PREFACE TO TH

I**N** this edition the etymologies ⟨...⟩ nd
for the most part rewritten, by ⟨G. W. S. Friedrichsen,⟩ to whom I
express my sincere thanks for undertaking a laborious task.

Numerous correspondents have sent in useful suggestions for
improving the dictionary, all of which are gratefully acknowledged
and many of which have been adopted in part or in full. Particular
mention must be made of the contributions of P. B. M. Allan, R. W.
Burchfield (who read through the proofs), the late Dr R. W. Chapman, L. F. Schooling, and G. C. Vanneck.

With regard to hyphening, some doubt is often felt when the
hyphen in a word coincides with the end of a line. To clarify the
matter a true hyphen is repeated at the beginning of the following
line.

E. McI., 1963

PREFACE TO THE FOURTH EDITION

I**N** this completely revised and reset edition numerous corrections
and additions have been made to bring the book up to date.
Thanks are due to the many correspondents who have pointed out
errors or suggested improvements. Especially must I express my
gratitude to Dr Scholes, Dr Honeyman, and Mr J. M. Wyllie for
the valuable assistance given for musical terms, chemical terms, and
many technical terms. The officials of the Clarendon Press too, past
and present, have throughout been most helpful.

In this edition the system of pronunciation devised for the *Pocket
Oxford Dictionary* has been adopted, the senses have been usually
numbered, the general abbreviations have been collected into an
appendix, and the swung dash has been freely employed.

Swung dash (∼).

To save space the 'swung dash' or 'tilde' is very frequently used
in the body of the article or the list of derivatives. It represents
either the complete word at the beginning of the article or the uninflected part of that word often marked by a vertical line. As, for
example, in the article **repeat,** ∼ stands for *repeat* (*or* repeat), ∼*ed*
for *repeated,* ∼ed**LY**[2] for repeated**LY**[2], ∼*ing* for *repeating,* ∼**ER**[1] for
repeat**ER**[1]; and in the article **reverber|ate** we have ∼*ating,* ∼ate,
∼ator**Y**, ∼**ATION**, ∼**ATIVE**, ∼**ANT** representing *reverberating,* reverberate, **reverberatORY, reverberATION, reverberATIVE, rever-
berANT.**

E. McI., 1950

From the
PREFACE TO THE FIFTH EDITION

From the
PREFACE TO THE THIRD EDITION

THE publication of the Supplement to the *Oxford English Diction-ary* in November 1933 makes important additions to the material which it is the aim of this book, as a dictionary of the living language, to present. Mr H. W. Fowler entrusted me with the preparation of this edition in February 1933, and until his death on the 26th December of that year I had the privilege of his guidance.

H. G. Le Mesurier, 1934

From the
PREFACE TO THE SECOND EDITION

WHEN we began, more than twenty years ago, the work that took shape as *The Concise Oxford Dictionary*, we were plunging into the sea of lexicography without having been first taught to swim. But lexicography for us was fortunately of the minor or dependent kind; and, fortunately also, the time was one at which the major or firsthand kind was reaching greater excellence than ever before, and the *Oxford English Dictionary*, four-fifths completed, already pro-vided popularizers with unlimited material.

The object we set before us, hinted at by the word *current* on our title-page, was to present as vivid a picture as the small dictionary could be made to give of the English that was being spoken and written at the time. The vividness was to be secured by allotting space to words more nearly in proportion to the frequency and variety of their use, and consequently to their practical value, than had been the custom; and further by an unprecedented abundance of illustrative quotation; define, and your reader gets a silhouette; illustrate, and he has it 'in the round'. That at least was our belief; and we hailed as confirmation of it one or two letters from persons unknown congratulating us on having 'produced a live dictionary', or 'treating English at last as a living language'.

A living language, however, does not remain unchanged through twenty years and a great war; our picture has needed, and received, a good deal of retouching before being again exhibited in public.

H. W. F., 1929

ACKNOWLEDGEMENTS

A DICTIONARY-MAKER, unless he is a monster of omniscience, must deal with a great many matters of which he has no firsthand knowledge. That he has been guilty of errors and omissions in some of these he will learn soon after publication, sometimes with gratitude to his enlightener, sometimes otherwise. The first letter we received after C.O.D. appeared was a demand for repayment of the book's cost, on the ground that it failed to give *gal(l)iot*, to settle the spelling of which it had been bought. Even for that announcement of an omission I am now grateful, as affording a good illustration of the less friendly form of correction, and reminding me to assure the public that to one revising for a new edition no correction is (ultimately) unwelcome; all is grist that comes to his mill. At the other end of the scale is the friend, known to me only by correspondence, who for years sent me fortnightly packets of foolscap devoted to perfecting a still contingent second edition—all this for love of the language not as a philological playground, but as the medium of exchange and bond of union among the English-speakers of the world. *Castigavit et emendavit Byron F. Caws* might have stood with justice at the foot of our title-page.

Other helpers have been many, some with systematic lists, others with a few isolated but valuable points; to all those in the list below I would fain offer—what some of them are no longer living to receive —my heartiest thanks:

Leslie J. Berlin Esq.; Major B. F. Caws; Dr R. W. Chapman; Mr S. K. N. Chaudhuri; *Sir Arthur Church K.C.V.O.; Rev. G. P. Ford; H. Gilbert-Carter Esq.; *Prof. Marcus Hartog; the Very Reverend Dr J. H. Hertz; Rev. J. Clare Hudson; Rev. F. E. Hutchinson; Lindsay Johnson M.D., F.R.S.; Rev. D. Evans Jones; Major C. V. N. Lyne; D. C. Macgregor Esq.; F. Morland Esq.; C. O. Ovington Esq.; George Pernet M.D.; Prof. Sir Flinders Petrie F.R.S.; Rev. S. de Saram; Kenneth Sisam Esq.; W. H. Thompson Esq.; B. H. Tower Esq.; F. F. Urquhart Esq.; *Rev. M. N. Walde; E. B. F. Wareing Esq.; *Dr F. H. P. van Wely; J. Beach Whitmore Esq.; Ernest W. Wignall Esq.; C. F. Williams F.G.S.; *Sir Dawson Williams C.B.E.

H. W. F.

* Those whose names are thus marked are known to me to be no longer living; and I fear the same may be true of some others, whom I have failed to reach by postal inquiries.

PREFACE TO THE FIRST EDITION

THE steady advance towards completion of the great *Oxford English Dictionary* has made it possible for the Delegates of the Clarendon Press to authorize the preparation and issue of this book, which in its own province and on its own scale uses the materials and follows the methods by which the Oxford editors have revolutionized lexicography. The book is designed as a dictionary, and not as an encyclopaedia; that is, the uses of words and phrases as such are its subject matter, and it is concerned with giving information about the things for which those words and phrases stand only so far as correct use of the words depends upon knowledge of the things. The degree of this dependence varies greatly with the kind of word treated, the difference between cyclopaedic and dictionary treatment varies with it, and the line of distinction is accordingly a fluctuating and dubious one. It is to the endeavour to discern and keep to this line that we attribute whatever peculiarities we are conscious of in this dictionary as compared with others of the same size. One of these peculiarities is the large amount of space given to the common words that no one goes through the day without using scores or hundreds of times, often disposed of in a line or two on the ground that they are plain and simple and that everyone knows all about them by the light of nature, but in fact entangled with other words in so many alliances and antipathies during their perpetual knocking about the world that the idiomatic use of them is far from easy; chief among such words are the prepositions, the conjunctions, the pronouns, and such 'simple' nouns and verbs as *hand* and *way*, *go* and *put*. Another peculiarity is the use, copious for so small a dictionary, of illustrative sentences as a necessary supplement to definition when a word has different senses between which the distinction is fine, or when a definition is obscure and unconvincing until exemplified; these sentences often are, but still more often are not, quotations from standard authors; they are meant to establish the sense of the definition by appeal not to external authority, but to the reader's own consciousness, and therefore their source, even when authoritative, is not named. A third and a fourth peculiarity are the direct results of the preceding ones; if common words are to be treated at length, and their uses to be copiously illustrated, space must be saved both by the curtest possible treatment of all that are either uncommon or fitter for the encyclopaedia than the dictionary, and by the severest economy of expression—amounting to the adoption of telegraphese—that readers can be expected to put up with.

In attaching this great importance to illustration, by the need of which the relative length of articles, and our manner of expressing ourselves on every page, are governed, we are merely acting, with the exaggeration imposed on us by our limited space, upon the principles of the O.E.D. That may be said to be the first dictionary for which the ideal procedure has been possible, that is, the approaching of each article with an open mind and a collection of examples large enough to be exhaustive, and the extraction from these of classified senses—the first dictionary, to put it another way, in which quotations have served not merely to adorn or convince, but as the indispensable raw material. This procedure—first the collection of sentences from all possible sources as raw material, and then the independent classification—we have often followed even in that part of our book (A–R) in which the O.E.D., with senses already classified and definitions provided, was before us, treating its articles rather as quarries to be drawn upon than as structures to be reproduced in little; and in the later part (S–Z), where we had no longer the O.E.D. to depend upon, it has been our practice still more often; for many of the more difficult (i.e. especially the common and 'simple') words, we have collected the quotations given in the best modern dictionaries (the *Imperial*, the *Century*, the *Standard*, Cassell's *Encyclopaedic*, Webster, etc.), added to these what we could get either from other external sources or from our own heads, and then framed our articles, often without reference to the arrangement that we found in any of our authorities. Proceeding in this manner, it was almost inevitable that we should be very much alive to the inadequacy of mere definition and the need of constant illustration. That our examples have some general tendency to the colloquial, and include many usages for which room has not been found in dictionaries many times as large as this, is in harmony with our design of on the one hand restricting ourselves for the most part to current English, and on the other hand omitting nothing to which that description may fairly be applied.

VOCABULARY

The words, or senses of words, given are meant to be such only as are current; 'current', however, is an elastic term; we might, but we do not, stretch it to include all words and senses used by Shakspere or in the Bible, on the ground that the whole of Shakspere and the whole of the Bible are still commonly read; thus the archaic senses of *addition* (title), *buxom* (pliant), *owe* (own), *sad* (serious), *sort* (suit), and the archaic words *shend* (scold), *wood* (mad), familiar as they are to readers of Elizabethan literature, are not given. We do stretch it to include many words and senses that are fossilized, having in themselves no life or capacity for further development, but kept extant by being enshrined in perhaps a single proverb or phrase that is still in use; of this sort are *coil* (confusion), preserved by 'shuffled off this mortal coil', and *scotch* (wound), preserved by 'we have scotched the snake, not killed it'.

Again, of the many thousands of old or new scientific and technical terms that have a limited currency some are carried by accident into the main stream of the language and become known temporarily or permanently, vaguely or precisely, to all ordinarily well-informed members of the modern newspaper-reading public. For the purposes of a dictionary that is not to be bulky and yet is to give a fuller treatment than is usual in dictionaries of its size to the undoubtedly current words forming the staple of the language, selection among these intruders is a difficult but very necessary task. The most that can be hoped for is that every one conversant with any special vocabulary may consider us, though sadly deficient on his subject, fairly copious on others; the meaning of many learned words that have been omitted as having no pretence to general currency may easily be gathered by reference first to the stem, which is often the subject of an article, or to another word of which the stem is clearly the same, and secondly to the suffix.

In another class of words and senses the test of currency has led us to diverge in the opposite direction from the practice usual in dictionaries of this size; if we give fewer scientific and technical terms, we admit colloquial, facetious, slang, and vulgar expressions with freedom, merely attaching a cautionary label; when a well-established usage of this kind is omitted, it is not because we consider it beneath the dignity of lexicography to record it, but because, not being recorded in the dictionaries from which our word-list is necessarily compiled, it has escaped our notice; we have not, however, consulted slang dictionaries nor made any attempt at completeness in this respect.

SPELLING

The spelling adopted is for the most part, but not invariably, that of the O.E.D. Such generally established spellings as *judgment*, *rhyme*, *axe*, have not been excluded in favour of the *judgement*, *rime*, *ax*, preferred by the O.E.D., but are retained at least as alternatives having the right to exist. In dealing with verbs such as *level*, *rivet*, *bias*, whose parts and derivatives are variously spelt, the final consonant being often doubled with no phonetic or other significance, we have as far as possible fallen in with the present tendency, which is to drop the useless letter, but stopped short of recognizing forms that at present strike every reader as Americanisms; thus we write *riveted*, *riveter*, but not *traveling*, *traveler*. On another point of varying usage—the insertion of a mute e in derivatives in *-able*, *-age*, *-ish*, etc., to indicate the 'long' sound of the stem vowel (*likable* or *likeable*, *milage* or *mileage*, *latish* or *lateish*)—we have thought ourselves justified in taking a bolder line, and have consistently omitted the *-e-*; it is against all analogy (or why not *smileing*, *Romeish*, *doteage*, *tideal*, *indescribeable*, *desireable*, *exciteable* ?), it is used chiefly in words not familiar or important enough to have their form respected as established, it obscures the different and more valuable use by which a soft g or c is indicated as in *manageable* and *serviceable*, and it tempts bad spellers to such monstrosities as *unpalateable*, *loveable*, and *moveable*. In words of the type *ardour*, *colour*, *favour*, where the O.E.D. recognizes both *-our* and *-or*, we have excluded the latter as being (except in particular words like *horror* and *torpor*, in which it is usually the only form) entirely non-British. Words in which *-y-* has intruded itself without completely dispossessing a more correct *-i-*, as *sylvan*, *tyro*, *tyre*, we have given with the *-i-* form either alone or placed first.

ORDER OF SENSES

From the order in which the senses of a word are here given no inference must be drawn as to their historical or other relations, the arrangement being freely varied according to the requirements or possibilities of the particular word. Sense-development cannot always be convincingly presented without abundant quotation from authorities, and the historical order is further precluded by the uniform omission of obsolete senses. Occasionally, when a rare but still current sense throws light on the commoner senses that follow or forms the connecting link with the etymology, it has been placed at the beginning; but more commonly the order adopted has been that of logical connexion or of comparative familiarity or importance.

DERIVATIVES

Hence introduces one or more of the direct derivatives of the word treated; *whence* introduces such derivatives under a particular sense to which they are restricted; *so* introduces words derived from another language; *hence or cogn.*, *whence or cogn.*, introduce groups of partly English and partly foreign derivation. The suffixes of such derivatives are commonly printed in small capitals, and are thus referred to the suffix article in its alphabetical place. The numbers enclosed in brackets indicate subdivisions of the suffix article, and are often used to distinguish among the possible senses of the derivative word those in which it is chiefly current.

REFERENCE BY SMALL CAPITALS

The use of small capitals for etymological purposes is explained above. In the same way reference is made:

(1) from the word treated to another word for the purpose of contrast, distinction, correlation, or the like. Of this kind are the references from *slander* to *libel* and *scandal*, from *creationism* to *evolution* and vice versa, and from *tenon* to *mortise* and vice versa;

(2) from any member of a group to the word under which the group is collected or further explained. *Ruby* (print.) is in this way referred to *type*; *order* (nat. hist.) to *class*[1]; and the *iron*[1], *golden*, and *silver ages* to *brazen*[1];

(3) from one or more words of a proverb or the like to that under which alone the proverb is explained. *Play*[1] and *drake*[2] contain such references to *duck*[1], *flesh* to *fish*[1];

(4) from a compound of the word treated to its other component for explanation. The sign (=) prefixed to such a reference indicates that the simple word treated is itself used in the sense of the compound. Thus, under *pie*[1], *sea-pie* is merely referred (SEA-~) to *sea*, but *magpie*, besides being referred to the article *magpie*, is recorded (= MAGPIE) as one of the senses of *pie*.

June, 1911

ETYMOLOGY

The etymology is given in square brackets at the end of each article when it is certainly known or regarded as probable. When, however, a proposed etymology rests on conjecture or hypothesis, it is ignored and the word is described as 'of unkn. orig.' or 'orig. unkn.'. References to other articles are in small capitals.

Words of Germanic (Gmc) origin that have come down from Old or Middle English are illustrated so far as possible by some or all of the forms recorded in the older stages of the cognate dialects, in the order Old Saxon (OS), Old High German (OHG), Old Norse (ON), and Gothic (Goth.). In Germanic inferred forms *th* and *dh* are used to denote the unvoiced and voiced dental spirants. In OE and ON words, as in OS and Gothic, the 'thorn' (þ) and the 'barred d' (ð) are represented by *th*, as hitherto. Thus OE *pæth* PATH, *thrāwan* THROW, ON *thveit* THWAITE, *garthr* GARTH. In OS words the plain b and d are used irrespective of their phonetic value in that dialect. The letters with superimposed macrons (*ā*, *ǣ*, etc.) in forms quoted from OE or other Gmc languages are long. For ON words the customary diacritic of length has been retained, as *á*, *ó*, etc.

'ME' includes the fifteenth century, no distinction being made between early and late ME. The use of this term will serve to distinguish words that were in use before 1500 from those whose documentation belongs to the sixteenth or later centuries.

Words of Romanic provenance are referred to their proximate origin, for the most part Old French, the earlier history of which, when known, is briefly indicated.

When OF or the like at the beginning of the etymology is not followed by the OF form, it is because the latter is identical in spelling with the English or differs from it only in some detail specified in brackets. Identity of ME and OF forms may be expressed as in 'ME *chartre* f. OF' (CHARTER[1]) or as in 'ME & OF *sidre*' (CIDER).

If the word is adopted from OF, the parent word is described as OF even though it survives in modern French in the same form, thus : 'ME *charge* f. OF'. Where the modern French differs appreciably from its OF form, this may be indicated as in 'ME & OF *prow* (mod. F *preux*)' (PROW[2]).

F, G, etc., must not be taken to imply that the word to which they are prefixed is current, or so spelt, in the modern language; nor does it follow from a word being given as OF that it is obsolete.

French nouns of Latin origin normally represent the Latin accusative case; nevertheless in this dictionary the Latin nominative is cited except when (e.g. in words ending in -*atio*) a change of stress is involved; thus, e.g., ORISON 'ME f. OF, f. L *orationem*'. For English words derived directly from Latin, the nominative case is cited, as in LIBATION 'f. L *libatio*'.

Many English words that have corresponding forms in both French and Latin present a special problem in that one cannot be certain whether the word was adopted from its French or from its Latin analogue. Sometimes, moreover, an earlier adoption from one source has been reinforced by a later adoption from, or conformation to, the other;

or, again, now one, now the other language has been laid under contribution by different individuals or groups of individuals. In such cases alternative origins have been given, which may mean either 'f. French or Latin' or 'f. French and Latin'.

In words derived from Latin, or from Greek through its latinized form, the age and standing of the Latin word are distinguished as Latin (L), late Latin (LL), medieval Latin (med. L), or modern Latin (mod. L). The dates here assumed are, for 'L', down to c. A.D. 200; for 'LL', from c. 200 to c. 600; for 'med. L', from c. 600 to c. 1500; for 'mod. L', from c. 1500.

The Latin form of a Greek word is usually omitted, and is to be inferred according to the rules of transliteration given below. Thus under PLEONASM 'f. L f. Gk *pleonasmos*' is to be read 'f. L *pleonasmus* f. Gk *pleonasmos*'.

A similar omission of a word in any other language implies identity of form.

Greek words are written with the corresponding English letters (φ, χ, ψ, ῥ, ῤῥ, = ph, kh, ps, rh, rrh, and ᾳ, η, ῳ = āi, ēi, ōi), and not according to the Latin transliteration, the rules for which are as follows: Greek k = Latin c; ai = ae, ou = u; u (except in diphthongs) = y; ei = i or e; oi = oe (but in nom. pl. = i); g (before g or k) = n; also, -ŏs (nom. masc.), -ŏn = -us, -um; -ēs, -ē (1st decl. nom.) = -a; -ōn (nom.) = -o; -ŏs (genit.) = -is; -a (accus. sing. masc. or fem.) = -em.

The first element of a compound word is often referred to a prefix article, and the remainder treated separately within brackets; meanings given within the bracket belong to the simple word, those of the compound being added if necessary outside it. Thus CONVENE is '[f. F *convenir* f. L CON(*venire vent-* come) assemble, agree, fit]'. The stem *vent-* and the sense 'agree, fit' are here added for the elucidation of CONVENTION and CONVENIENCE, which are referred to CONVENE.

The first element of a Greek compound similarly treated is sometimes written according to the current (Latin) transliteration, to facilitate reference to the prefix article; Greek *kakoepeia*, under CACOEPY, accordingly appears as CACO(*epeia*). Certain similar devices for saving needless repetition will, it is believed, explain themselves.

The etymological sections of all words, as also the prefix and the suffix articles, have been revised or redrafted for the present (fifth) edition. They are based in the first instance on the corresponding articles in the O.E.D., but we have also been privileged to make use of the proofs of the *Oxford Dictionary of English Etymology,* now nearing completion, by Dr. C. T. Onions, C.B.E. The great help and the many improvements afforded by this work are thankfully acknowledged.

G. W. S. F.

November, 1963

PRONUNCIATION

Phonetic respelling is placed in round brackets immediately after such words as require it, and the symbols in the PHONETIC SCHEME are primarily intended for this purpose. But respelling is often saved by employing the same symbols in the black type of the actual word; **bănĭsh**, for instance, has no respelling, and **dispōse** has only (-z).

Vowel symbols given in the Scheme with ⁻, ᴗ, —, or ᴖ, are also used without these marks to denote a vague indeterminate sound, which is almost identical for all vowels and (except in studied elocution) has no clear relation to the corresponding vowel marked ⁻ etc. (e.g., the a in *about* is like the o in *reason*, *proceed*, and is not like ā or ă). When so used in brackets, the indeterminates are printed in italics, thus: **ago** (*agō*), **proceed** (*prosēd*), **particular** (*partĭkūlar*). Used in the actual word, they are recognized by the absence of the marks ⁻, ᴗ, etc.; thus in **săcrament**, **cŏmmon**, **bĕggarly**, all the unmarked vowels (a; e; o; ar) are indeterminate. This does not apply to the last six symbols in the Scheme, which never have marks over them and are always distinct.

Indeterminate endings in -n, -m, -l or -le, when they require respelling, are also represented thus: **poison** (-zn), **fūsion** (-zhn), **tĕnsion** (-shn), **ōcean** (-shn), **lĭsten** (-sn), **bosom** (bŏŏzm), **hŭstle** (-sl), **official** (-shl), **weasel** (-zl), the vowel sound being that similarly indicated by the actual spelling of *spasm*, *prism*, etc.

PHONETIC SCHEME

Consonants: b; ch (chin); d; dh (dhe = the); f; g (go); h; j; k; l; m; n; ng (sing); ngg (finger); p; r; s (sip); sh (ship); t; th (thin); v; w; y; z; zh (vizhn = vision).

Vowels: ā ē ī ō ū ōō (mate mete mite mote mute moot)
ă ĕ ĭ ŏ ŭ ŏŏ (rack reck rick rock ruck rook)
ār ēr īr or ur (mare mere mire more mure)
ăr ĕr ŏr (part pert port)
ah aw oi oor ow owr (bah bawl boil boor brow bower)

Vowels marked ᴗ̲ may be pronounced either way, e.g. **pătriot** (pā- or pă-). In all vowel symbols with r (ār, ăr, etc.), the r, besides influencing the vowel sound, has its consonantal value when followed by a vowel in the next syllable of the word or in the following word (in *fearing* but not in *fearful*, in *far away* but not in *far gone*).

ACCENT

The main accent is shown by the mark ´, usually placed at the end of the stressed syllable; but, division into syllables being arbitrary in English, positions for the accent that would disguise the pronunciation are avoided; thus **stărr'ў** but **că'rrў**, **wŏŏll'en** but **cōōl'lў**, **lōc'al** but **vělō'cĭtў**, **ŏv'er** but **co'ver** (kŭ-), **mŭdd'ў** but **mŭd'dle**. The placing of two accents on a word means either (a) that the two marked syllables are equally stressed, as in ding'-dong', or (b) that among good speakers the one accentuation has as many adherents as the other, or (c) that the stress varies according to position in the sentence as explained in the dictionary article -ED². In the thousands of compounds given under their first elements among the alphabetically arranged combinations, accent is thus shown: if there is no hyphen separating the parts, the accent is always given (back'bone, backslide'); if there is a hyphen, the regular usage is for the first of the compounded words to be stressed, and the accent is then usually omitted (so oak-apple); if the stress falls, contrary to this rule, on the second component, it is marked (head-on′ adv.); if the stress is variable, each part has an accent (high-strung′).

PRONUNCIATION WITHOUT RESPELLING

All the further information necessary for the pronunciation of any word or part of a word that is not respelt is contained in the following six paragraphs; the assumptions made in these hold unless the contrary is shown in brackets.

1. Any letter or combination in the Phonetic Scheme has the value there shown; e.g., aw as in *awl*, not as in awake (awāk′); and ginger, linger, would be required to rhyme with *singer* unless ginger were followed by (-j-), and linger by (-ngg-).

2. The following additional symbols are used in the black type:

ė = ĭ (nāk′ėd, rėlŷ′, cŏll′ėge, prĭv′ėt)
ȋr, ûr, = ēr (bȋrth, bûrn)
ȳ, ў̆, = ī, ĭ (implŷ′, sŭnn′ў̆).

3. Final e unmarked is not indeterminate, but mute (sāne, ĭndŭc′tĭve; cf. rėcĭpė, dĭlėttän′tė).

4. A doubled consónant is pronounced as single (sĭll′ў̆, mănn′ĭsh, bŭtt′er), not as in cōōl′ly (-l-lĭ) or plain′nèss (-n-n-).

5. The following combinations and letters have the values shown:

Vowels.	Consonants.
ae = ē (aegis)	c is 'hard' and = k (cob, cry, talc), but
ai = ā (pain)	c before e, i, y, is 'soft' and = s (ice, icy,
air = āͬr (fair)	city)
au = aw (maul)	dg = j (judgement)
ay = ā (say)	g before e, i, y, is 'soft' and = j (age, gin,
ea, ee, = ē (mean, meet)	orgy)
ear, eer, = ēr (fear, beer)	kn = n at beginning of word or element of
eu, ew, = ū (feud, few)	compound (knot, unknot)
ie = ē (thief)	n before k, 'hard' c, q, x, = ng (zinc,
ier = ēr (pier)	uncle, tank, banquet, minx)
oa = ō (boat)	ph = f (photo)
ou = ow (bound)	qu = kw (quit)
oy = oi (coy)	tch = ch (batch)
	wr = r at beginning of word or element of
	compound (wry, awry)
	x = ks (fox)
	χ is the sound in Scots and German loch.

6. The following terminations have the values shown:

-age = -ĭj (garbage)	-sm = -zm (atheism, spasm)
-ate = -ĭt or -at (mandate)	-tion = -shon (salvation)
-ey = -ĭ (donkey)	-ture = -cher as well as- tūr, esp. in com-
-ous = -us (furious)	mon words.

INFLEXION

The rules assumed, exceptions to which are noted in a bracket placed after a word's grammatical description, are given below. The term 'sibilants' stands for words ending in -s, -x, -z, -sh or soft -ch, '-o wds' for all that end in -o, '-e wds' for all that end in mute -e, and '-y wds' for all that end in -y not preceded by a vowel (e.g. *deny*, *puppy*, but not *bray*, *donkey*).

1. Plural of nouns. Sibilants add -es (*boxes*, *porches*); -y wds change -y into -ies (*puppies*); the plural of -o wds is usually stated thus, photo n. (pl. ~*s*), potato n. (pl. ~*es*); other nouns add -s (*books*).

2. Possessive of nouns. Singular nouns take apostrophe, s (*man's, James's*); plurals, if they do not end in s, form the possessive by the same rule (*men's, geese's*), but, if they end in s, take an apostrophe only (*boys'*).

3. Comparative and superlative of adjectives and adverbs. In monosyllables and some disyllables (e.g. those in -y) add -er and -est (*bolder*), -e wds dropping the -e (*bravest*), and disyllables in -y having -ier and -iest (*happier, luckiest*); in other cases prefix *more* and *most* (*more beautiful, most splendid*). Monosyllables double a final single consonant (except x and w) if preceded by a single vowel (*grimmer*). This may be stated in the dictionary.

4. Third person singular present of verbs. Sibilants and -o wds add -es (*pushes, goes*); -y wds change -y into -ies (*cries*); other verbs add -s (*sings*).

5. Past and p.p. of verbs. -e wds add -d (*moved*); -y wds change -y into -ied (*relied*); other verbs add -ed (*trusted, vetoed*); if the final consonant is doubled, it is stated in the dictionary, thus: **glut**, v.t. (-tt-); **revel**, v.i. & t. (-ll-).

6. Participle of verbs. All verbs add -ing (*fishing*), -e wds dropping the -e (*dancing*); monosyllables double a final single consonant (except x) if preceded by a single vowel (*grabbing*).

7. Archaic 2nd and 3rd singular of verbs. The forms in -(e)st and -(e)th, being archaic, need only be mentioned, without rules; -(e)st is 2nd sing. present and past, -(e)th is 3rd sing. present; examples are *playest, dost, hear'st, madest, wouldst, saith, goeth.*

ABBREVIATIONS USED IN THE DICTIONARY

(For list of general abbreviations see Appendix I)

a., aa., adjective(s)
abbr./eviation etc.
abl./ative
abs./olute(ly)
acc., according, accusative
act./ive
adj./ective etc.
adjj., adjectives
adv./erb etc.
advv., adverbs
aeron./autics etc.
aesthet./ics etc.
AF, Anglo-French
Afr./ica(n)
AL, Anglo-Latin
alch./emy etc.
alg./ebra etc.
allus./ive etc.
alt./eration etc.
alw./ays
Amer./ica(n)
AN, Anglo-Norman
anal./ogy etc.
anat./omy etc.
Anglo-Ind./ian
anon./ymous etc.
ant./iquities
anthrop./ology etc.
ap./pendix
app./arently
Arab./ic
Aram./aic
arbitr./ary
arch./aic
archaeol./ogy etc.
archit./ecture etc.
arith./metic etc.

Ass./yrian
assim./ilated etc.
assoc./iated etc.
astrol./ogy etc.
astron./omy etc.
attrib./utive etc.
augment./ative etc.
Austral./ia(n)

b./orn
back form./ation
bef./ore
bibl./ical etc.
bibliog./raphy etc.
bill./iards
biog./raphy etc.
biol./ogy etc.
Boh./emian
bot./any etc.
Braz./il(ian)
Bret./on
Brit./ish
Bulg./aria(n)
Burm./ese
Byz./antine

c./entury
c./irca
cc., centuries
Celt./ic
cf., compare
chem./istry etc.
Chin./ese
chronol./ogy etc.
cinemat./ography etc.
cl./assical
cogn./ate

collect./ive(ly)
colloq./uial etc.
com./mon
comb./ination etc.
commerc./ial etc.
comp., compar./ative
compd, compound
compl./ement
compp., compounds
com./mon -Teut./onic
con./ics
conch./ology etc.
confus./ion
conj., conjunction, conjugation
conn./ect etc.
constr./uction etc.
contempt./uous etc.
contr./action etc.
cop./ulative
Copt./ic
Corn./ish
corr./ection etc.
correl./ative etc.
corresp./onding etc.
corrupt./ion
cp., compare
crick./et
cryst./allography
cu., cub., cubic
Cym./ric

d./ied
Da./nish
dat./ive
demonstr./ative
dent./istry

deriv./ative etc.
derog./atory etc.
dial./ect etc.
dict./ionary
diff./erent
different./iate etc.
dim./inutive etc.
dimm., diminutives
diplom./acy
dir./ect etc.
dissim./ilate etc.
dist./inct etc.
distrib./utive etc.
disyl./labic etc.
Dor./ic
Du./tch
dynam./ics etc.

E, English
eccl./esiastical etc.
EFris., East Frisian
Egyptol./ogy
E. Ind., East Indian
electr./icity etc.
ellipt./ical etc.
embryol./ogy
engin./eering etc.
Engl., England, English
entom./ology etc.
erron./eous(ly)
eschat./ology etc.
esp./ecial(ly)
eth./ics etc.
ethnol./ogy etc.
etym./ology etc.
euphem./ism etc.
Eur./ope(an)
ex./ample
exagg./eration etc.
exc./ept
exch./ange
excl., exclamation etc., exclusive etc.
excll., exclamations
expl./ain etc.
expr./essing etc.
exx., examples

F, French
f./rom
facet./ious etc.
fam./iliar etc.
fem./inine etc.
fenc./ing
fig./urative etc.
Fl./emish
foll./owing (word)
footb./all
form./ation
fortif./ication
Fr./ench
Frank./ish
freq./uent(ly)
frequent./ative(ly)
Fris./ian
ft, foot, feet
fut./ure

G, German
Gael./ic
gal./lon(s)
gen., general etc., genitive
geog./raphy etc.
geol./ogy etc.
geom./etry etc.
Gk, Greek
Gmc, Germanic
Goth./ic
gr., gram./mar etc.
gym./nastics etc.

Heb./rew
her./aldry etc.
Hind., Hindi, Hindustani
hist./orical etc., history
hort./iculture etc.
Hung./arian, -ary
hydrost./atics etc.

i., intransitive
Icel./andic
illit./erate etc.
imit./ative etc.
imper., imperat./ive
imperf./ect
impers./onal
improp./er(ly)
incept./ive
incl./uding, -usive
Ind./ia(n)
ind., indicative, indirect
indecl./inable
inf./initive
infl./uence etc.
instr./umental (case)
int./erjection
interrog./ative(ly)
intr./ansitive
Ir./ish
iron./ical(ly)
irreg./ular(ly)
It., Ital./ian
ital./ics

Jam./aica(n)
Jap./an(ese)
Jav./anese
Jew./ish
joc./ose, -ular(ly)

L, Latin
lang./uage
Lat./in
lexicog./raphy etc.
LG, Low German
lit./eral(ly)
Lith./uania(n)
LL, late Latin
log./ic etc.

M, middle (with languages)
magn./etism etc.
manuf./acture etc.
masc./uline
math./ematics etc.
MDu., middle Dutch
ME, middle English (1200-
1500)
mech./anics etc.
med./icine etc.
med.L, medieval Latin
metaph./or etc.
metaphys./ics etc.
metath./esis etc.
meteor./ology etc.
meton./ymy
Mex./ican
MHG, middle High German
mil./itary etc.
min./eralogy etc.
MLG, middle Low German
mod./ern
monosyl./labic etc.
morphol./ogy etc.
MSw., middle Swedish
mus./ic etc.
myth./ology etc.

n./oun
N. Amer., North American
nat. hist., natural history

nat. phil., natural philosophy
naut./ical etc.
nav./al etc.
neg./ative(ly)
neut./er
NFris., North Frisian
nn., nouns
nom./inative
Norm./an
north./ern
Norw./egian, -ay
N.T., New Testament
num./eral

O, old (with languages)
obj./ect etc.
obl./ique
obs./olete
obsc./ure etc.
obsolesc./ent
obstet./rics etc.
occas./ional(ly)
ODa., old Danish
OE, old English
OF, old French
OFris., old Frisian
OHG, old High German
OIr., old Irish
OLG, old Low German
ON, old Norse
ONF, old northern French
onomat./opoeic etc.
opp., (as) opposed (to)
OPr., old Provençal
opt., optative, optics etc.
ord./inary
orig./in(al(ly))
ornith./ology etc.
OS, old Saxon
OSl(av)., old Slavonic
OSp., old Spanish
O.T., Old Testament

p./age
paint./ing
Pal./estine
palaeog./raphy etc.
palaeont./ology etc.
parenth./etic etc.
Parl./iament(ary)
part., (present) participle
partic./ipial
pass./ive(ly)
path./ology etc.
pedant./ic(ally)
perf./ect (tense)
perh./aps
Pers./ia(n)
pers./on(al)
pert./aining
Peruv./ian
Pg., Portuguese
pharm./acy etc.
philol./ogy etc.
philos./ophy etc.
Phoen./icia(n)
phon., phonet./ics etc.
phonol./ogy etc.
photog./raphy etc.
phr./ase
phren./ology etc.
phrr., phrases
phys./ics etc.
physiol./ogy etc.
pl./ural
plup./erfect
poet./ical etc.
Pol./ish, -and

pol./itics etc.
pol. econ., political economy
polit./ics etc.
pop./ular etc.
Port./uguese
poss./essive, /ible etc.
p.p., past or passive participle
pp., pages
Pr./ovençal
pr./onounced etc.
prec., (the) preceding (word)
pred./icate etc.
pref./ix
prep./osition
pres./ent (tense)
pret./erite
print./ing
priv./ative
prob./able etc.
pron., pronoun etc., pronounced etc.
pronunc./iation
prop./er(ly)
pros./ody etc.
Prov./ençal
prov., proverb etc., provincial etc.
psych./ology etc.
psycho-an./alysis

R.-C., Roman Catholic
redupl./icated etc.
ref./erence
refash./ioned etc.
refl./exive(ly)
rel./ated, -ative
repl./acing etc.
repr./esent etc.
rhet./oric etc.
Rom., Roman, Romance, Romanic
Rom./an ant./iquities
Rom./an Cath./olic

Rom./an hist./ory
Russ./ia(n)

s./ingular
S. Afr., South Africa(n)
Sax./on
sb., substantive
Sc., Scotch, Scots, Scottish
Scand./inavia(n)
schol./astic
sci./ence etc.
Scot., Scotland, Scottish
sculp./ture
Sem./itic
sent./ence
Serb./ian
sing./ular
Skr., Sanskrit
sl./ang
Slav./onic
sociol./ogy etc.
Sp./anish
sp./elling
spec./ial(ly)
spirit./ualism etc.
sport./ing etc.
st./em
stat./ics etc.
subj., subject etc., subjunctive
subst./antive
suf./fix
sup., superl./ative
surg./ery etc.
surv./eying etc.
Sw./edish
syn./onym etc.

t., transitive
tech./nical(ly)
teleg./raphy etc.
term./ination
theatr./ical etc.
theol./ogy etc.
theos./ophy etc.

therm./ometry etc.
thr./ough
trans./itive etc.
transf., in transferred sense
transl./ation etc.
translit./eration etc.
trig./onometry etc.
Turk./ish, -ey
typ./ography etc.

ult./imate(ly)
uncert./ain
unexpl./ained
unkn./own
U.S., United States
usu./al(ly)

v./erb
var., variant, various
v. aux., verb auxiliary
vb, verb
vbl, verbal
v.i., verb intransitive
voc./ative
v.refl., verb reflexive
v.t., verb transitive
vulg./ar(ly)
vv., verbs

W, Welsh
w./ith
W. Afr., West Africa(n)
wd, word
wds, words
WFlem., West Flemish
WFris., West Frisian
WG, West Germanic
wh./ich
W.Ind., West Indian, -ies

yd, yard
yr(s), year(s)

zoogeog./raphy etc.
zool./ogy etc.

P = proprietary name. See below.
*, in etymologies, sign affixed to all forms not recorded but merely inferred.
*, other than in etymologies = (orig. or chiefly) U.S.
‖ = not U.S.
~ represents either the complete word at the beginning of the article or the uninflected part of that word often marked by a vertical line.

NOTE. The addition of etc. to the completion of an abbreviation means that it may be used not only for the exact form given, but for connected words or phrases; e.g. *bot./any etc.* means *botany, botanical, botanically, in botany*; *adv./erb etc.* means *adverb, adverbial, adverbially*; *transl./ation etc.* means *translated* as well as *translation*. Abbreviations given in the list with initial capital have always the capital in use; but those given with initial small letter have either form according to circumstances.

This dictionary includes some words which are or are asserted to be proprietary names or trade marks. Their inclusion does not imply either that they have acquired for legal purposes a non-proprietary or general significance or any other judgement concerning their legal status. In cases where the editor has some evidence that a word is used as a proprietary name or trade mark this is indicated by the symbol P, but no judgement concerning the legal status of such words is made or implied thereby.

A

A, letter (pl. *As*, A's, Aes). (Mus.) sixth note in scale of C major, & the corresponding scale. (In argument) first imaginary person or case. (Alg.) first known quantity. (Naut.) **A1** (ā wŭn), first-class vessel in Lloyd's Register of Shipping; (colloq.) excellent, best. (Naut.) *Æ*, third-class ship at Lloyd's.

a¹, an, (*a, an*; emphatic, ā, ăn), adj. (occas. called indefinite article. Before all consonants except silent *h*, use *a*; *a history*, *a historian*, though some still write *an* before *h* in unaccented syllable, but *an hour*: before all vowels except *eu*, *û*, use *an*; *an ŭlcer*, but *a ŭnit*, *a eulogy*; also *a one*. Placed after *many, such, what*, or any adj. preceded by *how, so, as, too*. Used with apparent plurals of number, *a dozen men* = a dozen of men; also with pl. adjj. *few, good many, great many*). (Unemphatic substitute for) one, some, any; one like (*a Daniel*); (after *all of, many of*, etc.) the same (*all of a size*); (distrib.) each (£40 *a year*, where *a* is orig. = foll.). [weakening of OE *ān* ONE]

a², prep. On, to, towards, into, in. Mostly now written as pref., or oftener omitted than expressed, or confused w. **A¹**. On: *abed, afoot*. To: *ashore*. Towards: *aback, afar, aside*. Into: *apart, asunder*. In: *now-a-days, twice a day*; w. vbl nouns, passively, *a-building*, actively, *was (a-) fighting*, and esp. w. *go, set*, as *he went a begging, they set the bells a ringing*. [weakening of OE prep. *an*, ON]

a-, pref. f. various sources. **1.** OE *a-*, orig. *ar-*, away, on, up, out, as *arise*. Occas. confused w. OF *a-* f. L *ad-, ac-, af-* etc. (No. 4), as *a(c)curse* etc. **2.** ME *a-* f. OE *an, on*, prep.; see prec. **3.** ME *a-* f. OE *of* prep., as *akin, a-clock*. **4.** ME *a-*, = OF pref. *a-* f. L *ad* to, at, either directly, as *ascend*, or thr. F *a-* as *agree*; many wds derived in the latter way have been later assim. to L spelling, as *a(d)dress, a(g)grieve*. **5.** ME *a-*, = OF *a-*, f. L *ab* from, away, as *abridge*. **6.** ME, AF *a-* = OF *e-, es* f. L *ex* out, utterly, as *amend, affray*. **7.** Gk *a-, an-*, not, without; directly, as *amorphous*, thr. L, as *acatalectic*, or thr. L & F, as *adamant*; compounded chiefly w. Gk words, but also w. others, as *a-moral*.

-a, suf. **1.** Nn. f. Gk, L, & Rom. fem. sing., as *idea* (Gk), *arena* (L), *piazza* (It.), *duenna* (Sp.), esp. Nat. Hist. terms, ancient or latinized mod. (*hyena, dahlia*), geogr. names (*Africa*), & names of women,

ancient or latinized mod. (*Lydia, Hilda*). **2.** Gk & L neut. pl. nouns (*genera, phenomena*), esp. names, often f. mod. L, of classes of animals (*mammalia*).

aard-vark (ärd′ värk), n. S.-African quadruped between armadillos & ant-eaters. [f. Du. *aarde* EARTH + *varken* pig; see FARROW]

aard-wolf (ärd′ wǒŏlf), n. S.-African carnivore between hyenas & civets. [see prec.]

Aar′on's beard (är-), n. Kinds of plant, esp. great St John's wort. [ref. to *Ps.* cxxxiii. 2]

Aar′on's rŏd (är-), n. Kinds of plant, esp. great mullein & golden rod. [ref. to *Num.* xvii. 8]

aasvogel (ah′sfōgl), n. S.-Afr. vulture. [S.-Afr. Du. (*aas* carrion + *vogel* bird)]

ab-, pref. repr. L *ab*, off, away, from, f. F, as *abuse*, or L, as *abduct*.

āb′a, abaya (abä′ya), nn. Sack-like outer garment worn by Arabs. [Arab.]

abăck′, adv. Backwards; (Naut.) of square sails pressed against mast by head wind; *taken ~*, of ship w. sails in that state, (fig.) surprised, discomfited. [A² + BACK¹]

ăb′acus, n. (pl. *-cī*, pr. -sī). **1.** Calculating frame w. balls sliding on wires, used before adoption of the nine figures & zero, & still in China etc., & in elementary teaching. **2.** (Archit.) upper member of capital, supporting architrave. [L *abacus* f. Gk *abax -akos* tablet]

Abăd′don, n. Hell; the devil (*Rev.* ix. 11). [Heb. word, destruction (*abad* he perished)]

abaft′ (-ah-), adv. & prep. (naut.). In stern half of ship; nearer the stern than, aft of. [A² + *baft*, OE *beæftan* f. *be* BY + *æftan* AFT]

•ăbalō′ně, n. Californian edible mollusc with ear-shaped shell lined with mother-of-pearl, sea-ear. [Sp.]

abăn′don¹, v.t. Give up to another's control or mercy; yield one*self* completely to a passion or impulse; give up (a possession or habit); forsake (a person, post). [ME, f. OF *abandoner* f. phr. *à bandon* under control f. Rom. *•bandonem* f. med. L *bandum*, var. LL *bannus, -um* BAN²]

abăn′don² (or as F, see Ap.), n. Careless freedom, letting oneself go. [F; see prec.]

abăn′doned (-ond), a. Profligate. [p.p. of ABANDON¹]

abăndonee′, n. (law). One to whom anything is relinquished. [ABANDON¹ + -EE]

aban'donment, n. Giving up or forsaking; being forsaken; self-surrender; careless freedom of manner, impulsiveness. [f. ABANDON[1] +-MENT, or F *abandonnement*]

abāse', v.t. Lower, humiliate, make base. Hence ~MENT (-sm-) n. [late ME *abesse* f. OF *abaissier* f. *a* (A- (4)) +*baissier* to lower f. Rom. **bassiare* f. LL *bassus* BASE[3], whence mod. form *abase*]

abāsh', v.t. Put out of countenance; (chiefly in pass.) be confounded. Hence ~MENT n. [ME *abaiss(e)* f. OF *esbair* f. *es-* = A- (6) +*bair* be astonished, of uncert. orig.; see -ISH[2]]

abask' (-bah-), adv. In warm light. [A[2] + BASK]

abāte', v.t. & i. 1. Diminish (t. & i.). 2. Do away with (nuisance); blunt (edge); lower (price); deduct (specified or unspecified part of price); mitigate (violence); weaken (energy). 3. (In law) quash (writ or action). 4. (Of flood or epidemic) grow less. So (f. OF) ~MENT (-tm-) n. [ME, f. OF *abatre* f. *a* = A (4)+*batre* beat f. Rom. **battere* for L *battuere*; cf. BATTLE[1]]

ăb'atis, abăt'is, n. Defence made of felled trees w. boughs pointing outwards. Hence **ăb'atis**ED[2] (-st) a. [F, f. *abatre* fell; see prec.]

abattoir (see Ap.), n. Slaughter-house. [F]

abăx'ial, a. (bot.). Away from the axis. [AB-, AXIS, -AL]

ăbb, n. Woof. [A- (1) +WEB]

Abb'a (ă-), n. Father. Used w. *Father* in invoking God (*Mark* xiv. 36). [Aram.]

ăbb'acy̆, n. Office, jurisdiction, or tenure, of an abbot. [earlier *abbatie* (see -ACY) f. LL *abbatia* (*abbat*- ABBOT)]

abbā'tial (-shal), a. Of an abbey, abbot, or abbess. [F, f. med.L *abbatialis* (*abbatia* ABBACY,|-AL)]

abbé (ăb'ā), n. Frenchman (orig. abbot) entitled to wear ecclesiastical dress, esp. without official duties. [F, f. LL *abbatem* nom. *-as* ABBOT]

ăbb'ess, n. Superior of abbey of enclosed nuns. [ME, f. OF *ab(b)esse* f. LL *abbatissa* (ABBOT, -ESS)]

ăbb'ey, n. (pl.~s). Building(s) occupied by monks or nuns under an abbot or abbess; the monks or nuns as a body; a church or house that was once an ~ or part of it (*the A~*, Westminster A~). [ME, f. OF *abbeie* etc. f. LL *abbatia* ABBACY]

ăbb'ot, n. Head of abbey of monks; *A~ of Misrule* or *of Unreason*, leader in medieval burlesque festivities. [OE *abbod*, f. LL *abbas* *-at-* f. Gk *abbas* (ABBA)]

abbrēv'iate[1], a. Relatively short (esp. in nat. hist.). [late ME f. LL *abbreviatus* p.p. of *-are* shorten (*ab* or *ad*+*brevis* short); cf. ABRIDGE]

abbrēv'i|āte[2], v.t. Make short (chiefly now of writing part of word for whole,

but also of visit, story, etc.). So (f. OF) ~ATION n. [f. as prec.; see -ATE[3]]

A B C (ābēsē'), n. The alphabet; rudiments of any subject; ‖ alphabetical railway guide.

Ab'derite (ă-), n. *The* ~, Democritus (see DEMOCRITEAN). [Gk *Abdērītēs* (*Abdēra*, a town, -ITE[1])]

ăb'dic|āte, v.t. Renounce formally or by default (a power, office, right; also abs. esp. of the crown). So (f. L) ~A'TION n., ~ātED[1](2) a. [f. L AB(*dicare* declare), -ATE[3]]

ăbdŏm'ĕn (*or* ăb'do-), n. 1. (anat.). Belly, including stomach, bowels, & other nutritive organs. 2. (zool.). Hinder part of insects, spiders, etc. [L]

ăbdŏm'inal, a. Of the abdomen in either sense; (of fish) having the ventral fins under the belly. [f. *abdomin-* stem of prec. +-AL]

ăbdŏm'inous, a. Corpulent. [as prec.+ -OUS]

abdū'cent, a. (anat.). Drawing away (of muscles that open or pull back the part they are fixed to). [f. L *abducent-* part. st. of AB(*ducere duct-* draw)]

abdŭct', v.t. Kidnap; take away (esp. a woman) by force or fraud; draw (limb etc.) from its natural position. [f. L *abduct-* see prec.]

abdŭc'tion, n. Illegal carrying off, esp. of a child, ward; forcible carrying off of any one, as of a voter; withdrawal of limb from natural position; shrinking of sides of a wound, causing it to gape. [f. LL *abductio* (prec., -ION)]

abdŭc'tor, n. Person who abducts another; (also ~*muscle*) muscle that abducts a limb. [as ABDUCT +-OR]

abeam', adv. On a line at right angles to the ship's or aircraft's length; ~ *of us*, opposite our centre, abreast. [A[2]+BEAM[1]]

abecedār'ian (ābīsī-), a. &n. 1. Arranged alphabetically, as the 119th Psalm; elementary, ignorant. 2. n. Pupil learning the alphabet (common in U.S.). [f. LL *abecedarius* (see -ARY[1]) +-AN]

abĕd', adv. In bed. [A[2]+BED[1]]

abele (abēl', ā'bl), n. The white poplar. [f. Du. *abeel* f. OF *abel* earlier *aubel* f. med. L *albellus* dim. of *albus* white]

ā'belmŏsk, n. Malvaceous N.-Afr. evergreen shrub yielding musk-seeds. [ult. f. Arab. *ḥabbu-'l-misk* grain of musk]

Aberdeen' (ă-), n. ~ *Angus*, Scottish breed of polled black cattle; ~ (*terrier*), rough-haired Scotch terrier. [*Aberdeen* in Scotland]

ăberdévine', n. Bird-fancier's name for the siskin. [orig. unkn.]

Aberdŏn'ian (ă-), a. & n. (Inhabitant, native) of Aberdeen. [f. med. L *Aberdonia* +-IAN]

aberglaube (ah'berglowbe), n. Excessive belief, superstition. [G]

Ab'ernĕthy̆ (ă-), n. Hard biscuit flavoured with caraway seeds. [orig. unkn.]

abĕ'rr|ant, a. Straying from moral stand-

ard; (in nat. hist.) diverging from normal
type. So ~ANCE, ~ANCY, nn. [f. L
aberrant- part. st. of AB(*errare* stray)]

äberrä'tion, n. **1.** A straying from the
path, lit. & fig.; breaking of rules; moral
slip; intellectual deficiency; temporary
lapse of memory; deviation from type.
2. (optics). Non-convergence of rays to
one focus. **3.** (astron.). Displacement of
heavenly body's true position to observer. [f. L *aberratio*; see prec., -ATION]

abĕt', v.t. (-tt-). Countenance or assist
(offence or offender; esp. *aid & ~*), incite.
So (f. AN) ~MENT, ~t'ER[1], ~t'OR, nn.
~*tor* is the legal & the commoner general
form. [ME, f. OF *abeter* (*à* to + *beter* BAIT[1])]

db ĕx'trä, adv. From outside. [LL]

abey'ance (-bā-), n. State of suspension,
dormant condition liable to revival, (of
rights etc.; mostly in phrr. *be in* or *fall
into ~*). [AF *abeiance* f. OF *abeer* f. *a* to
+ *beer* f. med.L *batare* gape]

abhŏr', v.t. (-rr-). Regard with disgust
& hatred (*Nature ~s a vacuum*). [ME, f.
L AB(*horrēre* shudder)]

abhŏ'rrence, n. Detestation; detested
thing (*flattery is my ~*). [foll.. -ENCE]

abhŏ'rrent, a. Inspiring disgust, hateful,
of conduct etc., often with *to* (person);
inconsistent (*from*); (arch.) feeling disgust (*of*), *as the Greeks were ~ of excess*.
[f. L *abhorrent-* part. st. see ABHOR]

abhŏr'rer, n. (hist.). Nickname of those
who signed addresses to Charles II in
1680. [ABHOR + -ER[1]]

abīd'ance, n. Continuance, dwelling (*in*),
abiding (*by* rules etc.). [ABIDE + -ANCE]

abīde', v.t. & i. (past & p.p. *abōde*, occas.
~*d*). **1.** Remain over; continue; dwell
(arch.); stand firm; (with *by*) remain
faithful to, act upon (terms). **2.** Wait for;
encounter, sustain; submit to, suffer;
(negatively as *I cannot, who can, ~*?) put
up with (noun or infinitive). [OE *abidan*
f. A-(1) + *bidan* BIDE]

abīd'ing, a. Permanent. Hence ~LY[2]
adv. [part. of ABIDE]

äbiĕt-, stem of several chemical terms. Of
resin, or fir. [L *abiet-* nom. *abies* fir-tree]

äb'ïgail, n. Lady's-maid. [character in
Beaumont & Fletcher's *Scornful Lady*,
perh. w. ref. to 1 *Sam.* xxv. 24–31]

abil'itỹ, n. Sufficient power, capacity (*to
do* something); legal competency (*to
act*); financial competency to meet a
demand; cleverness, mental faculty,
(general in sing., special in pl.). [ME
ablete f. OF f. L *habilitatem* (*habilis* deft,
-TY[1]) to wh. mod. sp. conforms]

db ïnït'ïō, adv. From the beginning. [L]

äb'ïogĕn'ēsis, n. Spontaneous generation. (Allied words) **äb'ïogĕnĕt'ic** a.,
connected w. the doctrine; **äb'ïogĕnĕt'-
ICALLY** adv., by spont. gen. or according
to the doctrine; **äbïŏ'gĕnIST** (2) n., one
who believes in it; **äbïŏ'gĕnous** a., so
produced; **äbïŏ'gĕn[1]** n., = abiogenesis.
[f. Gk *abios* f. A-(7) + *bios* life + GENESIS]

äb'jĕct, a. & n. **1.** Brought low, miserable;
craven, degraded, despicable. **2.** n. (Bibl.
& arch.) a person of the meanest condition. Hence ~LY[2] adv., ~NESS n. [ME, f.
L *abjectus* p.p. of AB(*jicĕre = jacĕre* throw)]

abjĕc'tion, n. Abasement, low estate.
[f. L *abjectio* (ABJECT, -ION)]

äbjurä'tion (-joor-), n. Action or form of
renunciation on oath, in all senses of
ABJURE (in hist. esp. of the Stuart claim).
[f. L *abjuratio* (ABJURE, -ATION)]

abjure' (-joor), v.t. Renounce on oath (an
opinion, heresy, cause, claim, or claimant);
swear perpetual absence from (one's
country etc.) [f. F *abjurer* or L AB(*jurare*
swear)]

äblactä'tion, n. Weaning from the
mother. [f. LL AB(*lactatio* f. *lactare*
suckle f. *lact-* nom. *lac* milk)]

äblä'tion, n. Removal (esp. in surgery, of
any part of body); (Geol.) waste of a
glacier or rock by melting or water action.
[f. LL *ablatio* f. AB(*lat-* p.p. st. of *ferre*
carry)]

äb'lative, a. & n. The case in Latin nouns
that expresses source, agent, cause, instrument, of action = *from* or *by* with the
noun (usu. noun; adj. with *case, sense,*
etc.); *~ ABSOLUTE*, a construction of noun
& participle in L Gram. giving time or
circumstances. [ME, f. OF (*-if, -ive*) or
L *ablativus* (prec., -IVE)]

äb'laut (-ow-), n. Vowel changes in the
parent Indo-European language, arising
out of differences of accent & stress, &
surviving e.g. in *drive, drove, driven.* [G]

ablāze', adv. & pred. a. On fire; glittering; excited. [A[2] + BLAZE[1]]

ā'ble, a. Talented, clever; competent,
having the means or power (*to*), esp. w.
parts of *be* to supply the deficiencies of
can; legally qualified; *~-bodied seaman*
(abbr. A.B.), of special class. Hence **āb'LY[2]**
adv. [ME, f. OF *hable; able*, (now *habile*)
f. L *habilis* handy (*habēre* to hold)]

-able, suf. f. F *-able* f. L *-a-* of first conjug.
+ *-bili-* see -BLE. In F extended to vbs of
all conjugg. In E now appended even to
native vbs as *bearable*, nouns as *clubbable*,
& phrase vbs as *get-at-able*; prob. f.
confusion w. the unrelated adj. *able.*
Now always w. pass. sense (*eatable*), but
in early wds freq. act. (*comfortable,
suitable*); cf. -BLE; *salable* (where no vb
exists) is an anal. of *debatable.*

∥äb'lĕt, äb'lĕn, n. Name for the freshwater fish bleak. [F *ablette* f. Rom. *abula*
for *albula* dim. of *alba* white]

äb'lings, äb'lins (-z), adv. (Sc. & north.).
Possibly, perhaps. [ABLE + -LINGS]

ablōōm', adv. & pred. a. In or into bloom.
[A[2] + BLOOM]

ablŭsh', adv. & pred. a. Blushing. [A[2] +
BLUSH]

ablu'tion (-lōō-), n. (usu. pl.). Ceremonial
washing of person, hands, or sacred
vessels; ordinary personal washing;
(sing.) water in which things have been

washed, esp. in Catholic Ritual. Hence ~ARY[1] a. [ME, f. OF, or LL AB(lutio f. luere lut- wash, -ION)]

ăb'nĕgāte, v.t. Deny oneself (something), renounce (a right or belief). [f. L AB(negare deny), -ATE[3]]

ăbnĕgā'tion, n. Denial; rejection (of doctrine); self-sacrifice (now oftener self-~~). [f. F, or LL abnegatio (prec., -ATION)]

abnŏrm'al, a. Exceptional, irregular, deviating from type. Hence **ăbnŏrmăl'ITY** n., the quality or an instance of it, ~LY[2] adv. [earlier & F anormal f. med. L anormalus corrupted f. Gk anōmalos ANOMALOUS; but now regarded as f. L abnormis, see foll.]

abnŏrm'ĭty, n. Irregularity; a monstrosity. [f. L AB(normis f. norma rule) see -TY]

aboard' (-ôrd), adv. & prep. On or into ship, train, etc. (ship etc. either expressed or omitted); alongside, near, esp. close or hard~. Lay (another ship) ~, place one's own alongside of her to fight; fall ~, fall foul of (another ship). [A[2]+BOARD]

abōde', n. Dwelling-place, house; stay, habit of dwelling, as in make one's ~. [vbl n. of ABIDE; cf. ride, rode, road]

aboil', adv. & pred. a. A-boiling, boiling. [A[2]+BOIL[2]]

abŏl'ĭsh, v.t. Do away with (customs, institutions). Hence ~ABLE a., ~ER[1], ~MENT, nn. [ME, f. F abolir (-ISH[2]) f. L abolēre destroy]

ăbolĭ'tion, n. Abolishing, being abolished. In the 18th & 19th cc. w. ref. to Negro slavery & the movement against it, whence also ~ISM(3), ~IST(2), (-shon-), nn. [f. F abolition or L abolitio (prec., -ION)]

A-bomb (ā'bŏm), n. Atomic bomb. [A for ATOMIC]

abŏm'ĭnable, a. Detestable, odious, morally or physically loathsome; (by conscious exaggeration) unpleasant. Hence ~leNESS (-ln-) n., ~LY[2] adv. [ME, f. OF, f. L abominabilis f. AB(ominari f. omen) deprecate; early sp. abh- due to assoc. w. L homo]

abŏm'ĭnāte[1], v.t. Loathe; (by exaggeration) dislike. [f. L abominat-; see prec.]

abŏm'ĭnāte[2], a. (poet.). Abominated. [f. L abominatus p.p., see ABOMINABLE]

abŏmĭnā'tion, n. Loathing; odious or degrading habit or act; an object of disgust (to). [ME, f. OF (ABOMINATE[1], -ATION)]

ăborĭ'gĭnal, a. & n. 1. Indigenous, existing in a land at the dawn of history, or before arrival of colonists (of races & natural objects). 2. n. (pl. ~s, but aborigines commoner). ~ inhabitant or (rarely) thing. Hence **ăborĭgĭnăl'ITY** n., ~LY[2] adv. [f. as ABORIGINES, +-AL]

ăborĭ'gĭnēs (-z), n. pl. (aboriginal usual for sing.; also the indefensible form aboriginĕ, & rarely abŏ'rĭgin or -en). First inhabitants, or those found in possession by colonists (also of native plants & animals). [L, f. phr. ab origine from the beginning]

abŏrt', v.i. Miscarry, have premature delivery of a child; (Biol.) become sterile, remain undeveloped, shrink away, (of plants & animals—the race, the individual, or part of the body). Hence ~IFA'CIENT (-āshent) a. & n., (drug or other agent) causing abortion. [f. L abort- p.p. st. of AB(oriri be born) miscarry]

abŏrt'ĕd, a. Untimely born, undeveloped; rudimentary (thorns are ~ branches). [ABORT+-ED[1] (2)]

abŏr'tion, n. Miscarriage of birth; the procuring of this, whence ~IST (1) (-shon-) n.; arrested development of any organ; a dwarfed or mis-shapen creature; failure of a project or action. [f. L abortio (ABORT, -ION)]

abŏr'tive, a. Premature (birth etc.); fruitless, unsuccessful; rudimentary (organ etc.), arrested in development. Hence ~LY[2] (-vi-) adv., ~NESS (-vn-) n. [ME, f. L abortivus (ABORT, -IVE)]

abou'lia (-ow-), abū'lia, n. Loss of will-power (as mental disorder). [f. Gk a- not +boulomai I will]

abound', v.i. 1. (Orig.) overflow, either of vessel or of liquid. 2. Be plentiful, be rich (in); teem or be infested (with). [ME, f. OF abunder etc. f. L AB(undare, f. unda wave); early sp. hab- due to assoc. w. L habēre have]

about'[1], adv. & prep. All round from outside, as compass it ~, He is ~ my path, beat ~ the bush; all round from a centre, as look or lay ~ you; somewhere round, as lie ~, hang ~ (the door), the fields ~ Oxford, people or objects ~ us, have not a penny ~ me; here and there (in a place, or abs.), as smallpox is ~, move or order ~, he put the tale ~, I was much put ~ (distracted), out & ~, restored to normal activity (after convalescence), dotted ~ the fields, man ~ town; near in number, scale, degree, etc., as ~ half, fifty, right, tired, midnight, my size (occas. much ~); facing round, as right~ turn (now ~ turn! as mil. word of command), the wrong way ~, put (the ship) or go ~; round a party, as take turns ~, read verse ~; occupied with, as ~ my father's business, send ~ his business, what are you ~?, go ~ to do, am ~ to do (so all fut. participles); in connexion with, as quarrels ~ trade, something wrong ~ it; circuitously, as he went a long way ~, I brought it ~, it came~. [OE onbūtan f. on (A[2]) +būtan BUT[1]]

about'[2], v.t. Change the course of (ship) to the other tack. [f. ABOUT adv.]

about'-slĕdge, n. Largest hammer used by smiths.

above' (-ŭv), adv., prep., a., & n. 1. adv. At a higher point (w. spec. meaning acc. to context); overhead, on high; up stream, upstairs; in heaven; on the upper side; earlier in a book or article (as was remarked ~; the ~-cited passages; the ~);

in addition (*over & ~*). **2.** prep. Over, on the top of, higher than (*~ par*; *~ oneself*, uppish, in unusual spirits etc.; *can't get ~ C*—in music), more than (*~ a hundred*), up stream from, projecting from (*head ~ water*; *heard ~ the tumult*; *~ ground* = alive), further north than, earlier in hist. than (*not traced ~ third century*), out of reach of (*~ criticism, measure, my understanding*), too great or good for (*~ meanness*, one's *station*), more important than (*~ all*), of higher rank than. **3.** adj. Preceding, previous, as *the ~ statements*. **4.** n. That which is *~*. [ME *abufan, abuven* f. A² + OE *bufan* (*be* by + *ufan* f. WG *ufana, *ubhana*, f. *uf, *ubh* UP)]

above'-board (-bōrd), adv. & pred. a. Undisguisedly; fair, open. [metaph. f. cards]

ăb ŏv'ŏ, adv. (Relating tediously) from the very beginning. [L; Hor. *A.P.* 147]

ăbracadăb'ra, n. Spell, magic formula; gibberish. Cabbalistic word supposed when written triangularly, & worn, to cure agues etc. [L (3rd c.), of unkn. orig.]

abrāde', v.t. Scrape off, injure, (skin etc.) by violent rubbing. [f. L AB(*radere ras-* scrape)]

A'brahăm-măn (ă-), n. (hist.). Wandering beggar of the 16th c., either a lunatic or feigning lunacy; hence *to sham Abram*, to feign illness or madness. [*Luke* xvi]

abrănc'hial(-ngk-), **abrănc'hiate** (-ngk-), aa. Without gills. [A-(7) + Gk *bragkhia* gills + -AL & -ATE²]

abrā'sion (-zhn), n. Scraping off (of skin etc.); the wounded place that results. So **abrās'IVE** a. & n., (substance) capable of rubbing or grinding down, tending to graze the skin. [f. LL *abrasio* ABRADE, -ION]

ăbrĕăc'tion, n. (psycho-an.). The removal by revival & expression of the emotion associated with forgotten, or repressed ideas of the event that first caused it. [AB-, REACTION; after G *abreagierung*]

abreast' (-rĕst), adv. On a level & facing the same way; keeping up, not behind, (*of* or *with* progress, thought, etc., or as prep., *~ the times*). [A² + BREAST¹]

abridge', v.t. Shorten (interview etc.); condense or epitomize (book etc.); curtail (liberty; of limbs etc. only now w. playful archaism); deprive (person *of*). [ME, f. OF *abregier* f. LL *abbreviare* ABBREVIATE¹]

abridge'ment, -**gment**, (-jm-), n. Shortening (of labour or time), curtailment (of rights); epitome, abstract. [ME, f. OF *abregement* f. *abregier* (prec., -MENT)]

abroach', adv. & pred. a. Pierced, so as to let the liquor run (of casks). [A² + BROACH²]

abroad' (-rawd), adv. Broadly, widely, in different directions; in motion (*there is a rumour ~; the schoolmaster is ~*, education is now becoming generally accessible); out of doors, in or to foreign lands; in error (*all ~*). Also treated as a noun

in *from ~*. [A² + BROAD a.; cf. *along, at large*]

ăb'rogāte, v.t. Repeal, cancel, (law or custom). So **ăbrogA'TION** n. [f. p.p. of L AB(*rogare* propose law); see -ATE³]

abrŭpt', a. Sudden, hasty, disconnected; steep, precipitous; (Bot.) truncated; suddenly cropping out (of geol. strata). Hence *~LY²* adv., *~NESS* n. [f. L *abruptus* p.p. of AB(*rumpere* break)]

abrŭp'tion, n. Breaking away of part from a mass. [f. L *abruptio* (ABRUPT, -ION)]

abs-, pref., variant, in L, of *ab*; see AB-.

ăb'scess (-sĕs), n. Collection of pus formed in a cavity of the body. [f. L *abscessus* a going away f. ABS(*cedere cess-* go)]

ăb'sciss(e) (-sĭs; pl. -*es*), **absci'ssa** (-sĭ-; pl. -*ae*), n. Portion of given line intercepted between fixed point within it & ordinate drawn to it from given point without it. [L *abscissa* (*linea*) p.p. of AB(*scindere sciss-* cut)]

absci'ssion (-sĭshn), n. (surg.). Cutting off, violent separation. [f. L *abscissio* (see prec., -ION)]

abscŏnd', v.i. Go away secretly, fly from the law. Hence *~ENCE, ~ER¹*, nn. [f. L ABS(*condere* stow, f. *dare* put)]

ăb'sence, n. Being away from a place or person; time of being away; nonexistence or want *of*; abstraction of thought (esp. *in phr. ~ of mind*); ‖ roll-call. [ME, f. OF *absence* f. L *absentia* (*absent-* ABSENT¹)]

ăb'sent¹, a. **1.** Not present; not existing. **2.** Abstracted in mind, whence *~LY²* adv., *~-min'*DED² a., *~-min'dĕdLY²* adv., *~-min'dĕd*NESS, *~NESS*, nn. [ME, f. OF *absent* f. L *absentem* part. of AB(*esse* be)]

absĕnt'², v.refl. Keep oneself away. [ME, f. F *absenter* f. LL *absentare* f. *absent-* ABSENT¹]

ăbsentee', n. A person not present; a person, esp. a landlord (& formerly parson), habitually living away from home. Hence *~ISM* (2) n., practice of being an *~*, practice of workers of absenting themselves from work, esp. frequently or without good reason. [ABSENT² + -EE]

ăb'sinth, n. Wormwood, the plant or its essence; a liqueur made (orig. at least) from wine & wormwood. [f. F *absinthe* f. L f. Gk *apsinthion*]

ăb'sĭt ŏm'ĕn, sent. May no ominous significance attach to the words, may my fears not be verified. [L]

ăb'solute (-ōōt, -ūt), a. Complete, perfect, pure (as *~ alcohol*), mere; unrestricted, independent; ruling arbitrarily; out of grammatical relation (*ablative ~* in L, *genitive ~* in Gk, *~ construction* in E, noun & participle used as adverbial clause, as *dinner being over we left the table*); real, not merely relative or comparative; unqualified, unconditional; self-existent & conceivable without relation to other things (*the ~*, as noun); *~ magnitude*

(Astron.), the magnitude of a star if at a standard distance of 10 parsecs : ~ *music*, self-dependent instrumental music devoid of literary suggestions; ~ *pitch* (Mus.), ability to recognize or reproduce the pitch of a note ; ~ ZERO. Hence ~NESS (-tn-) n. [ME, f. L *absolutus* p.p. see ABSOLVE]

ăb'solutely (-ōōtlĭ, -ūt-), adv. Independently, in & by itself ; arbitrarily, without external control ; without qualification ; without the usual accompaniments (as *a transitive vb used* ~, i.e. without its obj.) ; unconditionally ; positively, though you would not believe it ; conclusively, completely, quite ; at all (w. negatives) ; ‖ (colloq.) quite so, yes. [f. prec. +-LY²]

ăbsolu'tion (-lōō-, -lū-), n. Formal setting free from guilt, sentence, or obligation ; ecclesiastical declaration of forgiveness of sins ; remission of penance ; forgiveness. [ME, f. OF f. L *absolutionem* (ABSOLVE, -ION)]

ăb'solutism (-lōō-, -lū-), n. (Theol.) doctrine that God acts absolutely in the affair of salvation ; (Pol.) principle of absolute government. [ABSOLUTE +-ISM (3)]

ăb'solutist (-lōō-, -lū-), n. Partisan of political absolutism (also adj., as ~ *principles*) ; a metaphysician who identifies subject & object. [ABSOLUTE +-IST (2)]

absŏlve' (-s-, -z-), v.t. Set, pronounce, free (*from* blame etc., *of* sin, *from* obligation etc., or abs.) ; acquit, pronounce not guilty. [f. L AB(*solvere, solut-* loosen)]

ăb'sonant, a. Discordant, alien (*from*), unreasonable. [f. AB-+*sonant-* part. st. of L *sonare* sound on anal. of *dissonant, consonant*, & L *absonus*]

absŏrb', v.t. Swallow up, incorporate (*be* ~*ed by*, lose one's identity in) ; engross the attention of ; suck in (liquids) ; take in (heat, light, etc.) by chemical or molecular action. [f. F *absorber* f. L AB(*sorbēre sorpt-* suck in)]

absŏrb'|able, a. Easily sucked in. Hence ~ABIL'ITY n. [prec. + -ABLE]

absŏrbed' (-bd), a. Intensely engaged or interested. Hence ~LY² (-b'ĕdlĭ) adv. [p.p. of ABSORB]

absŏrbĕfā'cient (-shent), a. & n. Causing the absorption or drying up (e.g. of a tumour) ; agent that does this. [f. L *absorbēre* ABSORB +-FACIENT]

absŏrb'ent, a. & n. 1. Having tendency to suck in (abs., or *of*). 2. n. Substance of this kind ; one of the vessels in plants & animals (e.g. root tips) that absorb nutriment. [f. L *absorbent-* part. st. of *absorbēre* ABSORB]

absŏrb'ing, a. Engrossing, intensely interesting. Hence ~LY² adv. [part. of ABSORB]

absŏrp'tion, n. Disappearance through incorporation in something else ; natural or medical removal of tissues ; mental engrossment ; sucking in of fluid, light, etc., or nutriment. [f. LL *absorptio* (ABSORB, -ION)]

absŏrp'tive, a. Having a tendency to

suck in. Hence ~NESS (-vn-) n. [f. L *absorpt-* (ABSORB, -IVE)]

absquat'ūlāte (-ŏt-), v.i. Make off, decamp. [American-made jocular vb w. L pref. & suf.]

abstain', v.i. Keep oneself away, refrain, (*from*) ; refrain from alcohol, whence ~ER¹ n., ~ING² a. [ME, f. F *abstenir* f. L ABS(*tinēre tent-* = *tenēre* hold)]

abstēm'ious, a. Sparing, not self-indulgent, esp. in food and drink. Used of persons, habits, meals. Hence ~LY² adv., ~NESS n. [f. L *abstemius* +-OUS]

abstĕn'tion, n. Keeping off (abs., or *from* any pleasure) ; esp., not using one's vote. [F, f. L *abstent-* (ABSTAIN, -ION)]

abstĕr'gent, a. & n. Cleansing ; a cleansing substance. [f. L *abstergent-* part. st. of ABS(*tergēre ters-* wipe)]

abstĕr'sion (-shn), n. Cleansing, purgation. [f. L *absters-* (see ABSTERGENT) +-ION ; cf. LL *abstersio*]

abstĕr'sive, a. Cleansing. [as prec., -IVE]

ăb'stinence, n. Refraining (*from* any pleasure, or abs. in sense of continence, fasting, or, usu. *total* ~, going without alcohol) ; occas. = foll. [ME, f. OF, or L *abstinentia* (ABSTINENT, -ENCE)]

ăb'stinency, n. Habit of refraining from pleasures, esp. food. [see prec. & -ENCY]

ăb'stinent, a. Practising abstinence. Hence ~LY² adv. [ME, f. OF, or L *abstinent-* (ABSTAIN, -ENT)]

ăb'străct¹, a. Separated from matter, practice, or particular examples, not concrete ; ideal, not practical ; abstruse ; (with *the*, as noun) the ideal or theoretical way of regarding things (*in the* ~). Hence ~LY² adv., ~NESS n. [ME, f. L *abstractus* p.p. of ABS(*trahere* draw)]

ăb'străct², n. Essence, summary ; abstraction or abstract term. [see prec.]

abstrăct'³, v.t. Deduct, remove, (an obj. *much* etc. is occas. omitted) ; (euphem.) steal ; disengage (obj. *attention* etc. occas. omitted) *from* ; consider apart from the concrete ; summarize. [f. ABSTRACT¹]

abstrăct'ĕd, a. Withdrawn in thought, not attending. Hence ~NESS n. [-ED¹]

abstrăct'ĕdly, adv. In the abstract, ideally ; separately (*from*—esp. after *consider*) ; in an absent-minded way. [-LY²]

abstrăc'tion, n. Taking away, withdrawal ; (euphem.) stealing ; process of stripping an idea of its concrete accompaniments ; the idea so stripped, something visionary ; absence of mind. [f. F, or L *abstractio* (ABSTRACT¹, -ION)]

abstruse' (-ōōs), a. Hard to understand, profound. Hence ~LY² adv., ~NESS (-sn-) n. [f. F, or L ABS(*trusus* p.p. of *trudere* push)]

absŭrd', a. Incongruous, unreasonable, ridiculous, silly. Hence ~LY² adv. [f. F, or L *absurdus* (*ab-* +*surdus* deaf, dull)]

absŭrd'ity, n. Folly, unreasonableness ; an absurd statement or act. [f. F *absurdité* or LL *absurditas* (ABSURD, -ITY)] abŭn′dance, n. Quantity more than sufficient, plenty; overflowing emotion (~ *of the heart*); many people (*there are* ~ *who*); affluence, wealth. [ME, f. OF *abundance* f. L *abundantia* (as foll., -ANCE)]

abŭn′dant, a. More than sufficient, plentiful; rich (*in*). Hence ~LY² adv. [ME, f. OF *abundant* |f. L *abundant*- part. st. (ABOUND, -ANT)]

ăb urb′ě cŏn′dĭtā, adv. (abbr. A.U.C.). Counting from the foundation of Rome (753 B.C.). [L]

abūse′¹ (-z), v.t. Misuse, make bad use of; deceive (arch., but still used esp. in pass.); maltreat (arch.); revile. [ME, f. OF *abuser* f. Rom. **abusare* f. AB(*us*- p.p. st. of *uti* USE²)]

abūs|e′² (-s), n. Misuse, perversion (*of*); an established unjust or corrupt practice; reviling, whence ~′IVE a.,~′IVELY² (-vl-) adv.,~′IVENESS (-vn-) n. [ME, f. OF *abus* or L *abusus* n. f. *abus*- see prec.]

abŭt′, v.t.(-tt-). Have a common boundary with, border, (*upon*; or occas. without prep. as trans. vb; of estates or countries); end *on* or *against*, lean *on*, (of parts of a building). [sense 'border upon' f. OF *abouter* (*bout* end); sense 'end on' f. OF *abuter* (*but* end)]

abŭt′ment, n. A lateral support; (esp. in architecture) that on which an arch or bridge rests; point of junction between such support & thing supported. [ABUT +-MENT]

abŭtt′er, n. (In law) owner of the adjoining property. [ABUT +-ER¹]

abȳ(e)′, v.t. (arch.; past & p.p. *abought*). Redeem, pay the penalty of, (an offence); usu. w. *dearly, sore*). [OE *ābycgan*, f. A-(1) +BUY]

abȳsm′ (-z-), n. Earlier form, still used in poetical style, of ABYSS. [ME *abime* f. OF f. med. L *abysmus* (L *abyssus* +-ISM) ABYSS, to which the sp. later conforms]

abȳs′mal (-z-), a. Bottomless, esp. fig., as ~ *ignorance*. Hence ~LY² (-z-) adv. [ABYSM +-AL]

abȳss′, n. The primal chaos, bowels of the earth, lower world; a bottomless chasm, deep gorge; depth (~ *of light*). [f. LL *abyssus* f. Gk *abussos* bottomless]

abȳss′al, a. More than 300 fathoms below sea surface (water, zone, mud). [f. prec. +-AL; cf. F *abyssal*]

ac-, pref., assim. form of AD- before c-, k-, qu-. Occas. erron. for a- (of various orig.; see A-), as in *acknowledge*. See also AD-(2).

-ăc, suf. forming adjj., which are often also (if not only) used as nouns. From Gk -*akos*, the modification of adj. suf. -*kos* appended to nouns in -*ia*, -*ios*, -*ion*, & imitated in L. E wds in -*ac* may be f. Gk (-*akos*), L (-*acus*), or F (-*aque*).

acā′cia (-sha), n. Shrub or tree, of mimosa tribe, yielding gum arabic; the locust-tree or false~, grown for ornament; gum arabic. [L, f. Gk *akakia*]

ăc′adēme, n. (Prop.) = Academus (see ACADEMY); (used by mistake in poetic style for) the Gk Academy, a college, university. [Gk *Akadēmos* see ACADEMY; mistake perh. caused by Milton's 'grove of Academe', *P. R.* iv. 244]

ăcadĕm′ic, a. & n. 1. Belonging to or agreeing with the philosophic school of Plato (ACADEMY), (w. ref. to some of his successors' views) sceptical; an ancient Platonist. 2. Scholarly, (& by implication) abstract, unpractical, cold, merely logical; (as sing. noun) member of a university, one too much enslaved to the principles (in painting etc.) of an academy; (as pl. noun) merely theoretic arguments, university robes. 3. Of an academician or academy (~ *rank*). [f. L *academicus* (a. & n.); see ACADEMY; -IC]

ăcadĕm′ical, a. Belonging to a college or university; (as pl. noun) college costume (commoner than *academics*). [prec. +-AL]

ăcadĕm′ically, adv. Theoretically, unpractically; rarely also in any of the senses of the two precc. [prec. +-LY²]

acăd′emi′cian (-shn), n. Member of an Academy or art society, ǁ esp. of the Royal Academy of Arts. [f. F *académicien* f. L *academicus* ACADEMIC; see -IAN]

Acăd′emy, n. 1. The garden near Athens in which Plato taught; Plato's followers or philosophical system. 2. (a~). A place of study, including universities, ǁ but occas. used pretentiously or depreciatingly of something between a school & a university. 3. A place of training in a special art (Royal Military ~). 4. A society for cultivating literature, art, etc., of which membership is an honour, ǁ esp. the Royal ~ of Arts; ǁ the R.A.'s annual exhibition. [f. F *académie* or f. L f. Gk *akadēmeia* (*Akadēmos* the man or demigod f. whom Plato's garden was named)]

Acăd′ian, a. & n. Nova-Scotian. [f. F *Acadie* Nova Scotia +-AN]

ăc′ajou (-zhoo), n. CASHEW. [F, see CASHEW]

-acal, compd suf. = -AC +-AL. Adjj. in -*ac* being often used as nouns also, -*al* was appended to distinguish the adj. (*demoniac*, -*acal*), & even when there was no noun (*heliacal*). In adjj. -*acal* often differs f. -*ac* in suggesting looser connexion w. the orig. noun; e.g., *cardiac arteries* (*of the* heart), *cardiacal herbs* (*having influence on the* heart).

ăc′alēph, -ephe (-ěf), n. Jellyfish, medusa, sea-nettle. [Gk *akalēphē* nettle]

acăn′thus, n. Kinds of prickly-leaved plants, esp. bear's breech or brank-ursine; a conventional representation of its leaf used in Gk architecture. Hence acanth(o)-comb. form. [L, f. Gk *akanthos* (*akantha* thorn f. *akē* point)]

ăcăr′pĕll′ous, a. Without carpels. [A- (7), CARPEL, -OUS]

acărp′ous, a. (bot.). Not producing fruit. [A- (7) +Gk *karpos* fruit +-OUS]

acătălĕc′tic, a. & n. (A verse) not docked of a syllable, complete. [f. LL *acatalecticus* f. Gk *akatalēktos* (see A- (7), CATALECTIC)]

acăt′alĕpsў, n. Incomprehensibility (philos. term), the quality in the object answering to agnosticism in the subject. So **acătalĕp′tic a.** [f. med. L f. Gk *akatalēpsia* f. A- (7) + *katalambanō* grasp]

acaul′ous, a. (also -ĕs′cent, -īne, -ōse). (bot.). Apparently stemless, having very short stem. [A- (7) + L *caulis* stem + -OUS]

Accăd′īan, a. & n. 1. Of Accad in Shinar (*Gen.* x. 10). **2.** n. A language preserved in cuneiform inscriptions. [-IAN]

accēde′ (aks-), v.i. Enter upon an office; join a party; assent to an opinion or policy. Abs., or w. *to* if the office etc. is stated, in all senses. [f. L AC(*cedere* cess-come)]

accĕlerăn′dō (aks-), musical direction. Gradually increase speed. [It.]

accĕl′erāte (aks-), v.t. & i. Make quicker; cause to happen earlier; become swifter (of a motion or process); put on pace. [f. p.p. of L AC(*celerare* f. *celer* swift); see -ATE² ′ ³]

accĕl′erātĕd (aks-), a. (phys.). Progressively quicker (~ *motion*). Hence ~LY² adv. [p.p. of prec.]

accĕl′erāting (aks-), a. Causing progressively quicker motion (~ *force*). [-ING²]

accĕlerā′tion (aks-), n. 1. Making quicker; being made quicker. **2.** (phys.). Rate of increase of velocity per time unit, as with falling bodies. **3.** (astron.). ~ *of stars*, time gained daily by them over sun; ~ *of planets*, increased velocity from aphelion to perihelion; ~ *of moon*, increase in speed of mean motion; ~ *of tides*, amount of local advance on calculated time. [f. L *acceleratio* (ACCELERATE, -ION) or F *accélération*]

accĕl′erātive, a. Tending to increase speed, quickening. [f. ACCELERATE + -IVE]

accĕl′erātor (aks-), n. Person or thing that increases anything's speed, esp. an attachment in motor-cars for this purpose; one of a class of nerves & muscles. [ACCELERATE + -OR]

ăc′cent¹ (áks-), n. 1. Prominence given to a syllable, whether by higher musical pitch (ancient Gk & L, Swedish & Norw.), or by stress (most mod. languages, but perh. not F). Three marks called *acute* (′), *grave* (`), & *circumflex* (^ or ^) accents (systematically employed in Gk, & to a less degree in F) used for various purposes, e.g. to indicate syllabic pitch (Gk), quality of vowel sound (F), etymological hist. (F, E), metrical stress, syllabic stress (dictionaries etc.), the fact of a letter's not being silent, or conventional distinction between homonyms (F). **2.** Individual, local, or national mode of pronunciation; modulation to express feeling;

in pl., speech (poet.). **3.** (In prosody) rhythmical stress. **4.** (mus.). Stress recurring at intervals, regular or otherwise. **5.** (fig.). Intensity, sharp distinction. [F, or f. L *accentus* (*cantus* song) repr. Gk *prosōidia* (PROSODY)]

accent′ ¹(aks-), v.t. Pronounce with accent, emphasize (word or syllable); put the written accents on; heighten, make conspicuous. [f. obs. F *accenter* see prec.]

accĕn′tor (aks-), n. Kinds of bird (= WARBLER), esp. the hedge-sparrow, which name is now occas. avoided as misleading. [cf. LL *accentor*, f. *ad* to + *cantor* singer]

accĕn′tūal (aks-), a. Of accent; *prosody* or *verse*, of which the principle is accent or stress, not quantity. Hence ~LY² adv. [f. L *accentus* ACCENT¹ + -AL]

accĕn′tūāte (aks-), v.t. = ACCENT², but more used than it in the fig. sense. [f. F *accentuer* or its source med. L *accentuare* (ACCENT¹, -ATE³)]

accĕntūā′tion (aks-), n. Accenting (all senses from ACCENT). [f. as prec., -ION; cf. med. L *accentuatio*]

accĕpt′ (aks-), v.t. Consent to receive (gift), answer affirmatively (offer, invitation, suitor); regard with favour (esp. unfair favour, as ~ *the person of*, ~ *persons*); receive as adequate (~ *service of writ*), allow the truth of, believe; undertake (office); take responsibility for, agree to meet, (bill of exchange). *Of* may be added (exc. w, *service of writ*, *bill*) with a slight suggestion of formality or condescension. Hence ~ER¹ n. [ME, f. OF *accepter* or L *acceptare* frequent. of AC(*cipere* = *capere* take)]

accĕpt′|able (aks-), a. Worth accepting, pleasing, welcome. Hence or cogn. ~abLY² adv., ~abIL′ITY, ~ableNESS, nn. [ME, f. OF, or LL *acceptabilis* (ACCEPT, -ABLE)]

accĕpt′ance (aks-), n. Consent to receive (gift, payment, pleasure, duty); favourable reception (act. & pass.), approval, belief; ~ *of persons*, partiality; engagement to meet a bill; a bill so accepted. [F, see ACCEPT & -ANCE]

accĕptā′tion (äks-), n. A particular sense given to a word or phrase; its generally recognized meaning. [ME, f. OF, f. LL *acceptatio* (ACCEPT, -ATION)]

accĕpt′ĕd (aks-), a. Generally recognized or believed in (*Free & A~ Masons*, see FREE¹-*mason*). Hence ~LY² adv. [-ED¹]

accĕpt′or (aks-), n. One who accepts a bill (preferred to *accepter* in this sense). [f. ACCEPT; see -OR]

ăc′cĕss (-ks-; *also* aksĕs′), n. Approach; addition; right or means of approaching (*to*); being approached (*easy of* ~); advance (~ *& recess*); passage, channel, doorway; adhesion, growth, (usu. now *accession*); attack or outburst (*of* illness, anger, emotion). [ME, f. OF *aces, acces* or L *accessus* f. AC(*cedere* cess- come)]

accessarў (aksĕs′-, ăk′sĭs-), n. & pred. a.

(see also ACCESSORY). Helper in any act, one privy *to* it (as pred. a., *be* ~, *were made* ~); accompaniment, adjunct. [f. med. L *accessarius* (ACCEDE, -ARY¹); freq. confused w. *accessory*]

accĕss′i|ble (aks-), a. Able to be reached or entered (abs., or *to*); open to influence, to the influence of, (*to*). Hence ~BIL′ITY n., ~bLY² adv. [F, or LL *accessibilis* (ACCEDE, -BLE)]

accession (aksĕ′shn), n. Coming into presence or contact; coming into an office (esp. the throne) or condition (as manhood); being added; assent; thing added, addition; (in law) improvement or natural growth of property. [F, f. L *accessionem* (ACCEDE, -ION)]

accessor|ў (aksĕs′-, ăk′sĭs-), a. & n. (see also ACCESSARY). **1.** Additional, subordinately contributive (of things), adventitious. **2.** n. Thing of that character, esp. in pl. *the* ~*ies*. [f. med. L *accessorius* (ACCEDE, -ORY)]

acciaccatura (achahkatoor′a), n. (mus.). Grace-note performed quickly before an essential note of a melody. [It.]

ac′cĭdence (ăks-), n. The part of grammar, or a book, dealing with the variable forms of words; the elements of any subject. [f. L *accidentia* (tr. Gk *parepomena*) neut. pl. of *accidens* (ACCIDENT, -ENCE)]

ac′cident (ăks-), n. Event without apparent cause, unexpected (so *chapter of* ~*s*, unforeseen course of events); unintentional act, chance, fortune, (*by* ~); mishap; irregularity in structure; a property not essential to our conception of a substance (so of material qualities of bread & wine after transubstantiation; a mere accessory. [ME, f. OF f. L *accident-* part. st. of AC(*cidere* = *cadere* fall)]

accidĕn′tal (ăks-), a. & n. **1.** Happening by chance, undesignedly, or unexpectedly; occasional; not essential to a conception (so also *an*~ as n.); subsidiary. **2.** (mus.). ~ *sharps, flats, naturals,* & ~ as noun, signs attached to single notes, not in signature. **3.** (optics). ~ *colours,* those presented by subjective sensation, not external. **4.** (painting) ~ *lights,* & ~*s* as n., effects of other than ordinary daylight. [ME, f. OF (now -el), f. LL *accidentalis* (prec., -AL)]

accidĕn′tally (ăks-), adv. By chance, unintentionally. [-LY²]

ac′cĭdie (ăks-), acĕd′ia, nn. Sloth, torpor; despair. [ME, f. AN *accidie* f. med. L *accidia* alt. f. LL *acedia* f. Gk *akēdia* (A- (7), *kēdos* care)]

accip′itral (aks-), a. Hawklike; rapacious; keensighted. [f. L *accipitr-* nom. *-ter* hawk +-AL]

acclaim′¹, v.t. Applaud loudly or enthusiastically; (w. obj. & compl.) hail as (king, winner, saviour; ~*ed him king*). [ME, f. L AC(*clamare* shout), spelling assimilated to CLAIM]

acclaim′², n. Shout of applause. [f. prec.]

ācclamā′tion, n. Loud & eager assent to a proposal (*voted, carried, by* ~); shouting in a person's honour (usu. pl.). [f. L *acclamatio* (prec., -ATION)]

ăcclimā′tion, n. = acclimatization (see foll.), or distinguished from it as a natural process, not imposed on animals by man. [irreg. f. *acclimate* (foll.)]

|| **acclim′atīze, -ise** (-īz; also, esp. U.S., ăcc′limăte), v.t. & i. Habituate (animals, plants, one*self*) to new climate; (rarely) become so habituated. Hence || **acclimatīzA′TION** (also, esp. U.S., **acclimatā′-tion)** n. [f. F *acclimater* (earlier adopted as *acclimate*) +-IZE]

accliv′itў, n. Upward slope of a hill (cf. DECLIVITY). [f. L *acclivitas* f. AC(*clivis* f. *clivus* slope)]

ăccolāde′ (or -ahd), n. **1.** Sign at bestowal of knighthood, whether embrace, kiss, or stroke on shoulder with flat of sword. **2.** (mus.). Vertical line or brace coupling staves. [F, f. Prov. *accollada* n. from p.p. st. of Rom. *accollare* (AC-+L *collum* neck)]

accŏmm′odāte, v.t. Adapt (thing or person *to* another); prove such adaptation in, harmonize, (prova. w. implication of sophistry); reconcile, settle differences between; compose (quarrel); equip, supply, (person *with*); oblige, confer favour on; find lodging for. [f. p.p. of L AC(*commodare -at-* f. *commodus* fitting), -ATE², ³]

accŏmm′odāting, a. Obliging, easy to deal with, pliable, lax. Hence ~LY² adv. [-ING²]

accŏmmodā′tion, n. Adjustment (e.g. of eyes for various distances); adaptation of anything to a purpose or meaning different from the original; self-adaptation; settlement, compromise; serviceable thing, convenience (so in comp. as ~*-road;* ~*-ladder,* up ship's side); lodgings, entertainment; money loan (so in ~-BILL⁴); ~ *unit,* a home. [F, or f. L *accommodatio* (ACCOMMODATE, -ION)]

accom′paniment (-ŭm-), n. **1.** Appendage, thing that attends another. **2.** (mus.).Subsidiary part, usu. instrumental, supporting solo instrument or voice, choir, etc. [f. foll.+-MENT, after F *accompagnement*]

accom′pan|ў (-ŭm-), v.t. **1.** Supplement (a thing *with,* as word w. blow); go with, escort, attend; coexist with (of things), characterize. **2.** (mus.). Support (singer, player, chorus) by performing subsidiary part, whence ~(ў)IST (-ŭm-) n. After pass., *by* has almost ousted older *with,* now only used when ~*ied* = *combined.* [ME, f. OF *acompagner* (à to +*compaing* COMPANION)]

accŏm′plice (or -ŭm-), n. Partner, usu. subordinate, in crime. [late ME, f. earlier & F *complice* (prob. by assoc. w. foll.), f. LL *complic-em;* see COMPLICITY]

accŏm'plish (*or* -ŭm-), v.t. **1.** Fulfil, perform, complete, finish. **2.** Perfect (a person) in graceful acquirements, whence ~ED[1] (-sht) a. [ME, f. OF *acomplir* f. L *complēre* COMPLETE; see AC-, -ISH[2]]

accŏm'plishment (*or* -ŭm-), n. Fulfilment, completion; thing done or attained, achievement; faculty that perfects a person for society, (derog.) merely superficial acquirement. [late ME, f. F *accomplissement*; see prec., -MENT]

accompt, -ant, arch. for ACCOUNT, -ANT.

accŏrd'[1], v.t. & i. Be in harmony or consistent (abs., or *with*; chiefly of things); grant (indulgence, request, welcome, etc.). [ME, f. OF *acorder* f. Rom. *AC-(cordare* f. *cor cordis* heart)]

accŏrd'[2], n. Consent (*with one* ~), mutual agreement; treaty of peace; harmonious correspondence in colour, pitch, tone; volition (*of one's own* ~). [ME, f. OF *acord* (prec.)]

accŏrd'ance, n. Conformity, agreement, esp. in phr. *in* ~ *with*. [ME, f. OF *acordance* (as prec., -ANCE)]

accŏrd'ant, a. In tune, agreeing, (abs., or *with*). Hence ~LY[2] adv. [ME, f. OF *acordant* (as prec., -ANT)]

accŏrd'ing, adv. (only now in the compd conj. ~ *as,* & the compd prep. ~ *to*). ~ *as*: in proportion as (of a process varying w. another); in a manner depending on which of certain alternatives is true. ~ *to*: in a manner consistent with or degree proportioned to; as stated by. [-ING[2]]

accŏrd'inglў, adv. As the (stated) circumstances suggest; therefore; ~ *as*=*according as.* [-LY[2]]

accŏrd'ion, n. Portable musical instrument having bellows, metal reeds, & keyboard &/or buttons. Hence ~IST (3) n. [f. G *akkordion*]

accŏst'[1], v.t. Make up to & address, open conversation with; (of prostitute) solicit. [f. F *accoster* f. It. *accostare* f. Rom. *AC(costare* f. *costa* rib; see COAST)]

accŏst'[2], n. Greeting, opening remark. [f. prec.]

accouchement (see Ap.), n. Lying-in, delivery in childbed. [F]

accoucheur (see Ap.), n. (fem. *-euse*). Man-midwife, midwife. [F]

account'[1], v.t. & i. Consider, regard as, (followed by obj. & compl. or inf.; ~ *him a hero, wise, to be guilty*). *Be* ~*ed of,* be esteemed (alw. w. *little, much,* etc.). ~ *for,* give reckoning of (money held in trust); answer for (conduct, performance of duty); explain the cause of; serve as explanation of (*that* ~*s for it*); (sport) be responsible for the death of, kill. [ME, f. OF *aconter* f. *a-* AC- +*conter* COUNT[2]]

account'[2], n. **1.** Counting, calculation, in phrr. *cast* ~*s* (reckon up), *money of* ~ (names not of coins, but of sums, as guinea). **2.** Reckoning of debit & credit, in money or service; statement of money received & expended, with balance; so *open* or *close an* ~ *with,* render or send in, pay or settle, *an* ~; ~ *current* (whence a/c = account), one kept going w. occasional entries (now usu. *current* ·~); ~ *rendered,* used when a bill previously sent in, but left unpaid, is sent again; *joint* ~*s,* in which two persons not otherwise partners count as one; *keep* ~*s,* enter all expenditure for comparison w. income; *balance* or *square* ~*s with* person, receive or pay the balance due; *cash, profit-&-loss,* etc., ~, headings of subdivision in ledger; ∥ *sale for the* ~, on the Stock Exch., not for cash, but payable at next periodic settlement; *A in* ~ *with B,* having credit relations with; *for* ~ *of,* to be sold for (person); *on* ~, as interim payment; *on one's* ~, for his service; *on one's own* ~, for & at one's own purposes & risk, whence generally *on* ~ *of,* because of, & *on no* ~, by no means, certainly not. *A favourable result of the reckoning, profit; find one's* ~ *in,* profit by, *turn to* ~, make useful. *Statement of administration as required by creditor; ask, demand, yield, render, an* ~, *call* or *bring to* ~, extended from money to conduct generally, so *the great* ~, Day of Judgement, *gone to his* ~, dead; *give* ~ *of,* find cause of, explain, (in sport) *give a good* ~ *of oneself,* be successful. **3.** Estimation; person or thing *of,* or *held in, some* or *no* ~; *make little* ~ *of*; *take into, leave out of,* ~; *take* ~ *of*; *lay* ~*s with,* include in one's calculations, expect. **4.** Narration, report, description, of event, person, etc. [ME, f. OF *acont*; see prec. & COUNT[2]]

account'|able, a. Bound to give account, responsible, (*for* things, *to* persons, or abs.); explicable (occas. followed by *for*). Hence ~ABIL'ITY, ~ableNESS, nn. [f. ACCOUNT[1] +-ABLE]

accoun'tant, n. **1.** (Law) one liable to render account; defendant in an action of account. **2.** Professional keeper & inspector of accounts; ~*-general,* chief ~ in public offices. Hence accoun'tANCY n., profession of an ~, ~SHIP n., office of an ~. [f. part. of OF *aconter* ACCOUNT[1]; see -ANT]

accou'tre (-ōoter), v.t. (*-tring, -tred*). Attire, equip, esp. w. special costume (chiefly used in p.p.). [f. F *accoutrer* (OF *-coust-*) of uncert. orig.]

accou'trement (-ōot-), n. (usu. in pl.). Equipment, trappings; (Mil.) soldier's outfit other than arms & garments. [F (prec., -MENT]

accrĕd'it, v.t. Gain belief or influence for (adviser, advice); send out (ambassador etc.) with credentials *to* person, *to* or *at a* court or government; ~ *thing* (saying, policy) *to* person, or ~ *him with* it, put it down to him. [f. F AC(*créditer* f. *crédit* CREDIT)]

accrĕd'ited, a. Officially recognized (persons); generally accepted, orthodox, (beliefs). [p.p. of prec.]

accrēte'¹, v.t. & i. Grow together or into one; form round or on to, as round a nucleus; attract (such additions). [f. L *accret-* p.p. st. of AC(*crescere* grow)]

accrēte'², a. (bot.). Grown into one with something else. [f.L *accretus* p.p. see prec.]

accrē'tion, n. Growth by organic enlargement; the growing of separate things (as particles) into one; the whole resulting from this; adhesion of extraneous matter to anything; the matter so added; (Law) = ACCESSION, also increase of legacy etc. by share of failing co-legatee. [f. L *accretio* (ACCRETE¹, -ION)]

accru|e' (-ōō), v.i. Fall (to one, from a thing) as a natural growth, advantage, result; esp. of interest on invested money. Hence ~ED¹ (-ōōd') a. [late ME, f. OF *accreu(e)*, p.p. of *acreistre* (mod. *accroître*) f. L *accrescere* ACCRETE¹]

accūm'ūlāte, v.t. & i. Heap up, gain by degrees, (usu. fig., a fortune, ill will, etc., or abs.), amass, make money; ‖ take (University degrees) by accumulation (obj. expressed, or abs.), i.e. more than one step at a time; grow numerous, form an increasing mass or heap (lit. & fig., as *dirt, disasters, had ~d*). [f. p.p. of L AC(*cumulare* f. *cumulus* heap), -ATE², ³]

accūmūlā'tion, n. Collection (act. or pass.), amassing; money-making; growth of capital by continued interest; combination of distinct acts into one (degrees, see prec., or church services etc.); a mass (as snow, papers, property). [F, or f. med. L *accumulatio* (prec., -ION)]

accūm'ūlative, a. Arising from accumulation (~ *proof*, *evidence*, now being ousted by *cumulative*); so arranged as to accumulate (sinking fund); acquisitive, given to hoarding. Hence ~LY² (-vl-) adv. [as prec. +-IVE]

accūm'ūlātor, n. One who collects; money-maker; ‖ taker of degrees by accumulation; ‖ storage cell, battery. [L (as prec., -OR)]

ăcc'ūr|ate, a. Careful, precise, in exact conformity with a standard or with truth. Hence ~ACY n., ~atelY² (-tl-) adv. [f. L AC(*curare* f. *cura* care), -ATE²]

accūrs'ĕd, accūrst', a. Lying under a curse, ill-fated; involving misery, execrable, detestable. [ME f. CURSE, with *a-* (= A- 1) as intensive, on anal. of *awake, arise*]

accūs'al (-z-), n. Sometimes used for foll. [f. ACCUSE +-AL (2)]

ăccūsā'tion (-z-), n. Accusing; being accused; a charge of offence or crime; indictment. [ME, f. OF, f. L *accuṣationem* (ACCUSE, -ION)]

accūs'ative (-z-), a. & n. ~ *case* (or ~ as n.), the grammatical case used in Gk & L for the goal of motion or obj. of action; in uninflected languages, applied to the wd that stands as obj., though with no mark of case. Hence **accūsativ'AL** (-z-) adj., ~LY² (-z-; -vl-) adv. [ME, f. OF (-*if*, -*ive*)

or L (*casus*) *accusalivus*, transl. Gk (*ptōsis*) *aitiatikē*]

accūsatōr'ial (-z-), a. ~ *procedure* etc., in which prosecutor & judge are not the same, opposed to *inquisitorial*. [as foll. +-AL]

accūs'atory (-z-), a. ~ *language, manner*, etc., conveying or implying accusation. [f. L *accusatorius* (foll., -ORY)]

accūs|e' (-z), v.t. **1.** Charge with a fault, indict, (person), whence p.p. as noun, *the ~ed*; blame, lay the fault on, (person or thing, as *the times*); ~e as offender, of offence. **2.** Point to (subj. *evidence* etc., obj. a person). Hence ~'ER¹ (-z-) n., ~'ingLY² (-z-) adv. [ME *acuse* f. OF *acuser* f. L AC(*cusare* f. *causa* CAUSE)]

accūs'tom, v.t. Habituate (oneself, person, or thing, *to* do or *to*; commoner in pass.). [late ME, f. OF *acostumer* f. a-AC- +*costume* CUSTOM]

accūs'tomed (-md), a. In vbl senses; also, usual. [p.p. of prec. in obs. sense *make usual*]

āce, n. **1.** The one on dice (*ambs-~*, throw of two ones; *deuce ~*, throw of two & one, formerly two ones); the one on cards or dominoes; card etc. so marked. **2.** One point at rackets, lawn tennis, etc.; (Tennis) service that beats opponent. **3.** The smallest possible amount, hair's breadth, as *within an ~ of*. **4.** (Orig. French) airman who has brought down 10 or more hostile aircraft; one who excels at something, champion; also attrib. [ME *as* f. OF f. L *as* unity]

-acea (-ā'sha), L suf. freely used to form names (neut. pl. agreeing w. *animalia*) for families of animals; the names are L & pl., the sing. being supplied by E adjj. in -ACEAN used as noun; so *the crustacea, a crustacean*. [f. L *-aceus* (-*ac-*+*-e-us*) compd adj. formative]

-aceae (-ā'siē), L suf. freely used to form names (fem. pl. agreeing w. *plantae*) for families of plants. [f. *-aceus* see prec.]

-acean (-ā'shan), a. & n. suf. As adj., = -ACEOUS; as n., see -ACEA. [f. L *-aceus* see -ACEA +-AN]

acēd'ia, n. See ACCIDIE.

Acĕl'dama (ak-), n. Field of bloodshed, scene of slaughter. [*Acts* i. 19]

-aceous (-ā'shŭs), suf. freely used to form adjj. to the Nat.-Hist. nouns in -ACEA, -ACEAE, as *crustaceous, rosaceous*. [f. L *-aceus* see -ACEA +-OUS]

acephal-, beginning of several bot., zool., & eccl. terms. Headless. [f. LL f. Gk *akephalos* f. A- (7) +*kephalē* head]

aceph'alous (asĕf'-), a. Headless; recognizing no chief; (Zool.) having no part of body specially organized as head; (Bot.) with head aborted or cut off; (in prosody), (verse) wanting the regular first syllable. [as prec. +-OUS]

ā'cerbāte, v.t. Sometimes used for EX-ACERBATE.

acĕrb'itȳ, n. Astringent sourness, harsh

taste; bitterness of speech, manner, or temper. [f.' F *acerbité* or L *acerbitas* (*acerbus* sour-tasting, -TY)]

acèrv'ate, a. Growing in compact clusters (of spines etc.). [f. L *acervare* (*acervus* a heap), -ATE²]

acès'cent, a. Turning sour, rather sour, lit. & fig. [F, or f. L *acescent*- f. *acère* be sour, -ENT]

acet-, = ACETO-, before a vowel, as ~ *amide*.

ăcètăb'ūlum, n. (pl. *-la*). 1. (Rom. Ant.) cup to hold vinegar. 2. (Zool.) cup-shaped sucker of cuttle-fish etc.; socket of thigh-bone, or of joints in insects. [ME, f. L, f. *acetum* vinegar + -*abulum* dim. of -*abrum* receptacle]

ă'cétāte, n. Salt or ester of acetic acid. [f. ACET(IC) + -ATE¹ (3)]

acèt'ic, a. Pertaining to vinegar; ~ *acid*, the acid contained in vinegar. [f. L *acetum* vinegar + -IC]

acèt'i|fÿ, v.t. & i. Convert into vinegar; become sour. Hence ~FICA'TION, ~fiER¹ (2), nn. [as prec. + -FY]

aceto-, chem. in comb., = ACETIC, ACETYL, before a consonant (cf. ACET-), as ~ *chloride*.

ă'cétōne, n. Colourless limpid liquid valuable as a solvent of organic compounds. [as prec. + -ONE]

ă'cètous, a. Having the qualities of vinegar; sour. [as prec. + -OUS]

ă'cétÿl, n. (chem.). The radical of acetic acid. [f. ACET(IC) + -YL]

acèt'ÿlēne, n. A colourless gas, burning with a bright flame. [as prec., see -YL & -ENE]

Achaean (akē'an), a. & n. (Inhabitant) of Achaea (district of the Northern Peloponnesus; also, in Homeric use, Greece generally). [f. L f. Gk *Akhaios*]

acharnement (see Ap.), n. Ferocity; gusto. [F]

Achates (akāt'ēz), n. Faithful friend of Aeneas (Virg. *Aen.*); any faithful friend.

ache¹ (āk), v.i. Suffer continuous or prolonged pain. [OE *acan*, ME *aken*; mod. sp. assim. to foll.]

ache² (āk), n. Continuous pain. [OE *æce*, ME *eche, ache*; mod. pronunc. assim. to prec.]

ache³ (āch), n. Name of letter H.

Acheulian (ashūl'ian), a. Of the palaeolithic epoch represented by remains found at St Acheul in France. [-AN]

achiev|e', v.t. Accomplish, carry out; acquire; reach (an end). Hence ~'ABLE a. [ME *acheve* f. OF *achever* f. phr. *a chief* to a head; see A- (4), CHIEF]

achieve'ment (-vm-), n. Completion, accomplishment; thing accomplished; escutcheon or ensign armorial in memory of a distinguished feat; = HATCHMENT. [f. prec. + -MENT or f. F *achèvement*]

Achilles and Patrŏc'lus (akĭl'ēz), phr. Pair of devoted friends (in Homer's *Iliad*); TENDON of *Achilles*.

achīl'ous (ak-), a. (bot.). Without lips. [f. Gk *a*- A- (7) + *kheilos* lip + -OUS]

achlamÿd'ëous (ăklam-), a. (bot.). Without calyx or corolla. [f. Gk *a*- A- (7) + *khlamus* -*udos* cloak + -EOUS]

ăchromăt'|ic (ăk-), a. (opt.). Free from colour; transmitting light without decomposing it. Hence ~ICALLY adv., ~i'CITY (ak-), ~ISM (2) (akrōm²), nn., ~IZE (3) (akrōm²) v.t. [f. Gk *akhrōmatos* + -IC; see A- (7), CHROMATIC]

ă'cid¹, a. Sour (~ *drops*, kind of sweets); (Chem.) with the essential properties of an ACID⁵. So **acid'ITY** n. [f. F *acide* or L *acidus* (*acère* be sour)]

ă'cid², n. A sour substance; (Chem.) one of a class of substances that neutralize & are neutralized by alkalis, & are compounded of hydrogen & another element or elements, & of which the principal types are sour & turn vegetable blues to reds; ~ *test* (in which ~ is applied to test composition etc.; often fig. in morals etc.). Hence **acid'ic** a. (chem.). [f. prec.]

acid'i|fÿ, v.t. & i. Make, become, sour; (Chem.) convert into an acid, render acid. Hence ~fiABLE a., ~FICA'TION, ~fiER¹ (2), nn. [as ACID, see -FY]

ăcidim'éter, n. Instrument for measuring strength of acids. [as prec., see -METER]

ăcidōs'is, n. (path.). Acid condition of blood (esp. in diabetes). [hybrid formation f. ACID + -OSIS]

acid'ūlātéd, a. Made somewhat acid. [f. as foll. + -ATE³]

acid'ūlous, a. Somewhat acid. [f. L *acidulus* (dim. of *acidus* sour) + -OUS]

ă'cinus, n. (pl. *acini*). One of the small berries that make up a compound fruit such as the blackberry; the compound fruit itself; seed of a grape or berry; (Anat.) racemose gland. Hence **acin'i**-FORM a. [L, = berry, seed]

-acious (-ā'shus), suf. forming adjj. meaning 'inclined to', 'abounding in'. [f. L -*ax* -*acis*, added to vb stems to form adjj., + -OUS]

-ăcitÿ, suf. forming nouns of quality corresponding to adjj. in -ACIOUS directly f. L -*acitat*- or thr. F -*acité*.

ăck⁻ăck', a. (colloq.). Anti-aircraft (gun etc.). [formerly signallers' name for letters A.A.]

ăck ĕmm'a, adv. & n. (colloq.). *Ante meridiem*; air-mechanic. [formerly signallers' name for letters A.M.]

acknowledge (aknŏl'ij), v.t. Admit the truth of; own (person etc. *to be* something); own to knowing, take notice of; recognize the authority or claims of; recognize in legal form; express appreciation of; announce receipt of; reward (a service). [A- (2) + KNOWLEDGE; or from the obs. noun *acknowledge*]

acknowl'edgement, -gment, (-nŏlijm-), n. Act of acknowledging; thing given or done in return for a service, message, etc. [prec. + -MENT]

aclin'ic, a. ~ *line*, magnetic equator, on which magnetic needle has no dip. [f. Gk *aklinēs* (a- not + *klinō* bend) + -IC]

ăc'mė, n. Highest point, point of perfection. [Gk, = point]

ăc'nė, n. Pimple; disease marked by pimples. [erron. for Gk *akmē* (prec.)]

acŏck', adv. (Of the hat) in cocked fashion. [A prep. + COCK² v.]

ăc'olyte, n. Inferior officer in the church; attendant, assistant; novice. [ME, f. med.L *acolit(h)us* corrupt. of LL *acoluthus* f. Gk *akolouthos* follower]

ăc'onite, n. Monk's-hood or wolf's-bane, a poisonous plant; extract from this. Hence **ăcŏnit'IC a.**, **acŏn'itINE⁵ n.** [f. F *aconit* or L *aconitum* f. Gk *akoniton*]

ăc'ŏrn, n. Fruit of the oak; ~-*shell*, multi-valve cirriped, allied to barnacles. [OE *æcern*, Gmc, of disputed orig. The mod. form by erron. assoc. w. *corn*¹]

acŏtylēd'on, n. Plant with no distinct seed-lobes. Hence ~OUS a. [f. mod. L *acotyledonēs*; see A- (7), COTYLEDON]

acou'chy (-ōoshī), **n.** Small rodent allied to guinea-pig. [f. F *acouchi*, perh. f. native name in Guiana]

acous't|ĭc (-ōo-, -ow-), **a.** Relating to the sense of hearing; (of a mine) that can be exploded by sound waves transmitted under water. Hence ~ICAL a., ~icALLY adv., ~I'CIAN (-shn) n., ~ICS n. pl., science of sound, ~ical properties (of room). [f. Gk *akoustikos* (*akouō* hear)]

acquaint', v.t. Make (person, one*self*) aware (*of* or *with* facts, *that*, *how*, etc.); make one*self* familiar (*with* circumstances etc.); (pass.) have personal knowledge (*with* person or thing). [ME *acointe* etc., f. OF *acointer* f. med. L *accognitare* f. *cognit-* p.p. st. of CO(*gnoscere* come to know)]

acquain'tance, n. Knowledge of (*with*) person etc. more than mere recognition & less than intimacy; person(s) with whom one is acquainted (pl. now usu. ~s in this sense). Hence ~SHIP (-s-sh-) n. [ME, f. OF *acointance* (prec., -ANCE)]

acquĕst', n. Thing acquired; (Law) property gained otherwise than by inheritance. [f. OF *acquest* f. LL *acquistum* (whence Eng. var. *acquist*), f. L *acquisitum* (see ACQUIRE)]

ăcquiĕsc|e', v.i. Agree tacitly; ~*e in*, accept (arrangements, conclusions). So ~'ENCE n., ~'ENT a. [f. L AC(*quiescere* rest)]

acquire', v.t. Gain by oneself & for oneself; (of qualities etc.) win (person a good name etc.); come into possession of; *an* ~*d taste* (not natural). Hence ~MENT (-ī'rm-) n., ~*d* mental faculty. [f. OF *acquere* f. OF *acquerre* v. Rom. *acquaerere for L AC(*quirere quisit-* = *quaerere* seek); mod. sp. after L & *require*]

ăcquisi'tion (-zĭ-), **n.** Act of acquiring; thing acquired, welcome addition. So **acquis'itIVE** (-zĭ-) **a.**, **acquis'itivENESS** (-zĭ-; -vn-) **n.** [f. L *acquisitio* (as prec., see -ION)]

acquit', v.t. (-tt-). Pay (a debt); declare (person) not guilty (*of* offence); discharge one*self of* (duty, responsibility); ~ one*self* (perform one's part) *well, ill,* etc. [ME, f. OF *aquiter* f. Rom. *acquitare (AC-, QUIT²)]

acquitt'al, n. Discharge from debt; deliverance from a charge by verdict etc.; performance (of duty). [prec. + -AL (2)]

acquitt'ance, n. Payment of debt; release from debt; receipt in full. [ME, f. OF *aquitance* (ACQUIT, -ANCE)]

ā'cre (-ker), **n.** Measure of land, 4,840 sq. yds.; piece of tilled or enclosed land, field (only in special uses, as *broad* ~*s*, *God's* *A*~, *Long* *A*~). Hence (~)ā'crED² (-erd) a. [OE *æcer* = OHG *ackar*, ON *akr*, Goth. *akrs*, f. Gmc *akraz; cf. L *ager*, Gk *agros*]

ā'creage (-ker-), **n.** Amount of acres; acres collectively or in the abstract. [ACRE + -AGE]

ăc'rid, a. Bitterly pungent, irritating, corrosive; of bitter temper or manner. Hence **acrid'ITY n.** [irreg. f. L *acer -cris* + -ID, perh. after *acid*]

ăc'rimony, n. Bitterness of temper or manner. So **ăcrimōn'ioUS a.**, **ăcrimōn'iousLY² adv.** [f. F *acrimonie* or L *acrimonia* (prec., -MONY)]

Ac'rita (ăk-), **n. pl.** (zool.). Animals with no distinct nervous system. [mod. L f. Gk *akritos* undistinguishable]

ăcro- in comb. Highest, topmost, terminal; tipped with; at the point or extremity of. [f. Gk *akros* topmost, outermost]

ăc'robăt, n. Rope-dancer, tumbler; politician, reasoner, etc., who changes position nimbly. Hence **ăcrobăt'IC a.**, **ăcrobăt'ICALLY adv.**, ~ISM n. [f. F *acrobate* f. Gk *akrobatēs* (ACRO-, Gk *bainō* walk)]

ăc'rogĕn, n. (bot.). Cryptogamous plant having perennial stem with growing point at extremity, as ferns & mosses. Hence **acrŏ'gĕnoUS a.** [ACRO- + -GEN]

ăc'rolith, n. Statue with head & extremities of stone. [L f. Gk (ACRO-, -LITH)]

acrŏn'yc(h)al (-īk-), **a.** Happening at nightfall (esp. of rising or setting of stars). Hence ~LY² adv. [f. Gk *akronukhos* (ACRO- + *nux nuktos* night) + -AL]

ăc'ronym, n. Word formed from initial letters of other words (e.g. *Anzac, Nato, radar*). [ACRO- + Gk -ōnum- = *onoma* name]

acrŏp'ĕtal, a. Developing from below upwards. Hence ~LY² adv. [ACRO- + L *petere* seek + -AL]

ăcrophōb'ia, n. Morbid dread of heights. [ACRO-, -PHOBIA]

acrŏp'olis, n. Citadel or elevated part of a Greek city, esp. of Athens. [Gk *akropolis* (ACRO- + *polis* city)]

across' (-aws, -ŏ-), **adv. & prep.** In the form of a cross, as *with arms* ~; forming a cross with, making angles with, (object expressed or understood), as *a line drawn* ~ (*the road*); into contact with, as *came* ~

a tiger, an instance; from side to side (of), as *run ~ (the road)*; on the other side (of), as *by this time he is ~ (the Channel)*. Put *it ~* a person (sl.), get even with, impose on, deceive. [orig. adv f. F *à croix, en croix*, later apprehended as f. **A** prep. + CROSS¹]

acros'tic, n. Poem or other composition in which the initial (*single ~*), the initial & final (*double ~*), or the initial, middle, & final (*triple ~*) letters of the lines make words; word-puzzle so made; Hebrew poem of which the lines begin with the successive letters of the alphabet. Hence **acros'tic** a., **acros'tically** adv. [f. Gk *akrostikhis* (ACRO-, Gk *stikhos* row, line of verse)]

act¹, n. Thing done, deed, this as outward sign of a condition etc. (*~ of faith, contrition*); process of doing, operation, as *in the very ~ of, Act of God* (operation of uncontrollable natural forces); *Acts* (of *the Apostles*), N.T. book; decree passed by a legislative body etc.; *~ & deed*, binding legal instrument (esp. *I deliver this as my ~ & deed* said at time of signing); main division of a play; one of a series of short performances in circus or variety programme (*put on an ~*, sl., show off, talk for display); ‖ (formerly, in Universities) thesis maintained by candidate for degree etc. [ME, f. OF *acte* & L *actus, -um*; see foll.]

act², v.t. & i. Carry out (an incident or story) in mimicry, represent, perform a play or part; personate (character in a play or in life), as *~ Othello, ~ the fool*; perform actions, behave, as *~* (behave) *generously, ~* (serve) *as interpreter, ~ upon* (execute) *a suggestion, ~ up to* (put into practice) *a principle*; perform special functions, as *the policeman declined to ~, the brake refused to ~, alcohol ~s on the brain.* [partly f. L *act-* p.p. st. of *agere* do, partly f. prec.]

ac'ting, a. & n. In vbl senses, esp.: doing duty temporarily, as *A~ Captain*; doing alone duties nominally shared with others, as *A~ Manager, Trustee; ~ copy* (for players' use, with stage-directions & cuts). [ACT² + -ING²,¹]

Actin'ia (ăk-), n. (pl. *-ae, -as*). Genus of zoophytes belonging to the family Actiniadae; (pop.) sea anemone. [mod. L f. Gk *aktis -inos* ray]

ac'tinism, n. That property of the sun's rays by which chemical changes are produced, as in photography. So **actin'ic** a. [as prec. + -ISM]

actin'ium, n. Radio-active element found in pitchblende. [as prec. + -IUM]

actino-, comb. form of Gk *aktis -inos* ray, as **actinom'eter** n., instrument for measuring intensity of sun's heating rays; **actinothe'rapy** n., treatment of disease by light rays.

ac'tion, n., & v.t. **1.** Process of acting, exertion of energy or influence, as *men of*

~, put in ~, ~ of an acid; thing done, act; (in drama) series of events represented; mode of acting, management of body, etc., as *~ of a player, horse*; mechanism of piano or other instrument; legal process; engagement between troops etc.; *~ committee*, one chosen to take active steps; *~ stations*, positions taken up by troops etc. before going into *~*. **2.** v.t. Bring a legal *~* against. [ME, f. OF, f. L *actionem* (as ACT², see -ION)]

ac'tionab|le (-shon-), a. Affording ground for an action at law. Hence **~LY²** adv. [ACTION + -ABLE]

ac'tivate, v.t. Make active (*~d carbon*, carbon, esp. charcoal, treated to increase its adsorptive power; *~d sludge*, aerated sewage containing aerobic bacteria); (Phys.) make radio-active. [-ATE³]

ac'tive, a. **1.** Given to outward action; working, effective; energetic, diligent; acting of one's own accord, acting upon others. **2.** (gram.). The *~ voice* comprises all forms of intransitive verbs, & those forms of transitive verbs that attribute the verbal action to the person or thing whence it proceeds (the logical subject), as *We punished him*; not, like the forms of the passive voice, to the person or thing to whom it is directed (the logical object), as *He was punished by us*. Taken correctly, verbs are themselves called *~*. Hence **~LY²**(-vl-) adv. [ME, f. OF *actif* & L *activus* (ACT², -IVE)]

activ'ity, n. Exertion of energy; quality of being active, diligence, nimbleness; (pl.) active forces, spheres of action. [f. F *activité* & med. L *activitas* (in LL also = active form of verb); see prec., -TY]

ac'ton, n. Jacket of quilted cotton worn under mail; mail-plated jacket of leather etc. [ME, f. OF *auqueton* (mod. *hoqueton*) padding, padded jacket, f. Sp. *alcoton* (mod. *algodon*) cotton f. Arab. *al-qutun* the cotton]

ac'tor, n. Dramatic performer, whence **ac'tress¹** n.; (rarely) doer. [L, = doer, actor (as ACT², see -OR)]

ac'tual, a. Existing in fact, real; present, current. [ME, f. OF *actuel* f. LL *actualis* (*actus* vbl n. f. *agere* ACT²; see -AL)]

actual'ity, n. Reality; realism; (pl.) existing conditions. [f. as prec. + -ITY; in early use f. med. L *actualitas*]

ac'tualiz|e (-is|e (-iz), v.t. Realize in action; describe realistically. Hence **~A'TION** n. [ACTUAL + -IZE]

ac'tually, adv. In actual fact, really; for the time being; even (strange as it may seem). [-LY²]

ac'tuary, n. Expert in theory & practice of statistics, esp. of mortality, sickness, retirement, & unemployment; (formerly) registrar, notary. Hence **actuar'ial** a. [f. L *actuarius* amanuensis, book-keeper (*actus*; see ACTUAL & -ARY¹)]

ac'tuate, v.t. Communicate motion to (a machine etc.); serve as motive to (person). Hence **ăctŭA'TION** n. [f. med. L *actuare* (*actus*, as prec., see -ATE³)]

acŭ'ĭtў, n. Sharpness, acuteness (as of needle, acid, disease, wit). [f. F *acuité* or med. L *acuitas* (*acus -ūs* needle; see -ITY)]

acūl'ĕate, a. (Zool.) having a sting; (Bot.) prickly; incisive. [f. L *aculeatus* (ACULEUS, see -ATE²)]

acūl'ĕus, n. (pl. *-ēī*). (Zool.) sting; (bot.) prickle. [L *aculeus* sting, dim. of *acus* needle]

acŭm'ĕn, n. Keen discernment, penetration. [L *acumen -minis* anything sharp (*acuere* sharpen)]

acŭm'ĭnate¹, a. (nat. hist.). Tapering to a point. [f. L *acuminare* (prec.), see -ATE²]

acŭm'ĭnate², v.t. Sharpen, point; give poignancy to. Hence **acŭmĭnA'TION** n. [as prec., see -ATE³]

‖**acu'shla** (-ŏŏ-), n. Darling. [f. Ir. *ā cuisle* O pulse (of my heart) !]

acūte', a. Sharp, pointed; (of angles) less than a right angle; (of diseases) coming sharply to a crisis, opp. to *chronic*; (of controversy, difficulty) critical, serious; (of sensations, senses, intellect) keen; (of sounds) high, shrill; (of letters) bearing the ~ ACCENT. Hence ~LY² (-tl-) adv., ~NESS (-tn-) n. [f. L *acutus* p.p. of *acuere* sharpen]

acūt'ĭ- in comb. Sharp, as ~*foliate* sharp-leaved, ~*lobate* sharp-lobed. [L comb. form of *acutus* ACUTE]

-acў, branch of the wider suf. -CY forming nouns of state or quality from or modelled on L -*acia* or -*atia* or Gk -*ateia*. **1.** N. of quality f. L -*aci-a* f. adjj. in -*aci-*; *fall-* deceive *fallaci-* deceitful *fall-aci-a* fallacy. **2.** N. of state or quality f. L -*ati-a* f. nouns in -*at-* (nom. -*as*, -*i-* being part of stem or connecting link): med. L *primat-* *primati-a* primacy; & by analogy *supremacy*. **3.** N. of state f. med. L -*ati-a* f. nouns in -*atus*: *advocat-us* *advocat-ia* advocacy; & by analogy *curacy*. This formation was extended to adjj. f. L -*atus* to form *accuracy*, *obstinacy*, from *accurate*, *obstinate*, where L has nouns in -*atio*; hence other L words in -*atio* appear in E with -*acy* where E has no corresponding adj. in -*ate*, as *conspiracy*; similarly, E -*acy* for L -*atus* (n. of 4th decl.), as *magistratus* magistracy, gives rise to *episcopacy* as if f. E *episcopate*; & *lunacy* is formed to match *lunatic* on anal. of *diplomacy* diplomatic. **4.** N. of state, through L, f. Gk -*ateia* f. nn. in -*atēs* or vbs in -*ateuein*; *peiratēs peirateia* piracy.

ăd, n. (colloq.). Advertisement; **ăd'man**, publicist, propagandist. [abbr.]

ad-, pref. **1.** f. L *ad* to, w. sense of motion or direction to, change into, addition, adherence, increase, or mere intensification. Assim. before *c*, *f*, *g*, *l*, *n*, *p*, *q*, *r*, *s*, *t*, & prob. before *b*; reduced to *a* before *sc*, *sp*, *st*. In OF, L *ad* was regularly reduced to *a*, *a-*. Later the spelling was refash-

after L, as also in E f. the 15th c. Subsequent adoptions conform to L spelling. (The use of *ad-*, *ab-*, in pairs like *adoral* & *aboral*, situated *at* & *away from* mouth, is unknown to L). **2.** The substitution of *ad-* (*ac-* etc.) for *a-* was occas. applied where *a-* repr. other preff., as L *ab* (*advance*), OF *es-*, L *ex-* (*affray*), OE *a-* (*accurse*), see A-. So *admiral* f. Arab. *amiral*.

-ad, suf. of nouns. **1.** f. Gk -*ad-* (nom. -*as*), in collective numerals (*monad*, *dyad*, *triad*, *chiliad*, *myriad*); in fem. patronymics (*Dryad*, *Naiad*); in names of poems (*Iliad*, & by anal. *Dunciad*, *Rosciad*); & in family names of plants (*liliad*). **2.** f. F -*ade*; see the more usual -ADE. **3.** suf. invented to form adjj. & advv. in the sense of 'towards' (the part indicated by main element of word), as *cauad* towards the tail [L *cauda* tail]

ăd'age, n. Traditional maxim, proverb. [F, f. L *adagium* (*ad* to + *agi-*, root of *aio* I say)]

adagio (adahj'yŏ), adv., a., n. (mus. & dancing). Slow(ly); (n.)~movement. [It.]

Ad'am¹ (ă-), n. The first man (*not know one from ~*, have no knowledge of his looks); *old ~* (unregenerate condition), ~*'s ale* or *wine* (water), ~*'s apple* (projection of the thyroid cartilage of the larynx). [Heb. *a-dam* man]

Ad'am² (ă-), a. (At first in pl.) of the decorative style created by the brothers Robert & James *Adam* in the 18th c.

ăd'amant, n. A thing impenetrably hard (*be ~*, stubbornly refuse compliance with requests); (formerly) loadstone; diamond. Hence **ădamăn'tINE²** a. [f. OF *adamaunt* f. L *adamantem* (nom. -*mas*) f. Gk *adamas -mantos* untamable (*a-* not + *damaō* I tame)]

Ad'amīte (ă-), n. Child of Adam, human being; unclothed man; (Eccl.) name of sects who imitated Adam in this respect; (pl.) a section of humanity supposed by some to be alone derived from Adam. [f. med. L *Adamita* (ADAM¹, -ITE)]

adăpt', v.t. Fit (a thing *to* another); make suitable (*to* or *for* a purpose); modify, alter, (~*ed for* broadcasting). Hence or cogn. ~ABIL'ITY, ădaptA'TION, ~ER¹, nn., ~ABLE, ~IVE, aa. [f. F *adapter* f. L AD(*aptare* f. *aptus* fit)]

ăd căptăn'dum (vŭl'gus), adv. & a. (Calculated) to take the fancy (of the rabble). [L]

ădd, v.t. & i. Join (one thing *to* another), as ~ *your entreaties to mine*, ~ *insult to injury*, *this* ~*s to* (increases) *our difficulties*, *he* ~*ed* (stated further) *that—*, ~ *up together* (find the sum of), ~ (perform the process of summation) *correctly*, ~ *in* (include). [ME, f. L AD(*dere dit-* = *dare* put); see DO¹]

ădd'ăx, n. Large N.-African & Arabian antelope with twisted horns. [L, f. African wd]

addĕn'dum, n. (pl. *-da*). Thing to be added; appendix, addition. [L gerundive of *addere* ADD]

ădd'er, n. Small venomous snake, esp. common viper; *puff, death, horned, ~, *species of Viperidae; *flying ~*, dragon-fly; *~'s tongue*, kind of fern. [f. OE *nǣdre*, Gmc = OS *nādra*, OHG *nātara*, ON *nathra*, Goth. *nadrs*; n- lost in ME by wrong division of *a naddre*; cf. APRON]

addict', v.t. Devote, apply habitually, (*to* a practice), as *his tastes ~ him, he ~s himself* or *his mind, he is ~ed, to*; (Rom. Law) deliver over by sentence of a judge. So **ădd'ict** n., person ~ed to a habit esp. the taking of a specified drug etc. (*opium ~*), **addic'tion** n. [f. L AD(*dicere dict-* say) assign]

Add'ison's disease' (ă-; -zēz), n. Disease characterized by progressive anaemia & debility & brown discoloration of skin. [T. *Addison* discoverer, 1855]

addi'tion, n. Process of adding (*in ~ to*, as well as); thing added (*a useful ~*). [ME, f. OF, or L *additio* (as ADD, see -ION)]

addi'tional (-shon-), a. Added, supplementary. Hence **~LY²** adv. [prec. + -AL]

ădd'itive, a. & n. (Thing) to be added; characterized by addition (*~ process*). [f. LL *additivus*, see ADD]

ădd'le¹, a. ~ *egg*, rotten one, one that produces no chicken; empty, vain; muddled, unsound, as *~-brained, -head, -pated*. [f. OE *adela* mire (cf. MLG *adele*, G *adel*); now used only as adj.]

ădd'le², v.t. & i. Muddle, confuse; (of eggs) grow addle. [f. prec.]

ădd'dled (-ld), a. Made addle. [ADDLE a. assim. to p.p. form, apparently before ADDLE v. existed]

addrĕss'¹, v.t. Direct in speech or writing (*~ remarks, a protest, petition*, etc. *to* person; *~ oneself to*, speak or write to); write directions for delivery on cover of (letter, parcel, etc.); speak or write to, esp. deliver a speech to, (person, audience); apply (*oneself to* a task); (Golf) adjust club head behind (ball) before playing stroke. [ME, f. OF *adresser* f. Rom. *AD(drictiare* f. **drictum = L directum* DIRECT]

addrĕss'², n. Readiness, skill, dexterity, adroitness; superscription of letter, name of place to which person's letters are directed, whence **~OGRAPH** (2) n. **P**, machine for printing ~es; act of dispatching a ship; manner, bearing, in conversation; discourse delivered to audience; (pl.) courteous approach, courtship (*pay one's ~es to*). [f. prec. & f. F *adresse* n. f. *adresser*]

ăddrĕssee', n. Person to whom a letter is addressed. [ADDRESS¹ + -EE]

addŭce|e**', v.t. Cite as proof or instance. Hence ~e'ABLE, ~'IBLE, aa. [f. L AD(*ducere duct-* lead)]

addŭ'cent, a. (physiol.). (Of muscles)

drawing to a common centre. [as prec., see -ENT]

addŭct', v.t. (physiol.). Draw to a common centre. [as ADDUCE]

addŭc'tion, n. Act of adducing; act of adducting. [f. as ADDUCE; see -ION; cf. F *adduction*, LL *adductio*]

-āde, suf. of nouns. **1.** f. F *-ade*, the form in which Pr., Sp., or Port. wds in *-ada* f. L *-ata* (fem. sing. p.p. of verbs in *-are*) were adopted in F, often supplanting native F *-ée* direct f. L, as in *accolade* OF *acolée*. Now a living suf. both in F wds, many of which are borrowed by E (*tirade, gasconnade*), & in E (*blockade, orangeade*); E drops F *e* in *ballad, salad*. Meanings: action done (*tirade, fusillade*), body concerned in action or process (*ambuscade, cavalcade*), thing produced by action or from material (*masquerade, lemonade*). **2.** f. F *-ade* f. Gk *-ada* (nom. *-as*), as *decade*; but in E usu. -AD. **3.** f. Sp. or Port. *-ado*, masc. form corresp. to **1** above, with similar meaning (*brocade*), or that of the person concerned (*renegade*).

ăd'enoids (-z), n. pl. Mass of spongy tissue between back of nose & throat, often hindering inflation of lungs. Hence **ădenoid'AL** a. [f. Gk *adēn -enos* acorn, gland; see -OID]

adĕpt', n. & a. (One who is) thoroughly proficient (*in* anything); skilled alchemist. [f. L *adeptus* p.p. of AD(*ipisci* attain)]

ăd'equ|ate, a. Proportionate (*to* the requirements); sufficient, satisfactory. Hence **~ACY** n., **~ateLY²** (-tl-) adv. [f. L AD*aequare* make equal (*aequus*), see -ATE³]

adĕs'pota, n. pl. Literary works not attributed to (or claimed by) an author. [neut. pl. of Gk *adespota* without owner (*a-* not + *despotēs* master)]

ăd eūn'dem, adv. *Admitted ~ (gradum)*, to the same (degree at another univ.). [L]

à deux (see Ap.), adv. & a. For two; between two. [F]

adhēre' (-h-), v.i. Stick fast, cleave, *to* a substance, person, party, opinion). [f. F *adhérer* or L AD(*haerēre haes-* stick)]

adhēr'|ent (-h-), a. & n. Sticking (*to* substance); due *to*; connected with (*to*); (n.) supporter (*of* party etc.). So **~ENCE** (-h-) n. [f. F *adhérent* (as prec., see -ENT)]

adhē'sion (-hēzhn), n. Adhering (lit. & fig.); (Path.) unnatural union of surfaces due to inflammation. [f. F *adhésion* or L *adhaesio* (as ADHERE, see -ION)]

adhēs'ive (-h-), a. & n. Having the property of adhering; sticky; (n.) ~ substance. Hence **~LY²** (-h-; -vl-) adv. [f. F *adhésif, -ive* (as ADHERE, see -IVE)]

adhib'it (-h-), v.t. Put on, affix; apply, administer, (remedies). So **ădhibi'tion** (-h-) n. [f. L AD(*hibēre hibit- = habēre* hold) employ]

ăd hŏc, a. Arranged for this purpose, special. [L]

ăd hŏm'ĭnĕm, adv. & a. To the man, personal; ARGUMENT*um ~*. [L]

ădiabăt´ic, a. (phys.). Impassable to heat; occurring without heat entering or leaving system. [f. Gk *adiabatos* impassable (*a-* not +*diabainō* pass)]

ădiăn´tum, n. Kinds of ferns including the true maidenhair; (pop.) black maidenhair. [L, f. Gk *adianton* maidenhair]

ădiăph´or|ism, n. Latitudinarianism. So ~**IST n.** [f. Gk *adiaphoros* (*a-* not +*diaphoros* different) +-ISM]

adieu (adū´), int. & n. (pl. ~*s*, ~*x*, pr. adūz´). Good-bye; *make, take,* one's ~, say good-bye. [ME, f. OF (*à* to + *Dieu* God)]

ăd ĭnfīnĭt´um, adv. Without limit, for ever. [L]

ăd ĭn´terĭm, adv. & a. For the meantime. [L]

ăd´ipocēre, n. Greyish fatty substance generated in dead bodies subjected to moisture. [f. F *adipocire* (L *adeps -ipis* fat +-o- +*cire* wax f. L *cera*)]

ăd´ipōse, a. & n. Pertaining to fat, fatty; (n.) animal fat. Hence **ădĭpŏs´ITY n.** [f. L *adeps -ipis* fat +-OSE]

ăd´it, n. Approach; (of mines) horizontal entrance; act of approaching. [f. L *ADitus -ūs* (*ire it-* go)]

adjā´c|ent, a. Lying near, contiguous. So ~**ENCY n.** [ME, f. L AD(*jacēre* lie), see -ENT]

ădj´ective, a. & n. Additional, not standing by itself, dependent: ~ *colours* (not permanent without a basis); *Law A*~ (subsidiary part of law, procedure); (Gram.) ~, *noun* ~, the name of an attribute, added to the name of a thing to describe the thing more fully. Hence **ădjèctiv´AL a., ădjèctiv´alLY², ~LY²** (-vl-), advv. [ME, f. LL *adjectivus* f. AD(*jicĕre ject- = jacēre* throw), see -IVE]

adjoin´, v.t. Join, unite, (one thing *to* another); be contiguous with. [ME, f. OF *ajoindre, ajoign-* f. L AD(*jungere junct-* join)]

adjourn (ajĕrn´), **v.t. & i.** Put off, postpone; break off for later resumption; (intr., of persons met together) suspend joint proceedings & separate; change the place of meeting. Hence ~´MENT (ajĕr-) L. [ME, f. OF *ajorner* f. *a* AD- +*jorn* day f. LL *diurnum* day f. L *diurnus* DIURNAL; cf. JOURNAL, JOURNEY]

adjŭdge´, v.t. Adjudicate upon (a matter); pronounce judicially (*that* a thing *is* or a thing *to be*); condemn (person *to* penalty or *to* do); award judicially (thing *to* person). Hence ~´MENT (-jm-) n. [ME, f. OF *ajuger* (as foll.)]

adjud´ic|āte (ajōō-), **v.t. & i.** (Of a judge or court) decide upon (claim etc.); pronounce (person *to be* something); (intr.) sit in judgement & pronounce sentence. Hence ~A´TION, ~ātor, nn., ~ătive a., (ajōō-). [f. L AD(*judicare* f. *judex -icis* judge), see -ATE³]

ădj´unct, n. Subordinate or incidental thing, accompaniment (*to, of*); (Gram.) amplification of the predicate, subject,

etc.; (Logic) non-essential attribute. Hence **adjŭnc´tIVE a., adjŭnc´tiveLY³** (-vl-) adv. [f. L as ADJOIN]

adjure (ajoor´), **v.t.** Charge (a person) under oath or penalty of curse (*to* do); request earnestly. Hence **adjurA´TION** (ăjoor-) n. [ME, f. L AD(*jurare* swear) in LL sense 'put person to an oath']

adjŭst´, v.t. Arrange, put in order; harmonize (discrepancies); adapt (*to* standard or purpose). Hence~ABLE a., ~MENT n. [f. F *adjuster* (now *ajuster*) a refashioning, after *juste* JUST, of OF *ajoster* (mod. *ajouter,* = obs. E *adjoust*) f. Rom. *°adjuxtare,* f. L *juxta* near]

adjutage, aj-, (ăj´ōō-), n. Mouthpiece of an artificial fountain. [f. F. *aj(o)utage* (*ajouter* add, join; see prec. & -AGE)]

adj´ut|ant (ăjōō-), **a.** & n. **1.** Assistant; (Mil.) army etc. officer who assists superior officers by communicating orders, conducting correspondence, etc., whence~ANCY n. **2.** Gigantic Indian stork. [f. L *adjutare* frequent. as foll., see -ANT]

adj´uvant (ăjōō-), **a. & n.** Helpful, auxiliary; person, thing, that helps. [f. L AD(*juvare jut-* help), see -ANT]

ăd lĭb´ĭtum, adv. (abbr. **ad lib.**). At pleasure, to any extent; *ăd´-lĭb,* v.i. (colloq.), speak extempore. [L]

ăd´măss, n. That section of the community easily influenced by mass methods of publicity and entertainment or considered as likely to be so influenced. [f. AD advertisement +MASS²]

admeasure (-mĕzh´er), **v.t.** Apportion, assign in due shares. [ME, f. OF *amesurer* f. med. L AD(*mensurare* MEASURE)]

admeasurement (-mĕzh´erm-), n. Process of admeasuring; comparison; dimensions. [f. OF *amesurement* (as prec., see -MENT)]

admin´icle, n. A help; (Law) corroboratory evidence. So **ădminic´ŭlAR¹ a.** [f. L *adminiculum* prop; see -CULE]

admin´ister, v.t. & i. Manage (affairs); dispense (justice, sacraments, *to*); tender (oath *to*); furnish, give, (thing *to*); apply (remedies *to*); (intr.) act as administrator; contribute *to* (one's comfort etc.). Hence **admin´istRABLE a.** [ME, f. OF *aministrer* f. L AD(*ministrare* MINISTER)]

administrā´tion, n. Management (*of* business); management of public affairs, government; the ministry, the Government (chiefly U.S.); (Law) management of deceased person's estate; *Letters of A*~, authority to administer estate of an intestate, opp. to *probate*; dispensation (*of* justice etc.); tendering (*of* oath); application (*of* remedies). [ME f. OF, or L *administratio* (as prec., see -ATION)]

admin´istrātive, a. Pertaining to management of affairs; executive. Hence ~LY² (-vl-) adv. [f. L *administrativus* (as prec., see -IVE)]

admin´istrātor, n. Manager; one capable of organizing; one who performs official duties (of religion, justice, etc.); applier or giver (*of*); one authorized to manage estates for legal owner during minority etc., or estates of one who dies without appointing competent executors. Hence ~torship n., ~trix n. (pl. ~*trices*, pron. -ĭsĭz *or* -ĭs'ĕz). [L, as ADMINISTER, see -OR]

ăd'mirab|le, a. Surprisingly good, excellent; *A~le Crichton* (krīt'on), å prodigy, one who excels in many things (from James Crichton, 'The A~le Crichton', 1560–85, Scottish scholar, poet, athlete). Hence ~LY² adv. [F, or f. L *admirabilis* (as ADMIRE, see -ABLE)]

ăd'miral, n. Commander-in-chief of a country's navy (in England, formerly *Lord High A~*); naval officer of highest rank, commander of fleet or squadron; *A~ of the Fleet*, *A~*, *Vice-A~*, *Rear-A~*, the four grades of A~ in British Navy; privileged commander of fishing or merchant fleet; ship that carries the ~, Flagship; *Red A~*, *White A~*, two European species of butterfly. Hence~SHIP n. [ME *amyrayl* etc., *admirail* etc., f. OF *a(d)mira(i)l* etc., med. L *a(d)miralis* etc., f. Arab. *amir* commander; see AMEER, EMIR]

ăd'miraltў, n. Office of admiral; the department administering the Navy (in Britain, *Lords Commissioners of A~*); (Rhet.) command of the seas (esp. *the price of ~*); *Court of A~*, tribunal for trial & decision of maritime questions & offences. [ME *a(d)myralte* etc. f. OF *ad-miralte* (prec., -TY)]

ădmirā'tion, n. Pleased contemplation; (formerly) wonder; *the ~ of*, admired by; *note of ~* (!). [F, or f. L *admiratio* (as foll., see -ATION)]

admīre', v.t. Regard with pleased surprise or approval; (also, colloq.) express admiration of (*forgot to ~ her cat*); (formerly) wonder at. [f. F *admirer* or L AD(*mirari* wonder at)]

admīr'er, n. One that admires; lover. [ADMIRE + -ER¹]

admiss'i|ble, a. (Of idea or plan) worthy to be entertained; (Law) allowable as judicial proof; capable of being admitted (*to* office or position). Hence ~BIL'ITY n. [F, f. med. L *admissibilis* (ADMIT, -BLE)]

admi'ssion (-shn), n. Admitting, being admitted, (*to* society of persons or class of things); acknowledgement (*of* thing as true, *that* it is true). [late ME, f. L *admissio* (as foll., see -ION)]

admiss'ive, a. Tending to admit. [f. med. L *admissivus* (as foll., see -IVE)]

admit', v.t. & i. (-tt-). Allow (person etc.) entrance or access (*to* place, class, privileges, etc.); accept as valid or true, whence ~t'ĕdLY² adv.; acknowledge (thing *to be*, *that* it is); (abs.) *this, I ~, was wrong*; (of enclosed spaces) have room for; ~ *of*, leave room for (doubt, improvement). [ME, f. L AD(*mittere miss-let go*)]

admitt'able, a. Capable of being admitted (usu. to a place). [prec. + -ABLE]

admitt'ance, n. Admitting, being admitted (usu. to a place). [ADMIT + -ANCE]

admix', v.t. & i. Add as an ingredient; mingle (*with* something). So ~TURE n. [now f. AD- + MIX]

admŏn'ish, v.t. Exhort (person *to do*, *that* he should do); give advice; warn (*of* a thing); inform, remind, (*of* a thing, *that*). Hence ~MENT n. [ME *amonest(e)* f. OF *amonester* f. Rom. **admonestare* unexpl. alt. of L AD(*monēre monit-* warn); mod. E form irreg. assim. to L *admonēre* and -ISH]

admŏni'tion, n. Admonishing; warning, reproof. So admŏn'itorў a. [ME, f. OF *amonition* f. L *admonitionem* (as prec., see -ION)]

ăd naus'ĕăm, adv. To a disgusting extent. [L]

ădnŏm'inal, a. Belonging to an adnoun; attached to a noun. [f. L *ad + nomen* + -AL, after PRONOMINAL; cf. foll.]

ăd'noun, n. Adjective, word added to a noun substantive; adjective used substantively. [f. L *ad* to + NOUN on anal. of *adverb*]

ado (adŏō'), n. Action, business, fuss; difficulty; *much ado* prop. = *much to do*; but *much* being' taken as adj., *ado* is treated as n. [f. northern ME *at do* (= *to do*) f. ON *at* AT as sign of infin. + DO]

-ado, suf. of nouns. 1. f. Sp. or Port. -*ado* f. L -*atus* p.p. of vbs in -*are*, as *desperado* L *desperatus* (*desperare*); occas. changed in E to -*ade*, as *renegado*, now *renegade*. 2. Ignorant refashioning of nouns in -*ade* f. F -*ade* = Sp. -*ada* It. -*ata*, as *crusado* Sp. *cruzada*, *scalado* Sp. *escalada*.

adŏb'ė (*or* -ŏb'), n. Unburnt sun-dried brick. [Sp.]

ădolĕs'c|ent, n. & a. (Person) growing up, between childhood & manhood or womanhood. So~ENCE, ~ENCY, nn. [ME, f. OF, f. L AD(*olescere ult-* grow up), see -ENT]

Adŏn'is, n. Beautiful youth loved by Venus; beau, dandy; (Bot.) genus including pheasant's eye; || (Entom.) the butterfly Clifden Blue. [Gk, f. Phoen. *adōn* lord, title of a divinity]

ăd'onize, -ise (-ĭz), v. refl. & i. Adorn, dandify, (one*self*), play the Adonis. [f. F *adoniser* (prec., -IZE)]

adŏpt', v.t. Take (person) into a relationship he did not previously occupy; take (idea etc.) from some one else; choose. Hence ~ABIL'ITY, adŏp'tION, nn., ~ABLE a. [f. F *adopter* or L AD(*optare* choose)]

adŏp'tive, a. Due to adoption, as ~ *son*, *father*; apt to adopt. Hence ~LY² (-vl-) adv. [ME, f. OF (-*if*, -*ive*), f. L *adoptivus*; see prec. and -IVE]

adōr|e', v.t. Regard with the utmost respect & affection; (poet.) worship as a deity; (in R. C. Church) reverence with representative honours (the Host etc.).

So ~'ABLE a., ~'ABLY² adv., ădorA'TION n. [ME aoure, later adoure, f. OF aorer, later adorer, f. L adorare worship]

ador̄'er, n. Worshipper; ardent admirer, lover. [prec. +-ER¹]

adōrn', v.t. Add beauty or lustre to: furnish with ornaments. So ~MENT n. [ME aourne, later adourne f. OF aourner, later adorner, f. L AD(ornare furnish, deck)]

adown', adv. & prep. (arch., poet.). = DOWN³. [f. OE of dūne off the mount (A-(3), DOWN¹ n.)]

ăd rĕm, adv. & pred. a. To the point; to the purpose. [L]

ădrĕn'alin, n. A hormone secreted by the adrenal ductless glands & affecting circulation & muscular action; this extracted from animals for medicinal use. [AD-+RENAL+-IN]

adrift', adv. In a drifting condition, at the mercy of wind & tide or of circumstances; (Naut.) unfastened. [A prep.+DRIFT¹]

adroit', a. Having address, dexterous. Hence ~LY² adv., ~NESS n. [F phr. à droit rightly]

ădsciti'tious (-sītĭshus), a. Adopted from without; supplemental. [f. L AD(sciscere scit- inceptive of scire know) +-ITIOUS]

ădscrīp'tus glēb'ae, a. & n. (Serf) attached to the soil. [L]

adsŏrb', v.t. (Of a solid) attract (molecules of a gas or liquid) to its surface (cf. ABSORB). So adsŏrp'TION n. [f. AD-+L sorbēre sorpt- suck in]

ăd'sŭm, v.i. I am here. [L]

ăd'ūljāte, v.t. Flatter basely. So~A'TION, ~ātoR, nn., ~ātoRY a. [f. L adulari fawn on, see -ATE³]

Adŭll'amite, n. M.P. seceding from Liberal Party in 1866. [f. cave of Adullam (1 Sam. xxii. 1, 2) +-ITE]

adŭlt' (or ăd², esp. as n.), a. & n. (One who is) grown up; mature. [f. L adultus p.p. of adolescere; see ADOLESCENT]

adŭl'terant, a. & n. (Thing) employed in adulterating. [as foll., see -ANT]

adŭl'terate¹, a. Stained (in conduct or in birth) by adultery; (of things) spurious, counterfeit. [as foll., see -ATE²]

adŭl'ter|āte², v.t. Falsify by admixture of baser ingredients. So~A'TION, ~ātoR, nn. [f. L adulterare corrupt (f. adulter adulterer), see -ATE³; replacing obs. vb adulter (f. F adultérer or L adulterare), itself replacing ME avoutre (f. OF avoutrer f. L adulterare)]

adŭl'ter|er, n. One guilty of adultery. So ~ESS¹ n. [f. obs. adulter vb (orig. avoutre; see prec.) +-ER¹]

adŭl'terine, a. Of, born of, adultery; adulterated, counterfeit; illegal, unlicensed. [f. L adulterinus born of adultery, spurious (adulter adulterer, see -INE¹)]

adŭl'ter|y̆, n. Voluntary sexual intercourse of married person with one of the opposite sex other than his or her spouse. So ~OUS a., ~OUSLY² adv. [re-

placing ME avoutrie f. OF avoutrie etc., the mod. F adultère being, like E adultery, directly f. L adulterium]

adŭm'bral, a. Overshadowing, shady. [f. AD-+L umbra shade +-AL]

ăd'umbrāte (or adŭm²), v.t. Represent in outline; faintly indicate; typify, foreshadow; overshadow. Hence or cogn. ădumbra'TION n., adŭm'brATIVE a. [f. L AD(umbrare f. umbra shade), see -ATE³]

ăd ŭng'uem (-nggw-) (fᾰc'tus), a. Highly finished. [L]

adŭst', a. Scorched, dried up, parched; sunburnt; atrabilious, gloomy. [f. F aduste or L adustus p.p. of AD-(urere ustburn)]

ăd valōr'ĕm, adv. & a. (Of taxes) in proportion to estimated value of goods. [L]

advance'¹ (-vah-), v.t. & i. 1. Move or put forward; promote (plans, persons); bring forward (claims, suggestions); accelerate (events); pay (money) before it is due; lend; raise (price). 2. v.i. Move forward; make progress; rise (in price); (p.p.) far on in progress, as ~d studies, ideas. So ~'MENT (-ahnsm-) n. (esp. of promotion of plan or person). [ME avaunce f. OF avancer f. Rom. *abantiare f. LL abante in front (ab away + ante before); see AD-]

advance'² (-vah-), n. Going forward; progress; personal approach, overture; rise in price; payment beforehand, loan; ~ copy of book etc., supplied before publication; in ~, before (of place or time). [f. prec. & f. F avance n. (as prec.)]

advan'tage¹ (-vah-), n. Better position, precedence, superiority; favourable circumstance, whence ădvantā'geous (-jus) a., ădvantā'geousLY² (-jus-) adv.; (in Tennis) next point or game won after deuce points or games; have the ~ of, gain an ~ over, have, acquire, a better position than (you have the ~ of me, esp., you know me & I do not know you); take ~ (avail oneself) of a circumstance; take ~ of (overreach) a person; take a person at ~ (by surprise); to ~, in a way to exhibit the merits (was seen, heard, to ~); ~-ground (usu. vantage-), position that gives superiority. [f. OF avantage f. avant (see ADVANCE¹) +-age -AGE, see -AD]

advan'tage² (-vah-), v.t. Be beneficial to; be an advantage to; further, promote. [late ME, f. prec. or F avantager]

Ad'vent (ăd-), n. Season before the Nativity; coming of Christ, Incarnation; second coming of Christ; (a~) any (important) arrival. Hence ~ISM (3) n., ~IST (2) n., (tenets of) member of a sect holding millenarian views. [late OE, ME advent f. L adventus arrival f. AD(venire vent- come)]

ădventi'tious (-shus), a. ·Coming from without; accidental, casual; ‖ (Law, of property) coming from a stranger or by collateral, not direct, succession. Hence ~LY² adv. [f. L adventicius; see prec. & -ITIOUS¹]

adven′ture[1], n. Risk, danger; daring enterprise; unexpected incident; commercial speculation; hazardous activity. [ME *aventure* f. OF f. Rom. *adventura (sc. *res* thing) about to happen (ADVENT); see AD-]

adven′ture[2], v.t. & i. Hazard, imperil, (oneself, thing); incur risk; dare to go or come (*into, in, upon,* a place); dare to enter *on, upon,* (undertaking). [ME, f. OF *aventurer* (as prec.)]

adven′turer (-cher-), n. One who seeks adventures; soldier of fortune; speculator; one who lives by his wits. [f. F *aventurier* (as ADVENTURE[1], see -ER[1])]

adven′turesome (-cher-), a. Given to adventures. [ADVENTURE[2] + -SOME]

adven′turess (-cher-), n. Female adventurer; woman who lives by her wits. [f. ADVENTURER, see -ESS]

adven′turous (-cher-), a. Rash, venturesome; enterprising. Hence ~LY[2] adv. [ME, f. OF *aventuros* (as ADVENTURE[1], see -OUS)]

ad′verb, n. Word that modifies or qualifies an adjective, verb, or other adverb, expressing a relation etc. (e.g. *gently, so, now, where, why*). [f. F *adverbe* or L *adverbium* (*verbum* word, VERB) transl. of Gk *epirrhēma*]

adverb′ial, a. Pertaining to an adverb; of the nature of an adverb. Hence ~LY[2] adv. [f. F, or LL *adverbialis*; see -AL]

ăd verb′um, adv. & a. Word for word. [L]

ad′versary, n. Opponent, antagonist, enemy; *the A~*, the Devil. [ME, f. AF *adverser*, OF *adversier, -aire* f. L *adversarius*; see ADVERSE & -ARY[1]]

adver′sative, a. (Of words etc.) expressing opposition or antithesis. Hence ~LY[2] (-vl-) adv. [f. LL *adversativus* (*adversari* oppose, see foll. & -IVE)]

ad′verse, a. Contrary, hostile, (*to*); hurtful, injurious, (*to*); placed opposite. Hence~LY[2] (-sl-) adv. [ME, f. OF *adverse* (earlier *avers*) f. L *adversus* p.p. of AD- (*vertere vers-* turn)]

adver′sity, n. Condition of adverse fortune; misfortune. [ME, f. OF *adversite* (earlier *av-*) f. L *adversitatem* (as prec., see -TY)]

advert′, v.i. Refer *to* (in speaking or writing). [ME *avert* f. OF *avertir* f. Rom. *advertire for L *advertere* (ADVERSE) whence mod. form *advert*]

ad′vertise (-z), v.t. & i. Notify, warn, inform, (person *of* thing, *that*); make generally known (thing *by* circular, *in* journal, also abs.); ~ *for*, ask for by public notice. [ME *avertise* f. OF *avertir* (st. *-iss-*); see ADVERT]

advert′isement (-zm-), n. Public announcement (usu. by placards or in journals). [earlier *avert-* f. F *avertissement* (as prec., see -MENT)]

advice′, n. Opinion given or offered as to

action, counsel; information given, news; (pl.) communications from a distance; (Commerc.) formal notice of transactions. [ME *avis* f. OF f. Rom. *advisum (*ad* to + *visum* p.p. of *vidēre* see; see AD-]

advis′|able (-z-), a. To be recommended; expedient. Hence ~ABIL′ITY, ~ABLENESS, nn., ~abLY[2] adv. [f. foll. + -ABLE]

advise′ (-z), v.t. & i. Offer counsel to; recommend (*the doctor ~s a change of air*); (Commerc.) inform, notify; take counsel *with*. Hence advis′ER[1] (-z-) n., esp. person habitually consulted. [ME *avise* f. OF *aviser* f. Rom. *advisare (see ADVICE)]

advised′ (-zd), a. Deliberate, considered, whence ~LY[2] (-iz′ĕdli) adv.; judicious; *ill-~*, injudicious. [p.p. of prec.]

advis′ory (-z-), a. Giving advice; consisting in giving advice. [ADVISE + -ORY]

ăd vīt′ăm aut cŭl′păm, adv. During good behaviour. [L]

ad′vocacy, n. Function of an advocate; pleading in support of. [ME, f. OF *advocacie, -tie*, f. med. L *advocatia* (as foll., see -ACY)]

ad′vocate[1], n. One who pleads for another; one who speaks in behalf of (proposal etc.); professional pleader in courts of justice; *Faculty of A~s*, Scots bar; *Lord A~*, principal law-officer of crown in Scotland; *Devil's ~* (also, L, *advocatus diaboli*), one who pleads against a candidate for canonization. Hence ~SHIP (-ts-) n., *advocat* f. L *advocātory* a. [ME *avocat* f. OF f. L *advocatus* p.p. (as n.) of AD(*vocare* call)]

ad′vocate[2], v.t. Plead for, defend, recommend publicly. [f. prec.]

||**advows′on** (-z-), n. Right of presentation to a benefice. [ME (AF) *avowesoun* etc. f. OF *avoeson* f. L *advocationem* (as prec., see -ION)]

adynam′ia, n. Want of vital force; physical prostration. Hence **adynam′ic** a. [Gk *adunamia* (*a-* not + *dunamis* power)]

ad′ytum, n. (pl. *-ta*). Innermost part of a temple; private chamber, sanctum. [L f. Gk *aduton* not to be entered (*a-* not + *duton* vbl adj. of *duō* enter)]

adze, n. & v.t. Tool for cutting away surface of wood, like axe with arched blade at right angles to handle; (vb) cut with ~. [OE *adesa* of unkn. orig.]

æ, ae, symbol repr. a vowel sound betw. *a* & *e*. 1. In OE short *æ* repr. orig. Teut. short *a*, the sound of *'a* in *man*; replaced after 1100 usu. by *a* sometimes by *e*. Long *æ* repr. same sound prolonged, & was replaced in 13th c. by *e* or *ee*. 2. In 16th c. *æ* was reintroduced to repr. L or Gk *ai*; as, *ædify* (L *aedificare*), *æther* (Gk *aithēr*). In familiar wds *æ* gave place to *e*, (*edify, ether*), being kept (pron. *ē*) in some Gk & L proper names (*Æneas, Cæsar*, but *Judea, Etna*), in names of Gk & Roman antiquities (*ædile, ægis*), & in some scientific terms (*ætiology, phænogamous*, but *phenomenon, museum*).

-æ, -ae, pl. suf. of L nouns of 1st decl. in *-a*, & L form of Gk *-ai* pl. of nouns of 1st decl. in *-ē, -a, -ēs, -as*; kept in non-naturalized words (*laminae, larvae*), esp. in proper names (*Heraclidae*) & names of animal & plant orders (*Felidae, Rosidae*) varying with *-as* in some wds acc. to degree of familiarity (*actiniae, -as*) or of technicality (mathematical *formulae*, theological *formulas*); familiar wds take *-as* (*areas, hyenas, Julias*).

aed'ile, n. Roman magistrate who superintended public buildings, shows, police, etc. Hence ~SHIP (-lsh-) n. [f. L *aedilis* (*aedes* house, see -ILE)]

‖ **ae'ger, n.** (In Eng. univv.) note certifying that student is ill. [L, = sick]

ae'gis, n. Protection, impregnable defence; (Myth.) shield of Zeus or Athene. [L, f. Gk *aigis*]

‖ **aegrōt'āt, n.** (In Eng. univv.) certificate that student is too ill to attend examination etc. [L, = he is sick (*aeger*)]

Aeol'ian, a. 1. Of Aeōlis, district of Asia Minor colonized by ancient Greeks; (Mus.) ~ *mode*, ancient Greek MODE, ninth of the church modes (with A as final & E as dominant). **2.** Of Aeolus, god of winds; ~ *harp*, stringed instrument producing musical sounds on exposure to wind. [f. L *Aeolius* (1. *Aeolis* Gk *Aiolis*; 2. *Aeolus* Gk *Aiolos*) + -AN]

Aeol'ic, a. & n. Aeolian (dialect). [f. L f. Gk *aiolikos* (as prec., see -IC)]

ae'olipȳle, -pile, (or ēōl²), n. Instrument for showing force of steam escaping through narrow aperture. [f. F *æolipyle* f. L *Aeoli pylae* f. Gk *Aiolou pulai* gates of Aeolus, god of winds]

aeolŏt'ropȳ, n. Change of physical qualities consequent on change of position. [f. Gk *aiolos* changeful + *-tropia* turning]

ae'on, ē'on, n. An age of the universe, immeasurable period; eternity; (Platonic philosophy) a power existing from eternity, emanation or phase of the supreme deity. [LL *aeon* f. Gk *aiōn* age]

ā'erāte, v.t. Expose to mechanical or chemical action of air; charge with carbonic acid gas (formerly called *fixed air*). Hence **āerA'TION n.** [f. L *aer* air + -ATE³, after F *aérer*]

āēr'ial (or āī²), a. & n. **1.** Of air, gaseous; thin as air, ethereal; immaterial, imaginary; of or in the atmosphere, atmospheric; existing, moving, in the air; ~ *railway, ropeway*, system of overhead cables from which cars or containers are suspended, usu. driven electrically; ~ *Derby*, annual air-race. **2.** n. (pron. āī²). ~ wire or antenna as used in wireless. Hence ~ITY (-āl²) n., ~LY² adv. [f. L f. Gk *aerios* (*aēr* air) + -AL]

aerie, aery, eyrie, eyry, (ū'erĭ, ĭī'ĭ), n. Nest of bird of prey, esp. eagle, or of raven or other bird that builds high up; human residence perched high on mountain; brood of bird of prey. [f. med. L

aeria, aerea, f. OF *aire* (= Prov. *agre* nest) f. L *ager agri*]

ā'erifōrm (or āī²), a. Of the form of air, gaseous; unsubstantial, unreal. [f. L *aer* air + -FORM]

aero- (āī'o, ā'ero) in comb. Air, of aircraft, as: ~*băt'ics*, feats of expert aviation [after *acrobatics*]; ~*biŏl'ogy*, study of airborne micro-organisms or spores; ~*dȳnăm'ics*, the physics of gases in motion & their mechanical effects; ~*dȳne*, heavier-than-air aircraft; ~*foil*, aeroplane wing, tailplane, or fin; ‖~*grăm*, wireless message; ~*lite, ~lith*, meteorite; ~*naut*, one who navigates a (lighter-than-air) flying machine; ~*naut'ic(al)* aa.; ~*naut'ics*, science, art, or practice of aerial navigation; ~*plănk'ton*, collective name for all the forms of minute organic life drifting in the air; ~*stăt*, lighter-than-air aircraft; ~*stăt'ics*, physics of gases in equilibrium, science of air-navigation. [Gk comb.-form of *aēr* air]

ā'erōbe, n. Any microbe that lives on free oxygen from the air. Hence **āerōb'IAN, āerōb'IC, aa.** [AERO-, Gk *bios* life]

‖ **aerodrōme** (āī²), n. Large tract of open level ground, including all buildings & fixtures, for the operation of aircraft. [AERO-, -DROME]

‖ **aeroplāne** (āī²), n. Mechanically driven heavier-than-air flying machine. [f. F *aéroplane* (AERO-, Gk *planos* wandering)]

aeru'ginous (ērŏō-), a. Of the nature or colour of verdigris, or copper-rust. [f. L *aeruginosus* (*aerugo -inis* verdigris f. *aes aeris* brass, see -OUS)]

Aescūlāp'ius, n. God of medicine; physician. Hence ~IAN a. [L]

aes'thēte, n. Professed appreciator of the beautiful. [f. Gk *aisthētēs* one who perceives (as foll.)]

aesthĕt'‖ic, a. Belonging to the appreciation of the beautiful; having such appreciation; in accordance with principles of good taste. Hence ~ICAL a., ~icalLY² adv., ~ICISM, ~ICS, nn. [f. Gk *aisthētikos* (*aisthanomai* perceive, see -IC)]

aestho-physiŏl'ogȳ (-z-), n. Scientific study of the organs of sensation. [irreg. f. Gk *aisth-* perceive + PHYSIOLOGY]

aestival, (esp. U.S.) **estival,** (ĕs'tĭval, ĕstĭv'al), a. Belonging to, appearing in, summer. [ME *estival* f. OF f. L *aestivalis* f. *aestivus* (*aestas* heat), see -IVE, -AL]

aes'tivāte (ĕst-, ēst-), v.i. Spend the summer, esp. (Zool.) in state of torpor. [f. L *aestivare*, see -ATE³]

aestivā'tion (ĕst-, ēst-), n. (Zool.) aestivating; (Bot.) arrangement of petals in flower-bud before expansion. [f. prec., see -ATION]

aetāt'is, aet'āt., aet. Of or at the age of (*aet.* 17); *anno* ~ *suae —*, in the —th year of his age. [L]

aetiŏl'ogȳ, n. Assignment of a cause; philosophy of causation; (Med.) science of the causes of disease. So **aetiolŏ'gICAL**

a., aetiolŏ'gicalLY[2] adv. [f. LL f. Gk *aitiologia* (*aitia* cause, see -LOGY)]

af-, pref. = AD- before *f*.

afār', adv. At, to, a distance (usu. ~ *off*; *from* ~, from a distance). [ME *of feor, on ferr,* see A- (2, 3), FAR]

ăff'able, a. Easy of address, courteous, complaisant. Hence or cogn. **ăffa**BIL'ITY n., **ăff'abl**Y[2] adv. [F, f. L *affabilis* f. AF(*fari* speak), see -BLE]

affair', n. Thing to be done; concern, business, matter, as *that is my* ~; love ~; (pl.) ordinary pursuits of life; ~ *of honour,* duel; (colloq., of material things) *a gorgeous* etc. ~. ·[ME, f. OF *afaire* (*à faire* to do), cf. ADO]

affaire (de cœur) (see Ap.), n. Love affair. [F]

affect'[1], v.t. Practise, use, as ~ *a costume*; (of things) tend to assume (form, shape, etc.); assume (character), as ~ *the free-thinker*; pretend to have or feel (indifference etc.); pretend (*to* do). [f. F *affecter* or L *affectare* aim at, frequent. of AF(*ficere fect-* = *facere* do)]

affect'[2], v.t. Attack (as disease); move, touch, (in mind), whence ~**ing**LY[2] adv.; produce (material) effect on; (pass., arch.) be assigned, allotted, (*to* particular service etc.). [f. F *affecter* or L *affect-* p.p. stem of *afficere* act on,·influence; see prec.]

ăff'ĕct[3], n. (psych.). Feeling, emotion, desire. [f. L *affectus* disposition f. *afficere* (prec.)]

ăffĕctā'tion, n. Studied display *of*; artificiality of manner; pretence; (rare) declared occupation or employment (*all ships, whatever their* ~). [F, or f. L *affectatio* (as AFFECT[1], see -ATION)]

affĕc'tĕd, a. Artificially assumed or displayed; pretended; (of persons) full of affectation, artificial, whence ~LY[2] adv., ~NESS n.; (with adv.) disposed, inclined, (*towards* or abs.); attacked (as by disease); moved in the feelings; acted upon physically. [AFFECT[1, 2] +-ED[1]]

affĕc'tion, n. Affecting; mental state, emotion, whence ~AL a.; disposition (*towards*); goodwill, love, (*towards*); bodily state due to any influence; malady, disease; mode of living; property, quality, attribute. [ME, f. OF f. L *affectionem* (as AFFECT[2], see -ION)]

affĕc'tionate (-shon-), a. Loving; fond; (of things) showing love or tenderness. Hence ~LY[2] (-tl-) adv., ~NESS (-tn-) n. [f. F *affectionné* or med. L *affectionatus*; see -ATE[3]]

affĕc'tive, a. Pertaining to the affections, emotional. [f. F *affectif* f. LL *affectivus* (as AFFECT[2], see -IVE)]

ăff'erent, a. Conducting inwards or towards, as ~ *nerves,* ~ *vessels.* [f. L AF-(*ferre* bring), see -ENT]

ŏffĕttuŏ'sŏ (-tōō-), adv. (mus.). Feelingly. [It.]

affi'ance[1], n. Faith, trust (*in*); pledging of faith, esp. plighting of troth in mar-

riage. [ME, f. OF *afiancè* f. *afier* f. med. L AF*fidare* (*fidus* trusty), see -ANCE]

affi'ance[2], v.t. Promise solemnly in marriage (usu. pass.). [ME, f. OF *afiancer* f. *afiance*, see prec.]

affiche (ăfēsh'), n. Notice-paper affixed to wall, poster. [F, f. *afficher* post up]

ăffĭdāv'ĭt, n. Written statement, confirmed by oath, to be used as judicial proof. (Strictly, deponent *swears* an ~, judge *takes* it; but in pop. use deponent *makes* or *takes* it). [med. L, = has stated on oath, f. AF*fidare*, see AFFIANCE[1]]

affil'iāte, v.t. (Of an institution) adopt (persons as members, societies as branches); attach (persons, societies) *to*, connect (them) *with*, (a society); (Law) fix paternity of (illegitimate child *on* putative father) for purpose of maintenance; ascribe (child) *to* its parent; father (a thing) *upon*, trace (it) *to*. So **affilia'**TION n. [f. med. L AF*filiare* adopt (*filius* son), see -ATE[3]]

affined' (-nd), a. Related, connected. [f. F *affiné* (*affin* f. L *affinis*, see foll.) + -ED[1]; no vb in F or E]

affin'ĭtÿ, n. Relationship, relations, by marriage; relations, kindred, in general; structural resemblance (between animals, plants, languages); (fig.) similarity of character suggesting relationship, family likeness; liking; attraction; (Chem.) tendency of certain elements to unite with others. [ME, f. OF *afinite* f. L *affinitatem* (AF*finis* related, lit. bordering on, f. *finis* end, see -TY)]

affĭrm', v.t. & i. Assert strongly, aver; make formal declaration, (Law) make AFFIRMATION; (Logic, Gram.) state in the affirmative; (Law) confirm, ratify, (judgement). Hence ~ABLE, ~atORY, aa. [ME *af(f)erm(e)* f. OF *afermer* f. L AF*firmare* (*firmus* strong)]

affĭrmā'tion, n. Affirming, esp. (Law) solemn declaration by person who conscientiously declines taking an oath. [F, or f. L *affirmatio* (as prec., see -ATION)]

affĭrm'ative, a. & n. Affirming, answering yes; (Logic) expressing agreement of the two terms of a proposition; *answer in the* ~, answer yes, say that a thing is so. Hence ~LY[2] (-vl-) adv. [ME, f. OF *affirmatif* or LL *affirmativus* (as prec., see -IVE)]

affix'[1], v.t. Fix, fasten, (thing *to, on*); impress (seal, stamp); add in writing (signature, postscript); attach (censure, salary). [f. obs. F *affixer* or med. L *affixare* frequent. of L AF(*figere fix-* fix)]

ăff'ix[2], n. Appendage, addition; (Gram.) addition placed at the beginning or end of root, stem, or word, or in body of word, to modify its meaning. [f. F *affixe* f. L *affigere* (see prec.)]

affix'ture, n. Affixing. [f. AFFIX[1] after FIXTURE]

afflāt'us, n. Communication of supernatural knowledge; divine impulse, poetic or other; inspiration. [L vbl n. f. AF(*flare flat-* blow)]

afflict', v.t. Distress with bodily or mental suffering. [f. obs. *afflict* adj., f. OF *afflict*, earlier *afflit*, f. L AF(*fligere flict-* dash)]

afflic'tļion, n. Misery, distress; pain, calamity. So ~IVE a. [ME, f. OF f. L *afflictionem* (as prec., see -ION)]

ăff'luļent¹ (-lŏŏ-), a. Flowing freely, copious; abounding (esp. in riches), wealthy. Hence or cogn. ~ENCE n., ~entLY² adv. [ME, f. OF, f. L AF(*fluere flux-* flow), see -ENT]

ăff'luent² (-lŏŏ-), n. Tributary stream. [f. prec., prob. after F]

ăff'lŭx, n. Flow towards a point, esp. of humours; accession. [f. F, or med. L *affluxus -ūs*, vbl n. as AFFLUENT¹]

afford', v.t. (With *can*) have the means, be rich enough, (*to* do), manage to spare; furnish, bestow; (of things) yield supply of. [OE *geforthian* further (f. Y-+*forthian* (FORTH), ME *i-forthen, aforthe.* Mod. sp. assim. to wds in AF-; for *-d-* cf. BURDEN]

affo'rest, v.t. Convert into forest or (formerly) hunting-ground. So ~A'TION n. [f. med. L AF*forestare* (*foresta* FOREST)]

affrăn'chise (-z), v.t. Free from servitude or obligation. [f. F *affranchir*, as EN-FRANCHISE, with pref. A- (4)]

affray', n. Breach of the peace, caused by fighting or riot in a public place. [ME, f. OF *effrei* f. *esfreer*, vb f. Rom. **exfri-dare* (Rom. **fridus* f. Gmc **fridhu* peace); cf. AFRAID]

affreight'ment (-rāt-), n. The chartering of a ship to carry cargo (usu. *contract of* ~). [f. F *affrètement*, with sp. alt. after FREIGHT]

ăff'ricate, n. (phonet.). Combination of explosive consonant with an immediately following fricative or spirant, as G *pf*, *z*(= ts). So **affric'ative** a. & n. [f. L *affricatus*, cf. FRICATIVE]

affright'¹ (-īt), v.t. (arch.). Frighten. [late formation on FRIGHT v., partly due to obs. *affright* p.p. of OE **afyrhtan* (a-intensive)]

affright'² (-īt), n. (arch.). Alarm, terror. [f. prec.]

affront'¹ (-ŭnt), v.t. Insult openly: put to the blush, offend the modesty or self--respect of; face, confront. [ME, f. OF *afronter* slap in the face, insult, f. Rom. **AFfrontare* (*frons frontis* face)]

affront'² (-ŭnt), n. Open insult, as *put* ~ *upon, offer an* ~ *to, feel it an* ~. [f. prec.]

affū'sion (-zhn), n. Pouring on, esp. of water on the body in one kind of baptism; (Med.) pouring of water, usually 50° to 70° Fahr., upon fever patients. [f. LL *affusio* f. L AF(*fundere fus-* pour), see -ION]

Afghan (ăf'gàn), n. Native, language, of ~istan; (*a~*) knitted woollen coverlet.

afield', adv. On or in the field (esp. of labour or battle); to the field; away from home, at a distance, as *far* ~. [OE, f. A²]

afīre', adv. & pred. a. On fire (lit. & fig.). [ME, f. A²]

aflāme', adv. & pred. a. In flame, in a glow of light, (lit. & fig.). [f. A²]

afloat', adv. & pred. a. In a floating condition; at sea, on board ship, in naval service; full of water; floating in the air; out of debt, paying one's way; in full swing; in general circulation, current; (Commerc.) in currency as negotiable document; unsettled, adrift. [OE, f. A²]

à fond (see Ap.), adv. Thoroughly, fully. [F]

afŏŏt', adv. & pred. a. On one's own feet; astir, on the move; in operation or employment. [ME, f. A²]

afōre', adv. & prep. (Naut.) in front, in front of, as ~ *the mast*; (arch.) previously. [OE, f. A²+FORE²]

afōre- in comb. Before, previously, as ~*cited,* ~*going,* ~*named,* ~*said;* ~*thought,* premeditated, as *malice* ~*thought;* ~*time,* previously. [prec.]

ā fōrtiōr'ī, adv. With stronger reason, more conclusively. [L]

afraid', pred. a. Alarmed, frightened, (abs. or *of*); ~ (of the consequences, & therefore unwilling) *to do* a thing, ~ *of* a thing's *happening,* ~ *lest it should happen,* ~ (*that*) *it will happen; I'm* ~ (colloq.), I have to admit with regret (*I'm* ~ *I'm late; I'm* ~ *there's none left*). [p.p. of obs. vb *affray* f. OF *esfreer*, see AFFRAY]

ăf'reet, -rit, -rite, (-rēt), n. Evil demon in Mohammedan mythology. [Arab. *ifrīt*]

afrĕsh', adv. Anew, with fresh beginning. [A- (3)+FRESH]

Af'rican (ăf-), a. & n. (Native) of Africa. Hence ~ISM (4) n., ~IZE (3) v.t. [see -AN]

Afrikaans' (ăf-; -ahns), n. S.-African or Cape Dutch. [= Du. *Afrikaansch*]

Afrikăn'der (ăf-), n. S.-African breed of cattle; (formerly) Afrikaner. [f. Afrikaans *Afrikaander* alt. of Du. *Afrikaner* after *Hollander* etc.]

Afrika'ner (ăfrĭkahn-), n. Native of S. Africa born of European (esp. Dutch) settlers. [Du., = African]

Af'r(ō)- (ăf-), comb. form of *African.*

aft (ahft), adv. (naut.). In or near stern of ship; towards the stern; *fore & ~*, from stem to stern, lengthwise (also as adj. *fore-&-~*). [hist. before 1600 obsc.; prob. alt. f. ME *baft* (see ABAFT) on anal. of *after*]

af'ter¹ (ah-), adv., prep., & conj. **1.** adv. Behind in place, later in time, (*Jill came tumbling* ~; *look before & ~; soon, a week,* ~). **2.** prep. In pursuit or quest of, as *run, inquire,* ~ *him;* about, concerning, as *look* ~ *him,* take care of, keep an eye on, him; for, as *hanker* ~; following in point of time, later than, (~ *you*, formula in yielding precedence; ~ *you with,* colloq. request for next turn at; ~ *six months,* when six months have or had elapsed); in view of, as ~ *such behaviour*; next in importance to; according to (~ a FASHION; ~ one's *own heart*, such as one loves); in imitation of (person), as *a picture* ~ *Rubens*; in allusion to, as *named* ~; ~ *all*, in spite of all that has happened or has been said etc. (~ *all, what does it matter?*) or of one's exertions, expectations, etc. (*he tried for an hour & failed* ~ *all*; *so you have come* ~ *all!*). **3.** conj. In, at, the time subsequent to that at which, as ~ *he went, goes, has gone, had gone.* [OE *æfter*, Gmc f. *af-*(cogn. w. L *ab*, Gk *apo*) +compar. suf. *-ter* (see -THER)]

af′ter² (ah-), a. Later, following, as ~ *years*; (Naut.) hinder, posterior, as ~ *cabin, masts*. [f. prec.]

af′terbirth, n. Membrane enveloping the foetus in the womb, so called because its extrusion follows that of the infant, placenta. [AFTER a.]

af′ter-care, n. Attention bestowed on an individual or class after a certain period of treatment etc.; freq. attrib., as ~ *association*. [AFTER a.]

af′terdamp, n. Choke-damp, gas left in mine after explosion of fire-damp. [AFTER a.]

af′ter-effect, n. Effect that follows after an interval. [AFTER a.]

af′terglow, n. Glow in the west after sunset. [AFTER a.]

af′ter-grass, n. Grass that grows after first crop has been mown for hay, or among stubble after harvest. [AFTER a.]

af′terlight, n. Light of what is known afterwards, hindsight. [AFTER a.]

af′termáth, n. After-grass; (fig.) consequences, fruits, results, as *the* ~ *of war*. [AFTER a.+*math* mowing, OE *mǽth* f. Gmc *mǽ*-MOW]

af′termost (ah-), a. (naut.). Nearest the stern, most aft. [f. AFTER +-MOST]

afternoon′, n. The time from noon to evening, as *in, during, the* ~, *on Wednesday* ~, (fig.) *the* ~ *of life*. [AFTER prep.]

af′terpiece, n. Farce or smaller entertainment after a play. [AFTER a.]

af′ters (ah-), n. pl. (colloq.). Course following main course esp. at midday meal. [AFTER a. or adv.]

af′terthought, n. Reflection after the act; later expedient or explanation. [AFTER a. or adv.]

af′terwards (ah-; -z), adv. Later, subsequently. [OE *æftanweard*, a. (*æftan* AFT +-WARD), late OE *æfterweard*, ME *-ward*(s): see -ES]

ag-, pref. = AD- before *g*.

ag̃a (äg′a, agah′), n. Commander, chief officer in Mohammedan countries. [Turk. *agha* master]

again′ (*or* agèn′), adv. Another time, once more; ~ *& ~*, *time & ~*, repeatedly; *ever & ~*, *now & ~*, occasionally; *as much* ~, twice as much; *half as much* ~, one-&-a-half times as much; further, besides;

on the other hand, as *these* ~ *are more expensive*; *back* ~ (to the original position or condition); in return, as *answer* ~; in response, as *rocks echoed* ~, *glasses rang* ~; proportionately to specified act or condition, as *the loaded table groaned* ~. [OE *ongēan, ongægn*, etc., ME *ayen* etc., & (orig. north.) *again*; Gmc f. ON + *gag-an-* straight]

against′ (*or* agènst′), prep. & conj. **1.** In opposition to, as *fight* ~, *I am* ~ *reform*; in contrast to, as ~ *a dark background*; in anticipation of, as ~ *his coming*, ~ *a rainy day*; in preparation for, as *warned* ~ *pickpockets*; into collision with, as *ran* ~ *a rock*, (colloq.) *ran* ~ (chanced to meet) *a friend*; opposite to, as ~ *the horsepond* (usu. *over* ~). **2.** conj. (arch.). By the time that (*be ready* ~ *he comes*). [early ME *ayenes* etc., f. *ayen* (AGAIN) +-ES, with later (southern) inorganic -*t* as in *amidst, amongst, betwixt, whilst*]

ăg′ama, n. African & Indian lizard of the iguana type. [Carib]

ăg′ami, n. Tropical American bird, the trumpeter. [native name in Guiana]

agăm′ic, a. (zool.). Characterized by absence of sexual action. [as foll.+-IC]

ăgamo|gĕn′esis, n. Asexual reproduction. So ~gĕnĕt′IC a., ~gĕnĕt′ICALLY adv. [as foll.+*genesis* birth]

ăg′amous, a. (biol.). Without (distinguishable) sexual organs. [f. Gk *agamos* (*a*- not +*gamos* marriage)+-OUS]

agăpe′¹, adv. & pred. a. On the gape; open-mouthed with wonder or expectation. [A prep.]

ăg′apē², n. Love-feast held by early Christians in connexion with Lord's Supper; (Theol.) Christian love, charity (opp. *erōs* earthly or sexual love). [Gk, = brotherly love]

Agapemon|e (ăgapĕm′onǐ), n. Love-abode (usu. with sinister implication). Hence ~ITE¹ n. & a., (member) of a sect or association founded in Somerset *c.* 1850, pop. believed to practise free love. [irreg. f. Gk *agapē* love +*monē* abode]

ăg′ăr(-ăg′är), n. Solidifying agent in culture-media for bacteria prepared from certain seaweeds. [Malay]

ăg′aric (*or* agä²), n. Mushroom; name of various fungi. [f. L f. Gk *agarikon*]

ăg′ate, n. Name of several varieties of precious stone (semipellucid variegated chalcedonies); burnishing instrument of gold-wiredrawers; *the printing-type called in England *ruby*. [f. F *agate*, *-the*, It. *agata, -tha*, f. L f. Gk *akhatēs*, whence earlier F *achate*, in ME *achate*]

Agäv′e, n. (bot.). Genus of plants including American aloe. [f. L f. Gk *Agauē*, prop. name in myth.]

agäze′, adv. On the gaze. [A prep.]

āge¹, n. Length of life or of existence; *moon's* ~, time elapsed since new moon; duration of life required for a purpose, as *come of* ~, *full* ~ (in Eng. Law, 21 years),

~ *of discretion* (14), *over* ~; latter part of life, as *peevishness of* ~, ~ *before honesty*, children must give precedence to their elders; a generation; ~ *of* CONSENT; BRAZEN [1] etc.~; (Hist., Geol.) great period, as *Patriarchal A*~, *Ice A*~; (colloq.) long time, as *waiting for*~s. [ME, f. OF f. Rom. **ætaticum* f. L *aetas -atis* age; see -AGE]

āge[2], v.t. & i. (part. ~*ing*, *aging*). (Cause to) grow old. [f. prec.]

-age, suf. OF f. L *-aticum*, neut. of adj. suf. *-aticus* -ATIC (e.g. L *viaticum* journey-money, (later) journey. In Romanic greatly extended to form abst. nn. of appurtenance, & collectives, as **aeta-ticum* AGE, **coraticum* COURAGE. In med. L, the OF *-age* appears as *-agium*, e.g. OF *homage*, med. L *homagium*. After-wards added as living suf. in F & in E. Meaning: (1) collective belongings or aggregate of (*cellarage*); (2) function, condition, (*baronage*, *bondage*); (3) action (*breakage*); (4) fees payable for, cost of using, (*cartage*, *demurrage*).

aged, a. **1.** (āj'Id). Having lived long, old. **2.** (ājd). Of the age of, as ~ *ten*; (of horses) over six years old. Hence **ā'gĕd-**NESS n. [f. AGE v. + -ED [1]]

āge'less (-jl-), a. Never growing old. [AGE n. + -LESS]

ā'gencÿ, n. Active operation, action, as *moral, free,* ~; instrumentality, as *by the* ~ *of*; action personified, as *an invisible* ~; (Commerc.) office of agent; establishment for business purposes, as *Reuter's A*~. [f. med. L *agentia* (L *agere* do, see -ENCE)]

agĕn'da, n. Things to be done, (list of) items of business to be considered at a meeting; memorandum book. [L, neut. pl. of gerundive of *agere* do]

ā'gēne, n. Nitrogen trichloride, used for whitening flour. [P]

ā'gent, n. One who exerts power or produces an effect; (of things) efficient cause; a natural force acting on matter, as *chemical* ~; one who does the actual work, esp. one who represents a person or firm in business (*who is your* ~ *in Paris?*); *estate-, house-, land-,* ~. So **agĕn'tIAL** (-shl) a. [as ACT[2], -ENT]

agent provocateur (see Ap.), n. Person employed to detect suspected offenders by tempting them to overt action. [F]

agglŏm'er|āte[1], v.t. & i. Collect into a mass. Hence ~A'TION n., ~ātive a. [f. L *AGglomerare* (*glomus -meris* ball), see -ATE[3]]

agglŏm'erāte[2], a. & n. (Collected into) a mass; (Geol.) mass of volcanic fragments united under heat, opp. to con-glomerate. [as prec., see -ATE[2]]

agglŭt'ināte[1] (-lōō-), a. Glued together; consisting of simple words combined into compounds without change of form or loss of meaning. [f. L *AGglutinare* (*gluten -tinis* glue) see -ATE[2]]

agglŭt'in|āte[2] (-lōō-), v.t. & i. Unite as with glue; combine simple words to express compound ideas; (t. & i.) turn

into glue. Hence ~A'TION n., ~ātive a. [as prec., see -ATE[3]]

ăgg'randize, -ise (-īz), v.t. Increase the power, rank, wealth, of (person, State); exaggerate, embellish. Hence **aggrän'-dizeMENT, -ise-,** (-zm-) n. [f. F *agrandir* (st. *-iss-*) prob. f. It. AG(*grandire* f. L *grandis* large, the ending being assim. to vbs in -IZE)]

ăgg'rav|āte, v.t. Increase the gravity of (burden, offence, etc.); (colloq.) exasperate (person). So ~A'TION n. [f. L *AGgravare* make heavy (*gravis*) or F *aggraver*; see -ATE[3]]

ăgg'rēgate[1], a. & n. **1.** Collected into one body; collective, total; (Law) composed of associated individuals, as *cor-poration* ~. **2.** n. Sum total; assemblage; broken stone etc. used in making concrete; (Phys.) mass of homogeneous particles; *in the* ~, as a whole. [f. L *AGgregare* herd together (*grex gregis* flock), see -ATE[1, 2]]

ăgg'rĕg|āte[2], v.t. & i. Collect together; (trans.) unite (individual to company); amount to (specified total). Hence ~A'TION n., ~ātive a. [f. as prec., -ATE[3]]

aggrĕss', v.i. (rare). Begin a (or the) quarrel. So ~ION (-shn), ~OR, nn. [f. p.p. of L AG(*gredi gress- = gradi* step) or F *ag(g)resser*; later back-form. f. *aggression*]

aggrĕss'ive, a. & n. Of attack; offensive; disposed to attack; forceful; *assume the* ~, begin the quarrel. Hence ~LY[2] (-vl-) adv., ~NESS (-vn-) n. [as prec., see -IVE]

aggrieve', v.t. Grieve, distress, oppress, (usu. pass.). [ME *agreve* f. OF *agrever* f. L *aggravare* AGGRAVATE; mod. sp. after L, & GRIEVE]

aghast' (-gahst, -găst), a. Terrified; struck with amazement. [ME p.p. of obs. vb *agast* (A- (1) + *gasten*, obs. *gast* to alarm); sp. after *ghastly*]

ā'gĭle, a. Quick-moving, nimble, active. Hence or cogn. **agil'ITY** n., ~LY[2] (-l-lI) adv. [ME, f. OF f. L *agilis* (*agere* do)]

ā'giŏ, n. Percentage charged on exchange of paper-money into cash, or of one currency into another more valuable; excess value of one currency over another; exchange business. [It., = ease]

ā'giotage, n. Exchange business; speculation in stocks; stock-jobbing. [F, f. *agioter* (prec. + connecting *-t-*); see -AGE]

agist', v.t. Take in live stock to feed; charge (land or its owner) with a public burden. So ~MENT n. [f. OF *agister* (à to + *gister* lodge f. Rom. **jacitare* frequent. of *jacēre* lie)]

ā'gĭtāte, v.t. Move, shake; disturb, excite, (feelings, persons); revolve mentally, discuss, debate, (plans etc.); (abs.) keep up an agitation (*for*). [f. L *agitare* or F *agiter*; see -ATE[3]]

ăgĭtā'tion, n. Moving, shaking; commotion, disturbance, (mental or physical); debate, discussion; keeping of a matter constantly before the public; public excitement. [F, or f. L *agitatio* (as prec., see -ATION)]

ăgĭta′tō (-tah-), adv. (mus.). In an agitated manner. [It.]

ă′gĭtātor, n. One who agitates, esp. politically; apparatus for shaking or mixing. [L (see AGITATE & -OR)]

Aglaia (ăgli′a), n. One of the Graces. [Gk]

ăg′lĕt, aig′lĕt, n. Metal tag of a lace; spangle or other metallic ornament of dress; tagged point hanging from shoulder upon breast of some uniforms (usu. *aiguillette*); catkin of hazel, birch, etc. [ME, f. F *aiguillette* dim. of *aiguille* needle f. LL *acucula* dim. of *acus* needle]

agley′ (-ā), adv. (Sc.). Askew, awry. [A prep. +Sc. *gley* squint]

aglow′ (-ō), adv. & pred. a. In a glow. [A prep.]

ăg′nail, n. Torn skin at root of finger-nail; (formerly) corn on toe or foot. [OE *angnægl* f. *ang-* (cf. Goth. *aggwus*) tight, painful, +*nægl* nail (of iron etc.), hard excrescence fixed in the flesh; mod. sense, & forms *hang-nail*, (Sc.) *anger-nail*, result from pop. etym., *nail* being taken as finger-nail]

ăg′nāte, n. & a. (One who is) descended by male links (also, by male or female links) from same male ancestor (cf. COGNATE); sprung from same forefather, of same clan or nation; (fig.) akin, of same nature. So **ăgnăt′ĭc** a., **ăgnā′tĭon** n. [f. F *agnat* or L *agnatus* (*ad* to +*gnatus* born p.p. of (*g*)*nasci* f. stem *gen*-beget)]

ăgnōm′ĕn, n. A fourth name occas. given to Romans (cf. COGNOMEN); (loosely) nickname. [L (*ad* to +(*g*)*nomen* name)]

agnŏs′tĭc, n. & a. 1. One who holds that nothing is known, or likely to be known, of the existence of a God or of anything beyond material phenomena. 2. adj. Pertaining to this theory. Hence ~ISM n. [f. Gk *agnōstos* unknown (*a-* not +*gnō-* know); see -IC]

Ag′nus Căs′tus (ă-), n. Tree once held a preservative of chastity. [L, f. Gk *agnos* (name of tree), confused w. *hagnos* chaste, whence L *castus* is added]

Ag′nus Dē′ī (ă-), n. Part of Mass beginning *Agnus Dei*; figure of lamb bearing cross or flag; cake of wax stamped with such figure & blessed by Pope. [L, = lamb of God]

agō′, a. & adv. (Adj., always following noun) past, gone by, as *ten years* ~; (adv.) *long* ~, long since. [ME *ago, agone* p.p. of obs. vb *ago* (A-(1)+GO)]

agŏg′, adv. & pred. a. On the move, eager, expectant. [perh. f. OF *en gogues* (*gogue* fun, orig. unkn.)]

agŏn′ĭc, a. Making no angle; ~ *line*, line of no magnetic variation. [f. Gk *agōnios* without angle (*a-* not +*gōnia* angle)+-IC]

ăgŏnĭs′tĭc, a. Pertaining to athletic contests (esp. of Ancient Greece); (Rhet.) polemic, combative; strained, aiming at

effect. Hence ~AL a., ~aLLY² adv. [f. Gk *agōnistikos* f. *agōnistēs* combatant (*agōnes* games); cf. LL *agonisticus*]

ăg′onĭz|e, -is|e (-īz), v.t. & f. Torture; suffer agony, writhe in anguish; contend in arena, wrestle (lit. & fig.); make desperate efforts for effect. Hence ~īngLY² adv. [f. F *agoniser* or LL *agonizare* f. Gk *agōnizomai* contend (*agōn*, see prec.)]

ăg′onў, n. Mental anguish; ~ *column* (colloq.), = PERSONAL *column*; paroxysm of pleasure; pangs of death; extreme bodily suffering; struggle. [ME, f. OF *agonie* or LL *agonia* f. Gk *agōnia* f. *agōn* contest; see -Y¹]

ăgoraphŏb′ia, n. Dread in, and of, open spaces. [Gk *agora* assembly, -PHOBIA]

agou′tĭ, -tў, (-gōō-), n. Genus of rodents of cavy or guinea-pig family, esp. a hare-like animal of W. Indies. [f. F *agouti* or Sp. *aguti* f. native Ind. *aguti*]

ăg′rapha, n. pl. Sayings of Christ not recorded in the Gospels. [Gk, = unwritten things]

agrār′ian, a. & n. 1. Relating to landed property; ~ *outrage* (arising from discord between landlords & tenants); relating to cultivated land. 2. n. Advocate of redistribution of landed property, whence ~ISM n., ~IZE v.t. & i. [f. L *agrarius* (*ager agri* land, see -ARY¹) +-AN]

agree′, v.i. & t. Consent (*to* proposal, statement, *to* do); concur (*with* person *that*); become, be, in harmony (*with* person); (pl.) ~ *together, cannot* ~, get on with one another; suit the constitution of, as *work, lobster, does not* ~ *with him*; (Gram.) take some number, gender, case, person; (trans.) bring (balance, items of accounts) into harmony; consent to or approve of (proposal, terms, etc.). [ME, f. OF *agreer* f. Rom. *aggratare* make agreeable (*gratus*)]

agree′ab|le (-rĭabl), a. Pleasing (*to* or abs.); (colloq., of persons) well-disposed (*to* a thing, *to* do, or abs.); conformable *to*, as ~*le to all experience*. Hence ~leNESS n., ~LY² adv. [ME, f. OF *agreable* (*agreer* AGREE, see -ABLE)]

agree′ment, n. Mutual understanding, covenant, treaty; (Law) contract legally binding on parties; accordance in opinion; (Gram.) concord in gender, number, case, person. [ME, partly OF, partly f. AGREE +-MENT]

agréments (agrā′mahṅ), n. pl. Agreeable qualities or surroundings; (Mus.) ornamental notes embellishing a melody. [F]

agrĕs′tic, a. Rural, rustic; uncouth. [f. L *agrestis* (*ager* field) +-IC]

ăg′rĭcŭlture, n. Cultivation of the soil. Hence ăgrĭcŭl′turAL (-cher-) a., ăgrĭcŭl′tur(al)IST (-cher-) nn. [F, or f. L *agri cultura* (*ager agri* field +*cultura* CULTURE)]

ăg′rimonў, n. Kinds of plants, esp. *Agrimonia eupatoria* with small yellow flowers. [ME *egrimoigne* etc. f. OF *aigremoine* f. L *agrimonia*, whence OE & mod. forms]

ăg′rimōtor, n. Agricultural motor tractor. [f. L *ager agri* field + MOTOR]

agrŏn′om|ў, n. Rural economy, husbandry. So **ăgronŏm′ic(AL)** aa., **ăgronŏm′ics,** ~IST, nn. [f. Gk *agronomos* overseer of land (*agros* land + -*nomos* f. *nemō* dispense), see -Y¹]

aground′, adv. & pred. a. Upon the bottom of shallow water, as *be, run,* ~ (of ships). [ME, f. A prep. + GROUND]

āg′ūe, n. Malarial fever, with cold, hot, & sweating stages; shivering fit; quaking (lit. & fig.); ~-*cake,* enlargement of spleen or liver caused by ~. Hence **āg′ūED²** (-ūd) a. [ME, f. OF f. L *acuta* (sc. *febris* fever) ACUTE]

āg′ūish, a. Of the nature of ague; tending to produce ague; subject to ague; ague-like, quaking; coming by fits & starts. Hence ~LY² adv. [f. prec. + -ISH¹]

ah, int. expr. sorrow, regret, surprise, admiration, entreaty, remonstrance, dislike, contempt, mockery. [not in OE; ME has *a,* perh. f. OF *a, ah*]

aha′ (ahhah′), int. expr. surprise, triumph, mockery, irony. [f. AH + HA¹; formerly written *a ha*]

aha², n. See HA-HA n.

ahead (ahĕd′), adv. & pred. a. In advance; in the direct line of one's forward motion, as *breakers* ~; straight forwards; forward at a rapid pace, as *go* ~; in advance *of* (lit. & fig.). [f. A prep. + HEAD¹]

ahĕm′ (*a*-h-), int. used to attract attention or gain time. [lengthened form of *hem*]

ahimsa (a-hĭm′sah), n. Non-violence or non-killing acclaimed in Hindu Scriptures as the highest form of duty. [f. Skr. *a* without, *himsa* injury]

ahoy′ (*a*-h-), int. Nautical call used in hailing. [obs. *a* int. + HOY²]

Ah′riman. See ZOROASTRIAN.

à huis clos (ah wē klō), adv. With closed doors, in private. [F]

ahŭll′ (*a*-h-), adv. (naut.). With sails taken in & helm lashed on lee side. [f. A prep. + HULL²]

ai (ah′ī), n. Three-toed sloth of S. America. [f. Braz. *aï,* repr. its cry]

aiblins. See ABLINS.

aid¹, v.t. Help (person *to* do, or abs.); promote (recovery etc.). [ME, f. OF *aid(i)er* f. L *adjutare* frequent. of AD-(*juvare jut-*)]

aid², n. Help; (Law) help claimed by defendant from one who has joint-interest; (hist.) grant of subsidy or tax to king, (later) exchequer loan; helper; material source of help (usu. pl.), as ~*s & appliances; what's* (all) *this in* ~ *of?* (colloq.), what's your object? [ME, f. OF *aide* f. Rom. *adjuta* fem. p.p. of *adjuvare* AID¹ used as n.; cf. LL *adjutus* help]

aide (ād), n. = foll. [abbr.]

aide-de-camp (ād′ekong, & see AD.),

n. (pl. *aides-de-camp* pron. ād′ekŏngz). Officer assisting general by carrying orders etc. [F]

aide-mémoire (ād′māmwahr), n. (Book, document, serving as) an aid to the memory (esp. in diplomatic use). [F, f. *aider* to help + *mémoire* memory]

aig′rĕtte, n. Lesser white heron (usu. EGRET); tuft of feathers or hair; spray of gems etc. [F, see EGRET]

aig′uille (-gw-), n. Sharp peak of rock, esp. in Alps. Hence ~ESQUE′ a. [F, see AGLET]

aiguillette (āgwĭlĕt′), n. See AGLET.

ail, v.t. & i. Trouble, afflict, as *what* ~*s him?*; be ill. Hence **ail′**MENT n. [f. OE *eglan* (cogn. w. Goth. *agljan*) f. *egle* troublesome (Goth. *aglus*)]

ail′erŏn, n. (usu. pl.). Lateral-control flap(s) at rear of aeroplane's wingtip(s). [F]

aim¹, v.t. & i. Direct (blow, missile, *at*) point (gun etc.) towards (*at*); direct an act or proceeding against (*at*); (intr.) deliver blow, discharge missile, (*at*); take aim (abs.); form designs (abs.); *intend or try to* do. [ME, prob. f. two vbs (1) Picard. *amer,* OF & Prov. *esmer,* f. L *aestimare* reckon, (2) OF *aësmer* f. Rom. *adaestimare*; ME sense was *estimate*]

aim², n. Direction of a missile at an object, as *take* ~; design, purpose, object, whence **aim′LESS** a., **aim′lĕssLY²** adv., **aim′lĕssNESS** n. [ME, f. prec.]

ain't. See BE.

air¹, n. **1.** Gaseous substance enveloping earth, mixture of oxygen & nitrogen, breathed by all land animals & plants; atmosphere; free space overhead, as *birds of the* ~; unconfined space, as *open* ~; *fresh* ~, also simply ~, ~ not exhausted of its oxygen; breeze, light wind; *take* ~, become known; (of projects etc.) *quite in the* ~ (uncertain); (of opinions, feelings) *in the* ~, spreading about; *castles in the* ~, visionary projects; *give person the* ~ (sl.), dismiss him; *on the* ~, broadcast(ing) by radio. **2.** Appearance, as *an* ~ *of absurdity*; mien, gesture, as *with a triumphant* ~; affected manner (esp. in pl.), as *gave himself* ~*s,* ~*s & graces*; (Mus.) melody, tune, esp., in harmonized composition, predominant (usu. soprano) part. **3.** Combb.: ~-*ball(oon),* inflated toy; ~-*bed,* inflated mattress; ~-*bladder,* one filled with ~, in animals or plants; ~*'borne:* transported by ~; specially picked & trained for ~ operations, as *an* ~*borne division*; (of ~craft) (the ~, having taken off, as *the squadron was soon* ~*borne*; ~-*brake* (worked by ~ pressure); ~-*brick* (perforated for ventilation); ~-*bridge,* link between points provided by ~ transport; ~-*chamber* (in hydraulic machines, for equalizing pressure); *Air Chief Marshal, Air Commodore,* see *Air Force*; ~-*conditioned,* (of a room, building, etc.) having the ~ in it washed & brought to standard humidity (& temperature); ~-*cooled* (by a current of cool ~); ~'*craft*, aeroplane(s), ~*ship*(s), & balloon(s); ~*craft carrier*, ship that carries & serves as a base for aeroplanes; ~*craftman*, see *Air Force*; ~*craftwoman*, lowest rank in Women's Royal Air Force; ~ *crew* (of an ~craft); ~*cushion* (inflated with ~); *~'*drome*, aerodrome; ~-*engine* (actuated by heated ~); ~'*field*, aerodrome; *Air Force* (*the Royal Air Force*, abbr. *R.A.F.*), the ~craft service co-ordinate with Navy & Army, with officers as follows: *Marshal of the R.A.F., Air Chief Marshal, Air Marshal, Air Vice-Marshal, Air Commodore, Group Captain, Wing Commander, Squadron Leader, Flight Lieutenant, Flying Officer, Pilot Officer*; the non-commissioned ranks are *warrant officer, flight sergeant, sergeant, corporal,* (*leading*) ~*craftman*, ~-*mechanic*; ~-*frame*, body of ~craft as dist. from engine(s); ~'*graph*, system of transmitting letters etc. by ~ mail in the form of microfilms to save space, letter etc. so transmitted; ~-*gun* (using compressed ~ as propelling force); ~ *hostess*, stewardess on ~ *liner*; ~-*jacket* (inflated, to support wearer in water); ~-*lift*, transport of troops, supplies, etc. by ~; ~'*line*, line of ~craft for public service; ~ *liner*, large passenger ~craft; ~-*lock*, stoppage of flow in pump etc., caused by ~; ~ *mail* (carried by ~); ~'*man*, one who flies in an ~craft, esp. as pilot or member of crew; *Air Marshal*, ~-*mechanic*, see *Air Force*; ~-*minded*, interested in aviation; *Air Officer*, R.A.F. officer above the rank of Group Captain; *~'*plane*, aeroplane; ~-*pocket*, apparent vacuum in ~ causing ~craft to drop some distance; ~'*port*, aerodrome, esp. one fully equipped, usu. with customs-house, at which passengers by ~ liners embark or disembark; *~*post*, ~mail; ~-*pump* (for exhausting a vessel of its ~); ~'*raid*, attack by ~craft (freq. attrib., as ~-*raid precautions, warden, warning*); ~'*screw*, propeller of ~craft; ~'*ship*, flying machine lighter than ~; ~'*speed*, speed of ~craft relative to the ~ through which it is moving; ~-*stop*, helicopter passenger station; ~ *strip*, strip of ground used or usable for an ~field; ~ *thermometer* (with ~ instead of mercury); ~'*threads*, gossamer; ~-*tight* impermeable to ~; ~-*to*~, from one ~craft to another; *Air Training Corps* (formed in 1941 for youths aged 15–18; abbr. *A.T.C.*); ~ *umbrella*, a force of ~craft used to give ~ protection to a military operation; ~'*way*: ventilating passage in mine; route regularly followed by ~craft; ~'*worthy*, (of ~craft) fit to fly; ~'*worthiness* n. [1. ME *eir, ayre* f. OF *air* f. L *āerem* f. Gk *āēr*. 2. developed in F, & taken into E about 1600]

air¹, v.t. Expose to open air, ventilate; dry at fire or in ~ing cupboard; (refl.) go out into fresh air; parade (qualities, grievances, theories, fine clothes). [f. prec.]

Aire'dāle (ārd-), n. Large rough-coated terrier. [place in Yorks.]

air'less, a. Stuffy; breezeless, still. [AIR¹ +-LESS]

air'ȳ, a. Aerial, lofty; breezy; immaterial; of thin texture; light in movement; sprightly; graceful, delicate; unsubstantial; superficial, flippant; ~*fairy* (colloq.), delicate or light as a fairy. Hence **air'ILY²** adv., **air'INESS** n. [AIR¹ +-Y²]

aisle (īl), n. Division of church, esp. one parallel to & divided by pillars from the main nave, choir, or transept; passage between rows of pews. Hence **aisl**ED² (īld) a. [ME *ele* f. OF f. L *ala* wing; later forms i(s)le by assoc. w. *island*; *aisle* after mod. F *aile*]

‖ **ait** (āt), n. Small isle, esp. in a river. [OE *iggath, igeoth*, perh. dim. of *ieg, ig* island; the ME *eyt* is unexpl.; mod. *eyet, eyot* artificial sp. after *islet* & F *îlot*]

aitch, n. = ACHE³.

‖ **aitch'bone**, n. (Cut of beef lying over) buttock or rump bone. [orig. *nage-, nache-*bone (w. loss of *n-* as in ADDER), f. OF *nage, nache* buttock f. LL (pl.) *naticae* f. L *natis, -es* buttock(s); pop. etym. gives *H-, ice-, edge-, bone*]

ajâr'¹, adv. (Of doors) slightly open. [A prep. +*char* (OE *cerr* a turn)]

ajâr'², adv. In a jarring state. [A prep. + JAR¹ n.]

ajutage. See ADJUTAGE.

akim'bō, adv. (Of the arms) with hands on hips & elbows turned outwards. [in 15th c. *in kenebowe*, later *on kenbow, a kenbow*, of unkn. orig.]

akin', pred. a. Related by blood; (fig.) of similar or kindred character. [A prep.]

al-¹, pref. = AD- before *l*.

al-², pref. The Arab. article *the*, as in *alcohol* etc.

-al, suf. 1. Adj. f. L *-alis* (adj. suf. varying w. cogn. *-aris* -AR¹ which was always used when *l* preceded, as *regularis* but *generalis*) direct or through F *-el* (later refash. after L *-al-* in E); now appended freely to L nouns (*cordial*), Gk nouns (*colossal*), L adjj. (*individual*), & Gk adjj. in *-kos, -oidēs* (*comical, rhomboidal*); *-ical* indicates vaguer connexion w. the orig. n. than *-ic* (*comic* paper, *comical* story), cf. -ACAL; other suff. are occas. appended, as *generality, centralize*. 2. Nouns f. L *-alis, -al, -ales, -alia*, parts of above used as nouns (*rival, animal, annals, Saturnalia*), with new imitations (*cardinal, regimentals*). *-alia* became in F *-aille*, in E *-aille, -ail, -al* (L *sponsalia*, OF *espousaille*, E *spousaille* now *espousal*), the last now freely imitated to form vbl nn. (*reprisal, recital, bestowal*); in BRIDAL, BURIAL, the suf. is of diff. orig.

à la (ah lah), prep. After the manner of, as *à la Russe, à la Reform.* [F, for *à la mode*]

al'abaster (-bah-), n. & a. **1.** Name of several varieties of carbonate or sulphate of lime; (Min.) massive fine-grained sulphate of lime (*modern, gypseous, ~*), as distinct from the carbonates used by the ancients for holding unguents (*oriental, calcareous, ~*); box made of *~.* **2.** adj. Of *~,* like *~* in whiteness or smoothness. So **àlabas'trINE**[1] (-bah-) a. [ME, f. OF *alabastre* f. L *alabaster* f. Gk *alabast(r)os*]

à la carte (ah lah kärt), adv. By the bill of fare. [F]

alāck', int. (arch.) expressing regret or surprise, esp. in phr. *~-a-day.* [prob. f. *a* int. +*lak* LACK]

alāc'rity, n. Briskness, cheerful readiness. [f. L *alacritas* (*alacer* brisk, see -TY)]

Alǎdd'in's lǎmp, n. Talisman enabling holder to gratify any wish. [*Arabian Nights*]

à'lamōde, *à la mode* (ah lah mōd), adv. & a. In the fashion, fashionable; *~ beef,* piece of beef larded & stewed; *~ silk* (also as n., *alamode*), a thin glossy black silk. [F (*à la mode*), = in the fashion]

āl'ar, a. Pertaining to wings; winglike, wing-shaped; (Bot. & Physiol.) axillary. [f. L *alaris* (*ala* wing, see -AR[1])]

alǎrm'[1], n. Call to arms; warning sound giving notice of danger; warning, as *give, take, the~;* excited anticipation of danger; (Fencing) stamp on ground made with advancing foot; *~-post,* place for troops to assemble in case of *~;* mechanism that sounds the *~* (usu. *alǎ'rum*); *alarum--clock,* one with apparatus that rings at appointed hour; *alar(u)ms & excursions* (joc.), noise & bustle. [ME, f. OF *alarme* f. It. *allarme* (*all' arme!* to arms); form *alarum* now only of *~*-signal]

alǎrm'[2], v.t. Arouse to sense of danger; disturb; agitate, excite with fear. Hence *~ingLY*[2] adv. [f. prec.]

alǎrm'list, n. One who raises alarms on slight grounds (often attrib., as *these ~ist reports*); panic-monger. So *~ISM* n. [ALARM + -IST]

alǎ'rum, n. See ALARM n.

āl'ary, a. Pertaining to wings or winglike parts. [f. L *alarius* (*ala* wing, see -ARY[1])]

alas' (-ahs), int. expressing grief, pity, concern. [ME, f. OF (*h*)*a las* (mod. *hélas*) f. *ha* ah +*las*(*se*) wretched f. L *lassus* weary]

Alas'tor (-ahs-), n. Avenging deity, nemesis. [Gk (*a-* not +*last-* f. *lath-* forget)]

āl'āte, āl'ātèd, a. Having wings or wing-like appendages. [f. L *alatus* (*ala* wing, see -ATE[2])]

ālb, n. White vestment reaching to feet, worn by priests, & by some consecrated kings. [OE, ME *albe* (later also *aube* f. F) f. LL *alba* white (sc. *tunica, vestis*)]

āl'bacōre, n. Large species of tunny; other fish of same genus. [f. Port.

albacor (F *albicore*, also used in E) f. Arab. *al* the +*bukr* young camel, heifer]

Albān'ian (ǎl-), a. & n. (Native) of Albania; (native) of Scotland (hist.). [(1) f. med. Gk *Albania*; (2) f. med. L *Albania* Scotland (Ir. *Alban* gen. of *Albu*)]

albat'a, n. White metal, German silver. [f. L *albata* whitened (*albus* white)]

āl'batrŏss, n. Family of birds allied to petrels, inhabiting Pacific & Southern Oceans; esp. *wandering ~,* largest of sea-fowls. [alt., after L *albus* white, of obs. (17th c.) *alcatras* frigate-bird etc., f. Sp. & Pg. *alcatraz,* var. of Pg. *alcatruz* f. Arab. *alqadus* the bucket, Arab. name for the pelican, from its supposed water-carrying habit]

albē'it (awl-), conj. Though, as *~ that he failed, ~ he failed, he tried ~ without success.* [= all though it be that]

āl'bert, n. (Also *A~ chain*) kind of watch--chain. [f. Prince *Albert* consort of Queen Victoria]

Albert Hall, in Kensington, used for concerts, demonstrations, etc. [as prec.]

ālbĕs'cent, a. Growing white, shading into white. [f. L *albescere* (*albus* white), see -ENT]

Albigĕn'sēs (ǎl-, -z), n.pl. Heretics of 12th–14th cc. in S. France. [L *Albiga* Albi in S. France, -ESE]

ālbi'nō (-bē-), n. (pl. *-os*). Human being marked by congenital absence of colouring pigment in skin & hair, which are white, & eyes, which are pink & unable to bear ordinary light; any animal so distinguished; plant lacking the normal colouring. Hence **ālbi'nESS**[1] (-bē-), **āl'bINISM**, nn. [Port., orig. of white Negroes, f. L *albus* white]

Al'bion (ǎl-), n. (poet.). (Greek & Roman name for) Britain. [F, f. L *Albion* of uncert. orig.]

āl'bīte, n. White or soda feldspar. [f. L *albus* white +-ITE[1]]

āl'bum, n. Book for insertion of autographs, photographs, names, etc. [L, neut. sing. of *albus* white]

ālbūm'|ĕn (or ǎl-), n. White of egg; a constituent of animal solids & fluids, of seeds, & of tuberous or fleshy roots, found nearly pure in white of egg; (Bot.) substance found between skin & embryo of many seeds, usu. the eatable part. Hence *~īnOSE, ~īnOUS,* aa. [L *albumen -minis* white of egg (*albus* white) see -MEN]

ālbūm'enīze, -ise (-īz), v.t. (photog.). Coat (paper) with an albuminous solution. [prec. + -IZE]

ālbūm'inoid, a. & n. Like albumen; (n. pl.) proteins, class of organic compounds forming chief part of organs & tissues of animals & plants. Hence **ālbūminoid'AL** a. [f. albumen +-OID]

ālbūminūr'ia, n. Presence of albumen in the urine, usu. as symptom of kidney disease. [ALBUMEN, URINE, -IA[1]]

ālbŭrn'|um, n. Recently formed wood in

exogenous trees, sap-wood. Hence -OUS a. [L *alburnum* (*albus* white)]

|| **alcahest.** See ALKAHEST.

Alcā'ic (-ă-), a. & n. Pertaining to Alcaeus (Gk lyric poet, 600 B.C.), or to the metre he invented; (n. pl.)~ strophes. [f. LL f. Gk *Alkaikos* (*Alkaios*)]

alcalde (ahlkah'ldă), n. Magistrate or mayor in Spanish, Portuguese, or Latin--American town. [Sp., ult. f. Arab. *qādi* judge, CADI]

ălchĕm'ic (-k-), a. Pertaining to alchemy. Hence ~AL (-k-) a., ~alLY² (-k-) adv. [f. med. L. *alchimicus* or F *alchimique*: see ALCHEMY and -IC]

ăl'chemist (-k-), n. One who studies or practises alchemy. Hence **ălchemis'tic-** (AL) (-k-) aa. [f. OF *alquemiste* or med. L *alchemista*; see ALCHEMY and -IST]

ăl'chemize (-k-), -ise (-īz), v.t. Change as by alchemy; transmute. [back-formation on prec.]

ăl'chemy (-k-), n. Chemistry of the middle ages; esp., pursuit of the transmutation of baser metals into gold (also fig.). [ME, f. OF *alquimie* f. med. L *alchimia* f. Arab. *al-kimia*, *al* the +*kimia*, apparently = *khemía* (Gk form of native name of Egypt, but confused with Gk *khumeia* pouring f. *khu-* perf. st. of *kheō* pour, whence the spelling *alchymy*)]

ăl'cohŏl, n. Pure spirit of wine; any liquor containing this; (Chem.) large class of compounds of same type as spirits of wine. Hence ~ATE¹(3) n. [med. L, f. Arab. *al* the +*koh'l* powder for staining eyelids (*kahala* v. stain)]

ălcohŏl'ic, a. & n. **1.** Of, relating to, containing, caused by, alcohol. **2.** n. Person addicted to excessive consumption of alcohol. [prec. + -IC]

ăl'cohŏlism, n. Action of alcohol on human system. [ALCOHOL + -ISM]

ăl'cohŏl|ize, -ise (-īz), v.t. Saturate with alcohol; subject to alcoholic influence. Hence ~ĪZA'TION n. [ALCOHOL + -IZE]

ălcohŏlŏ|m'ĕter, n. Instrument for measuring alcoholic strength of spirits. Hence ~M'ETRY n. [f. ALCOHOL + -O- + METER]

Alcoran (ălkorahn', ălᴸ), n. Koran. Hence ~IC (-ănᴸ) a. [ME, f. OF f. Arab. *al-qoran* the reading; see KORAN]

ăl'cŏve, n. Vaulted recess in room-wall, esp. (in Spain) recess for bed; recess in garden wall or hedge; summer-house. [F, f. Sp. *alcova*, -*ba*, f. Arab. *al-qobbah* the vault (*qubba* v. vault)]

ăl'dĕhyde, n. Colourless volatile fluid of suffocating smell, obtained by oxidation of alcohol; class of compounds of this type. Hence **ăldĕhyd'ic** a. [abbr. of mod. L *alcohol dehydrogenatum* (deprived of hydrogen)]

al'der (awl-), n. Tree related to birch; other trees not related, as *black, white, red,* ~. [OE *alor, aler* (cf. ON *ölr, elrir,* OHG *elira,* mod. G *erle, eller*) w. phonetic *d*]

al'derman (awl-), n. Co-opted member of an English county or borough council, next in dignity to Mayor. Hence ~IC (-măn'-) a., ~SHIP n. [f. OE *aldor* patriarch (*ald* old + -*or* noun suf.) + -MAN]

al'dermanrȳ (awl-), n. Ward, district of a borough having its own alderman; rank of alderman. [prec. + -RY]

Al'derney (awl-), a. & n. **1.** Of cattle bred in ~ in the Channel Islands; (pop.) of cattle bred in the Channel Islands. **2.** n. Individual of either kind.

Al'dershŏt (awl-), n. (Used for) the permanent military camp at ~ in Hampshire.

Al'dine (awl-), a. Printed by Aldus Manutius, Venetian printer of 16th cent., who .introduced italic type; name of certain style of type. [f. *Aldus* + -INE¹]

Al'dis (awl-), a. ~ *lamp* (for signalling); ~ *lens* (for hand cameras); ~ *unit sight* (for aircraft). [A. C. W. *Aldis*, inventor]

āle, n. Liquor made from an infusion of malt by fermentation, flavoured with hops etc. || *merry-making at which* ~ *was drunk*; *alecost*, costmary; ~-*house*, one at which ~ is retailed; ~-*wife*, woman who keeps an ~-house; American fish allied to herring. [OE *alu,* ON *öl*]

āl'ēatorȳ, a. Depending on the throw of a die or on chance. [f. L *aleatorius* (*aleator* dice-player f. *alea* die)]

āle'cŏnner (ălk-), n. (hist.). Inspector of ale & ale-measures (now a titular office only). [ALE + CON¹ + -ER¹]

alee', adv. & pred. a. On the lee or sheltered side of ship; to leeward. [ME (rare before 16th c.) f. A² + LEE]

āl'ĕgar, n. Sour ale; malt vinegar. [f. (after *vinegar*) ALE + *egre* (= F *aigre* sour, see EAGER)]

alĕm'bic, n. Apparatus formerly used in distilling; also fig., as ~ *of fancy.* [ME *alambic* f. OF f. med. L *alembicus* f. Arab. *al-anbīq* the still f. Gk *ambix -ikos* cup, cap of a still; *lembick, limbeck,* were usu. in 15th–17th cc.]

alērt', a., n., & v.t. **1.** Watchful, vigilant; lively, nimble. **2.** n. Warning call, alarm; (period of) air-raid warning; *on the* ~, on the look-out. **3.** v.t. Make ~, put on the ~. Hence ~LY² adv., ~NESS n. [f. F *alerte* f. It. *all' erta* (*alla* to the +*erta* watch-tower, fem. p.p. of *ergere* f. L *erigere* ERECT)]

aleur'on, aleur'ōne, (-lūr-), n. Albuminoid substance found in seeds of plants etc. [Gk *aleuron* flour]

Alĕxăn'drian (ăl-), a. Relating to the late Greek civilization of Alexandria in Egypt. [-AN]

Alĕxăn'drine (ăl-), a. & n. ~ (*verse*), iambic line of six feet or twelve syllables. [f. F *alexandrin,* of disputed orig.]

alĕx'in, n. One of a class of substances found in blood serum capable of destroying bacteria. [G, f. Gk *alexō* ward off, -IN].

alexiphar'mic, a. & n. (Having the quality of) an antidote. [earlier -ac f. F *alexipharmaque* f. Gk *alexipharmakon* remedy for poison (*alexō* ward off + *pharmakon* poison)]

alfal'fa, n. Lucerne. [Sp., f. Arab.]

alfrĕs'cō, adv. & a. In the open air; open-air, as ~ *lunch*. [f. It. *al fresco* in the fresh (air)]

al'g|a, n. (pl. ~*ae*, pr. -jē). Seaweed. Hence ~AL, ~OID, ~OLŎ'GICAL, aa., ~IST (3) (-J-), ~ŎL'OGIST, ~ŎL'OGY, nn. [L]

al'gĕbr|a, n. Investigation of the properties of numbers & quantities by means of general symbols; *quadruple~a*, quaternions. Hence ~ā'IC(AL) aa., ~ā'icaLLY adv., ~(ā)IST nn. [It., f. Arab. *aljebr* reunion of broken parts (*jabara* reunite), bone-setting (obs. sense in E)]

al'gid, a. Cold, esp. of cold stage of ague. Hence **algĭd'ITY** n. [f. F *algide* or L *algidus* (*algēre* be cold, see -ID[1])]

al'gorism, n. Arabic (decimal) notation; *cipher in~*, 0, mere dummy. [ME *augrim*, later *algorisme*, f. OF *augorime*, *algorisme*, f. med. L *algorismus* f. Arab. *al-Khowarazmi* the man of Khiva, surname of a mathematician]

alguazil' (-gw-), n. Spanish warrant-officer or sergeant. [Sp. (now -*cil*) f. Arab. *al-wazir* the VIZIER, minister (*wazara*)]

al'gum, n. Tree mentioned in Bible (2 *Chron.* ii. 8; in 1 *Kings* x. 11 wrongly given as *almug*), prob. a kind of sandal-wood. [Heb.]

Alhăm'bra, n. Palace of Moorish kings at Granada. Hence **ălhambresQUE'** (-ĕsk) a. [f. Sp. f. Arab. *al-hamra'* the red (house)]

al'ias, adv. & n. (pl. ~*es*). (Name by which one is called) on other occasions. [L, = at another time, otherwise]

al'ibī, adv. & n. (The plea that when an alleged act took place one was) elsewhere; *excuse* (colloq.). [L, = elsewhere]

alicyc'lic, a. (chem.). Combining the properties of aliphatic & cyclic compounds. [f. *aliphatic* + *cyclic*]

al'idāde, -ād, n. Index of astrolabe, quadrant, etc., showing the degrees cut off on the arc. [F; earlier *allidatha* (ME), *alhidada*, f. med. L, f. Arab. *al-'idadah* the revolving radius ('*add* upper arm)]

al'ien[1], a. & n. 1. Not one's own; foreign, under foreign allegiance; differing in nature (*from*); repugnant (*to*). 2. n. Stranger; non-naturalized foreigner; one excluded *from*; (Law) ~-*friend*, -*enemy*, alien owing allegiance to friendly, hostile, country. Hence ~ISM (2) n., study & treatment of mental diseases, ~IST n., specialist in such diseases. [ME, f. OF f. L *alienus* belonging to another (*alius*)]

al'ien[2], v.t. (Poet.) estrange; (Law) transfer ownership of. Hence ~ABLE a., ~ABIL'ITY n. [ME, f. OF *aliener* f. L *alienare* (as prec.)]

al'ienāt|e, v.t. Estrange; transfer owner-ship of; turn away, divert (*from*). Hence ~OR n. [ME, f. L as prec., see -ATE[2]]

aliĕnā'tion, n. Estrangement; transference of ownership; diversion to different purpose; (*mental*) ~, insanity. [ME, f. OF, or f. L *alienatio* (as prec., see -ATION)]

alienee', n. One to whom transfer of property is made. [ALIEN[2] + -EE]

al'iform, a. Wing-shaped. [f. L *ala* wing + -FORM]

alight'[1] (-ĭt), v.i. Dismount (*from* horse), descend (*from* carriage); settle, come to earth, from the air. [OE *ālîhtan* (A- (1) + *lîhtan* LIGHT[5])]

alight'[2] (-ĭt), a. Kindled; on fire; lighted up. [p.p. of obs. *alight* kindle; now only used predicatively, on anal. of *a-blaze* & other adv. compds]

align' (-īn), *aline*, v.t. & i. Place, lay, in a line; bring into line; esp. bring three or more points into a straight line, as ~ *the sights* (of rifle) & *bull's-eye*; (intr.) form in line (as troops). Hence ~MENT (-īn'm-) n. [f. F *aligner* f. phr. *à ligne* in a LINE[2]]

alike', pred. a. & adv. Similar, like; (adv.) in like manner. [ME *ilike*, *alike*, etc., combining OE *gelic* (Y- & LIKE[1]) & ON *dlîkr* (= OE *anlîc*, see A-(2))]

al'iment, n. Food; (fig.) support, mental sustenance. Hence **ălimĕn'taL** a., **ălimĕn'taLLY[2]** adv. [late ME, f. F, or f. L *alimentum* (*alere* nourish, see -MENT]

ălimĕn'tary, a. Nourishing; performing functions of nutrition, as ~ *canal*; providing maintenance. [f. L *alimentarius* (as prec., see -ARY[1])]

ălimentā'tion, n. Nourishment; maintenance. [f. med. L *alimentatio* (*alimentare* as ALIMENT, see -ATION)]

al'imonȳ, n. Nourishment; maintenance; allowance due to wife from husband's estate, on separation from certain causes. [f. L *alimonia* nutriment (*alere* nourish, see -MONY)]

al'ipĕd, a. & n. 1. Wing-footed. 2. n. ~ animal, e.g. bat. [f. L *ala* wing, *pes pedis* foot]

ăliphăt'ic, a. (chem.). Of fat (as epithet of certain organic compounds). [f. Gk *aleiphar* -*atos* unguent, -IC]

al'iquŏt, a. ~ (*part*), part contained by the whole an integral number of times, integral factor. [f. F *aliquote* f. L *aliquot* some, so many]

-ality, compd noun-suf. = -AL + -TY. Quality, or instance of it, as (*a*) *generality*.

alive', adv. & pred a., In life, living; fully susceptible *to* (an idea etc.); active, brisk, as (colloq.) *look* ~, be brisk; swarming *with*, as *river* ~ *with boats*; *any man* ~ (whatever); *man* ~! (colloq. expletive). [OE *on life*, ME *on live*; see A[2] prep., LIFE]

aliz'arin, n. Red colouring matter of madder. [f. F *alizari* madder prob. f. Arab. *al* the + *açarah* extract ('*açara* v. press); see -IN]

ăl′kahĕst, n. Alchemist's supposed universal solvent (also fig.). [sham Arab., prob. invented by Paracelsus]

ălkalĕs′c|ent, a. & n. Incipiently or slightly alkaline (substance). Hence ~ENCE, ~ENCY, nn. [f. foll., see -ESCENT]

ăl′kali, n. (pl. ~s, ~es). (Chem.) series of compounds called bases, including soda, potash, & ammonia, highly soluble in water, producing caustic or corrosive solutions that neutralize strong acids, & turn vegetable yellows to brown, reds to blue, purples to green; (Commerce.) caustic soda, caustic potash, other alkaline products. Hence ~fĭ′ABLE a., ~FY v.t. [ME, f. med. L f. Arab. al-qalīy calcined ashes (qalay fry)]

ălkalĭm′ĕtrў, n. Measurement of strength of alkalis. [ALKALI + -METRY]

ăl′kaline, a. Of alkalis; of the nature of an alkali; ~ metals, those whose hydroxides are alkalis. [f. ALKALI + -INE¹, or f. F]

ăl′kaloid, n. Any nitrogenous base of vegetable origin. Hence **ălkaloid′**AL a. [f. G, as prec. + -OID]

ăl′kanĕt, n. (Plant whose root yields) a red dye. [ME, f. Sp. alcaneta, dim. of alcana f. Arab. al-henna the henna shrub]

all (awl), a., n., & adv. **1.** adj. (w. noun etc. expressed or understood). The whole amount, quantity, or extent of, as ~ day, ~ England, ~ his life, & ~ that, take it ~, ~ whom I saw; the greatest possible, as ~ speed; (w. pl.) the entire number of, as ~ men, ~ the others; ~ kind(s) of, every kind of; any whatever, as renounce ~ connexion; ~ the TIME¹; ~-time high, (low), a record high, (low), level or figure. **2.** n. ~ men, as ~ were agreed; (in scoring at games) for both sides (the score was two ~; love ~, no score to either side); (w. of) the whole, every one, as ~ of it, ~ of us; everything (that is ~; ~ is lost); one's whole property, as he lost his ~; ~ along of (vulg.), owing to; ~ but, everything short of (used adv.), as ~ but impossible, he was ~ but drowned; ~-in, inclusive of ~, as ~-in wrestling, unrestricted style; ~ in ~, of paramount or exclusive importance; ~ one, just the same, as it is ~ one to me; ~-up, (of aircraft) total (weight) of machine, crew, passengers, cargo, etc. when in air; ~ very fine or well, colloq. formula of dissatisfaction, as ~ very fine, but I shall stand it no longer; at ~, in any way, as not at ~, did you speak at ~? (not in affirmative sent.); in ~, in total number; one & ~, ~ & some (arch.), ~ & sundry, ~ individually & collectively. **3.** adv. Wholly, quite, as dressed ~ (orig. an adj.) in white, ~ covered with mud, ~ the better, ~ at once, ~ too soon; All Blacks (colloq.), New Zealand rugby football international team; ~-clear, signal that danger is over, esp. from enemy aircraft; *~-fired (sl.), extreme(ly), excessive(ly); ~ in, exhausted; ~ out, involving ~ one's

strength or resources, as he was going ~ out, at full speed; ~ OVER; ~-overish (colloq.), indisposed ~ over the body; || ~-red, (of cable, line, etc.) British throughout; ~ right, (adv.) as desired, satisfactorily, certainly (that's the man ~ right), (pred. a.) safe & sound, in good state, satisfactory, (sent.) I consent, ~ is well, (also iron. in threats, as ~ right! you shall repent this); ~-round adj., having ability in many departments, as an ~--round sportsman, so ~-rounder, n.; ~ there (colloq.), sane, in one's senses, as he's not quite ~ there; ~ the same: just the same, making no difference, (it's ~ the same to me whether he comes or not; if it's ~ the same to you, if you don't mind); in spite of this, notwithstanding, however, (he was punished ~ the same, in spite of extenuating circumstances etc.; ~ the same I wish you hadn't done it). **4.** Combb.: All-father, Odin, God; All Fools' Day, first of April; All Hallows (arch.), All Saints' Day, general celebration of saints, November 1st; All Souls' Day, day of supplication for souls of faithful deceased, Nov. 2nd. All is prefixed to many adjj., as ~-bountiful, ~-righteous, ~-sufficient, & esp. to partt., as ~-sufficing, ~-seeing, ~-knowing. [OE all, eall, Gmc]

Allah (ăl′a) n. Name of God among Mohammedans. [Arab. allah contr. of al-ilah (al the + ilah god = Heb. eloah)]

allay, v.t. Put down, repress; alleviate (pain etc.); diminish (pleasure etc.). [OE alecgan f. A- (1) + LAY³; ME alegge, aleye, alaye confused w. obs. allege alleviate & obs. allay ALLOY]

ăllĕgā′tion, n. Alleging; assertion (esp. one not proved). [ME, f. OF, or f. L allegatio (allegare allege, see -ATION)]

allĕg|e′, v.t. Affirm; advance as argument or excuse. Hence ~ed′ (-ĕjd) a., ~′ĕdLУ² adv., (used in statements for which author disclaims responsibility). [f. AF alegier, OF esligier f. Rom. *ex-litigare clear at law; confused in sense w. L allegare (see prec.)]

allĕ′giance (-jans), n. Duty of subject to sovereign or government; loyalty (lit. & fig.). [ME var. (+ A- (4), by confusion of form w. obs. allegeance (prec.) allegation, or of form & sense w. med. L alligantia ALLIANCE), of ligeaunce f. OF f. lige (LIEGE, -ANCE)]

ăllĕgŏ′rĭc, a. Pertaining to, of the nature of, allegory. Hence ~AL a., ~ALУ² adv. [ME, f. F -ique or LL allegoricus f. Gk (as foll., see -IC)]

ăll′ĕgor|ize, -ise (-ĭz), v.t. & i. Treat as an allegory; make allegories. Hence ~IST n. [f. F -iser or LL allegorizare f. Gk (as foll., see -IZE)]

ăll′ĕgorў, n. Narrative description of a subject under guise of another suggestively similar; emblem. [ME, f. OF -ie or L f. Gk allēgoria (allos other + -agoria speaking)]

allégrett'ō, adv. (mus.). Somewhat briskly. [It.]

allég'rō (-lā-), a., adv., n. (mus.). Lively, gay; (movement) in brisk time. [It.]

allélu'ia (-lōōya), n. Song of praise to God. [f. LL f. (Septuagint) Gk *allēlouïa* .f. Heb. *halleluyah* praise ye Jehovah]

äll'emände, n. Name of several German dances; country dance figure. [F. = German]

äll'ergy̆, n. (med.). Changed reactivity produced by a subsequent inoculation or treatment with the same thing, (more widely) sensitiveness to the action of particular foods, pollens, insect-bites, etc. Hence **allēr'gic** a., relating to or characterized by ~, (colloq.) sensitive (esp. antipathetic) *to*. [in G *allergie*, f. Gk *allos* other, after *energie* ENERGY]

allēv'i̇āte, v.t. Relieve, mitigate. Hence ~A'TION, ~ātōr, nn., ~ātive, ~ātoRY, aa. [f. LL *alleviare* lighten (*levis* light), see -ATE³]

äll'ey, n. (pl. ~s). Walk, passage, esp. in park or garden; narrow street; *blind* ~, one closed at end, enclosure for skittles etc. [ME, f. OF *alee*, walking, passage, f. *aler* go]

Alleyn'ian (alěn-), n. Member of Dulwich College. [E. *Alleyn*, founder (d. 1626)]

All-hăll'ow(s) (-ō, -ōz), n. All saints (in heaven), as *All hallows' day*, *Allhallowmass*. [ALL + HALLOW¹]

älliā'ceous (-shᵘs), a. Of the genus *Allium*, including garlic, onions, & leeks; smelling, tasting, of garlic etc. [f. L *allium* garlic + -ACEOUS]

alli'ance, n. Union by marriage; relationship; confederation (esp. between States); community in nature or qualities; (Bot.) group of allied families. [ME, f. OF *aliance* (as ALLY¹, see -ANCE)₁

äll'igātor, n. Genus of saurian reptiles of crocodile family, found in America; other large American saurians; ~ *apple*, *pear*, fruit of W. Indian trees; ~ *tortoise*, snapping turtle. [16th c. (a)*lagarto*.f. Sp. *el lagarto* the lizard f. L *lacertus*]

allit'erāt|e, v.i. (Use words that) begin with the same letter or sound. Hence ~IVE a., ~īveLY² (-yl-) adv. [back-form. f. foll.]

allitera'tion, n. Commencement of words in close connexion (esp. in early Teut. poetry, of accented syllables) with the same letter or sound. [f. med. L (15th c.) *alliteratio*; cf. F *allitération*]

ällo-, comb. form of Gk *allos* other.

äll'oc|āte, v.t. Assign, devote, (*to* person or object); locate. Hence or cogn. ~ABLE a., ~A'TION n. [f. med. L AL*locare* (*locus* place), see -ATE³]

ällocū'tion, n. Formal hortatory address (esp. one delivered by the Pope). [f. L *allocutio* -onis f. *alloqui* exhort]

al(l)ōd'i̇|um, n. Estate held in absolute ownership, without acknowledgement to a superior (opp. to *feudum*). Hence ~AL a., ~alLY² adv., ~alism, ~alist, nn. [f.

med. L f. Frankish *allōd* entire property (ALL + ōd estate); also anglicized *allod*, *allody*]

ällŏg'amy̆, n. (bot.). Cross-fertilization. [f. ALLO- + -GAMY]

ällŏp'athi̇y̆, n. Curing of a diseased action by inducing another action of a different kind (opp. to *homoeopathy*). Hence **ällopäth'ic** a., **ällopäth'icalLY** adv., ~ist n. [in G *allopathie*, f. ALLO- + -*pathie* -PATHY]

ällophy̆l'ian, a. & n. (One whose native tongue is) neither Aryan nor Semitic. [f. LL f. Gk *allophulos* (ALLO- + *phulē* tribe) + -IAN]

allŏt', v.t. (-tt-). Distribute by lot or with authority; assign (*to*). [f. OF *aloter* f. *à to* + *lot*; see LOT]

äll'othēism, n. Worship of strange gods. [f. ALLO- + Gk *theos* god + -ISM]

allŏt'ment, n. Apportioning; lot in life; share allotted to one; ‖ small portion of land let out for cultivation. [f. F *allotement* (*aloter*, see ALLOT & -MENT)]

ällŏt'rop|y̆, n. Variation of physical properties without change of substance. Hence **ällotrŏp'ic(AL)** aa., **ällotrŏp'icalLY²** adv., ~ism n. [f. Gk *allotropia* f. *allotropos* (ALLO- + *tropos* manner f. *trepō* turn)]

ällŏttee', n. One to whom allotment is made. [f. ALLOT + -EE]

allow', v.t. & i. Admit (thing *to* be, *that*); permit (practice, person *to* do); (refl.) indulge one*self* in (conduct); (intr.) admit *of*; give (limited periodical sum), as ~ *him £200 a year*; add, deduct, in consideration of something; ~ *for*, take into consideration, make addition or deduction corresponding to; ~ *me* (formula in offering services). Hence ~ABLE a., ~abLY² adv.; ~ĕdLY² adv., admittedly. [ME, f. OF *alouer* f. (1) L AL*laudare* praise, (2) med. L AL*locare* place]

allow'ance¹, n. Permission; tolerance (*of*); a limited portion or sum esp. of money or food; deduction, discount; *make* ~ *for*, allow for. [ME, f. OF *alouance* (as prec., see -ANCE)]

allow'ance², v.t. Make allowance to (person); supply (thing) in limited quantities. [f. prec.]

alloy'¹ (or äl'oi), n. Standard, quality, (of gold or silver); inferior metal mixed esp. with gold or silver (also fig.); mixture of metals. [f. F *aloi*, OF *alei* (whence obs. E *allay*), f. *aleier* combine f. L AL*ligare* bind]

alloy'², v.t. Mix with baser metal; mix (metals); debase; moderate. [f. F *aloyer*, OF *aleier*, see prec.]

all'seed (awl-), n. Name of various plants producing much seed.

all'spice (awl-), n. Jamaica pepper, pimento, supposed to combine flavour of cinnamon, nutmeg, and cloves; other aromatic shrubs, as *Carolina* ~, *Japan* ~, *wild* ~.

allude' (-ōō-, -ū-), v.i. Refer covertly, indirectly, *to*; (improp.) ~ *to*, mean. [f. L AL(*ludere lus-* play)]

allure', v.t., & n. Tempt, entice, win over, (*to*, *from*, person, place, conduct); fascinate, charm; (n.) charm, attractiveness. Hence ~MENT (-ūr'm-) n. [ME, f. OF *al(e)urer* attract (*a* AD-+*leurre* LURE)]

allu'sion (-lōōzhn, -lū-), n. Covert, implied, indirect, reference (*to*). [f. F, or LL *allusio* (as ALLUDE, see -ION)]

allus'ive (-lōōs-, -lūs-), a. Containing an allusion (*to*); abounding in allusions; (Her.) ~ (canting) arms. Hence ~LY² (-vl-) adv., ~NESS (-vn-) n. [as prec., see -IVE]

alluv'ion (-ōō-, -ū-), n. Wash of sea, river, against shore, banks; flood; matter deposited by flood; (Law) formation of new land by water's action. [F, f. L AL*luvionem* (nom. -*vio*) f. *luere* wash]

alluv'i|um (-ōō-, -ū-), n. (pl. ~*a*, ~ums). Deposit of earth, sand, etc., left by flood. Hence ~AL a. [LL, neut. of adj. AL*luvius* (*luere* wash)]

ally'¹ (or ăl'ĭ), v.t. Combine, unite, for special object *to*, *with*, (esp. of marriage & alliance with foreign states); (of things) *allied to*, connected with. [ME, f. OF *alier* (*aleier*) f. L AL*ligare* bind, cf. ALLOY¹]

ăll'ȳ² (or ali'), n. Person, state, etc., allied with another. [f. prec.]

ăll'ȳ³, *ăll'ey*, n. Choice playing-marble of marble or alabaster. [perh. dim. of *alabaster*]

ăl'ma(h), n. Egyptian dancing-girl. [Arab. *'almah* knowing (*'alama* know)]

ăl'magĕst, n. Great astronomical treatise of Ptolemy; other books on astrology & alchemy. [ME, f. OF f. Arab. *al the* +*majisti* = Gk *megistē* greatest]

Al'ma Māt'er (ā-), n. Name used of Universities & schools. [L, = bounteous mother]

al'manăc, -ăck, (awl-), n. Annual calendar of months & days, with astronomical & other data. [14th c. *almenak* = 13th c. med. L *almanac(h)*, F -*ach*, Sp. -*que*, It. -*acco*, of unkn. orig.]

ăl'mandīne, n. A garnet of violet tint. [F, alt. of obs. *alabandine* f. LL *alabandina* (*Alabanda*, city in Caria)]

almi'ghty (awlmīt'ĭ), a. & adv. All-powerful, esp. *A~God, the A~*; (sl.)great, (adv.) exceedingly. Hence almi'ghtiNESS n. [OE *ælmiehtig* (ALL adv.+ MIGHTY)]

almīr'ah (-*a*), n. (Anglo-Ind.). Wardrobe, movable cupboard. [Hind., f. Port. *almario* f. L *armarium* (see AMBRY)]

alm'ond (ahm-), n. Kernel of a stone--fruit borne by two trees (*sweet*, *bitter*, ~) allied to plum & peach; anything ~-shaped. [ME *almand(e)* etc. f. OF f. med. L *amandula* f. L *amygdala*, Gk *amugdalē*]

almoner (ahm'oner, ăl¹-), n. Official distributor of alms; *Hereditary Grand A~*, *Lord High A~*, (officers in royal household

of Great Britain); medico-social worker attached to a hospital. [ME *aumoner* etc., f. AF *aumoner*, OF -*ier*, f. Rom. *almosinarius* f. med. L *eleemosynarius* (as ALMS, see -ARY¹)]

al'mōst (awl-), adv. All but, very nearly (qualifying v., adv., adj.; also noun, as *his ~ impudence*). [f. ALL + MOST adv.]

alms (ahmz), n. (usu. as sing.). Charitable relief ·of the poor; donation; ~-*folk*, *almsman*, (supported by charity); ~-*giving*; ~-*house*, ∥ one founded by charity for reception of poor. [OE *ælmysse* f. pop. L (Rom.) *alimosina*, altered f. LL *eleemosyna*, *elemosina*, f. Gk *eleēmosunē* compassionateness (*eleēmōn* adj. f. *eleos* compassion)]

ăl'mŭg. See ALGUM.

ăl'ōe, n. Genus of plants with erect spikes of flowers & bitter juice; (pl.) purgative drug procured from juice of ~s; other plants, as *American ~*, Agave. [OE *aluwe* f. L f. Gk *aloē*]

ălŏĕt'ic, a. & n. (Medicine) containing aloes. [f. Gk *aloē* aloe on false anal. of *diuretic* etc.]

alŏft' (or -aw-), adv. & pred. a. High up (lit. & fig.); upward. [ME, f. ON *á lopt* (*á* in, on, to, +*lopt* air); cf. LIFT, LOFT]

alōne', pred. a. & adv. Solitary; standing by oneself (*in opinion* etc.); *LET*, *leave*, ~, abstain from interfering with; (adv.) only, exclusively. [ME, f. ALL adv. + ONE]

alŏng', adv. & prep. From end to end of; through any part of the length of; onward, as *get~*; ~ *with*, in company with, in conjunction with; *all ~*, all the time; (*all*) ~ *of* (vulg.), owing to; ∥ ~-*ships*, directed fore & aft; ~-*shore*, ~ by the shore, ~ & on the shore; ~*side*, close to side of ship; ~*side of*, side by side with (lit. & fig.). [OE *anllang* (*and-* against, facing, +*lang* LONG¹), orig. adj.]

alŏof', adv. & pred. a. Away, apart, (lit. & fig.), as *stand*, *keep*, *hold ~*; (Naut.) away to windward, as *spring ~* (cf. LUFF). Hence ~NESS n. [f. A prep. + LUFF]

alōpē'cia, n. (med.). Baldness. [f. L, f. Gk *alōpekía* fox-mange f. *alōpēx* fox]

aloud', adv. Loudly; not in a whisper; (colloq.) noticeably, as *reeks~*. [f. A prep. + LOUD]

alow' (-ō), adv. (naut.). In, into, lower part of vessel. [f. A prep. + LOW a.]

ălp, n. Mountain-peak; (in Switzerland) green pasture-land on mountain-side; *Alps*, mountain ranges separating France & Italy. [(pl.) f. F *Alpes* f. L]

ălpăc'a, n. Kind of llama with long woolly hair; its wool; fabric thence made. [f. Sp. f. *paco*, native Peruv. name]

ăl'penstŏck, n. Long iron-shod staff used in climbing Alps etc. [G, = Alp-stick]

ăl'pha, n. Greek letter A (A, α); *A~ and Omega*, beginning & end; (Astron.) chief star of constellation; ~ *particles*, *rays*, helium nuclei emitted by radio-active substances (orig. regarded as rays); ~

plus, superlatively good. [ME, f. Gk, f. Heb. *aleph* ox, leader]

ăl′phabĕt, n. Set of letters used in a language; first rudiments. Hence **ălphabĕt′ic** a. [f. LL *alphabetum* (Gk *alpha, bēta*, first two letters of alphabet)]

ălphabĕt′ical, a. Of the alphabet, as ~ *order*. Hence ~LY² adv. [as prec. +-ICAL]

Al′pine (ă-), a. & n. Of the Alps or any lofty mountains; (n.) ~ plant. [f. L *Alpinus* (*Alpes*, see ALP & -INE¹)]

Al′pinist (ă-), n. Alpine climber. [f. F *alpiniste* (as prec., see -IST)]

already (awlrĕd′ĭ), adv. Beforehand; by this time, thus early. [f. ALL adv. +READY]

Alsati|a (ălsāsh′a), **Alsace** (ăl′săs), nn. Province west of Rhine, re-ceded by Germany to France 1919; White Friars in London, once sanctuary for lawbreakers. Hence ~AN (-shan) a.; ~*an* (*wolf-hound*), a breed of dog. [L form of G *Elsass*, F *Alsace*]

ăl′sike, n. Kind of clover. [*Alsike* in Sweden]

al′sō (awl-), adv. In addition, besides; ~*-ran* n., horse not placed in first three in race, person(s) that failed to win distinction. [comb. of ALL = altogether, wholly, +sō (OE *al*+*swā*)]

ălt, n. (Mus.) high note, esp. *in* ~, in octave above treble stave beginning with G; (fig.) *in* ~, in an exalted frame of mind; ~*-horn*, brass wind-instrument of saxhorn type. [f. It. *alto* ALTO f. L *altus* (cf. G *alt* 1540)]

al′tar (awl-), n. Flat-topped block for offerings to deity; Communion Table; *lead to the* ~, marry; ~*-cloth*, (prop.) linen cloth used at Communion or Mass, (loosely) silk frontal & super-frontal; ~*-piece*, reredos, esp. a painting. [OE *altar, -er* f. LL *altar(e), -ium* (*altus* high)]

al′tarwise (awl-), adv. In the manner of an altar.

ăltăz′imuth, n. Instrument for determining altitude & azimuth of heavenly bodies. [*alt-* for *altitude*+AZIMUTH]

al′ter (awl-), v.t. & i. Change in character, position, etc. Hence or cogn. ~ABIL′ITY, ~A′TION, nn., ~ABLE a. [ME, f. OF *alterer* f. LL *alterare* (L *alter* other)]

al′terative (awl-), a. & n. Tending to alter; (n.) medicine, treatment, that alters processes of nutrition. [ME, f. med. L *alterativus* (prec., -ATIVE)]

al′terc|āte (ălt-, awlt-), v.i. Dispute hotly, wrangle, (*with*). So ~A′TION n. [f. L *altercari*, see -ATE³]

ăl′ter ĕg′ō, n. One's other self, intimate friend. [L, = second I]

altĕrn′ant (ălt-, awlt-), a. & n. Alternating; (Min.) of alternating layers; (n.) ~ quantity. [F, part. of *alterner* f. L *alternare* ALTERNATE]

altĕrn′ate¹ (awl-), a. & n. 1. (Of things of two kinds) coming each after one of the other kind; (Biol.) ~ *generation* (by ~ processes, as first by budding, next by

sexual reproduction); ~ *leaves, angles* (placed alternately on the two sides of stem, line). 2. n. (awl⁴). *Deputy, substitute. Hence ~LY² (-tl-) adv. [f. L *alternare* do one thing after the other (*alternus* every other f. *alter* other), see -ATE²]

al′tern|āte² (awl-), v.t. & i. Arrange, perform, (two sets of things) alternately; interchange (one thing) alternately *with*, *by*, another; (of two things) succeed each other by turns; (of a whole) consist of alternate things; (of one class of things) appear alternately with another. So ~A′TION n.; ~ātor n., dynamo giving an ~*ating current* (reversing its direction at regular intervals). [f. prec.]

altĕrn′ative (awl-), a. & n. 1. (Of two things) mutually exclusive. 2. n. (Strictly) permission to choose between two things; (loosely) either of two possible courses, as *I had no* (*other*) ~; one of more than two possibilities. Hence ~LY² (-vl-) adv. [f. med. L *alternativus* (as prec., see -ATIVE)]

although (awldhō′), conj. Though. [ME, f. ALL adv. +THOUGH]

ăltim′ĕter, n. Aeronautical aneroid for showing height above sea level. [L *altus* high, -METER]

ăl′titūde, n. Height; depth; (Geom.) length of perpendicular from vertex to base; height above sea level; (usu. in pl.) high place; (fig.) eminence. [ME, f. L *altitudo* (*altus* high), see -TUDE]

ăl′tō, n. (mus.). Highest male voice, counter-tenor; its musical part; female voice of similar range, contralto; its part; singer with ~ voice; tenor violin; ~*-clarinet, -trombone*, instruments similar to the clarinet, trombone. [It. *alto* (*canto*) high (singing); cf. earlier (16th c.) ALT]

altogether (awltogĕdh′er), adv. & n. Totally; on the whole; (n.) *an* ~, a whole; *the* ~ (colloq.), the nude. [early ME f. ALL +TOGETHER]

ăl′tō-réliev′ō (-lē-), n. (sculp.). High relief. [It. *alto-rilievo*]

ăl′tru|ism (-rŏŏ-), n. Regard for others as a principle of action. Hence ~IST n., ~ĭs′tĭc a., ~ĭs′tĭcALLY adv. [f. F *altruisme* f. It. *altrui* (= F *autrui*) somebody else; see -ISM]

ăl′um, n. A double sulphate of aluminium & potassium; series of salts including this; family of compounds including these; (Min.) various native minerals, alums proper & pseudo-alums. [ME, f. OF, f. L *alumen alumin-*]

alum′ina (-lŏŏ-), n. One of the earths, the only oxide of aluminium. [f. L *alumen* alum, on type of *soda* etc.]

ălūmin′ium, *al*ūm′inum, n. White light sonorous ductile malleable metal, not tarnished by air, used for instruments & as an alloy; ~ *bronze*, alloy of ~ & copper. [altered (after *sodium* etc.) f. *aluminum*, earlier *alumium*; see ALUM, -IUM]

alum′inous (-lōŏ-), a. Of the nature of alum or alumina. [f. F *alumineux* or L *aluminosus* (*alumen* ALUM, see -OUS)]

alŭm′n|us, n. (pl. ~ī; fem. ~a, pl. ~ae). (Former) pupil or student. [L, = foster--child]

ălvĕ′olate, a. Honeycombed, pitted with small cavities. [f. L *alveolatus* f. foll., see -ATE²]

ălvĕ′ol|us, n. Small cavity; socket of tooth, whence ~AR¹ a.; cell of honey-comb; conical chamber of a belemnite. [L, dim. of *alveus* cavity]

always (awl′wăz, -ĭz), adv. At all times; on all occasions (~ *excepting*, *provided*, etc., legal formulae). [OE (acc. case) *alne weg*, now (arch, or poet.) *alway*; super-seded in ME by (gen. case) *alle(s) weis* always]

am. See BE.

ămadavăt′, ăv-, n. Small Indian song--bird. [place-name]

ăm′adou (-ōō), n. German tinder, pre-pared from fungi, used as a match & styptic. [F, f. Pr. f. L *amatorem* lover (*amare*, see -OR)]

amah (ah′ma), n. (S. India, formerly) wet-nurse; (China & Far East) child's (native) nurse. [f. Port. *ama* nurse]

amain′, adv. (arch., poet.). Vehemently; in all haste. [A prep.+MAIN²]

amăl′gam, n. Mixture of a metal with mercury, as *gold* ~; plastic mixture of any substances (also fig.). [late ME, f. F *amalgame* or med. L *amalgama*, prob. f. L f. Gk *malagma* an emollient]

amăl′gamate¹, a. Combined, esp. of languages. [f. prec.+-ATE²]

amăl′gam|āte², v.t. & i. Mix; unite (classes, societies, companies, ideas, etc.); (of metals) combine with mercury. Hence ~A′TION n., ~ating or being ~ated, merging of two or more business concerns into one; ~ātoR n., ~ātive a. [f. prec., see -ATE³]

amănüĕn′sis, n. (pl. *-nsēs*). One who writes from dictation or copies manu-script. [L, adj. used as n., f. (*servus*) *a manu* secretary+*-ensis* belonging to]

ăm′arănt(h), n. Imaginary unfading flower; genus, including prince's feather & love-lies-bleeding; purple colour. Hence **ămarăn′t(h)ıne¹** a. [f. F *ama-rante* f. L f. Gk *amarantos* everlasting (*a-* not+*mainō* wither); *h* by confusion with Gk *anthos* flower]

ămarȳll′is, n. Kinds of bulbous plant. [L, f. Gk *Amarullis*, name of a country girl]

amăss′, v.t. Heap together; accumulate (esp. riches). [f. F *amasser* f. *a* (= A-(4))+*masser* (f. *masse* MASS²)]

ăm′ateur (-tūr or ămatē′r), n. One who is fond *of*; one who cultivates a thing as a pastime. Hence **ămateur′ısh** (-tūr-) a., **ămateur′ıshly²** adv., **ămateur′ısh-ness, ămateur′ısm**, nn. [F, f. L *amatorem* (*amare* love, see -OR)]

Amati (ahmah′tē), n. Violin or violoncello made by a member of the *Amati* family of Cremona (fl. *c.* 1570 onwards)

ăm′ative, a. Disposed to loving. Hence ~NESS (-vn-) n. [f. L *amare* love, see -ATIVE]

ăm′atŏl, n. High explosive made from TNT & ammonium nitrate. [irreg. f. AM(MONIUM)+(TRINITRO)TOL(UENE)]

ăm′atory, a. Pertaining to a lover or to sexual love. Hence **ămatŏr′ıal** a. [f. L *amatorius* (*amare* love, see -ORY)]

ămaur|ōs′is (-or-), n. Partial or total loss of sight from disease of optic nerve. Hence ~ŏt′ıc a. [f. LL f. Gk, f. *amauroō* darken (*amauros* dark), see -OSIS]

amāz|e′¹, v.t. Overwhelm with wonder. Hence ~′ĕdLY², ~′ıngLY², advv., ~e′-MENT (-zm-) n. [ME, perh. f. OE *āmasian* (once); see MAZE]

amāze′², n. (poet.). = AMAZEMENT. [f. prec.]

Am′azon (ă-), n. Fabulous race of female warriors in Scythia; female warrior (lit. & fig.); masculine woman. Hence **Amazŏn′ıan** (ă-) a. [ME, f. L f. Gk (prob. foreign word, but explained by Greeks as *a-* not+*mazos* breast, from removal of right breast to facilitate use of bow)]

ămbā′ges (-jĕz), n. pl. Roundabout ways. [ME, f. OF f. L *ambages* circuits; in mod. use as direct f. L]

ăm′băn, n. Chinese resident official in Tibet. [Manchu, = minister]

ămbăss′ador, n. Minister sent by one sovereign or State on mission to another (usu. *A~ Extraordinary*); minister of highest rank permanently representing sovereign or State at foreign court or government (*Ordinary*, *Resident*, *A~*; formerly *A~ Leger*); *A~ Plenipotentiary* (with full power to sign treaties etc.); official messenger. Hence **ămbăssa-dŏr′ıal** a. [ME; many early forms; mod. sp. f. F *ambassadeur* f. Rom. **ambactiatorem* f. **ambactiare* f. med. L *ambactia* charge, office, f. L *ambactus* servant, of Celtic orig.]

ămbăss′adréss, n. Female ambassador; ambassador's wife. [f. prec.+-ESS¹]

ăm′ber, n. & a. **1**. Yellow translucent fossil resin, found chiefly on S. shore of Baltic; ~ *Fauna*, *Flora*, animals, plants, of which remains are found in ~; (of) the intermediate cautionary traffic light between red (= stop) and green (= go). **2**. adj. Made of, coloured like, ~. [ME, f. OF *ambre* or med. L *ambra* etc. f. Arab. *'anbar* ambergris, to which the name orig. belonged]

ăm′bergris (-ēs), n. Wax-like substance found floating in tropical seas, & in intestines of sperm-whale, odoriferous & used in perfumery, formerly in cookery. [late ME, f. OF *ambre gris* grey amber]

ămbidĕx′ter, a. & n. (Person) able to use left hand as well as right, double-dealing. Hence **ămbĭdĕxtě'rĭty** n. [LL (*amb-* on both sides+*dexter* right-handed)] **ămbĭdĕx't(e)rous**, a.=prec. Hence ~LY² adv., ~NESS n. [as prec.+-OUS]

ăm'bĭent, a. Surrounding, circumfused. [f. L *ambiens -entis* part. of *ambire* go about (*amb-* on both sides+*ire* go)]

ămbĭgŭ'ĭtў, n. Double meaning; expression capable of more than one meaning. [ME, f. OF *ambiguite* or L *ambiguitas* (as foll., see -TY)]

ămbĭg'ŭous, a. Obscure; of double meaning; of doubtful classification; of uncertain issue. Hence ~LY² adv., ~NESS n. [f. L *ambiguus* doubtful f. *ambigere* (*amb-* both ways+*agere* drive)+-OUS]

ăm'bĭt, n. Precincts; bounds; compass, extent. [f. L *ambitus* a going round (*ambire*, see AMBIENT)]

ămbĭ'tĭon, n. Ardent desire for distinction; aspiration (*to be, to* do); object of such desire. [ME, f. OF f. L *ambitionem* (*ambire -it-*, canvass for votes, see AMBIENT & -ION)]

ămbĭ'tĭous (-shŭs), a. Full of ambition; strongly desirous (*of* a thing, *to* do); showing ambition, as *an ~ attempt*. Hence ~LY² adv., ~NESS n. [ME, f. OF *ambitious* or L *ambitiosus* (as prec., see -OUS)]

ămbĭv'al|ence, n. Co-existence in one person of the emotional attitudes of love and hate towards the same object. So ~ENT a. [f. L *ambo* both, after *equivalence*]

ăm'ble¹, v.i. (Of horses etc.) move by lifting two feet on one side together; ride an ambling horse, ride at an easy pace; move in a way suggesting an ambling horse. [ME, f. OF *ambler* f. L *ambulare* walk]

ăm'ble², n. Pace of an ambling horse; easy pace. [ME, f. OF f. *ambler*, see prec.]

ămblў|ŏp'ĭa, n. Impaired vision. Hence ~ŏp'ĭc a. [Gk, f. *ambluōpos* a. (*amblus* dull+*ōps ōpos* eye)]

ăm'bō, n. (pl. ~s, ~*nes* pr. -ōn'ēs). Pulpit in early Christian churches. [med. L, f. Gk *ambōn* rim, (med. Gk pulpit)]

ămboy'na (wŏod), n. Finely marked wood of an Asian tree. [*Amboyna* Island]

ămbrō'sĭa (-zĭa, -zhya), n. (Myth.) food of the gods; anything delightful to taste or smell; bee-bread. [f. L f. Gk, elixir of life, f. *ambrotos* (*a-* not+(m)*brotos* mortal)]

ămbrō'sĭal (-zĭal, -zhyal), a. Divinely fragrant; divine. Hence ~LY² adv. [f. L f. Gk *ambrosios* divine+-AL]

ăm'brў, aum-, n. (arch.). Pantry; wall--press; dresser; closed recess in wall of church. [ME *ar-, almarie*, later *aumery, aumbry*, f. OF, f. med. L *ar-, almarium* (-*ia*) f. L *armarium* closet, chest]

ambs-ace (ămz ās'), n. Both aces, lowest throw at dice; bad luck; worthlessness. [ME, f. OF *ambes as* f. L *ambo* both; see ACE; also written *ames-*]

ăm'būlance, n. Moving hospital following army; conveyance for sick or wounded persons. [F (L *ambulare* walk, see -ANCE)]

ăm'būlant, a. (path.). (Of a disease) shifting from one part of the body to another, not confining patients to bed; (of treatment) involving exercise on part of patient. [f. part. of L *ambulare* walk, see -ANT]

ăm'būlatorў, a. & n. 1. Pertaining to walking; adapted for walking; movable; not permanent. 2. n. Place for walking; arcade, cloister. [f. L *ambulatorius* (as prec., see -ORY)]

ămbuscāde'¹, n. Ambush. [f. F *embuscade* f. It. *imboscata* or Sp. *emboscada* (*imboscare*, see AMBUSH v. and -ADE)]

ămbuscāde'², v.t. & i. Lie, conceal, in ambush. [f. prec.]

ăm'bush¹ (-ŏŏsh), n. Concealment of troops, troops concealed, in a wood etc.; (generally) lying in wait; *make, lay, an ~, lie in ~*. [earlier *en-, em-,* f. OF *embusche* (as foll.)]

ăm'bush² (-ŏŏsh), v.t. & i. Conceal (troops, only in p.p.); lie in wait for; attack from ambush; (intr.) lie in wait. [earlier *en-, em-,* etc. f. OF *embuscher, -buissier,* f. Rom. *IMboscare (*boscus* BUSH)]

âme damnée (see Ap.), n. Tool, devoted adherent. [F]

ameer', amir' (-ēr), n. Title of various Mohammedan rulers in Scinde & Afghanistan. [Arab. *amir* commander (*amara* command); cf. EMIR]

amēl'ĭor|āte, v.t. & i. (Cause to) become better. Hence ~A'TION, ~ātor, nn., ~ātĭve a. [f. earlier MELIORATE after F *améliorer* alt. f. OF *ameillorer* (*meilleur,* L *meliorem* better)]

amĕn' (ā-, ah-), int. So be it. [f. LL f. Gk f. Heb. *amen* certainty, certainly (*aman* strength)]

amēn'|able, a. (Of persons) responsible (*to* law etc. or abs.); (of things) liable *to*; capable of being tested by (*to*); responsive, tractable. Hence ~abIL'ITY, ~able-NESS, nn., ~abLY² adv. [AF (Law Fr.), f. F *amener* bring to (*à to* +*mener* bring f. L *minare* threaten), see -ABLE]

amĕnd', v.i. & t. Abandon evil ways; (arch.) improve in health; correct an error in (legal document), make professed improvements in (measure before Parliament); make better. Hence ~ABLE a., ~MENT n. [ME, f. OF *amender* f. Rom. *admendare* for L *emendare* EMEND]

amende honorable (see Ap.), n. Public apology & reparation. [F]

amĕnds' (-z), n. Reparation, restitution, compensation, as *make ~*. [ME, f. OF *amendes* penalties, fine, pl. of *amende* reparation f. *amender* AMEND; pl. now treated in E as sing.]

amēn'ĭtў, n. Pleasantness (of places, persons, etc.); (pl.) pleasant ways. [ME, f. OF

amenite or . L *amoenitas*, f. *amoenus* pleasant, see -TY]

ā mĕn'sā ĕt tŏr'ō, adv. From board & bed. [L]

amĕn'tia (-sha), n. Imbecility. [L, f. *amens* (*a* = *ab* +*mens mentis* mind)]

amĕn'tum, **amĕnt'**, n. Catkin. Hence **ămentā'ceous**, **ămentĭf'erous**, **amĕn'tĭform**, aa. [L, = thong]

amĕrce', v.t. Fine; (loosely) punish. So **amĕr'ciable** a., ∼ment (-sm-), **amĕr'ciament**, nn. [ME *amercy* f. AF *amercier* (*à* at +*merci* MERCY)]

Amĕr'ican, a. & n. 1. Belonging to continent of America or to United States; ∼ *Beauty*, hybrid perpetual rose; ‖ ∼ *cloth*, *leather*, glazed cloth used for covering tables etc.; ∼ *organ*, small organ with suction-operated reeds instead of blown pipes. 2. n. Native of America of European descent; citizen of United States. [-AN]

Amĕr'icanism, n. Word or sense or phrase peculiar to or extending from United States; attachment to, sympathy with, United States. [prec. +-ISM]

Amĕr'icanize, -**ise** (-īz), v.t. & i. Naturalize as an American; make American in character; become American in character; use Americanisms. [as prec. + -IZE]

ămeri'cium (-ĭsĭ-, -ĭshĭ-), n. Radio-active transuranic metallic element. [f. *Americ(a)* +-IUM]

ames-ace. See AMBS-ACE.

ăm'ĕthyst, n. Precious stone, kind of quartz, purple or violet; *Oriental A∼*, rare violet variety of sapphire. So **ămĕthys'tine**[1] a. [ME *ametist* f. OF *ametiste* f. L f. Gk *amethustos* not drunken, the stone being supposed to prevent intoxication]

Amhă'ric (ă-), n. Official & court language of Abyssinia. [f. *Amhara*, Abyssinian province]

ăm'iable, a. Feeling & inspiring friendliness; lovable. Hence **ămiabil'ity**, ∼ness, nn., **ăm'iably**[2] adv. [ME, f. OF, f. LL *amicabilis* AMICABLE; confused with OF *amable* (mod. F *aimable*) f. L *amabilis* lovable (*amare* love, see -BLE)]

ămiăn't(h)us, n. Mineral variety of asbestos, splitting into flexible fibres; green fibrous chrysolite. [L, f. Gk *amiantos* undefiled, i.e. purified by fire, being incombustible; for -*h*- cf. AMARANTH]

ăm'ic|able, a. Friendly; done in a friendly spirit. Hence ∼abil'ity, ∼ableness, nn., ∼ably[2] adv. [f. LL *amicabilis* f. *amicus* friend, see -BLE]

ăm'ice[1], n. Square of white linen worn by celebrant priests, formerly on head, now on shoulders. [earlier *amyt* f. OF *amit* f. L *amictus* garment; -*ce*, or -*s*, perh. due to confus. w. foll.]

ăm'ice[2], n. Cap, hood, cape, of religious orders; badge worn by French canons on left arm. [ME, f. OF *aumusse* f. med.

L *almussa* etc. of unkn. orig.; early confused w. prec.]

amic'us cūr'iae, n. Friend of the court, disinterested adviser. [L]

amid', **amidst'**, prep. In the middle of (lit. & fig.); in the course of. [OE *on middan* etc. (i.e. *on* ON +oblique case of MID[1]), ME *amidde*, later *amiddes* (see -ES), & *amidst* with inorganic -*t* as in *against*]

ăm'idin, n. Soluble matter of starch; starch in state of solution. [f. *amid-* com.- -Rom. form of L *amylum* starch (med. L *amidum*, F *amidon*) + -IN]

amid'ships, adv. In middle of ship. [f. AMID +SHIP +-ES]

ăm'ildār, n. Native revenue-collector in India. [f. Pers.]

ăm'ine, n. (chem.). Compound formed from ammonia by replacing one or more hydrogen atoms by alcohol or other base-radicals. [f. AM(MONIA) +-INE[5]]

amir, n. See AMEER.

amiss', adv. & pred. a. Not up to the mark; out of order; wrongly; untowardly, as *come* ∼; *take* ∼, take offence at; *not* ∼, appropriate. [A prep. +MISS n.]

ăm'ity, n. Friendship, friendly relations. [ME, f. OF *amitie* f. Rom. *amicitatem* f. L *amicus* friend, see -TY]

ăm'meter, n. Instrument for measuring electric current in amperes. [f. AM(PERE) +-METER]

ăm'mō, n. (sl.). Ammunition. [abbr.]

ăm'monal, n. High explosive made from ammonium nitrate & aluminium. [f. AMMON(IUM) +AL(UMINIUM)]

ammōn'ia, n. A colourless gas with pungent smell & strong alkaline reaction, spirit of hartshorn; *liquid* ∼, (Chem.) liquefied ∼; ∼ *liquor*, solution of ∼ in water. [f. foll.]

ammōn'iăc, a. & n. Of the nature of ammonia; *sal* ∼, hard white crystalline salt, said to have been prepared from camels' dung near temple of Jupiter Ammon; (*gum*) ∼, a gum resin used in medicine & as cement. Hence **ămmoni'acal** a. [ME *armoniak* f. med. L *armoniacus*, -*um* f. L f. Gk *ammōniakon* belonging to Ammon]

ammōn'iātĕd, a. Combined with ammonia. [f. prec. +-ATE[1] (3) +-ED[1]]

ămm'onite, n. Fossil genus of Cephalopods. [f. mod. L *ammonites*, after med. L *cornu Ammonis*, L *Ammonis cornu* (Pliny), horn of (Jupiter) Ammon, see -ITE[1] (2)]

ammōn'ium, n. Univalent radical of ammonia salts; ∼ *chloride*, *sal* AMMONIAC; ∼ *carbonate*, rock ammonia (see SAL VOLATILE). [-IUM]

ămmūni'tion, n. Military stores (formerly of all kinds, now of bullets, shells, grenades, etc.); (fig.) facts, arguments, etc. used in attack or defence. [f. F (obs.) *amunition*, an army corruption of (*la*) *munition* MUNITION]

ămnês'ĭa, n. Loss of memory. [Gk, = forgetfulness]

ăm'nĕstў, n. & v.t. Intentional overlooking; act of oblivion, general pardon; (v.t.) give ~ to. [f. F *amnestie* or L f. Gk *amnēstia* oblivion f. *amnēstos* (-*mnē*- remember)]

ăm'nĭŏn, n. (pl. -*ia*). Innermost membrane enclosing foetus before birth. Hence **ămnĭŏt'ĭc** a. [Gk, = caul (dim. of *amnos* lamb)]

amoeb'|a (-mē-), n. Microscopic animalcule perpetually changing shape. Hence ~**ĭFORM**, ~**OID**, aa. [f. Gk *amoibē* change]

amoebaean (ămēbē'an), a. Alternately answering, esp. of dialogue in verse. [f. L f. Gk *amoibaios* interchanging (*amoibē* change), see -**AN**]

amŏk'. See AMUCK.

among(st)' (-mŭ-), prep. In the assemblage of, surrounded by; in the number of; within the limits of (collectively or distributively), as *five shillings ~ us*, *divided ~ us*; in comparison with, as *one ~ many*; by joint action of, as *kill him ~ you*; reciprocally, as *quarrelled ~ themselves.* [OE *on gemang* (i.e. on ON + *gemang* assembly, cf. MINGLE), ME *among(e)*, later *amonges* (see -**ES**), & *amongst* with inorganic -*t* as in *against*]

Amontillado (ahmŏntĭlyah'dō), n. (Formerly) a specially dry sherry; (now) sherry of a matured type; (fig., attrib.) of dry speech or manner. [Sp., f. *Montilla* (in Spain) + *ado* (= -**ATE**²)]

amŏ'ral, a. Unconcerned with, out of the sphere of, morals, non-moral. [A- (7) + AMPHIBIA + -OUS]

‖ **amŏrce'**, n. Priming charge; percussion cap for toy pistol. [F, f. OF *amordre* bite]

ăm'orist, n. One who professes (esp. sexual) love, a gallant. [f. L *amor* love + -**IST**]

ăm'orous, a. Inclined to love; in love; of, pertaining to, love. Hence ~**LY**² adv., ~**NESS** n. [ME, f. OF *amorous* (*amor* love, see -**OUS**)]

amŏrph'|ous, a. Shapeless; anomalous; (Min., Chem.) uncrystallized; unorganized. Hence ~**ISM**, ~**OUSNESS**, nn. [f. Gk *amorphos* shapeless (a- not + *morphē* form) + -**OUS**]

amŏrt'|ĭze, -ise (-ĭz), v.t. Alienate in mortmain; extinguish (debt, usu. by means of sinking fund), whence ~**ĭZA'TION** n. [ME, f. OF *amortir* (st. -*iss*-) f. Rom. **admortire* (*ad* to + *mort*- death)]

amount'¹, v.t. Come *to* (so much); be equivalent (in significance) *to*. [ME, f. OF *amonter* f. *amont* upward (lit. uphill, f. L *ad montem*)]

amount'², n. Total to which a thing amounts; full value, significance, etc.; quantity, as *a considerable ~ (of).* [f. prec.]

amour' (-oor), n. Love-affair; intrigue. [F, = love f. L *amorem*]

amourĕtte' (-oor-), n. Petty love-affair. [F, dim. of *amour*]

amour-propre (ăm'oor-prŏp'r), n. Self-esteem. [F]

ămp, n. Ampere. [abbr.]

ămpĕlŏp'sis, n. Climbing plant allied to vine. [Gk *ampelos* vine, *opsis* appearance]

ăm'pere (-ēr, -ār), n. (electr.). Current that one volt can send through one ohm, unit of current. [name (*Ampère*) of physicist (d. 1836)]

ămpersănd', n. The sign & (*and*, L *et*). [corrupt. of '*and* per se (i.e. by itself) *and*' the old way of spelling & naming the character &]

amphi- in comb. Both, of both kinds, on both sides, around. [Gk, prep.]

Amphĭb'ĭa (ă-), n. pl. Division of Vertebrata, intermediate between reptiles & fishes, as frogs, newts, etc. [f. L f. Gk *amphibia* (*zōa*) (animals) living in both elements (AMPHI- + *bios* life)]

ămphĭb'ĭan, a. & n. (Animal) living both on land & in water; (Zool.) member of the Amphibia; (tank or other vehicle) adapted for both land & water; an aircraft designed to rise from & alight on either land or water. [as prec. + -**AN**]

ămphĭbĭŏl'ogў, n. Branch of zoology treating of Amphibia. [as prec. + -**LOGY**]

ămphĭb'ĭous, a. Living both on land & in water; connected with both land & water; (Mil.) involving co-operation of sea & land (& occas. air) forces organized for invasion, (of forces) trained for such action; having two lives, connected with two classes, etc. Hence ~**LY**² adv. [f. AMPHIBIA + -**OUS**]

ămphĭbŏl'ogў, n. Quibble; ambiguous wording. Hence **ămphĭbolŏ'gĭcal** a. [f. F *amphibologie* or LL -*logia*, f. L f. Gk AMPHI(*bolia* f. *ballō* throw); assim. to words in -**LOGY**]

ămphic'tўons, n. pl. Deputies from ancient Greek states forming council. So **ămphĭctўŏn'ĭc** a. [f. Gk *amphiktuones* neighbours]

ăm'phĭgăm, n. (bot.). Plant with no distinct sexual organs. Hence **ămphĭg'-amous** a. [f. F *amphigame* (AMPHI- + Gk *gamos* marriage)]

ămphĭgour'ĭ (-oorĭ), **ăm'phĭgorў,** n. Nonsensical composition. [F *amphigouri*, orig. unkn.]

ămphĭmix'ĭs, n. (biol.). Mingling of two individuals, or of their germs, as in sexual reproduction. [AMPHI- + Gk *mixis* mingling]

ămphĭŏx'us, n. The fish lancelet. [f. AMPHI- + Gk *oxus* sharp]

ămphĭp'od|a, n. pl. Order of Crustacea, with feet of two kinds. Hence **ăm'-phĭpŏd** n., ~**AN**, ~**OUS**, aa. [AMPHI- + Gk *pous podos* foot]

ămphĭp'rostўle, a. With portico at both

ends. [F, f. L f. Gk *amphiprostulos* (AMPHI-+*prostulos* PROSTYLE)]

ămphisbaen'a, n. Fabulous serpent with head at each end; (Zool.) genus of worm-like lizards. [L, f. Gk *amphisbaina* (*amphis* both ways+*bainō* go)]

ăm'phithēātre (-*ater*), n. Oval or circular building, with seats rising behind & above each other round a central open space; large circular hollow; part of a theatre; (fig.) scene of a contest. Hence **ămphithēăt'rICAL** a. [f. L f. Gk *amphitheatron* (see AMPHI- & THEATRE)]

Amphit'rўon (ă-), n. Host, entertainer. [Molière, *Amphitryon*, iii. 5]

ăm'phora, n. (pl. -*ae*, -*as*). Greek or Roman two-handled vessel. [L, f. Gk *amphoreus* for AMPHI(*phoreus* f. *pherō* bear)]

ămphŏ'rĭc, a. (med.). · Like the sound produced by blowing into large vessel with small mouth. [f. prec.+-IC]

ămphotĕ'rĭc, a. Acting both ways, esp. (Chem.) capable of reacting as acid & base, or as electropositive & electronegative. [f. Gk *amphoteros* both, +-IC]

ăm'ple, a. (-er, -est). Spacious; extensive; abundant; copious; quite enough. Hence **ăm'pLY²** adv., **~NESS** (-ln-) n. [f. F f. L *amplus*]

ăm'pliative, a. (logic). Extending a simple conception. [f. L *ampliare* widen (*amplus*), see -ATIVE]

ămplĭfĭcā'tion, n. Extension, enlargement; making the most of a thing. [F, or f. L *amplificatio* (as foll., see -ATION)]

ăm'plĭf|ў, v.t. & i. Enhance; enlarge (story, statement); expatiate. Hence **~IER¹** n., (esp.) appliance increasing loudness of sounds, strength of wireless signals, etc. [ME, f. OF *amplifier* or L *amplificare* (as AMPLE, see -FY)]

ăm'plĭtūde, n. Breadth; abundance; wide range; dignity; (Astron.) space by which celestial body rises, sets, wide of due east, west; (Phys.) extent of vibration or oscillation; (Electr.) maximum departure from average of alternating current or wave. [F, or f. L *amplitudo* (as AMPLE, see -TUDE)]

ăm'poule (-ōōl), n. Small glass vessel for containing esp. hypodermic injection. [F, cf. foll.]

ămpŭll'a, n. (pl. -*ae*). Roman two-handled flask; vessel for sacred uses; (Biol.) dilated end of vessel, canal, duct, in an animal. Hence **ămpullA'cEOUS** (-āshus) a. [L]

ăm'pŭt|āte, v.t. Cut off (part of animal body etc. or abs.). Hence **~A'TION**, **~ātOR**, **~EE**, nn. [f. L *amputare* (amb-about+*putare* prune), see -ATE³]

amŭck', amŏk', adv. *Run* ~, run about in frenzied thirst for blood (also fig.). [f. Malay *amok* rushing in frenzy]

ăm'ŭlĕt, n. Thing worn as charm against evil (lit. & fig.). [f. L *amuletum*, orig. unkn.]

amŭs|e' (-z), v.t. Divert from serious business (*with* trifles, *by* trifling); tickle the fancy of; *be* ~*ed with*, *by*, *at*. So **~'ABLE**, **~'IVE**, aa. [ME, f. OF *amuser* cause to MUSE² (causal *à* to +*muser* stare)]

amūse'ment (-zm-), n. Pleasant diversion; excitement of risible faculty; pastime. [f. F *amusement* (*amuser*, see prec. and -MENT)]

ămўgdăl'ĭc, a. Of almonds, as ~ *acid*. [f. L *amygdala* ALMOND+-IC]

ămўg'daloid, a. & n. (Igneous rock containing mineral nodules) of almond shape. [f. Gk *amugdalē* ALMOND+-OID]

ăm'ўl, n. (chem.). The radical of various alcohols some of which are constituents of fusel oil. Hence **amўl'ĭc** a. [f. L *am(ylum)* starch+-YL; named as discovered in distilling fusel oil from starch]

ămўlā'ceous (-shus), a. Of starch, starchy. [f. L *amylum* starch+-ACEOUS]

ăm'ўloid, a. & n. Starchy (food). [as prec.+-OID]

ămўlŏp'sin, n. Ferment of the pancreatic juice that converts starch into sugar. [f. Gk *amulon* starch, after *pepsin*]

an¹, a. See A, adj.

an², conj. (arch., colloq., dial.). If. [weakening of *and*]

an-, pref. f. var. sources. 1. OE, ME *an* = on, as in *anon*, *anent*. 2. f. L *ad* before *n*, see AD-. 3. f. L *an-* = *ambi-*, as in *anfractuosity*. 4. f. Gk ANA-, as in *anode*. 5. f. Gk *an-* = *a-* not (before vowel), as in *anarchy*.

-an, suf. of adjj. (often used as nn.), f. L -*anus* direct or through F -*ain*, -(*i)en*, the ME forms, (retained in *certain*, *captain*, *chaplain*), but later refashioned after L as -*an*, or It., Sp., Port., -*ano*, & freely used in new words; added esp. to names of place, system, zool. order, or founder (*Chilian*, *Anglican*, *reptilian*, *Lutheran*); often as E termination to L adjj. in -*ius*, giving -IAN as a mere phonetic variant (cf. *Christ-ian*, *Mohammed-an*). See also -ANE, -EAN.

ăn'a, n. (With pl. ~*s*) collection of person's memorable sayings; (collect. pl.) anecdotes, lit. gossip, about a person. [=-ANA]

ăna-, pref. = Gk *ana* up, back, again, anew; before a vowel *an-*.

-ana, suf. Neut. pl. of L adjj. in -*anus* (see -AN) appended in 16th-c. F to names = the sayings of; in E from 18th c., now including anecdotes about, publications bearing on, places or persons, as *Tunbrigiana*, *Shakespeareana*.

ănabăp'tism, n. Re-baptism; doctrine of anabaptists. [f. LL f. Gk *anabaptismos* (ANA-+*baptismos* BAPTISM)]

ănabăp't|ist n. One who baptizes over again; (opprobriously) = BAPTIST. Hence **~is'tICAL** a. [f. F *anabaptiste* or mod. L *anabaptista* (prec., -IST)]

ăn'abăs, n. Kinds of fishes that leave water & ascend trees. [Gk part. of *anabainō* walk up]

anăb′asis, n. Up-country march, esp. that of Cyrus the younger into Asia, narrated by Xenophon. [Gk, = ascent f. ANA(*bainō* go)]

ănabăt′ic, a. (meteor.). (Of winds) caused by air flowing upwards, cf. KATABATIC. [as prec.+-IC]

anăb′olism, n. (biol.). Constructive metabolism (opp. KATABOLISM). So **ănabŏl′ic** a. [f. Gk *anabolē* ascent+-ISM]

ăn′abranch (-ahn-). n. A stream that turns out of, &, lower down, re-enters, a river. [ANA-+BRANCH]

ănachrŏn′ic(-k-), a. Involving anachronism, out of date. [f. ANA-+Gk *khronos* time+-IC]

anăch′ron|ism (-k-), n. Error in computing time; thing out of harmony with the present, esp. the relation of an event, custom, or circumstance to a wrong period of time; building etc. out of harmony with its surroundings in point of time. So ∼**is′tic** a. [f. F *anachronisme* or Gk *anakhronismos* f. *anakhronizō* (as prec.)]

ănaclăs′tic, a. Pertaining to refraction; springing back with crackling sound, as ∼ *glasses*. [f. Gk *anaklastos* refracted f. ANA(*klaō* bend)]

ănacolūth′on, n. (pl. *-tha*). Sentence, words, lacking grammatical sequence. [f. Gk *anakolouthon* (AN- (5)+*akolouthos* following)]

ănacŏn′da, n. Large snake of Ceylon; large S.-American Boa; any large snake that crushes its prey. [orig. unkn.]

anăcrĕŏn′tic, a. & n. (Poem) in the manner or metre(∪∪–∪|–∪–∪–∪)of Anacreon's lyrics; convivial & amatory. [f. LL *Anacreonticus* (Gk *Anakreōn*, name of poet)]

ănacrus′is (-ōō-), n. (pros.). Unstressed syllable at beginning of verse. [f. Gk *anakrousis* (ANA*krouō* strike up)]

anăd′romous, a. (Of fishes) ascending rivers to spawn. [f. Gk ANA(*dromos* running)+-OUS]

anaem′|ia, n. (med.). Lack of blood, unhealthy paleness; PERNICIOUS ∼. Hence ∼**ic** a. [f. Gk *anaimia* (AN- (5)+*haima* blood); see -IA¹]

anaerobe (ană′erŏb), n. Minute organism that can live without free oxygen. Hence **anaerŏb′ian**, **anaerŏb′ic**, aa. [f. AN- (5)+Gk *aēr* air+*bios* life]

ănaesthēs′ia, n. Insensibility (lit.). [f. Gk *anaisthēsia* (AN- (5)+*aisthēsis* sensation f. st. *aisthe-* perceive)]

ănaesthĕt′|ic, a. & n. (Agent) that produces insensibility. Hence ∼**ICALLY** adv. [f. Gk *anaisthētos* insensible (as prec.)+-IC]

anaes′thet|ize, **-ise** (-īz), v.t. Render insensible (lit. & fig.). Hence ∼**IST** (1), ∼**īza′TION**, nn. [as prec.+-IZE]

ăn′aglўph, n. Embossed ornament in low relief; (Photog.) composite stereoscopic picture printed in superimposed com-plementary colours. Hence **ănaglўph′ic** a. [f. Gk ANA*gluphē* (*gluphō* carve); cf. LL *anaglyphus* a.]

ănagnŏ′risis, n. Recognition, dénouement in a drama. [Gk, f. *anagnōrizō* recognize]

ănagŏ′gē, n. Spiritual or allegorical interpretation. So **ănagŏ′gic**(AL) aa., **ănagŏ′gical**LY² adv. [LL, f. Gk f. *anagō* lead up (AN- 4)]

ăn′agrăm, n. Transposition of letters of word or phrase, to form new word or phrase. Hence **ănagrammăt′ic**(AL) aa., **ănagrammăt′ical**LY² adv. [f. F *anagramme* after Gk *anagrammatizō* transpose letters; see -GRAM]

ănagrămm′at|ize, **-ise** (-īz), v.t. Form into an anagram. Hence -ISM, ∼-IST, nn. [f. Gk *anagrammatizō*(prec., see -IZE)]

ăn′al, a. Pertaining to, situated near, the anus. [f. ANUS+-AL]

ăn′alĕcts, **ănalĕc′ta**, n. pl. Literary gleanings. [f. Gk *analekta* things gathered (ANA*legō* pick up)]

ănalĕp′tic, a. & n. Restorative (medicine). [f. LL f. Gk *analēptikos* f. ANA-(*lambanō* take) restore, see -IC]

ănălgēs′ia, n. Absence of pain. So **ănălgĕt′ic**, (irreg.) **ănălgēs′ic**, aa., giving ∼, & nn., such drug. [Gk (-*gēs*-), f. *an*- (5), *algeō* feel pain]

ănalŏ′gic, a. Of analogy. [f. L f. Gk *analogikos* (as ANALOGY, see -IC)]

ănalŏ′gical, a. According to analogy; expressing an analogy. Hence ∼LY² adv. [as prec., see -ICAL]

anăl′ogist, n. One occupied with analogies; philosopher who saw in words images of the things they expressed. [as foll., see -IST]

anăl′ogize, **-ise** (-īz), v.t. & i. Represent by analogy; show to be analogous; employ analogy; be in harmony (*with*). [f. ANALOGY+-IZE]

anăl′ogous, a. Similar, parallel, (*to*). Hence ∼LY² adv., ∼NESS n. [f. L f. Gk *analogos* (*ana* up to+*logos* proportion)+-OUS]

ăn′alogue (-ŏg), n. Analogous, parallel, word or thing. [F, f. Gk *analogon* neut. adj., see prec.]

anăl′ogў, n. (Math.) proportion; agreement, similarity, (*to*, *with*, *between*); analogue; (Logic) process of reasoning from parallel cases; (Lang.) imitation of inflexion or construction of existing words in forming inflexions or constructions of others, without intervention of the formative steps through which these at first arose; (Nat. Hist.) resemblance of form or function between organs essentially different. [f. F *analogie* or L -*ia* f. Gk *analogia* proportion (as ANALOGOUS)]

ăn′alўs|e (-z), *-ўz|e, v.t. Examine minutely the constitution of; (Chem., Phys.) ascertain the elements of (a compound); find, show, the essence of (treatise etc.); (Gram.) resolve (sentence) into its grammatical elements. Hence ~ABLE a. [f. F *analyser* (*analyse*, as foll.); also -*yze* in E by assim. to vbs in -IZE].

anǎl'ỹsis, n. (pl. -*ysēs*). Resolution into simple elements (in all senses of prec.); *bowling* ~, register of the result of each ball, ratio of balls bowled to wickets taken. [med. L f. Gk *analusis* f. ANA(*luō* loose)]

ǎn'alỹst, n. One skilled in (usu. chemical) analysis. [f. F *analyste* f. *analyser* ANALYSE, on anal. of nouns in -*iste* -IST f. vbs in -*iser* -IZE]

ǎnalỹt'ic, a. Pertaining to analysis. Hence **ǎnalỹt'ics** n. [f. LL f. Gk *analutikos* (as ANALYSIS, see -IC)]

ǎnalỹt'ical, a. Employing the analytic method;~(co-ordinate) *geometry*; (Lang.) using separate words instead of inflexions. Hence ~LY² adv. [as prec., see -ICAL]

ǎnamnēs'is, n. Recollection (esp. of a previous existence). [Gk (ANA*mimnēskō* remind)]

ǎnamŏrph'osis, n. Distorted drawing appearing regular from óne point; (Bot.) abnormal transformation. [Gk (ANA-*morphoō* transform f. *morphē* form, see -OSIS)]

anǎn'as (*or* -ahn-), n. Pineapple. [F or Sp. *ananas, anana*; f. Guarani *nana*]

anǎn'drous, a. (bot.). Without stamens. [f. Gk *anandros* husbandless (AN- (5) + *anēr andros* male) + -OUS]

Ananī'as (ǎ-), n. A liar. [see *Acts* v. 1–5]

ǎn'apaest, n. (Prosody) foot consisting of two short syllables followed by one long. Hence **ǎnapaes'tic** a. [f. L f. Gk *anapaistos* reversed (ANA- + *paiō* strike)]

anǎph'ora, n. Repetition of word or phrase in successive clauses. [LL, f. Gk *anaphora* = carrying back f. ANA(*pherō* bear)]

ǎn'arch (-k), n. (poet.). Leader of revolt. [f. Gk *anarkhos* without ruler (AN- (5) + *arkhos*)]

anǎrch'ic(al) (-k-), aa. Lawless. Hence **anǎrch'icalLY²** adv. [as prec. + -IC, -ICAL]

ǎn'arch|ist (-k-), n. Advocate of anarchy. So ~ISM (-k-) n. [as prec. + -IST]

ǎn'archỹ (-k-), n. Absence of government; disorder; confusion. [f. med. L f. Gk *anarkhia* (as prec.)]

anǎr'throus, a. (Gk Gram.) used without the article; (Physiol.) jointless. [f. AN- (5) + Gk *arthron*, joint, article, + -OUS]

ǎnasǎr'c|a, n. A dropsical affection. Hence ~OUS a. [f. Gk *ana* up + *sarka* (nom. *sarx*) flesh]

ǎnastǎt'ic, a. In relief; ~ *printing* (from reliefs on zinc plates). [f. Gk *anastatos* set up (ANA*sta*- stánd up) + -IC]

ǎnastigmǎt'ic, a. Free from astigmatism (used esp. of photographic lenses in which this error is corrected. So (by back--formation thr. G) **anastig'mǎt** n., lens, or lens-system, so corrected. [AN- (5) + ASTIGMATIC]

anǎs'tomōse (-z), v.i. Communicate by anastomosis. [f. F *anastomoser* (*anastomose* = foll.)]

anǎstomōs'is, n. (pl. -*osēs*). Cross connexion of arteries, branches, rivers, etc. [Gk, f. *anastomooō* furnish with mouth (*stoma*), see -OSIS]

ǎnǎs'trophē, n. (rhet.). Inversion or unusual order of words or clauses. [Gk (ANA-, *strophē* turning f. *strephō* turn)]

anǎth'ēma, n. Accursed thing; curse of God; curse of the church, excommunicating a person or denouncing a doctrine; imprecation. [eccl. L, = excommunicated person, excommunication, f. Gk *anathema* thing devoted, (later) accursed thing (ANA*tithēmi* set up)]

anǎth'ēmatize, -ise (-iz), v.t. & i. Curse. [f. F *anathématiser* or LL f. Gk *anathematizō* (as prec., see -IZE)]

ǎnatŏm'ical, a. Belonging to anatomy; structural. Hence ~LY² adv. [f. F *anatomique* or LL f. Gk *anatomikos* (as ANATOMY); see -ICAL]

anǎt'omist, n. Dissecter of bodies; one skilled in anatomy; (fig.) analyser. [f. F *anatomiste*, as foll., see -IST]

anǎt'omize, -ise (-iz), v.t. & i. Dissect; (fig.) analyse. [f. F *anatomiser*, as foll., see -IZE]

anǎt'omỹ, n. Dissection; science of bodily structure; anatomical structure; analysis; (pop.) skeleton, mummy, emaciated creature. [f. F *anatomie* or LL f. Gk *anatomia* (ANA-, -TOMY)]

anǎt'ta, -tō, n. Orange-red dye, used for colouring cheese. [f. Carib *annoto*, name of tree]

ǎn'burỹ, ǎmb-, n. Soft tumour on horses & oxen; disease of turnips & allied plants. [perh. = *ang-berry* (OE *ang-*painful, cf. AGNAIL)]

-ance, suf. forming nn. of quality or action, chiefly thr. F -*ance* f. L -*antia* & -*entia* (see -ENCE) f. L pres. part. in -*ant*-, -*ent*- (nom. -*ans*, -*ens*). OF gave -*ance* both for existing L -*antia*, -*entia*, & for wds formed in F on same model; thus, *assistance*, *nuisance*, where L would have -*entia*. Later F followed L vowel; *élégance*, *tempérance* (L -*antia*), but *diligence*, *prudence* (L -*entia*). E adopted F forms of both kinds, & usu. retains F form; but after 1500 -*ence* was in some wds restored where L would have -*entia*, & mod. formations follow L vowel. F -*ance* also became living suf. in E on native vbs as *furtherance*, *forbearance*, *riddance*.

ǎn'cest|or, n. Any of those from whom one's father or mother is descended, forefather. Hence ~rESS¹ n. [ME, f. OF *ancestre*, *ancessor*, f. L. *antecessor*, -*orem*, f. ANTE(*cedere cess*- go), see -OR]

ǎncěs'tral, a. Belonging to, inherited from, ancestors. [16th c., f. OF *ancestrel*, mod. F -*al*; see prec. & -AL]

ǎn'cěstrỹ, n. Ancestral lineage; ancient

descent; ancestors. [ME, alt. f. OF *ancesserie* (as ANCESTOR, see -Y[1])]

anchithere (ăng'kĭthēr), n. Fossil animal, size of small pony, regarded as ancestor of the horse. [f. Gk *agkhi* near + *thērion* wild beast]

ănc'hor[1] (-k-), n. Heavy iron, composed of long shank, with ring at one end to which cable is fastened, & at other end two flukes, used for mooring ship to bottom of sea etc.; *sheet, bower, kedge*, ~~, (largest, middle, smallest size); (fig.) source of confidence; *cast, weigh,* ~, let down, take up, ~; *at* ~, anchored; *come to (an)* ~, anchor; *swallow the* ~ (Naut. sl.), retire from seafaring life; ~*-plate*, heavy piece of timber or metal serving as point of support for cables of suspension-bridge etc.; ~*-stroke* (Bill.), a kind of cannon; ~*-watch*, watch set while ship lies at ~. [OE *ancor* f. L *ancora* (not *anch*-) f. Gk *agkura* (st. *agk-* hook); later reinforced by OF *ancre*]

anc'hor[2] (-k-), v.t. & i. Secure (ship) with anchor; (fig.) fix firmly; (intr.) cast anchor, come to anchor. [ME, f. prec. or OF *ancrer*]

ănc'horage (-k-), n. Anchoring; lying at anchor; ~-ground; (fig.) thing to depend upon; ~-dues. [prec. + -AGE; cf. F *ancrage*]

ănc'horéss, ănc'réss, (-k-), n. Female anchorite. [f. obs. *anchor* (OE *ancra*, short form of LL *anachoreta* (med. L *-ita*) f. Gk *anakhōrētēs* (ANAkhōreō retire, see -ETE), influenced by the forms of *anchor*, see prec.]

ănc'horite, -rĕt, (-k-), n. Hermit; person of secluded habits. Hence **ănchorĕt'ic** (-k-) a. [f. LL *anachoreta* (med. L *-ita*) f. Gk *anakhōrētēs* (ANAkhōreō retire, see -ETE), influenced by the forms of *anchor*, see prec.]

ăn'chŏvy (or ănchō'), n. Small fish of herring family; ~-paste & ~-sauce, ~-toast, (made, spread, with anchovies); ~-pear, W.-Indian fruit eaten like mango. [f. Sp., Pg. *anchova*, of disputed orig.]

anchusa (ăngkŭs'a), n. Kinds of hairy-stemmed plant, such as alkanet & bugloss. [L]

ănc'hylose (-kĭlōz), v.t. & i. (Of joints, bones) stiffen, unite. [f. foll.]

anchylōs'is (ăngkĭ-), n. Formation of stiff joint by consolidation of articulating surfaces. [f. Gk *agkulōsis* (*agkuloō* crook f. *agkulos*, see -OSIS); *-ch-* for *-c-* to preserve hard sound]

ancien régime (see Ap.), n. Time before French Revolution; (transf.) the old order. [F]

ăn'cient[1] (-shent), a. & n. Belonging to times long past (esp. before fall of Western Roman Empire); having existed, lived, long (~ *lights*, window that neighbour may not deprive of light by building); *the A~ of Days*, God; *the* ~*s*, civilized nations of antiquity. Hence ~LY[2] adv., ~NESS n. [ME *auncien* etc. f. OF *ancien* f. Rom. **anti-, anteanus* (*ante* before, see -AN); *-t* after wds in -ENT; cf. *tyrant*]

ăn'cient[2] (-shent), n. (arch.). = ENSIGN. [corrupt. due to confusion of early forms of ENSIGN & ANCIENT[1]]

ăn'cientry (-shen-), n. Ancientness; old-fashioned style. [ANCIENT[1] + -RY]

ăncill'arỹ (or ăn'-), a. Subservient, subordinate, (to). [f. L *ancillaris* (*ancilla* handmaid, see -ARY[2])]

ancon (ăng'kon), n. (Physiol.) elbow; (Archit.) quoin of wall or rafter, console, pretended support to cornice; *A~ sheep*, kind with long bodies & short legs, the fore-legs crooked. [L, f. Gk *agkōn* bend, elbow]

-ancỹ, suf., in mod. E f. L *-antia* (as -ENCY f. L *-entia*) used partly to form new wds direct f. L, partly to refashion earlier wds in *-ance*, to denote quality or state, as opposed to *-ance*, which has besides this meaning that of action or process. See -CY.

and (and, *emphat.* ănd), conj. connecting words, clauses, and sentences, as *cakes ~ buns, black ~ brown bread, buy ~ sell*. Special uses: *four ~ twenty* (but *twenty-four*); *two hundred ~ forty, two thousand ~ forty* (but *two thousand four hundred*); *two ~ ten pence, two pounds ~ ten pence* (but *two pound ten*); *miles ~* (= innumerable) *miles; nice ~* (= nicely) *thin; try ~* (to) *come, mind ~* (to) *bring; there are books ~* (different kinds of, good & bad) *books; two ~ two*, by twos; *stir, ~* (= if you stir) *you are a dead man; and/or,* formula allowing reader to take either or both of two expressions (*contributions in money and/or garments*). [OE *and, ond* (Gmc **anda*), end (Gmc **andi*)]

Andalu'sian (ăndalōō'shn), n. & a. (Native) of Andalusia, a province of Spain; || ~ *wool*, fine soft kind; ~ (*fowl*), bluish-black domestic fowl. [-AN]

ăndăn'tè, adv. & n. (mus.). (Movement) in moderately slow time. [It.]

ăndanti'nō (-tē-), adv. & n. (Movement) rather quicker (orig. slower) than *andante*. [It., dim. of prec.]

An'derson shĕl'ter (ăn-), n. Portable arched corrugated-steel air-raid shelter. [Sir J. *Anderson*, Home Secretary (1939–40)]

ăn'diron (-ĭrn), n. Firedog, for supporting burning wood on hearth. [ME *aundyre*, *-yrne*, f. OF *andier*, of unkn. orig.; assim. in form to *iron*]

ăndroe'cium (-rē-), n. (bot.). The stamens taken collectively. [f. Gk *andro-* male + *oikion* house]

ăn'drogĕn, n. Any substance (e.g. a male sex hormone) capable of developing & maintaining many male sexual characteristics. [f. Gk *andro-* male + -GEN]

ăndrŏg'ỹn|ous, a. Hermaphrodite, whence ~Y[1] n.; (Bot.). with stamens & pistils in same flower or on same plant. [f. L f. Gk *androgunos* (*anēr andros* male + *gunē* woman) + -OUS]

-āne, suf. 1. Var. of -AN, usu. w. differentiation (*germane, urbane, humane*), but occas. alone (*mundane*). **2.** (Chem.) formed to give a series with Gk -ENE, -INE, -ONE, for naming hydrocarbon types.

ăn'ĕcdŏtage, n. Anecdotes; (joc.) garrulous old age. [-AGE]

ăn'ĕcdŏt|e, n. Narrative of detached incident; (pl. ~a) unpublished details of history. Hence ~IST n., ~AL, ānĕcdŏt-IC(AL), aa. [orig. pl. f. F *anecdotes* f. Gk *anekdota* things unpublished (AN- (5) + *ekdotos* f. *ekdidōmi* publish)]

anēle', v.t. (arch.) Anoint; give extreme unction to. [ME *anelien* (AN- (1) + *elien* oil f. OE *ele*, n. f. L *oleum*)]

anĕm'o|graph (-ahf), n. Instrument for recording on paper the direction & force of wind. Hence ~**grăph'IC** a. [f. Gk *anemos* wind + -GRAPH]

anĕmŏm'ĕter, n. Instrument for measuring force of wind, whence **ănĕmomĕt'rIC** a., **ănĕmŏm'ETRY** n.; apparatus for showing wind-pressure in organ. [as prec. + -METER]

anĕm'onĕ, n. Kinds of plants, esp. ~ *nemorosa* (also called *wind-flower*); sea ~, popular name of various actinoid zoophytes. [f. L f. Gk *anemōnē* daughter of the wind (as prec. + -ōnē patronymic suf.)]

ănĕmŏph'ilous, a. Wind-fertilized. [f. Gk *anemos* wind, see -PHILOUS]

anĕnt', prep. (arch., Sc.). Concerning. [= OE *on efen* on a level with]

-ānĕous, suf. f. L adjj. in -*aneus* (-*an-* + -*eo-*) + -OUS.

ăn'eroid, a. & n. ~ (*barometer*), one that measures air-pressure by its action on elastic lid of box exhausted of air, not by height of fluid column. [f. F *anéroïde* (Gk *a-* not + *nēros* wet, see -OID)]

ăn'eurўsm, -ism (-nūr-), n. Morbid dilatation of an artery; abnormal enlargement. Hence **ăneurўs'mAL, -is'mAL** (-nūrĭz-), a. [f. Gk *aneurusma* (*aneurunō* widen out f. *eurus* wide); cf. LL -*isma*]

anew', adv. Again; in a different way. [A- (3) + NEW]

ănfrăctūŏs'itў, n. Circuitousness, intricacy, (lit. & fig.); (usu. pl.) winding passage. [f. F *anfractuosité* f. LL *anfractuosus* f. L *anfractus* a bending, see -OSE & -TY]

ăng'arў (-ngg-), n. (law). Belligerent's right (subject to compensation) of seizing or destroying neutral property under stress of military necessity. [f. F *angarie* or LL *angaria* f. Gk *aggareia* (*aggaros* Persian courier)]

ăn'gel (-j-), n. Divine messenger; *visits, like those of ~s, short & far between*; *entertain an ~ unawares*, do service to one who proves to be an important person etc. (Heb. xiii. 2); lovely or innocent being; minister of loving offices; (sl.) financial backer of enterprise; old English gold coin (in full ~-*noble*), from

6s. 8d. to 10s., showing Michael piercing dragon; *good, evil,* ~, attendant spirits; ~ (*messenger*) *of death*; ~*-fish*, kind of shark; ~*s, devils, -on-horseback,* savoury of oysters wrapped in slices of bacon. [OE *engel* (f. **angil*) Gmc f. LL *angelus* f. Gk *aggelos*; in ME reinforced & superseded by OF *angele, angle* (mod. *ange*)]

ăngĕl'ic (-j-), a. Pertaining to angels; like an angel, of superhuman qualities; *A~ Doctor,* Thomas Aquinas. Hence ~AL a., ~alIcTY² adv. [f. F *angélique* or LL f. Gk *aggelikos* (as prec., see -IC)]

ăngĕl'ica (-j-), n. Aromatic plant, used in cooking & medicine; candied ~ root. [f. med. L (*herba*) *angelica* angelic herb]

ăn'gĕlus (-j-), n. Devotional exercise commemorating Incarnation, said by Roman Catholics at morning, noon, & sunset, at sound of bell (~-*bell* or ~). [f. opening words *Angelus domini*]

ăng'er¹ (-ngg-), n. Rage, hot displeasure. [ME, f. ON *angr* trouble (root **ang* strait)]

ăng'er² (-ngg-), v.t. Make angry, enrage. [ME, f. ON *angra* vex (as prec.)]

An'gĕvin (ănj-), a. & n. Of Anjou, of the Plantagenets, including English kings from Henry II to Richard II; (n.) a Plantagenet. [F]

ăngin'a (-j-), n. Quinsy; ~ *pĕc'torĭs,* spasm of chest resulting from over-exertion when heart is diseased. [L, = quinsy, f. Gk *agkhonē* strangling]

ăn'gio- (-j-), comb. form of Gk *aggeion* vessel dim. of *aggos* chest, chiefly in terms relating to seed- or blood-vessels.

angle¹ (ăng'gl), n. Space between two meeting lines or planes; inclination of two lines to each other; ACUTE, OBTUSE, RIGHT, ~; corner; sharp projection; (fig.) point of view; ~*-iron,* L-shaped piece of iron to strengthen framework; ~*-wise,* angularly. Hence (-)**anglED²** (ăng'gld) a. [ME, f. OF *angle* or L *angulus* dim. of **angus,* cf. Gk *agkos* bend]

angle² (ăng'gl), n., & v.i. Fish-hook (obs. exc. in *brother of the ~,* angler); (vb) fish with hook & bait (*for* or abs.), lit. & fig. [OE *angul* (= OHG *angul,* ON *öngull*) f. Gmc **ang-*; cf. prec.]

Angle³ (ăng'gl), n. (Pl.) Low-German tribe settled in Northumbria, Mercia, & E. Anglia. [f. L *Anglus* f. Gmc **angli-* (OE *Engle,* cf. ENGLISH) f. *Angul* a district of Holstein (as prec.)]

ăng'ler (-ngg-) n. One who angles; (Zool.) a British fish that preys upon small fish, attracting them by filaments attached to head & mouth. [f. ANGLE² + -ER¹]

Ang'lican (ăngg-), a. & n. (Adherent) of the reformed church of England; ~ *chant,* short harmonized melody in two or more phrases each beginning with a reciting note, for singing to unmetrical words (psalms, canticles). Hence ~ISM n. [f. med. L *Anglicanus* (Magna Carta) f. *Anglicus* (Bede) f. *Anglus* ANGLE³]

Anglice (ăng'glĭsē), adv. In English. [L]

Ang′licism (ăngg-), n. English idiom; English political principles. [f. foll., see -ISM]

Ang′licize (ăngg-), -ise (-iz), v.t. Make English in form or character. [f. med. L *Anglicus* English +-IZE]

Ang′lo- (ăngg-) in comb. English, as ~-*Catholic*; of English origin, as ~-*American*; half English & half —, as ~-*French* (*entente* etc.); ~-*Indian* a. & n., of British birth but living or having lived long in India, (in Eurasian use) Eurasian; ~-*Norman* n., the French language of the Normans as used in England after the Conquest, also adj. [comb. form of L *Anglus* English]

Anglo-Căth′olic, a. & n. (Member) of the party that insists on the catholicity of the Church of England & repudiates the epithet *protestant*. [prec.]

Anglomān′ia (ăngg-), n. Excessive admiration of English customs. So **Ang′lo-**PHIL, **Ang′lo**PHOBE, **Anglo**PHOB′IA (ăngg-), nn. [ANGLO- +-MANIA]

Anglo-Săx′on, n. & a. English Saxon (as distinct from Old Saxons of the continent), Old English (people, language) before Norman Conquest (in this dictionary called OE); of English descent (wherever found), whence ~DOM n. [f. mod. L *Anglo-Saxones* (Camden), app. after OE *Angul-Seaxan* (pl.), in med. L *Angli Saxones* (8th c.)]

Anglo-Săx′onism (ăngg-), n. Belief in claims of the Anglo-Saxon race. [prec. + -ISM]

ăngōl′a, ăngōr′a, (-ngg-), n. Fabric made from wool of angora goat; ~ *cat* (long-haired variety). [f. *Angora* (mod. form of ancient Gk *Agkura*, town in Asia Minor; *angola* is corrupt]

ăngostūr′a, ăngus-, (-ngg-), a. & n. Aromatic bark formerly used as febrifuge & tonic. [f. *Angostura*, town in Venezuela on the Orinoco, now Ciudad Bolivar]

ăng′r|ў (-ngg-), a. Enraged, wrathful, resentful, (*at, about,* thing, *at, with,* person); irritable, passionate; (of wound, sore, etc.) inflamed, painful. Hence ~iLY[2] adv. [ME, f. ANGER n. +-Y[2]]

Ång′ström (ăng′strĕrm or ŏng-) **ün′it,** n. A hundred-millionth of a centimetre, used in expressing short wave-lengths (abbr. A.U.). [A. J. *Ångström,* Swedish physicist (d. 1874)]

ăng′uine (-nggw-), a. Snake-like. [f. L *anguinus* (*anguis* snake), see -INE[1]]

ăng′uish (-nggw-), n. Severe bodily or mental pain. [ME *anguisse, -ish* f. OF *anguisse* choking f. L *angustia* tightness]

ăng′ular (-ngg-), a. Having angles; sharp-cornered; placed in, at, an angle; measured by angle, as ~ *divergence*; wanting plumpness; wanting suavity. Hence **ăngŭlā′rITY** (-ngg-) n., ~LY[2] (-ngg-) adv. [f. L *angularis* (*angulus* ANGLE[1], see -AR[1])]

ăng′ŭl|ate (-ngg-), a. Formed with

corners. Hence ~ATE[3] (-ngg-) v.t., ~A′-TION (-ngg-) n. [f. L *angulatus* (ANGLE[1], -ATE[2])]

ăngŭs′ti- (-ngg-) in comb. With narrow —, as -*foliate, -rostrate,* (leaves, beak). [L *angustus* narrow]

ănhy̆d′rous, a. (chem.). Without water of crystallization. [f. Gk *anudros* (AN- (5) +*hudōr* water) +-OUS]

ănicŏn′ic, a. (Gk ant.). (Of idols & symbols) not shaped in human or animal form. [AN- (5) +ICONIC]

ăn′icŭt, ann-, n. (Anglo-Ind.). River-dam in S. India built for irrigation purposes. [f. Tamil *anai-kattu* dam-building]

anigh (*ani′*), adv. & prep. Near. [mod. f. NIGH, after *anear, afar*]

ăn′il, n. Indigo (shrub & dye). [F or Pg. *anil* f. Arab. *an-nil* (*al* the +Arab.-Pers. *nil* f. Skr. *nili* indigo)]

ăn′ile, a. Old-womanish; imbecile. [f. L *anilis* (*anus* old woman, see -ILE)]

ăn′iline, n. A chemical base, the source of many dyes, obtained originally from indigo, now chiefly from coal-tar. [ANIL +-INE[5]]

anil′ity̆, n. Dotage. [f. L *anilitas* (ANILE, see -TY)]

ănimadver′sion (-shn), n. Criticism; censure. [f. L *animadversio* (*animadvertere -vers-,* see foll. and -ION)]

ănimadvert′, v.i. Pass criticism or censure *on* (conduct, fault, etc.). [f. L *animadvertere* f. *animus* mind +AD(*vertere vers-* turn)]

ăn′imal, n. & a. **1.** Organized being endowed (more or less perceptibly) with life, sensation, & voluntary motion; other ~ than man; quadruped; a brutish man. **2.** adj. Pertaining to the functions of ~s, as ~ *spirits* (natural buoyancy), ~ *magnetism* (mesmerism); pertaining to ~s as opp. to vegetables; carnal. Hence ~LY[2] adv. [L, for *animale* neut. of *animalis* having breath (*anima* breath, see -AL); the adj. orig. f. L adj.]

ănimăl′cŭle, n. Microscopic animal. [f. L *animalculum* (*animal,* see prec. & -CULE)]

ănimăl′cŭl|ism, n. Reference of physiological phenomena to agency of animalcules. So ~IST n. [f. prec. +-ISM]

ăn′imalism, n. Animal activity; sensuality; doctrine that men are mere animals. [ANIMAL +-ISM]

ănimăl′ity̆, n. Animal nature or system; merely animal nature; the animal world. [f. F *animalité* (*animal* a., see -TY)]

ăn′imaliz|e, -is|e (-iz), v.t. Convert into animal substance, sensualize. Hence ~A′TION n. [ANIMAL +-IZE]

ăn′imate[1], a. Living; lively. [f. L *animare* quicken, see -ATE[2]]

ăn′imăt|e[2], v.t. Breathe life into; enliven, make lively, as *an ~ed discussion;* inspirit (esp. in p.p.); inspire, actuate. Hence or cogn. ~ĕDLY[2] adv., **ănima′TION** n., (esp.) ardour, vivacity, ~OR n., (also,

Cinemat.) artist who prepares ~ed cartoons. [f. prec., see -ATE³]

ăn′ĭmè (-mā), n. A W. Indian resin used in making varnish; other resins. [F, of unkn. orig.]

ăn′ĭm|ĭsm, n. Doctrine of the *anima mundi* (that phenomena of animal life are produced by an immaterial soul); attribution of living soul to inanimate objects & natural phenomena; spiritualism (as opposed to materialism). Hence ~IST n., ~ĭs′TIC a. [f. L *anima* life, soul +-ISM]

ănĭmŏs′ĭtў, n. Active enmity (*against, between*). [ME, f. OF *animosite* or LL *animositas* (*animosus* spirited f. foll., see -OSE & -TY)]

ăn′ĭmus, n. (no pl.). Animating spirit; animosity. [L, = soul, mind, mental impulse]

ăn′ĭon, n. Electro-negative element evolved at anode during electrolysis (opp. CATION). [f. ANA- +ION]

ăn′ĭse, n. Umbelliferous plant with aromatic seeds. [ME, f. OF *anis* f. L f. Gk *anison* anise, dill]

ăn′ĭseed, n. Seed of anise, used as a carminative.

ănĭsĕtte′ (-z-), n. Liqueur flavoured with aniseed. [F, dim. of *anis* anise]

ănĭs|o- in comb. Unequal, as ~*ŏm′erous*, unsymmetrical, ~*ŏp′ia*, inequality of vision in the eyes. [f. Gk *anisos* (AN-(5) +*isos* equal)]

ănk′er, n. Measure of wine & spirits in Holland, N. Germany, Denmark, Sweden, Russia, & formerly in England (8½ imp. gals); cask holding the quantity. [Du., of unkn. orig.]

ankh (ăngk), n. (Egypt. ant.). Key-like cross as symbol of enduring life & generative energy. [Egyptian, = life]

ankle (ăng′kl), n. Joint connecting foot with leg; slender part between this & calf. [ME *ankel* prob. f. ON (cf. OSw. *ankol*) f. Gmc **ank-* (Aryan **ang-* as in ANGLE¹), whence also, app., OE *anclēow*]

ănk′lèt, n. Ornament or support for ankle. [prec. +-LET]

ănn′a, n. Formerly, a unit of currency in India and Pakistan, the sixteenth part of a RUPEE (now replaced by a decimal coinage); see PIE⁴, PICE. [Hind. *ana*]

ănn′alist, n. Writer of annals. Hence **ănnalĭs′tĭc** a. [f. foll. +-IST]

ănn′als (-z), n. pl. Narrative of events year by year; historical records. [f. L *annales* (*libri*) yearly (books) f. *annus* year, -AL]

ănn′ātes (-ts), n. pl. (Rom. Cath.) first year's revenue of see or benefice, paid to Pope. [f. F *annate* f. med. L *annata* year's proceeds (*annus*, see -ADE)]

anneal′ (-ēl), v.t. Toughen by gradually diminishing heat, temper (lit. & fig.). [OE *onǣlan* f. *on* AN- (1) +*ǣlan* burn, bake]

annĕc′tent, a. Connecting, as ~ *link*. [f. L as ANNEX, see -ENT]

Annĕl′ĭda, n. pl. (zool.). The class of segmented worms. Hence **ănn′elĭD³** n., **annĕl′ĭDAN** a. [mod. L, f. F *annelés* ringed (OF *annel* ring f. L *a(n)nellus* dim. of *anulus* ring) +*ida*, cf. -ID³]

annĕx′, v.t. Add as subordinate part; append (*to* book etc.); take possession of (territory etc.); attach as an attribute, addition, or consequence. Hence or cogn. ~ABLE a., **ănnĕxA′TION** n. [ME, f. OF *annexer* f. *annexe* thing joined f. L AN- (*nectere nex-* bind)]

ănn′ĕx(e), n. Addition to a document; supplementary building. [F (-*xe*), see prec.]

annī′hĭlāt|e (-nī-), v.t. Blot out of existence. Hence ~OR n. [f. LL AN-*nihilare* (*nihil* nothing), see -ATE²]

annĭhĭlā′tion (-nī-), n. Utter destruction; (Theol.) destruction of soul as well as body, whence ~ISM, ~IST, nn. [F, or f. LL *annihilatio*, see prec. & -ATION]

ănnĭvĕrs′arў, n. Yearly return of a date; celebration of this. [ME, f. L *anniversarius* (*annus* year +*versus* turned, see -ARY¹)]

ănn′ō aetāt′ĭs sū′ae, phr. In the — year of his or her age. [L]

Ann′ō Dŏm′ĭnī (ā-), phr. In the year of our Lord, of the Christian era, (usu. A.D.). [L (colloq., as n.) advancing age (~ *is the trouble*). [L]

ănn′ot|āte, v.t. & i. Furnish with notes (book, author); (v.i.) make notes (*on*). So ~A′TION, ~ātOR, nn. [f. L AN*notare* (*nota* mark), see -ATE³]

announce′, v.t. Proclaim; intimate the approach of; make known (without words) to senses or mind. Hence ~MENT (-sm-), **announ′CER¹** (esp. of items broadcast), nn. [late ME, f. OF *anoncer* f. L AN*nunciare* (*nuntius* messenger)]

annoy′¹, n. (arch., poet.). Annoyance. [ME, f. OF *anui*, *anoi* f. Rom. *inodio* f. L phr. *in odio* in hatred, hateful]

annoy′², v.t. Irritate; molest, harass. [ME, f. OF *anuier* etc. f. Rom. *inodiare*, f. as prec.]

annoy′ance, n. Molestation; vexation; disgust. [ME, f. OF *anuiance*, *anoiance* (*anuier*, see prec. & -ANCE)]

ănn′ūal, a. & n. Reckoned by the year; recurring yearly; lasting for one year; (plant) that lives only for a year; (book etc.) published in yearly numbers. Hence ~LY² adv. [ME *annuel* f. OF f. LL *annualis* = cl. L *annalis* (*annus* year, see -AL)]

annū′ĭtant, n. One who holds an annuity. [f. foll. +-ANT, by assim. to *accountant* etc.]

annū′ĭtў, n. Sum payable in respect of a particular year; yearly grant; investment of money entitling investor to series of equal annual sums; life, terminable, perpetual, ~ (ceasing at death of investor, after specified term, on repayment of principal); *immediate, deferred* or *reversionary*, ~ (commencing at end of first interval of payment after investment, after specified interval or event). [ME, f. OF *annuite* f. med. L *annuitatem* (*annuus* yearly, see -TY)]

annul', v.t. (-ll-). Annihilate; abolish, cancel; declare invalid. Hence ~MENT n. [ME, f. OF *anuller* f. LL ANnullare (*nullus* none)]

ănn'ūlar, a. Ring-like; ~ *space* (between inner & outer surface of cylinder); ~ *ligament* (girding wrist & ankle); ~ *eclipse* of sun (when moon, projected on sun's disc, leaves ring of light visible). Hence ~LY² adv. [f. F *annulaire* or L *an(n)ularis* (*an(n)ulus* ring, see -AR¹)]

ănn'ūlate, -āted, aa. Furnished, marked, with rings; formed of rings. Hence ănnūlaᵀTION n. [f. L *an(n)ulatus* (as foll., see -ATE²)]

ănn'ūlĕt, n. Small ring; (Archit.) small fillet encircling column. [f. L *an(n)ulus* ring + -ET¹]

ănn'ūloid, a. Ring-like. So ănn'ūlOSE¹ a. [as prec. + -OID]

annūn'ciāte (-shǐ-), v.t. Proclaim; intimate as coming or ready. [f. LL *annuntiare* ANNOUNCE, see -ATE³]

annūnciā'tion (-sǐ-), n. Announcement; (*A*~) that of the incarnation, made by the angel Gabriel to the Virgin Mary, festival commemorating this, Lady-day, March 25th. [ME, f. OF *annonciation* or LL *annuntiatio* (as prec., see -ATION)]

annūn'ciātor (-shǐ-), n. Announcer; indicator showing in which direction attendance summoned by bell or telephone is needed. [f. LL *annuntiator* (as prec., see -OR)]

ăno-, pref. = Gk *anō* adv., upward; in scientific terms, as ~*car'pous*, (of ferns) having fructification on upper part of frond; ~*gĕn'ic*, developed upwardly or inwardly.

ăn'ōde, n. (electr.). Positive pole (cf. CATHODE). [f. Gk *anodos* way up (*ana* up + *hodos* way)]

ăn'odȳne, a. & n. (Medicine, drug) able to assuage pain; (anything) mentally soothing. [f. L f. Gk *anōdunos* painless (AN- (5) + *odunē* pain)]

ănŏĕt'ic, a. (psych.). Characterized by ănōēs'is, consciousness with sensation but without thought. [f. A- (7) + Gk *noētos* perceptible + -IC]

anoint', v.t. Apply ointment, oil, to (esp. as religious ceremony at baptism or on consecration as priest or king); moisten, rub; *the Lord's Anointed*, (also) king by divine right. [f. obs. adj. *anoint* f. OF *enoint* p.p. of *enoindre* f. L IN(*unguere unct-*)]

anŏmalis'tic, a. (astron.). ~ *year*, time earth takes to pass from perihelion to perihelion; ~ *month*, time moon takes to pass from perigee to perigee. [f. Gk *anōmalos* ANOMALOUS + -IST + -IC]

anŏm'alous, a. Irregular; abnormal. Hence ~LY² adv., ~NESS n. [f. LL f. Gk *anōmalos* (AN-(5) + *homalos* even) + -OUS]

anŏm'alūre, n. African scale-tailed squirrel. [f. Gk *anōmalos* anomalous + *oura* tail]

anŏm'alȳ, n. Unevenness of motion etc.; irregularity (Astron.) angular distance of planet or satellite from its last perihelion or perigee. [f. L f. Gk *anōmalia* (*anōmalos* see prec.)]

ăn'omo- in comb. Irregular, as ~*carp'ous*, bearing unusual fruit, ~*phýll'ous*, with leaves irregularly placed. [f. Gk *anomos* without law (*a*- not + *nomos*)]

anŏn', adv. Soon, presently; (of contrast) now again; *ever & ~*, every now & then. [OE *on ān* into one, *on āne* in one (body, mind, state, way, movement, moment)]

ănona'ceous (-ā'shus), a. Pertaining to the custard-apple family *Annonaceae* (formerly *Anonaceae*). [-ACEOUS]

ăn'onȳm, n. Person who remains nameless; pseudonym. [f. F *anonyme* (as foll.)]

anonȳm'itȳ, n. State of being anonymous. [as foll., see -TY]

anŏn'ȳmous, a. (abbr. *anon.*). Of unknown name; of unknown or undeclared authorship. Hence ~LY² adv., ~NESS n. [f. L f. Gk *anōnumos* nameless (AN- (5) + *onoma* name)]

anŏph'elēs (-z), n. Kinds of (esp. malarial) mosquito. [Gk, = hurtful (*an*- not, *ōpheleō* benefit)]

ăn'orăk, n. Jacket of skin or cloth with hood attached, worn esp. in arctic regions. [f. Eskimo *dnorâq*]

anŏs'mia, n. Loss of sense of smell. [mod. L f. AN- (5) + Gk *osmē* smell + -IA¹]

anoth'er (-ŭdh-), pron. & a. (pl. *other* a., *others* pron.). An additional (one), as *try* ~ *pear, try* ~; ‖ unnamed additional party to legal action (*X versus Y & ~*); ‖ (in list of cricket eleven etc., written *A. N. Other*) anonymous player or one still to be selected; a counterpart to, as ~ *Solomon; such* ~, ~ of the same sort; a different (one), as *take this towel away & bring me* ~; (contrasted or coupled with *one*) *one man's meat is* ~ *man's poison, taken one with* ~; ONE ~. [AN + OTHER; in ME superseding OE *ōther* used by itself]

anour'ous (-oor-), a. Tailless. [f. AN- (5) + Gk *oura* tail + -OUS]

anŏx'ia, n. (med.). Deficiency of oxygen. [f. AN- (5), OX(YGEN), -IA¹]

anschluss (ăn'shlŏŏs), n. Union. [G]

ăn'serine, a. Of, like, a goose; silly. [f. L *anserinus* (*anser* goose, see -INE¹)]

answer¹ (ahn'ser), n. Reply; defence; solution; thing done in return. [orig. = solemn affirmation to rebut a charge, OE *andswaru* f. Gmc *andswarō* (*and*-against + *swar*- f. *swarjan*, OE *swerian* swear)]

answer² (ahn'ser), v.t. & i. Reply to or *to*, as ~ *me, my question, to me, to my question*;

~ *to* (acknowledge, have) *the name of X*; ~ (summons to) *the door*; reply to (charge); be responsible (*for* person or thing); ~ (correspond to, also ~ *to*) *my hopes, your description*; ~ (fulfil) *my purpose*; *will not* ~ (do, succeed); ~ *back* (vulg.), ~ rebuke saucily. [OE *andswarian* (as prec.)]

answerable (ahn'ser-), **a.** Responsible (*to* person, *for* act); (arch.) corresponding (*to*). [prec. + -ABLE]

ănt, n. A small social hymenopterous insect celebrated for industry, emmet, pismire; ~-*bear*, the great ~-*eater*; ~-*eggs*, larvae of ~s; ~-*catcher*, ~-*thrush*, bird of thrush family living on ~s; ~-*eater*, name of various animals that live on ~s; ~-*fly*, winged ~, used as bait in angling; ~-*hill*, mound over ~s'-nest, conical nest of termites; *White Ant*, termite, destructive social insect of neuropterous order. [OE *ǽmete, émete,* f. WG *ǎmaitjô* (ǎ off + *maitan* cut); *ǽmete* became *ant, émete* EMMET]

an't (ahnt). See BE.

ant- = ANTI- before unaspirated vowel.

-ant, suf. forming adjj. (& nn.) f. F *-ant* (or direct) f. L *-antem, -ĕntem, -ĭentem,* accus. of pres. part. (nom. *-ans, -ens*). OF levelled all L partt. under ending *-ant*, though later F preserved L *-ent-*. ME adopted OF *-ant* as *-aunt, -ant.* Most old wds retain *-ant,* but since 1500 some have been refash., universally (*apparent*) or partly (*dependent, -ant*); see -ENT. Mod. wds in *-ant* are f. L *-ant-,* direct or thr. F, or on L anal. (rarely where no vb exists, as *benignant* on anal. of *malignant*). Noun meanings: (1) personal agent, (2) thing, esp. drug, producing effect.

ăntă'cid, a. & n. Preventive of acidity (esp. in stomach). [ANT- + ACID]

ăntăg'onĭsm, n. Active opposition (*to, against,* thing; *between* two; *come into* ~ *with*); opposing principle. [f. as foll., see -ISM (cf. F *-isme*)]

ăntăg'on|ĭst, n. Opponent, adversary; (Phys.) counteracting muscle. Hence ~is'tic a., ~is'tICALLY adv. [f. F *-iste* or LL *-ista* f. Gk *antagōnistēs* (as foll., see -IST)]

ăntăg'onĭze, -ise (-iz), **v.t.** (Of a force etc.) counteract, tend to neutralize, (another); evoke hostility in, provoke to opposition, make into an enemy; *oppose,* resist. [f. Gk ANTa*gōnizomai* (*agōn* contest, see -IZE)]

ăntăl'kal|i, n. Substance that counteracts an alkali. Hence ~INE[1] **a.** [ANT- + ALKALI]

ăntăphrodĭs'iăc (-z-), **a. & n.** Preventive of venereal desire. [f. ANT- + APHRODISIAC]

ăntărc'tĭc, a. Southern, of south polar regions; *A~ Pole,* S. pole of earth or heavens; *A~ Circle,* parallel of 66° 32' S. [ME *antartik* f. OF *-ique* f. L f. Gk ANT- (*arktikos* ARCTIC)]

ăn'tĕ, n., & **v.t.** Stake put up by poker-player before drawing new cards; (v.t.) put up (an ~); *(transf.) to bet, stake, pay up. [L, = before]

ăn'tĕ-, pref. = L *ante* before, prep. & adv., used in E to form nn. & adjj. with or without adj. ending. 1. nn. (main stress on *an'te*), as ~-*room.* 2. adjj. (main stress not on *ante*), as ~-*reforma'tion(al)*; ~*nup'tial*; ~-*Commun'ion* (Service), Anglican Communion Service to end of prayer for the 'Church militant'.

ăntĕcēd'ence, n. Precedence, priority, (in time or causal relation); (Astron.) retrograde motion. [f. L *antecedere,* see foll. & -ENCE]

ăntĕcēd'ent, a. & n. 1. Previous (*to*); presumptive, *a priori.* **2.** n. Preceding thing or circumstance; (Logic) the part of a conditional proposition on which the other depends; (Gram.) noun, clause, sentence, to which a following (esp. relative) pronoun or adverb refers; (Math.) first term of a ratio; (pl.) past history (esp. of persons). Hence ~LY[2] adv. [f. F, or L *antecedent-,* part. of ANTE- (*cedere* go), see -ENT]

ăn'tĕchămber, n. Room leading to chief apartment. [earlier *anti-,* f. F *antichambre,* f. It. *anticamera* (ANTE-, CHAMBER)]

ăn'tĕchăpel, n. Outer part at west end of chapel. [ANTE- + CHAPEL]

ăn'tĕdāte[1], n. Date before the true time (esp. of writing). [ANTE- + DATE[2] n.]

ăntĕdāte'[2], v.t. Affix, assign, an earlier than the true date to (document, event); precede; anticipate. [f. prec.]

ăntĕdiluv'ian (-lŏŏ-), **a. & n.** Belonging, referring, appropriate, to the time before the flood; (colloq.) utterly out of date; (n.) old-fashioned person or thing, (also) very old person. [f. ANTE- + L *diluvium* DELUGE + -AN]

ăn'tĕlōpe, n. Deer-like ruminant kinds of animals. [ME, f. OF *antelop* or med. L *ant(h)alopus* f. Gk *antholops* of unkn. orig.]

ăn'te mĕrĭd'ĭĕm, phr. (abbr. *a.m.*), Between midnight & noon, as *7.30 a.m.* [L]

ăntĕmŭn'dāne, a. Existing, occurring, before creation of world. [f. ANTE- + L *mundus* world + -ANE]

ăntĕnāt'al, a. Previous to birth. [ANTE- + NATAL]

ăntĕnn'|a, n. (pl. ~ae). Sensory organ found in pairs on heads of insects & crustacea, feeler; (Bot.) irritable processes in male flower of some orchids; (Radio) = AERIAL n. Hence ~AL, ~ARY[1], ~ĭf'EROUS, ~ĭFORM, aa. [L, = sail-yard]

ăntĕnup'tial (-shl), **a.** Born, occurring, etc., before marriage. [f. LL ANTE(*nuptialis* NUPTIAL)]

ăntĕpĕn'dĭum, n. Veil for front of altar. [med. L (ANTE-, *pendĕre* hang)]

ăntèpĕnŭlt' (*or* -pēn⁴), a. & n. Last but two (orig. & usu. of syllables). [abbr. of LL (*syllaba*) *antepaenultima*, see foll.]

ăntèpĕnŭl'timate, a. & n. = prec. [f. LL ANTE(*paenultimus* PENULT) + -ATE²]

ănte-pŏst', a. (Of racing bets) made before the runners' numbers are hoisted on the board. [ANTE-]

ăntèprăn'dial, a. Before-dinner. [f. ANTE- + L *prandium* + -AL]

ăntēr'ior, a. More to the front; prior (*to*). Hence **ăntēriō'rITY** n., ~LY² adv. [f. F *antérieur* or LL *anterior*, compar. f. *ante* ANTE-]

ăn'tè-rōōm, n. Room leading to another; (Mil.) sitting-room in officers' mess. [ANTE- + ROOM, after earlier ANTECHAMBER]

anth- pref. = ANTI- before aspirate.

ănthĕl'ion, n. (pl. -*ia*). Luminous ring projected on cloud or fog bank opposite to sun. [late Gk, neut. of *anthēlios* opposite to sun (ANTH- + *hēlios* sun)]

ănthĕlmin'tic, a. & n. (Medicine) of use against intestinal worms. [f. ANTH- + Gk *helmins -minthos* worm + -IC]

ăn'them, n. Composition for church use sung antiphonally; non-metrical composition (usu. from Scriptures or Liturgy) set to sacred music; song of praise or gladness. [OE *antefne* f. med. L *antefana* f. LL *antiphona*, *antefana* ANTIPHON, E development being *antef'ne*, *antem'ne*, *an'tem*, *an'them*]

ăn'ther, n. (bot.). Part of stamen containing pollen; ~-*dust*, pollen; ~-*valve*, opening by which pollen is shed. Hence ~AL, ~IF'EROUS, ~OID, aa. [f. F *anthère* or mod. L *anthera*, in cl. L medicine extracted from flowers f. Gk *anthēra* flowery, fem. adj. f. *anthos*]

ănthŏl'ogǁy̆, n. A choice collection of passages from literature; *the* (*Greek*) *A*~*y*, a collection of about 4,500 poems, inscriptions, etc. by more than 300 writers (5th c. B.C.–6th c. A.D.). Hence ~IST n. [late Gk use of *anthologia* (*anthos* flower + -*logia* collection f. *legō* gather]

An'thony̆ (ăn'to-), n. *St* ~, patron of swineherds; ~, smallest pig of litter; (*St*) ~'*s fire*, erysipelas.

ăn'thracēnē, n. Complex hydrocarbon obtained in the distillation of coal-tar, the ultimate source of synthetic alizarin. [f. Gk *anthrax -akos* coal + -ENE]

ăn'thracǁite, n. Non-bituminous variety of coal. Hence ~ĬT'IC, ~ĬTOUS, aa. [f. Gk *anthrakitis* a kind of coal, or as prec. + -ITE¹]

ăn'thrăx, n. Malignant boil; splenic fever of sheep & cattle; malignant pustule caused in man by infection from animals so affected. [L f. Gk, = carbuncle]

ănthropǁo- in comb. = Gk *anthrōpos* man, as: ~*ocen'tric*, centring in man; ~*ŏg'eny*, study of origin of man; ~*ŏg'raphy*, science of geographical distribution of mankind; ~*olite*, ~*olith*, (-ŏp⁴), fossil man; ~*ŏm'etry*

measurement of human body; ~*ŏph'agous*, ~*ŏph'agy*, man-eating.

ăn'thropoid, a. & n. Man-like; (n.) being that is human in form only, esp. ~ ape. [f. Gk *anthrōpoeidēs* (ANTHROPO-, see -OID)]

ănthropŏl'ogy̆, n. Whole science of man; physiological & psychological science of man; study of man as an animal. Hence **ănthropŏlŏ'gICAL** a., **ănthropŏlŏ'gicalLY²** adv., **ănthropŏl'OGIST** n. [as prec. + -LOGY]

ănthropomŏrph'ic, a. Of the nature of anthropomorphism. [as foll. + -IC]

ănthropomŏrph'ǁize, -ise (-īz), v.t. Attribute human form or personality to (God etc. or abs.). Hence ~ISM, ~IST, nn. [as foll. + -IZE]

ănthropomŏrph'ous, a. Of human form. [f. Gk ANTHROPO*morphos* (*morphē* form) + -OUS]

anti-, pref. = Gk *anti* (before unaspir. vowel *ant-*, before aspirate *anth-*) opposite, against, in exchange, instead, rivalling. In wds f. Gk, or modelled on them, as -*thesis*, -*climax*. As living pref. in E (1) combining with nouns to form nouns, *anti-* having adj. force = rival (-*pope*, -*king*), opposing, counter, (-*chorus*, -*league*), reverse of (-*climax*); main stress is on *an'ti-*. (2) forming adjj. on nouns governed by *anti-* (-*slavery* society, -*vaccination* league) or on adjj. implying a noun so governed (-*national*, -*ritualistic*), with sense 'opposed to'; many of these are also nouns, esp. names of medicines (-*dysenteric*); main stress is not on ~. (3) forming derivative nouns & adjj. by addition of a suff., esp. -*ist*, (-*alcoholist*, -*tobacconist*, -*sabbatarian*) with sense 'one opposed to', also corresponding abstract nn. in -*ism* (-*Darwinism*); main stress is not on ~.

ănti-air'craft (-ah-), a. ~ *gun* etc. (for shooting down hostile aircraft). [prec.]

ăn'tiar, n. Upas tree of Java; poison thence obtained. [Jav. *antjar*]

ăntibil'ious, a. Of use against biliousness. [ANTI- (2)]

ăntibiŏt'ic, a. & n. **1.** Capable of destroying or injuring living organisms, esp. bacteria. **2.** n. ~ substance. [ANTI-(2), Gk *biōtikos* fit for life (*bios* life, -IC)]

ăn'tibŏdy̆, n. (physiol.). Kinds of substance in the blood tending to neutralize others that are harmful. [ANTI- (1)]

ăn'tic, a. & n. **1.** (arch.). Grotesque, bizarre. **2.** n. Grotesque posture (usu. pl.); (arch.) mountebank, clown. [f. It. *antico* f. L *antiquus* ancient, apparently from ascription of GROTESQUE work to the ancients]

ăn'tichrist (-k-), n. Enemy of Christ; (*A*~, *the A*~) great personal opponent of Christ expected by early church to appear before end of world. [ME, f. LL *antichristus* f. Gk *antikhristos* (ANTI- (1) + *khristos* CHRIST)]

ăntichris'tian (-k-), a. **Pertaining to** Antichrist; **opposed to Christianity.**

Hence ~ISM (-k-) n. [f. prec., with extended meaning]

ănti′cip|āte, v.t. Use in advance; forestall (person or thing); accelerate, as ~*ate* one's *ruin*; discuss, consider, realize, beforehand; (pop.) look forward to, expect, (event, *that* it will happen). Hence ~ANT a. & n., ~ātive a., ~ātively² (-vl-) adv. [f. L *anticipare* (*anti-* for ANTE-+ -*cipare* f. *capere* take) see -ATE³]

ănticipā′tion, n. Action of anticipating (in senses of the vb); *thanking you in* ~, closing formula in letter of inquiry or request; (Med.) occurrence of phenomena before usual time; (Mus.) introduction beforehand of part of chord about to follow. [f. L *anticipatio* (as prec., see -ATION)]

ănti′cipāt|or, n. One who anticipates. Hence ~ORY a. [L (as prec., see -OR)]

ăn′ticlimăx, n. Opposite of climax, addition of a particular that weakens the effect; descent contrasting with previous rise. [ANTI- (1)]

ănticlin′al, a. (Geol.) forming ridge on which strata lean against each other, & from which they slope down in opposite directions; (Anat.) with upright spine towards which spines on both sides incline. [f. ANTI- + Gk *klinō* lean + -AL]

ănticyc′lōne, n. Rotary outward flow of air from atmospheric area of high pressure; whole system of pressure & outward flow. [ANTI- (1)]

ăn′tidōt|e, n. Medicine given to counteract poison or disease (*against*, *for*, *to*); (fig.) something that counteracts an evil. Hence ~AL a. [f. L f. Gk *antidoton* neut. of ANTI*dotos* given against]

ăn′tigen, n. Substance introduced into the blood to stimulate production of antibodies. [ANTI(BODY) + -GEN (1)]

ăntigrŏp′ĕlŏs (-z), n. pl. Waterproof leggings. [perh. for *anthygropelos* (ANTI-(2) + Gk *hugros* wet + *pēlos* mud)]

ănti-Jăc′obĭn, a. & n. (One) opposed to the Jacobins (revolutionary party in France, 1789) or the French revolution. [ANTI- (2)]

ăntilŏg′arithm, n. Number to which a logarithm belongs, as *100 is the* ~ *of 2*. [ANTI- (1)]

ăntil′ogў, n. Contradiction in terms. [f. Gk *antilogia* (ANTI- + -*logia* -LOGY)]

ăntimacăss′ar, n. Covering thrown over chairs etc., as protection from grease or as an ornament. [ANTI- (2) + MACASSAR]

ăn′timasque, -mask, (-mahsk), n. Grotesque interlude between acts of masque. [ANTI- (1)]

ăntimŏnarch′ical (-k-), a. Opposed to monarchy. [ANTI- (2)]

ăn′timonў, n. Brittle metallic substance, bluish-white, of flaky crystalline texture. [late ME, f. med. L *antimonium*, of unkn. orig.]

ăntinŏm′ian, a. & n. **1.** Opposed to the obligatoriness of moral law; pertaining to A~s. **2.** n. (*A*~) one who maintains

that the moral law is not binding on Christians. [f. med. L *Antinomi*, name of sect in Germany (1535) alleged to hold above opinion (ANTI- + Gk *nomos* law) + -AN]

ăntin′omў, n. Contradiction in a law, or between two laws; conflict of authority; paradox. [f. L f. Gk ANTI*nomia* (*nomos* law)]

ăntipathĕt′ic, a. Opposed in nature or disposition (*to*). Hence ~AL a., ~aLlY² adv. [f. Gk ANTI*patheō* (as ANTIPATHY), see -ETIC]

ăntipăth′ic, a. Of contrary character (*to*); (Med.) having, producing, contrary symptoms. [f. F *antipathique* f. *antipathie* (as foll.)]

ăntip′athў, n. Constitutional or settled aversion (*against*, *to*, *between* persons). [f. F *antipathie* or L -*pathia* f. Gk -*patheia* f. ANTI*pathēs* opposed in feeling (*pathos* -*eos*)]

ănti-pĕrsonnĕl′, a. (Of bombs etc.) designed to kill or injure human beings. [ANTI- (2)]

ăntiphlogĭs′t|ic, a. & n. (Medicine, paste, etc.) reducing inflammation. So ~INE¹ n. P. [ANTI- (2)]

ăn′tiphon, n. Verse of psalm etc. intoned or sung responsively by alternating choirs during Divine Office before or after psalm; similar passage sung independently of psalm & not necessarily responsively. [f. LL *antiphona*, fem. sing., f. Gk ANTI*phōna* (neut. pl. of *antiphōnos* responsive) f. *phōnē* sound]

ăntiph′onal, a. & n. Sung alternately; responsive; (n.) collection of antiphons. Hence ~LY² adv. [as prec. + -AL]

ăntiph′onarў, n. Book of antiphons. [f. med. L *antiphonarium* (as ANTIPHON, see -ARY¹)]

ăntiph′onў, n. Antiphon; antiphonal singing response, echo. [f. Gk *antiphōnos*, see ANTIPHON & -Y¹]

ăntip′od|ēs (-z), n. pl. Place(s) diametrically opposite (to each other), esp. region opposite to our own; (sing. *ăn′tipŏde*) exact opposite (*of*, *to*). Hence ~AL, ~ĕ′AN aa. [f. LL f. Gk *antipodes* having the feet opposite, pl. of ANTI*pous* adj. (*pous podos* foot)]

ăn′tipōle, n. Opposite pole; direct opposite. [ANTI- (1)]

ăn′tipōpe, n. Pope elected in opposition to one (held to be) canonically chosen. [f. F *antipape* f. med. L *antipapa*; assim. to *pope*]

ăn′tiprōtŏn, n. Negative proton. [ANTI- (1)]

ăntipўrĕt′ic, a. & n. (Drug) allaying or preventing fever. So **ăntipўr′in** n. P, a derivative ~. [ANTI- (2); see PYRETIC]

ăntiquār′ian, n. Connected with study of antiquities; large size of drawing paper; antiquary, whence ~ISM n., ~IZE v.i. [as foll. + -AN]

ăn′tiquarў, n. Student, collector, of antiquities. [f. L *antiquarius* (*antiquus* ancient, see -ARY¹)]

ăn'tiquăte, v.t. Make obsolete (esp. in p.p.), abolish as out of date; make antique. [f. obs. adj. *antiquate* (L *antiquare* f. *antiquus* ancient, see -ATE²)]

ăntique' (-ēk), a. & n. **1.** Of old times; existing since old times; old-fashioned; after the manner of the ancients; archaic. **2.** n. Relic of ancient art or of old times; *the* ∼, n. style. Hence ∼NESS (-kn-) n. [F, or f. L *antiquus, anticus*, former, ancient (*ante* before); cf. ANTIC]

ănti'quity̆, n. Ancientness; old times, esp. time before middle ages; the ancients; (pl.) customs, events, precedents, of ancient times; (usu. pl.) ancient relics. [ME, f. OF *antiquite* f. L *antiquitatem* (*antiquus*, see prec. & -TY)]

ăntirrhi̇̆n'um (-rĭ-), n. Kinds of plant, snapdragon. [L, f. Gk *antirrhinon* (*anti* counterfeiting +*rhis rhinos* nose)]

ăntisăbbatār'ian, a. & n. (Person) opposed to observance of Sabbath. [ANTI- (3)]

ăntiscōrbūt'ic, a. & n. (Medicine) against scurvy. [ANTI- (2)]

ăntiscrip'tural (-chŏŏ-), a. Opposed to Scripture. [ANTI- (2)]

ănti-Sĕm'|īte, a. & n. (Person) hostile to Jews. So **ănti-Sĕmīt'ic** a., ∼ĭtīSM n. [ANTI- (2)]

ăntisĕp't|ic, a. & n. (Agent) counteracting putrefaction (lit. & fig.). Hence ∼ICALLY adv. [f. ANTI- (3) +SEPTIC]

ăntisō'cial (-shl), a. Opposed to principles on which society is based. [ANTI-(2)]

ănti'strophė, n. (Lines sung during) returning movement in Greek choruses (cf. STROPHE); inverse relation. [LL, f. Gk, = turning about (ANTI*strephō* turn against)]

ăntistrŏph'ic, a. Pertaining to antistrophes. [f. Gk *antistrophikos* (as prec., see -IC)]

ăn'ti-tănk, a. (Of gun etc.) for use against tanks. [ANTI- (2)]

ăntithē'|ist, n. One opposed to belief in existence of a God. Hence ∼ISM n. [ANTI- (3)]

ăntith'ĕsis, n. (pl. *-thesēs*). Contrast of ideas expressed by parallelism of strongly contrasted words; opposition, contrast, (*of, between*, two things); direct opposite (*of, to*). [LL f. Gk (vbl n. f. ANTI*tithēmi* set against)]

ăntithĕt'ic, a. Of the nature of antithesis; contrasted; consisting of two opposites. Hence ∼AL a., ∼aLLY² adv. [f. Gk *antithetikos* (as prec., see -IC)]

ăntitŏx'|in, n. A serum serving to neutralize a toxin. So ∼IC a. [ANTI- (2)]

ăn'ti-trāde, a. & n. ∼ (*wind*), one that blows in opposite direction to trade wind. [ANTI- (2)]

ăntitrinitār'ian, a. & n. (One) opposed to doctrine of the Trinity. Hence ∼ISM n. [ANTI- (3)]

ăn'tity̆pe, n. That which a type or symbol represents. Hence **ăntity̆p'ICAL** a. [f. Gk ANTI*tupos* responding as an impression to the die (*tupos* stamp)]

ăntivĕnēne', n. Antitoxin, esp. a snake-poison antidote. [f. ANTI- + L *venenum* poison]

ănt'ler, n. Branched horn, branch of a horn, of stag or other deer. Hence ∼ED² (-lerd) a. [late ME *auntelere* f. OF *antoillier* (mod. *andouiller*) of unkn. orig.]

ăntonomās'ia (-z-), n. Substitution of epithet etc. for proper name (e.g. *the Iron Duke*); use of proper name to express general idea (e.g. *a Solomon*). [L f. Gk, f. ANTO*nomazō* name instead (*onoma* name)]

ăn'tony̆m, n. A word of contrary meaning to another, as *bad* to *good* (opp. *synonym*). [ANTI- +(SYN)ONYM]

ăn'trum, n. (pl. *-tra*). Cavity in the body (esp. one in the upper jaw-bone). [f. L, f. Gk *antron* cave]

Ant'wĕrp (ă-), n. ∼ (*pigeon*), kind of homing or carrier pigeon. [*Antwerp* in Belgium]

ăn'us, n. Posterior opening of alimentary canal in animals. [L]

ăn'vil, n. Block (usu. iron) on which smith works metal; (Physiol.) a bone of the ear. [OE *onfilti, anfelte* (= OHG *anafalz*) of uncert. orig.]

anxi'ety̆ (ăngz-), n. Uneasiness, concern; solicitous desire (*for* a thing, *to* do). [f. F *anxieté* or L *anxietas -atis* (as foll., see -TY)]

anxious (ăngk'shus), a. Troubled, uneasy (*about*); earnestly desirous (*for* a thing, *to* do); causing anxiety, as *an* ∼ *business*. Hence ∼LY² adv. [f. L *anxius* (*angere* choke) +-OUS; cf. LL *anxiosus*]

any (ĕn'ĭ), a., pron., & adv. (With interrog.) one, some, (no matter which), as *have you* ∼ *wool?* *have you* ∼ *of them?* *were* ∼ *Frenchmen there?*; (after negative expr. or implied) *cannot see* ∼ *difference, to prevent* ∼ *loss, cannot find* ∼ *of them*; (in affirmative sent.) whichever (of all) is chosen, every, as ∼ *chemist will tell you, at* ∼ *rate*; *anyone* (pron.), whatever individual is chosen; ∼ *one* or *anyone* (adj.), ∼ *person*, anybody; (adv., w. compar. in neg. or interrog. context) at all, in ∼ degree, (*is that* ∼ *better?*; *without being* ∼ *the wiser*). [OE *ǣnig* (= OHG *einig*) f. *ān* ONE + -*ig* (see -Y²)]

an'y̆bŏdy̆ (ĕn-), n. or pron. Any person; *if you wish to be* ∼ (of any importance); *two or three anybodies* (ordinary people).

an'y̆how (ĕn-), adv. & conj. In any way whatever; in any case, at any rate; at haphazard, as *does his work* ∼, *things are all* ∼.

an'y̆thing (ĕn-), pron. & n. Whatever thing; a thing, no matter which; a thing of any kind.

an'y̆way (ĕn-), adv. & conj. = ANYHOW.

anywhere (ĕn'iwār), adv. In any place.

an'y̆wise (ĕn-; -z), adv. In any wise.

An'zăc (ă-), n. & a. (Pl.) *the* Australian & New Zealand Army Corps in the war of 1914–18; (sing.) member of the ~s; (adj.) of the ~s. [= A. & N.-Z. A.C.]

ā'orist, a. & n. (Gram.) indefinite, implying no limitation; (Gk Gram.) ~ (*tense*), one denoting simply occurrence (in indicative, with AUGMENT[1], past), without limitations as to continuance etc. So **āoris'tic** a. [f. Gk *aoristos* indefinite (*a*- not + *horizō* limit)]

āōrt'|a, n. Great artery or trunk of the arterial system, issuing from left ventricle of heart. Hence~ic a. [f. med. L f. Gk *aortē* that which is hung (*aeirō* lift)]

à outrance (see Ap.), phr. To the death, to the bitter end. [F]

ap-, pref. = AD- before *p*, & see APO-.

apāce', adv. Swiftly, quickly. [A prep. + PACE[1]]

apache' (-ahsh), n. Violent street ruffian in Paris; (*A*~, pr. apăch'i) member of N.-Amer. tribe. [F, f. native name, lit. = enemy]

ăp'anage, ăpp-, n. Provision for maintenance of younger children of kings etc., (orig. province or lucrative office); perquisite; (of territory) dependency; natural accompaniment or attribute. [F, f. med. L *appanagium* f. APpanare (*panis* bread) endow with means of subsistence, see -AGE]

apārt', adv. Aside, separately, independently, (*from*); asunder; *set* ~, devote, reserve (*for*); *jesting* ~ (laid aside). [ME, f. OF *apart* (à *to*, *part* side)]

apārt'heid (-t-hāt), n. (S. Afr.). Racial segregation. [Afrikaans (APART, -HOOD)]

apārt'ment, n. Single room of a house; (pl., & arch. & U.S. sing.) set of rooms (*~house*, block of flats). [f. F *appartement* f. It. *appartamento* f. *appartare* separate]

ăpathĕt'|ic, a. Insensible to emotion; indifferent. Hence ~ICALLY adv. [f. foll., after PATHETIC]

ăp'athў, n. Insensibility to suffering; passionless existence; indolence of mind. [f. F *apathie* f. L f. Gk *apatheia* f. *apathēs* without feeling (*a*- not + *pathos* suffering)]

āpe¹, n. Tailless monkey (gorilla, chimpanzee, orang-outan, gibbons); imitator, mimic; *play the* ~, mimic; *sea* ~, fish (sea fox). [OE *apa*, OHG *affo*, ON *api*, Gmc; ult. orig. unkn.]

āpe², v.t. Imitate, mimic. [f. prec.]

apeak' (-ēk), adv. & pred. a. (naut.). Vertical, as *oars* ~. [f. F à *pic* (à *to*, at, *pic*, summit, see PEAK)]

ăpĕp'sў, n. Lack of digestive power. [f. Gk *apepsia* (*a*- not + *peptō* digest)]

aperçu (see Ap.), n. Summary exposition, conspectus. [F, p.p. of *apercevoir* perceive]

apē'rient (*or* -ēr-), a. & n. Laxative (medicine). [f. L *aperire* open, see -ENT]

apē'ritif (*or* ahpărētēf'), n. Alcoholic appetizer. [F (-ér-), f. med. L *aperitivus*

variant of LL *apertivus* (L *aperire* open, see -IVE)]

apē'ritive, a. & n. = APERIENT. [f. F *apéritif* (prec.)]

ăp'erture, n. Opening, gap; space through which light passes in optical instruments. [f. L *apertura* (as prec., see -URE)]

āp'erў, n. Mimicry; apish performance; ape-house. [APE n. + -RY]

apĕt'alous, a. Without petals. [f. Gk *apetalos* leafless (*a*- not + *petalon* leaf) + -OUS]

āp'ex, n. (pl. -*icēs*, -*exes*). Tip, top, peak; vertex (of triangle, cone). [L, = peak, tip]

aph-. See APO-.

aphaer'esis (-fēr-), n. (gram.). The taking away of a letter or syllable at the beginning of a word. [Gk (APH-, *haireō* take)]

aphās'ia (-zya), n. Loss of speech, as result of cerebral affection. Hence **aphās'ic** (-z-) a. & n. [Gk, f. *aphatos* speechless (*a*- not + *pha*- speak)]

aphēl'ion, n. (pl. -*ia*). Point farthest from sun (of planet's or comet's orbit). [Graecized f. mod. L *aphelium* f. Gk *aph' hēliou* from the sun, after *apogaeum* APOGEE]

aphēliotrŏp'|ic, a. (bot.). Turning from the sun. Hence ~ICALLY adv., **aphēliŏt'ropism** n. [f. Gk as prec. + *tropikos* turning (*trepō*)]

aph'esis, n. Gradual loss of unaccented vowel at beginning of word, as in (e)*squire*. [Gk, = letting go, f. *aphiēmi* (*apo* away + *hiēmi* send)]

aphĕt'ic, a. Pertaining to aphesis. Hence **ăph'etize** v.t. [f. Gk *aphetos* vbl adj. (as prec.) + -IC]

ăph'is, n. (pl. *ăph'ĭdēs*). Plant-louse, minute insect, the food of ladybirds, & tended by ants for the honey-dew it yields. Hence **aphid'ian** a. [mod. L (Linnaeus) of unkn. orig.]

aphōn'ia, n. Total loss of voice. [Gk, f. *aphōnos* voiceless (*a*- not + *phōnē* voice)]

ăph'orism, n. Short pithy maxim. Hence or cogn. **ăphoris'mic**, **ăphoris'tic** [-IST], aa., **ăphoris'tically** adv. [f. F *aphorisme*, (obs.) *aff*-, or med. L f. Gk *aphorismos* definition, f. *aphorizō* (*horos* boundary), see -ISM]

ăphrodis'iăc (-z-), a. & n. Venereal; (drug) producing venereal desire. [f. Gk *aphrodisiakos* f. *aphrodisios* (*Aphroditē* Venus), see -AC]

aphŷll'ous, a. (bot.). Naturally leafless. [f. Gk *aphullos* (*a*- not + *phullon* leaf) + -OUS]

āpiār'ian, a. Pertaining to bee-keeping. [as foll. + -AN]

āp'iar|ў, n. Place where bees are kept. Hence ~IST n. [f. L *apiarium* (*apis* bee, see -ARY¹)]

āp'ical, a. Belonging to an apex; placed at the tip. Hence ~LY² adv. [f. L *apex* -*icis* + -AL]

ăp'iculture, n. Bee-keeping. [f. L *apis* bee + CULTURE]

apiece', adv. Severally, each, as *five pounds ~*. [orig. *a piece*]

ăp'ish, a. Of the nature, appearance, of an ape; ape-like in manner, silly. Hence ~LY² adv., ~NESS n. [f. APE n. + -ISH]

ăp'lanăt, n. (photog.). Symmetrical achromatic doublet lens comparatively free from spherical aberration. So **ăplanăt'ic** a., (of lens) free from certain aberrations. [G, f. Gk *a-* not + *planaō* wander; adj. f. Gk *aplanētos* free from error + -IC]

aplomb (see Ap.), n. Perpendicularity; self-possession. [F, = *à plomb* according to plummet]

ăpnoe'a (-nēa), n. Suspension of breathing. [mod. L f. Gk *apnoia* f. *apnoos* breathless (*a-* not + *pnoē* breath)]

ăpo-, pref. (before unaspirated vowel *ap-*, before aspirate *aph-*), = Gk *apo* prep. off, from, away, un-, quite; in compds f. Gk, & in mod. scientific wds with sense 'detached, separate'.

apŏc'alýpse, n. Revelation, esp. that made to St John in island of Patmos; book recording this. So **apŏcalýp'tic(AL)** aa., **apŏcalýp'ticALLY²** adv. [f. LL f. Gk *apokalupsis* (APO*kaluptō* uncover)]

apŏc'opė, n. Cutting off of last letter or syllable of word. [LL, f. Gk (APO*koptō* cut off)]

apŏc'rýpha, n. Books of Old Testament included in Septuagint & Vulgate, but not originally written in Hebrew, nor counted genuine by Jews, & excluded from Canon at Reformation; Christian gospels & epistles not admitted to the New Testament. [ME, f. LL *apocrypha* (*scripta*) hidden writings f. Gk *apokruphos* (APO*kruptō* hide away); treated in E as sing., with pl. *-as*]

apŏc'rýphal, a. Of the apocrypha; of doubtful authenticity; sham, false. [as prec. + -AL]

ăp'ŏd, n. Bird, reptile, fish, without (or with undeveloped) feet or ventral fins. Hence **ăp'odAL** a. [f. Gk *apous* footless (*a-* not + *pous podos* foot)]

ăpodĭc'tic, -deic'tic (-dī-), a. Of clear demonstration; clearly established. Hence **ăpodĭc'ticALLY** adv. [f. L f. Gk *apodeiktikos* (APO*deiknumi* show, see -IC)]

apŏd'osis, n. (pl. *-dosēs*). Concluding clause of sentence (cf. PROTASIS); consequent clause of conditional sentence, wherever placed. [LL, f. Gk (APO*didōmi* give back)]

ăp'ogee, n. Point (in orbit of moon or any planet) farthest from earth; greatest distance of sun from earth when latter is in aphelion; (fig.) most distant spot highest point. Hence **ăpogē'AN** a. [f. F *apogée* or med. L f. Gk APO*geion* away from earth (*gē* (*gai-, gei-*) earth)]

ăpolaus'tic, a. Self-indulgent. [f. Gk *apolaustikos* (APO*lauō* enjoy, see -IC)]

Apŏllinăr'is, n. Mineral water exported from the ~ spring in Rhenish Prussia.

Apŏll'ō, n. (pl. *-os*). Greek sun-god; (poet.) the sun; man of great beauty. [L, f. Gk *Apollōn*]

Apŏll'yon (*or* -ĭon), n. The Devil. [LL (Vulg.), f. Gk *apolluōn* part. of *apolluō* (APO- + *olluō* destroy)]

apŏlogĕt'ic, a. & n. Regretfully acknowledging, excusing, fault or failure; vindicatory; (n., usu. pl.) argumentative defence, esp. of Christianity. Hence ~AL a., ~alLY² adv. [f. F *apologétique* f. LL f. Gk *apologētikos* (*apologeomai* speak in defence, see APOLOGY & -IC)]

apolō'gia, n. Written defence of the conduct or opinions of the writer. [Gk; see APOLOGY]

apŏl'ogist, n. One who defends (esp. Christianity) by argument. [f. F *apologiste* f. Gk *apologia*, see APOLOGY & -IST]

apŏl'ogīze, -ise (-īz), v.i. Make an apology (*for*). [f. APOLOGY + -IZE]

ăp'ologue (-ŏg), n. Moral fable. [F, or f. L f. Gk *apologos* fable]

apŏl'ogý, n. Regretful acknowledgement of offence; assurance that no offence was intended; explanation, vindication; ~ *for*, poor or scanty specimen of (*this ~ for a letter*). [f. F *apologie* or L f. Gk *apologia* speech in defence]

ăp'ophthegm (-ofthĕm, -othĕm), n. Terse saying; pithy maxim. Hence ~ăt'ic (-ofthĕg-, -othĕg-) a., ~ăt'icALLY adv. [f. Gk *apophthegma* -matos* (APO*phtheggomai* speak out)]

ăpoplĕc't|ic, a. Pertaining to, causing, apoplexy; suffering from, tending to, apoplexy. Hence ~icALLY adv. [f. F *apoplectique* or LL f. Gk *apoplēktikos* (APO*plēssō* strike completely, see -IC)]

ăp'oplĕxý, n. Malady arresting powers of sense & motion, usu. caused by effusion of blood or serum in brain. [ME, f. OF *apoplexie* or LL f. Gk *apoplēxia* (as prec.)]

ăposiopēs'is, n. (rhet.; pl. *-pēsēs*). Sudden breaking-off in speech. [L, f. Gk f. APO(*siōpaō* keep silent)]

apŏs'tasý, n. Abandonment of religious faith, vows, principles, or party. [ME, f. LL f. late Gk *apostasia* (APO*sta-* withdraw)]

apŏs'tate, n. & a. (One) guilty of apostasy. So **ăpostăt'icAL** a. [ME, f. OF, or LL *apostata* f. late Gk *apostatēs* (as prec.)]

apŏs'tatize, -ise (-īz), v.i. Become an apostate (*from* one *to* another). [f. as APOSTATE + -IZE; cf. LL *apostatare*, med. L *-izare*]

ā pŏstĕriŏr'i (*or* -ĕr'-), adv. & adj. phr. (Reasoning) from effects to causes; inductive. [L, = from what comes after]

apŏs'til, n. Marginal note. [f. F *apostille* f. *-iller* = med. L *-illare* (A-(4), POSTIL)]

apŏs'tle (-sl), n. Messenger, esp. any of the twelve whom Christ sent forth t preach Gospel; A~s' Creed, earliest form of Christian creed, anciently ascribed to the ~s; first successful Christian missionary in a country, as ~ *of Germany*; leader of reform, as ~ *of tempèrance*; ~ *spoons* (with figures of ~s on handles). Hence ~SHIP n. [OE *apostol* (ME *apostel*) f. LL f. Gk *apostolos* (APO*stellō* send forth); later sp. (ME) f. OF *apostle* (mod. *apôtre*)]

apŏs′tolate, n. Apostleship; leadership in a propaganda. [f. LL *apostolatus* (as prec., see -ATE[1])]

ăpostŏl′ĭc, a. Pertaining to the Apostles; of the character of an apostle; of the Pope, papal, as *A~ See*, *succession*. Hence ~AL a., ~aLLY[2] adv. [f. F *-ique* or LL f. Gk *apostolikos* (as APOSTLE, see -IC)]

apŏs′troph|ĕ[1], n. (rhet.). Exclamatory address, in course of public speech or in poem, to particular person (often dead or absent). Hence **ăpostrŏph′IC** a., ~IZE v.t. & i. [L f. Gk, lit. turning away (as foll.)]

apŏs′trophĕ[2], n. Sign of omission of letter, or of possessive case, (e.g. *can′t*, *boy′s*). Hence **ăpostrŏph′IC** a. [F, or LL f. Gk *apostrophos* adj. as n., accent of elision (APO*strephō* turn away); assim. in pron. to prec.]

apŏth′ĕcarў, n. (arch.). Druggist, pharmaceutical chemist, as *Apothecaries′ Company*. [ME *apot*(*h*)*ecarie* f. OF *apotecaire* f. LL *apothecarius* f. L *apotheca* f. Gk *apothēkē* store-house (APO*tithēmi* lay away), see -ARY[1]]

apŏthĕōs′ĭs, n. (pl. *-osēs*). Deification (lit. & fig.); canonization; deified ideal; (loosely) release from earthly life. Hence **apŏth′ĕosize** v.t. [LL, f. Gk (APO*theoō* make a god of, f. *theos* god, see -OSIS)]

appal′ (-awl), v.t. (-ll-). Dismay, terrify. Hence ~l′ĭngLY[2] adv. [ME, f. OF *apalir* wax pale; cf. PALL[2]]

appanage. See APANAGE.

ăpparăt′us, n. (pl. *-uses*). Mechanical requisites, *an* appliance, for doing something; organs by which natural processes are carried on; ~ *criticus*, list of variant readings, materials for textual study of document. [L (AP*parare* make ready for, see -ATE[1])]

appă′rel[1], v.t. (-ll-). Attire, dress. [ME, f. OF *apareiller* f. Rom. *AD*pariculare* make fit (*pariculum* dim. of *par* equal)]

appă′rel[2], n. Ornamental embroidery on ecclesiastical vestments; (arch.) clothing, dress. [ME, f. OF *aparail, -eil* f. *apareiller*, see prec.]

appăr′ent (*or* -ă′r-), a. Manifest, palpable; seeming; *heir* ~ (whose right cannot be superseded by birth of nearer heir, cf. PRESUMPTIVE). Hence ~LY[2] adv. [ME, f. OF *aparant* f. L as APPEAR, see -ENT]

ăppari′tion, n. Appearance, esp. of a supernatural being; ghost. [late ME, f. F, or f. L *apparitio* (as APPEAR, see -ION)]

appă′ritor, n. Public servant of Roman magistrate; officer of civil or ecclesiastical court; herald, usher. [L (as prec., see -OR)]

appeal′[1] (-ēl), v.i. & t. Call *to* (higher tribunal) for deliverance from decision of lower (also abs.); ~ *to the country* (i.e. from parliament), dissolve parliament; remove (case) to higher court; call attention *to* (evidence); make earnest request (*to* person, *for* thing or *to* do); *pictures* ~ (address themselves) *to the eye*, *do not* ~ (prove attractive) *to me*. [ME, f. OF *apeler* f. L AP*pellare* address]

appeal′[2] (-ēl), n. Act of appealing; right of appealing; *Court of A~* (hearing cases previously tried in inferior courts). [ME, f. OF *apel* (as prec.)]

appeal′able (-ēl-), a. That can be appealed against; that can be appealed *to*. [APPEAL v. + -ABLE]

appear′, v.i. Become, be, visible; present oneself formally, publicly be published; be manifest; seem (occas. with implication of illusion). [ME, f. *aper-* st. of OF *apareir* f. L AP*parēre -rit-* come in sight]

appear′ance, n. Act of appearing (in vbl senses; *put in an* ~, show oneself); look, aspect; semblance; *to all* ~ (so far as can be seen); *save*, *keep up*, ~*s* (outward show etc.); apparition, phantom. [ME *aparaunce* f. OF *-ance, -ence*, f. LL *apparentia* (as prec., see -ENCE)]

appeas|e′ (-z), v.t. Pacify, quiet, (strife, anger, person); try to conciliate or bribe (a potential aggressor) by making concessions, freq. with implication of sacrifice of principles; soothe; satisfy (appetite, prejudice). So ~′ABLE (-z-) a., ~e′MENT (-zm-) n. [ME *apese* f. OF *apeser*, *apaisier* (*à* to + *pais* PEACE)]

appĕl′lant, a. & n. 1. Appealing; (Law) concerned with appeals. 2. n. One who appeals to higher court. [late ME, f. F (as APPEAL[1], see -ANT)]

appĕl′late, a. Taking cognizance of appeals, as ~ *jurisdiction*. [f. L as foll., see -ATE[2]]

ăppellā′tion, n. Name, title; nomenclature. [ME, f. OF, f. L as APPEAL[1], see -ATION]

appĕl′lative, a. & n. (Of words) designating a class, common (as opp. to *proper*); common noun, applicable to any member of a class; appellation. Hence ~LY[2] (-vl-) adv. [f. LL *appelativus* as APPEAL[1], see -ATIVE]

appĕnd′, v.t. Hang on, annex; add in writing. [f. L AP*pendere*]

appĕn′dage, n. Thing attached; addition; accompaniment. [prec. + -AGE]

appĕn′dant, a. & n. (Possession, thing, person) attached in subordinate capacity (*to* another). [F, part. of *appendre* f. L *-icis* (AP*pendĕre* APPEND)]

appĕn′d|ix, n. (pl. ~*icēs*, ~*ixes*). Subsidiary addition (*to* book or document); small process developed from surface of any organ, esp. *vermiform* ~*ix* (of the intestine), whence ~iciT′IS n. [L *appendix* *-icis* (AP*pendĕre* APPEND)]

ăpperceive′ (-sēv), v.t. (psych.). Unite and assimilate (a perception) to a mass of ideas already possessed, & so comprehend & interpret it. [ME, f. OF *aperceveir* (Rom. **appercipere* f. AP-+L *percipere* PERCEIVE)]

äppercĕp′tion, n. Mind's perception of itself; mental perception; (Psych.) action or fact of becoming conscious by subsequent reflection of a perception already experienced; process by which the mind apperceives. [f. F *aperception* (as prec., see -ION)]

äppertain′, v.i. Belong as possession or right to; be appropriate *to*; relate *to*. [ME, f. OF *apertenir* (mod. *appar-*) f. LL AP(*pertinēre* PERTAIN)]

äpp′ĕtence, -cў, n. Longing after, desire, (*of, for, after*); affinity (*for*). [f. F *appétence* or L *appetentia* (AP*petere* seek after) see -ENCE, -ENCY]

äpp′ĕtent, a. Eagerly desirous (*after, of*). [ME, f. L *appetere*, see prec. & -ENT]

äpp′ĕtīte, n. Desire, inclination, (*for*); desire to satisfy natural necessities, esp. hunger; relish. So **appĕt′ĬTIVE** a. [ME *apetyte* f. OF *apetit* f. L *appetitus* (as prec., see -ITE²)]

äpp′ĕtĭz|e, -is|e (-īz), v.t. (Of things) give appetite (only in part. ∼*ing*). Hence ∼ER¹ (2) n. [f. F *appétissant* part. irreg. f. *appétit* (as prec.), assim. to vbs in -IZE]

applaud′, v.i. & t. Express approval loudly, as by clapping hands; (v.t.) express approval of, praise. [f. L AP*plaudere -plaus-* clap hands]

applaus|e′ (-z), n. Approbation loudly expressed; marked approval. Hence ∼′IVE (-s-), a., ∼′IVELY² (-sĭvlĭ) adv. [f. med. L *applausus, -ūs* (as prec.)]

äp′ple, n. Round firm fleshy fruit of a rosaceous tree; (Bot.) any inferior fleshy many-celled fruit; ∼ *of discord,* golden ∼ contended for by Juno, Minerva, & Venus; ∼ *of Sodom, Dead Sea*∼, fruit dissolving into ashes; ∼ *of the eye,* the pupil, eyeball, any cherished object; ∼ *brandy,* spirit distilled from cider; ∼ *butter,* sauce of ∼s stewed in cider; ∼*-cart* (upset person's ∼*-cart,* spoil his plans); ∼ *cheese,* compressed ∼ pomace; ∼ *dumpling,* ∼ cooked in paste; ∼ *green,* a colour; ∼ *pomace,* pulp remaining after juice is expressed; ∼*-jack,* Amer. name for ∼ brandy; ∼*-john,* kind of ∼ said to keep two years & to be best when withered; ∼*-pie bed,* one with sheets so folded that one's legs cannot get down; ∼*-pie order,* perfect order; ***∼ *sauce* (sl.), insincere flattery (also as int. = nonsense!). [OE *æppel,* OHG *apful,* ON *epli,* Gmc **aplu-*]

appli′ance, n. Applying; thing applied as means to an end. [f. APPLY + -ANCE]

äpp′lica|ble, a. Capable of being applied; having reference, appropriate, (*to*). Hence ∼BIL′ITY n. [f. L *applicare* (APPLY) + -ABLE; cf. F. *applicable*]

äpp′licant, n. One who applies (*for*). [as prec., see -ANT]

äpplică′tion, n. Putting of one thing *to* another; employment of means; (∼ of) plaster, liniment, etc.; bringing (*of* a general rule etc.) to bear upon particular case; relevancy; diligence; making of a request; request made. [late ME, f. F, f. L *applicationem* (as APPLY, see -ATION)]

appliqué (äplē′kā), n., & v.t. Ornamental work cut out from one material & applied to the surface of another (esp. in dressmaking); (vb) ornament thus. [F p.p. of *appliquer* apply (L *applicare*)]

applў′, v.t. & i. Put close (*to*); administer (remedy etc. *to*; lit. & fig.); devote (*to*); make use of; use as relative or suitable (*to*), set one*self* closely (*to* task, *to* do); have reference (*to*); attend closely (*to*); address oneself (*for* help etc. *to*); make application (*for* situation); *applied,* put to practical use, practical (opp. *theoretical* or *pure*). [ME, f. OF *aplier* f. L AP*plicare* fold, fasten to]

appoggiatur′a (-ŏjatoora), n. (mus.). A grace consisting of the note above the principal note, interpolated before it & momentarily taking its place in the rhythm of the passage. [It.]

appoint′, v.t. Fix (time, place, *for* purpose); prescribe (thing, *that*): (Law) declare the destination of (property, also abs.); nominate, as ∼ *him governor, to govern, to be governor,* ∼ *him*; (p.p.) *well, badly,* ∼*ed,* so equipped. Hence ∼EE′ n. [ME, f. OF *apointer* (*à point* to the point)]

appoint′ment, n. Appointing; engagement, assignation; decree, ordinance; office assigned; (usu. pl.) outfit; *keep, break, an* ∼, appear, fail to appear, at fixed place & time. [ME, f. OF *apointement* (as prec., see -MENT)]

appŏr′tion, v.t. Assign as due share (*to*); portion out. Hence ∼MENT (-shon-) n. [f. OF *aportionner* (*à* to+*portionner* f. PORTION)]

äpp′osite (-z-), a. Well put; appropriate (*to*). Hence ∼LY² (-tl-) adv., ∼NESS (-tn-) n. [f. L AP(*ponere posit-* put)]

äpposi′tion (-z-), n. Application (of seal); placing side by side; (Gram.) placing of word in syntactic parallelism with another, esp. addition of one noun to another. Hence ∼AL (-zĭsho-) a. [ME, f. F, or f. LL *appositio* (as prec., see -ION)]

apprais|e′ (-z), v.t. (Esp. of official valuer) fix price for; estimate. Hence ∼′AL (-z-), ∼e′MENT (-zm-), nn., ∼′ABLE (-z-) a. [f. PRAISE v. (formerly used in the same sense), on anal. of *prize, apprize*]

apprĕ′ciab|le (-sha-), a. Capable of being estimated; perceptible, sensible. Hence ∼LY² adv. [as foll., see -BLE]

apprĕ′ci|āte (-shĭ-), v.t. & i. Estimate worth, quality, amount, of; estimate aright; be sensitive to; esteem highly; raise in value; rise in value. Hence ∼ATIVE, ∼ATORY, (-sha-), aa., ∼ATIVELY² (-vĭ-) adv. [f. LL AP*pretiare* appraise (*pretium* price), see -ATE³]

apprĕciā'tion (*or* -shĭ-), n. Estimation, judgement; perception; adequate recognition; rise in value; critique. [OF, f. LL *appretiationem* (as prec., see -ATION)]

ăpprĕhĕnd', v.t. Seize, arrest; perceive (by senses or intellect); understand; fear (thing, *that*). [f. F *appréhender* or L AP(*prehendere* -*hens*- lay hold of), whence also F *apprendre* learn]

ăpprĕhĕn'si|ble, a. Capable of being grasped (by senses or intellect). Hence ~BIL'ITY n. [f. LL *apprehensibilis* (as prec., see -BLE)]

ăpprĕhĕn'sion (-shn), n. Seizure, arrest; grasping (of ideas), conception; understanding; dread. [F, or f. LL *apprehensio* (as prec., see -ION)]

ăpprĕhĕn'sive, a. Pertaining to sensuous or mental perception; perceptive (*of*); intelligent; uneasy, fearful, (*of* thing, *that* it may happen, *for* person, *for* his safety). Hence ~LY² (-vl-) adv., ~NESS (-vn-) n. [f. F *appréhensif* or med. L *apprehensivus* (as prec., see -IVE)]

apprĕn'tice¹, n. Learner of a craft, bound to serve, & entitled to instruction from, his employer for specified term; tiro. Hence ~SHIP (-ssh-) n. [ME, f. OF *aprentis* f. *apprendre* (see APPRE-HEND), suggested by words in -*tis*, -*tif*, f. L -*tivus* (see -IVE)]

apprĕn'tice², v.t. Bind as apprentice. [f. prec.]

apprise' (-z), v.t. Inform; (pass.) be aware *of*. [f. F *appris* -*ise* p.p. of *apprendre* learn, teach, (see APPREHEND)]

apprize', v.t. (arch.). Appraise; appreciate. [ME, f. OF *aprisier* (à to +*prisier* PRAISE, PRIZE)]

‖ **ăp'prō**, n. *On* ~, (of goods supplied) to be returned if not satisfactory. [= *approval* or *approbation*]

approach'¹, v.t. & i. Come near(er); (Golf) play the approach shot; approximate in character etc. *to*; come near to; approximate to'; (Commerc.) make overtures or proposals to. Hence ~ABIL'ITY n., ~ABLE a. [ME, f. OF *aprochier* f. LL AD*propiare* draw near (*propius* compar. of *prope* near)]

approach'², n. Act of approaching; approximation; access, passage, (lit. & fig.); (Golf) stroke, not from a tee, played for the green. [f. prec.]

*app'robāte, v.t. Approve formally, sanction. [late ME, f. L AP(*probare* test f. *probus* good) see -ATE³]

ăpprobā'tion, n. Sanction; approval. So **ăpp'robātORY** a. [ME, f. OF f. L *approbationem* (as prec., see -ATION)]

approp'riate¹, a. Belonging, peculiar, (*to*); suitable, proper, (*to*, *for*). Hence ~LY² (-tl-) adv., ~NESS (-tn-) n. [f. LL AP*propriare* (*proprius* own), see -ATE²]

approp'ri|āte², v.t. Take possession of; take to oneself; devote to special purposes. Hence *or* cogn. ~A'TION, ~ātOR, nn., ~atIVE a. [f. prec., see -ATE³]

approv'al (-ōō-), n. Approbation; sanction. [f. foll. + -AL (2)]

approve' (-ōōv), v.t. & i. Give evidence of (quality); (refl.) show one*self* to be; confirm, sanction; commend; ~ *of*, pronounce, consider, good; (p.p.) pronounced satisfactory, accepted, (of persons, reasons, etc.; ~*d school*, State school for young offenders). [ME, f. OF *aprover* f. L as APPROBATE]

approv'er (-ōō-), n. One who approves; one who turns Queen's evidence. [f. prec. +-ER¹]

approx'imate¹, a. Very near; closely resembling; fairly correct. Hence ~LY² (-tl-) adv. [f. LL A*pproximare* (*proximus*, very near), see -ATE²]

approx'im|āte², v.t. & i. Bring, come, near (*to* thing, esp. in quality, number, etc.). Hence ~A'TION n., ~atIVE a., ~atIVELY² adv. [f. prec., see -ATE³]

ăppui' (-wē), n. (Mil.) defensive support; *point of* ~ (F *point d'*~), fixed object on which troops deploy into line, also fig. [F, f. *appuyer* support]

appŭrt'ĕnance, n. Belonging; appendage; accessory. [f. AF *apurtenance* (OF *aper-*, *apar-*) f. Rom. *appertinentia (as APPERTAIN, see -ANCE)]

appŭrt'ĕnant, a. & n. (Thing) belonging, appertaining, pertinent, (*to*). [ME, f. OF *apartenant* part. as APPERTAIN]

ăp'ricŏt, n. Orange-coloured stone-fruit allied to plum. [(earliest forms *abrecock*, *apricock*) f. Sp. *albar(i)coque* f. Arab. *al* the +*burquq* f. Gk *praikokion* prob. f. L *praecoquum* variant of *praecox* early-ripe, -*cot* by assim. to F *abricot*]

Ap'ril (ā-), n. Fourth month of year; ~-*fool*, one sportively imposed upon on ~-*fool-day* (April 1). [ME *averil* f. OF *avril*, & *aprille* dir. f. L *aprilis*]

ā priō'rĭ, adv. & a. (Reasoning) from cause to effect; deductively; (loosely) presumptively, as far as one knows. Hence **ā-priō'r**ITY n. [L, = from what is before]

ăp'ron, n. Garment worn in front of body to protect clothes; official dress, as *bishop's*, *dean's*, *freemason's*, ~; leather covering for legs in open carriage; skin covering stuffing of roast goose or duck; *tied to* ~-*strings* of (wife, mother, etc.), unduly controlled by; hard-surfaced area on airfield, used for handling & (un)loading aircraft; (Theatr.) advanced strip of stage for playing scenes before curtain. Hence ~ED² (-nd) a., ~FUL (-ŏŏl) n. [ME *naperon* etc., f. OF dim. of *nape* table-cloth f. L *mappa* (cf. MAP¹); for loss of n- (*a napron* = *an apron*) cf. ADDER]

ăpropos' (-pŏ), adv., a., n. To the purpose; in respect of; appropriate(ness). [F, *à* to +*propos* PURPOSE]

ăpse, n. Semicircular or polygonal recess, arched or dome-roofed, esp. in church. [f. APSIS]

ăp'sidal, a. Of the form of an apse; of the apsides. [f. foll. +-AL]

ăp'sis, n. (pl. *ăp'sidēs*, *ăpsĭd'ēs*). Aphelion, perihelion, of planet; apogee, perigee, of moon; *line of apsides*, straight line joining these. [L, f. Gk (*h*)*apsis -idos* fastening, felloe of wheel, vault, (*haptō* join)]

ăpt, a. Suitable, appropriate; having a tendency (*to* do or be); quick-witted (*at*). Hence ~'LY² adv., ~'NESS n. [ME, f. L *aptus* fitted p.p. of *apere* fasten]

ăp'terous, a. Wingless; (Bot.) having no membranous expansions. [f. Gk *apteros* (*a-* not +*pteron* wing) +-OUS]

ăp'terўx, n. New Zealand bird with rudimentary wings & no tail. [f. Gk *a-* not +*pterux* wing]

ăp'titūde, n. Fitness; natural propensity (*for*); ability. [F, f. LL *aptitudinem* (as APT, see -TUDE)]

ä'qua, n. (chem.). Liquid, solution, as ~ *fort'īs*, nitric acid, ~ *rē'gia*, mixture of nitric & hydrochloric acids, able to dissolve gold & platinum. [L, = water]

ä'qualŭng, n. Portable diving apparatus consisting of cylinders of compressed air strapped on back & feeding air automatically to diver as he requires it. [f. L *aqua* water +LUNG]

äquamarine' (-ēn), n. Bluish-green beryl; bluish green (also as adj.). [f. L *aqua marina* sea-water]

ä'quaplāne, n., & v.i. (Ride on) plank towed behind speedboat. [f. L *aqua* water +PLANE³]

äquarĕlle', n. Kind of painting with Chinese ink & thin water-colours. [F, f. It. *acquerella* water-colour dim. of *acqua* f. L *aqua* water]

aquar'ium, n. (pl. *-iums*, *-ia*). Artificial pond or tank for the keeping of live aquatic plants & animals; place of public entertainment containing such tanks. Hence **ä'quarıST** (3) n., keeper of an ~. [L (*aqua* water, see -ARIUM)]

Aquar'ius, n. Zodiacal constellation; eleventh sign of Zodiac. [L, = water--carrier (as prec., see -ARY¹)]

aquăt'ic, a. & n. (Plant, animal) growing, living, in or near water; (of sports) conducted in or upon water. [late ME, f. F *aquatique* or L *aquaticus* (*aqua* water, see -ATIC)]

ä'quatint, n. Method of engraving on copper by use of a resinous solution & nitric acid; engraving so made. [f. F *aqua-tinte* f. It. *acqua tinta*]

äqua-vit'ae, n. Ardent spirits, esp. of the first distillation. [L, = water of life]

ä'quĕdŭct, n. Artificial channel, esp. elevated structure of masonry, for conveyance of water; conduit; (Physiol.) small canal, esp. in head of mammals. [f. L *aquae ductus* conduit (*ducere duct-* lead)]

ä'quĕous, a. Of water, watery; (Geol.) produced by water, as ~ *rocks*. [irreg. f. L *aqua* water +-EOUS]

äquilē'gia, n. (Kinds of) plant of buttercup type; columbine. [mod. L, etym. unkn.]

ä'quiline, a. Of an eagle; eagle-like, as ~ *nose* (hooked). [f. L *aquilinus* (*aquila* eagle, see -INE¹)]

aquŏs' itў, n. Wateriness. [f. L *aquosus* (*aqua* water), see -OSE & -TY; cf. LL *aquositas*]

ar-, pref. = AD- before *r*.

-ar¹, suf. (1) adj. suf. f. L *-aris* (varying w. cogn. *-alis* -AL) taken direct or thr. F, or formed on L nouns. The OF form of L *-arem* was *-er*, later *-ier*; ME adoptives had *-er* (see -ER²), later assim. to L with *-ar* (e.g. ME *scoler*, now *scholar*). For F learned adoptives in *-aire*, see -ARY¹. (2) noun suf., f. L-*are*, *-ar*, neut. of above (e.g. *exemplar*) or thr. F (ME *piler*, now *pillar*).

-ar², suf. Occas. repr. L *-arius*, *-arium* (normally repr. by -ER², -ARY¹). Generally, of refash. (after -AR¹) of earlier *-er* f. OF *-ier* (e.g. OF *mortier*, ME *morter*, now *mortar*), or after F *-aire* (e.g. *vicar*, ME *viker* & *vicary* f. OF *vicaire*, L *-arius*).

-ar³, suf. Casual var. of -ER¹, -OR in nouns (e.g. *beggar*, *liar*, *pedlar*), prob. on anal. of *scholar*, *pillar*, *vicar* (see -AR¹, ²).

A'rab (ă-), n. & a. One of the Semitic race inhabiting Saudi Arabia & neighbouring countries; ~ *horse*; *street arab*, homeless child; (adj.) Arabian. [f. F *Arabe* f. L *Arabem* (nom. *-bs*) f. Gk *Araps -abos*]

ärabĕsque' (-k), a. & n. 1. Arabian; fantastic. 2. n. Decoration in colour or low relief, with fanciful intertwining of leaves, scroll-work, etc.; (Mus.) florid melodic figure, composition based on such figures; ballet dancer's posture in which body is bent forward on one leg with the other leg extended horizontally backwards. [F, = Arabian, see -ESQUE]

Aräb'ian, a. & n. 1. Of Arabia; ~ *Nights' Entertainments* (or *The Thousand and One Nights*), collection of fabulous stories; ~ *bird*, phoenix. 2. n. = Arab. [f. *Arabia* +-AN]

A'rabic (ă-), a. & n. 1. Arabian; *gum* ~ (exuded by some kinds of acacia); ~ *numerals*, 1, 2, 3, etc. 2. n. Language of the Arabs. [ME, f. OF *Arabic* f. L *Arabicus* (*Arabs* ARAB, see -IC)]

A'rabist (ă-), n. Student of Arabic. [ARAB +-IST]

ä'rable, a. & n. (Land) fit for tillage. [f. F, or f. L *arabilis* (*arare* plough, see -BLE)]

aräch'nid (-k-), n. (zool.). Member of the *Arachnida*, class comprising spiders, scorpions, & mites. [f. mod. L *arachnida* f. Gk *arakhnē* spider +-ID³]

aräch'noid (-k-), a. & n. 1.(bot.). Covered with long cobweb-like hairs. 2. n. Serous membrane lining the dura mater, & enveloping brain & spinal cord. [f. Gk *arakhnoeidēs* (*arakhnē* cobweb, see -OID)]

Aramā'ic (ä-), a. & n. (Language) of Aram or Syria; northern branch of

Semitic family of languages, including Syriac & Chaldee. [f. L f. Gk *Aramaios* of Aram + -IC]

Arane'idan (ă-), a. & n. (Member) of the *Araneida* or spiders. [f. mod. L *araneida* (*aranea* spider), see -ID³, -AN]

arapai'ma (-pī-), n. S.-American food-fish (largest freshwater fish). [Brazilian]

Araucâr'ia (ă-), n. Genus of trees including monkey-puzzle. [*Arauco*, name of province in Chile]

arb'alĕst, arb'last (-ah-), n. Crossbow. [f. OF *arbaleste* f. LL *arcuballista* (*arcus* bow + *ballista* military engine)]

arb'iter, n. Judge; one appointed by two parties to settle dispute, umpire; one who has entire control (*of*); ~ *elĕgantiar'um* (-shī-), judge of taste (lit. of elegance). [L]

arb'itrage, n. Traffic in bills of exchange or stocks to take advantage of different prices in other markets. [F, f. *arbitrer* as ARBITRATE, see -AGE]

arb'itral, a. Pertaining to arbitration. [F, f. LL *arbitralis*, see ARBITER & -AL]

arbit'rament, -ement, n. Deciding of dispute by arbiter; authoritative decision [ME, f. OF *arbitrement* (*arbitrer*, see ARBITRAGE & -MENT)]

arb'itrar|y̆, a. Derived from mere opinion; capricious; unrestrained; despotic; (Law) discretionary. Hence ~iLY² adv., ~iNESS n. [f. L *arbitrarius* or F *arbitraire*, see ARBITER & -ARY¹]

arb'itrāte, v.t. & i. Decide by arbitration. [f. L *arbitrari* judge, see ARBITER & -ATE³]

arbitrā'tion, n. Settlement of a dispute by an arbiter; ~ *of exchange*, determination of rate of indirect exchange between two currencies. [ME, f. OF, f. L *arbitrationem* (as prec., see -ATION)]

arb'itrātor, n. (Now the legal term for) arbiter. Hence ~SHIP n. [ME, f. OF *arbitratour* f. LL *arbitratorem* (as ARBITRATE, see -OR)]

arb'itrĕss, n. Female arbiter, mediatress; absolute mistress. [ME, f. OF *arbitresse* fem. of *arbitre* f. L ARBITER, see -ESS¹]

arb'or, n. Main support of machine; axle or spindle on which wheel revolves. [f. F *arbre* tree, axis, f. L *arbor*; refash. on L]

arborā'ceous (-shus), a. Tree-like; wooded. [f. L *arbor* tree, see -ACEOUS]

Arb'or Day (är-), n. Day set apart annually in U.S., S. Australia, & elsewhere for public tree-planting. [L *arbor* tree]

arbor'eal, a. Of, living in, connected with, trees. [f. L *arboreus* (*arbor* tree, see -AL)]

arbor'eous, a. Wooded; arboreal; arborescent. [as prec., see -OUS]

arborĕs'c|ent, a. Tree-like in growth or general appearance; (Archit.) branching out. Hence ~ENCE n., ~entLY² adv. [f. L *arborescere* grow into a tree (*arbor*), see -ENT]

arborēt'um, n. (pl. -*ta*). A botanical tree-garden. [L, f. *arbor* tree]

arb'ori|culture, n. Cultivation of trees & shrubs. Hence ~cŭl'turAL a., ~cŭl'turIST n. [f. L *arbor* -*oris* tree + CULTURE]

arborizā'tion, n. Tree-like appearance (Min., Chem.) in aggregation of crystals, (Anat.) from distension or injection of capillary vessels. [as prec. + -IZE + -ATION]

arb'or vit'ae, n. Popular name of several evergreens. [L, = tree of life]

arb'our (-er), n. Bower, shady retreat with sides & roof formed by trees or lattice-work covered with climbing plants. Hence ~ED² (-erd) a. [ME (h)*erber* f. OF (h)*erbier* grass lawn f. L *herbarium* (*herba* grass, herb, see -ARIUM), phonetic change to *ar-* being assisted by assoc. with L *arbor* tree]

Arb'ūtus (är-), n. Genus of evergreens including strawberry-tree. [L]

arc, n. Part of circumference of circle or other curve; *diurnal, nocturnal,* ~, part of circle that a heavenly body appears to pass through above, below, horizon; belt contained between parallel curves; (Electr.) luminous bridge formed between two separate carbon poles; ~-*lamp*, -*light*, using this. [ME, f. OF, f. L *arcus* bow, curve]

arcāde', n. Passage arched over; any covered walk, esp. with shops along one or both sides; (Archit.) series of arches on same plane. Hence **arcād'ED²** a. [F, f. Prov. *arcada* f. Rom. *arca ARCH, see -ADE]

Arcades ăm'bō (ärk'adĕz), sent. Blackguards both (cf. Byron *D. Juan*, iv. 93). [joc. application of Virg. *Ecl.* vii. 4]

Arcād'ian (är-), a. & n. Ideal(ly) rustic. [f. L *Arcadius* (Gk *Arkadia* mountain district in Peloponnese) + -AN]

Arc'ady̆, Arcād'ia (är-), n. (poet.). Ideal rustic paradise. [f. Gk *Arkadia*, see prec.]

arcān'um, n. (Usu. in pl. -*na*) mystery, secret. [L, neut. of *arcanus* (*arca* chest, see -AN)]

arch¹, n. Curved structure supporting bridge, floor, etc., or merely ornamental; curve; curvature in shape of ~, as *fallen* ~ (of foot); vault; *Court of Arches,* ecclesiastical court of appeal for the province of Canterbury, orig. held in the church of St Mary-le-Bow (or 'of the Arches'); ~'*way,* vaulted passage, arched entrance. Hence ~'wISE adv. [ME, f. OF *arche* f. Rom. **arca,* n. pl. by-form of L *arcus* ARC]

arch², v.t. & i. Furnish with an arch; form into an arch; overarch, span; (intr.) form an arch. [ME, f. OF *archer* (as prec.)]

arch³, a. (sup. -*est*). Chief, pre-eminent, as ~ *rogue, knave, impostor,* (but now usu. ~-); facetiously serious, innocently roguish, whence ~'LY² adv., ~'NESS n. [= foll.]

arch-, pref. = Gk *arkhi-, arkh-, arkhe-,* comb. form of *arkhos* chief. Hence L *archi-* whence OE *arce-,* ME *arche-,* coinciding w. OF *arche*. From these, *arch-* became a living formative. In mod. literary wds f. Gk or L directly, or thr. F, the form *archi-* is retained; cf. *arch-deacon* but *archidiaconal*. Meaning: (1) in titles of office etc. 'chief, superior', as *archbishop*, *-duke*, esp. in titles of Holy Roman or German empire, as *-butler*, *-chamberlain*; (2) 'pre-eminent, leading', as *-antiquary*, *-builder*, *-prophet*, *-wag*; esp. 'extreme, worst', as *-buffoon*, *-knave*, *-liar*; (3) chiefly archaic = 'first, original', as *-founder*, *-messenger*; (4) of things, 'chief', as *-diocese*.

Arch′aean (ark-), a. Of the earliest geological period. [f. Gk *arkhaios* ancient (*arkhē* beginning) +-AN]

ǎrchae|ŏl′ogў (-kĭ-), n. Study of antiquities, esp. of the prehistoric period. So ~olŏ′gic(AL) (-kĭo-) aa., ~olŏ′gicalłȳ² adv., ~ŏl′ogist (-kĭ-) n. [f. Gk *arkhaiologia* (as prec., see -LOGY)]

ǎrchaeŏp′terўx (-k-), n. Oldest known (fossil) bird, a link between birds & reptiles. [f. Gk *arkhaios* ancient + *pterux* wing]

archā′ic (-k-), a. Primitive, antiquated; (of language) no longer in common use, though retained for special purposes. Hence ~ICALLY adv. [f. Gk *arkhaïkos* (as prec., see -IC)]

ǎrch′ā|ism (-k-), n. Retention, imitation, of what is old or obsolete (esp. in language & art); archaic word or expression. Hence ~IST n., ~is′tic a., (-k-). [f. Gk *irkhaïsmos* (*arkhaïzō*, see foll. & -ISM)]

ǎrch′āize (-k-), -ise (-īz), v.t. & i. Imitate, affect, the archaic; (trans.) render archaistic. [f. Gk *arkhaïzō* copy the ancients (*arkhaios* ancient, see -IZE)]

ǎrch′ǎngel (-k-), n. Angel of highest rank; kind of dead-nettle; kind of pigeon. Hence **ǎrchǎngěl′ic** (-k-) a. [ME f. OF, or f. LL f. Gk *arkhaggelos* (see ARCH- & ANGEL)]

ǎrch′bish′op, n. Chief bishop; metropolitan. Hence **ǎrch**BISH′OPRIC n. [OE *ærce-* (ME *erche-*) *biscop*, f. Rom. *arcebiscopo* f. LL *archiepiscopus* (see ARCH- & BISHOP)]

ǎrch′deac′on, n. Ecclesiastical dignitary next below bishop, superintending rural deans & holding lowest ecclesiastical court, with power of spiritual censure. Hence **ǎrchdeac′on**SHIP n. [OE *arce-*, *ercediacon*, f. LL *archidiaconus* (see ARCH- & DEACON)]

ǎrchdeac′onrў, n. Jurisdiction, rank, residence, of archdeacon. [prec. + -RY]

ǎrchdi′ocēse, n. See of an archbishop. [ARCH- (4)]

ǎrch′dŭch′ěss, n. (hist.). Wife of an archduke; daughter of Emperor of Austria. [f. F *archiduchesse* (see ARCH- & DUCHESS)]

ǎrch′dŭke, n. (hist.), Son of Emperor of Austria. So **ǎrch**DŬC′AL a., **ǎrch′**DUCHY n. [f. OF *archeduc*, in med. L *archidux* (see ARCH- & DUKE)]

ǎrch′-ĕn′emў, n. Chief enemy; Satan. [ARCH- (2)]

ǎrch′|er, n. One that shoots with bow & arrows; Sagittarius, ninth zodiacal constellation. So ~ERY (2), AF, f. OF *archier* f. Rom. *arcarius* (*arcus* bow, see -ARY[1])]

ǎrch′ětўp|e (-k-), n. Original model, prototype. Hence ~AL a., ~alłȳ² adv. [f. L f. Gk *arkhetupon* (*arkhe-* ARCH- + *tupos* stamp)]

ǎrch′-fiend′, n. Satan. [ARCH- (2)]

archi-. See ARCH-.

|| **ǎrch′ibald** (-awld). See ARCHIE.

ǎrchidiǎc′onal (-kĭ-), a. Pertaining to an archdeacon. [f. LL *archidiaconus* ARCHDEACON + -AL]

|| **ǎrch′ie, -ibald**, nn. (sl.). Anti-aircraft gun. [f. name in pop. song]

ǎrchiĕpis′copal (-k-), a. Pertaining to an archbishop. [f. LL *archiepiscopus* ARCHBISHOP + -AL]

ǎrch′il (or -k-), n. (Violet dye from) various kinds of lichen. [corrupt. of ORCHIL]

ǎrchimǎn′drite (-k-), n. Superior of monastery or convent in Greek church. [f. LL *archimandrita* f. late Gk *arkhimandritēs* (*arkhi-* ARCH- + *mandra* monastery)]

Archimēd′ean (ark-), a. Of Archimedes (Greek mathematician); ~ *screw*, instrument raising water by tube in form of screw wound round cylinder. [f. L *Archimedeus* + -AN]

ǎrchipěl′agō (-k-), n. (pl. ~s). Aegean sea; sea with many islands; group of islands. [f. It. *arcipelago* (*arci-* ARCH- (4) + *pelago* gulf, pool, f. L f. Gk *pelagos* sea)]

ǎrch′itěct (-k-), n. Professor of building, who prepares plans & superintends work; designer of complex structure, esp. the Creator; (fig.) achiever, as ~ *of his own fortunes*. Hence ~IVE a. [f. F *architecte* or L *architectus* f. Gk *arkhitektōn* (*arkhi-* ARCH- + *tektōn* builder); some derivatives formed as if L *-tectus* were p.p. of *tegere* cover]

ǎrchitěctŏn′|ic (-k-), a. Of architecture or architects; constructive; controlling; pertaining to systematization of knowledge, whence ~ICS n., ~icAL a. [f. F *-ique* or L *-icus* f. Gk. *arkhitektonikos* (as prec., see IC)]

ǎrch′itěcture (-k-), n. Art or science of building; thing built, structure; style of building; construction. Hence **ǎrchitěc′**turAL (-k-; -cher-) a., **ǎrchitěc′tural**łȳ² adv. [F, or f. L *architectura* (*architectus* ARCHITECT, see -URE)]

ǎrch′itrāve (-k-), n. Epistyle, main beam resting immediately on the abacus on capital of column; the various parts surrounding doorway or window; moulding round exterior of arch. [F, f. It. *architrave* (*archi-* ARCH- + *trave* (f. L *trabs* *-abis*) beam)]

arch′ive (-k-), n. (usu. pl. ~s, pr. -kīvz). Place in which public records are kept; records so kept. [F (-*if*, -*ive*), f. LL *archi(v)um* f. Gk *arkheion* public office (*arkhē* government)]

arch′ivist (-k-), n. Keeper of archives. [f. prec. +-IST]

arch′ivolt (-k-), n. Lowest member of arch from impost to impost; mouldings decorating this. [f. F *archivolte* or It. *archivolio, arcovolta* (*arco* f. L *arcus* arch + *volta* VAULT, *volto* arched)]

arch′on (-k-), n. One of nine chief magistrates in ancient Athens; ruler, president. Hence ~SHIP n. [Gk (-ōn), = ruler (part. of *arkhō*)]

arc′tic, a. Of the north pole, northern; *A~ Circle* (of earth), parallel of 66° 32′ N. [ME *artik* f. OF *artique* f. L *ar(c)ticus* f. Gk *arktikos* (*arktos* bear, Ursa Major, see -IC)]

Arctūr′us (ār-), n. Brightest star in constellation Boötes. [ME, f. L, f. Gk *arktouros* (*arktos* bear + *ouros* guardian)]

arc′ūate, -āted, aa. Bent like a bow; arched. [f. L *arcuatus* (*arcuare* f. *arcus* bow; see -ATE²)]

arc′us senīl′īs, n. Narrow yellowish-white band gradually encircling the cornea with advancing age. [L, = bow of old age]

-ard, suf. forming nouns, usu. of censure (*sluggard, drunkard*), but cf. *standard* (orig. *stander*), *placard*; also spelt -*art* (*braggart*). [ME & OF, f. Gmc *-hart*, *-hard*, hardy, in proper names]

ard′ent, a. Burning, red-hot; parching; ~ *spirits* (prop. = inflammable, but now understood of their taste), alcoholic spirits; eager, zealous; fervent (of persons & feelings). Hence **ard′**ENCY n., ~LY² adv. [ME, f. OF *ardant* f. L *ardentem* (*ardēre* burn), see -ANT]

ard′our (-dẽr), n. Fierce heat; warm emotion; fervour, zeal, (*for*). [ME, f. OF, f. L *ardorem* (*ardēre* burn, see -OR)]

ard′ūous, a. Steep, hard to climb; hard to achieve, laborious; strenuous, energetic. Hence ~LY² adv., ~NESS n. [f. L *arduus* steep, difficult +-OUS]

are¹ (ār), n. French metric unit of square measure, square whose side is 10 metres (119·6 sq. yds). [F, f. L *area*]

are². See BE.

ar′ea, n. Vacant ground; level space; sunk court railed off from pavement & freq. giving access to basement of house, as ~ *bell*; superficial extent; region, tract; scope, range. [L, = vacant piece of ground in town]

ä′rēca, n. Kinds of palms; ~-*nut*, astringent seed of a species of ~. [Port., f. Tamil *adaikay* (*aḍai* close-clustering + *kay* nut)]

arēn′a, n. (pl. ~s). Central part of amphitheatre, in which combats take place; (fig.) scene of conflict, sphere of action. [L (*h*)*arena* sand, sand-strewn place of combat]

ărēnā′ceous (-shŭs), a. Sand-like; sandy. So **ărēnOSE′**¹ a. [f. L *arenaceus* (as prec., see -ACEOUS)]

aren′t (ärnt). See BE.

arē′ol|a, n. (pl. ~ae). Very small area, as that between veins of a leaf; interstice in tissue; circular spot, as that surrounding the human nipple; (Biol.) cell-nucleus of plant. Hence ~AR¹, ~ATE², aa., ~A′TION n. [L, dim. of AREA]

Arēŏp′agite (ă-, -jīt *or* -gīt) n. Member of the court of Areopagus. [f. L f. Gk *arciopagītēs* (see foll. & -ITE)]

Arēŏp′agus (-ă), n. Hill at Athens where highest judicial court sat. [L, f. Gk *Areios pagos* Mars′ hill]

arête (ărāt′), n. Sharp ascending ridge of mountain. [F, f. L *arista* ear of corn]

ar′gala, n. Adjutant-bird, gigantic Indian stork. [Hind. *hargīla*]

ar′gali, n. Asian wild sheep. [Mongol]

ar′gand, n. Lamp with tubular wick; gas-burner on same principle. [inventor]

ar′gent, n. & a. Silver (colour, esp. in armorial bearings). [F, f. L *argentum*]

argentif′erous, a. Yielding silver. [f. L *argentum* + -FEROUS]

ar′gentine, a. & n. Of silver; silvery; imitation silver; silvery lamellae on scales of fish; (Zool.) kinds of small fishes; (Min.) slate-spar. [f. F *argentin* (L *argentum* +-*in*; see -INE¹)]

ar′gil, n. Clay (esp. potter's). So ~IA′CEOUS a. [f. F *argille* f. L *argilla* f. Gk *argillos* (*argēs* white)]

Argive (ār′gĭv, -j-), a. & n. 1. Of Argos in ancient Greece, Greek. 2. n. An inhabitant of Argos, a Greek. [f. L *Argivus* f. Gk *Argeios*]

ar′gle-bar′gle, v.i., & n., (joc.). Debate. [corrupt. & redupl. of *argue*]

ar′gol, n. Tartar deposited from fermented wines, which when purified becomes cream of tartar. [ME *argoyle*, of unkn. orig.]

ar′gon, n. (chem.). A gas, an inert constituent of the atmosphere. [neut. of Gk *argos* idle (A- (7), *ergon* work)]

Ar′gonaut (ār-), n. 1. (pl.). Legendary heroes who sailed with Jason in the Argo for the golden fleece. 2. Genus of cephalopod molluscs including paper nautilus. [f. L (-*ta*) f. Gk *Argonautēs* sailor in the *Argō*]

ar′gosy̆, n. (hist., poet.). Large merchant-vessel, esp. of Ragusa & Venice; (poet.) ship, venture. [earlier *ragusye*, prob. f. It. *Ragusea* (*nave*) Ragusan (vessel)]

ar′got (-gō), n. Jargon, slang, of a class, esp. of thieves. [F, of unkn. orig.]

ar′gūe, v.t. & i. Prove, indicate, as *it ~s him (to be) a rogue, that he is a rogue, roguery in him*; maintain by reasons (*that*), whence **ar′g**ūABLE a.; treat (matter) by reasoning; ~ *it away*, get rid of it by argument; ~ (persuade) person *into, out of*; reason (*with, against*, person, *for, against, about*, thing). [ME, f. OF *arguer* f. L *argutare* frequent. of *arguere* make clear, prove, accuse]

ăr′gŭment, n. Reason advanced (*for, against*, proposition or course); (Logic) middle term in syllogism; reasoning process; debate; summary of subject-matter of book; ~ (usu. *argumĕn′tum*) *ad hominem*, one that takes advantage of character or situation of particular opponent, *ad crumenam*, of his avarice, *ad ignorantiam*, of his ignorance of the facts, *ex silentio*, of his silence. [ME, f. F f. L *argumentum* (*arguere*, see prec. & -MENT)]

ărgŭmĕntā′tion, n. Methodical reasoning; debate. [f. F, or L *argumentatio* f. *argumentari* (as prec.), see -ATION]

ărgŭmĕn′tative, a. Logical; fond of arguing. Hence ~LY² (-vl-) adv., ~NESS (-vn-) n. [F (-*if*, -*ive*), or f. LL *argumentativus*, as prec., see -ATIVE]

Ar′gus (ār′-), n. Fabulous person with a hundred eyes; watchful guardian; ~-*eyed*, vigilant; *argus-shell*, oculated porcelain-shell. [ME, f. L, f. Gk *Argos*]

ărgūte′, a. Sharp, shrewd; (of sounds) shrill. [ME, f. L *argutus* p.p. of *arguere*, see ARGUE]

argyr-, argyro-, in comb. = Gk *arguros* silver, as *argyran′thous*, with silvery flowers, *argyrophyll′ous*, silvery-leaved.

ar′ia (ahr-), n. (mus.). Extended song in three sections common in 18th-c. opera & oratorio. [It.]

Ar′ian (ār′-), a. & n. (Holder) of the doctrine of Arius of Alexandria (4th c.), who denied consubstantiality of Christ. Hence ~ISM n., ~IZE v.t. & i. [f. LL *Arianus* (*Arius* f. Gk *Arios, Areios*, see -AN)]

-ār′ian, suf. forming adjj. & nn., f. L -*arius* -ARY¹ + -AN. First in 16th c. (*disciplin*~, *quinquagen*~, etc.), later (17th c.) & now chiefly denoting (member of a) sect etc., as *millen*~, *Trinit*~, etc.

ă′rid, a. Dry, parched, (lit. & fig.); (of ground) barren, bare. Hence *arid′*ITY, ~NESS, nn. [f. F *aride* or L *aridus* (*arere* be dry)]

ār′iel, n. Species of gazelle in Western Asia & Africa. [f. Arab. *aryil* var. of *ayyil* stag]

Aries (ār′iēz), n. The Ram, first zodiacal constellation. [ME, f. L, = ram]

aright′ (-it), adv. Rightly. [A prep. + RIGHT n.]

ă′ril, n. Accessory seed-covering in certain plants. [f. mod. L *arillus* f. med. L *arilli* dried grapes]

-ār′ious, compd adj. suf. = L -*arius* (-ARY¹) + -OUS.

arise′ (-z), v.i. (*arōse, arisen*, pr. -z, -z-). (Arch.) rise, get up; (poet.) rise from the dead; (arch.) be heard (of sounds); originate; be born; come into notice; result (*from*); present itself. [A- (1) + RISE v.]

aris′ta, n. (pl. -*ae*). Awn, beard, of grain & grasses. [L]

aris′tate, a. Awned, bearded. [f. L *aristatus* (ARISTA, see -ATE²)]

ăristŏc′racȳ, n. Government by the best citizens; supremacy of privileged order, oligarchy; state so governed; ruling body of nobles; class from which ruling body is drawn, nobles; the best representatives of (intellect etc.). [f. F *aristocratie* or f. LL f. Gk *aristokratia* (*aristos* best, see -CRACY)]

ă′ristocrăt, n. One of a ruling oligarchy; one of the class of nobles. Hence **ăristŏc′ratISM** n. [f. F *aristocrate* (as foll.)]

ăristocrăt′ic, a. Pertaining to, attached to, aristocracy; grand, stylish. Hence ~AL a., ~aLLY² adv. [f. F *aristocratique* f. Gk *aristokratikos* (as ARISTOCRACY, see -IC)]

Aristotēl′ian (ă-), a. & n. (Disciple or student) of the Greek philosopher Aristotle. [f. L f. Gk *Aristoteles* Aristotle + -IAN]

arith′metic, n. Science of numbers; arithmetical knowledge, computation; treatise on computation. Hence **arithmĕti′CIAN** (-ishn) n. [ME, f. OF *arismetique* f. Rom. **arismetica* for L *arithmetica* f. Gk *arithmētikē* (*tekhnē*) (art) of counting f. *arithmeō* count (*arithmos* number), see -IC; corrupted in ME to *arsmetrike*, as if f. L *ars metrica* art of measure]

ărithmĕt′ical, a. Of arithmetic; ~ *progression*, (series of numbers showing) increase, decrease, by a constant quantity (e.g. 1, 2, 3, 4, etc., 9, 7, 5, 3, etc.). Hence ~LY² adv. [f. L *arithmeticus* + -AL]

-ār′ium, noun suf. (= 'place for') f. L neut. of adjj. in -*arius* (-ARY¹), chiefly in antiquarian words as *sacrarium*, occas. popularized, as *aquarium*.

ārk, n. Chest, box; *Ark of the Covenant, Ark of Testimony*, wooden coffer containing tables of Jewish law; covered floating vessel in which Noah was saved at the Deluge; *Noah's* ~, toy ~ with animals. [OE *ærc*, OHG *archa*, ON *örk*, Goth. *arka*, Gmc **arka* f. L *arca* chest]

arles (ārlz), n. pl. (dial.). Earnest-money. [see EARNEST²]

ārm¹, n. Upper limb of human body from shoulder to hand; *fore-*~(from elbow to hand); fore limb of an animal; large branch of tree; sleeve; thing resembling ~, as ~ *of the sea, ~′chair′* (with side supports), ~ *of lever, balance* (part from fulcrum to point of application of power or weight); ~′*hole* in garment, hole, through which ~ is put; ~′*pit*, hollow under ~ at shoulder; ~-*in*~ (of two persons with ~s interlinked); *infant in* ~s (too young to walk); *with open* ~s, cordially; *keep at* ~'s *length*, avoid familiarity with; *secular* ~, authority of secular tribunal. Hence **ārm′**FUL (-ōol) n., **ārm′lĕss¹** [-LESS] a. [OE *arm, earm*, OHG *arm*, ON *armr*, Goth. *arms*, Gmc **armaz*, cogn. w. L *armus* shoulder]

arm[2], n. (usu. pl.). Weapon(s); *fire-~s* (requiring explosive); *small ~s*, portable fire-arms, esp. rifles, pistols, light machine guns, sub-machine guns, etc.; *stand of ~s*, set for one soldier; (sing.) particular kind of weapon; *take up ~s*, arm oneself (often fig.), *bear ~s*, serve as soldier; *lay down ~s*, cease hostilities; *in ~s*, armed; *up in ~s*, actively engaged in rebellion etc. (also fig.); *under ~s*, in battle array; military profession; (sing. & pl.) each kind of troops, infantry, cavalry, etc.; heraldic devices, as *coat of ~s*; *King-of-Arms*, Chief Herald. Hence **ǎrm′lèss**[2] [-LESS] a. [ME, f. OF *armes* f. L *arma* arms, fittings]

arm[3], v.t. & i. Furnish with arms; *~ed neutrality* (of nations prepared for war); furnish with tools or other requisites; plate (*with* anything); furnish (magnet) with an armature; (intr.) *~* oneself, take up arms. [ME, f. OF *armer* f. L *armare* (*arma*)]

ǎrmãd′a, n. Fleet of ships of war, esp. *the* (*Invincible*) *A~* sent by Philip II of Spain against England in 1588. [Sp., f. L *armata* (*armare*) ARM v., see -ADE]

ǎrmadǐll′ō, n. (pl. *-os*). Burrowing animal of S. America, with body encased in bony armour, & habit of rolling itself into ball when captured; kinds of small terrestrial Crustacea with same habit, allied to wood-louse. [Sp., dim. of *armado* one armed f. L as ARM[3], see -ADO]

Armagědd′on (ǎr-, -g-), n. (Scene of) supreme conflict between the nations. [*Rev.* xvi. 16]

ǎrm′ament, n. Force (usu. naval) equipped for war; military equipments, guns on warship; process of equipping for war. [f. L *armamentum* (as ARM[2], see -MENT), partly through F *armement*]

ǎrm′ature, n. Arms, armour; defensive covering of animals or plants; piece of soft iron placed in contact with poles of magnet, preserving its power; essential part of a dynamo. [F, or f. L *armatura* (as prec., see -URE)]

arme blanche (see Ap.), n. Cavalry sword or lance; cavalry. [F, = white arm]

Armēn′ian (ǎr-), a. & n. **1.** Of Armenia; *~ bole*, red *~ earth*, used medicinally; *~ stone*, blue carbonate of copper. **2.** n. Native of Armenia; adherent of *~* church. [-AN]

ǎrm′iger, n. Esquire, one entitled to bear heraldic arms. [L, = bearing arms (*crma* arms + *gerere* bear)]

ǎrmill′ary, a. Pertaining to bracelets; *~ sphere*, skeleton celestial globe of metal rings representing equator, tropics, etc. [f. L *armilla* bracelet, see -ARY[2]]

Armin′ian (ǎr-), a. & n. (Adherent of the doctrine of Arminius (d. 1609), Dutch protestant theologian, who opposed the views of Calvin, esp. on predestination. Hence *~*ISM (ǎr-) n. [f. *Arminius*, Latiniz. of *Harmensen* + -AN]

ǎrm′istice, n. Cessation from hostilities (lit. & fig.); short truce; *A~ Day*, 11th Nov., kept as anniversary of the *~* (1918) that ended hostilities in the war of 1914-18. [F, or f. mod. L *armistitium* (*arma* arms + *-stitium* as in SOLSTICE)]

ǎrm′lèt, n. Band worn round arm; small inlet of sea or branch of river. [ARM[1] + -LET]

ǎrmōr′ial, a. & n. (Book) pertaining to heraldic arms. [ARMORY + -AL(1)]

ǎrm′or|y̌, n. Heraldry. Hence *~*IST n. [f. OF *armoirie* f. *armoier* blazoner f. *armoire* v. = It. *armeggiare* f. L *arma* arms]

ǎrm′our[1] (-mer-), n. **1.** Defensive covering for the body worn in fighting (*~-bearer*, one who carries another's *~*). **2.** Metal sheathing of ship of war, composed of *~-plates* (*~-clad*, furnished with this); steel plates etc. protecting cars, tanks, etc. from projectiles; armoured vehicles collectively, e.g. tanks, armoured cars, etc. **3.** Diver's suit. **4.** Protective covering of animals or plants. **5.** Heraldic insignia. [ME, f. OF *armēure* f. L *armatura* ARMATURE]

ǎrm′our[2] (-mer), v.t. Furnish with protective covering; *~ed* CRUISER; *~ed car, train*, etc., one supplied with protective plates of steel etc., & (usu.) guns; *~ed column, corps, division, force*, etc., one equipped with *~ed* cars, tanks, etc. [f. prec.]

ǎrm′ourer (-mer-), n. Manufacturer of arms; official in charge of ship's, regiment's, arms. [f. AF *armurer*, OF *-urier*, f. as above, see prec. & -ER[2]]

ǎrm′oury̌ (-mer-), n. Place where arms are kept, arsenal; *armourer's workshop. [perh. as ARMORY, but treated as f. ARMOUR + -Y[1]]

ǎrm′y̌, n. Organized body of men armed for war; *standing ~*, one of professional soldiers permanently in existence; *the ~*, the military service; vast host; organized body of men, as *Salvation A~*, *Church A~*, *Blue Ribbon A~*; *~ broker, contractor* (carrying on business in connexion with the *~*); *~ corps*, main subdivision of *~* in the field consisting usu. of two or three divisions with technical, administrative, supply, etc. formations; *~-list*, official list of officers; *~-worm*, larva of cotton-moth. [ME, f. OF *armee* f. L *armata* fem. p.p. of *armare* arm; see -Y[4]]

ǎrn′ica, n. Kinds of plants including mountain tobacco; medicine, esp. tincture, prepared from this. [mod. L of unkn. orig.]

aroint′, **-oy-**, v. or int. (arch.). *~ thee*, begone. [ME, orig. unkn.]

arōm′a, n. (pl. *-as*). Fragrance, sweet smell; subtle pervasive quality. [ME *aromat* f. OF f. L *aromata* (pl.) f. Gk *arōma -atos*; later conform. to L *aroma*]

ǎromǎt′ic, a. Fragrant; spicy; (of smell) pleasantly pungent. [ME, f. F *aromatique* f. LL f. Gk *arōmatikos* (AROMA, see -IC)]

arose. See ARISE.

around', adv. & prep. **1.** On every side, in every direction; *round, round round about; *about, here & there, at random, as *fool ~.* **2.** prep. On, along, the circuit of; about, enveloping. [f. A-(2)+ROUND]

arouse' (-z), v.t. Awaken; stir up into activity. [A-(1)+ROUSE², on anal. of *rise*, *arise*]

arpe'ggio (-ĕjō), n. (pl. *-os*), (mus.). Striking of notes of chord in (usu. upward) succession; chord so struck. [It.]

arquebus. See HARQUEBUS.

a'rrack (or arăk'), n. Eastern name for any native spirituous liquor, esp. that distilled from the coco-palm, or from rice & sugar. [f. Arab. *'araq* juice]

a'rrah (-ra), int. An Anglo-Irish expletive.

arraign' (-ān), v.t. Indict before a tribunal; accuse; find fault with, call in question, (action, statement). So ~MENT (-ān-) n. [f. AF *arainer* f. OF *araisnier* f. Rom. *ADrationare* reason, talk reasonably (*ratio -onis* reason, discourse)]

arrange', v.t. & i. Put into order, adjust; draw up (army); (Mus.) adapt (composition) for new medium, instrumental or vocal; adapt (play etc.) for broadcasting; settle (dispute etc.); settle beforehand the order, manner, of; (intr.) take steps, form plans, give instructions, (~ *to be there, for the car to be there*; ~ *about it*); come to agreement (*with* person, *about* thing, *to do, that,* or abs.). [ME, f. OF *arangier* (à to + *rangier* RANGE¹)]

arrange'ment (-jm-), n. Arranging; thing arranged; settlement of dispute etc.; (pl.) plans, measures, as *make your own ~s.* [F, as prec. +-MENT]

a'rrant, a. Notorious, downright, thoroughpaced, as ~ *knave, dunce, hypocrite, nonsense.* Hence ~LY² adv. [ME, variant of ERRANT, orig. in phrr. like ~ (= outlawed, roving) *thief*]

a'rras, n. Rich tapestry; hanging screen of this formerly hung round walls of rooms (often not too closely to admit person). Hence ~ED² (-st) a. [*Arras*, town in France famous for the fabric]

array'¹, v.t. Marshal, dispose, (forces); (Law) impanel (a jury); dress, esp. with display; (refl.) dress one*self* up; adorn; (fig.) clothe (in qualities etc.). [f. AF *arayer* = OF *areyer* f. Rom. *arredare* f. *ad* to + Gmc *ræđh-* READY]

array'², n. Order, as *battle* ~; (hist.) arming of militia, as *Commission of A~*; military force; imposing series *of* persons or things; order of impanelling jury; (poet.) outfit, dress. [ME, f. AF *arai*= OF *arei* f. *areyer*, see prec.]

arrear', n. (Arch.) hinder part, esp. of procession; (pl.) outstanding debts, what remains undone (~*s of work*); *in* ~s or ~, behindhand, esp. in payment; *in* ~ *of,* behind. [ME, orig. adv. f. OF *arere* (mod. F *arrière*) f. Rom. *aretro* (*ab* from + *retro* backwards); first used in phr. *in* ~]

arrear'age, n. Backwardness; unpaid balance; thing in reserve; (pl.) debts. [ME, f. OF *arerage* f. *arere*, see prec. & -AGE]

arrĕct', a. (arch. & poet.). (Of the ears) pricked up; (fig.) on the alert. [f. L *arrectus* p.p. of ARrigere raise up (*regere* straighten)]

arrest'¹, v.t. Stop (person, cannon-ball, decay); (Law) ~ *judgement*, stay proceedings after verdict, on ground of error; seize (person), esp. by legal authority; catch (attention); catch attention of. Hence ~IVE a., ~MENT, ~OR, nn. (~*or hook,* hook-like device for catching on cables on deck of aircraft carrier & checking speed of aircraft as they land). [ME, f. OF *arester* f. Rom. *ADrestare* remain, stop; see REST]

arrest'², n. Stoppage, check; ~ *of judgement* (see prec.); seizure; legal apprehension; imprisonment; *under* ~ (legal restraint). [ME, f. OF *arest* f. *arester*, see prec.]

arrêt (arā'), n. (hist.). Authoritative sentence or decree of the King or Parliament of France; (loosely) judgement, order. [F, f. OF *arest* (prec.)]

arride', v.t. (literary). Please, gratify. [f. L ARridēre smile upon, be pleasing to]

arrière-ban (ă'rier-), n. Summoning of vassals to military service by Frankish king; body thus summoned or liable to be summoned; noblesse; (improp.) summoning of inferior (*arrière-*) vassals. [F, f. OF *ariere-ban* for *herban, arban* f. Frankish **hari* army + **ban* edict, BAN (cf. OHG *heriban*), altered in form & sense by pop. etym., whence *ban* et *arrière-ban* summoning of superior & inferior vassals]

arrière-pensée (see Ap.), n. Ulterior motive; mental reservation. [F]

a'rris, n. Sharp edge formed by angular contact of two plane or curved surfaces, as ~*-gutter* (V-shaped), ~*-wise*, ridgewise. [corrupt. f. OF *areste*, mod. ARÊTE]

arriv'al, n. Act of coming to end of journey or destination (lit. & fig.); appearance upon scene; person, thing, that has arrived; (colloq.) new-born child; cargo to be delivered when ship arrives. [ME f. AF *arivaille* (*ariver*, see foll. & -AL (2))]

arrive', v.i. Come to destination (lit. & fig.) or end of journey (*at* Bath, *in* Paris, *upon* scene, *at* conclusion); (as Gallicism) establish one's repute or position; (of things) be brought; (of time) come; (of events) come about. [ME, f. OF *ariver* f. Rom. **arripare* come to shore (L *ripa*)]

arriviste (ărēvēst'), n. Careerist, parvenu. [F]

a'rrogant, a. Overbearing; presumptuous; haughty. Hence or cogn. ~ANCE, ~ANCY, nn., ~antLY² adv. [ME, f. OF (as foll., see -ANT)]

a'rrogate, v.t. Claim unduly (thing, *to* one*self* a thing); claim unduly that one possesses (a quality); claim unduly for (*to*) some one else. [f. L AR(*rogare* ask), see -ATE[3]]

ărrogā′tion, n. Unjust claim (*of* or abs.); unwarrantable assumption. [f. L *arrogatio* (as prec., see -ATION)]

arrondissement (see Ap.), n. Administrative subdivision of French department. [F]

ă′rrow (-ō), n. Pointed missile shot from bow; index, pin, ornament, of similar shape; ‖ broad ∼, mark distinguishing British Government stores; ∼-*stitch*, triangular set of stitches securing whalebone in stays; ∼-*headed characters*, cuneiform; ∼-*root*, plant from which a nutritious starch is prepared. Hence ∼Y[2] (-ŏi) a. [OE *earh*, *arwe*, f. Gmc **arhw*-, cf. Goth. *arhwazna*; cogn. w. L *arcus* bow]

ărse, n. (not now in polite use). Buttocks, rump. [OE *ærs*, OHG, ON *ars*, Gmc **arsaz*, cogn. w. Gk *orrhos*]

ărs′enal, n. Public establishment for storage or manufacture of weapons & ammunition (also fig.). [f. It. *arsenale*, earlier *arzenà* f. Arab. *dar accina'ah* (*dar* house + *al* the + *çina'ah* art f. *çana'a* fabricate); *d*- dropped perh. by confus. w. *de* prep.; -*ale* added in It.]

ărs′enic[1], n. (Chem.) brittle steel-grey semi-metallic substance, crystallizing in rhombohedrons, & volatilizing without fusion with odour of garlic; (pop.) trioxide of ∼, white mineral substance, a violent poison; *flowers of* ∼, same sublimed. Hence **ărsěn′**ICAL a. [OF, f. L f. Gk *arsenikon* yellow orpiment (identified with *arsenikos* male, but in fact) f. Arab. *az-zernikh* the orpiment f. Pers. *zerni* (*zar* gold)]

ărsěn′ic[2], a. Of, belonging to, arsenic; esp. (Chem.) applied to compounds in which arsenic combines as a pentad. [f. prec., -*ic* being identified with -IC (1)]

ărsěn′ious, a. Containing arsenic; esp. applied to compounds in which arsenic combines as a triad. [f. ARSENIC n. + -IOUS; see also -OUS]

ărs′is, n. (pl. *arsēs*). Accented syllable in English scansion (cf. *thesis*). [f. LL f. Gk, = lifting f. *airō* lift; in what sense, & whether orig. of voice or foot (in beating time), is disputed]

ărs′on, n. Wilful setting on fire of another's house or similar property or one's own when insured. Hence **∼*IST n., incendiary. [legal AF *arso(u)n* (13th c.) = OF *arson* f. Rom. **arsionem* f. L *ardēre ars*- burn]

art·, v. See BE.

ărt[2], n. Skill, esp. human skill as opposed to nature; skilful execution as an object in itself; skill applied to imitation & design, as in painting etc.; (attrib.) of artistic design etc. (chiefly shop use: ∼ *needlework*, *carpet*, *curtain*); thing in which skill may be exercised; esp. (pl.) certain branches of learning serving as intellectual instruments for more advanced studies, as *Bachelor*, *Master*, *of Arts*, one who has obtained standard of proficiency in these; *black* ∼, magic; practical application of any science; industrial pursuit, craft; guild, company of craftsmen; *fine* ∼*s*, those in which mind & imagination are chiefly concerned; knack; cunning; stratagem; ∼ *&* (*or*) *part*, design & (or) execution, as *be* ∼ *& part in* (accessory in both respects). [ME, f. OF *art* f. L *artem*]

ărt′ĕfăct, ărt′ĭ-, n. A product of human art & workmanship; (Archaeol.) a product of prehistoric art as dist. from a similar object naturally produced. [f. L *arte* (abl. of *ars* art) + *factum* (neut. p.p. of *facere* make)]

ărtěl′, n. Collective enterprise of peasants or workers in the Soviet Union. [Russ.]

ărtēr′ial, a. Belonging to, of the nature of, resembling, an artery (now freq. of important main roads, & lines of transport or communication, as ∼ *railway*, *road*, *traffic*). [F *artère* ARTERY, see -AL]

ărtēr′ialĭe, ărtē|ǐa|c|e (-ĭz), v.t. Convert venous into arterial (blood) by exposure to oxygen in lungs; furnish with arterial system. Hence ∼A′TION n. [prec. + -IZE]

ărtēriōscler̄ōs′is, n. Hardening of the arteries, esp. as concomitant of old age. [see ARTERY, SCLER(O)-, -OSIS]

ărtēriŏt′omў, n. Opening of artery for blood-letting; dissection of arteries. [f. LL f. Gk *artēriotomia* (as foll., see -TOMY)]

ărt′er|ў, n. Tube forming part of system by which blood is conveyed from heart (cf. VEIN) to all parts of body (also fig.). Hence ∼IT′IS n. [ME, f. L f. Gk *artēria* prob. f. *airō* raise]

ărtē′sian (-zhn), a. ∼ *well*, perpendicular boring into strata, producing constant supply of water rising spontaneously to surface. [f. F *artésien* (*Artois*, old French province)]

ărt′ful, a. Cunning, crafty, deceitful, (of persons & actions). Hence ∼LY[2] adv., ∼NESS n. [ART[2] + -FUL]

ărthr|ĭt′is, n. Inflammation of joint; gout. So ∼ĭt′IC a. [L f. Gk (*arthron* joint, see -ITIS)]

ărthro-, comb. form of Gk *arthron* joint, as in *arthrōp′athy*, painful affection of joints, *arthrōs′is*, articulation.

ăr′thrōpŏd, n. (zool.). Member of *Arthrōp′oda*, consisting of animals with jointed body & limbs. [prec. + Gk *pous podos* foot]

Arthūr′ian (är-), a. Relating to King Arthur or his knights. [-IAN]

ărt′ĭchōke, n. Plant (of which bottom of flower & bases of its scales are edible) allied to thistles, native of Barbary; *Jerusalem* (corrupt. of *girasole*, sunflower) ∼, species of sunflower with edible tuberous roots. [f. It. *articiocco* corrupt. of **alcarcioffo* (mod. It. *carciofo*, OSp. *alcarchofa*) f. Arab. *alkharshuf*]

ärt′icle[1], n. Separate portion of anything written; separate clause (of agreement etc.) as *Thirty-nine A∼s, A∼s of war, Apprenticeship, Association*; literary composition forming part of magazine etc. but independent; *leading* ∼ in newspaper, ∼ expressing editorial opinion; particular; particular thing, as *the next* ∼; (Gram.) *definite* ∼, 'the', *indefinite* ∼, 'a, an'; *in the* ∼ (moment) *of death* (usu. *in artic′ulo mortis*). [ME, f. OF, f. L *articulus*, dim. of *artus* limb]

ärt′icle[2], v.t. Set forth in articles; indict; bind by articles of apprenticeship. [f. prec.]

ärtic′ūlar, a. Pertaining to the joints. [ME, f. L *articularis* (as ARTICLE[1], see -AR[1])]

ärtic′ūlate[1], a. & n. Jointed; distinctly jointed, distinguishable, as ∼ *speech*; (n.) ∼ animal. Hence ∼LY[2] (-tl-) adv., ∼NESS (-tn-) n. [f. L *articulatus* (as prec., see -ATE[2])]

ärtic′ūlāt|e[2], v.t. & i. Connect by joints, mark with apparent joints (usu. pass.); divide into words, pronounce distinctly; (intr.) speak distinctly. Hence ∼ORY a. [f. prec., see -ATE[3]]

ärticūlā′tion, n. Act, mode, of jointing; joint; articulate utterance, speech; consonant. [F, or f. L *articulatio* (*articulare* joint as ARTICLE[1], see -ATION)]

ärt′ifice, n. Device, contrivance; address, skill. [F, f. L *artificium* (*ars artis* art + -*ficium* making f. *facere* make)]

ärtif′icer, n. Craftsman; inventor (*of*). [ME, of uncert. orig.; OF had *artificien*, of which this may be an alteration]

ärtifi′cial (-shal), a. Made by art; not natural; not real, as ∼ *flowers*; real, but produced by art, as ∼ *ice*; ∼ *horizon*, device indicating attitude of aircraft to horizon; ∼ *respiration*, inducing of respiration by manual or mechanical means. Hence **ärtificiäl′ITY** (-shI-), ∼NESS, nn., ∼IZE v.t., ∼LY[2] adv. [ME, f. F -*el*, or L *artificialis* (as ARTIFICE, see -AL)]

ärtill′erў, n. Anti-aircraft, anti-tank, field, medium, heavy, & mountain guns used by an army; branch or arm of the service that uses these; ∼-*train*, ordnance mounted on carriages & ready for marching. Hence **ärtill′erIST**,∼**man**, nn. [ME, f. OF *artillerie* f. *artiller* equip, arm; see -ERY]

ärtisăn′ (-z-), n. Mechanic, handicraftsman. [F, f. It. *artigiano* f. Rom. **artitianus* (*artitus* p.p. of *artire* instruct in arts, see -AN)]

ärt′ist, n. One who practises one of the fine arts, esp. painting; ∼'s *proof*, copy of engraving taken for ∼'s approval or correction & valued as fresher than ordinary copies; one who makes his craft a fine art (∼ *in words* etc.). Hence **ärtis′tic**(AL) aa., **ärtis′tically**[2] adv., ∼RY n. [f. F *artiste* f. It. *artista* (*arte* ART, see -IST)]

ärtiste′ (-tē-), n. Professional singer, dancer, etc. [F, see prec.]

ärt′less, a. Unskilful, uncultured; clumsy; natural; guileless, ingenuous. Hence ∼LY[2] adv., ∼NESS n. [ART[2] + -LESS]

ärt′ў, a. (colloq.). Pretentiously artistic; (of persons) aping the artistic; ∼-&-*crafty*, (joc., usu. of furniture) remarkable rather for specially artistic style than for usefulness or comfort (after the *Arts & Crafts* Exhibition Society). [-Y[2]]

ar′um, n. Kinds of monocotyledonous plants including wake-robin; ∼ *lily* (tall & white-spathed). [L, f. Gk *aron*]

-arў[1], suf. forming adjj. & nn. f. L -*arius*, -*arium* taken directly, or thr. later F learned-adoptives in -*aire*, or formed in E on L nn.; adjj. as *arbitrary, contrary, primary*; nn. = -*arius*, as *actuary, adversary*, = -*arium*, as *dictionary*, = -*aria*, as *fritillary*. The popular forms in OF ended in -*ier* (*premier* PREMIER). OF -*ier* = AF -*er*, whence ME -*er* as in *danger, carpenter* (-ER[2]), *mortar, vicar* (-AR[2]).

-arў[2], suf. Occas. in adjj. f. L-*aris* instead of regular -AR[1], thr. F learned adoptives in -*aire*, which repr. both L -*arius* (e.g. L *contrarius*, F- *aire*, E -ARY[1]) & L -*aris* (e.g. L *militaris*, F -*aire*, E -ARY[2]).

Ar′yan (ār-), a. & n. **1.** Applied by some to family of languages (also called *Indo-European, Indo-Germanic*) that includes Sanskrit, Iranian, Greek, Latin, Celtic, Germanic, Slavonic, with their modern representatives, by others only to the Indo-Iranian portion of these. **2.** n. Member of ∼ family; in Nazi Germany esp. contrasted with SEMITE. [f. Skr. *arya* noble (in earlier use a national name comprising worshippers of the gods of the Brahmans); earlier *Arian* is f. L *Arianus* of Aria (f. Gk *Areia* eastern Persia)]

as[1] (ăz, az), adv., conj., rel. pron. **1.** adv. (in main sentence, foll. by *as* in subord. clause expressed or understood) in the same degree, as *I came as soon as I could, I know that as well as you, you might as well help me, as* FAR[1] *as*. **2.** rel. adv. or conj. in subord. clause, with or without antecedent *as, so*, expressing manner, degree, etc., of the principal sentence; (degree) *you are as good as he, it is not so* (or *as*) *easy as you think, quick as thought he jumped out, fair as* (= though) *she is*; (manner) *do as you like, according as we decide, he looks as if he had seen a ghost, treat him as a stranger, you are, as it were* (= as if it were actually so), *compromised, they rose as one man, late as usual, he smiled, as who should say* (= as a man would smile who); (time) *it struck me as I was speaking*; (reason) *as you are not ready, we must go on*; (result) *he so arranged matters as to suit everyone, be so good as to come*; (illustration) *cathedral cities, as Norwich*. **3.** rel. pron. That, who, which, as *I had the same trouble as you*, *such countries as Spain*; (with antecedent inferred from main sentence) *he was a foreigner, as* (which fact) *they perceived from his accent.* **4.** Special phrases: *as for*, with regard to; *as from* (in formal dating, as *coal will be decontrolled as from 31st March*); *as regards*, so far as it concerns; *as to*, with respect to (*said nothing as to hours, as to when he would come; as to you, I despise you*); *as yet*, up to this time; *I thought as much*, I thought so; *as well (as)*, in addition (to); *as good as dead*, practically dead. **5.** Phrases in *(as) . . . as* expressing by reference to a proverbial type the highest or a high degree of some quality, & in alliterative or punning phrr. modelled on these: *bald as a coot, black as pitch, blind as a bat, bold as brass, brave as a lion, bright as a new pin, brown as a berry, busy as a bee, cold as charity, common as dirt, cool as a cucumber, cross as two sticks, dead as a doornail, dead as mutton, deaf as a post, drunk as a fiddler, drunk as a lord, dry as a bone, dull as ditchwater, easy as ABC, easy as lying, fit as a fiddle, flat as a pancake, good as gold* (of children's conduct), *good as a play* (amusing), *hard as nails, heavy as lead, hungry as a hunter, jolly as a sandboy, keen as mustard, large as life, light as air, mad as a hatter, mad as a March hare, meek as Moses, merry as a grig, old as the hills, pale as a ghost, plain as a pikestaff, pleased as Punch, plentiful as blackberries, plump as a partridge, proud as a peacock, proud as Lucifer, quick as thought, quiet as a mouse, right as a trivet, right as rain, safe as a house, sharp as a needle, silent as the grave, snug as a bug in a rug, soft as butter, soft as velvet, sound as a bell, stiff as a poker, straight as a die, strong as a horse, stubborn as a mule, sure as fate, thick as thieves, thin as a lath, tight as a drum, true as steel, ugly as sin, warm as (a) toast, weak as a rat, weak as water, white as a sheet.* [worn-down form of OE *al(l)swā* ALSO, later *alsa, als*]

ăs², n. Roman copper coin, orig. weighing 12 oz., but finally reduced to ½ oz. [L]

as-, pref. = AD- before *s*.

ăsafoet′ida (-fēt-) n. Concreted resinous gum with strong smell of garlic used in medicine and cookery. [med. L (*asa* f. Pers. *aza* mastic +FETID)]

asbĕs′tine (ăz-), a. Of, like, asbestos, incombustible (lit. & fig.). [f. L f. Gk *asbestinos* f. foll., see -INE²]

asbĕs′t|ŏs (ăz-), n. Fibrous mineral that can be woven into an incombustible fabric (also fig.). Hence ~IC, ~OID, aa. [f. L f. Gk, = unquenchable (*a-* not +*sbestos* f. *sbennumi* quench)]

ascĕnd′, v.t. & i. Go, come, up; (of things) rise, be raised; slope upwards, lie along ~ing slope; rise in thought, rank, degree of quality; (of sounds) rise in pitch; go back in point of time; (trans.)

go up, climb; ~ *a river*, go along it towards its source; mount upon, as ~ *the throne*. [ME, f. L *ascendere*, AD(*scendere scens-* = *scandere* climb)]

ascĕn′dancy̆, -ency̆, n. Dominant control, sway, (*over*). [f. after foll., see -ANCY]

ascĕn′dant, -ent, a. & n. **1.** Rising; (Astron.) rising towards zenith; (Astrol.) just above eastern horizon; predominant. **2.** n. Horoscope; point of ecliptic or degree of zodiac that (esp. at birth of child) is just rising above eastern horizon; *house of the* ~ (from 5 degrees of zodiac above this point to 25 below it); *lord of the* ~, any planet within this; *in the* ~, supreme, dominating, (improp.) rising; supremacy; ancestor. [ME, f. OF (*-ant*) f. L as ASCEND, see -ENT]

ascĕn′sion (-shon), n. Act of ascending; ascent of Christ on fortieth day after resurrection; *A~-day*, Holy Thursday, on which this is commemorated; *A~tide*, period of ten days from *A~-day* to Whitsun Eve; rising of a celestial body, as *right* ~ (celestial longitude). Hence ~AL a. [f. L *ascensio* (as ASCEND, see -ION)]

ascĕn′sive, a. Rising, progressive; (Gram.) intensive. [as prec., see -IVE]

ascĕnt′, n. Act of ascending; upward movement, rise, (lit. & fig.); way by which one may ascend, slope, flight of steps. [f. ASCEND on anal. of *descent*]

ăscertain′, v.t. Find out (for certain), get to know. Hence ~ABLE a., ~MENT n. [ME, f. OF *acertener*, st. *acertaine-* (à to +CERTAIN)]

ascĕt′ic, a. & n. Severely abstinent, austere; (n.) one who practises severe self-discipline, esp. (Eccl. Hist.) one who retired into solitude for this purpose. Hence ~AL a., ~alLY² adv., ~ISM (-sĭzm) n. [f. Gk *askētikos* f. *askētēs* monk (*askeō* exercise), see -ETE and -IC]

ascid′ium (asĭd-), n. Kinds of marine organism with leathery enveloping tunic, regarded as link in development of Vertebrata. [mod. L, f. Gk *askidion* dim. of *askos* wine-skin]

Asclēp′iad, n. (Gk and Lat. Prosody) verse consisting of a spondee, two or three choriambi, & an iambus. Hence ~ē′AN a. [f. LL f. Gk *Asklēpiadeios* (*Asklēpiadēs*, Greek poet, the inventor)]

As′cot (ă-), n. Racecourse on ~ Heath, Berks.; race-meeting at ~.

ascribe′, v.t. Attribute, impute, (*to*); consider as belonging (*to* person or thing). Hence or cogn. **ascrib′ABLE** a., **ascrip′-tion** n., (esp.) preacher's words ascribing praise to God at end of sermon. [ME *ascrive* f. OF *ascriv-* st. of *ascrire* f. L AD(*scribere script-* write)]

As′dic (ăz-), n. Device for detecting submarine. [f. initials of *Allied Submarine Detection Investigation Committee*]

āsē′ity̆, n. (metaphys.). Underived existence, the being uncreate. [f. med. L *aseitas* f. L *a se* from oneself; see -ITY]

asĕp′sis, n. Absence of putrefactive matter or harmful bacteria; the aseptic method in surgery. [A- (7) + Gk *sēpsis* decay (*sēpō*, see foll.)]

asĕp′tic, a. & n. Free from putrefaction or blood-poisoning; surgically sterile, sterilized, (of wounds, instruments, dressings); (of method etc.) seeking the absence (rather than counteraction, cf. *antiseptic*) of septic matter; (n.) non-putrescent substance. [A- (7) + Gk *sēptikos* putrefying (*sēpō* rot, see -IC)]

asĕx′ūal, a. (biol.). Without sex. Hence **asĕxūăl′ITY** n. [A- (7) + SEXUAL]

ăsh¹, n. Forest-tree with silver-grey bark, pinnate foliage, & close-grained wood; wood of this; ~-*fly*, ~-*grub*, (found on ~ & used by anglers); ~-*key*, winged seed of the ~; ~-*leaf*, an early potato; *mountain* ~, rowan-tree. [OE *æsc*, OHG *ask*, ON *askr*, f. Gmc *ask-az*]

ăsh², n. (usu. pl.). Powdery residue left after combustion of any substance; (pl.) remains of human body after cremation (lit. & fig.); *lay in* ~*es*, burn to the ground; *sackcloth & ~es* (symbol of repentance); || *bring back the ~es* (Crick.), wipe out defeat in series of test matches between England & Australia; * ~′*can*, dustbin; ~-*fire*, low fire used in chemical operations; ~-*furnace* (used in glass-making); *Ash Wednesday*, first day of Lent (from Rom. Cath. custom of sprinkling ~es on penitents' heads). [OE *asce*, OHG *asca*, ON *aska*, Goth. *azgo*, f. Gmc *azgon*]

ashāmed′ (-md), pred. a. Abashed, disconcerted, by consciousness of guilt; ~ *of* (conduct); ~ *for* (on account of) *you*; ~ *to do* (implying reluctance, but not always abstention). [p.p. of obs. vb *ashame* (A- (1) + OE *scamian* SHAME)]

ăsh′en¹, a. Pertaining to an ash-tree; made of ash. [ASH¹ + -EN⁵]

ăsh′en², a. Of ashes; ash-coloured, pale. [ASH² + -EN⁵]

ăsh′et, n. (Sc.). Big (usu. oval) plate. [f. F *assiette*]

Ashkenazim (ăshkĭnahz′ĭm), n. pl. Polish-German Jews (as dist. from SEPHARDIM). [mod. Heb., f. *Askenaz* (*Gen.* x. 3)]

ăsh′lar, n. Square hewn stone(s); masonry constructed of this; similar masonry as facing to rubble or brick wall. [ME, f. OF *aisel(i)er* (-ER²) supporting beam, ult. f. L *axis*, *assis* axle, board; see -AR²]

ăsh′laring, n. Short upright boarding in garrets, cutting off acute angle formed by roof with floor; ashlar masonry. [prec. + -ING¹]

ashōre′, adv. To, on to, on, shore. [A prep.]

ăsh′y̆, a. Of ashes; covered with ashes; ash-coloured, pale. [ASH² + -Y²]

Asian (āsh′an), a. & n. (Native) of Asia (now preferred to *Asiatic*). [f. L f. Gk *Asianos* (*Asia*, see -AN)]

Asiăt′ic (āshǐ-), a. & n. Asian. [f. L f. Gk *Asiatikos* (*Asiatēs* f. *Asia*, see -IC)]

aside′, adv. & n. **1.** To, on, one side,

away; * ~ (apart) *from*; *set* ~, quash (verdict); *speak* ~ (apart, in privacy). **2.** n. Words spoken ~, esp. spoken by an actor & supposed not to be heard by other performers; indirect effort. [orig. *on side*, see A prep.]

ăs′inine, a. Pertaining to asses; stupid. Hence **ăsinin′ITY** n. [f. L *asininus* (*asinus* ass, -INE¹)]

-asis, suf. forming names of diseases. [L -*āsis* f. Gk -*āsis* in nouns of stat . vbs in -*aō*]

ask (ah-), v.t. & i. Call for an answer to, as ~ (*him*) *a question*, ~ (*him*) *this*, (*him*) *who it is*, ~ *him the time*, ~ *a question of a person*, ~ *him about a thing*; make a request (for), as ~ *a favour of him*, ~ (*him*) *a favour*, ~ (*him*) *for it*, *ask* (abs.), ~ *him to do it*, ~ *that it may be done*, ~ *to have time given one*; invite (person *to* dinner etc., or *out*); (of things) demand, require, as *it* ~*s* (*for*) *attention*; ~ (publish) *the banns*; (pop.) *be* ~*ed in church*, have one's banns called; ~ *for trouble*, ~ *for it* (sl.), court trouble; *if you* ~ *me*, in my opinion. [OE *āscian*, *ācsian*, OHG *eiscon*, f. WG *aiskojan*; *æx* was usu. literary form to 1600]

askănce′, -ănt′, adv. Sideways, asquint; with indirect meaning; *look* ~ *at*, view suspiciously. [etym. unkn.]

ăskar′i (-ahr-), n. European-trained African native soldier. [Arab. *'askarī* soldier; pl. occas. as sing.]

askew′, adv. & pred. a. Obliquely; *look* ~ (not straight in the face); (adj.) oblique. [A prep. + SKEW]

aslant′ (-ahnt), adv. & prep. Obliquely; (prep.) slantingly across, athwart. [A prep. + SLANT]

asleep′, adv. & pred. a. In, into, a state of sleep (lit. & fig.); (of limbs) benumbed; (of top) spinning without apparent motion. [A prep. + SLEEP]

aslōpe′, adv. & pred. a. Sloping, crosswise. [perh. f. OE *aslopen* p.p. of *aslupan* slip away]

ăsp¹, n. (also *aspen*). Kind of poplar with specially tremulous leaves. [OE *æspe*, OHG *aspa*, f. WG *aspōn*]

ăsp², n. Small venomous hooded serpent of Egypt and Libya; (poet.) any venomous serpent. [ME, f. L f. Gk *aspis*]

aspā′ragus, n. Plant, whose vernal shoots are a table delicacy. [L, f. Gk *asparagos*]

ăs′pĕct, n. Way of looking; a looking, fronting, in a given direction; side so fronting; phase; look, expression; appearance (esp. to the mind); (Gram.) a verbal form expressing action or being in respect of its inception, duration, or completion. [ME, f. L *aspectus -ūs* (AD-*spicere -spect-* look at)]

ăs′pĕn, a. & n. Of, like, the asp (tree); quivering; (n.) = ASP¹. [ASP¹ + -EN; wrongly taken as noun used attrib. in *aspen leaf* etc.]

äspergill'um, n. Brush for sprinkling holy water. [med. L, f. *aspergere* (*ad* to + *spargere* sprinkle) + *-illum* dim. suf.]

äspe͞'rit̯y̆, n. Roughness; severity (of weather); harshness, sharpness, (of temper). [ME *asprete* f. OF f. L *asperitatem* (*asper* rough, see -TY), whence mod. form]

aspe͞rse', v.t. Besprinkle (*with*); bespatter (person, character, *with* damaging reports); calumniate. So **aspe͞r'sion** (-shn) n. [f. L *aspergere -ers-*, see ASPER-GILLUM]

äspersör'ium, n. Vessel for holy water. [med. L (as prec., see -ORY)]

äs'phält[1], n. A smooth hard bituminous substance; mixture of bitumen, pitch, & sand, for pavements etc.; similar mixture of coal-tar with sand etc. Hence **äsphäl'tic** a. [ME, ult. f. LL *asphaltum*, *-um*, f. Gk *asphaltos* of foreign orig.]

äs'phält[2], v.t. Lay (road) with asphalt. [f. prec.]

äs'phodĕl, n. Plant of lily family; (poet.) immortal flower in Elysium. [f. L f. Gk *asphodelos*; earlier *affodil*, whence DAFFO-DIL]

äsphyx'i̯|a, -x'y̆, n. Suspended animation due to lack of oxygen in blood, suffocation. Hence ~AL a., ~ATE[3] v.t., ~A'TION n. [mod. L f. Gk *asphuxia* (*a-* not + *sphuxis* pulse)]

äs'pic[1], n. (poet.). = ASP[2]. [F, f. L *aspidem*, nom. *-is*, w. unexpl. *-ic*]

äs'pic[2], n. Savoury meat jelly with cold game, eggs, etc., in it. [F, of disputed etym.]

äspidis'tra, n. Foliage plant with broad taper leaves, freq. grown as a house plant. [mod. L f. Gk *aspis* shield]

äs'pirant (*or* aspīr[2]-), a. & n. (One) who aspires (*to, after, for*). [F, or f. L as foll., see -ANT]

äs'pirate[1], a. & n. (Consonant) pronounced with a breathing, blended with sound of *h*; the sound of *h*. [f. L *aspirare*, see ASPIRE and -ATE[2]]

äs'pirate[2], v.t. Pronounce with a breathing; draw out (gas) from vessel. [as prec., see -ATE[3]]

äspirā'tion, n. Drawing of breath; desire (*for, after*); action of aspirating. [f. OF, or f. L *aspiratio* (as prec., see -ATION)]

äs'pirātor, n. Apparatus for drawing air, gas, through tube; instrument for drawing pus from abscesses; winnowing--machine. [f. L *aspirare*, see foll. and -OR]

aspīre', v.i. Desire earnestly (*to, after, at, to do,* or abs.); mount up (usu. fig.). [f. F, or L AD(*spirare* breathe)]

äs'pirin, n. An analgetic & febrifuge. [P]

asquint', adv. & pred. a. (With *look* or similar vb) obliquely, out at the corner of the eyes (esp. through defect in the eyes). [hist. & etym. unkn.; w. second element cf. Du. *schuinte* slant, slope]

äss (*or* ahs), n. Quadruped of horse family with long ears & tuft at end of tail (used esp. as type of ignorance, stupidity, etc.); *make an ~ of*, stultify (one*self*, or another); *asses' bridge* (*pons asinorum*), Euclid I, 5 'The angles at the base of an isosceles triangle are equal to one another'. [f. OE *assa*, not repr. outside OE, f. (thr. Celt.) L *asinus*, whence also OE *esol, eosol*, (OHG *esil*, Goth. *asilus*) which did not survive]

äss'agai, -sĕgai, (-gī), n. Slender spear of hard wood, esp. a missile of S. African tribes. [f. obs. F *azagaye* (mod. *zagaie*) f. Arab. *azzaghayah* (*al* the + Berber word *zaghayah*)]

assa'i (-ah-ē), adv. (mus.). Very. [It.]

assail', v.t. Make hostile attack upon (lit. & fig.); approach resolutely (task); overwhelm (*with* questions etc.). Hence ~ABLE a., ~ANT n. [ME, f. OF *asalir*, *asaillir*, f. med. L *assalire* f. L ASsilire (*salire salt-* leap)]

assäss'in, n. One who undertakes to kill treacherously; (hist.) Moslem fanatic in time of Crusades, sent by the Old Man of the Mountains to murder Christians. [F, or f. med. L *assassinus* f. Arab. *ḥashshash, ḥashishiyy* hashish-eater]

assäss'in|āte, v.t. Kill by treacherous violence. Hence ~A'TION, ~ātor, nn. [f. med. L *assassinare* (*assassinus*), see prec. and -ATE[3]]

assault'[1], n. Hostile attack (lit. & fig.); *~ of, at, arms*, attack in fencing, display of military exercises; rush against walls of fortress etc., as *carry by ~*; (Law) unlawful personal attack (including menacing words), as *~ & battery*; (euphem. for) rape (of woman). [ME, f. OF *asaut* f. Rom. **assaltus* (as ASSAIL)]

assault'[2], v.t. Make violent attack upon (lit. & fig.); assail; (euphem. for) rape (woman); attack (fortress) by sudden rush. Hence ~ABLE a. [ME, f. OF *asauter* f. Rom. **assaltare* spring at, for L **AS(sultare* frequent. of *salire sali-* leap)]

assay'[1], n. Trial of metals, esp. of fineness of coin or bullion; metal to be so tried; (arch.) attempt. [ME, f. OF *assai*, var. of *essai* (see ESSAY[1]), f. LL *exagium* weighing (*exigere, -agere,* weigh, try)]

assay'[2], v.t. & i. Try the purity of (precious metals, also fig.); attempt (anything difficult, *to do*). Hence ~ABLE a. [ME, f. OF *asayer, essayer* (see ESSAY[2]) f. Rom. **exagiare* (*exagium,* see prec.)]

assĕm'blage, n. Bringing, coming, together; concourse of persons; collection. [F (*assembler*, see foll. and -AGE)]

assĕm'ble, v.t. & i. Gather together, collect; (Mech.) fit together the parts of (machine, structure). [ME, f. OF *asembler* f. L ASsimulare in the (late) sense of bring together (*simul*)]

assĕm'bly̆, n. Gathering together, concourse, esp. deliberative body, legislative council; military call by drum or bugle; assembling a machine or its parts; ~ *line*, group of machines & workers operating on some product to be assembled; ~ *room*: room in which balls etc. are given; (also ~ *shop*) place where a machine or its parts are assembled. [ME, f. OF *asemblée* fem. p.p. of *asembler*, see prec.]

assent'[1], v.i. Agree (*to* proposal), defer (*to* a desire); express agreement (*to* statement or opinion, or abs.). Hence ~OR n. [ME, f. OF *asenter* f. L *assentari*, irreg. frequent. of Assentiri agree to (*sentire* think)]

assent'[2], n. (Official) concurrence, sanction, as *royal* ~ (of sovereign to bill passed by Parliament); mental acceptance. [ME, f. OF *asent(e)* (*asenter*, see prec.)]

assenta'tion, n. Obsequious concurrence. [F, f. L *assentationem* (as ASSENT, see -ATION)]

assen'tient (-shǐ-), a. & n. (Person) that assents. [f. L *assentient-* (*assentiri*, see ASSENT[1], -ENT)]

assert', v.t. Vindicate a claim to (rights); ~ *oneself*, insist upon one's rights; declare. Hence ~ABLE, ~IVE, aa., ~ively[2] (-vl-) adv., ~iveness (-vn-) n. [f. L As(*serere sert-* join) put one's hand on slave's head to free him]

asser'tion, n. Insistence upon a right; *self-*~, insistence on recognition of one's claims; affirmation, positive statement. [F, or f. L *assertio* (as prec., see -ION)]

assert'or, n. One who asserts; champion, advocate, (*of*). [L (as prec., see -OR)]

assess', v.t. Fix amount of (taxes, fine); fix amount of & impose (*upon* person or community); fine, tax, (person, community, property, *in*, *at*, so much); estimate value of (property) for taxation. Hence ~ABLE a., ~ably[2] adv., ~MENT n. [ME, f. OF *assesser* f. med. L *assessare* frequent. of As(*sidēre sess-* = *sedēre* sit)]

assess'or, n. One who sits as assistant, adviser, to judge or magistrate; one who assesses taxes or estimates value of property for taxation. [ME, f. OF *assessour* f. L *assessorem* assistant-judge (as prec., see -OR)]

ass'ets, n. pl. (sing. *-et*). (Law) enough goods to enable heir to discharge debts & legacies of testator; property liable to be so applied; effects of insolvent debtor; property of person or company that may be made liable for debts; (sing.) item of this in balance-sheet, (loosely) any possession, (colloq.) any useful quality. [f. AF *asetz* f. OF *asez* enough f. Rom. **assatis* (L *ad* to +*satis* enough)]

assev'er|āte, v.t. Solemnly declare. So ~A'TION n. [f. L Asseverare (*severus* serious), see -ATE[3]]

assib'il|āte, v.t. Give a hissing sound to. Hence ~A'TION n. [f. L Assibilare hiss, see -ATE[3]]

assidū'itý, n. Close attention; (pl.) constant attentions. [f. L *assiduitas* (*assiduus*, see foll. and -TY)].

assid'ūous, a. Persevering, diligent. Hence ~LY[2] adv., ~NESS n. [f. L *assiduus* (as ASSESS)+-OUS]

assign'[1] (-īn), v.t. Allot as a share (*to*); make over (esp. personal property, *to*); appoint (place etc. *to*); fix, specify; ascribe, refer, (event *to* date); ascribe (reason *to*, *for*, thing). Hence ~ABLE (-īn-) a., **assign'or'** (-īn-) n. [ME, f. OF *assigner* f. L Assignare mark out to (*signum* sign)]

assign'[2] (-īn), n. One to whom property, right, is legally transferred. [ME *assigne* (three syllables) f. F *assigné* p.p. of *assigner* (see prec.) gives both *assign* & *assignee*]

ass'ignāt, n. Paper money issued by revolutionary government (1790–95) of France. [F, f. L *assignatum*, neut. p.p. of *assignare* assign]

assignā'tion, n. Apportionment; formal transference; appointment (of time & place); *illicit love meeting. [ME, f. OF *assignacion* f. L *assignationem* (as ASSIGN[1], see -ATION)]

assignee' (-īn-), n. One appointed to act for another; assign; ~*s in bankruptcy*, persons charged with management of bankrupt's estate. [ME, f. OF *a(s)signé*, see ASSIGN n.]

assign'ment (-īn-), n. Allotment; legal transference; document effecting this; attribution; statement (of reasons); *task allotted to person. [ME, f. OF *assignement* f. med. L *assignamentum* (as ASSIGN[1], see -MENT)]

assim'il|āte, v.t. & i. Make like (*to*, *with*); (now rare) compare (*to*, *with*); absorb into the system (lit. & fig.); (intr.) be so absorbed. Hence or cogn. ~ABIL'ITY, ~A'TION, ~ātOR, nn., ~ABLE, ~ātive, ~ātORY aa. [f. L *assimilare*, by-form of *assimulare* (see ASSEMBLE) after *similis* like; see -ATE[3]]

assist', v.t. & i., & n. **1.** Help (person, process, person in doing), whence ~ANT a. & n., ~ANCE n. **2.** v.i. Take part (*in*); be present (*at*). **3.** n. *(Baseball) score credited to fielder who stops & throws in the ball to player nearest the base to which an opponent is running, so helping to put him out. [f. F *assister* f. L Assistere take one's stand by]

assize', n. Statutory price (of bread and ale); trial in which sworn assessors decide questions of fact, ‖esp. periodical sessions in each county of England & Wales for administration of civil & criminal justice; *great* ~, last judgement. [ME, f. OF *asise*, fem. sing. p.p. (as n.) of *asēeir* (mod. F. *asseoir*) sit at f. L *assidēre*, cf. ASSESS]

asso'ci|able (-sha-), a. That can be connected in thought (*with*). Hence ~ABIL'ITY n. [F, f. associer (as foll., see -ABLE)]

asso'ciate[1] (-shǐ-), a. & n. **1.** Joined in companionship, function, or dignity; allied. **2.** n. Partner; companion; colleague; subordinate member of a body, institute, etc.; thing connected with another. Hence ~SHIP n. [f. L Associare (socius sharing, allied), see -ATE²]

asso'ciat|e² (-shi-), v.t. & i. Join (persons, things, or one with another); connect in idea; make oneself a partner in (a matter); (intr.) combine for common purpose; have intercourse (with). Hence ~IVE, ~ORY, aa., ~OR n. [as prec., see -ATE³]

associa'tion, n. Act of associating (in all senses); organized body of persons; ‖ deed of ~, document giving particulars of limited liability company; fellowship, intimacy; ~ of ideas, mental connexion between an object & ideas related to it; ‖ ~ football (abbr. soccer), kind played with round ball, which may not be handled except by goalkeeper (cf. RUGBY). [F, or f. med. L associatio (as prec., see -ATION)]

assoil', v.t. (arch.). Absolve from sin, pardon; acquit; release; atone for. [ME, f. OF a(s)soil-, tonic stem of a(s)soldre f. L AB(solvere loose); Sc. has assoilzie (pron. -yī) still used in sense 'acquit']

ass'on|ance, n. Resemblance of sound between two syllables; rhyming of one word with another in the accented vowel & those that follow, but not in the consonants (e.g. sonnet, porridge); partial correspondence. So ~ANT a. [F, f. L assonare respond to (sonus sound), see -ANCE]

assort', v.t. & i. Classify, arrange in sorts; group with others; furnish (store, shop) with an assortment; (intr.) associate with; fall into a class; suit well or ill with. [f. OF assorter (à to + sorte SORT)]

assort'ment, n. Assorting; assorted set of goods of one or several classes. [-MENT]

assuage' (-sw-), v.t. Calm, soothe, (person, feelings, pain); appease (appetite, desire). Hence ~MENT (aswāj'm-) n. [ME, f. OF asouager f. Rom. *Assuaviare (suavis sweet)]

assum|e', v.t. Take upon oneself (aspect, air); ~ing, taking much upon oneself, arrogant; undertake (office, duty); usurp; simulate; take for granted.(thing, thing to be, that). Hence ~'ABLE a., ~'abLY² adv. [ME, f. L AS(sumere sumpt- take)]

assump'tion, n. Act of assuming (in all senses); (A~) reception of Virgin Mary into heaven, feast in honour of this; thing assumed; arrogance. [ME, f. L assumptio (as ASSUME, see -ION)]

assump'tive, a. Taken for granted; arrogant. [f. L assumptivus (as prec., see -IVE)]

assur'ance (ashoor-), n. Formal guarantee; positive declaration; (Law) securing of a title; compact securing value of property in the event of its being lost, or payment of specified sum on person's death (usu. life-~, fire-, marine-, insurance); certainty (make ~ double sure, remove all possible doubt, Shakesp.,

Macb. IV. i. 83); self-confidence; impudence. [ME, f. OF aseûrance (aseûrer, see foll. & -ANCE)]

assure (ashoor'), v.t. Make safe; ~ life (see prec.); make certain, ensure the happening etc. of; make (person) sure (of fact); tell (person) confidently (of a thing, of its being so, that it is so). Hence assur'édLY² adv., assur'édNESS n., (-shoor-). [ME, f. OF aseûrer f. Rom. *AS-securare (securus safe)]

assu'rgent, a. Rising; (Bot.) rising obliquely; aggressive. [f. L Assurgere rise, see -ENT]

Assy̆rio̱|l'ogy̆, n. Study of language, history, antiquities, of Assyria. Hence ~L'OGIST n. [f. L f. Gk Assuria + -LOGY]

astat'ic, a. Not tending to keep one position; ~ galvanometer, one in which the effect on the needle of the earth's magnetic field is greatly reduced; ~ needle (unaffected by earth's magnetism). [f. Gk astatos unstable (a- not + sta-stand) + -IC]

äs'ter, n. Kinds of plants with showy radiated flowers; China ~, flower allied to this. [L, f. Gk astēr star]

-aster, suf. expressing contempt, added to L and Rom. nn., as oleaster, poetaster, meaning 'petty, sham, would-be'. [L, as in philosophaster]

äs'terisk, n., & v.t. Star (*) used to mark words for reference or distinction; (v.t.) mark with ~. [f. LL f. Gk asteriskos dim. as ASTER]

äs'terism, n. Cluster of stars; three asterisks (*₀*), calling attention. [f. Gk asterismos (ASTER, see -ISM)]

astern', adv. (naut.). In, at, the stern; away behind; ~ of, behind (a ship, boat); backwards. [A prep. + STERN²]

äs'teroid, a. & n. 1. Star-shaped. 2. n. Name of small planets revolving round sun between orbits of Mars and Jupiter; kind of firework. Hence ~AL (-oid²) a. [f. Gk asteroeidēs (ASTER, see -OID)]

ästhen'ia (or -ēnī'a), n. (med.). Loss of strength, debility. Hence ästhen'ic a. & n. [mod. L f. Gk (A- (7) + sthenos strength) + -IA¹]

ästh'ma (-sm-), n. A disease of respiration, characterized by difficult breathing, cough, etc. [ME asma f. med. L asma f. Gk asthma -matos]

ästhmät'ic (-sm-), a. & n. Pertaining to, suffering from, good against, asthma; (n.) person suffering from asthma. Hence ~AL a., ~alLY² adv. [f. L f. Gk asthmatikos (as prec., see -IC)]

‖ asthore', n. (voc.). Darling. [Ir., voc. of stōr treasure]

astig'matism, n. Structural defect in the eye or a lens, preventing rays of light from being brought to common focus. So ästigmät'ic a. [A- (7) + Gk STIGMA -matos point + -IC]

astir', adv. & pred. a. In motion; out of bed; in excitement. [A prep. + STIR n.]

astŏn'ish, v.t. Amaze, surprise; *astonied* (arch. p.p. of *astony*, see etym.), dazed, dismayed. Hence ~MENT n. [altered f. obs. *astony* unexpl. form of obs. *astone* apparently f. OF *estoner*, *estuner* (mod. *étonner*), stupefy, shock, f. Gallo-Rom. *EX*tonare* (alt. f. L *attonare* strike with thunderbolt, stun); relation to STUN and G *staunen* is uncertain]

astound', v.t. Shock with alarm or surprise; amaze. [f. obs. *astound* a.=*astoned* p.p. of obs. *astone*, see prec.]

astrăd'dle, adv. & pred. a. In a straddling position. [A prep.+STRADDLE v.]

ăs'tragal, n. (Archit.) small moulding round top or bottom of columns; (Gunnery) ring round cannon near mouth. [f. foll.]

astrăg'alus, n. Ball of ankle-joint; kinds of leguminous plants including milk-vetch. [L, f. Gk *astragalos* huckle-bone, moulding, plant]

ăstrakhăn' (-kăn), n. Skin of young lambs from Astrakhan in Russia, with wool like fur.

ăs'tral, a. Connected with, consisting of, stars; ~ *spirits* (supposed to live in stars); ~ *body*, spiritual appearance of the human form; ~ *hatch*, dome-shaped window in aircraft through which the navigator takes astronomical observations; ~ *lamp* (throwing no shadow on table below). [f. LL *astralis* (*astrum* star, see -AL)]

astray', adv. or pred. a. Out of the right way (lit. & fig.). [OF *estraié* p.p. of *estraier* f. Rom. *extravagare wander out of bounds; but confused w. forms like *a-float*, *a-sleep*; no early noun *stray*]

astrict', v.t. (rare). Bind tightly; make costive; bind morally, legally; restrict (*to*). So **astric'tion** n. [f. L *astringere* -*ict*- (*ad* to +*stringere* bind)]

astric'tive, a. Tending to contract organic tissue; astringent, styptic. [as prec., see -IVE]

astride', adv., pred. a., & prep. In striding position; with legs on each side (*of*); ~ *of the road* etc., (Mil.) posted across it; (prep.) ~ of. [A prep.+STRIDE n.]

astringe' (-nj), v.t. Bind together; compress; constipate. [as ASTRICT]

astrin'gent (-nj-), a. & n. Binding, styptic; severe; austere; (n.) medicine. Hence ~LY² adv., **astrin'gency** n. [as prec., see -ENT]

astro-, in comb.=Gk *astron* star; in wds f. Gk, as ASTRONOMY, & mod. formations as *astrŏg'onў*, stellar cosmogony, *ăstro-lithŏl'ogў*, study of meteoric stones; *ăs'trodŏme*, *ăs'trohătch*, = ASTRAL *hatch*; *ăs'tronaut*, student or devotee of *ăstronaut'ics*, science of aerial navigation in space; *ăstrophўs'ics*, branch of astronomy dealing with the physics & chemistry of the heavenly bodies.

ăs'troïte, n. Gem known to the ancients;

kind of madrepore. [f. L f. Gk *astroïtes* (see prec. and -ITE¹)]

ăs'trolăbe, n. Instrument formerly used for taking altitudes etc. [ME, f. OF *astrelabe* f. med. L *astrolabium* f. Gk ASTRO-(*lab-* take)]

astrŏl'ogў, n. (Formerly) practical astronomy (also called *natural* ~); art of judging of reputed occult influence of stars upon human affairs (*judicial* ~). So **astrŏl'oger** n., **ăstrolŏ'gic**(AL) aa., **ăstrolŏ'gical**LY² adv. [ME, f. OF *astrologie* f. L f. Gk ASTRO(*logia* -LOGY)]

astrŏn'om|**ў**, n. Science of the heavenly bodies. So ~ER¹ (3) n., student of ~y, **ăstronŏm'ic**(AL) aa. (~*ical figures*, *distances*, as enormous as those familiar to ~ers), **ăstronŏm'ical**LY² adv. [ME, f. OF *astronomie* f. L f. Gk *astronomia* f. ASTRO*nomos* a. star-arranging (*nemō* arrange)]

astūte', a. Shrewd, sagacious; crafty. Hence ~LY² (-tl-) adv., ~NESS (-tn-) n. [f. obs. F *astut* or L *astutus* f. *astus* craft]

asŭn'der, adv. (Of two or more things) apart (in motion or position); *tear* ~, tear to pieces. [OE *on sundran*, see A prep. & SUNDER]

asȳl'um, n. Sanctuary, place of refuge, esp. for criminals or debtors; shelter, refuge; institution for shelter & support of afflicted or destitute persons, esp. lunatics (now *mental home*). [ME, f. L f. Gk *asulon* refuge]

asȳm'metrў, n. Want of symmetry. [A-(7)+SYMMETRY]

ăs'ymptŏte, n. Line that approaches nearer & nearer to given curve but does not meet it within a finite distance. [f. Gk *asumptōtos* not falling together (*a-* not+*sum-* together+*ptōtos* falling f. *piptō*)]

asȳn'dĕton, n. (pl. *-ta*). A rhetorical figure esp. in Greek & Latin, omitting the particle that normally begins a sentence. [LL f. Gk *asundeton* unconnected (*a-* not+*sundetos* f. *sundeō* bind together)]

ăt¹ (or at), prep. 1. Expressing exact, approximate, or vague position, lit. & fig., as *meet at a point*, *wait at the corner*, *at the top*, *at Bath* (or any town except London and that in which the speaker is, cf. IN¹), *at school*, *at sea*, *at a distance*, *at arm's length*, *out at elbows*, *at work*, *at dinner*, *play at fighting*, *good at repartee*, *at daggers drawn*, *at a disadvantage*, *at his mercy*, *at a low price*, *at midday*, *at first*, *at least*, *at all events*, *annoyed at finding*, *impatient at delay*; *at 10 High Street*, = c/o Mr. A., 10 High Street. 2. Expr. motion towards, lit. & fig., as *arrive at a place*, *get*, *rush*, *shoot*, *laugh*, *grumble*, *hint*, *snatch*, *aim*, *at*. 3. *At all*, in any degree (in neg. context); *at best*, *worst*, assuming best, worst, result etc.; *at one*, in harmony or agreement (*with*); *at that*, at that estimate (*will take it at that*, accept that account of the matter), moreover, into the bargain (*lost an arm, & the right arm at that*). [OE *æt*, OHG *az*, ON, Goth. *at*, Gmc cogn. w. L *ad* to]

‖ **At²** (ăt), n. (colloq.). Member of the (Women's) *A*uxiliary *T*erritorial *S*ervice (now W.R.A.C.). [f. initials A.T.S. ăts) treated as pl.]

at-, pref. = AD- before *t*.

ăt'arăxy, -ăx'ia, n. Stoical indifference. [f. mod. L f. Gk *ataraxia* (*a*- not + *tarassō* disturb)]

ăt'avism, n. Resemblance to remote ancestors, reversion to earlier type; recurrence of disease after intermission of some generations. Hence **ătavis'tic** [-IST, -IC] a. [f. F *atavisme* f. L *atavus* great-grandfather's grandfather, see -ISM]

atăx'ic, a. Characterized by ataxy; ~ *fever*, malignant typhus fever. [f. foll. + -IC]

atăx'y, n. Irregularity of animal functions; *locomotor* ~, morbid unsteadiness in use of legs, arms, etc. [f. mod. L f. Gk *ataxia* (*a*- not + *taxis* order f. *tassō* arrange)]

ate. See EAT.

-ate¹, suf. forming nn. orig. f. L *-atus* (gen. *-ūs*) in nouns of state from p.p. stems or nouns, or f. L *-atus*, *-ata*, *-atum* see -ATE²), which in OF became *-é* (*-ée*), but in learned words, & later in many reformed words, *-at*, as *prélat*, *primat*, *magistrat*. E having adopted *-at* afterwards added *-e* to mark quantity of *a*, & later words took *-ate* at once. E also formed wds either directly on L as *curate* or by anal. as *aldermanate*. Most nn. in *-ate* are (1) nn. of office, as *marquisate*, *syndicate*, (2) participial nn., as *legate* one deputed, *precipitate* what is thrown down, (3) chem. terms denoting salts formed by action of an acid on a base, as *nitrate*, *sulphate*.

-ate², suf. forming adjj. (1) chiefly (thr. F) f. L p.p. in *-atus* (1st conjug.), which (cf. prec.) became successively *-at*, *-ate*, as *desolate*. Many such adjj. formed causative vbs (see foll.) & served as p.p. to them, till later the native *-ed* was added; *-ated* also appears without intervention of vb, as *annulated*, and as alternative form to *-ate*; (2) L participial adjj. were also formed on nn., as *caudatus* tailed, & on adjj. as *candidatus* whiterobed; these were largely adopted in E, & others formed on anal. Many nouns in *-ATE¹* were orig. adjj. In *cordate*, *ovate*, etc., the sense is 'shaped like'.

-ate³, suf. forming vbs to correspond to adjj. in *-ATE²*, and subsequently to repr. the corresp. L vb in *-are* (p.p. *-atus*), as *separate*, *aggravate*. As these vbs usu. have F equivalents in *-er*, *-ate* was further used to form vbs on model of F vbs in *-er*, as *isolate* (F *isoler*). *-ate* was also used to form vbs that L might have formed, but did not, on nouns, as *felicitate* (L

felicitas -atis), & even vbs on nouns not of L orig., as *camphorate*.

atelier (see Ap.), n. Workshop, studio. [F]

ăt'elo- in comb. = Gk *atelēs* imperfect (*a*- not + *telos* end), as *-glossia*, *-gnathia*, *-stomia*, imperfect development of tongue, jaws, mouth.

Athanā'sian (á-, -shn), a. Of Athanasius (archbishop of Alexandria in reign of Constantine); ~ *creed* (that beginning *Quicunque vult*, = *Whosoever will*). [f. LL *Athanasius*, see -AN]

ăth'ě|ism, n. Disbelief in the existence of a God; godlessness. So ~IST n., ~**is'tic** a., ~**is'tically** adv. [f. F *athéisme* f. Gk *atheos* without God (*a*- not + *theos* God), see -ISM]

ăthěnae'um, n. Literary or scientific club (‖ esp. *the A*~, in London); reading-room, library. [L, f. Gk *Athēnaion* temple of *Athēnē*, goddess of wisdom]

athīrst', pred. a. Thirsty; eager (*for*). [OE *ofthyrst* for *ofthyrsted* p.p. of *ofthyrstan* be thirsty]

ăth'lēte, n. Competitor in physical exercises; robust, vigorous, man; ~*'s foot*, contagious skin-disease of the feet. [f. L *athleta* f. Gk *athlētēs* f. *athleō* contend for prize (*athlon*), see -ET²]

ăthlět'|ic, a. & n. Pertaining to athletes; physically powerful; (n. pl.) practice of physical exercises, ~ *sports*. Hence ~**ICALLY** adv., ~**ĭCISM** n. [f. L f. Gk *athlētikos* (as prec., see -IC)]

at-hōme', n. Reception of visitors within certain hours during which host or hostess or both have announced that they will be at home, a party.

athwart' (*-ôrt*), adv. & prep. Across from side to side (usu. obliquely); crosswise, perversely; in opposition to; (of ship) ~*-hawse*, across stem of another ship at anchor. [A prep. + THWART]

-atic, adj. suf. (= F *-atique*) f. L *-aticus* (orig. *-at*- of p.p. stems + -IC, but extended to nouns as *fanaticus* f. *fanum*), surviving phonetically in F & E *-AGE*; in many mo͏͏ᵉᵗⁿ formations, as *lunatic*, *lymphatic*; but in many apparent exx. (*dramatic*, *piratic*) the suf. is *-ic*, & *-at-* part of the stem.

-atile, adj. suf. like -ATIC in orig. & use = *-at-* + -ILE, as *volatile*, *fluviatile*.

a-tilt', adv. Tilted; *run*, *ride*, ~ (in encounter on horseback with thrust of lance, usu. fig.). [A prep. + TILT]

-ation, suf. of nn. thr. F *-ation* (or direct) f. *-ationem* (nom. *-atio*), the particular form of the compd suf. *-tio* (-TION) f. L p.p. in *-at-* of 1st conj., + *-io* (-ION). The phonetic descendant of L *-ationem* in OF was *-aison*, *-eison*, surviving in E *orison*, *reason*, etc. All F wds in *-ation* are learned adoptions f. L, & may be paralleled by vbs ending in *-er* (= L *-are*), which far outnumber all other vbs &, constitute the type of all new wds in F. Hence F nouns in *-ation* exceed in number all the other members of the group (*-tion*, *-ition*, *-sion*), & so they do in E. Some of these have no accompanying vb in E use, as *lunation*, *constellation*; the great majority have a vb in *-ate* as *create*, *creation*; some are formed on Gk vbs in -IZE or their imitations, as *organize*, *-ation*; the remainder have a vb without suf., as *alteration*, *causation*, etc. These last having the appearance of being formed immediately on the vbs *alter*, *cause*, etc., *-ation* assumes the character of a living E suf., & is applied even to vbs not of F orig., as in *starvation*, *flirtation*. Meanings: (1) vbl action; (2) an instance of this; (3) resulting state; (4) concrete result (*plantation*).

-ative, adj. suf. f. F *-atif*, *-ative* f. L *-ativus* f. *-ivus* -IVE appended to p.p. stems in *-at-* (cf. -ATIC). The use of L *-ativus* was extended in LL & med. L, & its representatives are freely used in the mod. langg. In E, adjj. in *-ative* are usu. paired by vbs in *-ate*; the anal. of pairs such as *affirm*, *-ative* gave *talkative* f. *talk*; after such as *quality*, *-ative* (f. L *-itas*, LL *-ativus*), we have *authoritative* formed dir. on AUTHORITY.

atlăn′tes (-ēz), n. pl. (archit.). Sculptured male figures serving as pillars. [Gk, pl. of ATLAS]

Atlăn′tic, a. & n. **1.** Pertaining to mount Atlas in Libya; hence applied to sea near western shore of Africa, & later to whole ocean between Europe & Africa on east & America on west. **2.** n. ~ ocean. [f. L f. Gk *Atlantikos* f. ATLAS]

atlăn′tosaur′us, n. (palaeont.). (Kinds of) gigantic fossil reptile. [f. ATLAS + Gk *sauros* lizard]

ăt′las, n. Volume of maps; large size of drawing paper; (Physiol.) uppermost cervical vertebra, supporting skull. [*Atlas -antos* (1) Greek god of the older family, who held up pillars of universe; (2) the mountain in N. Africa, regarded as supporting the heavens]

atmo- in comp. = Gk *atmos* vapour, as *atmŏl′ogў*, science of aqueous vapour, *atmŏl′ўsis*, separation of vapours, *atmŏm′eter* (for measuring evaporation).

ăt′mosphēre, n. Spheroidal gaseous envelope surrounding heavenly body; that surrounding earth; one surrounding any substance; mental or moral environment esp. artistic or emotional; air (in any place); (w. pl.) pressure of 15 lb. on square inch (that exerted by ~ on earth's surface). Hence **ătmosphĕ′ric**(AL) aa., **ătmosphĕ′ricaly**[2] adv.; **ătmosphĕ′rics** n. pl., interference with wireless reception due to electric disturbance in~. [f. mod. L *atmosphaera*, see ATMO-, SPHERE]

atŏll′ (*or* ăt′ŏl), n. Ring-shaped coral reef enclosing lagoon. [Maldive *atollon, atoll*, prob. = Malayalam *adal* closing]

ăt′om, n. **1.** Particle of matter indivisible

chemically; *physical* ~, supposed ultimate particle of matter (now held to consist of a positively charged nucleus, in which is concentrated most of the mass of the ~, round which revolve negatively charged electrons); *chemical* ~*s*, smallest particles in which elements combine with themselves or with each other; ~ *bomb*, ATOMIC *bomb*. **2.** Minute portion; small thing. [f. L f. Gk *atomos* indivisible (*a*-not + *-tomos* cut f. *temnō*), later reinforced by F *atome*]

atŏm′ic, a. Of, relating to, an atom or atoms; ~ *bomb* (deriving its destructiveness from the disintegration and partial conversion into energy of ~ nuclei); ~ *energy*, energy produced by changes in the ~ nuclei of uranium or similar metals; ~ *number*, (of a chemical element) number of unit positive charges carried by the nucleus of its atom; ~ *philosophy*, doctrine of formation of all things from indivisible particles endued with gravity & motion; (Chem.) ~ *theory* (that elemental bodies consist of indivisible atoms of definite relative weight, & that atoms of different elements unite with each other in fixed proportions, which determine the proportions in which elements & compounds enter into chemical combination); ~ *warfare* (in which ~ bombs are used); ~ *weight*, (now usu.) ratio between the weight of one atom of the element & $\frac{1}{16}$ of the weight of an atom of oxygen, (formerly) weight of an atom of the element as compared with that of an atom of hydrogen. Hence ~AL a., ~aLY[2] adv. [prec. + -IC]

ătomi′citў, n. The number of atoms in the molecule of an element; (formerly) = VALENCY. [f. prec., see -TY]

ăt′omism, n. Atomic philosophy; doctrine of action of individual atoms. [ATOM + -ISM]

ăt′om|ist, n. Holder of atomic theory or philosophy. Hence~**is′tic**a. [ATOM + -IST]

ăt′omiz|e, -is|e (-īz), v.t. Reduce to atoms. Hence ~a′TION n. [ATOM + -IZE]

ăt′omizer, n. Instrument for reducing liquids to fine spray. [prec. + -ER[1]]

ăt′omў[1], n. Skeleton; emaciated body. [f. ANATOMY, *an-* being taken as article]

ăt′omў[2], n. Atom, tiny being. [f. *atomi* pl. of L *atomus* ATOM]

atŏn′ai, a. (mus.). Not conforming to any system of key or mode. [A- (7) + TONAL]

atōne′, v.i. & t. **1.** Make amends (esp. ~ *for*, expiate). **2.** v.t. (arch.). Reconcile (enemies), compose (quarrel). [back form. f. foll.]

atōne′ment (-nm-), n. Atoning; expiation, reparation for wrong or injury; reconciliation of God & man, propitiation of God by expiation of sin; *Day of A*~, most solemn religious fast of Jewish year. [f. AT ONE + -MENT, after earlier *onement* f. obs. vb *one* unite]

atŏn'ic, a. & n. Unaccented, unstressed; (Path.) wanting tone; (n.) unaccented word (esp. in Gk Gram.). [f. med. L *atonicus* f. Gk ἄτονος toneless (*a-* not + *tonos* TONE), see -IC]

atŏp', adv. On the top (*of*). [A prep.]

ătrabil'ious (-lyus), a. Affected by black bile; melancholy; acrimonious. Hence ~NESS n. [f. L *atra bilis* (black bile, transl. Gk*melagkholia* MELANCHOLY) + -OUS]

atrip', adv. (Of anchor) just lifted from ground in weighing. [A prep. + TRIP]

āt'rium, n. (pl. *-a*, *-ums*). Central court of Roman house; covered portico, esp. before church door. [L]

atrō'cious (-shus), a. Heinously wicked; very bad, as ~ *pun*. Hence ~LY² adv., ~NESS n. [f. L *atrox -ocis* (*ater* black) + -OUS]

atrō'cĭtў, n. Heinous wickedness; atrocious deed; bad blunder. [f. L *atrocitas* (as prec., see -TY)]

ăt'rophў, n. Wasting away through imperfect nourishment; emaciation (lit. & fig.). Hence **ăt'rophў** v.t. & i. [f. LL f. Gk *atrophia* f. *atrophos* ill-fed (*a-* not + *trophē* food)]

ăt'ropine (-ēn), n. Poisonous alkaloid found in deadly nightshade. [f. mod. L *atropa* deadly nightshade f. Gk *Atropos* inflexible, name of one of the Fates, see -INE⁵]

•**ătt'aboy**, int. Exclamation expressive of encouragement or admiration. [corrupt. of *that's the boy!*]

ăttăch', v.t. & i. Fasten (thing *to* another); join one*self* (*to* person, company, expedition); bind in friendship, make devoted, (*has the gift of ~ing people to him*; *is deeply ~ed to her*); affix (immaterial things, name, liability, etc., *to*); attribute (importance etc. *to*); (Law) seize (person, property) by legal authority; adhere, be incident, as *no blame ~es to*. Hence ~ABLE a. [ME, f. OF *atachier* (mod. *attacher*, It. *attaccare*) f. *à to* + root found in Genevese *tache*, Sp. and Port. *tacha*, nail, TACK]

attaché (ătăsh'ā), n. One attached to ambassador's suite; ~ *case*, small rectangular valise ostensibly for carrying documents. [F, p.p. of *attacher* (as prec.)]

attăch'ment, n. Act of attaching; thing attached; means of attaching; affection; legal seizure, esp. *foreign* ~ (of foreigner's goods, to satisfy his creditors). [ME, f. F *attachement* (*attacher* ATTACH, see -MENT)]

attăck'¹, v.t. Fall upon, assault, (lit. & fig.); (of physical agents or diseases) act destructively upon. Hence ~ABLE a. [f. F *attaquer* f. It. *attaccare*, see ATTACH]

attăck'², n. Act of attacking (lit. & fig.); offensive operation. [f. prec., or F *attaque* n.]

attain', v.t. & i. Arrive at, reach; gain, accomplish; (intr.) ~ *to*, arrive at. Hence ~ABIL'ITY n., ~ABLE a., ~ableNESS n. [ME, f. OF *ataign-* st. of *ataindre* f. L ATtingere (*tangere* touch)]

attain'der, n. Consequences of sentence of death or outlawry (forfeiture of estate, corruption of blood, extinction of civil rights). [AF, = OF *ataindre* ATTAIN used as n. (see -ER⁴); meaning influenced by confus. w. OF *taindre* TAINT]

attain'ment, n. Act of attaining; thing attained, esp. personal accomplishment. [ME, ATTAIN + -MENT]

attaint', v.t. Subject to attainder; (of diseases etc.) strike, affect; infect; sully. [f. obs. *attaint* a. f. OF *ataint* p.p. as ATTAIN; confused in meaning with TAINT]

ătt'ar, n. Fragrant essential oil from rose-petals. [f. Pers. *'aṭar(-gul)* essence (of roses) f. Arab. *'uṭūr* aroma f. *'aṭara* breathe perfume; see OTTO]

attĕm'per, v.t. Qualify by admixture; modify temperature of; soothe, mollify; accommodate *to*; attune *to*; temper (metal). Hence ~MENT n. [ME, f. OF *atemprer* f. L AT(*temperare* TEMPER)]

attĕmpt'¹, v.t. Try (thing, action, *to* do); try to master (mountain, fortress); ~ *the life of*, try to kill. Hence ~ABLE a. [f. OF *attempter*, f. L AT(*temptare* TEMPT)]

attĕmpt'², n. Attempting; endeavour. [f. prec.]

attĕnd', v.t. & i. Turn the mind *to*; apply oneself (*to* or abs.); be present (*at*); wait upon; (trans.) wait upon; escort, accompany; be present at (lecture etc.). [ME, f. OF *atendre* f. L ATtendere *-tent-* stretch]

attĕn'dance, n. Act of attending (*upon* person, *at* lecture); *dance* ~ *on*, attend the convenience of; body of persons present. [ME, f. OF *atendance* (as prec., see -ANCE)]

attĕn'dant, a. & n. **1.** Waiting (*upon*); accompanying, as ~ *circumstances*; present, as ~ *crowd*. **2.** n. Servant, satellite. [ME, f. OF, part. as ATTEND]

attĕn'tion, n. & int. Act of attending, as *pay, give,* ~; faculty of attending, as *attract, call,* ~; consideration, care; (pl.) ceremonious politeness (*pay one's ~s to*, court); *come to, stand at,* ~ (military attitude; *A~!*, order to assume it, also *'shun!*). [ME, f. L *attentio* (as ATTEND, see -ION)]

attĕn'tive, a. Heedful, observant; polite, assiduous. Hence ~LY² (-vl-) adv., ~NESS (-vn-) n. [F (*-if, -ive*), f. L as ATTEND, see -IVE]

attĕn'ū|āte¹, v.t. Make slender; make thin in consistence; reduce in force or value. So ~A'TION n. [f. L ATtenuare (*tenuis* thin), see -ATE³]

attĕn'ūate², a. Slender; rarefied. [as prec., see -ATE²]

attĕst', v.t. & i. Testify, certify (~*ed cattle*, certified free from the tubercle bacillus); put (person) on oath or solemn declaration; administer oath of allegiance to (recruit); (intr.) bear witness *to*. Hence ~OR n. [f. F *attester* f. L ATtestari (*testis* witness)]

ăttĕstā'tion, n. Act of testifying; testimony; evidence; formal confirmation by signature, oath, etc.; administration of an oath. [F, or LL *attestatio* (as prec., see -ATION)]

Att'ic(á-), a. & n. Of Athens or Attica; ~ (*dialect*), Greek spoken by the Athenians; ~ *salt*, *wit*, refined wit; ~ *order*, with square column of any of the five ORDERS. [f. L f. Gk *Attikos*]

ätt'ic[2], n. Structure consisting of small order placed above another of greater height (usu. *Attic*); highest storey of house; room in this. [f. F *attique*, as prec.]

ätt'ic|**ism**, n. Style, idiom, of Athens; refined amenity of speech; attachment to Athens. So ~IZE (2) v.i. [f. Gk *attikismos*]

attīre', v.t., & n. Dress, array. [ME, f. OF *atirer* f. *à to + tire*, of unkn. orig.; cf. TIRE[3]]

ätt'itūde, n. Disposition of figure (in painting etc.); posture of body, as *strike an* ~ (assume it theatrically); settled behaviour, as indicating opinion; ~ *of mind*, settled mode of thinking. [F, f. It. *attitudine* fitness, posture, f. med. L *aptitudinem* (*aptus* fit, see -TUDE)]

ättitūd'inize, -ise (-īz), v.i. Practise attitudes; speak, write, behave, affectedly. [f. prec. + -IZE]

attorn' (-êrn), v.t. & i. (law). Transfer; make legal acknowledgement of new landlord. Hence ~MENT n. [ME, f. OF *atorner* (*à to + torner* TURN)]

attorn'ey[1](-tér-), n. One appointed to act for another in business or legal matters; barrister or solicitor (now joc. or derog., exc. in U.S.); *A*~ *General*, (in England & U.S.) legal officer empowered to act in all cases in which the State is a party; *abuse plaintiff's* ~ (iron. advice to lawyer with a weak case). Hence ~SHIP n. [ME, f. OF *atorné* p.p. as ATTORN; see -Y[4]]

attorn'ey[2] (-tér-), n. *Letter, warrant, of* ~ (by which person appoints another to act for him); *power of* ~, authority thus conferred. [ME, f. OF *atornée* fem. p.p., see prec.]

attrăct', v.t. Draw to oneself (esp. of physical forces); excite the pleasurable emotions of (person); draw forth & fix upon oneself (attention etc.). Hence ~ABIL'ITY n., ~ABLE a. [f. L AT(*trahere tract-* draw)]

attrăc'tion, n. Act, faculty, of drawing to oneself (lit. & fig.); drawing force; thing that attracts (fig.); ~ *of gravity* (existing between all bodies, & varying directly as their masses, inversely as the square of their distance apart); *magnetic* ~, action of magnet in drawing iron; *molecular* ~ (between molecules of bodies, acting only at infinitesimal distances); *capillary* ~ (by which liquid is drawn up through hairlike tube). [F, or f. L *attractio* (as prec., see -ION)]

attrăc'tive, a. Attracting, capable of at-

tracting (esp. fig.). Hence ~LY[2] (-vl-) adv., ~NESS (-vn-) n. [F(*-if, -ive*), as prec., see -IVE]

ätt'ribute[1], n. Quality ascribed to anything; material object recognized as appropriate to person or office; characteristic quality; (Gram.) attributive word. [ME, f. F *attribut* or L *attributum* (ATtribuere *-ut-* assign)]

attrib'ūt|**e**[2], v.t. Ascribe as belonging or appropriate *to*; refer (effect *to* its cause); assign (*to* time or place). Hence ~ABLE a. [as prec.]

ättribū'tion, n. Act of attributing; authority granted (*to* a ruler etc.). [ME, f. OF, f. L *attributionem* (as prec., see -ION)]

attrib'ūtive, a. & n. 1. (Logic) assigning an attribute to a subject; (Gram.) expressing an attribute (e.g. *old* in *the old dog* but not in *the dog is old*). 2. n. Word denoting an attribute (usu. an adjective or its equivalent). Hence ~LY[2] (-vl-) adv. [F (*-if, -ive*), as ATTRIBUTE[1], see -IVE]

attrit'éd, a. Worn by friction. [f. L AT(*terere trit-* rub)]

attri'tion, n. Friction; wearing out (*war of* ~, turning on which side can last longest); abrasion; (Theol.) sorrow for sin (short of *contrition*). [ME, f. LL *attritio* (as prec., see -ION)]

attūne', v.t. Bring into musical accord (*to*, lit. & fig.); tune (instrument). [AT- + TUNE v.]

atȳp'ical, a. Not conforming to type. [A- (7) + TYPICAL]

aubade (ōbahd'), n. Musical announcement of dawn; sunrise song. [F]

auberge (ōbâ'rzh'), n. Inn. [F]

aubergine (ōb'êrzhēn), n. Purple fruit of egg-plant. [F]

aubrietia (ōbrēsh'*a*) (erron.) **-retia**, n. (Kinds of) spring-flowering dwarf perennial plant. [f. Claude *Aubriet* (French artist), see -IA[1]]

aub'urn (-ern), a. Golden-brown (usu. of hair). [ME, f. OF *auborne* f. L *alburnus* whitish]

au courant (ō kōō'rahn), pred. a. Acquainted *with* what is going on; well-informed. [F]

auc'tion, n., & v.t. 1. Public sale in which articles are sold to the highest of successive bidders; *Dutch* ~, sale in which price is reduced by auctioneer till a purchaser is found; ~ *bridge*, form of bridge in which players bid for right to play the hand. 2. v.t. Sell by ~. [f. L *auctio* increase, auction (*augēre auct-*, see -ION)]

auc'tioneer' (-shon-), n., & v.i. (One whose business is to) conduct auctions. [-EER]

audā'cious (-shus), a. Daring, bold; impudent. Hence -LY[2] adv., ~NESS n., **audā'**CITY (-ās-) n. [f. L *audax* (*audēre* dare, see -ACIOUS)]

aud'ib|**le**, a. Perceptible to the ear. Hence ~LY[2] adv., **audiBIL'ITY**, ~le**NESS**

(-ĭn-), nn. [f. LL *audibilis* (*audire* hear, see -BLE)]

aud′ience, n. Hearing; *give* ~, listen; formal interview; persons within hearing; assembly of listeners; (of a book) readers. [ME f. OF, f. L *audientia* (*audire* hear, see -ENCE)]

aud′ile, a. & n. (Usu. of supernormal phenomena) received through the auditory nerves; (person) specially sensitive to auditory impressions. [irreg. f. L *audire* hear +-ILE]

aud′iō-frē′quency, n. & a. (Of, using) frequency comparable to that of sound. [f. L *audire* hear +-O-+FREQUENCY]

audiŏm′ēter, n. Instrument for testing hearing-power. [f. L *audire* hear +-O- +-METER]

aud′iphōne, n. Instrument that, pressed against upper teeth, assists hearing. [improp. f. L *audire* hear +Gk *phōnē* sound, on *telephone*]

aud′it, n. Official examination of accounts; searching examination, esp. Day of Judgement; periodical settlement of accounts between landlord & tenants; ~ *ale* (of special quality, formerly brewed in English colleges, orig. for use on day of ~); ~ *house*, *-room* (attached to Cathedral for transaction of business). [ME, f. L *auditus -ūs* hearing (*audire -it-*)]

aud′it[2], v.t. Examine (accounts) officially. [f. prec.]

audi′tion, n., & v.t. & i. Power of hearing; listening; trial hearing of applicant for employment as singer etc.; (vb) give an ~ (to). [F, or f. L *auditio* (*audire -it-*, see -ION)]

aud′itive, a. Concerned with hearing. [F (-*if*, -*ive*), as prec., see -IVE]

aud′it|or, n. Listener; one who audits accounts. Hence ~ORSHIP, ~RESS[1], nn. [f. AF *auditour* f. L *auditorem* (as prec., see -OR)]

auditōr′ial, a. Connected with an audit. [f. prec. +-IAL]

aud′itory, a. & n. **1.** Connected with hearing; received by the ear. **2.** n. Assembly of hearers, audience; (now usu. **auditōr′ium**) part of building occupied by audience. [f. L *auditorius*, -*um* (as prec., see -ORY)]

au fait (ō fā′), pred. a. Conversant, instructed; *put a person* ~ *with*, instruct him in. [F]

au fond (see Ap.), adv. At bottom (cf. *à fond*). [F]

Augē′an, a. Filthy, like the stables of Augeas, which Hercules cleansed by turning river Alpheus through them. [f. L *Augeas* f. Gk *Augeias* +-AN]

aug′er (-g-), n. Tool for boring holes in wood, having long shank with cutting edge & screw point, & handle at right angles; instrument for boring in soil or strata, with stem that can be lengthened. [OE *nafugār* (*nafu* NAVE[1]+*gār* piercer), cf.

OHG *nabuger*, Du. *avegaar*; for loss of *n*- cf. ADDER]

aught (awt), n. & adv. Anything; (adv., arch.) in any degree or respect. [OE *āwiht* (*ā* ever +*wiht* wight, whit); OE contr. *āht*, gives mod. *ought*, now less usu. form]

aug′ment[1], n. Vowel (in Sanskrit *a*, in Greek *ě*) prefixed to past tenses in the older Aryan languages. [ME, f. OF, or f. LL *augmentum* increase (*augēre*, see -MENT)]

augmĕnt′[2], v.t. & i. Make greater, increase; prefix the augment to; (intr.) increase. [ME, f. F *augmenter* or LL *augmentare* increase; see prec.]

augmentā′tion, n. Enlargement; growth, increase; addition; (Mus.) repetition of a passage in notes longer than those of the original. [ME, f. OF, f. LL *augmentationem* (*augmentare*, see prec. and -ATION)]

augmĕn′tative, a. & n. Having the property of increasing; (Gram., of affixes or derived words) increasing in force the idea of the original word; (n.) ~ word. [F (-*if*, -*ive*), f. L as AUGMENT[2], see -ATIVE]

au grand sérieux (see Ap.), adv. Very seriously (*take* it, him, etc., ~). [F]

aug′ur[1] (-er), n. Roman religious official who foretold future events by omens derived from the actions of birds etc.; soothsayer. Hence ~SHIP n. [L, prob. f. *avis* bird; cf. AUSPICE]

aug′ur[2] (-er), v.t. & i. Forebode, anticipate; ~ *well*, *ill*, have good or bad expectations *of*, *for*; *it* ~*s* (promises) *ill*. [f. prec.]

aug′ural, a. Pertaining to augurs; significant of the future. [f. L *auguralis* (AUGUR[1], see -AL)]

aug′ury, n. Divination by omens; augural ceremony; omen; presentiment; promise. [ME, f. OF *augurie* or L *augurium* (AUGUR[1])]

augŭst′[1], a. Majestic, venerable. Hence ~LY[2] adv., ~NESS n. [f. F *auguste* or L *augustus* consecrated, venerable]

Aug′ust[2], n. Eighth month of year, named after Augustus Caesar. [OE *august* f. L *augustus* (see prec.); in ME also *aust* f. OF *aoust*]

Augŭs′tan, a. & n. Connected with reign of Augustus Caesar, best period of Latin literature; (of any national literature) classical (in Eng. literature *c*. 18th c.); ~ *confession* (drawn up by Luther & Melanchthon at Augusta Vindelicorum or Augsburg); (n.) writer of the ~ age of any literature. [f. L *Augustanus*, see -AN]

Augŭs′tine (*or* awg²), n. An Augustinian monk. [f. L *Augustinus*, name of the Latin father]

Augŭstin′ian, a. & n. **1.** Of or relating to St Augustine (d. 430) or his doctrines; belonging to the order of Augustines. **2.** n. Adherent of the doctrines of St Augustine; one of the order of Augustines. Hence ~ISM (3) n. [f. L *Augustinus* (prec.) +-IAN]

auk, n. Kinds of black and white gregarious sea-bird, including the flightless and extinct *Great Auk*. [f. ON *álka* (cf. Sw. *alka*, Da. *alke*)]

aul'ic, a. Pertaining to a court; *A~ Council*, (in old German empire) personal council of emperor, (later) council managing Austrian war-department. [f. F *aulique* or L f. Gk *aulikos* (*aulē* court, see -IC)]

aum'brў, var. of AMBRY.

au naturel (see Ap.), adv. or pred. a. (Cooked) in the simplest way. [F]

aunt (ahnt), n. Father's, mother's, sister; uncle's wife; *A~ Sally*, game at fairs, in which players throw sticks at pipe in mouth of wooden woman's head, also fig. [ME, f. OF *aunte* f. L *amita*; E up to 17th c. had also *naunt* (my naunt = mine aunt), still used in dial.]

au pair (ō pār'), a. (Of arrangements between two parties) paid for by mutual services (no money passing). [F]

au pied de la lettre (ō pyā' de lah lĕt'r), adv. Literally. [F]

aur'a, n. Subtle emanation (from flowers etc.); atmosphere diffused by or attending a person etc. (esp. in mystical or spiritualistic use as a definite envelope of body or spirit); (Electr.) current of air caused by discharge of electricity from a sharp point; (Path.) sensation as of current of cold air rising from some part of body to head, premonitory symptom in epilepsy & hysterics. Hence **aur'al**[1] [-AL] a. [f. L f. Gk, = breeze, breath]

aur'al[2], a. Pertaining to organ of hearing; received by the ear. Hence ~LY[2] adv. [f. L *auris* ear + -AL]

aur'éate, a. Golden, gold-coloured; resplendent. [ME, f. L *aureatus* f. *aureus* golden f. *aurum* gold, -ATE[2]]

aurēl'ia, n. (Formerly) chrysalis, esp. of butterfly; (Zool.) kinds of phosphorescent marine animals. [It., = silkworm, fem. of *aurelio* golden f. L *aurum* gold]

aurēl'ian, a. & n. Of an aurelia; golden; (n.) collector, breeder, of insects. [prec. + -AN]

aurē'ola, n. Celestial crown won by martyr, virgin, doctor, by victory over world, flesh, or devil; = foll. [L (~ *corona*) golden (crown) fem. of *aureolus* f. *aureus* (*aurum* gold)]

aur'éole, n. Aureola; (prop.) gold disc surrounding head in early pictures; circle of light depicted round head; oblong glory surrounding divine figures; actual halo, esp. that seen in eclipses. [OF, f. prec.]

au revoir (ō revwahr'), adv. (Good-bye) till we meet again. [F]

aur'ic, a. Pertaining to gold; (Chem.) in which gold is trivalent. [f. L *aurum* gold, see -IC]

aur'icl|e, n. External ear of animals; process shaped like lower lobe of ear; either of the two upper cavities of the heart. Hence ~ED[2] (-ld) a. [f. foll.]

auric'ūla, n. Species of primula, bear's--ear; genus of molluscs. [L, = external ear, dim. of *auris* ear]

auric'ular, a. Pertaining to the ear; told privately in the ear, as ~ *confession*; ~ *witness*, one who tells what he has heard; pertaining to auricle of heart; shaped like an auricle. Hence ~LY[2] adv. [f. LL *auricularis* (AURICULA, see -AR[1])]

auric'ūlate, a. With ear-shaped projections. [as prec., see -ATE[2]]

aurif'erous, a. Yielding gold. [f. L *aurifer* (*aurum* gold); see -FEROUS]

aur'iform, n. Ear-shaped. [f. L *auris* ear + -FORM]

Auri'ga, n. Northern constellation, the Waggoner. [L, = charioteer]

Aurignā'cian (-shn), a. Of the palaeolithic epoch represented by remains found in the Aurignac cave of the Pyrenees. [-AN]

aur'ilāve, n. Instrument for cleaning ears. [f. L *auris* ear + *lavare* wash]

aur'ist, n. Ear specialist. [as prec. + -IST]

aurochs (owr'ŏks, aw-), n. Extinct wild ox; (improp.) European bison. [f. G *aurochs* (mod. *auerochs*) f. OHG *ûr-ohso* f. *ûr*- URUS + *ohso* OX]

aurōr'a, n. Luminous atmospheric (prob. electrical) phenomenon radiating from earth's northern (~ *borēal'is*) or southern (*austrāl'is*) magnetic pole; dawn; colour of sky at sunrise; *A~*, Roman goddess of dawn. Hence **aurōr'AL** a. [L, = dawn, goddess of dawn]

aur'ous, a. (chem.). In which gold is univalent. [f. L *aurum* + -OUS]

aur'um, n. Gold; ~ *ful'minans*, fulminate of gold; ~ *mosā'icum*, bisulphide of tin, bronze-powder. [L]

auscultā'tion, n. Act of listening, esp. (Med.) to movement of heart, lungs, etc. So **aus'cultātor** n., **auscul'tatory** a. [f. L *auscultatio* f. *auscultare* listen to, see -ATION]

Ausgleich (see Ap.), n. (hist.). Political agreement between Austria & Hungary, renewable every tenth year. [G]

aus'picāte, v.t. & i. Inaugurate, initiate; (intr.) augur. [f. L *auspicari* (*auspex* -*icis* observer of birds for *avispex* f. *avis* bird + -*spec*- observe), see -ATE[3]]

aus'pice, n. Observation of birds for purposes of taking omens; prognostic; prosperous lead, patronage, as *under the ~s of*. [F, or f. L *auspicium* (*auspex*, see prec.)]

auspi'cious (-shus), a. Of good omen, favourable; prosperous. Hence ~LY[2] adv., ~NESS n. [as prec. + -OUS]

Auss'ie n. (sl.). Australia(n). [abbr.]

austēre', a. Harsh, stern; stringently moral, strict, severely simple; harsh in flavour. Hence ~LY[2] (-ēr'l-) adv., ~NESS (-ēr'n-) n., **austē'rITY** n. (also attrib., severely simple). [ME, f. OF, f. L f. Gk *austēros* drying, harsh (*auō* v. dry)]

Aus'tin, n. & n. Contr. f. AUGUSTINE.

aus'tral, a. Southern. [f. L *australis* (*Auster* south wind, see -AL)]

Australā′sian (-shn), a. & n. (Native) of Australasia (Australia & adjoining islands). [f. *Australasia* f. F *Australasie* (L *australis*, see prec. +*Asia*)+-AN]

Austrāl′ian, n. & a. Native of, resident in, Australia ; (adj.) of Australia. [f. F *Australien* f. L as AUSTRAL]

aut′archy (-kĭ), n. Absolute sovereignty. Hence **autärch′ic**(AL) (-k-) aa. [f. Gk *autarkhia* (AUTO-, *arkhō* rule)]

aut′arkў, n. Self-sufficiency. Hence **autärk′ic**(AL) aa., **aut′arkIST** n. [f. Gk *autarkeia* (AUTO-, *arkeō* suffice)]

authĕn′t|ĭc, a. Reliable, trustworthy ; of undisputed origin, genuine ; (Mus., of ecclesiastical modes) having their sounds comprised within an octave from the final. Hence ∼ICALLY adv., ∼i′CITY n. [ME, f. OF *autentique* f. LL f. Gk *authentikos* f. *authentēs* one who does a thing himself (AUTO-+-*hentēs*, cf. *sunentēs* fellow-worker), see -IC]

authĕn′tic|āte, v.t. Establish the truth of ; establish the authorship of ; make valid. Hence ∼A′TION, ∼ātor, nn. [f. med. L *authenticare* (*authenticus*), see prec. and -ATE³]

auth′or, n. Originator (*of* a condition of things, event, etc.) ; writer of book, treatise, etc. ; (loosely) ∼′s writings. Hence ∼ESS¹ n., **authŏr′IAL** a. [ME *autour* f. AF, OF *autor*, *-teur* f. L *auctor* (*augēre auct-* increase, originate, promote, see -OR) ; *auth-* appears as scribal var. of *aut-* in Eng. c. 1550]

authŏritār′ian, a. & n. (Esp. Pol.) favouring obedience to authority as opp. to individual liberty ; (n.) supporter of this principle. [f. as foll. +-ARIAN]

authŏ′ritătive, a. Commanding, imperative ; possessing authority ; proceeding from competent authority. Hence ∼LY² (-vl-)adv., ∼NESS(-vl-)n. [f.foll.+-ATIVE]

authŏ′ritў, n. Power, right, to enforce obedience ; delegated power (*to do*, *for* an act, or abs.) ; person or body having authority ; personal influence, esp. over opinion ; weight of testimony ; book, quotation, considered to settle a question ; evidence, declaration, that may be cited in support of a statement (*on the* ∼ *of Plato*) ; person whose opinion is accepted, esp. expert in (*on*) a subject. [ME, f. OF *autorite* or L *auctoritas* (*auctor*, see AUTHOR and -TY)]

auth′oriz|e, -is|e (-īz), v.t. Sanction ; give ground for, justify, (thing) ; give authority to, commission, (person *to* do). *Authorized Version* (abbr. A.V.), **King James's Bible* or *Version*, the Bible of 1611. Hence ∼ABLE a., ∼A′TION n. [ME, f. OF *autoriser* f. med. L *auctorizare* (*auctor*, see AUTHOR and -IZE)]

auth′orship, n. Occupation, career, as a writer ; origin (of book). [-SHIP]

aut′ism, n. Morbid self-admiration,

absorption in phantasy. Hence **autis′tIC** a. [f. foll. +-ISM]

auto- in comb. = Gk *auto-* (*autos* self), in sense 'self, one's own, by oneself, independent(ly)', in wds f. Gk & new formations, as -*car′pous*, consisting of pericarp alone, -*gamy*, self-fertilization, -*genous*, self-producing, -*geny*, -*gony*, spontaneous generation, -*phagous*, -*phagy*, feeding on oneself (by absorption of tissues, during starvation), -*plasty*, repair of wounds with tissue from same body ; -*sugges′tion*, hypnotic suggestion proceeding from the subject himself.

aut′obahn, n. (pl. ∼*en*). German arterial road. [G (*auto* motor-car, *bahn* road)]

autobiŏg′rapher, n. One who writes his own history. [AUTO-]

autobiogrăph′ic, a. Pertaining to, engaged in, autobiography. Hence ∼AL a., ∼alLY² adv. [AUTO-]

autobiŏg′raphў, n. Writing the story of one's own life ; story so written. [AUTO-]

aut′ocār, n. Road vehicle driven by mechanical power. [AUTO-]

autocĕph′alous, a. Having its own head ; (of bishop, church) independent. [f. Gk *autokephalos*(AUTO-+*kephalē* head)+-OUS]

autŏch′thon (-k-), n. (usu. pl. ; -*onēs*, -*ons*). Original, earliest known, inhabitants ; aborigines. Hence ∼AL, autochthŏn′IC, ∼OUS, aa., ∼ISM, ∼Y¹, nn. [Gk, = sprung from that land itself (AUTO-+ *khthōn* -*onos* land)]

autŏc′racў, n. Absolute government ; controlling influence. [f. Gk *autokrateia* (as AUTOCRAT)]

aut′ocrăt, n. Absolute ruler. So **autocrăt′ic**(AL) aa., **autocrăt′icalLY²** adv. [f. F *autocrate* f. Gk *autokratēs* (AUTO-+ *kratos* might)]

aut′o-da-fé′ (-dahfā), n. (pl. *autos-da-fé*). Sentence of the Inquisition ; execution of this, esp. burning of heretic. [Port., = act of the faith ; also Sp. -*de-fé*]

aut′odidăct, n. Self-taught person. [AUTO-, DIDACT(IC)]

aut′o-ĕ′rotism, n. Spontaneous sexual emotion generated without external stimulus. [AUTO-+EROTISM]

autogĭr′ō, n. Kind of GYROPLANE. [patented name ; AUTO-, GYRO-]

aut′ograph¹ (-ahf), n. Author's own manuscript ; person's own handwriting, esp. signature ; copy produced by autography. Hence **autogrăph′ic**(AL) aa., **autogrăph′icalLY²** adv. [F, or f. L f. Gk *autographon* neut. of *autographos* (AUTO-+-*graphos* written)]

aut′ograph²(-ahf), v.t. Write with one's own hand ; copy by autography ; sign. [f. prec.]

autŏg′raphў, n. Writing with one's own hand ; author's own handwriting ; reproduction in facsimile of writing or drawing. [as prec., see -Y¹]

(For other words in *auto-* see AUTO-.)

aut′ohârp, n. Kind of zither with mechanical contrivance making playing of chords possible. [AUTO-]

autŏl′ўsĭs, n. Destruction of cells of the body by the action of its own serum. [f. AUTO- + Gk *lusis* dissolution]

*****aut′omăt**, n. Café or restaurant in which meals etc. are provided in slot--machines. [G; see AUTOMATON]

automăt′ic, a. & n. **1.** Self-acting; working of itself, (of a firearm) having mechanism for loading, firing, & ejecting until the ammunition is exhausted, or until the pressure on the trigger etc. is released; (n.) ~ firearm. **2.** Mechanical, unconscious; unintelligent, merely mechanical. **3.** (psych.). Performed unconsciously or subconsciously. Hence ~AL a., ~alLY² adv., **autŏmati′CITY** n. [as AUTOMATON + -IC]

automā′tion, n. Automatic control of the manufacture of a product through successive stages, (loosely) use of machinery to save mental & manual labour. [irreg. f. prec.]

autŏm′atism, n. Involuntary action; doctrine attributing this to animals; unthinking routine; faculty of originating action or motion; (Psych.) action performed unconsciously or subconsciously. [f. foll. + -ISM]

autŏm′at|on, n. (pl. ~a, ~ons). Thing endued with spontaneous motion; living being viewed materially; piece of mechanism with concealed motive power; living being whose actions are involuntary or without active intelligence. Hence ~ous a. [f. Gk (also L) AUTO*maton*, neut. adj., acting of itself]

*****automobile′** (-ēl), n. Motor-car. [F]

autŏn′omous, a. Of, possessed of, autonomy. [f. Gk AUTO(*nomos* law) + -OUS]

autŏn′om|ў, n. Right of self-government; personal freedom; freedom of the will (in Kantian doctrine); a self-governing community. So **autonŏm′IC** a., ~IST n. [f. Gk *autonomia*, as prec., see -Y¹]

autŏp′sў (*or* awt²), n. Personal inspection; post-mortem examination; (fig.) critical dissection. So **autŏp′tIC(AL) aa.** [f. mod. L f. Gk *autopsia* f. *autoptos* (AUTO- + *op-* see); cf. F *autopsie*]

autostrad|a (owtostrah′dah), n. (pl. ~e, pr. -ā). Italian arterial road. [It., = motor-car road]

autotŏx′|ĭn, n. Poisonous substance produced by changes within the organism. So ~IC a., ~ĭcA′TION n., poisoning by a virus generated within the body. [AUTO-, TOXIN, TOXIC]

aut′otўpe, n. Facsimile; photographic printing process for reproducing in monochrome. Hence **aut′otўpe** v.t. [AUTO-]

aut′umn (-m), n. Third season of the year, September–November (Astron., from autumnal equinox to winter solstice); (fig.) season of incipient decay. [ME *autumpne* f. OF f. L *autumnus*]

autŭm′nal, a. Of autumn; ~ *crocus*, MEADOW saffron; ~ *equinox*, time when sun crosses equator as it proceeds southward (Sept. 23); maturing, blooming, in autumn; past prime of life. [f. L *autumnalis* (as prec., see -AL)]

auxanŏm′eter, n. Instrument for measuring growth in plants. [f. Gk *auxanō* increase + -o- + -METER]

auxil′iar|ў (-lya-), a. & n. (One who is) helpful *to*; (Mil.) ~*y troops*, ~*ies*, foreign or allied troops in a nation's service; (Gram.) ~*y* (*verb*), one used to form tenses, moods, voices, of other verbs. [f. L *auxiliarius* (*auxilium* help, see -ARY¹)]

aux′in, n. Substance which stimulates growth, growth hormone. [f. Gk *auxanō* increase, -IN]

avadavat. See AMADAVAT.

avail′¹, v.t. & i. Afford help; be of value or profit; (trans.) help, benefit; ~ one*self of*, profit by, take advantage of. [ME; f. obs. *vail* vb f. OF *valoir* be worth f. L *valēre*]

avail′², n. Use, profit, only in phrr. *of* ~, *of no* ~, *without* ~, *to little* ~. [f. prec., cf. VAIL²]

avail′a|ble, a. Capable of being used, at one's disposal, within one's reach. Hence ~BIL′ITY, ~bleNESS (-ln-), nn., ~bLY² adv. [AVAIL v. + -ABLE]

av′alanche (-ahnsh), n. Mass of snow, earth, & ice, descending swiftly from mountain (also fig.). [F, dialect. form of *avalance* f. *avaler* descend, see -ANCE]

ăvani′a (-nēa), n. (hist.). (Extortionate) tax levied by Turks. [orig. unkn.; common in Levant]

avant-courier (avŏng′-kŏŏr′ĭer), n. One who runs, rides, before; esp. (pl.) scouts, advance-guard. [f. F *avant-coureur* (*avant* before + *coureur* runner, after COURIER]

avant-garde (avŏng′-gârd′), n. The pioneers or innovators in any art in a particular period. [F, = vanguard]

ăv′arice, n. Greed of gain, cupidity; (fig.) eager desire to get or keep. Hence **ăvari′cious** (-shus) a., **ăvari′cious**LY² adv. [ME, f. OF, f. L *avaritia* (*avarus* greedy, see -ICE)]

avast′ (-ahst), int. (naut.). Stop; cease. [f. Du. *houd vast* hold fast]

ăv′atâr, n. (Hindu Myth.) descent of deity to earth in incarnate form; incarnation; manifestation, display; phase. [f. Skr. *avatara* descent (*ava* down + *tar-* pass over)]

avaunt′, int. (arch., joc.). Begone. [ME, f. OF *avant* f. Rom. **abante* before (L *ab* from + *ante* before)]

āv′ē, int. & n. Welcome; farewell; shout of welcome or farewell; ~ *ăt′que* VALE², hail & farewell; *Ave Maria* (Hail, Mary), devotional recitation (cf. *Luke* i. 28) & prayer to the Virgin; ~-*bell*, rung when this is to be said. [L, 2nd sing. imper. of *avēre* fare well]

avenge' (-j), v.t. Inflict retribution, exact satisfaction, on behalf of (person, violated right, etc.); *be* ~*d*, ~ oneself; take vengeance for (injury). [ME, f. OF *avengier* (*à* to +*vengier* f. L *vindicare*)]

av'ens (-nz), n. *Wood* ~, herb bennet; *water* ~, plant of same genus. [ME *avence* f. OF (med. L *avencia*) of unkn. orig.]

avèn'tūrine, -in, n. Brownish glass with copper crystals, manufactured first at Murano near Venice; variety of quartz resembling this. [F, f. It. *avventurino* (*avventura* chance, from its accidental discovery)]

av'ĕnŭe, n. Way of approach (usu. fig.); approach to country house bordered by trees; roadway marked by trees or other objects at regular intervals; (esp. in U.S.) wide street. [F, fem. p.p. (used as n.) of *avenir* f. L ADvenire come to]

aver', v.t. (-rr-). Assert, affirm; (Law) prove (a plea). Hence ~RABLE a. [ME, f. OF *averer* f. Rom. *ADverare* verify (*verus* true)]

av'erage[1], n. Generally prevailing rate, degree, or amount; ordinary standard; medial estimate, as *on the* or *an* ~; apportionment of loss of ship, cargo, or freight, through unavoidable accident (*particular* ~) or through intentional damage to ship or sacrifice of cargo (*general* ~), among the owners or insurers; (Cricket) *batting* ~, aggregate number of runs made by batsman divided by the number of times he has been dismissed, *bowling* ~, cost of runs per wicket taken by bowler, calculated by dividing the number of runs scored off his bowling by the number of wickets he has taken. [Eng. c. 1500, corresp. to OF *avarie*, Cat., Sp. *averia*, Pg., It. *avaria*, Du. *avarij*, G *havarie*; ult. (thr. It.) f. Arab. *'āwariya* damaged goods f. *'awār* damage; the Eng. form -*age* is by assoc. w. allied concepts, e.g. *damage*, *primage*]

av'erage[2], v.t. Estimated by average; of the usual standard. Hence ~LY[2] (-jl-) adv. [f. prec.]

av'erage[3], v.t. Estimate the average of (by dividing the aggregate of several quantities by the number of quantities); estimate the general standard of; amount on an average to; ~ (work on an average) *six hours a day*. [as prec.]

aver'ment, n. Positive statement, affirmation; (Law) offer to prove, proof of, a plea. [ME, f. OF *averement* (as AVER)]

averrŭncat'or (-ŭngk-), n. Instrument for cutting off branches of trees high above head. [f. obs. vb *averruncate*, f. L *averruncare* ward off (*a* off +*verruncare* turn), but wrongly explained as f. *eruncare* weed out]

averse', a. Opposed, disinclined, (*to*, *from*); unwilling (*to* do). Hence ~NESS (-sn-) n. [f. L as AVERT]

aver'sion (-shn), n. Dislike, antipathy, (*to*, *from*, *for*); unwillingness (*to* do); ob-

ject of dislike, as *pet* ~. [F, or f. L *aversio* (as AVERT, see -ION)]

avert', v.t. Turn away (eyes, thoughts, *from*); ward off. Hence ~IBLE, ~ABLE, aa. [ME, f. L *avertere* (*a* AB- away +*vertere* *vers*- turn); partly f. OF *avertir* f. Rom. *avertire*; cf. ADVERT]

āv'ian, a. Pertaining to birds. [f. L *avis* bird +-AN]

āv'iarŷ, n. Place for keeping birds. [f. L *aviarium* (as prec., see -ARY[1])]

āv'iāte, v.i. Fly in or pilot an aircraft. [back form. f. foll.]

āviā'tion, n. Art or practice of operating a heavier-than-air aircraft. So ~OR n. [F, irreg. f. L *avis* bird, see -ATION]

av'id, a. Eager, greedy (*of*, *for*). Hence ~LY[2] adv. [f. F *avide* or L *avidus* (*avēre* crave)]

avid'itŷ, n. Ardent desire, greed. [ME, f. OF *avidite* or L *aviditas* (as prec., see -TY)]

āv'ifauna, n. Birds (of district, country) collectively. [f. L *avis* bird +FAUNA]

avion (see Ap.), n. Aeroplane. [F]

avi'so (-ēzō), n. Boat for carrying despatches. [Sp., f. L *advisum*, see ADVICE]

avĭzăn'dum, n. (Sc. Law). Private consideration. [med. L, gerund of *avizare* consider]

ăvoca'dō (-ah-), n. (pl. ~s). (Also ~ *pear*) pear-shaped tropical fruit, the ALLIGATOR pear. [Sp., =advocate (pop. rendering of Mex. *ahuacatl*)]

ăvoca'tion, n. Distraction; minor occupation; (loosely) vocation, calling. [f. L *avocatio* (*avocare* call away, see -ATION)]

ăv'ocet, -sĕt, n. Wading bird with upturned bill. [f. F *avocette* f. It. *avosetta*]

avoid', v.t. Shun, refrain from (thing, doing); escape, evade; (Law) defeat (pleading), quash (sentence). Hence ~ABLE a. [f. AF *avoider* = OF *evuider* clear out, get quit of (*es* out +*vuidier* f. *vuit*, *vuide*, VOID)]

avoid'ance, n. Act of avoiding; vacancy (of office, benefice). [prec. +-ANCE]

avoirdupois (ăverdŭpoiz'), a. & n. ~ (*weight*), system of weights used in English-speaking countries for all goods except precious metals & stones, & medicines; ~ *pound* contains 7,000 grains; *weight*, heaviness. [ME *aver* (*avoir*) *de peis* (*pois*), f. AF, OF *aveir de pois* goods of weight (*aveir* f. L *habēre* + *peis*, *pois*, see POISE); sp. -*du*- from *c.* 1650]

avouch', v.t. & i. Guarantee; affirm; confess. Hence ~MENT n. [ME, f. OF *avochier* f. L ADvocare (in legal use) call upon as defender]

avow', v.t. Admit, confess; (refl. & pass.) admit oneself to be, as ~*ed himself the author, the* ~*ed author*. Hence **avow'-**ABLE a., **avow'AL** n., **avow'ĕdLY**[2] adv. [ME, f. OF *avouer* f. L *advocare*; see ADVOCATE]

avŭl'sion (-shn), n. Tearing away; (Law) sudden removal of land by flood etc. to another person's estate. [f. L *avulsio* (*avellere -vuls-* pluck away)]

avŭnc'ŭlar, a. Of, resembling, an uncle. [f. L *avunculus* maternal uncle (dim. of *avus* grandfather) + -AR¹]

await' (*a*-), v.t. Wait for; (of things) be in store for. [ME, f. ONF *awaitier* (*à* to + *waitier*, OF *guaitier*, see WAIT v.)]

awāke'¹ (*a*-), v.t. & i. (past *awoke*, p.p. *awoke*, ~*d*). Cease to sleep; (fig.) become active; ~ *to*, become conscious of; rouse from sleep (lit. & fig.). [(1) OE *awæcnan*, *awŏc*, *awacen*, (*a*- prob. = on); of which present tense was early treated as weak vb, with past *awæcnede*, whence AWAKEN, *awakened*; (2) late OE *awacian*, *awacode*, in form a compd of *wacian* watch, but in sense = *awæcnan*; (3) in OE these were intr., the trans. sense being given by *awecc*(*e*)*an*, ME *awecche*, Goth. *uswakjan*, G *erwecken*, ousted by *awake*, trans., before 1300; see WAKE¹]

awāke'² (*a*-), pred. a. Roused from sleep; not asleep; vigilant; ~ *to*, aware of. [short for *awaken*, orig. p.p. of prec.]

awāk'en (*a*-), v.t. & i. = AWAKE¹ (lit. & fig.) esp. (fig.) arouse (*to* a sense of). [see AWAKE¹ (1)]

award'¹ (*awŏrd'*), v.t. Adjudge; grant, assign. [f. AF *awarder* f. ONF *eswarder* = OF *esguarder*, f. Rom. *EXwardare f. WG *ward-; see WARD, GUARD]

award'² (*awŏrd'*), n. Judicial decision; payment, penalty, assigned by this. [AF, f. *awarder*; see prec.]

awāre' (*a*-), pred. a. Conscious, knowing, (*of*, *that*). Hence ~NESS (*awār'n*-) n., condition of being ~ (*of* something or *that* something is). [OE *gewær* (OS *giwar*, OHG *gawar*) f. *ge*-Y-, +*wær* WARE²]

awash' (*-wŏ-*), pred. a. Flush with or washed by the waves. [A- (2)]

away' (*a*-), adv. To, at, a distance from the place, person, thing, in question (lit. & fig.), as *go* ~, *throw* ~, *give* ~, *he is* ~, *waste* ~, *fool* ~, *explain* ~; *out & ~*, beyond comparison; constantly, continuously, as *work* ~, *peg* ~; without delay, as *fire* ~; = go away (imper.); ~ *with* (imper.), go ~ with, take ~; *get* ~ *with it* (colloq.), do something with impunity; *make* ~ *with*, destroy; quasi-adj. in ~ *game*, *match*, *win*. [OE *onweg*, later *aweg* on (the, his, one's) way; f. A² prep. + WAY]

awe'¹, n. Reverential fear or wonder, as *stand in* ~ *of*, hold, keep, *in* ~; ~'*struck*, struck with ~. Hence ~'LESS (awl-), ~'SOME (aws-), aa. [ME *age* f. ON *agi* wh. replaced OE, ME *ege*, both f. Gmc *ag-; cf. Goth. *agis* fear]

awe'², v.t. Inspire with awe. [f. prec.]

awe'³, n. One of the float-boards of an undershot water-wheel. [orig. unkn.]

aweigh (*awā'*), adv. (Of anchor) just lifted from ground in weighing. [A² prep. + WEIGH]

awf'ul, a. Inspiring awe; worthy of profound respect; solemnly impressive;

(arch.) reverential; (sl.) notable in its kind, as ~ *scrawl*, *bore*, *relief*, *something* ~. Hence ~LY² adv., (also, sl.) extremely, ~NESS n. [AWE¹ + -FUL]

awhile (*awil'*), adv. For a short time. [OE *āne hwīle* a while]

awk'ward, a. Ill-adapted for use; clumsy (person, thing); bungling; embarrassing; difficult, dangerous, to deal with. Hence ~ISH¹ (2) a., ~LY² adv., ~NESS n. [f. obs. adj. *awk* backhanded, untoward (ME, f. ON *afug* turned the wrong way) + -WARD]

awl, n. Small tool for pricking, pricker, esp. that used by shoemakers. [OE *æl*, OHG *ala*, ON *alr*]

awn, n. Spinous process, beard, terminating grain-sheath of barley, oats, etc. Hence ~ed¹ (-nd) [-ED²], ~'LESS, aa. [ME, f. ON *ögn* pl. *agnar*, OHG *agana*, Goth. *ahana*]

awn'ing, n. Canvas roof, esp. above deck of vessel; (Naut.) poop-deck beyond bulkhead of cabin; shelter. Hence awned² (-nd) [-ED²] a. [orig. unkn.]

awry (*arī'*), adv. & a. Crookedly, askew; *look* ~, look askance (lit. & fig.); amiss, improperly; *go*, *run*, *tread*, ~, do wrong; (adj., usu. pred.) crooked (lit. & fig.). [A prep. + WRY]

ăxe, ăx, n., & v.t. Chopping-tool, usually iron with steel edge & wooden handle; *put the* ~ *in the helve*, solve a puzzle; (orig. U.S. pol.) *an* ~ *to grind*, private ends to serve; (vb) cut down (costs, services). [OE *æx*, OS *akus*, OHG *ackus*, ON *öx*, Goth. *aqizi*; cf. Gk *axinē*]

ăx'ial, a. Forming, belonging to, an axis; round an axis. Hence **ăxiăl'ITY** n., ~LY² adv. [f. AXIS + -AL]

ăx'il, n. Upper angle between leaf & stem it springs from, or between branch & trunk. [f. L *axilla* armpit]

ăx'ile, a. (bot., physiol.). Belonging to the axis. [f. AXIS, see -IL]

ăx'illary, a. Pertaining to the armpit; (Bot.) in, growing from, the axil. [f. F *axillaire* (see AXIL, -ARY)]

ăx'iom, n. Established principle; (rare) maxim; self-evident truth (esp. in geom.). [f. F *axiome* or L f. Gk *axiōma* (*axioō* hold worthy f. *axios*, see -M)]

ăxiomăt'ic(al), aa. Self-evident; characterized by axioms; (rare) full of maxims, aphoristic. Hence **ăxiomăt'icalLY²** adv. [f. Gk *axiomatikos* (*axiōma -matos*), see prec. & -IC, -AL]

ăx'is, n. (pl. *axēs*). **1.** Imaginary line about which a body rotates, or by revolution about which a plane is conceived as generating a solid (sphere. cone, cylinder); line dividing regular figure symmetrically. **2.** Straight line from end to end of a body, as ~ *of equator* (polar diameter of earth). **3.** (bot.). Central column of inflorescence or other whorl of growth. **4.** (opt.). Ray passing through centre of eye or lens, or falling perpendicularly on it. **5.** (physiol.). Central core of organ or organism. **6.** (pol.). Agreement between two or more countries intended to form a centre round which like-minded nations may rally; *the Axis* (hist., orig. *the Rome– –Berlin Axis*), (pact between) Germany & Italy, later extended to include Japan (*Rome–Berlin–Tokyo Axis*); attrib., as *Axis intrigues, powers, propaganda.* [L, = axle, pivot]

ă′xle, n. Spindle upon or with which wheel revolves; (in carriages, prop.) slender end of ~*-tree* (whole bar connecting wheels), (loosely) ~*-tree*; *wheel & ~,* a MECHANICAL power; ~*-box* (in which ends of ~s revolve); ~*-journal,* polished end of ~ revolving under bearing in ~*-box.* Hence **ă′xlED²** (-ld) a. [earliest in ME *axel-tre* f. ON *öxul-tré,* replacing the native ME *ax-tre* f. OE *æx, eax*]

Ax′minster (ă-), a. ~ *carpet,* kind formerly hand-woven at ~, now made at Wilton.

ăx′olŏtl, n. Newt-like amphibian found in Mexican lakes. [Aztec]

ăx′ŏn (zool.). Appendage of the nerve cell which carries signals from the cell. [f. Gk *axōn* axle]

ay (ī), int. & n. (pl. *ayes*). Yes; (n.) affirmative answer; *the ayes have it,* affirmative voters are in majority. [appears suddenly *c.* 1575; orig. unkn.]

ayah (i′a), n. Native Indian nurse or lady's maid. [Ind. vernacular *āya* f. Port. *aia* nurse, fem. of *aio* tutor]

aye (ă), adv. Ever, always; on all occasions; *for* ~, for ever. [ME *agg, ai, ei,* f. ON *ei, ey,* cogn. w. Goth. *aiw* f. Gmc *•aiwaz,* cogn. w. L *aevum* age; cf. Gk *aei* always]

aye-aye (i′ī), n. Squirrel-like animal of the size of a cat, found only in Madagascar. [F, f. Malagasy *aiay*]

Azăl′ĕa, n. Genus of flowering shrubby plants, natives of northern hemisphere. [mod. L, f. Gk *azalea* fem. of *azaleos* dry (from its dry wood or the dry soil in which it flourishes)]

Azil′ian, a. Of the transitional period between the palaeolithic & neolithic ages. [f. *Mas d'Azil* in French Pyrenees, where remains were found]

ăz′imuth, n. Arc of the heavens extending from the zenith to the horizon, which it cuts at right angles; ~*-circle,* one of which this is a quadrant, passing through zenith & nadir; *true ~* of a heavenly body, arc of horizon intercepted between north (in Southern hemisphere, south) point of horizon & the point where the great circle passing through the body cuts the horizon; *magnetic ~,* arc intercepted between this circle & magnetic meridian. Hence **ăzimŭth′AL** a., **ăzimŭth′allY²** adv. [ME, f OF *azimut* f. Arab. *assumut* (*al* the +*sumut* pl. of *samt* way, direction)]

azŏ′ic, a. Having no trace of life; (Geol.) containing no organic remains. [irreg. f. Gk *azōos* (*a-* not +*zōē* life) +-IC]

ăz′ōte, n. Former name of nitrogen. Hence **azŏt′IC** a., **ăz′otIZE** (3) v.t. [F, f. Gk *a-* not +*zōō* (for *zaō*) live, from its inability to support life]

Az′tĕc (ă-), a. & n. (One) of the Aztecs, the Mexican people dominant till the conquest of Cortes (1519).

ă′zure (-zher, -zhyer), n. & a., & v.t. **1.** Sky blue; (Her.) blue; unclouded vault of heaven; bright blue pigment; lapis lazuli. **2.** adj. Sky-blue, (fig.) cloudless, serene. **3.** v.t. Make ~. [ME, f. OF *azur* f. med. L *azura* f. Arab. *al* the +*lazward* f. Pers. *lazhward* lapis lazuli]

ăz′ȳgous, a. & n. (physiol.). (An organic part) not existing in pairs. [f. Gk *azugos* unyoked (*a-* not +*zugon* yoke) +-OUS]

B

B (bē), letter (pl. *Bs,* B's, Bees). (Mus.) seventh note in scale of C major (*B flat,* jocular euphem. for bug). (In argument) second hypothetical person or thing. (Alg.) second known quantity.

baa (bah), n., & v.i. (*baaing, baaed* or *baa'd*). = BLEAT. ~*-lamb,* nursery name for lamb. [imit.]

Bă′al, n. (pl. ~*im*). Phoenician god; (transf.) a false god. Hence ~ISM (3), ~IST (2), ~ITE (1), nn. [ME, f. Heb. *ba'al* lord]

baas (bahs), n. (S. Africa). Master (freq. as form of address). [Du., see BOSS²]

ba′bacōote (bah-), n. Species of lemur (Madagascar). [Malagasy *babakoto*]

Băbb′itt-mĕt′al, n. Soft alloy of tin, antimony, & copper. [*I. Babbitt* inventor (d. 1862)]

băb′ble¹, v.i. & t. Talk half articulately, incoherently, or excessively; murmur (of streams etc.); repeat foolishly; let out (secrets). Hence ~MENT (-lm-) n. [imit. of infant's *ba, ba,* +-LE (3); cf. F *babiller,* MLG *babbelen,* G *pappeln*]

băb′ble², n. Imperfect speech; idle talk; murmur of water etc. [prec.]

băb′bler, n. Chatterer; teller of secrets; long-legged thrush. [-ER¹]

băbe, n. (poet.). Young child, baby; inexperienced or guileless person (in pl. often ~s & sucklings). [ME, imit. of child's speech, cf. BABBLE]

băb′el, n. (*B~*) the tower in Shinar (*Gen.* xi); a high structure; visionary plan; scene of confusion, confusion of tongues, noisy assembly, meaningless noise. [ME, perh. f. Ass. *bab-ilu* gate of God]

băbirous′sa, -rus′sa, (-rōō-), n. E.- -Asian wild hog with upturned horn-like tusks. [Malay *babi* hog +*rusa* deer]

Bab′ism (bah-), n. Doctrine of a Persian mystical & pantheistic sect (*Babi*) founded in 1844. [f. Pers. *Bab-ed-Din,* gate (= intermediary) of the Faith, whence the founder's usual title of (the) Bab]

baboon′, n. Large African & S.-Asian monkey. [ME, f. OF babuin or med. L babewynus, of unkn. orig.]

babouche′ (-ōōsh), n. Oriental slipper. [F, f. Arab babush f. Pers. paposh (pa foot + posh covering); for p = b cf. pasha & bashaw]

ba′bu (bah′bōō), -bōō, n. (As Hindu title) Mr; Hindu (esp. Bengali) gentleman; Indian English-writing clerk, hence derog., ~ English. [Hind. babu]

babul′ (-ōōl), n. Gum-arabic tree of India and Arabia. [Hind. & Pers.]

bāb′y̆, n. Very young child; childish person, whence ~ISH[1] a., ~ishNESS, ~ISM (2), nn.; thing small of its kind; •girl, sweetheart, (sl.); ~ car, motor-car of small size and power; •~ carriage, perambulator; ~-farmer, one who contracts to keep babies; ~ grand, small grand piano; ||~-jumper, hanging frame in which child is fastened to exercise limbs; ~-sitter, person sitting with or looking after a ~ while its parents are out; hold the ~, carry the ~, (be left to) assume an undesired responsibility. Hence ~HOOD n. [ME, BABE, -Y[3]]

Băb′y̆lon, n. Capital of Chaldean empire; any great empire or vicious city; Rome, the papacy (ref. to Rev. xvii etc.), London, etc. Hence **Băbȳlōn′IAN** a. & n. [L, f. Gk Babulōn f. Heb. Babel BABEL]

băccalaur′ĕate, n. University degree of bachelor. [f. med. L baccalaureatus f. baccalareus BACHELOR; see -ATE[1]]

băcc′ara(t) (-rah), n. Gambling card game. [F]

băcc′āte, a. (bot.). Bearing berries, berry-shaped. [f. mod. L baccatus berried (bacca berry, -ATE[2])]

Băcc′hanal (-ka-), a. & n. 1. Of, like, Bacchus or his rites; riotous, roistering. 2. n. Priest, priestess, votary, of Bacchus; drunken reveller; dance or song in honour of Bacchus. [f. L bacchanalis (L f. Gk Bakkhos god of wine, -AL)]

Băcchanăl′ia (-ka-), n. pl. Festival of Bacchus; drunken revelry. [L neut. pl. of bacchanalis = prec.]

Băcchanăl′ian (-ka-), a. & n. Of Bacchanals; riotous, drunken; (n.) a Bacchanal, tippler. [f. L bacchanalis BACCHANAL + -AN]

Băcc′hant (-ka-), n. masc. or fem., & a.; **Bacchante** (băk′ant, bakánt′, bakǎn′ti), n. fem. Priest, priestess, votary of Bacchus; Bacchus-worshipping, wine-loving. Hence **Bacchăn′tIC** (-kǎ-) a. [(-nte F) f. L bacchari (-ANT) f. Gk bakkhaō celebrate Bacchic rites]

Băcc′hic (-kĭk), a. = BACCHANAL (adj. meanings). [f. L f. Gk bakkhikos of Bacchus]

Băcc′hus (-kus), n. Greek god of wine. [L, f. Gk Bakkhos]

băccif′erous, băcc′ifōrm, băcciv′orous, (băks-), aa. Berry-bearing, -shaped, -eating. [L baccifer (-FEROUS); L bacca berry + -FORM, -VOROUS]

||băcc′y̆ (-k-), n. (colloq.) Tobacco. [abbr.]

băch′elor, n. Young knight serving under another's banner (hist.); hence now, knight ~, simple knight not belonging to a special order; man or woman who has taken a university degree below Master; unmarried man. ~'s buttons, various button-shaped flowers esp. double buttercup, also small ratafia biscuits, also buttons attachable without sewing; ~ girl (unmarried and living independently); ~ (seal), young male fur-seal with no mate. Hence ~HOOD, ~SHIP, ~ISM(4), nn. [ME bacheler f. OF f. Rom. *baccalāris of unascert. orig. In the academic sense this was allied to baccalārius, & further (prob. by a word-play on bacca lauri laurel berry) to baccalaureus]

bacill′ary, a. Of little rods (tissue, membrane); connected with bacilli (disease, research). [BACILLUS + -ARY[1]]

bacill′ifōrm, a. Rod-shaped. [foll. + -FORM]

bacill′us, n. (pl. -lī). A rodlike bacterium, esp. one of the various types that cause disease by entering and multiplying in animal and other tissues. [LL dim. of L baculus stick]

băck[1], n. & a. 1. Hinder surface of human body (at the ~ of, behind in support, pursuit, or concealment; BEHIND one's ~; give, make, a ~, bend down at leapfrog; turn one's ~ upon, run away from, abandon; on one's ~, laid up; with one's ~ to wall, hard pressed); body as needing clothes (~ & belly, clothing & food) or as weight-carrier (~ equal to burden; have on one's ~, be burdened with; put, get, set, person's ~ up, make him angry; break one's ~, overburden him, & break[1] ~ of); surface of things corresponding to human ~ (less visible, active, or important; ~ of hand, leg, door, book, knife), side away from spectator; upper surface of animal's body, surface corresponding to this (ridge-shaped, etc.; ~ of hill, ship esp. in broke her ~; on the ~ of, in addition to); football player stationed behind (full, three-quarter, half, ~); the Backs, grounds on the Cam at the ~ of certain Colleges at Cambridge, of noted beauty; ~'band, over cart-saddle to keep shafts up; ~'board, at ~ of cart, also strapped across child's ~ to straighten it; ~'bone, spine (whence ~'bōnED[2] (-nd) a.; to the ~bone, thoroughly), main support, axis, watershed, chief strength, firmness of character; ~'fall, throw on ~ in wrestling; ~'sword, with only one edge, also singlestick. 2. adj. (no comp., superl. ~'most). Situated behind, remote, inferior, (take ~ seat, humble oneself); overdue (~ rent); reversed, counter, (~ current); ||~-bench(er), (occupant of) a seat in the House of Commons or similar assembly used by a member not entitled to a front-bench seat (~-bench freq. used attrib.); ||~-blocks, (Austral.) land in the remote & sparsely-inhabited interior; ~-chat (colloq.), retort(s), recrimination; ~-cloth, (Theatr.) painted cloth at ~ of stage as main part of scenery; ~'door, lit., & fig. secret means or approach, (adj.) clandestine, underhand; ~-drop, ~-cloth; ||~-end, late autumn; ~-fire, premature explosion in the cylinder of an internal-combustion engine (also as vb); ~ formation, making from a supposed derivative (as lazy, banting) of the non-existent word (laze, bant) from which it might have come; ~'ground, part of scene, picture, or description, that serves as setting to chief figures or objects & foreground, obscurity, retirement, (fig.) person's cultural knowledge, education, experience, etc.; ~'hand(ed), delivered with ~ of hand or in direction counter to the usual, indirect, unexpected, (~'hander, such blow, indirect attack, extra glass got by bottle's travelling wrong way); ~'log, reserves, arrears of unfulfilled orders; ~-marker, scratch man in race etc.; ~ number (of magazine etc.), (sl.) out-of-date method or person; ~ play (Cricket), see BACK³; ~-room boys (colloq.), men engaged in (secret) research; ~-seat driver, one who attempts to control without responsibility; ~'set, counter-current, check, reverse; ~'side, posterior, rump; ~-sight, that nearer stock of rifle etc., (Surv.) sight taken backwards; ~ slang, form of low slang in which words are spelt & pronounced backwards (e.g. ynnep for penny); ~'stage adj. & adv., behind the curtain in a theatre (freq. in the wings or dressing-rooms), (fig.) behind the scenes; ~'stairs n. & a., ~'stair a., ~'door above; ~'stays, ropes slanting abaft from mast-head to a lower point; ~'stroke, return or backhand stroke; ~'wash, motion of receding wave (lit. & fig.); ~'water, water dammed back, currentless water beside stream & fed by its backflow, stagnant condition of things, creek communicating with sea by barred outlets, water cast from ship's paddles, loss of power caused by this; ~'woods n. & a., ~'wood a., (connected with) remote uncleared forest land (so ~'woodsman); ~'woodsman, ||(also, fig.) peer who rarely or never attends House of Lords. [a. f. n., OE bæc, OS, ON bak, f. Gmc *bakam; now almost confined to E; cf. BACON]

băck², v.t. & i. Put, or be, a back, lining, support, or background, to; assist with countenance, money, or argument, bet upon, whence ~'ER¹ n.; (of sporting dogs) follow suit to one that points; ~ up, help by subordinate action, esp. in cricket; ride upon, break in to the saddle; countersign, endorse; cause to move back (horse, boat, engine, etc.; ~ a sail,

yard, lay it aback, i.e. to face wind; ~ water, reverse boat's forward motion with oars); go backwards; (of wind) change counter-sunwise (cf. VEER); ~ out (of), withdraw (from undertaking etc.); ~ down, abandon claim. [f. prec.]

băck³, adv. To the rear (often with omission of vb, esp. in imperative), away from what is considered the front (push the bolt ~); play ~ (Cricket), step ~ to play a defensive stroke; away from a promise (go ~ from or upon one's word); into the past, into or in an earlier position or condition, home; in return (answer ~ = retort; pay ~); at a distance (~ from the road); in a checked condition (keep ~); = ago; reckoning backwards (for years ~); behindhand; ~ & forth = to & fro; *~ of, = behind; ~'bite, slander, speak ill of, whence ~'bĭTER¹ n.; ~'lash(ing), irregular recoil of wheels in machinery due to defects or sudden pressure; ~'pedal, work pedal backwards, (fig.) check a forward movement, reverse one's action; ~slide' v.i., relapse into sin, whence ~slid'ER¹, ~slid'ING¹, nn.; ~'stitch n. & v.t. & i., sew(ing) with overlapping stitches. [aphetic f. ABACK]

băck⁴, n. Shallow vat used in brewing, dyeing, etc. [f. Du. bak tub, = LG back; cf. also F bac tub, ferry-boat, punt, med. L bac(c)us ferry-boat, LL bacca tub, of uncert. relationships]

băckgămm'on, n. Game played on special double board with draughts & dice; most complete form of win in this. [BACK³ (because pieces go back or re-enter), GAME¹]

băck'ing, n. In vbl senses; esp.: body of supporters; material used to form thing's back or support. [BACK², -ING¹]

backsheesh. See BAKSHEESH.

băck'ward(s), adv., **băck'ward**, a. 1. Away from one's front (look, lean, etc.); back foremost (walk etc.); back to starting-point (flow, roll, etc.); not of living things exc. in ~ & forwards); into a worse state (go etc.); into the past (reckon etc.); the reverse way (spell etc.; ring the bells ~, from bass upwards). 2. adj. Directed to rear or starting-point; reversed; reluctant, shy, behindhand, dull, whence **băck'wardNESS** n. [aphetic f. abackward, later referred to BACK¹; see -WARD, -WARDS]

||**băckwardā'tion**, n. (St. Exch.). Percentage paid by seller of stock for right of delaying delivery (cf. CONTANGO). [f. prec. used as vb +-ATION]

bāc'on, n. Cured back & sides of pig (save one's ~, escape death or injury); bring home the ~ (sl.), succeed in one's undertaking. [ME, f. OF f. Frank. bako = OHG bahho, bacho, buttock, ham, flitch, f. Gmc *bakon-; cf. BACK¹]

Bacōn'ian, a. & n. Of Francis Bacon or his philosophy, experimental, inductive; (n.) follower of Bacon; believer in ~

authorship of Shakespeare's plays. [*Bacon* (d. 1626) +-IAN]

băctĕri̇|ŏl′y̆sis, n. Artificial liquefaction of solid sewage by bacterial agency; destruction of bacteria by a serum. So ~**olȳt′ic** a., capable of destroying bacteria. [f. BACTERIUM + Gk *lusis* dissolution]

băcter′iophage (-fahzh, -fāj), n. Minute organism which destroys bacteria. [f. foll. + Gk *phagein* eat]

băctēr′|ium, n. (pl. *-ria*). Kinds of microscopic unicellular organism found almost everywhere, some of which cause disease. Hence ~IAL a., ~IŎL′OGY, ~IŎL′OGIST, nn. [mod. L, f. Gk *baktērion* dim. of *baktron* stick]

băc′ūline, a. Of the stick or flogging (esp. ~ *argument*). [f. L *baculum* stick + -INE¹]

băd, a. (worse, worst), & n. **1.** (Negatively) worthless, inferior, deficient, of poor quality, incorrect, not valid, (~ *air*, corrupt; ~ *coin*, debased; ~ *debt*, not recoverable; ~ *food*, not nourishing; **~ lands,* extensive barren uncultivable tracts; *go* ~, decay; *with* ~ *grace*, reluctantly; ~ *shot*, wrong guess; ~ *law*, not sustainable; ~ *form*, want of breeding; *in a* ~ *sense*, unfavourable); ~ *egg*, ~ *hat*, (sl.) person or ~ character. **2.** (Positively) noxious, depraved, vicious, offensive, painful (~ *blood*, ill feeling; ~ *for*, injurious to); in ill health, injured, in pain, (*she is* ~, *worse, today*; *a* ~ *leg*); (colloq. of things in no case good) notable, decided, pronounced, (~ *blunder*, *headache*, *falling-off*). **3.** n. Ill fortune (*take the* ~ *with the good*), wrong side of account (*£500 to the* ~), ruin (*go to the* ~). Hence **bădd′ISH¹** (2) a. [ME *badde*, perh. f. OE *bæddel* hermaphrodite, womanish man; for loss of *l* cf. *mycel* MUCH]

bade. See BID¹.

bădge, n. Distinctive mark, formerly of knight, now worn as sign of office or licensed employment or membership of a society; symbol, something that betrays a quality or condition. [ME *bage*, cf. rare OF *bage*; orig. unkn.]

bădg′er¹, n. (dial.). Hawker, esp. of provisions. [orig. unkn.; cf. obs. vb *badge* to hawk]

bădg′er², n. Grey-coated strong-jawed nocturnal hibernating plantigrade quadruped between weasels & bears; fishing--fly, & painting or other brush, made of its hair; ~-*baiting, -drawing*, setting dogs to draw it from its burrow or a cask; ~--*legged*, with legs of unequal length (popular error). [16th c. (older *brock*, *bauson*, *gray*) perh. f. BADGE + -ARD (earlier forms *bageard*, *badgerd*) with ref. to its white forehead mark]

bădg′er³, v.t. Bait like a badger, worry, tease. [f. prec.]

băd′īnage (-ahzh), n. Light raillery. [F]

băd′lȳ, adv. (worse, worst). Defectively, unsuccessfully, faultily, wickedly, cruelly,

dangerously, by much (*beaten*), very much (*want a thing* ~). [-LY²]

bădmash (bŭd′mahsh), bŭd′, n. (Anglo--Ind.). Rascal, bad character. [Pers. & Urdu]

băd′minton, n. A summer drink (claret, soda, sugar); game with net, rackets, & shuttlecocks. [Duke of Beaufort's seat]

băd′nĕss, n. Poor quality or condition; faultiness, invalidity; wickedness, noxiousness, adverseness. [-NESS]

Baed′eker (bād-), n. Guide-book published by firm founded by Karl *Baedeker*; ~ *raids*, German reprisal air-raids in 1942 on (cathedral) cities in England starred in ~.

bā′el, n. Indian tree, the orange-like fruit of which is a specific for diarrhoea etc. [f. Hind. *bel*]

băf′fle, v.t., & n. Foil, reduce to perplexity, bar progress of, (person, curiosity, faculties, efforts, ship); *baffling winds*, variable, preventing a straight course; (n.) ~ or ~-*plate*, plate hindering or regulating passage of fluid or gas through outlet or inlet (e.g. a damper); ~-*board*, *wall*, devices to prevent spread of noise. Hence ~r n., ~-plate. [hist. complex & uncert.; perh. f. obs. F *beffler*, mod. *bafouer* hoodwink etc.; also in obs. sense 'disgrace', cf. Sc. *bauchle*]

băff′y̆, n. Wooden golf club for lofting. [cf. Sc. *baff* a blow]

băg¹, n. Receptacle of flexible material with opening at top (‖green or *blue* ~, barrister's for briefs; hyphened with nouns showing contents or purpose etc., as *mail-*~, *travelling-*~, *hand*~, VANITY ~; also alone for such compp., e.g. for money-~, so ~s = wealth, or for game-~, also for game-~'s contents or all a sportsman has shot or caught; ~ *of bones*, lean creature; *whole* ~ *of tricks*, every device, everything, all the lot; *in bottom of* ~, as last resource; *in the* ~ (colloq.), in one's possession or power, (as good as) secured; *let cat out of* ~, reveal secret, esp. involuntarily; ~ *& baggage*, with all belongings, esp. of utter expulsion), whence ~g′ING¹ (3) n.; cow's udder; sac in body containing honey, poison, etc.; baggy place under eyes etc.; ‖(sl.) ~s, trousers; ~ *fox*, one brought, not found; ‖~′*man*, commercial traveller, also = ~ fox; ~′*pipe(s)*, reed-pipe wind instrument with bag as receptacle for air, melody pipe (chanter), & fixed-note pipes (drones), used in Scotland &, with variations, in Ireland & N. England; ~-*sleeve*, loose except at wrist; ~-*wig*, 18th-c. wig with back hair enclosed in ~. Hence ~′FUL (2) n. [ME *bagge*; cf. ON *baggi*, also OF *bague*, Pr. *bagua* baggage, med. L *baga* sack. The Engl. was possibly f. ON, but the source of this, & its relation to the Romanic, are unkn.]

băg², v.i. & t. (-gg-). Swell, bulge: ‖(Naut.) drop away from course; hang loosely;

put in a bag, secure (game, whether lit. bagged or not), take possession of, (euphem.) steal; ||(school sl.) claim on the ground of being first to claim (*I* ~, but usu. ~*s I* or ~*s, first innings!*). [prec.]

băg³, v.t. (-gg-). Cut (wheat etc.) with a hook. [also *badge*; orig. unkn.]

bagásse′, n. Residue after extracting juice from sugar-cane & sugar-beet. [F]

băgatĕlle′, n. Trifle, negligible amount; short unpretentious piece of music; minor game of billiard kind. [F, f. It. *bagatella* dim. perh. f. *baga* BAGGAGE]

băgg′age, n. Belongings with which one travels (now ousted exc. in U.S. by *luggage*; *~ car*, luggage van; *~ room*, cloak-room; *~ tag*, luggage label); portable equipment of army; good-for--nothing woman (now only used playfully), saucy girl. [ME, f. OF *bagage* f. *baguer* tie up or *bagues* bundles pl. of *bague* = It. & med. L *baga* sack, chest, see BAG¹]

băgg′|y̆, a. Puffed out, hanging in loose folds. Hence ~ĭNESS n. [BAG¹ + -Y²]

bagnio (băn′yŏ), n. Bathing-house (now only in Italy & Turkey); oriental prison; brothel. [f. It. *bagno* f. L *balneum* bath]

băguette′ (-gĕt), n. (Archit.) small moulding of semicircular section, like an astragal; gem cut in a long rectangular shape. [F]

bah, int. of contempt. [F]

Bahadur (bəhahd′er), n. Title of respect appended in India to a person's name (& other titles). [Hind., = gallant]

baignoire (bĕnwahr′), n. Box at theatre on level of stalls. [F, = bath]

bail¹, n. Security for prisoner's appearance, on giving which he is released pending trial (*forfeit* one's ~, fail to appear; *save* one's ~, appear); (joc.) *give leg* ~, run away; person(s) who become(s) surety for prisoner's appearance (*be, become, go,* ~; *go* ~ *for,* guarantee truth of anything; magistrate *accepts, admits to, allows, holds to, takes,* ~; prisoner *gives, offers, surrenders to his,* ~; his ~ *surrender, render, bring in, produce,* him). [ME, f. OF *bail* custody f. *baillier* take charge of f. L *bajulare* bear a burden (*bajulus* porter)]

bail², v.t. **1.** Deliver (goods) in trust. **2.** Admit to bail, release on security given for appearance, (of magistrate; arch.); secure liberation of, by becoming bail or security for (~ *out* if already in prison). [sense 1 f. F *bailler* deliver; sense 2 f. BAIL¹]

bail³, n. **1.** (hist.). Outer line of fortification formed of stakes; wall of castle court, or court itself (cf. BAILEY). **2.** (mod.). Bar separating horses in open stable; *swinging* ~, slung from manger to ceiling; (Cricket) one of the cross pieces (orig. one not two) over stumps. [ME, f. OF *bail, bail(l)e* perh. f. *bailler* enclose, of unkn. orig.]

bail⁴, n. Half-hoop for supporting wagon-

-tilt etc.; hoop-handle of kettle etc.; ||(Australia) frame holding cow's head at milking. [ME *beyl* f. ON *beygla* sword--guard etc. (*beygya* = OE *bēgan* to bend)]

bail⁵, v.t. Confine (arch.); || ~ *up*, secure (cow; see prec.); (of bush-rangers) make hold up the arms to rob, (intr. of victim) throw up the arms. [app. f. OF *bailler* enclose, cf. BAIL³]

bail⁶, **bāle**, v.t. & i. Throw water out of boat with pails etc. (~ *water out,* ~ *out boat,* or abs.); *bale out,* (of airman) make parachute descent esp. from damaged aircraft. Hence **bail′er**¹ [-ER¹ (2)] n. [f. obs. n. *bail* bucket f. F *baille* f. Rom. **bajula* fem. of L *bajulus* BAIL¹]

bail′able, a. Admitting of bail (offence). [BAIL¹, ² + -ABLE]

bailee′, n. One to whom goods are entrusted for a purpose. [BAIL² + -EE]

bail′er², n. Ball that hits bails at cricket. [BAIL³ + -ER¹]

bail′ey, n. Outer wall of castle; also any of its inner defensive circuits, or any of the courts enclosed between these; *Old B~,* London Central Criminal Court, standing in ancient ~ of city wall. [ME variant of BAIL³]

Bail′ey bridge, n. Emergency bridge designed for rapid construction. [Sir D. *Bailey* (b. 1901), designer]

||**bail′ie** (-li), n. Scottish municipal magistrate = Eng. alderman. [ME *bailli* f. OF *baillis* BAILIFF]

bail′iff, n. (Orig.) King's representative in a district (including mayor, sheriff, etc.), esp. chief officer of a hundred (still in *High-B~* of *Westminster, B~* of *Dover Castle,* etc.; used as Eng. equivalent of F *bailli,* G *landvogt,* Channel-I. *bailly* or first civil officer); officer under sheriff for writs, processes, arrests; agent of lord of manor; landholder's steward. [ME, f. OF *baillif* obj. case of *baillis* f. *baillir* administer f. *bail* BAIL¹]

bail′iwick, n. District, jurisdiction, of bailie or bailiff; (joc.) person's sphere of operations. [BAILIE + WICK²]

bail′ment, n. Delivery of goods in trust; bailing of prisoner. [OF *baillement* see BAIL² & -MENT]

bail′or, n. One who delivers goods to another for a stated purpose. [BAIL² + -OR]

bails′man (-z-), n. One who gives bail for another. [f. *bail's* (BAIL¹) + MAN]

bain-marie (băn′marē′), n. Vessel of hot water in which stewpans are stood to warm. [F, transl. med. L *balneum Mariae,* whence earlier (15th c.) *balne, balneum*]

Bairam (bīrahm′), n. Mohammedan festival (twice a year, Lesser & Greater). [Turk. & Pers.]

bairn, n. Child (Sc. & N.-Eng. form now borrowed into literary Eng., the E *berne* having perished, & *barne* become dialectal). [OE *bearn,* Gmc **barn-* f. *beran* BEAR³]

bait[1], v.t. & i. (Orig.) cause to bite. **1.** Worry (chained animal) by setting dogs at it (*with* dogs, or abs.; also of the dogs), whence (*bear, bull*, etc.) -**baiting**[1] n.; torment (helpless person) with jeers etc. **2.** Give food to, take food, (of horses on journey); stop at inn (orig. to feed horses, then also for rest or refreshment). **3.** Put food (real or sham) on or in (hook, trap, fishing-place). [ME *beylen* f. ON *beita* causal of *bíta* BITE[1]; w. sense 1 cf. OF *beter* (f. ON); sense 3 prob. f. foll.]

bait[2], n. Food to entice prey (*live ~*, small fish so used); (fig.) an allurement, temptation; halt in journey for refreshment or rest. [partly f. ON *beita* food, partly f. prec.]

bait[3]. See BATE[3].

baize, n. Coarse woollen stuff with long nap used for coverings. [f. F *baies* pl. fem. of *bai* chestnut-coloured, BAY[6], treated as sing.; cf. BODICE]

bake, v.t. & i. Cook by dry heat in closed place or on hot surface (not by direct exposure to fire), whence **bak′ing**[1] (5) n.; harden by heat; *half~d*, immature, half-witted; (of sun) ripen (fruit), tan (skin); (intr.) undergo the process, be cooked, hardened, tanned, by heat; ||*~′house*, house or room for baking bread, or for making loaf-sugar; *~′stone*, flat stone, slate, or iron plate, on which cakes are baked in oven; *baking-powder*, substitute for yeast. [OE *bacan*, OHG *bachan*, ON *baka*, f. Gmc **bak-*]

bak′elite, n. Widely-used synthetic resin or plastic made from formaldehyde & phenol. [G *bakelit*; f. L. H. *Baekeland* inventor (d. 1944); P]

bak′er, n. Professional breadmaker (*pull devil, pull ~*, encouragement to both sides; *~′s dozen*, thirteen, 13th loaf being huckster's profit; *~-legged*, knock-kneed); (Fishing) kind of artificial fly. Hence *~ESS*[1], **bak′ERY** (3), nn. [OE *bæcere* (*bacan* BAKE + -ER[1])]

bak′sheesh, bak′shish (-ēsh), n. Gratuity, tip, (article not used). [Pers., f. *bakhshīdan* give]

Bal′aam (-lăm), n. Disappointing prophet or ally; || (Journalism) matter kept in stock to fill up gaps in newspaper (*Numb.* xxii. 28 or 38; *~-box*, receptacle for this).

Bălaclav′a (-ahva), n. Site of Crimean battle; || *~ helmet*, woollen covering for head & shoulders worn esp. by soldiers etc. on active service.

bălalaik′a (-līka), n. Triangular guitar-like musical instrument, popular in Slav countries. [Russ.]

băl′ance[1], n. **1.** Weighing-apparatus with central pivot, beam, & two scales; spring or lever substitute for this; regulating gear of clock or watch; zodiac constellation (usu. *Libra* or *The Scales*), & (not now corresponding) seventh sign of zodiac. **2.** The weighing of actions or opinions, the wavering of fortune or chance, power to decide (*hold the ~*); counterpoise, set-off; equilibrium (*~ of power*, no State greatly preponderant); (Art) harmony of design & proportion; steady position (*lose one's ~*, fall physically or be upset mentally); *~-wheel*, in watch, regulating the beat); preponderating weight or amount (*the ~ of advantage lies with him*). **3.** (Accounts) difference between Cr & Dr, statement of this (*strike a ~*, determine it; *~-sheet*, written statement of it with details); *~ of payments*, difference of value between payments into & out of a country, including invisible items such as tourist expenditure etc.; *~ of trade*, difference between exports & imports; *~ in hand*, amount over after realizing assets & meeting liabilities; *~ due*, deficiency; *on ~*, taking everything into consideration; *the remainder of anything.* [ME, f. OF f. Rom. **bilancia* f. LL (*libra*) *bilanx -lancis* two-scaled (balance)]

băl′ance[2], v.t. & i. **1.** Weigh (a question, two arguments etc. against each other); match (thing) *with, by, against*, another; bring (thing, one*self*) into, or keep in, equilibrium; equal or neutralize weight of, make up for; oscillate, waver; (Dancing) move conversely with one's partner. **2.** (Accounts) compare Dr & Cr, make the entry necessary to equalize them; *account ~s*, two sides are equal; settle (account) by paying deficit. [f. F *balancer* (*balance* = prec.)]

băl′as, n. Red spinel resembling ruby. [ME, f. OF *balais* f. med. L *balascus* ult. f. Pers. *Badakhshan* district of origin]

Bălbrig′gan, n. Knitted cotton fabric used in hose, underwear, etc. [~ in Ireland]

băl′con|y̆, n. Outside balustraded platform with access from upper-floor window; (Theatre) tier of seats generally between dress-circle & gallery. Hence *~ĭED*[2] (-nĭd) a. [f. It. *balcone* f. Gmc **balkon* = BALK[1] + -*one* -OON]

bald (bawld), a. With scalp wholly or partly hairless (*go ~-headed* (sl.), stake everything, disregard consequences); (of animals etc.) hairless, featherless, treeless, leafless, napless; (of horses) marked with white, esp. on face (*~-faced*); (of style) meagre, dull, jejune, monotonous, (of bad qualities) undisguised, whence *~′LY*[2] adv.; *~′head, ~′pate*, (person) with *~ head*, kinds of duck (*pate* only) & pigeon; *~′ing* adj., becoming *~*. Hence *~′NESS* n. [ME *ballede* perh. f. obs. *ball* white spot (cf. W (*ceffyl*) *bâl* (horse) with white forehead, Ir. & Gael. *bal* spot), + -ED[2]]

băl′dachin (-k-), **-quin**, n. (Orig.) rich brocade; (now) canopy projecting, suspended, or on pillars, over altar, throne, etc. [f. F & Sp. *baldaquin* & It. *baldacchino*, in med. L *baldakinus*, f. *Baldacco*, It. form of *Bagdad*, place of origin]

bald-coot, bald'icoot, (bawl-), n. The coot, from its bare white forehead (pop.); bald person.

bal'derdash (bawl-), n. (Formerly) frothy liquid, mixture of liquors; (now) jumble of words, nonsense. [orig. unkn.]

baldmoney (bawld'mŭnĭ), n. Yellow--flowered umbelliferous plant. [orig. unkn.]

băl'dric (bawl-), n. Belt for sword, bugle, etc., hung from shoulder to opposite hip. Hence ~-WISE adv. [orig. & hist. obsc.; ME *baudry* f. OF *baudrei*; w. *baldric* cf. MHG *balderich* & med. L *baldringus*]

băle¹, n. Evil, destruction, woe, pain, misery, (poet. & arch.). Hence ~'FUL (-lf-) a., ~'fuLLY² adv. [OE, OS *balu*, OHG *balo*, ON *böl*, f. Gmc **balw-*]

băle², n., & v.t. (Make up into) package of merchandise usu. done up in canvas & corded or metal-hooped. [ME *bale* f. MDu. *bale* (Du. *baal*) or its prob. source OF *bale* (mod. *balle*) f. Frank. **balla* f. Gmc **ballon*; see BALL¹]

băle³. See BAIL⁵.

baleen' (-lf-), n. & a. Whalebone. [ME *baleyne* f. OF *baleine* f. L *balaena* whale]

băle'fire (-lf-), n. Great fire in the open; funeral pyre; beaconfire (*fire* added only in 19th c.); bonfire. [f. ON *bál* (= OE *bæl* great fire) + FIRE]

balk¹, baulk, (bawk), n. Ridge left unploughed; stumbling-block, hindrance; sanctuary area on billiard table; roughly squared timber beam; tie-beam of a house; headline of fishing-net. [OE *balc* f. ON *balkr* f. Gmc **balkuz*]

balk², baulk, (bawk), v.t. & i. Shirk, miss, (topic, turn, duty, chance); jib, shy, pull up; hinder, thwart, disappoint, discourage, startle. [f. prec.]

Bal'kan (bawl-), a. Of the peninsula bounded by the Adriatic, Aegean, and Black Seas, or of its peoples and countries. So ~IZE (3) v.t., divide (an area) into small antagonistic states.

ball¹ (bawl), n. Solid or hollow sphere; (with distinctive adj.) any of the heavenly bodies; hard or soft, inflated or solid, large or small, sphere used in games; (Cricket) single delivery of it by bowler (*no* ~, delivery breaking rules); solid missile (not always spherical) for cannon, rifle, pistol, etc. (*load with* ~, opposed to blank cartridge); (pl., vulg.) nonsense (*make a* ~*s of*, do badly, make a mess of); = BALLOT n., & see BLACK¹; ~ *of eye*, eye within lids; material gathered or wound in round mass, as snow, medicine (veterinary), wool, or string; ~ *of foot*, rounded part at base of great toe, so ~ *of thumb*. (Phr.) *have the* ~ *at* one's feet, have one's opportunity; *keep up the* ~, *keep the* ~ *rolling*, do one's part in talk etc.; *the* ~ *is with you*, it is your turn; ~ *& socket*, joint with greatest possible freedom; ‖ *three* ~*s*, pawnbroker's sign; ~*-firing*, with ~ cartridge; ~-PROOF; ~-*bearings*, axle fittings avoiding friction by use of small ~s; ~-*cock*, *-tap*, automatic cistern-tap with floating ~; ~-*flower*, archit. ornament resembling a ~ within a hollow flower; ~-*point*, (of fountain pen) having a tiny ~ as its writing point. [ME *bal* f. ON *böllr* f. Gmc **balluz*]

ball² (bawl), n. Social assembly for dancing (so ~-*room*; *give a* ~, of the entertainer; *open the* ~, lead first dance, fig. commence operations). [f. F *bal* f. obs. *baler, baller*, f. LL *ballare* to dance]

ball³ (bawl), v.t. & i. Squeeze or wind into a ball; ~ *up* (sl.), muddle; grow into a lump or lumps. [BALL¹]

băl'lad, n. Simple song, esp. sentimental composition of several verses, each sung to same melody, with accompaniment merely subordinate; poem in short stanzas narrating popular story. Hence ~-MONGER, ~RY (5), nn. [ME & OF *balade* (F *ball-*) f. Pr. *balada* dancing-song f. *balar* (BALL²), -ADE (1)]

ballade' (balahd), n. Poem of one or more triplets of seven-lined or eight-lined stanzas, each ending with same refrain line, & envoy; poem of equal (usu. seven or eight line) stanzas; ~ *royal*, stanzas of seven or eight ten-syllable lines (also *rhyme royal*). [earlier spelling & pron. of prec., now used technically]

băll'ast, n. Heavy material placed in ship's hold to secure stability; *in* ~, in the hold, (of ship) laden with ~ only or unladen, (of material) as ~; experience, principles, etc., that give stability to character; slag etc. used to form bed of railroad or substratum of road. [of doubtful orig.; f. LG or OSw., ODa. *ballast*; earlier form of latter, *barlast* may be = *bar* bare + *last* load]

băll'ast², v.t. Furnish with, render steady by means of, ballast (lit. & fig.); fill in (railroad bed) with ballast. Hence ~ING¹ (3) n. [f. prec.]

băllerin'a (-ēnah), n. Female ballet--dancer, esp. dancer taking one of the five leading classical female roles in ballet. [It.]

băll'et (-lā), n. Combined performance of professional dancers on the stage having a sustained continuous theme. Hence **băllétománe', băllétoMAN'IA,** nn., enthusiast, enthusiasm, for ~ performances. [F, dim. of *bal* BALL²]

ballis'ta, n. (pl. *-ae*). Ancient military engine for hurling great stones etc. [L, f. Gk *ballō* throw]

ballis'tic, a. Of projectiles. of hurling--power. Hence ~ICS n. [prec. + -IC]

ballon d'essai (see Ap), n. Experiment to see whether the public, or foreign States, will tolerate a new departure in policy etc., kite. [F]

băll'onĕt, n. Air compartment in envelope of balloon or airship. [F (*-nnet*) as foll.]

balloon'¹, n. (Archit.) large ball crowning pillar, spire, etc.; round or pear-shaped airtight envelope inflated with gas lighter than air & rising skywards, whence ~IST (3) n.; anything hollow & inflated; shape into which, or frame on which, trees & plants are trained; (colloq.) ~-shaped line enclosing words spoken by characters in strip cartoons etc.; ~ *barrage*, anti--aircraft barrier of steel cables supported in an almost vertical position each by a captive ~ (*barrage* ~); ~ *tire*, low--pressure tire of large section. [f. It. *ballone* large ball (*balla* see BALE² + -*one* see -OON)]

balloon'², v.t. Ascend in balloon, whence ~ER¹ n.; swell out like balloon (gowns etc.). [f. prec.]

ball'ot¹, n. (Small ball, ticket, or paper— also ~-*paper*—used in) secret voting; votes so recorded; lot-drawing (whether by balls or not); ~-*box*, used in voting or lot-drawing. [f. It. *ballotta* dim. of *balla* BALL¹]

ball'ot², v.i. Give secret vote; ~ *for*, select (officials etc.) by secret vote; draw lots (*for* precedence, esp. in H. of Commons for right of moving resolutions etc.). [f. It. *ballottare* (*ballotta* BALLOT¹)]

¶ **ball'y**, a. & adv. (sl.) expr. speaker's disgust or satisfaction (*stung by a* ~ *wasp*; *too* ~ *tired*; *whose* ~ *fault is that?*; *won the* ~ *lot*). [pronunciation of *bl—y*=*bloody*]

ballyhoo', n. (orig. U.S.). Trumped-up publicity of a vulgar or misleading kind; barker's harangue. [orig. unkn.]

ball'yrag, v.t. & i. (sl.; -gg-). Maltreat by hustling, jeering, or playing practical jokes on; indulge in horseplay. Hence ~GING¹ (-g-) n. [orig. unkn.; also *bully-rag*]

balm (bahm), n. Fragrant & medicinal exudation from certain trees; ointment for anointing, soothing pain, or healing; perfume, fragrance; healing or soothing influence, consolation; tree yielding ~ (Asia & N. Africa); ~ *gentle* or ~-*mint*, *bastard* ~, *field* ~, fragrant herbs; ~ *of Gilead* or *of Mecca*, golden oleo-resin once much used as antiseptic, artificial imitation of this. [ME *basme*, *ba(u)me*, f. OF f. L *balsamum* BALSAM; sp. variously adjusted to the L, whence mod. -*l*-]

balm'cricket (bahm-), n. Cicada. [earlier *baum*-; f. G *baumgrille* tree-cricket]

balmo'ral, n. Kinds of laced boot, petticoat, Scotch cap. [*B~ Castle*, royal residence in Aberdeenshire, Scotland]

balm|y (bahm'i), a. Yielding balm; fragrant, soft, mild, soothing, healing; (sl.) = BARMY. Hence ~iLY² adv., ~iNESS n. [BALM + -Y¹]

balneŏl'ogȳ, n. Scientific study of bathing and medicinal springs. [f. L *balneum* bath + -o- + -LOGY]

bal'sa (*or* bawl-), n. American tropical tree yielding light strong wood, cork-wood; raft or float. [Sp.]

bal'sam (bawl-), n. Resinous product= BALM; *true* ~ or ~ *of Mecca* = BALM *of Gilead*; other medicinal oleo-resins; *Canada* ~, used in mounting for microscope; artificial oily or resinous ointment, esp. various substances dissolved in oil or turpentine, e.g. ~ *of aniseed*; (fig.) healing or soothing agency; (Chem.) compounds of resins & volatile oils, insoluble in water; tree yielding ~; flowering plant of genus *Impatiens*; ~ *apple*, gourdlike plant with highly coloured fruit. Hence **balsăm'IC** (bawl- *or* băl-) a., **balsăm'ICALLY** adv., **balsamIF'EROUS** a., ~Y² (bawl-) a. [f. L *balsamum*; from *c.* 1000 to 1600 either variants of *basme* were used, or the full L; *balsam* before & after those dates]

bal'timore (bawl-), n. N.-Amer. orange & black starling. [colours of Lord Baltimore's (proprietor of Maryland) coat of arms]

băl'uster, n. Short pillar, slender above, pear-shaped below; post helping to support rail; (pl.) set of these supporting handrail of staircase (now usu. *banisters*). [f. F *balustre* f. It. *balaustro* f. L f. Gk *balaustion* wild-pomegranate flower (from shape of its calyx-tube)]

bălustr|āde', n. Row of balusters with rail or coping as ornamental parapet to terrace, balcony, etc. Hence ~ād'ED² a. [F, see prec., -ADE]

băm, v.t. & n. (sl., arch.). Hoax. [cf. BAMBOOZLE]

bămbin'ō (-ē-), n. (pl. -*ni*). Image of infant Jesus in swaddling-clothes shown in Italian churches at Christmas. [It., = baby]

bămboo', n. (pl. -*oos*). Kinds of tropical giant grasses; the stem, used as stick or material. [16th c., app. unexpl. alt. f. Pg. f. Malay *mambu*]

bămboo'zle, v.t. (sl.). Hoax, mystify, cheat *into* doing something or *out of* property etc. Hence ~MENT (-zelm-) n. [with BAM from *c.* 1700, of unkn. orig.]

băn¹, v.t. & i. (-nn-). Curse (t. & i., arch.); prohibit, interdict. [OE *bannan* summon, OHG *bannan*, ON *banna* interdict, curse, f. Gmc **bannan*]

băn², n. Ecclesiastical anathema, interdict; curse supposed to have supernatural power; angry execration (arch.); formal prohibition; sentence of outlawry, esp. *Ban of the* (Holy Roman) *Empire*; tacit prohibition by public opinion (*under a* ~). [OF, f. LL *bannum* f. Gmc **ban* proclamation with penalties; see prec. & cf. ABANDON]

băn³, n. (hist.). Viceroy of districts in Hungary, Croatia, etc., commanding in war. [Pers., = lord]

bănal' (-ahl, *or* băn'al, -ăl'), a. Commonplace, trite. [F (BAN³, -AL); orig. a feudal word; the use of the lord's mill was compulsory for all tenants (*bannal mill*), whence the sense *common to all*]

banăl′itў, n. Triteness; a commonplace. [f. F *banalité* f. prec., see -ALITY]

bana′na (-nah-), n. Tropical & subtropical fruit-tree; its fruit, finger-shaped with yellow rind, in clusters (*hand of* ∼*s*, bunch). [Port. or Sp. f. the native name in Guinea]

banaus′ic, a. (derog.). Suitable for a mere mechanic, illiberal. [f. Gk *banausikos* (*banausos* working by fire f. *baunos* forge, -IC)]

‖ **Băn′burў căke,** n. Spiced cake made at Banbury, Oxfordshire.

banc (băngk), **banco** (băngk′ō), n. Used in phrases *in banc, in banco,* = on the bench, applied to sittings of a Superior Court of Common Law as a full court (not Nisi Prius or circuit). [*banco* L abl. of *bancus* bench; see BANK⁵]

bănd¹, n. **1.** Thing that restrains, binds together, connects or unites (chiefly arch., now ousted by the orig. identical BOND); (Bookbinding) straps at back holding sheets together; ∼*-stone,* one passing through dry-stone wall & binding it. **2.** Flat strip of thin material; hoop round anything (of iron, elastic, etc.); strap forming part of a garment (shirt, waist, hat, etc.), (pl.) development of neckband or collar into two pendent strips (clerical, legal, academic); *reef-*∼, strip sewn on sail at eyelet holes for strength; (Mech.) belt connecting wheels; stripe of colour or distinguishable material on object; ∼*′box,* of paper-covered chip or cardboard for millinery (orig. for clerical ∼s ; *look as if* one *came out of* ∼*box,* of extreme neatness); ∼*-saw,* endless saw running over wheels; ∼*-wheel,* worked by strap from another. **3.** Organized company of armed men, robbers, persons with common object (*B*∼ *of Hope,* total--abstinence association), body of musicians, esp. wind-instrument performers (*brass* ∼ ; *military* ∼ ; *dance* ∼ ; ∼*′master,* conductor; ∼*′stand,* platform; ∼*s′man,* member of ∼); *∼ wagon,* wagon for ∼ of musicians esp. in circus parade, (fig.) imaginary vehicle regarded as carrying a ∼ of political leaders likely to be successful (*climb on the* ∼ *wagon,* strive to be on the winning side). [senses 1 & 2 ult. f. Gmc **bindan* BIND¹. (1) (tie), ME *band* f. ON *band* f. Gmc **bandam*; (2) (strip), late ME *bande* f. OF *bande, bende* = Pr., It., med. L *benda* f. Gmc **bendōn*; (3) (company), 15th c. *bande* f. OF *bande* = Pr., Sp., It. *banda* ribbon f. WG **banda* cogn. w. Goth. *bandwa*; see BANNER]

bănd², v.t. Put a band on; mark with stripes; form into a league (usu. refl. or pass.). [f. F *bander* f. *bande,* see prec.]

băn′dag|e, n., & v.t. Strip of material for binding up limb, wound, etc., or anything used for blindfolding; (vb) tie up with ∼e, whence ∼ING¹ (3) n. [F, f. *bande* see prec., -AGE]

băndănn′a, -ăn′a, n. Richly coloured yellow or white spotted (orig. always silk) handkerchief. [Hind. *bandhnu* method of spot-dyeing]

băndeau′ (-dō), n. (pl. -*x,* pr. -z). Fillet for binding woman′s hair; fitting-band inside woman′s hat. [F]

băn′derŏl(e), n. Long narrow flag with cleft end flown at masthead; ornamental streamer on knight′s lance; ribbon-like scroll (Archit., stone band) with inscription; sometimes = BANNEROL. [F *banderole* f. It. *banderuola* dim. of *bandiera* BANNER]

băn′dicōot, n. (India) rat as large as cat; (Australia) insectivorous marsupial. [f. Telugu *pandi-kokku* pig rat]

băn′dĭt, n. (pl. -*its,* -*ĭtt′ĭ*). Outlaw; lawless robber, brigand, (usu. in organized gangs); *a banditti,* gang of brigands. [f. It. *bandito* p.p. of *bandire* = med. L *bannire* proclaim see BAN¹, ²]

‖ **băn′dŏg,** n. Chained dog; mastiff, bloodhound. [earlier *band-dog* f. BAND¹]

băndoleer′, -ier′ (-ēr), n. Shoulder-belt with cartridge-loops. [f. F *bandouillere* f. It. *bandoliera* or Sp. -*lera,* f. *bandola* dim. of *banda* BAND¹; cf. Du. *bandelier*]

băndolēr′ō, n. Highwayman. [Sp.]

băn′doline, n. Gummy preparation for fixing the hair or moustache. [perh. f. BANDEAU]

băn′dў¹, v.t. Throw, strike, pass, to & fro (ball, or fig. stories, epithets, etc.); often ∼ *about;* discuss (names etc.); give & take (blows etc.), exchange (something *with* some one). [orig. obsc.; cf. F *bander* 'bandie at Tennis' perh. f. *bande* side; -*y* unexplained]

băn′dў², n. (Orig.) special form of tennis; (now also ∼*-ball*) hockey; the stick, curved at end, used in the game. [perh. f. prec.]

băn′dў³, n. Indian cart or buggy. [f. Telugu *banḍi*]

băn′dў⁴, a. Wide apart at the knees (of legs); ∼*-legged,* (of persons or animals) having ∼ legs. [perh. f. BANDY² curved stick]

bāne, n. Poison (lit. now only in comb., as *rat′s-*∼); cause of ruin, esp. *the* ∼ *of;* ruin, woe, (poet.). Hence ∼′FUL (-nf-) a., ∼′fulLў² adv., ∼′fulNESS n. [OE *bana,* OHG *bano,* ON *bani,* f. Gmc **banon-*]

băng¹, v.t. & i. Strike (t. & i.) noisily; shut (t. & i. of door) with noise; make sound of blow or explosion; thrash; (sl.) surpass. [16th c., perh. f. Scand.; cf. ON *banga* to hammer, LG *bangen* strike]

băng², n. Sounding blow, sound of a blow, report of gun. [f. prec.]

băng³, adv. & int. With sudden impact, abruptly, completely, explosively; *go* ∼, explode; conventional imitation of gun-fire. [f. BANG¹]

băng⁴, v.t. & n. Cut (front hair) straight across forehead; (n.) fringe resulting; ∼*-tail,* horse with tail cut straight across. [f. prec.]

bangl|e (băng'gl), n. Ring bracelet or anklet. Hence ~ED[2] (-ld) a. [f. Hind. *bangri* glass wrist-ring]

băn′ian, băn′yan, n. Hindu trader; (Bengal) native broker to European house; Indian flannel jacket; (Naut.) ~ -*day*, on which no meat is served out; ~-*hospital*, for animals; ~-*tree* (or ~), Indian fig, branches of which root themselves over great extent. [Port. *banian* f. Arab. *banyan* f. Gujarati *vaṇiyo* man of trading caste. ~ *day*, *hospital*, from caste reverence for animal life; ~ *tree*, E name used first of a specimen under which ~s had built pagoda]

băn′ish, v.t. Condemn to exile (person *from* place, or double obj. as ~*ed him the court*, or obj. of person only); dismiss from one's presence or mind. Hence ~MENT n. [ME, f. OF *banir* (-ISH[2]) f. Rom. *bannire f. Gmc *bannjan f. *bann- BAN[1]]

băn′ister, n. (usu. pl.). Upright(s) supporting stair handrail (also in pl. for uprights & rail together). [corruption of BALUSTER]

băn′jō, n. (pl. -*os*, -*oes*). Stringed musical instrument with guitar neck & head, tambourine body, played with fingers. Hence ~IST (3) n. [Negro corruption of earlier *bandore* ult. f. Gk *pandoura*]

bănk[1], n. 1. Raised shelf of ground, slope, elevation in sea or river bed; artificial slope enabling car etc. to maintain speed round a curve; flat-topped mass of cloud, snow, etc. 2. Sloping margin of river, ground near river (*right, left,* ~, to one looking down stream); edge of hollow place (e.g. top of shaft in mining). [ME *banke* f. ON; cf. OIcel. *bakki* in same senses f. Gmc *bankon cf. BANK[5], BENCH]

bănk[2], v.t. & i. Contain as a bank, confine with bank(s); (of car or aeroplane or its occupant) travel with one side higher; confine watch-escapement (of ~ing-pins), strike against the ~ing-pins or abs.; of escapement); ~ *up*, heap or rise into banks (of snow, clouds), pack tightly (fire, for slow burning). [f. prec.]

bănk[3], n. Establishment for custody of money, which it pays out on customer's order; || *the B*~, B~ of England, managing the public debt, issuing legal-tender notes, & having the Government for chief customer; (Gaming) amount of money before keeper of table; ~-*bill*, drawn by one ~ on another; ~-*book*, containing customer's private copy of his account with ~; ~-*credit*, arrangement by which customer may overdraw on security given; || ~ *holiday*, day on which ~s are legally closed, usu. kept as general holiday also in England; ||~-*note*, banker's promissory note payable to bearer on demand & serving as money; ~-*rate*, announced percentage at which B~ of England is prepared to discount bills. [f. F *banque* or its source It. *banca* f. Gmc *bank BENCH, see BANK[1, 5]]

bănk[4], v.t. & i. Keep bank, trade in money (~-*ing-house*, commercial firm that does some ~ing); keep money at bank; deposit (money etc.) at bank; convert into money; (Gaming) hold table fund; ~ (*up*)*on*, base one's hopes on, count upon, reckon reliable. [f. prec.]

bănk[5], n. Galley-rower's bench; tier *of oars* in galley; row of organ keys; working-table in some trades. [ME, f. OF *banc* f. Gmc *bank-; see BANK[1], BENCH]

bănk′able, a. That will be received at a bank (securities etc.). [BANK[3] +-ABLE]

bănk′er[1], n. Proprietor or partner of private bank, governor, director, etc., of joint-stock bank, (*let me be your*~, lend the money you need); (Gaming) keeper of the bank; dealer in some games of chance; a gambling game of cards. [BANK[3] + -ER[1], after F *banquier*]

|| **bănk′er[2],** n. Labourer (Eastern counties); (Hunting) horse that jumps on & off banks too large to clear. [BANK[1] + -ER[1]]

bănk′er[3], n. Wooden or stone bench for trimming bricks or stone on; ~-*mark*, mason's sign manual (formerly engraved on a dressed stone before it left the ~). [perh. = It. *banco* statuary's bench]

bănk′ĕt, n. Auriferous conglomerate like pudding-stone found in S. Africa. [Du., = kind of hardbake (BANQUET)]

bănk′ing, n. In vbl senses of BANK[2, 4]; also, fishing on a sea bank (esp. Newfoundland). [BANK[1]]

bănk′rŭpt[1], n. (Law) insolvent person whose effects, on creditors' or his own petition to Bankruptcy Court, are administered & distributed for benefit of all creditors; (pop.) insolvent debtor. [16th c. *banke rota, bankrout,* etc. f. It. *banca rotta* broken bank (BANK[3], L *rupt*-p.p. of *rumpere* break); mod. sp. after L]

bănk′rŭpt[2], v.t. Reduce to bankruptcy. [f. prec.]

bănk′rŭpt[3], a. Under legal process because of insolvency; insolvent; bereft (*of* some quality etc.). [perh. the short p.p. of prec.]

bănk′ruptcy̆, n. Being declared bankrupt, being insolvent; utter loss (of something, e.g. reputation). [prec. + -CY, irreg. for -*rupcy*]

bănk′sia (-sha), n. Australian flowering shrub now grown in Europe. [Sir J. *Banks* (d. 1820), -IA[1]]

bănks′man, n. Coal-mine overlooker above ground. [BANK[1]]

bănn′er, n. Cloth flag on pole used as standard of emperor, king, lord, knight, for war; flag of a country etc. (*join, follow, the ~ of*; now chiefly fig.); ensign (esp. in frame, or with two poles) borne in religious or political demonstrations; anything used as symbol of principles; ~-*screen*, fire screen hung from standing pole or mantelpiece; (attrib.) pre-eminent, conspicuous, as ~ *headline* (in newspaper). Hence ~ED² (-*erd*) a. [ME, f. AF *banere*, OF -*iere*, f. Rom. **bandaria* (cf. It. *bandiera*) f. med. L *bandum* standard (BAND¹), cf. Goth. *bandwa* sign]

bănn′erĕt, n. Knight having vassals under his banner; one knighted on the field for valour. [ME & OF *baneret* (*baniere* see prec. + -*et* = -ATE²) lit. bannered]

bănn′erŏl, n. Banner borne at great men's funerals & placed over tomb; = BANDEROLE. [var. of BANDEROLE]

bănn′ock, n. Scotch & N.-Eng. home-made loaf, usu. unleavened, flat, & round or oval; oatcake. [OE *bannuc*, 15th c. -*ok* etc.; cf. Gael. *bannach*]

bănns (-z), n. pl. Notice in church of intended marriage, thrice read to give opportunity of objection (*ask, publish, put up, forbid, the* ~). [pl. of BAN²]

băn′quĕt¹, n. Sumptuous feast; dinner with speeches in celebration of something or to further a cause. [F, dim. of *banc* bench BANK³]

băn′quĕt², v.t. & i. Regale (person); feast, carouse, whence ~ER¹ n. [f. F *banqueter* (*banquet* = prec.)]

bănquette′ (-kĕt), n. Raised way behind rampart etc. for firing from; bench behind driver in French diligence. [F, f. It. *banchetta* dim. of *banca* bench see BANK³]

băn′shee, n. Spirit whose wail portends death in a house (Irish & Scotch). [Ir. *bean sidhe* f. OIr. *ben side* woman of the fairies]

bănt, v.i. See BANTING.

băn′tam, n. Small kind of domestic fowl, of which the cock is very pugnacious; small but spirited person (~ *battalion*, of men below normal standard of height enrolled for the war of 1914–18); ~-*weight* (Boxing) see BOX*ing weights*. [f. *Bantam* in Java whence they were perh. brought, though perh. orig. Japanese]

băn′ter, n., & v.t. & i. Humorous ridicule, good-humoured personalities; (vb) make fun of, rally; talk jestingly. [f. 17th c.; of unkn. orig.]

băn′ting, n. Treatment of obesity by abstinence from sugar, starch, & fat; **bănt** v.i., adopt this. [W. *B*~, d. 1878]

bănt′ling, n. Young child, brat. [late 16th c., perh. f. G *bänkling* (f. *bank* bench, cf. *bastard*)]

Bantu (bahntoo′), n. & a. Used to include many related African languages & races. [native, = people]

bănx′ring, n. Javanese squirrel-like insectivorous animal. [Javanese *bangsring*]

băn′yan. See BANIAN (used esp. for the tree).

bănzai′ (-zī), int. Form of greeting by Japanese to their Emperor, cheer used in battle, etc. [Jap., = ten thousand years (of life to you)]

bă′obăb, n. African tree called also monkey-bread with enormously thick stem. [mentioned 1592]

băp, n. (Sc.). Small loaf or roll of bread. [orig. unkn.]

băp′tism, n. Religious rite of immersing (person) in, or sprinkling with, water in sign of purification & (with Christians) of admission to the Church, generally accompanied by name-giving; (fig.) ~ *of blood*, martyrdom, ~ *of fire*, soldier's first battle; naming of church bells & ships. Hence **băptis′mal** (-z-) a., **băptis′mally** adv. [ME *bapieme* f. OF *baptesme* f. LL f. Gk *baptismos* (*baptizō* BAPTIZE)]

băp′tist, n. One who baptizes, esp. John the B~; one of a sect (formerly called ANABAPTISTS by opponents) objecting to infant baptism, & practising immersion. [ME, f. OF *baptiste*, f. LL *baptista* f. Gk *baptistēs* (*baptizō* BAPTIZE)]

băp′tist(e)rў, n. Part of church (or formerly separate building) used for baptism; (in Baptist chapel) immersion receptacle. [ME, f. OF *baptisterie* f. LL f. Gk *baptistērion* (*baptizō* BAPTIZE)]

băptīze′, -ise (-īz), v.t. Immerse in or sprinkle with water, as sign of purification or initiation, esp. into the Christian Church; christen; (abs.) administer baptism; (fig.) purify, elevate; name or nickname. [ME, f. OF *baptiser* f. LL *baptizare* f. Gk *baptizō* bathe (*baptō* dip)]

băr¹, n. **1.** Long piece of rigid material (metal, wood, soap, etc.; ~-*bell*, iron ~ with ball at each end used in gymnastics, cf. *dumb-bell*; ~′*wood*, red wood from Gaboon imported in ~s for dyeing etc.). **2.** Slip of silver below clasp of medal as additional distinction; band of colour etc. on surface, (Her.) two horizontal parallel lines across shield (~ *sinister*, by mistake for BEND or BATON, supposed sign of illegitimacy). **3.** Rod or pole used to confine or obstruct (*window, door, grate, gate,* -~); barrier of any shape (*Temple Bar, toll′*~); sandbank or shoal at mouth of harbour or estuary. **4.** (Mus.) vertical line across stave dividing piece into sections of equal time-value, such sections; immaterial barrier; (Law) plea arresting action or claim; moral obstacle. **5.** Barrier with some technical significance, as, in lawcourt, place at which prisoner stands; hence ~ *of conscience, opinion*, etc.; ‖ *trial at* ~, in Queen's Bench division; a particular court (*practise at parliamentary, Chancery,* etc., ~); ‖ *be called to the* ~ (i.e. that in Inns of Court separating benchers), be admitted a barrister; ‖ *be called within the* ~ (i.e. that in courts within which Q.C.s plead), be appointed Queen's Counsel; *the* ~, barristers, profession of barrister. **6.** ‖ (Parl.) rail dividing off space to which non-members may be admitted on business. **7.** (In an inn etc.) counter across which refreshments are handed, space behind or room containing it; ‖ ~′*man,* ~′*maid,* *~ *tender*, attendants at such counter. [ME *barre* f. OF f. Rom. *barra* of unkn. orig.]

bar², v.t. (-rr-). Fasten (door etc.) with bar(s); keep (person) *in* or *out* (*~ring-out*, schoolboy rebellion); obstruct (path etc.); stay (process or party) by legal objection; exclude from consideration (esp. in imperative used as prep., e.g. ~ *one* in betting); (sl.) object to, dislike, (person, habit, etc.); mark with stripe(s). [ME *barren* f. OF *barrer* (*barre* BAR¹)]

bar³, n. Large European sea-fish. [F]

bàrathē'a, n. Fine cloth made from wool (with or without silk or cotton). [orig. unkn.]

bă'rathrŭm, n. Pit at Athens into which criminals were thrown; abyss. [L, f. Gk *barathron*]

barb¹, n., & v.t. **1.** Beardlike feelers of barbel etc.; chin-piece of nun's headdress; lateral filament branching from shaft of feather; subordinate recurved point of arrow, fish-hook, etc., (fig.) sting. **2.** v.t. Furnish (arrow etc.) with ~; *~ed wire*, for fences & esp. as obstruction in war, with wire prickles at intervals. [ME, f. OF *barbe* f. L *barba* beard]

barb², n. Breeds of horse & pigeon imported from Barbary. [f. F *barbe* (*Barbarie*)]

barb'ara, first word of the scholastic mnemonic lines for figures & moods of the syllogism (some of these, esp. *barbara*, *barbara celarent*, are used allusively for logic or logical training).

barbār'ian, n. & a. (Foreigner) differing from speaker in language & customs, esp. in hist., (a) non-Greek, (one) outside the Roman Empire, (a) non-Christian; rude, wild, or uncultured (person). [f. obs. F *barbarien* f. *barbare* (BARBAROUS, -IAN)]

barbă'r|ic, a. Rude, rough, like or of barbarians & their art or taste. Hence ~ICALLY adv. [ME, f. OF *barbarique* or L f. Gk *barbarikos* (*barbaros* BARBAROUS, & see -IC)]

barb'arism, n. Mixing of foreign or vulgar expressions in talk or writing; such an expression; absence of culture, ignorance & rudeness; instance of this. [f. F *barbarisme* or L f. Gk *barbarismos* (*barbarizō* speak like a foreigner f. *barbaros* BARBAROUS, -IZE)]

barbă'rit̬ȳ, n. Savage cruelty, instance of it; barbaric style or taste, instance of it, (usu. *barbarism*). [f. as foll., see -TY]

barb'ariz|e, -is|e (-īz), v.t. & i. Make or become barbarous; corrupt (language). Hence ~A'TION n. [f. as foll., see -IZE]

barb'arous, a. (Lang.) not Greek, not Greek or Latin, not pure, illiterate; (people) non-Greek, beyond Roman Empire, non-Christian, outlandish; uncivilized; cruel; coarse. Hence ~LY² adv., ~NESS n. [f. L f. Gk *barbaros* foreign + -OUS]

Barb'arȳ āpe, n. Large tailless monkey

of N. Africa and Gibraltar. [*Barbary*, old name of N. Africa]

barb'āte, a. (bot., zool.). Having hairy tufts. [f. L *barbatus* bearded (*barba* beard, -ATE²)]

barb'ecūe, n. Large wooden or iron framework for smoking or broiling; hog, ox, etc., roasted whole, whence **barb'e-cūe** v.t.; *open-air party at which animals are roasted whole; floor for drying coffee-beans. [f. Sp. *barbacoa* f. Haitian *barba-còa* crate on posts]

barb'el, n. Large European fresh-water fish with fleshy filaments hanging from mouth; such filament in any fish, whence ~(l)ED² a. [ME, f. OF *barbel* f. Rom. *barbellus* dim. of *barbus* barbel (*barba* beard)]

barb'er, n. One who shaves & trims customers' beards & hair (now freq. *hairdresser*); *~'s block*, for making & displaying wigs; *~'s itch*, skin disease caused by a fungoid organism communicated by (unsterilized) shaving apparatus; *~'s pole*, spirally painted & used as sign. [ME & AF *barbour* f. OF *barbeor* f. L *barbatorem* (*barba* beard), see -OR]

barb'er(r)ȳ, **bēr-**, n. Shrub with spiny shoots, yellow flowers, & oblong red berries; its berry. [late ME *barbere*, 16th c. *bar-*, *berbery*, f. OF *berbere*, *berberis*, of unkn. orig.]

barb'ĕt, n. Bird with bristle-tufts at base of bill. [cf. F *barbet* (*barbe* beard, see -ET¹)]

barbĕtte', n. Platform within fort or in ship from which guns fire over parapet etc. without embrasure. [F dim. of *barbe* beard; see -ETTE]

barb'ican, n. Outer defence to city or castle, esp. double tower over gate or bridge. [ME, f. OF *barbacane*, com.-Rom. of disputed orig.; cf. Pers. *barbăr khānah* house on the wall]

barbitūr'|ic, a. (chem.). *~ic acid*, an acid from which various hypnotic and sedative drugs are derived. Hence ~ATE¹ (3) n. [f. F (*-ique*) f. G *barbitur(säure)*]

Bar'bizŏn, n. Village near Fontainebleau; *~ School*, coterie of French naturalistic painters (middle of 19th c.).

barbŏl'a, n. (Also *~ work*) the embellishment of small articles by attachment of coloured models of flowers, fruit, etc. made from a plastic paste. [orig. unkn.]

barb'ūle, n. Filament branching from barb (of feather) as barb from shaft. [f. L *barbula* dim. of *barba* beard]

barc'arōle, **-ŏlle**, n. Song of gondolier, imitation of it. [f. F *barcarolle* f. It. *barcaruola*, boatman's song (*barca* boat)]

Barcelōn'a, n. Spanish city, capital of Catalonia; ~ (*nut*), hazel-nut imported from Spain.

bard¹, n. Celtic minstrel, (Wales) poet recognized at Eisteddfod, whence ~'IC a.; early poet; lyric poet; poet, whence ~'LING¹ n. Hence ~ŏL'ATRY n., worship of Shakespeare, the 'B~ of Avon'. [f. Gael. & Ir. *bárd*]

bárd², n. Armour for breast & flanks of warhorse. Hence ~'ED² a. [f. F *barde*, rel. to Pr. *aubarda*, Sp., Pg. *albarda*, f. Arab. *al-barda'ah* stuffed packsaddle]

bāre¹, a. Unclothed, undisguised, uncovered, bald, unfurnished, unprovided, threadbare, unsheathed, ill-provided, empty, unadorned, scanty, mere; ~ᶜ *back* a. & adv., *-ed* a., with ~ back, on unsaddled horse; ~'*faced*, without beard etc., without mask, also undisguised, shameless, or impudent, whence **bāre**-**fā'cĕDLY²** adv., **bārefā'cĕd**NESS n.; ~ᶜ *foot* a. & adv., ~'*footed* a., without shoes or stockings; ~'*headed*, without hat or cap. Hence **bār'ISH¹(2)** a. [OE *bær*, OHG *bar*, ON *berr*]

bāre², v.t. Uncover, unsheathe, reveal, strip. [f. prec.]

barège' (-āzh), n. & a. (Of) silky gauze. [orig. made at Barèges]

barely (bār'lĭ), adv. Openly, explicitly; merely; only just; scarcely. [BARE¹ + -LY²]

bāre'ness (-rn-), n. Lack of covering, unadorned state. [BARE¹ + -NESS]

bāre'sark (-rs-), n. & adv. Wild Norse warrior; (adv.) without armour. [lit. bare shirt (SARK); mod. form embodying supposed etym. of BERSERKER]

bārg'ain¹ (-gĭn), n. Agreement on terms of give & take, compact, thing acquired by bargaining (*good*, *bad*, ~, result cheaply or dearly bought; *a* ~, thing acquired or offered cheap; *Dutch*, *wet*, ~, closed with drink; *into the* ~, beyond the strict terms, moreover; *strike a* ~, come to terms; *make the best of a bad* ~, take misfortune etc. cheerfully). [ME, f. OF *bargaine* f. *bargaigner*, see foll.]

bārg'ain² (-gĭn), v.i. & t. Haggle (*with* someone, or abs.) over terms of give & take; stipulate *with* person *for* thing or *to* receive, give, etc. ; ~ *for*, be prepared for, expect, (usu. with neg. or *more than*); (trans.) ~ *away*, part with for a consideration. Hence ~ER¹ n. [ME, f. OF *bargaigner*, = Pr. *bargagnar*, It. *bargagnare*, med. L *barcaniare*, of disputed but undetermined orig.]

bārge, n., & v.i. 1. Flat-bottomed freight-boat for canals & rivers, with or without sails; second boat of man-of-war, for use of chief officers; large ornamental oared vessel for state occasions, house-boat (e.g. *College* ~); ~-*pole* (for fending; *would not touch with a* ~-*pole*, regard with loathing). 2. v.i. Lurch or rush heavily *into*, *against*, *about*; ~ *in*, intrude. [ME, f. OF *barge*, f. med. L *barga* var. of *barca* BARK³]

bārge-, comb. form in architecture = gable. ~-*couple*, two gable beams; ~-*course*, roof projecting beyond them; ~-*board*, ornamental screen to them; ~-*stones*, forming sloping or stepped line of gable. [f. med. L *bargus* gallows]

|| **bārgee'**, n. Man in charge of barge; *swear like a* ~, fluently, forcibly; *lucky* ~ (colloq.), lucky fellow. [-EE]

bār'ic, a. Of or containing barium. [BARIUM + -IC]

barill'a, n. Plant (*Salsola Soda*) in Spain, Sicily, Canaries; impure alkali made by burning either this or kelp. [Sp.]

bă'ritōne, n. & a. (mus.). (Voice, singer with voice, music suited to voice) between tenor and bass; euphonium (or tenor tuba) or saxhorn in B flat or C. [var. of BARYTONE]

bār'ium, n. (chem.). White metallic element, basis of alkaline earth baryta. [BARYTA or obs. *baria* + -IUM]

bārk¹, n. Outer sheath of tree trunks & branches; tan; (arch.) quinine (also *Peruvian* or *Jesuits'* ~); (sl.) skin; ~-*bed*, hot-bed of tan; ~-*bound*, hindered in growth by tight ~; ~-*pit*, of ~ & water for tanning; ~-*tree*, E name of cinchona. [ME, f. Scand. *bark*- (ON *börkr*) f. Gmc **barkuz*]

bārk², v.t. Strip bark from (tree), kill (tree) by ring-cutting bark (also *ring*-~); abrade (one's knuckles etc.); encrust. [f. prec.]

bārk³, **barque** (-árk), n. Three-masted vessel with fore & main masts square-rigged; mizen fore-&-aft rigged (usu. *barque*); any ship or boat (poet., usu. *bark*). [f. F *barque* f. Pr., Sp., or It., *barca* f. LL *barca* ship's boat]

bārk⁴, n. Usual cry of dogs, foxes, squirrels; (fig.) sound of gunfire, or of cough; ~ *worse than bite*, of testy harmless person. [f. foll.]

bārk⁵, v.i. & t. Utter sharp explosive cry (of dogs & some other animals); speak (& ~ *out*, say) petulantly, imperiously; ~ *at*, abuse; ~ *up the wrong tree*, denounce wrong person etc.; (sl.) cough. [OE *beorcan*, repr. an earlier **berkan*, perh. metathetic var. of BREAK¹]

bārk'er, n. Noisy assailant; shop or auction or travelling-show tout; (sl.) pistol, cannon. [f. prec.]

bārl'ey, n. (pl. ~s). Hardy awned cereal used as food & in making malt liquors & spirits; its grain; *pearl* ~, the grain ground small; ~-*broth*, strong ale; ~-*corn*, grain of ~ (*John Barleycorn*, malt liquor personified), its length as measure, ⅓ inch, top of fore-sight on rifle; ~-*mow*, stack; ~ *sugar*, twisted sweetmeat; ~-*water*, soothing decoction of pearl ~ for invalids. [OE *bærlic* adj. form; for *bær*- cf. obs. *bear* barley (f. Gmc **bariz*; so Goth. *barizeins* of barley); *-lic* = -LY¹]

*bārl'ow (-ō), n. (Also ~ *knife*) large single-bladed pocket-knife. [*B*~, orig. maker]

bārm, n. Froth on fermenting malt liquor, yeast, leaven. [OE *beorma*; cogn. w. Fris., LG *barm*]

Bārm'ecīde, n. & a. (Giver of benefits that are) illusory, imaginary, disappointing. [name of Arabian-Nights prince whose feast to beggar was rich dish-covers with nothing below]

bärm'ў, a. Full of barm; frothy; (sl., also ~ *on the crumpet*) wrong in the head, cracked. [-Y²]

bärn, n. Covered building for storing grain etc.; (derog.) unadorned building; ~ *dance*, (orig. U.S.) dance in which partners advance side by side & then dance a schottische step; ~*-door*, lit., & fig. target too large to be missed, also adj. of fowls = reared at the ~-door; ~*-owl*, = white, church, screech, -owl; ~*-stormer*, strolling player, ranting actor; ~*yard*, farmyard. [OE *bern, berern*, f. *bere-ern* (*bere* barley + *-ærn* place)]

Bärn'abў, n. (Saint) Barnabas; ~ *bright*, St Barnabas' day, 11th June (longest day in Old Style reckoning). [f. F *Barnabé* = LL (f. Heb.) *Barnabas*]

bärn'acle¹, n. (Usu. pl.) pincers placed on horse's nose to coerce him into quiet for shoeing etc.; (sl.; pl.) spectacles. [ME *bernac, barnacle, ber-*, f. OF *bernac* muzzle, of unkn. orig.; later form app. Eng. dim., see -LE]

bärn'acle², n. **1.** Arctic goose visiting Britain in winter (also *bernacle* for distinction from 2). **2.** Stalked cirriped clinging by fleshy foot-stalk to ship's bottom; follower who cannot be shaken off. [hist. & etym. unkn.; ME *bernekke, bernake* = OF *bernaque*, med. L *bernaca, -eca*; later *ber-, barnacle* = mod. F *ber-, barnacle, bernicle*]

bä'rograph (-ahf), n. Self-recording aneroid. [f. Gk *baros* weight + -GRAPH(2)]

barŏm'ĕter, n. Instrument measuring atmospheric pressure used for forecasting weather & ascertaining height above sea-level; *siphon, wheel, aneroid, ~*, various systems; (fig.) ~ *of opinion* etc. Hence **bärŏmĕt'rĭC(AL)** aa., **bärŏmĕt'rĭCAL**ʏ² adv., **barŏM'ETRY** n. [as prec. + -METER]

bä'ron, n. **1.** (hist.). One who held by military or other honourable service from the king or other superior (restricted later to king's ~s, & again to those, *Great Barons*, attending Great Council or summoned to Parliament; hence, peer). **2.** (mod.). One of the lowest order of nobility; holder of foreign title (called *Baron* ——, not, like English ~, *Lord* ——); (orig. U.S.) a great merchant in a (designated) commodity, (*beef* ~; *beer* ~); ~ *of beef*, double sirloin undivided. [ME & AF *barun*, OF *baron* f. med. L *baronem* nom. *baro* man (as in *king's man*) etc., f. Frankish *baro* (Salic Law; cf. MHG *bar*)]

bä'ronage, n. Barons or great vassals of Crown collectively; the nobility; book with list of peers & comments. [ME & OF *barnage* (prec., -AGE)]

bä'roness, n. Baron's wife; lady holding baronial title in her own right. [ME, f. OF *barnesse, -onesse*, see BARON, -ESS¹]

bä'ronĕt¹, n. Member of lowest heredi-

tary titled order, commoner with precedence of all knights exc. K.G.s; abbr. *bart*, added to name, as *Sir John Jones, Bart.* [ME, dim. of BARON; see -ET]

bä'ronĕt², v.t. Raise to rank of baronet. [f. prec. on anal. of *knight*]

bä'ronĕtage, n. Baronets collectively; book with list of them & comments. [-AGE; cf. BARONAGE].

bä'ronĕtcў, n. Baronet's patent or rank. [-CY]

barŏn'ial, a. Of, belonging to, befitting, baron(s). [foll. + -AL]

bä'ronў, n. Baron's domain, rank, tenure; (Ireland) division of county; (Scotland) large manor. [ME, f. OF *baronie* (BARON, -Y¹); cf. med. L *baronia*]

baroque' (-ŏk), a. & n. **1.** (Of) certain stylistic tendencies in 17th–18th c. arts. **2.** Grotesque, whimsical. [F, f. Pg., It. *barroco*, Sp. *barrueco*, of unkn. orig.]

barouche' (-ōōsh), n. Four-wheeled carriage with collapsible half-head, for four occupants & driver. [f. G (dial.) *barutsche* f. It. *barocchio* (Sp. *barrocho*) f. LL *birotus* (BI- 1a + *rota* wheel)]

bärque, n. See BARK³.

barquentine, bark-, (bärk'entēn), n. Vessel with foremast square-rigged, main & mizen fore-&-aft rigged. [f. BARK³ after BRIGANTINE]

bä'rrack, n., & v.t. **1.** Permanent building(s) in which soldiers are lodged (usu. pl.); (transf.) building in which others (e.g. children) are similarly herded together; building of severely dull or plain appearance. **2.** v.t. Place in ~s; hoot, jeer at, (players in cricket-match etc.). [f. F *baraque* f. It. *baracca* or Sp. *barraca* 'souldier's tent' (1617) orig. unkn.]

bärracōōn', n. Set of sheds or enclosure for slaves, convicts, etc. [f. Sp. *barracon* (as prec.; see -OON)]

bärracud'a (-ōōd-), **-cōōt'a, -cout'a** (-ōōt-), n. Large W.-Ind. sea-fish. [Sp.]

bärr'age, n. **1.** Damming; dam (esp. of those in Nile). **2.** (Mil., freq. bä'rahzh) barrier to offensive or defensive action on the part of an enemy usu. in the form of a line, area, or volume into which a large number of guns fire shells either continuously or for pre-arranged periods (*anti--aircraft* ~, barrier of shellfire against hostile aircraft; BALLOON ~; *box* ~, one laid down usu. on three sides in order to isolate a particular area; *creeping* ~, one laid down in front of & moving with one's own advancing troops; attrib., as ~ BALLOON. [F, f. *barre* BAR¹; see -AGE]

bä'rrator, -er, n. (legal). Vexatious litigant; malicious raiser of discord. [ME, f. AF *baratour*, OF *-eor* trickster f. *barat* (obs. Eng. *barrat*) of unkn. orig.]

bä'rratr|ў, n. (Marine law) fraud or gross negligence of master or crew to prejudice of ship's owners; (Law) vexatious litigation or incitement to it. Hence ~ous a. [ME, f. OF *baraterie* (*barat* see prec., -ERY)]

barred (bărd), a. In vbl senses; also [BAR[1]] marked with bars, (of harbour) obstructed with sandbar.

bă'rrel[1], n. Flat-ended cylindrical wooden vessel of hooped staves, cask; varying measure of capacity (~-*bulk*, 5 cub. ft); revolving cylinder in capstan, watch, & other machines; cylindrical body or trunk of an object, belly & loins of horse, etc.; metal tube of gun; *barrel-*, cylindrical or semi-cylindrical, as ~-*drain*, -*vault*; ~-*organ*, with pin-studded cylinder turned by handle & mechanism opening the pipes as required. [ME, f. OF *baril* of unkn. orig.]

bă'rrel[2], v.t. (-ll-). Put in barrel(s); ~*led*, (also) = *barrel-shaped*. [f. prec.]

bă'rren, a. (-est), & n. Not bearing, or incapable of bearing, children, young, fruit, vegetation, or produce; meagre, unprofitable, dull; (n.) ~ tract of land; ~*wort*, purple-&-yellow-flowered wood plant. Hence ~LY[2] adv., ~NESS n. [ME *barain* etc. f. OF *baraine* (fem.) etc. of unkn. orig.]

bă'rrėt, n. Flat cap, esp. the biretta. [f. F *barrette* BIRETTA]

bărricāde'[1], (now rarely) **-ā'dō**, n. Hastily erected rampart across street etc. of barrels, carts, stones, furniture; any barrier, lit. or fig. [f. F *barricade* or Sp. *barricada* (whence earlier Eng. *barricado*; see -ADO) f. F *barrique* (Sp. *barrica*) cask]

bărricāde'[2], (now rarely) **-ā'dō**, v.t. Block (street etc.) with barricade; defend (place or person) with barricade. [f. prec].

bă'rrier[1], n. Fence barring advance or preventing access; (ancient chariot-races) barred starting-cells; (foreign towns) gate at which customs are collected; (tilting) the lists or enclosing palisade, also railing parallel to which, but on opposite sides, tilters charged reaching their lances across; any obstacle, boundary, or agency that keeps apart. [ME & AF *barrere*, OF *barrière* f. Rom. **barraria* (**barra* BAR[1]) later assim. to F spelling]

bă'rrier[2], v.t. Close or shut in with barrier (usu. with *off*, *in*). [f. prec.]

băr'ring, prep. Except, not including. [part. of BAR[2]]

‖ **bă'rrister**, n. Law student called to bar & having right of practising as advocate in superior courts (in full, ~-*at-law*); *revising-*~, one appointed to revise lists of voters at parliamentary elections. [16th c. *bar(r)ester* f. BAR[1]; second element unexpl.]

bă'rrow[1] (-ō), n. (In local names) hill; (Archaeol.) grave-mound, tumulus. [OE *beorg*, OS, OHG *berg*, f. Gmc **bergaz*]

bă'rrow[2] (-ō), n. (Also *hand-*~) rectangular frame with short shafts used by two or more men for carrying loads on, stretcher, bier; (also *wheel-*~) shallow box with shafts & one wheel for similar use by one man; ‖ (also *coster's* ~) two-wheeled handcart (~-*boy*, coster); a ~ful. [ME *barewe* f. Gmc **barwā* f. *beran* BEAR[3]; cf. BIER]

bă'rrow[3] (-ō), n. (dial.). Castrated boar. [OE *bearg*, = OS, OHG *baruh* (G *barch*) f. Gmc **barguz*, -*gwaz*]

bar̂t'er[1], v.t. & i. Exchange (goods or immaterial things) *for* other goods (occas. *away*); part with for a (usu. unworthy) consideration (usu. *away*), whence ~ER[1] n.; trade by exchange. [f. OF *barater* trick, exchange, f. *barat*; see BARRATOR]

bar̂t'er[2], n. Traffic by exchange, truck, (also fig., e.g. of talk); (Arith.) reckoning of quantity of one commodity to be given for another, values being known. [f. prec.]

bar̂tizăn', n. Battlemented parapet, or overhanging battlemented corner turret, at top of church tower or castle. [spurious form (Scott) f. *bertisene* illit. spelling of *bratticing* see BRATTICE]

bar̂t'on, n. Farmyard; farm not let with rest of manor, but retained by owner. [OE *bere-tūn* (*bere* barley + *tūn* enclosure see TOWN)]

Bar̂t's, n. St Bartholomew's Hospital in London. [abbr.]

barȳt'|a, n. Oxide or hydroxide of barium. Hence ~IC a., ~O- comb. form. [f. foll.]

barȳt'ēs (-z), n. Native sulphate of barium, called also *heavy spar*, used in some white paints. [f. Gk *barus* heavy, partly assim. to mineral names in -ITES]

bă'rȳtōne, n. & a. (Gk gr.). (Word) with no or grave accent on last syllable. [f. F *baryton* or It. *baritono* & Gk *barutonos* (*barus* heavy + *tonos* TONE)]

bās'al, a. Of, at, or forming, the base; fundamental. [f. BASE[1] + -AL]

basalt (băs'awlt, basawlt'), n. Dark green or brown igneous rock often in columnar strata, whence **basal'tic**, **basal'tiform**, (-sawl-), aa.; black porcelain invented by Wedgwood. [f. L *basaltes* (in MSS. of Pliny) var. of *basanites* f. Gk (*basanos* touchstone)]

băs'an (-z-), **băz'an**, n. Sheepskin tanned in oak or larch bark (also *basil*). [f. F *basane* f. Pr. *bazana* f. Sp. *badana* f. Arab. *biṭanah* lining]

bas bleu (see Ap.), n. Bluestocking. [F]

băs'cūle, n. Lever apparatus used in ~-*bridge*, kind of drawbridge raised & lowered with counterpoise. [F, formerly *bacule* see-saw (*battre* bump + *cul* buttocks)]

bāse[1], n. **1.** That on which anything stands or depends, support, bottom, foundation, principle, groundwork, starting-point (~'*ball*, U.S. national game, more elaborate rounders, also ball used in it). **2.** (archit.). Part of column between shaft & pedestal or pavement. **3.** (bot. & zool.). End at which an organ is attached to trunk. **4.** (geom.). Line or surface on

which plane or solid figure is held to stand. **5.** (chem.). Correlative of ACID, substance capable of combining with an acid to form a salt (including, but wider than, ALKALI). **6.** (mil.). Town or other area in rear of an army where drafts, stores, hospitals, etc., are concentrated (also ~ *of operations*). **7.** (surv.). Known line used as geometrical ~ for trigonometry. **8.** (math.). Starting-number for system of numeration or logarithms (as 10 in decimal counting). [F, or f. L f. Gk *basis* (*bainō* step, stand)]

bāse², v.t. Found (something) *on*; establish (with adv., as *firmly*); ~ one*self on*, rely upon (in argument etc.). [f. prec.]

bāse³, a. (Orig.) of small height (now only in plant names as ~-*rocket*); morally low, cowardly, selfish, mean, despicable, whence ~'LY² (-sl-) adv.; menial; ‖ (Law) ~ *tenure*, *estate*, *fee*, not absolute, but determinable on fulfilment of contingent qualification; (Lang.) not classical (~ *Latinity*); ~-*born*, of low birth, illegitimate; ~-*court*, outer court of castle or court behind farmhouse; ~ *metals*, opposed to precious; ~ *coin*, spurious, alloyed. Hence ~'NESS (-sn-) n. [f. F *bas* f. LL *bassus* short (in L as cognomen)]

bāse'less (-sl-), a. Groundless, unfounded. Hence ~NESS n. [BASE¹, -LESS]

bāse'ment (-sm-), n. Lowest or fundamental part of structure; inhabited storey sunk below ground level. [BASE n. or v. +-MENT]

băsh, v.t., & n. **1.** Strike heavily so as to smash in (often *in*). **2.** n. Heavy blow; *have a* ~ *at it* (sl.), attempt it. [perh. imit. cf. *bang*, *smash*; or = Sw. *basa* flog, Da. *baske* cudgel]

bashaw', n. Earlier form of PASHA.

băsh'ful, a. Shy; shamefaced, sheepish. Hence ~LY² adv., ~NESS n. [f. obs. *bash* vb for ABASH +-FUL]

băshi-bazouk' (-ōok), n. Mercenary of Turkish irregulars, notorious for pillage & brutality. Hence ~ERY (4, 5) n. [mod. Turk., lit. brain-turned]

bāsi-, stem of many adjj. in Physiol. Of, at, forming, the base of. [BASE¹, BASIS]

bās'ic, a. Of, at, forming, base; fundamental; (Chem.) having the properties of or containing a base; (Min.) slightly silicated (igneous rock); prepared by non-siliceous process (steel); ~ *English*, select vocabulary of 850 words; ~ *slag*, fertilizer containing phosphates produced as by-products in the ~ process of steel manufacture. [BASE¹ +-IC]

basi'city̆, n. An acid's relative power of combining with bases. [prec. +-TY]

băs'il¹ (-z-), n. Kinds of aromatic herb, esp. *common* or *sweet* ~ & *bush* or *lesser* ~, both culinary. [ME, f. OF *basile* f. LL *basilisca* (*basiliscus* BASILISK), the Gk name *basilikon* (= royal) being misinterpreted as antidote for basilisk's venom]

băs'il² (-z-), n. Corruption of BASAN.

basil'ic, a. (Of vein) starting from elbow & discharging into axillary vein. [f. F *basilique* f. L f. Gk *basilikos* royal (as formerly thought of special importance)]

basil'ica, n. (Orig.) royal palace; hence, oblong hall with double colonnade & apse used for lawcourt & assemblies; such a building used as Christian church; (in Rome) one of the seven churches founded by Constantine. [L, f. Gk *basilikē* (*oikia*, *stoa*) royal (house, portico) f. *basileus* king, -IC]

basil'icon, -um, n. Kinds of ointment. [-on Gk, -um L, f. Gk *basilikos* as in prec.; so called as a 'royal' remedy]

băs'ilisk (-z-), n. Fabulous reptile (also *cockatrice*) hatched by serpent from cock's egg, blasting by its breath or look; (fig.) ~-*glance* etc., evil eye, person or thing that blasts (reputation etc.); (Zool.) small American lizard with hollow crest inflated at will. [f. L f. Gk *basiliskos* (dim. of *basileus* king) kinglet, serpent, golden-crested wren]

bās'in, n. Hollow round metal or pottery vessel, less deep than wide, & contracting downwards, for holding water etc., bowl; hollow depression; dock with flood-gates; land-locked harbour; tract of country drained by river & tributaries; circular or oval valley; (Geol.) formation with strata dipping towards centre, the deposit (e.g. coal) contained in this. Hence ~FUL (2) n. [ME & OF *bacin* (F *bassin*) f. Rom. *bac(c)hinus* f. LL *bacca* BACK⁴]

băs'inĕt, băs'nĕt, n. Light steel headpiece. [ME *basnet*, *bacinet* f. OF *bacinet* dim. of *bacin* BASIN]

bās'is, n. (pl. *bāsēs*). = BASE¹ (chiefly in fig. senses); main ingredient, foundation, beginning, determining principle; common ground for negotiation etc.; military base. [L = BASE¹]

băsk (bah-), v.i. Revel in warmth & light (usu. *in* the sun, firelight, etc.); ~-*ing-shark*, largest species of shark (also *sunfish* & *sailfish*). [app. f. ON *bathask* refl. of *batha* BATHE¹]

bas'kĕt¹ (bah-), n. Wicker vessel of osiers, cane, rushes, etc.; the quantity contained in it (also ~*ful*); wicker singlestick handguard; *pick of the* ~, best of the lot; ~-*ball*, game played with large inflated ball, a goal being scored when it is thrown into a ~ fixed 10 ft above ground at opponents' end; *basket-*, of ~ shape as ~-*hilt*, of ~ material or fashion as ~-*carriage*, -*work*. Hence ~RY(5) n. [orig. unkn.]

bas'kĕt² (bah-), v.t. Put in a basket, waste-paper or other. [f. prec.]

bās'on¹, n. (arch.). = BASIN.

bās'on², n., & v.t. Bench for felting hat material; (vb) felt. [perh. = BASIN]

basque (bahsk), n. & a. **1.** Biscayan, (native or language) of Western Pyrenees (*B*~). **2.** Short continuation of bodice below waist; bodice having this. [F, f. L *Vasco -onis*]

băs-rélief′, băss-, n. (Piece of) shallow carving or sculpture on background (less than half the true depth). [earlier *basse relieve*, f. It. *basso rilievo*, later alt. to F *bas-relief*]

băss[1], n. Common perch; *black* ~, perch of Lake Huron; European sea-fish (also *sea-wolf* and *sea-dace*). [earlier *barse* f. OE *bærs* = MHG *bars*, f. Gmc root *bærs-*, *bors-* bristle]

băss[2], n. Inner bark of lime, used for mats, hassocks, & baskets, & for tying plants, flowers, etc.; ~*-broom*, coarse fibre broom for rough work; ~*-wood*, Amer. lime, its wood. [alt. f. BAST]

băss[3], a. & n. Deep-sounding; (of, suited to) lowest part in harmonized music; (man with) ~ voice; *thorough-*~, *figured* ~, ~ part with shorthand indications below of the proper harmony, hence theory of harmony; ~*-viol*, *viola da gamba* or violoncello. [ME *bas*, *basc* see BASE[3]; now *bass* after It. *basso*]

băss′ét[1], n. Short-legged badger-dog. [F, dim. of *bas*, *basse* low; see BASE[3]]

băss′ét[2], n. Obsolete card-game. [f. It. *bassetta* f. *bassetto* dim. of *basso* BASE[3]]

băss′ét[3], n., & v.i. (geol.). Edge of stratum cropping out; (vb) crop out. [orig. unkn.]

băss′ét-hŏrn, n. Tenor clarinet. [transl. of F *cor de bassette* f. It. *corno di bassetto* see BASSET[2]]

băssinĕt′, n. Hooded wicker cradle or perambulator. [F, dim. of *bassin* BASIN]

băss′ō, n. = BASS[3] (second and third senses); ~ *profundo* (or *-on-*), (singer with) specially deep bass voice. [It., = (deep) bass]

bassōōn′, n. Wooden double-reed instrument used as bass to oboe; organ & harmonium stop of similar quality. Hence ~IST(3) n. [f. F *basson* (*bas* BASE[3] +-*on* see -OON)]

băssō-rĕliev′ō (-lyä-), n. (pl. *-os*). = BAS-RELIEF. [It.]

băst, n. Inner bark of lime (see BASS[2]); other flexible fibrous barks. [OE *bæst*, MHG, ON *bast* f. Gmc *bastaz*]

băs′tard, n. & a. (Child) born out of wedlock or of adultery, illegitimate; (of things) unauthorized, hybrid, counterfeit; ~ *file* (with serrations of medium coarseness); ~ *slip*, sucker of tree (also fig., = *bastard* n.); (Bot.) nearly resembling another species (~ BALM); (Zool.) ~ *wing*, rudimentary extra digit with quill-feathers. [ME, f. OF f. *bast* (BAT[2]) packsaddle (used as bed by muleteer) + -ARD; cf. BANTLING]

băs′tardīz|e, -is|e (-īz), v.t. Declare illegitimate. Hence ~A′TION n. [prec. + -IZE]

băs′tardў, n. Illegitimacy; ~ *order*, for support of illegitimate child by putative father. [f. AF & OF *bastardie*; see BASTARD, -Y[1]]

băste[1], v.t. Stitch together, tack, (as prelim. to regular sewing). [ME, f. OF

bastir sew lightly f. Gmc *bastjan* (cf. OHG *besten* lace, tie) f. *bast-* BAST]

băste[2], v.t. Moisten (roasting meat) with fat to prevent burning; pour melted wax etc. on (wicks in candlemaking). [orig. unkn.]

băste[3], v.t. Thrash, cudgel. [perh. = Sw. *basa* (see BASH) thr. past or p.p. *basit*, *baste*, *baist* in early exx.; cf. HOIST[1], [2]; or fig. use of prec. (cf. 'dry basting' Shakesp.)]

băstille′ (-ēl), n. Fortress; Paris prison-fortress destroyed 1789; prison. [ME *bastele*, *-ile*, *-el* f. OF *bastille*, for older *bastide* f. Pr. *bastida* fortification f. p.p. of *bastir* build]

băstinād′ō, n. (pl. *~es*), & v.t. (Punish with) caning on soles of feet. [f. Sp. *bastonada* (*baston* BATON) see -ADO(2)]

băs′tion, n. Projecting part of fortification, irregular pentagon with its base in the line (or at an angle) of the main works. Hence ~ED[2] (-nd) a. [F, f. It. *bastione* f. *bastire* build; cf. BASTILLE]

băt[1], n. Nocturnal mouse-like quadruped with fingers extended as frame of membranous wings; *have ~s in the belfry*, be crazy or eccentric. [f. 1575, alt. of ME *bakke* f. Scand.; earlier wds were *rearmouse* (f. OE), *flittermouse* (f. Du.)]

băt[2], n., & v.i. & t. **1.** Implement for striking ball in cricket, baseball, etc. (*off one's own* ~, in cricket, also fig., unaided; *carry one's* ~, be not out at end of innings); ~*sman* (*a good* etc. ~); ~*s′man* (*-an*), performer with cricket etc. ~, also one who signals with ~s in his hands to guide aircraft landing on ship's deck. **2.** vb. (-tt-). Use ~, have innings; strike (as) with ~. [ME, f. OF *batte* club (*battre* strike, see ABATE)]

băt[3], n. (sl.). Pace of stroke or step (*went off at a rare* ~). [orig. unkn.]

bat[4], n. (baht). (Anglo-Ind., colloq.). *The* ~, spoken language (orig. of India, now extended); *sling the* ~ (Army sl.), speak the lingo (in this use freq. pron. băt). [Hind., = speech, word]

băt[5], v.t. To wink (*never ~ted an eyelid*, did not sleep a wink, betrayed no emotion). [var. of obs. *bate* to flutter]

băt-, bât- (băt- (băt, baht), comb. form. For officers' baggage on campaign; ~*-horse* (for carrying baggage); ~*-pay*, baggage allowance. [f. OF *bast*, mod. *bât* packsaddle f. Rom. *bastum* perh. f. Gk *bastazō* lift]

batat′a (-ahta), n. W.-Indian plant, sweet or Spanish potato. [Sp. & Port. f. native American]

Batāv′ian, a. & n. (Inhabitant) of ancient Batavia (between Rhine & Waal) or of modern Holland, Dutch(man); of, inhabitant of, Batavia in Java. [f. L *Batavia* (*Batavi* pl.)]

bătch, n. Loaves produced at one baking; quantity or number of anything coming at once or treated as a set. [ME *bache* (*bæcan* BAKE) cf. *wake*, *watch*, *make*, *match*]

bāte¹, v.t. & i. Let down (~ *hope* etc.), restrain (~*d breath*); deduct (part of; usu. with neg., esp. *not* ~ *a jot* etc.); fall off in force. [aphetic f. ABATE]

bāte², n., & v.t. Alkaline lye for softening hides; (vb) steep in this. [cf. Sw. *beta* to tan, G *beize* maceration f. *beizen* cause to bite BAIT¹]

∥ **bāte³**, **bait³**, n. (sl.). Rage (*was in an awful* ~). [perh. = obs. *bate* var. of *debate*; or f. BAIT¹ = state of baited person]

bath¹ (bahth; *pl. pron.* -dhz), Bath, n. **1.** Washing; immersion in liquid, air, etc.(*air-* ~, *sun-* ~, exposure of naked body to air, sun; *mud-* ~, of mud for rheumatism; ~ *of blood*, carnage); water etc. for bathing, wash, lotion, surrounding medium; vessel (*sitz-* ~, like HIP-~ but with broad flat bottom [G *sitzbad* sitting bath]; *sponge-* ~, esp. of broad flat saucer shape to facilitate sponging), room (also ~-*room*), or building, for bathing in (see TURKISH); town resorted to for medical bathing; *°~robe*, dressing-gown. **2.** Order of knighthood (B~; for C.B., K.C.B., G.C.B., see abbreviations) named from the ~ preceding installation. **3.** Town in Somerset named from hot springs (B~ *bun*; B~ *Oliver*, biscuit invented by Dr W. Oliver of B~, d. 1764; B~ *brick*, preparation for cleaning metal; ∥ B~ *chair*, wheeled for invalid; ∥ B~ CHAP²; B~ *stone*, oolite building-stone). [OE *bæth*, OHG *bad*, ON *bath*, f. Gmc *batham*]

bath² (-ah- *or* -ā- *in all parts*), v.t. Subject to washing in bath (child or invalid, of nurse etc.). [f. prec.]

bath|e¹ (-dh), v.t. & i. Immerse (in liquid, air, light, etc.); (of person, liquid, etc.) moisten all over; (of sunlight etc.) envelop; take a bath or bathe, so ~*ing-costume*, -*dress*, ∥ -*drawers*, *trunks*; ~*ing-machine*, wheeled dressing-box drawn into sea for ~*ing* from. [OE *bathian*, OHG *badōn*, ON *batha*, f. Gmc *bathōn*]

bāthe² (-dh), **bāth'er** (-dh-), nn. Taking, taker, of a bath, esp. in sea, river, swimming-bath. [f. prec. in intr. sense]

bathĕt'ic, a. Marked by bathos. [irreg. f. Gk BATHOS after *pathos*, *pathetic*]

bathŏm'ēter, n. Instrument used to ascertain depth of water. [f. Gk *bathos* depth + -METER]

Bathōn'ian, a. & n. (Inhabitant) of Bath. [mod. L *Bathonia* Bath, -AN]

băth'ŏs, n. Fall from sublime to ridiculous; anticlimax; performance absurdly below occasion. [Gk, = depth]

bathy-, comb. form of Gk *bathus* deep.

bathȳb'ius, n. Slimy gelatinous substance dredged from great ocean depths (once believed to be protoplasmic, now known to be inorganic). [f. BATHY- + Gk *bios* life]

bathȳmĕtr-, stem of scientific words. Of depth-measurement. [f. BATHY- + -METER]

băth'ȳscaphe (-âf), n. = foll. [f. BATHY- + Gk *skaphē* boat]

băth'ȳsphēre, n. Large strong submersible sphere for deep-sea observation. [f. BATHY- + SPHERE]

băt'ik, n. Method (orig. Javan) of printing coloured designs on textiles by waxing parts not to be dyed. [Javanese *mbatik* drawing]

bāt'ing, prep. Except. [part. of BATE¹]

batiste' (-ēst), n. & a. (Of) fine light fabric like cambric in texture. [F, f. *Baptiste* of Cambrai, first maker]

∥ **băt'man**, n. (mil.). An officer's servant, so *băt'woman*; (orig.) one who looked after a baggage animal. [BAT-]

băt'on, n., & v.t. Staff of office, esp. *Marshal's* ~; constable's truncheon (vb, strike with this); wooden tube carried in relay race; (Her.) truncheon in shield (~ *sinister*, badge of bastardy); (Mus.) conductor's wand for beating time. [F *bâton*]

batra'chian (-k-), a. & n. Of frogs; (one) of the *Batrachia*, or animals that discard gills & tail. [f. Gk *batrakheios* (*batrakhos* frog) + -AN]

battǎl'ion (-yon), n. Large body of men in battle array (*God is for the big* ~s, force prevails); unit of infantry composed of several companies & forming part of regiment or brigade. [f. F *battaillon* (now *bata-*) f. It. *battaglione* f. *battaglia* BATTLE¹]

∥ **bătt'els**, n. pl. College account at Oxford for board & provisions supplied, or for all college expenses. [perh. f. obs. vb *battle* fatten f. obs. adj. *battle* nutritious cf. BATTEN¹]

bătt'en¹, n. Piece of square-sawn softwood timber 2 in. to 4 in. thick & 5 in. to 8 in. wide; bar of wood used for clamping boards of door etc.; strip of wood carrying electric lamps; (Naut.) strip of wood nailed on spar to save rubbing, or securing hatchway tarpaulin. Hence ~ING¹(6) n. [var. of BATON]

bătt'en², v.t. Strengthen with battens; (Naut.) ~ *down*, close the hatches (see BATTEN¹). [f. prec.]

bătt'en³, n. Bar in silk-loom striking in the weft. [f. F *battant* (*battre* strike, -ANT)]

bătt'en⁴, v.i. Feed gluttonously *on*, revel *in*, (often implying morbid taste); grow fat. [f. ON *batna* get better (*bati* advantage cf. BETTER¹, BOOT²); see -EN⁶]

bătt'er¹, v.t. & i. Strike repeatedly so as to bruise or break (person, thing, or abs.; also with advv. *about*, *down*, *in*; & intr., ~ *at the door*); operate against (walls etc.) with artillery; (fig.) handle severely (theories, persons); beat out of shape, indent; (Printing) deface (type) by use; ~*ing-charge*, full charge of powder for cannon; ~*ing-ram*, swinging beam anciently used for breaching walls, sometimes with ram's-head end; ~*ing-train*, set of siege guns. [ME, f. *bat-* in OF *batre* (BAT²) + -ER⁵]

bătt′er[2], n. Mixture of ingredients beaten up with liquid for cooking; defect in printing-type or stereotype plate. [ME *batour*, *-owre* f. OF *bat(e)ure* beating]

bătt′er[3], v.i., & n. (Have) receding slope from ground upwards (of walls narrower at top). [orig. unkn.]

bătt′erў, n. (Law) infliction of blows, or of the least menacing touch to clothes or person (esp. in phr. *assault & ~*); (Mil.) emplacement for one or more guns, artillery unit of regiment, consisting usu. of two sections & forming subdivision of regiment, (fig.) *turn a man's ~ against himself* (in argument); (in various sciences & arts) set of similar or connected cells, instruments, or utensils (electric, galvanic, optical, cooking); series of nesting-boxes, cages, etc., in which laying hens are confined for intensive laying or poultry reared & fattened; hammered brass or copper vessels. [f. F *batterie* (*battre* strike, & see -ERY)]

bătt′ing, n. In vbl senses; also, cotton fibre prepared in sheets for quilts etc. [BAT[2] + -ING[1]]

bă′tle[1], n. Combat, esp. between large organized forces (*general's ~*, decided by strategy or tactics, *soldier's ~*, by courage & skill; *pitched ~*, fought by common consent; *~ royal*, in which several combatants or all available forces engage, free fight); victory (*the ~ is to the strong*, *youth is half the ~*); *join, give, refuse, accept, offer, do, ~*; *~-axe*, medieval weapon, (colloq.) formidable (usu. middle-aged) woman; *~-cruiser*, heavy-gunned ship of higher speed & lighter armour than ~ ship; *~ dress*, soldier's etc. uniform of belted blouse & trousers; *~-piece*, picture or literary description of a ~-scene; *line of ~*, troops or ships drawn up to fight; *line-of-~ ship*, (obs.) of 74 or more guns; *~-ship* (mod.), most heavily armed and armoured warship, designed to meet the most powerful ships in ~. [ME *batayle* f. OF *bataille* f. Rom. **battalia* f. LL *battualia* pl. gladiatorial exercises f. L *battuere* beat]

bă′tle[2], v.i. Struggle *with* or *against* (difficulties, the waves, etc.). [f. F *batailler* (*bataille* = prec.)]

bă′tledŏre (-teld-), n. Wooden instrument like canoe paddle used in washing, baking, etc.; wooden, stringed, or parchmented bat used with shuttlecock in the game *~ & shuttlecock*. [from 1440; perh. f. Pr. *batedor* beater (*batre* beat + *-dor* = -TOR)]

bă′tlement (-tel-), n. (usu. in pl.). Indented parapet (raised parts, *cops* or *merlons*; gaps, *embrasures* or *crenelles*); parapet & enclosed roof. Hence *~ED*[2] a. [Eng. formation (+ -MENT) on OF *bataille*, *bateillier* furnish with turrets of defence, also, furnish with ramparts or bastions (whence ME p.p. *batayld*)]

battue (see Ap.), n. Driving of game by beaters to the sportsmen's station; shooting party on this plan; wholesale slaughter. [F]

bătt′ў, a. (sl.). Crazy. [f. BAT[1] + -Y[2]]

bau′ble, n. Showy trinket; court fool's emblem, a stick with ass-eared head carved on it; trifle, toy, thing of no worth. [ME *babel, babulle*, f. OF *babel, baubel* child's toy, of unkn. orig.]

baulk. See BALK.

baux′ite, n. (min.). Earthy compound containing varying proportions of alumina, the chief commercial source of aluminium. [f. *Les Baux* in France + -ITE[1](2)]

baw′bee, n. (Sc.). Halfpenny. [f. name of the laird of Sillebawby, mint-master under James V]

bawd, n. Procuress; obscene talk. [shortened form of ME *bawdstrot* f. OF *baudestrote, baudetrot* female pander]

bawd′ў, a. & n. Obscene (talk); *~y-house*, brothel. Hence *~iNESS* n. [f. prec.]

bawl, v.t. & i. Say, speak, in a noisy way (often with *out*, also with *at, against*, etc.). [imit.; cf. med. L *baulare* bark, Icel. *baula* (Sw. *böla*) to low]

‖ **bawl′ey**, n. (dial.). Fishing smack peculiar to Essex and Kentish coasts. [orig. unkn.]

bawn, n. Court of a castle; cattlefold. [f. Ir. *bábhun*]

bay[1], n. Kind of tree or shrub; (pl.) wreath of its leaves worn by conquerors or poets, heroic or poetic fame; *~'berry*, a West Indian tree, (also) candleberry or its fruit; *~ rum*, a perfume distilled from bayberry leaves. [f. OF *baie* f. L *baca* berry]

bay[2], n. Part of sea filling wide-mouthed opening of land; recess in mountain range; *Bay State*, Massachusetts. [ME, f. OF *baie* f. Sp. *bahia* f. LL *baia*]

bay[3], n. Division of wall between columns or buttresses; recess (*horse-~*), stall; *sick-~*, part of main deck used as hospital); space added to room by advancing window from wall line (*~ window*, filling such space); (Mil.) passing-place in a trench; ‖ railway platform having a cul-de-sac & acting as starting-point or terminus for a side-line, the cul-de-sac of such a platform, (*~-line*, side-line starting from this). [ME, f. OF *baée* f. *baer* to gape f. Rom. **batare*]

bay[4], n. Bark of large dog, of hounds in pursuit, esp. the chorus raised as they draw close; (in phrr. lit. of hounds & quarry, fig. of persecutors & victim, applied to the hunted animal) *stand* or *be at, turn to, hold hounds* etc. *at, ~*, show fight; (applied to hounds) *hold* or *have at, bring* or *drive to, ~*, come to close quarters with (quarry). [ME, f. (1) OF *tenir a bay* = It. *tenere a bada* hold agape or in suspense (see prec.) & (2) OF *abai*, in *tenir a bay* (mod. *aux abois*) f. *bayer*, foll.]

bay[5], v.i. & t. (Of large dogs) bark or howl; bark at, esp. ~ *the moon*. [ME, f. OF *bayer* (mod. *aboyer*) bark, (imit., of uncert. orig.), later infl. by BAY[4]]

bay[6], a. & n. Reddish-brown (horse). [f. F *bai* f. L *badius*]

bayadère' (-dār), n. Hindu dancing-girl (esp. one attached to a S.-Indian temple); striped textile fabric. [F, f. Port. *bailadeira* ballet-dancer]

Bay'ard, n. Chivalrous person. [French hero, 'chevalier sans peur et sans reproche', 1475–1524]

bay'onêt[1], n. Stabbing blade attachable to rifle-muzzle; *the* ~, or ~*s*, military force; (with prefixed number) so many infantry (cf. SABRE); *Spanish* ~, a plant, kind of yucca. [f. F *baionnette* perh. f. *Bayonne* as made or first used there]

bay'onêt, v.t. Stab with bayonet; ~ *into*, coerce by military force (or fig. by pressure) into. [f. prec.]

bayou (bī'ū), n. Marshy offshoot of river in southern N. America. [Amer. F, cf. Choctaw *báyuk* branch in a delta]

bay'-salt (sawlt), n. Salt in large crystals obtained by evaporation. [f. BAY[2]]

bazaar' (-zār), n. Oriental market; fancy fair in imitation of this, esp. sale of goods for charities. [f. Pers. *bazar* prob. through Turk. & It.]

•bazook'a, n. Anti-tank rocket-gun. [U.S., f. arbitr. name of comical mus. instrument]

bdell'ium (d-), n. Balsam-bearing tree; its resin. [L, f. Gk *bdellion* trans. of Heb. *b'dolakh* of uncertain meaning (carbuncle or crystal or pearl)]

be (bē, bi), v. substantive, copulative, & auxiliary (pres. ind.: *am*, pr. ăm, am; *art* arch., pr. ārt, art; *is*, pr. ĭz; pl. *are*, pr. ār, *ar*, & *be* arch.; past ind.: 1 & 3 *was*, pr. wŏz, woz; 2 *wast* arch., pr. wŏst, wost; pl. *were*, pr. wĕr, wār, wer; pres. subj. *be*; past subj. *were*, exc. 2 sing. *wert* arch., pr. wărt, wert; imperat. *be*; part. *being*, pr. bē'ĭng; p.p. *been*, pr. bĕn, bĭn; colloq. clipped forms '*m* = *am*, '*s* = *is*, '*re* = *are*. *Isn't*, *wasn't*, *aren't* pl., *weren't*, are legitimate in actual or printed talk; *ain't* is colloq. for *am not* & vulg. for *is* or *are not*. **1.** vb subst. Exist, occur, live, (often with *there*; *God is, there is a God;* *for the time being*, temporarily; *to be or not to be*, see *Haml*. III. i. 56—often joc. in trivial applications); remain, continue, (*let it be, do not be long*); (with advv. or adv. phrr.) occupy such a position, experience such a condition, have gone to such a place, busy oneself so, hold such a view, be bound for such a place, (*is in the garden, has been to Rome, be off, how is he?, what are you at?, I am for tariff reform, for London*); *been* colloq., called here, paid a visit, (*has anyone been?, has not been for orders*); *been and*, colloq. expletive of protest or surprise (*you have been & moved my papers!*); (with dat.) befall (*woe is me*).

2. vb cop. (With nouns, adjj., or adj. phrr.) belong under such a description (*I am a man, sick, of good courage*); coincide in identity with, amount to, cost, signify, (*thou art the man, twice two is four, it is nothing to me, what are these pears?*). **3.** vb aux. With p.p. of trans. vbs forming passives (*this was done*); with p.p. of some intr. vbs, as *fall, come, grow*, forming perfects (*the sun is set, Babylon is fallen*); with pres. part. act. forming continuous tenses act. & pass. (*he is building a house, the house was building*); with pres. part. pass. forming continuous tenses pass. (*the house was being built*); with infin. expressing duty, intention, possibility, (*I am to inform you, he is to be there, the house is to let, he is to be hanged, it was not to be found*); *were* with infin. in hypotheses (*if I were, or were I, to tell you*). **4.** Parts used as adjj., advv., nouns: *may-be*, perhaps, a possibility; *the to-be*, the future; *might-have-beens*, past possibilities; *would-be*, that yearns, or fancies himself, to be; *be-all*, whole being, essence. [f. four roots (1) Aryan *es-*, Gk, L, & Gmc *es-*, Skr. *as-*, to be; (2) Gmc **wes-*, Skr. *vas-*, remain; (3) Skr. *bhu-*, Gk *phu-*, L *fu-*, Gmc **beo-*, become; (4) Gmc **ar-* (f. *or-*) of unkn. orig. From (1) come *am* (cf. Gk *esmi*); from (2) come *was, wast, wert, were*; from (3) come *be, being, been*; from (4) come *art, are*]

be- (bĭ-), pref. f. OE *be-*, weak or stressless form of prep. & adv. *bī* BY, accented form of which appears in *by-law, by-word, by-gone*, etc. The orig. meaning was *about*, the various developments of which may be seen in the following groups of uses. **1.** Adding notion of all over, all round, to trans. vb, as *beset, besmear*. **2.** Adding notion of thoroughness, excess, to trans. vb, as *bedrug, bescorch*. **3.** Making intr. vbs trans., as *bemoan, bestraddle*. **4.** Forming trans. vbs = *to make* from adjj. & nouns, as *befoul, bedim, bebishop*. **5.** Making trans. vbs = *to call so & so* from nouns, as *bedevil, bemadam*. **6.** Making trans. vbs = *to surround with, to affect with, to treat in the manner of*, from nouns, as *becloud, beguile, befriend*. **7.** Making adjj. in -ED[2], from nouns, as *bewigged, beflagged*, (usu. with some contempt).

beach[1], n. Water-worn pebbles or sand; sea-shore covered with these; shore between high & low water mark; ~*-comber*, white man in Pacific Islands etc. who lives by collecting jetsam, longshore vagrant; ~*-head*, fortified position established on~ by landing forces [after *bridge-head*]; ~*-master*, officer superintending disembarkation of troops; ~*-rest*, chair--back for sitting against on ~. [16th c. *beach, bache*, of unkn. orig.]

beach[2], v.t. Run (ship, boat) ashore, haul up. [f. prec.]

‖ **beach-la-mār'** (-lah-), n. Jargon English used in Western Pacific. [corrupt. f. Port. *bicho do mar* BÊCHE-DE-MER]

beac'on[1], n. Signal, signal-fire on pole or hill; signal station; conspicuous hill (in names); lighthouse; guide or warning; BELISHA ~. [OE *bēacn*, OS *bōkan*, OHG *bouhhan* f. WG *baukn* cf. BECKON]

beac'on[2], v.t. Give light to, guide; supply (district) with beacons. [f. prec.]

bead[1], n. 1. (Orig.) prayer. 2. Small perforated ball for threading with others on string, used in counting one's prayers (*tell one's ~s*); the same used for ornament; drop of liquid, bubble; small knob in foresight of gun (*draw a ~ on*, take aim at); (Archit.) moulding like a bead series, or small one of semicircular section; ~*-roll*, list of names, long series, (orig. of persons to be prayed for); ~*s'man*, pensioner bound to pray for benefactor, almsman. [ME *bede* (f. *ibede*, OE *gebed* prayer), OS *beda*, OHG *beta*, Goth. *bida*, f. Gmc *beth-* see BID[1]]

bead[2], v.t. & i. Furnish with beads; string together; form or grow into beads. [f. prec.]

bead'ing, n. In vbl senses; also, a bead moulding. [BEAD[1]; see -ING[1]]

‖ **bea'dle**, n. Ceremonial officer of church, college, city company, etc.; parish officer appointed by vestry; (Sc.) church officer attending on the minister. Hence ~SHIP (-dels-) n. [(a) ME *budel*, *bidel* f. OE *bydel* = OHG *butil* f. WG *buthilaz* (see BID[1]); superseded by (b) ME *bedel*, f. OF *bedel* (med. L *bedellus*, *bidellus*) f. same Gmc source]

bea'dledom (-deld-), n. Stupid officiousness. [-DOM]

bead'y, a. (Of eyes) small & bright; covered with beads or drops. [BEAD[1]]

bea'gle, n. The smallest English hound, used for hare hunting when field follows on foot; spy etc.; *beagling*, hunting with ~s. [ME, perh. f. OF *bé-gueule* open throat (BAY gape)]

beak[1], n. Bird's bill (esp. in birds of prey, & when strong & hooked); similar mandible-end of other animals, as turtle; hooked nose; protection at prow of ancient warship; spout. Hence ~ED[2] (-kt) a. [ME *bec*, beak f. OF *bec* f. pop. L *beccus* f Gaulish origin]

‖ **beak**[2], n. (sl.). Magistrate; schoolmaster. [orig. unkn.]

beak'er, n. Large drinking-cup; lipped glass vessel for scientific experiments; tall wide-mouthed pottery drinking-vessel found in Bronze Age graves (~*-folk*, *-people*) [ME *biker* f. ON *bikarr* = OS *bikeri*, OHG *behhāri*, f. Gmc *bikar-jam*, f. med. L *bicarium* perh. f. Gk *bikos* drinking bowl. See PITCHER]

beam[1], n. Long piece of squared timber supported at both ends; cylinder in loom on which warp, cloth, is wound; chief timber of plough; bar of balance (*kick the~*, prove the lighter, be defeated); shank of anchor; lever in engine connecting piston-rod & crank; (pl.) horizontal cross-timbers of ship supporting deck & joining sides (*starboard*, *port*, ~, right & left sides, as *land on port ~* etc.); = ship's breadth (*on her ~-ends*, on her side, almost capsizing, in danger, at a loss); ray or pencil of light, or of electric radiation (~ *system*, wireless telegraphy in which transmission in a particular direction is achieved by reflecting a short-wave ~ from a parabolic arrangement of wires charged with static electricity); radiance, bright look, smile. [OE *bēam* tree, OS *bōm*, OHG *boum* f. WG *baumaz*; cf. ON *bathmr*, Goth. *bagms*]

beam[2], v.t. & i. Emit (light, affection, etc.); shine; smile radiantly. Hence ~'ING[2] a. [f. prec.]

beam'y, a. Radiant (rare); (poet., of spears etc.) huge; broad (of ships). [BEAM[1], -Y[2]]

bean, n. (Kinds of leguminous plants bearing) smooth kidney-shaped seed in long pods; similar seed of other plants, as coffee; coin (sl.; *I haven't a ~*, I'm stony-broke); *full of ~s*, ~*-fed*, in high spirits; ‖ OLD ~; *give* one ~*s* (sl.), punish or scold him; SPILL[1] *the ~s*. [OE *bēan*, OS, OHG *bōna*, ON *baun*, f. Gmc *baund*]

‖ **bean'feast**, **bean'o** (sl., pl. *-os*), n. Employer's annual dinner to workpeople, fête, merry time. [f. prec. (beans & bacon being orig. considered an indispensable dish)]

bear[1] (bâr), n. Heavy partly carnivorous thick-furred plantigrade quadruped; rough unmannerly person, whence ~*'-ISH*[1] a., ~*'ishNESS* n.; *Great Little*, *B~*, northern constellations; (St. Exch.) speculator for a fall, one who sells stock for future delivery hoping to buy it cheap meanwhile, & therefore tries to bring prices down (cf. BULL, & see foll.); heavy punching-machine; ~*'s-breech*, acanthus; ~*'s-foot*, kinds of hellebore; ~*'garden*, scene of tumult; ~*'s-grease*, pomade; ~*'skin*, (wrap etc.) of ~'s skin, Guards' tall furry cap; ~*'leader*, travelling tutor. [OE *bera*, OHG *bero*, f. WG *beron*]

bear[2] (bâr), v.i. & i., n. (St. Exch.). Speculate for a fall; produce fall in price of (stocks etc.); (n.) this operation. [f. prec., perh. w. ref. to selling the bear's skin before killing the bear]

bear[3] (bâr), v.t. & i. (*bore*, *borne* or *born*, see below†). 1. Carry (poet. or formal, exc. in the senses or contexts following); ~ *or* ~ *away*, win (the palm, bell, prize); carry visibly, show, be known by, (banner, device, arms, the marks *of*, name, relation or ratio *to*); ~ *oneself well* etc., behave); bring at need (~ *witness*, *company*; ~ *a hand*, help); wield (office, rule); carry internally (~ *a grudge*; ~ *in mind*, remember); wear (~ *arms*, the *sword*); ~ *out*, confirm; *be borne away* (by external force or influence, or internal impulse); *is borne in upon* one, becomes one's conviction. **2.** Sustain (weight, responsibility, cost; ~ *a part in*, share); stand (test etc.), endure (*grin* & ~ *it*), tolerate, put up with (*cannot* ~ *him*), whence ~'ABLE a.; be capable of upholding (*ice* ~s); be fit for (*his language won't* ~ *repeating*); ~ *with*, treat forbearingly; ~ *up*, (trans.) uphold, (intr.) not despair; *borne on the books of*, paid by. **3.** Thrust, strive, apply weight, tend, (~ *down*, overthrow; ~ *hard on*, oppress; ~ *upon*, be relevant to; *bring to* ~, apply; ~ *to the right, away, off*, incline; ~ *down*, swoop; ~ *up*, keep ship farther away from wind; ~ *up for*, change ship's course so as to sail towards). **4.** Produce, yield, give birth to. †The p.p. is *borne*, exc. that *born* is used in pass. parts referring to human & other mammal birth; even then *borne* is used before *by* with the mother (*has borne a child*; *born 1901*; *born of, borne by, Eve*). [OE, OS, OHG *beran*, ON *bera*, Goth. *bairan*, f. Gmc **ber-*, Aryan **bher-* (L *ferre*, Gk *pherein*)]

beard[1], n. Hair of lower face (excluding usu. the moustache, & occas. the whiskers); chin tuft of animals; gills of oyster; attachment threads of some shellfish; beak-bristles of birds; awn of grasses; *old-man's* ~, = traveller's joy. Hence ~'ED[2], ~'LESS, aa., ~'lèssNESS n. [OE *beard*, OHG *bart* f. WG **bardaz*]

beard[2], v.t. Oppose openly, defy, (~ *the lion in his den*). [f. prec.]

bear'er (bâr[4]), n. Person or thing that carries; part-carrier of coffin; (India) palanquin-carrier, body-servant; native carrier; bringer of letters or message, presenter of cheque; (with adj. *good* etc.) plant etc. that produces well etc.; ~ *company* (Mil.), medical unit organized to tend & bring in wounded on field service. [BEAR[3] + -ER[1]]

bear'ing (bâr-), n. In vbl senses; also or esp.: outward behaviour; heraldic charge or device; relation, aspect, (*consider it in all its* ~s; *what is the* ~ *of this on the argument?*); (pl.) parts of machine that bear the friction; compass direction in which a place etc. lies, (pl.) relative position (*have lost my* ~s, do not know where I am); ~*rein*, fixed rein from bit to saddle, forcing horse to arch its neck. [BEAR[3], ING[1]]

beast, n. Animal; quadruped; (Farming) bovine animal, esp. fatting-cattle (collect. pl. *beast*); animal for riding or driving; brutal man; person whom one dislikes; *The B*~, Antichrist; *the* ~, the animal nature in man. [ME, f. OF *beste* f. Rom. *besta* f. L *bestia*]

beast'liness, n. Gluttony, drunkenness, obscenity; disgusting food or drink. [f. foll.]

beast'ly[1], a. Like a beast or its ways: unfit for human use, dirty; (colloq.) undesirable. [-LY[1]]

beast'ly[2], adv. (sl.). (Intensifying adjj.

& advv. used in bad sense; cf. JOLLY) very, regrettably, (~ *drunk, wet; raining* ~ *hard*). [-LY[2]]

beat[1], v.t. & i. (past *beat*; p.p. *beaten*, but *beat* in *dead-beat*, often in sense *surpassed*, & occas. in other senses). Strike repeatedly (t. & i.; ~ *the breast*, in mourning; ~ *black & blue*, bruise; ~ *the air*, strive in vain; ~ *at door*, knock loudly; ~ *path*, make it by trampling), inflict blows on, (of sun, rain, wind) strike (*upon* something, or abs.); ~ *up*, ~ (person) severely; overcome, surpass (~ *hollow*, easily; ~ *person to it*, get there first, lit. & fig.; ~*s cockfighting*, is extremely exhilarating), be too hard for, perplex; move up & down (t. & i. of wings); move rhythmically (*heart* etc. ~*s*, ~ *time, seconds*, etc.); (Phys. etc.) create pulsation (see foll.); shift, drive, alter, deform, by blows (~ *down, back, away, off*; ~ *in*, crush; ~ *down price* or *seller*, cheapen or bargain with; ~ *up eggs* etc., reduce to froth, powder, paste; ~ *or* ~ *out metal*, forge); (Naut.) ~ *up, about*, strive, tack, against wind; strike (bushes, water) to rouse game (~ *about the bush*, approach subject slowly, shilly-shally; ~ *up recruits* etc., collect; ~ *up the quarters of*, visit; ~ *one's brains*, search for ideas; ‖ ~ *the bounds*, mark parish boundaries by striking certain points with rods); play on drum (~ *a parley, a retreat*, propose terms, retire); *~ *it* (sl.), go away. [OE *beātan*, OHG *bōzan*, ON *bauta*, f. Gmc **bautan*]

beat[2], n. Stroke on drum, signal so given; movement of conductor's baton; measured sequence of strokes or sounds; throbbing; (Phys. etc.) pulsation due to combination of two sounds or electric currents of (slightly) different frequencies; sentinel's or constable's appointed course; one's habitual round; sportsman's range. [f. prec.]

beat'en, a. In vbl senses; also or esp.: worn hard, trite; shaped by the hammer; exhausted, dejected. [p.p. of BEAT[1]]

beat'er, n. In vbl senses; esp.: man employed to rouse game; implement for beating flat. [BEAT[1] + -ER[1]]

bēatif'ic, a. Making blessed. [f. F *béatifique* or L *beatificus* (*beatus* p.p. of *beare* bless, & see -FIC)]

bēatificā'tion, n. Making or being blessed; (R.-C. Ch.) first step to canonization, announcement that dead person is in bliss. [F, or f. LL *beatificatio* (prec., -ATION)]

bēat'ify, v.t. Make happy; (R.-C. Ch.) announce as in prec. [f. F *béatifier* or LL *beatificare* (prec., -FY)]

beat'ing, n. In vbl senses; esp.: a chastisement; a defeat. [f. BEAT[1]]

bēat'itūde, n. Blessedness; (pl.) the blessings in *Matt.* v. 3-11. [F, or f. L *beati tudo* (*beatus* see BEATIFIC, -TUDE)]

beau (bō), n. (pl.~*x*, pr. bōz). Fop, dandy; lady's-man, admirer. [F]

Beauf'ort scāle (bōf-), n. Scale of wind velocity ranging from 0 (calm) to 12–17 (hurricane ; 75 miles an hour or over). [Sir F. *Beaufort*, English admiral (d. 1857)]

beau geste (bōzhĕst'), n. A display of magnanimity. [F]

beau īdē'al (bō), n. One's highest type of excellence or beauty. [F (*-éal*), = the ideal Beautiful (often misconceived in E as a beautiful ideal) ; see BEAU & IDEAL a.]

beau monde (see Ap.), n. Fashionable society. [F]

Beaune (bōn), n. A red Burgundy. [place]

beaut'ēous (bū-), a. (poet.). Beautiful. [ME *beaute* BEAUTY + -OUS ; cf. *plenteous*]

beaut'iful (bū-), a. Delighting the eye or ear, gratifying any taste, (~ *face, voice, poem, picture, soup, batting*) ; morally or intellectually impressive, charming, or satisfactory (~ *patience, organization, specimen*). Hence ~LY² adv. [BEAUTY + -FUL]

beaut'if|ȳ (bū-), v.t. Make beautiful ; adorn. Hence ~īER¹ (1, 2) n. [BEAUTY + -FY]

beaut'ȳ (bū-), n. Combination of qualities, as shape, proportion, colour, in human face or form, or in other objects, that delights the sight (~ *is but skin deep*, one cannot judge by appearances) ; combined qualities delighting the other senses, the moral sense, or the intellect ; a ~, beautiful person or thing (often ironical), exceptionally good specimen (*here is a* ~) ; beautiful women ; a beautiful trait or feature, ornament, (*that's the* ~ *of it*, the particular point that gives satisfaction) ; ~ *parlour* (orig. U.S.), establishment in which the art or trade of face-massage, face-lifting, applying cosmetics, etc. is carried on, whence *beauti'*CIAN (bū-) n., one who runs a ~ parlour ; ~*-sleep*, before midnight ; ~*-spot*, small patch placed on lady's face as foil to complexion, beautiful scene. [ME *beaute* etc. f. OF f. Rom, *bellitatem* f. L *bellus* pretty ; see -TY]

beaux yeux (bōzyȫ'), n. *For the* ~ *of*, just to gratify (person). [F, = fine eyes]

beav'er¹, n. Amphibious broad-tailed soft-furred rodent, building huts & dams ; its fur ; hat of this. [OE *beofor*, MDu. *bever*, OHG *biber*, ON *bjórr*, f. Gmc **bebruz*, cogn. w. L *fiber*]

beav'er², n. Lower face-guard of helmet. [ME & OF *bavière* bib (*bave* saliva)]

beav'erteen, n. Cotton twilled cloth with pile of loops. [f. BEAVER¹ after *velveteen*]

*bēb'ŏp, n. Kind of jazz music. [imit.]

bēcall' (-kawl), v.t. (arch. or vulg.). Call (person) names. [BE-(2)]

bēcalm' (-ahm), v.t. **1.** Make calm (sea etc.). **2.** Deprive (ship) of wind. [(1) BE-(2) +CALM v., (2) BE-(6) +CALM n.]

became. See BECOME.

bēcause' (-ŏz, -awz), adv. & conj. For the reason (*that* & clause, arch.) ; by reason, on account, (*of* & noun) ; for the

reason that, inasmuch as, since. [BY prep. + *cause* n., after OF *par cause de* the conj. use arises by omission of *that*]

bĕccafic'ō (-fē-), n. (pl. -os). Small migrant bird eaten in Italy. [It. (*beccare* peck + *fico* fig)]

bē'chamĕl (bĕsh-), n. Kind of white sauce. [inventor's name]

bêche-de-mer (see Ap.), n. Sea-slug, a Chinese dainty. [quasi-F of Eng. orig., alt. from *biche de mer* f. Pg. *bicho do mar*, lit. sea-worm]

‖ **bĕck¹**, n. Brook, mountain stream, (in northern England). [ME, f. ON *bekkr* cogn. w. OHG *bah*]

bĕck², n. Significant gesture, nod, etc. ; the order implied (*have at* one's ~, *be at* person's ~ & *call*, of entire dominion & obedience). [f. foll.]

bĕck³, v.t. & i. (poet.). Make mute signal, signal mutely to. [f. dial. *beck* v., shortened f. BECKON]

bĕck'ĕt, n. (naut.). Contrivance for securing loose ropes, tackle, or spars, (rope-loop, hook, bracket, etc.). [orig. unkn.]

bĕck'on, v.t. & i. Summon, call attention of, by gesture ; make mute signal (*to* person). [OE *biecnan, bēcnan*, OS *bōknian*, OHG *bouhhanjan* f. WG **bauknjan* f. *baukn-* BEACON]

bēcloud', v.t. Cover with clouds ; obscure. [BE-(6) + CLOUD n.]

bēcom|e' (-ŭm), v.i. & t. (-came, -come). Come into being ; *what has* ~*e of* (happened to) *him?* ; (copulative) begin to be (followed by n., adj., or adj. phr.) ; suit, befit, adorn, look well on, whence ~'ING² a., ~'ingLY² adv., ~'ingNESS n., (-kū-). [OE *becuman* (BE- + *cuman* COME) arrive, attain, = OHG *biquiman*, Goth. *biqiman*]

Becquerel rays (bĕk'rel rāz), n. pl. Rays emitted by radio-active substances (now usu. called *alpha, beta, gamma, rays*). [A. H. *Becquerel*, French physicist (d. 1878)]

bĕd¹, n. **1.** Thing to sleep on, mattress (*feather* ~ etc.), frame-work with mattress & coverings ; animal's resting place, litter ; (elliptical for) use of ~, being in ~ ; ~ & *board*, entertainment, connubial relations ; *narrow* ~, the grave ; ~ *of down, flowers, roses*, easy position ; ~ *of sickness*, invalid state ; *brought to* ~, in child-birth, *of child* or abs. ; *die in* one's ~, of natural causes ; *go to* ~, retire for the night (imperat., sl., cease talking etc.) ; *take to, keep*, one's ~, become, be, ill ; *make the* ~, arrange the coverings ; *lie in the* ~ *one has made*, take consequences of one's acts ; *got out of* ~ *on wrong side*, is bad-tempered for the day ; ~'*chamber* (arch. exc. of royal, as *Groom, Lady*, etc., *of the* ~*chamber*), ~*room* ; ~*-clothes*, sheets, pillows, etc., of ~ ; ~'*fellow*, sharer of ~, (fig.) associate ; ~*-jacket* (for sitting up in ~) ; ~*-key*, wrench for (un)fastening ~*stead* ; ~*-lift*, appliance for raising invalid to sitting position; ||~'**maker**, man tending college rooms at Oxf. & Camb.; ~-**pan**, invalid's chamber utensil for use in ~; ~'**post**, upright support of ~ (*in twinkling of ~post*, prob. transf. f. ~-**staff**, loose cross-piece of old ~steads often used as handy weapon; *between you & me & the ~post*, in confidence); ~'-**rid**(*den*), confined to ~ by infirmity, decrepit. [OE *bedreda* (*rida* rider), -*en* by confusion w. p.p.]; ~'**room**, for sleeping in; ~'**side**, side of esp. invalid's ~ (*good ~side manner*, of tactful doctors); ~-**sitting room**, (colloq.) ~-**sitter**, combined ~room & sitting room; ~'**sore**, developed in invalid by lying in ~; ~'**spread**, coverlet; ~'**stead**, framework of ~; ~'**straw**, herbaceous plant once used as straw for ~s, esp. (*Our*) *Lady's ~straw*; ~'**tick**, quadrangular bag holding feathers etc. for ~; ~'**time**, hour for going to ~. **2.** Flat base on which anything rests; ~-**plate**, metal plate forming base of machine; garden plot filled with plants, swamp with osiers; bottom of sea, river, etc. (~-**rock**, solid rock underlying alluvial deposits etc., fig. ultimate facts or principles of a theory, character, etc.); foundation of road or railway; slates etc. of billiard table; central part of gun-carriage; stratum; layer of oysters etc. [OE *bed*(*d*), OS *bed*, *beddi*, OHG *betti*, Goth. *badi* f. Gmc **badjam*]

běd², v.t. & i. (-dd-). Put or go to bed (poet. or arch. exc. of horses etc.); plant (esp. ~ *out*); cover up or fix firmly in something; arrange as, be or form, a layer. [f. prec.]

bědăb'ble, v.t. Stain, splash, with dirty liquid, blood, etc. [BE-(1) + DABBLE]

bědăd', int. (Irish etc. for) by GAD¹.

bědaub', v.t. Smear with paint etc.; bedizen. [BE-(1) + DAUB v.]

bědd'er, n. In vbl senses; also, plant suited for flower-bed. [-ER¹]

bědd'ing, n. In vbl senses; also: mattress, bedclothes, etc.; litter for cattle; bottom layer; (Geol.) stratification. [-ING¹]

běděck', v.t. Adorn. [BE-(1) + DECK v.]

běd'ěguar (-gär), n. Mosslike excrescence on rose-bush produced by insect's puncture. [f. F *bédeguar* f. Pers. *badawar* wind-brought]

|| **běd'el**(l) (*or* bedēl'), n. Official at Oxf. & Camb. with duties chiefly processional. [= BEADLE]

běděv'il, v.t. (-ll-, -l-). Treat with diabolical violence or abuse; possess, bewitch; spoil, confound; call devil. [BE-(5, 6) + DEVIL n.]

běděv'ilment, n. Possession by devil; maddening trouble, confusion. [prec. + -MENT]

bědew', v.t. Cover with drops, sprinkle. [BE-(6) + DEW]

bědight' (-īt), v.t. (past & p.p. *bedight*). Array, adorn, (arch.; usu. in p.p.). [BE-(1) + DIGHT]

bědim', v.t. (-mm-). Make (eyes, mind) dim. [BE-(4) + DIM a.]

bědiz'en, v.t. Dress out gaudily. [BE-(2) + DIZEN]

běd'lam, n. (*B~*) hospital of St Mary of Bethlehem used as lunatic asylum; any madhouse; scene of uproar. [f. *Bethlehem*; hospital founded as priory 1247, converted to asylum 1547]

běd'lamite, n. & a. Lunatic. [-ITE¹ (1)]

Běd'lington, n. (Also ~ *terrier*) short-haired, narrow-headed sporting terrier. [~ in Northumberland]

běd'ouin (-ōō-; *or* -ēn), n. (pl. same) & a. (Arab) of the desert, wandering; gipsy. [ME *bedoyn* f. OF *beduin* f. Arab. *badawin* pl. of *badawiy* dweller in the desert (*badw* desert); -*n* is prop the pl. sign]

bědrăb'bled (-ld), a. Dirty with rain & mud. [BE-(1), & see DRABBLE]

bědrăg'gle, v.t. Wet (dress etc.) by trailing it, or so that it trails or hangs limp. [BE-(1) + DRAGGLE]

bee, n. Four-winged stinging social insect (queen, drones, & workers) producing wax & honey; allied insects (*humble*, *mason*, *carpenter*, etc., ~); poet; busy worker; meeting for combined work or amusement (chiefly U.S., exc. *spelling-~*); *have a ~ in* one's bonnet, be obsessed on some point; ~-**bread**, (honey &) pollen used as food by ~s; ~-**eater**, kinds of foreign bird; ~HIVE; ~-**line**, straight between two places; ~-**master**, -*mistress*, keepers of ~s; ~ *orchis*, with ~-shaped flowers; ||~-**skep**, straw hive; ~'**s'wax**, secreted by ~s as comb material, (v.t.) polish with this. [OE *bēo*, OHG *bía*, ON *bý* f. Gmc **biðn*, cogn. w. OHG *bini* (G *biene*)]

beech, n. Smooth-barked glossy-leaved mast-bearing forest tree; its wood; ~-*fern*, kind of polypody; ~ *marten*, (also *stone marten*) white-breasted marten found in S. Europe; ~'*mast*, fruit of ~. Hence ~'EN⁵ a. [OE *bōcce*, *bēce* f. Gmc **bōkjōn*, also **bōkā-*, whence OE *bōc* (cf. *buckmast*, *buckwheat*), ON *bók*, OHG *buohha*]

beef, n. (pl. -*ves*), & v.i. **1.** Flesh of ox, bull, or cow; (in men) size, muscle; (usu. pl.) ox(en), esp. fattened, or their carcasses; ||~'*eater*, yeoman of guard, warder of Tower of London, (f. obs. sense well-fed menial); ~ *tea*, stewed ~ juice for invalids; ~STEAK; ~-*wood*, red timber of various trees. **2.** v.i. *(sl.)*. Complain. [ME *boef*, *beef* f. OF *boef* f. L *bovem* nom. *bos* ox]

beef'|y̌, a. Like beef; solid, muscular; stolid. Hence ~iNESS n. [-Y²]

Běěl'zěbŭb, n. The Devil; a devil. [OE, ME, f. L (Vulg.) f. Gk *beelzeboub* f. Heb. *ba'alz'bŭb* fly-lord]

been. See BE.

beer¹, n. Alcoholic liquor from fermented malt etc. flavoured with hops etc., including ale (pale) & porter (dark); other fermented drinks, as *nettle-~*;

GINGER-~; *small* ~, (lit., weak ~, (fig.) trifling matters (*think no small* ~ *of*, have high opinion of); ~*-engine*, for drawing ~ at a distance; ‖ ~'*house*, licensed for ~, not spirits; ‖ ~*-money*, servant's allowance in lieu of ~; ~*-pull*, handle of ~-engine. [OE *bēor*, MDu. *bēr*, OHG *bior*, com.-WG, whence prob. ON *bjórr*]

beer[2], n. One of the ends (so many threads) into which a warp is divided. [= BIER, cf. *porter* in same sense in Scotland]

beer'y̆, a. Of, like, beer; esp., betraying influence of beer. [-Y[2]]

bees'tings (-z), n. pl. First milk after calving. [OE *bȳsting* f. OE *bēost* (obs. *beest*), OHG *biost*, of unkn. orig.]

bees'wing (-z-), n. Second crust in long-kept port; old wine. [BEE + WING, from its filmy look]

beet, n. Two plants with succulent root, *red* ~ used for salad, *white* ~ for making sugar; ~*-root*; ‖ ~'*root*, root of ~. [OE *bēte*, LG *beete*, OHG *bieza*, WG f. L *beta*]

bee'tle[1], n., & v.t. Tool with heavy head & handle for ramming, crushing, smoothing, etc. (vb, beat with this); *three-man* ~, requiring three to lift it; ~*-brain* etc., blockhead. [OE *bietel* f. Gmc **bautilaz* f. *bautan* BEAT[1]; see -LE(1)]

bee'tle[2], n. Insect having upper wings converted to hard wing-cases (pop. only of the black & large varieties, also wrongly of insects like them, as the *black-* ~ or cockroach); short-sighted person (cf. ~*-eyed*, *blind as a* ~); ~*-crusher*, large boot or foot. [OE *bitula* biter f. *bītan* BITE[1]]

bee'tle,[3] a. Projecting, shaggy, scowling, (~ *brows*, ~*-browed*). [prob. f. prec. w. ref. to tufted antennae of some beetles]

bee'tle[4], v.i. Overhang (of brows, cliffs), hang threateningly (of fate etc.). [f. prec.]

beeves. See BEEF.

beez'er, n. (sl.). Nose. [orig. unkn.]

běfáll' (-awl), v.t. & i. (-fell, -fallen). Happen; happen to (person etc.). [OE *befeallan* f. BE-(2) + *feallan* FALL; cf. OS, OHG *bifallan*]

běfit', v.t. (-tt-). Suit, be fitted for; be incumbent on; be right for. Hence ~t'ING[2] a., ~t'ingLY[2] adv. [BE-(2) + FIT v.]

běfŏg', v.t. (-gg-). Envelop in fog; obscure. [BE-(6) + FOG[2] n.]

běfóol', v.t. Dupe. [BE-(5) + FOOL[1] n.]

běfóre', adv., prep., & conj. **1.** adv. Ahead (*go* ~); on the front (~ *& behind*); previous to time in question, already, in the past, (*long* ~). **2.** prep. In front of (~ *the mast*, of common sailors berthed forward), ahead of; under the impulse of (~ *the wind*, *recoil* ~, *carry all* ~ *you*); in presence of (*appear* ~ *judge*, *bow* ~ *authority*; ~ *God* = as God sees me; *the question* ~ *us*); awaiting (*world all* ~ *them*); earlier than (~ *Christ*, usu. abbr. B.C., appended to dates reckoned backwards from birth of Christ; this side the coming of (future event); farther on than; rather than (*would die* ~ *lying*). **3.** conj. Previous to the time when; rather than (*would die* ~ *I lied*). [OE *beforan* (BE- + *foran* adv. f. Gmc **fora* FOR)]

běfóre'hănd (-rh-), adv. In anticipation, in readiness; *be* ~ *with*, anticipate, forestall; ~ *with the world*, having money in hand. [ME, orig. two wds; cf. L *prae manu*, *manibus* at hand]

běfóul', v.t. Make foul (lit. or fig.); ~ *one's own* NEST. [BE-(4) + FOUL]

běfriend' (-rĕnd), v.t. Help, favour. [BE-(6) + FRIEND n.]

běg, v.t. & i. (-gg-). Ask for (food, money, etc.); (abs.) ask alms; ask (*for alms* etc.); live by alms; (of dog) sit up with forepaws raised expectantly; ask earnestly or humbly (thing, *for* thing, *of* person, person *to* do, *of* person *to* do, *that* something may be done); (in formal & courteous phrr.) ~ *pardon*, *leave*; ~ *off*, get (person) excused penalty etc.; ~ *to* do, take leave to do, take the liberty of doing, (*I* ~ *to differ*, *enclose*, *announce*, etc.); ~ *the question*, assume the truth of matter in dispute; *go* (*a-*)*begging*, (of situations, opportunities, etc.) find no accepter. [of uncert. orig.; perh. shortened f. F *béguiner* be a *beghard* or *béguin*, lay brother of mendicant order named f. Lambert Bègue]

běgăd', int. = by God (in fam. speech).

běgăn'. See BEGIN.

běgĕt' (-g-), v.t. (-tt-, -got, arch.-gat, -gotten). Procreate (usu. of father, sometimes of father & mother, cf. BEAR[3]); give rise to, occasion. Hence ~t'ER[1] n. [OE *begitan*; see BE-(2) & GET; cf. Goth. *bigitan*]

běgg'ar[1], n. One who begs; one who lives by begging; poor man or woman (~*s must not be choosers*, must take what is offered); (depreciatingly) fellow; (playfully) *little* ~, youngster etc.; *a good* ~ (= *begger*), good at collecting for charities etc. [perh. = *beghard* see BEG & -ARD]

běgg'ar[2], v.t. Reduce to poverty; outshine, reduce to silence (~ *description*); ~*-my-neighbour*, card game. [f. prec.]

běgg'ar|ly̆, a. Indigent; intellectually poor; mean, sordid. Hence ~liNESS n [BEGGAR[1] + -LY[1]]

běgg'ary̆, n. Extreme poverty. [-Y[1]]

běgin' (-g-), v.t. & i. (-nn-, began, begun). Commence (*to* do, *doing*, *work*, etc., or abs.; in pass. sense either *it has begun to be done*, or *it has been begun*); be the first to do something; take the first step (~ *to* colloq., appear likely ever to, make any attempt to); start speaking; ~ *at*, start from; ~ *with*, take first; *to* ~ *with*, in the first place; ~ *upon*, set to work at; come into being, arise; have its commencement, nearest boundary, etc. (at some point in space or time); ~ *the world*, start in life.

[OE *beginnan*, OS, OHG *biginnan*, WG f. *bi-* BE + Gmc *-ginnan*, of unkn. orig.]

běginn'er (-g-), n. In vbl senses; also, tiro. [-ER[1]]

běginn'ing (-g-), n. In vbl senses; also or esp.: time at which anything begins; source, origin; first part; *the ~ of the end*, first clear sign of final result. [-ING[1] (1)]

běgĭrd' (-g-), v.t. (-irt). Gird round or encircle. [BE-(1) + GIRD[1]]

běgone' (-awn, -ŏn), vb imperat. = be gone (more peremptory than *go*).

běgōn'ia, n. Kinds of plant with coloured perianths but no petals. [Michel *Begon* (d. 1710), -IA[1]]

běgŏr'ra, int. (Irish corruption of) by God!

běgŏt'(ten). See BEGET.

běgrīme', v.t. Soil deeply. [BE-(6) + GRIME]

běgrŭdge', v.t. Feel or show dissatisfaction at (thing), envy (one) the possession of. [BE-(2) + GRUDGE v.]

běguil|e' (-gĭl), v.t. Delude; cheat (person *of*, *out of*, or *into doing*); charm, amuse; divert attention from (toil, passage of time). Hence ~ER[1], ~e'MENT (-gĭlm-), nn. [BE-(2) + obs. vb *guile*, see GUILE]

beguinage (běg'ĭnahzh), n. House of beguines. [foll. + -AGE]

běg'uine (-gĕn), n. Member of Netherlands lay sisterhood not bound by vows. [Lambert *Bègue*, founder 1180]

běg'um, n. Mohammedan princess or lady of high rank. [Hind. *begam* f. East Turk. *bigim* fem. of *big* prince (BEY)]

běgŭn'. See BEGIN.

běhalf' (-ahf), n. (Only in phrr. 'on *or* in my etc. ~', 'on *or* in ——'s ~', 'on *or* in ~ of ——') *on* the part *of*, on account *of*, (a person); *in* the interest of (person or principle etc.). [mixture of earlier phrr. *on his halve* & *bihalve him*, either = on his side; see HALF]

běhāve', v.i. & refl. (Intr., usu. with adv.) conduct oneself, act, (rarely abs., esp. to or of children) conduct oneself with propriety, ~ *towards*, treat (*well* etc.); (refl., freq. of or to children, & usu. without adv.) show good manners; (of machines etc., intr. or refl.) work (*well*, *badly*, etc.); ~d p.p. (with *well-*, *ill-*), having good, bad, manners or conduct. [BE-(2) + HAVE]

běhāv'iour (-yer), n. Deportment, manners; moral conduct, treatment shown to or towards others; *be on* one's *good* or *best* ~, do one's best under probation; way in which ship, machine, substance, etc., acts or works. [f. prec., the ending due to confusion w. obs. *aver*, *havour*, *havyoure*, possession, = F *avoir*]

běhāv'iourism (-yer-), n. (psych.). Doctrine that, given adequate knowledge, all human actions admit of analysis into stimulus & response, & that ability to predict them depends on exhaustive study of behaviour in that light. [f. prec. + -ISM]

běhead' (-hěd), v.t. Cut the head from; kill in that way. [OE *behéafdian* f. be- (from) about + *héafod* HEAD n.]

beheld. See BEHOLD.

běhēm'oth (or bē'I-), n. Enormous creature. [perh. Egyptian *p-ehe-mau* water-ox (hippopotamus) assimilated to Heb pl. (of dignity) of *b'hemah* beast, see *Job* xl. 15]

běhěst', n. Command (poet.). [OE *behæs* (see HEST) f. *behátan* f. *be* BE- + *hátan* HIGHT]

běhind', adv., prep., & n. In or to the rear (of), on the farther side (of), hidden (by), at one's back; towards what are one's rear, farther back in place or time (than), past in relation to, too late, in concealment, in reserve, in support of, in an inferior position (to), under the defence of, in the tracks (of), outdone (by), in arrear (with); (n.) the posterior. Phrr.: *stay*, *leave*, ~, after others', one's own, departure or death; *fall* ~, not keep up; ~ *the scenes*, in private; *put* ~ one, refuse to consider; *go* ~ one's *words* etc., look for secret motives on his part; ~ one's *back*, without his knowledge; ~ *time*, unpunctual; ~ *the times*, antiquated. [OE *behindan* f. *be-* BE- + *hindan* HIND[3]]

běhind'hǎnd, adv. & pred. a. In arrear (*with* payments etc.); out of date, behind time; ill-provided (*with*). [prec. + HAND, cf. BEFOREHAND]

běhōld', v.t. (beheld). See, become aware of by sight; (abs. in imperat.) take notice, attend. Hence ~ER[1] n. [OE *bihaldan* f. BE-(2) + *haldan* HOLD.]

běhōl'den, pred. a. Under obligation (*to*). [p.p. (obs. exc. in this use) of prec. = bound]

běhōof', n. (arch.). (In phrr. *to*, *for*, *on* ~, or *the* ~, *of*) use, advantage. [OE *behóf*, OFris. *bihóf*, MHG *behuof* f. Gmc *bihafjan*; see HEAVE[1]]

běhōve', -hōove', v.t. impers. Be incumbent on (person) *to* (do something). [OE *behófian* f. prec.]

beige (bāzh), n. Kinds of fabric made of undyed and unbleached wool; colour of this. [F, of unkn. orig.]

bē'ing, n. In vbl senses; also or esp.: existence (*in* ~, existing); constitution, nature, essence; anything that exists (*the Supreme B*~, God); a person. [BE, -ING[1,2]]

běl, n. Unit (= ten decibels) used in the comparison of two levels of power in an electrical communication circuit. [f. A. G. *Bell* (d. 1922), inventor of telephone]

bělāb'our (-ber), v.t. Thrash (lit. & fig.). [BE-(3) + LABOUR v. (exert one's strength upon)]

bělāt'ĕd, a. Overtaken by darkness; coming too late. [p.p. of obs. *belate* f. BE-(4) + LATE]

bělaud', v.t. Load with praise. [BE-(2) + LAUD v.]

bělay', v.t. Make fast (running rope) round cleat etc. to secure it; (sailor's sl.

in imperat.) stop!, enough!; ~*ing-pin*, wooden or iron pin for ~*ing* on. [in naut. sense f. LG, Du. *beleggen* (in OE *belecgan*) surround, f. BE- (1) + *lecgan* LAY³]

běl can'tō (kah-), n. Singing characterized by full rich broad tone & accomplished technique. [It., = fine song]

belch¹, v.i. & t. Emit wind noisily from throat; utter noisily or drunkenly (abusive, blasphemous, or foul talk); (of gun or volcano) send out or up. [repr. OE *b(i)elcan*]

belch², n. Eructation; sound of gun, volcano; burst of flame. [f. prec.]

běl'cher, n. Parti-coloured neckerchief. [Jim *B*~, pugilist]

běl'dam(e), n. Old woman, hag; virago. [an Eng. formation, in ME = 'grandmother', f. *bel-* (BEAU) as in *belsire* + *dame* DAM²]

běleag'uer (-*ger*), v.t. Besiege (lit. & fig.). [f. Du. *belegeren* camp round f. BE- (6) + *leger* a camp; see LEAGUER¹]

běl'emníte, n. Tapering sharp-pointed fossil bone of extinct cuttlefish. [f. Gk *belemnon* dart + -ITE¹ (2)]

běl ěsprit' (-rē), n. (pl. *beaux esprits* pr. bōz ěsprē'). A wit. [F]

běl'fr|ȳ, n. Bell tower, attached or separate; bell space in church tower; BATS *in the* ~*y*. Hence ~IED² (-Id) a. [ME *berfrey* f. OF *berfrei* f. Gmc *berpfrith* f. *bergan* protect + *frithuz* peace; mod. sp. chiefly due to assoc. w. *bell*]

běl'ga, n. Belgian unit of exchange. [L fem. of *Belgus* Belgian (sc. *pecunia*)]

Běl'gian, a. & n. (Native) of Belgium; ~ *hare*, kind of domestic rabbit. [-AN]

Běl'gic, a. Of the Netherlands or Belgium; of the ancient Belgae. [f. L *Belgicus* (*Belgae*, -IC)]

Bělgrāv'|ia, n. Fashionable residential part of London south of Knightsbridge containing Belgrave Square. Hence ~IAN a.

Běl'ial, n. The devil; the spirit of evil; *man of* ~, reprobate. [f. Heb. *b'li-ya'al* (*b'li* not + *ya'al* use) worthlessness]

bělie', v.t. (-lying). Give false notion of; fail to act up to (promise etc.); fail to justify (hope etc.). [OE *beléogan* f. BE-(3) + *léogan* LIE²]

belief', n. Trust or confidence (*in*); acceptance of any received theology; acceptance as true or existing (of any fact, statement, etc.; *in*, or *of*, with nn., *that* with clause; *to the best of my* ~, in my genuine opinion); thing believed, religion, opinion, intuition; *The B*~, Apostles' Creed. [ME *bileafe* (f. OE *geléafa*; see foll.), = OS *gilôbho*, OHG *giloubo*, Goth. *galaubeins*]

bělieve|', v.t. & i. Have faith *in*, trust word of (person); put trust *in* truth of a statement, efficacy of a principle, system, machine, etc., existence of anything; give credence to (person, statement, etc., or *that*-clause; ~*e it or not*,

colloq., it is surprising but true); be of opinion *that*; *make* ~*e*, pretend. Hence ~'ABLE a., ~'ER¹ n., ~'ING² a. [early ME *bileven* f., by substitution of pref., OE *geléafan*, = OS *gilôbhian*, OHG *gilouben*, Goth. *galaubjan* f. Gmc *galaubhjan*, f. same root as in LEAVE¹, LIEF, LOVE]

bělíke', adv. (arch.). Probably, perhaps, (often iron.). [*be-* = BY prep. + LIKE a. (by what is likely)]

Belish'a (-ēsh-) **beac'on**, n. Post with yellow globe on top marking street crossing-place for pedestrians. [L. Hore-Belisha, Minister of Transport 1934]

bělit'tle, v.t. Make small, dwarf; depreciate. [BE-(4) + LITTLE]

bell¹, n. Hollow body of cast metal in deep cup shape widening at lip made to emit musical sound when struck; (Naut.) *one to eight* ~*s*, half hours of watch; ~-shaped object, as flower corolla (BLUE¹, CANTERBURY, ~). *Bear, carry away, the* ~, be first, win; ~, *book, & candle, bell* in allusion to eccles. cursing formula; *sound, clear, as a* ~, quite sound or clear (in other senses besides the acoustic), ~-*bird*, Brazilian and Austral. kinds with ~-like note; ~-*buoy*, with warning ~ rung by waves' motion; ~-*flower*, any plant of genus *Campanula*; ~-*founder*, -*founding*, -*foundry*, caster, casting, & manufactory, of ~*s*; ~-*glass*, ~-shaped as cover for plants; ~-*hanger*, one who puts up ~*s* & wires; ~-*heather*, heath; *~-hop* (sl.), hotel page; ~-*metal*, alloy of copper & tin (more tin than in bronze) for ~*s*; ~-*pull*, cord or handle attached to ~-*wire*, ~-*ringer*, -*ringing* (of church ~*s* with changes etc.); ~-*wether*, leading sheep of flock with ~ on neck, ringleader. [OE *belle*, MDu., MLG *belle*, Du *bel*; a LG wd perh. related to BELL²]

bell², v.t. Furnish with bell(s); ~ *the cat*, take the danger of a common enterprise on oneself (fable of cat & mice). [f. prec.]

bell³, n., & v.i. (Make the) cry of stag or buck at rutting-time. [OE *bellan* bark, bellow, OHG *bellan*; cf. ON *belja* & BELLOW]

bělladǒnn'a, n. (Bot.) deadly nightshade, a poisonous plant with purple flowers & purple-black berries; (Med.) drug prepared from this. [mod. L f. It., = fair lady, perh. because a cosmetic is made from it]

bělle, n. Handsome woman; reigning beauty (*the* ~ *of* any place). [F, f. L *bella* fem. of *bellus* pretty see BEAU]

belles-lettres (běl-lět'r), n. Studies, writings, of the purely literary kind. Hence **běllět'rIST** (3) (-l-l-) n., **běllětris'tIC** (-l-l-) a. [F]

bělli'cōse, a. Inclined to fighting. Hence ~ōs'ITY n. [f. L *bellicosus* (*bellum* war, -IC, -OSE¹)]

bělli'gerencȳ, n. Status of a belligerent. [f. foll., see -ENCY]

bělli'gerent, a. & n. (Nation, party, or

person) waging regular war as recognized by the law of nations; of such nation etc.; (loosely) any opponent engaged in conflict. [f. F *belligérant* or L *belligerare* wage war (*bellum* + *gerere*), -ANT]

Bĕllōn′a, n. War personified; woman of commanding presence. [L, = goddess of war f. *bellum* war]

bĕll′ow (-ō), v.i. & t., & n. **1.** Roar as a bull; shout, roar with pain; utter loudly and angrily (often *out, forth*); (of thunder, cannon, etc.) reverberate, roar. **2.** n. ~ing sound. [ME *belwe*, of uncert. orig.; perh. related to BELL³]

bĕll′ows (-ŏz), n. pl. Portable or fixed contrivance for driving air into a fire or through pipes of organ, reeds of harmonium, etc.; *pair of* ~, two-handled for fire; means used to fan passion etc.; the lungs (~ *to mend*, of broken-winded horse); expansible part of photographic camera. [OE *blæstbell(i)g*, later *bel(i)g*, whence ME *beli, bely*; see BELLY; also (north.) *belu, belw*, whence mod. *bellow(s)*]

bĕll′ȳ¹, n. Cavity of human body below diaphragm with stomach & bowels & other contents, abdomen; (externally) lower front of body; corresponding parts of animals; stomach; the body as food-consumer (cf. BACK¹), appetite, gluttony; the womb; cavity of anything; bulging part (concave or convex); front, inner, or lower surface; surface of violin etc. across which strings pass; ~*-band* (below horse's ~, checking play of shafts); ~*-worship*, gluttony; ~*-timber*, food; ~*-pinched*, starving; ~*-ache*, (n.) colic, (v.i., sl.) complain bitterly. Hence ·bĕll′iED (-id) a. [ME *bali, bely* f. OE *belig*, earlier *belg* bag, skin, = ON *belgr*, OHG *balg*, Goth. *balgs* f. Gmc **balgiz* f. *balg-, belg-* to swell: cf. BELLOWS]

bĕll′ȳ², v.t. & i. Swell out (usu of sails, & with *out*). [f. prec.]

bĕll′ȳful (-ŏŏl), n. As much as one wants of anything, esp. of fighting. [-FUL(2)]

bĕlŏng′, v.i. Pertain, be proper, *to* (as duty, right, possession, natural or right accompaniment, example in classification, characteristic, part, member, inhabitant, appendage); be rightly a member of club, coterie, household, grade of society, etc.; **be resident in*, connected *with*; ~ *under* or *in*, be rightly classified among; ~ *here* etc., live here, be rightly placed under this heading etc.; *where it* ~*s*, in its proper place. [ME, app. an intensive, f. BE- (2), of ME *longen*, obs. in this sense; cf. OHG *bilangēn* in same sense]

bĕlŏng′ings (-z), n. pl. A person's property, relatives, or luggage; everything connected with a subject. [f. prec.]

bĕlŏved (*as adj. or n. usu.* -ŭv′id; *as vb* -ŭvd′), p.p., a., & n. (Forming pass. parts of vb obs. in act.) dearly loved (followed by *of* or *by*, or abs.); (n.) darling (common

in voc., & with *my, his*, etc.). [BE-(2) + LOVE v.]

bĕlow′ (-ō), adv. & prep. **1.** adv. At or to lower level; on earth; in hell; downstairs (esp. Naut. *go* ~, from deck); down stream; in lower rank (*the court* ~); at foot of page, or farther on in book. **2.** prep. Lower than (~*-stairs*, arch., downstairs); too low to be affected by (~ *flattery*); down stream from; on inferior side of dividing line (~ *par*, ~ *the gangway*); at or to greater depth than; covered by; lower in amount, degree, etc., than (~ one's *breath*, less audibly than); of lower rank etc. than; unworthy of. Cf. BENEATH, UNDER. [*be-* = BY + LOW a.]

bĕlt¹, n. Encircling strip of leather etc. worn round waist or baldric-wise to confine or support clothes or weapons etc. (*hit below the* ~, fight unfairly); cincture of earl or knight; strip of colour, special surface, trees, etc., round or on anything; zone (*cotton, wheat, fever*, ~); endless strap connecting wheels; row of armour plates under water-line; *Great & Little B*~, channels into Baltic. [OE *belt*, = OHG *balz*, ON *belti*, f. Gmc **baltjaz* f. L *balteus*]

bĕlt², v.t. Put belt round (~*ed cruiser*, with belt & metal-covered deck); fasten on with belt; mark with belt of colour etc.; thrash with belt. [f. prec.]

bĕl′tāne, n. (Ancient Celtic festival on) May-day. [ult. f. Gael. *beilltainn*]

bĕl′vĕdēre, n. Raised turret to view scenery from. [It (*bel* beautiful, see BEAU, +*vedere* see)]

bĕlȳ′ing. See BELIE.

bēm′a, n. Platform in ancient Athenian public assembly. [Gk]

bĕmīre′, v.t. Cover or stain with mud; (pass.) be stuck in the mud [BE-(6) + MIRE n.]

bĕmoan′, v.t. Weep or express sorrow for or over. [OE *bemǣnan* f. BE-(3) + *mǣnan* MOAN]

bĕmūse′ (-z), v.t. Stupefy. [BE-(2) + MUSE v.]

‖ **bĕn**, n. (Sc.). Inner room (usu. of two-roomed cottage); *but & ~*, the outer & inner room. [ellipt. use of *ben* adv., within (OE *binnan*)]

bĕnch, n., & v.t. **1.** Long seat of wood or stone; boat-thwart; judge's seat, office of judge, law-court (*King's, Queen's, B*~); (collect.) judges, magistrates; ‖ (Parl.) seats appropriated to certain groups etc. (*Treasury*, FRONT¹, BACK¹, CROSS³, *bishops'*, ~*es*); *be raised to, be on, the* ~, be (made) a judge or bishop; working-table of carpenter etc.; ledge in masonry or earthwork; ~*-table*, stone seat in cloister etc.; ~*-mark*, cut by surveyors to mark point in line of levels; ~*-warrant*, one issued by a judge (opp. justice's warrant). **2.** v.t. Exhibit (dog) at show. [OE *benc*, = OS *banc*, OHG *bank*, ON *bekkr*, f. Gmc **bankiz*; cf. BANK¹]

‖ **bĕn'cher**, n. Senior member, sharing management, of Inn of Court. [-ER¹]

bĕnd¹, n. (Naut.) knot of various kinds (*fisherman's, weaver's,* etc.); (Her.) parallel lines from dexter chief to sinister base (~ *sinister* in opposite direction, sign of bastardy); shape (half BUTT) in which hides are tanned (~*-leather,* the thickest, used for soles). [OE *bend* band, bond, = OS *band,* OHG *bant,* Goth. *bandi,* f. Gmc **band-,* past stem of *bindan* BIND¹; see also BAND¹, BOND¹]

bĕnd², n. Bending, curve; bent part of anything; *the* ~*s* (colloq.), caisson disease. [f. foll.]

bĕnd³, v.t. & i. (past *bent,* p.p. *bent* exc. in ~*ed* knees). Force out of straightness, impart to (rigid object) or receive a curved or angular shape; arch (brows); tighten up, bring to bear, (energies etc. *on, to*); (pass.) be determined (*on* with gerund or noun); attach with knot (cable, sail); turn (t. & i.) in new direction (steps, eyes); incline (t. & i.) from the perpendicular (head), bow, stoop, submit, (*to* or *before*), force to submit (will etc.). Hence ~'ER¹ n., esp. (sl.) ‖ sixpenny bit, *spree. [OE *bendan* bind, = ON *benda* join, strain f. Gmc **bandjan* f. *band-,* see BEND¹]

bĕneaped' (-pt), a. Left aground by neap-tide. [p.p. f. unused *beneap* see BE-(6) & NEAP]

bĕneath', adv. & prep. Below, under, underneath, (poetic, arch., & literary, but usual in) ~ *contempt* etc., not worth despising etc., ~ *one,* unworthy of him. [OE *beneothan* = BE- +*neothan* = OS *nithana,* OHG *nidana,* ON *nethan* f. Gmc **nith-,* cf. NETHER]

bĕnĕdi'citè, n. Blessing invoked; grace at table; *the B*~, one of the canticles. [L, = *bless ye,* imperat. of *benedicere -dict-* bless (*bene* well + *dicere* speak)]

bĕn'ĕdick, n. Newly married man, esp. confirmed bachelor who marries. [Shakesp., *Much Ado*]

Bĕnĕdic'tine, a. & n. (Monk) of the order founded 529 by St Benedict, black monk; a liqueur. [f. F *bénédictin* f. L *benedictus* p.p. see BENEDICITE]

bĕnĕdic'tion, n. Utterance of a blessing, generally at table, at end of church service, or as special R.-C. service; a blessing, blessedness. [f. L *benedictio* (BENEDICITE, -ION)]

bĕnĕdic'tory, a. Of, expressing, benediction. [f. L *benedictus,* see prec. & -ORY, after *valedictory*]

bĕnĕdic'tus, n. One of the canticles. [first word in L version; see BENEDICITE]

bĕnĕfāc'tion, n. Doing good; gift for charitable purpose. [f. LL *benefactio* (BENEFIT¹, -ION)]

bĕn'ĕfăctor, n. Person who has given one friendly aid; patron of or donor to a cause or charitable institution. Hence ~RESS¹ n. [ME, f. LL *benefactor* (BENEFIT¹, -OR)]

bĕn'ĕfic|e, n. Church living; property held by an ecclesiastical officer esp. rector or vicar. Hence ~ED² (-st) a. [ME f. OF, f. L *beneficium* (*bene* well + *-fic-* f. *facere* do)]

bĕnĕf'icence, n., **bĕnĕf'icent**, a. Doing good, (showing) active kindness. Hence **bĕnĕf'icently²** adv. [f. F, or L *beneficentia* prec., -ENCE)]

bĕnĕfi'cial (-shl), a. Advantageous; (Law) of, having, the usufruct of property. Hence ~LY² adv. [ME, f. F *bénéficial* f. LL *beneficialis* (BENEFICE, -AL)]

bĕnĕfi'ciarў (-sha-), a. & n. (Law) holder, holding or held, by feudal tenure; holder of a living; receiver of benefits. [f. L *beneficiarius,* see BENEFICE, -ARY¹]

bĕn'ĕfit¹, n. Advantage (*for the* ~ *of,* on behalf of; *the* ~ *of the doubt,* assuming innocence rather than guilt); allowance, pension, attendance, to which person is entitled under Nat. Insurance Act or as member of benefit society etc. (*maternity, medical,* ~); exemption from ordinary courts by the privilege of one's order (~ *of* CLERGY, *peerage*); performance at theatre, game, etc., of which proceeds go to particular players (~*'s* ~, ~*-night,* ~*-match*); ~*-club,* -*society,* for mutual insurance against illness or age. [ME f. AF *benfet* f. L *benefactum* neut. p.p. of *benefacere* do well]

bĕn'ĕfit², v.t. & i. Do good to; receive benefit (*by* thing). [f. prec.]

Bĕn'ĕlŭx, n. Belgium, the Netherlands, & Luxembourg in association as a regional economic group; freq. attrib., as *the* ~ *countries.* [f. Belgium, Netherlands, Luxembourg]

bĕnĕv'olence, n. Desire to do good, charitable feeling; (Eng. Hist.) forced loan. [ME, f. OF *benivolence* f. L *benevolentia* f. *benevolens -entis* = foll.]

bĕnĕv'olent, a. Desirous of doing good, charitable. Hence ~LY² adv. [ME, f. OF *benivolent* f. L *bene volentem* nom. -*ens* well wishing (*velle* wish)]

Bĕngal' (-bĕnggawl), a. ~ *light,* firework used for signals; ~ *stripes,* striped gingham, orig. from ~; ~ *tiger,* the tiger proper. [former Indian province]

Bĕngali (bĕnggawl'ĭ), n. & a. (Native, language) of Bengal. [f. native *Bangali*]

bĕnight'ĕd (-nīt-), p.p. & a. (Forming pass., of vb obs. in act.) overtaken by night; involved in intellectual or moral darkness, ignorant. [BE-(6) + NIGHT]

bĕnign' (-īn), a. Gracious, gentle; fortunate, salutary; (of diseases) mild, not malignant. Hence ~LY² adv. [ME *benigne* f. OF f. L *benignus*; cf. *malign*]

bĕnig'n|ant, a. Kind, kindly, to inferiors; gracious; salutary. Hence ~ANCY n., ~antLY² adv. [recent formation f. prec. on anal. of MALIGNANT]

bĕnig'nitў, n. Kindliness, kindness, (usu. in the old). [ME, f. OF *benignite* f. L *benignitatem* (BENIGN, -TY)]

bĕn′īson (-zn), n. (arch.). A blessing. [ME *beneysun* etc. f. OF *beneiçun* etc. f. L *benedictionem* BENEDICTION]

Bĕnj′amïn[1], n. Youngest child, darling; ~*'s mess*, large share. [*Gen.* xlii. 4]

bĕnj′amïn[2], n. = BENZOIN; ~ *tree*, (a) that yielding benzoin, (b) a N.-Amer. shrub with aromatic bark. [corruption of BENZOIN]

bĕnn′ĕt, n. See HERB ~, & foll.

bĕnt[1], n. Stiff-stemmed grass of various kinds (with pl., or collect.); (also *bennet*) stiff flower-stalk, old stalk, of grasses; couch-grass; *way* ~, *stool* ~, etc., kinds of plant; heath, unenclosed pasture. [ME *bent*, repr. OE *beonet*- (in place-names), OS *binet*, OHG *binuz*, f. WG *binut*-]

bĕnt[2], n. Twist, inclination, bias, tendency; *to the top of* one's ~, *to heart's content*. [prob. f. BEND[2] on anal. of *descend*, *descent*, etc.]

bĕnt[3]. See BEND[3].

Bĕn′tham|ism (-ta-), n. Greatest happiness of the greatest number as guiding principle of ethics. So ~ITE[1] (1) n. [Jeremy *Bentham*, 1748–1832; see -ISM (3)]

bĕn′thŏs, n. (biol.). Flora & fauna found at the ocean bottom. [Gk, = depth]

bĕn trŏva′tŏ (-ah-), a. Well invented, characteristic if not true. [It.]

bēnŭmb′ (-m), v.t. Make torpid, insensible, powerless, (usu. of cold); paralyse (mind, action). [OE *beniman* deprive, p.p. *benuman*, whence ME *benomen*, whence 16th c. *benum* vb., later *benumb* (cf. *dumb*, *limb*)]

bĕn′zĕdrine (-ēn), n. Drug used to relieve respiratory trouble by inhalation, and internally as a nerve stimulant. [P]

bĕn′zĕn|e, n. An aromatic hydrocarbon got from coal-tar & represented by derivatives in all coal-tar products (formerly, & still in trade use, called *benzol*, *-ole*). Hence ~OID a. [BENZ(O)- + -ENE]

bĕn′zïne (-ēn), n. Mixture of liquid hydrocarbons got from mineral oils & used for removing grease-stains (in trade use often called *benzoline* or *benzene*). [foll. + -INE[5]]

benz(o)-, forming derivatives of foll.

bĕn′zŏïn (*or* -oin), n. (Also *gum* ~, *benjamin*) fragrant aromatic resin of Javanese tree. Hence **bĕnzō′ïc** a. [earlier *benjoin* through F, Sp., It., f. Arab. *luban jawi* frankincense of Java (*lo*- being dropped in Rom. as if the article)]

bĕn′zŏl, -ōle, n. = BENZENE. [BENZ(O)- + -OL]

bĕn′zoline (-ēn, -ïn), n. = BENZINE. [prec. + -INE[5]]

bĕqueath′ (-dh), v.t. Leave (*to* person) by will (personalty; cf. DEVISE); transmit to posterity (example etc.). [OE *becwethan* f. BE-(3) + *cwethan* say, see QUOTH]

bĕquĕst′, n. Bequeathing; thing bequeathed. [ME *biquyste* f. bi- BE + *cwis* saying cf. prec.: for -*t* cf. BEHEST]

bĕrāte′, v.t. Scold. [BE- + RATE[3]]

Bĕrb′er, n. & a. (Member) of the N.-African stock including the aboriginal races of Barbary, speaking allied languages. [f. Arab. *barbar* f. *barbara* talk confusedly, of unkn. orig.]

bĕrberry̆, n. See BARBERRY.

berceuse (bērsẽrz′), n. Cradle-song. [F]

|| **bēre**, n. Barley, esp. of six-rowed or four-rowed kinds. [OE]

bĕreave′, v.t. (~*d* or *bereft*). Rob, dispossess, *of* (usu. of immaterial things, as life, hope); leave desolate (esp. in p.p., usu. ~*d* in this sense); (of death etc.) deprive of a relation, wife, etc., whence ~MENT (-vm-) n. [OE *berēafian*, see BE-(2), REAVE]

beret (bĕ′rā), n. Round flat cap worn by Basque peasants; similar cap worn by men & women with sports & holiday clothes; service military headdress. [F, f. Pr. *berret* f. med. L *birretum* cap, dim. of LL *birrus* cloak; see BIRETTA]

bĕrg[1], n. = ICEBERG.

bĕrg[2], n. (S. Africa). Mountain or hill (esp. in comb.); ~ *wind*, hot northerly wind blowing in Cape Colony in May & August. [Afrikaans f. Du.]

bĕrg′amot[1], n. Tree of the citrus family; perfume extracted from its rind; an aromatic herb. [f. *Bergamo* town in Italy]

bĕrg′amot[2], n. Kind of pear. [f. F *bergamotte* f. It. *bergamotta* f. Turk. *beg-armudi* prince's pear]

bĕrg′mehl (-māl), n. Greyish-white flour-like geological deposit composed of infusorial shells, an abrasive & absorbent. [G, = mountain-flour]

berg′schrund (bārk′shrõont), n. (mountaineering). Crevasse or gap at junction of steep upper slope with glacier or nevé. [G]

bĕrhyme′ (-rīm), v.t. Write verses about, lampoon; put (matter) into rhymed form. [BE- (6) + RHYME n.]

bĕ′ribĕri, n. Deficiency disease common in the East. [Sinhalese, f. *beri* weakness]

Berkeleian (bārklē′an), n. & a. (Follower) of Berkeley or his philosophy, which denied the objective existence of the material world. [Bishop *Berkeley*, d. 1753; see -EAN]

bĕrkĕl′ium, n. Radio-active transuranic element. [f. *Berkel(ey)* in California + -IUM]

Bĕrlin′, n. & a. Four-wheeled covered carriage with hooded seat behind (also *berline*); ~ *black*, iron-varnish; ~ *iron*, for casts; ~ *warehouse*, shop for ~ *wool*, fine dyed knitting wool; ~ *gloves*, knitted. [~ in Germany]

bĕrm, n. Ledge in fortification between ditch & base of parapet. [f. F *berme* f. Du. *berm*, prob. cogn. w. ON *barmr* brim]

Bĕrmūd′ian, a. & n. (Inhabitant) of the *Bermudas*; ~ *rigged*, fitted with a high tapering sail. [-IAN]

Bĕrn′ardine, a. & n. = CISTERCIAN.

bĕ′rry̆[1], n. (Pop.) any small roundish juicy fruit without stone; (Bot.) fruit with seeds enclosed in pulp; grain of wheat etc.; egg in fish-roe (*in* ~, of henlobster carrying eggs). Hence (-)**bĕ′rri-ED²** (-id) a. [OE *beri(g)e*, OS *beri*, OHG *beri*, ON *ber*, Goth. (*weina*) *basi*, f. Gmc *basjam*, *bazjam*]

bĕ′rry², v.i. Come into berry, fill out; go gathering berries. [f. prec.]

bersaglieri (see Ap.), n. pl. Crack Italian infantry, orig. riflemen. [It.]

bĕrs′ĕrk(er), n Wild Norse warrior fighting with mad frenzy. [f. Icel. *ber-serkr* prob. = bear-sark, bear-coat]

bĕrth¹, n. Convenient sea-room (*give wide* ~ *to*, avoid); room for ship to swing at anchor; ship's place at wharf; proper place for anything; sleeping-place in ship, train, etc.; situation, appointment. [of uncert. orig.; prob. f. naut. use of BEAR³ vb + -TH¹]

bĕrth², v.t. Moor (ship) in suitable place; provide sleeping-place for. [f. prec.]

bĕrth′a, bĕrthe, n. Deep falling (usu. lace) collar to low-necked dress. *Big Bertha*, German gun of vast range used in bombarding Paris in the war of 1914–18. [F (-*e*), the woman's name]

Bĕrth′on boat, n. Collapsible boat. [E. L. *Berthon* inventor, d. 1899]

Bĕrtill′on sȳs′tĕm, n. Method of identifying criminals by measurements. [A. *Bertillon*, French anthropologist, d. 1914]

bĕ′rȳl, n. Precious stone, pale-green passing into light blue, yellow, & white; mineral species including also the emerald. [ME, f. OF f. L f. Gk *bērullos*]

bĕryll′ium, n. Hard white metallic element. [prec. + -IUM]

bĕseech′, v.t. (-*sought* pr. -sawt). Ask earnestly for (esp. *leave* etc.); entreat (person, person *that* or *to* do or *for* thing). [BE-(2) + ME *secen*, *sechen*, *seken*, SEEK]

bĕseech′ing, a. Suppliant (of look, tone, etc.). Hence ~LY² adv. [-ING²]

bĕseem′, v.t. Suit, be fitting or creditable to, (abs., or with *well*, *ill*, etc.). Hence ~ingLY² adv. [BE-(2) + SEEM]

bĕsĕt′, v.t. (-*tting*, past & p.p. -*set*). Hem in, set upon, (person); occupy & make impassable (road etc.); (of difficulties, temptations, etc.) assail, encompass. (~*ting sin*, that most frequently tempts one). [OE *besettan* BE-(1), & see SET v.)]

bĕsĕt′ment, n. Besetting sin; being hemmed in. [prec. + -MENT]

bĕshrew′ (-rōō), v.t. (Now only as mock-heroic imprecation) plague take (*me*, person, or thing). [BE-(2) + ME *schrewen* to curse f. SHREW]

bĕside′, prep. (formerly also adv. = foll.). Close to, by, near; on a level with, compared with; wide of (*mark*, *question*, etc.); ~ one*self*, out of one's wits. [OE *be sīdan* (BY, SIDE n.)]

bĕsides′ (-dz), adv. & prep. In addition (to), moreover; otherwise, else, (than); (neg. & interrog.) except. [prec. + -ES]

bĕsieg|e′, v.t. Invest, lay siege to; crowd round; assail with requests. Hence ~′ER¹ n. [f. ME *asege* by substitution of pref. BE-, f. ŎF *asegier* f. Rom. **assediare* f. *sedium* SIEGE]

bĕslāv′er, v.t. Cover with slaver; flatter fulsomely. [BE-(1) + SLAVER v.]

bĕslŏbb′er, v.t. = prec.; also, kiss effusively. [BE-(1) + SLOBBER v.]

bĕslŭbb′er, v.t. Besmear. [BE-(1) + SLUBBER]

bĕsmear′, v.t. Smear with greasy or sticky stuff (also of the stuff as subj.). [OE *bismierwan* see BE-(1) & SMEAR v.]

bĕsmĭrch′, v.t. Soil, discolour; dim brightness of. [BE-(1) + SMIRCH v.]

bĕs′om¹ (-z-), n., & v.t. (Sweep with) bundle of twigs tied round stick for sweeping, kind of broom. [OE *besema*, OHG *besamo*, f. WG **besmon*]

bĕs′om² (-z-), n. (Sc.). (Term of abuse for) woman. [orig. unkn.]

bĕsŏt′, v.t. (-tt-). Stupefy mentally or morally (chiefly in p.p.). [BE-(4) + SOT]

bĕsought′. See BESEECH.

bĕspangle (-ăng′gl), v.t. Set about with spangles. [BE-(6) + SPANGLE]

bĕspătt′er, v.t. Spatter (object) all over; spatter (liquid etc.) about; cover with abuse or flattery. [BE-(1) + SPATTER]

bĕspeak′, v.t. (past -*spoke*, p.p. -*spoke*, -*spoken*). Engage beforehand; order (goods); stipulate for; speak to (poet.); suggest, be evidence of; ‖ *bespoke boot-maker* etc. (prop. *bespoke-boot maker*), opposed to ready-made dealer. [OE, OS *bisprecan*, OHG *bisprehhan*, see BE-(3) & SPEAK]

bĕsprĕnt′, p.p. (poet.). Sprinkled (*with*); scattered about. [f. OE *besprengan* f. BE-(1) + *sprengan* sprinkle f. Gmc **sprangjan* causal of *springan* v.]

bĕsprinkle (-ĭng′kl), v.t. Sprinkle or strew over (*with*; lit. & fig.; also with the liquid etc. as subj. or obj.). [ME *besprengil* frequent. of OE *besprengan*, see prec. & -LE]

Bĕss′emer, a. & n. ~ *process*, for removing carbon, silicon, etc. from pig-iron by passing currents of air through it when molten & so making ~ *iron*, ~ *steel*, or ~. [Sir H. ~, inventor 1856]

bĕst¹, a. & adv. (superl. of *good*, *well*). Of, in, the most excellent kind, way (often, like *good*, *well*, used for specific adjj. & advv. as *kindest*, *most skilfully*). Phrr.: *the* ~ *part*, most; *had* ~, would find it wisest to; one's ~ *girl*, sweetheart; ~ *man*, bridegroom's supporter; ~ *seller*, (author of) popular book; *put* ~ *leg* or *foot foremost*, go at full pace, also fig.; *bad is the* ~, no good event possible; *with the* ~, as well as anyone; *do* one's ~, all one can; *be at* one's ~, in the ~ state; one's ~ *or Sunday* ~, ~ *clothes*; *have the* ~ *of it*, win in argument etc.; *make the* ~ *of things*, be contented; ~ *abused* (colloq.), most violently or generally abused (*the* ~ *abused book of the year*); *make the* ~ *of* one's *way*, go as fast as possible; *at* ∼, on the most hopeful view; *did it for the* ∼, with good intentions; *to the* ∼ *of* one's *power* etc., as far as one's power etc. allows; *the* ∼ *is the enemy of the good*, too high standard bars progress. [OE *betst*, OS *best*, OHG *bezzist*, ON *bazt*, *bezt*, Goth. *batist*, f. Gmc **batist-*, superl. of **bat-*; cf. BETTER & see -EST]

bĕst², v.t. (colloq.). Get the better of, circumvent, worst. [f. prec.]

bĕstead' (-ĕd), v.t. & i. Avail, help. [BE-(2)+*stead* v. f. STEAD]

bĕstĕd', p.p. (With *ill*, *hard*, *sore*, etc.) situated, circumstanced, pressed. [ME *bistad* f. BE-(2)+*stad* f. ON *staddr* p.p. of *stethja* place]

bĕs'tial, a. Of, like, a beast or beasts esp. quadrupeds; brutish, barbarous; depraved, lustful, obscene. Hence or cogn. ∼ITY (-ăl⁴) n., ∼IZE(3) v.t., ∼LY² adv. [ME, f. OF f. LL *bestialis* (*bestia* BEAST +-AL)]

bĕs'tiary̆, n. Medieval moralizing treatise on beasts. [f. med. L *bestiarium* f. L *bestia* beast]

bĕstir', v. refl. (-rr-). Exert, rouse, (oneself). [f. BE-(2)+STIR v.]

bĕstow' (-ō), v.t. Deposit; provide with lodging; confer (thing) *upon* (person) as gift. Hence ∼AL(2) (-ōal) n. [ME *bistowen*, see BE-(2), STOW]

bĕstrew'. (-rōō), v.t. (p.p. ∼*ed* or ∼n). Strew (surface) *with*; scatter (things) about; lie scattered over. [OE *bistrēowian* see BE-(1) & STREW; p.p. *-ewn* is recent, but now common]

bĕstride', v.t. (past *-ode*; p.p. *-idden*, *-id*, *-ode*). Get or sit upon (horse, chair) with legs astride; stand astride over (place or fallen friend or enemy; also fig. of rainbow etc.). [OE *bistrīdan*, see BE-(3), STRIDE v.]

bĕt, n., & v.i. & t. (*bet*, ∼*ted*). (Engagement to) risk one's money etc., risk (an amount etc.) against another's on the result of a doubtful event (*on* or *against* result or competitor, *that* so-&-so will happen; *you* ∼, you may take it as certain; ∼*ting-book*, for entering ∼s in. [of uncert. orig.; perh. f. ABET n., in sense 'instigation, support of a cause', w. *bet* vb f. *bet* n.]

bĕt'a, n. Second letter (B, β) of Gk alphabet, used as name of second star in a constellation, & in other numberings; ∼ *plus*, *minus*, rather better, worse, than second-class; ∼ *rays*, fast-moving electrons emitted by radio-active substances, orig. regarded as rays. [Gk]

bĕtake', v. refl. (*-took*, *-taken*). Commit one*self to* (i.e. try) some course or means; convey one*self to* (i.e. go to) a place or person. [ME; BE-, TAKE]

bĕt'atrŏn, n. (phys.). Apparatus for accelerating speed of electrons. [f. BETA +(ELEC)TRON]

bĕt'el, n. Leaf of *Piper betle*, which In-

dians chew with areca-nut parings; (hence by mistake) ∼*nut*, the areca nut. [Port. f. Malayalam *veṭṭila*]

bête noire (bāt nwahr), n. (One's) abomination. [F]

bĕth'el, n. Hallowed spot (*Gen.* xxviii. 19); ‖ nonconformist chapel; seamen's church (ashore or floating). [Heb. *beth-el* house of God]

‖**bĕthĕs'da** (-z-), n. Nonconformist chapel, [*John* v. 2; Heb., = house of mercy]

bĕthink', v. refl. (*-thought*) (alw. with *self* or arch. refl. *me*, *him*, etc.). Reflect, stop to think; remind one*self of*, *how*, or *that*; take into one's head *to*. [OE *bethencan*, see BE-(3), THINK]

bĕtide', v.i. & t. (only in 3 sing. pres. subj.). Happen (*whate'er* ∼); happen to (*woe* ∼ *him* etc.). [ME *bitiden* see BE-(2), TIDE v.]

bĕtimes' (-mz), adv. Early in day, year, life, etc.; in good time. [*by time* (ME) +-ES]

bĕtise (bātēz'), n. Foolish, ill-timed, remark or action. [F]

bĕtŏk'en, v.t. Augur, indicate, suggest. [ME *bitacnien* see BE-, TOKEN]

bĕt'on, n. (Orig. lime, now any kind of) concrete. [f. F *béton* ult. f. L *bitumen* mineral pitch]

bĕt'ony̆, n. Purple-flowered plant. [ME, f. OF *betoine* f. pop. L **betonica* for L *betonica* f. L *vettonica* f. name of Spanish tribe]

betook. See BETAKE.

bĕtray', v.t. Give up treacherously (person or thing *to* enemy); be disloyal to; lead astray; reveal treacherously; reveal involuntarily; be evidence or symptom of. Hence ∼AL(2), ∼ER¹, nn. [ME *betraien* f. BE-(2)+obs *tray* f. OF *traïr* f. L *tradere* hand over]

bĕtrŏth' (-ōdh), v.t. Bind with a promise to marry (usu. in p.p.). Hence ∼AL(2) n., ∼ED¹ a. & n. [ME *betreuthe*, *betrowthe* f. BE-(6)+*treuthe* TRUTH, later assimilated to TROTH]

bĕt'er¹, a., adv., & n. (comp. of *good*, *well*). Of, in, a more excellent kind, way (often, like *good*, *well*, for specific wd as *more virtuous*, *more plentifully*). Phrr.: *no* ∼ *than*, practically; *no* ∼ *than she should be*, (usu.) of easy virtue; one's ∼ *feelings*, higher self; ∼ *part*, most; one's ∼ *half*, wife; *for* ∼ *for* worse, on terms of accepting all results (see Prayer Book, Marriage Service); ∼ *than* (with number etc.), above; *had* ∼, would find it wiser to; *be*, *get*, ∼, less unwell; ∼ *than* one's *word*, more liberal than one promised to be; one's ∼, more skilful person; one's ∼s, people of higher rank; *get the* ∼ *of*, defeat, outwit; *know* ∼, refuse to accept statement, not be so foolish (as to do something); *think* ∼ *of it*, change one's mind; *change for the* ∼; ∼ *off*, richer, more comfortable; *the* ∼ *the day the* ∼ *the deed* (retort to charge of Sabbath-

-breaking). [OE *betera*, OS *betiro*, OHG *beziro*, ON *betri*, Goth. *batiza*, f. Gmc **batizon* f. **bat-*, cogn. w. **bŏt-* see BOOT³, -ER³]

bětt′er², v.t. & i. Amend, improve; surpass (a feat etc.); ~ *oneself*, get better situation, wages, etc. Hence ~MENT n., (also) enhanced value (of real property) arising from local improvements. [ME f. prec.]

bětt′er³, **-or, n.** One who bets. [BET +-ER¹]

bětween′, prep. & adv. (the orig. restriction to relations involving only *two* limits etc. still tends to be observed wherever AMONG is adequate for higher numbers). In, into, along, or across, a space, line, or route, bounded by (two or more points, lines, etc.); in, into, along, or across, an interval; separating; connecting; intermediately in place, time, or order (to); owing partly to, partaking of, shared by, (each); to & fro (*go-*~); to & from (*plies* ~ *London & Brighton*); reciprocally on the part of; confined to (~ *ourselves*, ~ *you & me*); by combination of, taking one & rejecting the other of (*choose* ~). *Far* ~, at wide intervals; ~ *cup & lip*, of dashed hopes; ‖~-*maid* (now usu. *tweeny*), servant assisting two others, e.g. cook & housemaid; ~ *wind & water*, at a vulnerable point; ~ *the devil & the deep sea*, with no escape; *betwixt &* ~, half-&-half; *stand* ~, mediate, be protector; ~ *whiles*, in the intervals. [OE *betwēonum* (also, orig. acc., *betwēon*) f. *be* BY+*twēonum*, dat. pl. (corresp. to Goth. *tweihnaim*, nom. *tweihnai*, distrib. num. formed w. *n-* suff. (cf. L *bini*) on the cardinal num.)]

bětwixt′, prep. & adv. (Poet., arch., or dial., for) BETWEEN. [ME *betwix*, later *betwixt*, OE *betweohs*, *betweox*, etc. (prob. shortened f. *betweoxum*, cf. prec.) f. *be* BY +**twisk-* (= OS *twisc*, OHG *zwiski* two each, G *zwischen*) f. **twā* TWO+**-isk-* -ISH¹]

‖ **Beu′lah, n.** Nonconformist chapel. [*Is.* lxii. 4]

běv′el¹, n. Joiner's & mason's tool for setting off angles; a slope from the horizontal or vertical, surface so sloping; ~ *edge*, as in a chisel; ~-*gear*, working one shaft from another at angle to it by ~-*wheels*, cogged wheels with working face oblique to axis. [f. OF **bevel* (mod. *biveau*) of unkn. orig.; cf. OF *bever* (arch.) give bias to]

běv′el², v.t. & i. (-ll-). Reduce (square edge) to, take, a slope. [f. prec.]

běv′erage, n. Drinking-liquor. [ME, f. OF *bevrage* f. Rom. **biberaticum* f. L *bibere* drink, see -AGE²]

běv′y, n. Company (prop. of ladies, roes, quails, larks). [orig. unkn.]

běwail′, v.t. & i. Wail (over), mourn (for). [BE-(3)+WAIL v.]

běware′, v.i. & t. (not inflected, & used only where *be* is the vbl part required, as

I will ~, but not *I* ~). Be cautious, take heed; take heed *of*, *lest*, *how that not*. [f. BE v.+WARE²]

běwil′der, v.t. Lead astray, perplex, confuse. Hence ~INGLY² adv., ~MENT n. [f. BE-(3)+obs. WILDER lose one's way]

běwitch′, v.t. Affect by magic, put a spell on; delight exceedingly, whence ~ING² a., ~INGLY² adv., ~MENT n. [ME *biwicchen* f. BE-(2)+OE *wiccian* enchant f. *wicca* WITCH n.]

bewray (birā′), v.t. (arch.). Reveal, esp. involuntarily. [ME *bewreien* f. BE-(2)+ *wreien* (OE *wrēgan* accuse)]

bey (bā), **bey′lic** (bā-), nn. (*Bey*) Turkish governor; (*beylic*) his district; *Bey* of *Tunis*, ruler of Tunisia. [f. Osmanli *bey*, formerly *beg*; cf. BEGUM]

běyönd′, adv., prep., & n. 1. At, to, the farther side (of), past, outside, besides; later than; out of reach, comprehension, or range, of (~ *measure*, exceedingly); surpassing; more than (with objective case, as *you have prospered* ~ *me*); (neg. & interrog.) except. **2.** *n*. *The* ~, the future life, the unknown; *the back of* ~, the remotest corner of the world. [OE *begeondan* f. *be* BY+*geondan* f. Gmc **jand* (see YON, YONDER)+-*ana* adv. suff.]

běz′ant (or bizǎnt′), n. Gold coin current in Europe from 9th c.; also silver. [f. OF *besan* f. L *Byzantius* (*nummus* coin) of Byzantium]

běz′el, n. Sloped edge of chisel etc.; oblique faces of cut gem; groove holding watch-glass or gem. [f. OF **bezel* (mod. *biseau*) of unkn. orig.]

bězique′ (-ēk), n. Card-game for two or four; combination of queen of spades & knave of diamonds. [f. F *besigue* of unkn. orig.]

běz′oar (-ōr), n. Concretion with hard nucleus found in stomach or intestines of certain animals (chiefly ruminants), formerly believed antidotal. [ult. f. Pers. *pādzahr* antidote, Arab. *bāzahr*]

bězŏn′ian, n. (arch.). Rascal, beggarly fellow. [earlier *besonio*, f. It. *bisogno* need, want]

bhāng (bā-). **n.** Indian hemp used as narcotic & intoxicant (smoked, chewed, eaten, & drunk). [earlier *bangue*, *bang*; f. Hind. etc. *bhang*]

bhis′tī, bhees′ty, (bēs-), n. (Anglo-Ind.) Indian water-carrier. [Urdu *bhistī* f. Pers. *bihisht* paradise (prob. joc. origin)]

bi-, pref. f. L *bi-*, twice, doubly, having two-, two-, freely used in English, esp. with wds f. L, but also with E wds (*bi-weekly*); see also BIN-. **1.** Adj., (a) having two ——, as *bilateral*, *bilingual*; (b) doubly, in two ways, as *bi-concave*; (c) in Bot. & Zool., twice over, i.e. divided into similarly divided parts, as *bipinnate*; (d) lasting for two ——, appearing every two ——, as *biennial*; (e) appearing twice in a ——, as *biannual*, *bi-monthly*; many wds are ambiguous between this & the last,

& *semi-*, *half-*, would be better here; (f) joining two ——, as *bi-parietal.* 2. Nouns, double, as *bi-millionaire.* 3. Chem. nouns & adjj., having twice the proportion of acid, base, etc., indicated by the simple wd, as *bicarbonate.* Now usu. superseded by *di-*.

bī′as¹, n. (In bowls) lopsided form of a bowl, its oblique course, the inserted plug of metal or influence deflecting, it; (metaph. from bowls) inclination, predisposition (*towards*), prejudice, influence; (Dressmaking etc.; as a., n., & adv.) *cut on the ~, cut ~,* cut obliquely across the texture, *~ band* etc., band so cut. [16th c., f. F *biais* = Pr. *biais*, Cat. *bialx, biais*, of unkn. orig.]

bī′as², v.t. (-s- *or* -ss-). Give a bias to, influence (usu. unfairly), inspire with prejudice. [f. prec.]

biāx′ial, a. With two (optic) axes. [BI-(1 a) + AXIAL]

bib¹, v.i. (-bb-). Drink much or often. [ME, perh. f. L *bibere* drink]

bib², n. Child's chin-cloth to keep dress-front clean; adult's apron-top (*best ~ & tucker*, best clothes). [perh. f. prec.]

bib³, n. A fish, the whiting-pout. [from an inflatable membrane on head resembling prec.]

bibb′er, n., **bibb′ing,** n. & a. Tippler, tippling, (usu. in comb., as *wine* etc. *-~*). [BIB V., -ER¹, -ING¹, ²]

bib′cŏck′, n. Tap or faucet with a bent nozzle fixed at the end of a pipe (dist. STOPCOCK). [perh. f. BIB²]

bibelot (bēb′lō), n. Small curio or artistic trinket. [F]

Bī′ble, n. Scriptures of the Old & New Testament, a copy of them, a particular edition of them (BREECHES, PRINTERS', VINEGAR, WICKED, ~); authoritative book; *~-oath*, taken on the ~; ‖*~-reader*, one employed to read the ~ from house to house; *~-Christian*, a member of sect so called; *~-clerk*, student at some Oxford colleges who reads lessons in chapel. [ME, f. OF f. LL f. Gk *biblia* books pl. of *biblion* dim. of *biblos, bublos* papyrus]

bib′lical, a. Of, concerning, contained in, the Bible. [f. med. L *ḅiblicus* (see -IC, -AL)]

bib′lico-, comb. of BIBLICAL, as *biblico-poetical.* [-O-]

bib′lio-, comb. form of *biblion* see BIBLE. Of books or the Bible.

bibliograph-. See foll., & -GRAPH, -GRAPHER, -GRAPHIC, -GRAPHY.

bibliŏg′raphȳ, n. History or description of books, their authorship, editions, etc.; book containing such details; list of books of any author, printer, country, subject. [f. Gk *bibliographia*; see BIBLIO-, -GRAPHY]

bibliŏl′ater, n., **bibliŏl′atrous,** a., **bibliŏl′atry,** n. Worshipper of, worshipping, worship of, books, a book, or the Bible. [BIBLIO-, -LATRY]

bibliomān′ia, bibliomān′iăc, nn. Rage for collecting, enthusiastic collector of,

books. [after F *bibliomanie*; see BIBLIO-, -MANIA]

bib′liophil(e), n. Book-fancier, -lover. Hence **bibliŏph′ilīsm**(3), **bibliŏph′ilĭst** (3), nn. [F *bibliophile* (BIBLIO-, -PHIL)]

bib′liopōle, bibliŏp′olȳ, nn. Seller, selling, of (esp. rare) books. [f. L (-*la*) f. Gk *bibliopōlēs* (BIBLIO-, -*pōlēs* -seller)]

bib′ūlous, a. Absorbent; addicted to drink. Hence *~*LY² adv. [f. L *bibulus* freely drinking (*bibere* drink) + -OUS]

bicăm′eral, a. With two (legislative) chambers. [BI-(1 a) + L *camera* CHAMBER + -AL]

bicărb′onate. See BI-(3).

bice, n. *~ or blue ~, green ~,* pigments made from blue, green, hydrocarbonate of copper; similar pigment made from smalt etc.; dull shades of blue & green given by these. [f. F *bis* brownish-grey, of unkn. orig.]

bicĕn′tenarȳ (*also* -tĕn²), a. & n. (Festival) of the two-hundredth anniversary. [BI-(1 a) + L *centenarius* CENTENARY; used of years by confusion with *centennial*]

bicĕntĕnn′ial, a. & n. Lasting, occurring every, two hundred years; (n.) = prec. [BI-(1 d) + CENTENNIAL]

bicĕph′alous, a. Two-headed. [BI-(1 a) + -CEPHALOUS]

bī′cĕps, n. (pl. *-es*). Muscle with double head or attachment, esp. the upper-arm flexor; muscularity. [L, = two-headed f. BI-(1 a) + -*ceps* = *caput* head]

bichlōr′ide (-kl-), n. Compound in which double proportion of chlorine combines with metal etc. (now usu. *dichloride*). [BI-(3)]

bichrōm′ate (-kr-), n. Salt with double proportion of chromic acid (now usu. *dichromate*). [BI-(3)]

bick′er, v.i. Quarrel; (of stream, rain, etc.) brawl, patter; (of flame, light, etc.) flash, glitter. [ME *biker, beker* of unkn. orig.; perh. a frequent. formation]

bicŭs′pĭd, a. & n. (Tooth) with two cusps. [BI-(1 a) + L *cuspis -idis* point]

bī′cȳcle, n., & v.i. (Ride on) two-wheeled pedal-driven vehicle. Hence **bī′cȳclĭst**(1) n. [F, f. BI-(1 a) + Gk *kuklos* wheel]

bid¹, v.t. & i. (past *bad, bade, bid*, p.p. *bidden, bid*). Command to (usu. without *to*; now literary, arch., or poet., for *tell* with *to*; also abs., as *do as you are ~*); invite (esp. in *~den guest*); salute (person) with *welcome, farewell,* etc.; (esp. at an auction) offer price, offer (a certain price) *for* (past & p.p. *bid*), whence *~d′ER¹* n.; (Bridge) make a BID² of or in, make a bid; proclaim (*defiance, the banns*); *~ fair to do,* show promise of doing; ‖ *~ding-prayer,* inviting congregation to join. [(a) the standard forms are those of OE *biddan* beg, pray, etc., OS *biddian,* OHG (G) *bitten,* ON *biðhja,* Goth. *bidjan,* f. Gmc **bidhjan*; (b) the meanings include some from OE *bēodan* offer, command, etc.,

OS *biodan*, OHG *biotan* (G *bieten*), ON *bjóða*, Goth. *biudan*, Gmc **beudhan*]

bid², n. Offer of price, esp. at auction; (Bridge) statement of number of tricks player proposes to win in specified suit or no-trumps; *make a ~ for*, (fig.) make an attempt to secure (favour, the prize, etc.). [f. prec.]

bidd'able, a. Obedient; (of hand or suit at cards) capable of being bid. [-ABLE]

bidd'ing, n. In vbl senses; esp. the offers at auction; a command. [-ING¹ (1)]

bidd'ỹ, n. (dial.). Chicken. [orig. unkn.]

bide, v.t. & i. (Arch. & poet. for ABIDE, but the regular wd in) *~ one's time*, await best opportunity. [OE, OS *bīdan*, OHG *bītan*, ON *bītha*, Goth. *beidan* f. Gmc **bīdan*]

bidet (bēd'ā), n. Raised narrow bath that can be bestridden. [F, = pony]

bienn'ial, a. & n. Lasting, recurring every, two years; (n., Bot.) plant that springs one year, or flowers, fructifies, & perishes, the next. Hence ~LY² adv. [f. L *biennis* f. BI-(1 d) + *annus* year + -AL]

bier, n. Movable stand on which coffin (or corpse) is taken to grave. [OE *bær*, OS, OHG *bāra* f. WG **bērō* f. *beran* BEAR³; mod. sp. app. after F *bière* f. same source]

biff, n., & v.t., (sl.). A smart blow; (vb) strike (person). [imit.]

‖ **biff'in**, n. Deep-red cooking-apple. [= *beefing* f. BEEF + -ING(3) with ref. to the colour]

bi'fid, a. Divided by a deep cleft into two parts. [f. L BI(*fidus* f. st. of *findere* cut)]

bifōc'al, a. & n. pl. 1. Having two foci (esp. of combined distant & near vision spectacles). 2. n. pl. ~ spectacles. [BI-(1 a)]

bifōl'iate, a. Of two leaves. [BI-(1 a) + L *folium* leaf + -ATE² (2)]

bi'furcate¹ (-ferk-), v.t. & i. Divide into two branches, fork. [f. foll., first in p.p. -*ated*]

bi'furcate² (-ferk-), a. Forked (esp. in Bot.). [f. med. L BI(*furcatus* f. *furca* fork, -ATE²)]

bifurcā'tion (-ferk-), n. Division into two branches; the point of division; the branches or one of them. [f. BIFURCATE¹]

big, a. & adv. Large; grown up; pregnant (*~ with young*, also *~-bellied*, & esp. fig. as *~ with fate*, *news*); important (*a ~ man; the Big Three, Five*, etc., the predominant few in any affair; *get, grow, too ~ for* one's *boots*, sl., become conceited, put on airs); boastful(ly) (*~ words, looks; look or talk ~*); (as distinctive epithet) *~ drum, toe, game; Big Ben*, great bell in the Houses of Parliament; *~ bug* (sl.), *= ~wig; ~ business*, commerce on the grand scale (freq. with sinister implication); *~ end*, end of the connecting-rod that encircles the crank-pin; *~-horn*, Rocky-Mountain sheep; **~ noise* (sl.), *=~wig; ~ stick*, display of force; *~'wig*, person of importance. Hence *~'NESS* n. [orig. unkn.]

big'amist, n. Man (woman) with two wives (husbands). [see BIGAMY, -IST]

big'amous, a. Guilty of, involving, bigamy. [f. as foll. + -OUS]

big'amỹ, n. Having two wives or husbands at once. [ME, f. OF *bigamie* (-Y¹) f. *bigame* bigamous f. LL *bigamus* (earlier *di-*, see DIGAMY)]

‖ **bigg, big**, n. Four-rowed barley. [f. ON *bygg*, corresp. to OE *bēow* grain, f. Gmc **beuwom*]

bight (bīt), n. Loop of a rope; curve, recess, of coast, river, etc., bay. [OE *byht*, MLG (G) *bucht* f. Gmc **bugan*, see BOW³]

big'ot, n. One who holds irrespective of reason, & attaches disproportionate weight to, some creed or view. Hence ~ED² a. [16th c. f. F; orig. unkn.]

big'otrỹ, n. Conduct, mental state, act, of a bigot. [f. F *bigoterie*; see BIGOT, -RY]

bijou (bēzh'ōō), n. (pl. -*oux*, pr. -ōō) & a. Jewel, trinket; small & elegant. [F]

bijouterie (bēzhōōt'erē), n. Jewelry, trinkets, etc. [F, see prec. & -RY]

bike, n., & v.i. (Colloq. abbr. for) BICYCLE.

bikin'i (-ēn'ē), n. Scanty two-piece beach garment worn by women. [f. *B~*, atoll in Marshall Islands in Pacific]

bilăt'eral, a. Of, on, with, two sides; affecting, between, two parties. Hence ~LY² adv. [BI-(1 a) + L *latus -eris* side + -AL]

bil'berrỹ, n. Fruit of dwarf hardy N.-European shrub growing on heaths & in mountain woods (also *blaeberry, whortleberry*). [cf. Da. *böllebær*]

bil'bō, n. (hist.; pl. -*os*). Sword. [f. *Bilbao* in Spain]

bil'boes (-ōz), n. pl. Iron bar with sliding shackles for prisoner. [orig. unkn.]

bile, n. Brownish-yellow bitter fluid secreted by the liver to aid digestion; derangement of the~; peevishness; *~-stone*, calculus in gall-bladder. [F, f. L *bilis*]

bilge¹, n. Nearly horizontal part of ship's bottom, inside or out; the foulness that collects inside the ~; (sl.) nonsense, rot; belly of barrel; *~-keel*, timber fastened under ~ to prevent rolling; *~-water*, stinking water collected in ~. [prob. var. of BULGE]

bilge², v.t. & i. Stave in the bilge of, spring a leak in the bilge; bulge, swell out. [f. prec.]

bilhărz'i|a, n. Flat-worm parasitic in the blood & bladder of residents in tropical countries (esp. Egypt). Hence *~AS'IS* n., chronic disease produced by its presence. [T. *Bilharz*, discoverer]

bil'iarỹ (-lya-), a. Of the bile. [f. F *biliaire*, see BILE, -ARY²]

biling'ual (-inggwal), a. Having, speaking, spoken or written in, two languages. [f. L *bilinguis* f. BI-(1 a) + *lingua* tongue + -AL]

bil'ious (-lyus), a. Liable to, affected by, arising from, derangement of the bile;

peevish. Hence ~LY² adv., ~NESS n. [f. F *bilieux* f. L *biliosus*; see BILE, -OSE¹, -OUS]
-bility, suf. See -BLE.

bilk, v.t. Evade payment of (creditor, bill); cheat, give the slip to. [orig. uncert.; perh. = BALK²; earliest use in cribbage; = spoil opponent's score]

bill¹, n. Obsolete weapon, halberd; (also ~'hook) concave-edged lopping implement for pruning etc. [OE, OS *bil*, OHG *bill* f. WG *biljam*]

bill², n. Bird's beak (esp. when slender, flattened, or weak, & in pigeons & web--footed birds); muzzle of platypus; narrow promontory (*Portland B*~ etc.); point of anchor-fluke. Hence ~ED² (-ld) a. [OE *bile* of unkn. orig.; not elsewhere in Gmc]

bill³, v.i. Stroke bill with bill (of doves); exchange caresses (esp. ~ & *coo*). [f. prec.]

bill⁴, n. Draft of proposed Act of Parliament; (Law) written statement of (esp. plaintiff's) case (*find a true* ~, *ignore the* ~, forms by which Grand Jury sends, does not send, case for trial); note of charges for goods delivered or services rendered; *bank or treasury note; poster, placard, programme of entertainment; (also ~ *of exchange*) written order by drawer to drawee to pay sum on given date to drawer or to named payee (if drawn not against value received, but to raise money on credit, the ~ is known as an *accommodation* ~); ~ *of fare*, list of dishes to be served, menu, (fig.) programme; ~ *of health*, certificate regarding infectious disease on ship or in port at time of sailing (*clean* ~ *of health*, no disease); ‖~ *of lading*, ship-master's detailed receipt to consignor; ‖~ *of quantities*, detailed statement of work, prices, dimensions, etc., involved in the erection of a building; ~ *of sale*, transferring personal property, or authorizing its seizure by lender of money if payment is delayed; ~*s of mortality* (hist.), weekly return of deaths in London & district (*within the* ~*s of mortality*, in or near London); *~'board*, hoarding; ~-*poster*, -*sticker*, man who pastes up placards; ~-*broker*, -*discounter*, dealer in, discounter of, ~s of exchange. [ME, AF *bille*, AL *billa*, Eng. alt. of L *bulla* in medieval sense of *seal*, *sealed document*, BULL³; see BILLET¹]

bill⁵, v.t. Announce, put in the programme; ~*ed to appear* etc., announced as going to; plaster with placards. [f. prec.]

bill'abŏng, n. (Austral.). Branch of river that comes to a dead end. [native]

bill'ét¹, n. Order requiring person to board & lodge the soldier etc. bearing it (*every bullet has its* ~, hits only by providential order), place where troops etc. are lodged; destination; appointment, situation. [ME, AF *billette*, AL *billetta*, dim. of *billa* BILL¹; cf. also OF *billete*, var. of *bullete*, med. L *bulletta*, dim. of *bulla*]

bill'ét², v.t. Quarter (soldiers etc.) *on* (town, householder, etc.), *in*, *at*; (of householder) provide (soldier etc.) with board & lodging. Hence ~EE, ~OR, nn. [f. prec.]

bill'ét³, n. Thick piece of firewood; small bar of metal; short roll inserted at intervals in hollow moulding (Norman archit.). [ME, f. F *billette* & *billot* dim. of *bille* tree-trunk f. med. L *billa*, *billus* prob. of Celt. orig.]

billet-doux (bĭlĭdōō'), n. Love-letter (joc.). [F]

bill'iards (-lyărdz), n. pl. Game played with cues & ivory balls on cloth-covered table; *billiard-marker*, attendant keeping the score. [f. F *billard* cue dim. of *bille* see BILLET³]

bill'ingsgate (-z-), n. Abuse, violent invective. [from the scolding of fishwomen in *Billingsgate* market]

bill'ion (-yon), n. A million millions; (in U.S.) a thousand millions. [F, coined in 16th c. out of BI- & *million* to denote the second power of a million; meaning afterwards changed in France (so U.S.) but not in Britain]

bill'on, n. Alloy of gold or silver with a predominating amount of some base metal. [F, f. *bille* BILLET³]

bill'ow¹ (-ō), n. Great wave; (poet.) *the* sea; (fig.) anything that sweeps along, as sound, troops. Hence ~Y² (-ōĭ) a. [f. ON *bylgja* f. Gmc *belgan* swell]

bill'ow² (-ō), v.i. Rise, move, in billows. [f. prec.]

bill'ȳ, n. (Austral.). Tin can used as kettle etc. in camping out. [prob. the male name]

‖ **bill'ȳboy**, n. River or coasting trading barge. [orig. unkn.]

‖ **bill'ycŏck**, n. Round-crowned hard felt hat, bowler. [said to have been orig. designed for *William Coke* 1850]

bill'ȳ-goat, n. Male goat. [*Billy* male name]

bill'ȳ-(h)ō, n. (Colloq., used in the intensive phr.) *like* ~; *raining like* ~ (cats & dogs); *fighting like* ~ (fiercely). [orig. unkn.]

bilŏb'ate, **bi'lobed** (-ōbd), aa. With two lobes. [BI-(1 a), & see LOBE, -ATE²(2), -ED²]

bil'tŏng, n. Strips of sun-dried meat. [Afrikaans f. *bil* buttock (from which it is cut) + *tong* tongue (which it looks like)]

Bim, n. (colloq.). Inhabitant of Barbados.

bim'anal, **bim'anous**, aa., **bim'āne**, n. (Individual) of the *Bimana* or two-handed order of mammalia, two-handed. [*bimane* F f. BI-(1 a) + L *manus* hand, & see -AL, -OUS]

bimbash'i (-ah-), n. Turkish military captain or commander; (formerly) British officer in Egyptian service. [Turk., = head of a thousand]

bimĕtăll'ic, a., **bimĕt'allism**, n., **bimĕt'allist**, n. & a. Of, system of, advocate of, using both gold & silver as legal tender to any amount at fixed ratio to each other. [f. F *bimétallique* 1869; see BI-(1 a), METALLIC, -ISM(3), -IST(2)]

bin, n. Receptacle (orig. of wicker, now usu. fixed, of wood) for corn, coal, dust, bottled wine, etc.; wine from a special ~; ‖ canvas receptacle used in hop-picking. [OE *binne* f. OBrit. **benna,* or f. med.L *benna* = OF *banne* f. Gaulish *benna*]

bin-, pref., treated as a euphonic form of BI- before vowels. Prob. orig. in F *binocle* (cf. BINOCULAR) & extended in E esp. to chem. compounds; cf. *bichloride, biniodide.*

bin'ary, a. Dual, of or involving pairs; (Mus.) ~ *measure,* of two beats to bar; ~ *form,* of movement in two sections; (Astron.) ~ *system,* two stars revolving round common centre or each other; (Chem.) ~ *compound,* of two elements; (Math.) ~ *scale,* with 2 (not 10) as base of notation. [f. LL *binarius* f. *bini* two together]

bin'ate, a. In pairs. [f. L *bini* two together+-ATE²(2)]

binaur'al, a. Of, used with, both ears, as ~ *stethoscope.* [BIN-+AURAL]

bind¹, v.t. & i. (*bound,* pr. bow-; also arch. p.p. in *bounden duty*). Tie; fasten, attach, *to, on*; put in bonds, restrain; fasten or hold together; be obligatory, exercise authority, impose constraint or duty, upon, (pass.) be required by duty *to* (do something); subject to legal obligation (esp. ~ *over to appear, to good behaviour, to keep the peace*; fig., *I'll be bound,* go bail for statement), indenture as apprentice; ratify (~ *the bargain*); make costive; bandage (usu. ~ *up*); wreathe (head etc.) *with,* (material) *round, about, on*; edge with braid, iron, etc.; cohere (of snow etc.); (Bookbind.) fasten (sheets) into stiff, orig. leather, vellum, etc., now usu. cloth, cover (*half-bound,* with leather at back & corners only), ~ *up,* together in one vol. [OE, OS *bindan,* OHG *bintan,* ON *binda,* Goth. *bindan* f. Gmc **bindan*]

bind², n. Indurated clay between coal strata; (Mus.) curved line between two notes to be held as one; = BINE. [f. prec.]

bin'der, n. In vbl senses; also or esp.: book~; obstetric apparatus; long fencing-withe; tie beam; through-stone in wall; wisp of straw, part of reaping-machine, for sheaf-binding; loose cover for unbound newspapers etc. [-ER¹]

bin'ding¹, a. Obligatory (*on*). [-ING²]

bin'ding², n. In vbl senses; also, book-cover; braid etc. for protecting raw edges. [-ING¹]

bind'weed, n. Kinds of convolvulus & other climbing plants. [BIND¹+WEED]

bine, n. Flexible shoot; stem of climbing plant, esp. the hop. [orig. dial. form of, & now replacing, BIND²]

binge (-j), n. (sl.). Drinking-bout, spree. [orig. dial., = soak]

bing'ō (-ngg-), n. Popular gambling game played with cards divided into numbered squares. [orig. unkn.]

binn'acle, n. Receptacle for ship's compass. [17th c. *bittacle* etc., f. Sp. or Pg. *bitácula* f. L *habitaculum* habitation]

binŏc'ular, a. & n. (Field or opera glass) adapted for two eyes (in. now usu. pl.). [f. L *bini* two together+*oculus* eye+-AR¹]

binōm'ial, a. & n. Consisting of two terms; ~ *theorem,* formula for finding any power of a ~ without multiplying at length; (n.) algebraic expression of two terms joined by + or −. [f. mod. L *binomium* (+-AL), a 16th c. application of med. L *binomius* having two personal names, irreg. f. BI- (1 a)+*nomen* name]

binōm'inal, a. Of two names (esp. ~ *system,* of scientific nomenclature by genus & species). [f. L *binominis* (BI- 1 (a) +*nomen -inis* name)+-AL]

bin'tŭrŏng, n. S.-Asian prehensile-tailed civet. [Malay]

bio-, comb. form of Gk *bios* (course of) life, which meaning it has in actual borrowings f. Gk, as *biography*; in mod. formations it is extended to include organic life (Gk *zōē*).

biochem'istry (-kĕ-), n. Study of the chemical or physico-chemical processes & products involved in the life phenomena of plants & animals. [prec.]

biogĕn'ésis, n. Hypothesis that living matter arises always from living matter. [BIO-+Gk GENESIS]

bi'ograph (-ahf), n. Early form of cinematograph. [trade name of U.S. machine exhibited in London in 1897]

biŏg'raphў, n. Written life of a person; branch of literature dealing with persons' lives; life-course of a living being. So **biŏg'RAPHER** n., **bīOGRAPH'IC(AL)** aa., **biōgrăph'icallY²** adv. [f. mod. L f. med. Gk *biographia* see BIO-, -GRAPHY]

biŏl'ogў, n. Science of physical life, dealing with the morphology, physiology, origin, & distribution, of animals & plants. So **biolŏ'gIC(AL)** aa., **biolŏ'gicalLY²** adv., **biŏl'ogIST** n. [f. F, G *biologie* see BIO-, -LOGY]

biŏm'etrў, n., **biomĕt'rics,** n. pl. Science of the application of statistical methods to biological facts. So **biomĕt'rIC(AL)** aa., **biomĕtrI'CIAN** n. [BIO-, -METRY]

bionŏm'ics, n. pl. Branch of biology dealing with the habits of life of organisms in their natural surroundings, relationship of forms of life to one another, etc. (cf. OECOLOGY). [f. BIO-, after ECONOMICS]

biophўs'ic|s (-z-), n. pl. Science of the application of the laws of physics to biological phenomena. Hence ~IST (-z-) n. [BIO-]

bi'oplăsm (-zm), **bi'oplăst,** nn. The

germinal matter, a small separate portion of it, from which all living things spring. [BIO- + Gk *plasma* see PLASMA]

bi'opsy, n. (surg.). Examination of tissue cut from the living body. [f. BIO-, & see OPTIC]

bi'oscōpe, n. = BIOGRAPH; (S.-Afr.) cinema. [BIO-, -SCOPE]

bipartisan' (-z-; *or* -pärt²), a. Of or involving two (political) parties. [BI-1 (a) + PARTISAN¹]

bipart'ite, a. 1. (Bot., of leaves) divided into two parts. 2. (Law, of treaties, contracts, etc.) drawn up in two corresponding parts. [BI-, PARTITE]

bi'pĕd, a. & n., bi'pĕdal, a. Two-footed (animal). [f. L *bipes* -*edis* f. BI-(1 a) + *pes pedis* foot]

bipinn'ate, a. Having lobes that themselves have lobes. [BI-(1 c) + PINNATE]

bi'plāne, n. Two-winged aeroplane. [BI-]

bipōl'ar, a. With two poles or extremities. [BI-(1 a)]

Bipon'tine, a. Printed at Zweibrücken (editions of classics). [BI- two + L *pons pontis* bridge (transl. of the name) + -INE¹]

biquadrăt'ic, a. & n. (Number) of the fourth power, square of a square; ~ (*equation*), in which there is a ~ variable. [BI-(1 b)]

birch¹, n. Kinds of smooth-barked slender-branched northern forest tree; (also ~-*rod*) bundle of its twigs used for flogging schoolboys etc. Hence ~'EN⁵ a. [OE *bierce*, OHG *birihha* f. Gmc *berkjōn*; also OE *berc* (whence north. dial. *birk*), ON *björk* f. Gmc *berkō*]

birch², v.t. Flog with a birch. [f. prec.]

bird, n. Feathered vertebrate; game ~; (sl.) girl: *little* ~, unnamed informant; *old* ~, wary person; ~*s of a feather*, people of like character; *a* ~ *in the hand, in the bush*, certainty, contingency; ~ *is flown*, prisoner etc. escaped; *kill two* ~*s with one stone*, gain two ends at once; *give one*, *get, the* ~ (sl.), hiss him, be hissed; ~ *of Jove*, eagle, *of Juno*, peacock, *of paradise*, New Guinea family with beautiful plumage, *of passage*, migratory (also fig. of sojourner), *of prey*, member of orders *Raptores* & *Accipitres*, as hawk, eagle, owl; ~-*bath*, basin in garden etc. for ~s to bathe in; ~-*cage*, for ~ or ~s; ~-*fancier*, one who knows about, collects, breeds, or deals in, ~s; ~-*lime*, sticky stuff spread on twigs to catch ~s; ~-*seed*, special seeds given to caged ~s; ~*'s-eye*, kinds of plant with small bright round flowers as mealy primrose or germander speedwell, (tobacco) in which ribs are cut as well as fibre, ~*'s-eye view*, conspectus of town, district, etc., as seen from above, or résumé of subject, (of pattern etc.) marked with spots; ~*'s-foot*, kinds of vetch, fern, trefoil, & starfish; ~*'s mouth*, reentrant angle cut in wood or stone; ~*'s nest*, ~-*nest*, nest of ~, kinds of plant

as *wild carrot*, ~-*nest orchid*, (v.i., esp. in gerund) hunt for nests, (of horse) turn head from side to side; ~-*table* (for wild ~s to feed on); ~-*watcher*, one who observes or identifies wild ~s, ~-*watching*, this practice; ~-*watch* v.i. [OE *brid* young bird, later superseding *fowl* in gen. sense ·(*any*) *feathered animal*; excl. E, etym. unkn.]

bird'ie, n. (golf). Hole done in one under *par* or *bogey*. [prec. + -Y³]

bir'ĕme, n. Ancient galley with two banks of oars. [f. L *biremis* f. BI-(1 a) + *remus* oar]

birĕtt'a, n. Square cap worn by R.-C. & some Anglican clerics. [f. It. *berretta* or Sp. *birreta* fem. forms corresp. to med. L *birretum*; see BERET]

Bir'rel(l)ism, n. Passing comment on life, pungent yet kindly, of a type characteristic of the writings & sayings of Augustine *Birrell*, English wit & essayist (d. 1933). [-ISM]

birth, n. Bringing forth of offspring (so many *at a* ~); coming into the world (*give* ~ *to*); origin, beginning; parentage, descent, inherited position; noble lineage, high-born people; *new* ~, regeneration; ~-*control*, methods of preventing undesired sexual conception, practice of these; ~*'day*, (anniversary of) day of one's ~ (~*day present*, given on this; ~*day book*, for entering friends' ~days; ~*day suit* joc., one's skin; ~*day honours*, titles etc. given on sovereign's ~day); ~-*mark*, peculiar mark on one's body at or from ~, usu. an irregularly-shaped blotch of skin dark red in colour; ~-*place*, at which one was born; ~-*rate*, births per thousand of population; ~-*right*, rights belonging to one as eldest son, as born in a certain station or country, or as a human being. [ME *burth(e), byrth(e)* f. ON *burthr* = Goth. *gabaurths* f. Gmc *(ga)burthiz* f. stem of *beran* BEAR³ + -TH¹]

bis, adv. 1. (mus.). Over again, repeat. 2. Twice (calling attention to a double occurrence in references etc.). [F & It. f. L, = twice]

bis'cuit (-kit), n. & a. ‖ Piece of unleavened bread of various materials, usu. crisp, dry, hard, & in small flat thin cakes; *soft round cake*; porcelain etc. after baking but before glazing & painting; ‖ half-piece or third of soldier's mattress; (of) light-brown colour; ~-*throw* (Naut.), short distance. [earlier *bisket* (now assim. to mod. F) f. OF *bescoit* (L BIS, *coctus* p.p. of *coquere* cook)]

bis dăt quī cit'ō dăt, sent. He gives twice who gives quickly. (formula in charity appeals.) [L]

bise (bēz), n. Keen dry N. wind in Switzerland, S. France, etc. [F]

bisĕct', v.t. Cut or divide into two (prop. equal) parts. Hence bisĕc'tion n. [BI-, L *secare sect-* cut]

bisĕc'tor, n. Bisecting line. [-OR]

bisĕx'ūal, a. Of two sexes; having both sexes in one individual. [BI-(1 a)+ SEXUAL]

bish'op, n. Clergyman consecrated as eccl. governor of a diocese & possessing powers of confirming, instituting, & ordaining; ~ SUFFRAGAN; mitre-shaped piece in chess; mulled & spiced wine; *Bishops' Bible*, version of 1568; ~'s-cap, -hat, -leaves, -weed, various plants. [OE *biscop*, OS *biskop*, OHG *biscof*, ON *biskup* f. pop. L **biscopo* (cf. Pg. *bispo*, It. *vescovo*) f. LL f. Gk *episkopos* (whence Goth. *aipiskaupus*) overseer (EPI- + -skopos -looking)]

bish'opric, n. Office of bishop. [OE *bisceoprīce* (prec.+*rīce* realm cf. G *reich*)]

bisk, n. Rich soup made by boiling down birds etc. [f. F *bisque* crayfish soup]

Bis'ley (-z-), n. (Used for) the ranges or the shooting competitions of the Nat. Rifle Association at ~ in Surrey.

Bismil'lah (-a), int. In the name of Allah! (common ejaculation of Moslems before action). [Arab. *bi-'sm-illāhi*]

bis'muth (-z-), n. A reddish-white metal. [f. mod. L *bisemutum*, latinization (1530) of G *wismut* of unkn. orig.]

bis'on, n. Wild ox of two species, (also *aurochs*) formerly over Europe, & still in Lithuania, (also *buffalo*) about Rocky Mountains. [f. L *bison -ontis* f. Gmc **wisand* cf. OE *wesend*, OHG *wisunt*]

bisque¹ (-k), n. (Tennis) right of scoring one point without winning it at any time in the set; (Croquet) right of playing extra turn; (Golf) stroke to be taken when desired. [F, etym. unkn.].

bisque² (-k), n. Unglazed white porcelain used in statuettes. [f. BISCUIT]

bissĕx'tile, a. & n. Leap(-year). [f. LL *bi(s)sextilis* (*annus*), (year) containing the *bis sextus dies* or doubled 24th Feb. (the sixth day before the calends of March)]

bis'tort, n. Herb with cylindrical spike of flesh-coloured flowers. [f. med. L *bistorta* (*bis* twice+*torta* fem. p.p. of *torquēre* twist) w. ref. to twisted form of root]

bis'toury (-torĭ), n. Surgeon's scalpel. [f. F *bistouri*, orig. unkn.]

bis'tre (-ter), n. & a. Brown pigment prepared from soot; colour(ed) like this. [F, etym. unkn.]

bit¹, n. Something to eat (*a* ~ & *a sup*); boring-piece of drill, cutting-iron of plane, nipping-part of pincers etc., part of key that grips lock-lever; mouthpiece of bridle, (fig.) control, (*draw* ~, slacken pace; *take* ~ *between teeth*, reject control). [OE *bite*, OS *biti*, OHG *biz*, ON *bit* f. Gmc **bitiz* f. **bitan* BITE¹]

bit², n. Morsel of food (*dainty* ~, *til'*~); small piece of anything (~ *by* ~, gradually; *give a* ~ *of* one's *mind*, speak candidly; *do* one's ~, contribute service or money to a cause); piece of scenery actual or painted; short passage in book etc.; ~*s & pieces* (colloq.), odds & ends; ~*s of*, poor little (*children, furniture*); *a* ~ *of a*, rather a (*coward* etc.); *a* ~, rather, *not a* ~ (*of it*), not at all, *every* ~ *as*, quite as; *a short time* (*wait a* ~); small coin (U.S., of fractions of Spanish dollar; in Britain, *threepenny* ~, etc.). [OE *bita*, OHG *bizzo*, ON *biti* f. Gmc **biton* f. **bitan* BITE¹]

bit³, v.t. (-tt-). Put bit into mouth of (horse); accustom to the bit; restrain. [f. BIT¹]

bitch, n. Female of dog, fox, wolf, (usu. ~ *fox*, & ~ *wolf*); (derog.) woman, esp. a lewd or catty or treacherous one. [OE *bicce*, ON *bikkja*, relation & etym. unkn.]

bite¹, v.t. & i. (past *bit*; p.p. *bitten* sometimes *bit*). Cut into or nip with the teeth; (with *off* etc.) detach with the teeth; snap *at*; (of serpents, fleas, etc.) sting, suck; accept bait (lit. & fig.); (of sword etc.) penetrate; cause glowing, smarting, etc., pain to (*frost-bitten*); corrode; (of wheels, anchor, etc.) grip; (now only in pass.) take in, swindle, (*were you bitten?*); ~ *the dust* or *ground*, fall & die; ~ one's *lips*, to control anger etc.; ~ *off more than one can chew*, attempt too great a task; *bitten with*, infected with (a mania, enthusiasm, etc.). [OE, OS *bitan*, OHG *bīzan*, ON *bíta*, Goth. *beitan* f. Gmc **bītan*]

bite², n. Act of, wound made by, piece detached by, biting; food to eat (~ & *sup*); taking of bait by fish; grip, hold, (lit. & fig.); herbage for cattle; (fig.) incisiveness, pungency. [f. prec.]

bit'er, n. In vbl senses; also, swindler (now only in *the* ~ *bit*). [-ER¹]

bit'ing, a. In vbl senses; esp., pungent, stinging, sarcastic. Hence ~LY² adv. [part. of BITE¹]

bitt'er, a., adv., & n. 1. Tasting like wormwood or quinine, opposite to sweet (~ -*cup*, cup of quassia wood giving ~ tonic property to liquid drunk from it); unpalatable to the mind, full of affliction; virulent, relentless; biting, harsh; piercingly cold (also as adv., *it was* ~ *cold*); *to the* ~ *end*, last extremity; hence ~ISH¹ (2) a., ~LY² adv., ~NESS n. 2. n. ~*ness* (*the* ~ *with the sweet, the* ~*s of life*); (pl.) liquors impregnated with wormwood etc. taken as stomachics; = ~ *beer*, opp. *mild*; ~*-sweet*, sweet(ness) with ~ after-taste or element (lit. & fig.), woody nightshade. [OE *biter*, OS, OHG *bittar*, ON *bitr*, Goth. *baitrs*, prob. f. Gmc **bitan* BITE¹; *the* ~ *end* may be f. Naut., where the wds mean the last part of a cable left round the BITTS when the rest is overboard, *bitter* being the turn at any moment on the bitts]

bitt'erling, n. Small carp-like freshwater fish of Central Europe. [G, f. *bitter* bitter +*ling* -LING¹]

bitt'ern, n. Kinds of marsh bird allied to herons, esp. one known for its booming note. [ME *botor* etc. f. OF *butor* f. Rom. *butitaurus* f. L *butio* bittern+*taurus* bull]

‖ bitt'ock, n. (dial.). Little bit. [BIT²+ -OCK]

bitts, n. pl. Pair of posts on deck for fastening cables etc. [ME (*c.* 1300), f. ON *biti* cross-beam; cf. LG, Du. *beting*]

bit'ūm|ěn, n. Mineral pitch, asphalt; kinds of native oxygenated hydrocarbon, as naphtha, petroleum. Hence ~iniˈEROUS, bitūm'inous, aa. [L, genit. *-minis*]

bitūm'iniz|e, -is|e (-īz), v.t. Convert into, impregnate or varnish with, bitumen. Hence ~AˈTION n. [prec.+-IZE (3, 5)]

bi'valent, a. = DIVALENT.

bi'vălve, a. & n., bi'vălved (-vd), bĭvăl'vŭlar, aa. With two valves; (mollusc) with hinged double shell; oyster. [BI-(1 a)+VALVE, *valv*ED², & see -ULE, -AR¹]

bĭv'ouăc (-ŏŏ-), v.i. & n. (-*acking*, -*acked*). (Remain, esp. for the night, in) temporary encampment without tents; *bivouacked*, in ~, see -ED¹ (2). [F, prob. f. G *beiwacht* (BY, WATCH) additional guard at night (in Argau & Zürich)]

bĭz, n. (colloq.). Business. [abbr.]

bizăr|re', a. Eccentric, fantastic, grotesque, mixed in style, half barbaric. So ~'rerie (-rē) [-ERY] n. [F; cf. Sp. *bizarro* handsome, brave, It. *bizzarro* choleric perh. f. Basque *bizarra* beard]

blăb, v.t. & i. (-bb-), & n. **1.** Talk or tell foolishly or indiscreetly, reveal, let out, (secrets etc., or esp.); hence ~b'ER¹ n. **2.** n. Person who~s. [imit., cf. BABBLE; ME *blabbe* n., babbler (whence later *blab* vb) & ME *blabber* vb; cf. OHG *blabbizōn*, ON *blubbra*, G *plappern*]

blăck¹, a. **1.** Opposite to white, colourless from the absence or complete absorption of all light; so near this as to have no distinguishable colour; very dark--coloured (~ *in the face*, purple with strangulation or passion); dark-skinned; dark-clothed; (of sky, deep water, etc.) dusky, gloomy; (of hands, linen) dirty; (as specific epithet) ~ *bear, currant, snake, heart-cherry*; deadly, sinister, wicked, hateful, (~-*hearted*; ~ *ingratitude*; *crimes of* ~*est dye*); dismal (~ *despair*); angry, sulky, threatening, (~-*browed*; ~ *looks*; *look* ~); implying disgrace or condemnation (~ *mark*, of discredit against one's name; ~ *book, list*, of persons suspect, tabooed, etc.; *deep in* one's ~ *books*, quite out of his favour); (of goods etc.) not to be handled by workers on strike. **2.** = ~ *blue*, discoloured with bruise; ~ & *tan*, (dog) so coloured, *B*~ & *Tans*, ex-service recruits of the R.I.C. against Sinn-Feiners 1921 named from mixture of military & constabulary uniforms; ~ & *white*, ink drawing (*down in* ~ & *white*, recorded in writing or print); ~ *art*, magic [~ partly in sense *wicked*, partly by assoc. w. med.

L *nigromantia* corrupt. of NECROMANCY]; ~ *ball*, used to reject candidate in club ballot, whence ~-*ball* v.t.; ~-*beetle*, cockroach; ~'*berry*, bramble or its fruit (*plentiful as* ~*berries*, as can be; ~*berrying*, gathering them); ~'*bird*, European song-bird, kidnapped Negro on slave-ship (~*birding*, trade in these); ~-*board*, in lecture-room for demonstrations in chalk; ‖ ~ *cap*, put on by judge in sentencing to death; ~'*cap*, kinds of bird, esp. the ~-warbler; ~ CATTLE; ‖ ~-*coat worker*, clerk etc. (opp. industrial employee); ~'*cock*, male (opp. *grey-hen*) of ~ grouse; ~ *coffee* (without milk, usu. strong); ‖ *B*~ *Country*, smoky district in Staffs. & War.; ~ *dog*, sulks; ~ *draught*, an aperient; ~ *eye*, discoloured with bruise, also with dark iris whence ~-*eye*ED² (-īd) a.; ~'*face*, dark--faced sheep; ~'*fellow*, Australian aboriginal; ~-*fish*, a species, also salmon just after spawning; ~ *flag*, used by pirates, also signal of execution completed; *Black'foot* (pl. -*feet*), member of a tribe of N.-Amer. Indians; ~ *friar*, Dominican; ~ *frost*, hard frost without snow or rime; ~ *game*, ~ grouse (& see ~*cock*); ~*guard* (blăg'ărd), (n. & a.) scoundrel(ly), foul--mouthed (person), whence ~*guard*ly¹ (-ăg²) a., (v.t.) call ~*guard*, abuse scurrilously [orig. collect. n., applied at various times to menials of royal household, camp-followers, bodyguard, criminal class, & vagrants]; *B*~ *Hand*, secret organization of Italian ~*mailers* & thugs in U.S.; ~-*head*, kinds of bird, esp. kind of gull, (also) kind of pimple on the skin; ~ *hole*, military lock-up (so *B*~ *Hole of Calcutta*); ~ *jack*, tarred-leather wine-bottle, also pirates' ~ flag, also flexible loaded life-preserver; ~-*lead*, (polish with) PLUMBAGO [named from marking like lead]; ~'*leg*, swindler esp. on turf, ‖ workman who works for master whose men are on strike (v.i. & t., act as ~leg, betray or injure thus) [orig. of senses unknown]; ~ *letter*, old type like the German; ~ *list* (of persons under suspicion, liable to punishment, etc.); ~*list'* (v.t.), enter name of (person) on ~ list; ~'*mail*, (hist.) tribute exacted by freebooters for protection & immunity, (mod., v.t. & n.) (force to make) payment for not revealing discreditable secrets etc., whence ~*mail*'ER¹ n. [obs. *mail* rent, OE *māl* f. ON *māl* agreement perh. = OHG *mahal* assembly]; ~ *Maria*, vehicle for taking prisoners from & to gaol; ~ *market*, illegitimate traffic in officially controlled goods or currencies or in commodities in short supply (~ *marketeer*, one who engages in this), place where this traffic is carried on; ~ *mass*, travesty of the mass said to be used in the cult of Satanism (also Eccl., a Requiem Mass); ~ *monk*, Benedictine; ~ *pudding*, sausage-shaped of blood, suet, etc.; ‖ *B*~ *Rod*, gentleman usher of Lord

Chamberlain's department, House of Lords, & Garter; ~ *sheep*, scoundrel; ~*-shirts*, fascists; ~*smith*, smith working in iron (cf. WHITESmith); ~*thorn*, thorny shrub bearing white flowers before leaves & small plums or sloes (~*thorn winter*, time of its flowering, cold with NE winds), cudgel or walking-stick of this; ~ *velvet*, mixture of stout & champagne; ‖ B~ WATCH[1], 42nd Highlanders [f. orig. uniform]; ~*-water fever*, tropical disease with bloody urine etc.; ~ *widow*, common Amer. spider, the female of which devours its mate. Hence ~'ISH[1] (2) a., ~'NESS n. [OE *blæc, blac*, OHG *blah-, blach-* (in comb.) of unkn. orig.]

black[2], n. Black colour; black paint, dye, varnish; black speck; fungus, smut, in wheat etc.; particle of soot; black cloth(es); Negro or negrito, whence ~'Y[3] n. [f. prec.]

black[3], v.t. Make black; polish with BLACKING; ~ *out*: obliterate or obscure; obscure (windows etc.) to prevent any light being seen from outside, esp. from the air, also abs.; ~*-out* n.: ~ing out or being ~ed out (also attrib., as ~*-out material, offences, time*); (fig.) condition of obscuration; temporary complete failure of memory; in flying, temporary blindness etc. resulting from centrifugal force when a sudden turn is made (v.i., suffer this). [f. BLACK[1]]

black'amoor, n. Negro; dark-skinned person. [BLACK[1]+MOOR[2]]

black'avised (-ĭzd) a. (arch.). Dark-complexioned. [BLACK[1]+F *vis* face]

black'en, v.t. & i. Make, grow, black or dark; speak evil of (person's character). [ME *blaknen* (BLACK[1], -EN[6])]

black'ing, n. In vbl senses; also, paste or liquid for blacking boots. [-ING[1]]

bladd'er, n. Membranous bag in human & other animal bodies (esp. the urinary ~, also gall, air, swimming, ~~); the same or part of it prepared for various uses, inflated etc.; (fig.) anything inflated & hollow, wordy man, windbag; inflated pericarp or vesicle in plants & seaweeds (~*-wrack*, common seaweed with these in its fronds). Hence ~Y[2] a. [OE *blædre*, OS *blādra*, OHG *blātara*, ON *blathra* f. Gmc *blædram* f. *blæ-* BLOW[1]]

blade, n. (Vague & poet.) leaf; flat lanceolate leaf esp. of grass & cereals; whole of such plants before ear comes (*in the* ~); (Bot.) expanded part of leaf apart from foot-stalk; flattened part of instrument, as oar, bat, spade, paddle-wheel; cutting-piece of edged tool, as sword, chisel, knife; sword; (also ~*-bone*) flat bone, esp. shoulder-~ as joint of meat or otherwise; jovial, hectoring, gay, etc., fellow (usu. with epithet). Hence (-)blād'ED[2] a. [OE *blæd*, OHG *blat*, ON *blath* f. Gmc *bladham* f. *blō* see BLOW[1]]

‡**blae'berry** (blā-), n. = BILBERRY. [f.

blae (Sc. & north. dial. f. ME *blo* f. ON *blár*; see BLUE) +BERRY]

blague (-ahg), n. Humbug, claptrap. [F]

*blah, n. (colloq.). Hyperbolic & frothy talk or writing. [orig. unkn.]

blain, n. Inflamed sore on skin, pustule. [OE *blegen* cf. Du. *blein*]

blame, v.t. Find fault with (*for offence* etc.); fix the responsibility on; *be to* ~*e*, deserve censure. Hence ~'ABLE a., ~'ABLY[2] adv. [f. OF *bla(s)mer*, ult. f. LL *blasphemare* BLASPHEME]

blame[2], n. Censure; responsibility for bad result (*lay the* ~ *on, bear the* ~). [f. OF *bla(s)me* cf. prec.]

blame'ful (-mf-), a. (Rare) conveying, (usu.) deserving, censure. [-FUL]

blame'less (-ml-), a. Innocent. Hence ~LY[2] adv., ~NESS n. [-LESS]

blame'worth|y (-mwěrdh-), a. Deserving blame. Hence ~iNESS n.

blanch (-ah-), v.t. & i. Make white by withdrawing colour, peeling (almonds), or depriving of light (plants); make or grow pale with fear, cold, etc.; ~ *over*, palliate by misrepresentation. [ME, f. OF *blanchir* (*blanc* BLANK)]

blancmange (blamahnzh'), n. Opaque white jelly of isinglass, gelatine, or corn-flour, & milk. [ME *blancmanger* f. OF (*blanc* BLANK +*manger* eat f. L *manducare* MANDUCATE)]

bländ, a. Gentle, polite, in manner; ironical; balmy, mild. Hence ~'LY[2] adv., ~'NESS n. [f. L *blandus*]

blän'dish, v.t. Flatter, coax. Hence ~MENT n. (usu. in pl.). [ME, f. OF *blandir* (-ISH[2]) f. L *blandiri* (*blandus*)]

blank[1], a. Not written or printed on (of paper); (of document) with spaces left for signature or details (*in* ~, *drawn in* ~, so prepared); ~ *cheque*, with amount left for payee to fill in, hence = CARTE BLANCHE); empty, not filled, (~ *space* etc.; ~ *cartridge*, without ball); void of interest, incident, result, or expression; *look* ~, nonplussed; unrelieved, sheer; unrhymed (~ *verse*, esp. the five-foot iambic). Hence ~'NESS n. [f. OF *blanc* white f. Rom. *blancus* f. Gmc *blankaz*]

blank[2], n. Lottery ticket that gains no prize; space left to be filled up in document, empty surface (one's *mind, memory* etc., *is a* ~, has no sensations etc.); *document having blank space(s) to be filled up; words printed in italics in Parl bills; time without incident, thing without meaning; coin-disc before stamping; = ~ *cartridge* (*20 rounds of* ~); dash written instead of word or letter, whence ~, ~*y*, ~*ed*, as substitutes for abusive nouns and adjj. [uses of prec.]

blänk'et[1], n. & a. 1. Large woollen sheet used for bed covering, for horse-cloth, & by savages for clothes; *wet* ~, person who extinguishes conversation; *born on the wrong side of the* ~, illegitimate. *2. adj. General rather than individual, covering all cases or classes. [ME, f. OF *blanquette* (*blanc* BLANK + -ETTE)]

blank'et², v.t. Cover with a blanket; stifle, keep quiet, (scandal, question, etc.); toss in a blanket as punishment; take wind from sails of (another craft) by passing to windward. [f. prec.]

biänk'lỹ, adv. Without expression, vacuously, (*look* ~ etc.); flatly (*deny* ~ etc.). [BLANK¹ + -LY²]

blanquette (blahnkět'), n. (cookery). White dish, such as a fricassee with white sauce. [F]

blāre, v.i. & t., & n. (Make) sound of trumpet; utter loudly. [ME *bleren*, imit.; cf. MDu. *blaren*, MHG *blêren*, *blerren*, G *plärren*]

blārn'ey, n., & v.t. & i. (Use, assail with) cajoling talk. [*Blarney*, Irish castle near Cork with stone conferring a cajoling tongue on whoever kisses it]

blasé (-ahz'ā), a. Cloyed, tired of pleasure. [F]

blāsphēm|e', v.i. & t. Talk impiously; utter profanity about, revile. So ~'ER² (4), blās'phēmY¹, nn., blās'phēmousa., biäs'phēmousLY² adv. [ME *blasfemen* f. OF *blasfemer* f. LL *blasphemare* f. Gk *blasphēmeō*; cf. BLAME]

blast¹ (-ah-), n. Strong gust of wind; sound of wind-instrument; current of air in smelting etc. (*in, out of*, ~, of furnace working or not); quantity of explosive used in blasting operation; destructive wave of highly compressed air spreading outwards from an explosion; ~*-furnace*, smelting furnace into which compressed hot air is driven by engine. [OE *blǣst*, OHG *blāst*, ON *blāstr* f. Gmc *blǣst*- f. *blǣsan* blow see BLAZE⁵]

blast² (-ah-), v.t. Blow up (rocks etc.) with explosives; wither, shrivel, blight, (plant, animal, limb, prosperity, character; esp., with subj. *God* understood, in curses, whence ~*ed*, damnable). [f. prec.]

blasto-, first element in many biological terms, meaning germ, bud. [f. Gk *blastos* sprout]

blās'todērm, n. Disc of cells found in the early segmentation of a fertilized ovum (as differentiated from *blastula*, hollow ball of cells, & *morula*, solid ball). [prec. + Gk *derma* skin]

blāt'ant, a. Noisy, vulgarly clamorous; flagrant, palpable. Hence ~LY² adv., blāt'ANCY n. [a Spenserian wd (*blattant*) of uncert. orig.; perh. after Sc. *blatand* = bleating]

blather(skite). See BLETHER.

blāze¹, n. Bright flame or fire (*in a* ~, on fire); (sl.) ~*s* = hell (*go to* ~*s*, *what the* ~*s*! *like* ~*s*, impetuously); violent outburst (~ *of passion* etc.); glow of colour, bright display; full light (~ *of publicity*). [OE *blase*, *blǣse* torch, f. Gmc *blasōn*; cf. MHG *blas* torch; ult. cogn. w. BLAZE³]

blāze², v.i. Burn with flame (~ *up*, burst into blaze); be brilliantly lighted; burn with excitement etc. (~ *up*, burst out in anger); show bright colours; emit light; ~ *away*, fire continuously with rifles etc., work enthusiastically at anything; *blazing indiscretion*, rash & conspicuous piece of candour; (Hunting) *blazing scent*, very strong (opp. to *cold scent*). [f. prec.]

blāze³, n. White mark on horse's or ox's face, or made on tree by chipping bark to mark route. [f. 17th c.; = ON *blesi*, OHG *blassa* (G *blesse*), MDu. *blesse* in same sense; stem *blas*- cogn. w. MHG *blas* bald, G *blass* pale)]

blāze⁴, v.t. Mark (tree, & so path) by chipping bark, esp. ~ *a trail*, also fig. [f. prec.]

blāze⁵, v.t. Proclaim as with trumpet, esp. ~ *abroad*, spread (news) about. [ME *blasen* blow prob. f. ON *blása* = OHG *blāsan*, Goth. *-blēsan* f. Gmc *blǣsan* (cf. BLAST) f. *blǣ-* (BLOW¹); later sense 'proclaim' f. MLG, MDu. *blāzen*]

blāz'er, n. Coloured jacket for boating, golf, etc. [BLAZE² + -ER¹]

blāz'on¹, n. Heraldic shield, coat of arms, bearings, or banner; correct description of these; record, description, esp. of virtues etc. [ME, f. OF *blason* shield, of unkn. orig.]

blāz'on², v.t. Describe or paint (arms) heraldically; inscribe (object) with arms, names, etc., in colours or ornamentally; give lustre to; set forth in fitting words; proclaim. Hence ~MENT n. [f. prec. partly confused in sense with BLAZE⁵]

blāz'onrỹ, n. (Art of describing or painting) heraldic devices, armorial bearings; brightly coloured display. [prec. + -RY]

-ble, suf. OF f. L *-bilis* forming vbl adjj. active or passive (*penetrabilis* penetrating or penetrable) f. vb or p.p. stems. L has *-ab.*, *-eb.*, *-ib.*, or *-ib.*, acc. to conjug. (*-ib.* also f. p.p. stems as *flexibilis*). Mod. F in making new wds uses only *-able*; E vacillates between this & using *-ible* wherever there was or might be a L *-ibilis*; to this confusion is added that between *-able & -eable*; *-eable* is necessary after soft *-c*, *-g*, (cf. *navigable*, *manageable*); it is also used in some wds to affect the vowel of the previous syllable (*tameable*). See also -ABLE, -IBLE. The E meaning in new wds is always passive, but some older wds (*capable*, *durable*) have active meaning after the older F (f. L) tradition. From adjj. in *-ble* are formed nouns in *-bility* (L *-bilitas*, see -TY) as well as in *-bleness*.

bleach, v.t. & i. Whiten by exposure to sunlight or by chemical process; ~*ing-powder*, chloride of lime. Hence ~'ER¹ n.; one who ~es (esp. textiles); vessel or chemical used in ~ing; *(usu. pl.) outdoor uncovered plank-seat for spectators at sports grounds. [OE *blǣcan*, ON *bleikja*, OHG *bleichēn* f. Gmc *blaikjan* f. *blaik*- white]

bleak[1], n. Small river fish, & allied sea-fish, of various species. [15th c. *bleke*; cf. ON *bleikja*, OHG *bleicha* f. Gmc *blaikjōn f. *blaik-* white]

bleak[2], a. Wanting colour; bare, exposed, windswept; chilly; dreary. [16th c., of obsc. phonology; rel. to obs. *bleach*, obs. *blake* (= OE *blāc*, ON *bleikr*) pale, ult. f. Gmc *blaik-*; see BLEACH]

blear, a., & v.t. (Make) dim-sighted, dull, filmy, (eyes or mind); (make) indistinct in outline; ~-*eyed*, having ~ eyes or wits. Hence ~[Y][2] a. [ME *blere* a. & vb, cogn. w. MHG *blerre* blurred vision, LG *blarr-*, *blerr-oged* blear-eyed]

bleat, v.i. & t., & n. (Make) sheep's, goat's, or calf's, cry; speak (& ~ *out*, say) feebly or foolishly or plaintively. [imit.; OE *blǣtan*, OHG *blāzen*, Du. *blaten*]

blеb, n. Small blister or bubble on skin, in water or glass. [imit. of making bubble with lips, cf. *blab*, *blob*, *blubber*]

bleed, v.i. & t. (*bled*). Emit blood (*heart* ~*s*, is in acute distress); suffer wounds or violent death (often *for* cause etc.); (of plants) emit sap; part with money, pay lavishly, suffer extortion; draw blood surgically from; extort money from; ‖ (part., vulg. euphem., cf. *blinking*, *blooming*, for) bloody; ~*ing heart*, pop. name of various plants, as wallflower. Hence ~[ER][1] n., person inclined to ~ excessively from a slight injury. [OE *blēdan*, ON *blǣtha* f. Gmc *blōdhjan* f. *blōdham* BLOOD]

bleep, n., & v.i. 1. (Sound of) radio signal transmitted from Russian earth satellite launched in 1957. 2. v.i. Transmit this signal. [imit.]

blem′ish[1], v.t. Mar, spoil the beauty or perfection of, sully. [ME, f. OF *ble(s)mir* (-ISH[2]) f. *ble(s)me* pale, of Gmc orig.]

blem′ish[2], n. Physical or moral defect, stain, flaw. [f. prec.]

blench, v.i. & t. Start aside, flinch, quail; close the eyes to, disguise from oneself. [hist. obsc.; perh. f. OE *blencan*, ON *blekkja* deceive; w. later senses cf. BLINK]

blend[1], v.t. & i. (~*ed* or *blent*). Mix (things) together (esp. sorts of tea, spirit, to get certain quality); mingle (t., & i. of element) intimately *with*; mix (components) so as to be inseparable & indistinguishable; become one, form harmonious compound; pass imperceptibly into each other (esp. of colours). [ME, f. ON *blanda* mix, not continuous w. cogn. OE (= OS, Goth.) *blandan*, OHG *blantan*]

blend[2], n. Mixture made of various sorts of tea, spirits, etc. [f. prec.]

blende, n. Native sulphide of zinc. [G *blende* f. *blenden* deceive, also *blendendes Erz* deceiving ore 'because while often resembling galena it yielded no lead']

Blen′heim (-ĕnĭm), n. & a. Kind of spaniel; ‖ ~ *Orange*, golden-coloured apple. [Duke of Marlborough's seat at Woodstock]

blenno-, **blenn-**, stem of many wds in pathology. Of mucus. [Gk *blennos* mucus]

blеnn′ў, n. Small spiny-finned sea-fish. [as prec. (through L *blennius*) from mucous coating of its scales]

blent. See BLEND[1].

bleph′aro-, stem of pathological words. Of the eyelids. [f. Gk *blepharon* eyelid]

bles′bŏk, n. Large S.-African antelope. [Afrikaans, f. *bles* BLAZE[3] (from white mark on forehead) + *bok* goat]

bless, v.t. (past & p.p. ~*ed*, sometimes *blest*, & see under BLESSED). Consecrate (esp. food; *not a penny to* ~ *oneself with*, w. ref. to cross on silver penny); call holy, adore, (God); attribute good fortune to (esp. one's stars); pronounce words that bring supernatural favour upon (of father, priest, etc.); invoke God's favour on; make happy or successful (abs. or *with* something); *God* ~ *me*, ~ *me, God* ~ *you*, ~ *you*, ~ *the boy*, ~ *my soul, I'm blest*, exclamations of surprise or indignation; (euphem.)=damn, curse, etc. [excl. E; OE *blǣdsian*, *blēdsian*, *blētsian*, f. Gmc *blōdhisōjan* f. *blōdham* BLOOD (mark with blood, consecrate); meaning influenced (1) by the word's being used at the Eng. conversion to translate L *benedicere*, (2) by confusion with the independent BLISS]

bless′ed, **blest**, (for pronunc. see under etym.), a. Consecrated; revered; fortunate; ~ *with*, fortunate in the possession of (esp. iron.); in paradise (esp. as n., *the* ~); blissful, bringing happiness (~ *ignorance* etc.); (euphem.) cursed. [p.p. of prec.; as p.p. & past tense *blessed* is usu. monosyl., as adj. disyl.; of the adj. forms *blessed* is the ordinary, *blest* the poet., also used in some phrr. as *Isles of the Blest*]

bless′ednéss, n. Happiness; enjoyment of divine favour; *single* ~, jocular phr. for being unmarried (perversion of Shakesp. *M.N.D.*, I. i. 78). [prec. + -NESS]

bless′ing, n. Declaration, invocation, or bestowal, of divine favour; grace before or after food (*ask a* ~); gift of God, nature, etc., thing one is glad of; ~ *in disguise*, unwelcome but salutary experience etc. [BLESS + -ING[1]]

blěth′er, **blǎth′er**, (-dh-), v.i., & n. (Talk) loquacious nonsense. Hence blǎth′er-skīte, blěth′erskǎte, nn. (dial.), blethering person. [ME *blather* f. ON *blathra* talk nonsense (*blathr* nonsense); *blether* is the Scots form adopted from Burns etc.]

blew, past of BLOW[1], [2].

blew′it (-ōō-), n. A late edible mushroom with lilac stem. [prob. f. *blue*, cf. dial. name *blue-legs*]

blight[1] (-īt), n. Disease of unknown or atmospheric origin affecting plants; plant disease caused by fungoid parasites, mildew, rust, smut; species of aphis; hazy close state of atmosphere;

any obscure malignant influence. [17th c., of unkn. orig.]

blight² (-īt), v.t. Exert baleful influence on, nip in the bud, wither, mar. Hence ~ER¹ (-īt-) n., esp. (sl.) annoying person. [f. prec.]

∥ **Blight'y** (-īt-), n. (army sl.). England, home, after foreign service (a ~ one, wound that ensures return to ~). [Anglo-Ind. corruption of Hind. *wilāyatī, bilātī*, European, English (*wilāyat* country, cf. Turk. VILAYET)]

∥ **blim'ey**, int. (vulg.) of surprise etc. [= God blind me!]

blimp, n. 1. Small non-rigid airship. 2. (Col.) *Blimp*, character invented by the cartoonist David Low (b. 1891), representing a pompous, obese, elderly figure pop. interpreted as type of diehard or reactionary. Hence ~ERY (4), ~'ishNESS, nn. [perh. f. LIMP²]

blind¹, a. Without sight (~ *in one eye*, ~ *of an eye*, having one eye ~; *turn a* or *one's ~ eye to*, affect not to see); without foresight, discernment, or moral or intellectual light (~ *to*, incapable of appreciating; *one's ~ side*, direction in which one is unguarded); reckless; mechanical, not ruled by purpose, (~ *forces*); hard to trace (~ *track*); (Post Office) ~ *letter, man, reader*, of ill-addressed letters and the officials dealing with them; concealed (~ *ditch*; ~*-stitch*, sewing visible only on one side, also as v.t. & i. sew thus); ~ *door* etc., walled up; closed at one end (~ *alley*; ~*-alley occupations*, such as fail to fit one for anything further); (sl.) drunk (also ~ *drunk*, ~ *to the world*); ~ *flying*, flying without sight of the ground, or guidance from (directional) wireless signals; ~ *hazard, hookey*, card-games; ~*-man's-buff*, game in which blindfold player tries to catch others, who push him about [f. obs. *buff* = *buffet*]; ~ *stamping, tooling* (in bookbinding without use of ink or goldleaf); ~*-story*, TRIFORIUM admitting no light; ~ *man's holiday*, time before candles are lighted; ~ *coal*, burning without flame, anthracite; ~*-worm*, = SLOW-*worm* (f. small size of eyes). [OE, OS *blind*, OHG *blint*, ON *blindr*, Goth. *blinds* f. Gmc *blindaz*]

blind², v.t. & i. Deprive of sight permanently or temporarily; rob of judgement, deceive; (v.i., sl.) go blindly or heedlessly (chiefly of reckless motorists); ~*ing* (vbl. n.), process of covering newly made road with fine material to fill interstices, material used for this purpose. [f. prec.]

blind³, n. Obstruction to sight or light; screen for windows, esp. on roller (*Venetian* ~, of laths running on webbing); (Fortif.) = foll.; pretext, stalking-horse; (sl.) drinking-bout. [f. prec.]

blind'age, n. Screen for troops in fortification, sieges, etc. [-AGE]

blind'fold¹, v.t. Deprive (eyes, person) of sight with bandage (also fig.). [replacing (through notion of folding) ME *blindfellen* (FELL v.) strike blind, chiefly used in p.p. whence the -*d*, which helped the confusion]

blind'fold², a. & adv. With eyes bandaged; without circumspection. [p.p., earlier *blindfelled* see prec.]

blind'ly, adv. Without seeing, gropingly; recklessly. [-LY²]

blind'ness, n. Want of sight; want of intellectual or moral sense, folly, recklessness. [-NESS]

blink¹, v.i. & t. Move the eyelids; look with eyes opening & shutting; shut the eyes for a moment; shine with unsteady light, cast momentary gleam; ignore, shirk consideration of, (esp. *the fact*); (part., vulg. euphem., cf. *bleeding, blooming*, for) bloody. [hist. & relations obsc.; in ME a rare var. of northern *blenk* = BLENCH; common f. late 16th c., coinciding w. MDu., Du., G *blinken*]

blink², n. Momentary gleam or glimpse; (also *ice*-~) whiteness about horizon, reflection of distant ice-fields. [f. prec.]

blink'er, n. In vbl senses; also, (usu. pl.) screen(s) preventing horse from seeing sideways. [-ER¹]

bliss, n. Gladness, enjoyment; perfect joy, blessedness; being in heaven. Hence ~'FUL a., ~'fuLLY² adv., ~'fulNESS n. [OE *bliths, bliss*, OS *blidsea* f. BLITHE + suf. -*sja*-; sense 'heavenly joy' by assoc. w. BLESS]

blis'ter, n., & v.t. & i. 1. Vesicle on skin filled with serum, caused by friction, burning, etc.; similar swelling on surface of plant, metal, painted wood; (Med.) anything applied to raise a ~; ~ (almost pure) *copper*; ~ *gas*, poison gas causing ~s on skin. 2. vb. Raise ~ on; become covered with ~s. [ME *blister, blester*, of unkn. orig.; cf. OF *blestre, blo(u)stre* swelling, pimple]

blithe(-dh), a. Gay, joyous, (chiefly poet.). Hence ~'LY² (-dhl-) adv., ~'SOME (-dhs-) adj. [OE *blithe*, OS *blithi*, OHG *blidi*, ON *blithr*, Goth. *bleiths* f. Gmc *blithiz*]

blith'ering (-dh-), a. (colloq.). Senselessly talkative; consummate (~ *idiot*); contemptible. [part. of *blither*, var. of BLETHER]

blitz, n., & v.t., (colloq.). 1. Intensive (esp. air) attack. 2. v.t. Damage or destroy in ~ (esp. in pass., as ~*ed areas, cities*). [abbr. of foll.]

blitz'krieg (-krēg), n. A violent campaign intended to bring about speedy victory. [G, = lightning war]

blizz'ard, n. Blinding snow-storm. [U.S. 'violent blow' (1829), 'snow-storm' (1870), orig. unkn.; cf. *blizz* downpour (of rain, 1770)]

bloat¹, v.t., v.i. & n., & **bloat'er**, n. Cure (herring) by salting & smoking slightly into *bloated* herring or *bloater*. [f. obs. adj.

bloat, earlier *blote*; orig. obsc., rel. to foll. uncert.; w. 16–17th c. *blo(a)te* herring cf. ON *blautr fiskr* soft fish]

bloat², v.t. & i., **bloat'ĕd**, a. Inflate, swell (t. & i.); (chiefly in p.p. as adj.) puffed up, esp. with gluttony, overgrown, too big, pampered (esp. *bloated aristocrat*, *armaments*). [f. obs. adj. *blaute*, *blowt(e)*, later (? after prec.) *bloat*, perh. f. ON *blautr* soft, flabby; cf. prec.]

blŏb, n. Drop of liquid; small roundish mass; spot of colour; (Cricket) = duck's egg. [imit., cf. BLEB]

blŏbb'er-lipped (-ĭpt), a. With thick protruding lips. [imit., cf. BLEB; *blabber*, *blubber*, are found in same sense]

blŏc, n. Combination of parties to support a government; (transf.) combination of nations, groups, etc., to foster a particular interest, as *sterling ~* (of countries with currencies tied to sterling). [F, = BLOCK¹]

block¹, n. **1.** Log of wood, tree-stump, (*chip of the old ~*, child like his father esp. in character; *cut ~s with razor*, waste ingenuity etc.); large piece of wood for chopping or hammering on (*the ~*, death by beheading) or mounting horse from; mound for shaping hats on, shape; *barber's ~*, wooden head for wigs. **2.** Pulley, system of pulleys mounted in case. **3.** Piece of wood (also *wood-~*) or metal engraved for printing. **4.** Bulky piece of anything; unhewn lump of rock; prepared piece of building-stone. **5.** Compact mass of buildings bounded by (usu. four) streets (*~-buster* sl., huge bomb capable of destroying this); *area in town or suburb. **6.** Stolid or hard-hearted person, whence *~ish¹* a. **7.** Obstruction, (Parl.) notice that a bill will be opposed, which prevents its being taken at certain times & so often kills it; ‖ (Traffic) jammed vehicles unable to proceed; *~ system* on railways, by which no train may enter a section till it is clear. **8.** (Cricket) spot on which batsman blocks ball & rests bat before playing. **9.** Tract of land offered to individual settler by government. **10.** Large quantity of shares etc. **11.** (Austral.) fashionable city promenade. **12.** *~-chain*, kind of endless chain used in bicycle etc.; *~'head*, dolt; *~'house*, detached fort (orig. one blocking passage), occas. one of connected chain of posts, also one-storeyed timber building with loopholes, also house of squared logs; ‖ *~ letters*, *writing* (with each letter separate as in print, & usu. in capitals); *~ tin*, refined tin cast in ingots. [ME, f. OF *bloc* f. MDu. *blok* of unkn. orig.]

block², v.t. Obstruct (passage etc.); put obstacles in way of (progress etc.; *~ up*, *in*, confine; (Parl.) announce opposition to (bill; see prec.); restrict use or expenditure of (currency or other asset; chiefly in p.p.); (Cricket) stop (ball) with bat; shape (hats); emboss (book cover);

~ out, *in*, sketch roughly, plan, (work). Hence *~'AGE* (3) n., a *~ed* (up) state. [f. prec., or F *bloquer* f. *bloc* see prec.]

blockāde'¹, n. Shutting-up, total or on land or sea side, of a place by hostile forces in order to starve it into surrender or prevent egress & ingress (*paper ~*, one declared but not made effective; *raise ~*, cease blockading, compel blockaders to cease; *run ~*, evade blockading force; *~-runner*, ship, captain, etc., doing this); imprisonment by snow etc. [f. prec. on anal. of F wds in -ADE]

blockād|e'², v.t. Subject to blockade (see prec.); obstruct (door, view, etc.). Hence *~'ER¹* n. [f. prec.]

blōke, n. (colloq.). Man, fellow, chap; dull or rustic person; *the ~* (Nav. sl.), ship's commander. [etym. unkn.]

blŏnd, **blŏnde** (see etym.), a. & n. (Of hair) light-auburn-coloured; (of complexion) fair (n., person with such hair & skin; (also *~ lace*) silk lace of two threads in hexagonal meshes (orig. of raw-silk colour, now white or black). [ME, a. F *blond*, fem. *blonde*, = Sp. *blondo*, It. *biondo*, med. L *blundus*, *blondus* perh. of Gmc orig.; *blonde* is used of the lace, & of the adj. & n. as applied to a woman, *blond* elsewhere]

blood¹ (blŭd), n. **1.** Red liquid circulating in veins of higher animals, corresponding liquid in lower animals, (*flesh & ~*, the animal nature; *let ~*, surgically); (fig.) sap, grape-juice, etc. **2.** Taking of life, murder, sacrifice, guilt of bloodshed. **3.** Passion, temperament, mettle, (*bad ~*, ill feeling; *his ~ is up*, he is in fighting mood; *~ out of a stone*, pity from the pitiless; *in cold ~*, deliberately). **4.** Race (*blue ~*, high birth; *fresh ~*, new members admitted to family, society, etc.; *~ royal*, royal family; *Prince* etc. *of the ~ royal* or *of the ~*, of royal race; *runs in the ~*, is a family trait). **5.** Relationship, relations, (*own flesh & ~*; *~ is thicker than water*, the tie of kindred is real); descent, good parentage, (of men, horses, etc.; *bit of ~*, *~-horse*, thoroughbred. **6.** Dandy, man of fashion, (*young ~*, either in this sense, or as personal form of *fresh ~* above, =younger member of party). **7.** *~ & iron*, relentless use of force (esp. as motto of Bismarckian policy); *~-&-*THUNDER; *~ ally*, red-veined ALLY³; *~ bank*, place where supply of *~* for transfusion is stored; *~ count*, counting of the number of corpuscles in a definite volume of *~*; *~-curdling*, so horrific as to tend to curdle the *~*; *~ feud*, between families of which one has spilt the other's *~*; *~ group*, any one of the (usu. four) types into which *~* may be divided according to its compatibility in transfusion; *~-guilty*, responsible for murder or death; *~-heat*, ordinary heat of human *~* in health, 98·4° F.; *~'hound*, large keen-scented dog with which cattle, slaves, etc., used to be tracked, detective spy; ~-*letting*, surgical removal of some of patient's ~, (joc.) ~shed; ~-*money*, reward to witness for securing capital sentence, fine paid to next of kin for slaughter of relative; ~ *orange*, with red juice; ~-*poisoning*, state resulting from introduction of septic matter into ~ esp. through wound; ~-*red*, red as ~; ~ -*relation*, one related by ~, not marriage; ~'*shed*, spilling of ~, slaughter [f. phr. *to shed* ~]; ~'*shot*, (of eye) suffused, tinged, with ~ (*see things* ~*shot*, find incitements to slaughter or traces of ~ in them); ~ *sports*, those involving ~shed or the killing of animals; ~-*stained*, stained with ~, disgraced by ~shed; ~'*stone*, kinds of precious stone spotted or streaked with red, esp. heliotrope; ~'*stock*, thoroughbred horses collectively; ~-*sucker*, leech, extortioner; ~'*thirsty*, eager for ~shed, whence ~'thi'rstiNESS n.; ~-*transfusion*, see TRANSFUSE; ~-*vessel*, flexible tube (vein or artery) conveying ~; ~'*worm*, bright-red kind used in fishing; ~-*wort*, kinds of plant with red roots or leaves, esp. bloody dock. [OE, OS *blōd*, OHG *bluot*, ON, Goth. *blōth*, f. Gmc *blōðham*]

blood² (blŭd), v.t. (Surg.) remove a little of the blood of (usu. *bleed*); allow first taste of blood to (hound); also fig. of inciting persons). [f. prec.]

blood'less (-ŭ-), a. Without blood; unfeeling; pale; without bloodshed, whence ~LY² adv. [-LESS]

bloody¹ (blŭd'ĭ), a. & adv. Of, like, running or smeared with, blood (~ *nose*, bleeding; ~ *flux*, dysentery); red (~ *hand*, armorial device of baronet); involving, loving, resulting from, bloodshed; (also ~-*minded*) sanguinary, cruel; ‖ (in strong language) = *damned* etc., or as mere intensive (*not a* ~ *one*); ‖ (similarly as adv.) = confoundedly, very; (in pop. plant names) ~ *finger*, *foxglove*. Hence blood'ILY² adv., blood'INESS n. [OE *blōdig*, see BLOOD, -Y²]

bloody² (blŭd'ĭ), v.t. Make bloody, stain with blood. [f. prec.]

bloom¹, n. Flower, esp. of plants grown or admired chiefly for the flower, florescence (*in* ~); prime, perfection; flush, glow; powdery deposit on grapes, plums, etc., freshness, (*take the* ~ *off*, stale); kind of raisin. [ME *blom*, *blome* f. ON *blóm*, *blómi*, OS *blōmo*, OHG *bluomo*, -*ma*, Goth. *blōma* f. Gmc *blōmon*, -*ōn* f. *blō*- BLOW³; cf. BLOSSOM]

bloom², v.i. Bear flowers, be in flower; come into be in, full beauty; culminate, flourish. [f. prec.]

bloom³, n. Mass of puddled iron hammered or squeezed into thick bar. [OE *blōma* in same sense]

bloom⁴, v.t. Make (puddled iron) into a BLOOM³. Hence ~'ERY (3) (also -*ary*) n. [f. prec.]

bloom'er¹, n. & a. (Obsolete female costume) of short skirt & trousers (as n., usu. pl.); (n. pl.) knickerbockers worn by girls & women for cycling, games, etc., with or without skirt. [Mrs *B*~, American editress, who advocated the use of the costume]

bloom'er², n. (sl.). Blunder. [= *blooming* (see foll.) *error*; -ER¹]

bloom'ing, a. In vbl senses (BLOOM²); also sl., euphemistic substitute for vulgar BLOODY. [-ING²]

Blooms'bury (-zberĭ), n. Part of London containing British Museum, formerly a fashionable residential (& later a literary) quarter.

bloss'om¹, n. Flower, esp. as promising fruit; mass of flowers on fruit-tree etc. (*in* ~); early stage of growth, promise; ~-*faced*, -*nosed*, bloated. Hence ~Y², ~LESS, aa. [OE *blōstm*, -*ma*, cogn. w. MDu. *bloesem*, MLG *blosem*, *blossem* (cf. also ON *blómstr*), prob. f. *blōs*-, extended form of *blō*-; see BLOOM]

bloss'om², v.i. Open into flower (lit., & fig., as ~ *out into a statesman*). [OE *blōstmian* cf. prec]

blot¹, n. Spot of ink etc., dark patch; disfigurement, blemish (esp. *on the scutcheon*), defect; disgraceful act or quality in good character. [14th c., of unkn. orig.; cf. ON *blettr* spot, stain]

blot², v.t. & i. (-tt-). Spot with ink (~ one's *copybook*, colloq., stain one's character, commit an indiscretion); smudge; (of pen, ink) make blots; cover with worthless writing; sully, detract from, (fair fame); ~ *out*, obliterate (writing), exterminate, destroy; dry with ~*ting-paper*, absorbent paper for drying wet ink-marks (~*ting-book*, -*case*, -*pad*, arrangements of this), whence ~t'ER¹ (2) n. (*also, record, file*). [f. prec.]

blot³, n. Exposed piece in backgammon; weak point in strategy etc. [16th c., of unkn. orig., possibly f. Du. *bloot* naked, exposed]

blotch, n. Inflamed patch, boil, etc., on skin; dab of ink or colour. Hence ~ED² (-cht), ~'Y², aa. [f. 1600; excl. E, perh. compounded f. *blot* & *botch* (obs. n.), *plotch* (obs.); cf. also SPLOTCH]

blottesque' (-sk), a. & n. (Piece of painting or description) done with heavy blotted touches. [-ESQUE]

blott'o, a. (sl.). Fuddled with drink. [orig. unkn.]

blouse (-owz), n. Workman's loose linen or cotton upper garment usu. belted at waist (chiefly French); woman's loose light bodice visible only to waist, & there belted. [F, of unkn. orig.]

blow¹ (-ō), v.i. & t. (*blew* pr. blō, ~*n* & in sense 'cursed', ~*ed*). (Of wind, air, 'it') move along, act as air-current, (~ *great guns*, violent gale); send strong air-current from mouth (~ *hot & cold*, vacillate), puff, pant; make or shape (bubble, glass) by ~ing; (of whales) eject air & water; (of electr. fuse) melt when over-loaded; cause air-current by means of (~ bellows); work bellows of (organ); exhaust of breath (esp. in pass.); send out by breathing (~ air into; ~ off steam, get rid of superfluous energy); (with advv. & prepp.) drive, be driven, by ~ing (~ over, pass off; ~ in sl., come in breezily, drop in); sound (wind instrument, note or signal on or with it, or with it as subject to blow t. or i.; ~ one's own trumpet, praise oneself); direct air--current at (~ fingers, fire; ~ out, extinguish); clear by air-current (nose, egg); break in or send flying off or out or up by explosion (~ out one's brains, shoot him, or usu. oneself); ~ up, inflate, shatter or be shattered by explosion, reprove, lose one's temper, enlarge (map, print); (sl.) betray (~ the GAFF²); (of flies) deposit eggs in; (sl.) curse, confound, (I'll be ~ed if etc.; ~ the expense, spend recklessly); (sl.) squander, spend (sum) recklessly, cf. BLUE³; ~ upon, stale, discredit, tell tales of; ~ ball, seed-head of dandelion etc.; ~fly, the meat fly; ~'hole, nostril of whale etc., vent for air, smoke, etc., in tunnel etc.; ~'lamp (for directing condensed heat on a selected spot); ~'pipe, tube for heating flame by blowing air or other gas into it, tube used in glass-blowing, Amer.-Ind. dart tube. [OE blāwan, OHG blā(h)an, blājan; not otherwise recorded in Gmc]

blow² (-ō), n. Blowing, taste of fresh air; blowing of flute, one's nose, etc.; =FLY¹--blow; ~-out, burst in a pneumatic tire, (Electr.) blowing of a fuse, (sl.) abundant meal or feed; ~-up, enlargement of picture etc. [f. prec.]

blow³ (-ō), v.i. (blew pr. blŏō, ~n). Burst into, be in, flower. [OE blāwan, OS blōjan, OHG bluojan f. *blō-; see BLADE, BLOOM]

blow⁴ (-ō), n. Blossoming (in full ~ etc.). [f. prec.]

blow⁵ (-ō), n. Hard stroke with fist, instrument, etc.; disaster, shock; come to, exchange, ~s, fight; strike a ~ for, against, help, oppose; at one ~, in one operation. [f. 15th c., of unkn. orig.]

blow'er (-ōer), n. In vbl senses of BLOW¹,³; also: apparatus for increasing a fire's draught, esp. sheet of iron before grate--front; escape of gas, or fissure allowing it, in coal mine. [BLOW¹, -ER¹]

blow'y (-ōi), a. Windy, wind-swept. [BLOW¹, -Y²]

blowzed (-zd), **blowz'y** (-zi), aa. Red-faced, coarse-looking, dishevelled. [f. obs. n. blouze beggar's wench; orig. unkn.]

blüb, v.i. (-bb-; sl.). Shed tears. [short for BLUBBER³]

blübb'er¹, n. Whale fat; jelly-fish (sailor's name); weeping. [ME blober; prob. imit. (obs. meanings foaming, bubble), cf. BLEB, BUBBLE]

blübb'er², a. Swollen, protruding, (of lips). [as prec.]

blübb'er³, v.t. & i. Utter with sobs, weep noisily; wet, disfigure, swell, (face) with weeping. [as prec.]

bluchers (blōōk'erz), n. pl. Old-fashioned low boots or high shoes. [named after the Prussian Field Marshal Blücher (d. 1819)]

blüdg'eon (-ŭjn), n., & v.t. (Strike repeatedly with) heavy-headed stick. [f. 18th c., of unkn. orig.]

blue¹ (blōō), a. Of the colour between green & violet in the spectrum, coloured like the sky or deep sea (also of things much paler, darker, etc., as smoke, distant hills, moonlight, bruise; & qualified by or qualifying other colours etc., as ~-black, deep ~, NAVY ~, Prussian ~); look ~, nervous, depressed (things looked ~, depressing); ~ funk, uncontrollable fear; true ~, faithful; dressed in ~ (Foot--Guards B~); the B~ (Squadron), one of three divisions (Red, White, B~) of Navy (hist.); belonging to a particular political party, usu. Tory; (of women) learned (see BLUESTOCKING); (of talk etc.) indecent; drink till all's ~, to drunkenness. ~'bell, (Scotland & N. Eng.) light-blue-flowered Campanula growing in dry places & flowering in summer & autumn, harebell, (S. Eng.) wild hyacinth with ~ or white flower growing in moist places & flowering in spring; ~ blood, high birth; ~-book, ‖ Parliamentary or Privy-Council report, *book giving personal details of U.S. government officials; ~'bottle, ~ cornflower, meat fly or blowfly; ~-chip attrib., (St. Exch. of shares) constituting a fairly reliable investment, though less secure than gilt-edged; ‖~-coat boy, scholar in charity school, esp. Christ's Hospital; ~ devils, depression; ~-eyed boy (colloq.), pet, favourite; ~ gum, kind of eucalyptus tree; ‖~-'jacket, seaman in Navy; *~ laws, severe Puritanic laws alleged to have been in force among early colonists of Connecticut; ~ light, flare with bluish light used for signals; B~ Mantle, one of four pursuivants of College of Arms; once in a ~ moon, very rarely; ~ mould, in certain cheeses when mature; ~ murder (colloq. in intensive phrr. as like ~ murder, at top speed); B~-nose (colloq.), Nova--Scotian; ~ pencil, used in marking corrections, obliterations, etc.; ~-pencil v.t., mark etc. with a ~ pencil, make cuts in, censor; B~ Peter, ~ flag with white square, hoisted before sailing; ~ pill, mercurial & antibilious; ~ print, ~ photographic print representing final stage of engineering or other plans, (fig.) detailed plan of work to be done; ~ ribbon, ribbon of the Garter, greatest honour in any sphere, sign of teetotalism; ~ rock, kind of pigeon; ~ ruin, bad gin; ~'stocking, woman having or affecting literary tastes & learning [Blue Stocking Society (in sense 'not in full evening dress') name given to meetings about 1750 at houses of Mrs Montague etc. to talk on literature etc. instead of playing cards; blue--worsted, i.e. ordinary, stockings were worn by some of the men attending instead of black silk]; ~-*stone*, sulphate of copper; ~ *water*, open sea; ~'*throat*, kind of small bird allied to warblers; ~-*water school*, strategists regarding the fleet as sufficient defence for Gt Britain. Hence **blu'ish**[1] (2) (blōo-) a., ~'NESS (-ŏon-) n. [ME *blue, blew(e)* f. OF *bleu* f. Rom. **blāvus* f. Gmc **blǣwaz* (whence OE *blǣ-*, OHG *blao, blaw-,* ON *bldr*)]

blue[2] (blōo), n. Blue colour (*Oxford* ~, dark; *Cambridge* ~, light; *the light, dark,* ~*s,* representatives or supporters of Cambridge, Oxford, in sporting contests); ~ pigment; ~ powder used by laundresses; ~ cloth etc.; *the* sky (BOLT[1] *from the* ~); *the* sea; (pl.) *the* Royal Horseguards; *the Blues* or *Blues trot,* dance of fox-trot kind; colour, member, of a political party; ‖ one who has represented his university in athletics etc. (*win* one's ~, be chosen as representative); = BLUE[1] *stocking*; (pl.) *the* dumps; (pl.) kind of (usu. sad) song of Negro origin. [f. prec.]

blue[3] (blōo), v.t. Make blue; treat with laundress's blue; (sl.) squander (money). [f. BLUE[1]]

Blue'beard (blōo-), n. Husband of many wives. [hero of popular story, who hung up in locked chamber the bodies of his murdered wives]

bluff[1], a. With perpendicular broad front (of ship's bows, cliffs); (of person, manner) abrupt, blunt, frank, hearty. Hence ~'LY[2] adv., ~'NESS n. [17th c. naut. wd of unkn. orig.; obs. Du. *blaf,* in same senses, only in Kilian (1599)]

bluff[2], n. Headland with perpendicular broad face. [f. prec.]

bluff[3], v.t. & i. (Game of poker) impose upon (opponent) as to value of one's hand & induce him to throw up his cards; treat (political opponents or rival States) so; practise this policy. [orig. unkn.; w. earlier sense *blindfold,* goes w. foll.]

bluff[4], n. Act of bluffing (*call* person's ~, make him show his cards, also fig.); overbearing demeanour, threats designed to operate without action. [w. earlier senses *horse's blinker, excuse* (sl.), goes w. prec.]

blun'der[1], v.i. & t. Move blindly, stumble, (often *on, along*); ~ *upon,* find by fluke; make gross mistake; mismanage (a business etc.); ~ *out,* utter thoughtlessly; ~ *away,* waste by mismanagement. Hence ~ER[1] n;, ~ingLY[2] adv. [ME *blondren, blundren,* of uncert. orig.; perh. frequent. (-ER[5]) of obs. *blond (bland;* see BLEND), or f. Icel. *blonda* doze, MSw. *blundra* shut the eyes]

blun'der[2], n. Stupid or careless mistake. [prob. f. prec., but found earlier]

blun'derbüss, n. Ancient short gun with large bore firing many balls. [perverted f. Du. *donderbus* thunder gun]

blun'derhead (-hĕd), n. = DUNDERHEAD (cf. prec.)

blünge (-j), v.t. (Pottery) mix (clay, flint-powder, etc.) up with water by revolving machinery. [after *plunge, blend*]

blunt[1], a. & n. **1.** Dull, not sensitive; without edge or point; plain-spoken; hence ~'ISH[1] (2) a. **2.** n. Short thick needle; (sl.) ready money. [ME *blunt,* orig. unkn.]

blunt[2], v.t. Make less sharp or sensitive. [f. prec.]

blunt'lУ, adv. Obtusely (shaped etc.); rudely, curtly. [-LY[2]]

blunt'ness, n. Dullness of point or edge; outspokenness. [-NESS]

blur[1], n. Smear of ink etc.; dimness, confused effect. [16th c.; orig. & relation to vb uncert.]

blur[2], v.t. & i. (-rr-). Smear (clear writing etc.) with ink etc.; sully, disfigure; make indistinct; efface; dim (perception etc.). [see prec.]

blurb, n. Publisher's (usu. eulogistic) description of book printed on jacket or in advertisements elsewhere. [orig. U.S. sl.]

blurt, v.t. Burst *out* with, utter abruptly. [imit. after *blow, spurt,* etc.]

blush[1], v.i. Become red (in the face; also with *face* etc. as subj.) with shame or other emotion (*at* sight or word, *with* or *for* joy or shame, *for* another); be ashamed (~ *to own* etc.); be red, pink. Hence ~'ingLY[2] adv. [ME *blusche, blysche* f. OE *blyscan,* cf. MLG *bloschen,* LG *blüsken;* cf. also OE *-blysian* MDu. *blōzen*]

blush[2], n. Glance, glimpse, (*at the first* ~, prima facie); reddening of face in shame etc. (*put to the* ~); rosy glow, flush of light; ~-, pink, rosy, (~-*rose,* ~-*tint,* etc.). [f. prec.]

blus'ter[1], v.i. & t. Storm boisterously (of wind, waves, persons); (trans. with *out, forth*) utter overbearingly; (refl.) storm (one*self*) *into* (anger etc.). Hence ~ER[1] n., ~ingLY[2] adv. [c. 1500; imit., as on *blow, blast,* etc.]

blus'ter[2], n. Boisterous blowing, noisy self-asserting talk, threats. Hence ~OUS, ~Y[2], aa. [f. prec.]

bō[1], **boh** (bō), int. used to startle (*can't say bo to a goose,* of shy or timid person).

*bō[2], n. (Hailing word corresponding to) mate, old chap. [orig. unkn.]

bō'a, n. S.-Amer. kinds of large non--poisonous snakes killing by compression (pop. extended to Old-World pythons; so also ~ *constrictor,* prop. a Brazilian species of ~); lady's long fur or feather throat-wrap. [L *boa* (Pliny)]

Bōaner'gēs (-z), n. Loud-voiced preacher or orator. [Gk, f. Heb. *b'ney regesh* sons of thunder (*Mark* iii. 17)]

boar (bōr), n. Male uncastrated pig; its flesh; ~'s *head*, esp. as dish at Christmas or on festive occasion. [OE *bār*, OS *bērswīn*, OHG *bēr* (G *bär*) f. WG **bair-*, ult. orig. unkn.]

board[1] (bōrd), n. 1. Long thin usu. narrow piece of sawn timber (strictly, over 4 in. broad, under 2½ thick); wooden slab (of one or more breadths of ~ bare or covered with leather etc.) used for various purposes, as in games, for posting notices, etc.; (pl.) the stage (*on the* ~*s*, employed as actor); (also *straw*-~) thick stiff paper used in bookbinding (covered with paper, 'in ~*s*', or cloth, 'cloth ~*s*'), & for other purposes. 2. Table (only in spec. senses or contexts); *above* ~, *open-*(ly); *sweep the* ~, take all the cards or stakes; table spread for meals (*bed & ~*, conjugal relations; *groaning* ~, plentiful meal); food served, daily meals provided at contract price or in return for services (~*money*, -*wages*, servant's pay in lieu of food; esp. ~ *& lodging*); council-table, councillors, committee; ‖*B*~ *of Trade*, *B*~ *of Customs and Excise*, *B*~ *of Inland Revenue*, government departments; ~*-school* (before 1902), managed by ~ according to Elementary Education Act of 1870. 3. Ship's side (only in spec. phrases, cf. *over*~), *go by the* ~, (of masts etc.) fall over~, also fig., *on* ~ ∎ ABOARD (in various senses), usu. now **on** or into ship (orig. meaning within the **sides**, not on the deck), train, coach, etc. 4. Tack (naut.). [OE *bord* combined two distinct Gmc words meaning (1) board (2) border, respectively f. Gmc *bordham & *bordhaz; the second was adopted in Romanic, &, thr. F, influenced the ME sense-development]

board[2] (bōrd), v.t. & i. 1. (f. prec.=wood) cover with boards (~ *up*, close with ~*s*). 2. (f. prec. = table) provide (lodger or daily guest) with, receive, stated meals at fixed rate; examine before a medical board (~*-out* v.t., invalid out of army etc.); ~ *with*, be entertained for pay in the house of. 3. (f. prec. = ship's side) come alongside (usu. to attack); force one's way on board (ship or abs.); embark on. 4. (Of ship) tack. [f. prec., with influence of F *aborder*]

board'er (bōr-), n. One who boards with someone (prec. 2), esp. boy or girl at boarding-school (opp. *day-boy*, -*girl*). [prec. + -ER[1]]

board'ing (bōr-), n. In vbl senses; also or esp.: erection of boards; ~*-house*, -*school*, in which persons, boys, board (BOARD[1,] 2); ‖~*-out*, (intr.) feeding elsewhere than at home, (trans.) placing (destitute children) in families; ~*-ship* (examining neutrals for contraband). [BOARD[1,2] + -ING[1]]

boast[1], n. Vainglorious statement; self--exaltation in words; fact one is proud of; *make* ~ *of*, announce proudly. Hence ~'FUL a., ~'FULLY[2] adv., ~'FULNESS n.

[ME *bost* n., *bosten* vb; mutual relation & orig. unkn.]

boast[2], v.i. & t. Extol oneself (also refl.), brag *of* or *about*; vaunt, brag of, brag *that*; possess as thing to be proud of. Hence ~'ER[1] n. [see prec.]

boat[1], n. Small open oared or sailing vessel, fishing-vessel, mail packet, or small steamer (*take* ~, embark; *have an oar in everyone's* ~, of busybodies; *in the same* ~, with like risks etc.); ~-shaped utensil for sauce etc.; ~*-hook*, long pole with hook & spike; ~*-house*, shed at water's edge for keeping ~; *ship's* ~, carried on board ship; ~ *train*, timed to catch or meet ship; ~*-fly*, water-bug swimming on water on its back; ~*-man*, hirer-out or rower or sailer of ~ for hire; ~*-bill*, S.-Amer. heron; ~*-race*, between rowing ~*s*; ~*-swain* (bō'sn), *bō's'n*, *bō'sun*, ship's officer in charge of sails, rigging, etc., & summoning men to duty with whistle [late OE *bātswegen*, cf. Icel. *sveinn* & see SWAIN]. Hence ~'AGE (4), ~'FUL (2), nn. [OE *bāt*, corr. to ON *beit* (ON *bátr* is f. OE), f. Gmc. **bail-* not otherwise represented; borrowed in other Gmc langg. f. these, & possibly in Rom. also (F *bateau* etc.)]

boat[2], v.i. & t. Go in a boat, amuse oneself so (~*ing man*); place, carry, in a boat. Hence ~'ER[1] n., hard straw hat (as worn in ~*ing*). [f. prec.]

bob[1], n., & v.t. (-bb-). Weight on pendulum, plumb-line, or kite-tail; knot of hair, tassel-shaped curl (~*-wig*, also ~, with short curls, opp. to full-bottomed; cf. CHERRY-*bob*); horse's docked tail; bunch of lob-worms; (Metre) short line at end of stanza; (vb) cut (woman's hair) to hang short of shoulders (*wear it* ~*bed*), (n.) ~bed hair. [f. 14th c.; orig. unkn.]

bob[2], v.i. (-bb-). Fish (*for* eels) with bunch (cf. prec.) of lob-worms.

bob[3], v.i. (-bb-). Move up & down, dance, rebound; ~ *up like a cork*, become active or conspicuous again after defeat; catch with the mouth (*for* cherries etc. floating or hanging); curtsy. [f. 14th c.; app. imit.]

bob[4], n. Jerk, bounding movement; curtsy; (Bellringing) kinds of change in long peals (*treble* ~ in which treble bell has a dodging course, ~ *minor* on 6 bells, *triple* on 7, *major* on 8, *royal* on 10, *maximis* on 12). [f. prec.]

‖ **bob**[5], n. *Dry*, *wet*,- ~, cricketing, boating, Etonian; *light*-~, soldier of light infantry. [prob. = *Robert*]

‖ **bob**[6], n. (sl.; pl. same). Shilling. [quoted f. 1812; orig. unkn.]

bob[7], v.t. (-bb-). Rap, jerk. [ME *boben*; orig. unkn.]

Bŏb'adil, n. Braggart. [Jonson, *Every Man in his Humour*]

bŏb'bery, n. & a. 1. Disturbance, row, fuss. 2. adj. Noisy, troublesome, skittish, (~ *pack*, scratch pack of hounds &

dogs of various breeds, usu. for hunting jackals). [Hind. *bap re* O father! int. of dismay]

bŏbb′in, n. Cylinder for holding thread, yarn, wire, etc., & giving it off as wanted, reel, spool; small bar & string for raising door-latch. [f. F *bobine*]

bŏbb′inĕt, n. Machine-made cotton net imitating lace made with bobbins on pillow. [prec., *net*]

bŏbb′ish, a. (sl.). Brisk, well, (esp. *pretty* ~). [BOB³ + -ISH¹]

‖ **bŏbb′y**, n. (sl.). Policeman. [as BOB⁵ + -Y³ (Sir *Robert* Peel, Home Sec. 1828)]

*•**bŏbb′y-sŏx**, n. pl. Short socks covering ankle. Hence ~ER¹(3) n., adolescent girl, esp. in early teens, wearing ~. [orig. unkn.]

*•**bŏb′căt**, n. American lynx. [BOB¹ (from shortness of tail)]

bŏb′olink, n. N.-Amer. songbird. [orig. *Bob* (o') *Lincoln*; imit.]

bŏb′-slĕd, -sleigh (slā), n. Two short sleighs coupled, used for drawing logs, & in tobogganing. [U.S. & Canadian wd, now also Anglo-Swiss]

bŏb′stay, n. Rope holding bowsprit down. [f. BOB (uncert. in what sense) + STAY²]

bŏb′tail, n. & a. Docked tail; with this; horse or dog with this; *ragtag* (or *tagrag*) *& ~*, the rabble. [BOB¹]

Bŏche (-sh), n. & a. (sl.). (Contempt. for) German. [F, perh. abbr. of *Alboche* (*Allemand* German & *-boche* substituted in contempt for other endings)]

bŏck, n. Strong dark-coloured German beer; (loosely) a glass of (any) beer. [F, f. G *bock* (in full *bockbier* f. *Einbecker bier* f. *Einbeck* in Hanover]

bŏde, v.t. & i. Foresee, foretell, (evil); portend, foreshow; promise *well* or *ill*. Hence **bŏd′ingLY²** adv., ~′MENT (-dm-) n. [OE *bodian* f. *boda* messenger.]

bŏde′ful (-df-), a. Ominous. [mod. formation f. prec. or obs. n. *bode* omen + -FUL(1)]

bodēg′a, n. Cellar or shop selling wine. [Sp., f. L f. Gk *apothēkē* see APOTHECARY]

bŏd′ice, n. Close-fitting upper part of woman's dress, down to waist; also, inner vest over stays. [orig. *pair of bodies* (cf. pair of stays), being a whalebone corset; now spelt & understood as sing.; cf. BAIZE]

bŏd′ied (-dĭd), a. Possessed of body or a body, embodied; esp. in comb., as *full-~*, *able-~*. [BODY¹ + -ED²]

bŏd′ilĕss, a. Incorporeal; separated from the body. [-LESS]

bŏd′ily¹, a. Of, affecting, the human body or physical nature; ~ *fear*, of physical harm. [BODY¹ + -LY¹]

bŏd′ily², adv. In the body, in person; with the whole bulk, as a whole. [BODY¹, -LY²]

bŏd′kin, n. Pointless thick needle with large eye for drawing tape etc. through hem; long pin for fastening hair; dagger;

person squeezed between two others (*ride, sit, ~*). [ME *boidekyn* etc.; orig. unkn.]

Bŏdleian (-lē′an), a. & n. The ~ (*library*), (also, colloq., *Bodley*) the Oxford University Library, founded by Sir Thomas Bodley (d. 1613). [-IAN]

bŏd′y¹, n. **1.** Man or animal as material organism (*keep ~ & soul together*, remain alive); corpse (*~-snatcher*, exhumer of corpses for dissection); *~ of Christ*, sacramental bread; *~-servant*, valet; *~-guard*, (rarely, member of) dignitary's retinue, escort, personal guard. **2.** Trunk, main portion (stem, hull, nave, etc., acc. to context); upper garment (minus sleeves & collar, or = bodice); document minus preamble etc.; majority. **3.** Human being, person, (*heir of* one's ~, *good sort of~, any ~*, etc.); *~-line bowling* (Cricket), fast bowling delivered persistently on the leg side. **4.** Aggregate of persons or things (*in a ~*, all together; ~ *politic*, State); society, league, military force; collection of precepts, information, etc. **5.** Piece of matter (*heavenly ~*, sun, star, etc.), quantity; comparative solidity or substantial character (*~-colour*, opaque; *wine of good ~*), thing perceptible to senses. [OE *bodig*, corresp. to OHG *potah, botah* (Bav. dial. *bottech*); orig. unkn.]

bŏd′y², v.t. **1.** Provide with body (rare). **2.** (Usu. with *forth*) give mental shape to; exhibit in outward shape; typify. [f. prec.]

Boeotian (bēō′shn), a. & n. Crass, dull, (person). [of Gk nation derided by Athenians]

Bō′er (or boor), n. & a. (Of) Dutch or Dutch-descended S.-African(s). [Du., see BOOR]

bŏff′in, n. (sl.). Man engaged in research, scientist. [orig. unkn.]

Bŏf′ors ·(-orz), n. ~ (*gun*), light anti--aircraft gun. [~ in Sweden]

bŏg¹, n. (Piece of) wet spongy ground, morass (in many plant names as ~ *violet*, BUTTERwort, *~-berry*, cranberry); *~ butter*, fatty hydrocarbon found in Irish peat-~; ~ *oak*, ancient preserved in black state in peat; *~-trotter*, Irishman. Hence ~g′Y² (-g-) a., ~g′INESS (-g-) n. [16th c., f. Ir. or Gael. *bogach* (*bog* soft)]

bŏg², v.t. (-gg-). Submerge in bog (usu. in pass.).

bŏg′ey (-gĭ), **Colonel Bogey**, n. Score that good golf-player should do hole or course in. [f. BOGY as imaginary person?]

bŏg′gle, v.i. Start with fright, shy; hesitate, demur, *at* or *about*; equivocate; fumble. [var. of BOGLE used as vb]

‖ **bŏg′ie** (-gĭ), n. Under-carriage with two or more wheel-pairs, pivoted below end of locomotive or railway-car; *~-car* etc., fitted on these. [northern dial. ~wd of unkn. orig.]

bō′gle, n. Phantom, goblin; bugbear; scarecrow. [Sc. since 1500; cf. 16th c. (obs.) *bog*, north. *boggard*, ME *bugge* (BUGBEAR), but mutual relations & orig. unkn.]

bŏg′us, a. Sham, fictitious. [U.S. wd, orig. unkn.]

bŏg′y̆, -gey, (-gĭ), n. (pl. -*ies*, -*eys*). The devil; goblin (nursery, *the ~ man*); bugbear. [early 19th c., perh. southern var. of BOGLE]

bōhea′ (-hē), n. Black tea of lowest quality (last crop of season). [f. Chin. *Wu-i* name of district]

Bōhēm′ian, a. & n. **1.** (Native) of Bohemia, a former kingdom now part of Czechoslovakia, Czech. **2.** Socially & unconventional (person); of free-&-easy habits, manners, & sometimes morals (esp. of artists etc.). Hence **bōhēm′ianISM** (2) n., **bōhēm′ianIZE** (4) v.i. [f. F *bohémien* gipsy]

boil¹, n. Hard inflamed suppurating tumour. [OE *býl*, *býle* (whence dial. *bile*), OS *bûla*, OHG *bûlla* (G *beule*) f. WG **bûljā̆* f. **bûl*-; mod. *boil* f. 16th c.]

boil², v.t. & i. Bubble up, undulate, (of liquid at the heat that converts it to gas; also of containing vessel); ~ *over* (of liquid or vessel), overflow or be overflowed thus; seethe, be agitated, like boiling water or its vessel (of sea etc., feelings, feeling person); bring (liquid, vessel) to heat at which it boils; subject to heat of ~ing water, cook thus; undergo cookery by ~ing; ~ *down*, *away*, reduce, convert to vapour, by ~ing; *keep the pot* ~*ing*, get a living; ~*ing hot*, ~ing, (colloq.) very hot; *blood* ~s, with indignation; ~*ed shirt* (sl.), cotton or linen shirt with starched front. [ME *boille* f. OF *boillir* f. L *bullire* (*bulla* bubble)]

boil³, n. = boiling, boiling-point, (esp. *on, at, to, the* ~). [f. prec.]

boil′er, n. One who boils; vessel for boiling, esp. large vessel of riveted wrought-iron plates for making steam in engine; tank attached to kitchen range; laundry vessel; vegetable etc. suited to boiling; ~*-iron*, *-plate*, rolled iron ¼ to ½ in. thick; ~*-tube*, internal air-pipe carrying heat through ~. [-ER¹]

boil′ing, n. In vbl senses; esp.: *the whole* ~ (sl.), all the lot; ~*-point*, temperature at which anything boils (water at sea-level, 212° F., 100° C.), high excitement. [-ING¹]

bois′terous, a. Violent, rough, (wind, sea, behaviour, speech, persons); noisily cheerful. Hence ~LY² adv. [16th c. var. of ME (obs.) *boistous*, prob. thr. the later form *boisteous*, -*uous*, of unkn. orig.; deriv. f. AF *boistous*, OF -*eus* lame is semantically impossible]

‖ **bŏk′ō**, n. (sl.). Nose. [orig. unkn.]

bōl′as, n. (sing. & pl.). S.-Amer. missile consisting of balls connected by a strong cord (when thrown bringing down quarry by entangling limbs). [Sp., pl. of *bola*

bōld, a. Courageous, enterprising, confident; *make* (*so*) ~ (*as*), presume, venture (*to* do); forward, immodest; vigorous, free, well-marked, clear, (imagination, drawing, description, features, headland, etc.); (of type, also ~*-faced*) having a heavy or conspicuous face. Hence ~′LY² adv., ~′NESS n. [OE, OS, OHG *bald* (G *bald* soon), ON *ballr* f. Gmc **balthaz*; cf. Goth. *balthei* ~ness]

bōle, n. Stem, trunk. [ME, f. ON *bolr* cf. G *bohle* plank]

bolĕc′tion, a. & n. (Moulding) raised above panel etc. [orig. unkn.]

boler′o (-ār′ō), n. Spanish dance; (freq. pr. bŏl′erō) woman's short jacket with or without sleeves resembling zouave jacket. [Sp.]

bŏl′ide, n. Large meteor, fire-ball. [F, f. L f. Gk *bolis -idos* (*ballō* throw)]

bŏll, n. Rounded seed-vessel, as in flax or cotton; ~*-weevil*, small destructive insect infesting cotton-plant. [f. MDu. *bolle*; see BOWL¹]

bŏll′ard, n. Post on ship or quay for securing ropes to; post on traffic island. [ME *bollarde* (c. 1300) f. ON *bolr* BOLE + -ARD]

bolŏm′eter, n. Radiation-measurer. [Gk *bolē* ray + -o- + -METER]

*bolŏn′ey, n. (sl.). Humbug, nonsense, trash. [orig. unkn.]

Bŏl′shĕv|ik, n. Advocate of proletarian dictatorship in Russia by soviets, Russian communist; (pop.) any revolutionary. Hence ~ISM n., ~IST n. & a., **Bŏl′shy̆** (sl.) n. & a. [f. Russ. *bolsheviki* n. pl. majority within the party]

bōl′ster¹, n. Long stuffed (esp. under-) pillow of bed or couch; pad or support in many machines & instruments. [OE *bolster*, OHG *bolstar*, ON *bolstr* f. Gmc **bolstraz* f. **bûl*- swell]

bōl′ster², v.t. & i. (Usu. with *up*) support with bolster, prop, aid & abet, countenance, preserve from (merited) destruction; pad; (with schoolboys) belabour with bolster, (intr.) have bolster-fight. [f. prec.]

bōlt¹, n. Short heavy arrow of crossbow, quarrel, (*my* ~ *is shot*, I have done all I can); discharge of lightning (~ *from the blue*, complete surprise); door-fastening of sliding bar & staple, sliding piece of lock; headed metal pin for holding things together, usu. riveted or with nut; (as measure) roll of canvas etc., bundle of osiers; ~*-line*, *-position*, (Mil.) defensive position at angle to main position to prevent a successful attack on some point of the main position from spreading farther; ~*-rope* (round sail-edge to prevent tearing). [OE *bolt*, MLG *bolte*, OHG *bolz*, ult. orig. unkn.]

bōlt², v.i. & t. Dart off or away, (of horse) break from control; gulp down unchewed; fasten (door etc.) with bolt, ~ *in* or *out*, shut in, exclude, by ~ing door; fasten together with bolts; *(Pol.) break away from (one's party), refuse to support one's party or a policy. [f. prec.]

bŏlt[3], n. Sudden start; running away. [f. prec.]

bŏlt[1], adv. (With *upright*) = as a bolt, quite. [f. L *bonus*]

bŏlt[5], boult (bōlt), v.t. Sift; investigate. [ME *bull(e)* f. OF *buller*, *buleter*, thr. *bureter* = It. *burattare*, of unkn. orig.]

bŏl'ter, n. In vbl senses of BOLT[2, 5]; esp.: horse given to bolting; (also *boulter*) sieve, sifting machine. [-ER[1]]

bŏl'us, n. Large pill. [mod. L, f. Gk *bōlos* clod]

bōm'a, n. (Central Africa). Defensible enclosure; police or military post; magistrate's office. [Swahili]

bomb (-ŏm), n., & v.t. & i. 1. A high-explosive or incendiary or smoke or gas etc. projectile fired from a mortar, or thrown or deposited by hand, or dropped from an aeroplane, & exploded by percussion or by time mechanism; ATOMIC, FLYING, ~; ~-*bay*, compartment in aircraft for holding ~s; ~-*disposal*, removal & detonation of unexploded & delayed-action ~s; ~-*load*, weight of ~s carried by aircraft; ~-*proof*, (shelter) strong enough to resist ~s; ~-*shell*, artillery ~ (now usu. *shell* exc. in similes, as *fell like a* ~-*shell* etc.); ~-*sight*, device in aircraft for aiming ~s. 2. v.t. & i. Assail with ~s, throw ~s; ~ *out*, drive by ~s out of a building etc.; ~ *up*, load (aircraft) with ~s. Hence ~'ER[1] (-mer) n., soldier trained in, aircraft used for, ~ing (also attrib., as *Bomber Command*). [f. F *bombe* f. It. *bomba* f. L f. Gk *bombos* hum]

bŏmbărd', v.t. Batter with shot & shell (esp. of warships attacking town); (Phys.) subject (atoms etc.) to a stream of high-speed particles; (fig.) assail persistently with abuse, argument, etc. Hence ~MENT n. [f. F *bombarder* f. *bombarde* f. med. L *bombarda* stone-throwing engine prob. f. L *bombus* hum]

bŏmbardier' (or bŭm-), n. 1. ‖ Artillery non-commissioned officer below sergeant. 2. *Bomb-aimer in aircraft. [F, see prec. & -IER]

bŏm'bardon, n. Low-pitched brass instrument or organ stop imitating this. [It. (-one), f. *bombardo* + -one, see BOMBARD, -OON]

bom'basine (-ŏm- or -ŭm-; -zĕn), n. Twilled dress-material of worsted with silk, with cotton, or alone, much used for mourning. [f. F *bombasin* f. LL *bombycinus* silken (*bombyx -ycis* silk or silk-worm f. Gk *bombux*)]

bŏm'bast, n. Turgid language, tall talk. Hence **bombăs'TIC** a., **bombăs'TICALLY** adv. [alt. f. earlier *bombace* f. F f. LL *bombacem* alt. f. *bombyx* see prec.]

Bom'bay duck, n. Small fish of S.-Asian coasts, eaten dried with curry. [corrupt. of *bombil*, see BUMMALO]

bombe (bawn̄b), n. (cookery). Any cone-shaped dish or confection, as *apricot, fish*, ~. [F]

bon, bonne, (F; see Ap.), a. French for *good*, common in some senses & phrases. [f. L *bonus*]

bŏn'a fid'ĕ, a. & adv. Genuine(ly), sincere(ly). [L abl. s. of foll.; as adj. it may be hyphened, not as adv.]

bŏn'a fid'ēs, n. (legal). Honest intention, sincerity. [L,=good faith; not hyphened]

bonăn'za, n. & a. (Prop.) prosperity, good luck; (pop.) greatly prospering, a large output (esp. of mines), worked with all best appliances (*a* ~ *farm*), a run of luck (*in* ~). [U.S. f. Sp., = fair weather f. L *bonus* good]

bon-bon (see Ap.), n. Sweetmeat. [BON]

‖ **bŏnce**, n. Large playing-marble. [orig. unkn.]

bŏnd[1], n. Thing restraining bodily freedom, imprisonment, (rare, only in pl., esp. *in*~s); faggot-withe; restraining or uniting force; binding engagement, agreement; deed by which A binds himself & his heirs etc. to pay a sum to B & his; government's or public company's documentary promise to pay borrowed money, debenture, (~'*holder*, person holding such document); (Sc.) mortgage; (Customs, of goods) *in* ~, stored under charge of Customs in 'bonded warehouse' till importer pays duty (*take out of* ~); (Bricklaying) various methods (*English* ~, *Flemish* ~, etc.) of holding wall together by making bricks overlap; ~ (*paper*), superior kind of writing-paper (suitable for ~s & similar documents); ~-*stone*, stone or brick running through wall. [ME var. of BAND[1]]

bŏnd[2], v.t. Bind together (bricks etc., see prec.), put customable goods into bond (see prec.), whence ~'ER[1] n., person who puts goods into bond, binding stone or brick; encumber with bonded debt (see BONDED). [f. prec.]

bŏnd[3], n. League, confederation. [Du.]

bŏnd[4], a. In slavery, not free, (arch.). Hence ~'*man*, ~'*maid*, ~'*servant*, ~'*service*, ~'*slave*, nn. [adj. use of ME *bonde* f. OE *bonda, bunda* husbandman f. ON *bóndi* = *bóandi*, part. of *búa, bóa* dwell; later infl. by BOND[1]]

bŏn'dage, n. Serfdom, slavery; confinement; subjection to constraint, influence, obligation, etc. [ME f. AF, or f. AL *bondagium*; see prec. & -AGE]

bŏnd'ĕd, a. (Of goods) placed in bond, (of warehouse) for such goods, (BOND[2]); (of debt) secured by bonds (BOND[1]). [BOND[1], -ED[2]]

bŏnds'man, n. Villein, serf; slave (lit. & fig.). [var. of *bondman* (BOND[4]) as though f. *bond's* genit. of BOND[1]]

Bŏnd Street, n. A London street, esp. as

resort of fashionable loungers (a ~ *exquisite*).

bōne¹, n. One of the parts making up vertebrate animal's skeleton; (pl.) the body (*my old ~s* etc.), its remains (*his ~s were laid*); the body's hard, solid, or essential part (*flesh & ~*; *skin & ~*, thin person; *horse with plenty of ~*, well developed frame; *bred in the ~*, ineradicable; *to the ~*, penetrating, of cold, wound, etc.); material of which ~s consist; similar substance, as ivory, dentine, whalebone; thing made of ~, as (pl.) dice, castanets, stay-ribs; a small or nearly finished joint of meat (*knuckle-~*, *broiled ~s*); subject of dispute (~ *of contention*, ~ *to pick with someone*); *make no ~s of*, *about*, *or to*, not hesitate; *will never make old ~s*, live long; *feel in* one's ~*s*, be quite sure; ~*-dry*, quite dry, (of country etc.) teetotal; ~*-head* (sl.), blockhead; ~*-idle*, *-lazy*, utterly idle or lazy; ~*-meal*, crushed or ground ~s used esp. as fertilizer; ~*-setter*, one who sets broken or dislocated bones, esp. without being qualified surgeon; ~*-shaker*, bicycle without rubber tires; ~*-spavin*, callous growth in horse's leg becoming as hard as ~. [OE *bān*, OS *bēn*, OHG, ON *bein* f. Gmc *bainam*]

bōne², v.t. **1.** Take out the bones from (meat, fish). **2.** (sl.). Steal. [1 f. prec., & perh. 2 (as dog makes off with bone)]

bōne³, v.t. (surv.). Take or test the level of (usu. as part.); *boning rod*, wooden rod used in levelling operations. [orig. unkn.].

bōne'fīre, n. Large open-air fire in celebration of some event; fire for consuming rubbish (*make a ~ of*, destroy). [earlier *bonefire* f. BONE n., bones being the chief material formerly used]

bŏn'gō (-ngg-), n. Large striped African antelope. [native]

bonhomie (bŏn'omē), n. Geniality. [F, f. *bonhomme* good fellow + *-ie*=-Y¹]

Bŏn'ifāce, n. Innkeeper. [Farquhar, *Beaux' Stratagem* (1707)]

bŏn'jism, n. Doctrine that the world is good, but not the best possible. So ~IST (2) n. [f. L *bonus* good + -ISM, after OPTIMISM of which it is the positive form]

bŏnit'ō (-ē-), n. (Kinds of) large mackerel-shaped fish, the striped tunny. [Sp.]

bon mot (bawn mō), n. (pl. *bons mots*), Witty saying. [F]

bŏnne, n. (French) nursemaid, maid. [BON]

bŏnne bouche (-ōōsh), n. Titbit, esp. to end up with. [F (BON, *bouche* mouth)]

bonnes fortunes (see Ap.), n. Ladies' favours, as a thing to boast of or pride oneself on. [F]

bŏnn'et¹, n. (Man's) Scotch cap; woman's outdoor head-dress without brim, with strings, & covering no part of forehead; ~ *rouge* (F, *pr.* bŏnă rōōzh), red cap as revolutionary symbol; (Naut.) additional

canvas laced to sail-foot; cowl of chimney etc., protective cap in various machines, ‖ hinged cover over motor of car; (Gaming, Auctions, etc.) accomplice, decoy; BEE *in ~*, an obsession; ~*-laird* (Sc.), petty landowner (who wore a ~, & not the hat of the gentry). Hence ~ED² a. [ME, f. OF *bonet* short for *chapel de ~* cap of (med. L) *bon(n)etus* some kind of material]

bŏnn'et², v.t. Put bonnet on (person); crush down hat over the eyes of (person). [f. prec.]

bŏnn'ȳ, a. (chiefly Sc.). Comely, healthy--looking; satisfactory. Hence ~ILY² adv. [orig. unkn.; perh. f. BON]

bŏn'spiel, n. (Sc.). Curling-match (usu. between clubs). [perh. f. Du. *bond* league, *spel* game]

bon ton (see Ap.), n. Good breeding, the fashionable world, (arch.). [F]

bŏn'us, n. Something to the good, into the bargain; esp. extra dividend to shareholders of company, distribution of profits to insurance-policy-holders, gratuity to workmen beyond their wages. [jocular or ignorant use of L *bonus* good (thing)]

bon vivant (see Ap.), n. Gourmand. [F]

bŏn'ȳ, a. Of, like, bone(s); big-boned; with little flesh. [BONE¹+-Y²]

bŏnze, n. Japanese or Chinese Buddhist priest. [F, f. Port. *bonzo* perh. f. Jap. *bonzō* f. Chin. *fan seng* religious person]

bŏn'zer, a. (Austral. sl.). Excellent, first-rate. [perh. f. BONANZA]

bōō, int., n., & v.t. & i. (Make) sound of disapproval or contempt; hoot (speaker, announcement, etc.). [imit. of cow's lowing]

bōōb, n. Simpleton. [contr. of foll.]

bōōb'ȳ, n. Silly dull-witted fool, lout; kinds of gannet; ~ *prize*, awarded to the last or lowest scorer in a contest of any kind; ~ *trap*, things placed on top of door ajar to fall on first opener, (Mil.) kinds of apparently harmless device concealing an explosive charge designed to go off when tampered with; ~*-trap* v.t. Hence ~ISH¹ a. [prob. f. Sp. *bobo* (both fool & bird) f. L *balbus* stammering]

bōō'dle, n. Crowd, pack, lot, (*the whole ~* or *caboodle*); money for political bribery etc.; a card-game. [now U.S.; 17th c. f. Du. *boedel* possessions, *the whole ~* = Du. *de heele boedel*, LG *de ganze bōdel*; cf. CABOODLE]

bōō'gie-wōō'gie (-gi-), n. Style of playing blues on the piano marked by a persistent bass rhythm. [orig. unkn.]

bōōhōō', n., & v.i. (Make) sound of noisy weeping. [imit.]

bōōk¹, n. **1.** Portable written or printed treatise filling a number of sheets fastened together (forming roll, or usu. with sheets sewn or pasted hingewise & enclosed in cover); literary composition that would fill such a set of sheets (or several) if printed; (fig.) anything from which one may learn, also imaginary record, list, etc., (~ *of fate*; ~ *of life*, list of those who shall be saved); the Bible (esp. *swear on the* ~); main division of literary work (*Bk I* etc.), or of Bible (*B~ of Genesis*); = LIBRETTO; back-hinged set of blank sheets for writing accounts, notes, exercises, etc., in (pl., merchant's accounts): (Turf) one's bets on a race or at a meeting (*won't suit my* ~, transf., is inconvenient); set of tickets, stamps, cheques, tricks at cards, etc., bound up or collected. 2. ~ *of reference*, not read continuously but used intermittently for information; *speak like a* ~, in formal phrases, *by the* ~, with correct information; *take a leaf out of* ——*'s* ~, imitate him; *without* ~, without authority, from memory; *on the* ~s, entered in list of members etc. (so *take* one's *name off the* ~s); *in* ——*'s bad* or *black, good,* ~s, in disfavour or favour with him; *bring to* ~, call to account. 3. ~*'binder, -ding*, binder, binding, of ~s; ~*'case* (-k-k-), case containing ~shelves; ~ *ends*, pair of ornamental props used to keep a row of unshelved ~s upright; ~*-keeper, -ping*, one who keeps, art of keeping, the accounts of a merchant, public office, etc.; ~*-learning* or *-lore, -learnĕd*, mere theory, knowing ~s but not life, so ~'ISH[1] a., ~'ISHLY[2] adv., ~'ISHNESS n.; ~*-maker, -king*, compiler, compiling, of ~s (esp. for mercenary motives), also professional betting man or ~*'ie* [-Y[3]] n., his profession; ~*'man*, literary man; ~*-mark(er)*, thing to keep place in ~; ~*-muslin*, fine kind folded in ~like way when sold; ~*-plate*, label with owner's name, crest, etc., for pasting into ~s; ~*-rest*, adjustable support for ~ on table; ~*'seller*; ~*'slide*, expanding stand for a few ~s; ‖~*'stall* (of ~s exposed for sale out of doors);~~ *token*, voucher for a sum of money to buy ~(s); ~ *value*, value of a commodity as entered in a firm's ~s (opp. *market value*); ~*-work*, study of rules or text~s (opp. to working sums, chemical analysis, etc.); ~*'worm*, maggot eating its way through~s, person devoted to reading. Hence ~*'LET* n. [OE, OS *bōc*, OHG *buoh*, ON *bók*, Goth. *bokos* (pl.) f. Gmc **bōk-*, usu. identified w. BEECH]

book[2], v.t. Enter in book or list; engage (seat etc.) by previous payment, (guest, supporter, etc.) for some occasion; enter name of (person engaging seat etc.), issue railway ticket to; ‖ take railway ticket; give, take down, address of (goods to be transmitted); *I'm* ~*ed*, caught, cannot escape; ‖~*ing-clerk, -office*, person, place, for buying tickets from. [OE *bōcian* f. prec.]

book'land, n. (hist.). Part of common land granted by charter (under the sovereign's orders) to a private owner. [OE *bōcland*, f. *bōc* document]

boom[1], n. Long spar with one end attached stretching sail-foot; floating barrier of timber across river or harbour mouth. [Du., = BEAM]

boom[2], v.i. & n. (Make) deep resonant sound; hum, buzz; (make) bittern's cry. [imit.]

boom[3], v.t. & i., & n. (Show) sudden activity, development, (esp. of commercial ventures, prices, etc., cf. SLUMP); (win) sudden popularity for (an' invention, cause, etc.) by advertising etc., launch with éclat. [U.S. wd, perh. f. prec. (cf. *make things hum*)]

boom'er, n. Large male kangaroo; (trappers' name for) N.-Amer. mountain beaver. [orig. unkn.]

boom'erang, n., & v.i. 1. Australian curved hardwood missile with convex edge returning to its thrower; (fig.) argument or proposal that recoils on its author. 2. v.i. Act as a ~, recoil. [native name, perh. modified]

boon[1], n. Request, thing asked for; favour, gift; blessing, advantage. [f. ON *bón*=OE *bēn* prayer f. Gmc **bōniz* of unkn. orig.; the change f. prayer to gift prob. helped by confusion with foll.]

boon[2], a. Bounteous, benign, (poet.: of nature, air, life, etc.); congenial, jolly, (~ *companion*). [f. BON; from 14th c.]

boor, n. Peasant; clumsy or ill-bred fellow. Hence ~'ISH[1] a., ~'ISHLY[2] adv., ~'ISHNESS n. [f. LG *būr* or Du. *boer* peasant; cf. BOWER[1]]

boost, v.t., & n. 1. (colloq.). Shove, hoist. 2. Increase the reputation, value, etc. cf (person, scheme, commodity, etc.) by advertising etc., boom. 3. (mech.). Raise the electromotive force in (electric circuit, battery, etc.), whence ~'ER[1] (2) n. 4. n. Scheme of advertisement; resulting advance in value etc. [U.S., orig. unkn.]

boot[1], n., & v.t. 1. Outer foot-covering, usu. all or partly of leather, coming above ankle; (hist.) instrument of torture, luggage-receptacle in coach under guard's & coachman's seat; luggage-receptacle at back of body of motor-car; *the* ~ *is on the other leg*, truth or responsibility just the other way round; *like old* ~s (sl.), tremendously; *over shoes over* ~s, as well risk much as little; *heart in* one's ~s, in terror; *die in* one's ~s, not in bed; ~ *& saddle* [perversion of F *boute-selle* 'place saddle'], cavalry signal to mount; ~*'jack*, for pulling ~s off; ‖~*'lace*, string or leather strip for lacing ~s; ~*'legger*, liquor-smuggler in U.S.; ~*'licker*, toady; ~*'maker*; ~*-trees*, moulds for keeping ~s in shape; (sl.) *get, give, the* ~, be dismissed, dismiss, from employment. 2. v.t. Kick; (sl.) kick (person) *out* (of the house, of employment, etc.). Hence ~'ED[2] a. [ME, f. OF *bote* of unkn. orig.]

boot[2], n. Good, advantage, (now only in *to* ~, as well, to the good, additionally). [OE *bōt*, OS *bōta*, OHG *buoza*, ON *bót*,

Goth. *bôta*, f. Gmc **bôtă-* f. root **bat-*BETTER]

bôôt³, v.t. (arch.; usu. impers. & abs.). Do good (*to*), avail, as, *what ~s* (*it*) *to*, (*it*) *little ~s*, (*it*) *~s* (*me*) *not*. [ME *boten* f. *bot* BOOT²]

bôôtee', n. Kind of lady's boot; infant's wool boot. [cf. *coatee*, see -EE]

bôôth (-dh), n. Temporary shelter of canvas etc.; covered stall in market, tent at fair, etc.; *polling-~*, for voting at elections. [ME *bôthe* f. ODa. **bôth* (whence Sw., Da. *bod* stall) f. East Norse *bóa* dwell (cf. OIcel. *búth* f. *búa*), cf. BOWER¹]

bôôt'less, a. Unavailing. [OE *bôtlĕas*, see BOOT², -LESS]

bôôts, n. Hotel-servant who cleans boots, conveys luggage, etc.

bôôt'ў, n. Plunder or profit acquired in common & to be divided; gain, a prize; *play ~*, act as decoy for confederates, practise collusion. [f. F *butin* f. *butiner* f. MLG *buyten* to plunder; ult. orig. unkn.]

bôôze, v.i., & n. Drink deeply, go on drinking; (n.) drink, a drinking-bout. [ME *bouse*, 16th c. *bowse*, f. MDu. *busen*, early mod. Du. *buizen* drink to excess]

bôôz'ў, a. Addicted to drink; fuddled. [prec. +-Y²]

bô-peep', n. Game of hiding & suddenly appearing to child; *play ~*, of elusive politicians, arguers, etc. [BO +PEEP v.]

bôr'a¹, n. Cold dry N.-E. wind blowing seasonally in the upper Adriatic. [dial. It., f. L BOREAS]

bôr'a², n. Mohammedan trader or hawker. [Hind. *bohra*]

bôrả'cic, a. Of borax (*~ acid*, = BORIO acid). [-IC]

bo'rage (bŭ-), n. Blue-flowered hairy-leaved plant used to flavour claret-cup etc. [f. OF *bourrache* f. med. L *borrago* f. Arab. *abu -rashsh* 'father of sweat' from its use as a diaphoretic]

bôr'ăx, n. A native salt of BORON, in white powder or crystal when pure. [ME & OF *boras* f. med. L *borax* f. Arab. *buraq* prob. f. Pers. *burah*]

Bôrdeaux' (-dō), n. Wine from ~ in S.W. France, claret. [place]

*bôrdĕll'ô, n. Brothel. [It.]

bôrd'er¹, n. & a. Side, edge, boundary or part near it; frontier of country, (pl. after *within, out of*, etc.) territory; *the B~*, boundary & adjoining districts between England & Scotland, **frontier of civilization*, (also *Border* adj. in these senses); continuous bed round garden or part of it, distinct edging for strength or ornament or definition round anything; *~land*, district on either side of *~*, (fig.) intermediate condition (as between sleeping & waking), debatable ground; *~ line*, line of demarcation; *~(-)line* adj., on the *~ line*, as *a ~-line case*, (esp., Psych.) one verging on insanity. [ME *bordure*, f. OF f. Rom. **bordare* whence F *border*; see BOARD¹, -URE]

bôrd'er², v.t. & i. Put or be a border to, whence *~ING¹* (3) n.; adjoin (trans., or intr. with *on, upon*); *~ upon*, resemble. [f. prec.]

bôrd'erer, n. Dweller on or near frontier, esp. that of England & Scotland. [BORDER n. +-ER¹ (4)]

bôre¹, v.t. & i. 1. Make hole in usu. with revolving tool, hollow out evenly (tube etc.), whence *bôr'ING¹* (2) n.; make (a hole, one's way), by boring, persistent pushing, or excavation. 2. (Of horse) thrust the head out; (Racing) push (another) out of the course. [OE *borian*, OHG *borōn*, ON *bora* f. Gmc **borōn* f. **boraz* (whence OE, ON *bor* auger)]

bôre², n. Hollow of gun-barrel; diameter of this, calibre; small deep hole made in earth to find water etc. [partly f. prec., partly f., or cogn. w., ON *bora* bore-hole]

bôre³, n. Nuisance (usu. as pred.); tiresome person, twaddler. [f. 1750, orig. unkn.; early quotations imply F deriv.]

bôre⁴, v.t. Weary by tedious talk or dullness. [app. f. BORE³, w. which it is contemporary, but relations uncert.]

bôre⁵, n. Great tide-wave with precipitous front moving up some estuaries. [perh. f. ON *bára* wave]

bôre⁶. See BEAR³.

bôr'ẻal, a. Of the North or north wind. [ME, f. LL *borealis* (foll., -AL)]

Bôr'ẻas, n. (God of) the north wind. [L f. Gk]

bore'côle (-ōrk-), n. = KALE. [f. Du. *boerenkool* peasant's cabbage]

bore'dom (-ôrd-), n. Being bored, ennui. [BORE³ +-DOM]

bôr'er, n. Person, tool, or machine, that bores holes; horse that bores; kinds of boring insect. [BORE¹ +-ER¹]

bô'ric, a. Of boron (*~ acid*, a preservative & mild antiseptic). [-IC]

bôrn, p.p. & a. *Be ~*, come into the world by birth; *~ of*, owing origin to; *~ again*, regenerate; (with compl.) destined to be (*~ rich, tired, to be hanged, a poet*); cf. also *~ orator, an orator ~*, etc.); *~ with a silver spoon in* one's *mouth, under a lucky star*, destined to wealth, good luck; *in all my ~ days*, my life; *~ fool, idiot* (utter, hopeless); often in comb. with adjj. & advv., as *base, first, ~*. [p.p. of BEAR³]

bôrne. See BEAR³.

borné (bôrn'ā), a. Having limitations, of limited ideas, narrow-minded. [F]

boro-, comb. form of foll.

bôr'ŏn, n. Non-metallic solid element (a brown amorphous powder or yellow crystals). [f. BORAX with ending of *carbon*, which it resembles in some respects]

borough (bŭ'ru), n. ‖ (Munic.) town with corporation & privileges conferred by royal charter; (Parl.) town sending member(s) to parliament; *the B~*, of Southwark; (hist.) *own, buy, ~*, power of controlling election of member, *close, pocket, ~*, so controlled, *rotten ~*, no longer (be-

fore 1832) having real constituency. [OE
burg, burh, OS *burg*, OHG *burug*, ON *borg*,
Goth. *baurgs* f. Gmc **burgs* cogn. w.
bergan shelter; cf. BURGH]

borough-Eng′lish (bŭ′rǔ Ĭngg-), n. (hist.).
Tenure in some parts of England, by
which all lands & tenements fell to youngest son. [f. AF *tenure en Burgh Engloys*
(i.e. not French, but existing in some
English boroughs)]

bŏ′rrow (-ō), v.t. & i. Get temporary use
of (money etc. to be returned; *of* or *from*
person); adopt, use without being the
true or original owner or inventor, derive
from another, import from an alien
source; (Golf) play ball up-hill to roll
back, (also) allow for wind or slope; ~*ed
light*, internal window; ~*ed* PLUMES;
~*-pit* (from which material has been
taken for filling or embanking). Hence
~ER[1], ~ING[1](2), nn. [OE *borgian* give a
pledge (= OHG *borgen* take heed. MHG,
G *borgen* borrow) f. *borg, borh* (= OS *borg*,
MHG *borc*) pledge, f. root of Gmc **bergan*
protect (see BOROUGH)]

bŏrsch (-sh), n. Highly seasoned Russian
soup of various ingredients including
beetroot. [Russ. *borshch*]

Bŏrs′tal, n. ~ *system*, of imprisonment
for young criminals, based on the INDE-
TERMINATE sentence; ~ *Association*, for
help of ~ prisoners on discharge; ~ *Institution*, formerly ~ *Prison*, at~ in Kent.

bŏrt, n. Diamond fragments made in
cutting; diamond malformed in the
making. [f. Du. *boort*]

bŏrz′oi, n. Russian wolf-hound. [f. Russ.
borzoy a. = swift, & n.]

‖ **bŏs, bŏss**, n., & v.t. & i., (sl.). (Also
~*-shot*) bad shot or guess, miss; bungle,
mess; ‖ ~*-eyed* (sl.), blind in one eye,
cross-eyed, crooked, one-sided; (vb; -ss-)
miss, bungle. [orig. unkn.]

bŏs′cage, -kage, n. Masses of trees
or shrubs. [ME, f. OF *boscage* f. *bosc*
wood (see BUSH[1]) +*-age* -AGE]

bŏsh[1], n. & int. (sl.). Nonsense, foolish
talk, folly. [Turk., = empty; introduced
by Morier's novel *Ayesha* (1834)]

‖ **bŏsh**[2], v.t. (school sl.). Make a fool of,
tease. [f. prec.]

bŏsh[3], n. Lower sloping part of blast-
-furnace shaft, from belly to hearth.
[orig. unkn.]

bŏsk, bŏs′kĕt, -quĕt (-k-), nn. Thicket,
plantation. [(a) ME *bosk* var. of *busk*
BUSH[1], in mod. use back form. f. BOSKY;
(b) *bosket* f. F *bosquet* f. It. *boschetto* dim.
of *bosco* wood; cf. BOUQUET]

bŏs′kȳ, a. Wooded, bushy. [f. ME *bosk*
(prec.) +-Y[2]]

bo′s′n. See BOAT[1]*swain*.

bosom (bŏŏ′zm), n. Person's breast; enclosure formed by breast & arms (*wife of
one's* ~); breast of dress, space between
dress & breast, old equivalent of pocket
(*put in one's* ~); *shirt-front; surface of
lake, ground, etc.; the midst (~ *of one's*

family, of the church); the heart, thoughts,
desires, etc. (*comes home to* one's ~, ~
-friend). [OE *bōsm*, OS *bōsom*, OHG
buosam f. WG **bōsm-* of unkn. orig.]

bŏss[1], n. Protuberance; round metal
knob or stud on centre of shield or ornamental work; (Archit.) carved or sculptured projection at intersecting-point of
ribs; (Mech.) enlarged part of shaft.
Hence ~ED[2] (-st), ~′Y[2], aa. [ME *boce* f.
OF *boce* (mod. *bosse*) of unkn. orig.]

bŏss[2], n. (sl.). Master, person in authority;
**manager of political organization;
person or thing that is best at any thing,
champion. [U.S. wd f. Du. *baas* master,
of unkn. orig.]

bŏss[3], v.t. (sl.). Be master or manager
of (~ *the show*, make all arrangements).
[f. prec.]

Bŏs′ton, n. Variation of the waltz. [~
in U.S.]

bo′sun. See BOAT[1]*swain*.

Bŏs′well (-z-), n. Biographer like James
~ (1740-95), writer of Johnson's life.
Hence **Boswĕll′IAN** a., ~ISM(3) n., ~IZE(4)
v.i.

bŏt, bŏtt, n. Parasitic worm; *the botts*,
horse disease caused by it; ~*-fly*, insect
whose eggs produce the ~s. [16th c.
bottes prob. of LG orig., cf. Du. *bot*,
WFris. *botten* (pl.), WFlem. *botse*, of
unkn. orig.]

bŏt′anist, n. Student of botany. [f. F
botaniste, see BOTANY, -IST(3)]

bŏt′anize, -ise (-īz), v.i. Study plants,
esp. by seeking them as they grow. [f.
Gk *botanizō* gather plants, see BOTANY,
-IZE]

bŏt′any[1], n. Science of plants. Hence
botăn′ICAL a. (also **botăn′IC** in names
of old societies), **botăn′ICALLY** adv.
[(a) *botany* f. *botanic* on anal. of *astronomy
-ic* etc., see -Y[1]; (b) *botanic* f. F *botanique*
or LL f. Gk *botanikos* f. *botanē* plant, see
-IC]

Bŏt′any[2], a. & n. ~ (*wool*), Australian
wool; ~ *yarn*, yarn made from this. [f.
~ *Bay*, early convict settlement in N.S.
Wales named from the variety of its flora]

botăr′gō, n. (pl. -*oes*, -*os*). Relish of
mullet or tunny roe. [It., f. Arab.
buṭarkhah f. Copt. *outarakhon* (Copt. *ou-
indef. art.* +Gk *tarikhion* pickle)]

bŏtch, n., & v.t. & i. (Make a) clumsy
patch; bungle(d) work; repair badly.
Hence ~′ER[1] n. [ME *bocche*, of unkn.
orig.]

bŏth, a., pron., & adv. 1. adj. The two
——s & not only one, as ~ (*the*) *brothers
are dead* (*have it* ~ *ways*, choose now one
now the other of alternatives or contradictories to suit one's argument etc.).
2. pron. The two & not only one (a) with
no n., as ~ *are dead*; (b) with *of* & n. or
pron., as ~ *of them* (or *of the brothers*) *are
dead*; (c) with n. or pron. as subj., & ~ in
the pred. in apposition, as *they* (or *the*
brothers) *are~ dead, they were gentlemen ~*.

3. adv. With equal truth in two cases (a) where ~ might still be held pronominal, as ~ *brother & sister are dead*; (b) clearly adv., as *she is ~ dead & buried*; (c) of more than two nouns etc., as ~ *God & man & beast*. [ME *bathe* f. ON *báthar* (= OS *bēthia*, OHG *bede*, *beide*), extended form of the simple wd repr. by OE *begen*, *bā* (ME *bō*), Goth. *bai*, *ba*]

both′er[1] (-dh-), **v.t. & i.** Pester, worry; be troublesome; worry oneself, take trouble; (subjunct. as mild imprecation) confound. [orig. unkn.; first in Irish writers, Sheridan, Swift, Sterne, & prob. of Anglo-Ir. orig.]

both′er[2] (-dh-), **n.** Worry, fuss, petty trouble. [f. prec.]

botherā′tion (-dh-), **n. & int. = prec.; (int.)** confound it! [BOTHER v. + -ATION]

both′ersome (-dh-), **a.** Annoying, troublesome. [-SOME]

both′ӯ, -ie (-th-) **n.** (Sc.). Hut, cottage; one--roomed building in which workmen are lodged. [orig. unkn.; perh. related to BOOTH]

bō′-tree, n. Sacred pipal tree of India, beneath which Gautama, by enlightenment, became the Buddha. [repr. Sinhalese *bogaha* f. *bo* = Pali & Skr. *bodhi* perfect knowledge + *gaha* tree]

bŏt′tle[1], **n.** Narrow-necked vessel, usu. of glass, for storing liquid; the amount of liquid in it; *the ~*, drinking, *over a ~*, while drinking; *bring up on the ~*, of child not fed from the breast; *~-brush*, cylindrical brush for cleaning *~s*, kinds of plant as horsetail; *~-glass*, coarse dark--green glass; *~-green*, dark green; *~-holder*, pugilist's attendant at prizefight, second, supporter, understrapper; *~-neck*, narrow stretch or restricted outlet of road, (fig.) anything obstructing an even flow of production etc.; *~-nose*, swollen nose, *~-nosed* whale; *~-party*, to which each guest brings a bottle of wine etc. (freq. extended to any gathering at which the licensing laws are defied); *~-washer* (colloq.), factotum, underling. [ME *botel*, *-ell(e)* f. OF *botele*, *bouteille* f. med. L *butticula* dim. of *butis*, *buttis* BUTT[1]]

bŏt′tle[2], **v.t.** Store in bottles; *~ up*, conceal, restrain for a time, (resentment etc.). [f. prec.]

bŏt′tle[3], **n.** Bundle of hay or straw (*look for needle in ~ of hay*, of hopeless search). [ME, f. OF *botel* dim. of *botte* bundle]

bŏt′tle[4], **n.** Blue, white, yellow, *~*, *~ of all sorts*, kinds of plant. [partly corruption of *buddle* corn-marigold, partly from shape of ovary or calyx]

bŏtt′om[1], **n. & a.** 1. Lowest part, part on which thing rests (*stand on own ~*, be independent; *~ up*, upside-down); the posterior; seat (of chair); ground under water of lake etc. (*go*, *send*, *to the ~*, sink; *touch ~*, be at the lowest point or on firm facts; *lo, from, ~ of heart*, genuinely, pro-

foundly); river-basin etc., low-lying land; less honourable end of table, class, etc.; person occupying this; farthest or inmost point (*~ of bay*); keel, horizontal part near keel, hull, ship esp. as cargo-carrier (*in British ~s*); foundation, basis, origin, (*be at the ~ of*, cause); essential character, reality, (*search to the ~*, *get to the ~ of*; *at ~*); stamina. **2. adj.** Lowest, last (*bet one's ~ dollar*, stake all); *~ drawer*, drawer in chest of drawers etc., in which a woman stores clothes etc. in preparation for marriage; ‖ *~* GEAR; fundamental; hence *~MOST* (-m-m-) **a.** [OE *botm*, OS *bodom*, OHG *bodam*, ON *botn* repr. Gmc **buthm-*, **buthn-*]

bŏtt′om[2], **v.t. & i.** Put bottom to (saucepan, chair); base (argument etc.) *upon*; touch bottom of sea etc.; touch bottom of, sound, find the extent or real nature of. [f. prec.]

bŏtt′omless, a. Without bottom (chair etc.); unfathomable. [-LESS]

bŏtt′omry[1], **n.** System of lending money to shipowner for purposes of voyage on security of ship, lender losing the money if ship is lost. [BOTTOM n. = ship + -RY after Du. *bodmerij*]

bŏtt′omry[2], **v.t.** Pledge (ship; see prec.).

bŏt′ülism, n. (med.). Sausage-poisoning or poisoning by infected tinned or other food. [f. L *botulus* sausage, -ISM]

boudoir (bŏŏd′wär), **n.** Lady's small private room. [F, lit. sulking-place f. *bouder* sulk]

Bou′gainvillae′a, -vil′ia, (bŏŏgan-), **n.** Tropical plant with large bright-coloured bracts. [*Bougainville*, French navigator, d. 1811]

bough (-ow), **n.** Tree-branch (if on tree, one of the chief branches). [OE *bōg*, *bōh*, OHG *buog*, ON *bógr* shoulder of an animal (the sense 'limb of a tree' is excl. Eng.) f. Gmc **bōguz*; see BOW[5]]

bought, See BUY. Var. *~en* (baw′ten), (in dial. & U.S. use) purchased at a shop (opp. *home-made*).

bougie (bŏŏzh′ē), **n.** Wax candle; thin flexible surgical instrument for exploring, dilating, etc., the passages of the body. [F, f. Arab. *Bujiyah* Algerian town with wax trade]

bouillabaisse (bŏŏlyabās′), **n.** French (esp. Marseilles) dish, rich fish-stew. [F]

bouilli (bŏŏyē′), **n.** Stewed or boiled meat. [F]

bouillon (see Ap.), **n.** Broth, soup; (Dress) puffed fold. [F, f. *bouillir* BOIL]

boul′der (bōl-), **n.** Water-worn rounded stone, cobble; large erratic block of weather-worn stone (in mining, of detached ore); *~-clay*, *-drift*, *-formation*, *-period*, geol. terms w. ref. to the Ice Age. [short for *boulderstone*, ME *bulderston* of Scand. orig.; cf. Sw. dial. *bullersten* large stone in a stream that makes a noise (Sw. *buller* noise, cf. G *bollern* rumble)]

Boule (bow′lē), **n.** Legislative council of

ancient Greece; modern Greek legislature. [Gk *boulē* senate (*boulomai* choose)]

boulevard (bōōl'vahr,* -ahrd), n. Broad street with rows of trees; *broad main road. [F, f. G *bollwerk* BULWARK orig. promenade on demolished fortification]

boul'ter (bōl-), n. Long fishing-line with many hooks. [orig. unkn.]

bounce[1], v.i. & t. (Cause to) rebound; (sl., of cheque) be returned to drawer when there are no funds to meet it; throw oneself about; burst noisily, angrily, etc., *into* or *out of* (room), *in* or *out*; talk big; hustle (person) by bluff or assumptions *into* do*ing* or *out of* (something); *bouncing girl* etc., big, hearty, bustling, noisy. [ME *bunsen* beat, thump, of unkn. orig., perh. imit.; cf. however LG *bunsen*, Du. *bonzen* beat, thump, Du. *bons* thump]

bounce[2], n. Rebound; boast, exaggeration, swagger. [f. prec.]

bounce[3], adv. Suddenly, noisily, (*come ~ against* etc. cf. BANG). [as prec.]

boun'cer, n. In vbl senses; also: unblushing lie; thing big of its kind; *chucker-out (sl.). [-ER¹]

bound[1], n. Limit of territory or estate; (usu. pl.) limitation, restriction, (*out of ~s*, beyond limits set by school etc. rules; *go beyond the ~s of reason, put ~s to*). [ME *bunne*, *bound*, etc. f. AF *bounde*, OF *bodne* etc., f. med. L *bodina* earlier *butina* of unkn. orig.]

bound[2], v.t. Set bounds to, limit, (esp. in pass. with *by*); be the boundary of. [f. prec.]

bound[3], v.i. (Of ball etc.) recoil from wall or ground, bounce; (of living thing, wave, etc.) spring, leap, advance lightly. [f. F *bondir* (orig. of sound) f. Rom. *bombitire* var. of LL *bombitare* (L *bombus* hum)]

bound[4], n. Springy movement upward or forward; (*advance by leaps & ~s*, with startling speed); (of ball etc.) recoil (*on the first ~*, between first two touchings of ground). [f. prec.]

bound[5], a. Ready to start, having started, *for* (or with preceding adv. as *homeward ~*). [ME *bun*(e), *boun*(e) f. ON *búinn* p.p. of *búa* get ready; *-d* phonetic, or partly after foll.]

bound[6], p.p. of BIND. In vbl senses; esp. *~ up with*, having the same interests as, closely connected with; *~ to win* etc., certain.

boun'dary, n. Limit-line; (Cricket) hit to limit of field scoring 4 or 6 runs. [BOUND¹+-ARY¹]

boun'den. See BIND¹.

boun'der, n. In vbl senses of BOUND²,³; esp., (sl.) cheerfully or noisily ill-bred person. [-ER¹]

bound'less, a. Unlimited. Hence ~LY² adv., ~NESS n. [BOUND¹+-LESS]

boun'teous, a. Beneficent, liberal; freely bestowed. Hence ~LY² adv., ~NESS n. [ME *bontyvous* f. OF *bontif* (*bonté* BOUNTY)

+-ous, altered later as though f. *bounté* BOUNTY+-OUS; cf. PLENTEOUS]

boun'tiful, a.=prec. (*lady ~*, beneficent lady of a neighbourhood); also, ample. Hence ~LY² adv. [foll.+-FUL]

boun'ty, n. Munificence, liberality in giving; gift (*king's, queen's, ~*), grant made to mother of triplets; *Queen Anne's ~*, former fund for augmenting poor benefices); gratuity to soldiers etc. on joining etc.; sum paid to manufacturers & producers to encourage trade enterprise. [ME, f. OF *bonte* f. L *bonitalem* f. *bonus* good (BON, -TY)]

bouquet' (bōōkā'), n. Bunch of flowers; perfume of wine. [F, f. dial. var. of OF *bos*, *bois* wood; see -ET]

bouquetin (bōōk²), n. The Alpine ibex. [F]

*bour'bon¹ (bēr-, boor-), n. Kind of whisky distilled from Indian corn & rye. [f. *Bourbon* County, Ky, where first made]

*Bour'bon² (boor-), n. Reactionary. [f. the ~ family, whose descendants founded dynasties in France & Spain]

bour'don (boor-), n. Low-pitched (16 ft) stop in organ; similar stop in harmonium; lowest bell in peal of bells; drone pipe of bagpipes. [F, = bagpipe-drone]

bourgeois¹ (boorzh'wah), n. & a. (Member) of middle class, (person) of humdrum or conventional middle-class ideas. [F, see BURGESS]

bourgeois² (berjois'), n. & a. (Printing) type) between long primer & brevier. [perh. a French printer's name]

bourgeoisie (boorzhwahzē'), n. The middle class. [F]

bourgeon. See BURGEON.

bourn¹ (boorn), n. Small stream. [southern var. of BURN¹]

bourn(e)² (boorn), n. Limit, goal. [f. F *borne* f. OF *bodne* BOUND¹]

bourse (boors), n. Foreign money-market, esp. that of Paris. [F]

boustrophed'on, a. & adv. (Written) from right to left & from left to right in alternate lines. [Gk, adv. = as ox turns in ploughing (f. *bous* ox, *-strophos* turning, *-don* adv. suf.)]

bout, n. Spell of or turn at work or exercise; fit of drinking or illness; trial of strength; *this ~*, on this occasion. [16th c. *bout*, *bowt* app. same as obs. *bought* (*bout*) bending]

boutonnière (bōōtŏnyār'), n. (Spray of flowers worn in) buttonhole. [F]

bouts rimés (bōō rēmā'), n. pl. Rhymed ends; versifying to set rhymes. [F]

bov'ine a. Of, like, an ox; inert, dull. [f. LL *bovinus* (*bos bovis* ox, see -INE¹)]

‖ **bov'ril**, n. A meat extract used like beef tea. [P]

bow¹ (bō), n. Curve; rainbow; weapon for shooting arrows (*bend, draw, the ~*; *two strings to one's ~*, a second resource; *draw the long ~*, exaggerate);=SADDLE-~; rod with stretched horse-hair for playing violin etc., single passage of this across strings; = BAIL⁴; = BOW-WINDOW; slip-knot with single or double loop, ribbon etc. so tied; ~s, ~compass(es), compass with jointed legs; ~-head, Greenland whale; ~-legged, bandy; ~-saw, narrow saw stretched like bowstring on wooden frame; ~'shot, distance to which ~ can send arrow; ~'string, (strangle with) string of ~ (former Turkish method of execution). [OE boga, OS, OHG bogo, ON bogi f. Gmc *bugon f. *bug- BOW³]

bow² (bō), v.t. Use the bow on (violin etc.; also abs.). [f. prec.]

bow³, v.i. & t. Submit (to the inevitable etc.), bend or kneel in sign of submission or reverence to or before (often with down); incline head in salutation, assent, etc. (~ing acquaintance, that stops at this, slight); express (thanks etc.), usher in or out, by ~ing; cause to bend (lit. & fig., knee, back etc. for burden, will); ~ down, crush, make stoop, (esp. ~ed down by care etc.). [OE būgan, cf. OHG biogan, ON *bjúga, Goth. biugan f. Gmc *beugan, f. *beug-, *bug-, cf. BOW¹]

bow⁴, n. Bending of head or body in salutation, respect, consent, etc.; make one's ~, retire. [f. prec.]

bow⁵, n. Fore-end of boat or ship from where it begins to arch inwards (often pl.); on the ~, of objects within 45° of the point right ahead; rower nearest the ~ (~-oar, his oar or himself); ~-chaser, see CHASE¹. [17th c. f. LG boog, Du. boeg, = Da. boug, Sw. bog, G bug, all = shoulder, ship's bow, the same wd as BOUGH; the naut. sense was developed in LG & Du.]

Bow bells (bō), n. Within the sound of ~, in City of London. [f. St Mary le Bow]

bowd'ler|ize, -ise (-iz), v.t. Expurgate (book, author). Hence ~ISM(3), ~IZA-TION, nn. [T. Bowdler (d. 1825), expurgator of Shakespeare, +-IZE(4)]

bow'el, n. Division of alimentary canal below stomach, intestine, gut, (sing. only in med. use); (pl.) entrails, inside of body; pity, tender feelings, (~s of mercy etc.); interior of anything. [ME buel, bouel f. OF buel f. L botellus dim. of botulus sausage]

bow'er¹, n. Dwelling, abode, (poet.); inner room, boudoir, (poet.); place closed in with foliage, arbour, summerhouse, whence ~Y² a.; ~-bird, Australian bird of the bird-of-paradise family constructing elaborate runs adorned with feathers, shells, etc. [OE (OS, OHG, ON) būr f. Gmc *būr- f. *bū dwell, cf. BOOR]

bow'er², n. (Also ~-anchor, -cable) either of two anchors (best & small) carried at ship's bow or of their cables. [BOW⁵ +-ER¹]

bow'er³, n. One of two cards (right ~, knave of trumps, left ~, knave of same colour) at euchre. [f. G bauer peasant, knave at cards, cogn. w. Du. boer; see BOOR]

*bow'ery, n. Farm, plantation; the B~, a wide street in New York City. [f. Du. bouwerij]

bow'ie-knife (bō'ī-), n. Long knife with 10–15 in. blade double-edged at point used as weapon in wild parts of U.S. [Col. J. Bowie (d. 1836)]

bowl¹ (bōl), n. Basin (hist., deep-shaped basin; now differing only as more dignified or poetic wd); drinking-vessel (the ~, conviviality); contents of a ~; ~-shaped part of tobacco-pipe, spoon, balance, etc. Hence~FUL(2)(bōl'fŏŏl) n. [ME bolle f. OE (OS, OHG) bolla, ON bolli f. Gmc *bŭl-swell; cf. BOLL]

bowl² (bōl), n. 1. Wooden ball made slightly out of spherical shape or weighted on one side to make it run curved course (BIAS). 2. Flattened or spherical wooden ball at skittles. 3. pl. Game played with ~s (sense 1) on grass, or with round balls in room. 4. pl. Skittles (dial.). [ME & F boule f. L bulla bubble; bowl² has taken its pronunc. f. bowl¹, & bowl¹ its spelling f. bowl²]

bowl³ (bōl), v.t. & i. Play bowls; trundle (ball, hoop, etc.) along ground; go along by revolving or by means of wheels, esp. ~ along, go fast & smoothly; (Cricket) deliver (ball, over, or abs.), knock off (bails) or down (wicket), dismiss (batsman; out or abs.), whence bowl'er¹ [-ER¹] n.; ~ over, knock down, (fig.) disconcert, render helpless. [f. prec.]

|| bowl'er² (bō-), n. = BILLYCOCK; ~-hat n., ~, v.t. (sl., -tt-), retire from the army etc. [f. B~, hatter, who designed it 1850]

bowline (bō'lin), n. Rope from weather side of square sail to bow; (also ~-knot) simple knot for forming a non-slipping loop at end of rope. [ME bouline etc. f. MLG bōline = MDu. boechlijne (BOW⁵, LINE²); early borrowing accounts for pronunc. diff. from that of BOW⁵; see also BOWSPRIT]

bowl'ing (bō-), n. In vbl senses; esp.: ~-crease, line from behind which bowler delivers ball; ~-alley, long enclosure for playing skittles; ~-green, lawn for playing bowls. [-ING¹]

bow'man¹ (bō-), n. (pl. -men). Archer. [BOW¹]

bow'man² (bō-), n. (pl. -men). Man stationed in bow of boat. [BOW⁵]

bow'sprit (bō-) n. Spar running out from ship's stem, to which forestays are fastened. [ME bouspret etc. f. MLG bōgsprēt = MDu. boechspriet (BOW⁵, SPRIT); see also BOWLINE]

Bow-street (bō-), n. & a. Street near Covent Garden with chief metropolitan police-court; B.-runner, -officer, old names for police officer.

bow win'dow (bō-; -dō), n. Curved (not angular) bay window; (sl.) large belly. Hence ~ED² (-ŏd) a. [BOW¹]

bow-wow, int. & n. Dog's bark; imitation of it; (nursery talk etc.) dog; the (*big*) ~ *style*, dogmatic manner in talk or writing.

bow'yer (bō-), n. Maker, seller, of bows. [BOW¹+-YER]

bŏx¹, n. Kinds of evergreen shrub, esp. one with small dark leathery leaves, much used in garden borders; (also ~*wood*) its wood, used by turners & engravers; (with qualification) similar plant (*bastard* ~ etc.). [OE *box* f. L *buxus*, Gk *puxos*]

bŏx², n. 1. Receptacle (usu. lidded, rectangular or cylindrical, & for solids) of wood, cardboard, metal, etc. (*in the same* ~, i.e. predicament); driver's seat on carriage or coach (from the ~ under it); = ~*ful* as quantity; money-~ (*put in the* ~); separate compartment at theatre, in tavern, etc., in stable or railway truck for horse (*loose* ~, in which it can move about); = JURY-~, ‖ WITNESS-~; hut for sentry or signalman; *fishing*, *shooting*, etc., -~, small country house for such temporary uses; protective case in various machines; *in the wrong* ~, awkward position. 2. ~ BARRAGE; ~ *bed*, with wooden roof & sides opening with sliding panels, also bed made to fold up & look like ~; ~*cloth*, close-woven cloth like buff; ~*coat*, heavy overcoat (for driving); ~*drain*, of quadrangular section; ~*iron*, for ironing, hollow for reception of heater; ~*keeper*, attendant on theatre ~es; ~*kite*, scientific kite consisting of two light rectangular ~es secured together horizontally; ~*office*, in theatre etc. for booking seats; ~*pleat*, double fold in cloth; ~ *spanner* (with socket head); ~*wallah* (Anglo-Ind. colloq.), pedlar, (sl.) European commercial man in India (in derogatory sense). Hence ~'FUL(2) n. [OE *box* prob. f. *buxem* acc. (for *buxidem*) of LL *buxis* (whence OHG *buhsa* f. WG *buhsja*) f. L *pyxis* PYX]

bŏx³, v.t. Provide with, put into, a box; ~ *up*, confine uncomfortably, squeeze together; ‖ lodge (document) in Law Court; divide off from other compartments; ~ *the compass*, (Naut.) rehearse the points in correct order, (fig.) make complete revolution & end where one began (in politics, argument, etc.). [f. prec.]

bŏx⁴, n. Slap with hand *on the ear*(s). [ME *box* of unkn. orig.]

bŏx⁵, v.t. & i. Slap person's *ears*; fight (someone, or intr.) with fists (usu. in padded gloves & merely for exercise); ~*ing-glove*, padded glove worn in boxing; ~*ing*-weights (amateur given first, professional in brackets), *heavy-weight* over 12 st. 10 (over 12 st. 7), *light heavy* (or *cruiser*)*-weight* 12 st. 10 (12 st. 7), *middle-weight* 11 st. 11 (11 st. 6), *light middle--weight* 11 st. 2 (not a professional category), *welter-weight* 10 st. 8 (10 st. 7), *light welter-weight* 10 st. (not a professional category), *light-weight* 9 st. 7 (9 st. 9), *feather-weight* 9 st. (9 st.), *bantam-weight* 8 st. 7 (8 st. 6), *fly-weight* 8 st. (8 st.). [f. prec.]

Bŏx and Cŏx, n. Two persons who are never together, never at home at the same time. [name of play adapted from the French in 1847 by J. M. Morton]

bŏx'calf' (-kahf), n. Chrome-tanned calfskin with hatched grain. [after Joseph *Box*, London bootmaker]

bŏx'er, n. Pugilist; (*B*~) member of Chinese anti-foreign secret society (hist.); medium-sized smooth-haired kind of dog derived from German bulldog. [BOX⁵, -ER¹]

bŏx'haul, v.i. Veer ship round on her keel (for want of room). [BOX³]

‖ **Bŏx'ing-day**, n. First week-day after Christmas. [on which CHRISTMAS-*boxes* are given, f. obs. sense of BOX³ f. (money)·BOX²]

boy, n. Male child (strictly till puberty, loosely till 19 or 20, 'the ~s' also of grown-up sons of a family); person who retains tastes or simplicity of boyhood; servant, slave, native labourer; male native, in various countries with subject races (cf. POST²-~ etc.); (familiar voc.) *old*, *my*, ~; ~, often = male (~*friend*, girl's or woman's favourite ~), young (~*husband*); = SCOUT¹; ‖ ~*'s-love*, southernwood. [ME *boi*, *boy*, the orig. of which, subject of involved conjectures, remains unascertained]

boyc'ott, v.t., & n. 1. Punish, coerce, (person, class, nation) by systematic refusal of social or commercial relations; combine in abstaining from (goods etc.) with this aim. 2. n. Such treatment. [Capt. *B*~, Irish land-agent so treated; f. 1880]

boy'hood, n. Boyish age; boys. [-HOOD]

boy'ish, a. Proper to boys; as of a boy, spirited, puerile. Hence ~LY² adv., ~NESS n. [-ISH¹(1)]

bra (-ah), n. (colloq.), Brassière. [abbr.]

brăb'ble, v.t., & n., (arch.). (Engage in) paltry noisy quarrel. [orig. obsc.; cf. Du. *brabbelen* jabber, stammer]

brāce¹, n. Thing that clasps, tightens, unites, secures; ‖ (pl.) suspenders for trousers; thong for tuning drum; ‖ strap suspending carriage-body from springs; connecting mark in printing ({); pair, couple, (dogs, game, derog. persons; pl. 3, 20, etc., *brace*); strengthening piece of iron or timber in building; ~ *& bit*, revolving tool for boring, screw-driving, etc.; (Naut.) rope attached to yard for trimming sail (*splice the* MAIN³ ~). [ME, orig. f. OF *brace* the two arms, f. L *bracchia* (pl.) arms; some senses f. foll. the naut. meaning perh. f. F *bras* arm]

brāce², v.t. Fasten tightly, stretch, string up, give firmness to, (~ *oneself up*, ~ one's *energies*, etc.; *bracing air*, opp. *relaxing*); support; couple together, (Naut.) move (sail) by braces. Hence

*brā′cer[1] n. (sl.), pick-me-up. [ME, partly f. OF *bracier* embrace, partly f. prec.; the naut. perh. f. F *brasser*]

brāce′lĕt (-sl-), n. Ornamental band, chain, etc., for wrist or arm; (sl.) hand-cuff. Hence ~ED[2] a. [ME, f. OF, dim. of *bracel* f. L *bracchiale* f. *bracchium* arm, see -ET[1], -LET]

brā′cer[2], n. Wrist-guard in archery & fencing. [ME, f. OF *brasseüre* f. *bras* arm +-*eure* -URE]

brăch, n. (arch.). Bitch hound. [ME *braches* pl. f. OF *braches*, -*ez*, pl. of *brachet* (whence ME *brachet*) dim. of *brac* f. WG; cf. OHG *braccho*, med. L *braccus*]

bra′chial (-ăk-), a. Of the, like an, arm. [f. L *bracchialis* (*bracchium* arm) see -AL]

bra′chiate (-ăk-), a. (bot.). With branches in pairs at right angles to stem, each pair at right angles to the last. [f. L *bracchiatus* see prec. & -ATE[2] (1)]

brăchy- (-k-), comb. form of Gk *brakhus* short, in many scientific terms.

brăchycephăl′ic (-kĭsĕ-), a. Short-headed (of skulls with breadth at least four-fifths of length; or of person or race with such skull). [prec.+-CEPHALIC]

brăchyĭl′ogў (-kĭ-), n. Conciseness of speech, condensed expression, incorrect-ness of speech due to excessive condensa-tion. [f. Gk *brakhulogia*, see BRACHY-, -LOGY]

brăck′en, n. A fern abundant on heaths, hillsides, etc.; (collect.) mass of ferns. [northern ME f. ON *brakni whence Sw. *bräken*, Da. *bregne* fern]

brăck′ĕt[1], n. Flat-topped projection from wall serving as support to statue, arch, etc.; shelf with slanting under-prop for hanging against wall; wooden or metal angular support; side-piece of gun--carriage supporting trunnion; support projecting from wall of gas or other lamp; pairs of marks, ( ), [ ], { } (cf. BRACE), used for enclosing words, figures, etc. (~-*turn* in skating, like one of the third pairs); (Mil.) distance between two shots in ranging (see foll.); group bracketed together (*income-~, class of tax-payers grouped according to income). [16th c. *bragget* f. F *braguette* or Sp. *bragueta* dim. of *brague*, *braga* f. L *braca* sing. of *bracae* breeches; sense-hist. obsc., perh. infl. by L *bracchium* arm]

brăck′ĕt[2], v.t. Enclose in brackets as parenthetic, spurious, (Math.) having spec. relations to what precedes or follows, etc.; couple (names etc.) with a brace, imply connexion or equality between (~-*ed*, equal); (Mil.) drop two shots one short & one beyond (target) in range--finding. [f. prec.]

brăck′ish, a. Between salt & fresh (of water). [f. obs. adj. *brack* f. Du. *brak*, -ISH[1]]

brăct, n. Small leaf or scale below calyx. So brăc′tĕAL, brăc′tĕATE[2](2), aa. [f. L *bractea* thin plate, gold leaf]

brăd, n. Thin flat slightly-headed nail. [later var. of ME *brod* goad, pointed instrument, f. ON *broddr* (= OE *brord*-OHG *brort*) spike]

brăd′awl, n. Small non-spiral boring-tool. [perh. f. prec.+AWL]

‖ Brăd′shaw, n. (Used for) ~'s *Railway Guide*, a time-table of all passenger trains running in Great Britain. [orig. issued in 1839 by George *Bradshaw*, printer]

‖ brae (-ā), n. Steep bank, hill-side. [ME *brā* f. ON *brí* (= OE *brǣw*) eyelid, = OS, OHG *brāwa* eyebrow f. Gmc *brǣw-; not related to BROW]

brăg, n., & v.i. & t. (-gg-). (Indulge in) boastful talk; boast of or of, boast *that*; card-game like poker. [ME, of unkn orig.; cf. (16th c.) F *braguer* etc.]

brăggadŏ′cio (-shĭŏ), n. Empty vaunt-ing. [formed by Spenser (meaning *boaster*) on prec. & It. augmentative -*occhio*]

brăgg′art, n. & a. (Person) given to brag-ging. [f. 16th c. F *bragard* f. *braguer* BRAG+-ARD]

brahmaput′ra (-ōot-), brah′ma, n. Kind of domestic fowl. [river *Brahmaputra* whence brought]

brah′min, -man, n. Member of Hindu priestly caste; *Brahmin (colloq., usu. derog.), highly cultured or intellectual person. Hence brahmin′ic(AL), -man-ic(AL), aa., brah′minISM(3), -manISM(3), n. [f. Skr. *brahmaṇa* f. *brahman* wor-ship]

brah′minee, a. Belonging to brahmin caste etc.; ~ *bull*, *ox*, sacred (humped) cattle, immune from slaughter. [f. prec.]

Brah′mōism, n. Reformed theistic Hinduism. So Brah′mō(IST) n., adherent of ~. [f. *Brahmo* in *Brahmo Samaj* (religious society founded in 1830), -ISM]

braid[1], n. Entwined hair, plait; band etc entwined with the hair; silk, thread, etc., woven into a band. Hence ~′ING[1] (3, 6) n. [see foll.]

braid[2], v.t. Plait, interweave, (hair, flowers, thread); arrange (hair) in braids: confine (hair etc.) with ribbon etc.; trim, edge, with braid. [OE, OS *bregdan*, OHG *brettan*, ON *bregtha* f. Gmc *bregdhan move to & fro]

brail, n., & v.t. (Haul *up* with) small rope(s) on sail-edges for trussing sails be-fore furling. [ME, f. OF *brail*, *braiel* f. LL *bracale* (also -*ile*) girdle (*bracae* breeches) see -AL(2)]

braille, B-, (-ăl), n., & v.t. 1. System of writing & printing for the blind, in which the characters are represented by raised dots. 2. v.t. Print or transcribe in ~ characters. [M. *Braille*, French in-ventor, 1834]

brain, n., & v.t. 1. Convoluted nervous substance in skull of vertebrates (sing. of the whole as an organ, pl. of the sub-stance; *blow out* one's ~s, shoot him in the head); centre of sensation, thought, etc. (usu. pl., sing. with dignified or exalted effect; *cudgel* etc. one's ~s, think hard; *have something on the* ~, be crazy about it; *turn* one's ~, make him vain & silly); intellectual power (*suck, pick,* one's ~, extract & use his ideas); ~-*fag,* nervous exhaustion; ~ *fever,* inflammation of the ~; ~-*fever bird,* Indian cuckoo (with maddeningly persistent cry sounding like '~fever'); ~-*pan* (colloq.), skull; ~ *sauce* (joc.), intelligence; ~-*sick,* mad; ~- *storm,* temporary mental upset marked by uncontrolled emotion & violent action; *Brains Trust,* *group of experts guiding or advising the government, (transf.) any group of experts, ‖ a body, consisting mainly of experts, broadcasting impromptu answers to selected questions from listeners; ~-*washing,* clearing the mind of established ideas by persistent suggestion & indoctrination; ~ *wave* (colloq.), sudden inspiration or bright idea; hence ~'LESS a. 2. v.t. Dash out ~s of. [OE *brægen* = MDu., LG *bregen,* Du., Fris. *brein,* not elsewhere in Gmc]

brain′y, a. Clever. [-Y²]

‖ **braird,** n., & v.i. (Sc.).(Come up in) fresh shoots. [same wd as obs. (Sc.) *brerd* f. OE *brerd* brim; cf. OE *brord* point, see BRAD]

braise (-z), v.t. Stew (prop. with fire above & below) tender with bacon, herbs, etc. [f. F *braiser* (*braise* hot coals)]

brake¹, n. = BRACKEN. [ME, perh. shortened f. *bracken,* -*en* being taken to be the pl. ending]

brake², n. Thicket, brushwood. [16th c., orig. unkn.]

brake³, n. Toothed instrument for braking flax & hemp; (also ~-*harrow*) heavy harrow; instrument for peeling of willow- -bark. [15th c. = MLG, MDu. *brake,* flax-brake f. *breken* BREAK¹]

brake⁴, v.t. Crush (flax, hemp) by beating. [f. prec.]

brake⁵, n. Apparatus for checking wheel's motion; (also ~-*van*) railway-carriage from which ~s of a train can be controlled, guard's compartment. Hence ~'LESS (-kl-) a. [18th c., of uncert. orig.; perh. transferred use of obs. *brake* bridle, curb (15th c.), of uncert. orig.; cf. F *frein* curb, also brake, G. *bremse* barnacle, also brake]

brake⁶, v.t. Apply brake to (wheel, car, train). [f. prec.]

brake⁷. See BREAK³.

*****brake′man** (-km-), ‖ **brākes′man** (-ks-), n. Man in charge of BRAKE⁵.

Brăm′ah-. (Lock, press, pen, etc.) invented by J. *Bramah* c. 1790.

brăm′ble, n. Rough prickly shrub with long trailing shoots; blackberry-bush; blackberry. Hence **brăm′bly²** a. [OE *bræmbel* (for earlier *bræmel,* cf. *slumber*), f. WG *bræm-,* *brăm-* (see BROOM)+-LE (1); cf. OS *brāmalbusc*]

brăm′bling, n. The mountain finch. [prec. + -LING¹ (1)]

brăn, n. Husks of grain separated from flour after grinding; ~ *pie,* form of LUCKY¹-*bag.* [ME *bren,* bran f. OF f. Gaulish *brennos* bran]

brăn′card (-ngk-), n. A horse-litter. [F. = litter (foll., -ARD)]

branch¹ (-ah-), n. Limb springing from tree or bough (*bough,* ~, *twig,* is the order, but ~ occas. for either of the others); lateral extension or subdivision of mountain-range, river, road, family, genus, subject of knowledge, argument, legislature, bank or other business, etc.; *root-&-* ~ adj., *root & ~* adv., thorough(ly), radical(ly). Hence (-)~ED³ (-cht), ~LESS, aa., ~′LET n. [ME, f. OF *branche* branch f. LL *branca* paw]

branch² (-ah-), v.i. Put branches *out, forth;* spring *out,* spread *forth,* tend *away or off,* diverge *into.* [f. prec.]

brăn′chi|ae, -ĭ|a, (-ngk-), n. pl. Gills. Hence ~AL, ~ATE²(2), ~F′EROUS, ~FORM, aa., ~O- comb. form. [L *branchia,* pl. *·ae,* f. Gk *bragkhia* pl.]

brăn′chy (-ah-), a. With many branches. [-Y²]

brănd¹, n. Burning or charred log or stick (~ *from the burning,* rescued person, convert), torch (poet.); mark made by hot iron; stigma (*the ~ of Cain,* blood- -guiltiness); trade-mark, particular kind of goods; iron stamp for burning a mark in; kind of blight (leaves etc. with burnt look); sword (poet.; perh. as flashing). [OE *brand,* OHG *brant,* ON *brandr* f. Gmc *brandaz* (*bran-* pret. st. of *brinnan* BURN²)]

brănd², v.t. Burn with hot iron (surgically, penally, or showing ownership or quality); impress on memory; stigmatize. [f. prec.]

brăn′dish, v.t. Wave about, flourish, (weapon, threat) as preliminary to action or in display. [f. OF *brandir* (-ISH²) f. Rom. *brandire* f. Gmc *brand-* BRAND² sword]

brănd′ling, n. Red worm with brighter rings used as bait. [BRAND¹ + -LING¹(1)]

brănd′-new′, brăn-, a. Conspicuously new. [f. BRAND¹, as if freshly stamped]

brăn′drĕth, n. Wooden stand for cask, hay-rick, etc. [ME, f. ON *brandreith* grate (*brandr* BRAND¹ + *reith* carriage)]

brăn′dy, n. Strong spirit distilled from wine; ‖~-*ball,* kind of sweet; ‖ ~ *pawnee* [Hind. *pani* water], ~ & water; ~-*snap,* gingerbread wafer. [17th c *brandwine, brandewine,* f. Du. *brandewz,* n = burnt (distilled) wine]

brănk-ŭrs′ine (-ngk-), n. Bear's breech, acanthus. [f. med. L *branca ursina* bear's claw cf. BRANCH]

brăn-new. See BRAND-NEW.

brănt(-goose). See BRENT.

brăsh¹, n. Loose broken rock or ice; hedge refuse, clippings, etc. [of unkn. orig.; cf. Du. *bras* (G *brass*) heap, lot, rubbish]

brash², a. (colloq.). Rash, cheeky, saucy. [orig. unkn.]

brass (-ahs), n., a., & v.t. & i. 1. (Hist.) alloy of copper with tin, zinc, or other base metal; (mod.) yellow alloy of ⅔ copper with ⅓ zinc (cf. BRONZE); inscribed sepulchral table of ~; *the* ~, the ~ instruments of a band; (sl.) money; effrontery, shamelessness. 2. adj. Made of ~; ~ *band*, set of musicians with ~ instruments; ~ *farthing*, least possible amount, esp. *don't care a ~ farthing*; ||~ *hat*, (mil. sl.) officer of high rank with gold braid on his hat; ||~ *plate*, on door, gate, or window-ledge, with name, trade, etc.; ||~ *rags*, sailors' cleaning cloths, as *part ~ rags* (Naut. sl.), dissolve intimacy *with*; ~ *tacks*, (sl.) actual details, real business, esp. *get down to ~ tacks*. 3. v.t. & i. (sl.). Pay *up*. [OE *bræs* of unkn. orig.; cf. MLG *bras* metal]

brass′age, n. Mint-charge for coining money. [F, f. *brasser* stir melted metals together; see -AGE]

brass′ard, n. Badge worn on arm. [F (*bras* arm & see -ARD)]

brass′erie, n. Beer-saloon or beer-garden (usu. supplying eatables also). [F, = brewery (*brasser* brew)]

brassière (brås′yār), n. Woman's undergarment worn to support breasts. [F]

brass′y (-ah-), a. & n. 1. Like brass in colour, sound, taste; impudent; pretentious; hence ~ILY² adv., ~INESS n. 2. n. (Also ~ie) brass-soled golf-club. [-Y²]

brat, n. Child (usu. derog.). [c. 1500 Sc., perh. short. f. Sc. *bratchart* = *bratchet* hound, brach, dim. of BRACH]

bratt′ice, bratt′icing, nn. (Coal-mining) wooden partition or shaft-lining. [ME *brutaske* etc. temporary breastwork on parapet f. ONF *breteske* = OF *bretesche* (mod. -*èche*) f. med. L *brittisca* of unkn. orig.]

brava′dō (-vah-), n. (pl. -*oes*, -*os*). Show of courage, bold front. [f. Sp. *bravada*, F *bravade*; see foll., -ADO (2), -ADE(1)]

brāve¹, a. & n. 1. Courageous (*the* ~, ~ *men*); (archaic-literary) finely dressed, showy, worthy, honest, admirable; hence ~′LY² adv. 2. n. Red-Indian warrior. [ME, f. F, It. *bravo*, f. Rom. *brabus*, f. *brabarus*, f. L *barbarus* BAR-BAROUS]

brāve², v.t. Defy, encounter with courage; ~ *it out*, carry oneself defiantly under suspicion or blame. [f. F *braver* see prec.]

brāv′ery, n. Daring; splendour, ostentation, finery. [16th c. also = *bravado*, f. F *braverie* or It. -*ia* (prec., -ERY)]

bra′vō¹ (-ah-), n. (pl. -*oes*, -*os*). Hired assassin, desperado. [It., see BRAVE¹]

bra′vō² (-ah-), n. & int. Cry of approval, esp. to actors etc. (occas. *brava*, *bravi*, to actress, company; also *bravissimo* superl.). [It. = BRAVE¹]

bravur′a (-oora), n. Brilliant or ambitious execution, forced display; style of (esp.

vocal) music requiring exceptional powers. [It.]

brawl, v. i., & n. Squabble, (engage in) noisy quarrel; (of streams) murmur. Hence ~′ER¹ n. [ME, of unkn. orig.]

brawn, n. Muscle; pickled or potted boar's flesh. [ME *braun(e)* f. AF *braun*, OF *braon* (Pr. *bradon*) f. WG *brādo* (*brādan* = G *braten* roast); sense *boar's flesh* is excl. E]

brawn′ (ĭ̄ȳ, a. Strong, muscular. Hence ~INESS n. [-Y²]

brăx′y, n. & a. (Sc.). Splenic apoplexy in sheep; (adj.) suffering from ~, (of meat) of a ~ sheep (also abs. as n., = ~ meat). [orig. unkn.; cf. OE *bræc* catarrh]

bray¹, n., & v.i. & t. (Make) the cry, or a sound like the cry, of ass or trumpet; ~ *out*, utter harshly. [ME, f. OF *braire*]

bray², v.t. Pound, beat small, esp. with pestle & mortar. [ME, f. OF *breier* (=Pr., Sp. *bregar*, It. *brigare*) f. Gmc *brekan* BREAK¹]

brāze¹, v.t. Colour like brass. [16th c., not continuous w. late OE *brasian* (*bræs* BRASS), but prob. formed anew on anal. of *glaze*, *glass*]

brāze², v.t. Solder with alloy of brass & zinc. [f. F *braser* solder]

brāz′en¹, a. Made of brass; strong, yellow, or harsh-sounding, as brass; (also ~-*faced*) shameless, whence ~LY² adv.; ~ *age*, third stage in human deterioration (golden, silver, ~, iron). [OE *bræsen* (*bræs* BRASS + -EN⁴)]

brāz′en², v.t. ~ *out*, carry off impudently ('it', matter, deed); make shameless. [f. prec.]

brā′zier¹ (-zher), n. Worker in brass. Hence **brā′ziERY**(1) n. [f. BRASS + -ier, on anal. of *glass*, *glazier*]

brā′zier²(-zher), n. Pan for holding lighted coal. [f. F *brasier* (*braise* hot coal)]

Brazil′, n. & a. (Also ~-*wood*) kinds of hard red S.-Amer. wood yielding dyes; ~-*nut*, large three-sided nut. [ME *brasile*, orig. Sp., Port., & F name of E.-Ind. wood, transferred to S.-Amer. similar species & thence to the country]

breach¹, n. (Naut.) breaking of waves (*clear* ~, rolling over without breaking; *clean* ~, carrying away of masts & everything on deck); breaking or neglect (*of* rule, duty, contract, someone's privileged rights, or promise, esp. to marry); ~ *of close*, trespass, *of the peace*, riot or affray; breaking of relations, separation, alienation, quarrel; broken state; gap, esp. in fortifications made by artillery (*stand in the* ~, bear brunt of attack, lit. or fig.); whale's leap clear out of water. [ME *breche* f. OF *breche* f. Frank. *breka*, Gmc *brekan* BREAK; superseding OE *bryce*, ME *bruche* (Gmc *brukiz* f. *brekan*)]

breach², v.t. & i. Break through, make gap in; (of whale) leap clear out of water [f. prec.]

bread (-ĕd), n. Flour moistened, kneaded, & baked, usu. with leaven (*white*, BROWN, *black*, ~; *standard* ~, wheaten of mixed flours; *break* ~, take food, join in Lord's supper; ~ *& butter*, ~ slices spread with butter, necessary food, a livelihood; ~-*&-butter letter*, ROOFER; ~-*&-butter miss*, school-girl; ~ *& scrape*, stingily buttered bread; *ship's* ~ (Naut.), hard biscuit; ~ *& cheese*, simple food, a livelihood; ~ *& milk*, broken ~ in boiling milk; ~ *& wine*, Lord's supper; ~ *of life* (see *John* vi. 35); *know which side one's* ~ *is buttered*, where one's interest lies; ~ *buttered on both sides*, easy prosperity; *take the* ~ *out of one's mouth*, take away his living by competition etc.; *eat the* ~ *of idleness*, *affliction*, be idle, afflicted; *daily* ~, livelihood; *make one's* ~, earn a living); ~-*basket*, (sl.) stomach; ~-*crumb*, inner part of loaf,~ crumbled for use in cooking; ~-*fruit*, -*tree*, South-Sea tree with farinaceous fruit; *~-line*, queue of poor people waiting to receive food; ~-*stuffs*, grain, flour; ~-*ticket* (entitling to ration); ~-*winner*, person (also art, trade, tool) that supports a family. Hence ~'LESS a. [OE *brēad*, OS *brōd*, OHG *brōt*, ON *brauth* f. Gmc *braudh- of unkn. orig., the orig. Gmc name for *bread* being LOAF]

breadth (-ĕd-), n. Broadness, measure from side to side, (*to a hair's* ~, exactly); piece (of cloth etc.) of full ~; extent, distance, room; largeness (*of mind*, view, etc.), liberality, catholicity, toleration; bold effect. Hence ~'WAYS, -WISE, advv. [16th c., f. obs. *brede*, OE *brǣdu*, +-TH[1] on anal. of *length* etc.]

break[1] (-āk), v.t. & i. (*broke* & in Bible *brake*; *broken* occas. *broke* see BROKE[2]). **1.** (Of a whole) make or become discontinuous otherwise than by cutting, divide into two or more parts, (~ BULK[1]; ~ *a set*, sell parts separately; ~ *a lance with*, argue against; ~ *bread with*, be entertained by; ~ *Priscian's head*, use bad grammar; ~ *person on wheel*, of medieval execution; ~ *butterfly on wheel*, waste power; ~ *ground*, plough, begin siege, or fig. any, operations; ~ *the ice*, get over initial shyness or reserve; ~ *the ranks*, disorder by leaving them; *troops* ~, disperse in confusion; *clouds* ~, show gap); crack, graze, (~ *a head*); shatter; dislocate (neck; ~ *the neck* or *back of*, kill, dispose of); make by separating obstacles (*a way* etc.); penetrate by ~ing (~ *open*); interrupt, change, (*gloom*, *spell*, *journey*, *silence*, one's *fast*; *voice* ~s, with emotion or at manhood; disrupt (*broken bonds* etc.); solve (a cipher); (Boxing, usu. as command from referee) come out of a clinch; ~ *out*, open up (receptacle) & remove contents (esp. Naut., of cargo). **2.** (Of a part) disconnect or depart from something otherwise than by cutting (~ *bough from tree*, *person of habit*; ~ *with*,

have breach or cease relations with; ~ *an officer*, dismiss; ~ *piece off*; *ball* ~s, changes from its course, *back* from *off*, *in* from *leg*, side). **3.** Make a way, come, produce, with effort, suddenness, violence, etc. (~ *into* house, *out of* prison, *through* obstacles; ~ *in*, intrude, interpose; *disease*, *war*, ~ *out*; ~ *out*, exclaim; ~ *news*, *a jest*, reveal it; ~ WIND[1]; *day* ~s; *abscess* ~s); escape, emerge from, (prison, bounds, covert; ~ *free* or *loose*; ~ *away from*). **4.** Make or become weak, disable, discourage, ruin, destroy, cease, exhaust, (~ *the heart*, *heart* ~s; *frost*, *weather*, ~s; ~ *bank*, exhaust its resources; *merchant* ~s, is bankrupt; ~ *blow*, *fall*, weaken its effect; tame, discipline, overpower, (with *in*, *to*, or abs.; ~ *a horse*, ~ *a horse to the rein*; ~ *in child*; ~ *one's will*, *spirit*; ~ *resistance*, *a rebellion*, *a strike*); make of no effect, transgress, violate, neglect, (*law*, *Sabbath*, *contract*, *promise*, one's *word*). **5.** ~ *down*, collapse, fail; demolish; analyse (cost, total, etc.) into its component items; ~ *even*, emerge with neither gain nor loss; ~ *off*, detach by ~ing, bring to an end; cease; ~ *out*, burst from restraint or concealment, release (flag when run up) from its trussed state, open up (receptacle) & remove contents (esp. Naut., of cargo); ~ *up*, dismiss, depart, ~ *small*, (of person) become feeble, show signs of decay. Hence ~'ABLE a. (also as n. pl., things easily broken), ~'AGE(3) n. [OE *brecan*, OS *brekan*, OHG *brehhan*, Goth. *brikan* f. Gmc *brekan]

break[2] (-āk), n. Breaking; ~ *of day*, dawn; (Cricket) deviation of ball on pitching (~-*back*, f. off side); (Billiards) points scored continuously; gap, broken place, interruption of continuity; short spell of recreation between lessons; (colloq.) a chance; (Mus.) point of separation between different registers of voice; irregularity; *a bad* ~ (colloq.), unfortunate remark or ill-judged action. [f. prec.]

break[3] (-āk), n. Carriage-frame with no body for breaking in young horses; large wagonette. [f. BREAK[1] or = *brake* framework, of unkn. orig.]

break'down (-āk-), n. Collapse, stoppage; failure of health or power; analysis of cost etc. into its component items; Negro dance. [f. BREAK[1], DOWN[3]]

break'er[1] (-āk-), n. In vbl senses (esp. in comb. as *horse*-~); also, heavy ocean-wave breaking on coast or over reefs. [-ER[1]]

break'er[2] (-āk-), n. (naut.). Small keg. [f. Sp. *barreca*, *barrica* cask]

break'fast (brĕk-), n., & v.i. & t. (Take, entertain at) first meal of day. Hence ~LESS a. [BREAK[1] interrupt + FAST n.]

break'neck (-ākn-), a. Dangerous (~ *pace*, *road*, *climb*).

break'-up (-āk-), n. Disintegration, decay, collapse, dispersal. [f. phr. *to break up*] break'water (-ākwaw-), n. Object breaking, mole etc. built to break, force of waves.

bream[1], n. Yellowish arch-backed freshwater fish; (also sea-~) a salt-water variety of this. [ME breme f. OF bre(s)me f. WG, as OS bressemo (= OHG brahsema, G brassen)]

bream[2], v.t. Clear (ship's bottom) by singeing with burning furze etc. [perh. f. Du. brem BROOM, furze]

breast[1] (-ĕst), n. Either milk-secreting organ in woman, corresponding rudiment in man, (occas. of beast's dug); (fig.) source of nourishment; upper front of human body or of coat, dress, etc.; corresponding part of animals; heart, emotions, thoughts, (make a clean ~ of, confess); ~'bone, thin flat vertical bone in chest connecting ribs; ~-drill, -hoe, etc., pushed with ~; ~-fed, -feeding; ~-harness, with ~-band instead of collar; ~-high, high as the ~, (submerged) to the ~, (of scent) so strong that hounds race with heads up; ~-pin, jewelled etc,. worn in tie; ~'plate, piece of armour covering ~, lower shell of turtle, tortoise, etc., inscription-plate on coffin; ~ stroke, stroke made while swimming on the ~ by extending the arms in front & sweeping them back; ~-wall, confining a bank of earth; ~-wheel, water-wheel with water admitted near axle; ~'work, temporary defence or parapet a few feet high. Hence ~'ED[2] a. [OE brēost, OS briost, ON brjóst f. Gmc *breustam, also OHG brust, Goth. brusts (Gmc *brusts)]

breast[2] (-ĕst), v.t. Oppose the breast to, face, contend with, (waves, hill). [f. prec.]

breast'summer (-ĕst-), brĕss'ummer, n. Beam across broad opening, sustaining superstructure. [BREAST[1]+SUMMER[2]]

breath (-ĕth), n. Exhalation as perceptible to sight or smell; slight movement of air; whiff of perfume etc.; air taken into and expelled from lungs (draw ~, breathe, live; a ~ of fresh air; spend, waste, ~, talk vainly; keep ~ to cool porridge, abstain from talk; ~ of life, nostrils, a necessity; take away person's ~, render him breathless with astonishment); respiration (catch, hold, one's ~, in fear or absorbing emotion); one respiration (say inconsistent things in one or the same ~); power of breathing (out of ~, not able to breathe quick enough; take ~, pause, rest); whisper, murmur, (not a ~ heard; also below one's ~, in a whisper). [OE brǣth f. WG *brāth-, whence OHG brādam (G brodem)]

breathe (-ēdh), v.i. & t. Use the lungs; live; seem alive; take breath, pause, (~ again, freely, recover from fear etc., be at ease); sound, speak, (of wind) blow, softly (~ upon, tarnish, taint); send out (new life into; fragrance; ~ one's last breath or last, die); take in (~ foul, wholesome, air); utter softly, also passionately

(~ strife), exhibit (~ simplicity); allow to ~, give rest to; force to ~, exercise, tire. [ME brethen f. prec.]

breath'er (-ĕdh-), n. In vbl senses; esp., short spell of exercise; brief pause for rest. [-ER[1]]

breath'ing (-ēdh-), n. In vbl senses; esp.: (Gk Gram.) rough, smooth, ~, signs ('), ('), indicating that initial vowel is or is not aspirated; ~-space, time to breathe, pause. [-ING[1]]

breath'ing[2] (-ēdh-), a. In vbl senses; esp., lifelike (statue etc.). [-ING[2]]

breath'less (-ĕth-), a. Lifeless; panting; holding the breath; unstirred by wind. [-LESS]

breath'lessly (-ĕth-), adv. Pantingly; in suspense. [-LY[2]]

breath'|y (-ĕth-), a. (Of singing-voice) not clear-cut at beginning of sound, using breath before vocal chords are tense. Hence ~iNESS n. [-Y[2]]

brĕc'cia (-cha), n. Rock of angular stones etc. cemented by lime etc. [It., whence F brèche f. Gmc = BREAK]

bred. See BREED[1].

breech, n., & v.t. 1. pl. ~es (-ich'iz) or pair of ~es, short trousers fastened below knee (Breeches Bible, Geneva Bible of 1560 with ~es for aprons in Gen. iii. 7) and (now) used esp. for riding or in court costume etc. (cf. KNICKERBOCKERS); (loosely) trousers or knickerbockers; wear the ~es, of wife ruling her husband; (sing. arch.) posterior. 2. (Gunnery) part of gun behind bore, back part of rifle or gun barrel; ~-block, closing ~ aperture in guns; ~-loader, -loading, (gun) loaded at ~, not through muzzle; ~es-buoy, lifebuoy with canvas ~es for user's legs. 3. v.t. (arch.). Put (boy) into ~es instead of petticoats. Hence ~ED[2] a., (-icht) wearing ~es, (-ĕcht) having a ~. [OE brēc pl., OS brōk, OHG bruoh, ON brók f. Gmc *brōks; relation to Gaul. brāca, whence L braca, doubtful; double pl. breeches since ME]

breech'ing (-ich-), n. Leather strap round shaft-horse's or wheeler's hindquarters for pushing back; (Naut.) rope securing gun to ship's side. [f. prec. +-ING[1]]

breech'less (-ich-), a. Without breeches. [-LESS]

breed[1], v.t. & i. (brĕd). Bear, generate, (offspring); cherish in womb or egg; propagate; be pregnant; yield, produce, result in; make propagate, raise, (cattle, domestic animals); train up; fit for being, adapt to, (~ him a lawyer, bred to the law), bring up; arise, spread; ~ in & in, always marry near relations; what is bred in the bone, hereditary traits. Hence ~'ER[1] n, (~er reactor, nuclear reactor that can create more fissile material than it consumes in the chain reaction). [OE brēdan, OHG bruotan f. WG *brōdjan f. *brōd-BROOD]

breed², n. Race, stock, strain; family with hereditary qualities. [f. prec.]

breed'ing, n. In vbl senses; esp., result of training, behaviour, good manners. [-ING¹]

breeze¹, n. Gad-fly. [OE *briosa* of unkn. orig.]

breeze², n., & v.i. 1. Gentle wind; wind off land, or sea, at certain hours; (sl.) quarrel, display of temper. 2. v.i. (sl.). Go like a ~, move *along* in lively manner. Hence ~'LESS (-zl-) a. [16th c. *brize*, *brieze*, app. f. OSp., Pg. *briza* NE wind, whence (18th c.) F *brise*; connexion w. F *bise* doubtful]

breeze³, n. Small cinders used with cement in making ~ *blocks* (light-weight concrete building blocks). [f. F BRAISE]

breez'|ў, a. Wind-swept; pleasantly windy; fresh, lively, jovial. Hence ~ILY² adv., ~INESS n. [-Y²]

Brĕ'hon, n. & a. Ancient Irish judge; ~ *law*, Irish code abolished under James I. [f. OIr. *brithem* judge]

Brĕn, n. (In full ~ *gun*) a light-weight machine-gun; ~ *carrier*, small bullet-proof tracked vehicle. [f. *Brno* in Czechoslovakia (where orig. made) + Enfield in England]

brĕnt(-goose), brănt-, n. Smallest species of wild goose, visiting Britain in winter. [deriv. & orig. application uncert.; cf. ON *brandgás*, G *brandgans*]

brĕr, n. (U.S. Negro dial. contraction for) brother (esp. in beast-fable personifications, as B~ *Fox*, *Rabbit*).

brĕss'ŭmmer. See BREASTSUMMER.

breth'ren (-ĕdhrĭn). See BROTHER.

Brĕt'on, a. & n. (Native or language) of Brittany in France. [F, = BRITON]

Brĕtwai'da (-ŏl-), n. Lord of the Britons, title given to Egbert & Old Eng. kings of various States who held supremacy or real supremacy over the rest.

brĕve, n. (Hist.) authoritative letter from sovereign or pope; (Mus.) note = two semibreves now rarely used (*alla* ~, time signature indicating 2 or 4 minim beats in bar); short prosody mark (˘) in printing. [var. of ME *bref(e)* BRIEF¹]

brĕv'ĕt, n., & v.t. Document conferring a privilege from sovereign or government, esp. rank without corresponding pay in army (~ *rank*, ~ *major*); honorary, nominal, position; (vb) confer ~ rank on. [ME f. OF, dim. of *bref* BRIEF¹]

brevi-, comb. form in scientific terms of L *brevis* short, as *brevirostrate* short-beaked.

brĕv'iarў, n. (R.-C. Ch.) book containing the Divine Office for each day, to be recited by those in orders. [f. L *breviarium* summary (*brevis* short, -ARY¹)]

brĕvier', n. Printing-type size between bourgeois & minion. [f. Du. or G *brevier* f. L *breviarium* (prec.)]

brĕv'itў, n. Shortness of expression, conciseness; short span (*of* life). [f. AF

brevete f. L *brevitatem* (*brevis* short, -TY)]

brew¹ (-ŏŏ), v.t. & i. Make (beer etc.) by infusion, boiling, & fermentation (*drink as you have* ~*ed*, take consequences); make (tea, punch) by infusion or mixture; undergo these processes; concoct, bring about, set in train, grow to ripeness, fester, gather force, (usu. of evil results; *mischief is* ~*ing*, ~ *rebellion*); ~*-house*, = brewery (but now less used). Hence ~'ER¹, ~'ERY (3), (-ŏŏ-), nn. [OE *brēowan*, OS *breuwan*, OHG *briuwan*, ON *brugga* f. Gmc *breuwan]

brew² (-ŏŏ), n. Process of brewing; amount brewed at once; quality of stuff brewed (*a good strong* ~). [f. prec.]

brew'age (-ŏŏ-), n. Concocted drink; process or result of concoction (lit. & fig.). [-AGE]

brew'is (-ŏŏ-), n. Broth (arch. & dial.). [MF *browes* f. OF *brouez* nom. of *brouet* dim. of *bro*, *breu* f. WG **broth-*; see BROSE, BROTH]

‖ **Brew'ster Sĕ'ssions** (-ŏŏ-; -shns), n. Sessions for issue of licences to trade in alcoholic liquors. [f. obs. *brewster* (orig. female) brewer, see -STER]

bri'ar. See BRIER.

Briār'eus, n. Many-handed person. [Gk mythol.]

bribe¹, n. Money etc. offered to procure (often illegal or dishonest) action in favour of the giver. [f. foll.]

brib|e², v.t. Pervert by gifts or other inducements the action or judgement of; (abs.) practise bribery. Hence ~'ER¹, ~EE', ~ABIL'ITY, ~'ERY(4), nn., ~'ABLE a. [ME, f. OF *briber*, *brimber* beg etc., of unkn. orig.]

bric'a-brăc, n. Curiosities, old furniture, china, fans, etc. [F, perh. = *de bric et de broc* by hook or by crook]

brick¹, n. & a. 1. Clay kneaded, moulded, & baked by fire or sun; block (usu. rectangular & about 9 in. × 4½ × 2¾) of this (*like a ton of* ~*s* colloq., with crushing weight or force); ~*-shaped* loaf, block of tea, etc.; child's toy building-block; (sl.), generous or loyal person; *drop a* ~ (sl.), commit an indiscretion; ~*-bat*, piece of ~, esp. as missile [BAT²]; ~*-dust*, powdered ~, colour like it; ~*-field*, *-kiln*, in which ~s are made, baked; ~*'layer*, workman building in ~; ~*'work*, building in ~; hence (rare) ~*'EN⁵* a. 2. adj. Built of ~. [15th c., f. MLG, MDu. *bricke*, *brik(e)*, of unkn. orig., whence also F *brique*]

brick², v.t. ~ *up*, block (window etc.) with brickwork (& used with other advv.). [f. prec.]

brick'ў, a. Littered with, coloured or looking like, bricks. [-Y²]

bric'ole (-ĭkl), n. Stroke off wall or cushion in tennis & billiards. [16th c., F, of unkn. orig.]

brid'al, n. & a. 1. Wedding-feast, wedding. 2. adj. Of bride or wedding (~

cheer, veil); hence ~LY² adv. [=*bride* ALE or festivity; OE *brȳd-ealo*; the prevailing adj. use results f. confusion with -AL]

bride¹, n. Woman on her wedding-day & for some days or weeks before & after it; ~'*cake*, rich cake eaten at wedding, sent round to friends etc. [OE *brȳd*, OS *brūd*, OHG *brūt*, ON *brúthr*, Goth. *brúths* f. Gmc *brúdhiz*]

bride², n. Delicate network connecting the patterns in lace; bonnet-string. [F, = BRIDLE¹, f. Teut.]

bride'groom (-dg-), n. Man at or soon before or after his marriage. [OE *brȳd-guma*, f. BRIDE¹ + *guma* man, = OS *brúdi-*, OHG *brútigomo*, ON *brúthgumi*; later assim. to GROOM]

brides'maid (-dz-), n. Unmarried woman (usu. one of several) attending bride at wedding. [16th c. *bridemaid*, cf. *bridegroom*]

brides'man (-dz-), n. Bridegroom's attendant, best man. [earlier *brideman*, cf. prec.]

‖ **bride'well** (-dw-), n. House of correction, gaol. [St Bride's Well, near the London~]

bridge¹, n. (northern form, in writers for local colour, *brig*). Structure carrying road or path across stream, ravine, road, etc. (~ *of boats*, over boats moored abreast; ~ *of gold*, *golden* ~, easy retreat provided for beaten enemy); (Naut.) raised platform from which ship is conned; upper bony part of nose; movable piece over which strings of violin etc. are stretched; (Billiards) support for cue formed with left hand; ~*-head*, post held on far side of river giving one access to enemy's position; ~*-train*, Mil. Engineers with material for building floating ~s. Hence ~LESS (-jl-) a. [OE *brycg*, OS *bruggia*, OHG *brucca*, ON *bryggja* f. Gmc *brugjo*]

bridge², v.t. Span as, with, or as with, a bridge. [OE *brycgian* see prec.]

bridge³, n. Card-game of Russian origin resembling whist, in which a player looks on while his exposed hand is played by his partner; AUCTION ~; CONTRACT¹ ~ [orig. unkn.]

bri'dle¹, n. Head-gear of harness, including head-stall, bit, & rein (*give horse the* ~, *lay* ~ *on his neck*, abandon control; *horse going well up to* ~, willing goer); restraint, curb; (Naut.) mooring-cable; (Physiol.) ligament checking motion of a part; ~*-bridge*, *-path*, *road*, etc., fit for riders but not for vehicles. [OE *bridel*, OHG *brittel*, f. Gmc *bregdan* see BRAID² + -LE(1)]

bri'dle², v.t. & i. Put bridle on (horse etc.); curb, hold *in*, bring under control; express offence, vanity, etc., by throwing up head & drawing in chin (often ~ *up*). [OE *brídlian* see prec.]

bridoon', n. Snaffle & rein of military bridle. [f. F *bridon* (BRIDE², -OON)]

Brie (brē), n. A soft cheese. [~, in northern France]

brief¹, n. Pope's letter on matter of discipline to person or community (less formal than bull); ‖ (Law) summary of facts & law-points of a case drawn up for counsel (*hold* ~ *for*, be retained as counsel for, argue in favour of); size of writing-paper, typewriter, etc.; instructions given to air crews etc.; *watching*~, of barrister who watches case for client indirectly concerned; ‖~*-case*, small leather hand bag; ‖ *a* ~, piece of employment for barrister, whence ~*LESS* a. [ME & OF *bref* f. L *breve* dispatch, note, neut. of *brevis* short]

brief², v.t. (Law) reduce (facts etc.) to a brief; instruct (barrister) by brief, employ; instruct (air crews etc.) with regard to raid etc. (~*-ing-room*, where such instructions are given); instruct thoroughly in advance. [f. prec.]

brief³, a. & n. Of short duration; concise (*be* ~, speak shortly; *in* ~, in short; (pl., colloq.) shorts, women's panties. Hence ~LY² adv., ~NESS n. [ME & OF *bref* f. L *brevis* short]

bri'er¹, **bri'ar**, n. (also *brere* arch.) Prickly bush, esp. of wild rose; *sweet* ~, wild rose with fragrant leaves & flowers, ~*-rose*, dog-rose. Hence ~Y² a. [OE *brǣr*, *brēr*, of unkn. orig.; cf. *frere*, FRIAR]

bri'er², **bri'ar**, n. The white heath, of which the root is used for tobacco pipes, pipe made from this root. [orig. (c. 1859) *bruyer* f. F *bruyère* heath]

brig¹, n. Two-masted square-rigged vessel, but with additional lower fore-&-aft sail on gaff & boom to mainmast. [abbr. of BRIGANTINE]

brig². Northern form of BRIDGE¹.

brigade'¹, n. **1.** Subdivision of army, varying in different countries & times; infantry unit consisting usu. of 3 battalions (with freq. a regiment of field artillery) & forming part of a division, corresponding armoured unit; ‖ *the B*~ (of Guards). **2.** Organized or uniformed band of workers (*Boys*', *Church*, etc., *B*~, organizations on military model for disciplining & occupying boys etc.). [F, f. It. *brigata* company (*brigare* brawl, *briga* strife); see -ADE]

brigade'², v.t. Form into brigade or brigades; join (regiment etc.) *with* others into a brigade. [f. prec.]

brigadier', n. (Formerly *Brigadier-General*) officer commanding a brigade, (titular rank granted to) staff officer of similar standing. [F, see -IER]

brig'and, n. Bandit, robber. Hence or cogn. ~AGE(3), ~ISM(2), nn., ~ISH¹ a. [ME f. OF, f. It. *brigante* (*brigare* see BRIGADE¹)]

brig'antine (-ēn), n. Two-masted vessel with square-sailed fore-mast & fore-&-aft mainmast. [16th c. *-din(e)* f. F brigandin (now *-tin*) t. It. *brigantino* t. *brigante* see prec.]

bright[1] (-ĭt), a. Emitting or reflecting much light, shining; lit up with joy, hope, etc.; vivid (~ *red* etc.); illustrious; vivacious, quick-witted, (often iron.; ~ *young things*). Hence ~'EN[6] v.t. & i., ~'ISH[1] (2) a., ~'LY[2] adv., ~'NESS n., (-ĭt-). [OE *beorht*, OS, OHG *beraht*, ON *bjartr*, Goth. *bairhts* f. Gmc *berhtaz*]

bright[2] (-ĭt), adv.=brightly (*shine* ~, ~*-beaming*, etc.). [OE *beorhte* (prec.)]

Bright's disease' (-ĭts; -zēz), n. Granular degeneration of the kidneys. [Dr R. *Bright* (d. 1858)]

brill, n. Flat-fish resembling turbot. [orig. unkn.]

brill'iant[1] (-lyă-), a. Bright, sparkling; illustrious, striking; talented, showy. Hence ~ANCE, ~ANCY, nn., ~antLY[2] adv. (-lyă-). [f. F *brillant* part. of *briller* shine, f. It. *brillare*, of unkn. orig.]

brill'iant[2] (-lyă-), n. Diamond of finest cut & brilliance (~ *shape* has two horizontal tables, joined by facets); a size of TYPE. [f. F as prec. used as n.]

brill'iantine (-yantēn), n. Cosmetic for hair. [f. F *brillantine* see BRILLIANT[1] +-INE[4]]

brim[1], n. Edge or lip of cup, bowl, or hollow; projecting edge of hat; ~*-full*, to the ~. Hence ~'LESS, ~MED[2] (-md), aa. [ME *brimme* of unkn. orig.; cf. ON *barmr* brim, MHG *brem* (G *bräme*) border]

brim[2], v.t. & i. (-mm-). Fill, be full, to the brim (lit. & fig.); ~ *over*, overflow. [f. prec.]

brimm'er, n. Full cup. [BRIM[2]+-ER[1]]

brim'stone, n. (Old name for) sulphur (||~ *& treacle*, nursery medicine); fuel of hell-fire; ~ *butterfly*, *moth*, sulphur-coloured species. Hence **brim'stony**[2] a. [ME *brin-*, *bren-*, etc. (BURN[2]+STONE)]

brin'dled (-dld), **brin'dle**, a. Brownish or tawny with streaks of other colour. [*brindled* (whence back form. *brindle*) alt. of *brinded* (also *branded*) f. (15th c.) *brended* f. *brend*, perh. of Sc. orig.]

brine[1], n. Salt water; the sea; tears (poet.); ~*-pan*, iron vessel or shallow pit for getting salt by evaporation. Hence **brin'y**[2] a. (*the briny*, sl., the sea). [OE *brȳne* of unkn. orig.; cf. MDu. *brine*, Du. *brijn*]

brine[2], v.t. Steep or pickle in, or wet with, brine. [f. prec.]

bring, v.t. & i. (*brought*, pr. -awt). 1. Cause to come, come with or conveying whether by carrying, leading, impelling, or attracting, (*take* expresses the corresponding notions with *go* for *come*); cause, result in; prefer (charge), adduce (argument); ~ *home to*, convict or convince of; ~ *into play*, cause to operate; ~ *into the world*, give birth to; cause to become (~ *low*); ~ *to bear*, apply (influence etc.); ~ *to book*, exact account from (offender);

~ *to mind*, recall; ~ *to pass*, cause to happen; persuade (*cannot* ~ *myself to believe*). 2. ~ *about*, cause to happen, reverse (ship); ~ *back*, call to mind; ~ *down*, kill or wound, cause penalty to alight *on*, abase, lower (price), continue (record) *to a* point, (Theatr.) ~ *down the house*, elicit tumultuous applause, ~ *forth*, give birth to, cause; ~ *forward*, carry sum of page's figures to next page, ~ *in*, introduce (custom), produce as profit, adduce, pronounce (*guilty, not guilty*), ~ *off*, rescue from wreck etc., conduct (enterprise) to success; ~ *on*, lead to, cause discussion of; ~ *out*, express, exhibit clearly, introduce (girl) to society, publish; ~ *over*, convert; ~ *round*, restore to consciousness, win over (*to other person's opinion*); ~ *through*, save (sick person); ~ *to*, check motion of, come to a stop, restore to conscious; ~ *under*, subdue; ~ *up*, educate, rear, sue in court, anchor (ship), come to a stop, call attention to, cause (person) to rise & speak, continue (accounts etc.) to a further point; ~ *up the rear*, come last. [OE, OS, OHG *bringan*, Goth. *briggan* f. Gmc *brengan*]

brink, n. Edge of steep place or abyss (*on* ~ *of grave*, soon to die); border of water, esp. when steep (*shiver on the* ~, hesitate to plunge, usu. fig.); verge (*of discovery*, ruin, eternity, etc.); ~*manship*, art of advancing to the very ~ of war but not engaging in it. [ME also *brenk*, f. Scand., cf. OIcel. *brekka* slope (Sw., Da. *brink*) MLG *brink* edge of field, MDu. *brinc*]

bri'o (-ēō), n. Vivacity. [It.]

briquette' (-kĕt), **bri'quet** (-kĕt), n. Block of compressed coal-dust. [F (*-ette*), dim. of *brique* BRICK]

brisk[1], a. Active, lively, (usu. of movement; ~ *pace*, *trade*, *wind*, etc.); enlivening, keen, (champagne, air, etc.). Hence ~'LY[2] adv., ~'NESS n. [16th c., f. F BRUSQUE]

brisk[2], v.t. & i. Make or become brisk (usu. with *up*). [f. prec.]

brisk'et, n. Breast of animals (esp. as joint of meat). [15th c. *brusket(te)* f. OF *bruschet* etc. (mod. *bréchet*)]

bri'stle[1] (-ĭsl), n. One of stiff hairs on hog's back & sides; short stiff hair of other animals, man's short-cropped beard, or plants; *set up* one's, another's, ~*s*, show or rouse temper. Hence **bri'stly**[2] (-ĭsli), **bri'stl**ED[2] (-ĭsld), aa. [ME *brustel* f OE *byrst* (= OHG, ON *burst* +-LE (1)]

bri'stle[2] (-ĭsl), v.i. & t. (Cause to) stand upright (hair etc.), raise or rise like bristles or into roughness, (often with *up*); show temper, prepare for fight; be thickly set *with* hair, difficulties, etc. [f. prec.]

bris'(t)ling, n. A small sardine-like fish [Norw. *brisling* sprat]

Bris'tol, n. (attrib.). ~ *board*, kind of cardboard for drawing on; (*shipshape & ~ fashion* (Naut., & transf.), with all in good order: ~ *cream, milk,* P, kinds of sherry.

Brit'ain (-Itn), n. (Also *Great* ~) England, Wales, & Scotland; *North* ~, Scotland; *Greater* ~ (descriptive, not official), Gt ~ & the colonies. [ME *Bretayne* f. OF *Bretaigne* f. L *Brittania*]

Britănn'ia (-ya), n. Personification of Britain; ~ *metal*, alloy of tin & regulus of antimony resembling silver. [L, anciently *Brittan(n)ia* = Gk *Brettania* f. *Brettanoi* Britons; see BRITISH]

Britănn'ic, a. Of Britain (chiefly in phr. *Her* or *His* ~ *Majesty*). [f. L *Britannicus* or F *britannique* (prec., -IC)]

Brit'icism, n. = BRITISHISM. [U.S. wd, f. *Brit*(ish) + -ISM(4), after *Gallicism*]

Brit'ish, a. Of the ancient Britons & their language; of Great Britain or its inhabitants (esp. in political or imperial connexion, & in botany etc.); *the* ~, soldiers, people, etc.; ~ *Academy*, chartered body of 200 for promotion of historical, philosophical, & philological studies; ~ *Association* (for advancement of science); ~ COMMONWEALTH (*of Nations*); ~ *Expeditionary* Force (abbr. B.E.F.), any of the armies sent abroad in wartime, esp. Sir J. French's original force in France in 1914; ~ *Museum*, national museum of antiquities, books, natural history, etc., in London; ~ *warm*, kind of short military overcoat. [OE *Brettisc, Bryttisc.* f. *Bret, Bryt* (f. OCelt. *Brett-, *Britt-*) + -ISH[1]]

Brit'isher, n. (U.S. etc. term for) British subject of British descent. [-ER[1]; cf. *foreigner*]

Brit'ishism, n. Idiom used in Gt Britain & not in U.S. etc. [-ISM (4)]

Brit'on, n. One of the race found by Romans in England; native of Great Britain or the British Empire (poet., melodramatic, etc.). [ME & OF *breton* f. L *Brittōnem* nom. *Britto*, f. OCelt. name, see BRITISH]

brit'tle, a. Apt to break, fragile. Hence ~NESS (-ln-) n. [ME *britul* f. *brut-* stem of OE *brēotan* break]

brit'zka, -tzska, (-'itska), n. Open carriage with calash top & space for reclining. [f. Pol. *bryczka* dim. of *bryka* wagon]

brize (-ēz). = BREEZE[1].

broach[1], n. Roasting-spit; church spire rising from tower without parapet; boring-bit. [ME & OF *broche* f. Rom. *brocca* spike f. L *brocc(h)us* in *brocci dentes* projecting teeth; see BROOCH]

broach[2], v.t. Pierce (cask) to draw liquor, begin drawing (liquor); open & start using (bale, box, cargo, etc.); begin discussion of, moot, (subject). [f. prec.]

broach[3], v.t. & i. (Usu. ~ *to*) veer or cause (ship) to veer & present side to wind & waves. [c. 1700; orig. unkn.]

broad (-awd), a., n., & adv. 1. Large across, wide, not narrow; = in breadth (6 *ft* ~); extensive (~ *acres*); full, clear,

main, explicit, (~ *daylight, facts, distinction, hint*); coarse (~ *story*); downright in sound, not mincing, (~ *Yorkshire, Scotch*); generalized (~ *rule*); tolerant (B~ *Church*, churchmen favouring comprehension & not pressing doctrines); bold in effect or style; *as* ~ *as it is long*, indifferent; || ~ ARROW; ~ *bean* (the common flat variety); ||~*cloth*, fine plain-weave double-width dressed black cloth [phr. in Act of Parl. 1482 kept as name for quality rather than width]; ~ GAUGE; ~*mind'ed*(*ness*), (the condition of) being tolerant in thought or opinion; ~*sheet*, large sheet of paper printed on one side only; ~*side*, ship's side above water between bow & quarter (~*side on, to,* with this presented), (discharge of) all guns on one side of ship, also = ~sheet; ~*silk*, -*weaver*, (of) silk in piece not in ribbons; ~*sword*, ~-*bladed* cutting-sword. 2. n. The ~ part (~ *of the back*); || (E. Anglia) large piece of water formed by widening of river; (sl.) woman, prostitute. 3. adv. = ~ly (*speak* ~, ~ *awake*); ~*blown*, in full bloom. Hence ~*EN*[6] v.t. & i., ~*LY*[2], ~*WAYS*, ~*WISE*, advv. [OE *brād*, OS *brēd*, OHG *breit*, ON *breithr*, Goth. *braiths* f. Gmc *braidhaz*]

broad'cast (-awdkah-), a., adv., v.t. & i. (past -*casted*, p.p. -*cast*), & n. (Of seed) scattered freely, not in drills or rows, (adv.) in this manner, (v.i. & t.) sow thus, (all also fig. of information, propaganda, etc.); (Radio, v.t.) disseminate (news, music, any audible matter) by wireless telephony, (v.i.) speak, sing, play, etc., for such transmission, (n., esp. attrib.) the practice etc. of ~ing (*today's* ~ *programme*). [f. prec. + *cast* p.p.]

Broad'moor (braw-), n. Asylum in Berkshire for criminal lunatics.

broad'ness (-aw-), n. (Superseded by *breadth,* exc. in sense) indelicacy (of speech). [-NESS]

Brŏb'dingnăg, n. Land of giants. Hence ~*IAN* (-ăg[4]) a. [Swift, *Gulliver's Travels*]

brocāde[1], n. Fabric woven with raised patterns; Indian cloth of gold & silver. [f. Sp. & Port. *brocado* f. It. *broccato*]

brocāde[2], v.t. Work with raised pattern. [f. prec.]

brŏc'(c)oli, n. Cultivated cabbage with edible flower head, hardy variety of cauliflower. [It., pl. of *broccolo* cabbage-top dim. of *brocco* see BROACH[1]]

|| **broch** (-ŏχ), n. Prehistoric circular stone tower in the north of Scotland. [f. ON *borg* castle]

brŏ'ché (-shā), a. & n. (Of fabrics, esp. silk) embossed, woven with a pattern on the surface; (n.) such fabric. [F, p.p. of *brocher* stitch]

brŏchure' (-shoor), n. Stitched booklet, pamphlet. [F]

brŏck, n. Badger; stinking fellow. [OE *broc* f. Celt.]

brŏck'ĕt, n. Second-year stag with

straight horns. [ME, f. AF *broquet* f. *broque* (= OF *broche* BROACH[1]) +*-et* -ET[1]; cf. F *brocard*]

broderie Anglaise (brŏd'rĭ ahṅglăz'), n. Open embroidery on white linen or cambric. [F, = English embroidery]

brogue[1] (-ōg), n. Rude Irish & Scotch- -Highland shoe of untanned leather; *fishing-~s*, waterproof leggings with feet; nailed & goloshed shoe for golf etc. [f. Gael. & Ir. *brōg* f. OIr. *brōce* shoe]

brogue[2] n. Dialectal, esp. Irish, accent. [orig. unkn.; perh. allusively f. prec.]

broid'er, v.t., **broid'erў**, n. (Poet. & arch. for) EMBROIDER(Y).

broil[1], n. Quarrel, tumult. [f. obs. vb *broil* mix, quarrel (cf. EMBROIL) f. OF *brouiller*]

broil[2], v.t. & i. Cook (meat) or be cooked on fire or gridiron; make, be, very hot (of person in sun etc.). Hence ~'ER[1] n., young chicken reared for ~ing. [ME *brule* f. OF *bruler*; ME *bruyle*, *broyle* corresp. formally to OF *bruillir* which, however, is intr.]

broil[3], n. Broiled meat. [f. prec.]

brŏke[1], n. Short-stapled wool on certain parts of fleece. [OE *broc* f. *brecan* BREAK]

brŏke[2], p.p. of BREAK, still often used in some spec. senses, as = ruined (esp., sl., *stony-~*), & *dismissed the service*.

brŏk'en, a. In vbl senses of BREAK[1]; also or esp., ~ *meat* etc., remains; ~ *tea*, *siftings*; ~ *water*, choppy; ~ *ground*, uneven; ~ *sleep*, intermittent; ~ *weather*, uncertain; ~ *English*, imperfect; ~- *-hearted*, crushed by grief; ~ *man*, reduced to despair; ~ REED; ~ *time*, (esp. working) time which has been reduced by interruptions; ~*-winded*, (of horse) incapacitated for hard work by ruptured air- -cells. [p.p. of BREAK]

brŏk'enly, adv. Spasmodically, by jerks, with breaks. [prec. +-LY[2]]

brŏk'er, n. ‖ Dealer in second-hand furniture etc.; middleman in bargains; agent, commissioner; ‖ person licensed to sell or appraise distrained goods. Hence ~AGE(4) n. [ME & AF *brocour* = OF *brocheor* broacher, retailer of wine (BROACH[1])]

brŏk'ing, n. Broker's trade, acting as broker. [f. obs. vb *broke* cf. prec.]

‖ **brŏll'ў**, n. (sl.). Umbrella. [abbr.]

brŏm'al, n. Compound produced by action of bromine on alcohol. [BROM(INE) +*al-* of ALCOHOL]

brŏm'ic, a. Containing bromine in chem. combination. Hence **brŏm'**ATE[1](3) n. [BROMINE, -IC]

brŏm'ide, n. Compound (see -IDE) of bromine, used in various preparations as sedative; a commonplace bore, trite remark, conventionalism, (orig. U.S. sl.); ~ *paper*, photographic printing & enlarging paper coated with silver ~ emulsion. [foll. +-IDE]

brŏm'ĭne, n. Non-metallic element, a poisonous dark liquid with rank smell. Hence **brŏm'**IZE (5) v.t., **brŏm'**ISM (5) n. [f. F *brome* f. Gk *bromos* stink +-INE[3]]

bromo-, brŏm-, comb. forms of *bromine* as in *bromobenzoic*, *bromacetic*. [-O-]

brŏn'chĭ, brŏn'chĭa, (-ngk-), nn. pl. (From -*i*, with *ei'ag*. -*us*) two main divisions of wind pipe; (-*ia*) ramifications of these in lungs. Hence **brŏn'chĭ**AL a., **brŏn'chĭo-, brŏn'cho-** (-ngk-) comb. forms, **brŏn'cho-** PNEUMONIA, **brŏnchŏ**T'OMIST, -ŏT'OMY, nn. [LL; f. Gk *brogkhia*]

brŏnch|it'is (-ngk-), n. Inflammation of bronchial mucous membrane. Hence ~it'IC a. [prec. +-ITIS]

brŏn'cŏ (-ngk-), n. (pl. -os). Wild or half- -tamed horse of California etc.; ~*-buster* (sl.), breaker in of ~s. [Sp., = rough]

Brŏntosaur'us, n. Genus of huge prehistoric dinosaurian reptiles of the Jurassic & Cretaceous periods. [f. Gk *brontē* thunder +*sauros* lizard]

brŏnze[1], n. & a. 1. Brown alloy chiefly of copper & tin (about 8:1; *the ~ age*, in which weapons and tools were made of ~); work of art made of this; colour of ~; hence **brŏnz'ў**[2] a. 2. adj. Made of, coloured like, ~. [F. f. It. *bronzo*, = med. L *brundium*; orig. unkn.]

brŏnze[2], v.t. & i. Give bronze-like surface to; make or become brown, tan. [f. prec.]

brooch (-ō-), n. Ornamental jewelled, etc., safety-pin for fastening some part of female dress, esp. the neck. [ME *broche* = BROACH[1]]

brōod[1], n. Hatch of young birds or other egg-produced animals; (usu. derog.) human family, children; swarm, crew, of men, animals, or things; ~, for breeding (~*-mare*, *-hen*). [OE *brōd*, cogn. w. Du. *broed*, OHG *bruot* f. Gmc *brō-* warm, heat]

brōod[2], v.i. Sit as hen on eggs; hang close *over* or *on* (of night etc.); meditate *on* or *over* (esp. insults, ill designs, etc.); meditate (often sullenly). [f. prec.]

brōod'jў, a. Wishing to sit or incubate (of hen). Hence ~INESS n. [BROOD[1] +-Y[2]]

brŏok[1], n. Small stream; ~*'lime*, kind of speedwell common in ditches [OE *hleomoc* name of the plant]. Hence ~*'LET* n. [OE *brōc*, MLG *brōk*, OHG *bruoh* marsh, WG of unkn. orig.]

brŏok[2], v.t. Put up with, tolerate, (in neg. context). [OE *brūcan*, OHG *brūhhan*, Goth. *brūkjan* f. Gmc *brūk-* use]

broom, n., & v.t. Yellow-flowered shrub growing on sandy banks etc.; genus to which it belongs; sweeping-implement usu. on long handle (vb, sweep with this); *new ~*, newly appointed official eager to sweep away abuses; ~*'rape*, kinds of parasitic herbs on roots of broom etc.; ~*'stick*, handle of ~ (ridden on through the air by witches, & jumped over by parties to sham marriage). [OE *brōm*, OS *-brāmio*, OHG *brāmo* f. WG **brām-* cf. BRAMBLE]

‖ **bröse** (-z), n. Dish of oatmeal with boiling water or milk poured on it; *Athole ~*, mixture of whisky & honey. [Sc. form of BREWIS]

broth (-ŏ-, -aw-), n. Water in which something, esp. meat, has been boiled, thin soup; (Irish) *~ of a boy*, good fellow. [OE, *broth*, ON *broth*, OHG *brod* f. Gmc **brotham* f. **bru-* BREW + -TH[1]]

bröth'el, n. House of ill fame, bawdy-house. [ME *brothel* worthless man, prostitute, f. OE *brēothan* go to ruin; hence 16th c. *brothel(-house)*, confused w. & replacing ME *bordel* (OF f. *bord* BOARD)]

broth'er (-ŭdh-), n. (pl. ~*s* & in some senses *breth'ren* pr. -ĕdhrĭn, see below). Son of same parents or (strictly *half-~*) parent as another person (the latter usu. specified by *my* etc. or a possessive case; pl. abbr. *Bros*, in title of firm, as *Smith Bros & Co.*); (Bibl.) kinsman; close friend; fellow citizen, countryman, or man, equal, (*a man & a ~*, esp. of Negro slaves); fellow member of religious society (pl. *brethren*); fellow member of guild, order, profession, etc. (pl. *brethren*); official of certain companies etc. (*Elder B~*, *Brethren*, member(s) of Trinity House Corporation); companion, associate, (pl. ~*s*) often with specification as *~ in arms*, *of the angle*; member of religious order (also title; either pl.); *~ german*, on both sides, *~ uterine*, of same mother only; *~-in-law*, *~ of* one's husband or wife, husband of one's sister. Hence ~LESS a., ~LIKE a. & adv., ~LY[1][2] a. & adv., ~LINESS n. [OE *brōthor*, OS *-ar*, OHG *bruodar*, ON *brōthir*, Goth. *brōthar* f. Gmc **brōthar* cogn. w. L *frater*]

broth'erhŏŏd (-ŭdh-), n. Fraternal tie; companionship; (members of) association for mutual help etc.; community of feeling. [ME *brotherhede* alt. f. ME *brotherrede* (f. OE *brōthor-rǣden*; cf. (KIND)RED) after wds in -HEAD]

brougham (-ōŏm, -ōŏ'am), n. One-horse (or electric) closed carriage. [Lord *B~* (d. 1868)]

brought. See BRING.

brou'haha (-rōŏ-), n. Commotion, to-do, sensation; hubbub, uproar. [F]

brow[1], n. Arch of hair over eye (usu. in pl. & usu. *eye~s*; *knit*, *bend*, one's ~*s*, frown); forehead (*~-ague*, megrim); edge, projection, of cliff etc., top of hill in road. Hence *~ED[2]* (-wd) a. [OE *brū* f. Gmc **brūs*, cf. ON *brún* eyebrow; not related to BRAE]

brow[2], n. (naut.). Gangway, inclined plane of planks. [app. f. Da., Sw. *bru* bridge]

brow'beat, v.t. Bully, bear down, with looks & words, [BROW[1]]

brown[1], a. Of the colour given by mixing

orange & black or by toasting bread; as distinctive epithet of species etc. (*~ bear*, *willow*; *~ coal*, lignite; *~ bread*, of unbolted flour; *~ paper*, coarse unbleached kind used for parcels etc.; *~ shirt*, a Nazi; *~ sugar*, half refined; *~ ware*, common sort of pottery); dark-skinned, tanned; ‖ (sl.) *do ~*, take in, cheat; *~ study*, reverie. Hence *~'ISH[1]* (2) a., *~'NESS* (-nn-) n., *~ӯ-* comb. form. [OE *brūn*, OS, OHG *brūn*, ON *brúnn* f. Gmc **brūnaz*]

brown[2], n. Brown colour; brown pigment; (ellipt. for) brown butterfly, fishing-fly, clothes; ‖ (sl.) copper coin; ‖ *the ~*, brown mass of flying game-birds; ‖ *fire into the ~*, let fly into a covey without singling out a bird (also transf., fire, launch missile, indiscriminately into a mass). [f. prec.]

brown[3], v.t. & i. Make or become brown by roasting, sunburn, or (gun-barrel etc.) chemical process; ‖ *~ed off* (sl.), bored, fed up. [f. BROWN[1]]

brown'ie, n. Benevolent shaggy goblin haunting house & doing household work secretly; junior member (ages 8–11) of GIRL *guides*. [BROWN[1] + -Y[3]]

Brown'ing, n. Kind of automatic rifle. [J. M. *~*, Amer. inventor (d. 1926)]

*brown'stŏne, n. Kind of reddish-brown sandstone used for building (esp. in front elevation); *~ district*, quarter occupied by the well-to-do. [BROWN[1]]

browse[1] (-z), n. Twigs, young shoots. etc., as fodder for cattle; act of browsing. [16th c., f. F *broust* & foll.]

browse[2] (-z), v.i. & t. Feed *on*, crop, (leaves, twigs, scanty vegetation); (abs.) feed thus, (fig.) read for enjoyment. [16th c., f. F *brouster* (mod. *brouter*) f. *broust* (mod. *brout*) young shoot f. Frank. **brust*; cf. OS *brustian* sprout]

Bru'in (-ōŏ-), n. (Personifying name for) bear. [MDu., = BROWN[1], name in *Reynard the Fox*]

bruise[1] (-ōŏz), n. Injury by blow to body (also to fruit etc.) discolouring skin. [f. foll.]

bruise[2] (-ōŏz), v.t. & i. Injure by blow that discolours skin without breaking it or any bone, contuse, (human or animal body, also fruit, plant, etc.); dint, batter, (wood, metal); (fig.) disable; pound, bray, grind small; (Hunting) ride recklessly; (with *easily* etc.) show effects of blow. [ME *brise*, *bruse* f. OE *brӯsan* crush; reinforced by AF *bruser*, OF *bruisier* (mod. *briser*) break]

bruis'er (-ōŏz-), n. In vbl senses; esp., prizefighter. [-ER[1]]

bruit[1] (-ōŏt), n. (arch.). Report, rumour. [F, = noise (*bruire* roar)]

bruit[2] (-ōŏt), v.t. (arch. & U.S.). Spread (report) *abroad*, *about*, make famous, celebrate. [f. prec.]

brŭmb'ӯ, n. (Austral. colloq.). Unbroken horse. [orig. unkn.]

brume (-ōō-), n. (poet.). Mist, fog. [F, f. L *bruma* shortest day, winter]

Brŭmm'agém, n. & a. (Dial. & derog. form of) Birmingham; (article) made at ~ counterfeit, cheap & showy. [allusion to counterfeit groats made there in 17th c., & to its plated goods]

brum'ous (-ōō-); a. Wintry, foggy. [f. F *brumeux* f. LL *brumosus* rainy (*bruma* BRUME, see -OUS)]

brŭnch, n. (sl.). Single meal in lieu of breakfast & lunch. [portmanteau wd]

brunĕtte' (-ōō-), n. & a. Dark-skinned & black- or brown-haired (woman). [F, fem. of *brunet* dim. of *brun* BROWN[1] see -ETTE]

Brŭns'wick (-z-), a. From~ in Germany; esp., ~ *line*, of Eng. sovereigns from George I; ~ *black*, a varnish. [f. LG *Brunswik* = G *Braunschweig*]

brŭnt, n. Chief stress (usu. *of* the attack etc., & in phr. *bear the* ~ *of*). [ME, orig. unkn.]

brush[1], n. **1.** (Arch. & U.S., Austral., etc.) brushwood or underwood, thicket, small trees & shrubs growing or (in U.S.) cut in faggots. **2.** Implement of bristles, hair, wire, etc., set in wood etc. for scrubbing or sweeping; bunch of hairs etc. in straight handle, quill, etc., *for* painting etc.; *the* ~, art of painting; ~, painter's style, painter (*from the same* ~). **3.** Tail, esp. of fox; ~-like tuft. **4.** (electr.). ~-like discharge of sparks, piece of carbon or metal ending in wires or strips securing good metallic connexion, (also) movable strip of conductible material for making & breaking connexion. **5.** (optics). Bright or dark figure with vague edge. **6.** Application of ~, brushing, esp. ~ *up* [f. foll.]; short smart encounter, skirmish, graze, abrasion, [f. foll.]. **7.** ~'*fire* (small frontier) *war*; ~-*pencil*, artist's colour-~; ~*wood*, undergrowth, thicket; ~-*work*, painter's (style of) manipulation. Hence ~'Y[2] a. [(sense ~*wood*) ME *brusche* f. OF *brosse*, *broce*, (other senses) ME *brusshe* f. OF *brosse*, *broisse* of uncert. orig.; *broce* & *broisse* have been identified, & related to Gmc **borst-*, **barst-* BRISTLE]

brŭsh[2], v.t. & i. Move briskly, esp. *by*, *through*, *against*; sweep or scrub clean, put in order, with brush; ~ *up*, furbish, (fig.) renew one's memory of; ~ *over*, paint lightly; graze or touch in passing; remove (dust etc.) with brush; ~ *aside*, *away* (fig.), ignore, pass over; injure by grazing. [f. prec.]

brusque (-ōōsk, -ŭsk), a. Blunt, offhand, (of or in manner, speech). Hence ~'LY[2] (-kl-) adv., ~'NESS (-kn-), ~rie (-ōōskerē') [-ERY], nn. [F, f. It. *brusco* sour]

Brüss'els (-z-), a. Made or grown at, or adopted from, ~, as ~ *carpet*, *lace*, *sprouts* (edible buds of kind of cabbage).

brŭt, a. (Of wines) unsweetened. [F]

brut'al (-ōō-), a. Sensual, rude, coarse, savagely cruel. Hence ~ISM(2), brutăl'ITY, nn., ~LY[2] adv., (-ōō-). [f. F *brutal* or LL *brutalis* (*brutus* BRUTE, -AL)]

brut'alize, **-is**(e) (-iz), v.t. & i. (-ōō-). Make (*rarely* grow) brutal. Hence ~A'TION n. [prec. +-IZE(3)]

brut|e (-ōōt), a. & n. (Beast) not gifted with reason; stupid, sensual, unspirited, beast-like, cruel, or passionate (person; & in same adj. senses of acts, motives, etc.); unconscious, merely material, (~ *force*, *matter*); lower animal; lower nature in man. Hence ~e'HOOD (-t-h-) n., ~'ISH[1](1) a., ~'ishLY[2] adv., ~'ishNESS n., ~'iFY v.t., ~'iFICA'TION n., (-ōō-). [15th c. (adj.) f. F *brut* f. L *brutus* stupid]

brut'um fŭl'mĕn (-ōō-) n. Empty threat, blank cartridge (fig.). [L]

Brut'us (-ōō-), n. Style of wig (19th cent.). [F name in honour of Roman hero]

bryŏl'ogist, **-l'ogў**, nn. Person learned in, the lore of, mosses. [Gk *bruon* kind of seaweed +-LOGIST, -LOGY]

brў'onў, n. Kinds of climbing plants; *red or white* ~, common species; *black* ~, *bastard* ~, plants resembling but not belonging to the genus. [f. L f. Gk *bruōnia*]

bŭb'al,n. A N.-African antelope. [f. L f. Gk *boubalos* ox-like antelope]

bŭb'ble[1], n. Spherical or hemispherical envelope of liquid enclosing air etc.; air- -filled cavity in solidified liquid, as glass, amber; unsubstantial or visionary project, enterprise, etc. (also adj. in this sense; *prick the* ~, unmask futility, pretension, etc.); SOUTH *Sea B*~; sound or appearance of boiling; ~-*&-squeak*, cold meat fried with chopped vegetables; ~-*car*, miniature motor-car with glass-like dome. Hence **bŭb'blY[2]** a. (also ǁ n., sl., champagne). [f. foll.]

bŭb'ble[2], v.i. & t. Send up, rise in, make the sound of, bubbles (lit., & fig. as ~ *over*, or ~, *with* laughter, wrath); delude (arch.). [14th c., imit.; cf. BLEB, BLUBBER, & obs. *burble*]

ǁ **bŭb'blў-jŏck**, n. (Sc.). Turkey-cock. [*bubbly* (BUBBLE[1]) +*Jock* = *Jack*]

bŭb'|o, n. (pl. *-oes*). Inflamed swelling in glandular part, esp. groin or armpit. Hence ~ŏn'IC a. (esp. ~*onic plague*). [L, f. Gk *boubōn* groin]

bŭbōn'ocele (-sēl), n. Hernia of groin. [prec., -CELE]

bŭccaneer', n., & v.i. (Be a) sea-rover, pirate, esp. of the Spanish-American coasts; adventurer. Hence ~ISH[1] (-nēr-) a. [f. F *boucanier* f. *boucaner* cure meat on a *boucan* (i.e. barbecue) a Braz. wd]

buc'cinātor (-bŭks-), n. Flat thin cheek- -muscle. [L, f. *buccinare* blow the trumpet f. *buccina*, -TOR)]

Bŭcĕph'alus, n. Riding-horse (joc.). [charger of Alexander of Macedon]

Buch'man|ism (bōōk-, bŭk-), n. Religious system, occas. called the *Oxford Group* (*Movement*) & (in U.S.) the *Moral Rearmament Movement*, introduced c. 1921

by F. *Buchman*. So ~ITE[1] a. & n.
[-ISM]

bŭck[1], n. Male of fallow-deer, reindeer,
chamois, antelope, hare, rabbit; dandy
(also *old* ~, vocative=old fellow), whence
~ISH[1] a., ~ishLY[2] adv.; (attrib., sl.)
male, of or for males, (~ *nigger* etc.);
~-*horn*, as material for knife handles etc.
(also ~-, as ~-*handled*); ~-*hound*, small
variety of staghound (not now used for
hunting); ~-*shot*, coarse shot; ~-*skin*,
(leather made of) ~'s skin, (pl.) breeches
of it; ~-*thorn*, thorny shrub with cathartic
berries; ~-*tooth*, one that projects. [OE
buc, OHG *bocch* (G *bock*), ON *bukkr*, f.
Gmc **bukkaz*]

bŭck[2], v.i. & t. (Of horse) jump vertically
with back arched & feet drawn together
(also ~-*jump*, whence ~-*jŭmpER[1]* n.);
~ *off*, throw (rider) thus. Hence ~ER[1] n.
[f. prec.]

bŭck[3], v.i. & t. (sl.). (With *up*) make
haste, become or make vigorous or
cheerful, (esp. intr. in imperat.). [f. BUCK[1]
in sense *dandy*]

‖ **bŭck[4]**, n. Basket for trapping eels.
[orig. unkn.]

bŭck[5], n. Body of cart (chiefly in comb.
as ~-*board*, ~-*cart*, in various local
senses). [perh. f. obs. *bouk* belly, f. OE *bûc*]

bŭck[6], n., & v.i., (orig. Anglo-Ind.). Conversation, boastful talk; (v.i.) chat,
swagger, brag (*about*); ~-*stick* (sl.),
braggart. [f. Hind. *baknā* talk freely]

•**bŭck[7]**, n. (sl.). Article placed as a
reminder before a player whose turn it
is to deal at poker; *pass the* ~ *to*, shift
responsibility to (another), make a dupe
of (person). [orig. unkn.]

•**bŭck[8]**, n. (sl.). Dollar. [orig. unkn.]

•**bŭck[9]**, n. Frame on which wood is
cross-cut. [f. Du. *zaag-boc*]

bŭck'bean, n. Water plant with pinkish
racemes. [transl. (1578) of Flem. *bocks
boonen* goats' beans]

bŭck'ĕt[1], n. Wooden or other vessel for
drawing or carrying water; piston of
pump; compartment of water-wheel,
scoop of dredging-machine or grain-
-elevator; socket for whip, carbine,
wooden leg, etc.; *kick the* ~ (sl.), die (but
perh. f. obs. *bucket* beam, yoke); ~-*shop*,
(orig. U.S.) office for gambling in stocks,
speculating on markets, etc. [accidental
story connected with elevator of office
first so called]. Hence ~FUL(2) (-ŏŏl)
n. [ME, AF *buket, buquet*, perh, f. OE
bûc pitcher]

bŭck'ĕt[2], v.i. & t. Ride hard (horse, or
abs.); ‖ (Rowing) hurry the forward
swing, row hurried stroke. [f. prec., cf.
pump = exhaust]

Bŭck'ingham Păl'ace, n. London
residence of the Sovereign. [place]

bŭck'le[1], n. Metal rim with hinged spiked
tongue for securing strap, ribbon, etc.
[ME *bocle* f. OF *boucle* f. L *buccula* beaver
of helmet (*bucca* cheek, see -ULE)]

bŭc'kle[2], v.t. & i. Fasten with buckle
(often *up, on*, etc.); ~ *to* (with *to* prep.)
prepare for, set about, (with *to* adv.) get
to work, start vigorously; (cause to) give
way, crumple up, under longitudinal
pressure (t. & i. of wheel, saw, etc.). [f.
prec.; the last sense perh. f. F *boucler*
bulge]

bŭck'ler, n., & v.t. Small round shield
usu. held by handle; protection, protector, (vb, protect); also technically in
various naut., zool., & anat. senses. [ME
boc(e)ler f. OF *bocler* lit. 'having a boss'
f. *boucle* boss, see BUCKLE[1], -ER[2]]

bŭck'ō, a. & n. (naut. sl.). Swaggering
(fellow). [f. BUCK[1]]

bŭck'ra, a. & n. (Negro dial.). Characteristic of, belonging to, the white man;
(n.) white man, master. [f. Surinam
Negro patois *bakra* master]

bŭck'ram, n. & a. Coarse linen or cloth
stiffened with gum or paste; stiffness,
stiff, (of manner); strong, strength, in
appearance only; *men in* ~, ~ *men*, non-
existent (1 *Hen. IV*, II. iv. 210-50). [ME,
f. AF *bukeram*, OF *boquerant*, of unkn.
orig.]

‖ **bŭck'shee**, n., a., & adv., (sl., orig.
army). 1. Something in addition to the
usual allowance, as extra rations. 2. adj.
& adv. Gratuitous(ly), free. [corrupt. of
BAKSHEESH]

bŭck'wheat (-wēt), n. A cereal plant with
seed used for horse & poultry food, & in
U.S. for breakfast cakes. [f. MDu.
boecweite beech wheat]

bŭcŏl'ic, a. & n. Of shepherds, pastoral,
rustic; (usu. pl.) pastoral poems (*the
B~s*, those of Virgil). Hence bŭcŏl'-
ICALLY adv. [f. L f. Gk *boukolikos* f.
boukolos herdsman]

bŭd[1], n. Rudiment of branch, leaf-
-cluster, or flower; flower not fully open;
(Zool.) animal forming by GEMMATION,
anything still undeveloped; (in ~),
putting forth buds; *nip in the* ~, destroy
at early stage (fig.). Hence ~LESS a.,
~LET n. [late ME *budde, bodde*, of unkn.
orig.]

bŭd[2], v.i. & t. (-dd-). Put forth buds,
spring forth; begin to grow or develop
(~*ding horns, lawyer, cricketer*); (Zool.)
produce, be produced, by GEMMATION;
(Gardening) ingraft (trans. or abs.) into
alien stock. [f. prec.]

bŭdd'ĕd, p.p. In vbl senses; esp., that
has budded, is in bud. [-ED[1](2)]

Buddh|a (bŏŏd'a), n. The Enlightened,
title of successive teachers past & future
of the Asian religion ~ISM(3) (bŏŏd'I-)
n., but applied esp. to Sakyamuni, Gautama, or Siddartha (5th c. B.C., in N.
India). Hence ~IST(2) (bŏŏd'I-) n. & a.,
~is'tic(AL) aa. [Skr., p.p. of *budh* know]

bŭdd'leia (-lĭa), n. Kinds of shrub with
lilac or yellow flowers of various forms.
[A. *Buddle*, botanist (d. 1715), -IA[1]]

•**bŭdd'ў**, n. (colloq.). (Usu. as familiar

form of address) brother, chum, mate. [dim. of *bud*, childish pronunc. of *brother*]

budge, v.i. & t. Make the slightest movement, force to do this, (in neg. sentences). [f. F *bouger* stir perh. (cf. Pr. *bolegar*)= It. *bulicare* f. Rom. *bullicare frequent. of *bullire* boil]

budg'erigar', n. The grass parakeet, or Australian love-bird. [native name]

budg'et, n., & v.i. Contents of a bag or bundle (mostly fig., esp. of news, & as title of newspapers); annual estimate of revenue & expenditure of a country (in Great Britain by Chancellor of Exchequer in House of Commons); private person's similar estimate; (v.i.) ~ *for*, allow or arrange for in ~. Hence ~ARY[1] a. [ME, f. OF *bougette* dim. of *bouge* leather bag f. L *bulga* (f. Gallic) knapsack; see BULGE]

buff[1], n. & a. (Of) stout velvety dull--yellow leather of buffalo or ox-hide; the human skin (*in* ~, naked); (of) dull--yellow colour (*the B~s*, East Kent Regt, from colour of the facings); (Path.) coagulated coating on blood drawn from fever patients, whence ~'Y[2] a.; ~-*coat*, -*jerkin*, formerly worn by soldiers as proof against sword-cut; ~-*stick*, -*wheel*, polishing tools covered with ~; ~-*tip*, kind of moth. [f. F *buffle* BUFFALO]

buff[2], v.t. Polish (metal) with buff; make (leather) velvety like buff. [f. prec.]

buff'alō, n. (pl. -*oes*). Kinds of ox (*Bos bubalus*, India, Asia, Europe, N. Africa; *Bos caffer*, S. Africa; American BISON); amphibious tank. [prob. f. Port. *bufalo*, f. LL *bufalus* f. L f. Gk *boubalos* antelope]

buff'er[1], n. Apparatus for deadening by springs or padding, or sustaining by strength of beams etc., a concussion, esp. of railway vans; ~ *State*, small State between two large ones diminishing chance of hostilities. [f. obs. vb *buff* (imit. of sound made by soft body struck, cf. PUFF & F *bouffer*) +-ER[1]]

buff'er[2], n. (sl.). (Usu. *old* ~) old-fashioned or incompetent fellow; (Nav.) chief boatswain's mate. [18th c., of obsc. orig.]

buff'et[1], n., & v.t. & i. (Strike with) blow of the hand; (of fate etc.) knock, hurt, plague; contend with (waves); contend *with*. Hence ~ING[1] (1, 2) n., beating, repeated blows, (Aeron.) irregular oscillation, caused by air eddies, of any part of an aircraft. [ME, f. OF, dim. of *buffe* blow (whence obs. E *buff* cf. BLIND[1]-*man's--buff*)]

buff'et[2], n. **1.** Sideboard, recessed cupboard, for china, plate, etc. **2.** (pr. bŏŏf'ā) refreshment bar. [18th c., F, of unkn. orig.]

buffo (bŏŏf'ō), n. & a. Burlesque, comic, (actor). [It.]

buffoon', n., & v.i. (Play the) wag, jester, mocker. Hence ~ERY(4) n. [f. F *buffon* f. It. *buffone* (*buffa* jest, *buffare* to puff), -OON]

bug, n. Flat ill-smelling blood-sucking

insect infesting beds; (loosely) small insect (often with defining word as *harvest, May, -~*; ~-*hunter* etc., entomologist); *any insect; *big* ~ (sl.), person of importance. Hence ~g'Y[2] (-g-) a. [orig. unkn.]

bug'abōō, bug'bear (-bār), nn. Fancied object of fear; false belief used to intimidate or dissuade. [16th c. *bugbear* f. obs. *bug* +BEAR[1]; *bugaboo* undetermined; cf. BOGLE, BOGY]

bugg'er (-g-), n., & v.t. (Law) sodomite, man having unnatural intercourse with beast or man, whence **bugg'ERY**(4) n.; (in foul or low talk, abusively or humorously): fellow, beggar, chap, beast; (v.t.) ~ *about*, hound from pillar to post. [f. F *bougre* f. med.L *Bulgarus* 11th-c. heretic from Bulgaria, supposed capable of any crime]

bugg'y (-g-), n. Light vehicle for one or two persons (esp. in U.S., India, colonies). [orig. unkn.]

bu'gle[1], n., & v.i. & t. Brass instrument like small trumpet used for military signals; (vb) sound ~, sound (call) on ~. Hence **bug'lER**[1] n. [ME, short for ~-*horn* f. OF *bugle*, f. L *buculus* dim. of *bos* ox]

bu'gle[2], n. Kinds of creeping plant with blue flowers. [F, f. LL *bugula*]

bu'gle[3], n. Tube-shaped glass bead sewn on dress etc. for ornament. [orig. unkn.]

bug'let, n. Small (cyclist's) bugle. [-ET[1]]

bug'loss, n. Kinds of plant allied with borage. [f. F *buglosse* or L f. Gk *bouglōssos* ox-tongued]

buhl (bŏŏl), n. & a. (Inlaid with) brass, tortoise-shell, etc., cut in ornamental patterns for inlaying. [Germanized f. *Boule* name of carver (d. 1732)]

build[1] (bĭl-), v.t. & i. (*built*). Construct by putting parts or material rightly together (house, ship, carriage, organ, engine, nest, or other structure large relatively to the builder); (abs.) be busy making one's house or nest; ~ *up, round, in*, surround (person, place, etc.) with houses etc., block up; (with material as obj.) lay *in(to* wall etc.) in ~*ing*; establish, make gradually, (often with *up*; system, empire, reputation); base (hopes etc.) *upon*, rely *upon*; *built* (with preceding adv. etc.), of such & such a BUILD[2]. [ME *bulden* f. OE *byldan*, f. *bold* dwelling f. Gmc **bu-* dwell, cf. BOWER[1], BOOTH]

build[2] (bĭl-), n. Style of construction, make; proportions of human body (*sturdy* ~ etc.); ~-*up*, favourable publicity designed to popularize a person, product, etc. [prec.]

buil'der (bĭl-), n. In vbl senses; esp.: master-builder, contractor for building houses. [-ER[1]]

buil'ding (bĭl-), n. In vbl senses; esp.: house, edifice; ~-*lease*, permitting lessee to build on the land; ‖~-*society*, of contributors to fund for loan to members when needing house. [-ING[1]]

bulb[1], n. Nearly spherical underground stem of lily, onion, etc., sending roots downwards & leaves etc. upwards; leaf-bud detaching itself from stem & becoming separate plant; (Anat.) roundish swelling of any cylindrical organ, as of hair-root or spinal cord; dilated part of glass tube (~-*tube*, ending in a ~); electric-light container. Hence ~ED[2] (-bd), ~IF'EROUS, bŭl'bIFORM, aa., bŭl'bo-comb. form. [f. L *bulbus* f. Gk *bolbos* onion]

bulb[2], v.i. Swell into bulb(s). [f. prec.]

bŭl'bous, a. Of, having, like, springing from, a bulb. [f. L *bulbosus* (BULB[1], -OUS)]

bulbul (bŏŏl'bŏŏl), n. Eastern song-thrush; singer, poet. [Pers. f. Arab.]

bŭlge[1], n. Convex part, irregular swelling, tendency to swell out, on flat or flatter surface; temporary increase in volume or numbers; =BILGE; (sl.) advantage (chiefly in phr. *have*, or *get*, *the* ~ *on*, have, get, the advantage over). Hence bŭl'gY[2] a., bŭl'gINESS n. [ME, f. OF *boulge*, *bouge*, or f. L *bulga* see BUDGET]

bŭlge[2], v.i. & t. Swell outwards irregularly & usu. faultily; extend (bag etc.) by stuffing it. [f. prec.]

bŭl'imỹ, **bŭlĭm'ia**, n. (Med.) morbid hunger; (fig.) voracity (for books etc.). [16th c. f. Gk *boulimia* (whence usu. mod. form) f. *bous* ox +*limos* hunger]

bŭlk[1], n. Cargo (*break* ~, begin unloading; ~ *not equal to sample*; *in* ~, loose, not in package; *load in* ~, put grain etc. in loose; *sell in* ~, in large quantities, as it is in the hold); large shape, person, body; size, magnitude; great size; mass, large mass; *the* greater part or number of; ~ *buying*, purchase by one buyer of all or most of a producer's output. [sense 'cargo' f. OIcel. *bulki*; sense 'mass' etc. perh. alt. f. obs. *bouk* (cf. BUCK[5])]

bŭlk[2], v.i. & t. Seem in respect of size or importance (~ *large*, *larger*); ~ *up*, form considerable sum etc., amount *to*; pile in heaps (fish); (Customs) ascertain weight of (tea etc.) by emptying out of chest. [f. prec.]

bŭlk'head (-hĕd), n. Upright partition dividing ship's cabins or water-tight compartments; compartment, stall. [15th c. *bulke hede* f. *bulke* (loose) cargo (BULK[1]) +HEAD[1]]

bŭl'k|ỹ, a. Large; too large. Hence ~INESS n. [BULK[1] +-Y[2]]

bull[1] (bŏŏl), n. & a. 1. Uncastrated male of ox or any bovine animal (~ *in china shop*, reckless or clumsy destroyer; *take* ~ *by the horns*, meet not evade difficulty); male of whale, elephant, & other large animals (usu. ~ *whale* or *whale*- etc.); constellation & sign Taurus. 2. (St. Exch.). Person trying to raise prices (see BEAR[1]). 3. = BULL'S-*eye* (of target). 4. adj. Like that of a ~ (~ *head*, *neck*, *voice*; also ~ *operations* on St. Exch.). 5. ~-*calf*, male calf, simpleton; ||~-*corner* (local),

barred refuge, usu. at junction of fields, from ~'*s attack*; ~-*dog*, powerful & courageous large-headed smooth-haired breed of dog, tenacious & courageous (person), || University proctor's attendant; **~-doze*, v.t. (sl.), cow, coerce; **~-dozer*, powerful caterpillar tractor pushing broad steel blade in front, used for removing obstacles, levelling uneven surfaces, etc.; ~-*fight*, Spanish sport of baiting ~ with horsemen etc.; ~-*finch*, strong-beaked handsome-plumaged song-bird, also [perh.=~ *fence*, cf. *minch* dial. for *mince*] quickset hedge with ditch; ~-*frog*, large Amer. species; ~-*head*, small big-headed fish = miller's thumb; ~-*headed*, obstinate, impetuous, blundering; ~-*of-the-bog*, bittern; ~-*puncher*,(Austral.) bullock-driver; ~-*pup*, -*bitch*, young, female, ~-*dog*; ~-*ring*, arena for ~-fight; ~-*roarer*, flat strip of wood tied to a string, making a roaring sound when whirled round; ~-*s-eye*, boss of glass formed at centre of blown glass sheet, hemispherical piece or thick disc of glass as light in ship's side, hemispherical lens, (lantern) with such lens, small circular window, centre of target, kind of sweetmeat; ~-*terrier*, cross between ~-dog & terrier; ~-*trout*, fish of salmon tribe. [ME *bole* f. ON *boli* = MLG, MDu. *bulle*; see BULLOCK]

bull[2](bŏŏl), v.i. & t. (St. Exch.). Speculate for the rise; try to raise price of (stocks). [f. prec.; BULL[1,2] perh. merely correl. to the more explicable BEAR[1,2]]

bull[3] (bŏŏl), n. Papal edict. [ME, f. OF *bulle* f. L *bulla*. cf. BILL[4]]

bull[4] (bŏŏl), n. (Often *Irish* ~) expression containing contradiction in terms or implying ludicrous inconsistency (often an intelligible statement made absurd by compression). [orig. unkn.]

bull[5] (bŏŏl), n. Drink made of water flavoured in empty spirit cask. [orig. unkn.]

Bull[6]. = JOHN *Bull*.

bull[7] (bŏŏl), n. Deck-game in which small flat sandbags are thrown on an inclined board marked with numbered squares. [orig. unkn.]

bullace (bŏŏl'ĭs), n. Wild (or semi-cultivated) plum tree or fruit. [ME *bolace* f. OF *beloce* f. Gaulish **bulluca* sloe]

bŭll'āte, a. (bot., physiol.). Puffy, blistered-looking. [f. L *bulla* bubble +-ATE[2]]

bull'ét (bŏŏ-), n. Missile of lead etc., spherical or conical, used in rifles (*dum-dum, expanding, soft-nosed, explosive,* ~, varieties so shaped etc. as to inflict complicated wound); ~-*head*, -*headed*, (with) round & presumably thick head; ~-*PROOF*. [f. F *boulette* dim. of *boule* ball f. L *bulla* knob]

bull'étin (bŏŏ-), n. Short official statement of public event or news or of invalid's condition. [F. f. It. *bullettino* dim. of *bulletta* lottery ticket dim: of *bulla* seal, BULL³]

bullion¹ (bŏŏl'yon), n. & a. Gold or silver before (or as valued apart from) coining or manufacture; (made of) solid or real gold or silver. [f. AF *bullion* mint, formally = OF *bouillon* f. Rom. *bullionem* f. *bullīre* BOIL²; meanings excl. E]

bullion² (bŏŏl'yon), n. Fringe of gold & silver thread twists. [f. F *bouillon*, see prec., in sense *bubble*]

bull'ock (bŏŏ-), n. Castrated bull, ox. [OE *bulluc*, dim. (-OCK) of *bulla* BULL¹]

bull'y¹ (bŏŏ-), n. Blusterer, tyrant (esp. among boys), coward & tyrant; hired ruffian; man who lives on prostitute's earnings. [16th c. as term of endearment, gallant, etc., prob. f. MDu. *boele* (G *buhle*)]

bull'y² (bŏŏ-), v.t. Persecute, oppress, tease, physically or morally; frighten *into* or *out of*; (abs.) play the bully; ~ *off*, perform preliminary crossing of clubs in hockey. [f. prec.]

bull'y³ (bŏŏ-), a. & int. (esp. U.S.). Capital, first-rate; ~ *for you, him,* etc., = bravo. [f. BULLY¹]

‖ **bull'y⁴** (bŏŏ-), n. Scrummage in (prop. Eton) football.

bull'y⁵ (bŏŏ-), n. (colloq.). (Also ~ *beef*) corned beef. [f. F *bouilli* boiled beef f. *bouillir* BOIL²]

bull'yrăg (bŏŏ-). See BALLYRAG.

bul'rush (bŏŏ-), n. Kinds of tall rush (pop. the cat's tail; in Bible, papyrus). [f. BULL¹, as in *bullfrog, bulltrout,* etc.]

bul'wark (bŏŏ-), n. Rampart, earthwork, etc.; mole, breakwater; person, principle, etc., that acts as a defence; ship's side above deck. [15th c., = rampart, corresp. to (prob. f.) MDu. *bolwerk*; see BOLE, WORK¹]

bŭm¹, n. Backside, buttocks; ‖ ~*-bailiff* (also ~), employed for arrests (from touching debtor on the back); ~*-boat,* plying with fresh provisions for ships (orig. scavenger boat). [ME *bom*, of unkn. orig.; prob. imit., cf. BUMP]

bŭm², n., a., & v.i. & t., (sl.). **1.** Habitual loafer (*go on the ~,* sponge on the community). **2.** adj. Of poor quality. **3.** vb (-mm-). Loaf, sponge, wander *around*; obtain by sponging, scrounge. [perh. back-formation f. BUMMER]

‖ **bŭm'ble**, n. Beadle; consequential jack-in-office. Hence ~DOM (-ld-) n. [name of beadle in *Oliver Twist*]

bŭm'ble-bee, n. Large kind of bee. [f. obs. vb *bumble* (BOOM, or obs. var. *bum,* + -LE)]

bŭm'ble-pŭppy, n. Whist, tennis, etc., played unscientifically; game with tennis-ball slung to post. [orig. unkn.]

bŭm'bō, n. Cold rum-punch. [cf. It. *bombo* child's wd for drink]

bŭmm'alō, n. Small fish of S.-Asian coasts. [f. Mahratti *bombil(a)*]

‖ **bŭmmaree'**, n. Middleman at Billings-gate fish-market; licensed porter at Smithfield meat-market in London. [orig. unkn.]

bŭmm'er, n. Idler, loafer. [cf. G *bummler*]

bŭmp¹, v.t. & i., & adv. **1.** Push, throw down, (box etc.) *against* or *on* (wall, person, floor, etc.); hurt (one's head etc.) by striking it (*against, on,* or abs.); seize by arms & legs & strike the posterior of (person) against floor, wall, etc.; come with a bump *against*; go along with repeated bumps; (Boat-racing, see foll.) overtake; (of cricket-ball) rise abruptly on pitching; *~ off* (sl.), remove by violence, murder. **2.** adv. With a bump, suddenly, violently, (*come, go,* etc., ~, cf. BANG, BOUNCE). [expressing sound of blow; by extension, the resulting swelling]

bŭmp², n. Dull-sounding blow, knock, collision; swelling caused by it; (Phrenol.) prominence on skull, faculty indicated by it; (Boat-racing) touching of boat by next, a win for latter (*~-supper,* in celebration of this); (Aviation) vertical air current causing irregularity in aircraft's motion, jolt experienced by aircraft in flight; *~-ball* (Cricket; pr. bǔm'bawl) ball hit hard on ground close to bat, coming with a long hop to fieldsman (so looking like a possible catch). [f. prec.]

bŭmp³, n., & v.i. (Make) bittern's cry. [imit.]

bŭm'per, n. In vbl senses; also, brim-full glass of wine; anything unusually large or abundant (harvest, full theatre); (Whist) score of two games against nil; (Motoring) spring fender for mitigating collisions. [-ER¹]

bŭmp'kin, n. Country or awkward or bashful fellow. [perh. f. Du. *boomken* little tree or MDu. *bommekijn* little barrel]

bŭmp'tious (-shus), a. Self-assertive. Hence ~LY adv., ~NESS n. [jocular form, on BUMP² & e.g. *fractious*]

bŭmp'y, a. Full of bumps, causing jolts, (esp. of road or cricket pitch or air in aviation). Hence ~INESS n. [-Y²]

bŭn¹, n. Small soft round sweet cake with a few currants (the usu. Eng. sense, but with local variations); *hot cross ~,* marked with cross & eaten on Good Friday; hair dressed in ~ shape. [ME *bunne*, cf. OF *bugne, buigne*; see BUNION]

‖ **bŭn²**, n. (Personifying name of) squirrel, rabbit. [16th c., of unkn. orig.]

bŭn'a (or bŏŏ-), n. Synthetic rubber made by the polymerization of butadiene. [f. *bu(tadiene* + *na(trium)* sodium]

bŭnch¹, n. Cluster of things growing or fastened together (flowers, grapes, keys); lot (*best of the ~*); (sl.) gang, group; ~ *grass,* kinds of N.-Amer. grass growing in tufts. Hence ~'Y² a. [orig. unkn.]

bŭnch², v.t. & i. Make into bunch(es), gather (dress) into folds; come or cling together, (Mil., of skirmishers) fail to keep intervals. [f. prec.]

*bŭnc'ō, n., & v.t., (sl.). (To) swindle (esp. by card-sharping or the confidence trick); ~-*steerer*, swindler. [cf. Sp. *banca* a card-game]

bŭn'combe. See BUNKUM.

bŭnd, n. (Anglo-Ind.). Embankment, causeway, quay. [Hind. *band*, of Persian orig.]

bŭn'der, n. (Anglo-Ind.). Landing-place, quay, harbour; ~-*boat* (used for coasting & harbour work). [Hind.]

bŭn'dle[1], n. Collection of things fastened together (esp. clothes & odds & ends in handkerchief); set of sticks, iron rods, etc., bound up; set of parallel fibres, nerves, etc.; 20 hanks of linen yarn. [ME *bundel* not continuous w. OE *byndele* a binding (Gmc **bund-* BIND) but f. MDu. *bondel*, LG, Du. *bundel*]

bŭn'dle[2], v.t. & i. Tie in, make *up* into, a bundle; throw confusedly *in* to any receptacle; go, put or send (esp. a person), in a hurry or unceremoniously *out*, *off*, *away*, etc. [f. prec.]

bŭng[1], n. Stopper, esp. large cork stopping hole in cask; ~-*hole*, for filling cask. [f. MDu. *bonghe* (= Du. *bom*)]

bŭng[2], v.t. Stop (cask) with bung; *eyes* ~*ed up*, closed with swelling from blow, or sealed with rheum; (sl.) throw (stones). [f. prec.]

bŭng'al|ow (-nggalō), n. One-storeyed house, orig. lightly built or temporary. Hence ~OID a., having the style or appearance of a ~ow. [f. Hind. *bangla* belonging to Bengal]

bungl|e (bŭng'gl), v.i. & t., & n. (Make) clumsy work, confusion; blunder over, fail to accomplish, (task). Hence ~ER[1] n; [imit., cf. obs. *bumble* in same sense]

bŭn'ion (-yon), n. Inflamed swelling on foot. [f. It. *bugnone* (*bugno* boil, lump) or OF *buignon* (f. *buigne*, mod. *bigne*) swelling]

bŭnk[1], n. Sleeping-berth. [orig. unkn.]

bŭnk[2], v.i., & n., (sl.). ~, *do a* ~, make off, vanish. [orig. unkn.]

*bŭnk[3], n. (sl.). Humbug, balderdash. [contr. of BUNKUM]

bŭnk'er, n., & v.t. Ship's coal-bin; (Golf) sandpit on course constituting a HAZARD; (Mil.) underground shelter; (v.t., usu. in p.p.) entangle in ~, (fig.) bring into difficulties. [orig. unkn.]

bŭnk'um, -combe (-km), n. Humbug, claptrap, sophistry. [anecdotic; member for Buncombe in N. Carolina speaking needlessly in Congress (1819-21) to impress his constituents]

bŭnn'ia (-ya), n. (Anglo-Ind.). Indian (prop. Hindu) trader or shopkeeper. [Hind. *banya*; see BANIAN]

bŭnn'y̆, n. Pet name for rabbit; ~-*hug*, an American dance. [BUN[2]+-Y[3]]

Bun'sen('s) (bǒon-, bŭn-), a. Invented by R. W. *Bunsen* (d. 1899), German chemist

(~ *burner*, *lamp*, burning air with gas for heating & blow-pipe work; ~ *battery*, *cell*, voltaic of spec. kind).

bŭnt[1], n. Cavity, baggy part, of fishing-net, sail, etc.; ~-*line* (confining ~ in furling sail). [orig. unkn.]

bŭnt[2], n. (Also *smut-ball*) disease of wheat. [orig. unkn.]

bŭnt[3], v.t. & i., & n. 1. (Chiefly dial.) push with the head or horns, butt. 2. (In baseball) stop (ball) with bat without swinging. 3. n. Act of ~ing; (in baseball) a ~ed ball, hit made by ~ing. [orig. unkn.; cf. BUTT[4]]

bŭn'ting[1], n. Sub-family of birds including *common* or *corn* ~, *yellow* ~ (or *yellow-hammer*), *black-headed*, *reed*, *snow*, etc., ~; grey shrimp. [orig. unkn.]

bŭn'ting[2], n. (Open-made worsted stuff used for) flags. [orig. unkn.]

buoy[1] (boi), n. Anchored float showing navigable course or reefs etc.; (also *life-*~) something to keep person afloat; also fig. in both senses. [15/16th c. *boye*, *buie* f. MDu. f. OF *boie* (mod. *bouée*) f. Frank. *bōkan; see BEACON]

buoy[2] (boi), v.t. 1. (Usu. with *up*) keep afloat; bring to surface of water; sustain (person, courage, etc.), uplift. 2. (Without *up*, sometimes with *out*) mark with buoy(s). [last meaning f. prec.; sense *float* etc. f. Sp. *boyar*; see BUOYANT]

buoy'age (boi-), n. Providing of buoys; series of buoys. [-AGE]

buoy'ancy̆ (boi-), n. Floating power on liquid or in air; (Hydrost.) loss of weight by immersion in liquid; elasticity, recuperative power, (of spirits, also of prices, etc.). [f. foll.; see -ANCY]

buoy'ant (boi-), a. Apt to float, rise, keep up, or recover, springy; able to keep things up; light-hearted. Hence ~LY[2] adv. [16th c. f. Sp. *boyante* p.p. of *boyar* float (cf. obs. F *bouyant* f. *boya* BUOY[1]]

bŭr, bŭrr, n. (Any plant with) clinging seed-vessel or flower; female hop-catkin; person hard to shake off. [ME, = Da. *borre* bur, burdock, Sw. *kard-borre* burdock]

Bŭr'berry, n. A kind of waterproof cloth, coat etc. of this, made by a company of that name. [P]

bŭr'ble, v.i. Simmer (*with* rage, mirth). [19th c., imit.; but cf. ME (obs.) *burble* bubble]

bŭrb'ot, n. Eel-like flat-headed bearded freshwater fish. [f. F *bourbotte*]

bŭrd'en[1], bŭrth'en (-dh-), n. (usu. -*den* exc. = *tonnage*). Load (lit., or of labour, duty, sorrow, etc.; ~ *of proof*, obligation to prove falling on maker of statement); obligatory expense; ship's carrying-capacity, tonnage; bearing of loads (*ship*, *beast*, *of* ~); (Bibl.) oracle, heavy fate; (= obs. senses of BOURDON) refrain, chorus, of song, chief theme or gist of poem, book, speech, etc. [OE *byrthen*,

OS *burthinnia* f. WG **burthi-* BIRTH + EN[3]; for *-d-* cf. *murder* etc.]

būrd'en[2], būrth'en (-dh-), v.t. Load (lit. & fig.), encumber, oppress, tax. [f. prec.]

būrd'ensome, a. Oppressive, wearying. Hence ~NESS (-mn-) n. [-SOME]

būr'dŏck, n. Coarse plant with prickly flower-heads (BUR) & dock-like leaves. [BUR + DOCK[1]]

bureau (būrō', bū[2]), n. (pl. *-eaux*, pr. *-ōz*). || Writing-desk with drawers, escritoire; *chest of drawers; office or department for transacting business, government department. [F, = desk, orig. the baize covering, f. OF *burel* f. *bure* coarse cloth]

būreau'|cracy̆ (-rō-), n. Government by bureaux, centralization; officialism; officials. Allied wds: ~CRAT (bū'ro-) n., ~crăt'IC a., ~crăt'ICALLY adv., ~'crat-ISM(2), ~'cratIST(2), nn. [f. prec. + -CRACY]

būrĕtte', n. Graduated glass tube for measuring small quantities of liquid. [F]

***būrg**, n. (colloq.). Town or city. [see BOROUGH]

|| **būr'gage**, n. An ancient tenure (*hold in* ~). [f. med. L *burgagium* (*burgus* see BOROUGH, -AGE)]

būrgee', n. Triangular flag bearing the colours or emblem of a yacht club or sailing club. [orig. unkn.]

bur'geon, bour'geon (bēr'jn), n., & v.i. (Put forth, spring forth as) young shoot(s), bud, begin to grow, (poet., & also in Zool. of GEMMATION). [ME, f. OF *bor-, burjon*, of unkn. orig.]

būr'gĕss, n. Inhabitant of borough with full municipal rights, citizen; (chiefly hist.) member of parliament for borough, corporate town, or university. [ME, f. OF *burgeis* f. Rom. **burgensis* f. *burgus* f. Gmc **burgs* BOROUGH]

burgh (bū'ru), n. (Sc.). Scots chartered town (used in E in writing of Scots borough). [Sc. form of BOROUGH]

burgher (bēr'ger), n. Freeman or citizen of a burgh or borough; (S. Afr.) citizen of European descent, wherever resident. [16th c., f. G or Du. *burger* f. *burg* BOROUGH]

būrg'lar, n. One who breaks into house by night with intent to commit felony. Hence ~Y[1] n., burglār'ıous a., burg-lār'ıously[2] adv. [c. 1500 *burgular, burglour*, = AL *burg(u)lator*, f. earlier *burgator* (= AF *burgesour*, cf. OF *burgur* thief); formation & orig. obsc.]

būr'gle, v.i. & t. Commit burglary; enter or rob (house) burglariously. [19th c. back form. f. prec.]

būrg'omaster (-ah-), n. Mayor of Dutch or Flemish or German town. [f. Du. *burgemeester* (BOROUGH)]

būrg'onĕt, n. (hist.). Visored helmet; steel cap. [f. OF *bourguignotte* f. *Bour-gogne* Burgundy]

būrgoo', n. (naut. sl.). Porridge. [orig. unkn.]

bŭrg'undy̆, n. Kinds of (usu. red) wine of Burgundy in France.

bū'r(h)el, n. Himalayan wild sheep. [f. Hind. *bharal*]

bu'rial (bĕ-), n. Depositing under earth, burying, esp. of dead body, funeral; ~-*ground*, cemetery; ~-*service*, religious form at funeral. [ME *buryel*, erron. formed as sing. of OE *byrgels* (cf. OS *burgisli*) f. **burg-* BURY + -*els* as in RIDDLE]

būr'in, n. Tool for engraving on copper. Hence ~IST(1) n. [F]

būrke[1], v.t. Avoid, smother, (publicity, inquiry); hush up, suppress, (rumour, book). [*Burke* executed 1829 for smothering people to sell bodies for dissection]

Būrke[2], n. (Used for) ~'s Peerage etc. [John ~, compiler (d. 1848)]

būrl, n., & v.t. Knot in wool or cloth; (vb) clear of ~s. [f. OF *bourle*]

būrl'ăp, n. Coarse canvas. [perh. f. Du. *boenlap* rubbing-cloth, confused w. *boer* BOOR]

būrlĕsque' (-k), a. & n., & v.t. Imitative, imitation, imitate, for purpose of deriding or amusing; bombast(ic), mock--serious(ness); caricature, parody, esp. (of) literary & dramatic work; *(vulgar) variety show freq. featuring comic strip--tease. [F, f. It. *burlesco* (*burla* mockery, -ESQUE)]

Bŭrl'ington House, n. Building in London used as headquarters of the Royal Academy, British Academy, British Association, Royal Soc., Geological Soc., Chemical Soc., & Linnean Soc.

būrl'y̆, a. Sturdy, corpulent. Hence ~INESS n. [ME *borlich* prob. f. OE **būrlic* (cf. OHG *būrlih* exalted) fit for the BOWER[1], see -LY[1]]

Būrmēse' (-z), a. & n. Of Burma; (n.) ~ native (pl. same) or language. **Būrm'an** a. & n., = ~. [*Burma* +-ESE, -AN]

būrn[1], n. (Sc., north., poet.). Small stream. [OE *burna*, MDu. *borne*, metathetic forms f. Gmc **brunnōn, -az*, cf. OS, OHG *brunno, -az* OS, ON *brunnr*, Goth. *brunna*; cf. BOURN[1]]

būrn[2], v.t. & i. (~t, occas. ~ed). **1.** Consume, waste, by fire (t. & i., the heat, heating person, or heated thing, being subject; ~ *away, out,* to nothing, to extinction; ~ *up,* get rid of by fire; ~ *out,* consume contents of; ~ one's *boats,* commit oneself irrevocably to a course); blaze, glow, with fire (~ *up,* flash into blaze; ~ *down, low,* less vigorously as fuel fails). **2.** Give, make to give, light (lamp, candles, gas, oil, etc.; ~ *blue* etc., give blue etc. light; ~ *candle at both ends,* not husband energy; ~ *daylight,* use artificial light by day; ~ *the midnight oil,* work late). **3.** Put, be put, to death by fire. **4.** Harden, produce, (bricks, lime, charcoal) by heat. **5.** Make (hole etc.) by heat (*money* ~*s hole in pocket,* clamours to be spent). **6.** Injure, be injured, by fire or great heat (~ one's *fingers*, suffer for meddling or rashness); char, scorch, in cooking (t. & i.), adhere to saucepan etc.; cauterize, brand, (~ *in*, *into*, impress indelibly); eat, make acid etc. eat, its way (*into* material, material, or abs.). **7.** Parch, freckle, tan, colour, (t. & i.; abs. or with *brown*, *dry*, etc.). **8.** Give, feel, sensation or pain (as) of heat (~*t child dreads fire*; *ears*~, when one is talked of; ~, get near discovery or truth, as in child's game). **9.** Make, be, hot or passionate, glow, blaze, rage, yearn. **10.** Utilize nuclear energy of (uranium etc.). **11.** ~ person *out*, expel him by fire; ~ *the water*, spear salmon by torchlight; ~*ing-glass*, convex lens or concave mirror concentrating sun's rays enough to ignite object at focus; ~*t almond* (enclosed in burnt sugar); ~*t ochre*, *sienna* (calcined); ~*t offering*, sacrifice made by ~ing. [OE *birnan* intr., *bærnan* trans., metathetic forms f. Gmc **brennan* (= OE, OS, OHG, Goth. *brinnan*), **brannjan* (= OS, OHG *brennan*, ON *brenna*, Goth. *brannjan*)]

burn³, n. Sore, mark, on body made by burning. [f. prec.]

burn'er, n. In vbl senses, esp. in comb. as *brick*-~; also, part of lamp etc. that shapes the flame. [-ER¹]

burn'et, n. Kinds of brown-flowered plant. [f. obs. adj. *burnet* f. OF *burnete* see BRUNETTE]

burn'ing, a. In vbl senses; also : ardent (~ *desire*); flagrant (~ *shame*, *disgrace*); hotly discussed, exciting, (~ *question*); ~ *scent* (in hunting), strong. [-ING²]

burn'ish, v.t. & i. Polish by friction; (with *well* etc.) take a polish. Hence ~ER¹ (2) n. [ME, f. OF *burnir* = *brunir* (*brun* BROWN), see -ISH²]

burnous(e) (-ōōs, -ōōz), n. Arab, Moorish, & lady's, hooded cloak. [F (-s), f. Arab. *burnus*]

burp, n., & v.i (sl.). Belch. [imit.]

burr¹, n. **1.** Nebulous disc round moon or star. **2.** Rough ridge left on cut or punched metal or paper (~-*drill*, dentist's). **3.** Siliceous rock used for millstones; whetstone; kinds of limestone. **4.** Rough sounding of letter *r* as in Northumberland ; whirring sound. [(1) var. of earlier *burrow* (Sc. var. *brough*); (2) app. same wd as BUR]

burr², v.t. & i. Pronounce with sound of Northumbrian *r*, also of French *r*; speak without clear articulation. [cf. prec.]

*burro (bŏŏ'rō), n. (colloq.). Small donkey used as pack-animal. [Sp.]

bu'rrow (-ō), n., & v.i. & t. (Make, live in) hole excavated in earth, as of foxes, rabbits, etc.; make by excavating (hole, one's way); retire out of sight; (fig.) investigate mysteries etc. Hence ~ER¹ n. [ME, app. var. of = BOROUGH]

burs'|a, n. (pl. ~ae, ~as). (anat., zool.). A sac or saclike cavity to lessen friction. Hence ~AL a. [med. L]

burs'ar, n. Treasurer, esp. of a college; exhibitioner esp. in Scots University or school, whence ~Y¹ n. [f. med. L *bursarius* (*bursa* bag, see PURSE)]

bursar'ial, a. Of bursar(y). [-AL]

burst¹, v.t. & i. (past & p.p. burst). **1.** Fly by expansion of contents, send (containing case), violently asunder, split, (powder, shell, etc.; exaggeratively, ~ *with food* or *emotion*, *heart* ~*s*). **2.** Get away from or through, make way *out* or *in*, express one's feelings, by force or suddenly (*river* ~*s banks*; ~ *in*, come into room, interrupt; ~ *out*, exclaim; ~ *into tears*, *out laughing*, break into tears, laughter). **3.** Open, come open, be opened, forcibly (*boil*, *bud*, *cloud*, ~; ~ *door*, *door* ~*s*, *in* or *open*). **4.** Fill, be full, to overflowing (*grain* ~*s granary*, *granary* ~*ing*; ~ *with joy*, *envy*, *pride*, *a secret*). **5.** Appear suddenly (~ *into flame*, *upon the view*; *sun*, *war*, *disease*, ~ *out*); suffer ~ing of (some part; ~ *a blood-vessel*, one's *heart*, *sides with laughing*, *buttons with food*); ~ *up*, explode, bring or come to utter collapse, (colloq., & often spelt *bust up*); *go bust* (colloq.), become bankrupt etc. [OE *berstan*, OS, OHG *brestan*, ON *bresta* f. Gmc **brestan*]

burst², n. Bursting, split; ~-*up* (often *bust*- colloq.), collapse; sudden issuing forth (~ *of flame*), explosion, outbreak, (lit. & fig.); spurt; continuous gallop; bout of drunkenness etc. (often vulg. *bust*; *on the bust*). [f. prec.]

burth'en (-dh-). See BURDEN.

burt'on (-tn), n. Light handy two-block tackle. [1495 *Breton*, *Brytton* (*tackles*)]

bury (bĕ'rĭ), v.t. Deposit in, commit to, earth, tomb, or sea (corpse); (of relatives) *to have buried*, lost; perform burial rites over; put under ground (~ *alive*; ~ *the hatchet*, renounce quarrel); put away, forget; (chiefly refl. & pass.) consign to obscurity; hide in earth (treasure etc.), cover up, submerge; withdraw from view (face in hands, hands in pockets); (p.p.) immersed (*buried in sloth*); ~*ing-ground*, -*place*, graveyard, cemetery. [OE *byrgan* f. WG **burgjan* f. *burg*- st. of.Gme **bergan* shelter, protect, see BURIAL]

bus, n. (pl. ~*es*), & v.i. **1.** Omnibus; (sl.) aeroplane, motor-car, motor-cycle; *miss the* ~, lose an opportunity, fail in an undertaking; ~ *driver*, ~'*man*, driver of an omnibus (~*man's holiday*, leisure time spent in the same kind of occupation as one's regular work). **2.** v.i. Go by ~. [abbr.]

‖ **bus'by** (-z-), n. Tall fur cap of Hussars & R.H.A. [orig. unkn.; cf. obs. *buzz*, see BUZZ⁴]

bush¹ (-ŏŏ-), n. Shrub, clump of shrubs; bunch of ivy as ancient vintner's sign (*good wine needs no* ~); luxuriant growth of hair, whisker, etc.; woodland, untilled district, (esp. of partly-settled countries:

take to the ~, become bush-ranger); BEAT[1] *about the* ~; ~- in many bird, beast, & plant names; ~-*fighter*, *-ing*, (person used to) fighting in the ~, guerilla warfare; ~-*harrow*, heavy frame with bars between which branches are inserted for harrowing grass land or covering seed, (vb) harrow with this; ~'*man*, aboriginal of a S.-Afr. tribe, dweller, farmer, or traveller in the Australian ~, whence bush'manSHIP(3) n. [after Du. *boschjesman* (*bosch* bush); ~-*ranger*, Australian brigand (at first escaped convict) living in the bush; ~-*rope*, tropical wild vine netting trees together; ~-*telegraph*, rapid spreading of information, rumour, etc. [ME *busk* f. ON *buskr* = OS, late OHG *busc*, f. Gmc *busk-*, whence med. L *buscus, boscus*, Rom. *bosco*, OF *bos, bosc, bois* wood]

bush² (-ŏŏ-), v.t. Set (ground) with bushes to frustrate net-poaching; bush-harrow (ground). [prec.]

bush³ (-ŏŏ-), n., & v.t. Metal lining of axle-hole or other circular orifice, perforated plug; (vb) furnish with ~. [f. MDu. *busse* BOX²]

bush'el (-ŏŏ-), n. Measure of capacity (8 gal.) for corn, fruit, etc. (*not hide* one's *light* or *candle under a* ~, set example; *measure others' corn by* one's *own* ~, judge others by oneself). Hence ~FUL(2) n. [ME *boyschel* f. OF *boissel* of Gaulish orig.]

Bushido (bŏŏsh'ĕdō), n. The code of honour & morals evolved by the samurai. [Jap., = military knight way]

bushveld (bŏŏsh'fĕlt), n. Veld composed largely of bush; low country of Transvaal. [f. Du. *boschveld*, see BUSH¹ & VELD]

bush'|y̌ (-ŏŏ-), a. Abounding in bushes; growing thickly. Hence ~iNESS n. [-Y²]

business (bĭz'nĭs), n. **1.** Being busy (orig. sense, now obs., see BUSYNESS). **2.** Task, duty, province, (*make it* one's ~ *to*, undertake); cause of coming (*what is your* ~?). **3.** Habitual occupation, profession, trade; serious work (*means* ~, is in earnest; *on* ~, with definite purpose; ~ *as usual*, things will proceed in spite of disturbing circumstances; ~ *end* (of tool, weapon, etc.), operative part; ~ *hours, hours of* ~, of regular work, open shop or office, etc.). **4.** Thing needing attention, agenda, (*the* ~ *of the day, meeting*, etc.); dealings with men & matters (~ *man*, one used to these, & see below; *man of* ~, agent, attorney). **5.** Difficult matter (*what a* ~ *it is!*, *make a great* ~ *of it*). **6.** Thing that concerns one, that one may meddle with, (*mind your own, go about your, send about his*, ~, reproof or dismissal; *has no* ~ *to*, no right). **7.** (Contempt.) device, machine, process, concern, course of events, (*sick of the whole* ~; *a lath-&-plaster* ~). **8.** (Theatr.) action, dumb-show. **9.** Buying & selling, bargaining, (*doing a great* ~; *good stroke of* ~; ~*man*, engaged in commerce, also

see above). **10.** Commercial house, firm. [OE *bisignis* (BUSY¹ + -NESS)]

business-like, a. Systematic, practical, prompt, well-ordered. [-LIKE]

busk, n. Rigid strip stiffening corset-front. [f. F *busc* f. It. *busco* splinter, rel. to F *bûche* log f. Gmc *busk-* see BUSH¹]

bus'ker, n. Itinerant musician or actor. [f. *busk* peddle etc. (perh. f. obs. F *busquer* to prowl)]

bus'kin, n. Boot reaching to calf or knee; thick-soled boot lending height to tragic actor in ancient times; the tragic vein, tragedy, (see SOCK; *put on the* ~, write or act tragedy). Hence ~ED² (-nd) a. [c. 1500, f. OF *bouzequin*, var. of *brousequin*, = OSp. *boszegui*, of unkn. orig.]

büss, n., & v.t. (arch.). Kiss. [earlier *bass* n. & v.; cf. F *baiser*, f. L *basiare*]

bust¹, n. Sculpture of person's head, shoulders, & chest; upper front of body, bosom, esp. of woman. [f. F *buste* f. It. *busto* of unkn. orig.]

bust². See BURST¹,². Hence **büs'tER²** (1, 2) n. (sl.), freq. in comb., as BLOCK¹-, BRONCO-, TANK-, ~*er*.

büst'ard, n. Kinds of large swift-running birds. [late ME; perh. mixture of OF *bistarde, oustarde*, both f. L *avis tarda* slow bird (the inappropriate adj. unexplained)]

bü'stle¹ (-sl), v.i. & t. Bestir oneself; make show of activity, hurry *about*; make (others) hurry or work hard. [perh. var. of obs. *buskle* f. obs. *busk* prepare (ON *búask* refl. of *búa* prepare cf. BOUND⁵)]

bü'stle² (-sl), n. Excited activity, fuss. [f. prec.]

bü'stle³ (-sl), n. Pad or frame puffing out top of woman's skirt behind. [orig. unkn.]

busy¹ (bĭz'ĭ), a. & n. **1.** Occupied, working, engaged, with attention concentrated, (~ *in, with, at*; also, prep. being dropped, with vbl n. now looking like part., as *he was* ~ *packing*); (of telephone line) engaged; unresting, ever employed, stirring, (~ *as a bee*); fussy, meddlesome, prying, mischievous; ~ *idle*(*ness*), spending energy on trifles; ~-*body*, meddlesome person, mischief-maker. Hence busILY² (bĭz'ĭ-) adv. **2.** n. (sl.). Detective. [OE *bisig*, ME *bisi* etc.; only E & MLG, MDu. *besich* (Du. *bezig*), of unkn. orig.]

busy² (bĭz'ĭ), v.t. Occupy (esp. *oneself*, one's *hands, eyes*, etc.), keep busy, (*with, in, at, about*, or with *-ing*, or abs.). [OE *bisgian* see prec.]

busy̌ness (bĭz'-), n. State or quality of being busy. [mod. form differentiated in spelling & pronunc. f. BUSINESS]

büt¹ (orig. adv. & prep. = outside, without; developed into conj., under which most mod. uses belong; but it is now adv., prep., negative rel. pron., subord. & co-ord. conj.; clear distinction of these is not here possible). **1.** Only (*she is* ~ *a child, I can* ~ *do it*). **2.** Except, if not, short of, except that, if it were not that, short of the condition that, *(they are all wrong ~ he, him; no one ~ me, I; never ~ once; he all ~ did it; what can he do ~ die; nothing would content him ~ I must come).* **3.** Otherwise than *(cannot choose ~, cannot ~, do it).* **4.** Who or that not *(no one ~ knows that).* **5.** Without the result etc. that *(never rains ~ it pours; justice was never done ~ someone complained).* **6.** Rather than so-&-so shall prove untrue *(it shall go hard ~ I will get there; ten to one ~ it was you)*; that not *(not such a fool ~—also ~ that, ~ what—he can see that; it is impossible ~ that offences will come).* **7.** To say (that) not *(not ~ that—also what—he believed it himself)*; *~ for this* etc., were it not so, without this; *~ then,* ~ on the other hand *(it is hot, no doubt, ~ then the heat is dry).* **8.** (After neg.) that *(I don't deny, doubt, ~ that).* **9.** On the contrary, nevertheless, however, on the other hand, moreover, yet. [OE *be-ūtan, būtan, būta* (BE-, OUT) outside, without, = OS *biūtan,* OHG *biūzan*]

bŭt², n., & v.t. An objection; (vb) utter, use, (~s ; *me no ~s).* [uses of prec.]

bŭtadï'ēne, n. (chem.). Gas used in making synthetic rubber. [f. BUTA(NE) +DI-² +-ENE; see BUNA]

bŭt'āne, n. (chem.). Hydrocarbon of the methane series. [f. BUT(YR-) +-ANE]

butch'er¹ (bŏŏ-), n. Slaughterer of animals for food; dealer in meat *(the ~, the baker, the candlestick-maker,* people of all trades); judge, general, etc., who has men killed needlessly or brutally; a salmon--fly; *~-bird,* kind of shrike; *~'s-broom,* low spiny-leaved evergreen; *~'s meat,* excluding poultry, game, & bacon etc. [ME *bocher* f. OF *bochier* (*boc* BUCK¹) lit. dealer in goat's flesh]

butch'er² (bŏŏ-), v.t. Slaughter (people) wantonly or cruelly; ruin by bad reading or editing, damage by harsh criticism. [f. prec.]

butch'erlў (bŏŏ-), a. Fit for, like, a butcher, coarse, brutal, bloody. [-LY¹]

butch'erў (bŏŏ-), n. Shambles (in barracks, camp, ship, etc.); (attrib.) butcher's trade *(~ trade, business,* etc.); needless or cruel slaughter of people. [f. OF *boucherie* (BUTCHER¹, -Y¹)]

bŭt'ler, n. Servant in charge of wine-cellar & plate etc.; principal manservant. [ME, f. AF *buteler,* OF *bouteillier,* see BOTTLE¹, -ER²(2)]

bŭtt¹, n. Wine or ale cask (108–140 gals); any barrel. [15th c. *butt* (AF *but*) f. OF *bot* (mod. *botte*) f. LL f. Gk *bytis* cask; see BOTTLE¹]

bŭtt², n. Thicker end, esp. of tool or weapon *(give fish the ~,* turn ~ of rod towards him for firmer hold); trunk of tree just above ground; ~ or *~-end,* remnant *(~-end* also = thicker end); base of leaf-stalk; kinds of flat-fish, as sole,

plaice, turbot; hide of back & flanks trimmed to rectangle, thickest leather (cf. BEND¹); square end of plank meeting a similar end (also *~-end).* [ME, (a) f. MLG, MDu. *butt* (G *butte*) flat fish; see HALIBUT, TURBOT; (b) = LG *but,* Du. *bot* stumpy, Sw. *but* stump; see BUTTOCK]

bŭtt³, n. Mound behind target; grouse--shooter's stand screened by low turf or stone wall; (pl.) shooting-range; target; end, aim, object; object of (ridicule etc.), object of teasing & ridicule. [14th c., f. OF *but* goal, of unkn. orig.]

bŭtt⁴, v.i. & t., & n. Push (v. & n.) with the head *(come ~ or full ~ against,* run into; ~ *in,* fig., intervene, meddle); meet end to end *(~ against, upon)*; come, place (timber etc.), with end flat *against* wall etc. [ME, f. OF *boter* f. WG **buttan* sprout (cf. MDu. *botten* strike, sprout); see BUTTON; E senses partly infl. by ABUT, BUTT²]

*butte (bŭt), n. Conspicuous isolated hill, esp. one with steep or cliff-like sides. [F, = knoll]

bŭtt'er¹, n. Fatty substance made from cream by churning *(look as if ~ would not melt in mouth,* demure; *melted ~,* sauce of ~, flour, etc.); kinds of substance of similar consistence or look, as ~ *of almonds;* fulsome flattery; *~-&-eggs,* kinds of plant with two yellows in flower, as toadflax; *~-bean,* yellow-pod kind usu. cooked in the pod unsliced, wax-pod, (also) large dried haricot bean; *~-boat,* sauce-boat; *~-knife,* blunt, of silver etc., for cutting ~; *~-scotch,* kind of toffee; *~bur,* plant with large soft leaves; *~cup,* kinds of yellow-flowered ranunculus; *~-fingers, -fingered,* (person) unable to hold things, esp. a catch at cricket; *~milk,* liquid left after churning ~; ‖ *~ muslin,* thin loosely woven cloth with fine mesh, used primarily as a wrapping for ~; *~-nut,* N.-Amer. oily nut (-tree); *~-print,* wooden stamp for marking ~; *~-wort,* fleshy-leaved violet--flowered bog-plant. Hence *~Y²* a., *~INESS* n. [OE *butere,* OS, OHG *butera,* WG f. L *butyrum* f. Gk *bouturon*]

bŭtt'er², v.t. Spread, cook, sauce, with butter *(fine words ~ no parsnips,* mere professions are valueless); for other phrr. see BREAD; (also ~ *up*) flatter. [f. prec.]

‖ **bŭtt'erbŭmp,** n.= BITTERN. [see BUMP³]

bŭtt'erflў, n. & a. Diurnal erect-winged insect with knobbed antennae; showy or fickle (person), trifler; *~-nut, -screw* (Mech.), with wings to be turned by thumb & finger; BREAK¹ ~ *on wheel;* (colloq.) *butterflies* (nervous tremors) *in the stomach* or *tummy.* [OE *buttor-flēoge* cf. Du. *botervlieg*]

bŭtt'erine (-ēn), n. Imitation butter of oleo-margarine & milk. [-INE¹]

bŭtt'eris, n. Farrier's tool for paring hoof. [cf. F *boutoir* & obs. E *butter*]

bŭtt'erў, n. Place in colleges etc. where

bread & ale, butter, etc., are kept; ~-
-*hatch*, half-door over which provisions
are issued. [ME, = AF *boterie* butt-store,
f. BUTT¹+-ERY; cf. ME *botelerie* = OF
bouteillerie bottle-store]

butt′ock¹, n. Half of rump (usu. in pl.);
manœuvre in wrestling (usu. *cross*-~,
running-~, etc.); ~-*steak*, = rumpsteak.
[f. BUTT²+-OCK, but recorded much earlier]

butt′ock², v.t. Throw by using buttock.
[f. prec.]

butt′on¹, n. Knob.or disc sewn to garment to fasten it by passing through
~hole, or for ornament (*boy in* ~*s*, page;
take by the ~, detain, see ~*hole* below);
bud; unopened mushroom; in plant
names, as BACHELOR'*s* ~; knob, handle,
catch, as in electric bell; small bar
revolving on pivot as door-fastening;
small rounded body; terminal knob (on
foil, making it harmless; also as ornament); ‖ ~-*boot*, fastened with ~*s*; ~*hole*,
slit made to receive fastening ~, (fig.)
small mouth, ‖ flower(s) worn in ~*hole*,
(vb) make ~holes (in), hold by a coat or
waistcoat ~, detain, (reluctant listener),
whence **butt′onhōlER¹** n. [last sense by
confusion with earlier ~*hold*]; ~*hook*, for
pulling ~ into place; ~-*stick*, appliance
for ~-polishing. Hence (·)~ED² (-nd),
~LESS, aa., ~*lessNESS* n. [ME, f. OF
boton f. Rom. *bottonem f. *bottare f. WG
*buttan sprout; see BUTT⁴]

butt′on², v.t. & i. Furnish with button(s);
fasten (t. & i.) with buttons (often *up*);
enclose within ~ed garment (person, or
object carried with one; usu. *up*). [f.
prec.]

butt′ons, n. Liveried page. [pl. of
BUTTON¹]

butt′onў, a. With many buttons. [-Y²]

butt′ress, n., & v.t. Support built against
wall etc. (FLYING ~); prop (lit. & fig.); ~-
-like projection of hill; (vb) support (lit.
& fig., often with *up*) with ~, by argument, etc. [ME, f. OF (*ars*) *bouterez* (cf.
mod. F *arc-boutant*) pl. of *bouteret* f.
bouter BUTT⁴]

butt′ў, n. (Colloq.) mate, chum, companion; (Mining) middleman between
mine-proprietor & miners; ~-*gang* (of
men undertaking part of large job, sharing profits equally). [orig. unkn.]

butyr-, būtyro-, st. & comb. form of
technical wds as *butyrA*′CEOUS, *butў′rIC*,
butyroacĕt′ic; of BUTTER, esp. in its chem.
aspect.

bŭx′om, a. Plump, comely. Hence
~NESS n. [earlier sense *pliant*; ME
buhsum f. st. of *būgan* BOW³+-SOME]

buy (bī), v.t. (bought), pr. bawt), & n. **1.**
Obtain by paying a (usu. money) price;
serve to procure (*money cannot*~); get by
some sacrifice (*dearly bought*); gain over
(person) by bribery etc.; *I'll* ~ *it* (sl.),
I give it up, I don't know (in reply to a
riddle or question); ~ *in*, ~ a stock of,
withdraw at auction by naming higher

price than highest offered; ~ *into*, ~
stock or shares in (the Funds or a
company); ~ *off*, get rid by payment of
(claim, claimant, blackmailer); ~ *out*,
pay person to give up post, property,
etc.; ~ *over*, bribe; ~ *up*, ~ as much as
possible of, absorb (other firm etc.) by
purchase; ~ *a pig in a poke*, commit oneself
inconsiderately. Hence ~′ABLE a., ~′ER¹
n., (esp.) agent who selects & purchases
stock for a large shop etc. (~*ers' market*,
one in which goods are plentiful & low
prices favour ~ers). **2.** n. A purchase (*a
good* ~, a bargain). [OE *bycgan*, OS
buggian, ON *byggja*, Goth *bugjan* of unkn.
orig.]

bŭz(z)¹, int. = Stale news!

bŭzz², v.i. & t. Make humming sound;
signal with buzzer; move, hover, *about*
(person or abs.) annoyingly like bluebottle; (sl.) go *off* or *away* quickly; (of a
company or place) sound confusedly;
circulate (t. & i. of rumour etc.); utter by
speaking together (~ *applause*); throw
hard (~ *stones*); interfere with by flying
very close to (aircraft). [imit.]

bŭzz³, n. Hum of bee etc.; sound of
people talking, stir, general movement;
*circular saw. [f. prec.]

bŭzz⁴, n. Downy beetle, fishing-fly like
it. [perh. as expressive, cf. FUZZY & obs.
buzz (large bushy) *wig*]

‖ **bŭzz⁵**, v.t. Finish (bottle of wine). [orig.
unkn.]

bŭzz′ard, n. Kinds of raptorial (*bald* ~ or
osprey, *honey* ~, *moor* ~, etc.). [ME, f.
OF *busard*, alt. f. *buson* f. L *buteonem*
falcon+-ARD]

bŭzz′er, n. In vbl senses; esp. steam-
-whistle, (also) electric buzzing-machine
for sending signals, (army sl.) signaller.
[BUZZ³, -ER¹]

bwa′na (-ah-), n. (Africa). Master, sir.
[Swahili]

by¹, prep. & adv. **1.** prep. (bĭ, *sometimes*
bī). Near, at or to side of, in postal
district of, about person or in possession
of, in company of, in region of, slightly
inclining to, (*Bromley-by-Bow, Coniston-
-by-Ambleside; come here by me; stand by,*
be faithful to, help; *abide by*, accept,
observe; *have not got it by me; come by*,
obtain; *by* oneself, alone; *North by East*,
between N & NNE; *by the head, stern*,
deeper in water there; *by land & sea*,
adventures by flood & field). **2.** Along, in
passing along, through, via, avoiding,
passing, out-stripping, (*by nearest road;
by the way*, as one goes, parenthetically;
so *by the by*, esp. as formula introducing
digression; *travel by Bâle, Paris*; *pass
him by, go by him*). **3.** During, in the
circumstances of, (*by day, night, daylight*;
by the space of, biblical for *during*). **4.**
Through the agency, means, instrumentality, or causation, of, owing to, in
such a manner, with, (*by* oneself, without
help or prompting; *know, say, by* HEART;

multiply, divide, by; *3 ft by 2 ft*; *lead by the hand*; *set by the ears*, egg on to quarrel; *go, be known, by the name of ——*; *what do you mean by that?*; *travel by rail*; *by all, no, means*; *live by bread*; *do it by one's deputy*; *have children by such a father, mother*; *authorized, hanged, made, by*; *no gas to read by*; *case goes by default*; *begin, end, by ——ing*; *by way of a joke*; *be by way of knowing everybody*, profess or be supposed to; *cautious by nature*; *by cheque, £6. 5. 4*, in Cr entries; *by chance*; *by dint of*; *by reason of*). **5.** As soon as, not later than, (*by now, next week, tomorrow, the time*—with or oftener without—*that*); according to, after, from, (*by rote*; *by right*; *by rights*, if right were done; *take warning, ·example, by*; *by your leave*; *judge by appearances*; *sell, buy, by retail, measure, the yard, packet*). **6.** With succession of, succeeding, (*by degrees, by hundreds, man by man, little by little*). **7.** To the extent of (*missed by a foot, too moral by half, better by far, much*). **8.** Concerning, in respect of, (*do one's duty by*; *French by blood, Jones by name*; *pull up by the roots*). **9.** As surely as I believe in (*by God*; *swear by all one holds sacred*; *swear by vegetarianism*, declare complete belief in it). **10.** adv. (bī). Near (*stand by*, be inactive. also be ready for action, esp. Naut.). **11.** Aside, in reserve, (*put, lay, set, by*, abandon or store up). **12.** Past (*they marched by*; *all that is gone by*). **13.** ~ *& large*, on the whole, everything considered, (orig. Naut., to the wind & off it). [OE *bī, bi, be*, OS, OHG *bī, bi*, Goth. *bi*; in OE the prep. was occas..*be*; in mod. E the adv. is always *bȳ*, the prep. usu. *bȳ* occas. *bȳ*, & the pref. either *bȳ-* or BE-]

bȳ², **bȳe**, a. Subordinate, incidental, secondary, side, out-of-the-way, secret, as *by(e) road*, *the by(e) effects*, *a by(e) consideration*; ~-ELECTION. [*by* adv. used attrib.; often hyphened with noun; usu. *by* when this is done, & *bye* as sep. wd]

bȳ³, n. = BYE (*-e* usu. exc. in *by the by*).

by-, the prep., adv., or adj. BY in composition. In mod. use chiefly (1) with adj. force; it may be written as separate wd (*by path* or *bye path*), hyphened (*by-path*), or, if the combination is often used, as one wd with the other (*bypath*); (2) with adv. force, as in *bystander, bygone*.

bȳ' and **bȳ'**, adv. & n. Before long, presently; (n.) the future. [prob. f. BY prep. denoting succession (*one by one* etc.)]

bȳ-blow (-ō), n. Side blow at someone else than the main opponent; bastard child. [BY a.]

bȳe, n. Something subordinate (*by the by* or *bye*, incidentally, parenthetically); (Cricket) run scored for ball that passes batsman and wicket-keeper, *leg-*~, for one that touches batsman; (Golf) hole(s) remaining after decision of match & played as a new game; (in games where competitors are paired off) odd man, being odd man. [BY¹ as n.]

bȳe'-bȳe¹, n. (Nursery word for) sleep, bed. [sound used in lullabies cf. *hushaby, lullaby, bye baby bunting*]

bȳe-bȳe'², int. = Good-bye. [colloq. & childish clipping of *good-bye*]

bȳ'ĕnd, n. Side or secret purpose. [BY a.]

bȳ'gone (-aw-), a. & n. Past, departed; antiquated; (pl. n.) the past, past offences (*let ~s be ~s*, forgive & forget). [BY adv.]

bȳ'lāne, n. See BY-.

bȳ'law, **bȳe'law** (bīl-), n. Regulation made by local authority or corporation, as town or railway company. [prob. f. obs. *byrlaw* local custom (ON *bȳjar* genit. sing. of *bȳr*, OE *bȳ* town, cf. *Derby* etc.), but associated with BY a.]

bȳ'nāme, n. Secondary name, sobriquet; nickname. [BY a.]

bȳ'pass (-ah-), n., & v.t. **1.** Secondary gas-jet always alight from which main ·jet is lit when wanted. **2.** Road usu. passing round, or through outskirts of, town etc., & designed to relieve traffic congestion by providing an alternative route for through traffic. **3.** v.t. Furnish with a ~, make détour round (town etc.), also fig. [BY a.]

bȳ'past (-ah-), a. Gone by, elapsed. [BY adv.]

bȳ'path (-ah-), n. Retired path (lit., & fig. as ~*s of history*). [BY a.]

bȳ'play, n. Action apart from the main course of events; esp., dumb show of minor characters on stage. [BY a.]

bȳ'product, n. Thing produced incidentally in manufacturing something else. [BY a.]

bȳre, n. Cow-house. [OE *bȳre* perh. cogn. w. *būr* BOWER¹]

bȳ'road, n. Little-frequented road. [BY a.]

bȳss'|us, n. Fine ancient textile fibre & fabric of flax; tuft of silky filaments by which some molluscs adhere to rock. Hence ~A'CEOUS, ~AL, ~IF'EROUS, ~INE², ~OID, aa. [L, f. Gk *bussos*]

bȳ'stander, n. Spectator. [BY adv.]

bȳ'street, n. Out-of-the-way street. [BY a.]

bȳ'way, n. Secluded road or track (often *highway & ~*); short cut; less known department of any subject. [BY a.]

bȳ'word (-wĕrd), n. Proverb; person, place, etc. taken as type of some (usu. bad) quality (esp. *a ~ for iniquity* etc.). [BY a.]

bȳ'work (-wĕrk), n. Work done by the way, at leisure moments. [BY a.]

Bȳzăn't|ine, a. & n. (Inhabitant) of Byzantium or Constantinople (~*ine historians*, of Eastern Empire from 6th to 15th c.); of the style in architecture etc. developed in the Eastern Empire (round arch, cross, dome, circle, mosaic). Hence ~INESQUE' (-ĕsk) a., ~INISM n., ~INIZE(²) v.t. [f. LL *Byzantinus* f. L f. Gk *Byzantion*]

C

C (sē), letter (pl. *C*s, *C*'s, *Cees*). *C springs*, see CEE. (Mus.) first note of natural major scale. (In argument) third hypothetical person or thing. (Alg.) third known quantity.

Caaba (kah′*aba*), n. Sacred building at Mecca, Mohammedan Holy of Holies containing the black stone. [Arab. *ka'bah*]

cab, n., & v.i. (-bb-). (Go in a) hackney carriage or taxi; driver's shelter on locomotive; ∼′*man*, driver of ∼; ‖∼-*rank*, row of ∼s on ∼′*stand*, where ∼s are authorized to wait; ‖∼-*runner*, -*tout*, men earning pay by fetching, or unloading luggage from, ∼s. Hence ∼′LESS a. [short for CABRIOLET]

cabăl′, n., & v.i. (-ll-). (Join in a) secret intrigue; clique, faction; (hist.) *the C*∼, 'Committee for Foreign Affairs' under Charles II, esp. Clifford, Arlington, Buckingham, Ashley, & Lauderdale (1672), precursor of modern Cabinet. Hence ∼′ER[1] n. [f. F *cabale*(*r*) f. med. L *cabala* CABBALA; not f. initials of Clifford etc., being quoted from 1646]

cäballer′o (-yär′ō), n. (pl. ∼s). A Spanish gentleman. [Sp.; see CAVALIER]

cäb′aret (-ā), n. French tavern; (in England, U.S., etc.) entertainment provided in restaurant etc. while guests are at table. [F]

cäbb′age, n. Kinds of cultivated vegetable with round heart or head; *sea* ∼, sea KALE; ∼ *butterfly*, ∼ *white*, large white or small white; ∼-*net*, for boiling ∼ in; ∼-*rose*, double red rose with large compact round flower; ∼-*tree*, various trees, esp. certain palms with terminal bud eaten like ∼. [15th c. *cabache*, -*oche* f. *caboche*, head, Picard form of OF *caboce*, of unkn. orig.]

cäb(b)′al‖a, n. Jewish oral tradition; mystic interpretation, esoteric doctrine; occult lore. Hence ∼ISM(3), ∼IST(2), nn., ∼IS′TIC a., ∼IS′TICALLY adv. [med. L, f. Heb. *qabbalah* tradition]

cäbb′y̆, n. (colloq.). Cab-driver. [-Y[3]]

cäb′er, n. Roughly trimmed pine-trunk used in Sc. Highland sport of *tossing the* ∼. [f. Gael. *cabar* pole]

cäb′in, n., & v.t. Small rude dwelling; room or compartment in ship for sleeping or eating in, officer's or passenger's room; ∼-*boy*, waiting on officers or passengers; ∼ *cruiser*, power-driven vessel with ∼ & living accommodation; (vb, chiefly in p.p.) confine in small space, cramp. [ME & OF *cabane* f. LL (Gaulish) *capanna*]

cäb′inĕt, n. & a. 1. Small private room, closet; case with drawers etc. for keeping valuables or displaying curiosities. 2. ‖(Pol.) council-room of inner circle of ministers controlling Government policy; those ministers collectively; ∼ *council*,

one of their meetings; ‖ *C*∼ *Minister*, one of them; ‖∼ *crisis*, difficulties involving change of government or resignation of some member(s) of ∼; *shadow* ∼ (formed by Oppc sition leaders from prospective holders of portfolios). 3. ‖∼ *edition*, between library & popular in cost etc.; ‖∼ *photograph*, size larger than carte-de-visite; ∼ *pudding*, made of sponge-cakes, eggs, milk, etc.; ∼-*maker*, -*making*, skilled joiner, joinery, (also of prime minister forming new government). [CABIN + -ET[1], influenced also by F *cabinet*]

cä′ble[1], n. Strong thick rope (Naut., 10 in. or more in circumf., cf. CABLET, HAWSER) of hemp or wire strands; (Naut.) rope or chain of anchor, (as measure) 100 fathoms; submarine or underground line containing insulated wires, also = CABLE-GRAM; (Archit. & goldsmith's work) rope-shaped ornament; ∼-*car*, one moved by an endless ∼; ∼-*laid rope*, of three triple strands; ∼ *railway*, *tramway*, one along which carriages are drawn by an endless ∼. [ME, OF *cable* f. LL *capulum* halter]

cä′ble[2], v.t. & i. Furnish, fasten, with cable; (Archit.) fill lower part of flutings of (column) with convex mouldings; transmit (message), communicate, inform (person), by cable. [16th c., f. prec.]

cä′blegräm (-lg-), n. Message by submarine cable. [CABLE[1] + -GRAM]

cä′blĕt, n. Cable-laid rope under 10 in. in circumference. [16th c., -ET[1]]

caboŏbs′, n. pl. Meat cooked in small pieces with ginger, garlic, etc. [Arab. *kabab*]

cäbochŏn′ (-sh-), n. Gem polished but not shaped or faceted; *en* ∼, (of a gem) so treated. [f. F *caboche*; see CABBAGE]

caboō′dle, n. (sl.). *The whole* ∼, all the lot (persons or things). [U.S., of unkn. orig.; cf. BOODLE]

caboōse′, n. Cooking-room on ship's deck; 'guard's van or car on goods train for workmen etc. [f. earlier Du. *cabuse* (*combuse*, cf. G *kabüse*, *kombüse*, F *cambuse*) mod. Du. *kabuis*, *kombuis*, of unkn. orig.]

cäb′otage, n. Coasting-trade; reservation to a country of ground & surface & air traffic within its territory. [F, f. *caboter* to coast, of unkn. orig.]

cäb′riŏle, n. & a. Kind of curved leg characteristic of Queen Anne & Chippendale furniture (often attrib.), from resemblance to goat's foreleg. [as foll., from resemblance to goat's foreleg]

cäbriolet′ (-lā), n. Light two-wheeled hooded one-horse chaise; motor-car with fixed sides & folding top. [F, f. *cabriole* goat's leap; see CAPRIOLE]

ca′cănn′y̆ (kah-). See CANNY.

cacä′o, n. & a. Seed of tropical Amer. tree, giving cocoa & chocolate; the tree (also ∼-*tree*). [Sp., f. Mex. *caca*(*uatl* tree)]

cäch′alot (-shalŏt, -shalō), n. Kinds of whale with teeth in lower jaw, esp.

common ~, sperm whale. [F, f. Sp., Pg. *cachalote*; ult. orig. unkn.]

cache (kăsh), n., & v.t. Hiding-place for treasure, provisions, ammunition, etc., esp. as used by explorers; the hiding (*make a* ~) or stores hidden; (vb) place in ~. [F, f. *cacher* to hide]

cachec'tic (-k-), a. Of, suffering from, CACHEXY. [f. L f. Gk *kakhektikos*; cf. F *cachectique*]

căch'et (-shā), n. Stamp (fig.), distinguishing mark, internal evidence of authenticity; (Med.) small case (made of gelatine etc.) enclosing dose of (nauseous) medicine. [F, f. *cacher* press]

cachĕx'y (-k-), n. Ill-conditioned state of body or mind. [f. LL *cachexia* f. Gk *kakhexia* (CACO- +*hexis* habit); cf. F *cachexie*]

căch'inn|āte (-k-), v.i. Laugh loudly. So ~A'TION n., ~ātORY a. [f. L *cachinnare*, -ATE³]

căch'olŏng, n. Kind of opal. [f. Kalmuck *kaschtschilon* beautiful stone]

căch'ou (-shōō), n. = CATECHU; pill used by smokers to sweeten breath. [F, f. Malay *kachu*; see CATECHU]

cachu'cha (-ōō-), n. A Spanish solo dance. [Sp.]

cacique' (-sēk), n. W.-Indian & Amer.--Indian native chief; (Spanish pol.) political boss. Hence **caciqu'ISM** (-sēk²-) n., local government on Tammany lines. [Sp., f. Haytian]

căc'kl|e, v.i. & t., & n. (Make) clucking of hen after laying; (indulge in) glib noisy inconsequent talk; boast; chuckle; ~e *out* etc., say ~ingly. Hence ~ER¹ n. [ME *cakelen*; imit., cf. Du. *kakelen*, G *gackeln*]

căco-, comb. form of Gk *kakos* bad, found in some wds taken direct or through L (& F) f. Gk; & prefixed in med. terms (=*disease of*, as *cacophthalmia* eye--disease, or *mal-*, as *cacomorphia* malformation) usu. to Gk components, rarely to L as *cacodorous* ill-smelling.

căcodēm'on, -aem'on, n. Evil spirit; malignant person. [f. Gk *kakodaimōn* (prec. +*daimōn* spirit)]

căc'odȳl, n. Stinking poisonous compound of arsenic & methyl. Hence **căcodȳl'ic** a. [Gk *kakōdēs* stinking (CACO- + *od-* root of *ozō* to smell) + -YL]

caco'ĕpȳ, n. Bad pronunciation (cf. ORTHOEPY). [f. Gk CACO(*epeia* f. *epos* word, see -Y¹)]

căcoëth'es (-ēz), n. Ill habit, itch for doing something unadvisable, usu. in *scribendi* ~, scribbling-mania. [f. L f. Gk *kakoēthes* neut. adj. (CACO- +*ēthos* disposition)]

cacŏg'raphȳ, n. Bad handwriting or spelling. Hence **cacŏg'RAPHER** n., **căcoGRAPH'IC(AL)** aa. [CACO-, after *orthography*]

cacŏl'ogȳ, n. Bad choice of words or pronunciation. [f. LL f. Gk *kakologia* vituperation (CACO-, -LOGY)]

cacōōn', n. Large flat polished bean of tropical shrub with 6–8 ft pods. [African?]

cacŏph'onous, a. Ill-sounding. [f. Gk *kakophōnos* (as foll.) +-OUS]

cacŏph'onȳ, n. Ill sound (cf. EUPHONY); discord (lit. & fig.). [f. Gk *kakophōnia* (CACO-, *phōnē* sound, see -Y¹)]

căc't|us, n. Kinds of succulent plant with thick fleshy stem, usu. no leaves, & clusters of spines. Hence ~A'CEOUS (-shus), ~AL, ~OID, aa. [L, f. Gk *kaktos* cardoon]

cacūm'inal, a. (phonet.). (Of sounds) produced with the tip of the tongue inverted or curled upwards towards the hard palate. [f. L *cacumen -minis* top, extremity +-AL]

căd, n. Person of low manners; person guilty or capable of ungentlemanly conduct, blackguard, whence ~d'ISH¹ a.; (obs.) hanger-on employed about (esp. school & college) games; (obs.) omnibus conductor. [abbr. of CADET]

cadăs'tral, a. Of, showing, the extent, value, & ownership, of land for taxation (esp. ~ *survey*). [f. F *cadastre* f. mod. Pr. *cadastro* f. It. *catast(r)o*, earlier *catastico* f. late Gk *katastikhon* list, register]

cădavĕ'ric, a. (med. & physiol.). Characteristic of a corpse. [f. L *cadaver* +-IC]

cadăv'erous, a. Corpse-like; deadly pale. [f. L *cadaverosus* (*cadaver* corpse) +-OUS]

căd'die, n. Golf-player's attendant for carrying clubs etc. [f. F *cadet* CADET]

cădd'is, n. ~-*fly*, feebly flying freq. nocturnal insect living near water; ~-*worm*, larva of ~-*fly* etc., living in water & making cylindrical case of sticks etc., used as bait. [of unkn. orig.]

cădd'ȳ, n. (Also *tea-*~) small box for holding tea. [f. Malay *kati* weight = 1⅓ lb.]

cād'ence, n. Rhythm; measured movement, esp. of sound; fall of voice, esp. at end of period; intonation; close of musical phrase. Hence (-)**cād'encED²** (-st) a. [F, f. It. *cadenza* f. pop. L **cadentia*; see CHANCE¹]

cād'encȳ, n. Descent of younger branch, cadetship. [as prec., -ENCY]

cadĕn'za (-tsa), n. (mus.). Flourish of voice or instrument at close of movement. [It.]

cadĕt', n. Younger son; student in naval or military or air force college, whence ~-SHIP n.; ~ *corps*, company of schoolboys receiving elementary military training. [f. F *cadet* f. 15th-c. Gascon *capdet* = Prov. *capdel* f. LL *capitellum* dim. of L *caput* head = little chief]

cădge, v.i. & t. Go about peddling or begging; get by begging. [etym. unkn.]

cădg'er, n. Carrier; itinerant dealer in eggs, butter, etc., between remote farms & towns; street hawker; beggar, loafer. [-ER¹]

cad'ī (kah-, kā-), n. Civil judge, usu. of town etc., among Turks, Arabs, Persians. [f. Arab. *qadi* f. *qada* judge]

Cădmē'an. See VICTORY. [f. L f. Gk *Kadmeios* +-AN]

căd'mium, n. Bluish-white metal resembling tin; ~-*yellow*, intense yellow pigment. Hence **cădmiF'EROUS, căd'mic,** aa. [f. obs. *cadmia* CALAMINE f. L f. Gk *kadmia (gē)* Cadmean (earth), -IUM]

cadre (kah'dr), n. Framework, scheme; (Mil.) permanent establishment of unit forming nucleus for expansion at need. [F, f. It. *quadro* f. L *quadrus* SQUARE]

cadŭ'cĕus, n. (pl. -*ĕi*). Ancient herald's wand, esp. as carried by messenger-god Hermes or Mercury. [L, f. Gk *karukion (kērux* herald)]

cadŭ'cĭtў, n., **cadŭc'ous,** a. Fleeting (nature); perishable(ness); (Zool. & Bot., of organs & parts) falling off (n. & a.) when work is done. [n. thr. F *caducité* (-TY), a. f. L *caducus* falling (*cadere* fall) + -OUS]

caec'|um (sē-), n. (pl. -*ca*). The blind gut, first part of large intestine in mammals etc.; any tube with closed end. Hence ~AL, ~IFORM, aa., ~ALLY² adv., ~IT'IS n. [L, for *intestinum caecum* f. *caecus* blind]

Caesar (sēz'ar), n. Roman Emperor from Augustus to Hadrian; heir presumptive of later Roman Emperor; (loosely) any Roman Emperor; an autocrat; the civil power (*Matt.* xxii. 21); ~'s *wife*, person required to be above suspicion. [L, family name of C. Julius]

Caesā'rèan, -ian, (sĭz-), a. & n. Of Caesar or the Caesars, imperial; ~ *birth, operation*, delivery of child by cutting walls of abdomen (from the improbable belief that Julius was so delivered); (n.) adherent of Caesar or an autocratic system. [f. L *Caesarianus* see -EAN]

Caes'arism, -ist, (sēz-), nn. (Believer in) autocracy. [-ISM(3), -IST(2)]

caes'ious (sēz-), a. (bot.). Bluish or greyish green. [f. L *caesius* +-OUS]

caes'ium (sēz-), n. (chem.). An alkali-metal. [as prec. f. its spectrum lines]

caesūr'|a (sĭz-), n. (Cl. prosody) break between words within a metrical foot; (Eng. prosody) pause about middle of line. Hence ~AL a. [L (*caedere caes-* cut, -URE)]

café¹ (kăf'ā), n. Coffee-house, restaurant (esp. foreign; ~ *chantant* (see Ap.), with music & entertainments, often in open air. [F, = coffee(-house)]

café² (kafā'), n. Coffee; ~ *au lait* (ō lā), with milk; ~ *noir* (nwahr), without milk. [F]

căfétēr'ia, n. Restaurant in which customers fetch what they want from the counters. [Sp., = coffee-shop]

căffe'ic, a. (chem.). Of coffee (esp. ~ *acid*). [f. F *caféique,* see CAFÉ², -IC]

căff'éine (-ēn), n. Vegetable alkaloid found in coffee & tea plants. [f. F *caféine* (CAFÉ², -INE⁵)]

Caffre. See KAFIR.

căf'tan (*also* kăftahn'), n. Eastern long under-tunic with waist girdle. Hence

~ED² (-nd) a. [f. Turk. *kaftan* (in earlier use thr. F)]

cāge, n., & v.t. Fixed or portable prison, of wire or barred, esp. for birds or beasts or prisoners of war; prison (lit. or fig.); (Mining) frame for hoisting & lowering cars; open framework of various kinds; (vb) place or keep in ~. [ME, f. OF f. L *cavea*]

***cā'gey** (-jĭ), a. Shrewd; not forthcoming, unapproachable, self-contained. Hence **cā'gĭLY²** adv. [orig. uncert.]

***cahoot** (ka-hōōt'), n. (sl.). Company, partnership; *go* ~*s*, go shares; *in* ~*s*, in collusion. [prob. f. F *cahute* cabin]

caiman. See CAYMAN.

Cain, n. Fratricide, murderer; *raise* ~, make a disturbance. [*Gen.* iv]

cainozō'ic (kīn-), a. (geol.). Of the third geological period (= *tertiary,* cf. *palaeo-zoic, mesozoic*). [f. Gk *kainos* new +*zōon* animal (cf. ZOO-) +-IC]

caique (ka-ēk'), n. Light Bosporan row-boat; Levantine sailing-ship. [F, f. Turk. *kaik*]

cairn, n. Pyramid of rough stones as memorial, sepulchre, landmark, etc.; (also ~ *terrier* small short-legged long-bodied shaggy-coated terrier (from its being used to hunt among ~s). [f. Gael. *carn*]

cairngōrm', n. (Also ~ *stone*) yellow or wine-coloured semi-precious stone. [found on C~, Scotch mountain (Gael. *carn gorm* blue cairn)]

caiss'on, n. Ammunition chest or wagon; large watertight case open at bottom, from which water is kept out by air pressure, used in laying foundations under water; boat-shaped vessel used as dock gate; ~ *disease* (of workers in compressed air, as in ~s etc.). [F (*caisse* f. L *capsa* CASE², -OON)]

cait'iff, n. & a. (poet. & arch.). Base, despicable, (person); coward(ly). [ME, f. ONF *caitif* f. L *captivus* CAPTIVE]

cajŏl|e', v.t. Persuade or soothe by flattery, deceit, etc. (also ~*e* person *into doing, out of,* something; or ~*e* something *out of* person). Hence ~*e*'MENT (-lm-), ~'ER¹, ~'ERY(4), nn., ~'inGLУ² adv. [f. F *cajoler* of uncert. orig.]

cāke, n., & v.i. & t. **1.** Small flattish loaf of bread (arch., as in *King Alfred & the* ~s); thin oaten bread (Sc. & north.; also *oat*~; *land of* ~*s,* Scotland); (usu. Eng. sense) bread with other ingredients besides flour, as currants, spice, eggs, sugar —the substance (~) or (*a* ~) a portion of it baked in a thick disc or ornamental shape—; flattish compact mass of other food (*fish*-~, PAN¹-~) or of any compressed substance (~ *of soap, wax, tobacco*); ~*s & ale,* merry-making; ~-*walk,* kinds of dance developed from Negro contest in graceful walking with ~ for prize; *a piece of* ~ (colloq.), something easy or pleasant; *take the* ~, carry off the honours; *cannot* *eat your* ~ *and have it*, cannot enjoy the two alternatives; hence **căk′y²** a. 2. v.t. & i. Form into compact flattish mass. [ME, prob. f. ON *kaka* (cf. OHG *kuocho*)]

cǎlabār′ bean, n. Poisonous seed of African climbing plant yielding an extract valuable in medicine & surgery. [*Calabar* on W. coast of Africa]

cǎl′abăsh, n. Kinds of gourd whose shell serves for holding liquid; fruit of American ~-tree, so used; pipe etc. made from these or of like shape. [f. F *calebasse* f. Sp. *calabaça*, Sicil. *caravazza*, perh. f. Pers. *kharbuz* melon]

cǎl′aber, -ar, n. Fur of grey squirrel. [ME, f. med. L *calabris, calabrum* f. Calabria]

*cǎlabōōse′ (-s), n. Common prison, lock-up. [f. Sp. *calabozo* dungeon]

cǎlamǎn′cō, n. Glossy Flemish woollen stuff much used in 18th c. [etym. unkn.; cf. Du. *kalamink*, F *calmande*]

cǎlamǎn′der, n. Hard cabinet wood of Ceylon & India. [etym. unkn.]

cǎl′amarў, n. Kinds of cuttlefish with pen-shaped internal shell. [f. L *calamarius* (*calamus* pen, -ARY¹)]

cǎl′amǐne, n. A zinc ore found in England. [F, f. med. L *calamina* alt. f. L *cadmia* CADMIUM]

cǎl′amǐnt, n. Kinds of aromatic herb. [ME, f. OF *calament* ult. f. Gk *kalaminthē*]

cǎl′amǐte, n. Fossil plant allied to mare's tail. [f. L *calamus* reed + -ITE¹(2)]

calǎm′itous, a. Marked by, causing, calamity. Hence ~LY² adv. [f. F *calamiteux* or L *calamitosus* see foll., & -ITOUS]

calǎm′itў, n. Adversity, deep distress; grievous disaster. [f. F *calamité* f. L *calamitatem* (-TY)]

calǎn′dō, mus. direction. Diminish tone & pace gradually. [It.]

calǎsh′, n. 1. Light low-wheeled carriage with removable folding hood; carriage hood. 2. (hist.). Woman's hooped silk hood. [f. F *calèche* f. Slav. (Czech *kolèsa* etc.)]

cǎlc- comb. form=lime; ~*-sinter*, crystalline deposit from lime-springs; ~*-spar*, crystallized carbonate of lime; ~*-tuff*, porous calcareous deposit. [f. G *kalk* f. L *calx -cis*]

cǎlcār′eous, -ious, a. Of, containing, carbonate of lime or limestone. Hence **cǎlcār′eo-**, comb. form. [f. L *calcarius* (CALC-, -ARY¹) + -OUS; first spelling wrong but usu.]

cǎlcěolār′ia, n. Kinds of plant with slipper-shaped flower. [f. L *calceolus* dim. of *calceus* shoe, -ARY¹]

cǎl′cěolāte, a. (bot.). Slipper-shaped. [as prec., -ATE²]

cǎl′cǐc, a. Of calcium. [-IC]

cǎlcǐf′erous, a. Yielding carbonate of lime. [f. L *calx -cis* lime, + -FEROUS]

cǎl′cⅰfў, v.t. & i. Convert, be converted,

into lime; replace by lime; harden by deposit of salts of lime; petrify. Hence ~ⅰF′ⅰC a., ~ⅰFⅰCA′TⅠON n. [as prec. + -FY]

cǎl′cimǐne, n., & v.t. White or tinted wash for ceilings & walls; (vb) distemper with ~. [P; f. L *calx -cis* lime + factitious ending]

cǎl′cǐn|e, v.t. & i. Reduce to quicklime or friable substance by roasting or burning; desiccate; refine by consuming grosser part; burn to ashes; (intr.) suffer these processes. Hence ~A′TION, ~ER¹(2), nn. [ME, f. OF *calciner* or med.L *calcinare* f. LL *calcina* lime]

cǎl′cǐte, n. Native carbonate of lime. [f. L *calx -cis* lime + -ITE¹]

cǎl′cⅰum, n. Chemical element, greyish white metal, the basis of lime (in many compd terms, as ~ *chloride*). Hence **cǎl′cⅰo-** comb. form. [as prec. + -IUM]

cǎl′cŭl|able, a. That may be reckoned, measured, computed, or relied upon. Hence ~ABIL′ITY n. [f. as foll. + -ABLE]

cǎl′cŭl|āte, v.t. & i. Compute (w. noun or clause, or abs.) by figures (~*ating-machine*, that does sums automatically); ascertain beforehand (event, date, etc.) by exact reckoning; plan deliberately (t. & i., esp. in intr. part. & p.p.) = cold-blooded, self-ish); (usu. pass.) arrange, adapt, (conduct, apparatus, etc.) *for* (purpose), *to* (do); (in p.p.) fit, suitable, *to* do; rely *upon*; *(colloq.) suppose, believe. Hence ~ATⅠVE a. [f. LL *calculare* (CALCULUS), -ATE³]

cǎlcŭlā′tion, n. (Result got by) reckoning; forecast. [ME, f. OF f. LL *calculationem* (prec., -ATION)]

cǎl′cŭlātor, n. In vbl senses; also: set of tables for use in calculation; calculating-machine. [L (CALCULATE, -OR)]

cǎl′cŭlous, a. Of, suffering from, stone or calculus. [f. L *calculosus* (foll., -OUS)]

cǎl′cŭlus, n. (pl. *-lī*, in math. sense freq. ~*es*). 1. (med.). Stone, concretion in some part of body (*renal* etc. ~ f. the particular part; *uric acid* etc. ~ f. its composition). 2. (math.). Particular method of calculation, as *differential, integral*, ~. [L, = small stone (-ULE) used in reckoning on abacus]

cǎldār′ium, n. (archaeol.). Roman hot bath room. [L, f. *calidus* hot, see -ARY¹]

caldron. See CAULDRON.

caldera (kahldār′a), n. (geol.). Deep cauldron-like cavity on summit of volcano. [Sp., = cauldron]

Cǎlēdōn′ian, a. & n. (Native) of ancient Scotland (also used in mod. titles of clubs etc., & joc.=Scotch or Scot). [f. L *Caledonia* northern Britain, -AN]

cǎlēfā′cient (-shent), a. & n. (Medical agent) producing warmth. [f. L *calefacere* (*calēre* be warm, *facere* make), -ENT, -ANT]

cǎlēfǎc′tory, a. & n. Producing warmth; (Archaeol.) warm room in monastery. [f. LL *calefactorius* see prec., -TORY]

cǎl′endar¹, n. System by which beginning, length, & subdivision, of civil year are fixed, esp. the GREGORIAN ~, used in Engl. from 1752; JULIAN ~; table(s) with months, weeks, & festivals etc., of a given year, or with dates important for certain classes, as *Gardener's* ~; register, list, esp. of canonized saints, prisoners for trial, or documents chronologically arranged with summaries; ~ MONTH. [ME, f. AF *calender*, (OF *-ier*), f. L *calendarium* account-book (CALENDS, -AR²)]

căl'endar², v.t. Register, enter in list; arrange, analyse, & index (documents), whence ~ER¹ n. [15th c., f. prec.]

căl'ender¹, v.t., & n. Press (cloth, paper, etc.) in a ~ or roller-machine to smooth it; steam mangle; (arch.) person who ~s. Hence **căl'ĕnd**RY n. [f. F *calendre(r)*, f. med. L *ca-, celendra*, corr. of L f. Gk *kulindros*]

căl'ender², n. Mendicant dervish in Turkey or Persia. [f. Pers. *qalandar*]

căl'ĕnds, k-, n. pl. First of month in Roman calendar; *on the Greek C*~, never. [ME, f. L *kalendae*, acc. *-as*, or OF *calendes*]

căl'enture, n. Tropical fever or delirium in which sailors etc. leap into sea. [F, f. Sp. *calentura* fever f. part. st. of L. *calēre* be hot, -URE]

calf¹ (kahf), n. (pl. *-ves*). Young of bovine animal, esp. domestic cow, for first year (*cow in, with,* ~, pregnant; *slip her* ~, suffer abortion); *golden* ~, wealth as object of worship (*Ex.* xxxii); stupid fellow; MOON-~; child (so ~-*love,* childish love affair); (also ~*skin*)=~-leather, esp. in bookbinding (~-*bound*) & shoemaking (*willow* ~, superior brown leather used in shoemaking; young of elephant, whale, deer, etc.; *sea*-~, seal; (Naut.) floating piece of ice; ~-*knee,* knock-knee; || ~'s *teeth,* milk teeth; *calves-foot jelly.* Hence ~'HOOD n., ~'ISH¹(1) a. [OE *cælf*, OS *calf*, OHG *chalb*, ON *kalfr*, Goth. *kalbō* f. Gmc *•kalbh-*]

calf² (kahf), n. (pl. *-ves*). Fleshy hinder part of leg-shank; ~ part of stocking. Hence ~'LESS, -CALVED² (kahvd), aa. [f. ON *kálfi* of unkn. orig.]

Căl'iban, n. Man of degraded bestial nature. [Shakesp., *Tempest,* & see CANNIBAL]

căl'ibr|āte, v.t. Find calibre of; calculate irregularities of (tube, gauge) before graduating. Hence ~A'TION n. [foll. +-ATE³]

căl'ibre (*-er*), **căl'iber**, n. Internal diameter of gun or any tube; weight of character, standing, importance; ability. Hence -**căl'ibr**ED²(-erd) a. [F (*-bre*), f. It. *calibro* or Sp. *-bre* f. Arab. *qalib* mould]

căl'icle, n. (biol.). Small cup-like body. So calic'ulAR¹ a. [f. L *caliculus* dim. of *calix* cup]

căl'icō, n. & a. (pl. ~*es*). ||(Of) cotton cloth, esp. plain white unprinted, bleached or unbleached (~-*ball,* dance at which only cotton dresses are worn); ~-*printer, -ting,* producer, production, of coloured patterns on ~. '[orig. *Calicut*-(etc.) *cloth* f. town on Malabar coast]

cālifōrn'ium, n. Radio-active transuranic element. [f. *Californ(ia)* +-IUM]

cāliŏl'ogy̆, n. Study of birds' nests. [f. Gk *kalia* hut, nest, -o-, -LOGY]

căl'ipăsh, căl'ipee, nn. Gelatinous substances in turtle regarded as dainties (*-ash,* dull green next upper shell; *-ee,* light yellow next lower shell). [perh. W.-Ind.; perh. *-ash* = CARAPACE]

căl'iph, -if, n. Successor (e.g. of Mohammed), (title of) Mohammedan chief civil & religious ruler. Hence **căl'iph**ATE¹ n. [f. OF *caliphe* f. Arab. *khalifah* successor]

căl'ix, n. (anat.;: pl. *-īcēs*). Cup-like cavity or organ. [L, = cup, cf. CALYX]

calk¹ (kawk), v.t., & n. (Provide with) sharp iron to prevent horse-shoe or boot from slipping. [app. ult. f. L *calx calcis* heel, cf. CALKIN].

calk² (kawk), v.t. Trace by colouring back of design & pressing along outlines. [f. F *calquer* f. It. & L *calcare* tread]

cal'kin (kaw-, *also* kál-), n. Turned-down heels of horse-shoe, also turned edge in front, esp. when sharpened in frost; iron guards on boots or shoes. [f. OF *calcain* f. LL *calcaneum* (*calx -cis* heel); 15th c. *kakun* f. Du. *kalkoen*]

call¹ (kawl), v.t. & i. **1.** Cry, shout, speak loudly, (lit. & fig. etc., as): (bird, trumpet, etc.) utter characteristic note; cry *out;* cry *to* (person); signal (*for* trumps); pay brief visit (*at* house, *on* person); read *over* (names to ascertain presence); ~ *for,* order, demand, need, go & fetch; ~ *on,* invoke, appeal to; ~ *off,* cancel (engagement etc.). **2.** Summon (lit. & fig. etc., as): demand presence of (cab, witness, actor after curtain); broadcast (to); (Cards) direct opponent to play (exposed or other card); ~ *into being,* create; ~ *to* ACCOUNT²; ~ *into play,* give scope for; ~ *in question,* dispute; ~ *to mind* etc., also ~ *up,* recollect; ~ *away, off,* divert, distract; ~ *in* money lent, doctor etc. for advice; ~ *forth,* elicit; ~ *out,* elicit, challenge to duel, summon (troops) esp. to aid the civil authorities; ~ *over the* COALS; ~ *up,* imagine, summon to talk by telephone, summon to serve in army etc. (so ~-*up* n.); rouse from sleep; fix the moment for (~ *case* in law-court); ~ *a halt;* ~ *a meeting);* urge, invite, nominate, (*duty, pleasure,* ~*s; many are* ~*ed;* || ~ *to the* BAR¹, *-ministry;* ~ *attention to;* ~ *to witness).* **3.** (With n. or adj. as compl.) name, describe as, (~ *a* SPADE *a spade;* ~ *him John,* ~ *him by the name of John;* ~ person *names,* abuse him; ~ COUSINS *with);* consider, regard as, (~ *that mean;* ~ *it a day,* regard the day's work as being finished); ~ (thing) one's *own,* possess; *•*~ *down* (colloq.), reprimand, challenge.

[late OE *ceallian* f. ON *kalla*; cf. MLG, MDu. *kallen*, OHG *challōn*]

call² (kawl), n. Shout, cry; (also ∼-*over*) =ROLL-∼; special cry of bird etc., imitation of this, instrument imitating it; signal on bugle etc., signalling-whistle; looking-in on business (so *house of* ∼); short formal visit (*pay* ∼, make one); invitation, summons, (to actor for applause; ‖ to the BAR¹; from God, conscience, or congregation, to be pastor); duty, need, occasion, (*no* ∼ *to blush*); demand for money, esp. for unpaid capital from company shareholders; (St. Exch.) option of claiming stock at given date; (Bridge) player's right or turn to make a bid, bid thus made, conventional signal to partner to lead trumps; a ring on or conversation over the telephone; ∼-*loan*, -*money*, lent subject to recall without notice; *at, within*, ∼, ready for orders; ∼-*boy*, prompter's attendant summoning actors; ∼-*day*, -*night*, at Inns of Court, for calling students to bar; ∼-*girl*, prostitute accepting appointments by telephone; ∼-*over*: (Betting) reading aloud a list of prices (in sporting club etc.); roll-∼ at schools. [f. prec.]

call'a, n. (bot.). (Also ∼-*lily*) marsh plant of N. Europe. [orig. unkn.]

call'er¹ (kaw-), n. In vbl senses; esp., person who pays call or visit. [-ER¹]

call'er², a. (Sc.). Fresh, not decaying, (of herring etc.); cool (of air). [Sc. var. of ME *calver*; ult. hist. obsc.]

callig'raph|y, n. Beautiful handwriting; (improp.) handwriting. So **callig'RAPHER**, ∼IST(1), nn., **cällïGRAPH'IC** a. [ult. f. Gk *kalligraphia* (*kallos* beauty, -GRAPHY)]

call'ing (kaw-), n. In vbl senses; also or esp.: divine summons to salvation or self--devotion; impulse to do something as right; occupation, profession, trade; persons following a particular business. [-ING¹]

Calli'opĕ, n. Muse of epic poetry; (*c*∼) set of steam whistles played by a keyboard like that of an organ. [Gk *Kalliopē* beautiful-voiced]

căl(l)'iper, n. & a., & v.t. ∼ *compasses* or ∼*s*, compasses with bowed legs for measuring diameter of convex bodies, or with out-turned points for measuring calibre; ∼ (*splint*), metal support for leg; ∼-*square*, rule with movable cross-heads for taking internal or external diameters; (vb) measure with ∼s. [app. = CALIBRE]

callisthĕn'|ic, a. Suitable for producing strength with beauty (esp. of girls' gymnastics). Hence ∼ICS n. [f. Gk *kallos* beauty + *sthenos* strength + -IC]

callös'itÿ, n. Abnormal hardness & thickness of skin; hardened insensible part, lump, (from friction, or natural as on horses' legs). [f. F *callosité* or L *callositas* (see foll., -TY)]

call'ous, a. (Physiol., Zool.) hardened, hard, (of parts of skin); (of person, heart,

etc.) unfeeling, insensible, whence ∼NESS n. [f. L *callosus* (CALLUS, -OUS) or F *calleux*]

call'ow (-ō), a. Unfledged; downy like young birds; raw, inexperienced; (Irish, a. & n.) low-lying, often flooded, (meadow). [OE *calu* f. WG **kalw-* (cf. G *kahl*) perh. f. L *calvus* bald]

call'us, n.(physiol., path., bot.). Thickened part of skin or soft tissue; bony material formed while bone-fracture heals. [L]

calm¹ (kahm), n. Stillness, serenity, (of weather, air, sea, the mind, social or political conditions); *a*∼, windless period. [ME & OF *calme* f. It. (= Sp., Pg.) *calma*, app. f. LL *cauma* f. (w. infl. of L *calor* heat) Gk *kauma* heat (*kaiō* burn)]

calm² (kahm), a., & v.t. & i. **1.** Tranquil, quiet, windless, (lit. & fig.); (colloq.) impudent (*pretty* ∼ *of him*); hence ∼'LY² adv., ∼'NESS n. **2.** v.t. Make ∼, pacify; (v.i.; alw. w. *down*) become ∼. [f. F *calme* n. & a., see prec.]

căl'mative (*also* kahm-), a. & n. (med.). Calming (agent), sedative. [prec. + -ATIVE]

căl'omĕl, n. (med.). Mercurous chloride used as purgative. [F, f. Gk *kalos* fair, *melas* black (explained anecdotically in various ways)]

cälorĕs'cence, n. (physics). Change of heat-rays to light-rays. [irreg. f. L *calor* heat after wds in -*escence*]

calori-, comb. form of L *calor* heat in Physics & Physiol. Hence **calŏ'riFA'CIENT**, **călorïF'IC**, **calŏ'riMET'RIC(AL)**, aa., **călorïF'ICALLY** adv., **calŏ'riFICA'TION**, **călorïM'ETER**, -METRY, nn., **calŏ'riFY** v.t.

calŏ'ric, n. Heat; ∼-*engine*, driven by hot air. [f. F *calorique* (L *calor* heat, -IC)]

căl'orie, n. (physics). Unit of quantity of heat; amount of heat required to raise temperature of one gram (*small* ∼) or one kilogram (*large* or *great* ∼) of water 1° C. (the latter used as a unit in expressing energy value of foods). [F, irreg. f. L *calor*]

calŏtte', n. Skull-cap of priests etc. [F]

călp, n. Irish dark-grey limestone. [orig. unkn.]

căl'trop, n. Four-spiked iron ball, formerly thrown on ground, to maim cavalry horses; kinds of plant with spined ∼-like flower heads. [OE *calcatrippe*, ME *calketrappe*, corresp. to OF *kauketrape* etc.; ult. referred to L *calx* -*cis* heel + TRAP, but hist. & interrelations obsc.]

căl'umĕt, n. Amer.-Ind. clay-bowled reed-stemmed tobacco-pipe; symbol of peace; *smoke the* ∼ *together*, make peace. [F (esp. Fr.-Canadian) dial. var. of mod. F *chalumeau* f. LL *calamellus* dim. of *calamus* reed]

calŭm'ni|ăte, v.t. Slander. Hence or cogn. ∼A'TION, ∼ätor, nn., ∼ätory a. [f. L *calumniari*, see -ATE³]

calŭm'nious, a. Given to, marked by, calumny. Hence ∼LY² adv. [f. L *calumniosus* or F *calomnieux* (foll., -OUS)]

căl'umnў, n. Malicious misrepresentation; false charge; slanderous report. [f. L *calumnia* or F *calomnie*]

Căl'varў, n. Place, (R.-C. Ch.) representation, of Crucifixion. [OF, f. LL *calvaria* skull transl. of *Golgotha*, *Matt.* xxvii. 33]

calve (kahv), v.i. & t. Give birth to a calf; (esp. in pass. of calf) give birth to; (of iceberg etc.) throw off mass of ice. [OE *cealfian* (CALF[1])] **-calved.** See CALF².

Căl'vin|ism, n. Calvin's theology (esp. the doctrines of particular election & redemption, moral inability in a fallen state, irresistible grace, final perseverance); adherence to this. ~IST(2) n. & a., ~is'TIC(AL) aa., ~is'ticalLY² adv., ~IZE(4) v.i. & t. [f. F *calvinisme* or mod. L *-ismus* (John *Calvin*, 1509–64)]

călx, n. (pl. *căl'cēs*). Powder or friable substance left when a metal or mineral has been burnt, residuum. [L *calx -cis* lime]

calyc-, calyci-, comb. form of CALYX. **călўciflor'AL, -flor'ATE², -flor'OUS, aa.,** with stamens & petals inserted in calyx; **căl'ўciFORM a.; calўc'inAL, căl'ўcinE³, aa.,** having a, on the calyx; **calўc'inAR a., = -al,** also (of flower) double by increase of calyx-lobes; **căl'ўcOID, calўcoid'EOUS, aa.**

căl'ўcl|e, n. (bot.). Row of bracts surrounding calyx-base; adherent crown of seed. Hence or cogn. ~ED² (-ld), **calўc'ūlAR¹, calўc'ūlATE², aa.** [f. L *calyculus* dim. of CALYX (-ULE)]

calўp'sō, n. Spontaneous topical W.-Ind. song. [etym. unkn.]

calўptr-, st. of bot. terms=having, like, a hood. [f. Gk *kaluptra* veil (*kaluptō* to cover)]

căl'ўx, n. (pl. *-ycēs, -yxes*). (Bot.) whorl of leaves (SEPAL) forming outer case of bud (for derivatives see CALYC-); (Physiol. & Biol.) = CALIX. [L, f. Gk *kalux* (cf. *kaluptō* to cover) case of bud, husk]

căm, n. Projecting part of wheel etc. in machinery, grooved, toothed, or otherwise adapted to convert circular into reciprocal or variable motion. [f. Du. *kam* COMB, cf. Du. *kamrad* cog-wheel]

cămaraderie' (-ahderē), n. The intimacy, mutual trust, & sociability, of comrades. [F]

cămarĭll'a, n. Cabal, clique, junto. [Sp.]

căm'aron, n. Large freshwater prawn resembling crayfish. [Sp., = shrimp]

căm'ber, n., & v.i. & t. Slight convexity above, arched form, (of beam, deck, road, etc.); (also ~-beam) slightly arched beam; small dock or tidal basin; (vb) have, impart to (beam etc.), such convexity. [f. F *cambre* f. L *camur* curved inwards; so F *cambrer* vb]

Căm'berwĕll Beaut'ў (bū-), n. A butterfly. [*Camberwell* in Surrey]

căm'bĭst, n. Expert in, manual of, exchanges; dealer in bills of exchange. [F (-*iste*) f. It. *-ista* f. *cambio* CHANGE]

căm'bĭum, n. Cellular tissue, below bark of exogens, in which annual growth of wood & bark occurs. [L, = (ex)CHANGE]

‖ căm'brel, n. Butcher's bent wood or iron for slinging carcasses by ankles. [orig. uncert.]

Căm'brĭan, a. & n. Welsh(man); (Geol.) (of) palaeozoic rocks lying above the Archaean in Wales & Cumberland. [f. L *Cambria* var. of *Cumbria* f. Celt. *Cymry* Welshman or *Cymru* Wales (OCelt. *Combroges* compatriots)]

căm'bric, a. & n. (Of) fine white linen; handkerchiefs. [f. *Kamerijk*, Flemish form of *Cambrai* in N. France, orig. place of making]

‖ Căm'bridge, n. University town in England; ~ *blue*, light blue; ~ *Platonists*, 17th c. group of philosophical divines at ~ University, influenced by aspects of (neo-) Platonism.

căme¹, n. Grooved slip of lead as used in lattice windows. [app.= Sc. *calm* casting-mould]

căme². See COMB.

căm'el, n. Large hornless ruminant long-necked cushion-footed quadruped with (Arabian) one hump or (Bactrian) two humps; thing hard to believe or put up with (*Matt.* xxiii. 24); machine for floating ship over shoals etc.; ‖ ~-*brown*, fishing-fly; ~'s-*hair*, made of ~'s hair or (paint-brushes) of squirrel's tail hairs. [late OE *camel*(l) f. L Gk *kamēlos* f. Semit. (cf. Heb. *gāmāl* camel); in MĒ reinforced by OF *cameil* etc.]

cămeleer', n. Camel-driver. [-EER]

cămĕll'ĭa, n. Flowering evergreen from China & Japan. [*Kamel*, 17th c. Jesuit & botanist, -IA¹]

camĕl'opărd (or kăm²), n. = the now usu. GIRAFFE. [f. L *camelopardus* f. Gk *camelopardalis* (CAMEL, PARD)]

căm'elrў, n. Troops on camels. [-RY]

Căm'embert (-ār), n. Small soft rich Normandy cheese. [name of village]

căm'ĕo, n. (pl. ~*s*). Piece of relief-carving in stone (sardonyx, agate, etc.) with colour-layers utilized to give background (cf. INTAGLIO). [f. It. *cam*(*m*)*eo*, whence F *camée*; OF also *cameu* (F *camaïeu*) whence earlier Eng. form, corresp. to med.L *cammaeus, camahutus*; ult. orig. unkn.]

căm'era, n. *In camera* (Lat.), in the judge's private room, not in open court; (orig. ~ *obscura*) photographing-apparatus; ~ *obscūr'a, lŭ'cĭda* (L, = dark, light, chamber), two kinds of apparatus projecting on paper, for tracing, image of distant object. [L,=vault, f. Gk *kamara* anything with arched cover]

cămerling'o (-nggŏ), -lĕn-, n. The Pope's chamberlain & financial secretary; treasurer of the Sacred College. [It. (-*ingo*); see CHAMBERLAIN]

Cămeron'ĭan, a. & n. (Follower) of Richard Cameron or his doctrines; Scottish reformed presbyterian; ‖ (pl.) battalion(s) of the Scottish Rifles (formed in 1689 orig. of ~s). [-IAN]

‖ **cămĭ-knick′ers**, n. pl. Woman's under-garment of camisole & knickers combined. [*cami(sole)* + *knicker(bocker)s*]

căm′ĭon, n. Low flat four-wheeled horse or motor truck. [F]

căm′isŏle, n. Under-bodice, usu. embroidered etc. [F, f. Sp. *camisola* (*camisa* CHEMISE)]

căm′lĕt, n. Light cloth of various materials for cloaks etc. [orig. a costly Eastern stuff of silk & camel's hair; 15th c. *chamlett*, -(e)*lot* f. OF *cham-*, *camelot* perh. ult. f. Arab. *khaml* nap, in assoc. w. CAMEL]

cămm′ock, n. Rest-harrow; kinds of yellow-flowered plant. [OE *cammoc* of unkn. orig.]

căm′omile, ch- (pr. k-), n. Aromatic creeping composite plant with daisy-like flowers used as tonic; allied kinds · of plant, *dog's*, *stinking*, *purple*, ~; ~ *tea*, infusion of the flowers. [ME, f. OF *camomille* f. LL *c(h)amomilla* f. Gk *khamaimēlon* earth-apple]

Camŏ′rra, n. Secret society in Naples etc. [It.]

căm′ouflage (-ŏoflahzh), n., & v.t. Disguise of guns, ships, etc., effected by obscuring outline with splashes of various colours; use of smoke-screens, boughs, etc., for same purpose; (transf.) means of throwing people off the scent; (vb) hide by ~; [F, f. *camoufler* disguise]

camouflet (kahmŏoflĕ′), n. Subterranean cavity formed by bomb exploding beneath surface of earth. [F]

camp[1], n. Place where troops are lodged in tents etc.; army on campaign; military life (*courts & ~s*); temporary quarters of nomads, gypsies, travellers; camping-out; persons camping out; (S. Afr.) portion of natural veld fenced off for pasture on farms; adherents of a doctrine; ~*-bed*, *-chair*, *-stool*, folding & portable; ~*-colour*, flag used in marking out ~; ~*-fever*, esp. typhus; ~*-follower*, non-military hanger-on of camp, male or female; ~*-meeting*, American religious open-air or tent meeting lasting several days. [F, f. It. *campo* f. L *campus* level ground]

camp[2], v.i. & t. Encamp, lodge in camp; (also ~ *out*) lodge in tent or the open, take up quarters; station (troops) in camp. [f. F *camper* (prec.)]

Campagna (-ah′nya), n. *The ~*, Italian plain S.E. of Tiber. [It., f. L *Campania* (CAMP[1])]

campaign′ (-ān), n., & v.i. 1. Series of military operations in a definite theatre or with one objective or from taking the field to a temporary or final cessation of hostilities (*the Burma, Moscow, 1704, ~*); organized course of action, esp. (Pol.) attempt to rouse public opinion for or against a policy. 2. v.i. Serve on or conduct a ~; hence ~ER[1] n. (*old ~er*, person

practised in adapting himself to circumstances). [f. F *campagne* open country, campaign, f. It. CAMPAGNA]

campanil′é (-nē-), n. Bell-tower, usu. detached, esp. in Italy. [It., f. *campana* bell]

campan|ŏl′ogў, n. The subject of bells (founding, ringing etc.). Hence ~ŏl′OGER, ~ŏl′OGIST, nn., ~olŏ′gĭcAL a. [f. LL *campana* bell + -LOGY]

campăn′ūl|a, n. Kinds of plant with bell-shaped flowers, usu. blue or white, as Canterbury bell. Hence ~A′CEOUS a. [mod. L, f. as prec., + -ula -ULE]

campăn′ūlāte, a. (zool. & bot.). Bell-shaped. [as prec. + -ATE[2]]

căm′phor, n. Whitish translucent crystalline volatile substance with aromatic smell & bitter taste. Hence **camphŏ′rɪc** a. [15th c. *camphire* etc., f. OF *camphore* or med. L *camphora*, f. Arab. *kafur*]

căm′phorāte, v.t. Impregnate or treat with camphor. [-ATE[3]]

căm′pion, n. Kinds of flowering plant, esp. the red & the white ~ & ragged robin. [etym. unkn.]

căm′pŏ săn′tŏ, n. Cemetery in Italy. [It., = sacred field]

‖ **camp′shĕd**, v.t. Face with campshot, revet. [etym. unkn.]

‖ **camp′shŏt**, ‖ **camp′shĕdding**, ‖ **camp′sheeting**, nn. Facing of piles & boarding to resist water-action on, or out-thrust of, a bank, revetting. [etym. unkn.]

***căm′pus**, n. Grounds of a school or college; the college as a teaching etc. institution. [L, = field]

căm′pўlo-, comb. form in bot. terms = bent-. [f. Gk *kampulos*]

căm′wŏŏd, n. Hard red W.-African wood yielding dye. [perh. native *kambi*]

căn[1], n., & v.t. Vessel for liquids, usu. of metal, esp. tin, & with handle over top, whence ~′FUL(2) n.; *carry the ~* (sl.), bear the responsibility; ~*-buoy*, large conical buoy over sands etc.; ~*-dock*, water-lily; (put in a) tin-plate box for hermetic sealing (meat, fish, fruit, etc.), whence (-)~n′ER[1] n., ~n′ERY (3) n., ~*ning-factory*; ~*ned* (sl.), drunk; ~*ned music* (sl.), music recorded for reproduction esp. on gramophone. [OE *canne* (once) = OHG *channa*, ON *kanna*, also LL *canna* f. Gmc; ME *canne*, *kan* prob. f. MDu. *kanne*, Du. *kan*]

căn[2], v. aux. (2 s., *canst* (poet.); 3 s., *can*; neg., *cannot*, *can't* (kahnt); past & condit., *could* (kŏŏd), (poet.) *couldst* or *couldest*; infin., part., & p.p., wanting; defective parts supplied f. *be able to*). Be able to; have the right to; be permitted to (*you ~ go*; also as mild imperat.); *could*, feel inclined to (*could laugh for joy*; *really couldn't think of it*; ~*not* AWAY *with*; (with ellipse) *will do what I~.* [OE *cunnan* = OS *cunnan*, OHG *kunnan*, ON *kunna*, Goth. *kunnan*, pret.-pres. vbs. meaning *know*, cogn. w. KEN, KNOW, & w. L (*g*)*nosco*, Gk *gignōskō*]

Căn'aan (-nan), n. Land of promise, paradise. [O.-T. name of Palestine]

Căn'ada, a. Of, from, ~ (in names of plants, animals, products, as ~ BALSAM).

Canăd'ian, a. & n. (Native) of Canada. [-IAN]

canaille (kanah'ē), n. The rabble. [F]

canăl', n., & v.t. (-ll-). Duct in plant or animal body for food, liquid, air, etc.; artificial watercourse for inland navigation (~s of Mars, markings of doubtful nature on planet Mars); artificial irrigation channel; (Zool.) groove in shell for protrusion of breathing-tube; (v.t.; rare) make ~ through; provide with ~s. [ME, f. OF canal f. L canalis; see CHANNEL]

canalic'ŭlate, -ātĕd, aa. (nat. hist.). With longitudinal groove(s); striated. [f. L canaliculus dim. of CANALIS + -ATE²,³]

căn'alīz|e, -is|e (-īz), v.t.=CANAL vb; convert (river) into canal by embanking, straightening course, locks, etc.; (fig.) give desired direction etc. to. Hence ~Ā'TION n. [prob. f. F canaliser (CANAL + -IZE)]

căn'apé (-ā), n. Piece of fried bread with anchovies etc. [F]

canărd' (or kăn'ăr), n. False report, hoax. [F]

Canarese. See KANARESE.

canăr'ȳ, a. & n. From the C~ Islands; (also ~-bird) yellow-feathered song-bird (green in wild state); (also C~-wine) a favourite wine in 16th–18th cc.; yellow fishing-fly; ~-coloured, bright yellow; ~ convolvulus, tree yielding RHODIUM¹; ~ creeper, yellow-flowered climbing plant; ~-seed, used as food for the bird. [f. F Canarie f. Sp. & L Canaria (canis dog), one of the islands being noted in Roman times for large dogs]

canăs'ta, n. Card game of S.-Amer. origin resembling rummy. [Sp., = basket]

canăs'ter, n. Tobacco prepared by coarsely breaking the dried leaves. [orig. the rush basket container; f. Sp. canastro, ult. f. Gk kanastron; see CANISTER]

cancan (see Ap.), n. High-kicking dance. [F]

căn'cel¹, v.t. & i. (-ll-). Obliterate, cross out, annul, make void, abolish, countermand, neutralize, balance, make up for, (v.i., ~ out or ~, of items) neutralize each other; (Math.) strike out (same factor) from numerator & denominator, from two sides of equation, etc. Hence ~lĀ'TION n. [late ME, f. OF canceller f. L cancĕllare (cancelli cross-bars, lattice; see CHANCEL)]

căn'cel², n. Countermand; suppression & reprinting of leaf or leaves set up, the suppressed or the substituted leaf or leaves. [f. prec.]

căn'cellate, -ātĕd, aa. (bot. & zool.). Marked with crossing lines, reticulated; (of bone) formed of interlacing fibres & plates with cavities, porous. [f. L cancellatus (CANCEL¹, -ATE²,³)]

căn'cellous, a. (Of bone)=prec. [-OUS]

căn'cer, C-, n. Zodiacal constellation the Crab (C~); fourth sign of zodiac (C~); TROPIC of C~; malignant tumour eating the part it is in, spreading indefinitely, & tending to recur when removed, (fig.) evil (sloth, bribery, etc.) acting similarly, whence ~ED² (-erd), ~OUS, aa. [ME, f. L cancer crab, cancer; see CANKER]

cănc'roid, a. & n. 1. Crab-like; like cancer. 2. n. Crustacean of crab family; disease like cancer. [as prec. + -OID]

cândélāb'rum (also -ä-, -ah-), n. (pl. -bra; also sing. -bra, pl. -bras). Large, usu. branched, candlestick or lampstand. [L (-um), f. candela CANDLE]

cândĕs'c|ent, a. Glowing (as) with white heat. Hence ~ENCE n. [f. L candescĕre (candēre be white, -ESCENT)]

căn'did, a. Unbiased; not censorious; frank; ~ camera, small camera for taking informal pictures of persons freq. without their knowledge; ~ friend, nominal friend glad to tell home-truths. Hence ~LY² adv., ~NESS n. [f. L candidus white, or F candide; see prec.]

căn'didate, n. One who puts himself or is put forward for appointment to an office or honour; person thought likely to gain any position; examinee. [f. L candidatus, as prec., -ATE² (2), orig. white-robed (Roman ~s wearing white)]

căn'did|ature, n. Standing for election, being candidate. So ~ACY n. [F, as prec. +-URE]

căn'died (-dĭd). See CANDY (p.p.).

căn'dle, n. Cylinder of wax, tallow, spermaceti, etc., enclosing wick, for giving light; (also ~-power) unit of light-measurement; Roman ~, firework, tube discharging coloured balls; can't, is not fit to, hold a ~ to, is not to be compared with; sell by inch of ~, by auction, last bid before small ~ expires winning (hist.); BELL, book, & ~; game not worth the ~, result not justifying the cost or trouble; BURN² ~ at both ends; hide~ under BUSHEL; ~berry-myrtle (N.-Amer.), ~berry-tree (Moluccas), yielding wax & nut-kernels used for ~s; ~-ends, remnants of ~, odds-&-ends hoarded by the stingy; ~-light, light of ~s, any artificial light, evening; ~stick, support for (usu. single) ~; ~-tree, Amer., with ~-like fruit some feet long. [OE candel f. L candela (candēre shine), in ME reinforced by AN, OF candel(l)e]

Căn'dlemas (-lm-), n. Feast of purification of Virgin Mary, when candles are blessed; (as date) 2nd Feb.; quarter-day in Scotland. [OE Candelmæsse (CANDLE, MASS¹)]

căn'dour (-der), n. Open-mindedness, impartiality; freedom from malice; frankness. [f. L candor whiteness (candēre shine, -OUR)]

căn'dȳ, n., & v.t. & i. 1. Crystallized sugar made by repeated boiling & slow evaporation (also *sugar-~*); *(w. pl.) sweets; ~-FLOSS, sweet confection, usu. pink, of fluffy spun sugar; ~-*stripe(d),* pattern(ed) in alternate stripes of white & colour. 2. vb. Preserve by coating with ~; form (t. & i.) into crystals; (p.p.) glistening, (arch.) honeyed, flattering. [for earlier (15th c.) *sugar candy* f. F *sucre candi* f. Arab.-Pers. *sukkar qandi* (*qand* sugar)]

căn'dўtŭft, n. Plant with white, pink, or purple flowers in flat tufts. [f. obs. *Candy* (*Candia* Crete)+TUFT]

cāne¹, n. Hollow jointed stem of giant reeds & grasses (bamboo, sugar ~) or solid stem of slender palms (rattan, Malacca, etc.) collectively & as material (~), or with pl. (*a* ~, ~*s*) of the stem or a length of it used for walking-stick or instrument of punishment; ‖ any slender walking-stick; stick of sealing-wax, sulphur, glass; ~-*apple,* strawberry-tree; ~-*brake,* kinds of grasses, (also) tract of land overgrown with ~s; ~ *chair,* with seat of woven ~ strips; ~-*sugar* (obtained from the sugar-~). Hence cān'Y² a. [ME *can(n)e,* f. OF *cane* f. L f. Gk *kanna* reed f. Semit. cf. Heb. *qaneh*]

cāne², v.t. Beat with cane, whence cān'- ING¹ (1) n.; drive (lesson) *into* (person) with cane; insert cane into (chair-frame etc.). [f. prec.]

caneph'orus, n. (pl. -*ri*). Sculptured Greek youth or maid bearing basket on head. [L, f. Gk *kanēphoros* (*kaneon* basket, *pherō* carry)]

cangue (kăng), căng, n. Heavy wooden board worn round neck by Chinese criminals. [F (-*gue*), f. Pg. *canga* yoke]

căn'ine (also kanīn'), a. & n. Of, as of, a dog or dogs; ~ *tooth* or ~, one of the four strong pointed teeth between incisors & molars. [f. F *canin,* -*e* or L *caninus* (*canis* dog, -INE¹)]

căn'ister, n. Small box usu. of metal for tea, shot, etc.; (R.-C. Ch.) vessel holding wafers before consecration; ~-*shot* or ~, = CASE²-*shot.* [f. L *canistrum* f. Gk *kanastron* wicker basket (*kanna* CANE¹)]

cănk'er, n., & v.t. 1. Ulcerous disease of human mouth; disease of horse's foot; disease of trees; (fig.) corrupting influence, rotten tendency; ~-*worm* or ~, caterpillar or larva destroying leaves or buds; ~-*rash,* variety of scarlet fever with ulcerated throat; hence ~OUS a. 2. v.t. Consume with canker, infect, corrupt; (p.p.) soured, malignant, crabbed. [ME *cancre* f. ONF f. L *cancer* (whence OE *cancer*); see CANCER, CHANCRE]

căn'a, n. Plant with bright yellow, red, or orange flowers & ornamental leaves. [L (CANE¹)]

cănn'el, n. (Also ~-*coal*) bituminous coal burning with bright flame & used in making coal oils & gas. [orig. unkn.]

cănn'ibal, n. & a. 1. Man who eats human flesh; animal feeding on its own species;

hence ~ISM(2) n., ~is'TIC a. 2. adj. Of, having, these habits. [16th-c. E & Sp. *Canibales* pl., var. of Carib name of W.- -Ind. nation; *Caliban* is prob. another variant]

cănn'ibalize, -ise (-·īz), v.t. Use (one of a number of similar machines) to provide spare parts for the others. [prec., -IZE(4)]

cănn'ikin, n. Small can. [-KIN]

cănn'on¹, n. 1. (Now *gun*) piece of ordnance, gun of the kind that needs mounting, (collect. sing. usu. instead of pl.); aircraft's heavy automatic gun, firing explosive shell; ~-*ball* (hist.), projectile; ~- *bone,* tube-shaped bone between hough & fetlock; ~-*clock,* fired at noon by burning-glass; ~-*fodder,* men regarded as material to be consumed in war. 2. (Mech.) hollow cylinder moving independently on shaft; watchkey barrel. 3. (Also ~-*bit*) smooth round bit for horse. 4. ‖ (Billiards) hitting of two balls successively by player's ball. 5. (Also ~-*curl*) sausage-shaped, prop. horizontal, curl. [f. F *canon* f. It. *cannone* great tube (*canna* CANE¹, -OON); in sense 4 f. older *carom* short for *carambole* (F, f. Sp.—*bola*); in sense 5 f. Sp. *cañon*]

cănn'on², v.i. ‖ Make a cannon at billiards (of player or ball); come into collision, strike obliquely, *against, into, with.* [f. prec.]

cănnonāde', n., & v.t. & i. Continuous gunfire; (vb) fire continuously; bombard, fire fast at. [F, f. It. *cannonata* (prec., -ADE)]

cannot. See CAN².

cănn'ūla, n. (surg.). Small tube for inserting into a cavity or tumour to allow fluid to escape. [L, dim. of *canna* CANE¹]

cănn'|ў, a. Shrewd, worldly-wise; natural, safe to meddle with, (esp. w. neg.); (esp. of Scots) thrifty; gentle, quiet, circumspect, (*ca' ~y,* Sc. for *drive* or *go gently,* as name for trade-union policy of limiting output); sly, pawky. Hence ~ĭLY² adv., ~ĭNESS n. [f. CAN² know + -Y²]

canoe' (-ōō), n., & v.i. (Go in, paddle) boat propelled with paddle(s). Hence ~'IST(3) (-ōō-) n. [f. Sp. & Haytian *canoa*]

căn'on, n. Church decree; ~ *law,* eccl. law; general law governing treatment of a subject; criterion; list of Bible books accepted by Church; list of recognized genuine works of a particular author (*the Shakespearian ~*); part of Mass containing words of consecration; (Mus.) piece with different parts taking up same subject successively in strict imitation; (Typ.) largest size of type with specific name; metal loop on bell for hanging it; member of cathedral CHAPTER, whence ~RY(2) n.; MINOR ~. [OE, f. L f. Gk *kanōn* rule (*kanna* CANE¹); in ME re- -introduced f. AN, OF *canun,* -*on*; in last sense short for CANONIC, in OE *canonic* f.

LL *canonicus*, whence OF *canonie*, *chanoine*, etc., whence ME *canun* etc.]

cañon. See CANYON.

canŏn′ical, a. & n., **canŏn′ic,** a. (arch.). Appointed by canon law (~ *hours*, for prayer, or for celebration of marriage, 8 a.m. to 3 p.m.; ~ *dress*, of clergy, also ~s as n. pl.); included in canon of Scripture; C~ *Epistles*, the seven of Peter, James, John, Jude; authoritative, standard, accepted; (Mus.) in canon form; of a cathedral chapter or a member of it. Hence **canŏn′icaly[2]** adv. [f. OF *canonique* or LL *canonicus*, med. L *canonicalis*; see CANON, -IC, -AL]

canŏn′icate, n. = CANON*ry*. [f. med. L *canonicatus* (as prec., -ATE¹)]

cănoni′city̆, n. Status as canonical book. [f. *canonicus* CANONICAL, -TY]

căn′on|ist, n. Canon-lawyer. Hence ~**is′tic**(AL) aa. [f. F *canoniste* f. med. L *canonista*, see CANON, -IST]

căn′oniz|e, -is|e (-ĭz), v.t. Admit formally to calendar of saints; regard as a saint; recognize (book) as canonical; sanction by church authority. So ~**A′TION** n. [ME, f. LL *canonizare* (CANON, -IZE)]

*•**canoō′dle,** v.i. & t. (sl.). Cuddle, fondle. [U.S., of unkn. orig.]

Canŏp′ic, a. Of *Canopus*, town of ancient Egypt; ~ *jar, vase*, urn used for holding the entrails of an embalmed body in ancient Egyptian burial. [f. L *Canopicus*]

căn′opy̆, n., & v.t. Covering suspended or held over throne, bed, person, etc. (also fig. of any overhanging shelter, sky, etc.); (Archit.) roof-like projection over niche etc.; cover of cockpit in aircraft; (vb) supply, be, such a covering to. [ME *canape, -ope*, f. med. L *canopeum* f. L f. Gk *kōnōpeion* mosquito-net (*kōnōps* gnat)]

canŏr′ous, a. Melodious, resonant. [f. L *canorus* (*canor* song f. *canere* sing) + -OUS]

cănt¹, n. Bevel, oblique face, of crystal, bank, etc.; push, toss, movement, that partly or quite upsets; tilted or sideways position; ~-*board*, sloping board. [app. f. MLG *kant, kante*, MDu. *cant*, point, side, edge, obsc. rel. to OF *cant* (mod. *chant, champ*), It., Sp. *canto* f. Rom. *•canto* of obsc. orig.]

cănt², v.t. & i. (Trans.) bevel off; tilt; turn *over*, turn upside down; push, pitch, sideways; (v.i.) take inclined position; lie aslant; (Naut.) swing round; ~-*hook*, iron hook at end of long handle, used for rolling logs. [f. prec.]

cănt³, n. & a., & v.i. 1. Peculiar language of class, profession, sect, etc., jargon; temporary catchwords (esp. as adj., ~ *phrase* etc.); words used for fashion without being meant, unreal use of words implying piety; hypocrisy. 2. v.i. Use talk of these kinds; (Her.) ~*ing arms, heraldry, coat*, containing allusion to name of bearer; hence ~′ER¹ n. [earlier of musical sound, of intonation, & of beggars' whining, perh. f. singing of religious mendicants; prob. f. L *cantus* song, *cantare* frequent. of *canere* sing]

can't (kahnt). See CAN².

Căn′tăb, n. (colloq.), **Căntabri′ğian,** n. & a. (Member) of Cambridge University. [f. L *Cantabrigia* Cambridge + -AN]

căn′taloup (-ōōp), n. Kind of melon. [F, f. It. *Cantalupo* in Italy]

căntănk′erous, a. Cross-grained, quarrelsome. Hence ~LY² adv., ~NESS n. [perh. f. ME *contak* contention on anal. of *traitorous, rancorous*]

cănta′ta (-tah-), n. (mus.). Choral work, kind of short oratorio, or lyric drama set to music but not acted; (formerly) elaborate vocal solo. [It. (*cantare* sing, *-ata* -ADE)]

Cănta′te (-ahtĕ), n. Psalm xcviii (O sing—) as a canticle. [L, = sing ye]

căntatri′ce (-ĕ′chā, -ēs′), n. Professional woman singer. [It. & F]

cănteen′, n. ‖ Provision & liquor shop in camp or barracks (*dry, wet*, ~, without; chiefly for, liquor); box of cooking-utensils for use in camp, soldier's mess-tin; soldier's water-vessel of tin, wood, etc.; bar, lunch-counter, etc. at outdoor entertainments & in large public & private institutions; case or chest of plate & cutlery for domestic use. [f. F *cantine* f. It. *cantina* cellar]

căn′ter, n., & v.i. & t. 1. Easy gallop (*win in a* ~, easily). 2. ~b. Go at this pace (of horse or rider); make (horse) go thus. [short for *Canterbury pace, gallop, trot*, etc., f. easy pace of Canterbury pilgrims]

căn′terbŭry̆, n. Stand with partitions for music etc.

Căn′terbŭry̆ bĕll, n. Kind of campanula. [f. bells of Canterbury pilgrims' horses]

cănthā′rĭdēs (-z), n. pl. (med.). Dried Spanish fly. [L, pl. of L f. Gk *kantharis* blister-fly]

căn′thus, n. Outer or inner corner of eye, where lids meet. [L f. Gk *kanthos*]

căn′tĭcle, n. Little song, hymn; one of the Prayer-Book hymns, as the *Benedicite, Nunc Dimittis, Te Deum; Canticles*, Song of Solomon. [ME, f. OF *canticle*, var. of *cantique* f. L *canticum* (*cantus* song f. *canere* sing); in 16th c. reinforced by L dim. *canticulum*]

căn′tilĕver, n. Bracket (of length many times breadth & more than twice depth) projecting from wall to support balcony etc.; ~ *bridge*, with piers each of which has two ~s, with long girders connecting ~s of adjacent piers. [f. LEVER; the significance of the first element is unkn.]

căn′tle, n. ‖ Piece, slice, cut off; hind-bow of saddle. [ONF *cantel* dim. of CANT¹]

căn′tŏ, n. (pl. *-os*). Division of long poem. [It., = song, as CANT³]

căn′ton¹ (*also* kăntŏn′), n. Subdivision of country; State of Swiss confederation:

(Her.) square division less than a quarter in upper corner of shield. Hence ~AL a. [OF, = corner (CANT¹, -OON)]

cantŏn'² (*also* -tŏon'), v.t. Divide into cantons (-tŏn); (-tŏon) quarter (soldiers). [f. F *cantonner*, partly prec.]

cănton'ment (-ōon-, -ŏn-), n. Lodging assigned to troops (formerly in India also permanent military station). [f. F *cantonnement* (prec., -MENT)]

căn'tor, n. 1. Leader of singing in church, precentor. 2. Precentor in synagogue. [L]

cantŏr'ial, a. Of the precentor, of N. side of choir (cf. DECANAL). [f. L as foll. + -AL]

căntŏr'is, mus. direction. To be sung by cantorial side in antiphonal singing. [L, genit. of *cantor* precentor (*canere* cantsing, -OR)]

căn'trip, n. (Sc.). Witch's trick; piece of mischief, playful act. [orig. unkn.]

Canŭck', n. & a. (sl.). French Canadian; *Canadian. [U.S. word]

căn'vas, n. Strong unbleached cloth of hemp or flax, for sails, tents, painting on; open kind used as basis for tapestry & embroidery; *under* ~, in tent(s), with sails spread; racing-boat's covered end; picture; ~-*back*, N.-Amer. duck (f. colour of back feathers). [ME & ONF *canevas* f. Rom. *cannabaceus* (L f. Gk *kannabis* hemp, -ACEOUS)]

căn'vass, v.t. & i., & n. Discuss thoroughly; solicit votes, solicit votes from (constituency), ascertain sentiments of, ask custom of, whence ~ER¹ n.; (n.) ~ing for votes. [f. prec., orig. sense being toss in a sheet, & so shake up, agitate, etc.]

căn'yon, cañon (kăn'yon), n. Deep gorge freq. with stream. [f. Sp. *cañon* tube (*caña* f. L *canna* CANE¹)]

cănzonĕt', n. Short light song; kind of madrigal. [f. It. *canzonetta* (*canzone* f. L *cantionem* f. *canere* sing)]

caoutchouc (kowch'ōok), n. & a. (Of) unvulcanized rubber. [F, f. Carib. *cahuchu*]

căp¹, n. Head-dress (woman's, esp. of muslin etc. worn indoors, but also now, like man's or boy's, for outdoor use, brimless & of cloth or soft material; ~ *in hand*, humbly; ~ *fits*, person feels that general remark is true of him; *set* one's ~ *at*, try to attract as suitor); special head-dress (*college* or *square* ~; *steel* ~, helmet; *Scotch* ~, part of Highland costume; *football* ~, of velvet etc., ‖ sign of inclusion in team; ~ *of MAINTENANCE*; ~ *of liberty*, conical, given to Roman slave on emancipation, now Republican symbol; ~ *& bells*, jester's insignia; FOOL's~); caplike covering, natural (mushroom top, knee-~, etc.), or added for various purposes (windmill top, toe-~, inner watchcase; *percussion* ~, for igniting explosive in cartridges etc.); (Naut.) doubly pierced block for lengthening mast by extra spar; conical paper bag, cornet; (Fox-hunting etc.) recognized payment by non-sub-

scriber for day's hunting (collected in ~), whence ~p'ER¹ n., the authorized collector; ~-*paper*, whity-brown for packing, also a size of writing-paper; ~-*stone*, top stone, coping. [OE *cæppe* f. LL *cappa*, of unkn. orig.; cf. CAPE¹, COPE¹]

căp², v.t. & i. (-pp-). Put cap upon; (Sc. Univv.) confer degree on; put percussion cap on nipple of (gun); protect(end of beam etc.) with metal etc., whence ~p'ING¹ (3) a.; lie on top of, crown; award (a player) his cap (for football etc.); outdo (~ *anecdote*, *quotation*, etc., produce a better or another apposite one; ~ *verses*, reply with one beginning with the last's last letter); touch or take off one's hat to (also intr. with *to*); injure at point (*horse* ~s *its hocks*). [f. prec.]

căpabil'itў, n. Power *of* (action etc., acting etc.), *for* (being done something to), *to* (do something); undeveloped faculty (*has* ~*ies*). [foll., -BILITY]

căp'ab|le, a. Susceptible (*of*, or abs.); having the power or fitness for (*of*); wicked enough for (*of*); gifted, able. Hence ~LY² adv. [F, f. LL *capabilis* (L *capere* hold, -BLE)]

capā'cious (-shus), a. Roomy. Hence ~NESS n. [L *capax* (*capere* hold), -ACIOUS]

capā'citance, n. (electr.). 1. Ratio of the change in an electric charge to the corresponding change in potential. 2. Ability to store a charge of electricity, CAPACITY. [f. CAPACIT(Y) + -ANCE]

capā'citāte, v.t. Render capable (*for, to* do); make legally competent. [CAPACITY, -ATE³]

capā'citor, n. (electr.). Device for storing electric charges. [f. CAPACIT(Y) + -OR]

capā'citў, n. Holding-power, receiving--power, (*for* happiness, heat, moisture; *filled to* ~, quite full; ~ *house*, packed theatre etc.); producing-power; cubic content (*measure of* ~, for vessels & liquids, grain, etc.); mental power, faculty; capability, opportunity, *to* do, *of* doing, etc. (rare); position, relative character, (*in a civil* ~; *in my* ~ *as critic*); legal competency; (Electr.) power of an apparatus to store electricity, CAPACITANCE. [f. F *capacité* f. L *·capacitatem* (CAPACIOUS, -TY)]

căp-à-pie' (-apē), adv. From head to foot, (armed, ready, etc.). [f. OF *cap a pie*]

capā'rison, n. (freq. pl.), & v.t. Horse's trappings; equipment, outfit; (vb) put ~ upon. [f. F *caparasson* (now -*açon*) f. Pr. -*assoun* f. -*asso* ult. f. LL *cappa* CAP¹; cf. med. L *caparo* (capa CAPE¹)]

cāpe¹, n. Short sleeveless cloak, either as separate garment or as fixed or detachable part of longer cloak or coat. Hence **cāpED²** (-pt) a. [16th c. f. F, f. Pr. *capa* (= OF *chape*) f. LL *cappa* CAP¹]

cāpe², C-, n. & a. Headland, promontory; *the C*~, of Good Hope, also = C~ Province (*C*~ *boy*, S.-African of mixed black

& white descent), & as adj. of its products (*C~ wine* etc.; *C~ doctor*, strong S.-E. wind peculiar to S. Africa; *C~ Dutch*, S.-Afr. Dutch, Afrikaans; *C~ gooseberry*, kind of winter cherry; *C~ smoke*, S.-African brandy). [14th c. *cape* f. F f. Pr. *cap* f. Rom. **capo* f. L *caput* head]

cǎp'(e)lin, n. Small smelt-like fish used as cod-bait. [F *cap(e)lan*, *-in*]

cǎp'er¹, n. Bramble-like S.-European shrub; (pl.) its flower-buds pickled (esp. *~ sauce*); English *~s*, seed vessels of nasturtium pickled. [ME *caperis*, *caperes*, (sing.) f. L f. Gk *kapparis*; for loss of *-s* cf. CHERRY, PEA]

cǎp'er², n., & v.i. (Give a) frisky movement, leap; fantastic proceeding; *cut a~*, *~s*, = *~* vb. [short for CAPRIOLE]

cǎpercaill'ie, -l'zie (-lyĭ, -lzĭ), n. Wood-grouse, largest European gallinaceous bird (Scotland etc.). [f. Gael. *capull coille* horse of the wood]

cǎp'erer, n. In vbl senses; esp., caddis-fly (from its flight). [CAPER², -ER¹]

cǎp'ful (-ŏŏl), n. Enough to fill a cap; esp., *~ of wind*, passing gust. [-FUL (2)]

cǎp'ĭǎs n. Writ of arrest. [L, = arrest]

cǎpillǎ'rĭtў, n. (Power of exerting) capillary attraction or repulsion. [f. F *capillarité* see foll., -TY]

capill'arў (*also* kǎp'-), a. & n. Of hair; hair-like, thin as a hair; (tube, blood-vessel) of minute or hair-like diameter (e.g. one of ramified blood-vessels intervening between arteries & veins); so *~* ATTRACTION, REPULSION. [f. L *capillaris* (-ARY²) f. *capillus* hair; cf. F *capillaire*]

cǎp'ĭtal¹, n. Head or cornice of pillar or column. [ME, f. OF *capitel* f. L *capitellum* dim. of *capitulum* dim. of *caput* head]

cǎp'ĭtal², a. & n. Involving loss of life, punishable by death, (*~ sentence, offence*) vitally injurious, fatal, (*~ error*); standing at the head (*~ letter*, also *~* as noun); chief (*~ manor*, held in capite or direct from king; *~ messuage*, occupied by owner of estate with several messuages; *~ town* or *city*, or *~* as.noun, head town of country, county, etc.); important, leading, first-class, (*~ ship*, battleship or battle cruiser); excellent, first-rate, (often as interj. of approval); original, principal, (*~ fund* or *~*, stock with which company or person enters into business, accumulated wealth used in producing more, holders of this as a class, *C~ & Labour*; *~ goods*, goods (to be) used in producing commodities, opp. *consumer goods*; *fixed ~*, machinery etc., *circulating* or *floating ~*, goods, money, etc.; so fig., *make ~ out of*, turn to account). Hence *~LY²* adv. [ME, f. OF f. L *capitalis* (*caput -itis* head, -AL)]

cǎp'ĭtalism, cǎp'ĭtalist, (*also* kǎp'-), nn. Possession or influence or system, possessor, of capital or fund used in production, (mod.,Pol.) dominance of private capitalists (opp. *socialism*). Hence cǎpi-

talĭs'tĭc a. [prec., -ISM(3), -IST(3), after F *-isme, -iste*]

cǎp'ĭtalĭz|e, -is|e (-ĭz; *also* kapĭt-), v.t. Convert into, use as, capital; compute or realize present value of (income); (fig.) turn to account, make use of to one's advantage. Hence *~A'TION* n. [-IZE(3); cf. F *-iser*]

cǎp'ĭtāte, -ātĕd, aa. (nat. hist.). Having distinct head; with clustered flowers etc. [f. L *capitatus* headed (*caput -itis*, -ATE²)]

cǎpĭtā'tion, n. (Levying of) tax or fee of so much a head; *~ grant*, of so much for every person fulfilling conditions. [F, or f. LL *capitatio* poll-tax (*caput -itis* head, -ATION)]

Cǎp'ĭtol, n. Roman temple of 'Jupiter on Tarpeian hill (later *~ine hill* or *~ine*); *Congress or State legislature building. [ME, f. ONF *capitolie*, OF *-oile*, f. L *capitolium* (*caput* head), whence mod. sp.]

capit'ular, a. Of a cathedral chapter; (Physiol.) of a terminal protuberance of bone. [f. med. L *capitularis* (L *capitulum* CHAPTER, -AR¹)]

capit'ularў, n. Collection of ordinances, esp. of Frankish kings. [f. med. L *capitularius, -ium* (as prec., -ARY¹)]

capit'ŭlāte, v.i. Surrender esp. on terms. [f. med. L *capitulare* draw up under heads (*capitulum*), see -ATE³]

capitŭlā'tion, n. Stating heads of subject; agreement, conditions, (esp. *the C~s*, hist., by which foreign residents in Turkey had exterritoriality); surrender on terms, instrument containing these. [F, or f. LL *capitulatio* (prec., -ATION)]

cǎp'on, n. Castrated edible cock. Hence *~IZE(3)* v.t. [late OE *capun* f. AN *capun, -on*, f. Rom. **cappone* f. L *caponem* (nom. *capo*)]

cǎponier', n. Covered passage across ditch of fort. [f. F *caponnière* f. Sp. *caponera* orig. a capon-cote (see prec.)]

cǎp'oral (-ahl), n. A French tobacco. [F]

capŏt', n., & v.t. (-tt-). (In piquet) winning of all tricks by one player; (vb) do this against (opponent). [F]

capŏte', n. Soldier's, traveller's, etc., long cloak with hood. [F, dim. of *cape* CAPE¹]

cǎp'ric, a. (chem.). *~ acid*, obtained from butter, coco-nut oil, etc. [f. L *caper -pri* goat + -IC (from its goatlike smell)]

cǎpric'cio (-ēchō), n. (mus.). Lively (usu. short) musical composition. [It., see foll.]

caprice' (-ēs), n. Unaccountable change of mind or conduct, fancy, freak; inclination to these; work of sportive fancy in art etc. [F, f. It. *capriccio* sudden start, orig. 'horror'; mod. sense f. *capra* goat]

capri'cious (-shŭs), a. Guided by whim, inconstant, irregular, incalculable. Hence *~LY²* adv., *~NESS* n. [f. F *capricieux* f. It. *capriccioso* (prec., -OUS)]

Cǎp'ricŏrn, n. Zodiacal constellation Goat; tenth sign of zodiac; TROPIC *of ~*. [f. OF *-corne* or L *capricornus* (*caper -pri* goat, *cornu* horn)]

D

căprĭfĭcā'tion, n. Hastening of ripeness in figs by subjecting them to puncture by wild-fig gall-insects. [f. L *caprificatio* f. *caprificus* wild fig (*caper* goat, *ficus* fig), -ATION]

căp'rĭne, a. Of, like, a goat. [f. L *caprinus* (*caper* -*pri*, -INE[1])]

căp'rĭŏle, n., & v.i. (Give a) leap, caper, esp. (in manège) horse's high leap & kick without advancing. [F (now *cab*-), or f. It. *capriola*, *capriolare* leap (L *capreolus* dim. of *caper* goat)]

căprō'ĭc, a. (chem.). ~ *acid*, found with capric & butyric acids in butter etc. [var. of CAPRIC for differentiation]

căps, abbr. of *capitals* (capital letters) in direction to printers etc.

căp'sĭcum, n. Kinds of plant with hot capsules & seeds; the prepared fruit. [mod. L, perh. f. L *capsa* CASE[2]]

căpsĭz|e', n., & v.t. & i. Upset, overturn, (of ship, boat). Hence ~'AL(2) n. [f. *cap*- as in Pr. *capvirar* = F *chavirer* capsize (cf. It. *capovolgere*, Sp. *capuzar*); 2nd elem. unexpl.]

căp'stan, n. Revolving barrel, worked by men walking round & pushing horizontal levers, or by steam etc., for winding cable in, hoisting heavy sails, etc. [f. Pr. *cabestan*, earlier *cabestran*, f. *cabestre* halter f. L *capistrum* f. *capere* hold]

căp'sŭl|e, n. (Physiol.) membranous envelope; (Bot.) dry seed-case opening when ripe by parting of valves; (Chem.) shallow saucer for evaporating etc.; (Med.) gelatine envelope enclosing dose; metallic top for bottle; detachable nose--cone of rocket or space missile containing instruments for recording & transmitting scientific data. Hence ~AR[1], ~ĭFORM, aa., ~ĭ- comb. form. [F, f. L *capsula* (CASE[2], -ULE)]

căp'tain[1] (-tĭn), n. Chief, leader; great soldier, strategist, experienced commander; (Army) OFFICER of rank next below major & above lieutenant, normally commanding a company or troop; (Navy) officer commanding man-of-war (also used; by courtesy, of commander); *C~ of the Fleet*, adjutant-general of a force, with rear-admiral's uniform; chief sailor of special gang (~ *of forecastle* etc.); Master of merchant ship; manager of Cornish mine; foreman; ‖ head boy or girl at school; leader of side in games; = grey GURNARD; ~'*s biscuit*, partly fermented ship's biscuit of superior quality. Hence ~CY, ~SHIP, nn., ~LESS a., (-tĭn-). [ME & OF *capitain* f. LL *capitaneus* chief (L *caput capit*- head); cf. CHIEFTAIN]

căp'tain[2] (-tĭn), v.t. Be captain of, lead. [f. prec.]

căptā'tion, n. Use of *ad captandum* arguments or appeals. [f. L *captatio* (*captare* catch at, frequent. of *capere* take, -ATION)]

căp'tion, n. ‖ Legal arrest; (Law) certificate attached to or written on document; heading of chapter, article, etc.; wording on cinema screen, cartoon, etc. [f. L *captio* (*capere* take, -TION)]

căp'tious (-shŭs), a. Fallacious, sophistical; fond of taking exception, trying to catch people in their words. Hence ~LY[2] adv., ~NESS n. [f. F *captieux* or L *captiosus* (prec., -OUS)]

căp'tiv|āte, v.t. Fascinate, charm. Hence ~ᴀ'TION n. [f. LL *captivare* take CAPTIVE, -ATE[3]]

căp'tive, a. & n. (Person, animal) taken prisoner kept in confinement, under restraint, unable to escape; of, like, prisoner (~ *state*); lead, take, hold, ~; ~ *balloon*, held by rope from ground. So **căptiv'ITY** n. [ME, f. OF *captif* f. L *captivus* (*capere capt*- take, -IVE)]

căp'tor, n., **căp'tress**, n. fem. One who takes a captive or prize. [-*or* LL (as prec., -OR); & see -ESS[1]]

căp'tur|e, n., & v.t. Seizing, taking possession of; thing or person seized; (v.t.) take prisoner, seize as prize; hence ~ER[1] n. [F, f. L *captura* as prec., -URE]

Căp'ŭchĭn, n. & a. Franciscan (friar) of new rule of 1528; woman's cloak & hood; ~ *monkey*, *pigeon*, kinds with head hair or feathers like cowl. [F (now -*cin*), f. It. *capucino* (*capuccio* cowl f. *cappa* CAP[1])]

căp'ut mŏr'tŭŭm, n. Worthless residue. [L, = dead head; alch. term for residuum of any substance after distillation or sublimation]

căpўbär'a, n. Large S.-Amer. rodent allied to guinea-pig. [Brazilian]

căr, n. Wheeled vehicle (chiefly poet. = chariot; ~ *of the sun*, *triumphal* ~, ~ *of Juggernaut*, etc.; or with specification as JAUNT'*ing*-~, MOTOR-~, *tramway*-~, *dining*-~; in U.S. of any railway carriage or van; in Engl. also of motor-car, of low two--wheeled truck for hogsheads etc., & of other low heavy carts); pendant of airship or balloon holding passengers; ~'*man*, driver of van or jaunting-~, carter, carrier. Hence ~'FUL(2) n. [ME & ONF *carre* f. Rom. *carra, = L *carrus*, -*um* four-wheeled vehicle, f. Celt. *karrom, -*os* (OIr., OWelsh *karr*)]

cărabineer', **cărb-**, n. Soldier with carbine; *The C~s*, (now) the 3rd Dragoon Guards. [f. F *carabinier* (CARBINE, -EER)]

că'racăl, n. Kind of lynx. [F, f. Turk. *qarah-qulaq* black-ear]

că'racŏle, -ŏl, n., & v.i. (Execute) half--turn(s) to right or left (of horse or rider). [f. F *caracole(r)*]

că'racul (-ōŏl), n. Kind of astrakhan fur; cloth imitating this. [Russ.]

carafe' (-ahf), n. Glass water-bottle for table. [F, f. It. *caraffa* prob. f. Sp. *garrafa* f. Arab. *gharafa* draw water]

că'ramĕl, n. Burnt sugar used for colouring spirits etc.; a sweetmeat; the colour of ~, a light brown. [F, f. Sp. *caramelo*]

că'rapăce, n. Upper shell of tortoise & crustaceans. [F, f. Sp. *carapacho*]

că'rat, n. Measure of weight for precious

stones, about 3½ grains; measure of purity of gold, pure gold being 24 ~. [F, f. It. *carato* f. Arab. *qiral* f. Gk *keration* fruit of carob (dim. of *keras* horn)]

că'ravăn (*or* -vän'), n. Eastern or N.-African company of merchants, pilgrims, etc., travelling together for safety, esp. through desert; covered cart or carriage, house on wheels. [16th-c. *carouan* f. Pers. *karwan*, later assim. to F *caravane*]

căravăn'serai (-rī), ' -sera, -sary, n. Eastern quadrangular inn with great inner court where caravans put up. [f. Pers. *karwansarai* (prec., *sara* mansion)]

că'ravel, cărv'el, n. (hist.). Small light fast ship, chiefly Spanish & Portuguese of 15th–17th cc. [15th c. *carvel* etc. f. OF *carvelle* f. Pg. *caravela*, ult. f. LL f. Gk *karabos* crab, light ship; 16th c. *caravel* f. F *-velle* or It. *-vella*]

că'raway (-a-w-), n. Umbelliferous plant with fruit (~-*seeds*) used in cakes. [15th c., immediate source uncert.; f. OSp. *alcarahueya* f. Arab. *alkaraviya*; in med. L, F, It., Sp. *carvi* (whence Sc. *carvy*); ult. orig. perh. L f. Gk. *karon, kareon* cummin]

cărb-, cărbo-, comb. forms of CARBON. Hence **cărb'IDE** n. (often for *calcium carbide* used in making acetylene gas).

cărb'ine, că'ra-, n. Short fire-arm for cavalry use. [f. F *carabine*, weapon of the *carabin* a mounted musketeer]

cărbŏhȳd'rate, n. (chem.). Energy-producing organic compound of carbon with oxygen & hydrogen (starch, sugar, glucose).

cărbŏl'ĭc, a. (chem.). ~ *acid*, powerful antiseptic & disinfectant. Hence **cărb'o-lĪZE**(5) v.t. [CARB-, -OL, -IC]

cărb'on, n. (chem.). Non-metallic element occurring as diamond, graphite, & charcoal, in carbonic acid gas, the carbonates, & all organic compounds; (Electr.) charcoal pencil used in one form of electric lighting; = ~ *copy* (made with ~ paper); ~ *dioxide*, carbonic acid gas; ~ *monoxide*, very poisonous, colourless, almost odourless gas formed during incomplete combustion of coke, charcoal, etc., occurring in coal-gas & in the exhaust fumes of motor engines; ~ *printing, process*, producing permanent prints in various colours; ~ *paper*, for taking copies of letters etc. Hence ~ATE[1](3) n. [f. F *carbone* f. L *carbonem* nom. *-o* charcoal]

cărbŏnā'ceous (-shus), a. Of, like, coal or charcoal; consisting of or containing carbon. [as prec., -ACEOUS]

carbŏnā'rĭ (-rē), n. (hist.). Neapolitan secret society of republican revolutionists. [It. pl. of *carbonaro* charcoal-burner, the name assumed by the society]

cărb'onāte, v.t. (chem.). Form into a carbonate; impregnate with carbonic acid gas, aerate. [f. *carbonate* n. see CARBON, -ATE[3]]

cărbŏn'ĭc, a. (chem.). Of carbon; ~ *acid* (*gas*), the gas formed in combustion of carbon, given out in breathing, & constituting choke-damp. [-IC]

cărbonĭf'erous, a. Producing coal; (Geol.) ~ *strata, system, formation,* palaeozoic next above old red sandstone; ~ *age, era, period,* in which these strata were deposited. [CARBON, -I-, -FEROUS]

cărb'onĭz|e, -is|e (-īz), v.t. Convert into carbon; reduce to charcoal or coke; cover (paper) with carbon for taking copies. Hence ~A'TION n. [-IZE(3, 5)]

cărborŭn'dum, n. Silicon carbide used for polishing by abrasion. [P; CARBON + CORUNDUM]

cărb'oy, n. Large globular glass bottle usually protected with a frame. [f. Pers. *qarabah*]

cărb'ŭncl|e, n. Red precious stone (formerly of many kinds, e.g. ruby; now garnet cut in boss shape); malignant tumour, anthrax, pimple on nose or face, whence ~ED[2] (-ld), **cărbŭnc'ŭlAR**[1], aa. [ME *charbucle* etc., f. OF f. L *carbunculus* small coal (CARBON, -UNCLE); mod. forms assim. to L]

cărbŭrĕt', v.t. (-tt-). Combine (any element) chemically with carbon; charge with carbon. Hence ~t'OR or ~t'ER[1] (2) n., apparatus mixing air with petrol vapour for combustion in motor engines. [CARBON, -URET]

căr'cajou (-jōō, -zhōō), n. American glutton, wolverene. [N.-Amer. F, app. of Ind. orig.]

căr'cass, -ase, n. Dead body (of human body now only with contempt); (with butchers) beast's trunk without head or offal (~ *meat*, raw meat as dist. from corned or tinned meat); mere body, dead or alive (*to save* one's ~), worthless remains (*of*); skeleton, framework, (of house, ship, etc.); (Mil.) kind of fire-ball from gun for igniting buildings. [ME *carcois* etc. f. AF (OF *charcois* etc.) = med. L *carcosium*; 16th c. *carcasse* f. F = It. *carcassa*; ult. orig. unkn.]

cărcin'ogen, n. (med.). Any cancer--producing substance. [f. Gk *karkinos* crab, cancer + -GEN]

cărcinō'ma, n. (pl. *-ata*). (med.). (A form of) cancer. [L, f. Gk *karkinōma* ulcer f. *karkinos* (prec.)]

cărd[1], n., & v.t. (Cleanse, comb, get into order, also scratch or torture, with) toothed instrument, wire-brush, or wire--set rubber or vulcanite strip, for raising nap on cloth or preparing wool, hemp, etc.; ~-*thistle*, teasel; ~*ing-machine*, with card-strips fixed on rollers. [ME, f. OF *carde* f. Pr. *carda* f. *cardar* f. Rom. *caritare f. L *carere* card; vb f. OF *carder* f. Pr. *cardar*]

cărd[2], n. (Also *playing-*~) one of pack of 52 oblong pieces of pasteboard used in games (COURT[1]-~; *house of* ~*s*, (lit.) child's game, (fig.) insecure scheme etc.; ~*s*, card-playing; *sure, safe, doubtful,* etc.,

~, such a plan, expedient; *knowing, queer,* ~, such a person; *put (all) one's ~s on the table,* disclose all one's resources, plans, etc.; *throw up, show,* one's ~s, give up, let out, one's plan; ~ *up* one's *sleeve,* plan in reserve; *on the ~s,* likely, possible); flat piece of thick paper or pasteboard for various purposes (*speak by the ~,* with precision, f. obs. use = mariner's compass; ‖ POST²~; (colloq.) an eccentric person, a character; *correspondence ~,* for short notes; = ticket of admission; = invitation; ~ or *visiting ~,* with name etc., sent or left in lieu of formal visit, so *leave a ~ on; wedding, Christmas,* etc., ~, sent in notification or compliment to friends; *collecting ~,* for entering subscribers to charities; programme of events at race-meetings etc., or of cricket scores, esp. *correct ~; the ~,* the correct thing, what is expected; printed or written notice, rules, etc., for hanging in window or on wall); ~*-case,* for carrying visiting ~s; ~*-basket, -rack,* for keeping visitors' ~s; ~*board,* pasteboard for cutting ~s from or making boxes etc.; ~ *index* (in which each item is entered on separate ~); ~*index* (v.t.), make a ~ index of; ~*-sharper,* swindler at ~*-games;* ‖ ~ *vote* (of delegates each counting for the number of his constituents). [f. F *carte* f. L *charta* f. Gk *khartēs* papyrus-leaf; *-d* for *-te* unexplained]

card'amom, n. Spice from seed-capsules of E.-Ind. plants. [f. L *cardamomum* or F *cardamome* f. Gk *kardamōmon* (*kardamon* cress, *amōmon* a spice plant)]

card'an, a. (engineering). ~ *joint,* UNIVERSAL joint; ~ *shaft* (with universal joint at one or both ends). [f. G. *Cardano,* Italian mathematician (d. 1576)]

card'iac, a. & n. Of the heart (esp. path., as ~ *symptoms,* of heart-disease); of upper orifice of stomach; (n.) heart-stimulant, cordial. [f. L *cardiacus* (esp. in *cardiaca passio*), f. Gk *kardiakos* f. *kardia* heart; cf. F *cardiaque*]

card'igan, n. Knitted woollen jacket with or without sleeves. [named after Earl of C~ c. 1855]

card'inal, C-, a. & n. On which something hinges, fundamental, important, (~ *virtues,* the four natural & three theological, see VIRTUE; ~ *numerals,* the primitive ones, one, two, three, etc., as opp. to the ordinal ones, first, second, third, etc.; ~ *points* (of compass), N., S., E., W.; ~ *church,* hist., one of principal churches in Rome, to which others were subordinate, whence C~, noun, orig. person in charge of one of these, now one of seventy princes of R.-C. Ch., members of Pope's council of 6 ~ bishops, 50 ~ priests, & 14 ~ deacons, & electors of new Pope, whence ~ATE¹, ~SHIP, nn.; also prefixed to other titles, as C~*-Legate*), whence ~LY² adv.; of deep scarlet; woman's short hooded (orig. scarlet) cloak; small scarlet bird;

(Zool.) of the hinge of a bivalve; ~*-flower,* scarlet lobelia. [ME, f. OF f. L *cardinalis* (*cardo -inis* hinge, -AL); n. f. OF in later eccl. uses of the Latin]

car̆dio-, comb. form of Gk *kardia* heart.

car̆dŏŏn', n. Composite vegetable allied to artichoke. [f. F *cardon* f. *carde* artichoke (-OON) f. Pr. *carda, -do,* f. Rom. **carda* for L *cardu(u)s* thistle. See CARD¹]

care¹, n. Solicitude, anxiety; occasion for these; serious attention, heed, caution, pains, (*take, have a,* ~, be cautious); charge, protection, (A, c/o or ~ of B, in addresses; *have the, take,* ~ *of; in, under,* one's ~); thing to be done or seen to (~*s of State* etc.; *that shall be my* ~); ~*-laden, -worn,* with anxieties; ~*'taker,* person hired to take charge, esp. of house in owner's absence, (adj.) exercising temporary control, as *a ~taker* (stopgap) *government.* [OE *caru,* OS *cara,* OHG *chara,* ON *kŏr,* Goth. *kara* f. Gmc **karō*]

care², v.i. Feel concern or interest *for* or *about;* provide food, attendance, etc., *for* (children, invalids, etc.); (w. neg. expressed or implied) feel regard, deference, affection, *for,* be concerned *whether* etc., (often with expletive *a pin, a damn, a farthing, a tinker's cuss; couldn't ~ less,* colloq., be utterly indifferent; *I don't ~ if I do,* am willing); be willing or wishful *to* (*should not ~ to be seen with him; do you ~ to try them?*). [OE *carian* f. Gmc **karō-jan* (prec.)]

careen', v.t. & i. Turn (ship) on one side for cleaning, caulking, etc.; (cause to) heel over; ***(of vehicle etc.) career wildly. [ult. f. L *carina* keel]

careen'age, n. Careening a ship; expense of it; place for it. [f. prec. + -AGE]

career', n., & v.t. 1. Swift course, impetus, (*in full, mid,* etc., ~); course or progress through life; development & success of party, principle, nation, etc.; way of making a livelihood (*a ~ diplomat,* a professional); hence ~IST (3) n., one intent mainly on personal advancement & success in life. 2. v.i. Go swiftly or wildly (often *about*). [f. F *carrière* f. It. *-iera* f. Rom. **carraria (via)* carriage-(road) f. L *carrus* CAR¹]

care'ful (-ārf-), a. Concerned *for,* taking care *of;* painstaking, watchful, cautious, (*to do, that, what, whether,* etc.); done with or showing care. Hence ~LY² adv., ~NESS n. [OE *carful;* see -FUL]

care'less (-ārl-), a. Unconcerned, lighthearted; 'inattentive, negligent (*of*), thoughtless; inaccurate. Hence ~LY² adv., ~NESS n. [OE *carlēas;* see -LESS]

caress', n., & v.t. 1. Fondling touch, kiss; blandishment. 2. v.t. Bestow these on; pet, make much of; hence ~inGLY² adv. [f. F *caresse(r)* f. It. *carezza(re)* f. L *carus* dear]

car̆'ret (or kār̆ᵗ) n. Mark (∧) placed below line to show place of omission. [L, = is wanting]

car'go, n. (pl. ~es). Freight of ship. [f. Sp. *cargo* f. *cargar* f. LL *car(ri)care* CHARGE²]

Că'rib, n. & a. (One) of aboriginal inhabitants of Southern W.-Ind. islands. So ~bē'an a. [f. Sp. *Caribe* cf. CANNIBAL]

că̆ribou' (-ōō), -boo', n. N.Amer. reindeer. [-*ou* Canad. F, prob. f. native wd]

că̆ricatŭr|e', n., & v.t. Grotesque representation of person or thing by over-emphasis on characteristic traits (pictorial, literary, or mimetic); hence ~ɪsᴛ(1) n.; (v.t.) make, give, a ~e of; hence ~'ABLE a. [F, f. It. *caricatura* (in 17th c. Eng. use)]

car'ies (-z), n. Decay (of bones or teeth). [L]

că̆'rĭllŏn (-lyon, *or* karĭl'yon), n. Set of bells sounded either from keyboard or mechanically; air played on bells; instrument (or part of organ) imitating peal of bells. [F]

carin'|a, n. (zool. & bot.) Ridge-shaped structure, Hence ~AL, **car'inATE²**, aa., ~o- comb. form. [L, =keel]

car'ious, a. Decayed (esp. of bones, teeth). [f. L *cariosus* (CARIES, -OSE¹)]

cark'ing, a. Burdensome (alw. with *care*). [f. obs. vb *cark* f. ONF *carkier* f. Rom. *°carcare* f. LL *carricare* CHARGE²]

‖ **carl(e)**, n. (Sc.). Man, fellow. [OE in comb. as *hūs-carl* f. ON *karl* cogn. w. CHURL]

‖ **carl'ine¹**, n. (Sc.). Old woman. [ME & ON *kerling* fem. of prec.]

carl'ine², n. Kinds of composite plants allied to thistle. [F, f. med. L *carlina* for *Carolina* reputedly named f. *Carolus* Charlemagne]

Carlovin'gian, Carolin'gian, (-j-), a. & n. (One) of second French dynasty founded by Charlemagne (d. 814). [f. F *carlovingien* after *mérovingien* MEROVINGIAN]

Carlȳl'|ism, n. Principles, literary manner, a mannerism, of Carlyle. So ~E'AN, ~IAN, aa., ~ESE' a. & n. [Thomas *Carlyle* 1795–1881; -ISM(3, 4)]

Carm'agnole (-anyŏl), n. Song & dance among French revolutionists of 1793. [F]

Carm'elite, n. & a. (Member) of mendicant order of friars (also *White Friars* f. their white cloak); fine woollen stuff, usu. grey. [F, or f. med. L *carmelita* (Mt *Carmel* in Palestine, place of foundation in 12th c., -ITE¹(1))]

carm'inative, a. & n. (Drug) curing flatulence. [f. F -*if or* med. L *carminativus* f. *carminare* heal (by incantation); see CHARM, -ATIVE]

carm'ine, n. & a. (Coloured like, colour of) crimson pigment made from cochineal. [f. F or Sp. *carmin*, f. med. L *carminium*, f. *carmesinum* CRIMSON + *minium* cinnobar]

carn'age, n. Great slaughter, esp. of men. [F, f. It. *carnaggio* (L *caro carnis* flesh, -AGE)]

carn'al, a. Sensual, fleshly; sexual (*have* ~ *knowledge of*, have sexual intercourse with); unsanctified, worldly. Hence ~ISM(2), **carnăl'ĭᴛʏ**, nn., ~ɪᴢᴇ(3) v.t., ~ʟʏ² adv. [f. LL *carnalis* (*caro* see prec., -AL)]

carnā'tion¹, n. & a. (Of) rosy pink (orig. flesh-) colour. [F, f. LL *carnationem* (as prec., -ATION) fleshiness]

carnā'tion², n. Cultivated kinds of clove pink. [in 16th c. also *coronation*, perh. the orig. form, later assim. to prec.]

carnau'ba (-naōō-, -now-), n. Brazilian wax palm; also *Brazilian wax*) its yellowish wax. [Braz. Port.]

carnĕl'ian. = CORNELIAN. [late 17th c. var. of CORNELIAN, after L *caro* etc., as flesh-coloured]

carn'i|fȳ, v.t. & i. (path.). Change (t. & i. of bone, lungs, etc.) to structure of flesh or muscle. Hence ~FICA'TION n. [L *caro carnis* flesh, -FY]

carn'ival, n. Half-week or week before Lent; festivities usual during this in R.-C. countries; riotous revelry; reckless indulgence in something (*of*; ~ *of blood-shed* etc.). [16th c., f. It. *carne-, carnovale* f. med.L *carnelevarium* etc. Shrovetide, f. *carn-* (*caro*) flesh + *levare* put away]

carniv'ora, n. Large order of flesh-eating mammalia, including cats, dogs, etc. [L neut. pl. see CARNIVOROUS]

carn'ivŏre, n. Carnivorous animal or plant. [F, as foll.]

carniv'orous, a. Feeding on flesh (esp. of the CARNIVORA, & of plants digesting animal substance). [f. L *carnivorus* (*caro carnis* flesh, -VOROUS)]

‖ **carn'ȳ, -ey**, v.t. (colloq.). Coax, wheedle. [orig. unkn.]

ca'rob, n. Horn-like pod of Mediterranean ~-tree. [16th c., f. F *carobe* (now -*oube*) f. Arab. *kharrubah* bean-pod]

ca'rol, n., & v.t. & i. (-ll-). i. Joyous song, human or of birds, esp. Christmas hymn. 2. vb. Utter, celebrate with, these; hence ~ɪᴇʀ¹ n. [ME, f. OF *carole*(r) of unkn. orig.]

Că'roline, a. Of Charlemagne; of the time of Charles I & II of England. [f. L *Carolus* Charles + -INE¹]

Carolingian. See CARLOVINGIAN.

°că̆'rom, n. Cannon at billiards. [see CANNON¹]

carŏt'id, a. & n. Of, near, the two great arteries carrying blood to head; (n.) one of these. [f. F *carotide* f. Gk *karōtides* pl. (*karoō* stupefy, compression of these arteries being thought to do this)]

carous|e' (-z), v.i., & n. (Have, engage in) a drinking-bout; drink deep. Hence ~'ᴀʟ(2) n. [orig. as adv. = right out, in phr. *drink* ~ f. G *gar aus trinken*]

carousĕl' (-ōōz-), cărr-, n. Tournament (hist.); °roundabout, merry-go-round. [f. F *carrousel*]

carp[1], n. A freshwater fish usu. bred in ponds. [ME, f. OF *carpe* f. Pr. f. LL *carpa*, perh. f. Gmc orig.; cf. OHG *karpfo*]

carp[2], v.i. Talk querulously, find fault, (usu. *at*); esp. *~ing tongue, criticism,* captious. [obs. ME senses *talk, say, sing,* f. ON *karpa* to brag, but mod. sense (16th c.) f. or infl. by L *carpere* pluck at, slander]

carp'al, a. Of the CARPUS. [CARPUS, -AL]

carp'el, n. (bot.). Pistil-cell, whether pistil is one cell or several. Hence ~LARY[1] a. [f. F *carpelle* f. Gk *karpos* fruit, see -LE (2)]

carp'enter, n., & v.i. & t. 1. Artificer in woodwork (esp. of rough solid kinds as in ship or house building, cf. JOINER, CABINET-*maker*; *the ~'s son*, Jesus); ~*-ant, -bee,* kinds boring into trees; ~*-scene,* played before a painted scene (also ~*-scene*) to give ~ time for preparing elaborate scene behind; so **carp'entry** (2, 5) n. 2. vb. Do, make by, ~'s work. [ME & AF *carpenter* (OF -*ier*) f. LL *carpentarius* (*carpentum* wagon f. Celt.)]

carp'et, n., & v.t. 1. Thick woven or felted fabric for covering floor & stairs (at first of table-covering, whence *on the ~*, under discussion; & as floor-covering long a boudoir luxury, whence ~*-knight,* stay-at-home soldier, ladies' man); *on the ~*, (also, colloq.) being reprimanded; smooth, soft, or bright expanse of grass, flowers, etc.; ~*-bed,* garden bed with dwarf plants arranged in pattern; ~*-dance,* informal; ~*-rods,* keeping stair-~ in place; ~*-snake,* variegated Australian kind; ~*-bag,* travelling-bag, orig. made of ~; ‖~*-bagger,* candidate for election or political agitator unconnected with district; hence ~LESS a. 2. v.t. Cover (as) with a carpet, whence ~ING[1] (3) n.; ‖ summon (servant etc.) into the room for reprimand, reprove. [ME, f. OF *carpite* or med. L -*ita,* corresp. to OF *charpie* lint, f. Rom. **carpire* f. L *carpere* pluck, pull to pieces]

carphŏl'ogy, n. Delirious fumbling with bed-clothes etc. [f. Gk *karphologia* (*karphos* twig, *legō* pick, -Y[1])]

carpo-[1], comb. form of CARPUS.

carpo-[2], comb. form of Gk *karpos* fruit. Hence **carpŏl'ogy** n.

carp'us, n. (anat.; pl. -*pī*). Part of skeleton that unites hand etc. to fore-arm, eight small bones in higher vertebrates (in man, wrist; in horse, knee). [f. Gk *karpos* wrist]

carrageen (kǎ'rageˇn), n. An edible seaweed found in N. Europe, Irish moss. [f. *Carragheen* in Ireland]

cǎ'rrel, n. 1. (hist.). Small enclosure or study in cloister. 2. Small cubicle in (stackroom of) library. [f. OF *carole,* med. L *carola,* of unkn. orig.]

cǎ'rriage (-rij), n. Conveying, transport; cost of conveying (~-FREE; ‖~-*forward,*

not prepaid); management (*of* enterprise etc.); passing (*of* Parl. motion etc.); manner of carrying (~ *of head, body,* etc.), bearing, deportment; wheeled vehicle for persons (*hackney, railway,* ~), esp. four-wheeled private vehicle with two (~ *& pair*) or more horses (~*-company, -folk,* who keep these), whence ~FUL (-rijf-) (2) n.; wheeled support of gun (usu. *gun-~*); wheeled framework of vehicle apart from body; (Mech.) sliding etc. part of machinery for shifting position of other parts; ~ *clock* (going in any position); ~*-dog,* spotted Dalmatian; ~*-drive,* road in parks etc.; ~*-way,* part of road intended for vehicular traffic. Hence ~LESS (-rijl-) a. [f. ONF *cariage* f. *carier* (CARRY, -AGE)]

cǎ'rriageable (-ija-), a. Available for carriages (of road). [-ABLE]

cǎ'rrick bĕnd, n. (naut.). Kind of knot or splice. [BEND[1]; *carrick* perh. f. obs. *carrack* armed merchant ship]

cǎ'rrier, n. In vbl senses; esp.: person undertaking for hire the conveyance of parcels (*common ~,* legal term including also railway and steamship companies etc.); part of bicycle etc. for carrying luggage; person or animal that without suffering from a disease conveys its germs; = *Bren ~, aircraft ~,* etc.; ~*-PIGEON;* ~*-nation* etc., conducting oversea trade for others; ~ *wave,* continuous electromagnetic wave motion emitted by radio transmitter. [CARRY + -ER[1]]

cǎ'rriŏle, n. Small open carriage for one; covered light cart; Canadian sledge. [F]

cǎ'rrion, n. & a. Dead putrefying flesh; anything vile, garbage, filth; ~*-crow,* between raven & rook, feeding on ~, small animals, etc.; (adj.) rotten, loathsome. [ME, f. AN, ONF *caroine, -oigne* (F *charogne*), f. Rom. **caronia* f. L *caro* flesh]

cǎrronade', n. (hist.). Short large-calibred ship's gun. [*Carron* (in Stirlingshire, Scotland) orig. place of making + -ADE]

cǎ'rrot, n. (Plant with) tapering orange-coloured edible root; (pl., sl.) red hair, red-haired person, whence ~Y[2] a. [f. F *carotte* f. L *carota* f. Gk *karōton*]

cǎ'rry[1], v.t. & i. 1. Convey in vehicle, ship, hand, or head (as *news*), or on person (also of vehicle etc., or water, wind, etc., as subject; ~ *corn,* from field to stack; *fetch & ~,* be underling; ~ *all before one,* succeed, overcome all opposition; ~ *weight,* be handicapped in horse-racing or fig.). 2. Conduct (*pipes ~ water, wires ~ sound*; ~ *into effect*; ~ *one back,* in fancy to earlier times; ~ *off to prison, to dine*). 3. Transfer (figures to column of higher notation; ~ *conviction,* implant one's own in other minds; ~ *over, forward,* entries to new page or account). 4. Propel to specified distance (of gun etc., with obj. usu. omitted; also intr.=*go* of missile).

5. Cause or enable to go *to* (of motive, journey-money, etc.). **6.** Bring *to* (of day's journey etc.). **7.** Prolong, continue, *to* (~ *tower to 500 ft. modesty to excess*). **8.** Win (prize; ~ *it, the day*, succeed; ~ *fortress* etc., capture; ~ *hearers with* one, persuade); win victory for (candidate; ~ one's *point, a motion, bill*). **9.** Wear, have with one, possess, involve, (arms, a watch, etc.; ~ one's BAT²; ~ *weight, authority*, be influential; ~ *with* one, remember; *loans* ~ *interest, principles* ~ *consequences*); stock (goods for sale). **10.** Hold in a certain way (~ one's *head, body, oneself*; ~ *sword*, in saluting-position). **11.** Endure weight of, support, (*ships* ~ *sail, piers* ~ *dome*). **12.** ~ *away*, inspire, transport, deprive of self-control, (Naut.) lose (mast etc.) by breakage, break off or away; ~ *off*, remove from life, win, render passable, ~ *it off* (*well*), make brave show; ~ *on*, advance (process) a stage, continue, manage (business), (v.i.) go on with what one is doing, (colloq.) behave strangely, flirt or have amorous intrigue (*with*); ~ *out*, put (principles, instructions, etc.) in practice; ~ *over* (St. Exch.), keep over to next settling-day; ~ *through*, bring safely out of difficulties, complete. [f. ONF *carier* (F *charrier*) f. *car* CAR]

că′rrў², n. (Mil.) *the* position of carrying sword; (Golf) ball's flight before pitching; portage between rivers etc.; range of gun etc.; ~*over* (St. Exch.), process of carrying or amount carried over. [prec.]

cărt, n., & v.t. & i. **1.** Strong two-wheeled vehicle (cf. WAGON) used in farming & for heavy goods, (also *spring, mail, dog, ~*) light two-wheeled one-horse vehicle for driving in, (*put ~ before horse*, reverse order, take effect for cause); *in the ~* (sl.), in a fix, in an awkward or losing position; ~*-horse*, thickset & fit for heavy work; ~*-ladder*, rack at sides or ends for increasing capacity; ~*-load*, = ~ful, also large quantity of anything; ~*-road, -way*, too rough for carriages; ~*-wheel*, wheel of ~, large coin as crown etc., lateral somersault (*turn* ~*-wheel*); ~*-whip*, long & heavy; ~*-wright*, maker of ~s; hence ~*-*AGE(4), ~*-*ER¹, ~*-*FUL(2) (-ŏŏl), nn. **2.** vb. Carry in a ~; work with a ~ [ME, f. ON *kartr* cart; relation to OE *cræt* is uncert.]

cărte, quarte (kărt), n. Fencing position (~ *& tierce*, sword-play). [F (*q-*), f. It. *quarta* fourth]

carte blanche (see Ap.), n. Blank paper given to person to write his own terms on; full discretionary power. [F, (CARD², BLANK)]

cărte-de-visite (vïzēt′), n. Photograph 3½ in. × 2¼. [F, = visiting card, its orig. purpose]

cărt′el, n. Written challenge to duel; (agreement for) exchange of prisoners; (also *kartell*) manufacturers' union to control production, marketing arrangements, prices, etc. Hence ~IZE (3) v.t. &

i., combine to form a (business) ~. [F, f. It. *cartello* dim.´of *carta* CARD²]

Cărte′sian (-zhn), a. & n. (Follower) of Descartes or his philosophy or mathematical methods. Hence ~ISM (-zĭan-) (3) n. [*Cartesius* mod. L name of René Descartes, 1596–1650, -IAN]

Cărthū′sian (-zhn), a. & n. (Member) of order of monks founded by St Bruno 1086; (member) of Charterhouse school founded on site of ~ monastery. [f. med. L *carthusianus* f. L *Carl(h)usia* (*Chartreuse*, near Grenoble) + -AN; see CHARTERHOUSE]

cărt′ilage, n. (Structure, part, in vertebrates, of) firm elastic tissue gristle, (*temporary* ~, in the young, changing later to bone). So **cărtilă′ginoid** a. [F, f. L *cartilago -inis*]

cărtilă′ginous, a. Of, like, cartilage (~ *fish*, with ~ skeleton). [f. F *cartilagineux* or L *-osus* (see prec., -OUS)]

cărtŏg′raphў, n. Map-drawing. So **cărtŏg′RAPHER** n., **cărtographIC(AL) aa.** [f. F *-ie*, see CARD², -GRAPHY]

cărtŏl′ogў, n. Study of maps & charts. So **cărtolŏ′gICAL a.** [f. F *-ie*, see CARD², -OLOGY]

cărt′omăncў, n. Fortune-telling by playing-cards. [f. It. *carta* CARD², -MANCY]

cărt′on, n. White disc within bull's-eye of target; cardboard box for holding goods or the cardboard used for these. [f. F as foll.]

cărtoon′, n., & v.i. & t. **1.** Drawing on stout paper as design for painting, tapestry, mosaic, etc.; full-page (or large) illustration, esp. on politics in a paper; hence ~IST(3) n.; *animated* ~, film made from a succession of drawings simulating a cinematographic film of living persons. **2.** vb. Draw ~, represent (person etc.) in a ~. [f. F *carton* or It. *cartone* (*carta* CARD², -OON)]

cărtouche′ (-ōōsh), n. (Archit.) scroll ornament, e.g. volute of Ionic capital; tablet imitating, or drawing of, scroll with rolled-up ends, used ornamentally or bearing inscription; (Archaeol.) oval ring containing hieroglyphic names & titles of Egyptian kings etc. [F, f. It. *cartoccio* augmentative of *carta* CARD²]

cărt′ridge, n. Charge of propellant explosive for fire-arms or blasting made up in case of paper, flannel, metal, etc. (*small-arm ball* ~, or ~, contains bullet also, *blank* ~ the explosive only); ~*-belt*, with sockets for ~s; ~*-paper*, thick & rough, used also for drawing & for strong envelopes. [16th c. *cartage* etc., corrupt. of prec.]

cărt′ularў, n. Collection of records; register. [f. med. L *c(h)artularium* f. L *chartula* dim. of *c(h)arta* CARD², -ARY¹]

că′runcle (*also* karū̆′), n. Fleshy excrescence, as turkeycock's wattles. [F, f. L *caruncula* (*caro carnis* flesh, -UNCLE)]

cărve, v.t. & i. (p.p. *-ed*, arch. *-en*). Cut (in gen. sense now only fig., as ~ one's *way*); produce by cutting (statue, portrait, representation in relief or intaglio, inscription, design, *out of, in,* or *on,* material), change by cutting (material *into* something), cover or adorn (material *with* figures cut in it, cut designs etc., whence cărv'ING¹(2) n.; cut up meat, cut up (meat etc.), at or for table (*carving knife,* long for this purpose); subdivide (usu. *up*); ~ *out,* take from larger whole, acquire esp. by the sword. [OE *ceorfan* f. WG *kerfan*]

cărv'el, = CARAVEL; ~-*built,* with planks flush (cf. CLINKER-BUILT).

cărv'er, n. In vbl senses; also, carving knife, (pl.) carving knife & fork. [-ER¹]

căryăt'id, n. Female figure used as pillar. [f. L f. Gk *karuatis -idos* priestess at Caryae]

căscăde', n., & v.i. (Fall like a) waterfall, or one section of large broken waterfall; wavy fall of lace etc. [F, f. It. *cascata* (*cascare* to fall f. L *cas-* see CASE¹)]

căscăr'a (sagrá'da) (-ahd-), n. Laxative drug from the bark of a tree. [Sp., = sacred bark]

căse¹, n. 1. Instance of thing's occurring; actual state of affairs (*is, is not, the* ~, is true, false); position, circumstances, in which one is, plight, (*in good, evil,* ~, well, badly, off); (Med.) person's diseased condition; instance of any disease. 2. (Law) cause, suit, for trial; statement of facts in cause *sub judice,* drawn up for higher court's consideration (*judge states a* ~); cause that has been decided & may be cited (*leading* ~, one often cited & governing subsequent decisions); sum of arguments on one side (*that is our* ~; *make out* one's ~, prove it); (fig.) ~ *of conscience,* matter in which conscience has to decide between conflicting principles. 3. (Gram.) form of noun, adj., or pronoun, in inflected languages expressing relation to some other word in sentence (in uninflected languages, this relation itself apart from form). 4. *In* ~, if, in the event that, lest; *in* ~ *of,* in the event of; *in the* ~ *of,* as regards (*in the* ~ *of Jones an exception was made*); *put* (*the*) ~ *that,* suppose; *in any* ~, whatever the fact is, whatever may happen; *in that* ~, if that is true, should happen; ~ *history,* record of person's ancestry, personal history, etc., for use in determining necessary treatment etc., ~-*law,* law as settled by precedent; ~'*work,* social work concerned with the individual. [ME & OF *cas* f. L *casus -ūs* fall (*cadere cas-* fall)]

căse², n., & v.t. 1. Enclosure of something, box, bag, sheath, etc.; glass box for showing specimens, curiosities, etc.; outer protective covering (of watch, sausage, seed-vessel, book, etc.); box with proper contents (*dressing-*~); (Print.) receptacle with compartments (*upper* ~, capitals, *lower* ~, small letters); ~-*bottle,* square for fitting into ~ with others;

~-*harden* v.t., harden surface of, esp. give steel surface to (iron) by carbonizing, (fig.) render callous; ~-*knife,* worn in sheath; ~-*shot,* or ~ (hist.), bullets in tin box fired from cannon without fuse, also = SHRAPNEL; ~-*worm,* = CADDIS. 2. v.t. Enclose in case, surround *with,* (also with *up, over*); hence căs'ING¹ (3) n. [f. ONF *casse* (F *châsse*) f. L *capsa* (*capere* hold)]

căs'ein, n. Protein of milk, the basis of cheese. [L *caseus* cheese + -IN]

căse'măt|e (-sm-), n. Vaulted chamber in thickness of wall of fortress, with embrasures; armoured enclosure for guns in warship. Hence ~ED² a. [16th c. *casamat*(e) f. It. *casamatta* or Sp.-*mata,* f. *casa* house (second element uncert.); mod. sp. f. F *casemate*]

căse'ment (-zm-, -sm-), n. Metal or wooden hinged frame with glass forming (part of) window (often ~-*window*); (poet. etc.) window; ~ *cloth,* cotton cloth used for curtains & as dress material etc. [15th c., of unkn. orig.]

căs'éous, a. Of, like, cheese. [f. L *caseus* cheese + -OUS]

casérn(e)' (-z-), n. (Usu. pl.) barracks. [F (-e), f. Pr. *cazerna* f. Rom. **quaderna* (place) for four f. L *quaterna*]

căsh¹, n. (no pl.), & v.t. 1. Ready money (*in, out of,* ~, having, not having, money; ~ *down,* paid on the spot); || ~ *on delivery* (abbr. C.O.D.), forwarding of goods against ~ to be paid to postman; (Banking etc.) specie, or specie & bank-notes; (Book-keeping) ~-*account,* to which only ~ is carried, & from which all payments are made, ~-*book,* for record of ~ received & paid; ~ *payment,* in ready money; ~ *price,* lowest, for ready money; ~ *register,* mechanical till visibly recording amount of each purchase, totalling receipts, etc.; hence ~'LESS a. 2. v.t. Give or obtain ~ for (note, cheque, etc.); ~ *in* (colloq.), die, ~ *in on,* realize profit on, (fig. use of poker phr.). [f. F *casse* (now *caisse*) box, or its source It. *cassa* f. L *capsa* CASE²]

căsh², n. (hist.; pl. *cash*). Kinds of E.-Ind. & Chinese small coin, esp. a former Chinese coin perforated for stringing = ₁⁄₁₀₀₀ of tael. [ult. f. Tamil *kasu* a small coin by confusion with CASH¹]

căsh'ew (-ōō), n. W.-Ind. etc. tree with kidney-shaped nut (~-*nut*). [f Pg. *caju* (*acaju,* whence F *acajou* mahogany), f. Tupi (*a*)*caju*]

cashier'¹, n. Person in charge of bank's or merchant's cash. [f. Du. *cassier* or its source F *caissier* (CASH¹, -IER)]

cashier'², v.t. Dismiss from service, depose; discard. [c. 1600 *casseer* etc., f. Flem. *kassereñ* disband, revoke, f. F *casser* = It. *cassare* quash f. LL *cassare* annul; see QUASH]

căsh'mēre, n. (Also ~ *shawl*) shawl of fine soft wool of Cashmere goat; the material; imitation of it. [f. *Kashmir* in N. India]

casi'nō (-sē-), n. (pl. *-os*). Public music or dancing or gambling room; old card-game. [It., dim. of *casa* house f. L *casa* cottage]

cask (-ah-), n. Wooden vessel (=BARREL[1]); this & its contents; varying measure of capacity. [16th c. *cask*(e) app. f. F *casque* helmet; sense 'barrel' is only Eng., & unexpl.]

cas'kĕt (-ah-), n. Small box, often of precious material & workmanship, for jewels, letters, cremated ashes, etc. [15th c., in form a dim. of prec., of obsc. orig.]

Căs'lon (-z-), n. (typ.). ~ *type*, old-face type cut in the foundry established by William~ (d. 1766), or in imitation of this.

casque (kăsk), n. (hist., poet.). Helmet. [F, f. Sp. *casco*]

Cassăn'dra, n. Prophet of ill; unregarded prophet. [Trojan prophetess fated to prophesy truly & be disbelieved]

cassā'tion, n. Annulment; *Court of C~*, court of appeal in France. [F, f. *casser*; see QUASH, -ATION]

cassa'va (-sah-), n. W.-Ind. etc. plant with tuberous roots; its starch or flour, bread made from these. [16th c. *cas*(s)*avi* etc., f. Haytian]

căs'erōle, n. A heat-proof earthenware vessel in which meat etc. is cooked & served (*en* ~, so served). [F]

că'ssia (*also* -sha), n. Inferior kind of cinnamon; kinds of plants yielding senna-leaves. [f. L f. Gk *kasia* f. Heb. *q'tsi'ah* (*qatsa'* cut off bark)]

căs'sock, n. Long close tunic worn by all clergy including seminarists and altar servers. Hence ~ED[2] (-kt) a. [f. F *casaque* long coat, f. It. *casacca* horseman's coat; ult. orig. uncert.]

căssolĕtte', n. Vessel for burning perfumes; perfume-box with perforated top. [F, dim. of *cassole* dim. of *casse* pan]

căss'owarў (-o-w-), n. Kinds of large running bird related to ostrich. [f. Malay *kasuari*]

cast[1] (-ah-), v.t. & i. (*cast*)). 1. Throw (poet. or arch. exc. in spec. uses, as: ~ *dice*; ~ *a vote*, give or deposit it; ~ LOTS; ~ *ashore*; ~ *net*, *hook*, *fly*; ~*ing-net*, once thrown & at once drawn in; ~ *the* LEAD[1], in sounding; ~ *anchor*; ~ *in one's teeth*, reproach him with, *that*; ~ *an eye*, *glance*, *look*; ~ *a spell on*, bewitch; ~ *light*, a *shadow*, *on*; ~ *blame*, one's *cares*, *upon*; ~ *into prison*). 2. Overthrow in a lawsuit. 3. Throw off, get rid of, lose, (~ *not a* CLOUT *till May be out*; ~ *calf*, *fruit*, *etc*.). Hence ~A'TION, ~ATOR, nn., ~ATORY a. [f. L *castigare* (see -ATE[3])]

Căstile' (-ēl) soap, n. Hard soap, usu. mottled, made with olive oil & soda. [*Castile*, in Spain]

Castil'ian, a. & n. (Native or inhabitant) of Castile; language of Castile, standard Spanish. [f. as prec. + -IAN]

found, (molten metal) *into* some shape, (figure etc.) *of* metal, whence ~'ING[1](2) n. 7. ~ *about*, go this way & that in search, devise means, (*for*, *to* do, *how*); ~ *away*, reject, (pass., of ship) be wrecked; ~ *back*, revert; ~ *down*, depress; ~ *in* one's *lot with*, share fortunes of; ~ *off*, abandon, (Knitting) close loops & make selvedge, (Naut.) loose & throw off (rope etc.), (Printing) estimate space taken in print by MS. copy; ~ *up*, calculate. [ME, f. ON *kasta*; it displaced OE *weorpan*, & has been displaced in ordinary literary use by *throw*]

cast[2] (-ah-), n. 1. Throw of missile etc., distance so attained; throw, number thrown, at dice, whence chance or try; throw of net, sounding-lead, or fishing-line (also, in fishing, the fly with hook & gut; & *good*, *bad*, etc. place for casting). 2. Casual lift in cart etc. 3. Undigested food thrown up by hawk, owl, etc. 4. Calculation, adding of columns in account. 5. Set of actors taking the parts in play, or the distribution among them. 6. Form into which any work is thrown; model made by running molten metal or pressing soft material into mould (also the negative mould itself). 7. Twist, inclination, (~ *in eye*, slight squint). 8. Tinge, shade, of colour. 9. Type, quality, (esp. ~ *of features*, ~ *of mind*). [f. prec.]

Căs'talў, n. (poet.). Fount of poesy. So **Căstāl'ian** a. [f. L f. Gk *Kastalia* fountain of the Muses]

căs'tanĕt (*or* -ĕt'), n. (Usu. pl.) hardwood or ivory instrument(s) used in pairs to rattle in time with dancing. [f. Sp. *castañeta* dim. of *castaña* f. L *castanea* chestnut]

cast'away (kahsta-), n. & a. Shipwrecked (person); reprobate. [p.p. of CAST[1], AWAY]

caste (-ah-), n. Hindu hereditary class, with members socially equal, united in religion, & usu. following same trade, having no social intercourse with persons of other ~s; hereditary more or less exclusive class elsewhere; this system, the position it confers (*lose*, *renounce*, ~, descend in social scale). Hence ~'LESS (-tl-) a. [f. Sp. & Port. *casta* lineage, race, breed, fem. of *casto* pure, CHASTE]

căs'tellan, n. Governor of castle. [ME & ONF *castelain* f. L *castellanus* (CASTLE, -AN)]

căs'tellātĕd, a. Castle-like; battlemented; (of district etc.) having castles. [f. med. L *castellatus* (CASTLE, -ATE[2])]

căs'tĭg|āte, v.t. Chastise, punish with blows or words; correct & emend (book etc.). Hence ~A'TION, ~ĀtOR, nn., ~ĀTORY a. [f. L *castigare* (see -ATE[3])]

cast′ing-vōte (-ah-), n. Vote that decides between two equal parties. [part. of CAST¹ in obs. sense 'turn the scale']

cast iron, n., **cast-iron**, a. Iron shaped by being run into mould; (adj.) made of ~; hard, untiring, rigid, unadaptable.

castle¹ (kah′sl, kà′sl), n. Large fortified building or set of buildings, stronghold; mansion that was once such; (Ireland) *The C~* (hist.), government system (f. Dublin C~), seat of vice-regal court & government); *Englishman's house his ~*, none may force entrance; (Chess) piece made with battlemented top, also *Rook*; *~ in the air*, *~ in Spain*, visionary project, day-dream, (so *~-builder*); *~-nut*, one with notched extension for locking pin. Hence **ca′stlED²** (-ld) a., **~WISE** (-lw-) adv. [late OE, ME *castel* stronghold f. ONF f. L *castellum* dim. of *castrum* fort]

ca′stle² (kah′sl, kà′sl), v.t. & i. (chess). Move castle next king and king round castle (*~ the king*, or abs.). [f. prec.]

cas′tor¹ (-ah-), n. Substance obtained from beaver used in medicine & perfumery; (sl.) hat. [F or L, f. Gk *kastōr* beaver]

cas′tor², **-er**, (-ah-), n. **1.** Condiment-bottle for table, (pl.) cruet-stand; *~ sugar*, white, finely granulated. **2.** Small swivelled wheel on leg of chair, table, etc. [CAST¹+-OR, -ER¹; sense 1, 17th c.; sense 2, 18th c.]

cas′tor³ (-ah-), n. Horny external knob inside horse's leg (also *chestnut*). [orig. unkn.]

cas′tor oil (-ah-), n. Nauseous vegetable oil used as purgative (*cold-drawn ~*, expressed from seeds without heat) & lubricant. [orig. uncert.; perh. so called as having succeeded CASTOR¹ in med. use]

cãstramĕta′tion, n. (archaeol.). Laying out of camps. [F, f. L *castra* camp, *metari* measure, -ATION]

cãstr|āte′, v.t. Remove testicles of, geld; deprive of *vigour*; expurgate (book). Hence **~A′TION** n. [f. L *castrare*, -ATE³]

cãstra′tō (-rah-), n. (pl. *-ti*, pr. *-tē*). A male singer castrated in boyhood so as to retain a soprano or alto voice. [It.]

ca′sual (-zhŏŏ-, -zū-), a. & n. Accidental; irregular; undesigned; unmethodical, careless; (colloq.) unceremonious; *~ labourer*, who works when the chance comes; ||*~ poor*, who sometimes need poor-relief (also *~ as noun*); ||*~-ward*, for their relief in workhouse; *~ water*, (Golf) temporary accumulation of water (i.e. not one of the recognized hazards of the course). Hence **~LY²** adv., **~NESS** n. [ME, f. OF *casuel* & L *casualis* (*casus* CASE¹, -AL)]

ca′sualtў (-zhŏŏ-, -zū-), n. Accident, mishap, disaster, esp. (pl.) list or number of killed, wounded, & invalided, in a battle, march, war, etc., (sing.) wounded etc. person. [15th c. f. prec.+-TY; after *royalty* etc. (also 16th c. (obs.) *casuality*, f. F *casualité*, med. L *casualitas*)]

cãsūarin′a (*also -ēn²a*), n. (Kinds of) Australian & E.-Indian tree with jointed leafless branches resembling gigantic horse-tails. [f. mod. L *casuarius* cassowary (from resemblance between branches & feathers)]

ca′su|ist (-zhŏŏ-, -zū-), n. Person, esp. theologian, who lays down application of ethical rules to special cases, weighs conflicting obligations, classifies exceptions, & draws distinctions; quibbler. Hence **~is′tic(AL)** aa., **~is′ticallY²** adv., **~istrY** n. [f. F *casuiste* f. L *casus* CASE¹, -IST(3)]

cãs′us, L n. *~ bĕll′ī*, act justifying war; *~ foed′eris* (fēd-), circumstances contemplated in treaty as requiring the action of the parties when they arise.

cãt¹, n. **1.** Small domesticated carnivorous quadruped (male, *Tom-~*); *wild ~*, larger native British kind; spiteful woman, scratching child; (Zool.) any member of genus *Felis*, as lion, tiger, panther, leopard (esp. *the Cats, the great Cats*); *~-like* animal of other species (*civet, musk, ~*). **2.** (hist.). Pent-house in sieges. **3.** (also *~′head*) horizontal beam from each side of ship's bow for raising & carrying anchor. **4.** (Also *~-o′--nine-tails*) rope whip with nine knotted lashes formerly used for flogging sailors & soldiers. **5.** Six-legged tripod always standing on three of its legs. **6.** Tapered short stick in game tip-*~*. **7.** *Turn ~ in pan*, change sides, be turncoat; *a ~ may look at a king*, rebuke to the exclusive; *care killed the ~* (for all its nine lives; therefore be cheerful); *wait for the ~ to jump, see which way the ~ jumps*, cult of the jumping *~*, etc., of politician refusing to advise until public opinion has declared itself; *fight like Kilkenny ~s*, to mutual destruction; *·BELL³ the ~*; *not room to swing a ~*, confined space; *~-&-dog life* etc., full of quarrels, esp. that of husband & wife; *rain ~s & dogs*, very hard. **8.** *~-bird*, Amer. thrush; ||*~ burglar* (who enters by climbing); *~-call*, shrill whistle (sound or instrument) expressing disapproval at theatre etc. (also as v.i. & t., use, reprove with, this); *~-eyed*, able to see in dark; *~-fish*, of various kinds, esp. large Amer. river-fish; *~-head*, see sense 3; *~-ice*, milky-looking, bubbly, not solid, irregular; ||*~-lap*, slops, tea, etc.; *~--mint*, blue-flowered aromatic plant; *~nap*, -sleep, brief, in chair etc.; *~'s--cradle*, child's game with transfers of string between fingers of two players; *~'s-eye*, precious stone of Ceylon & Malabar, reflector stud on road; *~'s-foot*, ground-ivy; ||*~'s-meat*, horse's or other flesh prepared & sold as food for *~s*; *~'s-paw*, person used as tool by another, slight breeze rippling water in places; *~'s-tail*, various plants, as reed-mace; *~-walk*, narrow footway along a bridge, among large engines, etc. Hence ~'HOOD n., ~'LIKE a. [OE *catte*, = OHG *kazza*, ON *köttr*, f. LL *cattus, catta*; ME *catt(e)* reinforced by ONF *cat* (F *chat*) f. same source]

cǎt², v.i. & t. (-tt-). ‖ Vomit (colloq.); (Naut.) raise (the anchor) from the surface of the water to the cathead. [f. prec.]

cata-, cat-, cath-, pref. in wds taken from Greek, & in others formed with Gk materials or on Gk analogy; meanings: down, away, wrongly, mis-, entirely, down upon, according to, alongside of, thoroughly. [f. Gk *kata* prep.]

catabolism. Var. of KATABOLISM.

catachr|ĕs'is (-k-), n. Perversion, improper use, of words. So ~ĕs'tIC(AL) aa., ~ĕs'ticaLLY² adv. [L, f. Gk CATA- (*khrēsis* f. *khraomai* use)]

cǎt'aclǎsm, n. Violent break, disruption. [f. Gk CATA(*klasma* f. *klaō* to break)]

cǎt'aclȳsm, n. Deluge (esp. in Geol. as required by theory of school that believed in repeated destructions of all life followed by new creations); political or social upheaval. Hence ~AL, ~IC, aa., ~IST(3) n., (all -Iz-). [f. F *cataclysme* f. Gk CATA(*klusmos* flood f. *kluzō* wash)]

cǎt'acomb (-kōm), n. Subterranean cemetery (orig. that under basilica of St Sebastian near Rome, supposed burying-place of Peter & Paul); (usu. pl.) the many Roman subterranean galleries with recesses excavated in sides for tombs; similar works elsewhere (in Paris; worked-out stone-quarries with bones from emptied churchyards); wine-cellar. [f. F *catacombes* f. LL *catacumbas* (name given to the cemetery of St Sebastian), of unkn. orig.; the ~s generally, while in use, were not so called]

catǎd'romous, a. (zool.). Descending to lower river or sea to spawn. [f. Gk CATA- (*dromos* -running) + -OUS]

cǎt'afǎlque (-k), n. Decorated stage for coffin or effigy of distinguished person during funeral service; open hearse. [F, f. It. *catafalco* of unkn. orig.; see SCAFFOLD]

Cǎt'alan, a. & n. (Native, language) of Catalonia in Spain.

cǎtalěc'tic, a. Wanting a syllable in last foot (of verse). [f. LL f. Gk CATA(*lēktikos* ceasing f. *lēgō* cease)]

cǎt'alěpsȳ, n. Suspension of sensation & consciousness accompanied by rigidity of the body. [f. LL *catalepsia* f. Gk CATA(*lēpsis* seizure) see foll.]

cǎtalěp'tic, a. & n. Of, subject to, the disease catalepsy (n., ~ person); (Philos.) of mental apprehension. [f. LL *catalepticus* f. Gk CATA(*lēptikos* seizing f. *lambanō* seize)]

cǎt'alŏgu|e (-g), °-lŏg, n., & v.t. (Enumerate, enter, in a) complete list, usu. alphabetical or under headings, & often with particulars added to items; °uni-

versity calendar; ~*e raisonné* (-zonā'), descriptive ~e arranged according to subjects or branches of subject. Hence ~ER¹ n. [F, f. LL f. Gk *katalogos* f. CATA- (*lĕgō* choose) enrol]

catǎl'pa, n. Kinds of tree with heart-shaped leaves & trumpet-shaped flowers. [N.-Amer. (Creek)]

catǎl'ẏsis, n. (chem.). Effect produced by a substance that without undergoing change itself aids a chemical change in other bodies. So cǎt'alȳst n., agent in ~, cǎtalȳt'ic a. [f. Gk CATA(*lusis* loosing f. *luō* loose) dissolution] •

cǎtamarǎn', n. Raft or float of logs tied side by side, longest in middle, used for communication with shore or short voyage; raft of two boats fastened side by side; quarrelsome woman. [f. Tamil *kaṭṭa-maram* tied tree]

cǎt'amite, n. Sodomite's minion. [f. L *catamitus* f. Gk *Ganumēdēs* cup-bearer of Zeus]

cǎtamoun'tain (-tǐn), cǎt-o'-m-, n. Leopard; wild quarrelsome person. [15th c., of Eng. formation]

cǎt'aplǎsm, n. (med.). Poultice. [F, or f. LL f. Gk *kataplasma* (*kataplassō* spread, smear over)]

cǎt'apǔlt, n., & v.t. & i. Ancient engine worked by lever & ropes for discharging darts, stones, etc.; ‖ boy's shooting contrivance of forked stick & elastic; mechanical contrivance for launching aircraft from deck of ship etc.; (vb) shoot or pepper (bird etc., or abs.) with ~, launch (aircraft). [f. F *catapulte* or L *catapulta* f. Gk *katapeltēs* perh. f. CATA- + *pallō* hurl]

cǎt'arǎct, n. Waterfall (prop. large & sheer, cf. CASCADE); downpour of rain, rush of water; (Path.) eye-complaint producing partial blindness; (Mech.) steam-engine governor acting by flow of water. [f. L *cataracta* f. Gk *katarrhaktēs* f. CAT(*arassō* dash); the path. sense prob. f. obs. sense *portcullis*]

catarrh' (-är), n. Inflammation of mucous membrane, a cold. Hence catär'rhAL (-ral) a. [f. F *catarrhe* f. LL *catarrhus* f. Gk *katarrhous* f. *katarreō* (CATA-, *rheō* to flow)]

cǎt'a(r)rhine (-rīn), a. & n. (zool.). (Monkey) having nostrils close together, oblique, & directed downwards, & opposable thumbs on all limbs. [f. Gk CATA-, *rhis rhinos* nostril]

catǎs'troph|ė, n. Dénouement of drama; disastrous end, ruin; event subverting system of things, esp. in Geol. (cf. CLYSM, UNIFORMITARIAN), whence catǎstrŏph'IC(AL) aa., ~ISM(3), ~IST(2), nn.; sudden, widespread, or signal disaster. [f. Gk CATA(*strophē* turning f. *strephō* to turn)]

Cataw'ba, c-, n. U.S. grape & wine. [river ~]

cǎt'boat, n. Sailing-boat with single mast

placed well forward, carrying one sail only. [prob. f. obs. *cat(t)*, vessel formerly used on the N.-E. coast]

catch[1], v.t. & i. (*caught* pr. kawt). **1.** Capture, ensnare (~ *a* CRAB[1]), overtake (also ~ *up*; *caught in storm*), lay hold of (also ~ *hold of*; ~ *a* TARTAR; ~ *up habit* etc., adopt), be in time for (train etc.). **2.** Surprise, detect, (*at* or *in*, or *doing*; ~ *me!*, *him!*, you may be sure we shall not). **3.** Hit (usu. with part specified; *caught him on the nose*; also *caught him a blow* or *one*). **4.** (Of fire or combustible) ignite, be ignited, (~ *fire* or ~). **5.** Be entangled, take hold, (usu. ~ *in* a thing; *bolt* ~*es*; ~ *on*, become popular). **6.** Snatch (pest. ~ *up*, *away*; ~ *at*, often fig. = be glad to get). **7.** Intercept motion of (nail ~es dress; at cricket, ~ *ball*, prevent its touching ground off bat, also ~ or ~ *out* batsman, dismiss by doing this); ~ *out*, (fig.) ~ in a mistake etc., ~ *napping*. **8.** Check suddenly (~ one's *breath*; ~ *up* speaker, interrupt): **9.** Receive, incur, be infected with, (cold, a cold, a fever; a scolding, thrashing, or 'it'; enthusiasm, a habit, an accent; ~ one's DEATH; *pond* etc. ~*es*, is coated with ice). **10.** Grasp with senses or mind (meaning, sound, tune; ~ *a likeness*, see & reproduce it; ~ *a glimpse of*, see for a moment; *don't* ~ *on*, fail to see meaning. **11.** Arrest, captivate, (attention, eye, fancy; ~ *Speaker's eye*, succeed in being called on to speak in H. of Commons). **12.** ~-*as*— -*can*, Lancashire wrestling style; ~-*drain*, along hillside to prevent water's running off; || ~-*'em-alive-o*, sticky flypaper; ~- -*fly*, a sticky-stemmed plant; ~'*penny* (adj.), claptrap, intended merely to sell; ~'*weed*, goosegrass; ~'*word*, word so placed as to draw attention, e.g. first of dictionary article, rhyming word in verse, last word (cue) of actor's speech, first word of page anticipated at foot of previous one, also word or phrase caught up & repeated esp. in connexion with party politics, slogan. Hence ~'ABLE a., (·)~'ER (1, 2) n. [ME *cac(c)hen* f. ONF *cachier* (= OF *chacier*, whence CHASE[2]), f. Rom. **captiare* for L *captare* f. *capere capt-* seize; the gen. sense of *catch* (*take*, not *pursue*) is excl. E, the orig. meanings (still in Rom.) having been taken by the later adoption CHASE[2]]

catch[2], n. **1.** Act of catching; amount of fish caught. **2.** Chance of, success in, catching at cricket (also *a good*, *safe*, ~, one skilful at it). **3.** Cunning question, deception, surprise; ~-*out*, act of catching out, circumstance that upsets calculations. **4.** Contrivance for checking motion of door etc. **5.** Thing or person caught or worth catching (*no* ~, bad bargain, unwelcome acquisition). **6.** (mus.). Composition for three or more equal voices, occas. so devised as to produce punning or other humorous verbal combinations. [f. prec.]

catch'ing, a. In vbl senses; esp.: infectious; attractive. [-ING[2]]

catch'ment, n. ~-*basin*, -*area*, from which rainfall flows into river, reservoir, etc. [CATCH[1], -MENT]

catch'pole, -*poll*, n. (hist.). Sheriff's officer, bum-bailiff. [late OE (once) *kæcepol*, ME *cachepol*, f. ONF **cachepol* (= OF *chacepol*) or AL *cacepollus* chase- -fowl (CATCH[1], L *pullus* fowl)]

catch'up, mis-spelling of KETCHUP.

catch'ỹ, a. Attractive; easily caught up (of tune etc.). [CATCH[1] + -Y[2]]

cate, n. (arch.; usu. pl.). Choice food. [for obs. *acate* f. OF *acat* purchase f. *acater* now *acheter* buy f. Rom. **AC(capt)are* frequent. of L *capere* take) catch at]

catechet'ic(al) (-kĕ-), aa. Of, by, oral teaching; according to a, or the Church, catechism; consisting of, proceeding by, question & answer. Hence **catechet'i**caLY[2] adv. [f. Gk *katēkhētikos* f. *katēkhētēs* oral teacher (foll.)]

cat'echism (-k-), n. Instruction by question & answer; published example of this, esp. on religious doctrine (*Church* C~, the Anglican; *Longer* & *Shorter* C~, of Presbyterians); series of questions put to anyone. Hence **catechis'**MAL (·k·) a. [f. LL *catechismus* (foll., -ISM)]

cat'ech|ize (-k-), -*ise* (-iz), v.t. Instruct by question & answer, or by use of Church Catechism; put questions to, examine. Hence or cogn. ~IST(1), ~iZER[1], (·k·), nn. [f. LL *catechizare* f. Gk *katēkhizō* f. CAT(*ēkheō* sound) make hear]

cat'echu (-ōō), n. Astringent substances with much tannin from bark, wood, or fruits, of Eastern plants. [app. f. Malay *kachu*; cf. CACHOU]

catechum'en (-kū-), n. A convert under instruction before baptism. [f. LL *catechumenus* (so F *catéchumène*) f. pass. part. of Gk *katēkheō* CATECHIZE]

catego'rical, a. (Logic: of proposition) unconditional, absolute; explicit, direct, plain-speaking; (Ethics) ~ *imperative*, bidding of conscience as ultimate moral law. Hence ~LY[2] adv. [f. LL f. Gk *katēgorikos* f. CAT(*ēgoros* -speaking) + -AL]

cat'egor|ỹ, n. (Orig. Gk meaning, *statement*) one of a possibly exhaustive set of classes among which all things might be distributed (the ~ies of Aristotle are: substance, quantity, quality, relation, place, time, posture, possession, action, passion); one of the *a priori* conceptions applied by the mind as frames to material supplied by sense; class, division. [f. LL f. Gk *katēgoria* statement as prec.]

catēn'a, n. Connected series. [L, = chain]

caten'arỹ, **catēnār'ian**, aa. & nn. (Like) curve formed by uniform chain hanging freely from two points not in one vertical line (~ *bridge*, suspension, hung from such chains). [f. L *catenarius* (prec., -ARY[1], -AN)]

cat'en|āte, v.t. Connect like links. So ~A'TION n. [f. L *catenare* as prec., -ATE[3]]

căt'er, v.i. Purvey food (usu. *for*); provide amusement etc. *for*. Hence ~ER¹ n. [f. obs. noun *cater* (now *caterer*), aphetic f. *acater* f. AN *acatour* buyer (CATE, -OR)]

căt'eran, n. (hist.). Highland fighting-man, marauder, cattle-lifter. [f. Gael. *ceathairne* peasantry]

căt'er-cousin (kŭz-), n. (arch.). Intimate; *be* ~s, on good or familiar terms. [perh. f. CATER as feeding together]

căt'erpillar, n. Larva of butterfly or moth; rapacious person; (Mech.) endless articulated steel band passing round & worked by two wheels of a tank, tractor, or vehicle required to cope with rough ground. [perh. f. OF *chatepelose* lit. hairy-cat, with -s dropped as pl. sign, & spelling influenced by vb *pill* rob, strip]

căt'erwaul, v.i., & n. (Make) cat's screaming; quarrel like cats. [of uncert. hist.; generally referred to CAT¹ & WAUL]

căt'gŭt, n. Material used for strings of fiddle etc. made of twisted intestines of sheep, horse, or ass (not cat); stringed instruments. [reason for appellation (*cat-*) unkn.]

cath-. See CATA-.

cathár'sis, n. (Med.) purgation; outlet to emotion afforded by drama (ref. to Arist., *Poet.* 6). [f. Gk *katharsis* (*katharō* cleanse f. *katharos* clean)]

cathárt'ic, a. & n. (med.). Purgative (medicine). [f. LL f. Gk *kathartikos* as prec.]

Cathay', n. (Arch. & poet. for) China. [f. med. L *Cat(h)aia*, f. *Kitah*, race name]

cathēd'ral, a. & n. (Orig. ~ *church*) principal church of diocese, with bishop's throne; ~ *utterance* etc., delivered EX CATHEDRA. [ME adj. f. OF *cathedral* or its source LL *cathedralis* f. L f. Gk CAT(*hedra* chair f. *hed-* sit), -AL]

Căth'erine-wheel, n. Circular spoked window or window-compartment; rotating firework; lateral somersault (*turn* ~s). [spiked wheel in St Catherine's martyrdom]

căth'eter, n. (med.). Tubular instrument for passing into bladder. [LL, f. Gk *kathetēr* f. CAT(*hiēmi* send)]

căth'ōde, n. (electr.). Negative pole of current; ~ *ray*, beam of electrons from ~ of high-vacuum tube under the impulse of an electron field. [f. Gk CAT(*hodos* way) descent]

căth'olic (*or* kah-), a. & n. **1.** Universal; of interest or use to all men; all-embracing, of wide sympathies, broad-minded, tolerant; *C~ Epistles*, encyclical (those of James, Peter, Jude, & John—2 & 3 *John* being irregularly included—; cf. CANONICAL). **2.** (Eccl.) *C~ Church*, whole body of Christians; ~, belonging (a) to this, (b) to the church before separation into Greek or Eastern & Latin or Western, (c) to the Latin church after that separation (cf. ORTHODOX), (d) to the part of the Latin church that remained under the

Roman obedience after the reformation, (e) to any church (as the Anglican) claiming continuity with (b); orthodox, in accord with the church in any of above senses, esp. = ROMAN CATHOLIC as (d) in contrast with Protestant, Reformed, Lutheran, etc.; *C~ King, his C~ Majesty*, of Spain (hist.); hence cathŏl'ICALLY, ~LY², advv., cathŏl'icISM(2, 3) n., cathŏl'icIZE(3), v.t., cathŏl'ico- comb. form. **3.** n. Member of Holy Catholic Apostolic and Roman Church accepting jurisdiction of Pope as supreme Head of that Church. [f. LL *catholicus* & F *catholique* f. Gk *katholikos* f. CATH- *holou* on the whole, universally]

cătholi'citý, n. Comprehensiveness, freedom from prejudice; wide prevalence; agreement with Catholic or R.-C. Church doctrine, catholicism. [prec., -ITY]

cathŏl'icŏn, n. Panacea. [F & med. L, f. Gk *katholikon* neut. CATHOLIC]

Căt'iline, n. Profligate conspirator. [*Catilina* Roman noble d. 63 B.C.]

căt'iŏn, n. Electro-positive element evolved at cathode in electrolysis (opp. ANION). [Gk, = going down (CAT-, *eimi* go)]

căt'kin, n. Downy hanging inflorescence of willow, hazel, etc. [f. Du. *katteken* (CAT¹, -KIN)]

căt'ling, n. Small cat; fine catgut; amputating knife. [-LING¹(2); surg. sense unexpl.]

catŏp'tr|ic, a. Of mirror, reflector, or reflexion. Hence ~ICS.n. [f. Gk *katoptrikos* f. CAT(*optron* f. *op-* see, -*tron* instr. suf.)]

căt'sup. Var. of KETCHUP.

cătt'ish, cătt'ý, aa. Catlike; (esp. fig.) sly and spiteful. [CAT¹]

căt'tle, n. Live-stock; oxen (as ~ *& sheep*); (occas.) horses; *black* ~, oxen of Scotch & Welsh highland breeds, orig. black; contemptible persons; ~*-feeder*, machine regulating amount of food for ~; ~*-leader*, nose-ring; ~*-lifter*, ~*-stealer*; ~*-PEN*¹; ~*-piece*, picture with ~; ~*-plague*, contagious disease of ~, rinderpest; *~*-rustler*, ~*-thief*. [ME & ONF *catel* (= OF *chatel*; see CHATTEL) f. med. L *capitale* CAPITAL²]

Caucā'sian (-shn), a. & n. (Member) of the white race, Indo-European; inhabitant of the Caucasus. [the *Caucasus*, supposed starting-place, +-IAN]

cauc'us, n., & v.t. & i. **1.** ‖ Local political usu. elective party committee for fighting elections, defining policy, etc. (gen. used only of opponents' organization); *the* ~, ~ system as a political power; hence ~DOM n. **2.** vb. Use the ~ system; organize, dictate to, by its means; hence ~ER¹ n. [U.S. wd (in sense *meeting*) of unkn. orig.]

caud'al, a. Of, at, like, tail. Hence or cogn. ~LY² adv., caud'ATE² a. [f. L *cauda* tail +-AL]

caudillo (kowdēl'yō), n. (pl. ~s). (In Spanish-speaking countries) leader. [Sp.]

cau'dle, n. Warm gruel with spice, sugar, & wine, for invalids, esp. women in child-bed. [f. ONF *caudel* (OF *chaudel*) f. LL *caldellum* dim. of L *caldum* hot drink (*calidus* warm)]

caught. See CATCH[1].

caul, n. Plain part at back of woman's cap; membrane enclosing foetus; portion of this occas. found on child's head (good omen, & charm against drowning); = OMENTUM. [ME *calle* perh. f. OF *calé* small cap]

caul'dron, căl-, n. Large boiling-vessel (usu. of deep basin shape with hoop handle & removable lid). [ME *caud(e)ron* f. ONF (OF *ch*-) augment. (see -OON) f. LL *caldaria* pot for boiling (L *calidus* warm, -ARY[1]); for the etymologizing -*l*- cf. FAULT]

caulës'cent, a. (bot.). With visible stem. [f. L *caulis* stalk after *arborescent* etc.]

caul'iflower (kŏl-), n. Cabbage with large fleshy flower-head. [16th c. *cole-florie* etc., f. F *chou-fleuri*; the first element was later assim. to COLE & L *caulis*, the second to FLOWER]

caul'ine, a. (bot.). Of, on, stem. [f. L *caulis* stem, -INE[1]]

caulk (kawk), v.t. Stop up seams of (ship), stop up (seams), with oakum & melted pitch (or, in iron ship, by striking plate--junctions with blunt chisel). Hence ~'ER[1] n. (in vbl senses, &, sl., = final dram). [f. OF *cauquer* tread, press with force, f. L *calcare* tread (*calx* heel)]

caulo-, comb. form of Gk *kaulos* or L *caulis* stem. [-O-]

caus'al (-z-), a. Of, acting as, expressing, due to, a cause or causes; of the nature of cause & effect. Hence ~LY[2] adv. [f. LL *causalis* (*causa*, -AL)]

causăl'ity (-z-), n. The being, having, or acting as, a cause; relation of cause & effect, doctrine that everything has cause(s). [prec., -ITY]

causa'tion (-z-), n. Causing, producing an effect; relation of cause & effect; doctrine that all things have causes, whence ~ISM(3), ~IST(2), nn. [f. LL *causatio* pretext etc., but w. sense f. med. L *causare* CAUSE[2], -ATION]

caus'ative (-z-), a. Acting as cause, productive *of*; (Gram.) expressing cause. Hence ~LY[2] (-vl-) adv. [ME, f. OF *causatif* or LL *causativus* (*causari* give as pretext, -IVE)]

cause[1] (-z), n. 1. What produces an effect; antecedent(s) invariably & uncondition-ally followed by a certain phenomenon; person who, agent that, occasions something; ground, reason, motive, for action; adequate motive or justification (esp. *show* ~); *efficient* ~, producing force, *material* ~, the requisite matter, *formal* ~, the idea or definition, *final* ~, purpose; *First C*~, the Creator. 2. (Law, & from law) matter about which person goes to law; his case (*plead a*~); law-suit; side of any dispute espoused by person or

party, militant movement, propaganda (*make common* ~ *with*); ǁ ~*list*, of cases awaiting trial. [ME, f. OF f. L *causa*]

cause[2] (-z), v.t. Effect, bring about, produce; induce, make, (person or thing *to* do, *to be* done something to). Hence **caus'ER**[1] n. [ME, f. med. L *causare* (or F *causer*) f. L *causa* CAUSE[1]]

cause célèbre (kōz sĕlĕ'br), n. (pl. *causes célèbres*, pr. as sing.). Law-suit that ex-cites much attention. [F]

cause'less (-zl-), a. Fortuitous; without natural cause; unjustifiable, groundless, whence ~LY[2] adv. [-LESS]

causerie (kōzerē'), n. (pl. -*s*, pr. as sing.). Newspaper article (or spoken address) of an informal or conversational kind, esp. on literary subjects. [F]

cause'way (-zw-), caus'ey (-z-), n., & v.t. Raised road across low or wet place or piece of water; raised footway by road; (v.t.) provide with ~. [alt. (by assoc. w. WAY) f. ME *caucé* (mod. dial. *causey*) f. ONF *caucié(e)* (mod. F *chaussée*), f. Rom. **calciata* (sc. *via*) f. L *calx* -*cis* CHALK]

caus'tic, a. & n. (Substance) that burns or corrodes organic tissue (*common or lunar* ~*ic*, nitrate of silver for surg. use; ~ *potash*, potassium hydroxide; ~ *soda*, sodium hydroxide); sarcastic, biting, whence ~ICALLY adv.; (Math.) (surface, curve) formed by intersection of rays reflected or refracted from curved sur-face. Hence ~i'CITY n. [f. F (-*ique*) or L f. Gk *kaustikos* (*kaustos* burnt f. *kaiō* burn), -IC]

cau'ter̆ize, -ise (-īz), v.t. Sear with hot iron or caustic; (fig.) make callous. Hence ~īzA'TION n. [f. LL *cauterizare* f. Gk *kautērion* branding-iron (*kaiō* burn); cf. F *cautériser*]

caut'er̆y, n. Metal instrument for searing tissue; cauterizing. [f. L f. Gk *kautērion* see prec.]

cau'tion, n., & v.t. 1. Prudence, taking care, avoidance of rashness, attention to safety, (ǁ ~ *money*, deposited as security for good conduct, esp. at Universities & Inns of Court), whence **cau'tious**(-shus), a., **cau'tiously**[2] adv.; warning (in drill, preliminary word of command), fact that acts as warning, warning with reprimand (*dismissed with a*~), whence ~ARY[1] (-sho-), a.; (colloq.) extraordinary thing, hideous or strange person. 2. v.t. Warn (person, often *against*, *to* or *not to* do); warn & reprove. [ME, f. OF f. L *cautionem* (*cavēre caut*- take heed, -ION)]

cavalcade', n. Company of riders. [F, f. It. *cavalcata* f. *cavalcare* ride f. LL *caballicare* f. L *caballus* horse; see -ADE]

cavalier', n. & a. 1. Horseman; courtly gentleman, gallant, esp. as escorting a lady, whence **cavalier'** v.t.; 17th-c. royalist. 2. adj. Offhand, curt, super-cilious, whence ~LY[2] adv. [earlier -*llero*, -*liero*, f. Sp.; present form F, f. It. *cavaliere*; see CHEVALIER]

cavăll'y̆, n. Kinds of tropical fish, horse-mackerel. [f. Sp. *cavalla* mackerel]

căv'alry̆, n. Horse-soldiers (usu. w. pl. vb). [f. F *cavallerie* f. It. *cavalleria* (*cavallo* f. L *caballus* horse, -ERY)]

căvati'na (-tē-), **n.** Short simple song; similar piece of instrumental music, usu. slow & emotional. [It.]

cāve¹, n. Underground hollow usu. with horizontal opening, den; IDOLS *of the ~*; || (Pol.) secession of part of party on some question (ADULLAMITE), the seceders; *~- -dweller*, esp. of prehistoric men living in *~s*; *~-fish, -man, -rat, -spider, -swallow,* kinds living in *~s* (also *~-bear* etc. of extinct kinds whose remains are found in *~s*); *~-man*, (in modern use) man of primitive passions, instincts, & behaviour. Hence *~'LET* (-vl-) n. [ME, f. OF f. L *cava* f. *cavus* hollow]

cāve², v.t. & i. Hollow out, make into a cave; || form political CAVE¹; *~ in*: subside, recede, (of earth etc. over hollow; of wall yielding inwards cf. BULGE); yield to pressure, submit, withdraw opposition; smash in (esp. person's hat or head), spoil shape of. [f. prec.; but *in~ in* may be f. U.S.— *in*, app. f. E. Anglian dial. *calve in*; cf. Flem. *inkalven* Du. *afkalven*, in similar sense]

căv'e³, int. (schoolboy sl.). Look out! (warning of master's approach). [L, = beware]

căv'ĕăt, n. 1. (Law) process to suspend proceedings (*enter, put in, a~*). **2.** Warning; proviso. [L, = let him beware]

căv'ĕăt ĕmp'tŏr, L sent. (= let the buyer see to it) disclaiming responsibility for buyer's disappointment.

căv'endish, n. Tobacco softened, sweetened, & pressed into cake, negro-head. [orig. unkn.]

căv'ĕrn, n. Underground hollow (rhet.). [ME, f. F *caverne* f. L *caverna* (*cavus* hollow)]

căv'ĕrned (-nd), **a.** Like, in, with, cavern(s). [-ED²]

căv'ĕrnous, a. Full of caverns; as of, huge or deep as, a cavern (*~ darkness, mouth, eyes*); porous. [f. L *cavernosus* (CAVERN, -OSE¹)]

căv'ĕ(s)son, n. Strong nose-band used in breaking troublesome horses. [f. F *caveçon* f. It. *cavezzone* augment. of *cavezza* halter]

căviār(e)' (*or* kăv'-), **n.** Sturgeon-roe pickled, eaten as relish; *~ to the general,* good thing unappreciated by the ignorant. [early forms represent It. *caviale* (obs. F *cavial*); later *caviar* etc., It. *caviaro*, F, Pg. *caviar*, f. Turk. *khāvyār*; relations & ult. orig. uncert.]

căv'il, v.i. (-ll-), **& n.** (Raise) captious objection (*at, about*). Hence *~IER¹* n. [f. obs. F *caviller* f. L *cavillari* (*cavilla* mockery)]

căv'ity̆, n. A hollow place, a hollow. Hence **căvĭta'TION** n., formation of *~* in

a structure, or of bubbles in a liquid, or of a vacuum. [f. F *cavité* or LL *cavitas* (L *cavus* hollow, -TY)]

*cavŏrt', v.i. (sl.). Prance. [orig. unkn.]

căv'y̆, n. Amer. rodent. [f. *cabiai* native name in French Guiana]

caw, n. & int., & v.i. & t. (Make) rook's, crow's, raven's, cry; *~ out,* utter in *~*ing tone. [imit.]

Căx'ton, n. Book printed by W. *~* (first Engl. printer, d. 1492); printing-type in imitation of *~*'s.

cay, n. Insular bank or reef of coral, sand, etc., cf. KEY³. [f. Sp. *cayo* shoal, reef; see KEY³, QUAY]

cayenne (kăĕn'), **n.** (Also *~ pepper*) pungent red pepper of capsicum. [f. Braz. *kyynha* assim. to *Cayenne* capital of French Guiana]

cay'man, cai'man, n. Kinds of large saurian of crocodile family (prop. an American genus with round short muzzle). [f. Sp., Pg. *caiman,* f. Carib *acayuman*]

*cayuse (kī'ūs), **n.** Indian pony. [Amer.- -Ind.]

|| cd, || cmd, = COMMAND² paper.

cē, = CEE.

cĕanŏth'us, n. A flowering shrub. [Gk]

cease¹, v.i. & t. Desist *from*; stop doing, being, etc., also w. inf.; (of feelings, actions) come to an end; bring to an end (strife, endeavours, etc.); (Mil.) *~ fire,* discontinue firing. [ME, f. OF *cesser* f. L *cessare* frequent. of *cedere* cess- yield]

cease², n. Ceasing (obs. exc. in *without ~,* incessantly). Hence *~'LESS* (-sl-) a., *~'LESSLY²* adv., *~'LESSNESS* n. [f. OF *ces* (*cesser* see prec.)]

cē'city̆, n. Blindness (usu. fig.). [f. L *caecitas* (*caecus* blind, -TY)]

cĕd'ar, n. Kinds of cone-bearing tree with fragrant durable wood including *~* of Lebanon, Atlas *~*, & deodar; various trees resembling *~*; *Japanese ~*, crypto-meria; *= ~-wood.* Hence (poet.) *~n* [-EN⁵] a. [ME & OF *cedre* f. L (whence directly OE *ceder*) f. Gk *kedros*]

cēde, v.t. Give up, grant, admit, surrender (territory). [f. F *céder* or L *cedere* yield]

cĕdill'a, n. Mark (⸲) written under *c* to show that it is sibilant. [f. Sp. *cedilla, zedilla* (= It. *ce-, zediglia,* F *cédille*) dim. of *zeda* f. Gk *zēta* letter Z]

cee, n. The letter C; *~ spring, C-spring,* spring so shaped supporting carriage body.

ceil (sēl), **v.t.** Line roof of (room). Hence **ceil'ING¹(2)** n.: such lining; (Aviation) maximum altitude a given aeroplane can attain, maximum altitude in particular weather conditions; upper limit of prices, wages, etc. [*ceiling* (14th c. *celynge*) f. *ceil* vb (in 15th c. cover w. wainscot, plaster, etc., cf. obs. *celure* canopy, hangings)+-ING¹(2); ult. orig. undetermined]

‖ **ceilidh** (kāl'ĭ), n. (Sc.). Informal gathering for song & story. [Gael.]

cěl'adŏn, n. & a. Willow green: grey green glaze used on some pottery. [F, f. name of character in D'Urfé's *Astrée*]

cěl'andĭne, n. Two yellow-flowered plants, *greater ~*, & *lesser ~* (also PILE⁶-*wort*). [ME & OF *celidoine* f. LL *celidonia*, for L *chelidonia* f. Gk *khelidonion* (*khelidōn* swallow); for -*n*- cf. *passenger*]

cělanēse' (-z), n. Kind of artificial silk. [P]

-cele (sēl), in medical compound words, = tumour of the —. [f. Gk *kēlē* tumour]

cěl'ébrant, n. Officiating priest, esp. at Eucharist. [F, or f. L *celebrare* (foll.), -ANT]

cěl'ébr|āte, v.t. & f. Perform publicly & duly (religious ceremony etc.); officiate at Eucharist; observe, honour, with rites, festivities, etc. (festival, events); publish abroad, praise, extol, (p.p.) famous. So ~A'TION n. [f. L *celebrare* (*celeber* -*bris* frequented, renowned); see -ATE³]

cělěb'rity, n. Being famous; well-known person (also attrib., as ~ *concert*). [f. L *celebritas* (*celeber* see prec., -TY)]

cěl'riăc, n. Turnip-rooted celery. [f. CELERY, -ac unexplained]

cělě'rity, n. Swiftness, dispatch (of living movement or agency). [ME & OF *celerite* f. L *celeritatem* (*celer* swift, -TY)]

cěl'ery, n. Plant of which blanched stem is used as salad & vegetable. [f. F *céleri* ult. f. Gk *selinon* parsley]

cělěste', n. & a. Sky blue: (also *voix* ~) organ & harmonium stop; (adj.) sky-blue. [f. F *céleste* f. L *caelestis* (*caelum* heaven)]

cělěs'tial, a. & n. Of the sky (~ *globe*, *map*); heavenly, divine, divinely good, beautiful, etc., whence ~LY² adv.; *C~ Empire* (hist.), China (transl. of native title; so *C~* (joc.) = Chinese, a. & n.). [ME, f. OF f. L *caelestis* (see prec., -AL)]

cěl'ibate, a. & n. (Person) not married, bound or resolved not to marry; unmarried (of life, habits). So **cěl'ibacy** n., **cělibatAR'IAN** a. & n. [F, or f. L *caelibatus* unmarried state (*caelebs* -*ibis*); see -ATE¹]

cěll, n. 1. Dependent nunnery or monastery (hist.); anchoret's one-roomed dwelling; cottage (poet.); grave (poet.); single person's small room in monastery or prison (*condemned ~*, for one condemned to death); compartment in bees' comb; (Electr.) voltaic apparatus with only one pair of metallic elements, unit of battery. 2. Enclosed cavity in organism or mineral (~*s of brain*, imaginary compartments assigned to various faculties); (Biol.) portion of protoplasm usu. enclosed in membrane, ultimate element of organic structures; (Zoophytes) cup-like cavity of individual polype in compound polypidom; (fig., of persons) centre or nucleus of (revolutionary) activities. Hence (-)cellED² (-ld), ~'IFORM, aa. [ME *celle* f. OF, or L

cella small room; late OE *cell* perh. dir. f. L]

cěll'ar, n., & v.t. (Put, store, in an) underground room; (also *wine-~*) place in which wine is kept, one's stock of wine (*keeps a good ~*); ~*-flap*, trapdoor into ~; ~*-plate*, in pavement over hole into coal-~. Hence ~AGE n. [ME *celer* f. AF, = OF *celier* f. LL *cellarium* (prec., -AR², -ARY¹)]

cěll'arer, n. Monastic keeper of wine & provisions. [ME *cel(l)erer* f. AF, = OF -*ier* f. LL *cellerarius* (see prec., -ER² (2))]

cěllarět', n. Case or sideboard for keeping winebottles in dining-room. [-ET¹]

cěll'|ō (ch-), 'c-, n. (pl. -os). (Short for) VIOLONCELLO. Hence ~AGE n. [It]

cěll'ophāne, n. Transparent wrapping material made from viscose. [P]

cěll'ūlar, a. Of, having, small single rooms or compartments or cavities; ~ *shirt* etc. (of open texture); (Physiol.) consisting of cells (as ~ *tissue*); ~ *plant*, without distinct stem, leaves, etc. Hence **cěllūlä'rity** n. [f. F *cellulaire*, see foll., -AR¹]

cěll'ūl|e, n. (anat.). Cell or cavity (see CELL, 2; the derivatives are formed from *cellule*, not *cell*). Hence or cogn. ~ATE², -ātěd, ~IF'EROUS, ~OUS, aa., ~A'TION n., ~O- comb. form. [f. L *cellula* (*cella* CELL, -ULE)]

cěll'ūloid, a. & n. Like cells; (n.) plastic made from camphor & cellulose nitrate. [irreg. f. CELLULOSE² +-OID]

cěll'ūlōse¹, a. Consisting of cells. Hence **cěllūlōs'ity** n. [CELLULE, -OSE¹]

cěll'ūlōse², n. (chem.). Substance forming solid framework of plants; (in pop. usage for) ~ *acetate* or ~ *nitrate*, solutions of which give the ~ finish used in varnishing metal, woodwork, etc., (also v.t., treat with ~). [F, f. L *cellula* CELLULE +-OSE²]

Cěl'sius. See CENTIGRADE.

Cělt¹, Kělt, n. Member of one of the peoples akin to the ancient Gauls (Bretons, Cornish, Gaels, Irish, Manx, Welsh). [f. F *Celte* f. L *Celta*; cf. Gk *Keltoi, Keltai,* pl.]

cělt², n. (archaeol.). Bronze or stone (or iron) chisel-edged prehistoric implement. [wd founded on the reading of the Clementine Vulgate in *Job* XIX. 24—*stylo ferreo, et plumbi lamina, vel celte* (v.l. *certe*) *sculpantur*]

Cěl'tic, K-, a. & n. (Language) of the Celts; *the ~ fringe*, the Scots, Irish, Welsh, & Cornish, in relation to the U.K. Hence **cěl'ticALLY** adv., **cěl'ticISM**(2, 4) n., **cěl'ticIZE**(2, 3) v.i. & t. [f. L *celticus* (CELT¹, -IC) or F *celtique*]

cělto-, comb. form of CELT¹. Hence **cěltŏL'OGIST, cěltoMAN'IAC, cěl'toPHIL,** nn. [-O-]

cěmĕnt', n., & v.t. 1. Substance applied as paste & hardening into stony consistence for binding together stones or bricks &

for forming floors, walls, etc., strong mortar of calcinated lime & clay (*hydraulic* ~, hardening under water); any substance applied soft for sticking things together; (fig.) principle of union; substance for stopping teeth; bony crust of tooth-fang. 2. v.t. Unite (as) with ~; apply ~ to, line or cover with ~. [ME *siment* f. OF *ciment* f. L *caementum* quarry stone (*caedere* cut, -MENT)]

cĕm′étery̆, n. Place for burials, not being a churchyard. [f. LL f. Gk *koimētērion* dormitory (*koimaō* put to sleep)]

cĕn′obite. See COENOBITE.

cĕn′otaph (-ahf), n. Sepulchral monument to person whose body is elsewhere; *the C~*, that in Whitehall commemorating the dead of the 1914–18 and 1939–45 wars; tomb from which one has risen. [f. F *cénotaphe* f. LL f. Gk *kenotaphion* (*kenos* empty, *taphos* tomb)]

cĕnse, v.t. Perfume, worship, with burning incense. [f. obs. *cense* noun (aphetic f. INCENSE[1]) or short for INCENSE[2]]

cĕn′ser, n. Vessel in which incense is burnt. [ME *censer* f. AF, = OF *censier* f. *encensier* f. *encense* INCENSE[1], -ER[2] (2)]

cĕn′sor, n., & v.t. 1. Ancient-Roman magistrate drawing up register or census of citizens & supervising public morals; person expressing opinions on others' morals & conduct. 2. Official licensing, or suppressing as immoral, seditious, or inopportune, books, plays, letters, news, or military intelligence (vb, exercise such control over, make excisions or changes in). 3. Various university officials. 4. (Psycho-anal.) ~(*ship*), a power by which elements of the Unconscious are inhibited from emerging into the consciousness. Hence or cogn. **cĕnsōr′IAL** a., ~SHIP n. [L, f. *censēre* tax, -OR]

cĕnsōr′ious, a. Fault-finding, over-critical. Hence ~LY[2] adv., ~NESS n. [f. L *censorius* (CENSOR, -ORY)+-OUS]

cĕn′sur|e (-sher), n., & v.t. 1. Adverse judgement, expression of disapproval, reprimand. 2. v.t. Blame, criticize unfavourably, reprove; hence ~ABLE a. [ME, f. OF *censure* f. L *censura* (*censēre* assess, -URE); vb f. F *censurer*]

cĕn′sus, n. Official numbering of population with various statistics (in Gt Britain taken every ten years); ~-*paper*, form left at every house to be filled up with names, ages, etc., of inmates. [L, f. *censēre* to rate]

cĕnt, n. *Per* ~, for, to, in, every hundred (in stating proportion, esp. of interest); *three* etc. *per* ~*s*, public securities at 3% etc.; ~ *per* ~, interest equal to principal; (U.S. etc.) hundredth of a dollar; typical small coin (*don't care a* ~). [f. F *cent*, or L *centum*, or It. *cento* hundred]

cĕn′tal, n. Weight of 100 lb. used for corn. [f. L *centum* hundred, perh. after QUINTAL]

cĕn′taur (-tŏr), n. Horse with human body, arms, & head, taking the place of its neck & head; hybrid creation, person or thing of double nature; (*C*~) name of a constellation; perfect horseman. Hence ~ESS[1] n. [f. L f. Gk *kentauros* of unkn. etym.]

cĕn′taury̆, n. Name of various plants. [f. LL *centauria* f. L f. Gk *kentaurion* (*kentauros* see prec.)]

cĕnta′vō (-ah-), n. (pl. ~*s*). 1/100 of a peso or similar currency unit in some S.-Amer. republics; 1/100 of an escudo in Portugal. [Amer.-Sp.]

cĕntĕnār′ian, a. & n. (Person) a hundred years old. [as foll.+-AN]

cĕntĕn′ary̆ (*also* sĕn′těn-), a. & n. 1. Of a hundred years. 2. n. Space of a hundred years reckoned from any point in a century; centennial anniversary, celebration of it. [f. L *centenarius* (*centeni* a hundred each, -ARY[1])]

cĕntĕnn′ial, a. & n. Of, having lived or lasted, completing, a hundred years; (of) the hundredth anniversary. [f. L *centum* hundred, & as BIENNIAL]

cĕntĕs′imal, a. Reckoning, reckoned, by hundredths. Hence ~LY[2] adv. [f. L *centesimus* hundredth (*centum* hundred) +-AL]

cĕn′ti-, comb. form of L *centum* hundred, = 1/100 of the denomination in the metric system. Hence ~GRAM, ~LITRE (-lēter), ~METRE (-mēter), nn.

cĕn′tigrăde, a. Having a hundred degrees (of Celsius's thermometer, with freezing-point of water 0° & boiling-point 100°). [F, f. L *centum* a hundred +*gradus* step]

‖ **cĕntill′ion** (-yon), n. Hundredth power of a million (1 with 600 ciphers). [*centum* (prec.), BILLION]

centime (sahntēm′), n. (hist.). French & Swiss coin = 1/100 of a franc. [F]

cĕn′tipēde, n. Many-footed wingless crawling animal. [f. L *centipeda* (*centum* hundred, *pes pedis* foot) or F *centipède*; earlier *centipie*, *centapee* prob. f. Sp.]

cĕnt′ner, n. German weight, about 1 cwt. [G, f. L *centenarius* CENTENARY]

cĕn′tō, n. (pl. -*os*). Composition made up of scraps from other authors. [L, = patch-work garment]

cĕn′tral, a. Of, in, at, from, containing, the centre; leading, principal, dominant; *C*~ *Empires*, *Powers*, (hist.), Germany & Austria-Hungary; ~ *heating*, method of warming a building by hot water or hot air or steam conveyed by pipes from ~ source. Hence **cĕntrāl′ITY** n., ~LY[2] adv., ~NESS n. [f. L *centralis* (*centrum* CENTRE, -AL) or F *central*]

cĕn′tralism, **cĕn′tralist**, nn. (Upholder of) a centralizing system. [prec. +-ISM(3), -IST(2)]

cĕn′traliz|e, **-is|e** (-īz), v.i. & t. Come, bring, to a centre; concentrate (administration) at single centre; subject (State etc.) to this system. Hence ~A'TION n. [CENTRAL, -IZE(3), or f. F *centraliser*]

cen'tre[1] (*-ter*), **cen'ter,** n. & a. **1.** Middle point (strictly, equidistant from ends of line measuring along it, or from extremities of regular surface or body, or from all points in circumference of circle or sphere, & at mean distance from all points in periphery of irregular surface or body). **2.** Point, pivot, axis, of revolution (of machine tool, short rod with cone--shaped point and tapered shank, one of pair between which rotating workpiece may be supported). **3.** Point of concentration or dispersion, nucleus, source. **4.** (Fenians etc.) organizer, leader, (esp. *head-*~). **5.** = INNER. **6.** (Archit.) wooden mould for arch or dome while building. **7.** (Mil.) main body of troops between wings. **8.** (Pol.; orig. f. French) *the C~*, men of moderate opinions (*left-*~, *left*, radical grades; *right-*~, *right*, reactionary). **9.** (Assoc. footb., Hockey) middle player in forward line (also ~ *forward*), kick or hit from wing to ~. **10.** ~ *of attraction*, (Physics) to which bodies tend by gravity, (fig.) drawing general attention; ~ *of gravity*, that point in body which being supported body remains at rest in any position; ~ *of mass*, point (in relation to body) any plane passing through which divides body into two parts of equal weight; DEAD ~; ~-*piece*, ornament for middle of table; ~-*rail*, third rail on mountain railways for cogged wheel etc.; ~-*second*(*s*), seconds hand mounted on centre arbor of clock or watch; ~-*bit*, boring-tool with ~ point & side cutters; ~-*board*, (flat-bottomed boat with) board for lowering through keel to prevent leeway: hence ~LESS, **cen'tric**(AL), aa., **cen'trically**[2] adv., **centri'city** n. **11.** adj. At, of, the ~; hence ~MOST (*-erm-*) a. [ME, f. OF *centre* or L *centrum* f. Gk *kentron* sharp point]

cen'tre[2] (*-ter*), **cen'ter,** v.i. & t. Be concentrated *in, on, at, round, about*; place in centre; mark with a centre; concentrate *in* etc.; find centre of; (Assoc. footb., Hockey) kick or hit (ball) from wing to centre. [f. prec.]

cen'tr(e)ing (*-ter-*), n. Temporary framing used to support arch, dome, etc., while under construction. [CENTRE[1] + -ING[1]]

centrif'ugal, a. Flying, tending to fly, from centre; ~ *force*, with which body revolving round centre tends to fly off, inertia; ~ *machine* etc., in which ~ force is utilized; (Bot.) ~ *inflorescence*, in which end flower opens first & side ones in downward order. Hence ~LY[2] adv. [f. L *centrum* CENTRE[1] + -*fugus* -fleeing (*fugere* flee) + -AL]

cen'trifuge, n. Centrifugal machine rotating at very high speed, designed to separate solids from liquids, or liquids from other liquids (e.g. cream from milk). [F; see prec.]

centrip'etal. a. Tending towards centre; ~ *force, machine* etc., *inflorescence*, opposite of CENTRIFUGAL. Hence ~LY[2] adv. [f. L *-petus* -seeking (*petere* seek) & as CENTRE[1]]

cen'tro-, comb. form of L *centrum* & Gk *kentron* CENTRE[1], = centre-, central, centrally.

cen'tuple, a., n., & v.t. Hundredfold; (vb) multiply by a hundred. [f. F *centuple* or LL *centuplus* for L *centuplex* (*centum* hundred, -*plic-* fold)]

centup'licate, a. & n. (*-at*), & v.t. (*-āt*). = prec., esp. *in* ~, of things of which a hundred copies are produced. [f. L *centuplicare* as prec., -ATE[2,3]]

centur'ion, n. Commander of century in Roman army. [ME, f. L *centurio -onis* (foll.)]

cen'tury, n. **1.** (Rom. hist.) company in army, orig. of 100 men; political division for voting. **2.** A hundred of something (esp., 100 runs at cricket); one of the hundred-year periods counting from a received epoch, esp. from birth of Christ (*first* ~, 1–100, *nineteenth* ~, 1801–1900, etc.); any hundred successive years, centenary. [f. L *centuria* (*centum* hundred)]

cephal'ic, a. Of, in, the head. [f. F *céphalique* f. L f. Gk *kephalikos* (*kephalē* head, -IC)]

-cephal'ic, = -CEPHALOUS.

ceph'alo-, comb. form = head-, head-& ——. [see CEPHALIC, -O-]

ceph'alopod, n. Mollusc with distinct tentacled head. [prec. + Gk *pous podos* foot]

cephalothor'ax, n. Coalesced head & thorax of spider, crab, etc. [CEPHALO-, THORAX]

-ceph'alous, last element esp. of anthropological terms = -headed, as *brachy-*~, with short head. [f. Gk *kephalē* head + -OUS]

ceram'/ic, k-, a. Of the art of pottery. Hence ~ICS, **ce'ramist**(2), nn. [f. Gk *keramikos* (*keramos* pottery, -IC)]

cerás'tes (*-ēz*), n. The horned viper of N. Africa. [L f. Gk *kerastēs* (*keras* horn)]

cerás'tium, n. Kinds of herb with horn--shaped capsules. [mod. L, f. Gk *kerastēs* horned (*keras* horn)]

ce'rato-, comb. form of Gk *keras -atos* horn, = horn-&- ——, horny-, & esp. of the cornea.

Cerb'erus, n. Three-headed dog guarding entrance to Hades (*sop to* ~, something to propitiate an official, guard, etc.). [L, f. Gk *Kerberos*]

cere, n. Naked wax-like membrane at base of some birds' beaks. [f. L *cera* wax]

cer'eal, a. & n. Of corn or edible grain; (n., usu. pl.) kind(s) of grain used for human food; article of diet made from wheat, maize, or other ~ (usu. as breakfast dish). [f. L *Cerealis* (*Ceres* goddess of corn, -AL)]

cĕrĕbĕll'um, n. Little or hinder brain. [L, dim. of CEREBRUM]

cĕ'rĕbral, a. Of the brain; (of literature, music, etc.) appealing to intellectual appreciation; = *letter*, consonant sounded by turning tongue-tip to top of palate. [CEREBRUM + -AL; cf. F *cérébral*]

cĕrĕbrā'tion, n. Working of the brain, esp. *unconscious* ~, of results reached without conscious thought. [CEREBRUM + -ATION]

cĕ'rĕbrum, n. The brain proper, in front of & above the cerebellum. Hence **cĕ'rĕbro-** comb. form; *cerebro-spin'al*, of brain & spine (*cerebro-spinal meningitis*, spotted fever). [L]

cere'cloth (sērklaw-), n. Cloth impregnated with wax etc., used as waterproof covering or (esp.) winding-sheet. [15th c. *cered cloth* f. *cere* to wax f. L *cerare* f. *cera* wax]

cere'ment (sērm-), n. (hist.; usu. pl.). Grave-clothes. [app. a Shakespearian alt. of prec. (-MENT)]

cĕrĕmōn'ial, a. & n. **1.** With or of ritual or ceremony, formal; hence ~ISM(3), ~IST(2), nn., ~LY[2] adv. **2.** n. System of rites; formalities proper to any occasion; observance of conventions; (R.-C. Ch.) book of ritual. [f. LL *ceremonialis* (CEREMONY, -AL)]

cĕrĕmōn'ious, a. Addicted or showing addiction to ceremony, punctilious. Hence ~LY[2] adv., ~NESS n. [F *cérémonieux* or LL *ceremoniosus* (foll., -OUS)]

cĕ'remon|y̆, n. Outward religious rite or polite observance; empty form; stately usage; formalities; punctilious behaviour (*without* ~*y*, offhand; *stand upon* ~*y*, insist on conventions, keep one's distance); *Master of the C~ies*, superintending forms observed on state or public occasions. [ME, f. OF *cerimonie* or L *caerimonia*]

cĕ'riph, (now rare for) SERIF.

cerise' (-ēz), a. & n. (Of) a light clear red. [F, = CHERRY]

cĕr'ium, n. A metallic element. Hence **cĕr'IC**(1), **cĕr'OUS,** aa. [f. planet *Ceres*, discovered (1801) just before, + -IUM]

cēro-, comb. form of L *cera* or Gk *kēros* wax.

cēroplăs't|ic, a. Modelled, of modelling, in wax. Hence ~ICS n. [f. Gk *kēro-* = CERO(*plastikos* adj. f. *plassō* to mould)]

cĕrt, n. (sl.). Event or result certain to happen. [abbr. *certain*]

cĕrt'ain (-tn, -tin), a. Settled, unfailing; unerring, reliable; sure to happen; indisputable; convinced (*of, that*); destined, undoubtedly going, to do; that might but need not or should not be specified (*a* ~ *person, lady of a* ~ *age*, some though perhaps not much (*felt a* ~ *reluctance*), existing but probably unknown to hearer (*a* ~ *John Smith*); *for* ~, assuredly. [ME, f. OF f. Rom. *certanus* f. L *certus* f. *cernere* decide, -AN]

cĕrt'ainly̆ (-tn-), adv. Indubitably; infallibly; confidently; admittedly; (in answers) I admit it, no doubt, yes. [prec. + -LY[2]]

cĕrt'ainty̆ (-tn-), n. Undoubted fact (*bet on a* ~, usu. dishonestly with secret knowledge of result), indubitable prospect; thing in actual possession; absolute conviction (*of, that*); *to, for, a* ~, beyond possibility of doubt. [ME & AF *certainte*, OF -*ete* (CERTAIN, -TY)]

cĕrt'ĕs (-z), adv. (arch.). Assuredly, I assure you. [ME, f. OF (*a*) *certes*, prob. f. Rom. *°(ad) certas* of a certainty]

certif'icate, n., & v.t. **1.** (-it). Document formally attesting a fact; esp. the bearer's status, acquirements, fulfilment of conditions, right to company shares, etc.; ‖ *bankrupt's* ~, stating that he has satisfied legal requirements & may recommence business. **2.** v.t. (-āt). Furnish with, license by, ~; hence **cĕrtifica'TION** n. [f. F *certificat* or its source med. L *certificatum* neut. p.p. (foll.)]

cĕrt'if|y̆, v.t. Attest formally, declare by certificate; ‖ (of doctor) officially declare (person) insane, whence ~IABLE a.; inform certainly, assure; ~*ied milk,* guaranteed free from tubercle bacillus. Hence ~IER[1] n. [ME, f. OF *certifier* f. med. L *certificare* f. L *certus* CERTAIN (-FY)]

cĕrtiorār'i (-shī-), n. Writ from higher court for records of case tried in lower. [L, = L *certiorem facere* inform]

cĕrt'itude, n. Feeling certain, conviction. [F, or f. LL *certitudo* (CERTAIN, -TUDE)]

cerul'ean (-ōō-), a. Deep-blue. [f. L *caeruleus* + -AN]

cerum'ĕn (-ōō-), n. Ear-wax. So **cerum'inous** (-ōō-) a. [f. L *cera* wax on anal. of *albumen*]

cĕr'use (-ōōs), n. (Also *white lead*) a white paint from carbonate & hydrate of lead, esp. as cosmetic. [ME, f. OF *ceruse* or L *cerussa*]

cĕrv'ical (or sĕrvīk[2]), a. (physiol.). Of the neck. So **cĕrvic'o-** comb. form. [F, or mod. L, f. L *cervix -icis* neck + -AL]

cĕrv'ine, a. Of, like, deer. [f. L *cervinus* (*cervus* deer + -INE[1])]

Cèsa'rèvitch, -witch, (-z-), n. Tsar's eldest son (hist.); ‖ (-w-) horse-race run annually at Newmarket. [Russ.]

‖ **cĕss,** n. Tax, rate, (now displaced by *rate* in Engl., but used in various senses in Ireland & Scotland). [prop. *sess* for obs. *assess* n. see ASSESS]

cĕssā'tion, n. Ceasing; pause. [f. L *cessatio* (*cessare* CEASE[1], -ATION)]

cĕss'er, n. (legal). Coming to an end, cessation, (of term, liability, etc.). [F (CEASE[1], -ER[4])]

cĕ'ssion (-shn), n. Ceding, giving up, (of rights, property, or esp. of territory by State). [F, or f. L *cessio* (*cedere cess-* go away, -ION)]

cĕ'ssionary̆ (-shon-), n. = ASSIGN[2]. [f. LL *cessionarius* as prec. + -ARY[1]]

cess'pit, n. Midden. [see foll.]

cess'pool, n. Well sunk for soil from water-closet etc., retaining solids & letting liquid escape (also fig., as ~ of *iniquity*). [alt., after POOL¹, f. 16th c. *cesperalle, susprall* ~, = 15th c. *suspiral* vent, water-pipe, f. OF *souspirail* (SUS-PIRE, -AL(2)]

ces'toid, a. & n. (zool.). Ribbon-like (intestinal worm, as tapeworm). [f. L f. Gk *kestos* girdle + -OID]

ces'tus, n. Loaded bull-hide hand--covering worn by Roman boxers. [L *caestus* (*caedere* strike)]

cet-, comb. form = of spermaceti, in chem. names. [f. L f. Gk *kētos* whale]

cetā'cean (-shn), a. & n. (Member) of the mammalian order containing whales. So **cetā'ceous** (-āshᵾs) a. [as prec., -ACEAN]

cet'eosaur (-ōr), ‖**saur'us**, n. Fossil saurian. [f. Gk *kētos -eos* whale & *sauros* lizard]

cet'erach (-k), n. Kinds of fern with frond-backs covered with scales. [med. L, prob. f. Arab.]

cet'eris pa'ribus, adv. Other things being equal. [L]

Chablis (shăb'lē), n. A French white Burgundy. [~ in France]

Chăd'bănd, n. Unctuous hypocrite. [person in Dickens's *Bleak House*]

chāfe, v.t. & i., & n. 1. Rub (skin, to restore warmth); make, become, sore by rubbing; (of beast, river) rub itself *against* (bars, rocks); irritate; show irritation, fume, fret. 2. n. (Sore made by) friction; state of irritation, pet, (*in a* ~). [ME *chaufe* f. OF *chaufer* f. Rom. *calefare* f. L *-facere* (*calēre* be hot, *facere* make)]

chāf'er, n. Kinds of beetle, usu. the COCK-CHAFER. [OE *ceafor*; also OE *cefer*, OS *kever*, OHG *chevar*; f. WG *kabhr-*, *kebhr-*, prob. cogn. w. JOWL]

chaff (-ahf), n., & v.t. 1. Separated grain--husks; chopped hay & straw; bracts of grass-flower; spurious substitute (*caught with* ~, easily deceived or trapped); worthless stuff; ~-*cutter*, machine chopping fodder; hence ~'y² (-ahf-) a.; (vb) chop (straw etc.). 2. Banter (n. & v.t.). [OE *ceaf*, OHG *cheva* husk, prob. f. Gmc *kaf-*, *kef-* gnaw (prec.); sense 2 of sl. uncert. orig.]

chăff'er, v.i. & t., & n. 1. Haggle, bargain (~ *away*, = BARGAIN *away*); hence ~ER¹ n. 2. n. = ~*ing*. [ME *ch(e)apfare* f. OE *cēap* see CHAPMAN + *faru* FARE]

‖**chăff'inch**, n. Common British small bird. [ME, f. CHAFF (f. haunting barndoor) + FINCH]

chāf'ing-dish, n. Vessel with burning charcoal etc. inside for keeping warm things placed on it. [f. obs. sense of CHAFE = warm]

chagrin (shagrēn'), n., & v.t. (Affect with) acute disappointment or mortification. [f. F *chagrin(er)*, of uncert. orig.]

chain, n., & v.t. 1. Connected series of metal or other links (ENDLESS ~); fetters, confinement, restraining force; necklace, watchguard, etc. 2. Sequence, series, set, (*of* proof, events, posts, mountains; *ladies'* ~, movement in quadrille). 3. Jointed metal-rod measuring-line, its length (66 ft). 4. (Also ~*-shot*) two balls or half balls joined by ~ for cutting masts etc. (hist.). 5. (naut.). Fastening for shrouds below CHANNEL² (also ~*-plate*), *the* ~s, whole contrivance (channel, ~--plate, & DEAD-eyes) for widening basis of shrouds; (pl.) leadsman's platform. 6. ~ *armour, mail*, made of interlaced rings; ~ *bridge*, = suspension; ~ *coupling*, extra coupling of railway vans in case of accident to screw coupling; ~*-gang* (of convicts ~ed together, or forced to work in ~s); ~*-letter*, a letter of which the recipient is asked to make copies to be sent to a (named) number of others (these doing the like in their turn); ~ *moulding*, archit. ornament with link carving; ~ *reaction*, chem. reaction forming intermediate products which react with the original substance & are repeatedly renewed; ~ *-smoker* (who lights another cigarette or cigar from the stump of the one last smoked); ~*-stitch*, ornamental sewing like ~, (sewing machine) simple sewing (cf. LOCK²*-stitch*); ~*-store*, one of a series of shops owned by one firm & selling the same goods; ~*-wale*, = CHANNEL²; ~*-wheel*, transmitting power by ~ fitted to its edge; hence ~'LESS a., ~'LET n. 7. v.t. Secure, confine, with chain (lit. & fig.). [ME *chayne*, f. OF *chaeine* f. L *catena*]

chair, n., & v.t. 1. Separate seat for one, of various forms (ARM¹ or *elbow*, BATH¹, CURULE, DECK¹, EASY¹; *take a* ~, sit down). 2. Seat of authority; professorship; ‖ mayoralty (*past or above the* ~, *below the* ~, of alderman who has, has not, been mayor). 3. Seat, office, of person presiding at meeting, public dinner, etc (*take, leave, the* ~, begin, end, the proceedings); chairman (*address, appeal to, the* ~; '*chair! chair!*', protest against disorder). 4. (Railway) iron or steel socket holding rail in place. 5. (hist.). = SEDAN. 6. *ELECTRIC* ~. 7. v.t. Install in CHAIR of authority; ‖ place in ~ & carry aloft (winner of contest, election, etc.); act as chairman of, preside over, (meeting). [ME, f. OF *chaière* f. L f. Gk *kathedra* (CATHEDRAL)]

chair'man, n. (pl. *-men*; fem. *chair--woman*. Person chosen to preside over meeting, permanent president of committee, board, etc. (C~ *of Committees*, in Houses of Parl., presiding instead of Lord Chancellor & Speaker when House is in Committee), whence ~SHIP n.; one who keeps or propels a Bath chair; (hist.) one of two sedan-bearers.

chaise (shāz), n. Pleasure or travelling carriage of various shapes, usu. now low, four-wheeled, & open, with one or two ponies; ~ *longue* (lŏngg; F, = long chair), kind of sofa with a rest for the back at one end only; POST-~. [F, var. of *chaire* f. OF *chaiĕre* CHAIR]

chălcĕd'onў (k-), cal-, n. Precious stone of quartz kind with many varieties as agate, cornelian, chrysoprase. [f. L c(h)*alcedonius* f. Gk *khalkēdōn*]

chălco- (k-), comb. form esp. in mineralogical terms = copper-, brass-. [f. Gk *khalkos*]

chălcŏg'raphў (k-), n. Art of engraving on copper. [prec., -GRAPHY]

chălcopyr'ite (k-; -ĭr-), n. A copper ore, yellow or copper pyrites. [CHALCO-, PYRITE]

Chaldĕ'an, Chaldee', (kăl-), ♁. & n. (Native) of Chaldea or Babylon; soothsayer, astrologer. [f. L f. Gk *khaldaios* + -AN]

chald'ron (-awl-), n. Coal measure, 36 bushels. [f. OF *chauderon*, w. -*l*- as in CAULDRON]

chalet (shăl'ā), n. Swiss mountain dairy-hut; Swiss peasant's wooden cottage; small villa. [Swiss-F]

chăl'ice, n. Goblet; eucharistic wine-cup (*mixed*~, with water ceremonially added); (poet.) flower-cup, whence **chăl'iced** (-st) a. [ME, f. OF (now *calice*), f. L CALIX]

chalk[1] (-awk), n. White soft earthy limestone used for burning into lime & for writing & drawing; coloured preparation of like texture used in crayons for drawing; *as like as* ~ *& cheese*, unlike in essentials; *by a long* ~, by far (f. use of ~ to score points in games); ~-*bed*, stratum of ~; ~-*pit*, quarry in which ~ is dug; ~-*stone*, gouty concretion like ~ in tissues & joints esp. of hands & feet. [OE *cealc*, OS *calc*, OHG *kalk* f. L *calx*-*cis* lime]

chalk[2] (-awk), v.t. Rub, mark, draw, write, write *up*, with chalk; ~ *it up*, put it down to my account; ~ *out*, sketch, plan as thing to be accomplished (often *for oneself*). [f. prec.]

chalk'|ў (-awk-), a. Abounding in, white as, chalk; like or containing chalk-stones. Hence ~INESS n. [-Y[2]]

chăll'ĕnge[1] (-j), n. Calling to account (*sentry's* ~, 'Who goes there?'); exception taken (e.g. to juryman); summons to trial or contest, esp. to duel, defiance; signal requiring recognition signal to be displayed by ship, aircraft, etc. [ME & OF *ca-*, *chalenge*, *-lange*, f. L *calumnia* CALUMNY]

chăll'ĕnge[2] (-j), v.t. Call to account (of sentry, & fig.); take exception to (evidence, juryman), dispute, deny; claim (attention, admiration, etc.); invite to contest, game, or duel, defy. Hence ~EABLE a., ~ER[1] n. [f. OF *ca-*, *chalenger* f. L *calumniari* (CALUMNY)]

chăll'is, n. Lady's-dress fabric. [perh. f. surname]

chalyb'ēate (ka-), a. Impregnated with iron (of mineral water or spring). [irreg.

for *chalybate* f. L f. Gk *khalups* -*ubos* steel + -ATE[2]]

cham (kăm), n. Great ~, autocrat (of dominant critic etc., esp. Dr Johnson). [f. earlier F & med. L form of KHAN[1]]

chamade (shamahd'), n. Signal for retreat on drum or trumpet. [F, f. Port. *chamada* (*chamar* f. L *clamare* call, -ADE)]

chamār', n. Member of the very low Indian caste of leather-workers: tanner, shoemaker. [Hind.]

chăm'ber, n. Room, esp. bedroom (poet. or arch.; but ~ *music*, for small instrumental combinations; ~ *concert*, of such music; ~ *orchestra*, *organ*, small); (pl.) set of rooms in larger building, esp. in Inns of Court, let separately, judge's room for hearing cases not needing to be taken in court; (hall used by) deliberative or judicial body, one of the houses of a parliament (esp. *second* ~); C~ *of Commerce*, *Agriculture*, board organized to forward these in a district; C~ *of* HORRORS; (also ~-*pot*) vessel for urine; ~ *counsel*, lawyer giving opinions in private, not practising in court; ~-*maid*, housemaid at inn or hotel, *housemaid; enclosed space in body of animal or plant, or in machinery etc. (esp. part of gun-bore, of larger diameter in some guns, separate in revolver, that contains charge). Hence (-)~ED[2] (-erd) a., ~ING[1] n. (arch.), licentiousness. [ME & OF *chambre* f. L *camera* vault]

chăm'berlain (-lĭn), n. Officer managing household of sovereign or great noble; Lord Great C~ *of England*, hereditary holder of ceremonial office; Lord C~ *of the Household*, with part management of Royal Household, & licenser of plays. Hence ~SHIP n. [ME, f. OF *chamberlain* etc., = med. L *camerlingus*, f. OFrank. *kamarling* (= OHG *chamarlinc*) f. *kamara* CHAMBER, -LING[1]]

chamēl'é|on (ka-), n. Small prehensile--tailed long-tongued lizard with power of changing colour & of living long without food; inconstant person. Hence ~ŏn'IC a., ~on-LIKE, a. & adv. [f. L f. Gk *khamaileón* (*khamai* on ground, *leōn* lion)]

chăm'fer, v.t., & n. Bevel symmetrically (right-angled edge or corner); (n.) surface so given (*hollow* or *concave* ~, made as with gouge instead of chisel); channel, flute, (v.t. & n.). [ult. f. F *chanfraindre* (lit. break-corner; CANT[1], L *frangere*); perh. back form. f. *chamfering*, f. F *chanfrain* etc. f. -*fraindre*]

chamois (shăm'wah, *in sense* 2 shăm'ĭ), n. 1. Wild mountain antelope of goat size. 2. (Also ~-*leather*, *shammy*, *shammy-leather*) soft pliable leather from sheep, goats, deer, etc. [F, = LL *camox*; ult. orig. unkn.]

chăm'omile, = CAMOMILE.

chămp, v.t. & i., & n. Munch (fodder noisily; work (bit) noisily in teeth; (make chewing action or noise. [prob. imit.]

champagne (shămpān'), n. Kinds of wine from E. France (usu. white & sparkling). [name of province, cf. foll.]

chăm'paign (-ăn), n. (Expanse of) open country. [ME, f. OF *champagne, -paigne* f. L *Campania*; see CAMPAIGN]

chăm'pert|y, n. (law). The offence of assisting a party in a suit in which one is not naturally interested with a view to receiving a share of the disputed property. So ~ous a. [ME & AF *champartie*, f. OF *champart* feudal lord's part of produce, f. L *campus* field, *pars* part]

chăm'pion, n. & a., & v.t. 1. Person who fights, argues, etc., for another or for a cause (*King's, Queen's, C~*, or *C~ of England*, hereditary official at coronations). 2. Athlete etc., animal, plant, etc., that has defeated all competitors (often as adj., ~ *boxer*, ~ *turnip*); (as adj. or adv., dial. or vulg.) first-class, prime, top-hole, splendidly. Hence ~LESS a., ~SHIP n. 3. v.t. Maintain the cause of. [ME, f. OF f. med. L *campionem* fighter (L *campus* CAMP[1])]

champlevé (shămp'levā), a. & n. ~ *enamel* or ~, enamel in which the colours are filled into hollows made in the surface (cf. CLOISONNÉ). [F, = raised field]

chance[1] (-ahns), n. & a. 1. Way things fall out, fortune; undesigned occurrence; opportunity; (Cricket) opportunity of dismissing a batsman given to a fieldsman (esp. in phr. *give a* ~); possibility; probability (esp. in pl., as *the ~s are against it*); absence of design or discoverable cause; course of events regarded as a power, fate; *by* ~, as it falls or fell out, without design; *on the* ~, in view of the possibility (*of, that*); *take* one's ~, let things go as they may, consent to take what comes; *the main* ~, that of getting rich; *stand a* (*good, fair*) ~, have a prospect; *chance-*, = *by* ~, *as~-sown tree*. 2. adj. Fortuitous (*a* ~ *companion, meeting*). [ME & OF *cheance* f. *cheoir* fall (Rom. *~cadére* f. L *cadere*+-ANCE)]

chance[2] (-ahns), v.i. & t. Happen (arch. in abs. use, getting rare in constr. *it* ~*d that, he* ~*d to* do); ~ *upon*, happen to find, meet, or come upon; (colloq.) risk (esp. ~ *it*); ~ one's *arm* (colloq.), take one's chance of doing something successfully (prob. orig. Army sl., from a N.C.O.'s risking the loss of his stripes). [f. prec.]

chan'cel (-ah-), n. Eastern part of church reserved for clergy, choir, etc., & usu. railed off. [ME, f. OF f. LL *cancellus* f. L *cancelli* lattice-bars]

chan'cellery (-ah-), -**ory**, n. Position, staff, department, official residence, of a chancellor; office attached to embassy or consulate. [f. OF *chancelerie* (*chancelier* see foll., -RY)]

chan'cellor (-ah-), n. State or law official of various kinds; *Lord C~* (also *C~ of England, Lord High C~*), presiding in H. of Lords & in Court of Appeal; *C~ of*

EXCHEQUER; *C~ of Duchy of Lancaster*, member of government (legally representative of King as Duke of Lancaster), often Cabinet minister employed on extra-departmental work; *C~ of bishop* or *diocese*, bishop's law officer; *C~ of Garter* or other order, who seals commissions etc.; non-resident head of university (Vice-C~ performing most duties); (Germany, Austria) chief minister of State. Hence~SHIP n. [ME, f. AF c(h)anceler, OF -*ier* (-OR) f. LL *cancellarius* law-court usher (*cancelli* CHANCEL)]

chance-med'ley (-ah-), n. (Law) action, esp. homicide, mainly but not entirely unintentional; inadvertency. [AF *chance medlée* (see MEDDLE) mixed chance]

chan'cery (-ah-), n. (*C~*) Lord Chancellor's court, a division of High Court of Justice (formerly a separate court of equity for cases with no remedy in common-law Courts, whence the meaning, still in U.S. & in literature, of court of equity); office for public records; (Boxing) *in* ~, with head held under opponent's arm being pommelled (from difficulty of getting clear of old Court of C~). [contracted f. CHANCELLERY]

chancre (shănk'er), n. Venereal ulcer. [16th c., F, f. L CANCER]

chan'cy (-ah-), a. Uncertain, risky. [CHANCE[1], -Y[2]]

chăndelier' (sh-), n. Branched hanging support for several lights. [F, see foll.]

chand'ler (-ah-), n. Dealer in candles, oil, soap, paint, & groceries (*corn-* ~, in corn; *ship-*~, in cordage, canvas, etc.). Hence **chand'lery**(1) (-ah-) n. [ME & AF *chandeler*, OF -*ier* (CANDLE, -ARY[1], -ER[2])]

chănge[1] (-j), n. Alteration; substitution of one for another, variety (*for a* ~); whence ~FUL(1) (-jf-), ~LESS (-jl-), aa.; *Change* (now freq. but wrongly '*Change*), place where merchants meet (*on C~*, engaged there); arrival of moon at fresh phase (prop. at new moon only); ~ (*of clothes*), second outfit in reserve; ~ *of life*, MENOpause; SEA ~; money given for money of a different value or currency; money returned as balance of that tendered for article (*take* one's, *the*, ~ *out of*, avenge oneself on); *get no* ~ *out of* (a person), fail to get the better of him (in business, argument, etc.); (Bell-ringing, usu. pl.) different orders in which peal can be rung (*ring the* ~s fig., vary ways of putting or doing thing); ~-*over*, alteration from one working system to another, reversal (of the situation in affairs, of opinions, etc.). [ME, f. AF *chaunge*, OF *change*, f. *changer* (foll.)]

chănge[2] (-j), v.t. & i. Take another instead of (~ one's *coat*); resign, get rid of, *for*; give or get money change for; put on different (esp. evening) clothes; go from one to another of (*thing* ~s *hands*, passes to different owner; ~ *houses*, *trains*; also abs. = ~ *trains, boats*, etc.); give & receive, exchange, (~ *places with, we ~d places*); make or become different (often *to, ·into, from*), (moon) arrive at fresh phase, esp. become new moon; ~ *colour*, turn pale or blush; ~ one's *feet* (colloq.), put on other shoes etc.; ~ *front*, take new position in argument etc.; ~ one's *condition*, marry; ~ one's *mind*, adopt new plan or opinion; ~ one's *note* or *tune*, become more humble, sad, etc.; ~ *step, foot, feet*, time other foot to drum in marching; ~ *up, down*, (Motoring) engage a higher, lower, gear. [ME, f. AF *chaunger*, OF *changer* f. L *cambiare, cambire* barter, of Celt. orig.]

change'a|ble (-ja-), a. Irregular, inconstant; alterable. Hence or cogn. ~**BIL'ITY** (-ja-), ~**bleNESS** (-ja-; -ln-), nn. [OF, as prec., -**ABLE**]

change'ling (-jl-), n. Thing or child substituted for another by stealth, esp. elf--child thus left by fairies. [CHANGE² + -LING¹]

chänn'el¹, n., & v.t. (-ll-). 1. Natural or artificial bed of running water; (Geog.) piece of water, wider than strait, joining two larger pieces, usu. seas (|| *the C~*, English C~); tubular passage for liquid; course in which anything moves, direction, line; medium, agency (esp. *through the usual ~s*); (Radio & Television) narrow band of frequencies sufficiently wide for transmission; groove, flute; ~ *iron* (or *bar*), rolled iron bar or beam flanged to form a ~ on one side. 2. v.t. Form ~s in, groove; cut out (*way* etc.). [ME & OF *chanel* f. L *canalis* CANAL]

chänn'el², n. Broad thick plank projecting horizontally from ship's side abreast of mast to broaden base for shrouds; (mod., sing. or pl.) level of deck (*rolling ~s under*). [for *chainwale* (WALE) cf. *gunnel* for *gunwale*]

chant (-ah-), n., & v.i. & t. 1. Song; (Mus.) short musical passage in two or more phrases each beginning with reciting note, for singing to psalms & canticles (*single, double, quadruple*, as one, two, four, verses are sung to it); measured monotonous song; sing-song intonation in talk. 2. vb. Sing; utter musically; intone, sing to a ~; ~ *the praises of*, constantly praise; ~ *horses*, sell fraudulently. [f. OF *chant*(er) song, sing, f. L *cantus -ūs, cantare*, (*canere cant-* sing)]

chan'ter (-ah-), n. In vbl senses; also; melody-pipe, with finger-holes, of bagpipe; (also *horse-~*) swindling horse--dealer. [-ER¹]

chanterëlle' (-ah-), n. Yellow edible fungus. [F, dim. f. L f. Gk *kantharos* drinking-cup]

chan'ticleer (-ah-), n. (Personal name for) domestic cock. [ME, f. OF *chantecler* (CHANT, CLEAR), name in *Reynard the Fox*]

chan'trèss (-ah-), n. Female singer (arch.

or poet.). [f. OF *chanteresse*, see CHANTER, -ESS¹]

chan'trў (-ah-), n. Endowment for priest(s) to sing masses for founder's soul; priests, chapel, altar, so endowed. [ME, f. OF *chanterie* (*chanter* CHANT, -ERY)]

chan'tў (-ah-) -tey. Varr. of SHANTY².

chā'ŏs (kā-), n. Formless void or great deep of primordial matter (*C~*, this personified as eldest of the gods); utter confusion. Hence (irreg.) **chăŏt'ic** a., **chăŏt'ICALLY** adv. (kā-). [L, f. Gk *khaos*, -*otic* after *erotic* etc.]

chăp¹, v.t. & i. (-pp-), & n. 1. Crack (t. & i.) in fissures (usu. of skin, by wind etc., also of dried-up earth etc.). 2. n. (Usu. pl.) crack(s), open seam(s), esp. in skin; hence ~**p'Y³** a. [vb & n. 14th c.; rel. & etym. obscure]

chăp², *chŏp*, n. (Pl.) jaws, esp. of beasts (*lick* one's ~s, w. relish or anticipation), cheeks (*fat-chops*, fat-faced person); (sing.) lower jaw or half of cheek, esp. of pig as food (*Bath chap*; ~*-fallen*, with jaw hanging down, dispirited, dejected); *chops of the Channel*, entrance from Atlantic to Channel. [16th c. var. of CHOP³; etym. & hist. obscure]

chăp³, n. (colloq.). Man, boy, fellow. [short for CHAPMAN cf. *customer*]

***chaparejos** (chahparā'hŏs), n. pl. Cowboy's leather or sheepskin overalls for legs. [Mex. Sp.; freq. abbr. as **chăps** (ch- or sh-)]

chăparrăl', n. (Thicket of) dwarf evergreen oak; ~*-cock*, fast-running bird. [Sp., f. *chaparra* evergreen oak]

chăp'-bŏŏk, n. (bibliog.). Specimen of popular literature (usu. small pamphlet of tales, ballads, tracts) formerly hawked by chapmen. [19th c., see CHAPMAN]

chăpe, n. Metal cap of scabbard-point; back-piece of buckle attaching it to strap etc.; || sliding loop on belt or strap. [ME, f. OF *chape* cope, hood; see CAPE¹]

chapeau-bras (shapŏ-brah'), n. (hist.). Three-cornered flat silk hat of 18th c. carried under arm. [F]

chăp'el, n. Place of Christian worship other than parish church or cathedral, esp. one attached to private house or institution (~ *royal*, of royal palace); oratory in larger building, with altar, esp. compartment of cathedral etc. separately dedicated (*Lady-~*, dedicated to Virgin, usu. E. of high altar); subordinate Anglican church, esp. ~ *of ease*, for convenience of remote parishioners; || place of worship of certain nonconformist bodies; ~ *service* or *attendance* at ~ (*keep a* ~, be present, in colleges); (Print.) printing--office, journeyman printers' association or meeting. [ME & OF *chapele* f. med.L *cappella* dim. of *cappa* cloak (CAPE¹); first ~ was sanctuary in which St Martin's sacred cloak was kept by *cappellani*]

chapelle ardente (shăpĕl' ardahnt'), n. Chamber prepared for lying-in-state of great personage & lit up with candles, torches, etc. [F]

chăp'elrў, n. District served by chapel. [-RY]

chăp'erŏn (sh-), n., &.v.t. 1. Married or elderly woman in charge of girl on social occasions; hence ~AGE n. **2.** v.t. Act as ~ to. [F, = hood, chaperon, dim. of *chape* cope (CAP¹)]

chăp'iter, n. (bibl.). Capital of column. [earlier form of CHAPTER]

chăp'lain (-lĭn), n. Clergyman officiating in private chapel of great person or institution, on board ship, or for regiment etc.; nun reciting inferior services in nunnery. Hence ~CY (-lĭn-) n. [ME, f. OF *chapelain* f. med. L *cappellanus* (CHAPEL, -AN)]

chăp'lĕt, n. Wreath of flowers, leaves, gold, gems, etc., for head; string of beads for counting prayers (one-third of rosary number), or as necklace; string of eggs in toad etc.; bead-moulding. Hence ~ED² a. [ME & OF *chapelet* dim. of *chapel* f. Rom. *cappellus* dim. of LL *cappa* CAP¹]

chăp'man, n. (hist; pl. *-men*). Pedlar. [OE *cēapmann* (= OHG *koufman*) f. *cēap* barter; see CHEAP]

chăpp'ie, -ў, n. (colloq.). Exquisite, man about town. [CHAP³ + -Y³]

chăp'ter, n. Main division of a book (abbr. *cap*, *ch.*, *c.*), (fig.) limited subject, piece of narrative, etc.; ‖ Act of Parl. numbered as part of session's statutes for reference (5 & 6 Will. IV. cap. 62 = Statutory Declarations Act 1835); general meeting, whole number, of canons of collegiate or cathedral church or members of monastic or knightly order (~-house, used for such meetings); ~ & verse, exact reference to passage, exact authority *for* statement; *to end of* ~, for ever; ~ *of* ACCIDENTS. [ME & OF *chapitre* f. L *capitulum* dim. of *caput -itis* head]

chăr¹, n. Hill trout of Wales etc. [etym. unkn.]

chăr², n., & v.i. (-r-, -rr-). 1. Odd job(s) of housework (usu. pl., & now usu. *chore*); (colloq.) ~woman; ~'woman, woman hired by the hour or day to do housework. **2.** v.i. Work by the hour or day at housecleaning, do odd jobs as ~woman. [OE *cerr*, *cerran* turn]

chăr³, v.t. & i. (-rr-). Burn (tr. & i.) to charcoal, scorch, blacken with fire. [app. back formation f. CHARCOAL]

‖ **chăr⁴, n.** (sl.). Tea. [f. Chin. *ch'a*]

char-à-banc(s) (shă'răbăng, or as in Ap.), n. Long vehicle, with many seats looking forward, for holiday etc. excursions. [F *char à bancs* = benched carriage]

chă'racter (kărĭk-), n.; & v.t. 1. Distinctive mark; (pl.) inscribed letters or figures; style of writing-symbols (*in the Roman*, *German*, ~); person's handwriting. **2.** Characteristic (esp. of species etc. in Nat. Hist.); collective peculiarities, sort, style; person's or race's idiosyncrasy, mental or

moral nature. **3.** Moral strength, backbone; reputation, good reputation; description of person's qualities; testimonial; status. **4.** Known person (usu. *public* ~); imaginary person created by novelist or dramatist; actor's or hypocrite's part (*in*, *out of*, ~, appropriate to these or not, also more widely of actions that are in accord or not with person's ~). **5.** Eccentric person (~ *actor*, who devotes himself to eccentricities). **6.** v.t. (poet. & arch.). Inscribe; describe. [ME *ca-* f. OF *caractere* f. L f. Gk *karaktēr* stamp, impress]

chăracteris't|ĭc (kă-), a. & n. Typical, distinctive, (trait, mark, quality), whence ~ICALLY adv.; (Math.) index of logarithm. [f. F *charactéristique* f. Gk *kharaktēristikos* (prec., -IST, -IC)]

chă'racteriz|e (kă-), -is|e (-ĭz), v.t. Describe character of; describe *as*; be characteristic of, impart character to. Hence ~A'TION n. [f. F or med. L f. Gk *kharaktērizō* (CHARACTER, -IZE)]

chă'racterlèss (kă-), a. Ordinary, undistinguished; without testimonial. [-LESS]

charade (sharahd'), n. Game of guessing word from written or acted clue given for each syllable & for the whole. [F, f. Pr. *charrado* (*charrà* chatter)]

chăr'coal, n. Black porous residue of partly burnt wood, bones, etc., form of carbon (occas. w. allus. to use of the fumes as method of suicide); ~*-burner*, maker of this. [perh. f. CHARE + COAL in sense (*wood*) *turned coal*]

chăre, n., & v.i. (Now rare var. of) CHAR².

chărge¹, n. 1. Material load; right quantity to put into thing, esp. of explosive for gun; figurative load. **2.** (Her.) device, bearing. **3.** Expense (*at his own* ~); price demanded for service or goods (*are his* ~*s reasonable?*). **4.** Task, duty, commission; care, custody, (*of*; *nurse in* ~ *of child*, *child in* ~ *of nurse*; CURATE *in* ~; ‖ *give* person *in* ~, hand over to police); *take* ~, (colloq., of things) get out of control (esp. with disastrous results); thing or person entrusted, minister's flock. **5.** Exhortation, directions, (*parting* ~, *bishop's* ~, *judge's* ~ *to jury*). **6.** Accusation (*lay to* one's ~, accuse him of; ‖ ~*-sheet*, record of cases at police station). **7.** Impetuous attack (*bayonet* ~), rush, (*return to the* ~, begin again, esp. in argument); (Mil.) signal sounded for such attack. [ME, f. OF *charge* f. Rom. *carrica* f. LL *car(ri)care* (foll.)]

chărge², v.t. & i. 1. Load, fill to the full or proper extent, (vessel, gun with explosive); saturate (air with vapour, water with chemicals, accumulator with electricity, memory with facts). **2.** Entrust *with* (~ oneself *with*, undertake). **3.** Command *to* do, exhort. **4.** Accuse, impute, (person *with* action, fault *upon* person); saddle *with* liability, place (liability) *on*; debit (~ *it to my account*). **5.** Demand

(price) *for* (also ~ *person price for*). **6.**
Attack (t. & i.) impetuously, esp. on
horseback. **7.** Place (weapon) in position
for use. [ME, f. ·OF *charg(i)er* f. LL
car(ri)care load f. L *carrus* CAR]

charge′able (-ja-), a. **1.** Expensive (arch.).
2. Liable to be charged *with* (accused of);
subject to a money demand; liable to be
made an expense; imputable to (*on*);
proper to be added *to* an account. Hence
chargeABIL′ITY (-ja-) n. [1 f. CHARGE[1],
2 f. CHARGE[2], +-ABLE]

chargé (*d'affaires*) (shärzh′ä dafär′), n.
(pl. *-ýés* pr. as sing.). Diplomatic agent;
representative at minor court or government. [F, = diplomatic representative]

char′ger[1], n. (arch.). Large flat dish.
[ME *chargeour* f. AF; see CHARGE[2], -OR]

char′ger[2], n. In vbl senses; esp., (Mil.)
officer's horse. [-ER[1]]

chā′riot, n., & v.t. Stately vehicle,
triumphal car, (poet. & esp. fig. of sun's
~ etc.); (hist.) four-wheeled carriage
with back seats only; (hist.) car used
in ancient fighting & racing, whence
chāriotEER′ n.; (vb) convey as or in ~.
[ME, f. OF, augment. of *char* CAR]

chā′ritab|**le**, a. Liberal in giving to the
poor; connected with such giving; wont
to judge favourably of persons, acts, &
motives. Hence ~**le**NESS (-ln-), n., ~**LY**[2]
adv. [OF *charité* = foll., -ABLE)]

chā′rity, n. Christian love of fellow men
(*in, out of,* ~ *with*); kindness, natural
affection, (~ *begins at home,* is due first
to kith & kin—freq. an excuse for not
subscribing etc.); candour, freedom from
censoriousness, imputing of good motives
when possible, leniency; beneficence,
liberality to the poor, alms-giving (pl.,
acts of this), alms; trust for advancement
of education; institution for helping
the helpless, help so given, (*cold as* ~, in
allusion to mechanical administration;
~*-boy, -girl,* brought up in such place);
Brother, Sister, of C~, member of religious
society devoted to relieving poor; *C~
Commission(ers)*, board created 1853 to
control charitable trusts. [ME, f. OF
charite f. L *caritatem* in its later sense
(*Christian*) *love*, f. *carus* dear+-TY]

chārivar′i (sh-), n. Medley of sounds,
hubbub (prop. a serenade of pans, trays,
etc., to unpopular person). [F, of unkn.
etym.]

chark′a, n. Country-made Indian spinning-wheel. [Hind. *charkha*]

|| **char′lādy**, n., var. of CHARWOMAN.

charl′atan (sh-), n. & a. Impostor in
medicine, quack; (of, as of) empty pretender to knowledge or skill. Hence
~ISH[1](1) a., ~ISM(2), ~RY, nn. [F, f. It.
ciarlatano (*ciarlare* patter)]

Charles's Wain (-lzïz), n. (Also *Plough,
Great Bear*) constellation *Ursa Major* or
its seven bright stars. [OE *Carles wægn*
the wain of Carl (Charles the Great,
Charlemagne)]

Charles′ton (-lz-), n., & v.i. An American
dance with side-kicks from the knee; (vb)
dance this, kick thus. [f. ~ in S. Carolina]

|| **Charl′ey,** n. (old colloq.). Night-watch-
man. [dim. of *Charles*]

charl′ock, n.. Field mustard, a common
yellow-flowered weed. [OE *cerlic*]

charl′otte (sh-), n. Kinds of pudding
made of stewed fruit with casing or
layers or covering of bread, biscuits,
sponge-cake, or bread-crumbs; ~ *russe,*
custard enclosed in sponge cake. [F]

charm[1], n. Verse, sentence, word, act,
or object having occult power (*against*),
spell; thing worn to avert evil etc.;
amulet; trinket on watch-chain etc.;
quality, feature, exciting love or admiration (~*s, beauty*); attractiveness, indefinable power of delighting. [ME & OF
charme f. L *carmen* song]

charm[2], v.t. Bewitch, influence (as) by
magic, (abs. or with pred. as ~ *asleep,
away*); ~ (*secret, consent,* etc.) *out of;*
endow with magic power (*bear a ~ed
life*); captivate, delight, (~*ed with*); give
pleasure to (*I shall be ~ed* as polite
formula); (part.) delightful, whence
~′**ing**LY[2] adv. [f. OF *charmer* f. *charme*
(prec.)]

charm′er, n. In vbl senses; esp., beautiful
woman (now joc. or arch.). [-ER[1]]

charmeuse (shärm′ĕrz), n. Soft smooth
silk dress-fabric. [F]

charn′el-house, n. House or vault in
which dead bodies or bones are piled.
[ME & OF *charnel* burying-place f.
med. L *carnale* f. LL *carnalis* CARNAL]

Chār′on (k-), n. Ferryman conveying
souls across Styx to Hades in Gk mythol.
(~'s *boat, ferry,* etc., phrr. for hour of
death). [f. Gk *Kharōn*]

chār′poy, n. (Anglo-Ind.). Light Indian
bedstead. [f. Hind. *charpai*]

chart, n., & v.t. **1.** Navigator's sea map,
with coast outlines, rocks, shoals, etc.;
outline map with conspectus of special
conditions, as *magnetic* ~; record by
curves etc. of fluctuations in temperature, prices, etc.; sheet of tabulated
information; hence ~′LESS a. **2.** v.t.
Make ~ of, map. [f. F *charte* & its source
L *c(h)arta* CARD[2]]

chart′er[1], n. Written grant of rights by
sovereign or legislature, esp. creation of
borough, company, etc. (*Great C~,* MAGNA
CHARTA); deed conveying land; =CHARTER-
-PARTY; privilege, admitted right; ~*-
-member,* original member of society,
incorporation, etc. [ME *chartre* f. OF f.
L *chartula* dim. of *charta* CARD[2]]

chart′er[2], v.t. Grant charter, give privi-
lege, to (||~*ed accountant,* member of Insti-
tute of Accountants with royal charter;
~*ed libertine,* one allowed to take liberties); hire (ship) by ~*-party,* (loosely) hire
(vehicle etc.), Hence ~ER[1] n. [f. prec.]

Chart′erhouse, n. Alms-house in London
for aged pensioners on site of Carthusian

monastery; (also ~ *School*) public school of same foundation now at Godalming. [alt. f. AF *Chartrouse* = OF *Chartreuse*, earlier *Charteuse* Carthusian monastery f. L *Cart(h)usia*; see CARTHUSIAN]

chǎrt'er-pǎrtў, n. Deed between shipowner & merchant for hire of ship & delivery of cargo. [f. F *charte partie* f. med. L *charta partita* divided charter]

chǎrt'ism, -ist, nn. (hist.). Principles, adherent, of reform movement of 1837–48. [f. L *charta* + -ISM(3), -IST(2), name taken from the democratic manifesto 'People's Charter']

chǎrtǒg'raphў (k-), etc. See car-.

chartreuse (see Ap.), **n.** Carthusian monastery; kinds (*green*, *yellow*, ~) of liqueur; pale apple-green colour. [made at La Grande *Chartreuse* (Carthusian monastery near Grenoble) f. place-name L *Cart(h)usia*; see CHARTERHOUSE]

chǎrt'ŭlarў (k-). See car-.

‖ **chǎr'woman (-wŏŏ-), n.** Woman hired by the day or hour for housework. [CHAR²]

chǎr'ў, a. Cautious; shy of, sparing *in*, *doing*; stingy *of* (~ *of praise*). Hence **chǎr'ILY² adv., chǎr'INESS n.** [OE *cearig*, OS *carag*, OHG *charag* f. Gmc *karō* CARE¹ + -Y²]

Charўb'dis (ka-), n. See SCYLLA.

chāse¹, n. Pursuit (*in* ~ *of*, pursuing; *give* ~, go in pursuit); hunting (*the* ~, hunting as sport); (also *chace*) unenclosed park-land; hunted animal or pursued ship; (Hist.) ~, ~*-port*, ~*-gun*, *chaser*, *bow-*~, *stern-*~, *bow*, *stern*, *-chaser*, gun, port, in bow or stern for use while chasing or being chased; (Tennis) a certain stroke. [ME & OF *chace* f. Rom. **captia* f. **captiare* CHASE²]

chāse², v.t. Pursue; drive *from*, *out of*, *to*, etc.; ~*r* (colloq.), tot of spirit taken after coffee, small quantity of water taken after drinking neat spirits (also fig.). [ME, f. OF *chacier* f. Rom. **captiare* for L *capiare* f. *capere* take; see CATCH¹]

chāse³, v.t. Emboss, engrave, (metal). [app. f. syn. *enchase* f. F *enchâsser* (EN-, CASE²)]

chāse⁴, n. Part of gun enclosing bore; groove cut to receive pipe etc. [f. F *chas* enclosed space f. L *capsus* enclosure etc., or f. *capsa* CASE²)]

chāse⁵, n. Iron frame holding composed type for page or sheet. [f. F *châsse* CASE²]

chasm (kǎ'zm), n. Deep fissure; break of continuity, hiatus; wide difference of feeling, interests, etc., between persons or parties; void, blank. Hence (poet.) ~**Y² a.** [f. L f. Gk *khasma*]

chasse (shahs), n. Liqueur after coffee etc. (also ~*-café*). [F]

chassé (shǎs'ā), n., & v.i. (Make) gliding step in dancing; ~ *croisé* (see Ap.: pl. *-s* *-s*), double ~, (fig.) idle manœuvring. [F]

chassis (shǎs'ē), n. (pl. the same). Base--frame of gun-carriage, motor-car, etc. [f. F *châssis* rel. to *châsse* (CHASE⁵)]

chāste, a. Abstaining from unlawful or immoral (also from all) sexual intercourse, pure, virgin; decent (of speech); restrained, severe, pure in taste or style, unadorned, simple. Hence ~**'LY² (-tl-) adv.** [ME, f. OF f. L *castus*]

chā'sten (-sn), v.t. Discipline, correct by suffering, (usu. of God, Providence, etc., or of trouble etc.); make chaste in style etc., refine; temper, subdue, (esp. in p.p.). Hence ~**ER¹ (-sener) n.** [f. obs. *chaste* vb (f. OF *chastier* f. L *castigare* CASTIGATE) + -EN⁶]

chǎstis|e' (-z), v.t. Punish; beat. Hence **chǎs'tisEMENT (-zm-), ~'ER¹, nn.** [ME, app. irreg. f. obs. vbs *chaste*, *chasty* (see prec.) + -IZE]

chǎs'titў, n. Continence; virginity, celibacy; simplicity of style or taste. [f. OF *chaslete* f. L *castitalem* (*castus* CHASTE, -TY)]

chǎs'ŭble (-z-), n. Sleeveless vestment of celebrant at Mass or Eucharist with colour regulated by the feast of the day. [ME. & OF *chesible*; later *-uble* f. F *chasuble* f. LL *casub(u)la* irreg. f. LL *casula* hooded cloak, dim. of *casa* house]

chǎt¹, v.i. (-tt-), & n. (Indulge in) easy familiar talk. Hence ~**t'Y² a., ~t'INESS n.** [short for CHATTER]

chǎt², n. Kinds of bird, chiefly thrushes (usu. in comb. as *stone*, *whin*, *-*~). [f. prec.]

château (shah'tō), **n.** (pl. *-x*, pr. *-z*), Foreign country house; *C*~, used attrib. in names of French wines made near certain ~x. [F]

chǎt'elaine (sh-), n. Set of short chains attached to woman's belt for carrying keys, watch, pencil, etc.; mistress of country house; (esp. in journalistic use) hostess. [f. F *châtelaine*, fem. of *-ain* lord of a castle, f. L *castellanus* f. *castellum* CASTLE]

chǎt'el, n. Movable possession (usu. pl., esp. *goods & ~s*); ~ *mortgage*, conveyance of ~s by mortgage as security for debt. [ME & OF *chatel* see CATTLE]

chǎtt'er, v.i., & n. 1. (Of birds) utter quick series of short notes; (of persons) talk quickly, incessantly, foolishly, or inopportunely; (of teeth) rattle together (also of ill-adjusted parts of machine). **2. n.** Any of these sounds; ~*box*, child etc. given to ~. [ME *chater* etc., imit., see -ER⁵]

chaud-froid (shō'frwah'), n. Dish of filleted poultry etc. served cold in jelly or sauce. [F, lit. hot-cold]

chauff'er, n. Metal basket holding fire; portable furnace with air-holes. [19th c., also (18th c.) *choffer*, of uncert. orig.; cf. (obs.) ME *chafer*, *chaufer*, & OF *chaufoire*; see CHAFING-DISH]

chauffeur (shōf'er, shōfēr'), n. Professional driver of a motor-car. Hence **chauffeuse (shōfērz'), n., female ~.** [F]

chaulmoo'gra, n. East-Indian tree; ~ ;

oil, fat obtained from its seeds & used in treatment of leprosy. [native name]

chauv'in|ism (shŏv-), n. Bellicose patriotism, foreign jingoism. So ~**IST**(2) n. & a., ~**is'tic** a. [*Chauvin*, Napoleonic veteran, person in Cogniard's *Cocarde Tricolore* 1831]

chaw, v.t., & n. (now vulg.). Chew; •~ *up*, utterly defeat; ~*-bacon*, bumpkin; (n.) quid of tobacco. [var. of CHEW]

cheap, a. Inexpensive (of thing, price, shop, dealer; ~ *& nasty*, of low cost & bad quality); worth more than its cost; easily got; worth little account, staled, (*hold* ~, despise); (as pred.) = cheaply (*got it* ~ etc.); *dirt* ~, very ~; *feel* ~ (sl.), be out of sorts; *on the* ~, in ~ manner; *C*~ *Jack*, travelling hawker; ‖ ~ *trip*(*per*), excursion(ist) by rail etc. at reduced fares. Hence ~**'LY²** adv., ~**'ISH**²(2) a., ~**'NESS** n. [f. phr. *good cheap* f. obs. *cheap* n. f. OE *cēap* barter, OS *kōp*, OHG *kouf*, ON *kaup* (cf. Goth. *kaupōn* vb) f. L *caupo* innkeeper]

cheap'en, v.t. & i. Haggle for (arch.); make or become cheap, depreciate. [-**EN**⁶]

cheat, n., & v.t. & i. **1.** Trick, fraud; swindler, deceiver; card-game in which undetected cheating is licensed. **2.** vb. Deceive, trick (person *out of* thing); deal fraudulently; while away (time, fatigue). [ME *chete* vb, aphetic f. *achete*, var. of ESCHEAT]

chĕck¹, int. & n. **1.** (Announcement of) exposure of chess king to attack. **2.** Sudden arrest given to motion, rebuff, repulse; slight military reverse. **3.** (hunt.). Loss of the scent. **4.** Stoppage, pause; restraint on action (*keep in* ~, under control); person or thing that restrains. **5.** Control to secure accuracy; token of identification for left luggage, seat-holder, etc.; bill in restaurant. **6.** •Counter at cards (hence colloq., *hand in* one's ~*s*, die). **7.** ~*-action* in piano, restraining hammer from striking string twice; ~*-nut*, screwed on over nut to prevent its working loose; ~*-rein*, attaching one horse's rein to other's bit, also rein preventing horse from lowering head; ~*-string*, in carriage for signalling to driver to stop; ~*-taker*, collector of pass tokens in theatre etc.; ~*-till*, in shop, recording receipts. [ME *chek, chak* f. OF *eschec* ult. f. Arab. f. Pers. *shah* king]

chĕck², v.t. & i. **1.** Threaten opponent's king at chess. **2.** Suddenly arrest motion of. **3.** (Of hounds) stop on losing scent, or to make sure of it. **4.** Restrain, curb, (of superior) find fault with, rebuke. **5.** Test (statement, account, figures, employees) by comparison etc., examine accuracy of. [ME *chek*(*e*) f. OF *eschequier* play chess, check, as prec.]

chĕck³, n. Cross-lined pattern; fabric woven or printed with this. So ~**ED²** (-kt) a. [prob. short for CHEQUER]

chĕck⁴, n. = CHEQUE.

chĕck'er. See CHEQUER¹, ³.

•**chĕck'ers**, n. pl. The game of draughts. [see CHEQUER¹]

chĕckmate', int. & n., & v.t. (also *mate*, now more usu. in chess but not in fig. sense). (Announcement to opponent of) inextricable check of king at chess, final defeat at chess or in any enterprise; (vb) defeat, frustrate. [ME *chek mat*(*e*) f. OF *eschec mat* (see CHECK¹) f. Arab. *shah mata* king is dead]

Chĕdd'ar, n. Kind of cheese. (~ in Somerset]

chee'-chee', n. (Anglo-Ind.). The affected English accent attributed to Eurasians; a Eurasian. [f. Hind. *chhī-chhī* filth, fie!]

cheek, n., & v.t. Side-wall of mouth, side of face below eye, (~*-tooth*, molar; ~*-bone*, that below eye; ~ *by jowl*, close together, intimate; *to* one's *own* ~, not shared with others); saucy speech (vb, address saucily), whence ~**'Y²** a., ~**'ILY²** adv., ~**'INESS** n.; cool confidence, effrontery, (*have the* ~ *to*); side post of door etc.; (pl.) jaws of vice, side-pieces of various parts of machines arranged in lateral pairs. [ME *chek*(*e*) f. OE *cēce, cēace*, cogn. w. MDu. *kāke*, MLG *kāke, kēke* f. WG *•kǣkōn-*]

cheep, v.i., & n. (Utter) shrill feeble note as of young bird. (Of young bird esp. of game) ~**'ER**¹ n. [imit.]

cheer¹, n. Frame of mind (*what* ~*?*, how do you feel?; *be of good* ~, stout-hearted, hopeful); food, fare, (*make good* ~, feast; *the fewer the better* ~, more to eat); shout of encouragement or applause (*three* ~*s*, successive united hurrahs, often *for* person or thing honoured). [ME *chere* face etc. f. AF, = OF *chiere* f. LL *cara* face f. Gk *kara* head]

cheer², v.t. & i. Comfort, gladden; incite, urge *on*, esp. by shouts; applaud (t. & i.), shout for joy; ~ *up*, comfort, take comfort. [f. prec.]

cheer'ful, a. Contented, in good spirits, hopeful; animating, pleasant; willing, not reluctant. Hence ~**LY²** adv., ~**NESS** n. [CHEER¹ + -FUL]

cheer'less, a. Dull, gloomy, dreary, miserable. Hence ~**LY²** adv., ~**NESS** n. [CHEER¹ + -LESS]

cheer'lȳ, adv. (naut.). Heartily, with a will. [formerly adj. & adv. (see -LY²) f. CHEER¹]

cheer'|ȳ, a. Lively, in spirits, genial. Hence ~**ĪLY²** adv., ~**'INESS** n., ‖ ~**iō** (sl.), int. of encouragement. [-Y²]

cheese¹ (-z), n. Food made of pressed curds; *a* ~, complete cake or ball of this within rind; *green* ~, immature, not yet dried; BREAD *&* ~; CHALK *&* ~; fruit of mallow; the heavy flat wooden ball used in skittles; *damson, guava,* ~, conserve of the fruit pressed into consistency of ~; ~*-cloth*, butter muslin; ~*-cutter*, with broad curved blade; ~*-cake*, tartlet filled with sweet yellow compound of curds etc.; ~-*hopper*, maggot of ~-*fly*; ~-*monger*, dealer in ~, butter, etc.; ~-*paring*, stingy, stinginess, (pl.) worthless odds & ends; ~-*plate*, 5 or 6 in. in diameter, also large coat-button; ~-*rennet*, name for Lady's bedstraw; ~-*scoop*, *-taster*, instrument for extracting piece; ~-*straws*, savoury of grated cheese etc. made up into thin strips. [OE *cēse*, OS *kāsi*, *k(i)ēsi*, OHG *chāsi*, WG f. L *caseus*]

cheese[2] (-z), n. (obs. sl.). *The* ~, the correct thing. [f. Hind. & Pers. *chiz* thing]

cheese[3] (-z), v.t. (sl.). ~ *it*, stop, give over, (only as imperat.). [orig. unkn.]

chees'|**y** (-z-), a. Like, tasting of, cheese; (sl.) stylish. Hence ~**ÏNESS** n. [CHEESE[1,2], -Y[2]]

cheet'ah, n. Kind of leopard, tamed in India & trained to hunt deer. [f. Hind. *chīta* f. Skr. *chitraka* speckled]

chef (sh-), n. Head cook (male). [F]

chef-d'œuvre (shādēr'vr), n. (pl. *chefs-*, same pronunc.). -**A**, one's, masterpiece. [F]

cheil(o)- (kī-). = CHIL(O)-.

cheir(o)- (kīr-). = CHIR(O)-.

cheirŏp'teran, n., **cheirŏp'terous**, a., (kīr-). (Member) of mammal order with membraned hands serving as wings, the bats. [prec. + Gk *pteron* wing + -**AN**, -OUS]

chek'a (chā-), n. (Earlier name of) OGPU. [Russ., f. initials (*che*, *ka*) of *Chresvychainaya Kommissiya*, extraordinary commission]

chel'a[1] (chā-), n. Novice qualifying for initiation in esoteric Buddhism. [Hind., = pupil]

chel'|**a**[2] (kē-), n. (pl. *-lae*). The prehensile claw of crabs, lobsters, scorpions, etc. Hence ~**ATE**[2], ~**ÏFORM**, aa. [f. Gk *khēlē* claw]

Chēll'ēan (sh-), a. (archaeol.). Of the palaeolithic epoch represented by remains found at Chelles in France. [-**AN**]

Chĕl'sea (-sǐ), n. Artistic quarter of London; ~ *bun*, kind of rolled currant-*bun*; ‖ ~ *pensioner*, inmate of the ~ Royal Hospital for old or disabled soldiers; ~ *ware*, kind of porcelain made at ~ in 18th c. [place]

Chĕltŏn'ian, a. & n. (Member) of Cheltenham College. [-**IAN**]

chĕm'ical (kĕ-), a. & n. Of, made by, relating to, chemistry; ~ COMBINATION, (usu. pl.) substance obtained by or used in ~ process; *heavy* ~*s*, bulk ~*s* used in industry & agriculture (prop. only of manufactured ~s). Hence or cogn. ~**LY**[2] adv., **chĕm'ico-** comb. form. [16th c. *chimicall* f. F *chimique* or mod. L *chi-*, *chymicus* (for *alchimicus*; see **ALCHEMIC**) + -**AL**]

chemin de fer (shemăn' defēr'), n. A form of baccarat. [F, = railway]

chemise (shǐmēz'), n. Woman's body under-garment. [ME, f. OF f. LL *camisia* shirt; earlier *kemes* dir. f. LL]

chemisĕtte' (shĕmǐz-), n. Bodice with upper part like chemise; lace, muslin, etc., filling up opening of dress below throat. [F, dim. of prec.]

chĕm'ist (kĕ-), n. Person skilled in chemistry; ‖ dealer in medical drugs, apothecary. [16th c. *chym-*, *chimist* f. F *-iste* f. mod.L *-ista* for *alchimista* **AL-CHEMIST**]

chĕm'istry (kĕ-), n. Science of the elements & compounds & their laws of combination & behaviour under various conditions; *applied* or *practical* ~, art of utilizing this knowledge; (IN)ORGANIC ~; (fig.) mysterious change or process. [prec., -RY]

chĕm'itype (kĕ-), n. (Process for getting) relief cast of engraving. [CHEMICAL etc. + TYPE]

chĕmothĕ'rapy (kĕ-), n. Treatment of disease by chemical means. [f. CHEM-(ICAL) + -O- + -THERAPY]

chenille (shǐnēl'), n. Velvety cord used in trimming dresses & furniture. [F, = caterpillar f. L *canicula* small dog]

chĕque (-k), ***check**, n. Written order to banker to pay named sum on drawer's account to bearer or (order of) named person; BLANK[1] ~; CROSS[2]*ed* ~; ~-*book*, number of stamped & engraved forms for drawing ~s bound & issued to customer. [var. of CHECK[1] formerly used of counterfoils for checking forgery]

chĕ'quer[1] (-ker), **chĕck'er**, n. (Pl.) chess-board as inn-sign; (often pl.) pattern made of squares or with alternating colours, whence **chĕ'quer-WISE** (-ker-) adv.; ‖ *Chequers*, Prime Minister's official country house in Bucks. [ME, aphetic f. **EXCHEQUER**]

chĕ'quer[2] (-ker), **chĕck'er**, v.t. Mark with squares, esp. of alternate colours; variegate, break uniformity of, (often fig., esp. in p.p. as *chequered lot*, *fortunes*). [f. prec.]

chĕ'rish, v.t. Foster, nurse, keep warm; value, hold in one's heart, cling to, (esp. hopes, feelings, etc.). [ME, f. OF *cherir* (see -ISH[2]) f. *cher* f. L *carus* dear]

cherōōt' (sh-), n. Cigar with both ends open. [f. F *-route* f. Tamil *shuruṭṭu* roll]

chĕ'rry, n. & a. Small stone-fruit; tree bearing this (also ~-*tree*), its wood (also ~-*wood*); *cornelian* ~, cornel; *make two bites at a* ~, boggle, be unenterprising or formal; ‖ ~-*bob*, two cherries with joined stems (BOB[1]); ~ *brandy*, dark-red liqueur of brandy in which cherries have been steeped; ~-*pie*, garden heliotrope; ~ *ripe*, fruit hawker's cry; (adj.) red (~ *lips*, *ribbon*; ‖ ~-*breeches*, 11th Hussars). [ME *chiri*(*e*), *chery*(*e*) f. ONF *cherise* (treated as pl.; cf. PEASE) = OF *cerise*, f. Rom. **cerasia** f. L f. Gk *kerasos*; OE *ciris*, *cyrs* f. WG dir. f. pop. L]

chĕr'sonese (k-; -ēs), n. Peninsula. [f. L f. Gk *khersonēsos* (*khersos* dry, *nēsos* island)]

chĕrt, n. A flint-like quartz. [orig. unkn.]

chĕ'rub, n. (pl. -s, -im). Angelic being; one of the second order of ninefold celestial hierarchy, gifted with knowledge as the first (seraphim) with love; (Art) winged (head of) child; beautiful or innocent child. Hence cheru'bɪc (-ōō-) a. [OE, ME cherubin, ME & mod. cherub, f. F f. L f. Gk f. Heb. k'rub pl. k'rubim]

chĕr'vil, n. Garden herb used in soup, salad, etc. [OE cerfille, = OHG kervola f. L f. Gk khairephullon]

Chĕsh'ire (-er), n. ~ cheese, made in ~; ~ cat, person with fixed grin. [place in England; prov. grin like a ~ cat unexpl.]

chĕss[1], n. Game for two players with thirty-two pieces or ~-men on ~-board chequered with sixty-four squares. [ME ches f. OF esches pl. of eschec CHECK[1]]

chĕss[2], n. One of the flooring planks of a pontoon bridge. [orig. unkn.]

chĕss'el, n. Cheese-making mould. [app. f. CHEESE[1] + WELL[1]]

chĕst, n. 1. Large strong box; box for sailor's belongings; carpenter's, medicine, etc., ~, holding special requisites; treasury, coffer, of institution (usu. fig. for the sums in it); case of some commodity, esp. tea (& so as variable measure); ~ of drawers, (esp.) frame with drawers for keeping clothes in bedroom. 2. Part of human or lower animal's body enclosed in ribs (get thing off one's ~ sl., say & be quit of it), whence ~'ED[2] a.; ~-note, -voice, of lowest speaking or singing register; ~-protector, flannel etc. worn on ~; ~-trouble, lung disease esp. chronic. Hence ~'Y[2] a. (colloq.), inclined to, marked by, symptomatic of, ~ disease. [OE cest, cist, OHG, ON kista f. L f. Gk kistē]

chĕs'terfield, n. Kind of overcoat, also of couch. [19th-c. Earl of C~]

chĕst'nŭt (-sn-), n. & a. Tree (also ~-tree, Spanish ~, or sweet ~) or its edible fruit; =~-wood; = HORSE[1]-~; = CASTOR[3]; stale anecdote; (of) ~-colour, deep reddish-brown; horse of this colour. [f. obs. chesten (f. OF chastai(g)ne f. L f. Gk kastanea) + NUT]

chĕvăl'-glass (sh-; -ahs), n. Tall mirror swung on uprights. [f. F cheval horse, frame]

chĕvalier' (sh-), n. Member of certain orders of knighthood, & of French Legion of Honour etc.; (hist.) The C~ or C~ de St George, Old Pretender, The Young C~, Young Pretender; soldier cadet of old French noblesse; ~ of industry (oftener in F form ~ d'industrie, see Ap.), adventurer, swindler. [ME & AF chevaler (OF -ier) f. med. L caballarius f. L caballus horse, see -IER, -EER; mod. form f. F; cf. CAVALIER]

chevaux de frise (shevō'defrēz'), n. pl. Iron spikes set in timber etc. to repel cavalry etc. in war, or to guard palings in peace; natural protective line of hair in plants, eyelashes, etc. [F, lit. horses of Friesland, invented by 17th-c. Frisians who had no cavalry]

chevet (shevā'), n. Apse; group of apses. [F, f. L capitium (caput head)]

chĕv'iot, n. & a. (Wool cloth) got, made, from sheep of C~ hills in Northumberland.

chĕv'ron (sh-), n. Bent bar of inverted V shape, in escutcheons, as archit. ornament (~-moulding, consisting of series of these), & on sleeve of Service uniform indicating °rank (3 bars for sergeant, 2 for corporal, etc.), or ‖ length of service. [ME, f. OF chevron f. Rom. °capronem (nom. °capro) f. L caper goat]

chĕv'rotain, -tin, (sh-), n. Small musk deer. [F, dim. of OF chevrot (chèvre goat)]

chĕv'y̆, chi(v)v'y̆, (usu. spelt -e- & pron. -i-), n., & v.t. & i. Chase (n. & v.), scamper (n. & v.); game of prisoners' base. [prob. f. ballad Chevy Chase (place-name)]

chew (-ōō), v.t. & i., & n. 1. Work about between teeth, grind to pulp or indent with repeated biting; (abs.) ~ tobacco, whence ~'ER[1] n.; turn over in mind; meditate upon or over; ~ the cud, bring back half-digested food into mouth for further chewing, (fig., usu. with of reflection, fancy, etc.) meditate; ~ the rag or the fat (sl.), reiterate an old grievance, grouse; ~ing-gum, preparation of sweetened & flavoured gums (esp. CHICLE), used for prolonged ~ing. 2. n. Act of ~ing; quid of tobacco. [OE cēowan, OHG kiuwan, ON tyggva, -ja f. Gmc °keuw(j)an]

Chian'ti (kiah-), n. Dry red Ital. wine. [~ in Tuscany, Italy]

chiaroscuro (kyăroskoor'ō), n. & a. Treatment of light & shade in painting; light & shade effects in nature; variation, relief, handling of transitions, use of contrast, in literature etc.; (adj.) of ~; half-revealed. [It., see CLEAR; OBSCURE]

chias'mus (kiăz-), n. Inversion in second phrase of order followed in first (I cannot dig, to beg I am ashamed). Hence chiăs'tɪc (ki-) a. [f. Gk khiasmos crosswise arrangement (KHI)]

chib'ol, n. (dial.). Spring onion with green stalk attached. [ME chibol(l)e f. OF °chiboule (mod. ciboule), ult. f. L c(a)epa onion; see CHIVE]

chibouk', n. & a. (-ōōk), n. Long Turkish tobacco pipe. [f. Turk. chibuk tube]

chĭc (sh-), n. & a. Skill, effectiveness, style, stamp of superiority; (adj.) stylish, in the fashion. [F]

chicāne' (sh-), v.t. & i., & n. Use chicanery; cheat (person) into, out of, etc.; (n.) chicanery; (holding of) hand without any trumps in bridge. [f. F chicane(r)]

chicān'ery (sh-), n. Legal trickery, pettifogging; sophistry. [f. F chicanerie (prec., -ERY)]

chichi (shē'shē'), a. & n. Frilly (thing), fussy or effeminate (person). [F]

chick[1], n. Young bird before or after hatching; *the* ~s, children of a family (so ~*abidd'g̃*, term of endearment of or to child); ~*weed*, small plant. [ME *chike* short for CHICKEN]

chick[2], **chik**, n. (Anglo-Ind.). Screen-blind of finely-split bamboo laced with twine. [Hind. *chik*]

chick'en, n. (pl. ~s, ~). Young bird, esp. of domestic fowl, flesh of this; youthful person (esp. in *no* ~); *Mother Carey's* ~, stormy petrel; *count* one's ~s *before they are hatched*, be over-sanguine, precipitate; ~*breast(ed)*, (having) malformed projection of breast-bone; **~feed*, food for poultry, (fig.) poor or trifling stuff; ~ *hazard*, game at dice; ~*heart(ed)*, (with) no courage; ~*pox*, mild eruptive disease esp. of children. [OE *cicen*, cogn. w. COCK[1], cf. MDu. *kieken*, MLG *küken*, ON *kjúklingr*]

chick'ling, n. Common cultivated vetch. [16th c. *chicheling* dim. of ME & OF *chiche* ult. f. L *cicer*]

chick'-pea, n. Dwarf-pea. [16th c. *chich-pease* as prec. + PEASE]

chi'cle (-kl *or* -klē), n. Milky juice of the sapodilla, the basis of chewing-gum. [f. Mex. *tzictli*]

chic'ory, n. Blue-flowered plant cultivated for its salad leaves & its root; its root ground for use with or instead of coffee. [late ME *cicoree* f. OF *cichoree* (now *chico-*) f. med. L *cic(h)orea* f. L f. Gk *kikhorion* SUCCORY]

chide, v.t. & i. (literary; *chid, chidden or chid*). Make complaints, speak scoldingly, (esp. fig. of hounds, wind, etc.); scold, rebuke. [OE *cīdan*, of unkn. orig.]

chief[1], n. (Her.) upper third of shield; leader, ruler; head man of tribe, clan, etc., whence ~'ESS[1] n.; head of a department, highest official; *C~ of Staff*, senior staff officer of a commander; || *C~ of the Imperial General Staff*, senior military member of the Army Council; *in* ~, most of all, especially, (*for many reasons, & this one in* ~); *-in-*~, supreme, as *Commander, Colonel, -in-*~. Hence ~'DOM, ~'SHIP, nn., ~'LESS a. [ME & OF *chef*, *chief* f. Rom. **capum* f. L *caput* head]

chief[2], a. & adv. (*-er, -est*, now rare). First by title (*C~ Justice* etc.); first in importance, influence, etc.; prominent, leading; (adv.) chiefly, especially, (*but* ~ or ~*est of all, forget not*). [orig. CHIEF[1] used in apposition]

chief'ly[1], a. Proper for a chief. [CHIEF[1] + -LY[1]]

chief'ly[2], adv. Above all; mainly but not exclusively. [CHIEF[2] + -LY[2]]

chief'tain (-tǐn), n. Military leader (poet.); captain of robbers; chief of Highland clan or uncivilized tribe. Hence ~CY, ~ESS[1], ~RY, ~SHIP, (-tǐn-), nn. [ME

chevelaine etc. (later assim. to CHIEF) f. OF, f. LL *capitaneus* CAPTAIN]

chiff'-chaff, n. Bird of warbler family. [imit.]

chiffon (see Ap.), n. (Usu. pl.) adornments of female dress; (sing.) thin gauze. [F, f. *chiffe* rag]

chiffonier' (sh-), n. Movable low cupboard with sideboard top. [F (prec. -IER)]

chigg'er (-g-), n. = CHIGOE.

chignon (see Ap.), n. Mass of hair on pad at back of head. [F, orig. = nape of neck]

chig'oe, n. Tropical flea, burrowing into skin. [W.-Ind.]

Chihuahua (chǐwah'wah), n. Very small breed of dog, originating in Mexico. [Mex. state & city]

chil'blain, n. Itching sore on hand, foot, etc., from exposure to cold. Hence ~ED[2] (-nd), ~Y[2], aa. [CHILL + BLAIN]

child, n. (pl. *chǐl'dren*). Unborn or newborn human being (pronoun *it*, or *he, she*); boy or girl (*from a* ~, from childhood on); childish person; (sl.) *this* ~, I, me; son or daughter (at any age) of (or with *my* etc.), offspring; descendant lit. or fig. or follower or adherent of (~ *of God, of the devil*; ~*ren of Izaak Walton*, anglers; *fancy's* ~; ~ *of nature*); result *of*; (in arch. form *childe*) youth of noble birth (*Childe Harold, Roland*); *with* ~, pregnant; ~*'s-play*, easy task; BURN*t* ~ *dreads fire*; ~*'bed*, ~*'birth*, parturition; ~ *wife*, very young wife. Hence ~'LESS a., ~'less-NESS n. [OE *cild* cogn. w. Goth. *kilthei* womb]

Chil'dermas, n. Festival of Holy Innocents, 28th Dec. [OE *cildra* gen. pl. CHILD + MASS[1]]

child'hood, n. Child's state; time from birth to puberty; *second* ~, dotage. [-HOOD]

child'ish, a. Of, proper to, a child; puerile, improper for a grown person. Hence ~LY[2] adv., ~NESS n. [-ISH[1]]

child'like, a. Having good qualities of child, as innocence, frankness, etc. [-LIKE]

child'ly, a. & adv. (poet.). Like a child. [mod. revival of obs. wd; -LY[1,2]]

chil'e, ***chil'i**. Var. of CHILLI.

chil'iad (k-), n. A thousand; a thousand years. [f. LL f. Gk *khilias*, -AD(1)]

chil'iasm, **chil'iast**, (k-), nn. Doctrine of or belief in, believer in, the millennium. Hence **chiliăs'tic** a. [f. mod. Gk *khiliasmos*, LL f. Gk *-astēs* (prec.)]

chill[1], n. Cold sensation, lowered temperature of body, feverish shivering, (*catch a* ~; also of special part as *liver-*~); unpleasant coldness of air, water, etc. (*take* ~ *off water* or *claret*, warm slightly); depressing influence (*cast a* ~ *over*); coldness of manner. [OE *cele* cogn. w. COLD; but the noun, after giving CHILL[2,3], was dormant 1400–1600, & revived as deriv. of CHILL[3]]

chill[2], a. Unpleasantly cold to feel;

feeling cold; unfeeling, unemotional, abstract. Hence ~NESS n. [app. f. prec.]

chill[3], v.t. & i. Make, become, cold; deaden, blast, with cold; depress, dispirit; harden (molten iron) by contact of cold iron; (colloq.) take the chill off (liquid); ~ed beef etc., beef etc. preserved at moderately low temperature in cold storage (as distinct from frozen meat). [app. f. CHILL[1]]

chill'i, -y̆, n. Dried pod of capsicum (as relish, or made into cayenne). [f. Sp. chile, chili f. Mex.]

chill'y̆[1], a. Rather cold to feel; feeling rather cold; sensitive to cold; not genial, cold-mannered. Hence~iNESS n. [CHILL[1] +-Y[2]]

chil'ly̆[2] (-l-lĭ), adv. (rare). In cold manner (lit. & fig.). [CHILL[2]+-LY[2]]

chil(o)-, cheil(o)-, (k-), comb. form of Gk kheilos lip, in zool. terms as chilopod (having feet serving as jaws).

|| Chil'tern Hŭn'drĕds (-z), n. pl. Apply for, accept, the ~, resign seat in House of Commons. [a Crown manor, adminis- tration of which, being titular office under Crown, requires the member to vacate his or her seat]

chime[1], n. Set of attuned bells; series of sounds given by this; harmony, melody, rhythm, sing-song; agreement, correspondence. [ME chymbe ult. f. L f. Gk kumbalon CYMBAL]

chime[2], v.i. & t. Make (bell) sound; ring chimes (of person or bells); ring chimes on (bells); show (hour) by chiming (also of hour, = sound); summon by bells to; repeat mechanically; be in rhyme, make to rhyme; be in agreement (together, with, or abs.); join in, express eager agreement. [as prec.]

chime[3], chĭmb, (-m), n. Projecting rim at ends of cask. [ME chimbe; cf. MDu., MLG (G) kimme]

chimēr'a, -aer'a, (kĭ-), n. 1. Monster with lion's head, goat's body, & serpent's tail. 2. Bogy; thing of hybrid character; fanciful conception; whence chimĕr'- ICAL a., chimĕr'icaLY[2] adv., (kĭ-). [ME & OF chimere f. L f. Gk khimaira she-goat, chimaera, (khimaros goat); later assim. to L form]

chimēre', n. Bishop's robe. [ME chemer, chymer, rel. to OF chamarre, F simarre; see CYMAR]

chim'ney, n. Flue carrying off smoke or steam of fire, furnace, engine, etc.; (also ~-stalk, -top) part of flue above roof; glass tube providing draught for lamp- -flame; natural vent, e.g. of volcano; (Mountaineering) narrow cleft by which cliff may be climbed; ~-corner, warm seat within old-fashioned fire-place; ~- -jack, rotating cowl; ~-piece, = MANTEL; ~-pot, earthenware or metal pipe added to ~-top (||~-pot hat, tall silk hat); ~- -stack, united group of ~-stalks; ||~-

-stalk, see above, also = tall factory ~; ||~-swallow, common swallow; ~-sweep man who sweeps ~s; ~-sweeper, = ~- -sweep, also = jointed ~-cleaning brush. [ME chimenee etc. f. OF cheminee f. LL caminata (?sc. camera) fireplaced (cham- ber) f. L caminus oven f. Gk; see -Y[4]]

chimpănzee', n. African ape resembling man. [native name in Angola]

chin, n. Front of lower jaw; up to the ~, ~-deep, deeply immersed. Hence ~NED[2] (-nd) a. [OE cin, OS, OHG kinni, ON kinn, Goth. kinnus f. Gmc *kinn- cogn. w. L gena, Gk genus]

Chin'a, a., chin'a, n. & a. 1. (C~). From China (C~ crape, C~ ASTER, etc.; C~ orange, common orange, orig. from China; Chin'aman, (derog. for) a Chinese; China- town, section of a town (esp. a seaport) in which the Chinese live as a colony). 2. (c~). (Made of) a fine semi-transparent earthenware, porcelain; things made of this; whence ~MAN'IA(C) nn.; ~-closet, for keeping or displaying one's ~; ~-clay; KAOLIN; ~-man, (Cricket) left-handed bowler's off-break to right-handed bats- man. [ult. orig. unkn.; not native name; found in Skr. about 1st c.]

chinchill'a, n. Small S.-Amer. rodent; its soft grey fur. [Sp., dim. of chinche bug f. L cimex -icis (from supposed smell)]

|| chin-chin', int. of greeting & farewell (Anglo-Chin.; also as n. & vb). [Chin. ts'ing ts'ing]

|| chine[1], n. Deep narrow ravine (now only in Isle of Wight & Hampshire). [OE cinu chink etc., = MDu. kēne chap f. root ki- burst open; cf. CHINK[1]]

chine[2], n. Backbone; animal's backbone or part of it as joint; ridge, arête. [f. OF eschine f. OFrank. *skina SHIN]

Chinee', n. (sl.). Chinese; the heathen ~, (joc., w. ref. to Bret Harte's Truthful James, for) the typical Chinese. [due to taking Chinese for pl.]

Chinēse' (-z), a. & n. (pl. the same). (Native, language) of China; ~ lantern, collapsible of paper used esp. in illumi- nating; ~ white, a pigment, white oxide of zinc. [China+-ESE]

chink[1], n. Crevice; long narrow opening, slit, peep-hole. [16th c., obsc. rel. to CHINE[1], which it replaced]

chink[2], n., & v.i. & t. 1. Sound as of glasses or coins striking together; (sl.) ready money. 2. vb. Make this sound; cause (coin etc.) to make it. [imit.]

Chink[3], n. (sl.). A Chinese. [abbr.]

Chino-, comb. form of China, = SINO- [-o-]

chinook', n. Warm dry wind which blows over the Rocky Mountains. [native name]

chintz, n. & a. (Of) cotton cloth fast- -printed with particoloured pattern & usu. glazed. [earlier chints pl. f. Hind. chint f. Skr. chitra; for sing. use cf. BAIZE]

chip[1], n. Thin piece cut from wood or broken from stone etc.; thin slice of potato, fruit, etc.; (pl., colloq.) potato-~s fried (*fish & ~*s); wood split into strips for making hats etc. (*~ bonnet, basket*); *dry as a ~*, flavourless, uninteresting; *~* (scion) *of*, esp. *~ of old block*, son resembling father; place in china etc. from which a *~* has been knocked off; (sl.) counter, piece of money; *have a ~ on* one's *shoulder*, be quick to take offence; *~-shot* (Golf), short lofted approach-shot on to putting-green. [14th c., belongs to CHIP[2]; rel. obsc.]

chip[2], v.t. & i. (-pp-). Cut (wood), break stone, crockery, at surface or edge; shape thus; cut or break (piece etc.) *off*, *from*; be susceptible to breakage at edge; carve (inscription); crack (egg-shell; esp. of chickens); (colloq.) banter (a person); (colloq.) *~ in*, interrupt. [1407 in *chip-ax*, prob. repr. OE *cippian*; cf. EFris. *kippen* cut, MDu. *kippen* chip eggs, hatch; in mod. senses apprehended as dim. of CHOP[1], cf. *drip drop, tip top*]

chip[3], n., & v.t. (-pp-). Wrestling-trick; (vb) trip up. [18th c., north.; etym. obsc.; cf. Du. *kippen* ensnare]

chip'muck, -**ŭnk**, n. North-American squirrel. [Amer.-Ind.]

Chipp'endāle, n. A fine and solid style of furniture. [T. *~* (d. 1779), cabinet-maker]

chipp'|y̆, a. (sl.). Dry, uninteresting; parched & queasy after drunkenness etc.; irritable. Hence ~**INESS** n. [CHIP[1]+-Y[2]]

Chips, n. (naut. sl.). Ship's carpenter. [pl. of CHIP[1], cf. BUTTONS]

chir(o)-, cheir(o)-, (kīr-), comb. form of Gk *kheir* hand, as *chirŏG'RAPHY* handwriting, *chir'oMANCY* palmistry.

chir'ograph (kīr-; -ahf), n. Document of various kinds formally written or signed. [f. F *chirographe* f. L f. Gk *kheirographon* (prec., -GRAPH)]

chirŏp'odist, chirŏp'ody̆, (kīr-), nn. Treater, treatment, of feet, toe-nails, corns, bunions, etc. [1785, app. f. CHIRO-, Gk *pous podos* foot, -IST(3)]

chiroprăc't|ĭc (kīr-), n. Manipulation of spinal column as method of curing disease. Hence ~**OR** n., one who practises~ĭc. [f. CHIRO- + Gk *praktikos* (*prassō* do, see -IC)]

chĭrp, v.i. & t., & n. (Make) short sharp note (as) of small bird; utter (song), express (joy etc.); thus; talk merrily; speak feebly. [imit.; late ME modification of earlier *chirk, chirl*]

chĭrp'|y̆, a. Lively, cheerful. Hence ~**INESS** n. [prec., -Y[2]]

chĭrr, v.i., & n. (Make) prolonged trilling sound (as) of grasshopper. [imit.]

chĭ'rrup, v.i., & n. (Make) series of chirps, twittering; (make) imitative chirping to baby etc. [extension of CHIRP]

chĭs'el (-zl), n., & v.t. (-ll-). (Cut, shape, with) tool with square bevelled end for shaping wood, stone, or metal (*cold ~*, all of steel or iron for trimming cold iron; *~led features* etc., clear-cut); *the ~*, sculpture's *~*, (art of) sculpture; (sl.) defraud, unfair treatment. [ME, f. ONF *chisel*, OF *cisel*, f. Rom. **cisellum* (L *caedere caes*- cut, see -LE(2))]

chit[1], n. Young child; young, small, or slender woman (depreciatingly, esp. *~ of a girl*). [14th c. = whelp, cub, kitten; etym. unkn., but cf. Ches. dial. *chit*, Sc. *cheet* puss, *chitty, cheety* cat]

chit[2], **chitt'y̆**, n. (orig. Anglo-Ind.). Note or written paper, esp. character given to servant; note of sum owed for drink etc.; *~-system* (of giving vouchers in payment instead of cash down). [f. Hind. *chiṭṭhi* f. Skr. *chitra* mark]

chit'al (-ĕt-), n. The Indian spotted deer. [Hind.]

chit'-chăt', n. Light conversation; subjects of it, gossip. [redupl. of CHAT[1]]

chit'in (kī-), n. Substance forming horny cover of beetles & crustaceans. Hence ~**OUS** a. [f. F *chitine* irreg. f. Gk *khitōn* tunic + -IN]

chitt'ăck, n. Indian weight corresponding to the ounce. [Bengali *chhaṭāk*]

chitt'erling, n. (usu. pl.). Smaller intestines of beasts, esp. as cooked for food. [13th c., of unkn. orig.]

chitt'y̆. See CHIT[2].

chiv'alrous, (poet. etc.) **chiv'alrĭc** (*also* -ăl[L]), (see foll.), a. Of, as of, the Age of Chivalry; of, as of, the ideal knight, gallant, honourable, courteous, disinterested; quixotic. Hence **chiv'alrous**LY[2] adv. [ME, f. OF *chevalerous* (CHEVALIER, -OUS); *chivalric* f. foll. + -IC]

chiv'alry̆ (formerly *chiv-*; now usu. *sh-*, as though a recent F importation), n. Horsemen, cavalry, (arch.); gallant gentlemen; knightly skill (arch.); medieval knightly system with its religious, moral, & social code; ideal knight's characteristics; devotion to service of women; inclination to defend weaker party; *flower of ~*, pattern knight, élite of nation's soldiers. [ME & OF *chi-, chevalerie* etc. f. med. L *caballerius* for LL *caballarius* horseman (CAVALIER, -ERY)]

chive, cive (s-), n. Small herb allied to onion & leek. [ME *cive, chive* f. OF *cive*, n. dial. **chive*, f. L *cepa* leek; see CHIBOL]

chiv(v)'y̆. See CHEVY.

chlōr-[1,2]. = CHLORO-[1,2], used before vowel.

chlōr'al (kl-), n. *~ hydrate* or *~*, a hypnotic & anaesthetic. Hence ~**ISM**(5) n., ~**IZE**(5) v.t. [F *chloral* f. CHLOR(INE) + AL(COHOL)]

chlōr'ide (kl-), n. (Chem.) compound of chlorine (-IDE); (pop.) kinds of bleaching agent, as *~ of lime, soda, potash*. [CHLOR-[2], -IDE]

chlōr'in|āte (kl-), v.t. Impregnate with chlorine. Hence ~**A'TION** n., treatment with chlorine (esp. in the extraction of gold from certain ores). [CHLORINE + -ATE[3]]

chlŏr'ine (kl-), n. (chem.). Non-metallic element, a yellowish-green heavy ill--smelling gas. [f. Gk *khlōros* green + -INE⁵]

chlŏro-¹, chlŏr-, comb. form in bot. & mineral. terms of Gk *khlōros* green.

chlŏro-², chlŏr-, comb. form in chem. terms of CHLORINE etc. Hence **chlŏr'ATE** (3) n., **chlŏr'IC**(2), **chlŏr'ous** (chem.) aa., (kl-).

chlŏr'odȳne (kl-), n. Patent medicine, narcotic & anodyne. [foll. + Gk *odunē* pain]

chlŏr'ofōrm (kl-), n., & v.t. 1. Anaesthetic, thin colourless liquid whose inhaled vapour produces insensibility. 2. v.t. Treat (person) with, render insensible by, ~, whence ~IST (1) n.; soak (thing) in ~. [f. F *chloroforme* f. CHLORO-² + *form*(*yl*) see FORMIC]

chlŏromȳ'cétin (kl-), n. An antibiotic used in some diseases, e.g. typhus. [f. CHLORO-², Gk *mukēs -ētos* fungus, -IN]

chlŏr'ophȳll (kl-), n. Colouring-matter of green parts of plants. [F CHLORO¹(*phylle* f. Gk *phullon* leaf)]

chlŏr|ōs'is (kl-), n. (Hist.) green sickness, anaemic disease of young women, with greenish complexion; (Bot.) blanching of green parts, or turning green of petals etc. Hence ~OT'IC a. [CHLOR-¹, -OSIS]

chŏck¹, n. Block of wood, esp. wedge for stopping motion of cask or wheel, also in various senses on ship esp. of wedges supporting boat on deck; (Turning; earlier form of) CHUCK⁴. [w. CHUCK⁴ prob. f. ONF **choque* cf. repr. by mod. Pic. *choke*, Norm. *chouque* (= F *souche*)]

chŏck², v.t., & adv. Make fast with chocks; place (boat) on chocks; ~ *up*, wedge in tightly, encumber (room etc.) with furniture etc.; (adv.) closely, tightly, close up; ~-*a-block*, jammed together, crammed *with*, chock-full *of* (orig. naut., of two blocks brought close together in a tackle); ~-*full*, stuffed. [f. prec.; the var. *choke-full* for ~-*full* is prob. an etym. guess & misrepresents pronunc.]

chŏc'olate, n. & a. (Cake) of cacao-seed paste; drink of this in hot milk or water; dark brown (n. & a.); ~ *cream*, sweetmeat of ~ enclosing sweet paste. [f. F *chocolat* or Sp. -*ate* f. Mex. *chocolatl* (not f. *cacao* or *cocoa*)]

Chŏc'taw, n. 1. (Member of) N.-Amer. Indian tribe, now in Oklahoma. 2. (c~) skating). Step from either edge to edge on other foot in opposite direction. [native; cf. MOHAWK]

choice¹, n. Choosing, selection, (*make ~ of*, select; *take* one's ~, decide between possibilities; *the girl of* one's ~; *for* ~, by preference, if one must select); power, right, faculty, of choosing (*at ~*, at pleasure; *have* one's ~; *have no ~*, have no alternative, not care which; *Hobson's ~*, to take or leave the one offer); élite, flower, *of*; variety to choose from; thing

or person chosen; alternative (*have no ~ but*). [ME *chois* f. OF f. *choisir* f. Rom. *causire f. Gmo *kausjan choose]

choice², a. Of picked quality, exquisite; carefully chosen, appropriate. Hence ~'LY² (-sl-) adv., ~'NESS (-sn-) n. [f. prec.]

choir (kwīr), *quīre* (arch.), n., & v.t. & i. 1. Band of singers performing or leading in musical parts of church service; chancel of cathedral, minster, or large church; choral society, company of singers (also of birds, angels, etc.); band of dancers; ~-*organ* (corruption of *chair*-), softest of three parts (*great, swell, ~, organ*) making up large compound organ, with lowest of three keyboards; ~ *school*, school maintained by a cathedral or church for ~boys & other pupils. 2. vb. Sing in chorus (intr., or with *strain, hymn*, etc., as obj.). [ME *quer*(*e*) f. OF *cuer* (mod. *choeur*) f. L CHORUS. The sp. *choir* after F–L; for pr. *quire* cf. ME *frere* FRIAR]

chōke¹, v.t. & i., & n. Stop breath of, suffocate, temporarily or finally, by squeezing throat from without, blocking it up within, or (of water, smoke, etc.) being unbreathable; (fig., of emotion) paralyse (~-*pear*, fact, reproof, etc., hard to swallow); suffer temporary stoppage of breath, become speechless from anger etc., (n., this condition); smother, stifle, kill, (plant, fire, etc.) by deprivation of light, air, etc.; suppress (feelings); block up wholly or partly (tube by narrowing part of it; as n., the narrowed part, whence ~-*bore*, of gun with bore narrowing towards muzzle; also of channel with sand, stones, etc., *stones ~* or ~ *up channel*, *channel* ~*s*), fill chock-full; ~ *down*, swallow (food), conceal (emotion) with difficulty; ~ *off*, make (person) relinquish an attempt; ~-*damp*, carbonic acid gas in mines, wells, etc.; *choking coil* (Electr.), (also ~) inductance coil used to prevent the passage of an alternating current or to alter its phase. [ME *cheke*, *choke* (= *acheke, achoke*), f. late OE (once) *ācēocian*, f. *cēace, cēce* CHEEK]

chōke², n. Centre part of artichoke. [prob. confusion of ending w. prec.]

chŏk'er, n. In vbl senses; esp. clerical or other stand-up collar. [-ER¹]

chŏk'ra, n. (Anglo-Ind.). Boy (esp. one employed as domestic servant). [Hind. *chhokra*]

∥ **chŏk'y̆**, n. (orig. Anglo-Ind., sl.). Prison, lock-up. [Hind. *chaukī* shed]

chŏl(ē)- (k-), comb. form in med. & chem. wds repr. Gk *kholē* gall, bile.

chŏl'er (kŏ-), n. (Hist.) one of the four HUMOURS, bile; (poet., arch.) anger, irascibility. [ME & OF *colre, colere* bile, anger f. L f. Gk *kholera* diarrhoea, in LL = bile, anger (Gk *kholē* bile)]

chŏl'era (kŏ-), n. (Also *English, bilious, summer*, ~, or in L ~ *nostras* = of our country) bilious summer & autumn disorder with diarrhoea & vomiting; (also

Asian, epidemic, malignant, ~) non--bilious often fatal disease endemic in India & epidemic in Europe; *chicken ~*, infectious disease of fowls; *~-bell*, flannel or silk waistband worn as preventive. Hence **cholerā'ic** (kŏ-) a. [ME, f. L f. Gk *kholera*; see prec.]

chol'eric (kŏ-), a. Irascible; angry. [ME *colerik(e)* etc. f. OF f. L f. Gk *kholerikos* (see CHOLER, -IC)]

chol'erine (kŏ-; *also* -ēn), n. Summer cholera; diarrhoea often prevalent at same time as Asian cholera. [F (*-ē-*), f. *choléra* CHOLERA]

chol'iamb (kŏ-), n. = SCAZON. Hence *~*IC (-ăm²) a. [f. LL f. Gk *khōliambos* (*khōlos* lame, *iambos* IAMBUS)]

chondri-, -o-, (kŏ-), comb. form of Gk *khondros*, in Med. & Physiol. = cartilage-.

chōose (-z), v.t. & i. (*chōse, chōsen,* pr. -z-). Select out of greater number; (Theol., esp. in p.p.) destine to be saved (*the chosen people, race,* Jews); decide (*to do one thing rather than another*); think fit, be determined, *to do*; make choice *between*; *cannot ~ but*, must, have to, (arch.); (with compl.) select as (*was chosen king*); *pick & ~*, select carefully, be fastidious; *nothing* etc. *to ~ between them*, of things nearly equal. Hence **chōos'ER**[1] (-z-) n., **chōos'(e)y²** (-z-) a. (colloq.), fastidious. [OE *cēosan*, OS, OHG *kiosan*, ON *kjósa*, Goth *kiusan*, f. Gmc **keusan*]

chŏp[1], v.t. & i. (-pp-). Cut by a blow, usu. with axe (*~ up, ~ into small pieces*, mince; often *~ off, away, down*); deliver such blow *at*; make one's way by such blows *through*; mince (esp. in p.p.); (fig.) cut (words etc.) short or into distinct parts; *~ in* (colloq.), intervene in talk; *~ back*, reverse one's direction suddenly, double; (of strata) *~ up, out,* come to surface. [ME, var. of CHAP[1], etym. unkn.; in sense approx. = MDu., LG *kappen* lop off, sever]

chŏp², n. Cutting stroke with axe etc.; thick slice of meat, esp. mutton or pork, usu. including rib (*~-house,* cheap restaurant); broken surface of water usu. due to action of wind against tide, so *~p'ȳ*[1] [-y²] a. [f. prec.]

chŏp³. See CHAP². [16th c.; var. of CHAP²; rel. & etym. obsc.]

chŏp⁴, v.t. & i. (-pp-), & n. *~ & change* (emphatic for *change*, usu. intr.), vacillate, be inconstant, (n., *~s & changes,* variations); *~ round, about,* (esp. of wind) change direction suddenly; *~ logic,* bandy arguments. Hence *~p'ȳ*[2] [-y²] a. [vb 1391 in *choppe-church*; etym. obsc.]

‖ **chŏp⁵**, n. (India, China) seal, licence, passport, permit; (China) trade-mark, a brand of goods; (Anglo-Ind. & colloq.) *first, second, ~~,* first, second, -class. [f. Hind. *chhāp* stamp]

chŏp-chŏp', adv. & int. (pidgin Eng.). Quick, quickly. [f. Chin. *k'wai-k'wai*]

chŏpp'er, n. One who chops; large--bladed short axe; butcher's cleaver. [CHOP¹ + -ER¹]

chŏp'stick, n. Small slip of ivory etc. of which two held in one hand are used by Chinese as fork. [pidgin Eng. (*chop* = quick + STICK) equivalent of Chin. *k'wai-tsze* nimble ones]

chŏp-sū'ey, n. Dish of fried or stewed meat or chicken flavoured with sesame oil & served with rice, onions, etc. (in Chinese restaurant). [Chin., = mixed bits]

chŏr'al[1] (kŏ-), a. Of, sung by, choir (*~ service,* with canticles, anthems, etc., so sung; *full ~ service,* with versicles & responses also sung); of, with, chorus. Hence *~*LY² adv. [f. F, or med. L *choralis* (CHORUS, -AL)]

choral(e)² (korahl'), n. (Metrical hymn to) simple tune usu. sung in unison, orig. in German reformed church. [f. G *choral(gesang)*]

chŏr'alist (k-), n. Chorus singer. [CHORAL¹, -IST]

chŏrd[1] (k-), n. String of harp etc. (poet.; also fig., as *touch the right ~,* appeal skilfully to emotion); (Anat.) obs. spelling of CORD, as *vocal ~, spinal ~*; (Math.) straight line joining ends of arc. [16th-c. refash. of CORD¹ after L *chorda*]

chŏrd² (k-), n. (Mus.) group of notes sounded together, combined according to some harmonic system (*common ~,* any note with its major or minor third, perfect fifth, & octave; *break* or *spread ~,* play its notes successively); harmonious combination of colours. [orig. *cord* for ACCORD² later altered after CHORD¹]

chŏrd'al (k-), a. Of, like, etc., CHORD¹,², [-AL]

chōre, n. Odd job, (pl.) household tasks. [U.S. form of CHAR²]

chorē'a (k-), n. St Vitus's dance. [L]

chŏr'ee (k-), n. = TROCHEE. [f. L f. Gk *khoreios*]

cho'regraph etc. See CHOREOGRAPH etc.

chorē'ic (k-), a. Of, having, chorea; of, marked by, chorees. [-IC]

chŏr'eograph (kŏ-; -ahf), n. Designer of ballet. So **choreŏg'RAPHER**, **choreŏg²RAPHY**, nn., **choreographIC** a., (kŏ-). [f. Gk *khoreia* dancing (*khoros* dancing--company) + -GRAPH]

chori- (kŏ-), bef. a vowel **choris-** (kŏ-), f. Gk *khōri(s)* asunder, apart, used in bot. terms etc.

cho'riamb, choriam'bus (kŏ-), n. Metrical foot ($- \cup \cup -$). Hence **choriam'bIC** (kŏ-) a. [f. LL f. Gk *khoriambos* (CHOREE, IAMB)]

chŏr'ic (k-), a. Of, like, chorus in Greek play. [f. LL f. Gk *khorikos* (CHORUS, -IC)]

chŏr'ion (k-), n. Outer membrane of foetus. [f. Gk *khōrion*]

cho'rister (kŏ-), n. Member of choir, esp. choir-boy (also fig. of angels, birds). [ME *querestre, -istre* prob. f. AF **cueristre* (= OF *-istre*) f. *cuer* CHOIR; 16th c. refash.

after (now obs.) *chorist* (F *choriste*, med. L *chorista*)]

chorŏg′raphў (kŏ-), n. Describing, description, of districts (more limited than *geography*, less than *topography*). Hence or cogn. **chorŏG′RAPHER** n., **chor‑GRAPH′IC(AL)** aa., **chorŏgräph′icaLᴌў²** adv., (kŏ-). [f. F -*graphie* or L -*graphia* f. Gk (Gk *khōra* land, -GRAPHY)]

chŏr′oid (k-), a. & n. Like chorion in shape or vascularity, esp. ~ *coat* (or ~ as noun), membrane lining eyeball. [f. Gk *khoreidēs* for *khorio-* (CHORION, -OID)]

chorŏl′ogў (kŏ-), n. Local distribution of species etc. Hence **chorolŏg′ICAL** a. [f. Gk *khōra* land +-LOGY]

chŏr′tle, v.i., & n. (Utter) loud chuckle. [portmanteau wd (Lewis Carroll) app. f. *chuckle* +*snort*]

chŏr′us (k-), n., & v.t. & i. 1. (Gk Ant.) band of dancers & singers in religious ceremonies & dramatic performances (also representing interested spectators in play; so in some Eng. plays); (one of) their utterances. 2. Personage speaking prologue & commenting on action in Elizabethan plays. 3. Band of singers, choir; thing sung by many at once; any simultaneous utterance of many (*in* ~, all speaking etc. together). 4. (Mus.) composition in several (oftenest four) parts each sung by several voices; refrain of song in which audience joins. 5. vb. Sing, speak, say, in ~. [L, f. Gk *khoros*]

chose jugée (see Ap.), n. Thing it is idle to discuss, as already settled. [F]

chose(n). See CHOOSE.

chŏt′a haz(i)ri (hahz′rĭ), n. (Anglo-Ind.). Light early breakfast. [Hind. (*chh-*), = little breakfast]

chou (shōō), n. Rosette or ornamental knot of ribbon, chiffon, etc., on woman's hat or dress. [F, f. L *caulis* cabbage]

chough (chŭf), n. Red-legged crow. [ME *choghe* unexpl.; w. forms *c*(*h*)*owe* etc. cf. M Du. *kauwe*, ONF *cauwe*, OF *choue*]

chouse, v.t., & n., (colloq.). Swindle, trick. [usu. supposed to be the same wd as Turk. *chiaus* official messenger, in allusion to one of these who is alleged to have defrauded Turkish merchants in England 1609, but there is some doubt about the account]

chow, n. Dog of a Chinese breed; (sl.) food. [pidgin Eng.]

chow′-chow, n. Chinese preserve of orange-peel, ginger, etc. [pidgin Eng.]

chow′der, n. Newfoundland & New England dish, stew of fresh fish or clams with bacon, onions, biscuit, etc. [app. orig. in Brittany, in phr. *faire la chaudière* supply a pot etc. for cooking a stew of fish etc.]

chrēmatis′t|ic(k-), a. (derog.). Of money-making, economic. Hence —ICS n. [f. Gk *khrēmatistikos* of money-making]

chrēstŏm′athў (k-), n. Collection of choice passages. [f. F -*mathie* or Gk

khrēstomathela f. *khrēstos* useful +-*mathcia* learning]

chri′sm (k-), n. Consecrated oil, unguent, anointing, esp. in sacred rites. [(a) OE *crisma*, ME *crisme*, f. LL *c*(*h*)*risma* f. Gk *khrisma* unction, later *chrism*(*e*) after the L sp.; (b) ME *creme* f. OF *cresme*, mod. F *chrême* (f. same source), became obs. in 17th c.; see CREAM¹]

chris′om (k-), n. (hist.). (In full, ~-*cloth*, -*robe*, etc.) child's white robe at baptism, used as shroud if it died within a month; ~-*child*, in its first month. [a different., pop. pr. of CHRISM]

Christ (k-), n. Messiah or Lord's anointed of Jewish prophecy; (title, now treated as name given to) Jesus as fulfilling this; divine ruler, saviour, inspirer, (esp. *the* or *a* ~); *the* ~-*child*, ~ as a child. Hence ~′HOOD n., ~′LESS, ~′LIKE, ~′LY¹, aa., ~′lèssNESS, ~′likeNESS (-kn-), nn., ~′WARD(S) adv. [OE *crist* = OS, OHG *Krist*, Goth. *Xristus* f. L *Christus* f. Gk *khristos* anointed one(*khriō* anoint) transl. of Heb.; see MESSIAH]

Christ-cross-row, criss-, (kris-kraws-rō), n. (arch.). The alphabet. [*Christ's cross*, a cross before alphabet in horn-books, +ROW (of letters)]

christen (kri′sn), v.t. & i. Admit as Christian by baptism; administer baptism; give name to (person at baptism, or as nickname; ~ *him*, ~ *him John*; also ships, bells, etc., with analogous ceremony). [OE *cristnian* (ME *crist*(*l*)(*n*)*en*) make Christian f. OE *cristen* adj. Christian, f. WG *°cristin* f. L *Christianus* CHRISTIAN]

Christendom (kri′sn-), n. Christians; Christian countries. [OE *cristendom* f. *cristen* adj., see prec., +-DOM]

Christian (kris′tyan), a. & n. (Person) believing in, professing, or belonging to, the religion of Christ (also as adj. of communities); of Christ or his religion; (person) showing character consistent with Christ's teaching, of genuine piety, Christlike, (also as adj. of conduct, feelings, communities, etc.); human (person) as opposed to *brute, brutal*; (sl.) civilized, decent, (person); ~ *burial* (with the ceremonies of the church); ~ *name*, given (as) at baptism, personal name (cf. SURNAME); ~ *era*, reckoned from birth of Christ; ~ *Science, Scientist*, (adherent of) a system of combating disease etc. without medical treatment by mental effect of patient's ~ faith. Hence or cogn. ~IZE (2, 3) v.i. & t., ~ĪZA′TION n., ~LIKE a., ~LY¹·² a. & adv. [16th c., f. L *Christianus* (CHRIST, -IAN), replacing earlier *cristen* adj.; see CHRISTEN]

Christian′ia (k-; -ahn-), n. A turn in skiing, in which the skis are kept parallel (abbr. **Chris′tie**). [~ in Norway (now Oslo)]

Christiān′itў (k-), n. The Christian faith,

doctrines of Christ & his apostles; a Christian religious system; being a Christian, Christian quality or character. [ME *cristianite* replacing (after LL *christianitas*) earlier *cristiente*, *cristente* f. OF *crestiente* f. *crestien* CHRISTIAN; see -TY]

Christie's (krĭs'tĭz), n. A sale-room in London esp. for art sales.

Christmas (krĭs'm-), n. (abbr. *Xmas*). (Also ~-*day*) festival of Christ's birth, 25th Dec., devoted esp. to family reunion & merrymaking, & a quarter-day (*Father* ~, personification of family festivity); (also ~-*tide*) week or more beginning 24th Dec. (~ *eve*); (attrib.) appropriate to ~, as ~ *book, card* (of greeting by post), *number* (of magazine), *present, pudding*; ||~-*box* (cf. BOXING-DAY), money given at ~ to postman etc. in general acknowledgement of indefinite or continuous services; ~-*tree*, evergreen tree set up in room or in the open & hung with candles, presents, etc.; ~ *rose*, white-flowered hellebore blooming Dec.–Feb. Hence ~Y² a. [late OE *Cristes mæsse* (MASS¹)]

Christo- (k-), comb. form of L *Christus* or Gk *Khristos* CHRIST, as ~*phany* (-ŏf²), manifestation of Christ. Hence **Christó-L'ATRY**, **Christo**MAN'IAC (-mā-), **Christó-L'OGY**, **Christŏl'OGIST**, nn., **Christo-LO'GICAL** a.

Chris'tӯ min'strels (k-; -z), n. pl. Negro--song troupe with blacked faces. [E. P. *Christy* (d. 1862), originator]

chrŏm'āte (k-), n. (chem.). A salt of chromic acid. [-ATE¹ (3)]

chromăt'ic (k-), a. 1. Of, produced by, full of bright, colour (~ *printing*, from blocks inked with various colours; ~*s*, science of colour). 2. (mus.). Of, having, notes not included in diatonic scale; ~ *scale*, proceeding by semitones; ~ *semitone*, interval between note & its flat or sharp. Hence **chromăt'ICALLY** adv. [f. L *chromaticus* or Gk *khrōmatikos* (*khrōma* -*atos* colour, -IC)]

chrŏm'atin (k-), n.(biol.). Tissue that can be stained. [as CHROMATO- + -IN]

chrŏm'ato-, **chrŏm'o-**, (k-), comb. forms of Gk *khrōma* -*atos* colour, as in *chromatop'sy*, abnormally coloured vision, *chromophotograph(y)*, photograph(y) in the natural colours, *chrom'osphere*, red gaseous envelope of sun.

chrŏm'atrŏpe (k-), n. Lantern slide of two circular discs, one rotating in front of other, giving kaleidoscopic movement of colours. [irreg. f. prec. + Gk -*tropos* (*trepō* turn)]

chrōme (k-), n. (Also ~ *yellow*) yellow pigment & colour got from chromate of lead; ~ *green, orange, red*, pigments from other compounds of chromium. [F, orig. name of *chromium*, f. Gk *khrōma* colour]

chrŏm'ic (k-), a. Of chromium. [prec. + -IC]

chrŏm'ium (k-), n. (chem.). Metallic ele-

ment. Hence **chrŏm'ATE¹(3)** n. [CHROME + -IUM]

chromo-¹, comb. form of prec.

chromo-². See CHROMATO-.

chrŏm'ograph (k-; -ahf), n., & v.t. (Reproduce with) gelatine copying--apparatus in which aniline dye is used for ink. [CHROMO-², -GRAPH]

chrŏmolith'ograph (-ahf), **chrŏm'ō** (pl. -os), (k-), n. Picture printed in colours from stone. So **chrŏmolithŏG'RAPHER**, **chrŏmolithŏG'RAPHY**, nn., **chrŏm'oli-thoGRAPH'IC** a. [CHROMO-² + LITHOGRAPH]

chrŏm'osŏme (k-), n. (biol.). Rod-like or thread-like structure occurring in the nucleus of animal and plant cells, carrying genetic material. [f. G *chromosom* (CHROMO- + Gk *sōma* body)]

chrŏn'ic (k-), a. Lingering, lasting, inveterate, (of disease, cf. ACUTE; ~ *invalid*, with ~ complaint; also of other states as ~ *doubt, rebellion*); ||(vulg.) bad, intense, severe. Hence **chrŏn'ICALLY** adv., **chrŏni'CITY** n. [f. F *chronique* f. L *chronicus* (in LL of disease) f. Gk *khroni-kos* (*khronos* time, -IC)]

chrŏn'icle (k-), n., & v.t. (Enter, relate, in a) continuous register of events in order of time; *Chronicles*, two books of O.T.; narrative, account; C~, newspaper name. Hence **chrŏn'icler¹** n. [ME *cronikle* f. AF -*icle* var. of OF *cronique* f. LL *chronica* sing. f. L f. Gk *khronika* neut. pl. (prec.); *ch-* after L sp.]

chronique scandaleuse (see Ap.), n. Body of scandalous gossip current at any time & place. [F]

chrŏn'ogrăm (k-), n. Phrase etc. of which the Roman-numeral letters added give a date, as LorD haVe MerCIe Vpon Vs =50 + 500 + 5 + 1000 + 100 + 1 + 5 + 5 = 1666. Hence **chrŏnogrammăt'IO** a. [f. Gk *khronos* time + -GRAM; -*matic* after Gk *grammatikos* adj. f. *gramma*]

chrŏn'ograph (k-; -ahf), n. Instrument recording time with extreme accuracy; stop-watch. Hence **chrŏnoGRAPH'IC** a. [as prec. + -GRAPH]

chron|ŏl'ogӯ (k-), n. Science of computing dates; arrangements of events with dates, table or treatise displaying this. Hence or cogn. ~ŏL'OGER, ~ŏL'OGIST, nn., **chrŏnoLO'GICAL** a., **chrŏnolŏ'gicaLY²** adv., ~ŏl'ogIZE(3) v.t. [as prec. + -LOGY]

chronŏm'ēter (k-), n. Time-measuring instrument, esp. one with complete provision against disturbance by temperature, used for navigation by astronomical sights at sea. [as prec. + -METER]

chronŏm'etrӯ (k-), n. Scientific time--measurement. So **chrŏnoMET'RIC(AL)** aa., **chrŏnomĕt'ricaLY²** adv. [as prec. + -METRY]

chrŏn'oscope (k-), n. Apparatus measuring velocity of projectiles. [as prec. + -SCOPE]

chrӯs- (k-), comb. form of Gk *khrusos* gold, = yellow in chem. & mineral. wds, of gold, golden, yellow, etc., in general wds.

chrys'alis, -id, (k-), n. (pl. *-ises, -ids, chrysăl'ĭdēs*). Form taken by insect in the torpid stage of passive development between larva (caterpillar etc.) & imago (butterfly etc.); case then enclosing it; (fig.) preparatory or transition state. [f. L f. Gk *khrusallis -idos* (*khrusos* gold)]

chrȳsăn'thĕmum (k-), n. (Bot.) genus including corn marigold; (Gardening) cultivated varieties of this brought from Japan & blooming from Sept. to Dec.; *land of the ~,* Japan. [f. L f. Gk *khrusanthemon* (CHRYS-, *anthemon* flower)]

chrȳsĕlĕphăn'tine (k-), a. Overlaid with gold & ivory as by ancient Greek sculptors. [f. Gk *khruselephantinos* (CHRYS-, ELEPHANT, -INE²)]

chrȳso- (k-). = CHRYS-.

chrȳsobĕ'rȳl (k-), n. Yellowish-green gem. [f. L f. Gk *khrusobērullos* (CHRYSO-, BERYL)]

chrȳs'olite (k-), n. (Formerly) green gem of various kinds; (now) olivine. [ME & OF *crisolite* f. (med. L *cri-*) L f. Gk *khrusolithos* (CHRYSO-, *lithos* stone)]

chrȳs'oprāse (k-; -z), n. (N.T.) prob. a golden-green variety of beryl; (now) apple-green variety of chalcedony. [ME *crisopace, -pase* f. OF *-pace* f. L *chrysopassus* var. of L f. Gk *khrusoprasos* (CHRYSO-, *prason* leek)]

chŭb, n. Thick coarse-fleshed river fish of the carp family, dusky green above. [late ME *chubbe*, of unkn. orig.]

chŭbb'|y̆, a. Round-faced, plump. Hence ~**ĭNESS** n. [CHUB+-Y²]

chŭck¹, int., n., & v.i. (Make) call of fowl or person calling fowls or urging horse. [imit.]

chŭck², n. Term of endearment. Hence ~**y³** n. [prob. var. of CHICK]

chŭck³, v.t., & n. Jerk *under the chin* (n. & v.); fling, throw, (n. & v.) with contempt, carelessness, ease, (*the ~,* sl., dismissal, as *give one the ~*); ~ *away,* waste, lose (*chance* etc.); ~ *up the sponge,* give up contest or attempt; ~ *up,* abandon in disgust; ~ *out,* expel (troublesome person) from meeting, music-hall, etc., whence ||~**ER¹-out** n.; (sl.) ~ *it,* cease; ~*-farthing,* kind of quoit game with coins, also pitch and toss. [in 16th c. *chock,* of uncert. orig.; perh. f. F *choquer* to knock]

chŭck⁴, n., & v.t. Contrivance in lathe & the like for holding work to be operated on; (vb) fix (wood etc.) to this. [var. of CHOCK¹]

chŭck⁵, n. (sl.). Food, grub; *hard ~* (Naut.), ship's biscuit; **~-wagon,* provision-cart accompanying pioneers etc. [orig. unkn.]

chŭc'kle, v.i., & n. (Indulge in) suppressed laughter, laugh with closed mouth, (show) signs of glee; exult *over;* (make) hen's call. [f. CHUCK¹, -LE(3)]

chŭc'kle-head (-hĕd), n., **chŭc'kle-headĕd (-hĕd-),** a. Dolt(ish); stupid (fellow). [f. *chuckle* blockish, prob. rel. to CHUCK⁴]

chŭdd'ar, n. (Anglo-Ind.). Large sheet, worn as shawl or head-covering by Indian women. [Hind. *chadar*]

chŭg, n. Characteristic sound of oil-engine or small petrol-engine when running slowly (also as v.i., esp. of exhaust gases). [imit.]

chŭkk'er, chŭkk'a, n. (polo). Each of the periods into which the game is divided. [Hind. *chakar*]

chŭm, v.i. (-mm-), & n. **1.** Occupy rooms together, whence ~**m'ERY(3)** n.; be intimate; ~ *up* (colloq.), form intimacy (*with*). **2.** Familiar friend (esp. now among boys); (Australia) *new ~,* recent immigrant, greenhorn. [from 1684; prob. short for *chamber-fellow* (1580), esp. at Oxford]

chŭmp, n. Short thick lump of wood; || thick end, esp. of loin of mutton (so ~ *chop*); (colloq.) head, || esp. *off* one's ~, mad with excitement etc.; (sl.) fool, blockhead. [mod. form, combining perh. *chunk+lump* etc.]

chŭnk, n. (colloq.). Thick lump cut off (wood, bread, cheese, etc.). [prob. var. of CHUCK⁴]

chupătt'y̆, n. (Anglo-Ind.). Small flat cake of coarse unleavened bread. [Hind. *chapāti*]

church¹, n. Building for public Christian worship, || esp. according to established religion of country; all Christians (*C~ militant,* Christians on earth warring against evil); an organized Christian society of any time (*primitive C~*), country (*C~ of Scotland*), or distinguishing principle (*reformed C~*); *C~ of England,* English or *Anglican C~,* English branch of Western or Latin Church rejecting Pope's supremacy since reformation; *Established C~,* recognized by State, as *C~ of England, Scotland;* organization, clergy & other officers, of a religious society or corporation; clerical profession (*go into the C~,* take holy orders); HIGH, LOW¹, BROAD, ~, parties with different views of doctrine & discipline, whence ~'man, ~'ISM(3), nn.; public worship (*go to, after, ~;* ~*-time;* ~*-goer, -going*); *C~ Army,* C.E. mission to working classes founded by Preb. Carlile in 1882; *C~ Commissioners,* body administering the assets & revenue of *C~* of England; ~'man, ~'woman, ~'manship, member, membership, of ~; *poor as a ~ mouse,* of poor person; ||~*-rate,* levied by vestry for maintenance of parish ~ & its services; ~ *service,* public worship, || book with Common Prayer, proper lessons, etc.; ~*-text,* black letter in monumental inscriptions; ~*ward'en,* elected lay representative of parish (usu. one of two, elected one by incumbent, one by parishioners), ‖ also long clay pipe; ~'yard, enclosed ground in which ~ stands, sometimes used for burial (‖ ~-yard cough, heralding death; fat ~yard, many deaths). Hence~'LESS a., ~'WARD(S) adv. [OE cir(i)ce, OS kirika, OHG kirihha f. WG *kirika f. med. Gk kurikon f. Gk kuriakon (sc. dōma) Lord's (house) f. kurios lord; see KIRK]

church², v.t. Bring (woman) to church to have thanks offered for delivery of child. [f. prec.]

church|ly, a. Obtrusively or intolerantly devoted to church or opposed to dissent. Hence~ifY v.t.,~iness n. [-y²]

churl, n. Person of low birth (gentleman or ~); peasant, boor; ill-bred fellow; cross-grained or niggardly person, whence ~'ish¹ a., ~'ishly² adv., ~'ishness n. [OE ceorl, MLG kerle f. WG *kerl- man, cogn. w. CARL(E)]

churn, n., & v.t. & i. (Agitate milk or cream, produce butter, in) butter-making machine; work this machine; stir (liquid) about, make it froth; (of sea etc.) wash to and fro, foam, seethe; ‖ large milk-can of ~ shape; ~-dash(er), -staff, appliance for agitating milk in ~; a ~ing, amount of butter made at once. [OE cyrin, MDu., MLG kerne, ON kirna f. Gmc *kernjōn]

churr, v.i., & n. (Make) deep trill as of nightjar. [imit., cf. CHIRR]

chut, int. of impatience. [imit.]

chute (shoot), n. Smooth rapid descent of water over slope; sloping channel, slide, with or without water, for conveying things to lower level (also shoot); slope for shooting rubbish down; toboggan--slide. [conflation of F chute fall (of water etc.) w. some senses of SHOOT]

chut'ney (pl. ~s), -nee, n. Hot Indian condiment of fruits, chillies, etc. [f. Hind. chatni]

chyle (kil), n. White milky fluid formed by action of pancreatic juice & bile on chyme. [f. LL chylus f. Gk khulos juice (khu- pour)]

chylo- (ki-), comb. form of Gk khulos CHYLE.

chyme (kim), n. Food converted by gastric secretion into acid pulp. [f. LL f. Gk khumos juice (khu- pour); khumus & khulos, synonyms, were differentiated by Galen]

chym'ist(ry). Old spelling of CHEMIST(RY).

chymo- (ki-), comb. form of Gk khumus CHYME.

cibor'ium, n. (Archit.) canopy, canopied shrine; receptacle for reservation of Eucharist, shaped like shrine, or cup with arched cover. [f. LL f. Gk kibōrion seed-vessel of water-lily. cup so shaped]

cicad'a, cica'la, cīga'la, (-ah-). n. Transparent-winged shrill-chirping insect. [L cicada, It.-cala, F-gale]

cic'atrice, cicāt'rix, n. (-ix, pl. -ῑrĕs, L form in scientific use). Scar of healed wound; scar on tree bark; (Bot.) mark left on stem by fall of leaf etc., hilum of seed. Hence cicatri'ciaL (-shl), cicāt'ricose¹, aa. [ME, f. OF cicatrice or L cicatric- (nom. -ix)]

cicāt'ric(u)le, n. (Biol.) germ of chick, round white spot on yolk, tread; (Bot.) = prec. [f. L cicatricula (prec., -ULE)]

cic'atriz|e, -is|e (-īz), v.t. & i. Heal, skin over, (t. & i.); mark with scars. Hence ~A'TION n. [f. F cicatriser f. LL cicatricare (CICATRICE) w. assim. to -iser, -IZE]

ci'cely, n. Kinds of umbelliferous plant (sweet, wild, rough, ~). [f. L f. Gk seselis SESELI w. assim. to the woman's name (= Cecilia)]

cicerōn'e (sise-, chiche-), n. (pl. -oni pr. -ōnē), & v.t. (Conduct traveller etc. as) guide who understands & explains antiquities etc. [It., f. L Ciceronem nom. -o the Roman orator]

Cicerōn'ian, a. & n. Eloquent, classical, or rhythmical, as Cicero's style; (n.) person learned in or admiring Cicero. Hence ~ISM(3, 4) n. [f. L Ciceronianus (prec., -IAN)]

cicisbeo (chĭchĭzbā'ō), n. (pl. -bei pr. -bāĭ). Recognized gallant of married woman. So cicisbe'ISM(3) n. [It.]

Cid, n. The ~, title (lord) of Ruy Diaz, 11th-c. Christian champion against Moors, & of epic relating his deeds. [Sp., f. Arab. sayyid]

-cide, suf. forming nouns meaning (1) slayer of (F, f. L -cida) or (2) slaughter of (F, f. L -cidium) both f. L caedere kill; taken f. L as parricide, or formed on L nn. as regicide or Gk nn. as dendricide or loc. on E nn. as birdicide.

cid'er, n. Fermented drink from apple--juice; ~-CUP; ~-press, for squeezing juice from apples. [ME & OF sidre f. LL f. Gk sikera f. Heb. shekar strong drink]

ci-devant (see Ap.), a. or adv. Former(ly), that has been (with the earlier name·or state). [F]

cigala. See CICADA.

cigar', n. Roll of tobacco-leaf for smoking; ~-shaped, cylindrical with pointed end(s); ~-holder, mouthpiece holding ~. [f. Sp. cigarro]

cigarĕtte', n. Small cylinder of cut tobacco or of narcotic or medicated substance rolled in paper for smoking. [f. F dim. of cigare, -ETTE]

cil'i|a, n. pl. Eyelashes; similar fringe on leaf, insect's wing, etc.; (Physiol.) hair-like vibrating organs on animal & vegetable tissue, serving many lower water animals for locomotion. Hence ~ARY¹, ~ATE², ~āted, aa., ~A'TION n. [pl. of L cilium eyelash]

cil'ice, n. (Garment of) hair-cloth. [F, or f. L f. Gk kilikion (Kilikia Cilicia); OE cilic f. L]

Cimmē'rian, a. Thick, gloomy, (of darkness, night, etc.). [f. L f. Gk kimmerios (of Cimmerii, people in perpetual night)+-AN]

cinch, n., & v.t. **1.** Saddle-girth used in Mexico etc.; (sl.) sure thing, a certainty. **2.** v.t. Put ~ on. [Sp. *cincha*]

cinchon'a (-kō-), n. Kinds of evergreen tree yielding cinchona bark or Peruvian bark & quinine; the bark, drug made from it & highly esteemed as tonic & febrifuge. Hence cinchonA'CEOUS a., cin'choninE⁵, cin'chonISM(5), nn., cin'chonizE(5) v.t., (-ko-). [Countess of *Chinchon*, introducer of drug in Spain 1640]

Cincinnāt'us, n. Great man in retirement who can be called upon in a crisis. [Roman hero called from plough to dictatorship (5th c. B.C.)]

cinc'ture, n., & v.t. (Surround with or as with a) girdle, belt, fillet, border. [f. L *cinctura* (*cingere* cinct- gird, -URE)]

cin'der, n. Slag; residue of coal, wood, etc., that has ceased to flame (whether cold or not) but has still combustible matter in it; (loosely in pl.) ashes; ~-*path*, running-track laid with fine ~s; ~-*sifter*, for separating ~s from ashes. Hence~Y² a. [OE *sinder*, (= OHG *sintar*, ON *sindr*), w. assim. to the unconnected F *cendre* & L *cinis*]

Cinderĕll'a, n. Person of unrecognized merit or beauty; ~ *dance* or ~, dance closing at twelve o'clock. [allusions to fairy-tale]

cin'ē-, comb. form of CINEMA; so: ~-*camera* (for taking. cinematographic photographs); ~-*film*; ~-*projector*; ~-*variety*, vaudeville entertainment including a cinema show.

cin'ema, n. Cinematograph theatre; *the* ~, cinematography, moving pictures. Hence cinĕmăt'IC a., relating to, having the qualities characteristic of, the ~. [abbr. of foll.]

cinĕmăt'ograph (-ahf), n., & v.t. & i. **1.** Apparatus producing pictures of motion by the rapid projection on a screen of a great number of photographs taken successively on a long film; = prec. **2.** v.t. Make ~ film of (scene), film; (v.i.) use ~. Hence cinĕmătŏgrăph'IC a., -icALLY² adv., cinĕmătŏg'raphy¹ n. [f. F *cinématographe* f. Gk *kinēma -atos* movement (*kineō* move), see -GRAPH]

cinerār'ia, n. Bright-flowered composite plant, grown chiefly under glass. [f. L *cinerarius* of ashes f. *cinis -eris* ashes (ash-coloured down on leaves)]

cinerār'ium n. Recess in which a cinerary urn is deposited. [as prec.]

cin'erary, a. Of ashes (esp. ~ *urn*, holding ashes of dead after cremation). [as prec.]

cinēr'eous, a. Ashen-grey (esp. of birds or plumage). [f. L *cinereus* (*cinis -eris* ashes) + -OUS]

Cingalēse' (-nggalēz), a. & n. See SIN-HALESE.

cing'ulum (-ngg-), n. Belt (used technically in Surg., Anat., Zool., etc.). [L]

cinn'abăr, n. & a. Red mercuric sulphide,

vermilion (n. & a.). [f. L *cinnabaris* f. Gk *kinnabari* f. Oriental source]

cinn'amon, n. & a. (E.-Ind. tree with) aromatic inner bark used as spice; ~-*colour(ed)*, (of) yellowish-brown; ~ *bear*, ~-coloured variety of the common N.-American black bear; ~-*stone*, brown or yellow garnet. Hence or cogn. cinn'a-mATE¹(3) n., cinnamŏm'IC, cinna-mŏn'IC, aa. [ME *cin-*, *sinamome* f. OF *cinnamome* f. L f. Gk *kinnamōmon* f. Semit. (Heb. *qinnamom*); mod. form after later Gk (L) *kinnamon*]

cinque, cinq, (sĭnk), n. The five at dice & cards. [f. OF *cink* f. L *quinque* five]

cinquecen'tō, cinquecen'tist, (chǐnk-wǐ-chē-), nn. Italian style of art, artist, of the 16th c. (15-) with reversion to classical forms. [It. (-*o*, -*ista*) with omission (in It.) of *mil*]

cinq(ue)'foil (sǐnkf-), n. Kinds of plant with compound leaf of five leaflets; (Archit.) five-cusped ornament in circle or arch. [thr. OF f. L *quinquefolium* five-leaf]

Cinque Pŏrts (sĭnk), n. pl. Certain ports (orig. five only) on SE coast with ancient privileges. [ME *sink pors* repr. OF *cink porz*, L *quinque portus* five ports]

ciph'er¹, cȳ-, n. Arithmetical symbol (0) of no value in itself but multiplying number it is placed after, and dividing decimal number it is placed before, by ten; person or thing of no importance; any Arabic figure; secret writing, thing so written, key to it; interlaced initials of person, company, etc., monogram; continued sounding of organ-note owing to defective valve. [ME, f. OF *cyfre* f. Arab. *çifr* ZERO]

ciph'er², cȳ-, v.i. & t. Do arithmetic; work (usu. *out*) by arithmetic, calculate; put into secret writing (cf. DECIPHER); (of organ-note) sound on sounding when not pressed. [f. prec.]

cip'olin, n. Italian white-&-green marble. [F, or f. its source *cipollino* (*cipolla* onion)]

cir'ca, cir'cĭter, prepp. (abbr. *c.* or *circ.*). About (with dates). [L]

Circă'ssian (-shn), a. & n. (Member, language) of a group of tribes of Caucasian race living in the Kuban province of Russia. [f. *Circassia* f. Russ. *Tcherkess*]

Cir'cē, n. Enchantress, temptress. Hence Cîrcē'AN a. [proper name in Gk myth.]

cîr'cinate, a. (bot.). (With leaves) rolled up from apex to base, as in most ferns. [f. L *circinare* make round (*circinus* compasses, -ATE²)]

cîr'cle¹, n. **1.** (Line enclosing) perfectly round plane figure (*square the* ~, find square of same area as given ~, attempt impossibilities; *great, small,* ~ on surface of sphere whose plane passes, does not pass, through sphere's centre; POLAR, ARCTIC, ANTARCTIC, ~); (loosely) roundish enclosure; orbit of planet; ring;

road, railway, etc. whose ends meet, allowing traffic to circulate continuously; curved tier of seats at theatre etc. (*dress* ~, *upper* ~, more & less expensive); (Archaeol.) ring of stones as at Stonehenge; *run round in* ~*s* (colloq.), be fussily busy with little result. 2. Period, cycle, round, (*come full* ~, end at starting--point); circling-feat in gymnastics; complete series. 3. (Logic, often *vicious* ~) fallacy of proving proposition from another that rests on it for proof. 4. Action & reaction that intensify each other (often *vicious* ~). 5. Persons grouped round centre of interest; set, coterie, class, (*first*, *upper*, ~*s*; ~*s in which* one *moves*). 6. Area of influence, action, etc., sphere. Hence ~WISE (-lw-) adv. [ME & OF *cercle* f. L *circulus* dim. of *circus* ring; OE *circul*, & mod. sp., f. L]

cir'cle², v.t. & i. Encompass (poet.); encompass *round, about*; move in a circle *round, about*; (Gym.) revolve round bar in various ways; be passed round (of wine etc.); (Mil.) sweep round on moving flank (of cavalry, cf. WHEEL²); (p.p.) rounded, marked with circles. [ME, f. prec., or OF *cercler*]

cir'clet, n. Small circle; circular band, esp. of gold, jewelled, etc., worn on head or elsewhere. [f. F *cerclet* (CIRCLE¹, -ET)]

circs, n. pl. (colloq.). Circumstances. [abbr.]

cir'cuit (-kit), n. Line enclosing an area, distance round; area enclosed; roundabout journey; sequence of changes, acts, etc.; chain of theatres, cinemas, etc., under a single management; journey of judge in particular district to hold courts, this district (eight in Eng. & Wales), the barristers (*member of a* ~) making the ~; group of local Methodist churches forming a minor administrative unit (*~ rider*, itinerant preacher serving a ~); (Electr.) path of current (*short* ~, faulty shortening of a ~ by defective insulation). [ME, f. OF or L *circuitus* f. CIRCUM(*ire ii-go*)]

circu'itous, a. Roundabout, indirect. Hence ~LY² adv., ~NESS n. [f. LL *circuitosus* (CIRCUIT, -OSE¹)]

cir'cular, a. & n. Round in superficies; moving in a circle (|| ~ *tour*, ending where it began by different route, ~ *ticket*, for this); (Logic) of, using, the *vicious* CIRCLE¹; addressed to a circle of persons, customers, etc. (~ *note*, banker's letter of credit in traveller's favour to several foreign bankers; ~ *letter* or ~, notice, advertisement, etc., reproduced for distribution); of, like, the geometrical circle; ~ *saw*, toothed disc revolving by machinery for sawing. Hence circu-lä'rity n., ~LY² adv. [ME *circuler* f. AF -er (OF -ier) f. LL *circularis* (CIRCLE, -AR¹)]

cir'cularize, **-ise** (-iz), v.t. Send circulars to. [-IZE(1)]

circ'ūlāt|e, v.i. & t. Go round (blood ~es through veins, water in pipes, wine on table, newspaper to circle of readers); (of decimals) = RECUR; send round, give currency to, (book, report, scandal, etc.); ~*ing library*, with books taken by subscribers in succession; ~*ing medium*, notes, gold, etc., used in exchange. [f. L *circulare* (CIRCLE¹), -ATE³]

circūlā'tion, n. Movement of blood from and to heart, similar movement of sap etc.; movement to and fro (~ *of water, atmosphere*, etc.); transmission, distribution, (of news, books, etc.); number of copies sold, esp. of newspapers; currency, coin, etc. [F, or f. L *circulatio* (*circulare* see prec., -ATION)]

cir'culative, a. Inclined to, promoting, circulation. [as prec., -IVE]

cir'culātor, n. One who circulates news, coin, etc. [as prec., -OR; earlier also f. L *circulator* peddler, quack]

cir'culatory, a. Of circulation of blood or sap. [f. L *circulatorius* (as prec., -ORY)]

circum-, pref. = L adv. & prep. *circum* round, about, used (1) adverbially, as *circumvagant* wandering round or about; (2) prepositionally, as *circumocular* surrounding the eye. E wds are some f. L (direct, as *circumscribe*, or thr. F as *circumcise*), & some formed in E on L elements as *circumambient*.

circumăm'bi|ent, a. Surrounding (esp. of air or other fluid). Hence ~ENCY n. [CIRCUM-(1) + AMBIENT]

circumăm'būl|āte, v.t. & i. Walk round (place etc.); walk about; beat about the bush. Hence ~A'TION n., ~ātory a. [f. LL CIRCUM(*ambulare* walk), -ATE³]

circumbĕn'dibus, n. (joc.). Roundabout method; circumlocution. [CIRCUM-(1), BEND, ending of L abl. pl. case]

circ'umcīse (-z), v.t. Cut off foreskin of (as Jewish or Muhammedan rite, or surgically); purify (~ *the heart, passions*, etc.). [ME, f. OF *circonciser*, or *circoncis*-stem of *circoncire*, f. L CIRCUM(*cīdere -cis-* = *caedere* cut)]

circumcī'sion (-izhn), n. Act or rite of, spiritual purification by, circumcising; (Bibl.) *the* ~, the Jews; (Eccl.) festival of C~ of Christ, 1st Jan. Hence ~*ION* n. [ME, f. OF f. LL *circumcisionem* (as prec., -ION)]

circum'ference, n. Encompassing boundary, esp. of figure enclosed by curve, as circle; distance round. So **circum-ferĕn'tiAL** (-shl) a. [ME, f. OF f. L CIRCUM(*ferentia* f. *ferre* bear, -ENCE)]

cir'cumflĕx, a. & n., & v.t. ~ (*accent*), mark (ˆ or ˜ in Gk, ˆ elsewhere) placed over vowel to indicate contraction, length (e.g. *viâ*), or special quality (vb, mark thus); (Anat.) curved, bending round something else, (~ *artery, muscle*, etc.). [f. L CIRCUM(*flexus* p.p. of *flectere* bend) transl. of Gk *perispōmenos*; see PERISPOMENON]

circum'flu|ent (-lŏŏ-), a. Flowing round,

surrounding. Hence ~ENCE n. [f. L CIR-CUM (*fluens* f. *fluere* flow, -ENT)]

circŭm'fluous (-lŏŏ-), a. = prec.; surrounded by water. [f. L CIRCUM*fluus* flowing or flowed round (*fluere* flow) +-OUS]

cĭrcumfū|se' (-z), v.t. Pour (fluid) *about* or *round* (object); surround, bathe, (object *with*, or of fluid as subj.). So ~'SION (-zhn) n. [f. L CIRCUM(*fundere fus-*pour)]

cĭrcum|gy̆r'āte, v.i. Turn, wheel, travel, round. Hence ~gy̆rA'TION n. [CIRCUM-(1) +GYRATE]

cĭrcumjā'cent, a. Situated around. [f. L CIRCUM(*jacent-* part. st. of *jacēre* lie)]

cĭrcumlitt'oral, a. Bordering the shore. [CIRCUM-(2) +L *lit(l)us -oris* shore +-AL]

cĭrcumlocū'tion, n. Use of many words where few would do; evasive talk; a roundabout expression; C~ *Office*, dilatory Government office. Hence ~AL, ~ARY[1], (-shon-), cĭrcumlŏc'ūtory, aa., ~IST(1) (-shon-) n. [F, or f. L CIRCUM-(*locutio* LOCUTION)]

cĭrcumnăv'igāt|e, v.t. Sail round (esp. *the globe* or *world*). Hence ~OR n. [f. L CIRCUM (*navigare* NAVIGATE)]

cĭrcumnut'āte, v.i. (bot.). Bend towards all points of compass successively (of growing parts of plant). Hence ~A'TION n. [CIRCUM-(1), NUTATE]

cĭrcumpōl'ar, a. (Astron.) ~ *star, motion,* etc., above horizon throughout diurnal course; (Geog.) about, near, one of the earth's poles. [CIRCUM-(2), L *polus* POLE[2], -AR[1]]

cĭrc'umscrībe, v.t. Draw line round; (Geom.) describe (figure) round another touching it at points, but not cutting it; lay down limits of, confine, restrict; define logically; sign (round robin), whence cĭrcumscrīb'ER[1] n. [f. L CIR-CUM(*scribere script-* write)]

cĭrcumscrip'tion, n. Having, marking out, or imposing, of limits; boundary; limited district; definition; (Geom.) circumscribing (see prec.); inscription round coin etc. [f. L *circumscriptio* (prec.), -ION]

cĭrcumsōl'ar, a. Revolving round, being near, the sun. [CIRCUM-(2), SOL[1], -AR[1]]

cĭrc'umspĕct, a. Cautious, wary, taking everything into account. Hence or cogn. cĭrcumspĕc'tion, ~NESS, nn., ~IVE a., ~LY[2] adv. [f. L CIRCUM(*spicere speci-* = *specere* look)]

cĭrc'umstance, n. 1. (pl.). Time, place, manner, cause, occasion, etc., surroundings, of an act; external conditions affecting or that might affect an agent (*in, under, the ~s*, owing to or making allowance for them; *under no ~s*, not whatever happens, never); material welfare (*in good, bad, easy, reduced, straitened, ~s*). 2. (sing.). Full detail in narrative; ceremony, fuss, (*without ~, unceremoniously; pomp & ~*); incident, occurrence, fact (esp. *the ~ that*). Hence

cĭrc'umstancED[2] (-st) a. [ME f. OF, or f. L CIRCUM(*stantia* f. part. of *stare* stand)]

cĭrcumstăn'tial (-shl), a. Depending on subordinate details (~ *evidence*, establishing the doubtful main fact by inference from known facts otherwise hard to explain); adventitious, incidental; with many details (~ *story*). Hence cĭrcumstăntiāl'ITY (-shĭ-) n., ~LY[2] (-shal-) adv. [as prec. +-AL]

cĭrcumvăll'āte, v.t., cĭrcumvallā'tion, n. (Surround with) rampart or entrenchment; process of doing this. [f. L CIRCUM(*vallare* f. *vallum* rampart), see -ATE[3], -ATION]

cĭrcum|vĕnt', v.t. Entrap; overreach, outwit. So ~vĕn'tion n. [f. L CIRCUM-(*venire vent-* come)]

cĭrcumvolū'tion (-lŏŏ-), n. Rolling round; coil; period; sinuous movement. [f. L CIRCUM(*volvere volut-* roll), -ION]

cĭrc'us, n. Rounded or oval arena lined with tiers of seats for equestrian & other exhibitions; amphitheatre of hills; || open circle with streets converging on it; travelling show of horses, riders, etc. [L, = ring]

cĭrque (-k), n. Arena, natural amphitheatre, (chiefly poet. & rhet.). [F, f. L as prec.]

cirrhō'sis (sĭrō-), n. Disease of liver, chiefly alcoholic. [Gk *kirrhos* tawny, -OSIS]

cĭrri-, cĭrro-, comb. form of CIRRUS. Hence cĭrrĭf'EROUS, cĭ'rrĭFORM, aa., & names of cloud-forms as *cirro-cŭm'ulus*. [-I-, -O-]

cĭ'rripĕd, -ēde, n. Marine animal in valved shell attached to other bodies, with legs like curl of hair. [f. F CIRRI(*pede* f. L *pes pedis* foot)]

cĭ'rrus, n. (pl. *-rī*). (Bot.) tendril; (Zool.) slender appendage, as beard of fishes, feet of cirripeds; (Meteor.) form of cloud with diverging filaments like lock of hair or wool. Hence cĭrrōse'[1], cĭ'rrous, aa. [L, = curl]

cĭs-, pref.=on this side of, opp. to *trans-* or *ultra-*, retaining in some orig. L wds the Roman sense (*cispadane, cisalpine,* S. or Rome-wards of Po, Alps), but usu. w. ref. to speaker's or majority's position (*cismontane*, N. of Alps or non-Italian; *cis-Leithan*, W. of Leitha, Austrian, non--Hungarian; *cis-pontine*, in London, on northern or better-known side of bridges or Thames); prefixed to the adj. form of the second element; often used in wds made for the nonce in opposition to wds in *trans-* or *ultra-* (*transatlantic & cisatlantic*); also of time as *cis-Eliza-bethan.* [L prep.]

*ciss'y̆, sĭ-, n. (sl.). Effeminate person. [ult. f. SISTER]

cist, n. (archaeol.). Prehistoric stone or hollowed-tree coffin; round receptacle used esp. for sacred purposes. [f. L f. Gk *kistē* box]

Cister'cian (-shn), n. & a. (Monk) of order founded 1098 at Cistercium or Citeaux, stricter offshoot of Benedictines, also called *Bernardine* as patronized by St Bernard of Clairvaux. [·AN]

cis'tern, n. Reservoir for storing water, esp. one on upper storey or level with pipes supplying taps on lower levels (also fig., of pond). [f. OF *cisterne* f. L *cisterna* (*cista* see CIST) cf. *caverna*]

cis'tus, n. Kinds of shrub with large white or red flowers. [f. L f. Gk *kistos*]

cit, n. (arch.). Citizen (usu. in derogatory sense). [abbr. of *citizen*]

cit'adel, n. Fortress, esp. one guarding or dominating city; last retreat of hard--pressed party, belief, etc. [f. F *citadelle* f. It. *cittadella* dim. of *cittade* f. L *civitatem* CITY]

cite, v.t. Summon to appear in law-court; quote (passage, book, author) in support of a position; mention as example. Hence or cogn. **cit'ABLE** a., **cīta'tion** n., (also) *mention in an official dispatch. [f. F *citer* f. L *citare* f. *ciĕre* set moving]

cith'er, n. (arch. or poet.) = foll. [f. F *cithare* or G *zither*; see foll.]

cith'ern, **citt'ern**, n. (arch. or poet.). Wire-stringed lute-like instrument usu. played with plectrum. [16th c. Eng. form, w. assim. to GITTERN, of L *cithara*, Gk *kithara* harp]

cit'izen, n. Burgess, freeman, of city; townsman; *civilian; member, native or naturalized, of a State (usu. *of*; ~ *of the world*, cosmopolitan); inhabitant of. Hence ~HOOD, ~RY, ~SHIP, nn. [ME *cilesein* f. AF alt. (perh. after DENIZEN) of OF *citeain* (CITY, ·AN)]

citôle', n. (hist.). = CITHERN. [ME, OF, app. as CITHERN with dim. ending]

citr-, comb. form of foll. Hence **cit'rATE¹** (3) n.

cit'ric, a. (chem.). Of citron (esp. ~ *acid*). [f. F *citrique* f. L *citrus* CITRON + ·IC]

cit'rine, a. Lemon-coloured. [ME & OF *citrin* f. LL *citrinus* (CITRON, ·INE¹)]

citro-. = CITR-.

cit'ron, n. (Tree bearing) lemon-like but larger, less acid, & thicker-skinned fruit. [F, f. L *citrus*, after *limon* LEMON]

citronĕll'a, n. Fragrant ethereal oil obtained from a tropical grass, used for keeping insects away. [mod. L, as CITRON]

Cit'rus, n. The genus including the citron, lemon, lime, orange, etc. [L]

cittern. See CITHERN.

cit'y̆, n. (Loosely) important town; || (strictly) town created city by charter, esp. as containing cathedral (but not all cathedral towns are cities, nor vice versa); *municipal corporation occupying a definite area; ~ *of* REFUGE; *Holy* C~, Jerusalem, Heaven; *Eternal* C~, C~ *of the Seven Hills*, Rome; *Celestial* C~, *Heavenly* C~, C~ *of God*, Paradise; || *the*

C~, part of London governed by Lord Mayor & Corporation, business part of this, commercial circles, || (*C~ man*, in commerce or finance; *C~ article*, in newspaper on these; *C~ Company*, corporation representing ancient trade-guild); *C~ editor*, one who deals with the financial news of a daily or weekly journal; ~ *state*, a city that is also an independent sovereign state. Hence (-)**cĭtiED²** (-tĭd), ~LESS, aa., ~WARD(s) adv. [ME *cite* f. OF f. L *civitatem* (*civis* citizen, ·TY)]

civ'ĕt, n. (Also ~-*cat*) carnivorous quadruped between fox & weasel in size & look; strong musky perfume got from anal glands of this. [f. F *civette* ult. f. Arab. *zabad*]

civ'ic, a. Of, proper to, citizens (~ *crown*, oak-garland, Roman honour to one who saved fellow-citizen's life in war); of city, municipal (~ *guard*, policeman, -men, in Eire); of citizenship, civil, (~ *virtues*, *activity*), whence **civ'ics** n. Hence **civ'icALLY** adv. [f. L *civicus* (*civis* citizen, ·IC)]

civ(v)ies (-vĭz), n. pl. (sl.). Civilian clothes. [abbr.]

civ'il, a. 1. Of gregarious men (~ *society*, *life*); of a citizen community (~ *institutions*; ~ *war*, confined to this, between fellow-citizens, *The C~ War*, in Engl., between Charles I & Parliament, in U.S., War of Secession); ~ *disobedience* (India), refusal to pay taxes, obey laws, etc., as part of a political campaign; of, becoming, a citizen (~ *rights*, *liberty*; ~ *spirit*). 2. Polite, obliging, not rude, whence (with pl. = favours) **civil'ITY** n. 3. Not naval, military, etc. (~ *defence*, civilian organization for dealing esp. with air raids; ~ ENGINEER¹; *C~ Service*, all non--warlike branches of State administration, *C~ Servant*, member of one of them). 4. Not ecclesiastical (~ *magistrates*, & formerly ~ *law*; ~ *marriage*, solemnized as ~ contract without religious ceremony). 5. Not criminal (~ *law*, concerning questions of private rights merely). 6. Not natural or astronomical (~ *day*, *year*, as recognized for dating etc.). 7. *C~ Law*, Roman law (so D.C.L.; & see above); || ~ *list*, Parliamentary allowance for sovereign's household & royal pensions. Hence ~LY² adv. [F, f. L *civilis* (*civis* citizen, ·IL)]

civil'ian (-yan), n. & a. (Person) not in or of navy or army or air force. Hence ~IZE(3) v.t., convert (Service post) into a ~ one, ~IZA'TION n. [f. CIVIL + ·IAN; earlier (ME) 'one learned in Civil Law' f. OF *civilien*]

civiliza'tion, -is- (-ĭz-), n. Making or becoming civilized; stage, esp. advanced stage, in social development; civilized States. [f. foll. + ·ATION]

civ'ilize, -ise (-īz), v.t. Bring out of barbarism, enlighten, refine; ~*e away*, get rid of (barbarous habits etc.). Hence

~ABLE a., ~ER¹ n. [f. F *civiliser*, see CIVIL, -IZE(3)]

Civv'ỹ Street, n. (sl.), Civilian life. [abbr.]

clǎck, n., & v.i. 1. Sharp sound as of boards struck together; flap-valve in pumps etc.; clatter of tongues. 2. v.i. Chatter loudly; make sound as of clogs on stone. [ME *clack* to chatter, prate prob. f. ON *klaka* chatter, twitter; of imit. orig.; cf. OHG *klecken*, Du. *klakken*, F *claquer*.]

clad. See CLOTHE.

clǎd(o)-, comb. form of Gk *klados* young shoot, in bot. terms as *cladocarp'ous* with fruit on lateral branchlets.

claim¹, v.t. Demand as one's due (recognition etc., *to* be, *that* one should be, recognized etc.); represent oneself as having (~ *the victory, accuracy*); profess *to* (be the owner, *have told* the truth); demand recognition of the fact that; contend, assert; (of things) deserve (esp. *attention*). Hence ~'ABLE a., ~'ANT(1) n. [ME, f. OF *claim*-, tonic stem of *clamer* f. L *clamare* call out]

claim², n. Demand for something as due (*lay* ~ *to*); right, title, *to* thing, right to make demand *on* person; (Mining etc.) piece of land allotted; *~-jumper*, one who appropriates a mining ~ already taken by another. [ME, f. OF *claime* f. *clamer* see prec.]

clairvoy'ance, n. Faculty of seeing mentally what is happening or exists out of sight; exceptional insight. [F, f. *clairvoyant* (-ANCE, -ANT) f. *clair* CLEAR + part. of *voir* see]

clairvoy'ant, n. (occas. fem. *-te*), & a. (Person) having clairvoyance. [F, = clear-sighted, see prec.]

clǎm¹. var. of CLAMP¹ in tech. senses. [ME f. OE *clam* bond, fetter = OHG *klamma* (G dial. *klamm*), also MHG, G *klemme*, f. Gmc *klam*- press or squeeze together]

clǎm². n. Various bivalve shellfish, esp. the N.-Amer. hard or round, & soft or long, ~, used for food. [16th c. ~*-shell*, app. f. prec.]

clǎm'ant, a. Noisy, insistent; urgent. [f. L *clamare* cry out, -ANT]

clǎm'ber, v.i., & n. Climb with hands & feet; climb with difficulty or labour. [prob. f. *clamb* (obs. past tense of CLIMB) + -ER²; cf. obs. (16–17th c.) *climber*]

clǎmm'|ỹ, a. Moist, usu. cold, & sticky or slimy (of the hand, ill-baked bread, any surface). Hence ~iLY² adv., ~iNESS n. [f. obs. or dial. *clam* (vb smear, adj. 'clammy') + -Y²; (of things) OE *clām* clay]

clǎm'our (-mer), n., & v.i. & t. Shout(ing); (make) loud appeal, complaint, or demand (abs., or *for*, *against*, *to* do; also as v.t., ~ *down*, silence, ~ *out of*, *into*, force by ~); (make) confused noise. So clǎm'orous a., clǎm'orousLY² adv. [ME, f. OF f. L *clamorem* (*clamare* CLAIM¹)]

clǎmp¹, n., & v.t. (also *clam* in some tech-

nical uses of n.). 1. Brace, clasp, or band, usu. of iron, for strengthening other materials or holding things together; various appliances or tools with opposite sides connected by screw for holding or compressing. 2. v.t. Strengthen, fasten together, with ~ or ~s. [14th c., prob. f. MDu., MLG *klamp*(e), alt. f. same root as CLAM¹]

clǎmp², n., & v.t. 1. Pile (of bricks for burning, potatoes etc. under straw & earth, turf, peat, garden rubbish, etc.). 2. v.t. Pile (bricks etc.) *up*. [16th c., f. Du. *klamp* heap, in brick-making]

clǎn, n. Scottish Highlanders with common ancestor, esp. while under patriarchal control (~*s'man*, member, fellow member, of ~); tribe; family holding together, whence ~n'ISH¹ a., ~n'ishLY² adv., ~n'ishNESS n.; party, coterie; genus, species, class. [f. Gael. *clann* f. L PLANT*a*]

clǎndés'tine, a. Surreptitious, secret. Hence ~LY³ (-nl-) adv. [f. L *clandestinus* (*clam* secretly)]

clǎng, n., & v.i. & t. Loud resonant metallic sound (esp. of trumpet, arms, large bell, some birds); (vb) make, cause (thing) to make, this. [imit., but infl. by L *clangere* resound, *clangor* (of trumpets, birds)]

clǎng'our (-ngger), n. Succession, prevalence, of clanging noises. Hence clǎng'orous a., clǎng'orousLY² adv., (-ngg-). [f. L *clangor* (prec., -OR)]

clǎnk, n., & v.i. & t. Sound as of heavy chain rattling; (vb) make, cause (bucket, chain, etc.) to make, this. [imit.; cf. CLANG, CLINK, Du. *klank*]

clǎn'ship, n. The clan system; division into mutually jealous parties; devotion to a leader. [-SHIP]

clǎp¹, n. Explosive noise (of thunder, of hand-palms struck together); slap, pat, (arch.). [ME, app. f. foll.]

clǎp², v.i. & t. (-pp-). ~ one's *hands*, ~ (*t*. & *i*.), applaud by striking palms together loudly (also, usu. w. *hands*, strike them for warmth, as signal etc.); flap (wings) audibly; ~ *on the back*, slap so in encouragement or congratulation; put, place, quickly or energetically (spurs *to* horse, person *in* prison, duty *on* goods; ~ *on all sail*; ~ *up peace, bargain*, make hastily or carelessly; ~ *eyes on*, catch sight of, esp. w. neg.); ~*-net*, fowler's or entomologist's, shut by pulling string. [ME *clappe*(n), OE *clappian*, OHG *klapfon*, ON *klappa* f. Gmc *klapp*- of imit. orig.]

clǎp³, n. (not in decent use). Venereal disease, gonorrhoea. [orig. uncert.; cf. OF *clapoir*, obs. Du. *klapoore* bubo]

*clǎp'board (-bōrd), n. = WEATHER-*board*. [anglicized f. LG *klapphołt* cask-stave]

clǎpp'er, n. Tongue or striker of bell; hand or wind rattle for scaring birds. [CLAP² + -ER¹]

clăpp′erclaw, v.t. (arch.). Scratch & hit; abuse, criticize spitefully. [prec., CLAW]

clăp′trăp, n. & a. Language, sentiment, meant to catch applause; showy. [CLAP¹, TRAP]

claque (-ahk), **claqueur′** (-kêr′), nn. Hired body of applauders, hired applauder. [F]

clă′rabĕlla (-ahr-), n. Fluty organ-stop. [f. L clarus clear, bellus pretty]

clă′rence, n. Four-wheeled close carriage with seats for four inside & two on box, four-wheeler cab. [Duke of C~ (William IV)]

Clă′renc(i)eux (-sū), n. Second KING¹ of Arms. [AF (-ceux), f. Clarence (Clare in Suffolk), dukedom of Lionel son of Edw. III]

clă′rendon, a. & n. (typog.). Thick-faced (type), **thus,** of various sizes.

clă′ret, n. & a. Kinds of red French wine imported from Bordeaux (usu. blends of light wine with Benicarlo); (sl.) blood (*tap* one's ~, make his nose bleed with blow of fist); ~-colour(ed), reddish--violet; artificial salmon-fly so coloured; ~-CUP¹. [ME, f. OF (vin) claret (orig. of wines of light red colour) f. clair CLEAR]

clă′rify, v.t. & i. Make clear (obscure subject, mind, sight); free from impurities, make transparent, (liquid, butter, air, etc.); become transparent (lit., & fig. of literary style etc.). Hence **clărific-**A′TION n. [ME, f. OF clare-, clarifier or LL clarificare (clarus CLEAR, -FY)]

clă′rinĕt (also -ĕt′), n. Wood-wind instrument with single-reed mouthpiece, holes, & keys; organ-stop of like quality. So **clărinĕtt′ist(3)** n. [f. F clarinette dim. of clarine kind of bell]

clă′rion, n. & a. Shrill narrow-tubed trumpet formerly used in war; rousing sound; organ-stop of ~ quality; (adj.) clear & loud. [ME clarion, -ioun, var. of OF claron (ult. f. L clarus CLEAR, see -OON), cf. med. L clario(n-), claro(n-)]

clărionĕt′, n. = CLARINET. [alt. f. CLARINET, after CLARION]

clă′rity, n. Clearness. [ME & OF clarte f. L claritatem (clarus clear, -TY)]

clărk′ia, n. Kinds of plant with showy flowers. [W. Clarke, U.S. explorer, -IA¹]

clăr′y, n. Kind of pot-herb. [15th c. clary, somehow repr. med. L sclarea whence OE slarege, -ie]

clăsh, v.i. & t., & n. (Make) loud broken sound as of collision, striking weapons, cymbals, bells rung together; encounter, conflict, (v.i., & n.); disagree(ment); be at variance with; colours ~, are discordant; rush or charge (vb) into, against, upon; ring (bells) all together. [imit.; cf. clack, crack, crash]

clasp¹ (-ah-), n. Contrivance of interlocking parts for fastening, buckle, brooch; metal fastening of book-cover; embrace, reach; grasp, handshake; bar of silver on medal-ribbon with name of occasion (in campaign commemorated by medal) at which wearer was present; ~-knife, folding, with catch fixing blade when open. [ME clasp, clapse, etym. unkn.; cf. hasp, (hapse)]

clasp² (-ah-), v.t. & i. Fasten (clasp); fasten (t. & i.) with or as clasp; encircle, hold closely; embrace; grasp (another's hand; ~ hands, shake hands emotionally; make common cause; ~ one's hands, interlace fingers). [partly f. prec.; w some senses cf. grasp, grip, clasp, CLIP¹]

clas′per (-ah-), n. In vbl senses: esp. (pl.) appendages of some male fish & insects for holding the female. [-ER¹]

class (-ah-), n., & v.t. 1. Rank, order, of society (higher, upper, middle, lower, working, ~es; the~es, the rich or educated, opp. the masses); ~-con′scious(ness), esp. realizing & taking part in the conflict between the labouring & other ~es; caste system. 2. Set of students taught together, their time of meeting, their course of instruction, *all college students of same standing, (~-fellow, -mate, present or past member of same ~ with one; ~-book, used by ~; ~-room, where ~ is taught). 3. (In foreign armies) all the recruits of a year (the 1960 ~). 4. ‖ Division of candidates after examination (take a ~, gain honours; so ~′man opp. to pass-man; ‖~-list, issued by examiners). 5. Division according to quality (so high, low, first, second, etc., ~, as adjj. of praise or depreciation, & first, second, ~, of railway carriages etc.; no ~, sl., quite inferior). 6. Number of individuals having common name as like in any respect. 7. (Nat. Hist.) highest division (~, order, family, genus, species) of animal, vegetable, or mineral kingdom. 8. Distinction, high quality (also attrib.). 9. v.t. Place in a ~; hence ~′ABLE a. [f. F classe f. L classis assembly]

clăss′ic, a. & n. 1. Of the first class, of allowed excellence; of the standard ancient Latin & Greek authors, art, or culture; of Latin & Greek antiquity; in the ~ style, simple, harmonious, proportioned, & finished (cf. ROMANTIC); having literary associations (~ ground); ‖~ races, Two & One Thousand Guineas, Derby, Oaks, St Leger. 2. n. Writer, artist or work, example, of admitted excellence; ancient Greek or Latin writer; Latin and Greek scholar; follower of ~ models (cf. ROMANTIC); (pl.) classical studies. [f. F classique or L classicus; see -IC]

clăss′ical, a. Standard, first-class, esp. in literature; of ancient Greek or Latin standard authors or art; learned in these; based on these (~ education); in, following, the restrained style of ~ antiquity (as prec., cf. ROMANTIC). Hence ~ISM(3), ~ITY (-ăl²), nn., ~LY² adv. [f. L classicus +-AL]

clăss′icism, -ĭst, nn. Following, follower,

of classic style; classical scholar(ship); advocacy, advocate. of classical education; (-*ism*) a Latin or Greek idiom. [-ISM(3, 4), -IST(2, 3)]

cläs′icize, -ise (-īz), v.t. & i. Make classic; imitate the classical style. [-IZE (2, 3)]

clässico-, comb. form of L *classicus* w. senses of CLASSIC. Hence **clässicŏl′ATRY** n.

cläss′if|ȳ, v.t. Arrange in classes; assign to a class; ~*ied*, *officially designated as secret*. So ~**īABLE**, ~**īcĀtory**, aa., ~**īcA′tion**, ~**īER¹**, nn. [f. L CLASSIS+-FY]

class′ȳ (-ah-), a. (sl.). Superior. [-Y²]

cläs′tic, a. (geol.). Composed of broken pieces of older rocks; ~ *rocks*, conglomerates etc. [f. Gk *klastos* (*klaŏ* break)]

clätt′er, v.i. & t., & n. (Make) dry confused sound as of many plates struck together; (resound with) noisy talk; ~ *along*, *down*, etc., move, fall, with a ~; (v.t.) cause (plates etc.) to ~. [ME *clater*, OE **clatrian*, of imit. orig.; cf. Du. *klateren*]

clause (-z), n. Short sentence; (Gram.) distinct member of a sentence including subject & predicate; single proviso in treaty, law, or contract. [ME, f. OF f. med. L *clausa* = L *clausula* conclusion (*claudere claus-* shut, -ULE)]

claus′tral, a. Of the cloister, monastic, narrow. [f. LL *claustralis* (CLOISTER, -AL)]

claustrophŏb′ia, n. Morbid dread of closed places. [f. L *claustrum* (see CLOISTER)+-PHOBIA]

cläv′āte, a. (bot.). Club-shaped. [f. L *clava* club +-ATE²]

cläv′ĭchŏrd (-k-), n. Predecessor of piano, first string-instrument with keyboard. [f. med. L *clavichordium* (L *clavis* key, CHORD¹)]

cläv′icle, n. Collar-bone. So **clavic′ŭlAR¹** a. [f. L *clavicula* dim. of *clavis* key]

cläv′ifŏrm, a. Club-shaped. [L *clava*, -FORM]

claw¹, n. Pointed horny nail of beast's or bird's foot (*pare*, *cut*, *the ~s of*, disarm); foot so armed, pincers of shellfish; (contempt.) hand; contrivance for grappling, holding, etc. (~*-hammer*, with bent split end for extracting nails; ~*-hammer coat*, dress coat). Hence (-)**clawED²** (-awd) a. [OE *clawu* f. obl. cases of *clēa* (whence dial. *clee*), with OS *clāuua*, OHG *klāwa* f. Gmc **klawŏ*, **klǣwŏ*]

claw², v.t. & i. Scratch, tear, seize or pull towards one, with claws or hands (~ *me & I'll ~ thee*, of mutual flattery f. obs. sense, still Sc., *scratch gently*); (Naut.) beat to windward, esp. ~ *off*, away from shore. [OE *clawian*, OHG *klāwen*, f. prec.]

clay, n. Stiff tenacious earth, material of bricks, pottery, etc.; (material of) human body (*wet*, *moisten*, one's ~, drink); (also ~ *pipe*) tobacco-pipe made of ~ (*yard of ~*, long one); ~*-cold*, cold as ~ (usu. of

the dead). Hence (with *-e-* to separate *yy*, & comp. *more*, *most*) ~*eY²* a. [OE *clæg*, (M) Du., (M)LG *klei*, f. Gmc **klai-* (whence OE *clām* clay; see CLAMMY), **klei-*, **kli-* to stick, cogn. w. Gk *gloios*, L *glus*, *gluten*]

clay′mŏre, n. Ancient Scottish two-edged broadsword; (incorrectly) basket-hilted often single-edged broadsword introduced in 16th c. [f. Gael. *claidheamh mŏr* great sword]

clean¹, a. **1.** Free from dirt, unsoiled, clear, (land of weeds, ship of barnacles, paper of writing, printing-proof of corrections; ~ BILL¹; ~ *hands*, ~*-handed*, ~*-handedness*, innocence, innocent; ~*-fingered*, unbribed; ~ *slate*, fig., freedom from all commitments; ~ *tongue*, abstinence from foul talk; ~ BREAST¹; *come* ~ sl., own up, confess everything; *show a ~ pair of heels*, escape by speed; ~*-bred*, thoroughbred); (Bibl.) free of ceremonial defilement or of disease; (of beasts etc.) fit for food (esp. ~ *fish*, not at or soon after spawning). **2.** Hostile to dirt (~ *servant*), cleanly. **3.** Well-formed, shapely, (joints, figure, so ~*-limbed*; ~ *ship*, with tapering lines). **4.** Smart, adroit, not bungling, (~ *fielding*). **5.** Even, unobstructed, clear-cut, complete, (~ *sweep*, complete riddance; ~ *timber*, without knots). **6.** Free from impropriety, esp. *keep it* ~ (colloq.). Hence ~′NESS n. [OE *clǣne*, OS *klēni*, OHG *kleini* f. WG **klain-*, perh. f. **klai-* CLAY]

clean², adv. Completely, right, outright, altogether, simply, absolutely, (~ *gone*, ~ *bowled*, *cut ~ through*, ~ *mad*, ~ *wrong*); ~*-cut*, sharply outlined. [OE *clǣne* adv. f. prec.]

clean³, v.t., & n. **1.** Make clean (*of* dirt etc.); empty (one's plate); make *oneself*, make oneself, become, clean (also ~ *up*); ~ *up*, put things tidy, put (things) tidy, clear (mess) away, (colloq.) acquire as gain or profit; ~ *out*, empty, strip, (esp. sl., person of his money); ~ *down*, ~ *by* brushing or wiping; hence ~′ABLE a., (-)~′ER¹(1, 2), n. **2.** n. ~*ing* (*give it a* ~). [f. CLEAN¹]

clean′lȳ¹, adv. In clean way. [OE *clǣnlíc* (CLEAN¹+-LY²)]

clean′l|ȳ² (-ĕn-), a. Habitually clean, attentive to cleanness. Hence ~**ĬLY²** adv., ~**ĬNESS** n., (-ĕn-). [OE *clǣnlíc* (CLEAN¹+-LY¹)]

cleanse (-ĕnz), v.t. Make clean (now formal or arch. for *clean* in lit. sense); purify (*of* sin etc., or with *sin* etc. as obj.); (Bibl.) cure (leper etc.). [OE *clǣnsian* (*clǣne* CLEAN¹)]

clear¹, a. & adv. **1.** Unclouded, transparent, not turbid, lustrous, unspotted, (so ~*-starch* v.t., ~ *starch* weil*; ~ *conscience*, feeling that one is innocent); distinct, unambiguous, intelligible, not confused, manifest, (*in* ~, not in cipher or code); discerning, penetrating, (so ~-

-sighted, ~*-sightedness*, usu. fig.); confident, decided, certain, (*on point, of fact, that*); easily audible; without deduction; net; rid *of*; complete (*three ~ days*); open, unobstructed, (*coast is ~*, no one about to see or interfere); unengaged, free, unencumbered by debt. 2. adv. Clearly (*speak loud & ~*; well defined; *show, shine*, ~); quite (~ *away, off, out, through*; *three feet ~*); apart, without contact, (*stand, hang, steer, get,* ~). [ME & OF *cler* (F *clair*) f. L *clarus*]

clear², v.t. & i. Make, become, clear (*of*; ~ *the air*, lit. of sultriness, fig. of suspicion, constraint, sulks, etc.; ~ one's *throat*, by slight coughing); show or declare innocent (*of*); free from or of obstruction (~ *the decks for action*, make ready to fight; ~ *land*, cut down trees etc. before cultivating); remove (obstruction, esp. ~ *out of the way*); melt away (also sl. of persons, go away); empty, become empty; pass over or by without touching (esp. in jumping, ~ *6 ft, 22 ft, a gate*); (Naut.) free (ship) by paying all dues, (intr. of ship) sail; defray (prospective charges) by single payment; make (sum) as net gain; ~ *away*, remove, remove meal from table, (of mist etc.) disappear; ~ *off*, get rid of, melt away, (of intruders) go away; ~ *out*, empty, make off; ~ *up*, solve (mystery), make tidy, (of weather etc.) grow clear. [ME, f. prec.]

clear'ance, n. Making clear; removal of obstructions; passing of cheques through Clearing-House; (certificate of) clearing of ship at Custom-House; permit to leave government employ; (Mech.) space allowed for the passing of two parts; ‖ ~ *sale* (held to effect ~ of superfluous stock). [prec. + -ANCE]

clear'côle, n., & v.t. (Paint with) size and whiting or white-lead as first coat in house-painting. [f. F *claire colle* clear glue]

clear'ing, n. In vbl senses; esp.; piece of land in primeval forest cleared for cultivation; *C~ Hospital*, field hospital for temporary reception and treatment of sick and wounded; *C~House*, banker's institution in London at which cheques & bills are exchanged, the balances only being paid in cash; ~*-house* fig., agency for collecting & distributing. [CLEAR², -ING¹]

clear'ly, adv. Distinctly to, with, senses or mind; manifestly; undoubtedly, (in answers) yes, no doubt. [CLEAR¹, -LY²]

clear'ness, n. Transparence; distinctness to, of, senses or mind; freedom from obstruction. [CLEAR¹, -NESS]

cleat, n. Wedge; projecting piece bolted on spar, gangway, etc., to give footing or prevent rope from slipping; piece of wood or iron bolted on for fastening ropes to. [OE *clēat*, cogn. w. OHG *klōz* lump, Du. *kloot* ball, f. WG *klaut-*; see CLOT]

cleav'age, n. Way in which thing (mineral, party, opinion, State) tends to split (esp. *lines, planes, of* ~). [foll. + -AGE]

cleave¹, v.t. & i. (*clove* or *cleft*; *cloven* or *cleft*). Split (often *asunder, in two*); chop, break, or come, apart, esp. along the grain or line of cleavage (*cleft palate*, malformation in mouth; *in a cleft stick*, in tight place allowing neither retreat nor advance; *cloven hoof*, of ruminant quadrupeds, of god Pan, & so of devil, whence *show the cloven hoof*, reveal an evil nature); make way through (water, air); hold (ground, persons) apart (of chasm lit. & fig.). Hence **cleav'ABLE** a. [OE *clēofan, clīofan*, OS, OHG *klioban*, ON *kljúfa* f. Gmc *kleubh-*]

cleave², v.i. (~*d* or *clave*; ~*d*). Stick fast, adhere, *to* (arch. exc. in fig. sense of *be faithful*). [OE *cleofian, clifian*, = OS *clibōn*, OHG *klebēn*; OE *clifan* = OS, OHG *kliban*, ON *klifa*; Gmc *klibh-* f. *klī-* stick; see CLAY]

cleav'er, n. In vbl senses; esp. butcher's chopping-tool for carcasses. [CLEAVE¹ + -ER¹]

cleav'ers (-z), **cliv'**, n. (used as sing. or pl.). Goose-grass, creeper sticking to clothes. [OE *clife*, OS, OHG *klība*; ME *clivre* etc., f. CLEAVE² + -ER¹]

cleek, n. Iron-headed golf-club with almost straight narrow face. [15th c. Sc. *cleke*, rel. to north. dial, *cleck*, south. dial. *cleach, cleech* to grasp]

clef, n. One of the three symbols (*C, tenor,* or *alto*; *G* or *treble*; *F* or *bass*) indicating pitch of stave in music. [F, f. L *clavis* key]

cleft¹, n. Fissure, split. [ME *clift* f. OE *clyft* (cf. OHG, ON *kluft*) f. Gmc *klubh-* f. *kleubh-* CLEAVE¹, w. assim. to foll.]

cleft², see CLEAVE¹.

‖ **clĕg**, n. Large grey fly, horse-fly. [15th c., f. ON *kleggi*]

cleistogăm'ic (klī-), a. (bot.). Permanently closed & self-fertilizing (of certain flowers). [Gk *kleistos* closed (*kleiō*) + -*gamos* -married]

‖ **clĕm**, v.t. & i. (northern; -mm-). Starve. [16th c., repr. OE -*clemman*, OHG -*klemmen* (G *klemmen*) f. Gmc *klam-* see CLAM¹]

clĕm'atis, n. Kind of climbing shrub (British wild species, traveller's joy or old man's beard). [L, f. Gk *klēmatis*]

clĕm'ency, n., **clĕm'ent**, a. Mild(ness) of temper or weather; (showing) mercy. [f. L *clementia, clemens -entis*]

clĕnch, clinch, v.t. & i., & n. (choice between *e* & *i* as indicated). 1. Secure (nail, rivet) by driving point sideways when through (i, e); close (t. & i. of teeth or fingers) tightly (e); grasp firmly (e); (of boxers) come to quarters too close for full-arm blow (i); (Naut.) fasten (rope) with special bend (i); confirm, settle (argument, bargain) conclusively (i). 2. n. Any of above actions or the resulting state. [ME *clenche* (16th c. var. *clinch*) f.

OE *clenc(e)an*, OHG *klenkan*, f. Gmc *klankjan* f. *klink-*, *klank-*, *klunk-*, parallel to *kling-* see CLING]

clĕn′cher. See CLINCHER.

Clĕopăt′ra's nee′dle, n. Egyptian obelisk on Thames embankment.

clĕp′sўdra, n. Ancient time-measuring device worked by flow of water. [L, f. Gk *klepsudra* (*kleptō* steal, *hudōr* water)]

clere′stŏrў (-ōrs-), n. Part of wall of cathedral or large church, with series of windows, above aisle roofs. [ME, f. CLEAR[1]+STOR(E)Y]

clēr′gў, n. The clerical order, all persons ordained for religious service (*the ~* usu. has pl. vb; *a ~*, i.e. the *~* of a country or church, has usu. sing. vb); *~men* (*30 ~ were present*); (hist.) membership of, learning proper to, *~* (*benefit of ~*, exemption from trial by secular court, & later from sentence for first conviction, enjoyed by all who could read); *~man*, ordained minister, esp. of Established Church; *~man's week*, *fortnight*, holiday including all weekdays before & after 1, 2, Sundays; *~woman*, wife, daughter, etc., of *~man*, esp. if dominating parish. [ME *clergy*, *-gie*, *-ge*, partly f. OF *clergié* f. LL *clericatus*, partly f. OF *clergie* f. *clerc* CLERK+*-ie* = -Y[1], after *clergié*]

clē′ric, a. (arch.), & n. Clergyman; of clergy. Hence clē′rico- comb. form. [f. LL f. Gk *klērikos* (*klēros* lot, allus. to *Acts* i. 17)]

clē′rical, a. & n. Of clergy, clergyman, or clergymen; of, made by, clerk(s) (*~ error*, in writing out; *~ duties*, *staff*); (n.) member of *~* party in a parliament etc. Hence *~ISM*(3), *~IST*(2), nn., *~IZE*(3) v.t., *~ITY* (-ăl[2]) n., *~LY*[2] adv. [f. LL *clericalis* (prec., -AL)]

clē′rihew, n. Short witty, comic, or nonsensical verse, usu. in four lines of varying length. [E. *Clerihew* Bentley (d. 1958)]

clerk (‖ klărk, *klĕrk), n. (Also *~ in holy orders*) clergyman (arch., legal & sometimes appended to signature to show status of writer); lay officer of parish church with various duties; (*no*) *great ~*, (no) scholar (arch.); officer in charge of records etc., secretary, man of business, of town (*Town C~*), corporation, etc. (usu. a lawyer); person employed in bank, office, shop, etc., to make entries, copy letters, keep accounts, etc.; *shop-assistant*; *C~ of the Weather*, personification of meteorology; *~ of the works*, overseer of materials etc. in buildings done by contract. Hence *~′DOM*, *~′ESS*[1], *~′SHIP*(1, 3), nn., *~′LY*[1] a. [OE *cleric*, *clerc*, merging w. ME *clerc*, *clerk(e)* f. OF *clerc*, f. LL *clericus* CLERIC]

clĕv′er, a. Adroit, dexterous, neat in movement (*~ horse*, good fencer); skilful, talented; ingenious (of doer or thing done); *~~*, excessively *~*. Hence *~ISH*[1](2) a., *~LY*[2] adv., *~NESS* n. [early

hist. obsc., orig. unkn.; corresp. in form & sense to LG *klöver*, *klever*, MDu. *klever* sprightly, brisk, smart, suggests LG orig.]

clĕv′is, n. U-shaped iron at end of beam for attaching tackle. [etym. unkn.]

clew (-ōō), n., & v.t. 1. Ball of thread or yarn; this as used in mythol. story to guide through labyrinth; = CLUE. 2. (naut.). Small cords suspending hammock; lower or after corner of sail. 3. v.t. *~ up*, draw lower ends of (sails) to upper yard or mast ready for furling. [ME *clyw(e)*, *clew(e)*, OE *cliwen*, *cleowen*, = Du., MLG *kluwen*; prob. dim. of a wd corresp. to OHG *kliu*, *kliuwi* (whence G *knäuel* clew); loss of *-en* as in *eve*, *game*]

cliché (klēsh′ā), n. Metal cast esp. stereo or electro duplicate; hackneyed literary phrase. [F]

click, n., & v.i. (Make) slight sharp sound as of cocking gun; catch in machinery acting with this sound; (of horse) touch shoes of fore & hind feet (n., this fault); (S.-Afr. langg.) (make) sharp non-vocal sucking sound as articulation; (sl.) secure one's object, come to an agreement. So *~′ER*[1] n., foreman shoemaker who cuts out the leather and gives out work, ‖ (Printing) foreman of a companionship of compositors who distributes the copy etc. [imit., cf. Du. *klikken*, F *cliquer*]

cli′ent, n. (Rom. Ant.) plebeian under protection of noble; (arch.) dependant, hanger-on; employer of lawyer; employer of any professional man, customer. Hence *~AGE*, *~SHIP*, nn., *~LESS* a. [f. L *cliens -entis* (*cluere* hear, obey, -ENT)]

cli′entĕle, n. 1. Person's dependants, following. 2. Customers, supporters, (of physician, shop, theatre, etc.). [f. L *clientela* clientship; later reintroduced f. F *clientèle*]

cliff, n. Steep rock-face, usu. overhanging sea; *~s′man*, skilled climber. [OE *clif*, OS, ON *klif*, OHG *klep*, f. Gmc *klibhom*]

climăc′tĕric (or -ē′r-), a. & n. 1. Constituting a crisis, critical; (Physiol. & Med.) occurring at period of life (45–60) at which vital force begins to decline. 2. n. Critical period in life (multiples of 7, odd multiples of 7, etc.; *grand ~*, 63rd year). [f. L (& partly f. F *climatérique*) f. Gk *klimaktērikos* f. *klimaktēr* rung of ladder (*klimax*), -IC]

clim′ate, n. (Region with certain) conditions of temperature, dryness, wind, light, etc.; (fig.) trend or attitude of community or era, character of something. Hence **climăt′ic** a., **climăt′ic-ALLY** adv., **climatŏL′OGY** n., **clim′ato-LO′GICAL** a. [ME f. OF *climat* f. L f. Gk *klima -at-* (*klinō* slope, -M)]

clim′ăx, n., & v.i. & t. 1. Ascending scale; series of ideas or expressions so arranged; last term in these; culmination, apex; hence (irreg.) **climăc′tic** a. 2. vb. Come, bring, to a *~*. [LL, f. Gk *klimax -akos* ladder, climax]

climb (-īm), v.t. & i. (past ~*ed* & arch. *clomb* pr. -ōm), & n. **1.** Ascend, mount, go *up*, (t. & i.) esp. with help of hands; ~ *down* (t. & i.), descend (cliff etc., or abs.) similarly, (intr.) retreat from position taken up, give in; (of sun, aeroplane, etc.) go slowly up; (of plants) get support by tendrils or twining from tree, trellis, etc.; slope upwards; rise by effort in social rank, intellectual or moral strength, etc.; ~*ing-iron*, spikes attachable to boot for ~ing trees or ice slopes; hence cli'mb-ABLE (-ma-) a. **2.** n. Piece of ~ing (~-*down*, abandonment of declared intention), place (to be) ~ed. [OE *climban*, (M)Du., (M)LG *klimmen*, OHG *klimban* (G *klimmen*), f. WG *klimban f. nasalized var. of *klibh-* CLEAVE²]

cli'mber (-imer), n. In vbl senses; esp.: climbing plant; kinds of bird, usu. with two forward & two backward toes; person climbing socially. [-ER¹]

clime, n. (poet.). Tract, country, (with or without ref. to climate). [f. L *clima*; see CLIMATE]

clinch. See CLENCH.

clin'cher, clĕn'cher, n. In vbl senses; esp., remark, argument, that triumphantly settles a question; *clincher-built*= CLINKER-BUILT. [prec. +-ER¹]

cling, v.i. (*clung*). ~ *together*, remain in one body or in contact, resist separation; stick, adhere *to*, (whether by stickiness, suction, grasping, or embracing; ~*ing garments*, showing form of body or limbs); remain faithful *to* (friend, habit, idea); ~'*stone*, kind of peach or nectarine in which flesh adheres to stone. [OE *clingan*, MDu. *klingen* stick, f. Gmc *kling-*, *klang-*, *klung-* parallel to *klink-*, see CLENCH]

clin'ic, n. Teaching of medicine or surgery at the hospital bedside; class, institution, so taught, conducted; *SEMINAR (last two senses). [f. F *clinique* f. Gk *klinikē* (*tekhnē*) CLINICAL (art)]

clin'ical, a. (med.). Of, at, the sick-bed (esp. of lectures, teaching, so given; ~ *thermometer*, for taking patient's temperature). Hence ~LY² adv. [f. prec. + -AL]

clink¹, n., & v.i. & t. (Make, cause *glasses* etc. to make) sharp ringing sound; ‖ ~*ing* (sl. as a. & adv.), exceedingly (good, fine), as a ~*ing good*, or ~*ing good, race*; ~'*stone*, kinds of felspar (f. ringing like iron when struck). Hence ‖ ~'er¹ [-ER¹] n. (sl.), ~ing specimen. [ME, perh. f. MDu. *klinken*; cf. CLANG, CLANK]

clink², n. (sl.). Prison, lock-up, (esp. *in* ~). [16th c., orig. unkn.]

clink'er³, n. Very hard yellow Dutch brick; brick with surface vitrified by great heat; mass of bricks fused together or of slag or lava. [17th c. *clincard* etc. f. Du. *klinkaerd* (now *klinker*) f. *klinken* CLINK¹]

clink'er-built, a. (Of boats) made with external planks overlapping downwards & fastened with clinched copper nails. [f. *clink* north. var. of *clinch*; see CLENCH]

clinŏm'ĕter, n. Instrument for measuring slopes. [f. Gk *klinō* to slope, -o-, -METER]

Cli'ŏ, n. (The Muse of) history. [f. Gk *Kleiō* (*kleiō* celebrate)]

clip¹, v.t. (-pp-), & n. **1.** Surround closely, grip tightly. **2.** n. Appliance for holding things together or for attachment to object as mark; brooch; set of attached cartridges for magazine rifle. [OE *clyppan* embrace, = OFris. *kleppa*, f. WG *klupp-jan*]

clip², v.t. (-pp-), & n. **1.** Cut with shears or scissors, trim thus, take away part of (hair, wool) thus, remove hair or wool of (sheep, person) thus, (~ one's *wings*, disable him from pursuing his ambition); remove small piece of (railway, bus, etc. ticket) to show that it has been used, whence ~p'ie [-Y³] n. (colloq.), bus conductress; pare edge of (coin); omit letters or syllables of (words); omit (letter etc.; ~ *his gs*). **2.** n. Operation of shearing or hair-cutting; quantity of wool clipped from sheep, flock, etc.; smart blow with the hand, cut with the whip, etc. [ME *clippen* f. ON *klippa*]

clipp'er, n. In vbl senses; also or esp.: instrument for clipping hair; swift mover (esp. of horse or ship); ship with forward-raking bows & aft-raking masts; trans-oceanic flying-boat P; (sl.) thing excellent of its kind. [CLIP², -ER¹]

clipp'ing¹, n. In vbl senses; esp., piece clipped off, *newspaper cutting. [CLIP², -ING¹]

clipp'ing², a. In vbl senses; esp., (sl.) first-rate. [CLIP², -ING²]

clique (-ēk), n. Small exclusive party, set, coterie. Hence cli'quish¹ (-ēk-), cli'qu(e)y² (-ēkl), aa., cli'quishness, cli'quism(2), (-ēk-), nn. [F, f. *cliquer* CLICK¹]

clit'oris, n. Rudimentary internal part of female genitals analogous to penis. [Gk *kleitoris*]

clivers, n. See CLEAVERS.

cloā'ca, n. (pl. -ae). Sewer; excrementory cavity in birds, reptiles, etc.; gathering-place of moral evil. Hence cloā'cal a. [L]

cloak, (arch.) clōke, n., & v.i. & t. **1.** Loose usu. sleeveless outdoor upper garment; covering (~ *of snow*); pretence, pretext, (*under the* ~ *of*); ~*-room*, for leaving ~s, hats, etc., or any luggage. **2.** vb. Put on one's ~; put ~ on (one*self* or another); conceal, disguise. [ME, f. OF *cloke*, dial. var. of *cloche* bell, cloak (from its bell shape) f. med. L *clocca* bell; see CLOCK¹]

clŏbb'er, n. Black paste used to hide cracks in leather; (sl.) clothing, gear. [orig. unkn.]

cloche (klōsh), n. ~ (*hat*), woman's bell-shaped hat; (orig. bell-shaped) glass cover for forcing or *protecting* outdoor plants. [F, = bel!]

clŏck[1], n., & v.i. & t. **1.** Time-measuring instrument periodically wound up, kept in motion by springs or weights acting on wheels, & recording hours, minutes, etc., by hands on a dial (*o'clock* now usu. only appended to the actual hour, as *six o'clock*, but *quarter to six*, *six fifteen*, 7.25; *what o'clock is it?*, what is the time?; *of the clock* still in formal or facetious use; *put back the* ~, fig., go back to a past age); ~like device showing readings on a dial (*range* ~); (colloq.) stop-watch; downy head of dandelion etc.; ~'*wise, counter-* ~'*wise*, moving in curve from left to right, right to left, as seen by spectator at centre; ~'*work*, mechanism on ~ principle (*like* ~*work*, regularly, automatically), (attrib.) regular, mechanical. **2.** v.i. (Of factory hands etc.) ~ *in, on, out, off*, register one's entry or exit by means of an automatic ~; (v.t.; colloq.) time (race) with stop-watch. [f. MDu., MLG *klocke* (= OS *glogga*, OHG *glocka*, ON *klokka*) f. med. L *clocca*, see CLOAK; ult. f. Celt., cf. OIr. *cloc*]

clŏck[2], n. (shop pl., formerly, *clox*). Pattern worked in silk etc. on side of stocking. Hence (-)~ED[2] (-kt) a. [16th c.; orig. unkn.]

clŏck'ing, a. ~ *hen*, one sitting on eggs. [Sc. & north. var. of CLUCK*ing*]

clŏd, n., & v.t. (-dd-). Lump of earth etc.; lump of earth (vb, pelt with ~s); *the* ~, soil, land, mere matter; (also ~'*hopper*, ~'*pole*) bumpkin, lout, (so ~'*hopping*, loutish), whence ~d'ISH[1] a., ~d'ishNESS n.; coarse part of neck of ox as meat. [in ME syn. var. of CLOT (now different.), corresp. to OE *clod-* f. Gmc **klud-*, cogn. w. **klut-* CLOT; see CLOUD]

clŏg[1], n. Block of wood fastened to leg to impede motion; impediment, encumbrance; woman's wooden-soled overshoe for wet ground; wooden-soled shoe with metal rim; ~*dance*, performed in ~s. [ME, of unkn. orig.]

clŏg[2], v.t. & i. (-gg-). Confine (animal) with clog; be an encumbrance to, burden; impede, hamper; choke up, obstruct by stickiness; fill up with choking matter; stop or act badly from being choked up. [f. prec.]

clŏgg'ўy (-g-), a. Lumpy, knotty; sticky. [-Y[2]]

cloisonné (klwahzŏnã'), a. & n. ~ *enamel* or ~, enamel in which colours of pattern are kept apart by thin outline plates. [F]

clois'ter, n., & v.t. (Enclose, shut up, in) convent, monastic house, (*the* ~, monastic seclusion); covered walk, often round quadrangle with wall on outer & colonnade or windows on inner side, esp. of convent, college, cathedral buildings, whence ~ED[2] (-erd) a. Hence **clois'tral** a. [ME & OF *cloistre* f. L *claustrum, clostrum*]

clōke. See CLOAK.

clōne, n. A group of plants produced vegetatively from one original seedling or stock. Hence **clōn'AL** a. [f. Gk *klōn* twig, slip]

clōn'us, n. (path.). Spasm with violent successive muscular contractions & relaxations. Hence **clōn'ic** a. [f. Gk *klonos*]

clōop, n., & v.i. (Make) sound (as) of cork being drawn. [imit.]

clōse[1], a. & adv. **1.** Shut; (of vowels) pronounced with lips or mouth cavity contracted (e.g. *o* in *not* is open, in *note* ~); narrow, confined, contracted, stifling (~ *siege, prisoner, air*); covered, concealed, secret, given to secrecy (*keep, lie,* ~, be in hiding; ~*-stool*, chamber-pot mounted in stool with cover); niggardly (so ~*t -fist'*ED[2] a., ~*-fist'*ÉdNESS n,); restricted, limited, (~ *corporation* etc.; ‖ ~ *scholarship*, not open to all; ~ BOROUGH); under prohibition (‖ ~ *season, time*, in which something is forbidden, esp. killing of game etc.). **2.** Near; dense, compact, with no or slight intervals, (~ *texture, thicket, writing*; ~ *order, combat*; ~ *quarters*, immediate contact; ~ *reasoner, argument, analysis*, leaving no gaps or weak spots, coherent; also adv., as *shut* ~, ~ *ranked*; ~*-grained*, without visible interstices; *stand, sit,* ~); in or nearly in contact (~ *proximity*; *a* ~ *shave*, near the skin, also fig., narrow missing of collision etc.; ~*-hauled*, with sails hauled aft so as to sail ~ to the wind; SAIL ~ *to the wind*; esp. in adv. or prep. phrr. ~ *by*, ~ *to*, ~ *upon*, as *he was* ~ *by*, ~ *to the road*, ~ *upon two hundred*); fitting exactly (~ *cap*, ~ *resemblance*); near & dear; nearly equal (~ *.contest*); concentrated (~ *examination, attention*); ~ *call* (colloq.), a near thing, something almost fatal; ~*-up* n., part of cinema film taken at short range and showing person(s) etc. on large scale. Hence ~'LY[2] (-sl·) adv., ~'NESS (-sn·) n. [ME & OF *clos* f. L *clausus* p.p. of *claudere* shut]

clōse[2], n. Enclosed place (*break* one's ~, legal, trespass on his land); precinct of cathedral; school playground; (Sc.) entry from street to court at back. [ME & OF *clos* f. L *clausum* enclosure (prec.)]

clōse[3] (-z), v.t. & i., & n. **1.** Shut (t. & i. of lid or box, door or room or house; lit., or = declare or be declared not open, of place of business etc.; *closing-time*, at which shops etc. stop business; ~ *upon*, of hand, box, etc., grasp or imprison, also of eyes, lose sight of by shutting); ~*d shop*, a trade etc. restricted to members of a (particular) trade union. **2.** Be the boundary of, conclude, bring or come to an end, complete, settle, (~ one's *days*, die; ~ *bargain*; abs. stop speaking, often *with* the remark etc.). **3.** Bring or come into contact (~ *the ranks* or, intr., ~ *up*; ~ *electric current* or *circuit*, give it continuity), come within striking distance, grapple *with*, (Naut., as v.t.) approach or come alongside of (other ship etc.); (Mil., as v.i. to men in rank) *right ~*, *left ~*, move sideways to right, left. 4. Express (often eager) agreement *with* (offer, terms, or person offering them). 5. *~ in*, enclose, come nearer, (of days) get successively shorter; *~ up*, block, fill, coalesce. 6. n. Conclusion, end; grappling of combatants; (Mus.) cadence. [ME *close(n)* f. OF *clos-* st. of *clore* f. L *claudere* shut]

clŏs'ĕt (-z-), n., & v.t. Private or small room, esp. for private interviews (so vb, *be ~ed with*, *together*, hold consultation) or for study (*~ play*, to be read not acted; *~ strategist* etc., theoretical); cupboard, as *china-~*; = WATER-~. [ME, f. OF dim. of *clos* CLOSE², -ET¹]

clō'sure (-zher), n., & v.t. 1. Closing, closed condition. 2. (Parl.) decision by vote of House of Commons, under certain restrictions, to put the question without further debate; (v.t.) apply *~* to (motion, speakers, etc.). [ME, f. OF, f. L *clausura* (*claudere claus-*, -URE)]

clŏt, n., & v.i. & t. (-tt-). 1. Mass of material stuck together; semi-solid lump of coagulated liquid, esp. of blood (*~ of blood*, pop. name for THROMBOSIS); (sl.) stupid person. 2. vb. Form (t. & i.) into *~s* (*~ted hair*, stuck together in locks; *~ted cream*, got by scalding milk; *~ted nonsense*, utter absurdity). [OE *clot(t)* f. WG **klutt-* (= MHG *kloz*) f. **klut-*, weak grade of **klaut-* CLEAT]

cloth (-awth, -ŏth, *pl.* -awdhz, -ŏths), n. (*pl.* *~s*, & in differentiated sense CLOTHES). (Piece, used for any purpose, of) woven or felted stuff; (also *table-~*) covering for table, esp. of linen at meals (*lay the ~*, prepare table for meal); woollen woven fabric as used for clothes; each of the breadths of canvas in a sail; duster; *~ of gold*, *silver*, tissue of gold or silver threads interwoven with silk or wool; || *American ~*, enamelled *~* like leather; *cut coat according to ~*, adapt expenditure to resources; profession as shown by clothes, esp. clerical (*respect due to his ~*; also *the ~*, clergy); *~-binding*, cover of book in linen or cotton *~*; *~-yard shaft* (hist.), arrow a yard long. [OE *clǎth* of unkn. orig.; Gmc cognates only since 12th c., cf. G *kleid*]

clōthe (-dh), v.t. (*~d* or, arch. & literary, *clad*). Provide with clothes, put clothes upon; cover like or as with clothes or a cloth (*leaves ~ trees*; *~d with righteousness*, *with plantations*; *body ~s soul*; also *~ face in smiles*, *ideas in words*). Hence clōth'ING¹(4) (-dh-) n. [OE *clǎthian*, *clǽthan*, f. *clǎth* CLOTH]

clothes (-ōz, -ōdhz), n. pl. Wearing-apparel; BED¹-*~*; linen etc. to be washed (*~-bag*, *-basket*, for conveying this; *~-horse* for airing it on; *~-line*, *-post*, || *-prop*, || *-peg*, rope, supports of rope, wooden clip on rope, for drying it after washing; *~-brush*; *~-moth*, destructive to *~*; *~-press*, cupboard with shelves for *~*; (old-)*~-man*, dealer in usu. old *~*. [repr. OE *clǎthas*; *cloths* (since *c.* 1600) completely different. in 19th c.]

clŏth'ier (-dh-), n. (Formerly) maker of cloth; dealer in cloth or clothes. [ME *clother*, see -ER¹, -IER]

clou (kloo), n. Point of greatest interest, chief attraction, central idea. [F, = nail]

cloud, n., & v.t. & i. 1. (Mass of) visible condensed watery vapour (see CIRRUS, CUMULUS, NIMBUS, STRATUS) floating high above general level of ground (*~-drift*, *~* in motion; *~-rack*, pile of broken *~s*; *~-burst*, violent rainstorm; *~-capped*, of hill with top hidden by *~*; *~-scape*, picture, picturesque grouping, of *~s*; *~-kissing*, of high hill or building); unsubstantial or fleeting thing; mass of smoke or dust; local dimness or vague patch of colour in or on liquid or transparent body; great number of birds, insects, horsemen, arrows, moving together; light woollen scarf; obscurity (*under ~ of night*; *a ~ of words*); *in the ~s*, mystical, unreal, imaginary, (so *~-castle*, daydream; *~-land*, *~-world*, utopia, fairyland), (of person) abstracted, inattentive; state of gloom, trouble, suspicion, louring or depressed look, (*~ on brow*; *under a ~*, out of favour, discredited); *~'berry*, mountain shrub with white flower & orange-coloured fruit; C*~-cuckoo-land*, *-town*, ideal realm [transl. of Gk *Nephelokokkugia* (*nephelē* cloud + *kokkux* cuckoo) in Aristophanes' *Birds*]; hence *~'LESS* a., *~'lĕssLY²* adv., *~'lĕssNESS*, *~'LET*, nn., *~'Y²* a., *~'ILY²* adv., *~'INESS* n., *~'WARD*(s) adv. 2. v. tb. Overspread, darken, with *~s*, gloom, or trouble; variegate with vague patches of colour; become overcast or gloomy (*~ up*, *over*). [ME *clud*, *clod*, *cloud*, app. same wd as OE *clūd* mass of rock or earth, prob. cogn. w. CLOD]

clough (klŭf), n. Ravine, steep valley usu. with torrent bed. [OE *clōh*, rel. to OHG *klinga*, G dial. *klinge*]

clout n., & v.t. Patch (n. & v.); a cloth (esp. *dish-~*); piece of clothing; hit, cuff, (n. & v., esp. with open hand); iron plate on boot etc. to save wear, (also *~-nail*) broad-headed nail for attaching *~*; (hist.) canvas on frame as mark at archery (*in the ~*, a hit!). [OE *clūt*, f. Gmc **klūt-* cogn. w. CLOT, CLEAT]

clōve¹, clōven. See CLEAVE¹.

clōve², n. One of small bulbs making up compound bulb of garlic, shallot, etc. (usu. *of*). [OE *clufu* cogn. w. CLEAVE¹]

clōve³, n. (Pungent aromatic dried bud of) tropical tree (*oil of ~s*, extracted from *~s* & used in medicine); (also *~-gilly-flower*) *~-scented* pink, original of carnation & other double pinks. [ME *clove(e)* f. F *clou (de girofle)*; *girofle* (see GILLYFLOWER) was orig. name of the spice; *clou* (f. L *clavus* nail) *de girofle* (in Eng. ~-*gillyflower*) was used of it w. ref. to its shape, transferred to the similarly shaped bud of pink, & later divided into *clove* for the spice, & *gillyflower* for the pink]

clóve hitch, n. Hitch by which rope is secured at any intermediate part round spar or rope that it crosses at right angles. [old p.p. of CLEAVE[1], as showing parallel separate lines]

clóv'er, n. Kinds of trefoil used for fodder (*be, live, in* ~, in ease & luxury). [OE *cláfre* = MLG *kláver*, first syll. corresp. to OS *klé*, OHG *kléo* (G *klee*) f. WG *klaiw-*]

clown, n., & v.i. **1.** Rustic; ignorant or ill-bred man, whence ~'ISH[1] a., ~'ishLY[2] adv., ~'ishNESS n.; jester, esp. in pantomime or circus, whence ~'ERY(4) n. **2.** v.i. Play the ~. [16th c., of obsc., perh. LG orig.; cf. NFris. *klönne, klünne* clumsy fellow]

clóx. See CLOCK[2].

cloy, v.t. Satiate, weary, by richness, sweetness, sameness, excess, of food or pleasure (usu. *with*). [f. obs. *accloy* f. OF *encloyer* f. Rom. **inclavare*; cf. EN-CLAVE]

club[1], n. **1.** Stick with one thick end as weapon (*Indian* ~s, pair swung to develop muscles; ~*-law*, rule by physical force); kinds of stick used in games, esp. golf; structure or organ in. Bot. etc. with knob at end; ~*-foot*(ed), (with) congenitally distorted foot; ~*-moss*, kind with upright spikes of spore-cases; ~*-root*, disease of turnips etc.; playing-card of suit bearing black trefoil (~s, the suit). **2.** Association of persons united by some common interest, meeting periodically for co-operation (*Alpine, golf, yacht,* BENEFIT, ~) or conviviality; body of persons with cooperation by ballot combined for social purposes & having premises (~*-house*) for resort, meals, temporary residence, etc. (|| ~'*land*, St James's in London, where ~s cluster), whence ~'DOM n., ~'LESS a. [ME *clubbe, clobbe* f. ON *klubba* assim. form of *klumba* club, rel. to CLUMP]

club[2], v.t. & i. (-bb-). Beat with club; use butt of (gun) as club; bring, come, into a mass; contribute (money, ideas) to common stock; (v.i.) combine *together, with,* for joint action, making up a sum, etc.; (Mil.) get (one's men) into a confused mass. [f. prec.]

clúbb'able, a. Fit for membership of a club. [CLUB[1], -ABLE]

clúb'haul, v.t. Tack (*ship,* or abs.) by anchoring & cutting cable, as device for getting off lee-shore when there is not room to wear. [orig. unkn.]

clúck, n., & v.i. (Make) guttural cry of

hen. Hence ~'Y[2] a., = CLOCKING. [early 17th c.; cf. obs. & dial. *clock* f. OE *cloccian*; imit.]

clue (-ōō), n. Fact or principle that serves as guide, or suggests a line of inquiry, in any problem, investigation, or study; thread of story, train of thought; (also rarely in other senses of) CLEW. Hence ~'LESS (-ōō-) a. [different. sp. of CLEW]

clúm'ber, n. Kind of spaniel. [C~ in Notts.]

clump, n., & v.i. & t. **1.** Cluster of trees or shrubs (usu. *of*); (also ~-*sole*) extra thickness of leather added to sole, usu. nailed on. **2.** vb. Tread heavily; heap or plant together; provide (boot) with ~. [16th c., f. MLG *klumpe* (LG *klump,* Du. *klomp,* G *klumpen*); see CLUB[1]]

clúm's|y̆ (-z-), a. Awkward in movement or shape, ungainly; ill-contrived; without tact. Hence ~iLY[2] adv., ~iNESS n. [c. 1600, app. f. north. dial. *clumse* (14th c.) benumbed with cold, +-Y[2]; prob. of Scand. orig., cf. Sw. dial. *klumsen, klumsig*]

clúnch, n. Soft white limestone used for internal carving-work. [orig. unkn.]

clúng. See CLING.

clús'ter, n., & v.t. & i. **1.** Group of similar things, esp. such as grow together, bunch; swarm, group, of persons, animals, etc. **2.** vb. Bring or come into, be in, a ~ or ~s (~*ed columns, pillars, shafts,* several close together, or disposed round or half detached from pier). [OE *cluster* app. f. Gmc **klut-*; cf. CLOT]

clútch[1], v.t. & i. Seize eagerly, grasp tightly; snatch *at.* [ME *clucche* var. of *clicche* (dial. *clitch*) f. OE *clyccan* f. Gmc **klukjan*]

clútch[2], n. Tight grasp; (pl.) grasping hands, cruel grasp; a grasping *at*; (Mech.) arrangement for throwing working parts into or out of action, gripping-piece of crane. [f. prec., but hist. obsc.; ME *cloke, cloche* claw; later *clutch* f. vb]

clútch[3], n. Set of eggs; brood of chickens. [18th c., south. var. of north. *cletch* f. *cleck* to hatch f. ON *klekja,* assoc. w. CLUTCH[1]]

clútt'er, n., & v.i. & t. (Bustle, run, with) confused noise or movement, loss of self--possession; confused mass, untidy state, litter n. & (esp. in ~*ed up with*) v.t. [late 16th c.; in part, phon. var. of *clotter* (f. *clot*) coagulate; in part assoc. w. *cluster, clatter*]

Clydesdale (klīdz'dāl), a. & n. (Of) a breed of heavy draught-horses (orig. from *Clyde* district in Scotland).

clýp'é|ŭs, n. Shield-like part of insect's head. Hence ~AL, ~ATE[2], ~iFORM, aa., ~o- comb. form. [L, = shield]

clýs'ter, n., & v.t., (med., now rare). = EN-EMA; (vb) treat with ~. [ME, f. OF *clystere* or L. f. Gk *klustēr* syringe]

|| **cmd,** = CD.

co-, pref. L short form of *com-* (*cum* prep. with), used in L only before vowels, h, gn, & (in the correct classical form) n, but in E as living pref. before any letter. **1.** Prefixed to vbs.,=with other subjects (*co-operate*) or objects (*co-adjust*); to adjj. & advv., = jointly, together, mutually, (*coeternally, coadjacent*); & to nouns, = joint, mutual, (*coheir, coequality*). **2.** In some math. words, short for *complement*, = 'of the complement', 'complement of' as *cosine, co-declination.*

coäcerva′tion, n. Heaping together, pile. [f. L CO(*acervatio* f. *acervare* f. *acervus* heap, see -ATION)]

coach, n., & v.i. & t. **1.** State carriage; (also *stage-~*) large four-wheeled & usu. four-horsed close carriage with seats inside and on the roof carrying passengers at fixed rates & times with stoppages for meals & relays of horses; HACKNEY-~; MOURNING-~; SLOW-~; (official name for) railway carriage; long-distance bus; (Naut.) room near stern of man-of-war; private tutor; trainer of athletic team etc.; *drive ~ & six through Act of Parliament,* stultify it; *~-box,* driver's seat; *~-built,* (of motor-car bodies) built of wood by craftsmen; *~-dog,* = CARRIAGE-*dog*; *~-house,* outhouse for carriages; *~′man,* driver of any carriage, whence *~′man*SHIP(3) n.; hence *~′*FUL(2) n. **2.** vb. Travel in, go by, stage-~ (*in the old ~ing days*); tutor, train, (pupil for examination, crew for race); give hints to, prime with facts; (intr.) read with tutor. [f. F *coche* f. Hung. *kocsi* adj. f. *Kocs* place-name]

coädj′utor (-ŏŏ-; *also* -ajŏŏ-ᴸ), n. Assistant esp. to bishop or other ecclesiastic. [ME, f. OF *coadjuteur* f. L CO(*adjutorem* f. ADjuvare -jut- help, -OR)]

coäd′ūnate, a. (physiol. & bot.). Congenitally united. [f. LL CO(*adunatus* p.p. of ADunare make one f. *unus* one)]

coäg′ūl|āte, v.t. & i. Change (t. & i.) from fluid to more or less solid state, clot, curdle, set, solidify. Hence or cogn., ~A′TION, ~ātOR, ~ANT(2), nn. [f. L *coagulatus* p.p. of -*are*; see -ATE²,³]

coai′ta (kŏī-), n. Small S.-Amer. monkey (red-faced spider-monkey). [f. Braz. *coati*]

coal, n., & v.t. & i. **1.** Hard opaque black or blackish mineral or carbonized vegetable matter found in seams or strata below earth's surface & used as fuel & in manufacture of gas, tar, etc. (*~s*, pieces of it ready for supplying fire; chief kinds, ANTHRACITE, BITUMINOUS, LIGNITE; *heap ~s of fire,* return good for evil, cf. *Rom.* xii. 20; *blow the ~s,* fan flame of passion etc.; *haul, call, over the ~s,* reprimand; *~s to Newcastle,* superfluous action); *~-bed, -seam,* stratum of ~; *~-black,* quite; *~-box, -scuttle,* receptacle for ~ to supply

room fire (*~-scuttle bonnet,* with front projection as of inverted *~-box*); *~-*BUNKER; *~-dust,* small *~s*; ∥*~-factor,* middleman between *~-owners* & customers; *~-field,* district with series of *~* strata; *~-fish,* black cod; ∥*~-flap, -plate,* cover of *~-cellar* opening in pavement; *~-gas,* mixed gases extracted from *~* & used for lighting & heating; *~-heaver,* man employed in moving*~,* whence*~′ie* [-ȳ³]n.; *~-hole,* ∥ small *~-cellar*; *~-master, -owner,* owner or lessee of *~-mine* or *~-pit* = COLLIERY; *~-measures* (Geol.), series of rocks formed by seams of *~* & intervening strata; *•~-oil,* paraffin; *~-sack,* black patch in Milky Way (esp. one near Southern Cross); *~-screen,* frame for parting large from small *~s*; *~-tar,* TAR extracted from bituminous *~,* & yielding paraffin, naphtha, benzene, creosote, & aniline dyes; *~-tit,* = COALMOUSE; *~-whipper,* man, machine, raising *~* from ship's hold; hence *~′*LESS (-l-l-), *~′*Y², aa. **2.** vb. Put *~* into (ship etc.); take in supply of *~*. [OE *col,* MDu. MLG *kole,* OHG *kol*(*o*), ON *kol,* f. Gmc **kolom*]

coalĕs′|ce′, v.i. Come together & form one (of material or immaterial things); combine in a coalition (of statesmen, parties). So *~′*CENCE n., *~′*CENT a. [f. L CO(*alescere alit-* grow f. *alere* nourish)]

coali′tion, n. Union, fusion; ∥ (Pol.) temporary combination for special ends between parties that retain distinctive principles. Hence *~*IST(1) (-sho-) n. [f. med. L *coalitio* (prec., -ION)]

coal′mouse, cōle-, n. Small dark-coloured bird (also COAL-*tit*). [ME *colmose* f. OE *colmāse* (*col* coal+*māse* f. WG **maisa* kind of small bird)]

coam′ing, n. Raised border round hatches etc. of ship to keep out water. [orig. unkn.]

coarse (kŏrs), a. Common, inferior, (*~ fish, fare*); rough, loose, or large, in texture, grain, or features; not delicate in perception, manner, or taste, unrefined; rude, uncivil, vulgar; obscene (of language); *~-fibred, -grained,* lit. of things, also fig. of persons = without delicacy. Hence *~′*LY² (-sl-) adv., **coars′**EN⁴ v.t. & i., *~′*NESS (-sn-) n., **coars′**ISH(2) a. [15th c., of unkn. orig.; the suggested connexion w. *course* is unsubstantiated]

coast¹, n. (Also *sea-~*) border of land near sea, sea-shore; CLEAR¹*~*; (U.S. & Canada) toboggan slide; (hence through COAST²) downhill run on bicycle with feet up or still; *~′guard*(*sman*), Admiralty *~* police-(man); *~′line,* the line of the sea-shore esp. with regard to its configuration (*the rugged ~line of the island*); ∥∥*~ waiter,* custom-house officer who deals with goods carried *~*wise. Hence *~′*AL a., *~*WARD(S) adv., *~′*WISE a. & adv. [ME & OF *coste* f. L *costa* rib, flank, side]

For compounds of *co-* not given consult **co-**.

coast², v.i. Sail along coast, trade between ports on same coast; slide down hill on toboggan, bicycle down hill without pedalling. Hence ~'ER¹ n., ~ing vessel, silver tray for decanter, rest for the foot on front fork of bicycle. [ME *costay*, -*ey*, -*ie* f. OF *costeier* f. *coste* (prec.)]

coat, n., & v.t. 1. Man's sleeved usu. cloth body garment (*dress*-~, with swallow tails for the evening; ~ *of* MAIL; FROCK-~; *great*~, *top*-~, outdoor, worn over another; *red* ~, traditional uniform of British soldier; so *red'*-~, soldier; ~ *of arms*, herald's tabard, gentleman's heraldic bearings or shield; ~ *armour*, blazonry, heraldic arms; ~-*card*, now *court*-, playing-card with coated figure, king, queen, or knave; *trail* one's ~-*tails*, for someone to tread on, = seek to pick quarrel; *dust* one's ~, beat him; *turn* one's ~, change sides, desert); woman's outer garment, (also, esp. in ~ *& skirt*) overcoat, or short tailored jacket worn with skirt; petticoat (arch. & dial.; in literature esp. in KILT one's ~s). 2. Covering compared to garment; beast's hair, fur, etc.; (Physiol.) investing membrane etc. of organ; skin, rind, husk layer of bulb etc.; covering of paint etc. laid on at once; hence (-)~'ED², ~'LESS, aa. 3. v.t. Put or (with *paint* etc. as subj.) be ~ of paint, tin, etc., upon, (p.p.) covered over *with* dust etc. [ME, f. OF *cote* f. WG *kotta* (= OS *cot*, OHG *kozza*, *kozzo* (garment of) shaggy woollen stuff, in med. L *cotta*)]

coatee', n. Short-tailed coat. [-EE]

coa'ti (-ah-), n. American carnivorous mammal like civet & racoon with long flexible snout. [Braz. (*cua* cincture, *tim* nose)]

coat'ing, n. Layer of paint etc.; material for coats. [-ING¹]

coax, v.t. & i. Persuade by blandishments (*to do*, *into doing* or good temper etc.; ~ *thing out of* person; ~ *fire to light*, *key into lock*, etc.); ~ *away*, *out*, etc., entice; practise wheedling. Hence ~'ER¹ n. [16th c., 'make a cokes of', f. obs. *cokes* (16th c.) simpleton, of unkn. orig.]

coāx'al, -**ial**, a. (math.). Having common axis. [CO-, AXIS, -AL]

cob¹, n. Male swan; stout short-legged riding-horse, whence ~b'Y² a.; (also ~-*nut*) large kind of hazel-nut; roundish lump of coal etc.; round-headed loaf; CORN-~. [orig. unkn.]

‖ **cob²**, n. Composition of clay, gravel, & straw, used for building walls. [orig. unkn.]

cob'alt (-awlt), n. Silvery-white metal similar in many respects to nickel; deep-blue pigment made from it. Hence **cobal'TIC**, ~**IF'EROUS**, **cobal'TOUS** (chem.), aa., **cobal'to**- comb. form., (-awl-). [G, prob. = *kobold* goblin of mines]

cobb'er, n. (Austral. colloq.). Chum, pal. [orig. unkn.]

cŏb'ble¹, n., & v.t. (Also ~-*stone*) waterworn rounded stone of size used for paving (vb, pave with these); (pl.) coals of this size. [f. COB¹ + -LE]

cŏb'ble², v.t. Put together roughly; mend, patch *up*, (esp. shoes). [c. 1500, app. back form. f. foll.]

cŏbb'ler, n. Mender of shoes; clumsy workman; (often *sherry* ~) iced drink of wine, sugar, lemon, sucked through straw (orig. unkn.; from U.S.); *'fruit pie*; ~*'s wax*, resinous substance used for waxing thread. [ME, of unkn. orig.]

Cŏb'den|ism, n. Policy based on Free Trade, international cooperation, & retrenchment, peace, non-intervention, and opposition to Empire. Hence ~**ITE¹**(1) a. & n. [R. Cobden, d. 1865, -ISM]

cō'ble, n. Kinds of fishing-boat in Scotland & N.E. England. [ME *coble*, *ill* cf. W *ceubal*, Bret. *caubal*]

cŏb'ra (dē capĕll'ō), n. The venomous hooded snake of India, with neck dilated like hood under irritation. [Port.; *cobra* f. L *colubra* snake, *capello* hood f. med. L *capellus* f. *cappa* CAPE]

cŏb'wĕb, n. & a. Spider's network, material of it, thread of this; thing of flimsy texture (so adj., thin, flimsy), subtle fanciful reasoning; musty rubbish (esp. fig. as ~*s of the law, of antiquity*; *blow away the* ~*s*, take an airing); entanglement, mesh. Hence ~**BED²** (-bd), ~**bY²**, aa., ~**bERY**(5) n. [ME *cop(pe)web* f. (obs.) *coppe* spider + WEB]

cŏc'a, n. (Leaves of) Bolivian shrub (chewed as stimulant). [Sp., f. Peruv *cuca*]

*cŏc'a-cōl'a**, n. Aerated non-alcoholic drink. [P]

cocaine', n. Drug from coca producing local insensibility. Hence ~**'IZE**(5) v.t., ~**IZA'TION**, ~**'ISM**(5), nn. [-INE⁵]

cŏc'cagee (-gē), n. A cider apple, cider from it. [f. Ir. *cac a ghéidh* goose dung (so coloured)]

cŏc'cȳx (-ks-), n. Small triangular bone ending spinal column in man; analogous part in birds etc. Hence or cogn. **cŏc-cȳ'gēAL** a., **cŏccȳ'gēo-**, **cŏc'cȳg**(o)-, (-ks-), comb. forms. [L, f. Gk *kokkux* -*ugos* cuckoo (like its bill)]

cŏch'in-chin'a, n. & a. (Fowl) of Cochin China breed. [place]

cŏch'ineal, n. Dried bodies of insect reared on cactus in Mexico etc., used for making scarlet dye & carmine. [f. F *cochenille* f. Sp. *cochinilla* or It. *iglia* (*coccino* f. L *coccinus* scarlet f. *coccum* scarlet, orig. berry)]

cŏch'lěa (-k-), n. (pl. -*leae*). Spiral cavity of internal ear. [L, = snail]

cŏck¹, n. **1**. Male bird (alone of domestic fowl, as below, also of BLACK-~; of other birds only when aided by context; in comb. in bird-names, as PEACOCK, WOOD ~, & prefixed = male as ~ *robin*; ~

sparrow, male sparrow, small lively pugnacious person; ~ *of the wood*, capercaillie; || ~ *of the north*, brambling; ~*-nest*, built by some ~s, as wren, to roost in); (short for) woodcock (w. collect. sing. for pl.); male of domestic fowl (~*-a-doodle-doo*, its crow, child's name for ~); GAME¹-~; ~-*&-bull story*, idle invention, incredible tale; ~*-crow*, *-crowing*, dawn; ~*-fighting*, setting ~s to fight as sport; *this beats* ~*-fighting*, is inexpressibly delightful; *live like fighting* ~s, on best of fare; *that* ~ *won't fight*, that plea, plan, will not do; ~ *lobster*, *salmon*, male; ~*-shot*, *-shy*, object set up to be thrown at with sticks, stones, etc., as formerly ~s at Shrovetide, a throw at this; ~*s'-comb*, crest of ~, yellow rattle & other plants, & see COXCOMB; ~*s'foot*, a pasture grass; ~*s'head*, kinds of trefoil; ~*'spur*, ~*'s* spur, gas-burner of same shape; ~ *of the walk*, dominant person (so ~ *of the school* among boys); *old*~, familiar vocative. 2. Tapped spout, tap, (~*-metal*, two parts copper to one of lead); (not decent) penis; lever in gun raised ready to be released by trigger (*at half, full,* ~, of gun half-ready or ready to be let off); indicating-tongue of balance. [OE *coc(c)*, prob. f. med. L *coccus* (imit.), in ME reinforced by OF *coq* f. same source]

cŏck², v.t. & i. Erect, stick or stand *up*, jauntily or defiantly (~ *the ears*, in attention; ~ one's *nose*, in contempt; ~ *a* SNOOK; ~ one's *eye*, glance knowingly, wink); ~ one's *hat*, set it on aslant, also turn up the brim (~*ed hat*, formerly, with brim fixed so, now, brimless triangular hat pointed before, behind, & above, of various uniform costumes; *knock into a* ~*ed hat*, out of shape or recognition); raise cock of (gun) in readiness for firing. [f. prec. w. ref. to cock's comb, crowing-attitude, etc.]

cŏck³, n. Upward bend (of nose etc.); significant turn (of eye); way of cocking hat; cocked state of gun (see COCK¹). [f. prec.]

cŏck⁴, n., & v.t. (Heap *hay*, rarely *corn*, into) small conical heap(s) in the field. [14th c., perh. of Scand. orig., cf. Norw. *kok* heap, ON *kökkr* lump, G dial. *kocke* heap of hay]

cŏckabon'dȳ (-ŭn-), n. Kind of fishing-fly. [f. W *coch a bon ddu* red with black trunk]

cŏckăd|e′, n. Rosette etc. worn in hat as badge of office or party or part of livery, esp. black leather rosette (badge of House of Hanover) worn by servants of persons serving Crown. Hence ~*ED²* a. [earlier *cockard* f. F *cocarde* orig. in *bonnet à la cocarde*, f. fem. of *coquard* pert (*coq* COCK¹, *-ARD*)]

cŏck-a-hōōp′, a. & adv. Exultant(ly), with boastful crowing. [of unkn. orig.]

Cockaigne′ (-ān), -**ayne′**, n. Imaginary land of idleness and luxury; (punningly w. ref. to COCKNEY) London. [ME *cokaygn*(e) f. OF (*pais de*) *cocaigne* (mod. *cocagne*) lit. 'land of cakes' f. MLG *kokenje* sweet cake]

|| **cŏck-a-leek′ie**. = COCKY-LEEKY.

cŏckalōr′um, n. (colloq.). Self-important little man; || *high* ~, boy's game of leap-frog type. [arbitrary form, f. COCK¹]

cŏckatoō′, n. Kinds of parrot with movable crest. [f. Malay *kakatúa* w. assim. to COCK¹]

cŏck′atrice, n. = BASILISK. [ME *cocatris*, *-ice* f. OF *cocatris* etc. f. med. L **calca-tricem* (L *calcare* tread, track) rendering Gk *ikhneumōn* tracker (see ICHNEUMON)]

cŏck′boat, n. Small ship's boat. [f. obs. *cock* small boat (f. OF *coque*) + BOAT¹]

cŏck′chāfer, n. Greyish-chestnut beetle flying with loud whirring sound. [perh. f. COCK¹ as expr. size or vigour + CHAFER]

cŏck′er¹, v.t. Indulge, pamper, coddle, (child, invalid, etc.; usu. *up*). [orig. obsc.; perh. f. obs. *cock* vb in same sense; cf. also obs. *cockle* fondle]

Cŏck′er², n. *According to* ~, exact, correct. [E. ~, famous teacher of arithmetic d. 1675]

cŏck′er³, n. Breed of spaniel. [a 'cocking-dog', as starting woodcock etc.; see -ER¹]

cŏck′erel, n. Young cock; pugnacious youth. [dim. of COCK¹, cf. *pickerel*, *mongrel*]

cŏck′-eyed (-īd), a. (sl.). Squinting; crooked, set aslant, not level; stupid. [COCK³]

cŏck′-hŏrse, adv. (Also *a-cock-horse*, see A²) astride, mounted. [in 16th c. = toy horse]

cŏc′kle¹, n. (Also *corn-*~) purple-flowered plant growing among corn, esp. wheat; disease of wheat turning grains black. [OE *coccul*; excl. E.; perh. f. a dim. of L *coccum* berry]

cŏc′kle², n. An edible bivalve; its shell; small shallow boat (also ~*-shell*, ~*-boat*); ~s of the heart, one's feelings (*delight*, *warm*, *the* ~s etc.). [ME & OF *cokille* f. med. L **cochilia* for *conchylia* (pl.)]

cŏc′kle³, v.i. & t., & n. (Make to) bulge, curl up, pucker; (n.) bulge or wrinkle in paper, glass, etc. [f. F *coquiller* blister (of bread) f. *coquille*; see prec.]

cŏc′kle⁴, n. Radiating-stove for heating room. [perh. f. Du. *kakel*, *kachel* f. G *kachel* stove-tile]

cŏck′-loft (-aw-), n. Small upper loft. [orig. uncert.; perh. f. COCK¹ + LOFT]

cŏck′ney, n. & a. (pl. ~s). (Characteristic of a) native of London (usu. contemptuous, esp. ~ *accent*). Hence ~*DOM* (-nĭd-), ~*ESE′* (-nēz′), nn., ~*FY* (-nĭf-) v.t., ~*ISH¹* a., ~*ISM*(2, 4) n., (-nĭ-), ~*IZE*(3) (nĭ-) v.t. & i. [ME *coken-ey* cock's egg

For compounds of co- not given consult CO-.

(*coken* gen. pl., *ey* f. OE *æg*); orig. sense prob. small or ill-shaped egg (still *cock's egg* in dial., cf. G *hahnenei*); obs. senses are 'child that sucketh long', 'one made a wanton or nestle-cock of', townsman, the limitation to London being later]

cŏck′pit, n. Place made for cockfights; arena of any struggle (~ *of Europe*, Belgium); (hist.) after part of man-of-war's orlop deck, quarters of junior officers, used in action as hospital; (Aeronaut.) space for pilot etc. in fuselage of aeroplane.

cŏck′roach, n. Nocturnal voracious dark-brown beetle-like insect (also *blackbeetle*) infesting kitchens. [f. Sp. *cucaracha* w. assim. to COCK¹, ROACH¹]

cŏck-sure′ (-shoor), a. Certain to happen, undoubtedly about *to* do; quite convinced *of*, *about*; self-confident, dogmatic, presumptuous, whence ~NESS (-rn-) n. [COCK¹ used intensively, SURE]

cocksy, coxy, coxiness. = COCKY etc.

cŏck′tail, n. & a., **cŏck′tailed** (-ld) a. (Horse) with docked tail, of racing stamp but not thoroughbred; (person) placed above his birth or breeding; kind of beetle; drink of spirit with bitters, sugar, etc. (origin doubtful; from U.S.). [tail like that of cock, or that cocks up; sense *half-bred* f. docking of hunters & stagecoach horses]

cŏck′-up, n. (typog.). Initial letter much taller than the rest. [COCK²]

cŏck′y̆, cŏck′sy̆, cŏx′y̆, a. Conceited, pert. Hence cŏck′ĬLY², cŏx′i-, adv., cŏck′ĬNESS, cŏx′i-, n. [COCK¹, -Y²]

cŏck̆y̆-leek′y̆, n. Scotch soup of cock boiled with leeks.

cŏc′k̆yŏll′y̆ bĭrd, n. (Nursery phr. for) bird.

cŏc′ō (pl. *-os*), **cŏc′oa¹** (-kō), **cŏk′er,** n. (Also ~*nut*, ~*-tree*, ~*nut-tree*) tropical palm-tree; *coconut*, its large ovate brown hard-shelled seed with edible white lining enclosing whitish liquid (~*nut milk*), (sl.) human head; *that accounts for the milk in the ~nut*, (joc.) now all is explained; ~*nut butter*, the solid oil obtained from the lining of a ~nut, used in soap, candles, ointment, etc.; ~*nut matting*, made from fibre of nut's outer husk; *double* ~*nut*, much larger two-lobed seed of Seychelles palm. [f. Port. & Sp. *coco* grimace; *cocoa* esp. since Dr Johnson's dictionary (1755), in which the article *coco* was run together with the article *cocoa* (= *cacao*); *coker* (17th c.) still in commerc. use]

cŏc′oa² (-kō), n. Powder made from crushed cacao seeds often with other ingredients; drink made from this or from the seeds; ~ *bean*, cacao seed; ~ *nib*, cotyledon of this; ~ *powder*, kind of gunpowder. [alt. of CACAO]

cocōōn′, n., & v.t. & i. Silky case spun by larva to protect it as chrysalis, esp. that

of silkworm, whence ~ERY(3) n.; similar structure made by other animals; (vb) form, wrap (one*self*, thing etc.) in, ~; spray with plastic material. [f. F *cocon* f. Pr. *coucoun* dim. of *coca* shell]

cŏcŏtte′, n. Member of the Parisian demimonde; fashionable prostitute. [F]

cŏd¹, n. Large sea fish (also ~*′fish*); ~*-bank*, submarine bank frequented by it; ~*-liver oil*, used as medicine. [ME, of unkn. orig.]

cŏd², v.t. & i. (sl.; -dd-). Hoax, fool. [orig. unkn.]

cŏd′a, n. (mus.). Independent and often elaborate passage introduced after the natural conclusion of a movement (also fig.). [It., f. L *cauda* tail]

cŏd′dle, v.t., & n. Treat as invalid, keep from cold & exertion, feed *up*; (n.) person who coddles himself or others. [etym. uncert.; perh. same wd as CAUDLE, or (16th c.) *coddle* boil gently, stew]

cōde, n., & v.t. 1. Systematic collection of statutes, body of laws so arranged as to avoid inconsistency & overlapping, whence cŏd′ĬFY v.t., cŏd′ĬFĬER¹, cōdĬFĬCĀ′TĬON, nn.; set of rules on any subject; prevalent morality of a society or class (esp. ~ *of honour*); system of mil. etc. signals; (Telegr.) set of letter or figure or word groups with arbitrary meanings for brevity or secrecy. 2. v.t. (Also *codify*) put (message) into ~ words, whence cŏd′ĔR¹ n. [ME, f. OF f. L CODEX]

cō-dĕclĭnā′tĭon, n. (astron.). Complement of the declination, North-Polar distance. [CO-(2)]

cŏd′eine (-ēn, -ĭēn), n. Alkaloid in opium used as hypnotic. [f. Gk *kōdeia* poppyhead + -INE³]

cōd′ĕx, n. (pl. *cŏd′ĭcēs*). Manuscript volume, esp. of ancient Bible or classical texts. [L, earlier *caudex* tree-trunk, tablet, book]

cŏdg′er, n. (colloq.). Fellow, buffer, queer old person. [perh. var. of CADGER]

cŏd′ĭcĭl, n. Supplementary addition, esp. modifying or revoking will. So cŏdĭcĭll′-ARY¹ a. [f. L *codicillus* (usu. pl.) dim. of CODEX]

cŏd′lĭng¹, n. Small codfish. [-LING¹(2)]

cŏd′lĭn(g)², n. Kinds of apple of long tapering shape; ~*s-&-cream*, willow-herb. [15th c. *querd(e)lyng(e)* f. AN *quer de lion* lion-heart; cf. the surname *Querdelioun*, *Querdling*, wh. survives as *Quadling*, *Quodling* (C.T.O.)]

cŏd′piece, n. (hist.). Bagged appendage to the front of men's breeches. [f. OE *codd* bag + PIECE¹]

***cō′-ĕd′,** n. (colloq.). Girl or woman student at *co-educational* institution. [abbr.]

cō-ĕdūcā′tĭon, n. Education of boys & girls together. Hence ~AL (-sho-) a. [CO-]

cŏĕffĭ′cĭent (-shnt), n. Joint agent or factor; (Alg.) number placed before and multiplying another quantity known or unknown; (Physics) multiplier that measures some property (~ *of friction, expansion,* etc.); *differential* ~, quantity measuring rate of change of a function of any variable with respect to that variable. [CO-]

coel′acănth (sēl-), a. & n. (Fish) having a hollow spine. [f. COEL(O)-, Gk *akantha* spine, thorn]

coel′iăc (sēl-), a. (physiol.). Of the belly. [f. L f. Gk *koiliakos* (*koilia* belly)]

coel′(o)- (sēl-), in scientific wds, f. Gk *koilos* hollow & L *coelum* heaven.

coen′(o)- (sēn-), in comb. = Gk *koinos* common.

coen′obite (sēn-), cēn′, n. Member of monastic community. Hence c(o)eno-bit′IC(AL) aa., c(o)en′obitISM(3) n., (sēn-). [f. LL *coenobita* f. LL f. Gk *koinobion* convent (COENO-, *bios* life)]

cŏē′qual, a. & n. (Arch., theolog., or emphatic, for) equal. Hence cŏēqual′ITY (-kwŏl-) n., ~LY² adv. [15th c., f. L *coaequalis* (CO-, EQUAL)]

cŏêrce′, v.t. & i. Forcibly constrain or impel (person) into quiet, obedience, or any course (*into*, rarely *to* do, or abs.); use force, secure by force (*a~d obedience*). Hence cŏêr′cIBLE a. [f. L co(*ercēre ercit- = arcēre* shut up)]

cŏêr′cion (-shn), n. Controlling of voluntary agent or action by force; government by force. Hence ~ARY¹ a., ~IST(2) n. & a., (-sho-). [f. OF *cohercion, -tion* f. L *coer(c)tionem* (COERCE, -ION)]

cŏêr′cive, a. Of, acting by, exercising, coercion. Hence ~LY² (-vl-) adv., ~NESS (-vn-) n. [irreg. f. COERCE + -IVE]

cŏessĕn′tial (-shl), a. Of the same substance or essence. [f. LL *coessentialis,* alternative rendering, with *consub-stantialis,* of Gk *homoousios* (Gk *ousia* = L *substantia, essentia*)]

cŏētăn′eous, a. = COEVAL a. [f. LL co(*aetaneus* f. L *aetas* age)+-OUS]

cŏētêrn′al, a. Alike eternal. So ~LY² adv. [f. LL *coaeternus*+-AL]

cŏēv′al, a. & n. (Person) of same date of origin, of same age, existing at same epoch, of same duration. Hence ~ITY (-ăl-) n., ~LY² adv. [f. LL co(*aevus* f. *aevum* age)]

cŏ-ĕxĕc′ūtor, cŏ-ĕxĕc′ūtrix, (-gz-), nn. Joint executor, executrix. [CO-]

cŏĕxis|t′, v.i. Exist together or *with.* So ~′TENT a., ~′TENCE n. (*peaceful ~tence,* of peoples with different political & social systems, living in mutual toleration). [CO-]

cŏĕxtĕn′sive, a. Extending over same space or time. [CO-]

cŏff′ee (-fĭ), n. Drink made from seeds of a shrub roasted & ground; light meal with ~, ~ as final course at dinner; the shrub, its seeds raw, roasted, or ground; *~-bean,* the seed; *~-cup,* of special shape or size;

~-grounds, sediment after infusion; *~-house, -palace,* refreshment house; *~-mill,* for grinding seeds; *~-pot,* for making or serving ~ in; *~-room,* public dining-room of hotel; *~-tavern,* temperance refreshment house. [f. Turk. f. Arab. *qahveh* the drink]

cŏff′er, n. Box, esp. for valuables; (pl.) treasury, funds; sunk panel in ceiling etc.; *~-dam,* watertight case in bridge-building, caisson. [ME & OF *cofre* f. L f. Gk *kophinos* basket]

cŏff′in, n., & v.t. 1. Chest in which corpse is buried; *drive nail into* one's ~, hasten his, one's, death by annoyance, intemperance, etc.; *unseaworthy* ship; horse's hoof below coronet (*~-bone,* last phalangeal bone of foot; *~-joint* at top of hoof); *~-plate,* of metal in lid with deceased's name etc.; hence ~LESS a. 2. v.t. Put in ~, store away (e.g. books) inaccessibly. [ME, f. OF *cof(f)in* little basket etc. f. L *cophinus* (prec.)]

cŏff′le, n. Train of beasts, slaves, etc., fastened together. [f. Arab. *qāfilah* caravan]

cŏg¹, n. One of series of projections on edge of wheel or side of bar transferring motion by engaging with another series; *hunting* ~, extra ~ on one wheel etc. securing constant variation in the ~s engaged; *~-wheel,* with ~s. Hence *~gED²* (-gd) a. [ME *cogge,* app. rel. to Sw. *kugge,* Norw. *kug*]

cŏg², v.t. (-gg-). ~ *dice,* fraudulently control the way they fall (*~ged dice* for loaded dice is a mistake of modern archaists). [16th c. cant of unkn. orig.]

cō′gent, a. Forcible, convincing, (of argument, &, usu. now playfully as though by transf. from this, of motive, compulsion, etc.). Hence cō′gENCY n., ~LY² adv. [f. L *cogent-* part. st. of *cogere* compel]

cŏ′gitable, a. Able to be grasped by reason, conceivable. [f. L *cogitabilis* (foll., -ABLE)]

cŏ′git|āte, v.i. & t. Ponder, meditate; devise; (Philos.) form conception of. Hence or cogn. ~A′TION n., ~ATIVE a., ~ātiveLY² adv., ~ātiveNESS n. [f. L *cogi-tare* = co(*agitare* AGITATE) think, -ATE³]

cognac (kŏn′yăk), n. French brandy, prop. that distilled from ~ wine. [place-name]

cŏg′nate, a. & n. 1. Descended from common ancestor (cf. AGNATE), akin in origin, nature, or quality; a relative. 2. (philol.). Of same linguistic family; representing same original word; of parallel development in different allied languages (*father* is ~ with L *pater, paternal* is derived from it); a ~ word. 3. (gram.). ~ *object* or *accusative,* one of kindred meaning to vb, used adverbially, not as true object (in *die the death, death* is ~, in *he slew death* it is object). Hence ~NESS

(-tn-) n. [f. L co(*gnatus* born usu. *natus* f. *gn-, gen-, gon-,* beget)]

cŏgnā'tion, n. Cognate relationship, now esp. in philology. [ME, f. L *cognatio* (prec., -ION)]

cŏgni'tion, n. (philos.). Action or faculty of knowing, perceiving, conceiving, as opposed to emotion & volition; a perception, sensation, notion, or intuition. So ~AL (-sho-), cŏg'nitIVE, aa. [f. L *cognitio* f. co(*gnoscere -gnit-* apprehend f. *gno-* KNOW, usu. *noscere*)]

cŏg'nizab|le (*also* kŏn²), **-is-** (-Iz-), a. Perceptible; recognizable; within the jurisdiction of a court etc. Hence ~LY² adv. [f. foll. +-ABLE]

cŏg'nizance (*also* kŏn²), **-is-** (-Iz-), n. **1.** Being aware, notice, sphere of observation, (*have~ of*, know, esp. in a legitimate or official way; *take ~ of*, attend to, not allow to go unobserved; *fall within, be beyond,* one's ~, of things that fairly concern, do not concern, one). **2.** (Right of) dealing with a matter legally or judicially (with phrr. as above in legal sense). **3.** Distinctive mark, as crest, coat of arms, badge. [ME, f. OF *conis(s)aunce* f. Rom. *connoscentia f. L *cognoscent-* part. st. of *cognoscere* see COGNITION, -ANCE]

cŏg'nizant (*also* kŏn²), **-is-** (-Iz-), a. Having knowledge, being aware, *of*; (Philos.) having cognition. [f. prec.,/see -ANT]

cŏgnize, -ise' (-Iz), v.t. (philos.). Have cognition of. [on anal. of COGNIZANCE & RECOGNIZE & of vbs rightly ending in -IZE]

cŏgnōm'ĕn, n. Nickname; surname; name; (Rom. Ant.) third or family name, as Marcus Tullius *Cicero*, or fourth name or personal epithet, as Publius Cornelius Scipio *Africanus* (also called *agnomen*). [L, CO-, (*g*)*nomen* name f. st. of (*g*)*noscere* KNOW]

cognoscente (kŏnyoshĕn'tI), n. (pl.-*ti*). Connoisseur. [It., lit., one who knows]

cŏgnŏs'cible, a. Capable of being known (esp. Philos.). [f. LL *cognoscibilis* f. L *cognoscere* see COGNITION +-IBLE]

cŏgnŏv'ĭt, n. (legal). Defendant's acknowledgement, to save expense, that plaintiff's cause is just. [L, = he has acknowledged]

cohăb'it, v.i. Live together, esp. as husband & wife (usu. of persons not married). So ~A'TION n. [f. LL *cohabitare* f. L co(*habitare* dwell frequent. of *habēre* hold); cf. F *cohabiter*]

coheir', coheir'ĕss, (kōār-), nn. Male, female, joint heir. [CO-]

cohēre', v.i. Stick together, remain united, (of parts or whole); be consistent, well knit (of arguments, style, etc.). Hence cohēr'ER¹ n., detector of electric waves consisting of a glass cylinder containing metal filings which ~ when struck by a wave. [L co(*haerēre -haes-* stick)]

cohēr'|ent, a. Cohering; consistent, easily followed, not rambling or inconsequent, (of argument, narration, etc.). So ~ENCE,

~ENCY, nn.,~entLY² adv. [f. L *cohaerent-* part. st. of *cohaerēre* (prec., -ENT)]

cohē'ritor, n. = COHEIR. [CO-]

cohē'sion (-zhn), n. Sticking together, force with which molecules cohere; tendency to remain united. So cohēs'IVE a., cohēs'IVELY² (-vl-) adv., cohēs'iveNESS (-vn-) n. [f. L *cohaes-* (see COHERE, -ION), after *adhere, adhesion*]

cŏ'hŏrt, n. Division of Roman army; band of warriors; persons banded together. [f. L *cohors -hort-* or F *cohorte*]

coif, n. (hist.). Close cap covering top, back, and sides, of head; serjeant-at-law's white cap. [ME, f. OF *coif(f)e* f. LL *cofia, cufia,* of uncert. orig.]

coiffeur (see Ap.) n. Hairdresser. [F]

coiffure (see Ap.), n. Way one's hair is dressed. [F]

coign (koin), n. ~ *of vantage*, place affording good view of something. [old form of COIN, QUOIN, preserved by *Macb.* I. vi. 7]

coil¹, v.t. & i. Dispose (rope etc.) in concentric rings; twist (t. & i., often *up*) into circular or spiral shape; move sinuously. [f. OF *coillir* (mod. *cueillir*, also in same sense; cf. Pg. *colher un cabo* coil a cable) f. L *colligere* COLLECT²]

coil², n. Length of coiled rope, spring, etc.; arrangement, thing arranged, in concentric circles; single turn of coiled thing, e.g. snake; lock of hair twisted & coiled; wire, piping, etc., in circles or symmetric curves; (Electr.) spiral wire for passage of current. [f. prec.]

coil³, n. (arch. & poet.). Disturbance, much ado, noise, (*this mortal ~*, turmoil of life). [orig. unkn.]

coin¹, n. Piece of metal made into money by official stamp; metal money; money; *false ~*, imitation in base metal etc., (fig.) anything spurious; *pay one in his own ~*, give tit for tat. Hence ~'LESS a. [ME, f. OF *coi(g)n* wedge, stamping-die, f. L *cuneus* wedge]

coin², v.t. Make (money) by stamping metal (~ *money*, get money fast); make (metal) into money; make money by means of (one's *brains* etc.); invent, fabricate, (esp. new word). [ME, f. OF *coignier* f. *coin* see prec.]

coin'age, n. Coining; coins; system of coins in use (*decimal ~*, in which each value is ten times the next below); fabrication (*the ~ of* one's *brain*), invention, coined word. [ME, f. OF *coigniage* see prec., -AGE]

coïncide', v.i. Occupy same portion of space; occur at and occupy same time; agree together or *with*; concur in opinion etc. [f. med. L *coincidere* (used unchanged in Eng. contexts in 17th c.), or F *coïncider*]

coïn'cidence, n. (Instance of) being coincident; notable concurrence of events or circumstances without apparent causal connexion. [f. as prec. (see -ENCE) or F *coïncidence*]

cöïn'cident, a. Coinciding. Hence ~LY² adv. [f. as prec. (see -ENT) or F *coïncident*]

cöïncidĕn'tal, a. Of the nature of (a) coincidence. [f. prec. + -AL]

coin'er, n. In vbl senses; esp., maker of counterfeit coin. [COIN² + -ER¹]

cöïnstantăn'ĕous, a. Exactly at the same moment. [CO-]

coir (koi'er), n. Coconut fibre, used for ropes, matting, etc. [f. Malayalam *kayar* cord]

cöï'tion, n. Sexual copulation. [f. L *coitio* f. CO(*ire it-* go)]

cŏke, n., & v.t. (Convert *coal* into) solid substance left when volatile parts have been distilled from coal. [prob. f. north. dial. *colk* core, of unkn. orig.]

coker(nut). See COCO.

cŏl, n. Depression in mountain-chain. [F, = neck, col, f. L *collum* neck]

cŏl-, form taken by COM- before *l*.

cŏl'a, k-, n. W.-Afr. tree; (also ~-*nut*, -*seed*), its seed, used as condiment, tonic, and antidote to alcohol. [W.-Afr.]

col'ander (kŭ-), **cŭlī'ender,** n., & v.t. (Pass through a) perforated vessel used as strainer in cookery; similar appliance for casting shot. [15th c., perh. f. Pr. *colador (Sp. *colador*) f. Rom. *colatorem f. *colare* -*at-* f. *colum* strainer (-OR); cf. LL *colatorium*; for intrusive -*n*- cf. *passenger*]

cö-lăt'ĭtūde, n. (astron.) Complement of latitude, difference between it & 90°. [CO-(2)]

‖ **cŏlcănn'on,** n. Irish dish of cabbage and potatoes pounded and stewed. [orig. unkn.]

cŏl'chicum (or -kī-), n. Meadow-saffron; drug extracted from it used for gout. [L, f. Gk *kolkhikon* neut. adj. (*Kolkhis* on Black Sea, -IC)]

cŏl'cothar, n. Red peroxide of iron used in polishing glass etc. [f. Arab. *qolqotar*]

cŏld¹, a. **1.** Of low temperature, esp. when compared with human body or with that usual in things like the one in question (*ice, key, stone, ~, ~* as these); *~-blooded*, of fish & reptiles, also fig. of sluggish persons, & see below; *~-livered*, unemotional; *~ steel*, sword, bayonet, etc., opposed to fire-arms, *inch* or *few* etc. *inches of ~ steel*, thrust). **2.** Not heated or having cooled after heat (*~ water; throw ~ water on plan*, discourage it; *~ in death* or *~, dead; ~ pig*, water thrown on sleeper to wake him, also *~-pig* as v.t.; *~-hammer*, work metal in *~* state; *~-CHISEL; ~ without, ~* sugarless spirit & water; *~ meat*, that has cooled after cooking; *~ shoulder*, of roast mutton, *give the ~ shoulder to*, entertain poorly, show distaste for company of, also *~-shoulder* as v.t.; *in ~ blood*, without the excuse of heat or excitement, of cruelty etc., whence *~'blood'ED²* a., *~'blood'ĕd-NESS* n.); feeling *~*; slow to absorb heat (of clayey soil). **3.** Without ardour, friendliness, or affection, undemonstrative, apathetic, (so *~'heart'ED²* a., *~'heart'ĕdNESS* n., *~'heart'ĕdLY²* adv.; *idea leaves* one *~*, unmoved, not impressed). **4.** Chilling, depressing, uninteresting, (*~ comfort, counsel, news*). **5.** Faint (of scent in hunting). **6.** *~ colours*, blue, grey, etc., opp. red, yellow, etc.; *~-drawn* CASTOR OIL; *~ coil*, tube coiled round inflamed part with *~* water running in it; *~ blast*, of *~* air forced into furnace; *~* CREAM; *~ feet*, (orig. army sl.) funk, disinclination to fight or go to or remain at the front; *~ snap*, sudden spell of *~* weather; *have person ~* (at one's mercy); *~* WAR. Hence *~'ISH¹(2)* a., *~'LY²* adv., *~'NESS* n. [OE, OS *cald*, OHG *kalt*, ON *kaldr*, Goth. *kalds* f. Gmc *kaldaz cogn. w. L *gelu*]

cŏld², n. Prevalence in atmosphere, or rarely in any object, of low temperature (*left out in the ~*, not looked after); inflamed state of mucous membrane, with hoarseness, running at nose, sore throat, etc. (CATCH¹ *~; often ~ in the head*). Hence *~'PROOF* a. [OE *cald* neut. adj. see prec.]

cŏld-shŏrt, a. Brittle in its cold state (of iron). [f. Sw. *kallskör* (= Norw., Da. *koldskjör*) f. *kallr* COLD + *skjör* brittle, w. assim. to SHORT (sense 6); cf. *red-short*]

cŏle, n. (Old name, now rare exc. in comb., for) kinds of cabbage etc., as rape, sea kale; *~-seed*, plant from which colza oil is got. [ME *col(e)*, north. *cal* (KALE), f. ON *kál* (= OE *cawel*, OHG *kōl(i)*), f. L *caulis* cabbage]

cŏlĕŏp'terous, a. Of the order of *Coleoptera* or beetles, with front wings converted into sheaths for hinder. [f. Gk *koleopteros* (*koleos* sheath, *pteron* wing) + -OUS]

***cŏle-slaw** (-ls-), n. Salad of sliced cabbage. [f. Du. *koolsla* = *kool-salade* (*kool* cabbage)]

cŏl'ic, n. Severe griping pains in belly. Hence *~kY²* a. [15th c., f. LL f. Gk *kolikos* (COLON¹, -IC)]

Coliseum. Var. of COLOSSEUM.

colī'tis, n. Inflammation of the lining of the colon. [COLON¹ + -ITIS]

collăb'or|āte, v.i. Work in combination (*with*, or abs.) esp. at literary or artistic production; co-operate treacherously with the enemy. So *~A'TION, ~ātor*, nn. [f. F *collaborer* or L COL(*laborare* LABOUR²), -ATE³]

cŏllage' (-ahzh), n. An abstract form of art in which photographs, pieces of paper, matchsticks, etc. are placed in juxtaposition & glued to the pictorial surface. [F]

collăpse', n., & v.i. (Undergo, experience, a) falling in, sudden shrinking together, giving way, prostration by loss of nervous or muscular power, breakdown of mental energy, loss of courage. [vb back form. f. *collapsed* f. L *collapsus* p.p. of COL(*labi laps-* slip); n.f. medical *collapsus* n.]

collap'sible, -able, a. So made as to collapse when required for packing etc. [-BLE]

coll'ar¹, n. Neckband, upright or turned over, of coat, dress, shirt, etc.; band of linen, lace, etc., completing upper part of costume; ‖ neck-chain of order of knighthood; ‖ ~ *of SS* or *esses,* formerly badge of House of Lancaster, still in some officials' costume; leather or metal band round dog's or prisoner's neck; roll round horse's neck bearing weight of draught (~-*harness,* opp. BREAST¹-*harness;* ~-*work,* hard pulling esp. up hill, & fig. of severe effort, so also *against the* ~); restraining or connecting band, ring, pipe, in machines etc.; arrangement connecting several fishing-flies; coloured stripe round animal's neck; piece of meat, brawn, fish, tied in roll; ~-*beam,* horizontal beam connecting two rafters and forming with them an A-shaped roof--truss; ~-*bone,* joining breast-bone & shoulder-blade, clavicle. Hence (-)~ED² (-rd), ~LESS, aa. [ME & AF *coler* (OF *-ier*) f. L *collare* (*collum* neck, -AR¹)]

coll'ar², v.t. Seize (person) by the collar, capture; (Rugby footb.) lay hold of and stop (opponent holding ball); (sl.) appropriate; press (meat etc.) into roll. [f. prec.]

collaret(te)', n. Woman's collar of lace, fur, etc. [f. F *collerette* (*collier* COLLAR¹, -ETTE)]

collat|e', v.t. Compare in detail (copies of text or document, one copy *with* another); (Bibliog.) verify order of (sheets) by signatures; put together; appoint (clergyman) to benefice (only of the Ordinary). So ~'OR n. [f. L COL(*lat*-p.p. st. of *ferre* bring)]

collat'eral, a. & n. Side by side, parallel; subordinate but from same source, contributory, connected but aside from main subject, course, etc.; of common descent but by different line (so as noun =~ kinsman); ~ *security* or ~, property pledged as guarantee for repayment of money (opp. *personal* giving right of action for recovery). Hence ~LY² adv. [ME, f. med. L COL(*lateralis* LATERAL)]

colla'tion, n. In vbl senses of COLLATE; also: (R.-C. Ch.) light repast in evening of fast-day; light meal (usu. *cold* ~) often at exceptional time. [ME, f. OF f. L *collationem* (COLLATE, -ION); sense *repast* from Benedictine monastery readings of Lives of the Fathers (*collationes patrum;* *collatio* also of the reading & debate on it) followed by light repast]

coll'eague (-ĕg), n. One of two or more holders of joint office or (loosely) of position in a profession or business (usu. with *my* etc.). [f. F *collègue* f. L COL(*lega*)]

coll'ect¹, n. Short prayer of Common Prayer Book, esp. one of those appropriated to days or seasons & read before Epistle & in morning & evening prayer. [ME & OF *collecte* f. med. L *collecta* in similar senses = L *collecta* fem. p.p. of *colligere* COLLECT²]

collect'², v.t. & i. Assemble, accumulate, bring or come together; get (taxes, contributions) from a number of people; (colloq.) call for, fetch; secure (specimens, books, etc.) for addition to a set; regain control of, concentrate, recover, (one*self,* one's thoughts, energies, courage; ~*ed,* not distracted, cool, whence ~ĕDLY² adv.; ~ *a horse,* keep him in hand, not let him sprawl); infer, gather, conclude. Hence ~ABLE, -IBLE, a. [f. (partly) OF *collecter* (f. *collecte* n. COLLECT¹), or LL *collectare,* or obs. E *collect* adj. f. L *collectus* p.p. of COL(*ligere* = *legere* pick)]

collectän'ea, n. pl. Collected passages, miscellany. [L, neut. pl. adj.]

collec'tion, n. Collecting; collecting of money, money collected, at meeting or Church service for charitable or religious purpose; accumulation *of* water, dust, etc.; group of things collected & belonging together (literary materials, specimens, works of art, etc.); ‖ (pl.) college terminal examination at Oxford etc. [ME, f. OF f. L *collectionem* (COLLECT², -ION)]

collec'tive, a. & n. Formed by, constituting a, collection, taken as a whole, aggregate, (~ *fruit,* resulting from many flowers, as mulberry); of, from, many individuals, common, (~ *note,* signed by several States; ~ *ownership,* of land, means of production, etc., by all for benefit of all, whence collec'tivism, collec'tivist, nn.); (Gram. & Log.) ~ *noun,* ~ *idea,* or ~, used in sing. to express many individuals, as *cattle, troop, duck;* ~ *security,* (Pol.) policy or principle of the alliance of several countries in order to guarantee the security of each one. Hence ~LY² (-vl-) adv., collectiv'ITY n. [f. F *collectif* or L *collectivus* (as prec., -IVE)]

collec'tor, n. One who collects (specimens, curiosities, railway tickets at station, money due, esp. taxes, rent, & subscriptions); collecting-apparatus in various machines; in India, chief official of district collecting revenue & holding magisterial powers, whence (office & district) ~ATE¹ n. Hence ~SHIP n. [ME & AF *collectour* (F *-eur*) f. med. L *collectorem* (as prec., -OR)]

‖ **colleen',** n. (Anglo-Ir.) Girl. [Ir. *cailín,* dim. of *caile* country-woman]

coll'ege, n. Body of colleagues with common functions & privileges (*Sacred C~,* ~ *of cardinals,* the Pope's council of 70; *Heralds' C~,* or *C~ of Arms; C~ of Physicians, Preceptors,* etc.); ‖ independent corporation of scholars in university, usu. with master, fellows, scholars, & students not on foundation; ‖ similar foundation outside university (as Eton, Dulwich); small degree-giving university; institution for higher education affiliated to university; place of professional study (army, naval, or agriculture, etc.); || large public secondary school (Marlborough); (pretentious name for) private school; buildings of any of these; ||~ *living*, benefice in gift of a ~; ~ *pudding*, small plum pudding for one person. Hence **collē′gial** a. [ME, f. OF *colege* or L (*collegium* (*collega* COLLEAGUE).

|| **cŏll′ĕger**, n. One of seventy foundation scholars at Eton. [-ER¹]

collē′gian, n. Member of a college; || (old sl.) inmate of a prison. [f. med. L *collegianus* (*collegium*, -AN)]

collē′giate¹, a. Constituted as, belonging to, a college or body of colleagues, corporate; ~ *church*, endowed for chapter but with no see, (Sc. & U.S.) under joint pastorate; ~ *school*, of high pretensions. Hence ~**LY²** (-tl-) adv. [f. LL *collegiatus* (COLLEGE, -ATE²)]

collē′giāte², v.t. Make collegiate. [as prec., -ATE³]

cŏll′ĕt, n. Encompassing band, ferrule, socket, flange holding gem, bezel. [F, dim. of COL]

collide′, v.i. Come into collision; be in conflict. [f. L COL(*lidere lis- = laedere* hurt)]

cŏll′ie, -ў, n. Scotch sheep-dog. [perh. f. *coll* COAL+-Y³ (as orig. black)]

cŏll′ier (-yer), n. Coal-miner, whence **cŏll′iery(3)** (-ye-) n.; coal-ship; sailor on this. [ME *colier* f. COAL+-IER]

cŏll′ig|āte, v.t. Bring into connexion (esp. isolated facts by a generalization). So ~**A′TION** n. [f. L COL(*ligare* bind), see -ATE³]

cŏll′im|āte, v.t. Adjust line of sight of (telescope etc.), make parallel (telescopes, rays). Hence ~**A′TION** n. [*collimare* false reading in Cicero for COL(*lineare* f. *linea* line)]

cŏll′imātor, n. Small attached telescope for collimating an instrument; tube in spectroscope throwing parallel rays on prism. [-OR]

collin′ear, a. In same straight line. [COL-]

|| **Cŏll′ins** (-z), n. (colloq.). = ROOFER. [Jane Austen, *P. & P.*, ch. xxiii]

colli′sion (-zhn), n. Dashing together, violent encounter of moving body, esp. ship or railway train, with another; (fig.) harsh combination (of consonants); clashing of opposed interests etc. (esp. *in* ~, *come into* ~ *with*); (Naut.) ~*mat*, ready for putting over hole made by ~. [f. LL *collisio* (COLLIDE, -ION)]

cŏll′oc|āte, v.t. Place together; arrange; station, set in particular place. So ~**A′TION** n. [f. L COL(*locare* f. *locus* place); see -ATE³]

cŏll′ocūtor, n. Partaker in talk, as *my* ~ *said*. [LL, f. COL(*loqui locut-* talk), -OR]

collŏd′ion, n. Solution of gun-cotton in ether filming when exposed, used in photography & surgery. Hence ~**ED³** (-nd) a., ~**IZE(5)** v.t., **collŏd′io-** comb. form. [f. Gk *kollōdēs* (*kolla* glue, -ODE)]

collŏgue′ (-g), v.i. Talk confidentially (with suggestion of plotting, an obs. sense). [orig. obsc.; perh. f. F *colloque* conference assoc. w. L *colloqui* converse & obs. *colleague* vb plot]

cŏll′oid, n. & n. Gluey (substance); (Path.) ~ *tissue* etc., degenerated into homogeneous gelatinous consistence (also ~, such substance); (Chem.) non-crystalline substance with very large molecules; when dissolved the solution is viscous & sticky, e.g. starch, gelatine, & plastics. Hence **colloid′AL** a. [Gk *kolla* glue, -OID]

cŏll′op, n. Slice of meat; (Bibl.) fold of skin in fat person or animal. [14th c. (= fried bacon & eggs), of Scand. orig.; cf. Sw. *kalops* (dial. *kollops*) slices of beef stewed, OSwed. *kolhuppadher* roasted on coals (*kol* COAL, *huppa* leap)]

collō′quial, a. In or of talk, oral; belonging to familiar speech, not used in formal or elevated language. Hence ~**ISM(3, 4)**, ~**IST(1)**, nn., ~**LY²** adv. [f. L *colloquium* COLLOQUY, -AL]

cŏll′oquist, n. = COLLOCUTOR. [foll., -IST(1)]

cŏll′oquy, n. Converse; a conversation; judicial and legislative court in Presbyterian Church. [f. L COL(*loquium* f. *loqui* speak)]

cŏll′otype, n. Thin plate of gelatine etched by actinic rays & then printed from (~ *plate*, *process*, etc.). [f. Gk *kolla* glue +TYPE]

collude′ (-ōō-), v.i. (arch.). Practise collusion. [f. L COL(*ludere lus-* play)]

collu′sion (-ōōzhn), n. Fraudulent secret understanding, esp. between ostensible opponents as in law-suit. Hence **collus′-IVE** (-ōō-) a., **collus′iveLY²** adv. [ME, f. OF, or f. L *collusio* (prec., -ION)]

collў′rium, n. (pl. -ia). Eye-salve; suppository. [f. L f. Gk *kollurion* poultice]

cŏll′ўwŏbbles (-lz), n. pl. (colloq.). Rumbling in the intestines. [imit.]

cŏl′ocўnth, n. Bitter-apple, gourd plant with bitter-pulped fruit used as purgative drug; the drug. [f. L f. Gk *kolokunthis*]

cŏl′on¹, n. (anat.). Greater part of larger intestine, from caecum to rectum. Hence **colŏn′ic** a., ~**IT′IS** n. [ME, f. L f. Gk *kōlon*]

cŏl′on², n. Punctuation-mark (:) ranking between period and semicolon, & used esp. to mark antithesis, illustration, or (often with dash : —) quotation; in Greek (·). [f. L f. Gk *kōlon* limb, clause]

colŏn′ate, n. Serf system in later Roman Empire. [f. LL *colonatus* (L *colonus*, see COLONY, -ATE¹)]

colonel (kĕrn′el), n. Highest regimental

officer; (short for) lieutenant-~; C~ BLIMP; C~ *Commandant*, honorary rank of senior officers of R.A., R.E., etc. Hence ~CY (kĕrn²) n. [16–17th c. also *coronel* f. obs. F *coronel* (now *colonel*) f. It. *colonnello* (*colonna* COLUMN)]

colo̅nelship (kĕrn⁴), n. Being a colonel (cf. *colonelcy*, ordinary word for the office), [-SHIP]

colo̅n'ial, a. & n. (Inhabitant) of a colony, esp. of a British Crown Colony; C~ *Office*, State department in charge of the Colonies. Hence ~ISM(2, 4) n., (freq. derog.) alleged policy of exploitation of backward or weak peoples, ~LY² adv. [F, or f. L *colonia* COLONY +-AL]

co̅l'onist, n. Settler in, part-founder or inhabitant of, a colony. [COLONIZE, -IST]

co̅l'oni̅z|e, -is|e (-iz), v.t. & i. Establish colony in; establish in a colony; establish or join a colony; *(Pol.) plant voters in a district for party purposes. Hence ~A'TION,~ER¹,nn. [f. L *colon-us, colon-ia*, COLON-Y+-IZE]

co̅lonna̅d|e', n. Series of columns with entablature; row of trees. Hence ~'ED³ a. [F (*colonne* COLUMN, -ADE)]

co̅l'onȳ, n. (Gk hist.) independent city founded by emigrants; (Rom. hist.) settlement usu. of veterans in conquered territory acting as garrison; settlement, settlers, in new country forming community fully or partly subject to mother State; their territory; people of one nationality or occupation in a city, esp. if living more or less in isolation or in a special quarter (so of animals, ~ *of sparrows* etc.); (Biol.) aggregate of animals as in coral. [f. L *colonia* (*colonus* farmer f. *colere* till)]

co̅l'ophon, n. Tail-piece in old books, often ornamental, giving information now placed on title-page (*from tille-page to ~, from cover to cover*). [LL, f. Gk *kolophōn* summit]

colo̅ph'onȳ, n. Dark resin distilled from turpentine & water. Hence colo̅ph'on-ATE¹(3) n., coloph-, colophon-, comb. forms. [f. L *colophonia* (*resina* resin) of *Colophon* in Lydia]

co̅loquin'tida, n. = COLOCYNTH.

Co̅lora̅'do̅ bee'tle (-rah-), n. Yellow black--striped beetle, destructive to potato plant. [*Colorado* in U.S.]

colo(u)ra̅'tion (kŭ-, kŏ-), n. Colouring, method of putting on or arranging colour; natural, esp. variegated, colour of living or other things. [F, or f. LL *coloratio* f. *colorare* COLOUR², -ATION]

co̅loratu̅ra (-ahtoor'a), n. Florid passages in vocal music (often attrib., as ~*soprano*). [It., f. L *colorare* to colour]

co̅lorif'ic (*also* kŭ-), a. Producing colour; highly coloured. [f. F *colorifique* (COLOUR¹, -I-, -FIC)]

co̅lorim'eter (*also* kŭ-), n. Instrument measuring intensity of colour. [L *color*, -I-, -METER]

colo̅ss'al, a. Of, like, a colossus; gigantic, huge; (colloq., f. G) remarkable, splendid, delightful. Hence ~LY² adv. [F, or f. COLOSSUS +-AL]

Co̅losse̅'um, Co̅lise̅'um, nn. Amphitheatre in Rome begun by Vespasian in A.D. 72; scene of gladiatorial combats & the martyrdom of many Christians. [L]

colo̅ss'us, n. (pl. -ī, -uses). Statue of much more than life size; gigantic person or personified empire etc., esp. conceived (like C~ of Rhodes) as standing astride over dominions. [L, f. Gk *kolossos*]

colo̅t'omȳ, n. (surg.). Incision in COLON¹ to provide artificial anus in stricture etc. [COLON¹, -TOMY]

colour¹ (kŭl'er), n. 1. Sensation produced on eye by rays of decomposed light (cf. *black*, effect produced by no light or by surface reflecting no rays, & *white*, effect produced by rays of undecomposed light). 2. A particular hue, one, or any mixture, of the constituents into which light decomposes as in spectrum, including loosely black, white (ACCIDENTAL ~; *complementary* ~, that combined with given ~ makes white; *fundamental, primary, simple*, ~s, red, green, & violet, or with painters red, blue, & yellow, giving all others by mixture; *secondary* ~, mixture of two primary; ~-*blind*, unable to distinguish certain colours, see DALTONISM, also fig. in U.S., impartial between whites & blacks, whence ~-*blind*NESS n.; ~ *scheme*, ~-design on which the furnishing and decoration of a room or the planting of a flower garden is based; ~-*wash*, coloured distemper (also as v.t.); *see the* ~ *of* one's *money*, receive some payment from him); *man, woman*, etc., *of* ~, of non-white race, esp. Negro (~ *bar*, legal or social distinction between whites & people of ~). 3. Ruddiness of face (*lose, gain*, ~; *change* ~, turn pale or red). 4. Appearance, light, (*paint in bright, dark*, ~s; *see in its true* ~s; *put false* ~s *upon*). 5. (Art) colouring, ~--system, -perception, effects as of ~ got by light and shade in engraving, whence ~IST(3) (kŭl'er-) n., ~IS'TIC a.; pigment, paint, (~-*box*, of assorted artists' paints; WATER-~s; ~-*man*, dealer in paints). 6. (Pl.) coloured ribbon, dress, etc., worn as symbol of party, membership of club, etc. (‖ *get* one's, *give* one *his*, ~s, of inclusion in athletic team; *show* one's ~s, one's party or character); flag of ship, pair of silken flags (*King's* or *Queen's* ~, *regimental* ~) carried by regiment (TROOP-*ing of the* ~ or ~s; *with the* ~s, serving in army; *sail under false* ~s, fig. of hypocrite or impostor; *come off with flying* ~s, win credit; *nail* ~s *to mast*, persist, refuse to climb down; ~-*sergeant*, senior sergeant of infantry company, now *Company Sergeant-Major* or *Quartermaster Sergt*, with duty of guarding ~s); coloured dresses. **7.** Show of reason, pretext, false plea, (*give no ~ for saying*; *under ~ of*). **8.** (Mus.) timbre, quality, also variety of expression. **9.** (Gen.) character, tone, quality, mood, shade of meaning, (*take one's ~ from*). **10.** (Literature) picturesqueness, ornate style, (*local ~*, use of details giving verisimilitude, background, or atmosphere). Hence ~FUL (kŭler-) a., full of ~, bright, gay (often fig.). [ME, f. OF *color*, -*our* f. L *colorem*]

colour² (kŭl′er), v.t. & i. Give colour to; paint, stain, dye; disguise; misrepresent (*highly ~ed details*); imbue with its own colour (*motive ~s act*); take on colour; blush; ~*ed person* (not wholly of white descent, of mixed blood). [ME, f. OF *colo(u)rer* f. L *colorare* (*color* COLOUR¹)]

col′ourab|le (kŭler-), a. Specious, plausible; counterfeit. Hence ~LY² adv. [ME, f. COLOUR² +-ABLE or OF *colorable*]

col′ouring (kŭler-), n. In vbl senses; esp., style in which thing is coloured, or in which artist employs colour. [-ING¹]

col′ourless (kŭler-), a. Without colour; pale; dull-hued; wanting in character or vividness; neutral, impartial, indifferent. Hence ~LY² adv., ~NESS n. [-LESS]

col′oury (kŭl′erĭ), a. (commerc.). Having the colour that goes with good quality (of hops, coffee, etc.). [-Y²]

côlpŏrteur′ (-tér; *also* kŏl²), n. Book-hawker, esp. one employed by society to distribute Bibles. [F]

côlt¹, n., & v.t. Young male of horse from when it is taken from dam to age of 4 (with thoroughbreds 5); inexperienced person, ‖ esp. cricket professional in first season; (Naut.) rope used for chastisement (vb, thrash with ~); ~*s′foot*, common large-leaved yellow-flowered weed; ~*'s tail*, ragged-edged cloud. Hence ~HOOD n., ~′ISH¹ a. [OE *colt* of unkn. orig., but cf. Sw. *kult* etc. applied to half-grown animals & boys]

Côlt², n. (Used for) ~ revolver, automatic gun, or pistol. [S. ~, inventor (d. 1862)]

•côl′ter. See COULTER.

cŏl′ŭbrine, a. Snake-like; esp., of, like, the *Coluber* (genus of harmless snakes). [f. L *colubrinus* (*coluber* snake)]

cŏlumbār′ium, n. (pl. -*ia*). (In mod. use) building with tiers of niches for reception of cinerary urns. [L, = pigeon-house]

cŏl′umbine¹, n. Garden plant with flower like five clustered pigeons, kind of aquilegia. [ME, f. OF f. LL *columbina* (*herba*) f. L *columba* dove, -INE¹]

Cŏl′umbine², n. Mistress of Harlequin in pantomime. [f. F *Colombine* or It. -*ina* f. *colombino* dovelike]

cŏlŭmb′|ium, n. (chem.). = NIOBIUM. Hence ~ITE¹ n., native ore of ~ium. [f. *Columbia* in United States, -IUM]

cŏl′umn (-um), n. **1.** (Archit.) long vertical often slightly tapering cylinder usu.

supporting entablature or arch, or alone as monument, (fig.) support; ~-shaped object, organ in Anat. or Bot., part of machine, etc. (~ *of water, mercury*, confined vertical cylindrical mass; ~ *of smoke*, rising straight). **2.** Vertical division of page for figures etc., or to reduce length of lines esp. in newspapers (also part of newspaper, sometimes more or less than ~, devoted to special subject, as AGONY ~, *advertisement ~s*; *our ~s*, *the ~s of The Times*, contents of newspaper), whence ~IST n., journalist who regularly contributes to a newspaper a ~ of miscellaneous comment on people and events. **3.** Narrow-fronted deep arrangement of troops in successive lines (*in ~ of sections, platoons, companies*, with one section etc. forming each line & one section's etc. length between lines; *quarter ~*, with 6 paces between lines); FIFTH ~; body of ships, esp. following one another. Hence or cogn. **colŭm′nar**¹, ~ED² (-und), **colŭm′niform**, aa. [15th c. & OF *colompne* f. L *columna* pillar; mod. sp. f. L]

colŭre′, n. One of two great circles intersecting rectangularly at poles & dividing equinoctial & ecliptic into four equal parts, one passing through equinoctial, & one through solstitial, points of ecliptic. [f. LL f. Gk *kolouros* truncated]

côl′za, n. = COLE-*seed*; ~-*oil*, made from it & used in lamps. [F, f. LG *kōlsāt* COLE-seed]

com-, pref. = L *cum* in comb., retained as *com*- before b, p, m, & rarely before vowels, changed to *cor*- before r, *col*-before l, *co*- before vowels, h, & gn, & *con*-before other consonants; *com*- occurs in E also before f (*comfort*). Meaning, *with, together, altogether, completely.*

côm′a¹, n. Unnatural heavy sleep, stupor, lethargy. Hence ~TOSE a. [f. Gk *kōma -atos* deep sleep]

côm′a², n. (pl. -*ae*). (Bot.) tuft of silky hairs at end of seed; (Astron.) nebulous envelope round nucleus of comet. [L, f. Gk *komē* hair of head]

cŏmb¹ (-m), n. Toothed strip of horn, metal, ivory, etc., for arranging, cleaning, or confining the hair; = CURRY²-*comb*; thing of same shape, look, or purpose, in many machines, esp. for dressing wool, or collecting electricity, or in animal structure; red fleshy crest of fowl esp. cock, analogous growth in other birds, (*cut the ~ of*, humiliate); crest of hill or wave; = HONEYCOMB¹; ~-*out*, process or instance of COMB²ing out. Hence (-)cŏmbED² (-md) a. [OE, OS *camb*, OHG *kamb*, ON *kambr* f. Gmc *¹kambaz*]

cŏmb² (-m), v.t. & i. Draw comb through (hair), curry (horse), dress (wool, flax) with comb; search (place) thoroughly; (of wave) curl over; ~ *out*, secure or get rid of (as) by ~ing (esp. of getting recruits from among those previously exempted from service). [ME f. prec., replacing *kemb* see UNKEMPT]

com′bat (kŭ- or kŏ-), n., & v.t. & i. (Do) battle; *single~*, duel; (engage in) contest, struggle; oppose, strive against. [f. F *combat & combattre* f. LL (COM-, *battere, batuere*, fight), cf. BATTLE]

com′batant (kŭ- or kŏ-), a. & n. Fighting, fighter. [OF part. as prec.]

com′bative (kŭ- or kŏ-), a. Pugnacious. Hence ~LY² adv., ~NESS n. [COMBAT v. +-IVE]

combe. See COOMB.

comb′er (-mer), n. In vbl senses; esp.: machine for combing cotton or wool very fine; long curling wave, breaker. [-ER¹]

combinā′tion, n. Combining; combined state (*in ~ with*); combined set of things or persons; (Math., pl.) different collections possible of given number of individuals in groups of given smaller number; (Chem.) union of substances in compound with properties differing from theirs; united action; ‖(pl.) single under-garment for body & legs; motor-cycle with side-car attached (in full *motor-cycle ~*); ~ (*lock*), complicated locking arrangement used for safes, strong-rooms, etc.; ~-*room*, at Cambridge = COMMON¹-*room*. [16th c., f. obs. F *combination* or LL *combinatio* (COMBINE, -ATION)]

combine′, v.t. & i., & n. 1. Join together (persons or things material or other); possess (esp. qualities usu. separate) together; (cause to) coalesce in one substance, form chemical compound; co-operate; ~*d operation* (in which the fighting services co-operate); *combining form* (Gram.), special form of word used in combinations (e.g. *Anglo-* repr. *England* or *English*). 2. n. (*usu.* kŏm⁴). Combination of persons, esp. to raise prices or obstruct course of trade; (pr. kŏm′-) ~d reaping and threshing machine. So **cŏm′binātive** a. [ME, f. OF *combiner* or LL COM(*binare* f. L *bini* two together)]

cŏmb′ing (-mĭ-), n. In vbl senses; esp., (pl.) hairs combed off. [-ING¹]

combŭs′ti|ble, a. & n. (Matter, thing) capable of or used for burning; excitable. Hence ~BIL′ITY n. [f. F, or med. L *combustibilis* (foll., -IBLE)]

combŭs′tion (-schn), n. 1. Destruction by fire (SPONTANEOUS ~). 2. (Chem. etc.) development of light & heat going with chemical combination; oxidation of organic tissue. [OF, or LL *combustio* f. L *comburere -ust-* burn]

come¹ (kŭm), v.i. (*came, come*). 1. Start, move, arrive, towards or at a point, time, or result (often not specified because obvious, while point of departure, if it matters, is always specified; cf. GO; ~ *into world*, be born; ~ *of* AGE; ~ *to an end*, cease; ~ *to hand*, of letter etc., be delivered; ~ SHORT; ~ *to a point*, taper;

~ *to blows*, fight; ~ *home to*, be realized by; ~ *& go*, pass to & fro, pay brief visit, be transitory; *let 'em all ~ l*, sl. announcement of readiness; *light ~ light go*, what is easily won is soon lost; *coming nineteen*, in nineteenth year; *two years~ Christmas*, including time from now to Christmas). 2. Be brought (*the dinner came*; ~ *under notice, before judge*). 3. Fall, land, *on* (*came on my head*), 4. Move relatively by motion of beholder etc. towards one (~ *into sight, to* one's *knowledge, in* one's *way*; ~ *to light*, be revealed). 5. Reach point with hand, instrument, or missile. 6. Occur, fall *to* lot of, (~*s on such a page*; *one ~s before, after, another*; ~ *into* one's *head; the work, ill luck, ~s to me*). 7. Happen (*how ~s it that —?*; *to~* pred. adj., *future*; *for a year to —; the to-~*, the future; ~ *what may*, whatever happens). 8. Become present from future (~ *to pass; the time will ~ when*). 9. Spring *of*, be the result *of*, (*that's what ~s of grumbling*; ~ *of noble parents*). 10. Enter, be brought, *into* (collision, play, prominence; ~ *to harm*, be injured). 11. Amount *to* (~*s to* 2/6; *it ~s to this, that—*, is as much as to say that). 12. Take form (*the butter will not~*). 13. Find oneself under compulsion or in a position *to* (*have ~ to believe, has ~ to be used*). 14. (With cogn. obj.) traverse, accomplish, (*have ~ 3 miles, a long way*). 15. Play a part (sl.; ~ *the bully over*; ~ *it strong*, show vigour; ~ *it too strong*, overdo something, exaggerate). 16. Become, get to be, prove, (*string ~s untied, things ~ right, he came alive*; ~*s expensive, easy, true, natural*). 17. (Imperat. as exclamation) now then (encouraging), think again, don't be hasty. 18. ~ *about*, happen; ~ *across*, meet with; ~ *along*, (colloq.) make haste; ~ *at*, reach, discover, get access to; ~ *away*, get detached; ~ *back*, recur to memory, *retaliate or retort (sl.); (as n., ~-back) a return to, reinstatement in, one's former position (*stage a ~-back*); ~ *by* (prep.) obtain, (adv.) pass; ~ *clean*, confess; ~ *down*, extend downwards *to*, be handed down by tradition, fall, be humbled (esp. *in the world*, lose caste); ~ *down upon*, rebuke, punish, exact reparation from; ~ *down with*, pay (money); ~ *forward*, present oneself, answer appeal; ~ *in*, enter house or room, begin innings, take such a place in race etc. (~ *in third*), be elected, come to power, be received as income, become seasonable or fashionable, serve a purpose (esp. ~ *in useful*), find a place (*where does the joke ~ in?*; *where do I ~ in?* how are my interests advanced?); ~ *in for*, get share of, get; ~ *into*, receive possession of; ~ *near doing*, narrowly escape or fail; ~ *off*, be detached, extricate oneself from contest etc. in such state (*with flying* COLOURS, *badly*), be accomplished, fulfilled; ~ *off it* (colloq.), stop acting or talking like that, change your tune; ~ *on*, (prep.) = ~ *upon*, (adv.) continue coming, advance esp. to attack, progress, thrive, supervene (of wind, storm, disease), arise to be discussed, appear on stage, begin to bowl, (imperat.) follow me, I defy you; ~ *out*, go on strike, emerge from examination etc. with such success, emerge from clouds, be found out, be solved, show itself (of photograph, smallpox, arrogance), be published (~*s out on Saturdays*), make début on stage or in society; ~ *out with*, utter; ~ *over*, (prep.) master as an influence, (adv.) ~ from some distance or across obstacle (*came over with the Conqueror, over from London to see us*), change sides or opinion; ~ *round*, look in for casual visit, recover from ill temper, swoon, anaesthetic, etc., be converted from one view to its opposite; ~ *to*, (prep.) inherit, return to (one*self*, one's *senses* from fainting-fit or from folly), (adv.) cease moving, revive; ~ *under*, be classed as or among, be subjected to (influence); ~ *up*, ∥ join university, approach person for talk, get abreast *with*, spring out of ground, become fashionable, be mooted, be equal *to* standard etc., (imperat., to horse) go faster; ~ *upon*, attack by surprise, strike or lay hold of (mind), make demand on, be a burden to, meet by chance with. [OE, OS *cuman*, OHG *queman*, ON *koma*, Goth. *qiman* f. Gmc *kweman, kuman*, cogn. w. L *venire*, Gk *bainō*]

come[2] (kŭm), n. ~*-&-go*, passing to & fro; ~*-down*, downfall, degradation. [f. prec.]

come-ăt'-able (kŭm-), a. Accessible. [-ABLE]

coměd'ian, n. Actor, writer, of comedies. [f. F *comédien* f. *comédie* COMEDY]

comědiěnne', n. Comedy actress. [F]

cŏm'ĕdist, n. Writer of comedies. [foll., -IST(3)]

cŏm'ĕdў, n. Stage-play of light, amusing, & often satirical character, chiefly representing everyday life, & with happy ending (cf. TRAGEDY); branch of drama concerned with ordinary persons & employing familiar language; life, or an incident in it, regarded as a spectacle; *Old, Middle, New, C*~, classification of ancient Greek ~, the first farcical & largely political, the last corresponding to modern ~, & the second transitional. [ME, f. OF *comedie* f. L f. Gk *kōmōidia* f. *kōmōidos* comic poet f. *kōmos* revel]

come'l∥y (kŭm'li), a. Pleasant to look at (usu. of personal appearance, sometimes of behaviour or conduct). Hence ~i̯-NESS n. [ME *cumelich, cumli* prob. f. *becumelich* (BECOME + -LY); cf. MHG *komlich* suitable, G *bequem* (C.T.O.)]

cŏm'er (kŭ-), n. One who comes (usu. qualified, as *first* ~); *all* ~*s*, any one who applies, takes up a challenge, etc. [-ER[1]]

coměs'tĭble, n. (usu. pl.). Thing to eat. [F, f. med. L *comestibilis* f. L *comedere* eat up]

cŏm'ĕt, n. A hazy-looking object, occas. with a star-like nucleus, & occas. with a tail, moving in an elliptical or nearly parabolic path about the sun; ~*-year*, in which conspicuous ~ comes; ~*-wine*, made in ~*-year*, supposed of superior quality. Hence ~ARY[1], **comět'ic**, aa. [ME & OF *comete* f. L f. Gk *komētēs* long-haired (star); OE *cometa* f. L (*-ta*)]

com'fit (kŭ-), n. Sweetmeat, sugarplum. [ME f. OF *confit* f. L CON(*fectum* = *factum* neut. p.p. of *facere* make)]

com'fort (kŭ-), n., & v.t. **1.** Relief in affliction, consolation, being consoled; person who consoles one or saves one trouble; cause of satisfaction; conscious well-being, being comfortable; possession of ~*s*, things that make life easy; *creature* ~*s*, good food, clothes, etc.; *eiderdown quilt; *~ *station*, public lavatory. **2.** v.t. Soothe in grief, console; make comfortable; ~ *the king's enemies* (arch.), give them aid. [ME *confort* etc. f. OF *confort*(er) f. LL *confortare* strengthen f. L *fortis* strong]

com'fortable (kŭ-), a. & n. **1.** Such as to obviate hardship, save trouble, & promote content, ministering to comfort; at ease, free from hardship, pain, & trouble; tranquil, with easy conscience; *the C*~ *Words*, the four scriptural passages following the Absolution in the Communion Office. **2.** *n.* Eiderdown quilt. Hence **com'fortablY**[2] (kŭ-) adv. [ME, f. AF *confortable* (prec., -ABLE); cf. LL *confortabilis*]

com'forter (kŭ-), n. One who comforts (*the C*~, Holy Ghost; *Job's* ~, professed consoler who depresses); ∥ baby's dummy teat; ∥ woollen scarf; *eiderdown quilt. [ME, f. AF *confortour*, OF *-eor* (as prec., -ER[1])]

com'fortless (kŭ-), a. Dreary, without provision for comfort. [-LESS]

cŏm'frey (kŭ-), n. (pl. ~*s*). Tall rough-leaved ditch plant with clusters of whitish or purplish bells. [f. AF *cum-*, OF *confirie* of obsc. orig.]

com'fy (kŭ-), a. (colloq.). Comfortable. [abbr.]

cŏm'ic, a. & n. **1.** Of comedy (~ *opera*, with ~ treatment & much spoken dialogue, also mere burlesque set to music); mirth-provoking, laughable or meant to be so, facetious, burlesque, funny, (~ *song, paper*; ~ *history of Rome* etc.; ~ *strip*, set of drawings, forming part of a series, appearing regularly in a journal, usu. broadly humorous). **2.** n. (colloq.). Music-hall comedian (also, in F form, *comique*); ~ *paper*. Hence ~o- comb. form. [f. L f. Gk *kōmikos*]

cŏm'ical, a. Mirth-provoking, laughable;

odd, queer. Hence ~ITY (-ăl²) n., ~LY² adv. [as prec. + -AL]

Cŏm'infŏrm, n. International Communist organization (1947–56) established to carry on the propaganda formerly conducted by the Comintern. [f. first elements of Russ. forms of Com(munist) Inform(ation Bureau)]

Cŏm'intĕrn, n. Third INTERNATIONAL. [f. first elements of Russ. forms of Com(munist) Intern(ational)]

cŏmĭtădj'ĭ, n. Member of band of irregular soldiery in the Balkans. [common Balkan form = Turk. komita, f. F comité committee, + -dji; lit. 'member of a (revolutionary) committee']

cŏm'ĭtў, n. Courtesy; ~ of nations, friendly recognition as far as practicable of each other's laws & usages. [f. L cōmitas (cōmis courteous)]

cŏmm'a, n. Punctuation-mark (,) of the least separation indicated between parts of sentence, also used to separate figures etc.; (Mus.) definite minute interval or difference of pitch; inverted ~s, raised or superior ~s used to begin & end a quotation, the first (or first pair) inverted (he said 'no' or "no"); ~ bacillus, ~-shaped found in cholera; ~ butterfly, one with a white ~-shaped mark on the underside of the hind wing. [f. L f. Gk komma clause]

command'¹ (-ah-), v.t. & i. Order, bid, (what God ~s, ~s us, ~s us to do, ~s that we should do, ~s to be done; also ellipt., let us do as God ~s; & abs., God ~s & man obeys); have authority over, control of; be supreme; be in command; be in command of (ship, forces, etc.); ~ in chief, be commander-in-chief of, or abs.; restrain, master, (passions, oneself); have at disposal or within reach (sum, skill, person; so yours to ~, obediently); deserve & get (sympathy etc.); dominate (strategic position) from superior height, look down over. [ME, f. OF comander f. LL commandare COMMEND]

command'² (-ah-), n. Order, bidding, (word of ~, customary order for movement in drill; at or by one's ~, in pursuance of his bidding); ‖ ~ paper (usu. abbr. Cmd, formerly Cd, with register number, as Cd 5723), paper laid by ~ of the Crown before Parliament etc.; exercise or tenure of authority, esp. naval or military (in ~ of, commanding; under ~ of, commanded by); control, mastery, possession, (great ~ of language, skill in speech; at ~, ready to be used at will; ~ of the passes etc.); body of troops etc., district, under commander (the Nore, Southern, Bomber, C~); ~-in-chief, supreme ~; ‖ ~ night, with theatrical etc. performance given by royal ~; ‖ ~ performance, theatrical etc. performance given by royal ~; the HIGH(er) ~. [f. prec.]

cŏmmandănt', n. Commanding officer, esp. governor of fortress. Hence ~SHIP n. [17th c., F (COMMAND¹, -ANT)]

cŏmmandeer', v.t. Impress (men), seize (stores), for military service. [f. S.-Afr.-Du. kommanderen (-āʳ-) f. F as prec.]

comman'der (-ah-), n. In vbl senses; also or esp.: C~ of the Faithful, title of Caliph; C~, Lieut.-C~, naval OFFICERS; Wing C~, AIR¹-force officer; member of higher class in some Orders of Knighthood; large wooden mallet; C~-in-Chief, (Army) of all military land-forces of State, of portion of them quartered in colony, or of expedition in foreign country, (Navy) of all ships on a station. Hence ~SHIP(1) n. [ME, f. OF comandere, -eor (COMMAND¹, -ER¹)]

comman'ding (-ah-), a. In vbl senses; esp.: exalted, impressive, (of persons, looks, ability, etc.); with wide view (of hill, position). [-ING²]

command'ment (-ah-), n. Divine command (the ten ~s, Mosaic decalogue; eleventh ~, any precept jestingly classed with these). [ME, f. OF comandement (COMMAND¹, -MENT)]

comman'dŏ (-ah-), n. (pl. ~s). Party called out for military service, body of troops; (C~) unit of British & Imperial amphibious shock-troops raised orig. in the 1939–45 war, member of such unit. [Port., f. commandar COMMAND¹, wd used by S.-Afr. Dutch, & familiarized in Boer war]

comme il faut (kŏm ēl fō), pred. a. Well-bred. [F]

commĕm'orāt|e, v.t. Celebrate in speech or writing; preserve in memory by some celebration; (of things) be a memorial of. Hence ~IVE a. [f. L commemorare bring to remembrance, see -ATE³]

commĕmorā'tion, n. Act of commemorating; service, part of service, in memory of saint or sacred event; ‖ (Oxford Univ.) annual celebration in memory of founders. [ME, f. L commemoratio (as prec., see -ATION)]

commĕnce', v.t. & i. Begin (work, doing, to do); (arch.) start, set up, as (lawyer etc.); ‖ take the full degree of (M.A. etc.). [ME, f. OF comencer f. Rom. *cominitiare (COM-, initiare INITIATE)]

commĕnce'ment (-sm-), n. In vbl senses; also, ceremony when degrees of Master & Doctor are conferred at Cambridge, Dublin, & U.S. Univv. [ME, f. OF (prec., -MENT)]

commĕnd', v.t. Entrust for safe keeping (arch. exc. in ~ one's soul to God, ~ thing to person's care); praise; (arch.) ~ me to, remember me kindly to (person); ~ me to, give me by choice (often iron.). [ME, f. L com(mendare=mandare entrust, see MANDATE)]

commĕn'dab|le, a. Praiseworthy. Hence ~leNESS (-ln-) n., ~LY² adv. [ME, f. OF f. L commendabilis (prec., -BLE)]

commĕn'dăm, n. Tenure of benefice in absence of regular incumbent. [med. L (dare in) commendam give in trust]

commĕndā'tion, n. Praise; act of commending person to another's favour. [ME, f. OF f. L *commendationem* (as COMMEND, see -ATION)]

commĕn'datory, a. Commending, holding, held, in commendam. [f. LL *commendatorius* (as prec., see -ORY)]

commĕn'sal, a. & n. (One) who eats at the same table; (animal, plant) living as another's tenant & sharing its food (cf. PARASITE). Hence ~ISM, **cŏmmensăl'-ITY,** nn. [ME, f. OF, or f. med. L *commensalis* f. *mensa* table, see -AL]

commĕn'surable (-sher-), a. Measurable by the same standard (*with, to*); (of numbers) divisible without remainder by the same quantity; proportionate *to*. Hence~ABIL'ITY,~ableNESS, nn.,~abLY² adv., (-sher-). [f. LL COM(*mensurabilis,* as MEASURE, see -BLE)]

commĕn'surate (-sher-), a. Coextensive (*with*); proportionate (*to, with*). Hence ~LY² (-tl-) adv., ~NESS (-tn-) n. [f. LL COM(*mensuratus,* prec., -ATE²)]

cŏmm'ĕnt¹, n. Explanatory note ᴜᴄ remark; criticism; (fig., of events et ᴀ.) illustration. [f. L *commentum* contrivance (in LL also = interpretation) neut. ᴘ.p. of *comminisci* devise]

cŏmm'ĕnt², v.i. Write explanatory notes (*upon* a text); make (esp. unfavourable) remarks (*upon*). [f. prec. or F *commenter*]

cŏmm'entary, n. Expository treatise; set of running comments on a book or remarks on a speech or performance; comment. [f. L *commentarius, -ium,* sb. use of adj. (COMMENT¹, -ARY¹)]

commĕntā'tion, n. Making of comments. [f. L *commentatio* (*commentari* discuss, see COMMENT & -ATION)]

cŏmm'ĕntātor, n. Writer of commentary; eyewitness whose description of a ceremony, sporting event, etc., is broadcast. [L (as prec., see -OR)]

cŏmm'ĕrce, n. Exchange of merchandise, esp. on a large scale; CHAMBER *of* ~; intercourse (esp. sexual); card game. [F, or f. L COM(*mercium* f. *merx mercis* merchandise)]

commĕr'cial (-shl), a. & n. Of, engaged in, bearing on, commerce; ~ (*traveller*), trader's agent, showing samples & soliciting orders; ~ announcement or programme; ‖~ *room* (in hotel for ~ travellers). Hence ~ISM, ~IST, (-sha-), ~ITY (-shĭăl²), nn., ~IZE v.t., ~LY² adv., (-sha-). [f. prec.+-AL]

Cŏmm'ie, n. (colloq.). Communist. [abbr.]

cŏmminā'tion, n. Threatening of divine vengeance; recital of divine threats against sinners in Anglican Liturgy. [ME, f. L *comminatio* f. *comminari* threaten; see -ATION]

cŏmm'inatory, a. Threatening, denun-

ciatory. [f. med. L *comminatorius* (as prec., see -ORY)]

commin'gle (-nggl), v.t. & i. Mingle together. [COM-]

cŏmm'inūte, v.t. Reduce to small fragments; divide (property) into small portions. So **cŏmminū'tion** n. [f. L COM(*minuere -ut-* f. *minor* less)]

commis'er|āte (-z-), v.t. & i. Feel, express, pity for; condole *with.* Hence or cogn. '~A'TION n., ~ātIVE a., ~ātIVELY² adv. [f. L *commiserari* f. *miser*; see MISER¹, -ATE³]

cŏmmissār', n. (Former name of) head of a government department of the U.S.S.R. [Russ. *kommissar* f. F *commissaire* (as COMMISSARY)]

cŏmmissār'ial, a. Of a commissary. [-AL]

cŏmmissār'iat, n. Department (esp. Mil.) for supply of food etc.; a department of the Soviet Republic Civil Service. [as foll., see -ATE¹]

cŏmm'issary, n. Deputy, delegate; representative of a bishop in part of his diocese, or of absent bishop; officer charged with supply of food etc. for body of soldiers; *C~ general,* chief ~, esp. (Mil.) chief of a commissariat service. Hence ~SHIP n. [ME, f. med. L *commissarius* person in charge (COMMIT, COMMIT, -ARY¹)]

commi'ssion¹ (-shn), n. **1.** Command, instruction; authority, body of persons having authority, to perform certain duties; ‖~ *of the peace,* (authority given to) Justices of the Peace; *on the*~, having this; *royal* ~, ~ of inquiry or committee appointed by the Crown at the instance of the Government. **2.** Warrant conferring authority, esp. that of officers in the army, navy, and air force from lieutenant or pilot officer upwards. **3.** *In* ~, (of persons) having delegated authority, (of an office) placed by warrant in charge of a body of persons instead of the constitutional administrator, (of ship of war) manned, armed, & ready for sea. **4.** Entrusting of authority etc. to a person; charge, matter, entrusted to person to perform. **5.** Authority to act as agent for another in trade, as.*have goods on* ~; pay of a ~-agent, percentage on amount involved. **6.** Committing (*of* crime etc.); ‖~-*day,* opening day of assizes, when judge's ~ is read. [ME, f. OF f. L *commissionem* (as prec., -ION)]

commi'ssion² (-shn), v.t. Empower by commission; give (officer) command of ship; order (ship) for active service; (of officer) assume command of (ship); give (artist etc.) a commission for piece of work. [f. prec.]

commissionaire' (-shonār), n. ‖ Member of the *corps of C~s* organized in London for employment as messengers etc.; uniformed door attendant at theatres, cinemas, large shops, etc. [F, see COM-MISSIONER]

commi'ssioned (-shond), a. Authorized; (of officers) holding rank by commission; (of ships) put in commission. [-ED¹]

commi'ssioner (-sho-), n. One appointed by commission; member of a commission, esp. of government boards etc., as *Charity, Civil Service, C~*; representative of supreme authority in a district, department, etc.; *High C~*, chief representative in London of Commonwealth countries, also chief United Kingdom representative in Commonwealth countries; *Lord High C~*, representative of the Crown at the General Assembly of the Church of Scotland. Hence ~SHIP n. [ME, f. med. L *commissionarius* (COMMISSION, -ARY¹, -ER²(2))]

commi'ssūre, n. Juncture, seam; joint between two bones; line where lips, eyelids, meet; bands of nerve substance connecting hemispheres of brain, two sides of spinal cord, etc. So **commis-sūr'AL** a. [f. L *commissura* junction (as foll., see -URE)]

commit', v.t. (-tt-). Entrust, consign, for treatment or safe keeping (*to* person, his care, his judgement, *to* writing, memory, earth, the flames); ~ (*to* prison), consign officially to custody; refer (bill) to committee; perpetrate (crime, blunder), whence ~t'ABLE a.; compromise, involve, (character, honour, one*self*); bind one*self to* (a course). Hence ~t'AL n. (~ting to prison, reference to committee, ~ting of oneself), ~MENT n. (esp., engagement that restricts freedom of action). [ME, f. L *committere* join, entrust, f. *mittere miss-* send]

committ'ee (-ti), n. Body of persons appointed for special function by (& usu. out of) a (usu. larger) body, as (Parl.) *C~ of Supply, Ways & Means, House resolves itself into a C~, goes into C~, is in C~, C~ of the whole House; Standing C~* (permanent during existence of appointing body); *Joint C~* (of members nominated by different bodies); ~ -*man*, member of a ~; (Law, pron. kŏmĭtē') person entrusted with charge, as ~*s for lunatics*. [f. prec. + -EE]

commix', v.t. & i. (arch., poet.). Mix. So ~TURE n. [back formation f. *commixt*, as MIX f. MIXED]

commōde', n. Chest of drawers; chiffonier; (esp. *night-~*) close-stool. [F, f. L COM(*modus* measure) convenient]

commōd'ious, a. Roomy; (arch.) handy. Hence ~LY² adv., ~NESS n. [f. F *commodieux* or med. L *commodiosus* f. L *commodus*; see prec.]

commōd'itў, n. Useful thing; article of trade (*staple* ~); (arch.) convenience. [ME, f. OF *commodite* or L *commoditas* (COMMODE, -TY)]

commŏdōre, n. Naval officer above captain and below rear-admiral (in Brit.

navy a temporary rank); *Air C~*, officer of AIR¹ *Force*; (courtesy title) senior captain when three or more ships cruise together, captain of pilots, president of yacht-club; senior captain of a shipping line; ~'s ship. [17th c. *comma*(*n*)*dore*, prob. f. Du. *kommandeur* commander; present form unexpl.]

cŏmm'on¹, a. (-er, -est). 1. Belonging equally to, coming from, or done by, more than one, as *our ~ humanity*, ~ *cause, ~ consent*. 2. Belonging to, open to, affecting, the public, as ~ *crier, jail, alehouse, nuisance, scold*. 3. Of ordinary occurrence, as *a ~ experience* (~ *or garden*, sl., of the familiar kind); ordinary, of ordinary qualities, as ~ *honesty, no ~ mind*; without rank or position, as ~ *soldier, the ~ people*; of the most familiar type, as ~ *nightshade, snake*. 4. Of inferior quality; vulgar. 5. (Math.) belonging to two or more quantities, as ~ *factor, multiple*; (Gram.) ~ *noun*, name applicable to any one of a class, ~ *gender*, masculine or feminine; (Pros.) of variable quantity; (Mus.) ~ *time, measure*, (two or four beats in bar), ~ *chord*. 6. ~ *form¹*; ~ *ground*, basis for argument etc. accepted by both sides; ~ *law*, unwritten law of England, administered by the Queen's courts, purporting to be derived from ancient usage (~ *law wife*, concubine); ~ *metre*, hymn stanza of 4 lines (with 8, 6, 8, 6 syllables); *Court of C~ Pleas* (for trial of civil causes, abolished 1875); *C~ Prayer*, liturgy set forth in Book of C. P. of Edward VI; ‖ ~ *room*, (in some colleges, schools, etc.) room to which the members have ~ access for business or social purposes; ~ *sense*, normal understanding, good practical sense in everyday affairs, general feeling (of mankind or community), *philosophy of ~ sense* (accepting primary beliefs of mankind as ultimate criterion of truth); ~*sens'ical*, possessing, marked by, ~ sense; ~ *weal*, ~*weal*, arch., public welfare, (also) = COMMONWEALTH. Hence ~NESS (-n-n-) n. [ME & OF *comun* f. L *communis*]

cŏmm'on², n. Land belonging to a community, esp. unenclosed waste land; (*right of*) ~, a man's right over another's land, as ~ *of pasturage; out of the ~*, unusual; *in ~*, in joint use, shared; *in ~ with*, in the same way as (*in ~ with all sensible people I hold that . . .*). [prec. as n.]

cŏmm'onable, a. (Of animals) that may be pastured on common land; (of land) that may be held in common. [f. obs. vb *common* f. OF *comuner* (as COMMON¹) +-ABLE]

cŏmm'onage, n. Right of common; land, condition of land, held in common; commonalty. [-AGE]

cŏmm'onaltў, n. The common people; general body (of mankind etc.); body

corporate. [ME & OF *communalle, -aute,*
f. med. L *communalitatem*; see COMMON[1],
-AL, -TY]

¶ **cŏmm'oner,** n. One of the common
people (below rank of peer); (rarely)
member of House of Commons, esp. *the
great C~,* elder Wm Pitt, *First C~,* the
Speaker; (at Oxford University) student
not on foundation; one who has right
of common. [ME, f. COMMON[2] & obs. vb
common (see COMMONABLE) +-ER[1]]

cŏmm'oney, n. Inferior playing-marble.
[COMMON[1]+-Y[3]]

cŏmm'onlý, adv. Usually; to an ordinary
degree, as ~ *honest;* meanly, cheaply.
[-LY[2]]

cŏmm'onplăce[1], n. & a. **1.** Notable
passage, entered for use in a ~*-book;*
ordinary topic; everyday saying; platitude; anything common or trite. **2.** adj.
Lacking originality, trite. Hence ~NESS
(-sn-) n. [=L *locus communis*=Gk *koinos
topos* general theme]

cŏmm'onplăce[2], v.t. & i. Extract commonplaces from; enter in commonplace-
-book; utter commonplaces. [f. prec.]

cŏmm'ons (-z), n. pl. The common
people; third estate in English or other
similar constitution, represented by
Lower House of Parliament (*House of
C~*); provisions shared in common;
common table, as DOCTORS' COMMONS;
¶ (Oxf., Camb.) definite portion of food
supplied at fixed charge; daily fare, as
short ~. [ME, pl. of COMMON[2]]

cŏmm'onwealth (-wĕl-), n. Body politic,
independent community; republic (also
fig., as ~ *of learning*); republican government in England, 1649–60; title of
federated Australian States; *British C~
of Nations,* (term coined by Gen. Smuts
in 1919 for) British Empire, now usu.
(*British*) *C~* (*C~ Institute,* building in
London devoted to promoting wider
public knowledge of the life, scenery, &
industries of the C~; *C~ Relations Office,*
Government department responsible for
relations between Britain & the various
countries of the C~); company of actors
sharing receipts; (formerly) public welfare. [also *commonweal,* f. COMMON[1]+
WEALTH, WEAL; cf. F *bien public,* L *res
publica*]

commō'tion, n. Physical disturbance;
bustle, confusion; tumult, insurrection.
[ME, f. OF *comocion* or L *commotio* (as
foll., see -ION)]

commove' (-ōōv), v.t. Move violently
(lit. & fig.); excite. [ME *comm(o)eve,* f.
strong st. of OF *commo(u)voir* f. L COM-
(*movère mot-* MOVE)]

cŏmm'ūnal, a. Of a commune; of the
Paris Commune; of the commonalty, of
or for the community, for the common
use; (India) of the antagonistic religious
and racial communities in a district (~

voting, elections, disturbances, etc.). [F, f.
LL *communalis* (as COMMUNE, see -AL)]

cŏmm'ūnal|ism, n. Theory of govern-
ment by local autonomy. So ~IST n.,
~is'tic a. [prec.+-ISM]

cŏmm'ūnaliz|e, -is|e (-īz), v.t. Make
(thing) the property of a local community.
Hence ~A'TION n. [-IZE]

cŏmm'ūne[1], n. French territorial division, smallest for administrative purposes; similar division elsewhere; *The
C~* (*of Paris*), (1) usurping body during
the Reign of Terror, (2) communistic
government in 1871. [F, f. med. L *com-
muna* for *communia* neut. pl. of L *communis* COMMON[1]]

commūne'[2] (*or* kŏm[2]), v.i. Hold intimate
intercourse (*with* person, one's own heart,
together); *receive Holy Communion. [f.
OF *comuner* f. *comun* COMMON[1]]

commūn'ic|able, a. That can be im-
parted; communicative. Hence ~ABIL-
ITY, ~ableNESS, nn., ~abLY[2] adv. [f. LL
communicabilis (as foll., see -BLE); cf. F
communicable]

commūn'icant, n. One who (esp.
regularly) receives Holy Communion;
one who imparts information. [as foll.,
see -ANT]

commūn'icāte, v.t. & i. Impart, transmit,
(heat, motion, feeling, news, a discovery,
to); share (a thing) *with;* receive, administer, Holy Communion; hold intercourse *with;* (of rooms etc.) have common
door (*with*). [f. L *communicare* (as COM-
MON[1] +-ic- factitive suf.), see -ATE[3]]

commūnicā'tion, n. Act of imparting
(esp. news); information given; intercourse; common door or passage or road
or rail or telegraph or other connexion
between places, (Mil., pl.) connexion
between base & front. [ME, f. OF *comuni-
cacion* f. L *communicationem* (prec.,
-ATION)]

commūn'icātive, a. Ready to impart;
open, talkative. Hence ~LY[2] adv.,
~NESS n. [f. OF -*if, -ive,* as COMMUNICATE,
see -IVE]

commūn'icātor, n. Person, thing, that
communicates; part of telegraph instrument used in sending message; contrivance for communicating with guard or
driver of train. [L (as prec., see -OR)]

commūn'ion (-yon), n. Sharing, participation; fellowship (esp. between
branches of Catholic Church); body
professing one faith; intercourse; participation in Lord's Supper (also *Holy C~*);
close, open, ~, exclusion from, admission
to, ~ of persons not baptized according to
Baptist principles; ~*-cloth, -cup* (used
at Holy C~); ~*-rail* (in front of ~-table
in some churches); ~*-table* (used for
Holy C~). [ME, f. L *communio* (as
COMMON[1], see -ION) or OF *communion*]

commūn'ionist (-yon-), n. *Close, open, ~,*

adherent of close, open, communion; *fellow-~*, member of same communion. [-IST]

communiqué (see Ap.), n. Official intimation. [F]

cŏmm'ŭn|ĭsm, n. Vesting of property in the community, each member working according to his capacity and receiving according to his wants; (usu. *C~ism*) movement or political party advocating *~ism*, party affirming need for a dictatorship of the proletariat, associated with the Comintern (1919–43) & the Cominform (1947–56). Hence *~ist* n., *~is'tio* a. [f. F *communisme* f. *commun* COMMON¹, see -ISM]

communĭtār'ian, n. Member of community practising communism. [f. foll.+-ARIAN]

commŭn'ĭtў, n. Joint ownership, as *~ of goods*; identity of character; fellowship (*~ of interest* etc.; also attrib., as *~ singing*, in which all present join); organized political, municipal, or social body; body of people living in same locality (*~ centre*, place providing social & other facilities for a neighbourhood); body of men having religion, profession, etc., in common, as *the mercantile ~*, *the Jewish ~*; *the ~*, the public; monastic, socialistic, or other, body practising *~* of goods. [ME & OF *comunete* f. L *communitatem* (as COMMON¹, see -TY)]

cŏmm'ŭnĭz|e, **-ĭs|e** (-īz), v.t. Make (land etc.) common property. Hence *~A'TION* n. [f. L *communis* COMMON¹+-IZE]

commŭt'|able, a. Exchangeable; that can be compounded for. Hence *~ABIL'ITY* n. [f. L *commutabilis* (as foll., see -BLE)]

cŏmmŭtā'tion, n. Commuting; money paid by way of *~*; *C~ Act* (for *~* of tithes in England, 1836); *~ ticket*, season ticket. [F, or f. L *commutatio* (as foll., see -ATION)]

commŭt'ative (*also* kŏm'ŭtāt-), a. Relating to or involving substitution. [f. med. L *commutativus* (as foll., see -ATIVE)]

cŏmm'ŭtātor, n. Person, thing that commutes; contrivance for altering course of electric current. [as foll., see -OR]

commŭt|e', v.t. & i. Interchange (two things); buy off (one obligation) by (*for*, *into*) another; change (punishment *into* another less severe); change (one kind of payment *into*, *for*, another); *buy and use a season (commutation) ticket for travelling, esp. daily to and from work in a city, whence *~'ER* n. [f. L COM-*mutare -mutat-* exchange]

cŏmōse', a. Having a COMA²; hairy, downy. [f. L *comosus* (COMA², see -OSE¹)]

cŏmp, n. (colloq.). Compositor. [abbr.]

cŏm'păct¹, n. Agreement between parties; *general ~*, common consent; FAMILY, SOCIAL, *~*. [f. L COM(*pacisci pact-* covenant); cf. PACT]

compăct'², a. & n. **1.** Closely or neatly packed together; (of style) condensed, terse. Hence *~LY* adv., *~NESS* n. **2.** n. (kŏm'păkt). Miniature flat vanity case, or refill for it. [f. L COM(*pingere pact- = pangere* fasten)]

compăct'³, v.t. Join firmly together; condense; make up, compose, (*of*). [f. prec.]

compā'gēs, n. Framework, complex structure (lit. & fig.). [L COM(*pages* f. *pangere* fix)]

compā'gin|āte, v.t. Join firmly together. So *~A'TION* n. [f. LL *compaginare* (com-*pago -ginis* = prec.), see -ATE³]

compăn'ion¹ (-yon), n., & v.t. & i. One who accompanies another; associate *in*, sharer *of*, as *~ in arms*, fellow-soldier, *~ of his retreat*; title of handbooks, as *Gardener's C~*; || member of lowest grade of some orders of knighthood, as *C~ of the Bath*; *C~ of Honour* (of the order of *C~s* of Honour); person (usu. woman) paid to live with another; thing that matches another (also adj., as *~ volume*); (v.t.) accompany; (v.i.) consort *with*. Hence *~ATE²* a. (*~ate marriage*, marriage with birth-control & provision for divorce by mutual consent). [ME, f. OF *compai(g)non* f. Rom. **companionem* f. L *panis* bread]

compăn'ion² (-yon), n. (naut.). Raised frame on quarter-deck for lighting cabins etc. below; *~ hatch*, wooden covering over *~-way*; *~ hatchway*, opening in deck leading to cabin; *~-ladder* (from deck to cabin); *~-way*, staircase to cabin. [f. Du. *kompanje* (now *kam-*) quarter-deck, corresp. to OF *compagne*, It. (*camera della*) *compagna* pantry, caboose, ult. rel. to prec.]

compăn'ionab|le (-nyo-), a. Sociable. Hence *~LY²* adv., *~leNESS* (-ln-) n. [COM-PANION¹+-ABLE]

compăn'ionship (-nyo-) n. State of being companion(s); (Printing) company of compositors working together. [-SHIP]

cŏm'panў (kŭm-), n., & v.t. & i. Companionship; *in ~*, not alone; *bear*, *keep*, *a person ~*, accompany him; *part ~* (*with*), part (from); *weep for ~* (because one's companion weeps); *keep ~*, associate as lovers; number of persons assembled; one's usual associates, as *addicted to low ~*; *he is good, bad, ~* (a pleasant, dull, companion); social party; guests; *I sin in good ~*, better men have done the same; *~ manners*, the artificial behaviour put on before strangers; body of persons combined for common (esp. commercial) object, as JOINT² Stock *C~*, || *Limited Liability C~* (liability of each member limited usu. to amount subscribed by him), *John C~* (*East India C~*); partner(s) not named in title of firm, as *Smith & Co.*; party of players; subdivision of infantry battalion usu. commanded by major or captain (cf. TROOP, BATTERY; *~ officer*, captain or lower commissioned officer; *~ sergeant-major*, senior non-com. officer of *~*); unit of R.A.S.C., R.E., etc.; *ship's*

~, entire crew; (v.t., arch.) accompany; (v.i.) consort *with*. [ME, f. OF *compaignie* f. Rom. *compania* f. *companio* (COMPANION¹, -Y¹)]

com'parable, a. That can be compared (*with*); fit to be compared (*to*). [ME, f. OF f. L *comparabilis* (as COMPARE¹, see -BLE)]

compa'rative, a. & n. **1.** Of or involving comparison, as *the ~ method*, esp. of sciences, as ~ *anatomy*; (Gram.) ~ *adjective, adverb*, one in the ~ degree; expressing a higher degree of the quality denoted by the simple word; estimated by comparison, as *the ~ merits of*; perceptible by comparison, as *in ~ comfort*. **2.** n. ~ degree. Hence ~LY² (-vl-) adv. [ME, f. L *comparativus* (foll., -ATIVE)]

compare'¹, v.t. & i. Liken, pronounce similar, (*to*), esp. with negative, as *not to be ~d to*; estimate the similarity of (one thing *with*, *to*, another; two things together); observe the similarity or relation between (passages of book etc.; abbr. *cp.*); ~ *notes*, exchange views; (Gram.) form comparative & superlative degrees of (adjective, adverb); (v.i.) bear comparison, as *no lady can ~ with Sally*. [ME, f. OF *comperer* (later *-par-*) f. L *comparare* (*par* equal)]

compare'², n. Comparison, as *beyond, without, past*, ~. [app. f. (*without*) compare (obs. var. of COMPEER) being referred to COMPARE¹]

compa'rison, n. Act of comparing; simile, illustration; *in ~ with*, compared to; *degrees of* ~, positive, comparative, superlative, (of adjectives & adverbs). [ME, f. OF *compareson* f. L *comparationem* (as COMPARE¹)]

compart', v.t. Divide into compartments. [f. OF *compartir* or L *compartiri* (*pars partis* part)]

compart'ment, n. Division separated by partitions esp. of railway carriage; watertight division of ship; || (Pol.) separate portion of a bill, or business in hand, for discussion of which a limit of parliamentary time is allotted by Government. [f. F *compartiment* f. It. *-mento* (as prec., see -MENT)]

com'pass¹ (kŭm-), n. (*Pair of*) ~es, instrument for describing circles, with two legs connected at one end by movable joint; *beam-~es* (with sliding sockets, for large circles); *bow-~es* (with legs jointed to bend inwards); circumference, boundary; area, extent, (also fig., as *beyond my ~*); range of a voice; roundabout way, as *fetch, go, a ~*; instrument of navigation showing magnetic or true north & bearings from it (*mariners' ~, gyro-~*); BOX³ *the ~*; *~-plane* (convex, for planing concave surfaces); *~-saw* (with narrow blade, for curves); ~ *window*, semicircular bay window. [ME, f. OF *compas*, the relation

of wh. to Rom. collaterals & OF *compasser* (see foll.) is obsc.]

com'pass² (kŭm-), v.t. Go round; hem in; grasp mentally; contrive; accomplish. Hence ~ABLE a. [ME, f. OF *compasser*, f. Rom. *compassare* measure (COM-, *passus* PACE)]

compa'ssion (-shn), n. Pity inclining one to spare or help, as *have ~ on us*. [ME & OF *compassion*, f. LL *compassionem* f. LL COM(*pati* pass- suffer), see -ION]

compa'ssionate¹ (-sho-), a. Sympathetic, pitying; || ~ *allowance* (granted when an ordinary pension or allowance is not admissible under official rules); || ~ *leave* (granted out of compassion). Hence ~LY² (-tl-) adv., ~NESS (-tn-) n. [latinized f. F *compassionné* (-ATE²)]

compa'ssionate² (-sho-), v.t. Regard, treat, with compassion. [f. prec.]

compat'i|ble, a. Consistent, able to co-exist, (*with*). Hence or cogn. ~BIL'ITY n., ~BLY² adv. [F, f. med. L *compatibilis* (COM*pati* suffer with, -BLE)]

compat'ri|ot, n. Fellow-countryman. Hence ~ŏt'IC a. [f. F *compatriote* f. LL COM(*patriota* PATRIOT)]

compeer', n. Equal, peer; comrade. [ME & OF *comper*; see COM-, PEER¹]

compel', v.t. (-ll-). Constrain, force, (*to do, to a course*); bring about (an action) by force, as ~ *submission*; (poet.) drive forcibly; ~*ling* a., rousing strong interest or feeling of admiration. Hence ~l'ABLE a. [ME, f. L COM(*pellere puls-* drive)]

com'pend, n. = COMPENDIUM.

compen'dious, a. Brief but comprehensive (of works & authors). Hence ~LY² adv., ~NESS n. [ME, f. LL *compendiosus* (foll., see -OUS)]

compen'dium, n. (pl. *-ums, -a*). Abridgement; summary; abstract. [L, lit. what is weighed together f. COM(*pendĕre* weigh)]

com'pensāt|e, v.t. & i. **1.** Counterbalance; make amends (*for* thing, *to* person, *with, by*, another thing, or abs.); recompense (person *for* thing). **2.** (mech.). Provide (pendulum etc.) with mechanical compensation. Hence COMPEN'SATIVE a. & n., ~OR n., COMPEN'SATORY a. [f. L COM(*pensare* frequent. of *pendĕre pens-* weigh)]

compensā'tion, n. Compensating; thing given as recompense; ~*balance*, ~*-pendulum*, of chronometer (neutralizing effect of temperature). Hence ~AL a. [ME, f. OF, or f. L *compensatio* (as prec., see -ATION)]

com'père (-pâr), n., & v.t. **1.** Organizer of cabaret or broadcast entertainment who introduces the artistes, comments on the turns, etc. **2.** v.t. Act as ~ to. [F, = gossip]

compete', v.i. Strive (*with* another *for* thing, *in* doing, or abs.); vie (*with* another *in* a quality). [f. L COM(*petere -tit-* seek), in post-class. sense 'strive after or contend for (something)']

cŏm'pĕtence, -cў, nn. Sufficiency of means for living, easy circumstances; ability (*to do, for* a task); (of court, magistrate, etc.) legal capacity, right to take cognizance. [f. L *competentia* (as prec., see -ENCE, -ENCY)]

cŏm'pĕtent, a. Properly qualified (*to do, for* a task); legally qualified (judge, court, witness); (of things) belonging, permissible, *to,* as *it was ~ to him to refuse.* Hence ~LY² adv. [ME, f. OF *competent* or L *competent-* (as COMPETE, see -ENT)]

cŏmpĕti'tion, n. Act of competing (*for*), by examination, in market, etc. [f. LL *competitio* (as foll., see -ION)]

compĕt'itive, a. Of, by, offered for, competition. Hence ~LY² (-vl-) adv. [f. p.p. st. of L *competere* (COMPETE) + -IVE]

compĕt'it|or, n. One who competes, rival. Hence ~ORY a., ~RESS¹ n. [f. F *compétiteur* or L *competitor* (as prec., see -OR)]

cŏmpilā'tion, n. Compiling; thing compiled. [ME, f. OF f. L *compilationem* (foll., -ATION)]

compile', v.t. Collect (materials) into a volume; make up (volume) of such materials; (Cricket sl.) score (so many runs). [ME, f. OF *compiler* or app. source, L COM*pilare* plunder]

complā'cence, -cў, nn. Tranquil pleasure; self-satisfaction. [f. med. L *complacentia* f. L COM(*placēre* please), see -ENCE, -ENCY]

complā'cent, a. Self-satisfied. Hence ~LY² adv. [f. L *complacent-* part. st. of *complacēre,* see prec., -ENT]

complain', v.i. Express dissatisfaction with (*of*); announce that one is suffering from (*of* a headache etc.); state a grievance (*to* an authority of offender or offence), whence ~ANT (1) n., plaintiff in certain suits; (poet.) emit mournful sound. [ME, f. OF *complaindre* (st. *-aign-*) f. Rom. *COM(*plangere planct*-beat the breast) bewail; see PLAIN²]

complaint', n. Utterance of grievance; formal accusation; *plaintiff's case in civil action; subject, ground, of ~; bodily ailment. [ME, f. OF *complainte* (prec., COM-, PLAINT²)]

complais'|ance (-z-; *or* kŏm'plĭz-), n. Obligingness, politeness; deference. So ~ANT a. [F, formally = med. L *complacentia* COMPLACENCE; see PLEASANCE]

cŏm'plĕment¹, n. That which completes; (Gram.) ~ *of* (words completing) *the predicate;* full number required (to man ship, fill conveyance, etc.); (Math.) ~ *of an angle,* its deficiency from 90° (cf. SUPPLEMENT). Hence cŏmplĕmĕn'tAL a., cŏmplĕmĕn'talLY² adv. [ME, f. L com*plementum* (COMPLETE¹, -MENT)]

cŏmplĕmĕnt'², v.t. Complete, form complement to. [f. prec.]

cŏmplĕmĕn'tarў, a. Serving to complete; ~ *angles* (making up 90°); ~ COLOURS. [-ARY¹]

complēte'¹, a. Having all its parts, entire; finished; unqualified, as ~ *surprise*; (arch. of persons) accomplished, as ~ *horseman.* Hence ~LY² (-tl-) adv., ~NESS (-tn-) n. [ME, f. OF *complet* or L *completus* p.p. of COM*plēre* fill up]

complēte'², v.t. Finish; make whole or perfect; make up the amount of. So **complē'tion n., complēt'ive a.** [f. prec.]

cŏm'plĕx¹, n. Complex whole; (Psych.) kind of mental abnormality set up by suppressed tendencies or experience; (loosely) obsession. [f. L *complexus -ūs* embrace etc. (as foll.)]

cŏm'plĕx², a. Consisting of parts, composite; complicated; ~ *sentence,* one containing subordinate clause(s). Hence complĕx'ITY n., ~LY² adv. [f. F *complexe* or L *complexus* p.p. of *complectere* (-*i*) embrace; in some uses referred to *complexus* plaited]

complē'xion (-kshn), n. Natural colour, texture, & appearance, of the skin (esp. of face); (fig.) character, aspect, as *his conduct wears another ~.* Hence ~ED² (-kshond), ~LESS, aa. [OF, f. L *complexionem* (as prec., see -ION); orig. = combination of supposed qualities determining nature of a body]

compli'ance, n. Action in accordance with request, command, etc.; *in ~ with,* according to (wish etc.); base submission. [COMPLY, -ANCE]

compli'ant, a. Disposed to comply, yielding. Hence ~LY² adv. [-ANT]

cŏm'plicacў, n. Complexity; complicated structure. [f. L as foll., see -ACY]

cŏm'plicate, v.t. Mix up (*with* other things); make intricate (esp. in p.p.). [f. L COM(*plicare* fold), see -ATE³]

cŏmplicā'tion, n. Involved condition; entangled state of affairs; complicating circumstance, as *here is a further ~.* [f. LL *complicatio* (as prec., see -ATION)]

compli'citў, n. Partnership in an evil action. [f. F *complicité* or *complice* (see ACCOMPLICE) + -TY]

cŏm'pliment¹, n. Polite expression of praise, as *pay, make, a ~;* act implying praise; (pl.) formal greetings, as *make, pay, send,* one's *~s,* (as accompaniment to message, note, present, etc.) *with Mr —'s ~s;* ~s *of* (greetings appropriate to) *the season;* (arch.) gift, gratuity. Hence ~ARY¹ (-ĕn²) a. [F, f. It. *complimento* f. Sp. *cumplimiento* fulfilment of the duties of courtesy f. L as COMPLEMENT¹; cf. COMPLY]

cŏm'pliment'², v.t. Pay a compliment to (person *on* thing); present (person *with* thing) as mark of courtesy. [f. F *com-plimenter* (prec.)]

cŏm'plin(e), n. (Eccl.) last service of the day. [ME *cumplie* f. OF *complie* (mod.

complies) repr. LL *completa* (*hora*) COM-
PLETE; forms *-in,*. *-ines* after *matin,*
-in(e)s]

comply', v.i. Act in accordance (*with*
wish, command, etc., or abs.). [f. It.
complire ult. f. L *complēre* COMPLETE]

cŏm'pō, n. (pl. *-os*). Abbr. of COMPOSITION,
esp. = stucco, plaster.

compōn'ent, a. & n. **1.** Contributing to
the composition of a whole. **2.** n. ~ part.
[f. L COM(*ponere* put), -ENT]

compŏrt', v.t. & i. Conduct, behave,
one*self*; ~ *with*, suit, befit. [f. L COM-
(*portare* carry) & F *comporter*]

compōs|e' (-z), v.t. (Of elements) make
up, constitute, (esp. pass., *be* ~*ed of*);
construct in words, produce in literary
form, (poem etc., or abs.); (Mus.) invent
& put into proper form; set (words) to
music; (Print.) set up (type) to form
words & blocks of words, set up (article
etc.) in type; put together, arrange,
artistically; adjust (dispute etc.); arrange
in specified or understood manner, or
for specified purpose, as ~*e yourself to*
write, ~*e your countenance*, ~*e your*
thoughts for action; tranquillize (oneself,
passions, etc.), esp. in p.p., whence
~'ĕDLY[2] adv., ~'ĕDNESS n., (-z-). [f. F
composer; see POSE[1]]

compōs'er (-z-), n. One who composes
(usu. music). [prec.+-ER[1]]

compōs'ing (-z-), n. In vbl senses; ~-
machine (for setting up type); ~*-stick*,
metal instrument of adjustable width in
which type is set. [-ING[1]]

cŏm'posite (-zĭ- *or* -zĭ-), a. & n. (Thing)
made up of various parts; (Archit.) fifth
classical ORDER, Ionic & Corinthian
mixed; (plant) of the Natural Order
Compositae, in which the so-called flower
is a head of many flowers (as daisy, dandelion, etc.); (of ships) built of both wood
and iron; ‖ ~ (railway) *carriage*, one
with compartments of different classes;
~ *candle* (of stearic acid & stearin of
coconut oil); ~ *photograph* (produced by
accurately superimposing several por-
trait-heads). Hence ~LY[2] adv., ~NESS n.
[f. F *composite* or L *compositus* p.p. of
L COM(*ponere posit-* put)]

cŏmposi'tion (-z-), n. **1.** Act of putting together; formation, construction; formation of words into a compound word;
construction of sentences, art of literary
production; act, art, of composing music;
setting up of type. **2.** Mental constitution,
as a touch of madness in his ~. **3.** Arrangement (of the parts of a picture etc.); thing
composed, mixture; piece of music or
writing. **4.** Agreement for cessation of
hostilities; compromise. **5.** Compound
artificial substance, esp. one serving the
purpose of a natural one (often attrib.,
as ~ *billiard-balls*. **6.** Agreement for payment of sum in lieu of larger sum or other

obligation, as *made a* ~ *with his creditors*.
[ME, f. OF, f. L *compositiōnem* (prec.,
-ION)]

compŏs'itive (-z-), a. Combining. [f. LL
compositīvus (as prec., see -IVE)]

compŏs'itor (-z-), n. Type-setter. [f. AF
compositour f. L *compositōrem* (as prec.,
see -OR)]

cŏm'pŏs (*mĕn'tĭs*), a. In one's right
mind; *non* ~, not in one's right mind. [L]

compŏss'ible, a. Able to coexist (*with*).
[F, f. med. L COM(*possibilis* POSSIBLE)]

cŏm'pŏst[1], n. Compound manure; combination. [ME, f. OF, f. L *compositum*, as
COMPOSITE]

cŏm'pŏst[2], v.t. Treat with, make into,
compost. [ME, f. OF *composter* (prec.)]

compō'sure (-zher), n. Tranquil demeanour, calmness. [f. COMPOSE+-URE]

cŏmpotā'tion, n. Tippling together. So
cŏm'potātor n. [f. L *compotatio* (COM-,
POTATION)]

cŏm'pōte, n. Fruit preserved in syrup.
[F, f. OF *composte*, fem. form of *compost*
COMPOST]

compound'[1], v.t. & i. **1.** Mix (ingredients,
lit. & fig.); combine (verbal elements)
into a word; make up (a composite
whole). **2.** Settle (matter by mutual concession, debt by partial payment, subscription by lump sum, or abs.). **3.** Condone (liability, offence) for money etc.;
~ *a felony*, forbear prosecution on private
motive. **4.** v.i. Come to terms (*with*
person *for* forgoing claim etc., *for* offence).
Hence ~ABLE a. [ME *compoun(e)* f. OF
compondre f. L COM(*ponere* put), whence
obs. *compone*; *-d* as in EXPOUND]

cŏm'pound[2], a, & n. **1.** Made up of
several ingredients; consisting of several
parts; combined, collective; ~ *fracture*
(complicated with skin wound); ~ *addi-*
tion, *subtraction*, etc. (dealing with various
denominations); ~ INTEREST[1]; (Zool.,
Bot.) consisting of a combination of
organisms, or simple parts, as ~ *animal*,
~ *flower*; ‖ ~ *householder* (whose rates are
paid by landlord & included in rent).
2. n. Mixture of elements, ~ thing, esp.
~ word; (Chem.) substance consisting of
two or more elements chemically united
in definite proportions by weight. [orig.
p.p. of *compo(u)ne*, see prec.]

cŏm'pound[3], n. (In India, China, etc.)
enclosure in which house or factory
stands. [perh. f. Malay *kampong*]

cŏmpradŏr', n. (In China) chief agent or
factotum in European house of business.
[Port., = buyer, f. LL *comparatōrem* f.
COM(*parare* furnish), see -OR]

cŏmprĕhĕnd', v.t. Grasp mentally,
understand, (person, thing); include,
take in. [ME, f. L COM(*prehendere -hens-*
grasp) or OF *comprehender*]

cŏmprĕhĕn's|ible, a. That may be under-
stood; that may be comprised. Hence

~ĪBIL'ITY n., ~ĬBLY² adv. [ł. L *comprehensibilis* (as prec., see -BLE)]

cŏmprĕhĕn'sion (-shn), n. Act, faculty, of understanding; inclusive power, as a term of wide ~; toleration of divergent opinions (esp. Eccl.). [f. L *comprehensio* (as prec., see -ION) or F *compréhension*]

cŏmprĕhĕn'sive, a. Of understanding, as ~ *faculty*; including much, as ~ *term*, ~ *grasp* (fig. & lit.); ~ *school*, large secondary school providing courses of varied kinds & lengths. Hence ~LY² (-vl-) adv., ~NESS (-vn-) n. [f. LL *comprehensivus* (as prec., see -IVE) or F *compréhensif*]

comprĕss'¹, v.t. Squeeze together; condense (air, language, thoughts). Hence ~IVE a. [ME, f. OF *compresser* or L *compressare* f. COM(*primere press-* = *premere* press)]

cŏm'prĕss², n. Soft pad of lint etc. for compressing artery etc.; piece of wet cloth covered with waterproof bandage, for relief of inflammation. [f. F *compresse* f. L fem. p.p. as prec.]

comprĕss'|ible, a. That may be compressed. Hence ~ĪBIL'ITY n. [-IBLE]

comprĕ'ssion (-shn), n. Squeezing together, condensation, (lit. & fig.). So comprĕss'OR n. [ME, f. OF f. L *compressionem* (as COMPRESS¹, see -ION)]

compris|e' (-z), v.t. Include, comprehend; consist of, as *the house ~es 9 bedrooms* etc.; condense (*within* limits etc.). Hence ~'ABLE (-z-) a. [ME, f. OF *comprise* fem. p.p. of *comprendre* COMPREHEND, on anal. of SURPRISE (F *surprise*, *surprendre*)]

cŏm'promise¹ (-z), n. Settlement of dispute by mutual concession; adjustment of (*between*) conflicting opinions, courses, etc., by modification of each. [f. OF *compromis* f. L *compromissum* p.p. of COM(*promittere* PROMISE)]

cŏm'promise² (-z), v.t. & i. Settle (dispute) by mutual concession; (v.i.) make a compromise; bring (person, one*self*) under suspicion by indiscreet action. [f. prec.]

cŏmprovin'cial (-shl), a. & n. (Person, esp. bishop). of the same (esp. archiepiscopal) province. [f. LL *comprovincialis* (COM-, PROVINCE, -AL)]

comptrŏll'er (kont-), n. Spelling of CONTROLLER (by erron. assoc. w. LL *computus*, see COUNT¹), introduced c. 1500, & surviving in some titles, as *C~ and Auditor General*.

compŭl'sion (-shn), n. Constraint, obligation; *under*, *upon*, ~, because one is compelled. [ME, f. OF f. LL *compulsionem* (as COMPEL, see -ION)]

compŭl'sive, a. Tending to compel. Hence ~LY² adv. [f. L *compuls-* as COMPEL, -IVE]

compŭl'sor|ў, a. (Of action, agent) enforced; compelling (~*y legislation* etc., opp. *permissive*). Hence ~ĬLY² adv., ~ĬNESS n. [as prec., -ORY]

compŭnc't|ion, n. Pricking of conscience: slight regret, scruple, as *without* ~*ion*. Hence ~IOUŞ (-shus) a., ~IOUSLY² (-shus-) adv. [ME, f. OF f. LL *compunctionem* f. COM(*pungere* *punct-* prick), see -ION]

cŏmpŭrgā'tion, n. Clearing from a charge, vindication, esp. (Eng. Hist.) trial & purgation by oath. So cŏm'pŭrgātor n., compŭrg'atorY a. [f. LL *compurgatio* f. COM(*purgare* purify) see -ATION]

compūt|e', v.t. Reckon (number or amount often *at* figure, *that*, or abs.). So ~'ABLE (or kŏm²), ~'ATIVE (or kŏm²), aa., cŏmpūtā'TION n., ~'ER¹ n., calculator, electronic calculating machine. [f. F *computer* or L COM(*putare* reckon)]

comrade (kŭm'rĭd, kŏ-), n. Mate or fellow in work or play or fighting, equal with whom one is on familiar terms, (usu. of males, cf. *companion*); (as prefix) fellow member of trade union, communistic society, etc. (*C~ Smith*). Hence ~SHIP (-dsh-) n. [16th c. *cama-*, *camerade* f. F, f. Sp. *camarada* room-mate, lit. roomful (CHAMBER, -ADE)]

*Cŏm'stockerў, n. Opposition to naked realism in art or literature. [A. *Comstock*, U.S. neo-Puritan (d. 1915)]

Cŏm't|ism, n. = POSITIVISM. So ~IST n. [Auguste *Comte*, founder (d. 1857), +-ISM]

cŏn¹ (-nn-), v.t. ~ (*over*), study, learn by heart. [different. form of *cun*, ME *cunn* CAN²]

cŏn², *cŏnn, v.t. (-nn-). Direct steering of (ship, or abs.); *conning-tower*, armoured pilot-house of warship, superstructure of submarine from which steering, firing, etc., are directed when it is on or near the surface. [app. weakened form of *cond* (17th c.) f. F *conduire* f. L *conducere* CONDUCT v.]

cŏn³, prep. (It.). With (esp. Mus.), as ~ *brio* (spirit), *espressione* (expression), *fuoco* (fire), *moto* (spirited movement).

cŏn⁴. See CONTRA.

*cŏn⁵, n., & v.t. (In attrib. use) confidence (~ *game*, CONFIDENCE trick); (v.t.) swindle, dupe. [abbr.]

con-, pref. = L *cum* (see COM-) before *c d f g l n q s t v*.

cŏn'ācre (-ker) n. (In Ireland) letting by tenant of small portions of land prepared for crop. [CORN¹ + ACRE]

cŏn amŏr'ĕ, adv. Zealously. [It.]

conā'tion, n. (philos.). The exertion of willing that desire or aversion shall issue in action. Hence cŏn'ATIVE a. [f. L *conatio* (*conari* to try, -ATION)]

concăt'ĕn|āte (-n-k-), v.t. Link together (fig.). So ~A'TION n. & L CON(*catenare* f. *catena* chain), see -ATE³]

cŏnc'āve, a. & n. With outline or surface curved like interior of circle or sphere (cf. CONVEX); (n.) ~ surface, esp. vault of heaven. Hence or cogn. ~LY² (-vl-) adv., concăv'ITY n. [f. L CON(*cavus* hollow) or F *concave*]

concāv'ō-, in comb. Concavely, concave & —, as ~-*concave*, concave on both sides, ~-*convex*, concave one side, convex the other. [-O-]

conceal', v.t. Keep secret (*from*); hide. Hence ~MENT n. [ME, f. OF *conceler* f. L CON(*celare* hide)]

concēde', v.t. Admit, allow, (statement, *that*); grant (right, privilege, points or start in game etc.; *to* person); (Sport. sl.) lose (game etc.). [f. F *concéder* or L CON(*cedere*, -cess- yield)]

conceit'[1] (-sēt), n. Personal vanity; fanciful notion, far-fetched comparison or other euphuism; *in my own* ~ (judgement); *out of* ~, no longer pleased *with*. [ME, f. CONCEIVE on anal. of *deceit, deceive*, etc.]

conceit'[2] (-sēt), v.t. (arch.). Imagine; persuade oneself (*that*). [f. prec.]

conceit'ĕd (-sēt-), a. Vain (orig. *self-*~). Hence ~LY[2] adv. [CONCEIT[1]+-ED[2]]

conceiv'|able (-sēv-), a. That can be (mentally) conceived. Hence ~ABIL'ITY, ~ableness, nn., ~ablY[2] adv., (-sēv-). [f. foll. + -ABLE]

conceive' (-sēv), v.t. & i. Become pregnant with; become pregnant; form in the mind, imagine, (also ~ *of*); fancy, think, (*that*); formulate, express, (usu. pass., as ~*d in plain terms*). [ME, f. OF *conceiv-* stressed st. of *conceveir* f. L CON(*cipere cept-* = *capere* take)]

concĕl'ĕbr|āte, v.i. (R.-C. Ch., of newly ordained priest) celebrate mass with ordaining bishop. Hence ~A'TION n. [f. L CON(*celebrare* CELEBRATE)]

cŏn'centrāt|e, v.t. & i., & n. **1.** Bring together to one point (troops, power, attention); (Chem.) increase strength of (liquid etc.) by contracting its volume, (fig. in p.p. of hate etc.) intense; (v.i.) employ all one's power or attention (*upon*). **2.** n. ~ed form of something, product of ~ion. Hence **cŏncentrA'TION** n. (~*ion camp*, for the accommodation of political prisoners, internees, etc.); ~IVENESS, ~OR, nn., ~IVE a. [f. after CONCENTRE; see -ATE[3]]

concĕn'tre (-ter), v.t. & i. Bring, come, to a common centre. [f. F *concentrer*, f. con- CON-+*centre* CENTRE[1]]

concĕn'tr|ic, a. Having a common centre (*with* or abs.). Hence ~ICALLY adv., **cŏncĕntri'cITY** n. [ME, f. OF *concentrique* or med. L CON(*centricus*, as CENTRE)]

cŏn'cĕpt, n. Idea of a class of objects, general notion. [f. LL *conceptus* f. *concept-* (CONCEIVE)]

concĕp'tion, n. Conceiving (in all senses); thing conceived, idea. Hence ~AL (-sho-) a. [ME, f. OF f. L *conceptionem* (as prec., -ION)]

concĕp'tive, a. Conceiving (mentally), of conception. [f. LL *conceptivus* (as prec., see -IVE)]

concĕp'tūal, a. Of mental conceptions. [f. med. L *conceptualis* (*conceptus* -*ūs* as prec., -AL]

concĕp'tūal|ism, n. Doctrine that universals exist as mental concepts (only); doctrine that the mind can form ideas corresponding to abstract terms. So ~IST n. [-ISM]

concern'[1], v.t. Relate to, affect; interest oneself (*with*, *in*, *about*, matter, *to* do); *be* ~*ed* (take part) *in*; *I am not* ~*ed*, it is not my business (*to*); (in p.p.) troubled, as *a* ~*ed air, am* ~*ed to hear, at, for* person, *about*; ~*ing* (prep.), about. [f. F *concerner* & med. L sense 'regard, concern' of LL CON(*cernere* sift, discern) mix]

concern'[2], n. Relation, reference, (*with*); *have no* ~ (nothing to do) *with*; *have a* ~ (interest, share) *in*; anxiety, solicitous regard, as *asked with deep* ~; matter that affects one, as *no* ~ *of mine*; (pl.) affairs, as *meddling in my* ~*s*; business, firm, as *a flourishing* ~; (colloq.) thing, as *smashed the whole* ~. [f. prec.]

concern'ment, n. Affair, business; importance, as *of vital* ~; being concerned (*with*); anxiety. [-MENT]

cŏn'cert[1], n. Agreement, union, as *work in* ~ (*with*); combination of voices or sounds, as *voices raised in* ~; musical entertainment; ~ *grand*, grand piano of largest size for ~*s*; ~ *pitch* (slightly higher than the ordinary; transf., state of unusual efficiency or readiness. [f. F *concert* f. It. *concerto* f. *concertare*; see foll.]

concĕrt'[2], v.t. Arrange (by mutual agreement, also of one person). [f. F *concerter* f. It. *concertare* of obsc. orig.]

concĕrt'ĕd, a. In vbl senses; also (Mus.) arranged in parts for voices or instruments. [-ED[1]]

cŏncerti'na (-tē-), n. Portable musical instrument consisting of a pair of bellows with a set of studs at each end. [CONCERT[1]+-INA[2]]

concert'ō (-chĕr-), n. (pl. -*os*). Composition (usu. in three movements) for solo instrument(s) accompanied by orchestra. [It., see CONCERT[1]]

concĕ'ssion (-shn), n. Act of conceding; thing conceded, esp. (Diplom.) grant to CONCESSIONAIRE, piece of territory of which the occupation & use are granted to a State, company, or person. Hence ~ARY[1] (sho-) a. [F, or f. L *concessio* (as CONCEDE, see -ION)]

concĕssion(n)aire' (-sho-), n. Holder of concession, grant, etc., esp. of monopoly given by government to foreigner. [F (-*nn*-), prec., -ARY[1]]

concĕss'ive, a. Of, tending to, concession; (Gram.) expressing concession. [f. LL *concessivus* (as CONCEDE, see -IVE)]

concĕtt'ism (-chĕt-), n. Use of fanciful turns (It. *concetti*) in literature. [-ISM]

cŏnch (-ngk), n. Shellfish; shell of a mollusc, esp. (Rom. Myth.) as trumpet of a Triton; (Archit.) domed roof of semicircular apse; (also *concha*) external ear, its central concavity. [f. L *concha* shell f. Gk *kogkhē* mussel etc.]

cŏnchif'erous (-ngk-), a. (zool., geol.), Shell-bearing. [as prec., see -FEROUS]

cŏnchŏl'ogy̆ (-ngk-), n. Study of shells & shellfish. So **cŏnchŏlŏ'ġical** a., ~IST n. [as CONCH, see -LOGY]

∥ **cŏn'chy̆** (*or* -shǐ), n. (sl.). Conscientious objector. [abbr.]

concierge (see Ap.), n. (In France etc.) door-keeper, porter, (esp. of flats etc.). [F]

concil'iar, a. Of ecclesiastical councils. [f. L *concilium* COUNCIL + -AR¹]

concil'i|āte, v.t. Gain (esteem, goodwill); pacify; win over (*to* one's side etc.); reconcile (discrepant theories). Hence *or* cogn. ~ativE, ~atory, (-lya-), aa., ~ātoR, ~atoriNESS (-lya-), nn. [f. L *conciliare* (as prec.), see -ATE³]

conciliā'tion, n. Reconcilement; use of conciliating measures; *Court of ~* (offering parties a voluntary settlement). [f. L *conciliatio* (as prec., see -ATION)]

concinn'ity̆, n. Elegance, neatness, of literary style. [f. L *concinnitas* (*concinnus* well-adjusted, see -TY)]

concise', a. Brief in expression (of speech, style, person). Hence ~LY² (-sǐ-) adv., ~NESS (-sn-) n. [f. F *concis or* L *concisus* p.p. of CON(*cidere cis-*=*caedere* cut)]

conci'sion (-zhn), n. Mutilation (in *Phil.* iii. 2, = circumcision, contemptuously); conciseness. [ME, f. L *concisio* (as prec., see -ION)]

cŏn'clāve, n. Meeting-place, assembly, of cardinals for election of Pope; private assembly, as *in* ~. [ME, f. OF f. L CON(*clave* lock-up place f. *clavis* key)]

conclude' (-n-klōōd), v.t. & i. Bring to an end, make an end, (~ one's *speech* etc., or ~, *with* remark etc., *by saying* etc.); (of things) come to an end; infer (*from* premisses etc.); settle, arrange, (treaty etc.); resolve (*to* do). [ME, f. L CON(*cludere clus-* = *claudere* shut)]

conclu'sion (-n-klōōzhn), n. Termination; final result; *in* ~, lastly, to conclude; inference; decision; (Logic) proposition deduced from previous ones, esp. last of three forming a syllogism; *try* ~s *with*, engage in a trial of skill etc. with; settling, arrangement, (*of* peace etc.). [ME, f. OF *or* f. L *conclusio* (as prec., see -ION)]

conclus'ive, (-n-klōō-), a., Decisive, convincing. Hence ~LY² (-vǐ-) adv., ~NESS (-vn-) n. [f. LL *conclusivus* (as prec., see -IVE)]

concŏct', v.t. Make up of mixed ingredients (soup, drink, story, plot). Hence *or* cogn. concŏc'TION, concŏc'toR, nn., concŏc'tivE a. [f. L CON(*coquere cocticook*)]

concol'orous (-kŭl-), a. (nat. hist.). Of uniform colour. [f. L CON(*color* colour) + -OUS]

concŏm'itance, -cy̆, (-n-k-), n. Coexistence, esp. (-*ance*) of body & blood of Christ in each of the eucharistic elements. [f. med. L *concomitantia* (as foll., see -ANCE, -ANCY)]

concŏm'itant (-n-k-), a. & n. Going together, as ~ *circumstances*; (n.) accompanying thing. Hence ~LY² adv. [f. LL CON(*comitari* f. *comes -mitis* companion), see -ANT]

cŏnc'ŏrd, n. Agreement, harmony, between persons or things; treaty; (Mus.) chord satisfactory in itself without others to follow; (Gram.) agréement between words in gender, number, etc. [ME & OF *concorde* f. L *concordia* f. CON(*cors* f. *cor cordis* heart) of one mind]

concŏrd'ance (-n-k-), n. Agreement; alphabetical arrangement of chief words (*verbal* ~) or subjects (*real* ~) occurring in a book (esp. the Bible) or author, with citations of the passages concerned. [ME, f. OF, f. med. L *concordantia* (foll., -ANCE)]

concŏrd'ant (-n-k-), a. Agreeing, harmonious, (*with* or abs.); in musical concord. Hence ~LY² adv. [ME, f. OF, f. L *concordare* (concors), see CONCORD and -ANT]

concŏrd'ăt (-n-k-), n. Agreement between Church & State esp. one between Roman See (or Pope) and a secular government. [F, or f. its source L *concordatum* (Engl. since 17th c.) neut. p.p. as prec.]

cŏnc'ourse (-ōrs), n. Crowd; confluence of things, as *fortuitous* ~ *of atoms*. [ME, f. OF *concours* f. L *concursus -ūs* (as CONCUR)]

concrĕs'cence, n. (biol.). Coalescence, growing together. [f. L *concrescentia* (as foll., see -ENCE)]

cŏnc'rēte¹, a. & n. 1. (Gram., of noun) denoting a thing as opposed to a quality, state, or action, not ABSTRACT; existing in material form, real; *in the* ~, in sphere of reality. 2. n. ~ thing; composition of gravel, cement, etc., for building, (attrib.) made of this. Hence ~LY² (-tl-) adv. [f. L *concretus* p.p. of CON(*crescere cret-* grow)]

concrēte², v.t. & i. (-n-krēt') form into a mass, solidify; (kŏnk̇²) treat with concrete. [f. prec.]

concrē'tion (-n-k-), n. Coalescence; concrete mass, esp. (Path.) morbid formation in the body, stone, (Geol.) mass formed of solid particles, whence ~ARY¹ (-n-krēsho-) a.; embodiment in concrete form. [f. L *concretio* (CONCRETE¹, -ION)]

concūb'inage (-n-k-), n. Cohabiting of man and woman not legally married; having, being, a concubine. [ME, f. OF, as CONCUBINE, see -AGE]

concūb'inary̆ (-n-k-), a. & n. (Person) living in concubinage; of, sprung from, concubinage. [f. med. L *concubinarius* (as foll., see -ARY¹)]

cŏnc'ūbine, n. Woman who cohabits with a man, not being his wife; (among polygamous peoples) secondary wife. [ME, f. OF f. L CON(*cubina* f. *cubare* lie)]

concup'iscence (-n-k-), n. Sexual appetite; (N.T.) desire for worldly things. [ME, f. LL *concupiscentia* (as foll., see -ENCE)]

concup'iscent (-n-k-), a. Lustful, eagerly desirous. [f. L *concupiscere* inceptive of CON(*cupere* desire), see -ENT]

concur' (-n-k-), v.i. (-rr-). Happen together, coincide; (of circumstances etc.) co-operate (*with* or abs.); agree in opinion (*with*). So **concu'rrence** (-n-k-) n. [f. L CON(*currere curs-* run)]

concu'rrent (-n-k-), a. & n. Running together, as parallel lines; existing together; co-operating; agreeing; ~ *lease* (made before the former expires); ~ *fire insurance* (of which the risk is definitely proportioned among several companies); (n.) ~ circumstance. Hence ~LY² adv. [as CONCUR, see -ENT]

concuss' (-n-k-), v.t. Shake violently, agitate, (usu. fig.); intimidate. [f. L CON(*cutere cuss-* = *quatere* shake)]

concu'ssion (-n-kŭshn), n. Violent shaking; shock; (Surg.) injury to brain etc. caused by heavy blow etc.; ~*bellows*, self-acting reservoir regulating wind in organ; ~*fuse* (in shell, ignited by ~). [f. L *concussio* (as prec., see -ION)]

condemn' (-m), v.t. Censure, blame; give judgement against; bring about conviction of, as *his looks* ~ *him*; doom (*to* death, *to* be beheaded; also fig. *to* toil etc.); ~*ed cell* (for ~ed persons); pronounce forfeited (smuggled goods etc.), unfit for use, incurable. Hence **condem'-nable** (-mn-) a. [ME *condemp*, -*n(e)* f. OF *condem(p)ner* f. L CON(*demnare* = *damnare* DAMN)]

condemna'tion, n. Censure; judicial conviction; ground for condemning, as *his own conduct is his* ~. [f. L *condem-natio* (as prec., see -ATION)]

condem'natory, a. Expressing condemnation. [f. L as CONDEMN, see -ORY]

condensa'tion, n. Act of condensing (t. & i.); condensed mass; abridgement. [f. LL *condensatio* (as foll., see -ATION)]

conde'ns|e, v.t. & i. Compress; ~*ed milk* (reduced by evaporation); concentrate (rays of light); increase intensity of (electricity); reduce, be reduced, from gas or vapour to liquid; compress into few words, make concise. Hence or cogn. ~ABIL'ITY n., ~'ABLE a., ~'ERY (3) n., factory for ~ed milk. [f. F *condenser* or L CON(*densare* f. *densus* thick)]

conde'nser, n. In vbl senses; esp.: chamber in steam-engine in which steam is condensed on leaving cylinder; (electrical) CAPACITOR; lens, system of lenses, concentrating light. [-ER¹]

condescend', v.i. Deign, stoop, (*to* an act, *to* do); waive one's superiority (*to* a

person); ‖ (Sc.) ~ *upon*, specify (particulars). [ME, f. OF *condescendre* f. LL CON-(*descendere* DESCEND)]

condescend'ing, a. Showing condescension, esp. patronizing. Hence ~LY² adv. [prec. +-ING²]

condescen'sion (-shn), n. Affability to inferiors; patronizing manner. [f. LL *condescensio* (as CONDESCEND, see -ION)]

condign' (-īn), a. Severe & well-deserved (usu. of punishment). Hence ~LY² (-īnli) adv. [ME, f. OF *condigne* f. L CON(*dignus* worthy)]

con'diment, n. Thing used to give relish to food. Hence ~AL (-ĕn²) a. [f. L *condimentum* (*condire* pickle, see -MENT)]

condi'tion¹, n. Stipulation, thing upon the fulfilment of which depends that of another, (~ *precedent*, that must be fulfilled before a bequest etc. becomes valid); *on* ~ *that*, if, provided that; (Gram.) clause expressing a ~; (pl.) circumstances, esp. those essential to a thing's existence, as *the* ~*s of equilibrium, favourable* ~*s*, *under existing* ~*s*; state of being, as *eggs arrived in good* ~, *persons of humble* ~; *in, out of,* ~, in good, bad, ~; *change one's* ~, marry. [ME, f. OF *con-dicion* f. L *condicionem* f. CON(*dicere* say) agree upon, see -ION]

condi'tion², v.t. Stipulate (*that*); agree by stipulation (*to* do); *the size is* ~*ed by* (depends on) *the requirements*; *the two things* ~ (are essential to) *each other*; *they* ~ *the universe* (impose conditions on it) anew; (Commerc.) test the condition of (material); bring into desired state or condition; make fit (esp. dogs, horses, etc.). [f. OF *condicionner*, see prec.]

condi'tional (-sho-), a. & n. Not absolute, dependent (*on* or abs.); (Gram.) ~ *clause*, one expressing a condition, PROTASIS, ~ *mood* in French and Italian verbs, that used in the apodosis; (n.) ~ word, conjunction, mood, clause. Hence ~ITY (-shonăl²) n., ~LY² adv. [ME & OF *con-dicionel* or f. LL *condicionalis* (as CONDI-TION¹, see -AL)]

condi'tioned (-shond), a. 1. Having a (specified) disposition, as *ill, well,* ~; in a (specified) condition, as *well-*~ *ground, cattle*; circumstanced. 2. Subject to conditions. 3. ~ *reflex*, reflex action responding, through habit or training, to a stimulus not naturally connected with it, e.g. watering of dog's mouth at sound of feeding-bell. [CONDITION¹, ² +-ED², ¹]

condol'atory, a. Expressing condolence. [f. foll. on anal. of *consolatory* etc.]

condôle', v.i. Express sympathy (*with* or abs., *upon* loss etc.). Hence **condōl'ence** n. [f. LL CON(*dolēre* suffer)]

con'dom, n. Contraceptive sheath. [inventor]

condomin'ium, n. (diplom.). Joint control of a State's affairs vested in two or

For compounds of *co-* not given consult CO-.

more other States. [CON-, L *dominium*
DOMINION]

condōne', v.t. Forgive, overlook, (offence,
esp. matrimonial infidelity); (of actions)
atone for (offence). So **cŏndonA'TION** n.
[f. L CON(*donare* give)]

cŏn'dor, n. Large S.-Amer. kind of
vulture; *California C~*, great vulture of
California. [Sp., f. Peruvian *cuntur*]

cŏndŏttier'e (-tyǟrī), n. (pl. *-ri*, pron. -rē).
Leader of troop of mercenaries. [It.
f. *condotto* CONDUCT[1]]

condūce', v.i. (Usu. of events, rarely of
persons) lead, contribute, *to* (result).
Hence **condū'CIVE** a., **condū'CIVENESS**
(-vn-) n. [f. L CON(*ducere* lead)]

cŏn'duct[1], n. Leading, guidance, (cf.
SAFE-*conduct*); ~*money* (paid to a witness
for travelling expenses); manner of conducting (business etc.); (Art) mode of
treatment; behaviour (esp. in its moral
aspect, as *good, bad, ~*); *regimental, company,~ sheet*, record of a soldier's offences
and punishments. [ME & OF *conduit(e)*
f. L *conductus* (f. p.p. st. of *conducere*), also
Rom. *conducta* (*conduct* (15th c.) after L]

conduct'[2], v.t. & i. Lead, guide, *to*; (of
road) lead *to*; command (army); direct
(orchestra, choir, concert, or abs.); direct,
manage, (business etc.); ~ one*self*, behave
(*well, with* judgement, etc.); (Physics)
transmit (heat etc.). Hence ~ANCE n.
(electr.), ~ing power of specified conductor. [ME & OF *conduit(e)* p.p. of
conduire f. L CON(*ducere* duct- lead); later
assim. to L; see prec.]

¶ **cŏn'duct**[3], n. An Eton chaplain. [f. L
conductus hired (p.p. of *conducere* see
prec.)]

condūc'ti|ble, a. Capable of conducting
(heat etc.) or (rarely) being conducted.
Hence ~BIL'ITY n. [f. L *conduct-*; see
prec. & -DLE]

condūc't|ion, n. Transmission (of heat
by contact etc.); conducting (of liquid
through pipe etc., esp. of natural processes). So ~IVE a., **cŏnductīv'ITY** n.
[F, or f. L *conductio* (CONDUCT[2], -ION)]

condūc'tor, n. Leader, guide; manager,
director of orchestra, choir, etc.; official
in charge of passengers on omnibus, tram,
or (U.S.) train; thing that conducts or
transmits (esp. heat etc., as *good, bad,
non-, ~*); *lightning-~*, rod at top of
building, conducting electricity away into
earth. Hence ~SHIP, **condūc'tress**[1], nn.
[ME & OF *conduitour* f. L *conductorem*
(CONDUCT[2], -OR); later assim. to L]

conduit (kŭn'dĭt, kŏn[2]), n. Channel or
pipe for conveying liquids (or fig.); tube or
trough for protecting insulated electric
wires, length of this; ~ *system*, (electr.
traction) with conductor in underground
~, (house-lighting) with conducting wires
in lead piping. [ME, f. OF *conduit* (=
med. L *conductus* in same sense) CON-
DUCT[1]]

condūp'licate, a. (bot.). Folded length-

wise along middle. [f. L CON(*duplicare*
DUPLICATE)]

cŏn'dȳl|e, n. (anat.). Rounded process at
end of bone, forming articulation with
another bone. Hence ~OID a. [F, f. L f.
Gk *kondulos* knuckle]

Cŏn'dȳ('s fluid), n. A solution of potassium (per)manganate as disinfectant.
[H. B. *Condy*, Engl. physician]

cŏne, n., & v.t. & i. 1. Solid figure with
circular (or other curved) base, tapering
to a point (generated by straight line that
always passes through a fixed point, and
describes any fixed curve); fruit of pine
or fir; marine shell of genus *Conus*;
~-shaped thing, esp. (Meteorol.) foul-
-weather signal; ~*s*, fine flour used by
bakers for dusting troughs. 2. v.t. Shape
like ~; (pass., of aircraft) be picked up or
illuminated by many (hostile) search-
lights simultaneously; (v.i.) bear ~s. [f.
F *cône* or L f. Gk *kōnos*]

cŏn'ey. See CONY.

confāb', n., & v.i. Colloq. abbr. of CON-
FABULATION or foll.

confăb'ūl|āte, v.i. Converse, chat, (*with*
or abs.). Hence or cogn. ~A'TION n.,
~atORY a. [f. L CON(*fabulari* f. *fabula* tale),
see -ATE[3]]

confec'tion, n., & v.t. Mixing, compounding; thing compounded, esp. preserve,
sweetmeat, whence ~ARY[1] (-sho-) a.;
ready-made article of (usu. female) dress,
mantle, wrap, etc.; (v.t.) prepare, make,
(a ~). [ME, f. OF f. L *confectionem* f.
CON(*ficere fect-* = *facere* make), see -ION]

confēc'tion|er(-sho-), n. Maker of sweet-
meats, pastry, etc. (usu. for sale). Hence
~ERY(1, 2) n. [-ER[1]]

confed'eracȳ, n. League, alliance; conspiracy; collusion; body of confederate
persons or States, as *Southern C~*, Confederate States of America. [ME & AF
confederacie f. st. of LL *confoederatio*, as
foll.; see -ACY(3)]

confĕd'erate[1], a. & n. 1. Allied (lit. &
fig.); *C~ States* of America (seceding from
the Union, 1860-5). 2. n. Ally, esp. in bad
sense, accomplice. [f. LL CON(*foederare* f.
foedus -eris league), see -ATE[2]]

confĕd'er|āte[2], v.t. & i. Bring (person,
State, one*self*), come, into alliance (*with*).
So ~A'TION n. [as prec., see -ATE[3]]

cŏn'fēr[1], v. (imperat.). Compare (abbr.
cf.). [L]

confĕr'[2], v.t. & i. (-rr-). Grant, bestow,
(title, degree, favour, etc., *on*); (v.i.)
converse, take counsel, (*with* or abs.).
Hence ~MENT n., ~RABLE a. [f. L CON-
(*ferre* bring)]

cŏn'ference, n. Consultation; (esp.
annual) meeting of any organization,
association, etc. for consultation etc.;
annual assembly of Methodist Church. So
cŏnferĕn'tiAL (-shal) a. [f. F *conférence*
or med. L *conferentia* (as prec., see -ENCE)]

confĕss', v.t. & i. Acknowledge, as *I ~
my fault, that I did it, to doing it, to having*

done it, to a dread of spiders; formally declare one's sins, esp. to a priest, whence ∼ANT n.; (of priest) hear (penitent) ∼. Hence ∼èdLY[2] adv. [ME, f. OF *confesser* f. Rom. *confessare frequent. of L CON-(*fitēri fess-* = *fatēri* declare, avow)]

confe′ssion (-shn), n. Acknowledgement (of offence, fault, etc.); *auricular* ∼ (of sins to priest), whence ∼ARY[1] (-sho-) a.; thing confessed; ∼ *of faith*, declaration of religious doctrine, creed, statement of one's principles in any matter; (formerly) tomb of CONFESSOR. [ME, f. OF f. L *confessionem* (as prec., see -ION)]

confe′ssional (-sho-), a. & n. Of confession; (n.) stall in which priest hears confession, as *secrets of the* ∼. [(adj.) prec. +-AL; (n.) F, f. med. L *confessionale* (neut. adj. as n.)]

confe′ssionist (-sho-), n. Adherent of a creed, esp. of the Augsburg Confession (Lutheran). [f. F *confessioniste* (-IST)]

confess′or, n. One who confesses; one who avows his religion in face of danger, but does not suffer martyrdom; *The C*∼, King Edward the C∼; priest who hears confession. [ME, f. AF *confessur*, OF *-our*, f. L *confessorem* (as CONFESS, see -OR)]

confett′i, n. pl. Plaster bonbons, bits of coloured paper, used as missiles in the carnival, at weddings, etc. [It., = sweetmeats]

cŏnfidant′, n. (fem. ∼*e*, pron. -ănt). Person trusted with private (usu. love) affairs. [18th c.; perh. meant to repr. sound of F *confidente* (as foll., see -ANT)]

confide′, v.t. & i. Repose confidence *in*, (part.) unsuspicious; impart (secret *to*); entrust (object of care, task, *to*). [f. L CON(*fidere* trust)]

cŏn′fidence, n. Firm trust; assured expectation; boldness; impudence; imparting of private matters (*in* one's ∼, allowed to know his private affairs); thing so imparted; *told in* ∼ (as a secret); ‖∼ *trick*, persuading victim to entrust valuables to one as sign of ∼. [ME, f. L *confidentia* (as prec., see -ENCE)]

cŏn′fident, a. & n. Trusting, fully assured (*that, of*, or abs.), bold; impudent; (n.) confidant, sharer of (secret). Hence ∼LY[2] adv. [as CONFIDE, see -ENT]

cŏnfiden′tial (-shl), a. Spoken, written, in confidence; entrusted with secrets; charged with secret service. Hence ∼ITY (-shiăl[2]), ∼NESS, nn., ∼LY[2] adv., (-sha-). [as CONFIDENCE +-AL]

configūra′tion, n. Mode of arrangement, conformation, outline; (Astron.) relative position of planets etc. [f. LL *configuratio* (foll., -ATION)]

config′ure (-ger), v.t. Give shape to (usu. fig.). [f. L CON(*figurare* FIGURE)]

cŏn′fine[1], n. (usu. pl.). Border-land, esp. (fig.) between two classes of ideas etc. [f.

F *confins* pl. f. L CON(*finia* (neut. pl.) f. *finis* end, limit)]

confine′[2], v.t. & i. Keep (person, thing, oneself, *within, to*, limits); imprison; (pass.) be in childbed, be brought to bed. [f. F *confiner* f. *confins*, obs. *-ines*; see prec.]

confine′ment (-nm-), n. Imprisonment; being confined, esp. in childbed; limitation. [F (-MENT)]

confirm′, v.t. Establish more firmly (power, possession, person *in* possession); ratify (treaty); possession, title, *to* person); corroborate (statement, evidence), whence ∼ATIVE, ∼atoRY, aa., ∼atiVELY[2] adv.; establish, encourage, (person *in* habit, opinion, etc.); administer religious rite of confirmation to, whence cŏnfirm-ănd′ [-ND[1]] (candidate for ∼ation), cŏnfirmEE′, nn.; *a*∼*ed* (inveterate) *drunkard, disease*. [ME *conferme* f. OF *confermer* f. L CON(*firmare* f. *firmus* FIRM); later assim. to L]

cŏnfirmā′tion, n. Act of confirming; corroboration; rite administered to baptized persons in various Christian Churches. [ME, f. OF f. L *confirmationem* (as prec., see -ATION)]

cŏn′fiscāt|e, v.t. Appropriate to the public treasury (by way of penalty); seize as by authority. So confis′CABLE, confis′catoRY, aa., ∼OR n. [f. L CON-(*fiscare* f. *fiscus* treasury), see -ATE[3]]

cŏnfiscā′tion, n. Act of confiscating; (colloq.) legal robbery with sanction of ruling power. [f. L *confiscatio* (prec., -ATION)]

confit′eor n. (eccles.). Form of prayer or confession of sins. [L, = I confess (*confitēri*)]

cŏnflagrā′tion, n. Great & destructive fire (lit. & fig.). [f. L *conflagratio* (CON-*flagare* burn up, see FLAGRANT)]

conflā′tion, n. Fusing together esp. fig. of two variant texts or readings into one. [f. LL *conflatio* fusion f. L CON(*flare* blow), see -ATION)]

cŏn′flict[1], n. Fight, struggle, (lit. & fig.); collision; clashing (*of* opposed principles etc.); *in* ∼, discrepant (often *with*). [ME, f. L *conflict-ūs* (as foll.)]

conflict′[2], v.i. Struggle (*with* or abs., usu. fig.): clash, be incompatible, whence conflic′TION n. [ME, f. L CON(*fligere flict-*strike)]

cŏn′fluent (-ŏŏent), a. & n. 1. Flowing together, uniting, (of streams, roads, etc. & fig.), so cŏn′fluENCE (-ŏŏens) n.; ∼ *smallpox* (when vesicles run together). 2. n. Stream flowing with another (prop. of same size). [f. L CON(*fluere flux-* flow), -ENT]

cŏn′flux, n. Confluence. [f. LL *con-fluxus -ūs* (as prec.)]

conform′, v.t. & i. Form according to a pattern, make similar (*to*); adapt *oneself* to; (v.i.) comply with (to), be conformable (to or abs.). Hence ~ANCE n. [ME, f. OF conformer or, esp. in bibl. contexts, L CON(formare f. forma shape)]

conform'|able, a. Similar (to); consistent, adapted, (to); tractable. Hence ~ABIL'ITY n., ~abLY² adv. [-ABLE]

conforma'tion, n. Manner in which a thing is formed, structure; adaptation (to). [f. L conformatio (as CONFORM, see ·ATION)]

conform'ist, n. One who conforms to a practice or usage, esp. ∥ one who conforms to usages of Church of England. [-IST]

conform'ity, n. Likeness (to, with); compliance (with, to). [ME, f. OF conformite or LL conformitas, see CONFORM, -TY]

confound', v.t. Defeat (plan, hope); (mild oath)~ it, you, (= God ~), esp. in p.p. whence ~êdLY² adv.; (Bibl.) put to shame; throw into perplexity; throw (things) into disorder; mix up; confuse (in idea). [ME, f. OF confondre f. L CON-(fundere fus- pour) mix up]

confratern'ity, n. Brotherhood (esp. religious or charitable); body, gang. [ME, f. OF confraternite or med. L CON(fraternitas FRATERNITY)]

confrère (see Ap.), n. Fellow member of profession, scientific body, etc. [OF, later f. F confrère]

confront' (-ŭnt), v.t. Meet face to face, stand facing; be opposite to; face in hostility or defiance; (of difficulties etc.) oppose; bring (person) face to face with (accusers etc.); compare. Hence cônfronta'TION n. [f. F confronter f. med. L CON(frontare f. frons -ntis face)]

Confu'cian (-shn), a. & n. (Follower) of Confucius, the Chinese Philosopher. Hence ~ISM (-sha-) n. [f. Confucius, latiniz. of K'ung Fŭ tsze K'ung the master, +-AN]

confūs|e' (-z), v.t. Throw into disorder; mix up in the mind; abash, perplex, (usu. pass.). Hence ~êdLY² adv., ~'êdNESS n., (-z-). [19th c. back form. of confused (14th c.) f. F confus or its L source; see CONFOUND]

confu'sion (-zhn), n. Act of confusing; confused state; tumult; (as imprecation) ~ !, drink~ to; ~ worse confounded, made worse than it was. [ME, f. OF, or f. L confusio (as prec., see -ION)]

confute', v.t. Convict (person) of error by proof; prove (argument) false. So côn-fūtA'TION n. [f. L confutare]

congé (see Ap.), côn'gee (-ĭl), n. Dismissal without ceremony; (arch.) bow, esp. at parting, (F) congé d'élire (dălēr'), royal permission to elect bishop. Hence con'gé, -gee, v.t. & i. [ME congye f. OF congie f. L commeatus -ūs leave of absence f. COM(meare go) go & come: now usu. treated as mod. F]

congeal' (-j-), v.t. & i. Freeze, solidify by cooling; coagulate t. & i. of blood etc. or

fig.). Hence ~ABLE a., ~MENT n. [ME congele f. OF congeler f. L CON(gelare f. gelu frost)]

côngēlā'tion (-j-), n. Congealing; congealed state; congealed substance. [ME, f. OF, or L congelatio (as prec., see -ATION)]

côn'gener (-j-), n. & a. One of the same kind as (of) another; (adj.) akin, allied, (to). ·[f. L congener f. genus -eris kind]

côngēnĕ'ric (-j-), a. Of same genus, kind, race; allied in nature or origin. [as prec., -IC]

congĕn'erous (-j-), a. Of same genus or (loosely) family; of same kind;~ muscles (concurring in same action). [f. L congener CONGENER +-OUS]

congēn'ial (-j-), a. (Of persons, characters, etc.) kindred, sympathetic, (with, to); suited, agreeable, (to). Hence ~ITY (-ăl²) n., ~LY² adv. [app. f. CON-+ GENIAL]

congĕn'ital (-j-), a. Belonging to (with) one from birth (esp. of diseases, defects, etc.). Hence ~LY² adv. [f. L CON-(genitus p.p. of gigno beget) +-AL]

cŏng'er (-ngg-), n. Large sea eel (also ~ eel). [ME, f. OF congre f. L conger -gri f. Gk goggros]

congē'ries (-jĕrĭez), n. (pl. same). Collection, mass, heap. [L (as foll.)]

congĕst' (-j-), v.i. & t. (Intr.) accumulate to excess (esp. in p.p.); affect with congestion; ~ed district, area of land too crowded to support its population; (Med.) ~ed organ (overcharged with blood). Hence congĕs'tIVE a. [f. L CON(gerere gest- bring)]

conges'tion (-jĕschon), n. Abnormal accumulation of blood in a part of the body (fig. of population, traffic, etc.). [F, f. L congestionem (as prec., see -ION)]

côn'globāte (-n-g-), v.t. & i., & a. Form into a ball; (adj.) so formed. So ~A'TION n. [f. L CON(globare f. globus), see -ATE²,³ F]

conglōbe' (-n-g-), v.t. & i. = prec. [f. F conglobe or L conglobare, see prec.]

conglōm'erate¹ (-n-g-), a. & n. Gathered into a round mass; (Geol.) (pudding-stone, water-worn fragments of rock) cemented into a mass (cf. AGGLOMERATE). [f. L CON-(glomerare f. glomus -eris ball), see -ATE²]

conglōm'er|āte² (-n-g-), v.t. & i. Collect into a coherent mass (lit. & fig.). So ~A'TION n. [as prec. see -ATE³]

conglu'tin|āte (-n-glōō-), v.t. & i. Stick together (as) with glue. So ~A'TION n. [f. L CON(glutinare (gluten -inis glue), see -ATE³]

cŏng'ou (-nggōō, -ō), n. Kind of black Chinese tea. [f. Chin. kung-fu(-ch'a) labour (tea)]

congrăt'ul|āte (-n-g-), v.t. Address (person) with expressions of sympathetic joy (on an event); ~ate oneself, think oneself happy (on). Hence ~ANT a. & n., ~ātivE, ~ātory, aa., ~ātor n., (-n-g-). [f. L CON(gratulari f. gratus pleasing), see -ATE³]

congrătūlā'tion (-n-g-), n. Congratulating; (pl.) congratulatory expressions. [F, or f. L *congratulatio* (prec., -ATION)]

cŏng′rĕgàte (-ngg-), v.t. & i. Collect, gather, into a crowd (of persons) or mass (of things). [ME, f. L CON(*gregare* f. *grex gregis* flock), see -ATE³]

cŏngrĕgā′tion (-ngg-), n. Collection into a body or mass; assemblage; ‖ general assembly of (qualified) members of university; (Bibl.) collective body of Israelites in wilderness, also, public solemn assembly of the nation; (Bibl.) *C~ of Saints*, *the wicked*, etc., (whole body); body assembled for religious worship; permanent committee of Roman College of Cardinals, as *the C~ de propaganda fide*. [ME, f. OF, or f. L *congregatio* (as prec., see -ATION)]

cŏngrĕgā′tional (-ngg-; -sho-), a. Of a congregation; (*C~*) of, adhering to, Congregationalism. [-AL]

Cŏngrĕgā′tional|ism (-ngg-; -sho-), n. System of ecclesiastical polity that leaves legislative, disciplinary, and judicial functions to the individual church & congregation. So ~IST n., ~IZE v.t. [prec. +-ISM]

cŏng′rĕss (-ngg-), n. Coming together, meeting; formal meeting of delegates for discussion, esp. of persons engaged in special studies, as *Church C~*, annual meeting of Church of England, *Social Science C~*, etc.; (*C~*) national legislative body of U.S. or S. & Central Amer. republics; its session; *C~-man*, member of C~. [f. L *congressus -ūs* f. CON(*gredi gress-*=*gradi* walk)]

congrĕ′ssional (-nggrĕsho-), a. Of a congress. [f. L *congressio* (as prec., see -ION)+-AL]

Cŏng′rĕve (-ngg-), a. & n. ~ (*match*), kind of friction match; ~ (*rocket*), kind formerly used in war. [Sir W. ~, inventor (d. 1828)]

cŏng′ruence (-nggrōōens), -cў, n. Agreement, consistency, (of one *with* another, *between* two). [ME, f. L *congruentia* (as foll., see -ENCE, -ENCY)]

cŏng′ruent (-nggrōō-), a. Suitable, accordant, (*with*); (Geom.) of figures) coinciding exactly when superposed. [ME, f. L *congruens -ent-* part. of *congruere* agree]

cŏng′ruous (-nggrōō-), a. Accordant, conformable, (*with*); fitting. Hence or cogn. **congru′ITY** (-nggrōō-) n., **~LY²** adv. [f. L *congruus* (as prec.)+-OUS]

cōn′ĭc, a. & n. Cone-shaped; of a cone, as ~ *section*; (n. pl.) study of plane ~ sections. Hence ~AL a., ~aLLY³ adv., ~AINESS n. [f. Gk *kōnikos* (CONE, -IC)]

cōn′ĭco-, in comb. With a conical tendency, as ~-*cylindrical*. [as prec.]

cōn′ifer, n. Cone-bearing plant. Hence **conIF′EROUS** a. [L (as CONE, see -FEROUS)]

cōn′ifŏrm, a. Cone-shaped. [CONE, -FORM]

---

cōn′ïne, **cōn′ïïne**, n. An alkaloid, the poisonous principle of hemlock. [f. LL *conïum* f. Gk *kōneion* hemlock +-INE⁵]

conjĕc′tural (-kcher-), a. Involving, given to, conjecture. Hence ~LY² adv. [F, or f. L *conjecturalis* (as foll., see -AL)]

conjĕc′ture¹, n. Formation of opinion without sufficient grounds, guessing, esp. in textual criticism, of a reading not in the text; *a ~*, a guess, proposed reading. [OF, or f. L *conjectura* f. CON(*jicere ject-* = *jacĕre* throw), see -URE]

conjĕc′tur|e², v.t. & i. Guess; propose (a conjectural reading); (v.i.) make a guess. Hence ~ABLE a., ~abLY² adv., (-kcher-). [ME, f. OF -*er* or LL -*are* (prec.)]

conjoin′, v.t. & i. Join (t. & i.); combine. [ME, f. OF *conjoin-* pres. st. of *.conjoindre* f. L CON(*jungere junct-* join)]

conjoint′, a. United; associated. Hence ~LY² adv. [OF, p.p. as prec.]

cŏn′jugal (-ŏŏ-). a. Of marriage, as ~ *rights*; of husband and/or wife, as ~ *affection*. Hence ~ITY (-ăl²) n., ~LY² adv. [f. L *conjugalis* f. CON(*jux -jugis* f. root of *jungere* join) consort, see -AL]

cŏn′jugate¹ (-ŏŏ-), v.t. & i. (Gram.) inflect (verb) in voice, mood, tense, number, person; (v.i.) unite sexually; (Biol.) become fused. [f. L CON(*jugare* f. *jugum* YOKE) yoke together, see -ATE³]

cŏn′jugate² (-ŏŏ-), a. & n. Joined together, esp. coupled; (Gram.) derived from same root; (Math.) joined in a reciprocal relation; (Biol.) fused; (n.) word or thing. [as prec., see -ATE²]

cŏnjugā′tion (-ŏŏ-), n. Joining together; (Gram.) scheme of verbal inflexion; (Biol.) fusion of two (apparently) similar cells for reproduction. Hence ~AL (-ŏŏ-; -sho-) a. [f. L *conjugatio* (as prec., see -ATION)]

conjŭnct′, a. & n. Joined together; combined; associated, joint; (n.) ~ person or thing. Hence ~LY² adv. [ME, f. L *conjunctus*, see CONJOIN]

conjŭnc′tion, n. 1. Union, connexion; *in ~*, together (*with*). 2. (astrol., astron.). Apparent proximity of two heavenly bodies. 3. Combination of events or circumstances; number of associated persons or things. 4. (gram.). Uninflected word used to connect clauses or sentences, or to co-ordinate words in same clause. Hence ~AL a., ~LY² adv., (-sho-). [ME, f. OF f. L *conjunctionem* (as prec., see -ION)]

cōnjunctiv′a, n. Mucous membrane connecting inner eyelid & eyeball. Hence **conjūnctivIT′IS** (-itis) n.' [mod. L (for *membrana ~*) as foll.]

conjūnc′tive, a. & n. 1. Serving to join, as ~ *tissue*. 2. (gram.). Of the nature of a conjunction; uniting sense as well as construction, cf. DISJUNCTIVE; ~ *mood* of verb, one used only in conjunction with another verb, cf. SUBJUNCTIVE. 3. n. ~

word or mood. Hence ~LY² (-vl-) adv. [f. LL *conjunctivus* (as CONJOIN, see -IVE)]

conjūnc'ture, n. Combination of events, posture of affairs. [app. f. F *conjoncture* f. L as CONJOIN, see -URE]

cŏnjūrā'tion (-ōō-), n. Solemn appeal; incantation. [ME, f. OF f. L *conjurationem* (foll., -ATION)]

conjure, v.t. & i. 1. (konjoor'). Appeal solemnly to (person *to* do). 2. (kŭn'jer). Constrain (spirit) to appear by invocation (also ~ *up, down, out of* person); effect, bring *out,* convey *away,* by juggling; juggle, produce magical effects by natural means, perform marvels (*a name to* ~ *with,* of vast influence); *°~ man, woman,* witch (-doctor); ~ *up,* cause to appear to the fancy. [ME, f. OF *conjurer* f. L CON- (*jurare* swear) band together by oath]

con'jurer, -or, n. (kŭn'jerer). One who practises legerdemain, juggler; unusually clever person, as *he is no* ~. [(-er, 14th c.) f. prec.+-ER¹; (-or, 15th c.) f. AF *conjurour* (OF -eor) f. L *conjuratorem* (as prec., see -OR)]

cŏnk¹, n. (sl.). Nose. Hence ~'Y² a. & n., big-nosed (person). [perh. = CONCH]

‖ **cŏnk²,** v.i. (colloq.). Break down, give *out* (usu. of mechanism etc.). [orig. unkn.]

‖ **cŏnk'ers** (-z), n. pl. Boys' game played with horse-chestnuts (orig. with snail-shells) through which a string is threaded, the object being to break that held by opponent. [dial. *conker* snail-shell]

cŏnn'āte, a. Born with a person, innate (of two or more qualities etc.) born together, coeval in origin; (Bot., Zool.) congenitally united (of leaves united at base etc.). [f. L *connatus* var. of *cognatus* COGNATE]

connā'tural (-cher-), a. Innate, belonging naturally, (*to*); of like nature. Hence~LY³ adv. [f. LL CON(*naturalis* NATURAL)]

connĕct', v.t. & i. Join (two things, one *to* another); make coherent (arguments etc.); (pass.) have practical relations *with*; associate mentally *with*; unite *with* others in relationship etc. (usu. pass. or refl.); (v.i.) join on (*with*). Hence~ER¹(2), ~OR, nn., ~IBLE a. [f. L CON(*nectere nex* bind)]

connĕc'tĕd, a. In vbl senses, esp.: joined in sequence, coherent, whence ~LY² adv., ~NESS n.; related, as *well* ~ (with persons of good position). [-ED¹]

connĕc'tive, a. Serving, tending, to connect; ~ *tissue* of the body, fibrous tissue connecting & supporting the organs. [-IVE]

connĕ'xion (-kshon), **connĕc'tion,** n. Act of connecting; state of being connected (*cut the* ~, separate things, have no more to do with something); relation of thought, as *in this* ~; connecting part, as *hot water*~s; connecting train, steamer, etc. as *miss the* ~; personal intercourse; sexual relation, as *criminal* ~ (abbr. *crim. con.*); family relationship; relative;

religious body, whence ~AL (-sho-) a.; body of customers etc., as *business with a good* ~; *in* ~ *with,* connected with, esp. of trains, boats, etc., taking on passengers from others. [f. L *connexio* (as CONNECT, see -ION)

conning tower. See CON².

***connip'tion,** n. (sl.). (Usu. ~ *fit*) fit of rage or hysteria. [orig. unkn.]

conniv'ance, n. Conniving (*at, in*); tacit permission, as *done with his* ~. [f. F *connivence* or L *conniventia* (as foll., see -ENCE, -ANCE)]

connive', v.i. Wink *at* (what one ought to oppose). [f F *conniver* or L *connivēre* shut the eyes (to)]

conniv'ent, a. (nat. hist.). Gradually convergent. [as CONNIVE, see -ENT]

connoisseur (kŏnaser'), n. Critical judge (*of, in,* matters of taste). Hence ~SHIP n. [F (now -aiss-), f. pres. st. of *connoitre* (now -aître) +-eur -OR; cf. RECONNOITRE]

connŏt|e', v.t. (Of words) imply in addition to the primary meaning; (of facts etc.) imply as a consequence or condition; (Logic) imply the attributes while denoting the subject; (loosely) mean. Hence or cogn. **connotā'tion** n., ~'ative a., ~'atively² adv. [f. med. L CON(*notare* f. *nola* mark) mark in addition]

connūb'ial, a. Of marriage; of husband and/or wife. Hence ~ITY (-ăl²) n., ~LY² adv. [f. L *connubialis* f. CON(*nubium* f. *nubere* marry), see -AL]

cōn'oid, a. & n. Cone-shaped; (n.) solid generated by revolution of a conic section about its axis, also, any more or less cone-shaped body. Hence **conoid'**AL a. [f. LL f. Gk *kōnoeidēs* (as CONE, see -OID)]

cŏn'quer (-ngker), v.t. & i. Overcome by force; get the better of (habit, passion, etc.); *stoop to* ~, use indirect means for gaining one's end; acquire, subjugate, (land). Hence ~ABLE a. [ME, f. OF *conquerre* f. Rom. **conquerere* f. L CON-(*quirere = quaerere* seek, get)]

cŏn'queror (-ngke-), n. One who conquers; *the C~,* William I; (colloq.) *play the* ~ (decisive game); ‖ horse-chestnut that has broken others in boys' game of CONKERS. [ME, f. AF *conquerour* (OF -eor) f. *conquerre*; see prec. & -OR]

cŏn'quest, n. Subjugation (of country etc.); *the* (*Norman*) *C~,* acquisition of English crown by William of Normandy, 1066; conquered territory; person whose affections have been won; *make a* ~ (*of*), win (person's) affections. [ME, f. OF *conquest(e)* f. p.p. of Rom. **conquerere;* see CONQUER]

cōnquist'ador, n. Conqueror, esp. one of the Spanish conquerors of Mexico & Peru in 16th c. [Sp.]

consăng'uine (-nggwIn), a.=foll. [F (-in, -ine), as foll.]

consănguin'eous (-nggw-), a. Of the same blood, akin. [f. L CON(*sanguineus* f. *sanguis -inis* blood)+-OUS]

cŏnsănguin′ity (-nggw-), n. Blood-relationship (also fig.). [ME, f. L *consanguinitas* (as prec., see -TY)]

cŏn′science (-shens), n. Moral sense of right & wrong; *good* or *clear, bad* or *guilty,* ~, consciousness that one's actions are right, wrong; *have on* one's ~, feel guilty about; *in all* ~, *upon* one's ~, (forms of asseveration); *have the* ~ *to,* have the impudence to; *for* ~ (or ~′) *sake,* to satisfy one's ~; ~ *clause* in act, one ensuring respect for the ~s of those affected; ~ *money* (sent to relieve the ~, esp. in payment of evaded income-tax). Hence ~LESS a. [ME, f. OF f. L *conscientia* f. CON(*scire* know) be privy to, see -ENCE]

cŏnsciĕn′tious (-shi-; -shus), a. Obedient to conscience, scrupulous, (of persons or conduct); ~ *objector,* person who avails himself of CONSCIENCE *clause,* man (often abbr. *c.o.*) who pleads conscience & objects to military service. Hence ~LY² adv., ~NESS n., (-shus-). [f. F *consciencieux, -euse,* f. med. L *conscientiosus* (as prec., see -OUS)]

cŏn′scious (-shus), a. Aware, knowing, (*of* fact, *of* external circumstances, *that,* or abs.); with mental faculties awake; (of actions, emotions, etc.) realized by the actor etc. (*with* ~ *superiority; a hardly* ~ *movement*); ◼ SELF-CONSCIOUS. Hence ~LY² (-shus-) adv. [f. L *conscius* f. CON(*scire* know) be privy to + -OUS]

cŏn′sciousness (-shus-), n. State of being conscious; totality of a person's thoughts & feelings, or of a class of these, as *moral* ~; perception (*of, that*). [-NESS]

conscribe′, v.t. (now rare). Enlist by CONSCRIPTION. [f. L CON(*scribere scriptum*) enrol]

conscript′¹, v.t. ◼ prec. [orig. U.S., back form. f. CONSCRIPTION]

cŏn′script², a. Enrolled or formed by conscription; ~ *fathers* [L *patres conscripti,* orig. *patres et conscripti*], collective title of Roman senators. [f. L *conscriptus,* see CONSCRIBE]

cŏn′script³, n. One enrolled by conscription. [after F *conscrit*]

conscrip′tion, n. Compulsory enlistment for military or naval or air force service (esp. enrolment by lot); ~ *of wealth,* taxation or confiscation of property for war purposes to impose equality of sacrifice on non-conscripts. [after F *conscription* repr. L *conscriptionem,* see CONSCRIBE]

cŏn′secrāte¹, a. Consecrated. [ME, f. L CON(*secrare* f. *sacer* sacred), see -ATE²]

cŏn′secrāt|e², v.t. Set apart as sacred (*to*); devote *to* (purpose); sanctify. So ~OR n., ~ORY a. (prec., -ATE³]

cŏnsecrā′tion, n. Act of consecrating, dedication, esp. of church, churchyard, etc., by bishop; ordination to sacred office, esp. of bishop; devotion *to* (a pur-pose). [ME, f. L *consecratio* (as prec., see -ATION)]

consĕc′tary, n. Deduction, corollary. [f. L *consectarium* (neut. adj. as n.) f. *consectari* frequent. as foll.]

cŏnsecū′tion, n. Logical sequence; sequence of events; (Gram.) sequence of words, tenses, etc. [f. L *consecutio* f. CON(*sequi secut-* pursue) overtake, see -ION]

consĕc′ūtive, a. Following continuously; (Gram.) expressing consequence, as ~ *clause;* (Mus.) ~ *intervals* (of the same kind, occurring adjacently between the same two parts, esp. fifths or octaves). Hence ~LY² (-vl-) adv., ~NESS (-vn-) n. [f. F *consécutif, -ive* f. med. L *consecutivus* (as prec., see -IVE)]

cŏnsĕnĕs′cence, n. General decay by age. [f. L CON(*senescere* grow old f. *senex*), -ENCE]

consĕn′sual (-sŭ-, -shŏŏ-), a. (physiol.). Caused by sympathetic action. [f. foll. + -AL]

consĕn′sus, n. Agreement (*of* opinion, testimony, etc.); (Physiol.) agreement of different organs in effecting purpose. [L as foll.)]

consĕnt′¹, v.i. Acquiesce, agree, (*to* a thing, *to* do, *that,* or abs.). [ME, f. OF *consentir* f. L CON(*sentire sens-* feel) agree]

consĕnt′², n. Voluntary agreement, compliance; permission; *age of* ~ (at which ~, esp. of girl to seduction, is valid in law); (prov.) *silence gives* ~; *with one* ~, unanimously. [ME, f. OF *consente* f. *consentir* (prec.)]

cŏnsĕntā′neous, a. Accordant, suited, (*to, with*); unanimous, concurrent. Hence consĕntanē′ITY, ~NESS, nn., ~LY² adv. [f. L *consentaneus* (as CONSENT¹) + -OUS]

consĕn′tient (-shnt), a. Agreeing; concurrent; consenting (*to*). [f. L as CONSENT¹, see -ENT]

cŏn′sequence, n. Result (of something preceding; *take the* ~s, accept whatever results from one's choice or act); logical inference; *in* ~, as a result (*of*); importance; *of* (*no*) ~, (un)important; social distinction, rank, as *persons of* ~. [ME, f. OF f. L *consequentia* (as foll., -ENCE)]

cŏn′sequent¹, n. Event that follows another; second part of conditional proposition, dependent on the antecedent; (Math.) second of two numbers in a ratio, second & fourth of four proportionals. [as foll.]

cŏn′sequent², a. Following as a result (*on*); following logically; logically consistent. [f. F *conséquent* f. L CON(*sequi* follow), see -ENT]

cŏnsequĕn′tial (-shl), a. Following as a result or inference; following or resulting indirectly, as ~ *damages;* self-important. Hence ~ITY (-shlǎl-), n., ~LY² (-shal-) adv. [f. L *consequentia* CONSEQUENCE + -AL] cŏn'sèquently, adv. & conj. As a result; therefore. [-LY²]

‖ consĕrv'ancy, n. Commission, court, controlling a port, river, etc., as *Thames C~*; official preservation (of forests etc.). [18th c. alt. of (obs.) *conservacy* (16th c.) f. AF f. med. L *conservatia* (CONSERVE², -ACY)]

cŏnservā'tion, n. Preservation; ~ *of energy*, principle that total quantity of energy of any system of bodies (including the universe) is invariable. [ME, f. OF, or f. L *conservatio* (CONSERVE², -ATION)]

consĕrv'ative, a. & n. 1. Preservative (a. & n.); (*C~ party*, English political party) disposed to maintain existing institutions; (of estimate) moderate, cautious, purposely low. 2. n. One so disposed, (*C~*) member of the C~ party. So consĕrv'atism n. [ME, f. OF *conservatif* (CONSERVE², -IVE), f. LL *conservativus*]

consĕrvatoire' (-twahr), n. Public school of music & declamation (on Continent). [18th c. *-orio* f. It., whence F *-oire* (19th c. in Eng.)]

cŏn'servātor, n. Preserver; official custodian (of museum etc.); ‖ ~s *of the peace*, the King, Lord Chancellor, etc.; ‖ ~s *of a river* (see CONSERVANCY). [f. AF *-atour* (OF *-ateur*) f. L *conservatorem* (as foll., see -OR)]

consĕrv'atory, n. Greenhouse for tender plants; = CONSERVATOIRE. [f. LL *conservatorius*; partly f. F *-toire* (as foll., see -ORY)]

consĕrve'¹, n. (usu. pl.). Confection, preserve. [f. OF, = med. L *conserva* as foll.)]

consĕrve'², v.t. Keep from harm, decay, or loss. [ME, f. OF *conserver* or L CON-(*servare* keep)]

consid'er, v.t. & i. Contemplate mentally; weigh the merits of (course, claim, etc.); reflect (*that, whether*, etc., or abs.), reckon with, make allowance for; be of opinion (*that*); regard as, as *I ~ him (to be) a knave*, ~ *yourself under arrest*; (arch.) ~ *of*, think over. [ME, f. OF *considerer* f. L *considerare* examine]

consid'erab|le, a. Worth considering; (of persons) notable, important; (of immaterial things) much, no small, (trouble, annoyance, pleasure), whence ~LY² adv. [f. med. L *considerabilis* (prec., -ABLE)]

consid'erate, a. Thoughtful for others; (arch.) careful. Hence ~LY² (-tl-) adv., ~NESS (-tn-) n. [as prec., -ATE²]

considerā'tion, n. Act of considering; meditation; *take into ~*, consider; *under ~*, being considered; *in ~ of*, in return for, on account of; fact, thing, regarded as a reason, as *that is a ~*, *on no ~*; compensation, reward, as *for a ~*; (Law) thing given, done, as equivalent by person to whom a promise is made; thoughtfulness for others; importance (now rare). [OF, f. L *considerationem* (as prec., see -ATION)]

consid'ering, prep. In view of, as *it is excusable ~ his age, how young he is, (that)*

he has no experience; (ellipt.) *that is not so bad, ~* (the circumstances). [-ING²]

consign' (-īn), v.t. Hand over, deliver, *to* (misery, watery grave, person, person's care); transmit, send by rail etc., *to* (person), whence cŏnsignEE', cŏnsignOR', (-īn-), nn.; deposit (money *in* bank). Hence ~ABLE (-īn-) a. [f. F *consigner* or L *consignare* mark with a seal (*signum*)]

cŏnsignā'tion, n. Formal payment of money to person legally appointed; act of consigning goods; *to the~ of*, addressed to. [f. L *consignatio* (as prec., see -ATION)]

consign'ment (-īn-), n. Consigning; goods consigned. [-MENT]

consil'i|ent, a. (Of inductions from different phenomena) accordant. Hence ~ENCE n. [f. mod. L CON(*silire* = *salire* jump), see -ENT]

consist', v.i. Be composed *of* (esp. material things); be comprised *in*, as *virtue ~s in being uncomfortable*; harmonize *with*; (Bibl., Col. i. 17) exist. [f. L CON(*sistere* stop) exist]

consis'tence, -cy̆, n. Degree of density, esp. of thick liquids; firmness, solidity, (lit. & fig.); (-*cy*) state of being consistent, esp. of persons. [f. F *consistence* (now *-ance*) or LL *consistentia*, see prec., -ENCE, -ENCY]

consis'tent, a. Compatible, not contradictory, (*with*); (of person) constant to same principles. Hence ~LY² adv. [as prec., -ENT]

cŏn'sistory (*also* kŏnsĭs'), n. Senate composed of Pope & Cardinals; (*also C~ Court*) bishop's court for ecclesiastical causes & offences; Lutheran clerical board; court of presbyters. So cŏnsĭstōr'ĭAL a. [f. ONF *consistorie* (OF *-oire*) f. L *consistorium* (as CONSIST, see -ORY)]

consō'ciate¹ (-shĭ-), a. & n. Associate(d). [f. L CON(*sociare* f. *socius* fellow), see -ATE²]

consō'ciate² (-shĭ-), v.t. & i. Associate. So consōcĭā'tion n. [as prec., see -ATE³]

cŏnsolā'tion, n. Act of consoling; consoling circumstance; ~ *race, prize, stakes* (open to competitors unsuccessful in former events). [ME, f. OF f. L *consolationem* (as foll., see -ATION)]

cŏnsōl'ator|y̆, a. Tending, meant, to console. Hence ~ĭLY² adv. [ME, f. L *consolatorius* (as foll. see -ORY)]

cŏnsōl|e'¹, v.t. Comfort. Hence ~'ABLE a. [f. F *consoler* f. L CON*solare, -rī*]

cŏn'sōle², n. (Archit.) kind of bracket or corbel; frame containing keyboards, stops, etc., of organ; ~*-table, -mirror* (supported by bracket against wall). [F, of unkn. orig.]

cŏnsŏl'idāt|e, v.t. & i. Solidify (t. & i.); strengthen (usu. fig., power etc.); combine (territories, estates, companies, statutes, debts) into one whole; ‖ ~*ed annuities, consols*, Government securities of Great Britain, ~ed in 1751 into a single stock at 3% (now 2½), *C~ed Fund*, united product of various taxes etc., whence interest of national debt etc. is paid. Hence **consŏlida'tion**, **~or**, nn., **~ory** a. [f. L con(*solidare* f. *solidus*), see -ATE[3]]

∥consŏls' (-z), n. pl. See prec. [abbr.]

consommé (see Ap.), n. Strong meat soup [F]

cŏn'sonance, n. Recurrence of same or similar sounds in words, assonance; sounding of two notes in harmony; (Mus.) consonant interval, concord; (fig.) agreement, harmony. [ME, f. OF, or f. L *consonantia* (as foll., see -ANCE)]

cŏn'sonant[1], a. Agreeable *to*, consistent *with*; harmonious; agreeing in sound; (Mus.) making concord. Hence **~ly[2]** adv. [ME, f. F f. L con(*sonare* sound f. *sonus*), see -ANT]

cŏn'sonant[2], n. Alphabetical element other than vowel; sound that in forming a syllable is combined with vowel. Hence **cŏnsonān'tal** a. [ME, f. OF f. L con*sonantem* (*litteram* letter) sounding with another (as prec.)]

cŏn'sŏrt[1], n. 1. Husband or wife; *queen* ~, king's wife: *king, prince*, ~, queen's husband. 2. Ship sailing with another. [OF, f. L con(*sors* -*rtis* lot) sharer, comrade]

consŏrt'[2], v.t. & i. Class or bring together, keep company, (*with*); agree, harmonize, (*with*). [f. prec.; sense 'agree' prob. f. SORT[2](2)]

consŏr'tium (-shium), n. Temporary co-operation of several powers or large interests to effect some common purpose. [L, =partnership (*consors* sharing, sharer)]

conspĕc'tus, n. General view of subject, scene, etc.; tabulation of details, synopsis. [L, vbl n. f. con(*spicere* look at)]

conspic'uous, a. Clearly visible, striking to the eye; attracting notice, remarkable, as ~ *by its absence, for his loyalty*. Hence **cŏnspicu'ity** (now rare), **~ness**, nn., **~ly[2]** adv. [f. L *conspicuus* (as prec.) +-OUS]

conspi'racy, n. Act of conspiring (in good or bad sense); combination for unlawful purpose; plot. [ME, f. AF con*spiracie*, alt. f. OF -*ation* (whence ME -*ation*) f. L *conspirationem* (CONSPIRE, -ATION)]

conspi'rat|or, n. One engaged in a conspiracy. Hence **~ress[1]** n. [ME, f. AF -*tour*, OF -*teur*, f. as foll., see -OR]

conspire', v.i. & t. Combine privily for unlawful purpose, esp. treason, murder, sedition; combine, concur, (*to* do); plot, devise, as ~ *his ruin*, ~ *an attack*. [ME, f. OF *conspirer* f. L con(*spirare* breathe) agree, plot]

conspūe', v.t. (rare). Express detestation, clamour for the abandonment or abolition, of (person, policy, etc.). [f. F con*spuer* f. L con(*spuere* spit) spit upon]

con'stable (kŭn-), n. (Also *police* ~)

policeman; ∥*Chief* C~, head of police force of county etc.; *special* ~, person sworn in to act as ~ on special occasion; *outrun the* ~, run into debt; C~ *of France*, principal officer of household of early French kings, commander-in-chief in king's absence; C~ *of England, Lord High* C~, similar officer in English Royal household (now temporary officer on special occasions). [ME, f. OF *conestable* f. LL *comes stabuli* (med. L *conestabulus*) count of the stable]

constăb'ulary, a. & n. (Organized body) of constables. [f. med. L *constabularia* f. -*arius* (prec., -ARY[1])]

cŏn'stancy, n. Firmness, endurance; faithfulness; unchangingness. [f. L con*stantia* (as foll., see -ANCY)]

cŏn'stant, a. & n. 1. Unmoved, resolute; faithful (*to*); unchanging; unremittent, as ~ *attention, chatter*. 2. n. (Math.) quantity that does not vary; (Phys.) number expressing a relation, property, etc., that remains the same for same substance in same conditions, as ~ *of friction*. [ME, f. OF f. L con(*stare* stand), see -ANT]

Constăn'tia (-sha), n. Wine from the ~ farm near Cape Town.

cŏn'stantly, adv. Always; often. [-LY[2]]

cŏn'stellāte, v.t. & i. Form into a constellation. [f. LL *constellatus* f. L *stella* star, see -ATE[3]]

cŏnstellā'tion, n. Number of fixed stars grouped within an imaginary outline (also fig.). [OF, or f. LL *constellatio* (as prec., see -ATION)]

cŏn'sternāte, v.t. Dismay (usu. pass.). [f. L con(*sternare, -sternere*, throw down), see -ATE[3]]

cŏnsternā'tion, n. Dismay. [F, or f. L con*sternatio* (as prec., see -ATION)]

cŏn'stipāte, v.t. Confine (bowels); render costive. [f. L con(*stipare* press), see -ATE[3]]

cŏnstipā'tion, n. Costiveness. [ME, f. OF, or f. LL *constipatio* (as prec., see -ATION)]

constit'uency, n. Body of voters who elect a representative member; (division of) county or (division of) borough returning an M.P.; place, body of residents in place, so represented; body of customers, subscribers, etc. [f. foll., see -ENCY]

constit'uent, a. & n. 1. Composing, making up, a whole; appointing, electing; able to frame or alter a (political) constitution, as ~ *assembly, power*. 2. n. One who appoints another his agent; component part; member of a constituency. [f. L *constituent-* (partly thr. F -*ant*), as foll., see -ENT]

cŏn'stitūte, v.t. Appoint, as ~ *him president*, ~ *oneself a judge*; establish, found; give legal form to (assembly etc.); frame, form, (esp. pass. of bodily or mental constitution); make up, be the components of. [f. L con(*stituere* -*ut-*=*statuere* set up)]

For compounds of co- not given consult co-.

cŏnstitū'tion, n. Act, mode, of constituting; character of the body as regards health, strength, etc.; mental character; mode in which State is organized; body of fundamental principles according to which a State is governed; *written* ∼, document embodying these; (hist.) decree, ordinance, as *C∼s of Clarendon* (1164). [ME, f. OF, f. L *constitutionem* (as prec., see -ION)]

cŏnstitū'tional (-sho-), a. & n. 1. Of, inherent in, affecting, the bodily or mental constitution; essential; of, in harmony with, authorized by, the political constitution, as ∼ *sovereign, government* (limited by ∼ forms), whence ∼ITY (-shŏnăl²) n.; adhering to the political constitution. 2. n. ∼ walk, for health's sake. Hence ∼LY² adv. [-AL]

cŏnstitū'tionalism (-sho-), n. Constitutional government; adherence to constitutional principles. [-ISM]

cŏnstitū'tionalist (-sho-), n. Writer on the political constitution; adherent of constitutional principles. [-IST]

cŏnstitū'tionalize (-sho-), -ise (-iz), v.t. & i. Make constitutional; (intr.) take a constitutional. [-IZE]

cŏn'stitūtive, a. Constructive, formative; essential; component. Hence ∼LY² (-vl-) adv. [f. LL *constitutivus* (see CONSTITUTE, -IVE); cf. F *constitutif*]

cŏn'stitūtor, n. Person that constitutes. [L (as CONSTITUTE, see -OR)]

constrain', v.t. Compel (person *to do, to* course or state, or abs.); bring about by compulsion; confine forcibly, imprison (lit. & fig.); (p.p.) forced, embarrassed, as ∼*ed voice, manner*, whence ∼ĕDLY³ adv. [ME, f. OF *constreindre* f. L CON- (*stringere strict-* tie)]

constraint', n. Compulsion (*under* ∼); confinement; restraint of natural feelings, constrained manner. [f. OF *constreinte*, fem. p.p. as n., see prec.]

constrict', v.t. Contract, compress; cause (organic tissue) to contract. So constric'tion n., constric'tive a. [f. L as CONSTRAIN]

constric'tor, n. Muscle that draws together or narrows a part; compressor (surgical instrument); BOA-∼. [mod. L (as prec., see -OR)]

constrin|ge' (-j), v.t. Compress; cause (organic tissue) to contract. Hence ∼'gENCY n., ∼'gENT a., (-j-). [f. L con-*stringere* CONSTRAIN]

construct', v.t. Fit together, frame, build, (also fig.); (Gram.) combine (words) syntactically; draw, delineate, as ∼ *a triangle*. [f. L CON(*struere struct-* pile, build)]

construc'tion, n. Act, mode, of constructing; thing constructed; syntactical connexion between words; construing, explanation, (of words); interpretation (of conduct etc.), as *put a good, bad,* ∼

upon his refusal; ∼ *train* (conveying materials for the ∼ or upkeep of a railway). Hence ∼ISM (-sho-) n., artistic expression by means of mechanical structures (chiefly Theatr.). [ME, f. OF or L *constructio* (as prec., see -ION)]

construc'tional (-sho-) a. Of construction; structural, belonging to the original structure. [-AL]

construc'tive, a. Of construction; tending to construct, esp. opposed to *destructive* as *positive* to *negative*, as ∼ *criticism*; belonging to the structure of a building; inferred, not directly expressed, virtual, as *a* ∼ *denial, permission, blasphemy, treason*. Hence ∼LY² (-vl-) adv. [17th c., f. CONSTRUCT + -IVE; cf. F *constructif*, LL -*ivus*]

construc'tor, n. One who constructs, esp. supervisor of naval construction. Hence ∼SHIP n. [-OR]

cŏn'strue (-ōō, *also* konstrōō'), v.t. & i., & n. 1. Combine (words *with* others) grammatically, as '*rely*' *is* ∼*d with 'on*'; analyse (sentence), translate word for word; admit of grammatical analysis, as *this passage does not* ∼; expound, interpret, (words, actions). 2. n. (kŏn'). Passage to be translated word for word. [ME, f. L *construere* CONSTRUCT]

cŏnsubstăn'tial (-shl), a. Of the same substance, esp. of the three Persons in the Godhead. Hence ∼ITY (-shiăl²) n. [ME, f. LL *consubstantialis* (Tert.); see SUB-STANCE & -AL]

cŏnsubstăn'tiāte (-shi-), v.t. & i. Unite in one substance. [f. LL *consubstantiatus* (as prec., see -ATE², ³)]

cŏnsubstăntiā'tion (-shi-), n. (Doctrine of) real substantial presence of body & blood of Christ together with bread & wine in Eucharist (cf. TRANSUBSTANTIA-TION). [f. LL *consubstantiatio* (as prec., see -ATION)]

cŏn'suetūde (-sw-), n. Custom, esp. as having legal force; social intercourse. [ME, f. L *consuetudo*, see CUSTOM]

cŏnsuetūd'inary (-sw-), a. & n. Customary, as ∼ *law*; (n.) manual of customs, esp. of monastic house, cathedral, etc. [ME, f. LL *consuetudinarius* (as prec., see -ARY¹)]

cŏn'sul, n. Title of two annual magistrates exercising supreme authority in Roman republic; title of three chief magistrates of French Republic 1799–1804 (*First C∼*, Napoleon); State agent residing in foreign town and protecting subjects there. Hence ∼SHIP n. [ME, f. L *consul*; cf. CONSULT]

cŏn'sular, a. & n. Of a consul; (Roman) of ∼ rank. [ME, f. L *consularis* (as prec., see -AR¹)]

cŏn'sulate, n. Office, establishment, of a (modern) consul; (period of) consular government in France; office of (Roman) consul. [ME, f. L *consulatus* (as prec., see -ATE¹)]

consŭlt′, v.t. & i. Take counsel (*with* person or book, or abs.); seek information or advice from (person, book); ~ one's *pillow*, take a night for reflection; take into consideration (feelings, interests); ~*ing physician*, ⌐who is called in by colleagues or applied to by patients for advice in special cases). Hence **consŭl′tABLE, consŭl′tATIVE, aa., cŏnsultEE′** n. [f. F *consulter* or L *consultare* frequent. of *consulere* -*sult*-; cf. CONSUL]

consŭl′tant, n. One who consults; consulting physician. [as prec., see -ANT]

cŏnsultā′tion, n. Act of consulting; deliberation; conference. [ME, f. OF, or f. L *consultatio* (as prec., see -ATION)]

consŭme′, v.t. & i. Make away with; use up; eat, drink, up; spend, waste, (time, trouble, etc.); (p.p.) eaten up (*with envy*); (v.i.) waste away. Hence ~′ABLE a. & n. (usu. pl.), (article) intended for consumption (~*able ledger*, register of receipt and issue of such items). [ME, f. L CON(*sumere sumpt*- take up); partly thr. F *consumer*]

consŭm′edlÿ, adv. Excessively. [prec., -LY²]

consŭm′er, n. In vbl senses, esp. (Pol. Econ.) user of an article, opp. to *producer*; ~(*s*) *goods*, things which directly satisfy human wants and desires, e.g. food and clothing; ~ *resistance*, = SALES *resistance*. [-ER¹]

consŭmm′ate¹, a. Complete, perfect, as ~ *general, skill, ass.* Hence ~LY² (-tl-) adv. [f. L CON(*summare* complete f. *summus* utmost), see -ATE²]

cŏn′summăt|e², v.t. Accomplish, complete, esp. marriage (by sexual intercourse). Hence ~IVE a., ~OR n. [as prec., see -ATE³]

cŏnsummā′tion, n. Completion (esp. of marriage, see prec.); desired end, goal; perfection; perfected thing. [ME, f. OF *consommation* or L *consummatio* (as prec., see -ATION)]

consŭmp′tion, n. Using up; destruction; waste; amount consumed; wasting disease, esp. *pulmonary* ~, phthisis. [ME, f. L *consumptio* (as CONSUME, see -ION), or OF *consumption*]

consŭmp′tive, a. & n. Tending to consume; tending to, affected with, consumption, whence ~LY² (-vl-) adv., ~NESS (-vn-) n.; (n.) ~ patient. [17th c., f. CONSUMPT(ION)+-IVE, after *presumption, presumptive*, etc.]

cŏntabĕs′c|ence, n. (bot.). Suppression of pollen formation in anthers of flowers. So ~ENT a. [f. L CON(*tabescere* waste away f. *tabes* consumption), see -ENCE]

cŏn′tăct, n., & v.t. 1. State, condition, of touching, as *be in* ~ *with*; (fig.) *come into* ~ *with*, come across, meet; *make, break,* ~, complete, interrupt, electric circuit (so ~*maker, -breaker*); (Math.) touching of

straight line & curve, two curves, or two surfaces; (Med.) person likely to carry contagion through ~ with infected person; ~ *lenses,* glasses fitting inside eyelids; ~ *man,* intermediary esp. between a government department & the public. 2. v.t. (*also* kontăkt′), Get into touch with (person). [f. L *contactus -ūs* vbl n. f. CON(*tingere tact*- = *tangere* touch)]

contadi′no (-ahdē-), n. (fem. -*na*; pl. -*ni* pr. -nē, fem. -*ne* pr. -nā). Italian peasant. [It.]

contā′gion (-jn), n. Communication of disease from body to body; contagious disease; moral corruption; contagious influence (fig.). [ME, f. OF, or f. L CON(*tagio* f. *tangere* touch, -ION)]

contā′gionist (-jon-), n. One who thinks a disease (plague, cholera, etc.) contagious. [-IST]

contā′gious (-jus), a. Communicating disease by contact (lit. & fig.); (of diseases) so communicable (fig.) catching, infectious. Hence ~LY² adv., ~NESS n., (-jus-). [ME, f. OF *contagieus* or LL *contagiosus* (as CONTAGION, see -OUS)]

contain′, v.t. Have, hold, as contents; comprise, include; (of a measure) be equal to, as *a pound* ~*s 16 ounces*; (pass.) be included (*within* a space, *between* limits); (Geom.) enclose, form boundary of; (of numbers) be divisible by (number) without remainder; restrain, as *could not* ~ *himself for joy,* ~ *your anger*; (Mil.) keep (enemy force) from moving, esp. with a view to operations elsewhere. Hence ~ABLE a., ~ER¹ n., (esp.) vessel, box, etc., designed to ~ some particular article(s), ~MENT n., (esp.) policy of building up strength against a possible enemy in the hope of eventual agreement with him. [ME, f. OF *contenir* f. L CON(*tinere tent*-= *tenēre* hold)]

contăm′inate, v.t. Pollute, infect. So **contămina′tion** n. (*also,* in literary criticism, the blending of two plays, tales, etc., into one). [f. L *contaminare,* see -ATE³]

‖**contăng′ō** (-ngg-), n. (pl. -os). Percentage paid by buyer of stock for postponement of transfer (cf. BACKWARDATION); ~ (*also continuation*)-*day,* second day before settling-day. [etym. unkn.]

conte (kawñt), n. Short story (as a form of literary composition). [F]

contĕmn′ (-m), v.t. (literary). Despise, treat with disregard. Hence ~ER¹ (-mn-) n. [ME, f. OF *contemner* or L CON(*temnere tempt*- despise)]

cŏn′templ|āte, v.t. & i. Gaze upon; view mentally; expect; intend, purpose; (v.i.) meditate. So ~A′TION n. (*in* ~*ation,* intended), ~ātOR n. [f. L *contemplari,* see -ATE³]

cŏn′templātĭve (*also* kontĕm′pla-), a. Meditative, thoughtful; (of life in middle ages) given up to religious contemplation, opp. to *active*. Hence ~LY² (-vl-) adv., ~NESS (-vn-) n. [ME, f. OF -*if*, f. L *contemplativus* (prec., -IVE)]

contĕmporān'ēous, a. Existing, occurring, at the same time (*with*); covering the same time; of the same period. Hence contĕmporānē'ITY, ~NESS, nn., ~LY² adv. [f. L CON(*temporaneus* f. *tempus* -*oris* time, see -ANEOUS]

contĕm'porarў, a. & n. (Person) belonging to the same time; (person) equal in age; (newspaper) published during same period. [CON-+TEMPORARY; in 18th c. *cotemporary* was preferred]

contĕm'porīze, -ise (-īz), v.t. Make contemporary, cause to agree in time. [f. st. of prec.+-IZE]

contĕmpt', n. Act, mental attitude, of despising; condition of being despised; *have, hold, in* ~, *bring, fall, into* ~; (Law) disobedience to sovereign's lawful commands or to authority of Houses of Parliament or other legislative body, esp. ~ *of court*, disobedience to, interference with administration of justice by, courts of law. [ME, f. L *contemptus* -*ūs* (as CONTEMN)]

contĕmp'tible, a. Deserving contempt, despicable; *Old C*~*s*, Sir J. French's army of 1914 (w. ref. to Kaiser's alleged 'French's ~ little army'). Hence contĕmptIBIL'ITY, ~NESS, nn., contĕmp'tibLY² adv. [ME, f. LL *contemptibilis* (as CONTEMN, see -BLE)]

contĕmp'tūous, a. Showing contempt (*of*); scornful; insolent. Hence~LY² adv., ~NESS n. [as CONTEMPT+-OUS]

contĕnd', v.i. & t. Strive, fight, (*with* person *for* thing); struggle *with* (feelings, natural forces); compete, be in rivalry, as ~*ing passions*; argue (*with*); (v.t.) maintain (*that*). [f. OF *contendre* or L CON(*tendere* tent-stretch, strive)]

cŏn'tĕnt¹ (*formerly, & still occas.*, kontĕnt'), n. 1. (pl.)~*s of*, what is contained in (vessel etc., book, document); (*table of*) ~*s*, summary of subject-matter of book. 2. Capacity (of vessel), volume (of solid). 3. (sing. only). Constituent elements of a conception; substance (of cognition, art, etc.), opp. *form*; amount (of some particular constituent) contained (the *ester*~ of an oil), or yielded (the *sugar* ~ per acre of beet). [ME, repr. med. L *contentum*, -*ta* (as CONTAIN)]

contĕnt'², n. Contented state, satisfaction, esp. *to one's heart's* ~. [immed. source obsc.; perh. f. CONTENT v. or a.]

contĕnt'³, a. & n. Satisfied; willing (*to* do); *well*~, well pleased; ‖ (House of Lords ~, *not* ~, (= *ay*, *no*, in House of Commons); ‖ (n. pl.) those who vote '~'. [ME, f. OF f. L *contentus*, as CONTENT¹]

contĕnt'⁴, v.t. Satisfy; ~ *oneself*, be satisfied (*with* thing, *with* doing). Hence ~ĕdLY² adv., ~ĕdNESS, ~MENT, nn. [ME, f. OF *contenter* (as prec.)]

contĕn'tion, n. Strife, dispute, controversy; emulation; point contended for in argument. [ME, f. OF, or f. L *contentio* (as CONTEND, see -ION)]

contĕn'tious (-shus), a. Quarrelsome; involving contention. Hence ~LY² adv., ~NESS n., (-shus-). [ME, f. OF *contentieux* f. L *contentiosus* (as prec., see -IOUS)]

contĕr'minal, a. Having a common boundary. [as foll. +-AL]

contĕr'minous, a. Having a common boundary (*with, to*); (of two things) meeting at their ends; coextensive (in space, time, meaning). Hence ~LY² adv. [f. L CON(*terminus* boundary)+-OUS]

cŏn'tĕst¹, n. Debate, controversy; strife; (friendly) competition. [f. foll., or F *conteste*]

contĕst'², v.t. & i. Debate, dispute (point, statement, etc.); strive in argument (*with, against*); strive *for*; dispute with arms (field, victory, issue, battle); contend or compete for (seat in Parliament etc.). Hence contĕs'TABLE a. [f. F *contester* f. L CON(*testari* f. *testis* witness)]

contĕs'tant, n. One who contests. [F (-ANT)]

cŏntĕstā'tion, n. Disputation; assertion contended for; *in* ~, in dispute. [f. L *contestatio* (as CONTEST², see -ATION), & partly f. F -*ation*]

cŏn'tĕxt, n. Parts that precede or follow a passage & fix its meaning; *in this* ~ (connexion). So contĕx'tūaL a., contĕx'tūaLY² adv. [f. L *contextus* -*ūs* f. CON(*texere* text- weave)]

contĕx'ture, n. Act, mode, of weaving together; structure; fabric; mode of literary composition. [F (as prec., see -URE)]

contĭgū'ity, n. Contact; proximity; (Psych.) proximity of ideas or impressions in place or time, as principle of association. [f. LL *contiguitas* (as foll., see -TY), or F *contiguité*]

contĭg'ūous, a. Touching, adjoining, (*to*); next in order (*to*); neighbouring. Hence ~LY² adv. [f. L *contiguus* f. CON(*tingere=tangere* touch)+-OUS]

cŏn'tĭnent¹, a. Temperate; chaste. Hence or cogn. cŏn'tĭnENCE n., ~LY² adv. [ME, f. L as CONTAIN, see -ENT; cf. OF *continent*]

cŏn'tĭnent², n. Continuous land, mainland; ‖ the *C*~, mainland of Europe; one of the main continuous bodies of land (Europe, Asia, Africa, N. & S. America, Australia). [15th c. *continent land*, = F *terre continente*, L *terra continens* (as prec.)]

cŏntĭnĕn'tal, a. & n. 1. Of a continent; ~ *drift*, (Geol.) supposed slow movement of the continents on a deep-seated plastic substratum; belonging to, characteristic of, the Continent, whence ~ISM, ~IST, nn., ~IZE v.t., ~LY² adv. 2. n. Inhabitant of the Continent; *(sl.)* currency note of an early issue that rapidly depreciated (*I don't care a* ~). [-AL]

contin'gencў (-j-), n. Uncertainty of occurrence; chance occurrence; thing that may happen hereafter; thing dependent on an uncertain event; thing incident to another, incidental expense etc. [f. LL *contingentia* as foll., see -ENCY]

contin'gent (-j-), a. & n. 1. Of uncertain occurrence; accidental; incidental *to*; true only under existing conditions; non--essential; conditional. 2. n. Force contributed to form part of army etc. (or fig.). Hence ~LY² adv. [f. L CON(*tingere*= *tangere* touch), see -ENT]

contin'ual, a. Always going on; very frequent. Hence ~LY² adv. [ME & OF *continuel* f. L as CONTINUOUS, see -AL]

contin'uance, n. Going on, duration; *of long* ~, lasting long; remaining, stay, (*in* place, condition, etc.). [OF (CONTINUE, -ANCE)]

contin'uant, a. & n. (Consonant) of which the sound can be prolonged (as *f v s r*), opp. of stop or check. [F, or f. L as CONTINUE, see -ANT]

continuā'tion, n. Carrying on, resumption, (of an action, course, story, book, etc.); ‖ (Stock Exch.) carrying over an account to next ~ (or CONTANGO) *-day*; that by which a thing is continued, additional parts; gaiters continuous with knee--breeches; ~ *school* (for additional teaching in leisure time of those who have left primary and other schools). [ME, f. OF f. L *continuationem* (as prec., see -ATION)]

contin'uātive, a. Tending, serving, to continue. [f. LL *continuativus* (as prec., see -IVE)]

contin'uātor, n. One who writes continuation to another's work. [f. mod. L as foll., -OR]

contin'ue, v.t. & i. Maintain, keep up, (action etc.); retain (person *in* office etc.); take up, resume, (narrative etc. or abs.); (Law) adjourn; remain in existence; stay (*in, at*, place, *in* a state); *if you* ~*e* (are still) *obstinate*; not cease (*doing, to* do). Hence ~ABLE a. [ME, f. OF *continuer* f. L *continuare* as CONTINUOUS]

continu'itў, n. State of being continuous; (Cinemat.) scenario; *law of* ~ (that all changes in nature are continuous, not abrupt). [f. F *continuité* f. L *continuitatem* (as foll., see -TY)]

contin'uous, a. (Of material things) connected, unbroken; uninterrupted in time or sequence; ~ *brake* of train, ~ series of carriage brakes controlled from one point; (Archit.) ~ *style* (with mullions of window continued in tracery); ~ *voyage*, one which, though interrupted, is regarded as a single voyage in ref. to the object with which it was undertaken. Hence ~LY² adv., ~NESS n. [f. L *continuus* f. CON(*tinēre* = *tenere* hold) + -OUS]

contin'uum, n. (philos.). An unbroken mass or tissue or course of or of matter,

sensation, events, etc. (SPACE-*time* ~). [L, neut. of *continuus*, see prec.]

cont'line, n. Spiral interval between strands of rope; space between casks stowed side by side. [etym. unkn.]

contorn'iate, a. & n. (Medal) with deep furrow round disc within edge. [f. It. *contorniato*, f. *contorno* CONTOUR; so F *-iate*]

contort', v.t. Twist, distort. [f. L CON-(*torquēre* tort-)]

contor'tion, n. Twisting; twisted state (esp. of face or body). [f. L *contortio* (prec. -ION)]

contor'tionist (-sho-), n. Artist whose work, gymnast whose body, exhibits contortions. [-IST]

con'tour (-oor), n., & v.t. Outline; line separating differently coloured parts of design; artistic quality of outline; outline of coast, mountain mass, etc.; ~ *line*, one representing horizontal ~ of earth's surface at given elevation, as in a ~ *map*; (v.t.) mark with ~ lines, carry (road) round ~ of hill. [F, f. It. *contorno* f. *contornare* draw in outline f. *tornare* TURN]

con'tra, prep. & n. *Pro & ~* (usu. *con*), for & against; *pros & cons*, arguments for & against; (Bookkeeping) opposite side of account, esp. credit side. [L, as foll.]

contra-, pref. f. L adv. & prep. *contra* against, opposite, etc. In many E wds f. or after L or It. In names of mus. instruments & organ-stops, denoting a pitch of an octave below.

con'traband, n. & a. 1. Prohibited traffic, smuggling; smuggled goods; ~ *of war*, anything forbidden to be supplied by neutrals to belligerents (*absolute, conditional*, ~, things that may under no, some, circumstances be supplied, as, *absolute* ~, weapons, *conditional* ~, cotton). 2. adj. Forbidden to be imported or exported, as ~ *goods*; concerned with these, as ~ *trade*(*r*). [f. Sp. *contrabanda* f. It. CONTRA(*bando* proclamation), cf. BAN]

con'trabandist, n. Smuggler. [f. Sp. *contrabandista* (as prec., see -IST]

con'trabass, n. = DOUBLE¹-*bass*. [f. It. CONTRA(*basso* BASS)]

contracep'tive, a. & n. Preventive of uterine conception. So **contracep'tion** n., use of ~s. [CONTRA- + (CON)CEPTION]

con'tract¹, n. Agreement between parties, States, etc.; business agreement for supply of goods or performance of work at fixed price; agreement enforceable by law (NUDE ~); accepted promise to do or forbear; formal agreement for marriage; conveyance of property; (Bridge) undertaking to make so many tricks; ~ *bridge*, a form of auction bridge in which only tricks bid and won count towards game. [ME, f. OF f. L *contractus* contract (as foll.)]

contract'², v.t. & i. Enter into business or legal engagement (*to do, for doing, for* piece of work, or abs.); ~ one*self out of*, ~ *out of*, or abs. → *out*, for exemption or exclusion from provisions of (law etc.); ~ (enter into) *marriage*; form (friendship, habit); incur (debt); draw together (muscles, brow, etc.); make smaller, whence contracti**BIL'ITY** n., contrac't-**IBLE** a.; restrict, confine, (lit. & fig.); (Gram.) shorten (word) by combination or elision; shrink, become smaller; (p.p.) narrow, mean, (of ideas etc.). [f. L **CON-** (*trahere tract-* draw)]

contrac'tile (-ĭl, -il), a. Capable of or producing contraction, as ~ *muscles, metal, force*. So contractil'ITY n. [F (as prec., see -ILE)]

contrac'tion, n. Shrinking, contracting; restriction, confinement; shortening of word by combination or elision; contracted word; contracting (*of* debt, disease, habit). [F, f. L *contractionem* (as prec., see -ION)]

contrac'tive, a. Serving to contract. [-IVE]

contrac'tor, n. Undertaker of contract; contracting muscle. [LL (as CONTRACT², -OR)]

contrac'tual, a. Of (the nature of) a contract. [as CONTRACT¹ +-AL]

contradict', v.t. Deny (statement); deny the words of (person); be contrary to, as *these rumours* ~ *each other*. Hence or cogn. contradic'TABLE a., contradic'TOR n. [f. L CONTRA(*dicere dict-* say)]

contradic'tion, n. Denial; opposition; statement contradicting another; inconsistency; ~ *in terms*, plainly self-contradictory statement or words as '*almost quite ready*' *is a* ~ *in terms*. [ME, f. OF, f. L *contradictionem* (as prec., -ION)]

contradic'tious (-shŭs), a. Inclined to contradict; disputatious. Hence ~LY² adv., ~NESS n. [-IOUS]

contradic'tor|y̆, a. & n. Making denial; mutually opposed or inconsistent; contradictious; (n.) ~y̆ assertion. Hence ~ILY² adv., ~INESS n. [f. LL *contradic-torius* (as prec., see -ORY)]

contradistinc'tion, n. Distinction by contrast. [CONTRA-]

contradisting'uish (-nggw-), v.t. Distinguish (things, one *from* another) by contrast. [CONTRA-]

contral'tō, n. & a. (pl. *-os*). (Part assigned to, singer with) lowest female voice. [It. (CONTRA- +ALTO)]

contraposi'tion (-z-), n. Opposition, contrast; (Logic) a mode of conversion (*if all A is B, then by* ~ *all not-B is not-A*, *or no not-B is A*). So contrapos'itive (-z-) a. [f. LL *contrapositio* (Boeth.)]

con'traprŏp, n. Coaxial, oppositely rotating airscrew. [CONTRA-, PROP(ELLER)]

contrăp'tion, n. (sl.). Queer machine, makeshift contrivance. [perh. f. *contrive*, cf. *conceive, -ception*]

contrapŭn'tal, a. Of or in counterpoint. [f. It. *contra(p)punto* COUNTERPOINT +-AL]

contrapŭn'tist, n. One skilled in counterpoint. [f. It. *contra(p)puntista* (as prec., -IST)]

contrar'iant, a. Opposed (*to*). [ME, f. OF, f. LL *contrariare* (as CONTRARY), see -ANT]

contrari'ety̆, n. Opposition in nature, quality, or action; disagreement, inconsistency. [ME, f. OF *contrarete* f. LL *contrarietatem* (as CONTRARY, see -TY)]

contrar'ious, a. (arch.). Opposed; perverse; (of things) adverse. [ME, f. OF f. med. L *contrariosus* (as prec., see -OUS)]

con'trariwise (-z; *also* kontrār'-), adv. On the other hand; in the opposite way; perversely. [foll. +-WISE]

con'trary̆ (see below), a., n., adv. **1.** Opposed in nature or tendency (*to*); (of wind) impeding, unfavourable; *the* opposite (of two things); (pop., pron. kontrār'ĭ) perverse, self-willed, whence contrar'I-NESS n.; opposite in position or direction. **2.** n. *The* opposite; *on the* ~ (corroborating a denial expressed or understood, as *Have you nearly done?—On the* ~, *I have only just begun*); *interpret by contraries*, understand Yes for No etc.; *to the* ~, to the opposite effect, as *there is no evidence to the* ~. **3.** adv. In opposition *to*, as *act* ~ *to nature*. Hence con'trarily² adv. [ME, f. AF *contrarie* (OF *-aire*) f. L *contrarius* (CONTRA, see -ARY¹)]

contrast'¹ (-ah-), v.t. & i. Set (two things, one *with* another) in opposition, so as to show their differences; show striking difference on comparison (*with*). [f. F *contraster* f. It. f. med. L CONTRA(*stare* stand)]

con'trast² (-ah-), n. Juxtaposition (esp. of forms, colours, etc.) showing striking differences (*between*; *in* ~ *with*); thing showing such a difference (*to*). Hence contras'ty² (-ah-) a., exhibiting strong ~s (esp. of photographic negatives). [f. F *contraste* f. It. *contrasto* (see prec.)]

con'trate, a. ~ *wheel*, one with teeth at right angles to its plane. [CONTRA- +-ATE²]

contravalla'tion, n. Chain of redoubts and breastworks placed by besiegers between their camp and the town. [f. F *contre-*, It. *-vallazione* (CONTRA-, see CIR-CUMVALLATION)]

contravēne', v.t. Infringe (law); dispute (statement); (of things) conflict with. [f. F *contrevenir* or LL CONTRA(*venire vent-* come)]

contravĕn'tion, n. Infringement (*in* ~ *of*, violating). [F (as prec., see -ION)]

contretemps (see Ap.), n. Unlucky accident; hitch. [F]

contrib'ute, v.t. & i. Pay, furnish, (*to* common fund etc.); supply (literary article etc.); (v.i.) ~ *to*, help to bring about. [f. L CON(*tribuere -ut-* bestow)]

contribū'tion, n. Act of contributing; thing, help, literary article, contributed;

imposition levied for support of army in the field; *lay under* ~, exact ~s from. [ME, f. OF, or f. LL *contributio* (prec., -ION)]

contrib′utor, n. One who contributes (esp. literary articles). [f. AF *contributor* (as CONTRIBUTE, -OR)]

contrib′utory̆, a. & n. That contributes (~ *negligence*, of injured person who has failed to take proper precautions against accident; (n.) person liable, when a company fails, to share in paying off its debts. [f. med. L *contributorius* (as prec., -ORY)]

cŏn′trite, a. Broken in spirit by sense of sin, completely penitent; (of actions) showing a ~ spirit. Hence ~LY² (-tī-) adv. [ME, f. OF *contrit* or eccl. L *contritus* f. L CON(*terere trit-* rub) bruise]

contri′tion, n. Being contrite, penitence. [ME, f. OF, or f. eccl. L *contritio* (prec., -ION)]

contriv′ance, n. Act of contriving; deceitful practice; invention; mechanical device; inventive capacity. [-ANCE]

contriv|e′, v.t. Invent, devise; bring to pass, manage, (thing, *to* do); also of undesired event, as ~*e to make matters worse*; (abs.) manage household affairs (*well* etc.), whence ~*er¹* n. Hence ~′ABLE a. [ME *controve, -eve,* f. OF *controver* find, imagine; mod. *contrive* unexpl.]

contrŏl′¹, n. Power of directing, command; restraint; means of restraint, check; standard of comparison for checking inferences deduced from experiment; (Spirit.) personality actuating a medium; station at which aeroplanes, motors, etc., in races are allowed time to stop for overhauling etc.; section of road in which a (racing) motor vehicle has to observe certain instructions (as to speed etc.); (pl.) various devices in aircraft used to control altitude, direction, speed, etc. [corresp. to F *contrôle,* earlier *contrerolle* copy of a roll, as med. L CONTRA(*rotulus* see ROLL¹); in Eng. prob. f. foll.]

contrŏl′², v.t. (-ll-). Dominate, command; hold in check (one*self,* one's anger); check, verify; regulate (prices etc.). Hence ~l′ABLE a., ~MENT n. [ME, f. AF (= OF) *controreller* keep copy of roll of accounts, in mod. F *contrôler;* see prec.]

contrŏll′er, n. In vbl senses; also one who checks expenditure, steward, ‖ esp. of royal household, Mint, Navy, etc. (often spelt *compt-*). Hence ~SHIP n. [ME *counterroller* f. AF *contrerollour* (as prec., see -OR)]

cŏntrover′sial (-shl), a. Of, open to, given to, controversy. Hence ~ISM, ~IST, nn., ~LY² adv., (-sha-). [f. LL *controversialis* (as foll., -AL)]

cŏn′trover̆sy̆, n. Disputation; *without, beyond,* ~, unquestionably. [ME, f. L

controversia (as foll., see -Y¹); cf. obs. F *controversie*]

cŏn′trovert (*also* -vert′), v.t. Dispute about, discuss; dispute, deny. Hence ~IST n. [c. 1600 formed on contemporary *controverse* vb (f. L *controversus* disputed), on anal. of *convert, pervert,* etc.; cf. LL *controvertere* invert]

cŏntūma′cious (-shus), a. Insubordinate, disobedient, esp. to order of court. Hence or cogn. ~LY² adv., ~NESS, cŏn′tūMACY, nn. [f. L CON(*tumax -acis,* see -ACIOUS]

cŏntūmēl′ious, a. Opprobrious; insolent. Hence ~LY² adv. [ME, f. OF *contumelieus* f. L *contumeliosus* (as foll., see -OUS]

cŏn′tūmĕly̆, n. Insolent, reproachful, language or treatment; disgrace. [ME, f. OF *contumelie* f. L *contumelia*]

contūse′ (-z), v.t. Injure by blow without breaking skin, bruise. So contū′SION (-zhn) n. [f. L CON(*tundere tus-* thump)]

conŭn′drum, n. Riddle; hard question. [orig. unkn.]

cŏnūrbā′tion, n. Aggregation of urban districts. [CON-, L *urbs urbis* city, -ATION]

cŏnvalĕsce′, v.i. Regain health. [ME, f. L CON(*valescere* incept. of *valēre* be well)]

cŏnvalĕs′c|ent, a. & n. (Person) recovering from sickness; ~*ent hospital* (for ~ents). So ~ENCE n. [as prec., see -ENT]

convĕc′t|ion, n. Transportation of heat or electricity, by movement of heated or electrified substance. Hence ~OR n., heating apparatus for circulating warm air. [f. LL *convectio* f. CON(*vehere vect-* carry), see -ION]

convenance (see Ap.), n. (usu. pl.). Conventional propriety. [F]

convēn|e′, v.t. & i. Assemble (t. & i.); convoke (assembly); summon (person *before* tribunal). Hence ~′ABLE a. [ME, f. OF *convenir* or L CON(*venire vent-* come) assemble, agree, fit]

convēn′ience, n. Suitableness, commodiousness; material advantage, as *marriage of* ~; personal comfort, as *at your* ~, in a way, at a time, convenient to you; advantage, as *a great* ~; *make a* ~ of one, utilize him unconscionably, abuse his good nature; useful appliance; ‖ water-closet; (arch.) vehicle; (pl.) material comforts. [f. L *convenientia* (as prec., see -ENCE)]

convēn′ient, a. Suitable, commodious; not troublesome, as *if it is* ~ *to you*. Hence ~LY² adv. [as CONVENE, see -ENT]

cŏn′vent, n. Religious community (usu. women, cf. MONASTERY) living together; building occupied by this. [ME & AF *covent* = OF *convent* f. L *conventus* (as prec.), to wh. later (16th c.), sp. conforms]

‖ **convĕn′ticle**, n. (hist.). Clandestine religious meeting, esp. of Nonconformists or Dissenters; building used for this. [f. L *conventiculum* (place of) assembly, dim. as prec.]

For compounds of *co-* not given consult CO-.

convĕn'tion, n. Act of convening; formal assembly, esp. (Eng. Hist.) of Parliament without summons of King, 1660 & 1688; agreement between parties; general (often tacit) consent; practice based on this; accepted method of play (in leading, bidding, etc.) in various card games. [ME, f. OF or f. L *conventio* (as CONVENE, see -ION)]

convĕn'tional (-sho-), a. Depending on convention, not natural, not spontaneous; (Art) following traditions; (of bombs, weapons, etc.) other than atomic. Hence ∼ISM, ∼IST, ∼ITY (-ăl²), nn., ∼IZE v.t., ∼LY² adv. [f. F *conventionnel* or LL *conventionalis*]

convĕn'tionarỹ (-sho-), a. & n. (Tenant, tenure) on terms orig. fixed by convention, not by custom. [f. med. L *conventionarius* (as prec., -ARY¹)]

convĕn'tŭal, a. & n. (Member, inmate) of a convent; (member) of the less strict branch of Franciscans, living in large convents. [f. med. L *conventualis* (as CONVENT, see -AL; cf. F *conventuel*)]

convẽrge', v.i. & t. (Of lines) tend to meet in a point (also fig.); (Math., of series) approximate in the sum of its terms towards a definite limit; (trans.) cause to ∼. So **convẽr'gENCE, -ENCY, nn., convẽr'gENT a.** [f. LL CON(*vergere* VERGE)]

convẽrs'a̱ble, a. Easy, pleasant, in conversation; fit for social intercourse. Hence ∼IeNESS n., ∼LY² adv. [F, f. med. L *conversabilis* (as foll., see -BLE)]

cŏn'versance, -cỹ, n. Familiarity, acquaintance, (*with*). [as foll., see -ANCE]

cŏn'versant, a. Having frequent intercourse, well acquainted, (*with* person, subject, etc.); (of things) concerned (*in, about, with*). [ME, f. OF f. L *conversari* CONVERSE¹, see -ANT]

cŏnversā'tion, n. Talk, whence ∼IST (-sho-) n.; ∼ (*piece*), kind of genre painting of group of figures; sexual intercourse, as *criminal* ∼ (*crim. con.*, cf. CONNEXION). [OF, f. L *conversationem* (as prec., see -ATION)]

cŏnversā'tional (-sho-), a. Fond of, good at, pertaining to, conversation. Hence ∼IST n., ∼LY² adv. [-AL]

cŏnversaziōn'ė (-ăts-), n. (pl. *-nes, -ni* pr. -nē). Soirée given by learned or art society. [It., f. L as CONVERSATION]

convẽrse'¹, v.i. Talk (*with* person, *on, about,* subject). [f. OF *converser* f. L *conversari* keep company (with), frequent. as CONVERT¹]

cŏn'vẽrse², n. (arch.). Discourse; intercourse. [f. prec.]

cŏn'vẽrse³, a. & n. 1. Opposite, contrary. **2.** n. (Logic) converted proposition; form of words produced by transposition of some terms of another (*he had learning without wealth* is the ∼ of *he had wealth without learning*); (Math.) *this proposition is the ∼ of the former* (assumes its conclu-

sion & proves its datum). Hence ∼LY³ (-sl-) adv. [f. L p.p. *conversus*, see CONVERT¹]

conver'sion (-shn), n. Transposition, inversion, esp. (Logic) of subject & predicate (*if no A is B, then by* ∼ *no B is A*); bringing over (*to* an opinion, party, faith, etc.); turning of sinners to God; changing (*to, into*); change (of debentures, stocks, etc.) into others of different character. [ME, f. OF, f. L *conversionem* (foll., -ION)]

convẽrt'¹, v.t. Change (*into*); cause to turn (*to* opinion, faith, etc.), cf. PERVERT; turn to godliness; (Stocks etc.) see prec.; (Logic) see prec.; (Rugby football) complete (a try) by kicking goal (also abs.). Hence ∼ER¹ n., (esp.) large retort used in Bessemer steel process. [ME, f. OF *convertir* f. Rom. *convertire for L CON(*vertere vers-* turn) turn about; in some senses dir. f. L]

cŏn'vẽrt², n. Person converted, esp. to religious faith or life. [f. prec.]

convẽrt'ible, a. & n. 1. That may be converted; (of terms) synonymous; (of currency etc.) that may be converted into gold or dollars; (of motor-car etc.) capable of being converted from one class or type to another; ∼ *husbandry*, rotation of crops. **2.** n. A ∼ motor-car etc. Hence **convẽrtiBIL'ITY n., convẽrt'-iBLY² adv.** [OF, f. L *convertibilis* (as prec., see -BLE)]

cŏn'vĕx, a. Curved like the outside of circle or sphere (cf. CONCAVE). Hence or cogn. **convĕx'ITY n., ∼LY² adv.** [f. L *convexus*]

convĕx'o- in comb. Convex and —, as ∼-concave. [as prec., see -O-]

convey' (-vā), v.t. Transport, carry; transmit (sound, smell, etc.); impart, communicate, (idea, meaning); (Law) make over (property *to,* or abs.). Hence ∼ABLE (-ā'a-) a., ∼ER¹ (-ā'er), ∼OR (-ā'or), nn., (esp.) mechanical contrivance for ∼ing heavy articles or materials (*coal-* ∼*er;* ∼*or belt*). [ME, f. OF CON*veier*, mod. *convoyer* CONVOY¹ (*veie, voie,* f. L *via* way)]

convey'ance (-vā'a-), n. Carrying; transmission; communication of ideas etc.); (document effecting) transference of property; carriage, vehicle. [-ANCE]

convey'ancer (-vā'a-), n. Lawyer who prepares documents for conveyance of property. [-ER¹]

convey'ancing (-vā'a-), n. Work of prec. [-ING¹]

cŏn'vict¹, n. Condemned criminal undergoing penal servitude. Hence ∼ISM(3) n. [f. obs. adj. *convict* (as foll.)]

convict'², v.t. Prove guilty (*of* offence); declare guilty by verdict of jury or decision of judge; impress (person) with sense of error. Hence **convic'tıvE a.** [ME, f. L CON(*vincere vict-* conquer)]

convic'tion, n. Proving or finding guilty; *summary* ∼ (by judge or magistrates without jury); act of convincing; settled belief; (Theol.) awakened consciousness of sin. [f. LL *convictio* (as prec., see -ION)]

convinc|e', v.t. Firmly persuade (*of, that*; esp. pass.); produce in (person) a moral conviction (*of* sin etc.). Hence ~e'MENT (-sm-), ~'ingNESS, nn., ~'ingLY² adv. [as CONVICT²]

convin'cible, a. Open to conviction. [f. LL *convincibilis* (as prec., see -IBLE)]

conviv'ial, a. Of, befitting, a feast; festive, jovial. Hence~IST, conviviäl'ITY, nn., ~LY² adv. [f. L *convivialis* f. *convivium* feast]

cŏnvocā'tion, n. Calling together; assembly; ‖ (Ch. of Eng.) synod of clergy of province of Canterbury or York; ‖ legislative assembly of Oxford or Durham Univ. Hence~AL(-sho-)a. [ME, f. L *convocatio* (as foll., -ATION)]

convōke', v.t. Call together, summon to assemble. [f. L CON(*vocare* call)]

cŏn'volute (-ōŏt), a. & n. (bot., conch.). Rolled together, coiled; (n.) coil. [as CONVOLVE]

cŏn'volutĕd (-ōŏt-), a. (zool.). Coiled, twisted. [f. vb *convolute* (as prec.), otherwise rare]

cŏnvolu'tion (-ōŏ-), n. Coiling, twisting; fold, twist. [as foll., see -ION]

convŏlve', v.t. & i. Roll together, roll up, (esp. in p.p.). [f. L CON(*volvere voluti*-roll)]

convŏl'vūlus, n. (pl. *-luses*). Kinds of twining plant including bindweed. [L, as prec. with dim. suf.]

convoy'¹, v.t. (Of ship of war) escort (merchant or passenger vessel); escort with armed force; (arch.) conduct (guests, lady, etc.). [ME, f. OF *convoier*, var. of *conveier* CONVEY]

cŏn'voy², n. Act of convoying; protection; escort (for honour or protection); company, supply of provisions, etc., under escort; number of merchant ships sailing in company under escort. [f. F *convoi* f. *convoier* (prec.)]

convŭlse', v.t. Shake violently (lit. & fig.); throw into convulsions (usu. pass.); cause to be violently seized with laughter (usu. pass.). [f. L CON(*vellere vuls*- pull)]

convŭl'sion (-shn), n. Violent irregular motion of limb or body due to involuntary contraction of muscles (usu. pl., & esp. as a disorder of infants); (pl.) violent fit of laughter; violent social or political agitation; violent physical disturbance. Hence ~ARY² (-sho-) a. [F, or f. L *convulsio* (as prec., see -ION)]

convŭl'sive, a. Attended or affected with, producing, convulsions (lit. & fig.). Hence ~LY² (-vl-) adv. [CONVULSE, -IVE]

cŏn'ў, -ney, n. (pl. *-ies, -eys*). Rabbit (now used only in statutes etc., & as shop name for the fur); (Bibl.) hyrax; (arch.) ~-*catcher*, sharper. [ME *cunin* f. OF *conin*, parallel form of *conil* (f. L *cuni-*

culus), pl. *coniz, conis*, whence ME *conies* (pl.), whence sing. *cony*]

cōo, v.i. & t., & n. (Make) soft murmuring sound of or as of doves & pigeons; *bill & ~*, converse amorously; say ~ingly. [imit.]

cōo'ee, cōo'ey, n., & v.i. (Make) sound adopted as signal by Australian settlers from the aborigines. [imit.]

cŏŏk¹, n. One whose business is to cook food; *too many ~s spoil the broth*, one director is enough; **~-book*, cookery book; ~*-house*, camp kitchen, outdoor kitchen in warm countries, (on ship, also ~*-room*) galley; ~*-shop*, eating-house. [OE *cōc* f. pop. L *cōcus* for L *coquus*]

cŏŏk², v.t. & i. Prepare (food or abs.) by heat; (v.i.) undergo ~ing; (also ~ *up*) concoct (fig.); (colloq.) tamper with (accounts etc.); ‖ (sl.) of exertion etc.) exhaust (runner etc., esp. in p.p.); ~ *his goose*, do for him, settle his hash. [prec.]

cŏŏk'er, n. Cooking-apparatus, -stove; vessel food is cooked in; fruit etc. that cooks well; one who cooks (accounts etc.) or concocts. [-ER¹]

cŏŏk'erў, n. Art, practice, of cooking; ~*-book* (dealing with ~). [-ERY]

cŏŏk'ie, n. (Sc.) plain bun; **small flat cake, biscuit. [f. Du. *koekje* dim. of *koek* cake]

cŏŏk'ў, n. (colloq.). (Usu. female) cook. [-Y³]

cōol¹, a. & n. Moderately cold; (Hunt.) ~ *scent* (faint, weak); unexcited, calm; lacking zeal, lukewarm; wanting cordiality; calmly audacious, as *a ~ hand* (person); (complacently or emphat. of large sums of money) *it cost me a ~ thousand*; (n.) ~ air, ~ place, ~ness; ~*-headed*, not easily excited; ~ *tankard*, ~ing drink of wine, water, lemon-juice, etc. Hence ~'ISH¹ a., ~'LY² (-l-lī) adv., ~'NESS n. [OE *cōl* f. Gmc **kōluz* f. **kōl-* ablaut f. **kal-*, see COLD]

cōol², v.i. & t. Become cool (lit. & fig.; also ~ *down*); make cool (lit. & fig.); ~ one's COPPERs; ~ one's *heels*, be kept waiting. [OE *cōlian* (f. prec.)]

cōol'ant, n. Liquid applied to edge of cutting tool etc. to lessen friction. [COOL¹, -ANT]

cōol'er, n. Vessel in which a thing is cooled, as *wine, butter*, ~; **refrigerator*; (sl.) prison cell. [-ER¹]

cōol'ie, -lў, n. Indian or Chinese hired labourer. [f. Hind. *quli*]

cōolth, n. (now colloq. or joc.). Coolness. [f. COOL¹, after *warmth*]

‖ **coomb**, ‖ **combe**, (kōōm), n. Valley on flank of hill; short valley running up from coast; CWM. [OE *cumb*; cf. W *cwm* valley]

****cōon**, n. = RAC(C)OON; sly fellow; (contempt.) a Negro; *gone ~*, one whose case is hopeless. [abbr.]

For compounds of *co-* not given consult co-.

cōon⸱căn′, n. (Also *conquian*) simple two-handed card-game (orig. Mexican). [f. Sp. *con quien* with whom?]

cōop¹, n. Basket placed over sitting or fattening fowls; fowl-run; ‖ basket used in catching fish. [ME *cupe* basket f. MDu., MLG *kūpe*, ult. f. L *cūpa* cask]

cōop², v.t. Put in coop; confine (persons; also ~ *up*, *in*). [f. prec.]

‖ **cō-ōp′**, n. (colloq.). Co-operative society or store. [abbr.]

cōop′er¹, n., & v.t. Maker of casks for dry goods (*dry*~) or liquids (*wet*~); *white*~, maker of pails, tubs, etc.; (on ship) repairer of casks etc.; (also *wine*~) one who samples, bottles, or retails wine; equal mixture of stout & porter; (v.t.) repair (cask), stow in casks, furbish *up*. [f. MDu., MLG *kūper* f. *kūpe* COOP¹; see -ER¹]

cooper², see COPER².

cōop′erage. n. Cooper's work or workshop. So **cōop′ERY**(3) n. [-AGE]

cō(-)ōp′er|āte, v.i. Work together (*with* person *in* a work, *to* an end); (of things) concur in producing an effect. So ~ANT a. & n., ~ātoR n. [f. LL co(*operari* f. *opus operis* work), see -ATE³]

cō(-)ōperā′tion, n. Working together to same end; (Pol. Econ.) co-operative combination. [ME, f. L *cooperatio* (as prec., see -ION); partly thr. F *-tion*]

cō(-)ōp′erative, a. Of, tending to, co-operation; (Pol. Econ.) ~ *society* (for production or distribution of goods, profits being shared by members), ~ *store* (belonging to ~ society). Hence ~LY² (-vi-) adv. [f. LL *cooperativus* (as prec., see -IVE)]

cō-ōpt′, v.t. Elect into body by votes of existing members. So **cō-ōptā′TION** n. [f. L co(*optare* choose)]

cō-ōrd′inate, a. & n. **1.** Equal in rank, esp. (Gram.) of clauses of compound sentence (cf. SUBORDINATE); consisting of ~ things. **2.** n. ~ thing, esp. (Math.) each of a system of magnitudes used to fix position of point, line, or plane. Hence ~LY²(-tl-) adv. [f. CO-+L *ordinare* (*ordo -inis* or.ier), see -ATE²]

cō-ōrd′in|āte², v.t. Make co-ordinate; bring (parts) into proper relation. Hence ~A′TION n., ~ātive a. [prec., -ATE³]

cōot, n. Name of several swimming & diving birds, esp. the *bald* ~, web-footed bird with base of bill extended to form white plate on forehead, whence *bald as a* ~. [ME *cote*, *coote*, corresp. to Du. *koet*; ult. orig. unkn.]

cōot′ie, n. (Army sl.). Body-louse. [perh. f. Hind. *khuthi* scab]

cōp¹, n. (spinning). Conical ball of thread wound upon spindle. [OE *cop* top]

cōp², n. (sl.). Policeman. [cf. foll., COPPER²]

cōp³, v.t. (-pp-), & n., (sl.). **1.** Catch (~ *it*, catch it, be punished). **2.** n. Capture (chiefly in phr. *a fair*~). [etym. unkn.]

copaï′ba, **-va**, (-pī-, -pä-), n. Aromatic balsam used in medicine & the arts. [(-*ba*) Sp., f. Braz. *cupauba*]

cōp′al, n. Kinds of resin used for varnish. [Sp., f. Mex. *copalli* incense]

cōpär′cenäry, **-ery**, **cōpär′cener**, nn. = PARCENARY, PARCENER. [CO-]

cōpärt′ner, n. Partner, sharer, associate. Hence ~SHIP n. (*labour* ~*ship*, system designed to interest workmen in their business by means of profit-sharing). [CO-]

cōpärt′nery, n. Copartnership. [f. prec., see -ERY(2)]

cōpe¹, n. (Eccl.) long cloak worn by ecclesiastics in processions; (fig.) ~ (cloak) *of night*, ~ (canopy) *of heaven*; (Founding) outer portion of mould; = COPING; ~*-stone*, head stone of building, finishing touch. [ME *cāpe*, *cōpe*, repr. OE *-cāp*, *cāpe* (= ON *kápa*), f. med. L *cāpa* var. of LL *cappa* CAP¹, CAPE¹]

cōpe², v.t. & i. Furnish with a cope; cover (wall etc.) with COPING; cover as with a vault; (v.i.) ~ *over*, project like a coping. [f. prec.]

cōpe³, v.i. Contend evenly, grapple successfully, *with* (person, task). [f. OF *coper*, *colper*, (mod. F *couper*); see COUP]

cōp′ěck, n. Russian copper coin (the hundredth part of a rouble). [f. Russ. *kopeika* dim. of *kopyĕ* lance]

‖ **cōp′er¹**, n. (Also *horse*~) horse-dealer. [f. obs. *cope* buy, f. MDu., MLG *kōpen* (cogn. w. CHEAP), f. *cope*]

cōp′er², **coop′er²**(kō-), n. Floating grog-shop for North Sea fishers. [f. Flem. & Du. *kooper* f. *koopen* buy (prec.)]

Copěr′nican, a. ~ *system*, *theory*, (that the planets, including earth, move round sun). [f. *Copernicus* latinized f. *Kopper-nik*, astronomer (d. 1543) +-AN]

cōp′ing, n. Top (usu. sloping) course of masonry in wall; overhanging ledge protecting wall-fruit; ~*-stone* (used for ~). [COPE²+-ING¹]

cōp′ious, a. Plentiful; abounding in information; profuse in speech; (of languages) having large vocabulary. Hence ~LY² adv., ~NESS n. [ME, f. OF *copious* or L *copiosus* (*copia* plenty, see -OUS)]

cōpol′ÿmer, n. Compound analogous to a polymer but with units of more than one kind. So ~IZE(3) v.t., ~ĪZA′TION n. [CO-, POLYMER]

cŏpp′er¹, n., a., & v.t. **1.** Reddish malleable ductile metal; bronze (formerly ~) coin, penny, halfpenny, farthing; cooking or laundry boiler of iron or ~; *hot* ~*s*, mouth & throat parched by drinking, *cool* one's ~*s* (by drinking); ~ *beech* (kind with ~-coloured leaves); ~*-bit*, soldering tool pointed with ~; ~*-bottom* v.t., sheathe bottom of (ship) with ~ (esp. in p.p.); ‖~*captain*, sham captain; ~ *Indian*, red Indian of N. America; ~*-head*, venomous American snake; ~*plate*, polished ~ plate for engraving or etching, print from this, (adj., of writing) neat; ~*-smith*, one who works in ~. 2. v.t. Cover (ship's bottom etc.) with ~. Hence ~ʏ² a. (esp., ~-coloured). [OE *coper*, ON *kopar* f. *kupar* (also *kuppar* whence OHG *kupfar*) f. LL *cuprum* for L *cyprium aes* Cyprian metal]

‖ cŏpp'er², n. (sl.). Policeman. [cf. COP²]

cŏpp'eras, n. Sulphate of iron, green vitriol. [15th c. *coperose* f. OF *couperose* f. med. L *cup(e)rosa* perh. = *aqua cuprosa* copper water]

cŏpp'ice, n. Small wood of underwood & small trees, grown for periodical cutting; ~-*wood*, underwood. [f. OF *copeïz* f. Rom. *colpaticium* f. *colpare* cut f. med. L *col(a)pus* f. L f. Gk *kolaphos* blow, cuff]

cŏp'ra, n. Dried kernels of coconut. [Port., prob. f. Malayalam *koppara* coconut]

cŏp'ro- in. comb. = Gk *kopros* dung, as: -*lite*, fossil dung, so -*lĭt'ic* a.; -*logy* (-ŏl²), treatment of filthy subjects in literature etc.; -*phagous* (-ŏf²), (of beetles) dung-eating.

‖ cŏpse, n., & v.t. = COPPICE; ~'*wood*, underwood; (v.t.) treat as ~wood, cover with ~s. Hence cŏp'sʏ² a. [syncop. form of COPPICE]

Cŏpt, n. Native Egyptian Christian of Jacobite sect of Monophysites. [f. F *copte*; earlier (*c.* 1600) *Coptie*, *Copht(i)e* f. Arab. *qufṭ*, *qufṭi*, f. Copt. *gyptios*, *kyptaios*, f. Gk *Aiguptios* Egyptian]

Cŏp'tic, a. & n. (Language) of the Copts. [-IC]

cŏp'ŭl|a, n. (Logic, Gram.) verb *be* (as mere sign of predication); (Anat.) connecting part (bone, cartilage, ligament); (Mus.) short connecting passage. Hence ~ᴀʀ¹ a. [L]

cŏp'ŭl|āte, v.i. Unite sexually. Hence ~ᴀᴛᴏʀʏ a. [f. L *copulare* fasten together (prec.), see -ᴀᴛᴇ³]

cŏpŭlā'tion, n. Sexual union; grammatical or logical connexion. [ME, f. OF or L *copulatio* (as prec., see -ɪᴏɴ)]

cŏp'ŭlātive, a. & n. Serving to connect; (Gram.) connecting words or clauses that are connected in sense (cf. DISJUNCTIVE), also, connecting subject & predicate; (Zool., Anat.) relating to sexual union; (n.) ~ conjunction or particle. Hence ~ʟʏ² (-vl-) adv. [ME, f. OF (-*if*, -*ive*), or LL *copulativus* (as prec., see -ɪᴠᴇ)]

cŏp'ȳ¹, n. Reproduction (of writing, picture, etc.); imitation; page written after model (of penmanship); ‖ (Law) transcript of manorial court-roll, containing entries of admissions of tenants to land hence called COPYHOLD; written or printed specimen (of book etc.); *rough*, *foul*, ~, original draft; *fair*, *clean*, ~ (transcribed from rough ~); ~ *of verses*, short set as school exercise; *fair* ~, model version of this; model to be copied; manuscript or matter to be printed (*in-*

cident etc. *will make good* ~, lends itself to interesting narration in newspapers etc.); ~-*book*, one containing copies for learners to imitate (BLOT² one's ~-*book*); ~-*book maxims*, *morality* (commonplace); ~-*-writer*, one who writes or prepares advertising ~ for publication. [ME, f. OF *copie* f. L *copia* abundance &c., in med. L = transcript, from phr. *facere copiam describendi* give permission to transcribe]

cŏp'ȳ², v.t. & i. Transcribe (*from* original), whence ~ɪsᴛ n.; make copy of; imitate; crib from neighbour in examination; ~-*cat* (colloq.), slavish imitator. [ME, f. OF *copier* f. med. L *copiare* (as prec.)]

‖ cŏp'ȳhōld, n. & a. Tenure by COPY¹; (land) so held. Hence ~ᴇʀ¹ n.

cŏp'ȳright (-rīt), n. & a., & v.t. Exclusive right given by law for term of years to author, designer, etc., or his assignee to print, publish, or sell, copies of his original work; (adj.) protected by ~ (of books etc.); (v.t.) secure ~ for (book etc.).

coque (kŏk), n. Small loop of ribbon; (in mod. use, pr. kŏk, attrib.) applied to feathers used in trimming, in boas, etc. [F, = a shell]

coquet'¹ (-kět), a. Coquettish. [F (orig. noun, dim. of *coq* cock)]

coquet'², coquette', (-kět), v.i. (-tt-). Play the coquette; flirt (*with*); dally, trifle, *with* (matter, proposal, etc.). [f. F *coqueter* f. prec.]

cō'quetrȳ (-kit-), n. Coquettish behaviour or act; (fig.) trifling; attractive prettiness as result of art. [f. F *coquetterie* (*coqueter*, as prec., see -ᴇʀʏ)]

coquett|e' (-kět), n. Woman who trifles with man's affections; crested humming-bird. Hence ~ɪsʜ¹ a., ~'ɪsʜʟʏ² adv., (-kět-). [F, fem. of COQUET]

coqui'tō (-kē-), n. Chilian palm-tree yielding palm-honey. [Sp., dim. of *coco* coconut]

cor-, pref. = COM- before *r*.

‖ cŏ'racle, n. Wicker boat covered with watertight material used on Welsh & Irish lakes & rivers. [f. W *cwrwgl* f. *cwrwg* = Ir. *curach* boat]

cŏ'raco- in comb. (anat.). Of the *coracoid process* (beak-shaped process extending from shoulder-blade towards breast-bone). [f. Gk *korax* -*akos* crow]

cŏ'ral, n. & a. Hard calcareous substance (red, pink, white, etc.) secreted by many tribes of marine polyps for support & habitation; ~-*reef*, accumulation of this; toy of polished ~ for children cutting teeth; unimpregnated roe of lobster; (adj.) like ~, esp. red; ~-*island* (formed by growth of ~); ~-*rag*, limestone containing beds of petrified ~s. [ME, f. OF f. L *corallum* f. Gk *korallion*]

coralli- in comb. Coral, as -*ferous*, -*form*, bearing, shaped like, coral. [as prec., see -ɪ-]

cŏ'ralline¹, n. Kinds of seaweeds with calcareous jointed stem; (pop.) name of various plant-like compound animals; ~ zone of sea-depths, that in which these abound. [f. It. *corallina* dim. of *corallo* CORAL]

cŏ'ralline² (-ĭ-, -ī-), a. Coral-red; ~ *ware*, Italian red-paste pottery (17th–18th c.); like, composed of, coral. [F. or f. L *corallinus* (CORAL, -INE¹)]

cŏ'rallite, n. Fossil coral; coral skeleton of polyp; coralline marble. [-ITE¹]

cŏ'ralloid, a. & n. (Organism) like, akin to, coral. [-OID]

cŏr'ăm prep. (w. abl. case). In the presence of (*judice*, (jōod'isī), a judge, *pŏp'ŭlō*, the public, etc.). [L]

cor anglais (kŏr ahng'glā), n. The alto oboe. [F, = English horn]

cŏrb'el, n., & v.t. & i. (-ll-). (Archit.) projection of stone, timber, etc., jutting out from wall to support weight, whence ~led² (-ld) a.; (also ~-*block*) short timber laid on wall or pier longitudinally under beam; ~-*table*, projecting course resting on ~s; (v.t. & i.) ~ *out*, *off*, (cause to) project on ~s. [ME, f. OF dim. of *corp* (foll.); see -LE²]

cŏrb'ie, n. (Sc.). Raven; carrion crow; ~-*steps*, step-like projections on sloping sides of gable. [ME, f. OF *corbet*, -*in* (dim. of *corp* f. L *corvus* crow) + -Y³]

cŏrd, n., & v.t. Thin rope, thick string; (Anat.) ~-like structure in animal body, as SPINAL, UMBILICAL, ~, VOCAL ~s; ~-like rib on cloth; ribbed cloth, esp. corduroy; ~s, corduroy breeches or trousers; measure of cut wood (usu. 128 cub. ft); (fig.) ~s of discipline, fourfold ~ of evidence, etc.; (v.t.) bind with ~. [ME, f. OF *corde* f. L f. Gk *khordē* gut, string of musical instrument]

cŏrd'age, n. Cords, ropes, esp. in rigging of ship. [F (as prec. + -AGE]

cŏrd'āte, a. Heart-shaped. [f. L *cor cordis* heart, see -ATE²]

cŏrd'ĕd, a. Bound with cords; furnished with cords; (of cloth etc.) ribbed. [-ED²,¹]

cŏrdélier', n. Franciscan friar of strict rule (wearing knotted cord round waist). [ME, f. OF *cordeler*, -*ier* (*cordele* dim. as CORD, see -IER)]

cŏrd'ial, a. & n. (Medicine, food, drink) that stimulates the heart, esp. (Commerc.) aromatized & sweetened spirit; hearty, sincere; warm, friendly, whence ~ITY¹ (-ăl-) n., ~LY² adv. [ME, f. med. L *cordialis* (*cor cordis* heart, -AL)]

cŏrdĭller'a (-lyāra), n. Mountain ridge (one of parallel series), esp. of the Andes & same system in Central America & Mexico. [Sp.]

cŏrd'ite, n. A smokeless explosive. [f. CORD (from its appearance) + -ITE¹(2)]

cŏrd'on, n., & v.t. Projecting course of stone in wall; chain of military posts; line or circle of police etc.; (also *sanitary*

~) guarded line between infected & un-infected districts; ornamental cord or braid; (pron. as F) ribbon of knightly order (~ *bleu*, see Ap., joc., first-class cook); fruit-tree pruned to grow as single stem; (v.t., also ~ *off*) enclose with (military, police, etc.) ~. [16th c. *cordone* f. It.: later f. F *cordon* (as CORD, see -OON)]

cŏrd'ovan, a. & n. (Leather) of Cordova. [f. Sp. *cordovan*(o)]

cŏrd'uroy, n. & a. Coarse thick ribbed cotton stuff, orig. worn chiefly by labourers; (pl.) ~ trousers; ~ *road*, of tree-trunks laid across swamp. [late 18th c., app. f. *cord* ribbed fabric; remainder uncert.]

cŏrd'wain, n. (arch.). Spanish leather formerly used for shoes. [ME *cordewan*(e), *corduan*(e), f. OF *corduan*, -*ewan* of Cordova]

cŏrd'wainer, n. Shoemaker (now only as guild-name etc.). [AF *cordewaner*, OF *cordouanier* (prec., see -ER²)]

cōre, n., & v.t. Horny capsule containing seeds of apple, pear, etc.; central part cut out (esp. of rock in boring); bar of soft iron forming centre of electro-magnet or induction coil; internal mould filling space to be left hollow in a casting; central strand of rope; innermost part, as (fig.) *rotten at the* ~, *English to the* ~; heart; a disease, tumour, in sheep; (v.t.) remove ~ from, whence cōr'ER¹(2) n. Hence ~'LESS (-rl-) a. [ME *core*, of unkn. orig.]

cō'rela'tion. See CORRELATION.

cō-réli'gionist (-jo-), n. Adherent of same religion. [-IST]

cŏreŏp'sis, n. Plant with rayed usu. yellow flowers. [mod. L, f. Gk *koris* bug, *opsis* appearance, w. ref. to shape of seed]

cō-rèspŏn'dent, n. Person proceeded against together with the RESPONDENT in divorce suit. [CO-]

cŏrf, n. Large basket formerly used in mining; basket in which fish are kept alive in water. [f. MDu., MLG *korf* (= G *korb*) f. L *corbis*]

cŏrg'i (-gi), -gy, n. Small Welsh dog. [W]

cōriā'ceous (-shus), a. Like leather, leathery. [f. LL *coriaceus* (*corium* leather, see -ACEOUS)]

cŏriǎn'der, n. Annual plant with aromatic fruit (pop. called ~ *seed*) used for flavouring. [ME, f. OF *coriandre* f. L *coriandrum* f. Gk *koriannon*]

Cŏrin'thian, a. & n. (Native) of Corinth; (arch.) man of fashion & pleasure; *Epistles to the* ~s, books in N.T.; (Archit.) ~ *order*, one of the three Grecian ORDERS, having bell-shaped capital with rows of acanthus leaves, whence ~ESQUE' a. [f. L f. Gk *Korinthios* (*Korinthos*) + -AN]

cŏrk, n. & a., & v.t. 1. Bark of ~-oak (~-*tree*) of W. Europe; piece of ~ used as float for fishing line etc. (*like a* ~, buoyant, recovering quickly from depression etc.); bottle-stopper of ~; (Bot.) inner division of the bark in higher plants; (adj.) made of ~, as ~ *jacket* (for supporting person in water); ~*screw*, steel screw for drawing ~ from bottle, ~*screw curl* (spirally twisted), (v.t. & i.) move spirally; ~'*wood*, name of various light porous woods. 2. v.t. Stop, stop *up*, (as) with ~, blacken with burnt ~. [ME, f. Du., LG *kork*, f. Sp.-Arab. *alcorque*, of unkn. orig.]

cŏrk′age, n. Corking, uncorking, of bottles; hotel-keeper's charge for serving wine etc. not supplied by himself. [-AGE]

cŏrked (-kt), a. Stopped with, blackened with burnt, cork; (of wine) gone bad from defective corking. [-ED¹]

cŏrk′er, n. (sl.). Something that puts an end to a discussion, something astonishing, e.g. a monstrous lie, a 'whopper'. [-ER¹]

cŏrk′ў, a. Cork-like; (colloq.) frivolous, lively, skittish, restive. [-Y²]

cŏrm, n. (bot.). Bulb-like subterraneous stem, solid bulb. [f. Gk *kormos* trunk with boughs lopped off (*keirō* cut)]

cormo- in comb. Trunk, stem, (in terms referring to evolution of races etc.). [as prec.]

cŏrm′orant, n. Large lustrous-black voracious sea-bird; rapacious person. [ME, f. OF *cormaran* f. med. L *corvus marinus* sea-raven; for ending -ant cf. *peasant*, *tyrant*]

cŏrn¹, n. A grain, seed, esp. of cereals (also of pepper etc.); (collect. sing.) grain, also cereal plants while growing; *maize, Indian ~; ‖~-*chandler*, retail dealer in ~; ~-*cob*, part to which grains are attached in ear of maize; ~-*cob pipe* (made of this); ~-*COCKLE¹*; ~'*crake*, the bird landrail; ~-*exchange* (for trade in ~); ‖~-*factor*, dealer in ~; ~-*flag*, plant of genus Gladiolus; ‖~'*flour*, fine-ground Indian ~, also, flour of rice or other grain; ~'*flower*, name of various plants growing among ~; ‖~-*laws* (regulating ~-trade, esp. the English laws restricting importation, and repealed in 1846); ~ *marigold*, yellow-flowered ~field weed; ‖~-*rent* (paid in ~ or varying with price of ~); ‖~-*stalk* (colloq.), tall person (applied as nickname to persons of European descent born in Australia, esp. in N.S.W.). [OE *corn*, OS, OHG, ON *korn*, Goth. *kaurn* f. Gmc *kurnam* cogn. w. L *granum*]

cŏrn², v.t. Sprinkle, preserve, with salt (esp. in p.p.). [f. prec.]

cŏrn³, n. Horny place esp. on feet; *tread on my ~s*, hurt my feelings; ~-*plaster* (for application to ~s). [ME, f. OF f. L *cornu* horn]

cŏrn′brăsh, n. (geol.). Coarse calcareous sandstone. [f. CORN¹+BRASH¹]

cŏrn′ĕa, n. Transparent horny part of anterior covering of eyeball. [med. L *cornea* (*tela*) horny (web)]

cŏrn′el, n. Genus including cornelian cherry & common ~ or dogwood. [ult. f. L *cornus*]

cŏrnĕl′ian, căr-, n. Dull red or reddish--white chalcedony. [ME & OF *corneline*, refash. after med. L *cornelius*, earlier *corneolus*; cf. CARNELIAN]

cŏrn′ĕous, a. Horn-like, horny. [f. L *corneus* (*cornu* horn)+-OUS]

cŏrn′er, n., & v.t. & i. 1. Place where converging sides or edges meet; projecting angle, esp. where two streets meet; *turn the ~*, pass round it into another street, (fig.) pass critical point (in illness etc.); *cut off a ~*, avoid it by a short cut; ‖ (sl.) *the C~*, Tattersall's betting-rooms (orig. near Hyde Park C~); hollow angle enclosed by meeting walls etc.; *put* (child) *in the ~* (as punishment); (fig.) *drive into a ~* (difficult position from which there is no escape). 2. Secret or remote place, as *done in a ~*, *hole-&-~ transactions* (underhand); region, quarter, as *all the ~s of the earth*. 3. (Commerc.) buying up the whole of any stock in the market, so as to compel speculative sellers to buy from one to fulfil their engagements, (loosely) any combination to raise price by securing monopoly. 4. (Association football and Hockey) free kick, hit, from the ~-flag given when the ball has been kicked, hit, over his own goal-line by an opponent. 5. ~-*chisel*, -*punch*, etc. (angular, for cutting, cleaning, etc., ~s); ‖~-*boy*, -*man*¹, street rough, loafer; ‖~-*man*² (at either end of row of nigger minstrels, playing bones or tambourine & contributing comic effects); ~-*stone*, one in projecting angle of wall, foundation stone, (fig.) indispensable part, basis. 6. v.t. Furnish with ~s, set in ~, drive into ~ (esp. fig.), force (dealers) or control (commodity) by means of ~. 7. v.i. Form~ (*in* commodity). [ME, f. AF *corner* (OF -*ier*, -*iere*) f. Rom. *cornarium*, -*ia* f. L *cornu* horn, see -ER²(2)]

cŏrn′ĕt¹, n. (Also *cornet-à-piston(s)*, *cornopean*) brass musical instrument of trumpet class, with valves operated by pistons; ~-*player*, also ~IST n.; conically--rolled piece of paper for groceries etc.; conical wafer filled with ice-cream; *solo ~*, *echo ~*; organ-stops. [ME, f. OF *cornet*, dim. of Rom. *corno* f. L *cornu* horn]

cŏrn′ĕt², n. White head-dress of Sister of Charity; ‖ (formerly) fifth commissioned officer in cavalry troop, who carried the colours (from obs. sense *pennon*, *standard*), whence ~CY n. [f. F *cornette* dim. of *corne* f. Rom. *corna* f. L *cornua* horns]

cŏrn′ic|e, n. (Archit.) horizontal moulded projection crowning a building etc., esp. uppermost member of entablature of an

For compounds of *co-* not given consult CO-.

order, surmounting frieze; ornamental moulding round wall of room just below ceiling; (Mountaineering) overhanging mass of hardened snow at edge of precipice. Hence ~ED² (-st) a. [*cornice, -ish* f. F (16th c. -*ice, -ise, -iche*), f. It. *cornice*, prob. f. L *cornix -ic-* crow]

cŏrnif'erous, a. (geol.). Producing or containing hornstone. [f. L *cornifer* horn--bearing (*cornu* horn, see -FEROUS)]

Cŏrn'ish, a. & n. 1. Of Cornwall; ~ boiler, cylindrical flue-boiler; ~ CHOUGH, PASTY¹; ~ Riviera, coastal region of Cornwall, esp. the south coast. 2. n. The ~ language (extinct since 18th c.). [-ISH¹]

cŏrnŏp'ĕan. See CORNET¹.

cŏrn'stŏne, n. Mottled red and green limestone, subordinate bed in Old Red Sandstone formation. [CORN¹]

cŏrnūcōp'ĭ|a, n. (pl. -*as*). Horn of plenty; goat's horn represented in art as overflowing with flowers, fruit, and corn; ornamental vessel shaped like this; overflowing store, whence ~AN a. [LL, f. L *cornu copiae* horn of plenty]

cŏrnūt'ĕd, a. Having horns or horn-like projections. [f. obs. *cornute* f. L *cornutus* (*cornu* horn) +-ED¹]

cŏrn'ÿ¹, a. Of, abounding in, corn. [-Y²]

cŏrn'ÿ², a. Of, having, corns; (sl., of jokes etc.) out of date, old-fashioned. [CORN¹+-Y²]

corŏll'a, n. (bot.). Whorl of leaves (petals), separate or combined, forming inner envelope of flower. Hence cŏrolla'CEOUS (-ā'shus) a. [L, dim. of *corona* crown]

corŏll'arÿ, n. Proposition appended to one already demonstrated, as inference from it; immediate deduction; natural consequence, result. [f. L *corollarium* money paid for chaplet, gratuity, neut. adj. f. prec., -ARY¹]

corŏn'a¹, n. (pl. -*ae*). 1. Small disc of light round sun or moon; similar disc opposite sun, ANTHELION; halo of white light seen around disc of moon in total eclipse of sun (now known to belong to sun). 2. Circular chandelier hung from roof of a church. 3. (archit.). Member of cornice, with broad vertical face, usu. of considerable projection. 4. (anat.). Various crown-like parts of body. 5. (bot.). Appendage on top of seed or inner side of corolla. 6. Brush discharge of electricity. [L, = crown]

corŏn'a², n. A brand of Havana cigar. [Sp.; P]

‖ cŏ'ronach (-ăχ), n. Funeral-song, dirge, in Scottish Highlands and Ireland. [Ir., = Gael. *corranach* (*comh-* together +*ranach* outcry)]

cŏ'ronal¹, n. Circlet (esp. of gold or gems) for the head; wreath, garland. [ME, app. f. AF *coro(u)nal f. coroune CROWN¹+-AL]

corōn'al² (*also* kŏ⁻), a. (Anat.) ~ *suture*, transverse suture of skull separating frontal bone (~ *bone*) from parietal bones; of the crown of the head; (Bot.) of a

corōna. [F, or f. L *coronalis* (CORONA¹, see -AL)]

cŏ'ronarÿ, a. (anat.). Resembling, encircling like, a crown (~ *arteries*, those that supply the tissues of the heart with blood; ~ THROMBOSIS). [f. L *coronarius* (*corona* crown, -ARY¹)]

cŏ'ronate, -ātĕd, aa. (bot. & zool.). Furnished with a corona or crown--shaped part. [f. L *coronare* (CORONA¹, see -ATE²)]

cŏrona'tion, n. Ceremony of crowning sovereign or sovereign's consort; ~*oath*, taken by sovereign at ~. [ME, f. OF f. med. L *coronationem* (as prec., -ATION)]

cŏ'roner, n. Officer of county, district, or municipality, holding inquest on bodies of persons supposed to have died by violence or accident; ~*'s inquest*, inquiry held by ~*'s* court as to cause of death; official holding inquiry in cases of treasure trove; (orig.) officer charged with maintaining rights of private property of crown. Hence ~SHIP n. [ME, f. AF *cor(o)uner* f. *coroune* CROWN, see -ER²(2)]

cŏ'ronĕt, n. Small crown (implying dignity inferior to that of sovereign); fillet of precious materials, esp. as decorative part of woman's head-dress; garland; (Anat.) lowest part of horse's pastern. [f. OF *coronette* dim. of *corone* CROWN]

cŏ'ronĕtĕd, a. Wearing a coronet (esp. as belonging to peerage). [-ED²]

corōn'oid, a. (anat.). Curved like crow's beak (of processes of bones). [f. Gk *korōnē* crow +-OID]

corōz'ō, n. (pl. -*os*). S.-American tree, allied to palms; ~*nut*, its seed, from which vegetable ivory is made. [native]

cŏrp'oral¹, a. Of the human body, as ~ *punishment*; personal; (arch.) ~ *oath*, one ratified by touching a sacred object. Hence ~LY² adv. [ME, f. OF f. L *corporalis* (*corpus -oris* body, see -AL)]

cŏrp'oral², -as, n. Cloth on which consecrated elements are placed during celebration of mass. [14th c. -*al*, f. med. L *corporale* (sc. *pallium*) body cloth (as prec.); so OF *corporaus*, whence ME -*aus*, later *corporas*]

cŏrp'oral³, n. Non-commissioned officer ranking below sergeant (*the little C~*, Napoleon I); ‖ *ship's* ~, officer attending to police matters under master-at-arms. [obs. F, var. of *caporal* f. It. *caporale* prob. f. L *corporalis* (as prec.) confused w. *capo* head]

cŏrporăl'itÿ, n. Material existence; body; (pl.) bodily matters, wants, etc. [ME, f. LL *corporalitas* (as CORPORAL¹, see -TY)]

cŏrp'orate, a. Forming a body politic or corporation, as ~ *body, body* ~; ~ *town* (having municipal rights); forming one body of many individuals; of, belonging to, a body politic. Hence ~LY² (-tl-) adv. [f. L *corporare* form into a body (*corpus -oris*), see -ATE²]

cŏrpora'tion, n. United body of persons,

esp. one authorized to act as an individual; artificial person created by charter, prescription, or act of the legislature, comprising many persons (~ *aggregate*) or one (~ *sole*); *municipal* ~, civic authorities of borough, town, or city; (colloq.) abdomen, esp. when prominent. [f. LL *corporatio* (as prec., see -ATION)]

cŏrp′orative, a. Of a corporation. [f. CORPORATE + -IVE]

cŏrp′orātor, n. Member ŏf a corporation. [as CORPORATE, see -OR]

cŏrpōr′ĕal, a. Bodily; material; (Law) tangible, as ~ *hereditament* (of material objects). Hence ~ITY (-ăl²) n., ~LY² adv. [f. LL *corporealis* f. L *corporeus* (*corpus* -*oris* body) + -AL]

cŏrpore′itў, n. Quality of being or having a material body; bodily substance. [f. med. L *corporeitas* (as prec., see -TY)]

cŏrp′osant (-z-), n. Ball of light sometimes seen on ship during storm, St Elmo's fire. [f. OSp., It. *corpo santo* = L *corpus sanctum* holy body]

corps (kōr), n. (*pl. same, pr.* kōrz). **1.** = ARMY ~. **2.** Body of troops for special (medical, ordnance, intelligence, etc.) service. **3.** A students' society in a German university. **4.** ~ *d'armée* (ărmā′), army ~; ~ *de ballet* (see Ap.), the company of dancers in a ballet; *C*~ *diplomatique* (dēplōmahtĕk′), all the ambassadors & attachés of foreign states at a Court or capital. [F (as foll.)]

cŏrpse, n. Dead (usu. human) body; ~- *candle*, lambent flame seen in churchyard or over grave, regarded as omen of death. [ME *corps*, var. sp. of *cors* (CORSE), f. OF *cors* (mod. *corps*) f. L *corpus* body]

cŏrp′ŭl|ent, a. Bulky (of body); fat. So ~ENCE, -ENCY, nn. [ME, f. L *corpulentus* (*corpus* body, see -ULENT)]

cŏrp′us, n. (pl. -*pora*). Body, collection, of writings; ~ *juris* (joor′ĭs), body of law; ~ *delicti* (dĭlĭk′tĭ), all that goes to make a breach of law; (Physiol.) structure of special character in the animal body; *C*~ *Christi* (krĭs′tĭ), Feast of the body of Christ (Thursday after Trinity Sunday). [L, = body]

cŏrp′uscle (-sl), **cŏrpŭs′cule** (-kŭl), n. Minute body forming distinct part of the organism, esp. (pl.) those constituting large part of the blood in vertebrates; atom (esp. of electricity). [f. L *corpusculum* (as prec., see -CULE)]

cŏrpŭs′cūlar, a. Of corpuscles or atoms; ~ (EMISSION) *theory of light*. [as prec. + -AR¹]

corrăl′, n., & v.t. (-ll-). **1.** Pen for horses, cattle, etc. (in U.S. & Span. Amer.); defensive enclosure of wagons in encampment; enclosure for capturing wild animals. **2.** v.t. Form (wagons) into ~, confine in ~; *(colloq.) get hold of. [f. Sp. *corral*; cf. KRAAL]

correct′¹, v.t. Set right, amend; sub-

stitute right for (wrong); mark errors in (proof-sheet etc.) for amendment; admonish (person); cure (person) of fault; punish (person, fault); counteract (hurtful quality); bring into accordance with standard (reading of barometer etc.). [ME, f. L COR(*rigere rect-* = *regere* guide)]

correct′², a. True, accurate; right, proper, (of conduct, manners, etc.); in accordance with a good standard (of taste etc.). Hence ~LY² adv., ~NESS n. [F, as prec.]

correc′tion, n. Correcting; *I speak under* ~, I may be wrong; thing substituted for what is wrong; punishment, as *house of* ~ (bridewell). Hence ~AL (-sho-) a. [ME, f. OF f. L *correctionem* (as prec., see -ION)]

correc′titude, n. Correctness esp. of conduct. [mod., = *correct* + *rectitude*]

correc′tive, a. & n. (Thing) serving, tending, to correct or counteract what is harmful. Hence ~LY² (-vl-) adv. [F as CORRECT¹, see -IVE; cf. LL *correctivus*]

correc′tor, n. One who corrects; censor, critic; ||~ *of the press*, proof-reader; one who punishes. [ME, f. AF *corectour* f. L *correctorem* (as CORRECT¹, see -OR)]

co′rrĕlāte¹, n. Each of two related things (esp. so related that one implies the other). [f. as foll.]

co′rrĕlāte², v.i. & t. Have a mutual relation (*with, to*); bring (thing) into such relation (*with* another). [app. suggested by earlier *correlation, correlative* (16th c.)]

correl′ative, a. & n. Having a mutual relation (*with, to*); analogous; (Gram., of words) corresponding to each other & regularly used together, e.g. *either* & *or*; (n.) ~ word or thing. Hence or cogn. ~LY² adv. [f. med. L *correlativus* (-IVE); cf. F *corrélatif*]

corrĕlā′tion n., ~LY² (-vl-) adv., correlativ′ity n. [f. med. L *correlativus* (-IVE); cf. F *corrélatif*]

correspŏnd′, v.i. Be in harmony (*with, to*); be similar, analogous, (*to*); agree in amount, position, etc. (*to*); communicate by interchange of letters (*with*); ~*ing member* (of learned society etc.), honorary non-resident member with no voice in the society's affairs. Hence ~INGLY² adv. [f. F *correspondre* f. med. L COR(*respondere* RESPOND)]

correspŏnd′ence, n. Agreement, harmony, (*with, to; between* two); communication by letters; letters; ~ *school* (instructing by ~, and conducting ~ courses). [ME, f. OF f. med. L *correspondentia* (as prec., see -ENCE)]

correspŏnd′ent, n. & a. One who writes letters (to person or newspaper, esp. one employed for that purpose, as *our New York* ~, *war* ~); person, firm, having regular business relations with another esp. in another country; (adj.) corresponding (*to, with,* or *abs.*), whence ~LY² adv. [ME, f. OF, or f. med. L as prec., see -ENT] cŏ′rrĭdŏr, n. Main passage in large building, on which many rooms open; outside passage connecting parts of building; (Pol.) strip of a State's territory that runs through that of another & secures access to the sea etc.; ‖~ *train* (with narrow passage from end to end). [F, f. It. *corridore* corridor for *corridoio* (*correre* run +-*orio* -ORY) by confus. w. *corridore* runner]

‖ cŏ′rrie, n. (Sc.). Circular hollow on mountain side. [f. Gael. *coire* cauldron]

cŏrrigĕn′dum, n. (pl. -*da*). Thing to be corrected (esp. fault in printed book). [L (as CORRECT[1])]

cŏ′rrĭgĭble, a. Capable of being corrected; (of persons) submissive, open, to correction. [ME, f. OF (as CORRECT[1], see -BLE)]

corriv′al, n. = RIVAL. [F (as COR-, RIVAL)]

corrŏb′orant, a. & n. Strengthening (medicine); corroborating (fact). [F, or as foll., see -ANT]

corrŏb′or|āte, v.t. Confirm formally (law etc.); confirm (person, statement) by evidence etc. Hence or cogn. ~ative, ~atory, aa., ~ātor n. [f. L COR(*roborare* f. *robur* -*oris* hard wood) strengthen, -ATE[3]]

corrŏborā′tion, n. Confirmation by further evidence. [F, or f. LL *corroboratio* (as prec., see -ATION)]

corrŏb′oree, n. Native dance of Australian aborigines. [native]

corrŏde′, v.t. & i. Wear away, destroy gradually (of rust, chemical agents, diseases, & fig.); (v.i.) decay. So corrō′sion (-zhn) n. [ME, f. L COR(*rodere* ros-gnaw)]

corrōs′ive, a. & n. (Thing) tending to corrode (lit. & fig.); ~ *sublimate*, (Commerc.) mercuric chloride, a strong acrid poison. Hence ~LY[2] (-vl-) adv., ~NESS (-vn-) n. [ME, f. OF *corosif*, -*ive*, as CORRODE, see -IVE]

cŏ′rrugāte (-ŏŏ-), v.t. & i. Contract into wrinkles or folds (t. & i.); mark with, bend into, ridges, as ~*d iron*. Hence or cogn. cŏrrugA′TION (-ŏŏ-) n. [f. L COR-(*rugare* f. *ruga* wrinkle), -ATE[3]]

cŏ′rrugātor (-ŏŏ-), n. Muscle that contracts the brow in frowning. [mod. L as prec., see -OR]

corrŭpt′[1], a. Rotten; depraved, wicked; influenced by bribery; (of language, texts, etc.) vitiated by errors or alterations; ~ *practices*, forms of bribery esp. at elections. Hence ~LY[2] adv., ~NESS n. [ME, f. OF *cor(r)upt* or L COR(*rumpere rupt-* break)]

corrŭpt′[2], v.t. & i. Infect, taint, (lit. & fig.); bribe; destroy purity of (language); become corrupt. So corrŭp′tive a. [ME, f. prec., replacing (now obs.) *corrump*]

corrŭp′ti|ble, a. Liable to corruption, perishable; capable of moral corruption. Hence or cogn. ~BIL′ITY n., ~bLY[2] adv. [ME, f. LL *corruptibilis* (CORRUPT[1], -BLE)]

corrŭp′tion, n. Decomposition; moral deterioration; use of corrupt practices (bribery etc.); perversion (of language etc.) from its original state; deformation (of word); (Law) ~ *of blood*, effect of attainder upon person attainted. [ME, f OF, or f. L *corruptio* (as prec., see -ION)]

cŏrs′ăc, -ăk, n. (zool.). Tartar fox [Turki]

cŏrs′age (-ahzh or -ïj), n. Bodice or waist of woman's dress; *bouquet (to be) worn, orig. at waist. [ME, f. OF (*cors* body, see CORPSE & -AGE)]

cŏrs′air, n. Privateer, privateering vessel, esp. of Barbary; a pirate. [f. F *corsaire* f. med. L *cursarius* (*cursus* -*ūs* inroad, f. *currere* run, -ARY[1])]

cŏrse, n. (arch., poet.). See CORPSE.

cŏrs′ĕt, n. Woman's closely fitting inner bodice stiffened with whalebone & fastened by lacing, stays. Hence ~ED[2] a. [ME, f. OF, dim. of *cors* body, see CORPSE]

cŏrs′lĕt, -selĕt (-sl-), n. Piece of armour covering body; garment (usu. tight--fitting) covering body as distinct from limbs; (Zool.) insect's thorax, part between head & abdomen. [OF, as prec., see -LET]

cortège (kŏrtāzh′), n. Train of attendants; (esp. funeral) procession. [F]

Cŏr′tes, n. pl. Two chambers making legislative assembly of Spain or Portugal. [Sp., Port.]

cŏrt′ex, n. (pl. -*tĭcēs*). Bark; outer grey matter of brain, outer part of kidney. [L *cortex* -*icis* bark]

cŏrt′ical, a. (Bot.) of the bark or rind; (Anat., Zool.) forming the outer part of animal body or organ. [f. as prec. +-AL]

cŏrt′icate, -āted, aa. Having bark; bark-like. [f. L *corticatus* (as prec., see -ATE[2])]

cŏrt′isōne, n. One of a group of hormones produced by the cortex of the suprarenal gland. [P]

corŭn′dum, n. Crystallized mineral of same species as sapphire & ruby, blue, grey, brown, black; mineral species of crystallized alumina. [f. Tamil *kurundam*]

cŏ′ruscāte, v.i. Sparkle, flash, (lit., & fig. of wit etc.). So corŭs′cANT a., cŏrusca′TION n. [f. L *coruscare*, see -ATE[3]]

corvée′ (-vă), n. (feudal). Day's work of unpaid labour due by vassal; statute labour, e.g. that exacted of French peasants before 1776. [ME, f. OF f. med. L *corrogata* (sc. *opera*) f. COR(*rogare* ask)]

cŏrvĕtte′, n. (naut.). Flush-decked war--vessel with one tier of guns (hist.); small fast naval escort-vessel. [F, f. MDu. *korf* kind of ship, + dim. -ETTE]

cŏrv′ine, a. Of, akin to, the raven or crow. [f. L *corvinus* (*corvus* raven, see -INE[1])]

Cŏ′rybănt, n. (pl. -*s*, -*ēs*). Priest of Phrygian worship of Cybele, performed with extravagant dances. Hence Cŏrybăn-

tIAN, Cŏrўbăn'tIC, Cŏrўbăn'tINE, aa.
[ME, f. L f. Gk *Korubas -bant-*]

Cŏ'rўdon, n. Typical rustic in pastoral poetry. [L, f. Gk *Korudōn*]

cŏ'rўmb, n. (bot.). Species of inflorescence; raceme in which lower flower-stalks are proportionally longer. Hence ~OSE'[1] a. [f. L f. Gk *korumbos* cluster]

cŏrўphae'us, n. (pl. -*aei* pr. -ē'ī). Leader of a chorus (also fig.). [L, f. Gk *koruphaios* (*koruphē* head)]

cŏ'rўphée (-fā), n. A leading dancer in a ballet. [F, as prec.]

corўz'a, n. Catarrh. [LL, f. Gk *koruza* running at nose]

cŏs[1], n. (Also *Cos lettuce*) kind of lettuce introduced from Cos (now Stanchio). [f. Gk *kŏs*]

cŏs[2], n. Abbr. of COSINE.

cŏse (-z), v.i. Make oneself cosy. [back formation on COSY, cf. LAZE f. *lazy*]

cŏsĕc'ant, n. (trig.). Secant of complement of given angle (abbr. *cosec.*). [CO-]

cŏseis'mal (-sīz-), a. & n. (Line or curve connecting points) of simultaneous shock from earthquake wave. [CO-]

‖ **cŏsh,** n., & v.t., (sl.). Bludgeon, life-preserver (~-*boy*, youth or man armed with ~); (v.t.) strike with ~. [orig. unkn.]

cŏsh'er, v.t. Pamper, cocker *up*. [orig. unkn.]

cŏ-sĭg'natorў, a. & n. (Person) signing jointly with others. [CO-]

cŏ'sine, n. (trig.). Sine of complement of given angle (abbr. *cŏs*). [CO-]

cŏsmĕt'ic (·z-), a. & n. (Preparation) designed to beautify hair, skin, or complexion. [f. Gk *kosmētikos* (*kosmeō* adorn f. *kosmos* order, adornment, see -ETIC)]

cŏs'mic (-z-), a. Of the universe or COSMOS (esp. as distinguished from the earth); ~ *philosophy*, = foll.; ~ *rays*, radiations that reach the earth equally from all directions, characterized by enormous voltages and high penetrative power. Hence ~AL a., ~ALLУ[2] adv. [f. Gk *kosmikos* (*kosmos* world, see -IC)]

cŏs'mism (-z-), n. Conception of the cosmos as a self-acting whole. So **cŏs'm-IST** n. [COSMOS[1] + -ISM]

cosmo- in comb. = Gk *kosmos* universe, as -*geny*, evolution of the universe, -*logy*, -*logist*, -*lo'gical*, science of, student of, concerned with, the universe, -*plas'tic*, moulding the universe.

cŏsmŏg'onў (-z-), n. (Theory of) the creation of the universe. So **cŏsmŏgŏn'-IC(AL)** aa., ~IST(3) n., (-z-). [f. Gk *kosmogonia* (COSMO- + -*gonia* f. -*gonos* -begetting)]

cŏsmŏg'raphў (-z-); n. Description, mapping, of general features of universe or earth. So **cŏsmŏg'RAPHER** n., **cŏsmo-GRAPH'IC(AL)** aa., (-z-). [f. Gk *kosmographia*, see COSMO-, -GRAPHY]

cŏsmŏp'olIs (-z-), n. A cosmopolitan city. [f. COSMO- + Gk *polis* city]

cŏsmopŏl'itan (-z-), a. & n. Belonging to all parts of the world; (person) free from national limitations. Hence ~ISM n., ~IZE v.t. & i., (-z-). [f. foll. + -AN]

cŏsmŏp'olit|e (-z-), n. & a. Citizen of the world; (adj.) free from national prejudices. Hence ~ISM n. [f. Gk *kosmopolitēs* (COSMO- + *politēs* citizen)]

cŏsmopolit'ical (-z-), a. Belonging to universal polity. [f. prec. + -ICAL]

cŏsmora'ma (-z-; -ah-), n. Peep-show illustrating all parts of the world. Hence **cŏsmorăm'IC** a. [f. COSMO- + Gk *horama* spectacle (*horaō* see)]

cŏs'mŏs[1] (-z-), n. The universe as an ordered whole; ordered system of ideas, etc., sum-total of experience. [f. Gk *kosmos*]

cŏs'mŏs[2] (-z-), n. Plant bearing single dahlia-like blossoms of various colours. [f. Gk *kosmos* ornament]

Cŏss'ăck, n. Member of a people of south-eastern Russia, esp. as light horse in Russian army; ~ *post*, military outpost of a few mounted men. [f. F *cosaque* f. Turki *quzzaq* adventurer]

cŏss'ĕt, n., & v.t. Pet lamb; (v.t.) pet, pamper. [(vb f. n.) perh. = OE *cotsǣta* cot-sitter (i.e. animal brought up in house)]

cost[1] (kaw-, kŏ-), n. Price (to be) paid for thing; *prime* ~ (also ~ *price*), that at which merchant buys; (pl.) law expenses, esp. those allowed in favour of winning party; expenditure of time, labour, etc.; *at* ~, at the initial ~; *al all* ~*s*, cost what it may; *at the* ~ *of*, at the expense of losing; *count the* ~, consider the risks before action; *to a person's* ~, to his loss; ~ *accountant, clerk*, one who records every item of (esp. overhead) expenses in a business concern (with a view to checking wasteful expenditure); ~-*book* (showing expenses, profit, etc., of mine). Hence ~'LESS a. [ME, f. OF *cost, cousi* f. Rom. **costo* f. **costare* (foll.)]

cost[2] (kaw-, kŏ-), v.i. & t. (*cost*). Be acquirable at, involve expenditure of, as ~ *him five shillings*, ~ *the writer infinite labour*; result in the loss of, as ~ *him his crown*; ~ *him dear*(*ly*), involved a heavy penalty; (Commerc.) fix price of. The person is indirect object, the price is expressed adverbially, *in* being understood. [ME, f. OF *coster, couster* f. Rom. **costare* f. L CON(*stare* stand) stand firm, stand at a price]

cŏs'tal, a. Of the ribs. [F, f. L *costa* rib; see -AL; cf. LL *costalis*]

cŏs'tard, n. ‖ Large kind of apple; (arch.) head. [ME, perh. f. OF *coste* rib (as prec.,) + -ARD]

cŏs'tate, a. Ribbed, having ribs. [f. L *costatus* (*costa* rib, see -ATE[2])]

For compounds of *co-* not given consult CO-.

‖ **cŏstean′, -een, v.i.** (mining). Sink pits down to rock to find direction of lode. [f. Corn. *cothas stean* dropped tin]

‖ **cŏs′ter(monger)** (-ŭngg-), n. Man who sells fruit, fish, etc., from barrow in street. [COSTARD, MONGER]

cŏs′tive, a. With confined bowels, constipated; (fig.) niggardly. Hence ~NESS (-vn-) n. [ME *costif* f. OF *costive* f. L *constipatus* CONSTIPATED]

cost′l|y̆ (kaw-, kŏ-), a. Of great value; expensive. Hence ~iNESS n. [-LY¹]

cŏst′mary̆, n. Aromatic perennial plant, formerly used in medicine & for flavouring ale. [OE *cost* f. L f. Gk *kostos* +(St) *Mary*]

cŏst′ume (*also* -tūm′), n., & v.t. Style, fashion of dress or attire (including way of wearing hair); complete set of outer garments; ~ *jewellery,* artificial jewellery worn for decorative purposes; ~ *piece,* play in which actors wear historical ~; (v.t.) provide with ~. [F, f. It. *costume* f. L *consuetudinem* CUSTOM]

cŏstūm′ier, -ūm′er, n. Maker of, dealer in, costumes. [F (-*ier* as prec., see -EER]

cōs′y̆ (-z-), -zy̆, a. & n. Comfortable, snug, (of person or place); (n.) canopied corner seat for two (cf. F *causeuse*); *tea, egg,* ~, quilted covering to retain heat in teapot, egg. Hence **cōs′ily̆²** adv., **cōs′iness** n., (-z-). [etym. unkn.]

cŏt¹, n., & v.t. (-tt-). Small erection for shelter, as *bell-, sheep-,* ~; (poet.) cottage; (v.t.) put (sheep) in ~. [OE *cot,* = MDu., MLG, ON *kot,* f. Gmc **kutom,* cogn. w. COTE]

cŏt², n. (Anglo-Ind.) light bedstead; (Naut.) swinging bed for officers, sick persons, etc.; ‖ small (usu. swinging) bed for child; bed in children's hospital. [Anglo-Ind., f. Hind. *khaṭ* bedstead, bier]

cŏt³, n. Abbr. of foll.

cōtăn′gent (-j-), n. (trig.). Tangent of complement of given angle (abbr. *cŏt.* [CO-]

cōte, n. Shed, stall, shelter, esp. for animals as *dove-, hen-, sheep-,* ~. [OE *cote* = MLG *kote,* f. Gmc **kuton,* cogn. w. COT¹]

co-temporary etc. See CONTEMPORARY etc.

cō-tĕn′ant, n. Joint tenant. [CO-]

cŏt′erie, n. Circle, set, of persons associated by exclusive interests; select circle in society. [F, orig. = association of country people, f. *cotier* COTTAR, see -ERY]

cōtĕrm′inous, a. Var. of CONTERMINOUS. [CO-]

cothŭrn′us, n. (pl. -*ni*). Buskin, thick-soled boot of Athenian tragic actor (also fig., of elevated style etc.). [L, f. Gk *kothornos*]

cō-tīd′al, a. ~ *line* on map (connecting places at which high water occurs at same time). [CO-]

cotill′ion, -llon, (-lyon), n. Name of several dances; music for these. [F (-*llon*), = petticoat]

cŏtŏnĕăs′ter, n. (Kinds of) small tree or shrub of N. Europe, resembling hawthorn and bearing rose-red berries. [f. L *cotonea* quince +-ASTER]

cŏtt′a, n. Short surplice. [It., see COAT]

cŏtt′age, n. Labourer's or villager's small dwelling; small country residence; ~ *hospital* (in ~, without resident medical staff); ~ *loaf* of bread (of two round masses, smaller on top of larger); ~ *piano* (small upright). [ME, f. AF **cotage,* f. COT¹, COTE, see -AGE]

cŏtt′ager (-tǐ-), n. Inhabitant of a cottage. [-ER¹]

‖ **cŏtt′ar, -er¹, n.** Scots peasant occupying cottage on farm, and labouring on farm at fixed rate when required; = COTTIER. [partly f. med. L *cotarius* (see COTTIER), partly (16th c.) f. COT¹, see -AR², -ER²]

cŏtt′er², n. Key, wedge, bolt, for securing parts of machinery etc.; esp., split pin that opens after passing through hole; ~*-pin,* pin to keep ~ in place. [also, earlier, *cotterel*; orig. unkn.]

‖ **cŏtt′ier, n.** Cottager: Irish peasant holding under ~ *tenure* (letting of land in small portions at rent fixed by competition). [ME, f. OF *cotier,* f. med. L *cotarius* f. *cota*; see COT¹, COTE, -IER, -ER²]

cŏtt′on¹, n. White downy fibrous substance clothing seeds of ~-*plant,* used for making cloth, thread, etc.; ~-*plant;* thread spun from ~ yarn (also *sewing*~); cloth made of ~; GUN~; ~-*cake,* compressed ~ seed as food for cattle; ~-*grass,* kinds of plant with white silky hairs; ‖~-*lord,* magnate of ~ trade; ~-*spinner,* workman who spins ~, owner of ~ mill; ~-*tail,* common American rabbit, with white fluffy tail; ~ *waste,* refuse yarn used for cleaning machinery etc.; ‖~ *wool,* raw ~, esp. as prepared for wadding; ~ *yarn,* ~ prepared for weaving into fabrics. Hence ~y̆² a. [ME *coto(u)n* f. OF *coton* f. Arab. *qutun*]

cŏtt′on², v.i. Agree, harmonize, (*together, with* each other); ~ *up,* make friendly advances (*to* or abs.); become attached *to*; ~ *on to* (person, thing), take to him, it; ~ *on* (*to*), (sl.) understand. [f. prec.]

cŏttonŏc′racy̆, n. The magnates of the cotton trade. So **Cŏttonŏp′olis** n. (joc.), Manchester. [COTTON¹ + -o- + -CRACY, Gk *polis* city]

cŏty̆lĕd′on, n. Primary leaf in embryo of higher plants, seed-leaf; kinds of plants including navelwort or pennywort. [L, f. Gk *kotulēdōn* cup-shaped cavity (*kotulē* cup)]

cŏty̆lĕd′onous, a. Having cotyledons. [-OUS]

cŏt′y̆loid, a. (anat.). Cup-shaped. [f. Gk *kotuloeidēs* (*kotulē* cup, see -OID)]

couch¹, n. Bed; thing one sleeps on; lounge like sofa, but with half-back and head-end only; (Malting) bed in which grain germinates after steeping. [ME & OF *couche* f. *coucher* (foll.)]

couch[2], v.t. & i. Lay one*self* down (now only in p.p.); (Malting) lay (grain) on floor to germinate; lower (spear etc.) to position of attack; remove (cataract; also~person, person's *eye*, for cataract); express (thought etc. *in* words); veil (meaning *under* words); (of animals) lie (esp. in lair); crouch, cower; lie in ambush. [ME, f. OF *coucher* f. L COL(*locare* place)]

couch[3] (kow-, kŏō-), n. (More usu. ~-*grass*) kind of grass with long creeping roots, a common weed. [var. of QUITCH]

couch'ant, a. (her.). (Of animals) lying with body resting on legs and head raised. [F, part. as COUCH[2]; see -ANT]

Couéism (kŏō'ălzm), n. Systematic auto-suggestion of a sanguine kind. [Émile *Coué*, French psychologist (d. 1926), +-ISM]

coug'ar (kŏō-), n. Large American feline quadruped, puma. [f. F *couguar* repr. Guarani *guazu ara*]

cough[1] (kawf, kŏf), n. Act of coughing; tendency to cough, diseased condition of respiratory organs; ~-*drop*, -*lozenge*, medicated sweet to relieve ~. [f. foll.]

cough[2] (as prec.), v.i. & t. Expel air from lungs with violent effort and noise produced by abrupt opening of glottis; (trans.) ~ *out*, *up*, eject by, say with, cough; ~ *down*, silence (speaker) with ~*ing*; ~ *up* (sl.), blurt out, say with reluctance, bring out, produce. [ME *coghe*, *covhe*, rel. to OE *cohhetan*, MDu. *cuchen*, MHG *küchen* (G *keuchen*), of imit. orig.]

could. See CAN[2].

couleur' de rōse' (kōōlẽr; -z), a. & n. = ROSE-*colour(ed)*. [F]

coulisse (kōōlēs'), n. (Usu. pl.) wings in theatre; space between two of these; groove in which sluice-gate moves. [F]

couloir (kōōl'wahr), n. Steep gully on mountain side. [F]

coulomb (kōōlŏm'), n. Quantity of electricity conveyed in one second by current of one ampere. [*de C~*, French physicist (d. 1806)]

coul'ter (kōl-), *cŏl-, n. Iron blade fixed in front of share in plough. [OE *culter* f. L *culter*]

coum'arin (kōō-), n. Aromatic crystalline substance found in seeds of Tonka bean etc. [f. F *coumarine* (*cumarú*, name in Guiana of Tonka bean, see -IN)]

coun'cil, n. Ecclesiastical assembly, as *oecumenical*, *diocesan*, ~; (N.T.) Jewish Sanhedrin; advisory or deliberative assembly, as (hist.) Great *C~*, ~ of tenants-in-chief & great ecclesiastics (last summoned in 1640), CABINET ~; body of councillors, ‖ as PRIVY ~ (*the King*, *Queen*, *Crown*, *in C~*, Privy C~ as issuing

Orders in C~ or receiving appeal petitions from colonies etc.), *C~ of State* (of foreign countries); ‖ body assisting governor of British crown colony or dependency; local administrative body of town, city, or administrative county, as *County C~*; *C~ of War*, assembly of officers called in special emergency, (in some foreign countries) permanent military board; ~-*board*, table at which~ sits, ~ in session; ~-*chamber*, room in which ~ meets; ~-*house*, building in which~ meets, (also) house built by a municipal~. [This form represents OF *cuncile* f. L *concilium* convocation, assembly, f. *calare* summon (cf. Gk *kalein*); the form COUNSEL repr. OF *cunseil* f. L *consilium* advice. From ME both spellings were interchangeable; in 16th c. began the different. acc. to wh. *council* = any deliberative body, *counsel* = act of counselling, advice, &c.]

coun'cillor, n. Member of a (town etc.) council. Hence ~SHIP n. [16th-c. different. f. COUNSELLOR; see COUNCIL]

coun'sel[1], n. Consultation; *take* ~, consult (*with* or abs.); advice; (Theol.) ~ *of perfection*, injunction (orig. of Christ or Apostles) not regarded as universally binding (*Matt.* xix. 21); plan; *keep* one's (*own*) or *another's* ~ (secret); body of legal advisers in cause; barrister; *Queen's*, *King's*, *C~* (abbr. *Q.C.*, *K.C.*), ~ to the crown, taking precedence of other barristers. [ME, repr. OF *con-*, *cunseil* f. L *consilium* consultation, advice, rel. to *consulere* (cf. CONSUL), *consultare* CONSULT. See COUNCIL]

coun'sel[2], v.t. (-ll-). Advise (person *to* do); recommend (thing, *that*). [ME *conseil* f. OF *conseiller* f. L *consiliari* (as prec.)]

coun'sellor, n. Adviser; (also ~-*at-law*) advising barrister (now arch. in England). [ME *counseiller*, -*our*, f. OF *conseillere*, -*eor*, f. as COUNSEL[1] + -ER[2], -OR; cf. med. L *consiliaris*, -*ator*]

count[1], n. Counting; one's reckoning (*keep*, *lose*, ~, be aware, fail to know, how many there have been); sum total; (Law) each charge in an indictment; ~-*down*, counting of seconds before a missile etc. is fired; ‖ (H. of Commons) ~-*out*, adjournment when fewer than 40 members are present; ~-*out* (Boxing), counting of 10 sec. to give fallen man time to rise, failing which he loses the match. [ME, f. OF *conte* f. LL *computus* (as foll.)]

count[2], v.t. & i. Enumerate, reckon up; repeat numerals in order; ~ *up*, find the sum of; ~ *out*, ~ while taking from a stock; (of boxer) *be* ~*ed out*, fail to rise in time (see prec.); ‖~ *out the House*, procure adjournment (as prec.); include in reckoning; consider (a thing to be (so & so); ~ *on*, *upon*, expect confidently; be included in reckoning, as *that does not* ~ ;

~ for, be worth (much etc.); (Sc.) **~ kin** (*with*), be demonstrably related (to). [ME, f. OF *conter* f. L *computare* COMPUTE]

count³, n. Foreign noble corresp. to earl; **~ PALATINE.** Hence **~'ship** n. [f. OF *conte* f. L *comitem* (nom. *-mes*) companion]

count'énance¹, n. Expression of face, as *change* (one's) **~** (from emotion), *keep* one's **~,** maintain composure, esp. refrain from laughing; face; composure, as *put out of* **~,** disconcert, *keep* (person) *in* **~** (usu. by show of support). [ME, f. OF *contenance* f. L *continentia* (as CONTAIN, see -ENCE)]

count'énance², v.t. Sanction (act); encourage (person, practice, person *in* practice). [f. prec.]

coun'ter¹, n. 1. Small (usu. round) piece of metal, ivory, etc., used for keeping account in games, esp. cards; imitation coin. 2. Banker's table; table in shop on which money is counted out & across which goods are delivered; **~-jumper,** (derog.) shopman. [f. AF *cont(e)our,* OF *-(e)oir,* f. med. L *computatorium* (as COMPUTE, see -ORY(2))]

coun'ter², n. Part of horse's breast between shoulders and under neck; curved part of stern of ship. [orig. unkn.]

coun'ter³, n. (fencing). Circular parry in which hand retains same position while point describes a circle. [f. F *contre* COUNTER-]

coun'ter⁴, n. (shoemaking). Back part of shoe or boot round heel. [abbr. of COUNTERFORT]

coun'ter⁵, a. Opposed; opposite; duplicate; **~** (*rocking turn* or *rocker*), skating figure (see ROCK²). [arising f. combb. w. COUNTER-]

coun'ter⁶, v.t. & i. Oppose, contradict; (Chess) meet with counter move; (Boxing) give (opponent, or abs.) return blow while parrying. [ME, partly f. ENCOUNTER, partly f. COUNTER-]

coun'ter⁷, adv. In the opposite direction, as *hunt, run, go,* **~** (i.e. to direction taken by game); contrary, as *act, go,* **~** (*to* instructions etc.). [ME, f. F *contre* COUNTER-]

coun'ter⁸, n. (Abbr. for) counter rocking turn (see ROCK³).

coun'ter-, pref. in ME *countre-* f. OF f. L *contra* against, in return, orig. in words f. OF, F, or It., but now a living prefix of vbs, nouns, adjj., and advv., with sense (1) reciprocation, opposition, frustration, rivalry, (2) opposite position or direction, (3) correspondence, match, (of things having naturally two opposite parts), (4) duplicate, substitute.

counter|act', v.t. Hinder, defeat, by contrary action; neutralize. Hence **~ăc'tion** n., **~ăc'tive** a. [COUNTER(1)]

counter-a'gent, n. Counteracting agent or force. [COUNTER-(1)]

coun'ter-approach, n. (mil.). Work constructed by besieged outside permanent fortifications to check besiegers. [COUNTER-(1)]

coun'ter-attăck', n., & v.t. & i. Sortie, charge, etc., in reply to attack by enemy; (v.t. & i.) make **~** (upon). [COUNTER-(1)]

coun'ter-attrăc'tion, n. Attraction of contrary tendency; rival attraction. [COUNTER-(1)]

coun'terbăl'ance, n., & v.t. Weight balancing another; (v.t.) act as **~** to. [COUNTER-(1)]

coun'terblast (-ah-), n. Energetic declaration against something. [COUNTER-(1)]

counterchănge' (-j), v.t. & i. Interchange; chequer; (v.i.) change places or parts. [f. F *contrechanger* (see COUNTER-(1) and CHANGE v.)]

coun'terchárge, n. Charge in opposition to another, charge against accuser. [COUNTER-(1)]

coun'tercheck, n. Check that opposes a thing; check that operates against another; (arch.) retort (*the* **~** *quarrelsome,* see *As You Like It,* v. iv. 85). [COUNTER-(1)]

coun'ter-claim, n. Claim set up against another; claim set up by defendant in suit. [COUNTER-(1)]

counter-clŏck'wise (-z). See CLOCK¹.

coun'ter-ĕs'pionage (or -ahzh'), n. Spying directed against the enemy's spy system. [COUNTER-(1)]

coun'terfeit¹ (-fĭt, -fēt), a. & n. (Thing) made in imitation, not genuine, (of coins, writings, persons, etc.). [ME, f. OF *contrefet, -fait,* p.p. of *contrefaire* f. Rom. *CONTRA- (facere* make)]

coun'terfeit² (-fĭt, -fēt), v.t. Imitate; forge (coin, bank-notes, handwriting); simulate (feelings); (fig.) resemble closely. Hence **~ER¹** n. [ME, f. prec.]

coun'terfoil, n. Complementary part of bank cheque, official receipt, etc., with note of particulars, retained by drawer. [COUNTER-(3)]

coun'terfort, n. Buttress supporting wall or terrace. [f. F *contrefort* or It. *contraforte* (COUNTER-, FORT)]

counter-i'rritant, n. Thing used to produce surface irritation and thus counteract disease (also fig.). So **counter--irritā'tion** n. [COUNTER-(1)]

countermand' (-ah-), v.t., & n. Revoke (command); recall (person, forces, etc.) by contrary order; cancel order for (goods etc.); (n.) order revoking previous one. [ME, vb f. OF *contremander* f. med. L *CONTRA(mandare* order)]

coun'termárch, v.i. & t., & n. (Cause to) march in the contrary direction. [COUNTER-(2)]

coun'termárk, n. Additional mark, for greater security etc.; additional mark on bale of goods belonging to several merchants; hallmark added to that of the maker. [f. F *contremarque*, see COUNTER-(3) & MARK]

coun'termine, n., & v.t. & i. (Mil.) mine made to intercept that of besiegers; submarine mine sunk to explode enemy's mines by its explosion; (fig.) counterplot; (v.t.) oppose by ~; (v.i.) make a ~. [COUNTER-(1); cf. F *contremine(r)*, It. *contramina(re)*]

coun'termure, n. Wall raised within or behind another as reserve defence. [f. F *contremur* (It., Sp. *contramuro*)]

coun'terpane (-īn, -ăn), n. Outer covering of bed, coverlet, quilt. [alt. (w. assim. to PANE in obs. sense *cloth*) f. (now obs.) *counterpoint* f. OF *contrepointe* alt. f. *cou(l)tepointe* f. med. L *culcita puncta* quilted mattress]

coun'terpart, n. Duplicate; person, thing, forming natural complement to another; opposite part of INDENTURE. [COUNTER-(3), after OF *contrepartie*]

coun'terplot, n., & v.t. & i. (-tt-). Plot contrived to defeat another; (vb) frustrate by ~, devise ~ (against). [COUNTER-(1)]

coun'terpoint, n. (mus.). Melody added as accompaniment to given melody; art, mode, of adding melodies as accompaniment according to fixed rules; *double*, *triple*, etc. ~, invertible ~, in which the melodies can be changed in position above and below one another; *strict* ~ (acc. to code of rules as academic exercise, not as actual composition). [f. OF *contrepoint* f. med. L CONTRA*punctum* pricked opposite, i.e. to the original melody (*pungere punct-* prick)]

coun'terpoise[1] (-z), n. Counterbalancing weight; thing of equivalent force etc. on opposite side; equilibrium. [ME & OF *countrepeis* f. *contre* COUNTER- (1) + *peis*, later *pois*, f. L *pensum* weight; cf. POISE]

coun'terpoise[2] (-z), v.t. Counterbalance; compensate; bring into, keep in, equilibrium (lit. & fig.). [ME *countrepeise*, *-pese*, f. OF *contrepeser* (as prec.); later Eng. *-poise* assim. to prec.]

coun'ter-reforma'tion, n. Reformation running counter to another, esp. that in Church of Rome following on Protestant Reformation. [COUNTER-(1)]

coun'ter-revolu'tion (-lōō-, -lŭ-), n. A revolution opposed to a former one or reversing its results. Hence ~ARY[1] (-shon-) a. & n. [COUNTER-(1)]

coun'terscarp, n. (fortif.). Outer wall or slope of ditch, supporting covered way. [f. F *contrescarpe* f. It. CONTRA(*scarpa* SCARP)]

coun'tershaft (-ah-), n. Intermediate shaft driven from main shaft to transmit motion to particular parts of a system of machinery. [COUNTER- (1)]

coun'tersign[1] (-īn), n. Watchword, password, given to all men on guard (cf. PAROLE); mark used for identification etc.

coun'tersign[2] (-īn), v.t. Add signature to (document already signed); ratify. [f. F *contresigner* (as prec.)]

countersink', v.t. Bevel off (top of hole) to receive head of screw or bolt; sink (screw-head) in such hole. [COUNTER-(3)]

counter-ten'or, n. (mus.). (Part for, singer with) male voice higher than tenor, alto. [f. OF *contre-teneur* f. It. *contra-tenore* (see CONTRA- & TENOR)]

countervail', v.t. & i. Counterbalance (esp. in ~*ing duty*, one put on imports that are bounty-fed to give home goods an equal chance); avail against. [ME, f. OF *contrevaloir* f. L CONTRA *valēre*]

coun'terweight (-wāt), n. Counterbalancing weight. [COUNTER-(1)]

coun'terwork (-ẽrk), n., & v.t. & i. (Mil.) work raised in opposition to those of enemy; (gen.) opposing work; (v.t.) counteract, frustrate; (v.i.) work in opposition. [COUNTER-(1)]

coun'tess, n. Wife, widow, of count or earl; lady ranking with count or earl in her own right. [ME & OF *contesse* f. Rom. *comitissa* fem. of *comes* COUNT[3], see -ESS]

‖ coun'ting-house, n. Building, room, devoted to keeping accounts; office.

count'less, a. Too many to count. [-LESS]

coun'trified, -ryfied, (kŭn-; -īd), a. Rural, rustic, in appearance, manners, etc. [p.p. of *countrify*, else little used (COUNTRY + -FY)]

coun'try (kŭn-), n. Region; territory of a nation; land of a person's birth, citizenship, etc., fatherland; rural districts as opp. to towns, esp. the rest of a land as opp. to the capital; (Cricket sl.) *in the* ~, far from the wickets; ‖ APPEAL[1] *to the* ~ (body of electors); ~ *club* (orig. U.S.), club with its quarters in a rural district for the sake of outdoor sports; ~ *cousin*, relation or person of countrified manners or appearance; ~*-house*, *-seat*, residence of ~ gentleman; ‖ ~ *note*, banknote issued by local bank; ~ *party*, political party supporting agricultural against manufacturing interests; ~*side*, particular rural district, its inhabitants. [ME, f. OF *contree*, *cuntree*, f. med. L (Rom.) *contrata* (land) lying opposite (CONTRA); see -Y[4]]

coun'try dance, n. Any rural or native English dance, esp. those in which couples stand face to face in two long lines. [COUNTRY + DANCE; perverted to *contredanse* etc.]

coun'tryman, n. (fem. *coun'trywoman*). Man of one's own (or a specified) country; person living in rural parts.

coun'ty, n. Territorial division in Great Britain and Ireland, chief unit for administrative, judicial, and political purposes; administrative division in most British colonies; *political and administrative division next below State; people of a ~; ~ PALATINE; ‖ ~ *corporate*, city, town, ranking as administrative ~; ‖ ~ *borough*, large borough ranking as ~ for administrative purposes; ~ *council*, representative governing body of administrative ~; ~ *court*, ‖ judicial court for civil action, whence ~-*court* (v.t. colloq.), sue in this; ‖ ~ *family* (with ancestral seat in a ~); ~ *town*, one in which business of ~ is (or was orig.) transacted; ‖ *the* ~, ~ families, so ~ attrib. [ME, f. AF *counte* f. L *comitatus* (as COUNT³, see -ATE¹)]

coup (kōō), n. Notable or successful stroke or move; (Billiards) direct holing of ball; ~ *d'état* (dĕtah'), violent or illegal change in government; ~ *de grâce* (de grahs), finishing stroke; ~ *de main* (see Ap.), sudden vigorous attack; ~ *d'œil* (dŭ'ē), comprehensive glance, general view; ~ *de théâtre* (tāah'tr), dramatically sudden or sensational act. [F, f. med. L *col(a)pus* f. L f. Gk *kolaphos* blow]

coupé (kōōp'ā), n. Four-wheeled closed carriage for two inside & driver; ‖ half-compartment at end of railway carriage; covered motor-car seated for two. [F, p.p. of *couper* cut, as noun]

cou'ple¹ (kŭ-), n. Leash for holding two hounds together, whence (fig.) *go*, *hunt*, *run*, *in* ~s; pair, brace, esp. of hunting dogs (collect. sing. for pl., as *15* ~); approximately two, a few; wedded or engaged pair; pair of partners in dance; *a* ~ *of*, two; pair of rafters; (Dynam.) pair of equal and parallel forces acting in opposite directions. [ME, f. OF *cople* f. L COPULA]

cou'ple² (kŭ-), v.t. & i. Fasten, link, together (dogs in pairs); connect (railway carriages) by a coupling; unite, bring together, (persons); marry (t. & i.); associate in thought or speech (two things *together*, one *with* another); (v.i.) unite sexually. [ME, f. OF *copler* (as prec.)]

coup'ler (kŭ-), n. In vbl senses; esp. contrivance for connecting two manuals, or manual with pedals, or notes with their octaves above or below (*octave* ~), of organ. [prec. + -ER¹]

coup'let (kŭ-), n. Pair of successive lines of verse. [F, dim. of COUPLE]

coup'ling (kŭ-), n. In vbl senses; esp.: link connecting railway carriages; contrivance for connecting parts of machinery. [-ING¹]

coup'on (kōō-), n. Detachable ticket entitling holder to periodical payments of interest, services of excursion agency, ration of food, cloth, clothes, etc. when controlled; ‖ (Pol. sl.) party leader's recognition of parliamentary candidate as deserving election; voucher given with retail purchase, a certain number of which entitle holder to a 'free gift' (so ~

system). [F, = *piece cut off* (*couper*, see COUPÉ, -OON)]

cou'rage (kŭ-), n. Bravery, boldness, as *take*, *pluck up*, *lose*, ~; *take* one's ~ *in both hands*, nerve oneself to a venture; *Dutch* ~ (induced by drinking); ~ *of one's opinions*, ~ to act up to them. [ME & OF *corage* f. Rom. *coraticum* f. L *cor* heart; see -AGE]

courågeous (kŭrāj'ŭs), a. Brave, fearless. Hence ~LY² adv., ~NESS n. [ME & AF *corageous* (OF *-eus*), f. prec., see -OUS]

cou'rier (kŏŏ-), n. Servant employed to make travelling arrangements on continent; title of newspapers, as *Liverpool C*~; running messenger. [(1)ME *corour* f. OF *coreor* f. Rom. *curritorem* (L *currere* run); (2) 16th c. *currior*, *-ier* f. F, f. It. *corriere* (med. L *currerius*)]

cour'lan (koor-), n. Long-billed rail-like wading bird of tropical America, noted for its dismal cry; limpkin. [F]

course¹ (kōrs), n. 1. Onward movement; pursuit of game esp. of hares with (grey)-hounds; direction taken, as *hold*, *take*, *change*, one's ~, *ship's* ~, *a dangerous* ~ (line of conduct), ~ *of events*, ~ *of nature* (ordinary procedure); (pl.) *evil* ~s (behaviour). 2. Ground on which race is run (also *race-*~); channel in which water flows; golf links. 3. ~ *of* EXCHANGE. 4. Career; series (of lectures etc.); rota for duty among members of cathedral body. 5. Each of successive divisions of meal (esp. soup, fish, joint, etc.). 6. Continuous layer of stone etc. in building. 7. (naut.). *Fore*, *main*, -~, fore, main, -sail. 8. *In the* ~ *of*, during; *by* ~ *of*, according to ordinary procedure of (law etc.); *in due* ~, in the natural order; *of* ~, naturally, as was to be expected; *matter of* ~, natural thing. [ME & OF *co(u)rs* f. L *cursus* (*currere curs-* run); later reinforced by corresp. fem. form OF *course*]

course² (kōrs), v.t. & i. Pursue (game, as prec.); run about, run (esp. of liquids); give (horse) a run; use (hounds) in coursing. [f. prec.]

cours'er (kōr-), n. (poet.). Swift horse. [ME, f. OF *corsier* f. Rom. *cursarius* (*cursus* COURSE, see -ARY¹); orig. = war-horse, charger]

court¹ (kōrt), n. 1. (Also ~'*yard*) space enclosed by walls or buildings; ‖ (Camb. Univ.) college quadrangle; subdivision of an Exhibition building, museum, etc., open to the general roof; ‖ confined yard opening off street; (in a town) yard surrounded by houses & communicating with street by an entry. 2. Enclosed quadrangular area, open or covered, for games, as *tennis*, *fives*, ~; plot of ground marked out for lawn-tennis. 3. ‖ Sovereign's residence; his establishment and retinue; the body of courtiers; ‖ sovereign and his councillors as ruling power, as *C*~ *of St James's* (British sovereign's ~); assembly held by sovereign, state recep-

tion; *High C~* (assembly) *of Parliament.*
4. Assembly of judges or other persons
acting as tribunal, as ~ *of law, law-~, ~
of justice,~ of judicature,* COUNTY, *criminal,*
POLICE, ~; place, hall, in which justice
is administered; *out of ~,* (of plaintiff, and
fig. of arguments) not entitled to be heard.
5. (Meeting of) qualified members of company or corporation; (in some friendly
societies) = LODGE¹. 6. Attention paid to
one whose favour, affection, interest, is
sought, as *pay ~ to.* 7. ‖~*card,* king,
queen, knave; ‖~ *circular,* daily report
of ~ doings published in newspapers; ‖~
guide, directory containing (theoretically)
names of those who have been presented
at ~; ~ *martial,* judicial ~ of naval,
military, or air force officers, (v.t., ~-
-*martial*) try by this; *drumhead ~ martial*
(held round upturned drum in time of
war); ~ *plaster,* sticking-plaster for cuts
etc. (formerly used by ladies as ~ for
face-patches); ~ *roll,* manorial-court
register of holdings (see COPY¹). [ME, f.
OF *cort* f. LL, med. L *cortis, curtis, -us* f.
L *cohortem* (nom. *-ors*), yard, COHORT; the
senses of assembly, judicial court, by
confus. in F with L *curia*]

court² (kōrt), v.t. Pay court to; make love
to (also abs.) with a view to matrimony;
entice (person, *into, to, from,* etc.); seek
to win (applause etc.); invite (inquiry
etc.; *you are ~ing disaster*). [prec.]

court'éous (kŏr-, kĕr-), a. Polite, kind,
considerate, in manner or address. Hence
~LY² adv., ~NESS n. [ME & OF *cort-,
curteis* f. Rom. **cortensis* (prec., -ESE);
assim. to wds in -OUS]

courtesan, -zan (kŏrtĭzăn'), n. Prostitute. [f. F *courtisane* f. It. *cortigiana,*
fem. adj. as n. (as prec. + -*ana* -AN)]

court'ésў (kŏr-, kĕr-), n. Courteous
behaviour or disposition; *by ~,* by
favour, not of right; ‖~ *title,* one held by
~, having no legal validity; ‖(Law) ~ *of
England, Scotland,* husband's tenure after
wife's death of certain kinds of property
inherited by her; = CURTSY. [ME, f. OF
curt-, cortesie f. *corteis* COURTEOUS; see -Y¹]

court'ier (kōr-), n. Attendant at, frequenter of, sovereign's court. [ME
courteour, app. f. AF **corte(i)our,* f. OF
cortoyer vb f. *cort* COURT¹]

court'lỹ (kōr-), a. Polished, refined, in
manners; obsequious, flattering. Hence
~ĬNESS n. [-LY¹]

court'ship (kōr-), n. Courting, wooing,
with view to marriage. [-SHIP]

couscous(sou) (kōō'skōōsōō), n. African
dish of granulated flour steamed over
broth, freq. with meat added. [F, f. Arab.
kuskus (*kaskasa* bruise)]

cous'in (kŭzn), n. (Also *first ~, ~ german*)
child of one's uncle or aunt; *my second ~,*
my parent's first ~'s child; *my first
(second* etc.) ~ *once* (*twice* etc.) *removed,*

my first (second etc.) ~'s child (grandchild etc.), also, my parent's (grandparent's etc.) first (second etc.) ~; *call
~s,* claim kinship (*with*); title used by
sovereign in addressing another sovereign
or a nobleman of same country. Hence
~HOOD, ~SHIP, nn., ~LY¹ a., (kŭzn-). [ME,
f. OF *cosin, cusin,* f. L *consobrinus* cousin
by the mother's side]

coûte que coûte (kōōtkekōōt'), adv. At
all costs. [F]

coutur|e (kōō'tūr), n. Dressmaking.
Hence ~*ier* (kōōtūr'ēā), fem. ~*ière*
(kōōtūrўār'), nn., dressmaker. [F]

couvade (kōōvahd'), n. Primitive people's
custom by which husband feigns illness
and is put to bed when his wife lies in.
[obs. F, f. *couver* hatch]

cōve¹, n. Small bay or creek; sheltered
recess; (Archit.) concave arch, curved
junction of wall with ceiling or floor.
[OE *cofa,* MLG *cove,* MHG *kobe,* ON *kofi*
f. Gmc **kubhon*]

cōve², v.t. Arch (esp. ceiling at junction
with wall); slope (fireplace sides) inwards.
[prec.]

cōve³, n. (sl.). Fellow, chap. [16th c. *cofe.*
cant of unkn. orig.]

‖**co'ven** (kŭ-), n. (Sc.). Assembly of
witches. [var. of AF *covent,* see CONVENT]

co'vènant (kŭ-), n., & v.t. & i. Compact,
bargain; (Law) contract under seal, clause
of this; (Bibl.) compact between God and
the Israelites, as ARK *of the ~, land of the
~* (Canaan); *Solemn League and C~*
(establishing Presbyterianism in England
and Scotland, 1643); *C~ of the League of
Nations,* document constituting the
League, incorporated in the Treaty of
Versailles & other treaties concluding
the first world war (1919); (v.t. & i.) agree
(*with* person *for* thing, *to do, that*). [ME,
f. OF, part. of *co(n)venir,* see CONVENE]

co'vènantéd (kŭ-), a. Bound by a
covenant. [-ED¹]

co'vènanter (kŭ-), n. One who covenants,
esp. (Sc. Hist.) adherent of the National
Covenant (1638) or Solemn League &
COVENANT. [-ER¹]

Cŏv'ent Gãrd'en (*also* kŭ-), n. (Used for)
the ~ fruit and vegetable market in
London.

Cŏv'entrỹ (*also* kŭ-), n. Town in Warwickshire; *send* person *to ~,* refuse to
associate with him.

co'ver¹ (kŭ-), v.t. Overspread, overlay,
(*with* cloth, lid, etc., also fig. *with* disgrace
etc.); strew thoroughly (*with*); lie over,
be a covering to; extend over, occupy
the surface of; protect; ~*ing letter,*
explanatory one with enclosure; (of
fortress, guns, etc.) command (territory);
conceal (feelings etc.); ~ *with gun,* present
gun at; (Mil., Cricket) stand behind
(front-rank man, another player to stop
balls he misses; ~*point,* fielder ~*ing*

For compounds of *co-* not given consult *co-*.

point, his place); include, comprise; deal with (subject); (Journalism) report (proceedings of a meeting, public dinner, etc.); suffice to defray (expenses); protect by insurance; (of stallion) copulate with; ~ *in*, complete the covering of, fill in (grave etc.) with earth; ~ *up*, conceal, esp. by wrapping up. Hence ~ING[1](3) n. [ME, f. OF *covrir, cuvrir* f. L CO(*operire opert-*)]

co'ver[2] (kŭ-), n. Thing that covers; lid; binding of book; either board of this, as *from ~ to ~*; wrapper, envelope, of letter, as *address* person *under ~ to another*; case of bicycle tire; hiding-place, shelter, (*take ~*, Mil., utilize lie of ground for protection); protection from attack (*cloud ~*); a force of aircraft for protecting a land or sea operation (*air, fighter, ~*); screen, pretence, as *under* (*the*) ~ *of humility*; woods or undergrowth sheltering game, COVERT[2]; (Commerc.) funds to meet liability or secure against contingent loss; plate, napkin, etc., laid for each person at table; ~ *girl*, girl or woman whose picture illustrates ~ of magazine etc. [f. prec.]

co'verage (kŭ-), n. Area or amount covered, section of community reached by a particular advertising medium, risk covered by insurance policy. [-AGE]

co'verlet, -lid, (kŭ-), n. Counterpane, quilt; covering. [ME *coverlite* etc. app. repr. OF **covre-lit* (as COVER[1] + *lit* bed)]

co'vert[1] (kŭ-), a. (Of threat, glance, etc.) secret, disguised. Hence ~LY[2] adv. [ME, f. OF, p.p. of *covrir* COVER[1]]

co'vert[2] (kŭ'vert, -er), n. Shelter, esp. thicket hiding game; ~ *coat*, short light overcoat. [ME, f. OF *covert* p.p. as n. (COVER[1])]

co'verture (kŭ-), n. Covering, cover; shelter; condition of married woman under husband's protection. [ME, f. OF as prec., see -URE]

co'vet (kŭ-), v.t. Desire eagerly (usu. what belongs to another). Hence ~ABLE a. [ME, f. OF *cu-, coveitier* f. Rom. **cupiditare* (as CUPIDITY)]

co'vetous (kŭ-), a. Eagerly desirous (*of* another's property etc.); grasping, avaricious. Hence ~LY[2] adv., ~NESS n. [ME, f. OF *coveitous* (as prec., see -OUS)]

co'vey (kŭ-), n. (pl. ~s). Brood of partridges; family, party, set. [ME, f. OF *covee* p.p. of *cover* hatch f. L *cubare*, see -Y[4]]

co'vin (kŭ-), n. (legal, arch.). Conspiracy, collusion. [ME, f. OF *covin(e)* f. med. L *convenium, -ia* f. *convenire* (as CONVENE)]

cō'ving (kŭ-), n. Arched piece of building; (pl.) curved sides of fire-place. [COVE[2] + -ING[1]]

cow[1], n. (pl. ~s, arch. *kīne*). Female of any bovine animal, esp. of the domestic species; female of elephant, rhinoceros, whale, seal, etc.; ~-*bane*, water hemlock; ~-*boy*, boy in charge of ~s, *man in charge of grazing cattle on ranch; *~-

-*catcher*, apparatus fixed in front of locomotive engine to remove cattle & other obstructions; ~-*fish*, (1) sea-cow, (2) Indian & American fish with horn-like spines over eyes; ~-*grass*, wild species of trefoil; ~-*heel*, foot of ~ or ox stewed to jelly; ~'*herd*, one who tends ~s at pasture; ~-*hide*, (leather, whip, made of) ~'s hide; ~'*itch*, = COWAGE; *~-*puncher*, = ~-*boy*; ~'*shot* (Cricket sl.), violent pull made in crouching position; ~-*tree*, S.-American tree with milk-like juice. Hence ~ISH[1] a. [OE *cū*, OS *kō*, OHG *kuo*, ON *kȳr*, Gmc **kōuz, *kōz*, cogn. w. L *bos*, Gk *bous*]

cow[2], v.t. Intimidate. [perh. f. ON *kuga*]

cow'age, cowh-, n. Tropical plant with stinging hairs on pod. [f. Hind. *kawanch*]

‖ **cow'an,** n. (Sc.). Working but unqualified mason; (hence) intruder on a freemasons' lodge. [orig. unkn.]

cow'ard, n. & a. Faint-hearted, pusillanimous, (person). Hence ~LINESS n., ~LY[1] a., ~LY[2] adv. [ME, f. OF *coart* (= It. *codardo*), f. L *cauda*; see -ARD]

cow'ardice, n. Faint-heartedness; *moral ~*, fear of disapproval. [ME, f. OF *couardise* (as prec., see -ICE)]

cow'er, v.i. Stand, squat, in bent position; crouch, esp. from fear. [ME, f. MLG *kūren* lie in wait, of unkn. orig.]

cowl[1], n. Monk's hooded garment; hood of this; hood-shaped covering of chimney or ventilating shaft. Hence cowlED[2] (-ld) a. [(1) OE *cugele* f. LL *cucula* f. L *cucullus* hood of cloak; (2) OE *cufle* cogn. w. Du. *keuvel*, conn. w. Icel. *kofl* cowl]

‖ **cowl**[2], **coul** (-ow-), n. Tub for water, esp. one with two ears, carried by two men on ~-*staff*. [ME *cuvel(e)* app. f. OF *cuvele* f. L *cupella* dim. of *cupa* barrel]

cow-pŏx, n. Disease on teats of cows, communicated to human beings by vaccination.

cowr'ie, -ŷ, n. Shell of small gastropod found in Indian Ocean, used as money in Africa & S. Asia; the animal; kinds of gastropod including *common ~* of British coast. [f. Hind. *kauri*]

cow'slip, n. ‖ Wild plant growing in pastures, with fragrant yellow flowers; ‖ ~ *tea, wine* (made from these). [OE *cū-slyppe* f. *cū* cow + *slyppe* slimy substance (i.e. cow-dung)]

cŏx, n., & v.t. & i., (colloq.). = COXSWAIN, esp. of racing boat; (vb) act as ~ (of). [abbr.]

cŏx'a, n. (pl. -*ae*). Hip. Hence cŏx'AL a. [L]

cŏx'comb (-ōm), n. Conceited showy person. Hence cŏxcŏmb'ICAL (-mĭ-) a. [= *cock's comb*; orig. (cap worn by) professional fool]

cŏx'combry (-komrĭ), n. Foppery, behaviour of a coxcomb. [-RY]

cŏx'swain (-kswān, -ksn), n. (abbr. COX). Helmsman of boat; person on board ship permanently in charge of, & (unless superior officer is present) commanding, boat & crew. Hence ~LESS a., ~SHIP n. [ME, f. cock (see COCKBOAT)+SWAIN; cf. BOATSWAIN]

coxy. See COCKY.

coy, a. Modest, shy, (usu. of girl); (of place) secluded; ~ of, backward, reserved, in (speech etc.). Hence ~'LY² adv., ~'NESS n. [ME, f. OF coi (fem. coite) f. Rom. *quetus f. L quietus QUIET]

coyot'e (ko-, also ki'ōt), n. N.-American prairie-wolf. [Mex. Sp., f. Mex. coyotl]

coypu (koi'pōō), n. S.-American aquatic beaver-like rodent (cf. NUTRIA). [native name]

coz (kŭz), n. (arch.). Abbr. of COUSIN.

cōze, v.i., & n (Have a) chat. [(vb) prob. f. F causer; n. perh. influenced by COSY]

co'zen (kŭ-), v.t. & i. (literary). Cheat, defraud, (of, out of); beguile (into doing); act deceitfully. Hence ~AGE(3) n. [16th c. cant, of unkn. orig.]

cōz'ȳ, a. See COSY.

crăb¹, n. Kinds of ten-footed crustacean, esp. edible species found near most sea-coasts; zodiacal constellation, CANCER; machine (orig. with claws) for hoisting heavy weights; (pl.) lowest throw at hazard, two aces, whence turn out ~s, end in failure; catch a ~ in rowing, get oar jammed under water by faulty stroke; ~'s eyes, round concretion of carbonate of lime, found in stomach of crayfish; ~(-louse), parasitic insect infesting human body; ~-pot, wicker trap for ~s. Hence ~'LET n., ~'LIKE a. & adv. [OE crabba, MDu., MLG krabbe, ON krabbi, rel. to OS krebil etc., see CRAYFISH]

crăb², v.t. & i. (-bb-). (Of hawks) scratch, claw, fight with, (each other or abs.); (colloq.) cry down, pull to pieces. [f. MLG krabben, rel. to prec.]

crăb³, n. (Also ~-apple) wild apple (fruit & tree); sour person. [perh. alt. (after CRABBED) of 15th c. (now Sc. & north.) scrab, of Scand. orig.; cf. Sw. dial. skrabba wild apple]

crăbb'ĕd, a. Cross-grained, perverse, churlish, irritable; (of writings or authors) ruggedly intricate, difficult to make out; (of handwriting) ill-formed & hard to decipher; sour, harsh. Hence ~LY² adv., ~NESS n. Also (in first two senses only) crăbb'ȳ a. [ME; CRAB¹ +-ED², influenced in sense by CRAB³]

crăck¹, n. & a. Sudden sharp noise (of whip, rifle, thunder); ~ of doom, thunder-peal of Day of Judgement; sharp blow, as a ~ on the head; in a ~, in a moment; (arch., sl.) boast, lie; ‖ (Sc. & North.) brisk talk, (pl.) news; (sl.) = WISE¹ ~; fissure formed by breakage; partial fracture (the parts still cohering); good player, horse, etc.; burglar, house-breaking; (adj., colloq.) first-rate; ~-

brained, crazy. [ME crak, goes w. foll.; so OHG krach]

crăck², v.t. & i. (Cause to) make sharp noise, as ~ a whip, whips ~; (utter) a joke; chat;* ~ down on (sl.), take severe measures against; ~ up, praise; break (nut, skull, etc.) with sudden sharp report; ~ a bottle, empty, drink it; (sl.) ~ a crib, break into a house; break (t. & i.) without complete separation of parts; voice ~s, is ~ed (becomes dissonant, esp. at age of puberty); damage, ruin, (credit etc.); decompose (heavy oils) by heat and pressure to produce lighter hydrocarbons (such as petrol); (p.p., colloq.) crazy, insane; ~-jaw (colloq.), (word) difficult to pronounce. Hence ~'ABLE a. [OE cracian, Du. kraken, OHG krahhōn f. WG *krakōjan]

crăck'er, n. In vbl senses; also or esp.: firework exploding with sharp report; explosive bon-bon; instrument for cracking, as nut~s; thin hard biscuit; *biscuit; smash, breakdown; (school sl.) lie; *~jack (sl.), exceptionally fine or expert (thing or person); ~s, pred. a. (sl.), crazy, mad. [-ER¹]

crăc'kle, v.i., & n. Emit slight cracking sound; (n.) such sound, (also ~-china, -glass, -ware) china, glass, with appearance of minute cracks. [f. CRACK² +-LE(3)]

crăck'ling, n. In vbl senses; also, crisp skin of roast pork. [-ING¹]

crăck'nel, n. Light crisp kind of biscuit. [f. F craquelin f. MDu. krākeling f. krāken CRACK²]

cracks'man, n. Burglar. [CRACK¹, MAN]

crăck'ȳ, a. Full of cracks; apt to crack; (colloq.) crazy. [-Y²]

-cracy, noun suf. added to Gk stems (and as -ocracy to E wds), meaning 'rule of, ruling body of, class influential by'; thus demo~ = popular government, the demo~ = the lower classes as political power; pluto~ = government by the rich, the pluto~, those whose wealth gives them power; so cottono~ etc. [f. F -cratie f. Gk -kratia (kratos power); see -CY]

crā'dle, n., & v.t. 1. Bed, cot, for infant, mounted on rockers; from the ~, from infancy; (fig.) place in which thing is nurtured in earliest stage, as ~ of an art, of a nation; framework resembling ~, esp. (Naut.) that on which ship or boat rests during construction or repairs; frame attached to scythe to lay corn evenly; (Engraving) kind of serrated chisel, rocking-tool; (Mining) trough on rockers in which auriferous earth is shaken in water; CAT's-~. 2. v.t. Place in (child's, ship's) ~, contain or shelter as ~; mow (corn) with ~-scythe. [OE cradol cogn. w. OHG kratto basket]

crād'ling, n. In vbl senses; also (Archit.) wood or iron framework. [prec. +-ING¹]

craft (-ah-), n. Skill; cunning, deceit; art,

trade, (esp. in combb., as *handi*~, *priest*~, *state*~); *the gentle* ~, angling; members of a ~; *the C*~, brotherhood of Freemasons; boat, vessel, (pl. *craft*); ~-*brother*, -*guild*, workman, guild of workmen, of same trade; ~*s'man*, one who practises a ~, whence ~*s'*man** SHIP**(3) (-ah-) n., (also) private in the R.E.M.E. [OE *cræft*, OS, OHG *kraft*, ON *kraptr* strength]

craf't|ў (-ah-), a. Cunning, artful, wily. Hence ~**ĬLY**[2] adv., ~**ĬNESS** n. [f. prec. +-**Y**[2]]

cräg[1], n. Steep or rugged rock; ~*s'man*, skilled climber of ~s. Hence ~g'**ED**[2], ~g'**Y**[2], aa., ~g'**EDNESS**, ~g'**ĬNESS**, nn., (-g-). [of Celt. orig.]

∥ **cräg**[2], n. (geol.). Deposits of shelly sand found in Norfolk, Suffolk, Essex. [orig. unkn.]

cräke, n., & v.i. Kinds of bird including **CORN**~; cry of the corn~; (v.i.) utter this. [ME; n. f. ON *krāka* crow, or f. the vb (imit., cf. **CROAK**)]

cräm, v.t. & i. (-mm-), &n. **1.** Fill overfull; force (thing *into*, *down*; ~ *down* one's *throat*, tell him repeatedly); stuff (poultry etc. *with* food); eat greedily; (fig.) prepare (t. & i.) for examination; learn, get up, (subject) for special purpose; ~*full*, as full as ~ming can make it. **2.** n. Crowd, ~ming for examination; (sl.) lie. [OE *crammian* (=ON *kremja* squeeze), cogn. w. *crimman* cram, OHG *krimman* press etc.]

cräm'bō, n. Game in which one player gives word to which each of the others must find rhyme; *dumb* ~, game in which one side must guess word, a rhyme to which is given, by representing other rhymes to it in dumb show. [16th c. *crambe*, app. allus. L *crambe repetita* cabbage served up again]

crämm'er, n. In vbl senses, esp.: one who crams (esp. pupils); lie. [-**ER**[1]]

cräm'oisў, -m'es**ў**, (-z-), a. & n. (arch.). Crimson (cloth). [15th c. *cremesi* &c., f. early It. *cremesi* & OF *crameisi* (mod. *cramoisi*) f. Arab. *qirmazi* of the **KERMES**; see **CRIMSON**]

crämp[1], n. Contraction of muscles from sudden chill, strain, etc.; ~*fish*, electric ray, torpedo. [ME, f. OF *crampe* f. MDu., MLG *kramp* f. same root as **CRAM**]

crämp[2], n. (Also ~*-iron*) metal bar with bent ends for holding masonry etc. together; portable tool for pressing two planks etc. together; restraint. [f. MDu. *krampe*, as prec.]

crämp[3], a. Hard to make out, as ~ *word*, *handwriting*; contracted, cramped. Hence ~'**NESS** n. [perh. f. **CRAMP**[1, 4], but cf. F *crampe* curved]

crämp[4], v.t. Affect with **CRAMP**[1]; confine narrowly (also ~ *up*); (fig.) restrict (energies etc.); fasten with **CRAMP**[2]. Hence ~'**EDNESS** n. [f. **CRAMP**[1,2]]

cräm'pon, n. Metal hook, grappling-iron; iron plate with spikes for walking

on ice etc. [ME; F, f. as **CRAMP**[2], see -**OON**]

∥ **crän**, n. (Sc.). Measure for fresh herrings (37½ gal.). [= Gael. *crann* of unkn. orig.]

crän'age, n. Use of crane; dues paid for this. [**CRANE**[1]+-**AGE**]

crän'berrў, n. Small dark-red acid berry, fruit of dwarf shrub native of Britain, N. Europe, N. America, etc. [17th c., named by Amer. colonists f. G *kranbeere*, LG *kranebere* crane-berry]

cräne[1], n. Large wading bird with long legs, neck, and bill; machine for moving heavy weights; siphon; (also *water-*~) tube for supplying water to locomotive; ~*-fly*, daddy-long-legs; ~*'s-bill*, various species of geranium. [OE *cran*, OS, OHG *krano*; w. suff., OE *cranoc*, OHG *chranuh* (G *kranich*)]

cräne[2], v.t. & i. Move with crane; stretch (neck), stretch neck, like crane; ~ *at*, pull up at, shrink from, (hedge, difficulty). [f. prec.]

cränĭō- in comb. = foll., as *cranio*LO'**GI**CAL, -**LOGIST**, -**LOGY** (-ŏl[2]), -**METRY** (-ŏm[2]).

crän'ium, n. (pl. *-ia*, *-iums*). Bones enclosing the brain; bones of the whole head, skull. Hence **crän'IAL** a. [med. L, f. Gk *kranion* skull]

cränk[1], n., & v.t. **1.** Part of axle or shaft bent at right angles for converting reciprocal into circular motion, or vice versa; elbow shaped connexion in bell-hanging; revolving disc turned by criminals as punishment. **2.** v.t. Bend into ~ shape, furnish or fasten with ~; ~ *up*, set (engine of motor-car) going by turning a ~ (also abs.). [OE *cranc*, app. f. *crincan* bў-form of *cringan* fall in battle, orig. 'curl up']

cränk[2], n. Fanciful turn of speech; eccentric idea or act; eccentric person. [different. f. prec.]

cränk[3], a. Weak, shaky, (usu. of machinery). [f. **CRANK**[1]]

cränk[4], a. (naut.). Liable to capsize. [perh. rel. to prec.]

crankle (-ăng'kl), v.i., & n. Bend in and out, twist; (n.) bend, twist. [f. **CRANK**[1]+-**LE**]

cränk'|ў, a. Sickly; shaky, crazy; capricious; crotchety, eccentric; full of twists; (Naut.) = **CRANK**[4]. Hence ~**ĬLY**[2] adv., ~**ĬNESS** n. [**CRANK**[1,2,3,4]+-**Y**[2]]

crän'nog, n. Ancient lake-dwelling in Scotland or Ireland. [Ir. (*crann* tree, beam)]

cränn'|ў, n. Chink, crevice, crack. Hence ~**ĬED**[2] (-ĭd) a. [15th c., perh. rel. to OF *cran*, *cren* notch; cf. **CRENEL**]

cräpe, n., & v.t. Gauze-like fabric with wrinkled surface, usu. of black silk or imitation silk (of other colour or material now usu. **CRÊPE**), used for mourning dress; band of this round hat etc. as sign of mourning; ~*-cloth*, ~-like woollen material; (v.t.) cover, clothe, drape, with ~. Hence **cräp'Y**[2] a. [anglicized sp. of **CRÊPE**]

cräped (-pt), a. In vbl senses; also, crisped, crimped. [CRAPE + -ED², ¹]

*cräps, n. pl. Game of chance played with dice; *shoot* ~, play this. [orig. unkn.; cf. *crabs* (CRAB¹)]

cräp'ül|ent, a. Given to, suffering from effects of, resulting from, intemperance. Hence or cogn. ~ENCE n., ~OUS a. [f. LL *crapulentus* f. L *crapula* inebriation, see -LENT]

cräsh¹, v.i. & t., & n. 1. Make a ~ (see n.); move, go, with a ~, (of aircraft or airman) fall to earth; (v.t.) dash in pieces, throw, force, drive, with a ~; *go, fall,* ~ (with a ~). 2. n. Noise as of broken crockery, thunder, loud music, etc., violent percussion or breakage, (fig.) ruin, collapse of mercantile credit; ~-*dive,* (of submarine) dive hastily and steeply in an emergency (also as n.); ~-*helmet,* protective helmet of motor cyclist etc.; ~-*land,* (of aircraft or airman) land hurriedly with a ~, usu. without lowering undercarriage. [imit., cf. CLASH]

cräsh², n. Coarse linen for towels etc. [f. Russ. *krashenina* coloured linen]

cräs'ïs, n. (Gk gram.). Combination of the vowels of two syllables (as *kagô* for *kai egô*). [Gk, = mixture (*kerannumi* mix)]

cräss, a. Thick, gross; (fig.) gross, as ~ *stupidity*; grossly stupid. Hence ~'LY² adv., ~'NESS n. [f. L *crassus* solid, thick]

cräss'itüde, n. Grossness; gross stupidity. [f. L *crassitudo* (as prec., see -TUDE)]

-crat, noun suf. = supporter, member, of a -CRACY, & used & appended similarly (-*crat, -ocrat*). Hence -crät'IC(AL) adj. suff. [f. F -*crate* formed f. adjj. in -*cratique* (on anal. of Gk *autokratēs* or independently) f. Gk -*kratia* -CRACY]

crätch, n. Rack for feeding beasts out of doors. [ME *crecche* f. OF *creche* f. Rom. *creppja f. WG *krippja CRIB]

cräte, n. Large open-work case or basket for carrying glass, crockery, fruit, etc. Hence ~'FUL (-tf-) n. [perh. f. Du. *krat* basket etc.]

crät'er, n. Mouth of volcano; bowl--shaped cavity, esp. that made by explosion of shell or bomb. Hence ~ïFORM a. [L, f. Gk *kratēr* mixing-bowl]

cravät', n. Neckcloth, tie (now arch. or shop). Hence ~t'ED² a. [f. F *cravate* f. Croatian *Hrvat* Croat]

cräve, v.t. & i. Beg for; long for; beg, long, *for.* Hence **cräv'ING¹** n., strong desire, intense longing, (*for*). [OE *crafian,* rel. to ON *krefja*]

cräv'en, a. & n. Cowardly, abject, (person); *cry* ~, surrender. Hence ~LY² adv. [ME *cravant, -and(e),* of unkn. orig.]

craw, n. Crop of birds or insects. [ME *crawe* f. OE **craga,* cogn. w. MDu. *crāghe,* MLG *krāge,* MHG *krage* neck, throat]

crawfish. See CRAYFISH.

crawl¹, n. Pen in shallow water for fish, turtles, etc.; = KRAAL. [f. Du. KRAAL]

crawl², v.i., & n. 1. Move slowly, dragging body along close to ground, or on hands & knees; walk, move, slowly; creep abjectly; (of ground etc.) be alive *with* crawling things; feel creepy sensation, whence ~'Y² a. 2. n. ~ing; *the* ~, a high-speed swimming stroke. [ME *creule, croule,* later *craule,* of unkn. orig.; cf. Da., Norw. *kravle,* G *krabbeln* crawl]

crawl'er, n. In vbl senses; esp.: baby's overall; louse; cab moving slowly in search of fare. [-ER¹]

cray'fish, craw-, n. Small lobster-like freshwater crustacean; spiny lobster. [ME & OF *crevice* f. WG **krabitja,* **krebitja,* whence OS *krebit,* OHG *krebiz* (G *krebs*); see CRAB]

cray'on, n., & v.t. Stick, pencil, or coloured chalk or other material for drawing; carbon point in electric arc lamp; (v.t.) draw with ~s, (fig.) sketch. [F, f. *craie* chalk, see -OON]

cräze, v.t. & i., & n. Render insane (usu. in p.p.); produce small cracks on (pottery); (v.i.) have such cracks; (n.) insane fancy, mania, crazy condition, (*be the* ~, be generally sought or affected). [ME; (n. f. vb) orig. = break, shatter, perh. f. ON *krasa (Sw. *krasa* crunch, *slå i kras* dash to pieces)]

cräz'ing, n. In vbl senses; ~-*mill* (for crushing tin ore). [-ING¹]

cräz'|ÿ, a. (Of ship, building, etc.) unsound, shaky; sickly; insane, mad; (colloq.) extremely enthusiastic (*about*); (of paving, quilts, etc.) made of irregular pieces fitted together; *~*y bone,* funny bone. Hence ~ïLY² adv., ~ïNESS n. [CRAZE + -Y²]

creak, n., & v.i. Harsh strident noise, as of unoiled hinge, new boots, etc.; (v.i.) make this. Hence ~'Y² a. [ME, imit., cf. CRAKE, CROAK]

cream¹, n. Oily part of milk, which gathers on the top, & by churning is made into butter; CLOTted (also *Devonshire* or *Cornish*) ~; fancy dish, sweet, like or made of ~; best part of anything, esp. the point of an anecdote; part of a liquid that gathers at the top; ~ *of tartar,* purified & crystallized bitartrate of potassium, used in medicine etc.; ~ *of lime* (pure slaked); ~-like preparation, as *cold* ~ (cooling unguent); ~-coloured *horse;* ~ *cheese,* soft rich kind made of unskimmed milk & ~; ~-*fruit,* a ~-like fruit of Sierra Leone; ~-*coloured,* yellowish white; ~-*laid, -wove, paper,* laid, wove, paper of ~ colour; ~ *separator,* machine for separating ~ from milk. Hence ~'Y² a., ~'ïNESS n. [ME *creme* f. OF *cresme* (mod. F *crème* f.), a pop. application of the orig. sense CHRISM (mod. F *chrême* m.); see CHRISM]

cream², v.i. & t. (Of milk & liquids) form cream or scum; cause (milk) to ~; take cream from (milk); take the best part of (anything); add cream to (tea etc.). [f. prec.]

cream'er, n. Flat dish for skimming cream off milk; machine for separating cream. [-ER¹]

cream'ery, n. Butter-factory; shop where milk, cream, etc., are sold. [-ERY]

crease, n., & v.t. & i. Line caused by folding, fold, wrinkle; (Cricket) line defining position of bowler & batsman, as *bowling* ~ (from behind which bowler delivers ball); POPPING ~; (v.t.) make ~s in (material); (v.i.) fall into ~s. Hence **creas'y²** a. [in 16th c. form *creast*(e) the same wd as CREST (in 15th c. also *creast*); cf. obs. crest (of cloth), middle line of fold]

creat|e', v.t. & i. Bring into existence, give rise to; originate, as (of actor) ~*e a part*; invest (person) with rank, as ~*e a man a peer*, ~*e a peer*; (v.i., sl.) make a fuss. Hence ~'IVE a., ~'IVELY² adv., ~'IVENESS n. [ME, f. L *creare*, see -ATE³]

cre'atine, n. An organic base found in the juice of flesh. [f. Gk *kreas -atos* meat +-INE⁵]

crea'tion, n. Act of creating (esp. the world); investing with title, rank, etc. (~ *of peers*, ultimate means of overcoming resistance of House of Lords to will of Commons); all created things; a production of the human (esp. dressmaker's, actor's) intelligence, esp. of the imagination. [ME, f. OF f. L *creationem* (as CREATE, see -ATION)]

crea'tion|ism (-sho-), n. Theory that God creates a soul for every human being at birth; theory that attributes origin of matter & species to special creation (not EVOLUTION). So ~IST n. [-ISM]

creat'or, n. The C~, the Supreme Being; one who creates, whence **creat'ress¹** n. [ME, f. OF *creator, -ur, -our*, f. L *creatorem* (as CREATE, see -OR)]

crea'ture, n. Created thing; animate being (often as distinct from man); human being, person, (often expr. admiration, contempt, patronage, etc.); one who owes his fortune to another; mere instrument; *the* ~ (often spelt as Ir., *cratur* etc.), whisky or other intoxicant; ~ COMFORTS. [ME, f. OF f. LL *creatura* (as prec., see -URE)]

crea'turely (-rl-), a. Of creatures. [-LY¹]

crèche (krāsh), n. Public nursery for infants; model of the manger-scene at Bethlehem. [F (as CRATCH)]

cred'at Judae'us (*Apell'a*) (jōō-), sent. expressing incredulity. [L, = let the Jew Apella believe it, see Hor. *Sat.* I, v. 100]

cred'ence, n. Belief; *give* ~ *to*, believe; *letter of* ~ (introduction); small side table for eucharistic elements before consecration. [ME, f. OF or f. med. L *credentia* (*credere* believe, see -ENCE)]

creden'tial, n. (usu. pl.; -shalz). Letter(s) of introduction (also fig.). [f. med. L *credentialis* (as prec., see -AL)]

cred'i|ble, a. (Of persons or statements) believable, worthy of belief. Hence or cogn. ~BIL'ITY n., ~bLY² adv. [ME, f. L *credibilis* (as CREDENCE, see -BLE)]

cred'it¹, n. Belief, trust; *give* ~ *to*, believe (story); good reputation; power derived from this; acknowledgement of merit, as *have the* ~ *of*, *get* ~ *for*; source of honour, as *a* ~ *to the school*, *it does him* ~; trust in person's ability & intention to pay, as *give* ~, *deal on* ~, *long* ~; reputation of solvency & honesty; sum placed at person's disposal in books of a bank etc.; *letter of* ~ (authorizing person to draw money from writer's correspondent in another place); (Bookkeeping) acknowledgement of payment by entry in account, sum entered on ~ side of account (cf. DEBIT), this side; *give* person ~ *for*, enter (sum) to his ~, (fig.) ascribe (quality) to him. [f. F *crédit* f. It. *credito* f. L *credere -it-* believe, trust]

cred'it², v.t. Believe; carry to credit side of account (~ *amount to* person, person *with* amount); (fig.) ~ person *with*, think he has (a quality). [f. prec.]

cred'itab|le, a. That brings credit or honour (*to*). Hence ~LY² adv. [-ABLE]

cred'itor, n. One to whom a debt is owing; (Bookkeeping) ~ (abbr. *Cr*) *side* of account, right-hand side. [ME & AF *creditour* (OF *-eur*) f. L *creditorem* (as CREDIT¹, see -OR)]

cred'ō, n. (pl. -os). Creed (esp. Apostles' & Nicene, beginning in Latin with ~); musical setting of Nicene Creed. [ME; L, = I believe]

cred'ulous, a. Too ready to believe; (of things) showing such readiness. Hence or cogn. **credūl'ITY**, ~NESS, nn., ~LY² adv. [f. L *credulus* (*credere* believe)]

creed, n. Brief formal summary of Christian doctrine, esp. *Apostles'* (also *the C~*), *Nicene*, *Athanasian*, *C~*; system of religious belief; set of opinions on any subject. Hence ~'LESS a. [OE *crēda*, f. L CREDO]

creek, n. ‖ Inlet on sea-coast; small harbour; short arm of river; (U.S. & Colon.) tributary river; narrow plain between mountains. [(1) ME *crike* f. ON *kriki* (or partly f. OF *crique*, f. ON); (2) ME *crēke* f. MDu. *crēke* (or f. *crike*, by lengthening); ult. orig. unkn.]

creel, n. Large wicker basket for fish; angler's fishing-basket. [orig. Sc., of unkn. orig.]

creep, v.i. (*crēpt*), & n. **1.** Move with body prone & close to ground; move timidly, slowly, or stealthily; ~*ing* BARRAGE; insinuate oneself *into*, come in, *up*, unobserved; proceed, exist, abjectly; (of plants) grow along ground, wall, etc.; *flesh* ~*s*, feels as if things were ~*ing* over it (result of fear, repugnance, etc.); (Naut.) drag with creeper at bottom of water; ~*mouse* (adj.), timid, shy. **2.** n. ~*ing*; shrinking horror, as (colloq. pl.)

gave me the ~*s*; low arch under railway embankment; opening in hedge etc.; (Geol.) gradual movement of disintegrated rock due to atmospheric changes etc. [OE *crēopan*, OS *criopan*, ON *krūpja* f. Gmc **kreupan*]

creep'er, n. In vbl senses, esp.: plant that creeps along ground or up wall; grapnel for dragging bottom of water. [-ER¹]

creep'ỹ, a. Having a creeping of the flesh; productive of this; given to creeping. So ~**-crawl'ỹ** a. [-Y²]

creese, crease, kris (-ēs, -ĭs), n. Malay dagger with wavy blade. [Malay (*kcris, kres*)]

crem|āte', v.t. Consume (esp. corpse) by fire. So ~**A'TION**, ~**ā'tionIST**(2) (-sho-), nn. [back form. f. *cremation* (17th c.) f. L *crematio* f. *cremare* burn]

cremāt'or, n. Person, furnace, cremating corpses or rubbish. Hence **crematōr'ium** (pl. *-s, -ia*), **crem'atory**(2), nn. [f. as prec., see -OR]

crème (-ām), n. ~ *de menthe* (demahnt), peppermint liqueur; ~ *de la* ~ (-dlah-), the very pick, élite. [F]

cremōn'a, n. Violin made at C~; cromorne. [place]

crēn'ate, -āted, a. (bot., zool.). With notched or toothed edge. Hence **crēnA'TION** n. [f. mod. L *crenatus* f. pop. L (= It.) *crena* notch, see -ATE²]

crēn'ature, n. Rounded tooth on edge of leaf etc. [as prec. see -URE]

crēn'el, crēnĕlle', n. Open space in embattled parapet, for shooting through etc. [ME, f. OF *crenel*, dim. of *cren, cran*; cf. It. f. pop. L *crena* notch; see CRANNY, CRENATE]

crēn'e(l)lāte, v.t. Furnish with battlements or loopholes. Hence **crēnellA'TION** n. [f. F *créneler* (as prec.), see -ATE³]

crē'ōle, n. & a. (Descendant of) European (also ~ *white*) or Negro (~ *Negro*) settler in W. Indies, Mauritius, etc.; (adj.) of such descent, (of animals etc.) naturalized in W. Indies etc. [F *créole* f. Sp. *criollo*, app. ult. f. *criar* breed (cf. Sp. *criado* domestic), f. L *creare* CREATE]

crē'osōte, n. Colourless oily fluid distilled from wood-tar, a strong antiseptic; (Commerc.) carbolic acid. Hence **crēs'OL** n., caustic liquid obtained by distillation of coal tar. [f. Gk *kreas* meat + *sōzō* save]

crêpe (-āp), n. Crapy fabric other than black mourning crape; ~ *de Chine* (deshēn), of silk kind; ~ *rubber*, very durable rubber used for shoe soles etc. [F, f. L *crispa* curled; see CRAPE]

crep'it|āte, v.i. Make crackling sound; (of beetles) eject pungent fluid with sharp report. So ~**ANT** a., ~**A'TION** n. [f. L *crepitare* frequent. of *crepare* creak, see -ATE³]

crĕp'on (krĕp'ŏn), n. Stuff like crape, but of firmer substance. [F (as CRÊPE, see -OON)]

crĕpt. See CREEP.

crĕpŭs'cular, a. Of twilight; (Zool.) appearing, active, in twilight; dim, not yet fully enlightened. [f. L *crepusculum* twilight + -AR¹]

crescĕn'dō (krĕsh-), adv., n., & a. (mus.). (Passage of music to be played) with gradually increasing volume (abbr. *cres., cresc.*); (fig.) progress towards a climax. [It., part. of *crescere* grow (as foll.)]

crĕs'cent, n. & a. 1. Increasing moon, figure of moon in first or last quarter; this as badge of Turkish Sultans; the Turkish power; the Moslem religion; any figure of ~ shape, ‖ esp. row of houses. 2. adj. Increasing, ~-shaped. [ME & AF *cressant*, OF *creissant*, f. L *crescere* grow, see -ENT]

crĕss, n. Name of various plants usu. with pungent edible leaves, as *garden* ~, WATER¹~; *Indian* ~, tropaeolum. [OE *cresse, cressa* = OHG *kressa, -o*, f. WG **krasjō-* creep]

crĕss'et, n. Metal vessel for holding grease or oil for light, usu. mounted on pole; (mod.) fire-basket for lighting wharf etc. [ME, f. OF *cresset, craisset*, f. *craisse* = *graisse* GREASE]

crĕst, n., & v.t. & i. 1. Comb or tuft on animal's head; ~-*fallen*, with drooping ~, dejected, abashed; plume, tuft, of feathers; (apex of) helmet; head, top, esp. of mountain; surface line of neck in animals; mane. 2. (anat.). Ridge along surface of bone, as *frontal, occipital, ~ of skull*. 3. (her.). Device above shield & helmet on coat of arms, or separately, as on seal, notepaper, etc. 4. v.t. Furnish with ~, serve as ~ to, reach ~ of (hill, wave); (v.i., of waves) form into a ~. [ME, f. OF *creste* f. L *crista* tuft]

crētā'ceous (-shus), a. Of (the nature of) chalk; C~ *system* (Geol.), third & final system of the Mesozoic group of rocks. [f. L *cretaceus* (*creta* chalk, see -ACEOUS)]

crēt'ic, n. Metrical foot (- ‿ -). [f. L f. Gk *Krētikos* (*Krētē* Crete, see -IC)]

crēt'in, n. Deformed idiot of a kind found esp. in Alpine valleys. Hence ~**ISM** (2) n., ~**IZE** v.t., ~**OUS** a. [f. F *crétin* f. Swiss F *creitin, crestin* f. L *Christianus* CHRISTIAN in mod. Rom. sense 'human creature']

crĕt'ŏnne (*also* -ĕtŏn'), n. Stout unglazed cotton cloth with pattern printed on one or both sides. [F]

crēvăsse', n. Deep fissure in ice of glacier. [F, readopted as different. f. foll.]

crĕv'ice, n. Chink, fissure. [ME *crevace, -isse* f. OF *crevace* (mod. -*asse*) f. *crever* burst (L *crepare*) + -*asse* = L -*aceo*, see -ACEOUS]

crew¹ (-ōō), n. Whole body of men manning ship or boat; associated body, company, of persons; set, gang, mob; ~ *cut*, man's hair cut short all over. [ME *crue* f. OF *creue* increase fem. p.p. (as n.) of *croistre* grow f. L *crescere*]

crew². See CROW³.

crew'el (-ōō-), n. Thin worsted yarn for

tapestry & embroidery; ~-*work*, design in worsted on linen or cloth ground. [15th c. *crule*; orig. unkn.]

crib[1], n. Barred receptacle for fodder; hovel, hut; small bed for child, with barred sides; wicker salmon-trap; framework lining shaft of mine; (also ~-*work*) heavy crossed timbers used in foundations in loose soil etc.; *bin for maize, salt, etc.; set of cards given to dealer at cribbage, taken from other players' hands; (colloq.) plagiarism; translation for (esp. illegitimate) use of students; CRACK[2] *a* ~; ~-*biting* (of horses), habit of seizing manger in teeth & at same time noisily drawing in breath. [OE *crib(b)*, OS *kribbia*, OHG *kripp(e)a* f. WG **kribjōn*]

crib[2], v.t. (-bb-). Confine in small space; furnish (cowshed etc.) with cribs; pilfer; copy unfairly or without acknowledgement. [f. prec.]

crib'bage, n. Card game for two, three, or four persons. [f. CRIB[1] + -AGE]

crib'riform, a. (anat., bot.). Having small holes, like a sieve. [f. L *cribrum* sieve + -FORM]

crick, n., & v.t. Spasmodic affection of muscles of neck, back, etc., sudden stiffness; (v.t.) produce ~ in (neck etc.). [15th c., of unkn. orig.]

crick'et[1], n. (Also *house*-~) a jumping chirping insect. [ME, f. OF *criquet* f. *criquer* creak etc.; imit.]

crick'et[2], n., & v.i. Open-air game played with ball, bats, & wickets, between two sides of 11 players each (|| *not* ~ colloq., infringing the codes of fair play between honourable opponents in any sphere); (v.i.) play ~. Hence ~ER[1] n. [from 1598, of uncert. orig.; cf. OF *criquet* stick to aim at in the game of bowls; cf. Flem. *krick(e)* stick]

cric'oid, a. & n. Ring-shaped (cartilage of larynx). [f. Gk *krikoeidēs* (*krikos* ring, -OID)]

cri de cœur (krē' de kö̃r'), n. A passionate appeal, complaint, or protest. [F, = cry from the heart]

cri'er, n. One who cries; officer who makes public announcements in court of justice or (*town* ~) in a town. [ME & OF *criere*, nom. of *crieur* (*crier* CRY, see -OR)]

crik'ey, int. (sl.), expr. astonishment. [euphem. for *Christ*]

crime, n., & v.t. 1. Act (usu. grave offence) punishable by law; evil act, sin; ~-*sheet*, record of soldier's offences against regulations. Hence ~'LESS (-ml-) a. 2. v.t. (mil.). Charge with or convict of military offence. [ME, f. OF f. L *crimen* -*minis* judgement, offence]

crime passionnel (krēm' pásyŏ̃něl'), n. Crime due to jealousy. [F, = crime of passion]

crim'inal, a. & n. Of (the nature of) crime; ~ CONVERSATION, CONNEXION; (person) guilty of crime. Hence or cogn.

crimin'al'ITY n., ~LY[2] adv. [ME, f. OF *criminel* f. LL *criminalis* (as CRIME, see -AL)]

crim'in|āte, v.t. Charge with crime; prove (one*self* etc.) guilty of crime; censure. Hence or cogn. ~A'TION n., ~āTIVE, ~āTORY, aa. [f. L *criminari* (*crimen* CRIME), see -ATE[3]]

crim'ině, -nў, int. (arch.), expr. astonishment. [euphem. for *Christ*]]

criminŏl'ogў, n. Science of crime. [f. L *crimen* -*minis* CRIME + -O- + -LOGY]

crim'inous, a. Guilty of crime, only in phr. ~ *clerk* (clergyman). [f. AF *criminous* (OF -*eux*) f. L *criminosus* (as prec., see -OUS)]

crimp[1], n., & v.t. Agent who entraps men for seamen or soldiers (also fig.); (v.t.) entrap thus, impress, (seamen, soldiers). [17th c., of unkn. orig.]

crimp[2], v.t. Compress into plaits or folds, frill; make flutings in, corrugate; contract (flesh of freshly-caught fish) by gashing; mould, bend, into shape. [prob. f. MDu., MLG *krimpen*, = MHG *krimpfen*; cogn. w. CRAMP[1, 2]]

crim'son (-z-), a. & n., & v.t. & i. Deep-red (colour); ~ RAMBLER; (v.t. & i.) turn ~. [15th c. *cremesin* = early Sp. *cremesin*, early It. -*ino*, med. L -*inus*, metathetic alt. (+ -*in(o)* -INE[1]) of *ker*-, *car*- f. Arab. *qirmazi*: see CRAMOISY]

cringe (-j), v.i., & n. Cower; bow servilely; behave obsequiously (*to*); (n.) fawning obeisance, cringing. [ME *crenge*, causal deriv. of OE *cringan, crincan*, see CRANK[1]]

cringle (krĭng'gl), n. (naut.). Eye of rope containing thimble for another rope to pass through. [f. LG *kringel* dim. of *kring* ring f. root of CRANK[1]]

crin'ite, a. (bot., zool.). Hairy. [f. L *crinitus* (*crinis* hair)]

crinkl|e (krĭng'kl), v.t. & i., & n. Twist, wrinkle. Hence ~Y[2] a. [ME, frequent. f. st. of OE *crincan*, see CRINGE, CRANK[1], -LE(3)]

crink'um-crank'um, n. & a. (Thing) full of twists & turns (lit. & fig.). [playful f. CRANK[1]]

crin'oid, a. & n. (zool.). Lily-shaped (echinoderm). Hence **crinoid'AL** a. [f. Gk *krinoeidēs* (*krinon* lily, see -OID)]

crinolětte', n. Contrivance for distending back of woman's skirt. [dim. f. foll.]

crin'oline (also -ēn), n. Stiff fabric of horsehair etc. formerly used for skirts; hooped petticoat; netting round warship as defence against torpedoes. [F (L *crinis* hair + *linum* thread)]

crio-, comb. form of Gk *krios* ram, as -*sphinx* (ram-headed), -*ceratite*, ram's--horn ammonite.

crip'ple, n., & v.t. & i. Lame person; staging for cleaning windows etc.; (v.t.) lame, (fig.) disable, impair; (v.i.) hobble, walk lamely, (*along* etc.). Hence ~DOM (-ld-), ~HOOD (-lh-), nn. [OE *crypel*, MHG *krüppel*, ON *kryppill* f. Gmc **krup*- (**kreupan* CREEP)] cris. = CREESE.

cris'is, n. (pl. cris'es, pr. -ēz). Turning-point, esp. of disease; moment of danger or suspense in politics, commerce, etc., as *cabinet, financial,* ~. [L, f. Gk *krisis* decision (*krino* decide)]

crisp, a., n., & v.t. & i. Hard but fragile, brittle; bracing, as ~ *air*; brisk, decisive, as ~ *manner, style,* etc.; (of hair etc.) curly; ‖ (n. pl.) thin fried and dried slices of potato (marketed in packets); (v.t. & i.) curl in short stiff folds, make or become ~. Hence ~'LY² adv., ~'NESS n. [OE *crisp* adj. f. L *crispus* curled]

cris'pāte, a. Crisped, (Bot., Zool.) with wavy margin. [f. L *crispare*, -ATE²]

crispā'tion, n. Curling; undulation; contraction (esp. = GOOSE-*skin*). [as prec., -ATION]

crisp'ỹ, a. Curly; brittle; brisk. [-Y²]

criss'-cross (-aws), n., a., adv., & v.i. & t. 1. Crossing lines, currents, etc. (for ~ *row* see CHRIST-CROSS-ROW). 2. adj. In cross lines (~ *pattern, traffic*), (of persons or temper) peevish. 3. adv. Crosswise, at cross purposes (*everything went* ~). 4. vb. Move crosswise, work with ~ pattern. [orig. (15th c.) f. *Christ's Cross*; later apprehended as redupl. of *cross*]

cris'tāte, a. (nat. hist.). Having a crest. [f. L *cristatus* (as CREST, see -ATE²)]

crite'rion, n. (pl. -*ia*). Principle, standard, a thing is judged by. [f. Gk *kriterion* as foll.]

crit'ic, n. One who pronounces judgement; censurer; judge of literary or artistic works; one skilled in textual criticism. Hence ~ASTER n. [f. L f. Gk *kritikos* (*krites* judge f. *krino,* see -IC)]

crit'ical, a. Censorious, fault-finding; skilful, engaged, in criticism; belonging to criticism; involving risk or suspense, as ~ *condition, operation*; (Math., Physics) marking transition from one state etc. to another, as ~ *angle, temperature.* Hence ~LY² adv. [-AL]

crit'icism, n. Work of a critic; critical essay or remark; *textual* ~ (dealing with text of an author); *the higher* ~ (dealing with origin, character, etc., of texts, esp. of Biblical writings). [-ISM]

crit'iciz|e, -is|e (-īz), v.t. Discuss critically (often abs.); censure. Hence ~ABLE a. [-IZE]

crit'ico- in comb. = critically, critical & —, as *-historical.* [CRITIC + -O-]

critique' (-ēk), n. Critical essay or notice; art of criticism. [alt., after F *critique,* of CRITIC in obs. sense *criticism*]

croak, n., & v.i. & t. Deep hoarse sound of frog or raven; (v.i.) utter ~, forebode evil, (sl.) die; (v.t.) utter dismally, *(sl.) kill. Hence ~'Y² a. [16th c. (cf. 15th c. *crok*), imit.; cf. CRAKE, CREAK]

croak'er, n. In vbl senses; esp., prophet of evil. [-ER¹]

Crō'at, n. Member of the people from which Croatia is named. [Slav.]

crō'ceāte (-sī-), a. Saffron, saffron-coloured. [f. L *croceus* (CROCUS), see -ATE²]

crō'chet (-shī), n., & v.t. (-*cheted* pr. -shīd). Knitting (material or work) done with hooked needle; (v.t.) make (shawl etc. or abs.) in ~. [F, dim. of *croc* hook]

crō'cidolite, n. A fibrous silicate of iron & sodium, blue asbestos; yellow mineral produced from this, used for ornament. [f. Gk *krokis -idos* nap of cloth + -LITE]

crock¹, n. Earthen pot or jar; ‖ (dial.) metal pot; broken piece of earthenware used for covering hole in flowerpot. [OE *croc, crocca,* rel. to ON *krukka*; also rel. to OE *crōg* (G *krug*), OE *crūce* (MHG *krūche*)]

crock², n., & v.i. & t. (Sl.) Inefficient or broken-down or worn-out person; broken-down horse; ‖ (Sc.) old ewe; (v.i. sl.) ~ *up,* break down; (v.t.) disable (usu. in p.p.). [orig. Sc., cf. Norw. *krake* sickly beast, MDu. *kraecke* broken-down horse or house; app. cogn. w. CRACK]

crock'erỹ, n. Earthenware vessels. [f. obs. (14th c.) *crocker* potter (CROCK¹), see -ERY]

crock'ét, n. Small ornament (usu. bud or curled leaf) on inclined sides of pinnacles etc. [f. AF *crokel,* = OF CROCHET; see CROQUET, CROTCHET]

crŏc'odile, n. Large amphibious saurian reptile (esp. the Nile species); ~ *tears* (hypocritical, from belief that the crocodile wept while devouring, or to allure, its victim); ‖ (colloq.) schoolgirls walking two & two. Hence crŏcodil'IAN (-yan) a. [ME & OF *cocodrille* f. LL *cocodrillus* f. L f. Gk *krokodeilos*]

crō'cus, n. Kinds of dwarf bulbous plants with brilliant (usu. yellow or purple) flowers; ~ *sativus,* species of this yielding saffron; AUTUMNAL ~; a peroxide of iron used for polishing. [L, f. Gk *krokos* crocus, saffron]

Croes'us (krēs-), n. Wealthy person. [~, king of Lydia]

‖ croft (-aw-, -ŏ-), n. Enclosed piece of (usu. arable) land; small holding of CROFTER. [OE *croft,* of unkn. orig.]

‖ crof'ter (-aw-, -ŏ-), n. One who rents a small holding, esp. joint tenant of Scotch divided farm. [-ER¹]

Crō-Magnon (-măn'yon), a. Of a prehistoric tall long-headed European race, remains of which were found in ~, a cave in Dordogne, France.

crŏm'lĕch (-k), n. (In Wales & now rarely in England) megalithic tomb; (in France) circle of upright prehistoric stones; (formerly in England) megalithic tomb or stone circle. [W (*crom* bent, *llech* flat stone)]

cromōrne', crèmōn'a, n. An organ reed-stop. [F, f. G *krummhorn* crooked horn]

crōne, n. Withered old woman; old ewe. [ME, f. ONF *carogne* CARRION or MDu. *c(a)roonje,* f. same source]

crōn'ỹ, n. Intimate friend. [17th c.,

Camb. Univ. sl., f. Gk *khronios* of long standing, chronic, f. *khronos* time]

crook, n. & a., & v.t. & i. Shepherd's, bishop's, hooked staff; anything hooked; hook; bend, curve; act of bending; (sl.) rogue, swindler; *by* HOOK *or by* ~; (sl.) *on the* ~, dishonestly; ~-*back(ed)*, hunchback(ed); (adj.) = CROOKED; (v.t. & i.) bend, curve. [ME *crōc* f. ON *krókr* hook etc.]

crook′ed, a. Not straight, bent, twisted; deformed; bent with age; (fig.) not straightforward, dishonest; (of stick, pr. -ŏŏkt) having a cross handle, crutched. Hence ~LY[2] adv., ~NESS n. [ME, f. prec. +-ED[1]]

Crookes (-ks), n. Name of Sir William ~ (d. 1919), English scientist, used attrib. (or in gen.) to designate apparatus invented by him etc. So: ~ *rays*, cathode rays; ~'s *tube*, glass vacuum tube for illustrating high rarefaction phenomena; ~'s *vacuum* (extremely high one).

croon, v.t. & i., & n. (Hum, sing, mutter, in) low undertone. Hence ~′ER[1] n., soft singer of highly sentimental songs. [ME, orig. Sc. & north., f. MDu., MLG *krōnen* groan, lament, (Du. *kreunen*)]

crop[1], n. Pouch-like enlargement of gullet in birds, where food is prepared for digestion; stock, handle, of whip; (also *hunting*-~) short whipstock with loop instead of lash; produce of cultivated plants, esp. cereals; *in, under, out of*, ~ (cultivation); season's total yield (of cereal etc.); entire hide of animal tanned; cropping of hair; style of wearing hair cut short; piece cut off end; name of some cuts of meat; NECK *& ~*; ~-*eared*, with ears (also, hair) cut short; ~-*over*, annual junketings at end of the W.-Indian sugar-cane harvest. [OE *crop(p)*, MDu., MLG *kropp*, OHG *kropf*, ON *kroppr*]

crop[2], v.t. & i. (-pp-). Cut off; (of animals) bite off (tops of plants); gather, reap; cut short (ears, tail, hair, nap of cloth, edges of book); sow, plant, (land *with* barley etc.); (v.i.) bear a crop; turn *up* unexpectedly; ~ *out, forth*, appear; (Geol.) ~ *up, out*, come to surface. [f. prec.]

cropp′er, n. Person, thing, that crops; pigeon with large crop, pouter; *good, heavy, light*, ~, plant yielding good etc. crop; (sl.) heavy fall, as *came a* ~. [CROP[1,2] + -ER[1]]

cropp′y, n. Person with short cropped hair, esp. (hist.) Irish rebel, sympathizer with French revolution, in 1798. [CROP[1] +-Y[2]]

cro″quet[1] (-kā, -kǐ, *krokā′), n. Game, played on lawn, in which wooden balls are driven with mallets through hoops; act of croqueting a ball. [perh. North. F, dial. form of CROCHET]

cro′quet[2] (-kǐ), v.t. (~*ing*, ~*ed*, pr. -kǐng, -kǐd). (In game of croquet) drive away (opponent's ball or abs.) by placing the

two together & striking one's own (cf. ROQUET). [f. prec.]

croquette′ (-kět), n. Seasoned & fried ball of rice, potato, meat, etc. [F (*croquer* crunch)]

crōre, n. (Anglo-Ind.). Ten millions, one hundred lakhs (usu. of rupees). [f. Hind. *kror*]

crō′sier, -zier, (-zhyer), n. Bishop's, abbot's, pastoral staff; (improp.) archbishop's cross. [orig.=bearer of a crook, ME *croser*, f. OF *crossier* f. *crosse* CROOK; confused w. OF *croisier* (ME *croiser*) cross-bearer, f. *croiz* CROSS + -IER; mod. *crosier* = ~'s *staff* (16th c.)]

cross[1] (-aw-, -ŏ-), n. 1. Stake (usu. with transverse bar) used by the ancients for crucifixion, esp. that on which Christ was crucified; model of this as religious emblem; sign of ~ made with right hand as religious act; staff surmounted with ~ & borne before archbishop or in processions, ~-*bearer*, person who carries this: monument in form of ~, esp. (also *market*-~) one in centre of town; Christian religion. 2. Trial, affliction; annoyance. 3. ~-shaped thing; (*Southern*) C~, a constellation; *Greek* ~ (+); *Latin* ~ (†); *St Andrew's* ~ (×); *Tau* ~, ~ *of St Anthony*, (T); *Maltese* ~ (⊕); *fiery* ~, Scots signal (orig. two bloody sticks) sent through district to rouse inhabitants. 4. Decoration in orders of knighthood (*Grand* C~, highest degree of this): decoration for personal valour, as *Victoria, George, Distinguished Service, Military, Distinguished Flying*, C~. 5. Intermixture of breeds; animal resulting from this; mixture, compromise, *between* two things; (sl.) fraud, swindle; *on the* ~, diagonally. Hence ~′LET n., ~′WISE adv. [(a) This (surviving) form is OE *cros* f. ON *kross* f. OIr. *cros*; there were also (b) OE *crūc*, ME *cr(o)uche*, = OHG *krūzi*; (c) ME *croiz* f. OF *croiz*; (d) later Norse *cors* surviving in Sc., all ult. f. L *crux*, *crucis*]

cross[2] (-aw-, -ŏ-), v.t. & i. Place crosswise, as ~ *swords* (in fighting, also fig.); ~ one's *fingers, keep* one's *fingers* ~*ed*, crook one finger over another to bring good luck; make sign of cross on or over (esp. *oneself*, as sign of awe, to invoke divine protection, etc.); ~ *fortune-teller's hand with*, give her (coin); draw line across, as ~ *out, off*, cancel, ‖ ~ *cheque* (with two lines usu. filled up with *& Co.* or name of bank through whom alone it may be paid); write across (what is already written, a letter); go across (road, river, sea, or abs.); bestride (saddle, horse); carry, move, across; meet and pass (*each other* or abs.); *two persons' letters* ~ (each being dispatched before receipt of the other); ~ one's *mind*, occur to one; ~ *the path of*, meet with, thwart; thwart (person, will, plans); (cause to) interbreed; cross-fertilize (plants). [f. prec.]

cross³ (-aw-, -ŏ-), a. Passing from side to side, transverse, (||~ *bench*, in the House of Lords, for independent members who do not vote with the Government or the official Opposition; so ~*bench*, adj., impartial, as *the ~-bench mind*; ~ *voting*, when in Parliamentary divisions etc. some of either or each side vote against their own party, as *there was no ~ voting*); intersecting; contrary, opposed, (*to a purpose* etc., or abs.); (colloq.) peevish, out of humour, as *be ~ with* one, *as ~ as two sticks*, whence ~LY² adv., ~'NESS n.; ~*patch*, ill-natured person; ~ *reference* (from one part of book to another for further information); (Bookkeeping) ~ *entry* (transferring amount to different account or neutralizing previous entry); ~*bred*, hybrid; (sl.) dishonest, dishonestly got. [partly f. CROSS¹, partly thr. (obs.) *cross* adv.]

cross- in comb. 1. f. CROSS n., objectively, as ~*bearer*, or attrib. = having a transverse part, as CROSS-BOW, marked with a ~, as ~*BUN*. 2. f. CROSS a. = crossing, transverse, as ~*bar*, *-beam*, *-keys*, *-piece*, CROSS-SECTION, CROSS-BONES. 3. Adv., in vbs as ~*breed*, *-fertilize* (animals, plants, from individuals of different species), CROSS-EXAMINE, CROSS-QUESTION; in vbl nouns as ~*fire*, firing in two crossing directions. 4. Prep. = across, as ~*country*, adj., across fields, not following roads.

cross'belt, n. Belt for cartridges etc. from shoulder to opposite hip. [CROSS-(2)]

cross'bill, n. Bird the mandibles of whose bill cross when bill is closed. [CROSS-(2)]

cross'bones, n. pl. Figure of two thigh--bones laid across each other, usu. under skull as emblem of death. [CROSS-(2)]

cross'bow (-bō), n. Bow fixed across wooden stock, with groove for the missile (stone, arrow, etc.) and mechanism for holding and releasing string. [CROSS-(1)]

cross'butt'ock, n., & v.t. Throw over the hip, in wrestling. [CROSS-(4)]

cross'coun'ter, n. (boxing). Blow at head delivered across opponent's lead-off with the other hand. [CROSS- (4)]

cross'cut, n. & a. Diagonal cut, path, etc.; figure in skating; (adj.) adapted for cutting across the grain (chiefly in ~ *saw*). [CROSS-(2)]

crŏsse, n. Long racquet-like implement used in LACROSSE. [F, f. OF *croce*, *croc*, hook]

cross-exam'ine, v.t. Examine (esp. witness in legal action) minutely, with a view to checking previous examination or eliciting suppressed facts. Hence cross--examinA'TION n. [CROSS-(3)]

cross'garnet, n. T-shaped hinge, fixed to door etc. by the long shank. [CROSS-(1) +*garnet* kind of tackle or purchase]

cross'grain, n. Grain running across the regular grain. [CROSS-(2)]

cross'grained (-nd), a. (Of wood) with grain running irregularly or in crossing directions; (fig.) perverse, intractable. [-ED²]

cross'hatch, v.t. Engrave with intersecting series of parallel lines. [CROSS-(3)]

cross head(ing), n. (In newspaper etc.) indication of the contents of the following passage inserted here & there across the column for the reader's guidance in an article or report. [CROSS-(2)]

cross'ing (-aw-, -ŏ-), n. In vbl senses; also or esp.: intersection of two roads, railways, etc., as || *level ~* (of road and railway, or two railways, on same level); place where street is crossed; ~*sweeper*, one who sweeps this. [-ING¹]

cross'legged (-gd), a. (Of person squatting) with legs crossed; (of person sitting on chair) with one leg laid across the other. [CROSS-(3)]

cross'light, n. Light that crosses another; (fig.) illustration of subject from another point of view. [CROSS-(2)]

cross purposes, n. pl. Contrary or conflicting purposes; name of a game; *be at ~*, misunderstand one another, (also) have conflicting plans with same object. [CROSS-(2)]

cross question, n. Question asked in CROSS-QUESTIONing; ~*s & crooked answers*, game in which each question gets answer written for another.

cross-ques'tion, v.t. Question in order to elicit details or test accuracy. [CROSS-(3)]

cross'road, n. Road that crosses another or joins two main roads; (also *cross roads*) intersection of two roads; *at the ~s* (fig.), at a critical turning-point (in person's life etc.). [CROSS-(2)]

cross'ruff, n., & v.i. (Whist, Bridge). Alternate trumping by partners (see RUFF⁴); (vb) play a ~o. [CROSS-(3)]

cross'sec'tion, n. A transverse section, (fig.) a comprehensive representative sample. [CROSS-(2)]

cross'stitch, n. Stitch formed of two crossing each other; kind of needlework characterized by these. [CROSS-(2)]

*cross'tie, n. Railway sleeper. [CROSS-(2)]

cross'trees, n. pl. Two horizontal cross--timbers bolted to head of lower mast to support mast above. [CROSS-(2)]

cross'word, n. Puzzle in which words crossing vertically & horizontally according to a chequered pattern have to be filled in from clues. [CROSS²]

crŏtch, n. Bifurcation, fork (esp. of the human body). [perh. = ME & OF *croche*, *croc* hook f. ON *krókr* CROOK]

crŏtch'ĕt, n. || (Mus.) black-headed note with stem, half of minim; whimsical fancy, whence ~EER², ~iNESS, nn., ~Y² a.; hook. [ME, f. OF, dim. of *croc* hook (prec.), see CROCKET]

Crŏt'on, n. Genus of plants, from one species of which *c~ oil*, a drastic purgative, is obtained. [f. Gk *krotōn* tick, croton]

crouch, v.i., & n. Stoop, bend, esp. timidly or servilely; (n.) ~ing. [ME, perh. f. OF *crochir* be bent, f. *croc* CROOK]

croup[1], -pe, (-ōō-), n. Rump, hindquarters, (esp. of horse). [ME & OF *croupe* f. WG **krupp*- rel. to CROP[1]]

croup[2] (-ōō-), n. Inflammatory disease in larynx & trachea of children, marked by sharp cough. [f. (now dial.) vb *croup* croak (imit.)]

croup'ier (-ōō-), n. Raker in of money at gaming table; assistant chairman at public dinner. [F, orig.= rider on the CROUP[1]]

croûton (krōō'tawn), n. Small piece of fried bread served with soups. [F]

crow[1] (-ō), n. Kinds of birds, esp. *carrion* ~, large black bird; *white* ~, a rarity; *as the* ~ *flies*, straight; **eat* ~, submit to humiliation; ~ (*-bar*), bar of iron (usu. with beak-like end) used as lever; ~'-*berry*, fruit of a small heath-like shrub; ~-*bill*, forceps for extracting bullets etc.; ~'*foot*, name of various plants, esp. species of buttercup, (Naut.) arrangement of small ropes for suspending awning, (Mil. also ~'s-*foot*) caltrop; ~'s-*footed*, marked with ~'s-feet; ~-*quill*, ~'s quill or steel pen for fine writing; ~'s-*foot*, wrinkle at outer corner of eye; ~s-*nest*, barrel fixed at mast-head of whaler etc. as shelter for look-out man; ~-*toe*, ‖ bluebell (& other flowers, as buttercup). [OE *crāwe*, OS *krāia*, OHG *krāja* etc., f. CROW[3]]

crow[2] (-ō), n. Crowing of cock; joyful cry of infant. [ME, f. foll.]

crow[3] (-ō), v.i. (past *crew* pr. krōō, or ~*ed* pr. krōd, p.p. ~*ed*). Utter loud cry of cock; (of child) utter joyful cry; exult loudly; ~ *over*, triumph over. [OE *crāwan*, OHG *krājan*, *krāen*, WG of imit. orig.]

crowd[1], n. Throng, dense multitude, (*would pass in a* ~, is not conspicuously defective; *the* ~, the masses; (colloq.) company, set, lot; large number (of things); (Naut.) ~ *of sail*, large number of sails hoisted. [f. foll.]

crowd[2], v.i. & t. Collect (t. & i.) in a crowd; fill, occupy, cram, (space etc. *with*); fill (place etc.) as a crowd does; force one's way *into*, *through*, etc. (confined space etc. or abs.); force (thing, person) *into* etc.; ~ *out*, exclude by ~ing; (Naut., of ship or crew) hasten on; ~ *sail*, hoist unusual number of sails. [OE *crūdan* press, drive, corresp. to MDu., MLG *crūden* press, push]

crown[1], n. 1. Wreath of flowers etc. worn on head, esp. as emblem of victory, (also fig. as *martyr's* ~, *no cross no* ~). 2. Monarch's head-covering of gold etc. & jewels; (fig.) king or queen, regal power, supreme governing power in a monarchy. 3. Any ~-shaped ornament. 4. (British coin worth) five shillings; foreign coin, esp.= KRONE. 5. Top part, esp. of skull; whole head; upper part of cut gem above girdle; highest or central part of arch or arched structure, as ~ *of the causeway*; top of hat; part of tooth projecting from gum. 6. Size of paper, 15" × 20". 7. ~ *& anchor*, popular gambling game played with dice marked with ~s, anchors, etc., and a corresponding board; ~-*glass*, made in circular sheets without lead or iron and used chiefly for windows; ‖ ~-*land* (belonging to the C~); C~ *Colony* (controlled by the C~); ~ *Derby*, kind of china made at Derby & often marked with ~ surmounting D; ‖ ~ *law*, criminal law; ‖ ~ *lawyer* (in service of the C~); C~ *office* (transacting common law business of Chancery); C~ *prince*, heir--apparent or designate to a sovereign throne; C~ *princess*, his wife; ~-*wheel*, CONTRATE wheel. [ME *corune*, *crune*, etc., f. ONF *corune* (OF *corone*) f. L *corona*]

crown[2], v.t. 1. Place crown on (person, head); invest (person) with regal crown or dignity (~ *him*, ~ *him king*; ~*ed heads*, kings & queens); (fig.) reward; occupy the head of, form chief ornament to, (lit. & fig.); put finishing touch to, as *to* ~ *all*; bring (efforts) to happy issue. 2. (Draughts) make (piece) a king. 3. (Dent.) ~ *a tooth*, protect its remains with a gold etc. cap cemented on. [ME *c(o)rune* etc., f. AF *coruner* (OF *coroner*) f. L *coronare*]

crowned (-nd), a. In vbl senses; (of hat) *high, low*, ~, with high, low, crown.

‖ **crown'er**, n. (obs. or dial.). = CORONER.
[pop. by-form of CORONER, assim. to CROWN]

cru'cial (-ōōshl), a. Decisive, critical, (case, point, test, etc.); (Anat.) cross--shaped, as ~ *incision*. [F, f. L *crux crucis* cross +-AL]

cru'cian, -sian, (-ōōshn), n. Yellow fish allied to carp. [f. LG *karusse* +-AN]

cru'ciate (-ōōsh-), a. (zool., bot.). Cross--shaped. [f. L *crux crucis* cross; see -ATE[2](2)]

cru'cible (-ōō-), n. Melting-pot (usu. of earthenware); (fig.) severe trial. [ME, f. med. L *crucibulum* night-lamp, crucible, app. f. *crux crucis* CROSS]

crucif'erous (-ōō-), a. Wearing, adorned with, a cross; (Bot.) of the family *Cruciferae*, having flowers with four equal petals arranged crosswise. [f. LL *crucifer* (as CRUCIAL, see -FEROUS)]

cru'cifix (-ōō-), n. Image of Christ on the cross; (improp.) cross. [ME, f. LL *crucifixus* f. *crux crucis* cross; see FIX]

crucifi'xion (-ōō-; -kshon), n. Crucifying; *the* C~ (of Christ); picture of this. [f. LL *crucifixio* (as prec., see -ION)]

cru'ciform (-ōō-), a. Cross-shaped. [f. L *crux crucis* cross, see -FORM]

cru'cify (-ōō-), v.t. Put to death by fastening to a cross; (fig.) mortify (passions, sins, flesh); (Mil.) tie up (soldier) with arms out in field punishment. [ME, f. OF *crucifier* f. Rom. **crucificare* (see -FY) for LL *crucifigere* (see CRUCIFIX)]

crude (-ōō-), a. In the natural or raw state; (of food etc.) not digested; unripe; (of diseases etc.) not matured; (fig.) ill--digested, unpolished, lacking finish; rude, blunt, (action, statement, manners); (Gram., of form of word) uninflected. Hence or cogn. ~'LY² (-dl-) adv., ~'NESS (-dn-), crud'ITY, nn., (-ōō-). [ME, f. L *crudus* raw]

cru'él (-ōō-), a. Indifferent to, delighting in, another's pain; (of actions) showing such ·indifference or pleasure; painful, distressing. Hence or cogn. ~LY² adv., ~TY n., (-ōō-). [ME, f. OF, f. L *crudelis*]

cru'ét (-ōō-), n. Small glass bottle with stopper for vinegar, oil, etc., for table; small vessel for wine or water in celebration of Eucharist; ~-*stand* (for ~s & castors). [ME *cruel(t)e* app. f. AF *cruel(e)* dim. OF *crue, cruie* pot, f. OLG *cruca* (CROCK¹)]

cruise (-ōōz), v.i., & n. 1. Sail to & fro on look-out for ships, for protection of commerce in time of war. for plunder, or for pleasure, making for no particular port (also fig.); (of aircraft) fly at *cruising speed* (economic travelling speed, less than top speed). 2. n. Cruising voyage. [f. Du. *kruisen* (f. *kruis* CROSS); cf. Sp., Port. *cruzar*, F *croiser*]

cruis'er (-ōōz-), n. Warship of high speed & medium armament; *armoured* ~ (with lighter armour than battleship); BATTLE¹, BELT²*ed*, ~; (*un)protected* ~, one with(out) protective deck; ~ *weight* (Boxing), 'light-heavy' weight, 12 st. 10 lb. (amateur), 12st. 7 lb. (professional). [f. Du. *kruiser* (as prec., see -ER¹)]

‖ **cruive** (-ōōv), n. (Sc.). Wicker salmon--trap. [15th c., of unkn. orig.]

*°**crüll'er**, n. A small cake made of dough containing eggs, butter, sugar, etc., twisted or curled & fried in fat. [f. Du. *krullen* curl]

crümb (-m), n., & v.t. Small fragment, esp. of bread; (fig.) small particle, atom, (of comfort etc.); soft inner part of bread; ~-*cloth* (laid over carpet, esp. under table); (v.t.) cover, thicken, with ~s, break into ~s. Hence ~'Y² (-mǐ) a. [OE *crūma*, MDu. *crūme*, MDu., MLG *crōme*, Icel. *krumr, kraumr*]

crüm'ble, v.t. & i. Break, fall, into crumbs or fragments (lit. & fig.). [earlier *crimble* f. OE *crūma*; assim. to CRUMB]

crüm'blỹ, a. Apt to crumble (intr.). [CRUMB +-LY¹; now treated as f. prec. + -Y²]

crümp, v.t., & n. (colloq.). Hit (esp. cricket-ball) hard; (n.) hard hit, heavy fall, (army sl.) bursting shell; sound of bursting bomb or shell. [imit.]

crüm'pét, n. Soft cake of a yeast mixture, baked on iron plate; (sl.) head (BARMY *on the* ~). [17th c., of unkn. orig.]

crüm'ple, v.t. & i. Crush together or *up* into creased state; ruffle, wrinkle; become creased; (fig.) collapse, give way (usu.

with *up*). [f. obs. *crump* v. & a. (make, become) curved +-LE(3)]

crünch, v.t. & i., & n. 1. Crush with teeth, esp. noisily; grind under foot (gravel etc.); make one's way (*up, through*, etc.) thus. 2. n. ~*ing* (noise). [replaces *cra(u)nch*, imit.]

crüpp'er, n. Strap buckled to back of saddle & looped under horse's tail; hind-quarters of horse. [ME, f. AF *cropere* (OF *-iere*), f. WG *kropp- CROP¹; see CROUP¹, -ER²]

crur'al (-oor-), a. (anat.). Of the leg. [f. L *cruralis* (*crus cruris* leg, see -AL)]

crusáde' (-ōō-), n., & v.i. (Hist.) Christian expedition to recover Holy Land from Mohammedans; war instigated by Church for alleged religious ends; (fig.) aggressive movement against public evil etc., as *Temperance* ~; (v.i.) engage in ~. Hence **crusād'ER¹** n. [in 16th c. *croisade* (F, f. *croix*), later *crusado, -ada* (Sp., f. *cruz*), 18th c. *crusade*; see CROSS, -ADE]

*crusād'ō (-ōō-), n. Portuguese coin. [f. Port. *cruzado* marked with cross]

cruse (-ōōs, -ōōz), n. (arch.). Pot, jar, of earthenware (WIDOW'S ~). [15th c. *crowse* corresp. to OE *crūse* (cf. OHG *krūselin*, MHG *krūse*); *cruse* perh. f. MLG *krūs*]

crüsh¹, v.t. & i. Compress with violence, so as to break, bruise, etc.; crumple (dress etc.) by rough handling; (fig.) subdue, overwhelm, as *a* ~*ing defeat, reply*; ~ *out*, extinguish, stamp out; ~ *a cup of wine*, drink it; (v.i.) squeeze one's way (*into* etc.). [ME, f. OF *croissir, cruissir*, of unkn. orig.]

crüsh², n. Act of crushing; crowded mass (esp. of persons); (colloq.) crowded social gathering; (Austral.) fenced passage with funnel-shaped end along which cattle are driven in single file for branding; similar but shorter closed passage for dealing with single animal; ~-*room* in theatre etc. (for promenade during intervals); ~ *hat*, collapsible opera hat with spring; *have a* ~ *on* (sl.), be in love with. [f. prec.]

crüst, n., & v.t. & i. 1. Hard outer part of bread; similar casing of anything, e.g. harder layer over soft snow (~-*hunt* n. & v.t. & i., of hunting elks etc. over a ~ that supports hunters but not quarry); hard dry·scrap of bread; pastry covering pie; hard dry formation, scab, on skin; (Geol.) outer portion of earth; coating, deposit, on surface of anything; ~ *of wine*, deposit on sides of bottle; hard external covering of animal or plant; (fig.) anything superficial; (sl.) impudence. 2. v.t. Cover with, form into, ~; (v.i.) become covered with ~. [ME *crouste, cruste*, partly f. OF *crouste*, partly f. its source, L *crusta*]

Crüstā'cea (-sha), n. pl. Large class of animals, mostly aquatic, with hard shell, as crabs, lobsters, shrimps. Hence **crüstā'CEAN** (-āshn) a. & n.; **crüstā-**

cèŏL'OGY n. [neut. pl. of mod. L CRUST-(*aceus* -ACEOUS)]

crŭstā'ceous (-shŭs), a. Crust-like; (of animals) having a hard covering, esp. (Zool.) belonging to the *Crustacea*. [f. mod. L *crustaceus* (CRUST, -ACEOUS)]

crŭs'tĕd, a. Having a crust; (of wine) having deposited a crust; (fig.) antiquated, venerable, as ~ *prejudice, theory*. [-ED²]

crŭs'tǁ̆y, a. Crust-like, hard; irritable; curt. Hence ~ĭLY² adv., ~ĭNESS n. [-Y²]

crŭtch, n. Staff (usu. with crosspiece at top) for lame person (usu. *pair of* ~*es*); forked rest for leg in a side-saddle; fork of the human body (cf. CROTCH); (Naut.) various forked contrivances; crosspiece, whence ~ED² (-cht) a. [OE *crycc,* OS *krukka,* OHG *krucka* ON *krykkja* f. Gmc. **kruk-* bend]

Crŭtch'ĕd Fri'ars, n. pl. Minor order of friars wearing a cross; site of their convent in London. [f. ME *crouch* CROSS¹ + -ED²]

crŭx, n. Difficult matter, puzzle; ~ *ansāt'a,* ANKH (lit. = handled cross). [L, = cross]

cruzeiro (krŏŏzā͞ir'ō), n. The monetary unit of Brazil. [Pg., f. *cruz* cross]

crȳ¹, n. Loud inarticulate utterance of grief, pain, fear, joy, etc.; loud excited utterance of words; appeal, entreaty; proclamation of wares to be sold in streets; rumour; voice of the public; watchword, as *war-*~, *battle-*~; fit of weeping; yelping of hounds (also fig.), as *full* ~ (pursuit); *within* ~, within calling distance (*of*); *a far* ~, a long way; ~-*baby*, one who cries childishly; *follow in the* ~, be in the following crowd of nobodies; *much* ~ *& little wool*, fuss to no purpose, as when pigs are shorn. [ME & OF *cri* f. *crier* CRY²]

crȳ², v.t. & i. (*cried*). Utter loudly, exclaim, (with sentence as object, or *that*); make loud utterance, as ~ *out,* ~ *to* (person etc.); announce for sale, as ~ *muffins;* ~ *stinking fish,* condemn one's own wares; weep (*bitter tears,* one's *heart out,* one*self to sleep,* or abs.; ~ *over spilt milk,* waste regrets); (of animals, esp. birds) make loud call; (of hounds) yelp; ask *for* (esp. ~ *for the moon*); ~ *down,* disparage; ~ *off,* withdraw *from* bargain; ~ *up,* praise, extol; ~ CRAVEN; ~ *halves,* claim share (*in*); ~ QUARTER, QUITS; ~ *shame upon,* protest against (act, person). [ME *crie* f. OF *crier* f. L *quiritare*]

crȳ'ing, a. In vbl senses; esp. (of evils) calling for notice, flagrant. [-ING²]

crȳ'ogĕn, n. (chem.). Freezing-mixture; thing mixed with ice to make this. [f. Gk *kruos* frost + -GEN(1)]

crȳ'olite, n. Lustrous mineral of considerable industrial value found abundantly in Greenland, consisting mainly of sodium-aluminium fluoride. [f. Gk *kruos* frost + -LITE]

crȳpt, n. Underground cell, vault, esp. one beneath church, used as burial-place. [f. L f. Gk *kruptē* (*kruptos* hidden)]

crȳptaesthēs'ia, n. Supernormal knowledge, whether telepathic or clairvoyant. [CRYPTO- + Gk *aisthēsis* perception + -IA¹]

crȳp'tic, a. Secret, mystical. [f. LL f. Gk *kruptikos* (as CRYPT, see -IC)]

crȳp't(**ō**)**-,** comb. form of Gk *kruptos* hidden, secret, as ~*obranchiate* with concealed gills, ~*o-Communist* secret sympathizer with Communism, ~*ōl'ogy* enigmatical language.

crȳp'tō, n. (colloq.). Person owing secret allegiance to a political creed etc.; esp. short for ~-*Communist.* [as prec.]

crȳp'togăm, n. Plant having no stamens or pistils, & therefore no proper flowers. Hence **crȳptogăm'ic, crȳptŏg'amous,** aa., **crȳptŏg'amist**(3), **crȳptŏg'amy¹,** nn. [f. F *cryptogame* (CRYPTO- + Gk -*gamos* wedded), after Linnaean class-name *Cryptogamia*]

crȳp'togrăm, -graph (-ahf), nn. Thing written in cipher. So **crȳptŏg'RAPHER, crȳptŏG'RAPHY,** nn., **crȳptoGRAPH'IC a.** [CRYPTO- + -GRAM, -GRAPH]

crȳptomēr'ia, n. Evergreen tree of the cypress type; Japanese cedar. [CRYPTO- + Gk *meros* part (because the seeds are enclosed by scales)]

crȳs'tal, n. & a. **1.** A clear transparent ice-like mineral; *rock-*~, a form of pure quartz; piece of this; ~ *set,* simple form of receiving apparatus in broadcasting using a ~ rectifier; (poet.) any clear transparent thing, esp. water; ~-*gazing,* concentration of one's gaze on ball of rock-~, pool of ink, etc., for the purpose of inducing a hallucinatory picture of future or distant events (~, colloq., view of the future thus obtained, prophetic utterance); (also ~ *glass*) glass of very transparent quality; vessel etc. of this; *C~ Palace,* building of glass & iron built in Hyde Park for the 1851 Exhibition & re-erected at Sydenham & destroyed by fire in 1936; (Chem., Min.) aggregation of molecules with definite internal structure & external form of solid enclosed by symmetrically arranged plane faces. **2.** adj. Made of, like, clear as, ~. [ME, f. OF *cristal* f. L f. Gk *krustallos* ice, crystal]

crȳs'talline, a. Made of, clear as, like, crystal; ~ *heaven* (in Ptolemaic system, between primum mobile & firmament, assumed to explain precession of equinox etc.); ~ *lens* of eye, transparent body in membranous capsule behind iris. [ME, f. OF -*in* or L f. Gk *krustallinos* (as prec.), see -INE²]

crȳs'tallizǀe, -isǀe (-ĭz), v.t. & i. Form into crystals or (fig.) definite or permanent shape; ~*ed fruit* (preserved by impregnation with sugar, and coated with sugar crystals). Hence ~ABLE a., ~A'TION n. [-IZE]

crȳstallǀo-, comb. form of Gk *krustallos* CRYSTAL, as ~*ogen'ic,* ~*ō'geny,* forming, formation of, crystals, ~ŏg'rapher, ~o-graph'ic, ~ŏg'raphy, student of, pertaining to, science of, crystal structure.

crys'talloid, a. & n. Crystal-like; (body) of crystalline structure (cf. COLLOID). [-OID]

ctĕn'oid (t-), a. & n. (Fish with scales or teeth) like a comb. [f. Gk klenoeidēs (kleis ktenos comb, see -OID)]

cŭb, n., & v.t. & i. (-bb-). 1. Young of fox, as ~-hunting; young of bear or other wild beast; unpolished youth (usu. unlicked ~); (colloq., short for) ~ reporter, young or inexperienced newspaper reporter; = WOLF-~ (junior boy scout). 2. vb. Bring forth (~s, or abs.). Hence ~b'ISH¹ a., ~'HOOD n. [of unkn. orig.]

cŭb'age, n. (Finding of) cubic content. [CUBE + -AGE]

cŭb'ature, n. = prec. [f. CUBE after QUADRATURE; cf. F cubature]

cŭbb'ing, n. CUB-hunting. [CUB + -ING¹]

cŭbb'y, n. Snug place (usu. ~-hole). [f. obs. or dial. cub, stall, pen; cf. LG kübje linhay]

cŭbe, n., & v.t. 1. Solid contained by squares; block of anything so or similarly shaped; product of a number multiplied by its square (~ of 2, alg. symbol 2³, = 8, ~ root of 8, alg. symbol ³√ 8, = 2). 2. v.t. Find ~ of (number); find cubic content of (solid); pave with ~s. [F, or f. L f. Gk kubos]

cŭb'ĕb, n. Pungent berry of a Javan shrub, used in medicine & cookery, & when crushed in medicated cigarettes. [ME, f. OF cubebe, quibibe, f. Arab. kababah]

cŭb'ic, a. Cube-shaped; of three dimensions; ~ foot, inch, volume of a cube whose edge is one foot, inch; ~ content of solid, its volume expressed in ~ feet etc.; involving the cubes of quantities, as ~ equation. Hence ~AL a., ~alLY² adv. [f. F cubique or L f. Gk kubikos (as CUBE, see -IC)]

cŭb'icle, n. Small separate sleeping-compartment in schools etc. [f. L cubiculum (cubare lie down)]

cŭb'iform, a. Cube-shaped. [-I-, -FORM]

cŭb'ism, n. A style in art in which objects are so presented as to give the effect of an assemblage of geometrical figures. So cŭb'IST n. [CUBE, -ISM]

cŭb'it, n. Ancient measure of length, 18 to 22 in. [ME, f. L cubitum elbow, length of forearm]

cŭb'ital, a. Of the forearm or corresponding part in animals. [ME, f. L cubitalis (prec. -AL)]

cŭb'oid, a. & n. Cube-shaped, like a cube, as ~ bone (of the foot); (n.) rectangular parallelepiped. Hence cŭboid'AL a. [f. Gk kuboeidēs (as CUBE, see -OID)]

cŭck'ing-stool, n. (hist.). Chair in which disorderly women etc. were ducked as punishment. [ME; orig. also cuck-stool, f. obs. cuck f. ON kúka void excrement]

cŭck'old, n., & v.t. Husband of unfaithful wife; (v.t.) make a ~ of. [ME cuke-weld, -wold, f. OF cucuault (cucu CUCKOO)]

cu'ckoo (kŏo-), n. & pred. a. 1. Migratory bird reaching British Islands in April & depositing its eggs in nests of small birds; simpleton; ~ clock (striking with sound like ~'s note); ~-flower, meadow plant with lilac-white flower, lady-smock; ~-pint, common arum, wake-robin; ~-spit, froth exuded by the larvae of certain insects as a protection. 2. adj. (sl.). Crazy, barmy. [ME cuccu etc. (superseding OE gēac, ME geke) f. OF cucu]

cŭc'ŭllate, -ātĕd, a. (bot., zool.). Shaped like, covered with, a hood. [f. LL cucullatus (cucullus hood, see -ATE²)]

cŭc'ŭmber, n. (Creeping plant with) long fleshy fruit eaten in thin slices as salad; cool as a ~, quite cool, self-possessed. [14th c. cucumer f. L; 15th c. cocomber etc. f. OF cocombre f. L cucumerem (nom. -mis)]

tŭcŭrb'it, n. Gourd. Hence ~A'CEOUS (-āshus) a. [f. L cucurbita]

cŭd, n. Food that ruminating animal brings back from first stomach into mouth & chews at leisure; (fig.) chew the ~, reflect, ruminate. [OE cwidu, cudu; app. cogn. w. OHG chuti, quili, glue]

cŭd'bear (-bār), n. Purple or violet dyeing-powder prepared from various lichens; kind of lichen. [named by Cuthbert Gordon, patentee]

cŭd'dl|e, v.t. & i., & n. 1. Hug, embrace, fondle; lie close & snug; nestle together; curl oneself up. 2. n. Hug, embrace. Hence ~eSOME (-ls-), ~Y², aa., given to ~ing or tempting to ~e. [orig. unkn.]

cŭdd'y¹, n. Cabin of half-decked boat, (hist.) saloon of large ship; closet, cupboard. [perh. f. early mod. Du. kajute]

∥cŭdd'y², n. (Sc.). Donkey; fool, ass; young of the coal-fish; lever on tripod for lifting stones etc. [perh. f. pet form of Cuthbert, as DICKY, NEDDY]

cŭd'gel, n., & v.t. (-ll-). 1. Short thick stick used as weapon; ~-play, contest with ~s; (fig.) take up the ~s for, defend vigorously. 2. v.t. Beat with ~, esp., fig., ~ one's brains for, try to think of. [(vb f. n.) OE cycgel, of unkn. orig.]

cŭd'weed, n. Composite plant with chaffy scales round flower-heads, given to cattle that had lost their cud. [f. CUD]

cŭe¹, n. Last words of a speech in a play, serving as signal to another actor to enter or speak; (Mus.) similar guide to singer or player; hint how to act; proper course to take. [orig. unkn.]

cŭe², n. Pigtail (also QUEUE); long straight tapering leather-tipped rod for striking ball in billiards etc. [f. F queue QUEUE]

cue'ist (kū'ist), n. Billiard-player. [prec. + -IST(3)]

cŭff¹, n. Ornamental bottom part of sleeve; separate band of linen worn round wrist; *trouser turn-up; off the ~

extempore, without preparation. Hence
(-)cŭffED² (-ft) a. [orig. unkn.]

cŭff², v.t. & n. 1. Strike with open hand.
2. n. Such blow. [orig. unkn.; cf. Sw.
kuffa thrust, G *kuffen* thrash]

Cŭf'ic, K-, a. & n. (Of) rude form of the
Arabic alphabet found chiefly in inscriptions. [f. *Cufa*, city S. of Bagdad, -IC]

cui bŏn'ŏ? (kī), sentence. Who profited by
it? (i.e. who is most likely to have brought
it about?); (pop.) to what purpose? [L]

cuirăss' (kw-), n. Body armour, breast-
plate & back-plate fastened together;
woman's close-fitting sleeveless bodice.
[ME, f. OF *cuirasse* f. It. *corazza* f. Rom.
coriacea f. LL *coriaceus* (*corium* leather,
see -ACEOUS)]

cuirassier (kwĭrasē̆r', kū̆r-), n. Horse-
-soldier wearing cuirass. [F (as prec., see
-EER)]

cuisine (kwĭzēn'), n. Kitchen arrangements; style of cooking. [F, f. L *coquina*
(*coquere* cook)]

cuisse (kwĭs), cuĭsh (kw-), n. (hist.).
Thigh armour (usu. pl.). [14th c. *quys-
sewes*, *cuissues*, f. OF pl. of *cuissel* f. LL
coxale (*coxa* hip)]

cul-de-sac (see Ap.), n. Blind alley;
(Anat.) tube etc. open at one end only.
[F]

-cule, dim. suf. = F -*cule* f. L -*culus*, -*cula*,
-*culum*; the L suf. appears in E as -cle, as
-cule, or in full: *article, corpuscule, corpuscle, fasciculus, Auricula, vasculum.*

cŭl'inarў, a. Pertaining to a kitchen or
cooking; fit for cooking, as ~ plants. [f.
L *culinarius* (*culina* kitchen, see -ARY¹)]

cŭll, v.t. & n. Pick (flower etc.); select;
(n.) animal removed from flock (& usu.
fattened) as inferior or too old for breeding. [ME, f. OF *cuillir* etc., ult. f. L
colligere COLLECT]

cullender. See COLANDER.

cŭll'ĕt, n. Refuse glass with which
crucibles are replenished; broken glass.
[later form of COLLET now disused in this
sense]

‖ cŭll'ў, n. (sl.). Dupe, simpleton; mate,
pal. [prob. cant, of unkn. orig.]

cŭlm¹, n. Coal-dust (esp. of anthracite).
[orig. unkn.]

cŭlm², n. (bot.). Stem of plant (esp. of
grasses). So ~IF'EROUS a. [f. L *culmus*]

cŭl'minant, a. At, forming, the top; (of
heavenly body) on the meridian. [foll.,
-ANT]

cŭl'min|āte, v.i. Reach its highest point
(*in*; lit. & fig.); (Astron.) be on the meridian. Hence ~A'TION n. [f. LL *culminare*
(*culmen* summit) see -ATE³]

cŭl'pab|le, a. Criminal, blameworthy, as
~*le negligence, hold him* ~*le.* Hence
cŭlpabIL'ITY, ~lENESS (-ln-), nn., ~LY²
adv. [ME & OF *coupable* f. L *culpabilis*
(*culpa* blame, see -ABLE); later assim. to L]

cŭl'prĭt, n. Offender; prisoner at the bar.
[17th c.; orig. in formula *Culprit, how
will you be tried?,* said by Clerk of Crown

to prisoner pleading Not Guilty; abbr. of
Culpable: prest d'averrer etc. (You are)
guilty: (I am) ready to prove etc.]

cŭlt, n. System of religious worship;
devotion, homage, to person or thing
(*the* ~ *of*). [f. F *culte* or L *cultus -ūs* worship (*colere cult-* till, worship)]

cŭl'tivāte, v.t. Till, whence cŭl'tivABLE,
cŭltivāt'ABLE, aa.; (fig.) improve, develop, (person, mind, manners; esp. in
p.p.); pay attention to, cherish, (faculty,
art, person, his acquaintance); prepare
(ground) with CULTIVATOR. [f. med. L
cultivare f. *cultiva* (*terra*) tilled (land), as
prec., -IVE, -ATE³]

cŭltivā'tion, n. Cultivating, cultivated
state, (lit. & fig.). [F (as CULTIVATE, see
-ATION)]

cŭl'tivātor, n. One who cultivates; implement for breaking up ground & up-
rooting weeds. [-OR]

cŭl'trate, a. (nat. hist.). Knife-edged. So
cŭl'trifORM a. [f. L *cultratus* (*culter* -*tri*
knife, -ATE²)]

cŭl'tur|e, n., & v.t. Tillage; rearing, pro-
duction, (of bees, oysters, fish, silk,
bacteria); set of bacteria thus produced;
improvement by (mental or physical)
training; intellectual development; (v.t.)
cultivate (lit. & fig., chiefly in p.p. ~ed
pr. -cherd). Hence ~AL a., ~IST(2) n.,
(-cher-). [ME, f. OF, or f. L *cultura* (as
CULT, see -URE); vb (16th c.) f. n., or F
culturer]

‖ cŭl'ver, n. (dial.). Wood-pigeon; ~*keys,*
cowslip, other plants. [OE *culfre*, of
unascert. orig.]

cŭl'verin, n. (hist.). Large cannon, small
firearm. [ME, f. OF *coulevrine* snake (L
colubra, -INE¹)]

cŭl'vert, n. Channel, conduit, carrying
water across under road, canal, etc.;
channel for electric cable. [c. 1770, of
unkn. orig.]

cŭm, prep. With; ~ *grano* (*salis*) (grăn'ŏ
săl'ĭs), with caution or reserve (lit. with
a grain of salt); ~ *dividend* (abbr. ~ *div.*),
including dividend about to be paid;
also in names of combined parishes, as
Stow-~-Quy. [L]

cŭm'ber, v.t., & n. Hamper, hinder;
burden; (n.) hindrance, obstruction.
[ME, prob. aphetic f. ENCUMBER or obs.
acumber]

cŭm'bersome, a. Unwieldy, clumsy.
Hence ~LY² (-ml-) adv., ~NESS (-mn-) n.
[-SOME]

Cŭm'brian, a. & n. (Native) of Cumberland; of the ancient British kingdom of
Cumbria. [-AN]

cŭm'brous, a. = CUMBERSOME. Hence
~LY² adv., ~NESS n. [CUMBER + -OUS]

cŭm'in, -mm-, n. Umbelliferous plant
like fennel, with aromatic seed. [ME, f.
OF *cumin, comin* f. L f. Gk *kuminon*; OE
cymen (OHG *kumin, -il,* G *kümmel*) dir.
f. L]

‖ cŭmm'er, kĭmm'er, n. (Sc.). Godmother of one's child or godchild; female companion; woman. [ME, f. OF *comniere* f. LL *commater*]

cŭmm′erbŭnd, n. (Anglo-Ind.). Waist sash. [f. Hind. & Pers. *kamar-band* loin band]

cŭm′quat (-ŏt), n. Plum-sized orange--like fruit with sweet rind and acid pulp, used in preserves. [dial. form of Chin. *kin kü* golden orange]

cŭm′shaw, n. (pidgin-Eng.). Present, tip, baksheesh. [dial. form of Chin. *kan hsieh* grateful thanks]

cŭm′ulate, a. Heaped up, massed. [as foll., see -ATE²]

cŭm′ul|āte², v.t. & i. Accumulate. Hence ~A′TION n. [f. L *cumulare* (*cumulus* heap), see -ATE³]

cŭm′ūlātive, a. Tending to accumulate; increasing in force etc. by successive additions, as ~ *evidence*; ~ *voting*, system in which each voter has as many votes as there are representatives, & may give all to one candidate; ~ *preference shares* (entitling holder to arrears of interest before other shares receive any on current year). Hence ~LY² (-vl-) adv., ~NESS (-vn-) n. [f. prec. + -IVE]

cŭm′ulus, n. (pl. *-lī*). Heap; set of rounded masses of cloud heaped on each other & resting on horizontal base. So **cŭm′ūlo-** comb. form, **cŭm′ūlous** a. [L]

cŭn′eate, a. Wedge-shaped. [f. L *cuneare* (*cuneus* wedge), see -ATE²]

cŭn′eiform (*also* kūnē′I-), a. & n. 1. Wedge-shaped. 2. n. ~ writing in ancient inscriptions of Persia, Assyria, etc. [f. L *cuneus* wedge, -FORM]

cŭnĕtte′, n. (fortif.). Central trench sunk in fort ditch, serving as drain. [F, f. It. *cunetta*, aphetic f. *lacunetta* dim. of *lacuna* ditch etc., see LACUNA]

cŭnn′ing¹, n. Artfulness, craft; (arch.) ability, dexterity. [ME (not in OE), app. f. ON *kunnandi* f. *kunna* know, see CAN²]

cŭnn′ing², a. Artful, crafty; (arch.) skilful, ingenious; able. Hence ~LY² adv. [ME (not in OE), f. ON as prec.; see -ING²]

cŭp¹, n. Drinking-vessel, with or without handle & stem, as *tea, coffee,* ~; *challenge* ~ (prize for race etc., usu. of gold or silver, esp. one held by winner only until next race etc.); rounded cavity, esp. calyx of flower, socket of some bones, etc.; cupful, as ~ *of tea, half a* ~; one's ~ *of tea* (colloq.), what interests or suits one; chalice used, wine taken, at Communion; fate, portion, experience, as *a bitter* ~, *his* ~ *was full* (happiness, misery, was complete); *the* ~*s that cheer but not inebriate*, tea (Cowper *Task* iv. 39); *in* one's ~*s*, while (getting) drunk; 'wine, cider, etc., with various flavourings, as *claret-*~; ~ *& ball*, = at end of stem, with attached ball to be thrown & caught in ~ or on spiked end of stem; ~*-bearer*, one who serves wine, esp. officer of royal or noble

household; ~*-moss*, lichen with ~-shaped processes arising from the thallus; ~*-shake*, opening between two concentric layers of timber. Hence ~′FUL (-ŏŏl) n. (pl. *-ls*). [OE *cuppe* f. pop. L *cuppa* cup, different. f. L *cūpa* cask]

cŭp², v.t. (-pp-). Bleed (person) by means of a ~*ping-glass*. [f. prec.]

cupboard (kŭb′erd), n. Shelved closet or cabinet for crockery, provisions, etc.; SKELETON *in the* ~; ~ *love* (simulated for sake of what one can get by it). [CUP¹ + BOARD]

cŭp′el, n., & v.t. (-ll-). Small flat circular vessel used in assaying gold or silver with lead; (v.t.) assay in ~. Hence ~LA′TION n. [f. F *coupelle* dim. of *coupe* CUP¹]

Cŭp′id, n. Roman god of love; beautiful boy; ~*'s bow*, (upper edge of) upper lip, which is shaped like the conventional double-curved bow carried by ~. [f. L *Cupido* (*cupere* desire)]

cŭpid′ity, n. Greed of gain. [ME, f. OF *cupidite* or L *cupiditas* (*cupidus* desirous, see -TY)]

cŭp′ola, n. Small rounded dome forming roof; ceiling of dome; (also ~*-furnace*) furnace for melting metals; revolving dome protecting mounted guns on warship; (Anat., Zool.) dome-like organ or process. [It., f. LL *cupula* dim. of *cūpa* cask, see CUP¹]

cŭp′reous, a. Of or like copper. [f. LL *cupreus* (LL *cuprum* COPPER) + -OUS]

cŭp′ric, a. Containing divalent copper. So **cŭprif′erous**, **cŭp′rous**, aa., **cŭp′ro-** comb. form. [f. LL *cuprum*, -IC(1)]

cŭp′ūle, n. (bot., zool.). Cup-shaped organ, receptacle, etc. [f. L as CUPOLA]

cŭr, n. Worthless, low-bred, or snappish dog; surly, ill-bred, or cowardly fellow. [ME *curre*, earlier *kur-dogge*, = MDu. *korre*; perh. ult. f. ON *kurra* grumble]

cŭr′açao, **-çoa**, (-sō), n. Liqueur of spirits flavoured with peel of bitter oranges. [Du. island in Caribbean sea; *-çoa* is E mis-spelling]

cŭr′acy̆, n. Curate's office; benefice of perpetual curate. [f. CURATE, see -ACY(3)]

cŭrár′e, **-i**, n. Resinous bitter substance from some S. American plants, paralysing the motor nerves, used by Indians to poison arrows. Hence **cŭr′arine** n., **cŭr′arize**(5) v.t. [native *wurali* etc.]

cŭr′assow (-ō), n. Turkey-like bird of Central & S. America. [= CURAÇAO]

cŭr′ate, n. Assistant to parish priest; ~*-in-charge*, clergyman appointed to take charge of parish during incapacity or suspension of incumbent. [f. med. L *curatus* f. *cura* CURE]

cŭr′ative, a. & n. (Thing) tending to cure (esp. disease). [F (-*if*, -*ive*), f. L *curare* CURE², see -ATIVE]

cŭrāt′or, n. Person in charge, manager; keeper, custodian, of museum; ‖ member of board managing property or having general superintendence in University;

‖ (Sc. law; kŭr′a-) guardian of minor, lunatic, etc. Hence **cūratŏr′IAL** a., **~SHIP** n. [ME, f. AF *curatour* (OF *-eur*) or L *curator* (as prec., -OR)]

cŭrb, n., & v.t. **1.** Chain, strap, passing under lower jaw of horse, used as a check; (fig.) check, restraint; hard swelling on horse's leg, whence ~′Y² n.; frame round top of well; timber or iron plate round edge of circular structure; = KERB; ~ *roof*, one of which each face has two slopes, the lower one steeper. **2.** v.t. Put ~ on (horse), (fig.) restrain. [ME, f. OF *courbe* adj. & *courber* vb f. L *curvus* bent]

cŭrc′ŭma, n. Turmeric, substance used in curry-powder, as test for alkalis (~ *paper*), etc.; kinds of tuberous plants yielding this & other commercial substances. [med. or mod. L, f. Arab. *kurkum* saffron, turmeric]

cŭrd, n. Coagulated substance formed (naturally or artificially) by action of acids on milk, and made into cheese or eaten (often pl.; ~*s & whey*, junket); fatty substance found between flakes of boiled salmon; ~ *soap* (white, of tallow & soda). Hence ~′Y² a. [ME *crud(de)*, *crod(de)*, of unkn. orig.]

cŭr′dle, v.t. & i. Congeal, form into curd; (fig.) ~ *the blood* (with horror). [f. *curd* vb (f. prec.) +-LE(3)]

cūre¹, n. Remedy; course of medical or other treatment (esp. of specified kind, as *grape*, *milk*, -~), success with this; spiritual charge, as ~ *of souls*; vulcanization. Hence ~′LESS (kūr̄l) a. [ME, f. OF f. L *cura* care]

cūre², v.t. & i. Restore to health (also fig.); remedy (an evil); preserve (meat, fruit, tobacco) by salting, drying, etc. (also intr.); vulcanize (rubber), (of rubber) become vulcanized. Hence **cūrABIL′ITY** n., **cūr′ABLE** a. [ME, f. OF *curer* f. L *curare* take care of (*cura*)]

cūre³, n. (sl.). Odd or eccentric person. [abbr. of CURIOUS]

curé (see Ap.), n. Parish priest in France etc. [F]

curette′, n., & v.t. & i. Surgeon's small scraping-instrument; (vb) scrape with ~. [F, f. *curer* cleanse (CURE²)]

cŭrf′ew, n. Medieval regulation for extinction of fires at fixed hour in evening; hour for this; (also ~*-bell*) bell announcing it; ringing of bell at fixed evening hour, still surviving in some towns; (under martial law etc.) signal or time after which inhabitants may not be abroad. [ME, f. AF *coverfu*, = OF *cuevrefeu*, f. imper. of *covrir* COVER +*feu* fire]

cūr′ia, n. One of the ten divisions of any of the three ancient Roman tribes; its place of worship; Roman senate-house; senate of ancient Italian towns; court of justice (esp. under feudal organization); the Papal court. [L]

cūr′ial, a. Of a curia; of the Papal court, whence ~ISM n. [OF, f. L *curialis* (CURIA, see -AL)]

cūr′io, n. (pl. *-os*). Curious object of art. [19th c. abbr. of foll.]

cūriŏs′itȳ, n. Desire to know; inquisitiveness; strangeness; *a* ~, strange or rare object. [f. OF *curiosete* f. L *curiositatem* (as foll., see -TY)]

cūr′ious, a. Eager to learn; inquisitive; minutely careful, as ~ *inquiry*; strange, surprising, odd; erotic, pornographic (as euphemism in booksellers' catalogues). Hence ~LY² adv., ~NESS n. [ME, f. OF *curios* f. L *curiosus* f. *cura* care, see -IOUS(1)]

cūr′ium, n. (chem.). Radio-active transuranic element. [f. Marie & Pierre *Cur(ie)*, French scientists, +-IUM]

cŭrl¹, n. Spiral lock of hair; ~*-paper* (used for twisting hair into ~s); anything spiral or incurved; act of curling, as ~ *of the lip* (expressing scorn); state of being curled, as *keep the hair in* ~; disease of potatoes etc. in which shoots or leaves are curled up. [f. foll.]

cŭrl², v.t. & i. Bend, coil, into spiral shape (t. & i.); ~ *up*, roll up into a curl, (intr., sl.) collapse; move in spiral form (of smoke etc.); play at CURLING; ~*ing*-*irons*, *-tongs*, instruments (heated before use) for ~ing the hair; ~*ing-pins*, folding clips used (cold) for similar purpose. [earliest in 14th c. *crolled*, *crulled*, f. obs. adj. *crolle*, *crulle* curly, f. MDu. *krul*; cf. vbs G *kröllen*, *krollen*, LG, Du., EFris. *krullen* curl]

cŭrl′ew, n. Wading bird with long slender curved bill. [ME *curlu* f. OF *corlieu*, *corlio*, orig. imit., but assim. to OF *corlieu* courier]

cŭrl′ing, n. In vbl senses; esp.: Scots game played on ice with large round stones; ~*-irons*, *-tongs*, *-pins*, see CURL². [-ING¹]

cŭrl′ȳ, a. Having, arranged in, curls; ~*-pate*, ~*-headed* person. Hence **cŭrl′iNESS** n. [-Y²]

cŭrmŭdg′eon (*-jn*), n. Churlish or miserly fellow. Hence ~LY¹ (*-jn-*) a. [orig. unkn.]

cŭ′rrach (*-ra*), n. Coracle. [f. Ir. *curach*, cf. CORACLE]

cŭ′rrant, n. Dried fruit of a seedless variety of grape grown in the Levant, much used in cookery; *red*, *white*, *black*, ~, (fruit of) species of Ribes; *flowering* ~, grown for ornament. [ME *raisins of Corauntz* (Corinth), f. AF, as in mod. F *raisins de Corinthe*]

cŭ′rrency, n. Time during which a thing is current; (of money) circulation; money current in actual use in a country (‖ ~ *note*, inconvertible legal-tender note for £1 or 10s. issued by Treasury during & after the 1914–18 war, replaced in 1928 by Bank of England notes); prevalence (of words, ideas, reports). [f. foll., see -ENCY]

cŭ′rrent¹, a. In general circulation or use

(of money, opinions, rumours, words); pass, go, run, ~, be generally accepted as true or genuine; (of time) now passing, as ~ week, month; belonging to the ~ time, as ~ issue (of journal); ~ handwriting, cursive. Hence ~LY² adv. [ME cora(u)nt f. OF part. of corre (courir) f. L currere run]

cǔ'rrent², n. Running stream; water, air, etc., moving in given direction; course, tendency, (of events, opinions, etc.); transmission of electric force through a body. [prec. as n.]

cǔ'rricle, n. Light two-wheeled carriage (usu. for two horses abreast). [f. foll. L]

curric'ul|um, n. (pl. ~a). Course (of study). Hence ~AR¹ a. [L, = course, race-chariot, f. currere run]

cǔ'rrier, n. One who dresses & colours tanned leather. [ME & OF corier f. L coriarius (corium leather, see -ARY¹, -ER²)]

cǔr'rish, a. Like a cur; snappish; mean-spirited. Hence ~LY² adv., ~NESS n. [-ISH¹]

cǔ'rry¹, n., & v.t. 1. Dish of meat etc. cooked with bruised spices & turmeric; ~-paste, -powder, preparations of turmeric etc. for making ~. 2. v.t. Prepare, flavour, with ~-powder. [f. Tamil kari sauce]

cǔ'rry², v.t. Rub down or dress (horse etc.) with ~-comb; dress (tanned leather); (fig.) thrash; ~ favour (orig. favel f. OF faveau, favel, the chestnut horse), ingratiate oneself (with person) by officiousness etc. [ME, f. OF correier f. Rom. *conredare f. Gmc (cf. Goth. garaidjan prepare); see READY]

cǔrse¹, n. Utterance of deity or person invoking deity, consigning person or thing to destruction, divine vengeance, etc. (~s come home to roost, injure the curser; under a ~, feeling or liable to its effects); sentence of excommunication; profane oath, imprecation; accursed object; evil inflicted in response to a ~; great evil, bane; (Cards) ~ of Scotland, nine of diamonds. [late OE curs, isolated & of unkn. orig.]

cǔrse², v.t. & i. Utter curse against; excommunicate; blaspheme; afflict with (esp. in pass.); (v.i.) utter curses. [late OE cursian, f. prec.]

cǔrs'ěd, -st, a. & adv. In vbl senses; also: damnable, abominable, (arch.; usu. curst) cantankerous; (adv.) cursedly. Hence cǔrs'ědLY² adv., cǔrs'ědNESS n. [ME, p.p. of prec.]

cǔrs'ive, a. & n. Running (writing in manuscript), opp. to UNCIAL. [f. med. L (scriptura) cursiva (L currere curs- run, see -IVE)]

cǔrs'or, n. Transparent slide engraved with hair-line forming part of slide-rule. [L, as CURSIVE]

cǔrsōr'ial, a. Having limbs adapted for running (~ birds etc.). [as CURSORY, -AL]

cǔrs'or|y̆, a. Hasty, hurried, (~y inspec-

tion). Hence ~ILY² adv., ~INESS n. [f. L cursorius of a runner (as CURSIVE, see -ORY)]

cūrs'us, n. Race-course; stated order of daily prayer; course of studies. [L]

cǔrt, a. Discourteously brief; terse, concise; (literary) short. Hence ~'LY² adv., ~'NESS n. [f. L curtus short]

curtail', v.t. Cut short (lit. & fig.); deprive of. Hence ~MENT n. [f. obs. curtal horse with docked tail f. F courtault (OF cortald, f. court short (CURT) + Gmc. suff. *-ald); assim. to tail]

cǔrt'ail-stěp, n. Lowest step of stair, with outer end carried round. [orig. unkn.]

cǔrt'ain (-tn), n., & v.t. 1. Suspended cloth used as screen; draw the ~ (back or aside to reveal objects, forward to conceal them); screen separating stage of theatre from auditorium (~ falls, drops, is dropped, at end of action, rises, is raised, at beginning; also fig.; ~ l, narrator's word drawing attention to dramatic situation just described, = tableau); fire-proof ~ in theatre, metal sheet cutting off stage; plain wall of fortified place, connecting two towers etc.; piece of plain wall not supporting a roof; partition, cover, in various technical senses; ~-fire, = BARRAGE (Mil.); ~ lecture, wife's reproof to husband in bed; ~-raiser in theatre, short opening piece. 2. v.t. Furnish, cover, shut off, with ~s. [ME & OF cortine f. LL cortina rend. Gk aulaia (aulē court]

cǔrtā'na (or -ah-), n. Pointless sword borne before kings of England at Coronation, as emblem of mercy. [ME, f. Anglo-L curtana (sc. spatha sword) f. curtus CURT, see -AN]

cǔrt'ilage, n. (law, dial.). Area attached to dwelling-house. [ME, f. AF f. OF cortil small COURT +-AGE]

cǔrt'sy̆, -sey, n., & v.i. 1. Feminine salutation made by bending knees & lowering body; make, drop, a ~. 2. v.i. Make ~ (to person). [var. of COURTESY]

cūr'ule (-ōōl), a. Pertaining to any high civic dignity; (Rom. Ant.) ~ chair, one like camp-stool, inlaid with ivory; ~ magistrate, one entitled to this. [f. L curulis f. currus chariot]

cūrv'ature, n. Curving; curved form; (Geom.) deviation (of curve) from straight line. [f. L curvatura (as foll., see -URE)]

curve¹, v.t. & i. Bend so as to form a curve. [L curvare (as foll.)]

curve², n. Line of which no part is straight; curved form or thing; (Statistics etc.) line presenting diagrammatically a continuous variation of quantity, force, etc., graph. [f. L curvus bent]

cǔrvět' (also kěrv'it), n., & v.i. (-tt-, -t-). Horse's leap with fore-legs raised together & hind-legs raised with spring before fore-legs reach ground; (v.i., of horse or rider) make ~. [vb f. It. cor-

vettare) f. It. *corvetta* dim. of *corva* curve as prec.)]

curvi-, comb. form of L *curvus* curved, as *-caudate*, *-costate*, *-dentate*, *-rostral*, with curved tail, ribs, teeth, beak; *-foliate*, with leaves bent back; *-form*, of curved shape; *-nervate* (of leaves), with veins diverging from mid-rib & converging towards margin.

curvilin'ear, a. Contained by, consisting of, curved line(s). Hence ~LY² adv. [prec. +-LINEAR]

cŭs'cŭs, n. Aromatic root of an Indian grass, used for fans etc. [f. Hind. *khas khas*]

cū'sĕc, n. (Flow of) one cubic foot (of water) per second (unit in irrigation engineering). [abbr. of *'cubic foot per second'*]

cŭsh'at, n. (Sc., dial.). Wood-pigeon, ring-dove. [OE *cūscute*, of unkn. orig.]

cushion¹ (kŏŏ'shn), n. **1.** Mass of soft material stuffed into cloth or silk covering, for sitting, kneeling, reclining, on; PIN-~. **2.** Pad worn by woman under hair; pad beneath skirt of woman's dress. **3.** Elastic lining of sides of billiard table; steam left in cylinders as buffer to piston; fleshy part of buttock (of pig etc.); frog of horse's hoof; sweet in ~ shape; ~-*tire* of bicycle (rubber tubing stuffed with rubber shreds). Hence ~Y² (-sho-) a. [(a) 14th c. *cuisshin* etc. f. OF *coissin*; (b) 14th c. *cusshin* etc. f. OF *coussin*; OF forms of uncert. orig.; ult. f. L *culcita*]

cushion² (kŏŏ'shn), v.t. Furnish with cushions; protect with cushions (also fig.); suppress quietly (complaints etc); (Billiards) place, leave, (ball) against cushion. [f. prec.]

cush'y (kŏŏ-), a. (sl.). (Of a post, task, etc.) easy, pleasant, comfortable. [Anglo-Ind., f. Hind. *khush* pleasant]

cŭsp, n. Apex, peak; (Geom.) point at which two branches of curve meet & stop; (Archit.) projecting point between small arcs in Gothic tracery; (Bot.) pointed end, esp. of leaf. Hence ~ED² (-pt) a. [f. L *cuspis -idis* point]

cŭs'pid|al, a. Of (the nature of) a cusp. So ~ate, ~ātĕd, [-ATE²(2)] aa. [as prec., -AL]

*cŭs'pidŏr, n. Spittoon. [Port., = spitter (*cuspir* f. L CONSpuere, see -OR)]

*cŭss, n. Curse; person, creature, (often disparaging). [vulg. pron. of CURSE¹]

cŭss'ĕdnĕss, n. Perversity, esp. *pure* ~. [vulg. pron. of *cursedness*]

cŭs'tard, n. Mixture of eggs & milk, baked or served liquid; ~*-apple*, W. Indian fruit with pulp like ~. [in ME a kind of pie; alt. f. obs. *crustade*, f. AF, f. *cruste* CRUST, see -ADE]

cŭstŏd'ial, a. Relating to custody. [-AL]

cŭstŏd'ian, n. Guardian, keeper. So **cŭstŏd'ĭER¹** n. [as foll. + -AN]

cŭs'tody, n. Guardianship, care, (*parent has* ~ *of child*, *child is in the* ~ *of father*);

imprisonment, esp. *take into* ~, arrest. [f. L *custodia* (*custos -odis* guardian, see -Y¹)]

cŭs'tom, n. Usual practice; (Law) established usage having the force of law; (pl.) duty levied upon imports from foreign countries; ~*-house*, office (esp. in seaport) at which ~s are collected; business patronage or support; *the C-~s*, department of the Civil Service that deals with the levying of ~s; *~ *clothes* (made to measure; so ~*-built*, *-made*, etc.) [ME & OF *custume* (see COSTUME) f. Rom. *costumae f. *costudne f. L *consuetudinem*]

cŭs'tomar|ỹ, a. & n. Usual; (Law) subject to, held by, custom (of the manor etc.); (n., also *-tumary*) written collection of the customs of a manor. Hence ~ILY² adv., ~INESS n. [f. med. L *custumarius* f. *custuma* f. AF *custume* (as prec., see -ARY¹)]

cŭs'tomer, n. Buyer; client of bank; (colloq.) *queer, awkward, etc.,* ~ (person to deal with), ~ (person to deal with). [ME, f. as prec.; in mod. senses f. CUSTOM + -ER¹]

cŭs'tŏs, n. Guardian, keeper; ~ *rŏtŭlōr'um*, keeper of the rolls, principal justice of the peace in a county. [L]

cŭt¹, n. Act of cutting; stroke, blow, with knife, sword, whip; ~ *& thrust*, hand-to-hand struggle; excision (of part of a play etc.); act, speech, that wounds the feelings; particular stroke in cricket, tennis, croquet, etc.; refusal to recognize an acquaintance (esp. *give one the* ~ *direct*); *short* ~, crossing that shortens the distance; fashion, style, (of clothes, hair, etc.; *the* ~ *of one's* JIB¹); *a* ~ (degree, stage) *above*; wound made by cutting; railway cutting; narrow opening in floor of stage of theatre, by which scenes are moved up & down; = WOODcut; piece (esp. of meat) cut off; reduction (in wages, prices, etc.); *draw* ~s, draw lots with sticks of unequal length (a different word, of unkn. orig.); ~*-off*, device to prevent feeding of cartridges from magazine of rifle; ~*-out*, device in motor-car for releasing gas rapidly without passage through silencer. [f. foll.]

cŭt², v.t. & i. (*cŭt*). **1.** Penetrate, wound, with edged instrument, as *the knife* ~ *his finger*, *he* ~ *his finger with a knife*, (fig.) *argument* ~s *both ways* (tells for both sides); (fig.) *a* ~*ting wind*, ~*ting retort*, *it* ~ *him to the heart*, whence ~*t'ingLY²* adv.; divide with knife etc. *in two, in* or *into* pieces (~ *the knot*, fig., solve problem in irregular but efficient way, cf. GORDIAN); (fig.) ~ (renounce) *a connexion*; detach by ~ting; carve (meat); cross, intersect, as *two lines* ~ *each other*; (intr.) pass *through, across*, etc., (sl.) run (~ *& run*, run away); reduce by ~ting (hair etc.); reduce (wages, prices, time, etc.; ~ *it fine*, allow only the minimum; ~ *a loss*, abandon

losing speculation in good time; ~ *the
record*, reduce the recorded shortest time
for race etc., or surpass record otherwise); shape, fashion, by ~ting (coat,
gem, etc.); perform, execute, make, as ~
a CAPER, DASH, FIGURE, *joke*; divide (pack
of cards, or abs.) to select dealer, prevent
cheating, etc.; hit (ball, or abs.) in certain
way, in cricket etc.; renounce acquaintance of (person), decline to recognize
him, esp. ~ *him dead*; absent oneself
from, avoid, renounce, as ~ *a lecture*, ~
the whole concern; ~ *a tooth*, have it
appear through gum (~ one's *eye or
wisdom teeth*, fig., develop insight or
wisdom); ~ *short*, shorten by ~ting (lit.
& fig.), also interrupt; ~ one's *stick*, go;
~ *coat according to* CLOTH. 2. ~ *back*
(Cinemat.), repeat, for dramatic reasons,
portions of scenes already shown on
screen (also as n., ~*back*); ~ *down*, bring
or throw down by ~ting, (fig.) reduce
(expenses); ~ *in* (intr.), enter abruptly,
interpose (in conversation), (Cards) join
in game by taking place of player who
~s *out*, (Motoring) obstruct path of
vehicle one has just overtaken by
returning to one's own side of the road
too soon; ~ *no ice* (sl.), effect little or
nothing; ~ *off*, remove by ~ting, bring
to abrupt end or (esp. early) death, intercept (supplies, communications), exclude
(*from* access etc.); ~ *off with a shilling*,
disinherit by bequeathing a shilling; ~
out, remove by ~ting, stop doing or using
(something), (fig.) out-do or supplant
(rival), fashion or shape (lit. & fig.), *detach (animal) from the herd, (Cards, intr.)
be excluded from game as result of
~ting, (Nav.) capture (enemy ship) by
getting between it & shore, (Motoring)
obstruct path of oncoming vehicle by
moving out from one's own side of the
road, esp. in order to overtake another
vehicle; ~ *up*, ~ in pieces, destroy utterly,
(fig.) criticize severely, (usu. pass.) distress
greatly, ~ *up* (*well*), leave (large) fortune,
~ *up rough*, show resentment; ~*-&-come-
-again*, abundance; ~ *& dried or dry* (of
opinions etc.), ready-made, lacking freshness; ~*'purse*, thief; ~*'throat*, murderer,
(adj., of competition) intensive, merciless,
(of bridge, euchre, etc.) three-handed.
[ME *cutte, kitte, kette*, without cogn.
in WG or Rom.; cf. however, Swed. dial.
kåta, (*kutå*), from source of which the ME
wd may derive]

cütan′ĕous, a. Of the skin. [f. mod. L
cutaneus (*cutis* skin, see -ANEOUS)]

cŭt′away, a. & n. (Coat) with skirt cut
back from the waist.

cŭtch′a, a. (Anglo-Ind.). Of poor quality;
makeshift (opp. PUCKA); (of bricks) sun-
-dried. [Hind. *kachcha* raw]

cutchĕ′rry, cŭtch′ery, n. (Anglo-Ind.).
Public office, court-house; office of
planter etc. [f. Hind. *kachahri*]

cūte, a. (colloq.). Clever, shrewd; inge-

nious; *attractive. Hence ~′LY² (-tl-)
adv., ~′NESS (-tn-) n. [for ACUTE]

cŭt′icle, n. Epidermis or other superficial skin; (Bot.) superficial film of
plants. Hence **cŭtic′ūlAR¹** a. [f. L
cuticula dim. of CUTIS]

cŭt′is, n. (anat.). True skin, underlying
the epidermis. [L, = skin]

cŭt′lass, n. Short sword with wide
slightly curved blade, esp. that used by
sailors. [f. F *coutelas* augment. of *couteau*
(*coutel*; see foll.)]

cŭt′ler, n. One who makes or deals in
knives & similar utensils. [ME, f. OF
coutelier f. *coutel* (f. L *cultellus* dim. of
culter COULTER), see -ER²(2)]

cŭt′lery, n. Trade of the cutler; things
made or sold by cutlers. [ME, f. OF
coutelerie (as prec., see -ERY]

cŭt′lĕt, n. Neck-chop of mutton, small
piece of veal, broiled or fried in bread-
-crumbs; imitation of mutton-~ in
minced fish etc. [f. F *côtelette* double dim.
of *côte* rib f. L *costa*]

cŭtt′er, n. Person, thing, that cuts;
superior kind of brick that can be cut;
boat belonging to ship of war, fitted for
rowing & sailing; small single-masted
vessel rigged like sloop, but with running
bowsprit. [-ER¹]

cŭtt′ing, n. In vbl senses; ∥ esp. excavation of high ground for railway, road, etc.;
∥ *press* ~, paragraph etc. cut from newspaper. [-ING¹]

cŭt′tle, n. (Usu. ~*-fish*) mollusc ejecting
black fluid when pursued; ~*-bone*, its
internal shell, used for polishing. [OE
cudele, of uncert. orig.]

∥ **cŭtt′y̆**, a. & n. (Sc. & north.). Cut short,
abnormally short; (n.) short pipe; ~
-stool, seat in Sc. churches where unchaste
women sat to receive public rebuke
during service. [CUT², -Y²]

cŭt′water (-waw-), n. Knee of head of
ship, dividing water before it reaches
bow; forward edge of prow; wedge-
-shaped end of pier of bridge.

cŭt′worm (-wẽrm), n. Caterpillar that
cuts off young plants level with the
ground.

cwm (kōōm), n. Var. of COOMB.

-cȳ, suf., special form of the abstract suf.
-Y¹, repr. L -*cia*, -*tia*, & Gk -*kia*, -*keia*,
-*tia*, -*teia* (in E occurring chiefly in the
combined forms -ACY, -ANCY, -ENCY,
-CRACY, -MANCY). On anal. of wds in -*acy*,
-*ncy*, with corresp. nn. in -*ate*, -*nt*, -*cy*
was extended to wds in -*n*, as *chaplaincy,
captaincy*, after *incumbency, lieutenancy*,
&, being thus regarded as independent
suf. = -*ship*, to other wds as *colonelcy*; it
is even added to wds ending in -*t* (where
-*c*- should have been substituted for -*t*-),
as *bankruptcy, idiotcy*, normal form being
idiocy f. Gk *idióteia*.

cȳăn′ic, a. Blue; (Chem.) of, containing,
cyanogen. [as foll. +-IC]

cyan|(o)-, comb. form of Gk *kuanos*, a dark-blue mineral. *kuaneos* dark-blue. Meaning (1) dark-blue, as ~*ōm'eter*, instrument for measuring blueness of sky; (2) of, containing, cyanogen.

cyăn'ogĕn, n. (chem.). Compound of two radicals each consisting of one atom of nitrogen and one of carbon. Hence **cy'an**IDE n. (*cyanide process*, method of extracting a precious metal from its ore by treatment with a dilute solution of potassium cyanide). [f. F *cyanogène* (as prec. +-GEN)]

cyanŏs'is, n. Blue discoloration, due to circulation of imperfectly oxygenated blood. [f. Gk *kuanōsis* (as prec., see -OSIS)]

cybernĕt'ics, n. Study of system of control & communications in animals & electrically operated devices such as calculating machines. [f. Gk *kubernētēs* steersman, -ICS]

cy'cad, n. (bot.). Kinds of palm-like plant. [f. mod. L *cycas cycad-* f. supposed Gk *kukas*, scribal error for *koïkas*, pl. of *koïx* Egyptian palm]

cyc'lamĕn, n. Kinds of plant cultivated for their early-blooming flowers. [L, irreg. f. Gk *kuklaminos*]

cy'cle, n., & v.i. **1.** Recurrent period (of events, phenomena, etc.); *Metonic* or *Lunar* ~, one of 19 years, used for finding date of Easter; period of a thing's completion; complete set or series; series of poems or songs (*song* ~) collected round a central event or idea; bicycle, tricycle, or similar machine; ~-*car*, very light motor vehicle of simplified design with 3 (rarely 4) wheels, usu. fitted with chain drive & engine of 1 or 2 cylinders. **2.** v.i. Revolve in ~s; ride ~. [ME, f. OF or f. LL f. Gk *kuklos* circle]

cyc'lic, -ical, aa. Recurring in cycles; belonging to a chronological cycle; (-*ic*) of a cycle of poems, as ~ *poet*; (Gk Ant., -*ic*) ~ *chorus*, dithyrambic chorus, danced in ring round altar; (Bot., of flower) with its parts arranged in whorls; (Org. Chem., -*ic*) with the constituent atoms in a ring formation. [f. F *cyclique* or L f. Gk *kuklikos* (prec., -IC)]

cyc'list, n. Rider of a cycle. [CYCLE +-IST]

cyclo-, comb. form of Gk *kuklos* circle, as ~*graph*, instrument for tracing circular arcs, ~*meter* (-ŏm²), instrument for measuring (1) circular arcs (2) distance traversed by bicycle etc., ~*stomous* (-ŏs²), with round mouth, ~*ra'ma* (-ah-), circular panorama.

cyc'loid, n. Curve traced by a point on a radius of a circle within (*prolate* ~), on (*common* ~), or without (*curtate* ~), its circumference, as the circle rolls along a straight line. Hence **cycloid'al** a. [f. Gk *kukloeidēs* (as CYCLE, see -OID)]

cyc'lōne, n. System of winds rotating round a centre of minimum barometric pressure; violent hurricane of limited diameter. Hence **cyclŏn'ic** a. [as *cyclome*

prob. repr. Gk *kuklōma* wheel, coil of snake, f. *kuklos* CYCLE]

cyclop(a)ed'|ia (-pĕd-), n. = ENCYCLOPAEDIA. Hence ~IC a. [abbr. of ENCYCLOPAEDIA]

Cyclope'an, -clōp'ian, a. Of, like, a Cyclops; huge; ~ *masonry*, an ancient style made with huge irregular stones. [f. L *Cyclopeus*, -*pius*, f. Gk *kuklōpeios*, -*pios*, (as foll.)]

Cyc'lōp(s), n. (pl. -*ops*, -*opses*, -*ōp'ēs*). (Gk Myth.) one-eyed giant; one-eyed person. [L (-*s*), f. Gk *kuklōps* (*kuklos* circle + *ōps* eye)]

cyc'lostȳle, n., & v.t. Apparatus printing copies of writing from stencil-plate cut by pen with small toothed wheel; (v.t.) reproduce with this. [CYCLO-]

cyc'lotrŏn, n. (phys.). Apparatus for electro-magnetic acceleration of charged atoms, atomic nuclei, etc. [f. CYCLO- + (ELEC)TRON]

cyd'er. See CIDER.

cyg'nĕt, n. Young swan. [ME, f. OF *cygne* or L *cygnus* +-ET¹]

cyl'inder, n. (Geom.) solid generated by straight line moving parallel to itself and describing with its ends any fixed curve, esp. circle; roller-shaped body, hollow or solid; barrel-shaped object of baked clay covered with cuneiform writing and buried under Babylonian or Assyrian temple; stone of similar shape used as seal by Assyrians; cylindrical part of various machines, esp. chamber in which steam acts upon piston; metal roller used in printing. [f. L f. Gk *kulindros* (*kulindō* roll)]

cylin'drical, a. Cylinder-shaped. [mod. L, f. Gk *kulindrikos* (as prec., see -IC) +-AL]

cyl'indroid, a. & n. (Figure) like a cylinder. [f. Gk *kulindroeidēs* (as prec., -OID)]

cym'a, n. (pl. -*mas*). Ogee moulding of cornice (~ *recta* with concave, ~ *reversa* with convex, curve uppermost); = CYME. [mod. L, f. Gk *kuma* wave, anything swollen]

cymăr', n. Woman's loose light garment esp. under-garment. [f. F *simarre*; see CHIMERE]

cym'bal, n. One of a pair of concave brass or bronze plates, struck together to make ringing sound. Hence ~IST n. [ME, f. OF *symbale* or L f. Gk *kumbalon* (*kumbē* cup)]

cym'balō (pl. -*os*), -lŏn, nn. = DULCIMER. [f. It. *cembalo*, as prec.]

cym'bifŏrm, a. (anat., bot.). Boat-shaped. [f. L *cumba*, *cymba* f. Gk *kumbē* boat +-FORM]

cyme, n. (bot.). Inflorescence in which primary axis bears single terminal flower that develops first, system being continued by axes of secondary and higher orders (cf. RACEME). Hence **cymose**¹ a. [F *cyme*, var. of *cime* summit, f. pop. L *cima*, L f. Gk *kuma* CYMA]

Cўm′ric (k-), a. Welsh. [f. W *Cymru* Wales]

cўn′ic, a. & n. 1. Of, characteristic of, the Cynic philosophers; = foll. 2. n. (*C*~) philosopher of sect founded by Antisthenes, marked by ostentatious contempt for pleasure. 3. Sneering fault-finder. Hence ~ism n. [f. L f. Gk *kunikos* (*kuōn kunos* dog, nickname for Cynic)]

cўn′ical, a. Churlish; captious; incredulous of human goodness; sneering. Hence ~LY² adv. [-AL]

cўno- = Gk *kuno-*, comb. form of *kuōn* dog, as ~*phob′ia*, dread of dogs.

cўnoceph′alus, n. Fabulous dog-headed man; (Zool.) dog-faced baboon. [L, f. Gk *kunokephalos* (prec. +*kephalē* head)]

cўn′osūre (*or* -shoor), n. (Constellation containing) Pole-star, Little Bear; guiding star; centre of attraction or admiration. [F, or f. L f. Gk *kunosoura* dog's tail, Little Bear]

cypher. See CIPHER.

cy pres (sēprā′), adv., n., & a. (Law) as near as possible (to testator's intentions); (adj.) approximate; (n.) approximation. [AF, = F *si près* so near (as etc.)]

cўp′ress, n. Coniferous tree with hard wood and dark foliage; branch of this as symbol of mourning. [ME, f. OF *cipres* f. LL *cypressus* (= L *cu-*) f. Gk *kuparissos*]

Cўp′rian, a. & n. (Inhabitant, native) of Cyprus; licentious (person). [f. L *Cyprius* (*Cyprus*) +-AN]

Cўp′riot, -ōte, a. & n.=prec. (first sense). [-OT²]

Cyrenā′ic (sīr-), a. & n. (Philosopher) of the hedonistic school of Aristippus of Cyrene. [f. L f. Gk *Kurēnaikos* (*Kurēnē*)]

Cўrill′ic, a. ~ *alphabet*, that used by Slavonic peoples of the Eastern Church. [St *Cyril*, reputed author, +-IC]

cyrto- (sêr-), comb. form of Gk *kurtos* curved, as ~*meter* (-ŏm′-), instrument measuring chest.

cўst, n. (Biol.) hollow organ, bladder, etc., in animal or plant, containing liquid secretion; (Path.) sac containing morbid matter, parasitic larva, etc.; cell containing embryos etc. [f. LL & med. L *cystis* (so in 16th c. Eng.), f. Gk *kustis* bladder]

cўst-, cўstī-, cўsto-, comb. form of Gk *kustis, kustē*, bladder, as *cystiform*, bladder-shaped, *cysto*CELE, -SCOPE, -TOMY.

cўs′tic, a. Of the urinary bladder; of the gall-bladder; of the nature of a cyst. [f. as CYST +-IC]

cўstīt′is, n. Inflammation of the bladder. [CYST-, -ITIS]

-cўte, suf. in biol. wds meaning *cell*, as LEUCO*cyte*. [f. Gk *kutos* vessel]

cўto-, comb. form of Gk *kutos* vessel, as ~*blast*, protoplasmic nucleus of a cell; ~*plasm*, protoplasmic content of cell other than the nucleus.

cўtŏl′ogў, n.(biol.). Study of cells. Hence **cўtŏl′ogist** n. [CYTO-]

czar etc. See TSAR etc.

Czech, -kh, (chĕk), n. & a. (Native or language) of Bohemia. [f. Boh. *Cech*]

Czechoslovak (chĕkōslŏv′ăk), a. & n. (Native) of the State called *Czechoslovakia*, including Bohemia, Moravia, part of Silesia, Slovakia, and formerly Carpathian Ruthenia. [*Czech, Slovak*, native race-names, -o-]

D

D (dē), letter (pl. *Ds*, *D's*, Dees); *D block, trap, valve*, shaped like the letter; also **D=**DEE; (Mus.) second note of natural major scale.

'd. Colloq. clipping of *had* & *would*, chiefly after *I*, *we*, *you*, *he*, *she*, *they*.

-d, p.p. suf. (*heard* etc.); see -ED¹.

da. See DAD.

dăb¹, v.t. & i. (-bb-). Strike lightly or undecidedly, hit feebly *at*, tap, peck; press but not rub (surface) with sponge etc., whence ~b′ER¹(2) n.; press (brush, dabber, etc.) against surface. [f. 1300, of unkn. orig.]

dăb², n. Slight or undecided but sudden blow, tap, peck; brief application of sponge, handkerchief, etc., to surface without rubbing; moisture, colour, etc., so applied. [f. prec.]

dăb³, n. Kind of flat-fish. [16th c., of unkn. orig.]

dăb⁴, n. & a. (colloq.). Adept (*at* games etc., do*ing*); *he is a* ~ *hand* (*at*). [f. 1690, of unkn. orig.]

dăb′ble, v.t. & i. Wet intermittently, slightly, or partly, soil, moisten, splash; move the feet, hands, bill, about in water; engage *in* or *at* pursuit etc. as a hobby, whence **dăb′bl**ER¹ n. [16th c., f. Du. *dabbelen*]

dăb′chick, n. Water-bird, the little grebe. [16th c. *dap-, dop-*, later *dip-*; perh. cogn. w. DIP]

dăb′ster, n. = DAB⁴; = DAUB*ster*. [-STER]

da ca′pō (dahkah-), mus. direction. Repeat from the beginning. [It.]

dāce, n. Small freshwater fish. [ME *darse* f. OF *dars* f. med. L (8th c.) *darsus*, of Gaulish orig.]

dachs′hund (dahks-hŏont), n. Short-legged breed of dog. [G, = badger-dog]

dacoit′, n. Member of Indian or Burmese armed robber band. [f. Hind. *ḍakait* f. *ḍaka* gang-robbery]

dacoit′y̆, n. (Act of) gang-robbery. [f. Hind. *ḍakaiti* as prec.]

dăc′tyl, n. Metrical foot ~⌣⌣. [f. L f. Gk *daktulos* finger]

dăctyl′ic, a. & n. Of dactyls; (noun, usu. pl.) ~ verse(s). [f. L f. Gk *daktulikos* (prec., -IC)]

dăd, da (dah), **dăd′a, dădd′y̆**, nn. (colloq.). Father (esp. as voc.); *daddy-long′legs*, crane-fly. [f. 16th c.; infantile sound]

dād′ō, n. (pl. *-os*). Cube of pedestal between base & cornice; lower few feet of room-wall when faced with wood or coloured differently from upper part. Hence ~ED² (-ōd) a. [It., = DIE¹]

daed′al, a. (poet.). Skilful, inventive; mazy; manifold, complex, mysterious. [f. L f. Gk *daidalos* skilful, variegated]

Daedāl′ian, -ēan, a. In the manner of Daedalus the Greek artificer; intricate; labyrinthine. [f. L *Daedaleus* of Daedalus (cf. Gk *daidaleos* cunningly wrought) + -AN]

daemonic. See dem-.

daff (dah-), v.t. (arch.). Put aside, waive. [var. of DOFF, preserved by 1 *Hen. IV*, IV. i. 96]

dăff′odil (also **dăffodill′y, dăff′adowndill′y**, in poetry etc.), n. & a. Lent lily, pale-yellow-flowered narcissus (alternative to leek as Welsh national emblem); pale yellow (n. & a.). [f. earlier *affodill* (d- unexplained) f. L f. Gk *asphodelos* ASPHODEL]

dăft (dah-), a. (esp. Sc.). Foolish, reckless, wild, crazy. [ME *daffte* = OE *gedæfte* mild, meek; orig. sense (cf. Goth. *gadaban* be fit) fitting, suitable (cf. DEFT; for change of meaning cf. SILLY]

dăgg′er (-g-), n. Stabbing-weapon with short pointed and edged blade (*at* ~*s drawn*, on the point of fighting, in strained relations, *with* person, or abs.; *look, speak,* ~*s* bitterly, so as to wound); (Print.) (*double*) ~, = (*double*) OBELISK. [ME, app. an E form.; prob. related to *dag* stab (14th c.) & OF, F *dague* dagger]

•dăg′ō, n. (pl. ~*s*, ~*es*). (Term of contempt for) a Spaniard, Portuguese, or Italian. [f. Sp. *Diego* = James]

dague′rreotȳpe (-gēro-), n. (Portrait taken by) early photographic process. [*Daguerre* 1839 inventor, -O-, TYPE]

dah, n. Burmese sword-knife. [Burmese]

dahabee′yah (dah-ha-), **-bī′ah** (-bē-), n. Nile sailing-boat. [Arab., = the golden, orig. sense *gilded barge*]

dahl′ia (dāl-), n. Mexican composite plant cultivated in Europe for its many-coloured single & double flowers (*blue* ~, impossibility); shade of red. [*Dahl* d. 1789, botanist, -IA¹]

dai (dī), n. (Anglo-Ind.). Wet-nurse. [Hind.; cf. Pers. *dāyah*]

Dail (Eireann) (doil(yĕ′ran)), n. Chamber of Deputies in the Irish Republic legislature. [Ir., = assembly of Ireland]

dail′y, a., adv. & n. **1.** (Recurring, appearing, done) every day or week-day, from day to day, constant, often; ~ *bread,* one's necessary food or livelihood. **2.** n. A ~ newspaper (pl. *dailies*); ∥ (colloq.) non-resident maid-servant. [OE *-dæglīc* (DAY, -LY¹)]

dai′mĭŏ (dī-), n. (pl. *-os*). Japanese feudal vassal, noble, (hist.). [Jap., f. Chin. *dai* great, *myo* name]

dain′tў,¹ n. Choice morsel, dish, etc.,

delicacy, tit-bit, (lit. & fig.). [f. OF *dainte, -tie* f. L *dignitatem* (*dignus* worthy, -TY)]

dain′t|ў², a. Delicate, choice; tasteful, pretty, of delicate beauty, scrupulously clean; particular, nice, of delicate tastes & sensibility, fastidious; inclined to luxury. Hence ~iLY² adv., ~iNESS n. [f. prec.]

•daiquiri (dĭk′ĭrĭ, dăk⁴), n. Kind of cocktail. [Cuban]

dair′ў, n. Room or building for keeping milk & cream & making butter etc. (~*maid*, in charge of this); the milk department in farming; shop for milk etc. (~*man,* dealer in milk etc.); cows of a farm. Hence (f. rare vb) ~ING¹ n. [ME *deierie* f. obs. *dey* (OE *dæge* 'kneader of DOUGH') dairymaid +-ERY]

dā′is (*or* dās), n. Raised platform, esp. at end of hall for high table, throne, etc., or terrace. [ME, f. OF *deis* f. L *discus* DISC, DISH, in med. L sense *table*]

dais′ў (-z-), n. Small European wild & garden flower; other plants resembling it, esp. the larger ox-eye ~; (sl.) first-rate specimen of anything; ~*-chain,* string of daisies fastened together; ~*-cutter,* horse lifting feet very little, ball travelling along ground at cricket. Hence **dais′iED²** (-zĭd) a. [OE *dæges ēage* day's eye]

dak, dâk. See DAWK.

dal (dahl). See DHAL.

dāle, n. Valley (esp. in north; also in poet. use, as *hill & ~*); ~*s′man,* inhabitant of ~s in north. [OE *dæl,* OS *dal,* OHG *tal,* ON *dalr,* Goth. *dal(s)* f. Gmc *dal-*; see DELL]

dăll′ў, v.i. & t. Amuse oneself, make sport; toy amorously (*with* or abs.); coquet *with* temptation etc.; be evasive *with* person or business; idle, loiter, delay; ~ *away,* consume (time, opportunity) to no purpose. Hence **dăll′iANCE** n. [f. OF *dalier* chat]

Dălmā′tian (-shn), n. (Also ~ *dog*) spotted dog kept to run with carriage. [*Dalmatia,* -AN]

dălmăt′ic, n. Wide-sleeved loose long vestment with slit sides worn by deacons & bishops on some occasions, & by kings & emperors esp. at coronation. [ME, f. OF *dalmatique* or LL *dalmatica* (*vestis* robe) of Dalmatia]

dăl segno (sān′yō), mus. direction (abbr. *D.S.*). Repeat from point indicated. [It.]

dalt′onĭsm (dawl-), n. Colour-blindness, esp. inability to distinguish green from red. [f. F *daltonisme* f. John *Dalton,* Eng. chemist so affected, d. 1844, -ISM(2)]

dăm¹, n., & v.t. **1.** Barrier constructed to hold back water & raise its level, to form a reservoir, or to prevent flooding; causeway; water confined by~. **2.** v.t. (-mm-). Furnish or confine with ~ (usu. *up*); block *up,* obstruct, (lit. & fig.). [12th c., app. f. MLG, MDu. *dam* (= OFris. *dam*, MHG *tam*, ON *dammr*), cf. (f. same stem but not directly related) OE *fordemman* (ME *demme*), = Goth. *faurdammjan* stop up, shut off]

dăm², n. Mother (usu. of beast); *the devil & his ~*, the powers of evil. [ME; var. DAME]

dăm'age, n., & v.t. 1. Harm (*to one's great ~*), injury impairing value or usefulness; (Law; pl.) sum of money claimed or adjudged in compensation for loss or injury; (sl.) cost (*what's the ~?*). 2. v.t. Injure (usu. thing) so as to diminish value; detract from reputation of (person etc.; *trying to ~ the Government*; *a damaging admission*); hence ~ABLE (-Ija-) a. [ME, f. OF *damage*(r) f. *dam* loss f. L *damnum* +-AGE]

dămascēne', -skeen', v.t. Ornament (metal) with inlaid gold or silver; ornament (steel) with watered pattern produced in welding. [f. *Damascus*, -*cene* thr. L f. Gk *damaskēnos*,-*keen* thr. F & It.]

dăm'ask, n. & a., & v.t. 1. ~ *rose*, old variety brought from Damascus; its colour; figured woven material (prop. of silk); twilled table-linen with woven designs shown by reflection of light; steel of or as of Damascus, with wavy surface-pattern due to special welding of iron & steel together. 2. adj. Coloured like ~ rose, blush-red; made of or resembling the silk, linen, or steel. 3. v.t. Weave with figured designs; = DAMASCENE; ornament with pattern; make (cheek etc.) red. [ME, f. AF **damasc* f. L *Damascus*]

dāme, n. (Arch., poet., or joc., for) lady; ∥ keeper, male or female, of Eton boarding house; (Law; ∥ prefixed title of) wife of knight or baronet (*Lady* in ordinary use; cf. *D~ Fortune*, *D~ Nature*); ∥ lady member of Order of British Empire (also as prefix corresp. *Sir*); *D~ Commander*, *D~ Grand Cross*, (ranks in Order of B.E. & in R.V.O.); ∥ higher female member of Primrose League; ∥ *~-school*, primary school of the kind formerly kept by old women; *~'s violet*, cruciferous plant with pale lilac flowers that have no scent until evening. [ME, f. OF f. L *domina* mistress]

dămm'ar, n. Resin obtained from certain Indian and Australasian coniferous trees, used in varnish-making. [Malay *damar*]

dămn (-m), v.t. & i., & n. 1. Condemn, censure, (*~ a person's character*); (Theatr., of audience) receive coldly, secure the withdrawal of, (play); bring condemnation upon, be the ruin of; ~ *with faint praise*, commend so frigidly as to suggest disapproval; doom to hell (so in optative, often *d——*, = *may God ~* person or thing, or with object omitted; *~ed*, or *I'll be ~ed, if I know* etc., colloq. negation); cause the damnation of, (person or thing, or abs.; esp. ~ *your eyes*, or *impudence !*). 2. n. An uttered curse; a

negligible amount (*don't care, not worth, a~*). [ME, f. OF *damner* f. L *damnare* (*damnum* loss, harm)]

dăm'nab|le, a. Subject to, deserving damnation; hateful, confounded, annoying. Hence ~LY² adv. [ME, f. OF f. LL *damnabilis* as prec., -ABLE]

dămnā'tion, n. & int. Damning of play; (condemnation to) eternal punishment in hell; (int.) = may ~ take a person or thing. [ME, f. OF f. L *damnationem* (DAMN, -ATION)]

dăm'natory, a. Conveying, causing, censure or damnation. [f. L *damnatorius* (*damnare* DAMN, -ORY)]

dămned (-md), a. & adv. In vbl senses; also or esp.: *the ~*, souls in hell; damnable, infernal, unwelcome; confoundedly, extremely, (~ or *d—d* or *damn' hot, funny*, etc.). [-ED¹]

dăm'ni|fy, v.t. (legal). Cause injury to. Hence ~FICA'TION n. [f. OF *damnifier* f. LL *damnificare* (*damnum* loss, -FY)]

dămn'ing¹ (-mī-), n. In vbl senses; esp., cursing. [-ING¹]

dămn'ing² (-mn-, -mī-), a. In vbl senses; esp., ~ *evidence*, that secures conviction. [-ING²]

dămnōs'a herēd'itās, n. Inheritance that brings more burden than profit. [L]

Dăm'oclēs (-z), n. *Sword of ~*, imminent danger in midst of prosperity. [Greek who was feasted with sword hung by a hair over him]

Dăm'on and Pȳth'iās, n. & a. (As of) devoted friends (~ *friendship*). [Gk tale]

dăm'osĕl (-z-), -zĕl, n. (arch.). Var. of DAMSEL.

dămp, n., a., & v.t. 1. 1. = CHOKE¹-~ (also *black~*); = FIRE¹-~; moisture in air, on surface, or diffused through solid; dejection, chill, discouragement, (*cast* or *strike a ~ over* or *into*); ~(-*proof*) *course*, layer of slate etc. in wall to keep ~ from rising; hence ~²PROOF a. 2. adj. Slightly wet; hence ~'EN³ v.t. & i. (chiefly U.S.), ~'ISH¹(2) a., ~'LY² adv., ~'NESS n. 3. vb. Stifle, choke, dull, extinguish, (~ *down a fire*, heap with ashes etc., to check combustion); (Mus.) stop vibration of (string); discourage, depress, (zeal, hopes); moisten; (Gardening) ~ *off*, rot, & fall off from ~. [late 15th c., f. MLG *damp* vapour etc., = OHG *dampf*]

dăm'per, n. Person or thing that depresses; (Piano) pad silencing string except when removed by pedal or by note's being struck; metal plate in flue controlling combustion; contrivance for wetting paper, stamps, etc.; (Austral.) unleavened cake baked in wood ashes. [-ER¹]

dăm'sel (-zl), n. (arch. & literary). Young unmarried woman. [ME, f. OF *dameisele* f. Rom. **domnicella* dim. of L *domina* mistress]

dăm'son (-z-), n. & a. Small dark-purple plum (~ *plum*, larger but similar); tree bearing it; ~ *cheese*, solid conserve of ~s & sugar; (adj.) ~-coloured. [ME *damascene* f. L *damascenum* (*prunum* plum) of Damascus]

dăn, n. (Also ~ *buoy*) small buoy used as a mark in deep-sea fishing; steel canister attached to a long flagged pole showing limits of area cleared by mine-sweepers (~*n'er*, ~-*layer*, vessel laying these). [orig. unkn.]

Danaos. See TIMEO.

dance[1] (dah-), v.i. & t. Move with rhythmical steps, glides, leaps, revolutions, gestures, etc., usu. to music, alone or with a partner or set (~ *to* one's *tune* or *pipe*, follow his lead); jump about, skip, move in lively way (of heart, blood, etc.); bob up and down on water etc. (~ *upon nothing*, be hanged); perform (minuet, waltz, etc.); ~ *attendance* (*upon* person), be kept waiting (by), follow about; cause to ~ (bears etc.); toss up & down, dandle, (baby); ~ *away, off, into*, etc., lose, bring, etc., by dancing (*his head off, his chance away, herself into favour*). [ME, f. OF *danser* f. Rom. *dansare* of unkn. orig.]

dance[2] (dah-), n. Dancing motion (see prec.); some special form of this; single round or turn of one; tune for dancing to, or in ~ rhythm; dancing-party; *lead* (person) *a* ~, cause him much trouble; *D*~ *of Death* or *of Macabre*, medieval picture-subject of Death leading all ranks to grave; *St Vitus's* ~, disorder chiefly in children with convulsive involuntary movements. [ME, f. OF f. *danser* (prec.)]

dan'cer (dah-), n. In vbl senses; esp.: one who dances in public for money; ‖ *merry* ~*s*, aurora borealis. [-ER[1]]

dăn'dĕlion, n. Yellow-flowered composite plant with widely toothed leaves. [f. F *dent de lion* lion's tooth]

dăn'der, n. (colloq., esp. U.S.). Temper, anger, indignation, (*get* one's ~ *up*, grow, make him, angry). [orig. unkn.]

Dăn'die Din'mont. Breed of terrier. [character in *Guy Mannering*]

dăn'dle, v.t. Dance (child) on knee or in arms; pet. [16th c., of unkn. orig.; cf. It. *dandolare* waggle]

dăn'druff, -iff, n. Dead skin in small scales among the hair, scurf. [also -*riff*, -*raff, dander*, of unkn. orig.]

dăn'dy[1], n. & a. (Person) devoted to smartness esp. of costume, neat, smart, decorated, whence **dăndi'ACAL** a., **dăn'dify** v.t., **dăndifICA'TION** n., ~ISH[1] a., ~ISM(2) n.; *(colloq.) very good of its kind, splendid, first-rate; sloop with special rig; ‖ (also ~-*cart*) spring-cart used by milkmen; ~-*brush*, of whalebone etc. for cleaning horse. [1780 in Scotland, where *Dandy* also stands for *Andrew*]

dăn'dy[2], n. = DENGUE. [W.-Ind. Negro corrupt.]

dăn'dy[3], n. (Anglo-Ind.). Strong cloth hammock slung from bamboo pole, car-

ried shoulder-high by two or more men (a common means of transport in hilly districts). [Hind. *ḍanḍī* (*ḍaṇḍ* staff)]

Dāne, n. Native of Denmark; (hist.) Northman invader of England; (also *Great* ~) powerful short-haired breed of dog. [ME, f. ON *Danir* (in OE *Dene*, as in *Denmark*), LL *Dani*]

Dāne'gĕld, -gĕlt, (-ng-), n. (Hist.) annual tax prob. imposed orig. in 10th c. to provide funds to protect England against the Danes, & later continued as a land tax; (transf.) appeasement by bribery. [f. prec. +ON *gjeld* payment]

dăn'ger (-j-), n. Liability or exposure to harm, risk, peril, (*of* one's *life, of* death or other evil; *in* ~ *of*, likely to incur etc.); position of railway signal directing stoppage or caution (*signal is at* ~); thing that causes peril (*a* ~ *to the peace of Europe, to navigation*). So ~OUS a., ~OUSLY[2] adv., (-j-). [earlier sense *power* f. OF *dangier* f. Rom. *dominiarium* f. L *dominus* lord]

dang'le (dang'gl), v.i. & t. Be suspended & sway to & fro; hold or carry (thing) swaying loosely; hold (hopes etc.) as temptation *before* person, *in* his sight, etc.; hover *after, round, about*, person as a follower, lover, etc., whence ~ER[1] n. [16th c., of unkn. orig.; cf. Da. *dangle*]

Dăn'iel (-yel), n. Upright judge, person of infallible wisdom. [*Dan.* i–vi, & *Merchant of Venice*, IV. i. 223, 333]

Dăn'ish, a. & n. (Language) of Denmark or the Danes. [OE *Denisc* (-ISH[1]), altered after DANE]

dănk, a. Soaked, oozy; unpleasantly or unwholesomely damp (of air, weather, etc.). [ME, prob. f. Scand.; cf. Sw. *dank* marshy spot]

Dănte'an, a. & n. (Student) of Dante; in Dante's style or recalling his descriptions. So **Dăntesque'** a., **Dăn'tist**(3) n. [-AN]

dăp, v.i. & t. (-pp-), n. Fish by letting bait bob on water; dip lightly; make (ball) bounce, (of ball) bounce, on ground; (n.) bounce of ball. [cf. DAB[1]]

dăph'nĕ, n. Kinds of flowering shrub. [Gk (-ē), = laurel]

dăpp'er, a. Neat, smart, in appearance or movement. [ME, f. MDu. *dapper* strong, stout, cogn. w. OHG *tapfar*]

dăp'ple, v.t. & i., & n. Variegate, become variegated, with rounded spots or patches of colour or shade; (n.) ~d effect; ~-*grey*, (horse) of grey with darker spots. [of unkn. orig; ON *apalgrár*, G *apfelgrau*, F *gris-pommelé*, & other parallels, suggest some connexion with *apple*]

dărb'ies (-biz), n. pl. (sl.). Handcuffs. [allus. use of *Father Darby's bands*, some rigid form of band for debtors (16th c.)]

Dărb'y and Joan, n. Devoted old married couple. [perh. f. poem 1735 in *Gentleman's Mag.*]

dāre, v.t. (before expressed or implied infin. without *to*, the 3 sing. pres. is usu.

~, the past & conditional often *durst*; otherwise ~*s*, ~*d*; infin. without *to* is usual only after the sense *venture* in negative or virtually negative sentence), & n. **1.** Venture (to), have the courage or impudence (to), (*I ~ swear*, feel sure that; *~ he do it? he ~s* to insult me; *I would if I durst* or ~*d*; *they ~d* or *durst not come, did not ~ to come*); attempt, take the risks of, (*~ all things, a leap, the event*, person's *anger*); defy (person); challenge (person) *to do, to it*, etc.; *I ~ say* (rare exc. in 1st person; 3rd sing. in reported speech, *he ~s* to say, past *he ~d say* or *to say*), am prepared to believe, do not deny, = very likely (often iron.); ~'*devil*, reckless (person). **2.** n. Act of daring, challenge. [a Gmc preterite-present (cf. CAN); OE *durran*, OS *gidurran*, OHG *giturran*, Goth. *gadaursan*, f. Gmc. **ders-*, **dars-*, **durs-*; cf. Gk *tharseŏ* be bold]

|| **darg**, n. (Sc.). A day's work, a definite amount of work. [contr. f. *daywerk* or *daywark* day-work]

dar'ĭ, n. = DURRA.

dar'ing[1], n. In vbl senses; esp., adventurous courage. [-ING[1]]

dar'ing[2], a. In vbl senses; esp., adventurous, bold. Hence ~LY[2] adv. [-ING[2]]

dark[1], a. With no or relatively little light, unilluminated (*~ lantern*, that can have its light covered), gloomy, sombre; of colour more or less near black (esp. as pref. to adjj. of colour as ~-*brown*; ~ BLUE[2]s); brown-complexioned, not fair; evil, atrocious; cheerless (~ *side of things*); sad, sullen (*a ~ humour*), frowning; obscure (~ *saying*, ~ *oblivion*); secret (*keep* thing ~; *keep* ~, remain in hiding); little known of (~ *horse*, one of whose racing form little is known, & fig. of persons); unenlightened (*in the ~est ignorance*; *the ~ ages*, Middle Ages, also, & esp., the period between the break-up of the Roman Empire (A.D. 395) & the end of the 10th c.); *the D~ Continent* (in last two senses), Africa; ~ *room*, with actinic rays excluded for treating photographic films. Hence ~'ISH[1](2) a., ~'LY[2] adv., ~'NESS n. (*Prince of ~ness*, the Devil). [OE *deorc*; as adj. exclusively E, but cf. OHG *tarchanjan* to hide]

dark[2], n. Absence of light (esp. *in the ~*); nightfall (*at ~*); dark colour (esp. in art, *the lights and ~s of a picture*); want of knowledge (*am in the ~ about it*; *leap in the ~*, rash step or enterprise). Hence ~'SOME a. (poet.). [f. prec.]

dark'en, v.t. & i. Make or become DARK[1]; ~ one's *door*, pay him a visit (usu. neg.); ~ *counsel*, make perplexity worse. [-EN[6]]

dark'le, v.i. Lie concealed; grow dark. [mod. back formation f. foll. misunderstood as part.]

dark'ling, adv. & a. In the dark. [-LING[2]]

dark'ỹ, -ey, n. (colloq.). Negro. [-Y[3]]

dar'ling, n. & a. Loved, best loved, lovable, (person or animal). [OE *dēorling* (DEAR, -LING[1])]

darn[1], v.t., & n. **1.** Mend (esp. knitting) by interweaving yarn with needle across hole, whence ~'ING[1](5) n.; ~'*ing-ball*, *last*, for stretching work during operation. **2.** n. Place so mended. [c. 1600, perh. f. MDu. *dernen* stop holes in (a dike)]

darn[2], v.t. (sl.). Damn (as imprecation). [deformation of DAMN]

darn'el, n. Kind of grass growing as weed among corn. [prob. f. Walloon *darnelle*]

dart, n., & v.t. & i. **1.** Pointed missile, esp. light javelin, || (pl.) indoor game with toy ~s & target; sting of insect etc.; sudden rapid motion; act of throwing missile. **2.** vb. Throw (missile), throw missile; emit suddenly (glance, flash, anger); start rapidly in some direction. [ME, f. OF *dart* (mod. *dard*) f. Frank. *daroth]

dart'er, n. In vbl senses; also: web-footed bird of pelican tribe; (pl.) order of birds including kingfishers & bee-eaters; kinds of fish. [-ER[1]]

dar'tle, v.t. & i. Keep on darting. [-LE(3)]

Dart'moor, n. (Used for) ~ convict prison near Princetown, Devon.

Dart'mouth (-mu-), n. (Used for) Royal Naval College, ~, Devon.

dar'tre (-ter), n. Kinds of skin disease, esp. herpes. So **dar'trous** a. [F, in OF *dertre*, med. L *derbita* f. Gaulish ~*dervita*]

Darwin'ian, a. & n. Of, person believing in, Charles Darwin (d. 1882) or his doctrines esp. on evolution of species. So **Dar'winism**(3) n., **Dar'winist**(2) n. & a., **Darwinis'tic** a., **Dar'winite**[1](1) n. & a., **Dar'winize**(2, 4) v.t. & i.

dash[1], v.t. & i. Shatter *to pieces* (rarely abs., as *flowers ~ed by rain*); knock, drive, throw, or thrust, *away, off, out, down*, etc.; fling, drive, splash, (thing or person) *against, upon, into*; bespatter *with* water etc. (~'*board*, of wood or leather in front of vehicle to keep out mud, board beneath motor-car windscreen containing instruments; ~*ed with colour*); dilute, qualify, (water *with* spirit, joy *with* pain); frustrate (~ one's *hopes*), daunt, discourage, confound; write *down* or throw *off* rapidly (composition, sketch); underline; (sl.) = *damn* as mild imprecation; fall, move, throw oneself, with violence; come into collision *against, upon*; ride, run, or drive *up*, move about, behave, with spirit or display, whence ~'ING[2] a., ~'ingLY[2] adv. [ME *dasse*, *dasche*, prob. imit.; cf. Sw. *daska* to beat]

dash[2], n. Sound of water striking or struck; splash of colour; infusion (~ *of brandy, of good blood*); hasty pen-stroke; horizontal stroke in writing or printing to mark a break in sense, a parenthesis (two ~es), omitted letters or words, etc.; rush, onset, sudden advance; (capacity for) vigorous action; showy appearance or behaviour (*cut a ~*, make a brilliant show). [f. prec.]

dăsh'er, n. In vbl senses; esp., contrivance for agitating cream in churn. [-ER¹]

dăs'tard, n. Coward skulker, esp. one who commits brutal act without endangering himself. Hence ~LY¹ a., ~liness n. [prob. f. *dazed* p.p. +-ARD]

dă'sўūre, n. (Kinds of) small ferocious arboreal cat-like carnivorous marsupial found in Australia and Tasmania. [Gk *dasus* rough + *oura* tail]

dāt'a. See DATUM.

‖ **dăt'aller, day'taler**, n. Workman engaged and paid by the day. [DAY, TALE in sense *reckoning*, -ER¹]

dāte¹, n. W.-Asian & N.-Afr. tree (also ~-*palm*), or its fruit, an oblong single--seeded berry. [ME, f. OF, f. L f. Gk *daktulos* finger]

dāte², n. Statement in document, letter, book, or inscription, of the time (& often place) of execution, writing, publication, etc.; time at which thing happens or is to happen; *(colloq.)* engagement, appointment; period to which antiquities etc. belong; person's age, duration, term of life, (arch. or poet.); (*go*) *out of* ~, (become) obsolete; *up to* ~ (f. book--keeping phr. for accounts completed to current day, now as adj. & adv.), meeting, according to, the latest requirements of knowledge; ~-*line*, meridian 180° from Greenwich, east & west of which the ~ differs, line in newspaper at head of message, special article, etc., giving ~ & place of dispatch. [ME, f. F f. L *data* fem. p.p. of *dare* = (letter) given (at such a time & place)]

dāte³, v.t. & i. Mark (letter etc.) with date (~*d from London*), whence dāt'ER¹(2) n.; refer (event) to a time;* (colloq.) make an appointment with; count time, reckon, (*dating from the Creation*); bear date, be ~d; have origin *from* (*church* ~s *from the 14th c.*); (of art, style, etc.) become· recognizable as of a past or particular period; be or become out of date. Hence dāt'ABLE a. [f. prec.]

dāte'less (-tl-), a. Undated; endless; immemorial. [f. DATE², ³, -LESS]

dāt'ive, a. & n. ~ (*case*), the case in nouns, pronouns, & adjj., proper to the remoter object or recipient. So dativ'AL a., ~LY³ (-vl-) adv. [f. OF (-*if, -ive*) or L *dativus* (*dare dat-* give, -IVE)]

dāt'um, n. (pl. -*ta*). Thing known or granted, assumption or premiss from which inferences may be drawn; fixed starting-point of scale etc. (ORDNANCE ~); (pl.) facts of any kind, notes. [L, neut. p.p. of *dare* give]

datūr'a, n. Kinds of poisonous plant, including stramonium, yielding strong narcotic. [f. Hind. *dhatura*]

daub, v.t. & i., & n. Coat (wall etc.) *with* plaster, clay, etc. (n., the material); smear (surface; n., a smear), lay on

(greasy or sticky stuff); soil, stain; paint (t. & i.) inartistically, lay (colours) *on* so, (n., a coarse painting), whence ~ER¹, ~'STER, nn., ~Y² a. [ME, f. OF *dauber* f. L DE(*albare* f. *albus* white) whitewash]

daught'er (dawt-), n. One's female child; female descendant, female member of family, race, etc.; woman who is the spiritual or intellectual product of person or thing; product personified as female (*Carthage ~ of Tyre; Fortune and its ~ Confidence*; ~-*language*, as French of Latin); ~-*in-law*, son's wife, (loosely) step~. Hence ~HOOD n., ~LY¹ a. [OE *dohtor*, OS -*ar*, OHG *tochter*, ON *dóttir*, Goth. *dauhtar*, cogn. w. Gk *thugatēr*]

daunt, v.t. Discourage, intimidate; press (herrings) down in barrel. [ME, f. OF *danter* (now *dompter*) f. L *domitare* frequent. of *domare* tame]

daunt'less, a. Intrepid, persevering. Hence ~LY² adv., ~NESS n. [perh. f. obs. *daunt* a check f. prec. +-LESS]

dauph'in, dauph'iness, nn. (hist:). (Wife of) King of France's eldest son. [ME; family name (f. L *delphinus* DOLPHIN) of lords of Dauphiné, last of whom ceded it on condition of *dauphin*'s being accepted as French heir-apparent's title]

‖ **dăv'enpŏrt**, n. Escritoire with drawers & hinged writing-slab. [prob. maker's name]

Dăv'id and Jŏn'athan, n. Any pair of devoted friends. [1 *Sam.* xviii etc.]

dăv'it, n. Crane on board ship used for hoisting anchor, torpedo, etc. inboard or outboard; one of pair of cranes for suspending or lowering ship's boat. [ME, f. OF *daviot* (mod. *davier*), dim. of OF *Davi* David]

Dăv'ў (lămp), n. Miner's wire-gauze safety lamp. [Sir H. *Davy* (d. 1829), inventor]

dăv'ў, n. (sl.). Take one's ~, swear (*that, to* fact). [short for AFFIDAVIT]

Dăv'ў Jone's's lŏck'er (jōnzĭz), n. The deep, a watery grave (in the sea). [f. 1751; allusion unkn.]

daw, n. = JACKDAW. [ME, corresp. to OE *dawa*, OHG *tāha* (G *dohle*)]

daw'dl|e, v.i. & t., & n. Idle, dally; ~e *away* (time etc.), waste; hence ~ER¹ n.; (n.) ~ing person. [cf. dial. *daddle, doddle*, in same sense]

dawk, dâk, dak, (dawk), n. (Anglo-Ind.). Post or transport by relays of men or horses; relay; ~ *bungalow*, house for travellers at ~ station. [Hind.]

dawn, v.i., & n. 1. Begin to appear or grow light (of day, daylight, morning, country shone upon, things becoming evident to mind, intelligence, civilization, etc.); *first* ~*ings* etc., beginning; ~*ing*, the East; ~ *upon*, begin to be perceptible to. 2. n. First light, daybreak, rise or incipient gleam of anything. [*dawn* vb (whence the n.) deduced f. *dawning* (c. 1300), app. f. ON (cf. OSw. *daghning*);

these wds replaced older *daw* vb (OE *dagian*), *dawing* (OE *dagung*)]

day, n. **1.** Time while sun is above horizon, (loosely) including twilights (~ *& night*, adv., throughout these or in both alike; *all*~, *all the*~, adv., throughout it; ~'*break*, *break of* ~, dawn; ~*-dream*, *-ing*, *-er*, reverie or castle in air, indulgence, indulger, in them); dawn (*before*, *at*, ~); daylight (*by* ~; *was broad* ~; *clear as* ~). **2.** Twenty-four hours (*solar* or *astronomical* ~, from noon; *civil* ~, from midnight; *sidereal* ~, between two meridional transits of first point of Aries, about 4' shorter than *solar*; *natural* ~, = sidereal, also in first sense above). **3.** Civil ~ as point of time, date, etc. (*one* ~, adv., on an unspecified date past or future; *the other* ~, on a ~ not long ago; *one of these* ~*s* or *fine* ~*s*, before long, in prophecy or promise; *some* ~, adv., in the future; *on one's* ~, when he is at his best; ~ *of* GRACE). **4.** Date of specified festival etc. (*first* ~, Sunday; *Christmas* ~, *birth*~, *pay*~, *last Day* or *Day of* JUDGEMENT). **5.** Date agreed upon (*keep* one's ~, be punctual; *one's* ~, for being at home to guests, esp. *once a week*). **6.** Victory (*carry*, *win*, *lose*, *the* ~). **7.** Period (often pl., *in the* ~*s of*, *the* ~*s of old*, *in* ~*s to come*, *men of other* ~*s*; *better* ~*s*, when one was or will be better off; *fallen on evil* ~*s*, in misfortune; sing., *at*, *to*, *this* ~; *present*~, adj. = modern; *these*~*s*, adv., nowadays; *the* ~, the current ~; *sufficient for the* ~ *is the evil thereof*, do not anticipate trouble; *men of the* ~, persons of importance at any time; *creature of a* ~, short-lived). **8.** One's ~, lifetime, period of prosperity, activity, power, etc., (also pl. *end* one's ~*s*, die; *every dog has his* ~, no one always unlucky). **9.** *This* ~ *week*, *month*, *year*, reckoning forward or back from *to*~; ~ *about*, on alternate ~*s*; ~ *by* ~, ~ *after*, *from* ~ *to* ~, *every* ~, advv. of daily repetition or progress; *twice* etc. *a* ~, in each ~ (see A²); *call it a* ~, consider that one has done a ~'s work; *know the time of* ~, be wide awake, knowing; *the* ~ *before*, *after*, *the fair*, advv., too early, late, for opportunity. **10.** ∥~*-boarder*, schoolboy feeding but not sleeping at school; ~*-book* in book-keeping, book in which esp. sale transactions are entered at once for later transfer to ledger; ∥~*-boy*, schoolboy living at home;~*-fly*, ephemerid;~*-labourer*, hired by ~ at fixed wage; ~*-long* a. & adv., (lasting) for whole ~; ~*-owl*, hawk-owl hunting by ~; ~*-room*, used by ~ only, esp. common living-room at schools; ~*-school*, opp. Sunday, evening, or boarding school; ~*-spring*, dawn (poet.); ~*-ticket*, covering return on same~; ~*-time*, not night, esp. *in the* ~*-time*. [OE *dæg*,

OS *dag*, OHG *tac*, ON *dagr*, Goth. *dags* f. Gmc **dagaz*]

day'light (*-lit*), n. Light of day (BURN³ ~); openness, publicity; *let* ~ *into* (sl.), stab or shoot; dawn (*before*, *at*, ~); visible interval as between boats in race, wine & glass-rim (*no* ~, fill up), or rider & saddle; ~*-saving*, use of fictitious time in summer prolonging ~ working hours.

daze, v.t. & n. **1.** Stupefy, bewilder; dazzle; hence **dāz'ĕdLY²** adv. **2.** n. Stupefaction, bewilderment. [ME *dasen* f. ON; cf. Icel. *dasask* refl. vb become weary]

dăz'zl|e, v.t., & n. **1.** Confuse or dim (sight, eye, person) with excess of light, intricate motion, incalculable number, etc.; confound or surprise (mind, person) by brilliant display lit. or fig.; ~*ed with* or *by*; ~*e lamps* or *lights* (over-bright, on motor-car); ~*e paint* (so patterned on ship as to deceive enemy about her type or course); hence ~**EMENT** (*-lm-*) n., ~**ǐngLY³** adv. **2.** n. Glitter. [f. prec. + -LE(3)]

D-Day, n. Day (6 June 1944) on which British and American forces invaded N. France. [*D* for day]

de-, pref. f. L adv. & prep. *de*. As an etymological element: (1) in senses down (*depend*), away (*defend*, *deduce*), completely (*declare*, *denude*), in a bad sense (*deceive*, *deride*); (2) repr. L *dis-* (in privative sense, largely replacing *de-*), thr. Rom., OF *des-*, later *de-* (mod. F *dé-*). Early adoptives in E retained OF *des-* later refash. *dis-* (as in *disarm*); later wds have *de-* wh. was treated as identical with *de-* f. L *de-*; hence (3) as a living pref. with privative force forming compd vbs (with derivatives) as *de-acidify*, *decentralize*, *demoralize*, *denazify* (*-ication*).

deac'on, n. (Primitive Church) appointed minister of charity (*Acts* vi. 1–6); (Episcopal) member of third order of ministry below bishop & priest; (Baptist, Congregational, Presbyterian) officer attending to congregation's secular affairs. Hence ~**SHIP** n. [OE, f. LL f. Gk *diakonos* servant]

deac'oness, n. Woman in primitive & some modern Churches with functions analogous to deacon's. [f. LL *diaconissa* (prec., -ESS¹)]

dead (dĕd), a., n., & adv. **1.** That has ceased to live (*the* ~, n., ~ person or persons, or all who have ever died; *from the* ~, from among these; ~ *men tell no tales*, argument for killing possessor of secret; ~*house*, mortuary; ~ *march*, march-like funeral music; ~*-office*, funeral service; ~ *as a doornail*, quite ~; ~ *& gone*; *wait for* ~ *men's* SHOES; FLOG ~ *horse*; ~ *men* or *marines*, empty bottles; ~ *man's finger*, *hand*, *thumb*, kinds of orchid; ~ *man's handle*, the controlling handle in electric trains which must be held and pressed down for current to pass, so that slackening by death or illness cuts the current & stops the train). 2. Benumbed, insensible, (of hands etc.; also ~ *to*, unconscious or unappreciative of, hardened against). 3. Without spiritual life. 4. Obsolete, past, not effective, (~ *language*, one no longer in ordinary use, e.g. ancient Gk; ~ *letter*, law no longer observed, unclaimed or undelivered letter at post office). 5. Inanimate (~ *fence*, of timber etc., opp. *quickset*; ~ *matter*): extinct, dull, lustreless, without force, muffled, (~ *brand*, *coal*; ~ *gold*, unburnished; ~ *colour*, first layer in picture, cold & pale; ~-*nettle*, non-stinging weed like nettle; ~-*alive*, spiritless; ~ *sound*, not resonant). 6. Inactive, motionless, idle, (D~ *Sea*; ~ *point* or ~ *centre*, least & greatest extension of piston or crank, where it exerts no effective power; ~ *weight*, inert, of lifeless matter, also fig. of debt etc.; ~ *pull*, *lift*, at thing too heavy for one to move; ~ *freight*, sum paid in chartering ship for part not occupied by cargo; ~ *arch*, *window*, etc., sham; ~ *end*, terminus of branch line of railway etc.; ~ *hand*, = MORTMAIN, usu. implying protest; ~ *hours*, still, in night; ~ *season*; ~ *stock*, unemployed capital, unsalable goods; ~ *ball*, out of play; *wind falls* ~; as n., = ~ *time*, *at* ~ *of night*, *in the* ~ *of winter*). 7. Abrupt, complete, unrelieved, exact, (*come to* ~ *stop*; *a* ~ *faint*; *on a* ~ *level*; ~ *heat*, exact equality in race, ~-*heat* v.i. & t.; ~ *spit* (colloq.), very counterpart *of*; *a* ~ *calm*; ~ *loss*, without compensation; *be in* ~ *earnest*; *a* ~ *certainty*; ~ *on the target*, quite straight, so ~ *shot*, unerring; ~'*lock*, utter standstill, also as v.t.). 8. (Golf, of ball) very close to hole, within certain holing distance. 9. ~-*alive*, (of place, occupation, etc.) dull, tedious, monotonous; ~-*eye* (Naut.), round flat three-holed block for extending shrouds; ~-*fire*, St Elmo's fire, as presaging death; ~ *ground*, *water* (out of reach of a fort's guns, infantry fire, etc.); ~'*head*, non-paying theatre-goer or passenger; ~'*light* (Naut.), shutter inside porthole to prevent light showing out; ~ (-) *line*, line beyond which it is not permitted or possible to go, fixed limit of time, (U.S. prisons) painted line across exercise-yard on crossing which a prisoner is liable to be shot; ~ *man's* (or *men's*) *fingers*, finger-like divisions of gills in lobster or crab; *~ pan* (sl.), expressionless immobile face; ~ *reckoning* (Naut.), of ship's position by log, compass, etc., when observations are impossible; D~-*Sea* APPLE; hence ~'NESS n. 10. adv. Profoundly, absolutely, completely, (~ *asleep*, *level*, *straight*, *tired*, *drunk*; ~-*beat*, tired out, (Mech.) without recoil, *(n., sl.) worthless sponger; CUT² ~; ~ *against*, directly opposite to). [OE *dēad*, OS *dōd*, OHG

tōt, ON *dauthr*, Goth. *dauths* f. Gmc *dauthaz* f. *dau-* DIE²]

dead′en (dĕd-), v.t. & i. Deprive of or lose vitality, force, brightness, feeling, etc.; make insensible *to*. [-EN⁶]

dead′ly¹ (dĕd-), a. Causing fatal injury; of poisonous nature (~ *nightshade*); entailing damnation (~ *sin*); implacable, internecine; deathlike (~ *paleness*, *faintness*, *gloom*); intense (*in* ~ *haste*; ~ *dullness*). Hence **dead′liNESS** n. [OE *dēadlic* (DEAD, -LY¹)]

dead′ly² (dĕd-), adv. As if dead (~ *white*, *faint*); extremely (~ *tired*, *dull*). [OE *dēadlice* (DEAD, -LY²)]

deaf (dĕf), a. Wholly or partly without hearing (*the* ~, ~ *people*; ~ *of an*, *or in one*, *ear*; ~ *as an adder* or *a post*; *none so* ~ *as those that won't hear*); insensible *to* harmony, rhythm, etc.; not giving ear *to*, uncompliant, (*turn a* ~ *ear to*); ~ *nut*, with no kernel; ~-*&-dumb alphabet*, *language*, etc., signs for communication by the ~; ~ *mute*, ~ *& dumb person*. Hence ~'LY² adv., ~'NESS n. [OE *dēaf*, OS *dof*, OHG *toup*, ON *daufr*, Goth. *daufs* f. Gmc *daubhaz*]

deaf′en (dĕf-), v.t. Deprive of hearing by noise; make (sound) inaudible by louder one; make (floor etc.) impervious to sound. [-EN⁶]

deal¹, n. *A great*, *good*, ~, large, considerable, amount; (sl.) *a* ~, = a great ~; (same phrases used adv.) to a large, considerable, extent, (esp. with comparative or superl.) by much, considerably. [OE *dǣl*, OS *dēl*, OHG *teil*, Goth. *dails*, f. Gmc *dailiz*; cf. DOLE¹]

deal², v.t. & i. (~*t* pr. dĕlt), & n. 1. Distribute, give *out*, (gifts etc.) among several; deliver as his share or deserts to person (esp. of Providence etc.; ~*t him happiness*, *good measure*; of persons, esp. ~ *a blow*, abs. or with *at*, lit. & fig.). 2. Distribute cards to players for a game or round (n., such distribution, player's turn for it, as *my* ~, or round played after it), give (card, hand, etc.) to player. 3. Associate *with* (esp. neg. as *refuse to* ~ *with*); do business *with* person, *in* goods (n., colloq., a bargain or transaction; also dishonest job); *New D~*, the programme of social and economic reform planned by the Roosevelt administration of 1932 and subsequent years; *raw* ~ (colloq.), unfair treatment; *square* ~ (colloq.), justice, fair treatment. 4. Occupy oneself, grapple by way of discussion or refutation, take measures, *with*; (with adv.) behave (~ *honourably*, *cruelly*, esp. *with* or *by* person). Hence ~'ING¹(1) n. [OE *dǣlan* as prec.]

deal³, n. Piece of sawn fir or pine wood between 7 & 9 in. broad & 6 ft long, & 3 in. thick; a quantity of these; fir or pine wood. [c. 1400; f. MLG *dele* plank; see THILL]

deal′er, n. In vbl senses; esp. player

dealing at cards; trader, usu. in comb. as *corn~*. [-ER¹]

dĕămbŭlā'tion, n., **dĕăm'bŭlatŏry̆**, a. Walking. [f. L *deambulatio, deambulatorium*, f. DE(*ambulare* walk), -ATION, -ORY]

dean¹, n. Head of cathedral or collegiate--church chapter; ‖(also *rural~*) clergyman exercising supervision over group of parochial clergy within division of arch-deaconry; (colleges) resident fellow, or one of several, with disciplinary & other functions; (foreign, Scots, & modern universities) president of a faculty; =DOYEN; *D~* of *Faculty*, president of the Faculty of Advocates in Scotland. [ME *deen, dene*, f. OF *deien* f. LL *decanus* f. Gk *dekanos* one set over ten]

dean², **dēne**, n. Vale (esp. in names ending in *-dean, -dene, -den*). [OE *denu*, cogn. w. DEN]

dean'ery̆, n. Office, house, of dean; ‖ group of parishes presided over by rural dean. [-ERY]

dear, a., n., adv., & int. **1.** Beloved (often as merely polite or even ironical form in talk, esp. *my ~ sir, my ~ Jones*, & now used at beginning of most letters not intended to be markedly business-like; as n., *~* or *~'est*, esp. in voc., *= ~ one*; a *~*, esp. in coaxing formulae). **2.** Precious *to*; one's cherished (*for ~ life*, as though life were at stake). **3.** High-priced, costly, (as adv., *sell, buy, pay*, COST² one, *~*; *~ year, shop*, in which prices run high); hence *~'*LY² adv., *~'*NESS n. **4.** int. *~, ~l, ~ mel, oh ~l*, expressing surprise, distress, sympathy, etc. [OE *dēore*, OS *diuri*, OHG *tiuri*, ON *dȳrr* f. Gmc *deurjaz*]

dearth (dĕr-), n. Scarcity & dearness of food; scanty supply of. [ME *derthe* (prec., -TH¹)]

dear'ȳ, -ie, n. (usu. voc.). Dear one. [-Y³]

death (dĕth), n. **1.** Dying (DIE² *the ~*; *~'-bed*, on which one dies, *~bed repentance*, fig., change of policy made too late to bear fruit; *~-rattle*, sound in dying person's throat; *~-roll*, list of the killed or dead; *~-watch*, kinds of insect whose ticking portends *~*). **2.** End of life (*civil ~*, ceasing to count as citizen by outlawry, banishment, etc.; *catch one's ~*, i.e. fatal chill etc.; *~-duties*, tax levied before property passes to heir; *~-rate*, yearly number of *~s* to 1,000 of population; *~-trap*, unwholesome or dangerous place). **3.** Being killed or killing (*field of ~*, battlefield etc.; *be the ~ of*, kill; *do, put, stone*, etc., *to ~*; *war to the ~*, *~-feud*, till one kills or is killed; *it is, we make it, ~ to*, *~* is the penalty; *be in at the ~*, see fox killed, or fig. any enterprise ended; *be ~ on* (sl.), skilful at killing game etc., or fig. at doing anything; *sick unto, tickled to, tired to, ~*, to utmost limit; *~-adder*, kinds of venomous snake; *~-blow*, mortal,

lit. & fig.; *~-warrant*, for criminal's execution, abolition of custom etc.). **4.** Ceasing to be, annihilation, personified power that annihilates, (*at ~'s door*, soon to die; *~'s-head*, skull as emblem of mortality, also kind of moth with skull marked on back; *sure, pale, as ~*; *hold on like grim ~*; *~ on rats*, good rat-killer, of dogs; *~l*, archaic imprecation). **5.** Being dead (*~-mask*, cast taken of dead person's face; *eyes closed in ~*). **6.** Want of spiritual life (*everlasting ~*, damnation). **7.** *Black D~*, (mod. name, transl. f. G for) great pestilence of Oriental Plague in Europe in 14th c. Hence *~'*LESS a., *~'lĕ*ssLY² adv., *~'lĕ*ssNESS n., *~'*LIKE a. & adv., *~'*LY¹ a. & adv., *~'*WARD(S) a. & adv., (dĕth-). [OE *dēath*, OS *dōth*, OHG *tōd*, ON *dauthr*, Goth. *dauthus* f. Gmc *dau-* DIE², -TH¹]

°dĕb, n. (colloq.). Débutante. [abbr.]

dĕbâcle (dībah'kl), n. Break-up of ice in river; (Geol.) sudden rush of water carrying along blocks of stone and other debris; confused rush, rout, stampede; collapse, downfall, e.g. of a government. [F]

dĕbăg', v.t. (sl.; -gg-). Remove the 'bags' (= trousers) from. [DE-, BAG¹]

dĕbâr', v.t. (-rr-). Exclude *from* admission or right (also *~* person *the crown* etc.); (rare) prevent, bar, (entrance etc.). [ME, f. F *débarrer* (OF *des-*), f. *des-* DE- +*barrer* BAR²]

dĕbârk', v.t. & i. = DISEMBARK. Hence **dĕbârkA'TION** n. [f. F *débarquer* (DE-, BARK³)]

dĕbâse', v.t. Lower in quality, value, or character; adulterate (coin). Hence *~*MENT (-sm-) n. [DE- + obs. *base* for ABASE]

dĕbât'able, a. Questionable, subject to dispute, (*~ ground* lit. or fig., for which parties contend, borderland). [OF (foll., -ABLE)]

dĕbāt|e', v.t. & i., & n. **1.** Contest, fight for, (*long ~ed the victory*); dispute about, discuss, (a question); hold argument, esp. in Parliament or public meeting (*~ing--society*, for practice); consider, ponder, (t. & i.); hence *~'*ER¹ n. (esp. of one skilled rather in argument than in oratory). **2.** n. Controversy, discussion, public argument. [ME, f. OF *debat, debattre* f. Rom. *°debattere* (DE-, see BATTLE)]

dĕbauch', v.t., & n. **1.** Pervert from virtue or morality; make intemperate or sensual; seduce (woman); vitiate (taste, judgement); hence *~*ABLE a. **2.** n. Bout or habit of sensual indulgence; hence *~*ERY(4) n. [f. F *débaucher*, of unkn. orig.]

dĕbauchee' (-bosh-), n. Viciously sensual person. [f. F *débauché* p.p. see prec., -EE]

dĕbĕn'ture, n. **1.** ‖(Arch. or techn.) voucher given to person supplying goods to Royal Household or Government Office, entitling him to payment, Custom--House certificate to exporter of amount due to him as drawback or bounty. **2.** ‖ (Ord. sense) sealed bond of corporation or company acknowledging sum on which interest is due till principal is repaid, esp. fixed interest constituting prior charge on assets; ‖~ *stock*, ~s consolidated or created as stock whose nominal capital represents debt of which interest only is secured as perpetual annuity. [ME; early sp. *-ur*, app. = L *debentur* are owing]

debil'itate, v.t. Enfeeble (constitution etc.). [f. L *debilitare*, see foll., -ATE³]

debil'ity, n. Feebleness (of health, purpose, etc.). [ME, f. OF *debilite* f. L *debilitatem* (*debilis* weak, -TY)]

deb'it, n., & v.t. **1.** Entry in account of sum owing; side of account (left-hand) in which these entries are made (cf. CREDIT). **2.** v.t. Charge (person) *with* sum; enter (sum) *against* or *to* person. [f. L *debitum* DEBT]

débonair', a. Genial, pleasant, unembarrassed. [ME, f. OF *debonaire* = *de bon air* of good disposition]

débóshed' (-sht), a. (Arch. for) debauched.

débouch' (-sh; *also* -ōōsh), v.i. Issue from ravine, wood, etc., into open ground (of troops; also of stream). So~MENT (-ōōsh-) n. [f. F *déboucher* f. *dé-* DE-+*bouche* mouth]

Debrett', n. (Used for) ~'s Peerage etc. [John ~, compiler]

debris, dé-, (deb'rē), n. Scattered fragments, wreckage, drifted accumulation. [F (*dé-*), f. obs. *débriser* break down]

debt (det), n. Money, goods, or service, owing (~ *of honour*, not legally recoverable, esp. of sum lost in gambling; ‖~--*collector*, one whose business it is to collect ~s for creditors; ~ *of nature*, death; *National D*~, money owed by State in its corporate capacity; *funded*~, the part of this converted into fund of which interest only is to be paid; *floating* ~, part of it repayable on demand, or at stated time; *small* ~, of limited amount recoverable in County Court); being under obligation to pay something (*in*, *out of*, *get into*, ~ or *person's*~). [ME & OF *dette* f. Rom. *°debita* f. L *debitum* p.p. of *debēre* owe]

debt'or (det-), n. One who owes money or an obligation or duty; (Book-keeping) *Debtor, Dr*, heading of left-hand or debit side of account. [ME & OF *dettour* f. L *debitorem* (prec., -OR)]

°débunk', v.t. (colloq.). Remove the false sentiment from (person, reputation, institution, cult, etc.); remove (celebrity) from his pedestal. [DE-, BUNK³]

‖ **débus'**, v.t. & i. (-ss-). Unload (men, stores) or alight from motor vehicles. [DE-+BUS, after *detrain*]

début (see Ap.), n. First appearance in society, or on stage etc. as performer. [F] **débutant, débutante** (see Ap.), nn. Male or female performer making début; (fem.) girl coming out or being presented. [F]

deca-, dec-, pref. f. Gk *deka* ten in many technical terms as *decag'ynous* with ten pistils, *decahěd'ral* ten-sided (*-hedron*, such solid), *decān'drous* with ten stamens, *děc'astyle* ten-columned (portico); esp. in French metric system = ten of the specified unit (cf. DECI-), whence **děc'-agram, dec'alitre** (-ēter), **dec'amètre** (-ter).

děc'ade, n. Set, series, of ten; ten years; ten books (1–10, 11–20, etc.) of Livy. So **dec'adAL, decad'ic,** aa. [F *décade* f. LL *decas* -*ad*- (also *decada* fem.) f. Gk (*deka* ten), see -AD, -ADE(2)]

dec'adence, n., **dec'adent,** a. & n. Falling away, declining, deteriorating, (used esp. of a period of art or literature after culmination); (literary sl.) *decadent*, (writer or artist) affecting certain vices, obscurities, & turgidities of style. [F, f. med. L *decadentia* f. med. L *decadēre* (DECAY), see -ENCE]

dec'agon, n. Plane figure with ten sides and angles. So **decag'onAL** a. [f. med. L *decagonum* (DECA-, -GON)]

decăl'cify, v.t. Deprive (bone etc.) of its lime. [DE-]

děc'alogue (-ŏg), n. The ten commandments. [ME, f. OF, or LL f. Gk *dekalogos* (after *hoi deka logoi* the ten precepts)]

děcăm'eron, n. Collection of tales like the D~ of Boccaccio (100 tales told by a company in ten days). [f. It. *decamerone* after med. L *Hexameron*]

děcămp', v.i. Break up or leave camp; go away suddenly, take oneself off, abscond. So~MENT n. [f. F *décamper* (DE-, CAMP¹)]

děcăn'al (*or* děk'a-), a. Of dean, deanery, or south side, on which dean sits, of choir. [f. LL *decanus* DEAN¹+-AL]

děcān'i, mus. direction. To be sung by decanal side in antiphonal singing (cf. CANTORIS). [L genit. as prec.]

děcănt', v.t. Pour off (liquid or solution) by gradual inclination of vessel without disturbing sediment; pour (wine) similarly from bottle into decanter; (fig.) move or transfer as if by pouring. [f. med. L DE(*canthare* f. L. f. Gk *kanthos* CANT¹ used of lip of beaker)]

děcăn'ter, n. Stoppered glass bottle in which wine or spirit is brought to table. [-ER¹]

děcăp'itāte, v.t. Behead (esp. as legal punishment); take the head or end from. So ~ABLE a., ~A'TION n. [f. F *décapiter* or LL DE(*capitare* f. *caput -itis* head)]

děc'apŏd, n. Ten-footed crustacean. [f. F *décapode* f. Gk DECA(*pous -podos* foot)]

děcărb'onize, -ise (-īz), v.t. Deprive of its carbon or carbonic acid. [DE-]

děcă'sualize (-zhŏŏ-, -zū-), **-is|e** (-īz), v.t. Do away with the casual employment of (labour). Hence ~A′TION n. [DE-, -IZE]

dĕcas**yl̄lăb′ic**, a. & n., dĕcas**yl̄l′able**, n. & a. (Line) of ten syllables. [DECA-]

dĕcay′¹, v.i. & t. Deteriorate, lose quality, decline in power, wealth, energy, beauty, etc.; rot (t. & i.); cause to deteriorate. [ME, f. OF decair f. Rom. *DE(cadēre for L cadēre fall)]

dĕcay′², n. Decline, falling off; ruinous state, wasting away (phonetic ~, wearing down of word-forms); break-up of health, decomposition; rotten tissue (remove the ~). [f. prec.]

dĕceas|e′, n., & v.i. (Esp. in legal and formal use for) death, die, depart(ure) from life. Hence ~ED¹(2) (-ēst′) a. and n. (with or without the). [ME, f. OF deces f. L DE(cessus n. f. cedere cess-′go)]

dĕceit′ (-sēt), n. Misrepresentation, deceiving; trick, stratagem; the vice of deceitfulness; misleading appearance. Hence ~FUL a., ~fuLY² adv., ~fulNESS n., (-sēt-). [ME, f. OF deceite n. f. fem. p.p. of deceveir f. L DE(cipere -cept- = capere take) deceive]

dĕceiv|e′ (-sēv), v.t. & i. Persuade of what is false, mislead, (~e oneself, juggle with one's own convictions, also be mistaken); use deceit; disappoint (esp. hopes). So ~′ABLE a., ~′ER¹ n., (-sēv-). [ME, f. OF deceveir f. L as prec.]

dĕcĕl′erāte, v.t. Diminish speed of, cause to slow down (also abs.). [DE-, after ACCELERATE]

Dĕcĕm′b|er, n. Twelfth month of year. Hence ~RIST n., member of Russian revolutionary conspiracy in ~er 1825. [ME, f. OF decembre f. L December (decem ten) orig. tenth month of Roman year]

dĕcĕm′vir (-er), n. (pl. ~s, ~ī). (Rom. Hist.) member of board of ten acting as council or ruling power, esp. that appointed 451 B.C. to draw up laws of Twelve Tables; member of any ruling body of ten, as at Venice. So ~AL a., ~ATE¹ n. [L, f. decem viri ten men]

dĕ′cenc|y, n. Propriety of behaviour; what is required by good taste or delicacy; avoidance of obscene language & gestures & of undue exposure of person; respectability; the ~ies, decorous observances, requirements of a decent life. [f. L decentia (decēre be fitting, -ENCY)]

dĕcĕnn′ar̆y, a. & n. ·(Of) period of ten years. [f. L decennis (decem, annus) ten- -year + -ARY¹]

dĕcĕnn′iad, dĕcĕnn′ium (pl. -ia), n. Ten-year period. [-ad irreg. f. L (-um) f. decennis (prec.); see -AD]

dĕcĕnn′ial, a. Of ten-year period; recurring in ten years. Hence ~LY² adv. [f. L decennium see prec. + -AL¹]

dĕ′cent, a. Seemly, not immodest or obscene or indelicate; respectable; passable, good enough, tolerable, whence

~ISH¹(2) a.; ‖ (school sl.) kind, not severe or censorious. Hence ~LY² adv. [f. L decēre beseem, -ENT]

dĕcĕn′traliz|e, -is|e (-īz), v.t. Undo the centralization of; confer local government on. Hence ~A′TION n. [DE-]

dĕcĕp′tion, n. Deceiving, being deceived; thing that deceives, trick, sham. [ME, f. OF, or LL deceptio (decipere see DECEIT, -ION)]

dĕcĕp′tive, a. Apt to deceive, easily mistaken. Hence ~LY² (-vl-) adv., ~NESS (-vn-) n. [f. F déceptif (prec., -IVE); cf. LL deceptivus]

dĕchris′tianize (-krĭscha-), -ise (-īz), v.t. Divest of its christianity. [DE-]

dĕci-, pref. shortened from L decimus tenth, used (as déci- in F) esp. in French metric system in sense 1/10 of specified unit. So dĕ′cĭbĕl (unit for measuring relative intensities of sounds), dĕ′cĭgrăm, dĕ′cĭlitre (-ēter), dĕ′cĭmêtre (-er), nn.

dĕcīde′, v.t. & i. Settle (question, issue, dispute) by giving victory to one side; give judgement (between, for, in favour of, against, or abs.); bring, come, to a resolution (that ~s me; ~ to do, on, for, or against doing). Hence dĕcīd′ABLE a. [ME, f. OF decider or L DE(cīdere cis- = caedere cut)]

dĕcīd′ĕd, a. In vbl senses; also: definite, unquestionable, (a ~ difference); (of persons) of clear opinions or vigorous initiative, not vacillating. Hence ~LY² adv. [-ED¹]

dĕcīd′er, n. In vbl senses; also, (Racing) heat in which tie is run off. [-ER¹]

dĕcīd′uous, a. Shed periodically or normally (of leaves, teeth, horns, etc.); shedding its leaves annually; shedding its wings after copulation (of ants etc.); fleeting, transitory. [f. L deciduus f. DE-(cĭdere = cadere fall)+-OUS]

dĕcill′ion (-yon), n. ‖ Tenth power of million (1 with 60 ciphers). Hence ~TH³ a. & n. [f. L decem ten & million, see BILLION]

dĕ′cimal, a. & n. Of tenths or ten, proceeding by tens, (~ numeration, ordinary counting-system with ten for basis, reckoned by decades; ~ system, of weights and measures, with denominations rising by tens; ~ notation, counting in tens; ~ arithmetic, using this notation, also in narrower sense that, also called ~s, treating of ~ fractions; ~ fraction or ~, one whose denominator is a power of ten, esp. when expressed by figures written to right of the ~ point or dot placed after the unit figure, & denoting tenths, hundredths, etc., according to their place; RECURring ~, ~ COINAGE); of ~ coinage, whence ~IST(2) n. Hence ~IZE(3) v.t., ~ĭzA′TION n., ~LY² adv. [c. 1600 (math.) f. L decimus tenth, -AL]

dĕ′cĭmāte, v.t. Put to death one in ten

of (mutinous or cowardly soldiers); destroy tenth or large proportion of (esp. of epidemic or other visitation). So **děcima′tion** n. [f. L *decimare* take the tenth man (*decimus*), see -ATE²]

dĕ′cimō-sĕx′tō. = SEXTODECIMO.

dĕ′cimus. See PRIMUS¹.

dĕciph′er, v.t. & n. Turn into ordinary writing or make out with key (thing written in cipher); make out meaning of (bad writing, hieroglyphics, anything perplexing); (n.) interpretation of cipher document. Hence ~ABLE a., ~MENT n. [DE-]

dĕci′sion (-ĭzhn), n. Settlement (*of* question etc.), conclusion, formal judgement; making up one's mind, resolve; resoluteness, decided character. [ME, f. OF, or L *decisio* (DECIDE, -ION)]

dĕcis′ive, a. Deciding, conclusive, (esp. ~ *battle*); = DECIDED (~ *character,* ~ *superiority*). Hence ~LY² (-vl-) adv., ~NESS (-vn-) n. [F (DECIDE, -IVE)]

dĕciv′ilize, -ise (-ĭz), v.t. Divest of civilization. [DE-]

dĕck¹, n. 1. Platform of planks or wood-covered iron extending from side to side of ship or part of it (in large ships *main, middle, lower,* ~s, also *upper* or *spar* ~ above *main,* & ORLOP below *lower; poop* & *forecastle* ~s, short ones in stern & bow); (sl.) the ground; CLEAR² *the* ~s; *on* ~, not below; ~*-chair,* camp-stool, also long-armed reclining chair, used in passenger steamers; ~*-hand,* man employed on vessel's ~ in cleaning and odd jobs; ~*-house,* room erected on ~. 2. Pack of cards (now chiefly U.S.). [15th c. 'covering' f. MDu. *dec* (cf. foll.); naut. use (*c.* 1500) app. an Eng. development]

dĕck², v.t. Array, adorn; furnish with, cover as, a deck. [*c.* 1500 f. MDu. *dekken* cover; see THATCH]

dĕc′kle, n. Contrivance in papermaking-machine for limiting size of sheet (~*-edge,* rough uncut edge). [f. G *deckel* dim. of *decke* cover]

dĕclaim′, v.i. & t. Speak rhetorically (often *against,* = inveigh), practise speaking or recitation; deliver impassioned rather than reasoned speech; utter rhetorically. Hence ~ER¹ n. [16th c. *declame* f. F *declamer* or L *declamare;* see CLAIM]

dĕclamā′tion, n. Act or art of declaiming; rhetorical exercise, set speech; impassioned speech, harangue. So **dĕclăm′atory** a. [f. F, or L *declamatio* (prec., -ATION)]

dĕclăr′ant, n. One who makes legal declaration. [f. L *declarare* DECLARE, -ANT]

dĕclarā′tion, n. Stating, announcing; positive, emphatic, solemn, or legal assertion, announcement, or proclamation (~ *of war,* before beginning hostilities, not now usual; ~ *of the poll,* of vote-totals of election-candidates); manifesto, written announcement of

intentions, terms of agreement, etc. (*D*~ *of* INDULGENCE; *D*~ *of* RIGHTS; *D*~ *of Independence,* of 4th July 1776 by N.-Amer. British colonies; *D*~ *of Paris* 1856, *of London* 1909 unratified by Gt Britain, international agreements on maritime law); (Law) plaintiff's statement of claim, affirmation in lieu of oath, Custom-House statement (see foll.); (Cards) a bid, pass, double, etc., the winning bid. [ME, f. L *declaratio* (foll., -ATION)]

dĕclāre′, v.t. & i. 1. Make known, proclaim publicly, formally, or explicitly, (~ *war, a dividend*); (abs.) *Well, I* ~ (excl. of incredulity, surprise, or vexation). 2. Pronounce (person etc.) to be something, as ~ *him* (*to be*) *an enemy to humankind;* ~ *oneself,* avow intentions, reveal character; ~ *for, against,* side with, against; ~ *innings closed,* or ~, elect to cease batting as though all were out; ~ *off,* break off (bargain etc., or abs.). 3. (Customs) name (dutiable goods) as in one's possession. 4. (Bridge) name the trump suit, or call 'No trumps'; (other card games) announce that one holds (certain combinations of cards etc.). Hence or cogn. **dĕclā′rative, dĕclā′ratory,** aa., **dĕclā′ratively², dĕclār′ĕdly²,** advv., **dĕclār′er¹** n. (esp. at cards). [ME, f. L DE(*clarare* f. *clarus* clear)]

déclassé (dāklās′ā), a. (fem. -*ée*). That has lost caste or sunk in social scale. [F]

dĕclăss′ify, v.t. Remove from classified or secret list. [DE-]

dĕclĕn′sion (-shn), n. Deviation *from* uprightness etc.; deterioration, decay; (Gram.) case-inflexion, one of the noun-classes distinguished by their different methods of case-inflexion, declining. [irreg. f. OF *declinaison* f. L *declinationem,* whence obs. E *declination* in same sense]

dĕclinā′tion, n. Downward bend; (Astron.) angular distance of star etc. north or south of celestial equator, celestial latitude; (Compass) angular deviation of needle, E. or W., from true north. Hence ~AL (-sho-) a. [ME, f. OF or f. L *declinatio* (foll., -ATION)]

dĕcline′¹, v.i. & t. Slope downwards (usu. intr.); bend, droop, (i., & also t. as *with head* ~*d,* ~*s its blossoms*); (of day, life, etc.) draw to close; sink morally (~ *on,* descend to); fall off, decay, decrease, deteriorate; turn away from, refuse, (discussion, challenge, battle; ~ *to do, doing, to be* treated in such a way); say one cannot accept (invitation etc., or abs.; ~ *with thanks* freq. iron., reject scornfully); (Gram.) inflect, recite the cases of, whence **dĕclin′able** a. [ME, f. OF *decliner* or L DE(*clinare* bend)]

dĕcline′², n. Sinking, gradual loss of vigour or excellence, decay, deterioration; phthisis, consumption; fall in price; setting, last part of course, (of sun, life, etc.). [ME, f. prec. & OF *declin*]

děclĭnŏm'ĕter, n. Instrument for measuring magnetic declination. [irreg. f. L *declinare* see DECLINE + -METER]

děcliv'it|y̆, n. Downward slope. Hence ~OUS a. [f. L *declivitas* f. DE(*clivis* f. *clivus* slope), -TY (cf. DEFORMITY)]

děcliv'ous, a. Sloping down (esp. in Zool. of profile). [f. L *declivis* see prec. + -OUS]

děclŭtch', v.i Disengage clutch esp. of motor-car. [DE-]

děcŏc'tion, n. Boiling down so as to extract essence; liquor resulting. [ME, f. OF or L DE(*coctio* f. *coquere coct-* boil, -ION)]

děcōde', v.t. Decipher (code telegram etc.). [DE-]

děcŏll'āte, v.t. Behead, truncate (p.p., of spiral shell without apex). So děcoll-A'TION n. [LL DE(*collare* f. *collum* neck), -ATE³]

décolletage (dākŏl'tahzh), n. (Exposure of neck and shoulders by) low-cut neck of bodice. [F (DE-, *collet* collar of dress)]

décolleté (dākŏl'tā), a. (fem. *-ée*). Low-necked (of dress); wearing low-necked dress. [F, as prec.]

děcol'o(u)rĭz|e (-kŭler-), **-is|e** (-ĭz), v.t. Deprive of colour. Hence ~A'TION, ~ER¹(2), nn. [DE-, COLOUR¹, -IZE(3)]

dē'cŏmplĕx, a. Doubly complex, having complex parts. [DE-]

děcompōs|e' (-z), v.t. & i. Separate into its elements (substance, light, etc.); analyse (thought, motive); rot (t. & i.). Hence ~'ABLE a., ~'ER¹(2), děcŏmposī'-TION, nn., (-z-). [f. F *décomposer* (DE-, COMPOSE)]

děcŏm'posite (-z-), a. & n. (Substance, word, etc.) made by compounding a compound with another element, further composite. [f. LL *decompositus* transl. of Gk *parasunthetos* used of words derived from compounds; see DE-]

dē'compound, a. & n. = DECOMPOSITE (esp. in Bot.). [DE-]

děcomprĕss', v.t. Relieve pressure on (underwater or other worker) by means of an air-lock. Hence **děcomprĕ'ssion** (-shn) n., ~OR n., contrivance for relieving pressure in motor engine. [DE-]

děcon'sĕcrāte, v.t. Secularize. [DE-]

děcontăm'in|āte, v.t. Remove contamination from (esp. areas, clothes, etc., affected by poison-gas or radio-activity). Hence ~A'TION n. [DE-]

děcontrŏl', v.t. (-ll-), & n. Release from (esp. war-time) control by Government etc. [DE-]

décor (dākōr'), n. All that makes up the appearance of a room or the stage. [F]

děc'orāt|e, v.t. Furnish with adornments (esp. church with flowers etc.); serve as adornment to; invest with order, medal, etc.; ~ed as adj. or n., (of) third English STYLE of architecture. Hence ~IVE a.

[f. L *decorare* (*decus -oris* beauty), -ATE³]

děcorā'tion, n. In vbl senses; esp.: (pl.) flags, wreaths, etc., put up on occasion of public rejoicing; medal, star, etc., worn as honour. [F, or f. LL *decoratio* (prec., -ATION)]

děc'orātor, n. In vbl senses; esp., tradesman who papers, paints, etc., houses. [-OR]

děc'orous (or dĭkōr'-), a. Not violating good taste or propriety, dignified and decent. Hence ~LY² adv. [f. L *decōrus* (*decor* f. *decēre* be fit, -OR) + -OUS]

děcort'icāte, v.t. Remove the bark, rind, or husk from. [f. L DE(*corticare* f. *cortex* bark), -ATE³]

děcōr'um, n. Seemliness, propriety, etiquette; particular usage required by politeness or decency. [L, neut. adj. as DECOROUS]

děcoy', n., & v.t. (Entice, esp. by help of trained bird etc., into) pond with narrow netted arms into which wild duck may be tempted and caught; allure *into, out of, away*, etc., ensnare; bird etc. trained to entice others; (also ~-*duck*) swindler's confederate, tempter; bait, enticement. [17th c., f. MDu. *de kooi* 'the coy', whence also, without the article, obs. (now dial.) E *coy*; *kooi* f. WG *ca(u)wia* f. L *cavea* CAGE]

děcrease', v.i. & t., **děc'rease**, n. 1. Lessen, diminish, (i. & t.); hence **děcreas'-ingly²** adv. 2. n. Diminution, lessening. [ME *dis-, de-*, f. OF *de(s)creiss-*, pres. stem of *de(s)creistre* f. Rom. *discrescere* (in LL w. sense 'grow in different directions') f. L DE(*crescere cret-* grow); n. f. OF *de(s)creis*]

děcree', n., & v.t. 1. Ordinance or edict set forth by authority; decision (in other courts called *judgement*) in Admiralty cases, (in Divorce cases) order declaring nullity or dissolution or giving judicial separation (‖ ~ *nīs'ĭ*, order for divorce unless cause to the contrary is shown within a period, orig. six months, later six-weeks); will, as shown by result, of God, Providence, Nature, etc. 2. v.t. Ordain by ~. [ME, f. OF *decre* f. L DE(*cretum* neut. p.p. of *cernere* sift) thing decided]

děc'rĕment, n. Decrease, amount lost by diminution or waste, (esp. as scientific term opp. INCREMENT). [f. L *decrementum* (DECREASE, -MENT)]

děcrĕp'it, a. Wasted, worn out, enfeebled with age & infirmities, (of persons or institutions). So **děcrĕp'ĭTUDE** n. [ME, f OF *decrepit* or L DE(*crepitus* p.p. of *crepare* creak)]

děcrĕp'it|āte, v.t. & i. Calcine (mineral or salt) till it ceases to crackle in fire; crackle under heat. Hence ~A'TION n. [DE-, L *crepitare* frequent. of *crepare* creak]

decrescĕn'dō (dākrĕsh-). = DIMINUENDO. [It.]

For compounds of *de-* not given consult DE-.

dĕcrĕs′cent, a. Waning, decreasing, (usu. of moon). [f. L *decrescens* (DECREASE, -ENT)]

dĕcrēt′al, n. Papal decree; (pl.) collection of these, forming part of canon law. [ME, f. OF *decretal* f. LL *decretalis* (letter) of DECREE, -AL]

dĕcrȳ′, v.t. Disparage, cry down. [f. F *décrier* (DE-, CRY²)]

dĕc′ūman, a. Especially large or powerful (usu. of wave lit. or fig.). [f. L *decumanus*, used of main gate of camp where tenth cohort was quartered (*decimus* tenth, -AN)]

dĕcŭm′bent, a. (bot. & zool.). Lying along ground or body (of plant, shoot, bristles). [f. L DE(*cumbere* lie), -ENT]

dĕc′ūple, a., n., & v.t. & i. Tenfold (amount); (vb) multiply by ten. [F (*dé-*), f. LL *decuplus* (*decem* ten, *-plus* cf. *duplus* DOUBLE)]

dĕcŭss′ate, a. (-at), & v.t. & i. (-āt). 1. X-shaped, intersecting; (Bot.) with pairs of opposite shoots, each at right angles to pair below; (Rhet.) marked by chiasmus. 2. vb. Arrange in these ways; intersect; hence **dĕcŭssā′TION** n. [f. L *decussare* (*decussis* number ten, X), -ATE², ³]

dedans (dedahń′), n. (tennis). Open gallery at end of service-side of a court; (transf., *the* ~) spectators watching a tennis match. [F, = inside]

dĕd′icāt|e, v.t. Devote with solemn rites (*to* God or *to* sacred use; of church etc. esp. without certain forms necessary for legally consecrating ground or buildings); give up (*to* special purpose); inscribe (book etc.) *to* patron or friend. So ~OR, ~EE′, nn., ~IVE, ~ORY, aa. [f. L DE(*dicare* declare), -ATE³]

dĕdicā′tion, n. In vbl senses; also, dedicatory inscription on building etc. or in book. [ME, f. OF, or f. L *dedicatio* (prec., -ION)]

dĕdūc|e′, v.t. Bring down (annals etc.) *from* or *to* a time; trace descent of (person etc.) *from*; infer, draw as conclusion, *from*. So ~′IBLE a. [f. L DE(*ducere* duci- lead)]

dĕdŭct′, v.t. Take away, put aside, (amount, portion, etc., *subtract* being now used of numbers) *from* (or abs.). [f. L *deduct-* see prec.]

dĕdŭc′tion, n. Deducting; amount deducted; deducing, inference from general to particular, *a priori* reasoning, (cf. INDUCTION); thing deduced. [ME, f. OF, or L *deductio* (DEDUCE, -ION)]

dĕdŭc′tive, a. Of, reasoning by, deduction, *a priori*. Hence ~LY² (vl-) adv. [f. L *deductivus* (DEDUCE, -IVE)]

dee, n. Letter D; D-shaped harness-ring.

deed, n. Thing done intentionally; brave, skilful, or conspicuous act; actual fact, performance, (*in word & ~*; *in ~ & not in name*, whence INDEED; *in very ~*); (Law) written or printed instrument effecting legal disposition & sealed & delivered by disposing party (in practice now always signed also but not always delivered); ~*-poll*, deed made & executed by one party only (paper polled or cut even, not indented). Hence ~′LESS a. [OE *dǣd*, OS *dād*, OHG *tāt*, ON *dáth*, Goth.*-deths* f. Gmc *dǣdiz*, cogn. w. DO¹]

deem, v.t. Believe, consider, judge, count, (abs. in parenthesis, as *it was, I ~ed, time to go*; ~ *highly of*, have high opinion of; ~ *it* one's *duty*; *was ~ed sufficient*, *to suffice*; ~*ed that this would do*). [OE *dēman*, OS *dōmian*, OHG *tuomen*, ON *dœma*, Goth. *domjan* f. Gmc *dōmas* DOOM]

deem′ster, n. One of two justices of Isle of Man. [prec., -STER]

deep¹, a. 1. Going far down from top (~ *hole, water, draught, drink, drinker, gambling, gambler*; *go* (in) *off the* ~ END¹; *in* ~ *waters*, plunged in grief etc.); going far in from surface or edge (~ *wound, shelf, border*; ~ *mourning*, expressed by wide crape etc.; ~ *plunge*; ~ *reader, thinker*). 2. Hard to fathom, profound, not superficial, penetrating, (~ *dissimulation*; *a* ~ *one*, sl., cunning or secretive; *the* ~*er causes*; ~ *learning, study*; ~ *influence*; ~ *insight*). 3. Heartfelt, absorbing, absorbed, (~ *feelings, interest, curses*; ~ *in a pursuit*, dead to everything else). 4. Intense, vivid, extreme, heinous, (~ *disgrace, sleep, night, sin, colour*; ~ *-red* etc.). 5. Going or placed (so) far down, back, or in (*water 6 ft* ~; *ankle-* ~ *in mud*; *drawn up six* ~; *ship* ~ *in the water, hands* ~ *in pockets*; ~ *in debt*; ~ *in the human heart*, fully versed in it). 6. Brought from far down (~ *sigh*); not shrill, low-pitched, full-toned, (note, bell, voice; ~*-mouthed*, of dog). Hence ~′EN⁶ v.t. & i., ~LY³ adv., ~′MOST a., (rare, for *depth*) ~′NESS n. [OE *dēop*, OS *diop*, OHG *tiuf*, ON *djúpr*, Goth. *diups* f. Gmc *deupaz* cogn. w. DIP¹]

deep², n. *The* ~ (poet.), the sea; (Cricket, *the* ~) position of fieldsmen stationed behind the bowler at or near boundary (*the* ~ *field*); (usu. pl.) deep part(s) of the sea; abyss, pit, cavity; mysterious region of thought or feeling. [as prec. (neut. adj. in OE)]

deep³, adv. Deeply, far in, (*read* ~ *into the night*; *still waters run* ~, real feeling or knowledge not showy); esp. in comb. as ~*-drawn* (of sighs), ~*-laid* (of scheme, secret & elaborate), ~*-rooted* (esp. of prejudice), ~*-seated* (of emotion or disease). [OE *dīope, dēope*, (DEEP¹)]

deep′ing, n. Section, one fathom deep, of fishing-net. [-ING³]

deer, n. (collect. sing. usu. for pl.). Kinds of ruminant quadruped with deciduous branching horns (*small* ~, insignificant animals or things collectively, cf. *King Lear* III iv. 144); ~*-hound*, large rough greyhound; ~*-forest*, normally treeless wild land reserved for stalking ~; ~·*lick*, spring or damp spot impregnated with salt etc. where ~ come to lick; ~·*neck*, horse's thin neck; || ~·*s-foot*, a fine grass; ~·*skin*, (made of) ~'s skin; ~·*stalker*, sportsman stalking ~, cloth cap peaked before and behind. [OE *dēor*, OS *dior*, OHG *tiur*, ON *dȳr*, Goth. *dius* f. Gmc *deuzom*]

deface', v.t. Mar appearance or beauty of, disfigure; discredit; make illegible. Hence ~ABLE (-sa-) a., ~MENT (-sm-) n. [ME, f. OF *def-*, *desfacer* (DE-, FACE[1])]

dē fāc'tō, a. & adv. In fact, whether by right (DE JURE) or not (*king* ~, *the* ~ *king*). [L]

dēf'alcāt|e, v.i. Commit defalcations, misappropriate property in one's charge. So ~OR n. [f. med. L DE(*falcare* lop f. L *falx* -*cis* scythe), -ATE[3]]

defalcā'tion, n. Defection, shortcoming; fraudulent deficiency of money owing to breach of trust, misappropriation, amount misappropriated. [f. med. L *defalcatio* (prec., -ATION)]

dēfāme', v.t. Attack the good fame of, speak ill of. So **dēfama'TION** n., **dēfām'a-TORY** a. [ME *dif-*, *de-*, f. OF *diffamer* f. L *diffamare* spread abroad (DIS-, *fama* report), see DE-; form *de-* after L *defamis*, -*atus* infamous]

dēfātt'ěd, a. Deprived of its fat. [DE-]

dēfault'[1], n. Want, absence, (*in* ~ *of*, if or since such a thing is wanting); failure to act or appear, neglect, (*make* ~; *judgement by* ~, given for plaintiff on defendant's failure to plead); failure to pay, defaulting. [ME, f. OF *defaute* f. *defaillir* see foll. & cf. FAULT]

dēfault'[2], v.i. & t. 1. Make, be guilty of, default; fail to appear in court; not meet money calls, break; hence ~ER[1] n., (also Mil.) soldier guilty of military offence (~*er sheet*, record of such offences, now *conduct sheet*). 2. Declare (party) in default & give judgement against him. [ME, f. prec. & OF *defaillir* (3 sing. *default*) f. DE-, L *fallere* deceive]

dēfeas'ance (-fēz-), n. Rendering null & void. [ME, f. OF *defesance* f. *de(s)faire* undo, DEFEAT, -ANCE]

dēfeas'i|ble (-fēz-), a. Capable of annulment, liable to forfeiture. Hence ~BIL'ITY n. [AF, as prec., -IBLE]

dēfeat', v.t., & n. Frustrate, frustration; (Law) annul(ment); (arch.) disappoint *of*; overthrow (v. & n.) in contest esp. in battle. [ME; n. prob. f. vb, which is f. OF *defait* p.p. of *desfaire* f. med. L *disfacere* (DE-, L *facere* do)]

dēfeat'|ism, n. Conduct tending to bring about acceptance of defeat, esp. by action on civilian opinion. So ~IST n. & a. [f. F *défaitisme* (as prec., -ISM)]

dēf'ēcāte, v.t. Clear of dregs, refine, purify, (lit. & fig.); get rid of (dregs, ex-

crement, sin). Hence ~A'TION, ~ātor, nn. [f. L DE(*fecare* f. *faex* -*cis* dregs), -ATE[3]]

dēfēct', n., & v.i. Lack of something essential to completeness; shortcoming, failing, (*has the* ~*s of his qualities*, the particular ones that often accompany his particular virtues); blemish; amount by which thing falls short; (v.i.) desert. [f. L *defectus* n. f. DE(*ficere fect-* = *facere* do) desert, fail]

dēfēc'tion, n. Falling away from allegiance to leader, party, religion, or duty; desertion, apostasy. [f. L *defectio* (prec., -ION)]

dēfēc'tive, a. & n. 1. Having defect(s), incomplete, faulty, wanting or deficient (*in* some respect); (Gram.) not having all the usual inflexions. 2. n. A ~ person. Hence ~LY[2] (-vl-) adv., ~NESS (-vn-) n. [ME, f. OF *defectif* or LL *defectivus* as prec., -IVE]

|| **dēfence'**, *dēfense'*, n. Defending from, resistance against, attack (cf. OFFENCE; *best* ~ *is offence*, advantage goes with the initiative; in cricket, guarding of one's wicket, also batting as opposed to bowling; *science* or *art of* ~, boxing or fencing); (Mil., pl.) fortifications (also *line of* ~, series of fortified posts); ~ *in depth*, system of ~ comprising successive areas of resistance; thing that protects; justification, vindication, speech or writing used to this end; (Law) accused party's denial, pleading, & proceedings, counsel for the ~; || *D*~ *of the Realm Act* (abbr. D.O.R.A., joc. *Dŏr'a*), Act of August, 1914, providing Government with wide powers during war. Hence ~LESS (-sl-) a., ~lèssLY[2] adv., ~lèssNESS n. [ME *defens*, *defense*, f. OF f. LL *defensum*, -*a*, p.p. see foll.]

dēfēnd', v.t. & i. Forbid, avert, (arch.; still in *God* ~!); ward off attack from, keep safe, protect (*against, from*); uphold by argument, vindicate, speak or write in favour of; (Law) make defence in court (~ *oneself*, conduct one's own defence), (of counsel) appear for defendant, conduct defence of. [ME, f. OF *defendre* f. L DE(*fendere -fens-* FEND)]

dēfēn'dant, n. Person sued in law-suit (cf. *plaintiff*); (attrib.) holding this relation (*the* ~ *company*). [ME, f. OF *defendant* part. (prec., -ANT)]

dēfēn'der, n. One who defends; *D*~ *of the Faith*, title of Eng. Sovereigns from Henry VIII, who received it from Pope for writing against Luther; (Sport) holder of championship etc. defending the title (opp. *challenger*). [ME & AF *defendour*, OF -*eor* (DEFEND, -OR)]

dēfēnestrā'tion, n. Action of throwing out of a window. [DE-, L *fenestra* window, -ATION]

defense. See DEFENCE.

For compounds of *de-* not given consult DE-.

defen'si|ble, a. Easily defended (in war or argument); justifiable. Hence **~BIL'ITY** n., **~bLY²** adv. [ME *-able* f. OF f. LL *-abilis*; later *-ible* f. LL *-ibilis*; see DEFEND, -ABLE, -IBLE]

defen'sive, a. & n. **1.** Serving, used, done, for defence, protective, not aggressive; hence **~LY²** (vl-) adv. **2.** n. State or position of defence (esp. *be, stand, act, on the ~*). [ME, f. F *défensif* f. med. L *defensivus* (DEFEND, -IVE)]

defer'¹, v.t. & i. (-rr-). Put off, postpone, (*~red* ANNUITY; *~red pay,* part of soldier's pay formerly held over to be paid at discharge or death; *~red* SHARE's); procrastinate, be dilatory. Hence **~MENT** n. [later, differentiated form of ME *differre*; see DIFFER]

defer'², v.i. (-rr-). Submit or make concessions in opinion or action *to* (person). [f. F *déférer* f. L DE(*ferre* bring)]

def'erence, n. Compliance with advice etc. of one superior in wisdom or position (*pay* etc. ~ *to*); respect, manifestation of desire to comply, courteous regard, (*in ~ to,* out of respect for authority of). So **deferen'tiAL** (-shl) a., **deferen'tiaLly²** (-shal-) adv. [f. F *déférence* (prec., -ENCE)]

def'erent, a. (Physiol.) conveying to a destination (of ducts etc.); (rare for) deferential. [first sense (f. F or direct) f. L *deferens* part. of DE(*ferre* carry); second f. DEFER², -ENT]

defi'ance, n. Challenge to fight or maintain cause, assertion, etc.; open disobedience, setting at nought, (*bid ~ to, set at ~, in ~ of*). [ME, f. OF (DEFY, -ANCE)]

defi'ant, a. Openly disobedient; rejecting advances, suspicious and reserved. Hence **~LY²** adv. [f. F *défiant* (DEFY, -ANT)]

defi'ciency (-Ishn-), n. Being deficient; want, lack; thing wanting; amount by which thing, esp. revenue, falls short; *~ disease* (caused by lack of some essential element in the diet). [f. LL *deficientia* (*deficere* see DEFECT, -ENCY)]

defi'cient (-Ishnt), a. Incomplete, defective, wanting *in* specified quality; insufficient in quantity, force, etc.; half-witted. Hence **~LY²** adv. [f. L *deficiens* (*deficere* see DEFECT, -ENT)]

def'icit, n. Amount by which esp. sum of money is too small; excess of liabilities over assets. [f. F *déficit* f. L *deficit* 3 sing. pres. of *deficere* see DEFECT]

dē fid'é, pred. a. Required to be held as article of faith. [L]

defi'er, n. One who defies. [DEFY, -ER¹]

defilade', v.t., & n. Secure (fortification) against enfilading fire; (n.) this precaution or arrangement (also *defilement*). [Eng. formations after ENFILADE vb & n.]

defile'¹, v.i., **def'ile,** n. **1.** March by files, in file. **2.** n. Narrow way through which troops can only march so, gorge. [f. F *défiler* & *défilé* p.p. (DE-, *file* FILE³)]

defile'², v.t. Make dirty, befoul; pollute,

---

corrupt; desecrate, profane; make ceremonially unclean. Hence **~MENT** n. (see DEFILADE). [ME *defoul* f. OF *defouler* trample down, outrage (DE-, *fouler* FULL²); altered after obs. *file, befile* f. OE (*be*)*fȳlan* f. *ful* FOUL]

defin|e', v.t. Settle limits of; make clear, esp. in outline (*well-~ed image; ~e* one's *position,* state it precisely); set forth essence of, declare exact meaning of, (also abs., frame definitions); (of properties) make up total character of. Hence **~'ABLE** a. [ME, f. OF *definer* f. Rom. **definare* for L DE(*finire* f. *finis* end)]

def'inite, a. With exact limits; determinate, distinct, precise, not vague; (Gram.) **~ inflexions,** those of German and early E adjj. used after **~** article & similar wds; **~** *article,* the; *past* or *preterite ~,* simple past tense in French, as *il vint* he came. Hence **~LY²** (-tl-) adv. (also, in loose colloq. use, yes, certainly), **~NESS** (-tn-) n. [f. L *definitus* p.p. see prec.]

defini'tion, n. Stating the precise nature of a thing or meaning of a word; form of words in which this is done; making or being distinct, degree of distinctness, in outline (esp. of image given by lens or shown in photograph); degree of accuracy of sound reproduction in radio or of picture reproduction in television. [ME, f. OF (-*cion*) or L DE(*finitio* f. *finire* f. *finis* end, -ION]

defin'itive, a. Decisive, unconditional, final, (of answer, treaty, verdict, etc.). Hence **~LY²** (-vl-) adv. [ME, f. OF *definitif* f. L *definitivus* (prec., -IVE)]

dē'flagr|āte, v.t. & i. Burn away with rapid flame. Hence **~A'TION, ~ātOR,** nn. [f. L DE(*flagrare* blaze), -ATE³]

deflāte', v.t. Let inflating air etc. out of (pneumatic tire etc.); (Finance) reduce the inflation of (State's currency), (abs.) adopt this policy. Hence **deflā'tion** n. [f. DE- +(IN)FLATE]

deflēc|t', v.t. & i. Bend aside or (rarely) down, (make) deviate (*from*). Hence **~'tOR** n. [f. L DE(*flectere flex*- bend)]

deflē'xion (-kshn), **-ēc'tion,** n. Lateral or downward bend, deviation, (lit. & fig.; in Electr. & Magn., of needle from its zero). [f. L *deflex*- (prec., -ION)]

deflorā'tion, n. Deflowering. [ME, f. OF f. LL *deflorationem* (foll., -ATION)]

deflow'er, v.t. Deprive of virginity, ravish; ravage, spoil; strip of flowers. [ME, f. OF *desflorer* f. Rom. **disflorare** f. LL DE(*florare* (*flos floris* flower)]

dē'fluent (-lōō-), a. & n. Down-flowing (part; e.g. lower end of glacier). [f. L DE(*fluere* flow), -ENT]

dēfo'rest, v.t. **=** DISFOREST. [f. DE- + FOREST]

deform', v.t. Make ugly, deface; put out of shape, mis-shape, (esp. in p.p. of person with mis-shapen body or limb). [ME, f. OF *deformer* f. L DE(*formare* f. *forma* shape)]

dēfŏrmā′tion, n. Disfigurement; change for the worse (esp. as opponent's name for Reformation); perverted form of word (*dang* for *damn* etc.); (Physics) changed shape *of*. [ME, f. OF f. L *deformationem* (prec., -ATION)]

dēfŏrm′itў, n. Being deformed, ugliness, disfigurement, (physical or moral); a malformation esp. of body or limb. [ME, f. OF (-*te*) f. L *deformitatem* f. DE(*formis* f. *forma* shape), -TY]

dēfraud′, v.t. Cheat (person, person *of*, or abs.). [ME, f. OF *defrauder* or L *defraudare* (DE-, *fraus* FRAUD)]

dēfray′, v.t. Settle, discharge by payment, (cost, expense). Hence ∼ABLE a., ∼AL(2) n. [f. F *défrayer* f. *frai*(*l*) (now pl. *frais*) cost, f. LL *fritus*, *fretus*, *fredus* f. OFrank. *frithu* peace; cf. AFFRAY]

dēfrŏck′, v.t. = UNFROCK.

dĕft, a. Dextrous, skilful, handling things neatly. Hence ∼LY[3] adv., ∼′NESS n. [ME; var. of DAFT]

dēfŭnct′, a. Dead (*the* ∼, way of mentioning a particular dead person), no longer existing. [f. L DE(*functus* p.p. of *fungi* perform) dead]

dēfў′, v.t. Challenge to combat or competition (arch. or joc.); challenge *to* do or prove something; resist openly, set at naught; (of things) present insuperable obstacles .*to* (*defies definition*, *capture*, *attack*, etc.). [ME, f. OF *defier* f. Rom. *DIS(fidare* trust f. *fidus* faithful)]

dégagé (see Ap.), a. (fem. -*ée*). Easy, unconstrained. [F]

dēgauss′ (-gows), v.t. Neutralize the magnetization of (ship etc.) with an encircling current-carrying conductor (∼*ing belt*), esp. as precaution against magnetic mines. [DE-, GAUSS]

dēgĕn′erate[1], a. & n. **1.** Having lost qualities proper to race, sunk from former excellence; (Biol.) having reverted to lower type; hence **dēgĕn′erACY** n. **2.** n. ∼ person or animal. [f. L p.p. see foll., -ATE[2]]

dēgĕn′erāte[2], v.i. Become degenerate (see prec.). [f. L *degenerare*, f. DE(*gener* f. *genus -eris* race) ignoble, -ATE[3]]

dēgĕnerā′tion, n. Becoming degenerate; (Path.) morbid disintegration of tissue or change in its structure (esp. *fatty* ∼ *of heart*). [f. F, or LL *degeneratio* (prec., -ION)]

dēgluti′tion (-glōō-), n. Swallowing. [f. F *déglutition* f. L DE(*glutire* swallow), -ION]

dēgrāde′, v.t. & i. Reduce to lower rank; depose as punishment; lower in estimation, debase morally, whence **dēgrād′ING[3]** a.; reduce (Biol.) to lower organic type, (Physics) to less convertible form (energy), (Geol.) to disintegration (rocks etc.); degenerate; ‖ (Camb. Univ.) put off entering for honours examination

for a year beyond regular time. So **dēgradA′TION** n. [ME, f. OF *degrader* f. LL DE*gradare* (*gradus* step)]

dēgree′, n. **1.** Step (as) of staircase (arch.; perh. so in 2 *Kings* xx. 9, & in Psalm-title *Song of D*∼*s*, Ps. 120–134); thing placed like step in series, tier, row; stage in ascending or descending scale or process (*by* ∼*s*, gradually; *fine by* ∼*s* & *beautifully less*, see Prior, *Henry & Emma*, 431; often misquoted *small by* etc.); step in direct genealogical descent (*prohibited* ∼*s*, number of these too low to allow of marriage, i.e. first, second, & third, reckoning from one party to common ancestor & down to the other). **2.** Social or official rank; relative condition (*each good in its*∼); stage in intensity or amount (*to a high or the last* ∼, also colloq. in latter sense *to a* ∼; in law, *principal in the first*, *second*, ∼). **3.** Academic rank conferred as guarantee of proficiency, or (*honorary* ∼) on distinguished person; masonic rank. **4.** (Gram.) stage (POSITIVE, COMPARATIVE, SUPERLATIVE) in comparison of adjj. & advv. **5.** (Geom. etc.) unit of angular or circular-arc measurement, 1/90 of right angle or 1/360 of circumference (symbol °, as 45°; ∼ *of* LATITUDE, about 69 miles); (Therm.) unit of temperature in any scale. **6.** *'Third* ∼, severe and protracted examination of accused person by the police to extract information or confession (also attrib.). Hence ∼LESS a. [ME, f. OF *degre* f. Rom. *DE-(gradus* step)]

dēgrē′ssion (-shn), n. A going down; (esp. decrease in the rate of taxation on sums below a certain limit). [in mod. use after *pro-*, *regression*]

de haut en bas (see Ap.), adv. In a condescending or superior manner. [F]

dēhis|ce′ (-ĭs), v.i. Gape, burst open, (esp. in Bot. of seed-vessels, & in Physiol.). So ∼′CENCE n., ∼′CENT a. [f. L DE(*hiscere* incept. of *hiare* gape)]

dēhŏrt′ative, a. & n. Dissuasive; thing meant to dissuade. [f. LL DE(*hortativus* f. *hortari* exhort, -IVE)]

dēhūm′anīze, -ise (-ĭz), v.t. Divest of human characteristics. [DE-]

dēhўd′rāte, -ise (-ĭz), v.t. (chem.). Deprive (substance) of water or its elements. [f. DE- + HYDRATE]

dēhўp′notīze, -ise (-ĭz), v.t. Rouse, release, from hypnotic state. [DE-]

dē-ī′cer, n. Composition applied to aircraft's wings to prevent formation of ice, or any mechanical or electrical device for the same purpose. So **dē-ice′** v.t., free (aircraft) from ice. [DE-]

dē′icide, n. Killer, killing, of a God. [f. LL *deicida* (*deus* god, -*i*-, -CIDE)]

deic′tic (dīk-), a. (philol., gram.). Pointing, demonstrative. [f. Gk *deiktikos* (*deiktos* f. *deiknumi* show, -IC)]

---

dē'ifórm, a. Godlike in form or nature. [f. med. L *deiformis* (*deus* god, -I-, -FORM)]

dē'ify, v.t. Make a god of; make godlike; regard as a god, worship. Hence **dēi-FICA'TION** n. [ME, f. OF *deifier* f. LL *deificare* (*deus* god, -FY)]

deign (dān), v.t. Think fit, condescend, (*to* do; condescend to give (answer etc.). [ME, f. OF *degnier* f. L *dignare*, -*ari* deem worthy]

dē'ī grā'tiā (-shī-), adv. By God's grace. [L]

dē īn'tĕgrō, adv. Afresh. [L]

dē'ism, dē'ist, nn. Belief, believer, in the existence of a god without accepting revelation; (adherent of) natural religion. Hence **dēis'TIC(AL)** aa. [f. F *déisme*, *déiste*, f. L *deus* god + -ISM(3), -IST(2)]

dē'itȳ, n. Divine status, quality, or nature; a god; *the D~*, the Creator, God. [ME, f. OF *deite* f. LL *deitatem* (*deus* god, -TY)]

dějĕct', v.t. Dispirit, depress (usu. in p.p.). Hence **~ĕdLY²** adv. [ME, f. L DE(*jicĕre* -*ject*- = *jacĕre* throw)]

dějĕc'ta, n. pl. Person's or animal's excrements. [L, neut. pl. p.p. as prec.]

dějĕc'tion, n. Downcast state, low spirits; (Med.) evacuation of bowels, excrement. [ME, f. OF, or L *dejectio* (prec., ION)]

déjeuner (dě'zhonā), n. Breakfast; lunch, esp. of ceremonial kind. [F]

dē jūre (joor'i), a. & adv. Rightful, by right, (king etc. ~; *the ~ king*; cf. DE FACTO). [L]

dĕkk'ō, n. (sl.). A look (*let's have a ~*). [Hind. *dekho* imp. of *dekhnā* look]

dělaine', n. Light dress-fabric. [f. F (*mousseline*) *de laine* woollen (muslin)]

dělāte', v.t. Inform against, impeach, (person); report (offence). So **dělā'tion**, **dělāt'ōr**, nn. [f. L DE(*lat*- p.p. st. of *ferre* carry)]

dělay', v.t. & i., & n. Postpone(ment), defer(ring), put(ting) off, loiter(ing), be(ing) tardy, wait; hinder, hindrance. [ME; (n. f. OF *delai*) f. OF *delaier* f. *laier* leave]

dĕl crĕd'erĕ (-ād-), a., adv., & n. (commerc.). Under, charge made for, selling agent's guarantee that buyer is solvent. [It.]

dĕl'ē, printing direction (abbr. *d*). Delete indicated letter, word, or passage (written in margin). [L, imperat. of *delēre* DELETE]

dělĕc'table, a. Delightful, pleasant. [ME, f. OF f. L *delectabilis* f. *delectare* DELIGHT]

dělĕctā'tion, n. Enjoyment (usu. *for* one's ~). [ME f. OF (prec., -ATION)]

dělĕc'tus, n. School reading-book of selected passages. [L, n. f. DE(*ligere lect*- = *legere* choose)]

dĕl'ėgacȳ, n. System of delegating; appointment as delegate; body of delegates. [foll., -ACY]

dĕl'ėgate¹, n. Deputy, commissioner;

elected representative sent to conference. [ME, f. OF *delegat* f. L *delegatus* (foll., -ATE²)]

dĕl'ėgate², v.t. Depute (person), send as representative; commit (authority etc.) to or *to* agent; *~d legislation*, delegation to Ministers, by Acts of Parliament, of the power to make orders & regulations which have the force of law. [f. L DE(*legare* depute), -ATE³]

dělėgā'tion, n. Entrusting of authority to deputy; body of delegates (*Congress representatives of a single State; Austro-Hungary, the D~s* (hist.), two bodies appointed by Austrian & Hungarian Parliaments to deal jointly with imperial questions). [f. L DE(*legatio* LEGATION)]

dělēte', v.t. Strike out, obliterate, (letter, word, passage; also fig.). So **dělē'tion** n. [f. L *delēre* -*let*-]

dělēt'ērious, a. Noxious physically or morally, injurious. Hence **~LY²** adv. [f. Gk *dēlētērios* f. *dēletēr* destroyer (*dēleomai* injure) + -OUS]

dĕlf(t), n. Glazed earthenware made at Delft (earlier *Delf*) in Holland. [place]

dělib'erate¹, a. Intentional; considered, not impulsive; slow in deciding, cautious; leisurely, not hurried, (of movement etc.). Hence **~LY²** (-tl-) adv., **~NESS** (-tn-) n. [f. L *deliberatus* (foll., -ATE²)]

dělib'erāte², v.i. & t. Consider, think carefully, (intr., or with indirect question *how it might be done, what to do*); take counsel, consult, hold debate. [f. L DE(*liberare* = *librare* weigh f. *libra* balance), -ATE³]

dělibera'tion, n. Weighing in mind, careful consideration; discussion of reasons for & against, debate; care, avoidance of precipitancy; slowness of movement. [ME, f. OF *deliberation* f. L *deliberationem* (prec., -ATION)]

dělib'erative, a. Of, appointed for purpose of, deliberation or debate (usu. *~ assembly* or *functions*). Hence **~LY²** (-vl-) adv. [F (-*if*, -*ive*) or f. L *deliberativus* (DELIBERATE², -IVE)]

dĕl'icacȳ, n. Fineness of texture, graceful slightness, tender beauty; weakliness, susceptibility to disease or injury, need of care, discretion, or skill; nicety of perception, sensitiveness, (of persons, senses, or instruments); consideration for others' feelings; shrinking from, avoidance of, the immodest or offensive; choice kind of food, dainty; a nicety. [ME; foll., -ACY]

dĕl'icate, a.. Delightful (poet.); palatable, dainty, (of food); sheltered, luxurious, effeminate, (*~ living, nurture, upbringing*); fine of texture, soft, slender, slight; of exquisite quality or workmanship; subdued (of colour); subtle, hard to appreciate; easily injured, liable to illness; requiring nice handling, critical, ticklish; subtly sensitive (of persons or instruments); deft (*a ~ touch*); avoiding the offensive or immodest; considerate (esp. of actions). Hence ~LY² (-tl-) adv. [ME, f. OF delicat or L delicatus]

•**dèlicatèss'en,** n. pl. (Shop selling) delicacies or relishes for the table. [G delikatessen f. F délicatesse]

dèli'cious (-shus), a. Highly delightful, esp. to taste, smell, or the sense of humour. Hence ~LY² adv., ~NESS n. [ME, f. OF f. LL deliciosus f. L deliciae delight f. DE(licere = lacere allure), -OUS]

dèlict', n. Violation of law, offence, (in flagrant ~, = IN FLAGRANTE DELICTO). [f. L delictum neut. p.p. of DE(linquere leave) come short]

dèlight' (-ít), v.t. & i., & n. **1.** Please highly (shall be ~ed to, in accepting invitation; was ~ed with or at the result); take, find, great pleasure in (so in p.p., the books ~ed in by the many), be inclined and accustomed to do. **2.** n. High pleasure, thing that causes it; hence~FUL a., ~fulLY² adv., ~SOME a. (literary), (-ít). [ME delíten f. OF delitier f. L delectare see DELECTABLE; sp. -gh- since 16th c., after light &c.]

Dèlil'ah (-la), Da~, n. Temptress, false & wily woman. [Judges xvi]

dèlim'it(āte), vv.t. Determine limits or territorial boundary of. So **dèlimit-A'TION** n. [-it thr. F délimiter, -itate direct, f. L DE(limitare f. limes -itis boundary), -ATE³]

dèlin'è|āte, v.t. Show by drawing or description, portray. So ~A'TION, ~ātor, nn. [f. L DE(lineare f. linea line), -ATE³]

dèlinèāv'it, -vēr'unt, L vb sing. & pl. (usu. abbr. del.). So-&-so drew this. [f. L as prec.]

dèlin'quencȳ, n. Neglect of duty; guilt; a sin of omission; misdeed. [f. LL delinquentia f. delinquens part. (DELICT, -ENCY)]

dèlin'quent, a. & n. **1.** Defaulting, guilty. **2.** n. Offender. [f. L delinquens (prec. -ENT)]

dèliquès|ce', v.i. Become liquid, melt, (fig.) melt away; (Chem.) absorb enough water from the air to dissolve itself. So ~'CENT a., ~'CENCE n. [f. L DE(liquescere incept. of liquere be liquid)]

dèli'rious, a. Affected with delirium, temporarily or apparently mad, raving; wildly excited, ecstatic; betraying delirium or ecstasy. Hence ~LY² adv. [as foll. +-OUS]

dèli'rium, n. Disordered state of mind with incoherent speech, hallucinations, & frenzied excitement; great excitement, ecstasy; ~ trèm'ens (abbr. d.t.), special form of ~ with terrifying delusions to which heavy drinkers are liable. [L, f. DElirare (lira furrow)]

dèlitès'cent, a., **dèlitès'cence,** n. Latent (state). [f. L DE(litescere incept. of -litère = latère lie hid), -ENT, -ENCE]

dèliv'er, v.t. Rescue, save, set free from;

disburden (woman in parturition) of child (usu. pass.; also fig. was ~ed of a sonnet); unburden oneself (of esp. a long-suppressed opinion etc.) in discourse; (of judge) pronounce (judgement); give up or over, abandon, resign, hand on to another; distribute (letters, parcels, ordered goods) to addressee or purchaser (~ the goods, fig., carry out one's part of agreement); present, render, (account); (Law) hand over formally (esp. sealed deed to grantee, so seal & ~); launch, aim, (blow, ball, attack; ~ batile, accept opportunity of engaging); recite (well- -~ed sermon). Hence ~ABLE a. [ME, f. OF delivrer f. LL deliberare (DE-, L liberare f. liber free)]

dèliv'erance, n. Rescue; emphatically or formally delivered opinion, (in jurors' oath) verdict. [ME, f. OF délivrance (prec., -ANCE)]

dèliv'erer, n. In vbl senses; esp., saviour, rescuer. [ME, f. DELIVER +-ER³]

dèliv'erȳ, n. Childbirth; surrender of; delivering of letters etc., a periodical performance of this (the first, the two- -o'clock, ~); (Law) formal handing over of property, transfer of deed (formerly essential for validity) to grantee or third party; sending forth of missile, esp. of cricket-ball in bowling, action shown in doing this (a good, high, ~); uttering of speech etc. (its ~ took two hours), manner of doing this (a telling ~). [ME, f. AF delivree fem. part. used as n. of delivrer DELIVER, -Y⁴]

dèll, n. Small hollow or valley usu. with tree-clad sides. [ME delle, MLG, MDu. delle, MHG telle f. WG *daljō (as in Goth. ibdalja slope); cf. DALE]

Dèll'a Crùs'can, a. & n. (Member) of the Florentine Academy della Crusca, a society for purifying the Italian language, which issued an authoritative dictionary; following artificial literary methods; member of a late 18th-c. artificial English school of poetry. [f. It. (Accademia) della Crusca (Academy) of the bran (i.e. sitting) +-AN]

dèlouse', v.t. Rid of lice, & fig. of booby- -traps, mines, etc. [DE-]

Dèl'phian, Dèl'phic, aa. (As) of the oracle of Delphi; obscure, ambiguous. [-ic f. L f. Gk Delphikos, -ian f. L f. Gk Delphoi +-IAN]

Dèl'phin, a. The ~ classics or text, in an edition prepared for the Dauphin, son of Louis XIV. [L f. Gk, = dolphin; see DAUPHIN]

dèl'phinine, n. (chem.). A poisonous alkaloid used medically. [f. bot. L f. Gk delphinion (dim. of delphin dolphin) larkspur +-INE⁵]

dèlphin'ium, n. (Kinds of) ranunculaceous plant, including the larkspur. [as prec.]

For compounds of **de-** not given consult **DE-**.

děl'phinoid, n. & a. (Member) of the family including dolphins, porpoises, grampuses, etc. [f. Gk *delphin* dolphin, -OID]

děl'ta, n. Letter D (Δ, δ) of Greek alphabet; triangular alluvial tract at mouth of river enclosed or traversed by its diverging branches, esp. that of Nile, whence **děltā'ɪc** a.; ~ *metal*, alloy of copper, zinc, and ferro-manganese; ~ *rays*, rays of low penetrative power emitted by radium, polonium, uranium, etc., consisting of low-velocity electrons knocked from an atom during a collision with some other particles; ~ *wing*, triangular swept-back wing of aircraft. [Gk]

děl'toid, a. & n. Triangular; ~ *muscle* or ~, muscle of shoulder lifting upper arm; like a river delta. [f. F *deltoïde*, mod. L *deltoides* (prec., -OID)]

dělude' (-ōōd, -ūd), v.t. Impose upon, deceive. [f. L DE(*ludere lus*- play)]

děl'ūge, n., & v.t. 1. Great flood, inundation, (*the D*~, Noah's flood); heavy fall of rain; flood of words etc. 2. vb. Flood, inundate, (lit. & fig.). [ME, f. OF f. L *diluvium* (*diluere* DILUTE)]

dělu'sion (-ōōzhn, -ū-), n. Imposing or being imposed upon; false impression or opinion, esp. as symptom or form of madness, whence ~AL a. [ME, f. LL *delusio* (DELUDE, -ION)]

dělus'ive (-ōō-, -ū-), a. Deceptive, disappointing, unreal. Hence ~LY[2] adv., ~NESS n. [DELUDE, -IVE]

de luxe (lōōks), a. & adv. Luxurious(ly), sumptuous(ly); of superior kind. [F]

dělve, v.t. & i., & n., (arch., poet., & dial.). 1. Dig; make research in documents etc.; (of road etc.) make sudden dip. 2. n. Cavity; depression of surface, wrinkle. [OE *delfan*, OS -*delban*, OHG -*telban* f. WG *delbh*-]

děmăg'nětĭz|e, -**ĭs|e** (-ĭz), v.t. Deprive of magnetic quality. Hence ~ᴀ'TION n. [DE-]

děm'agŏg|ue (-g), n. Popular leader; political agitator appealing to cupidity or prejudice of the masses, factious orator. Hence or cogn. **děmagŏg'ɪo** (-gĭk) a., ~ISM(2), ~Y[1] nn., (-g-). [f. Gk *dēmagōgos* (DEMOS, *agōgos* leading)]

děmand'[1] (-ah-), n. Request made as of right or peremptorily, thing so asked, (*payable on* ~ as the ~ is made); call of would-be purchasers *for* commodity (*laws of supply and* ~ in Pol. Econ.; *in* ~, sought after); urgent claim (*many* ~*s on my time*). [ME, f. OF *demande* f. *demander* see foll.]

děmand'[2] (-ah-), v.t. Ask for (thing) as a right or peremptorily or urgently (*of* or *from* person; obj. a noun, infin., or *that*- -clause); require, need (*piety* ~*s it*; *task* ~*s skill*); ask to be, insist on being, told (~ *one's business*, what he wants). Hence or cogn. ~ABLE a., ~ANT(1) n. [ME, f. AF, OF *demander* f. L DE(*mandare* order cf. MANDATE)]

děmārcā'tion, n. Marking of boundary, esp. *line of* ~. Hence (by back formation) **dē'mārcāte** v.t. [Sp. (-*cion*), f. *demarcar* mark bounds of (DE-, MARK)]

děmarche (dēmärsh'), n. (In E diplomatic journalese) political step or proceeding. [F]

děmatēr'ialize, -**ise** (-ĭz), v.t. & i. Make, become, non-material, spiritual. [DE-]

dēme, n. (Gk hist.) township of ancient Attica. [f. Gk *dēmos*]

dēmean'[1], v. refl. ~ *oneself*, behave, conduct oneself, (always w. adv. or adv. phr.). [ME, f. OF *demener* f. DE-+*mener* lead f. post-class. L *minare* drive cattle f. *minari* threaten]

dēmean'[2], v.t. (usu. refl.). Lower in dignity. [DE-, MEAN[3]]

děmean'our (-ner), n. Bearing, outward behaviour. [f. DEMEAN[1]; earlier -*ure*, -*er*]

děměnt', v.t. Drive mad, craze, (usu. in p.p.). Hence **děměn'tědly**[2] adv. [f. LL *dementare* f. DEmens out of one's mind (*mens mentis*)]

děmenti (see Ap.), n. Official denial of rumour etc. [F]

děměn'tia (*or* -sha), n. (med.). Species of insanity consisting in feebleness of mind. [L (*demens* see DEMENT)]

děmerār'a (*or* -ah'ra), n. Kind of brown raw cane sugar in large crystals from Demerara. [place]

děmě'rit, n. Ill desert; fault, defect. Hence ~ōr'ious [-ORY, -OUS] a. [OF *de(s)merite* or f. L *demeritum* neut. p.p. of DEmereri deserve; orig. sense desert (good or bad, like *merit*); the two have now been fixed to opposite senses]

děmesne' (-ēn *or* -ān), n. 1. (Law) possession (of real property) as one's own (esp. *hold in* ~); an estate held in ~, all of an owner's land not held of him by freehold tenants, or all that he actually occupies himself; *Royal* ~, Crown lands; *State* ~, land held by State. 2. Sovereign's or State's territory, domain; landed property, estate; region, sphere, *of*. [ME, f. AF, OF *demeine* (later AF *demesne* perh. by assoc. w. MESNE *or mansio*) f. L *dominicus*; see DOMAIN]

děm'i-, pref. usu. written with the hyphen, still used as living pref. to form temporary words, but largely superseded by SEMI-. Half-size, half, imperfect, partial(ly), semi-; ~*tasse* (F), small cup (of black coffee). [F, f. L *dimidius*, -*um*]

děm'igŏd, n. Partly divine being, son of god and mortal, or deified man. [prec.]

děm'ijohn (-jŏn), n. Bulging narrow-necked bottle of 3–10 gal., usu. cased in wicker & with wicker handles. [corrupt. of F *dame-jeanne* Dame Jane; found in many langg., but earliest in F, prob. as playful personification]

děmil'itarize, -**ise** (-ĭz), v.t. Take away the military organization from (frontier, zone, etc.). [DE-]

děm'ilune (-ōōn), n. (fortif.). Outwork

protecting bastion or curtain. [F, = half moon]

dĕm'ĭ-mŏnd|e, n. Class of women on outskirts of society, of doubtful reputation & standing. Hence **~aine'** n., woman of the **~e**. [F, = half world]

dĕm'ĭ-rĕp, n. Woman of suspected chastity. [abbr. for *demi-reputable*]

dėmise' (-z), v.t., & n. Convey, grant, (estate) by will or lease (n., this process); transmit (title etc.) by death or abdication (n., this event, esp. *~ of the Crown*; transf., death). Hence **dėmis'ABLE** (-z-) a. [vb f. n., AF use of p.p. of OF *desmettre* DISMISS, in refl. abdicate]

dĕm'ĭsĕmiquāv'er, n. (mus.). Note, with three-hooked symbol, equal to half a semiquaver. [DEMI-]

dėmi'ssion (-shn), n. Resigning, abdication, *of*. [f. F *démission* f. L DI(*missionem* f. *mittere miss-* send, -ION)]

dėmit', v.t. & i. (-tt-). Resign (office, or abs.). [f. F *démettre* f. L DE(*mittere* send)]

dĕm'iūrge, n. Creator of world (in Platonic philosophy; also of Christian God, & of supposed subordinate agents in creation). Hence **dėmiūr'gic** a. [f. LL f. Gk *dēmiourgos* craftsman (*dēmios* f. DEMOS, *-ergos* working)]

dėmōb', v.t. (-bb-). Demobilize (esp. in p.p. of individuals released by demobilization). [abbr.]

dėmōb'iliz|e, -is|e (-ĭz), v.t. Release from mobilized state, disband, (troops, ships). Hence **~A'TION** n. [DE-]

dėmŏc'racy̆, n. (State practising) government by the people, direct or representative; *the* politically unprivileged class. [f. F *démocratie* f. LL f. Gk *dēmokratia* (DEMOS, -CRACY)]

dĕm'ŏcrăt, n. Advocate of democracy; **(D~)* member of Democratic party. Hence **dĕmŏc'ratISM**(3) n. [f. F *démocrate* (prec.)]

dĕmŏcrăt'ĭc, a. Of, like, practising, advocating, democracy; **D~party*, opposed to REPUBLICAN & supporting State, local, & individual liberty against federal powers. So **dĕmocrăt'ICALLY** adv., **dĕmŏc'ratIZE**(3) v.t. & i., **dĕmŏcratīZA'TION** n. [f. F *démocratique* (as prec.)]

Dėmŏc'ritě'an, a. Of Democritus, his humour, or his theory of atoms. [f. L f. Gk *Dēmokriteios* of Democritus (Gk philosopher of 5th c. B.C. called the laughing philosopher, & an atomistic physicist) +-AN]

dėmodé (dāmōd'ā), a. Out of fashion. [F]

Dėmogŏrg'on, n. A mysterious & terrible infernal deity. [LL; perh. assim. of some Oriental name to Gk DEMOS, *gorgos* grim]

dėmŏg'raphy̆, n. Vital statistics, illustrating condition of communities. Hence

dėmŏg'RAPHER n., **dėmŏGRAPH'IC** a. [DEMOS, -GRAPHY]

demoiselle (dĕm'wazĕl'), n. The Numidian crane. [F, = DAMSEL]

dėmŏl'ĭsh, v.t. Pull or throw down (building), destroy; overthrow (institution, theory); eat up. So **dėmoli'TION** n. [f. F *démolir* (-ISH²) f. L DE(*moliri* construct f. *moles* mass)]

dĕm'on, dae-, n. (Gk myth.; often *dae-*) supernatural being, inferior deity, spirit, ghost, indwelling or attendant spirit, genius; evil spirit (as in demoniacs); heathen deity; devil; malignant supernatural being; cruel, malignant, destructive, or fierce person (*~ bowler*, very fast; *is a ~ for work*, works strenuously); personified vice or passion. Hence **dėmono-** comb. form, **dėmonŏl'ATRY**, **dėmonŏL'OGY**, nn. [f. L f. Gk *daimōn* deity, w. sense also of L f. Gk *daimonion* divine (power etc.) neut. adj.]

dėmŏn'ėtīze, -ise (-ĭz; *or* -mŭ-), v.t. Deprive (metal etc.) of its status as money. [f. F *démonétiser* (DE-, L *moneta* MONEY, -IZE)]

dėmŏn'iăc, a. & n. (Person) possessed by an evil spirit; of such possession; devilish; fiercely energetic, frenzied. [ME, f. LL *daemoniacus* (Gk *daimonion* see DEMON, -AC)]

dėmoni'acal, a. = prec. adj. (esp. in phr. *~ possession*, & in sense *devilish*). [prec.+-AL]

dėmŏn'ĭc, dae-, a. = prec, inspired, of supernatural genius or impulses. [f. LL f. Gk *daimonikos* (DEMON, -IC)]

dĕm'onism, n. Belief in the power of demons. [-ISM(3)]

dĕm'onīze, -ise (-ĭz), v.t. Make into or like, represent as, a demon. [f. med. L *daemonizare* (DEMON, -IZE)]

dėmŏn'stra|ble (*or* dĕm'on-), a. Capable of being shown or logically proved. Hence **~BIL'ITY** n., **~bLY²** adv. [ME, f. OF or L *demonstrabilis* (foll., -ABLE)]

dĕm'onstrāte, v.t. & i. Show (feelings etc.); describe & explain by help of specimens or experiments, teach as a demonstrator; logically prove the truth of; be a proof of the existence of; make a military demonstration; take part in a demonstration by public meeting, whence **dėmon'strATE**(1) n. [f. L DE-(*monstrare* show, see MONSTER, -ATE³]

dĕmonstrā'tion, n. Outward exhibition *of* feeling etc.; logical proving, clear proof, (*to ~*, conclusively); thing serving as proof; exhibition & explanation of specimens or experiments as way of teaching; show of military force to intimidate, to mask other operations, or in peace to show readiness for war; exhibition of opinion on political or other question, esp. public meeting or procession, whence **~IST**(1) (-sho-) n. Hence

For compounds of *de-* not given consult DE-.

~AL (-sho·) a. [ME, f. OF, or L *demonstratio* (prec., -ION)]

demŏn'strative, a. & n. Serving to point out or exhibit (esp. in Gram., ~ *pronoun* or *adjective*, or ~ as noun, this etc.); giving proof *of*; logically conclusive; concerned with proof; given to or marked by open expression of feelings (~ *person*, *behaviour*, *affection*, etc.). Hence ~LY² (-vl-) adv., ~NESS (-vn-) n. [f. F *démonstratif* or L *demonstrativus* (as prec., -IVE)]

dĕm'onstrātor, n. One who demonstrates; teacher by demonstration, assistant to professor doing practical work with students; partaker in demonstration by public meeting. [L (DEMONSTRATE, -OR)]

dĕmŏ'ralĭz|e, -ĭs|e (-ĭz), v.t. Corrupt morals of, deprave; destroy the discipline, cohesion, courage, or endurance of (esp. troops; see MORALE). Hence ~A'TION n. [f. F *démoraliser* (DE-, MORAL, -IZE)]

dĕ mŏrt'ŭĭs nĭl nĭs'ĭ bŏn'ŭm, sent. Nothing but good should be spoken of the dead. [L]

Dĕm'ŏs, n. Personification of the populace or democracy. [Gk, = people]

Dĕmosthĕn'ĭc, a. Like Demosthenes or his oratory; eloquent, patriotic, denunciatory, (of speech). [f. Gk *Dēmosthenikos* of Demosthenes (Attic orator 4th c. B.C.)]

*•**dĕmōte'**, v.t. Reduce to lower rank or class. Hence **dĕmŏ'tion** n. [f. DE-+(PRO)MOTE]

dĕmŏt'ĭc, a. Popular, vulgar; (Archaeol.) in the popular form (opp. *hieratic*) of ancient Egyptian writing. [f. Gk *dēmotikos* (*dēmotēs* one of the DEMOS+-IC)]

dĕmŭl'cent, a. & n. Soothing (medicine). [f. L DE(*mulcēre* soothe), -ENT]

dĕmŭr', v.i. (-rr-), & n. **1.** Make difficulties, raise scruples or objections *to* or *at*; (Law) put in a demurrer, whence **dĕmŭr'rant**(1) n. **2.** n. Objecting, objection, (usu. *without*, *no*, ~). [f. OF *demorer* f. Rom. *DE(*morare* f. L *-i* delay]

dĕmūre', a. Sober, grave, composed; ironically reserved; affectedly coy, prudish. Hence ~LY² (-rl-) adv., ~NESS (-rn-) n. [ME; perh. f. AF *demuré* f. OF *demorer* (prec.), w. sense-development as *staid*; infl. by obs. *mure* in same sense f. OF *meur* f. L *maturus* ripe]

dĕmŭr'rable, a. That may be demurred to, open to objection, (esp. legal). [DEMUR, -ABLE]

dĕmŭr'rage, n. Rate or amount payable to shipowner by charterer for failure to load or discharge ship within time allowed, similar charge on railway trucks; detention, delay; charge (1½*d*. per oz) of Bank of Engl. deducted in giving notes or gold for bullion. [f. DEMUR+-AGE]

dĕmŭr'rer, n. Legal objection to relevance of opponent's point even if granted, which stays action till relevance is settled; exception taken. [f. AF *demurrer* infin. = DEMUR; -ER⁴]

dĕmy', n. (pl. *-ies*, pr. -ĭz). Size of paper (printing, 17½ x 22½; writing, 15½ x 20); ‖ scholar of Magd. Coll., Oxford (orig. w. half fellow's allowance), whence ~SHIP n. [var. of DEMI-]

dĕn, n. Wild beast's lair; lurking-place of thieves etc.; small room unfit to live in; room in which person secludes himself to work etc. [OE *denn*, MLG *denne*, OHG *tenni*, f. WG *dannja, *-jō*; cogn. w. DEAN²]

dēnār'ĭus, n. (pl. *-ĭī*). Ancient-Roman silver coin (orig. about 8*d*.), whence Engl. *d*. for penny. [f. *deni* ten each, -ARY¹; *denarius* (*numus*) = (coin) of ten (*asses*)]

dĕn'ary, a. Of ten, decimal. [f. L (prec.)]

dēnā'tionalĭz|e, -ĭs|e (-ĭz; -sho-), v.t. Deprive (nation) of its status or characteristics, (person) of membership or characteristics of his nation, (institution) of its position as national property. Hence ~A'TION n. [f. F *dénationaliser* (DE-, NATIONAL, -IZE)]

dēnā'turalĭz|e, -ĭs|e (-ĭz; -cher-), v.t. Change nature of, make unnatural; (usu. refl.) divest of citizenship or membership of State. Hence ~A'TION n. [DE-, NATURAL, -IZE(3); also DE-+NATURALIZE]

dēnā'ture, v.t. Change nature or essential qualities of (esp. tea or alcohol by adulteration). So **dēnā'turant** (-chŏo-) n., substance used in denaturing. [f. F *dénaturer* (DE-, NATURE)]

dēna'zĭ|fў (-ahts-), v.t. Rid of Nazism & its influence. Hence ~FICA'TION n. [DE-]

dĕn'drīte, n. (Stone or mineral with) natural tree-like or moss-like marking. Hence **dĕndrĭt'ĭc** a. [F, f. Gk *dendritēs* adj. (*dendron* tree), -ITE¹]

dendr(o)-, -i-, comb. forms, f. Gk *dendron* tree. Hence **dĕn'drĭform**, **dĕn'drŏid**, aa., **dĕndrŏl'ogy**, **dĕndrŏl'ogist**, nn., **dĕn'drophĭl(e)**, **dĕn'drophobe**, aa. & nn.

‖ **dēne¹**, n. Bare sandy tract, low sandhill, by sea. [perh. related to LG, Fris. *düne*, Du. *duin*, F *dune*]

dēne². See DEAN².

dēnĕgā'tion, n. (arch.). Denial. [F (*déné-*), f. LL DE(*negationem* f. *negare* deny, -ATION)]

dēne-hōle, **dāne-**, n. (archaeol.). Artificial cave in chalk entered by vertical shaft often 60 ft deep. [orig. ŭncert.; perh. f. DANE]

dĕng'ue '-nggĭ), n. Infectious eruptive fever causing acute pains in joints. [prob. f. Swahili name, w. assim. to Sp. *dengue* prudery, w. ref. to stiffness of patient's neck & shoulders]

dĕni'able, a. That one can deny. [-ABLE]

dĕni'al, n. Refusal of request; = SELF-~; statement that thing is not true (*meet charge with flat* ~) or existent, contradiction; disavowal of person as one's leader etc. [DENY, -AL(2)]

dĕni'er¹, n. One who denies. [DENY, -ER¹]

dènier'² (-nē̃r), n. **1.** (arch. or obs.). Very small sum or coin. **2.** (commerc.; also **dèn'yer**, dēn'iā). Unit of weight by which silk & rayon yarn is weighed & its fineness estimated. [OF, 1/12 of sou, f. DENARIUS]

dèn'igr̄āte, v.t. Blacken; defame, whence or cogn. ~ātor, ~a'tion, nn. [f. L DE(nigrare f. niger black)]

dèn'im, n. Twilled cotton fabric used for overalls etc. [for serge de Nim (Nîmes in France)]

dènit'r̄āte, dènit'rifȳ, vv.t. Free of nitric or nitrous acid or nitrates. [DE-]

dèn'izen, n., & v.t. **1.** Inhabitant, occupant, (of place); foreigner admitted to residence & certain rights; naturalized foreign word, animal, or plant; hence ~ship n. **2.** v.t. Admit as ~ (usu. pass.). [ME, f. AF deinzein (deinz = F dans f. L DE-, intus within, -aneus see -ANEOUS)]

dènŏm'ināte, v.t. Give name to, call or describe as so-&-so (w. obj. & compl.). [f. L DE(nominare NOMINATE)]

dènōmīnā'tion, n. Name, designation, esp. characteristic or class name; class of units in numbers, weights, money, etc. (reduce to the same ~; money of small ~s); class, kind, with specific name; religious sect, whence ~AL (-sho-) a. (~al education, according to principles of a Church or sect, whence ~aLize(3) (-sho-) v.t.). [ME, f. OF, or L denominatio (prec., -ATION)]

dènŏm'ināitive, a. Serving as, giving, a name. [f. F -if, or L denominativus (as prec., -ATIVE)]

dènŏm'inātor, n. Number below line in vulgar fraction, divisor; common~, (least) common multiple of the ~s of a number of fractions, also fig. [f. F -teur, or LL denominator (as prec., -OR]

dènōtā'tion, n. Denoting; expression by marks or symbols; sign, indication; designation; meaning of a term; (Log.) aggregate of objects that may be included under a word (cf. CONNOTATION), extension. [f. F, or L denotatio (DENOTE, -ATION)]

dènōt'ative, a. Indicative of; (Log.) merely designating, implying no attributes, (cf. CONNOTATIVE). Hence ~LY (-vl-) adv. [DENOTE, -ATIVE]

dènōte', v.t. Mark out, distinguish, be the sign of; indicate, give to understand, (esp. that-clause); stand as name for; (Log.) be a name for, be predicated of, (the word white ~s all white things, as snow, paper, foam). Hence ~MENT (-tm-) n. [f. F dénoter or L DE(notare mark f. nota NOTE¹)]

dènouement (see Ap.), n. Unravelling of plot or complications, catastrophe, final solution, in play, novel, etc. [F (dénouer unknot, f. DE-, L nodare f. nodus knot, -MENT)]

dènounce', v.t. Prophesy (woe, vengeance); inform against; openly inveigh

against; give notice of termination of (armistice, treaty). Hence ~MENT (-sm-) n. [ME, f. OF denoncier f. L DE(nuntiare f. nuntius messenger)]

de nouveau (de nōōvō'), adv. Afresh, starting again. [F]

dē nōv'ō, adv. = prec. [L]

dènse, a. Closely compacted in substance; crowded together; crass, stupid. Hence ~'LY² (-sl-) adv., ~'NESS (-sn-) n. [f. F, or L densus]

dèn'sitȳ, n. Closeness of substance; (Physics) degree of consistence measured by ratio of mass to volume or by quantity of matter in unit of bulk; crowded state; stupidity. [f. F densité or L densitas (prec., -TY)]

dènt, n., & v.t. (To mark with a) surface impression (as) from the blow of a blunt-edged instrument. [ME; var. of DINT]

dèn'tal, a. & n. Of tooth, teeth, or dentistry; ~ letter or ~, made with tongue-tip against upper front teeth (as th) or front of palate (as d, t), whence ~IZE(3) v.t. [f. med. L dentalis f. L dens dentis tooth +-AL]

dèn'tāte, a. (bot. & zool.). Toothed, with tooth-like notches. So **dèntA'tion** n., **dèntāt'o-** comb. form. [f. L dentatus (prec., -ATE²)]

dèn'ti-, comb. form of L dens dentis tooth, as ~lingual formed by teeth & tongue. Hence ~FORM, dènti'GEROUS, aa.

dèn'ticle, n. Small tooth or tooth-like projection; = DENTIL. So dèntic'ūlAR¹, dèntic'ūlATE² (-at) or -ātĕd, aa., dènticūlA'tion n. [f. L denticulus (prec., -CULE)]

dèn'tifrice, n. Powder, paste, etc., for tooth-cleaning. [F, f. L DENTI(fricium f. fricare rub)]

dèn'til, n. One of series of small rect-angular blocks under bed-moulding of cornice in classical architecture (often ~-cornice, -band, -moulding). [f. obs. F dentille dim. of dent tooth f. L dens dentis]

dèn'tine, n. Hard dense tissue forming main part of teeth. [f. L as prec. +-INE⁴]

dèn'tist, n. One whose profession it is to treat diseases of the teeth, extract them, insert artificial ones, etc. Hence ~RY n. [f. F dentiste f. dent see DENTIL, -IST(3)]

dènti'tion, n. Cutting of teeth, teething; characteristic arrangement of teeth in animal. [f. L dentitio (dentire to teethe, -ION)]

dèn'ture, n. Set of (usu. artificial) teeth. [F, f. dent tooth (see DENTIL) +-URE]

dènūde' v.t. Make naked; strip of clothing, covering, possession, attribute; (Geol.) lay (rock, formation) bare by removal of what lies above. Hence dènūdā'tion n., dènūd'ATIVE a. [f. L DE(nudare f. nudus naked)]

dènŭnciā'tion, n. Denouncing; invec-tive. So dènŭn'ciative, dènŭn'ciatorȳ,

(-sha-) aa., **děnŭn′ciātor** (-shǐ-) n. [F, or f. L *denuntiatio* (DENOUNCE, -ATION)]

děnȳ′, v.t. Declare untrue or non-existent (~ *the charge, the possibility, that it is so, this to be the case*; rarely with *but* after neg., *I don't ~ but he may have thought so*); disavow, repudiate, (~ *one's word, signature, faith, leader*); refuse (person, thing, person a thing, thing *to* person; *I was denied this, this was denied me* or *to me*); ~ *oneself*, be abstinent; report as not at home, refuse access to, (person visited). [ME, f. OF *denier* f. L DE(*negare* say no)]

‖ **dě′odănd**, n. (hist.). Thing forfeited to Crown to be used in alms etc. as having caused a human death. [f. L *deo dandum* thing to be given to God]

dě′odār, n. Himalayan cedar. [f. Hind. *de'odar* f. Skr. *deva-dara* divine tree]

děŏd′orīz|e (*or* -ōd-), -is|e (-īz), v.t. Deprive of odour, disinfect. Hence ~A′TION, ~ER¹(2), nn. [DE-, L *odor* smell, -IZE]

děöntŏl′ogȳ, n. Science of duty, ethics. So **děŏntOLO′GICAL** a., **děŏntŏL′OGIST** n. [f. Gk *deont*- part. st. of *dei* it is right, -o-, -LOGY]

Dē′ō ŏp′tǐmō măx′ǐmō, phr. To God the best & greatest (in dedications). [L]

Dē′ō volĕn′tĕ adv. (abbr. D.V.). God willing; if nothing occurs to prevent it. [L]

děpart′, v.i. & t. (Poet., arch., etc.) go away (*from*), take one's leave; set out, start, leave, (esp. in time-tables, as *dep. 6.30 a.m.*); die, leave by death, (~ *from life*, ~ *this life*); diverge, deviate, (~ *from received account, custom*). [ME, f. OF DE(*partir* f. L *partire* divide)]

děpart′ed, a. & n. Bygone (~ *greatness*); deceased (person; esp. *the* ~). [-ED¹(2)]

děpart′ment, n. Separate part of complex whole, branch, esp. of municipal or State administration; French administrative district; *~ *store*, large shop supplying all kinds of goods. So **děpart′měn′tAL** a., **děpartměn′talY²** adv. [f. F *département* (DEPART, -MENT)]

děpar′ture, n. Going away; deviation *from* (truth, standard); starting, esp. of train (*the* ~ *platform*); setting out on course of action or thought (esp. *new* ~); (Naut.) amount of ship's change of longitude in sailing. [f. OF *-eure* (DEPART, -URE)]

děpa′stur|e (-ah-), v.t. & i. (Of cattle) graze upon, graze; put (cattle) to graze; (of land) feed (cattle). Hence ~AGE n. [DE-]

děpaup′erīze, -ise (-īz), v.t. Raise from, rid of, pauperism. [DE-, PAUPER, -IZE]

děpěnd′, v.i. Hang down (poet., arch., etc.); be contingent (*it* ~*s upon himself*, i.e. upon his efforts, skill, wisdom, etc.; also abs. in *that* ~*s*, i.e. can only be answered conditionally); be grammatically dependent (*up*)*on*; rest for maintenance etc. *upon* (*she* ~*s upon her own efforts, her pen, her mother, my help*); reckon confidently *upon* (esp. in imperat.,

~ *upon it*, you may be sure); be waiting for settlement (of lawsuit, Bill, etc.). [ME, f. OF DE(*pendre* f. L *pendĕre* suspend but with sense of *pendēre* be suspended)]

děpěn′dab|le, a. That may be depended on. Hence ~leNESS (-ln-) n., ~LY² adv. [-ABLE]

děpěn′dant, -ent¹, n. One who depends on another for support, retainer, servant. [f. F *dépendant* part. (DEPEND, -ANT)]

děpěn′dence, n. Depending (*upon*), being conditioned or subordinate or subject; living at another's cost; reliance, confident trust; thing relied on. [f. F *dépendance* (prec., -ANCE)]

děpěn′dencȳ, n. Something subordinate or dependent, esp. country or province controlled by another. [as prec., -ANCY, -ENCY]

děpěn′dent², a. Depending (*on*), contingent, subordinate, subject; maintained at another's cost; (Gram. of *clause, phrase*, or *word*) in subordinate relation to a sentence or word. [earlier *-ant* = DEPENDANT]

děpic|t′, v.t. Represent in drawing or colours; portray in words, describe. Hence or cogn. ~′tER¹, ~′tOR, ~′tION, nn., ~′tIVE a. [f. L DE(*pingere pict*- paint)]

děpic′ture, v.t. Picture, depict. [DE-+PICTURE v.]

děp′il|āte, v.t. Remove hair from. Hence ~A′TION, ~ātOR, nn., depil′atORY a. & n. [f. L DE(*pilare* f. *pilus* hair), -ATE³]

děplēt|e′, v.t. Empty out, exhaust; relieve of congestion. So **děplē′tION** n., ~′IVE a. & n., ~′ORY a. [f. L DE(*plēre* -*plet*- fill)]

děplōr|e′, v.t. Bewail, grieve over, regret; be scandalized by. Hence ~′ABLE a., ~′abLY² adv., ~′ABIL′ITY, ~′ableNESS, nn. [f. F *déplorer* or L DE(*plorare* bewail)]

děploy′, v.t. & i., & n., (mil.). 1. Spread out (t. & i. of troops) from column into line; so ~MENT n. 2. n. Doing this. [f. F *déployer* f. L DIS(*plicare* fold), cf. DISPLAY]

děplume′ (-oo-), v.t. Pluck, strip of feathers. [ME, f. OF *deplumer* or med. L *deplumare* (DE-, L *pluma* feather)]

děpŏl′arīz|e, -is|e (-īz), v.t. (Opt.) change direction of polarization of (ray); (Electr. & Magn.) deprive of polarity; (fig.) disturb, shake loose, dissolve, (convictions, prejudices). Hence ~A′TION, ~ER′(2), nn. [DE-]

děpōn′ent, a. & n. 1. (L & Gk gram.) (verb) passive (or, in Gk, middle) in form but active in sense (named from notion that they had laid aside the pass. sense). 2. Person making deposition under oath or giving written testimony for use in court etc. [f. L DE(*ponere posit*- place), -ENT]

děpŏp′ŭl|āte, v.t. & i. Reduce population of; decline in population. So ~A′TION n. [f. L DE(*populari* lay waste f. *populus* people), -ATE³; see DISPEOPLE]

dĕpôrt', v.t. **1.** Bear or conduct one*self* in such a manner. **2.** Remove, esp. into exile, banish, whence **dĕpôrtᴀ'tion** n., **dĕpôrtᴇᴇ'** n., person who is or has been ~ed. [sense 1 f. OF *deporter* (ᴅᴇ-, *porter* carry f. L *portare*); sense 2 f. F *déporter* f. L ᴅᴇ(*portare* carry)]

dĕpôrt'ment, n. Bearing, demeanour, manners; way a thing (e.g. metal in chem. experiment) behaves. [F (*-ement*), as prec. 1, -ᴍᴇɴᴛ]

dĕpōs|e' (-z), v.t. & i. Remove from office, esp. dethrone, whence ~'ᴀʙʟᴇ (-z-) a.; bear witness *that*, testify *to*, esp. on oath in court. [ME, f. OF *deposer* (ᴅᴇ-+*poser*); cf. LL *deponere* in same sense & see ᴘᴏsᴇ¹]

dĕpŏs'it¹ (-z-), n. Thing stored or entrusted for safe keeping; sum placed in bank, ‖ usu. at interest & not to be drawn on without notice (*on* ~, so disposed of; *has a current & a* ~ *account*); sum required and paid as pledge or earnest or first instalment; layer of precipitated matter, natural accumulation. [f. L ᴅᴇ(*positum* neut. p.p. of *ponere* place)]

dĕpŏs'it² (-z-), v.t. Lay down in a (usu. specified) place; lay (eggs; usu. with adv. etc.); (of water or natural agency) leave (layer of matter) lying; store or entrust for keeping (esp. sum at interest in bank); pay as pledge for fulfilment of contract or further payment. [f. obs. F *dépositer* or med. L *depositare* frequent. of L *deponere* see prec.]

dĕpŏs'itary (-z-), n. Person to whom thing is committed, trustee. [f. LL *depositarius* (ᴅᴇᴘᴏsɪᴛ¹, -ᴀʀʏ¹)]

dĕposi'tion (-z-), n. (Picture of) taking down of Christ from the cross; deposing from office, esp. dethronement; (giving of) sworn evidence, allegation, (usu. dĕ-); depositing. [ME, f. OF, f. L *depositionem* f. *deponere* (ᴅᴇᴘᴏsɪᴛ¹, -ɪᴏɴ), used as n. of action of *depose, deposit*]

dĕpŏs'itor (-z-), n. Person who deposits money, property, etc.; apparatus for depositing some substance. [f. ᴅᴇᴘᴏsɪᴛ+-ᴏʀ]

dĕpŏs'itory (-z-), n. Storehouse (lit. & fig.); = ᴅᴇᴘᴏsɪᴛᴀʀʏ. [f. LL *depositorium* (ᴅᴇᴘᴏsɪᴛ¹, -ᴏʀʏ)]

dĕp'ot (-ō), n. **1.** (Mil.) place for stores; headquarters of regiment; recruit-drilling station; ‖ part of regiment not on foreign service. **2.** Storehouse, emporium; *(pr. dē'pō)* railway station. [f. F *dépôt* f. L as ᴅᴇᴘᴏsɪᴛ¹]

dĕprāve', v.t. Make bad, deteriorate, pervert, corrupt, esp. in moral character or habits. So **dĕpravᴀ'tion** n. [ME, f. OF *depraver* or L ᴅᴇ(*pravare* f. *pravus* crooked)]

dĕprăv'itў, n. Moral perversion, viciousness; (Theol.) innate corruption of man. [ᴅᴇ-+obs. *pravity* f. L *pravitas* (prec., -ᴛʏ)]

dĕp'rĕcāt|e, v.t. Plead against (~*e one's*

anger, beseech him not to be angry); express wish against or disapproval of (~*e war, hasty action, panic*). Hence or cogn. ~**inɢʟʏ²** adv., **dĕprĕcᴀ'tion** n., ~**ɪᴠᴇ**, ~**ᴏʀʏ**, aa. [f. LL ᴅᴇ(*precari* pray), -ᴀᴛᴇ³]

dĕprē'ciāt|e (-shɪ-), v.t. & i. Diminish (t. & i.) in value; lower market price of; reduce purchasing power of (money); disparage, belittle. Hence ~**inɢʟʏ²** adv., ~**ᴏʀʏ** (-sha-) a. [f. L ᴅᴇ(*pretiare* f. *pretium* price), -ᴀᴛᴇ³]

dĕprĕciā'tion (-ēsɪ-, -ēshɪ-), n. Depreciating or being depreciated; allowance made in valuations, estimates, and balance sheets, for wear & tear. [prec., -ᴀᴛɪᴏɴ]

dĕprĕdā'tion, n. (usu. pl.). Spoliation, ravages. [F (*dé-*), f. LL ᴅᴇ(*praedationem* f. *praedare* f. *praeda* prey, -ᴀᴛɪᴏɴ)]

dĕp'rĕdātor, n. Spoiler, pillager. [f. LL *depraedator* (prec., -ᴏʀ)]

dĕprĕss', v.t. Push or pull down, lower; bring low, humble; reduce activity of (esp. trade); lower (voice) in pitch; dispirit, deject; ~*ed classes* (Indian pol.), persons of the lowest Indian castes, untouchables. So ~**ɪʙʟᴇ** a. [f. OF *depresser* f. LL ᴅᴇ(*pressare* frequent. of *premere* ᴘʀᴇss²)]

dĕprĕss'ant, a. & n. (med.). Lowering, sedative, (medicine). [prec. + -ᴀɴᴛ]

dĕprē'ssion (-shn), n. Lowering, sinking; (Astron.) angular distance of star etc. below horizon; sunk place, hollow, on surface; reduction in vigour (esp. of trade), in pitch (of voice), vitality, or spirits; (Meteorol.) lowering of barometer or atmospheric pressure, esp. centre of minimum pressure or system of winds round it. [ME, f. OF, or LL ᴅᴇ(*pressio* f. *premere* ᴘʀᴇss- press, -ɪᴏɴ)]

dĕprĕss'or, n. (anat.). ~ *muscle* or ~, one pulling down some organ etc. [LL (prec., -ᴏʀ)]

dĕprivā'tion (or -ī-), n. Loss, being deprived, *of*; deposition from esp. ecclesiastical office; felt loss (*that is a great* ~). [f. med. L *deprivatio* (foll., -ᴀᴛɪᴏɴ)]

dĕprīv|e', v.t. Strip, bereave, debar from enjoyment, *of*; depose (esp. clergyman) from office. Hence ~'ᴀʙʟᴇ a., ~'ᴀʟ(2) n. [ME, f. OF *depriver* f. med. L ᴅᴇ(*privare* f. L *privare* deprive)]

dē profŭn'dīs, n. & adv. (Cry) from the depths of sorrow etc. [initial L wds of *Ps*. cxxx]

dĕpth, n. Being ᴅᴇᴇᴘ; measurement from top down, from surface inwards, or from front to back; abstruseness; sagacity; intensity of colour, darkness, etc.; (pl.) deep water, deep place, abyss, lowest or inmost part; middle (*in the* ~ *of winter*); deep or mysterious region of thought, feeling, etc. (*cry from the* ~*s*, ~ *of inspiration*, ~*s of degradation*); *out of* one's

~, in water too deep to stand in, (fig.) engaged on too hard a task or subject; ~*-charge*, bomb for dropping on submerged submarine, set to explode at desired ~. [ME; DEEP, -TH¹]

dĕp'ūr|āte, v.t. & i. Make, become, free from impurities. So ~A'TION, ~ātŏr, nn., **dĕpūr'ATIVE** a. & n. [f. med. L DE(*purare* f. L *purus* pure)]

dĕpūtā'tion, n. Body of persons appointed to represent others. [f. LL *deputatio* (foll., -ATION)]

dĕpūte', v.t. Commit (task, authority) to substitute; appoint as one's substitute. [ME, f. OF *deputer* f. L DE(*putare* think) regard as, allot]

dĕp'ūtīze, -ise (-īz), v.t. Act as deputy or understudy (*for*), esp. in musical engagements. [foll. +-IZE]

dĕp'ūtý, n. Person appointed to act for another or others (*by* ~, by proxy; ~ *lieutenant*, abbr. D. L., ~ of Lord Lieutenant of county); member of deputation; parliamentary representative (*Chamber of Deputies*, lower house in French & other Parliaments); ‖ manager of doss-house; ~-, deputed, acting-. Hence ~SHIP(1) n. [ME, f. OF *depute* p.p. of *deputer* DEPUTE, -Y⁴]

dĕră'cĭnāte, v.t. Tear up by the roots. [f. F *déraciner* (DE-, *racine* f. LL *radicina* dim. of *radix* root), -ATE³]

dĕrail', v.t. & i. Cause (train etc.) to leave the rails (usu. pass.); (rarely) leave the rails. So ~MENT n. [f. F *dérailler* (DE-, *rail* rail)]

dĕrānge' (-j), v.t. Throw into confusion or out of gear, disorganize, cause to act irregularly; make insane (esp. in p.p.); disturb, interrupt. So ~MENT (-jm-) n. [f. F *déranger* (DE-, *rang* rank)]

dĕrāte', v.t. Remove proportion of rates incident on (*derating scheme, bill*). [DE-]

dĕrā'tion, v.t. Remove (food etc.) from rationed category. [DE-]

Der'bý (dār-), n. **1.** Annual horse-race at Epsom; ~ *day*, of the race; ~ *dog*, any dog straying on course, (fig.) trivial untimely interruption. *2. (*d*~; pron. dẽr-) bowler hat. [Earl of ~ founder 1780]

Der'bÿshire (dār-; -sher), a. ~ *neck*, goitre, bronchocele; ~ *spar*, fluor-spar. *de règle* (rā'gl), pred. a. Customary, proper. [F]

dĕ'rĕlict, a. & n. Abandoned, ownerless, (esp. of ship at sea); abandoned property, esp. ship; person abandoned by society. [f. L DE(*relict*- see RELINQUISH)]

dĕrĕlic'tion, n. Abandoning, being abandoned; retreat of sea exposing new land; neglect of *duty*; failure in duty, short-coming. [f. L *derelictio* (prec., -ION)]

dĕrĕquisi'tion (-z-), v.t. Free (requisitioned property). [DE-]

dĕrīde', v.t. Laugh to scorn. [f. L DE(*ridēre* ris- laugh)]

de rigueur (rēgẽr'), pred. a. Required by etiquette (*evening dress is* ~). [F]

dĕrĭ'sion (-zhn), n. Ridicule, mockery, (*hold, have, in* ~, mock at; *be in* ~, be mocked at; *bring into* ~); laughing-stock. [ME, f. OF, f. LL *derisionem* (DERIDE, -ION)]

dĕris'īve, dĕris'orý, aa. Scoffing (~ *cheers*, ironical); (*-ory* only; of offer etc.) ridiculously futile, not to be taken seriously. Hence **dĕris'īvelÿ²** (-vǐ-) adv. [f. L *deris*- see DERIDE, +-IVE, -ORY]

dĕrĭvā'tion, n. Obtaining from a source; extraction, descent; formation of word from word or root, tracing or statement of this (cf. COGNATE); theory of evolution, whence ~IST(2) n. [f. F, or L *derivatio* (DERIVE, -ATION)]

dĕrĭv'ative, a. & n. (Thing, wòrd, chemical substance) derived from a source, not primitive or original. Hence ~LÝ² (-vǐ-) adv. [f. F *dérivatif* f. LL *derivativus* (foll., -IVE)]

dĕrīve', v.t. & i. Get, obtain, (*from* a source, or ·with the source present in thought); have one's or its *origin* etc. *from*; gather, deduce, (knowledge, truth, ideas, etc.) *from*; (pass., refl., & intr.) be descended or have one's origin *from*; (pass., of words) be formed *from*; trace, show, or assert, descent, origin, or formation, of (person, thing, word) *from*. Hence ~'ABLE a. [f. OF *deriver* or L *derivare* (DE-, *rivus* stream) divert, derive]

dĕrm, n. Skin; true skin or layer of tissue below epidermis. Hence or cogn. ~'AL, ~'IC, aa., ~'at(o)-, ~'o-, comb. forms, ~atīt'IS n., inflammation of the skin, ~atŏl'ogÿ, ~atŏl'ogist, nn. [f. Gk *derma* skin (*derō* flay, -M)]

dern. = DARN².

dernier ressort (dẽrnyā' resōr'), n. Last resort, desperate expedient. [F]

dĕ'rogāte, v.i. Detract, take away part, *from* (a merit, right, etc.); sink in the scale, do something derogatory. [f. L DE(*rogare* ask), -ATE³]

dĕrogā'tion, n. Lessening or impairment of law, authority, position, dignity, etc.; deterioration, debasement. [ME, f. OF, or L *derogatio* (prec., -ATION)]

dĕrŏg'atorÿ, a. Tending to detract *from*, involving impairment, disparagement, or discredit, *to*; lowering, unsuited to one's dignity or position; depreciatory. [f. LL *derogatorius* (DEROGATE, -ORY)]

dĕ'rrick, n. Contrivance for moving or hoisting heavy weights, kind of crane with adjustable arm pivoted at foot to central post, deck, or floor; framework over oil-well or similar boring. [obs. senses *hangman, gallows*, f. name of hangman *c.* 1600]

dĕ'rring-dō', n. (pseudo-arch.). Desperate courage. [f. Chaucer's *In dorrying don that longeth to a knyght* (in daring to do that which belongeth etc.) misinterpreted by Spenser]

dĕ'rringer (-j-), n. Small large-bore pistol. [U.S. inventor's name]

dĕ′rris, n. Kinds of tall tropical woody climbers; insecticide made from the powdered tuberous root of some of these. [Gk. ~ leather covering]

dērv, n. Fuel oil used in heavy road vehicles. [f. diesel-engined road vehicle]

dĕr′vish, n. Moslem friar vowed to poverty & austerity (*dancing* or *whirling* ~, *howling* ~, according to the practice of his order). [f. Pers. *darvesh* poor]

dĕs′cant¹, n. (Poet.) melody, song; (Mus.) melodic independent treble accompaniment. [ME, f. OF *deschant* f. med. L DIS(*cantus* CHANT)]

dĕscánt′², v.i. Talk at large, dwell freely, upon (esp. in praise, ~ *upon the beauties of*). [f. OF *deschanter* f. med. L *discantare* (prec.)]

dĕscénd′, v.i. & t. Come or go down, sink, fall, (~*ing letter* in Typ., with tail below line); slope downwards; make sudden attack *upon*; proceed in narrative etc. from earlier to later time, from greater to less (so Math., ~*ing series of* numbers), from general to particular; stoop *to do*; (rare) be DESCENDED *from*; be transmitted by inheritance *from* (of qualities, property, privileges), pass (*to* heir, or abs.); go down (hill, stairs). Hence ~ER¹ n., ~*ing* letter. [ME, f. OF *descendre* f. L DE(*scendere* = *scandere* climb)]

dĕscén′dant, n. Person or thing DESCENDED (*of*, or with *his* etc.). [F (prec., -ANT)]

dĕscén′dĕd, p.p. Sprung, having origin, *from* ancestor or stock (*is* ~ etc. usual instead of the rare *descends* etc.). [-ED¹(2)]

dĕscén′dible, -able, a. Transmissible by inheritance. [OF (-*able*); see -BLE]

dĕscént′, n. Descending, downward motion; downward slope; way down; sudden attack, esp. from sea; decline, sinking in scale, fall; being descended, lineage; single generation (*lineal succession of four* ~s); transmission of property, title, or quality, by inheritance. [ME, f. OF *descente* (*descendre* DESCEND)]

dĕscríb|e′, v.t. Set forth in words, recite the characteristics of; qualify *as* (*should* ~ *e him as a scoundrel*); mark out, draw, (esp. geom. figure); move in (such a line, curve); (abs.) deal in, give a, description. Hence ~′ABLE a. [f. L DE(*scribere* *script-* write)]

dĕscríp′tion, n. Describing, verbal portrait(ure), of person, object, or event (*answers to the* ~, has the qualities specified), more or less complete definition; sort, kind, class, (*no food of any* ~, *tyrant of the worst* ~). [ME, f. OF, f. L *descriptionem* (DESCRIBE, -ION)]

dĕscríp′tive, a. Serving to describe (~ *touches*), fond of describing (~ *writer*). Hence ~LY² (-vl-) adv. [f. LL *descriptivus* (DESCRIBE, -IVE)]

dĕscrý′, v.t. Catch sight of, succeed in discerning (lit. & fig.). [ME; prob. var. of obs. *descrive* f. OF *descrivre* DESCRIBE, & confused in early use with DECRY]

dĕs′ĕcr|āte, v.t. Deprive of sacred character; outrage, profane, (sacred thing); dedicate *to* (evil). Hence ~A′TION, ~ātor, nn. [DE-+(CON)SECRATE]

*dĕsĕg′rēgāte, v.t. Abolish racial segregation in (schools etc.). [DE-]

dĕsén′sitīze, -ise (-īz), v.t. Reduce or destroy the sensitiveness of (photographic plates etc.). [DE-]

dĕsert′¹ (-z-), n. Deserving, worthiness of recompense good or bad; character that deserves good, virtue, whence ~LESS a.; deserving people; (pl.) acts or qualities deserving good or bad recompense, such recompense, (*reward him according to, give him, he has got, his* ~s). [ME, f. OF obs. p.p. of *deservir* DESERVE]

dĕs′ert² (-z-), a. & n. 1. Uninhabited, desolate; uncultivated, barren. 2. n. Waterless & treeless region, (fig.) uninteresting or barren subject, period, etc.; ~ *rat* (colloq.), soldier of 7th (British) armoured division, which had a jerboa's figure as divisional sign, & which fought in the ~ campaign in N. Africa (1941-2). [ME; OF a. f. LL p.p. see foll.; n. f. LL *desertum* (cl. L *deserta* neut. pl.)]

dĕsert′³ (-z-), v.t. & i. Abandon, give up, (thing); depart from (place, haunt); forsake (person or thing having claims on one, as *wife, post, the colours, ship*); fail (*his presence of mind* ~*ed him*); run away (esp. from service in armed forces), whence ~ER¹ (-z-) n. So dĕser′tion (-z-) n. [f. F *déserter* f. LL *desertare* frequent. of L DE(*serere sert-* join)]

dĕsérv|e′ (-z-), v.t. & i. Be entitled by conduct or qualities to (good or bad); have established a claim to be *well* or *ill* treated at the hands *of*. Hence ~′ĕdLY² (-z-) adv. [ME, f. OF *deservir* f. L DE-(*servire* serve)]

dĕsérv′ing (-z-), a. Meritorious; worthy (*of* praise, censure, etc.). [-ING²]

déshabillé (see Ap.), n. = DISHABILLE. [F]

dĕs′icc|āte, v.t. Dry, dry up, (esp. milk etc. for preservation). So ~A′TION, ~ātor, nn., ~ATIVE a. [f. L DE (*siccare* f. *siccus* dry), -ATE³]

dĕsíd′erāte, v.t. (pedant.). Feel to be missing, regret absence of, wish to have. [f. L DE(*siderare* see CONSIDER), -ATE³]

dĕsíd′erative, a. & n. (gram.). (Verb, conjugation, etc.) formed on another verb etc. & expressing desire of doing the action. [f. LL *desiderativus* (prec., -IVE)]

dĕsīderāt′um, n. (pl. -*ta*). Thing missing, felt want. [L (neut. p.p. see DESIDERATE)]

dĕsígn′¹ (-zīn), n. Mental plan; scheme of attack *upon* (*has* ~s *upon me*); purpose (*whether by accident or* ~); end in view; adaptation of means to ends (*the argu-*

ment from ~, maintaining existence of a God by pointing to such adaptation); preliminary sketch for picture etc.; delineation, pattern; artistic or literary groundwork, general idea, construction, plot, faculty of evolving these, invention. [f. 15th-c. F *desseing* f. *desseigner* see foll.]

dèsign'² (-zīn), v.t. & i. Set (thing) apart *for* person; destine (person, thing) *for a* service; contrive, plan; purpose, intend, (~*s an attack, to do, doing,* or *that —*, thing or person *to* be or do something), whence ~**èdLY²** (-zïn-) adv.; make preliminary sketch of (picture); draw plan of (building etc. to be executed by others); be a designer; conceive mental plan for, construct the groundwork or plot of, (book, work of art). [f. F *désigner* appoint f. L *designare* DESIGNATE², with senses also of obs. F *desseigner* purpose & mod..F *dessiner* draw]

dès'ignate¹ (-z-), a. (placed after its noun). Appointed to office but not yet installed (*bishop* ~ etc.). [f. L p.p. (foll., -ATE²)]

dès'ignate² (-z-), v.t. Specify, particularize; serve as name or distinctive mark of; style, describe as; appoint to office (*as, to, for*). [f. L DE(*signare* f. *signum* mark), -ATE³]

dèsignā'tion (-z-), n. Appointing to office; name, description, title. [f. L as prec., -ATION]

dèsign'er (-zīn-), n. In vbl senses; esp. draughtsman who makes plans for manufacturers. [-ER¹]

dèsign'ing (-zīn-), a. In vbl senses; esp. crafty, artful, scheming. [-ING²]

dèsip'ience, n. Trifling, silliness. [f. L *desipientia* f. DE(*sipere = sapere* be wise)]

dèsir'a|ble (-z-), a. Worth wishing for. Hence ~**BIL'ITY**, ~**bleNESS**, nn., ~**bLY²** adv., (-z-). [ME, f. OF (DESIRE², -ABLE)]

dèsïre'¹ (-z-), n. Unsatisfied appetite, longing, wish, craving; request; thing desired. [ME, f. OF *desir*, f. vb (foll.)]

dèsïre'² (-z-), v.t. Long for, crave, wish, (noun, infin., noun & infin., or *that-*-clause); (abs.) feel desire; ask for; pray, entreat, command, (~ *him to wait*; *she ~d we would wait*). [ME, f. OF *desirer* f. L *desiderare* DESIDERATE]

dèsïr'ous (-z-), pred. a. Wishful *to do*, ambitious *of* (success etc.), having the desire *of doing*, wishful *that*. [f. AF *-ous*, = OF *-eus*, f. Rom. *desiderosus (prec., -OUS)]

dèsist' (-zī-, -sī-), v.i. Cease (*from doing, from* sin). [f. OF *desister* f. L DE(*sistere* stop)]

dèsk, n. Fixed or movable piece of furniture or box having (often in combination with drawers, seat, etc.) a board usu. sloped serving as rest for writing or reading at; the ~, clerical, office, or literary work. Hence ~**FUL(2)** n. [ME, f. med. L *desca* f. L *discus* disc]

dès'man, n. Aquatic insectivorous shrew--like mammal of Russia and the Pyrenees. [F & G, f. Sw. *desman-råtta* musk-rat]

dès'olate¹, a. Left alone, solitary; uninhabited; ruinous, neglected, barren, dreary; forlorn, disconsolate, wretched. Hence ~**LY²** (-tl-) adv., ~**NESS** (-tn-) n. [ME, f. L DE(*solare* f. *solus* alone), -ATE²]

dès'olāt|e², v.t. Depopulate; devastate; make (person) wretched. Hence ~**OR** n. [ME, f. prec., see -ATE³]

dèsolā'tion, n. Desolating; neglected, ruined, solitary, or barren state; being forsaken, loneliness; dreary sorrow. [ME, f. LL *desolatio* (as prec., -ATION)]

dèspair', n., & v.i. 1. Loss, utter want, of hope; thing that causes this, whether by badness or unapproachable excellence. 2. v.i. Lose, be without, hope (*of*, or abs.; *his life is* ~*ed of*); hence ~**īngLY²** adv. [ME, f. OF *despeir-* stressed st. of *desperer* f. L DE(*sperare* hope)]

‖ **despatch.** See disp-.

dèsperad'ō (-ahd-, -ād-), n. (pl. -*oes*). Person ready for or given to reckless, esp. criminal, undertakings. [OSp. (adj. only), f. L *desperatus* see foll.]

dès'perate, a. Leaving no or little room for hope, extremely dangerous or serious, utterly impracticable; reckless from despair, violent, lawless, staking all on a small chance, so **dèsperA'TION** n.; extremely bad (*a* ~ *night, storm,* etc.); very great (~ *fear, a* ~ *fool*). So ~**LY³** (-tl-) adv., ~**NESS** (-tn-) n. [ME, f. L DE(*sperare* hope), -ATE²]

dès'picab|le, a. Vile, contemptible. Hence ~**LY²** adv. [f. LL *despicabilis* f. DE(*spicari* cf. *specere* look at), -BLE]

dèspise' (-z), v.t. Look down upon, contemn. [ME; f. *despis-* st. of OF *despire* f. L DE(*spicere = specere* look at)]

dèspite', n. & prep. Outrage, injury, contumely, (arch.); malice, spite, offended pride (*died of mere* ~); *in* ~ *of,* = *of,* ~, notwithstanding the opposition of, in the teeth of, in spite of, (also *in my* etc. ~, in spite of my etc. efforts, arch.). Hence ~**FUL** a., ~**fulLY²** adv., (-tf-). [ME, f. OF *despit* f. L *despectus -ūs* f. *despicere* see prec.]

dèspoil', v.t. Plunder, spoil, rob, deprive, (person or place; often *of*). Hence or cogn. ~**ER¹**, ~**MENT**, **dèspŏliā'TION**, nn. [ME, f. OF *despoiller* (now *dépouiller*) f. L DE(*spoliare* spoil)]

dèspŏnd', v.i., & n. 1. Lose heart, be dejected; so ~**ENCY** n., ~**ENT** a., ~**entLY²**, ~**īngLY²**, advv. 2. n. (Arch., only in SLOUGH *of D*~) dejection. [f. L DE(*spondēre* promise) give up, resign]

dès'pot, n. Absolute ruler, whence ~**IST**(2) n.; tyrant, oppressor. So **dèspŏt'IC** a., **dèspŏt'ICALLY** adv. [f. F *despote* f. med. L *despota* f. Gk *despotēs*]

dès'potism, n. Arbitrary rule; State under a despot. [f. F *despotisme* (prec., -ISM)]

dès'quam|āte, v.i. Come off in scales. Hence ~**A'TION** n., **dèsquăm'atīve**, dèsquăm'atory, aa. [f. L DE(*squamare* f. *squama* scale)]

dèssért' (-z-), n. ‖ Course of fruit, sweets, etc., at end of dinner; ~-SPOON. [F, f. *desservir* (des- f. L *dis-*, *servir* SERVE) clear the table]

dèstĭnā'tion, n. Place for which person or thing is bound. [OF, or f. L *destinatio* (foll., -ATION)]

dès'tĭne, v.t. Appoint, fore-ordain, devote, set apart, (person or thing to do, *to* or *for* a service, achievement, etc.; of God, Fate, etc., or of persons; but chiefly in pass.); *was* ~*d to*, was, as we now know, to. [ME, f. F *destiner* f. L DE(*stinare* prob. causative of *stare* stand)]

dès'tĭny, n. Predetermined events; person's, country's, etc., appointed or ultimate lot; power that fore-ordains, invincible necessity. [ME, f. OF *destinee* (prec., -Y⁴)]

dès'tĭtūte, a. Without resources, in want of necessaries; devoid *of*. So dèstĭtū'-TION n. [f. L DE(*stituere* -*tut-* = *statuere* place) forsake]

dès'trĭer, n. (hist.). War-horse. [OF, f. Gallo-Rom. *dextrarius* hand-led (DEXTER, -ARY¹)]

dèstroy', v.t. Pull down, demolish, undo, make useless, kill, annihilate, nullify, neutralize effect of. Hence ~ABLE a. [ME, f. OF *destruire* f. Rom. *destrugere* f. L DE(*struere struct-* build)]

dèstroy'er, n. In vbl senses; esp. (orig. *torpedo-boat* ~) a warship designed to attack the enemy with torpedoes and to protect her own fleet from attacks by enemy light surface craft and submarines. [-ER¹]

dèstrŭc'tĭ|ble, a. Able to be destroyed. Hence ~BIL'ITY n. [f. LL *destructibilis* (DESTROY, -BLE)]

dèstrŭc'tion, n. DESTROYING or being destroyed; what destroys, cause of ruin, (*is our* ~). [ME, f. OF f. L *destructionem* (DESTROY, -ION)]

dèstrŭc'tive, a. & n. **1.** Destroying; deadly *to*, causing destruction *of*; (of criticism or policy) merely negative, refuting etc. without amending, not constructive; hence ~LY² (-vl-) adv., ~NESS (-vn-) n. **2.** n. Person, thing, that aims at or effects destruction. [ME, f. OF (-*if*, -*ive*), f. LL *destructivus* (DESTROY, -IVE)]

‖ dèstrŭc'tor, n. Refuse-burning furnace. [LL, = destroyer (DESTROY, -OR)]

dès'uetūde (-swī-), n. Passing into, state of, disuse. [f. F *désuétude* or L DE(*suetudo* f. *suescere suet-* be wont, -TUDE)]

dèsŭl'phurĭz|e (-fer-), -is|e (-ĭz), v.t. Free from sulphur. Hence ~A'TION n. [DE-]

dès'ultor|y̆, a. Skipping from one subject to another, disconnected, unmethodical. Hence ~ĭLY² adv., ~ĭNESS n. [f. L

dèsultōrius f. *desultor* circus-rider f. DE(*sult-* = *salt-* p.p. st. of *salire* leap)]

dèsy̆nŏn'y̆mize, -ise (-ĭz), v.t. Differentiate in sense (synonymous words). [DE-, SYNONYM, -IZE]

dètăch', v.t. Unfasten & remove (*from*, or abs.; ~*ed mind, view,* etc., regarding things impartially, free from prejudice; ~*ed house*, not joined to another on either side); (Mil. & Nav.) send (ship, regiment, etc.) on separate mission. Hence ~ABLE a., ~ĕDLY² adv., ~ĕDNESS n. [f. F *détacher*; see DE-, ATTACH]

dètăch'ment, n. Detaching; portion of army etc., or large body, separately employed; standing aloof from or unaffected by surroundings, public opinion, etc., independence of judgement, selfish isolation. [f. F *détachement* (prec., -MENT)]

dèt'ail¹, n. Dealing with things item by item (*in* ~; *go into* ~, give the items separately); minute account, number of particulars; item, small or subordinate particular, (*but that is a* ~, often iron. to call special attention), whence ~ED² (-ld) a., with particulars; minor decoration in building, picture, etc., way of treating this; (Mil.) distribution of orders of the day, small detachment. [f. F *détail* f. *détailler* see foll.]

dètail'², v.t. Give the particulars of, relate circumstantially; (Mil.) tell off for special duty. [f. F *détailler* (DE-, *tailler* cut, see TAILOR)]

dètain', v.t. Keep in confinement; withhold (money due etc.); keep waiting, hinder. Hence ~EE n., person ~ed in custody, usu. on political grounds. [f. OF *detenir* f. Rom. *detenēre* f. L DE(*tinēre* -*tent-* = *tenēre* hold)]

dètain'er, n. (legal). Detaining of goods taken from owner for distraint etc.; keeping of person in confinement; writ by which person already arrested may be detained on another suit. [f. AF *detener* f. OF *detenir* see prec., -ER⁴]

dètèct', v.t. Find out (guilty person, person *in doing*); discover existence or presence of. Hence or cogn. dètĕc'TABLE a., dètĕc'TION n. [f. L DE(*legere lect-* cover)]

dètĕc'tive, a. & n. **1.** Serving to detect. **2.** n. Policeman employed to investigate special cases (*private* ~, person undertaking special inquiries for pay; *amateur* ~, person who sets up theories on police cases); ~ *story* etc. (that tempts readers to solve ~ problems). [prec., -IVE]

dètĕc'tor, n. In vbl senses; also or esp.: coherer used in wireless telegraphy; valve in wireless receiving set. [-OR]

dètĕnt', n. Catch by removal of which machinery is set working, (in clocks etc.) catch that regulates striking. [f. F *détente* f. *détendre* slacken (DE-, L *tendere* stretch)]

For compounds of *de*- not given consult DE-.

détente (see Ap.), n. Easing of strained relations esp. between States. [F, as prec.]

dētĕn'tion, n. Detaining, being detained; arrest, confinement, (*House of D~*, lock-up); compulsory delay; (at schools) keeping in as punishment; *~ barracks*, military prison. [F, or f. LL *detentio* (DETAIN, -ION)]

détenu (dātenōō'), n. Person detained in custody. [F, p.p. of *détenir* detain]

dētĕr', v.t. (-rr-). Discourage or hinder (*from*, or abs.) by or as fear, dislike of trouble, etc. Hence **dētĕ'rrENCE,** **~MENT,** nn. [f. L DE(*terrēre* frighten)]

dētĕr'gent, a. & n. Cleansing (agent). [f. L DE(*tergēre ters-* wipe), -ENT]

dētēr'ior|āte, v.t. & i. Make, grow, worse. Hence or cogn. **~A'TION** n., **~ātive** a. [f. L *deteriorare* (*deterior* worse f. *de* down), -ATE[3]]

dētĕrm'inant, a. & n. Determining, decisive, conditioning, defining, (agent, factor, element, word). [DETERMINE, -ANT]

dētĕrm'inate, a. Limited, definite, distinct, finite, definitive. Hence **~LY[2]** (-tl-) adv., **~NESS** (-tn-) n. [ME, f. L p.p. (DETERMINE, -ATE[2])]

dētĕrminā'tion, n. (Law) cessation of estate or interest; conclusion of debate; judicial sentence; fixing of date etc.; delimitation, definition; exact ascertainment *of* amount etc.; fixed direction, decisive bias; (*~ of blood to* some part, tendency to flow there); settling of purpose, fixed intention; resoluteness. [ME, f. OF, or L *determinatio* (DETERMINE, -ATION)]

dētĕrm'inātive, a. & n. (Thing) that impels in a certain direction; (attribute, mark, symbol) serving to define or qualify. [f. F *déterminatif* (foll., -IVE)]

dētĕrm'in|e, v.t. & i. Bring, come, to an end (esp. in law); limit in scope, define; fix beforehand (date); settle, decide, (dispute, person's fate, *what* is to be done, *that —*, *whether*, etc.), come to a conclusion, give decision; be the decisive factor in regard to (*demand ~es supply*); ascertain precisely, fix; give an aim to, direct, impel *to*; decide (person) *to do*; resolve (*to do*, *that —*, *on doing*, on a course; *be ~ed*, have resolved). Hence **~ABLE** a. [f. OF *determiner* f. L DE(*terminare* f. *terminus* end)]

dētĕrm'ined (-nd), a. In verbal senses; also, resolute, unflinching. [-ED[1]]

dētĕrm'in|ism, n. Theory that human action is not free but determined by motives regarded as external forces acting on the will. So **~IST**(2) n. & a., **~is'tic** a. [f. F *-isme* or G *-ismus* (Kant)]

dētĕrs'ive, a. & n. Cleansing (substance). [f. F *détersif* (DETERGENT, -IVE)]

dētĕst', v.t. Abhor, dislike intensely. Hence or cogn. **~ABLE** a., **~ableNESS** (-ln-) n., **~abLY[2]** adv. [f. L DE*testari* call God to witness against]

dētĕstā'tion, n. Abhorrence (*have, hold, in ~*, abhor); detested person or thing. [F, or f. L *detestatio* (prec., -ATION)]

dēthrōne', v.t. Depose (ruler, dominant influence). Hence **~MENT** (-nm-) n. [DE-]

dēt'inūe, n. (legal). *Action of ~*, suit for recovery of thing wrongfully detained. [f. OF *detenue* f. p.p. of *detenir* DETAIN]

dĕt'on|āte (or dē-), v.i. & t. (Cause to) explode with loud report. Hence or cogn. **~A'TION** n., **~ātive** a. [f. L DE(*tonare* thunder), -ATE[3]]

dĕt'onātor, n. Detonating contrivance, esp. as part of bomb or shell; railway fog-signal. [-OR]

detour (dītoor'), **détour** (F), n. Deviation, roundabout way, digression, (esp. *make a ~*). [F (*dé-*), f. *détourner* (DE-, TURN)]

dētrăct', v.t. & i. Take away (*much, something*, etc., or abs.) *from* a whole (esp. in sense *reduce the credit due to, depreciate*). Hence or cogn. **dētrăc'tion, dētrăc'tor,** nn., **dētrăc'tive** a. [f. L DE(*trahere tract-* draw)]

dētrain', v.t. & i. Discharge, alight, from train (troops etc.; cf. ENTRAIN). [DE- + TRAIN n.]

dētrīb'aliz|e, -is|e (-īz), v.t. (anthrop.). Break up (tribal organization), also abs. So **~A'TION** n. [DE-]

dĕt'riment, n. Harm, damage, (esp. *without ~ to*). [ME, f. OF or L DE(*trimentum* f. *terere trit-* rub, wear, -MENT)]

dētrimĕn'tal, a. & n. Harmful, causing loss, whence **~LY[2]** adv.; (n., sl.) undesirable suitor, e.g. younger son. [-AL]

dētrīt'ĕd, a. (geol.). Disintegrated, formed as detritus. [DETRITUS as p.p. + -ED[1]]

dētrī'tion, n. Wearing away by rubbing. [f. L *detrit-* see DETRIMENT, -ION]

dētrīt'|us, n. Matter produced by detrition, as gravel, sand, silt; debris. Hence **~AL** a. [L *detritus -ūs* = wearing down, see DETRIMENT]

de trop (de trō'), pred. a. Not wanted, unwelcome, in the way. [F]

deuce[1], n. The two at dice or cards; (Tennis) state of score (40 all, games all) at which either party must gain two consecutive points or games to win. [f. OF *deus* (mod. *deux*) f. L *duos* nom. *-o* two]

deuce[2], n. Plague, mischief; the devil (*~ take it*; *who, where, what*, etc., *the ~?*; *the ~ is in it if I cannot*, I certainly can; *play the ~ with*, spoil, ruin; *the ~ to pay*, trouble to be expected; *a ~ of a mess*; *~ knows*; *~ a bit*, not at all; *the ~ he isn't*, it is incredible that he is not). [f. LG *duus*, = G *daus*, f. as prec., the two at dice being the worst throw]

deu'cĕd (dū-, dōō-), a. & adv. Confounded(ly); great (*in a ~ hurry*). Hence **~LY[2]** adv. [-ED[2]]

dē'us ĕx măch'inā (-k-), n. Power, event,

that comes in the nick of time to solve difficulty, providential interposition, esp. in novel or play. [L, = god from the machinery (by which in ancient theatre gods were shown in air)]

dē'us misĕrēāt'ur (-z-), n. The canticle God be merciful, Psalm 67. [L]

deuterăg'onist, n. Person of next importance to PROTAGONIST in drama. [f. Gk *deuteragōnistēs* (DEUTERO-, *agōnistēs* actor)]

deutēr'ium, n. Heavy isotope of hydrogen with mass about double that of ordinary hydrogen; so **deut'eron** n., nucleus of the~ atom. [DEUTERON-+-IUM; *deuteron* after PROTON]

deut'ero-, comb. form of Gk *deuteros* second, as ~*-Isaiah,* supposed later author of *Isaiah* xl–lv, ~*-canon'ical* of Bible books, admitted later to Canon, *deuterŏg'amỹ,* second marriage.

Deuterŏn'omist, n. Author, joint--authors, or compiler, of *Deuteronomy.* [-IST]

Deuterŏn'omỹ, n. Fifth book of Pentateuch. Hence Deuteronŏm'ic(AL) aa. [f. LL f. Gk DEUTERO(*nomion* f. *nomos* law) second book of law]

deut'zia (*also* doit-), n. White-flowered shrub. [J. *Deutz* fl. 1781, -IA[1]]

deux-temps (see Ap.), n. Kind of waltz more rapid than the trois-temps. [F, = two-time]

dĕvăl'ūJe, v.t. Reduce the value of. Hence ~A'TION n. [DE-]

dĕv'ast|āte, v.t. Lay waste, ravage. Hence or cogn. ~A'TION, ~ātoR, nn. [f. L DE(*vastare* f. *vastus* waste), -ATE[3]]

dĕvěl'op, v.t. & i. Unfold (t. & i.), reveal, bring or come from a latent to an active or visible state; (Mil.) open (an attack); make or become fuller, more elaborate or systematic, or bigger; (Photog.) treat (plate, film) so as to make picture visible; make progress; exhibit (*has ~ed a tendency to*), come or bring to maturity. Hence ~ABLE a., ~ER[1] (1, 2) n. [late 16th c. dis- f. F de(s)*velopper* f. Rom. **volup-, *velup-* of unkn. orig.]

dĕvěl'opment, n. Gradual unfolding, fuller working out; growth; evolution (of animal & plant races); well-grown state; stage of advancement; product; more elaborate form; developing of photograph; ‖ ~ *area,* one suffering from or liable to severe unemployment. [f. F (prec., -MENT]

dĕvělopmĕn'tal, a. Incidental to growth (~ *diseases*); evolutionary. Hence ~LY[3] adv. [-AL]

dĕv'iāte, v.i. Turn aside, diverge, (*from* course, rule, truth, etc., or abs.), digress. [f. LL DE(*viare* f. *via* way), -ATE[3]]

dĕviā'tion, n. In vbl senses; esp.; deflexion of compass-needle by iron in ship etc.; divergence of optic axis from normal position. Hence ~IST (-sho-) n.,

one who departs from strict Communist doctrine. [f. F, or LL *deviatio*]

dĕvice', n. Make, look, (arch.; *things of rare, strange,* ~); (pl.) fancy, will, (*left to one's own ~s*); plan, scheme, trick; contrivance, invention, thing adapted for a purpose; drawing, design, figure; emblematic or heraldic design; motto. [ME & OF *devis, devise,* f. L *divisum, -a,* neut. & fem. p.p. of *dividere* DIVIDE]

dĕv'il[1], n. 1. *The D~,* supreme spirit of evil, tempter of mankind, enemy of God, Satan. ' 2. Heathen god; evil spirit possessing demoniac; superhuman malignant being. 3. Wicked or cruel person; mischievously energetic, clever, knavish, or self-willed person, luckless or wretched person (usu. *poor ~*); vicious animal. 4. Junior legal counsel working for a leader (*Attorney-General's* ~, junior Counsel to Treasury). 5. Literary hack doing what his employer takes the credit and pay for; *printer's* ~ (hist.), errand--boy in printing-office. 6. Personified evil quality (*the~ of greed* etc.); fighting-spirit, energy or dash in attack. 7. (Name of) kinds of animal, bird, firework, & implement; violent S.-African dust-storm (also *dust* ~); highly seasoned dish, esp. uevilled bones. 8. Phrases (see also those in DEUCE[2], in all of which ~ may be substituted): *a ~ of a ~* —, one of an unwelcome or remarkable or amusing kind; — *is the* ~, a great difficulty or nuisance; *like the* ~, with great energy etc.; *go to the* ~, be ruined, (imperat.) be off; *the* ~*/,* excl. of annoyance or surprise; ~ *a one,* not one; *the* ~ *& all,* everything bad; *between the* ~ *& the deep sea,* in a dilemma; ~*s-on-horseback,* see ANGEL; ~ *take the hindmost* (motto of selfish competition); *give the* ~ *his* DUE; *the* ~ *to pay,* trouble ahead; *talk of the* ~ (*& he will appear*), said when one comes just after being mentioned; ‖ *the* ~ *among the tailors,* row, disturbance; ~*'s advocate, -acy* (one who puts) the ~'s case against canonization, (transf.) depreciator, depreciation; ~*'s bones,* dice; ~*'s books,* cards; ‖ *D~'s Own,* 88th Foot, Inns of Court Volunteers; ~*'s* TATTOO; ~*'s in* many plant-names, esp. ~*'s-bit,* kind of scabious; ~*'s coach-horse,* large cocktail beetle; ‖~*'s dust,* shoddy. 9. ~*-dodger,* preacher, parson; ~*-fish,* name of many kinds; ~*-may-care,* reckless, rollicking. Hence ~DOM, ~HOOD, nn., ~WARD(S) adv. [OE *dēofol,* OS *diubul,* OHG *tiufal,* ON *djöfull,* Goth. *diabaulus* f. LL f. Gk *diabolos* slanderer, in LXX rendering Heb. *sātān* SATAN]

dĕv'il[2], v.i. & t. (-ll-). Work as lawyer's or author's devil (usu. *for* principal); grill with hot condiments. [f. prec.]

dĕv'ilish, a., & adv. 1. Like, worthy of, the devil, damnable; hence ~LY[2] adv.,

---

For compounds of *de-* not given consult DE-.

~NESS n. 2. adv. (colloq.). Very. [-ISH¹]

děv'ilism, n. Devilish quality or conduct; worship of devils. [-ISM]

děv'ilment, n. Mischief, wild spirits; devilish or strange phenomenon. [-MENT]

děv'ilry, -try, n. Diabolical art, magic; the devil and his works; wickedness, cruelty; reckless mischief, daring, or hilarity; demonology; devils. [-RY]

děv'ious, a. Remote, sequestered; winding, circuitous, erratic; erring. Hence ~LY² adv., ~NESS n. [f. L DE(*vius* f. *via* way) + -OUS]

děvīs|e' (-z), v.t., & n. (Law) assign, give (realty; cf. BEQUEATH) by will (n., this act, clause effecting it), whence ~'OR, ~EE', (-z-), nn.; plan, contrive, invent, plot, scheme, (thing, *how*, or abs.). Hence or cogn. ~'ABLE a., ~'ER² (4) n., (-z-). [ME, f. OF *deviser* f. Rom. **divisare* frequent. of L *dīvidere* -vis- DIVIDE]

děvīt'aliz|e, -is|e (-iz), v.t. Make lifeless or effete. Hence ~A'TION n. [DE-]

děvīt'ri|fy, v.t. Deprive of vitreous quality, make (glass or vitreous rock) opaque & crystalline. Hence ~FICA'TION n. [DE-]

děvoid', a. Destitute, empty, *of*. [ME; short p.p. of obs. *devoid* f. OF DE(*voidier* f. *voide* VOID)]

děv'oir (-vwŭr), n. Duty, one's best, (*do* one's ~); (pl.) courteous attentions (*pay* one's ~*s to*). [ME & AF *dever* = OF *deveir* f. L *debēre* owe]

děv'olute (-ŏŏt), v.t. Transfer by devolution, depute, (work). [f. L p.p. st. see DEVOLVE]

děvolu'tion (-lŏŏ-), n. Descent through a series of changes; descent of property by due succession; lapse of unexercised right to ultimate owner; (Biol.) degradation of species (cf. EVOLUTION); deputing, delegation, of work or power (esp. by House of Parliament to its committees). [f. LL *devolutio* (foll., -ION)]

děvŏlve', v.t. & i. Throw (duty, work), (of duties) be thrown, fall, descend, *upon* (deputy, or one who must act for want of others); descend, fall by succession, (*to*, *upon*, or abs.). [f. L DE(*volvere volut-*roll)]

Děvōn'ian, a. & n. (Native) of Devonshire, (Geol.) (of) the formation lying above the Silurian & below the Carboniferous. [-IAN]

Děv'onshire (-er), n. ~ (i.e. clotted) *cream*.

děvōte', v.t. Consecrate, dedicate, give up exclusively, (one*self*, another, thing, esp. abilities etc.) *to* (God, person, pursuit, purpose); give over to destruction etc. Hence ~MENT (-tm-) n. [f. L DE(*vovēre vot-* vow)]

děvōt'ĕd, a. In vbl senses; esp.: zealously loyal (~ *friend*), whence ~LY² adv.; doomed (esp. ~ *head*). [-ED¹]

děvōtee', n. Votary *of*, one devoted *to*; zealously or fanatically pious person. [-EE]

děvō'tion, n. Devoutness; devoting;

divine worship, (pl.) prayers, praying, (*was at his* ~*s*), whence ~AL a., ~alLY² adv., ~alISM(3), ~alIST(2), nn., (-sho-), enthusiastic addiction or loyalty (*to*, or abs.). [ME, f. OF, f. L *devotionem* (DEVOTE, -ION)]

děvour' (-owr), v.t. Eat (of beasts); eat like a beast or ravenously; (Bibl.) consume recklessly, waste, destroy, pillage, (substance, property, or its owners); kill, decimate, (of fire, sword, plague, etc.), engulf; take in greedily with ears or eyes (book, story, beauty or beautiful person); absorb the attention of (~*ed by anxiety*); (poet.) ~ *the way* etc., go fast, esp. of horses. Hence ~inglY² adv. [ME, f. OF *devourer* f. L DE(*vorare* swallow)]

děvout', a. Reverential, religious, pious, (of person, act, etc.), whence ~NESS n.; earnest, hearty, genuine. Hence ~LY² adv. [ME, f. OF *devot* f. L p.p. (DEVOTE)]

dew¹, n. Atmospheric vapour condensed in small drops on cool surfaces from evening to morning; freshness, refreshing or gently stealing influence, (usu. *of* sleep, eloquence, youth, music, etc.); any beaded or glistening moisture, esp. tears, sweat; *mountain* ~, illicitly distilled whisky; ~'*berry*, kind of blackberry; ~-*claw*, rudimentary inner toe of some dogs; ~-*drop*; ~-*fall*, time when ~ begins to form, evening; ~-*point*, temperature at which it forms; ‖ ~-*pond*, shallow, usu. artificial, pond fed by atmospheric condensation, (chiefly) found or constructed on English downs; ~-*rake*, for surface of grass or stubble; ~-*ret* v.t., RET by exposure to ~ instead of steeping in water; ~-*worm*, large garden worm. Hence ~'LESS, ~'Y², aa., ~'ilY² adv., ~'iNESS n. [OE *dēaw*, OS *dau*, OHG *tou*, ON *dǫgg* f. Gmc **dawwa-*]

dew², v.t. & i. (Impers.) form or fall as dew (*it is beginning to* ~); (poet.) bedew, moisten. [ME *dewen* as prec.]

dēwān' (-wahn), n. Head financial minister of Indian state; prime minister of a native state. [Arab. & Pers. *dīwān* (= *devan*, see DIVAN)]

dew'lăp, n. Fold of loose skin hanging from throat of cattle (& transf. of other animals or men). Hence ~PED² (-pt) a. [ME; f. LAP¹; first element of unkn. orig.; cf. Du., Norw. *doglæp*, Sw. *drōglapp*]

dĕx'ter, a. Of or on the right-hand side (in Her., to the spectator's left). [L]

dĕxtĕ'rity, n. Manual or mental adroitness, skill, neatness of handling; right-handedness, using of right hand. [f. F (-té) or L DEXTER(*itas* -ITY)]

dĕx'trin, n. (chem.). Soluble gummy substance obtained from starch & used on adhesive stamps etc. [as foll. + -IN]

dĕx'tro-, comb. form of L DEXTER, esp. in terms concerned w. chem. property of causing plane of polarized light ray to rotate to right (opp. LAEVO-, which see for compounds).

dex′trose, n. (chem.). Dextro-rotatory form of glucose. [prec., -OSE²]

děx′trous, -ter-, a. Neat-handed, deft; mentally adroit, clever; using right hand by preference. Hence **děx′t(e)rously²** adv. [DEXTER + -OUS]; ′-tr- correct but less common]

Dey (dā), n. (hist.). Commander of janizaries at Algiers; governor of Algiers or Tripoli. [F, f. Turk. *dāī* maternal uncle]

d(h)al (dahl), n. Split pulse, a common foodstuff in India. [Hind.]

dhar′ma (dăr-, dĕr-), n. (India). Right behaviour, virtue; (in Buddhism) the law. [Skr., = a decree, custom]

dharmsala (dărmsah′la), n. (India). Building devoted to charitable uses (esp. a travellers' rest-house). [Skr., f. *dhárma* custom, *sālā* house]

dhōb′i (dō-), n. Indian native washerman; ~('s) *itch*, troublesome oriental form of eczema. [Hind., f. *dhōb* washing]

dhōt′i (dō-), n. Loin-cloth worn by male Hindus. [Hind.]

d(h)ow (dow), n. Single-masted Arabian-Sea ship of about 200 tons; any Arab ship, esp. as used in E.-Afr. slave-trading. [in Arab. *dāw*, but orig. lang. unkn.]

d(h)u′rrie (dŭr-), n. A thick coarse durable Indian cotton cloth fringed square used for floor-coverings etc. [f. Hind. *dari*]

di-¹, pref. Form of L .DIS- (which see for meaning) used before *b, d, l, m, n, r, s* + cons., *v,* usu. *g,* & sometimes *j.* In LL & Rom. often replaced by *dis-* (so *dismiss*), in OF & ME often varying with *de-* (so *defer¹* f. L *differre*). Not a living pref. in E.

di-², pref. f. Gk *di-* for *dis* twice, two-, double-. In many E wds, & as living pref. in Chem. with various special uses.

di-³, pref. = foll. before vowel.

di(a)-, repr. Gk *dia-, di-,* the prep. *dia* through, thorough(ly), apart, across. In Gk words taken direct, or through L or F & L; also in many scientific words made with Gk elements or on Gk analogy.

diabēt′es (-z), n. Disease with excessive glucose-charged urine, thirst, &. emaciation. [LL f. Gk, f. DIA(*bainō* go)]

diabēt′ic, a. & n. Of diabetes; (person) suffering from diabetes. [f. prec. + -IC]

dia′blerie (-ahblerĕ), n. Devil's business; sorcery; wild recklessness; devil-lore. [F (*diable* f. L *diabolus* DEVIL, -RY)]

diabŏl′ic(al), aa. Of, having to do with, proceeding from, externally like, the devil (usu. *-ic*); fiendish, atrociously cruel or wicked, (usu. *-ical*). Hence **diabŏl′ically²** adv. [ME, f. OF *diabolique* or LL f. Gk *diabolikos* (DEVIL, -IC) + -AL]

diăb′olism, n. Sorcery; devilish conduct or nature; belief in or worship of the devil. [f. Gk *diabolos* DEVIL + -ISM]

diăb′olize, -ise (-īz), v.t. Make into, represent as, a devil. [as prec. + -IZE]

diăb′olō (or dī-), n. Game with two-headed top & sticks. [fancy formation]

diachrŏn′|ic (-k-), a. (Of the approach to the study of a subject, esp. linguistics) historical (opp. *synchronic,* which seeks to describe it as it is found to exist). Hence ~ICAL, ~ist′ic, diăch′ronous (-k-), aa. [DIA- + Gk *khronos* time + -IC]

diăch′ylon, -hylum, (-k-), -ūlum, n. Sticking-plaster of litharge, olive oil, & water, on linen. [ME, f. OF *diaculon* etc. or LL *diachylon* f. Gk *dia khulōn* by juices]

diăc′onal, a. Of a deacon. [f. LL *diaconalis* (DEACON, -AL)]

diăc′onate, n. Office of, one's time as, deacon; deacons. [f. LL ◁(-*tus*), as DEACON, -ATE¹]

diacrit′ical, a. Distinguishing, distinctive, esp.~*marks* used to indicate different sounds of a letter, accents, diaeresis, cedilla, etc.; capable of seeing distinctions. [f. Gk DIA(*kritikos* see CRITIC) + -AL]

diăctin′ic, a. Transmitting, transparent to, the actinic rays. [DI-³, Gk *aktis -inos* ray, -IC]

diadĕl′phous, a. (bot.). With stamens united in two bundles (cf. MONADELPHOUS, POLYadelphous). [DI-², Gk *adelphos* brother]

di′adĕm, n. Crown, or plain or jewelled fillet, as badge of sovereignty; wreath of leaves or flowers worn round head; sovereignty; crowning distinction or glory. Hence ~ED² (-md) a. [ME, f. OF *diademe* f. L f. Gk DIA(*dēma* f. *deō* bind, -M)]

diaer′esis, n. (pl. *-esēs*). Mark (as in *aërate*) over second of two vowels indicating that they are not one sound. [LL, f. Gk *diairesis* (DI-³, *haireō* take) separation]

diagnōse′ (-z), v.t. Determine from symptoms the nature of (a disease). [f. foll.]

diagnōs′is, n. (pl. *-osēs*). Identification of disease by means of patient's symptoms etc., formal statement of this; classification of person's character, assignment of species etc. [f. Gk (DIA-, *gignōskō* recognize)]

diagnōs′t|ic, a. & n. Of, assisting, diagnosis; (n.) symptom. Hence ~ICS n., ~ICALLY adv., ~I′CIAN (-shn) n. [f. Gk DIA(*gnōstikos* f. *gnōstos* known, prec., -IC)]

diăg′onal, a. & n. (Straight line) joining two non-adjacent angles of rectilineal figure or solid contained by planes; obliquely placed like the ~ of a parallelogram (~ *row* or ~, as of the squares of the same colour on chess-board); inclined at other than a right angle, having some part so inclined (~ *cloth* or ~, twilled diagram　　　　　　　337　　　　　　diapason

with ridges oblique to the lists). Hence ~LY[2] adv. [f. L *diagonalis* f. Gk DIA(*gōnios* f. *gōnia* angle), -AL]

di'agrăm, n. (Geom.) figure made of lines used in proving etc.; sketch showing the features of an object needed for exposition; symbolic representation, by lines, of process, force, etc. Hence or cogn. **diagrammăt'ic** a., **diagrammăt'ically** adv., **diagrămm'atize(1)** v.t. [f. F *diagramme* or L f. Gk DIA(*gramma -atos* f. *graphō* write, -M)]

di'agraph (-ahf), n. Instrument for drawing projections, enlarging maps, etc., mechanically. [f. F *diagraphe* (prec., -GRAPH)]

di'al, n., & v.t. & i. (-ll-). 1. (Usu. *sun*-~) instrument showing hour by sun's shadow on graduated plate; (also ~-*plate*) face of clock or watch; plate in steam-gauge, gas-meter, etc., on which pressure, consumption, etc., are indicated by index-finger; (sl.) face. 2. vb. Measure, indicate, (as) with~; (automatic telephony) make a call by moving disc from successive numbers or letters to fixed point and letting it return, ring up (number etc.) thus. [ME, f. med. L *dialis* f. L *dies* day; ult. hist. obsc.]

di'alĕct, n. Form of speech peculiar to a district, class, or person, subordinate variety of a language with distinguishable vocabulary, pronunciation, or idioms. Hence **dialĕc'tAL** a., **dialĕc'talLY**[2] adv., **dialĕctŏL'OGY**, **dialĕctŏl'OGIST**, nn. [f. F *dialecte* or L f. Gk *dialektos* f. DIA*legomai* converse]

dialĕc'tic[1], n. (often in pl.). Art of investigating the truth of opinions, testing of truth by discussion, logical disputation; (Mod. Philos.; not in pl.) criticism dealing with metaphysical contradictions & their solutions. So **dialĕcti'CIAN** (-shn) n. [f. OF *dialectique* or L f. Gk *dialektikē* (*tekhnē* art) of debate (prec., -IC)]

dialĕc'tic[2], a. & n. Logical, of disputation; (person) skilled in critical inquiry by discussion; = DIALECT*al*. [f. L or Gk *dialektikos* (-IC)]

dialĕc'tical, a. = DIALECTIC[2] (adj.); = DIALECT*al*; belonging to DIALECTIC[1] in mod.-philos. sense. Hence ~LY[2] adv. [-AL]

dialŏ'gic, a. In, of, dialogue. [f. LL *dialogicus* (DIALOGUE, -IC)]

diăl'ogist, n. Speaker in, writer of, dialogue. [f. LL f. Gk *dialogistēs* (foll., -IST)]

di'alogue (-ŏg), n. Conversation; piece of written work in conversational form, this kind of composition (*written in* ~); the conversational part in a novel. [ME, f. OF *dialoge* f. L f. Gk *dialogos* (DIA*legomai* converse)]

diăl'ysis, n. (pl. -*yses*). Parting of colloid from crystalloid parts of mixture by filtration through parchment floating in

water. Hence, **di'alȳse** (-z) v.t. [f. Gk DIA(*lusis* f. *luō* loose)]

dialȳt'ic, a. (chem.). Of, by, dialysis. [f. Gk DIA(*lutikos* f. *lutos* loosed f. *luō* loose, -IC)]

diamăgnĕt'|ic, a. & n. Tending to lie E. & W., across the magnetic axis, when suspended freely & acted on by magnetism; of ~ic bodies or diamagnetism; a ~ ic body or substance. Hence ~ICALLY adv., **diamăg'nĕtIZE(3)** v.t. [DIA-]

diamăg'nĕtism, n. Diamagnetic tendency; the diamagnetic branch of magnetism. [DIA-]

diamantė (dēamahǹ'tǎ), a. & n. (Material) scintillating with powdered crystal etc. [F, see DIAMOND]

diamăntif'erous, a. Diamond-yielding. [f. F *diamant* DIAMOND, -I-, -FEROUS]

diăm'ĕt|er, n. Straight line passing from side to side of any body or geom. figure through centre (with special geom. applications for curves), transverse measurement, width, thickness; unit of linear measurement of magnifying-power (*lens magnifying 2000* ~*ers*). So ~rAL a., ~ralLY[2] adv. [f. OF *diametre* f. L f. Gk DIA*metros* (*grammē* line) measuring across f. *metron* measure]

diamĕt'rical, a. Of, along, a diameter, diametral; (of opposition, difference, etc.) direct, complete, like that between opposite ends of diameter. Hence ~LY[2] adv. [f. Gk *diametrikos* (prec., -IC) +-AL]

di'amond, n., a., & v.t. 1. Colourless or tinted precious stone of pure carbon crystallized in octahedrons & allied forms, harder than any other known substance (cut into TABLE, ROSE, & BRILLIANT[2]; *Bristol, Cornish*, etc., ~, kinds of rock crystal; *black* ~, dark-coloured ~, coal; *rough* ~, not-yet cut, person of intrinsic worth but rough manners; ~ *cut* ~, of persons well matched in wit or cunning). 2. Glittering particle or point. 3. (Usu. *glazier's* or *cutting* ~) tool with small ~ for glass-cutting. 4. Figure shaped like section of ~, rhomb (~ *panes*, small panes so shaped set in lead), playing-card bearing this (~*s*, the suit; *a small* ~, one of lower cards). 5. A printing TYPE. 6. ~-*back*, kinds of moth & turtle; ~ *cement*, for setting ~s; ~-*drill*, set with ~s for boring hard substance; ~-*field*, tract yielding ~s; ~-*point*, ~-tipped stylus used in engraving, (usu. pl.) place where two lines or rails intersect obliquely; ~-*snake*, Australian python; ~ *wedding*, 60th anniversary; hence ~**iF'EROUS** a., ~-**WISE** adv. 7. adj. Made of, set with, ~s, rhomb-shaped. 8. v.t. Adorn with ~s, dewdrops, etc. [ME & OF *diamant* f. med. L *diamas* -*mant*- var. of L f. Gk *adamas* ADAMANT]

Diăn'a, n. Horsewoman, lady who hunts; woman bent on remaining single. [L, goddess of hunting & chastity]

diapās'on (-zn), n. Combination of notes

or parts in harmonious whole; melody, strain, esp. grand swelling burst of harmony; compass of voice or instrument; range, scope; fixed standard of musical pitch; *open, stopped,* ~, two chief foundation-stops in organ. [L, f. Gk DIA *pasŏn (khordŏn)* through all (strings) f. *pas* all]

di'aper, n., & v.t. Linen fabric with small diamond pattern; baby's napkin of this; sanitary towel; ornamental design of diamond reticulation for panels, walls, etc. (vb, decorate with this). [ME, f. OF *diapre* f. med. L f. Byzant. Gk *diaspros* adj. f. DIA-, *aspros* white]

diăph'anous, a. Transparent. [f. med. L *diaphanus* f. Gk DIA(*phanēs* -showing f. *phainō* show)+-OUS]

diaphorĕt'ic, a. & n. (Drug, treatment) productive of perspiration. [f. LL f. Gk *diaphorētikos* f. DIA(*phoreō* carry f. *pherō*), -ETIC]

di'aphragm (-ăm), n. Muscular & tendinous partition separating thorax from abdomen in mammals; partition in shellfish, plant tissues, & various instruments, esp., in optics, telephony, & wireless, disc pierced with circular hole; So diaphrăgmăt'ic a. [ME, f. LL f. Gk DIA(*phragma -atos* f. *phrassō* hedge in, -M)]

di'archy (-ki), dy-, n. Government by two independent authorities, esp. the reformed Indian constitution started in 1921. [DI-², Gk *archō* rule; *dy-* less correct]

di'arist, n. One who keeps a diary. Hence diaris'tic a. [DIARY+-IST]

di'arize, -ise (-iz), v.i. & t. Keep, enter in, a diary. [DIARY, -IZE]

diarrhoe'|a (-rēa), n. Excessive evacuation of too fluid faeces. Hence ~'AL, ~IC, aa. [f. LL f. Gk DIA(*rrhoia* f. *rheō* flow)]

di'ary, n. Daily record of events, journal; book prepared for keeping this in; calendar with daily memoranda esp. for persons of a particular profession. Hence diar'IAL a. [f. L *diarium (dies day,* -ARY¹)]

Diăs'pora, n. The DISPERSION (of the Jews). [Gk, f. DIA(*speirō* scatter)]

di'astāse, n. (chem.). A ferment converting starch to glucose, important in digestion. So diastăt'ic, (irreg.) -ăs'ic, aa. [F, f. Gk *diastasis* separation (DIA-, *histēmi* set)]

diăs'tolĕ, n. Dilatation of heart or artery alternating with systole, & with it forming pulse (*systole & ~ often fig. of reaction, fluctuation, etc.). [LL f. Gk, f. DIA(*stellō* send)]

diatĕss'arŏn, n. Harmony of the four gospels. [f. LL f. Gk *dia tessarōn* composed of four]

diathĕrm'ancy, n. diathĕrm'anous, diathĕrm'ic, aa. (Having the) quality of transmitting radiant heat. [f. F *diathermansic, diathermane*+-OUS, *dia-thermique,* f. Gk DIA(*thermansis* f. *thermainō* f. *thermos* warm)]

di'athĕrmy, n. Application of electric

currents to produce heat in the deeper tissues of the body. [DIA-+Gk *thermē* heat+-Y¹]

diăth'ĕsis, n. (med.; pl. *-esĕs).* Constitutional predisposition, habit. [Gk, f. DIA-(*tithēmi* place)]

di'atŏm, n. Member of genus *Diatoma,* microscopic unicellular algae found esp. at bottom of sea & forming fossil deposits. So diatomA'CEOUS (-ăshus) a. [f. Gk DIA(*tomos* f. *temnō* cut) alluding to the cells' being connected in easily separable chains]

diatom'ic, a. (chem.). Consisting of two atoms; having two replaceable atoms of hydrogen. [DI-², ATOM, IC]

diatŏn'ic, a. (mus.). (Of scale) proceeding by notes proper to key without chromatic alteration; (of melodies & harmonies) constructed from such a scale. [f. F *diatonique* or LL f. Gk DIA(*tonikos* TONIC) with intervals of a tone]

di'atribe, n. Piece of bitter criticism, invective, denunciation. [F, f. L f. Gk (*-ē*) = wearing away of time, discourse, f. DIA(*tribō* rub)]

dib, v.i. (-bb-). = DAP. [var. of DAB¹, whence also *dap*]

dibăs'ic, a. (chem.). Having two bases or two atoms of a base. [DI-², BASE¹]

dibb'er, n. Instrument for dibbling, dibble. [f. DIB, now used thus only in *dibbing-stick*]

dib'ble, n., & v.t. & i. 1. Instrument for making holes in ground for seeds etc. 2. vb. Prepare (soil) with this; sow or plant thus; use a ~. [ME; perh. f. DIB +-LE(1), but found much earlier]

dibs (-z), n. pl. (Child's game with) sheep's knuckle-bones; counters at cards; (sl.) money. [prob. f. DIB; cf. earlier *dib-stones*]

dic'ast, dicăs'tery, nn. (Gk Ant.). (Member of) Athenian jury (*-ery),* which gave both verdict & sentence. [f. Gk *dikastēs, dikastērion, dikazō* I judge f. *dikē* right]

dice¹, n. pl. See DIE¹.

dice², v.i. & t. Play DICE¹, whence di'CER¹ n.; gamble *away* at dice; chequer, mark with squares; (Cookery) cut (meat etc.) into small cubes. [f. prec.]

dice'box, n. Box of hour-glass shape from which dice are thrown; ~ *insulator,* piece of porcelain so shaped supporting telegraph wire.

dichlōr'ide (-kl-), n. (Now usu. chem. form of) BICHLORIDE. [DI-²]

dichŏg'amous (-k-), a. (bot.). Having stamens & pistils that mature at different times, so that self-fertilization is impossible. [f. Gk *dikho-* asunder, *-gamos* -married]

dichŏt'om|y (-k-), n. Division into two; binary classification; (Bot. & Zool.) repeated bifurcation. So dichotŏm'IC, ~OUS, aa., ~IST(1) n., ~IZE (1, 3) v.t. & i., ~OUSLY² adv., (-k-). [as prec., *-TOMY]

dichrō'ic (-k-), a. Showing two colours

(esp. of doubly refracting crystals). [f. Gk DI²(*khroos* f. *khrōs* colour) + -IC]

dichrōm′ate (-k-), n. (Now usu. chem. form of) BICHROMATE. [DI-²]

dichrōmăt′ic (-k-), a. Two-coloured (esp. of animal species of which individuals show different colorations). [DI-² + Gk *khrōmatikos* (*khrōma* -*atos* colour, -IC)]

dichrōm′ic (-k-), a. With only two colours (esp. of colour-blind vision seeing two of three primary colours. [Gk *dikhrōmos* (prec.) + -IC]

dick¹, n. (sl.). *Take* one's ~ *that* or to *it*, swear, affirm. [short for *declaration*]

*•**dick²**, n. (sl.). Detective.

dick′ens (-z), n. (colloq.). Devil, deuce. [from 1598; prob. use of *Dickon* = Richard, or the surname *Dickens*, as alliterative substitute for *devil*]

dick′er¹ (in commerce.). Half-score, ten, esp. of hides. [ME *dyker* f. WG *decura* f. L *decuria* set of ten (*decem*)]

*•**dick′er²**, v.i. Trade by barter, chaffer, haggle. [prob. f. prec. through the barter in skins with Indians]

dick′y̆¹, -ey, n. (colloq. & sl.). Donkey; (also ~-*bird*) small bird; false shirt-front; pinafore or apron; driver's seat; ‖ servant's seat at back of carriage. [some senses f. the male name]

‖ **dick′y̆²**, a. (sl.). Unsound, shaky. [orig. unkn.]

dĭcŏty̆lĕd′on, n. Flowering plant with two cotyledons. Hence ~OUS a. [DI-²]

dic′taphōne, n. Machine recording, for subsequent reproduction in type, what is spoken into it. [P, f. foll. + PHONE¹]

dic′tāte¹, n. Authoritative direction (usu. of reason, conscience, nature, etc.; often pl.). [f. L *dictatum* neut. p.p. see foll.]

dictāte′², v.t. & i. Say or read aloud (matter to be written down, often *to* writer; also abs.); prescribe, lay down authoritatively, (terms, thing to be done); of person, also of motive etc.); lay down the law, give orders, (*will not be* ~*d to*). So **dicta′tion** n. [f. L *dictare* frequent. of *dicere dict*- say, -ATE³]

dictāt′or, n. Absolute ruler, usu. temporary or irregular, of a State, esp. one who suppresses or succeeds a democratic government; person with absolute authority in any sphere; one who dictates to writer. Hence ~SHIP, **dictāt′ress¹**, nn. [ME; L (prec., -OR)]

dictātŏr′ial, a. Of dictator; imperious, overbearing. Hence ~LY² adv. [f. L *dictatorius* f. prec. + -AL]

dic′tion, n. Wording & phrasing, verbal style. [f. F, or L *dictio* (*dicere dict*- say, -ION)]

dic′tionary̆ (-sho-), n. Book dealing, usu. in alphabetical order, with the words of a language or of some special subject, author, etc., wordbook, lexicon, (*French-English* etc. ~, of French etc. words with English etc. explanation; ~ *of architecture* or the *Bible*, *Shakespeare* ~, etc.);

walking or *living* ~, well-informed person; ~ *English*, *style*, etc., over-correct, pedantic. [f. med. L *dictionarium* (prec., -ARY¹)]

dic′tograph (-ahf), n. Apparatus reproducing in one room the sounds made in another, loud-speaking internal telephone. [P, irreg. f. foll. + -GRAPH]

dic′tum, n. (pl. -*a*, -*ums*). Formal saying, pronouncement; (Law) judge's expression of opinion not having legal validity; maxim, current saying. [L, neut. p.p. of *dicere* say]

did. See DO¹.

didăc′t|ic (or dī-), a. Meant to instruct; having the manner of a teacher. Hence ~ICALLY adv., ~ICISM n. [f. Gk *didaktikos* (*didaskō* teach)]

did′apper, n. Small diving water-fowl. [for *dive-dapper* f. earlier *divedap* f. OE *dufedoppa* (*dūfan* dive + *doppa* cf. *dip*)]

did′dle, v.t. (sl.). Cheat, swindle. [perh. back formation f. *Jeremy Diddler* in Kenney's *Raising the Wind*, 1803]

didgeridoo′, -y̆doo′, n. Australian aboriginal musical instrument of tubular shape. [native]

*•**did′ō**, n. (colloq.). (pl. -*oes*). Antic, caper, prank (esp. in phr. *cut* (*up*) ~*es*). [orig. unkn.]

didst. 2 sing. past of DO¹.

didy̆m′ium, n. (chem.). A rare metal. [f. Gk *didumos* twin + -IUM (from its being always found with lanthanum)]

die¹, n. (pl. *dice*, ~*s*). **1.** (Pl. *dice*) small cube with faces bearing 1–6 spots used in games of chance; *dice*, game played with these; *the* ~ *is cast*, course irrevocably decided; *upon the* ~, at stake; *as straight*, *true*, *as a* ~. **2.** (Pl. ~*s*): (Archit.) plinth, cubic part of pedestal between base & cornice; engraved stamp for coining, striking medal, embossing paper, etc.; ~-*sinker*, engraver of ~*s*. [ME & OF *de* f. L *datum* neut. p.p. of *dare* give; sp. *dice* as in *mice*, *ice*]

die², v.i. (*dȳ′ing*). Cease to live, expire, (*of* illness, hunger, etc., *by* violence, the sword, one's own hand, *from* wound etc., *through* neglect, *on* scaffold, *at* the stake, *in* battle, *for* friend, cause, etc., *in* poverty; ~ *a beggar*, *martyr*; ~ *a glorious*, *dog's*, *death*; ~ *the death*, be put to death, arch. or jocular; ~ *game*, fighting, not tamely; ~ *hard*, not without struggle; ~ *in* one's *bed*, of age or illness, *in* one's *boots* or *shoes*, by violence, *in harness*, while still at work, *in last ditch*, desperately defending something; *never say* ~, not give in, keep up courage); (Bibl.) suffer as in death (*I* ~ *daily*), suffer spiritual death, ~ *unto*, escape thraldom of (sin); *be dying for*, *to* do, have great desire; ~ *of laughing*, laugh to exhaustion; (of plants etc.) lose vital force, decay; come to an end, cease to exist, go out, disappear, be forgotten, fade away, (of flame, fame, sound, etc.; *secret* ~*s with* one; often *away, down, off, out*); ~*-away* adj., languishing; ~*-hard*, person who dies hard or resists compulsion etc. to the last, obstinate politician etc.; ‖ *Die--hards*, 57th Regiment of Foot. [ME *deghen*, prob. f. ON *deyja* = OS *dōian*, OHG *touwan*, f. Gmc **dawjan*; cf. DEAD]

dĭĕlĕc'trĭc, a. & n. Insulating (medium or substance), non-conductive, non-conductor. [DI-[3] +ELECTRIC = through which electricity is transmitted (without conduction)]

dies'el (dēz-), n. (attrib.). ~ *engine*, type of oil-engine invented by Dr R. *D*~ of Munich (d. 1913), in which ignition of fuel is produced by the heat of air suddenly compressed. [person]

dī'ēs (-z) ĭr'ae, n. Day of Judgement; Latin hymn beginning so. [L, = day of wrath]

dī'ēs (-z) nŏn, n. (Law) day on which no legal business is done; (transf.) day that does not count or cannot be used. [L, short for ~ *juridicus* non-judicial day]

dī'et[1], n., & v.t. 1. Way of feeding; prescribed course of food, regimen, whence dĭĕti'tian, -i'cian, (-shn), n., one versed in or practising dietetics (prop. -*ician*, after *physician*); one's habitual food. 2. v.t. Feed (person, one*self*) on special food as medical regimen or punishment. [ME, f. OF *diete*(*r*) f. L f. Gk *diaita* way of life]

dī'et[3], n. Conference, congress, on national or international business; meeting of the estates of the realm or confederation (esp. as Engl. name for foreign parliamentary assemblies). [ME, f. med. L *dieta* day's work, assembly, etc.; prob. f. *diaita* DIET[1] confused with *dies* day]

dī'etary̆, n. & a. (Course) of diet; allowance or character of food in large institutions. [ME f. med. L *diaetarium* (DIET[1], -ARY[1])]

dĭĕtĕt'ĭc, a. Of diet. Hence ~ICS n., ~ICALLY adv. [f. LL f. Gk *diaitētikos* (DIET[1], -IC)]

dif-, pref. = DIS- before *f* in L wds. Repr. in OF by *de-* (mod. F *dé-*), which occas. survives in E, as in *defer*, *defy*.

diff'er, v.i. Be unlike; be distinguishable *from*; be at variance, disagree, (*from, with*, or abs.; *agree to* ~, give up attempt to convince each other). [ME *differre* f. OF *differer* f. L DIF(*ferre* bear, tend), all used in senses (a) *differ*, (b) *defer*; in E, sense (b) was differentiated as DEFER[1] esp. since 1500]

diff'erence, n., & v.t. Being different, dissimilarity, non-identity (DISTINCTION *without* ~); point in which things differ; quantity by which amounts differ, remainder after subtraction, (*split the* ~, come to compromise); change in price of stocks etc. between certain dates (*pay, meet, the* ~); disagreement in opinion, dispute, quarrel; characteristic mark distinguishing individual or species,

differentia (vb., serve as distinguishing mark of, differentiate); *make a* ~ *between*, treat differently; *it makes a great* ~, is important. [ME, f. OF *difference* f. L *differentia* (foll., -ENCE)]

diff'erent, a. Not the same, unlike, of other nature, form, or quality, (*from, to, than*, all used by good writers past and present, *than* chiefly where a prep. is inconvenient). Hence ~LY[2] adv. [ME, f. OF *different* f. L *different-* part. st. (DIFFER, -ENT)]

differĕn'tia (-shĭa), n. (pl. *-ae*). Distinguishing mark, esp. of species within a genus. [L, see DIFFERENCE]

differĕn'tial (-shl), a. & n. 1. Of, exhibiting, depending on, a difference (~ *duties, charges, tariff*, that differ according to circumstances). 2. Constituting a specific difference, distinctive, relating to specific differences (~ *diagnosis*). 3. (Phys., Mech.) concerning the difference of two or more motions, pressures, etc. (~ *gear*, or ~ as n., gear enabling car's hind-wheels to revolve at different speeds in rounding corners). 4. n. (Math.) infinitesimal difference between consecutive values of continuously varying quantity (~ *calculus*, method of calculating this); difference in wage between industries or between skilled & unskilled workers in same industry. Hence ~LY[2] (-sha-) adv. [f. mod. L *differentialis* (DIFFERENCE, -AL)]

differĕn'ti|āte (-shi-), v.t. & i. Constitute the difference between, of, or in; develop (t. & i.) into unlikeness, specialize, (species, organs, functions, synonyms); discriminate, discriminate between. Hence ~A'TION (-si-) n. [f. DIFFERENCE; see -ATE[3]]

diff'icile (-ēl), a. Unaccommodating, exigent, hard to deal with, persuade, etc. [F]

diff'icult, a. Hard to do or practise, troublesome, perplexing, (often ~ *of access, to answer*, etc.); = prec. [back formation f. foll.]

diff'icult|y̆, n. Being hard to do (*with* ~*y*, often as adv. = not easily) or obscure; something hard or obscure; hindrance; embarrassment of affairs, esp. want of money; reluctance, demur, objection, (*make* ~*ies*, be unaccommodating). [ME, f. OF *difficulte* or L DIF(*ficultas* = *facultas* FACULTY)]

diff'idence, n. Self-distrust, excessive modesty, shyness. [f. (obs.) F, or L *diffidentia* (foll., -ENCE)]

diff'ident, a. Wanting in self-confidence, bashful. Hence ~LY[2] adv. [f. L DIF(*fidere* trust), -ENT]

diff'luence, n., diff'luent, a., (-lŏŏ-). Flowing apart, becoming fluid; deliquescence, deliquescent. [f. L DIF(*fluere* flow), -ENT, -ENCE]

diffrăct', v.t. (opt.). (Of edge of opaque body) break up (beam of light) into series of dark and light bands or coloured spectra. So **diffrăc'tion** n, **diffrăc'tive** a., **diffrăc'tively**² (-vl-) adv. [f. L DIF(*fringere* = *frangere fract-* break)]

diffūse'¹ (-s), a. Spread out, diffused, not concentrated, (of light, inflammation, etc.); not concise, long-winded. Hence ~**LY**² (-sl-) adv., ~**NESS** (-sn-) n. [ME, f. OF *diffus* or L DIF(*fundere fus-* pour)]

diffūs|e'² (-z), v.t. & i. Send forth, shed abroad, (light, particles, heat, geniality, knowledge, rumour); (Chem.) intermingle (t. & i. of gases or fluids) by diffusion, whence ~'**IBLE** (-z-) a., ~**IBIL'ITY** (-z-) n. Hence or cogn. **diffū'sion** (-zhn) n., ~'**IVE** (-s-) a., ~'**IVELY**² (-sĭvl-) adv., ~'**IVENESS** n. [f. L *diffus-* see prec.]

dĭg, v.t. & i. (*dug*, formerly also ~*ged*; *-gg-*), & n. **1.** Use spade or mattock, claws, hands, or snout, in excavating or turning over ground; make research (*for* information, *into* author etc.); make way by ~ging *into, through, under*; excavate or turn up (ground) with spade etc.; make (hole etc.) by ~ging (~ *a pit for*, fig., try to entrap); get by ~ging (potatoes); thrust (spurs, one's nails, feet, point of weapon) *into* something or *in*; poke (person *in the ribs*); ~ (-*self, -selves*, or abs.) *in*, prepare defensive trench or pit; ~ *out*, get, find, make, by ~ging; ~ *up*, break up (fallow land). **2.** n. Piece of ~ging; (colloq.) archaeological excavation; thrust, poke, (esp. *in the ribs*; also fig. ~ *at*, remark directed against). [14th c. *digge*; deriv. f. OE *dician* (f. DIKE) presents phonological, connexion w. F *diguer* semantic, difficulties]

dĭgămm'a, n. Sixth letter (ϝ, in sound = w) of original Gk alphabet, later disused, but important in philology from correspondences with cognate languages. [L f. Gk (DI-², GAMMA, i.e. double gamma (ϝ) from its shape)]

dĭg'am|y̆, n. Taking, having, a second spouse. Hence or cogn. ~**IST**(1) n., ~**OUS** a. [f. LL f. Gk DI²(*gamia* f. *-gamos* -married)]

dĭgăs'tric, a. & n. (anat.). With two swelling ends (of muscles); muscle of lower jaw. [DI-², Gk *gastēr -tr-* belly, -IC]

dī'gĕst¹, n. Methodical compendium or summary, esp. of a body of laws (the *D*~, that compiled by order of Justinian); periodical synopsis of current literature or news. [ME, f. L *digesta* neut. pl. p.p. see foll.]

dĭgĕst'², v.t. & i. Reduce into systematic form, classify; summarize; think over, arrange in the mind; prepare (food) in stomach and bowels for assimilation (intr. of food, admit of digestion; ~ *well, will not* ~); (of drugs, wine, etc.) promote digestion of; assimilate (conquered territory etc.); brook, endure, be reconciled to, (insult, opinion); get mental nourishment from. Hence ~**IBLE** a., ~**IBIL'ITY** n., ~**IBLY**² adv. [ME, f. L DI¹(*gerere gest-* carry) sort]

dĭgĕs'ter, n. In vbl senses; esp. in cookery, stock-pot (cf. foll.). [-ER¹]

dĭgĕs'tion (-schon), n. Digesting (*hard, easy, of* ~) of physical or mental food; power of digesting (*a good, weak,* ~); long steeping in hot fluid to extract essence, stewing. [ME, f. OF f. L *digestionem* (DIGEST², -ION)]

dĭgĕs'tive, a. & n. Of, promoting, digestion; substance aiding digestion; ointment to promote suppuration. Hence ~**LY**² (-vl-) adv. [ME, f. OF (-*if*, -*ive*), f. LL *digestivus* (DIGEST², -IVE)]

dĭgg'er (-g-), n. In vbl senses; also or esp.: (also *gold*~) one who digs or searches for gold in gold-fields; (sl.) Australian; *D*~*s*, N.- Amer. Indians living on roots; digging-part of various machines; (also ~*wasp*) division of *Hymenoptera*. [-ER¹]

dĭgg'ing (-g-), n. In vbl senses; also or esp.: (pl., occas. *a* ~*s*) mine or goldfield; ‖ (pl., colloq., also abbr. *digs*) lodgings. [-ING¹]

dight (dīt), v.t. (arch., & chiefly in p.p. *dight*). Clothe, array, adorn; make ready. [OE *dihtan* f. L *dictare* DICTATE, = OHG *tihtōn*, ON *dikta*; obs. in 18th c., revived by Scott etc.]

dĭ'gĭt, n. Finger or toe (joc., or in zool. or anat.); finger's breadth; any numeral from 0 to 9; (Astron.) twelfth part of sun's or moon's diameter (in measuring eclipse). So ~**AL** a. [ME, f. L *digitus*]

dĭgĭtāl'is, n. Medicine prepared from foxglove. [L, naming the foxglove (1542) after its G name *fingerhut* thimble (DIGIT, -AL)]

dĭ'gĭtate, -ātĕd, a. (zool., bot.). With divided fingers or toes; with deep radiating divisions. Hence **dĭgĭta'tion** n., **dĭgĭta'to-** comb. form. [f. L *digitatus* (DIGIT, -ATE²)]

dĭ'gĭtigrāde, a. (zool.). Walking on toes, not touching ground with heel, (cf. PLANTIGRADE). [F (L *digitus*, -I-, *-gradus* -walking)]

dĭg'nif|y̆, v.t. Make worthy; confer dignity upon, ennoble; make stately (p.p., marked by dignity, self-respecting, stately); speak of by high-flown title (*school* ~*ied with name of college*). [f. OF *dignifier* f. LL *dignificare* (*dignus* worthy, -FY)]

dĭg'nitary̆, n. Person holding high office, esp. ecclesiastical. [f. foll. +-ARY¹]

dĭg'nity̆, n. True worth, excellence, (*the* ~ *of labour*); high estate or estimation (*beneath* one's ~, unfit for one to do); honourable office, rank, or title; elevation of manner, proper stateliness; ~ *ball*, Negro public dance (from its elaborate formality). [ME & OF *dignete* f. L *dignitatem* (*dignus* worthy, -TY); cf. DAINTY]

dĭg'răph, n. Group of two letters expressing one sound, as *ch, ea*. [DI-², Gk *graphē* writing]

dĭgrĕss' (or dī-), v.i. Diverge from the

track, stray; depart from or *from* the main subject temporarily in speech or writing. .Hence or cogn. digrĕ′ssion (-shn) n., ~ive a. [f. L DI¹(*gredi = gradı* walk *gress-*)]

dihĕd′ral, a. Having or contained by two plane faces; ~ *angle*, (esp.) angle formed by wing pairs of an aeroplane. [f. DI-² + Gk *hedra* seat, base, +-AL (1)]

dīke, dȳke, n., & v.t. **1.** Ditch; ‖ natural watercourse; ‖ low wall esp. of turf; embankment, long ridge, dam, against flooding, esp. those in Holland against sea; causeway; (fig.) barrier, obstacle, defence; (Mining & Geol.) fissure in stratum filled with deposited matter, this matter; ‖ ~*reeve*, officer in charge of drains, sluices, & sea-banks, of fen district. **2.** v.t. Provide, defend, with ~(s). [ME, f. ON *dík* & MLG *dīk* dam, MDu. *dijc* ditch, dam; see DITCH]

dilăp′idāte, v.t. & i. Bring, come, into disrepair or decay (building, furniture, clothing, estate, fortune). [f. L. DI¹(*lapidare* f. *lapis* stone) squander; the E sense based on a peculiarly E application of the L]

dilăpidā′tion, n. Squandering; bringing or coming into, being in, disrepair; ‖ sum charged against incumbent etc. for wear & tear during his tenancy; falling away of cliffs etc., debris resulting. [ME, f. LL *dilapidatio* (prec., -ATION)]

dilāt|e′ (dī-, di-), v.t. & i. Make or become wider or larger, expand, widen, enlarge, (*with* ~*ed eyes*), whence ~′ABLE a., ~ABIL′ITY n., dilatā′TION (& irreg. dilā′tion) n.; expatiate, speak or write at large (usu. *upon*). [ME, f. OF *dilater* f. L DI¹(*latare* f. *latus* wide)]

dīlāt′or, n. (anat.). (Also ~ *muscle*) muscle that dilates an organ (cf. CONSTRICTOR). [irreg. for less used *dilatator*; see prec. -OR]

dil′ator|y̆, a. Tending to; designed to cause, given to, delay. Hence ~ILY² adv., ~INESS n. [f. LL *dilatorius* (DI¹*lat-* p.p. st. of *differre* DEFER¹, -ORY)]

dilĕmm′a (or dī-), n. Argument forcing opponent to choose one of two alternatives (*horns of the* ~) both unfavourable to him; position that leaves only a choice between equal evils. So dilĕmmăt′ic a. [LL, f. Gk DI²(*lēmma -atos* assumption f. root of *lambanō* take, -M)]

dilĕttăn′|tè, n. (pl. *-ti*, pr. *-tē*) & a. **1.** Lover of the fine arts; amateur; smatterer, one who toys with subject or concentrates on nothing; hence ~TISH¹ a., ~TISM(1) n. **2.** adj. Trifling, not thorough, amateur. [It., f. *dilettare* f. L *delectare* DELIGHT, -ANT]

dil′igence¹, n. `Persistent effort or work; industrious character. [ME, f. OF (DILIGENT, -ENCE)]

dil′igence² (*occas.* dēlēzhahns′), n. Foreign public stage-coach. [F, as prec.]

dil′igent, a. Hard-working, steady in

application, industrious, attentive to duties. Hence ~LY² adv. [ME, f. OF, f. L DI¹(*ligere lect-* = *legere* choose) love, take delight in, -ENT]

dill, n. Umbelliferous annual yellow--flowered herb. [OE *dile*, OS *dilli*, OHG *tilli*, ON *dylla*, of unkn. orig.]

dill′y̆-dăll̆y̆, v.i. (colloq.). Vacillate; loiter. [redupl. of DALLY]

dil′uent (or -ōō-), a. & n. Diluting (agent); (substance) increasing proportion of water in the blood etc. [f. L *diluere* DILUTE², -ENT]

dil′ūte¹, a. Weakened by addition of water; (of colour) washed-out, faded; (fig.) watery, watered down. [f. L *dilutus* p.p. see foll.]

dilūte′², v.t. Reduce strength of (fluid) by adding water; diminish brilliance of (colour); water down (doctrine, zeal); ~ *labour*, substitute a proportion of women or unskilled men (*dilutees*) for skilled men. So dilu′TION (-ōō-) n. [f. L DI¹(*luere lut-* wash)]

dilu′vial, -al, -ŭ-), a. **1.** Of a flood, esp. of the Flood in Genesis. **2.** (Geol.) ~ *theory, changes*, etc., depending on general deluge or catastrophic water-action, whence ~IST(2) n.; of the drift formation now called Glacial Drift. [f. LL *diluvialis* (*diluvium* DELUGE, -AL)]

dim, a., & v.i. & t. (-mm-). **1.** Faintly luminous or visible; not bright, clear, or well-defined; obscure; seeing or seen, hearing or heard, apprehending or apprehended, indistinctly (*take a* ~ *view of* (colloq.), regard with pessimism; hence ~LY² adv., ~m′ISH¹ (2) a., ~′NESS n. **2.** vb. Become or make~, becloud, outshine. [OE *dim(m)*, ON *dimmr*, cogn. w. OHG *timbar*, of unkn. orig.]

*dime, n. Silver coin, 1/10 of dollar (~ *novel*, cheap shocker). [obs. sense *tithe*, f. OF *disme* f. L *decima* fem. of *decimus* tenth]

dimĕn′sion (-shn), n. Measurable extent of any kind, as length, breadth, thickness, area, volume, (usu. pl.; of *great* ~s, very large); *the three* ~s, length, breadth, & thickness (point has no ~s, line one, surface two, body three; *fourth* in math. speculations, property of matter that should be to solids as solids are to planes); (Alg.) number of unknown quantities contained as factors in a product (*x³*, *x²y*, *xyz*, all of three ~s). Hence ~AL, ~LESS, aa., (-sho-). [ME, f. OF f. L. DI¹(*mensionem* f. *metiri mensus* measure, -ION)]

dim′erous, a. (bot., entom.). With two parts. [DI-², -MEROUS]

dim′eter, n. Verse of two measures (measure in some metres has one foot; in others two). [f. LL f. Gk DI²(*metros* f. *metron* measure)]

dimid′iate, a. Halved, split in two. [f. L (-*diare*) f. DI¹(*midium* f. *medius* mid), -ATE²]

dimin′ish, v.t. & i. Make or become,

actually or in appearance, less (*hide* one's ~*ed head*, i.e. reduced power etc.; in Mus., ~*ed*, of intervals less by a chromatic semitone than the full, as ~*ed fifth* etc.); (t. & i.); ~*ed responsibility* (Law), limitation of criminal responsibility on the ground of mental weakness or abnormality. Hence ~ABLE a., ~ɪɴɢLY² adv. [ME; conflation of MINISH & obs. *diminue* f. OF *diminuer* f. L DI¹*minuere* -*minut*- cf. *minor* less]

dīmĭn'ŭĕn'dō, mus. direction (abbr. *dim.*) & n. Gradually decrease loudness (cf. CRESCENDO); gradual decrease, musical passage marked by it, (also fig.). [It.]

diminū'tion, n. Diminishing, amount of it; (Mus.) repetition of passage in notes shorter than those previously used. [ME, f. OF f. LL *di*- (cl. L *de*-) *minutionem* (DIMINISH, -ION)]

dimin'ūtive, a. & n. (Gram.) (word) describing small specimen of the thing denoted by corresponding primitive word; remarkably small, tiny. Hence **dimin'ūtĭv'AL** a. (gram.), ~LY² (-vl-) adv., ~NESS (-vn-) n. [ME, f. OF f. LL *di*- (*de*-) *minutivus* (DIMINISH, -IVE)]

dim'issory̆, a. Sending away; permitting to depart; *letters* ~ (Eccl.), bishop's authorization of a candidate's ordination outside his own see. [f. LL *dimissorius* (*dimittere* send away)]

dim'ity̆, n. Stout cotton fabric woven with raised stripes or fancy figures used for bedroom hangings etc. [ME, f. It. *dimito* or f. med. L *dimitum* f. Gk DI²(*mitos* warp-thread)]

dimörph'ĭc, dimörph'ous, aa. (bot., zool., chem., mineral.). Exhibiting, occurring in, two distinct forms. So **dimörph'ISM(2)** n. [f. Gk DI²(*morphos* f. *morphē* form) +-IC, -OUS]

dim'ple, n., & v.t. & i. 1. Small hollow esp. in cheek or chin; ripple in water, hollow in ground; hence **dim'plY²** a. 2. vb. Produce ~s in, show ~s. [c. 1400, formally corresp. to OHG *tumpfilo* (G *tümpel*) pool]

din, n., & v.t. & i. (-nn-). 1. Continued confused stunning or distracting noise. 2. vb. Assail with ~; repeat ad nauseam *into* person or person's *ears*; make a ~. [vb f. n., OE *dyne*, OHG *tuni*, ON *dynr*]

dinär' (dē-), n. Unit of currency in Iraq & Jugoslavia. [Arab. *dīnār* f. L DENARIUS]

dine, v.i. & t. Take dinner (~ *out*, away from home; ~ *off* or *on*, have for dinner; ~ *with Duke Humphrey*, go without dinner—perh. w. allusion to those who walked during dinner-time in Duke Humphrey's Walk in St Paul's); entertain (persons) at dinner, (of room etc.) provide dining-accommodation for (some number); *dining-room*, used for meals. [ME, f. OF *di(s)ner* f. Rom. **dis(je)junare* f. DIS- + LL *jejunare* f. *jejunus* fasting]

din'er, n. One who dines; railway dining--car; ~*out*, one who often dines from

home, esp. one much invited for his social qualities. [-ER¹]

ding'-dong', adv., n., & a. (With) alternating strokes as of two bells (*hammer away at it* ~; ~ *race*, *game*, etc., in which each has the better alternately); sound of bell(s); jingle of rhyme. [imit.]

dinghy, dingey, (ding'gi), n. Small ship's--boat; small pleasure rowing-boat; aircraft's small inflatable rubber boat. [orig. native rowing-boat on Indian rivers, f. Hind. *ḍẽṅgī*]

dingle (ding'gl), n. Deep dell, usu. shaded with trees. [orig. unkn.]

ding'ō (-ngg-), n. (pl. ~*es*). Wild or half--domesticated Australian dog. [native]

din'gly̆ (-j-), a. Dull-coloured, grimy, dirty-looking. Hence ~ɪLY² adv., ~ɪNESS n. [perh. f. DUNG +-Y²]

|| **dink'um**, a. & n. (Austral. dial. or sl.). Genuine, real (~ *oil*, the honest truth); (n.) work, toil. [orig. unkn.]

dink'y̆, a. (colloq.). Pretty, neat, of engaging appearance. [f. 16th c. Sc. *dink* trim (of unkn. orig.) +-Y²]

dinn'er, n. Chief meal of day, whether at midday or evening (formal meal with distinct courses); public feast in honour of person or event; ~*-bell*, *-hour*, *-time*, *-party*; || ~*-jacket*, tailless dress coat; ~*-set*, of plates, dishes, etc.; ~*-wagon*, movable tray on castored legs. Hence ~LESS a. [ME, f. OF *di(s)ner*; see DINE, -ER⁴]

dīnŏ'ceras, n. Extinct elephant-sized ungulate mammal with three pairs of horns. [f. Gk *deinos* terrible + *keras* horn]

dīnörn'ĭs, n. Extinct ostrich-sized New Zealand flightless bird, the moa. [f. Gk *deinos* terrible + *ornis* bird]

din'osaur (-ör), n. Reptile (freq. huge) of Mesozoic era. Hence **dinosaur'IAN** (-ör'-) a. & n. [f. Gk *deinos* terrible + *sauros* lizard]

din'othēre, n. Huge extinct proboscidean quadruped. [f. Gk *deinos* terrible + *thērion* wild beast]

dint, n., & v.t. 1. (Arch.) stroke, blow, (whence, mod.) *by* ~ *of*, by force or means of; mark made by blow or pressure, dent. 2. v.t. Mark with ~s, dent. [OE *dynt*, & partly f. cogn. ON *dyntr*; ult. orig. unkn.]

dīŏ'cĕsan (-zn), a. & n. 1. Of a diocese. 2. n. Bishop in relation to diocese or clergy; || member of diocese in relation to bishop (corresp. to *parishioner*). [ME, f. OF *diocesain*, LL *diœcesanus* (foll., -AN)]

di'ocese (-ĕs, -ēs), n. Bishop's district. [ME & OF *diocise* f. L f. Gk DI³(*oikēsis* f. *oikeō* inhabit) administration]

di'ōde, n. Electronic valve having two electrodes. [DI-², Gk *hodos* way]

diœ'cious (-ēshus), a. (Bot.) having the male & female flowers on separate plants; (Zool.) with the two sexes in separate individuals. [DI-², Gk *-oikos* -housed, -OUS]

Dĭonȳs'ĭan, -ĭăc, a. Of *Dionȳsus*, the Greek god of wine, or his worship. [-*ian* f. L *Dionysius*+-AN; -*iac* f. LL f. Gk *Dionusiakos* f. *Dionusia* the feast of Dionysus]

dĭŏp'ter, -tre (-*ter*), n. Refractive power of a lens having a focal length of one metre (used as unit of refractive power; thus a lens of +5 ~s is a positive lens with a focal length of 20 cm.). [f. F *dioptre* f. L f. Gk *dioptra* (see foll.)]

dĭŏp'tr|ĭc, a. & n. **1.** Serving as medium for sight, assisting sight by refraction, (~*ic glass, lens, system*); of refraction, refractive; of ~*ics*; hence ~ICALLY adv. **2.** n. Unit of refractive power, power of lens with focal distance one metre; (pl.) part of optics dealing with refraction (cf. CATOPTRICS). [f. Gk *dioptrikos* f. DI[3](*optra* f. *op*- see +instr. suf. -*tra*) optical instrument, -IC]

dĭora'ma (-*rah*-), n. Spectacular painting in which, by changes in the colour & direction of light thrown on or through it, effects of such natural processes as sunrise are produced. Hence (irreg.) **dĭoram'ĭc** a. [DI-[3], Gk *horama -atos* (*horaō* see, -M)]

dĭŏx'ĭde, n. (chem.). Oxide formed by combination of two atoms of oxygen with one of metal or non-metal (*carbon* ~ etc.). [DI-[2]]

dip[1], v.t. & i. (-pp-). **1.** Put or let down into liquid, immerse, (~ *one's pen in gall*, write bitterly); dye thus; make (candles) by immersing wick in hot tallow; wash (sheep) in vermin-killing liquid; take *up* (liquid, grain, etc.) in scoop, pan, etc. **2.** Lower (flag, sail, scale of balance) for a moment. **3.** Involve in debt (colloq.). **4.** Go under water & emerge quickly; put hand, ladle, etc., *into* to take something out (~ *into* one's *purse* etc., spend freely); go below any surface or level (*sun* ~*s below horizon*; *bird* ~*s & rises in flight*; *scale* ~*s*). **5.** Extend downwards; have downward slope (esp. of magnetic needle, & of strata; ~*ping-needle*, one so mounted as to measure magnetic dip). **6.** Make investigations (~ *deep into the future*): look cursorily or skippingly *into* (book). [OE *dyppan* f. Gmo *dupjan* cogn. w. DEEP]

dip[2], n. **1.** A dipping (see prec.); quantity dipped up; (colloq.) bathe in sea etc.; amount of submergence. **2.** (Astron., Surv.) apparent depression of horizon due to observer's elevation; angle made by magnetic needle with horizon. **3.** Downward slope of stratum; depression of skyline etc. **4.** Tallow candle. **5.** Washing-preparation for sheep etc. **6.** ~ -*needle,* = dipping-needle (see prec.); ~ -*net,* small fishing-net with long handle; ~-*pipe,* ‖ -*trap,* arranged to cut off communication of gas etc. by downward bend in which liquid stands; ~-*stick,* rod for measuring depth of liquid. [f. prec.]

dĭphthēr'ĭa, dĭphtherīt'ĭs, (-*fth*-), nn. Acute infectious disease with inflammation of a mucous membrane esp. of throat, & exudation forming a false membrane. Hence **dĭphthēr'ĭal, dĭphthē'rĭc, dĭphtherīt'ĭc, dĭph'theroĭd,** aa. [f. F *diphthérie, diphthérite* (earlier name), f. Gk *diphthera* hide, -Y[1], -ITIS]

dĭph'thŏng (-*fth*-), n. Union of two vowels pronounced in one syllable (ou, oi); two vowel characters representing sound of single vowel (ea in *feat*), digraph; compound vowel character, ligature, (æ). Hence **dĭphthŏng'al** a., ~IZE (3) v.t., (-ngg-). [f. F *diphthongue* f. LL f. Gk DI[2](*phthoggos* -sounded f. *phthoggos* voice)]

dĭpl(o)-, comb. form of Gk *diplous* double, in many scientific words as *diploblas'tic* with two germinal layers, *diplocard'iac* with right & left sides of heart separate.

dĭplŏd'ocus, n. Gigantic extinct N.-American herbivorous dinosaur. [f. prec. +Gk *dokos* wooden beam]

dĭplōm'a, n. (pl. -*s,* rarely -*ta*). State paper, official document, charter; document conferring honour or privilege, esp. University or College certificate of degree, whence ~'d, ~ED[2] (-mad), ~LESS, aa.· [L f. Gk (-*ō*-), f. *diploō* (*diplous* double), -M; orig. folded paper]

dĭplōm'acȳ, n. Management of, skill in managing, international relations; DOLLAR ~; adroitness, artful management, tact. [f. F *diplomatie* f. *diplomate* see foll., -Y[1]]

dĭp'lomăt, n. = DIPLOMATIST. ·[f. F *diplomate* back formation f. *diplomatique* see foll.]

dĭplomăt'ĭc, a. & n. (Palaeographic examination) of official or original documents, charters, etc. (freq. pl. in n.); of diplomacy (~ *body,* ambassadors & legation-officials at a court; ~ *agent, service*); skilled in diplomacy; proceeding by negotiation; (of statements, dealings, persons) uncandid, subtle. Hence **dĭplomăt'ICALLY** adv. [f. mod. L *diplomaticus* & F -*ique* f. Gk DIPLOMA -*atos,* -IC]

dĭplōm'atist, n. One officially engaged in diplomacy; adroit negotiator. [DIPLOMAT, -IST]

dĭplōm'atize, -ise (-ĭz), v.i. Act as diplomatist; use diplomatic arts. [DIPLOMAT, -IZE]

dĭp'nōan, a. & n. (Fish) having both gills and lungs. [f. Gk *dipnoos* with two breathing-apertures (DI-[2]+*pnoē* breath)]

dī'pōle, n. (phys. & chem.). Object oppositely charged at two points or poles; molecule in which centre of action of positive portions (protons) does not coincide with that of negative portions (electrons). Hence **dĭpōl'AR[1]** a., having two poles, as a magnet. [DI-[2], POLE[2]]

dĭpp'er, n. In vbl senses; also or esp.: Anabaptist or Baptist; kinds of bird, esp. water ouzel; kind of ladle; (Photog.)

apparatus for immersing negatives; *the D~*, the Great Bear. [DIP¹, -ER¹]

‖ dipp'ỹ, a. (sl.). Crazy. [orig. unkn.]

dipsomān'ia, n. Morbid craving for alcohol. Hence dipsoMAN'IAC n. [Gk *dipso-* (*dipsa* thirst, -O-), -MANIA]

dip'teral, a. With double peristyle. [f. L f. Gk DI²(*pteros*-winged f. *pteron* wing), -AL]

dip'terous, a. (Entom.) two-winged, belonging to the order *Diptera* (insects with one pair of membranous wings); (Bot.) with two wing-like appendages. [as prec. + -OUS]

dip'tých (-ĭk), n. Ancient hinged two-leaved writing-tablet with inner sides waxed; painting, esp. altarpiece, of two leaves closing like book. [f. LL *diptycha*, -*um* f. Gk DI²(*ptukha* neut. pl. of -*ptukhos* -folding)]

dīre, a. Dreadful, calamitous, (~ *sisters*, the Furies). Hence ~'LY² (-īrĭ-) adv. [f. L *dirus*]

direct'¹, v.t. & i. Address (letter, parcel, *to* person or place); utter or write *to* or *to* be conveyed *to* (*I ~ my remarks to you*); control, govern the movements of, (*soul*, ~*s body, commander troops*); turn (thing, person, eyes, attention) straight *to* something; tell (person) the way (*to*; ~*ing-post*, = FINGER-*post*); guide as adviser, principle (*duty ~s my actions*), etc.; order (person) *to* do, thing *to* be done; give orders (*that* or abs.). So direc'tive a. (also n.), general instruction for the carrying out of military etc. operations). [f. L DI¹(*rigere rect-=regere* put straight)]

direct'², a. & adv. Straight, not crooked-(ly) or round about, (*the ~ road*; *went ~ to heaven*; ~ *action*, exertion of pressure on the community by strikes instead of on Parliament by votes to force political measures on the Government; ~ *ray*, not reflected or refracted; ~ *shot*, *hit*, without ricochet); (Astron.) proceeding from W. to E., not retrograde; (of descent) lineal(ly), not collateral(ly); (of argument) following uninterrupted chain of cause & effect etc.; diametrical (~ *opposite*, *contrary*, *contradiction*); (Mus.) not inverted (of interval, chord), not contrary (of motion); straightforward, frank, going straight to the point, not ambiguous; immediate(ly), personal(ly), not by proxy; (Gram.) ~ *speech* or *oration*, the words as actually spoken, not modified (cf. OBLIQUE, INDIRECT) in reporting; ~ *current*, electric current flowing always in the same direction; ~ *method*, method of teaching a language through use of the language itself without translation & without study of formal grammar; ~ *tax*, levied originally (income tax etc.) on person who bears the burden ultimately (cf. INDIRECT). Hence ~NESS n. [f. L *directus* p.p. see prec.]

direc'tion, n. Directing, aiming, guiding, managing; = DIRECTORATE; instruction

what to do, order, (usu. pl.); address on letter or parcel; course pursued by moving body, point to which one moves or looks, (*in the ~ of London*, Londonwards); scope, sphere, subject, (*new ~s of inquiry*, *improvement in many ~s*); ~*-finder*, wireless receiving device for finding bearings of transmitting stations. Hence ~AL (-shon-) a. (esp. of wireless transmitted over a narrow angle). [ME, f. OF, or L *directio* (DIRECT¹, -ION)]

direct'lỹ, adv. & conj. In a DIRECT² manner; at once, without delay; presently, in no long time; (colloq.) as soon as (*went ~ I knew*). [-LY²]

Direc'toire (-twär), a. (Dressmaking) in imitation of styles prevalent during the French Directory. [F; see DIRECTORY²]

direc'tor, n. Superintendent, manager, esp. member of managing-board of commercial company; (Cinemat.) stage-manager and producer of a film; (Fr. Hist.) member of Directory; (Eccl.) priest acting as spiritual adviser; apparatus controlling direction in instruments etc.; elaborate gun-sight for co-ordinating fire of several guns. Hence direct̄ōr'IAL a., ~SHIP, direc'tRESS¹, nn. [f. AF *directour*, OF -*eur*, f. LL *director* (DIRECT¹, -OR)]

direc'torate, n. Office of director; board of directors. [-ATE¹]

direc'torỹ¹, a. Directive, advisory, (esp. of part of law advising procedure omission of which does not invalidate action). [ME, f. LL *directorius* (DIRECT¹, -ORY)]

direc'torỹ², n. Book of rules, esp. for public or private worship; book with lists of inhabitants of district, members of professions, etc., with various details; (Fr. Hist.) revolutionary executive of five directors in power 1795–9 (D~). [f. LL *directorium* neut. adj. see prec.]

direc'trix, n. (pl. -*ices*). = DIRECTRESS; (Geom.) fixed line used in describing curve or surface. [DIRECTOR, -TRIX]

dire'ful (-īrf-), a. Terrible, dread. Hence ~LY² adv. [DIRE, -FUL(1)]

dĭrge, n. Song sung at burial, or in commemoration of the dead; lament. [ME, f. L *dirige* imperat. of *dirigere* DIRECT¹, first wd. in Latin antiphon in Matins part of Office of the Dead]

di'rigible, a. & n. Capable of being guided (esp. of balloons); (n.) ~ balloon or airship as opp. *aeroplane*. [as DIRECT¹, -IBLE]

dirigisme (dērēzhĭzm'), n. Policy of State direction & control in economic & social matters. [F (*diriger* DIRECT¹)]

dī'riment, a. Nullifying (~ *impediment*, making marriage null & void from the first). [f. L *dirimere* (DIS-, *emere* take), -ENT]

dĭrk, n., & v.t. Kind of dagger (esp. of Highlanders); (vb) stab with this. [17th--18th c. *durk*, of unkn. orig.]

dĭrn'dl, n. Kind of dress imitating Alpine peasant costume with bodice & full skirt;

(also ~ *skirt*) full skirt with tight waistband. [G, dim. of *dirne* girl]

dirt, n. Unclean matter that soils, wet mud (~ *pie*, made by children in gutters etc.); anything worthless (*yellow* ~, gold; ~, scornful name for land; ~-*cheap*, very cheap); earth, soil; dirtiness; foul talk; *fling* ~, talk abusively or slanderously; *eat* ~, put up with insult etc.; ~-*eating*, disease with morbid craving to eat earth; ~ *track*, a course made of rolled cinders, brickdust, etc., for motor-cycle racing, or of earth for flat-racing; *~ wagon*, dust-cart. [ME *drit* f. ON *drit* excrement]

dirt′y, a., & v.t. & i. 1. Soiled, foul, mixed with or like or connected with dirt, (*D~ Shirts*, 101st Foot, from fighting in shirt-sleeves at Delhi); unclean, obscene; sordid, mean, despicable; *do the* ~ (sl.), play a shabby trick; ~ *work*, esp. dishonourable proceedings, (also) drudgery (*do person's* ~ *work for him*); ill-gotten, esp.~*money*; (of weather) rough, squally; (of colour) not pure or clear; *D~ Allan*, sea-bird getting food by forcing gulls etc. to disgorge: hence **dirt′ILY²** adv., **dirt′I-NESS** n., **~ISH¹**(2) a. 2. vb. Make; become, ~. [-Y²]

dirz′i, n. (Anglo-Ind.). Indian native tailor. [Hind. f. Pers. *darzi* (Pers. *darī* sewing)]

dis-, pref. f. L *dis-* (which was changed to DI-¹ or DIF- before certain letters; see also DE-) related to *bis* (orig. *dvis* = Gk *dis* twice) & *duo* two. In E, *dis-* appears (1) in wds taken direct f. L or f. F wds similarly adopted; (2) as repr. OF *des-* (mod. F *dé-*, *des-*) the inherited form of L *dis-*; (3) as repr. LL *dis-* for L *de-* (see DE-); (4) as a living pref. with privative force. Meanings: asunder, away, apart or between, one by one, utterly (in wds already negative, as *disannul*), un-, not, the reverse of, deprivation of, expulsion from.

disabil′ity, n. Thing, want, that prevents one's doing something, esp. legal disqualification. [f. obs. adj. DIS*able* (= *unable*), -BILITY]

disa′ble, v.t. Incapacitate *from doing* or *for* work etc.; cripple, deprive of power of acting; disqualify legally, pronounce incapable, hinder. Hence **~MENT** (-blm-) n. [DIS-, ABLE]

disabuse′ (-z), v.t. Undeceive, disillusion. [DIS-]

disaccord′, n., & v.i. Disagree(ment), (be at) variance. [ME; DIS-]

†isadvan′tage (-vah-), n. Unfavourable condition (*taken at a* ~): loss, injury. [f. F *désavantage* (DIS-, ADVANTAGE)]

disad′vanta′geous (-*jus*), a. Involving disadvantage or discredit, derogatory. Hence **~LY²** adv. [DIS-]

disaffec′ted, a. Estranged, unfriendly, disloyal, esp. to Government. [p.p. of vb DIS*affect*, dislike]

disaffec′tion, n. Political discontent, disloyalty. [as prec. after AFFECTION]

disaffirm′; v.t. (legal). Reverse (previous decision); repudiate (settlement). Hence **disaffirma′TION** n. [DIS-]

disaffo′rest, v.t. ‖ Reduce from legal state of forest to ordinary land. Hence **~A′TION** n. [f. AL DIS(AFFORESTare)]

disagree′, v.i. Differ, be unlike, not correspond; differ in opinion, dissent, quarrel; (of food, climate, etc.) prove unsuitable, have bad effects, (*with* person, his health, digestion, etc.). Hence **~MENT** n. [ME, f. OF *desagreer* (DIS-, AGREE)]

disagree′ab|le (-gria-), a. & n. 1. Not to one's taste, unpleasant; unamiable, bad-tempered; hence **~leNESS** (-ln-) n., **~LY²** adv. 2. n. (Usu. pl.) unpleasant experience(s), trouble(s), worries. [ME, f. OF *desagreable* (DIS-, AGREEable)]

disallow′, v.t. Refuse to sanction or accept as reasonable or admit, prohibit. [ME, f. OF *desalouer* (DIS-, ALLOW)]

disannul′, v.t. (-ll-). Cancel, annul. [DIS-]

disappear′, v.i. Cease to be visible, vanish, die away from sight or existence, be lost. Hence **~ANCE** n. [DIS-]

disappoint′, v.t. Not fulfil desire or expectation of, break appointment with, (person; *~ed a!, in, of, with*; *agreeably* etc. *~ed*, glad to find one's fears groundless); belie, frustrate, (hope, purpose, etc.). Hence **~ING²** a., **~edLY²**, **~ingLY²** advv., **~MENT** n., event etc. that ~s, distress resulting. [f. F *désappointer* (DIS-, APPOINT)]

disapproba′tion, n. Disapproval. So **disapp′robative, disapp′robatory,** aa. [DIS-]

disapprov|e′ (-ōōv), v.t. & i. Have, express, unfavourable opinion of or *of*. Hence **~′AL**(2) n., **~′ingLY²** adv., (-ōō-). [DIS-]

disarm′, v.t. & i. Deprive of weapons; deprive of weapons (esp. in fencing, jerk foil etc. out of hand of); dismantle (city, ship), reduce, be reduced, to peace footing (of army), abandon or cut down military establishment, whence **disARM′A-MENT** n.; deprive of power to injure; pacify hostility or suspicions of. [ME, f. OF *desarmer* (DIS-, ARM³)]

disarrange′ (-j), v.t. Put into disorder, disorganize. Hence **~MENT** (-jm-) n. [DIS-]

disarray′, n., & v.t. (Throw into) disorder; (poet.) unclothe. [ME; DIS-]

disartic′ul|ate, v.t. Separate, undo the articulation of, take to pieces. Hence **~A′TION** n. [DIS-]

disassimila′tion, n. (physiol.). Conversion of assimilated into less complex or waste substances. [DIS-]

disassocia′tion, n. = DISSOCIATION (esp. in psych. senses: *~ of a personality*). [DIS-]

disas′t|er (-zah-), n. Sudden or great misfortune, calamity; ill luck (*a record of* ~*er*). So **~rous** a., **~rousLY²** adv., (-zah-).

For compounds of *dis-* not given consult DIS-.

[f. F *désastre* (DIS-, *astre* f. L f. Gk *astron* star)]

disavow', v.t. Say one does not know or approve of, repudiate. Hence ~AL(2) n. [ME, f. OF *desavouer* (DIS-, AVOW)]

disband', v.t. & i. Break up, disperse, (t. & i. of troops etc.). Hence ~MENT n. [f. 16th-c. F *desbander* see DIS-, BAND¹ (3)]

disbar', v.t. (-rr-). Expel from membership of the bar, deprive of status of barrister. Hence ~MENT n. [DIS-, BAR¹]

disbelieve', v.t. & i. Refuse credence to (person or statement etc.); be a sceptic; have no faith *in*. So **disBELIEF'** n. [DIS-]

|| **disbench'**, v.t. Deprive of status of bencher. [DIS-, BENCH n.]

disbranch' (-ah-), v.t. Strip of branches. [DIS-]

disbud', v.t. (-dd-). Remove (esp. the superfluous) buds of. [DIS-]

disburd'en, v.t. Relieve of or of a burden; get rid of, discharge, (load, thoughts). [DIS-]

disburse', v.t. & i. Expend, defray; pay money. Hence ~MENT (-sm-) n. [f. OF *desbourser* (DIS-, BOURSE)]

disc, disk, n. Thin circular plate (e.g. coin); round flat or apparently flat surface (*sun's* ~) or mark; round flattened part in body, plant, etc.; gramophone record (*~jockey* sl., compère of radio programme of gramophone records). [f. L f. Gk *diskos* DISCUS]

discal'ceate, a. & n., **discal'ceated, discalced'** (-st), aa. Barefooted or only sandalled (friar, nun). [(-ed anglicized) f. L DIS(*calceatus* p.p. of *calceare* f. *calceus* shoe)]

discard', v.t. & i., & n. **1.** Throw out or reject from hand at cards (specified card, or abs. of playing non-trump that does not follow lead); cast aside, give up, (clothes, habit, belief, etc.); dismiss, cashier. **2.** n. (dis'-). ~ing at cards, ~ed card. [DIS-, CARD²]

discarn'ate, a. Parted from the flesh, disembodied. [DIS-, (IN)CARNATE]

discern' (-s-, -z-), v.t. & i. **1.** (arch.). Distinguish, see the difference between, (good & bad, good *from* bad, *between* good & bad). **2.** Perceive clearly with the mind or senses, make out by thought or by gazing, listening, etc.; so ~IBLE a., ~IBLY² adv. [ME, f. OF *discerner* f. L DIS(*cernere cret-* sift)]

discern'ing (-s-, -z-), a. Having quick or true insight, penetrating. [-ING²]

discern'ment (-s-, -z-), n. Discerning; keenness of perception, penetration, insight. [-MENT]

discerp'ti|ble, a. That can be plucked apart, not indestructibly one. Hence ~BIL'ITY n. [f. LL DIS(*cerpere -cerpt-* = *carpere* pluck) +-IBLE]

discerp'tion, n. Pulling apart, severance; severed piece. [f. LL *discerptio* (prec., -ION)]

discharge'¹, v.t. & i. Relieve of load (ship etc.; ~ *gun*, fire it off; ~ *bankrupt*, relieve him of further liability), withdraw electricity from; dismiss, cashier, (*was ~d from*, or rarely ~*d*, *the service*); release (prisoner), let go (patient, jury); put forth, get rid of, send out, emit, unload from ship, (cargo, missile, liquid, purulent matter, abuse; also abs., as *ship*, *abscess*, *has ~d*); (of river, refl. or intr.) disembogue; (Law) cancel (order of court); acquit oneself of, pay, perform, (duty, debt, vow); (Dyeing) remove (colour), undye (fabric). [ME, f. OF *descharger* (DIS-, CHARGE²)]

discharge'², n. Unloading (*of* ship or cargo); firing off of gun etc. (*a* ~ *of arrows*, several arrows shot); emission (of liquid, electricity, purulent matter); release, exoneration, exemption, acquittal, written certificate of these; dismissal; liberation; payment (*of* debt); performance (*of* obligation); (Dyeing) process of, composition used in, discharging. [ME, f. prec.]

dischar'ger, n. In vbl senses; esp., appliance for producing electric discharge. [-ER¹]

disci'ple, n. One of Christ's personal followers, esp. one of the Twelve; any early believer in Christ; follower, adherent, of any leader of thought, art, etc. Hence ~SHIP (-lsh-) n., **discip'ulAR¹** a. [OE *discipul* (ME *deciple* f. OF) f. L *discipulus* (*discere* learn)]

disciplinar'ian, n. Maintainer of discipline (*strict*, *good*, *poor*, *no*, ~). [as foll. + -AN]

dis'ciplinary (*also* -lin'-), a. Of, promoting, discipline; of the nature of mental training. [f. med. L *disciplinarius* (foll., -ARY¹)]

dis'cipline¹, n. Branch of instruction; mental & moral training, adversity as effecting this; military training, drill, (arch.); trained condition; order maintained among schoolboys, soldiers, prisoners, etc.; system of rules for conduct; control exercised over members of church; chastisement; (Eccl.) mortification by penance. So **dis'ciplinAL** (*or* -lin'-) a. [ME, f. OF f. L *disciplina* (*discipulus* DISCIPLE, -INE²)]

dis'ciplin|e², v.t. Bring under control, train to obedience & order, drill, whence ~ABLE a.; chastise. [ME, f. LL (-*nare*) as prec.]

disclaim', v.t. & i. Renounce legal claim to, renounce claim; disown, disavow, (authorship, character). [AF *desclamer* (DIS-, CLAIM¹)]

disclaim'er, n. Act of disclaiming; renunciation, disavowal. [AF (= prec. as n., -ER⁴)]

disclose' (-z), v.t. Remove cover from, expose to view, make known, reveal. [ME, f. OF *desclore* (DIS-, L *claudere claus-* shut)]

disclo'sure (-zher), n. Disclosing; thing disclosed. [-URE]

discŏb′olus, n. (pl. *-lī*). Ancient quoit--thrower; statue of one in act of throwing. [L, f. Gk *diskobolos* (*diskos* stone or metal quoit, *-bolos* -throwing f. *ballō* throw)]

discŏg′raphў, n. Catalogue raisonné of gramophone records. [DISC, -O-, -GRAPHY]

dis′coid, a. Disc-shaped. [f. LL f. Gk *diskoeidēs* (DISC, -OID)]

discol′our (-ŭler), v.t. & i. Change or spoil the colour of, stain, tarnish; become stained etc. Hence or cogn. **discolo(u)rᴬ-TION,** ∼MENT, (-ŭler-), nn. [ME, f. OF *descolorer* or LL DIScolorare = L DE-(colorare COLOUR²)]

discom′fit (-ŭm-), v.t. Defeat in battle; thwart, disconcert. So ∼URE n. [ME *disconfit* f. OF p.p. of *desconfire* (DIS-, COMFIT)]

discom′fort (-ŭm-), n., & v.t. Uneasiness of body or mind; want of comfort; (vb) make uneasy. [ME, f. OF *desconfort(er)* (DIS-, COMFORT)]

discommŏde′, v.t. Put to inconvenience. [DIS- + obs. *commode* f. L *commodare* (*commodus* see COMMODE)]

discŏmm′on, v.t. ‖ Debar (tradesman) from serving undergraduates; enclose (common land). [DIS-, COMMON¹, ²]

‖ **discŏmm′ons** (-z), v.t. Deprive (member of college) of commons; discommon (tradesman). [DIS-, COMMONS]

discompōs|e′ (-z), v.t. Disturb composure of, ruffle, agitate. Hence ∼′eᴅLY², ∼′iɴɢLY², (-z-), advv., **discompō′sᴜRE** (-zher) n. [DIS-]

disconcert′, v.t. Derange, spoil, upset, (plan, concerted measures); disturb self--possession of, ruffle, fluster. Hence ∼MENT n. [f. obs. F DIS(*concerter* CON-CERT²)]

disconnect′, v.t. Sever the connexion of (thing *from*, *with*, another) or between. [DIS-]

disconnec′ted, a. In vbl senses; esp. (of speech or writing) incoherent, with bad connexion or transitions, whence ∼LY² adv., ∼NESS n. [-ED¹]

disconnĕ′xion, -ction (-kshn), n. Disconnecting; want of connexion, disconnectedness. [DIS-]

discŏn′solate, a. Forlorn, inconsolable, unhappy, disappointed. Hence ∼LY² (-tl-) adv. [ME, f. med. L DIS(*consolatus* p.p. of L *consolari* CONSOLE¹)]

discontĕnt′, n., a., & v.t. 1. Dissatisfaction, want of contentment; grievance. 2. adj. (rare). Not content, dissatisfied, (*with*). 3. v.t. (Usu. in p.p.) make dissatisfied; hence ∼eᴅLY² adv., ∼eᴅNESS, ∼MENT, nn. [DIS-, CONTENT ², ³, ⁴]

discontig′ūous, a. (With parts) not in contact. [DIS-]

discontin′ū|e, v.t. & i. (Cause to) cease; cease from, give up, (do*ing*, habit etc.); cease taking, paying (newspaper, subscription). So ∼ANCE n. [ME, f. OF *dis-*

continuer f. med. L DIS(*continuare* CONTINUE)]

discontin′ūous, a. Wanting continuity in space or time, having interstices, intermittent. Hence or cogn. **discŏntinū′ITY** n., ∼LY² adv. [f. med. L DIS(*continuus* CONTINUOUS) + -OUS]

dis′cŏrd¹, n. 1. Disagreement, variance, strife; harsh noise, clashing sounds; whence or cogn. **discŏrd′ANT a., discŏrd′ANCE n., discŏrd′antLY² adv.** 2. (mus.). Want of harmony between notes sounded together; chord unpleasing or unsatisfactory in itself & requiring to be resolved by another; any interval except unison, octave, perfect fifth and fourth, major & minor third & sixth, & their octaves; single note dissonant with another. [ME, f. OF *descord* (foll.)]

discŏrd′², v.i. Disagree, quarrel, be different or inconsistent (*with*, *from*); be dissonant, jar, clash. [ME, f. OF *descorder* f. L *discordare* f. DIS(*cors -cord-* -hearted f. *cor -dis* heart)]

dis′count¹, n. Deduction from amount due or price of goods in consideration of its being paid promptly or in advance; deduction from amount of bill of exchange etc. by one who gives value for it before it is due; discounting; allowance for exaggeration in accepting story; *at a* ∼, below par, depreciated, not in demand. [17th c., f. F *descompte*, *-conte* (foll.)]

discount′², v.t. Give or get present worth of (bill not yet due); leave out of account; lessen, detract from; part with for immediate but smaller good; allow for exaggeration in; use up effect of (news etc.) beforehand, stale by anticipation. Hence ∼ABLE a. [f. OF *desconter*, *-compter*, f. med. L DIS(*computare* L=COMPUTE)]

discount′ĕnance, v.t. Refuse to countenance, discourage, show disapproval of. [partly f. obs. F *descontenancer* (DIS-, COUNTENANCE²)]

discou′rag|e (-kŭ-), v.t. Deprive of courage, confidence, or energy; deter *from*; discountenance. Hence ∼eMENT n., ∼iɴɢLY² adv., (-kŭrij-). [ME, f. OF *descoragier* (DIS-, COURAGE)]

discŏ′urse¹ (-ôrs), n. Talk, conversation, (arch.); dissertation, treatise, sermon. [ME, f. OF *discours* f. L DIS(*cursus* COURSE¹)]

discourse′² (-ôrs), v.i. & t. Talk, converse; hold forth in speech or writing on a subject (*of*, *upon*, or abs.); give forth (some kind of music; ref. to *Hamlet* III. ii. 374). [f. prec., partly f. F *discourir*]

discourt′eous, a., **discourt′esў,** n., (-kér-, -kôr-). Rude(ness), uncivil, incivility. Hence **discourt′eousLY²** adv. [DIS-]

discŏ′ver (-kŭ-), v.t. Disclose, expose to view, reveal, make known, exhibit, manifest, betrayў; (Chess) ∼ *check*, check by removing piece or pawn; find out (fact etc., *that* etc., unknown country), suddenly realize, whence or cogn. ~ABLE a., ~ER¹ n. [ME, f. OF *descovrir* f. LL DIS-(*cooperire* COVER¹)]

disco'vert (-kŭ-), a. (legal). Unmarried or widowed (of woman). [f. OF *descovert* p.p. (prec.)]

disco'very (-kŭ-), n. Revealing, disclosure, (in Law, compulsory disclosure by party to action of facts or documents on which he relies; in play, poem, etc., revelation unravelling plot); finding out, making known; thing found out. [f. DISCOVER on anal. of *recover*, *recovery*]

discrě'dit¹, n. Loss of repute, thing involving this; doubt, lack of credibility, (*throws* ~ *upon*); loss of commercial credit. [DIS-]

discrě'dit², v.t. Refuse to believe; bring disbelief or disrepute upon. [DIS-]

discrě'dit|ble, a. Bringing discredit, shameful. Hence ~LY² adv. [DIS-]

discreet', a. Judicious, prudent, circumspect, not speaking out at inopportune times. Hence ~LY² adv. [ME, f. OF *discret* f. L DIS(*cretus* p.p. of *cernere* sift) separate, with LL sense f. its derivative *discretio* discernment]

dis'crěpant (*or* -rěp'-), a. Different, inconsistent, (of stories etc.). So discrěp-ANCY n. [f. L DIS(*crepāre* sound), -ANT]

dis'crěte, a. Separate, individually distinct, discontinuous; (Metaphys.) abstract, not concrete. Hence ~NESS (-tn-) n. [ME, f. L *discretus* see DISCREET]

discrě'tion, n. Liberty of deciding as one thinks fit, absolutely or within limits (*it is within* one's ~ *to*; *at the* ~ *of*, to be settled or disposed of by the wish of; *at* ~, at one's own pleasure; *surrender at* ~, unconditionally), whence ~ARY¹ (-sho-) a.; discernment, prudence, judgement, (*years*, *age*, *of* ~, time at which one is fit to manage oneself—in Eng. law, 14; ~ *is the better part of valour*, used as joc. excuse for cowardice). [ME, f. OF *discrecion* f. L *discretionem* (DISCREET, -ION)]

discrim'in|ate, v.t. & i. Be, set up, or observe, a difference between (also intr. with *between*), distinguish *from* another; make a distinction (~*ate against*, distinguish unfavourably, of taxes etc.), observe distinctions carefully. So ~A'TION n., ~ATIVE a. [f. L *discriminare* (*discrimen* distinction f. *discernere* DISCERN), -ATE³]

discrim'inating, a. In vbl senses; esp.: discerning, acute; ~ *duty*, *rate*, varying in amount according to country sending goods or person rated, differential. [-ING²]

discrown', v.t. Take crown from, depose, (sovereign lit. or fig.). [DIS-]

discur'sive, a. Rambling, digressive, expatiating; proceeding by argument or reasoning, not intuitive. Hence ~LY² (-vl-) adv., ~NESS (-vn-) n. [f. med. L *discursivus* f. L DIS(*currere curs-* run), -IVE]

dis'cus, n. Heavy disc thrown in ancient Roman & Greek athletic exercises & modern Olympic Games & other sports. [L f. Gk *diskos* quoit]

discüss', v.t. Examine by argument, debate, whence ~IBLE a.; consume with enjoyment (food, wine, meal). [ME, f. L DIS(*cutere* -*cuss-* = *quatere* shake)]

discü'ssion (-shn), n. Examination by argument; a debate; consumption with enjoyment *of* food. [ME, f. OF f. LL *discussionem* (prec., -ION)]

disdain', n., & v.t. Scorn, (regard with) contempt; think beneath oneself (*to do*, *doing*, or noun) or one's notice. Hence ~FUL a., ~fuLLY² adv. [ME, f. OF *desdeign(er)* f. L DE(*dignari* f. *dignus* worthy)]

disease' (-zēz), n. Morbid condition of body, plant, or some part of them, illness, sickness; any particular kind of this with special symptoms & name; deranged or depraved state of mind or morals. [ME, f. OF *desaise* (DIS-, EASE n.)]

diseased' (-zēzd), a. Affected with disease; morbid, depraved. [ME, p.p. of *disease* vb (now rare) f. OF *desaaisier* as prec.]

disěmbark', v.t. & i. Put, go, ashore. Hence disěmbarka'TION n. [f. F *désembarquer*, or It., or Sp. (DIS-, EMBARK)]

disěmbă'rrass, v.t. Free from embarrassment, rid or relieve (*of*); disentangle (*from*). Hence ~MENT n. [DIS-]

disěmbŏd'|ȳ, v.t. Separate, free, (soul, idea) from body or the concrete; disband (troops). Hence ~iMENT n. [DIS-]

disěmbŏgue' (-g), v.i. & t. (Of river etc.) pour forth at mouth (intr., or *itself*, waters, etc.); (fig.) discharge, pour forth, (t. & i. of speech, crowd, etc.). [f. Sp. *desembocar* (DIS-, *en* in, *boca* mouth)]

disěmbos'om (-ŏoz-), v.t. & i. Disclose, reveal; unburden oneself, make confidences. [DIS-]

disěmbow'el, v.t. (-ll-). Remove entrails of, rip up so as to cause bowels to protrude. Hence ~MENT n. [DIS-]

disěmbroil', v.t. Extricate from confusion or entanglement. [DIS-]

disěnchant' (-ah-), v.t. Free from enchantment or illusion. Hence ~MENT (-ah-) n. [f. F *désenchanter* (DIS-, ENCHANT)]

disěncüm'ber, v.t. Free from encumbrance. [f. F *désencombrer* (DIS-, ENCUMBER)]

disěndow', v.t. Strip (esp. Church) of endowments. Hence ~MENT n. [DIS-]

disěngāge', v.t. & i., & n. Detach, liberate, loosen; (Fencing) pass point of sword to other side of opponent's (n., this movement); come apart, break contact. [DIS-]

disěngāged' (-jd), a. In vbl senses; esp.: at leisure to attend to any visitor or business that comes; vacant, not bespoken. [-ED¹]

disěngāge'ment (-jm-), n. Disengaging; liberation (of chem. component); freedom from ties, detachment; easy natural manner; dissolution of engagement to marry; (Fencing)=DISENGAGE n. [-MENT]

disèntail', v.t. (legal). Free from entail, break the entail of. [DIS-]

disèntăng'le (-nggl), v.t. & i. Extricate, free from complications; unravel, untwist; come clear of tangle. Hence ~MENT (-nggelm-) n. [DIS-]

disènthral(l)' (-awl), v.t. (-ll-). Free from bondage. Hence **disènthral'**MENT (-awl-) n. [DIS-]

disèntomb' (-ōōm), v.t. Take out of tomb; unearth, find by research. [DIS-]

disèquilib'rium, n. Lack or loss of equilibrium, instability. [DIS-]

disèstăb'lish, v.t. Undo establishment of; deprive (Church) of State connexion, depose from official position. Hence ~MENT n. [DIS-]

diseur (dēzér'), n. (fem. *-euse*, pr. -ér̄z'). Artiste entertaining with monologue. [F, = talker]

disfăv'our (-ver), n., & v.t. Dislike, disapproval; being disliked (*fall into, be in*, ~); (vb) regard, treat, with ~. [DIS-]

disfea'ture, v.t. Mar features of, disfigure. [DIS-]

disfig'ure (-ger), v.t. Mar beauty of, deform, deface, sully. Hence **disfigŭrA'**TION, ~MENT (-germ-), nn. [ME, f. OF *desfigurer* (DIS-, L *figurare* f. *figura* FIGURE[1])]

disfŏ'rèst, v.t. = DISAFFOREST; clear of forests. [f. OF *desforester* (DIS-, FOREST)]

disfrăn'chise (-iz), v.t. Deprive of citizen rights; deprive (place) of right of sending, (person) of right of voting for, parliamentary representative. Hence ~MENT (-izm-) n. [DIS-, obs. *franchise* vb = ENFRANCHISE]

disfrŏck', v.t. Deprive of clerical (garb &) status. [DIS-]

disgŏrge', v.t. & i. Eject (as) from throat (esp. fig., trans. or abs., of giving up ill-gotten gains, booty, etc.); (of river etc., trans., refl., or intr.) disembogue, discharge (waters). [ME, f. OF *desgorger* (DIS-, GORGE[1])]

disgrāce'[1], n. Loss of favour, downfall from position of honour; ignominy, shame; thing involving dishonour, cause of reproach. Hence ~FUL a., ~fulLY adv., ~fulNESS n., (-sf-). [f. F *disgrâce* f. It. *disgrazia* (DIS-, GRACE)]

disgrāce'[2], v.t. Dismiss from favour, degrade from position; bring shame or discredit upon, be a disgrace to. [f. F *disgracier* as prec.]

disgrŭn'tled (-ld), a. Discontented, moody. [from 17th c.; DIS-, *gruntle* obs. frequent. of GRUNT]

disguise'[1] (-gĭz), v.t. Conceal identity of (~ *oneself*, person or thing, *as* someone or something else, *by doing, with* false beard etc., *in* costume etc.); misrepresent, show in false colours; conceal, cloak, (~ *one's intention, opinion*). Hence ~MENT (-izm-) n. [ME, f. OF *desguisier* (DIS-, Rom. *guisa* GUISE)]

disguise'[2] (-gĭz), n. Use of changed dress or appearance for concealment's sake, disguised condition (*blessing in* ~, one that seems to be a misfortune); garb used to deceive; artificial manner, deception. [ME, f. prec.]

disgŭst'[1], n. Loathing, nausea, repugnance, strong aversion, (*at, for, towards, against*). [f. OF *desgoust* or It. *disgusto* (DIS-, GUST[2])]

disgŭst'[2], v.t. Excite loathing, aversion, or indignation, in (~*ed with, at, by*). Hence ~èdLY[2], ~ingLY[2], advv. [f. OF *desgouster* or It. *disgustare* (prec.)]

disgŭst'ful, a. Disgusting, repulsive; (of contempt, curiosity, etc.) inspired by, full of, disgust. [-FUL]

dish[1], n. Shallow flat-bottomed usu. oval or oblong vessel of earthenware, glass, or metal, for holding food at meals; food so held, particular kind of food (SIDE-~; *made* ~, of various ingredients; *standing* ~, that appears daily, also fig.); ‖ (arch.) cup, esp. ~ *of tea*, tea-drinking, whence ~ *of gossip*, a chat; ~-shaped receptacle used for any purpose; ~-*cover*, of metal etc. for keeping food in ~ hot; ~-*cloth* & (arch.) -*clout*, for washing ~es & plates; ~-*wash*, -*water*, in which ~es have been washed; ~-*washer*, water wagtail. [OE *disc*, OS *disk*, OHG *tisc*, ON *diskr* f. L *discus* DISC]

dish[2], v.t. & i. Put (food) into dish ready for serving; ~ *up*, serve meal, (fig.) present (facts, argument) attractively; make concave or dish-shaped; (of horse) move fore-feet not straight but with scooping motion; circumvent, outmanœuvre, (esp., Pol.) defeat (opponents) by adopting their policy (~*ing the Whigs*, of Reform Bill 1867). [f. prec.]

dishabille' (-sabĕl), n. Being negligently or partly dressed, undress, (usu. *in* ~); undress garment or costume. [f. F *déshabillé* p.p. of *déshabiller* (DIS-, *habiller* clothe)]

dishabit'ūāte (-s-h-), v.t. Make (person) unaccustomed (*for* etc.). [DIS-]

dishărm'onize (-s-h-), ~ise (-iz), v.t. Put out of harmony, make discordant. [DIS-]

dishărm'onȳ (-s-h-), n. Discord, dissonance. So **dishărmŏn'ious** a. [DIS-]

disheart'en (-s-hár-), v.t. Make despondent, rob of courage. Hence ~MENT n. [DIS-]

‖**dishè'rison** (-s-h-), n. Disinheriting. [ME, f. OF *desheriteisun* f. *desheriter* (ME *disherit*) f. DIS- +LL *hereditare* INHERIT]

dishèv'elled (-ld), a. With disordered hair; (of hair) loose, flung about, unconfined; (of person) untidy, ruffled, unkempt. Hence **dishèv'el**MENT n. [ME *dischevel, -ee*, f. OF *descheveler* (DIS-, *chevel* hair f. L *capillus*) +-ED[1]]

dishon'èst (-sŏ-), a. Fraudulent, knavish, insincere, (of person, . act, statement),

For compounds of *dis-* not given consult DIS-.

Hence ~LY² adv. [ME. f. OF *deshoneste* (DIS-, HONEST)]

dishon'ĕstỹ (·sŏ-), n. Want of honesty, knavery, deceitfulness, fraud. [ME, f. OF *deshoneste* (prec., -Y¹)]

dishon'our¹ (·s-ŏner), n. State of shame or disgrace, discredit; thing that involves this; refusal to honour cheque, bill of exchange, etc. [ME, f. OF *deshonor* (DIS-, L *honorem* HONOUR¹)]

dishon'our² (·s-ŏner), v.t. Treat with indignity; violate chastity of; disgrace; refuse to accept or pay (cheque, bill of exchange). [ME, f. OF *deshonorer* f. LL DIS(*honorare* L = HONOUR²)]

dishon'ourab|le (·s-ŏner-), a. Involving disgrace, ignominious; unprincipled, base, against dictates of honour. Hence ~leNESS n., ~LY² adv. [DIS-]

dishorn' (·s-h-), v.t. Cut off horns of. [DIS-]

disillu'sion, n., & v.t., **disillu'sion|ize,** -ise (·ız), v.t., (·ōōzho-). Disenchant(ment), free(dom) from illusions. Hence ~MENT n. [DIS-, -IZE]

disincĕn'tive, a. & n. Deterrent. [DIS-]

disinclinā'tion, n. Want of liking or willingness (*for* or *to* course, *to* do). [DIS-]

disincline', v.t. Make indisposed (*to* do, *for* or *to* course). [DIS-]

disincorp'orāte, v.t. Dissolve (corporate body). [DIS-]

disinfĕct', v.t. Cleanse (room, clothes, etc.) of infection. Hence or cogn. **disinfĕc'tANT(2)** a. & n., **disinfĕc'tION** n. [DIS-]

disinflā'tion, n. (econ.). Deflation. Hence ~ARY¹ (·sho-) a. [DIS-]

disingĕn'ūous (·j-), a. Insincere, having secret motives, not candid. Hence ~LY² adv., ~NESS n. [DIS-]

disinhĕ'rit, v.t. Reject as heir, deprive of inheritance. Hence ~ANCE n. [ME; DIS-, *inherit* in obs. sense *make heir*]

disin'tĕgrāte, v.t. & i. Separate into component parts, deprive of or lose cohesion. Hence ~A'TION, ~ātOR, nn. [DIS-]

disintĕr', v.t. (·rr-). Unbury, exhume, unearth. Hence ~MENT n. [f. F *désenterrer* (DIS-, INTER¹)]

disin'terĕst, v.t. & refl. To divest of interest, (refl.) cease to concern one*self* (esp., in Diplom., renounce intention or right of intervening etc.). [DIS-]

disin'terĕstĕd, a. Not biased by self--seeking, impartial; ~ *management* (of public house by manager who does not profit by sale of liquor). Hence ~LY² adv., ~NESS n. [DIS-]

disinvĕst'ment, n. Realization of a country's assets. [DIS-]

disjĕc'ta mĕm'bra, n. pl. Fragments, scattered remains. [L]

disjoin', v.t. Separate, disunite, part. [ME., f. OF *desjoindre* f. L DIS(*jungere* *junct-* join)]

disjoint', v.t. Dislocate, disturb working or connexion of (p.p., esp. of talk, inco-

herent, desultory, whence ~ĕdLY¹ adv., ~ĕdNESS n.); take to pieces at the joints. [ME, f. obs. *disjoint* adj. f. p.p. of OF as prec.]

disjoin'tion, n. Disjoining, separation. [ME, f. OF or L *disjunctio* (DISJOIN, -ION)]

disjunc'tive, a. & n. Disjoining, involving separation; (Log., Gram.) alternative (adj.), involving choice between two words etc., (n., ~ proposition or conjunction). Hence ~LY² (·vl-) adv. [f. L *disjunctivus* (DISJOIN, -IVE)]

disk. See DISC.

dislike', v.t., & n. 1. Not like, have aversion or objection to. 2. n. Aversion (*to, of, for*). [DIS-]

dis'locāte, v.t. Put out of joint (limb, or fig. machinery, affairs); (Geol.) make (strata) discontinuous; displace. So **dislocA'TION** n. [f. med. L DIS(*locare* L = place), -ATE³]

dislŏdg|e', v.t. Remove, turn out, (esp. fortified enemy) from position. Hence ~(e)'MENT (·jm-) n. [ME, f. OF *desloger* (DIS-, LODGE v.)]

disloy'al, a. Unfaithful to or *to* friendship etc.; untrue to allegiance, disaffected to government, whence ~IST(2) n. .& a. Hence or cogn. ~LY² adv., ~TY n.· [ME, f. OF *desloial* (DIS-, LOYAL)]

dis'mal (·z-), a., **dis'mal|s,** n. pl. Depressing, miserable, sombre, dreary; hence ~LY² adv., ~NESS n.; *the ~ science,* political economy; *the ~s,* low spirits, dumps. [orig. noun = unlucky days f. AF *dis mal* f. L *dies mali* ill days; these were two special days in each month in medieval calendars]

dismăn'tle, v.t. Strip of covering, protection, etc.; deprive (fortress, ship, etc.) of defences, rigging, equipment. Hence ~MENT (·lm-) n. [f. obs. F *desmanteller* (DIS, MANTLE n.)]

dismast' (·ah-), v.t. Deprive (ship) of mast(s). [DIS-]

dismay', v.t., & n. (Fill with) consternation, discourage(ment). [ME, f. OF *desmaier* (cf. Pr. *desmaiar*) f. Rom. *dismagare* f. DIS-+Gmo *mag-*; cf. MIGHT¹]

dismĕm'ber, v.t. Tear or cut limb from limb; partition (empire, country), divide up. Hence ~MENT n. [ME, f. OF *desmembrer* (DIS-, L *membrum* limb)]

dismiss', v.t., & n. Send away, disperse, disband, (assembly, army; Mil., imperat., word of command closing drill, also as n., *the ~,* release at end of drill); allow to go; discharge, cashier, from service or office (*was ~ed the,* or *from the, army*); send away from one's presence; put out of one's thoughts, cease to feel; treat (subject) summarily; (Law) send out of court, refuse further hearing to, (case); (Cricket, of batsman) send (ball), send ball of (bowler), usu. *to boundary* or *for four* etc., (of fielding side) put (batsman, side) out (usu. *for* score). Hence ~AL(2), (now rare)

dismi′ssion (-shn), nn., ~IBLE a. [ME; superseding obs. *dismit*, after OF *desmis* (p.p. of *desmettre*) or its source, med. L *dismissus* (DIS-, L *mittere miss-* send)]

dismount′, v.i. & t., & n. Alight, cause to alight, from or *from* horseback etc. (n., alighting); unseat, unhorse, (of horse, enemy, or stumble etc.); remove (thing) from its mount (esp. gun from carriage). [DIS-]

disobed′ience, n., **disobed′ient**, a. Disobeying (~ *to* orders, master, etc.), rebellious(ness), rule-breaking. Hence **disobed′ientLY**² adv. [ME, f. OF (*des-*), see DIS-, OBEDIENCE, OBEDIENT]

disobey′ (-bā), v.i. & t. Disregard orders, break rules; not obey (person, law). [ME, f. OF *desobeir* (DIS-, OBEY)]

disoblig|e′, v.t. Refuse to consult convenience or wishes of. Hence ~′ING² a., ~′ingLY² adv., ~′ingNESS n. [f. F *désobliger* (DIS-, OBLIGE)]

disord′er¹, n. Want of order, confusion; tumult, riot, commotion; ailment, disease. [f. F *désordre* (DIS-, ORDER)]

disord′er², v.t. Disarrange, throw into confusion; put out of health, upset. [ME; assim. to ORDER v. of earlier *disordain* f. OF *desordener* (DIS-, ORDAIN)]

disord′erl|ў, a. 1. Untidy, confused; irregular, unruly, riotous; hence ~iNESS n. 2. Constituting public nuisance (~*y house*, bawdy, gaming, or betting, -house). [DISORDER¹, -LY¹]

disorg′aniz|e, -ise (-īz), v.t. Destroy system etc. of, throw into confusion. Hence ~A′TION n. [f. F *désorganiser* (DIS-, ORGANIZE)]

disō′rient|āte, v.t. Place (church) with chancel not directly eastwards; confuse (person) as to his bearings (lit. & fig.). Hence ~A′TION n. [DIS-]

disown′ (-ōn), v.t. Refuse to recognize, repudiate, disclaim; renounce allegiance to. [DIS-]

dispa′rag|e, v.t. Bring discredit on, lower; speak slightingly of, depreciate. So ~EMENT (-|)m-) n., ~ingLY² (-|)-) adv. [ME, f. OF *desparagier* marry unequally (DIS-, *parage* equality f. L *par* equal, -AGE)]

dis′parate, a. & n. 1. Essentially different, diverse in kind, incommensurable, without relation; hence ~LY² (-tl-) adv., ~NESS (-tn-) n. 2. n. (usu. pl.). Thing(s) so unlike that there is no basis for comparison. [f. L DIS(*paratus* p.p. of *parare* provide) separate, influenced in sense by L *dispar* unequal]

dispa′rity, n. Inequality, difference, incongruity. [f. F *disparité* f. LL *disparitalem* (DIS-, PARITY)]

dispark′, v.t. Convert (park-land) to other uses. [DIS-]

dispart′¹, n. (gunnery). Difference between semidiameters of gun at base-ring and at muzzle, to be allowed for in aiming; sight making the allowance. [orig. unascertained: cf. foll.]

dispart′², v.t. & i. (poet.). Separate, part asunder, (t. & i.); go in different directions; distribute. [f. L DIS(*partire* f. *pars* part) distribute]

dispa′ssionate (-sho-), a. Free from emotion, calm, impartial. Hence ~LY² (-tl-) adv., ~NESS (-tn-) n. [DIS-]

dispatch′¹, dès-, v.t. & i. Send off to a destination or for a purpose; give the death-blow to, kill; get (task, business) promptly done, settle, finish off; eat (food, meal) quickly; (arch.) make haste. [f. It. *dispacciare* or Sp. *despachar* expedite; not connected w. F *dépécher*]

dispatch′², dès-, n. Sending off (of messenger, letter, etc.); putting to death (*happy* ~, suicide as practised by Japanese); prompt settlement of business, promptitude, efficiency, rapidity; written message, esp. official communication on State affairs (~*-box*, for carrying these & other documents); (*D-~*) title of newspaper; agency for conveying goods etc.; ~*-rider*, esp. motor-cyclist or horseman carrying military messages. [f. prec., or It. *dispaccio*, Sp. *despacho*]

dispel′, v.t. (-ll-). Dissipate, disperse, (fears, darkness). [f. L DIS(*pellere* drive)]

dispen′sable, a. That can be relaxed in special cases (canon, law, oath); not necessary, that can be done without. [f. med. L *dispensabilis* (DISPENSE, -ABLE)]

dispen′sarў, n. Place, esp. charitable institution, where medicines are dispensed. [f. med. L *dispensarius*; see -ARY¹]

dispensā′tion, n. Distributing, dealing out; ordering, management, esp. of the world by Providence; arrangement made by Nature or Providence; special dealing of Providence with community or person; religious system prevalent at a period (*Mosaic, O.T., Christian,* ~); exemption from penalty or duty laid down in esp. eccl. law (*with, from*); doing without (*with*). [ME, f. OF, or L *dispensatio* (foll., -ATION)]

dispense′, v.t. & i. 1. Distribute, deal out; administer (sacrament, justice); make up & give out (medicine); grant dispensations; release *from* obligation. 2. ~ *with*: relax, give exemption from, (rule); annul binding force of (oath); render needless (usu. *the need* of etc.); do without. So **dispen′ser**¹ n., (esp.) professional maker-up of medical prescriptions. [ME, f. OF *despenser* f. L *dispensare* frequent. of DIS(*pendĕre pens-* weigh)]

dispeo′ple (-pēp-), v.t. Depopulate. [ME, f. OF *despeupler* (DIS-, PEOPLE)]

dispers|e′, v.t. & i. Scatter (t. & i.), drive, go, throw or send, in different directions, rout, dispel, be dispelled; send to or station at separate points; put in circulation, disseminate; (Opt.) divide (white light) into its coloured rays. Hence ~AL(2) n., ~'ĕDLY² adv., ~'IVE a., ~'ive-LY² adv., ~'iveness n. [ME, f. OF *disperser* f. L DI¹(*spergere* -*spers*- = *spargere* scatter)]

disper'sion (-shn), n. Dispersing (see prec.); *the D*~, the Jews dispersed among Gentiles after Captivity. [ME, f. LL *dispersio* (prec., -ION) transl. Gk *diaspora*]

dispi'rit, v.t. Make despondent, depress. Hence ~ĕDLY² adv. [DIS-]

dispit'eous, a. Pitiless. [19th-c. revival with changed sense as if f. DIS-, PITEOUS, of 16th-c. *despiteous* (DESPITE)]

displāce', v.t. Shift from its place (~*d person*, one who has been expelled or has escaped from his native country as a result of annexation, transfer of population, etc.; abbr. D.P.); remove from office; oust, take the place of, put something else in the place of, replace. [f. OF *desplacer* (DIS-, PLACE n.)]

displāce'ment (-sm-), n. Displacing, being displaced; amount by which thing is shifted from its place; ousting, replacement by something else; amount or weight of fluid displaced by solid floating or immersed in it, (*a ship with a* ~ *of 11,000 tons*). [prec., -MENT]

display'¹, v.t. Exhibit, expose to view, show; show ostentatiously; reveal, betray, allow to appear. [ME, f. OF *despleier* f. L DIS(*plicare* fold) cf. DEPLOY]

display'², n. Displaying; exhibition, show; ostentation; (Print.) arrangement of type with a view to calling attention. [f. prec.]

displeas|e' (-z), v.t. Offend, annoy, make indignant or angry, be disagreeable to; *be* ~*ed* (*at, with*, or abs), disapprove, be indignant or dissatisfied. Hence ~'ING² a., ~'INGLY² adv., (-zi-). [ME, f. OF *desplaisir* (DIS-, L *placēre* PLEASE]

displea'sure (-lězher), n., & v.t. Displeased feeling, dissatisfaction, disapproval, anger; (vb) cause ~ to, annoy. [ME, f. OF as prec., assim. to PLEASURE]

displume' (-ōō-), v.t. (poet.). Strip of feathers, lit. & fig. [DIS-]

dispŏrt', v. refl. & i., & n. 1. Frolic, gambol, enjoy one*self*, display one*self* sportively. 2. n. (arch.). Relaxation, pastime. [ME, f. OF *desport*(er) f. DIS-, *porter* carry; see SPORT]

dispōs'a|ble (-za-), a. That can be disposed of, got rid of, made over, or used; at disposal. Hence ~BIL'ITY n. [DISPOSE, -ABLE]

dispōs'al (-zl), n. Disposing of, getting rid of, settling, dealing with, bestowal, assignment; sale; control, management, (*at* one's~); placing, disposition, arrangement. [foll., -AL(2)]

dispōse' (-z), v.t. & i. 1. Place suitably, at intervals, or in order; bring (person, mind) into certain state (esp. in p.p. *well-ill-*,~*d*); incline, make willing or desirous, *to* something or *to* do; give (thing)

tendency *to*; determine course of events (*man proposes, God*~*s*). 2. ~ *of*: do what one will with, regulate; get off one's hands, stow away, settle, finish, kill, demolish (claim, argument, opponent), dismiss (cricket XI *for* certain score), consume (food); sell. [ME, f. OF DIS-(*poser* see POSE¹) confused with L *disponere* thr. such derivatives as foll.]

disposi'tion (-zi-), n. Setting in order, arrangement, relative position of parts; (usu. pl.) plan, preparations, stationing of troops ready for attack, defence, etc.; ordinance, dispensation, (*a* ~ *of Providence* etc.); bestowal by deed or will; control, disposal, (*at* one's ~); bent, temperament, natural tendency; inclination *to*. [ME, f. OF f. L DIS(*positionem* f. *ponere posit-* place)]

dispossĕss' (-oz-), v.t. Oust, dislodge, (person); deprive *of*; rid (person) of or *of* evil spirit (obs.). Hence dispossĕ's-SION (-shn), ~OR (-oz-), nn. [f. OF *despossesser* (DIS-, POSSESS)]

dispraise' (-z), v.t., & n. Disparage(ment), censure. [ME; n.f. vb, f. OF *despreisier* f. LL DE*pretiare* DEPRECIATE]

disprōōf', n. Refutation; thing that disproves. [DIS-]

dispropŏr'tion, n. Want of proportion; being out of proportion. Hence ~ED³ (-shond) a. [DIS-]

dispropŏr'tionate (-sho-), a. Wanting proportion; relatively too large or small. Hence ~LY² (-tl-) adv. [DIS-]

disprove' (-ōōv), v.t. (p.p. ~*d*, rarely ~*n*). Prove false, show fallacy of, refute. [ME, f. OF *desprover* (DIS-, PROVE)]

dis'pūtab|le, a. Open to question, uncertain. Hence ~LY² adv. [F, or f. L *disputabilis* (DISPUTE¹, -ABLE)]

dispūt|ā'tion, n. Argument, controversy. Hence ~ā'TIOUS (-shus) a., ~ā'tious-LY² adv.,~ā'tiousNESS n. (-shus-). [ME, f. OF, or L *disputatio* (foll., -ATION)]

dispūte'¹ v.t. & i. Argue, hold disputation, (*with, against*, person, *on, about*, subject), whence dis'pūtANT(1) n. & a.; quarrel, have altercation; discuss (*whether, how*, etc.); point, question; controvert, call in question, (statement, fact); resist (landing, advance, etc.); contend for, strive to win, (pre-eminence, victory, every inch of ground). [ME *despute* f. OF *desputer* f. L DIS(*putare* reckon)]

dispūte'², n. Controversy, debate, (*in* ~, being argued about; *beyond, past, without*, ~, certainly, indisputably); heated contention, quarrel, difference of opinion. [f. prec.]

disqualificā'tion (-ŏl-), n. In vbl senses; esp., thing that disqualifies. [foll., -FICATION]

disqual'ify (-ŏl-), v.t. Unfit, disable, (*for* some purpose or office); incapacitate legally, pronounce unqualified; debar from competition because of infringement of rules. [DIS-]

disqui′et, v.t., a., & n. Deprive of peace, worry; (adj.) uneasy, disturbed, whence **disqui′ɛtude**, **~ness**, nn.; (n.) anxiety, unrest. [DIS-]

disquisi′tion (-zĭ-), n. (Arch.) Investigation, inquiry; (mod.) long or elaborate treatise or discourse *on* subject. Hence **~al** a. [f. L DIS(*quisitio* f. *-quirere -quisit- = quaerere* seek, -ION)]

disrāte′, v.t. (naut.). Reduce to lower rating or rank. [DIS-]

disregârd′, v.t., & n. 1. Pay no attention to, ignore, treat as of no importance. 2. n. Indifference, neglect (*of, for*). [DIS-]

disrĕl′ish, n., & v.t. Dislike, (regard with) distaste, aversion. [DIS-]

disrĕmĕm′ber, v.t. (dial. etc.). Fail to remember. [DIS-]

disrepair′, n. Bad condition for want of repairs (usu. *is* etc. *in ~*). [DIS-]

disrĕp′utab|le, a. Discreditable; of bad repute, not respectable in character or appearance. Hence **~leness** (-ln-) n., **~ly²** adv. [DIS-]

disrepūte′, n. Ill repute, discredit. [DIS-]

disrespĕct′, n. Rudeness, want of respect. So **~ful** a., **~fully²** adv., **~fulness** n. [DIS-]

disrōbe′, v.t. & i. Divest of robe or garment (also fig.); undress (refl. or intr.). [DIS-]

disrŏot′, v.t. Uproot; dislodge. [DIS-]

disrŭpt′, v.t. Shatter, separate forcibly. [19th-c. vb f. L *disrupt-* see foll.]

disrŭp′tion, n. Bursting asunder, violent dissolution, rent condition; *the D~*, split in Church of Scotland 1843. So **disrŭp′tive** a. [f. L DIS(*ruptio* f. *rumpere rupt-* break, -ION)]

dissăt′isfy, v.t. Fail to satisfy, make discontented (*dissatisfied with, at*). So **dissatisfac′tion** n. [DIS-]

dissāve′, v.i. Spend one's savings. [DIS-]

disseat′, v.t. Unseat. [DIS-]

dissĕct′, v.t. Cut in pieces; anatomize, cut up, (animal, plant) to show its structure etc.; examine part by part, analyse, criticize in detail. Hence or cogn. **dissĕc′tion**, **dissĕc′tor**, nn. [f. L DIS(*secare sect-* cut)]

disseise′, -ze, (-sēz), v.t. Oust, dispossess, of estates (or fig.). [ME, f. AF = OF *dessaisir* (DIS-, SEIZE)]

disseis′in (-zĭn, (-sēz-), n. (legal). Disseising, wrongful dispossession of real property. [ME, f. AF = OF *dessaisine* (DIS-, SEIZIN)]

dissĕm′bl|e, v.t. & i. Cloak, disguise, conceal, (character, feeling, intention, act); pretend not to see, ignore, (insult etc.; arch.); fail to mention (fact); conceal one's motives etc., be a hypocrite, whence **~er¹** n. [perh. assim. to *resemble* of obs. *dissimule* f. OF *dissimuler* f. L DIS(*simulare* SIMULATE)]

dissĕm′in|āte, v.t. Scatter abroad, sow in various places, (lit., seed; usu. fig., doctrines, sedition, etc.); **~ated** *sclerosis*, disease of central nervous system resulting in various forms of paralysis. So **~a′tion**, **~ātor**, nn. [f. L DIS(*seminare* f. *semen -inis* seed), -ATE³]

dissĕn′sion (-shn), n. Discord arising from difference in opinion. [ME, f. OF f. L DIS(*sensionem* f. *sentire sens-* feel, -ION)]

dissĕnt′¹, v.i. Refuse to assent; disagree, think differently or express such difference (*from*), ‖ esp. in religious doctrine from an established church (*~ing minister*, nonconformist clergyman). Hence **~ing-ly²** adv. [ME, f. L DIS(*sentire* feel)]

dissĕnt′², n. (Expression of) difference of opinion; ‖ refusal to accept doctrines of established church, nonconformity, (coll.) dissenters. [f. prec.]

dissĕn′ter, n. One who dissents, esp. from a national church; ‖ member of a sect that has separated itself from the Church of England. [-ER¹]

dissĕn′tient (-shĭ-, -shnt), a. & n. (One) disagreeing with a majority or official view. [f. L DIS(*sentire* feel), -ENT]

dissĕp′iment, n. (bot. & zool.). Partition, septum. [f. L DIS(*saepimentum* f. *saepire* f. *saepes* hedge, -MENT]

dissĕrt′, **diss′ertāte**, vv.i. Discourse, give an exposition, disquisition, or dissertā′tion n. [f. p.p. stems of L DIS(*serere sert-* join) & its frequent. *dissertare*, -ATE³]

dissĕrve′, v.t. Do an ill turn to. So **disservice** n. [DIS-]

dissĕv′er, v.t. & i. Sever, divide. [ME, f. AF f. OF *deseverer* f. LL *disseparare* (DIS-, SEPARATE)]

diss′idence, n. Disagreement, dissent. [f. L *dissidentia* (foll., -ENCE)]

diss′ident, a. & n. Disagreeing, at variance; dissentient (a. & n.); dissenter. [F, or f. L DIS(*sidēre = sedēre* sit), -ENT]

dissim′ilar, a. Unlike (*to*, also rarely *from, with*). Hence **dissimilă′rity** n., **~ly²** adv. [DIS-]

dissim′il|āte, v.t. (philol.). Make unlike (sounds repeating each other, as in cinnamon, orig. cinnamom). Hence **~a′tion** n. [f. L DIS(*similis* like), after ASSIMILATE]

dissimil′itude, n. Unlikeness. [f. L *dissimilitudo* (prec., -TUDE)]

dissim′ul|āte, v.t. Pretend not to have or feel (cf. SIMULATE); dissemble, be hypocritical. So **~a′tion**, **~ātor**, nn. [f. L DIS(*simulare* SIMULATE), -ATE³]

diss′ipāt|e, v.t. & i. Disperse, dispel or disappear, (cloud, vapour, care, fear, darkness); dissolve to atoms, bring or come to nothing; squander (money); fritter away (energy, attention); engage in frivolous or dissolute pleasures (*people go there to ~e*). Hence **~ive** a. [f. L DIS(*sipare* throw), -ATE³]

For compounds of *dis-* not given consult DIS-.

diss'ipātĕd, a. In vbl senses: esp., given to dissipation, dissolute. [-ED¹]

dissipā'tion, n. Scattering, dispersion, disintegration; wasteful expenditure *of*; distraction, want of concentration, *of* faculties etc.; frivolous amusement; intemperate or vicious living. [f. F, or L *dissipatio* (DISSIPATE, -ION)]

disso'cialize (-sha-), **-ise** (-īz), v.t. Make unsocial, disincline for society. [DIS-, SOCIAL, -IZE]

disso'ciāte (-shi-), v.t. Disconnect, separate, in thought or in fact (*from*); (Chem.) decompose, e.g. by heat; (Psych.) cause (person's mind) to develop more than one centre of consciousness (~*ated personality*, co-existence of two or more distinct personalities in the same person). So ~A'TION (-si-), n., ~ABLE, ~ATIVE, (-sha-), aa. [f. L DIS(*sociare* f. *socius* comrade), -ATE³]

diss'olu|ble (-ŏŏbl; or dĭsŏl'ūbl), a. That can be disintegrated, untied, or disconnected. Hence ~BIL'ITY (-lŏŏ-) n. [f. F, or L DIS(*solubilis* SOLUBLE)]

diss'olute (-ōŏt), a. Lax in morals, licentious. Hence ~LY² (-tl-) adv., ~NESS (-tn-) n. [f. L *dissolūtus* p.p. (DISSOLVE)]

dissolu'tion (-lŏŏ-), n. Disintegration, decomposition; liquefaction (of ice or snow); undoing *of* bond, partnership, marriage, or alliance; dismissal of assembly, ‖ esp. ending of a Parliament with a view to fresh election; death; coming to an end, fading away, disappearance. [ME, f. OF, or L *dissolutio* (foll., -ION)]

dissŏlve'e (-z-), v.t. & i. Decompose (t. & i.); make or become liquid esp. by immersion in liquid (~*ed in tears*, weeping copiously), relax, enervate; vanish (~*ing views*, of magic lantern, one fading while another replaces it); disperse (t. & i.), ‖ esp. ~*e Parliament* or ~*e*, declare DISSOLUTION; put an end to (partnership etc.), annul. Hence ~'ABLE a. [ME, f. L DIS(*solvere solut-* loosen)]

dissŏl'vent (-z-), a. & n. (Thing) that dissolves something (usu. *of*). [-ENT]

diss'onant, a. Discordant, harsh-toned, incongruous. Hence or cogn. **diss'o-naNCE** n., ~LY² adv. [ME, f. OF, or L DIS(*sonare* sound), -ANT]

dissuade' (-swād), v.t. Advise against, deprecate, (action); give advice to hinder, divert, (person *from*). So **dissua'SION** (-wăzhn) n., **dissuās'IVE** (-sw-) a. [ME, f. L DIS(*suadēre suas-* persuade)]

dissyllable etc. See disy- etc.

dissȳmmĕt'rical, a., **dissȳmm'ĕtrȳ**, n. Symmetrical, symmetry, in opposite directions, as in the two hands (esp. of crystals with two corresponding forms). [DIS-]

dis'taff (-ahf), n. Cleft stick about 3 ft long on which wool or flax was wound for spinning by hand; corresponding part of spinning-wheel; woman's work; ~ *side*, female branch of family (cf. *spear-side*

for the male). [OE *distæf*, f. STAFF¹, the first element being app. = LG *diesse* bunch of flax; cf. DIZEN]

dis'tal, a. (anat., bot.). Away from centre of body or point of attachment, terminal. [irreg. f. DISTANT, -AL]

dis'tance, n., & v.t. 1. Being far off, remoteness; extent of space between, interval, (*within striking-*~, near enough to deliver blow); avoidance of familiarity, reserve, (esp. *keep* one's ~); distant point (*at, to, from, a* ~); remoter field of vision (*in the* ~; *middle* ~, in painted or actual landscape, between foreground & far part); space of time (*at this* ~ *of time*); (in adv. phrr.) *a good* etc. ~ *off*; (Racing) a length of 240 yds (i.e. the ~ of the ~-*post*, used in (obs.) heat-racing, from the winning-post); *beaten by a* ~ (by about that ~). 2. v.t. Place or make seem far off; leave far behind in race or competition. [ME, f. OF *destance* f. L *distantia* (DI¹*stare* stand apart)]

dis'tant, a. Far, or a specified distance, away or *from* (*three miles* ~); remote, far apart, in position, time, resemblance, etc. (*a* ~ *likeness, connexion*; ~ *ages*; ~ *signal* on railway, one in advance of home signal to give warning); not intimate, reserved, cool. Hence ~LY² adv. [ME, f. OF, or L *distant-* part. st. see DISTANCE]

distāste', n. Dislike, repugnance, slight aversion, (*for*). [DIS-]

distāste'ful (-tf-), a. Disagreeable, repellent, (*to*). Hence ~NESS n. [-FUL]

distĕm'per¹, v.t. (arch., usu. in p.p.). Upset, derange, in health or sanity (*a* ~*ed fancy*). [ME, f. LL DIS(TEMPER*are* L)]

distĕm'per², n. Derangement, an ailment, of body or mind; dog-disease with catarrh, cough, & weakness; political disorder. [f. prec.]

distĕm'per³, n., & v.t. 1. Method of painting on plaster or chalk with colours mixed with yolk of egg, size, etc., instead of oil, used for scene-painting & internal walls (*paint in* ~). 2. v.t. Paint (wall etc., or abs.) thus. [n. f. vb, f. OF *destemprer* f. LL as DISTEMPER¹]

distĕnd', v.t. & i. Swell out by pressure from within (balloon, vein, nostrils, etc.). So **distĕn'SIBLE** a., **distĕnsibIL'ITY**, **distĕn'SION** (-shn), nn. [f. L DIS(*tendere tens-* stretch)]

dis'tich (-k), n. Pair of verse lines, couplet. [f. L f. Gk DI²(*stikhon* f. *stikhos* line) neut. adj.]

dis'tichous (-k-), a. (bot.). (Having fruit etc.) arranged in two vertical lines on opposite sides of stem. [f. L f. Gk *distikhos*, as prec., -OUS]

distil', v.i. & t. (-ll-). Trickle down; come or give forth in drops, exude; turn to vapour by heat, condense by cold, & recollect (liquid); extract essence of (plant etc., or fig. doctrine etc.); drive (volatile constituent) *off* or *out* by heat; make (whisky, essence) by distillation; undergo distillation. So ~IA'TION n., ~l'aTORY a. [ME, f. OF *distiller*, or L DI¹(*stillare* drop)]

dis'tillate, n. Product of distillation. [as prec., -ATE²]

distill'er, n. One who distils, esp. alcoholic spirit, whence~ ERY(3) n.; apparatus for distilling salt water at sea. [-ER¹]

distinct', a. Not identical, separate, individual, different in quality or kind, unlike, (*from*, or abs.); clearly perceptible, plain, definite; unmistakable, decided, positive. Hence ~LY² adv., ~NESS n. [ME, f. L *distinctus* p.p. see DISTINGUISH]

distinc'tion, n. Making of a difference, discrimination, the difference made (~ *without a difference*, a merely nominal or artificial one); being different; thing that differentiates, mark, name, title; showing of special consideration, mark of honour; distinguished character, excellence, eminence; (of literary style) individuality. [ME, f. OF f. L *distinctionem* (DISTINGUISH, -ION)]

distinc'tive, a. Distinguishing, characteristic. Hence ~LY² (-vi-) adv., ~NESS (-vn-) n. [f. LL *distinctivus*; see -IVE]

distingué (see Ap.), a. Of distinguished air, features, manners, etc. [F]

disting'uish (-nggw-), v.t. & i. Divide *into* classes etc.; be, see, or point out, the difference of (thing, thing *from* another; also intr. with *between*), differentiate, draw distinctions; characterize, be a mark or property of; make out by listening, looking, etc., recognize; make one*self* prominent (often *by* gallantry etc.). Hence ~ABLE a., ~abLY² adv. [f. F *distinguer* or L DI¹(*stinguere stinct*- extinguish) with irreg. use of -ISH²]

disting'uished (-nggwisht), a. In vbl senses; esp.: remarkable (*for* or *by* quality etc.), eminent, famous, of high standing; = DISTINGUÉ. [-ED¹]

distort', v.t. Put out of shape, make crooked or unshapely, (actually or, as by curved mirror etc., apparently); misrepresent (motives, facts, statements). Hence or cogn. ~èdLY² adv., distor'tION n., (also) lack of clearness and correctness in sounds transmitted by telephone or wireless, distor'tionAL (-sho-) a. [f. L DIS(*torquēre tort*- twist)]

distor'tionist (-sho-), n. Caricaturist; acrobat who distorts his body. [-IST]

distract', v.t. Divert, draw away, (attention, the mind, usu. *from*); draw in different directions, divide or confuse the attention of, (often p.p. with *between*) bewilder, perplex; (chiefly p.p.) drive mad or infuriate (~*ed with, by, at*). Hence ~èdLY², ~ingLY², advv. [ME, f. L DIS(*trahere tract*- draw)]

distrac'tion, n. Diversion of, thing that diverts, the mind; interruption; lack of concentration; amusement, relief from over-absorption; confusion, perplexity, internal conflict, dissension; frenzy, madness, (*to* ~, to a mad degree). [f. L *distractio* (prec., -ION)]

distrain', v.i. (legal). Levy a distress (*upon* person or his goods, or abs.), seize chattels to compel person to pay money due (esp. rent) or meet an obligation, or to attain satisfaction by sale of the chattels. Hence ~ER¹, ~OR, ~EE', ~MENT & (in same sense) distraint', nn. [ME, f. OF *destreindre* f. L DI¹(*stringere strictsqueeze*)]

distrait' (-rā), a. (fem. -*te*, pr. -āt). Absent-minded, not attending. [F]

distraught' (-awt), a. Violently agitated; crazy. [ME; alt. of obs. *distract* a. after *straught*, p.p. of *stretch*]

distress'¹, n. Severe pressure of pain, sorrow, etc., anguish; want of money or necessaries; straits, dangerous position; exhaustion, being tired out, breathlessness; (Law) = DISTRAINT; ~*gun*, -*rocket*, signals from ship in danger; ~*warrant*, authorizing distraint. Hence ~FUL a. [ME, f. OF *destrece* f. Gallo-Rom. *districtia (= LL *districtio* DISTRAIN, -Y¹)]

distress'², v.t. Subject to severe strain, exhaust, afflict; cause anxiety to, vex, make unhappy. Hence ~ingLY² adv. [ME, f. AF *destresser* f. -*ecier*, f. prec.]

distrib'utary, n. River branch that does not return to main stream after leaving it (as in a delta). [foll. +-ARY¹]

distrib'ut|e, v.t. Deal out, give share of to each of a number; spread abroad, scatter, put at different points; divide into parts, arrange, classify; (Print.) separate (type that has been set up) & return each letter to its proper box in the case; (Log.) use (term) in its full extension so that it includes every individual of the class. Hence (orig. -*er*) ~OR n., ~ABLE a. [ME, f. L DIS(*tribuere tribut*assign)]

distribu'tion, n. Distributing, apportionment; (Pol. Econ.) dispersal among consumers effected by commerce, also extent to which individuals or classes share in aggregate products of community; spreading abroad, dispersing, scattered situation or arrangement; division into parts, arranging, classification; (Print.) act or process of distributing type; (Log.) application of term to all individuals of the class. Hence ~AL (-sho-) a. [ME, f. OF, or L *distributio* (prec., -ION)]

distrib'utive, a. & n. 1. Of, concerned with, produced by, distribution; (Log., Gram.) referring to each individual of a class, not to the class collectively. 2. n. (Gram.) ~ word (as *each, neither, every*). Hence ~LY² (-vl-) adv. [ME, f. F (-*if*, -*ive*), or LL -*ivus* (DISTRIBUTE, -IVE)]

dis'trict, n., & v.t. 1. Territory marked

off for special administrative purpose; ‖ division of parish with its own church or chapel & clergyman; ‖ urban or rural division of county with D~ Council; assigned sphere of operations; tract of country with common characteristics, region; *~ *attorney*, prosecuting officer of a ~; ‖~ *visitor*, person working under clergyman's direction in section of parish. 2. v.t. Divide into ~s. [F, f. med. L *districtus* jurisdiction f. L *district-* see DISTRAIN]

distring′äs (-ngg-), n. (law). Writ bidding the sheriff or other officer distrain in certain cases. [L, = thou shalt DISTRAIN]

distrust′[1], n. Want of trust, doubt, suspicion. Hence ~FUL a. (*of*), ~fulLY[2] adv. [DIS-]

distrust′[2], v.t. Have no confidence in, doubt, not rely on. [DIS-]

disturb′, v.t. Agitate, trouble, disquiet, unsettle; perplex. [ME, f. OF *destorber* f. L DIS(*turbare* f. *turba* crowd)]

disturb′ance, n. Interruption of tranquillity, agitation; tumult, uproar, outbreak; (Law) molestation, interference with rights or property. [ME, f. OF *destorbance* (prec., -ANCE)]

disun′ion (-yon), n. Separation, want of union, dissension. So **disUNITE′** v.t. & i. [DIS-]

disuse′[1] (-s), n. Discontinuance, want of use or practice, desuetude. [f. foll.]

disuse′[2] (-z), v.t. Cease to use. [f. OF *desuser* (DIS-, USE)]

disyll′|able, diss-, n. Word, metrical foot, of two syllables. So ~**äb′ic** a., ~**äb′icALLY** adv. [f. F *dissyllabe* (DI-[2], SYLLABLE); -ss- in F as sign of hard sound]

ditch, n., & v.i. & t. 1. Long narrow excavation, esp. to hold or conduct water or serve as boundary; watercourse; *the D~*, English Channel or North Sea (R.A.F. sl.); DIE[2] *in last* ~; ~*-water*, stagnant in ~ (esp. *dull as* ~*-water*). 2. vb. Make or repair ~es (esp. *hedging & ~ing*), whence ~*′ER*[1] (1, 2) n.; provide with ~es, drain; (sl.) leave in the lurch; (sl., of airman) make forced landing on sea, bring (aircraft) down thus; (pass., of vehicle) stick in a ~. [OE *dic*, OS *dik*, MHG. *tich*, ON *diki*, of unkn. orig., see DIKE]

di′theism, n. Religious dualism, belief in independent principles of good & evil. [DI-[2]]

dith′er (-dh-), v.i., & n. Tremble, quiver, vacillate. [imit.]

dith′yramb (-ăm), n. Greek choric hymn of wild character; Bacchanalian song; vehement or inflated poem, speech or writing. So **dithyräm′bic** a. & n. [f. L f. Gk *dithurambos*]

ditt′any, n. A herb, formerly of medicinal repute. [ME, f. OF *ditan* f. L f. Gk *diktamnon* perh. f. *Diktē* in Crete]

ditt′ō, a. & n. (*abbr.* d°, do; pl. -*os*). The aforesaid, the same, (in accounts, inventories, & commerc. or colloq. talk, instead of repeating word); duplicate, similar thing, (~ *suit, suit* of ~*s*, clothes all of one material); *say* ~ *to*, agree with, endorse opinion of. [It. (now *detto*), f. L *dictus* p.p. of *dicere* say]

dittog′raphy, n. Copyist's mistaken repetition of letter, word, or phrase, cf. HAPLOGRAPHY. Hence **dittogräph′ic** a. [f. Gk *dittos* double, -GRAPHY]

ditt′y, n. Short simple song. [ME, f. OF *dite* f. L *dictatum* neut. p.p. of *dictare* DICTATE[2]]

ditt′y-bäg, -böx, nn. Sailor's, fisherman's, receptacle for odds & ends. [orig. unkn.]

diurēt′ic, a. & n. (Substance) exciting discharge of urine. [ME, f. OF -*ique*, or LL f. Gk *diourētikos* f. DI[3](*oureō* make water), -IC]

diurn′al, a. (Astron.) occupying one day; (arch.) daily, of each day; of the day, not nocturnal. Hence ~LY[2] adv. [ME, f. LL *diurnalis* (*dies* day)]

div (dĕv), n. Evil spirit in Persian mythology. [Pers., = Skr. *deva* god]

di′va (dē-), n. Great woman singer, prima donna. [It. f. L, = goddess]

div′ag|āte, v.i. Stray, digress. Hence ~A′TION n. [f. L DI[1](*vagari* wander), -ATE[3]]

di′valent, a. Combining with two atoms of hydrogen etc., having two combining equivalents. [DI-[2], L *valēre* be worth, -ENT]

divăn′, n. Oriental council of State, esp. Turkish privy council; oriental council-chamber, court of justice; long seat against room-wall; smoking-room, cigar-shop. [Turk., f. Pers. *devan* brochure, account-book, custom-house(see DOUANE), tribunal, senate, bench]

divä′ric|āte (*or* dī-), v.i. Diverge, branch, (of roads, branches, etc.). Hence or cogn. ~A′TION n., ~ATE[2] (-at) a. (bot., zool.). [f. L DI[1](*varicare* f. *varicus* straddling), -ATE[3]]

dive, v.i. & n. 1. Plunge, esp. head foremost, into water etc.; (of aircraft) plunge steeply downwards, (of submarine) submerge; go down or out of sight suddenly; put one's hand *into* water, vessel, pocket; penetrate or search mentally *into*; *diving-bell*, open-bottomed box or bell in which person can be let down into deep water. 2. n. Plunge, header, swim under water; submerging of submarine, aircraft's steep descent; sudden dart out of sight; *drinking-den*; a basement or underground room in which some particular commodity is sold (*oyster* ~); hiding-place or sanctuary for the disreputable; ~*-bomber*, aircraft specially designed to aim bombs at target by diving towards it and release them while diving, so ~*-bomb* v.t. & i. [repr. OE *dūfan* (intr.) dive, sink, & *dyfan* (trans.) immerse; f. Gmc *dūbh-*, cogn. w. DEEP, DIP]

div′er, n. In vbl senses; esp.: person who dives for pearls, to examine sunk ships, etc.; kinds of diving bird. [-ER[1]]

diver|ge' (*or* dĭ-), v.i. & t. Proceed in different directions from point or each other; go aside *from* track; differ, deviate; make ~ge, deflect. Hence ~'ɢᴇɴᴄᴇ, ~'ɢᴇɴᴄʏ, nn., ~'ɢᴇɴᴛ a., ~'ɢᴇɴᴛʟʏ² adv. [f. med. L *divergere* f. ᴅɪ-¹, L *vergere* ᴠᴇʀɢᴇ v.]

div'ers (-z), a. (arch. or joc.). Sundry, several, more than one. [ME, f. OF f. L ᴅɪ¹ (*versus* p.p. of *vertere* turn) = foll.]

diverse' (*or* dĭ-). a. Unlike in nature or qualities; varied, changeful. Hence or cogn. ~ʟʏ² (-sl-) adv., divers'iꜰᴏʀᴍ a. [ME, as prec.]

divers'i|fў (*or* dĭ-), v.t. Make diverse, vary, modify, variegate. So ~ꜰɪᴄᴀ'ᴛɪᴏɴ n. [ME, f. OF *diversifier* f. med. L *diversificare* (prec., -ꜰʏ)]

diver'sion (*or* dĭ-; -shn), n. Deflecting, deviation; diverting of attention, manœuvre to secure this, feint; recreation, pleasant distraction, pastime. [f. LL *diversio* (ᴅɪᴠᴇʀᴛ, -ɪᴏɴ)]

divers'ity (*or* dĭ-), n. Being diverse, unlikeness; different kind; variety. [ME, f. OF *diversite* f. L *diversitatem* (ᴅɪᴠᴇʀs, -ɪᴛʏ)]

divert' (*or* dĭ-), v.t. Turn aside, deflect, (stream etc., *from, to,* or abs.); turn elsewhere, get rid of, ward off; draw off attention of (*from* one thing *to* another), distract; entertain, amuse, whence ~ɪɴɢ³ a., ~ɪɴɢʟʏ² adv. [f. OF *divertir* f. L ᴅɪ¹*vertere* & ᴅᴇ*vertere* -*vers*- turn in different directions, turn away]

divertissement (dēvĕrtēs'mahŭ), n. Short ballet etc. between the acts of a play. [F]

Div'ēs (-z), n. (Typical name for) rich man; ‖ (Law) ~ *costs*, costs on higher scale (opp. *pauper costs*). [L, = rich, ref. to *Luke* xvi. 19, where Vulgate has ~]

divest' (*or* dĭ-), v.t. Unclothe; strip of garment etc.; deprive, rid, *of* (~ *oneself of*, abandon). Hence ~ᴍᴇɴᴛ, ~ɪᴛᴜʀᴇ, nn. [16th c. *devest* f. OF *desvestir* (ᴅɪs-, L *vestire* f. *vestis* garment)]

‖ **div'i,** divv'ў, n. (Co-op. societies' sl.). Dividend. [abbr.]

divide'¹, v.t. & i. Separate (t. & i.) into or in(to) parts, split or break up; sunder, part, cut off, (things, thing *from*); cause to disagree, set at variance, distract; distribute, deal out, (*among, between*); share *with* others; (Math.) see how often number contains another (~ 20 *by* 3), do ᴅɪᴠɪsɪᴏɴ, (of number) go into (number) without remainder; part (t. & i. of House of Parliament, meeting, etc.) into two sets in voting. (*Mr X did not* ~ *the House; the House*~*d*). [ME, f. L ᴅɪ¹(*videre -vis-*)]

divide'², n. (U.S. etc.). Watershed. [f. prec.]

div'idend, n. (Math.) number to be divided by ᴅɪᴠɪsᴏʀ; sum payable as interest on loan or as profit of joint-stock company (ᴇx ~, ᴄᴜᴍ ~) or to creditors of insolvent estate; individual's share of it (‖ ~-*warrant,* order to pay this); ~ *stripping,* evasion of tax on ~s by an arrangement between a company liable to pay tax and another able to claim repayment of tax. [f. F *dividende* or L *dividendum* (ᴅɪᴠɪᴅᴇ¹, -ɴᴅ¹)]

divid'er, n. In vbl senses: esp., (pl.) measuring-compasses, esp. those provided with screw for setting to small intervals. [-ᴇʀ¹]

div'i-div'ĭ, n. Curved pods of a small tropical-American tree, used in tanning; this tree. [Carib]

divid'ual, a. Separate; separable. Hence ~ʟʏ² adv. [f. L *dividuus*+-ᴀʟ]

divinā'tion, n. Divining, insight into or discovery of the unknown or future by supernatural means; skilful forecast, good guess. [ME, f. OF f. L *divinationem* (ᴅɪᴠɪɴᴇ², -ᴀᴛɪᴏɴ)]

divine'¹, a. (-er, -est), & n. 1. Of, from, like, God or a god (~ *right of kings,* independent of their subjects' will); devoted to God, sacred, (~ *service,* public worship); superhumanly excellent, gifted, or beautiful; hence ~ʟʏ² (-nl-) adv. 2. n. Person (usu. cleric) skilled in theology. [ME, f. OF *devin* f. L *divinus* f. *divus* godlike]

divin|e'², v.t. & i. Make out by inspiration, magic, intuition, or guessing, foresee, predict, conjecture; practise divination; ~*ing-rod,* see ᴅᴏᴡsɪɴɢ. Hence ~'ᴇʀ⁸ (4) n. [ME, f. F *deviner* f. L *divinare* (*divinus* ᴅɪᴠɪɴᴇ¹)]

divin'ity, n. Being divine, godhood; a god, godhead; *the D*~, God; adorable or adored person; theology, University theological faculty; (Bookbind.) ~ *calf* (dark brown with *blind* ᴛᴏᴏʟɪɴɢ). [ME, f. OF *devinite* f. L *divinitatem* (ᴅɪᴠɪɴᴇ¹, -ᴛʏ)]

divin|ĭz|e, -is|e (-ĭz), v.t. Deify. Hence ~ᴀ'ᴛɪᴏɴ n. [f. F *diviniser* f. *divin* ᴅɪᴠɪɴᴇ¹]

divis'ible (-z-), a. Capable of being divided actually or in thought; (Math.) ~ *by,* containing (a number) some number of times without remainder. Hence ᴅɪᴠɪsɪʙɪʟ'ɪᴛʏ (-z-) n. [f. F, or LL *divisibilis* (ᴅɪᴠɪᴅᴇ¹, -ɪʙʟᴇ)]

divi'sion (-zhn), n. 1. Dividing or being divided, severance; distribution, sharing, (~ *of labour,* time-saving arrangement giving different parts of manufacturing process etc. to different persons). 2. Disagreement, discord. 3. (Math.) process of dividing number by another (*long, short,* ~, methods usual with divisors greater, not greater, than 12; *symbol of* ~, ÷, as 3÷4 = ¾). 4. (Log.) classification, enumeration of parts, distinction of meanings. 5. (Parl.) separation of House into two sets for counting votes. 6. Dividing line, boundary; part, section. 7. Administrative etc. district, definite part, under single command, of army or fleet, esp. (Mil.) formation of an army, commanded by a Major-General, and (*infantry* ~) usu. consisting of three infantry brigades, with cavalry (now armoured car regiment), artillery, engineers, signals, **R.A.S.C.**, **R.A.M.C.**, and **R.A.O.C.**; *airborne, armoured, parachute,* ~; ‖ part of county or borough returning a Member of Parliament. **8.** (Nat. Hist.) section of kingdom, order, genus, etc. **9.** ‖ (Prison) *1st, 2nd, 3rd,* ~, lenient, medium, severe, treatment in prison prescribed by judge. Hence ~AL (-zho-) a., ~alLY² adv. [ME, f. OF f. L *divisionem* (DIVIDE¹, -ION)]

divīs'or (-z-), n. (math.). Number by which another (the DIVIDEND) is to be divided; number that divides another without remainder. [ME, f. F *diviseur* or L *divisor* (DIVIDE¹, -OR)]

divōrce'¹, n. Legal dissolution of marriage (~ *ā vin'cŭlō matrimōn'iī,* i.e. from the bonds of marriage) opp. to judicial separation of married pair (~ *ā men'sā et tho'ro,* i.e. from board and bed); (loosely) decree of nullity of marriage; (fig.) severance, sundering. [ME, f. OF f. L *divortium* f. DI¹(*vortere* later *vertere* turn)]

divōrce'², v.t. Legally dissolve marriage between; separate (spouse) by divorce *from*; put away, repudiate, (spouse); dissolve (union); sever (things, thing *from*). Hence **di-** or **divōrcEE'** (also F *divorcé* masc., *-ée* fem.). ~MƐNT (-sm-), nn. [ME, f. OF *divorcer* f. LL *divortiare* (prec.)]

div'ot, n. (Sc., north.). ‖ A turf, sod; (Golf) piece of turf cut out in making a stroke. [orig. unkn.]

divŭl‖ge' (-j), v.t. Let out, reveal. Hence or cogn. **divŭlgA'TION**, ~ge'MENT (-jm-), ~'gENCE, nn. [f. L DI¹(*vulgare* publish f. *vulgus* people)]

‖ divv'y̆, n. Var. of DIVI.

Dix'ie('s länd), n. The U.S.A. south of Mason & Dixon's line, the former slave States. [corrupt. of *Dixon,* surveyor?]

dix'y̆, dix'ie, n. Large iron pot in which stew, tea, etc., are made or carried on campaign. [f. Hind. *degchī* cooking pot]

diz'en (*or* dī-), v.t. (rare). Array with finery, deck *out or up,* bedizen. [dress (distaff) with flax (1530): app. identical with first element in DISTAFF]

dizz'y̆, a., & v.t. **1.** Giddy, dazed, unsteady, tottering, confused; making giddy; (of mountain, tower, etc.) very high; (of stream, wheel, etc.) whirling rapidly; hence ~ILY² adv., ~ĭNESS n. **2.** v.t. Make ~y, bewilder. [OE *dysig,* OFris. *dusig,* MDu. *dosech,* LG *dusig, dōsig,* OHG *tusic* f. WG **dus-*]

djibba(h). See JIBBA(H).

do¹ (dŏō), v.t. & i. & aux. (sing. pres. **2,** *doest* pr. dŏō'īst as t. & i., *dost* pr. dŭst as aux.; **3,** *does* pr. dŭz & arch. *doth* pr. dŭ-, *doeth* pr. dŏō'īth; past *did, dĭdst;* p.p. *done* pr. dŭn; *dŏn't, didn't,* are common for *do not, did not; doesn't,* & vulg. *dŏn't,* for *does not*). **1.** v.t. Put (arch.; now only in *do to death*); bestow, impart, grant, render, give, (*does him credit, does credit to his intelligence; does me good, harm; did a service to his country; do*

justice to); perform, carry out, effect, bring to pass, (thing, work, good, right, wrong, duty, bidding, penance; *it isn't done,* is bad form), whence **do'ING**¹(1) (dŏō-) n., (esp., pl.) what happens on an occasion or is done by or befalls a person, (sl.) adjuncts, things needed; (p.p. & perf.) complete, bring to an end, (*it is, I have, done*); exert, use, (*do one's endeavour,* one's *best,* &, sl., one's *damnedest*); produce, make, (*have done six copies*); operate on, deal with, repair, set in order, (*does the French books for the Athenaeum; paper-hanger does a house, housemaid a room; do one's hair*); cook, roast, etc., to the right degree (*chop done to a turn; well, over, under,* -*done*); solve (sum, problem); translate *into* English etc.; work at (lesson); play the part of (*did Lear, the cicerone;* hence *do the polite* etc.); exhaust, tire out; (sl.) cheat (also *do in the eye*); traverse (such a distance); (colloq.) see the sights of (city, museum); (sl.) undergo (term of punishment); (with noun of action as compd vb) *do battle* etc., fight etc.; ‖(sl.) provide food etc. for (*they do you very well; do oneself well,* make liberal provision for one's own comfort). **2.** v.i. (With adv. or advl phr.) act, proceed, (*do as they do at Rome; would do wisely to withdraw*); perform deeds (*do or die*); make an end (*have done!,* cease; *let us have done with it*); fare, get on, (well, badly, etc.; of person or thing; *how do you do?* or *how d'ye do?*); be suitable, answer purpose, serve, suffice. **3.** v. substitute: (a) replacing vb and taking its construction, as *I chose my wife as she did her gown;* (b) replacing vb & obj. etc., as *if you saw the truth as clearly as I do;* (c) as elliptical auxiliary, as '*did you see him?*' '*I did*'; (d) with *so, it, which,* etc., as: *I wanted to see him, & I did so; in passing through the market, which he seldom did; if you want to tell him, do it now.* **4.** v. aux. Used with infin. for simple pres. & past (a) when special emphasis is to be laid on a fact, as *I do so wish I could,* esp. in contrast with what has preceded, as *but I did see him;* also for imperat. in urgent petitions, as *do tell me, do but think;* or when the pronoun is inserted & emphasized, as *do you go rather;* (b) when inversion is desired, as *rarely does it happen that;* (c) the usual form in questions except with *have, be,* & some monosyl. vbs, as *did you recognize her?, do you dare?* or *dare you?*; (d) usual in *not* statements except with *be, have, dare, need,* etc.; also in *not* commands. **5.** Phrr. etc.: *a to-do,* bustle, fuss; *well-to-do,* rich enough, thriving; *have to do with,* be concerned or connected or have dealings with; *nothing doing,* going on; *done,* used in accepting offer or bet; *do-nothing,* a. & n., idle(r). **6.** With prepp.: *do by,* treat, deal with, in such a way; *do for* (colloq.), ‖ act as housekeeper etc. for, ruin, destroy, kill; *do to, unto*, = do by; *do with*, get on with, tolerate (joc., *could do with a drink*), find sufficient; *do without*, dispense with. **7.** With advv.; *do away (with)*, abolish; *do in* (sl.), kil¹; *do up*, restore, repair, wrap up (parcel), tire out. Hence do'ABLE (dōō-) a., do'ER¹ (dōō-) n. [OE & OS *dōn*, OHG *tuon*, f. WG •*dō-* cogn. w. Gk *tithēmi*]

do² (dōō), n. (sl.). Swindle, imposture, hoax; ∥ (colloq.) entertainment, jollification (*there's a big do on at No. 2*), (in pl.) share (*fair do's!* share fairly). [f. prec.]

do³, doh, (dō), n. (mus.).· Key-note of scale (*movable do*); the note C (*fixed do*). [arbitrary]

dō⁴, abbr. of DITTO.

doat. See DOTE.

dŏbb'in, n. Draught or farm horse. [pet--name = Robert]

Docĕt'ic, a., **Docĕt'ist, Docĕt'ism**, nn. (Of, holder of) the heresy that Christ's body was not human but phantasmal or of celestial substance. [mediæ. L f. Gk *dokētai* (*dokéō* seem)+-IC, -IST, -ISM]

doch'-an-dŏ'ris (dŏx-, see Ap., dŏk-), n. Stirrup-cup, last drink. [f. Gael. *deoch--an-doruis* a drink at the door]

doch'miăc (dŏk-), a. & n. Composed of dochmii (dochmius, ∪−−∪−); (n., usu. pl.) line(s) so composed. [f. L f. Gk *dokhmiakos* f. *dokhmios* oblique]

dŏ'cĭle, a. Teachable; submissive; easily managed. So docil'ITY n. [ME, f. OF, or L *docilis* (*docēre* teach, -IL)]

dŏck¹, n. Kinds of coarse weedy herb, popular antidote for nettle stings. [OE *docce*, cf. MDu. *dockeblaederen*]

dŏck², n. Solid fleshy part of animal's tail; crupper of saddle or harness. [ME, = mod. Icel. *dockr*; ult. orig. unkn.]

dŏck³, v.t. Cut short (animal in tail, person in hair; or tail etc.); lessen, deprive *of*, put limits on (person, supplies); (Law) ~ *the entail*, cut it off; ~*-tailed*, with tail~ed. [f. prec.]

dŏck⁴, n., & v.t. & i. **1.** Basin with flood--gates in which ships may be loaded, unloaded, or repaired (*dry or graving* ~, for repairing or building, water being pumped out; *wet* ~, with water kept at high-tide level; *floating* ~, floating structure usable as dry ~); (usu. pl.) range of ~ basins with wharves and offices, dockyard; •ship's berth, wharf; (Railway) ∥ platform-enclosure in which line terminates; ~*-dues*, charge for use of ~, also ~'AGE(4) n.; ~*-glass* (large, for wine--tasting); ~*-master*, superintendent of ~'*yard* or enclosure with ~s & all ship-building & repairing appliances, ∥ esp. in connexion with Navy. **2.** vb. Bring(ship), (of ship) come, into ~; furnish with ~s. [c. 1500, f. MDu. *docke*, of unkn. orig.]

dŏck⁵, n. Enclosure in criminal court for prisoner; ∥ ~ *brief* (undertaken gratis by barrister in court selected by poor prisoner in ~). [16th c., prob. = Flem. *dok* cage, of unkn. orig.]

dŏck'er, n. Labourer in DOCK⁴. [-ER¹]

dŏck'ĕt, n., & v.t. ∥ (Law) register of legal judgements (vb, enter in this); endorsement on letter or document showing its contents or subject (vb, endorse thus); ∥ Custom-House warrant certifying payment of duty; ∥ certificate of cotton clearing-house entitling presenter to delivery; ∥ permit to buy controlled or scarce goods. [15th c., of unkn. orig.]

dŏck'ize, -is|e (-ĭz), v.t. Make (river) into range of docks. Hence ~A'TION n. [-IZE]

dŏc'tor¹, n. (Arch.) teacher, learned man, (*D~s of the Church*, certain, esp. four Eastern & four Western, early fathers; *who shall decide when* ~*s disagree?*); holder of the highest university degree in any faculty (often honorary; used as prefix to surname, usu. abbr. *Dr*), esp. ~ of medicine male or female (also pop. of any medical man, M.D. or not, esp. in voc.); (Naut. sl.) ship's cook; kinds of mechanical appliance for regulating etc.; artificial fly; ~*'s stuff*, physic. Hence or cogn. ~AL, dŏctōr'IAL, ~LESS, aa., ~ATE¹, ~SHIP(1, 3), ~HOOD, **dŏc'tress¹** (joc. etc. for usu. ~ fem.), nn. [ME, f. OF f. L (*docēre doct-* teach, -OR)]

dŏc'tor², v.t. & i. Confer degree of doctor on; treat (patient, one*self*) medically; castrate; patch up (machinery etc.); adulterate, falsify; practise as physician (esp. in gerund). [f. prec.]

Dŏc'tors' Cŏmm'ons, n. pl. Common table, buildings (in which certain courts were held), of former College of Doctors of Civil Law in London (frequent literary allusions to probate, marriage-licence, & divorce business once transacted there). [COMMONS]

dŏctrinaire', **dŏctrinār'ian**, nn. & aa. **1.** Pedantic theorist, person who'applies principle without allowance for circumstances; hence **dŏctrinair'ism**(2), **dŏctrinār'ian**ism(2), nn. **2.** adj. Theoretic and unpractical. [-*aire* F (L *doctrina* DOC-TRINE, -ARY¹) name of French political party 1815; -ARIAN]

dŏc'trinal (*or* dŏktrīn²), a. Of, inculcating, doctrine(s). Hence ~LY² adv. [f. LL *doctrinalis* (foll., -AL)]

dŏc'trin|e, n. What is taught, body of instruction; religious, political, scientific, etc., belief, dogma, or tenet (*Monroe* ~*e*, U.S. policy foreshadowed by President Monroe 1823 discountenancing European State interference in America). Hence ~ISM(1), ~IST(1), nn., ~IZE(2) v.i. [ME, f. OF f. L *doctrina* (DOCTOR¹, -INE⁴)]

dŏc'ŭment, n., & v.t. **1.** Thing, esp. deed, writing, or inscription, that furnishes evidence (*human* ~, description, incident, etc., illustrating human nature); hence **dŏcŭmĕn'tARY¹** a., (also n., film dealing with a natural history, archaeological, industrial, travel, or similar subject, usu. accompanied by an explanatory talk). **2. v.t.** Prove by, provide with, ~s or evidence; so **docŭmĕntaᵀᴵᴼᴺ** n. [ME, f. OF f. L *documentum* (*docēre* teach, -MENT)]

dŏdd'er¹, n. Kinds of slender leafless threadlike parasitic plant. [ME *doder* = MLG *dod(d)er*, MHG *toter* (G *dotter*)]

dŏdd'er², v.i. Tremble, nod, with frailty, palsy, etc. (~-*grass*, quaking-grass); totter, potter, be feeble. Hence ~ᴇʀ¹ n., infirm, feeble, or inept person. [orig. unkn.; cf. obs. (15th c.) *dadder*]

dŏdd'ered (-*erd*), a. Having lost the top or branches (of oaks & other trees). [prob. f. frequent. of obs. vb *dod* poll, lop]

dōdec(a)-, comb. form = twelve-, as *ĕ'odĕc'agon*, plane figure of twelve sides, *dōdĕcahē'dron*, solid figure of twelve faces, *dōdĕcasyll'able*, verse of twelve syllables. [f. Gk *dōdeka* twelve]

dŏdge¹, v.i. & t. **1. v.i.** Move to & fro, change position, shuffle; move quickly *round*, *about* or *behind*, obstacle so as to elude pursuer, blow, etc.; play fast & loose, quibble, prevaricate; (of bell in chime) sound one place out of the normal order. **2. v.t.** Baffle by finesse, trifle with; elude (pursuer, opponent, blow) by sideward deviation etc.; move (thing) to & fro; ask (person) questions in unexpected order. [orig. unkn.]

dŏdge², n. Piece of dodging, quick side-movement; trick, artifice; (colloq.) clever expedient, mechanical etc. contrivance; sounding of bell out of normal place in chimes. Hence **dŏdg'yˣ²** a. [f. prec.]

dŏdg'er, n. In vbl senses; esp., artful or elusive person; (colloq.) screen on ship's bridge as protection from spray etc.; *small handbill; *Indian-meal cake (*corn~*). [-ᴇʀ¹]

dōd'ō, n. (pl. *-oes*, *-os*). Large extinct bird of Mauritius. [f. Port. *doudo* simpleton]

doe (dō), n. Female of fallow deer (cf. ʙᴜᴄᴋ¹), hare or rabbit; ~*skin* (-ōs-), skin of ~, leather of this, fine cloth resembling it. [OE *dā*, of unkn. orig.]

does, doest. See ᴅᴏ¹.

dŏff, v.t. Take off (hat, clothing); (rarely) abandon, discard, (custom, condition). [ME, = *do off*]

dŏg¹, n. **1.** Quadruped of many breeds wild & domesticated; hunting-dog (fig., ~*s of war*, havoc, rapine); male of ~, wolf (also ~*wolf*), (fem. *bitch*), or fox (also ~*fox*). **2.** Worthless or surly person; fellow (*sly*, *lucky*, *jolly*, ~; ꜱᴇᴀ-~). **3.** (astron.). *Greater* or *Lesser Dog*, constellations, also Sirius or Procyon, chief star in either (also ~*star*, usu. Sirius; ~*days*, hottest part of year in July & Aug., variously dated with ref. to rising of Sirius). **4.** Kinds of mechanical device for gripping etc.; short iron bar with upturned spike at each end in common use for joining heavy timbering; (pl., also *fire-~s*) pair of

metal supports for burning wood, or for grate, or for fire-irons. **5.** (Also *sea-~*) light near horizon portending storm; *sun-~*, parhelion. **6.** Phrr.; *go to the ~s*, be ruined; *throw to the ~s*, throw away, sacrifice; *not have* ᴡᴏʀᴅ¹ *to throw at ~*; *every ~ has his* ᴅᴀʏ; *love me, love my ~*, accept my friends as yours; *rain* ᴄᴀᴛꜱ & ~*s*; *die like a ~*, *a ~'s death*, miserably, shamefully; *not a ~'s chance*, not even the least chance; *take hair of ~ that bit you*, drink more to cure effects of drink; *help lame ~ over stile*, be friend in need; *lead, lead one, a ~'s life*, a life of misery or of miserable subservience; *give ~ ill name & hang him*, of power of nickname or slander; *let sleeping ~s lie*, let well alone; *put on ~* (colloq.), assume airs of importance; ‖ *the ~s* (colloq.), greyhound race-meeting; ~ *in the manger*, one who prevents others enjoying what is useless to him; ~ *in a blanket*, rolled currant dumpling or jam pudding. **7.** ~'*berry*, fruit of ~*wood*; ~-*biscuit*, for feeding ~s; ‖~*box*, railway van for ~s; ~'*cart*, two-wheeled driving-cart with cross seats back to back; ~-*cheap*, very; ~-*collar*, lit., & fig. of person's straight high collar divided at back, clerical collar; ~-*faced*, epithet of kind of baboon; ~-*fall*, in which wrestlers touch ground together; ~-*fennel*, stinking camomile; ~'*fight*, a fight (as) between ~s, (colloq.) a fight between aircraft; ~'*fish*, kinds of small shark & other fish; ~('s)-*grass*, couch-grass; ~-*hole*, -*hutch*, mean room; ~'-*house* (*in the ~house*, sl., in disgrace); ~ *latin*, incorrect, mongrel; ~-*lead*, string etc. for leading ~; ~-*leg(ged) staircase*, going back & forward without well-hole; ~'*rose*, wild hedgerose; ~('s)-*ear* n. & v.t., corner of page turned down with use, fill (book) with these; ~'s-*body*, (Naut. sl.) dried pease boiled in a cloth, a junior officer, drudge; ~'*shore*, wooden prop supporting ship's weight during building and cut away before launching; ~'*skin*, leather of or imitating ~'s skin used for gloves; ~-*sleep*, light & fitful; ~'s *letter*, r (f. snarling sound); ~'s-*meat*, horseflesh, offal; ~'s-*nose*, mixed drink of beer & gin; ~('s)-*tail*, kind of grass; ~'s-*tongue*, plants of borage kind; ~'s-*tooth*, plant with speckled leaves & flowers; ~-*tired*, tired out; ~-*tooth*, small pyramidal ornament esp. in Norman & Early English architecture; ~-*violet*, scentless kind; ~-*watch* (Naut.), short half watch of two hours (4–6, 6–8, p.m.); ~-*whip*, for keeping ~s in order; ~'*wood*, wild cornel; *kind of flowering shrub. Hence ~g'ɪꜱʜ¹, ~'ʟᴇss, ~'ʟɪᴋᴇ, aa., ~g'ȳ¹ or ~g'ie (-g-) [-ʏ³], ~'ʜᴏᴏᴅ, nn. [late OE *docga*, of unkn. orig.]

dŏg², v.t. (-gg-). Follow closely, pursue, track, (person, his *steps*; of person or calamity etc.); (Mech.) grip with dog. [f. prec.]

dŏg'āte, n. Office of doge. [f. F *dogat* f. It. *dogato* (foll., -ATE¹)]

dōge (-j), n. (hist.). Chief magistrate of Venice, Genoa. [F f. It., f. L *ducem* nom. *dux* leader]

dŏgg'ĕd (-g-), a. Obstinate, tenacious, persistent, unyielding, (*it's* ~ *does it*, persistency succeeds). Hence ~LY² adv., ~NESS n. [ME; -ED²]

dŏgg'er (-g-), n. Two-masted bluff--bowed Dutch fishing-boat. [ME, f. MDu. *dogger* fishing-boat, cf. *ten dogge varen* to go to the cod-fishing]

dŏgg'erel (-ge-), a. & n. Trivial, mean, halting, or irregular, (verse). [ME, app. f. DOG¹ (as in *dog latin* etc.)]

dŏgg'ō, adv. (sl.). Lie ~ (motionless, making no sign). [*dog*]

dŏgg'|ȳ² (-g-), a. (for *doggy¹* see DOG¹). Of dogs; devoted to dogs. Hence ~INESS n. [-Y²]

dŏg'ma, n. (pl. ~s, rarely ~ta). Principle, tenet, doctrinal system, esp. as laid down by authority of Church; arrogant declaration of opinion. [L f. Gk (*dogma* -*mat-* opinion, f. *dokeō* seem, -M]

dŏgmăt'|ic (rarely ~ical), a. Of dogma(s), doctrinal; based on *a priori* principles, not on induction; (of person, book, etc.) authoritative, laying down the law, arrogant. Hence ~ICS n., ~ICALLY adv. [f. LL f. Gk *dogmatikos* (prec., -IC)]

dŏg'mat|ize, -t|ise (-īz), v.i. & t. Deal in positive unsupported assertions, speak authoritatively; express (principle etc.) as a dogma. So ~ISM(1), ~IST (1), nn. [f. F *dogmatiser* or LL f. Gk *dogmatizō* (DOGMA, -IZE)]

do'gŏŏd'er (dŏŏ-), n. (colloq., freq. derog.). Earnest, idealistic, would-be reformer. [-ER¹]

doh. See DO³.

doil'ȳ, n. Small napkin placed below finger-glass etc. [fabric named from 17th--c. London linen-draper]

do'ing (dŏŏ-). See DO¹.

doit, n. Very small sum or coin; merest trifle (esp. *don't care a* ~). [16th c., f. MLG *doyt*, MDu. *duit*, of unkn. orig.]

doit'ĕd, a. (Sc.). Crazed, esp. with age. [ME; orig. unkn.]

dŏl'ce fār nĭ̆ent'ĕ (-chā), n. Pleasant idleness. [It., = sweet doing nothing]

dŏl'drums (-z), n. pl. Dullness, dumps, depression; (of ship, usu. *in the* ~) becalmed state; region of calms & light baffling winds near equator. [prob. formed on *dull*, cf. *tantrums*]

dōle¹, n., & v.t. 1. (arch.). Lot, destiny, (*happy man be his* ~, may he be happy). 2. Charitable distribution; charitable (esp. sparing, niggardly) gift of food, clothes, or money; ‖ *the* ~ (colloq.), relief claimable by the unemployed. 3. v.t. Deal *out* sparingly, esp. as alms. [OE *dāl*, f. Gmc **dailaz*, see DEAL¹]

dōle², n. (poet.). Grief, woe; lamentation.

[ME *dol* etc. f. OF *dol*, *doel*, etc. f. Rom. **dolus* f. L *dolēre* grieve]

dōle'ful (-lf-), a. Dreary, dismal; sad, discontented, melancholy. Hence ~LY² adv., ~NESS n. [ME; prec., -FUL]

dŏl'erīte, n. Coarse basaltic rock much used as road-metal. [F (-é-), f. Gk *doleros* deceptive (because easily confused with true greenstone)]

dŏl'ichocĕphăl'ic (-ko-), a. Long-headed (of skull with breadth less than ⅘ of length; or of person or race with such skull). [f. Gk *dolikhos* long + -CEPHALIC]

dŏll, n., & v.t. & i. 1. Toy baby, puppet; (~*'s house*, miniature toy house for ~s, tiny dwelling-house); pretty but silly woman (so ~*'s face*). Hence ~'ISH¹ a., ~'ishLY² adv., ~'ishNESS n. 2. v.t. & i. (colloq.). Dress *up* smartly, deck up. [short for *Dorothy*]

dŏll'ar, n. (Orig.) English name for German thaler, also for Spanish piece of eight; unit of U.S. gold & silver coinage = 100 cents (symbol or ~ *sign*, $; *the almighty* ~, money, mammon); corresponding coin in Canada, etc.; ‖ (sl.) five--shilling piece, crown; *half a* ~ (sl.), half a crown; ~ *area* (in which currency is linked to U.S. ~); ~ *diplomacy* (that seeks to further the commercial and financial interests of a country abroad and to extend its influence in international relations by means of these interests). [16th c. *daler* etc. f. LG & early mod. Du. *daler* f. G *taler* f. *Joachimstaler* coin from silver mine of the *Joachimstal*]

dŏll'op, n. (colloq.). Clumsy or shapeless lump of food etc. [orig. obsc.; cf. Norw. dial. *dolp* lump]

dŏll'ȳ, n. (Pet-name, esp. in voc., for) doll; kinds of appliance in ·clothes--washing, ore-washing, pile-driving, iron--punching, polishing, etc.; ~*-shop*, marine store. [-Y³]

Dŏll'ȳ Vār'den, n. Kinds of woman's hat & dress. [character in *Barnaby Rudge*]

dŏl'man, n. Long Turkish robe open in front; hussar's jacket worn with sleeves hanging loose; woman's mantle with flaps for sleeves. [ult. f. Turk. *dolaman*]

dŏl'mĕn, n. Megalithic tomb. [F, perh. f. Cornish (*doll* hole, *men* stone)]

dŏl'omite, n. Kind of rock (double carbonate of lime & magnesia); *The D~s*, mountains of this, esp. those in Tyrol. Hence dŏlomīt'IC a. [*Dolomieu*, French geologist 1794, -ITE¹]

dŏl'orous, a. (usu. poet. or joc.). Distressing, painful; dismal, doleful; distressed. Hence ~LY² adv. [ME, f. OF f. LL *dolorosus* (DOLOUR, -OUS)]

dolōse', a. (legal). Having criminal intent; intentionally deceitful. [f. L *dolosus* (*dolus* guile, -OSE¹)]

dŏl'our (-ler), n. (poet.). Sorrow, distress. [ME, f. OF, f. L *dolorem* nom. *-or*]

dŏl'phin, n. Sea animal of the whale order resembling porpoise but larger &

with beak-like snout; the fish dorado, which changes to many colours in dying; curved fish in heraldry, sculpture, etc.; bollard or mooring-post or buoy. [ME also *delphin* f. L *delphinus* f. Gk *delphis -inos*; cf. DELPHIN]

dolt, n. Dull fellow, blockhead. Hence ~'ISH[1] a., ~'ISHNESS n. [app. related to *dol, dold*, obs. var. of DULL, *dull_d*]

Dom, title prefixed to names of R.-C. dignitaries, and Benedictine & Carthusian monks, and in Portugal & Brazil to Christian names of persons of the royal family, cardinals, bishops, etc. [abbr. of L *dominus* lord]

-dom, suf. forming nouns expressing rank, condition, domain, f. nn. or adjj. (*earldom, freedom, kingdom*), & (f. nouns) used collectively for the pl. or = the ways of (*officialdom*). [OE, OS *-dōm*, OHG *-tuom* (G-*tum*), orig. an independent n. = DOOM[1]]

domain', n. Estate, lands, dominions; district under rule, realm, sphere of influence; scope, field, province, of thought or action; (Internat. & U.S. law) *Eminent D~*, lordship of sovereign power over all property in State, with right of expropriation. So **domān'IAL** a. [f. F *domaine*, earlier OF *demeine* DEMESNE]

dōme, n., & v.t. 1. Stately building, mansion, (poet.); rounded vault as roof, with circular, elliptical, or polygonal base, large cupola; natural vault, canopy, (of sky, trees, etc.); rounded summit of hill etc.; hence **dōmED²** (-md), **dōm'IC(AL)**, ~'LIKE (-ml-), **dōm'Y²**, aa. 2. v.t. Cover with, shape as, ~. [F, f. It. *duomo* cathedral, dome, (& direct) f. L *domus* house]

Domes'day (Bŏŏk) (dŏōmz-), n. Record of Will. I's Great Inquisition of lands of England made 1086. [ME, = DOOM[1]*sday*, pop. name given to the book as final authority]

domĕs'tǀǀc, a. & n. 1. Of the home, household, or family affairs; of one's own country, not foreign; native, home-made; (of animals) kept by or living with man; home-keeping, fond of home; hence ~ICALLY adv. 2. n. Household servant. [f. F *domestique* f. L *domesticus* (*domus* home)]

domĕs'ticǀāte, v.t. Naturalize (colonists, animals); make fond of home (esp. in p.p.); bring (animals) under human control, tame; civilize (savages). So ~ABLE a., ~A'TION n. [f. med. L *domesticare* (prec., -ATE[3])]

dŏmĕstǀ'cǀt̆ǀȳ (or dŏ-), n. Domestic character; home life or privacy; homeliness; *the* ~*ies*; domestic affairs; domesticated state. [-ITY]

dŏm'ĕtt, n. Fabric of wool & cotton used for shrouds etc. [orig. unkn.]

dŏm'icǀle (or -ǀl), n., & v.t. & i. 1. Dwelling-place, home; (Law) place of perman-

ent residence, fact of residing; place at which bill of exchange is made payable (v.t., make payable *at* a place). 2. vb. (Also **dŏmicil'IATE²**) establish, settle (t. & i.), in a place; so **dŏmiciLIA'TION** n. [ME, f. OF f. L *domicilium* f. *domus* home]

dŏmicil'iarȳ (-lya-), a. Of a dwelling--place (~ *visit*, of officials to search or inspect private house). [as prec., -ARY[1]]

dŏm'inant, a. & n. 1. Ruling, prevailing, most influential; (of heights) outstanding, overlooking others. 2. (mus.). Fifth note of scale of any key (adj., of this, as ~ *chord, seventh*, etc.); reciting note in eccles. modes, usu. fifth from final. 3. (Mendelism) main characteristic appearing in the first generation of hybrids inherited from one only of the parents (adj., of this). Hence **dŏm'INANCE** n., ~LY² adv. [F, f. L *dominari* see foll., -ANT]

dŏm'ināte, v.t. & i. Have commanding influence over (also intr. with *over*); be the most influential or conspicuous (of person, power, sound, feature of scene); (of heights) overlook, hold commanding position *over*. [f. L *dominari* (*dominus* lord), -ATE³]

dŏminā'tion, n. Ascendancy, sway, control; (pl.) angelic powers of fourth rank (see ORDER[1] prec., -ATION). [ME, f. OF f. L *dominationem* (prec., -ATION)]

dŏmineer', v.i. Act imperiously, tyrannize, be overbearing. Hence ~ingLY² adv. [f. Du. (-*neren*) f. F *dominer* DOMINATE]

domin'ical, a. Of the Lord (Christ; ~ *year*, dat̪a̪ A.D.); of the Lord's day, Sunday-, (~ *letter*, the one of the seven A-G denoting Sundays in any year). [f. LL & med. L *dominicalis* f. LL *dominicus* (L *dominus* lord, -IC) +-*alis* -AL]

Domin'ican, a. & n. 1. Of St Dominic or his order of preaching friars. 2. n. Black or ~ friar. [f. med. L *Dominicanus* f. *Dominicus* L name of *Domingo* de Guzman-+-AN]

‖ **dŏm'inie**, n. (Sc.). Schoolmaster. [later sp. of (16th c.) *domine* sir voc. of L *dominus* lord]

domin'ion (-yon), n. Lordship, sovereignty, control; domains of feudal lord, territory of sovereign or government (*D~ of Canada*, name given to Canadian colonies united 1867; *D~ of New Zealand*, title given 1907; *D~ of Ceylon* 1948); (Law) right of possession. [ME, f. OF f. med. L *dominionem* nom. -o f. L *dominium* (*dominus* lord)]

dŏm'inō, n. (pl. ~*es*). 1. Loose cloak with half-mask worn to conceal identity esp. at masquerade, whence ~ED² (-ōd) a.; person wearing this~. 2. One of 28 small brick-shaped pieces marked with pips used in game of ~es. [F, prob. f. L *dominus* lord, but unexplained]

dŏn¹, n. 1. Spanish title prefixed to

Christian name (*Don Juan*, rake, libertine; *Don* QUIXOTE); Spanish gentleman, Spaniard. 2. Distinguished person; adept *at* something. 3. Head, fellow, or tutor, of college, whence ~n'ISH[1] a., ~n'ISHNESS n. [Sp., f. L *dominus* lord]

don², v.t. (-nn-). Put on (garment). [= *do on*]

dŏn'a(h), n. (sl.). Woman; sweetheart. [f. Sp. *doña* or Port. *dona* f. L *domina* lady]

dona'tion, n. Bestowal, presenting; thing presented, gift (esp. of money given to institution), whence *donate'* v.t., present. [ME, f. OF f. L *donationem* (*donare* give, -ATION)]

dŏn'ative (*or* dŏ-), a. & n. (Benefice) given directly, not involving presentation to or investment by the Ordinary; gift, present, esp. official largess. [ME, f. L *donativum* gift (OF *donatif*); adj. use later (L *donare* give, -ATIVE)]

dŏn'atorў, n. Recipient of donation. [f. med. L *donatorius* (*donare* give, -ORY)]

done (dŭn), p.p. of DO¹. ~ *brown*, duped, swindled; ~ *up*, tired.

dōnee', n. Recipient of gift. [as DONOR, -EE]

∥ **dŏn'ga** (-ngga), n. Gully, ravine. [S.-Afr.]

dŏn'jŏn (*also* dŭ-), n. Great tower of castle, keep. [var. spelling of DUNGEON]

dŏnk'ey, n. (pl. ~s). (Usual word for) ass; stupid person; ~-*engine*, hauling or hoisting steam-engine on ship's deck; ~'s *years* (sl.), a very long time. [18th c., perh. f. DUN¹, or proper name *Duncan* (cf. *dicky*, *neddy*)]

dŏnn'a, n. Italian or Spanish or Portuguese lady. [It., f. L *domina* mistress]

Dŏnn'ybrŏŏk (Fair), n. Scene of uproar, free fight. [*Donnybrook* in Ireland]

dŏn'or, n. Giver (esp. of blood for transfusion). [ME, f. OF *doneur* f. L *donatorem* (*donare* give, -OR)]

dŏn't¹. See DO¹.

dŏn't², n.(joc.). Prohibition. [use of prec.]

dōō'dle, v.i. & n. 1. Scrawl or draw absent-mindedly. 2. n. Scrawl or drawing so made; ~-*bug*, *(larva of)* tiger beetle, *unscientific device for locating minerals, ∥ flying-bomb (colloq.). [orig. unkn.]

dōōl'ie, -ў, n. Simple form of Indian litter used as army ambulance. [f. Hind. *doli* (Skr. *dul-* to swing)]

dōōm¹, n. (Hist.) Statute, law, decree; (arch.) decision, sentence, condemnation; fate, destiny, (usu. evil); ruin, death; the Last Judgement (now only in *crack*, *day*, *of* ~, & in ~'s *day*; *till* ~'s*day*, for ever; cf. DOMESDAY). [OE, OS *dōm*, OHG *tuom*, ON *dómr*, Goth. *dōms* f. Gmc *dōmaz* f. *do-* DO¹]

dōōm², v.t. Pronounce sentence against, condemn *to* some fate, *to* do; consign to misfortune or destruction (esp. in p.p.); (arch.) decree (~*ed his death*). [f. prec.]

door (dōr), n. 1. Hinged or sliding barrier usu. of wood or metal for closing entrance to building, room, safe, etc. (*front* ~, *chief* ~ from house to street etc.; *lives* etc. *next* ~, in next house or room; so *three* ~*s off* etc.; *next* ~ *to* fig., nearly, almost, near to; so *at death's* ~). 2. Entrance, access, exit, (*show one the* ~, expel him; *open a* ~ *to*, *close the* ~ *upon*, make possible, impossible). 3. *Out of* ~*s*, abroad, in the open air; *within* ~*s*, in the house; *lay*, *lie, at the* ~ *of*, impute, be imputable to; DARKEN ~. 4. ~'*bell*, inside bell worked by handle or button outside ~; ∥ ~-*case*, -*frame*, structure in which ~ is fitted; ∥ ~-*keeper*, porter; ~'*mat*, for rubbing off mud from shoes; ~-*money*, taken at ~ of place·of entertainment; ~'*nail*, with which ~s used to be studded (*dead*, *deaf*, etc., *as a* ~*nail*); ~-*plate*, usu. of brass bearing occupant's name; ~-*post*, upright of ~-case; ~'*step*, leading up to usu. outer ~; ~-*stone*, slab in front of ~; ~'*way*, opening filled by ~. Hence (-)~ED² (-ōrd), ~LESS (-ōrl-), aa. [OE, OS *duru* (*dor*), OHG *turi* (*tor*), ON *dyrr*, Goth. *daur* f. Gmc *dur-* cogn. w. L *fores*, Gk *thura*]

dŏp, n. Cheap S.-Afr. brandy; a dram of liquor. [Du., = shell, husk]

dōpe, n., & v.t. 1. Thick liquid used as food or lubricant; kinds of varnish esp. in aeroplane manufacture; narcotic, stupefying drink; drug etc. given to horse or greyhound to try to make it win; *(sl.) information about a racehorse's past performances or form, information of use to journalists etc. 2. v.t. Administer ~ to, drug, (cf. NOBBLE). [f. Du. *doop* sauce (*doopen* to dip)]

doppel-gänger. See DOUBLE¹-*ganger*.

dŏpp'er, n. (Derog. for) member of the Gereformeerde Kerk of S. Afr., in communion with the Christian Reformed Church of Holland. [f. Du. *dooper* baptist, f. *doopen* dip]

dŏr, n. Insect flying with loud humming noise; black dung-beetle, cockchafer, rose-beetle, etc. [OE *dora* orig. unkn.]

∥ **Dŏr'a**, n. See DEFENCE.

dora'dō (-ah-), n. (pl. ~s). Splendidly coloured sea-fish, dolphin. [Sp., f. L DE(*auratus* gilt f. *aurum* gold. -ATE²)]

Dŏrc'as, n. Meeting of ladies to make clothes for the poor. [*Acts* ix. 36]

Dŏr'ian, a. & n. (Inhabitant) of Doris, district of ancient Greece; (member) of one of three divisions (*Aeolian*, *Ionian*, ~) of ancient Greeks (~ *mode*: ancient Greek MODE, reputedly simple & solemn in character; first of eccles. modes, with D as final & A as dominant). [f. L f. Gk *Dōrios* (*Dōris* as above) + -AN]

Dŏ'ric, a. & n. 1. = prec. adj.; ~ ORDER (also ~ as n.); (of dialect) broad, rustic. 2. n. Dialect of ancient Greece (cf. *Attic*, *Ionic*, *Aeolic*), rustic English or esp. Scots. [f. L f. Gk *Dōrikos* (prec., -IC)]

Dork'ing, a. & n. (Fowl) of the ~ breed. [~ in Surrey]

dorm'ant, a. Lying inactive as in sleep (of some animals through winter, undeveloped buds, potential faculties); (Her., of beast) with head on paws; not acting, in abeyance, (often *lie* ~; ~ *warrant* etc., drawn in blank; ~ *partner*, sleeping). Hence **dorm'ancy** n. [ME, f. OF (*dormir* f. L *dormire* sleep, -ANT)]

dorm'er, n. (Also ~-*window*) projecting upright window in sloping roof. [f. OF *dormeor* f. L *dormitorium* (prec., -ORY)]

dorm'itory, n. Sleeping-room with several beds & sometimes cubicles; suburban or country district of city people's residences. [ME, f. L (DORMER)]

dorm'ouse, n. (pl. *-mice*). Small hibernating rodent between mouse and squirrel. [ME; orig. obsc.; pop. referred to F *dormir* & MOUSE since 16th c.]

dorm'y, a. (golf). (Of player or side) as many holes ahead as there are holes to play (~ *one*, *five*, etc.). [orig. unkn.]

‖ **do'rothy bag,** n. Lady's open-topped handbag slung by loops from wrist. [fem. name]

Do'rothy Perk'ins (-z), n. Climbing rose bearing clusters of double pink flowers. [personal name]

dorp, n. (S. Africa). Village, small township. [Du.; see THORP]

dors'al, a. (Anat., Zool., Bot.) of, on, near, the back; ridge-shaped. Hence ~LY² adv. [F, or f. LL *dorsalis* (foll., -AL)]

dors(o)-, comb. form = back-&-, as in *dorsabdom'inal* of back & belly, *dorsolat'eral* of back & sides. [L *dorsum* back, -O-]

dort'our (-ter), **-ter,** n. (hist.). Bedroom, dormitory, esp. in monastery. [ME, f. OF (-*our*), as DORMER]

dor'y¹, n. (Also *John D~*) sea-fish used as food. [ME, f. OF *doree* fem. p.p. of *dorer* gild, as DORADO]

dor'y², n. Flat-bottomed skiff, esp. fishing-vessel's boat in U.S. [orig. unkn.]

dos'age, n. Giving of medicine in doses; size of dose. [-AGE]

dose, n., & v.t. 1. Amount of medicine to be taken at once (also fig. of flattery, punishment, etc.). 2. v.t. Give physic to (person), adulterate, blend, (esp. wine with spirit). [vb f. noun, F, f. LL f. Gk *dosis* (*didōmi* give)]

‖ **doss,** n., & v.i., (sl.). Bed in ~-*house* or common lodging-house; (v.i.) sleep in this; hence ~'ER¹ n. [18th c. *dorse* f. L *dorsum* back; cf. dial. *hoss* for *horse*]

doss'al, n. Hanging behind altar or round chancel. [f. med. L *dossale* f. LL *dorsalis* DORSAL]

doss'ier (-syā, -sier), n. Set of documents, esp. record of person's antecedents. [F, so called f. label on back (*dos*); see -ER²(2)]

dost. See DO¹.

dot¹, n. Small spot, speck, roundish penmark; (Orthogr.) period, point over *i* or *j*, point used as diacritical mark; (Mus. writing) point used with various meanings; small child, tiny object; ~-*&-dash*, using ~s & dashes, as in Morse code; ~-*wheel*, used for making dotted line; ‖ *off* one's ~ (sl.), half-witted, (temporarily) crazy; *on the* ~, exactly on time. [16th c., perh. repr. OE *dott* head of boil, cogn. w. OHG *tutto* nipple]

dot², v.t. (-tt-). Mark with dot(s); place dot over (letter *i*; ~ *the is & cross the ts*, fill in details, make meaning quite clear); (Mus.) ~*ted* crotchet etc., with time value increased by half; diversify as with dots (*sea* ~*ted with ships*); scatter (*about*, *all over*) like dots; ‖ (sl.) hit (~*ted him one in the eye*); ~ *& carry* (one), child's formula for remembering to carry in addition sum; ~ *& go one*, n., a., & adv., limp, limping(ly). [f. prec.]

dot³, n. Woman's marriage portion. [F]

dot'ard, n. One in his dotage. [foll., -ARD]

dote, doat, v.i. Be silly, deranged, infatuated, or feeble-minded, esp. from age, whence **dot'AGE** n.; concentrate one's affections, bestow excessive fondness, (*up*)*on*. Hence **dot'ingLY²** adv. [ME *doten* corresp. to MDu. *doten* be silly, whence OF *redoter* (mod. *ra-*)]

doth. See DO¹.

dott'(e)rel, n. Kind of plover. [ME; DOTE + -REL, named from the ease with which it is caught]

dot'tle, -tel, n. Plug of tobacco left unsmoked in pipe. [DOT¹, -LE]

dott'y, a. Dotted about, sporadic, marked with dots; (colloq.) shaky of gait (~ *on his legs*), feeble-minded, half idiotic. [DOT¹ + -Y²]

Dou'ai, -ay, (doō'ā, dow'ā), n. ~ *version*, *Bible*, English translation of the Bible used in the R.C. Church. The Old Testament was completed at ~ in France early in the 17th c.

dou'ane (doō'ahn), n. Foreign custom-house. [F, f. Arab. *diwan* DIVAN]

dou'ble¹ (dŭ-), a. & adv. 1. adj. Consisting of two members, things, layers, etc., forming a pair, twofold (~ *chin*, with roll of fat below chin proper); folded, bent, stooping much; with some part ~ (~ *axe*, with two edges, ~ *eagle*, with two heads); (of flowers) with petals multiplied by conversion of stamens etc.; having twofold relation, dual, ambiguous (~ *meaning*, = DOUBLE ENTENDRE); twice as much or many (*of*, *or*, with prep. omitted, seeming to govern following wd); of twofold or extra size, strength, value, etc. (~ *ale*, ~ *florin*); (Mus.) lower in pitch by an octave (~ *bassoon* etc.; ~ *bass*, lowest-pitched stringed instrument); (Mil.) ~ *time* (also formerly, & still in general use, ~-*quick time*), regulation running pace; deceitful, hypocritical; ~ ENTRY; ‖ ~ *first*, (person who has taken) first-class University honours in two subjects; ~ *star*, two stars so close as to seem one, esp. when forming connected pair; *work* ~ TIDES; hence ~NESS (-ĭn-) n., doub'LY² adv. 2. adv. To twice the amount etc. (~ *as bright*; *see* ~, two things when there is only one, esp. of drunken man); two together (*ride* ~, two on horse; *sleep* ~, two in bed). 3. ~-, a. or adv., is freely used in new or obvious compounds, as well as in the following; ~-*acting*, in two ways, directions, etc., esp. of engine in which steam acts on both sides of piston; ~-*banking*, leaving a vehicle alongside another stationary vehicle; ~-*barrel*, = ~-*barrelled*, or ~-barrelled gun; ~-*barrelled*, with two barrels (also fig. = ambiguous, of compliment etc.; & of compound surname); ~-*bass*, lowest-pitched stringed instrument; ~-*bedded*, with two beds or ~ *bed*; ~-*bitt* v.t. (Naut.), pass (cable) twice round bitts or round two pairs of bitts; ~-*breasted*, (of coat or waistcoat) made to button on either side; *~-cross'* (sL.), (v.t.) cheat (each of two parties, usu. by pretended collusion with both), (n.) act of this nature; hence ~-*cross'er*; ~-*dealer*, ~-*ling* n. & a., deceiver, deceit(ful); ~-*dyed* usu. fig., deeply stained with guilt (~-*dyed scoundrel*); ~-*edged*, with two cutting edges, (of argument, sarcasm, etc.) telling against as well as for one; ~-*faced*, insincere; ~-*gänger* (-ng-), wraith of living person [f. G *doppel-gänger* double-goer]; ~ *harness* (fig.), matrimony; ~-*jointed*, having joints that allow unusual bending movements to limb; ~-*leaded* (-lĕd-), of printed matter with wide spaces between lines to draw attention; ~-*lock* v.t., turn key of (some locks) twice; ~-*quick* (see ~ *time* above; also) adv., very quickly; ~-*reef* v.t. (Naut.), contract spread of (sail) by two reefs; ~-*refine*, refine twice over. [ME, f. OF f. L *duplus* (*duo* two)]

dou'ble² ·(dŭ-), n. Double quantity, double measure of spirits etc., twice as much or many (~ *or quits*, game, throw, toss, deciding whether person shall pay twice his loss or debt or nothing); counterpart of thing or person; wraith; (Mil.) *at the* ~, running; (Bridge) doubling of a bid; score (short whist) of five to less than three, (long whist) of ten to nothing, (stake being doubled); (Lawn-tennis etc.) game between two pairs; (Darts) a throw on the narrow space enclosed by the two outer circles of a dartboard; (Racing) a bet on two horses etc. in different races, the winnings & stake from one race being carried forward & bet on the second; sharp turn of hunted animal, or of river. [f. prec. & foll.]

dou'ble³ (dŭ-), v.t. & i. 1. Make double, increase twofold, multiply by two; (Bridge) ~ value of points to be won or lost on (adversary's bid); amount to

twice as much as; (Mus.) add same note in higher or lower octave to; (of actor) ~ *part(s)*, play two in same piece. 2. (mil.) Move in double time, run. 3. Put (passenger etc.) in same quarters with another (also ~ *up*). 4. Bend, turn, (paper, cloth) over upon itself (often *up*). 5. ~ *up*, bend one's body into stooping or curled-up position, cause (another) to do this by blow, (of paper, leaf, etc.) become folded. 6. Clench (fist). 7. (billiards). Rebound, make to rebound. 8. (naut). Get round (headland). 9. Turn sharply in flight, pursue tortuous course. [ME, f. OF *dobler*, *dubler* f. LL *duplare* (L *duplus* DOUBLE¹)]

double entendre (see Ap.), n. Ambiguous expression, phrase with two meanings, one usu. indecent; use of such phrases. [from 1673; obs. F (now *double entente*, which is often needlessly substituted in E for the established ~)]

doub'let (dŭ-), n. 1. (hist). Close-fitting body-garment worn by men with or without sleeves & short skirts (~ *& hose*, masculine attire, also light attire without cloak). 2. One of a pair, esp. one of two words of same derivation but different sense (*fashion & faction*). 3. pl. Same number on two dice thrown at once. 4. Two birds killed with double-barrel. 5. (Microscope etc.) combination of two simple lenses. [ME, f. F (DOUBLE¹, -ET)]

dou'bleton (dŭ'bltŏn), n. Two cards only of a suit (dealt to a player). [f. DOUBLE¹, after *singleton*]

doubloon' (dŭ-), n. (hist). Spanish gold coin, double pistole (orig. 33-36s., later slightly over £1). [f. F *doublon* or Sp. *doblon* (DOUBLE¹, -OON)]

doublure (dōoblūr'), n. Ornamental usu. leather lining inside book-cover. [F]

doubt¹ (dowt), n. Feeling of uncertainty (*about*), undecided frame of mind, inclination to disbelieve (*of*, *about*; *have no* ~ *that . . .*), hesitation; uncertain state of things, want of full proof (*give one the benefit of the* ~, assume his innocence rather than guilt) or of clear signs of the future; *make no* ~, feel sure; *no* ~, certainly, admittedly; *without* ~, certainly. [ME, f. OF *doute* f. *douter* DOUBT²]

doubt² (dowt), v.i. & t. Feel uncertain (about); waver; be undecided about or *about*, hesitate to believe or trust, call in question, (person, fact expressèd by noun or by clause with *whether*, *if*, or, in negative or interrog. sentences, *that*, *but*, *but that*; *I* ~ *whether*, *I don't* ~ *that*, *can you* ~ *that*, *he will win*); have doubts of (esp. w. neg., as *never* ~*ed of success*); || (arch. & dial.) be afraid, rather think, suspect, (that *I* ~ *we are late*). [ME *dute* f. OF *doter*, *duter* f. L *dubitare*; mod. sp. after L]

doubt'ful (-owt-), a. Of uncertain meaning, character, truth, or issue, undecided, ambiguous, questionable, (~ *syllable*, *letter*, that can be either long or short); unsettled in opinion, uncertain, hesitating. Hence ~LY² adv., ~NESS n. [-FUL]

doubt′less (-owt-), adv. Certainly, no doubt, I admit, (usu. concessive, cf. UNDOUBTEDLY). [-LESS]

¶ **douce** (doos), a. (Sc.). Sober, gentle, sedate. [ME, f. OF *doux* fem. *douce* f. L *dulcis* sweet]

douceur (see Ap.), n. Gratuity; bribe. [F]

douche (doosh), n., & v.t. & i. 1. Jet of water applied to body externally or internally as form of bathing or for medicinal purpose. 2. vb. Administer ~ to, take ~. [F, f. It. *doccia* pipe f. L *ductio* conduit (*ducere* lead)]

dough (dō), n. Kneaded flour, bread-paste; pasty mass; (sl.) money; ~′*boy*, boiled dumpling, (sl.) U.S. infantryman; ~′*nut*, cake of ~ sweetened & fried. Hence ~Y² (dō′Ĭ) a., ~′ĬNESS (dō′Ĭ-) n. [OE *dāg*, OHG *teic*, ON *deig*, Goth. *daigs* f. Gmc *°daigaz*]

dought′ỹ (dowt-), a. (arch. or joc.). Valiant, stout, formidable. Hence ~ĬLY² adv., ~ĬNESS n. [OE *dohtig* var. of *dyhtig* = MLG, MDu. *duchtich*, MHG *tühtic* f. Gmc *°dugan* be strong]

Dou′khobŏrs (dōōko-), n. pl. Religious sect, with some likeness in doctrines to Quakers, of which large numbers migrated from Russia to Canada after persecutions for refusing military service. [f. Russ. = spirit-fighters]

doum (dowm, dōōm), n. (Also ~-*palm*) Egyptian palm-tree. [f. Arab. *daum*, *dum*]

¶ **dour** (-oor), a. (Sc.). Severe, stern, obstinate. Hence ~′LY² adv., ~′NESS n. [ME; poss. f. L *durus* hard]

douse, dowse, v.t. (Naut.) lower (sail), close (port-hole); extinguish (light; ~ *the glim*, arch., put out the light); throw water over, drench. [orig. uncert.]

dove (dŭv), n. Kinds of pigeon (*cushat*, *ground*, *ring*, *rock*, *stock*, *turtle*, *wood*, ~~); the Holy Spirit; type of gentleness or innocence (so ~-*eyed*); messenger of good news or peace (*Gen.* viii); darling (esp. *my* ~); ~-*colour(ed)*, (of) warm grey; ~'s-*foot*, kinds of crane's-bill; ~~-*hawk*, hen-harrier (from its colour); ~′-*col(e)*, pigeon-house (*flutter the* ~*cots*, alarm quiet people). Hence ~LIKE (dŭvl-) a. [ME *duve*, OS *dūba*, ON *dúfa*, OHG *tūba*, Goth *dūbo* f. Gmc *°dūbhōn*]

Dŏv′er′s powd′er, n. (pharm.). Preparation of opium, ipecacuanha, and sulphate of potash or sugar of milk, an anodyne diaphoretic. [Dr. Thos. *Dover* (d. 1742)]

dove′tail (dŭvt-), n., & v.t. & i. 1. Tenon shaped like dove's spread tail or reversed wedge, fitting into corresponding mortise & forming joint; such a joint. 2. vb. Put together with ~s; (fig.) fit together (t. & i.) compactly.

dow. See D(H)OW.

dow′ager, n. ‖ Woman with title or pro-

perty derived from her late husband (often in comb. as *Queen* ~, ~ *countess* or *countess* ~; ~ *duchess*); (colloq.) dignified elderly lady. [f. OF *douagere* f. *douage* DOWER, -ER²(2)]

dowd′(l̄y, n. & a. (Woman) shabbily, badly, or unfashionably dressed; (of dress etc.) unattractive, unfashionable. Hence ~ĬLY² adv., ~ĬNESS, ~ŸISM(2), nn., ~ŸISH¹ a. [f. obs. *dowd* slut, of unkn. orig.]

dow′el, n., & v.t. Headless pin of wood, metal, etc., for keeping two pieces of wood, stone, etc., in their relative position; (vb) fasten with ~. [ME, f. MLG *dovel* (whence G *döbel*), = OHG *tubili*; see THOLE²]

dow′er, n., & v.t. 1. Widow's share for life of husband's estate; property or money brought by wife to husband, dowry; endowment, gift of nature, talent. Hence ~LESS a. 2. v.t. Give dowry to; endow *with* talent etc. [ME; vb f. n., OF *douaire* f. med. L *dotarium* (L *dos dotis*, -ARY¹)]

‖ **dowl′as**, n. Kind of strong calico or linen. [*Doulas* in Brittany]

down¹, n. Open high land, ‖ esp. (pl.) treeless undulating chalk uplands of S. England used for pasture; = DUNE; ‖ *The D*~*s*, part of sea (opposite North D~s) within Goodwin Sands. [OE *dūn*, OS *dūna* (MDu. *dūne*); see DUNE]

down², n. First covering of young birds; bird's under plumage, used in cushions etc.; fine short hair, esp. first hair on face, also on fruit etc.; fluffy substance. [ME f. ON *dúnn*, whence LG *dūne*, G *daune*]

down³, adv. (superl., a. or adv., ~′*most*). 1. (Motion): from above, to lower place, to ground, (*come* ~, from bedroom; *knock*, *fall*, ~; *sun*, *ship*, *goes* ~, sets, sinks; *food goes* ~, is swallowed; *get* ~, swallow, alight; *book* etc. *goes* ~, finds acceptance; *get*, *set*, ~, from carriage etc.; *brought* ~ *by river*; *money* ~, *pay* ~, at once, as though on counter; *write*, *set*, *put*, *take*, *copy*, ~, on paper; so *Bill* ~ *for second reading today*); to place regarded as lower, into helpless position, with current or wind, southwards, ‖ from capital or university, (*Lords' amendments sent* ~ *to Commons*; *bear* ~, sail to leeward; *run*, *ride*, *hunt*, ~, bring to bay; *shout*, *hiss*, ~, silence; ~ *to Norfolk* from Scotland, *to Scotland* or *the country* from London; ‖ *go* ~, for vacation or at end of university life; ‖ *send* ~, university punishment; *up & ~*, to & fro); (ellipt. for imperat. of) lie, get, put, etc., ~ (~, *Ponto!*; ~ *helm*, put the HELM ~; & with *with*, ~ *with the aristocrats!*). 2. (Station): in lower place (*blinds were* ~; *is not* ~ *yet*, i.e. out of his bedroom); ‖ not up in capital or university; in fallen posture, prostrate, at low level, in depression, humiliation, etc., (*hit man who is* ~; *many* ~ *with fever*; *sun*, *tide*, *are* ~; ~ *in* *the mouth* or ~ or ~-*hearted*, dispirited; *are we* ~-*hearted?*, sl. assertion of confidence; *bread is* ~, cheaper). 3. (Order, time, quality): inclusively of lower limit in series (*from King* ~ *to cobbler*); from earlier to later time (*custom handed* ~); to finer consistence (*boil, grind, wear, thin,* ~); into quiescence (*calm* ~). 4.(Phrases): *be* ~ *on*, pounce upon, treat severely; ~ *to the ground*, completely; ~ *at* HEEL; ~ *on* one's LUCK; ~ *&- out*, unable to resume the fight in boxing, beaten in the struggle of life, done for; ~-*&-out* in, ~ *under*, at the antipodes, in Australia etc. [OE *dūne* aphetic f. *adūne* ADOWN]

down[4], prep. Downwards along, through, or into; from top to bottom of; at a lower part of (*situated* ~ *the Thames*); *up &* ~, to & fro along; ~ *town*, into the town from higher or outlying part, *to or in the business part of a city; ~ *the wind*, with it (*let go* ~ *the wind*, abandon, discard). [f. prec.]

down[5], a. (not compared). Directed downwards (~ *leap, look;* ~ *grade*, descending slope in railroad, fig. deterioration); ~ *draught*, downward draught, esp. one driving down chimney into room; ~ *payment*, made in cash; ~ *train*, going, coming, from London, ~ *platform*, for such train's departure or arrival. [f. DOWN³]

down[6], v.t. (colloq.). Put, throw, knock, (usu. person or aeroplane) down; ~ *tools*, cease work for the day etc., go on strike. [f. DOWN³]

down[7], n. Reverse of fortune (usu. *ups & ~s*); (Dominoes) = POSE¹; *have a ~ on*, dislike, tend to be down on, (colloq.). [f. DOWN³]

down'cast[1] (-ah-), n. (Also ~-*shaft*) shaft for introducing fresh air into mine. [DOWN³ + CAST²]

down'cast[2] (-ah-), a. (Of looks) directed downwards; dejected.

down'fall (-awl), n. Great fall of rain etc.; fall from prosperity, ruin.

downhill, n., adj. & adv. (N., down'hil') downward slope, decline, (~ *of life*, later half); (adj., down²) sloping down, declining; (adv., -hil') in descending direction, on a decline.

Down'ing Street, n. Street in London containing important government offices, esp. the Prime Minister's official residence (No. 10), the Government of the day (*does not find favour in* ~; ~ *disapproves*).

down'pour (-pōr), n. Heavy fall of rain etc.

down'right (-rīt; downrīt' *if placed late*), a. & adv. 1. (Arch.) vertical; plain, definite, straightforward, blunt, whence ~NESS (-rīt²) n.; not short of, out-&-out, (*a* ~ *lie, atheist;* ~ *nonsense*). 2. adv. Thoroughly, positively, quite, (~ *scared, insolent*). [ME, DOWN³ + RIGHT a. & adv.]

downstairs', adv., down'stair(s), a. Down the stairs; to, on, of, a lower floor.

down'throw (-ō), n. (geol.). Depression of strata on one side of fault.

down'trödden, a. Oppressed, kept under.

down'ward, a. & adv., **down'wards** (-z), adv. (Moving, pointing, leading) towards what is lower, inferior, or later. [OE *adūnweard* (DOWN³, -WARD)]

down'y̆[1], a. Like, of, downs. [DOWN¹, -Y²]

down'|y̆[2], a. Of, like, covered with, down; (sl.) wide awake, knowing. So ~ĭLY² adv., ~ĬNESS n. [DOWN², -Y²]

dowr'y̆, n. Portion woman brings to her husband; talent, natural gift. [ME, f. AF *dowarie*, OF *douaire* DOWER]

dows'ing (-z-), n. Searching for latent water or minerals with the ~- (or *divin- ing-*) rod, a forked twig held by the **dows'er** (-z-) & dipping over the right spot. [orig. unkn.]

dŏxŏl'ogy̆, n. Liturgical formula of praise to God, as *Glory be to* etc. [f. med. L f. Gk *doxologia* (*doxa* glory, -LOGY)]

dŏx'y̆[1], n. Beggar's wench, paramour. [16th c. cant, of unkn. orig.]

dŏx'y̆[2], n. Opinion, esp. on theology. [joc. use of end of *orthodoxy, heterodoxy*]

doyen (see Ap.), n. Senior member of a body, esp. senior ambassador at a court. [F, f. L as DEAN¹]

doyley. See DOILY.

dōze, v.i. & n. 1. Sleep drowsily, be half asleep; ~ *off*, fall lightly asleep. 2. n. Short slumber. [cf. ON *dúsa* doze, Da. *dōse* make drowsy]

do'zen (dŭ-), n. (Pl. ~, used adjectively or as noun, when with numeral or equivalent except *some*) twelve, as *a, three, several, how many,* ~ *figs* or *of the best figs, of these,* but *some* ~s *of people*, cf. *some* (about a) ~ (*of*) *people,* ~s *of* (= many) *times*; (pl. ~s) set of twelve, as *pack them in* ~s; *baker's, devil's, long, printer's,* ~, thirteen; ‖ *talk nineteen to the* ~, incessantly. [ME, f. OF *dozeine* (L *duodecim* twelve)]

drăb[1], n., & v.i. (-bb-). Slut, slattern; prostitute; (vb) whore. [perh. related to LG *drabbe* mire, Du. *drab* dregs]

drăb[2], a. & n. (Of) dull light brown colour; dull, monotonous; monotony. [prob. f. obs. & F *drap* cloth]

‖ **drăbb'et**, n. Drab twilled linen used for smock-frocks. [prec., -ET¹]

drăb'ble, v.i. & t. Go splashing *through*, make dirty and wet with, water or mud. [ME, f. LG *drabbelen* paddle in water or mire; cf. DRAB¹]

Dracaen'a (-sĕn-), n. Genus of liliaceous trees, including the *dragon tree* (yielding DRAGON's-blood). [mod. L f. Gk *drakaina* fem. of *drakōn* dragon]

drachm (-ăm), n. Ancient Greek silver coin, drachma; (Apoth. wt) 60 grains, ⅛ oz; (Avoird.) 27¹⁄₃ grains, ¹⁄₁₆ oz; small quantity. [ME *dragme* f. OF, or f. LL *dragma* f. L f. Gk *drakhmē*]

drăch'ma (-k-), n. (pl. ~s, ~e). Ancient

Greek coin (see prec.); modern Greek coin. [L, f. Gk *drakhmē(drassomai* grasp)]

Dracōn'ian, Dracŏn'ic, aa. (Of laws) rigorous, harsh, cruel. [*Drakōn* Athenian legislator 621 B.C. + -IAN, -IC]

draff (-ahf), n. Dregs, lees; hog's-wash; refuse of malt after brewing. [ME, = MLG, Icel., Sw. *draf*, OHG pl. *trebir* (G *treber*)]

draft[1] (-ah-), n. **1.** (Selection of) detachment of men from larger body for special duty, contingent, reinforcement; *(Mil.) call-up, conscription. **2.** Drawing of money by written order (*make a ~ on* fund etc., also fig. *on* person's confidence, friendship, etc.), bill or cheque drawn, esp. by one branch of bank on another. **3.** Sketch of work to be executed; rough copy of document. **4.** (masonry). Chisel-dressing along margin of stone's surface. [var. of DRAUGHT[1]]

draft[2] (-ah-), v.t. **1.** Draw off (part of larger body, esp. of troops) for special purpose; *conscript. **2.** Prepare, make rough copy of, (document, esp. Parliamentary Bill), whence *~ER*[1] n. **3.** (masonry). Cut draft on (stone). [f. prec.]

drafts'man (-ahf-), n. One who makes drawings or designs; one who drafts documents or Parliamentary Bills. [= DRAUGHTSMAN]

drăg[1], v.t. & i. (-gg-). Pull along with force, difficulty, or friction; allow (feet, tail, etc.) to trail; *~* one's *feet*, (fig.) be slow or reluctant to do something; *ship ~s her anchor, anchor ~s*, anchor fails to hold; *~ in*, introduce (subject) needlessly (*why ~ in Velasquez?*); also *~ in by the head & shoulders*); (Mus.) go too slowly, be wanting in life; trail, go heavily; *~ on*, continue (t. & i.) tediously; *~ out*, protract; use grapnel or drag (often *for* drowned person or lost object), dredge, search bottom of, (river etc.) with grapnels, nets, etc.; harrow (land); apply drag to(wheel, vehicle); (colloq.) *~ up* (child), rear roughly. [ME, f. OE *dragan* or ON *draga* DRAW]

drăg[2], n. Heavy harrow; rough sledge; four-horsed private vehicle like stage coach; (also *~-net*) net drawn over bottom of river etc. or surface of field to enclose all fish or game; *(sl.) influence, pull; apparatus for dredging or recovering drowned persons etc.; muckrake; iron shoe for retarding vehicle downhill; obstruction to progress; strong-smelling lure for hounds in lieu of fox (so *~-hounds*), club for pursuing this sport; slow motion, impeded progress; *~-anchor*, floating frame on hawser to check leeway of drifting ship; *~-chain*, used to retard vehicle by fixing wheel, (fig.) impediment. [f. prec.]

dragée (drah'zhā), n. Sugar-coated almond, small silver ball for decorating cake, sweet (often one serving as vehicle for a drug). [F, see DREDGE[2]]

drăg'gle, v.t. & i. Make wet, limp, & dirty, by trailing; hang trailing; lag, straggle in rear; *~-tail(ed)*, (woman) with *~d* or untidily trailing skirts. [f. DRAG[1] + -LE(3)]

drăg'oman, n. (pl. *-ans, -en*). Interpreter, esp. in Arabic, Turkish, or Persian. [f. F f. O Arab. *targuman*, cf. TARGUM]

drăg'on, n. Mythical monster like crocodile or snake with wings & claws & often breathing fire; (with allusion to legends) guardian of treasure etc. or of female chastity, watchful person, duenna; (Bibl.) whale or ·shark, serpent, crocodile, jackal; *the old D~*, Satan; kinds of lizard & pigeon; *~-fly*, neuropterous insect with long slender body & two pairs of large wings; *~'s-blood*, bright red gum exuding from kind of palm fruit (*~ tree*); *~'s teeth*, anti-tank obstacles resembling teeth pointed upwards. [ME, f. OF f. L *draconem* nom. *-o* f. Gk *drakōn* serpent]

drăgonnāde', n., & v.t. (Pl.) persecutions of Protestants under Louis XIV by quartering dragoons on them; persecution carried on by means of troops; (vb) persecute thus. [F (*dragon* DRAGOON, -ADE)]

dragōōn', n., & v.t. **1.** Cavalryman (orig. mounted infantryman armed with carbine called *~*; later of certain cavalry regiments that were formerly mounted infantry); rough fierce fellow; kind of pigeon (also *dragon*). **2.** v.t. Set *~s* upon, persecute (see prec.), force *into* a course by persecution. [f. F *dragon* carbine, so named as breathing fire (DRAGON)]

drail, n. Fish-hook & line weighted with lead for dragging at depth through water. [app. f. TRAIL, infl. by *draw* etc.]

drain[1], v.t. & i. Draw (liquid) *off* or *away* by conduit, *~-pipes* etc. (also fig., *~ the wealth of England*); drink (liquid), empty (vessel), to the dregs; dry (land etc.) by withdrawing moisture; (of river) carry off superfluous water of (district); deprive (person, thing) *of* property, strength, etc.; trickle *through*, flow *off* or *away*; (of wet cloth, vessel, etc.) get rid of moisture by its flowing away (*set it there to ~*). [OE *drēahnian* cogn. w. DRY]

drain[2], n. Channel carrying off liquid, artificial conduit for water, sewage, etc.; (Surg.) tube for drawing off discharge from abscess etc.; constant outlet, withdrawal, demand, or expenditure (*a great ~ on my resources*); (sl.) small draught, drink; *~-pipe*, pipe for carrying off surplus water or liquid sewage from a building, (attrib., colloq., of trousers) very narrow; *~-pipes* (colloq.), such trousers. [f. prec.]

drain'age, n. Draining; system of drains, artificial or natural; *~-basin*, district drained by river; what is drained off, sewage. [-AGE]

drain'er, n. In vbl senses; esp., vessel in which things are put to drain. [-ER¹]

drāke¹, n. Kinds of ephemeral fly used in fishing (green ~, common day-fly). [OE *draca*, MLG, MDu. *drake*, OHG *trahho*, WG f. L *draco* DRAGON]

drāke², n. Male duck (play DUCK¹s & ~s). [ME; corresp. to LG *drake*, G dial. *drache*, *trech*, repr. second element in OHG *anutrehho* (G *enterich*) f. *anut* (G *ente*); ult. orig. unkn.]

drăm, n. A weight (see DRACHM); small draught of spirit etc. (~-drinker, -ing, tippler, -ing; ~-shop, public-house). [ME; for DRACHM]

dra'ma (-ah-), n. Stage-play; *the* ~, the dramatic art, composition & presentation of plays; set of events having the unity & progress of a play & leading to catastrophe or consummation. [LL f. Gk (gen. -*atos*), f. draŏ do, -M]

drămăt'|ic, a. Of drama; as of a play-actor, theatrical; fit for theatrical representation, sudden, striking, impressive; (of utterances etc.) not to be taken as one's own, representing another person's thoughts. Hence ~ICALLY adv. [f. LL f. Gk *dramatikos* (prec., -IC)]

drăm'atĭs persŏn'ae, n. pl. (often with sing.-constr.). (List of) characters in a play. [L]

drăm'atist, n. Playwright. [DRAMA, -IST]

drăm'atiz|e (-is|e (-ĭz), v.t. & i. Convert (novel etc.) into a play, admit of such conversion; make a dramatic scene of. Hence ~A'TION n. [DRAMA, -IZE]

drăm'atŭrg|e, n. Playwright. So **drāmatŭr'gĭc** a., ~IST(1), ~Y¹, nn. [F, f. Gk *dramatourgos* (DRAMA, -*ergos* -working)]

drank. See DRINK¹.

drāpe, v.t. & n. 1. Cover, hang, adorn, with cloth etc.; arrange (clothes, hangings) in graceful folds. 2. n. Piece of drapery, curtain. [ME, f. OF *draper* (*drap* f. LL *drappus* cloth)]

drāp'er, n. Dealer in cloth, linen, etc. [ME, f. AF *draper* (OF -*ier*), see prec., -IER]

drāp'er|y̆, n. Cloth & linen & cotton fabrics; draper's trade; arrangement of clothing in sculpture etc.; clothing or hangings disposed in folds, whence ~IED² (-Id) a. [ME, f. OF *draperie* (*drap* cloth, -ERY)]

drăs't|ic, a. Acting strongly, vigorous, violent, esp. (Med.) strongly purgative. Hence ~ICALLY adv. [f. Gk *drastikos* (*drastos* vbl adj. of draŏ do, -IC)]

drăt, v.t. 3 sing. subjunct. (vulg.). Confound, curse, bother, (as woman's imprecation). Hence ~t'ED¹ a. [for '*od* (God) *rot*]

draught¹ (-ahft), n. (also *draft* in some senses, as stated). 1. Drawing, traction, (*beast of* ~, ~-*horse*, etc., for drawing cart, plough, etc.). 2. Drawing of net for fish etc., take of fish at one drawing. 3. Single act of drinking, amount so

drunk, (also fig. of joy, love, pain, etc.); dose of liquid medicine (*black* ~, a purgative). 4. (naut.). Depth of water ship draws or requires to float her. 5. pl. ‖ Game with 24 similar pieces on ~ (same as *chess*) -*board*. 6. Current of air in room, chimney, etc. (*forced* ~, of furnace, made by rarefying air above or compressing it below; ‖ *feel the* ~, sl., suffer from adverse, usu. financial, conditions), whence ~'Y² a., ~'INESS n., (-ahf-). 7. Outline, preliminary drawing for work of art; plan of something to be constructed (also -*ft*); rough copy, first conception, of document (usu. -*ft*). 8. (Selection of) military detachment, party, reinforcement, (usu. -*ft*). 9. (Written order for) withdrawing of money from fund in bank etc., cheque, bill of exchange, (now -*ft*). 10. Drawing of liquor from vessel (*beer on* ~, in tapped cask; so ‖ ~ *beer*, opp. *bottled*). [ME *draht*, f. unrecorded OE, or f. ON *drahtr*, *drattr*, = MDu. *dragt*, OHG *traht* f. Gmc *dragan* DRAW]

draught² (-ahft), v.t. Draw off (party for military service etc.) from larger body (now *draft*); make plan or sketch of (also -*aft*). [f. prec.]

draughts'man (-ahft-), n. (pl. -*men*). One who makes drawings, plans, or sketches (*good*, *bad*, *no*, ~, one who draws well etc), whence ~SHIP(3) n., **draughts'woman** (-ahftswŏo-) n. fem.; (usu. *draftsman*) person who drafts document, esp. Parliamentary Bill; piece in game of draughts. [*draught's* +*man*]

Dravid'ian, a. & n. (Member, language) of one of the non-Aryan races of Southern India and Ceylon (including Tamils & Kanarese). [f. Skr. *Dravida*, a province of S. India]

draw¹, v.t. & i. (*drew*, *drawn*). 1. Pull (boat up from water, hat over face, belt tighter, pen across paper, friend aside); pull after one (plough, cart, cartload, etc.); drag (criminal) on hurdle etc. to execution; contract, distort, (*with* ~*n face*); haul in (net); bend (bow; ~ *a* BEAD¹ *on*); pull at (~ *bit*, *bridle*, *rein*, check horse, & fig. oneself); pull (curtain, veil) open or shut; ~ *cloth*, clear table after meal; (Cricket) divert (ball) to on side with bat; (Golf) drive (ball) too much to left (of right-handed player). 2. Attract, bring to one, take in, (*drew a deep breath*; & abs., *chimney*, *pipe*, ~*swell*, promotes, allows, draught; *I felt* ~*n to him*; *drew my attention*; ~ *him into talk*, *out of temptation*; ~*s customers*, & abs., attracts attention or custom); induce *to* do; be attracted, assemble, *round* or *about* some centre (*drew round the table*); bring about, entail, (*drew after it great consequences*; ~ *ruin upon oneself*). 3. Extract (cork, tooth, gun-charge, nail, cricket-stumps from ground, card from pack; pistol, sword from sheath, also abs.= ~ one's sword or pistol; ~ *one's* *sword against*, attack; ~ LOTS, also abs. = ~ lots, & trans. = obtain by lot, as *drew the winner*; drag (badger, fox) from hole; haul up (water) from well; bring out (liquid, blood) from vessel, bung (~ *it mild*, i.e. orig. beer, now = be moderate, not exaggerate); extract essence of (~ *the tea*, also intr. *the tea* ~*s*); (of poultice) drain (gathering etc.); take, get from a source (~ *inspiration*, one's *salary*; *tax* ~*s well*, ~*s from the rich only*); (Cards) cause to be played (~ *all the trumps*); bring (person) out, make him reveal information, talent, irritation, etc.; deduce, infer, (conclusion); extract something from, empty, drain (*calf* ~*s cow*), disembowel (*hanged*, ~*n*, & *quartered*, of criminal; ~ *fowl* before cooking); (Hunt.) search (covert) for game (~ *blank*, find none). 4. Protract, stretch, elongate, (*long*-~*n agony*; ~*-plate*, hard steel plate pierced with graduated apertures through which rods or wires are ~n during manufacture; ~ *wire*, make it by pulling piece of metal through successively smaller holes); (Naut., intr. of sail) swell out with wind. 5. Trace (furrow, figure, line; ~ *the line at*, refuse to go as far as or beyond); delineate, make (picture), represent (object), by ~ing lines, (abs.) use pencil thus; describe in words; practise delineation; frame (document) in due form, compose, (often *up*, *out*); formulate, institute, (comparisons, distinctions); write out (bill, cheque, draft, *on* banker etc.), (abs.) make call *on* person or his faith, memory, etc., *for* money or service. 6. Make way, move, *towards*, *near*, *off*, *back*, etc. (~ *to an end* or *close*); (Racing) get farther *away* to the front, come *level*, gain *on*. 7. (Of doubtful origin); (of ship) require (such a depth of water) to float; ~ *game* or *battle*, part without deciding it. 8. (With advv. in special senses); ~ *back*, withdraw from undertaking; ~ *in*, entice, persuade to join, (of day) close in, (of successive days) become shorter; ~ *off*, withdraw (troops; or intr. of troops etc.); ~ *on*, lead to, bring about, allure, approach (intr.); ~ *out*, lead out, detach, or array (troops), prolong, elicit, induce to talk, write out in proper form, (of days) become longer; ~ *up*, (refl.) assume stiff attitude, (intr.) come up *with* or *to* = overtake, come to a stand, (t. & i. of troops) bring or come into regular order, (trans.) compose (document etc.). [OE, OS *dragan*, OHG *tragan*, ON *draga*, Goth. *gadragan*]

draw², n. Act of DRAWING; esp.: strain, pull; attractive effect, person or thing that draws custom, attention, etc.; drawing of lots, raffle; drawn game; remark etc. meant to elicit information or set person off on pet subject; act of whipping out revolver in order to shoot (*quick on the* ~); *movable part of draw-bridge. [f. prec.]

draw'băck, n. Amount of excise or import duty paid back or remitted on goods exported; deduction *from*; thing that qualifies satisfaction, disadvantage; ~ *lock*, with spring bolt that can be drawn back by inside knob. [DRAW¹]

draw'bridge, n. Bridge hinged at one end for drawing up to prevent passage or to open channel. [ME; DRAW¹]

Drawcăn'sir (*-er*), n. & a. (Person) formidable both to friend and foe; fierce swashbuckler. [name of character in Villiers's *Rehearsal*]

drawee', n. Person on whom draft or bill is drawn. [-EE]

draw'er, n. In vbl senses; also or esp. (arch.) tapster; receptacle sliding in & out of special frame (~*s* or *chest of* ~*s*) or of table etc., for holding clothes, papers, etc., whence ~FUL(2) n.; (pl.) two-legged (usu. under-) garment suspended from waist. [-ER¹]

draw'ing, n. In vbl senses; esp.: art of representing by line, delineation without colour or with single colour, (*out of* ~, incorrectly drawn); product of this, black-&-white or monochrome sketch; ~*-block*, of detachable leaves of ~-paper adhering at edges; ~*-board*, for stretching ~-paper on; ~*-compass(es)*, with pen or pencil substituted for one point; || ~*-pin*, for fastening ~-paper to ~-board. [-ING¹]

draw'ing-rōom, n. Room for reception of company, to which ladies retire after dinner; levee, formal reception esp. at court. [for 16th c. *withdrawing-*]

drawl, v.i. & t., & n. 1. Speak, utter (often *out*), with indolent or affected slowness; (of words, esp. in part.) be so uttered; hence ~'ingLY² adv. 2. n. Slow utterance. [16th c. cant, f. LG, Du. *dralen* delay, linger, EFris. *draulen* loiter]

drawn, p.p. of DRAW¹; ~*-work*, fancy work in linen etc. done by drawing out threads.

draw'wĕll, n. Deep well with rope and bucket. [ME; DRAW¹]

dray, n. Low esp. brewer's cart without sides for heavy loads (~*-horse*, large & powerful; ~*'man*, brewer's driver). [ME, f. OE *dragan* DRAW¹; cf. MLG *drage* litter, Sw. *drög* dray]

dread¹ (-ĕd), v.t., & n. 1. Be in great fear of; shrink from, look forward to with terror; fear greatly (*that*, *to* learn etc.), be afraid (*to* do). 2. n. Great fear, awe, apprehension; object of fear or awe. [n. f. vb, ME *dreden* f. OE *a-*, *ondrǣdan*, OS *antdrādan*, OHG *inttrātan*, ult. orig. unkn.]

dread² (-ĕd), a. Dreaded, dreadful; awful, revered. [ME p.p. of DREAD¹]

dread'ful (-ĕd-), a. Terrible, awe-inspiring (|| *penny* ~ ellipt., hist., story-book full of horrors); troublesome, disagreeable, boring, very bad or long, horrid. Hence ~LY² adv. [-FUL]

dread'nought (-ŏdnawt), n. (Cloth used for) thick coat for stormy weather; (D~) early type of 20th-c. battleship greatly superior in tonnage & power to all pre-decessors (f. name of first built in 1906).

dream[1], n. Vision, series of pictures or events, presented to sleeping person; act, time, of seeing such vision; *waking* ~, similar experience of one awake; con-scious indulgence of fancy, reverie, castle in the air, (also *day*~); thing (ideal, person, dress, dish, etc.) of ~like goodness, beauty, or refinement; ~*reader*, inter-preter of ~s; ~*world*, *-land*, region out-side the laws of nature. Hence ~'LESS, ~'LIKE, aa. [ME *dream* corresp. to OE *drēam*, OS *drôm*, OHG *troum*]

dream[2], v.i. & t. (~*t* pr. -ĕmt, or ~*ed*). Have visions in sleep; see, hear, etc., in sleep (~*t a dream, did you* ~ *it?*, ~ *that . . .*); imagine as in a dream, think possible; (with negative etc.) think *of* even in a dream, so much as contemplate possibility *of*, have any conception *of*; fall into reverie; form imaginary visions *of*; be inactive or unpractical (& trans. ~ *away* one's *time*). Hence ~'ER[1] n. [ME; as prec.]

dream'-hole, n. Hole left in wall of tower etc. to admit light. [perh. f. OE *drēam* mirth, music (the holes letting sound of bells issue)]

dream'|ỹ, a. Full of dreams (rare or poet.); given to reverie, fanciful, un-practical; dreamlike, vague, misty. Hence ~ILY[2] adv., ~INESS n. [-Y[2]]

drear'|ỹ, (poet.) drear, a. Dismal, gloomy, dull. Hence ~(i)LY[2] adv., ~(i)-NESS n. [OE *drēorig* (*drēor* gore). cogn. w. *drēosan* to drop & G *traurig* sad]

dredge[1], n., & v.t. & i. 1. Apparatus for bringing up oysters, specimens, etc., or clearing out mud etc., from river or sea bottom. 2. vb. Bring *up*, clear *away* or *out*, with ~; clean out (harbour, river) with ~; use ~; hence dredg'er[1] [-ER[1] (1, 2)] n. [15th c. Sc. *dreg*, perh. rel. to MDu. *dregghe*, or to DRAG[1]]

dredge[2], v.t. Sprinkle with flour or other powder; sprinkle (flour etc.) *over*; dredg-*ing-box*, = foll. [16th c., f. obs. *dredge* sweetmeat, f. OF *dragee* f. L f. Gk *tragēma*. (*trōgō* chew)]

dredg'er[2], n. (for *dredger*[1] see DREDGE[1]). Box with perforated lid for sprinkling flour etc. [prec., -ER[1]]

‖ **dree**, v.t. (arch.). Endure (still in ~ one's *weird*, submit to one's lot). [OE *drēogan*]

dreg, n. (usu. pl.). Sediment, grounds, lees, (*drink, drain, to the* ~*s*, leaving nothing); worthless part, refuse; (sing.) small remnant (esp. *not a* ~). Hence ~g'y[2] (-g-) a. [ME; prob. f. ON: cf. Icel. *dreggjar*, Sw. *drägg* pl., lees]

Dreibund (drī'bŏont), n. = TRIPLE *Alliance* (3). [G (*drei* three, *bund* league)]

drench[1], n. Draught or dose administered to animal; (arch.) large, medicinal, or poisonous draught; a soaking or down pour. [OE *drenc* f. Gmc *drank-* f. *drinkan* DRINK]

drench[2], v.t. Make to drink largely; force (animal) to take draught of medicine; (Sheep-washing, Tanning) steep, soak; wet all over with falling liquid (or of the liquid; ~*ed with, by*). [OE *drencan* f. Gmc *drankjan* causative of *drinkan* DRINK]

dren'cher, n. In vbl senses; esp.: drench-ing shower; apparatus for giving drench to beast. [-ER[1]]

Dres'den (-z-), n. ~ *china, porcelain*, kind produced in Saxony esp. in 18th c.

dress[1], v.t. & i. 1. (mil.). Correct the alignment of (companies etc. in relation to each other, or men in line), (intr.) come into correct place in line etc. (*up*, i.e. for-ward, *back*, or abs.). 2. Array, clothe, (~*ed in black, serge*, etc.); provide oneself with clothes (~ *well* etc.); put on one's clothes; put on evening dress (esp. ~ *for dinner*); ~ *up*, attire oneself, attire (an-other), elaborately or in masquerade: ~ *out*, attire conspicuously. 3. Deck, adorn, (ship with flags, shop-window with tempting wares); provide (play) with costumes. 4. Treat (wound, wounded man) with remedies, apply dressing to. 5. Subject to cleansing, trimming, smoothing, etc.; brush, comb, do up, (hair); curry (horse, leather; & fig., often ~ *down*, thrash, scold). 6. Finish surface of (textile fabrics, building-stone). 7. Prepare, cook, (food); prune (plant); manure. [ME, f. OF *dresser* f. Rom. *directiare* f. L *directus* DIRECT]

dress[2], n. 1. Clothing, esp. the visible part of it, costume (*full* ~, that worn on great occasions; *evening* ~, or ~, that worn at dinners or evening parties; *morn-ing* ~, ordinary; *a* ~, lady's gown, frock). 2. External covering, outward form. (*birds in their winter* ~, French dogs appearing in English ~). 3. ‖ ~ *circle*, first gallery in theatres, in which evening-~ was once required; ~ *coat*, swallow-tailed for evening ~; ~*-guard*, on bicycle etc. to protect ~; ~*-improver*, = BUSTLE[3]; ~*'maker, -king*, (woman) making women's ~es; ~ *rehearsal*, final one in costume; ~*-shield, -preserver*, piece of waterproof material fastened under the arms of a bodice. [f. prec.]

dress'age (-ahzh), n. Training of horse in obedience & deportment. [F, f. *dresser* train]

dress'er[1], n. Kitchen sideboard with shelves for dishes etc.; *dressing-table. [ME, f. OF *dresseur* (dresser DRESS[1]); cf. med. L *directorium*]

dress'er[2], n. In vbl senses; esp.: sur-geon's assistant in hospital operations, whence ~SHIP(1) n.; one who helps to dress actors or actresses, looks after costumes, etc. [-ER[1]]

drĕss'ing, n. In vbl senses; esp.: scolding or thrashing (usu. with *down*); sauce, stuffing, etc.; manure; bandages, ointments, etc., for wound; stiffening used in finishing fabrics; ~-*bell* etc., signal to dress for dinner; ~-*case*, of toilet necessaries; ~-*gown*, worn while making toilet or in dishabille; ~-*room*, attached to bedroom for toilet; ~-*table*, for looking-glass etc. [-ING¹]

drĕss'|y̆, a. Fond of, smart in, dress; (of clothes) stylish. Hence ~ĭNESS n. [·Y²]

drew. See DRAW¹.

drey (drā), n. Squirrel's nest. [orig. unkn.]

drĭb'bl|e, v.t. & i., & n. 1. Flow, let flow, in drops or trickling stream (n., such flow); (of child, idiot, etc.) run at the mouth. 2. (Football) work (ball) forward with slight touches of alternate or different players' feet (n., piece of ~ing). 3. (Billiards) make (ball) just roll (or intr. of ball) into pocket. Hence ~ER¹ n. [frequent. of obs. *drib* vb. var. of DRIP; see -LE(3)]

drĭb(b)'lĕt, n. Small quantity, petty sum, (esp. *by* ~s). [f. *drib* see prec. +-LET]

dried, drier. See DRY², ¹.

drift¹, n. 1. Being driven by current; slow course or current; ship's deviation due to currents (~-*anchor*, = DRAG²-*anchor*). 2. Projectile's deviation due to rotation. 3. ‖ (Forest Law) driving of cattle to one place on appointed day to determine ownership etc. 4. Natural or unperceived progress, tendency. 5. Waiting on events, inaction, (esp., contempt., *the policy of* ~). 6. Purpose, meaning, tenor, or scope, of person or his words. 7. Shower, driving mass; snow, sand, etc., accumulated by wind; (also ~-*ice*, -*wood*, etc.) matter driven by water; (Geol.) superficial deposit made by current of water or air (*D*~·, Pleistocene ice detritus, boulder clay). 8. (Also ~-*net*) large net for herrings etc. allowed to drift with tide. 9. (Mining) horizontal passage following mineral vein. 10. S.-Afr. ford. 11. Tool for enlarging or shaping hole in metal. 12. The horizontal component of the aerodynamic pressure on all exposed surfaces of an aeroplane in flight (cf. LIFT). [ME, vbl n. f. DRIVE¹]

drift², v.i. & t. Be carried (as) by current of air or water, (of current) carry; go passively or aimlessly; pile, be piled, by wind into drifts; cover (field, road) with drifts; form or enlarge hole (see prec.). Hence ~'AGE(1) n., ~'ER¹ n., (esp.) boat used in drift-net fishing (much also in mine-sweeping during the 1914–18 war). [f. prec.]

drill¹, n., & v.t. & i. 1. Pointed steel etc. tool, or machine, for boring holes (vb, bore, of person or tool, with *metal* etc., or *hole* etc., as obj.; also intr., ~ *through*, perforate); boring shellfish. 2. Instruction or exercise in military evolutions (~-*sergeant*, instructor in ~, also fig.), rigorous discipline, exact routine, (vb,

subject to, or undergo, such discipline; *B Company will ~ tomorrow*; ~ *him in what he is to say*, *in Latin Grammar*). [f. MDu. *drillen* vb, *dril* n., of unkn. orig.]

drill², n., & v.t. Small furrow for sowing seed in, ridge with such furrow on top, row of plants so sown; machine for furrowing, sowing, & covering seed; (vb) sow (seed) thus, plant (ground) in ~s. [perh. f. obs. *drill* rill, of unkn. orig.]

drill³, n. Kind of baboon. [prob. W.-Afr.]

drill⁴, n. Coarse twilled linen or cotton fabric. [earlier *drilling* f. G *drillich* f. L *trilicem* nom. -*ix* (*tri*- three-, *licium* thread)]

dril'y̆. See DRY¹.

drink¹, v.t. & i. (*drănk*; *drŭnk* & poet. *drŭnk'en*). Swallow (liquid); take (*the waters* at a spa) medicinally; ~ *off*, *up*, ~ the whole of at once; (of plants, porous things, etc.) absorb (moisture; often *up* or *in*); (fig.) ~ *in*, contemplate, listen to, with delight; empty (vessel, *the cup of* pain or joy); spend (wages etc.) on drink; swallow liquid, take draught, (often *of* a source; ~ *deep*, take large draught, or be great ~er as in next sense); take spirituous liquor esp. to excess, tipple, be a drunkard, (~ *hard*, *heavily*, *like a fish*; ~*ing*-BOUT; ~*ing*-*water* (reserved, pure enough, for ~ing); ~ *one*self *drunk*, *to death*, *out of a situation*; ~ *down* or *under the table*, outlast in retaining control of oneself while ~ing); ~ *to*, pledge, toast; wish good etc. to in ~ing (~ *one's health*, ~ *success* or *confusion to*). Hence (·) ~ER¹ n. [OE *drincan*, OS *drinkan*, OHG *trinkan*, ON *drekka*, Goth. *drigkan* f. Gmc *drenk*-]

drink², n. Liquid swallowed or absorbed; beverage; intoxicating liquor (also *strong* ~), excessive indulgence in it, intemperance (*on the* ~, giving way to this; *in* ~, drunk); glass etc. or portion of liquor (STAND¹ *a round*); ~-*offering*, libation; *the* ~ (R.A.F. sl.), the sea. Hence ~'LESS a. [OE *drinc* & *drinca* f. *drincan*= prec.]

drink'able, a. & n. Good to drink; (n., esp. in pl.) thing(s) to drink. [-ABLE]

drip¹, v.i. & t. (-pp-). Fall, let fall, in drops; let drops fall, be so wet (*with* blood etc.) as to shed drops (~*ping wet*, very wet). [cogn. w. DROP, but of uncert. hist., poss. f. Scand., cf. MDa. *drippe*]

drip², n. Act of dripping; dripping liquid; (sl.) boring person; (Archit.) projection keeping rain from parts below (so ~-*moulding*, ~'*stone*); ~-*drop*, persistent dripping. Hence ~p'y̆² a. [f. prec.]

dripp'ing, n. In vbl senses; also: fat melted from roasting meat, & used for frying or as food; ~s, water, grease, etc., dripping from anything. [-ING¹]

drive¹, v.t. & i. (*drŏve*, *drĭven*). 1. Urge in some direction by blows, threats, violence, etc. (usu. with adv. or prep. as *away*, *back*, *in*, *out*, *from*, *to*, *through*; ~

out, oust, take place of); chase or frighten (game, wild beasts, enemy esp. in guerrilla warfare) from over large area into small in order to kill or capture. 2. Scour (district), ‖ (Forest Law) hold a DRIFT¹. 3. (Urge &c) direct course of (animal drawing vehicle or plough, vehicle etc., or locomotive); convey in vehicle; act as driver of vehicle; travel, go, in car or carriage at one's disposal (cf. *ride* in omnibus, tram, train). 4. Impel forcibly, constrain, compel, (*to*, *into*, *to* do; ~ *mad*, *out of* one's *senses*); overwork (*was very hard ~n*). 5. Impel, carry along (of wind, water), throw, propel, send in some direction, (inanimate things); (Cricket) return (ball) from freely swung bat to or past bowler; (Golf) strike (ball, or abs.) with DRIVER from tee (also ~ *off*). 6. Force (stake, nail, etc.) *into* ground etc. with blows; bore (tunnel, horizontal cavity); (also *let* ~) aim blow or missile (*at*). 7. (Of steam or other power) set or keep (machinery) going (also of person, ~ *a quill*, *pen*, write). 8. Carry on, effect, conclude, (*drove a roaring trade, good bargain*). 9. Defer (~ *it to the last minute*). 10. Dash, rush, hasten; work hard *at*. 11. Float along, drift, tend, (*driving rain*; ~ *at*, seek, intend, mean; *what is he driving at?*). [OE *drīfan*, OS *drīban*, OHG *trīban*, ON *drīfa*, Goth. *dreiban* f. Gmc *dribhan*]

drive², n. Excursion in vehicle (see prec.); driving of game or enemy (see prec.); stroke at cricket, golf, etc. (see prec.); energy, push; tendency; organized effort to achieve a special purpose; carriage-road, ‖ esp. private road to house; WHIST³~. [f. prec.]

driv'el, v.i. & t. (-ll-), & n. 1. Run at mouth or nose like child; talk childishly or idiotically; fritter *away*; hence ~IER¹ n. 2. n. Silly nonsense, twaddle. [ME *drevele*, *dravele*, OE *dreflian*, perh. cogn. w. DRAFF]

driv'er, n. One who drives (DRIVE¹), coachman (also *cab-~*, *engine-~*, etc.; *slave-~*, overseer of slave gang); (Golf) straight-faced wooden club for driving from tee; (Mech.) driving-wheel or other part that receives power directly; *front*, *rear*, ~, bicycle in which power is applied to front, rear, wheel; QUILL-~. Hence ~LESS a. [-ER¹]

driv'ing-wheel, n. Wheel communicating motion to other parts of machine; large wheel of locomotive; cycle wheel that is directly worked.

driz'zle, v.i., & n. (Fall in, be wet with) spray-like rain (subj., *the day*, *rain*, *it*). Hence **driz'zl**Y² a. [16th c.; perh. f. ME *drese* (OE *drēosan* fall) +-LE(3)]

drō'gher (-ger), n. W.-Ind. coasting vessel; slow heavy craft. [18th c., f. F *drogueur* f. Du. *drogher* (*droogen* to dry) named from drying herrings]

drōgue (-ōg), n. Buoy at end of harpoon

line; sea anchor, a bag-like contrivance used to retard the drifting of a boat & keep her head to the wind; = WIND¹*sock*. [perh. var. of DRAG²]

droit (or drwah), n. Right, due, legal perquisite, (esp. ~*s of Admiralty*, proceeds of enemy's ships, wrecks, etc.). [ME, f. OF f. L *directum* DIRECT²]

drŏll, a., n., & v.i. Facetious, amusing; queer, odd, surprising; hence **drŏl'**LY⁸ (-ŏl-ll) adv., ~'NESS n.; (n., now rare) jester, wag; (v.i., now rare) play the buffoon, jest *with*, *at*, *on*. [f. F *drôle(r)* of unkn. orig.]

drŏll'erȳ, n. Jesting; a facetious composition; quaint humour. [-ERY]

drōme, n. (colloq.). Aerodrome. [abbr.] **-drōme**, suf. repr. Gk *dromos* course, used in Gk compounds such as *hippodrome*, in modern words such as *aerodrome*, and (loosely) in *picturedrome*.

drŏm'edarȳ (*also* -ŭm-), n. Light fleet usu. Arabian or one-humped camel bred for riding. [ME, f. OF *dromedaire* f. LL *dromedarius* f. L f. Gk *dromas -ados* runner, -ARY¹]

drŏm'ond, n. (hist.). Large medieval ship for war or commerce. [ME, f. OF *dromon*(t) f. LL f. Byz. Gk *dromōn*]

drōne, n., & v.i. & t. 1. Male of honey-bee, which does not work; idler; deep humming sound; monotonous speech or speaker; bass-pipe of bagpipe; fixed continuous tone emitted by this. 2. vb. Buzz like bee or bagpipe, talk or utter monotonously, whence **drŏn'**INGLY⁸ adv.; idle; idle *away* (life etc.). [OE *drān*, *drǣn*, OS *drān*, OHG *treno* of obsc. phonology; f. WG *dran-*, *dren-*, *drun-*, *boom*]

drōōl, v.i. (U.S. & dial.). Drivel, slobber. [contr. f. DRIVEL]

drŏŏp, v.i. & t., & n. 1. Hang down, slope, incline, as in weariness; (of eyes) look downwards; (poet., of sun etc.) sink; languish, decline, flag, lose heart; let (head, face, eyes) fall forward or down; hence ~'ingLY² adv. 2. n. ~ing attitude, loss of spirit, fall of tone. [ME, f. ON *drūpa* vb cogn. w. foll.]

drŏp¹, n. 1. Round, pear-shaped, or hemispherical portion of liquid such as hangs or falls separately or adheres to surface (*of* water, tears, sweat, dew, rain, blood, or abs. in these senses); (Med.) smallest separable quantity of a liquid (in pl., liquid medicine to be measured by ~s); minute quantity (~ *in bucket* or *ocean*, infinitesimal factor); glass etc. of intoxicating liquor (*take a* ~; *has taken a* ~ *too much*, is drunk; *have a* ~ *in* one's *eye*, show signs of having drunk); pendant, hanging ornament, (*ear-~s*, ear-rings; ~*s of* glass chandelier); sugar-plum (*acid*, *pear* etc., ~*s*); hence ~LET n. 2. Act of dropping, fall, social come-down, descent in prices, temperature, etc.; thing that drops or is dropped, as

(Theatr.) painted curtain let down between acts (also ~-*curtain*), (in gallows) platform withdrawn from under feet of condemned (also, distance he is allowed to fall, as ~ *of 3 ft*); abrupt fall in level of surface, amount of this; (also ~-*kick*) kick at football made by dropping ball and kicking it as it rises (~-*off*, such kick to start play after goal, try, or touch-down). 3. ~-*forging* (also *die-forging*), the system of forcing a piece of white-hot metal through an open-ended die of the required shape; ~-*hammer* (also ~-*press*), forging-machine using the power of a dropped weight; ~-*shot* (Lawn Tennis), shot dropping abruptly after clearing net; ~-*shutter*, appliance for giving instantaneous exposure in photography; ~-*sulphur*, -*tin*, granulated by being dropped molten into water; ~'*wort*, kinds of plant with tuberous root fibres. [OE *dropa*, OS *dropo*, ON *dropi*, cogn. w. OHG *tropfo*; f. Gmc **dreup-*, **draup-*, **drup-*, whence DRIP, DROOP]

drŏp², v.i. & t. (-pp-). 1. Fall in drops; give off moisture in drops. 2. Fall by force of gravity from not being held etc., (fig.) be uttered casually (the remark ~*ped from him*), disappear (a letter has ~*ped out*). 3. Sink to ground exhausted, wounded, etc. (~ on one's knee, kneel), (of setter) crouch at sight of game. 4. Fall naturally *asleep*, (*back*) *into* habit etc.; die; cease, lapse, (*affair was allowed to* ~; the correspondence ~*ped*). 5. Fall in direction, condition, amount, degree, pitch, (*prices, voices,* ~); go *down* stream; fall *behind, to the rear*, etc. 6. Come or go casually *in* as visitor, *into* place, *across* person; ~ *on* or *across*, reprimand or punish. 7. Let fall (liquid, tears) in drops, shed; let go, relinquish, cease to hold, (~ *anchor*, anchor ship); give birth to (esp. lambs). 8. Utter casually as if unconsciously (esp. ~ *a hint*; so ~ *a postcard, line, note*). 9. Lose (money, esp. in gaming). 10. Fell with axe, blow of fist, or bullet. 11. Set down (passenger, parcel). 12. Omit (*letter*, one's *hs, syllable*) in speech. 13. Let (eyes) droop; lower (voice); ~ CURTSY. 14. (Football) send (ball), make (goal), by drop-kick (see prec.; also intr. = take drop-kick). 15. Cease to associate with, have done with (~ *it!*, stop that). 16. ~ *away, in,* depart, enter, one by one; ~ *off*, = ~ away, also fall asleep. [OE *dropian*, see prec.]

drŏpp'ings (-z), n. pl. What falls or has fallen in drops, e.g. wax from candles; dung of beasts or birds. [-ING¹]

drŏp'-scène, n. = drop-curtain (DROP¹); final scene, finale, of drama in real life.

drŏp's|ў, n. Disease in which watery fluid collects in cavities or tissue of body, (fig.) overswollen state. Hence ~ICAL a., ~ICALly² adv. [ME, apphetic form of HYDROPSY]

drŏs(h)'kў, n. Russian low four-wheeled

carriage; cab in German towns. [f. Russ. *drozhki* dim. of *drogi* wagon (*droga* shaft)]

Drosŏph'ila, n. Genus of flies, used extensively in genetic research; common fruit-fly. [mod. L, f. Gk *drosos* dew, moisture, -PHIL]

drŏss, n. Scum thrown off from metals in melting; foreign matter mixed with anything, impurities; refuse, rubbish. Hence ~'Y² a. [OE *drŏs*, MDu. *droese* dregs; cf. MLG *drōsem*, OHG *truosana* (G *drusen*)]

drought (-owt), (poet., Sc., U.S.) **drouth**, n. (Arch.) dryness, lack of moisture, also thirst; continuous dry weather, want of rain. Hence drought'Y² (-owt-), drouth'Y², a. [OE *drūgath* (*drȳge* DRY¹, -TH¹)]

drŏve¹, n. 1. Herd, flock, being driven or moving together; crowd, multitude, shoal, large number, esp. as moving together. 2. Mason's broad chisel. [OE *drāf* (*drīfan* DRIVE¹)]

drŏve². See DRIVE¹.

drŏv'er, n. Driver of droves to market, cattle-dealer. Hence drŏve³ v.t., drŏv'ING¹ n. [ME; DROVE¹+-ER¹]

drown, v.i. & t. 1. Suffer death by suffocation in liquid (often now usu. *be* ~*ed*; but ~*ing man* etc.); suffocate (person, animal) by submersion (subj., person etc., or the liquid); submerge, flood, drench, (esp. fig. ~*ed in tears, sleep, wine*; *like* ~*ed rat*, in soaked condition; ~ *out*, drive out by flood). 2. Deaden (grief etc.) with or in drink; overpower (esp. of louder sound making voice etc. inaudible). [ME (orig. north.) *drun, droune*, pointing to an OE **drūnian*; orig. obsc.]

drowse (-z), v.i. & t., & n. Be dull & sleepy, half asleep; be sluggish; make drowsy; pass *away* (time) in drowsing; (n.) half-asleep condition. [back form. f. foll.]

drow's|ў (-z-), a. Sleepy, half asleep, dozing; lulling, soporific; sluggish; ~*y-head*, sleepy person. Hence ~'IHEAD (arch.), ~'INESS, nn., ~'ILY² adv. [early 16th c., prob. rel. to OE *drūsian* sink, become slow, cogn. w. *drēosan*, see DREARY]

drŭb, v.t. (-bb-). Cudgel, thump, belabour; beat in fight; beat (notion) *into, out of*, person. Hence ~b'ING¹ n. [earlier sense *bastinado*, perh. f. Arab. *darb* beating]

drŭdg|e, n., & v.i. 1. Servile worker, slave, hack; hence ~'ERY(2, 5) n. 2. v.i. Work slavishly at distasteful work; hence ~'ingLY² adv. [orig. unkn.]

drŭg, n., & v.t. & i. (-gg-). 1. Original simple medicinal substance, organic or inorganic, used alone or as ingredient (*the* ~ *habit*, of taking opiates etc.); unsalable commodity, thing no longer in demand (usu. ~ *in the market*); ***~-*store*, chemist's shop; hence ~g'Y² (-g-) a. 2. vb. Adulterate with ~, esp. with narcotic or poison; administer ~s, esp. narcotics, to; indulge in narcotics etc.; nauseate, cloy. [ME, f. OF *drogue* of ancient orig.]

drŭgg′et (-g-), n. (Over-carpet or floor-cloth of) coarse woollen stuff used for floor or table coverings. [f. F *droguet* of unkn. orig.]

drŭgg′ist (-g-), n. Dealer in drugs, pharmaceutical chemist. [f. F *droguiste* (DRUG, -IST)]

Dru′id (-ōō-), n. Priest, magician, soothsayer, among Celts of ancient Gaul & Britain; officer of Welsh Gorsedd or national assembly. Hence ~ESS[1], ~ISM (3), nn., Druid′IC(AL) aa., (-ōō-). [f. F *druide* or L pl. *druidae*, *-des*, f. OCelt. *druid-* magician]

drŭm[1], n. 1. Musical instrument sounded by striking & made of hollow cylinder or hemisphere with parchment stretched over opening(s) (*bass, tenor, big,* KETTLE, etc., ~). 2. (zool.). Natural organ giving resonance, as howling monkey's hyoid bone. 3. Sound (as) of ~, esp. bittern's cry; player of ~, drummer. 4. Cylindrical structure (~ *of ear,* hollow part of middle ear) or object, cylinder or barrel in machinery on which something is wound or for other purposes; solid part of Corinthian or composite capital; stone block forming section of shaft; cylindrical receptacle for packing dried fruit, holding oil, etc. 5. Evening or afternoon-tea party (hist.). 6. (Also ~-*fish*) kinds of American fish able to make drumming noise. 7. ~′*fire,* heavy continuous rapid artillery fire usu. heralding infantry attack; ~′*head,* skin or membrane of ~ (~*head* COURT[1] *martial*), membrane across ~ of ear, circular top of capstan; ~ *major,* N.C.O. commanding drummers of regiment; ~′*stick,* stick with knob or pad for beating ~, lower joint of cooked fowl's leg. [f. 16th c. (obs.) *drombeslade, drombyllsclad,* f. LG *trommelslag* drum- beat f. *trommel* f. *trum(b)e,* Du. *trom*]

drŭm[2], v.i. & t. (-mm-). Play the drum, whence ~m′ER[1] n., player of drum, *commercial traveller; beat, tap, or thump, continuously on something (on piano, *at* door; *feet* ~ *on floor; a* ~*ming in the ears*); (of birds, insects) make loud hollow noise with quivering wings; summon, beat *up,* as by ~*ming;* ~ *out,* cashier by beat of drum; drive (person) *into* apathy etc., (lesson) *into* person, by persistence; strike (hands etc.) repeatedly (*up)on* something; play (tune etc.) on or as on drum. [f. prec.]

drŭm[3], **drŭm′lin,** nn. (geol.). Long oval mound of drift or diluvial formation. [f. Gael. & Ir. *druim* ridge; *-lin* perh. for -LING[1]]

Drŭmm′ond light (lĭt), n. Limelight or oxyhydrogen light. [Capt. T. *Drummond,* inventor *c.* 1825]

drŭnk, pred. a. & n. (also p.p. of DRINK[1]). 1. Intoxicated, overcome with liquor, (*beastly, blind, dead, half,* etc., ~; ~ *as a*

fiddler or *lord;* also fig., ~ *with joy, success, rage*); hence ~′ARD n. 2. n. (sl.). Drinking-bout, drunken fit; (from police charge-sheets) case of drunkenness (hence gen.) man charged with drunkenness, drunken man. [p.p. of DRINK[1]]

drŭnk′en, a. (rarely pred., cf. prec.). Intoxicated; given to drinking, often drunk; caused by or exhibiting drunkenness (~ *frolic, brawl*). Hence ~LY[2] adv., ~NESS n. [as prec. -en EN[1]]

drupe (-ōō-), n. Stone-fruit, fleshy or pulpy fruit enclosing stone or nut with kernel, as olive, plum, cherry. Hence drupA′CEOUS (-ōōpā′shus) a. [f. L f. Gk *druppa* over-ripe (olive)]

drup′el (-ōō-), **drupe′let** (-ōōpl-), nn. Small drupe in compound fruit, as blackberry. [-EL, -LET]

druse[1] (-ōōz), n. Crust of crystals lining rock-cavity, cavity so lined. [G]

Druse[2] (-ōōz), n. Member of political & religious sect of Mohammedan origin about Mt Lebanon. [Ismail al-*Darazi,* founder 1040]

drȳ[1], a. (*drier, -est*). 1. Without moisture (~ *eyes,* free from tears; ~ SHAMPOO); not rainy, with deficient rainfall. 2. Parched, dried up, (colloq.) thirsty, (of liquid) having disappeared by evaporation, draining, wiping, etc.; (of country, state, legislation, etc.) teetotal, prohibiting sale of intoxicants (*go* ~, accept such legislation). 3. Not yielding water, milk, etc. (*cow, well, is* ~). 4. Without butter (~ *bread, toast*). 5. Solid, not liquid, (~ *goods,* see below; ~ *measure,* measure of capacity for these). 6. (Of wine) free from sweetness & fruity flavour. 7. Unconnected with liquid (*die a* ~ *death,* not by drowning or bloodshed; ~ *cough,* without phlegm; || ~-BOB[3]). 8. Impassive, unsympathetic, stiff, hard, cold, (~ *jest, sarcasm, humour,* expressed in matter-of-fact tone with show of unconsciousness). 9. Meagre, plain, bare, not enlarged upon, (~ *facts, thanks*); uninteresting, dull, unprofitable. 10. Untinged by prejudice or interest (~ *light*). 11. ~-*bulb thermometer,* one of pair in hygrometer with wet & ~ bulbs; ~-*clean,* clean (clothes etc.), by means of spirit etc., without using water, so ~-*cleaner, -cleaning;* ~ *cooper,* maker of casks for ~ goods; ~-*cure,* cure (meat etc.) without pickling in liquid; ~-DOCK[4]; ~-*fly* a. & v.i. (fish) with fly floating lightly on water; ~ *goods,* non-liquid goods, as corn, also (esp. U.S.) drapery, mercery, haberdashery; ~ *lodging,* without board; ~-*nurse,* tending but not suckling child, (v.t.) bring up by hand; ~ *pile,* electric pile or battery in which no liquid is used; ~-*plate,* photographic plate with sensitized film hard & ~ for convenience of keeping, developing at leisure, etc.; ~-*point,* needle for engraving without acid on bare copper plate (also v.i. use this process, & n., engraving produced so); **~-rot**, decayed state of wood not exposed to air caused by fungi, also the fungi, (fig.) unsuspected moral or social decay; **~-salt** v.t., = **~-cure**; **~-salter**(y), dealer, dealing or shop that deals, in drugs, dyes, gums, oils, pickles, tinned meats, etc.; **~-shod** a. or adv., without wetting the feet; **~-walling** without mortar). Hence **~ISH**[1] (2) a., **dri'LY**[2] (or **~'lӯ**) adv. (esp. in fig. senses), **~NESS** n. [OE *drȳge*, rel. to MLG *dröge*, MDu. *druge*, *dröghe*, Du. *droog* f. WG **drŭg-*, whence also G *trocken*]

drȳ', v.t. & i. Make or become dry by wiping, evaporation, draining, etc.; cause (cow) to cease giving milk; **~** *up*, make utterly dry, (of moisture) disappear utterly, (of well etc.) cease to yield water, (colloq., esp. in imperat.) cease talking or doing something, (Theatr.) forget one's lines. Hence **dri'ER**[1] (1, 2) (or **~'er**) n., (also) substance mixed with oil-paints to expedite **~ing**. [OE *drȳgean* (*drȳge* DRY[1])]

drȳ'ăd, n. Nymph inhabiting tree, wood--nymph. [f. L f. Gk *druas -ados* (*drus* tree)]

Drȳ'asdŭst (*-az-*), n., d-, a. Dull laborious antiquary or historian; (adj.) very dry, uninteresting. [Dr **~**, fictitious person (*dry as dust*) to whom Scott dedicated]

'dst, clipping of *wouldst*, *hadst*.

dŭ'ăd, n. (Incorrect for) DYAD.

dŭ'al, a. & n. **1**. Of two, twofold, divided in two, double, (**~** *ownership*, *skirt*); *the D~ Monarchy*, former Austro-Hungarian Empire; shared by two, joint, as **~** *control*. **2**. (gram.). **~** *number* or **~**, inflected form proper to two persons or things (additional to *singular* & *plural*). So **dŭäl'ITY** n., **~IZE**(3) v.t., **~LY**[2] adv. [f. L *dualis* (*duo* two, -AL)]

dŭ'alin, n. Powerful explosive of nitre, nitroglycerin, & sawdust. [prec. (dual nitre) +-IN]

dŭ'al|ism, n. Duality; use of dual number; theory recognizing two independent principles (mind & matter, cf. *idealism* & *materialism*; good & evil in the universe; two personalities in Christ), so **~IST** (2) n., **~is'tic** a., **~is'tically** adv. [DUAL +-ISM]

⫷ **dŭb'**[1], n. Deep pool in northern streams; a puddle (sl.). [16th c. Sc., orig. unkn.]

dŭb'[2], v.t. (-bb-). **1**. Make (person) into *a knight* by striking shoulders with sword; invest with (new title), name, nickname, (person or thing, with complement; **~bed** *me Doctor*, *quack*, *a scribbler*). **2**. Dress (artificial fishing-fly). **3**. Smear (leather) with grease. [late OE *dubbian*, aphetic f. OF *aduber*, *adober*, com.-Rom. of unkn. orig.]

dŭb'[3], v.t. (-bb-). Make another recording of sound-track of (film) esp. in a different language, add (sound effects or music) to a film, or to a radio or television production. [abbr. of *double*]

dŭbb'ing, n. In vbl senses; esp., prepared

grease for leather (also *dŭbb'in*). [-ING[1]]

dŭbī'etӯ, n. Feeling of doubt; doubtful matter. [f. LL *dubietas* (*dubius* doubtful, -TY)]

dŭb'ious, a. Indistinct (**~** *light*), vague, unreliable (**~** *friend*), of questionable value or truth (*a* **~** *compliment*); of doubtful issue (**~** *undertaking*, *struggle*); of suspected character (**~** *gains*, *company*); hesitating, doubting. Hence **~LY**[2] adv., **~NESS** n. [f. L *dubiosus* (*dubium* doubt, -OSE[1])]

dŭbita'tion, n. Doubt, hesitation. [ME, f. OF, or L *dubitatio* (*dubitare* DOUBT[2], -ATION)]

dŭb'itative, a. Of, expressing, inclined to, doubt or hesitation. Hence **~LY**[3] (-vl-) adv. [f. LL *dubitativus* as prec. +-IVE]

dŭc'al, a. Of, like, bearing title of, duke. [F, f. LL *ducalis* (*dux* DUKE, -AL)]

dŭc'at, n. Gold coin, formerly current in most European countries; coin, (pl.) money. [ME, f. It. *ducato* f. med. L *ducatus* DUCHY (prob. named from Duke of Apulia 1140)]

Duce (dōō'chā), n. Chief (*Il*, or *the*, **~**, Mussolini as Fascist leader). [It., f. L *dux ducis*]

dŭch'ess, n. Duke's wife or widow; lady holding a duchy in her own right; imposing woman; ‖ (sl.) costermonger's wife (abbr. *dŭtch*). [ME, f. OF (-e), f. med. L *ducissa* (DUKE, -ESS[1])]

duchesse (dōōshĕs'), n. Kind of satin; **~** *lace*, kind of Brussels pillow-lace. [F, = duchess]

dŭch'ӯ, n. Territory of reigning duke or duchess; royal dukedom of Cornwall or Lancaster, each' with certain estates, revenues, & jurisdiction of its own. [ME, f. OF *duche*(e) f. med. L *ducatus* (DUKE, -Y[4])]

dŭck'[1], n. (pl. often **~** collective; also **~s**). **1**. Kinds of swimming-bird, esp. the domesticated form of the mallard or wild-**~** (*like* **~** *in thunderstorm*, with upturned eyes, looking flabbergasted, faint, etc.; *like water off* **~**'*s back*, producing no effect; *take to anything like* **~** *to water*; *fine day for young* **~s**, rainy weather; *lame* **~**, disabled person, defaulter on Stock Exchange; *in two shakes of* **~**'*s tail*, in an instant); female of this (cf. DRAKE[2]); its flesh. **2**. Darling (esp. in voc.), whence **~**'*y*[2] n. (also **~***y diamond*). **3**. (Cricket; also **~**'*s-egg*) batsman's score of 0. **4**. *Bombay* **~**, BUMMALO ; **~** *&* *drake*, game of making flat stone skip along water (*make* **~s** *& drakes of*, *play* **~s** *etc. with*, squander); **~**'*-billed* PLATYP*pus* or ORNITHO*rhynchus*; **~**-*boards*, narrow path of wooden slats. in trench or over mud; **~**-*hawk*, marsh harrier; **~**-*shot*, of size for shooting wild **~**; **~**'*weed*, plant that carpets surface of still water. Hence **~'LING**[1](2) n. (UGLY **~***ling*). [OE *duce*, *dŭce* f. *dŭcan dive (foll.)]

dŭck³, v.i. & t., & n. **1.** Plunge, dive, dip head, under water & emerge; bend quickly, bob, to avoid blow etc. or by way of bow or curtsy; plunge (person etc.) momentarily *in* water, or abs., whence ~'ING¹(1) n. (*~ing-stool*, chair at end of oscillating pole, formerly used for ~ing scolds and other objectionable persons); lower (head) suddenly. **2.** n. Quick dip below water in bathing, or lowering of head. [ME *d*(*o*)*uke* f. OE **dūcan*, (= MLG, MDu. *dūken*, OHG *tūhhan*)]

dŭck³, n. Strong untwilled linen or cotton fabric for small sails & outer clothing esp. of sailors; (pl.) trousers of this. [f. MDu. *doek*, = OS *dōk*, OHG *tuoh*, of unkn. orig.]

dŭck⁴, n. (colloq.). Amphibious landing craft. [f. DUKWS, official designation]

dŭck'er¹, n. Kinds of diving-bird, esp. dabchick & water ouzel. [DUCK², -ER¹]

dŭck'er², n. Breeder of ducks. [DUCK¹, -ER¹]

dŭct, n. Conduit, tube, for conveying liquid; tube or canal in body conveying chyle, lymph, or secretions (named from function, as *biliary ~*, or from discoverer, as *Eustachian ~*, *~s of Bellini*); vessel of plant's vascular tissue holding air, water, etc. Hence ~'LESS a. (*~less glands*, of which the secretion is not carried off by a ~, but acts directly on the blood). [f. L *ductus* leading, aqueduct (*ducere duct-* lead)]

dŭc'tile, a. (Of metals) malleable, flexible, not brittle, (in technical use) capable of being drawn out into wire, tough; plastic (of clay etc., or of person or character), pliable, tractable, docile. Hence **dŭctīl'ITY** n. [ME, f. OF f. L *ductilis* (*ducere* see prec., -IL)]

dŭd, n. & a. (sl.). **1.** (Pl.) clothes, rags; (sing.) scarecrow (also ~'*man*), shell etc. that fails to go off, futile plan or person. **2.** adj. Counterfeit, useless, unsatisfactory, futile. [orig. unkn.]

*dūde, n. (sl.). Fastidious aesthetic person, often imitating English speech, dress, & manners; dandy, swell. Hence .dūd'ISH¹ a. [orig. unkn.]

dŭdg'eon (-jn), n. Resentment, feeling of offence, (usu. in ~). [orig. unkn.]

dud(h)een' (dŏŏ-), n. (Ir.). Short clay pipe. [f. Ir. *dúidín*, dim. of *dúd* pipe]

dūe¹, a. & adv. **1.** Owing, payable, as a debt or obligation (*fall, become,* ~, as bill reaching maturity); that ought to be given to person (*first place is ~ to Milton, it is ~ to him to say*), merited, appropriate (*has his ~ reward*), rightful, proper, adequate (*after ~ consideration*), to be looked for, calculated or foreseen (*in ~ time*; to be ascribed *to* cause, agent, etc. (*the difficulty is ~ to our ignorance; the discovery is ~ to Newton;* the advl use of ~ *owing,* as *I came late ~ to an accident,* is incorrect); under engagement *to* do something (*is ~ to speak tonight*) or to arrive

at certain time (*train ~ at 7.30, already ~ & over~*). **2.** adv. (Of points of compass) exactly, directly, (*went ~ east, a ~ N. wind*). [ME, f. OF *deü* (p.p. of *devoir* owe) f. Rom. **debutus* f. L *debitus* (*debēre* owe)]

dūe², n. Person's right, what is owed him, (*give one, esp. the devil, his ~*, not be unjust to him, even though he deserves little or is no friend); what one owes (*pay one's ~s*); (usu. pl.) toll, fee, legally demandable (*harbour, light, tonnage, university, ~s*); (Naut.) *for a full ~*, for good, thoroughly, completely. [f. prec., & OF *deu*]

dū'el, n., & v.i. (-ll-). **1.** Fight with deadly weapons between two persons, in presence of two seconds, to settle quarrel (*the ~,*' ~*ling* & its code of rules); any contest between two persons, animals, parties, causes; hence ~LIST(1) n. **2.** v.i. Fight ~(s). [f. med. L (AL) *duellum* (arch. f. L *bellum* war) single combat; cf. LL *duellare* fight a duel]

dŭenn'a, n. Elderly woman acting as governess & companion in charge of girls (orig. & esp. in Spanish family); chaperon. [f. Sp. *dueña* f. L *domina* mistress]

dūet', -tt, n. Musical composition for two voices or performers; (fig.) dialogue, scolding-match; pair, couple. Hence **dūett'IST**(1) n. [f. It. *duetto* dim. of *duo* duet f. L *duo* two]

|| dŭff¹, n. (Dial. etc. for) DOUGH; PLUM-~.

dŭff², v.t. (sl.). Fake up (goods), give look of newness etc. to, (|| ~*ing*, counterfeit); (Austral.) steal & alter brands on (cattle); (Golf) mishit (shot, ball). [perh. back form. f. DUFFER]

dŭff'el, **dŭf'fle**, n. Coarse woollen cloth with thick nap (*~ coat,* overcoat of ~ with toggle fastenings instead of buttons); **kit of sportsman or camper-out.* [*Duffel* in Brabant]

dŭff'er, n. || One who sells trash as valuable, pretending to be smuggled, stolen, etc.; || pedlar, hawker; faker of sham articles; counterfeit coin, picture, etc.; unproductive mine; thing of which no use can be made; inefficient, useless, or stupid person. [goes with DUFF²]

dŭg¹, n. Udder of female mammals, also teat, nipple, (not now used of women exc. contempt.). [orig. unkn.; cf. Sw. *dægga* suckle]

dŭg². See DIG¹.

dŭg'ŏng (dŏŏ-), n. (pl. often ~). Large herbivorous mammal of Indian seas. [f. Malay *duyong*]

dŭg'-out, n. Canoe made by hollowing tree-trunk; underground shelter esp. for troops in trenches; || (sl.) retired officer etc. recalled to service.

duik'er, **duy-**, n. (dīk-), n. Small S.-African antelope. [Du. *duiker* (in full *duikerbok*)]

dūke, n. **1.** (Hist.) provincial military commander under later Roman emperors; (Bibl.) chief of tribe. **2.** (In some parts of Europe) sovereign prince ruling duchy or small State; (Gt Britain & some other countries) person holding highest hereditary title of nobility outside royal family (also *royal* ~, ~ who is also royal prince, with precedence); DINE *with D~ Humphrey.* 3. Kind of cherry. 4. (sl.). Hand, fist. [ME, f. OF *duc* f. L *dux ducis* leader]

duke'dom (-kd-), n. Territory ruled by, dignity of, duke. [-DOM]

Dŭk'eries (-ĭz), n. pl. District in Notts. containing several ducal estates. [-ERY]

Dul'ăg (dŏo-), n. Camp for prisoners of war in transit. [G abbr. of *Durchgangslager*]

dŭl'cĕt, a. Sweet, soothing, (esp. of sounds). [15th c. also *doucet* f. OF dim. of *doux* f. L *dulcis* sweet]

dŭl'cĭ|fȳ, v.t. Sweeten, make gentle. Hence ~FICA'TION n. [f. LL *dulcificare* (*dulcis* sweet, -FY)]

dŭl'cĭmer, n. Musical instrument with strings of graduated length over sounding board or box struck with hammers, prototype of piano. [f. OF *doulcimer* said to repr. L *dulce melos* sweet song]

Dŭlcĭnē'a (*or* -sĭn'ĭa), n. Idolized & idealized mistress. [name of Don Quixote's mistress]

dŭll, a., & v.t. & i. 1. Slow of understanding, obtuse, stupid, whence ~ARD n.; (of ears, eyes, etc.) without keen perception; (of inanimate things) insensible; (of pain etc.) indistinctly felt; sluggish, slow- -moving, stagnant, (of person, animal, trade); (of goods, stocks) not easily salable, not in demand; listless, depressed; tedious, monotonous; blunt (esp. of edge); (of colour, light, sound, taste) not bright, vivid, or keen; (of weather) overcast, gloomy; hence ~ISH¹ a., dŭl(l)'NESS n., dŭl'LY² (dŭl-lĭ) adv. 2. vb. Make ~ (~ *the edge of*, blunt, make less sensitive, interesting, effective); lose force, intensity, clearness, or keenness. [ME *dul*, also (obs.) *dil*, f. OE *dol* (*dyll*), corresp. to MLG, MDu. *dul*, OS (Du.) *dol*, OHG *tol* f. WG *dul-*]

dŭlse, n. Edible kind of sea-weed. [f. Ir. & Gael. *duileasg*]

dŭl'ȳ, adv. Rightly, properly, fitly; sufficiently; punctually. [ME; DUE¹+-LY²]

du'ma (dŏo-), n. Russian parliament, 1906–17. [previously name of elective municipal councils]

dŭmb¹ (-m), a. (compar. & superl., pron. -mer, -mĭst). Unable to speak, abnormally (of human beings) *the* ~, *the deaf & * ~, as nouns) or normally (~ *animals*, used in pity or contempt); inarticulate, having no voice in government etc., (*the ~ millions*); silenced by surprise, shyness, etc. (esp. *strike* ~; ~ *in mixed company*); taciturn, reticent, (*Nature is ~ on the point*; *English a * ~ *people*); *stupid; without speech (~ *crambo*; ~ *show*, significant gestures, part of play given in early drama without words);

unheard, giving no sound; without the voice, sound, or other property, usual in things of the name (~ *piano*, set of keys for exercising fingers; ~*waiter*, ‖ an upright with revolving shelves enabling waiter to be dispensed with in dining- -room, *food-lift; ‖~ *barge, craft*, without sails or motive power; ~*bell*, short bar with weight at each end used in pairs for exercising muscles, (v.i.) use these; ~ *well*, sunk merely to carry off surface water); ~*iron*, one of the two curved forward ends of the side-members of a motor-car chassis. Hence ~'LY² (-ml-) adv., ~'NESS (-mn-) n. [OE, OS *dumb*, OHG *tump* stupid, ON *dumbr*, Goth. *dumbs* mute, of unkn. orig.]

dŭmb², v.t. Make dumb. [f. prec.]

dŭmbfound' (-mf-), v.t. Strike dumb, confound, nonplus. [*dumb, confound*]

‖ **dŭm'bledōre** (-ld-), n. (dial.). Bumble- bee; cockchafer. [f. *dumble-* (cf. *bumble-*, *drumble-*; *humble-bee*)+DOR]

dŭm'dŭm, a. & n. ~ (*bullet*), kind of soft- -nosed bullet that expands & inflicts laceration. [*D*~ in India, with cantonment & arsenal]

dŭmm'ȳ, n. & a. 1. (Whist) imaginary fourth player whose hand is turned up & played by partner (~ *whist* or ~, game so played; *double* ~, game with two such hands); (Bridge) the partner of the player who makes the first call in the accepted declaration, or his (exposed) hand. 2. Person taking no real part, or present only for show, figurehead, mere tool, man of straw; dolt, blockhead. 3. Counterfeit object, sham package etc., clothes-block, lay figure, man's figure as target; baby's indiarubber teat; *sell the * ~ (Rugby football), deceive opponent by feigning to pass ball. 4. adj. Sham. [DUMB¹+-Y³]

dŭmp¹, n. ‖ Short thick object of various kinds; ‖ leaden counter used in games; obs. Australian coin, (sl.) small coin (*not worth a* ~); ‖ kind of bolt in ship-building; rope quoit for game on board ship; kind of skittle; kind of sweetmeat; short stout person. [18th c., orig. unkn.; goes with DUMPY]

dŭmp², v.t. & n. 1. Shoot, deposit, tilt down, (rubbish); let fall with a bump; (Commerc.) send (goods unsalable at high price in home market) to foreign market for sale at low price, to avoid lowering home price & capture new market; drop down (t. & i.) with a thud; land (superfluous immigrants) in foreign country; hence ~'ER¹ n. 2. n. Dull blow, thud; heap of refuse, place for shooting this; (Mil.) temporary depot of munitions. [ME, perh. of Norse orig., cf. Da. *dumpe*, Norw. *dumpa*, Sw. dial. *dompa*, fall plump]

dŭmp'ling, n. Mass of dough boiled or baked either plain or enclosing apple etc. [c. 1600; in sense, as f. DUMP¹+-LING¹, but is recorded very much earlier]

dumps, n. pl. Depression, melancholy, (usu. *in the* ~). [16th c., of obsc. orig.; perh. f. MDu. *dump* exhalation, haze, mist]

dum'p|y, a. & n. **1.** Short & stout (~*y level*, kind used in surveying); hence ~iNESS n. **2.** n. ‖ Short-legged Scotch breed of fowls. [18th c., orig. unkn.; goes w. DUMP[1]; for the sense, cf. DUMPLING]

dun[1], a. & n. (Of) dull greyish-brown colour as of ass or mouse (~-*bird*, ‖ pochard; ~ *diver*, ‖ female or young male of goosander); (poet.) dark, dusky; ~ *horse*; kinds of artificial fishing-fly. [OE *dun*(n), = OS *dun* reddish brown]

dun[2] n., & v.t. (-nn-). **1.** Importunate creditor; debt-collector; demand for payment. **2.** v.t. Importune for payment of debt; pester. [perh. var. of DIN]

dunce, n. One slow at learning, dullard, (~*'s cap*, paper cone put on head of ~ at school). [f. John *Duns* Scotus, schoolman, d. 1308, whose followers were ridiculed by 16th-c. humanists and reformers as enemies of learning]

dun'derhead (-ĕd), n., **dun'der-headed** (-ĕd-), a. Blockhead; stupid (person). [17th c., orig. unkn.]

Dundrear'y, n. ~ *whiskers*, long side whiskers worn without beard. [~, character in T. Taylor's comedy *Our American Cousin*]

dune, n. Mound or ridge of loose sand on coast. [f. F *dune* f. MDu. *dûne*; see DOWN[1]]

dung, n., & v.t. **1.** Manure; excrement of animals (rarely of man; ~-*beetle*, whose larvae develop in ~; ~-*fly*, feeding in it; ~-*worm*, found in cow-~ & used as bait; ~-*cart*, *-fork*, for conveying, loading, & spreading, manure); moral filth. **2.** v.t. Manure (land; of farmer, grazing animals, or the manure). [OE *dung*, OHG *tunga* (G *dung*, *dünger*), also Icel. *dyngja*]

dung'aree (-ngg-), n. Coarse Indian calico; (pl.) overalls etc. of ~. [f. Hind. *dungrī*]

dun'geon (-jn), n., & v.t. (Now usu. *donjon*) great tower of castle in innermost court or bailey; strong subterranean cell for prisoners; (vb) shut *up*, imprison in ~. [ME, f. OF *donjon* f. Gallo-Rom. *domnionem f. L *dominus* lord]

dung'hill, n. Heap of dung or refuse in farmyard (*cock on his own* ~, household, parish, etc., tyrant or bully; ~ *cock* etc., barn-door not game, whence ~ as adj., craven).

‖ dun'iwassal (dŏŏ-), n. (Sc.). Highland gentleman of secondary rank. [Gael. *duine* man, *uasal* noble]

*dunk, v.t. & i. Dip (bread, cake, etc.) into soup or a beverage while eating. [f. G *tunken* (var. *dunken*) dip]

Dunkirk', n. (Scene of) evacuation of a defeated army by sea like that of the British from ~ in May 1940. [port in France]

dun'lin, n. Red-backed sandpiper. [-LING[1]]

dunn'age, n. Mats, brushwood, gratings, etc., stowed under or among cargo to prevent moisture & chafing. [17th c. *dinnage*; orig. unkn.]

‖ dunn'ock, n. Hedge-sparrow. [DUN[1], -OCK]

dunt, n. Blow given to aircraft by a vertical current of air suddenly encountered. [orig. Sc., prob. var. of DINT]

du'o, n. (In music-hall usage) pair of artistes (*comedy* ~). [L, = two]

duode'cimal, a. & n. Of twelve or twelfths, proceeding by twelves; (n. pl.) cross-multiplication, method used for dimensions given in feet, inches, & twelfths of inch, used by quantity surveyors etc. [f. L *duodecimus* twelfth +-AL]

duode'cimo, n. (usu. 12mo). Book-size in which each leaf is 1/12 of printing-sheet; book of this size; diminutive thing or person. [L (*in*) *duodecimo* abl. see prec.]

duoden'ary, a. Proceeding by twelves, in sets of twelve. [f. L *duodenarius* (*duodeni* twelve at once, -ARY[1])]

duoden'|um, n. (anat.). First portion of small intestine immediately below stomach. Hence ~AL a., ~IT'IS (-ĭt-) n. [ME, f. med. L (*duodeni* see prec., from its length of 12 in.)]

du'ologue (-ŏg), n. Conversation between two persons, dramatic piece with two actors. [irreg. f. Gk *duo* two, after *monologue*]

duŏm'o (dw-), n. (pl. ~s). Italian cathedral. [It.]

dup|e, n., & v.t. **1.** Victim of deception, gull; hence ~ERY(2) n. **2.** v.t. Cheat, make a fool of; hence ~'ABLE a., ~aBIL'ITY, ~'ER[1], nn. [F *dupe* (dial.) hoopoe, from the bird's stupid appearance]

du'ple, a. Double (now only in: ~ *ratio*, that of 2 to 1; ~ *time*, *rhythm*, of two beats to the bar). [f. L *duplus* (*duo* two, *-plus* f. *ple-* fill)]

du'plex, a. Of two elements, twofold, (~ *gas-burner*, with two jets combining into one flame; ~ *lamp*, with two wicks); ~ *telegraphy*, by which one wire transmits messages both ways at once. [L, gen. *-plicis* (*duo* two, *plic-* fold)]

du'plicate, a. & n. **1.** With two corresponding parts, existing in two examples; doubled, twice as large or many; ~ *proportion*, *ratio*, proportion of squares in relation to that of their radicals; exactly like a thing already existing (of any number of copies or specimens). **2.** n. One of two things exactly alike, esp. that made after the other; second copy, with equal legal force, of letter or document; second copy of bill drawn in two parts, second of exchange; pawnbroker's ticket; one of two or more specimens of thing exactly or virtually alike; synonym; exact correspondence between two things (*made in* ~). [ME, f. L as foll., -ATE[2]]

dŭp′lic|āte², v.t. Double, multiply by two; make in duplicate, make exact copy of, produce copies of, whence ~**ātor** n. Hence ~**a′tion** n. [f. L *duplicare* (DUPLEX, -ATE³)]

dŭpli′city, n. Double-dealing, deceitfulness; doubleness. [ME, f. OF *duplicite* or LL *duplicitas* (DUPLEX, -TY)]

dŭr′ab|le, a. Lasting, not transitory; resisting wear, decay, etc. Hence **dūrabil′ity**, ~**leness** (-ln-), nn., ~**ly²** adv. [ME, f. OF f. L *durabilis* (*durare* f. *durus* hard, -ABLE)]

dūrăl′umin, n. An aluminium alloy remarkable for its strength and hardness, used for aircraft etc. [P, f. *Dür(en)* in the Rhineland + ALUMIN(IUM)]

dūr′a māt′er, n. (anat.). Tough outer membrane enveloping brain & spinal cord. [med. L, = hard mother, transl. of Arab. phrase]

dūrăm′en, n. Heart-wood of exogenous tree. [L, f. *durare* harden]

dūr′ance, n. Imprisonment (usu. *in ~ vile*). [F (*durer* last f. L *durare* see DURABLE, -ANCE)]

dūrā′tion, n. Continuance in, length of, time; time for which thing continues (*for the ~*), phr. common in war-time contracts). [ME, f. OF f. med. L *durationem* (prec., -ATION)]

dŭrb′ar, n. Indian ruler's court; public levee of Indian prince or (hist.) Anglo-Ind. governor or viceroy. [f. Pers. & Hind. *darbar* court]

dūrĕss(e)′ (or .dŭr′ĕs), n. Forcible restraint, imprisonment; compulsion, esp. imprisonment, threats, or violence, illegally used to force person to do something (*under ~; plea of ~*, for voiding contract so made). [ME, f. OF *duresse* f. L *duritia* (*durus* hard, -ESS²)]

dŭr′ian (door⁴), n. S.-E. Asian tree bearing a large oval fruit containing pulp notable for its fetid smell and agreeable taste; its fruit. [Malay]

dūr′ing, prep. Throughout, at some point in, the continuance of. [ME (-ING²) f. OF *durant* after L abl. abs. constr., as *durante vita* (or *vita durante*)]

dŭrm′ast (-ah-), n. Kind of oak. [*dur*-(perh. erron. for *dun*) + MAST²]

dŭrn, v.t. = DARN².

du′rra, dh-, (dŏŏ-), n. Indian millet. [f. Arab. *durah*]

dŭrst. See DARE.

dŭsk, n., a., & v.i. & t. **1.** Shade, gloom; darker stage of twilight. **2.** adj. (poet.). Shadowy, dim, dark-coloured, whence ~**′ish¹** a., & (in ordinary use) ~**′y²** a., ~**′ily²** adv., ~**′iness** n. **3.** vb. (poet.). Become, look, make, dim or dark or shadowy. [ME *dosk*, later *dusk*, f. OE *dox* swarthy; *-sk* is abnormal]

dŭst¹, n. **1.** Finely powdered earth or other matter lying on ground or on surfaces or carried about in clouds by wind (*shake off the ~ of one's feet*, depart in-

dignantly; *throw ~ in* one's *eyes*, mislead him by misrepresentation or diverting attention from point; *bite the ~*, fall wounded or slain). **2.** || Household refuse (~-*bin*, receptacle for this; ~-*man*, man who empties this & removes the ~ in ~-*cart*). **3.** Pollen. **4.** (With *a*) cloud of ~ (*what a ~!, a great ~, make* or raise *a ~*). **5.** Dead person's remains (*honoured ~*; also *in the ~*, dead); the human body, man. **6.** Humiliation (*humbled in, to, the ~*). **7.** Confusion, turmoil, excitement, row, contest, (~ *& heat*, the burden of a struggle). **8.** (sl.). Cash. **9.** *~-bowl*, area denuded of vegetation by drought & overcropping & so reduced to desert; ~-*brand*, disease of corn, smut; ~-*cloak*, -*coat*, -*gown*, -*wrap*, -*cloth*, worn or put over objects to keep off ~; ~-*colour*, dull light brown; ~-*cover*, -*jacket*, book's jacket; ~-*guard*, in machine, or on bicycle to protect dress; ~-*man*, = SAND-*man*; ~-*pan*, into which ~ is brushed from floor; ~- *shot*, smallest-sized shot. Hence ~**LESS** a. [OE *dūst*, MDu. *dūst* (LG *dust*, Du. *duist* fine flour), ON *dust* f, Gmc *dunst-* (whence G *dunst* vapour)]

dŭst², v.t. & i. Sprinkle with dust or powder (intr., of birds, take dust-bath; ~ *the eyes of*, deceive, take in); make dusty; sprinkle (dust, powder); clear of dust by brushing, wiping, or beating (~ one's *jacket*, beat him); clear away (dust etc.), clear furniture of dust. [f. prec.]

dŭs′ter, n. Cloth for dusting furniture etc.; person who does this. [-ER¹]

dŭs′ting, n. In vbl senses; esp. (sl.), thrashing, tossing in storm at sea. [ING¹]

dŭs′t|y, a. Full of, strewn with, finely powdered like, dust; dry as dust, uninteresting; vague, indefinite, (~*y answer*); || (sl.) *not so* ~*y*, fairly good; ~*y miller*, plant auricula (from white dust on leaves & flowers), artificial fishing-fly. Hence ~**ILY²** adv., ~**INESS** n. [-Y²]

Dŭtch¹, a. & n. **1.** (hist.). Of Germany including Netherlands (*High ~*, of Southern Germans; *Low ~*, of Germans of sea coast, Netherlands, & Flanders). **2.** Of the language or people of Holland & Netherlands (~ *school*, of painters distinguished by artistic treatment of everyday subjects; *the ~*, people of Holland & Netherlands). **3.** Coming from Holland, made or invented by the ~, (~ *clock, chair, cheese*, HOE, OVEN). **4.** Characteristic of or attributed to the ~ (~ AUCTION, COURAGE; *talk to* one like a ~ *uncle*, lecture him paternally; ~ *wife*, frame of cane etc. for resting the limbs in bed, long bolster similarly used). **5.** n. The German language in any of its forms (*High ~*, German; *Low ~*, Low German including language of Holland & other northern varieties) (hist.). **6.** Language of Holland & Netherlands (*double ~*, gibberish). [f. MDu. *dutsch* Hollandish,

Netherlandish, German, = OE *thēodisc*, OS *thiudisc*, OHG *diutisc* (G *deutsch* German) national, f. Gmc *theudā* people + -ISH[1]]

¶ dütch[2], n. See DUCHESS.

Dütch'man, n. (pl. -men, fem. -woman). Hollander or Netherlander (or *I'm a ~*, *I'm a ~ if—*, forms of positive & negative asseveration); Dutch ship (*Flying ~*, spectral ship).

düt'eous, a. Dutiful, obedient, (of person or conduct). Hence ~LY[2] adv., ~NESS n. [irreg. f. DUTY +-OUS (cf. *beauteous*) after *bounteous, plenteous*]

düt'iable, a. Liable to customs or other duties. [-ABLE]

düt'iful, a. Regular or willing in obedience & service. Hence ~LY[2] adv., ~NESS n. [foll. +-FUL]

düt'y, n. 1. Behaviour due to superior, deference, expression of respect. 2. Payment to public revenue levied on import, export, manufacture, or sale, of goods (CUSTOMS, EXCISE, *duties*), transfer of property (DEATH, PROBATE, *succession, stamp, duties*), licences, legal recognition of documents, etc. (~ is levied on article or transaction, tax usu. on persons). 3. Moral or legal obligation, what one is bound or ought to do (~ *call*, visit one would rather not but feels bound to pay). 4. Binding force of what is right. 5. Business, office, function, performance of or engagement in these (*on, off, ~*, actually so engaged or not), (Eccl.) performance of church services (*took my ~ for me*). 6. (mech.). Measure of engine's effectiveness in units of work done per unit of fuel. 7. *Do ~ for*, serve or pass for (something else); ~-*paid, -free*, of goods on which customs or excise ~ has been paid or is not leviable. [f. AF (not in OF) *duete*, see DUE[1], -TY]

düüm'vir (-er), n. (pl. ~s, ~ī). Member of board of two equal officials. Hence ~ATE[1] n. [L, lit. man of the two]

duvet (see Ap.), n. Eider-down quilt. [F]

¶ düx, n. (no pl.). Top pupil in class (chiefly Sc.). [L, = leader]

dwāle, n. Deadly nightshade. [prob. f. Scand. (ON *dvöl* delay, Sw. *dvala* trance)]

dwarf (-ôrf), n., a., & v.t. 1. Person, animal, or plant, much below ordinary size of species, whence ~'ISH[1]a., ~'ishLY[2] adv., ~'ishNESS n., (-ôrf-). 2. Small supernatural being in esp. Scandinavian mythology skilled in metal-working. 3. adj. Undersized (in many plant names); puny, stunted. 4. v.t. Stunt in growth, or in intellect etc.; make look small by contrast or distance. [OE *dweorg*, MLG, MDu. *dwerch*, OHG *twerg*, ON *dvergr* f. Gmc. *dwergaz*]

dwëll, v.i. (*dwëlt*), & n. 1. Keep one's attention fixed, write or speak at length, (*up*)on subject (~ *upon note, syllable*, etc.,

prolong it). 2. Make one's abode, spend one's time, live, *in, at, near, on,* etc. (now usu. *live* in talk). 3. (Of horse) be slow in raising feet, pause before taking fence. 4. n. Slight regular pause for some purpose in motion of machine. [OE *dwellan*, OS *-ian*, OHG *twellan*, ON *dvelja* delay etc., f. Gmc *dwaljan*]

dwëll'er, n. Inhabitant, resident *in, on,* etc.; horse that DWELLS at fence. [-ER[1]]

dwëll'ing, n. In vbl senses; also: place of residence, house; ~-*house*, used as residence, not as office, warehouse, etc.; ~-*place*, = ~. [-ING[1]]

dwin'dle, v.i. Become smaller, shrink, waste away; lose importance, decline, degenerate. [16th c., f. (now dial.) *dwine* fade away f. OE *dwīnan*, ON *dvīna* +-LE(3)]

dȳ'ad, n. The number two; group of two, couple. Hence dȳăd'IC a. [f. LL f. Gk *duas -ad-* (*duo* two, -AD)]

Dȳ'ăk, n. Aboriginal of Borneo. [Malay, = savage]

dyarchy. See DIARCHY.

dȳe[1], n. Colour produced by or as by dyeing, tinge, hue, (also fig., *crime, scoundrel, of blackest, deepest, ~*); matter used for dyeing, colouring-matter in solution; ~-*stuff, -ware, -wood*, yielding ~; ~-*house, -works*, where dyeing is done. [OE *dēag* (foll.)]

dȳe[2], v.t. & i. (~*d*; part. ~*ing*). Colour, stain, tinge; impregnate (tissue) with colouring-matter (~ *in the wool, in grain*, while material is in raw state, giving more permanent result); make (thing) such a colour (~ *cloth red, a rose colour*, etc.); (of material) take colour *well, badly*, etc. [OE *dēagian* of unkn. orig.]

dȳ'er, n. One who dyes cloth etc. (~*'s* in many names of plants yielding dye, as ~*'s bugloss, broom, oak, weed*). [-ER[1]]

dȳ'ing, n. In vbl senses of DIE[2]; esp. (attrib.) connected with, at time of, death (~ *bed, declaration, wish*; ~ *oath*, made at, or with solemnity proper to, death). [-ING[1]]

dyke. See DIKE.

dȳnăm'ic, a. & n. 1. Of motive force (cf. *static*); of force in actual operation (cf. *potential*); active, potent, energetic; of dynamics; (Med.) functional (cf. *organic*); (Philos.) accounting for matter or mind as being merely the action of forces, so dȳn'amISM(3), dȳn'amist[1] [-IST(2)] (& see DYNAMICS), nn. 2. n. Energizing or motive force. [f. F *dynamique* f. Gk *dunamikos* (*dunamis* power, -IC)]

dȳnăm'ical, a. Of dynamics; of force or mechanical power actively operative; (Theol., of inspiration) endowing with divine power, not impelling mechanically; of dynamism (see prec.). Hence ~LY[2] adv. [-AL]

dȳnăm'ics, n. pl. used as sing. 1. Branch of mechanics that treats of motion in itself, and of the motion of bodies or matter under the influence of forces (including KINEMATICS and KINETICS; opp. STATICS), whence **dỹn'amist²** [-IST(3)] (& see DYNAMIC) n.; branch (of any science) in which forces are considered (now often with a specific prefix, as in AERO*dynamics*). **2.** Moving forces, physical or moral, in any sphere. [-ICS]

dỹn'amite, n., & v.t. High explosive of nitro-glycerine mixed with inert absorbent; (vb) shatter with ~. [Gk *dunamis* force, -ITE]

dỹn'amit|er, n. User of explosive esp. for revolutionary purposes. So **dỹnamit'ic** a., ~ISM(1), ~IST(1), nn. [prec., -ER¹]

dỹn'amo-, comb. form of Gk *dunamis* power, as in *~-electric*=of current (formerly *dynamic*) electricity, also = converting mechanical into electric energy.

dỹn'amō, n. (pl. -os). Machine converting mechanical into electric energy by rotating coils of copper wire in magnetic field. [short for *~-electric machine*, see prec.]

dỹnamŏm'eter, n. Kinds of instrument measuring energy expended by animal, engine, or mechanical force; gauge for telescope's magnifying-power. [DYNAMO-, -METER]

dỹn'ast, n. Ruler, member of a dynasty. [f. L f. Gk *dunastēs* (*dunamai* am able)]

dỹn'astỹ, n. Line of hereditary rulers. So **dỹnäs'tic** a., **dỹnäs'tically** adv. [f. F *dynastie* or LL f. Gk *dunasteia* lordship (prec.)]

dỹne, n. (phys.). Unit of force (the amount that, acting for one second on one-gram mass, gives it velocity of one centimetre per second). [F, f. st. of Gk *dunamis* force]

dỹs-, pref.=Gk *dus-* bad-, opp. *eu-* good-, chiefly in medical or other scientific words taken f. Gk or made with Gk elements.

dỹs'entery, n. Disease with inflamed mucous membrane & intestinal glands, griping pains, & mucous & bloody evacuations. So **dỹsente'ric** a. [f. OF *dissenterie* or L f. Gk *dusenteria* (DYS-, *entera* bowels)]

dỹsgĕn'ic, a. Exerting a detrimental effect on the race (opp. EUGENIC). [f. DYS-+genés produce+-IC]

dỹslogis't|ic, a. Disapproving, opprobrious, (of sense in which term is used). Hence **~ICALLY** adv. [DYS-+(EU)LOGISTIC]

dỹspĕp'sia, n. Indigestion. So **dỹspĕp'tic** a. & n., (person) subject to ~ or the attendant depression. [L, f. Gk DYS(*pepsia* f. st. of *pessō* cook)]

dỹspnoe'|a (-nēa), n. (path.). Difficult breathing. Hence **~ic** a. [L, f. Gk *duspnoia* (DYS-, *pneō* breathe)]

dỹsprŏs'ium (-zi-), n. (chem.). Element of rare-earth group. [mod. L, f. Gk *dusprositos* hard to get at]

dỹsūr'ia, n. Painful urination. [LL, f. Gk *dusouria* (DYS-+*ouron* urine)]

E

E, e, (ē), letter (pl. *Es*, E's). (Mus.) note, & corresp. scale; second-class ship in Lloyd's register.

e-, pref. Shortened form of EX-(1).

each, a. & pron. (Of two or more) every (one) taken separately, as *~ man has two votes, ~ of us has two votes, we have two votes ~, they cost a penny ~, ~ is worse than the one before; they hate ~ other, ~ hates the other; sides of two triangles are equal ~ to ~* (a side of one to the corresponding side of the other). [OE *ǣlc*, = LG, Du. *elk*, OHG *eogilih* (G *jeglich*) f. WG *°aiwō galikaz* ever alike; see AYE, LIKE, ALIKE; OE had also *ylc* ILK; *gehwilc* = OHG *gihwelih* (see WHICH); *ǣghwilo* = OHG *eogihwelih*]

eag'er (-g-), a. Full of keen desire; strongly desirous (*to do, for, after, about,* etc.); (of passions etc.) keen, impatient; (arch.) ~ (cold) *air.* Hence **~LY²** adv., **~NESS** n. [ME, f. OF *aigre* keen, f. L *acrem* (nom. *acer*)]

ea'gle, n. **1.** Large bird of prey, with keen vision & powerful flight; figure of this, esp. as ensign of Roman or French army, or as lectern in church. **2.** (golf). Hole played in two strokes under par. **3.** *°Double* ~, coin worth twenty dollars; *~-eyed,* keen-sighted; *~-owl,* largest European owl. [f. OF *aigle* f. L *aquila*]

eag'let, n. Young eagle. [f. F *aiglette* (as prec., see -ET¹)]

eagre (āg'er, ē-), n. Large tidal wave, esp. in the Humber, Trent, & Severn. [orig. unkn.]

-ean, suf. of adjj. & nn. (also *-aean, -cian*), with sense ' of, belonging to, like '; = -AN w. end of stem, usu. Gk *-ai(os),* L *-ac(us),* or Gk *-ei(os),* L *-ei(us); -aean* chiefly in unfamiliar wds as *Ascraean, Achaean; -cian* (apart from Gk & L as *Pompeian* etc.) is used w. E names in *-ey, -y,* as *Bodleian, Rugbeian; -ean* is pron. with *ē* (*Tacitēan, empyrēan,* exc. in familiar adjj. as *Prŏt'ean, Hercūl'ean,* (-Ian), but cf. *pygmēan;* some have *-ean* incorrectly for *-ian-* (*antipodean*), & some vary betw. the two (*Aristotelean, -ian*).

ear¹, n. **1.** Organ of hearing, esp. external part of this; faculty of discriminating sound, as *an ~ for music; ~-*shaped thing, esp. handle of pitcher; *bring* (storm, hornets' nest, etc.) *about* one's *~s; prick up* one's *~s,* assume expectant attitude; *I would give my ~s,* make any sacrifice (*for* a thing, *to* do); *over head and ~s,* deeply immersed *in* (lit. & fig.); *set* (persons), *be, by the ~s* (at variance); *a word in your ~s* (in private); *be all ~s* (deeply attentive); *it goes in at one ~ & out at the other,* it leaves no impression; *give ~,* listen *to; have a person's ~* (favourable attention); *were your ~s burning last night?* (we were talking about you); *send*

him *away with a flea in his* ~, told him
some home truths etc. 2. ~-*ache*, pain in
drum of ~; ~'*mark*, (n.) mark on ~ of
sheep etc. as sign of ownership, (fig.) mark
of ownership, (v.t.) mark (sheep etc.) with
this, (fig.) assign (fund etc.) to definite
purpose; ~-*phone*, = HEAD-*phone*; ~-*ring*
(worn in lobe of ~ for ornament); ~'*shot*,
hearing distance, as *within, out of,* ~-*shot*;
~-*trumpet*, tube used by persons partly
deaf; ~-*wax*, viscid secretion in~. Hence
(-)~ED[2] (-rd), ~'LESS, aa. [OE *ēare*, OS,
OHG *ōra*, ON *eyra*, Goth. *auso*, cogn. w.
L *auris*, Gk *ous*]

ear², n. Spike, head, of corn, containing
its flowers or seeds. [OE *ēar*, OS *ahar*,
OHG *ahir*, ON *ax*, Goth. *ahs* cogn. w. L
acus -eris husk]

ear'ing, n. (naut.). Small rope (one of
several) fastening upper corner of sail to
yard. [EAR¹+-ING¹; or = *ear-ring*]

earl (ĕrl), n. (fem. *countess*). Nobleman
ranking between marquis & viscount (cf.
COUNT²); *E*~ *Marshal*, officer presiding
over Heralds' College etc. Hence ~'DOM
(ĕr-) n. [OE *eorl*, OS, OHG *erl*, ON *earl*,
JARL, of unkn. orig.]

earl'y (ĕr-), a. & adv. Absolutely or relatively near to the beginning of a portion
of time, as *an* ~ *visit,* ~ *risers, rise* ~,
keep ~ *hours* (rise & go to bed ~), ~
peaches (maturing ~ in the year), *E*~
English STYLE, *fix an* ~ *date* (not long
hence), *at your earliest convenience* (as
soon as you conveniently can), *the* ~ *part*
(beginning) *of the century; the* ~ *spring,
morning,* etc., *the* ~ *part* of spring etc.;
~ *bird,* (joc.) ~ *riser* (w. ref. to proverb *the
~ bird gets the worm*); ~-*Victorian* a. & n.,
(writer etc.) of or characteristic of Victoria's ~ *reign*; ~ *door,* theatre door
admitting audience before usual hour and
at enhanced price; *earlier on,* at an earlier
stage, previously (after *later on*). Hence
earl'iNESS (ĕr-) n. [(adj. f. adv.) OE
ǣrlīce (ar posit. degree of *ǣr* ERE,
-LY²)]

earn (ĕrn), v.t. (Of person, action, conduct, etc.) obtain as reward of labour or
merit. [OE *earnian* = OHG *arnēn* f. WG
aznōjan, cf. OE *esne*, Goth. *asneis* labourer, Goth. *asans* (G *ernte*) harvest]

earn'est¹ (ĕr-), a. & n. Serious, zealous,
not trifling; ardent (*desire* etc.); *in* ~,
serious(ly), not jesting(ly). Hence ~LY¹
adv., ~NESS n. [(a.f.n.) OE *cornust* = OHG
ernust (G *ernst*) f. ern- as in ON *ern*
vigorous]

earn'est² (ĕr-), n. Money paid as instalment, esp. to confirm contract etc.; foretaste, presage, betokening, (*is an', in,* ~ *of
what is to come*). [ME *ernes* prob. var. of
erles, arles f. OF *erles* f. Rom. *arrulas*
pl. dim. of L *arr(h)a* pledge]

earn'ing (ĕr-), n. In vbl senses, esp. (pl.)
money earned. [-ING¹]

earth¹ (ĕr-), n. (pl. only as below). 1. The
ground, as *it fell to* ~; (w. pl.) hole of

badger, fox, etc.; the dry land; land &
sea opp. the sky; this planet; this world
opp. heaven or hell (*why* etc. *on* ~ ? *why
EVER?*); (w. pl.) soil, mould; (Chem., w.
pl.) any of certain metallic oxides,
uninflammable, & having little taste
or smell; || (Electr., w. pl.) connection
with ~ as completion of circuit. 2. ~-
born, of mortal race, (Myth.) emerging
from ~ at birth; ~-(substitute for
WATER¹-) *closet*; ~-*light, -shine,* partial
illumination of dark part of moon by
light from ~; ~-*nut,* (roundish tuber of)
an umbelliferous woodland plant, other
plants; ~*work,* bank of ~ used in fortification; ~-*worm,* worm living in ground,
(fig.) grovelling person. Hence ~'WARD(S)
adv. [OE *eorthe,* OS *ertha,* OHG *erda,*
ON *jörth,* Goth. *airtha* f. Gmc **erthō*]

earth² (ĕr-), v.t. & i. Cover (roots of
plants) with heaped-up earth; drive (fox)
to earth; (intr., of fox) run to earth;
(Electr.) = GROUND³. [f. prec.]

earth'en (ĕr-), a. Made of earth; made of
baked clay. [-EN⁵]

earth'enware (ĕr-), n. (often attrib.).
Vessels etc. made of baked clay; baked
clay. [WARE¹]

earth'ly (ĕr-), a. Of the earth, terrestrial;
(colloq.) *no* ~*y use, reason, chance,* no use
etc. at all; || not an ~*y* (sl.), no chance
whatever. Hence ~INESS n. [-LY¹]

earth'quake (ĕr-), n. Volcanic convulsion
of earth's surface; (fig.) social or other
disturbance.

earth'y (ĕr-), a. Like, of, earth or soil;
(fig.) grossly material. Hence ~INESS n.
[-Y²]

ear'wig, n., & v.t. (-gg-). Insect once held
to get into the head through the ear;
(v.t.) influence (person) by secret communications. [OE *ēarwicga* (*ēare* EAR¹ +
wicga ~)]

ease¹ (ēz), n. Freedom from pain or
trouble; freedom from constraint, as *at
one's* ~; (Mil.) *stand at* ~ (in relaxed
attitude, with feet apart); relief from
pain; CHAPEL *of* ~; facility, esp. *with* ~.
Hence ~'LESS (-zl-) a. [ME, f. OF *eise,
aise* (cf. Prov. *aize,* It. *agio*) f. Rom.
*adjaces f. L *adjacens* ADJACENT]

ease² (ēz), v.t. & i. Relieve from pain
etc.; give mental ease to (person, one*self,*
one's *mind*); (joc.) rob (person *of* his purse
etc.); relax, adjust, (what is too tight);
(Naut.) slacken (rope, sail, *away, down,
off*), ~ *her,* reduce speed of engine; (v.i.)
~ *off,* become less burdensome. [ME, f.
OF *a(a)isier* (prec.)]

ease'ful (ēzf-), a. Comfortable, soothing;
at rest; slothful. Hence ~LY² adv., ~NESS
n. [-FUL]

eas'el (-z-), n. Wooden frame to support
picture, blackboard, etc. [f. Du. *ezel* = G
esel ASS]

ease'ment (-zm-), n. (Law) right of way
or similar right over another's ground;
supplementary building, shed, etc.;

(arch.) relief from pain or burden. [ME, f. OF *aisement* (as EASE², -MENT)]

east, adv., n., & a. (Towards, at, near) the point of the horizon where the sun rises (90° to right of North); *to the ~* (*of*), in an eastward direction (from); ~ (*wind*), wind blowing from the ~; eastern part of the world, orient; altar-end of church (whether truly oriented or not); *the E~*, (esp.) north-~ region of the U.S.; *Far E~*, China, Japan, etc.; *Middle E~*, (esp.) countries from Egypt to Iran inclusive; *Near E~*, Turkey & Balkan States; ‖ *E~ End*, eastern part of London; *E~ Side*, eastern part of New York. Hence ~'WARD a. & n., ~'WARD(s) adv. [OE *ēast*, OS, OHG *ōst-*, ON *aust-* f. Gmc *aus-to-*, *aus-tro* f. Aryan *aus* (L *aurora*, *auster*)]

Eas'ter, n. Festival of Christ's resurrection, corresponding to Passover, & observed on 1st Sunday (~ *day*, *Sunday*) after the first full moon on or after March 21 (also arch. ~*tide*); (also ~*week*) week commencing with ~ day; ~ *eggs* (painted & presented to friends at ~); ~ *eve*, day before ~ day; ~ *offering*(s), customary payments made to the incumbent on ~ day (now usually the collection proceeds). [OE *ēastre*, pl. *ēastron*, OHG *ōstarūn* app. f. *Eostre*, dawn-goddess (*aus*-, see prec.)]

eas'terly, a. & adv. In an eastern position or direction; (coming) from the east, as ~ *wind*. [f. obs. *easter* (perh. compar. of EAST) + -LY¹]

eas'tern, a. & n. Of, dwelling in, the east part of the world; *E~ Church* (Greek); lying towards the east; (n.) inhabitant of the East, member of E~ Church. Hence ~MOST a. [OE *ēasterne* (see EAST & -ERN)]

eas'ting, n. (naut.). Distance to the eastward; easterly direction. [-ING¹]

eas'y (-z-), a., adv., & n. **1.** Free from pain, discomfort, annoyance, anxiety, etc.; ~ *circumstances*, affluence; free from embarrassment or stiffness, as ~ *manners*, *free & ~* (not stiff, not strict); not difficult (*to do*, or abs.; ~ *of access*, easily got at); easily persuaded, compliant, (*woman of ~ virtue*, unchaste); (Commerc., of commodity) not much in demand, (of market) not showing eager demand, (cf. TIGHT). **2.** adv. In ~ manner, as *take it* ~, proceed comfortably; (as command) ~ *l*, move gently, ~ *all!*, stop (prop. rowing), whence *an* ~, a short rest; ‖ *stand* ~ *!* (Mil.), permission to squad standing at ease to relax attitude further. **3.** ~ *chair*, one designed for comfort, usu. with arms; ~*going*, (of horse) having an ~ gait, (of person) fond of comfort, indolent, taking things easily; ~*mark* (colloq.), simpleton; ~ *money* (not hard to earn). Hence **eas'ILY²** adv., **eas'INESS** n., (-z-). [ME, f. OF *aisie* p.p. of *aisier* EASE²]

eat, v.t. & i. (past *ate*, *eat*, pron. ĕt; p.p. *eaten*, pron. ētn). Masticate & swallow (solid food); **swallow** (soup); ~ one's *words*, retract them in humiliating manner; ‖ ~ one's *terms* or *dinners*, be studying for the bar; ~ HUMBLE *pie*; ~ (person) *out of house & home*, ruin him by ~ing (lit. & fig.) all he has; *horse* etc. ~s *its head off*, costs more to feed than it is worth; *well, don't* ~ *me!*, joc. reply to vehement protest etc.; (intr. as pass.) *the cakes ~ crisp*; destroy, consume, as ~ one's *heart out*, suffer bitterly; ~ *away*, destroy gradually (lit. & fig.); ~ *up*, consume completely, waste, (lit. & fig.), absorb, as ~*en up with pride*. Hence **eat'ABLE** a. & n. (usu. pl.), ~*ER¹* n., one who or that which ~s (*he is a big ~er*, *an opium-~er*), fruit that may be ~en raw. [OE, OS *etan*, OHG *ezzan*, ON *eta*, Goth. *itan* f. Gmc *etan* f. Aryan *ed-* (L *edere*)]

eat'ing, n. In vbl senses; ~*house*, restaurant. [-ING¹]

eats, n. pl. (sl.). Food. [pl. of obs. *eat*, something edible (OE *æt*), or fresh formation f. vb]

eau (ō), n. ~*-de-Cologne* (ōd'ekolōn'), perfume made at Cologne; ~*-de-Nil* (-denēl'), greenish colour (supposed to resemble Nile water); ~*-de-vie* (-devē'), brandy; ~ *sucrée* (see Ap.), water and sugar. [F, = water]

eaves (ēvz), n. (now pl.). Overhanging edge of roof or thatch; ~*'drop*, stand under this to listen to secrets, listen secretly to private conversation; ~*dropper*, one who does this (usu. fig.). [OE *efes*, cf. OHG *obasa* (G dial. *obsen*), f. same root as OVER; -s being now taken as pl. *eave* is occas. used for sing.]

ĕbb, n., & v.i. **1.** Reflux of tide, as ~ *& flow*, ~*tide*; decline, decay, as *at a low* ~. **2.** v.i. Flow back, recede, decline, decay. [OE (*ebbian* vb f.) *ebba* (Du. *eb*, *ebbe*), f. WG *abhjon*, *-ōn* f. *abh* OFF]

E'-boat, n. Enemy high-speed motor torpedo-boat. [E abbr. of *enemy*]

ĕb'on, a. (poet.). Made of, black as, ebony. [15th c. *eban* f. med. L *ebanus* f. L f. Gk *ebenos*]

ĕb'onīte, n. = VULCANITE. [f. foll. + -ITE¹]

ĕb'on|y̆, n. & a. **1.** Kinds of hard black wood. **2.** adj. Made of, black as, this. Hence ~IZE(3) v.t. [16th c., irreg. var. of *ebon*, perh. after *ivory*]

ēbrī'ety̆, n. (now rare). Drunkenness. [f. F *ébriété* or L *ebrietas* (as foll., see -TY)]

ĕb'rious, a. (now rare). Drunk; given to, of, drunkenness. [f. L *ebrius* + -OUS]

ēbŭll'i|ent, a. Boiling; exuberant. So ~ENCE, ~ENCY, nn. [f. L E(*bullire -it-* boil), -ENT]

ēbulli'tion, n. Boiling; effervescence; (fig.) sudden outburst (*of passion*, war, etc.). [f. L *ebullitio* (as prec., see -ION)]

écarté (ākärt'ā), n. Card-game for two persons in which cards may be discarded for others. [F (*écarter* discard)]

Ec'ce Hōm'ō (ĕksī), n. Picture of Christ

wearing crown of thorns. [L, = behold the man (*John* xix. 5)]

eccĕn'tric (-ks-), a. & n. 1. Not concentric (*to* another circle); not placed, not having its axis etc. placed, centrally; (of 'orbit) not circular; (of heavenly body) moving in an ~ orbit; irregular; odd, whimsical. 2. n. (Mech.) ~ contrivance for changing rotatory into backward-&-forward motion, esp. for slide-valve of steam-engine; odd, whimsical person. Hence **eccĕn'-trICALLY** adv., **ĕccentri'ciTY** n. [f. LL *eccentricus* f. Gk *ekkentros* (*ek* out of + *kentron* CENTRE[1]), see -IC]

ĕcclēs'ia (-z-), n. (Gk Ant.). General assembly (esp. of Athenian citizens), cf. BOULE. [L, f. Gk *ekklēsia* (*ekkaleō* call out); in later Gk & LL = church]

ĕcclēs'iăst (-z-), n. Member of Athenian ecclesia; 'the Preacher', Solomon (regarded as author of *Eccles.*). [f. LL, Gk *ekklēsiastēs* (as prec.)]

Ecclēsiăs'tēs (ĭ-, -zĭ-, -z), n. An O.T. book. [as ECCLESIAST]

ĕcclēsiăs'tic (-zĭ-), n. & a. Clergyman; (adj., now rare) = foll. [f. F *-ique* or LL f. Gk *ekklēsiastikos* (as prec.)]

ĕcclēsiăs'tic|al (-zĭ-), a. Of the church or the clergy; ‖*E~al Commission*(ers), body formerly administering part of Church of England revenues. Hence or cogn. ~aLLY[2] adv., ~ISM n. [-AL]

Ecclēsiăs'ticus (ĭ-, -zĭ-), n. A book of the Apocrypha. [as ECCLESIASTIC, = of (i.e. to be read in) church]

ĕcclēsiŏl'og|y (-zĭ-), n. Science of churches, esp. of church building & decoration. Hence **ĕcclēsiŏlŏ'gɪC(AL)** aa., ~IST n., (-zĭ-). [f. ECCLESIA + -O- + -LOGY]

ĕc'dўsis, n. (pl. *-sēs*). Casting off (esp. of slough in serpents etc.; also fig.); slough. [f. Gk *ekdusis* (*ekduō* put off)]

ĕ'chelon (-sh-), n., & v.t. Formation of troops in parallel divisions, each with its front clear of that in advance; *in* ~, so drawn up; (v.t.) draw up thus; grade in civilian organization. [(vb f. n.) f. F *échelon* (*échelle* ladder f. L *scala*, see -OON)]

ĕchid'na (-k-), n. Australian toothless burrowing animal like hedgehog. [f. Gk *ekhidna* viper]

ĕch'inite (-k-), n. Fossil echinoderm or sea-urchin. [f. ECHINUS + -ITE[1]]

echinodĕrm (ĭkĭn-, ĕk'ĭn-), n. Class of animals including sea-urchins. [as foll. + DERM]

ĕchīn'us (-k-), n. Sea-urchin, animal inhabiting spheroidal prickly shell. [f. L f. Gk *ekhinos* hedgehog, sea-urchin]

ĕch'ō[1] (-k-), n. (pl. ~*es*). Repetition of sound by reflexion of sound-waves (*cheer* person etc. *to the* ~, loudly); *E~*, cause of this personified; close imitation; obsequious imitator or adherent; artifice by which last syllables of one verse are taken up by next; conventional indication given to partner at bridge or whist of

the number of cards held in suit led etc.; ~*gram*, record of ~*-sounder* (sounding apparatus for determining depth of sea beneath ship). Hence ~LESS a. [ME, f. L f. Gk *ēkhō*, conn. w. *ēkhē* sound]

ĕch'ō[2] (-k-), v.i. & t. (Of places) resound with an echo; (of sounds) be repeated, resound; (Bridge etc.) play the echo (see prec.); (v.t.) repeat (sound) by echo; repeat (another's words), imitate the words or opinions of (person). [f. prec.]

ĕch'ō|ism (-k-), n. = ONOMATOPOEIA. So ~IC a. [-ISM]

ĕc'lair (āk'lâr), n. Small finger-shaped cake filled with cream and iced. [F]

éclaircissement (see Ap.), n. Clearing up, explanation, (of conduct etc.). [F]

ĕclămp'sia, n. Kind of epileptic convulsions caused by anatomical lesion to which pregnant women are specially liable. [ult. f. Gk *eklampō* shine forth (visual hallucination being a symptom)]

éclat (ĕklah'), n. Conspicuous success, general applause, as *with great* ~; social distinction. [F]

ĕclĕc'tĭc, a. & n. (Ancient philosopher) selecting such doctrines as pleased him in every school; (person) borrowing freely from various sources, not exclusive in opinion, taste, etc. Hence ~ICALLY adv., ~ĪCISM(3) n. [f. Gk *eklektikos* (*eklegō* pick out, see -IC)]

ĕclipse[1], n. Interception of the light of a luminous body (sun, moon, etc.), by intervention of another body between it & the eye or between the luminous body and what illuminates it; ANNULAR, PARTIAL, TOTAL, ~; deprivation of light; loss of brilliance or splendour (*in* ~, of birds, having lost the courting plumage); periodical obscuration of lighthouse light. [ME, f. OF f. L f. Gk *ekleipsis* vbl n. f. *ekleipō* fail to appear, be eclipsed (*leipō* leave)]

ĕclipse[2], v.t. (Of a heavenly body) obscure (another) by passing between it & spectator or between it and the source of its light; intercept (light, esp. of lighthouse); (fig.) deprive of lustre, outshine, surpass. [f. prec.]

ĕclip'tic, a. & n. Of eclipse; (n.) sun's apparent orbit. [f. L f. Gk *ekleiptikos* (ECLIPSE[1], -IC)]

ĕc'lŏgue (-g), n. Short poem, esp. pastoral dialogue, such as Virgil's Bucolics. [f. L f. Gk *eklogē* selection (*eklegō* pick out)]

ĕcŏl'ogy, oec- (ē-), n. Branch of biology dealing with living organisms' habits, modes of life, and relations to their surroundings. [f. G *ökologie* f. Gk *oikos* house, -LOGY]

ĕconŏm'ic, a. & n. 1. Of ~s; maintained for profit, on a business footing, paying expenses, (of rent) high enough to compensate builder, owner, etc.; connected with industrial arts; ~ *botany*, *geography*, etc., botany etc. studied from the utilitarian standpoint. **2.** n. pl. Practical science of the production & distribution of wealth, (also) condition of a country as to material prosperity. [f. F *-ique* or L f. Gk *oikonomikos* (see ECONOMY & -IC)]

ĕcŏnŏm′ical, a. Saving, thrifty, not wasteful (*of*); relating to economics or to political economy. [-AL]

ĕcŏnŏm′ically, adv. Thriftily; from an economic point of view. [-LY²]

ĕcŏn′omist, n. Manager (*of* money etc.); thrifty person; writer on economics or political economy. [as ECONOMY + -IST]

ĕcŏn′omīze, -ise (-īz), v.t. & i. Use sparingly; turn to the best account; (v.i.) practise economy, cut down expenses. Hence ~A′TION n. [as foll. + -IZE]

ĕcŏn′omȳ, n. **1.** Administration of concerns & resources of a community; *Political E~,* theory of production & distribution of wealth. **2.** Frugality; (w. pl.) instance of this. **3.** (theol.) Judicious handling of doctrine, whence (with play on sense *frugality*) ~ *of truth.* **4.** Organization; organized body, society, etc. [f. F *économie* or L f. Gk *oikonomia* f. *oikonomos* steward (*oikos* house + *-nomos* f. *nemō* manage)]

ĕcru′ (-ōō, or as F *écru*), n. Colour of unbleached linen. [F, = unbleached]

ĕc′stasize, -ise (-īz), v.t. & i. Throw, go, into ecstasies. [f. foll. + -IZE]

ĕc′stasȳ, n. Exalted state of feeling, rapture, (esp. of delight); (Med.) morbid state of nerves in which mind is occupied solely by one idea; trance; poetic frenzy. [ME, f. OF *extasie* f. LL f. Gk *ekstasis* vbl n. f. *existēmi* put (person) out of (his senses)]

ĕcstăt′|ĭc, a. Of, subject to, producing, ecstasies (esp. of joy). Hence ~ICALLY adv. [f. F *extatique* f. Gk *ekstatikos* (as prec., see -IC)]

ĕc′to- in comb., f. st. of Gk *ektos* outside, as, ~*blăst,* (Biol.) outer membrane of cell; ~*plăsm,* (Biol.) outer layer of protoplasm, supposed viscous substance exuding from body of spiritualistic medium during trance; ~*zōon,* external parasite.

ĕc′todĕrm, n. (biol.). Outer cellular membrane investing a multicellular animal. [ECTO-, DERM]

-ectomy, suf. f. Gk *ektomē* excision, in surgical terms denoting operations in which some part is removed, as *colectomy,* excision of part of the colon.

ecumenical. See OECUMENICAL.

ĕc′zēma, n. Inflammation of the skin, of several kinds. [f. Gk *ekzema* (*ek* out + *zeō* boil, see -M)]

-ed¹, (1) suf. forming p.p. of weak vbs (also *-d, -t,* as in *sold, bought*); -ed (now reduced in sound to *-d* or *-t* except in *-ded, -ted,* in some bibl. wds,·as *blessed,* & in *learned*) was in OE *-ed, -ad, -od,* acc. to vb class, *-d* alone being the participial element, f. Gmc -*dha*- f. Aryan *-to-* (cf..Gk vbl adj. *-tos,* L p.p. *-tus*); *-t* is used in vbs that shorten in p.p. a long vowel of stem, as *crept, dreamt* (dreamed if pronounced with ē), and in some ending in *-d* after *l, n, r,* as *gilt, sent, girt.* (2) p.pp. in *-ed* (and *-en*) are used (rarely f. intr., commonly from trans. vbs) as adjj., meaning when intr. 'that has done so-&-so' (*vanished hand, fallen idol, escaped convict*); a special use, w. resultant force, is seen in *outspoken, well-read;* occas. it is doubtful whether adjj. in *-ed* are trans. (or intr.) p.pp. or belong to foll.: *decayed* may be *that has been decayed, that has decayed,* or *that is affected with decay;* reference to -ED¹(2) is made only for the rare intr. p.p. adjj.

-ed² (as prec.), suf., distinct f. prec. in OE *-ede,* OS *-ōdi,* f. Gmc type -*ōdhja-* (functioning as L *-tus* in *caudatus*), appended to nn. to form adjj. meaning possessed of, affected with, etc., as *talented, wooded, diseased;* esp. used to make adj. out of adj. & n., usu. stressed (apart from demands of context) in attrib. use on first component (a *quick- -witted lad, mel′al-cornered chest*), in pred. use on second (*he seems quick-witt′ed enough*) exc. where this is more or less otiose (*ru′by, coff′ee,* etc., *-coloured* attrib. & pred.); occas. = 'having the ways of' instead of simply 'having', as *bigoted, crabbed, dogged;* occas. indisting. f. prec.(2).

Edā′cious (-shŭs), a. (pedant.). Of eating; greedy. So ĕdÀ′CITY n. [f. L *edax -acis* (*edere* eat, see -ACIOUS)]

Ed′ăm (ē-), n. Spherical Dutch cheese. [~, in Holland]

Edd′a (ĕ-), n. (*Older, Poetic,* ~) collection of ancient Icelandic poems; (*Younger, Prose,* ~)· miscellaneous handbook (c. 1230) to Icelandic poetry. [perh. f. a name in an ON poem]

ĕdd′|ȳ, n., & v.t. & i. **1.** Small whirlpool; wind, fog, smoke, moving like this. **2.** v.t. & i. Whirl round in ~ies. [orig. obsc.]

edelweiss (ād′elvīs), n. Alpine plant with white flower, growing in rocky places. [f. G *edel* noble + *weiss* white]

Ed′en (ē-), n. Abode of Adam & Eve at their creation; delightful abode; state of supreme happiness. [ME, f. LL f. Gk f. Heb. *'eden* orig. = delight]

ĕdĕn′tāte, a. & n. (Animal) without incisor & canine teeth; toothless (animal). [f. L E(*dentatus* f. *dens -ntis* tooth, see -ATE²)]

edge¹, n. Sharpened side of blade of cutting instrument or weapon; sharpness of this, as *the knife has no* ~; *take the* ~ *off,* blunt, weaken, dull, (appetite, argument, etc.); *be on* ~, be excited or irritable; *set* (person's) *teeth on* ~, jar his nerves, affect him with repulsion; ~- -shaped thing, esp. crest of a ridge; (fig.) critical position or moment; meeting-line of two surfaces of a solid; (Skating) *do the inside, outside,* ~, skate on the inner, outer, ~ of skates; boundary-line of surface; brink (of precipice); *have the* ~

on (sl.), have the advantage of; ~-*bone*, see AITCH-BONE; ~-*tool*, cutting-tool (in fig. sense also *edged tool*). Hence ~'LESS (-jl-) a. [OE *ecg*, OS *eggia*, OHG *ekka*, ON *egg* f. Gmc *agja* cogn. w. L *acies* edge]

ĕdge², v.t. & i. Sharpen (tool etc., also fig.); ~ *on*, =EGG² *on*; furnish with border, form border to; insinuate, push, (thing, oneself) *into, in, out, off,* etc., (v.i.) advance obliquely. [f. prec.]

ĕdge'ways, ~wise, (-jwăz, -jwīz), adv. With edge uppermost or foremost; (fig.) *get a word in* ~ (in talkative person's silent interval; (of two things) edge to edge. [-WAYS, -WISE]

ĕdg'ing, n. In vbl senses, esp. border, fringe; ~-*shears* (for trimming edges of lawn). [-ING¹]

ĕdg'y̆, a. Sharp-edged; (of painting) of too sharp outline; having one's nerves on edge, irritable. [-Y²]

ĕd'ible, a. & n. (Thing) fit to be eaten. Hence **ĕdĭBIL'ITY** n. [f. LL *edibilis* (*edere* eat, see -BLE)]

ĕd'ict, n. Order proclaimed by authority; *E~ of Nantes*, issued by Henry IV of France to grant toleration to Protestants, and revoked by Louis XIV. Hence **ĕdĭc'tAL** a. [ME; f. L *edictum* f. E(*dicere dict-* say) proclaim]

ĕd'ifice, n. Building (esp. large one; also fig.). [ME, f. OF *edifice* f. L *aedificium* (*aedis* temple + -*ficium* f. *facere* make)]

ĕd'ify, v.t. Benefit spiritually; improve morally (often iron.). So **ĕdĭFICA'TION** n. [ME, f. OF *edifier* f. L *aedificare* (as prec., see -FY)]

ĕd'it, v.t. Prepare an edition of (another's work); set in order for publication (material chiefly provided by others); garble, cook, (dispatches etc. in newspaper); act as editor of (paper etc.). [(1) f. F *éditer* f. L E(*dere dit-* = *dare* give) put out; (2) back formation f. EDITOR]

ĕdi'tion, n. Form in which a literary work is published (*library, cabinet, popular,* ~); whole number of copies of book, newspaper, etc., issued from same types & at same time (see also IMPRESSION); (fig.) production of the same type, person etc. resembling another (*a more charming* ~ *of her sister*). [f. F *édition* f. L *editionem* (as EDIT, see -ION)]

édition de luxe (see Ap.), n. Handsome edition. [F]

ĕdī'tĭŏ prīn'cĕps (-shĭŏ), n. First printed edition of a book. [L]

ĕd'itor, n. One who prepares the work of others for publication; one who conducts a newspaper or periodical. Hence ~SHIP, **ĕd'itRESS¹,** nn. [L (as EDIT, see -OR)]

ĕditōr'ial, a. & n. 1. Of an editor. 2. n. Newspaper article written by or under responsibility of the editor. Hence ~LY² adv. [-IAL]

ĕd'ŭc|āte, v.t. Bring up (young persons); give intellectual & moral training to; provide schooling for; train (person,

oneself, a faculty, *to* do); train (animals). Hence ~ABIL'ITY, ~ātOR, nn., ~ABLE, ~ātive, aa. [f. L *educare* conn. w. EDUCE, see -ATE³]

ĕdŭcā'tion, n. Bringing up (of the young); systematic instruction; course of this, as *classical, commercial, art,* ~; development of character or mental powers; training (of animals). Hence ~AL a., ~(al)IST(3) nn., ~alLY² adv., (-shon-). [f. F, or L *educatio* (as prec., see -ATION)]

ĕdūce', v.t. Bring out, develop, from latent or potential existence; (Chem.) disengage (substance) from a compound; infer (number, principle, *from* data). Hence **ĕdū'CIBLE** a. [f. L E(*ducere duct-* lead)]

ĕd'ŭct, n. (chem.). Body disengaged from another in which it previously existed; inference. [as prec.]

ĕdŭc'tion, n. Educing; (in steam-engine) ~-*pipe, -valve,* etc., EXHAUST¹-pipe etc. [f. L *eductio* (as prec., see -ION)]

ĕdŭl'cor|āte, v.t. Free from acid properties or from soluble particles, purify. Hence ~A'TION n. [f. med. L *edulcorare,* f. LL *dulcorare* (*dulcor* sweetness f. *dulcis*), see -ATE³]

Edward'ian (ĕdwŏrd-), a. & n. 1. Of the time of any of the Edwards, Kings of England; (esp.) characteristic of Edward VII's reign (1901-10). 2. n. Person belonging to this period. [-IAN]

-ee, suf. forming nn. expr. the person affected by the vbl action, corresp. to agent nn. in -*or,* prop. in legal terms on anal. of AF, as *appellor, appellee,* but extended to the indirect obj., as *lessee, vendee*; now also in non-techn. wds, & without corresp. -*or,* as *employee, payee*; & without consciousness of its meaning, as *bargee, absentee*; a few wds are adoptions f. mod. F -*é, -ié,* as *debauchee, refugee*. In *committee* (orig. a person), accent has changed with meaning. *Epopee* is not an instance; in *coatee, -ee* perh. = -Y³; in *settee, goatee, -ee* is unexplained. [AF -*é* of p.p. f. L -*atus*]

eel, n. A snake-like fish; (fig.) slippery creature; (pop.) minute animal found in vinegar & in sour paste; ‖~-BUCK⁴; ~-*spear* (for transfixing ~s). Hence ~'Y³ a. [OE *ǣl,* OS, OHG *ǣl,* ON *ǎll* f. Gmc *ǣlaz* of unkn. orig.]

e'en. See EVEN¹,³.

-eer, Anglicized form of F suf. -*ier* f. L -*arius* -ARY¹, expr. person concerned with; F -*ier* is retained in the less familiar wds (*muleteer* but *bombardier*); -*eer* is freely used for new nn., as *auctioneer, mountaineer,* often derog., as *sonneteer*. Vbs are also formed (*electioneer*) by back formation on *auctioneering* etc. See -IER.

e'er. See EVER.'

eer'|ie, -ry̆, a. Superstitiously timid; strange, weird. Hence ~ILY² adv., ~INESS n. [ME *eri,* of unkn. orig.]

ef-, pref. = EX-(1) before *f*.

efface', v.t. Rub out: (fig.) obliterate, wipe out; utterly surpass, eclipse; treat, regard, one*self* as unimportant. Hence ~ABLE a., ~MENT (-sm-) n. [f. F *effacer* f. *ef*- EF-+*face* FACE]

effect'¹, n. Result, consequence (*cause and* ~, causation); efficacy, as *of no* ~; combination of colour or form in picture etc., as *a pretty* ~; (pl.) property, as *personal* ~*s, no* ~*s* (written by banker on dishonoured cheque); *give* ~ *to, take* ~, make, become, operative; impression produced on spectator, hearer, etc., as *calculated for* ~; *bring to, carry into,* ~, accomplish; *in* ~, for practical purposes. Hence ~LESS a. [ME, f. OF, or L *effectus* -*ūs* f. EF(*ficere fect-* = *facere* make)]

effect'², v.t. Bring about, accomplish; ~ (take out) *a policy* (of insurance). [f. prec.]

effec'tive, a. & n. **1.** Having an effect; ~ *range* (of weapon), range within which it is ~; powerful in effect; striking; (of soldiers, sailors, etc.) fit for service; actual, existing. **2.** n. ~ soldier, ~ part of army. Hence ~LY² (-vl-) adv., ~NESS (-vn-) n. [f. OF (-*if*, -*ive*) or L *effectivus* (as EFFECT¹, see -IVE]

effec'tual, a. Answering its purpose; valid. Hence ~LY² adv., ~NESS n. [ME, f. OF *effectuel* f. med. L -*alis* (EFFECT¹, -AL)]

effec'tūāte, v.t. Bring to pass, accomplish. Hence ~A'TION n. [f. med. L *effectuare* (as EFFECT¹)]

effem'in|ate, a. Womanish, unmanly. Hence ~ACY n., ~ately² (-tl-) adv. [ME, f. L EF(*feminare* f. *femina* woman), see -ATE²]

effen'di, n. Turkish title of respect applied to government officials & members of learned professions. [f. Turk. *efendi* lord, corrupt. of Gk *authentēs* (see AUTHENTIC)]

eff'erent, a. (physiol.). Conveying outwards, discharging. [f. L EF(*ferre* carry), see -ENT]

effervĕs|ce', v.i. Give off bubbles of gas, bubble, (often fig. of persons); (of gas) issue in bubbles. Hence ~'CENCE, ~'CENCY, nn., ~'CENT a. [f. L EF(*fervescere* incept. of *fervēre* be hot)]

effēte', a. Exhausted, worn out; feeble, incapable. Hence ~NESS (-tn-) n. [f. L EF*fetus* worn out by breeding (*fetus*)]

effica'cious, a. (Of thing) producing, sure to produce, desired effect. Hence or cogn. ~LY² adv., ~NESS, effi'ic-ACY, nn. [f. L *efficax* (as foll., -ACIOUS)]

effi'cient (-shent), a. Productive of effect; (of persons) competent, capable; ~ CAUSE¹, that which makes a thing what it is. Hence or cogn. effi'ciENCY n. (also, Mech.) the ratio of useful work performed to the total energy expended, ~LY² adv. (-shen-). [ME, f. L *efficient-*, as EFFECT¹, see -ENT]

eff'igy, n. Portrait, image; *hang, burn,*

(person) *in* ~, hang, burn, his image. [f. L *effigies* (EF*fingere* fashion)]

efflores|ce', v.t. Burst out into flower (lit. & fig.); (Chem., of crystalline substance) turn to fine powder on exposure to air, (of salts) come to the surface & there crystallize, (of ground or wall) become covered with saline particles. So ~'CENCE n., ~'CENT a. [f. L EF(*florescere* FLOURISH)]

eff'luence (-lōō-), n. Flowing out (of light, electricity, etc., or fig.); what flows out. [foll., -ENCE]

eff'luent (-lōō-), a. & n. **1.** Flowing forth. **2.** n. Stream flowing from larger stream, lake, sewage tank, etc. [f. L EF(*fluere flux-* flow), see -ENT]

effluv'ium (-lōō-), n. (pl. -*ia*). Exhalation affecting lungs or sense of smell; (supposed) stream of minute particles emitted by magnet etc. [L, as prec.]

eff'lux, n. Flowing out (of liquid, air, gas; also fig.); that which flows out. Hence **efflu'xion** (-kshon) n. [f. L *effluxus* -*ūs* (as prec.)]

eff'ort, n. Strenuous exertion; (of oratory etc.) display of power; (colloq.) something accomplished involving concentration or special activity (*that's a pretty good* ~). [F, f. *efforcer* f. Rom. *EX(fortiare* f. *fortis* strong)]

eff'ortless, a. Making no effort, passive; (of skill etc.) without effort, easy. [-LESS]

effron'terÿ (-ŭnt-), n. Shameless audacity. [f. F *-erie* f. *effronté* f. Rom. *exfrontatus* f. LL EF(*frons -ntis* forehead) shameless; see -ATE², -ERY]

efful'g|ent, a. Radiant. Hence ~ENCE n., ~entLY² adv. [f. L EF(*fulgēre* shine), see -ENT]

effuse'¹ (-s), a. (Bot., of inflorescence) spreading loosely; (Conch.) with lips separated by groove. [as foll.]

effuse'² (-z), v.t. Pour forth (liquid, air, light, smell; also fig.). [ME, f. L EF(*fundere fus-* pour)]

effū'sion (-zhn), n. Pouring forth (lit. & fig.); unrestrained utterance (often contempt., of literary work). [ME, f. OF, or f. L *effusio* (as prec., see -ION)]

effū'sive, a. (Of speech or emotions) exuberant, demonstrative; (Geol., of an igneous rock) poured out when molten and later solidified. Hence ~LY² (-vl-) adv., ~NESS (-vn-) n. [as EFFUSE², see -IVE]

eft, n. Newt. [OE *efeta* NEWT, of unkn. orig.]

eftsoon(s)', adv. (arch.). Soon afterwards. [OE *eftsōna* (see AFT & SOON); -*s* = -ES]

egad', int. By God. [prob. orig. *aah +God*]

ēgălitār'ian, a. & n. **1.** Of, relating to, holding, the principle of the equality of mankind. **2.** ~ person. Hence ~ISM n. [f. F *égalitaire* f. *égal* equal]

Egēr'ia (ij-), n. A person's tutelary divinity. [name of a prophetic nymph of Roman legend, Numa's instructress]

egg[1], n. Spheroidal body produced by female of birds etc. esp. of domestic fowl, containing germ of a new individual; ADDLE, WIND[1], ~; *bad* ~, person, scheme, that comes to no good; *good* ~ (sl.), excellent person or thing (also as commendatory exclamation); *as sure as* ~*s is* ~*s*, undoubtedly; *teach your grandmother to suck* ~*s*, offer advice to persons more experienced than yourself; *have all your* ~*s in one basket*, risk all on a single venture;~ *& anchor, dart, tongue,* (Archit.) kinds of moulding; ~*-&-spoon race* (in which runners carry ~ in spoon); ~ *cleavage* (Biol.), process of cleavage in fertilized ~-shell; ~*-cup* (for holding ~ boiled in shell); ~*-dance*, dance blindfold among ~s, (fig.) intricate task; ~*-flip, -nog*, hot beer, cider, wine, etc., with ~s stirred in; *~-head* (sl.), intellectual; ~*-plant,* (fruit of), white-fruited *Solanum esculentum*; ~*-shell,* shell of ~, fragile thing (~*-shell china,* very thin kind); ~*-slice,* utensil for taking omelette from pan; ~*-spoon*, small spoon for eating boiled ~s; ~*-tooth*, protuberance on bill-sheath of embryo bird for cracking shell; ~*-whisk*, utensil for beating ~s. [ME *ey* f. OE *æg* (= OS, OHG *ei*) superseded by ME *eg* f. ON *egg*]

egg[2], v.t. Urge (person) *on* (*to* an act, *to* do). [f. ON *eggja* = EDGE v.]

egg'er, n. Kind of large moth common in Great Britain (also ~*-moth, oak* ~*-moth*). [prob. f. EGG[1] + -ER (owing to egg-like appearance of cocoon)]

ĕg'lantine, n. Sweetbriar. [ME, f. OF *eplantine* f. OF *aiglent* prob. f. L *acus* needle, see -LENT]

ĕg'ō, n. (metaphys.). The conscious thinking subject, opp. to the non-ego or object. [L, = I]

ĕgocĕn'tric, a. Centred in the ego; (loosely) self-centred, egoistic. [EGO + *centric* (CENTRE[1] + -IC), after *geocentric* etc.]

ĕg'ō|ĭsm, n. (Ethics) theory that treats self-interest as foundation of morality; systematic selfishness; self-opinionatedness; = foll. Hence ~ĭST n., ~ĭs'TIC(AL) aa., ~ĭs'tĭcalLy adv. [f. F *égoïsme* (as EGO, see -ISM)]

ĕg'ot|ĭsm, n. Too frequent use of 'I' & 'me'; practice of talking about oneself; self-conceit; selfishness. Hence ~ĭST n., ~ĭs'TIC(AL) aa., ~ĭs'tĭcalLy adv., ~ĭZE v.i. [f. EGO + -ISM; *-t-* perh. on F *idiotisme* etc.]

ĕgrē'gious (-jus), a. (Arch.) surpassing, (mod.) shocking, as ~ *folly, blunder, ass.* Hence ~LY[2] adv., ~NESS n. [f. L E(*gregius* f. *grex gregis* flock) lit. towering above the flock]

ĕg'rĕss, n. (Right of) going out; (Astron.) end of eclipse or transit; way out (lit. & fig.). [f. L *egressus -ūs* f. L E(*gredi gress-* = *gradi* step)]

ĕgrē'ssion (-shn), n. Going out or forth. [f. L *egressio* (as prec., see -ION)]

eg'rĕt (ēg- *or* ĕg-), n. Lesser white heron; feathery down on seeds of dandelion, thistle, etc. [ME; var. of AIGRETTE]

Egyp'tian (ĭjĭp'shn), a. & n. (Native) of Egypt; ||~*printing-type* (thick-stemmed); = GIPSY (obs.). [-IAN]

Egyptŏl|ī'ogў (-ŏ-), n. Study of Egyptian antiquities. So ~L'OGIST n. [-O-, -LOGY]

eh (ē), int. expr. inquiry or surprise, or inviting assent. [ME *ey*]

eid'er (ī-), n. A northern species of duck; ~ (*-down*), small soft feathers from breast of this (~*-down*, also, quilt stuffed with ~-down). [ult. f. Icel. *æðr*]

eid'ograph (ī-; -ahf), n. Instrument for enlarging or reducing drawings. [f. Gk *eidos* form + *graphō* write]

eidōl'on (ī-), n. (pl. *-ons, -a*). Spectre, phantom, cf. IDOL. [Gk, see IDOL]

eight (āt), a. & n. One more than seven (8, viii); (Skat.) figure of two adjacent circles; crew of ~ in rowing-boat; || *the* E~*s*, boat-races at Oxford & Cambridge between such crews; || *have one over the* ~ (sl.), get rather drunk. Hence **eighth**[2] (ătth) a. & n., ~h'LY[2] (ătth-) adv. [OE *eahta* OS, OHG *ahto*, ON *ătta*, Goth. *ah!au* f. Gmo *°ahtō-* cogn. w. L, Gk *oktō*]

eighteen' (āt-), a. & n; One more than seventeen (18, xviii); ~*mo*, = OCTODECIMO. Hence ~TH[2] a. & n. [OE *e(a)htatȳne, -tēne* (as prec., see -TEEN)]

eight'some (āt-), n. & a. ~ (*reel*), lively Scottish reel for eight dancers. [-SOME]

eight'ў (āt-), a. & n. Eight times ten (80, lxxx). Hence *eight'*IETH (āt-) a. & n. [OE *eahtatig* (as EIGHT + *-tig* -TY[2])]

eirēn'icŏn (ī-)ʒ n. Proposal tending to make peace. [Gk, neut. adj. (*eirēnē* peace, see -IC)]

eisteddfod (ăstĕdh'vod), n. (pl. ~*au*). Congress of Welsh bards; local gathering for musical competitions etc. [W, lit.= session f. *eistedd* sit]

eis wōōl (ī-), n. (Also *ice wool*) very fine glossy worsted wool of two-thread thickness. [G *eis* ice]

ei'ther (īdh-, ē-), adj., pron., & adv. (conj.). 1. Each of two, as *at* ~ *end was a lamp,* ~ *view is tenable,* ~ *is tenable*; one *.or* other of two, as *put the lamp at* ~ *end, there is no lamp at* ~ *end,* ~ *of you can go*. 2. adv. or conj. On one or other opposition, which way you will, as *he is* ~ *drunk or mad,* ~ *come in or go out,* (w. neg. or interrog.) any more than the other, as *if you do not go, I shall not* ~. [OE *ǣghwæther*, OHG *eogihwedar* f. WG *°aiwō gihwatharaz* ever each of two; cf. AYE, EACH, WHETHER]

ějăc'ŭl|āte, v.t. Utter suddenly (words or abs.); eject (fluids etc.) from the body. Hence ~A'TION n., ~ātORY a. [f. L E(*jaculari* f. *jaculum* javelin) dart]

ěječt'[1], v.t. Expel (*from* place, office, property), dispossess (tenant) by legal process; dart forth, emit. Hence or cogn. ĕjĕc'tion, ~ment, ĕjĕc'tor, nn. [f. L e(jicĕre ject- = jacĕre throw)]

ĕj'ĕct², n. Something inferred, not an actual nor a conceivable object of our own consciousness. [f. L ejectum neut. p.p. of ejicere (see prec.)]

ĕjĕc'tive, a. Tending to eject; pertaining to an eject. Hence ~ly² (-vl-) adv. [-ive]

ēke¹, v.t. ~ out: supplement (defective means etc. with); (improp.) contrive to make (livelihood) or support (existence). [OE *ēacan, OS ōkian, OHG ouhhōn, ON auka, Goth. aukan f. Gmc *aukan cogn. w. L augēre]

ēke², adv. (arch.). Also. [OE ēac, OS ōk, OHG ouh, ON, Goth. auk; of disputed orig., perh. cogn. w. prec.]

ĕkk'a, n. (Anglo-Ind.). Small one-horse Indian vehicle; similar cart drawn by bullock. [Hind.]

-el. See -le(1) & (2).

ĕlăb'orate¹, a. Carefully or minutely worked out; highly finished. Hence ~ly² (-tl-) adv., ~ness (-tn-) n. [f. L e(laborare f. labor work), see -ate²]

ĕlăb'or|āte², v.t. Produce by labour; work out (invention, theory, etc.) in detail; (of natural agencies) produce (substance etc.) from its elements or sources. Hence or cogn. ~a'tion n., ~ative a. [as prec., -ate³]

ĕlaeo-, comb. form of Gk elaion oil, as ~meter, instrument for determining purity of oils.

élan (see Ap.), n. Vivacity; impetuous rush. [F]

ĕl'and, n. S.-African antelope of heavy build. [Du., = elk]

ĕlăpse', v.i. (Of time) pass away. [f. L e(labi laps- glide)]

ĕlăs'tic (or -lah-), a. & n. 1. Spontaneously resuming its normal bulk or shape after contraction, dilatation, or distortion (of solids, liquids, & gases); springy; (of feelings or persons) buoyant; flexible, adaptable, as ~ conscience; ~-side boots or ~-sides, 19th-c. boots with ~ web at sides instead of buttons or laces. 2. n. ~ cord or string, usu. woven with india-rubber. Hence ĕlăs'tically adv., ĕlăsti'city n. [f. Gk elastikos impulsive (elaunō drive)]

ĕlāte', v.t., & a. 1. Inspirit, stimulate, (esp. in p.p.); make proud. 2. adj. (arch.). In high spirits, exultant, proud. So ĕlā'tion n. [ME, f. L e(ferre elat- raise]

ĕl'bow¹ (-ō), n. Outer part of joint between fore & upper arm; ~-shaped bend or corner; at one's ~, close at hand; lift one's ~, drink too much; up to the ~s, busily engaged in; out at ~s, (of coat) worn-out, (of person) poor; ~-grease, vigorous polishing, hard work; ~-room, plenty of room. [OE elnboga, OHG elinbogo, ON elnbogi f. Gmc *alino-bogan (see ell & bow¹)]

ĕl'bow² (-ō), v.t. & i. Thrust, jostle, (person, oneself, into, in, etc.; also intr.). [f. prec.]

ĕl'chee (-ĭ), n. Ambassador. [f. Turk. ilchi representative of a tribe (il)]

∥ ĕld, n. (arch., poet., dial.). Old age; the olden time. [OE eldo, OS eldī, OHG elti, ON elli f. Gmc *althī f. *althaz old]

ĕl'der¹, a. & n. 1. (The) senior (of relations, or of two indicated persons), as his ~ brother, which is the ~?; (Cards) ~ hand, first player; ∥ ~ brother of Trinity House, each of thirteen senior members of this corporation who sit as Nautical Assessors in navigation cases (usu. pl., ~ brethren); E~ statesman. 2. n. (Pl.) persons of greater age, as respect your ~s; person advanced in life; member of a senate; official in early Christian Church (= Gk presbuteros), & in some Protestant (esp. Presbyterian) churches, whence ~ship n. [OE eldra, comp. of old, see -er³]

ĕl'der², n. Low white-flowered tree; ~(-berry) wine (made from fruit of this). [OE ellærn, MLG ellern, elderne]

ĕl'derly, a. Getting old. [elder¹+-ly¹]

ĕl'dèst, a. First-born or oldest surviving (member of family, son, daughter, etc.). [OE eldest superl. of old, see -est]

El Dorad'o (ĕldorahd'ō), n. (pl. ~s). Fictitious country or city abounding in gold. [Sp., = the gilded]

ĕl'dritch, a. (Sc.). Weird, hideous. [orig. unkn.]

Elĕăt'ic (ĕl-), a. & n. 1. Relating to Elea, an ancient Greek city in S.W. Italy, or the school of philosophers who were born or lived there about the 6th c. B.C., esp. Zenophanes, Parmenides, & Zeno. 2. n. An ~ philosopher. [f. L Eleaticus f. Elea]

ĕlĕcămpāne', n. Plant with bitter aromatic leaves & root; sweetmeat flavoured with this. [corrupt. of med. L enula (for L inula) campana (prob. = of the fields)]

ĕlĕct'¹, a. Chosen; select, choice; (Theol.) chosen by God, as the ~; chosen to office etc., as bride ~. [ME, f. L e(ligere lect- = legere pick)]

ĕlĕct'², v.t. Choose (thing, to do); choose (person) by vote, as ~ a magistrate, ~ him to the magistracy, ~ him (to be) magistrate; (Theol., of God) choose (persons) ir preference to others for salvation. [as prec.]

ĕlĕc'tion, n. Choosing, esp. by vote; general ~ (of representatives, esp. members of House of Commons, throughout the country), ∥ by~ (of M.P. to fill vacancy); (Theol.) see prec. [ME, f. OF f. L electionem (as prec., see -ion)]

ĕlĕctioneer' (-shon-), v.i., & n. Busy oneself in political elections; (n.) one who ~s. [prec. +-eer]

ĕlĕc'tive, a. (Of official, office, authority) appointed by, filled up by, derived from, election; having power to elect; (Chem.) ~ affinity, tendency to combine with some substances rather than others. Hence ~ly² (-vl-) adv. [f. F électif -ive f. LL electivus (as elect¹, -ive)]

elěc′tor, n. One who has right of election (esp. of M.P.); (hist.) German Prince entitled to share in election of Emperor, Hence ~AL a., ~SHIP n. [ME; L (as ELECT[1], -OR)]

elěc′torate, n. Dignity, dominions, of German Elector; body of electors. [-ATE[1]]

elěc′trĕss, n. Female elector; wife of German Elector. [as prec. +-ESS[1]]

elěc′tric, a. & n. 1. Of, charged with, capable of developing, electricity; ~ blanket (heated by ~ current); ~ blue, steely blue; ~ chair (used in an electrocution); ~ eel, one able to give ~ shock; ~ light (produced by electricity); ~ shock, effect of sudden discharge of electricity; ~ storm, violent disturbance of the earth's electrical condition; ~ torch, portable ~ lamp operated by a dry battery in its holder. 2. n. Substance in which ~ force can be excited by friction. Hence **elěc′trICALLY** adv., **elěctrI′CIAN** (-shn) n. [f. mod. L electricus f. L f. Gk ēlektron amber, see -IC]

elěc′trical, a. Relating to electricity (rare in other senses of prec.). [-AL]

elěctri′cĭtў, n. 1. (Prop. static~) abnormal condition of the atoms or molecules of a body usu. due to an excess or deficiency of electrons; various kinds were formerly distinguished by the methods of production, as frictional ~ (by friction), galvanic ~ (by chemical action), thermal ~ (by heat), magnetic ~ (by magnetism), or by the substances in which they were produced, as vitreous ~ (in glass), resinous ~ (in resin); but only two kinds are now recognized in ordinary use, positive ~, a deficiency of electrons, and negative ~, an excess of electrons. 2. Movement of electrons or electrons moving along a conductor. 3. Science of static ~ or of electric currents. [-ITY]

elěctrĭficā′tion, n. Electrifying; conversion of steam railway into electric. [as foll., see -FICATION]

elěc′trĭfy, v.t. Charge (body) with electricity; subject (person etc.) to electric shock; convert (railways, transport, manufactures, etc.) to electric working; (fig.) startle, excite. [f. ELECTRIC + -FY]

elěc′trĭz|e, -**is|e** (-īz), v.t. = prec. Hence ~A′TION n. [as prec. +-IZE]

elěc′trō, n., & v.t., (colloq.). = ELECTRO-plate, type. [abbr.]

elěc′tro-, comb. form of Gk ēlektron, taken as meaning 'electricity'. Of, pertaining to, caused by, electricity, as: ~biol′ogy, science of the electrical phenomena of living beings; ~card′iogram, record of the sequence of electrical waves generated at each heartbeat, used in diagnosis of heart disorders, recorded by an ~card′iograph; ~chem′istry, electricity as applied to chemistry; ~dynăm′ics, dynamics of electricity; ~kinět′ics, science of electricity in motion; ~logy (-ŏl[2]), electric

science; ~lўsis (-ŏl[2]), chemical decomposition by electric action, science of this, (Surg.) breaking up of tumours or calculi by electric agency; ~lўse (-z), decompose thus; ~lўte, any liquid or solution chemically changed by passage of electric current, any substance forming such a solution with water or another liquid; ~magnět′ic, having both electrical and magnetic character or effects (applied esp. to waves or radiations which travel with the same velocity as light); ~măg′netism production of magnetism by electric current; ~meter (-ŏm[2]), instrument measuring electricity; ~mō′tion, motion of electric current, mechanical motion produced by electricity; ~mōt′ive, producing, tending to produce, an electric current; ~mōt′or, machine for using electricity as motive power; ~něg′ative, ~pos′itive, of negative, positive, electricity; ~pathy (-ŏp[2]), electrical treatment of disease; ~phŏre, ~phorus (-ŏf[2]), instrument for generating statical electricity by induction; ~plāte, (v.t.) coat with silver by ~lysis, (n.) ware thus produced; ~scōpe, instrument indicating presence or quality of electricity; ~stăt′ics, science of statical electricity; ~thě′rapy, cure of diseases by electrical treatment (hence ~thě′rapist); ~therm′al, relating to heat electrically derived; ~tonus (-ōt[2]), condition of motor nerve under electric current; ~tўpe, (n.) model, copy, formed by deposition of copper on a mould by electrolytic action, esp. for printing, (v.t.) copy thus.

elěctrocū′tion, n. Killing by electricity (as capital punishment); (transf.) death caused in any way by electricity. Hence **elěc′trocūte** v.t. [f. prec., suggested by execution]

elěc′trōde, n. Conductor through which electricity enters or leaves an electrolyte, gas, vacuum, or other medium. [ELECTRO- + Gk hodos way]

elěctrolier′, n. Cluster of electric lamps. [f. ELECTRO- on chandelier]

elěc′trŏn, n. (phys., chem.). Indivisible unit of negative electricity and one of the fundamental constituents of matter, normally rotating (in numbers constant for each element) about the positive nucleus of every atom. Hence **elěctrŏn′IC** a., also n. pl., branch of physics and technology dealing with behaviour of ~s esp. in a vacuum, e.g. in radio valves, X-ray tubes, etc. [f. ELECTRO- or ELECTRIC, with Gk -on appended]

elěc′trum, n. Alloy of silver & gold used by the ancients; (Mineral.) native argentiferous gold ore. [L, f. Gk ēlektron amber, ~]

elěc′tūarў, n. Medicinal powder etc. mixed with honey or syrup. [ME, f. LL electuarium perh. corrupt. of Gk ekleikton (ekleikhō lick out)]

elēěmŏs′ўnarў (or -z-), a. Of, dependent

on, alms; charitable; gratuitous. [f. med. L *eleemosynarius* (as ALMS, see -ARY[1])]

ĕl'ĕgant, a. & n. (Of movements, style, author, manners) graceful; tasteful; refined; (of modes of life etc.) of refined luxury; (vulg.) excellent; (n.) person with pretensions to taste & fashion. Hence or cogn. **ĕl'ĕgANCE** n., **~LY**[2] adv. [f. F *élégant* or L *elegant-*, cf. ELECT[1]]

ĕlĕgī'ăc, a. & n. 1. (Of metre) suited to elegies, esp. ~ *couplet* (usu. Gk or Lat.) dactylic hexameter & pentameter: mournful. 2. n. pl. ~ verses. [f. LL f. Gk *elegeiakos* (as ELEGY, see -AC)]

ĕl'ĕgīze, -ise (-iz), v.i. & t. Write an elegy (*upon*); write in mournful strain; write an elegy upon. [-IZE]

ĕl'ĕgȳ, n. Song of lamentation, esp. for the dead (often vaguely used of other poems); poem in elegiac metre. [f. F *élégie* f. L f. Gk *elegeia* (*elegos* mournful poem)]

ĕl'ĕment, n. 1. Component part, as *reduced to its* ~*s*, analysed, *the* ~*s of national wealth, there was an* ~ *of cant, cant was a notable* ~, *in his style*. 2. (chem.). Any of the substances that cannot be resolved by chemical means into simpler substances. 3. Any of *the four* ~*s*, viz. earth, water, air, fire (hist.); one of these as a being's abode or sphere, as (usu. fig.) *in, out, of, his* ~. 4. Atmospheric agencies, as *war of the* ~*s*. 5. (electr.). Resistance wire in an electric heater; electrode. 6. pl. Rudiments of learning (i.e. the A B C) or of an art or science; *Euclid's E* ~*s* (of Geometry). [ME, f. OF, f. L *elementum*]

ĕlĕmĕn'tal, a. & n. 1. Of the four elements; of the powers of nature, as ~ *worship*; comparable to these, as ~ *grandeur, tumult*; uncompounded; essential. 2. n. (theosoph.). Spirit of earth, air, etc. [prec. +-AL]

ĕlĕmĕn'tar|ў, a. Rudimentary, introductory; (Chem.) not decomposable. Hence ~ĬLY[2] adv., ~ĬNESS n. [f. L *elementarius* (as ELEMENT, see -ARY[1])]

ĕl'ĕmī, n. A stimulant resin used in ointments, varnish, etc. [= F *élémi*, Sp. *elemi*, f. Arab. *al-lami*]

ĕlĕn'chus (-ngk-), n. (pl. *-chi*). Logical refutation; *Socratic* ~, mode of eliciting truth by short question & answer. [L, f. Gk *elegkhos*]

ĕlĕnc'tic (-ngk-), a. Of, given to, refutation or cross-examination. [f. Gk *elegktikos* (*elegkhō* refute, as prec., see -IC)]

ĕl'ĕphant, n. 1. Huge four-footed pachyderm with proboscis & long curved ivory tusks; *white* ~, burdensome possession (from cost of maintenance). 2. Size of paper (28 × 23 in.; *double* ~, 40 × 26½). Hence **ĕlĕphăn'toID** a. [ME *oli-, ele-faunte* f. OF *oli-, elefant*, f. L *elephan-tus, -ntem* (nom. *-phas*), f. Gk *elephas -antos*]

ĕlĕphănti'asis, n. Skin disease causing

part affected to resemble elephant's hide. [L f. Gk (as prec., see -ASIS)]

ĕlĕphăn'tine, a. Of elephants; ~ *epoch* (when large pachydermata abounded); clumsy, unwieldy, as ~ *movements, humour, task*. [f. L f. Gk *elephantinos* (as prec., -INE[2])]

Eleusin'ian (ŏ-), a. ~ *mysteries* (of Demeter, celebrated at Eleusis in Attica). [f. L f. Gk *Eleusinios* (*Eleusis -inos* + -AN]

ĕleuth'ero- in comb. = Gk *eleutheros* free, as ~*mān'ia*, mad zeal for freedom, ~*phŷll'ous*, with distinct leaves.

ĕl'ĕvāt|e, v.t. Lift up; hold up (the Host) for adoration; raise (one's eyes, voice, hopes); raise axis of (gun); exalt in rank etc.; raise morally or intellectually (aims, style; esp. in p.p.); (p.p., colloq.) slightly drunk. Hence ~ORY a. [f. L E(*levare* lift f. *levis* light), see -ATE[3]]

ĕlĕvā'tion, n. Elevating, being elevated, (in all senses); angle (esp. of gun) with the horizontal; height above given (esp. sea) level; drawing made in projection on vertical plane, flat drawing of front, side, or back, of house etc.; grandeur, dignity. [f. OF, or L *elevatio* (as prec., see -ATION)]

ĕl'ĕvātor, n. Person, thing, device, that elevates; muscle that raises limb etc.; machine for hoisting grain etc.; *lift. [L (as prec., see -OR)]

ĕlĕv'en, a. & n. One more than ten (11, xi, XI); *an* ~, ~ *persons forming side at cricket etc.; the E~* (disciples, without Judas); ||~*s(es)* n. (colloq.), light refreshment about 11 a.m. So ~TH[3] a. & n. (*the* ~*th* HOUR). [OE *endleofon*, OS *elleban*, OHG *einlif*, ON *ellifu*, Goth. *ainlif* f. Gmc *ainaz* ONE + *lif* (perh. = one *left* over (ten))]

ĕlf, n. (pl. *elves*). (Teut. Myth.) a supernatural being; mischievous creature; dwarf; little creature; ~*boll*, flint arrow-head; ~*lock*, tangled mass of hair; ~*struck*, bewitched. Hence **ĕl'fISH**[1], **ĕl'v**-ISH[1], aa. [OE *elf* (= MHG *elbe*) & *ælf* = OS *alf*, MHG *alp*, ON *dlfr* f. Gmc *albh-*]

ĕl'fin, a. & n. Of elves, elfish; (n.) dwarf, child. [f. prec., *-in* unexpl.]

ĕli'cit, v.t. Draw forth (what is latent, usu. fig.); educe (truths *from* data), draw out, evoke, (admission, answer *from* person). [f. L E(*licere licit-* for *lacere* entice)]

ĕlīde', v.t. Omit (vowel, syllable) in pronunciation. [f. L E(*lidere lis-* = *laedere* dash)]

ĕl'igi|ble, a. Fit to be chosen (*for* office etc.); desirable, suitable. Hence ~BIL'ITY n., ~bLY[1] adv. [f. F *éligible* or LL *eligibilis* (ELECT[1], -BLE)]

ĕlim'in|āte, v.t. Remove, get rid of; (Physiol., Chem.) expel (waste matter *from* tissues, substance *from* a compound); ignore (part of question etc.); (Alg.) get rid of (quantities) from equation; (improp.) extract (desired element from compound, also fig.). So ~ABLE a., ~A'TION n., ~ātor n., (esp.) apparatus enabling a wireless set to use current from electric main, so ~ating any or all of its batteries. [f. L E(*liminare* f. *limen -minis* threshold), see -ATE³]

éli'sion (-zhn), n. Suppression of vowel or syllable in pronouncing, (rarely) of passage in book etc. [f. LL *elisio* (as ELIDE, see -ION)]

élite (ēlēt'), n. *The* choice part, *the* best, (*of*). [F]

élix'ir (-er), n. Alchemist's preparation designed to change metals into gold or (also ~ *of life*) to prolong life indefinitely; sovereign remedy; PAREGORIC ~. [ME, f. med. L, f. Arab. *aliksir* the elixir (*iksir* prob. f. late Gk *xērion* desiccative powder)]

Elizabēth'an (I-), a. & n. (Person, writer) of the time of Queen Elizabeth I. [-AN]

elk, n. Large animal of the deer kind found in N. Europe and (also *moose*) N. America; species of deer & antelope; ~*-hound*, large Scandinavian shaggy-coated hunting dog. [15th c. *elke* prob. repr. OE *elh, eolh*; further hist. obsc.]

ell, n. Measure of length (*English* ~, = 45 in.; now obs. as measure); *give him an inch* (a little) *& he'll take an* ~ (much). [OE *eln*, OHG *elina*, ON *öln*, Goth. *aleina* f. Gmc **alinā* cogn. w. L *ulna*]

ellipse'¹, n. Regular oval; figure produced when a cone is cut by a plane making smaller angle with the base than the side of the cone makes, whence **ellipti'city** n. — foll. Hence or cogn. **ellip'tic(al¹)** aa., -**ically¹** adv. [f. Gk *elleipsis* f. *elleipō* come short (*en* in + *leipō* leave)]

ellip'sis, ellipse'², n. (pl. -*pses*, pron. -*psēz*). Omission from sentence of words needed to complete construction or sense. So **ellip'tical²** a., -**ically²** adv. [as prec.; cf. ECLIPSE¹]

ellip'soid, n. Solid of which all plane sections through one axis are ellipses & through the other ellipses or circles. [-OID]

elm, n. Tree with rough doubly serrated leaves. Hence ~'Y² a. [OE, OHG *elm*, cogn. w. ON *almr*, L *ulmus*]

El'mō (ĕ-), n. *St* ~, pop. name for St Peter Gonzalez (d. 1246), Spanish Dominican preacher who became patron saint of seamen; *St* ~'s *fire*, CORPOSANT, interpreted as a sign of his protection, though occas. of impending disaster (*dead-fire*).

elocu'tion (ē- or ĕ-), n. Manner, style, art, of oral delivery. Hence ~ARY¹ a., ~IST(3) n., (-shon-). [f. L *elocutio* f. E(*loqui locut-* speak), see -ION]

éloge (ĕlōzh'), n. Discourse in honour of deceased person (esp. member of French Academy, pronounced by his successor). [F]

Elō'hist (ĕ-), n. Author(s) of the *elohistic* parts of the Hexateuch, marked by use

of *Elohim* for *Yahveh* (Jehovah). [f. Heb. *elohim* God + -IST]

el'ongate (-ngg-), v.t. & i., & a. 1. (-āt). Lengthen, prolong; (Bot.) be of slender or tapering form. 2.. adj. (-at; Bot., Zool.) long, slender, tapering. [f. LL E(*longare* f. *longus* long), see -ATE³,²]

elŏngā'tion (-ngg-), n. Lengthening; the part (of line etc.) produced; (Astron.) angular distance of planet from sun. [f. LL *elongatio* (as prec., see -ATION)]

élōpe', v.i. (Of woman) run away from husband or home (*with* paramour, lover); abscond. Hence ~MENT (-pm-) n. [AF *aloper* perh. f. ME **alope* p.p. of **aleapen* (*a-* = *and-* against + LEAP), cf. G *entlaufen* run away]

el'oquence, n. Fluent, forcible, & apt use of language; rhetoric. So **él'oquent** a., **él'oquently²** adv. [ME, f. OF f. L *eloquentia* f. E(*loqui* speak), see -ENCE]

élse, adv. (Following indef. or interrog. pron.) besides, in addition, as *any one, anybody, anything,* ~, *who* ~ *? who* ~'*s ?, whose* ~ *?;* (same constr.) instead, as *what — could I say ?;* otherwise, if not, as *run,* (or) ~ *you will be late;* ~'*where,* in, to, some other place. [OE, OHG *elles,* OSw. *äljes* gen. sing. cogn. w. Goth. *aljis* other, L *alius*]

elu'cid|āte (-ōō-, -ū-), v.t. Throw light on, explain. Hence ~A'TION, ~ātor, nn., ~ātive, ~ātory, aa. [f. LL E(*lucidare* f. *lucidus* bright f. *lux lucis* light)]

élude' (-ōōd, -ūd), v.t. Escape adroitly from (blow, danger, difficulty, person's grasp, person, inquiry, observation); avoid compliance with (law, request) or fulfilment of (obligation); escape from, baffle, (the understanding). So **elu'sion** (-lōōzhn *or* -lū-), **elus'iveness,** nn., **elus'ive, elus'ory,** aa., **elus'ively²** adv. (-lōō- *or* -lū-). [f. L E(*ludere lus-* play)]

él'van, n. Hard rock of igneous origin; broad vein or dyke of this. [perh. f. Corn. *elven* spark]

él'ver, n. A young eel. [var. of *eel*-FARE² = brood of young eels]

elvish. See ELF.

Élysée (ālēzā'), n. Official residence of French President. [F]

Elys'i|um (ĭlĭz-), n. (Gk Myth.) abode of the blessed after death; place, state, of ideal happiness. Hence ~AN a. [f. L f. Gk *Elusion* (ē-) (*pedion* plain)]

él'ytron, n. (pl. -*ra*). Outer hard wing-case of coleopterous insect; the vagina. [f. Gk *elutron* sheath (*eluō* roll round)]

El'zevir (ĕ-; -er), a. & n. (Book) printed by Elzevier family at Amsterdam, The Hague, etc. (1592–1680); a printing type.

ĕm, n. The letter M; (Typog.) unit for measuring amount of printed matter in line.

'em pron. (colloq.). Them. [orig. a form of ME *hem*, dat. & acc. 3rd pers. pl.; now regarded as abbr. of *them*]

em-, pref. = EN- before *b, p*, & (freq.) *m*.

Nearly all E wds with this pref. have (or formerly have. had) alternative forms in IM-.

ēmā′ci̱|āte (-shĭ-), v.t. Make lean, waste, (esp. in p.p.); impoverish (soil). So **~A′TION** (-sĭ-) n. [f. L E(*maciare* f. *macies* leanness), see -ATE³]

ĕm′anāte, v.i. Issue, originate, (*from* source, person, etc.); (of gases, light, etc.) proceed, issue, (*from*). [f. L E(*manare* flow), see -ATE³]

ĕmanā′tion, n. Issuing (*from*); thing proceeding from a source (esp. fig., of virtues, qualities, moral powers); person, thing, proceeding from the Divine Essence. So **ĕm′anāti̱ve** a. [f. LL *emanatio* (as prec., see -ATION)]

ēmăn′ci̱păt|e, v.t. (Rom. Law) release (child, wife) from power of *pater familias*; free from legal, social, political, intellectual, or moral restraint. Hence **~OR** n., **~ORY** a. [f. L E(*mancipare* f. *manceps* purchaser f. *manus* hand + *capere* take), -ATE³]

ēmăncipā′tion, n. Setting free, esp. from slavery or from legal disabilities, whence **~IST** (-shon-) n.; setting free, freedom, from intellectual or moral fetters. [f. L *emancipatio* (prec. -ATION)]

ēmăn′ci̱pist, n. (Austral.; hist.). Ex-convict who has served his term. [f. EMANCIPATE + -IST]

ēmăs′cūlate¹, a. Castrated; effeminate. [f. L E(*masculare* f. *masculus* dim. of *mas* male), see -ATE²]

ēmăs′cū̱l|āte², v.t. Castrate; weaken, make effeminate; impoverish (language); weaken (literary composition) by excisions. Hence **~A′TION** n., **~āti̱ve**, **~āto̱ry**, aa. [as prec., see -ATE³]

ĕmbalm′ (-ahm), v.t. Preserve (corpse) from decay orig. with spices, now by means of arterial injection; preserve from oblivion; endue with balmy fragrance. Hence **~MENT** (-ahm-m-) n. [ME *embaume* f. OF EM(*baumer*, as BALM)]

ĕmbănk′, v.t. Shut in, confine, (river etc.) by banks, raised stone structure, etc. Hence **~MENT** n., (also) structure of earth etc. to carry a railway, road, etc. [EM-]

ĕmbärg′ō, n. (pl. **~es**), & v.t. **1.** Order forbidding ships of a foreign power to enter, or any ships to leave, the country's ports; suspension of (a branch of) commerce, as *be under*, *lay on*, *an* **~**; impediment. **2.** v.t. Lay (ships, trade) under **~**; seize (ship, goods) for State service. [Sp., f. *embargar* f. Rom. *IM-barricare* (*barra* BAR¹)]

ĕmbärk′, v.t. & i. Put, go, on board ship (*for* destination), whence **ĕmbärkA′TION** n.; engage (*in*, *upon*, undertaking, war, etc.). [f. F *embarquer* f. en EM- + *barque* BARK³]

embarras de choix*, *de richesse (ahn-bahrah′ de shwah′, de rēshēs′), n. More alternatives, wealth, than one knows how to deal with. [F]

ĕmbă′rrass, v.t. Encumber, impede; (p.p.) encumbered with debts; complicate (question etc.); perplex. Hence **~ing̱LY²** adv., **~MENT** n. [f. F *embarrasser* f. Sp. *embarazar* (EM-, BAR²)]

ĕm′bassy̱, n. Ambassador's function or office; his residence; deputation to a sovereign etc. [f. OF *ambassee* f. med. L *ambasciata* (LL *ambascia* order. duty), f. Rom. *ambactiare* see AMBASSADOR]

ĕmbăt′tle¹, v.t. Set (army) in battle array. [ME, f. OF EM(*bataillier* f. *bataille* BATTLE)]

ĕmbăt′tle², v.t. Furnish (building, wall) with battlements. [ME, f. EM- + OF *bataillier* (-*eill*-), see BATTLEMENT]

ĕmbay′, v.t. Lay (vessel) within a bay; (of wind) force (vessel) into a bay; enclose as in a bay, shut in. Hence **~MENT** n. [EM-]

ĕmbĕd′, im-, v.t. (-dd-). Fix firmly in surrounding mass (esp. in p.p.); (of the mass) surround thus. [EM-]

ĕmbĕll′ish, v.t. Beautify, adorn; heighten (narrative) with fictitious additions. Hence **~MENT** n. [ME, f. OF EM(*bellir* f. *bel* f. L *bellus* handsome), see -ISH²]

ĕm′ber¹, n. (usu. pl.). Small piece of live coal or wood in dying fire (& fig.). [OE *æmerge*, OHG *eimuria* pyre, ON *eimyrja* embers; -b- as in *slumber*]

ĕm′ber², a. **~** *days*, days of fasting and prayer, the Wed., Fri., & Sat., after (1) 1st Sun. in Lent, (2) Whitsunday, (3) Holy Cross Day (Sep. 14), and (4) St Lucia's day (Dec. 13). [OE *ymbren* n. perh. f. *ymbryne* period (*ymb* about + *ryne* course)]

ĕm′ber³, n. (Usu. **~**-*goose*, -*diver*) an Orkney sea-fowl, the loon. [f. Norw. *emmer*]

ĕmbĕz′zle, v.t. Divert (money etc., also abs.) fraudulently to one's own use. Hence **~MENT** (-zelm-) n. [f. AF *enbesiler* f. OF *besillier* maltreat, ravage, of unkn. orig.]

ĕmbitt′er, v.t. Make bitter (fig.); aggravate (evil); exasperate (person, feeling). Hence **~MENT** n. [EM-]

ĕmblāz′on, v.t. Portray conspicuously, as on heraldic shield; adorn (shield) with heraldic devices (also fig.); celebrate, extol. Hence **~MENT** n. [EM-]

ĕmblāz′onry̱, n. = BLAZONRY. [EM-]

ĕm′blĕm, n., & v.t. **1.** Symbol, typical representation; (arch.) pictorial parable; (of person) type (of a quality); heraldic device. **2.** v.t. Symbolize, show forth by **~**. [(vb f. n.) f. L f. Gk *emblēma* -*matos* insertion f. EM(*ballō* throw)]

ĕmblĕmăt′ic(al), aa. Serving as a type (*of*). Hence **ĕmblĕmăt′ica̱LLY²** adv. [prec., -IC]

ĕmblĕm′atist, n. Maker of emblems or of allegories. [as prec. + -IST]

ĕmblĕm′atize, -ise (-īz), v.t. Serve as emblem of; represent by an emblem. [as prec. + -IZE]

ĕm′blèment, n. (legal; usu. pl.). Profits

of sown land; natural products of soil. [f. OF *emblaement* f. *emblaer* f. med. L IMB*ladare* sow with wheat (*bladum*), see -MENT]

embŏd'|ȳ, v.t. Clothe (spirit) with body; give concrete form to (ideas etc.); express tangibly (principles *in* actions etc.); (of things) be an expression of (ideas etc.); form into a body; include, comprise. Hence ~iMENT n. [EM-]

embŏg', v.t. (-gg-). Plunge into, hamper in, a bog (lit. & fig.). [EM-]

embŏl'den, v.t. Make bold, encourage (often *to* do). [EM- + BOLD + -EN⁶]

ĕm'bolism, n. Obstruction of artery etc. by clot of blood etc., esp. as cause of paralysis. [14th c. 'intercalation' f. LL f. Gk *embolismus*; in medical sense f. *embolus* (L f. Gk 'peg', 'stopper') + -ISM]

embonpoint (see Ap.), n. Plumpness (chiefly of women; usu. euphem.). [F, f. phr. *en bon point* in good condition]

embos'om (-ŏŏz-), v.t. Embrace; (p.p.) enclosed *in*, surrounded *with*, (trees, hills, etc.). [EM-]

embŏss', v.t. Carve, mould, in relief; cause figures etc. to stand out on (surface); make protuberant. Hence ~MENT n. [ME; prob. f. OF *EMbocer (see ROSS¹)]

embouchure (see Ap.), n. Mouth of river; opening of valley; (Mus.) part of musical instrument applied to mouth, mode of applying this. [F]

embow'el, v.t. (-ll-). Remove the bowels from (body). [f. OF ENboweler for *esboueler (es- = EX- + *bouel BOWEL)]

embow'er, v.t. Enclose as in bower. [EM-]

embrāce', v.t., & n. 1. Fold (person etc.; in pl. abs. = ~ one another) in the arms, usu. as sign of affection; clasp, enclose; accept eagerly (offer, opportunity, etc.); adopt (course of action, doctrine, party, cause); (of things) include, comprise; (of persons) comprise (thing *in* a formula, report, etc.); take in with eye or mind. 2. n. Folding in the arms, (euphem.) sexual intercourse. Hence ~ABLE a., ~MENT (-sm-) n. [ME; (n.: f. vb) f. OF EM(*bracer* f. L *bracchium* arm]

embranch'ment (-ah-), n. Branching out (of arm of river etc.). [EM- + BRANCH n. + -MENT]

embrăng'le (-nggl), *im*-, v.t. Entangle, confuse. Hence ~MENT (-nggelm-) n. [EM- + obs. *brangle*]

embrā'sure (-zher; *also* ĕmbrazhoor'), n. Bevelling off of wall at sides of door or window, splaying; opening in parapet for gun, widening from within. [F, f. *embraser* splay, of unkn. orig.]

ĕm'brocāte, v.t. Bathe, foment, (limb etc.) to mitigate disease. [f. LL *embrocare* f. *embrocha* f. Gk *embrokhē* f. EM(*brekhō* wet)]

embrocā'tion, n. Liquid used for rubbing affected part. [as prec., see -ATION]

embroid'er, v.t. Ornament (cloth etc.,

or abs.) with needlework; embellish (narrative) with fictitious additions. [ME, f. AF *enbrouder* = OF *brouder* whence *broider*; -er perh. after foll.]

embroid'er|ȳ, n. Embroidering; embroidered work; adventitious ornament. [ME, f. AF *enbrouderie* (prec., -ERY)]

embroil', v.t. Bring (affairs, narrative, etc.) into state of confusion; involve (person) in hostility (*with* another). Hence ~MENT n. [f. F EM(*brouiller*, see BROIL¹)]

embrown', v.t. Make brown. [EM-]

ĕm'bryŏ, n. & a. (pl. -os). 1. Offspring of animal before birth (or emergence from egg); thing in rudimentary stage; *in* ~, undeveloped. 2. adj. Undeveloped. Hence **ĕmbryŏn'ic** a. [LL *embryo* -*onis* erron. f. Gk EM(*bruōn* f. *bruō* swell, grow)]

ĕmbryŏ- in comb. = prec., as ~*ctony* (-ŏk⁴-), destruction of foetus in womb, ~*gĕn'esis*, formation of embryo, ~*logy* (-ŏl⁴-), science of the embryo, ~*tomy* (-ŏt⁴-), cutting up of foetus in womb.

‖ **ĕmbŭs'**, v.t. & i. (mil. etc.; -ss-). Put (men, stores) or get into motor vehicles. [EM- + BUS, after *entrain*]

emĕnd', v.t. (Seek to) remove errors from (text of book etc.). .Hence **ĕmĕndā'TION, ĕm'ĕndātor**, nn., ~**atORY** a. [f. L E(*mendare* f. *menda* fault)]

ĕm'erald, n. Bright-green precious stone; colour of this; size of TYPE; *E~ Isle*, Ireland. Hence ~INE¹ a. [ME, f. OF *emeraude* f. com.-Rom. *smaralda f. L f. Gk *smaragdos*]

emĕrge', v.i. Come up out of a liquid; come into view (*from* enclosed space etc.); issue (*from* state of suffering etc.); (of facts etc.) come out as result of inquiry; (of question, difficulty, etc.) crop up. So **emĕr'gENCE** n., **emĕr'gENT** a. [f. L E(*mergere mers*- dip)]

emĕr'genc|ȳ, n. Sudden juncture demanding immediate action; ~*y door, exit,* etc., for use in ~*ies* only, e.g., in case of fire. [f. LL *emergentia* (as prec., see -ENCY)]

emē'ritus, a. Honourably discharged from service, as ~ *professor* (retired). [L, p.p. of E(*merēri* earn)]

ĕm'erŏds, n. pl. (bibl.). = HAEMORRHOIDS.

emĕr'sion (-shn), n. Emerging; .reappearance of sun, moon, star, after eclipse or occultation. [f. LL *emersio* (EMERGE, -ION)]

ĕm'erȳ, n. Coarse corundum used for polishing metal, stones, etc.; ~*-cloth, -paper, -wheel* (covered with ~ powder). [f. F *émeri*(l) f. Rom. *smericulum* f. Gk *smēris* polishing powder]

emĕt'ic, a. & n. (Medicine) that causes vomiting (also fig.). [f. LL f. Gk *emetikos* (*emeō* vomit, see -ETIC)]

emeute (see Ap.), n. Popular rising. [F]

ĕm'igrāte, v.i. & t. Leave one country to settle in another; (colloq.) change one's place of abode; (v.t.) assist (person) to emigrate. So ~ANT a. & n., ~A'TION n., ~ātORY a. [f. L E(*migrare* MIGRATE)]

émigré (ĕm'ĭgrā), n. French emigrant, esp. Royalist who fled at French Revolution. [F]

ĕm'inence, n. **1.** Rising ground. **2.** Distinguished superiority (social, intellectual, etc.); (*E~*) cardinal's title. [f. L *eminentia* (as EMINENT, see -ENCE)]

éminence grise (ā'mĕnahŭs grēz'), n. Confidential agent, esp. one who exercises power unofficially (applied orig. to Cardinal Richelieu's private secretary). [F, = grey cardinal]

ĕm'inent, a. Exalted, distinguished; ~ DOMAIN; (of qualities) remarkable in degree, whence ~LY² adv. [f. L *eminēre* jut; see -ENT]

ĕmir' (-ēr), n. Saracen or Arab prince or governor; descendant of Mohammed. [f. F *émir* f. Sp. *emir* f. Arab. *amir* AMEER]

ĕm'issarў, n. Person sent on (usu.) an odious or underhand mission. [f. L *emissarius* (as EMIT, see -ARY¹)]

ĕmi'ssion (-shn), n. Giving off or out (*of* light, heat, smell, etc.); thing thus given out; ~ *theory* (that light is ~ of streams of imponderable particles from luminous bodies). So **ĕmiss'IVE** a. [f. L *emissio* (as foll., see -ION)]

ĕmit', v.t. (-tt-). Give out, send forth, (stream, light, heat, sound, opinion, paper currency, etc.). [f. L E(*mittere miss-* send)]

ĕmm'ĕt, n. (dial.). Ant. [OE; see ANT]

ĕmŏll'ient (-lye-), a. & n. (Application) that softens living animal textures (also fig.). [f. L E(*mollire* f. *mollis* soft), see -ENT]

ĕmŏl'ūment, n. Profit from office or employment, salary. [ME, f. OF, or f. L *ēmŏlumentum, ēmŏli-*, f. E(*mōlere* grind out), -MENT]

ĕmō'tion, n. Agitation of mind, feeling; excited mental state. Hence ~LESS a. [F, f. *émouvoir*, after *mouvoir* MOVE, *motion* MOTION]

ĕmō'tional (-shon-), a. Of the emotions; liable to emotion, whence ~ISM(1), ~IST(2), ~ITY (-shonăl'-), nn., ~LY² adv. [prec. + -AL]

ĕmōt'ive, a. Of, tending to excite, emotion. Hence ~LY² (-vl-) adv. [f. L *emovēre*, see EMOTION, -IVE]

ĕmpăn'el, ĭm-, v.t. (-ll-). Enter on panel, enrol, (jury). [f. AF EM(*paneller* PANEL)]

ĕm'pathў, n. (psych.). The power of projecting one's personality into (and so fully comprehending) the object of contemplation. [rendering of G *einfühlung* (*ein* in + *fühlung* feeling) after Gk *empatheia*]

ĕm'peror, n. (fem. **ĕm'prĕss**). Sovereign of Roman, Western, or Eastern Empire; head of Holy Roman Empire; sovereign (title superior in dignity to king); ~ *penguin*, largest known species of penguin of the Antarctic; *purple* ~, kind of butterfly. Hence ~SHIP n. [ME, f. OF *emperere,*

-pereor, f. L *imperator, -orem*, f. IM(*perare* = *parare* prepare, order) command, see -OR]

ĕm'phasis, n. Stress laid on word(s) to indicate special significance; vigour, intensity, of expression, feeling, action, etc.; importance assigned to a thing; prominence, sharpness of contour. [L f. Gk, f. EM(*phainō* show)].

ĕm'phasize, -ise (-īz), v.t. Lay stress upon (word in speaking); bring (fact etc.) into special prominence. [f. prec. + -IZE]

ĕmphăt'|ic, a. (Of language, tone, gesture) forcibly expressive; (of words) bearing the stress; (of person) expressing himself with emphasis; (of actions) forcible, significant. Hence ~ICALLY adv. [earlier *-ical* (16th c.) f. LL f. Gk *emphatikos* (as EMPHASIS, see -IC)]

ĕmphўsĕm'a, n. (path.). Enlargement of air vesicles of the lungs; swelling caused by presence of air in connective tissues of body. [f. LL f. Gk *emphusēma* (*emphusaō* puff up)]

ĕm'pīre, n. Supreme & wide (political) dominion; absolute control (*over*); government in which sovereign is called emperor; territory of an emperor; (hist.) *the E~*, (usu.) Holy Roman E~; *E~ Day* (now *Commonwealth Day*), May 24th, birthday of Q. Victoria; *E~ City, State* (of New York); (attrib., *E~*) denoting a style of furniture or dress fashionable during the first (1804–15) or second (1851–70) French E~. [ME, f. OF *empire* (earlier *emperie* whence E *empery*) f. L *imperium* conn. w. *imperare*, see EMPEROR]

ĕmpi'ric, a. & n. Based, acting, on observation & experiment, not on theory, whence ~IST(2) n.; (person) relying solely on experiment; quack. Hence ~AL a., ~alLY² adv., ~ISM n. [f. L f. Gk *empeirikos* f. *empeiria* experience]

ĕmplāce'ment (-sm-), n. Situation; placing; platform for guns. [F (EM- + PLACE + -MENT)]

ĕmplāne', v.i. & t. Go or put on board aeroplane. '[EM- + (AERO)*plane*]

ĕmploy', v.t., & n. **1.** Use (thing, one's power, etc., *for, in, on, about*, an object); use services of (person); keep (person) in one's service; busy, keep occupied, (oneself, others, *doing, in*, etc.). **2.** n. *In the* ~ *of*, ~ed by. Hence ~ABLE a., ~ER¹ n. [ME (n. f. F *emploi*) f. OF *employer* f. L IM(*plicare* fold), cf. IMPLY]

employé (ŏmploi'ā), n. (fem. *-ée*). Person employed for wages. [F p.p. (prec.)]

employee', n. = prec. [-EE]

employ'ment, n. In vbl senses: esp., one's regular trade or profession. [-MENT]

ĕmpois'on (-zn), v.t. Put poison into; taint; corrupt (fig.); embitter (person's mind *against*). [ME, f. OF EM(*poisonner* POISON)]

ĕmpōr'ium, n. Centre of commerce, mart; shop. [f. L f. Gk *emporion* f. EMporos merchant (*por-* journey)]

empow′er, v.t. Authorize, license, (person *to* do); enable. [EM-]

em′press, n. Wife of emperor; woman governing an empire or (fig.) having absolute power. [ME, f. OF *emperesse* fem. of *emperere* EMPEROR, see -ESS¹]

empressement (see Ap.), n. Display of cordiality. [F]

‖ **emprise′** (-z), n. (arch.). (Chivalrous) enterprise. [ME, f. OF fem. p.p. as n. of *emprendre* f. Rom. *IM(pre(he)ndre* take)]

emp′ty¹, a. & n. 1. Containing nothing; devoid *of* (qualities); (colloq.) hungry; (of house) devoid of furniture or inmates; (of van, ship, etc.) without load; (of persons, plans, etc.) lacking sense; meaningless. 2. n. ~ truck, box, etc. 3. ~-*handed*, bringing no gift, carrying nothing away; ~-*headed*, -*pated*, witless. Hence **emp′tiness** n. [OE *æmetig* f. *æmetta* leisure +-Y²]

emp′ty², v.t. & i. Remove contents of (vessel etc. *upon* etc.); transfer (contents of one thing *into* etc. another); (of river) discharge itself (*into*); (v.i.) become empty. [f. prec.]

empur′ple, v.t. Make purple, redden. [EM-]

empyre′an, a. & n. (Of the highest heaven, as the sphere of fire or as the abode of God; (of) the visible heavens. So **empy′real** a. [f. LL *empyreus* f. Gk EM(*puros* f. *pur* fire) + -AN]

em′u, n. Large Australian bird allied to the cassowary. [17th c. *emia*, *eme*, f. Port. *ema* crane, ostrich]

em′ul|āte, v.t. Try to equal or excel; rival; imitate zealously. So ~A′TION, ~ātor, nn., ~ātive a. [f. L *aemulari* (as foll.), see -ATE³]

em′ulous, a. Zealously, jealously, imitative (*of*); desirous (*of* renown etc.); actuated by spirit of rivalry. Hence ~LY² adv. [f. L *aemulus* +-OUS]

emul′sify, v.t. Convert into an emulsion. [f. L E(*mulgēre muls-* milk) +-FY]

emul′sion (-shn), n. Milky liquid with oily or resinous particles suspended in it; mixture of light-sensitive silver salts suspended in gelatine or collodion for coating photographic plates and films. Hence or cogn. ~IZE(3) v.t., **emul′sive** a. [F, or f. mod. L *emulsio* (as prec., see -ION)]

emunc′tory, a. & n. Of nose-blowing; (organ, duct) conveying waste matter from the body. [f. L E(*mungere munct-*), see -ORY]

en, n. Unit of width in printing, narrower than EM. [N]

en-¹, pref. The form assumed in F by L *in-* (see IN-¹); in E used chiefly in wds from F (*enamour*, *embarrass*, *engage*); before *b* & *p*, occas. before *m*, it is changed to *em-*; from 14th c. *in-* (*im-*) [or IN- (IM-)] has taken the place of *em-* (*em-*), & conversely; now used to form E vbs (a) on nouns, with sense ' put (the object) into

or on something ' (*embed*, *engulf*, *entrust*) or ' put something into or on (the object)' (*enjewel*); (b) on nn. or adjj., w. sense ' bring into such condition ' (*englad*, *enslave*); often with suf. -EN⁶ (*embolden*, *enlighten*); (c) on vbs with sense ' in ', ' into ', ' upon ', (*enfold*) or w. intensive force (*encarnalize*).

en-², pref. The form assumed by Gk *en-* (*em-* before *b*, *m*, *p*, *ph*; *el-*, *er-*, before *l*, *r*), w. sense ' in ' (*energy*, *enthusiasm*, *emphasis*).

-en¹, -n, suf. forming p.p. of strong vbs (*spoken*, *sworn*); often obs. or arch. (*gotten*, *graven*); freq. displaced by -*ed* (*shaped* for *shapen*); or surviving only in adj. sense (*drunken*, *lorn*). For adj. sense see -ED¹(2). [OE -*en*, OS, OHG -*an*, ON-*enn*, -*inn*, Goth. -*ans*, f. Gmc *-enaz*, *-anaz*]

-en², suf. forming dimm., as *chicken*, *maiden*. [Gmc *-ino(m)*, neut. of *-ino-* -EN⁵]

-en³, suf. forming femm. (now only in *vixen*), and found in some nouns, as *burden*. [f. WG* -*innja* f. Gmc *-inī*]

-en⁴, suf. seen in *oxen*; orig. part of stem in weak-decl. nouns, but retained only in pl., & added to other old plurals, as in *brethren*, *children*, *kine*, (earlier -*ther*, -*der*, *ky*). [OE -*an*]

-en⁵, -n, suf. forming adjj. f. nn., usu. expr. material; mostly obs. or arch. (*silvern*) or usu. in metaph. senses (*golden*), the noun being used as adj.; but *wooden*, *woollen*, & a few others, remain. [OE -*en*, OS, ON -*in*, OHG -*in*, Goth. -*ein-* f. Gmc *-ino-* cogn. w. L -*ino-* see -INE]

-en⁶, suf. forming vv.t. & i. from adjj. (*deepen*, *moisten*) on anal. of a few in OE (*fasten*), & f. nouns as *listen* (OE), *happen* (14th c.), *heighten*, *hearten*, etc., (mod.).

ena′ble, v.t. Authorize, empower, (person *to* do); supply (person etc.) with means (to do); ‖ *Enabling Act*, esp. that of 1920 conferring on the Established Church a certain measure of autonomy subject to parliamentary veto. [EN-¹]

enact′, v.t. 1. Ordain, decree, (thing, *that*), whence **enac′tion**, ~MENT, nn., **enac′tive**, **enac′tory**, aa.; ~*ing clauses* (containing new provisions). 2. Play (scene, part, on stage or in life). [EN-¹ + ACT n. & v.]

enam′el¹, n. Glass-like opaque or semi-transparent coating of metallic surfaces for ornament or as preservative lining (also fig.); any smooth hard coating; kinds of complexion-veneer; coating of teeth; painting done on ~; (poet.) smooth bright surface colouring, verdure, etc. [f. foll.]

enam′el², v.t. (-ll-). Inlay, encrust, (metal etc., the face or skin) with enamel; portray (figures etc.) with enamel; adorn with varied colours. [ME, f. AF EN¹-*ameler*, -*anailler*, f. OF *esmail*, alt. f. *esmaut* f. WG *small*- see SMELT¹]

enăm′our (-mer), v.t. Inspire with love (*of*, esp. in p.p.); charm, delight. [f. OF EN¹(*amourer* f. *amour* love f. L *amorem*, nom. *-or*)]

ěnăn′tiŏmŏrph, n. Mirror image, form related to another as an object is to its image in a mirror. [f. Gk *enantios* opposite, *morphē* form]

ěnăntiŏp′athy̌, n. = ALLOPATHY. [f. Gk *enantios* opposite + -PATHY]

ěnăr′thrōs′is, n. (anat.). Ball-&-socket joint. [Gk, f. EN²(*arthros* f. *arthron* joint), -OSIS]

en blŏc (ahǹ), adv. In a lump, wholesale. [F]

ěncaen′ia (-sēn-), n. Dedication festival; ‖(Oxf.) = COMMEMORATION. [L, f. Gk *egkainia* (EN-² + *kainos* new)]

ěncāge′, in-, v.t. Confine (as) in cage. [EN-¹]

ěncămp′, v.t. & i. (Of troops) settle (t. & i.) in camp; lodge (t. & i.) in the open in tents. [EN-¹]

ěncămp′ment, n. In vbl senses; also, place where troops are encamped. [-MENT]

ěncāse′, in-, v.t. Put into a case; surround as with a case. Hence ~MENT (-sm-), n. [EN-¹]

‖**ěncăsh′**, v.t. Convert (bills etc.) into cash; receive in form of cash, realize. Hence ~MENT n. [EN-¹]

ěncaus′tic, a. & n. (Painting, art of painting) by burning in; ~ *brick*, *tile*, (inlaid with coloured clays burnt in). [f. L f. Gk *egkaustikos*, see EN-², CAUSTIC]

-ence, suf. forming nn. of quality or action f. F *-ence* or direct f. L *-entia* f. L pres. part. in *-ent-* (nom. *-ens*); also f. earlier (M)E & F wds in *-ance*, after 1500 refash. after L *-entia*; see -ANCE, -ENCY.

enceinte (see Ap.), a. & n. 1. (Of women) pregnant. 2. n. Enclosure (in fortification). [F]

ěncěphăl′ic, a. Of the brain. [f. Gk *egkephalon* brain (EN-² + *kephalē* head) + -IC]

ěncěph′al‖(o)-, comb form of Gk *egkephalon* (prec.); ~*ît′is*, inflammation of the brain (see SICKNESS); ~*ogram*, an X-ray photograph of the brain; ~*ograph*, ~ogram, (also) instrument for recording brain waves; ~*ôg′raphy*; ~*ŏt′omy*, dissection of the brain.

ěncěph′alon, n. (anat.). The brain. [mod. L f. Gk (see ENCEPHALIC)]

ěnchain′, v.t. Chain up, fetter; hold fast (attention, emotions). Hence ~MENT n. [f. F EN¹(*chainer* CHAIN)]

ěnchant′ (-ah-), v.t. Bewitch (lit. & fig.); charm, delight. Hence or cogn. ~ER¹, ~MENT, ~RESS¹, incl. ~ĭngLY² adv., (-ah-). [ME, f. F *enchanter* f. L IN(*cantare* sing, frequent. of *canere* cant-)]

ěnchīrĭd′ion (-k-), n. Handbook. [f. LL f. Gk f. *en* in, *kheir* hand]

ěncīr′cle, v.t. Surround, encompass, (*with*); form a circle round. [EN-¹]

en clair (ahǹ), phr. (Of telegrams, official

messages, etc.) in ordinary language (not in code or cipher). [F]

ěnclasp′ (-ah-), v.t. Hold in clasp or embrace. [EN-¹]

ěnclāve′, n. Territory surrounded by foreign dominion. [F, f. *enclaver* f. Rom. *IN(clavare* f. *clavis* key)]

ěnclit′‖ic, a. & n. (gram.). (Word) so unemphatic as to be pronounced as part of preceding word, esp. (Gk) throwing its accent back on preceding word. Hence ~ICALLY adv. [f. LL f. Gk *egklitikos* (EN-² + *klinō* lean), see -IC]

ěnclōse′, in-, (-z), v.t. Surround, fence in, (land etc. *with*, *in*, walls etc.); shut up in receptacle (esp. something besides letter in envelope); bound on all sides, contain, (esp. Math.); hem in on all sides. [ME, f. OF *enclos* p.p. of *enclore*; see EN-¹, CLOSE³]

ěnclō′sure (-zher), n. Enclosing (esp. of common land, to make it private property, as E~ *Act*); enclosing fence etc.; enclosed place; paper etc. enclosed with letter in envelope. [AF, OF *enclosure* (prec., -URE)]

ěnclōthe′ (-dh), v.t. Clothe. [EN-¹]

ěncloud′, v.t. Envelop in cloud. [EN-¹]

ěncōde′, v.t. Put (message) into code or cipher. [EN-¹]

ěncōm′iăst, n. Composer of an encomium; flatterer. Hence ěncōmiăs′tic a. [f. Gk *egkōmiastēs* (*egkōmiazō*, as foll. *-ast* = -IST(1) w. vbs in *-azō*)]

ěncōm′ium, n. Formal or high-flown praise. [L, f. Gk *egkōmion* (EN-² + *kōmos* revelry)]

ěncom′pass (-ŭm-), v.t. Surround (esp. with friendly or hostile intention); contain. Hence ~MENT n. [EN-¹ + COMPASS n.]

encore (ŏngkōr′, *& see Ap.*), int., n., & v.t. 1. (Spectator's or auditor's demand for song etc. to be sung etc.) again, once more; further, item given in response. 2. v.t. Demand repetition of (song etc.), summon (performer) for this. [(vb f. n.) F, = once again]

ěncoun′ter, v.t., & n. 1. Meet hostilely; fall in with. 2. n. Meeting in conflict, falling in, (*with*). [ME; (n. f. OF *encontre* f. OF *encontrer* f. Rom. *IN(contrare* f. L *contra* against)]

ěncou′rag‖e (-kŭ-), v.t. Embolden; incite, advise, (person *to* do); promote, assist, (commerce, opinion, etc.). Hence or cogn. ~EMENT (-kŭrǐjm-) n., ~ĭngLY² adv. [ME, f. OF EN¹(*coragier*, as COURAGE)]

En′cratīte (ě-), n. Member of early Christian heretical sect abstaining from meat, wine, & marriage. [f. LL f. late Gk *egkratiēs* (*egkratēs* continent, -ITE¹)]

ěncrim′son (-z-), v.t. Make crimson. [EN-¹]

ěncroach′, v.i. Intrude usurpingly (*on* others' territory, rights, etc., or abs.). Hence ~MENT n. [f. OF EN¹(*crochier* f. *croc* hook); see CROOK]

ěncrust′, in-, v.t. & i. Cover with a crust; overlay (surface) with ornamental crust;

of precious material; (v.i.) form into a crust. Hence ~MENT n. [f. F *incruster* f. L IN(*crustare*, as CRUST); also f. EN-¹+ CRUST]

encŭm'ber, v.t. Hamper (person, movement, action, *with* burden, difficulty, etc.); burden (person, estate, *with* debts); fill, block, (place *with* lumber etc., lit. & fig.). Hence ~MENT n. [ME, f. OF EN¹- (*combrer* CUMBER)]

encŭm'brance, n. Burden; annoyance; impediment; *without* ~, having no children; claim, mortgage, etc., on property. [f. OF *encombrance* (as prec., see -ANCE)]

encŭm'brancer, n. One who has an encumbrance on another's estate. [-ER¹]

-ency̆, suf. f. L -*entia*, usu. denoting quality or state, not action; see -ANCE, -ANCY, -CY.

ency̆c'lic(al), aa. & nn. (Pope's letter) for extensive circulation. [f. LL *encyclicus*, for -*ius*, f. Gk *egkuklios* (EN-²+*kuklos* circle)]

ency̆clop(a)ed'|ĭa (-pē-), n. (pl. ~*ias*). Book giving information on all branches of knowledge or of one subject, usu. arranged alphabetically; esp. the French ~*ia* of Diderot, D'Alembert, and others; general course of instruction. Hence ~IC(AL) aa., ~ISM(3), ~IST(3), nn. [mod. L, f. pseudo-Gk *egkuklopaideia* for *egkuklios paideia* all-round education (as prec., *paideia* f. *paideuō* educate f. *pais paidos* boy)]

ency̆st', v.t. Enclose in a cyst. Hence ~A'TION, ~MENT, nn. [EN-¹]

end¹, n. 1. Limit, as *there is no* ~ *to it*; extremity (of line etc.); || *East, West, End* (part of London); surface bounding a thing at either extremity, head of cask etc.; remnant, as *candle* ~*s*, *odds & ~s*; *rope's* ~, short piece bound at ~s with thread for flogging; *shoemaker's* ~, length of thread armed with bristle. 2. Conclusion (of period, action, state, book, etc.); latter part; destruction; death. 3. Result, purpose, as *to gain his* ~*s*, *to what* ~ ?; object for which a thing exists, final cause. 4. *Place on* ~ (upright); *turn* ~ *for* ~, reverse; *world without* ~, for ever; *placed* ~ *to* ~ (lengthwise, continuously); ~ *on*, with its ~ fronting one; *no* ~, much, many, *of*; *on* ~, continuously (*for three weeks on* ~); *be at, come to, an* ~, be, become, exhausted or completed; *in the* ~, finally, after all; *at one's wits'* ~, quite perplexed; *put an* ~ *to*, stop, abolish; *keep one's* ~ *up*, acquit oneself well in conversation, bargain, etc.; *go* (*in*) *off the deep* ~ (sc. of swimming-bath) fig., take risks, (also) lose one's temper; *make an* ~ *of*, put a stop to; *at a loose* ~, unoccupied; *make both* ~*s meet*, live within one's income; *is at the* ~ *of his tether*, knows, can do, no more; ~-*iron*, movable plate changing size of grate in range; ~-*paper*, blank leaf pasted down on

boards or wrappers of book; ~-*product*, final product of a number of operations. [OE *ende*, OS *endi*, OHG *enti*, ON *endir*, Goth. *andeis* f. Gmc *andja*-]

end², v.t. & i. Bring (action, speech, life, etc.) to an end; put an end to, destroy; come to an end; ~ *by doing*, eventually do (*will* ~ *by marrying a duke*); result *in*; ~ *up*, conclude, finish. [OE *endian* (as prec.)]

endam'age, v.t. = DAMAGE. [EN-¹]

endan'ger (-j-), v.t. Cause danger to. [EN-¹]

endear', v.t. Render (person, thing, one*self*) dear (*to*). Hence ~INGLY² adv., ~MENT n. [EN-¹]

endeav'our (-dĕver), v.t. & i., & n. 1. Try (*to* do); strive *after*. 2. n. Attempt (*to do, at doing*). [EN- (n. f. vb) f. EN-¹+DEVOIR]

endĕm'|ĭc, a. & n. 1. Regularly found among (specified) people, in (specified) country. 2. n. ~ic disease. Hence ~ICALLY adv., endĕmi'CITY n. [f. F *endémique* f. Gk EN-²+*dēmos* people+-IC; cf. *epidemic*]

endĕrm'|ĭc, a. Acting on the skin. Hence ~ICALLY adv. [EN-²+DERM+-IC]

end'ing, n. In vbl senses, esp. latter part (of word, story, etc.). [-ING¹]

en'dive, n. Species of chicory, with curled leaves, used as salad. [ME, f. OF f. LL *endivia* f. L *intibus, -um*, Gk *entubon*]

end'less, a. Infinite; eternal; incessant; (Mech.) ~ *band, cable, chain* (with ends joined for continuous action over wheels etc.). Hence ~LY² adv., ~NESS n. [OE *endelēas*, see END¹ and -LESS]

en'do- (before a vowel end-), comb. form of Gk *endon* within, as; ~*card'ium*, lining membrane of heart; ~*cardit'is*, inflammation of this; ~*carp*, inmost layer of pericarp; ~*crāne*, inner surface of skull; ~*crine*, secreting internally, ductless, of the ~crine glands, [Gk *krinō* sift]; ~*carp*, inner layer of blastoderm; ~*gamous*, ~*gamy*, (-ŏg'-), (of) marrying within the tribe; ~*gen*, plant that develops wood in interior of stem; ~*genous* (-ŏj¹), growing from within; ~*lymph*, fluid in membranous labyrinth of ear; ~*metrit'is*, ~*mĕt'rium*, (inflammation of) lining membrane of womb; ~*morph*, mineral enclosed in another; ~*pä'rasite*, internal parasite; ~*plasm*, ~*sarc*, inner soft layer of protoplasm; ~*scope*, instrument for viewing internal parts of body; ~*skĕl'eton*, internal framework of vertebrates; ~*smōse* (-ŏz'm-), ~*smōs'is* (-ŏzm-), passage of a fluid inwards through a porous septum; ~*sperm*, albumen enclosed with embryo in seeds; ~*spore*, inner coat of spore, spore formed in a case; ~*thĕl'ium*, layer of cells lining blood-vessels etc.

endorse', in-, v.t. Write on back of (document), esp. sign one's name on back of (bill, cheque, etc.); write (explanation, comment, *on* back of document); ~ *over*, make over one's rights in (bill etc. *to* another person, also fig.); confirm (statement, opinion), (vulg. in advertisements) confirm advertiser's praise of (—'s pills etc.); ‖ motorist's, publican's, *licence is ~d*, has record of offence written on the back. Hence ~MENT (-sm-) n. [refash. on L; ME *endosse* f. OF *endosser* f. med. L IN(*dorsare* f. *dorsum* back)]

endow', v.t. Bequeath, give, permanent income to (person, institution); invest (person) *with* (privileges etc.); furnish (person) *with* (ability etc.; esp. in p.p.). Hence ~MENT n. (*~ment assurance*, payment of a fixed sum to an insured person on attaining an agreed age, or to his or her estate if death occurs earlier). [ME, f. AF *endouer* f. EN-¹+OF *douer* f. L *dotare* (as DOWER)]

endue', **in-**, v.t. Put on (clothes etc., also fig.); clothe (person) *with*; (usu. pass.) furnish (person *with* qualities etc.). [ME, f. OF *enduire* f. L IN(*ducere* lead, draw), associated in sense w. *induere* put on (clothes)]

endur'ance, n. Habit, power, of enduring; enduring. [OF, see -ANCE]

endur|e', v.t. & i. Undergo (pain etc.); submit to; bear (*to do*, esp. w. neg.); last. Hence ~ABLE a., ~'ING LY² adv., ~'INGNESS n. [ME, f. OF *endurer* f. L IN (*durare* harden f. *durus*)]

end'ways, **-wise**, (-z) adv. With the end turned towards the spectator or uppermost or foremost; end to end. [-WAYS, -WISE]

-ēne, suf. forming names of hydrocarbons, as *benzene, camphene*.

en'ema (or ĭnē²), n. Injection of liquid or gaseous substance into the rectum; the syringe used. [LL, f. Gk *enēma* f. *eniēmi* inject]

en'emy, n. & a. **1.** Hostile person; opponent (*of, to*, another); *the E~*, the Devil; member of hostile army or nation; hostile force or ship; (colloq.) *how goes the ~?*, what is the time? **2.** adj. Of, or belonging to, the ~ (*~ ships, aircraft, alien*; *destroyed by ~ action*). [ME, f. OF *enemi* f. L IN²(*imicus = amicus* friend)]

energet'|ic, a. & n. Strenuously active; forcible, vigorous; powerfully operative; (n. pl.) science of energy. Hence ~ICALLY adv. [f. Gk *energētikos* f. EN²(*ergeō* f. *ergon* work), see -IC]

ener'gic, a. (rare). = prec. [f. ENERGY + -IC]

en'ergize, -ise (-ĭz), v.t. & i. Infuse energy into (person, work); be in active operation. [-IZE]

energum'en, n. Demoniac; enthusiast, fanatic. [f. LL f. Gk *energoumenos* (pass. part., see ENERGETIC)]

en'ergy, n. **1.** Force, vigour, (of speech, action, person, etc.); active operation; (pl.) individual powers in exercise, as *devote your energies to this*; (latent) ability. **2.** (phys.). *Actual, kinetic, motive,*

~, a body's power of doing work by virtue of its motion (half product of mass into square of velocity); *potential, static, latent* ~, body's power of doing work by virtue of stresses resulting from its relation to other bodies; CONSERVATION *of ~*; *mass ~*, ~ which all bodies possess in virtue of their mass (product of mass into square of velocity of light), and of which a small portion is released (as radiations etc.) in radio-activity and other types of atomic disintegration. [f. LL f. Gk *energeia* f. EN²(*ergēs* f. *ergon* work)]

enerv'ate¹, a. Wanting in (physical, moral, literary, artistic) vigour. [f. L E(*nervare* f. *nervus* sinew), see -ATE²]

en'erv|āte², v.t. Weaken (physically etc as prec.). So ~A'TION n. [as prec. -ATE³]

enface', v.t. Write, print, stamp (form of words) on bill etc.; do this to (bill etc.). Hence ~MENT (-sm-) n. [EN-¹]

en famille (ahn famē'ye), adv. At home, among one's family. [F]

enfant terrible (see Ap.), n. Child who asks awkward questions, repeats what he has heard, etc. [F]

enfee'ble, v.t. Make feeble. Hence ~MENT (-belm-) n. [ME, f. OF EN¹ (*feblir* as FEEBLE)]

enfeoff' (-fĕf), v.t. Invest (person) with fief; (fig.) hand over. [ME, f. AF *enfeoffer* OF *enfeffer* (FIEF)]

enfeoff'ment (-fĕf-), n. Enfeoffing; document effecting this; fief. [-MENT]

en fête (ahn fāt), adv. & pred. a. Engaged in, attired etc. for, holiday-making. [F]

enfett'er, v.t. Bind in fetters (lit. & fig.); enslave (person *to*). [EN-¹]

enfilāde', n., & v.t. **1.** Fire from guns etc sweeping line of works or men from end to end. **2.** v.t. Subject (troops, road, etc.) to ~. [(vb f. n.) F, f. EN¹(*filer* f. *fil* thread) see -ADE]

enfold', **in-**, v.t. Wrap up (person etc. *in, with*); clasp, embrace; shape into folds [EN-¹]

enforce', v.t. Urge, press home, (argument, demand); impose (action, conduct, *upon* person etc.); compel observance of (law etc.). Hence or cogn. ~ABLE a., ~DLY² (-sĕd-) adv., ~MENT (-sm-) n. [ME, f. OF *enforcier* f. Rom. *infortiare f. *fortis* strong]

enfrāme', v.t. Set (picture etc.) in frame, serve as frame to. [EN-¹]

enfran'ch|ise (-z), v.t. Set free; invest (town) with municipal rights, ‖ esp. that of representation in parliament; admit (person) to electoral franchise. Hence ~iseMENT (-zm-) n. [f. obs. F EN¹(*franchir* f. *franc* FRANK a.), see -ISH²]

engāg|e' (-n-g-), v.t. & i. **1.** Bind by contract or promise (esp. of marriage, as *~ed couple*). **2.** Hire (servant); bespeak (seats, cabs, etc.). **3.** Pledge oneself (*to do, that*); *~e for*, guarantee, promise. **4.** Induce; attract, charm, (esp. in part.).

whence ~'ingLY² adv. **5.** (archit.). Fasten (pillar) into wall; interlock (thing *with* another). **6.** Hold fast (attention); employ busily (usu. pass.). **7.** Embark in (politics etc.). **8.** Bring (troops) into conflict; enter into conflict with (also *with*). Hence ~e'MENT (-jm-) n. [f. F EN¹(*gager* f. GAGE¹)]

en garçon (see Ap.), adv. & pred. a. As a bachelor, unmarried. [F]

engarl'and (-ng-), v.t. Put a garland upon; wreathe (*with* flowers etc.). [EN-¹]

engěn'der (-j-), v.t. Beget (now only fig.); (of situation, condition, etc.) bring about. [ME, f. OF *engendrer* f. L IN(*generare* GENERATE)]

ěn'gine (-j-), n., & v.t. **1.** Mechanical contrivance consisting of several parts; ≈ STEAM-~; FIRE-~; machine, instrument, used in war; instrument, means; ‖~-*driver* (of ~, esp. locomotive); ~-*lathe* (worked by machinery); ~-*turning*, engraving of symmetrical patterns on metals by machine. **2.** v.t. Fit (ship etc.) with ~(s). [(vb f. n.) f. OF *engin* f. L *ingenium* (see INGENIOUS)]

engineer'¹ (-j-), n. **1.** One who designs & constructs military works; soldier of branch of army called *E*~s, trained to engineering. **2.** (Also *civil* ~) one who designs works of public utility, bridges, canals, gas-works, etc.; maker of engines. **3.** One who has charge of engine; *engine-driver. Hence ~sḥip n. [ME, f. OF *enginneor* f. med. L *ingeniatorem* (*ingeniare*, as ENGINE, see -OR); ending later assim. to -EER]

engineer'² (-j-), v.i.& t. Act as engineer; construct, manage, (bridge, work, etc.) as engineer; (colloq.) arrange, contrive, bring about. [f. prec.]

ěn'ginerý (-j-), n. Engines; machinery (often fig.). [-ERY]

engír'd(le) (-n-g-), vv.t. Surround with or as with girdle. [EN-¹]

‖ **Eng'lander** (ingg-), n. *Little* ~, one opposed to imperial policy. [-ER¹]

Eng'lish¹ (ingg-), a. & n. **1.** Of England; *the* ~ (people, soldiers, etc.); ~*man*, ~*woman*, one who is ~ by birth, descent, or naturalization. **2.** Of, written or spoken in, the ~ language. **3.** n. The ~ language (also *the king's, queen's,* ~, as *mishandle the queen's* ~); *Old* ~, (ending about 1150), *Middle* ~ (ending 1500); *in plain* ~, in plain words. **4.** Size of TYPE; *Early* ~ STYLE. [OE *englisc, ænglisc,* OS *engelsch,* MHG *engel(i)sch,* ON *enskr* f. Gmc *anglisko* (*angli-* ANGLE³)]

‖ **english²** (ingg-), v.t. (arch., affected). Render into English. [f. prec.]

engōrge', v.t. Devour greedily; (pass.) be crammed, (Path.) be congested with blood. Hence ~MENT (-jm-) n. [f. F EN-¹ (*gorger* GORGE)]

engraft', **in-**, (-ah-), v.t. Insert (scion of one tree into, upon, another); implant (principles etc. *in* the mind etc.); incor-

porate (thing *into* another); add (adventitious thing *upon*). [EN-¹]

engrail', v.t. Indent the edge of, give serrated appearance to, (esp. Her.). [ME, f. OF EN¹*gresler* f. *gresle* hail]

engrain', **in-**, v.t. Cause (dye etc.) to sink deeply into a thing (usu. fig.); (p.p. cf. INGRAINED) inveterate, as *in* ~*ed* rogue. [ME, f. OF *engrainer* dye in grain (*en graine*); see GRAIN]

engrāve', v.t. Inscribe, ornament, (hard surface *with* incised marks); carve (figures etc. *upon* surface); (fig.) impress deeply (*upon* memory etc.); cut (figures etc.) in lines on metal plates for printing. [EN-¹ + GRAVE²]

engrāv'ing, n. In vbl senses, esp. copy of picture etc. from engraved plate. [-ING¹]

engrōss', v.t. Write (document) in large letters; express in legal form; (hist.) buy whole stock of (corn etc.) so as to get monopoly; monopolize (conversation etc.); absorb (person, his attention, time etc.; esp. in p.p. ~*ed in* subject etc.). Hence ~MENT n. [ME; (1) f. AF EN¹*grosser* (*grosse* f. med. L *grossa* large writing); (2) f. phr. *in gross* wholesale]

engŭlf', **in-**, v.t. Plunge into, swallow up (as) in, a gulf. Hence ~MENT n. [EN-¹]

enhance' (-hah-, -hā-), v.t. Heighten, intensify, (qualities, powers, etc.); exaggerate; raise (price). Hence ~MENT (-hahnsm-) n. [ME, f. AF *enhauncer* prob. alt. f. OF *enhaucer* f. Rom. *IN(*altiare* f. *altus* high)]

enhǎrmōn'|ic, a. (mus.). Of, having, intervals smaller than semitone (esp. such intervals as that between G sharp & A flat). Hence ~ICALLY adv. [f. LL f. Gk EN²*armonikos* (*harmonia* HARMONY, see -IC)]

enig'ma, n. Riddle; puzzling person or thing. Hence or cogn. **enigmăt'ic**(AL) aa., **enigmăt'icalLY** adv., ~tize(3) v.t. [f. L f. Gk *ainigma -matos* f. *ainissomai* speak allusively (*ainos* fable)]

enisle', **in-**, (-īl), v.t. (poet.). Make into an isle; place on an isle; isolate. [EN-¹]

enjämb'ment (-m-m-; *or* ahñzhahñ-bmahñ'), n. (pros.). Continuation of sentence beyond second line of couplet. [f. F *enjambement* f. EN¹(*jamber* f. *jambe* leg), see -MENT]

enjoin', v.t. Prescribe, impose, (action, conduct, *on* person); command (person *to* do); issue instructions (*that*); (Legal, esp. U.S.) prohibit by judicial order. [ME, f. OF *enjoindre* (st. *-joign-*) f. L IN(*jungere* join)]

enjoy', v.t. ~ one*self*, experience pleasure; take delight in, whence ~ABLE a., ~able-NESS n., ~abLY² adv.; have the use of (advantages etc.); experience, as ~ *poor health.* Hence ~MENT n. [ME, f. OF EN-¹ (*joier* f. *joie* JOY) give joy to, (refl.) enjoy; or f. OF EN¹(*joir* f. L *gaudere* rejoice)]

enkin'dle, v.t. Cause (flame, passions, war, etc.) to blaze up; inflame with passion. [EN-¹]

enlāce′, v.t. Encircle tightly; enfold; entwine. Hence ~MENT (-sm-) n. [ME, f. OF *enlacier* f. Rom. *inlaciare f. *lacius; see LACE²]

enlārge′, v.t. & i. Increase, extend; widen, expand, (mind, heart, ideas); (arch.) release; grow larger; expatiate *upon*; (Photog.) reproduce, be capable of reproduction, on larger scale. Hence ~MENT (-jm-) n., (esp.) such photographic reproduction, **enlār′gER**¹ n., apparatus for enlarging or reducing negatives or positives. [ME, f. OF EN¹*larger* (LARGE)]

enlight′en (-īt-), v.t. Instruct, inform, (person *on* subject); (poet.) shed light on (object), give light to (person); free (person) from prejudice or superstition (esp. in p.p.). Hence ~MENT (-īt-) n. [EN¹ + LIGHT n. + -EN⁶]

enlink′, v.t. Link together, connect closely, (*with*, *to*; lit. & fig.). [EN-¹]

enlist′, v.t. & i. Engage (t. & i.) for military service (*~*ed man*, private soldier); secure the co-operation or support of (persons, feelings, natural forces, sciences, etc., *in* enterprise etc.). Hence ~MENT n. [EN-¹]

enliv′en, v.t. Animate, inspirit, (persons, feelings, trade, etc.); brighten (picture, scene). [EN-¹ + LIFE + -EN⁶]

en māsse (ahn), adv. In a mass; all together. [F]

enmēsh′, v.t. Entangle in or as in a net. Hence enmēsh′MENT n. [EN-¹]

ēn′mitý, n. Hatred; state of hostility. [ME, f. OF *enemistie* f. Rom. *inimicitatem (as ENEMY, see -TY)]

ēnn′ead, n. Set of nine (discourses, books, points). [f. Gk *enneas* nine, see -AD)]

ennō′ble, v.t. Make (person) a noble; make noble, elevate. Hence ~MENT (-belm-) n. [f. F EN¹ *noblir* (NOBLE)]

ennui (ŏn′wē, *& see Ap.*), n. Mental weariness from lack of occupation or interest. Hence~ED² (ŏnwēd′), *ennuyé* (see *Ap.*, fem. *-ée*, pl. *-és*, *-ées*), aa. [F, f. L *in odio*, cf. ANNOY¹]

ēnōrm′itý, n. Monstrous wickedness; crime. [f. F *énormité* f. L *enormitatem* (as foll., see -TY)]

ēnōrm′ous, a. Huge, very large, as ~ *beast*, *difference*. Hence ~LY² adv., ~NESS n. [f. L E(*normis* f. *norma* pattern, standard) + -OUS]

ēn′osis, n. Union of Cyprus with Greece. [Gk *henōsis*]

enough′ (enŭf′), (poet.) **ēnow′**, a., n., & adv. Not less than the required number, quantity, degree, as (adj.) *we have apples ~*, *~ apples*, *beer ~*, *~ beer*, *he made ~ noise* (to justify supposition etc.), *~ noise to wake the dead*, *for his purpose*; (n.) *we have ~ of everything except beer*, *~ of* (stop) *this folly*, *~!* (say no more), *~ is as good as a feast*, *cry '~'* (acknowledge defeat), *I have had ~* (am tired) *of him*, *I had ~ to do* (my work cut out) *to catch the train*,

you have done more than ~, *~ and to spare* (pred.; adj. or n.) *five men are ~*, *five quarts is not ~*; (adv.) *it is boiled* (just) *~*, *he does not advertise ~*, *are you warm ~?*, *he does not ~* (usu. *sufficiently*) *realize the difficulties*, *she sings well ~* (tolerably) *you know well ~* (quite well) *what I mean*; *oddly ~* (to justify the term oddly), *he had lost his purse*; *sure ~* (to satisfy rational doubt), *there it was*. [OE *genōg*, OS *gi-*, OHG *ginuog*, ON *gnógr*, Goth. *ganōhs* cogn. w. Gmc **-nah-* in OE *geneah* it suffices]

ēnounce′, v.t. Enunciate; pronounce (words). Hence ~MENT (-sm-) n. [f. F *énoncer* (as ENUNCIATE)]

en passant (see *Ap.*), adv. By the way; (Chess) *take* (pawn that advances two squares at once) *~* (with your own pawn by which it could have been taken if it had advanced only one). [F]

en pension. See PENSION.

en prise (ahn prēz), phr. (Chess). In a position to be taken. [F]

‖ **enquire**, enquiry. See INQUIRE, INQUIRY.

enrāge′, v.t. Make furious (*~d at*, *by*, *with*). [f. F EN¹ *rager* (RAGE)]

en rapport (ahn rapŏrr′), adv. In touch (*with*). [F, see RAPPORT]

enrāp′ture, v.t. Delight intensely. [EN-¹]

enrē′giment (-jm-), v.t. Form (men) into a regiment; discipline. [f. F EN¹(*régimenter* f. *régiment* REGIMENT)]

en règle (ahn rāgl), adv. In due form. [F]

enrich′, v.t. Make rich; add to contents of (collection, museum, book); make richer in quality, flavour, etc. Hence ~MENT n. [ME, f. OF EN¹(*richir* f. *riche* RICH)]

enrōbe′, v.t. Put a robe upon. [EN-¹]

enrōl′, -ll, v.t. (-ll-). Write name of (person) on list, esp. of army; incorporate (person) as member (*in* society etc.), enter (deed etc.) among rolls of court of justice; record, celebrate. Hence **enrōl′-**MENT n. [ME, f. OF EN¹ *roller* f. *rolle* ROLL n.]

en route (ahn rŏŏt), adv. On the way (*to*, *for*, place etc. or abs.). [F]

ens (ĕnz), n. (pl. *entia*, pr. ĕn′shĭa). An entity (esp. as an abstract notion). [L, part. of *esse* be, suggested by *absens*; cf. ENTITY]

‖ **En′sa** (ĕ-), n. Organization for entertaining troops etc. [initials of *Entertainments National Service Association*]

ensăm′ple, n. (arch.). = EXAMPLE. [ME, f. AF *ensa(u)mple* f. OF *essemple* EXAMPLE]

ensăng′uined (-nggwĭnd), a. Bloodstained, bloody, (lit. & fig.) [EN-¹ + L *sanguis* *-inis* blood + -ED¹]

ensconce′, v.t. Establish (one*self* etc. in secret, safe, snug, etc., place). [EN-¹]

ensemble (see *Ap.*), n. (Also *tout ~*) thing viewed as a whole; general effect; (Mus.) concerted passage in which all performers unite (*good ~*, performance of such passage in which all performers are in tune & time with one another, with blend & balance of tone). [F]

enshrine′, v.t. Enclose (relic etc.) in shrine; serve as shrine for (precious thing, lit. & fig.). Hence ~MENT (-nm-) n. [EN-¹]

enshroud′, v.t. Cover completely, hide from view. [EN-¹]

en′siform, a. Sword-shaped; ~ cartilage (appended to the sternum). [f. L ensis sword + -FORM]

en′sign (-īn), n. **1.** Badge (of office etc.); banner, flag, ‖ esp. (Brit. naut.) white, blue, or red, flag with union in corner (white ~, of Royal Navy & Royal Yacht Squadron, blue ~, of naval reserve etc., red ~, of merchant service). **2.** Standard-bearer (formerly, lowest commissioned officer of foot, cf. ANCIENT²), whence ~CY (-īn-) n. [ME, f. OF enseigne f. L INSIGNIA]

en′silage, n., & v.t. Preservation of green fodder in silo or pit without drying; fodder thus preserved; (v.t.) treat (fodder) by ~. [(vb f. n.) F (as foll., see -AGE)]

ensile′, v.t. Put (fodder) into a silo: [f. F ensiler f. Sp. EN¹silar (SILO)]

enslave′, v.t. Make (person etc.) a slave (lit., or fig. to habit, superstition, etc.). Hence ~MENT (-vm-) n. [EN-¹]

enslav′er, n. In vbl senses, esp. woman by whose charms a man is enslaved. [-ER¹]

ensnare′, v.t. Entrap (lit. & fig.). [EN-¹]

ensoul′ (-sōl), in-, v.t. Infuse a soul into. [EN-¹]

ensphere′, v.t. Encircle, enclose. [EN-¹]

ensue′, v.i. & t. Happen afterwards: result (from, on); (Bibl.) seek after. [ME, f. OF ensuivre f. Rom. *IN(sequere = L seguī follow)]

ensure′ (-shoor), v.t. Make (person, thing) safe (against risks); make certain (thing, that it shall happen); secure (thing to, for, person etc.); (formerly)=INSURE. [f. AF EN¹seurer f. IN(assurer ASSURE]

enswathe′ (-dh), v.t. Bind, wrap, in bandage (lit. & fig.). Hence ~MENT (-dhm-) n. [EN-¹]

-ent, suf. forming adjj. & nn., f. F -ent (or direct) f. L -entem, acc. of pres. part. (nom. -ens) in 2nd, 3rd, & 4th conjj. Also f. earlier (M)E & F wds in -ant, refash. (since 1500) after L -ent-; see -ANT.

entab′lature, n. (archit.). The part of an order above the column, including architrave, frieze, & cornice. [f. It. intavolatura f. IN(tavolare f. tavola TABLE), see -URE]

enta′blement (-belm-), n. Horizontal platform(s) supporting statue, above dado & base. [F, f. EN¹tabler (TABLE), see -MENT]

entail′¹, n. Settlement of succession of landed estate so that it cannot be bequeathed at pleasure; estate so secured; (fig.) inalienable inheritance (of qualities, beliefs, etc.). [f. foll.]

entail′², v.t. Settle (land etc.) as in prec.; bestow (thing) as inalienable possession (on person); impose (expense, labour, on

person); necessitate. Hence ~MENT n. [ME; EN-¹ + TAIL²]

entan′gle (-nggl), v.t. Catch in snare or among obstacles; involve (person etc.) in difficulties; make (thing) tangled or intricate (lit. & fig.). Hence ~MENT (-nggelm-) n., (also, Mil.) barrier erected to impede the enemy's progress (esp. one formed of stakes and interlaced barbed wire). [EN-¹]

en′tasis, n. (archit.). Slight convexity of a column shaft (introduced to correct the visual illusion of concavity). [Gk, f. enteinō to stretch]

entel′echy (-ki), n. (philos.). Realization, the becoming or being actual of what was potential, developed perfection, (Aristotle defines the soul, the Form or E~ of an organized body); what gives perfection, informing spirit. [f. LL f. Gk entelekheia (en telei ekhein to be in perfection)]

entell′us, n. (Also ~ monkey) the sacred Indian bearded monkey. [proper name (Virg. Aen. v. 437–72)]

entente (see Ap.), n. (diplom.). Friendly understanding between States; group of States in such relation; E~ cordiale, of Gt Britain & France 1904; the (Triple) E~, of these with Russia 1908. [F, = understanding]

en′ter, v.i. & t. **1.** v.i. Go, come, in, (into place, room, etc., or abs.); (3rd pers. imperat. as stage direction) come upon stage, as E~ Macbeth; ~ into, engage in (conversation, relations, agreement, inquiry, etc.), sympathize with (person's feelings etc.), form part of (calculations, plans, etc.), bind oneself by (recognizances, treaty, contract); ~ (up)on, assume possession of (property), begin (process etc.), begin to deal with (subject). **2.** v.t. Go, come, into (place etc.); penetrate (flesh etc.); become member of (army, church, etc.); give initial training to (dog), break in (horse); write (name, details, etc., in list, book, etc.); record name of (person) as competitor for (contest, race, etc.; also intr., announce oneself as competitor); ~ an appearance, show oneself at a meeting etc.; (of minority in deliberative body, ‖ esp. House of Lords) ~ a protest, record it in journals or minutes, make it; admit, procure admission for, (pupil, member of a society); ~ up, complete series of entries in (account-books etc.). Hence ~ABLE a. [ME, f. OF entrer f. L intrare (intra within)]

enter′ic, a. & n. Of the intestines; ~ (fever), typhoid. So **enterit′is** n. [f. Gk enterikos (enteron intestine, see -IC)]

en′tero- (before a vowel en′ter-), comb. form of Gk enteron intestine, as ~lite, stony concretion of stomach etc., ~tomy (-ŏtᵻ) cutting open intestine.

en′terprise (-z), n. Undertaking, esp. bold or difficult one; courage, readiness, to engage in ~s, as he has no ~. [ME, f.

OF *entreprise* f. *entreprendre* (*entre* between +*prendre* take f. L *pre(he)ndere*)]

ĕn'terprising (-z-), a. Showing enterprise. Hence ~LY² adv. [part. of arch. vb *enterprise* (f. prec.)]

ĕntertain', v.t. Maintain (correspondence, discourse); amuse, occupy agreeably, (person etc., often iron.), whence ~ING² a., ~ingLY² adv.; receive hospitably (~ *angels unawares*, see *Heb.* xiii. 2; also abs., as *they* ~ *a great deal*); harbour, cherish, welcome or consider, (idea, feeling, proposal). [f. F *entretenir* f. Rom. *INTER(tenēre* hold)]

ĕntertain'ment, n. In vbl senses, esp.: amusement, as *much to my* ~; public performance or show (|| ~ *tax*, one levied on attendance at these). [-MENT]

ĕnthral(l)' (-awl), v.t. (-ll-). Enslave (usu. fig.); charm. Hence **ĕnthral'MENT** (-awl-) n. [EN-¹]

ĕnthrōne', v.t. Place (king, bishop, etc.) on throne, esp. as formal induction (also fig.). Hence ~MENT (-nm-) n. [*c.* 1600, replacing *enthronize* (foll.)]

ĕnthronizā'tion, n. Enthronement (lit. & fig.). [f. ME *en-, intronise* f. OF *introniser* f. LL (*in-*) f. Gk EN²(*thronizō* as THRONE, -IZE)]

ĕnthūse' (-z), v.i. (colloq.). Show enthusiasm, gush. [back formation on foll.]

ĕnthū'siăsm (-zĭ-), n. Ardent zeal (*for, about,* an object, cause, etc.). [f. LL f. Gk *enthousiasmos* f. *enthousiazō* f. EN²(*theos* god) possessed by a god]

ĕnthūs'iăst (-zĭ-), n. One who is full of enthusiasm (*for* cause etc.), whence ~IO a., ~ICALLY adv., (-zĭás⁴); visionary, self-deluded person. [f. LL f. Gk *enthousiastēs* (as prec.)]

ĕn'thȳmēme, n. (logic). Syllogism in which one premiss is suppressed. [f. L f. Gk *enthumēma* f. EN²(*thumeomai* consider (*thumos* mind)]

ĕntice', v.t. Allure (person etc. *from* place, course of conduct, etc., *into* another; *to* do). So ~MENT (-sm-) n. [ME, f. OF EN¹-*ticier* prob. lit. set on fire (L *titio* fire-brand)]

ĕntire', a. & n. Whole, complete; not broken or decayed; not castrated; unqualified, as ~ *affection*; mere, as *an* ~ *delusion*; all of one piece, continuous; pure, unmixed; (n., hist., || & on inn-signs) blend of former ale, beer, & twopenny. Hence ~NESS (-īrn-) n. [ME, f. OF *entier* f. L IN²(*teger*, f. *tag-, tangere* touch)]

entire'ly (-īrlĭ), adv. Wholly; solely. [-LY²]

entire't|y (-īrtĭ), n. Completeness, esp., *in its* ~*y*; sum total (*of*); (Law) *possession by* ~*ies* (undivided). [f. OF *entierete* f. L *integritalem* (as ENTIRE, see -TY)]

ĕnti'tle, v.t. Give (book etc.) the title of (*Adam Bede* etc.); give (person) the title of (sultan etc.); (of circumstances, qualities, etc.) give (person etc.) a claim (*to* a

thing, *to* do). [ME, f. OF *entiteler* f. LL IN-(*titulare,* as TITLE)]

ĕn'tity, n. A thing's existence, as opp. to its qualities or relations; thing that has real existence. So **ĕn'titATIVE** a. [f. F *entité* or med. L *entitas,* see ENS, -TY]

ĕn'to-, comb. form of Gk *entos* within, as -*pa'rasite, -zo'on,* internal parasite, -*phyte,* plant growing inside a plant or animal.

ĕntomb' (-ōōm), v.t. Place in tomb (lit. & fig.); serve as tomb for. Hence ~MENT (-ōōm-m-) n. [f. OF EN¹*oumber* (as TOMB)]

ĕntōm'ic, a. Of insects. [as foll. +-IC]

ĕntomo- in comb. Insect, as : ~*lite* (-ŏm⁴), fossil insect, ~*phagous* (-ŏf⁴-), insect-eating, ~*philous* (-ŏf⁴-), (Bot.) fertilized by means of insects, ~*tomy* (-ŏt⁴-), insect anatomy. [f. Gk EN(*tomos* f. *temnō* cut) cut up, in neut. pl. = insects]

ĕntomŏl'og|ȳ, n. Study of insects. Hence **ĕntomolō'gicAL** a., ~IST n., ~IZE v.i. [f. F ENTOMO(*logie* -LOGY)]

entourage (see Ap.), n. Surroundings; attendant persons. [F]

en-tout-cas (ahñ tōō kah), n. Umbrella-sunshade; kind of hard lawn-tennis court. [F, lit. in any case]

entr'acte (see Ap.), n. (Performance in) interval between acts of play. [F]

ĕn'trails (-z), n. pl. Bowels, intestines; (fig.) inner parts (*of* the earth etc.). [ME, f. OF *entrailles* f. med. L *intralia* alt. f. L *interanea* (neut. pl.) f. *inter* among]

ĕntrain', v.t. & i. Put (esp. troops), get, into a train. [EN-¹]

ĕntrămm'el, v.t. (-ll-). Entangle, hamper. [EN-¹]

ĕn'trance¹, n. Coming or going in; coming of actor upon stage; entering *into, upon* (office etc.); right of admission; (in full ~ *fee*) fee paid on admission to club, school, etc.; door, passage, etc., one enters by. [OF (as ENTER, -ANCE)]

ĕntrance'² (-ah-), v.t. Throw into a trance; overwhelm (*with* joy, fear); carry away as in trance (*from, to*). Hence ~MENT (-ahnsm-) n. [EN-¹]

ĕn'trant, n. One who enters room, profession, etc., or *for* (race etc.). [F, part. as ENTER]

ĕntrăp', v.t. (-pp-). Catch in or as in trap; beguile (person *to* destruction etc., *into* doing). [f. OF EN¹(*traper* TRAP¹)]

ĕntreat', v.t. (Also ~ *of*) ask (person) earnestly (*to* do, *that*), whence ~ingLY² adv.; (Bibl.) *evil* ~, treat ill. [ME, f. OF EN¹(*traiter* TREAT)]

ĕntreat'ȳ, n. Earnest request. [prec. + -Y⁴]

entrechat (ŏ'ntreshah), n. Striking together of the heels several times during leap from ground, in dancing. [F, f. It. (*capriola*) *intrecciata* complicated (caper)]

entrecôte (ŏ'ntrekŏt), n. (cookery). Steak cut off the ribs. [F]

entrée (ŏ'ntrā, & see Ap.), n. Right, privilege, of admission; || made dish served between fish & joint. [F, = ENTRY] *entremets* (see Ap.), n. A side dish or dainty. [F]

entrench', in-, v.t. & i. Surround (post, army, town) with trench (also fig., esp., one*self*); (rarely) encroach, trespass, *upon*. Hence ~MENT n. [EN-¹]

entre nous (see Ap.), adv. Between you & me. [F]

entrepôt (see Ap.), n. Storehouse for deposit; commercial centre for import & export, collection & distribution. [F]

entrepreneur (ahntreprenêr'), n. Person in effective control of commercial undertaking; contractor acting as intermediary. [F]

entresol (see Ap.), n. Low storey between first & ground floor. [F]

en'tropy, n. (phys.). Measure of the unavailability of a system's thermal energy for conversion into mechanical work. [f. G *entropie* f. EN-² + Gk *tropē* transformation, after *energie* ENERGY]

entrust', in-, v.t. Charge (person) *with* (duty, object of care); confide (duty, person, thing, its safety, *to* person). [EN-¹]

en'try, n. 1. Coming or going in; ceremonial entrance; (Law) taking possession; place of entrance, door, gate, lobby, mouth of river. 2. Registration in records, account-books, etc.; item so entered; *bookkeeping by double, single,* ~ (in which each item is entered twice, once, in ledger); list of competitors for race etc. [ME *entre(e)* f. OF *entree* f. Rom. *intrata* (as ENTER, -Y⁴)]

entwine', in-, v.t. Interweave (lit. & fig.); wreathe (thing *with, about, round,* another); embrace. [EN-¹]

entwist', in-, v.t. Clasp with, form into, a twist; twist (thing) in *with* (another). [EN-¹]

enuc'le|āte, v.t. Explain, clear up; (Surg.) extract (tumour etc.) from shell etc. Hence ~A'TION n. [f. L E(*nucleare* f. NUCLEUS)]

enūm'er|āte, v.t. Count; specify (items). Hence or cogn. ~A'TION, ~ātor, nn., ~ātive a. [f. L E(*numerare* NUMBER²)]

enūn'ci|āte (-shi-), v.t. Express definitely (proposition, theory); proclaim; pronounce (words). So ~A'TION (-si-), ~ātor (-shi-), nn., ~ātive (-sha-) a. [f. L E(*nuntiare* announce f. *nuntius* messenger), -ATE³]

enūre', v.i. (& t.). See INURE.

enūrēs'is, n. (path.). Incontinence of urine. [f. Gk *enoureō* urinate in (EN-² + *ouron* urine)]

envel'op, v.t. Wrap up (person, thing, subject, etc., *in* garment, flames, clouds, mystery, or w. *flame* etc. as subject); (Mil.) effect the surrounding of (enemy). Hence ~MENT n. [ME *envolupe* f. OF *envoluper* f. EN-¹ as DEVELOP]

en'velope (*or* ŏn-), n. Wrapper, covering, (lit. & fig.), esp. folded & gummed cover of letter. [f. F *enveloppe* (as prec.)]

envěn'om, v.t. Put poison on or into (weapon, air, etc.); infuse venom into (feelings, words, actions); corrupt (mind etc.). [ME -*im*, f. OF EN¹(*venimer* as VENOM)]

en'viab|le, a. Calculated to excite envy (said of desirable thing or its possessor). Hence ~LY² adv. [f. ENVY v. +-ABLE]

en'vious, a. Full of envy; feeling envy *of* (person, thing). Hence ~LY² adv. [ME, f. AF *envious*, OF *-eus*, f. L *invidiosus* (as ENVY¹, see -OUS)]

envir'on, v.t. (Of persons or things) form a ring, be stationed, round; surround (person, place, etc.) hostilely, protectively, as attendants, etc.; surround (person, thing, *with* others). [ME, f. OF *environer* f. adv. as ENVIRONS]

envir'onment, n. Surrounding; surrounding objects, region, or circumstances. [-MENT]

envir'ons (-z; *or* ěn'vǐronz), n. pl. District surrounding town etc. [17th c. f. F, f. OF *environ* (n. f. adv.) f. *viron* circuit, neighbourhood, f. *virer* VEER]

envis'age (-z-), v.t. Look in the face of; face (danger, facts); contemplate, esp. under particular aspect. Hence ~MENT (-jm-) n. [f. F EN¹*visager* (VISAGE)]

en'voy¹, n. (arch.). (Author's parting words, esp.) short stanza concluding certain arch. forms of poem (also *-oi*). [ME, f. OF f. *envoiier* send (*en voie* on the way f. L *via*)]

en'voy², n. Messenger, representative; esp. minister plenipotentiary, ranking below ambassador & above *chargé d'affaires*. Hence ~SHIP n. [f. F *envoyé*, p.p. as prec., loss of *-é* as in ASSIGN²]

en'vy¹, n. Grudging contemplation (*of* more fortunate persons, *of, at,* their advantages, or abs.; often playfully); object, ground, of this, as *she, her poodle, is the ~ of Bath*. [OF *envie* f. L *invidia* f. *invidus* f. IN(*vidēre* see) envy]

en'vy², v.t. Feel envy of, as *I ~ him, ~ his impudence, ~ him his impudence*. [ME, f. OF *envier* f. med. L *invidiare* (*invidia* ENVY¹)]

enwind', v.t. (Of thing) wind itself round (another). [EN-¹]

enwomb' (-ōom), v.t. Enclose (as) in womb. [EN-¹]

enwrăp', in-, v.t. (-pp-). Wrap, enfold, (*in*; lit. & fig.). [EN-¹]

enwreathe' (-dh), v.t. Surround as or (as) with wreath; intertwine. [EN-¹]

enzoöt'ic, a. & n. (Disease) regularly affecting cattle etc. in a particular district or at a particular season. [f. EN-², Gk *zōion* animal, -IC]

en'zyme, n. (chem.). An organic catalyst formed by living cells but not depending on their presence for its action. [f. G *enzym*, f. EN-² + Gk *zumē*, see ZYMOSIS]

E'ocēne (ē-), a. (geol.). Of the lowest division of Tertiary strata. [f. Gk *ēos* dawn + *kainos* new]

ēolith'ic, a. Of the period preceding the

PALAEOlithic age. [Gk *ēōs* dawn, *lithos* stone]

eon. See AEON.

ĕ'osin, n. Red fluorescent dye-stuff used (esp.) in microscopy and colour-photography [f. Gk *ēōs* dawn +-IN]

-eous, suf. = L *-eus* +-OUS, forming adjj. meaning ' of the nature of ', as *ligneous* like wood; in *righteous, courteous, gorgeous, -eous* is a corruption of another suf.; *bounteous, duteous* result from the addition of *-ous* to another suf.

ĕozō'ic, a. (geol.). (Of strata) showing the earliest indications of animal life. [Gk *ēōs* dawn, *zōion* animal]

ep- in comb. = EPI- before unaspirated vowels.

ĕp'ăct, n. Age of moon on Jan. 1; excess of solar over lunar year. [f. F *épacte* f. LL f. Gk *epaktai* f. EP(*agō* bring) intercalate]

ĕp'arch (-k), n. Governor, bishop, of an eparchy. [f. Gk EP(*arkhos* ruler)]

ĕp'archў (-k-), n. Subdivision of modern Greece; diocese in Russian (Greek) Church. [f. Gk *eparkhia* (as prec., see -Y[1])]

ĕpaule'ment (-awlm-), n. (fortif.). Breastwork (esp. as flank protection). [F, f. *épauler* protect with ~, f. *épaule* (as foll.)]

ĕp'aulĕt(te) (-pol-), n. Ornamental shoulder-piece of uniform; (of private soldier) *win his ~s*, earn promotion to rank of officer. [f. F *épaulette* dim. of *épaule* shoulder f. L *spatula*]

épée (āpā'), n. The sharp-pointed duelling-sword, used (blunted) in fencing. [F, = sword]

ĕpeirogĕn'esis (-pīr-), n. (geol.). Process of making continents. [f. Gk *ēpeiros* mainland, GENESIS]

ĕpĕn'thĕsis, n. Insertion of a letter or sound within a word. Hence **ĕpĕnthĕt'ic** a. [Gk]

epergne (ĕpĕrn'), n. Centre ornament (esp. in branched form) for dinner-table to hold flowers or fruit. [orig. unkn.]

ĕpĕxĕg|ĕs'is, n. Additional, addition of, words to make meaning clear (e.g. ' difficult *to do* '). So ~ĕt'IC(AL) aa., ~ĕt'icalLY[2] adv. [Gk (EP-+EXEGESIS)]

eph-, pref. = EPI- before h.

ĕphēbe', n. (Gk Ant.). Citizen aged 18 to 20. [f. L f. Gk EPHEbos (*hēbē* early manhood)]

ĕphĕm'era (pl. *-ras*), -eron (pl. *-rons, -ra*), nn. Insect living only a day; kinds of insects including mayfly; short-lived thing. [f. Gk EPHEmeros lasting only a day (*hēmera*)]

ĕphĕm'eral, a. (Of diseases) lasting only a day; (of insects, flowers, etc.) lasting a day or a few days; short-lived, transitory. Hence ~ITY (-ăl[4]) n. [f. Gk as prec. +-AL]

ĕphĕm'er|is, n. (pl. ~*ides*, pr. -ĕ'rĭdĕz). Astronomical almanac or table. [LL f. Gk (*-ĕm-*), = calendar (as prec.)]

ĕph'rod, n. Jewish priestly vestment. [ME; Heb., f. *aphad* put on]

ĕph'or, n. One of five Spartan magistrates controlling the kings; (in mod. Greece) overseer. [f. Gk EPHoros (*horaō* see)]

ĕpi-, pref. = Gk *epi* upon, at, on the ground of, in addition.

ĕp'iblăst, n. (biol.). Outermost layer of blastoderm. [f. EPI-+Gk *blastos* sprout, germ]

ĕp'ic, a. & n. (Poem) narrating continuously achievements of one or more heroes, as the *Iliad* & *Odyssey*; fit for recital in an ~, of heroic type or scale; *E~ dialect*, form of Gk in which the ~ poems were written; *national~*, poem of any form, embodying nation's conception of its past history. Hence ~AL a., ~aLLY' adv. [f. L f. Gk *epikos* (EPOS, -IC)]

ĕpicēd'ium, n. Funeral ode. [f. L f. Gk EPI(*kēdeion* f. *kēdos* care)]

ĕp'icēne, a. & n. (Lat. & Gk Gram.) denoting either sex without change of gender; for, used by, both sexes; (person) with characteristics of both sexes. [f. LL f. Gk EPI(*koinos* common)]

ĕpicĕn'trum, -tre (-ter), nn. Point at which earthquake breaks out. [f. Gk EPI(*kentros* a. as CENTRE)]

ĕpiclēs'is, -klēs'is, n. Invocation, esp. of the Holy Spirit to consecrate the elements in the Eucharist. [Gk (EPI-, *kaleō* call)]

ĕp'icūr|e, n. One who is choice & dainty in eating & drinking. Hence ~ISM (2) n. [f. med. L *epicurus*, appellative use of L f. Gk *Epikouros* Epicurus]

ĕpicūrē'an, a. & n. (Follower) of Epicurus, Athenian philosopher (300 B.C.) who taught that highest good was pleasure (i.e. practice of virtue); (person) devoted to pleasure, esp. refined sensuous enjoyment. Hence ~ISM(3) n. [f. L *epicurēus* (LL *-ius*) f. Gk *Epikoureios* (prec., -EAN)]

ĕp'icycle, n. (geom.). Small circle rolling on circumference of a greater. Hence **ĕpicўc'lic** a. [ME, f. L OF, or LL f. Gk EPI(*kuklos* circle)]

ĕpicўc'loid, n. Curve traced by point in circumference of a circle rolling on exterior of another. Hence ~AL (-oid[4]) a. [prec. +-OID]

ĕpideic'tic (-dīk-), a. Meant for display. [f. Gk *epideiktikos* f. EPI(*deiknumi* show), see -IC]

ĕpidĕm'ic, a. & n. (Disease, lit. & fig.) prevalent among community at special time, cf. ENDEMIC. Hence ~AL a., ~alLY[2] adv. [f. F *épidémique* f. *épidémie* f. LL f. Gk *epidēmia* f. *epidēmios* a. (*dēmos* people)]

ĕpidĕmiŏl'ogў, n. Science of epidemics. [f. Gk as prec., -LOGY]

ĕpidĕrm'|is, n. Outer layer of skin of animals, cuticle; outer animal integument of shell; true skin of plant below cuticle. Hence ~AL, ~IC, ~OID, **ĕpidĕr-moid'**AL, aa. [LL, f. Gk EPIdermis (DERM)]

ĕpĭdĭ'ascōpe, n. Optical lantern projecting images of both opaque & transparent objects. [EPI- + DIA- + -SCOPE]

ĕpĭgăs'tr|ĭum, n. Part of abdomen immediately over stomach. Hence ~IC a. [LL, f. Gk EPIgastrion (gastēr stomach)]

ĕp'ĭgĕne, a. (Geol.) produced on surface of earth; (of crystal) chemically altered since its formation. [f. F épigène f. Gk EPI(genēs born)]

ĕpĭgĕn'esis, n. Formation of organic germ as a new product; theory of ~ (that the germ is brought into existence, not merely developed, in process of reproduction). [EPI-]

ĕpĭglŏtt'|ĭs, n. Erect cartilage at root of tongue, depressed during swallowing to cover glottis. Hence ~IC a. [Gk EPI-(glōttis f. glōtta tongue)]

ĕp'ĭgŏne, n. One of a later (& less distinguished) generation. [f. L f. Gk epigonos (EPI- + root of gignomai be born]

ĕp'ĭgrăm, n. Short poem ending in witty turn of thought; pointed saying or mode of expression. So **ĕpĭgrammăt'ĭc** a., **ĕpĭgrammăt'ĭcALLY** adv., **ĕpĭgrămm'atĭst**(3) n., **ĕpĭgrămm'atĭze**(1, 2) v.t. & i. [f. F épigramme or L f. Gk EPI(gramma -GRAM)]

ĕp'ĭgraph (-ahf), n. Inscription on stone, statue, coin, etc., whence **ĕpĭgráph'ĭc** a., **ĕpĭg'raphĭst** (2), **ĕpĭg'raphy**[1], nn.; motto. [f. Gk EPI(graphē f. graphō write)]

ĕp'ĭlĕpsy̆, n. Nervous disease in which patient falls to ground unconscious, with or without convulsions. [f. F épilepsie or LL f. Gk epilēpsia f. EPI(lambanō take)]

ĕpĭlĕp'tĭc, a. & n. Of epilepsy; (person) subject to epilepsy. [f. F épileptique or LL f. Gk epilēptikos (as prec.)]

ĕpĭl'ogĭst, n. Writer, speaker, of epilogue. [f. foll. + -IST]

ĕp'ĭlōgue (-g), n. Concluding part of literary work; speech, short poem, addressed to spectators by actor at end of play; ‖ (Radio) short religious service towards the end of some B.B.C. programmes. [F, f. L f. Gk EPI(logos speech)]

ĕpĭph'any̆, n. Manifestation of Christ to the Magi; manifestation of a superhuman being. [ME; (1) f. OF epiphanie f. LL f. Gk epiphania (neut. pl. adj.) f. EPI(phainō show); (2) f. Gk epiphaneia manifestation]

ĕpĭphĕnŏm'ĕnon, n. (med., philos.; pl. -ena). Secondary symptom, mere concomitant of something else not regarded as its cause or result. [EPI-, PHENOMENON]

ĕp'ĭphy̆te, n. Plant growing on (usu. not fed by) another; vegetable parasite on animal body. Hence **ĕpĭphy̆t'AL,** **ĕpĭphy̆t'ĭc** aa. [f. EPI- + Gk phuton plant]

Epīr'ot (I-), n. Inhabitant of Epirus. [f. Gk ēpeirōtēs (ēpeiros, -OT[2])]

ĕpis'copacy̆, n. Government of church by bishops; the ~, the bishops. [as EPISCOPATE, -ACY, after prelacy]

ĕpis'copal, a. Of bishop(s); ~ church, constituted on principle of prec. Hence ~ISM(3) n., ~LY[2] adv. [f. F épiscopal or LL episcopalis (as BISHOP, see -AL)]

ĕpiscopāl'ian, a. & n. (Adherent) of episcopacy; (member) of episcopal church. Hence ~ISM(3) n. [f. L as prec. + -AN]

ĕpis'copate, n. Office, position, tenure, of bishop; the ~, the bishops. [f. LL episcopatus (episcopus BISHOP, see -ATE[1])]

ĕp'isōde, n. Part between two choric songs in Gk tragedy (orig. interpolation); incidental narrative or series of events. Hence **ĕpĭsŏd'ĭc**(AL) aa., **ĕpĭsŏd'ĭcalLY[2]** adv. [f. Gk EPeisodion f. eisodos entry (eis into + hodos way)]

ĕpispăs'tĭc, a. & n. (med.). Blistering (plaster, substance). [f. LL f. Gk epispastikos f. EPI(spaō draw), see -IC]

ĕpistēmŏl'ogy̆, n. Theory of the method or grounds of knowledge. [f. Gk epistēmē knowledge + -O- + -LOGY]

ĕpis'tle (-sl), n. Letter (now only joc. of ordinary modern letters), esp. one of an apostle, part of the canon of Scripture; the E~, extract from apostolical ~ read in Communion service; literary work, usu. verse, in form of letter. [ME, f. OF f. L f. Gk epistolē f. EPI(stellō send)]

ĕpis'tolary̆, a. Of, carried on by, suited to, letters. [f. F épistolaire or L epistolaris (as prec., see -ARY[2])]

ĕpis'toler, n. (eccl.). Reader (cf. GOSPELLER) of the Epistle. [f. OF epistolier or med. L epistolarius as prec., -ER[2] (2)]

ĕpis'trophe, n. (rhet.). Ending of several sentences or clauses with same word. [Gk EPI(strophē turning f. strephō)]

ĕp'ĭsty̆le, n. (archit.). = ARCHITRAVE. [f. L f. Gk EPI(stulion f. stulos pillar)]

ĕp'ĭtaph (-ahf), n. Words (supposed to be) inscribed on tomb. [ME, f. OF epitaphe or L f. Gk EPI(taphion f. taphos tomb)]

ĕpĭthalăm'ĭum, n. (pl. -iums, -ia). Nuptial song or poem. Hence ~ĭAL, **ĕpĭthalăm'ĭo,** aa. [f. L f. Gk EPI(thalamion f. thalamos bride-chamber)]

ĕpĭthēl'|ĭum, n. Tissue forming outer layer of mucous membrane; (Bot.) epidermis formed of young cells. Hence ~ĭAL a. [mod. L, f. EPI- + Gk thēlē teat]

ĕp'ĭthĕt, n. Adjective expressing quality or attribute; significant appellation. Hence ~IC(AL) aa., ~ĭcalLY[2] adv., (-ĕt-). [f. F épithète or L f. Gk EPI(theton f. EPI(tithēmi place)]

ĕpĭt'om|ĕ, n. Summary, abstract, of book; condensed account; (fig.) thing that represents another in miniature, as man, the world's ~e. Hence ~IST(1) n., ~IZE(3) v.t. [f. L f. Gk epitome f. EPI(temnō cut) abridge]

ĕpĭzō'ŏn, n. (pl. -oa). External parasite or commensal. [EPI-, Gk zō(i)on animal]

ĕp'ĭzoŏt'ĭc, a. & n. (Disease) temporarily prevalent among animals (cf. ENZOOTIC, EPIDEMIC). [prec., -IC]

ĕp'ŏch (-k), n. Beginning of era in history,

science, life, etc., as *this made an ~, an ~-making event*; date; period in history or life marked by special events. Hence

ĕp'ochal (-k-) a. [f. med. L f. Gk *epokhē* stoppage f. EP(*ekhō* hold)]

ĕp'ōde, n. Form of lyric poem, used by Horace; third division of Greek choral ode (see STROPHE). [f. F *épode* or L f. Gk *epō̆(i)dos* f. EP(*a(i)dō* sing)]

ĕp'onȳm, n. One who gives his name to a people, place, or institution. So **ĕpŏn'ȳmous** a. [f. Gk EP(*ŏnumos* f. *onoma* name)]

ĕp'opee, n. Epic poem or poetry. [f. F *épopée* f. Gk *epopoiïa* (foll. +*poieō* make)]

ĕp'ŏs, n. Early unwritten epic poetry; epic poem. [L f. Gk *epos* word, song]

ĕpsil'on, n. Greek letter (Ε, ε) ĕ (cf. ETA). [Gk (*psilos* bare)]

Ĕp'som (ĕ-), n. Town in Surrey; ~ *salt(s)*, magnesium sulphate; (used for) race-course at~, principal race-meeting there held, including Derby and Oaks.

ē'qua|ble, a. Uniform, even, not easily disturbed. Hence~BIL'ITY n.,~bLY² adv. [f. L *aequabilis* (as EQUATE, -BLE)]

ē'qual¹, a. & n. 1. The same in number, size, value, degree, etc. (*to, with*, or abs.), as *twice three is ~ to six, the totals are ~, talks French & Dutch with ~ ease, the two are ~ in ability*; having strength, courage, ability, etc., adequate *to* (*the occasion, a cup of tea, doing*, etc.); uniform in operation etc., as ~ *laws*; evenly balanced (fight etc.); ~ TEMPERAMENT. 2. n. Person ~ to another in rank etc., as *mix with your ~s*, or in power etc., as *he has no ~*; (pl.) ~ things, as *if ~s be added to ~s*. [ME, f. L *aequalis* (*aequus* even, see -AL)]

ē'qual², v.t. (-ll-). Be equal to (person, thing, in quality, number, etc.). [f. prec.]

ĕqual'itȳ (-ŏl-), n. Condition of being equal (*between* two or more; *with* person etc. *in* quality etc.; usu. abs.); *is on an ~ with*, is on equal terms with. [ME, f. OF *equalite* f. L *aequalitatem* (as EQUAL¹, see -TY)]

ē'qualiz|e, -is|e (-īz), v.t. & i. Make (thing etc.) equal (*to, with*; (Footb. etc.) bring score to equality with opponent's. Hence ~A'TION n. [-IZE]

ē'quallȳ, adv. In an equal degree; in equal shares; uniformly. [-LY²]

ĕquanim'itȳ, n. Evenness of mind or temper; composure; resignation. [f. F *équanimité* or L *aequanimitas* (*aequus* even +*animus* mind), see -TY]

ĕquāte', v.t. State equality of (thing *to, with*, another); treat as equivalent. [f. L *aequare* (*aequus* equal), see -ATE³]

equā'tion, n. 1. Making equal, balancing, (of demand & supply etc.). 2. (Amount or process of) compensation for inaccuracy, as (Astron.) *personal ~*, allowance for individual slowness in noting phenomena (also fig.), ~ (difference between mean & apparent places) *of the equinoxes*. 3. (math.). Formula affirming equivalence of

two expressions connected by the sign=. Hence ~AL a., ~ALLY² adv., (-shon-). [f. L *aequatio* (as prec., see -ATION)]

equāt'or, n. A great circle of the earth, equidistant from the poles; = EQUINOCTIAL; *magnetic ~*, ACLINIC line. [ME, f. med. L (as prec., -OR)]

equātōr'ial, a. Of, near, the equator; ~ *telescope* (attached to axle revolving in direction parallel to plane of equator). Hence ~LY² adv. [-IAL]

|| **ĕ'querrȳ** (*or* ĭkwĕ'rĭ), n. Officer of prince or noble charged with care of horses; officer of British royal household. [16th c. *esquiry* f. obs. F *escurie* stable (= med. L *scura, scuria*) perh. f. WG *skur* shed; confused in E w. L *equus* horse]

equĕst'rian, a. & n. 1. Of horse-riding; ~ *statue* (of person on horse); (Rom. Ant.) of the order of Equites or Knights. 2. n. Rider, performer, on horseback. [f. L *equestris* (*eques* horseman f. *equus* horse) +-AN]

equĕstriĕnne', n. Horsewoman; (esp.) female circus-rider. [pseudo-F, f. prec. with fem. suffix]

equi- = L *aequi-*, comb. form of L *aequus* equal, as ~*ang'ŭlar* (-ngg-), having equal angles.

equidis'tant, a. Separated by equal distance(s). [f. F *équidistant* f. LL *aequidistantem* (see EQUI- & DISTANT)]

equilăt'eral, a. Having all the sides equal. [f. LL *aequilateralis* (see EQUI- & LATERAL)]

equilib'r|āte, v.t. & i. Cause (two things) to balance; balance (t. & i.); counterpoise. Hence ~A'TION n. [f. LL *aequilibrare*, see -ATE³]

equil'ibrist, n. Rope-walker, acrobat. [f. F *équilibriste* (*équilibre* EQUILIBRIUM)]

equilib'rium, n. State of balance (lit. & fig.); *a body in stable ~* (tending to recover ~ after disturbance); neutrality of judgement etc. [L (EQUI-, *libra* balance)]

equimŭl'tiple, n. (usu. pl.). Number having a common factor with another. [EQUI-]

ē'quine, a. Of, like, a horse. [f. L *equinus* (*equus* horse, see -INE¹)]

ĕquinŏc'tial (-shal), a. & n. 1. Of equal day & night; ~ *line*, circle of celestial sphere whose plane is perpendicular to earth's axis; happening at or near time of equinox, as ~ *gales*; at, near, the (terrestrial) equator. 2. n. ~ line, (pl.) ~ gales. [ME, f. OF, or L *aequinoctialis* (as foll., see -AL)]

ē'quinŏx, n. Time at which sun crosses equator & day & night are equal (*vernal ~*, about March 20; *autumnal ~*, about Sep. 22 or 23); (pl.) two points at which sun crosses equator; PRECESSION *of ~es*. [ME, f. OF *equinoxe* or med. L *equinoxium* f. L *aequinoctium* (*nox* -*ctis* night, EQUI-)]

equip', v.t. (-pp-). Furnish (ship, army, person, *with* requisites); provide (one*self*

etc.) for journey etc. Hence ~MENT n.
[f. F *équiper*, *esq*- prob. f. ON *skipa* man
(ship) f. *skip* SHIP]

ē'quipage, n. Requisites for an undertaking; outfit for journey etc.; carriage
& horses with attendants. [f. F *équipage*
(as prec., -AGE)]

ē'quipoise (-z), n., & v.t. 1. Equilibrium
(often fig.); counterbalancing thing.
2. v.t. Counterbalance, hold (mind) in
suspense. [EQUI-]

ēquipŏll'|ent, a. & n. Equal in power,
force, etc.; practically equivalent; (n.)~
ent thing. So ~ENCE, ~ENCY, nn. [f. OF
equipolent f. L *aequipollentem* (EQUI-,
pollēre be strong)]

ēquipŏn'der|āte, v.t. Counterbalance. So
~ANT a. & n. [f. med. L *aequi(ponderare*
weigh f. *pondus -eris* weight), see EQUI-
& -ATE[3]]

ēquipotĕn'tial (-shl), a. (phys.). In which
the potential of a force is the same or
constant at all points. [EQUI-]

ē'quitab|le, a. Fair, just, whence ~leNESS
n., ~LY[2] adv.; (of claims etc.) valid in
equity as opposed to law. [f. F *équitable*
(as EQUITY + -ABLE)].

ēquitā'tion, n. (usu. joc.). Riding on
horse; horsemanship. [F, or f. L *equitatio*
f. *equitare* f. *eques -itis* horseman f. *equus*
horse, see -ATION]

ē'quitý, n. 1. Fairness; recourse to principles of justice to correct or supplement
law; system of law coexisting with and
superseding common and statute law.
2. ‖ (*E~*) actors' trade union. 3. pl.
‖ Stocks and shares not bearing fixed
interest. 4. Net value of mortgaged property after deduction of charges. [ME,
f. OF *equite* f. L *aequitatem* (*aequus* fair,
see -TY)]

ēquiv'al|ent, a. & n. 1. Equal in value
(*to*); (of words) meaning the same; (Chem.)
equal in combining value (*to*); having the
same result; corresponding. 2. n. ~ent
thing, amount, word, etc. So ~ENCE,
~ENCY, nn. [ME, f. OF or f. LL *aequi-
(valēre* be worth), see EQUI- & -ENT]

ēquiv'ocal, a. ‘ Of double meaning, ambiguous; of uncertain nature; ~ *generation* (spontaneous); undecided; (of persons, character, etc.) questionable, suspicious. Hence ~ITY(-ăl'-), ~NESS, nn., ~LY[2]
adv. [f. LL *aequivocus* (EQUI-, *vocare* call),
see -AL]

ēquiv'oc|āte, v.i. Use ambiguous words
to conceal the truth, prevaricate. Hence
or cogn. ~A'TION, ~ātoR, nn. [f. LL
aequivocare (as prec., see -ATE[2])]

ē'quivōque (-k), -ōke, n. Pun; ambiguity.
[f. LL *aequivocus* EQUIVOCAL; later also f.
F *équivoque*]

-er[1], suf. forming esp. agent nn. f. nn. &
vbs. Orig. = ‘ one who has to do with ’,
OE *-ere* f. Gmc *-arjaz*, the relation of
which to L *-arius* (-ARY[1]) is obsc.; so E
wds as *hatter*, *slater*; a few as *cottager*,
villager; also colloq. wds of action, as

header, *out-&-outer*, and of number, as
fiver, *tenner*; add *Londoner*, *foreigner*, etc.
As many wds so formed correspond to
vbs, *-er* took agent sense (*clothier* one
connected with cloth, one who clothes),
& can now be added to any vb unless
otherwise provided, as *correspond(ent)*,
translat(or); *-or* (*-our*, *-ier*) & *-er* may coexist, with or without differentiation
(*saviour*, *-er*; *assertor*, *-er*); some wds
app. double *-er* (*caterer*, *fruiterer*, *poulterer*); *-er* is occas. used to anglicize L
-us (*astronomer*, *biographer*, *chrono-
loger*). Meanings: (1) person, animal, that
does something; (2) instrument, machine,
occurrence, etc. (*poker*, *paper-cutter*, *deo-
dorizer*, *eye-opener*); (3) person concerned
with thing (*hatter*, *geographer*); (4) person
belonging to place etc. (*Londoner*,
Britisher); (5) sl. distortion of word with
other ending (*Rugger*, *Soccer*, *footer*,
Rugby, Association, football).

-er[2], suf. in nn. & adjj. f. OF, of var. orig.,
esp.: (1) OF, ME *-er* f. L *-arem*; ME *-er*
was later refash. w. *-ar*; see -AR[1]. (2) AF,
ME *-er* (OF *-ier*) f. L *-arius*, *-arium*, as in
butler, *carpenter*, *danger*; see -ARY[1]. (3)
OF *-ēure* f. L *-aturam = -*URE, as *border*.
(4) For interchange of *-er*, *-or*, see -OR.

-er[3], suf. forming comparatives; now (exc.
in poetry and mannered prose) only in
adjj. of one syllable, or of two ending in
-y, *-ly*, *-le*, *-er*, *-ow*, & a few others (esp. w.
accent on last syllable; see -EST), & in
advv., chiefly those identical with adjj.,
as *hard*; the vowel change seen in German
etc. now remains only in *elder*, BETTER.
[OE: (adj.) *-ra* f. Gmc *-izon-* & *-ōzon-*;
(adv.) *-or* f. Gmc *-ōz*]

-er[4], suf. esp. in Law terms, as *cesser*, *dis-
claimer*, *misnomer*, *user*; also *dinner*, *supper*. Meaning: (single instance of) the vbl
action, document effecting this. [AF, OF
inf.]

-er[5], suf. forming frequent. vbs f. others
(*wander*, *waver*, f. *vend*, *wave*) or on sound-
-imitations (*twitter*); *batter*, *flicker*, *shim-
mer*, *slumber*.

ēr'a, n. System of chronology starting
from some particular point of time, as
Christian~, ~ *of the* HEGIRA; historical or
other period; date forming commencement of this. [f. LL *aera* number expressed in figures (pl. of *aes aeris* money,
treated as fem. sing.)]

ērādiā'tion, n. Emission of rays. [E-]

ērăd'ic|āte, v.t. Tear up by roots; extir-
pate, get rid of. So ~ABLE a., ~A'TION n.
[f. L E(*radicare* f. *radix -icis* root), -ATE[3]]

ērāse' (-z), v.t. Rub out; obliterate.
Hence ērās'ABLE a., ērās'ER[2](2), ērā's-
URE (-zher), nn. [f. L E(*radere ras-*scrape)]

Erās'tian (I-), a. & n. (Adherent) of the
supposed doctrines of Erastus, subordin-
ating ecclesiastical to secular power.
Hence ~ISM(3) n., ~IZE(3) v.t. & i. [f.
Erastus, Heidelberg physician of 16th c.,
+ -IAN]

E′ratō (ĕ-), n. Muse of lyric poetry. [Gk]

ere (âr), prep. & conj. (poet., arch.). Before (of time); ~ *long*, before long; ~*while* (arch.), formerly. [OE *ǣr*, OS, OHG *ēr*, Goth. *airis* f. Gmc *airiz* compar. of *air* adv. early]

E′rebus (ĕ-), n. (Gk Myth.). Place of darkness between earth & Hades. [L, f. Gk *Erebos*]

ĕrĕct′[1], a. Upright, not stooping, (lit. & fig); vertical; (of hair etc.) set up, bristling. Hence ~LY[2] adv., ~NESS n. [ME, f. L E(*rigere rect-* = *regere* direct) set up]

ĕrĕct′[2], v.t. Raise, set upright, (oneself, body, etc.); build (lit. & fig.); form (persons, principles, etc.) *into* (class, system, etc.). [ME; as prec.]

ĕrĕc′tile, a. That can be erected; ~ *tissue* in animals (capable of being distended & becoming rigid under excitement). [f. F *érectile* (as ERECT[1], see -IL)]

ĕrĕc′tion, n. Erecting; building, structure, (lit. & fig.). [F, or f. L *erectio* (as prec., see -ION)]

ĕrĕc′tor, n. Person, thing, that erects, as ~-*muscle*. [-OR]

ĕ′rĕmite, ·n. Hermit (esp. of Christian solitaries from 3rd c. onwards). Hence **ĕrĕmit′IC(AL)** aa. [ME, f. OF or f. LL *eremita* HERMIT]

ĕ′rĕthism, n. (path.). Abnormal excitement (of organ or tissue, fig. of mind). [f. F *éréthisme* f. Gk *erethismos* (*erethizō* irritate, see -ISM)]

ĕrg, ĕrg′ŏn, n. (phys.). Unit of work or energy. (The work done by unit force, one dyne, on a body which moves 1 cm. in the direction of action of the force). [f. Gk *ergon* work]

ĕrgatŏc′racy, n. Rule of the workers. [Gk *ergatēs* worker, -O-, -CRACY]

ĕrg′ō, adv. (usu. joc.). Therefore. [L]

ĕrg′ot, n. Disease of rye etc. caused by fungus; diseased rye seed as medicine. [F, f. OF *argot* cock's spur, f. appearance produced]

ĕrg′otism, n. = prec.; disease produced by bread made from flour affected by this. [-ISM]

ĕrica′ceous (-shus), a. Belonging to the heath genus *Eric′a* or its family *Ericā′-ceae*. [f. L f. Gk *ereikē* heath, see -ACEOUS]

E′rin (ĕ-), n. (Ancient name of) Ireland.

Erin′ÿs (ĕ-), n. (pl. *Erinyes*, pr. ĕrĭn′lēz), A Fury. [Gk]

ĕris′tic, a, & n. (Art) of disputation; (of argument or arguer) aimed or aiming at victory rather than truth. [f. Gk *eristikos* (*erizō* f. *eris* strife, see -IC)]

ĕrl-king′, n. Bearded golden-crowned giant of Teutonic folk-lore who lures little children to the land of death. [f. G *erl-kŏnig* alder-king, a mistransl. of Da. *ellerkonge* king of the elves]

ĕrm′in|e, n. Animal of weasel tribe, whose fur is brown in summer & white (except black tail-tip) in winter; its fur, used in robes of judges & peers (often poet. as

emblem of purity), whence ~ED[2] (-nd). a; (Her.) white marked with black spots. [ME, f. OF (*h*)*ermine* of unkn. orig.]

-ern, suf. in *northern* etc. f. Gmc *-rōnja-* (*-ro-* + *-ōnja-* = L *-aneus*).

ĕrne, n. Sea eagle. [OE *earn*, OHG *arn*, ON *ǫrn* f. Gmc *arn-*]

‖ Ern′ie (ĕr-), n. Device for drawing prize-winning numbers of premium bonds. [f. initial letters of *electronic random number indicator equipment*]

ĕrōde′, v.t. (Of acids, currents, etc.) gnaw away, destroy gradually, wear out. So **ĕrō′sION** (-zhn) n., **ĕrōs′IVE** a. [f. F *éroder* or L (*rodere ros-* gnaw)]

Er′ōs (ĕr-), n. Love, god of love, Cupid. [Gk *ĕrōs*]

ĕrŏt′ic, a. & n. 1. Of love, amatory. 2. n. ~ poem or composition or person. Hence ~a n. pl., ~ *literature*, ~ISM n., ~ spirit or character. [f. F *érotique* or Gk *erōtikos* (*erōs -ōtos* sexual love, see -IC]

ĕ′rotism, n. Sexual desire or excitement, eroticism. [f. Gk *erōs* (as prec.) +-ISM]

ĕrōt′omān′ia, n. (path.). Melancholy, madness, arising from love. [f. Gk *erōs* (as prec.) +-MANIA]

ĕrr, v.i. Make mistakes; (of statements etc.) be incorrect; sin. [ME, f. OF *errer* f. L *errare*]

ĕ′rrand, n. Short journey on which an inferior is sent to carry message etc., as *run, go*, (on) ~*s*, ~-*boy*; object of journey; purpose. [OE *ǣrende*, OS *ārundi*, OHG *ārunti*, of obsc. orig.]

ĕ′rrant, a. & n. Roaming in quest of adventure, esp. KNIGHT-~; itinerant; erring, deviating from correct standard; whence **ĕ′rrANCY** n.; (n.) KNIGHT-~. [ME; (1) f. OF *errer, edrer*, f. LL *iterare* (*iter* journey), (2) as ERR; see -ANT]

ĕ′rrantry, n. Condition, conduct, notions, of a knight-errant. [-RY]

ĕrrăt′|ic, a. Uncertain in movement; (of diseases) moving from one part to another; irregular in conduct, habit, opinion; (Geol.) ~*ic blocks*, stray masses foreign to surrounding strata. Hence ~ICALLY adv. [ME, f. OF *erratique* f. L *erraticus* (as ERR), see -ATIC]

ĕrrăt′um, n. (pl. *-ta*). Error in printing or writing, esp. (pl.) errors noted in list attached to book. [L, neut. p.p. as prec.]

ĕrrōn′eous, a. Mistaken, incorrect. Hence ~LY[2] adv., ~NESS n. [ME, f. OF *erroneus* or L *erroneus* (*erro -onis* vagabond, as ERR) +-OUS]

ĕ′rror, n. Mistake, as *make, commit, an* ~, CLERICAL ~; condition of erring in opinion; wrong opinion; *in* ~, mistaken(ly), by *mistake*; ~ *of a planet*, difference between its observed & calculated positions; (Law) *writ of* ~ (to procure reversal of judgement on ground of ~); transgression. Hence ~LESS n. [ME, f. OF f. L *errorem* (as ERR, -OR)]

ersätz′ (âr-), n. & a. Substitute. [G]

Erse (ĕrs), a. & n. Highland Gaelic

(dialect); (unused & disliked in Ireland for) Irish. [early Sc. form of *Irish*]

ĕrst, adv. (arch.). (Also ~'*while*) formerly, of old. [OE *ǽrest* superl. of *ǽr*, see ERE]

ĕrubĕs'cent (-rŏŏ-), a. Reddening, blushing. [f. L E(*rubescere* incept. of *rubēre*), see -ENT]

ĕructā'tion, n. Belching (lit. & fig., esp. of volcano. [f. L *eructatio* (Eructare, see -ATION)]

ĕ'rudite (-rŏŏ-), a. (Of persons & writings) learned. Hence or cogn. ~LY² (-tl-) adv., **ĕrudi'tion** n., (-rŏŏ-). [ME, f. L *erudire* -*it*- train (*rudis* rude)]

ĕrŭpt', v.i. (Of teeth) break through gums; (of volcano) break out. [f. L E(*rumpere rupt*- break)]

ĕrŭp'tion, n. Outbreak (of volcano, whence ~AL (-shon-) a.; also of geyser, disease, war, passion, mirth, wit); (Path.) breaking out (of rash, pimples, etc.); (of teeth) breaking through gums. [F, or f. L *eruptio* (as prec., see -ION)]

ĕrŭp'tive, a. Bursting forth; tending to burst forth; of, formed by, forced up by, volcanic eruption. Hence ~LY² adv., ~NESS, **ĕruptiv'ITY**, nn. [f. as ERUPT +-IVE, or F *éruptif*]

-erȳ, -rȳ, suf. forming nouns, orig. after F -*erie*: (a) f. com.·Rom. -*aria* = L -*ario*- (F -*ier*, -*er*) +-*ia* -Y¹; F wds in -*ier* usu. denote person having some occupation, wds in -*erie* the class of goods he deals in, as *draperie*, his employment, as *archerie*, his place of work, as *boulangerie*; -*erie* was also used without existing wd in -*ier*, as *soierie* (*soie*) silk goods, *niaiserie* (*niais*) foolishness. (b) f. OF -*ere*, -*eor* (mod. F -*eur* f. L -*ator* +-*ie*. On anal. of wds thus formed, -*erie* was added to vb stems direct, w. sense class of actions (*tromperie* deceit), occupation (*confiserie* confectioner's business), place of this (*brasserie* brewery). Many E wds are f. F; others are formed on nn. in -*er* (*bakery, fishery, pottery*), or on others (*knavery, slavery, popery*). Meanings: (1) class of goods (*drapery*); (2) employment or condition (*archery, dupery*); (3) place of work or cultivation or breeding (*brewery, vinery, piggery*); (4) conduct (*foolery*); (5) all that has to do with (*popery*), things of the nature of.

ĕrȳsip'élas, n. (Also *St Anthony's fire, the rose*) local febrile disease producing deep red colour on skin. [f. L f. Gk *erusipelas*]

ĕrythēm'a, n. Superficial inflammation of the skin in patches. [f. Gk *eruthēma* f. *eruthainō* be red (*eruthros*)]

-es, old genit. termination used to give adv. force; appearing as -*s* (*needs*), -*ce* (*once*), & (w. excrescent -*t*) -*st* (*against*); also in the emphatic absolute forms *ours, yours, hers*, etc.

ĕscalāde', n. Scaling of walls with ladders. [F, f. Sp. *escalada* f. med. L *scalare* (*scala* ladder), see -ADE]

ĕs'calātor, n. Moving staircase for carrying passengers up or down. [as ESCALADE, -OR]

ĕscallŏn'ĭa, n. S.-Amer. kinds of flowering shrubs. [*Escallon*, discoverer, -IA¹]

ĕscăll'op. See SCALLOP.

ĕscapāde', n. Breaking loose from restraint; flighty piece of conduct. [F, f. Sp. *escapada* (as ESCAPE², see -ADE)]

ĕscāpe'¹, n. Act of escaping; fact of having escaped (*a narrow, hairbreadth*, ~); (means of) mental distraction or relief from reality (also attrib., as ~ *literature, reading*), whence **ĕscāp'ISM** n., **ĕscāp'IST** n. & a.; leakage (of gas etc.); garden plant growing wild; = FIRE-~; ~ *clause*, one specifying conditions under which contracting party is free from obligations; ~-*pipe, -valve* (for ~ of steam or water); ~-*shaft* (for ~ of miners when other shaft is blocked). [f. foll.]

ĕscāpe'², v.i. & t. Get free (*from* prison, person, etc.); (of steam, fluids, etc.) find a way out; get off safely, go unpunished; (v.t.) get clear away from (person, his grasp, etc.), avoid (unpleasant thing, *doing*); elude notice or recollection of, as *his name had* ~*d me*; (of words) issue unawares from (person, his lips). Hence **ĕscapEE'** n., one who has ~d. [ME *escape* f. AF, ONF *escaper*; ME *eschape* f. OF *eschaper* f. Rom. *excappare* f. *cappa* cloak (see CAP)]

ĕscāpe'ment (-pm-), n. Outlet; (of watch or clock) mechanism connecting motive power & regulator. [-MENT]

ĕscārp', n., & v.t. 1. Steep bank immediately in front of & below rampart; similar natural formation. 2. v.t. Cut into form of ~, so ~MENT n. [(vb f. F *escarper*) f. F *escarpe* f. It. *scarpa* SCARP]

-ĕs'cent, suf. forming adjj. f. L part. of inceptive vbs (-*escens -ntis*), as *effervescent*, & thence in wds usu. describing play of colour, as *iridescent, opalescent*, or merely adjectival, as *alkalescent*.

eschalĕt' (ĕsh-). See SHALLOT.

eschat|ŏl'ogȳ (ĕsk-), n. Doctrine of death, judgement, heaven, & hell. Hence ~olŏ'gICAL a. [f. Gk *eskhatos* last +-LOGY]

ĕscheat'¹, n. Lapsing of property to crown or lord of manor on owner's dying intestate without heirs; property so lapsing. [ME, f. OF *eschete* p.p. of *escheoir* f. Rom. *excadēre* f. L EX- (*cidere* = *cadere* fall)]

ĕscheat'², v.t. & i. Confiscate; hand over (property) as an escheat (*to* person, *into* his hands); revert by escheat (*to* or abs.). [prec.]

ĕschew' (-ŏŏ), v.t. Avoid, abstain from, (action, conduct, kind of food, etc.). [ME, f. OF *eschiver* f. Rom. *skivare* f. WG *skeuh*, see SHY¹]

eschschŏlt'zia (Ishŏl-), n. A plant with usu. yellow flowers, Noah's nightcap. [*Eschscholtz*, explorer, -IA¹]

esclandre (ĕsklahŭ'dr), n. Scandal; disturbance. [F]

es'cort[1], n. Body of armed men acting as guard to persons, baggage, etc.; person(s) accompanying another on journey for protection or guidance, or for courtesy's sake. [f. F *escorte* f. It. *scorta* f. *scorgere* conduct f. Rom. *EX(COR*rigere* f. *regere* direct)]

escort'[2], v.t. Act as escort to; ~ *carrier*, aircraft carrier for ~ing convoys. [f. prec.]

escribe', v.t. (math.). Describe (circle) so as to touch one side of triangle exteriorly & the other two produced. [f. E-+L *scribere* write]

es'critoire (-twahr), n. Writing-desk with drawers etc. for stationery. [F (now *éc-*), f. med. L *scriptorium* (as prec., see -ORY)]

escrow' (-ō), n. Written legal engagement to do something, kept in third person's custody until some condition has been fulfilled. [AF *escrowe*, OF *escroe*, f. med. L *scroda* f. Gmc *skraudh-*, see SCROLL, SHRED]

escudo', n. (pl. -os). Portuguese monetary unit & silver coin (applied also to various Spanish-American gold & silver coins). [Sp. & Port., f. L *scutum* shield]

es'culent, a. & n. (Thing) fit for food. [f. L *esculentus* (*esca* food, see -LENT)]

escutch'eon (-chon), n. Shield with armorial bearings (*a blot on his* ~ (stain on reputation); middle of ship's stern where name is placed; pivoted keyhole-cover. [f. ONF *escuchon* f. Rom. *scutionem* (L *scutum* shield, see -ION)]

-ese, suf. forming adjj. (& nn.), f. OF *-eis* f. L *-ensis* local suf. (freq. now *-ian*, as *Atheniensis* Athenian); applied to some foreign countries & towns (*Japanese, Milanese*), either as adj. or meaning ' inhabitant ' (pl. *-ese*) or ' language '; also used spec. (adj. or n.) of diction of mannered writers (*Carlylese*), as though a non-English language.

es'kar, -er, n. (geol.). Long ridge of post-glacial gravel in river valleys. [f. Ir. *eiscir*]

Eskimo, -quimau, (ĕs'kĭmō), n. (pl. *-os, -oes*, pr. *-mōz; -maux*, pr. *-mō, -mōz*). Member of a people in arctic coasts of America. [native]

esote'ric, a. (Of philosophical doctrines etc.) meant only for the initiated; (of disciples) initiated; private, confidential. Hence ~AL a., ~alLY[2] adv. [f. Gk *esōterikos* (*esōterō* compar. of *esō* within, see -IC)]

espagnolette' (-ănyŏlĕt), n. Fastening of French window. [F, dim. of *espagnol* Spanish]

espal'ier, n. Lattice-work on which trees or shrubs are trained; tree so trained. [F, f. It. *spalliera* (*spalla* shoulder)]

espart'o, n. (Also ~ *grass*) kinds of grass imported from Spain and N. Africa for paper-making. [Sp., f. L f. Gk *sparton* rope of the plant *spartos*]

espe'cial (-shl), a. Pre-eminent, excep-

tional, as *my* ~ *friend, thing of* ~ *importance*; particular (opp. to *ordinary*, cf. SPECIAL); belonging chiefly to one case (*for your* ~ *benefit*). Hence ~LY[2] (-sha-) adv. [ME, f. OF, f. L as SPECIAL]

Esperan'to (ĕ-), n. An artificial language designed as a medium for persons of all nations. [pen-name (f. L *spero* hope) of its inventor, Dr Zamenhof, 1887]

espi'al, n. Acting as a spy; watching, espying. [ME, f. OF *espiaille*, as ESPY, see -AL(2)]

espiègle'rie (see Ap.), n. Roguishness. [F]

es'pionage (-ĭj, -ahzh'), n. Practice of spying or using spies. [F (*-nn-*) f. *espionner* f. *espion* SPY]

esplanade', n. Level piece of ground, esp. one used for public promenade; level space separating citadel of fortress from town. [F, f. Sp. *esplanada* f. *esplanar* f. L EX*planare* make level (*planus*), see -ADE]

espous'al (-zl), n. (arch.). (Usu. pl.) marriage or betrothal; (fig.) espousing of (a cause etc.). [ME, f. OF *espousailles* f. L *sponsalia* neut. pl. (*sponsus* p.p. as foll. see -AL)]

espouse' (-z), v.t. (Usu. of man) marry, give (woman) in marriage (*to*); adopt, support, (doctrine, cause, etc.). [ME, f. OF *espouser* f. L *sponsare* (*sponsus* p.p. of *spondēre* betroth)]

espressiv'o (-ēvŏ), adv. (mus.). With expression. [It.]

espress'o, n. Apparatus for making coffee under pressure; coffee-bar equipped with this; also attrib. [It.]

esprit (ĕsprē'), n. Sprightliness; wit; ~ *de corps* (de kōr), regard for honour & interests of body one belongs to; ~ *fort* (fōrr), strong-minded person, free-thinker. [F, f. L as SPIRIT]

espy', v.t. Catch sight of; detect (flaw etc.). [ME, f. OF *espier* f. com.-Rom *spiare* f. Gmc *spehōn*, see SPY]

-esque, suf. forming adjj., = F *-esque* f. It. *-esco* f. med. L *-iscus* in Gmc wds; cf. OHG *-isc* (mod. *-isch*) = -ISH[1]; meaning ' after the manner of ', as *arabesque, burlesque, Dantesque*.

Esquimau. See ESKIMO.

esquire', n. ‖ Title appended to name of one regarded as gentleman by birth, position, or education, esp. in address of letter (abbr. *Esq.*); (arch.) = SQUIRE. [ME, f. OF *esquier* f. L *scutarius* shield-bearer (*scutum* shield, -ARY[1])]

ess, n. S(-shaped thing); COLLAR[1] *of* ~es. **-ess**[1], suf. forming female nn. f. F (*coun tess, lioness*) or on E wds (*goddess*); in 15th c. the OE fem. *-ster* (now only in *spinster*) came to be regarded as masculine, & could take fem. *-ess* (*seamstress*), agent nn. in *-ter, -tor*, regularly have *-tress* (*chantress*); other exx. are *authoress* etc. (*author* etc. now preferred), *giantess, quakeress; governess* (formed on vb) is irreg., perh. on anal. of *sorceress* (formed on old *sorcer* not on *sorcerer*, which has double agent suf.); euphony leads to same clipping in *adventuress, murderess*; *-tress* is now recognized angliciz. of F *-trice* (L *-trix -tricis*), though of diff. orig. [f. F *-esse* f. LL f. Gk *-issa*]

-**ess²**, suf. in abstr. nn. f. adjj., as *duress, largess; riches, laches*, are exx., mistaken for pl. [ME & OF *-esse* = It. *-ezza* f. L *-itia* -ICE]

ess'ay¹, n. Attempt (*at*); a literary composition (usu. prose & short) on any subject, whence ∼IST(3) n. [f. F *essai*, see ASSAY¹]

essay'², v.t. & i. Try, test, (person, thing); attempt (task, *to do*, or abs.). [refash. f. ASSAY² on F *essayer*]

ess'e, n. Essential being or nature (often contrasted with *bene esse* well-being). [L, = to be]

ess'enc|e, n. An existence or entity (spiritual or immaterial); absolute being, reality underlying phenomena; all that makes a thing what it is; intrinsic nature; indispensable quality or element; extract obtained by distillation etc. (lit. & fig.); perfume, scent, whence ∼ED² (-st) a. [ME, f. OF f. L *essentia* f. *essens -ntis* fictitious part. of *esse* be, repr. Gk *ousia*]

Essēne' (ē-), n. Member of an ancient Jewish sect, of mystical tenets & coenobitical life. [f. L f. Gk pl. *Essēnoi*]

essĕn'tial (-shl), a. & n. 1. Of, constituting, a thing's essence; indispensable (*to*); ∼ *proposition*, one that predicates of a subject what is implied in its definition; ∼ *character* (of species, genus, etc.), marks that distinguish it from others included with it in next superior division; ∼ *harmony* (belonging to one particular key); ∼ *oil*, volatile oil, marked by characteristic odour etc. 2. n. Indispensable element. Hence ∼ITY (-shiăl⁴) n., ∼LY² (-shal-) adv. [ME, f. LL *essentialis* (as ESSENCE, -AL)]

-**est**, suf. forming superl. adjj. & advv. (& FIRST, LAST); for limits of use see -ER³, but many adjj. can bear *-est* though not *-er*, as *awkward, barren, fragile, loyal, legible*, & many in *-id*, as *limpid*; in poetry & mannered prose *-est* is used w. almost any adj., & appended to advv. in *-ly*, as *quickliest*. [OE *-ost, -ust, -ast*, f. Gmc *-ōsto-*, & OE *-est, -st*, f. Gmc *-istaz* (compar. *-ōz-, -iz-*, +Aryan *-to-*), cf. Gk *-isto-; -iz-* required vowel change, now only in *eldest*, BEST]

estăb'lish, v.t. Set up (government, house of business, etc.) on permanent basis; settle (person, one*self*, *in* office etc.); secure permanent acceptance for (custom, precedent, belief, etc.); place beyond dispute (fact, *that*); make (church) legally national. [ME, f. OF *establir* (st. *-iss-*, see -ISH²) f. L *stabilire* (as STABLE a.)]

estăb'lishment, n. Establishing; *Church E∼, the E∼*, church system established by law; organized body of men maintained

for a purpose, as army, navy, civil service; *peace, war,* ∼, reduced, increased, army etc. in time of peace, war; staff of servants etc.; public institution, house of business; household, as *separate* ∼ (of man maintaining paramour). [-MENT]

estăblishmentar'ian, a. & n. (Person) adhering to, advocating the principle of, an established church. [-ARIAN]

estăm'inet (-nă), n. French café selling wine, beer, & coffee, or cottage with bar-room. [F]

estāte', n. 1. Order, class, forming part of body politic & sharing in government; ‖ *the Three E∼s* (in England), Lords Spiritual, Lords Temporal, Commons; *third ∼*, (usu.) French bourgeoisie before Revolution; ‖ (joc.) *fourth ∼*, the press. 2. Person's interest in landed property (*real ∼*) or movables (*personal ∼*), whence **estāt'**ED² a.; a landed property (‖*∼ agent*, steward of ∼, go-between in sales of houses & land); ∼ *car*, dual-purpose light saloon vehicle constructed or adapted for the carriage of both passengers & goods. 3. One's collective assets & liabilities. 4. (arch.). Condition, as *the holy ∼ of matrimony*. [ME, f. OF *estat* f. L as STATE]

estēem', v.t., & n. 1. Think highly of; consider, as *I shall ∼ it* (*as*) *a favour*. 2. n. Favourable opinion, regard, respect. [(n. f. vb) f. OF *estimer* f. L as ESTIMATE²; see AIM¹]

es'ter, n. (chem.). Compound formed by replacing the hydrogen of an acid by a hydrocarbon radical of the ethyl type. [coined by the German chemist L. Gmelin (d. 1853)]

es'timable, a. Worthy of esteem. [F, f. L *aestimabilis* (as ESTEEM, see -BLE)]

es'timate¹, n. Approximate judgement (of number, amount, etc.); quantity assigned by this; ‖ *the E∼s*, forecasts of national expenditure, presented annually to parliament; contractor's statement of sum for which he will undertake specified work; judgement of character or qualities. [f. foll. or L *aestimatus -ūs*]

es'timāte², v.t. Form an estimate of; fix (number etc.) by estimate *at* (so much); form an opinion of. So ∼ative a., ∼ātor n. [f. L *aestimare*, see -ATE³]

estimā'tion, n. Judgement of worth, as *in my ∼*; esteem, as *hold in ∼, be in ∼*. [ME, f. OF *estimacion* or L *aestimatio* (as prec., see -ATION)]

estival etc. See aest-.

estŏp', v.t. (law; -pp-). Bar, preclude, (*from* thing. *from* do*ing*). Hence∼p'AGE n. [f. AF, OF *estoper* f. *estoupe* f. L *stuppa* tow; see STOP¹]

estŏpp'el, n. (law). The being precluded from a course by previous action of one's own. [f. OF *estoupail* bung f. *estoper* (prec., -AL(2))]

estŏv'ers (-z), n. pl. Necessaries allowed by law (as wood for repairs or fuel taken by a tenant from his holding). [f. AF *estover*, OF -*eir* be necessary, f. L *est opus*]

estrade' (-ahd), n. Raised platform, dais. [F, f. Sp. *estrado* f. L *stratum* neut. p.p. of *sternere* spread (with carpets)]

èstrange' (-j), v.t. Alienate (person) in feeling (*from* another). Hence ~MENT (-jm-) n. [ME, f. OF *estranger* f. L *extraneare* (as STRANGE)]

èstreat', v.t. (law). Take out record of (fine, bail, etc.) & return it to Court of Exchequer to be prosecuted. [f. AF *estrete*, OF *estraite* fem. p.p. of *estraire* EXTRACT]

ès'tūar|y̌, n. Tidal mouth of large river. Hence ~INE¹ a. [f. L *aestuarium* neut. adj. as n. (*aestus* -*ūs* tide, see -ARY¹)]

èsūr'i|ent, a. (joc.). Hungry; needy & greedy. So ~ENCE, ~ENCY, nn. [f. L *esurire*, desiderative f. *edere es-* eat]

-èt¹, suf. forming (orig.) dimm., many not now realized as such; mostly in ME adoptions f. OF (*bullet, hatchet, sonnet*); double dim. -LET (F -*et* + -*et*) is living suf. [OF -*et* & -*ette* (dist. only in mod. E) = It. -*etto*, -*etta*, f. Rom. -*itto*, -*itta*, of unkn. orig.]

-èt², -ēte, suf. in agent nn. f. Gk, -*et* in older or familiar wds, as *poet, comet, anchoret, -ete* in newer or learned ones, as *athlete, aesthete, exegete*. [f. Gk -*ētēs*: *epithet, paracleie*, are not exx.; *diabetes* retains full form]

ēt'a, n. Greek letter (H, η)=ē (cf. EPSILON). [Gk]

et'acism (ā-), n. Pronunciation of Gk ē as English ā (cf. ITACISM). [f. Gk *ēta* letter *ē*, -ISM]

état-major (ătah' mahzhŏr'), n. (mil.). Staff, staff-office. [F]

ĕt cĕt'era, ĕtcĕt'era, phr. & n. (pl. -*as*). (Abbr. *etc.*, *&c.*) & the rest, & so on, as *I remain yours etc.*; (n. pl.) extras, sundries. [L]

ĕtch, v.t. & i. Reproduce (pictures etc.), portray (subject), by engraving metal--plate etc. by means of acids or corrosives, esp. for purpose of printing copies; (v.i.) practise this art. [f. Du. *etsen* f. G *ätzen* etch f. OHG *azzen* cause to eat or be eaten f. Gmc *atjan* causative of *elan* EAT]

ĕtch'ing, n. In vbl senses, esp. copy from etched plate; ~*needle*, used in ~. [-ING¹]

ètĕr'nal, a. That always (has existed &) will exist, as ~ *life, punishment; the E~, God; ~ CITY;* (colloq.) incessant, too frequent, as *these~ bickerings; the~ triangle,* two males & a female or *vice versa.* Hence or cogn. ètĕrn'(al)IZE(3) vv.t., ~LY² adv. [ME, f. OF f. LL *aeternalis* f. L *aeternus*, see -AL]

ètĕr'nity̌, n. Being eternal; immortal fame; (pl.) eternal truths; infinite time, esp. future; the future life. [ME, f. OF *eternite* f. L *aeternitatem* (*aeternus*, see prec. & -TY)]

Etesian (ītēzh'an), a. ~ *winds* (blowing annually in Mediterranean from N.W. for about 40 days in summer). [f. L f. Gk *etēsios* (*etos* year) + -AN]

-eth, suf. See -TH³.

ĕth'āne, n. A colourless and odourless gas insoluble in water and burning with a pale flame, ethyl hydride. [f. ETH(ER) + -ANE]

ĕth'er, n. 1. Clear sky, upper regions beyond clouds. 2. (phys.). A medium assumed to permeate space & fill interstices between particles of air & other matter, medium in which electro-magnetic waves are transmitted, whence ~IC a. 3. (chem.). Colourless light volatile liquid produced by action of sulphuric acid & other acids on alcohol, an anaesthetic. [f. L f. Gk *aithēr* f. root of *aithō* burn, shine]

ĕthēr'ĕal, -ial, a. 1. Light, airy; heavenly; of unearthly delicacy of substance, character, or appearance, whence ~ITY (-ăl'-), ~ĪZA'TION, nn., ~IZE(3) v.t., ~LY² adv. 2. (phys., chem.). Of, like, ETHER, so ĕth'erIFICA'TION n., ĕth'erIFY v.t.; ~ *oil*, essential or volatile oil. [f. L (*-eus, -ius*) f. Gk *aitherios* (as prec.) + -AL]

ĕth'eriz|e, -is|e (-īz), v.t. Put (patient) under influence of ether. Hence ~A'TION n. [-IZE]

ĕth'ic, a. & n. 1. (Now usu. ~*al*) relating to morals, treating of moral questions, *'moral; ~ dative* (of person indirectly interested, as *knock* me *at the door*). 2. n. pl., & rarely sing. Science of morals, treatise on this, moral principles, rules of conduct, whole field of moral science. Hence ~AL a. (also, of drugs, conforming to a recognized standard), ~ALY² adv., ~IZE(3) v.t. [f. F *éthique* or L f. Gk *ēthikos* (ETHOS, -IC)]

Ethiōp'ian (ē-), a. & n. (Native) of Ethiopia, esp. (Anthropol.) as epithet of one of the races into which human species is divided. [-AN]

ĕth'moid, a. Sieve-like; ~ *bone*, square--shaped bone at root of nose, through the many perforations of which the olfactory nerves pass to the nose. [f. Gk *ēthmoeidēs* (*ēthmos* sieve)]

ĕth'nārch (-k), n. Governor of a people or province. So ~Y¹ (-kĭ) n. [f. Gk *ethnos* nation + -*arkhēs* ruler]

ĕth'nic, -ic|al, aa. Pertaining to race, ethnological, whence ~ALY² adv.; (~) gentile, heathen, whence ~AlISM(2) n. [f. LL f. Gk *ethnikos* (*ethnos* nation, see -IC)]

ĕthnŏg'raphy̌, n. Scientific description of races of men. So ĕthnŏG'RAPHER n., ĕthnŏgrăph'IC(AL) aa., ĕthnŏgrăph'icalLY adv. [f. Gk *ethnos* nation + -GRAPHY]

ĕthnŏl'ogy̌, n. Science of races & their relations to one another & characteristics. So ĕthnŏlŏ'gIC(AL) aa. (-*ic frontier*, corresponding to a division of races), ĕthnŏlŏ'gicalLY² adv., ĕthnŏl'ogIST n. [as prec. + -LOGY]

ĕt hŏc gĕn'us ŏm'nĕ, phr. And all that kind of thing (often as ornamental substitute for *et cetera*). [L]

ĕthŏl′ogў, n. Science of character-formation. Hence ĕtholŏ′gICAL a. [f. L f. Gk *ēthologia* (ETHOS, see -LOGY)]

ĕth′ŏs, n. Characteristic spirit of community, people, or system. [Gk (*ē-*) = character, nature, disposition]

ĕth′ўl, n. (chem.) The hydrocarbon radical present in ordinary alcohol & ether. [f. ETH(ER), -YL]

-ĕt′ic, suf. of adjj. & nn. = Gk agent suf. *-ĕt-* or *-ēt-*+-IC, in wds f. Gk or on Gk models, as *emetic* (Gk *emĕtikos*), *ascetic* (Gk *askĕtikos*).

ĕt′iol|āte, v.t. Make (plant) pale by excluding light; give sickly hue to (person). Hence ∼A′TION n. [f. F *étioler* f. Norm. *étieuler* make into haùlm (*éteule* f. pop. L *stupila* f. L *stipula* straw)]

ētiology. See AETIOLOGY.

ĕtiquette′ (-kĕt), n. Conventional rules of personal behaviour in polite society; ceremonial of court; unwritten code restricting professional men in what concerns interests of their brethren or dignity of their profession, esp. *medical*, *legal*, ∼. [f. F *étiquette* TICKET, ∼]

ĕt′na, n. Vessel for heating small quantity of liquid by burning spirit. [f. the volcano]

Et′on (ē-), n. ∼ *collar* (broad, stiff, worn outside coat-collar); ∼ *crop*, cutting of woman's hair short like boy's; ∼ *jacket*, boy's short coat reaching only to waist. [f. ∼ College]

Etrŭs′can (I-) a. & n. (Native) of ancient Etruria. [f. L *Etruscus*+-AN]

ĕt sĕq(q)., *sĕquĕn′tĕs* (-z), *-tĭa*, (in reference to books etc.). And the words, pages, etc., that follow. [L]

-ĕtte, suf. forming dim. nn. (rarely adjj.), repr. OF *-ette*, the fem. corresp. to -ET[1]. (1) Older adoptions now have *-et*; *-ette* appears chiefly in wds introduced since 17th c., as *cigarette*, *etiquette*. (2) A mod. commerc. use, = 'sham', is seen in *leatherette*, *Brusselette* (carpet). (3) A mod. fem. suf., as *usherette*.

étude (ātūd′), n. A short musical composition or exercise. [F]

ĕtui′ (-wē), **ĕtwee′,** n. Small case for needles, toothpicks, etc. [f. F *étui*]

ĕtўmŏl′ogīze, -ise (-īz), v.t. & i. Give, trace, the etymology 'of'; suggest etymology for; study etymology. [16th c., f. F *-iser*, or med. L *ethimologizare* (as foll., -IZE)]

ĕtўmŏl′ogў, n. Account of, facts relating to, formation & meaning of word; branch of linguistic science concerned with this; part of grammar treating of individual words & their formation & inflexions. Hence or cogn. ĕtўmŏl′OGER, ĕtўmŏl′O-GIST, nn., ĕtўmŏlŏ′gIC(AL) aa., ĕtўmŏlŏ′gicalLY[2] adv. [f. OF *ethimologie* f. L f. Gk *etumologia* (as foll., -LOGY)]

ĕt′ўmŏn, n. Primary word that gives rise to a derivative. [L, f. Gk *etumon* (neut. of *etumos* true) literal sense, original form, of a word]

eu- in comb. = Gk *eu* well, cf. DYS-.

eucalŷp′tus, n. Kinds of plants including Australian gum tree; ∼ *oil*, a disinfectant. [f. EU-+Gk *kaluptos* covered (*kaluptō*), flower being protected by cap]

eu′charis (ūk-), n. (Also ∼ *lily*) S.-Amer. bulbous plant with white bell-shaped flowers. [Gk (*kharis* grace) pleasing]

Eu′charist (ūk-), n. Lord's Supper; consecrated elements, esp. the bread, as *give*, *receive*, the ∼. Hence ∼IC(AL) (-ĭs′-) aa. (∼*ic Congress*, international meeting of Roman Catholics in veneration of the Blessed Sacrament, originally held annually, later biennially). [ME, f. OF *eucariste* f. LL f. Gk *eukharistia* f. EU-(*kharistos* f. *kharizomai* offer willingly) grateful]

eu′chre (-ker), n., & v.t. 1. American card game for 2, 3, or 4 persons. 2. v.t. Gain advantage over (opponent) by his failure to take three tricks at ∼ (also fig.). [orig. unkn.]

Eu′clid, n. Alexandrian mathematician (c. 300 B.C.); his *Elements* or treatise on geometry, a copy of this; (obs.) geometry as a science or subject; (mod.) the geometry of ordinary experience, accepting ∼'s axioms as indisputable (cf. RELATIVITY). Hence Euclíd′EAN a. [f. Gk *Eukleidēs*]

eud(a)em′on|ism (-dēm-), n. System of ethics basing moral obligation on tendency of actions to produce happiness. So ∼IST(2) n. [f. Gk EU(*daimōn* guardian genius) happy, -ISM]

eudiŏm′ĕter, n. Graduated glass tube in which gases may be chemically combined by electric spark passing between metallic terminals at its closed end, used in chemical experiments. So **eudiomĕt′**RIC-(AL) aa., **eudiomĕt′ricalLY**[2] adv., **eudiŏ-M′ETRY** n. [f. Gk EU(*dios*, st. of *Zeus*, gen. *Dios*, god of the sky) clear+-METER]

eugĕn′ic, a. & n. 1. Of the production of fine (esp. human) offspring. 2. n. pl. Science of this. So **eu′gĕn**IST(2) n., student of ∼s. [f. EU-+Gk *gen-* produce+-IC]

euhēm′er|ism, n. Reference of myths to historical basis. So ∼IST(2) n., ∼is′TIC a., ∼IZE(4) v.t. & 1. [f. *Euhemerus*, Sicilian author c. 316 B.C., +-ISM]

eul′og|īze, -ise (-īz), v.t. & i. Extol, praise, in speech or writing. So ∼IST(1) n., ∼is′TIC a., ∼is′TICALLY adv. [f. foll.+-IZE]

eul′ogў, n. Speech, writing, in praise of person etc., as *pronounce his* ∼, *pronounce a* ∼ *on him*; praise. [f. med. L *eulogium* f. (app. by conf. w. L *elogium*) LL f. Gk *eulogia* (EU-, -LOGY)]

Eumĕn′ides (-ēz), n. pl. (Euphemistic name for) Furies. [Gk, = gracious ones]

eun′uch (-uk), n. Castrated male person, esp. one employed in harem, or (in Oriental courts & under Roman empire) employed in state affairs. [ME, f. L f. Gk *eunoukhos* lit. bedchamber attendant (*eunē* bed+*okh-* st. of *ekhō* hold)]

euŏn'ўmus, n. Kinds of shrubs including spindle-tree. [f. L f. Gk EU(*ŏnumos* f. *onoma* name) of lucky name]

eupĕp'tic, a. Of, having, good digestion. [f. Gk EU(*peptos* f. *pessō, peptō*, digest)+ -IC]

euph'ĕm|ism, n. Substitution of mild or vague expression for harsh or blunt one; expression thus substituted, as *'queer' is a ~ism for 'mad'*. So **~is'tic** a., **~is'tically** adv., **~ize**(1, 2) v.t. & i. [f. Gk *euphēmismos* f. EU(*phēmos* f. *phēmē* speaking, fame), see -ISM]

euphōn'ium, n. (mus.). Bass instrument of saxhorn family. [mod. L, f. Gk *euphōnos* see foll.]

euph'onў, n. Pleasing sound; quality of having this (usu. of words, phrases, etc.); tendency to phonetic change for ease of pronunciation. So **euphōn'ic, euphōn'i-ous**, aa., **euphōn'ically, euphōn'ious-ly**[2], advv., **euph'onize**(3) v.t. [f. F *euphonie* f. LL f. Gk *euphōnia* f. EU(*phōnē* sound)]

euphōr'bia, n. (Kinds of) widely distributed herb or shrub of the spurge family. [L (-*ea*), f. *Euphorbus* physician to Juba II, -IA[1]]

euphŏr'ia, euph'orў, nn. Feeling of well-being. Hence **euphŏr'ic** a. [f. Gk EU-(*phoria* f. *pherō* bear)]

euph'rasў, n. = EYEbright. [f. med. L f. Gk *euphrasia* cheerfulness f. EUphrain*ō* gladden (*phrēn* mind)]

Euphrŏs'ўnē (*or* -z-), n. One of the Graces. [Gk]

euph'u|ism, n. Artificial or affected style of writing (prop., in imitation of Lyly's *Euphues*, 1580); high-flown style. So **~ist** n., **~is'tic** a., **~is'tically** adv. [-ISM]

Eurasian (ūrāsh'an), a. & n. (Person) of mixed European & Asian parentage; of Europe & Asia. [f. *Europe*+*Asia*+-AN]

eurēk'a (ūr-), int. & n. (The exulting exclamation) 'I have (found) it!' [f. Gk *heurēka* 1st pers. perf. of *heuriskō* find]

eurhўth'mic(ūr-), a. In or of harmonious proportion (esp. in architecture). Hence **~s** n. pl., harmony of bodily movement, esp. as developed with the aid of music into a system used in education. [f. L f. Gk *euruthmia* good rhythm (see EU-, RHYTHM)+-IC]

Europe'an (ūr-), a. & n. (Native) of Europe; happening in, extending over, Europe, as *a~ reputation*. Hence **~ism**(2, 3, 4), **~iza'tion**, nn., **~ize**(3) v.t., (ūr-). [f. F *européen* f. L *Europaeus* (L f. Gk *Europē* Europe)+-AN]

eurōp'ium (ūr-), n. (chem.). A rare-earth metallic element. [mod. L, f. L *Europa* Europe, -IUM]

Eurovision (ūr'ōvĭzhn), n. Television of European range. [*Euro(pean)* (*tele*)*vision*]

eu'sŏl, n. Antiseptic and bactericide prepared from bleaching powder. [f. initial letters of *Edinburgh University solution of lime*]

Eustach'ian (-ăk-), a. Of Eustachius the Italian anatomist (d. 1574); *~ tube*, canal leading from the pharynx to the cavity of the middle ear. [-AN]

eutĕc'tic, a. (chem.). *~ mixture*, one in which the constituents are in such proportions as to solidify at one temperature (*~ temperature or point*) like a pure substance. [f. EU-+Gk *tēkō* melt+-IC]

Eutĕrp'ē, n. The MUSE[1] of music, whence *~an* a.; genus of palms. [Gk]

euthanās'ia (-z-, -s-), n. Gentle & easy death; bringing about of this, esp. in case of incurable & painful disease. [Gk (EU-+*thanatos* death)]

ēvăc'ū|āte, v.t. Empty (esp. stomach or bodily organ of contents), whence **~ant**(2) a. & n.; withdraw from (place; esp. of troops); remove (person) esp. from place considered to be dangerous, whence **~ee'** n., person so removed; discharge (excrement etc.; also fig.). So **~a'tion** n.- [f. L E(*vacuare* f. *vacuus* empty)]

ēvāde', v.t. Escape from, avoid, (attack, pursuit, designs, adversary, blow, obstacle, etc.); avoid doing (duty etc.), answering (question), yielding to (argument etc.); defeat intention of (law etc., esp. while complying with its letter); (of things) elude, baffle. Hence **ēvād'able** a. [f. F *évader* f. L E(*vadere vas*- go)]

ēvă'gin|āte, v.t. (physiol.). Turn (tubular organ) inside out. So **~a'tion** n. [f. L E(*vaginare* f. *vagina* sheath), see -ATE[3]]

ēvăl'ū|āte, v.t. Ascertain amount of; find numerical expression for. So **~a'tion** n. [f. F *évaluer* (*é-* EX, VALUE)]

ēvanĕsce', v.i. Fade out of sight; become effaced; disappear. [f. L E(*vanescere* VANISH)]

ēvanĕs'c|ent, a. (Of impression, appearance, etc.) quickly fading; (Math.) infinitesimal. Hence **~ence** n., **~ently**[2] adv. [f. F *évanescent* (as prec., see -ENT)]

ēvăn'gel (-j-), n. (arch.). The Gospel; any of the Four Gospels; doctrine, principle, (of politics etc.). [ME, f. OF *evangi(l)le* f. eccl. L f. Gk EU(*aggelion* cf. ANGEL) good news]

ēvăngĕl'ic, -ic|al, (-j-), aa. & nn. 1. Of, according to, the teaching of the Gospel or the Christian religion; esp. (usu. ~*al*) of the Protestant school maintaining that the essence of the Gospel consists in doctrine of salvation by faith, good works & sacraments having no saving efficacy, whence ~**alism**(3) n. 2. n. Member of this school. Hence **~ally**[2] adv. [f. LL f. eccl. Gk *euaggelikos* (as prec., see -IC, -AL)]

ēvăn'gelism (-j-), n. Preaching of the Gospel; = EVANGELICALISM. [-ISM]

ēvăn'gelist (-j-), n. One of the writers of the Four Gospels; preacher of the Gospel; layman doing home missionary work. [ME, f. OF *evangeliste* f. LL (-*ia*) f. Gk *euaggelistēs* (as EVANGELIZE, -IST)]

ĕvăngelis'tic (-j-), a. Of the Four Evangelists; of preachers of the Gospel; = EVANGELICAL. [-IC]

ĕvăn'gelĭz|e (-j-), -is|e (-īz), v.t. Preach the Gospel to (persons, also abs.); win over (person) to Christianity. Hence ~A'TION n. [f. LL evangelizare f. Gk euaggelizomai (as EVANGEL)]

ĕvăn'ĭsh, v.i. (literary). Vanish; die away. Hence ~MENT n. [ME, f. OF evanir (-ISH²) f. Rom. *exvanire = L evanescere EVANESCE]

ĕvăp'or|āte, v.t. & i. Turn (t. & i.) from solid or liquid into vapour (also fig.; esp. colloq. disappear, die); remove the liquid part of; (v.i.) exhale moisture. So ~ABLE, ~ATIVE, aa., ~A'TION, ~ĀTOR, nn. [f. L evaporare (as VAPOUR), see -ATE³]

ĕvā'sion (-zhn), n. Act, means, of evading; shuffling excuse. So ĕvās'ĭve a., ĕvās'ĭvelȳ² (-vl-) adv., ĕvās'ĭveness (-vn-) n. [ME, f. OF evasion f. LL evasionem (as EVADE, see -ION)]

Eve¹ (ēv), n. The first woman; daughter of ~, woman (often w. allusion to feminine curiosity etc.). [f. Heb. Havvah orig. = life, living]

ĕve², n. Evening or day before (of) a church festival or any date or event; time just before anything, as on the ~ of an election; (arch.) evening. [ME; = EVEN¹; for loss of -n cf. maid]

ĕvĕc'tion, n. Inequality in moon's longitude. [f. L evectio f. E(vehere vect- carry), -ION]

ē'ven¹, n. (poet.). Evening; ~song, evening prayer in Church of England; ~tide, evening. [OE æfen, OS, OHG āband of obsc. orig.]

ē'ven², a. (-er, -est). Level; smooth; uniform in quality; in same plane or line (with); equally balanced, as ~-handed justice; equal in number or amount; (Law, Commerc.) of ~ (same) date; (of temper etc.) equable, unruffled; ~ money (Betting), neither laying nor taking odds; (of numbers) integrally divisible by two, opp. to ODD; ODD & ~; be ~ with, have one's revenge on. Hence ~LY² adv., ~NESS n. [OE efen, OS, OHG eban, ON jafn, Goth. ibns f. Gmc *ebhnaz of unkn. orig.]

ē'ven³, adv. inviting comparison of the assertion, negation, etc., made with a less strong one that might have been made, as he disputes ~ the facts (not merely the inferences from them), I never ~ opened (much less read) it, does he ~ suspect (not to say realize) the danger?, ~ if my watch is right we shall be late (later if it is slow), this applies ~ more (not merely equally) to French (than to English); (arch.) neither more nor less than, just, simply, as ~ (quite) so, (emphasizing identity) that is, as God, ~ our own God. [OE efne, as prec.]

ē'ven⁴, v.t. Make even; treat as equal or comparable (to); ~ up, to balance; *~ up

on, requite, make return to (a person). [OE efnan, as prec.]

ēve'ning (-vn-), n. Close of day, esp. sunset to bedtime; this time spent in particular way, as musical ~s; (fig.) decline of life, closing period; ~ dress, that prescribed by fashion to be worn in the ~; ~ primrose (with pale yellow flowers that open in the ~); ~ star, Jupiter, Mercury, or other planet, & esp. (the ~ star) Venus, when seen in West after sunset. [OE æfnung vbl n. f. æfnian (as EVEN¹)]

ĕvĕnt', n. Fact of a thing's happening, as in the ~ of his death, his coming, if he dies, comes; thing that happens, esp. important thing, as quite an ~, whence ~FUL, ~LESS, aa.; (in doctrine of chances) any of several possible but mutually exclusive occurrences; double ~, combined occurrence of two ~s, esp. as subject of bets; (Sport.) something on the issue of which money is staked; result, outcome; in any or either ~, at all ~s, in any case. [f. L eventus -ūs f. E(venire come)]

ĕvĕn'tŭal, a. That will happen under certain circumstances; ultimately resulting, whence ~LY² adv. [f. prec., after actual]

ĕvĕntŭál'ĭty, n. Possible event. [·ITY]

ĕvĕn'tŭāte, v.i. Turn out (well, ill, etc.); result (in or abs.); *happen, come to pass. [f. L as EVENT, -ATE²]

ĕv'er, adv. Always, at all times, (arch. exc. as foll.); for ~ (& ~, & a day), for all future time, incessantly; ~more', always; ~ after, ~ since; ~ yours (in ending a letter). (arch.) & anon, now & then; (w. negative, question, condition, comparison) at any time, as nothing ~ happens, did you ~ hear such stuff?, if I ~ catch him, the best thing I ~ heard, as good as ~, better than ~; (strengthening as) be as quick as ~ you can; (emphasizing question, colloq.) what ~ (also whatever) does he want?, who ~ can it be?, which ~ Brown do you mean?, when, where, how, ~ did I drop it?, why ~ didn't you say so?; ~ so (earlier never so), very, as it is ~ so much easier; (appended to superl. as sl. ellipsis for that~ was or were: the back-benchers were the most docile ~); did you ~? (as complete sentence), did you ~ see or hear the like? [OE æfre, of unkn. orig.]

***ĕv'erglāde**, n. Marshy tract of land, esp. (pl.) swamp in S. Florida. [prec. +GLADE]

ĕv'ergreen, a. & n. Always green or fresh (lit. & fig.); (tree, shrub) having green leaves all the year round (cf. DECIDUOUS).

ĕverlas'ting (-ah-), a. & n. 1. Lasting for ever; lasting long; lasting too long, repeated too often; (of plants) keeping shape and colour when dried. 2. n. Eternity, as from ~; ~ flower; strong twilled woollen stuff. Hence ~LY² adv., ~NESS n. [ME; EVER+LASTING]

évert', v.t. (Physiol.) turn (organ etc.) inside out; (arch.) overthrow (goverment etc.). So **éver'sion** n. [f. L E(*vertere vers-* turn)]

èv'ery (-vr-), a. Each, all (w. sing. vb), as ~ *word of it is false*, (w. possess. pron.) *it engaged his ~ thought*, (of succession or alternation) *he comes ~ day, ~ other* (i.e. second) *day, ~ three days, ~ third day ; ~ now & then, ~ now & again, ~ so often*, from time to time; ~ *bit* (quite) *as much*; ~*body* (*else*), ~ (other) person; ~*day'* (adj.), occurring daily, worn or used on ordinary days, commonplace; ~ *one* each, as ~ *one of them is wrong*; ~*one* (also ~ *one*), ~ body, as ~*one likes to have his way*; ~*thing*, all things, as ~*thing depends on that*, thing of first importance, as *pace is ~thing; ~ time* (colloq.), without exception, without any hesitation; ~ *way*, in ~ way, in ~ respect; ~*where*, in ~ place. [OE *æfre ælc* EVER EACH]

Ev'erymän (èvr-), n. The ordinary or typical human being, the 'man in the street'. [character in 16th c. morality]

évict', v.t. Expel (person; esp. tenant *from* land etc.); recover (property, title to it, *of, from*, person) by legal process. So **èvic'tion**, **évic'tor**, nn. [f. L E(*vincere vict-* conquer)]

èv'idence, n., & v.t. **1.** Clearness, obviousness, esp. *in ~*, conspicuous. **2.** Indication, sign, (*of* quality, treatment, etc.); testimony, facts, making for (also *of*) a conclusion, esp. (pl.) *the E~s of Christianity*; INTERNAL, EXTERNAL, ~. **3.** (law). Information (given personally or drawn from documents etc.) tending to establish fact, as *call* (person) *in ~* (as a witness), CIRCUMSTANTIAL, PRESUMPTIVE, *verbal* ~; ‖ *turn King's, Queen's ~*, (of accomplice in crime) give ~ against one's accomplices; statements, proofs, admissible as testimony in court. **4.** v.t. Serve to indicate, attest. So **èviden'tial** (-shl), **èviden'tiary**[1] (-sha-), aa., **èviden'tialy**[2] (-sha-) adv. [OF, or f. L *evidentia* (as foll., see -ENCE)]

èv'ident, a. Obvious (to eyes or mind). Hence ~LY[2] adv. [OF, or f. L E(*vidēre* see), see -ENT]

èv'il (-vl, -vil), a., n., & adv. **1.** Bad, harmful; *the E~ One*, the Devil; *of* ~ (bad) *repute, an* ~ (slanderous) *tongue; ~ eye*, malicious look, pop. believed to do material harm. **2.** n. ~ thing, sin, harm, (*of two ~s choose the less*); ~*-doer*; *Aleppo* ~, a disease of boils; ~ = KING'S ~. **3.** adv. In ~ manner, as *speak ~ of*, (Bibl.) ~*entreat, ~-disposed*. Hence ~LY[2] adv. [OE *yfel*, OS, OHG *ubil*, Goth. *ubils* f. Gmc **ubhilaz*]

évince', v.t. Show, indicate, (quality etc., *that* etc.); show that one has (quality). Hence **èvin'cive** a. [as EVICT]

èv'ir|āte, v.t. Castrate (male); (fig.) deprive of manly qualities. So ~A'TION n. [f. L E(*virare* f. *vir* man), see -ATE[3]]

èvis'cer|āte, v.t. Disembowel; (fig.) empty (thing) of vital contents. Hence ~A'TION n. [f. L E*viscerare* (VISCERA), see -ATE[3]]

évōke', v.t. Call up (spirit from the dead, feelings, memories, energies); ‖ summon (cause) to higher court. So **èvoca'tion** n., **èvōc'ative, èvōc'atory** aa. [f. L E(*vocare* call), or f. earlier *evocation*]

èv'olute (-ōōt), a. & n. ~ (*curve*), locus of centres of curvature of another curve that is its INVOLUTE. [f. L p.p. as EVOLVE]

èvolu'tion (-lōō-), n. **1.** Opening out (of roll, bud, etc.; usu. fig.); appearance (of events etc.) in due succession; evolving, giving off, (of gas, heat, etc.). **2.** Unfolding of curve; (Math.) extraction of root from any given power (cf. INVOLUTION). **3.** Development (of organism, design, argument, etc.); *Theory of E~* (that the embryo is not created by fecundation, but developed from a pre-existing form); origination of species by development from earlier forms, not by special creation (cf. CREATIONISM), whence ~ISM, ~IST, nn., ~is'tic a., (-lōōshon-). **4.** Formation of heavenly bodies by concentration of cosmic matter. **5.** Change in disposition of troops or ships; wheeling about, movement, in dancing etc. Hence ~AL, ~ARY[1], aa., (-lōōshon-). [f. L *evolutio* (as EVOLVE, see -ION)]

èv'olutive (-lōō-), a. Tending to evolution. [-IVE]

évolve', v.t. & i. Unfold, open out, (fig.); set forth in due sequence; give off (heat etc.); develop, deduce, (theory, facts, etc.); develop (t. & i.) by natural process; ~ *from* one's *inner consciousness*, create imaginatively (often joc. of romancing etc.). Hence ~MENT (-vm-) n. f. L E(*volvere volut-* roll)].

èvul'sion, n. Forcible extraction. [f. L *evulsio* f. E(*vellere vuls-* pluck), see -ION]

ewe (ū), n. Female sheep; one's ~ *lamb*, one's most cherished possession (2 *Sam.* xii); ~*-necked*, (of horses) having a thin concave neck. [OE *éowu*, OS *ewwi*, OHG *ouwi*, ON *ær* f. Gmc **awi-* cogn. w. L *ovis*]

ew'er, n. Pitcher; water-jug with a wide mouth. [ME, f. AF **ewere* = OF *aiguiere* f. Rom. *aquaria*, fem. adj. as n. (*aqua* water, see -ARY[1])]

ewigkeit (ā'vigkīt), n. (joc.). *Into, in, the* ~, into thin air, in the unknown. [G, = eternity]

èx, prep. (commerc.). (Of goods) out of, sold from, (*ship, store*, etc.); (of stocks or shares) *èx div'idend* (abbr. *èx div.* or *x.d.*), not including next dividend. [L]

ex-[1], pref. **1.** = L *ex* before *h, c, p, q, s* (which is often dropped), and *t*; becoming *ef-* before *f*, *e-* before other consonants; forming vbs with sense 'out', 'forth', (*exclude, exit*), 'upward' (*extol*), 'thoroughly' (*excruciate*), 'make so-&-so' (*exasperate*), 'remove, expel, free, from' (*expatriate, -onerate, -coriate*), and adjj. w. sense 'not having', esp. in form *e-* (*ecaudate* tailless). 2. L *ex* is prefixed to nn. and rarely adjj. (orig. to titles of office etc.) in sense 'formerly', 'quondam', as *ex-chancellor, ex-Prime-Minister*.

ex-², pref. repr. Gk *ex* (*ek* before vowels) out, as *exodus, ecdysis*.

ĕxă'cerb|āte, v.t. Aggravate (pain, disease, anger); irritate (person etc.). So **~A'TION** n. [f. L EX¹(*acerbare* f. *acerbus* bitter)]

ĕxăct'¹ (-gz-), a. Precise, rigorous, (rules, order, etc.); (of person, judgement, description, report, answer, etc.) accurate, strictly correct; *~ sciences* (admitting of absolute precision). Hence or cogn. **ĕxăc'tITUDE, ~NESS**, nn., (-gz-). [f. L p.p. as foll.]

ĕxăct'² (-gz-), v.t. Demand & enforce payment of (money, fees, etc., *from, of*, person), insist upon (act, conduct, *from, of*), whence **~ING²** a.; (of circumstances) require urgently. Hence or cogn. **ĕxăc'tABLE** a., **ĕxăc'toR** n., (-gz-). [f. L EX¹ (*igere act- = agere* drive)]

ĕxăc'tion (-gz-), n. Exacting (*of money* etc.); sum, thing, thus exacted; illegal or exorbitant demand, extortion; arbitrary & excessive impost. [ME, f. L *exactio* (as prec., see -ION)]

ĕxăct'lỹ (-gz-), adv. In adj. senses, esp. (as answer or confirmation) quite so, just as you say. [-LY²]

exa'gger|āte (ĭgzăj-), v.t. Magnify (thing described, or abs.) beyond limits of truth; intensify, aggravate; make (physical features etc.) of abnormal size. Hence or cogn.**~ātĕdLY²,~atIvELY²,**advv.,**~A'TION, ~ātoR**, nn., **~atIve** a., (ĭgzăj-). [f. L EX¹ (*aggerare* heap up, f. *agger* heap), see -ATE³]

exalt' (ĭgzawlt'), v.t. Raise, place high in rank, power, etc.; praise, extol, (often *~ to the skies*); dignify, ennoble, (esp. in p.p.); intensify (colours etc.). [ME, f. L EX¹(*altare* f. *altus* high)]

ĕxaltā'tion (-awl-), n. Raising, lifting up, (usu. fig.); elation, rapturous emotion; intensification. [ME, f. OF, or f. LL *exaltatio* (prec., -ATION)]

ĕxăm' (-gz-), n. (colloq.). See foll.

ĕxăminā'tion (-gz-), n. Minute inspection (*of, into*); POST-MORTEM *~*; (colloq. abbr. *exam*) testing of knowledge or ability (of pupils, candidates) by questions oral or written; *~-paper*, series of such questions or of examinee's answers to them. Hence **~AL** (-shon-) a. [ME, f. OF, or f. L *examinatio* (as foll., see -ATION)]

ĕxăm'in|e (-gz-), v.t. & i. Investigate, scrutinize, (accounts, person *in* or *on* subject, organ, baggage for contraband goods, theory, statement, one's own conscience, *whether*); (intr.) inquire *into*. Hence **~ANT, ~EE', ~ER¹**, nn., **~atŏR'IAL** a., (-gz-). [ME, f. OF *examiner* or L *examinare* (*examen*, for *exagmen*, tongue of balance, examination, as EXACT²)]

exam'ple (ĭgzah-), n., & v.t. Fact, thing, illustrating general rule; problem, exercise, designed to do this; specimen of workmanship, picture, etc.; warning to others, as *make an ~ of* (punish) *him*; precedent, as *beyond, without, ~*; conduct as object of imitation, as *give, set, a good ~* (cf. EXEMPLARY); *take ~ by*, copy; (v.t., rare exc. in p.p.) exemplify. [ME; (vb f. n.) OF f. L *exemplum* (as EXEMPT¹)]

ĕxăn'imate (-gz-), a. Dead; lacking animation, spiritless. [f. L EX¹*animare* deprive of life (*anima*), see -ATE²]

ĕx ăn'imō, adv. & a. Heartily, sincere(ly). [L, = from the soul]

ĕx'ărch (-k), n. (Under Byzantine emperors) governor of distant province; (in Eastern Church) patriarch, bishop, patriarch's deputy. So **~ATE¹** (-k-) n. [f. LL f. Gk *exarkhos* f. EX²(*arkhō* rule)]

ĕxăs'per|āte (-gz-), v.t. Make worse (ill feeling, disease, pain); irritate (person; *~ated at, by*); provoke (person *to* ill, *to* do). Hence or cogn. **~ātingLY²** adv., **~A'TION** n., (-gz-). [f. L EX¹(*asperare* f. *asper* rough), see -ATE³]

ĕx cathĕd'rā, adv. & a. Authoritative(ly). [L, = from the (teacher's) chair]

ĕx'cav|āte, v.t. Make hollow; make (hole, channel) by digging; dig out (soil) leaving a hole; unearth, get out, by digging. Hence or cogn. **~A'TION, ~ātoR**, nn. [f. L EX¹(*cavare* f. *cavus* hollow), see -ATE³]

ĕxceed', v.t. & i. Do more than is warranted by (one's commission, rights, etc.); be greater than (quantity, thing, *by* so much); surpass (person etc. *in*); be pre-eminent, whence **~ING²** a. & (arch.) adv., **~ingLY²** adv.; be immoderate in feeding etc.; exaggerate. [ME, f. OF *exceder* f. L EX¹(*cedere cess-* go)]

ĕxcĕl', v.t. & i. (-ll-). Surpass (others *in* quality, *in doing*); be pre-eminent (*in, at*, thing, *in* quality, *in doing*). [ME, f. L EX¹(*cellere*, cf. *celsus* lofty)]

ĕx'cellence, n. Surpassing merit; thing in which person etc. excels. [ME, f. L *excellentia* (as prec., see -ENCE)]

ĕx'cellencỹ, n. Title (*Your, His, Her, E~*) of ambassadors, governors & their wives, & some other officers. [as prec., see -ENCY]

ĕx'cellent, a. Pre-eminent; very good. Hence **~LY²** adv. [OF (as prec., see -ENT)]

ĕxcĕl'sior, int. & n. Higher (as trade mark etc.); *soft shavings of wood for stuffing. [L, compar. of EX¹*celsus* lofty]

ĕxcĕpt'¹, v.t. & i. Exclude (thing) from enumeration, statement, etc., as *present company ~ed, ~ him from the general pardon*; make objection *against*. So **ĕxcĕp'tIve** a. [f. L EX¹(*cipere cept- = capere* take)]

ĕxcĕpt'², ĕxcĕp't|ĭng, prep. & conj. (*~ing* is required only after *not, without*, as *we are all fallible, except the pope*, but *not excepting the pope*; *~ing* is also usual after *always*). 1. Not including, but, as *we all* *failed ~ him, he is everywhere ~ in the right place, never to be found ~ in the wrong place, it is right ~ that the accents are omitted, ~ for the omission of accents.* 2. conj. (arch.). Unless, as ~ *he be born again.* [except ME; *except* orig. p.p. (f. L as prec.) in abs. constr. (~ *you = you being excepted*); ~*ing*, abs. use of part. of prec.]

excep'tion, n. Excepting; thing excepted, thing that does not follow the rule; *the ~ proves the rule,* the excepting of some cases shows that the rule exists, or that it applies to those not excepted; *with the ~ of,* except; *take ~,* object *to*; *subject, liable, to ~* (objection), whence ~ABLE (-shon-) a. [ME, f. OF, or f. L *exceptio* (EXCEPT[1], -ION)]

excep'tional (-shon-), a. Forming an exception; unusual, as ~ *advantages.* Hence ~ITY (-ǎl[4]) n., ~LY[2] adv. [-AL]

excerpt[1] (ěk'serpt *or* ĭksẽrpt'), n. Extract from book etc., article fróm learned society's Transactions etc. printed off separately for private circulation. [as foll.]

excẽrpt'[2], v.t. Extract, quote, (passage *from* book etc., *or* abs.). Hence *or* cogn. ~IBLE a., **excẽrp'tion** n. [f. L EX[1](*cerpere cerpt- = carpere* pluck)]

excẽss', n. (Usu. pl.) outrage; intemperance in eating or drinking; overstepping of due limits; fact of exceeding, esp. *in ~ of,* more than; amount by which one exceeds another; ~ *fare* on railway, payment due for travelling farther or in higher class than ticket warrants; ~ *luggage* (over the weight for free carriage); superabundance, extreme degree, (*of* cruelty etc.); exceeding of the proper amount or degree, esp. *in, to,* ~; ~ *profits duty, levy, tax,* tax on profits swollen by war conditions. So ~IVE a., ~IVELY[2] (-vĭ-) adv. [ME, f. OF *exces* f. L *excessus -ūs* (as EXCEED)]

exchãnge'[1], n. **1.** Act, process, of exchanging (*of* goods, prisoners of war, blows, words, etc.; ~ *is no robbery,* joc. excuse for unfair ~). **2.** Exchanging of coin for its equivalent in coin of same or another country; money-changer's trade; *par of ~,* standard value of coinage of one country in terms of that of another; (*rate, course, of*) ~, price at which bills drawn in a foreign currency may be bought, also, difference between this & par; system of settling debts between persons (esp. in different countries) without money, by *bills of ~* (*first, second, third, of ~,* separate bills of even tenor & date as security against miscarriage). **3.** Thing exchanged for another. **4.** Building where merchants assemble to transact business, as STOCK-~. **5.** || Central telephone office of a district where connexions are made for local or trunk calls. [ME, f. AF *eschaunge = OF eschange* (EX-[1], CHANGE[1]); later *ex-* after L]

exchãnge'[2], v.t. & i. Give, receive, (thing) in place of (*for*) another; interchange (blows, words, glances, etc.); (v.i., esp. of coin) be received as equivalent *for*; pass (*from* one regiment or ship *into* another) by exchange with another officer. [ME, f. OF *eschangier* (EX-[1], CHANGE[2])]

exchãn'gea|ble (-jabl), a. That may be exchanged (*for*); ~*ble value* (estimated by that of the goods for which a thing may be exchanged). Hence ~BIL'ITY (-jab-) n. [-ABLE]

exchẽ'quer (-ker), n. || Department of public service charged with receipt & custody of revenue; || *Chancellor of the E~,* finance minister of United Kingdom; royal or national treasury; money of private person etc.; || (also *Court of E~*) court of law, now merged in King's Bench Division (orig. using table with chequered cloth for accounts); || ~ *bill* (issued by authority of Parliament, bearing interest at current rate). [ME, AF *escheker,* OF *eschequier* f. med. L *scaccarium* chess-board, CHEQUER[1]; *ex-* by erron. assoc. w. EX-[1] in *exchange* etc.]

excíse'[1] (-z), n., & v.t. **1.** Duty or tax levied on goods & commodities produced or sold at home, & on various licences etc.; || government office collecting ~ (now *Board of Customs & E~*); || ~*'man,* officer collecting ~ & preventing infringement of ~ laws. **2.** v.t. Force (person) to pay ~, overcharge (also *fig.*). Hence **excís'ABLE** (-z-) a. [(vb f. n.) f. MDu. *excijs, accijs* f. OF *acceis* tax f. Rom. **accensum* f. **accēnsare* tax (CENSUS)]

excíse'[2] (-z), v.t. Cut out (passage of book, limb, organ, etc.). (Bot., Zool.) cut out, notch. So **excí'SION** (-zhon) n. [f. L EX[1](*cídere cis- = caedere* cut)]

excít|e', v.t. Set in motion, rouse up, (feelings, faculties, etc.); provoke, bring about, (action, active condition); promote activity of (bodily organs etc.) by stimulus; move (person) to strong emotion; (colloq. ellipt.) *don't ~e!,* keep cool!; (Electr., Magnet.) induce activity in (substance), set (current) in motion, whence **excíta'TION** n.; (Photog.) sensitize (plate). Hence *or* cogn. ~ABIL'ITY, ~e̱'MENT (-tm-), nn.; **ěx'cítANT** a. & n., ~t ABLE (esp., of persons, easily ~ed, unbalanced), ~'ATIVE, ~'ATORY, aa., ~'ědry[2] adv. [ME, f. OF *exciter* or L *excitare* frequent. of EX[1](*ciẽre* set in motion)]

excláim', v.i. & t. Cry out, esp. from pain, anger, etc.; utter (words quoted direct or with *that*) thus; ~ *against,* accuse loudly. [f. F *exclamer* or L *exclamare,* sp. after CLAIM]

exclamã'tion, n. Exclaiming; words exclaimed; *note of ~* (!). So **exclám'atory** a. [ME, f. OF, or f. L *exclamatio* (prec., -ATION)]

exclude' (-lo͞od), v.t. Shut out (person, thing, *from* place, society, privilege, etc.); prevent the occurrence of, make impossible, (doubt etc.); expel & shut out.

So **ĕxclu′sion** (-lōozhn) n. [ME, **f.** L EX¹(*cludere clus-* = *claudere* shut)]

ĕxclus′ive (-lōo-), a. Shutting out; not admitting *of*; desirous of excluding others, (of social circles etc.) chary of admitting members, select, whence **ĕxclus′ivism**(2) (-lōo-) n.; (shop, newspaper) not to be had, not published, elsewhere; (of terms etc.) excluding all but what is specified; employed, followed, to the exclusion of all else, as *his ~ occupation*; (quasi-adv.) not counting, as *20 men, ~ of our own*. Hence ~LY² (-lōosĭvl-) adv., ~NESS (-lōosĭvn-) n. [f. med. L *exclusivus* (prec., -IVE)]

ĕxcō′gĭt|āte, v.t. Think out, contrive. So ~A′TION n., ~ātIVE a. [f. L EX¹(*cogitare* COGITATE)]

ĕxcommūn′icăt|e, v.t. (eccl.) Cut off (person) from participation in sacraments, or from all communication with the Church. So **ĕxcommūnica′TION**, ~OR, nn., ~IVE, ~ORY, aa. [f. LL EX¹(*communicare* f. *communis* COMMON), see -ATE³]

ĕxcō′ri|āte, v.t. Remove part of skin of (person etc.) by abrasion etc.; strip, peel off, (skin). So ~A′TION n. [f. L EX¹*coriare* (*corium* hide), see -ATE³]

ĕx′crĕment, n. Waste matter discharged from bowels, dung, (often pl.). Hence or cogn. ~AL (-ĕn²), ~I′TIOUS¹ (-Ishus), aa. [f. F *excrément* or L *excrementum* (as EXCRETE, see -MENT)]

ĕxcrĕs′cence, n. Abnormal or morbid outgrowth on animal or vegetable body (also fig.). So **ĕxcrĕscĕn′tIAL** (-shal) a. [f. L *excrescentia* (as foll., see -ENCE)]

ĕxcrĕs′cent, a. Growing abnormally; redundant; (Gram., of sound in word) due merely to euphony. [f. L EX¹(*crescere cret-* grow), -ENT]

ĕxcrēt′a, n, pl. Waste expelled from body, esp. faeces & urine. [L, p.p. as foll.]

ĕxcrēt|e′, v.t. (Of animals or plants) separate & expel (waste matters, also abs.) from system. Hence or cogn. **ĕxcrē′tION** n., ~IVE, ~ORY, aa. [f. L EX¹(*cernere cret-* sift)]

ĕxcru′ciāt|e (-krōoshĭ-), v.t. Torment acutely (person's senses; now esp. in part. as adj.); torture mentally (now rare). Hence or cogn. ~ingLY² (-krōoshĭ-) adv., **ĕxcrucia′TION** n. (-krōo-) n. [f. L EX¹(*cruciare* torment f. *crux crucis* cross), see -ATE³]

ĕx′culpāte, v.t. Free from blame; clear (person *from* charge etc.). Hence **ĕxculpa′TION** n., **ĕxcul′patORY** a. [f. med. L EX¹(*culpare*, *culpa* blame), see -ATE³]

ĕxcŭ′rrent, a. Running out; (of blood) flowing from heart, arterial; affording an exit; (Bot.) projecting. [as foll., see -ENT]

ĕxcŭrs|e′, v.i. (rare). Wander, digress (usu. fig.); make an excursion. Hence ~IVE a., ~′IveLY² (-vl-) adv., ~′IveNESS (-vn-) n. [f. L EX¹(*currere curs-* run)]

ĕxcŭr′sion (-shon), n. Journey, ramble, with intention of returning (also fig.);

pleasure trip of number of persons, whence ~IST (-shon-) n.; ~ *train* (for~ists; usu. at reduced rates); (arch.) sortie (*alarms & ~s*); (Astron.) deviation from regular path. Hence ~AL, ~ARY¹, aa., (-shon-). [f. L *excursio* (as prec., see -ION)]

ĕxcŭrs′us, n. (pl. ~*es*). Detailed discussion of special point in book, usu. in appendix at end. [L vbl n. as EXCURSE]

ĕxcūs|e′¹ (-z), v.t. Attempt to lessen or blame attaching to (person, act); obtain exemption for (person, one*self*, *from* duty etc.); (of things) serve as exculpation of (person, act, person *for* act); release (person *from* a duty; also double obj., as *we ~e him the fee*); dispense with, as *we will ~e your presence*; *~e me* (as apology for lack of ceremony, interruption, etc.; also as form of dissent). So ~′ABLE, ~′atORY, aa., ~′abLY² adv., (-z-). [ME & OF *es-*, *excuse*(r) f. L EX¹*cusare* (*causa* CAUSE¹)]

ĕxcūse′² (-s), n. Apology offered, exculpation (usu. *in ~ of*); ground of this; plea for release from duty etc. [ME, f. OF (as prec.)]

‖ **ĕx′eăt**, n. (In schools, colleges, etc.) permission for temporary absence. [L, 3rd sing. subj. of EX¹(*ire* go)]

ĕx′ecrab|le, a. Abominable. Hence ~LY² adv. [f. L *execrabilis* (foll., -BLE)]

ĕx′ecrāt|e, v.t. & i. Express, feel, abhorrence for; (v.i.) utter curses. Hence or cogn. **ĕxecra′TION** n., ~IVE, ~ORY, aa. [f. L EX¹(s)*ecrari* (*sacrare* devote f. *sacer* sacred, accursed), see -ATE³]

ĕxĕc′ūtant (-gz-), n. One who executes, performer, (of music etc.). [f. F *exécutant*, part. as foll.]

ĕx′ecŭt|e, v.t. Carry (plan, command, law, judicial sentence, will) into effect; carry out design for (product of art or skill); perform (action, operation, etc.); make (legal instrument) valid by signing, sealing, etc.; ‖ convey (estate) in property; discharge (office, function); perform (musical composition); inflict capital punishment on. Hence ~ABLE a. [ME, f. OF *executer* f. med. L *executare* f. EX¹(*sequi secut-* follow)]

ĕxecū′tion, n. Carrying out, performance; dexterity in performing music; (of weapons) destructive effect, as *do ~* (also fig. of personal charms etc.); seizure of property or person of debtor in default of payment; infliction of capital punishment, whence ~ER¹ (-shon-) n.; ‖ *E~ Dock* (hist.), place on bank of Thames near Wapping where pirates were formerly hanged. [ME, f. OF *execution* f. L *execu-tionem* (as prec., -ION)]

ĕxĕc′ūtive (-gz-), a. & n. 1. Pertaining to, having the function of, executing. 2. (Branch of government) concerned with executing laws, decrees, & sentences (cf. JUDICIAL, *legislative*). 3. *Person in ~ position in business organization etc. [-IVE]

execūtor, n. **1.** (ĕk'sĭ-). One who carries out or performs. **2.** (ĭgzĕk⁴). Person appointed by testator to execute his will; *literary ~*, person charged with writer's unpublished works etc. Hence **exĕcū-tōr'ɪᴀʟ** a., **exĕc'ūtorsʜɪᴘ**, **exĕc'ūtrɪx** (pl. -*cūt'rĭces*), nn., (-gz-). [ME, f. AF *executour* f. L *executorem* (ᴇxᴇᴄᴜᴛᴇ, -ᴏʀ)]

exĕg|ēs'ĭs, n. Exposition esp. of Scripture. So **~ĕt'ɪᴄ**(ᴀʟ) aa., **~ĕt'ɪᴄᴀʟʏ²** adv. [Gk *exēgēsis* f. ᴇx²(*ēgeomai* lead)]

exĕm'plar (-gz-), n. Model, pattern; type (of a class); parallel instance. [ME, f. OF *exemplaire* f. LL *exemplarium* (ᴇxᴀᴍᴘʟᴇ, -ᴀʀʏ¹)]

exĕm'plar|y̆ (-gz-), a. Fit to be imitated; typical; illustrative; serving as a warning (*~y damages* in law, exceeding amount needed for compensation). Hence **~ɪʟʏ²** adv., **~ɪɴᴇss** n. [f. L *exemplaris* (as ᴇxᴀᴍᴘʟᴇ, see -ᴀʀʏ²)]

exĕm'pli|fy̆ (-gz-), v.t. Illustrate by example; be an example of; make attested copy of (document) under official seal. So **~ғɪᴄᴀ'ᴛɪᴏɴ** n. [ME, f. med. L *exemplificare* (ᴇxᴀᴍᴘʟᴇ, -ғʏ)]

exĕmpt'¹ (-gz-), a. & n. **1.** Free (*from* taxation, control, failings, etc.). **2.** n. Person exempted, esp. from tax; ‖ one of four officers sometimes commanding Yeomen of Guard (now usu. *exon*). [ME, f. OF f. L ᴇx¹(*imere empt- = emere* take)]

exĕmpt'² (-gz-), v.t. Free *from* (as prec.). So **exĕmp'ᴛɪᴏɴ** (-gz-) n. [prec.]

exĕn'ter|āte, v.t. Disembowel (only fig.). So **~ᴀ'ᴛɪᴏɴ** n. [f. L ᴇx¹*enterare* (Gk *enteron* intestine), see -ᴀᴛᴇ³]

exĕquāt'ur (-er), n. Recognition of a country's consul by a foreign government; temporal sovereign's authorization of bishop under Papal authority, or of publication of Papal bulls. [L, = he may perform]

ex'ĕquies (-kwĭz), n. pl. Funeral rites. [ME, f. OF f. L *exsequiae* f. ᴇx¹(*sequi* follow)]

ex'ercīse¹ (-z), n. Employment (of organ, faculty, power, right); practice (of virtues, profession, functions, religious rites); exertion of muscles, limbs, etc., esp. for health's sake; bodily, mental, or spiritual training; task set for this purpose; (pl.) military drill, athletics, etc.; academical declamation etc. required for degree; composition set to pupils: act of worship. [ME, f. OF *exercice* f. L *exercitium* f. ᴇx¹(*ercēre -cĭt- = arcēre* restrain) keep at work]

ex'ercīse|² (-z), v.t. & i. Employ (faculty, right, etc.); train (person etc.); tax the powers of; perplex, worry; discharge (functions); take, give (horse etc.), exercise. Hence **~ᴀʙʟᴇ** a. [ME; f. prec.]

exĕrcitā'tion (-gz-), n. Practice, training; literary or oratorical exercise. [f. L *exercitatio* f. *exercitare* frequent., as ᴇxᴇʀ-ᴄɪsᴇ¹, -ᴀᴛɪᴏɴ]

ex'ĕrgue (-g; *also* ĕgzẽrg'), n. Small space

usu. on reverse of coin or medal, below principal device; inscription there. Hence **exĕrg'uᴀʟ** (-gl) a. [F, f. med. L *exergum* f. Gk ᴇx-³+*ergon* work]

exĕrt' (-gz-), v.t. Exercise, bring to bear, (quality, force, influence); *~ oneself*, strive (*to do, for* object). So **exĕr'ᴛɪᴏɴ** n. (-gz-). [f. L ᴇx¹(*serere sert-* bind) put forth]

exes (ĕk'sĭz), n. pl. (colloq.). Expenses. [abbr.]

Ex'eter Hall (ĕ-; hawl), n. Building in Strand formerly used for May meetings etc. (see ᴍᴀʏ).

ex'ĕunt, v.i. (Stage direction) they (two or more actors) leave the stage; *~ om'nēs*, all leave the stage. [L, = they go out]

exfōl'i|āte, v.i. (Of bone, skin, minerals, etc.) come off in scales or layers; (of tree) throw off layers of bark. So **~ᴀ'ᴛɪᴏɴ** n. [f. L ᴇx¹(*foliare* f. *folium* leaf), see -ᴀᴛᴇ³]

ex grā'tia (-shĭa), phr. As an act of grace. [L]

exhalā'tion (ĕksa-), n. Evaporation; puff of breath; short burst (*of* anger etc.); mist, vapour; effluvium. [ME, f. L *exhalatio* (foll., -ᴀᴛɪᴏɴ)]

exhāle', v.t. & i. Give off (fumes etc., also fig.) in vapour; be thus given off, evaporate, (*from, out of*); (Path., of animal fluids) pass off in minute quantities through blood-vessel etc.; breathe out (life, soul, words, etc.); get rid of (anger etc.) as if by blowing. [ME, f. OF *exhaler* f. L ᴇx¹(*halare* breathe)]

exhaust'¹ (ĭgzaw-), n. (In hydraulic, steam, or internal-combustion engines) expulsion or exit of motive fluid, steam, or gaseous products of combustion from cylinder after completion of power stroke by piston; similar exit of spent fluid or gases from turbine; *~-pipe* etc. (for this); process of exhausting vessel of air; (apparatus for) production of outward current of air by creating partial vacuum. [f. foll.]

exhaust'² (ĭgzaw-), v.t. Draw off (air, also fig.); consume entirely; use, account for, the whole of; empty (vessel) of contents; say, find out, all that is worth knowing of (subject); drain (person, kingdom, etc.) of strength, resources, etc. esp. in p.p.); tire out. Hence **~ɪʙɪʟ'ɪᴛʏ** n., **~ɪʙʟᴇ** a. [f. L ᴇx¹(*haurire haust-* draw)]

exhaustion (ĭgzaws'chon), n. Exhausting (in all senses); total loss of strength; arrival at a conclusion by eliminating alternatives. [-ɪᴏɴ]

exhaus'tive (ĭgzaw-), a. Tending to exhaust esp. a subject; comprehensive. Hence **~ʟʏ²** (-vl-) adv., **~ɴᴇss** (-vn-) n. [-ɪᴠᴇ]

exhib'it¹ (ĭgzĭ-), n. Document or thing produced in lawcourt & referred to in written evidence; thing, collection of things, sent by person, firm, etc., to an exhibition; showing, display. [f. L neut. p.p. as foll.]

exhibit 424 exorbitant

exhĭb′it² (ĭgzĭ-), v.t. Show, display; submit for consideration; manifest (quality); show publicly (for amusement, in competition, etc.). So ~OR n., ~ORY a. [f. L EX¹(*hibēre hibit-* = *habēre* hold)]

exhibĭ′tion (ĕksĭ-), n. 1. Showing, display, (of thing); *make an ~ of* oneself, behave so as to excite contempt; public display of works of art etc.; *the Great E~*, first ~ on large scale, London, 1851. 2. ‖ Fixed sum given to student for term of years from funds of school, college, etc., whence ‖ ~ER¹ (ĕksĭbĭsh′on-) n., cf. SCHOLARSHIP. [OF, f. LL *exhibitionem* (as prec., see -ION); sense 2 f. LL use 'food, maintenance']

exhibĭ′tion|ism (ĕksĭbĭsh′on-), n. Tendency towards display or extravagant behaviour; (Path.) perverted mental condition characterized by indecent exposure of the person. So ~IST n. & a. [-ISM]

exhĭl′ar|āte (ĭgzĭ-), v.t. Enliven, gladden, (person, spirits). So ~ANT(2) a. & n., ~A′TION n., ~ātive a., (ĭgzĭ-). [f. L EX(*hilarare* f. *hilaris* cheerful), see -ATE³]

exhort (ĭgzört′), v.t. Admonish earnestly; urge (person *to do*, *to a* course); advocate (reform etc.). So ~′ative, ~′atORY, aa., (ĭgzört′-). [ME, f. OF *exhorter* or L EX¹-(*hortari* see HORTATORY)]

exhortā′tion (ĕksör-), n. Exhorting; formal, liturgical, address. [ME, f. OF, or f. L *exhortatio* (prec., -ATION)]

exhūm|e′, v.t. Dig out, unearth, (lit. & fig.). So ~A′TION n. [f. F *exhumer* f. med. L EX¹(*humare* f. *humus* ground)]

ex′igence, -cў (ĕksĭ-), n. Urgent need; emergency. [F, or LL *exigentia* (foll., -ENCY)]

ex′igent, a. Urgent, pressing; requiring much, exacting; ~ *of*, demanding. [f. L *exigere* EXACT², see -ENT]

ex′igible, a. That may be demanded or exacted (*against*, *from*, person). [as prec., -BLE]

exig′uous, a. Scanty, small. Hence or cogn. **exĭgū′ITY, ~NESS**, nn. [f. L *exiguus* (as prec.) +-OUS]

ex′ile¹, n. Penal banishment; long absence from one's country (also fig.). [ME, f. OF *exil* f. L EX¹*silium* (*salire* leap)]

ex′ile², n. Banished person (lit. & fig.). [ME, f. prec., or OF *exile*, & infl. by L *exul*]

ex′ile³, v.t. Bànish (person *from*; lit. & fig.). [ME, f. OF *exilier* f. LL *exiliare* (as EXILE¹)]

exil′ian, a. Of the Jews' exile in Babylon. So ~IC a. [f. L as EXILE¹ +-IAN]

exil′itў, n. (pedant.). Thinness; subtlety. [f. L *exilitas* (*exilis* thin, see -TY)]

exist′ (-gz-), v.i. Have place in the domain of reality; have being under specified conditions; ~ *as* (in the form of); (of circumstances etc.) occur, be found; live; continue in being. [c. 1600, back form. f. foll.; cf. F *exister*]

exis′tence (-gz-), n. Being, existing, esp. *in* ~; life, as *a wretched, precarious, ~*; mode of existing; existing thing; all that exists. [ME, f. OF, f. LL *existentia* f. L EX¹(*sistere* redupl. f. *stare* stand), see -ENCY]

exis′tent (-gz-), a. Existing, actual, current. [-ENT]

existĕn′tial (-gz-; -shl), a. Of or relating to existence; (Log., of a proposition) predicating existence. [f. LL *existentialis*, see EXISTENCE]

existĕn′tial|ism (-gz-; -shal-), n. An anti-intellectualist philosophy of life holding that man is free & responsible, based on the assumption that reality as existence can only be lived but can never become the object of thought. Hence ~IST a. & n. [f. F *existentialisme*, see prec. & -ISM]

ex′it¹, n. Departure of player from stage (also fig.); death; going out or forth; liberty to do this; passage to go out by. [f. L *exitus -ūs* going out (as foll.); partly also from foll.]

ex′it², v.i. (Stage direction) — goes off stage, as *E~ Macbeth* (also fig.). [3rd sing. pres. of L EX(*ire it-* go)]

ex-lib′ris, n. Book-plate, label with arms, crest, etc., & owner's name pasted into book. [L *ex libris* from library (of So-&-so)]

ex′o- in comb. = Gk *exō* outside, as: ~*derm*, outer layer of blastoderm; ~*gamous*, (-ŏg²), (of, following) custom compelling man to marry outside his own tribe; ~*gen* n., ~*genous* (-ŏj²) a., = DICOTYLEDON (*ous*), w. ref. to external growth of stem; ~*păth′ic*, (of disease) originating outside the body; ~*phagous*, ~*phagy*, (-ŏf²), not eating members of one's own tribe; ~*plasm*, outermost layer of protoplasm; ~*skĕl′eton*, external integument, bony or leathery; ~*smŏs′is*, passage of a fluid outwards through a porous septum.

ex′odus, n. Departure, going forth, (esp. of body of emigrants); departure of Israelites from Egypt; (*E~*) book of O.T. relating this. [LL, f. Gk EX²*odos* (*hodos* way)]

ex off′i′cio (-shĭŏ), adv. & a. In virtue of one's office, as ~ *members of committee*. [L]

‖ ex′ŏn, n. See EXEMPT¹. [repr. F pron.]

exŏn′er|āte (-gz-), v.t. Exculpate; free (person) *from* (blame etc.); release (person *from* duty etc.). Hence ~A′TION n., ~ātive a., (-gz-). [f. L EX¹(*onerare* f. *onus -eris* burden), see -ATE³]

exŏphthäl′m|us, -ŏs, n. Protrusion of eyeball. Hence ~IC a. [f. Gk EX²(*ophthalmos* eye) adj.]

exörb′it|ant (-gz-), a. Grossly excessive (of price, demand, ambition, person). Hence ~ANCE n., ~antLУ² adv., (-gz-). [f. LL EX¹*orbitare* go out of the wheel-track (ORBIT), -ANT]

exŏr'c|ize, -ise (-īz), v.t. Expel (evil spirit *from, out of,* person or place) by invocation or use of holy name; clear (person, place, *of* evil spirits). So ~ISM, -IST, nn. [f. LL *exorcizare* f. Gk EX²*orkizō* (*horkos* oath)]

exŏrd'ĭ|um, n. (pl. *-iums, -ia*). Beginning, introductory part, esp. of discourse or treatise. Hence ~AL a. [L, f. EX¹(*ordiri* begin)]

exŏtĕ'ric, a. & n. (Of doctrines, modes of speech, etc.) intelligible to outsiders (cf. ESOTERIC); (of disciples) not admitted to esoteric teaching; commonplace, ordinary, popular; (n. pl.) ~ doctrines or treatises. Hence ~AL a., ~alLY² adv. [f. LL f. Gk *exōterikos* (*exōterō* compar., see EXO-, -IC)]

exŏt'ic (-gz-), a. & n. 1. (Of plants, words, fashions) introduced from abroad; strange, bizarre. 2. n. ~ plant (also fig.). [f. L f. Gk *exōtikos* (see EXO-, -IC)]

expănd', v.t. & i. Spread out flat (t. & i.); expound, write out, in full (what is condensed or abbreviated, algebraical expression, etc.); develop (t. &-i.) *into;* swell, dilate, increase in bulk, (t. & i.); become genial, throw off reserve; ~*ed metal,* sheet metal slit and stretched into a lattice, used (esp.) to reinforce concrete. So **expănsi̇BIL'ITY** n., **expăn'si̇BLE** a. [f. L EX¹(*pandere pans-* spread)]

expănse', n. Wide area or extent; expansion. [as prec.]

expăn'sile, a. (Capable) of expansion. [-IL]

expăn'sion (-shn), n. Expanding; (Commerc.) extension of transactions; ~ (increase) *of the currency, of territory,* whence ~ISM(3), ~IST(2), nn. (-shon-); increase in bulk of steam in cylinder of engine; *triple-~ engine* (in which steam passes through 3 cylinders). [f. LL *expansio* (prec., -ION)]

expăn'sive, a. Able, tending, to expand (t. & i.); extensive; comprehensive; (of persons, feelings, speech) effusive. Hence ~LY² (-vl-) adv., ~NESS (-vn-), **expănsiv'ITY,** nn. [as prec., see -IVE]

ex̆ păr't'e, adv. & a. (law, & transf.). On, in the interests of, one side only; (adj., *ex-parte*) made or said thus, as *an ex-parte statement.* [L]

expā'ti̇|āte (-shi-), v.i. Speak, write, copiously (*on* subject); wander unrestrained (usu. fig.). Hence ~A'TION (-sī-) n.; ~atoRY (-sha-) a. [f. L EX¹(*spatiari* walk about, as SPACE), -ATE³]

expăt'ri̇|āte¹, v.t. Banish; (refl.) emigrate; (Law of Nations, refl.) renounce citizenship. Hence ~A'TION n. [f. med. L EX¹(*patriare* f. *patria* native land), see -ATE³]

expăt'ri̇ate², a. & n. Expatriated (person). [as prec., see -ATE¹,²]

expĕct', v.t. Look forward to, regard as likely, as *I ~ a storm, ~ to see him, ~ him to come, ~ (that) he will come, ~ him next*

week, don't ~ me, ~ payment today, not so bad as I ~ed (it to be), just what I ~ed of him; shall not ~ you till I etc. *see you,* leave you to arrive when you please; look for as due, as *I ~ you to be punctual, that you will be punctual, do you ~ payment for this?;* (colloq.) think, suppose, (*that*); (abs.) *she is ~ing* (colloq.), she is pregnant. [f. L EX¹(*spectare* look, frequent. of *specere* see)]

expĕc'tancy, n. State of expectation; prospect, esp. of future possession; prospective chance (*of*). [c. 1600, f. foll., see -ANCY]

expĕc'tant, a. & n. 1. Expecting (*of* or abs.; ~ *mother,* pregnant woman); having the prospect, in normal course, of possession, office, etc.; characterized by waiting for events, esp. (Med.) ~ *method;* (Law) reversionary. 2. n. One who expects, candidate for office etc. Hence ~LY² adv. [14th c., f. L *exspectare* EXPECT; see -ANT]

expĕctā'tion, n. Awaiting; anticipation, as *beyond, contrary to,* ~; ground for expecting (*of*); (pl.) prospects of inheritance; thing expected; ~ *of LIFE,* probability of a thing's happening. [f. L *expectatio* (as prec., see -ATION)]

expĕc'tative, a. Of reversion of benefices, reversionary. [f. med. L *expectativus* (prec., -ATIVE)]

expĕc'torant, a. & n. (Medicine) that promotes expectoration. [as foll., see -ANT]

expĕc'tor|āte, v.t. Eject (phlegm etc.) from chest or lungs by coughing or spitting; (abs.) spit. Hence ~A'TION n. [f. L EX¹*pectorare* (*pectus -oris* breast), -ATE³]

expēd'ient, a. & n. 1. (Usu. predic.) advantageous, suitable, as *do whatever is* ~, *it is ~ that he should go;* politic rather than just. 2. n. Contrivance, device. Hence or cogn. **expēd'IENCE,** -ENCY, nn., ~iAL (-ĕn'shal) a., ~LY² adv. [ME, f. OF, or f. L *expedient-* (as foll., see -ENT)]

ex'pĕdite, v.t. Assist the progress of (measure, process, etc.); dispatch (business). [f. L EX¹*pedire -dit-* (*pes pedis* foot)]

expĕdi'tion, n. Warlike enterprise; journey, voyage, for definite purpose; men, fleet, sent on this; promptness, speed. Hence ~ARY¹ a., ~IST(3) n., (-shon-). [ME, f. OF, or f. L *expeditio* (as prec., see -ION)]

expĕdi'tious (-shus), a. Doing or done speedily; suited for speedy performance. Hence ~LY² adv., ~NESS n., (-shus-). [f. prec., see -IOUS(2)]

expĕl', v.t. (-ll-). Eject (person *from* place, bullet *from* gun, etc.) by force; turn out (person *from* a community, school, etc.; also w. *from* omitted *was ~ed the school*). Hence ~l'ENT a. [ME, f. L EX¹(*pellere puls-* drive)]

expĕnd', v.t. Spend (money, care, time, *on* object, *in* doing); use up; (Naut.) wind (spare rope) round spar etc. Hence ~ABLE a., likely to be or meant to be sacrificed or destroyed. [ME, f. L EX¹(*pendĕre* pens-weigh)]

expen′diture, n. Laying out (*of money* etc.); consuming; amount expended. [after earlier (obs.) *expenditor* f. as prec. (med. L irreg. p.p. *penditus*; see -URE]

expense′, n. Expenditure; cost; (pl.) outlay in execution of commission etc., reimbursement of this, as *he paid my ~s, offered me £10 & ~s; at the ~* (cost) *of*, esp. (fig.) by bringing discredit etc. on, as *you defend his veracity at the ~ of his understanding*, if what he says is true he is a fool; *a laugh at his ~* (at him). [ME, f. AF (= OF es-), f. LL *expensa* fem. p.p. (as EXPEND)]

expen′sive, a. Costly. Hence ~LY² (-vl-) adv., ~NESS (-vn-) n. [EXPEND, -IVE]

exper′ience¹, n. Actual observation of or practical acquaintance with facts or events; knowledge resulting from this, whence **exper′ienced²** (-st) a.; event that affects one, as *an unpleasant ~*; fact, process, of being so affected, as *I learnt by ~*; (usu. pl.) state, phase, of religious emotion; *~ table*, table showing expectation of life at different ages etc. compiled from the ~ of life-assurance offices. [ME, f. OF *experience* f. L *experientia* f. EX¹*periri pert-* try; see -ENCE]

exper′ience², v.t. Meet with, feel, undergo, (pleasure, treatment, fate, etc.); learn, find; (*that, how,* etc.). [f. prec.]

experien′tial (-shal), a. Of experience; *~ philosophy* (treating all knowledge as based on experience), whence ~ISM, ~IST, nn., (-shal-). Hence ~LY² (-shal-) adv. [f. L as EXPERIENCE¹, see -AL]

expe′riment¹, n. Test, trial, (*of*); procedure adopted on chance of its succeeding or for testing hypothesis etc. [ME, f. OF, or L *experimentum* (as prec., see -MENT)]

expe′riment², v.i. Make experiment (*on, with*). Hence ~A′TION n. [prec.]

experimen′tal, a. Based on experience, not authority or conjecture; based on experiment, as *~ philosophy*, whence ~ISM, ~IST, nn.; tentative; used in experiments. Hence ~IZE(2) v.i., ~LY² adv. [-AL]

expert′¹, a. Trained by practice, skilful, (*at, in*). Hence ~LY² adv., ~NESS n. [ME, f. OF, f. L as EXPERIENCE¹]

ex′pert², n. Person having special skill or knowledge (*at, in*), as *mining ~*, (attrib.) *~ evidence*. [F (prec. as n.)]

expertise′ (-ēz), n. Expert opinion or skill or knowledge. [F]

expert′o cred′e, sent. You may take my word for it, because I have tried. [L, = believe one who has tried]

ex′piate, v.t. Pay the penalty of, make amends for, (sin). So ~ABLE, ~ātORY, aa., ~A′TION, ~ātOR, nn. [f. L EX¹(*piare* seek to appease f. *pius* devout), -ATE³]

expira′tion (-per-), n. Breathing out (*of air* etc.); termination (*of* period, truce, etc.). [f. L *expiratio* (as foll., see -ATION)]

expire′, v.t. & i. Breathe out (air *from* lungs, or abs.), whence **expir′atORY** a.; die; (of fire etc.) die out; (of period) come to an end; (of law, patent, truce, etc.) become void, reach its term; (of title etc.) become extinct. [ME, f. OF *expirer* f. L EX¹(*spirare* breathe)]

expir′y, n. Termination (of period, truce, etc.) [f. prec. + -Y⁴]

‖ **expis′cate,** v.t. (Sc.). Find by scrutiny etc. [f. L *expiscari* (EX-¹, *piscari* to fish)]

explain′, v.t. Make known in detail (thing, *that, how,* etc.); make intelligible (meaning, difficulty, etc., also abs.); account for (conduct etc.); *~ away*, modify, do away with, (esp. offensive language, awkward facts) by explanation; *~ one-self*, make one's meaning clear, (also) give an account of one's motives or conduct. Hence ~ABLE a. [f. L EX¹(*planare* f. *planus* flat)]

explana′tion, n. Explaining, esp. with view to mutual understanding or reconciliation; statement, circumstance, that explains. [ME, f. L *explanatio* (as prec., see -ATION)]

explan′ator|y̆, a. Serving, meant, to explain. Hence ~iLY² adv. [as EXPLAIN, see -ORY]

• **ex′pletive** (*or* īksplē-), a. & n. **1.** Serving to fill out (esp. sentence, metrical line etc.). **2.** n. = thing, word, etc., esp. oath or meaningless exclamation. [f. LL *expletivus* f. EX¹(*plēre* fill), -IVE]

ex′plic|ate, v.t. Develop (notion, principle, etc.), whence ~A′TION n.; (arch.) explain, whence ~ABLE, ~ātIVE, ~ātORY, aa. [f. L EX¹(*plicare plicat-* or *plicit-* fold) unfold. see -ATE³]

ex′plicit¹, v.i. Here ends (formerly written at end of book), cf. INCIPIT. [LL; prob. abbr. of p.p. as prec., but treated as 3rd sing.]

expli′cit², a. Stated in detail, leaving nothing merely implied; definite; (of persons) outspoken; *~ faith*, acceptance of doctrine with clear understanding of all it involves (cf. IMPLICIT). Hence ~LY² adv., ~NESS n. [f. F *explicite* or L *explicitus* (as EXPLICATE)]

explode′, v.t. & i. Expose, bring into disrepute, (theory, fallacy, etc.); (of gas, gunpowder, boiler, etc.) go off with loud noise; cause (these) to do this; *magneto ~r*, hand-operated portable electrical apparatus for detonating high-explosive charges. [f. L EX¹(*plodere plos-* = *plaudere* clap) hiss off stage]

ex′ploit¹, n. Brilliant achievement. [ME, f. OF *esploit(e)* f. L neut. & fem. p.p. as EXPLICATE]

exploit′², v.t. Work, turn to account, (mine etc.); utilize (person etc.) for one's own ends, esp. derog. of *~ing* colonial possessions, the working classes, etc. Hence or cogn. ~ABLE a., ~AGE, exploita′-TION, nn. [ME, f. OF *exploiter* f. Gallo-Rom. *explicitare* frequent. as prec.]

explōr|e', v.t. Inquire into, examine (wound) by touch; examine (country etc.) by going through it. Hence or cogn. **explora'TION**, **~'ER**[1], nn., **~'atIVE**, **~'atORY**, aa. [f. F *explorer* f. L *explorare*]

explō'sion (-zhn), n. Going off with loud noise; such noise; outbreak (of anger etc.). [f. L *explosio* (as EXPLODE, see -ION)]

explōs'ive, a. & n. **1.** Tending to eject something with loud noise; (of consonant sound) produced by explosion of breath, stopped; tending to explode or cause explosion (lit. & fig.). **2.** n. ~ agent or material, ~ letter; *high* ~ (abbr. H.E.), kinds having very violent shattering effect & used not as propellants but in shells, bombs, etc. Hence **~LY²** (-vl-) adv., **~NESS** (-vn-) n. [as EXPLODE, see -IVE]

expōn'ent, a. & n. (Person, thing) that sets forth or interprets; executant (of music etc.); type, representative; (Alg.) index, symbol indicating what power of a factor is to be taken, whence **ex̄ponēn'tIAL** (-shal) a. [f. L EX¹(*ponere posit-* put), see -ENT]

expōrt'[1], v.t. Send out (goods) to another country. Hence or cogn. **~ABLE** a., **~A'TION** n. [f. L EX¹(*portare* carry)]

ex'pōrt², n. Exported article; (usu. pl.) amount exported; exportation; ~ *duty* (paid on~). [f. prec.]

expōse' (-z), v.t. Leave (person, thing) unprotected (esp. from weather); subject *to* (risk etc.); (Photog.) subject (film etc.) to light; turn (child) out of doors to perish; (p.p.) open *to* (the East etc.); exhibit, display; put up for sale; disclose (secret, project, etc.); unmask (villain, villainy). [ME, f. OF EX¹(*poser*, see COMPOSE)]

exposé (ĕkspōz'ā), n. Statement of facts; showing up (of discreditable thing). [F, p.p. as prec.]

exposi'tion (-z-), n. Setting forth, description; explanation; commentary; = EXPOSURE; exhibition of goods etc. [ME, f. OF, or f. L *expositio* (as EXPONENT, see -ION)]

expos'it|ive (-z-), a. Descriptive; explanatory. So **~OR** n., **~ORY** a., (-z-). [as prec., see -IVE]

ex̄ pŏst făc'tō, a. Acting retrospectively, as ~ *law*. [L, = from what is made (i.e. enacted) afterwards]

expŏs'tul|āte, v.i. Make friendly remonstrance; remonstrate (*with* person *about*, *for*, *on*). Hence or cogn. **~A'TION** n., **~ātORY** a. [f. L EX¹(*postulare* POSTULATE)]

expō'sure (-zher), n. Exposing, being exposed, (*to* air, cold, danger, etc.); abandoning (of child); display, esp. of goods for sale; unmasking of imposture etc.; aspect, as *southern* ~; (Photog.) action of exposing plate or film to the light, duration of this action. [-URE]

expound', v.t. Set forth in detail (doc-trine etc.); explain, interpret, (esp. Scripture). [ME *expoune* f. OF *espondre* (as EXPONENT)]

express'[1], a., adv., & n. **1.** (Of likeness) exact; definitely stated, not merely implied; done, made, sent, for special purpose; ‖ ~ *train* (fast, stopping at few intermediate stations); ~ *rifle* (discharging bullet with high initial velocity & low trajectory); ~ *bullet* (expanding, for ~ rifle); ‖ ~ *delivery* (by special postal messenger). **2.** adv. With speed, by ~ messenger or train. **3.** n. ~ train, messenger, rifle. Hence **~LY²** adv. [ME, f. OF *expres, -esse* (as foll.)]

express'², v.t. Squeeze out (juice, air, *from*, *out of*); emit, exude; represent by symbols, as (Math.) (quantity) *in terms of* (another); reveal, betoken, (feelings, qualities); put (thought) into words; ~ one*self*, say what one means (*strongly* etc. *on* subject, *well*, *aptly*, etc.). Hence **~IBLE** a. [ME, f. OF EX¹(*presser* PRESS²)]

express'ion (-shn), n. Expressing (in all senses); wording, diction, word, phrase; (Alg.) collection of symbols expressing a quantity; aspect (of face), intonation (of voice), whence **~LESS** (-shon-) a.; (Art) mode of expressing character etc., whence **~IST(2)** (-shon-) n.; (Mus.) execution that expresses the feeling of a passage, as ~*mark*, sign, word, indicating~ required, ~*stop* (in harmonium, producing ~ by varied air-pressure). [ME, f. OF f. L *expressionem* f. EX¹(*primere* = *premere* PRESS², -ION)]

express'ional (-shon-), a. Of verbal, facial, or artistic expression. [-AL]

express'ionism (-shon-), n. Modern tendency among painters, dramatic authors, etc., to subordinate realism to the symbolic or stylistic expression of the artist's or character's inner experience; (Mus.) tendency to discard rules and conventions and thus obtain complete freedom for composer's self-expression (as in Schönberg). [-ISM]

express'ive, a. Serving to express (~ *of* motion etc.); (of word, gesture, etc.) significant. Hence **~LY²** (-vl-) adv., **~NESS** (-vn-) n. [F (-*if*, -*ive*), as EXPRESSION, see -IVE]

exprobrā'tion, n. Reproachful language. [f. L *exprobratio* f. EX¹(*probrare* f. *probrum* shameful deed), see -ATION]

exprŏp'ri|āte, v.t. Dispossess (*from* estate etc.); take away (property). So **~A'TION** n. [f. med. L EX¹(*propriare* f. *proprium* property), see PROPER & -ATE³]

expŭl'si|on (-shon), n. Expelling. So **~IVE** a. & n. (med.). [ME, f. L *expulsio* (as EXPEL, see -ION)]

expŭnge' (-j), v.t. Erase, omit, (name *from* list, passage *from* book, etc.). So **expŭnc'tION** n. [f. L EX¹(*pungere punct-* prick)]

ex'purg|āte (-per-), v.t. Purify (book etc.) by removing matter thought objectionable; clear away (such matter). Hence or cogn. ~A'TION. ~ātor, nn., ĕxpūrgā-tōr'IAL, ĕxpūrg'ātORY, aa. [f. L EX¹ (purgare cleanse), -ATE³]

ĕx'quisite (-z-), a. & n. 1. Of consummate excellence or beauty; acute (~ pain, pleasure); keen (~ sensibility etc.). 2. n. Coxcomb, fop. Hence ~LY² (-tī-) adv., ~NESS (-tn-) n. [f. L EX¹(quirere quisit-= quaerere seek)]

ĕxsăng'uināte (-nggwĭn-), v.t. Drain of blood. [f. L EX¹(sanguinatus f. sanguis -inis blood), see -ATE³]

ĕxsăng'uine (-nggwĭn) a. Lacking blood. [EX-¹]

ĕxscind', v.t. Cut out, excise, (lit. & fig.). [f. L EX¹(scindere cut)]

ĕxsĕrt', v.t. (biol.). Put forth. [= EXERT]

‖ ĕx-sĕrv'ice, a. That has been but is no longer in one of the fighting services.[EX-¹]

ĕx'siccate, v.t. Dry up; drain dry. [f. L EX¹(siccare f. siccus dry)]

ĕx'tant (or Ikstănt'), a. Still existing (esp. of documents etc.). [f. L EX¹(stare stand), see -ANT]

extasy. See ECSTASY.

ĕxtĕm'por|ē, adv. & a. (Spoken, done) without preparation; off-hand; speak ~e (without notes). Hence or cogn.~AN'EOUS, ~ARY¹, aa.,~ăn'ĕouslY², ~ariLY², advv., ~ăn'ĕousNESS n. [L ex tempore (tempus time) on the spur of the moment]

ĕxtĕm'poriz|e, -is|e (-īz), v.t. & i. Compose, produce, extempore; (intr.) speak extempore. Hence ~A'TION n. [f. prec +IZE]

ĕxtĕnd', v.t. & i. Lay out (esp. body, limbs, etc.) at full length; write out (shorthand 'etc.) at full length; (intr. & refl.) reach (to point, over, across, etc., space); cause to do this; prolong (period); enlarge (scope, meaning of word, etc.); (Mil., of line etc.) spread out into open order with regular intervals between men (trans., cause to~); (Sport. sl.) tax powers of (horse, athlete) to the utmost (usu. pass.); stretch forth (hand, arm); accord (kindness, patronage, to); (Law) value (land etc.), seize (land etc.) for debt. Hence or cogn. ĕxtĕnsiBIL'ITY n., ĕxtĕn'dIBLE, ĕxtĕn'sIBLE, aa. [ME, f. L EX¹(tendere tens- or tent- stretch)]

ĕxtĕn'sile, a. .Capable of being stretched out or protruded. [as prec., see -ILE]

ĕxtĕn'sion (-shn), n. Extending (in all senses exc. Law); extent, range; prolongation; enlargement; additional part (of railway, plan, theory, etc.); word(s) amplifying subject or predicate; University E~, extramural instruction conducted by a university or college. [f. L extentio, -sio, (as prec., see -ION)]

ĕxtĕn'sive, a. (Of space, purchase, operation, etc.) large; far-reaching, comprehensive; (of agricultural production etc.) depending on extension of area (cf. INTENSIVE). Hence ~LY² (-vl-) adv., ~NESS (-vn-) n. [f. LL extensivus (as prec., see -IVE)]

ĕxtĕn'sor, n. ~ (muscle), one that straightens out part of the body. [as EXTEND, see -OR]

ĕxtĕnt', n. Space over which a thing extends; width of application, scope, as to a great ~, to the full ~ of his power; large space, as a vast ~ of marsh; (Law) valuation (of land etc.); seizure, writ for seizure (of land etc.). [f. AF estente, ex-, p.p. of estendre (as EXTEND)]

ĕxtĕn'ūāt|e, v.t. Lessen seeming magnitude of (guilt, offence) by partial excuse, as we must not ~e, nothing can ~e, his baseness, whence ~ORY a.; (improp.) lessen seeming guilt of, as do not ~e yourself, his conduct; (arch.) make thin or weak. Hence ĕxtĕnūā'TION n. [f. L EX¹(tenuare f. tenuis thin), -ATE³]

ĕxtēr'ior, a. & n. 1. Outer; situated or coming from without; ~ angle, that between side of rectilineal figure & adjacent side produced. 2. n. Outward aspect or demeanour. Hence ~ITY (-ŏ'r-) n., ~LY² adv. [L, compar. of exterus outside]

ĕxtēr'ioriz|e, -is|e (-īz), v.t. Realize (conception) in outward form; attribute external existence to. Hence ~A'TION n. [-IZE]

ĕxtĕrm'in|āte, v.t. Root out (species, race, sect, opinion). Hence or cogn. ~A'TION, ~ātor, nn., ~ātory a. [f. L EX¹terminare (TERMINUS), -ATE³]

ĕxtĕrn'al, a. & n. 1. Situated outside; (of remedies etc.) applied to the outside of the body; (Theol.) consisting in outward acts, whence ~ISM(2) n.; belonging to the world of phenomena (~ world), outside the conscious subject; ~ evidence (derived from source independent of the thing discussed). 2. n. pl. Outward features or aspect, ~ circumstances, non-essentials. Hence ĕxtĕrnăl'ITY n., ~LY² adv. [f. L externus outward +-AL]

ĕxtĕrn'aliz|e, -is|e (-īz), v.t. Give, attribute, external existence to. Hence ~A'-TION n. [-IZE]

ĕxtĕrritōr'ial, a. = EXTRATERRITORIAL. So ~ITY (-ăl⁴-) n. [EX-¹]

ĕxtinct', a. (Of fire etc.) no longer burning; (of volcano) that has ceased eruption; (of life, hope, etc.) quenched; (of family, class, species) that has died out; (of office etc.) obsolete; (of title of nobility) having no qualified claimant. [ME, f. L EX¹(stinguere stinct- quench)]

ĕxtinc't|ion, n. Extinguishing; making, being, becoming, extinct; wiping out (of debt); annihilation. So ~IVE a. [f. L extinctio (as prec., see -ION)]

ĕxting'uish (-nggw-), v.t. Put out, quench, (light, hope, life, faculties); eclipse, obscure, (person) by superior brilliancy; reduce (opponent) to silence; destroy; wipe out (debt); annihilate. Hence ~ABLE a., ~MENT n. [irreg. f. L extinguere (as EXTINCT)+-ISH²; cf. distinguish]

ĕxtĭng'uĭsher (-nggw-}, n. In vbl senses, esp. *fire* ~, apparatus with jet for discharging liquid chemicals or foam to extinguish fire. [-ER¹].

ĕx'tĭrp|āte, v.t. Root out, destroy, (tree, weed, species, nation, tumour, heresy, etc.). So ~A'TION, ~ātor, nn. [f. L EX¹(s)*tirpare* (*stirps* stem), see -ATE³]

ĕxtŏl', v.t. (-ll-). Praise enthusiastically (~ *him to the skies*). [f. L EX¹(*tollere* raise)]

ĕxtŏrt', v.t. Obtain (money, promise, etc.) by violence, intimidation, importunity, etc. (*from*); extract forcibly (meaning, inference, *from* words, data). Hence **ĕxtŏr'tIVE** a. [f. L EX¹(*torquēre tort*- twist)]

ĕxtŏr'tion, n. Extorting, esp. of money; illegal exaction. Hence ~ER¹ (-shon-) n. [ME, f. LL *extortio* (as prec., see -ION)]

ĕxtŏr'tionate (-shon-), a. Using, given to, extortion; (of prices etc.) exorbitant. [-ATE²]

ĕx'tra, a., adv., & n. 1. Additional; larger than its name indicates, as ~ *foolscap, octavo*; of superior quality, as *calf* ~. 2. adv. More than usually, as ~ *strong*; additionally; ‖ ~-*special* (latest) *edition* (of evening paper). 3. n. ~ thing, one for which ~ charge is made, as *dancing is an* ~; (Crick.) run not scored off bat; additional dance; (Cinemat.) person engaged temporarily for a minor part or to be one of a crowd. [prob. for EXTRAORDINARY, perh. f. F]

ĕx'tra- in comb. = L *extra* in senses 'situated outside of a thing', 'not coming within its scope'; chiefly in wds f. med. L or mod. L (L has only *extraordinarius*), as: ~-*atmosphē'ric*, of the space beyond the atmosphere; ~*cos'mical*, acting outside the universe; ~*crā̆n'ial*, outside the skull; ~*curric'ular*, not coming within the curriculum; ~-*essĕn'tial*, not included in the essence of a thing; ~*judi'cial*, not belonging to the case before the court, not legally authorized, (of confession) not made in court; ~-*mun'dane*, outside of our world or of the universe; ~*mur'al*, outside the walls or boundaries (of town or city), outside the scope of ordinary university teaching or studies; ~-*offi'cial*, not pertaining to an office; ~*parŏch'ial*, outside, not concerned with, the parish; ~*phys'ical*, not subject to physical laws; ~ *spĕc'tral*, lying outside the visible spectrum; ~*terrĕs'trial*, outside the earth or its atmosphere.

ĕx'trăct¹, n. The tough or viscid matter got by treating a substance with solvents & then evaporating them; preparation containing the active principle of a substance in concentrated form; passage from book etc. [as foll.]

ĕxtrăct'², v.t. Copy out (passage in book etc.); make extracts from (book etc.); take out by force (teeth, anything firmly fixed); draw forth (money, admission, etc.) against person's will; obtain (juices etc.) by suction, pressure,

etc.; derive (pleasure etc. *from*); deduce (principle etc. *from*); (Math.) find (root of a number). Hence **ĕxtrăc'tABLE** a., **ĕxtrăc'tor** n. [f. L EX¹(*trahere tract*- draw)]

ĕxtrăc'tion, n. Extracting; lineage (of *Indian* ~); ~ *rate*, proportion of total weight of unground wheat which is converted into flour, & not into bran or sharps, expressed as a percentage of the weight unground. [F, or f. LL *extractio* (prec., -ION)]

ĕxtrăc'tive, a. & n. (Thing) of the nature of an extract; ~ *industries* (depending on mining & oil). [-IVE]

ĕxtradit'able, a. Liable to, (of crime) warranting, extradition. [f. foll. + -ABLE]

ĕx'tradite, v.t. Give up (fugitive foreign criminal) to the proper authorities; obtain the extradition of. [back formation f. foll.]

ĕxtradi'tion, n. Delivery of fugitive criminal to proper authorities; (Psych.) localizing of sensation at distance from the centre of sensation. [F (EX-¹, see TRADITION)]

ĕxtrā̆d'ŏs, n. Upper or outer curve of arch. [F EXTRA(*dos* back f. L *dorsum*)]

ĕxtrā̆n'ĕous, a. Of external origin; foreign *to* (object to which it is attached etc.); not belonging (*to* matter in hand, class). Hence ~LY² adv., ~NESS n. [f. L *extraneus* (*extra* outside) + -OUS]

ĕxtraŏr'dinar| y̆ (-trŏr-, -traŏr-), a. & n. Out of the usual course; (of officials etc.) additional, specially employed; *envoy*~*y*, diplomatic minister of second class, ranking next to ambassador; exceptional, surprising; unusually great; (n. pl.) extra allowances to troops (arch.). Hence ~ILY² adv., ~ĭNESS n. [f. L *extraordinarius* (*extra ordinem* outside the usual order. -ARY¹)]

ĕxtrăp'olāte, v.t. & i. (math.). Calculate from known terms a series of other terms which lie outside the range of the known terms (also fig.). So **ĕxtrapolA'TION** n. [EXTRA- + (INTER)POLATE]

ĕxtratĕrrĭtŏr'ial, a. (Of ambassadors etc.) free from jurisdiction of the territory in which one resides. So ~ITY (-ăl'-) n. [EXTRA-]

ĕxtrăv'agance, n. Being extravagant; absurd statement or action. [F (foll., -ANCE)]

ĕxtrăv'agant, a. Immoderate; exceeding the bounds of reason; profuse, wasteful; (of price etc.) exorbitant. Hence ~LY² adv. [f. med. L EXTRA(*vagari* wander), see -ANT, & F *extravagant*]

ĕxtrăvagăn'za, n. Fantastic composition (literary, musical, dramatic), language or behaviour. [f. It. *estravaganza* (prec., -ANCE)]

ĕxtrăv'agāte, v.i. (rare). Wander away (*from* right course, into error etc.); exceed due bounds. [as EXTRAVAGANT, see -ATE³]

ĕxtrăv'asāte, v.t. & i. Force out (fluid) from its proper vessel; flow out. Hence ĕx̆trăvăsā′TION n. [EXTRA-, L *vas* vessel, -ATE[3]]

ĕx′trăvĕrt, n. Var. of EXTROVERT.

extrēme′, a. & n. 1. Outermost, farthest from centre, situated at either end; *divided in ~ & mean ratio* (the whole being to one part as that part to the other); utmost; last, as (R.-C. Ch.) ~ *unction,* anointing by priest of dying person; reaching a high degree, as ~ *old age, in* ~ *danger; an* ~ *case* (having some characteristic in the utmost degree); (of actions, measures) severe, stringent; (of opinions, persons, etc.) going to great lengths, opp. to *moderate,* whence extrēm′ISM, extrēm′IST, nn.; *in the* ~, ~ly. 2. n. Thing at either end of anything, esp. (pl.) things as remote as as different as possible, as ~*s meet*; (Logic) subject or predicate in proposition, major or minor term in syllogism; (Math.) first, last, term of ratio or series; *run to an* ~, go *to* ~*s,* taken an ~ course. Hence ~LY[2] (-ml-) adv., ~NESS (-mn-) n. [ME, f. OF f. L *extremus* superl. of *exterus* outward]

extrēm′it|y̆, n. Extreme point, very end; *the* ~ *ies,* hands & feet; extreme adversity, embarrassment, etc., as *driven to* ~*y, what can we do in this* ~*y?*; (usu. pl.) extreme measure(s). [ME, f. OF *extremite* or L *extremitas* (prec., -TY)]

ĕx′tric|āte, v.t. Disentangle, release, (person, thing, *from* confinement, difficulty); (Chem.) liberate (gas etc.) from state of combination. Hence ~ABLE a., ~A′TION n. [f. L EX[1](*tricare* f. *tricae* perplexities), -ATE[3]]

extrin′s|ic, a. Lying outside, not belonging, (*to*); operating from without; not inherent or essential. Hence ~ICALLY adv. [f. LL adj. *extrinsicus,* f. L adv. *-secus* (*exter* outside + *-in* local suf. + *secus* beside)]

extrōrse′, a. (bot.). (Of anthers) turned outwards. [F, f. L *extrorsus* outwards (EXTRA- + *versus* towards)]

ĕx′trŏvĕrt, n. (psych.). Person not given to introspection (chiefly in antithesis with INTROVERT n.). So ĕxtrovĕr′SION (-shn) n. [f. L *extra* outside (w. assim. to INTRO- + *vertĕre* turn]

extrude′ (-rōō-), v.t. Thrust out (person, thing, *from*). Hence ĕxtru′SION (-rōōzhn) n., ĕxtrus′IVE (-rōō-) a. [f. L EX[1](*trudere trus-* thrust)]

exŭb′er|ant (-gz-), a. Luxuriantly prolific (lit. & fig.); growing luxuriantly; (of health, emotions, etc.) overflowing, abounding; (of persons, actions, etc.) effusive, overflowing with spirits; (of language) copious, lavish in ornament; abundant. Hence or cogn. ~ANCE n., ~antLY[2] adv., (-gz-). [F, or f. L EX[1](*uberare* be fruitful f. *uber* fertile), -ANT]

exŭb′erāte (-gz-), v.i. Abound, overflow; indulge freely *in.* [as prec., see -ATE[3]]

exūde′ (-gz-), v.i. & t. Ooze out, give off (moisture etc.), like sweat. Hence **or**

cogn. exūdā′TION n., exūd′atIVE (-gz-) a. [f. L EX[1](*sudare* sweat)]

exŭlt′ (-gz-), v.i. Rejoice exceedingly (*at, in,* thing, *to* find etc.); triumph (*over* person). Hence or cogn. exŭl′tANCY (-gz-), exŭltā′TION, nn., exŭl′tANT a., exŭl′tantLY[2] adv., (-gz). [f. F *exulter* or L EX[1]*ulere = saltare* frequent. of *salire salt-* leap)]

exūv′i|ae, n. pl. Animal's cast skin, shell, or covering, (recent or fossil, also fig.). Hence ~AL a. [L, = animal's skin, spoils of enemy, f. EX[1]*uere* divest oneself of]

exūv′i|āte, v.t. & i. Shed (exuviae, also fig.), slough. Hence ~A′TION n. [prec., -ATE[3]]

ex võt′õ, adv. & n. (Offering made) in pursuance of a vow. [L (as adv. phr.)]

eyas (i′as), n. Young hawk taken from nest for training, or not yet completely trained. [orig. *nyas* f. F *niais* f. Rom. *nid(i)acem* (nom. *-ax*) f. *nidus* nest; for loss of *n-* cf. ADDER]

eye[1] (i), n. Organ of sight; iris of this, as *blue, brown,* ~*s*; region of the ~*s,* as BLACK[1] ~; ~ *of day,* sun; EVIL ~; *in the wind's* ~ (direction of the wind); (Mil.) ~*s right, left, front,* (turn them thus); *mind your* ~, take care; (contempt.) *pipe, put* one's *finger in,* one's ~, weep; *beam, mote, in* one's ~ (*Matt.* vii. 3); ~ *for* ~, retaliation (*Exod.* xxi. 24); *clap, set,* ~*s on,* behold; *be all* ~*s,* watch intently; *up to the* ~*s,* deeply (engaged), as *up to the* ~*s in work,* mortgaged *up to the* ~*s; his* ~*s are bigger than his belly* (said of a person who has helped himself to more than he can eat); *made him open his* ~*s* (stare with astonishment); *open* one's ~*s to,* make him realize; *wipe the* ~ *of* (shooter), kill game he has missed; *all my* ~ (*& Betty Martin*), humbug, nonsense; *my* ~(*s*)*!,* int. expr. astonishment; *lose an* ~, (often) lose the sight of it; *if you had half an* ~ (were not wholly blind or dull); *saw with half an* ~ (at a glance); *the* NAKED ~; *have an* ~ *to,* have as one's object; *with an* ~ (a view) *to; keep an* ~ *on,* keep watch on (lit. & fig.); *have an* ~ *for* (a due sense of) *proportion* etc.; *in the* ~*s* (judgement *of*); *in the* ~ (from the point of view) *of the law; in the mind's* ~, in anticipation or imagination; *see* ~ *to* ~, agree entirely (*with*); *view with a friendly, jealous,* ~ (with such feelings); *throw* DUST *in the* ~*s of; make* ~*s* (look amorously) *at; cast* SHEEP's ~*s;* thing like an ~, as spot on peacock's tail, ~ *of needle* etc. (hole for thread etc.), *hook & ~* (kind of fastening for dress), loop of cord or rope, leafbud of potato; BULL[1]'s-~; *glass* ~ (artificial, of glass etc.); APPLE *of the* ~; ~*ball,* pupil of the ~, ~ itself within lids & socket; ~*-bath,* *-cup,* small glass for applying lotion etc. to ~; ~*-bolt,* bolt, bar, with ~ at end for hook etc.; ~*bright* (also *euphrasy*), plant formerly used to cure weak ~*s*; ~*brow,* fringe of hair over ~; ~-*glass*, lens for assisting defective sight, (pl.) pair of these held in position by hand or by spring on nose (cf. SPECTACLE); ~'*hole*, hole containing ~, hole to look through; ~'*lash*, hair, row of hairs, on edge of ~lid; ~'*lid*, upper or lower cover of ~, (fig.) *hang on by the* ~*lids*, have only slight hold; ~-*opener*, enlightening or surprising circumstance; ~'*piece*, lens(es) at ~-end of telescope etc.; ~-*servant* (working properly only under employer's ~); ~-*service* (performed only thus); ~'*shot*, seeing-distance, as *beyond, in, out of,* ~*shot (of)*; ~'*sight*, power, faculty, of seeing; ~'*sore*, ugly object, thing that offends the sight; ~-*splice* (made by turning up end of rope & interlacing its strands with those of upper part); ~'*strings*, muscles, nerves, tendons, of ~; ~-*tooth* (canine, just under or next to ~, in upper or lower jaw); ~'*wash*, lotion for ~, (sl.) bunkum, mere professions; ~'*water*, tears, lotion for ~, aqueous or vitreous humours of ~; ~'*witness*, one who can bear witness from his own observation. Hence (~)EYED² (id), ~'LESS (il-), aa. [OE *éage*, OS *ōga*, OHG *ouga*, ON *auga*, Goth. *augo* f. Gmc *augon]

eye² (ī), v.t. (part. *eying* or ~*ing*). Observe, watch, (*jealously, narrowly, with disgust*, ASKANCE, etc.). [f. prec.]

eye′let (il-), n. Small hole in cloth, sail, etc., for lace, ring, rope, etc.; loophole; ~-*hole*, small hole to look or shoot through; small eye. [ME *oilet* f. OF *oillet* dim. of *œil* eye f. L *oculus*]

eyot. See AIT.

eyre (ār), n. (hist.). Circuit, circuit court, as *Justices in E*~. [ME, f. OF *eire* f. L *iter* journey]

eyrie. See AERIE.

F

F (ĕf), letter (pl. *Fs*, *F's*). (Mus.; also *fa*) fourth note in diatonic scale of C major. (In MSS. a capital F was freq. written as **ff.** Hence, by a misunderstanding, the spelling of certain family names as *ffolkes, fforde*, etc.).

fa (fah), **fah**, n. Fourth note of octave in solmization. [first syl. of *famuli*, see GAMUT]

Fab′ian, a. Employing cautious & dilatory strategy to wear out an enemy (esp. ~ *policy*); ~ *Society* (of socialists following such policy). [f. L *Fabianus* (Q. Fabius Cunctator (= delayer), commander against Hannibal, -AN)]

fa′ble¹, n. Story, esp. of supernatural character, not founded on fact; (collect.) myths, legendary tales, idle talk (*old wives'* ~*s*); false statement, lie; thing only supposed to exist; short story, esp. with animals for characters, conveying a moral, apologue; plot of play etc. [ME, f. OF f. L *fabula* (*fari* speak)]

fa′ble², v.i. & t. (arch. & poet.). Romance, tell fictitious tales, whence **fāb′lER¹** n.; state fictitiously; (p.p.) celebrated in fable, legendary, fictitious. [ME, f. OF *fabler* f. L *fabulari* see prec.]

fáb′liau (-lō), n. (pl. -*x* pr. -z). Metrical tale of early French poetry. [F]

fáb′ric, n. Thing put together; edifice, building; frame, structure, (lit. & fig.); (often *textile* ~) woven material; construction, texture, tissue. [f. F *fabrique* f. L *fabrica* (*faber* artificer)]

fáb′ric|āte, v.t. Construct, manufacture, make; invent (facts), forge (document). So ~A′TION, ~ātoR, nn. [f. L *fabricare* as prec., -ATE³]

fáb′ulist, n. Composer of fables or apologues; liar. [f. F *fabuliste* (FABLE¹, -IST)]

fáb′ulous, a. Given to legend (~ *historians*); celebrated in fable; unhistorical, legendary, incredible, absurd, exaggerated. Hence or cogn. **fábŭlos′ITY**, ~NESS, nn., ~LY² adv. [f. F *fabuleux* or L *fabulosus* (FABLE¹, -OUS)]

façade′ (-sahd), n. Face of building towards street or open space; frontal or outward appearance. [F (foll., -ADE¹)]

fāce¹, n. 1. Front of head from forehead to chin (*look one in the* ~, confront him steadily; *show one's* ~, appear; ~ *to* ~, confronted; ~ *to* ~ *with*, confronting; *set one's* ~ *against*, oppose; *with wind, sun, in one's* ~, straight against one; *fly in the* ~ *of*, openly disobey; *in* ~ *of*, opposite to; *in the* ~ *of*, or *in* ~ *of*, despite; *to person's* ~, openly in his presence; *in the* ~ *of day*, openly; *her* ~ *is her fortune*, beauty her only dower. 2. Expression of countenance (*pull, wear, a long* ~, look serious or dismal); grimace (*make, pull, a* ~ or ~*s*). 3. Composure, coolness, effrontery, (*have the* ~, be shameless enough; *save one's* ~, forbear from or evade shaming him or oneself openly). 4. Outward show, aspect, (*on the* ~ *of it*, to judge by appearance; *put a new* ~ *on*, alter aspect of; *put a good, bold,* ~ *on matter*, make it look well, show courage in facing it); *lose* ~, be humiliated, lose one's credit or good name [transl. of Chin. *tiu lien*]. 5. Surface (*from the* ~ *of the earth*); front, façade, right side, obverse, dial-plate of clock etc., working surface of implement etc. 6. ~-*ache*, neuralgia; ~ *card*, king, queen, or knave; ~-*lift(ing)*, plastic surgery for making ~ firm, removing wrinkles, etc.; ~ *value*, nominal value as stated on coin, note, etc. Hence -fācED² (-st) a. [ME, f. OF f. Rom. *facia f. L *facies*]

fāce², v.t. & i. 1. Meet confidently or defiantly (~ *matter out*, carry it through; ~ *opponent down*, browbeat him), not shrink from (~ *up to*, confront), stand fronting, (~ *the music*, not quail at moment of trial); present itself to (*the problem that* ~*s us*). 2. Turn (card) face upwards. 3. (Of persons etc.) look, (of things) be situated, in a certain direction (*on, to,* or *North, Eastwards,* etc.). **4.** Front towards, be opposite to, (*to ~ page 20*). **5.** (Lacrosse, Ice hockey, etc.) place (ball, puck, etc.) between crosses, sticks, etc., of two opposing players as preliminary to commencement of game (so ~ *off*). **6.** (mil.). Turn in certain direction on one's ground (*left, about,* ~; also trans., *he ~d his men about*. **7.** Supply (garment) with FACINGS; cover (surface) with layer of other material; dress surface of; coat (tea) with colouring matter. [f. prec.]

fā′cer, n. Blow in the face; great & sudden difficulty. [FACE¹ + -ER¹]

fā′cĕt, n. One side of a many-sided body, esp. of a cut gem; one segment of a compound eye. Hence **~ED²** a. [f. F *facette* (FACE¹, -ETTE)]

facē′tiae (-shiē), n. pl. Pleasantries, witticisms; (book catalogues) books of humorous or erotic character. [L (*facetus* urbane)]

facē′tious (-shus), a. Addicted to or marked by pleasantry, waggish. Hence **~LY²** adv., **~NESS** n. (-shus-). [f. F *facétieux* (*facétie* f: L *facetia* sing. of prec.)]

fā′cia (-sha), n. Plate over shop-front with occupier's name etc. [var. of FASCIA]

fā′cial (-shl), a. & n. **1.** Of the face (esp. in Anat., as ~ *artery*); ~ *angle*, that formed by two lines from nostril to (1) ear & (2) forehead. **2.** n. Face massage. [f. med. L *facialis* (FACE¹, -AL)]

-fācient (-shnt), suf. forming adjj. representing L *-facient-* (*facere* make, -ENT) added to infin. in *-ē(re)*, as *calefacere, liquefacere,* w. sense *producing the action* of the vb. E forms, on strict anal. w. L, *absorbefacient* etc., &, loosely, *abortifacient, calorifacient,* etc., where L would have vbs in *-ficare,* adjj. in *-ficus* -FIC.

fā′cile, a. Easily done or won (now usu. derog.); working easily, ready, fluent; of easy temper, gentle, flexible, yielding. [F, or f. L *facilis* (*facere* do)]

fa′cĭlĕ prĭn′cĕps, pred. a. Easily first. [L]

facĭl′it|āte, v.t. Make easy, promote, help forward, (action or result). Hence **~A′TION** n. [f. F *faciliter* (FACILE, -ATE³)]

facĭl′itў̆, n. Being easy, absence of difficulty, unimpeded opportunity (*give ~ies for, of doing*); ease or readiness of speech etc., aptitude, dexterity, fluency; pliancy. [f. F *facilité* or L *facilitas* (FACILE, -TY)]

fā′cing, n. In vbl senses of FACE²; esp.: (pl.) cuffs, collar, etc., of soldier's jacket, differently coloured from rest; coating of different material, esp. of stone etc. on wall; turning in some direction (*put person through his ~s*, test his qualities, proficiency, etc.; *go through* one's *~s*, be thus tested). [-ING¹]

facsim′ĭlĕ, n., & v.t. Exact copy, esp. of writing, printing, picture, etc. (*reproduced in ~* exactly); (vb) make ~ of. [L *fac*

imperat. of *facere* make+neut. of *similis* like]

fact, n. Perpetration of act, occurrence of event, (now only in *before, after, the ~, confess the ~*); thing certainly known to have occurred or be true, datum of experience, (often with explanatory clause or phrase, as *the ~ that fire burns,* or *my having seen him*); *the ~s of* life (colloq.), details of animal reproduction, the realities of a situation; thing assumed as basis for inference (*his ~s are disputable*); (sing. without *a*) the true or existent, reality, (so *matter of ~,* independent of inference; MATTER¹-*of-~*; *in ~*; *as a matter of ~*; *in point of ~*; *the ~ of the matter is*); *in ~,* (also, in summarizing) in short; *~-finding* adj., engaged in finding out~s. [f. L *factum* neut. p.p. of *facere* do]

fac′tion, n. Self-interested, turbulent, or unscrupulous party, esp. in politics; prevalence of party spirit. Hence or cogn. **~AL** (-shon-), **fac′tious** (-shus), aa., **fac′tiously²** adv., **fac′tiousness** n., (-shus-). [F, f. L *factionem* (*facere* fact- do, -ION); see FASHION]

-faction, suf. repr. L *-factio,* forming nn. of action related to vv. in -FY, prop. only when *-fy* represents L *-facere,* F *-faire,* as in *satisfaction,* but also used (instead of -FICATION) when *-fy* represents L *-ficare,* F *-fier,* as in *petrifaction*.

factī′tious (-shus), a. Designedly got up, not natural, artificial. Hence **~LY²** adv., **~NESS** n. (-shus-). [f. L *facticius* (*facere* fact- make) +-OUS; see -ITIOUS]

fac′titive, a. (gram.). ~ *verb,* one with sense *make, call,* or *think,* that takes obj. & compl. (*he thought her mad*). [irreg. f. L *facere* fact- make, -IVE]

fac′tor, n. Agent, deputy; merchant buying & selling on commission, whence **~AGE**(4) n.; ‖ (Sc.) land agent, steward; (Math.) one of the components that make up a number or expression by multiplication; (Biol.) physiological unit determining hereditary character; circumstance, fact, or influence, contributing to a result; ~ *cost,* cost of product to producer; ~ *of safety* (Engineering), ratio of a material's strength to the maximum load etc. it may have to sustain. [f. F *facteur* or L *factor* (prec., -OR)]

factōr′ial, n. & a. (math.). Product of series of factors in arithmetical progression; product of an integer & all lower integers (adj., ~ 4, symbol $\lfloor 4$ or $4!$, = $4 \times 3 \times 2 \times 1$). [-IAL]

fac′tory, n. Merchant company's foreign trading station (hist.); manufactory, workshop, (‖ *F~ Acts,* regulating management in interest of the hands). [16th c., repr. Pg. *feitoria,* Sp. *factoria,* obs. F *factorie* (FACTOR, -Y¹)]

factōt′um, n. Man or woman of all work; servant managing his master's affairs. [med. L, as FACSIMILE+neut. of L *totus* whole]

fac′tŭal, a. Concerned with, of the nature of, fact. Hence ~LY² adv. [f. FACT, after ACTUAL]

fac′tum, n. Statement of facts or points in controversy, memorial. [L, see FACT]

fac′ŭl|a, n. (astron.; pl. *-ae*). Bright spot or streak on sun. Hence ~AR¹, ~OUS, aa. [L, dim. of *fax fac-* torch]

fac′ultātive, a. Permissive; optional; contingent; of a faculty. [F (*-if, -ive*); foll., -IVE]

fac′ult|ў, n. Aptitude for any special kind of action; executive ability (chiefly U.S.); power inherent in the body or an organ; a mental power, e.g. the will, reason; ‖ branch of art or science, department of University teaching (*the four ~ies*, Theology, Law, Medicine, Arts), Masters & Doctors in any of these (‖ pop., *The F~y*, members of medical profession); *staff of university or college; liberty of doing something given by law or a superior, authorization, licence, (esp. eccl.). [ME, f. OF *faculte* or f. L *facultas* (*facilis* easy)]

fad, n. Pet notion or rule of action, craze, piece of fancied enlightenment. Hence ~d′ISH¹, ~d′Y², aa., ~d′INESS, ~d′ISH-NESS, ~d′ISM(3), ~d′IST(2), nn. [dial., of unkn. orig.]

fade, v.i. & t. Droop, wither, lose freshness & vigour; (of colour etc.) grow dim or pale; cause to lose colour; disappear gradually; (Cinemat.) cause (picture) to pass gradually *in* or *out* (of view on the screen), (transf. of sound-films and broadcasting) increase or reduce (sound) from or to inaudibility, whence fād′ING¹ vbl n. Hence ~′LESS a., ~′lĕssLY² adv., (-dl-). [ME, f. OF *fader* (*fade* dull, insipid)]

fae′cēs (-z), n. pl. Sediment; excrement of the bowels. Hence faec′AL a. [L, pl. of *faex*]

Fä′erie, -rў, n. & a. Fairyland, the fairies, esp. as represented by Spenser; (attrib.) visionary, fancied. [var. of FAIRY]

fag, v.i. & t. (-gg-), & n. 1. Toil painfully; (of occupation)‛ tire, make weary; ‖ (at schools, of seniors) use the service of (juniors), (of juniors) do service for seniors; (Cricket) ~ *out*, field; ~*-end*, inferior or useless remnant. 2. n. ‖ Drudgery, unwelcome task (*what a ~ !*), exhaustion (*brain-~*); ‖ (at schools) junior who has to ~; (sl.) cigarette. [orig. unkn.; cf. FLAG⁵]

fagg′ot, fag′ot, n., & v.t. & i. 1. Bundle of sticks or twigs bound together as fuel; bundle of steel rods; ‖ dish of liver chopped, seasoned, & baked; ‖ ~*-vote* (hist.), manufactured by transferring sufficient property to unqualified person, so ~*-voler*. 2. vb. Bind in ~s, make ~(s). [ME, f. OF *fagot*]

Fahr′enheit (-hīt), a. (*abbr.* F.). ~ *thermometer*, with 32° & 212° for freezing & boiling points of water. [Prussian inventor d. 1736]

faience (see Ap.), n. Decorated earthenware & porcelain. [f. F *faïence* f. *Faenza* Italian town]

fail¹, n. Failure, one who fails, in an examination; *without ~*, for certain, irrespective of hindrances, emphasizing injunction‛ or promise). [ME, f. OF *fail(l)e* (*faillir* FAIL²)]

fail², v.i. & t. (strictly intr. with ind. obj.). Be missing (see FAILING²) or insufficient, not suffice for needs of (person), run short, (*time would ~ me to tell*; *words ~ me*, I cannot adequately describe etc.; *his heart ~ed him*); neglect, not remember or not choose, to (*he ~ed to appear*; *don′t ~ to let me know*); become extinct, die away; flag, break down; become weaker or less efficient; prove misleading, disappoint hopes of, (*the prophecy ~ed*; *the wind ~ed us*); be insufficiently equipped *in*, not succeed in the attainment *of*; not succeed (*in doing* or *to do*); miscarry, come to nothing; suspend payment, go bankrupt; be rejected as candidate; reject (candidate). [ME, f. OF *faillir* f. Rom. **fallire* = L *fallere* deceive]

fail′ing¹, n. In vbl senses; also, foible, shortcoming, weakness. [-ING¹]

fail′ing², prep. In default of (~ *this*, if this does not happen; *whom~* or ~ *whom* in proxy appointments). [-ING²]

faille (fāl), n. A light glossless ribbed silk dress-material. [F]

fail′ure (-yer), n. Non-occurrence, non--performance; running short, breaking down; ill success; unsuccessful person, thing, or attempt; insolvency. [17th c. *failer* f. AF = OF *faillir* FAIL², cf. -ER⁴, -URE]

fain¹, pred. a., & adv. Willing under the circumstances *to*; left with no alternative but *to*; (adv.) *would ~*, would be glad to. [OE *fægen*, OS *fagan*, ON *feginn*, cogn. w. OE *gefēon*, OHG *gifehan* rejoice]

‖ fain², fains (-z), **fĕn(s)** (-z), child's formula (usu. *fains I* as v.t.) stipulating for exemption from unwelcome office etc. (~ *I wicket-keeping!*). [with *fen, fens*, f. FEND in obs. sense ‘ forbid ’]

fainéant (see Ap.), n. & a. Idle(r), inactive (official). [F, perversion on *faire* do, *néant* nothing, of OF *faignant* sluggard (*faindre* skulk, FEIGN)]

faint¹, a. Sluggish; timid (~*-heart*, coward; so ~*-heart′*ED² (-härt-) a., ~*-heart′ed*LY² adv., ~*-heart′ed*NESS n.); feeble (*a ~ show of resistance*); dim, indistinct, pale (~ *or feint lines*, *ruled ~* or *feint*, of paper with lines to guide writing; *a ~ idea*, inadequate); giddy or languid with fear, hunger, etc., inclined to swoon; (of air, scents, etc.) sickly, oppressive. Hence ~′ISH¹(2) a., ~′LY² adv., ~′NESS n. [ME, f. OF, p.p. of *faindre* FEIGN]

faint², v.i. Lose courage, give way, (arch.); swoon (v. & n.; ~*ed away*; *in a dead ~*, utterly insensible). [f. prec.]

faints, n. pl. Impure spirit coming over at beginning & end of distillation. [f. FAINT¹]

fair[1], n. Periodical gathering for sale of goods, often with shows & entertainments, at place & time fixed by charter, statute, or custom (*a day after the ~, too late*); FANCY ~. [ME, f. OF *feire* (now *foire*) f. LL *feria* sing. f. L *feriae* holiday]

fair[2], a., n., & v.i. & t. **1.** Beautiful (*the ~ sex*, *the ~*, women; also arch. as n., *a ~ = a woman*); satisfactory, abundant, (*a ~ heritage*); specious (*~ speeches*); blond, not dark, (*a ~ man*, *complexion*, *hair*, whence ~'haiRED[2] a.); clean, clear, unblemished, (*~ water*; *~ COPY*[1]; *~ fame*); just, unbiased, equitable, legitimate, (*~ & square* a. & adv., without finesse, above-board; *~ trade*, principle that reciprocity should be the condition of free trade; *a ~ FIELD*[1] *& no favour*; *all's ~ in love & war*; *by ~ means or foul*; *~ play*, equal conditions for all); of moderate quality, not bad, pretty good, whence ~'ISH[1](2) a.; favourable, promising, gentle, unobstructed, (*~ or foul weather*; *~-weather friends*, not good in a crisis; *in a ~ way to succeed*; *by ~ means*, without violence or fraud; *~way*, navigable channel, regular course or track of ship, prepared part of golf-links free from hazards between tee and green); ‖ *~-light*, = TRANSOM *window*; *~-maid*, = FUMADE; *February Fair-maids*, snowdrops. **2.** v.i. (Of weather) become ~; (v.t.) make ~ copy of (document); (Shipbuilding etc.) make smooth and regular. Hence ~'NESS n. [OE *fæger*, OS, OHG *fagar*, ON *fagr*, Goth. *fagrs* f. Gmc **fagraz*]

fair[3], adv. *Speak* one ~, address him courteously; *~-spoken*, (of person) courteous, bland; *write out* ~, as FAIR[2] copy; *hit*, *fight*, ~, according to the rules; BID[1] ~; *~ & softly*, gently, not so fast, (esp. as protest against assumptions etc.); (with *strike*, *fall*, etc.) straight, plump, clean. [OE *fægre* (prec.)]

fair'ing[1], n. Present bought at a fair. [-ING[1]]

fair'ing[2], n. The making of an aircraft's surface smooth and streamlined; any light structure added for this purpose. [f. FAIR[2] as v.t. + -ING[1]]

Fair Isle (il), n. One of the Shetlands; ‖ *~ (sweater*, *pull-over*, etc.), jersey knitted in designs said to be Moorish.

fair'ly, adv. In adj. senses; (also) utterly, completely, (*~ beside himself*; there is sometimes doubt between this sense & that of *rather*, *tolerably*, as in *~ good*). [-LY[2]]

fair'|y, n. & a. **1.** Small supernatural being with magical powers; *~y lamps*, *lights* (of glass, for esp. outdoor decoration); *Fairyland*, home of *~ies*, enchanted region; *~y ring*, circular band of darker grass caused by fungi & attributed to *~y* dancing; *~y-tale*, about *~ies*, also account of strange incident, coincidence, marvellous progress, etc., fabrication, fib; hence *~y-*

DOM, *~ŷHOOD*, *~ŷISM*, nn. **2.** adj. Of *~ies*; imaginary, fictitious; *~y-like*, beautiful & delicate or small, whence *~iLY*[2] adv. [ME, f. OF *faerie* (now *féerie*) f. *fae* FAY; see *-ERY*]

fait accompli (see Ap.), n. Thing done & no longer worth arguing against. [F]

faith, n. Reliance, trust, in; belief founded on authority (*pin one's ~ to or upon*, believe implicitly); (Theol.) belief in religious doctrines, esp. such as affects character & conduct, spiritual apprehension of divine truth apart from proof; system of religious belief (*the Christian*, *Jewish*, *~*; DEFENDER *of the F~*; *the ~*, the true religion); things (to be) believed; warrant (*on the ~ of*); promise, engagement, (*give*, *pledge*, *plight*, *keep*, *break*, *violate*, one's *~*); loyalty, fidelity, (*good ~*, honesty of intention; *bad ~*, intent to deceive; *Punic ~*, treachery); *~-cure*, *-curer*, *-healing*, *-healer*, acting by prayer, not drugs etc. [ME *feith*, f. OF *feid* (pron. *feith*), later *fei* (mod. *foi*) whence arch. (*by my*) *fay*, f. L *fidem*]

faith'ful, a. Loyal, constant, (*to person*, one's word), conscientious; trustworthy; true to fact, the original, etc., accurate; *the ~* (pl.), true believers, esp. Mohammedans. Hence *~NESS* n. [-FUL]

faith'fully, adv. In adj. senses; esp.: *yours ~*, customary formula for closing business or formal letter; *deal ~ with*, speak home truths to or of; *promise ~*, emphatically (colloq.). [-LY[2]]

faith'less, a. Unbelieving; perfidious, false to promises; unreliable. Hence *~LY*[2] adv., *~NESS* n. [-LESS]

fake[1], v.t., & n. (naut.). Coil (rope); (n.) one round of a coil. [orig. unkn.]

fake[2], v.t., & n. **1.** Do *up*, make presentable or specious, contrive out of poor material. **2.** n. Piece of faking, thing *~d up* (esp. sham antique), dodge, cooked report. Hence *~MENT* (-km-) n., *~*. [perh. f. obs. *feak*, *feague* thrash, prob. f. G *fegen* sweep, thrash]

fakir (-ēr), n. Moslem (or Hindu) religious mendicant, devotee. [f. Arab. *faqir* poor man]

Falan'gist, n. Member of a Spanish Fascist organization *Falán'ge* (-ghā). [Sp. *~a* f. *falange* phalanx]

fal'bala, n. Flounce, trimming. [17th c. f. F, of unkn. orig.; see FURBELOW]

fal'cate, a. (anat., bot., zool.). Hooked, sickle-shaped. [f. L *falcatus* f. *falx* sickle, *-ATE*[2](2)]

fal'cated, a. (astron.). = prec. (of moon etc.). [as prec., see *-ATE*[2]]

falchion (fawl'chon), n. Broad curved convex-edged sword. [ME *fauchoun* f. OF *fauchon* f. Rom. **falcionem* (nom. *-cio*) f. L *falx* sickle]

fal'ciform, a. (anat.). Sickle-shaped. [f. L *falx -cis* sickle + -FORM]

falcon (faw'kn, fawl'kn), n. Small diurnal bird of prey, esp. as trained to hawk for sport (in ~ry the female only, cf. TERCEL). So ~RY(2, 5) n. [ME, f. OF *faucon* f. LL *falconem*]

falc′oner (fawk-), n. Keeper and trainer of hawks; one who hunts with hawks. [f. OF *faulconnier*, see prec., -ER²(2)]

falc′onet (fawk-), n. **1.** (hist.). Light cannon. **2.** Species of shrike. [first sense f. It. *falconetto* dim. of *falcone* FALCON; last f. FALCON +-ET¹]

fälderäl′, n. Gewgaw, trifle. [cf. the earlier *fal-lal*]

fald′stool (fawl-), n. Bishop's armless chair; ‖ movable desk for kneeling at; desk for litany to be said from. [f. med. L *faldistolium* f. WG *faldistōl* (*faldan* to fold, STOOL)]

Falḗr′ian, n. A famous wine of ancient Campania. [f. L (*vinum*) *Falernum* Falernian (wine) +-IAN]

fall¹ (fawl), v.i. & (dial. & U.S.) t. (*fell*; ~en often conjugated with *be*, see -ED¹(2), & used as adj.). **1.** Descend freely (~*ing star*, meteor), drop (*the remark fell from him*; *lambs* ~, are born), come down, lose high position (*statesmen* ~; ~*en angel*, one of those cast out of heaven), swoop (*vengeance fell*). **2.** Become detached, hang down; sink to lower level (*barometer, prices*, ~), decline, slope; disembogue *into*; subside, ebb, abate; show dismay (*faces* ~), droop (*eyes* ~). **3.** Cease to stand (~*ing sickness* arch., epilepsy), become prostrate, come to ground, sin, be overthrown, perish (~ *prostrate, flat*; *plans* ~ *to the ground*, are abandoned, fail; ~ *on one's sword*, in suicide; *wicket* ~s, batsman is out; *fortress* ~s, is taken; *woman* ~s, loses chastity; *many fell*, were killed in battle; *seven lions fell to his rifle*; ~*en on evil times*, in misfortune; ~ *a prey or sacrifice to*; ~ *into error*; *houses* ~, tumble in fragments; ~ *to pieces, in two, asunder*); (trans.) cause to ~, fell (tree). **4.** Take such a direction (*his eye fell upon me*), have such a place (*accent* ~*s on first syllable*), alight, come by chance etc., (*the lot fell upon me*; *it fell to my lot to*; *cost* ~*s to you*; *it fell in my way*; ~ *amongst thieves, upon a corrupt age*; *subject* ~*s into three divisions*). **5.** Pass into such a state (*fell into a rage*, in love), become so-&-so (~ *dumb, due*), lapse, revert, (*revenues* ~ *to the Crown*). **6.** Occur, have date, (*Easter* ~*s early*), find place (*what now* ~*s to be described*). **7.** With prepp.: ~ *a- —ing*, begin; ~ *behind*, be passed by; ~ *for* (colloq.), be captivated by, admire, yield to the charms or merits of; ~ *into*, (line) take one's place in the ranks, combine with others, (*conversation with*) begin talking to, (*habit* etc.) adopt it; ~ *(up)on*, assault, come across, (one's *feet* or *legs*) get well out of difficulty; ~ *to —ing*, take to, begin, (also ~ *to work*); ~ *under*, be classed among, be subjected to (*observation* etc.); ~ *within*, be included in. **8.** With advv.: ~ *astern*, (of ship) drop behind; ~ *away*, desert, revolt, apostatize, decay, vanish; ~ *back*, retreat; ~ *back upon*, have recourse to; ~ *behind*, lag; (colloq.) ~ *down* (*on*), fail (in); ~ *foul of*, come into collision with, quarrel with, attack; ~ *in*, (Mil.) take or cause to take places in line, (of buildings etc.) give way inwards, (of debt etc.) become due, (of land etc.) become available, (of lease) run out; ~ *in with*, happen to meet, accede to (views), agree with (person), coincide with, humour; ~ *off*, withdraw, decrease, degenerate (so ~*ing off*, n.), (of ship) refuse to answer helm, (of subjects) revolt; ~ *on*, join battle, begin feeding; ~ *out*, quarrel, come to pass, result *well* etc., (Mil.) leave the ranks; ~ *out of*, give up (habit) etc.; (fig.) ~ (LEAN²) *over backwards*; ~ *short*, become insufficient, (of missile) not go far enough; ~ *short of*, fail to obtain; ~ *through*, miscarry, fail; ~ *to*, begin eating or fighting. [OE *feallan*, OS, OHG *fallan*, ON *falla*]

fall² (fawl), n. Act of falling (see prec.); also or esp.: amount of rain etc. that falls; (now chiefly U.S.; also ~ *of the year or leaf*) autumn; number of lambs born; cataract, cascade, (often pl.); downward trend, amount of descent; wrestling-bout, throw in this, (*try a* ~, lit. & fig.); rope of hoisting-tackle; amount of timber cut down; succumbing to temptation (*the F~ of man*, Adam's sin and its results); kind of woman's veil; ~*out*, airborne particles of radio-active materials from explosion of atomic or hydrogen bomb. [f. prec.]

fäll′acy, n. Misleading argument, sophism, (Log.) flaw that vitiates syllogism, one of the types of such flaws; delusion, error, (PATHETIC ~); unsoundness, delusiveness, disappointing character, (of arguments, or beliefs). So **falla′CIOUS** (-āshus) a., **fallā′ciousLY** adv., **fallā′ciousNESS** n., (-shus-). [f. -L *fallacia* (*fallax* deceiving f. *fallere* deceive) see -ACY]

fäl-läl′, n. Piece of finery. Hence **fälläl(1)**²**ERY**(5) n. [(contemptuous) reduplication, cf. *gewgaw*, perh. f. FALBALA]

fäll′ible, a. Liable to err or be erroneous. Hence **fällIBIL′ITY** n. [f. med. L *fallibilis* (*fallere* deceive, -BLE)]

Fallōp′ian, a. Of Fallopius the Italian anatomist (d. 1562); ~ *tubes*, the human oviducts. [-AN]

fäll′ow¹ (-ō), n., a., & v.t. (Ground) ploughed and harrowed but left uncropped for a year; uncultivated (land); (vb) break up (land) for sowing or to destroy weeds. [ME *falwe*, rel. to OE *fealga* (pl.) harrows, *fealgian* break up land, MLG *valge*, G *felge*]

fäll′ow² (-ō), a. Of pale brownish or reddish yellow (now only in ~-*deer*, species smaller than red deer). [OE, OS *falu*, OHG *falo* (G *fahl, falb*), ON *fǫlr* f. Gmc *falwaz*]

false (fawls), a. & adv. **1.** Erroneous, wrong, incorrect, (~ *idea, verdict*; ~ *concord*, breach of agreement rules in grammar; ~ *quantity*, incorrect length of vowel in verse or pronunciation; ~ *note* in music; ~ *drawing*; ~ *imprisonment*, illegal; ~ *weights* etc.; ~ *pride, shame*, based on wrong notions; ~ *position*, one that tempts person to act against his principles; ~ *step*, stumble, transgression; ~ *start*, wrong start (in racing); lying, deceitful, treacherous, unfaithful *to*; deceptive (~ *mirror, medium*); spurious, sham, artificial, (~ *coin, god, prophet, hair, teeth*; ~ *colours*, flag one has no right to, lit. & fig.); improperly so called, pseudo-, (~ *acacia*; ~ *bottom*, horizontal partition in vessel, drawer, etc.; ~ KEEL[1]); ~ *alarm* (given without good cause, either to deceive or under apprehension of danger); ~ *card*, one played contrary to usual custom, in order to mislead opponents; ~ *pretences*, misrepresentations made with intent to deceive; hence or cogn. ~'LY[2] (-awlsl-) adv., ~'NESS (-awlsn-), fal'SITY (fawl-), nn. **2.** adv. *Play* person ~, cheat, betray.` [ME *fals(e)* f. OF *fals, faus* f. L *falsus* p.p. of *fallere* deceive; OE *fals* dir. f. L]

false'hood (fawls-h-), n. Falsity; something untrue, contrariety to fact; lying, lie(s). [-HOOD]

falsett'o (fawl-), n. (pl. *-os*). Head voice in men, as used by male altos (*in* ~, *a* ~ *tone*, etc., often of sham indignation). [It., dim. of *falso* FALSE]

fal'sif|y (fawl-), v.t. Fraudulently alter (document); misrepresent; make wrong, pervert; disappoint (hope, fear, etc.). So ~ICA'TION (fawl-) n. [f. F *falsifier* or LL *falsificare* (FALSE, -FY)]

Falstäff'ian (fawl-), a. Like or characteristic of Shakespeare's Falstaff, fat, jovial, & humorous. [-IAN]

fal'ter (fawl-), v.i. & t. Stumble, stagger, go unsteadily; stammer, speak hesitatingly, (~ *out*, utter, say, thus); waver, lose courage, flinch. Hence ~ingLY[2] adv. [orig. obsc.; perh. f. ME *falden* (FOLD[2]) in obs. sense *falter*, after *totter* etc.]

fame[1], n. Public report, rumour; reputation (*house of ill* ~, bawdy-house), good reputation; renown, celebrity. [ME, f. OF f. L *fama* = Gk *phēmē* (*fa-* speak)]

fame[2], v.t. (Pass.) be currently reported *as, for, to* be or do; (p.p.) famous, much spoken of, (*for valour* etc.). [ME, f. OF *famer* (prec.)]

famil'ial (-lyal), a. Of, occurring in, characteristic of, (member of) a family. [-IAL]

famil'iar (-lyar), a. & n. **1.** Of one's family (arch. for *family* attrib.); intimate (*with*), in close friendship (~ *spirit*, or ~ as n., demon attending & obeying witch etc.); closely acquainted *with* (some subject); well known, no longer novel, (*to*); common, current, usual; unceremonious, free, over-free; amorously or sexually intimate (*with*). **2.** n. (R.-C. Ch.) person rendering certain services in Pope's or bishop's household; intimate friend or associate; ~ spirit. Hence ~LY[2] adv. [ME, f. OF *familier* f. L *familiaris* (FAMILY, -AR[1])]

familiä'rity, n. Close intercourse, intimacy *with* person or some subject; amorous intimacy, (pl.) caresses etc.; unceremoniousness, treating of inferiors or superiors as equals, (~ *breeds contempt*). [ME, f. OF *familiarite* f. L *familiaritatem* (prec., -TY)]

famil'iariz|e, -is|e, (-lyariz), v.t. Make (thing) well known; make (person, person's *mind* etc., *oneself*) well acquainted or at home *with*. Hence ~A'TION n. [-IZE]

fam'ily, n. **1.** Members of a household, parents, children, servants, etc. (*happy* ~, animals of different kinds in one cage); set of parents & children, or of relations, living together or not (*Holy F*~, the Virgin, Jesus, St Joseph, & often St John Baptist & St Elizabeth, as grouped in pictures); person's children. **2.** All descendants of common ancestor, house, lineage, (*of* ~, well born); race, group of peoples from common stock. **3.** Brotherhood of persons or nations united by political or religious ties. **4.** Group of objects distinguished by common features. **5.** Group of allied genera, usu. subdivision of ORDER. **6.** ~ *allowance* (paid to employees or State-insured person in proportion to size of ~); ~ *butcher* etc., supplying families as opp. to the army etc.; ~ *hotel*, with special terms for families; *in a* ~ *way*, without ceremony; || *in the* ~ *way*, with child; ~ *Bible*, large Bible with fly-leaves for registering births etc.; || ~ *coach*, large closed carriage, a game of forfeits; ~ *likeness*, that between relations, vague resemblance; || ~ *living*, benefice in gift of head of ~; ~ *man*, one with ~, domestic person; ~ *planning*, birth control; ~ *tree*, genealogical chart. [f. L *familia* household (*famulus* servant, -Y[1])]

fam'ine, n. Extreme scarcity of food in a district etc.; dearth of something specified, as *water* ~ (~ *prices*, raised by scarcity); hunger, starvation, (*die of* ~). [ME, f. OF, f. *faim* f. L *fames* hunger, -INE[1]]

fam'ish, v.t. & i. Reduce, be reduced, to extreme hunger; (colloq.) *be* ~*ing*, feel hungry. [ME, f. *fame* (obs., f. OF *afamer* f. L *fames* hunger) +-ISH]

fam'ous, a. Celebrated (*for* quality etc.), well known; (colloq.) capital, excellent, whence ~LY[2] adv. [ME, f. AF *famous* f. OF *-eus* f. L *famosus* (FAME, -OSE[1])]

fam'ulus, n. (pl. *-li*). Attendant on magician. [L, = servant]

fan[1], n. Winnowing-machine; instrument, usu. folding & sector-shaped when spread out, on radiating ribs, for agitating air to cool face; anything so spread out, as bird's tail, wing, leaf, kind of ornamental vaulting (~ *tracery*); rotating apparatus giving current of air for ventilation etc.; (Naut.) (blade of) screw, propeller; (in windmill) small sail for keeping head towards wind; ‖ ~-*light*, ~-shaped window over door; ~-*tail*, ~-shaped tail or end, kind of pigeon, ‖ coal-heaver's hat or sou'-wester. [OE *fann* f. L *vannus* winnowing-basket]

fan², v.t. & i. (-nn-). Winnow (corn), whence ~n'ER¹(2) n.; winnow away (chaff), sweep away (as) by wind from fan; move (air) with fan; drive current of air (as) with fan upon, to cool (face etc.) or to kindle (flame, ~ *the flame*, increase excitement etc.); (of breeze) blow gently on, cool; spread out (t. & i.) in fan shape. [f. prec.]

fan³, n. (sl.). Devotee of a specified amusement, as *film* ~s, *football* ~s; ~ *mail*, letters from ~s. [abbr. of foll.]

fanāt'ic, a. & n. (Person) filled with excessive & mistaken enthusiasm, esp. in religion. Hence ~AL a., ~alLY² adv., ~ISM n., ~IZE(2, 3) v.i. & t. [f. F (-*ique*) or L *fanaticus* (*fanum* temple, -ATIC)]

fan'cier, n. Connoisseur in some article or animal (of which the name is usu. prefixed, as *dog*, *rose*, ~~). [FANCY², -ER¹]

fan'ciful, a. Indulging in fancies, whimsical, capricious; fantastically designed, ornamented, etc., odd-looking; imaginary, unreal. Hence ~LY² adv., ~NESS n. [-FUL]

fan'cÿ¹, n. & a. **1.** Delusion, unfounded belief; faculty of calling up things not present, of inventing imagery; mental image; arbitrary supposition; caprice, a whim; individual taste, inclination, (*take a* ~ *to*, *for*; *catch the* ~ *of*, please); *the* ~, those who have a certain hobby, = -*fanciers*, esp. the patrons of boxing; art of breeding animals with certain points of excellence; ~-*free*, not in love. **2.** adj. (not pred.). Ornamental, not plain, (~ *bread*; ~ *dress*, masquerade costume, so ~-*dress* or ~-*ball*; ~-*work*, ornamental sewing etc.; ‖ ~ *fair*, bazaar for sale of ~ goods); (of flowers etc.) particoloured; capricious, whimsical, extravagant, (*at a* ~ *price*; ‖ ~ *franchise*, based on complicated or arbitrary qualifications; ~ *dog*, *pigeon*, etc., bred for particular points of beauty etc.); based on imagination, not fact (~ *picture*); ~ *man*, sweetheart, (sl.) man living on earnings of a prostitute. [contraction of FANTASY]

fan'cÿ², v.t. Picture to oneself, conceive, imagine, (~ *oneself dead*; ~ *a blue dahlia*; ~ *him to be here*, *that he is here*; imperat. as excl. of surprise, ~!, ~ *his believing it!*); be inclined to suppose, rather think; (colloq.) have good conceit of (one*self*, one's *game* etc.); take a fancy to, like; breed, grow, (animals, plants) with attention to certain points. [f. prec.]

fándangle (-ăng'gl), n. Fantastic ornament, tomfoolery. [perh. f. foll.]

fándäng'ō (-ngg-), n. (pl. -*oes*). Lively Spanish dance; tune for this. [Sp.]

fāne, n. (poet.). Temple. [f. L *fanum*]

fǎn'fāre (& see Ap.), n. Flourish of trumpets, bugles, etc. [F]

fǎnfäronāde', n. Arrogant talk, brag; = prec. [f. F *fanfaronnade* f. *fanfaron* (prec., -OON), -ADE]

fǎng¹, n. Canine tooth, esp. of dogs & wolves; serpent's venom-tooth; spike of tool held in the stock; (prong of) root of tooth. Hence (-)~ED² (-gd), ~'LESS, a. [late OE *fang* f. ON (= OS, OHG) *fang* f. Gmc vb *fanhan to catch]

fǎng², v.t. Prime (pump) by pouring in water to start it. [f. prec.]

fǎn'tǎn', n. Chinese gambling game in which the number of coins etc. hidden under a bowl has to be guessed; gambling game played with cards, [Chin.]

fǎntāsia (-aze'a, -ä'zla, -ah²), n. Musical or other composition in which form is subservient to fancy. [It. = FANTASY]

fǎn'tǎst, ph-, n. Visionary, dreamer. [f. med. L f. Gk *phantastēs* (*phantazomai* make a show f. *phainō* show)]

fǎntǎs'tic, a. Fancied (rare); extravagantly fanciful, capricious, eccentric; grotesque or quaint in design etc. Hence (thr. obs. ~*al*) ~äl'ITY, ~alNESS, ~ISM, nn., ~alLY² adv. [ME, f. OF f. med. L *fantasticus* f. LL f. Gk *phantastikos* (prec., -IC)]

fǎn'tasÿ, ph-, n. Image-making faculty, esp. when extravagant or visionary; mental image; fantastic design; = FANTASIA; whimsical speculation. [ME, f. OF *fantasie* f. L f. Gk *phantasia* (see FANTAST)]

Fǎn'tee, n. Member, language, of a Negro tribe inhabiting the territory of Ghana; *go* ~, (of European) conform to native habits. [native]

fǎntocci'ni (-ochēnē), n. pl. Mechanically worked puppets; marionette show. [It.]

faquir. See FAKIR.

fär¹, adv. (FARTHER, -*thest*; FURTHER, -*thest*), & n. **1.** At a great distance, a long way off, (often with *away*, *off*, *out*; also fig., as ~, *so* ~, *from doing*, ~ *from it*; ~ *be it from me to*, I would on no account); to a great distance or advanced point (*driven* ~ *into the ground*; ~ *gone*, advanced (see below also); *he will go* ~, do much; *go* ~ *to effect* etc., nearly do so; by a great interval, by much, (~ *different*, *better*, *the best*; also ~ *& away*); *so* ~, to such a distance, (also) up to now; *how* ~, to what extent; *as* ~ *as*, right to, not short of, (place); *as* or *so* ~ *as*, in *so* ~ *as*, to whatever extent. **2.** ~-*away*, remote, long-past, (of look etc.) absent, dreamy; ~-*between*, infrequent; ~ EAST; ~-*famed*, widely known; ~-*fetched*, (of simile, illustration, etc.) studiously sought out, strained; ~-*flung* (rhet.), widely extended; ~ FORTH; ~ *gone*, very ill or mad or drunk or much in debt; ~ off, remote; ~-reaching, widely applicable, carrying many consequences; ~-seeing, -sighted, prescient, prudent, (-sighted) seeing distant things more clearly than near ones. 3. n. A distance (do you come from ~?); large amount (by ~, with compar. & superl., prefer, surpass, etc.). [OE feor(r), OS, OHG fer, ON fjarri, Goth. fairra f. Gmc *fer- cogn. w. Gk peran beyond]

fär², a. (farther, -est, further, -est). Distant, remote, (a ~ CRY¹). [OE feorr f. prec.]

fä'rad, n. (electr.). Electro-magnetic unit of capacity. [f. Faraday, physicist, d. 1867]

färadä'ic, a. (electr.). Inductive, induced, (of current). [as prec., -IC]

färce¹, n. Dramatic work merely to excite laughter; this species of drama; absurdly futile proceeding, pretence, mockery. Hence fär'CICAL a., fär'ciCALLY² adv., färcicäl'ITY n. [F, orig.= stuffing, f. L farcire to stuff, used metaph. of interludes etc.]

färce², v.t. (arch.). Season, spice, stuff, (in cookery, & fig. of literary compositions). [ME f. OF farsir f. L as prec.]

färceur' (-sẽr), n. Joker, wag. [F]

fär'cy, n. Disease, esp. of horses, allied to glanders; ~ bud, button, small tumour in this. [w. older farcin f. F farcin f. L farciminum (farcire stuff)]

¶ färd'el, n. (arch.). Bundle, burden. [ME, f. OF, dim. of farde burden f. Arab. fardah]

färe¹, n. 1. Cost of passenger's conveyance, passage-money; passenger in hired vehicle. 2. Food provided (usu. good, bad, plentiful, etc., ~; BILL⁴ of ~). [OE fær, = OHG, ON far, & OE faru = ON fọr, f. st. of foll.]

färe², v.i. Journey, go, travel, (poet.; so ~ forth, start); happen, turn out, (how ~s it?); get on well, ill, etc., have such luck; be entertained, be fed or feed oneself, well etc. [OE, OS, OHG, Goth., Gmc faran, f. far- cogn. w. Gk poros ford]

färewëll' (-rw-), int. & n. 1. Good-bye!, Adieu!, (~ to, no more of!). 2. n. Leave-taking, parting good wishes. [ME; imper. of prec.+well]

farin'a, n. Flour or meal of corn, nuts, or starchy roots; powdery substance; ∥ (Bot.) pollen; (Chem.) starch. Hence färina'CEOUS (-āshus) a. [L (far corn, -INE⁴)]

fä'rinõse, a. Mealy, sprinkled with powder. [f. LL farinosus (prec., -OSE¹)]

¶ färl, n. (Sc.). Thin cake, orig. quadrant--shaped, of oatmeal or flour. [for obs. fardel quarter (FOURTH, DEAL), cf. FARTHING]

färm¹, n. Tract of land used under one management for cultivation (orig. only of leased land; home ~, reserved & worked by owner of estate containing other ~s); (also ~-house) dwelling-place attached to ~; tract of water used as a

preserve (oyster-~); place where children are farmed (see foll.); ~-hand, worker on ~; ~'stead, ~ with buildings on it; ~yard', yard or enclosure attached to ~-house. [ME ferme f. OF f. med. L firma fixed payment (L firmare fix f. FIRMus)]

färm², v.t. & i. 1. Take proceeds of (tax, office, etc.) on payment of fixed sum; (also ~ out) let out proceeds of (tax etc.) to person for fixed sum. 2. Let the labour of (persons) for hire; contract to maintain and care for (persons, esp. children) for fixed sum. 3. Cultivate, till; till the soil, be a farmer. Hence ~'ER¹, ~'ING¹, nn. [f. prec.]

fär'õ, n. Gambling card-game. [f. Pharaoh (significance doubtful)]

farouche' (-ōōsh), a. Sullen, shy. [F]

farra'gõ (-rah-, -rā-), n. (pl. -os). Medley, hotch-potch. Hence farrä'ginous a. [L (genit. -inis), = mixed fodder (far corn)]

fä'rrier, n. Shoeing-smith; ∥ horse-doctor; N.C.O. in charge of cavalry regiment's horses. Hence fä'rriERY(2) n. [16th c. ferrier f. F f. L ferrarius f. ferrum iron, -ER²(2)]

fä'rrow (-ō), n., & v.t. & i. 1. Giving birth to, litter of, pigs (20 at one ~). 2. vb. Produce (pigs), produce pigs. [vb f. n., OE fearh, OHG farah f. Gmc *farhaz cogn. w. L porcus]

färt, n., & v.i. (indecent). Emission of, emit, wind from the anus. [Aryan, cf. Gk perdomai]

färth'er (-dh-), adv. & a. (used as comp. of FAR¹,², see etym.), & v.t. 1. To or at a more advanced point or greater extent or distance (I'll see you ~ or FURTHER first); in addition, also besides, moreover, (now usu. further). 2. adj. More extended, additional, more; more distant or advanced, whence~MOST a. 3. v.t. (rare).=FURTHER. [ME ferther, var. of FURTHER; both used as comp. of far, but with tendency to restrict ~ to lit. & further to secondary senses]

färth'ëst (-dh-), a. & adv. 1. Most distant (at the, at, ~, at the greatest distance, at latest, at most). 2. adv. To or at the greatest distance. [var., now more usu., of FURTHEST]

∥ färth'ing (-dh-), n. Quarter of a penny; least possible amount (doesn't matter a ~). [OE feorthing (feortha FOURTH, -ING³)]

färth'ingäle (-dhingg-), n. (hist.). Hooped petticoat. [16th c. (also vard-, verd-) f. F verdugale f. Sp. -ado (verdugo rod, -ADO)]

färt'lëk, n. (athletics). Method of training for middle & long-distance running, in which the athlete runs over country, mixing fast with slow work. [Sw., = speed-play]

fäs'cēs (-z), n. pl. (Rom. hist.). Bundle of rods with axe in the middle carried by lictor before high magistrate; ensigns of authority. [L (pl. of fascis bundle)]

fascia (fä'shIa), n. (Archit.) long flat surface of wood or stone under eaves or cornice, cf. FACIA; (Anat.) thin sheath of fibrous tissue; stripe, band, fillet, belt; (in full ~ *board*) instrument board of motor-car. [L]

făs'ciăted (-shǐ-), a. (Bot.; of contiguous parts) compressed, growing, into one (so **făscia'TION** n.); striped. [f. L *fasciatus* p.p. of *fasciare* swathe (prec.), -ATE²]

făs'cicle, -ĭcŭle, -ic'ŭlus, (făsĭ-), n. (Bot. etc., bunch, bundle, whence **făs'cicleD²** (-ld), **fascic'ŭlAR¹, fascic'ŭlATE²,** -ăted, aa., **fascĭcŭlA'TION** n.; one part of book published by instalments. [f. L *fasciculus* (FASCES, -CULE)]

făs'cin|ăte, v.t. Deprive (victim) of power of escape or resistance by one's look or presence (esp. of serpents); attract irresistibly, enchant, charm, whence ~**ātING²** a., ~**ātingLY²** adv. Hence or cogn. ~**A'TION,** ~**ātoR** (esp., ~ opera-hood), nn. [f. L *fascinare* (*fascinum* spell), -ATE³]

făscine' (-sēn), n. Long faggot used for engineering purposes & esp. in war for lining trenches, filling ditches, etc.; ~ *dwelling,* prehistoric lake dwelling supported by cross layers of sticks sunk below surface. [F, f. L *fascina* (*fascis* bundle, -INE¹)]

Făs'cism (făshǐ-, făsǐ-), **fasci'smo** (-shēzmō), n. Principles & organization of the patriotic & anti-communist movement in Italy started during the 1914–18 war, culminating in the dictatorship of Benito Mussolini (d. 1945), & imitated by Fascist or blackshirt associations in other countries. So **Făs'cist** (făshǐ-, făsǐ-), **fasci'sta** (-shē-, pl. *-ti* pron. *-tē*), n. [It. *fascismo* (*fascio* bundle, group, f. L as FASCES, see ISM)]

∥ **făsh,** v.t. (or refl.), & n. (Sc.). Bother, trouble, inconvenience. [n. f. vb, f. OF *fascher* (now *fâcher*)]

fǎ'shion (-shn), n. & v.t. 1. Make, shape, style, pattern, manner, (*after the ~ of,* like; so ~ = WISE, as *walk crab-~*); *after, in, a ~,* not satisfactorily, but somehow or other. 2. Prevailing custom, esp. in dress (~*-plate,* picture showing style of dress). 3. Conventional usages of upperclass society (*the ~,* whatever is in accord with these for the time being; *set the ~,* give the example in changing them; *the ~,* (also) admired & discussed person or thing; *in, out of, ~ or the ~,* agreeing or not with current usage; *man* etc. *of ~,* (hist. or joc.), of social standing, moving in & conforming with upper-class society); hence ~**ED²** (-ond) a. 4. v.t. Give shape to, form, mould, (*into, to,* or abs.). [ME *facīun, -soun* f. AF *fasun* (F *façon*), f. L *factionem* (*facere* fact- make, -ION)]

fǎ'shionab|le (-shon-), a. & n. 1. Following, suited to, the fashion; characteristic of, treating of, or patronized by, persons of fashion. Hence ~**leNESS** n., ~**LY²** adv. 2. n. ~*le* person. [prec. n., -ABLE]

fast¹ (fah-), v.i. 1. Abstain from all or some kinds of food as religious observance or in sign of mourning (~*-ing-day,* = FAST²-*day*). 2. Go without food. [OE *fæstan,* OHG *fastēn,* ON *fasta,* Goth. *fastan* orig. = keep, observe, hold FAST³]

fast² (fah-), n. Act of fasting (prec., 1); season or (also ~*-day, fasting-day*) day appointed for fasting; going without food (*break* one's ~ = BREAKFAST v.). [ME, f. ON *fasta* (OS, OHG *fasta*) as prec.]

fast³ (fah-), a. 1. Firmly fixed or attached (*stake ~ in the ground*); ~ *friend* or *friendship,* steady, close; *ship ~ aground*; ~ *asleep; a ~ prisoner;* ~ *colour,* unfading, not washing out; *make ~,* fasten; *play ~ & loose,* ignore obligations, be unreliable; *door is ~,* locked etc.; *take ~ hold of,* tight; ~ *with gout,* confined). 2. Rapid, quickmoving, producing quick motion, (~ *train;* ~ *cricket-pitch, racquet-court, putting-green,* on which ball bounds or runs smartly; *watch is ~,* shows too advanced time; ~ *person,* dissipated, see foll.). Hence ~**'ISH¹**(2) a. [OE *fæst,* OS *fast,* OHG *festi,* ON *fastr,* Gmc **fast-,* same base as FAST¹]

fast⁴ (fah-), adv. (-er, -est). Firmly, fixedly, tightly, securely, (*stand, sit, stick,* ~; ~ *bind,* ~ *find,* lock up what you would not lose; *eyes ~ shut; sleep ~,* soundly); (poet. & arch.) close *beside, by, upon,* etc.; quickly, in quick succession; *live ~,* live in a dissipated way, expend much energy in short time. [OE *fæste* (prec.)]

fa'sten (fah'sn), v.t. & i. Make fast, attach, fix, secure by some tie or bond, (*to, upon, on* adv. or prep., *together, up, in* adv. or prep.; or abs.; ~ *parcel, garment, door,* etc., or *string, bolt,* etc.; ~ *off thread* etc., secure with knot or otherwise; whence ~**ING¹**(4) (fah'sn-) n.; direct (look, thoughts, etc.) keenly (*up*)*on;* fix (nickname, imputation, etc.) (*up*)*on;* ~ *quarrel upon,* pick quarrel with; become fast (*door will not ~*); ~ (*up*)*on,* lay hold of, single out for attack, seize upon (pretext). Hence ~**ER¹**(2) (fah'sn-) n. [OE *fæstnian,* OS *fastnōn,* OHG *fastinōn,* f. Gmc **fastinōjan* f. **fast-* FAST³, -EN⁶]

făs'tī, n. pl. Chronological register of events, annals. [L, = calendar]

făstid'ious, a. Easily disgusted, carefully selective, hard to please. Hence ~**LY²** adv., ~**NESS** n. [f. L *fastidiosus* (*fastidium* loathing, see -OUS¹)]

făsti'giăte, a. (bot.). With conical or tapering outline. [f. L *fastigium* gable + -ATE²]

fast'ness (fah-), n. In adj. senses (FAST³); also, stronghold, fortress. [OE *fæstnes* f. FAST³ + -NESS]

făt, a., n., & v.t. & i. (-tt-). 1. Fed up for slaughter, fatted; well-fed, plump, (*cut up ~,* leave much money), corpulent; thick, substantial, (esp. of printing-type); greasy, oily, unctuous, (*cut it ~,* make a display); (of coal) bituminous; (of clay etc.) sticky; fertile, rich, yielding abundantly, (~ *lands, benefice, job; a ~ lot,* sl.,

a great deal usu. iron.=very little); slow-
-witted, indolent, (~-*head*, dolt; ~-*witted*,
stupid); ‖ ~-*guts*, corpulent person; ~-
-*hen*, kinds of GOOSE-*foot*; ~ *lime*, nearly
pure lime, slaking easily; hence~t'ISH¹(2)
a., ~ 'NESS n. 2. n. The ~ part of anything
(*live on the ~ of the land*, have the best of
everything); oily substance composing
~ parts of animal bodies (*the ~ is in the
fire*, there will be an explosion); (Theatr.)
part of role that enables actor to show
off; (Chem.) natural ester of glycerol &
acid; hence ~'LESS a. 3. vb. = FATTEN;
kill the fatted calf for, receive (returned
prodigal) with joy. [OE *fǣt*(t) (whence
fǣttian vb), OFris. *fatt, fett*, OHG *feizzit*
(G *feist*) f. WG *faitidhaz*, p.p. f. Gmc
faitjan fatten f. Gmc *faitaz* adj. fat]

fāt'al, a. Like fate, inevitable, necessary;
of, appointed by destiny (~ *sisters*, the
Fates; ~ *thread*, allotted length of life;
~ *shears*, death); fateful, important,
decisive; destructive, ruinous, ending
in death, (*to*); deadly, sure to kill; (by
exagg.) mischievous, ill-advised. Hence
~LY² adv., ~NESS n. [ME, f. OF *fatal* or
L *fatalis* (FATE, -AL)]

fāt'al|ism, n. Belief that all events are
predetermined by arbitrary decree; submission to all that happens as inevitable.
So ~IST(2) n. & a., ~IS'TIC a., ~IS'TICALLY
adv. [-ISM]

fatāl'itӯ, n. Subjection to, supremacy of,
fate, predestined liability to disaster;
fatal influence; misfortune, calamity;
death by accident, in war, etc. [f. F
fatalité or LL *fatalitas*, see FATAL, -ITY]

fāt'alize, -ise (-īz), v.i. & t. Incline to
fatalism; subject to government by fate.
[-IZE]

fa'ta morga'na (fah-, -gah-), n. Kind of
mirage seen esp. in strait of Messina. [It.
(*fata* FAY, *Morgana* female name)]

fāte, n., & v.t. 1. Power predetermining
events unalterably from eternity; (Myth.)
goddess, one of the three Greek goddesses
(*Clō'thō, Lăch'esis* (-k-), *At'rŏpos*), of
destiny; what is destined to happen;
appointed lot of person etc.; person's
ultimate condition (*decide, fix, seal*, one's
~); death, destruction. 2. v.t. (usu. pass.).
Preordain (*he was ~d to* do or be; *it was
~d that*); (p.p.) doomed to destruction.
[ME, f. L *fatum* neut. p.p. of *fari* speak]

fāte'ful (-tf-), a. Prophetic; fraught with
destiny, important, decisive; controlled
by, showing power of, fate. Hence ~LY²
adv. [-FUL]

fa'ther¹ (fahdh-), n. 1. Male parent (also
fig.; *the wish is ~ to the thought*, one
believes because one wishes to; *the child
is ~ to the man*, lays down the lines of his
development); = ~-*in-law*; = step-~;
(also *adoptive* ~), one who has adopted a
child. 2. Progenitor, forefather; originator, designer, early leader, (~ *of English
poetry*; *F~ of history*, Herodotus; *F~ of
lies*, the devil; *F~s of the Church* or *F~s*,

Christian writers of first five centuries).
3. One who deserves filial reverence (~ *of
his country*); religious teacher. 4. God;
First Person of the Trinity. 5. Confessor;
priest belonging to religious order,
superior of monastic house; *Right, Most,
Reverend F~ in God*, titles of bishop, archbishop; *The Holy F~*, the Pope; = *priest*
as prefixed title; venerable person, god,
(*F~ Christmas, Thames, Time*, personifications). 6. Oldest member, doyen, (*F~
of House of Commons*, member with longest
continuous service); (pl.) leading men,
elders, (*City F~s*; *Conscript F~s*, Roman
senators). 7. ~-*figure*, an older person
regarded as a trusted leader; ~-*in-law*, ~
of one's wife or husband; ~-*land*, native
country. Hence ~HOOD, ~SHIP, nn., ~LESS
a., ~LIKE, ~LY¹·², aa. & advv., ~LINESS n.,
(fahdh-). [OE *fæder*, OS *fadar*, OHG
fater, ON *faðir*, Goth. *fadar* f. Gmc
fader, cogn. w. L *pater*]

fa'ther² (fahdh-), v.t. Beget; be the father
of; originate (statement etc.); pass as,
confess oneself, the father, author, of
(child, book); govern paternally; fix
paternity of (child, book) *upon*. [f. prec.]

făth'om¹ (-dh-), n. (pl., with numbers,
often *fathom*). Measure of six feet, chiefly
used in soundings; ‖ quantity of wood 6 ft
square in section, whatever the length.
[OE *fæðm* the outstretched arms, cogn.
w. OS *fathmos*, OHG *fadum*, ON *fathmr*]

făth'om² (-dh-), v.t. Encircle with the
arms (arch.); measure with fathom-line,
sound, (depth of water); (fig.) get to the
bottom of, comprehend, whence ~LESS a.,
~lĕssLY² adv. [OE *fæthmian* (prec.)]

fathŏm'eter (-dh-), n. Instrument for
determining depth of sea by measuring
time taken by sound-wave to reach the
bottom and return. [FATHOM¹, -METER]

fatĭd'ical, a. Gifted with prophetic power.
[f. L *fatidicus* (FATE, -*dicus* -saying) + -AL]

fatigue' (-ēg), n., & v.t. 1. Weariness after
exertion; weakness in metals after repeated blows or long strain; task etc.
that wearies; soldier's non-combatant
duty (~-*party* or ~, party told off for this;
so ~-*dress*). 2. v.t. Tire, exhaust, whence
~LESS (-ēgl-), fati'guING² (-ēgĭ-), aa.;
weaken (metal; see above). [f. F *fatigue*(r)
f. L *fatigare*]

făt'ling, n. Young fatted animal. [-LING¹]

făt'ten, v.t. & i. Make fat (esp. animals
for slaughter); grow fat; enrich (soil).
[-EN⁶]

făt'tӯ¹, a. Like fat, unctuous, greasy;
consisting of fat, adipose; with morbid
deposition of fat (~ *degeneration* of heart
or kidney). [-Y²]

făt'tӯ², n. Fat child etc. (usu. voc.). [-Y³]

făt'uous, a. Vacantly silly, purposeless,
idiotic. Hence or cogn. fatū'ITY n., ~LY²
adv., ~NESS n. [f. L *fatuus* + -OUS]

faubourg (fōb'oorg), n. Suburb, esp. of
Paris. [F]

fauc'al, a. & n. (phonol.). Of the throat,

deeply guttural (sound). [f. L *fauces* throat +-AL]

fau′ces (-ēz), n. pl. (anat.). The cavity at the back of the mouth. [L]

fau′cet, n. (esp. U.S.). Tap for barrel etc.; any kind of tap. [f. OF *fausset* vent-peg]

faugh (faw), int. of disgust.

fault, n., & v. t. & i. **1.** Defect, imperfection, blemish, of character or of structure, appearance, etc. (*generous* etc. *to a* ~, excessively; *with all* ~*s*, at buyer's risk). **2.** Transgression, offence, thing wrongly done, (Racquets etc.) ball wrongly served; *find* ~ (*with*), complain (of), whence ~′fīnDER¹ n., ~′fīnDING¹,², n. & a. **3.** Responsibility for something wrong (*the* ~ *was mine*; *it will be our own* ~), defect that causes something (*the* ~ *is in the patient*); *in* ~, guilty, to blame, (*who is in* ~ ?). **4.** (hunt.). Loss of the scent, check so caused, (*be at* ~, also fig. = be puzzled, not know what to do). **5.** (geol.). Break in continuity of strata or vein. **6.** (telegr.). Imperfect insulation, leakage. **7.** vb. Find ~ with, blame; (Geol.) break continuity of (strata or vein), show such break. Hence ~′LESS a., ~′lĕssLY² adv., ~′lĕssNESS n., ~′y² a., ~′ĭLY² adv., ~′ĭNESS n. [ME & OF *faut*(*e*) f. Rom. *fallita* fem. p.p. of *fallere* FAIL²]

faun, n. One of a class of Latin rural deities with horns & tail. [ME, f. L *Faunus* Latin god identified w. Gk Pan]

faun′|a, n. (pl. ~*ae*, ~*as*). The animals of a region or epoch; treatise upon these. Hence ~AL a., ~IST(3) n., ~ĭs′tĭC(AL) aa. [mod. L, f. name of goddess sister of Faunus, see prec.]

fauteuil (see Ap.), n. Arm-chair; theatre stall. [F]

faux pas (fō pah), n. Act that compromises one's, esp. a woman's, reputation; an offence against social convention, an indiscreet speech or action. [F, = false step]

fāv′our¹ (-ver), n. **1.** Friendly regard, goodwill, (*find* ~ *in the eyes of*, be liked by; CURRY² ~), approval (*look with* ~ *on*), good graces (*be, stand high* etc., *in* person's ~); kindness beyond what is due (*should esteem it a* ~; *by* ~ *of* —, written on letter conveyed by friend; *do me the* ~ *of* —*ing*; *have received your* ~ *of yesterday*, letter; *woman bestows her* ~*s on lover*, yields). **2.** Leave, pardon, (arch.; *by your* ~; *under* ~, if one may venture to say so). **3.** Partiality, too lenient or generous treatment (FEAR¹ *or* ~). **4.** Aid, furtherance, (*under* ~ *of night*); *in* ~ *of*, on behalf or in support of, on the side of, to the advantage or account of, (*am in* ~ *of a five-day week*; *cheques to be drawn in* ~ *of the treasurer*). **5.** Thing given or worn as mark of ~, knot of ribbons, rosette, cockade, badge. **6.** (arch.). Looks, countenance, whence *well, ill, hard*, etc., ~ED² (-*crd*) a. [ME, f. OF, f. L *favorem* (*favēre* show kindness to, -OR)]

fāv′our² (-ver), v.t. **1.** Look kindly upon,

approve; treat kindly, countenance, (Journalism) choose to wear; oblige *with*. **2.** Treat with partiality, be unjust on behalf of. **3.** Aid, support; serve as confirmation of (theory etc.); prove advantageous to (person), facilitate (process etc.), whence ~ING² (-ver-) a. **4.** Resemble in features (~ *one's father*). **5.** (p.p.). Having unusual advantages (*most* ~*ed nation*, to which a State accords lowest scale of import duties); ~*ed by*, (of letter) by favour of. [ME, f. OF *favorer* f. med. L *favorare* as prec.]

fāv′ourab|le (-ver-), a. Well disposed, propitious; commendatory, approving; giving consent (~*le answer*); promising, auspicious, (~*le aspect*); helpful, suitable, (*to*). Hence ~leNESS n., ~LY² adv. [ME, f. OF *favorable* f. L *favorabilis* (FAVOUR¹, -ABLE)]

fāv′ourit|e (-ver-), n. & a. (Person or thing) preferred above others (*the* ~*e of, a* ~*e with or of*); (Racing) *the* ~*e*, competitor generally expected to win; person chosen as intimate by king or superior & unduly favoured, whence ~ISM(3) n. [f. obs. F *favorit* f. It. *favorito*, p.p. of *favorire* (= OF *favorir*) favour]

fawn¹, n., a., & v.i. & t. **1.** Young fallow deer, buck or doe of first year (*in* ~, pregnant); ~ or ~*-colour*(*ed*), (of) light yellowish brown. **2.** vb. (Of deer) bring forth (young, or abs.). [ME, f. OF *faon* f. Rom. *fetonem* nom. -o (FOETUS)]

fawn², v.i. (Of animals, esp. dog) show affection by tail-wagging, grovelling, etc. (~ *on, upon*, lavish caresses on); (of persons) behave servilely, cringe (*upon* patron, or abs.), whence ~′ING² a., ~′ĭnGLY² adv. [OE *fagnian, fægnian*, OS, OHG *faganôn*, ON *fagna*, Goth. *faginôn* rejoice, cogn. w. FAIN¹]

fay, n. (poet.). Fairy. [ME, f. OF *fae* f. Rom. *fata* sing. f. L *fata* pl. the fates]

fē′altў, n. Feudal tenant's or vassal's (acknowledgement of obligation of) fidelity to his lord (*do, make, receive, swear*, ~). [ME, f. OF *feaulte* f. L *fidelitatem* (*fidelis* f. *fides* faith, -TY)]

fear¹, n. Painful emotion caused by impending danger or evil, state of alarm (*was in* ~), dread *of, that*, or *lest*; *for* ~ *of*, (*that*), *lest*, in order that so-&-so may not occur; *without* ~ *or favour*, impartially; dread & reverence (*the* ~ *of God*); anxiety for the safety *of* (*in* ~ *of his life*); *no* ~, it is not likely. Hence ~′LESS a. (Of danger etc.), ~′lĕssLY² adv., ~′lĕssNESS n. [OE *fǣr*, corresp. to OS *vār*, OHG *fāra* (G *gefahr*), ON *fār* f. Gmc *fǣr-*]

fear², v.i. & t. Be afraid (also as arch. refl. in parenthesis, *I* ~ *me*; *never* ~, there is no danger of that); be afraid of; hesitate *to* do, shrink from *do*ing; revere (God); apprehend, have uneasy anticipation of; be afraid *that* (or with *that* omitted; also *need not* etc. ~ *but* or *but that*). [OE *fǣran* f. prec.]

fear'ful, a. Terrible, awful; (by exagg.) annoying etc. (*in a ~ mess*); frightened, timid; apprehensive *of*, *lest*, (*that*); wanting resolution *to*; reverential. Hence ~LY² adv., ~NESS n. [-FUL]

fear'nought (-awt), n. Stout woollen cloth used at sea for clothing & for protecting portholes etc. [FEAR², NOUGHT]

fear'some, a. Appalling, esp. in appearance (usu. joc.). Hence ~LY² (-ml-) adv., ~NESS (-mn-) n. [-SOME]

feas'i|ble (-z-), a. Practicable, possible; (loosely) manageable, convenient, serviceable, plausible. Hence ~BIL'ITY n. [ME, f. OF *faisable*, *-ible* f. *fais-* st. of *faire* f. L *facere* do +-IBLE]

feast, n., & v.i. & t. **1.** Joyful religious anniversary (*movable*, *immovable*, ~, recurring on different, same, date); annual village festival; sumptuous meal, esp. one given to number of guests and of public nature; (fig.) gratification to the senses or mind (*~ of reason*, intellectual talk). **2.** vb. Partake of ~, fare sumptuously, whence~'ER¹ n.; pass (night etc.) *away* in~ing; regale (guests, one's *eyes on* beauty etc.). [ME, f. OF *feste(r)* f. pop. L *festa* pl. of *festum* feast]

feat¹, n. Noteworthy act, esp. deed of valour (often ~ *of arms*); action showing dexterity or strength, surprising trick. [ME *faite*, *fete* f. OF *fait*, *fet* FACT]

‖ **feat²**, a. (arch.). Adroit, smart, dextrous, neat. Hence ~'LY² adv. [ME *fete* f. OF *fet* (prec.)]

feath'er¹ (-fĕdh-), n. **1.** One of the appendages growing from bird's skin, consisting of quill, shaft, & two vanes of barbs (*show the white ~*, betray cowardice—white ~ in game-bird's tail being mark of bad breeding—; *crop* one's~s, humiliate him; (collect.) plumage (*in high* or *full ~*, in good spirits etc.; *birds of a ~*, people of one sort); feathered game (*fur & ~*, game beasts & birds). **2.** Piece(s) of ~ attached to arrow; plume worn in hat etc. (*a ~ in* one's *cap*, something one may be proud of); very light object (*could have knocked me down with a ~*); ridge of upright hair; ~like flaw in gem. **3.** (rowing). Action of feathering (see foll.). **4.** ~ *bed*, mattress stuffed with ~s; ~-*bed* v.t. (-dd-), make things easy for, pamper; ~-*edge*, (n.) fine edge of wedge-shaped board, (v.t.) bring (board) to this; ~-*head*(ed), -*brain*(ed), -*pate*(d), silly (person); ~-*stitch*, ornamental zig-zag sewing; ~-*weight*, very light thing or person, esp. jockey not over 4 st. 7 lb., boxer 9 st. Hence (-) ~ED² (-ĕrd), ~LESS, ~Y², aa., ~INESS, ~LET, an., (fĕdh-). [OE *fether*, OS *fethara*, OHG *fedar*, ON *fjǫlhr* f. Gmc **fethrō*]

feath'er² (-fĕdh-), v.t. & i. **1.** Furnish, adorn, line, coat, with feathers (*~ an arrow*; ~ one's *nest*, enrich oneself; TAR *&~*); form featherlike ornamentation for. **2.** Float, move, or wave, like feathers. **3.** Turn (oar), turn oar, so as to pass

through the air edgeways, (Aeron.) make (propeller blades) rotate in such a way as to lessen air resistance. **4.** (Shoot.) knock feathers from (bird) without killing. **5.** (Hunt.; of hound) make quivering motion of body & tail while seeking scent. [OE *gefithrian* f. prec.]

feath'ering (-fĕdh-), n. In vbl senses; esp.. plumage; feathers of arrow; feathery structure in animal's coat; (Archit.) cusps in tracery; featherlike marking in flower. -ING¹

fea'ture, n., & v.t. **1.** (Usu. pl.) part(s) of the face, esp. with regard to shape & visible effect; distinctive or characteristic part of a thing, part that arrests attention; distinctive or prominent article etc. in newspaper etc.; ~ *film*, ~ *picture*, cinema drama of some length in several reels. **2.** v.t. Stand as distinctive mark upon; portray, sketch the prominent points of; *show on cinema screen, have as chief ~, give special prominence to. Hence -**fea'tureD²** (-cherd), ~LESS (-cherl-), aa. [ME, f. OF *fet-*, *faiture* f. L *factura* (*facere* fact- make, -URE)]

fĕb'rifūge, n. Medicine to reduce fever, cooling drink. Hence **fĕbrif'ūgAL** a. [f. F *fébrifuge* or LL *febrifuga*, *-ia* (f. *febris* fever, -FUGE)]

fĕb'rile, a. Of fever, feverish. [f. F *fébrile* or LL *febrīlis* (*febris* fever, -ILE)]

Fĕb'ruarў (-rŏŏ-), n. Second month of year (~ *fill-dike*, name referring to its rain & snow). [ME *feverer*, *februar*, f. OF *feverier* f. Rom. *febrarius*; mod. sp. after L *februarius*]

fē'cĭt, fēcēr'ŭnt (abbr. *fec.*), v. sing. & pl. 3rd pers. (So-&-so) made this picture etc. (used with artist's signature). [L, perf. of *facere* make]

fĕck'lĕss, a. Feeble, futile, inefficient. Hence ~LY² adv., ~NESS n. [Sc. *feck* (aphetic f. EFFECT) +-LESS]

fĕc'ŭl|ent, a. Turbid, fetid. So ~ENCE n. [F (*fé-*), or f. L *faeculentus* (FAECES, -ULENT)]

fĕc'ŭnd, a. Prolific, fertile; fertilizing. So **fĕcŭn'dITY** n. [ME, f. OF *fecond* or L *fecundus*]

fĕc'und|āte, v.t. Make fruitful; impregnate. Hence ~A'TION n. [L FECUND*are*, -ATE³]

fed. See FEED¹.

fĕd'eral, a. **1.** (theol.). Based on doctrine of Covenants. **2.** (pol.). Of the polity in which several States form a unity but remain independent in internal affairs; concerning this whole & not the separate parts. **3.** Relating to, favouring, central (as distinct from State) government. Hence ~ISM(3), ~IST(2), nn., ~IZE(3) v.t., ~IZA'TION n., ~LY² adv. [17th c. *foederal* f. L *foedus -eris* covenant +-AL]

fĕd'er|āte, v.t. & i. Band together (t. & i.) in league for some common object; organize (t. & i. of States) on a FEDERAL basis.

So ~ATE³ (-at), ~ATIVE, aa., ~atïveLY³ adv. [LL *foederare* (prec.), -ATE³]

fēderā'tion, n. Federating, whence ~IST(2) (-sho·) n.; federated society, esp. federal empire or group of States; IM-PERIAL~. [f. LL *foederatio* (prec., -ATION)]

fee, n., & v.t. (~'*d*, ~d). **1.** Fief, feudal benefice, (hist.). **2.** Inherited estate (~ *simple*, without limitation to particular class of heirs; ~-*tail*, with such limitation; *hold in* ~ *simple* or ~, have as absolute property). **3.** Sum payable to public officer for performing his function; remuneration of lawyer, physician, or any professional man (RETAIN*ing*-~); entrance money for examination, society, etc.; terminal payment for instruction at school; gratuity. **4.** vb. Pay ~ to, engage for a ~. [ME, f. AF *fee* = OF *fe, fieu*, etc. f. med. L *feodum, feudum*, prob. f. Frank. **fehod* cattle-property. See FEUD², FIEF]

fee'b|le, a. & n. **1.** Weak, infirm; deficient in character or intelligence; wanting in energy, force, or effect; dim., indistinct; hence ~leNESS (-ln-) n., ~lISH¹(2) a., ~LY³ adv. **2.** n. (Fenc.) = FOIBLE. [ME, OF *feble* f. L *flebilis* lamentable (*flēre* weep)]

feed¹, v.t. & i. (*fĕd*). Supply with food (~ *a cold*, eat plentifully when you have a cold); put food into mouth of (*cannot* ~ *himself*); graze (cattle); gratify (*vanity* etc., also *eyes* etc.), comfort (person) *with* hope etc.; take food, eat, (*at the high table*; *well, high,* etc.; often ~ *on*, consume); serve as food for; nourish, make grow, (~ *up*, fatten, also satiate; *fed up,* sl., having had too much of something, bored *with*); keep (reservoir, fire, etc.) supplied; supply (machine) with material (~-*pipe*, doing this); use (land) as pasture (often ~ *down, close*); deal out (fodder) *to* animals; supply (material)(*in*)*to* machine; (Theatr. sl.) supply (actor etc.) with cues; (Football) give a pass to; (of cattle) eat, eat *down*, (pasture); ~*ing-bottle*, for hand-fed infants. [OE *fēdan*, OS *fōdean*, OHG *fuotan*, ON *fœtha*, Goth. *fōdjan* f. Gmc **fōdhon* FOOD]

feed², n. Act of feeding, giving of food, (*two biscuits at one* ~; *out at* ~, turned out to graze; *off* one's ~, with no appetite; *on the* ~, of fish, feeding or looking out for food); pasturage, green crops; horse's allowance of oats etc.; fodder; (colloq.) meal, feast; feeding of machine, material supplied, charge of gun; ~-*tank, trough,* holding water for locomotive. [f. prec.]

feed³. See FEE.

feed'băck, n. (electr.). The return of a fraction of the output signal from one stage of a circuit, amplifier, etc. to the input of the same or a preceding stage (*positive, negative,* ~, tending to increase, decrease, the amplification etc.); (transf., esp. of biol., psych., and social systems) the carrying back of some of the effects

of some process to its source or to a preceding stage so as to strengthen or modify it; also attrib. [FEED², BACK³]

feed'er, n. In vbl senses: esp.: *large, quick, gross,* etc., ~, one who eats much etc.; child's feeding-bottle; || child's bib; tributary stream (also fig.); (Rounders etc.) player who tosses ball to striker; hopper or feeding apparatus in machine; ~ *line, railway,* branch line linking up outlying districts with main line. [-ER¹]

feed'ing, a. In vbl senses; also, ~ *storm,* one that constantly increases. [-ING²]

fee-faw-fŭm', int. & n. Ogreish exclamation; (n.) nonsense fit only to terrify child. [in *Jack the Giant-Killer*]

feel, v.t. & i. (*fĕlt*), & n. **1.** Explore by touch (~ *the pulse of*, lit., & fig.=cautiously ascertain sentiments of; ~ one's *way,* grope it out, proceed carefully); search (*about*) with hand *after, for*; try to ascertain by touch *whether, if, how;* (Mil.) reconnoitre (ground, enemy); perceive by touch (~ *a hard substance, heat, pain, a blow; I felt him move, moving, that he was cold;* ~ one's *legs* or *feet,* find firm standing, also fig., be at ease); have sensation of touch; be conscious of (sensation, emotion, conviction; *a felt want,* desideratum); be consciously (~ *well, warm, angry,* CHEAP; ~ *quite* conscious, be fit, self-possessed, etc.; ~ UP *to work* etc.; ~ *like* doing, have inclination to do); experience, undergo, (*he shall* ~ *my vengeance; felt the storm severely*), be affected by, behave as if conscious of, (*ship* ~s *her helm*); be emotionally affected by, have sympathy *with* or compassion *for,* (~ *the censure keenly*); have vague or emotional conviction (*that;* esp. ~ *in* one's *bones*); (quasi-pass.) be realized as, seem, produce impression of being, (*air* ~s *chilly;* ~s *like velvet*). **2.** n. Sense of touch (*firm to the* ~); testing by touch; sensation characterizing something. [OE *fēlan,* OS *-folian,* OHG *fuolen* f. WG **fōljan*]

feel'er, n. In vbl senses: esp.: organ in certain animals for testing things by touch or searching for food; (Mil.) scout; tentative proposal or hint, *ballon d'essai.* [-ER¹]

feel'ing¹, n. In vbl senses: esp.: sense of touch; physical sensation; emotion (often *of* hope, fear, etc.); (pl.) susceptibilities, sympathies, (*hurts my* ~s, offends me); readiness to feel, tenderness for others' sufferings, (*good* ~, avoidance of unkindness etc.); consciousness of (*had a* ~ *of safety*), conviction not based solely on reason; sentiment (*the general* ~ *was against it*); (Psych.; differently used by various writers) state of consciousness, sensation or desire or emotion (not perception or thought), element of pleasure or pain in any mental state, intuitive belief; (Art) general emotional effect produced. [-ING¹]

feel'ing², a. In vbl senses; esp.: sensitive;

sympathetic; showing emotion; heartfelt (a ~ *pleasure*). Hence ~LY² adv. [-ING²]

feet. See FOOT.

feign (fān), v.t. & i. Invent (excuse, story, accusation), forge (document), represent in fiction, imagine, (arch.); simulate, pretend, (~ *that one is mad, oneself mad, madness*); practise simulation. [ME, f. *feign-* st. of OF *feindre* f. L *fingere*]

feint¹ (fā-), n., & v.i. 1. Sham attack (blow, cut, thrust, or military assault) to divert attention or deceive opponent; pretence (*make a ~ of doing*). 2. v.i. Make ~ (*at, upon, against*). [f. F *feinte* (p.p. *feindre* FEIGN)]

‖ **feint²** (fā-), a. & adv. ~ *lines, ruled* ~, = FAINT¹. [old spelling often kept in this use]

fel(d)'spar, n. Kinds of crystalline white or flesh-red mineral. So **fel(d)späth'**ic a. [f. G *feldspat(h)* f. *feld* field, *spat(h)* spar; spelling *fels-*, commoner but incorrect, due to false deriv. f. G *fels* rock]

fel'ibrist, n. Member of the *Félibrige*, a society of Provençal poets & writers (Mistral etc.). [f. F *Félibrige*, -IST]

fel'icide, n. Cat-killing. [f. L *feles* cat + -CIDE]

felicif'ic, a. (eth.). Tending to happiness. [f. L *felix -icis* +-FIC]

feli'citate, v.t. Make happy (rare); congratulate (usu. *on*), whence (usu. pl.) ~A'TION n. [f. L *felicitare* (*felix* happy, -ATE³]

feli'citous, a. Blissful (rare); (of expression, quotation, civilities, or person in these connexions) strikingly apt, pleasantly ingenious. Hence ~LY² adv. [foll., -OUS]

feli'city, n. Being happy, intense happiness; a blessing; fortunate trait; happy faculty in expression, appropriateness; well chosen phrase. [ME, f. OF *felicite* f. L *felicitatem* (*felix* happy, -TY)]

fel'id, n. One of the *Felidae* or cat-tribe. [f. L *feles* cat, -ID³]

fel'ine, a. & n. Of cats; catlike (~ *amenities*, veiled spite, women's innocent-seeming thrusts), whence **felin'ity** n.; (n.) = prec. [f. L *felinus* (prec., -INE¹)]

fell¹, n. Animal's hide or skin with the hair (also transf. of human skin); thick or matted hair or wool, fleece, (~ *of hair*, unkempt hair of head); ~MONGER. [OE *fel(l)*, OS, OHG *fel*, ON *-fjall*, Goth. *-fill* f. Gmc *fellam* cogn. w. L *pellis*]

‖ **fell²**, n. Hill (in names, as *Sca F* ~); stretch of N.-English moorland. [f. ON *fiall* cogn. w. OHG *felis* (G *fels*) rock]

fell³, a. (poet.). Fierce, ruthless, terrible, destructive. [ME, f. OF *fel* f. Rom. *fello* FELON]

fell⁴, v.t., & n. Strike (person, animal) down by blow or cut; cut down (tree; n., amount of timber cut); stitch down (projection of seam). [OE *fellan* f. Gmc *falljan* causative of *fallan* FALL¹]

fell⁵. See FALL¹.

fell'ah (-a), n. (pl. ~*een*, ~s). Egyptian peasant. [Arab.]

fell'oe (-li, -lō), **fell'y**, n. Outer circle (or one piece of it) of wheel, attached by spokes. [OE *felg*, MLG, MDu. *velge*, OHG *felga* of unkn. orig.]

fell'ow (-ō), n. 1. One associated with another, comrade, (usu. in pl., as *separated from his* ~s; *good* ~, boon companion; HAIL²-~*well-met*; ~*-feeling*, sympathy). 2. Counterpart, match, other of pair, equal, one of same class, contemporary, (*stone dead hath no* ~, no keeper of secrets like a dead man; *shall never find his* ~; *passed all his* ~s). 3. Co-opted graduate incorporated member of college & in some colleges re-elected at intervals (~ *commoner*, undergraduate privileged to dine at ~s' table); elected graduate holding stipend for certain years on condition of research. 4. Member of governing body in some Universities; member of various learned Societies. 5. Man, boy, (*poor* ~ !, *my dear* or *good* ~, *old* ~; a ~, occas. = *one, I*, as *a* ~ *can't work all day long*; *the* ~, contemptuously). 6. (In comb. with nn.; ~ or ~-) belonging to same class (~ *creature*, person or animal also created by God), associated in joint action (~ *soldier*), in same relation to same object (~ *citizen*, whence ~*cit'izenship* n.; ~*-countryman*); ~*-traveller*, (also) non-Communist who sympathizes with aims and general policy of Communist party. [OE *fēolaga* f. ON *felagi* f. *fé* (= OE *feoh* FEE) +LAY³]

fell'owship (-lō-), n. Participation, sharing, community of interest; companionship, intercourse, friendliness, (often *good* ~); body of associates, company, (*right hand of* ~, sign of admission); guild, corporation; brotherhood, fraternity; dignity or emoluments of college fellow; *post-graduate scholarship. [-SHIP]

felly. See FELLOE.

fel'ō de sē, n. (pl. *felonēs, felos*). Self-murderer, (no pl.) self-murder. [Anglo-L, = FELON about himself]

fel'on¹, a. (poet.), & n. 1. Cruel, wicked, murderous. 2. n. One who has committed felony. [ME, f. OF f. med. L *fellonem* nom. *-o* of unkn. orig.]

fel'on², n. Small abscess esp. under or near nail, whitlow. [perh. as prec.]

felōn'ious, a. Criminal; (Law) of, involving, felony; who has committed felony. Hence ~LY² adv. [FELONY +-OUS]

fel'onry, n. The class or body of felons. [-RY]

fel'ony, n. Crime of kind legally graver than misdemeanour. [MF, f. OF *felonie* (FELON, -Y¹)]

felspar. See FELDSPAR.

fel'stone (-on), n. Compact felspar occurring in amorphous rock masses. [f. G *felsstein* (*fels* rock, *stein* stone)]

felt¹, n., & v.t. & i. 1. Kind of cloth made by rolling & pressing wool with lees or size; (attrib.) made of this (esp. ~ *hat*); hence~~Y²a. **2.** vb. Make into~, mat together; become matted; cover with ~. [OE *fell*, OS *filt*, OHG *filz* f. WG **fellta, -i*]

felt². See FEEL.

fel'teric, n. A horse-disease. [orig. unkn.]

felucc'a, n. Small Mediterranean coasting vessel with oars or lateen sails or both. [17th c. f. It., ult. f. Arab. *fulk* ship]

fem'ale, a. & n. **1.** Of the offspring-bearing sex (~ *child, slave, dog*); (of plants or their parts) fruit-bearing, having pistil & no stamens, (also used of some plants by mere metaphor suggested by their colour etc., as ~ *fern, bamboo, myrtle*); of women (~ *sex, education, suffrage, weakness*). **2.** Of inferior vigour etc. (~ *sapphire,* pale variety). **3.** (In instruments etc.) fitted to receive corresponding male part (~ *screw,* as in nuts). **4.** n. ~ person (*the law is harsh to all* ~*s*) or animal; (vulg.) woman, girl, (*a young* ~ *has called*). [ME & OF *femelle* n. f. L *femella* dim. of *femina* woman, w. assim. to *male*]

feme co'vert (fěm kŭ-), **feme sŏle,** nn. (legal). (*Covert*) married woman; (*sole*) spinster, widow, or married woman entirely independent of her husband as regards property. [AF *feme* woman, *covert* covered, *sole* single]

fěmin'ǎl'itў, n. Female nature; female peculiarity; woman's knick-knack etc. [obs. *feminal* f. OF (L *femina* woman, -AL) +-ITY]

fěminē'itў, n. Womanliness; womanishness. [f. L *femineus* (*femina* woman) +-ITY]

fěm'inine, a. Of female sex (rare); of women; womanly; (Gram.) having the gender proper to women's names; (Pros.) ~ *rhyme,* of two syllables, the second being unstressed (orig. in F verse, of words ending in mute *-e*), ~ *ending,* of line with last accent on penult, ~ *caesura,* not immediately following stress. Hence ~LY²adv.,~NESS, **fěminin'ITY,** nn. [ME, f. OF *feminin* or L *femininus* (*femina* woman, -INE¹)]

fěm'inǐsm, n. Advocacy, extended recognition, of the claims of women. So ~IST n. [f. L *femina* woman +-ISM]

fěmin'itў, n. = FEMININITY. [ME, f. OF *feminite* (L *femina* woman, -ITY)]

fěm'inǐz|e, -is|e (-ǐz), v.t. & i. Make or become feminine. Hence ~A'TION n. [f. L as prec. +-IZE]

femme de chambre (see Ap.), n. Lady's maid; chambermaid. [F]

fěm'ur (-er), n. (pl. ~s, *fěm'ora*). Thighbone; corresponding part of insect. So **fěm'orAL.** [L]

fěn¹, n. Low marshy or flooded tract of land (|| *the* ~*s,* low-lying districts in Cambs. etc.); ~*berry,* cranberry; ~*fire,* will-o'-the-wisp; ~*man,* inhabitant of ~*s;* || ~*pole,* for use in jumping ditches; || ~*reeve,* officer in charge of ~*lands;* ~-

-runners, kind of skates. Hence ~n'Y²a. [OE *fen(n)*, OFris. *fen(n)e*, OHG *fenna, -ni,* ON *fen,* Goth. *fani* f. Gmc **fanja-*] **fen²,** **fens.** See FAIN².

fence¹, n. Art of fencing, use of the sword, (*master of* ~, skilled swordsman, often fig. = good debater); (arch.) bulwark; hedge, wall, railing; etc., keeping out intruders from field etc. (*sunk* ~, placed along bottom of ditch; *sit on the* ~, remain neutral in contest, not take sides; *come etc. down on right side of* ~, join winner; PUT *horse at* ~); guard, guide, gauge, in various machines; receiver, receiving-house, of stolen goods; || ~*-month, -season, -time,* close time for game or fish. [ME, for DEFENCE]

fence², v.i. & t. Practise sword-play, use the sword scientifically, (~ *with question* or *questioner,* parry, evade answering); screen, shield, protect, (*from, against*); repel, keep *off* or *out;* surround (as) with fence, enclose, fortify, (~*d cities* in O.T.; often *about, in, round, up*); (of horse) leap fences; deal in stolen goods. Hence **fěn'CER¹** n. (esp. of swordsman, also of horse). [f. prec.]

fence'less (-sl-), a. Unenclosed (poet.) unfortified, defenceless. [FENCE¹ + -LESS]

fěn'cible, n. (hist.). Soldier liable only for home service. [for DEFENSIBLE]

fěn'cing, n. In vbl senses; also: railing; fences; material for fences. [-ING¹]

fěnd, v.t. & i. Ward *off,* keep *away,* repel *from;* provide *for* (usu. one*self*). [ME, for DEFEND]

fěn'der, n. Thing used to keep something off, prevent collision, etc.; (naut.) piece of old cable, matting, etc., hung over vessel's side; guard, esp. metal frame for fire to keep coals from rolling into room; || ~*-stool,* long footstool before ~. Hence ~LESS a. [-ER¹]

fěněstěll'a, n. (archit.). Niche in wall S. of altar holding piscina & often credence. [L, dim. of *fenestra* window]

fěněs'tra, n. (pl. *-ae*). Small hole or opening in bone etc., esp. one of two (~ *ovalis* and ~ *rotunda*) in internal ear. [L, = window]

fěněs'tr|ate, a. (bot., zool.). With small window-like perforations. So ~āTED² a., furnished with windows, pierced with hole(s), perforated. [f. L *fenestrare* (prec.), -ATE²]

fěněstrā'tion, n. (Archit.) arrangement of windows in a building; (Bot. & Zool.) being fenestrate; (Surg.) operation of making a 'window' in medial wall of middle ear, performed in some cases of deafness. [prec., -ATION]

Fēn'ian, n. & a. **1.** One of a league among the Irish in U.S. founded in 1858 for promoting revolution & overthrowing English government in Ireland; hence ~ISM(3) n. **2.** adj. Of ~s or ~ism. [f. OIr. *féne* name of ancient Irish people confused w. *fiann* guard of legendary kings]

fěnks, n. pl. Fibrous parts of whale's blubber, refuse of blubber when melted. [orig. unkn.]

fěnn'ĕc, n. Small N.-African fox notable for its huge pointed ears. [Arab.]

fěnn'el, n. Yellow-flowered fragrant umbelliferous herb used in sauces. [OE *finugl* f. L *faeniculum* (*faenum* hay, -CULE)]

fěn'ūgreek, n. Leguminous plant with seeds used in farriery. [ME, f. OF *fenugrec* f. L *faenugraecum* (*faenum* hay, *Graecus* Greek)]

feoff. See FIEF.

feoffee' (fěfē'), n. Person to whom freehold estate in land is conveyed by a feoffment; ~ *in* or *of trust*, trustee invested with such estate. [f. AF *feoffe* p.p. f. OF *fieffer* (FEE), see -EE]

feoff'ment (fěf-), n. Particular mode of conveying freehold estate. [as prec., -MENT]

feoff'or, -er, (fěf-), n. One who makes feoffment to another. [as FEOFFEE, -OR]

fer'ae natūr'ae, a. (pred. or placed after noun). Not domesticated, living in a wild state, (*hares are, the hare is,* ~; *animals* ~). [L, = of a wild nature]

fěr'al, a. Wild, untamed, uncultivated; brutal. [f. LL *feralis* (L *fera* wild beast, -AL)]

fer de lance (fărdelahns'), n. A large and peculiarly venomous snake of tropical S. America. [F, = iron head of lance]

fě'rėtory, n. Shrine for saint's relics, tomb; ‖ bier; chapel in which shrines were deposited. [ME *fertre* f. OF *fiertre* f. L *feretrum* f. Gk *pherètron* (*pherŏ* bear, w. assim. to -ORY]

fěr'ial, a. (eccl.). (Of day) ordinary, not appointed for festival or fast (~ *service* etc., for use on ~ day). [ME, f. OF *ferial* or med. L *ferialis* (*feria* week-day +-AL)]

fěr'īne, a. = FERAL. [f. L *ferinus* (*fera* wild beast, -INE[1])]

Fering'hee (-ĭnggĭ), n. (Indian term for) European, esp. Indian-born Portuguese. [corrupt. of FRANK[1]]

fěrm'ĕnt[1], n. Leaven, fermenting-agent; fermenting, fermentation; agitation, excitement, tumult. [ME, f. OF, or L *fermentum* (*fervēre* boil, -MENT)]

ferměnt'[2], v.i. & t. Suffer, subject to, fermentation; (make) effervesce; excite, stir up, foment. Hence ~ABLE a. [ME, f. OF *fermenter* or L *fermentare* (prec.)]

fěrměntā'tion, n. Process like that induced by leaven in dough, with effervescence, heat, & change of properties; agitation, excitement. Hence **ferměnt'ATIVE** a. [f. med. L *fermentatio* (prec., -ATION)]

fěrn, n. One of a large group of vascular cryptogams many of which have feathery fronds (also collect., *go through heath &* ~); ~-*owl*, nightjar. Hence ~ 'LESS, ~'Y[2], aa., ~'ERY(3) n. [OE *fearn*, MDu. *væren*, OHG *farn* f. WG **farna*]

ferō'cious (-shŭs), a. Fierce, savage,

cruel. Hence ~LY[2] (-shŭs-) adv. [f. L *ferox* -*ocis* +-OUS]

ferŏ'cǐty, n. Ferocious character or act. [f. F *férocité* or L *ferocitas* (prec., -TY)]

-ferous, suf. (in actual use -*iferous*, see -I-) forming adjj., f. L -*fer* -producing (*ferre* bear) +-OUS; in adjj. taken direct or thr. F -*fère* f. L as *auriferous*, & now a living suf., esp. in Nat. Hist., = -bearing, -having.

fě'rŏx, n. Great lake trout. [L name *Salmo ferox* fierce salmon]

fě'rrāte, n. A salt of ferric acid. [f. L *ferrum* iron +-ATE[1](3)]

fě'rrėous, a. Of, containing, iron. [f. L *ferreus* (prec.) +-OUS]

fě'rrėt[1], n. Half-tamed variety of polecat kept for driving rabbits from burrows, killing rats, etc.; searcher, detective. Hence ~Y[2] a. [ME, f. OF *fuiret, furet* alt. f. *fuiron, furon* f. LL *furionem, furonem* f. L *fur* thief]

fě'rrėt[2], v.i. & t. Hunt with ferrets (*go* ~ *ing*); clear out (holes, ground), take or drive away (rabbits etc.), with ferrets (*about, away, out,* etc.); rummage, search *about,* (*for*); search *out* (secrets, criminals, etc.). [f. prec.]

fě'rrėt[3], n. Stout cotton or silk tape. [f. It. *fioretti* floss-silk pl. of *fioretto* dim. of *fiore* f. L *flos* -*oris* flower]

fěrri-, comb. form used to indicate presence of iron in ferric compounds; see -IC.

fě'rrǐage, n. Conveyance by, charge for using, ferry. [-AGE]

fě'rrǐc, a. Of iron; (Chem.) containing iron in trivalent form (cf. FERROUS). [f. L *ferrum* iron +-IC]

fěrrif'erous, a. Iron-yielding. [as prec. + -FEROUS]

Fě'rris wheel, n. Giant revolving vertical wheel supporting passenger cars on its periphery, an attraction at exhibitions etc. [G. W. G. *Ferris*, U.S. engineer]

fěrro-, comb. form used to indicate presence of iron in ferrous compounds; see -OUS.

fěrro-măgnět'ic, a. Magnetic as opp. to diamagnetic. [prec.]

fě'rrotype, n. Positive photograph taken on thin iron plate; this process. [FERRO-, TYPE]

fě'rrous, a. Containing iron (~ *& non-*~ *metals*); (Chem.) containing iron in divalent form (cf. FERRIC). [f. L *ferrum* iron +-OUS]

ferru'gǐnous (-rōō-), a. Of, containing, iron-rust or iron as a chemical constituent; rust-coloured, reddish-brown. [f. L *ferrugo* -*ginis* rust (*ferrum* iron) +-OUS]

fě'rrule, -rel, n. Metal ring or cap strengthening end of stick or tube; band strengthening or forming joint. Hence **fě'rrulED**[2] (-ld) a. [15th c. *vyrelle*, 17th c. *verrel*, f. OF *virelle* etc., f. L *viriola* dim. of *viriae* bracelet, assim. to *ferrum* iron]

fě'rry̆, v.t. & i., & n. **1.** Convey or pass in boat, work (boat), (of boat) pass to &

fro, over river, canal, or strait; fly (air-craft) from factory to operational airfield (~ *pilot*, one who makes such flights). 2. n. Place, provision, for ~ing; (Law) right of ~ing & levying toll for it; ~ *boat*; ~*man*; ~*bridge*, large ~-boat transporting railway train entire. [vb OE, OS *ferian*, OHG *feren*, ON *ferja*, Goth. (= Gmc) *farjan* f. *far-* FARE[2]; n. (ME) f. ON *ferja* f. *far-* (prec.)]

fèrt'ile (-il, -il), a. Bearing abundantly, fruitful, (lit. & fig.; ~ *of*, *in*). So **fertil'ity** n. [ME, t OF *fertil* f. L *fertilis* (*ferre* bear)]

fèrt'iliz|e, -is|e (-iz), v.t. Make fertile or productive (esp. soil); (Bot. etc.) fecundate (individual, organ). Hence ~ABLE a., ~A'TION, ~ER[1](1, 2), nn. [-IZE]

fè'rula (-ōol-, -ŏol), nn. (Bot.) giant fennel (-*ula*); flat ruler with widened pierced end for punishing boys, whence **fè'rule** (-ŏol) v.t. [L (-*a*)]

fèrv'ent, a. Hot, glowing; ardent, intense, (~ *soul*, *lover*, *hatred*), so **fèrv'ency** n. Hence ~LY[2] adv [ME, f. OF f. L *fervēre* boil. -ENT]

fèrv'id, a. 1. (poet.) Hot, glowing. 2. Ardent, intense. Hence ~LY[2] adv. [f. L *fervidus* (prec.)]

fèrv'our (-er), n. Glowing condition, intense heat; vehemence, passion, zeal. [ME, f. OF *fervor* f. L *fervorem* nom. -*or* (FERVENT, -OR)]

Fès'cènnine, a. ~ *verses*, scurrilous lam-poons. [f. L *Fescenninus* (*Fescennio* town in Etruria, -INE[1])]

fès'cŭe, n. Small stick, teacher's pointer; kinds of grass, including some valuable for pasture & fodder. [ME *festu(e)* f. OF *festu* f. Rom. **festucum* f. L -*a*; *fescue* f. 16th c.]

fèsse, n. (her.). Two horizontal lines as bar across middle of field. [ME, f. OF, f. L FASCIA]

fès'tal, a. Of a feast; keeping holiday; gay. Hence ~LY[2] adv [f. OF, or LL *festalis* (FEAST, -AL)]

fès'ter, v.i. & t., & n. 1. (Of wound or sore) generate matter, ulcerate; (of poison, disease, grief) cause suppuration, rankle; putrefy, rot; cause festering in. 2. n. ~ing condition. [ME; f. obs. n. *fester* f. OF *festre* f. L FISTULA]

fès'tival, a. (not pred.), & n. Festal day, celebration, merry-making; periodic musical performance(s) of special impor-tance; (adj.) of a feast (-*day*). [ME (adj.) f. OF f. med. L *festivalis* (foll., -AL)]

fès'tive, a. Of a feast; joyous, fond of feasting, jovial. Hence ~LY[2] (-vl-) adv. [f. L *festivus* (*festum* FEAST, -IVE)]

fèstiv'ity, n. Gaiety, rejoicing; festive celebration, (pl.) festive proceedings. [ME, f. OF *festivite* or L *festivitas* (prec., -TY)]

fèstoōn', n., & v.t. 1. Chain of flowers or leaves, or ribbons etc., hung in curve between two points. 2. v.t. Adorn (as)

with, form into, ~s. Hence ~ERY(5) n. [f. F *feston* f. It. *festone* f. *festa* feast + -OON]

fètch[1], v.t. & i., & n. 1. (Go for &) bring back (person or thing; ~, or *go* & ~, a *doctor*; FAR[1]~*ed*; ~ & *carry*, run back-wards & forwards with things, be a servant); cause to come, draw forth, (blood, tears; ~ *up*, vomit); bring in, realize, sell for, (a price); move the feelings of, delight (whence ~'ING[3] a.) or irritate; heave (sigh), draw (breath); deal (blow; usu. with ind. obj., ~ *him a box on the ears*); ~ *a* COMPASS[1]; ~ *up*, come to a stand. 2. n. Far-reaching effort (arch.); dodge, trick; (Naut.) line of con-tinuous extent from point to point, e.g. of a bay or of open sea. [OE (*fecc(e)an* var. of *fetian* whence dial. *fet* in same sense]

fètch[2], n. Person's wraith or double [orig. unkn.]

fête (fāt), n., & v.t. 1. Festival, great entertainment, (~-*day*, appointed for ~); day of saint after whom child is named, observed in R.-C. countries like birth-day. 2. v.t. Entertain, make much of (person). [f. F *fête(r)* FEAST]

fête champêtre (see Ap.), n. Outdoor fête. [F]

fè'tial (-shl), a. & n. (Rom. ant.). 1. ~ *law*, of declarations of war & treaties of peace. 2. n. One of Roman college of priests who served as heralds. [f. L *fetialis*]

fèt'id, foe- (fē-), a. Stinking. Hence ~LY[2] adv., ~NESS n. [f. L *fetidus* (*fetēre* stink)]

fèt'ish, -ch(e) (-sh), n. Inanimate object worshipped by savages for its magical powers or as being inhabited by a spirit; principle etc. irrationally reverenced. Hence or cogn. ~EER', ~ER[1], ~ISM(3), ~IST(2), nn., ~IS'TIC a. [f. F *fétiche* f. Port. *feitiço* charm, orig. adj. = FACTITIOUS]

fèt'lock, n. Part of horse's leg where tuft of hair grows behind pastern-joint (~-*deep*, so as to cover ~s). [ME *fet(e)lak*, *fytlok*, corr. to MHG *vizzeloch*, G *fissloch*; rel. to G *fessel* & ult. to FOOT]

fèt'or, n. Stench. [L, see FETID, -OR]

fèt'ter, n., & v.t. 1. Shackle for the feet; bond, (pl.) captivity; check, restraint; ~*lock*, (heraldic representation of) D-shaped ~ for tethering horse by leg. 2. v.t. Bind (as) with ~s, impede, re-strain. Hence ~LESS a. [OE *feter*, OS *feteros*, OHG *fezzera*, ON *fjǫturr* f. Gmc **feter-* cogn. w. FOOT]

fèt'tle, n. Condition, trim, (*in good* etc. ~). [f. ME (now dial.) vb *fettle* make ready, f. OE (now dial.) n. *fetel* girdle]

fetus. See FOETUS.

fèt'wa, n. Decision given by Moslem judi-cial authority. [Arab.]

feu, n. (Sc.). Perpetual lease at fixed rent; piece of land so held. [var. of FEE]

feud[1], n. Lasting mutual hostility (*be at* ~ *with*), esp. (often *deadly* ~) between two tribes, families, etc., with murderous assaults in revenge for previous injury.

[ME *fede*, f. OF *faide*, *fede* f. Frank. *faida* = OHG *fêhida*, OE *fǣhthu* enmity: see FOE]

feud², n. Fief, feudal benefice. territory held in fee. [f. med. L as FEE]

feud'al, a. Of a feud or fief: ~ *system*, medieval European polity based on relation of vassal & superior arising from holding of lands in feud; of, resembling, according to, this system. Hence ~LY² adv., ~ISM(3), ~IST(2), nn., ~IS'TIC a., ~IZE(3) v.t., ~IZA'TION n. [f. med. L *feudalis* (prec., -AL)]

feudal'ity, n. Feudal system or principles; feudal holding, fief. [f. F *feodalité* (prec., -TY)]

feud'atory, a. & n. Feudally subject *to*, under overlordship; (n.) feudal vassal. [f. med. L *feudatorius* f. *feudare* (FEUD², -ORY)]

feu de joie (fĕ̅rdezhwah'), n. Salute of guns fired on ceremonial occasions. [F]

feuilleton (see Ap.), n. Ruled-off portion at foot of (esp. French) newspapers, devoted to fiction, criticism, light literature, etc. [F, = leaflet]

fev'er, n., & v.t. 1. Morbid condition with high temperature & excessive change & destruction of tissues; any of a group of diseases so characterized, each with distinctive name, as *scarlet*, *typhoid*, ~; nervous excitement, agitation; ~ *heat*, high temperature of body in ~; ~*trap*, place that collects ~germs. 2. v.t. Throw into ~ [OE *fēfor* = OHG *fiebar*, f. L *febris*]

fev'erfew, n. A herb formerly used in medicine. [OE *fēferfuge* f. LL; see FEBRIFUGE]

fev'erish, a. Having symptoms of fever; excited, fitful, restless; (of places) infested by fever, feverous. Hence ~LY² adv., ~NESS n. [-ISH¹]

fev'erous, a. Infested with or apt to cause fever; feverish. [-OUS]

few, a. & n. Not many (~ is opp. to *many*, *a ~ to none*, *only a ~ = ~*; *a man of ~ words*; *he spoke a ~ words*; *~ have such a chance*; *~, a ~, of his friends were there*; *a ~ know the truth*; *a faithful ~ remained*; *visitors are ~*); in ~ (arch.), in ~ words, briefly; *some ~*, no great number; *the ~*, the minority, the elect, etc.; *not a ~*, many; (colloq.) *a good ~*, fair number (of); *every ~ days* etc., once in every group of a ~ days. Hence ~'NESS n. [OE *fēawe*, OS, OHG *fao* (*faw-*), ON *fár*, Goth. *fawai* f. Gmc *faw*- cogn. w. L *pau-cus*]

fey (fā), a. (Sc.) ‖ Fated to die, at point of death; disordered in mind (often with over-confidence etc.) like person about to die. [OE *fǣge*, OS *fēgi*, OHG *feigi*, ON *feigr* f. Gmc *faigjaz*]

fez, n. Turkish cap, a tasselled dull-red truncated cone. [f. Turk. *fes* perh. f. *Fez*, town]

fiacre (fē'ahkr), n. French four-wheeled cab. [f. the Hôtel de St F~, Paris]

fiancé, -ée (see Ap.), n. One's betrothed, (-é) male, or (-ée) female. [F]

Fianna Fail (fē'ana fawl), n. Eamon de Valera's party, which entered the Dail Eireann in August 1927. [nom. pl. of Ir. *fian* + gen. of *Fál* Ireland; lit. = armed men of Ireland]

fiäs'cō, n. (pl. *-os*). Failure or break-down (orig. in dramatic etc. performance), ignominious result. [It., = bottle (unexplained allusion)]

fi'at (-at, -ăt), n., & v.t. Authorization; decree, order, (n., & rarely vb = authorize); *~ money*, inconvertible paper-money made legal tender by Government decree. [L, = be it done]

fib¹, n., & v.i. (-bb-). (Tell) trivial or venial lie. Hence ~b'ER¹, ~'STER, nn. [perh. f. obs. *fible-fable* nonsense, redupl. of FABLE]

‖ **fib²**, n., & v.t. (-bb-). A blow (vb, strike, hit about) in pugilism etc. [orig. unkn.]

fi'bre (-ber), n. Thread-like filament forming with others animal & vegetable tissue or textile substance; substance consisting of ~s; fibrous structure; structure, grain, character, (*man of coarse ~*); substance that can be spun, woven, or felted; small root or twig; ~*board*, building material made of wood or other plant ~s compressed into boards. Hence (-)fi'brED (-berd), ~LESS (-erl-), fib'riFORM, fib'ROUS, aa., fib'ROUSLY² adv., fib'ROUSNESS n., fibro- comb: form. [F, f. L *fibra*]

fib'ril, n. Small fibre; subdivision of fibre; ultimate subdivision of root. Hence ~IAR(Y), ~lATE², ~lātĕd, ~l'iFORM, ~lOSE¹, aa., ~lA'TION n. [also *fibrilla* mod. L dim. of prec.]

fib'rin, n. Coagulable lymph found in animal & vegetable matter. Hence ~o- comb. form, ~OUS a. [FIBRE + -IN]

fib'roid, a. & n. Of fibrous structure or appearance; (n.) ~ uterine tumour. [-OID]

fib'röin, n. Chemical substance of which silk & cobweb mainly consist. [FIBRO- + -IN]

fibrōm'a, n. (pl. *-ta*). Fibrous tumour. [mod. L (FIBRE, & cf. SARCOMA)]

fibrosit'is, n. (Rheumatic) inflammation of fibrous tissue. [f. mod. L *fibrosus* (FIBROUS) + -ITIS]

fib'ül|a, n. (pl. *-ae*, *-as*). Splint bone on outer side of leg; (Ant.) brooch or clasp. Hence ~AR¹ a. [L]

-fic, suf. (in actual use, *-ific*, see -I-) repr. L *-ficus* f. weakened root of *facere* make, do, forming adjj. f. nn. as *pacificus* peace-making, f. adjj. as *magnificus*, f. vv. as *horrificus*, & f. the advv. *male*, *bene*. E adopted many L adjj. of this type thr. F; & later formations, arising in various langg., are usu. of international currency, as *acidific*, *morbific*.

-fică'tion, suf. (in actual use *-ification*, see -I-) repr. L *-fication-* (nom. *-tio*), which formed nn. of action f. vv. in *-ficare* -FY. E adopted many pairs of words, n. & vb, f. L thr. F or of F formation, as *purify*, *purification*; hence *-fication* has become the recognized means of forming nn. corresp. to vv. in *-fy* exc. when these repr. L vv. in *-facere* (see -FACTION); as a rule the formation is based only on possible L types; exceptions are *beauti~*, *Frenchi~*, *transmogri~*.

ficelle', a. String-coloured. [F, = string]

fi'chu (-shōo), n. Woman's small triangular shawl of lace etc. for shoulders & neck. [F]

fic'kle, a. Inconstant, changeable. Hence ~NESS (-ln-) n. [OE *ficol* cf. *befician* deceive]

fic'tile, a. Made of earth or clay by potter, of pottery. [f. L *fictilis* (*fingere fict-* fashion, -IL)]

fic'tion, n. Feigning, invention, thing feigned or imagined, invented statement or narrative, literature consisting of such narrative, esp. novels, whence ~IST(3) (-shon-) n., conventionally accepted falsehood (esp. *legal*, *polite*, ~). Hence ~AL (-shon-) a. [F, f. L *fictionem* (prec., -ION)]

ficti'tious (-shus), a. Counterfeit, not genuine; (of name or character) assumed; imaginary, unreal; of, in, novels; regarded as what it is called by legal or conventional fiction. Hence ~LY[2] adv., ~NESS n., (-shus-). [f. L *ficticius* (prec.) +-OUS]

fic'tive, a. Creating, created, by imagination. [F (-*if*, -*ive*), see FICTION, -IVE]

fid, n. **1.** (naut.). Conical wooden pin used in splicing; (also ~'*pin*) square wooden or iron bar for supporting topmast. **2.** Small thick piece or wedge of anything. [orig. unkn.]

fid'dle, n., int., & v.i. & t. **1.** (Fam. or contempt. for) violin (*fit as a* ~, in good condition & spirits; *hang up* one's ~ *when one comes home*, be witty abroad & dull at home; *play first*, *second*, ~, take leading, subordinate, position; *face as long as a* ~, dismal). **2.** (naut.). Contrivance for stopping things from rolling off table. **3.** (sl.). An act of cheating. **4.** ~-BOW[1], ~-*case*, for holding ~; ~-*de-dee'*, int. & n., nonsense, ~-*faddle*, (n.) trivial matters, idler, (adj.) petty, fussy, (int.) nonsense, (v.i.) fuss, trifle; ~-*head*, carving at ship's bows; ~ *pattern*, of spoons & forks with ~-shaped heads; ~*stick*, (n.) = ~-bow, (also, usu. pl., as int.) nonsense! **5.** int. Nonsense! **6.** vb. Play the ~, play (tune etc.) on ~, be idle or frivolous, make aimless movements, (*about*, *at*, *with*, etc.); fritter *away*; (sl.) cheat, swindle. [ME, f. OE **fithele*, OHG *fidula*, ON *fithla*, Gmc **fithulōn* f. pop. L **vitula* VIOL]

fidd'ler, n. Player on fiddle, esp. for hire (*F~'s Green*, sailor's Elysium); kind of small crab. [OE *fithelere* (prec., -ER[1])]

fidd'ley, n. (naut.; pl. ~s). Iron framework round opening of stokehole. [orig. unkn.]

fidd'ling, a. In vbl senses; esp., petty, futile, contemptible, inconsiderable. [-ING[2]]

fidel'ity, n. Faithfulness, loyalty, (*to*); strict conformity to truth or fact; exact correspondence to the original; (Radio etc.) clarity of reproduction. [f. F *fidélité* or L *fidelitas* FEALTY]

fidg'et[1], n. **1.** Bodily uneasiness seeking relief in spasmodic movements (often *the* ~s); restless mood. **2.** One who fidgets or causes others to; act of bustling etc. rustle of dress etc. Hence ~Y[2] a., ~INESS n. [sense 1 f. obs. *fidge* to twitch sense 2 f. foll.]

fidg'et[2], v.i. & t. Move restlessly (often *about*); be uneasy, worry; make uncomfortable, worry, (person). [f. prec.]

fid'ibus, n. Paper spill for lighting candles, pipes, etc. [G students' slang]

Fid'ō, n. Device for enabling aircraft to land by dispersing fog by means of petrol -fired flame burners heating air over runway. [initials of *Fog Investigation Dispersal Operation*]

fidu'cial (-shl), a. (surv., astron., etc.). ~ *line*, *point*, etc., one assumed as fixed basis of comparison. [f. LL *fiducialis* (*fiducia* trust, -AL)]

fidu'ciary (-sha-), a. & n. **1.** Of trust or trustee(ship); held or given in trust; (of paper currency) depending for its value on public confidence or securities. **2.** n. Trustee. [f. L *fiduciarius* (prec., -ARY[1])]

fid'us Achat'es (akātēz), n. Devoted follower, henchman. [L, =faithful Achates, follower of Aeneas in *Aeneid*]

fie (fī), int. expr. sense of outraged propriety, usu. iron. or to children (often ~ *upon you!*). [ME, f. OF f. L *fī* excl. of disgust at stench]

fief (fēf), **feoff** (fēf), n. = FEUD[2].

fie'-fie (fī'fī), a. Improper, scandalous. [FIE]

field, n., & v.i. & t. **1.** (Piece of) ground, esp. one used for pasture or tillage, & usu. bounded by hedges etc.; tract abounding in some natural product (*diamond*, *coal*, etc., ~~). **2.** Ground on which battle is fought (often *battle-*~; also fig., *left his rival in possession of the* ~; *a fair* ~ *& no favour*, equal conditions in contest; *hold the* ~, not be superseded); scene of campaign (*in the* ~, campaigning; *take*, *keep*, *the* ~, begin, continue, campaign); battle (*hard-fought*, *stricken*, ~); *F~ of Cloth of Gold*, scene of meeting between Henry VIII & Francis I, 1520. **3.** Ground for playing cricket, football, etc.; players, partakers, in outdoor contest or sport; all competitors or all except the favourite (*a good* ~, many & good competitors). (Cricket) side not batting, one of this side (see also LONG[1]~). **4.** Large stretch expanse, of sea, sky, ice, snow, etc., also fig. (*the whole* ~ *of history*). **5.** (Her.) surface of escutcheon or of one of its divisions; groundwork of picture, coin, flag, etc. **6.** Area or sphere of operation.

observation. intellectual activities, etc. (*each supreme in his own ~, filled the ~ of the telescope. wide ~ of vision, outside the magnetic ~*, not near enough to be attracted) **7.** attrib. (In names of animals etc.) found in the open country (*~-mouse, ~-ash*) **8.** ~*-allowance*, to officer on campaign to meet increased expenditure; ~*-artillery, -battery, -gun or -piece*, light & mobile for use with armies in the ~, ~*-book* (used in ~ by surveyor for technical notes); ~*boot*, knee-length & close-fitting, ~*-cornet*, magistrate of township in Cape Colony etc.; ~*-day*, (Mil.) manœuvring-exercise or review, (fig.) great occasion, important debate; ~ *dressing*, appliances for wound in battle, ~ *events*, athletic sports such as weight-putting, jumping, discus-throwing, etc. (i.e. other than *races*); ~*-glass*, binocular telescope for outdoor use, one of the lenses of astronomical telescope or compound microscope, ~ *hospital*, ambulance, temporary hospital near battle-field; F~ *Marshal*, army officer of the highest rank, ~ *mustard*, charlock, ~*night*, = ~*-day* (fig. sense); ~*-officer*, above captain & below general; ~*-preacher, -preaching*, in open air; ~*-punishment* (Mil.), kinds of penal servitude for offences on campaign, ~*s'man*, ~*er* at cricket, ~*-sports*, outdoor, esp hunting, shooting, fishing, ~ *telegraph*, movable for use on campaign; ~*-work*, temporary fortification, outdoor work of surveyor etc., or of collector of scientific data, hence ~*'WARD(S)* adv. **9.** vb. Act as ~sman in cricket, baseball, or rounders; stop (& return) ball; put into the ~ (of football teams etc.); (Betting) back the ~ against the favourite; hence ~*'ER*[1] n. [OE, OS, OHG *feld* f WG *felthu*]

field′fare, n. Species of thrush spending winter in Britain. [MF *feldefare* perh. f FIELD + FARE[2]]

fiend, n. The devil; evil spirit, demon; person of superhuman wickedness, esp. cruelty (often jocular, as *the interviewer ~*), (with qualifying word) devotee or addict (*fresh-air ~, dope ~, morphia ~*). Hence ~*'ISH*[1] a., ~*'ishLY*[2] adv., ~*'ish-NESS* n., ~*'LIKE* a. [OE *féond*, OS *fiond*, OHG *fiant*, ON *fjándi*, Goth. *fijands* part. of Gmc **fijéjan* hate; cf. FRIEND]

fierce, a. Violent in hostility, angrily combative; raging, vehement, (of mechanism) violent, not smooth or easy in action, ardent, eager. Hence ~*'LY*[2] (-sl-) adv., ~*'NESS* (-sn-) n. [ME, f. OF *fiers* nom. of *fier* (F = proud) f. L *ferus* savage]

‖ **fi′eri fa′ciäs** (-shi-), n. (legal; abbr. *fi. fa.*) Writ to sheriff for executing judgement. [L, = see that (the sum) is made]

fier′|y̆ (fīr-), a. Consisting of, flaming with, fire; (of arrows etc.) fire-bearing; looking like fire, blazing-red; (of eyes) flashing, ardent; hot as fire; acting like fire,

inflaming, (~*y̆ taste* etc.); eager, pugnacious, spirited, irritable, (of horse) mettlesome; (of gas, mine, etc.) inflammable, liable to explosions; (of cricket-pitch) making ball rise dangerously, ~*y̆* CROSS[1] Hence ~*iLY*[2] adv., ~*iNESS* n. [ME; FIRE[1] + Y[1]]

fiesta (fē′ĕstah), n. Festivity, holiday [Sp., = feast]

fife, n., & v.i. & t. **1.** Kind of small shrill flute used with drum in military music; = ~r. **2.** vb. Play the ~; play (air etc.) on the ~; hence fif′ER[1] n. [f. G *pfeife* PIPE, or f F *fifre*]

fife-rail (-fr-), n. (naut.). Rail round mainmast with belaying-pins. [perh. f. prec. because fifer sat on it while anchor was weighing]

fifteen′ (*also* fif[2]), a. & n. One more than fourteen, 15, XV; (Rugby football) side of 15 players; *the F~*, Jacobite rising of 1715. Hence ~*TH*[2] a. & n. [OE *fífténe. -tÿne*, (FIVE, -TEEN)]

fifth, a. & n. **1.** Next after fourth (*smite under the ~ rib*, kill; ~ *wheel* of coach etc., something superfluous, also as name of two horizontal half-circles sliding one over the other when a carriage-front turns); ~ *part*, one of five equal parts into which thing is or might be divided. **2.** n. = ~ part; (Mus.) interval of which the span involves five alphabetical notes, harmonic combination of the notes thus separated; (pl.) ~*-rate material*. **3.** ~ *column*, organized body sympathizing with and working for the enemy within a country at war etc., (loosely) traitors, spies; ~*-column activities*, organized hindrance of the national effort by subversive propaganda on the part of ~*-columnists*; F~ *Monarchy*, last of the five great empires (*Dan.* ii. 44; ~*-monarchy-man*, 17th-c. zealot expecting immediate second coming of Christ & repudiating all other government); F~ REPUBLIC. [OE *fífta* (still *fÿt* in diall.); *fifth* f. 14th c. on analogy of FOURTH; see -TH[2]]

fifth′ly̆, adv. In the fifth place (in enumerations). [-LY[2]]

fif′t|y̆, a. & n. **1.** Five times ten, 50, L. (~*y̆-one, -seven*, etc.; ~*y̆-first, -third*, etc.); ~*y̆-~y̆*, half & half, equal shares (*go ~y̆-~y̆; on a ~y̆-~y̆ basis*); large indefinite number (*have ~y̆ things to tell you*); hence ~*y̆FOLD* a. & adv., ~*iETH* a. & n. **2.** n. Set of ~y persons or things (*hid them by ~ies in a cave; the ~ies*, years between 49 & 60 in life or century) [OE *fíftig* (FIVE, -TY[2])]

fig[1], n. (Broad-leaved tree, usu. ~*-tree*, bearing) soft pear-shaped many-seeded fruit eaten fresh (*green ~s*) or dried (esp. *Turkey or Smyrna ~s; pulled ~s*, superior hand-picked Turkey ~s); *under* one's *vine & ~-tree*, safe at home; anything valueless (*don't care a ~ for*; *also a ~ for ~!*, as excl.); ~*-leaf*, device for fig 451 filaria

concealing private parts (*Gen.* iii. 7); ~-*wort*, brown-flowered herb. [ME, f. OF *figue* f. Pr. *figa* f. Rom. **fica* f. L *ficus*]

fig², n. Dress, equipment, (*in full* ~)₁ condition, form, (*in good* ~). [f. foll.]

fig³, v.t. (-gg-). ~ *out* or *up* (horse), make lively, ~ *.out* (person), dress up, bedizen. [var. of obs. *feague* f. G *fegen*; see FAKE²]

fight¹ (fīt), v.i. & t. (*fought*, pr. fawt). Contend in battle or single combat (*against, with, for*, on behalf of person or to secure thing); maintain (cause, suit at law, quarrel) against opponent, contend over (question), win one's *way* by ~*ing*, contend with in battle or duel, or with the fists; set on (cocks, dogs) to ~ (~*ing*-COCK¹); handle (troops, ship) in battle; ~ *off*, repel with effort; ~ (dispute etc., or *it*) *out*, settle by ~*ing*; ~ *shy of*, keep aloof from (person, undertaking, etc.); ~*ing chance*, a possibility of success if strenuous effort is made; ~*ing-top*, circular gun-platform fixed high up on warship's mast. Hence ~'ER¹ (fīt-) (esp.) n. & a., (fast aircraft) designed primarily for aerial ~*ing* (~*er-bomber*, such aircraft used as a bomber. [OE *feohtan*, OS, OHG *fehtan* f. WG **fehtan*]

fight² (fīt), n. Act of fighting, (*give, make a*, ~, *valiant in* ~); battle; combat, esp. pugilistic or unpremeditated, between two or more persons, animals, or parties (*running* ~ kept up while one party flees & one pursues; ‖ *sham* ~, between troops for practice or display; *stand-up* ~₁ open & formal); (fig.) strife, conflict; appetite or ability for fighting (*has* ~ *in him yet*; *show* ~, not yield tamely). [f. prec.]

fig'ment, n. Invented statement; thing that has no existence except in imagination. [f. L *figmentum* (*fig-* see FIGURE¹, -MENT)]

fig'urant masc., -*ante* fem., **figŭrăn'tĕ** (pl -*ti*, pr. -*tě*), nn. Ballet-dancer. [F (first two forms) & It. (third)]

figŭrā'tion (*also* -ger-), n. Determination to a certain form; the resulting form; shape, outline; allegorical representation; ornamentation by designs; (Mus.) use of florid counterpoint. [f. F, or L *figuratio* (FIGURE², -ATION)]

fig'urative (-ger-, -gūr-), a. Emblematic, typical; pictorial or plastic; metaphorical, not literal; metaphorically so called; abounding in, addicted to, figures of speech. Hence ~LY² (-vl-) adv., ~NESS n. [ME. f. OF (-*if*, -*ive*), or LL *figurativus* (as prec., -ATIVE)]

fig'ure¹ (-ger), n. **1.** External form, shape; (Geom.) superficial space enclosed by line(s), or three-dimensional space enclosed by surface(s), any of the classes of these, as triangle, sphere; bodily shape (*has a well-developed* ~; *keep* one's ~, not grow stout); a person as seen (*saw a* ~ *leaning against the door*; ~ *of fun*, grotesque person); a person as contem-

plated mentally (*the most terrible* ~ *in our history*); conspicuous appearance (*make* or *cut a brilliant, poor*, ~, produce such impression; *person of* ~, distinguished). **2.** Image, likeness; representation of human form, statue, person in picture, emblem, type, simile. **3.** Diagram, illustrative drawing, (abbr. for ref. *fig.*), esp. *text-*~, dist. from *plate*; horoscope; decorative pattern; evolution in dancing, division of set dance; (Skating) movement, series of movements, beginning & ending at centre. **4.** Numerical symbol, esp. one of the ten in Arabic notation (*double* ~s, number between 9 & 100; *income of five* ~s, between £10,000 & £100,000; *reach three* ~s, in cricket, get century; *got it at a low, high*, ~, cheap, dear). **5.** (rhet.; *also* ~ *of speech*) recognized form of abnormal expression giving variety, force, etc., e.g. aposiopesis, hyperbole, metaphor, (~ *of speech* only) piece of exaggeration. **6.** (gram.). Permitted deviation from rules of construction, e.g. ellipse. **7.** (log.). Particular form of syllogism according to position of middle term. **8.** (mus.). Short succession of notes producing single impression, brief melodic or rhythmic formula out of which longer passages are developed. **9.** ~-*dance*, dance or dancing exhibition with distinct divisions, ~-*dancer*, performer in this; ~-*head*, carving, usu. bust or full-length ~, over ship's cutwater, nominal leader or president without real authority, (joc.) person's face. Hence ~LESS (-gerl-) a. [ME, f. OF f. L *figura* (*fig-* st. of *fingere* fashion, -URE)]

fig'ure² (-ger), v.t. & i. Represent in diagram or picture; picture mentally, imagine, (often *to* oneself; **I* ~ *it like this* colloq., this is my theory, explanation, etc.); be symbol of, represent typically, embellish with pattern (~*d satin*); mark with numbers or prices, do arithmetic, cipher (~ *up*, reckon amount of); ~ *out*, give result in figures (~*s out at £45*); make appearance, appear, (~ *as*, pass for, assume character of), be conspicuous. [ME, f. OF *figurer* f. L *figurare* (prec.)]

figŭrine' (-ēn), n. Statuette. [F, f. It. *figurina* dim. of *figura* FIGURE¹]

fil'ament, n. Slender thread-like body, fibre, (esp. in animal or vegetable structure); not easily fusible conductor in electric bulb or thermionic valve, heated or made incandescent by current; (of air, light, etc.) imaginary portion of stream, row of particles following each other. (Bot.) part of stamen that supports anther. Hence ~ARY¹ (-ěn²), ~ED², ~OUS (-ěn²), aa. [F or mod. L, f. LL *filare* spin f. L *filum* thread, -MENT]

filār'|ia, n. (pl. -*iae* pr. -ĭē). Parasitic worm introduced into the blood by certain flies and mosquitoes. Hence ~iAL a., **filari'asis** n. [mod. L f. L *filum* thread (-AR¹, -IA¹)] fil′ature, n. (Establishment for) reeling silk from cocoons. [F, as FILAMENT, -URE]

fil′bert, n. (Nut of) cultivated hazel. [short for ~-*nut* = dial. F *noix de filbert*, ripe about St *Philibert's* day (Aug. 22)]

filch, v.t. Steal, pilfer. [orig. unkn.]

file¹, n., & v.t. 1. Instrument usu. of steel with roughened surface(s) for reducing or smoothing objects (*bite, gnaw,* ~, attempt vain task); (sl.) artful person, dodger, (usu. *old, deep,* etc., ~), person. 2. v.t. Smooth, reduce surface of, with ~; elaborate to perfection (esp. literary work); ~ *away* (roughnesses etc.), remove with ~. [OE *fēol, fīl,* OS, OHG *fīla* f. WG *fīhala*]

file², n., & v.t. 1. Stiff pointed wire on which documents etc. are run for keeping; folder for holding papers arranged for reference; set of papers so kept, esp. in court of law referring to a cause; series of issues of a newspaper in order. 2. v.t. Place (papers) on ~ or among public records. [f. F *fil* f. L *filum* thread]

file³, n., & v.i. & t. 1. (Mil.) a front-rank man & the man or men straight behind him (*in* ~, marching with the men of a double line faced towards one of its ends; *single, Indian,* ~, similar formation of single line; RANK¹ *&* ~; *a* ~ *of men,* two told off for some purpose); row of persons or things one behind another; (Chess) line of squares from player to player (cf. RANK¹). 2. vb. March in ~; ~ *off, away,* go off by ~s; (v.t.) order (soldiers) to move *off* by ~s. [f. F *file* f. LL *filare* f. L *filum* thread]

fil′ĕmŏt, a. & n. Dead-leaf colour(ed), brownish yellow. [f. F *feuille morte* dead leaf]

filet (fĕl′ā), n. Kind of net with square mesh (~ *lace,* ~ *net*). [F, = thread]

fil′ial, a. Of, due from, son or daughter. Hence ~LY² adv. [f. F, or LL *filialis* (L *filius, -a,* son, daughter, -AL)]

fil′iāte, v.t. (Rare for) AFFILIATE.

filiā′tion, n. Being some one's child; descent (*from*); formation of offshoots, branch of a society or language; genealogical relation or arrangement. [f. F, or LL *filiatio* f. L *filius* son, -ATION]

fil′ibĕg, n (Sc.). Kilt. [f. Gael. *feileadh beag* little fold]

fil′ibŭster, n., & v.i. 1. One who engages in unauthorized warfare against foreign State, *obstructionist in legislative assembly 2. v.i. Act as ~. Hence ~ER¹ n., a ~, one who ~s. [ult. f. Du. *vrijbuiter* FREEBOOTER affected by F *flibustier.* Sp. *filibustero*. mutual rel. uncert.]

fil′igree, fil′a-, n. Ornamental work of fine gold or silver or copper wire formed into delicate tracery, fine metal openwork anything delicate, light, showy, & frail. Hence fil′igreeD² a. [f. F *filigrane* f It. *filigrana* (L *filum* thread, *granum* grain)]

fil′ing, n In vbl senses of FILE¹, also,

(usu. pl.) particle(s) rubbed off by file. [-ING¹]

fill, v.t. & i., & n. 1. Make or become full (*with; sails* ~, are distended with wind)· stock abundantly; occupy whole capacity or extent of, spread over, pervade, (~ *the bill,* be the only conspicuous item, also in U.S., do all that is required. suffice); (of dentist) block up (hollow tooth, cavity) with gold etc., whence ~′ING¹(4) n.; satisfy, satiate, (esp. in part., of kinds of food); hold (position), discharge duties of (office); execute (an order, commission, etc.); occupy (vacant time); appoint holder of (vacant post); adulterate (esp. cotton fabrics: usu. in p.p.); ~ *in,* complete (outline), add what is wanted to complete (unfinished document, blank cheque, etc.); ~ *out,* enlarge, become enlarged, to the proper limit; ~ *up,* ~ completely, supply vacant parts or places or deficiencies in, do away with (pond·etc.) by ~ing, grow full; FEBRUARY ~-*dike;* hence ~′ER¹(1, 2) n. 2. Full supply of drink or food (*drink, have,* etc., one's ~; also with intr. vbs, as *fret her*~); enough to ~ something (*a* ~ *of tobacco*). [OE *fyllan,* OS *fullian,* OHG *fullen,* ON *fylla,* Goth. *fulljan* f. Gmc *fulljaz* FULL¹]

fille (fē′ye), n. ~ *de chambre* (de shahn′br), chambermaid; ~ *de joie* (de zhwah), prostitute. [F, = daughter]

fill′ĕt, n., & v.t. 1. Head-band, ribbon, string, or narrow band, for binding the hair or worn round head; band, bandage; thin narrow strip of anything; (pl.) animal's loins; fleshy detachable piece of meat near loins or ribs, undercut of sirloin; one of the thick slices into which a fish may be divided; middle part of leg of veal boned, rolled, & tied up; piece of beef, fish, etc., similarly prepared; (Archit.) narrow flat band separating two mouldings, small band between flutes of column; (Her.) horizontal division of shield, quarter of CHIEF¹ in depth; raised rim or ridge on any surface; (Book-bind.) plain line impressed on cover. 2. v.t. Bind (hair, person as to hair) with ~; encircle with ornamental band; divide (fish) into ~s. [ME, f. OF *filet* f. L *filum* thread + -ET¹]

fill′ip, n., & v.t. & i. 1. Sudden release of finger or thumb when it has been bent & checked by thumb or finger; slight smart stroke thus given; stimulus, incentive; mere trifle (*not worth a* ~). 2. vb. Propel (coin, marble, etc.) with a ~, stimulate (~ one's *memory* or *wits*); strike slightly & smartly; make a ~ [prob. imit., cf. FLIP]

fill′ister, n. Rabbeting-plane for window-·sashes etc. [orig. unkn.]

fill′ȳ, n. Female foal (cf. COLT); (sl.) young lively girl. [f. ON *fylja* f. Gmc *fuljón* see FOAL]

film, n., & v.t. & i. 1. Thin skin, plate, coating, or layer· (Photog.) coating of collodion, gelatin, etc., spread on photographic paper or plate, or used instead of plate, celluloid roll used in cinematography, its contents as shown (~-FAN³; ~ *star*, eminent cinema actor or actress; ~ *test*, photographic test of would-be ~ actor; *the* ~*s*, cinema show); dimness over eyes; slight veil of haze etc.; fine thread or filament; hence fil′MY² a., fil′MILY² adv., fil′MINESS n. 2. vb. Cover, become covered, (as) with ~; reproduce (scene etc.) for the cinema; be (well or ill) suited for reproduction on the ~s. [OE *filmen* membrane = OFris. *filmene* skin, cogn. w. FELL¹]

fil′oselle, n. Floss silk. [F, f. It. *filosello* perh. f. Rom. **follicellus* cocoon, dim. of L *follis* bag, influenced by It. *filo* thread]

fils (fēs), n. The son, junior, (appended to name to distinguish between father & son of same names, cf. PÈRE). [F]

fil′ter, n., & v.t. & i. 1. Contrivance for freeing liquids from suspended impurities, esp. by passing them through stratum of sand, charcoal, etc.; (Photog.) screen (usu. of coloured glass or gelatine) for absorbing light of some colours; ~-*bed*, tank or pond with false bottom covered with sand etc. for ~ing large quantities; ~-*tip*, (of cigarettes) having a ~ at the mouth end. 2. vb. Pass (liquid), flow, through ~; (of ~) purify (liquid); make way *through, into*, etc., percolate, (of news etc.) leak *out* or come *through*; join another line of traffic at road junction etc.; obtain by ~ing. [vb f. n., f. F *filtre* f. med. L *filtrum* f. Gmc st. whence FELT¹ (earliest ~ being of felt)]

filth, n. Loathsome dirt; uninviting food, garbage; vileness, pollution, obscenity; foul language. Hence fil′thy² a. (~*y lucre*, dishonourable gain, also joc., money), fil′thILY² adv., fil′thINESS n. [OE *fylth*, OS *fūlitha*, OHG *fūlida* (FOUL¹, -TH¹)]

fil′trate¹, n. Filtered liquor. [FILTER v., -ATE¹(2)]

fil′tr|āte², v.t. & i. = FILTER v. So ~A′TION n. [f. mod. L *filtrare* (as prec., -ATE³)]

fim′briāte, -ātēd, aa. (bot., zool.). Fringed, bordered with hairs etc. [f. L *fimbriatus* f. *fimbriae* fringe; see +-ATE²]

fin, n. Organ for propelling & steering attached to fish & cetaceans at various parts of body (*anal, caudal, dorsal, pectoral, ventral*, etc.); sharp lateral projection on share or coulter of plough; small projecting surface on various parts of aircraft, for ensuring stability; (sl.) hand (*tip us your*~, shake hands). Hence (-)~NED² (-nd), ~′LESS, aa. [OE *finn*, MLG, MDu. *vinne*]

fin′al, a. & n. 1. At the end, coming last, ultimate; putting an end to doubt, conclusive, definitive, unalterable; concerned with the purpose or end aimed at (~ CAUSE¹; ~ *clause* in Gram., introduced

by *in order that, lest*, etc.); hence ~LY² adv. 2. n. Last or deciding heat or game in athletics, whence ~IST n., competitor in this; (sing. or pl.) last of a series of examinations; ǁ (colloq.) edition of newspaper published latest in the day; (Mus.) principal note in any mode. Hence ~IZE v.t., complete, bring to an end. [ME, f. OF, or L *finalis* (*finis* end, -AL)].

fina′lè (-nah-), n. (Mus.) last movement of instrumental composition, piece of music closing act in opera; close of drama etc.; conclusion, final catastrophe. [It., as prec.]

finăl′itÿ, n. Principle of final cause viewed as operative in the universe; being final; belief that something is final; final act, state, or utterance. [F (-té), f. LL *finalitatem* (FINAL, -TY)]

finance′, n., & v.t. & i. 1. (Pl.) pecuniary resources of sovereign, State, company, or person; management of (esp. public) money, science of revenue. 2. vb. Furnish with ~s, find capital for; engage in financial operations. [ME, f. OF (*finer* settle debt f. *fin* end; -ANCE)]

finăn′cial (-shl), a. Of revenue or money matters (~ *year*, annual period for which public accounts are made up). Hence ~LY² (-sha-) adv. [prec.+-IAL]

finăn′cier¹ (*also* finanser̄′), n. One skilled in levying & managing public money; capitalist. [F (FINANCE, -IER)]

financier′² (-sēr), v.i. & t. Conduct financial operations (usu. contempt.); *cheat, swindle, (~ money away; ~ one out of). [f. prec.]

finch, n. Kinds of small bird (usu. with distinctive epithet or prefix, as *mountain* ~, BULL¹~). [OE *finc*, OHG *fincho* f. WG *finkiz*, *finkjon*]

find, v.t. (*found*), & n. 1. Come across, fall in with, light upon, (*was found dead; we* ~ *St John saying; administer the law as you* ~ *it; found a treasure*): obtain, receive, (~ *favour, mercy,* one's ACCOUNT² *in*; ~ one's *feet*, get the use of them, develop one's powers); recognize as present, acknowledge or discover to be so-&-so, (*I* ~ *no sense in it*, ~ *the terms reasonable; how do you* ~ *yourself?; must take us as you* ~ *us*, put up with us as we are); discover by trial to be or do or (*that*) or to (*has been found wanting*; ~*s rest agreeable; is found to pay; I* ~ *it pays, pay*, or *to pay*, or *that it pays*; ~ *it impossible, necessary, to* —); discover by search; discover (game), discover game, in hunting; ~ *oneself*, discover one's vocation, & see below; succeed in obtaining (money, bail, sureties; *can't* ~ *time to read; found courage to* —; *could* ~ *it in my heart to* —, am inclined; ~ *expression, place, vent*); come home to, reach the conscience of; ascertain by study or calculation or inquiry (~ one's *way to*, contrive to reach, arrive at); (Law) determine & declare (*it*, i.e. the

offence, *murder*; person *guilty* etc.; *that*
—; ~ *true* BILL[3]), whence ~'ING[1](2) n.;
supply, provide, furnish, (*they found him
in clothes*; *hotel does not* ~ *tea*; *all found*,
with all necessaries provided, of servants'
wages; ~ one*self*, provide for one's own
needs, & see above); ~ *out*, discover,
devise, solve, detect in offence; hence
~'ABLE a. 2. n. ~ing of fox; discovery of
treasure, minerals, etc.; *sure* ~, place
where something (esp. fox) is sure to be
found. [OE, OS, OHG *findan*, ON *finna*,
Goth. *finthan*, Gmc *finthan*]

fin'der, n. In vbl senses; esp.: small
telescope attached to large one to find
object; contrivance for same purpose in
microscope & in photographic camera.
[-ER[1]]

fin de siècle (see Ap.), a. Characteristic
of end of nineteenth century, advanced,
modern; decadent. [F, = end of century]

fine[1], n., & v.i. & t. 1. End (now only in *in*
~, to sum up, finally, in short); ‖ sum
of money paid by in-coming tenant in
consideration of small rent; sum of money
fixed as penalty for offence. 2. vb. Pay consideration *for* privilege or appointment;
punish by a ~, whence fin'ABLE-a. [ME
& OF *fin* settlement of dispute f. L *finem*,
nom. *finis* end]

fine[2], a., n., adv., & v.t. & i. 1. Of high
quality; clear, pure, refined, (of gold or
silver) containing specified proportion
of pure metal, as *gold 22 carats* ~, *silver
11 oz* ~; delicate, subtle, exquisitely
fashioned, (of feelings) elevated; of
slender thread, in small particles, thin
(~ *pencil*, of hard lead for making ~
lines); sharp (~ *pen*, narrow-pointed);
(Athlet.) reduced to perfect condition;
capable of delicate perception or discrimination, perceptible only with difficulty (*a* ~ *distinction*); excellent, of
striking merit, good, satisfactory, fortunate, of good effect, (*had* ~ *sport*; *has
been a* ~ *thing for him*; often iron., as *a* ~
friend you have been!); well conceived or
expressed; of handsome appearance or
size, dignified, (~ *potatoes*; *a man of* ~
presence); free from precipitation or thick
fog & with some sunshine, (~ *weather*;
one ~ *day*, once upon a time; *one of these*
~ *days*, some day, in prophecies); ornate,
showy, smart, (~ *feathers*, gaudy plumage, lit. & fig., as ~ *feathers make* ~ *birds*);
fastidious, dainty, affecting refinement,
(of speech or writing) affectedly ornate;
complimentary, euphemistic, (*say* ~
things about person, *call things by* ~
names); ~ *arts*, those appealing to sense
of beauty, as poetry, music, & esp.
painting, sculpture, architecture; ~
chemicals, produced or used in small
quantities and in a state of comparative
purity (i.e. other than heavy chemicals,
dyestuffs, cellulose or sugar products,
etc.); ~*draw*, sew together (two pieces of
cloth, rent, garment) so that the join is

imperceptible; ~*drawn*, subtle, extremely thin, (Athlet.) trained down in
weight; ~ *gentleman*, *lady*, person of
fashion, person who thinks himself above
working; ~*spun*, delicate, flimsy, (of
theories etc.) excessively subtle, unpractical; hence fin'ISH[1](2) a., ~'LY[2]
(-nl-) adv., ~'NESS (-n-n-) n. 2. n. ~
weather (*in rain or* ~). 3. adv. ~ly (*talk
~*). 4. vb. Make (beer) clear (often *down*);
(of liquid) become clear; ~ *away*, *down*,
off, make or become ~r, thinner, less
coarse, (make) dwindle, taper. [ME, f.
OF *fin* f. Rom. *finus*, deduced f. *finire*
FINISH after *grossus*, *grossire* (GROSS)]

fine champagne (see Ap.), n. Liqueur
brandy. [F]

fin'ery[1], n. Smartness, stylishness, (rare);
showy dress or decoration. [FINE[2] adj.,
-ERY]

fin'ery[2], n. Hearth where cast iron is
made malleable or steel made from pig-
iron. [f. F *finerie* f. *finer* refine (FINE[2]4)]

finĕsse', n., & v.i. & t. 1. Delicate manipulation, subtle discrimination; artfulness,
cunning strategy; (Cards) attempt to
take trick by inferior card, with higher
one in reserve. 2. vb. Use ~; wheedle
into, trick *away*, manage by ~; (Cards)
make a ~, play (card) by way of ~. [F
(FINE[2], -ESS[2])]

fing'er (-ngg-), n., & v.t. 1. One of five
terminal members of hand (*thumb*, &
fore, *middle*, *ring*, & *little* ~s), or four
excluding thumb (usu. now numbered
thus, but cf. *fourth* ~, i.e. ring ~, in
marriage service), (*done by the* ~, i.e.
agency, *of God*; *more wit in his little* ~
than in your whole body; *lay*, *put*, *a* ~
upon, touch however slightly; *lay*, *put*,
one's ~ *on* ailing part or cause of evil,
point with precision to; *look through* one's
~*s at*, pretend not to see; *lift*, *stir*, *a* ~,
make the least effort; *turn* or *twist* person
round one's (*little*) ~, cajole him; *my* ~*s
itch*, I long, am impatient, *to do*; *his* ~*s are
all thumbs*, he is clumsy; *with a wet* ~, with
ease; BURN[2] one's ~*s*; CROSS[2] one's ~*s*;
have a ~ *in the pie*, take part in a matter;
let slip through one's ~*s*, lose hold of;
have at one's ~*tips* or ~*ends*, be versed
in, know familiarly; *to the* ~*nails*, completely); part of glove that holds ~; ~
like object, esp. such part of a fruit etc.,
& in various machines; ~*alphabet*,
language, conventional signs for talking
with the deaf; ~*bowl*, *glass*, for rinsing
~s after dessert; ~*fern*, kind of spleen-
wort; ~*fish*, starfish; ~*plate*, fastened
on door to prevent ~*marks*; ~*post*,
giving directions at parting of roads;
~*print*, impression of person's ~, used
for identifying criminals etc.; ~*stall*,
cover of leather or rubber to protect ~
in dissections etc. or when wounded;
hence ~LESS, (-)~ED[2] (-nggerd), aa. 2. v.t.
Touch with, turn about in, the ~s; take
(bribes etc.); play upon (instrument) with

the ~s, play (passage) with ~s used in particular way, mark (music) with signs showing which ~s are to be used, whence ~ing[1] (-ngg-) [-ING[1]] n. [OE *finger*, OS, OHG *-ar*, ON *fingr*, Goth. *figgrs* f. Gmc *fingraz*]

fing'ering[2] (-ngg-), n. (for *fingering*[1] see prec.). Wool for stockings. [17th c. *fingram*, perh. f. F *fin grain*, as GROGRAM f. *gros grain*]

‖ fing'erling (-ngg-), n. Parr. [FINGER n., -LING[1]]

fin'ial, n. (archit.). Ornament finishing off apex of roof, pediment, gable, tower--corner, canopy, etc. [14th c., var. of FINAL]

fin'ical, a. Over-nice, precise, fastidious; too much finished in details. Hence ~LY[2] adv., ~NESS, ~ITY (-ǎl[2]), nn. [perh. f. FINE[2], or var. of foll.]

fin'icking, fin'ikin, a. = prec. [perh. f. MDu. *fijnkens* accurately, neatly; rel. to prec. undetermined]

fin'is, n. (no. pl.). (At end of book) the end; end of anything, esp. of life. [L]

fin'ish, v.t. & i., & n. 1. Bring to an end, come to the end of (often ~ *doing*; ~ *off*, provide with an ending, complete; consume, get through, the whole or remainder of (food, book); kill, dispatch, overcome completely; perfect, put final or ~*ing* touches to, (~*ed manners, gentleman*; also with *off, up*); complete education of; (v.i.) reach the end, cease, leave *off*; have done *with*; end in something or *by doing*. 2. n. Last stage, termination, esp. of a fox-hunt (*be in at the* ~, often fig.); *fight to a* ~, till one party is completely worsted; what serves to give completeness; accomplished or completed state; mode of ~*ing* (esp. furniture, as *mahogany* ~). [ME *fenys* etc. f. OF *fenir* f. L *finire* (*finis* end), -ISH[2]]

fin'isher, n. In vbl senses; esp.: workman or machine doing last operation in manufacture; discomfiting thing, crushing blow, etc. [-ER[1]]

fin'ite, a. Bounded, limited, not infinite; (Gram.) limited by number and person, not infinitive. Hence ~NESS (-tn-) n. [f. L *finitus* p.p. of *finire* FINISH]

Fin(n), n. One of N.-Eastern European people who call their country *Suomi*. [OE *Finnas*, ON *Finnr*, L *Fenni*, Gk *Phinnoi*]

finn'an, n. (Also ~ *haddock*) haddock cured with smoke of green wood, turf, or peat. [f. *Findhorn* or *Findon*, Scotland]

finn'er, n. Kinds of whale, esp. rorqual, having dorsal fin. [-ER[1]]

Finn'ic, a. Of the group of peoples allied to the Finns; Finnish. [-IC]

Finn'ish, a. & n. (Language) of the Finns; Finnic. [-ISH[1]]

Finn'ō-Ug'ric (-ōog-), a. & n. (Belonging to) family of Ural-Altaic languages including Finnish, Estonian, Lapp, & Hungarian. So Finn'ō-Ug'rian (-ōog-) a. [UGRIAN]

finn'y, a. Having fins; like a fin; of, teeming with, fish. [FIN + -Y[2]]

fiord, fjord, (fy-), n. Long narrow arm of sea between high cliffs as in Norway. [Norw., ON *fjorthr*; see FIRTH]

fi'orin, n. Kind of grass. [f. Ir. *fiorthdn*]

fir, n. (Also ~*tree*) kinds of coniferous tree with needles placed singly on the shoots (*Scotch, silver, spruce,* ~); their wood; ~*-apple, -ball, -cone*, fruit of ~; ~*-needle*, its leaf. Hence ~r'y[2] a. [ME *firr(e)* f. OE **fyre* or ON *fyri*- f. Gmc **furhjōn-*]

fire, 1. Active principle operative in combustion, flame, incandescence, (*set* ~ *to*, kindle; *strike* ~, elicit sparks by friction or blow; *no smoke without* ~, always some ground for rumour). 2. State of combustion (*on* ~, burning, fig. excited; *set on* ~, ignite, excite; *set the Thames on* ~, do something remarkable; *catch, take,* ~, be ignited). 3. Burning fuel in grate, furnace, etc. (*heap* COALS *of* ~; *burnt child dreads the* ~; *out of the* FRYING-*pan into the* ~; FAT *is in the* ~), whence fir'ING[1](3) n. 4. Conflagration, destructive burning, (~*!*, call for aid at a ~; *pour oil on* ~, add to excitement; *go through* ~ *& water*, face all perils; ~ *& sword*, burning & slaughter); *Greek* ~ (hist.), combustible composition for igniting enemy's ships etc. 5. Luminosity, glow, (*St Elmo's* ~, corposant); burning heat, fever, *St Anthony's* ~, erysipelas. 6. Vehement emotion, fervour, spirit, lively imagination, vivacity, poetic inspiration. 7. Firing of guns (*open, cease,* ~; *running* ~, successive shots from line of troops etc., esp. fig. of criticism, objections, etc.; *between two* ~s, shot at from two directions; *line of* ~, path of bullet about to be shot; *under* ~, being shot at; HANG, MISS[2], ~). 8. ~*-alarm*, automatic arrangement for giving notice of ~; ~*-arm* (usu. pl.), rifle, gun, pistol, etc.; ~*-back*, Sumatran pheasant; ~*-ball*, large meteor, globular lightning, (Mil.) ball filled with combustibles (hist.); ~*-balloon*, made buoyant by heat of combustible burning at its mouth; ~*-bird*, kind of bee-eater; ~*-blast*, disease of plants; ~*-blight*, disease of hops; ~*-bomb*, incendiary; ~*-box*, fuel-chamber of steam-boiler; ~*-brand*, piece of burning wood, person or thing kindling strife; ~*-brick* (proof against ~, used in grates etc.); ‖ ~*-brigade*, organized body of ~*men*; *~*-bug* (colloq.), incendiary, pyromaniac; ~*-clay* (kind used for ~*-bricks*); ~*-control*, system of regulating ~ of ship's or fort's guns; ~*-crest*, very small bird akin to wren; ~*-cross*, = *fiery* CROSS[1]; ~*-damp*, miner's name for carburetted hydrogen, explosive when mixed in certain proportion with air; ~*-dog*, andiron; ~*-drake*, meteor, fiery dragon (in German myth.); ~*-eater*, juggler who eats fire, great fighter, duellist; ~*-engine*,

machine for throwing water to extinguish
~s ; ~*escape*, apparatus for saving people
in burning house ; ~*-eyed* (poet.), with
glowing eyes ; ‖ ~*-flair*, a fish, the sting-
-ray ; ~*-fly*, winged insect emitting phosphorescent light ; ‖ ~*-guard*, protective
frame or grating in front of ~ in room,
(also) = ~*-watcher* ; ~*-hose*, hose-pipe for
extinguishing ~s ; ~*-insurance*, against
losses by ~ ; ~*-irons*, tongs, poker, &
shovel ; ~*-light*, light from ~*-place* ; ~-
-lighter, prepared kindling-fuel ; ~'*lock*,
antiquated musket in which priming was
ignited by sparks ; ~'*man*, tender of
furnace or steam-engine ~, **man** employed
to extinguish ~s ; ~*-new* (arch.), = brand-
-new ; ‖ ~*-office*, insuring against ~ ; ~-
-opal, kind of opal with internal flame-
-coloured reflections, GIRASOLE ; ‖ ~*-pan*,
brazier ; ~*-place*, grate or hearth for
room-~ ; ~*-plug* (abbr. F.P.), connexion
in water-main for ~*-hose* ; ~*-policy*, ~-
-insurance office's certificate guarantee-
ing compensation in case of ~ ; ~*-raising*,
arson ; ~*-screen*, to keep off heat of ~ ;
~*-ship* (hist.), freighted with combustibles
and sent adrift to ignite enemy's ships
etc. ; ~*-side*, space round ~*-place*, home
life (*~*side chat*, radio talk by President
to the nation) ; ~*-step*, = firing-step
(FIRE²) ; ~*-stone*, kind that resists ~, used
for furnaces etc. ; ~*-teazer*, stoker ; ~*-trap*,
building without proper exits in case of
~ ; ~*-walking*, (religious) ceremony of
walking barefoot over white-hot stones,
wood-ashes, etc. ; ~*-watcher*, person keeping watch for ~s esp. those caused by
~*-bombs* ; ~*-water*, ardent spirits ; ~'-
wood, wood prepared for fuel ; ~'*work*,
kinds of apparatus giving spectacular
effects by use of combustibles etc.,
squib, rocket, etc., (fig., pl.) display of wit,
passion, etc. ; ~*-worship*, treatment of ~
as a deity. Hence ~'PROOF (-ĭrp-), ~'LESS
(-ĭrl-), aa. [OE *fÿr*, OS, OHG *fiur*, f. WG
fûir, cogn. w. Gk *pur*]

fire², v.t. & i. Set fire to with intention
of destroying ; kindle (explosives) ; (fig.)
stimulate (the imagination), fill (person)
with enthusiasm ; (of explosives, mines)
catch fire ; become heated or excited (~
up, show sudden anger) ; redden (t. & i.) ;
bake (pottery, bricks), cure (tea, tobacco)
by artificial heat ; (Farriery) cauterize ;
supply (furnace, engine) with fuel ; cause
(explosive, gun) to explode (often *off* ; ~
salute, discharge number of guns as salute ;
~ *broadside*, discharge all guns on one
side of ship), (abs.) shoot, discharge gun
etc. (*at*, *into*, *on*, *upon*), (fig.) ~ *away*, begin, go ahead ; (of gun etc.) go off ; propel
(missile) from gun etc. (fig. ~ *off a postcard*, *a remark*) ; *~ out* or ~, expel,
dismiss, reject, (person) ; *firing-party*,
-squad, squad detailed to ~ volleys at a
military funeral or carry out a military
execution ; *firing-step* (on which soldier in
trench stands to ~). [f. prec.]

fir′er, n. In vbl senses ; esp. *single* etc. ~,
gun that fires once etc. without reloading.
[-ER¹]

firkin, n. Small cask for liquids, butter,
fish, etc. ; (as measure) half of kilderkin.
[15th c. *ferdekyn* prob. f. MDu (*vierde*
fourth, -KIN)]

firm¹, n. Partners carrying on business
(‖ *long* ~, set of swindlers who obtain
goods & do not pay). [in 16th, 18th c.
signature, style, f. Sp. & It. f. Rom. **firma*
(L *firmare* confirm) ; cf. FARM¹]

firm², a., adv., & v.t. & i. **1.** Of solid or
compact structure ; fixed, stable ; steady,
not shaking ; established, immutable, (of
offer etc.) not liable to cancellation after
acceptance ; steadfast, unflinching, resolute ; constant *to* ; (Commerc., of prices,
goods) maintaining their level or value ;
hence ~'LY² adv., ~'NESS n. **2.** adv. ~ly
(*stand* ~, *hold* ~ *to*). **3.** vb. Solidify (t. &
i.), compact, (soil after planting etc.,
cheese) ; fix ~ly (plants in soil). [ME, f.
OF *ferme* f. L *firmus*]

firm′ament, n. Vault of heaven with its
clouds & stars. Hence ~AL (-ĕn⁴) a. [ME,
in med. L senses of L *firmamentum* (*firmare*
as prec., -MENT)]

firm′an, n. Oriental sovereign's edict,
grant, licence, passport. [f. Pers. *ferman*]

first, a., n., & adv. **1.** Earliest in time or
order (*at* ~ *sight*, *view*, or *blush*, prima
facie ; *F*~ CAUSE¹ ; *come in* ~, win race ;
shall do it ~ *thing*, colloq., before anything
else ; *in the* ~ *place*, to begin with ; *the two
etc.* ~, *the* ~ *two* etc., lit., or = the ~ &
second etc. ; often further defined, as *the
~ man you meet*, *was the* ~ *to do it*) ; foremost in position, rank, or importance
(*head* etc. ~, with the head etc. in front ;
the ~ *men in the country* ; ‖ *F*~ *Lord of the
TREASURY* ; ‖ *F*~ *Lord of the Admiralty*,
parliamentary chief of Navy ; ‖ *F*~ *Sea
Lord*, professional chief of Navy) ; coming
next after a specified or implied time
(*shall take the* ~ *train* ; *the* ~ *cuckoo*) ; (with
the) even one (*he doesn't know the* ~ *thing
about it*) ; unsupported by others, sufficient by itself, (*obeyed at her* ~ *word*) ; basic
or self-evident (~ *principles*). **2.** ~ *aid*,
help given to hurt person before doctor
comes ; ~*-born*, eldest (child) ; ~*-CHOP⁵* ;
~ *class*, set of persons or things grouped
together as better than others, ‖ *best*
accommodation in railway train etc.,
‖ highest division in examination list,
place in this ; ~*-class*, (adj.) belonging to
the ~ class, of best quality, very good,
(adv.) ‖ by the ~ class (*travels* ~*-class*) ;
~ *coat*, ~ layer of paint ; ~ *cost*, cost
not including profit ; ~*-day*, Sunday ; ~
floor, ‖ the one above ground-floor,
**ground-floor ; ‖ ~*-foot* (Sc.), ~ person to
cross threshold in the New Year (also as
vb) ; ~ *form*, lowest class in schools ; ~-
-fruit (usu. pl.), ~ products of agriculture
for the season esp. as offered to God, ~
results of work etc., (hist.) payment to

some superior by new holder of office; ~-
-hand, direct,without intermediate agency
(at ~ hand, directly); ~ name, Christian
name; ~-night(er), (habitual frequenter
of) ~ performance of plays; ~-offender
(against whom no previous conviction is
recorded); ~-rate, of the highest class (the
~-rate Powers, great States of ~-rate
importance), excellent, very well, (a ~-
-rate machine, feeling~-rate), (as n., Naut.)
line-of-battleship of the old type, three-
-decker (hist.); ~ violin, one of the players
taking the uppermost string part in
orchestral music, the leader of such
players, the leader of a string quartet.
3. n. The~, person or thing~mentioned;
from the~, from the beginning; from~ to
last, throughout; at~, at the beginning;
~ ~ day of June etc.; || the F~ of (Sep-
tember, when partridge-shooting begins);
(Commerc.) ~ of exchange, ~ of set of bills
of even tenor & date; place in ~ class in
examination, person who takes this; ~
place in race, winner of it; (pl.) best quality
of flour, butter, etc. **4.** adv. Before anyone or anything else (often ~ of all, ~ &
foremost; ~ come ~ served; ~ & last, taking one thing with another, on the whole;
~ or last, sooner or later); before some
specified or implied event, time, etc.
(must get this done ~); in preference,
rather, (will see him damned ~); for the
~ time (when did you see him ~?). [OE
fyrst, OS, OHG furist, ON fyrstr f. Gmc
*furist-, superl. f. *fur-, *for-; see FORE,
FORMER, etc.]

first'ling, n. (usu. pl.). First result of
anything, first-fruits; first offspring, first
born of season. [-LING¹]

first'ly, adv. In the first place, first, (only
in enumerating topics; & many writers
still prefer first). [-LY²]

firth, frith, n. Arm of sea; estuary. [15 c.
Sc., f. ON fjǫrthr FJORD]

fisc, fisk, n. Treasury of ancient Rome,
Roman emperor's privy-purse; (rare)
State treasury, exchequer. [f. L fiscus]

fis'cal, a. & n. **1.** Of public revenue (*~
year, financial year). **2.** n. Legal official
in some foreign countries; (Sc.) = PRO-
CURATOR~. Hence ~LY² adv. [f. F, or L
fiscalis (prec., -AL)]

fish¹, n. (pl. often fish). **1.** (Pop.) animal
living in the water, (strictly) vertebrate
cold-blooded animal having gills throughout life & limbs (if any) modified into
fins, (pretty kettle of ~, confusion, muddle;
~ out of water, person out of his element;
drunk, dull, mute, as a ~; drink like a ~,
excessively; feed the ~es, be drowned, be
seasick; all 's ~ that comes to his net, he
takes all he can get; there 's as good ~
in the sea as ever came out of it, no fear
of scarcity; FLAT, FLYING, GOLD, JELLY,
SHELL¹, SUN, SWORD, etc., ~); person
who is angled for; (colloq.) person of
specified kind (cool, loose, queer, etc., ~);
the flesh of ~ (~, flesh, & fowl; neither ~,

flesh, nor good red herring, thing of indefinite character; other ~ to fry, more important business to attend to); the F~ or
F~es, zodiac constellation. **2.** ~-carver,
knife for serving ~; ~-globe, for keeping
gold~ etc. in; ~-glue, isinglass; ~-hook,
used for catching ~, (Naut.) part of
anchor-raising tackle; ~-kettle, oval pan
for boiling ~; ~-knife, of silver etc. for
eating ~; ~-monger, dealer in ~; ~-pond,
in which ~ are kept, (joc.) the sea; ~-pot,
wicker trap for eels, lobsters, etc.; ~-slice,
carving-knife for ~, cook's implement for
turning or taking out ~; ~-sound, ~'s
swimming-bladder; ~-tail, shaped like
~'s tail (of jet of gas, whence ~-tail
burner), ~-tail wind in rifle shooting,
one blowing down range & varying in
direction; ~-torpedo shaped like ~ & with
automatic propulsion; ~'wife, woman
selling ~. Hence ~'LET, || ~'MONGER, nn.
[OE fisc, OS, OHG fisk, ON fiskr, Goth.
fisks f. Gmc *fiskaz cogn. w. L piscis]

fish², v.i. & t. Try to catch fish (~ in
troubled waters, make one's profit out
of disturbances), whence ~'ERY(2, 3) n.;
search for something in or under water;
seek by indirect means for (secrets, compliments, etc.), whence ~'ING² a.; (rare)
try to catch (fish) or get (coral etc.) from
below water; draw out of water, pocket,
etc., draw out; (Naut.) ~ the anchor, draw
flukes up to gunwale; try to catch fish in
(pool etc.; ~ out, exhaust the fish in),
whence ~'ABLE a.; get (fact, opinion,
secret) out; ~ing-rod, long tapering usu.
jointed rod to which~ing-line is attached.
[OE fiscian f. Gmc *fiskōjan (prec.)]

fish³, n., & v.t. **1.** (Naut.) piece of wood,
convex & concave, used to strengthen
mast etc.; flat plate of iron, wood, etc.
strengthening beam or joint (so ~-plate,
one of two holding rails together). **2.** v.t.
Mend or strengthen (spar etc.), join (rails)
with~. [(n. f. vb) 17th c. f. F ficher fix f.
Rom. *figicare f. L figere]

fish⁴, n. Piece of ivory etc. used as counter
in games. [f. F fiche f. ficher (prec.)]

fish'er, n. Fisherman (arch.; ~ of men,
evangelist, see Matt. iv. 19); fishing
animal; ~-man, man who lives by fishing,
angler, fishing-boat. [OE fiscere (FISH¹,
-ER¹)]

fish'y, a. Abounding in fish; like fish's
(~y eye, dull, vacant-looking); smelling or
tasting like fish; consisting of fish (a ~y
repast); (sl.) of dubious character, questionable. Hence ~ILY² adv., ~INESS n.
[-Y²]

fisk. See FISC.

fissi-, fisso-, comb. forms of L fissus see
FISSURE, as fissidac'tyl with digits divided,
fissip'arous reproducing by fission.

fiss'ile, a. Cleavable, tending to split.
Hence fissil'ITY n. [f. L fissilis (FISSURE,
-IL)]

fi'ssion (-shn), n. **1.** (biol.). Division of
cell etc. into new cells etc. as mode of

reproduction. 2. (phys.). Splitting of atomic nuclei (~ *bomb*, atom bomb). Hence ~ABLE (-sho-) a. [f. L *fissio* (foll., -ION)]

fi′ssure (-sher), n., & v.t. & i. Cleft made by splitting or separation of parts; (Bot., Anat.) narrow opening in organ etc., esp. depression between convolutions of brain; cleavage; (vb) split (t. & i.). [ME, f. OF, or L *fissura* (*findere fiss-* cleave, -URE)]

fist, n., & v.t. **1.** Clenched hand, esp. as used in boxing (~ *law*, the right of the strongest); (joc.) hand (*give us your* ~, shake hands); handwriting (*writes a good* ~; *I know his* ~); HAND¹ *over* ~. **2.** v.t. Strike with ~; (Naut.) handle (sail, oar, etc.). Hence ~′ED² a. [OE *fȳst*, MLG, OHG *fūst* f. WG **fūsti*]

fis′tic(al), aa. (joc.) Pugilistic. [-ICAL]

fis′ticuffs, n. pl. Fighting with the fists. [c. 1600, f. *fisty* + CUFF²]

fis′tul∣a, n. Long pipe-like ulcer with narrow mouth; natural pipe or spout in whales, insects, etc. Hence ~AR¹, ~OUS, aa. [L *fistula* pipe, flut♂; earlier *fystel* etc. f. OF]

fit¹, **fytte**, n. (arch.). Section of a poem. [OE *fitt*, orig. unkn.]

fit², n. Paroxysm of periodic ailment, sudden transitory attack of some illness; sudden seizure, with loss of consciousness or convulsions, of hysteria, apoplexy, fainting, paralysis, or epilepsy (*give one a* ~, surprise or outrage him; *beat one into*, *give one*, ~s, defeat him easily); sudden transitory state (*a* ~ *of energy*, *idleness*, *devotion*, *indifference*, etc., whence ~′FUL a., ~′fully² adv., ~′fulNESS n.; *by* ~s (*& starts*), spasmodically); caprice, mood, (*when the* ~ *was on him*). [ME *fit* position of danger, perh. = OE *fitt* (once)? conflict; orig. unkn.]

fit³, a. (-tt-). Well adapted or suited (*for* some purpose or status or *to* do or be; SURVIVAL *of the* ~*test*); good enough *for* (*a dinner* ~ *for a king*); becoming, proper, right, (*it is* ~ *that*; *see or think* ~ *to*, decide to); qualified, competent, worthy, *to* do (*not* ~ *to hold a* CANDLE *to*); in suitable condition, ready, *to* do or *for* (also vulg. as adv., *crying* ~ *to burst himself*); angry, troubled, or exhausted enough *to* (do something violent, sink to the ground, etc.); in good athletic condition or health (~ *as a* FIDDLE). Hence ~′LY² adv. [c. 1440, of unkn. orig.]

fit⁴, v.t. & i. (-tt-), & n. **1.** Be in harmony with, become, befit; be of right measure, shape, & size for (esp. of dress; often abs., *as the* CAP¹ ~*s*); fill up, exactly correspond to, (receptacle, fellow, etc., or abs.; often *in*, *into*, *in with*), make to do this; make suitable, adapt, *for*, to with n. or inf.; make competent *for* or *to*; ~ *on*, try on (garment); supply, furnish, (ship etc., rarely person) *with*; ~ *out*, *up*, equip; hence ~′tER¹ n., esp.: (Tailoring and Dressmaking) one who supervises cut-

ting, ~ting, altering, etc., of garments; mechanic who ~s (up) all kinds of machinery. **2.** n. Adaptation, adjustment, style in which garment ~s (*a tight*, *bad*, *excellent*, ~); ~*out*, equipment. [16th c., perh. f. prec.]

fitch, n. (Brush made of) polecat's hair. [16th c. = polecat, f. foll. or its MDu. source]

fitch′ew (-ōo), n. Foumart, polecat. [14th c., f. OF *fichau*, also *fissel*, f. MDu. *fisse*, *vitche*]

fit′ment, n. Piece of fixed furniture. [FIT⁴, -MENT]

fit′ness, n. Being fit; moral worthiness; propriety (*the* ~ *of things*, what is right or appropriate). [-NESS]

fitt′ing¹, n. In vbl senses; esp.: (usu. pl.) fixture(s), apparatus, furniture; (Engin.) ~*shop*, place where parts are put together. [-ING¹]

fitt′ing², a. In vbl senses; esp. becoming, proper, right, whence ~LY² adv. [-ING²]

fit′up, n. (Theatr. colloq.). Temporary or portable stage and stage-fittings; ~ (*company*), minor travelling theatrical troupe carrying makeshift scenery. [FIT⁴]

five, a. & n. One more than four, 5, v, V, (*twenty*-~, ~-*&*-*twenty*; ~ *o'clock*; *How old are you?*—*F*~); the number ~ (*twice* ~ *is ten*); set of ~ things; card, die, or domino with ~ pips; (also fiv′ER¹ n.) hit at cricket for ~ runs, ‖ £5 note; *bunch of* ~s, hand; (pl.) gloves, shoes, etc., of fifth size; (pl.) the ~-per-cents (colloq.); ~-*day week* (having ~ working days); ~-*finger exercise*, on piano for exercising all fingers, keeping them on same ~ notes all the time; ~-*finger*, kinds of plant (as cinquefoil, oxlip), also starfish; ‖ ~-*line(d) whip*, urgent summons to attend in House of Parliament (now disused); ~-*o'clock tea*, light afternoon meal; ~′*penny* (also pr. fîp-), costing, rated at, 5*d*; ‖ ~-*per-cents*, stock or shares paying 5%; ~-*year plan* (for the economic development of Russia in 5 years, inaugurated in 1928, later of other countries & repeated in Russia). Hence ~′FOLD (-vf-) a. & adv. [OE, OS *fíf*, OHG *fimf*, ON *fimm*, Goth. *fimf* f. Gmc **fimfi* cogn. w. L *quinque*, Gk *pente*]

fives (-vz), n. Ball-game played with hands or bat in court with two, three, or four walls. [pl. of *five* used as sing.; significance unknown]

fix¹, v.t. & i. Make firm or stable, fasten, secure, implant (principles, memory, etc.) (*in*, *on*, *to*, etc.); direct steadily, set, (eyes, gaze, affection, attention) *on* or *upon*; (of object) attract & hold (attention, eyes, etc.); make (eyes, features), or become, rigid; deprive of, lose volatility or fluidity, congeal (t. & i.); make (colour, photographic image) fast, whence ~′ER¹(2) n.; single out (person) *with* one's eyes etc.; place definitely or permanently, station, establish; take up one's position; settle one's choice, decide, (*up*)*on*; assign precise position of; refer (thing, person) to definite place or time; determine incidence of (liability etc.); settle, determine, specify, (price, date, place); arrest changes or development in (language, literature); mend, repair; *(freq. *up*)* arrange, organize, prepare; ~*ed focus* (Photog.), best position of lens for general snapshot work. [ME; ult. f. L *fixus* p.p. of *figere* fix; partly thr. obs. *fix* a. (OF *fix*), & med. L *fixare*]

fix², n. Dilemma, position hard to escape from; finding position, position found, by bearings or astronomical observations (*radio* ~, position of aircraft, ship, etc., found by radio). [f. prec.]

fixā′tion, n. Fixing, being fixed; process of rendering solid, coagulation; process of combining a gas with a solid; (Psycho-anal.) arrested mental development. [f. med. L *fixatio* (*fixare* see FIX¹, -ATION)]

fix′ative, a. & n. Tending to fix; (n.) substance used to fix colours or drawings. [-ATIVE]

fix′ature, n. Gummy preparation for fixing the hair. [as prec., -URE]

fixed (-kst), a. In vbl senses, esp.; ~ *idea*, one tending to become a monomania; ~ *acid* or *oil*, one not evaporable without decomposition; ~ *point*, where policeman is permanently stationed; ~ *star*, one seeming to keep same relative position to others (opp. *planet*); ~ CAPITAL²; ~ *property*, land & houses. [-ED¹]

fix′edly̆, adv. In fixed manner; esp. (of looking) intently. [-LY²]

fix′edness, n. Fixed state, immobility, permanence, steadfastness. [-NESS]

*****fix′ings** (-z), n. pl. Apparatus, equipment; trimming of dress or dish, adjuncts. [-ING¹]

fix′ity̆, n. Fixed state; (Phys.) property of enduring heat without being volatilized or losing weight; stability, permanence. [f. L *fixus* see FIX¹ + -ITY]

fix′ture, n. Thing fixed or fastened in position; (Law; pl.) articles of a personal nature annexed to house or land; person or thing confined to or established in one place (chiefly in pred., as *seems to be a*~); (Athlet. etc.) (date appointed for) meet, race, etc. [changed f. obs. *fixure* f. LL *fixura* (*figere fix-*, -URE)]

fiz′gig (-g-), n. & a. Giddy flirtatious young woman; kind of small firework, cracker; (adj.) flighty. [prob. f. FIZZ + *gig* (obs. = flighty girl)]

fizz, v.i., & n. (Make) hissing or spluttering sound, whence ~′y² a.; (sl.) champagne. [imit.]

fiz′zle, v.i., & n. Hiss or splutter feebly (n., this sound); ~ *out*, come to lame conclusion; (n.) fiasco. [f. as prec. + -LE(3)]

flăbb′ergast (-gah-), v.t. Dumbfound, so astonish as to incapacitate. [from 1722; perh. f. *flabby*, *aghast*]

flăbb′|y̆, a. Hanging down, flaccid, limp, (usu. of flesh); nerveless, feeble, (of language or character). Hence ~ĭNESS n. [alt. f. earlier *flappy* (FLAP, -Y²)]

flabĕll′ate, flabĕll′iform, aa. (bot. & zool.). Fan-shaped. [f. L *flabellum* fan (*flare* blow) + -ATE², -FORM]

flăc′cid (-ks-), a. Hanging loose or wrinkled, limp, flabby, (usu. of flesh); relaxed, drooping; wanting vigour, feeble. Hence flăccid′ity n. [f. F *flaccide* or L *flaccidus* (*flaccus* flabby)]

flăg¹, n. Kinds of plant with bladed leaf growing on moist ground, esp. various species of iris; ~s or ~ collect., kinds of coarse grass; long slender blade of a plant. Hence ~g′y³ (-g-) a. [ME; cf. Du. *vlag*, Da. *flæg*]

flăg², n., & v.t. (-gg-). (Also ~*stone*) flat slab of rock for paving, (pl.) pavement made of these, also ~g′ING¹(6) (-g-) n.; (vb) pave with ~s. [15th c. *sod*, cf. Icel. *flag* spot whence sod has been cut out, ON *flaga* slab of stone; cf. FLAW¹]

flăg³, n. (Also ~*feather*) quill-feather of bird's wing. [perh. f. obs. *flag* drooping f. OF *flac* f. L *flaccus* flabby]

flăg⁴, n., & v.t. (-gg-). **1.** Piece of bunting or other stuff, usu. oblong or square, attached by one edge to staff or halyard & used as standard, ensign, or signal (*black* ~, pirate's ensign, also ~ hoisted outside prison to announce execution of criminal; *white* ~, ~ of truce, disclaiming hostile intention; *yellow* ~, displayed by ship with infectious disease on board, hospital ship, or ship in quarantine; ~ *of convenience*, foreign ~ under which a ship is registered to avoid taxation etc. at home; ~ *of truce*, white, indicating desire to parley; DIP¹ ~; *hoist the* ~, as claim to discovered territory; *lower* or *strike* one's ~, take it down as salute or sign of surrender); (Naut.) ~ carried by ~ship as emblem of admiral's rank afloat (*hoist, strike,* one's ~, assume, relinquish, command); tail of setter or Newfoundland dog; ~*boat*, serving as mark in aquatic matches; || ~*captain*, captain of ~ship; ~*day* || (on which money is raised for a cause by sale to passers-by etc. of ~s to be worn as evidence of having given); *****F~ *Day*, June 14, anniversary of the adoption of the Stars and Stripes in 1777; ~*lieutenant*, admiral's A.D.C.; || ~*list*, roll of ~*officers*, i.e. admirals, vice-admirals, or rear-admirals; ~*man*, signaller at races etc.; ~*rank* (of ~-officers); ~*ship*, having admiral on board; ~*staff*, pole on which ~ is hung; ~*station*, where trains stop only if signalled; ~*wagging* (sl.), signalling; ~*waver*, agitator. **2.** v.t. Place ~ on or over; mark out with ~s; inform (person), communicate (information, *that*), by ~-signals. [orig. unkn.; perh. as FLAG³, FLAG⁵; earliest in E (15th-16th c.) whence perh. in other Teut. langg.]

flåg[5], v.i. (-gg-). Hang down, flap loosely; droop, fade, become limp; lag, lose vigour, grow languid; fall off in interest. [15 c., rel. to obs. *flag* (FLAG[3])]

flagĕll'ant (*also* flåj[2]), n. & a. (One) who scourges himself; given to flogging. [f. L *flagellare* (FLAGELLUM), -ANT]

flå'gell|āte[1], v.t. Scourge. Hence or cogn. ~A'TION, ~ātOR, nn., ~ātORY a. [as prec., -ATE[3]]

flagĕll'|um, n. (pl. ~a). (Bot.) runner, creeping shoot; (Zool. Biol.) lashlike appendage. Hence **flå'gellıate**[2] [-ATE[2]], ~ĭFORM, aa. [L, = whip]

flågeolĕt'[1] (-jol-; *also* flåj[2]), n. Small flute blown at end. [F, dim. of OF *flag(e)ol* of unkn. orig.]

flågeolĕt'[2] (-jol-; *also* -lå), n. Kind of kidney-bean. [F, = *fageolet* dim. of *fageol* f. L *faseolus*]

flagi'tious (-shus), a. Deeply criminal, atrocious, heinous, villainous. Hence ~LY[2] adv., ~NESS n., (-shus-). [ME, f. L *flagitiosus* (*flagitium* crime, -OUS)]

flåg'on, n. Large vessel usu. with handle, spout, & lid, to hold liquor for table; similar vessel for Eucharist; (Wine-trade) flattened globular glass bottle holding nearly two bottles. [ME *flakon* f. OF *flacon* (FLASK, -OON)]

flåg'rant, a. Glaring, notorious, scandalous, (of offence or offender). Hence or cogn. **flåg'rancy** n., ~LY[2] adv. [f. L *flagrare* (blaze, -ANT]

flail, n. Hand threshing-implement, wooden staff at end of which a short heavy stick hangs swinging. [OE *flegil*, OS *flegil*, OHG *flegel*, WG f. L *flagellum*]

flair, n. Selective instinct for what is excellent, paying, etc. [F (*flairer* to smell f. Rom. *flagrare* = *fragrare* see FRAGRANT)]

flåk, n. (German) anti-aircraft fire; ~ *ship*, German anti-aircraft vessel. [abbr. of F*liegerabwehrk*anone]

flåke[1], n. Rack for storing oatcake etc.; stage for drying fish etc. [ME *ficke* f. ON *flake*, *fleke* hurdle]

flåke[2], n., & v.i. & t. **1.** Light fleecy tuft, esp. of snow; portion of ignited matter thrown off; thin broad piece peeled off, chiplike piece (*corn*, *wheat*, ~); natural division of fish's flesh; layer; carnation with striped petals; ~-*white*, pigment made from white-lead in ~s; hence **flåk'y**[2] a. **2.** vb. Fall like, sprinkle as with, snow; take, come, *away* or *off* in ~s. [ME, orig. unkn.; cf. ON *flakna* flake off]

flåm, n. Sham story, trick, deception. [17th c., goes with earlier FLIM-FLAM]

flåm'beau (-bō), n. (pl. -s or -x, pr. -z). Torch, esp. of several thick waxed wicks. [F, f. *flambe* FLAME[1] (= med. L *flambellum*)]

flåmboy'ant, a. & n. **1.** Marked by wavy flamelike lines (of French 15th & 16th c. Archit.); floridly decorated; gorgeously

coloured; ostentatious, showy. **2.** n. Kinds of flame-coloured flower. [F, part. of *flamboyer* (*flambe* FLAME[1])]

flåme[1], n. (Portion of) ignited gas (*the* ~*s*, fire, esp. as consuming); visible combustion (*in* ~*s*; *burst into* ~ or ~*s*); bright light, brilliant colouring; passion, esp. of love (*fan the* ~, make it more intense); (joc.) sweetheart (*an old* ~ *of mine*); kinds of moth; ~-*projector* or *-thrower*, = FLAMMENWERFER. Hence ~'LESS (-ml-) (poet.), **flåm'y**[2], aa. [ME *flame*, *flaum(b)e* f. OF *flame* (f. L *flamma*) & *flambe* (f. L *flammula* dim. of *flamma*)]

flåme[2], v.i. & t. Emit flames, blaze, (often *away*, *forth*, *out*, *up*); (of passion) burst out; (of persons, break *out*, blaze *up*, into anger; shine, gleam, (~ *up*, blush violently); move like flame; send (signal) by fire; subject to action of flame (*sterilized by flaming*). [ME *flam(b)e* f. OF *flam(b)er* (prec.)]

flåm'ĕn, n. (Rom. Ant.). A god's priest. [L]

flåm'ing, a. In vbl senses; esp.: very hot (*a* ~ *sun*); bright-coloured; exaggerated, over-laudatory (*a* ~ *description*): ~ *onions*, anti-aircraft projectile resembling a chain of fire-balls. [-ING[2]]

flaming'ō (-ngg-), n. (pl. ~*es*). Tall long-necked web-footed (sub)tropical bird with pink, scarlet, & black plumage. [Port. (-*engo*) perh. f. Rom. *flama* flame + *-enc* = -ING[3]]

flåmm'able, a. (Rare, & chiefly in *non*-~, for) INFLAMMABLE.

flåmm'enwerfer (-värfer), n. Machine spouting liquid fire in war. [G, = flame-thrower]

flån, n. Pastry spread with jam, conserves, etc. [F]

flånerie (flah'nrē), **flåneur** (flah'nér), nn. Idling, idler. [F]

flånge (-j), n., & v.t. **1.** Projecting flat rim, collar, or rib. **2.** v.t. Provide with ~. [orig. uncert.; w. obs. *flanch* perh. rel. to OF *flanchir* (see FLANK), *flangir* bend]

flånk, n., & v.t. **1.** Fleshy part of side between ribs & hip; side of building, mountain, etc.; right or left side of army or body of troops (*in* ~, at the side; TURN[1] ~ *of*). **2.** v.t. Guard or strengthen on the ~, menace ~ of, take in ~, enfilade, rake; be posted or situated at ~ of; march past ~ of; OUT-~. [ME, f. OF *flanc* (*flanche*) f. Gallo-Rom. *flancum* (-*ca*) f. OFrank. *hlanca* side]

flånk'er, n. Fortification guarding or menacing flank; (Mil., usu. pl.) flank skirmisher(s); thing that flanks anything [-ER[1]]

flånn'el, n. & a. **1.** Woven woollen stuff, usu. without nap (pl., kinds of this, ~ goods); (pl.) underclothing of ~, = bandages, garments esp. trousers of ~ whence ~led[2] (-ld) a.; piece of ~ used in washing person or cleaning floor, whence **flånn'el** (-ll-) v.t.; hence ~ETTE[2] (2) n., ~LY[2] a. **2.** adj. Made of ~. [perh. f. W *gwlanen* (*gwlân* wool)]

flăp, v.t. & i. (-pp-), & n. **1.** Strike with something broad, drive (flies etc.) *away* or *off*; (of birds) strike (something) with flat of wing; swing or sway about, flutter, oscillate; move (t. & i. of wings) up & down; beat the wings. **2.** n. Light blow with something broad;ᐧmotion of wing etc.; (colloq.) state of excitement (*be in, get into, a* ~); broad hanging piece hinged or attached by one side only, e.g. trapdoor, pocket-cover, hat-brim, table-leaf, valve, fish's gill-cover, piece of skin left in amputations; open mushroom-top (cf. *button*). [ME, imit.]

flăpdoo'dle, n. Nonsense, bunkum. [orig. unkn.]

flăp'jăck, n. Small cake of flour fried in grease; flat vanity case for face-powder. [FLAP + JACK[1]]

flăpp'er n. Flat fly-killing instrument; bird-scaring clapper; young wild-duck or partridge; (sl.) girl in late teens; hinged or hanging piece, flap; broad fin; crustacean's tail; (sl.) hand; (w. ref. to Laputans) person, thing, that jogs one's memory or wits. [-ER[1]]

flāre, v.t. & i., & n. **1.** (Cause to) bulge gradually upwards (of ship's sides), spread outwards gradually (as the sides of a ship, a woman's skirt, etc.); blaze with bright unsteady flame, glow as with flame, (often *about, away, out*); part., gaudy, over-conspicuous); ~ *up*, burst into sudden blaze or anger. **2.** n. Dazzling irregular light, unshaded flame in open air; sudden outburst of flame; signal light used at sea; bright light used as signal; container of combustible material, dropped from aircraft to illuminate target area etc.; ~*-path*, area illuminatedᐧ to enable aircraft to land or take' off; ostentation; upward bulge in ship's sides; gradual widening (esp. of a skirt); ~*-up*, sudden breaking into flame, short brilliant popularity or display, burst of anger, uproarious merrymaking. [orig. unkn.]

flăsh[1], v.i. & t. Break suddenly into flame, give out flame or sparks, (~ *in the pan*, fail after showy start, like priming of old guns); emit or reflect light, gleam; send, reflect, (something) like a flash or in flashes (*eyes* ~ *fire*, ~ *back defiance*); burst suddenly into view or perception (~*ed upon me that* —); move swiftly; ~ *up* or *out*, show sudden passion; cause to gleam (~*ed his sword*; *had a torch* ~*ed in my face*); send by telegraph (*news was* ~*ed over England*); (Glass-making) spread out (t. & i.) into a sheet, cover (plain glass) with coloured film; (of water) rush along, rise & flow, fill or flood (stream etc.) with water; ~*-board*, for sending more water from mill-dam into mill-race; ~*-pipe*, extra pipe with'line of holes for lighting high gas-lamp; ~*ing-point*, temperature at which vapour from oil etc. may be ignited. [in 14th c. of the sea etc., of imit. orig.; cf. *clash, plash*]

flăsh[2], n. Sudden transitory blaze (~ *in the pan*, abortive effort; see prec.), time occupied by it, instant, (*in a* ~); ostentation; sudden short access of feeling (*a* ~ *of hope*); (Cinemat.) exposure of a scene, recapitulation of an earlier scene (also ~*'back*); preparation for colouring spirits; rush of water let down weir to take boat over shallows, contrivance for producing this; (Mil.) coloured patch of cloth as distinguishing emblem of division etc.; ~*-light*, used for signals & in lighthouses, also for photographing by night etc., (also) electric torch; ~*-point*, (now more usu. for) FLASH[1]*ing-point*, also fig. [f. prec.]

flăsh[3], a. Gaudy, showy, counterfeit (~ *notes, money*); cant, slang; connected with thieves, tramps, etc. [f. prec.]

flăsh'ing, n. Strip of metal to obviate flooding or soaking at joint of roofing etc. [18th c., = obs. *flash* (16th c.)]

flăsh'|ў, a. Brilliant but shallow or transitory, cheaply attractive; showy, gaudy; given to display. Hence ~**ĭLY[2]** adv., ~**ĭNESS** n. [-Y[2]]

flask (-ah-), n. (Also *powder-*~) leather or metal case for carrying sportsman's supply of gunpowder; Italian narrow-necked wickered wine or oil bottle; traveller's pocket bottle of metal or (usu. leather-covered) glass for wine, spirit, etc. [16th c. 'powder-flask' f. OF *flasque*, 17th c. 'bottle' f. It. *fiasco* f. LL *flasca*, *flasco*; ult. orig. unkn.]

flask'ĕt (-ah-), n. ‖ Long shallow basket (arch.); ‖ clothes-basket; small flask. [f. OF *flasquet* (*flasque* FLASK, -ET[1])]

flăt[1], n. Storey (now rare); suite of rooms on one floor as residence; *apartment; (Nav.) ship's compartment on to which cabins etc. open (*after cabin, wardroom*, ~). [alt. f. obs. *flet* = OE *flet* cogn. w. foll.]

flăt[2], a. & adv., n., & v.t. (-tt-). **1.** Horizontal, level; spread out, lying at full length, (*fell* ~; ~ *against the wall*; *with the* ~ *hand*); even, smooth, unbroken, without projection, (~ *tint*, uniform); with broad level surface & little depth; unqualified, plain, downright, (~ *denial*, *refusal*; ~ *nonsense, blasphemy*; *that's* ~, let there be no doubt about it); dull, lifeless, monotonous, (*fall* ~, prove a failure, not win applause; *market is, prices are,* ~, inactive, sluggish); slow-witted; dejected, without energy, (~ *beer*, that has lost its effervescence); (Mus.) below the true pitch (*B, D*, etc., ~, a semitone lower than B, D, etc.; *sings* ~); ~ *aback* (emphat. for ABACK naut. & fig.); ~*-boat*, with ~ bottom for transport in shallow water; ~ *candlestick*, with broad base & short stem for carrying about; ~*-fish*, family including sole, turbot, plaice, etc.; ~*-foot(ed)*, (having) foot not normally arched; ~*-iron*, for ironing linen etc.; ~ *out*, all out, at top speed, using all one'sᐧ

strength or resources; ~ *race*, over level ground (opp. hurdle-race or steeplechase); ~ *rate* (the same in all cases, not proportional etc.); hence ~'LY² adv., ~'NESS n., ~t'EN⁶ v.t. & i. (~*ten out*, bring aircraft parallel with ground), ~t'ISH¹(2) a., ~'WAYS, ~'WISE, advv. 2. n. What is ~ (*on, from, the* ~, of drawings etc. as opposed to sculpture), ~ part of anything (*the* ~ *of the hand, with the* ~ *of his sword*); level ground, plain, low land, swamp; ~-bottomed boat; shallow basket; (Theatr.) section of scenery mounted on frame (*join the* ~*s*, transf., make a thing into a coherent whole, preserve appearance of a consistent attitude); (sl.) duffer, dupe; (Mus.) note lowered a semitone below natural pitch, sign indicating this lowering, *sharps & ~s*, black notes on piano. 3. v.t. Make ~ (chiefly in manufacturing processes; elsewhere ~*ten*). [ME, f. ON *flatr* of unkn. orig.]

flätt'er, v.t. Court, fawn upon; compliment unduly, overpraise; gratify vanity of, make feel honoured; inspire with (esp. unfounded) hope; please one*self* with the belief (*that*); gratify (eye, ear, etc.); ~*ing unction*, salve one administers to one's own conscience or self-esteem (*Haml.* III. iv. 145); (of portrait, painter, etc.) exaggerate good looks of. Hence or cogn. ~ER¹, flätt'ERY(4, 5), nn., ~ingLY² adv. [ME; orig. obsc., ult. rel. to OF *flater* to smooth]

flät'ül|ent, a. Generating gas in the alimentary canal; caused by, attended with, troubled with, accumulation of such gas; inflated, puffed up, windy, pretentious. Hence or cogn. ~ENCE, ~ENCY, nn., ~entLY² adv. [F (foll., -ULENT)]

flät'us, n. Wind in stomach or bowels. [L, vbl n. (*flare* blow)]

flaunt, v.i. & t., & n. 1. Wave (t. & i.) proudly; display oneself or one's finery; show off, parade, (one*self*, finery, etc.); hence ~'ingLY² adv., ~'Y² a. 2. n. ~ing motion. [orig. unkn.]

flaut'ist, n. Flute-player. [f. It. *flautista* (*flauto* FLUTE)]

flavěs'cent, a. Turning yellow, yellowish. [f. L *flavescere* (*flavus* yellow, -ESCENT)]

flǎv'in, n. Surgical antiseptic, & yellow dye, got from dyer's oak. [L *flavus* yellow, -IN]

flǎv'ō-prōt'ėin (*or* -tēn), n. One of group of conjugated proteins which constitute the yellow oxidizable enzymes. [prec., PROTEIN]

flāv'our (-ver), n., & v.t. 1. Aroma, mingled sensation of smell & taste, distinctive taste; undefinable characteristic quality; hence flāv'orOUS, ~LESS, ~SOME, (-ver-), aa. 2. v.t. Give ~ to, season; hence ~ING¹(3) (-ver-) n. [ME, f. OF *flaur, fraor*, etc. (perh. f. L *fragrare* be FRAGRANT), w. assim. to *savour*]

flaw¹, n., & v.t. & i. 1. Crack, breach, rent; imperfection, blemish; (Law) in-

validating defect in document, procedure, evidence, etc.; hence ~'LESS a., ~'lèssLY³ adv., ~'lèssNESS n. 2. vb. Crack (t. & i.), damage, mar. [ME, perh. f. ON *flaga* slab cf. FLAG², FLAKE²]

flaw², n. Squall of wind; short storm. [16th c., prob. f. MDu. *vlāghe* (Du. *vlaag*), MLG *vlāge*]

|| **flawn**, n. (arch.). Kind of custard. [ME, f. OF *flaon* (now *flan*) f. LL *fladonem* nom. -o f. OFrank. *flado* flat cake]

flǎx, n. Blue-flowered plant cultivated for its textile fibre & its seeds called linseed; (with qualifying word prefixed or suffixed) kinds of similar plant, as *dwarf, toad-, -~, -dodder*; fibres of ~, dressed or undressed; cloth of ~, linen; ~-*lily*, New Zealand plant of lily family yielding a valuable fibre; ~-*seed*, linseed. [OE *flæx*, OS, OHG *flahs*, f. WG **flahsa*]

flǎx'en, a. Of flax; (of hair) coloured like dressed flax, pale yellowish-brown. [-EN⁵]

flay, v.t. Strip off skin or hide of; (fig.) criticize severely; pillage, plunder, (person); peel off (skin, bark, peel); pare off (turf); || ~-*flint*, extortioner, miser. [OE *flēan*, MDu, *vlae(gh)en*, ON *flā* f. Gmc **flahan*]

flea, n. Small wingless jumping insect feeding on human & other blood (*send one away with a ~ in his ear*, discomfited by a reproof or repulse); *sand*-~, *water*-~, small jumping crustaceans; = ~--beetle; small or contemptible creature; ~-*bag* (sl.), sleeping-bag; ~-*bane*, ~-*wort*, kinds of plant supposed to drive away~s; ~-*beetle*, jumping beetle infesting hops; ~-*bite*, lit., & fig. slight inconvenience or expense, mere trifle, also small reddish spot in animal's colouration (~-*bitten*, sprinkled with these on lighter ground; also lit.); *~ circus*, a show of performing ~s; ~-*dock*, butterbur; ~-*louse*, jumping plant-louse; ~-*pit* (sl.), allegedly verminous place of public assembly, e.g. cinema. [OE *flēah*, MDu. *vlō*, OHG *flōh*, ON *flō* f. Gmc **flauh-* or **thlauh-* (FLEE)]

fleam, n. Lancet for bleeding horses. [f. OF *flieme* f. Rom. **fleutomum* f. LL *flebotomus* f. Gk *phlebotomon* see PHLEBOTOMY]

flèche (-āsh), n. Slender spire perforated with windows, esp. at intersection of nave & transept. [F, orig. = arrow]

flěck, n., & v.t. 1. Spot in the skin, freckle; patch of colour or light; small particle, speck; hence ~'LESS a. 2. v.t. Mark with ~s, dapple, variegate. [f. ON *flekkr* n. *flekka* vb, or MLG, MDu. *vlecke*; cf. OHG *flec, fleccho* (G *fleck*)]

flěck'er, v.t. Dapple, variegate; scatter in patches. [prec. + -ER⁵]

fled. See FLEE.

flědge, v.t. Provide with feathers or plumage, wing for flight, deck with feathers or down. Hence ~'LESS (-jl-) a. [f. obs. adj. *fledge* corresp. to late OE (*un*)*fligge*,

MDu. *vlugge*, OHG *flucchi* f. WG **fluggja* (**flug-* FLY[5])]

fledg(e)ling (-jl-), n. Young bird; inexperienced person. [as prec. +-LING[1]]

flee, v.i. & t. (*fled*; *fly, flying*, are now usu. substituted for ~, ~*ing*; *is fled*, see ED[1](2), or *has fled*). Run away, seek safety in flight, (*from, before*); vanish, cease, pass away; run away from; leave abruptly; eschew, shun. [OE *fléon*, OS, OHG *fliohan*, ON *flý(j)a*, Goth. *thliuhan* f. Gmc **thleuhan*]

fleece, n., & v.t. 1. Woolly covering of sheep or similar animal (*Golden F~*, Austrian & Spanish order of Knighthood); quantity of wool shorn from a sheep at once; rough, abundant, or woolly head of hair; thing like a ~, white cloud, falling snow, etc.; (Carding) thin sheet of cotton or wool fibre; hence (-)fleecED[2] (-ĕst), flee′CY[2], aa. 2. v.t. Shear (sheep; rare); strip of money, property, etc. (also *of*), whence ~′ABLE a.; overspread as with ~ (*sky* ~*d with clouds*). [OE *fléos*, Du., MHG *vlies*, f. WG **fleus-*]

fleer, v.i., & n. 1. Laugh impudently or mockingly, gibe, jeer, sneer. 2. n. Mocking look or speech. [cf. Norw. & Sw. dial. *flira* to grin]

fleet[1], n. Naval armament, number of warships under one command-in-chief (*the* ~, the navy); number of ships or boats sailing in company; group of aircraft; ~ *of cabs, taxis*, etc., those owned by one proprietor; ‖ F~ *Air Arm*, aviation service of Royal Navy. [OE *fléot* ship, shipping (*fléotan* FLEET[5])]

‖ **fleet**[2], n. Creek, inlet; *The F~*, stream, now covered sewer, running into Thames E. of F~ Street, also the prison that stood near it (*F~ marriage*, performed by a *F~ parson* or disreputable clergyman in & about the *F~* ready to marry clandestinely); *F~ Street*, (used for) the press, London journalism. [OE *fleot*, MLG *flēt*, MDu., LG *vliet*, MHG *vliez(e)* ON *fljót* cogn. w. FLEET[5]]

fleet[3], a. (poet. or literary). Swift, nimble. Hence ~′LY[2] adv., ~′NESS n. [f. ON *fljótr*, cogn. w. FLEET[5]]

‖ **fleet**[4], a. & adv. Shallow (of water); at or to no great depth (*plough or sow* ~). [perh. repr. OE **fléat*, cogn. w. foll.]

fleet[5], v.i. Glide away, vanish, be transitory; pass rapidly, slip *away*; move swiftly, fly. Hence ~′ING[2] a., ~′INGLY[2] adv. [OE *fléotan*, OS *fliotan*, OHG *fliozan*, ON *fljóta* f. Gmc **fleutan*, cogn. w. FLOAT[2]]

Flem′ing, n. Inhabitant of Flanders. [f. MDu. *Vlāming*, w. assim. to foll.]

Flem′ish, a. & n. (Language) of Flanders; ~ BOND[1]. [f. MDu. *Vlaemisch* (prec., -ISH[1])]

flench, **flinch**[1], **flense**, v.t. Cut up (whale); flay (seal). [f. Da. *flense*, cf. Norw. *flinsa* flay]

flesh[1], n. 1. Soft substance between the skin & the bones, esp. the muscular part of animal bodies (~ & *blood*, the body or its material, mankind, human nature with its emotions & infirmities; as adj., actually living, not supernatural or imaginary; one's *own* ~ & *blood*, near relations, descendants; ~ & *fell*, the whole body; as adv., entirely; *one* ~, united as one personality, see *Gen.* ii. 24; *proud* ~, overgrowth of granulations springing on wound; *make his* ~ *creep*, frighten or horrify him esp. with dread of the supernatural). 2. Pulpy substance of fruit or plant. 3. Plumpness, fat, (*lose, put on*, ~, grow thin, fat); *in* ~, fat. 4. Tissue of animal bodies (excluding fish & sometimes fowls) as food, meat, (~*-feeding*, ~*-eater*, etc.; *neither* FISH[1], ~, *nor* etc). 5. Visible surface of human body (~*-colour, -ed*, yellowish pink); = ~ & *blood* above (*all* ~, whatever has bodily life; *the way of all* ~, the experience common to all men; *in the* ~, in bodily form, in life; *after the* ~, corporeally). 6. The sensual appetites (*sins of the* ~, unchastity). 7. ~*-brush*, *-glove*, for stimulating circulation by rubbing; ~*-fly*, depositing eggs or larvae in dead ~; ~*-pots* (w. ref. to *Exod.* xvi. 3), high living; ~ *side* or ~, side of a hide that adjoined the ~; ~ *tights*, fleshings; ~*-tints*, esp. painter's rendering of ~*-colour*; ~*-wound*, one not reaching bone or vital organ. Hence ~′LESS a. [OE *flǽsc*, OS *flêsk*, OHG *fleisc*, ON *flesk* f. Gmc **flaisk-*]

flesh[2], v.t. Incite (hound etc.) by taste of blood; initiate in bloodshed; inflame by foretaste of success; use *sword* etc. for first time on flesh (or fig. *pen, wit*, etc.). [f. prec.]

‖ **flesh′er**, n. (Sc.). Butcher. [f. FLESH + -ER[1]]

flesh′ings (-z), n. pl. Close flesh-coloured garment usu. of silk worn on stage etc. to represent natural skin. [FLESH[1], -ING[1]]

flesh′l|y, a. Carnal, lascivious, sensual, (esp. of appetites etc., rarely of persons); mortal, material, not divine or spiritual; worldly. Hence ~iNESS n. [OE *flǽsclic* (FLESH[1], -LIKE)]

flesh′|y, a. Plump, fat; of flesh, without bone; (of plant or fruit tissue) pulpy; like flesh. Hence ~iNESS n. [-Y[2]]

fleur-de-lis (flĕr′delē′; pl. *fleurs-* pr. as sing.), **flow′er-de-luce** (arch. & U.S.), n. Iris flower; heraldic lily; (sing. or pl.) royal arms of France, French royal family, France. [F (first form), = lily flower (*lis* lily); the arch. E form is unexpl.]

fleur′et (-oor-), n. Ornament like small flower. [f. F *fleurette* (*fleur* FLOWER, -ETTE)]

fleuron (flĕrawn′), n. Flower-shaped ornament in architecture or printing, on coins, etc. [F]

fleur′y (-oorĭ), **flor′y**, a. (her.). Decorated with fleurs-de-lis. [f. F *fleuré*, OF *flore* (*fleur* FLOWER, -Y[4])]

flew. See FLY[2].

flews (-z), n. pl. Hanging lips of blood-hound etc. [orig. unkn.]

flĕx[1], v.t. Bend (in scientific use of bending limb etc. by flexor, or in Geol. of distorted strata). [f. L *flectere flex*-]

flĕx[2], n. Flexible insulated wire used for conveying electric current. [abbr. of foll.]

flĕx'i|ble, a. That will bend without breaking, pliable, pliant; easily led, manageable; adaptable, versatile; supple, complaisant. Hence or cogn. ∼BIL'ITY n., ∼bLY[2] adv. [f. OF, or L *flexibilis* (FLEX[1], -IBLE)]

flĕx'ile, a. Supple, mobile; tractable; versatile. Hence **flĕxil'ITY** n. [f. L *flexilis* (FLEX[1], -IL)]

fiĕ'xion (-kshn), n. Bending, curvature, bent state, (esp. of limb or joint); bent part, curve; (Gram.)=inflexion, whence ∼AL, ∼LESS, (-kshon-), aa.; (Math.)=flexure. [f. L *flexio* (FLEX[1], -ION)]

flĕx'or, n. (Also = *muscle, tendon*) muscle that bends a part (opp. EXTENSOR). [FLEX[1], -OR]

flĕx'ūōse, a. (bot.). Serpentine, undulating. Hence **flĕxūōs'o-** comb. form. [f. L *flexuosus* (*flexus -ūs* a bend see FLEX[1], -OSE[2])]

flĕx'ūous, a. Full of bends, winding. Hence or cogn. **flĕxūos'ITY** (-ŏs²), n., ∼LY² adv. [as prec., -OUS]

fiĕ'xure (-ksher), n. Bending, curvature, bent state; bend, curve, turn; (Math.) curving of line or surface or, in theory of elasticity, of surface or solid (∼ *of a curve*, its bending to or from a straight line); (Geol.) bending of strata under pressure. [f. L *flexura* (FLEX[1], -URE)]

flĭbb'ertigĭbb'ĕt, n. Gossiping, flighty, frivolous, or restless person. [imit. of chatter]

flick, n., & v.t. 1. Light sharp blow with whiplash etc. shot out and withdrawn, or with finger-nail; sudden movement, jerk; slight sharp cracking sound; (sl.) cinema film, (pl.) cinema performance; ∼*-knife* (with blade springing out when button is pressed). 2. v.t. Strike with a ∼; dash or jerk (dust etc.) *away, off*; give a ∼ with (whip, towel, etc.). [imit.]

flick'er, v.i., & n. 1. Quiver, vibrate, wave to and fro, blow lightly & unsteadily, (of flags, leaves, serpents' tongues, wind, etc.); (of flame etc., & fig. of hope etc.) flash and die away by turns; hence ∼ingLY² adv. 2. n. ∼ing movement or light. [OE *flicorian* imit.]

flier. See FLYER.

flight[1] (-īt), n., & v.t. 1. Act or manner of flying through air (*take* one's or *a*, *wing* one's, ∼, fly), pursuit of game by hawk; migration, migrating body, flock, of birds or insects; swift movement of projectiles etc.; passage of projectile from gun to target; (of time) swift passage; soaring, excursion, sally, (of wit, fancy, ambition, etc.); distance that bird, aircraft, or missile, can fly; series (of stairs

between two landings, or *of* hurdles or rails for racing over); volley (*of* arrows etc.); *in the first* ∼, taking a leading place; oat-chaff; R.A.F. unit consisting of a few machines; ∼*-deck*, for taking-off from, and landing on, an aircraft-carrier; ∼-*feather*, -*muscle*, used in flying; ∼-*lieutenant*, -*sergeant*, see AIR[1] *Force*. 2. v.t. Shoot (wildfowl; also abs.) in ∼; vary trajectory and pace of (cricket-ball etc.). [OE *flyht*, OS *fluht*, f. WG **fluhti* f. **fleugan* FLY²]

flight[2] (-īt), n. Running away, hasty retreat, absconding, (*take*, *take to*, *betake* one*self to*, ∼, run away; *put to* ∼, rout). [OE **flyht*, OS, OHG *fluht*, ON *flótti* f. Gmc **thluhtiz* f. **thleuhan* FLEE]

flight'|ў (-īt-), a. Guided by whim or fancy, fickle; half-witted, crazy. Hence ∼iLY² adv., ∼iNESS n. [FLIGHT[1] + -Y²]

flim'flăm, n. Trifle, nonsense, idle talk; piece of humbug, deception. [16th c.; imit. redupl.; cf. FLAM & foll.]

flim's|ў (-z-), a. & n. 1. Easily destroyed, frail, slightly put together; paltry, trivial, frivolous, superficial; hence ∼iLY² adv., ∼iNESS n. 2. n. Banknote(s) (sl.); thin paper, reporter's copy. [17th c., goes w-prec. & FLAM]

flinch[2] (for *flinch*[1] see FLENCH), v.i. Give way, draw back, (*from* duty, course, etc.); wince. [f. OF *flenchir* f. WG (OFrank.) **hlankjan*; see LANK]

flin'ders (-z), n. pl. Fragments, splinters, (*break*, *fly*, *in* ∼). [15th c., cf. Norw *flindra* splinter]

fling, v.i. & t. (*flŭng*), & n. 1. Rush, go angrily or violently (∼ *out of the room*; *flŭng away in a rage*); (of horse etc.) kick and plunge (often *out*), (of person; usu. *out*) break into invective; throw, hurl, (often *about*, *aside*, *away*, *by*, *out*, *up*, *at*; rejected thing, missile, flotsam, dice); throw one*self into* person's arms, a boat, etc., *on* person's compassion etc., *into* an enterprise (i.e. take it up with all one's might); suddenly spread *out* (arms), kick *up* (heels); cast (one's eyes) carelessly (*up)on*; send, emit, (sound, smell, light); put (person) suddenly or violently *into* prison; launch (troops etc.) *on* enemy or *against* fortress or enemy; (of wrestler or ridden horse) throw to the ground; ∼ (fact etc.) *in* one's *teeth*, reproach him with it; ∼ (door etc.) *open* or *to*, open or shut violently. 2. n. Throw, cast, (*have a* ∼ *at*, make an attempt at, jeer at); impetuous dance (esp. *Highland* ∼); violent movement, plunge; spell of indulgence in impulse (*have* one's ∼). [ME, perh. f. ON **flinga*, whence *flengja* flog]

flint, n. Hard stone of nearly pure silica found in pebbly lumps steel-grey within & encrusted with white; anything hard and unyielding; piece of ∼ used with steel to produce fire (∼ *& steel*) esp. in ∼-lock gun; piece of an alloy of rare-earth metals used in automatic petrol lighters as the spark-producing element; pebble of ~ (*wring water from a* ~, work miracles; *skin a* ~, be miserly or avaricious; *set one's face like a* ~, be determined); ~*-glass*, pure lustrous kind orig. made with ~; ~*-lock*, (lock of) gun discharged by spark from~. Hence flin'tY² a., flin'ti-NESS n. [OE *flint*, MDu. *vlint*, OHG *flins*]

flip¹, v.t. & i. (-pp-), & n. 1. Put (pellet, coin) in motion with a fillip; fillip (person's ear, cheek, etc.), strike lightly; make a fillip with fingers; move (fan, whip, fishing-fly) about with sudden jerk(s); strike smartly *at* with whip etc. 2. n. Smart light blow, fillip, flick; (colloq.) a (short) flight in an aeroplane. [imit.]

flip², n. Beer and spirit mixed, sweetened, & heated with hot iron; EGG¹~. [perh. f. prec. in sense *whip up*]

flip-flăp, n. Kind of somersault; kind of firework, cracker; (in places of amusement) machine with passenger cars hung at ends of long moving arms. [imit.]

flipp'ant, a. Lacking in gravity, treating serious things lightly, disrespectful. Hence flipp'ANCY n., ~LY² adv. [from 1605, orig. = nimble, voluble, perh. f. FLIP¹, -ANT]

flipp'er, n. Limb used to swim with, as in turtle & penguin; (sl.) hand. [FLIP¹ + -ER¹]

flipp'ertў-flŏpp'ertў, a. Loose, dangling.

flirt, v.t. & i., & n. 1. Fillip, send with a jerk; wave or move briskly (fan, bird's tail); play at courtship (*with*), pretend to make love, whence ~A'TION n., ~ā'tious (-shŭs) a. 2. n. Sudden jerk, quick motion quickly checked; man who pays, or usu. woman who invites or accepts, attentions merely for amusement, whence ~'ISH¹, ~'Y², aa. [imit.]

flit, v.i. (-tt-), & n. 1. Migrate, be gone, depart; change one's abode, move; pass lightly, softly, or rapidly (often *about, by, to & fro*); fly lightly, make short flights, (of birds & esp. bats). 2. n. Change of abode. [ME, f. ON *flytja* cogn. w. FLEET⁵]

flitch, n., & v.t. 1. Side of hog salted and cured (~ *of Dunmow*, there given yearly to any couple proving conjugal harmony for year and day); square of blubber, steak of halibut; || slice (usu. outside one) of timber from tree-trunk; ~*-beam* (compound, esp. of iron plate between two slices of wood). 2. v.t. Cut (log or halibut) into ~es. [OE *flicce*, MLG *vli(c)ke*, ON *flikki*]

flitt'er, v.i. Flit about, flutter; ~*-mouse*, bat. [FLIT + -ER⁵]

*flivv'er, n. (sl.). Cheap motor-car. [orig. unkn.]

flix, n. Kinds of fur; beaver's down. [orig. unkn.]

float¹, n. || Floating (rare; *on the*~, afloat); mass of floating weeds, ice, etc.; raft; cork or quill used on fishing-line as indicator; cork supporting edge of fishing-net;

inflated part supporting fish etc.; hollow ball regulating cistern tap ; (Theatr.; sing. or pl.) footlights ; (also ~*-board*) one of the boards of water-wheel or paddle-wheel; kind of low-bodied cart; platform on wheels with show used in processions; tool for smoothing plaster (~*-stone*, for smoothing curved bricks, & cf. foll.); single-cut file; passing of weft-threads over part of warp without being interwoven, thread so passed; ~*-bridge*, of rafts; ~*-grass*, kind of aquatic grass. [partly f. OE *flot* floating state, OE *flota* ship, & foll.]

float², v.i. & t. Rest on surface of liquid; (of stranded ship) get afloat; move with moving liquid, drift; be suspended freely *in* liquid; move or be suspended in air as if buoyed up; hover *before* eye or mind; (Commerc., of acceptance) be in circulation, awaiting maturity; (Commerc.) bring (company, scheme) into favour, launch, (of scheme etc.) be launched; cover with liquid, inundate; (of water etc.) support, bear along, (buoyant object); set afloat; circulate (rumour); waft through air; ~*-stone*, kinds of light stone that ~ (& see prec.). [OE *flotian*, OS *flotōn*, ON *flota* cogn. w. FLEET⁵; in ME infl. by OF *floter*]

float'able, a. Capable of floating; (of stream) in which rafts etc. can float. [-ABLE]

float'age, n. Floating; || (right of appropriating) flotsam; ships etc. afloat on river; floating masses; buoyancy; part of ship above water-line. [-AGE]

floatā'tion, flot-, n. Floating (*centre of*~, of gravity in floating body); starting of company or enterprise. [*flot-* on anal. of *quotation* etc.; FLOAT², -ATION]

float'er, n. In vbl senses; esp. (St. Exch.) government stock certificate, railway bond, etc., recognized as security. [-ER¹]

float'ing, a. In vbl senses; esp. (Commerc.; of cargo) at sea (~ *trade, rates*, etc., concerned with cargoes at sea); ~ CAPI-TAL², DEBT, RIB; fluctuating, variable, (*the* ~ *population*); ~ *anchor* = DRAG²*-anchor*; ~ DOCK⁴; ~ *bridge*, kinds of bridge & ferry, also part of bridge that can be swung away on pontoon; ~ *kidney*, abnormal condition in which the kidneys are movable; ~ *light*, lightship, lifebuoy with lantern; ~ VOTE. [-ING²]

flŏcc'ōse, a. (bot.). Tufted. [f. LL *flocco-sus* (L *floccus* FLOCK¹, -OSE¹)]

flŏcc'ūle, n. Small portion of matter like flock of wool. [f. FLOCCULUS]

flŏcc'ūlent, -lōse, -lous, aa. Like tufts of wool; in, showing, tufts. Hence flŏcc'ūlENCE n. [foll., -ULENT, -OSE¹, -OUS]

flŏcc'ūlus, n. (pl. *-li*). = FLOCCULE; (Anat.) small lobe in under surface of cerebellum. [mod. L, dim. of foll.]

flŏcc'us, n. (pl. *-ci*, pr. -ŏksï). Tuft of woolly hairs or filaments. [L, = foll.]

flŏck¹, n. Lock, tuft, of wool, cotton, etc.;

(pl.) material for quilting & stuffing made of wool-refuse or torn-up cloth; (pl. or collect. sing) powdered wool or cloth for making ~-*paper*; (Chem.; pl.) light loose masses precipitated; ~-*bed*, stuffed with ~s; ~-*paper*, wallpaper sized & then powdered with ~ either all over or in patterns. Hence ~'Y² a. [f. OF *floc* f. L *floccus*]

flock², n., & v.i. **1.** Large number of people (chiefly in such phrr. as *come in* ~s); number of animals of one kind, esp. birds, feeding or travelling together; number of domestic animals, usu. sheep, goats, or geese, kept together (~s & *herds*, *sheep* & *cattle*); the Christian body; a congregation esp. in relation to its pastor; family of children, number of pupils, etc.; ~-*master*, sheep-farmer. **2.** v.i. Congregate, go in great numbers, troop, (often *about, after, into, to, in, out, together*). [OE *flocc*, MLG *vlocke*, ON *flokkr*]

floe, n. Sheet of floating ice. [prob. f. Norw. *flo*, ON *fló* layer]

flog, v.t.(-gg-). Beat with birch, cane, whip, etc., whence ~g'ING¹(1) (-g-) n.; drive (learning, laziness, etc.) *into* or *out of* person; urge (horse etc.) on with whip (~ *dead horse*, waste energy); (sl.) defeat, excel; (sl.) sell; cast fishing-line repeatedly over (stream). [17th c. cant; imit., or f. L *flagellare* to whip]

|| **flong**, n. Prepared paper for stereotyping. [f. F *flan* FLAWN]

flood (flŭd), n., & v.t. & i. **1.** (Also ~-*tide*) inflow of tide (opp. EBB); (poet.) river, stream, sea (~ & *field*, sea & land); irruption of water over land, inundation, (*the F~*, *Noah's F~*, that in Genesis), whence ~ŏM'ETER n.; outpouring of water, torrent, downpour, (~s *of rain*, a ~ *of tears* or *words*); ~-*gate*, opened & closed to admit or exclude water, esp. lower gate of lock, also sluice; ~-*light*, copious artificial light projected from many directions, eliminating all shadows in surface illuminated (so ~-*lighting*, ~-*lit*). **2.** vb. Inundate, cover with a ~ (also fig., *was* ~*ed with letters*); irrigate; deluge (burning house, mine) with water; (of rain) fill (river) to overflowing; come in great quantities (usu. *in*); have uterine haemorrhage. [OE, OS *flōd*, OHG *fluot*, ON *flóth*, Goth. *flōdus* f. Gmc *flōthuz*]

floor (-ōr), n., & v.t. **1.** Lower surface of room, (also ~*ing*) boards etc. of which it is made; bottom of sea, cave, etc.; part of House of Parliament where members sit and speak (*take the* ~, esp. U.S., speak in debate); set of rooms etc. on same level in house (|| *ground*~, on ground level, *first* ~, || *above this*), storey; level area; ~-*lamp*, mounted on metal etc. pillar standing on ~; ~-*cloth*, substitute for carpet; ~ *show*, entertainment presented not on stage but on ~ of night-club etc.; *·~-walker*, shopwalker; hence ~'LESS (-ōr'l-) a. **2.** vb. Furnish with ~, pave; serve as

~ of; bring to the ~ or ground, knock down; confound, nonplus; || (at school) tell (boy) to sit down as not knowing lesson; overcome, get the better of, (~ *the paper*, answer every question in it). [OE, ON *flór*, MHG *vluor* f. Gmc **flōruz*]

floor'er (-ōr-), n. Knock-down blow; disconcerting news or argument; paper or question hard to answer. [-ER¹]

flop, v.i. & t. (-pp-), n., int., & adv. **1.** Sway (intr.) about heavily; walk etc. in ungainly way; sit, kneel, lie, *down* awkwardly; throw *down* negligently or noisily; make dull sound of soft body falling or of flat thing slapping water; (sl., of book, play, etc.) fail, collapse; hence ~p'Y² a. **2.** n. ~ping motion, sound made by it; (sl.) failure (of book, play, etc.). **3.** int. & adv. With a ~. [var. of earlier FLAP]

flor'a, n. (pl. *-ae*, *-as*). (List of) plants of particular region or epoch (cf. FAUNA). [F. goddess of flowers (*flos* -*oris* flower)]

flor'al, a. Of flora(s) (~ *zone*, tract of earth with special vegetable characteristics); of flower(s). [f. L *floralis* of Flora (prec.)]

Flo'rentine, a. & n. (Inhabitant) of Florence in Tuscany (~ *iris*, white or pale blue one); kind of twilled silk. [f. L *Florentinus* (*Florentia* Florence, -INE¹)]

flores'cence, n. Flowering time or state. [f. L *florescere* (*florēre* bloom, -ESCENT, -ENCE)]

flor'et, n. (Bot.) one of small flowers making up a composite flower (~ *of the disc*, *the ray*, of the flower's centre or circumference); small flower, floweret. [17th c., f. L *flos* -*oris* +-ET]

flor'iate, v.t. Decorate with flower-designs etc. [as foll., -ATE³]

flor'iculture, n. Cultivation of flowers. Hence **floricul'tural** a., **floricul'turist** (3) n., (-cher-). [f. L *flos* -*oris* flower + CULTURE]

flor'id, a. Profusely adorned as with flowers, elaborately ornate, (of literary, artistic, or musical style); ostentatious, showy; ruddy, flushed, high-coloured. Hence **florid'ITY**, ~NESS, n., ~LY² adv. [f. F *floride* or L *floridus* (*flos* FLOWER)]

Flo'rida, n. State in U.S. (~ *water*, a perfume; ~ *wood*, kind used for inlaying).

florif'erous, a. (Of seeds or plants) producing many flowers. [f. L *florifer* (*flos* FLOWER, -FEROUS)]

florile'gium, n. (pl. *-ia*). Anthology. [transl. into mod. L (L *flos* FLOWER, *legere* gather) of Gk *anthologion* ANTHOLOGY]

flo'rin, n. Foreign coin of gold or silver current at different times; (hist.) English gold coin (6/8) of Edw. III; || current English coin (2/-). [ME, f. OF f. It. *fiorino* dim. of *fiore* f. L *florem* nom. *flos* FLOWER (stamped with lily)]

flor'ist (also flō⁴), n. One who deals in, raises, or studies flowers. [L**flos* -*oris* flower, -IST]

flŏr'uit (-ŏŏ-), n. Period (falling exact birth and death dates) at which a person was alive. [L, = he flourished]

flory. See FLEURY.

flŏs'cūlar, -lous, aa. Having florets, composite-flowered. [f. L *flosculus* (FLOWER, -CULE)]

flŏss, n. Rough silk enveloping silk-worm's cocoon (~ *silk*, this used in cheap silk goods; CANDY ~. Hence ~'Y² a. [f. F (*soie*) *floche* floss (-silk), ult. f. L *floccus* FLOCK¹]

flotation. See FLOATATION.

flotill'a, n. Small fleet; fleet of boats or small ships. [Sp., dim. of *flota* fleet]

flŏt'sam, n. Wreckage found floating (cf. JETSAM); oyster-spawn. [f. AF *floteson* (OF *floter* = FLOAT²)]

flounce¹, v.i., & n. **1.** Go with agitated or violent motion, flop, plunge, throw the body about, (*away, out, about, down, up*). **2.** n. Fling, jerk, of body or limb. [16th c., of unkn. orig.; perh. imit., as *bounce, pounce*]

flounce², n., & v.t. **1.** Strip gathered & sewn by upper edge round woman's skirt, & with lower edge hanging, as ornament. **2.** v.t. Trim with ~(s). [alt. of ME *frounce* fold, pleat, f. OF *fronce* f. *froncir* wrinkle f. WG (OFrank.) *hrunkjan*; cf. FLANK, FLINCH]

floun'der¹, n. A small flat-fish. [late ME, f. AF *floundre,* OF *flondre* of Scand. orig.; cf. OSwed. *flundra*]

floun'der², v.i., & n. **1.** Struggle & plunge (as) in mud or wading; make mistakes, manage business badly or with difficulty. **2.** n. Piece of ~ing, staggering attempts to get on. [imit., perh. assoc. w. *founder, blunder*]

flour (-owr), n., & v.t. **1.** Finer part of meal obtained by bolting; wheat meal; fine soft powder; ~-*box,* tin box for dredging ~; hence ~'Y² (-owr-) a. **2.** v.t. Sprinkle with ~; *grind into ~.* [different. sp. of FLOWER in sense *finest part*]

flou'rish¹ (flŭ-), v.i. & t. Grow vigorously; thrive, prosper, be successful; be in one's prime; spend one's life, be active, *in, at, about,* etc., a certain time (cf. FLORUIT); use flourishes in handwriting or literary work or speech; show ostentatiously; wave (weapon) about; throw (limbs) about; prelude fancifully in music etc. [ME, f. OF *florir* (-ISH²) f. L *florēre* (*flos* FLOWER)]

flou'rish² (flŭ-), n. **1.** Prosperity, vigour, (rare; *in full* ~). **2.** Ornament of flowing curves about letter or word in handwriting; rhetorical embellishment, florid expression; ostentatious waving of weapon, hand, etc. **3.** (mus.). Fanfare of brass instruments, florid passage, extemporized addition or prelude; hence ~'Y² a. [f. prec.]

flout, v.t. & i. Mock, insult, express contempt for by word or act; scoff *at*. [from 16th c.; perh. var. of FLUTE v.]

flow (-ō), v.i., & n. **1.** Glide along as a stream; (of blood) circulate; (of persons or things) come, go, in numbers; (of talk, literary style, etc.) move easily; (of garment, hair, etc.) hang easily, undulate; (Math.; of numbers) increase or diminish continuously by infinitesimal quantities; gush out, spring; (of blood) be spilt; result *from*; run full, be in flood (*ebb & ~;* *swim with the* ~*ing tide,* be on the winning side); (of wine) be poured out without stint; be plentifully supplied *with* (arch.; *land* ~*ing with milk & honey*). **2.** n. ~ing movement in stream; amount that ~s; ~ing liquid; (of dress, figure, etc.) undulation; outpouring, stream, copious supply; rise of tide (*ebb & ~*); overflowing of Nile etc.; ~ *of spirits,* habitual cheerfulness; ~ *of soul,* genial conversation (as complement to FEAST *of reason*). [OE *flōwan,* cogn. w. ON *flóa,* Du. *vloeijen,* f. Gmc *flō-* (FLOOD)]

flow'er (*also* flowr), n., & v.i. & t. **1.** (Bot.) reproductive organ in plant containing one or more pistils or stamens or both, & usu. a corolla & calyx, (pop.) coloured (i.e. not green) part of plant from which fruit or seed is later developed, whence ~AGE(1) n.; (Old Chem.; pl.) powder left after sublimation (~*s of sulphur* etc.); scum formed by fermentation (~*s of tan*); a blossom apart from the plant (*No* ~*s,* intimation that wreaths etc. are not desired at funeral); ~*ing* plant; (pl.) ornamental phrases (usu. ~*s of speech* often iron.); *the* pick or choice *of; the* best part, essence; *the* choicest embodiment *of;* state of blooming (*in* ~), prime (*in the* ~ *of his age*); ~-*de-luce,* see FLEUR-DE-LIS; ~-*girl,* who sells ~s; ~-*piece,* picture of ~s; ~-*pot,* usu. of red earthenware holding soil in which plant may be set; ~-*show,* competitive or other exhibition of ~s; hence (-)~ED² (-erd), ~LESS, aa., ~ET¹ n. **2.** vb. Produce ~s, bloom or blossom, whence ~ING² a. (~*ing fern,* osmund); (Gardening) cause or allow (plant) to ~; embellish with worked ~s or floral design. [ME & OF *flour, flur,* f. L *florem* nom. *flos*]

flow'erer, n. Plant that flowers at specified time etc. (*late, abundant,* ~). [-ER¹]

flow'er|y, a. Abounding in flowers; full of fine words, compliments, figures of speech, etc., whence ~INESS (-owr-) n. [-Y²]

flow'ing (-ō̆I-), a. In vbl senses; also or esp.: (of style) fluent, easy; (of lines, curves, contour) smoothly continuous, not abrupt; (Naut.) *with* ~ *sheet* or *sail,* sailing with lee clews eased off when wind is nearly across course. Hence ~LY² adv. [-ING²]

flown¹ (-ōn), a. (arch.). Swollen, puffed up, (~ *with insolence and wine-* Milt.). [obs. p.p. of FLOW]

flown². See FLY².

flŭc'tūāte, v.i. Move up & down like waves (rare); vary irregularly, rise & fall, be unstable; vacillate, waver. So ~A'TION n. [f. L *fluctuare* (*fluctus* *-ūs* wave f. *fluere* flow), -ATE³]

flue¹ (floō), n. Kind of fishing-net. [from 14th c.; cf. MDu. *vluwe*]

flue² (floō), n. Substance formed by loose particles of cotton etc., fluff. Hence ~'Y² (-ōō'ĭ) a. [16th c., cf. Flem. *vluwe* in same sense]

flue³ (floō), n. Smoke-duct in chimney; channel for conveying heat, esp. hot-air passage in wall, tube for heating water in some kinds of boiler; ~*-pipes* (mus.), organ-pipes other than reed-pipes. [perh. rel. to FLUE⁵]

flu(e)⁴ (floō), n. (colloq.). (Short for) IN-FLUENZA.

flue⁵ (floō), v.i. & t. Splay, make (opening) widen inwards or outwards. [f. obs. adj. *flue* splayed, expanded, of obsc. orig.]

flu'ency (floō-), n. Smooth easy flow, esp. in speech; ready utterance. [f. LL *fluentia* (f. foll.; see -ENCY]

flu'ent (floō-), a. & n. Flowing (rare in lit. sense); ready to flow, liquid, (rare); fluid, not settled, liable to change, (rare); (of motion, curves, etc.) graceful, easy; (of speech or style) copious, coming easily, ready; expressing oneself quickly & easily; (Math., in fluxions) that FLOWS (n., the variable quantity that flows). Hence ~LY² adv. [f. L *fluere* flow, see -ENT]

fluff, n., & v.t. 1. Light feathery stuff given off by blankets etc.; soft fur; soft downy mass or bunch; *bit of* ~ (sl.), girl, woman; soft short hair on lip or cheek; || (sl.) theatrical part imperfectly known; hence ~'Y² a., ~'INESS n. 2. v.t. Put soft surface on (flesh side of leather); make into ~; shake (oneself, one's feathers etc.) *up* or *out* into ~y mass; || (sl.) blunder in theatrical part. [perh. modification of FLUE²]

flu'id (floō-), a. & n. (Substance) consisting of particles that move freely among themselves & yield to the slightest pressure (including gases & liquids); moving readily, not solid or rigid, not stable; liquid constituent or secretion. Hence fluid'IFY v.t., fluid'ITY n., (floō-). [f. F *fluide* or L *fluidus* (*fluere* flow, -ID¹)]

fluke¹ (floōk), n. Kinds of flat-fish, the flounder, (now rare); kinds of parasitic worm found in sheep's liver; || kind of kidney potato. [OE *flōc*, cogn. w. ON *flōki* & G *flach* flat]

fluke² (floōk), n. Broad triangular plate on arm of anchor; barbed head of lance, harpoon, etc.; (pl.) whale's tail. [perh. f. prec.]

fluke³ (floōk), n., & v.i. & t. (Make) lucky accidental stroke; get, hit, etc., by ~e. Hence ~'Y² a., ~'ILY² adv., ~'INESS n., (floō-). [orig. unkn.; first in billards]

*flume (floōm), n., & v.i. & t. Artificial channel conveying water for industrial use; ravine with stream; (vb) build ~s,

convey down a ~. [ME, f. OF *flum* f. L *flumen* river (*fluere* flow)]

flumm'ery, n. Food made by boiling oatmeal down to a jelly (arch. or dial.); kinds of sweet dish made with milk, flour, eggs, etc.; empty compliments, trifles, nonsense. [f. W *llymru* (of unkn. orig.]

flumm'ox, n. & v.t. (sl.). Confound, bewilder, disconcert. [prob. dial., imit.]

flump, v.i. & t., & n. Fall or move heavily, set or throw *down*, with a dull noise (n., the action or sound). [imit.]

flung. See FLING v.

flunk'ey, n. (pl. ~s). Liveried servant, footman, (usu. contempt.); toady, snob. Hence ~DOM (-kĭd-), ~ISM (-kĭizm), nn. [orig. Sc.; perh. f. FLANK, with sense *sidesman, flanker*]

fluo(r)-, fluoro-, (floō-), comb. forms of FLUORINE, as *fluobŏ'ric*; *flu'oro*SCOPE, instrument with fluorescent screen used instead of dark room to show X-ray effects. [foll.]

flu'or (floō-), n. Kinds of gemlike readily fusible mineral containing fluorine; ~-*spar*, calcium fluoride. [mod. application of L, = flowing, flux (*fluere* flow, -OR)]

fluor|ĕs'cence (floō-), n. Coloured luminosity produced in certain substances by incident light or other electro-magnetic radiations of shorter wave-length, esp. violet and ultra-violet light and X-rays; property of absorbing light of short (invisible) wave-length and emitting light of longer (visible) wave-length. Hence ~ĕsce' v.i., exhibit ~escence, ~ES'CENT a., (floō-). [prec., -ESCENT, -ENCE]

flu'orine (floō-), n. Non-metallic element of the HALOGEN group. Hence flu'orIDE (floō-)·n. [F, (FLUOR, -INE⁵]

flu'rry, n., & v.t. 1. Gust, squall; commotion, excitement, nervous hurry, agitation; whale's death-throes. 2. v.t. Confuse by haste or noise, agitate. [imit.; cf. earlier *flurr, hurry*]

flush¹, v.i. & t., & n. 1. Take wing & fly away; cause to do this, put up, (birds). 2. Number of birds put up at once. [ME, imit.; cf. *fly, rush*]

flush², v.i. & t. Spurt, rush out; cleanse (drain etc.) by flow of water; flood (meadow); (of plant) throw out fresh shoots (also causative, *rain~es the plants*); glow with warm colour; (of blood) rush into & redden face; (of face) become red or hot, blush; cause to glow or blush; suffuse with warm colour; inflame with pride or passion, encourage, (~*ed with exercise, joy, victory, insolence*, etc.). [perh. = prec. influenced by *flash* & *blush*]

flush³, n. Rush of water; sudden abundance; stream from mill-wheel; rush of emotion, elation produced by it or by victory etc.; fresh growth of grass etc.; cleansing of drain by flushing; glow of light or colour; rush of blood to face, reddening caused by it; hot fit in fever; freshness, vigour. [f. prec.]

flush¹, a., & v.t. **1.** Full to overflowing, in flood; (usu. pred.) having plentiful supply of or of money etc., (of money) abundant; even, in same plane, level *with*, without projections or raised edges. **2.** v.t. Send, fill in (joint) level with surface. [prob. f. FLUSH²]

flush,⁵ n. Set of cards all of one suit; *straight ~*, set of cards in a regular sequence; *royal ~* (Poker), a straight ~ headed by ace. [f. OF *flus, flux* = Flem. *fluys*, Sp. *flux*, f. L FLUXus]

flus'ter, v.t. & i., & n. **1.** Confuse with drink, half-intoxicate; flurry, make nervous; be agitated, bustle. **2.** n. Flurry, flutter, agitation. [orig. unkn.; cf. Icel. *flaustr(a)* hurry, bustle]

flus'tra, n. (pl. *-ae, -as*). Sea-mat, polyzoic species resembling seaweed. [arbitrary mod., L coinage by Linnaeus]

flute (floot), n., & v.i. & t. **1.** Musical wind-instrument, long wooden pipe with holes along it stopped by fingers or keys, & blow-hole in side near upper end, whence **flut'IST**(3) (floo-) n. ; ~*-player*; organ stop with ~-like tone; semicylindrical vertical groove in pillar, similar groove elsewhere, e.g. in frills, whence **flut'ING**¹(6) (floo-) n. **2.** vb. Play ~; whistle, sing, or speak, in ~-like tones; play (air etc.) on ~; make ~s or grooves in. [ME, f. OF *fleüte, flaüte, flahute*, f. Pr. *flaüt*]

flutt'er, v.i. & t., & n. **1.** Flap wings, flap (wings), without flying or in short flights; come or go with quivering motion (usu. to the ground); go about restlessly, flit, hover; quiver, vibrate, (of pulse) beat feebly & irregularly; tremble with excitement, be agitated; move (flag etc.) irregularly, agitate, ruffle; throw (person) into confusion or agitation. **2.** n. ~*ing*; tremulous excitement (*be, put, in a ~*); stir, sensation, (*make a ~*); vibration (*wing, tail, ~*, defects of aircraft in flight); (sl.) modest gambling venture, speculation. [OE *flotorian* frequent. form cogn. w. OE *fléotan* FLEET⁵]

flut'y (floo-), a. Like flute in tone, soft & clear. [-Y²]

fluv'ial (floo-), a. Of, found in, river(s). [f. L *fluvialis (fluvius* river, -AL)]

fluv'iatile (floo-), a. Of, found in, produced by, river(s). [f. F, or L *fluviatilis* (prec., -ATILE)]

fluv'io- (floo-), comb. form of L *fluvius* river, as *fluvio-marine, fluviom'eter*.

flux, n., & v.i. & t. **1.** Morbid or excessive discharge of blood, excrement, etc., (formerly) dysentery; flowing out, issue; flowing; inflow of tide (usu. ~ *& reflux*, often fig.); flood of talk etc.; continuous succession of changes (*in a state of ~*); (Math.) continued motion (*line is the ~ of a point*); (Phys.) rate of flow of any fluid across given area, amount crossing in in given time; substance mixed with metal etc. to promote fusion. **2.** vb. Issue in a ~, flow copiously; make fluid,

fuse, treat with a fusing ~. [ME *flix(e), flux* f. OF *flux* or L *fluxus (fluere* flux-flow)]

flu'xion (-kshn), n. Flowing (rare); continuous change (rare); (Math.) rate or proportion at which a flowing or varying quantity increases its magnitude (*method of ~s*, the Newtonian calculus). Hence ~AL, ~ARY¹, aa., (-kshon-). [f. F, or L *fluxio* (prec., -ION)]

fly¹, n. Two-winged insect (*~ in amber*, curious relic; *~ on wheel*, person who over-estimates his own influence; *break ~ on wheel*, expend disproportionate energy; *a ~ in the ointment*, trifling circumstance that mars enjoyment; *no flies on him* etc., sl. praise of person's or thing's efficiency; HESSIAN, TSETSE, ~); kinds of plant-disease caused by various flies (*a good deal of ~ exists*); natural or artificial ~ used as fishing-bait; CATCH¹ ~; ~*-blow*, (n.) ~'s egg in meat etc., (v.t.) deposit eggs in, taint, (~*-blown*, tainted, lit. & fig.); ~*-book*, case for keeping fishing-flies in; ~*-catcher*, trap for flies, kinds of bird; ~*-fish* (v.i.), fish with ~; ~*-flap*, for driving away flies; ~*-net*, net or fringe protecting horse from flies; ~*-paper*, for catching or poisoning flies; ~*-trap*, for catching flies, also kinds of plant esp. *Venus's* ~*-trap*; ~*-weight* (BOX⁵); ~*-whisk*, for driving away flies. [OE *flyge, fléoge*, OS, OHG *flioga* f. WG *fleugōn* (foll.)]

fly², v.i. & t. (*flew*, pr. floo, *flown* pr. flōn; *is, has flown*, see -ED¹(2); *fly* is preferred in talk & ordinary prose for *flee*, but not *flew* or *flown* for *fled*). Move through air with wings (*~ high*, be ambitious; *high-flown*, exalted, turgid, bombastic; *as the* CROW¹ *flies*; *the bird is flown*, person wanted has escaped; often *about, away, forth, off, out*) or in aircraft; direct flight of (aircraft), transport (passengers) in aircraft; make (pigeon, hawk) ~; (Hawk.) soar by way of attack *at* (fig., ~ *at higher game*, have nobler ambitions); pass or rise quickly through air; jump clear over or over fence etc.; make (kite) rise & stay aloft (*~ a kite*, raise money by accommodation bill, also try how the wind blows, feel one's way by *ballon d'essai*); (of flag, hair, garment, etc.) wave; set or keep (flag) ~ing; travel swiftly, rush along, pass rapidly; spring, start, hasten, (*~ to arms*, take up arms eagerly); *~ in the* FACE¹ *of*; *~ at, upon*, attack violently; *~ into* a passion, raptures, etc.; *~ out*, burst into violent language or action); be driven or forced off suddenly (*made sparks ~; send ~ing; make the money ~*, spend quickly; *door flew open; glass etc. flies*, breaks in pieces); *let ~*, discharge (missile), (abs.) shoot, hit, or use strong language, *at*; run away, flee, flee from (*must ~ the country*); ~*-away*, (of garments) streaming, loose, négligé, (of persons) flighty; ~*-by-night*, one who makes night excursions or decamps by night; ~-*over* n., procession of aircraft, (also ~-*over bridge, viaduct*) bridge for carrying vehicles over traffic-congested areas, esp. over main roads; ~-*past* n., ceremonial flight of aircraft past some person or place, cf. MARCH⁴ *past*; ~-*the- -garter*, kind of leap-frog. [OE *flēogan*, OS, OHG *fliogan*, ON *fljúga* f. Gmc *fleugan*]

flȳ³, n. Flying, distance flown, (*on the* ~, on the wing, in motion); || one-horse hackney-carriage (obs.); lap on garment to contain or cover buttonholes, flap at entrance of tent; part of flag farthest from staff, also its breadth from staff to end; (Theatr.; pl.) space over proscenium; speed-regulating device in clockwork & machinery; ~-*leaf*, blank leaf at beginning or end of book, blank leaf of circular etc.; ~'*man*, || driver of ~ = carriage (obs.), man stationed in flies of theatre to work rope etc.; ~-*sheet*, 2 or 4 page circular etc.; ~-*wheel*, heavy- -rimmed on revolving shaft to regulate machinery or accumulate power. [f. prec.]

flȳ⁴, a. (sl.). Knowing, wide awake. [orig. unkn.]

flȳ'er, fli'er, n. Bird etc. that flies (usu. *high, poor*, etc., ~); (colloq.) ambitious person; animal, vehicle, etc., going with exceptional speed; airman; flying jump. [-ER¹]

flȳ'ing, a. In vbl senses; also or esp.: making movements like flight (~ *bed- stead*, experimental aircraft shaped like bedstead for testing methods of vertical take-off; ~ *boat*, form of SEAplane in which a boat serves as both fuselage & float; ~ *bomb*, aerial torpedo, pilotless aircraft with explosive war-head; ~-*dog*, kind of vampire-bat; ~ DUTCHMAN; ~ *fish*, kinds rising into air by wing-like pectoral fins, also nickname for native of Barbados; ~ *fox*, kinds of fruit-eating bat; ~ *man*, airman; *F*~ *Officer*, rank in AIR¹ Force; ~ *saucer*, saucer-like object occas. reported as having been seen flying at great speed & height; ~ *squad*, police detachment with motor-cars etc. for rapid pursuit; ~ *squirrel*, kinds floating in air by skin connecting fore & hind legs); hanging loose, fluttering, (~ *jib*, light sail set before jib on ~ jib-boom; *with* ~ COLOUR¹s); done or taken in passing (~ *jump*, with running start; ~ *handicap, mile, start*, in which starting-post is passed at full speed); passing, hasty, (~ *visit*); temporary (~ *bridge*); designed for rapid movement (~ *squadron, column*); ~ *but- tress*, slanting from pier etc. to wall & usu. carried on arch. [-ING²]

foal, n., & v.t. & i. 1. Young of horse, ass, etc., colt or filly, (*in, with*, ~, pregnant). 2. vb. Give birth to (~), give birth to ~. [OE *fola*, OHG *foli*, ON *foli*, Goth. *fula* f. Gmc *folon* cogn. w. L *pullus*]

foam, n., & v.i. 1. Collection of small bubbles formed in liquid by agitation, fermentation, etc.; froth of saliva or perspiration; (poet.) the sea; ~ *rubber*, ~like rubbery substance used esp. in upholstery. 2. v.i. Emit ~, froth at the mouth; (of water etc.) froth, gather ~, run ~ing *along, down, over*, etc., pass *off* or *away* in ~; (of cup etc.) be filled with ~ing liquor. Hence ~'LESS, ~'Y², aa. [OE *fām*, OHG *feim* f. WG *faima*]

fŏb¹, n., & v.t. (-bb-). Small pocket for watch etc. formerly made in waistband of breeches; (vb) put in one's ~, pocket. [17th c., cf. G dial. *fuppe* pocket]

fŏb², v.t. (-bb-). Cheat, take in; palm (something inferior) *off upon* (person); put (person) *off with* (something inferior). [16th c., cf. obs. *fop* to dupe & G *foppen* befool]

fō'cal, a. Of, situated or collected at, a focus; (Opt.) ~ *distance* or *length*, distance between centre of mirror or lens & its focus. [FOCUS, -AL]

fŏc'alize, -is|e (-īz), v.t. = FOCUS v.t. Hence ~A'TION n. [prec., -IZE]

fo'c's'le. See FORECASTLE.

fō'cus, n. (pl. -*ci* pr. -sī, -*uses*), & v.t. & i. (-s-, -ss-). 1. (Plane geom.) one of points from which distances to any point of given curve are connected by linear relation; (Opt., Heat, etc.) point at which rays meet after reflection or refraction, point from which rays appear to proceed, point at which object must be situated for image given by lens to be well defined (*in, out of, bring into*, ~), focal length of lens, adjustment of eye or eyeglass necessary to produce clear image; point to which sound-waves converge; principal seat (of disease, activity, etc.). 2. vb. Converge, make converge, to a ~; adjust ~ of (lens, eye); bring into ~. [L, = hearth]

fŏd'der, n., & v.t. 1. Dried food, hay, straw, etc., for stall-feeding cattle; CANNON¹-~; hence ~LESS a. 2. v.t. Give ~ to. [OE *fōdor*, OHG *fuotar*, ON *fóthr* f. Gmc *fōthram* (FOOD)]

fōe, n. (poet. etc.). Enemy, adversary, opponent, ill-wisher; ~'*man* (arch.), enemy in war. [OE *gefā* n. f. *gefāh* adj. (= OHG *gafēh* at feud with, f. WG *gafaiha*; cf. FEUD¹)]

foet'us (fēt-), **fēt'us**, n. Fully developed embryo in womb. Hence **f(o)et'AL** a., **f(o)et'ICIDE**(2) n., (fē-). [L *fœtus -ūs* offspring]

fŏg¹, n., & v.t. (-gg-). 1. Aftermath; long grass left standing in winter. 2. v.t. Leave (land) under ~; feed (cattle) on ~. [14th c., of unkn. orig.; cf. Norw. *fogg*]

fŏg², n., & v.t. & i. (-gg-). 1. Vapour suspended in atmosphere at or near earth's surface, obscurity caused by this (*in a* ~, puzzled, at a loss); abnormal darkened state of atmosphere; (Photog.) cloud on developed plate; ~-*bow*, like rainbow produced by light on ~; ~-*horn*, sounding instrument for warning ships in ~; ~-*signal*, detonator placed on railway line in ~ to guide driver. 2. *vb.* Envelop (as) with ~; bewilder, perplex; (Gardening) die *off* from damp; (Photog.) make (negative) obscure or cloudy; || (Railway) place ~-signals on line, whence || ~-g′ER¹ n. [perh. back form. f. FOGGY; from 16th c.]

fŏgg′|ў (-g-), a. Thick, murky; of, like, infested with, FOG²; obscure, dull, confused, (*has only a* ~*y idea of it*; *not the* ~*iest*, colloq., sc. *idea*); beclouded, indistinct. Hence ~ILY² *adv.*, ~INESS n. [f. FOG¹+-Y; earlier senses *covered with coarse grass*, *boggy*, *flabby* (flesh), *murky* (air); hence, poss., FOG²]

fŏ′gle, n. (thieves' sl.). Silk handkerchief. [orig. unkn.]

fŏg′ў, -gey, (-g-), n. (Usu. *old* ~) old-fashioned fellow, old man behind the times. Hence fŏg′(e)yDOM, fŏg′ўISM, nn., fŏg′ўISH¹ a., (-g-). [18th c., abbr. of *fogram*, of unkn. orig.]

Föhn (fĕrn), n. Hot southerly wind in the Alps. [G, ult. f. L *Favonius*]

foi′ble, n. Weak point, weakness of character, quality on which one mistakenly prides oneself; (Fenc.) part of sword-blade from middle to point (cf. FORTE). [F, obs. form of *faible* FEEBLE]

foil¹, n., & v.t. 1. (Archit.) arc or space between cusps of window (vb, ornament with ~s, as ~*ed arch*). 2. Metal hammered or rolled into thin sheet (usu. *gold*, *tin*, etc., ~); sheet of this, or now amalgam of tin & quicksilver, placed behind mirror-glass, backing; leaf of it placed under precious stone etc. to brighten or colour it or enhance its brightness by contrast (vb, supply with this). 3. Anything that sets something off by contrast (vb, set off thus). [ME, f. OF f. L *folium* leaf]

foil², v.t. & i., & n. 1. (Hunt.) run over or cross (scent, ground) so as to baffle hounds (also *abs.* of deer etc., spoil the scent thus); beat off, repulse, frustrate, parry, baffle. 2. n. Track of hunted animal (*run*, *run upon*, *the* ~, over same track a second time); (arch.) repulse, defeat, check. [f. OF *fouler* full cloth, trample; f. Rom. *fullare f. L *fullo* fuller]

foil³, n. Blunt-edged sword with button on point used in fencing. [16th c., of unkn. orig.]

|| **fois′on** (-zn), n. (arch.). Plenty. [ME, f. OF f. L *fusionem* (*fundere fus*- pour, -ION, -SON)]

foist, v.t. Introduce surreptitiously or unwarrantably *into* or *in* (adv.); palm (*off*) *on* or *upon*, father (composition) *upon*. [orig. of palming false die; prob. f. Du. dial. *vuisten* take in the hand (*vuist* fist)]

fold¹, n., & v.t. 1. (Usu. *sheep*-~) enclosure for sheep; (fig.) church, body of believers (also *true* ~). 2. v.t. Shut up (sheep etc.)

in ~; place sheep in ~ or ~s on (land) to manure it. [OE *fald* = MLG *valt*; unconnected w. foll.]

fold², v.t. & i., & n. 1. Double (flexible thing) over upon itself (also *in*, *over*, *together*; ~ *up*, make more compact by ~ing); bend portion of (thing) *back*, *down*; become, be able to be, ~ed (~*ing door*(s), in 2 parts, often themselves ~ing, hung on 2 jambs); wind, clasp, (arms etc.) *about*, *round*; lay together & interlace (arms), clasp (one's hands); swathe, envelop, (~ *it in paper*; *hills* ~*ed in mist*); embrace *in* arms or *to* breast. 2. n. Doubling of ~ed object; hollow between two thicknesses (*carried it in a* ~ *of her dress*), hollow or nook in mountain etc.; coil of serpent, string, etc.; ~ing (*another* ~ *gives 32mo*); line made by ~ing; (Geol.) the ~ing or curvature of strata. [OE *fealdan*, OHG *faltan*, ON *falda*, Goth. *falthan*, Gmc *falthan]

-fold, suf. (OE *-feald*, OS *-fald*, OHG *-falt*, ON *-faldr*, Goth. *-falths*) cogn. w. FOLD², Gk *-paltos*, *-plasios*, & *-plo-* in *haplos* single, & prob. L *-plex* (*simplex* etc.); added to cardinals to form adjj. w. sense *multiplied by* (orig. sense *folded in* —, *plaited in* — *strands*). Now largely superseded by wds f. L in *-ble*, *-ple*, (*treble*, *quadruple*), but retained in the advl use (*repaid tenfold*), & in adjj. when there is a plurality of things more or less different (*a twofold charm*).

fŏl′der, n. In vbl senses; esp.: paper-folding instrument; folded circular etc.; (pl.) folding eyeglasses. [-ER¹]

fōliā′ceous (-shus), a. Leaf-like; with organs like leaves; of leaves; laminated. [f. L *foliaceus* (*folium* leaf, -ACEOUS)]

fōl′iage, n. Leaves, leafage, (lit., or as represented in art; ~ *leaf*, excluding petals etc.; ~ *plant*, cultivated for ~, not for flowers). Hence (-)fōl′iagED² (-ĕjd) a. [f. F *feuillage* f. *feuille* (f. L *folia* pl. of *folium* FOIL¹)+-AGE]

fōl′iar, a. Of leaves. [f. L *folium* leaf, -AR¹]

fōl′iate¹, a. Leaf-like; having leaves; having specified number of leaflets (*1*, *5*, etc., ~). [f. L *foliatus* (*folium* leaf, -ATE²)]

fōl′i|āte², v.i. & t. Split (intr.) into laminae; decorate (arch, door-head) with foils; number leaves (not pages) of (volume) consecutively. So ~A′TION n. [f. L *folium* leaf, -ATE³]

fōl′iō, n. (pl. *-os*). Leaf of paper, parchment, etc., numbered only on front; (Bookkeep.) two opposite pages of ledger etc. used concurrently, page of ledger etc. used for both sides of account; leaf-number of printed book; number of words (72 or 90) taken as unit of reckoning length of document; sheet of paper folded once (*in* ~, of books on such paper); volume made of such sheets, largest-sized volume, (also attrib., *a* ~ *book*, *in six volumes* ~). [L, abl. of *folium* leaf (abl. f. use in reff., = *on leaf 50* etc.)]

fōl'iŏle, n. Division of compound leaf, leaflet. [F, f. LL *foliolum* dim. of *folium* leaf]

folk (fōk), n. (Arch.) a people, nation, race; (pl., the sing. being arch. or dial.) people in general, people of specified class, (now being ousted by *people*); ~, of the people (chiefly in compounds imitated f. German, as ~-*custom*, -*song*; ~-*etymology*, perversion of word's form to make it significant; ~'*lore*, traditional beliefs etc., study of these, ~'*lörist*, student of these), ~'*sў* a., friendly, sociable. [OE, OS, OHG *folc*, ON *folk* f. Gmc *folkam*]

fŏll'icle, n. Small sac or vesicle; cocoon. So **fŏllic'ūlAR**[1], **fŏllic'ūlātĕd** [-ATE[2]], aa. [f. L *folliculus* (*follis* bellows, -CULE)]

fŏll'ow (-ō), v.t. & i., & n. 1. Go or come after (moving thing or person; ~ *the hounds*, hunt; ~ *my leader*, game in which each player must do as leader does; ~ one's *nose*, leave one's route to chance; ~ *the plough*, be ploughman); go along (path); come after in order or time; accompany, serve; go after as admirer or FOLLOWER; result from, be the necessary consequence of, be involved in, (*trade* ~*s the flag*); strive after, aim at; treat or take as guide or master, obey, espouse opinions or cause of; conform to (~ SUIT), act upon, take as rule; practise (profession etc.; ~ *the sea*, be sailor); keep up with mentally, grasp the meaning of, (argument, speaker); go or come after person or thing (~ *in his steps*; ~ *in the wake of*); come next in order, as *his arguments are as* ~*s* (not ~); happen after something else, ensue; result, be deducible, (*it must* ~ *as the night the day*). 2. ~ *after* (prep. & adv.), = ~ (in most senses, but with slightly formal effect); (Cricket, of side) ~ *on*, go in again out of turn after getting less than opponents by certain number (n., ~-*on*, doing this); ~ *out*, pursue to the end; ~ *through* (Golf), carry stroke through to fullest possible extent after striking ball (~-*through* n., this action); ~ *up*, pursue steadily, add another blow etc. to (previous blow etc.), (Footb. etc.) keep near (player with) ball to support; ~-*up*, the continuation of an action, (esp.) a second advertising circular sent referring to an earlier one. 3. n. (Billiards) stroke causing player's ball to roll on after object-ball, motion so given; (at restaurants) supplementary portion of half the quantity. [OE *folgian*, OS -*ōn*, OHG -*ēn*, ON *fylgia* f. Gmc *fulg-*]

fŏll'ower (-ōer), n. In vbl senses; esp.: adherent, disciple; man courting maidservant. [-ER[1]]

fŏll'owing[1] (-ō-), n. In vbl senses; also, body of adherents, followers. [-ING[1]]

fŏll'owing[2] (-ō-), a. In vbl senses; esp., now to be mentioned (also as pron. sing. or pl., *the* ~ *are noteworthy*). [-ING[2]]

fŏll'ў, n. Being foolish, want of good

sense, unwise conduct; foolish act, idea, or practice, ridiculous thing; costly structure (considered) useless (usu. with originator's name, ~'*s F*~). [ME, f. OF *folie* f. *fol* mad, FOOL[1], see -Y[1]]

fōment', v.t. Bathe with warm or medicated lotions, apply warmth to; foster, stimulate, or instigate (sentiment, conduct, sedition, etc.), whence ~ER[1] n. [f. F *fomenter* f. LL *fomentare* f. L *fomentum* (*fovēre* cherish, -MENT)]

fōmĕntā'tion, n. In vbl senses; esp., (application of) warm flannels etc. for fomenting purposes. [f. LL *fomentatio* (prec., -ATION)]

fŏnd, a. Foolishly credulous or sanguine; over-affectionate, doting; tender, loving; ~ *of*, full of love for, much inclined to. Hence ~'LY[2] adv., ~'NESS n. [ME; p.p. of obs. *fon* be foolish]

fŏn'dant, n. Kind of sweetmeat. [F (*fondre* melt f. L *fundere* pour, -ANT)]

fŏn'dle, v.t. & i. Caress; toy amorously (*with*, *together*). [f. obs. *fond* vb (FOND), -LE(3)]

fŏns ĕt ŏrī'gō, phr. The source and origin (*of*). (L)

fŏnt, n. Receptacle for baptismal water; receptacle for holy water; oil-reservoir of lamp. [OE *font*, *fant*, ult. f. eccl. use of L *fons font-* spring]

fŏn'tal, a. Primary, original, of the fountain-head; baptismal. [f. OF, or LL *fontalis* (prec., -AL)]

fŏntanĕl(le)', n. Membranous space in infant's head at adjacent angles of parietal bones. [F (-*lle*), dim. of *fontaine* FOUNTAIN]

fōod, n. Victuals, nourishment, provisions, (*be* ~ *for worms*, dead; *be* ~ *for fishes*, drowned; ~ *for powder*, soldiers); edibles (~ *& drink*); particular kind of ~; nutriment of plants; material for the mind (*mental, intellectual*, ~; ~ *for thought* or *meditation*); ~-*stuff*, thing used as ~. Hence ~'LESS a. [OE *fōda*, cogn. w. ON *fœtha*, Goth. *fōdeins* f. Gmc *fōdh-*, *fadh-*; cf. FEED[1]]

fōol[1], n., a., & v.i. & t. 1. Silly person, simpleton, person whose conduct one disapproves of, (*be a* ~ *to*, be nothing in comparison with; *play the* ~, blunder, trifle; *no* ~ *like an old* ~, esp. of aged lover; ~'*s bolt is soon shot*, his stock of argument is soon exhausted; *man is* ~ *or physician at thirty*, sensible man needs no doctor); jester, clown, in medieval great house (*play the* ~, indulge in buffoonery); dupe (*make a* ~ *of*; *be a* ~ *for* one's *pains*, take trouble to no end; *All Fools' day*, 1st April; *April* ~, person taken in or sent on ~'s errand on that day; *send, go, on* ~'*s errand*, fruitless one; ~'*s* MATE[1]; ~'*s paradise*, illusory happiness); ~'*s-cap*, ~*s' cap*, cap with bells worn by medieval jester, dunce's conical paper cap, watermark of some old papermakers, writing paper 15–17 × 12–13½ in.; hence ~'ERY(4, 5),

~ŏC'RACY, nn., ~'ISH¹ a., ~'ishLY² adv.. ~-ishNESS n., ~'PROOF² a. (of rules etc. so plain as to defy misinterpretation). 2. •adj. (colloq.). ~ish, silly. 3. vb. Play the ~, idle, trifle, (also *about* & *around*); cheat (person) *out of* money etc. or *into doing*, get (money etc.) by cajolery *out of* person; throw (time, money) *away* ~ishly; make a ~ of, dupe, play tricks on. [ME, f. OF *fol* f. L *follis* bellows, later *empty- -headed person*]

fŏŏl², n. Creamy liquid of fruit stewed, crushed, & mixed with milk, cream, etc. (esp. *gooseberry* ~). [prob. f. prec.]

fŏŏl'hărd|y̆, a. Foolishly venturesome, delighting in needless risks. Hence ~i- NESS n. [f. OF *fol hardi* (FOOL¹, HARDY¹)]

fŏŏt¹, n. (pl. *feet*). 1. Termination of leg beginning at ankle (FIND one's *feet*; *have feet of clay*, be liable to overthrow, see *Dan.* ii. 33). 2. Step, pace, tread, (*swift of* ~; *has a light* ~). 3. Infantry (*the 4th* ~ or *regiment of* ~; ~-*soldier*; *a captain of* ~; *horse*, ~, *& artillery*). 4. Lower end of bed, table, grave, couch, etc. (opp. *head*), part of stocking etc. covering~. 5. Metri- cal unit with varying number of syllables one of which is accented. 6. Lineal measure of 12 in. (*10 feet long*; ā *ten-*~ *pole*; *six* ~ or *feet three*; see also SQUARE a., CUBIC). 7. Lower usu. projecting part, base. 8. (zool.). Kinds of loco- motive or adhesive organ in inverte- brates. 9. (bot.). Part by which petal is attached, root of hair. 10. Lowest part, bottom, of hill, ladder, wall, list, page, class, etc. 11. Dregs, oil refuse, coarse sugar, (pl. ~s). 12. Phrr. : *have one* ~ *in grave*, be near death; (*with one's*) *feet foremost*, being carried to burial; *find, know, length of* one's ~, learn his weak- nesses, be able to manage him; *measure another's* ~ *by* one's *own last*, judge others by oneself; *set, put, have*, one's ~ *on the neck of*, utterly subdue, hold in sub- jection; *on* one's *feet*, standing, in health, with a livelihood; *carry* one *off his feet*, make him enthusiastic, greatly excite; FALL¹ *on* one's *feet*; *keep* one's *feet*, not fall; *put* one's ~ *down*, take up firm position (fig.); *put* one's ~ *in it*, blunder; BEST¹ ~; CHANGE² ~ or *feet*; *at* one's *feet*, as his disciple, subject, or suppliant; *have* BALL¹ *at* one's *feet*; *with foal at* ~, of mare that has foaled; *on* ~, walking, not riding etc., also in motion (*set agitation, move- ment*, etc., *on* ~, start it), busy, projected, proceeding; *tread under* ~, oppress; *wet* etc. *under* ~, on the ground. 13. ~-*&- -mouth* (*disease*), kind of fever esp. in horned cattle; ~'*ball*, large round or elliptical inflated ball, game played with it, ~'*baller*, player at this; ~-*bath*, wash- ing of feet, small bath used for this; ~'*board*, ~*man's* platform at carriage- -back, board for getting in or out of carriage by, sloped board for driver's feet; ~'*boy*, page, boy servant in livery;

~-*bridge*, -*path*, -*road*, -*way*, etc., for ~-*passengers* only; ~-*drill*, -*pump*, etc., worked by or with help of ~; ~'*fall*, sound of ~*step*; ~-*fault* (Lawn Tennis), fault made by overstepping the base line while serving; ~-*gear*, boots, socks, etc.; ‖ *F*~ *Guards*, Grenadier, Coldstream, Scots, Irish, Welsh, Guards; ~-*hill*, lying at base of mountain; ~'*hold*, support for feet, surface for standing on, also fig.; ~'*lights*, screened lights in front of stage (GET¹ *across the* ~*lights*); ~'*man*, infantry- man, liveried servant for carriage, door, & table, trivet to hang on grate bars; ~-*mark*, ~*print*; ~-*muff*, for keeping feet warm; ~-*note*, inserted at ~ of page; ~-*pace*, walking pace, dais; ~'*pad*, un- mounted highwayman; ~-*page*, boy servant; ~-*pan*, for washing feet; ~- -*passenger*, one who walks, not rides or drives; ‖ ~-*path* (for ~-*passengers*); ~- -*plate*, driver's and fireman's platform in locomotive; ~-*pound*, quantity of energy that will raise 1 lb. to height of 1 ft; ~'*print*, impression left by ~; ~-*race*, running-match between persons; ~-*rot*, disease of ~ in sheep & cattle; ~-*rule*, rigid measure 1 ft long; ‖~-*slogger* (sl.), walker, infantryman, & so~-*slogging* n. & a.; ~'*sore*, having sore feet, esp. with walking; ~'*stalk*, (Bot.) stalk of leaf or peduncle of flower. (Zool.) attachment of barnacle etc.; ~'*step*, tread, footprint, (*follow in* one's ~*steps*, do as he did); ~-*stone*, foundation stone, stone at ~ of grave; ~'*stool*, for resting feet on; ~'*sure*, sure-footed; ~'*warmer*, thing to warm feet, esp. flat hot-water tin formerly used in railway carriages; ~-*wear*, = ~-*gear*. Hence (-)~'ED², ~'LESS, aa. [OE, OS *fōt*, OHG *fuoz*, ON *fótr*, Goth. *fōtus* f. Gmo •fōt- cogn. w. L *ped-*, Gk *pod-*]

fŏŏt², v.i. & t. ~, dance, (rare) pace, go; set foot on, traverse on foot (rare); put new foot to (stocking); add up or *up* (account); pay (bill); (of bill, items, etc.) mount *up to*. [f. prec.]

‖ fŏŏt'er, n. (sl.). The game football. [-ER¹]

fŏŏt'ing, n. Placing of feet, foothold; surface for standing on, secure position, (lit. & fig.); conditions, relations, position, status, in which person is towards others, degree of intimacy etc.; entrance on new position, admittance to trade, society, etc., (only in *pay for* or *pay* one's ~, i.e. a customary fee for it); projecting course at foot of wall etc.; (reckoning of) sum total of column of figures etc. [FOOT² + -ING¹]

fŏŏ'tl|e, v.i., & n. (sl.). 1. Trifle, play the fool; hence ~ING² a. 2. n. Twaddle, folly. [orig. unkn.]

fŏŏ'zle, v.t., & n. (sl., esp. golf). 1. Do clumsily, bungle, make a mess of. 2. n. Clumsy failure. [f. G dial. *fuseln* work badly or slowly; cf. FUSEL OIL]

fŏp, n. Dandy, exquisite, vain man. Hence ~'LING¹(2), ~p'ERY(4, 5), nn.

~p'ISH¹ a., ~p'ishLY² adv., ~p'ish-NESS n. [in 15th c. 'fool', whence perh. the 17th c. sense 'dandy']

for (fŏr, fŏr, fer, *according to position or emphasis required*), prep. & conj. **1.** prep. Representing, in place of, in exchange against, as price or penalty of, in requital of, (*sits* ~, *member* ~, *Liverpool*; *once* ~ *all*, instead of many repetitions, finally; *substituted* ~; *agent* ~; *got it* ~ *6d.*; *thrashed* ~ *his pains*; *do you take me* ~ *a fool?*); in defence or support or favour of, on side of, (*take my word* ~ *it*, be assured; *hurrah* ~ *person or thing*; *am* ~ *tariff-reform*); with a view to, in order to be, conducive(ly) to, (*go* ~ *a walk*; *went* ~ *a soldier*; *is*, did *it*, ~ *her good*; ~ *sale*, to be sold); to get, win, or save (*send*, *go*, ~ *a cab*; *would not do it* ~ *the world*; *not paid* ~; *play* ~ *penny points*; *was tried* ~ *his life*; *cannot do it* ~ *the life of me*; *run* ~ IT); to reach, arrive at, be received by, or belong to (*left*, *sailed*, ~ *India*; *made* ~ *shelter*; *go* ~ (sl.), attack; *getting on* ~ *two o'clock*; *bought shoes* ~ *the maids*; *won a name* ~ *himself*); (after vbs, adjj., nn., & interjections, of emotion, faculty, or fitness; after adjj. & advv. with *too*, *enough*; after expressions implying fitness etc.) as regards, in the direction of, (*don't care* ~ *games*; *a longing* ~ *praise*; *fit* ~ *nothing*; *ready* ~ *dinner*; *oh* ~ *wings!*; *now* ~ *it!*; *too beautiful* ~ *words*; *good enough* ~ *me*; *time* ~ *school*; *is not long* ~ *this world*, will soon die; *nothing* ~ *it but to submit*, submission the only course open; *is the man* ~ *the job*; *it is* ~ *you to make the move*; *the motive* ~ *retreating*); with the result, at the cost, to the amount, of (*all out* ~ *44*; *150* ~ *6 wickets*; *drew on him* ~ *£100*); to affect, as affecting, beneficially or the reverse (*they live* ~ *each other*; *can shift* ~ *myself*; *things look bad* ~ *you*; *it is bad* ~ *him to smoke*; & hence ~ with noun or pron. & infin. as neutral noun-phrase = Latin acc. & inf., *it is wicked* ~ *him to smoke*, *it is usual* ~ *hats to be worn* = that hats should be worn); in the character of, as, as being, (*hold it* ~ *certain*; *mistaken* ~ *him*; *be hanged* ~ *a pirate*; *take* ~ *granted*; *I* ~ *one do not believe it*; *did it* ~ *the second time*; ~ GOOD); by reason, under influence, because, on account, of (*did it* ~ *pure wantonness*; *avoid it* ~ *fear of accidents*; *I tremble* ~ *him*; *notorious* ~ *parsimony*; *do it* ~ *my sake*; *fie* ~ *shame!*; *alas* ~ *him!*); in spite of (~ *all that*, ~ *all you say*, ~ *all he seems to dislike me*, *I still like him*); on account of the hindrance of (*were it not*, *but*, *except*, ~ *one thing I might be happy*); corresponding to, in contrast with, (~ *one enemy he has a hundred friends*; *bulk* ~ *bulk*, taking equal bulk of each; *word* ~ *word*, literally, verbatim); so far as concerns, regarding, (~ *the rest*; ~ *my part*; ~ *all*, *aught*, *I know*; *hard up* ~ *money*; *wants* ~ *nothing*); considering, making

the allowance required by, the usual nature of (*a humane man* ~ *an executioner*; *very bright* ~ *a winter day*); during, over, to the extent of, (*has been so* ~ *months*; *walk* ~ *two miles*; *made comfortable* ~ *life*, ~ *the present*; *left him alone* ~ *once*); ~ *all the world*, exactly (*looked* ~ *all the world like a porpoise*; *be for it* (sl.), be destined for punishment. **2.** conj. (Introducing new sentence or series of sentences containing proof of or reason for believing what has been previously stated) seeing that, since, in order to be convinced of this observe or remember that . . . [OE, OS *for*, Goth. *faur*, prob. shortened f. Gmc *fora FORE²]

for-, pref. formerly very common, but remaining only in some dozen common words. Meanings: (1) away, off, apart, (~*by*, ~*get*, ~*give*); (2) prohibition (~*bid*, ~*fend*); (3) abstention, neglect, (~*bear*, ~*go*, ~*sake*, ~*swear*); (4) bad effect (~*do*); (5) excess, intensity (~*lorn*, ~*worn*). [OE *for-*, *fær-*, OS *for-*, OHG *fir-*, *far-*, Goth. *fair-*, *faur-*, cogn. w. Gk *peri*, *pro*, *para*, & L *per*, *pro*]

fŏ'rage, n., & v.t. & i. **1.** Food for horses & cattle, esp. for horses in army; foraging (*on the* ~ etc.); ‖ ~*-cap*, infantry undress cap. **2.** vb. Collect ~ from, ravage; search for ~ or (fig.) *for* anything, rummage, supply with ~; get by foraging; so **fŏ'rager** (-ĭj-) [-IER] n. [ME, f. OF *fourrage*(r) f. *fuerre* f. WG *fōder FODDER]

forăm'en, n. (pl. *-mǐna*). Orifice, hole, passage, (esp. in Anat., Zool., Bot.). Hence **forăm'in**ATE², **-āt̆ed**, aa. [L (*forare* bore, *-MEN*)]

fŏrasmuch' as (-*az*-; -*az*), conj. Seeing that, since. [= *for as much as*]

fŏ'ray, n., & v.i. (Go on, make) incursion, raid, inroad. [prob. n. f. vb f. ME *forayer* f. OF *fourrier* f. *fuerre* FODDER + *-ier* -ER¹]

forbear'¹ (fŏrb'ār, forbār'), n. (usu. pl.). Ancestor(s). [FORE- + obs. *beer* (BE, -ER¹)]

forbear'² (-bār'), v.t. & i. (-*bore*, -*borne*). Abstain or refrain from or *from*; not use or mention; be patient. Hence ~ANCE n., ~inGLY² adv., (-bār'-). [OE *forberan* (FOR-(3), BEAR²)]

forbid', v.t. (-*băd* or -*băde*; -*bĭdden*). Command (person etc.) not to do, (person etc.) not to go to (place), not allow (person etc. something; person or thing to exist or happen), (~ *him to go*, *him the court*, *him wine*; ~ *gladiators*, *bullfights*; *was* ~*den wine*): (of circumstances, hindrance, etc.) exclude, prevent, make undesirable, (*God* ~*!*, may it not happen!); ~*den* or *prohibited* DEGREES; ~*den fruit*, thing desired because not allowed. [OE *forbēodan*, see FOR-(2), BID]

forbid'ding, a. Repellent, of uninviting appearance. Hence ~LY² adv., ~NESS n. [-ING²]

forby(e), prep. & adv. (Sc. & arch.). Besides; not to mention; in addition. [FOR-(1) + BY; cf. G *vorbei*]

force[1], n. **1.** Strength, power, impetus, violence, intense effort; military strength; body of armed men, army, (pl.) troops; body of police (*the~*, the police); strength exerted on an object, coercion, (*by ~*, *per ~*, by compulsion). **2.** Mental or moral strength; influence, controlling power, efficacy, power to convince, vividness of effect, (*the ~ of circumstances brought it about*; *there is ~ in what you say*; *described with much ~*); (loose use) desirability, good sense, (*can't see the ~ of doing what one dislikes*). **3.** Binding power, validity, (*law remains in*, *comes into*, *~*; *put in ~*, enforce); real import, precise meaning. **4.** (phys.). Measurable and determinable influence inclining body to motion, intensity of this, (formerly) kinetic energy (CONSERVATION *of ~* or *energy*), (formerly) cause of any class of physical phenomena, e.g. of heat or motion, conceived as inherent in matter; (fig.) agency likened to these (*considers himself a ~ in the world*). **5.** *By ~ of*, by means of; (Mil.) *in ~*, in large numbers; *in great~*, vigorous, fit, lively; *~-pump*, that forces water beyond range of atmospheric pressure. Hence *~LESS* (-sl-) a. [ME, f. OF f. Rom. **fortia* (L *fortis* strong)]

force[2], v.t. **1.** Use violence to, ravish. **2.** Constrain, compel, (*~ one's hand*, compel him to act prematurely or adopt policy unwillingly), put strained sense upon (words), (Cards) compel (player) to trump or reveal his strength, compel player to play (certain card); *~d landing*, compulsory landing of aircraft owing to damage, engine failure, etc.; so *~-land* v.t. & i.; compel (person) *to do*, *into doing*, or *into* specified action. **3.** Strain to the utmost, urge, (*~ the pace* or *running*, adopt high speed in race to tire adversary out quickly; so *~ the bidding* at auction; *~ one's voice*, strain to get notes beyond usual compass or degree of loudness beyond what is easy or natural; *~d march*, requiring special effort; *~d DRAUGHT*[1]; *~ the game*, run risks to score quickly; *~ an analogy*, *simile*, etc., overstrain it). **4.** Overpower, capture, make way through, break open, (stronghold, defences, pass, lock, door) by force. **5.** Drive, propel. **6.** Impose, press, (thing) *upon* person (*~ a card*, in conjuring, make one choose a particular card unconsciously). **7.** Effect, produce, by effort (*~ a smile*, make oneself smile; *~ one's way*, *a passage*); take by force, extort, wring, (*~ it out of his hands*; *~d loan*; *~ tears from his eyes*, *the facts out of him*). **8.** Artificially hasten the maturity of (plant, scholar). Hence **fŏr′cĕd**LY[2] adv. [ME, f. OF *forcer* (prec.)]

¶ **force**[3], n. (northern). Waterfall. [f. ON *fors*]

force′ful (-sf-), a. (Arch. or literary or affected for) forcible. Hence *~LY*[2] adv., *~NESS* n. [-FUL]

force majeure (mahzhĕr′), n. Irresistible compulsion, coercion diplomatically recognized as irresistible; war, strike, act of God, etc., excusing fulfilment of contract. [F]

force′meat (-sm-), n. Meat chopped, spiced, & seasoned for stuffing. [f. obs. *force* alt. f. FARCE[2]]

fŏr′cĕps, n. sing. & pl. Surgical pincers; (Anat., Entom., Zool.) organ resembling *~*, whence **fŏr′cĭp**ATE[2] a. [L (genit. *-ipis*)]

fŏr′cible, a. Done by, involving, force; telling, vivid, convincing, (of acts, words, style, artist, etc.); *~-feeble*, disguising feebleness under show of force. Hence *~NESS* n., **fŏr′cibly**[2] adv. [AF, OF (FORCE, *-IBLE*)]

fŏrd, n., & v.t. & i. **1.** Shallow place where river etc. may be crossed by wading. **2.** vb. Cross (water), cross water, by wading. Hence *~ABLE*, *~LESS*, aa. [OE, OS *ford*, OHG *furt* f. WG **furd-*; cf. FARE]

fordo′ (-ōō), v.t. (arch.; *-did*, *-done* pr. dŭn). Kill, destroy, spoil; (p.p.) exhausted, tired out. [OE *fordōn* see FOR- (4), DO[1]]

fore[1], a. & v. **1.** Situated in front (opp. HIND, BACK, AFT). **2.** n. *~* part, bow of ship; (Naut.) *at the ~*, on the *~-royal* mast-head; *to the ~*, on the spot, ready to hand, available, alive, (recently) conspicuous (*come to the ~*, take leading part). [developed f. compounds w. FORE-]

fore[2], adv. & prep. **1.** adv. In front (still *in ~ & aft*, at bow & stern, all over ship, backwards & forwards or lengthwise in ship; *~-&-aft rigged*, having *~-&-aft* sails, i.e. sails set lengthwise, not to yards, as chief sails; *~-&-aft cap*, with peak at each end). **2.** prep. In presence of (in adjurations), as *~ George* = by George. [OE, ME *fore*, OS, OHG *fora*, Goth. *faura*; in mod. naut. use perh. f. LG; prep. often mistakenly '*fore* as if short for *before*]

fore[3], int. (golf), warning people in front of stroke. [prob. for BEFORE]

fore-, FORE[2] freely used as a pref. with vbs, their participial adjectives, vbl nouns, & nouns of action; also with other nouns. Meanings with vbs etc.: (1) in front (*~-runner*); (2) beforehand, in advance, (*~ordain*). Meanings with nouns other than verbal or of action: (3) in front, front-, (*~-quarter*); (4) front part of (*~-arm*); (5) of, near, or towards stem of ship or connected w. foremast (*~-castle*, *~-hold*); (6) anticipatory, precedent, (*~-knowledge*).

fore′arm[1] (fōr′ärm), n. Arm from elbow to wrist or finger-tips; corresponding part in foreleg or wing. [FORE-(4)]

forearm′[2] (fōrärm′), v.t. Arm beforehand. [FORE-(2)]

forebear (fōr′bār), n. = FORBEAR[1].

forebŏd|e (forb-), v.t. Predict (rare); betoken, portend; have presentiment of (usu. evil) or *that*. Hence *~′ing*LY[2] adv. [FORE-(2)]

foreboding (forb-), n. Prediction (rare), presage or omen, presentiment, (esp. of evil). [-ING[1]]

fore-cabin (fōr'k-), n. Cabin in fore part of ship, usu. for second-class passengers. [FORE-(5)]

forecast[1] (fōrkahst'), v.t. (*forecast* or ~*ed*, see in etym.). Estimate, conjecture, beforehand. [ME; FORE-(2)+CAST[1]; ~*ed* depends on mistaken assumption that the vb is derived f. foll.]

fore'cast[2] (fōr'kahst), n. Foresight, prudence, (rare); conjectural estimate of something future, esp. of coming weather. [f. prec.]

forecastle, fo'c's'le (fōk'sl), n. (Hist.) short raised deck at bow, (in warship, later but now obs.) part of upper deck forward of aftermost fore-shroud; (in modern ship) forward part under deck where sailors live. [FORE-(5)]

foreclos|**e** (fōrklōz'), v.t. & i. Bar, preclude, prevent, shut out from enjoyment *of*; (Mortgage Law) bar (person entitled to redeem) upon nonpayment of money due, bar (right of redemption), take away power of redeeming (mortgage), whence ~URE (fōrklōzh'er) n.; settle (arguable point etc.) by anticipation. [ME, f. OF *forclore*, p.p. *-clos* (OF *for* out f. L *foris*, CLOSE[3])]

fore'court (fōr'kōrt), n. Enclosed space before building, outer court. [FORE-(3)]

fore'edge (fōr'ej), n. Front or outer edge (esp. of book); ~ *painting*, decoration of the front (occas. the top) edge of book with coloured design. [FORE-(3)]

fore'father (fōr'fahdher), n. (Pl.) the persons, esp. in earlier generations, from whom one's father or mother is descended, (loosely) the past generations of a family or race; (sing., rare) man from whom one is descended. [FORE-(6)]

fore'finger (fōr'finnger), n. Finger next thumb (also called *first* or *index finger*). [FORE-(3)]

fore'foot (fōr'f-), n. One of beast's front feet; (Naut.) foremost piece of keel, course in front of this (*crossing our* ~). [FORE-(3, 5)]

fore'front (fōr'frŭnt), n. Very front, foremost part, van, (*in the* ~ *of the battle*). [FORE-(3)]

foregather. See FORGATHER.

‖ **fore'gift** (fōr'g-), n. (law). Premium for lease. [FORE-(6)]

forego[1] (fōrgō), v.t. & i. (-*went*, -*gone* pr. -gawn). Precede in place or time (~*ing*, previously mentioned); ~*ne conclusion*, decision or opinion come to in advance of the evidence or necessary facts, prejudice, result that can be or could have been foreseen. [ME; FORE-(2)]

forego[2]. See FORGO.

foregō'er (fōrg-), n. Predecessor. [FORE-(1)]

fore'ground (fōr'g-), n. Part of view, esp. in picture, nearest observer; most conspicuous position. [FORE-(3)]

fore'hand (fōr'h-), n. & a. 1. Part of horse in front of rider. 2. adj. (Of stroke at tennis etc.) not backhanded. [FORE-(3)]

forehead (fŏ'rĕd), n. Part of face above eyebrows & between temples. [OE *forhēafod* see FORE-(4), HEAD[1]]

fŏ'reign (-rĭn), a. Belonging to, proceeding from, other persons or things; alien *from* or *to*, irrelevant, dissimilar, or inappropriate, *to*; introduced from outside (esp. ~ *body* or *substance* in the tissues etc.); situated outside, coming from another district, parish, society, etc.; outside the country, not in one's own land; *of, in*, characteristic of, coming from, dealing with, some country not in the United Kingdom or English-speaking countries (~ *& home trade*; ~ *parts*, countries; *F*~ *Office*, department for ~ affairs or its building; ~ *letter-paper*, thin to reduce postage). Hence ~ISM(2, 4) n., ~IZE(3) v.t. & i., (-rĭn-). [ME *foren(e)* f. OF *forain* f. LL *foranus* (L *foras*, *-is* outside, -AN)]

fŏ'reigner (-rĭn-), n. Person born in foreign country or speaking foreign language; foreign ship, imported animal or article. [-ER[1]]

forejudge (fōrj-), v.t. Judge or determine before hearing the evidence. [FORE-(2)]

foreknow (fōrnō'), v.t. (-*knew*, -*known*). Know beforehand, have prescience of. So **foreKNOWLEDGE** (fōrnŏl'ij) n. [FORE-(2)]

fŏ'rel, fŏ'rrel, n. Vellum-like parchment for covering account-books. [ME, f. OF *forrel* f. *fuerre* sheath; see FUR]

fore'land (fōr'l-), n. Cape, promontory, strip of land in front of something. [FORE-(3)]

fore'leg (fōrl-), n. Beast's front leg. [FORE-(3)]

fore'lock[1] (fōrl-), n. Lock of hair growing just above forehead (*take time, occasion*, etc., *by the* ~, not let chance slip). [FORE-(3)]

fore'lock[2] (fōrl-), n., & v.t. Wedge put through hole in bolt to keep it in place; (vb) secure thus. [FORE-(3), LOCK[2]]

fore'man (fōrm-), n. President & spokesman of jury; principal workman superintending others (*working* ~, one who both works & supervises). [FORE-(3)]

fore'mast (fōrm-), n. Forward lower mast of ship (~ *man, seaman, hand*, sailor below rank of petty officer). [FORE-(5)]

fore'most (fōr'mōst, -ost), a. & adv. superl. 1. Most advanced in position, front, (*head, end*, etc., ~, with head etc. in front); most notable, best, chief. 2. adv. Before anything else in position, in the first place, (usu. *first & ~*). [OE *formest* (= Goth. *frumists*) f. *forma* (FORE[2])

+superl. -*m*, = OS *formo*. Goth. *fruma*) + -EST; assim. to *fore* & *most*]

fore′nāme (fŏrn-), n. First or Christian name. [FORE-(3)]

fore′nōōn (fŏrn-), n. The day till noon, morning. [FORE² + NOON]

forĕn′s|ic, a. Of, used in, courts of law (~*ic medicine*, medical jurisprudence). Hence ~ICALLY adv. [f. L *forensis* (FORUM) + -IC]

foreordain′ (fŏrŏr-), v.t. Predestinate, appoint beforehand. So **foreORDINA′TION** (fŏrŏr-) n. [FORE-(2)]

fore′peak (fōrp-), n. (naut.). End of fore-hold in angle of bows. [FORE-(5)]

fore′plāne (fōrp-), n. First plane used after saw or axe. [FORE-(6)]

fore-reach′ (fōr-r-), v.i. & t. Shoot ahead; gain upon, pass. [FORE-(1)]

fore-run′ (fōr-r-), v.t. (-nn-; -*ran*, -*run*). Be precursor of, foreshadow. Hence ~n′ER¹ (1, 2) n. [FORE-(1)]

fore′sail (fōr′sl, -sāl) n. Principal sail on foremast (lowest square sail, or fore-&-aft bent on mast, or triangular before mast). [FORE-(5)]

foresee′ (fōrsē′), v.t. (-*saw*, -*seen*). See beforehand, have prescience, of (*that*); exercise foresight (obs. exc. in ~ING² a., ~INGLY² adv.). [FORE-(2)]

foreshadow (fōrshăd′ō), v.t. Prefigure, serve as type or presage of. [FORE-(2)]

fore′sheets (fōrsh-), n. pl. Inner part of bows of boat with gratings for bowman. [FORE-(5)]

fore′shore (fōrsh-), n. Part of shore between high- & low-water marks, or between water & land cultivated or built on. [FORE-(4)]

foreshort′en (fōrsh-), v.t. Show, portray, (object) with the apparent shortening due to visual perspective. [FORE-(1)]

foreshow′ (fōrshō′), v.t. (p.p. ~*n*). Fore-tell; foreshadow, portend, prefigure. [OE *foresceáwian* see FORE-(1), SHOW]

fore′sight (fōr′sīt), n. Foreseeing, pre-vision; care for the future; front sight of gun. [FORE-(2, 3)]

fore′skin (fōrs-), n. Prepuce. [FORE-(3)]

fŏ′rĕst, n., & v.t. 1. Large tract covered with trees & undergrowth sometimes mixed with pasture, trees growing in it (lit., & fig. as *a ~ of masts*); DEER-~; (with proper name prefixed) district formerly ~ but now cultivated, as *Sherwood F~*; ‖ (Law) unenclosed woodland district kept for hunting usu. owned by sovereign; ~*tree*, of large growth fitted for ~. 2. v.t. Plant with trees, convert into ~. [ME, f. OF f. med. L *forestis* (*silva* wood) outside (walls of park) f. L *foris* outside]

forestall′ (fōrstawl′), v.t. (Hist.) buy up (goods) in order to profit by enhanced price; be beforehand with in action, anticipate and so baffle; deal with before the regular time, anticipate. [f. OE *foresteall* n. ambush, see FORE-(6), STALL¹]

fore′stay (fōrs-), n. Stay from foremast-

head to ship's stem to support the fore mast. [FORE-(5)]

fŏ′rĕster, n. Officer in charge of forest, or of growing timber; dweller in forest; (*F~*) member of the Ancient Order of F~s (friendly society); bird or beast of forest, e.g. New-Forest pony; kinds of moth. [ME, f. OF *forestier* (FOREST, -IER)]

fŏ′rĕstrỹ, n. Wooded country, forests; science & art of managing forests. [f. OF *foresterie* (FOREST, -ERY)]

fore′tāste¹ (fōr′t-), n. Partial enjoyment or suffering (*of*) in advance, anticipation. [FORE-(2)]

foretāste′² (fōrt-), v.t. Taste beforehand, anticipate enjoyment etc. of. [FORE-(2)]

foretĕll′ (fōlt-), v.t. (-*tŏld*). Predict, prophesy; presage, be precursor of. [FORE-(2)]

fore′thought (fōr′thawt), n. Previous contriving, deliberate intention; provident care. [FORE-(6)]

fore′time (fōrt-), n. The past, early days, old times. [FORE-(6)]

fore′tōken¹ (fōr′t-), n. Sign of something to come, prognostic. [FORE-(6)]

foretōk′en² (fōrt-), v.t. Portend, point to. [FORE-(2)]

fore′tŏp (fōrt-), n. TOP of foremast; *fore-top-gall′ant mast*, mast above *fore-top-mast*, i.e. mast above foremast; *fore-topgall′ant-sail*, sail above *fore-top′sail*, i.e. sail above foresail. [FORE-(5)]

forewarn′ (fōrwŏrn′), v.t. Warn before-hand (esp. in ~*ed is forearmed*). [FORE-(2)]

fore′woman (fōr′wŏŏman), n. President & spokeswoman of jury of matrons; chief workwoman supervising others. [FORE-(3)]

fore′word (fōr′wĕrd), n. Preface; intro-ductory remarks, esp. by another than the author of the book etc. [from 1842; mod. formation of the anti-Latinists, after G *vorwort*; FORE-(3)]

fore′yard (fōr′yǎrd), n. Lowest yard on FOREMAST.

fŏrf′eit (-fĭt), n. & a., & v.t. 1. (Thing) lost owing to crime or fault (*his life was the ~ or was ~, his ~ life*); penalty for breach of contract or neglect; fine; trivial fine for breach of rules in clubs etc. or in games (*play ~s*), article surrendered by player in game of ~s to be redeemed by performing ludicrous task; forfeiture. 2. v.t. Lose right to, be deprived of, have to pay, as penalty of crime, neglect, etc., or as necessary consequence of something; hence ~ABLE a., ~URE n., (-fĭt-). [ME, f. OF *forfait* p.p. of *forfaire* f. med. L *foris facere* transgress (L *foris* outside, *facere* do)]

fŏrfĕnd′, v.t. Avert, keep off, (usu. in *God ~ !*). [FOR-(2)]

fŏrf′icate, a. (zool.). Scissor-shaped. [f. L *forfex* -*icis* scissors + -ATE²]

fŏrgăth′er (-dh-), v.i. Assemble, meet together, associate, converse. [16th c. Sc., f. Du. *vergaderen*, w. assim. to FOR-(5), GATHER]

forgave. See FORGIVE.

forge[1], n. Smithy; blacksmith's hearth or fireplace with bellows; furnace or hearth for melting or refining metal, workshop containing it. [ME, f. OF f. L *fabrica* FABRIC]

forge[2], v.t. & i. Shape by heating in fire and hammering; fabricate, invent, (tale, lie); make in fraudulent imitation, esp. write (document, signature) in order to pass off as written by another, whence **for′ger**[1] n. Hence **for′geABLE** (-ja-) a. [ME, f. OF *forgier* f. L *fabricare* FABRICATE]

forge[3], v.i. Make way, advance, gradually or with difficulty, esp. ~ *ahead*, take lead in race, get start. [orig. unkn.]

for′gery, n. Forging, counterfeiting, or falsifying, of document; spurious thing esp. document or signature. [FORGE[2], -ERY]

forget′ (-g-), v.t. & i. (-*got*,-*gotten* & poet. -*got*; -tt-). Lose remembrance of or *about* (noun, *that, how to,* or abs.); neglect (usu. *to* do), inadvertently omit to bring or mention or attend to; put out of mind, cease to think of, (esp. *forgive &* ~); disregard, slight; ~ *oneself*, neglect one's own interests, act unbecomingly or unworthily, lose consciousness; ~*-me-not*, kinds of myosotis, esp. one with small yellow-eyed blue flowers (~*-me-not blue* as name of colour). Hence ~FUL a. (*of*), ~fulLY[2] adv., ~fulNESS n., ~t′ABLE a. [OE *forgietan*, OS *fargetan*, OHG *fargezzan* see FOR-(1), GET]

forgive′e′ (-g-), v.t. & i. (-*gāve*, -*given*). Remit, let off, (debt, person debt); pardon (offence, offender, offender offence, or abs.). Hence ~′ABLE a., ~e′ness (-gĭvn-) [~*en*+-NESS] n., ~ingLY[2] a., ~ingLY[2] adv., ~′ingNESS n., (-g-). [OE *forgiefan* see FOR-(1), GIVE]

forgo′, v.t. (-*wĕnt*, -*gone* pr. -gawn). Abstain from, go without, let go, omit to take or use, relinquish. [OE *forgān* see FOR-(3), GO]

fo′rint, n. Principal monetary unit of Hungary. [Hung.]

fork, n., & v.i. & t. 1. Pronged agricultural implement for digging, lifting, carrying, or throwing; two, three, or four, -pronged instrument used in eating at table or cooking; (also *tuning*~) steel instrument giving when struck a fixed musical note; stake with ~ed end used as prop for vines etc.; ~ing, bifurcation, e.g. that of human legs, of diverging roads, or of branches; flash of ~ed lightning; hence ~′Y[2] a. (poet.). 2. vb. Form ~, have or develop branches; lift, carry, dig, or throw with ~; (sl.) ~ *out* or *over* or *up*, hand over, pay. [OE *forca*, OS *furka*, OHG *furcha*, ON *forkr* f. L *furca*]

forked (-kt), a. With fork or fork-like end, branching, divergent, cleft, (*three*-~ etc., with three etc. prongs); two-legged. [-ED[2]]

forlorn′, a. Desperate, hopeless, (cf. foll.) abandoned, forsaken, (poet.) deprived *of,*

in pitiful condition, of wretched appearance. [p.p. of obs. *forlese*, OE *forlēosan* see FOR-(1), LOSE]

forlorn′ hope, n. Storming-party; desperate enterprise. [16th c., f. Du. *verloren hoop* lost troop (*hoop* = HEAP)]

form[1], n. 1. Shape, arrangement of parts, visible aspect (esp. apart from colour), shape of body (*face &* ~). 2. Person or animal as visible or tangible (*saw a* ~, the ~ *of* —, *before me*). 3. (philos.). That which makes anything (*matter*) a determinate species (Scholastic), conditions of thing's existence by knowing which we can produce it (Baconian), formative principle holding together the elements of thing (Kantian). 4. Mode in which thing exists or manifests itself (*in, under, take, the* ~ *of*), species, kind, variety. 5. (gram.). One of the shapes taken by a word in spelling, pronunciation, or inflexion, external characteristics of words apart from meaning. 6. ǁ Class in most (esp. the Public) schools (usu. numbered from *sixth* down to *first*). 7. Arrangement & style in literary or musical composition. 8. Customary method (*in due* ~; *that is common* ~, is of no special significance), set order of words, formula, regularly drawn document, ǁ document with blanks to be filled up. 9. Formality, mere piece of ceremony. 10. Behaviour according to rule or custom (*good, bad,* ~, satisfying or offending current ideals); correct procedure (*he knows the* ~). 11. Condition of health & training (*in, out of,* ~, fit or not for racing etc., of horses or athletes; *lose* one's ~), good spirits (*was in great* ~). 12. Long seat without back, bench. 13. (Print.; ǁ also ~*e*) body of type secured in chase for printing at one impression. 14. Hare's lair. [ME, f. OF *forme* f. L *forma*]

form[2], v.t. & i. 1. Fashion, mould, (*into* certain shape; *after, by, from, upon,* pattern; or abs.); assume shape, become solid. 2. Mould by discipline, train, instruct, (person, or faculty etc.); embody, organize, *into* a company etc. 3. Frame, make, produce; articulate (word); conceive, (idea, judgement), develop (habit); contract (alliance); be material of, make up, make *one* or *part of.* 4. (gram.). Construct (new word) by derivation, inflexion, etc. 5. (mil. etc.). Draw up (t. & i.; often *up*) in order, assume specified formation (~ *line, column*), ~ in a formation (*right, left,* ~). [ME, f. OF *fourmer* f. L *formare* (prec.)]

form-, comb. form of FORMIC or FORMYL, as *formAL′DEHYDE*, a disinfectant & antiseptic, *form′alIN* a solution of this.

-form, suf. (in actual use *-iform*, see -I-) f. F *-forme* f. L *-formis* (FORM[1]) giving adjj. (1) w. sense *having the form of* (*cruciform, cuneiform*), (2) referring to number of forms (*uniform, multiform, diversiform*). *Chloroform* does not contain this suf.

for'mal, a. **1.** (Metaphys.) of the essence of a thing (~ CAUSE[1]), essential not material; of the outward form, shape, appearance, arrangement, or external qualities, (Log.) concerned with the form, not the matter, of reasoning. **2.** Valid in virtue of its form, explicit and definite, not merely tacit. **3.** Ceremonial, required by convention (a ~ call), perfunctory, having the form without the spirit; observant of forms, precise, prim, excessively regular or symmetrical, stiff, methodical, whence ~ISM(2), ~IST(2), nn., ~is'tic a. Hence ~LY[2] adv. [ME, f. L formalis (FORM[1], -AL)]

for'mal'ity, n. Conformity to rules, propriety; ceremony, elaborate procedure; formal or ceremonial act, requirement of etiquette or custom; being formal, precision of manners, stiffness of design. [f. F formalité (prec., -TY)]

for'maliz|e, -is|e (-īz), v.t. Give definite shape or legal formality to; make ceremonious, precise, or rigid, imbue with formalism. Hence ~A'TION n. [-IZE]

for'mat (or -ah), n. Shape & size of book. [F]

forma'tion, n. Forming, being formed; thing formed; arrangement of parts, structure, (Mil.) disposition of troops; a number of aircraft flying in company, whence *for'māte[1] v.i., (of aircraft) fly in(to) ~; (Geol.) assemblage of rocks of series of strata having some common characteristic. [late ME, f. OF or f. L formatio (FORM[2], -ATION)]

for'mative, a. & n. Serving to fashion, of formation; (Gram., of flexional & derivative suffixes and prefixes) used in forming words, (n.) ~ element. [OF (-if, -ive) see FORM[2], -ATIVE]

‖ **forme,** n. (print.). See FORM[1].

for'mer, a. & pron. Of the past or an earlier period (in ~ times; more like her ~ self; our ~ haunts), whence ~LY[2] adv.; the ~ (with noun, or oftener as pron. with possessive the ~'s), the first or first mentioned of two (opp. LATTER). [ME, f. forme +-ER[3], after FOREMOST]

for'm|ic, a. (chem.). ~ic acid, colourless irritant volatile acid contained in fluid emitted by ants. Hence **for'm'ate[2]** [-ATE[1](3)], ~ENE, ~YL, nn. [irreg. f. L formica ant +-IC]

formica'tion, n. Sensation as of ants crawling over the skin. [f. L formicatio -onis tingling, f. formica ant]

form'idab|le, a. To be dreaded; likely to be hard to overcome, resist, or deal with. Hence ~leNESS n., ~LY[2] adv. [f. F, or L formidabilis (formidare fear, -ABLE)]

form'less, a. Shapeless, without determinate or regular form. Hence ~LY[2] adv., ~NESS n. [-LESS]

form'ul|a, n. (pl. -ae, -as). Set form of words, definition, enunciation of principle in form of words, statement prescribed for use on some occasion; rule unintelligently followed, conventional usage or belief, whence ~ISM(3), ~IST(2), nn., ~is'tic a.; recipe; principle serving to accommodate differences of aim or opinion (diplomatists seeking a ~a); (Math.) rule or statement in algebraic symbols; (Chem.) expression by symbols of substance's constituents; tabulation of certain facts by symbols & figures. Hence ~arIZE(3) [through obs. ~ar a.], ~IZE(3), vv.t.=FORMULATE, ~arIZA'TION, ~IZA'TION, nn. [L, dim. of forma FORM[1]]

for'mulary, n. & a. Collection of formulas; document or book of set forms esp. for belief or ritual; (adj.) in or of formulas. [f. F formulaire f. neut. of L formularius (prec., -ARY[1])]

for'mul|āte, v.t. Reduce to, express in, a formula; set forth systematically. Hence ~A'TION n. [FORMULA +-ATE[3]]

forn'icāt|e, v.i. Commit fornication. So ~OR n. [f. LL fornicari (fornix -icis brothel), -ATE[3]]

fornica'tion, n. Voluntary sexual intercourse between man (occas. restricted to unmarried man) & unmarried woman (cf. adultery). [ME, f. OF f. LL fornicationem (prec., -ION)]

‖ **forpined'** (-nd), a. (arch.). Wasted by hunger, torture, etc. [p.p. of obs. forpine see FOR-(5)]

forrader. See FORWARD[2].

forrel. See FOREL.

forsāke', v.t. (-sŏŏk, -sāken). Give up, break off from, renounce; withdraw one's help, friendship, or companionship from, desert, abandon. [OE forsacan (= OS forsakan, OHG firsahhan) deny, renounce, refuse, f. FOR-(3) +sacan contend; see SAKE]

forsooth', adv. Truly, in truth, no doubt, (used parenthet. always in irony). [OE forsóth (FOR, SOOTH)]

‖ **forspent',** a. (arch.). Tired out. [p.p. of obs. forspend see FOR-(5), SPEND]

forswear' (-wār), v.t. (-swŏre, -swŏrn). Abjure, renounce on oath; ~ oneself, swear falsely, perjure oneself; (p.p.) perjured. [OE forswerian, see FOR-(3, 1), SWEAR]

forsyth'ia, n. (Kinds of) spring-flowering ornamental shrub bearing bright-yellow flowers. [f. W. Forsyth (d. 1804), English botanist, +-IA[1]]

fort, n. Fortified place (usu. single building or set of connected military buildings, cf. FORTRESS); trading-station, orig. fortified (hist.). [F, abs. use of fort strong f. L fortis]

fort'alice, n. (Arch. & poet.) fortress; (mod.) small outwork of fortification, small fort. [f. med. L fortalitia (L fortis strong)]

forte[1], n. Person's strong point; (Fenc.) sword-blade from hilt to middle (cf. FOIBLE). [f. F fort abs. use of adj.= strong; for substitution of fem. form cf. morale, locale]

fort'e², mus. direction (abbr. *f.*). Loud; *~ ~* (abbr. *ff.*), very loud; *~ piano* (abbr. *fp.*), loud & then immediately soft. [It.]

forth, adv. & prep. 1. Forwards (now only in *back & ~*, & to & fro); onwards in time (now only in *from this time ~*, & in comb. as *hence~*); forward, into view, (*bring, come, show,* etc., *~*); out from home etc. (*sail, issue, ~*); out of doors (*cast ~*); *& so~*, & so on, & the like; *so far ~*, to that extent; *so far ~ as*, to whatever extent. 2. prep. (arch.). From out of. [OE, OS *forth*, MHG *vort* f. WG **fortha*]

forthcom'ing (-kŭ-), a. About or likely to come forth; approaching; ready to be produced when wanted. [prec., COME, -ING²]

forthright' (-rīt), adv., **forth'right** (-rīt), a. & n. 1. adv. Straight forward; straightway. 2. adj. Going straight; outspoken, unswerving; decisive, dextrous. 3. n. (arch.). Straight course (*~s & meanders*). [OE ; FORTH + RIGHT a. & adv.]

forthwith' (-th, -dh), adv. Immediately, without delay. [for *forth with* used abs.]

fortifica'tion, n. Fortifying; strengthening of wine with alcohol ; (Mil.) providing, art or science of providing, with defensive works, (usu. pl.) defensive work(s), wall(s), earthwork(s), tower(s), etc. [F, f. LL *fortificationem* act of strengthening (foll., -ATION)]

fort'if|ȳ, v.t. & i. Strengthen structure of; impart vigour or physical strength or endurance to, strengthen mentally or morally, encourage; increase nutritive value of (food); strengthen (liquors) with alcohol; corroborate, confirm, (statement); provide (town, army, one*self*) with defensive works; erect fortifications. Hence *~ĪABLE* a. [late ME, f. OF *fortifier* f. LL *fortificare* (*fortis* strong, -FY)]

fortiss'imo, mus. direction (abbr. *ff.*, *ffor., forss.*). Very loud. [It.]

fortiter. See SUAVITER.

fort'itude, n. Courage in pain or adversity. [F, f. L *fortitudo* (*fortis* strong, -TUDE)]

fort'night (-nīt), n. Period of two weeks (*today, this day, Monday,* etc., *~*, a *~* from today etc.; *would rather keep him* etc. *a week than a ~*, he etc. is a large eater). [OE *fēowertȳne niht* fourteen nights]

fort'nightly (-īt-), a. & adv. (Happening, appearing) once every fortnight. [-LY¹, ²]

fort'ress, n., & v.t. Military stronghold, esp. strongly fortified town fit for large garrison; (vb, poet.) serve as *~* to, protect. [ME, f. OF *forteresse* f. Rom. **fortaritia* (cf. FORTALICE), f. L *fortis* strong]

fortu'itism, fortu'itist, nn. Belief, believer, in chance & natural causes, not design, as causing adaptations in nature (cf. *teleology, -ist*). [foll.-ISM, -IST]

fortu'itous, a. Due to or characterized by chance, accidental, casual. Hence *~LY²* adv., *~NESS* n. [f. L *fortuitus* (*fors -tis* chance) + -OUS]

fortu'itȳ, n. Fortuitousness; a chance occurrence; accident; unstudied or unintended character. [irreg. f. on prec. (-ITY)]

fort'unate, a. Favoured by fortune, lucky, prosperous; auspicious, favourable. [ME, f. L *fortunatus* (FORTUNE, -ATE²)]

fort'unately (-tl-), adv. Luckily, successfully, (esp. as parenthesis qualifying whole sentence = it is a fortunate thing that). [-LY²]

fort'une¹ (-chŏon, -tūn), n. Chance, hap, luck, as a power in men's affairs (*F~*, this power personified as goddess; *try the ~ of war*, see what it will bring, risk it; SOLDIER *of ~*); luck good or bad that falls to anyone or to an enterprise etc. (in sing. or pl.; *try* one's *~*, take some risky step), coming lot (*tell* person his *~, tell ~s*, of gipsies etc., whence *~-tëllēr¹* n.); good luck; prosperity, prosperous condition, wealth, (*make* one's *~, prosper; make a ~*, become rich; *spent a small ~ on it*, large sum; *marry a ~*, heiress), whence *~LESS* (-nl-) a.; *~-hunter*, man seeking rich wife. [ME, f. OF f. L *fortuna*]

fort'une² (-chŏon, -tūn), v.i. (arch. & poet.). Chance, occur, (esp. impers., *it ~d that*); come by chance *upon*. [ME, f. OF *fortuner* f. L *fortunare* make fortunate (prec.)]

fort'ȳ, a. & n. 1. Four times ten, 40, xl, XL, (*~one, ~first,* etc.; *~ winks*, short nap esp. after dinner); hence **fort'ieth** a. & n. 2. n. Age of *~* years (*after ~, over ~; the forties*, years of life or century between 39 & 50; HUNGRY *Forties; roaring forties*, stormy ocean tracts between lat. 30° & 50° S.; || *the Forties*, sea area between N.E. coast of Scotland and S.W. coast of Norway (so named from its depth of *~* fathoms or more); ||*~-PENNY nail; the F~-five*, Jacobite rebellion of 1745. [OE *fēowertig* (FOUR, -TY²)]

for'um, n. (Rom. Ant.) public place, market-place, place of assembly for judicial & other business, esp. at Rome; place of public discussion; periodical etc. giving opportunity for debate etc.; court, the law courts, (fig. *the ~ of conscience* etc.). [L]

for'ward¹, a. & n. 1. (Naut.) belonging to fore part of ship; lying in one's line of motion (*the ~ horizon*), onward or towards the front (*the ~ path; ~ play* in cricket, see foll.; *~ movement*, special effort at political etc. progress; *~ school, party, opinions,* advanced or extreme). 2. (commerc.). Relating to future produce (*~ contract*). 3. Advanced, progressing to maturity or completion, (of plant, crop, season) well advanced or early; ready, prompt, eager, (often *to* do); precocious; presumptuous, pert, whence *~LY²* adv.; hence *~NESS* n. 4. n. One of the first-line players in football, hockey, etc. [OE *foreweard* (FORE², -WARD), a.]

fŏr′ward²(s), adv. (-d is added below to senses in which the -s form is rare or not used). Towards the future, continuously onwards, (-d; *from this time* ~; *look* ~, ahead; CARRIAGE ~; *date* ~, of commercial orders, post-date). 2. Towards the front in the direction one is facing, (Cricket; -d) *play*~, reach~ to play short-pitched ball; with continuous ~ motion (*rushing* ~), (Mil., as word of command, -d, = go ~, advance). 3. In advance, ahead, (-d; *send him* ~; ~*-looking*, progressive); *backward(s) & ~*, to & *fro*; to the front, into prominence, (-d; *bring* ~, draw attention to; *come* ~, offer oneself for task, post, etc.; *put or set* ~, allege, make *oneself* too conspicuous). 4. (naut.; -d). To, at, in, fore part of ship. 5. Onward so as to make progress (-d; *go* ~, be going on, progress; *can't get any forwarder*, or usu. colloq. *forrader*, make no progress). [OE *foreweard*, prob. neut. acc. of *prec.*]

fŏr′ward³, v.t. Help forward, promote; accelerate growth of; send (letter etc.) on to further destination, (loosely) dispatch (goods etc.). [f. prec.]

∥ **forwear′ied** (-ĭd), forwŏrn′, aa. (arch.). Tired out. [FOR-(5), WEARY, WEAR², vv.]

fŏsse, n. Long narrow excavation, canal, ditch, trench, esp. in fortification; (Anat.) groove, depression, also **fŏssette′** n. [ME, f. OF, f. L *fossa* orig. fem. p.p. of *fodere* dig]

fŏss′ick, v.i. (sl.). Rummage, search about. [dial. wd current in Austral. gold-mining=search in crevices or abandoned workings]

fŏss′il, a. & n. Found buried, dug up, (~ *fuel* etc.; now rare); (thing) preserved in strata of earth with more or less chemical or other change of texture & recognizable as remains or impressions of plant or animal of past (usu. prehistoric) ages (~ *bones, shells, ivory*; *hunting for* ~*s*; also fig., as *words are* ~ *thoughts*); (person or thing) belonging to the past, antiquated, incapable of further development. Hence ~ATE³ v.t., ~A′TION n., ~IF′EROUS a., ~IZE(3) v.t. & i., ~IZA′TION n. [f. F *fossile* f. L *fossilis* (*fodere* foss-dig, -IL)]

fŏssŏr′ial, a. (zool.). Burrowing; used in burrowing. [f. LL *fossorius* (*fossor* digger f. *fodere* see prec., -OR)+-AL]

fŏs′ter¹, n. Food (obs. exc. in comb., as ~*-child, -father, -mother, -parent, -son, -daughter, -brother, -sister*, = having the specified relationship not by blood, but in virtue of nursing or bringing up); acting or treated as —; ~*-mother*, (also) = INCUBATOR. [OE *fóstor* (FOOD, suf. *-tro-*)]

fŏs′ter², v.t. (Arch.) tend affectionately, cherish, keep warm (in bosom), promote growth of; encourage or harbour (feeling); (of circumstances) be favourable to. Hence~ER¹, fŏs′trESS¹, nn. [OE *fóstrian*, f. prec.]

fŏs′terage, n. Fostering; custom of employing foster-mothers. [-AGE]

fŏs′terling, n. Foster-child, nursling, protégé. [OE *fóslorling* (FOSTER¹, -LING¹)]

fougasse (fŏŏgahs′), n. Improvised mortar excavated in the ground, charged with stones, bits of iron, etc., and fired by gunpowder. [F]

fought. See FIGHT¹.

foul, a., n., adv., & v.i. & t. 1. Offensive to the senses, loathsome, stinking, (~ *brood*, a disease of larval bees); dirty, soiled (~ *linen*), filthy; (sl.) revolting, disgusting; defaced with corrections (~ *copy*); charged with noxious matter (~ *air, water*); clogged, choked, (~ *gun--barrel*); (of ship's bottom) overgrown with weed, barnacles, etc.; morally polluted, obscene, disgustingly abusive, (*the* ~ *fiend*, the devil; ~ *deed, motive, talk*; ~*-mouthed, -tongued*); (of fish at or after spawning) in bad condition; ugly (now dial. exc. in *fair or* ~); unfair, against rules of game etc., (~ *blow, stroke, riding*; ~ *play*, in games, & fig. treachery, murder or violence); (of weather) wet, rough, stormy; (of wind) contrary; in collision (FALL¹ ~ *of*); entangled (*rope is* ~). 2. n. Something ~ (*through* ~ *& fair*, through everything); collision, entanglement, esp. in riding, rowing, or running, irregular stroke or piece of play. 3. adv. In irregular way (*hit him* ~; *play one* ~, deal treacherously with him). 4. vb. Become ~, get clogged; make ~ or dirty (~ *one's own* NEST); pollute with guilt, dishonour; cause (anchor, cable) to become entangled, jam or block (crossing, railway line, traffic); become entangled; run ~ of, collide with. [OE, OS, OHG *fūl*, ON *fūll*, Goth. *fūls* f. Gmc *fūlaz*]

foul′ard (fŏŏl′ahr), n. Thin flexible material of silk or silk & cotton; handkerchief of it. [F]

foulé (fŏŏlā′), n. Light woollen dress material with glossy surface. [F, = pressed (cloth), p.p. of *fouler* FULL²]

foul′ly (-l-lĭ), adv. Abominably, cruelly, wickedly (*was* ~ *murdered*); with unmerited insult (~ *slandered*). [-LY²]

foul′nèss, n. Foul condition; foul matter; disgusting wickedness. [-NESS]

foum′art (fŏŏ-), n. Polecat. [ME *fulmard* (FOUL, *mearth* marten)]

found¹, v.t. & i. Lay base of (building etc.); be original builder, begin building, of (town, edifice); set up, establish (esp. with endowment), originate, initiate, (institution); construct, base, (tale, one's fortunes, classification, rule, etc.) (*up*)*on* some ground, support, principle, etc. (also *is* ~*ed in justice* etc.; *well, ill*, etc., ~*ed*, reasonable, justified, baseless, etc.); rely, base oneself, (of argument etc.) be based, (*up*)*on*. [ME, f. OF *fonder* f. L *fundare* (*fundus* bottom)]

found², v.t. Melt & mould (metal), fuse (materials for glass); make (thing of molten metal, glass) by melting. So **foun′dry**(3) n. [ME, f. OF *fondre* f. L *fundere fus-* pour]

found³. See FIND.

founda′tion, n. Establishing, constituting on permanent basis, esp. of an endowed institution; such institution, e.g. monastery, college, or hospital (*on the* ~, entitled to benefit by its funds, whence ‖ ~ER¹ (-shon-) n.), or its revenues; solid ground or base, natural or artificial, on which building rests, lowest part of building usu. below ground-level; basis, groundwork, underlying principle, (*report has no* ~; *base religion on a moral* ~); body or ground on which other parts are overlaid, e.g. underskirt, first set of stitches in crochet or knitting; ~ *garment,* woman's supporting undergarment, e.g. corset, corslet, girdle; ~-*muslin, -net,* gummed fabrics for stiffening dresses & bonnets; ~-*school,* endowed; ~-*stone,* esp. one laid with ceremony to celebrate founding of edifice. [ME, f. OF *fondation* or L *fundatio* (FOUND¹, -ATION)]

foun′der¹, n. In vbl senses of FOUND¹; esp., one who founds institutions (~-*member,* ‖ ~'s *kin,* relatives of ~ entitled to election or preference); ~'s *shares,* shares issued to ~s of public company as part-consideration for business taken over, & separate from ordinary capital. Hence ~SHIP, **foun′dress¹,** nn. [-ER¹]

foun′der², n. In vbl senses of FOUND¹. [-ER²]

foun′der³, v.i. & t., & n. 1. (Of earth, building, etc.) fall down or in, give way; (of horse; or with rider substituted as subject) fall from overwork, collapse, fall lame, stick fast in bog etc.; cause (horse) to break down by overwork; (of ship) fill with water & sink, cause (ship) to do this; (Golf) hit (ball) into ground. 2. n. Inflammation of horse's foot from overwork; (also *chest, body,* ~~) rheumatism of chest-muscles in horses. [ME, f. OF *fondrer* submerge, collapse, (L *fundus* bottom)]

found′ling, n. Deserted infant of unknown parents. [ME; p.p. of FIND + -LING¹]

fount¹, n. (poet. or rhet.). Spring, source, fountain; (shop) reservoir of oil in lamp or of ink in pen. [f. L *fons -tis* on anal. of *mount;* from late 16th c.]

‖fount² (*or* fŏnt), n. (print.). Set of type of same face & size. [f. F *fonte* (*fondre* FOUND²)]

foun′tain (-tĭn), n. Water-spring; source of river etc. (also fig., *Crown is the* ~ *of honour; poison the* ~s *of trust*); jet of water made to spout, structure provided for it, (also *drinking-*~) public erection with constant supply of drinking-water; reservoir in lamp, printing-press, etc., for oil, ink, etc. (~-*pen,* having this); ~-*head,* original source. Hence (-)~ED² (-Ind) a. [ME, f. OF *fontaine* f. LL *fontana* orig. fem. of L *fontanus* adj. (FOUNT¹, -AN)]

four (fŏr), a. & n. 1. One more than three, 4, iv, IV, (~ *corners of earth* etc., remotest parts; ~ *corners of document* etc., its scope; *within the* ~ *seas,* in Gt Britain; ~ *figures,* some number from 1000 to 9999; *twenty* etc. -~ *or* ~-*&-twenty* etc.; ~-*&- -twentieth* etc.); (ellipt.)~ hours (~*o'clock*), ~ horses (*carriage* etc. *&*~); ‖ ~-*ale* (hist.), sold at 4*d.* a quart; ~ *by two,* rifle pull- -through cloth; ~-*coupled,* with ~ coupled wheels; ~-*course,* with fourfold rotation (of crops); ~-DIMENSION*al,* *~-*flusher* (sl.), bluffer, humbug [orig. Poker term]; ~- -*footed,* quadruped (adj.); ‖ ~-*foot way,* space (4 ft. 8½ in.) between pair of rails; ~ FREEDOMS; ~-*handed,* (of monkeys) quadrumanous, (of games) for ~ persons, (of piece of music) for two players; ~- -*horse*(d), drawn by ~ horses; ~-*in-hand,* vehicle with ~ horses driven by one person on the box (also adv., *drive* etc. ~-*in-hand*); ~-*oar,* (boat) with ~ oars; ~ *o'clock,* the plant marvel of Peru; ~-*part,* arranged for ~ voices to sing; ~'*pence,* sum or coin = 4*d.*; ~'*penny,* costing 4*d.,* (obs.) silver coin = 4*d.*; ~- -*post* (of bed), having ~ posts to support canopy, ~-*poster,* such bed, (also) 4-mas- ted ship; ~-*pounder,* gun throwing 4-lb. shot; ~-*rowed barley,* with ~ rows of awns; ~-*score,* eighty, age of 80 years; ~- -*square,* square-shaped, solidly based or steady; ~-*stroke* (attrib., of internal- -combustion engines), having a cycle of ~ strokes (intake, compression, combus- tion, and exhaust); *the* ~ *hundred,* the exclusive social set of any place; ~-*wheel,* ~-wheeled carriage; ~-*wheeler,* ~-wheeled hackney carriage; hence ~-FOLD a. & adv., ~-TEEN¹ a., ~-teenTH¹ a. & n., (fŏr-). 2. n. The number ~; set of ~ persons or things, esp. ~-pipped card, domino, or side of die, ~-oared boat & crew (~s, races for these), hit etc. at cricket for ~ runs; *on all* ~s (earlier ~ = ~ limbs), crawling on hands & knees, (also, fig.) completely analogous or corresponding (*the cases are not on all* ~s; *is the simile on all* ~s *with the thing illustrated?*); ~- -*pennyworth of* spirits (hist.); (pl.) ~-*per- -cent. stock.* [OE *fēower,* OS *fiwar,* OHG *fior,* ON *fjórir,* Goth. *fidwōr,* cogn. w. Gk *tessares,* L *quatuor*]

fourgon (foor′gawn), n. Luggage-van. [F]

Four′ierism (fŏŏ-), n. Fourier's system for reorganization of society (PHALAN- STERY). [Charles *Fourier,* French socialist, 1772–1837]

four′some (fŏr-), n. Game of golf between two pairs, partners playing the same ball; (colloq.) a company or party of four persons. [FOUR, -SOME; orig. adj.]

fourth (fŏr-), a. & n. 1. Next after third (*the, a,* ~, ellipt. as n., esp. = 4th day of month; ~ *part,* quarter); ~ ESTATE; F~ *Republic* (in France 1947–58). 2. n. Quarter, ~ part; (Mus.) interval of which the span involves four alphabetical notes, harmonic combination of notes thus separated; F~ *of June*, principal annual celebration at Eton College, speech-day and procession of boats; F~ *of July*, U.S. anniversary of declaration of Independence; ~ *party* (hist.), Lord R. Churchill, Sir H. D. Wolff, Sir J. Gorst, Mr Balfour, and a few other Conservatives who (1880--5) attacked impartially the Liberal Government & the Conservative front bench; (pl.) articles of ~ quality. [OE *feortha*, OS *fiortho*, OHG *fiordo*, ON *fjórthi*, cogn. w. Gk *tetartos* L *quartus*]

fourth'ly (fōr-), adv. In the fourth place (in enumerations). [-LY²]

fōv'e|a, n. (anat. etc.; pl. ~ae pr. -ē). A small depression or pit. Hence ~AL, ~ATE², aa., pitted. [L]

fove'ola, n. (pl. -ae pr. -ē). A small fovea. Hence fōv'eolATE², -āted, aa., pitted. [L, dim. of prec.]

fowl, n., & v.i. 1. Bird (rare), birds (rare exc. in *wild-*~), their flesh as food (only in *fish, flesh,' & ~*); domestic cock or hen (often qualified, as *barn-door* ~, *game, guinea,* ~; ~*-pest*, infectious disease of ~s resembling chicken cholera; || ~*-run*, place where ~s may run, breeding establishment for ~s), its flesh as food. 2. v.i. Catch, hunt, shoot, or snare, wild~, whence ~'ER¹, ~'ING¹, nn.; ~*ing-piece*, light gun used in ~ing. [OE *fugol*, OS *-al*, OHG *fogal*, ON *fugl*, Goth. *fugls* f. Gmc **foglaz* perh. by dissim. f. **flugla*- (*flug-FLY²*)]

fŏx¹, n. (fem. VIXEN, also *bitch-*~). Red--furred sharp-snouted bushy-tailed quad-ruped preserved in England as beast of chase & proverbial for cunning; crafty person; northern constellation; FLYING ~; ~ *& geese*, game played on board; ~*-brush*, tail of ~; ~*-chase*, ~*-hunt*; ~*-EARTH¹*; ~*glove*, tall plant with purple or white flowers like glove fingers; ~*'hole* (Mil.), hole in ground used as shelter against missiles or as firing-point; ~*'hound*, kind bred & trained to hunt ~es; ~*-hunt* n. & v.i., chasing of, chase, ~ with hounds, whence ~'hÜntER¹ n.; ~*-hunting* a. & n., (given to) this sport; ~*'tail*, ~'s tail, kinds of grass; ~*-terrier*, short-haired for unearthing ~, but kept chiefly as pet; ~*'trot*, an American dance. [OE *fox*, OS *vuhs*, OHG *fuhs* f. WG **fuhs*]

fŏx², v.i. & t. Act craftily, dissemble; dis-colour (leaves of book, engraving, etc.) with brownish spots (esp. in p.p.); (sl.) deceive, trick. [f. prec.]

fŏx'|ý, a. Fox-like, crafty(-looking); red-dish-brown, (Paint.) over-hot in colour; damaged with mildew etc. Hence ~iNESS n. [-Y²]

|| *foyer* (fwah'yā), n. Large room in theatre etc. for audience's use during interval. [F]

fra (-ah), n. = FRATE as prefixed title. [It.]

fråc'as (-ah), n. (pl. same). Noisy quarrel, row. [F, f. It. *fracasso* uproar]

fråc'tion, n. 1. Dividing of Eucharistic bread. 2. (arith.). Numerical quantity that is not an integer, one or more aliquot parts, (*vulgar* ~, expressed by numerator above & denominator below a line; DECI-MAL~; *proper, improper,* ~, with numera-tor less, greater, than denominator). 3. Small piece or amount, scrap, (esp. *not a* ~). Hence ~AL ·(~*al distillation*, partial separation of liquids having different boiling-points by gradual heat-ing), ~ARY¹, aa.,·(-shon-). [ME, f. OF *fraction* f. LL *fractionem* (L *frangere fract-* break, -ION)]

fråc'tionāte (-shon-), v.t. Separate (mix-ture) into portions of different properties by distillation etc. [prec.+-ATE³]

fråc'tionize (-shon-), -ise (-ĭz), v.t. Break up into fractions (Math.), or portions. [-IZE]

fråc'tious (-shŭs), a. Unruly, cross, peev-ish. Hence ~LY² adv., ~NESS n., (-shŭs-). [f. FRACTION in obs. sense brawling +·-OUS, after *captious* etc.]

fråc'ture, n., & v.t. & i. 1. Breaking, breakage, esp. of bone or cartilage (COM-POUND² ~); surface shown by mineral when broken with hammer; substitution of diphthong, diphthong substituted, for simple vowel owing to influence of follow-ing consonant. 2. vb. Cause ~ in, break continuity of, crack (t. & i.). [f. F, or L *fractura* (FRACTION, -URE)]

fraen'um, frē-, n. (pl. -na). Small liga-ment checking motion of organ. [L, = bridle.]

frå'gile, a. Easily snapped or shattered, weak, perishable, of delicate frame or constitution. So fragil'ITY n. [f. F, or L *fragilis* (*frag-* root of *frangere* break)]

fråg'ment, n. Part broken off, detached piece; isolated or incomplete part, re-mainder of lost or destroyed whole, esp. extant remains or unfinished portion of a writing or work of art. Hence ~ARY¹ a., ~A'TION n. (~*ation bomb*, one breaking up into small~s when exploded). [f. F, or L *fragmentum* (as prec., -MENT)]

fråg'rant, a. Sweet-smelling. So fråg'-rANCE n. [f. obs. F, or L *fragrare* smell sweet, -ANT]

frail¹, n. Rush basket for packing figs, raisins, etc. [ME, f. OF *fraiel*, of unkn. orig.]

frail², a. Fragile; transient (~ *life, bliss,* etc.); in weak health; morally weak, un-able to resist temptation, (euphem., of women) unchaste. [ME, f. OF *fraile* FRAGILE]

frail'tý, n. Liability to err or yield to temptation; fault, weakness, foible. [ME, f. OF *frailete* f. L *fragilitatem* (FRAGILE, -TY)]

fraise¹ (-z), n. (fortif.). Horizontal or down-sloping palisade round berm. [F, orig. = mesentery of calf]

fraise² (-z), n. Tool for enlarging circular hole or cutting teeth in watch wheels. [F (*fraiser* enlarge hole f. *fraise* as prec.)]

framboes'ia (-bēz-), n. Contagious tropical disease with raspberry-like swellings, the yaws. [mod. L, f. F *framboise* raspberry + -IA¹]

frame¹, v.t. & i. Shape, direct, dispose, (thoughts, acts, another person) to a purpose (*for, to, to do*, or with adv.); give promise of being skilful etc. (usu. *well*); adapt, fit, *to* or *into*; construct by combination of parts or adaptation to design, contrive, devise, invent, compose, express, (complex article, plot, rule, story, theory); articulate (words); conceive, imagine; [f. foll.] set in a frame, serve as frame for (landscape ~*ed in an archway*), whence ~'ING¹(3) n.; (orig. U.S. sl.) concoct false charge against, devise plot with regard to; ~*e up* (orig. U.S. sl.), prearrange (event) with sinister intent, fake result of (race, election, etc.). Hence ~'ABLE a., ~'ER¹ n. [OE *framian* be helpful (*fram* forward, see FROM)]

frame², n. Construction, constitution, build; established order, plan, system, (*the ~ of society* or *government*); temporary state (*of* mind); framed work or structure (*the ~ of heaven* or *earth*), human or animal body (*sobs shook her ~, man of gigantic ~*); skeleton of building, underlying support or essential substructure of anything; case or border enclosing picture, pane of glass, etc., whence ~'LESS (-ml-) a.; single complete image or picture transmitted in series of lines by television; (Gardening) glazed portable box-like structure protecting plants from cold; ‖ (Mining) inclined board for washing ore; (Snooker) triangular ~ for setting up balls, balls so set up, round of play during which balls are pocketed; ~ *aerial*, revolving aerial composed of rectangles or loops of wire, adapted for directional reception; ~*-house*, of wooden skeleton covered with boards; ~*-saw*, stretched in ~ to make it rigid; *~-up*, conspiracy; ~'*work*, ~, structure, upon or into which casing or contents can be put (lit., fig.). [f. prec.]

franc, n. French, Belgian, & Swiss monetary unit. [ME, f. OF, f. *Francorum Rex* king of the FRANKS, legend on earliest gold coin so called (14th c.)]

fran'chise (-z), n. (Chiefly hist. & U.S.) legal immunity or exemption from some burden or jurisdiction, privilege or exceptional right, granted to person, corporation, etc.; full membership of corporation or State, citizenship; right of voting at public elections esp. for member of Parliament, principle of qualification for this (FANCY¹~). [ME, f. OF (*franc* FRANK², -ISE)]

Francis'can, a. & n. (Friar) of the order founded 1209 by St Francis of Assisi; of the ~s. [f. F *franciscain* f. med. L *Franciscus* Francis + -AN]

fran'cium, n. Radio-active metallic element. [f. *France* + -IUM]

Franc'o-, comb. form of med. L *Franci* the Franks, now used = French-&-, as ~*-German*. Hence ~PHIL(E̊), ~PHOBE, nn. & aa. [FRANK¹, -O-]

franc'olin, n. Kind of partridge resembling pheasant. [F, f. It. *francolino*]

franc tireur (see Ap.), n. (pl. *-cs -rs*). Man of irregular light-infantry corps; a guerrilla fighter. [F]

fran'gible (-j-), a. Breakable, fragile. [OF, f. L *frangere* to break + -IBLE]

fran'gipane, ~*äni*, (-j-), n. (Perfume of) red jasmine; kind of almond cream or paste. [F, prob. f. *Frangipani*, maker]

Frank¹, n. One of the Germanic nation or coalition that conquered France in 6th c.; (in Levantine use) person of Western nationality. Hence~'ISH¹a. [OE *Franca*, OFrank. *Franko*, (whence med. L *Francus*, OF *Franc*), perh. f. weapon (cf. OE *franca* javelin)]

frank², a. Ingenuous, open, candid, outspoken; undisguised, avowed. Hence ~'LY² adv., ~'NESS n. [f. OF *franc* f. med. L *francus* free f. prec. (full freedom being confined to the Franks)]

frank³, v.t. & n. 1. (Hist.) superscribe (letter etc.) with signature ensuring gratis conveyance; facilitate coming & going of (person), give social passport to; convey (person) gratuitously; exempt from future payment etc. (*a ~ing duty, imposition*); ~*ing machine* (for stamping letters etc. and recording cost of postage incurred). 2. n. (hist.). ~*ing* signature, ~*ed* cover. [f. prec. in obs. sense *free of charge*]

Frank'enstein (-tīn), n. ~*'s monster*, thing that becomes formidable to the person who has created it. [M. W. Shelley (d. 1851), *Frankenstein*]

Frank'fort black, n. Fine black pigment used in copperplate engraving. [German town]

***frank'furt(er)** (-fer-), n. Highly seasoned German sausage. [f. *Frankfurt* German town]

frank'incense, n. Aromatic gum resin (prop. from trees of genus *Boswellia*) used for burning as incense. [ME, f. OF *franc encens* (FRANK² in obs. sense *luxuriant*, INCENSE¹)]

frank'lin, n. (hist.). Land-owner of free but not noble birth in 14th & 15th cc. [ME *francoleyn* etc., as FRANK², w. second element of obsc. orig.]

frank'-pledge, n. (hist.). System by which each member of tithing was responsible for every other (also rarely fig.), e.g. of relation between members of a Government). [AF *franc plege* (FRANK², PLEDGE), mistransl. of OE *frithborh* peace-pledge (not free-pledge)]

fran'tic, a. Wildly excited, beside oneself with rage, pain, grief, etc.; showing frenzy, uncontrolled. Hence ~ICALLY,

~ĭcLY², advv. [ME *frentik, frantik* f. OF *frenetic* PHRENETIC]

fräp, v.t. (naut.). (-pp-). Bind tightly. [f. F *frapper* bind, strike]

frappé (-ăp'ā), a. (Esp. of wines) iced, cooled. [p.p. of F *frapper* strike]

fräss, n. Excrement of larvae; refuse left by boring insects. [f. G *frass* (*fressen* devour)]

frat'e (-ahtă), n. (pl. *-ti* pr. -tē). Friar. [It.]

frät'er, n. (hist.). = REFECTORY. [ME, f. OF *fraitur* for *refreitor* f. med. L *refectorium* REFECTORY]

fratern'al, a. (As) of brother(s), brotherly; *~ order*, FRIENDLY Society. [f. med. L *fraternalis* f. L *fraternus* (*frater* brother, -AL)]

fratern'itў, n. Being fraternal, brotherliness; religious body; guild, company with common interests, set of men of same class etc.; *students' society in university or college. [ME, f. OF *fraternite* f. L *fraternitatem* (prec., -TY)]

frät'erniz|e, -is|e (-iz), v.i. Associate, make friends, behave as intimates, (*with, together*, or abs.). So ~A'TION n. [f. F *fraterniser* (L *fraternus* FRATERNAL, -IZE)]

frät'ricid|e, n. Killing of one's, one who kills his, brother or sister. Hence ~AL a. [f. F, or L *fratricida*, LL *-cidium*, (*frater -tris* brother, -CIDE)]

Frau (frow), n. (Of German wife or widow) Mrs; German woman. [G]

fraud, n. Deceitfulness (rare); criminal deception, use of false representations, (in Law, *in ~, to the ~, of*, so as to defraud); dishonest artifice or trick (*pious ~*, deception intended to benefit deceived, & esp. to strengthen religious belief); person or thing not fulfilling expectation or description. [ME, f. OF *fraude* f. L *fraudem* nom. *fraus*]

fraud'ül|ent, a. Guilty of, of the nature of, characterized or effected by, fraud. Hence or cogn. ~ENCE n., ~entLY² adv. [ME, f. OF, or L *fraudulentus* (prec., -ULENT)]

fraught (frawt), a. Stored, equipped, *with* (poet.); (fig.) *~ with*, involving, attended with, full of, threatening or promising, destined to produce, woe, danger, meaning, etc. [ME, p.p. of obs. *fraught* vb load with cargo, f. MDu. *vrachten*; so obs. *fraught* n. f. *vracht* FREIGHT]

Fräul'ein (froil'in), n. (Of German spinster) Miss (with surname; also alone as voc.); German spinster; German governess. [G]

Fraun'höfer (frown-) lines, n. pl. The dark lines in the solar spectrum. [J. von *Fraunhofer*, Bavarian optician (d. 1826)]

fräxinell'a, n. Kinds of garden dittany. [mod. L, dim. of L *fraxinus* ash]

fray¹, n. Noisy quarrel, brawl; fight, conflict, (lit. or fig.; *eager for the ~*). [for AFFRAY]

fray², v.t. & i. (Of deer) *~ head*, or *~*, rub velvet off new horns; wear through by

rubbing, ravel *out* edge or end of, (usu. woven material); become ragged at edge. [f. F *frayer* f. L *fricare* rub]

frāzil', n. (Canad. & U.S.). Anchor-ice, ice crystals in a stream. [f. Can. F *frasil* snow floating in the water; cf. F *fraisil* cinders]

****fräz'zle**, n. Worn or exhausted state (esp. *worn, beaten, to a ~*). [perh. as FRAY²]

freak, n. Caprice, vagary; capriciousness (*out of mere~*); product of sportive fancy; (also *~ of nature*) monstrosity, abnormally developed specimen. Hence ~'ISH¹ a., ~'ishLY² adv., ~'ishNESS n. [16th c., orig. unkn.]

freaked (-kt), *a.* Oddly flecked or streaked. [-ED²]

frēc'kle, n., & v.t. & i. 1. Light brown spot on skin, (pl.) sporadic sunburn. 2. vb. Spot, be spotted, with ~s. [alt. f. ME *frecken* f. ON *freknur* pl.]

free¹, a. (*freer, freest*, pr. -ēer, -ēist), & adv. 1. Not in bondage to another, having personal rights & social & political liberty, (*~ labour*, of ~ men not slaves, & see 2); (of State, its citizens or institutions) subject neither to foreign domination nor to despotic government, having national & civil liberty; *~-born*, inheriting citizen rights & liberty; *~'hold*, (estate held by) tenure in fee simple or fee-tail or for term of life (also of corresponding tenure of office), (adj.) held by *~hold*; *~'holder*, possessor of *~hold* estate; *~'man*, person not slave or serf, citizen of ~ State (& see 4); *~'mason*, member of fraternity for mutual help & brotherly feeling called *F~ & Accepted Masons* having elaborate ritual & system of secret signs (the orig. ~ masons were prob. skilled masons emancipated & allowed to move from place to place in & after 14th c., & the *accepted* may have been honorary members of the ~ masons' societies); *~'masonry*, system & institutions of the ~masons, secret understanding between like characters, instinctive sympathy. 2. Loose (~ *wheel* in bicycle, driving-wheel able to revolve while pedals are at rest), unrestricted (~ *love*, sexual relations irrespective of marriage), at liberty, not confined, released from ties or duties, unimpeded (~ *trade*, left to its natural course without customs duties to restrict imports or protect home industries, this principle; *~-trader*, believer in it), unfettered in action (*have or give a ~ hand*, right of acting at discretion), permitted *to do*, independent (*F~ Church*, unconnected with State; *the F~ Churches*, nonconformists; *F~ Church of Scotland* (hist.), seceders of 1843 from Presbyterian establishment; *~ house*, public house not tied to a particular brewery; *~ lance*, medieval mercenary, modern politician or controversialist with no party allegiance, unattached journalist; *~ labour*, of workmen not belonging to trade unions, & see 1; ~-*thinker*, -*thinking* n. & a., -*thought*, rejector etc. of authority in religious belief, rationalist etc.), unconstrained(~ *step*, *gestures*); (of literary style) not observing strict laws of form (~ *verse*, = VERS LIBRE), (of translation) not literal; allowable (*it is ~ for* or *to him to do so*); open to all comers (~ *fight*, in which anyone present joins); clear of obstructions, clear *of* or *from* something undesirable, (of wind) not adverse; not fixed, not in contact, (Chem.) not combined, (of power or energy) disengaged or available; ~-*board*, part of ship's side between line of flotation & deck-level; ~-*hand*, (of drawing) done without artificial aid to the hand; ~-*stone*, kind of peach of which when ripe the stone is loose (& see 3); ~ *will*, power of directing our own actions without constraint by necessity or fate (& see 3). 3. Spontaneous, unforced, unearned, gratuitous, willing, (~ *grace*, unmerited favour of God; ~ *gift*, not in requital; *did it of my own ~ will*, & so ~-*will* adj., voluntary; ~ *quarters*, gratuitous entertainment; *am ~ to confess*, not unwilling); lavish, profuse, unstinted, copious, (~ *of his money*, open-handed; so ~-*handed*, liberal; ~ *flow of water*; ~ *liver*, *living*, indulger, indulgence, in pleasures esp. of the table); frank, unreserved, (~-*spoken*, not concealing one's opinions, blunt; ~ *& easy*, unceremonious, also as n., smoking-concert etc.), forward, familiar, impudent, (*make* or *be* ~, take liberties *with*); (of talk, stories, etc.) broad, not quite decent; ~'*stone*, fine-grained easily sawn sandstone or limestone (& see 2). 4. Released or exempt *from* (~ *from the ordinary rules*, *disease*, *difficulty*, etc.); having burgess rights (*made ~ of the city*), having the entrée & use *of* (~ *of the house*); not subject to tax, toll, duty, trade-restrictions, or fees (~ *port*, open to all traders alike; ~-*list*, of persons to be admitted ~, duty-~ articles, etc.; ~ *school*, with no fees charged; ~ *pass*, not paid for; also adv., *as the gallery is open* ~, & in comb. as *carriage*-~, without charge for conveyance); ~'*man*, one who has the freedom of a city, company, etc. (& see 1). 5. adv. ~*ly*, without cost or payment, (Naut.) not close-hauled. Hence ~'LY[2] adv. [OE *frēo*, OS, OHG *frī*, ON *frīr*, Goth. *freis* f. Gmc *frijaz*, cogn. w. FRIEND]

free[2], v.t. (~*d*). Make free, set at liberty, (~*d'man*, emancipated slave, esp. in Rom. Hist.); relieve *from*, rid or ease *of*; clear, disengage, distangle. [OE *frēon* (prec.)]

free'boot|er, n. Pirate, piratical adventurer. Hence by back formation free'-boot v.i., ~*-*ING[1,2] n. & a. [f. Du. *vrij-buiter* (FREE[1], BOOTY, -ER[1]); cf. FILIBUSTER]

free'dom, n. Personal liberty, non-slavery; civil liberty, independence; liberty of action, right *to* do; power of self-determination, independence of fate

or necessity; frankness, outspokenness, undue familiarity (*take* ~*s with*); facility, ease, in action; boldness of conception; (Physics) capability of motion; exemption *from* defect, disadvantage, burden, duty, etc.; privilege possessed by city or corporation; participation in privileges of membership *of* company etc. or citizenship *of* city (often given *honoris causa* to distinguished persons); unrestricted use *of* (*has the* ~ *of the library*); *the four* ~*s*, ~ *of speech and religion*, ~ *from fear and want*. [OE *frēodōm* (FREE[1], -DOM)]

free'mar̃tin, n. Hermaphrodite or imperfect female of ox kind. [orig. unkn.]

frees'ia (-z-), n. Kinds of iridaceous bulbous plant from Cape of Good Hope. [f. E. M. *Fries*, Sw. botanist (d. 1878) + -IA[1]]

freeze, v.i. & t. (*frōze*, *frōzen*), & n. 1. (Impers.) *it ~s* etc., there is etc. frost; be converted into or covered with ice; become rigid as result of cold; become fastened *to* or *together* by frost, (sl.) ~ *on to*, take or keep tight hold of; feel very cold (~ *to death*, die by frost); be chilled by fear; cause to congeal, form ice upon, (fluid or moist thing; often *in*, *over*, *up*), preserve (meat etc.) by refrigeration; make (credits, assets, etc.) temporarily or permanently unrealizable; peg or stabilize (prices, wages, etc.); (by exagg.) ~ *one's blood*, terrify him; chill (feelings), paralyse (powers); stiffen, harden, injure, kill, by chilling (*frozen to death*); (sl.) ~ *out*, exclude from business, society, etc., by competition or boycotting etc.; ~-*out*, variety of poker in which each player drops out as soon as he loses his capital; *freezing-mixture*, salt & snow or other mixture used to ~ liquids; *freezing-point*, temperature at which liquid, esp. water, ~*s*; *frozen limit* (colloq.), the extreme of the objectionable or unendurable. 2. n. State, coming, period, of frost; stabilization of prices, wages, etc. [OE *frēosan*, OHG *friosan*, ON *frjósa* f. Gmc *freusan*]

freez'ing, a. In vbl senses; esp.: (by exagg.) very cold; (of manners) chilling, distant. Hence ~LY[2] adv. [-ING[2]]

freight (frāt), n., & v.t. 1. Hire of ship for transporting goods; transport of goods by water (in U.S. by land also), charge for this, cargo, shipload; load, burden. 2. v.t. Load (ship) with cargo; hire or let out (ship) for carriage of goods & passengers. [f. MDu. *vrecht* var. of *vracht* see FRAUGHT]

freight'age (-āt-), n. Hire of ship for, cost of, conveyance of goods; freighting or hiring of ship; cargo. [-AGE]

freight'er (-āt-), n. One who (charters &) loads ship; one who consigns goods for carriage inland; one whose business is to receive & forward freight; cargo ship, freight-carrying aircraft. [-ER[1]]

Frênch, a. & n. 1. Of France or its people; having the qualities attributed to ~

people; ‖ ~ **bean**, kidney or haricot bean used as vegetable both in unripe sliced pods & in ripe seeds; ~ **bread**, kind of fancy bread; ~ **chalk**, kind of steatite used for marking cloth & removing grease & as dry lubricant; ~ **drain** (of rubble, letting water soak away); ~ **grey**, tint composed of white with ivory black, Indian red, & Chinese blue; so HORN¹; take ~ **leave**, depart, act, without asking leave or giving notice; ‖ ~ **letter**, a contraceptive sheath; ~'**man**, man of ~ birth or nationality, (*good* etc.) ~-speaker, ~ **ship**, the red-legged partridge; ~ **polish**, kind of polish for wood; ~-**polish** v.t., polish with this, whence ~-pŏl′ishᴇʀ¹ n.; ~ **roof**, mansard; ~ **toast**, fried bread; ~ **window**, glazed folding-door serving as window & door; ~'**woman**, woman of France. 2. n. The ~ language (~ *lesson*, *master*, etc., concerned with this); *the* ~ (pl.), the ~ people. Hence ~'ɴᴇss n., Frĕn′chy ²,³ a. & n. [OE *frencisc*, OHG *frenkisc* (FRANK¹, -ɪsʜ¹)]

Frĕnch′ĭ|fў, f-, v.t. Make French in form, character, or manners (usu. in p.p.). Hence ~FICA′TION n. [-FY]

Frĕnch′lĕss, a. Knowing no French. [-LESS]

frenetic. See PHRENETIC.

frenum. See FRAENUM.

frĕn′z|ў, n., & v.t. 1. Mental derangement, temporary insanity, paroxysm of mania, (rare) delirious fury or agitation, wild folly. 2. v.t. (usu. in p.p.). Drive to ~y, infuriate, (~*ied rage*, that of a ~ied person). [ME, f. OF *frenesie* f. med. L *phrenesia* for L f. Gk *-ĕsis* f. *phrĕn* mind; cf. FRANTIC]

frē′quency n. Frequent occurrence, commonness of occurrence (*word* ~), being repeated at short intervals, (of pulse) number of beats per minute; (Phys.) rate of recurrence (of vibration etc.), number of repetitions in given time esp. per second (*high, medium, low,* ~, aber. H.F., M.F., L.F., w. ref. to sound-waves, electro-magnetic waves, etc.); (Statistics) the ratio of the actual to the number of possible occurrences of an event; ~ *modulation* (Radio), varying the ~ of the carrier wave in accordance with speech or music, system of broadcasting using this method of modulation. [f. L *frequentia* (foll., -ᴇɴᴄʏ)]

frē′quent¹, a. Found near together, numerous, abundant; often occurring, common, happening in close succession, (of pulse) rapid, (*it is a* ~ *practice to*), whence ~-ʟʏ² adv.; (with agent-noun) habitual, constant, (*a* ~ *caller*). [f. F, or L *frequens -entis* crowded]

frēquĕnt′², v.t. Go often or habitually to (place, meetings, company, house). Hence or cogn. frēquĕnta′ᴛɪoɴ, ~ᴇʀ¹, nn. [f. F *fréquenter* or L *frequentare* (prec.)]

frēquĕn′tative, a. & n. (gram.). (Verb or verbal form or conjugation) expressing frequent repetition or intensity of action. [f. L *frequentativus* (prec., -ᴀᴛɪᴠᴇ)]

frĕs′cō, n. (pl. *-ōs, -oes*), & v.t. Method of painting (esp. *in* ~), picture, in water-colour laid on wall or ceiling before plaster is dry; (vb) paint (wall etc., picture or subject) thus. [It., orig. adj.= foll.]

frĕsh, a., adv., & n. 1. New, novel, not previously known, used, met with, or introduced, (*break* ~ *ground*, try something unhackneyed); additional, other, different, further, (*begin a* ~ *chapter*); recent, lately made or arrived, just come *from*; raw, inexperienced, (~'**man**, first-year man at University); not preserved by salting, pickling, smoking, tinning, etc. (~ *herrings, meat, fruit,* & see below; ~ *butter,* & see next sense); not salt (~ *water*; ~'*water* a., of ~ water, not of the sea, as ~*water fish, fishing, sailor*; ~ *butter*, not flavoured with salt, & see prec. sense), not salt or bitter, drinkable, (~ *water*); pure, untainted, invigorating, refreshing, cool, (of air, wind, water); not stale, musty, or vapid (~ *fish, meat, fruit,* & see above; ~ *egg*); not faded (~ *flowers, memories*); unsullied, bright & pure in colour (*a* ~ *complexion*), looking healthy or young; not weary, brisk, vigorous, fit, (*never felt* ~er; *as* ~ *as paint*, quite brisk, prob. a pun on the warning '~ paint'; *a* ~ *wind*, of some strength); excited with drink; *presumptuous, forward, cheeky, amorously impudent. 2. adv. Newly, esp. in comb. as ~-*caught, -coined*; ~-*run*, (of salmon) lately come up from the sea. 3. n. ~ part of day, year, etc. (*in the* ~ *of the morning*); rush of water in river, flood. Hence ~'ᴇɴ⁶ v.t. & i., ~'ɴᴇss n. [ME *fersse* f. OE *fersc* f. Gmo *friskas*; ME *fresch* f. OF *freis*, fem. *fresche*, f. same Gmo orig.]

‖ **frĕsh′er, n.** (sl.). = FRESHman. [-ᴇʀ¹]

frĕsh′ĕt, n. Rush of fresh water flowing into sea; flood of river from heavy rain or melted snow. [FRESH n. +-ᴇᴛ½ or f. OF *freschete* f. *frais* FRESH]

frĕsh′lў, adv. Recently (only with participles, = *fresh* adv.); afresh (rare); with unabated vigour; with fresh appearance, odour, etc. [-ʟʏ²]

frĕt¹, n., & v.t. (-tt-). **1.** Ornamental pattern made of continuous combinations of straight lines joined usu. at right angles (also *Greek*~). **2.** v.t. Variegate, chequer; adorn (esp. ceiling) with carved or embossed work; ~-*saw*, very narrow saw stretched on frame for cutting thin wood in ornamental patterns; ~'*work*, carved work in decorative patterns esp. of straight lines, also wood cut with ~-saw. [ME, f. OF *frete* trellis-work & *freter* vb]

frĕt², v.t. & i. (-tt-), & n. **1.** Gnaw, wear or consume or torment by gnawing, (of moths etc., horses champing bit, action of frost, rust, corrosives, friction, etc., or the passions); make (passage etc.) by wearing away; chafe, irritate, annoy, worry, distress; distress oneself with regret or discontent (*at*; ~ *away* or *out* one's *life* etc.); ~ *& fume*, show angry impatience; (of stream etc.) flow or rise in little waves, chafe; ruffle (water). 2. n. Irritation, vexation, querulousness, (*in a* ~; ~ *& fume*; *on the* ~); hence ~'FUL a., ~'fuLLY² adv., ~'fulNESS n., ~'t'Y² a. [OE *fretan*, OHG *frezzan*, Goth. *fra-itan* f. Gmc **fra-* FOR-(5) + *etan EAT]

fret³, n. Bar or ridge on fingerboard of some stringed instruments fixing positions of fingers to produce required notes. Hence ~t'ED² a. [orig. unkn.]

Freud'ian (froid-), a. & n. (Disciple) of Freud or his doctrines of PSYCHO-*analysis*. [Sigmund *Freud* (d. 1939) + -IAN]

fri'able, a. Easily crumbled. Hence or cogn. **friABIL'ITY,** ~NESS, nn. [f. F. or L *friabilis* (*friare* crumble)]

fri'ar, n. Member of certain religious orders esp. the four mendicant orders of Franciscans (*Grey F~s*), Augustinians (*Austin F~s*), Dominicans (*Black F~s*), & Carmelites (*White F~s*); ~'s *balsam*, tincture of benzoin. Hence ~LY¹ a. [ME & OF *frere* f. L *fratrem* nom. *-ter* brother; for *friar* cf. CHOIR]

fri'ary, n. Convent of friars. [14/15th c. *frary, freyry,* f. OF *frairie, frerie* (*frere* (prec.) + -Y¹) w. assim. to prec.]

frib'ble, v.i., & n. Trifle, be frivolous; (n.) trifler. [imit.; earlier senses *stammer, totter*]

fric'andeau (-dō), n. (pl. *-x* pr. *-z*), & v.t. (Slice of) fried or stewed meat, esp. veal, served with sauce; (vb) make into ~x. [F]

fricassee', n., & v.t. Meat cut up, fried or stewed, & served with sauce, esp., ragout of birds or small animals cut up; (vb) make ~ of. [F, p.p. of *fricasser*]

fric'ative, a. & n. (Consonant) made by friction of breath in narrow opening, as *f, th,* Scotch *ch.* [f. L *fricare* rub + -ATIVE]

fric'tion, n. Medical chafing; rubbing of two bodies, attrition; (Phys., Mech.) resistance body meets with in moving over another (*angle of* ~, maximum angle at which one will remain on another without sliding); (fig.) clash of wills, temperaments, opinions, etc. (usu. between two persons); ~*-ball,* used in bearings to lessen ~; ~*-clutch, -cone, -coupling, -disc, -gear(ing),* contrivances for transmitting motion by ~. Hence ~AL, ~LESS, aa., (-shon-). [F, f. L *frictionem* (*fricare* rub, -ION)]

Frid'ay (-dĭ), n. Sixth day of week (*Good* ~, ~ before Easter-day, commemorating Crucifixion; *Black* ~, used as name for various disasters that fell on ~). [OE *frīgedæg,* OHG *frīatag,* ON *frjádagr* day of *Frigg,* wife of Odin, com.-WG transl. of LL *Veneris dies* day of planet Venus)]

friend (frĕnd), n., & v.t. 1. One joined to another in intimacy & mutual benevo-

lence independently of sexual or family love; person who acts for one, e.g. as second in duel; (loosely) acquaintance, stranger that one comes across or has occasion to mention anew, (*my* ~ *in the brown hat now left me*; used in voc. as polite form or in irony, & by Quakers as ordinary address; preceding a name, as ~ *Jones, Dick*; || *my honourable* ~, of another M.P. in House of Commons; *my learned* ~, of another lawyer in court); (pl.) one's near relations, those responsible for one; sympathizer, helper, patron, (*no* ~ *of* or *to order, virtue,* etc.; *a* ~ *at court,* one whose influence may be made use of); helpful thing (*my shyness was here my best* ~); one who is not an enemy, who is on the same side; *be, keep, make,* ~*s,* be or get on good terms; (*F~*) Quaker (*Society of F~s,* the Quakers as a communion); hence ~'LESS a., ~'lĕssNESS n., (frŏ-). 2. v.t. (poet.). Befriend, help. [OE *frēond,* OS *friund,* OHG *friunt,* ON *frœndi,* Goth. *frijonds,* part. of Gmc *frijōjan f. *frijaz FREE; cf. FIEND, -ND²]

friend'ly (frĕ-), a., n., & adv. 1. Acting, disposed to act, as friend; characteristic of friends, expressing, showing, or prompted by, kindness (|| ~ *lead* among London poor, entertainment to raise funds for distressed person); not hostile, on amicable terms, (*a* ~ *nation*; ~ *action* at law, brought merely to get a point decided; ~ *match,* played for honour merely, not in competition for cup etc.); favourably disposed, ready to approve or help, (of things) serviceable, convenient, opportune; || *F~ Society,* for mutual insurance against distress in sickness or old age; hence **friend'liLY²** (rare) adv., **friend'liNESS** n., (frŏ-). 2. n. (w. pl.). Native of ~ tribe. 3. adv. (rare). In ~ manner (*used, received, us* ~). [-LY²]

friend'ship (frĕ-), n. Being friends, relation between friends; friendly disposition felt or shown. [-SHIP]

Friesian (frē'zhan), a. & n. (Of, one of) a breed of Friesland cattle. [var. of FRISIAN]

frieze¹, n. Coarse woollen cloth with nap usu. on one side only. [ME, f. OF (*drap de) frise* Frisian cloth]

frieze², n. Member of entablature coming between architrave & cornice; horizontal broad band of sculpture filling this; band of decoration elsewhere. [f. F *frise* f. med. L *frisium* f. L *Phrygium* (*opus* work) of Phrygia]

frig (-j), fri(d)ge, n. (colloq.). Refrigerator. [abbr.]

frig'ate, n. (Hist.) warship next in size & equipment to ships of the line, with 28–60 guns on main deck & raised quarter-deck & forecastle; corvette, sloop, small destroyer; (also ~*-bird*) large swift tropical bird of prey. [f. F *frégate* f. It. *fregata* of unkn. orig.]

fright (frīt), n., & v.t. 1. Sudden fear, violent terror, alarm; grotesque-looking or badly dressed person. **2.** v.t. (poet.). Frighten. [OE *fryhto* metathetic form of *fyrhto* = Goth. *faurhtei*, also OS, OHG *forhta*, f. Gmc **furht-* o? unkn. orig.]

fright'en (-it-), v.t. Throw into a fright, terrify, (often *out of, into, doing*); drive *away, out of* (place etc.), *into* (submission etc.), by fright; *~ed at* or *of* (*at* w. ref. to an occasion, *of* to habitual fear). [prec. (n.) +-EN[1]]

fright'ful (-it-), a. Frightening (arch.); dreadful, shocking, revolting; ugly, hideous, whence ~NESS n. (esp., as mistransl. of G *Schrecklichkeit* terrorizing of civilian population as military resource); (sl.) very great, awful. Hence ~LY[2] adv. [-FUL]

fri'gid, a. Cold (esp. of climate or air; ~ *zone*, region enclosed by either polar circle);without ardour, apathetic, formal, forced; sexually irresponsive; chilling, depressing; dull, flat, insipid. Hence or cogn. **frigid'ITY**, ~NESS, nn., ~LY[2] adv. [f. L *frigidus* (*frigēre* be cold f. *frigus* n. cold)]

frill, n., & v.t. & i. **1.** Ornamental edging of woven material, one side of strip being gathered & the other left loose with fluted appearance; similar paper ornament on ham-knuckle etc.; natural fringe of feathers, hair, etc., on bird, animal, or plant; (pl.) airs, affectation, (*puts on ~*s), useless embellishments or accomplishments; mesentery of animal; (Photog.) puckered gelatine film at edge of plate. **2.** vb. Decorate with a ~; (esp. Photog., of gelatine film) pucker at edges of plate etc. Hence ~ED[2] (-ld) a., ~'ERY(5), ~'ING[1] (3, 6), nn. [16th c., orig. unkn.]

frill'ies (-liz), n. pl. (colloq.). Frilled petticoats etc. [-Y[2] or -Y[3]]

fringe (-j), n., & v.t. **1.** Ornamental bordering of threads left loose or formed into tassels or twists; such bordering made separately; border, edging, (*Newgate ~*, beard allowed to grow below shaven chin); front hair cut short & allowed to hang over forehead; natural border of hair etc. in animal or plant; hence ~'LESS (-jl-), frin'gY[2], aa. **2.** v.t. Adorn or encircle with ~, serve as ~ to; hence frin'gING[1](3) n. [ME & OF *frenge* f. Rom. **frimbia* f. L *fimbria*]

fripp'erY, n. Finery, needless or tawdry adornment esp. in dress; empty display esp. in literary style; knick-knacks, trifles. [f. OF *freperie* (*frepe* rag, -ERY)]

*Fris'cō, n. San Francisco. [abbr.]

frisĕtte (-z-), n. Band of small artificial curls on forehead. [F (*friser* FRIZZ)]

friseur '(frēzẽr'), n. Hair-dresser. [as prec.]

Fris'ian (-z-), a. & n. (Native, language) of Friesland. [f. L *Frisii* pl. f. OFris. *Frise*+-AN]

frisk, v.i. & t., & n. **1.** Move sportively, gambol; **feel over, search, (person) for weapon etc. (sl.). **2.** n. Gambol. Hence

fris'kY[2] a., **fris'kILY**[2] adv., **fris'kiNESS** n. [f. obs. *frisk* a. f. OF *frisque* lively of unkn. orig.]

fris'kĕt, n. (print.). Thin iron frame keeping sheet in position while printing. [f. F *frisquette*]

frit, n., & v.t. (-tt-). **1.** Calcined mixture of sand & fluxes as material for glassmaking; vitreous composition from which soft porcelain is made. **2.** v.t. Make into ~, partially fuse, calcine. [f. It. *fritta* fem. p.p. of *friggere* FRY[2]]

frit-fly, n. Small fly destructive to wheat. [orig. unkn.]

frith. See FIRTH.

fritill'ary (or frit[2]), n. Kinds of liliaceous plant, esp. snakeshead; kinds of butterfly. [f. L *fritillus* dice-box +-ARY[1]]

fritt'er[1], n. Piece of fried batter often containing slices of fruit etc. (*apple, oyster*, etc.,~); (pl.) = FENKS. [ME, f. OF *friture* (L *frigere frict-* FRY[2], -URE), see -ER[2](3)]

fritt'er[2], v.t. Subdivide minutely; throw (time, money, energy, etc.) *away* on divided aims. [f. obs. n. *fritter(s)* = obs. *fitters* n. pl. f. obs. *fitter* v. of unkn. orig.]

Fritz, nickname for the Germans or a German [G, abbr. of *Friedrich* Frederick]

friv'ol, v.i. & t. (-ll-). Be a trifler, trifle; throw (money, time) *away* foolishly. [back formation f. foll.]

friv'olous, a. Paltry, trumpery, trifling, futile; given to trifling, not serious, silly. Hence or cogn. **frivōl'ITY**, ~NESS, nn., ~LY[2] adv. [f. L *frivolus* +-OUS]

friz(z)[1], v.t., & n. **1.** Curl, crisp, form into mass of small curls, (hair, or person etc. in regard to it); dress (wash-leather etc.) with pumice or scraping-knife. **2.** n. Frizzed state, frizzed hair, row of curls; hence **frizz'Y**[2] a. [f. F *friser*]

frizz[2], v.i. Make sputtering noise in frying. [f. FRY[2] w. imit. termin.]

friz'zle[1], v.t. & i., & n. **1.** Curl (t., & i. esp. with *up*, of hair etc.) in small crisp curls. **2.** n. ~d hair; hence **frizz'lY**[2] a. [orig. unkn.; earlier than FRIZZ[1]]

friz'zle[2], v.i. & t. Fry, toast, or grill, with sputtering noise. [FRIZZ[2]+-LE(3)]

frō, adv. Away (only in *to & ~*, backwards & forwards, or of repeated journeys between two places). [f. ON *frá* prep. = OE FROM]

frŏck, n., & v.t. **1.** Monk's long gown with loose sleeves, (fig.) priestly character; = SMOCK-~; sailor's woollen jersey; child's skirt & bodice as outer dress for indoor use; woman's dress; ‖ (also ~-*coat*) man's long-skirted coat not cut away in front; military coat of like shape. **2.** v.t. Invest with priestly office, cf. UNFROCK. [14th c. f OF *froc*, perh. f. WG (OFris., OS, OHG) *hroc*]

*frŏe, *frow (frō), n. Cleaving tool with handle at right angles to blade. [subst. use of FROWARD ' turned away ']

Froe'belism (frẽr[2]), n. Education of

young children on the kindergarten system. [F. W. A. *Froebel*, German educationalist (d. 1852), -ISM]

frŏg¹, n. Tailless amphibious animal developed from tadpole; (derog. for) Frenchman (as eating ~s), whence Frŏgg'y² (-g-) n.; ~-*eater*, Frenchman; ~-*fish*, kinds of fish esp. the angler; ~-*in- -the-throat*, hoarseness; ~'*man*, person equipped for underwater operations orig. against enemy shipping; ~'s, ~, -*march*, carrying of prisoner face downwards by four men holding a limb each; ~-*spawn*, lit., & as names for kinds of freshwater algae. Hence ~ğ'y² (-g-) a. (esp. = cold as a ~). [OE *frogga*, pet name for *forsc*, *frosc*, *frox* = OHG *frosc*, ON *froskr* f. Gmc *froskaz*]

frŏg², n. Elastic horny substance in middle of sole of horse's foot. [perh. f. prec.]

frŏg³, n. Attachment to waistbelt to support sword, bayonet, etc.; military coat- -fastening of spindle-shaped button & loop, whence ~ğED² (-gd) a. [orig. unkn.]

frŏg⁴, n. Grooved piece of iron at place in railway where tracks cross. [orig. unkn.]

frŏl'ic a. (arch.), v.i., & n. 1. Joyous, mirthful, sportive, full of pranks. 2. v.i. (-ck-). Play pranks, gambol. 3. n. Outburst of gaiety, prank, merriment, merrymaking, gay party. Hence ~SOME a., ~SOMELY² adv., ~SOMENESS n. [f. Du. *vrolijk* adj. cf. G *fröhlich* (MDu. *vrô* glad, -LIKE]

from (from, *emphatic or at end of clause* frŏm), prep. expressing separation & introducing:—1. Person, place, etc., whence motion takes place (*comes ~ the clouds*; *repeated ~ mouth to mouth*). 2. Starting-point (~ *title to colophon*, throughout book; ~ *2nd July*; ~ *day to day*, daily; ~ *time to time*, occasionally; ~ *a child*, since childhood). 3. Inferior limit (*saw ~ 10 to 20 boats*). 4. Object etc. whence distance or remoteness is reckoned or stated (*ten miles ~ Rome*; *am far ~ saying*; ~ *home*, out, away; *absent*, *away*, ~ *home*; *apart ~ its moral aspect*). 5. Thing or person got rid of, escaped, avoided, of which one is deprived etc., person or thing deprived, (*took his sword ~ him*; *released him ~ prison*; *cannot refrain ~ laughing*; *appeal ~ lower court*, *dissuade ~ folly*). 6. State changed for another (~ *being attacked became the aggressor*; *raise penalty ~ banishment to death*). 7. Thing distinguished (*doesn't know black ~ white*). 8. Source (*dig gravel ~ pit*; *draw conclusion ~ premisses*; *quotations ~ the fathers*). 9. Place of vantage etc. (*saw it ~ the roof*; ~ *his point of view*, as he sees things). 10. Giver, sender, etc. (*gifts ~ Providence*; *frocks ~ Worth's*; *things not required ~ me*). 11. Model (*painted ~ nature*). 12. Reason; cause, motive, (*died ~ fatigue*; *suffering~ dementia*; ~ *his looks*

you might suppose). 13. Advbs or advl phrr. of place or time (~ *long ago, of old*, *above*, etc.), or prepositions (~ *under her spectacles*; ~ *out the bed*). [OE *fram*, *from*, OS, OHG, Goth. *fram*, ON *frá* (FRO), f. Gmc *fra-* forward]

frŏnd, n. (Bot.) leaf-like organ formed by union of stem & foliage in certain flowerless plants, esp. ferns, & differing from leaf in usu. bearing fructification; (Zool.) leaf-like expansion in some animal organisms. Hence frŏn'dAGE(1) n., frŏn'dOSE¹ a. [f. L *frons* -*dis* leaf]

Fronde (-awnd), n. Party that rebelled against Mazarin & Court during minority of Louis XIV; malcontent party; violent political opposition. [F, orig. = sling]

front (-ŭnt), n. & a., & v.i. & t. 1. Forehead (poet.; *head & ~*, chief part or item); face (~ *to ~*; *have the ~*, be impudent enough usu. *to do*; *present*, *show*, *a bold ~*); (Mil.) foremost line or part of army etc., line of battle, part of ground towards real or imaginary enemy, scene of actual fighting (*go to the ~*, join troops on campaign), direction in which formed line faces (*change ~*); (fig.) organized body or department of activity (*home*, *kitchen*, *popular*, ~); (Archit.) any face of building, esp. that of main entrance; fore part of anything (opp. BACK); (Meteor.) boundary between cold & warm air masses (*cold*, *warm*, ~, forward boundary of a mass of advancing cold, warm, air); ‖ *the* promenade of a seaside resort; band of false hair, set of false curls, worn over woman's forehead; breast of man's shirt, also dicky; (with prep.) forward position (*in ~ of*, before, in advance of, confronting; *in ~*; *come to the ~*, become conspicuous); (ellipt.) = in ~ as adv. or adj. (*were beset ~ & rear*; *two-pair ~*, second-floor room in ~); hence ~'WARD a. & adv., ~'WARDS adv., (-ŭn-). 2. adj. Of the, situated in, ~ (‖ ~ *bench*, reserved for ministers or ex-ministers in Parliament houses; ~ *door*, chief entrance of house); ~ *page*, first page of newspaper (usu. attrib., of news of striking journalistic importance). 3. vb. Face, look, *to, towards*, (*up*)*on*; face, stand opposite to; have ~ on side of (street etc.); confront, meet, oppose; furnish with ~ (~*ed with stone*). [ME; n. OF, f. L *frons frontis*; vb f. OF *fronter*]

fron'tag|e (-ŭn-), n. Land abutting on street or water, land between front of building & road, whence ~ER¹(4) n.; extent of front; front of building; ground occupied by troops in camp or on parade; facing a certain way, exposure, outlook. [-AGE]

fron'tal¹ (-ŭn-), n. Covering for front of altar; façade. [ME, f. OF *frontel* f. L *frontale* (FRONT, -AL)]

fron'tal² (-ŭn-), a. Of forehead (~ *bone*, *artery*); of, on, front (~ *attack*, delivered direct, not on flank or rear). [-AL]

fron'tier (-ŭn-, -ŏn-), n. Part of a country that borders on another; the borders of civilization; (attrib.) of, on, the ~; ~*sman*, one living on or beyond the borders of civilization (*Legion of F~smen*, organization enrolling men with such experience). [ME, f. OF *frontier*, *-iere* f. *front* FRONT, see -ARY[1]]

Fron'tignac (-ĭnyăk), n. A muscat wine. [erron. for *-nan*, name of French town]

fron'tispiece (-ŭn-), n., & v.t. (Archit.) principal face of building, decorated entrance, pediment over door etc.; illustration facing title-page of book or one of its divisions (vb, supply *with* as ~). [f. F *frontispice* f. med. L *frontispicium* countenance (FRONT, *specere* look).w. assim. to *piece*]

front'less (-ŭn-), a. Unblushing (rare); without front. [-LESS]

front'let (-ŭn-),. n. Band worn on forehead; = PHYLACTERY; animal's forehead; cloth hanging over upper part of altar frontal. [f. OF *frontelet* (FRONTAL[1], -LET)]

fron'to-, comb. form of L *frons -tis*=of the forehead & —, as ~-*nasal*. [for *fronti-* (-I-, -O-)]

fron'ton (frŭ-), n. Pediment. [F, f. It. *frontone* (FRONT, -OON)]

frōre, a. (poet.). Frozen, frosty. [arch. p.p. of FREEZE]

frost (-aw-, -ŏ-), n., & v.t. 1. Freezing, prevalence of temperature below freezing-point of water (‖ *ten degrees of* ~, 22° Fahrenheit; *hard*, *sharp*, ~; *white* or *hoar*, *black*, ~, with, without, rime; *Jack F~*, ~ personified), frozen state or consistence (*there is still* ~ *in the ground*), frozen dew or vapour (*windows covered with*~); influence that chills, makes grey, etc.; (sl.) failure; ~-*bite*, inflammation or gangrene of & below skin from severe cold, ~-*bitten*, affected with this; ~-*work*, tracery made by ~ on glass etc.; hence ~'LESS a. 2. v.t. Nip, injure, (plants etc.) with ~; cover (as) with rime, powder with coating of sugar etc., whence ~-ING(3) n.; give roughened or finely granulated surface to (glass, metal); turn (hair) white; arm (horse's shoes) against slipping by nails etc. [OE, OS, OHG, ON *frost* f. Gmc **frust-* f. **freusan* FREEZE]

fros't|y (-aw-, -ŏ-), a. Cold with frost; cold, chilling, frigid, lacking in warmth of feeling; covered, seeming to be covered, with hoar-frost. Hence ~iLY[2] adv., ~i-NESS n. [-Y[2]]

froth (-ŏ-, -aw-), n., & v.i. & t. 1. Collection of small bubbles, foam; impure matter on liquid, scum; worthless matter, idle talk, etc.; ‖ ~-*blower* (joc.), beer-drinker (esp. as designation of member of a certain charitable Order); hence ~'Y[2] a., ~'iLY[2] adv., ~'iNESS n. 2. vb. Emit, gather, ~; cause (beer etc.) to foam. [ME, f. ON *frotha*, *frauth*, cogn. w. OE *āfrēothan* to~]

frou'-frou (-ōō-, -ōō), n. Rustling, esp. of dresses. [F, imit.]

frow[1], n. Dutchwoman. [ME, f. Du. *vrouw* = G *frau* woman]

*frow[2]. See FROE.

frō'ward, a. (arch.). Perverse, refractory. Hence ~LY[2] adv., ~NESS n. [FRO, -WARD]

frown, v.i. & t., & n. 1. Knit brows esp. to express displeasure or concentrate attention; (of things) present gloomy aspect; express disapprobation (*at, on, upon*); put (interrupter, interruption, etc.) *down* with ~; express (defiance etc.) with ~; hence ~'ingLY[2] adv. 2. n. Vertically furrowed state of brow; look expressing severity, disapproval, or deep thought. [ME, f. OF *frongnier*, *froignier*, of obsc. orig.]

frowst, n., & v.i. (colloq.). Fusty heat in room (‖ vb, stay in, enjoy, this). Hence **frows'tr**[2] a. [cf. earlier *frowzy*]

frowz'|y, a. Ill-smelling, fusty, musty, close; slatternly, unkempt, dingy. Hence ~iNESS n. [17th c., of unkn. orig.; cf. 16th c. *frowy*]

froze(n). See FREEZE.

frŭctif'erous, a. Bearing fruit. [f. L *fructifer* (FRUIT, -FEROUS)]

frŭctificā'tion, n. (bot.). Fructifying; reproductive parts of plant, esp. of ferns & mosses. [f. LL *fructificatio* (foll., -FICATION)]

frŭc'tify, v.i. & t. Bear fruit (lit. & fig.); make fruitful, impregnate. [ME, f. OF *fructifier* f. L *fructificare* (FRUIT, -FY)]

frŭc'tōse, n. Fruit sugar. [f. L *fructus* FRUIT + -OSE[2]]

frŭc'tūous, a. Full of, producing, fruit (lit. & fig.). [ME, f. OF, or L *fructuosus* (FRUIT, -OUS)]

frug'al (frōō-), a. Careful, sparing (*of*), economical, esp. as regards food; sparingly used or supplied, costing little. Hence or cogn. **frugăl'**ITY n., ~LY[2] adv., (frōō-). [f. L *frugalis*, see -AL]

frugiv'orous (frōō-), a. Feeding on fruit. [f. L *frux frugi-* fruit + -VOROUS]

fruit (frōōt), n., & v.i. & t. 1. (Usu. pl.) vegetable products fit for food (usu. ~*s of the earth*, so ~'AGE(1) (-ōŏt-) n.; plant's or tree's edible product of seed with its envelope (also collect. in sing., as *feeds on* ~); vegetable seed with envelope as means of reproduction; (Bibl.) offspring (usu. ~ *of the body, loins, womb*); produce of action, (pl.) revenues produced (*the* ~*s of industry*); (sing. or pl.) result, issue, consequence; ~-*cake*, containing currants etc.; ~ *clipper*, fast ship carrying ~; ~-*knife*, with silver etc. blade against acid; ~*machine*, coin-operated gaming machine. in which a player is successful who gets a certain combination of different coloured balls; ~-*piece*, picture of ~; ~ *salad*, of various ~s cut up & mixed in bowl often with cream etc.; ~ *sugar*, glucose, laevulose, or fructose; ~-*tree*, grown for its ~; hence (-)~'ED[2] a. 2. vb. Bear, make bear, ~. [ME, f. OF f. L *fructus -ūs* (*frui* enjoy)]

fruitār′ian (frŏŏ-), n. Feeder on fruit. [-ARIAN]

fruit′er (frŏŏt-), n. Fruit-ship; tree producing fruit (*a sure ~*); ‖ fruit-grower. [15th c., f. OF *fruitier*; later f. FRUIT +-ER¹]

‖ **fruit′erer** (frŏŏt-), ⸢n. Dealer in fruit. [15th c., f. prec. +-ER¹: cf. *poulterer*]

fruit′ful (frŏŏt-), a. Productive, fertile, causing fertility; productive of offspring, prolific, (lit. & fig.; *a session ~ in great measures*); beneficial, remunerative, whence ~LY² adv. Hence ~NESS n. [-FUL]

frui′tion (frŏŏ-), n. Enjoyment, attainment of thing desired, realization of hopes etc. [ME, f. OF f. LL *fruitionem* (*frui fruit-*, enjoy, -ION)]

fruit′less (frŏŏt-), a. Not bearing fruit; yielding no profit, ineffectual, useless, empty, vain. Hence ~LY² adv., ~NESS n. [-LESS]

fruit′lĕt (frŏŏt-), n. (bot.). =DRUPEL. [-LET]

fruit′|y̆ (frŏŏt-), a. Of fruit; (of wine) tasting of the grape, whence ~ĭNESS n.; (colloq.) suggestive, broad, full of rough humour or (usu. scandalous) interest. [-Y²]

frum′entȳ (frŏŏ-), **fŭrm′etȳ**, n. Hulled wheat boiled in milk & seasoned with cinnamon, sugar, etc. [ME, f. OF *frumentee* (*frument* f. L *frumentum* corn), -Y⁴]

frŭmp, n. Old-fashioned dowdily-dressed woman. Hence **frŭm′pISH¹**, **frŭm′pY²**, aa. [16th c., perh. f. (now dial.) *frumple* f. MDu. *verrompelen* RUMPLE]

frŭs′trāte¹, a. (arch.). Frustrated. [f. L *frustratus* (foll., -ATE²)]

frŭstr|āte′² (*also* frŭs-), v.t. Balk, baffle, neutralize, counteract, disappoint. So ~A′TION n. [f. L *frustrari* (*frustra* in vain), -ATE³]

frŭs′tule, n. Two-valved shell of diatom. [F, f. L *frustulum* (foll., -ULE)]

frŭs′tum, n. (pl. *-la*, *-tums*). Remainder of regular solid whose upper part has been cut off by plane parallel to base, or part intercepted between two planes. [L, = piece broken off]

frutĕs′cent (frŏŏ-), a. (bot.). Of the nature of a frutex. [for *fruticescent* (foll., -ESCENT)]

frut′ĕx (frŏŏ-), n. (bot.). (pl. *-icĕs*). Woody-stemmed plant smaller than tree, shrub. [L (genit. *-icis*)]

frut′icōse (frŏŏ-), a. (Bot.) shrubby; (of minerals, zoophytes, etc.) looking like shrub. [prec., -OSE¹]

frȳ¹, n. Young fishes fresh from the spawn; young of salmon in second year; young of other creatures produced in large numbers, e.g. bees or frogs; *small ~*, young or insignificant beings, children etc. [ME, f. ON *frjó* = Goth. *fraiw* seed]

frȳ², v.t. & i., & n. 1. Cook (t. & i.) in boiling fat (*other FISH¹* to *~*); *~ing-pan*, shallow pan used; *out of ~ing-pan into fire*, from bad to worse). 2. n. Fried meat; ‖ various internal parts of animals usu.

fried, esp. LAMB′s *~*. [ME, f. OF *frire* f. L *frigere*]

frȳ′er, **frī′er**, n. Vessel for frying fish; one who fries (fish). [-ER¹]

‖ **fŭb′sy̆** (-z-), a. Fat or squat. [f. obs. *fubs* small fat person]

fuchsia (fūsh′a), n. Drooping-flowered shrub. [mod. L (*Fuchs* 16th-c. German botanist, -IA¹)]

fuch′sine (fŏŏk-), n. Salt of rosaniline forming deep red dye. [prec. (f. resemblance of colour to flower) +-INE⁴]

fūc′us, n. (pl. *-ci* pr. *-sī*). Kinds of seaweed with flat leathery fronds. Hence **fūc′OID** a. [L, = rock-lichen, f. Gk *phukos*]

fŭd′dle, v.i. & t., & n. 1. Tipple, booze; intoxicate; stupefy, confuse. 2. n. Spell of drinking (*on the ~*), intoxication; confusion. [orig. unkn.]

fŭdd′y̆-dŭdd′y̆, a. & n. (colloq., joc.). Old-fashioned (person), ineffectual (old fogy). [orig. unkn.]

fŭdge¹, int. & n. Nonsense!; nonsense; piece of stop-press news inserted in newspaper page at the last minute by special means; soft-grained sweetmeat made with milk, sugar, chocolate, etc. [perh. f. foll.]

fŭdge², v.t. & i., & n. 1. Fit together, patch, make up, in a makeshift or dishonest way, cook, fake; practise such methods. 2. n. Piece of fudging. [perh. f. obs. *fadge* v.i., fit]

Fuehrer, Füh-, (fūr′-), n. Leader. [G]

fū′el, n., & v.t. & i. (-ll-). 1. Material for fires, firing, coal, wood, etc.; something that feeds or inflames passion etc. 2. vb. Supply (fire) with *~*; get *~*. [ME, f. OF *fouaille* f. Rom. **focalia* f. FOCUS, -AL]

fŭg, n., & v.i., (colloq.: -gg-). 1. Fustiness of air in room; fluff and dust collected in corners etc. 2. v.i. Enjoy a frowsty atmosphere. Hence ~g′Y² (-g-) a. [orig. unkn.]

fūgā′cious (-shus), a. Fleeting, evanescent, hard to capture or keep. So **fūgā′CITY** (-ăˊ) n. [f. L *fugax* (*fugere* flee, -ACIOUS)]

fūg′al, a. Of the nature of a fugue. Hence ~LY² adv. [-AL]

-fūge, suf. in adjj. & nn. f. mod. L in *-fugus*. Acc. to L anal. the sense should be *fleeing from* (*fugere*) as in L *lucifugus*, *erifuga*; but in the mod. formations it is *putting to flight* (*fugare*) as in *febrifuge*, *vermifuge*.

fū′gitive, a. & n. 1. Fleeing, running away, that has taken flight; flitting, shifting; evanescent, of short duration, quickly fading; (of literature) of passing interest, ephemeral, occasional. 2. n. One who flees esp. from danger, enemy, justice, or owner: exile, refugee. [ME, f. OF (*-if*, *-ive*), f. L *fugitivus* (*fugere fugit-* flee, -IVE)]

fū′gleman (-gel-), n. (pl. *-men*). ‖ Soldier placed in front of regiment etc. while drilling to show the motions & time;

fugue

leader, organizer, spokesman, whence by back formation **fū'gle** v.i. [f. G *flügel-mann* (*flügel* wing, *mann* man)]

fugue (fūg), n., & v.i. & t. **1.** Polyphonic composition in which a short melodic theme (' subject ') is introduced by one of the parts and successively taken up by the others, thereafter forming the main material of the texture (*double* ~, with two such themes), whence **fŭg'uIST**(1) (-gĭ-) n.; loss of memory coupled with disappearance from one's usual haunts. **2.** vb. Compose or perform ~ (*fuguing* or ~*d*, in the form of a ~). [f. F, or It. f. L *fuga* flight]

ful, suf. orig. =**FULL** a. **1.** Forming adj. f. nn., w. sense *full of* (*beautiful*), & sometimes *having qualities of* (*masterful*); also adj. f. adj. or f. L adj. stems (*direful, grateful, tristful*), perh. on anal. of older synonyms in *-ful*; also f. vv. (*forgetful*), arising perh. f. cases in which first component might in form be either n. or v. (*helpful*, & esp. *thankful* where the sing. n. being disused *thank* would naturally be taken for verb); a pass. sense is seen in *bashful*=abashable. **2.** Forming nn., w. sense *amount required to fill* (*handful*). *Handful* is a differentiation f. *hand full*, which in the Teut. langg. had orig. besides its literal sense that of *quantity that fills a hand*. The differentiation is not carried out equally in all langg., G *handvoll* etc. taking their gender f. first component, though written as single wds. In mod. E *-ful* is a living suf. freely added to nn. (*boxful, houseful, churchful*); a reminiscence of its orig. is seen in *spoons-ful, cupsful*, which are ambiguous & contrary to good mod. usage.

fŭl'crum, n. (pl. *-ra*). (Mech.) point against which lever is placed to get purchase or on which it turns or is supported; means by which influence etc. is brought to bear; (Bot.; usu. pl.) accessory organs, appendages, e.g. bracts, tendrils. [L, = post of couch (*fulcire* to prop)]

fulfil' (fŏŏl-), v.t. (-ll-). Bring to consummation, carry out (prophecy, promise), satisfy (desire, prayer); perform, execute, do, (command, law); answer (purpose), comply with (conditions); bring to an end, finish, complete, (period, work). Hence ~MENT (fŏŏl-) n. [OE *full-fyllan* (**FULL**[1], FILL)]

fŭl'gent, a. (poet. & rhet.). Shining, brilliant. [f. L *fulgēre* shine, -ENT]

fŭl'gŭrite, n. (Geol.) rocky substance fused or vitrified by lightning, tube made by passage of lightning into sand; an explosive. [f. L *fulgur* lightning +-ITE[1](2)]

ful'ham (fŏŏl'am), n. (hist.). Loaded DIE[1]. [orig. unkn.]

Ful'ham Păl'ace (fŏŏl'am), n. Official residence of the Bishop of London.

fŭli'ginous, a. Sooty, dusky. [f. LL *fuliginosus* (*fuligo -inis* soot, -OUS)]

full[1] (fŏŏl), a., v.t., & adv. **1.** Filled to utmost capacity, holding all (*of*, or abs.) its limits will allow, replete, (~ *to the brim, to overflowing*, & colloq. *up*); (of heart etc.) overcharged with emotion (~-*hearted*, stirred with deep feeling, also zealous, confident, courageous). **2.** Holding or having abundance *of*, crowded (*in a* ~ *house*, with a good proportion of members present), showing marked signs of (~ *of vitality*). **3.** Engrossed with the thought of (~ *of himself, of his subject*; ~ *of the news* etc., unable to keep from talking of it). **4.** Replete with food (arch. of persons; *a* ~ *stomach*); (chiefly Bibl.) having had one's fill of (~ *of years & honours*). **5.** Abundant, sufficient, copious, satisfactory, (*a* ~ *meal*; *turned it to* ~ *account*; *give* ~ *details*; *he is very* ~ *on this point*). **6.** Complete, entire, perfect, answering completely to its name, reaching the specified or usual limit, entirely visible, (~ *point* or *stop*, period in punctuation; ~ *daylight, membership*; ~ *brother, sister*, born of same father and mother; *of the* ~ *blood*, of pure descent, not hybrid, so ~-*blooded*, & see below; ~ *pay*, that allowed on active service; ~ *age*, after minority; ~ DRESS[2], & so ~-*dress rehearsal*; ~-*dress debate* in Parliament, prearranged on important question, not arising casually; ~ SWING n.; *at* ~ *length*, lying stretched out, also = *in* ~ below; ~-*length portrait* etc., of whole figure; ~ *moon*, with whole disc illuminated, also the time when this comes; ~ *face*, turned straight to spectator; *wailed a* ~ *hour*; *it was* ~ *summer*). **7.** (Of light) intense, (of colour) deep, (of motion etc.) vigorous (*a* ~ *pulse*; ~ *gallop, speed*, etc., used adv. with *come* etc.; ~ *speed ahead!*, order to pursue course with energy). **8.** Swelling, plump, protuberant, (of dress) containing superfluous material arranged in folds etc. (vb, make ~, gather, pleat). So ~-*back*, football player stationed behind; ~-*blooded*, vigorous, hearty, sensual, & see above; ~-*bodied*, esp. of wine with much BODY; ~-*bottomed*, (of wig) long behind, opp. BOB[1]; ~ *house, hand*, Poker hand with three of a kind and a pair; ~-*mouthed*, (of cattle) with ~ complement of teeth, (of dogs) baying loudly, (of oratory, style, etc.) sonorous, vigorous; ~ *pitch* (Cricket), a bowled ball pitched right up to the wicket without first touching the ground (also ~ *toss*); ~ *score* (Mus.), complete score comprising music for all performers; ‖ ~-*timer*, child who attends during all school-hours (opp. *half-timer*). **10.** (used abs. as n.) Whole (*cannot tell you the* ~ *of it*; *in* ~), without abridgement; *to the* ~, to the utmost extent, quite); height, acme, (*season, moon, is past the* ~); hence ~'ISH[1](2) a. **11.** adv. Very (chiefly poet.; ~ *fain*; ~ *many a*; *know it* ~ *well*); quite, fully, (~ *six miles*; ~ *as useful as*; often in comb.,

as ~-*blown*, of flowers, quite open, also
fig. as ~-*blown dignity* ; ~-*grown*, having
reached maturity); exactly (*hit him* ~ *on
the nose*); more than sufficiently (*this
chair is* ~ *high*). [OE *full*, OS *ful*, OHG
foll, ON *fullr*, Goth. *fulls* f. Gmc *fullaz*
cogn. w. Gk *polus*]

full[2] (fŏŏl), v.t. Cleanse & thicken (cloth).
[ME, back form. f. foll.; cf. OF *fouler*
FOIL[2]]

full'er[1] (fŏŏ-), n. One who fulls cloth;
~'*s· earth*, hydrous silicate of alumina.
[OE *fullere*, f. L *fullo* +-ER[1]]

full'er[2] (fŏŏ-), n., & v.t. Grooved tool on
which iron is shaped; groove made by
this esp. in horse-shoes; (vb) stamp with
~. [orig. unkn.]

ful(l)'ness (fŏŏl-), n. Being FULL[1]; esp.·
(Bibl.) *the~ of the heart*, emotion, genuine
feelings, *the* ~ *of time*, the destined time,
the ~ *of the world* etc., all that fills it; (of
sound, colour, etc.) richness, volume,
body. [-NESS]

full'ȳ (fŏŏ-), adv. Completely, without
deficiency; quite (esp. with numbers); ~
fashioned, (of women's stockings) seamed
& shaped. [-LY[2]]

ful'mar (fŏŏ-), n. Sea-bird of petrel kind
& gull's size. [perh. f. ON *fúll* FOUL[1]+
már MEW[1]]

fŭl'minant, a. Fulminating; (Path., of
diseases) developing suddenly. [f. L as
foll., -ANT]

fŭl'mināt|e[1], v.i. & t. Flash like lightning,
explode, detonate, (~*ing gold, mercury*,
etc., various fulminates, see FULMINIC);
thunder forth, utter or publish, (censure);
issue (usu. official) censures *against* (esp.
of Pope). Hence or cogn. fŭlminA'TION
n., ~ORY a. [f. L *fulminare* (*fulmen* lightning), -ATE[3]]

fŭl'mine, v.t. & i. (poet.). Send forth
(lightning, thunder); thunder (lit. & fig.).
[as prec.]

fŭlmin'ic, a. (chem.), ~ *acid*, the hypothetical parent of the fulminates, many
of which are explosive. Hence **fŭl'-
mināte**[2] [-ATE[1](3)] n. [f. L *fulmen -inis*
lightning +-IC]

ful'ness. See FULLNESS.

ful'some (fŭ-, fŏŏ-), a. Cloying, excessive,
disgusting by excess, (of flattery, servility, exaggerated affection). Hence
~LY[2] (-ml-) adv., ~NESS (-mn-) n. [FULL[1],
-SOME]

fŭl'vous, a. (nat. hist.). Reddish-yellow,
tawny. So **fŭlves'cent** a. [f. L *fulvus*+
-OUS]

fūmāde', n. Smoked pilchard. [f. Sp.
fumado smoked, f. L *fumare* FUME, -ADO(1)]

fūm'arōle, n. Crevice in cone of volcano
through which vapour issues. [f. F
fumarolle f. LL *fumariolum* dim. of L *fu-
marium* smoke-chamber (*fumus* smoke,
-ARY[1])]

fŭm'bl|e, v.i. & t., & n. 1. Use the hands
awkwardly, grope about (*at, with,*
fastening etc.); *for, after,* thing sought);

handle or deal with awkwardly or nervously (~*e the ball*, not stop it cleanly),
hence ~ER[1] n. 2. n. Bungling attempt.
[16th c., f. LG *fummeln*, Du. *fommelen*]

fūme, n., & v.t. & i. 1. Odorous smoke,
vapour, or exhalation; watery vapour;
noxious vapour supposed to rise from
stomach to brain (*the~s of wine* etc.); also
fig. of excitement, enthusiasm, etc.); fit
of anger (*in a* ~); hence fūm'Y[2] a. 2. vb
Perfume with incense; subject to chemical ~s esp. those of ammonia (photographic film, oak, to darken tints); emit
~s; (of vapour etc.) rise, be emitted; be
pettish, chafe (*at*). [ME; n. f. OF *fum*,
vb f. *fumer*, f. L *fumus, fumare,* smoke]

fūm'ig|āte, v.t. Apply fumes to; disinfect
or purify with fumes; perfume. Hence
~A'TION, ~A'TOR, nn. [f. L *fumigare* (*fumus*
smoke), -ATE[3]]

fūm'itorȳ, n. Herb formerly used in
medicine. [ME, f. OF *fumeterre* f. med. L
fumus terrae earth-smoke, w. assim. to
-ORY]

fŭn, n., & v.i. (-nn-). 1. Sport, amusement,
jocularity, drollery, (*make* ~ *of, poke* ~
at, ridicule; *for or in* ~, as a joke, not
seriously; *is good, great,* ~, very amusing; *like* ~, vigorously, quickly, much;
what ~!, how amusing!). 2. v.i. (rare).
Indulge in ~, joke. [f. obs. *fun* vb, var.
of *fon* befool; see FOND]

fūnăm'būlist, n. Rope-walker. [ult. f. L
funambulus (*funis* rope, *ambulare* walk),
-IST]

fŭnc'tion, n., & v.i. 1: Activity proper to
anything, mode of action by which it
fulfils its purpose; office-holder's duty,
employment, profession, calling ; religious or other public ceremony or occasion,
social meeting of formal or important
kind; (Math.) variable quantity in relation to other(s) in terms of which it may
be expressed or on which its value depends; hence ~LESS (-shon-) a. 2. v.i.
Fulfil a ~, operate, act. [F, f. L *func-
tionem* (*fungi funct-* perform, -ION)]

fŭnc'tional (-shon-), a. Official, merely
formal, (rare); (Physiol.) of, affecting, the
functions of an organ etc. only, not
structural or organic (esp. of diseases),
(of organ) having a function, not functionless or rudimentary; (Math.) of a
FUNCTION; (of building etc.) shaped or constructed with regard only to its function,
not to traditional or other theories of
design. Hence ~LY[2] adv. [-AL]

fŭnc'tionarȳ (-shon-), n. & a. 1. n. Official. 2. adj. = prec. (not in math. sense).
[-ARY[1]; n. f. F *fonctionnaire*]

fŭnc'tionāte (-shon-), v.i. = FUNCTION v.
[-ATE[3]]

fŭnd, n., & v.t. 1. Permanent stock of
something ready to be drawn upon (*a* ~
*of common sense, tenderness, labour, know-
ledge*); stock of money, esp. one set apart
for a purpose (SINK[1]*ing*~); (pl.) pecuniary
resources (*in* ~s, having money, flush);

|| *the* ~*s*, stock of national debt as mode of investment *(has £10,000 in the* ~*s*; || ~*-holder*, such investor). **2. v.t.** Convert (floating debt) into more or less permanent debt at fixed interest; put into a ~, collect, store, (rare); || invest (money) in the ~*s*. [f. L *fundus* bottom]

fŭn′dament, n. The buttocks. [ME, f. OF *fondement* f. L *fundamentum* (FOUND[1], -MENT)]

fŭndamĕn′tal, a. & n. **1.** Of the groundwork, going to the root of the matter, serving as base or foundation, essential, primary, original, from which others are derived, (*a* ~ *change*; *the* ~ *rules*; *the* ~ *form*); (Mus.) ~ *note*, lowest note of chord in its original (uninverted) form, ~ *tone*, produced by vibration of whole sonorous body (opp. *harmonics* produced by that of its parts); hence ~ITY (-ăl²) n., ~LY² adv. **2.** n. Principle, rule, article, serving as groundwork of system (usu. pl.); (Mus.) ~ note or tone. [ME, f. LL *fundamentalis* (prec., -AL)]

′fŭndamĕn′tal‖ism, n. Maintenance, in opposition to modernism, of traditional orthodox beliefs such as the inerrancy of Scripture & literal acceptance of the creeds as fundamentals of protestant Christianity. So ~IST n. & a. [prec. +-ISM]

fŭnēb′rial, a. (rare). Of funeral (*custom is* ~ *in origin*). [f. L *funebris* (*funus* see foll.) +-AL]

fŭn′eral, a. & n. **1.** Of, used etc. at, burial or cremation of the dead (~ *pile, pyre,* pile of wood etc. on which corpse is burnt; ~ *urn*, holding ashes of cremated dead; ~ *oration*). **2.** n. Burial of the dead with its observances, obsequies; burial procession; (colloq.) unpleasant concern; lookout (*that's your* ~). [ME; adj. OF, f. LL *funeralis* (L *funus -eris* funeral +-AL); n. f. OF *funeraille* f. med. L *funeralia* neut. pl. of *funeralis*, -AL(2)]

fŭn′erary̆, a. = FUNEBRIAL. [f. LL *funerarius* (prec., -ARY[1])]

fŭnēr′eal, a. Appropriate to funeral, gloomy, dismal, dark. Hence ~LY² adv. [f. L *funereus* (FUNERAL) +-AL]

fŭn′gible (-j-), a. (legal). That can serve for, or be replaced by, another answering to the same definition (of goods etc. 'contracted for, when an individual specimen is not meant). [f. med. L *fungibilis* f. *fungi* (*vice*) serve (turn), -IBLE]

fŭn′gicide (-j-), n. Fungus-destroying substance. [FUNGUS, -I-, -CIDE]

fŭng′ous (-ngg-), a. Of fungi, having nature of a fungus; springing up like a mushroom, transitory. [f. L *fungosus* (foll., -OSE[1])]

fŭng′‖us (-ngg-), n. (pl. ~*i* pr. -jī, ~*uses*). Mushroom, toadstool, or allied plant including moulds; (Bot.) cryptogamous plant without chlorophyll feeding on organic matter; thing of sudden growth; (Path.) spongy morbid growth or excrescence; skin-disease of fish. Hence ~AL (-ngg-), ~IFORM (-j-), ~IV′OROUS (-j-), ~OID, ~USY², (-ngg-), aa. [L, perh. cogn. w. Gk *sphoggos* SPONGE]

fūnic′ŭlar, a. Of a rope or its tension (~ *railway*, worked by cable & stationary engine). [f. L *funiculus* (*funis* cord, -CULE) +-AR[1]]

fŭnk, n., & v.i. & t., (sl.). **1.** Fear, panic, (*blue* ~, terror); coward; hence ~′Y² a.; || ~*-hole*, trench dug-out, employment used as pretext for evading military service. **2. vb.** Flinch, shrink, show cowardice; (try to) evade (undertaking), shirk; be afraid of; inspire fear in. [18th c. Oxford sl.; cf. contemporary Du. *fonck, in de fonck sijn*]

fŭnn′el, n. Diminishing tube, or truncated cone & tube, for conducting liquid, powder, etc., into small opening; ventilating or lighting shaft; metal chimney of steam engine or ship; ~-shaped lower part of chimney. Hence (-)~lED² (-ld) a. [ME *fonel* f. Pr. *fonilh*, (Sp. *fonil*) f. L *infundibulum* f. IN(*fundere* pour)]

fŭnn′iment, n. Joke, drollery. [foll., -MENT]

fŭnn′y̆[1], a. Affording fun, comical; curious, queer, perplexing, hard to account for; ~*y bone*, part of elbow over which ulnar nerve passes; ~*y-man*, professional jester. Hence ~ILY² adv., ~INESS n. [-Y²]

|| **fŭnn′y̆**[2], n. Narrow clinker-built boat for one sculler. [perh. f. prec.]

fŭr, n., & v.t. & i. (-rr-). **1.** Trimming or lining made of dressed coat of certain animals, e.g. ermine, beaver; coat of such animals, as material for trimming etc.; (usu. pl.) garment(s) of or having ~; short fine soft hair of certain animals distinguished from the longer hair, (pl.) skins of such animals with the ~; *make the* ~ *fly*, make a disturbance, stir up trouble, raise Cain; (collect.) furred animals (esp. ~ *& feather*; *hunt* ~, hares); crust adhering to surface, e.g. deposit of wine; coating formed on tongue in sickness; crust of carbonate of lime in kettle etc.; hence ~r′Y² a. **2. vb.** Provide (garment, animal), clothe (person), coat (tongue, inside of kettle; also intr., become coated), with ~; clean ~ from (boiler); (Carpent.) level (floor-timbers) by inserting strips of wood. [ME; n. f. vb, OF *forrer* f. *forre, fuerre* sheath f. WG *föder* (= OE *fōddor*, OHG *fuotar*, Goth. *fodr* f. Gmc *fothrom*)]

fŭrb′elow (-ō), n., & v.t. **1.** Flounce, pleated border of skirt or petticoat; (pl., contempt.) showy ornaments; || kind of wrinkled seaweed. **2. v.t.** Adorn with ~ (s). [18th c. var. of FALBALA]

fŭrb′ish, v.t. Remove rust from, polish *up*, burnish; give new look to, renovate, revive, (something antiquated; usu. *up*). [ME, f. OF *forbir* (-ISH²) f. WG, OS *furbian*; cf. MHG *vürben*, OHG *furben*]

fûrc'ate¹ (-ăt, -at), a. Forked, branched. Hence **fûrcāt'o-** comb. form. [f. LL *furcatus* (L *furca* fork, -ATE²)]

fûrc|āte'², v.i. Form a fork, divide. So **∼A'TION** n. [f. L *furca* fork + -ATE³]

fûrfurā'ceous (-ferăshus), a. Scurfy; (Bot.) covered with bran-like scales. [f. LL *furfuraceus* (L *furfur* bran, -ACEOUS)]

fū'rious, a. Full of fury, raging, frantic, violent; *fast & ∼*, (of mirth etc.) eager, uproarious. Hence **∼LY²** adv. [ME, f. OF *furieus* f. L *furiosus* (FURY, -OUS)]

fûrl, v.t. & i. Roll up & bind (sail) on yard or boom; close, fold up, draw away, relinquish (fan, umbrella, wings, curtain, hopes); become ∼ed, roll away like clouds. [16th c., f. F *ferler* f. OF *fer(m)* FIRM² + *lier* bind]

fûr'long, n. Eighth of mile. [OE *furlang* (*furh* furrow, LONG adj.); orig. = length of furrow in common field, regarded as square containing ten acres]

fûr'lough (-lō), n., & v.t. Leave of absence, esp. to soldier; (vb) grant ∼ to. [f. Du. *verlof* (after G *verlaub*) cogn. w. FOR-, LEAVE¹]

fûrm'ety. See FRUMENTY.

fûrn'ace (-ĭs), n., & v.t. **1.** Apparatus including chamber for combustibles in which minerals, metals, etc., may be subjected to continuous intense heat; hot plate; severe test (esp. *tried in the ∼*); closed fireplace for heating building by hot pipes. **2.** v.t. Heat in ∼. [ME, f. OF *fornais* f. L *fornacem* nom. *-ax* (*fornus* oven)]

fûrn'ish, v.t. Provide with (∼ed with, having); fit up (house, room) with all necessary appliances, esp. movable furniture (∼ed house, rooms, etc., esp. let with furniture); provide, afford, yield. [f. OF *furnir* (-ISH²) f. Rom. **fornire* ult. f. WG **frumjan* (OS *frummian*) promote, f. root of FROM]

fûrn'iture, n. Contents of receptacle (∼ of his pocket, money; ∼ of my shelves, books; ∼ of one's mind, knowledge & intelligence; harness etc. of horse etc. (arch.); movable contents of house or room, tables, chairs, etc.; (Print.) pieces of wood or metal placed round or between type to make blank spaces and fasten the matter in the chase. [f. F *fourniture* (*fournir* FURNISH]

fûrōr'e, n. Enthusiastic admiration, rage, craze. [It., f. L *furorem* (*furere* be mad, -OR¹)]

fû'rrier, n. Dealer in, dresser of, furs. [-IER]

fûrr'ing, n. In vbl senses; also (Ship-build.), doubling of planks on ship's side. [-ING¹]

fû'rrow (-ō), n., & v.t. **1.** Narrow trench made by plough; ship's track; rut, track, groove, long indentation, deep wrinkle, hollow between ridges; ∥∼*-slice*, slice of earth turned up by mould-board of plough; hence **∼LESS** (-ŏl-), **∼Y²** (-ŏi), aa.

2. v.t. Plough; make ∼s, grooves etc., in; mark with wrinkles. [OE *furh*, OHG *furuh*, ON *for* f. Gmc **furh-*]

fûrth'er (-dh-), adv. & a. (for usage of *fur-, far-*, see FARTHER etym.), & v.t. **1.** To or at more advanced point in space or time (*unsafe to proceed ∼*; *& then to lapse unless ∼ continued*); to greater extent, more, (*inquire ∼*); (also ∼*more*) in addition, moreover, also (esp. introducing fresh consideration in argument); at greater distance (*I'll see you ∼ first*, euphem. for *in hell*, as strong refusal of request). **2.** adj. Going beyond what exists or has been dealt with, additional, (*threats of ∼ punishment*; *till ∼ notice*, in announcing arrangement to continue during pleasure); more distant (*on the ∼ side*), whence ∼MOST a. .Help on, promote, favour, (undertaking, movement, cause); hence ∼ANCE n., ∼SOME a., (-dh-). [OE *furthor* adv., *furthra* adj., (FORE², -THER), *fyrthrian* vb]

fûrth'est (-dh-), a. & adv. = FARTHEST. [superl. formed f. prec.]

fûrt'ive, a. Done by stealth, clandestine, meant to escape notice; sly, stealthy, stolen, taken secretly; thievish, pilfering. Hence ∼LY² (-vl-) adv., ∼NESS (-vn-) n. [f. F (-*if, -ive*) or L *furtivus* (*furtum* theft, -IVE)]

fûr'unc|le (-ŭngkl), n. Boil, tumour. Hence ∼ūlAR, ∼ūlOUS, aa., (-ŭnk²). [f. L *furunculus* (*fur* thief, -UNCLE)]

fûr'y, n. Fierce passion, wild anger, rage, (*in a ∼*, fit of rage); impetuosity in battle etc. (*the Spanish F∼*, massacre by Spaniards at Antwerp 1576); violence of weather, disease, etc. (*like ∼*, furiously, hard); (usu. pl.) snake-haired goddess(es) of Gk myth (*Alēc'tō, Tisiph'onē, Megaer'a*) sent from Tartarus to punish crime, (fig.) avenging spirits, remorseful pangs, (*haunted by the furies of her father's blood*); virago, angry or malignant woman. [ME, f. OF *furie* f. L *furia* (*furere* be mad)]

fûrze, n. Spiny yellow-flowered evergreen shrub growing on European waste lands, gorse, whin. Hence **fûrz'y²** a. [OE *fyrs* of unkn. orig.]

fûs'cous, a. (nat. hist.). Sombre, dark, in colour. So **fûs'co-** comb. form. [L *fuscus*, -OUS]

fūse¹ (-z), v.t. & i., & n. **1.** Melt (t. & i. with intense heat; blend, amalgamate, (t. & i.) into one whole (as) by melting (of metals, living bones, institutions, motives, etc.); hence **fūs'IBLE** a., **fūsIBIL'ITY** n., (-z-). **2.** n. (electr.). Piece of easily-fusible wire, placed in main or branch circuit, designed to melt when overloaded and thus interrupt the current and prevent the section being loaded above the safety limit. [f. L *fundere fus-* pour]

fūse² (-z), n., & v.t. **1.** Tube, casing, cord, etc., filled or saturated with combustible matter for igniting bomb, blasting-charge, etc., component screwed into shell, mine, etc. designed to detonate explosive charge after an interval (*time*- ~) or on impact or when subjected to magnetic or vibratory stimulation. 2. v.t. Fit ~ to [f. It. *fuso* f. L *fusus* spindle]

fusee' (-z-), n. Conical pulley or wheel esp. in watch or clock; exostosis or bony tumour on horse's cannon-bone; large--headed match for lighting cigar or pipe in wind. [f. F *fusée* spindle, -EE]

fūs'elage (-z-), n. Framework of aeroplane. [F, f. *fuseler* cut in spindle form (*fuseau* dim. f. L *fusus*), -AGE]

fūs'el oil (-z-), n. Mixture of several alcohols, chiefly amyl, produced, usu. in small amounts, during alcoholic fermentation and making alcoholic liquors harmful or poisonous. [f. G *fusel* bad spirit, cf. *fuseln* FOOZLE]

fūs'iform (-z-), a. (nat. hist.). Shaped like spindle or cigar, tapering at both ends. [f. L *fusus* spindle, -I-, -FORM]

fūs'il (-z-), n. Obsolete light musket. [F, = It. *focile* (L *focus* hearth, fire, -IL)]

fūsilier' (-z-), n. (usu. pl.). (Man of) certain British regiments formerly armed with fusils. [F, (prec., -IER)]

fūsillāde' (-z-), n., & v.t. 1. (Wholesale execution by) continuous discharge of fire-arms. 2. v.t. Assault (place), shoot down (persons), by ~. [F *fusiller* shoot f. FUSIL, -ADE)]

fū'sion (-zhn), n. Fusing; fused mass; blending of different things into one; coalition, whence ~IST(2) (-zhon-) n.; ~ *bomb*, hydrogen bomb. [f. F, or L *fusio* (FUSE[1], -ION); cf. FOISON]

fūss, n., & v.i. & t. 1. Bustle, excessive commotion, ostentations or nervous activity; treatment of trifles as important; abundance of petty detail; ~-*pot* (colloq.), person who is always making a ~; hence ~'Y[2] a., ~'iLY[2] adv., ~'iNESS n. 2. vb. Make ~; busy oneself restlessly with trifles; move fussily *about, up & down*, etc.; agitate, worry, (person). [perh. imit. of sputtering or bubbling]

fūstanĕll'a, n. Man's white kilt in modern Greece. [It., dim. of mod. Gk *phoustani* prob. f. It. *fustagno* FUSTIAN]

fūs'tian, n. & a. 1. Thick twilled short--napped cotton cloth usu. dyed dark; turgid speech or writing, bombast. 2. adj. Made of ~, (fig.) bombastic, worthless, sorry, pretentious. [ME, f. OF *fustaigne* (med. L *fustaneus* adj. perh. = from *Fostat* suburb of Cairo)]

fūs'tic, n. Two kinds of wood yielding yellow dye (*young* ~, Venetian sumach; ~ or *old* ~, Amer. & W. Ind.); dye from these. [f. F f. Sp. *fustoc* f. Arab. *fustuq* f. Gk as PISTACHIO]

fūs'tigāte, v.t. (joc.). Cudgel. So ~A[L]TION n. [LL *fustigare* (*fustis* cudgel), -ATE[3]]

fūs't|ȳ, a. Stale-smelling, musty, mouldy; close, stuffy; antiquated, old-fashioned.

Hence ~iNESS n. [14th c., f. OF *fust*, smelling of the cask (*fust*, f. L *fustis* cudgel)]

fut. See PHUT.

fütch'el(l), n. One of timbers supporting shafts, pole, or axle-bar, of carriage. [orig. unkn.]

futh'orc (fōō-), n. Runic alphabet. [its first six letters (*th* being one)]

fūt'ile (-ī-, -ĭl-), a. Useless, ineffectual, vain, frivolous. Hence or cogn. fūtil'iTY n., (rare) ~LY[2] adv. [f. L *futilis* leaky, futile, f. *fud-* st. of *fundere* pour]

fütt'ock, n. One of ship's middle timbers between floor & top timbers; ~ *plates*, iron plates in a ship's top to which the ~ *shrouds* (lower ends of which are fastened to ring on mast below) are fixed, as well as the dead-eyes of the topmast rigging. [ME *fot(t)ekes, fot(t)eken*, etc., f. MLG f. *fōt* FOOT + -*ken* -KIN]

fū'ture, a. & n. 1. About to happen, that will be hereafter (~ *life, state*, existence after death), that will be something specified (*my* ~ *wife*); of time to come, (Gram., of tense) describing event yet to happen. 2. n. Time to come (*for the* ~, *in* ~, from now onwards; *past, present, & ~*); what will happen in the ~; person's, country's, etc., prospective condition; (Gram.) ~ tense; one's betrothed; (Commerc.; pl.) goods & stocks sold for ~ delivery, contracts for these; hence ~LESS (-cherl-) a. [OF (-*ur*, -*ure*), f. L *futurus* fut. part. of *esse* be f. st. *fu*-BE]

fū'turist (-che-), n. & a. 1. (theol.). (One) believing that the prophecies of the Apocalypse etc. are still to be fulfilled. 2. (art). Adherent of **fū'turism** (-che-) n., an early 20th-c. movement in (esp. Italian) art, literature, etc., marked by violent departure from traditional methods and by the use of arbitrary symbols in the expression of emotion. [-IST]

fūtū'rĭtȳ, n. Future time; (sing. or pl.) future events; future condition, existence after death; ~ *stakes*, stakes raced for long after entries or nominations are made. [-ITY]

füzz, n. Loose volatile matter, fluff; fluffy or frizzed hair; ~-*ball*, a fungus, the puff-ball. [17th c., goes w. foll.]

füzz'|ȳ, a. Frayed, fluffy; blurred, indistinct; frizzed. Hence ~iLY[2] adv., ~iNESS n. [17th c., prob. f. Du. *voos*, LG *fussig* spongy]

fy, fye. = FIE.

-fy, suf. forming vbs. In the older E vbs -*fy* represented F -*fier*, L -*ficare*. L formed vbs in -*ficare* (with or without intervention of adjj. in -*ficus*) f. nn., w. sense *make, produce*, (*pacificare*; orig. intr., *make peace*) or *make into* (*deificare* deify); f. adjj. w. sense *bring into a state* (*sanctificare*); & f. vb stems w. causative sense (*horrificare* horrify). In med. L -*ficare* was often substituted for -*facere*;

I

hence F & E vbs in *-fier*, *-fy*, occas. repr.
L vbs in *-facere* (F *stupéfier*, but p.p.
stupéfait as well as *stupéfié*, stupefy;
OF *satisfier*, but mod. F *satisfaire*; F
liquéfier liquefy, *rubéfier* rubefy). Apart
f. these in *-efy* E has always *-ify* (-I-),
which is freely added to E adjj. & nn. to
form vbs chiefly joc. or colloq. (*speechify*, *Frenchify*; also, on vb, the irreg.
argufy). Vbs formed on adjj. have often
intr. as well as trans. sense (*solidify* make
or become solid). Vbs in *-ify* have nn. in
-ification, those representing L vbs in
-facere have nn. in -FACTION; but E has
petrifaction where F has the correct
pétrification.

fyl'fot, n. Swastika, equal-armed cross of
which each arm is continued rectangularly, all clockwise or counterclockwise.
[name based on ancient direction for
design of painted window, in which ~
may mean either the particular pattern
or something to *fill the foot* of the window.]

fytte. See FIT¹.

G

G (jē), letter (pl. *Gs*, G's). (Mus.) fifth note
of diatonic scale of C major; corresponding scale or key; *G* CLEF.

gǎb, n. (colloq.). Talk, prattle, twaddle,
(*stop your ~*, hold your tongue; *gift of the
~*, talent for speaking, also loquacity).
[18th c. *gab* to talk, mouth = 17th c. *gob*
conversation, 16th c. *gob* mouth, perh. f.
Ir. *gob* beak, mouth]

gǎb'ardine (-ēn), n. Dress material of
cotton or silk with wool lining; material
for raincoats. [var. of GABERDINE]

gǎb'ble, v.i. & t., & n. 1. Talk volubly or
inarticulately, read aloud (t., often *over*,
& i.) too fast; utter too fast. 2. n. Voluble
confused unintelligible talk. [16th c., f.
MDu. *gabbelen*]

gǎb'bro, n. A basic igneous rock of
crystalline texture resembling dolerite
and granite. [It.]

gabelle', n. Tax (usu. foreign tax), esp.
the French pre-Revolution salt-tax. [F,
f. It. *gabella* ult. f. Arab. *qabála* tribute]

gǎb'erdine (-ēn), n. Loose long upper
garment esp. of Jews & almsmen; a fine
hard-laid cloth. [f. OF *gauvardine* perh.
f. MHG *wallevart* pilgrimage]

gǎb'ion, n. Cylinder of wicker or woven
metal bands to be filled with earth for
use in fortification or engineering. [F,
f. It. *gabbione* (*gabbia* CAGE, -OON)]

gǎbionāde', n. Line of gabions. [-ADE(1)]

gā'ble, n. Triangular upper part of wall
at end of ridged roof; (also *~-end*)
~-topped wall; ~-shaped canopy over
window or door, whence **gā'blET¹** n.
Hence (-)**gā'blED²** (-ld) a. [ME *gavel* f.
ON *gafl*; ME *gable* f. OF f. ON; cogn. w.
OE *geafol*, OHG *gabala* fork, OHG *gibil*
gable]

gǎb'y̆, n. Simpleton. [orig. unkn.]

gǎd¹, int. of surprise, asseveration, etc.
(also *by ~*, *begad*). [= GOD]

gǎd², v.i. (-dd-), & n. Go about idly, rove,
wander, (usu. *about*, *abroad*, *out*); (of
plants, esp. in part.) straggle; (*up*)*on the
~*, going about, on the move; *~'about*,
(person) given to ~ding. [perh. back
formation f. obs. *gadling* companion,
OE *gœdeling* (*gœd* fellowship, -LING¹)]

gǎd(d)i (gŭd'ī), n. Cushioned throne of
Indian ruler; (transf.) the regal position.
[Hind. *gaddi* cushion]

gǎd'-fly, n. Breeze, cattle-biting fly;
irritating or worrying person; violent
impulse, oestrum. [f. obs. *gad*·spike f.
ON *gaddr* cogn. w. YARD¹]

gǎdg'et, n. (colloq.). Small fitting or
contrivance in machinery etc.; (transf.)
dodge, device. [first in naut. use; orig.
unkn.]

Gadhěl'ic (-dĕ-), a. & n. = GAELIC in its
wider sense. [literary f. Ir. *Gaedheal*
Gael + -IC]

gǎd'oid, a. & n. (Fish) of the cod family.
[f. Gk *gados* cod + -OID]

gadroon', n. (usu. pl. or attrib.). Convex
curve(s) in series forming ornamental
edge like inverted fluting. [f. F *godron*;
cf. *goder* pucker]

gǎd'wall (-awl), n. A freshwater duck of
the north of Europe & America. [orig.
uncert.]

Gael.(gāl), n. Scottish Celt; (rarely) Irish
Celt. [f. Sc.-Gael. *Gaidheal*]

Gael'ic (gāl-, gǎl-), a. & n. (Language) of
Scottish Celts, of Scottish & Irish &
Manx Celts. [-IC]

gǎff¹, n., & v.t. 1. Barbed fishing-spear;
stick with iron hook for landing large
fish; spar extending top of fore-&-aft
sail not set on stays. 2. v.t. Seize (fish)
with ~. [f. F *gaffe* boat-hook]

gǎff², n. (sl.). *Blow the ~*, let out plot.
[orig. unkn.]

‖ **gǎff³**, n. (sl.). Public place of amusement, esp. (usu. *penny ~*) low theatre or
music-hall. [orig. unkn.]

gǎffe, n. Blunder, indiscreet act or remark, *faux pas*. [F]

gǎff'er, n. Elderly rustic, old fellow, (also
as prefix to name); ‖ foreman of gang.
[contr. of *godfather*, *ga*- by assoc. w.
grandfather; cf. GAMMER, GOSSIP]

gǎg, n., & v.t. & i. (-gg-). 1. Thing thrust
into mouth to prevent speech or outcry
or (Surg.) hold it open for operation,
(Parl.) closure or GUILLOTINE, (vb, apply
~ *to*, silence, deprive of free speech). 2.
Actor's interpolations in dramatic dialogue (vb, make these); (Theatr.) carefully
prepared comic effect or business introduced into music-hall sketch, stage-play,
etc., (vb, make these); *~-man*, professional deviser of *~s*. 3. *~-bit*, specially
powerful for horse-breaking, *~-rein*,
arranged to make bit more powerful,
(*gag*, v.t.) apply *~-bit* to (horse). 4. Joke.

hoax; (sl.) imposture, lie, (v.t., deceive; v.i., practise deceit). 5. Retch, choke. [vb 15th c., perh. imit. of choking sound]

găg′a (or gah-), a. (sl.). Fatuous, senile; dotty. [F.]

găge[1], n., & v.t. 1. Pledge, thing deposited as security; (glove thrown down as, any symbol of) challenge to fight. 2. v.t. Stake, pledge, offer as guarantee. [ME; n. f. OF gage (f. Frank. *waddi, = OHG wetti, Goth wadi; see WED); vb f. F gager of same orig., or for ENGAGE]

găge[2]. See GAUGE[1].

găge[3], n. Greengage. [abbr.]

găg′gle, n., & v.i. 1. Flock (of geese); (derog.) company (of women). 2. v.i. (Of geese) cackle. [14th c. imit.; cf. Du. gaggelen]

gai′ety, n. Being gay, mirth; (usu. pl.) merrymaking, festive occasion(s), amusements; bright appearance. [f. F gaieté (GAY, -TY)]

Gaik′war, Gaek-, (gīk-), n. Ruler of Baroda. [Marathi, = cowherd]

gail′y. See GAY.

gain[1], n. Increase of possessions etc., profit, advance, improvement; acquisition of wealth, lucre; (pl.) sums acquired by trade etc., emoluments, winnings; increase in amount. [OF (gaaignier GAIN[2])]

gain[2], v.t. & f. Obtain, secure, (desired or desirable thing; ~ time, obtain delay by pretexts or slow methods; ~ the ear of, get favourable hearing from); win (sum) as profits or as result of changed conditions, earn, whence ~′ings (-z) [-ING[1] (2)] n. pl.; make a profit, be benefited, improve or advance in some respect, be enhanced by comparison or contrast; win (land from sea, battle, victory; ~ the upper hand, be victorious); bring over to one's interest or views, win over, persuade, prevail upon; reach, arrive at, (desired place); ~ ground, progress, advance, encroach (up)on; ~ (ground) (up)on, get closer to (person or thing pursued); (of sea) encroach (up)on land; ~ (up)on, win the favour of. Hence ~′ABLE a., ~′ER[1] n. [f. OF gaaignier to till, acquire, f. Rom. *guadaniare f. WG *waithanjan (OHG weidenen graze, hunt) f. *waitha pasture (OE wǣth hunting)]

gain′ful, a. Lucrative, remunerative; bent on gain. [-FUL]

gainsay′, v.t. (arch., literary; past -said, pr. -ād or -ĕd). Deny, contradict. Hence ~ER[1] n. [f. obs. gain- pref. against f. ON gegn (see AGAIN)+SAY]

gainst, 'gainst. (Poet. for) AGAINST.

gait, n. Manner of walking, bearing or carriage as one walks. [var. of GATE[2]]

gait′er, n. Covering of cloth, leather, etc., for leg below knee or for ankle. Hence ~ED[2] (-erd) a. [f. F guêtre]

găl′a (or gah[2]), n. Festive occasion, fête, (often attrib., as ~ day, dress, etc.). [F f. It.]

galăc′tic, a. (astron.). Of the galaxy. [f. Gk galaktikos (foll., -IC)]

galăc′to-, comb. form of Gk gala -aktos milk, used in scientific terms as ~gogue, (substance) inducing a flow of milk.

găl′antine ·(-ēn), n. White meat boned, spiced, tied, boiled, & served cold. [ME, f. OF, altered f. galatine jellied meat]

galăn′ty show (-ō), n. Pantomime on screen made by shadows of puppets. [perh. f. It. galanti pl. of galante GALLANT]

gălate′a n. Superior striped cotton dress material (orig. used for children's sailor suits). [f. H.M.S. G~.]

găl′axy, n. Irregular luminous band of stars indistinguishable to naked eye encircling the heavens, Milky Way; brilliant company (of beauties, talent, etc.). [earlier also -ias, -ia f. OF galaxie & LL -ias, med. L -ia f. Gk galaxias (gala -aktos milk)]

găl′banum, n. Gum resin from some Persian species of ferula. [ME, f. L f. Gk khalbanē prob. f. Oriental wd]'

găle[1], n. (Also sweet~) bog-myrtle. [OE (also Du. & G) gagel]

găle[2], n. Very strong wind, (naut.) storm, (poet.) gentle breeze. [orig. obsc.; cf. Norw. galen bad (of weather)]

‖ **găle**[3], n. Periodical payment of rent (hanging~, arrears of rent). [contr. f. obs. gavel in GAVELKIND]

găl′e|a, n. (bot., zool.). Structure like helmet in shape, function, or position. So ~ATE[2], ~āted, aa. [L, = helmet]

‖ **galeen′y**, n. Guinea-fowl. [f. Sp. gallina (morisca Moorish) hen]

Gāl′en, n. (joc.). Physician. [f. L f. Gk Galēnos, Pergamene 2nd-c. A.D. physician]

galēn′a, n. Common lead ore, lead sulphide, lead glance. [L, = lead ore (in partly purified state)]

galēn′ic, a., **galēn′ical**, a. & n. Of, according to, Galen; esp. (remedy) made of vegetable, not synthetic, components. [Galen +-IC(AL)]

Galilē′an, a. Of the astronomer Galileo; ~ telescope (with bi-convex objective and bi-concave eyepiece). [-AN]

Găl′ilee, g-, n. Porch or chapel at entrance of church. [OF, = med. L galilaea, perh. as less sacred than church w. ref. to Galilee as opp. Judaea, or esp. to Matt. iv. 15 (~ of the Gentiles)]

gălima′tias (-āsiah), n. Confused or meaningless talk, rigmarole. [F, of unkn. orig.]

găl′ingale (-ngg-), n. Aromatic root of E.-Ind. plants used in cookery & medicine; (also English~) kind of sedge. [ME, f. OF galingal f. Arab. khalanjan perh. f. Chin. ko-liang-kiang mild ginger from Ko]

galiot. = GALLIOT.

găl′ipŏt, n. Kind of hardened turpentine. [F, of unkn. orig.]

gall[1] (gawl), n. Secretion of liver, bile, (now only of lower animals); (fig.) bitter substance, bitterness, (~ & wormwood); ~-bladder & its contents; asperity, rancour, (*dip* one's *pen in* ~, write violently), whence ~'-LESS (gawl²-l-) a.; *impudence (sl.); ~-bladder* vessel containing the ~; ~*stone*, calculous formation in ~-bladder. [OE *gealla*, ON *gal*, OS, OHG *galla* f. Gmc *gall-* cogn. w. Gk *kholē* & YELLOW]

gall² (gawl), n. Painful swelling, pustule, blister, esp. in horse; sore produced by chafing; mental soreness or its cause; place rubbed bare, flaw; bare spot in field or coppice. [ME, f. MLG, MDu. *galle* (= OE *gealla*)]

gall³ (gawl), v.t. & i. Rub sore, injure by rubbing; vex, annoy, harass, humiliate, whence ~'ING² a. [f. prec., orig. as back formation f. *gall*ED²]

gall⁴ (gawl), n. Excrescence produced by insect on trees, esp. on oak (also *oak-~*, used in making ink & tannin, & in dyeing & medicine); ~*-fly*, insect producing ~s; ~*-nut*, (in ~*ic acid*) **gall'ic¹** a. [ME, f. OF *galle* f. L *galla*]

gall'ant (also, *in senses indicated below, occas.* galǎnt'), a., n., & v.t. &i. **1.** Showy, finely dressed, (arch.); grand, fine, stately, (of ship, horse, etc.); brave, chivalrous, ‖ (also Parl., as conventional epithet of a member of the services, as *the honourable & ~ member*); markedly attentive to women (galǎnt'); concerned with love, amatory, (galǎnt'); hence ~LY² (*or as above* galǎnt²) adv. **2.** n. Man of fashion, fine gentleman; ladies' man, lover, paramour, (galǎnt'). **3.** vb (galǎnt'). Play the ~, flirt *with*, flirt with; escort, act as cavalier to, (lady). [ME, f. OF *galant* part. of *galer* make merry]

gall'antry, n. Bravery, dashing courage; courtliness, devotion to women; a polite or amorous act or speech; conduct of a gallant, amorous intercourse or intrigue, sexual immorality. [f. F *galanterie* (prec., -ERY)]

gall'eon, n. (hist.). Vessel shorter & higher than galley; ship of war (usu. Spanish); large Spanish ship used in American trade. [f. F *galion* (*galie* GALLEY), or Sp. *galeon*; see -OON]

gall'ery, n., & v.t. **1.** Covered space for walking in partly open at side, portico, colonnade; balcony long narrow passage in thickness of wall or supported on corbels, open towards interior of building; platform projecting from inner wall of church, hall, etc., providing extra room for audience or reserved for musicians (freq. *minstrels'* ~), reporters, strangers, etc.; (Theatr.) highest such balcony, persons there seated, least refined part of audience (*play to the* ~, appeal to lower taste, use claptrap); long narrow room (e.g. *shooting-~*, for indoor target practice or matches), passage, corridor; room or building used for showing works of art; chimney-holder of lamp; (Mil., Mining) horizontal underground passage; ~ *hit* (Cricket, & fig.,

from theatre) piece of showy play, so ~ *shot, stroke*; hence ~FUL(2) n. **2.** v.t. Provide, pierce, etc., with ~ or galleries. [f. F *galerie* f. It. f. med. L *galeria*]

gall'ey, n. (pl. ~s). **1.** (Chiefly hist.) low flat single-decked vessel using sails & oars, & usu. rowed by slaves or criminals; ancient Greek or Roman warship with one or more banks of oars; large open row-boat, e.g. that used by captain of man-of-war. **2.** Ship's kitchen. **3.** (print.). Oblong tray to which type is transferred from composing stick (~ *proof*, in slip form, not in sheets or pages). **4.** ~*-slave*, person condemned to row in ~, (fig.) drudge; ~*worm*, kind of many-footed insect (from likeness of its legs to oars). [ME, f. OF *galie*, *-ee* f. med. L *galea*, med. Gk *galaia*]

galliǎm'bic, a. & n. In the metre of e.g. Catullus's *Attis*; (n., usu. pl.) such verse(s). [f. L *gall*IAMBUS song of Galli or priests of Cybele +-IC]

gall'iard, n. (hist.). Quick & lively dance in triple time for two persons. [ME, f. OF *gaillard*]

Gall'ic² (for *gallic¹* see GALL⁴), a. Of the Gauls, Gaulish; (usu. joc.) French, whence **gall'ic**ISM(4) n., **gall'ic**IZE(2, 3) v.t. & i. [f. L *Gallicus* (*Gallus* Gaul, -IC)]

Gall'ican, a. & n. Of the ancient church of Gaul or France; (adherent) of the school of French Roman Catholics following Bossuet & claiming partial autonomy (opp. ULTRAMONTANE), whence **gall'ican**ISM(3), **gall'ican**IST(2), nn. [f. F, or L *Gallicanus* (prec., -AN)]

gall'icē (-sē), adv. In French (used in giving F for English phrase etc.). [L, =in Gaulish]

galligǎs'kins (-z), n. pl. (joc.). Breeches, trousers. [orig. wide hose of 16th & 17th cc., f. F *garguesque* for *greguesque* f. It. *grechesca* fem. of *grechesco* Greek (-ESQUE)]

gallimau'fry, n. Heterogeneous mixture, jumble, medley. [f. F *galimafrée*].

gallin|ā'ceous (-shus), a. Of the order *Gallinae* including domestic poultry, pheasants, partridges, etc. So ~A'CEAN (-āshan) a. & n. [f. L *gallinaceus* (*gallina* hen, -ACEOUS)]

gallina'zo (-ah-), n.(pl. ~s). An American vulture, the turkey buzzard. [f. Sp. *gallinaza* (L *gallina* hen, *-aza* augment.)]

Gall'iō, n. Person, esp. official, refusing to meddle outside his province. [*Acts* xviii]

gall'iot (-y-), n. Dutch cargo-boat or fishing-vessel; small (usu. Mediterranean) galley. [ME, f. OF *galiote* f. It. *galeotta* f. med. L *galea* GALLEY]

gall'ipot, n. Small earthen glazed pot used for ointments etc. [prob. f. GALLEY, as brought in galleys from the Mediterranean]

gall'ium, n. Soft bluish-white metal. [f. L *gallus* cock, transl. of *Lecoq* de Boisbaudran the discoverer 1875, + -IUM]

gallivant′, v.i. Gad about (usu. in part. or vbl n.). [perh. corruption of *gallant* v.]

Gallo-, comb. form=*French-*, as ~*-Briton*, ~*-German*, ~*-Roman*. Hence ~MAN′IA n., ~MAN′IAC a. & n., Gäll′ophil, Gäll′o-PHOBE, nn. & aa., ~PHOB′IA n. [*Gallus* GAUL, -O-]

gäll′on, n. A measure of capacity (‖ *imperial* ~, 277½ cubic inches; *wine* ~, 231) for liquids or corn etc. [ME, f. ONF *galon*, OF *jalon*, f. Rom. **gallone*, cf. med. L *galeta*, OF *jaloie*]

galloon′, n. Narrow close-woven braid for binding dresses etc., of gold, silver, silk, or cotton. [f. F *galon* f. *galonner* trim with braid, of unkn. orig.]

gäll′op, n., & v.i. & t. **1.** Horse's or other quadruped's fastest pace, with all feet off ground together in each stride (*full* ~, *at a* ~, going thus); a ride at this pace. **2.** vb. Go at a ~ (of horse, or with its rider as subj., or of other quadruped); make (horse etc.) ~; read, recite, or talk, fast (often *through*, *over*); move or progress rapidly (*in a* ~*ing consumption*). [f. F *galop(er)* f. WG, see WALLOP]

gällopäde′, n. Lively, orig. Hungarian, dance. [F, see GALOP, -ADE(1)]

gäll′oper, n. In vbl senses; esp., ‖ (Mil.) aide-de-camp, light field gun. [-ER¹]

Galliophil etc. See GALLO-.

Gällovid′ian, a. & n. (Native) of Galloway. [f. med. L *Gallovidia*+-AN]

gäll′oway (*-o-*), n. Horse of small strong breed from Galloway, SW. Scotland; small-sized horse; one of a breed of cattle peculiar to Galloway. [district]

gäll′ows (-ōz), n. pl. (usu. treated as sing.). Structure, usu. of two uprights & cross-piece, on which criminals are hanged; punishment of hanging (*a* ~ *look*, *have the* ~ *in* one's *face*, of sinister appearance); similar structure used for cookery, gymnastics, etc.; ~*-bird*, person fit to be hanged; ~*-ripe*, fit to be hanged; ~*-tree*, =~. [ME, f. ON *galgi*= OE *gealga*, OS, OHG *galgo*, Goth. *galga* f. Gmo **galgon*]

*Gäll′up pöll, n. Test of how representative sample of public is to vote, esp. as basis of forecasts. [G. H. *Gallup* (b. 1901)]

galoot′, n. (colloq.). Clumsy lout. [orig. unkn.]

gäl′op, n., & v.i. **1.** Lively dance in 2-4 time. **2.** Dance a ~. [vb f. n., F, see GALLOP]

galore′, adv. & n. (In) abundance (*with beef & ale* ~; ~ *of alcohol*; also *in* ~). [f. Ir. *go leór* to sufficiency]

galosh′, gol-, n. Overshoe usu. of rubber to keep shoes clean or dry; piece of leather etc. round lower part of boot or shoe uppers, whence ~ED² (-sht) a. [ME, f. OF *galoche*, f. LL *gallicula* small Gallic shoe]

galümph′, v.i. Go prancing in triumph. [made by L. Carroll perh. on *gallop*, *triumph*]

gälvän′|ic, a. 1. (hist.). Of, produced by, as of, electricity (~*ic battery*, *pile*, former names for types of primary battery; ~*ic electricity*, electricity from a primary battery). **2.** (fig.). (Of smile, movement, etc.) sudden & forced. Hence ~ICALLY adv. [foll., -IC]

gäl′van|ism, n. (hist.). Electricity from a primary battery; the use of this or other direct-current electricity for medical purposes. Hence ~ISɪ(3) n. [f. F *galvanisme* (L. *Galvani* discoverer 1792, -ISM)]

gäl′vaniz|e, -is|e (-īz), v.t. Stimulate by or as by electricity (also fig., ~*e into life*, rouse by shock or excitement); coat with metal by electrolysis; coat (iron) with zinc (usu. without the use of electricity) to protect it from rust. Hence ~A′TION, ~ER¹, nn. [f. F *galvaniser* (prec., -IZE)]

gäl′vano-, comb. form of GALVANIC, GALVANISM, as ~*graphy* (-ŏg²-), method of producing copperplate engravings by ~*plasty*, metal-coating by galvanism; ~*meter* (-ŏm²), instrument for measuring electric currents; ~SCOPE.

Gälwē′gian (-jn), a. & n. = GALLOVIDIAN. [f. *Galloway* on anal. of *Norwegian*]

gäm′ba, n. (Also ~ *stop*) organ stop with string tone. [earlier =, & short for, VIOLA¹ *da gamba*]

gämbäde′, -äd′ō (pl. *-os*, *-oes*), n. Horse's leap or bound; fantastic movement, freak, escapade. [-*ade* F (Scott); -*ado* f. Sp. *gambada* (*gamba* leg, -ADO)]

gäm′bier, n. Astringent extract of oriental plant used in tanning etc. [f. Malay *gambir* the plant]

gäm′bit, n. Kinds of opening in chess in which player sacrifices pawn or piece to secure certain ends, many ~s having special names as *King's*, *Queen's*, *Cunningham's*, ~; (fig.) opening move in some action etc. [17th c. *gambett* f. It. *gambetto* tripping up (*gamba* leg); -*it* = F *gambit*, Sp. -*ito*]

gäm′bl|e, v.i. & t., & n. 1. Play games of chance for money, esp. for high stakes (~*e away*, lose thus); take great risks to secure great results in war, finance, etc.; hence ~ER¹ n., ~ESOME (-ls-) a. **2.** n. ~ing (esp. *on the* ~*e*); risky undertaking or attempt. [f. obs. (16th c.) *gamel*, var. of ME *gamen* GAME¹]

gamboge′ (-ōozh), n. Gum resin from Cambodian & Siamese trees used as yellow pigment. [f. mod. L *gambogium* f. *Cambodia*]

gäm′bol, n., & v.i. (-ll-). Caper, frisk. [f. F GAMBADE]

game¹, n. 1. Jest (*make* ~ *of*, ridicule); diversion, spell of play (*a* ~ *of ball*); amusing incident (*what a* ~!). **2.** Contest played according to rules & decided by skill, strength, or luck (ROUND, SQUARE, ~; *be on*, *off*, one's ~, be in, out of, form; *have the* ~ *in* one's *hands*, be sure to win or able to direct it; *play the* ~ lit. & fig., observe the rules, behave honourably;

play a good, poor, ~, be skilful or not); (Gk & Rom. Ant.; pl.) athletic, dramatic, & musical contests, gladiatorial etc. shows; scheme, undertaking, etc., followed up like a ~ *(was playing a deep, double, winning, losing,* etc., ~; *the* ~ *is up,* success now impossible; *so that's your little* ~; *spoilt my* ~; *play* one's ~, advance his schemes unintentionally; ~ *not worth* CANDLE). 3. pl. Dodges, tricks, *(none of your* ~*s !*). 4. Single round in some contests, e.g. whist or tennis (~ *&* ~, one ~ scored to each side); (Commerc.) apparatus for a ~; winning score in ~ (~ *and,* short for ~ *& set* in tennis); state of ~ *(the* ~ *is four all, love three,* etc.). 5. Hunted animal, quarry, object of pursuit, *(fair* ~, legitimately to be pursued or attacked; so *forbidden* ~); (collect.) wild animals, birds, etc., hunted for sport or food, flesh of these. 6. Kept flock *of* swans. 7. ~*-act, -law* (usu. pl.), regulating the killing & preservation of ~; ~*-bag,* for holding ~ killed by sportsman; ~ *ball,* state of ~ in tennis etc. at which one point may win; ~*-chicken, -cock, -egg, -fowl,* of kind bred for c:ck-fighting; ~*-keeper,* man employed to breed ~, prevent poaching, etc.; ~*-licence,* to kill or deal in ~; ~*-preserver,* landowner etc. who breeds ~ & applies ~*-laws* strictly; ~*s'manship,* art of winning ~s by distracting one's opponent; ~*-tenant,* lessee of shooting or fishing. [OE *gamen,* OS, OHG, ON *gaman*]

gāme[2], a. Like a game-cock, spirited, (DIE[2] ~); having the spirit to do, *for* Hence ~LY[2] (-ml-) adv., ~'NESS (-mn-) n. [f. GAME[1]*-cock*]

gāme[3], v.i. & t. Play at games of chance for money, gamble; throw *away* in gambling; *gaming-house, -table,* frequented for gambling. Hence ~'STER (-ms-) n. [(1) ME *gamen* f. OE *gam(e)nian*; (2) ME *game* f. GAME[1]]

gāme[4], a. (Of leg, arm, etc.) lame, crippled. [18th c. dial., of unkn. orig.]

gāme'some (-ms-), a. Sportive. Hence ~LY[2] adv., ~'NESS n. [-SOME]

gāmēte', n. (biol.). Sexual protoplasmic body, which unites with another for reproduction. [f. Gk *gametē* wife, *gametēs* husband, (*gameō* marry]

gamin (see Ap.), n. (Street) urchin, neglected boy. [F]

gămm'a, n. Third letter (Γ, γ, = G) of Greek alphabet, used sometimes in enumerations to supplement 3 & c (~ *plus, minus,* rather better, worse, than third-class); kind of moth; ~ *rays,* X-rays of very short wave-length emitted by radio-active substances. [Gk]

gămmād'ion, n. = FYLFOT. [late Gk, dim. of prec., fylfot consisting of four gammas (Γ)]

gămm'er, n. (Rustic name for) old woman. [contr. of *godmother, ga-* by assoc. w. *grandmother*; cf. GAFFER, GOSSIP]

gămm'on[1], n., & v.t. 1. Bottom piece of flitch of bacon including hind leg (usu. ~ *of bacon);* smoked or cured ham; ~ *& spinach* (as dish, &, with pun on *gammon*[3], = humbug). 2. v.t. Cure (bacon). [f. ONF *gambon (gambe* leg, -OON)]

gămm'on[2], n., & v.t. 1. Kind of victory scoring two games at backgammon. 2. v.t. Defeat (adversary) thus. [app. = ME *gamen* GAME[1]]

gămm'on[3], n., int., & v.i. & t. 1. Humbug, deception; (int.) nonsense! 2. vb. Talk plausibly; feign (intr.); hoax, deceive. [perh. as prec.]

gămm'on[4], v.t., & n., (naut.). Lash (bowsprit) to stem; (n., also ~*ing*) the lashing. [orig. unkn.]

gămm'y, a. (sl.). = GAME[4]. [orig. unkn.]

gămo-, comb. form of Gk *gamos* marriage, used esp. in Bot. describing plants with specified parts united, as *gamopet'alous* with petals united; also *gamogen'esis* sexual reproduction.

gămp, n. (colloq.). Umbrella, esp. large untidy one. [f. Mrs *G*~ in Dickens' *Martin Chuzzlewit*]

găm'ut, n. 1. (hist.). Lowest note in medieval scale = modern G on lowest line of bass stave; the Great Scale consisting of all notes used in medieval music (G as above to E in highest space of treble). 2. (mod.). Whole series of recognized notes; major diatonic scale; people's or period's recognized scale; voice's or instrument's compass; whole range or scope of anything *(the whole* ~ *of crime; run up & down the* ~). [f. med. L *gamma ut* (GAMMA taken as name for note one tone lower than A of classical scale + *ut* first of six arbitrary names of notes forming hexachord, being the italicized syllables of a Sapphic stanza, *Ut* queant laxis *resonare fibris Mira gestorum famuli tuorum, Solve polluti labii reatum, Sancte Johannes*)]

găm'y, a. Abounding in game; = GAME[2] (rare); having flavour or scent of game kept till it is high. [-Y[2]]

găn'der, n. Male goose *(sauce for the goose is sauce for the* ~, used in retorting an argument etc. on its first user); fool, simpleton. [OE *gan(d)ra,* MLG *ganre,* LG, Du. *gander*; cogn. w. GANNET]

găng, n., & v.i. & t. 1. Company of workmen, or of slaves or prisoners; band of persons acting or going about together esp. for criminal purpose or one disapproved by speaker (*v.i.,* join *up,* act in concert, *with);* set *of* tools etc. arranged to work simultaneously (v.t., arrange (tools etc.) to work in co-ordination); ~*-board,* plank usu. with cleats nailed on it for walking into or out of boat. 2. v.i. (Sc.). Go; ~ *agley* (aglā'), (of plan etc.) go awry; ~ one's *ain gait,* take one's own course. [OE, OS, OHG *gang,* ON *gangr,* Goth. *gaggs,* Gmc f. *gangan* GO]

gănge (-j), v.t. Protect (fish-hook, part of fishing-line) with fine wire. Hence **găn′GING**[1] (-j-) n. [orig. unkn.]

găng′er, n. Foreman of gang. [-ER[1]]

Găngĕt′ic, a. Of the Ganges. [f. L *Gangeticus* (L f. Gk *Gaggēs*, -IC)]

găng′ling (-ngg-), a. Loosely built, straggling. [f. *°gangle* frequent. of GANG]

găng′li|on (-ngg-), n. (pl. *-lia*). Enlargement or knot on nerve, from which nerve--fibres radiate; mass of grey matter in central nervous system forming a nerve--nucleus (*~on-cell, -corpuscule, -globule,* nerve-cell in this); (fig.) centre of force, activity, or interest. Hence **~ātĕd, ~onātĕd,** [-ATE[2], -ED[1]], **~FORM, ~ŏn′IC,** aa. [f. Gk *gagglion*]

găng′rēne (-ngg-), n., & v.i. & t. **1.** Necrosis, usu. with decomposition, of part of the body (often fig.); hence **găng′rēnous** a. **2.** vb. Become affected, affect, with mortification. [f. L f. Gk *gaggraina*]

găng′ster, n. Member of a gang of violent criminals or roughs. [-STER]

gangue (găng), n. Earth etc., matrix, in which ore is found. [F, f. G *gang* lode = GANG]

găng′way, n. & int. Passage esp. between rows of seats (|| in House of Commons, cross-passage half-way down giving access to back benches; members *above, below, ~* are more, less, closely associated with official policy of their party); passage etc. on ship, esp. platform connecting quarterdeck & forecastle; opening in bulwarks by which ship is entered or left, bridge laid across from this to shore etc.; (int.) make way, please! [18th c., f. GANG + WAY]

găn′ister, n. Close-grained siliceous stone found, mixed with clay, in the lower coal--measures of Yorkshire, and used for furnace-linings. [orig. unkn.]

gănn′ĕt, n. A sea-bird, the solan (-goose). [OE *ganot,* OHG *ganazzo,* MHG *ganze*; cogn. w. GANDER]

găn′oid, a. & n. (Of fish-scale) enamelled, smooth & bright; (fish) having ~ scales. [f. F *ganoïde* f. Gk *ganos* brightness + -OID]

găn′trý, gaun′, n. Four-footed wooden stand for barrels; structure supporting travelling crane, railway signals, etc. [prob. f. obs. contr. of GALLON + *tree*]

Găn′ymēde, n. (Joc.) waiter, potboy; (Astron.) largest satellite of Jupiter. [f. L f. Gk *Ganumēdēs* cupbearer of Zeus]

gaol (jāl), jail, n., & v.t. (*g-* in official, *g-* & *j-* indifferently in literary use, *j-* in U.S.). **1.** Public prison for detention of persons committed by process of law, (without article) confinement in this; *~-bird,* prisoner, habitual criminal, rogue; *~-delivery,* clearing of ~ esp. at assizes by trying all prisoners awaiting trial; *~-fever,* virulent typhus formerly endemic in ~s. **2.** v.t. Put in ~ [ME, f. ONF

gaiole, OF *jaiole* (now *geôle*) f. Rom. dim. of L *cavea* CAGE]

gaol′er (jāl-), jail′er, jail′or, n. (see prec.). Man in charge of gaol or prisoners in it. Hence *~*ESS[1] n. [as prec. + -ER[2](2)]

găp, n. Breach in hedge or wall; gorge, pass; unfilled space or interval, blank, break in continuity, (*stop, fill, supply, a ~,* make up deficiency); wide divergence in views, sympathies, etc. Hence *~*PED[2] (-pt), *~*p′Y[2], aa. [ME, f. ON, = chasm, cogn. w. foll.]

gāpe, v.i., & n. **1.** Open mouth wide, (of mouth, oysters, wounds, chasm, etc.) open or be open wide, split, part asunder; stare, gaze curiously, *at;* yawn. **2.** n. Yawn; open-mouthed stare; *the ~s,* poultry disease with gaping as symptom, (joc.) fit of yawning; expanse of open mouth or beak, part of beak that opens; rent, opening; *~-seed* (joc.), staring, occasion for staring, thing stared at. [ME, f. ON *gapa* cogn. w. MHG *gaffen*]

gāp′er, n. In vbl senses; esp. kinds of bird, kind of mollusc. [-ER[1]]

gă′rage (*or* garahzh′), n., & v.t. **1.** Building or shed for storing or repair of motor--vehicles. **2.** v.t. Put (motor-car) in ~. [F]

gărb, n., & v.t. **1.** Dress, costume, esp. of distinctive kind, way one is dressed. **2.** v.t. Attire, put (esp. distinctive) clothes upon (person; usu. pass. or refl.). [f. obs. F *garbe* f. It. *garbo* f. Gmc, cogn. w. GEAR]

gărb′age (-ij), n. Offal used for food; refuse, filth; foul or worthless reading. [ME, orig. unkn.]

găr′ble, v.t. Select best in, take pick of, (rare); make (usu. unfair or malicious) selections from (facts, statements, etc., mutilate in order to misrepresent; (erron.) unintentionally distort or confuse (facts, statements). [f. It. *garbellare* f. Arab. *gharbala* sift cf. *kirbal* sieve]

gărb′oard (-berd), n. (Also ~ *strake*) first range of planks laid on ship's bottom next keel; corresponding plates in iron ship. [f. Du. *gaarboord* (GATHER, BOARD)]

gărçon (see Ap.), n. Waiter in French hotel etc. [F]

gărd′en, n., & v.i. **1.** Piece of ground devoted to growing flowers, fruit, or vegetables (KITCHEN, || MARKET, ~); (pl.) ornamental grounds for public resort (usu. *botanical, zoological,* etc., *~s*); specially fertile region (*the ~ of England,* Kent, Worcestershire, etc.); || (pl. with name prefixed as *Onslow, Spring, G~s*) set of houses in street, square, etc.; *the G~,* philosophy or school of Epicurus (cf. PORCH, ACADEMY); (attrib.; with or without hyphen) cultivated, not wild, (*~ plants, ~-cress; common or ~,* sl., ordinary), living in *~s* (*~-spider; ~-white,* kind of butterfly; *~-warbler,* kind of bird); ~ *city,* industrial or other town laid out systematically with a view to spacious and attractive surroundings; || *so ~ suburb;*

~-*frame*, forcing-frame for plants; ~-*glass*, bell-glass for covering plant; ~-*party*, social meeting on lawn or in ~; ~-*plot*, piece of ground used as ~; ~ *seat*, bench etc. for use in ~; ‖ ~-*stuff*, vegetables & fruit; (sl.) *lead up the* ~ (*path*), entice, mislead; hence ~ED² (-nd), ~ESQUE', aa., ~ING¹(1) n. 2. v.i. Cultivate a ~. [ME, f. ONF *gardin* (OF *jardin*) f. Rom. *gardinus f. WG *gardo+-*inus* -INE¹; see YARD]

gárd'ener, n. Person who gardens, esp. servant employed to tend a garden, also, esp. *jobbing* ~, employee working at intervals. [ME, f. ONF *gardinier (OF *jard-*) as prec. +-ER²(2)]

gárdĕn'ia, n. Kinds of trees & shrubs with large white or yellow flowers & usu. fragrant scent. [mod. L (Dr. A. *Garden* d. 1791, -IA¹)]

gāre'fowl (-rf-), n. The great auk. [f. ON *geirfugl* (*geir* of doubtful meaning)]

gaŕ'fish, n. Fish with long spearlike snout & green bones. [app. f. OE *gār* spear]

gaŕ'ganey, n. Kind of teal. [f. It. dial. var. of *garganello*]

gàrgăn'tŭan, a. Enormous, gigantic. [*Gargantua* giant in Rabelais +-AN]

gaŕg'ĕt (-g-), n. Inflamed state of head or throat in cattle, pigs, or poultry; inflammation of cow's or ewe's udder. [perh. f. obs. *garget* throat f. OF *gargate*, *-guette*]

gaŕ'gle, v.t. & i., & n. 1. Wash (throat), wash throat, with liquid kept in motion by breath. 2. n. Liquid used thus. [f. F *gargouiller* (foll.)]

gaŕg'oyle, gur-, n. Grotesque spout usu. with human or animal mouth, head, or body, projecting from gutter of (esp. Gothic) building to carry water clear of wall. [f. OF *gargouille* throat, gargoyle]

gàribăl'dĭ, n. Kind of woman's or child's blouse, orig. of bright red; ‖ biscuit containing currants. [f. red shirts of *G~* (Italian patriot 1807–82) & his followers]

gaŕ'ish, a. Obtrusively bright, showy, gaudy, over-decorated. Hence~LY² adv., ~NESS n. [16th c. *gaurish* app. irreg. f. obs. *gaure* stare +-ISH¹]

gaŕl'and, n., & v.t. 1. Wreath of flowers, leaves, etc., worn on head or hung on something as decoration; distinction, palm, prize, for victory etc.; (arch.) anthology, miscellany; metal etc. imitation of ~. 2. v.t. Crown with ~, deck with ~s, serve as ~ to. [ME, f. OF *ger-*, *garlande* of unkn. orig.]

gaŕl'ic, n. Plant with bulbous strong-smelling pungent-tasting root used as flavouring in cookery. Hence (esp. of smell) ~KY² a. [OE *gārlēac* (*gār* spear, LEEK)]

gaŕm'eht, n., & v.t. Article of dress, esp. gown or cloak, (pl.) clothes; outward and visible covering of anything; (vb) poet., usu. in p.p.) attire. [ME & OF *garni-*, *garnement* (GARNISH, -MENT)]

gàrn'er, n., & v.t. (poet. & rhet.). 1. Storehouse for corn, granary, (also fig.). 2. v.t. Store, deposit, collect. [ME, f. OF *gernier* f. L *granarium* GRANARY]

gàrn'ĕt, n. Vitreous mineral, of which a deep transparent red kind is used as gem. [ME, f. OF *grenat*, *-ate* f. med. L *granatum* POMEGRANATE]

gàrn'ish, v.t., & n. 1. Decorate, embellish, (esp. dish for table); (Law) serve notice on (person, called ~EE' n.) for purpose of attaching money belonging to debtor, summon (person) as party to litigation started between others; hence ~ER¹, ~MENT, nn. 2. n. (Also ~ING¹ n.) things used to decorate dish for table (also fig. of literary embellishments). [ME, f. OF *garnir* (-ISH²) f. WG *warnjan WARN]

gàrn'iture, n. Appurtenances, accessories; adornment, trimming esp. of dish; costume. [F (GARNISH, -URE)]

garotte. See GARROTTE.

gă'rrĕt¹, n. Room (usu. squalid) on top floor or partly or entirely in roof, attic. [ME, f. OF *garite* watch-tower (*garir* defend, f. WG *warjan; see WEIR)]

gă'rrĕt², v.t. (archit.). Insert small pieces of stone in joints of (coarse masonry). [orig. unkn.]

gàrrĕteer', n. Dweller in garret, esp. poor literary hack. [-EER]

gă'rrison, n., & v.t. 1. Troops stationed in fortress, town, etc., to defend it (~ *town*, having ~). 2. v.t. Furnish with, occupy as, ~; place (troops, soldier) on ~ duty. [ME, f. OF *garison* (*garir* see GARRET¹, defence, w. sense of F & obs. E *garnison* (GARNISH)]

gă'rron, n. Small inferior horse bred in Scotland & Ireland. [f. Gael. *gearran*]

gă'rrot, n. Kind of sea duck. [F]

gar(r)ŏtt|e', n., & v.t. 1. Spanish method of capital punishment by strangulation, apparatus used in it; highway robbery performed by throttling victim. 2. v.t. Execute by strangulation; throttle in order to rob, whence ~ER¹ n. [f. F *garrotter* or Sp. *garrotear* f. *garrote* a stick (used in twisting cord tight), of unkn. orig.]

gă'rrulous (-rŏŏ-), a. Given to talk, loquacious, wordy, (of bird, stream, etc.) chattering, babbling. Hence or cogn. garrul'ITY (-rŏŏ-), ~NESS, nn., ~LY² adv. [f. L *garrulus* (*garrire* chatter) +-OUS]

gaŕt'er, n., & v.t. 1. Band worn above or below knee to keep stocking up; ‖ *the G~*, (badge of) highest order of English knighthood, membership of this; (*G~*)= G~ King of Arms. 2. v.t. Fasten (stocking), encircle (leg), with ~. [ME, f. OF *gartier* (*garet*, now *jarret*, bend of knee, perh. f. Celt., cf. Breton *gâr*, W *gâr*, leg-bone)]

‖ gàrth, n. (arch. & dial). Close, yard, garden, paddock, open space within cloisters. [ME f. ON *garthr*= OE *geard* YARD²]

găs, n. (pl. *găses*), & v.t. & i. (-ss-). **1.** Any aeriform or completely elastic fluid (used chiefly of those that do not become liquid or solid at ordinary temperatures, other ~es being usu. called *vapours*); such fluid, esp. COAL-~ or various mixtures with carburetted hydrogen, used for lighting or heating; *(colloq.) petrol, gasoline, (step on the ~, accelerate motor engine by pressing down accelerator pedal with foot, also fig.); (Mining) explosive mixture of firedamp with air; hydrogen etc. used to fill balloon; nitrous oxide~ as anaesthetic(often *laughing-~); (also *poison-~) kinds used to asphyxiate enemy in war; jet of ~ used for lighting; empty talk, boasting, humbug, windbag eloquence. **2.** ~*-bag*, bag for holding ~, (derog.) empty talker, airship's ~-container, airship or balloon (opp. aeroplane); ~ *bracket*, pipe with burner(s) projecting from wall; ~*-coal*, bituminous from which ~ can be made; ~*-coke*, residuum of coal when ~ has been made from it; ~*-engine*, *-motor*, with pcwer obtained by production or rhythmical combustion and explosion of~ in closed cylinder; ~*-fitter*, tradesman or workman providing house with ~-*fittings*, apparatus for heating or lighting with ~; ~*-helmet*, ~*-mask*, kinds of appliance including respirator worn as defence against poison-~; ~*'holder*, large receptacle for storing ~, gasometer; ~*light*, light given by esp. coal-~, jet of burning ~ (~*light paper, plates*, photographic materials that can be developed in weak artificial light); ~*-main*, main pipe supplying ~; ~*-man*, manufacturer of ~, collector of sums due for ~-supply; ~*-mask* (as ~*-helmet*); ~*-meter*, apparatus registering amount of ~ consumed; ~*-oven* (heated by ~); ~*-ring*, perforated with small holes & fed with ~ for cooking etc.; ~*-shell* (charged with poison-~, usu. in liquid form); ~*-tar*, COAL-tar produced in making ~; ~*-works*, manufactory of ~; hence **găs'EOUS** a., **gase'ITY** n., ~'i-FORM, ~'LESS, aa., ~'IFY v.t., ~'iFIABLE a., ~iFICA'TION n. (also, underground production of ~ from unmined coal). **3.** vb. Supply (room, railway-carriage, etc.) with ~; project poison-~ upon (enemy, place), (pass.) be poisoned with ~; pass (thread, lace) through ~-flame to remove loose fibres; talk emptily or boastfully, whence ~s'ER[1] n. [wd invented by Van Helmont on Gk *khaos* CHAOS]

Găs'con, n. Native of Gascony; braggart. [F]

găsconāde', n., & v.i. Boast(ing). [f. F *gasconnade* (prec., -ADE)]

găsèlier', n. Gas-lamp, usu. suspended from ceiling, with several burners often on branches. [f. GAS after CHANDELIER]

găsh[1], n., & v.t. **1.** Long & deep slash, cut, or wound; cleft such as might be made by slashing cut; act of making such cut. **2.** v.t. Make ~ in, cut. [16th c., var. of

ME *garse* vb & n. f. OF **garse*, *garser* perh. f. LL *c(h)araxare* f. Gk *kharassō* incise]

‖ găsh[2], a. (naut. sl.). Spare, extra.

găs'kèt, n. Small cord for securing furled sail to yard; strip of tow etc. for packing piston or caulking joint. [orig. unkn.]

gasogene. See GAZOGENE.

găs'olēne, -ine (-ēn), n. Volatile inflammable liquid got in distilling petroleum & used for heating & lighting; *petrol. [GAS, -OL, -ENE, -INE[1]]

gasöm'ēter, n. (Chem.) vessel for holding gas; large reservoir in which gas is stored for distribution by pipes. [f. F *gazomètre* (gaz GAS, *mètre* f. Gk *metron* measure)]

gasp (gahsp), v.i. & t., & n. **1.** Catch breath, strain *for* air or breath, with open mouth as in exhaustion or astonishment; ~ *life* etc. *away* or *out*, expire; ~ *out*, utter with ~s; hence ~*'ingLY[2]* adv., ~*'ER[1]* n. (esp., sl.) ‖ cheap cigarette. **2.** n. Convulsive catching of breath (*at* one's *last* ~, at point of death). [ME, f. ON *geispa* to yawn cf. *geip* idle talk]

găss'|y̆, a. Of, full of, like, gas; (of talk etc.) empty, verbose. Hence ~iNESS n. [-Y[2]]

găs't(e)ropŏd, n. Mollusc (e.g. snail) with locomotive organ placed ventrally. So **găsterŏp'odous** a. [f. F *gastéropode* (GASTRO-, Gk *pous podos* foot)]

găstrae'a, n. (Assumed) primitive sac-like animal consisting of two layers (ectoderm & èndoderm) of cells. [mod. L (GASTRO-)]

găs'tric, a. Of the stomach (~ *fever*, enteric; ~ *juice*, thin clear acid nearly colourless fluid secreted by stomach glands & effecting digestion). [f. Gk as foll. + -IC]

găstr(o)-, comb. form of Gk *gastēr -(e)ros* stomach, as *gastro-entē'ric*, of stomach & intestines, *găs'troCELE*, *gastrŏT'OMY*, *gastrIT'IS.

găstr|ŏl'ogy̆, n. Science of cookery. So ~ŏL'OGER, ~ŏL'OGIST, nn. [f. Gk *gastro-logia* (prec., -LOGY)]

găs'tronôme, n. Judge of cookery. [F, back formati n f. *gastronomie* see foll.]

găstrŏn'om|y̆, n. Art & science of good eating. So ~ER[1] n., **găstronŏm'IC(AL)** aa., **găstronŏm'icalLY[2]** adv., ~IST(3) n. [f. F *gastronomie* (GASTRO-, after *astronomie* etc.)]

***găt**, n. (sl.). Gun, revolver. [abbr. of GATLING]

gāte[1], n., & v.t. **1.** Opening in wall of city or enclosure made for entrance & exit & capable of being closed with barrier; (Bibl.) place of judicial assembly in city; mountain pass; means of entrance or exit (~ *of ivory, horn*, by which false, true, dreams come; *Bosphorus & Hellespont are the two ~s of Constantinople*); barrier closing the opening of a wall, wooden or iron framework, solid or of bars or gratings, hung on hinges, turning on pivots, or sliding, single or double; contrivance regulating passage of water; number entering by payment at ~s to see football match etc., amount of money thus taken (also ~*-money*). 2. ||~*-bill* (Oxf. & Camb.), record of undergraduate's returns to college after hours, fines imposed for these; ~*-crasher* sl. (also *crasher*), uninvited intruder at party etc., so ~*-crash* v.i. & t.; ~*house*, lodge of park etc., room over city ~ often used as prison; ~*-keeper*, attendant at ~, || kind of butterfly; ~*-legged table* (with legs in ~*-like* frame swinging back to allow top to fold down); ~*-meeting*, at which money is taken for admission; ~*-post*, on which ~ is hung or against which it shuts (*between you & me & the* ~*-post*, or bed*-post*, in close confidence); ~*way*, = ~ (first sense), frame of or structure built over ~, means of entrance or exit; hence ~*LESS* (-tl-) a. 3. v.t. (Oxf. & Camb.). || Confine to college entirely or after certain hours. [OE *gæt*, *geat*, OS, ON *gat* f. Gmc *gatom*]

gāte², n. (With prefixed name in North etc.) street. [ME, f. ON *gata*, OHG *gazza*, Goth. *gatwō* f. Gmc *galwōn*-]

gắth'er (-dh-), v.t. & i. Bring together, cause to assemble, (*be* ~*ed* to one's *fathers*, die); acquire by collecting, amass; cull, pluck; collect (grain etc.) as harvest; receive addition of (*rolling stone* ~*s no moss*, change of calling does not pay; *complexion* ~*s colour*; *invalid* ~*s strength*; ~ *head*, acquire strength, swell as a festering sore; ~ *way*, begin to move, of ship); summon up (energies), gain or recover (breath); infer, deduce (*that*); draw (garment, brow) together in folds or wrinkles, esp. pucker (part of dress) by running thread through; pick *up* from ground; draw *up* (limbs, person) into smaller compass; sum *up* (scattered facts); summon *up* (thoughts, strength, etc.) for an effort; come together, congregate, form a mass; receive additions (*the tale* ~*ed, like a snowball*); come to a head, develop purulent swelling. [OE *gaderian*, cf. Du. *gaderen* gather & OE *geador* together]

gắth'ering (-dh-), n. In vbl senses; esp.: purulent swelling; assembly, meeting; ~*-coal*, large piece to keep fire in. [-ING²]

gắth'ers (-dherz), n. pl. Part of dress that is gathered or drawn in. [f. GATHER]

Gắt'ling, n. (Also ~ *gun*) machine gun with clustered barrels. [R.J. ~, inventor (d. 1903)]

gauche (gōsh), a. Tactless, without ease or grace, socially awkward. [F]

gaucherie (gōsherē'), n. Gauche manners, a gauche action. [F]

gauch'o (gow-, gaw-), n. (pl. -*os*). One of a mixed European & Amer.-Ind. people of mounted herdsmen. [Sp., prob. f. native S.-Amer. lang.]

gaud, n. Something gaudy, showy orna-

ment, gewgaw; (pl.) showy ceremonies, gaieties. [ME, f. OF *gaudir* make merry f. L *gaudēre* rejoice]

|| **gaud'y̆¹**, n. Grand entertainment, esp. annual college dinner to old members etc.; ~*-day*, day of rejoicing, day on which college ~ is held. [f. L *gaudium*, partly f. OF *gaudie* joy, wantonness]

gaud'y̆², a. Tastelessly or inappropriately fine, showy, or brilliant (of dress, decoration, literary style, etc.). Hence ~ILY² adv., ~INESS n. [most prob. f. GAUD+-Y²]

gauffer. See GOFFER.

*gaufre.** See GOFER.

gauge¹ (gāj), **gāge²** (in naut. sense), n. 1. Standard measure to which things must conform, esp. measure of capacity or contents of barrel, diameter of bullet, or thickness of sheet iron; capacity, extent, scope, (*take the* ~ *of*, estimate); distance between pair of rails (*broad, narrow,* ~, of more, less, than 4 ft. 8½ in., *standard* ~). 2. (naut.; *gage*). Relative position in respect to wind (*have the weather* ~ *of*, be to windward of, fig. have advantage of; also rarely *lee, southerly,* etc., ~). 3. Graduated instrument measuring force or quantity of rainfall, stream, tide, wind, etc.; contrivance attached to vessel to show height of its contents; instrument for testing and verifying dimensions of tools, wire, etc.; adjustable carpenter's tool for marking parallel lines; (Print.) strip regulating depth of margin etc.; means of estimating, criterion, test. [f. ONF *gauge* (OF *jauge*) of unkn. orig.]

gauge² (gāj), v.t. Measure exactly (esp. objects of standard size, as wire, bolts; fluctuating quantities or forces, as rainfall, wind; depth of liquid content); find capacity or content of (cask etc.) by measurement & calculation (*gauging-rod*, exciseman's instrument for this); estimate, take measure of, (person, character); make uniform, bring to standard size or shape. Hence ~'ABLE a., gau'GER¹ (1, 2) n., (gāj-). [f. ONF *gauger* (prec.)]

Gaul, n. Inhabitant of ancient Gaul; (joc.) Frenchman. [f. *Gaul* the country f. F *Gaule* f. Frank. *walha* foreigners; cf. WELSH]

Gauleiter (gow'līter), n. Nazi district political leader. [G]

Gaul'ish, a. & n. (Language) of ancient Gauls; (joc.) French (adj.). [f. GAUL+-ISH¹]

gault, n. (geol.). Series of clay and marl beds between upper & lower greensand. [orig. unkn.]

gaunt, a. Lean, haggard; grim or desolate looking. Hence ~'NESS n. [15th c., of unkn. orig.]

gaunt'lĕt¹, n. (Hist.) armoured glove (*fling, throw, down the* ~, issue challenge; *pick, take, up the* ~, accept challenge); stout glove with long wrist for driving, fencing, wicket-keeping, etc. Hence ~ED² a. [late ME, f. OF *gantelet* (*gant* glove f. WG *want-*, med. L *wantus*).]

gaunt′lĕt,² *gänt-, n. *Run the* ~, pass between rows of men who strike one with sticks, cords, etc., as military, naval, or school punishment (also fig. of being subjected to criticism). [earlier *gantlope* f. Sw. *gatlopp* (GATE², *lopp* course, cf. G *gassenlaufen*) w. assim. to prec.]

gauntry, -tree, See GANTRY.

gaur (gowr), n. The Indian wild ox. [Hind.]

gauss (gows), n. Unit of magnetic induction. Hence ~′AGE n. [after Karl *G~*, German mathematician (d. 1855)]

gauz|e, n. Thin transparent fabric of silk, cotton, wire, etc.; slight haze. Hence ~′Y² a., ~′iNESS n. [f. F *gaze* f. *Gaza* in Palestine]

gave. See GIVE¹.

*gav′el, n. Auctioneer's or chairman's or judge's hammer. [orig. unkn.]

‖ **gāv′elkind, n.** (legal). Land-tenure, especially in Kent, involving equal division of intestate's property among all his sons. [f. obs. *gavel*, OE *gafol*, tribute, cogn. w. GIVE¹, +KIND¹]

gavŏtte′, n. Slow dance of 18th c.; music for it; piece of music in common time, each phrase beginning on third beat of bar. [F, f. Pr. *gavoto* (*Gavot* native of Alps)]

gawk, n. Awkward or bashful person. [rel. to obs. (12th c.) *gaw* gaze (f. ON *gá* heed), & 18th c. *gawk* vb stare]

gawk′|ў, a. & n. Awkward, ungainly, bashful, (person). Hence ~iNESS n. [f. prec., or *gawk* vb]

gay, a. (~*er*, ~*est*). Full of or disposed to or indicating mirth, light-hearted, sportive; airy, offhand; *(sl.) cheeky, impertinent; (euphem.) dissolute, immoral, living by prostitution; showy, brilliant, bright-coloured, finely dressed, (*with*). Hence **gai′LY²** adv. [ME, f. OF *gai*, of unkn. orig.]

gāze, v.i., & n. 1. Look fixedly (*at, on, upon*); hence **gāz′ER¹** n. **2. n.** Intent look (*stand at~*, looking thus). [ME, orig. unkn., but cf. obs *gaw* (GAWK)]

gaze′bō, n. (pl.~*s*,~*es*, pr.~ōz). Structure whence a view may be had, belvedere, lantern, turret, balcony, etc. [perh. joc. formation f. prec. on L future (cf. LAVABO) or f. some Oriental word]

gazĕlle′, n. Small graceful soft-eyed kinds of antelope. [F, f. Arab. *ghazal*]

gazĕtte′, n., & v.t. 1. (Hist.) news-sheet, periodical publication giving current events; ‖ one of three official journals (*London, Edinburgh, Belfast, G~*) issued by authority twice a week with lists of government appointments & bankrupts & other public notices; (in newspaper titles as *Birmingham, Shields, G~*) newspaper. **2. v.t.** ‖ Publish in official ~ (esp. in pass. of officials so announced). [F, f. It. *gazzetta* f. *gazeta*, a Venetian small coin]

gazĕtteer′, n. Geographical dictionary.

[so called as first provided for gazette-writers, earlier sense of ~]

găz′ogēne, găs-, n. Apparatus for making aerated waters. [f. F *gazogène* (GAS -GEN)]

gean (gēn), n. (Fruit of) wild cherry. [f. F *guigne*, of unkn. orig.]

gear (gēr), n., & v.t. & i. 1. Equipment, apparel, etc. (arch.); harness of draught animals; apparatus, appliances, tackle, tools; combination of wheels, levers, etc.; wheels working on one another by teeth etc.; arrangements connecting motor with its work (*in, out of, ~*, connected or working, with connexion interrupted or not working; *high, low, ~*, by which driven part of bicycle, motor-car, etc., revolves faster, slower, relatively to driving part; similarly *top, bottom, ~* of the available extremes), whence ~′ING¹(6) (gēr-) n.; rigging; goods, household utensils; ~*box, -case*, enclosing ~ing of bicycle etc.; ~*-wheel*, cog-wheel, esp. that in bicycle which transmits motion of pedals to axle; hence ~′LESS (gēr-) a. **2. vb.** Harness (draught animal; often *up*); put (machinery) in ~, provide with ~ (~ *up, down*, provide with high, low, ~); make (an industry or factory) subservient or ancillary *to* another, or *to* a programme; (of cog-wheel) fit exactly *into*, be in ~ *with*. [ME, f. ON *gervi*, OS *gerwi*, OHG *garawi* f. Gmc *garwjan* prepare]

gĕck′ō (g-), n. (pl. ~*s*, ~*es*). House lizard found in warm climates. [f. Malay *gekoq*, imit. of its cry]

‖ **gee¹, gee²gee, n.** (colloq.). Horse. [orig. child's wd, f. foll.]

gee², gee²hō′, gee²(h)ŭp′, gee²wō′, intt. (Words of command to horse etc.) go on, go faster, (occas.) turn to right.

*gee³, int. of asseveration, discovery, etc. [abbr. of *Jesus*]

geese. See GOOSE.

geez′er (g-), n. (sl.). Old person, old creature. [dial. pronunc. of *guiser* mummer (as GUISE +-ER¹)]

Gĕhĕnn′a (g-), n. Hell; place of burning, torment, or misery. [eccl. L, f. Hellenistic Gk *geenna* f. Heb. *gehinnom* hell, orig. valley of Hinnom where children were sacrificed]

Geig′er coun′ter (gīg-), n. Cylindrical device for detecting and recording radio-activity. [f. *Geiger*, German physicist (1882–)]

gei′sha (gā-), n. Japanese dancing-girl. [Jap.]

Geiss′ler (gī-) tūbe, n. Sealed tube filled with rarefied gas that becomes incandescent when an electric current is passed through it. [H. *Geissler*, German physicist (d. 1879)]

geist (gi-), n. Intellectuality & sensibility, capacity for or tendency to mental fervour. [G, as GHOST]

gĕl, n., & v.i. (-ll-). (Form) a semi-solid

colloidal solution. [first syllable of *gelatin*]

gĕl'atin(e) (*also* -ēn), n. Amorphous brittle transparent tasteless slightly yellow substance, basis of the jellies resulting from stewing skin, tendons, ligaments, bone-matrix, etc. (*vegetable* ~, constituent of gluten identical with animal ~; *blasting* ~, an explosive nitro--glycerine compound; ~ *paper*, coated with sensitized ~ for photography). Hence **gēlatin'iFORM** a., **gĕlăt'inocomb.** form. [f. F *gélatine* f. It. *gelatina* (*gelata* JELLY, -IN)]

gĕlăt'in|ous, a. Jelly-like in consistence etc.; of gelatin. So ~ICE(3) v.t. & i., ~OID a. & n. [f. F *gélatineux* (prec., -OUS)]

gēla'tion, n. Solidification by freezing. [f. L *gelatio* (*gelare* freeze, -ATION)]

gĕld (g-), v.t. Deprive (usu. male animal) of generative power, castrate, excise testicles or ovaries of. Hence (-)~'ER¹ n. [ME, f. ON *gelda*]

gĕl'ding (g-), n. Gelded horse or other animal. [ME, f. ON *geldingr* (prec., -ING³)]

gĕl'id, a. Icy, ice-cold; chilly, cool. [f. L *gelidus* (*gelu* frost) cogn. w. COLD]

gĕl'ignite, n. A nitro-glycerine explosive. [f. GELATINE, L *ignis* fire, -ITE¹(2)]

gĕm, n., & v.t. (-mm-). 1. Precious stone, esp. when cut and polished; object of great beauty or worth, choicest part *of*, prized thing; precious or semi-precious stone with engraved design; hence ~m'Y² a. 2. v.t. Adorn (as) with ~s. [ME, f. L *gemma* bud, jewel]

Gĕmār'a (g-), n. Later part of Talmud, commentary on MISHNA. [Aram., = completion]

gĕm'inate¹, a. (nat. hist.). Combined in pairs. [f. L *geminare* (*geminus* twin), -ATE²]

gĕm'in|āte², v.t. Double, repeat, arrange in pairs. So ~A'TION n. [as prec., -ATE³]

Gĕm'inī, n. & (-ī) int. Constellation Castor and Pollux or the Twins, third sign of Zodiac, (also as arch. or vulg. int. of surprise, pr. jimini). [L, = twins]

gĕmm'a, n. (bot., zool.; pl. *-ae*). Leaf--bud; (in mosses etc.) small cellular body that separates from mother-plant & starts fresh one; (Zool.) bud-like growth on animal of low organization becoming detached & developing into individual. [L, see GEM]

gĕmm'ate¹, a. Having buds, reproducing by gemmation. [f. L *gemmatus* (prec., -ATE²)]

gĕmmāte'², v.i. Put forth buds, propagate by gemmation. [f. L *gemmare* (GEMMA), -ATE³]

gĕmmā'tion, n. Act, manner, of budding, arrangement of buds, reproduction by gemmae, formation of new individual by protrusion & separation of part of the parent. So **gĕmm'ATIVE** a. [F, f. L *gemmare* (as prec., -ATION)]

gĕmmif'erous, a. Producing precious stones; bearing buds = foll. [f. L *gemmifer* (GEMMA, -I-, -FEROUS)]

gĕmmip'arous, a. Of, propagating by, gemmation. Hence ~LY² adv. [GEMMA, L -r *rus* (*parere* bring forth)]

gĕmĭnŏ|l'ŏg̃y̆, n. Science of gems. Hence ~L'OGIST n. [f. L *gemma* GEM, -O-, -LOGY]

gĕmm'ūle, n. (biol.). Small gemma; one of the hypothetical units in Darwin's theory of pangenesis. [F, f. L *gemmula* (GEMMA, -ULE)]

gems'bŏk (gĕmz-), n. Large S.-African antelope with long slender straight horns. [Du.]

‖ **gĕn**, n. (sl.). Information etc. published for all ranks. [first syllable of *general information*]

-gĕn, suf. forming nn. in scientific use f. F -*gène* f. Gk -*genēs* -born, of such a kind, (*gen-*, *gn-*, seen in *gi-gn-omai* be born, become). (1) in *oxygen* & later chem. formations -*gen* has the sense *that which produces* (*hydrogen, nitrogen, cyanogen*); (2) in *endogen, exogen,* etc. (bot.) -*gen=* growth (*acrogen, thallogen*).

gĕnăppe', n. Smooth kind of worsted. [f. *Genappe* in Belgium]

gendarme (see Ap.), n. (pl. ~s). 1. Soldier, mounted or on foot, employed in police duties esp. in France. 2. (On a mountain) rock-tower occupying & blocking arête. [F]

gendarmerie (see Ap.), n. Force of gendarmes. [F]

gĕn'der¹, n. Grammatical classification (or one of the two, or three, classes) of objects roughly corresponding to the two sexes & sexlessness (MASCULINE, FEMININE, & NEUTER; see also COMMON¹, EPICENE), (of nouns & pronouns) property of belonging to such class, (of adjj.) appropriate form for accompanying a noun of any such class; (joc.) sex. Hence ~LESS a. [ME, f. OF *gen(d)re* f. L GENUS]

gĕn'der², v.t. (poet.). = ENGENDER. [ME, f. OF *gen(d)rer* f. L *generare* (prec.)]

gĕne, n. (biol.). One of the factors or elements of which a germ-cell contains a pair transmitted each from one parent. [mod. formation, cf. -GEN]

gĕnĕalŏ'gĭcal, a. Of genealogy; tracing family descent; ~ *tree*, table showing descent of family or of animal species in shape of tree with branches. Hence ~LY² adv. [f. F *généalogique* f. med. L f. Gk *genealogikos* (GENEALOGY, -IC)+-AL]

gĕnĕal'og̃|ize, -ise (-ĭz), v.t. & i. Trace genealogy of; draw up genealogies. Hence ~IST(1) n. [foll., -IZE]

gĕnĕal'og̃y̆, n. Account of descent from ancestor by enumeration of intermediate persons, pedigree; investigation of pedigrees; plant's or animal's line of development from earlier forms. [ME, f. OF (-*gie*) f. LL f. Gk *genealogia* (*genea* race, -LOGY)]

genera. See GENUS.

gĕn′eral, a. & n. 1. Completely or approximately universal, including or affecting all or nearly all parts, not partial, particular, local, or sectional, (~ *confession*, to be made by whole congregation; ~ ELECTION; *G~ Post Office*, ‖ head office in London; ~ *post*, first morning delivery, also name of indoor game); prevalent, widespread, usual, (*in a ~ way*, ordinarily); not limited in application, relating to whole class of objects, occasions, etc., true of all or (opp. *universal*) nearly all cases (*as a ~ rule*, in most cases), including points common to individuals of a class & neglecting differences (~ *word, term, notion*); not restricted to one department, not specialized, (‖ ~ *dealer*, trader in many articles; ~ *hospital*, large military hospital receiving sick and wounded from the field hospitals, one not specializing in any particular disease; ~ *practitioner*, doctor treating cases of all kinds; ‖ ~ *servant*, maid-of-all-work; ~ *reader*, of miscellaneous literature); roughly corresponding or'adequate, sufficient for practical purposes, (~ *resemblance, idea*); vague, indefinite, (*spoke only in ~ terms*); (Mil., of officer) above rank of colonel; (appended to titles, as ADJUTANT~, ATTORNEY ~, POST²-*master ~*) chief, head, with unrestricted authority or sphere, (also *joc.* with other nn., as *lover ~*, one who makes love to all women); *in~*, generally, in all ordinary cases, barring special exceptions, for the most part. **2. n.** *The ~* (arch.), the public; (pl.; now rare) ~ principles, notions, or rules; chief of religious order, e.g. of Jesuits, Dominicans; (Mil.) officer next below Field Marshal (also by courtesy of *lieutenant-~ & major-~*); commander of army; tactician, strategist, of specified merit (*a good, bad, great, ~; no ~*); ‖ = ~ servant above (colloq.). [ME, f. OF, f. L *generalis* (GENUS, -AL)]

gĕneraliss′imō, n. (pl. ~s). Commander of combined military & naval & air force, or of several armies. [It., superl. of *generale* GENERAL]

gĕnerăl′itў, n. Being general, applicability to whole class of instances; vagueness; general point, principle, law, or statement; main body, bulk, majority, of. [f. F *généralité* f. LL *generalitatem* (GENERAL, -TY)]

gĕneralīzā′tion, n. (Forming of) general notion or proposition obtained by induction (often used disparagingly, esp. *hasty ~*, one based on too few instances). [foll., -ATION]

gĕn′eralīz|e, -is|e (·ĭz), v.t. & i. Reduce to general laws, form into a general notion, give a general character to, call by a general name; infer (law, conclusion) by induction; base general statement upon (facts etc.); (Math., Philos.) throw into general form, extend application of;

form general notions by abstraction; (Paint.) render only the typical characteristics of; make vague, use generalities, speak vaguely; bring into general use. Hence ~ER¹ n. [-IZE]

gĕn′erallў, adv. For the most part, extensively; in a general sense, without regard to particulars, not specially, (~ *speaking*, in general); as a general rule, commonly. [-LY²]

gĕn′eralship, n. Office of a general; strategy, military skill; skilful management, tact, diplomacy. [-SHIP]

gĕn′erāte, v.t. Bring into existence, produce, evolve, (plants, animals, etc., usu. in pass.; heat, force, light, friction, electricity, etc.; result, state of things, state of mind, etc.); (Math.; of point, line, surface, conceived as moving) make (line, surface, solid). [f. L *generare* beget (GENUS), -ATE³]

gĕnerā′tion, n. Procreation, propagation of species, begetting or being begotten, (*equivocal* or SPONTANEOUS ~); production by natural or artificial process; single step in descent or pedigree (*have known them for three ~s*; *his descendant in the tenth ~*); whole body of persons born about same time (*my, the rising, ~*), average time in which children are ready to replace parents (reckoned at ⅓ of a century or at 30 years as a time-measure). [ME, f. OF, or L *generatio* (prec., -ATION)]

gĕn′erative (-ăt-, -at-), a. Of procreation; able to produce, productive. [ME, f. LL *generativus* (prec., -ATIVE)]

gĕn′erātor, n. Begetter; apparatus for producing gases, steam, electricity, etc. [L (GENERATE, -OR)]

gĕnē′r|ic, a. Characteristic of a genus or class; applied to (any individual of) a large group or class; general, not specific or special. Hence ~ICALLY adv. [f. F *générique* or med. L *genericus* (GENUS, -IC)]

gĕn′erous, a. Magnanimous, noble-minded, not mean or prejudiced, free in giving, munificent, so gĕneros′ITY n.; (of soil) fertile; ample, abundant, copious; (of diet, colour, wine) rich & full. Hence ~LY² adv. [f. F *généreux* or L *generosus* (GENUS, -OUS) well-born, generous]

gĕn′esis, n. First book of O.T., with account of the Creation (*G~*); origin, mode of formation or generation, (also in comb. as *abio-~, partheno-~*). [L f. Gk *gen-* become]

gĕn′ĕt, n. (Fur of) kind of civet-cat. [ME, f. OF *genete* f. Arab. *jarnait*]

gĕnĕt′|ic, a. Of, in, concerning, origin; of ~ics. Hence ~ICALLY adv., ~ICS n. pl., the study of heredity & variation, including loosely the physiology of reproduction & the art of breeding. [f. GENESIS on anal. of *antithesis* -etic]

gĕnĕv′a¹, n. Spirit distilled from grain & flavoured with juniper berries, Hollands. [f. Du. *genever* f. OF *genevre* f. L *juniperus* JUNIPER w. assim. to foll.]

Gĕnĕv'a², a. (attrib.), & n. Of, from, Geneva (~ *bands*, clerical BAND's like those of Swiss Calvinists; ~ *Conventions*, of 1864-5 neutralizing ambulances etc. in war; ~ *cross*, red Greek cross on white ground distinguishing ambulances etc. in war; ~ *gown*, black, worn by Calvinists & low-churchmen in pulpit; (as n., used for) the ~ Conventions, the League of Nations or its proceedings. Hence Gĕnĕv'AN, GĕnĕvESE', aa. & nn.

gĕn'ial¹, a. Nuptial, generative, (~ *bed*, *instinct*; rare); conducive to growth, mild, warm, (of air, climate, etc.); cheering, enlivening; jovial, kindly, sociable, whence **gĕniäl'ITY** n., ~IZE(3) v.t.; of genius (rare). Hence ~LY² adv. [f. L *genialis* (GENIUS, -AL)]

gĕni'al², a. (anat.). Of the chin. [f. Gk *geneion* chin (*genus* jaw cf. L *gena*)+ -AL]

gĕnic'ŭlate, -ātĕd, aa. (nat. hist.). Having knee-like joints. [f. L *geniculatus* (*geniculum* f. *genu* knee, -CULE, -ATE²)]

gĕn'ie, n. (pl. usu. *gĕnĭi*, see GENIUS). Jinnee, sprite or goblin of Arabian tales. [f. F *génie* f. L GENIUS]

gĕni'o-, comb. form of Gk *geneion* chin, as ~*hy'oid* of chin & hyoid bone.

gĕnis'ta, n. Kinds of yellow-flowered shrubs (including in some classifications the common broom). [L]

gĕn'ital, a., & n. (pl.). 1. Of animal generation. 2. n. pl. External organs of generation. [f. OF *genital*, *-ailles*, or L *genitalis*, *-alia* (*gignere. genit-* beget, -AL)]

gĕn'itive, a. & n. ~ *case* or ~, grammatical form of nouns, pronouns, adjectives, & participles, corresponding in inflected languages to *of*, *from*, & other prepositions with the noun representing, the source, possessor, etc. (~ ABSOLUTE, Gk construction corresponding to Latin ablative absolute). Hence **gĕnitiv'AL** a. [ME, f. OF *-if* or L *genitivus* (*casus* case) rendering Gk *genikē* (*ptōsis* case); as prec. +-IVE]

gĕn'ito-, comb. form of GENITAL, as ~-*urinary* of the genital & urinary organs.

gĕn'ius, n. (pl. *-iuses*, *-ii*). Tutelary spirit of person, place, or institution (*good, evil*, ~, two opposed spirits or angels working for person's salvation or damnation, also person who powerfully influences one for good or ill); (usu. pl., *genit*, w. sing. GENIE) demon(s), supernatural being(s); nation's, age's, etc., prevalent feeling, opinions, or taste; character, spirit, drift, method, of a language, law, etc.; associations or inspirations *of* a place; natural ability, special mental endowments; (no pl.) exalted intellectual power, instinctive & extraordinary imaginative, creative, or inventive capacity, (pl. *-iuses*) person having this; ~ *loci* (L; lō̄s'ī), presiding deity, associations, etc., of the place. [L, in first sense, f. root of *gignere* beget]

Gĕn'ōa, n. Italian city (~ *cake*, rich with almonds on top). Hence **GĕnōesE'** (*-ēz*) a. & n.

gĕn'ocīde, n. Extermination of a race. [f. Gk *genos* race, -CIDE(2)]

genre (see Ap.), n. Kind, style; (also ~-*painting*) portrayal of scenes etc. from ordinary life. [F]

Gĕn'rō, g-, n. pl. = Elder Statesmen (see STATESMAN). [Jap., = chief elders]

gĕns (-z), n. (Rom. Ant.; pl. *gentēs*). Clan, sept, among Greeks or Romans. [L, genit. *gentis* (*gignere* beget)]

gĕnt, n. Gentleman (vulg.); person pretending to status of gentleman (joc.). [short for GENTLEMAN]

gĕnteel', a. (usu. iron.; vulg. in serious use). Appropriate to, characteristic of, belonging to, the upper classes, stylish, fashionable, well-dressed, elegant. Hence ~ISM(4) n., word used instead of the ordinary natural word because it is thought to be more ~ (e.g. *lady-dog* for *bitch*, *perspire* for *sweat*), ~LY² (-l-li) adv. [16th c. *-ile*, re-adoption of F *gentil* GENTLE]

gĕn'tian (-shn, -tian), n. Kinds of usu. blue-flowered plant found esp. in mountain regions; ~-*bitter*, tonic extracted from its root; ~-*violet*, dye, used as antiseptic, esp. in treatment of burns. [ME, f. L *gentiana* (*Gentius* king of Illyria, -AN)]

Gĕn'tile, a. & n. (Person) not of Jewish race, (in Mormon use) non-Mormon, whence ~DOM (-ld-) n.; of a nation or tribe, (a. & n. in Gram.) (word) indicating nationality; heathen, pagan. [ME, f. L *gentilis* (GENS, -IL)]

gĕntili'tial (-shl), a. Of a nation, gens, or family (~ *noun, name, insignia*). [f. L *gentilitius* (*gentilis* GENTILE) +-AL]

gĕntil'itÿ, n. Gentle birth, status of gentleman or lady, (now rare); (usu. iron.) being genteel, social superiority, good manners, upper-class habits, (*shabby* ~, endeavour to keep up genteel appearances). [ME, f. OF *gentilite* (foll., -ITY)]

gĕn'tle, a. (*-er*, *-est*), n., & v.t. 1. Well-born, (Her.) having right to bear arms, (now only in ~ & *simple*, & in comb. as ~*folks*, GENTLEMAN); (of birth, blood, family, pursuits, etc.) honourable, belonging to or fit for the class of gentlemen; || (arch.) generous, noble, courteous (still playfully in ~ *reader*, author's apostrophe); tame, quiet, (*the* ~ *craft*, angling), easily managed; not stormy, rough, or violent; (of medicine) mild, not drastic; (of rule etc.) not severe; moderate (*a* ~ *heat*), gradual (*a* ~ *slope*); kind, mild, tender, (*the* ~ *sex*, women); ~*folk(s)*, people of good position & family. 2. n. Maggot, larva of flesh-fly or bluebottle, used as fishing-bait (f. obs. sense *soft* of adj.); (pl., vulg.) ~folk. 3. v.t. Break in (horse), handle (horse) firmly but gently. [ME, f. OF *gentil* f. L *gentilis* GENTILE; cf. JAUNTY]

gĕn'tlehŏŏd (-telh-), n. Position or character attaching to gentle birth. [from 1860; -HOOD]

gĕn'tleman (-telm-), n. Man entitled to bear arms but not included in the nobility (chiefly hist.); member of certain professions etc. (arch.); ‖ man of gentle birth attached to household of sovereign or great person (~ *in waiting* etc.; ~-*at-arms*, one of sovereign's bodyguard); man of chivalrous instincts, fine feelings, & good breeding (*the* ~'*s psalm*, Ps. xv); man of good social position, man of wealth & leisure (~ *at* LARGE); (courteous synonym for) man, (pl., in voc.) male members of audience, also in letters = Sirs; ‖ (pl. as sing. n.) men's public lavatory; (Law) man who has no occupation; (joc.) *old* ~, the devil, *my* ~, the fellow I was speaking of, ~'*s* ~, valet; ‖ ~ *commoner* (hist.), privileged undergraduate at Oxf. & Camb.; ~ *farmer*, country ~ who farms; ‖ ~ RANKER; ~ *usher*, ~ acting as usher to great person; ~'*s agreement* (binding in honour, but not enforceable at law). Hence ~HOOD, ~SHIP(1), nn. [GENTLE + MAN after OF *gentilz hom*]

gĕn'tlemanlike (-telm-), a. Appropriate to, resembling, a gentleman. [-LIKE]

gĕn'tleman‖ỹ (-telm-), a. Feeling, behaving, or looking, like a gentleman; befitting a gentleman. Hence ~INESS n. [-LY¹]

gĕn'tleness (-tel-), n. Kindliness, mildness; freedom from severity, suddenness, violence, steepness, etc. [-NESS]

gĕn'tlewoman (-telwŏŏman), n. (pl. -en). Woman of good birth or breeding, lady. Hence ~HOOD n., ~LIKE, ~LY¹, aa., ~līNESS n. [GENTLE + WOMAN after OF *gentil-femme*]

gĕn'tlỹ, adv. As gentleman or gentlewoman (only in ~ *born*, of gentle birth); quietly, moderately, softly, slowly,. (as remonstrance) not so fast etc.; mildly, tenderly, kindly. [-LY²]

gĕn'trỹ, n. People next below the nobility in position & birth; (derog., esp. *these* ~) people. [prob. f. obs. *gentrice* f. OF *genterise* var. of *gentelise* (*gentil* GENTLE)]

gĕn'ūal, a. Of the knee. [L *genu* knee, -AL]

gĕn'ūflĕct, v.i. Bend the knee, esp. in worship. Hence or cogn. ~OR, gĕnūflĕ'xION, nn., ~ORY a. [f. LL *genuflectere* -*flex*- (prec., *flectere* bend)]

gĕn'ūine, a. Of the original stock, pure-bred; really proceeding from its reputed source or author; having the supposed character, not counterfeit, properly so called. Hence ~LY² (-nl-) adv., ~NESS (-n-n-) n. [f. L *genuinus* innate, post-cl. authentic]

gĕn'us, n. (pl. *gĕn'era*). (Logic) kind of things including subordinate kinds or SPECIES (*highest* ~, not itself subordinated as species to higher ~; *subaltern* ~,

so subordinated); (Zool., .Bot.) group of animals or plants having common structural characteristics distinct from those of all other groups, & usu. containing several species (see CLASS); the generic & specific names, the former with capital initial, form the proper name; *the* ~ *Homo*, mankind); (loosely) kind, class, order, tribe. [f. L *genus* -*eris* cogn. w. KIN]

-gĕnỹ, suf. forming nn. indicating mode of production f. F -*génie* (-GEN), as *anthropō'geny* history of human evolution, often with corresp. nn. in -*genesis* & adjj. in -*genetic*.

gĕo-, comb. form of Gk *gĕ* earth (Gk *geō*-), as ~*dynām'ic* of the latent forces of the earth, ~*selēn'ic* of earth & moon.

gĕocĕn'tric, a. Considered as viewed from the earth's centre (~ *latitude of planet*, in which it would appear to observer at earth's centre); having or representing the earth as centre, not HELIOcentric. [prec., *centric* (CENTRE¹, -IC)]

gĕ'ōde, n. (Concretionary stone containing) cavity lined with crystals or other mineral matter. Hence **gĕŏd'IC** a. [f. F *géode* or L f. Gk *geōdēs* earthy (*gĕ* earth, -ODE)]

gĕŏd'|ĕsỹ, n. Branch of mathematics dealing with figure & area of the earth or large portions of it. So **gĕodēs'ic**, **gĕodĕt'IC**, aa. (~*esic*, ~*etic*, *line*, shortest possible on surface between two points), **gĕodĕt'icAL** a., **gĕodĕt'icaLLY²** adv., ~-ĕsIST(3) n. [f. F *géodésie* or mod. L f. Gk GEO(*daisia* f. *daiō* divide)]

gĕŏg'nosỹ, n. = GEOLOGY; geology of a district; knowledge of the mineral character, grouping, & distribution, of particular rocks. So **gĕognōs'tIC(AL)** aa. [f. F *géognosie* (GEO-, Gk *gnōsis* knowledge, *gnōstos* known]

gĕográph'ic, **-icAL**, aa. Of geography (~ *latitude*, angle made with plane of equator by perpendicular to earth's surface at any point; ~*al mile*, = 1' of longitude on equator or about 2,000 yds). Hence ~alLY² adv. [f. F (-*ique*) or LL f. Gk GEO(*graphikos* GRAPHIC) + -AL]

gĕŏg'raphỹ, n. Science of the earth's surface, form, physical features, natural & political divisions, climate, productions, population, etc. (*mathematical, physical*, & *political*, ~, the science in these aspects); subject-matter of ~; features, arrangement, of place; treatise or manual of ~. So **gĕŏg'RAPHER** n. [f. F *géographie* or L f. Gk GEO(*graphia* -GRAPHY)]

gĕŏl'ogīze, **-ise** (-īz), v.i. & t. Devote time to examining places geologically, collect specimens, etc.; examine (place) thus. [foll. + -IZE]

gĕŏl'ogỹ, n. Science of the earth's crust, its strata, & their relations & changes; geological features of district. Hence **gĕolō'gIC(AL)** aa. (-*ic* now only of things forming part of subject-matter of ~), gĕŏlŏ′gicalLY² adv., gĕŏL′OGIST n. [f. mod. L f. GEO-+-LOGY]

gĕ′ŏmănc|ỹ, n. Divination from figure given by handful of earth thrown down, & hence from figures given by dots made at random. Hence or cogn. ~ER¹ n., gĕŏmăn′tIC a. [ME, f. OF geomancie f. med. L f. Gk GEO(manteia -MANCY)]

gĕŏm′ĕter, n. Person skilled in geometry; kinds of caterpillar & corresp. moth (from caterpillar's seeming to measure ground by its mode of walking). [f. L f. Gk GEO(metrēs measurer)]

gĕŏmĕt′ric, -ic|al, aa. Of, according to, geometry (~al tracery, with openings of ~ form, as circles, trefoils, etc.; ~al proportion, involving equal ratios in its two parts, as 1 : 3 :: 4 : 12; ~al progression, with constant ratio between successive quantities, as 1 : 3 : 9 : 27 : 81; ~ spider, constructing web of ~ pattern). Hence ~alLY² adv. [f. L f. Gk geōmetrikos (prec. -IC)+-AL]

gĕŏm′ĕtrīze, -ise (-ĭz), v.i. & t. Work, form, by geometrical methods. [f. LL geometrizare (as foll., -IZE)]

gĕŏm′ĕtrỹ, n. Science of properties & relations of magnitudes (as lines, surfaces, solids) in space. So gĕŏmĕtri′cIAN (-ĭshn) n. [ME, f. OF geometrie f. L f. Gk GEO(metria measuring)]

gĕŏmŏr′phŏl′ogỹ, n. Study of the physical features of the (crust of the) earth & its geological structures. [GEO-, MORPHO-LOGY]

gĕŏph′ag|ỹ, n. = DIRT-eating. So ~IST(1) n. [GEO-, Gk -phagia -eating]

gĕŏphŷs′ic|s (-z-), n. The physics of the earth. Hence ~AL a., ~IST n. [GEO-]

gĕŏpŏl′itics, n. The politics of a country as determined by its geographical features. [GEO-]

gĕŏpŏn′ic, a. (pedantic or joc.). Agricultural. [f. Gk GEO(ponikos f. ponos toil + -IC)]

¶ Geor′dĭe (jôr-), n. (Sc. & north.). = COLLIER (all senses); native of Tyneside. [George, -Y³]

George (jôrj), n. 1. St ~, patron saint of England from time of Edw. III who chose him as patron of Order of the Garter (St ~'s day, 23rd April; St ~'s cross, vertical & horizontal red bars crossing in centre). 2. Jewel forming part of Garter insignia. 3. ‖ Automatic pilot of aircraft (sl.). 4. Brown ~, vessel of brown earthenware; by ~, oath .or exclamation; ‖~ Cross, Medal, (abbr. G.C., G.M.), decorations for gallantry instituted 1940. [f. L f. Gk Geōrgios supposed prince of Cappadocia martyred under Diocletian]

georgĕtte′ (jôr-), n. A thin silk dress-material. [f. dressmaker's name]

Geor′gian¹ (jôr-), a. Of the time of the first four Kings George of England; of the time of George V and VI. [-IAN]

Geor′gian² (jôr-), a. & n. (Inhabitant,

language) of Georgia in the Caucasus; (inhabitant) of Georgia in U.S. [-AN]

Geor′gic (jôr-), n. One book (first, fourth, ~) of the ~s, Virgil's poem on husbandry. [f. L f. Gk geōrgika pl. neut. adj. (geōrgos husbandman f. GEO-, erg- work, -IC)]

gĕŏstrŏph′ic, a. (meteorol.). Depending on the rotation of the earth. [GEO-+Gk strophikos f. strephō turn]

gĕŏt′ropism, n. Plant-growth in relation to gravity (positive ~, tendency of roots to grow towards, negative ~, of stems to grow away from, centre of earth). So gĕŏtrŏp′ic a.; gĕŏtrŏp′icALLY adv. [GEO-, Gk tropikos (tropē a turning f. trepō turn + -IC, -ISM)]

gĕrān′ium, n. Kinds of wild herbaceous plant bearing fruit like crane's bill, crane's-bill; kinds of cultivated pelargonium; colour of the scarlet ~. [L, f. Gk geranion (geranos crane)]

gĕr′falcon (-awkn, -awl-), n. Any large northern falcon, esp. the Icelandic. [ME, f. OF gerfaucon f. WG *gerfalco (= G gerfalke) f. ON geirfalki (for geir- cf. GAREFOWL), see FALCON]

gĕriăt′r|ic, a. Relating to ~ics n. pl., branch of medical science dealing with old age & its diseases. So gĕriatri′cIAN (-ĭshn), ~IST(3), ~Y¹, (jĕri′a-), nn. [f. Gk gēras old age, iatros physician, -IC]

gĕrm, n., & v.i. 1. Portion of organism capable of developing into a new one (~, usu. of female reproductive element, opp. sperm-), rudiment of animal or plant; micro-organism or microbe, esp. one of those supposed to cause disease (~-CARRIER); (fig.) that from which something may spring, elementary principle (in ~, not yet developed); ~-cell, cell in body of an organism which is specialized for reproductive purposes, and which, when united to one of the opposite sex, forms a new individual, gamete; ~-plasm, nuclear part of ~-cell by which, according to Weismann's theory, hereditary characteristics are transmitted. 2. v.i. Germinate, sprout, (fig. only). [f. F germe f. L germen]

gĕrm′an¹, a. (Now only as appended to BROTHER, SISTER, COUSIN) in the fullest sense of relationship; = GERMANE. [ME, f. OF germain f. L germanus of same parents]

Gĕrm′an², a. & n. 1. Of, characterizing, Germany or its inhabitants or language (~ measles, contagious disease like mild measles; ~ Ocean, North Sea; ~ sausage, large kind stuffed with spiced partly cooked meat; ~ text, black letter; ~ silver, white alloy of nickel, zinc, & copper). 2. n. Native, language, of Germany (High~, form of ~ orig. spoken in South, but now in literary use throughout Germany; Low ~, dialects of Germany that are not High~, also, all forms of WG, including English & Dutch, except High~). Hence ~ISH¹ a., ~ISM(2,

3, 4), ~IST(1, 3), nn., ~IZE(2, 3, 4) v.t. & i., ~ĪZA'TION, ~ĪZER¹, nn., Gĕ̄rmān'o-comb. form., Gĕ̄rmănoMAN'IA n., Gĕ̄rmăn²OPHIL, Gĕ̄rmăn'OPHOLE, aa. & nn., ~ŏph'ILIST, Gĕ̄rmănoPHOB'IA, nn. [f. L *Germanus* a. & n. of related peoples of central & N. Europe, name perh. given by Celts to their neighbours (cf. OIr. *gair* neighbour)]

gĕ̄rmăn'der, n. Kinds of plant esp. the blue-flowered ~ *speedwell*. [f. med. L *germandra* ult. f. late Gk *khamaidruon* f. *khamai* on the ground +*drus* oak]

gĕ̄rmăne', a. Relevant, pertinent, *to* the matter or subject. [var. of GERMAN¹]

Gĕ̄rmăn'ic, a. & n. ~ Of the Germans (chiefly hist. in ~ *Confederation*, ~ *Empire*); of the Teutonic race or any Teutonic people (of language, =primitive Teutonic; also with limiting word: *East* ~, Gothic & some almost lost languages as Burgundian & Vandal; *North* ~, Scandinavian; *West* ~, High & Low German, English, Frisian, Dutch, etc.; see also INDO-~). [f. L *Germanicus* (GERMAN², -IC)]

gĕ̄rmăn'ium, n. Brittle white metallic element. [mod. L, f. *Germanus* GERMAN² +·IUM]

gĕ̄rm'icĭde, n. & a. (Substance) having power to destroy (esp. disease-)germs. Hence gĕ̄rmicīd'AL a. [·I·, ·CIDE]

gĕ̄rm'inal, a. Of germs, in the nature of a germ; in the earliest stage of development. Hence ~LY² adv. [as GERM, ·AL]

gĕ̄rm'in|āte, v.i. & t. Sprout, bud, put forth shoots, (lit. & fig.); cause to shoot, develop (trans.), produce. Hence or cogn. ~ANT a. (intr. usu. fig.), ~A'TION, ~ātor, nn., ~ATIVE a. [f. L *germinare* (GERM), ·ATE³]

gĕ̄rm'on, n. Long-finned tunny. [F]

gĕ̄rŏntŏc'racў (g·, j·), n. Government by, governing body of, old men. [f. Gk *gerŏn -ontos* old man, -CRACY]

gĕ̄rŏntŏl'ogў (g·, j·), n. Scientific study of old age & its diseases. [f. Gk *gerŏn* (prec.), -LOGY]

-gerous, suf. (in use *-igerous*, see -I·) f. L *-ger* bearing (*gerere* bear) +·OUS; in some words taken f. L, & freely added to L stems, as in *frondigerous* leaf-bearing.

gĕ̄rrўmăn'der (g·), (erron.) ‖ jĕrrў-, v.t. & n. 1. Manipulate (constituency etc.) unfairly so as to secure disproportionate influence at election for some party or class; hence ~ER¹ n. 2. n. Such manipulation. [vb f. n., orig. U.S.; anecdotic; substitution of name of governor Gerry of Massachusetts for *sala*- in *salamander*]

gĕ̄'rund, n. Forms of Latin verb *-ndum*, *-ndi*, *-ndo* serving as cases of the infinitive in its noun use, constructed as nouns but able to govern like their verb; English verbal noun in -ING¹ when used distinctly as part of verb (*his doing this is doubtful*); ~-*grinder*, teacher of Latin. So gĕ̄run'dIAL a. [f. LL *gerundium* f.

gerundum, var. of *gerendum* gerund of *gerere* do = thing to be done, doing]

gĕ̄rŭn'dĭve, a. & n. Of, like, the gerund; (n.; in L Gram.) verbal adjective from gerund stem having sense *that should be done* etc. Hence gĕrundīv'AL a., ~LY² adv. [f. LL *gerundivus* (prec., -IVE)]

gĕss'ō, n. Plaster of Paris, gypsum, prepared for use in painting & in sculpture. [It., f. L GYPSUM]

gĕstalt' (gĕshtahlt), n. (psych.) An organized whole in which each individual part affects every other, the whole being more than a sum of its parts; chiefly attrib., as ~ *psychology*, *theory*. [G, = form, shape]

Gĕsta'pō (gestah-), n. German secret state police of Nazi régime. [f. initial letters of *Geheime Staats-Polizei*]

gĕstā'tion, n. Carrying or being carried in the womb between conception & birth, this period. [f. L *gestatio* (*gestare* frequent. of *gerere* carry, -ATION)]

gĕstatōr'ial, a. ~ *chair*, for carrying the Pope on certain occasions. [f. L *gestatorius* (*gestator* carrier as prec. +·OR, -ORY)]

gĕstĭc'ŭl|āte, v.i. & t. Use expressive motion of limbs or body with or instead of speech; express thus. So ~A'TION, ~ātor, nn., ~ATIVE, ~ātoRY, aa. [f. L *gesticulari* (*gesticulus* dim. of *gestus* GESTURE), -ATE³]

gĕs'ture, n., & v.i. & t. 1. Significant movement of limb or body; use of such movements as expression of feeling or rhetorical device; (transf.) step or move calculated to evoke response from another or to convey (esp. friendly) intention. 2. vb. = GESTICULATE. [ME, f. med. L *gestura* (L *gerere gest*- wield, -URE)]

gĕt¹ (g·), v.t. & i. (past *gŏt*; p.p. *gŏt*, & in comb. & arch. & U.S. *gŏtt'en*). 1. trans. Obtain, procure, by effort or contrivance (~ *coal*, extract it from mine), earn (*cannot ~ a living*), gain (*got little by it*), win (~ *the upper hand*, *start*, *advantage*, *sun*, *wind*, *better*, of a person; ~ *the best of it*, be victorious; ~ *fame*, *credit*, *glory*, etc.; ~ *knowledge* or *wind of*, learn, hear rumours of); learn *by heart* or *rote*; obtain as result of calculation (*we ~ 9·5 as the average*); receive as gift, wages, etc.; extract by prayer, demand, inquiry, etc. (*from*, *out of*; *could not ~ leave*, *any supper*); come to have (desired thing, as *rest*, one's *way*, *speech* of someone, *a sight of*, *possession of*; ~*religion*, be converted); contract (idea etc.; also ~ *it into* one's *head*, be convinced *that*; ~ *measles*; ~ person or thing *on the brain*, think of him exclusively, on one's *nerves*, be irritably affected by him); (of story etc.) ~ *wind*, become known; have inflicted on one, suffer, receive as one's lot or penalty, (*fall*, *blow*, *the worst of it*, *six months*; ~ *it*, be punished, scolded, etc.; ~ *the* BOOT¹, SACK¹, MITTEN); (with *for* or ind. obj.) procure, provide, (*got him a place*;

we can ~ *it for you*); catch (fish etc.); bring in, carry home, (crop); (colloq.) corner, puzzle, catch in argument, (esp. in perf. & past); (colloq.) understand (person or thing); (colloq.) take, eat, (dinner etc.); (colloq., in perf.) have (*have not got a penny; it has got to be done*, must); (now usu. only of animals) beget; (with compl.) succeed in bringing, placing, etc. (*got it over* or *across* see below, *through door, into room*, etc.), bring into some state (~ *with child*, make pregnant); ~ *them ready*; ~ person *upon* a subject, make him talk of it; ~ *ship under way*, start her; esp. with p.p. as ~ *it done, got the laws obeyed*); suffer injury etc. to some part of one (*got my wrist dislocated; shall ~ my feet wet*); induce, prevail upon, (person) *to do*. 2. intr. Succeed in coming or going *to, from, into, out of, through, over, here, there, as far as*, etc. (*where has it got to?*, what has become of it? ; ~ *across* or *over* (sc. the footlights), sl., reach audience, be effective; ~ *there*, sl., succeed); (sl.) be off, clear out; (with infin.) acquire habit (one *soon ~s to like it*); come to be doing (*they got talking*); become (~ *tired, hot, excited, drunk*; ~ *well, better*, recover from illness; ~ *clear, rid*, or *quit, of*; *~ *wise to*, become aware of; ~ *under way*, begin to sail; ~ *done with*, bring to an end; ~ *married, used to it, shelved*). 3. (With prepp.): ~ *at*, reach (whence ~-ăt̔ABLE a.), ~ hold of, ascertain, (sl.) tamper with, bribe, etc., (sl.) attack, banter, (*who are you ~ting at?*, often = trying to impose upon—expressing incredulity); ~ *into*, (colloq.) put on (boots, clothes), (of liquor) affect, confuse, (one's *head*); ~ *off*, dismount from, obtain release from (engagement etc.), not remain on (the grass etc.); ~ *on*, mount (horse etc.), rise on one's *feet* or *legs* to speak in public; ~ *over*, surmount (difficulty), show (evidence, argument) to be unconvincing, recover from (illness) or from surprise at, accomplish (distance, task, etc.), (sl.) circumvent; ~ *round*, cajole, evade; ~ *through*, bring to an end, (of Bill etc.) be passed by (Lords, Commons, etc.), while away (time etc.); ~ *to*, begin (business etc.); ~ *upon*, = ~ on. 4. (With advv.); ~ *about*, go from place to place, begin walking after illness etc., (of rumours) be circulated; ~ *abroad*, (of rumours) = ~ about; ~ *along*, advance, meet with success, fare *ill* or *well* etc., manage *without* something, live harmoniously *together* or *with*, (colloq.) ~ *along with you!*, be off!, nonsense!; ~ *away*, escape, start, (imperat.) be off!; ~ *away with it*, succeed in what one tries to do, escape retribution, act with impunity; ~ *back*, come home etc., recover (lost thing); ~ *back* one's or some of one's *own*, sl., have revenge; ~ *down*, dismount; ~ *in*, be elected as M.P., enter carriage, bring home (crop), collect (debts etc.), fit (work etc.) into given time, suc-

ceed in placing (blow), ~ one's *hand in*, become at home with some operation, *can't ~ in a word* EDGEWAYS; ~ *off*, escape (t. & i.), start, go to sleep, be acquitted or pardoned, be let off *with* or *for* specified penalty, procure acquittal or slight penalty for (person); ~ *off with*, become on friendly or amorous terms with member of opposite sex; ~ *on*, display (pace; ~ *a move on*, sl., make a start), advance, make progress (~ *on* or ~ *out*, work or go), prosper, fare, manage *without* something, agree or live sociably *with*, be ~*ting on for*, approaching (an age etc.); *~ *on to*, succeed in understanding; ~ *out*, (imperat.) be off!, nonsense!, transpire, elicit, succeed in uttering, publishing, etc., dismiss, be dismissed, in cricket; ~ *out of*, issue or escape from (*got out of bed on wrong side*, is in bad temper; ~ *out of sight*, one's *depth*, disappear, be in too deep water to stand; ~ *out of hand*, break from control, also finish *work* etc.), abandon (habit) gradually, evade do*ing*, elicit (information) or obtain (money) from (person); ~ *over*, bring (troublesome task) to an end; ~ *through*, bring to or reach destination, (of Bill) be passed in Parliament, succeed in an examination; ~ *through with*, succeed in doing or enduring; ~ *together*, collect (t. & i.), unite in discussion, promotion of plan, etc.; ~-*together* n., (social) assembly; ~ *under*, subdue (fire); ~ *up*, rise esp. from bed, mount esp. on horseback, (of fire, wind, sea) begin to be violent, (of game) rise from cover, (of cricket-ball) rise sharply from pitch, organize, set on foot, (of laundress) dress (linen), make presentable, arrange the appearance of, (hair, the person, mounting of play, binding & print of book), make rise (*I got my, his, back up*, became, made him, angry or stubborn), produce (~ *up steam*, enough to work engine, also fig. of working oneself into anger or energy; ||~ *the wind up*, sl., feel afraid), work up (factitious emotion, subject for examination etc.). Hence ~t̔ABLE a. [ME, f. ON *geta* = OE -*gietan* (cf. *beget, forget*), OS -*getan*, OHG -*gezzan*, Goth. *bigitan* f. Gmc *getan*]

gĕt², n. Begetting, offspring, (of animals, esp. in sporting talk). [f. prec.]

gĕt'away (-*a*-w-), n. (Esp. of thieves etc.) escape, as *make* one's ~. [GET¹]

gĕt-ŭp', n. Style of equipment or costume, style of production of book etc. [GET¹]

gē'um, n. Kinds of rosaceous plant, avens, as HERB-bennet. [L, prob. = herb-bennet]

gew'gaw (g-), n. Gaudy plaything or ornament, bauble; paltry showy trifle. [ME, of unkn. orig.]

gey (gā), adv. (Sc.). Very, considerably, (also adj. ~ *&* —), in same sense). [var. of GAY]

gey'ser (gāz-, gīz-), n. Intermittent hot spring throwing up column of water;

‖ (gēz- apparatus for heating water. [f. Ycel. *Geysir* name of a particular specimen in Iceland (*geysa* to gush)]

Ghanai'an (gahnā'*an*), a. & n. (Native) of Ghana (formerly Gold Coast colony). [-IAN]

gharry (gă'rǐ), n. (Anglo-Ind.). Indian carriage (usu. horse-drawn and plying for hire). [Hind, *gā̆rī*]

ghast'l‖y (gah-, gă-), a. & adv. Horrible, frightful, shocking; (colloq.) objectionable, deathlike, pale, wan, lurid; (of smile etc.) painfully forced; (adv., chiefly with adj. as ~ *pale*) ghastlily. Hence ~ILY² adv., ~INESS n. [ME *gastliche* f. obs. *gast* terrify (cf. OE *gǣstan* torment) +-LY¹; *gh-* after GHOST]

gha(u)t (gawt), n. (Anglo-Ind.). *Eastern, Western, G~s,* two mountain chains along E & W. sides of Southern Hindostan; mountain pass, defile; flight of steps leading to river landing-place; *burning-~,* level spot at the top of river ~ on which Hindus burn their dead. [Hind. *ghat*]

Gha'zǐ (gah-), n. Mohammedan anti-infidel. [Arab. p.p. of *ghaza* fight]

ghee (gē), n. Indian buffalo-milk butter clarified to resemble oil. [f. Hind. *ghī*]

gherk'in (gĕr-), n. Young green, or small kind of, cucumber used for pickling. [f. Du. **gurkkijn* (now *gurkje*) f. Slavonic, ult f. late Gk *aggourion*]

ghett'ō (gĕ-), n. (hist.; pl. ~s). Jews' quarter in city. [It.; orig. much conjectured, but unkn.]

Ghib'ellin‖e (gĭ-), n. & a. 1. One of emperor's faction (opp. GUELPH) in medieval Italian States; hence ~ISM(3) n. 2. adj. Adhering to ~es. [f. It. *Ghibellino* supposed to be f. G *Waiblingen* estate belonging to Hohenstaufen emperors]

ghōst (gō-), n., & v.t. & i. 1. Principle of life (now only in *give up the ~,* die); Spirit of God (now only in *Holy G~,* Third Person of Trinity). 2. Soul of dead person in Hades etc.; dead person appearing to the living (*raise, lay,* ~, cause it to appear or cease appearing), apparition, spectre; emaciated person; shadowy outline or semblance (*not the ~ of a chance,* none at all). 3. (opt.). Bright spot or secondary image in field of telescope due to defect of lens. 4. Artistic or literary hack doing the work for which his employer takes credit. 5. ~*-word,* one of which the existence is imaginary or based on a delusion, as CELT², FYLFOT; *the ~ walks* (Theatr. sl.), salaries are, or will be, paid; hence ~'HOOD n., ~'LIKE a. 6. vb. Haunt, prowl, act, as a ~; act as a ~ writer etc. (for). [OE *gāst,* OS *gēst,* OHG *geist* f. WG **gaist;* sp. *gh-* first in Caxton, prob. due to Flem. *gheest*]

ghōst'l‖y (gō-), a. (Arch.) spiritual, incorporeal, concerned with sacred or ecclesiastical matters, (*our ~y enemy,* the Devil; ~*y father, adviser, director,* etc., confessor;

~*y comfort, counsel,* etc., administered by priest; ~*y weapons,* religious arguments, ecclesiastical penalties, etc.); (as) of a ghost, spectral. Hence ~INESS n. [OE *gāstlic* (prec., -LY¹)]

ghoul (gōōl), n. Spirit preying on corpses in Eastern tales. Hence ~'ISH¹ a., ~'ishLY² adv., (gōō-). [f. Arab. *ghul* f. vb = seize]

‖ **ghyll,** var. of GILL².

gial'lō anti'cō (jahl-, ahntē-), n. Rich yellow marble found in Italian ruins. [It.]

gī'ant, n. & a. 1. Being of human form but superhuman stature, (Gk Myth.) one of the sons of Gaea (Earth) & Uranus (Heaven) or Tartarus (Hell) who warred against the Gods; agency of enormous power; abnormally tall person, animal, or plant; person of extraordinary ability, courage, strength, etc. (*there were ~s in those days,* our fathers were superior to us); ~ *cement,* specially tenacious kind; ~*-powder,* kind of dynamite; ‖~('s)*-stride,* gymnastic apparatus of pole with revolving head & hanging ropes enabling user to take huge strides round pole; hence ~ESS¹ n., ~ISM n., pathological condition characterized by abnormal growth, esp. of the bones, ~LIKE a. 2. adj. Of extraordinary size or force, gigantic, monstrous, (often in plant-names). [ME *geant* (afterwards affected by L) f. OF *geant* f. L f. Gk *gigant-* nom. *-gas*]

giaour (jowr), n. (Turkish contemptuous name for) infidel, esp. Christian. [f. Pers. *gaur*]

gib (g-, j-), n. Piece of wood or metal used to keep some part of a machine etc. in place; pin or wedge. [orig. unkn.]

gibb'er (j-, g-), v.i., & n. 1. Speak fast & inarticulately, chatter like an ape. 2. n. Such speed or sound. [imit.]

gibb'erish (g-, j-), n. Unintelligible speech, meaningless sounds, jargon, blundering or ungrammatical talk. [perh. f. prec. (but found earlier) +-ISH¹ as used in names of langg.]

gibb'ĕt, n., & v.t. 1. (Orig.) gallows; (later) upright post with arm on which bodies of executed criminals were hung up; death by hanging. 2. v.t. Put to death by hanging; expose on ~; hang up as on ~; hold up to infamy or contempt. [ME, f. OF *gibet* gallows dim. of *gibe* club]

gibb'on (g-), n. Kinds of long-armed ape esp. of Indian archipelago. [F (Buffon), alleged to be a native wd]

gibb'ous (g-), a. Convex, protuberant; (of moon or planet) having bright part greater than semicircle & less than circle; humped, hunchbacked. Hence or cogn. **gibbos'ity** (-ŏs²) n., **gibbōs'o-** comb. form, ~LY² adv., (g-). [f. L *gibbosus* f. *gibbus* hump, see -OUS]

gibe, jibe, v.i. & t., & n. Flout, jeer, mock, (as vb, with *at,* or trans., or abs.),

Hence **gĭb′ER¹** n., **gĭb′ĭngLY²** adv. [orig. unkn.]

gĭb′lĕts, n. pl. Parts of goose taken out or cut off before cooking, as liver, gizzard, pinions, feet; *giblet soup*, made with these. [f. OF *gibelet* ragout of game]

gĭb′us, n. Opera or crush hat. [*G~*,maker]

gĭdd′ȳ (g-), a., & v.t. & i. 1. Dizzy, disposed to fall, stagger, or spin round (*with* sickness, success, etc.); making dizzy (*a ~ precipice, maze, success*); circling with bewildering speed; mentally intoxicated, incapable of attention, excitable, frivolous (*play the ~ goat*, fool), inconstant, flighty; ||*~-go-round*, MERRY²-go-round; hence **gĭdd′ĭLY²** adv., **gĭdd′ĭNESS** n., (g-). 2. vb. Make or become ~. [OE *gidig* insane (GOD, -Y²) lit. 'possessed by a god', as Gk *entheos*]

gĭft (g-), n., & v.t. 1. Giving (*would not have it as a ~*, even gratis; *the living is in the ~ of —*, is his to bestow; *came to me by free ~*); (Law) voluntary transference of property without consideration; thing given, present, donation; faculty miraculously bestowed, virtue looked upon as emanation from heaven etc., (*~ of* TONGUES); natural endowment (*~ of the* GAB), talent, whence **gĭf′tED²** (g-) a.; *~-book*, one given or suitable for giving as present; *~ coupon*, voucher issued with certain commodities, a specified number of which entitles holder to a ~; *~-HORSE*, one given; hence **gĭf′tĭe** [-Y³] (g-) n. (Sc.; *the ~ie gie us to see oursels as others see us*). 2. v.t. Endow with ~s, present *with* as ~; bestow as ~ (*to* person; *away*). [ME, f. ON *gipt* = OE, OS, OHG *gift*, Goth. *-gifts* f. Gmc *geftiz* f. *gebh-* GIVE]

gĭg¹ (g-), n. 1. Light two-wheeled one-horsed carriage (*~-lamps*, sl., spectacles; *~′man*, person who keeps ~, member of GIGMANITY) 2. Light narrow clinker-built ship's-boat for oars or sails; rowing-boat chiefly used for racing. [f. 13th c. in var. senses; orig. unkn.]

gĭg² (g-), n. Kind of fish-spear. [short for *fizgig*, *fishgig* f. Sp. *fisga* harpoon]

gĭgăn′tĭc, a. Giant-like in size, stature, etc., abnormally large, huge. Hence or cogn. **~ESQUE′** (-ĕsk) a., **~ĭCALLY** adv. [f. L *gigas -antis* GIANT, -IC]

gĭg′gle (g-), v.i., & n. 1. Laugh like an affected, ill-bred, or undisciplined girl, titter, have small bursts of half-suppressed laughter. 2. n. Such laugh, freq. (*fit of*) *the ~s*. [imit.; cf. Du. *giechelen*, G *gickeln*]

gĭg′lĕt, -ot, (g-), n. Giggling girl. [14th c., f. obs. *gig* flighty girl (GIG¹), now associated with prec.]

gĭgmăn′ĭtȳ (g-), n. The respectable unimaginative middle classes, Philistines. [*gigman* (GIG¹) + -ITY (Carlylese wds)]

gĭg-mill (g-), n. Machine for raising nap on cloth; building in which these stand. [f. GIG¹]

gĭg′olō, n. (pl ~s) Professional male

dancing-partner. [F, formed as masc. of *gigole* dance-hall woman]

gĭg′ot, n. Leg of mutton; *~ sleeve* = LEG-*-of-mutton* sleeve. [F]

gila (hē′la) mŏn′ster, n. Large venomous lizard of Arizona, New Mexico, etc. [*Gila*, river of Southern U.S.]

Gilbert′ian (g-), a. Of the humorously topsy-turvy kind characteristic of Gilbert & Sullivan opera (*a ~ situation*). [W. S. *Gilbert*, librettist, d. 1911, -IAN]

gĭld¹ (g-), v.t. (p.p. usu. *~ed* in the fully verbal use & in fig. use as adj., *gilt* as adj. in lit. sense). Cover with thin layer of gold laid on as gold leaf or otherwise (*~pill*, soften down unpleasant necessity), whence **gĭl′dER¹**, **gĭl′dĭNG¹** (2, 4), nn.; make (condition etc.) tolerable or reputable by money (or with *money* etc. as subj.); tinge, adorn, with golden colour or light; give specious brilliance to by fair words; || *Gilded Chamber*, House of Lords; *~ed* or *gilt spurs*, emblem of knighthood; *~ed youth*, the young men of fashion & wealth; *gilt-cup*, buttercup. [OE *gyldan*, ON *gylla* f. Gmc. *gulthjan* (GOLD)]

gĭld². See GUILD.

gĭll¹ (g-), n. (usu. pl.), & v.t. 1. Respiratory organ(s) in fishes & other water-breathing animals; wattles or dewlap of fowls; vertical radiating plates on under side of mushrooms etc.; flesh below person's jaws & ears (*rosy about the ~s*, healthy-looking); *~-cover*, bony case protecting fish's *~s*; *~-net*, for entangling fishes by the *~s*; hence (-)*~ED²* (-ld) a. 2. v.t. Gut (fish); cut off *~s* of (mushroom); take in *~-net*. [ME f. ON, whence Sw. *gäl*, Da. *gjælle*]

|| **gĭll²** (g-), n. Deep usu. wooded ravine; narrow mountain torrent. [ME, f. ON *gil* glen]

gĭll³, n. Quarter-pint liquid measure (||in some parts half-pint). [ME, f. OF *gille*, med. L *gillo*]

Gill⁴, n. Female name; *Jack & ~* (or *Jill*), lad & lass. [ME, abbr. of *Gillian* pop. form f. OF *Juliane* f. L *Juliana* (*Julius*)]

gillarōō′ (g-), n. Irish trout. [f. Ir. *giolla* fellow, *ruadh* red]

gĭll′ie (g-), n. 1. (hist.). Highland chief's attendant. 2. Man or boy attending sportsman in Scotland. [f. Gael. *gille* lad, servant]

gĭll′ȳflower, n. (now rare). Clove-scented pink; other similarly scented flowers, as wallflower, white stock. [ME *gilofre* f. OF *gil-*, *girofle* f. med. L f. Gk *karuophullon* (*karuon* nut, *phullon* leaf) w. assim. to *flower*]

gĭlt¹ (g-). See GILD¹ (*cloth ~*, book-binding of cloth with ~ letters or tooling).

gĭlt² (g-), n. Gilding (*take the ~ off the gingerbread*, strip thing of adventitious attractions); *~-edged paper, securities, stocks*, etc., such investments as trustees prefer or are restricted to. [f. prec.]

gilt³ (g-), n. Young sow. [ME, f. ON *gyltr*]

gim'bal, n. (pl. exc. in comb. as ~*-ring* etc.). Contrivance (usu. of rings & pivots) for keeping articles (esp. compass & chronometer) horizontal at sea. [16th c. var. of *gimel* f. ME f. OF *gemel* double finger-ring, f. L *gemellus* dim. of *geminus* twin]

gim'crack, n. & a. 1. Trumpery article, knick-knack, useless ornament; hence ~ERY(5) n., ~Y² a. 2. adj. Showy & flimsy, worthless, trumpery. [ME *gibecrake* (? inlaid work), of unkn. orig.]

gim'let (g-), n. Kind of boring-tool (usu. semi-cylindrical with wooden crosspiece as handle & worm at pointed end). [ME, f. OF *guimbelet*, dim. f. WG *wem-*, whence LG *wemel* boring-tool & obs. *vimble*]

‖ **gimm'er** (g-), n. (dial.). Young ewe; (derog.) woman. [ME, f. ON *gymbr*]

*****gimm'ick** (g-), n. (sl.). Tricky device, device adopted for the purpose of attracting attention or publicity. [orig. unkn.]

gimp, **gÿmp**, (g-), n. Silk, worsted, or cotton twist with cord or wire running through it; fishing-line of silk etc. bound with wire; (Lacemaking) coarser thread outlining design. [f. Du. *gimp* of unkn. orig.]

gin¹, n., & v.t. (-nn-). 1. Snare, net, trap, (n. & v.t.). 2. Hoisting apparatus, kinds of crane & windlass. 3. Machine for separating cotton from its seeds (vb, remove seeds of with this). [ME; aphetic f. OF *engin* ENGINE]

gin², n. Spirit distilled from grain or malt, GENEVA¹; ~ & IT²; *pink* ~, ~ flavoured with angostura bitters; ‖~*-palace*, gaudily decorated public-house; ~ *sling*, American cold drink of ~ flavoured & sweetened. [short for GENEVA¹]

gin'gall (-gawl), j-, n. Musket fired from a rest, or light swivel gun, in China & India. [f. Hind. *janjal*]

gin'ger (-j-), n., a., & v.t. 1. (Plant with) hot spicy root used in cooking & medicine & preserved in syrup or candy as sweet (*black* ~, unscraped, from E. Indies; *white* ~, scraped, from Jamaica; ~ *shall be hot in the mouth*, the love of pleasure is immortal). 2. Mettle, spirit; stimulation (see vb; ‖~ *group* in Parliament, that urges Government to more decided action). 3. (Of) light reddish-yellow colour (n. & a.). 4. ~ *ale, beer, pop*, kinds of aerated ~-flavoured drink; ~ *brandy*, a cordial; ~*bread*, a cake made with treacle & flavoured with ~ (~*bread nut*, small button-like cake of it; *take the* GILT² *off the* ~*bread*), also (as adj., with allusion to fancy and often gilded shapes in which it was made) gaudy, showy, tawdry, (esp. ~*bread Gothic*); ~*-nut*, ~*bread nut*; ~*-race*, a root of ~, ~ *wine*, a British wine of fermented sugar, water, & bruised ~ hence ~Y² a. 5. v.t. Flavour with ~ put ~ up fundament of (horse) to produce liveliness, (fig.) rouse *up* (person). [OE & LL *gingiber* f. L *zingiber* f. Gk *ziggiberis* f. Skr. *çrngavera* (*çrnga* horn, *vera* body)]

gingerade' (-j-), n. = GINGER *beer*. [f. prec. after LEMONADE]

gin'gerly (-j-), adv. & a. With, showing, extreme caution so as to avoid making a noise or injuring oneself or what is touched or trodden on. [perh. f. OF *gensor* compar. of *gent* graceful f. L *genitus* (well-)born]

gingham (ging'am), n. Kind of cotton or linen cloth of dyed yarn often in stripes or checks; (colloq.) umbrella. [f. Du. *gingang* or F *guingan* ult. f. Malay *ginggang* (orig. adj. = striped)]

gin'gili, n. (E.-Ind. plant yielding) a sweet oil. [f. Hind. *jinjali* f. Arab. *juljulan*]

gingiv'al, a. Of the gums. [L *gingiva* gum +-AL]

gingko. Var. of GINKGO.

gin'glymus (g-, j-), n. (anat.). Hinge-like joint in body with motion only in two directions (e.g. elbow). [f. Gk *gigglumos* hinge]

*****gink** (g-), n. (sl.). (Queer) fellow, chap.

gink'go (gingk'gō), n. (pl. ~es). Chinese & Japanese tree with fan-shaped leaves. [f. Jap. *gingko* f. Chin. *yinhing* silver apricot]

gin'seng, n. (Root of) medicinal plant found in China, Nepal, Canada, & Eastern U.S. [f. Chin. *jên shên* (*jên* man) perh. = image of man, w. allusion to forked root]

‖ **gipp'ō**, n. (army sl.). Soup, gravy, stew.

‖ **gipp'ÿ**, n. (army sl.). Egyptian soldier. [abbr.]

gip'sy, **gÿ-**, n. Member of a wandering race (called by themselves *Romany*) of Hindu origin with dark skin and hair, living by basket-making, horse-dealing, fortune-telling etc., & speaking a much corrupted Hindi; (playful) mischievous or dark-complexioned woman; ~ *bonnet*, with large side flaps; ~ *moth*, European moth very destructive to foliage; ~ *rose, scabious*; ~ *table*, light round one on tripod. Hence ~DOM, ~HOOD, ~ISM(2), nn., ~ISH¹ a., ~FY (usu. in p.p. ~*fied*) v.t. [16th c. *gipcyan* for *Egyptian*, f. supposed orig. of the race when it appeared in England in early 16th c.]

giraffe' (-ahf, -āf), n. African ruminant quadruped with spotted skin & long neck & legs, camelopard. [ult. f. Arab. *zarafah*]

gi'randole, n. Revolving firework, discharge of rockets from revolving wheel; revolving jet of water; branched candle bracket or candlestick; ear-ring or pendant with large central stone surrounded by small ones. [F, f. It. *girandola* (*girare* see GYRATE)]

gi'rasol(e), n. Kind of opal reflecting reddish glow, fire-opal. [It. (-e), f. *girare* see prec. + *sole* sun, orig. = sunflower]

gird[1] (g-), v.t. (poet. or rhet.; ~*ed* or *girt*). Encircle (waist, person as to waist) with belt etc. esp. to confine clothes (~ one*self*, one's *loins*, prepare for action, often with *up*); invest *with* strength, power, etc.; equip *with* sword in belt; fasten (sword etc.) on with belt (*on* adv. or prep., *upon*, *to*); secure (clothes) on body with girdle or belt; put (cord etc.) *round*; encircle (town etc.) *with* besiegers or siege-works; (of belt, fence, etc.) encircle. [OE *gyrdan*, OS *gurdian*, OHG *gurten*, ON *gyrtha* f. Gmc *gurthjan* (GIRTH)]

gird[2] (g-), v.i., & n. Jeer, gibe, *at*. [ME strike etc., orig. unkn.]

gird′er (g-), n. Beam supporting joists of floor; iron or steel beam for like use; latticed or other compound structure of steel etc. forming span of bridge, roof, etc. [GIRD[1]+-ER[1]]

gir′dle[1] (g-), n., & v.t. 1. Belt or (now usu.) cord used to gird waist; (orig. U.S.) corset; something that surrounds like a ~; part of cut gem dividing crown from base & embraced by the setting; (Anat.) bony supports for upper & lower limbs (*shoulder* or *pectoral*, *pelvic* or *hip*, ~); ring round tree made by removal of bark. 2. v.t. Surround with ~ (often *about*, *in*, *round*); kill (tree) or make it more fruitful by girdling. [OE *gyrdel*, OHG *gurtil*, ON *gyrthill* (GIRD[1], -LE(1))]

‖ **gir′dle**[2] (g-), n. (Sc. & north.). Circular iron plate placed over fire for toasting cakes; ~-*cake*, so made. [var. of GRIDDLE]

girl (g-), n. Female child, unmarried woman, (*old* ~, affectionate or disrespectful address or description for woman, mare, etc.; *the* ~s, daughters of family, married or not); maidservant; man's sweetheart (often *best* ~); female (~ *friend*); ~ *guides*, organization parallel to *boy* SCOUT. Hence ~'HOOD, ~'ie [-Y[3]], nn., ~'ISH[1] a., ~'ishLY[2] adv., ~'ishNESS n., (g-). [ME *gurle*, *girle*, *gerle*, perh. cogn. w. LG *gör* child]

Giron′dist, n. & a. (Member) of moderate republican party in French assembly 1791–3; (person) of such views. [f. F *Girondiste* (*Gironde* French department from which leaders of party came)]

girt[1] (g-), n., & v.t. 1. Measurement across or round surface that is not flat, with account taken of elevations & depressions. 2. v.t. Measure ~ of; (of trees etc.) measure (so much) in ~. [var. of GIRTH]

girt[2]. See GIRD[1].

girth (g-), n., & v.t. & i. 1. Leather or cloth band tightened round body of horse etc. to secure saddle etc.; measurement round any more or less cylindrical thing; ~-*web*, woven material for ~s. 2. vb. Surround; encircle (horse etc.), secure (saddle etc.), with ~; measure (so much) in ~. [ME, f. ON *gjorth*, Goth. *gairda* f. Gmc *gerda*, cogn. w. GARTH, GIRD[1]]

gist (j-), n. Real ground or point, sub-

stance or pith of a matter. [OF, 3rd sing. pres. of *gesir* lie f. L *jacēre*]

gitt′ern (g-), n. Gut-stringed instrument, kind of early guitar. [ME, f. OF *guiterne*; cf. CITHERN, GUITAR]

give[1] (g-), v.t. & i. (*gāve*, *gĭv′en*). (General sense) make another the recipient of something in subject's possession or at subject's disposal (with obj. of thing given, & ind. obj. usu. preceding obj. If without *to* & following it if with *to*; in pass., either obj. may become subj., the other being retained without *to* if direct, with or without *to* if indirect. Thus : *I gave him a book*; *I gave £50 to the R.S.P.C.A.*; *I gave it him*; *he was ~n a book*; *a book was ~n him*; *the R.S.P.C.A. was ~n £50*: *£50 was ~n to*, or *~n*, *the R.S.P.C.A.* Corresponding constructions are to be assumed with the various senses unless they are inapplicable or exceptions are mentioned). 1. Bestow gratuitously, hand over as present, confer ownership of with or without actual delivery, render (benefit etc.) without payment, (abs.) bestow alms or donations (*to*); confer, grant, (favour, honour, etc.); accord (one's *heart*, affection, confidence); (of God etc.) grant (faculty etc., or *to* be or do; ~ *me*, in imperat., I prefer or admire, as ~ *me the good old times*); bequeath; sanction marriage of (daughter etc.; usu. *in marriage*). 2. Deliver, hand over, without reference to ownership, put (food etc.) before one, (~ MITTEN, SACK[1], BOOT[1], cf. GET), administer (medicine); deliver (message, love, compliments, etc.); commit, consign, entrust, (~ *into custody* or *in* CHARGE[1]); pledge, assign as guarantee, (one's *word*, *honour*, etc.). 3. Make over in exchange or payment, pay, sell *for* price, (~ *as good as one gets*), retort adequately in words or blows; so ~ *a* ROLAND *for an Oliver*; ~ *one his due*, admit any merits he may have; *would* ~ *the world*, one's *ears*, make any sacrifice *to* secure or *for* something, or *if*). 4. Devote, dedicate, addict, (*gave his life to it*; *much* ~*n to these pursuits*). 5. Put forth (some action or effort) to affect another or simply (~ *him a kick*; ~ *a jump*, *cry*, etc.; ~ *orders*; ~ person one's *blessing*; ~ *you joy*, prob. orig. with ellipse of *God*, now taken as = *wish* with *I* expressed or omitted ; ~ *the time of day*, say good morning, evening, etc.); deliver (judgement etc.) authoritatively (~ *the case*, or *it*, *for* or *against* person; in cricket, ~ *batsman out* or *not out*); (p.p., of document) dated; provide (ball, party, dinner) as host. 6. Present, offer, expose, hold out, show, (~ person one's *hand*; ~ *a back*, stand to be leapfrogged over; *The Times* ~s *the facts*; ~s *no sign of life*; *thermometer* ~s *80° in the shade*); read, recite, sing, act, perform, (piece etc.). 7. Make partaker of, impart, be source of, (*gave me his sore throat*; *gave its name to the* *battle*; ~ *a piece of* one's *mind*, scold, reproach; ~ *to the world*, publish; ~ person *to understand, know*, etc., inform, assure). **8.** Allot, assign, ascribe, grant, assume, (*he was* ~*n the contract, the name of John, quarters*; *under the* ~*n conditions*; ~*n health, the thing can be done*). **9.** Yield as product or result (*lamps* ~ *a bad light*; *analysis* ~*s the following figures*). **10.** Cause or allow to have (*solitude* ~*s it its only charm*; *gave me much pain*; *this* ~*s him a right to complain*; ~ one*self trouble*, take pains; ~ one*self airs*, be pretentious; *gave myself an hour to get there*; *was* ~*n a rest*). **11.** Collapse, lose firmness, yield to pressure, become relaxed, make room, shrink. **12.** (Of window, passage, etc.) look, lead, (*up*)*on, into*. **13.** (In phrr. with obj.): ‖ ~ *one best* (colloq.), admit his superiority; ~ *birth to*, bring forth (lit. & fig.); ~ *chase*, start in pursuit; ~ *ear*, listen; ~ *ground*, retreat; ~ *it him* etc., administer punishment (often *hot*); ~ *child* etc. *something to cry for*, chastise for causeless crying; ~ *one what for*, sl., punish or scold; ~ *place* (*to*), make room (for), yield precedence (to), be superseded (by); ~ *rise to*, occasion; ~ *TONGUE*; ~ *way*, retire, fail to resist, be superseded by (*to*), be dislodged, break down, make concessions, abandon oneself *to* grief etc., fall in price, begin to row or row harder. **14.** (With advv.); ~ *away*, alienate by gift, hand over (bride) to bridegroom, betray or expose to ridicule or detection (esp. sl. ~ *away the* SHOW²), distribute (prizes); ~ *back*, restore; ~ *forth*, emit, publish, report; ~ *in*, yield, cease fighting or arguing, hand in (document) to proper official, (p.p.) added as supplement; ~ *off*, emit (vapour etc.); ~ *out*, announce, emit, distribute, cease or break down from exhaustion etc., run short; ~ *over*, cease from do*ing*, abandon (habit etc.), desist, hand over (~*n over*, abandoned *to* evil courses etc.); ~ *up*, resign, surrender, part with (~ *up the* GHOST), deliver (fugitive etc.) into hands of pursuers etc., abandon one*self to* a feeling etc., cease to have to do with, cease from effort, (refl. & p.p.) devote or addict *to*, divulge (names of accomplices etc.), pronounce incurable or insoluble, renounce hope of. Hence **giv'ER¹** (g-) n. [OE *giefan*, OS, OHG *geban*, ON *gefa*, Goth. *giban* f. Gmc *gebhan*; initial *g*- due to Scand., as in GET]

give² (g-), n. Yielding to pressure, elasticity, (*there is no* ~ *in a stone floor*); ~ *& take*, mutual concession, compromise, exchange of talk. [f. prec.]

giv'en (g-), a. In vbl senses; ~ *name*, CHRISTIAN name. [p.p. of GIVE¹]

gizz'ard (g-), n. Bird's second stomach for grinding the food mixed in the first with gastric juice; specially muscular stomach of some fish, insects, & molluscs;

fret one's ~, worry; *sticks in* one's ~, is unpalatable (fig.). [ME *giser* f. OF *g(u)iser* f. L *gigeria* cooked entrails of fowl]

gläb'rous, a. (anat. etc.). Free from hair or down, smooth-skinned. [f. L *glaber* + -OUS]

gla'cé (-ah-sā), a. (Of cloth, leather, etc.) smooth, polished; (of fruits) iced, sugared. [F]

gla'cial (-āsial, -āshīal, -āshī), a. Of ice, icy; (Chem.) crystallized; (Geol.) characterized, produced, by the presence or agency of ice (~ *epoch, era, period*, when northern hemisphere was mostly covered with ice-sheet). Hence ~LY² adv. [f. F, or L *glacialis* (*glacies* ice, -AL)]

gla'ciated (-sǐ-, -shǐ-), a. Marked or polished by ice-action; covered with glaciers or ice-sheet. So **glācia'TION** n. [p.p. of *glaciate* f. L *glaciare* freeze, -ATE³]

gla'cier, n. Slowly moving river or mass of ice formed by accumulation of snow on high ground. Hence ~ED² (-erd) a. [F (*glace* ice)]

gla'cis (or *glahsē*), n. Bank sloping down from fort, on which attackers are exposed to fire. [F, orig. = slippery place (OF *glacier* to slip)]

glad, a., & v.t. (-dd-). **1.** Pleased (pred. only; *I am* ~, ~ *of it*, ~ *to hear it*, ~ *that it is so*, ~ *it is so, shall be* ~ *to come* etc.; iron., *should be* ~ *to know*); (of looks, feelings, etc.) marked by, filled with, expressing, joy; (of news or events) giving joy; (of nature etc.) bright, beautiful; *the* ~ *eye* (sl.), amorous or festive glance; ~ *hand* (orig. U.S.), the hand of welcome; ~ *rags* (sl.), Sunday or dress clothes; hence ~d'EN² v.t., ~'LY² adv., ~'NESS n., (poet.) ~'SOME a., ~'SOMELY² adv., ~'SOMENESS n. **2.** v.t. (arch.). Make ~. [OE *glæd*, OS *glad*, ON *glathr*, OHG *glat* smooth (the orig. sense), cogn. w. L *glaber*]

gläde, n. Clear open space or passage between forest trees. [orig. unkn.]

glad'iātor, n. Man trained to fight with sword or other weapon at ancient Roman shows; political etc. champion in argument, controversialist. So **glädiatōr'IAL** a. [L (*gladius* sword)]

glädiōl'us (or *gladī'o-*), n. (pl. -ī, -*luses*). Iridaceous plant with sword-shaped leaves & bright flower-spikes. [L, dim. of *gladius* sword]

Glad'stone, n. & a. ~ (*bag*), kind of light portmanteau; ~ *claret*, of cheap kinds that became common by Gladstone's reduction of duty 1860. [W.E. ~, statesman d. 1898]

glair, n., & v.t. **1.** White of egg; kinds of adhesive preparation made from it; any similar viscid substance; hence ~'EOUS, ~'Y² etc. aa. **2.** v.t. Smear with ~. [ME, f. OF *glaire*, ult. f. L *clara* fem. of *clarus* CLEAR]

glaive, n. (arch. & poet.). Broadsword, sword. [ME, OF, app. f. L *gladius* sword]

glam'our (*-er*), n., & v.t. **1.** Magic, enchantment, (*cast a ~ over*, enchant); delusive or alluring beauty or charm; hence **glâm'orous** a. **2.** v.t. Affect with ~, bewitch, enchant. [18th c. var. of GRAMMAR in sense GRAMARYE]

glance¹ (-ah-), v.i. & t., & n. **1.** (Of weapon) glide off object instead of striking it full (often *aside, off*); (of talk or talker) pass quickly *over*, glide *off* or *from*, subject; ~ *at*, make passing & usu. sarcastic allusion to; (of bright object or light) flash, dart, gleam; (of eye) cast momentary look, flash, (~ *at*, give brief look at); ~ *over*, read cursorily; ~ *down, up*, etc.; ~ one's *eye*, direct it *at, over*, etc.; hence **glan'cing**LY² (-ah-) adv. **2.** n. Swift oblique movement or impact, (Cricket) stroke with bat's face turned slantwise to ball; (sudden movement producing flash or gleam; brief look (*at, into, over*, etc.). [15 c. *glence* etc. prob. a nasalized form of obs. *glace* in same sense, f. OF *glacier* slip]

glance² (-ah-), n. Lustrous ore (*copper ~, native copper sulphide; lead ~*, GALENA). [f. G *glanz* lustre]

glând¹, n. (Physiol.) simple or complex organ composed of nucleated cells secreting constituents of the blood for use or ejection; (Bot.) secreting cell or group of cells on surface of plant-structure. So (see -UL-) **glân'dULE** n., **glân'dULAR¹**, ~uliF'EROUS, **glân'dULOSE¹** (Bot.), **glân'dULOUS**, ~LESS, aa. [f. F *glande* f. OF *glandre* f. L *glandula* (*glans -dis* acorn, -ULE)]

glând², n. (mech.). Sleeve used to press a packing tight on a piston. [orig. unkn.]

glân'der|s (-z), n. pl. Contagious horse-disease with swellings below jaw & mucous discharge from nostrils; the same communicated to man. Hence ~ED² (*-erd*),~ous, aa. [f. OF *glandre* see GLAND¹]

glândif'erous, a. Bearing acorns. [f. L *glandifer* (GLAND¹, -FEROUS)]

glân'difôrm, a. Acorn-shaped; like gland. [GLAND¹, -FORM]

glâr|e, v.i. & t., & n. **1.** Shine dazzlingly or disagreeably; be over-conspicuous or obtrusive, whence ~'ingLY² adv., ~'ingNESS n.; look fixedly or fiercely (*at, upon*); express (hate, defiance) by look. **2.** n. Strong fierce light, oppressive unrelieved sunshine; tawdry brilliance; fierce or fixed look; hence ~'Y² a. [ME, = MDu. & MLG *glaren*]

glass¹ (-ah-), n. **1.** Substance, usu. transparent, lustrous, hard, & brittle, made by fusing sand with soda or potash or both & other ingredients (CROWN¹, FLINT, PLATE, WATER¹, ~); substances of similar properties or composition, as ~ *of antimony*, vitreous oxy-sulphide fused. **2.** ~ utensils, ornaments, windows, greenhouses; ~ vessel esp. for drinking, amount of liquid contained in this, drink (*a friendly ~, fond of his ~; has had a ~ too much*,

is rather drunk); sand-~, hour-~; carriage window; plate of ~ covering picture; glazed frame for plants; looking-~; eye-~, (pl.) pair of spectacles; lens; ~ disc covering watch-face; telescope, spy-~, field-~, opera-~, microscope; barometer, weather-~. **3.** ~*-blower*, one who blows & shapes ~; ~ *case*, chiefly of ~ for exhibiting or protecting objects; ~*-cloth*, linen cloth for drying ~es, cloth covered with powdered ~ like ~-paper; ~ *cloth*, woven fabric of fine-spun ~; ~*-cutter*, workman, tool, cutting ~; ~*-culture*, of plants under ~; ~*-dust*, powdered ~ for polishing; ~ *eye*, false eye of ~, kind of blindness in horses; ~*'house*, building where ~ is made, greenhouse, ~*-roofed* photographing-room, ‖(sl.) military prison; ~*-paper*, covered with ~-dust; ~ *snake*, snake-like lizard of Southern U.S., with very brittle tail; ~*'ware*, articles made of ~; ~ *wool*, ~ in form of fine fibres for packing & insulation; ~*'wort*, kinds of plant formerly used in ~-making. Hence ~*'ful*(2) n., ~*'less* a. [OE *glæs*, OS, OHG *glas* f. WG *glas*]

glass² (-ah-), v.t. Fit with glass, glaze, (rare); enclose in glass (rare); make (the eye) glassy (rare); mirror, occasion reflection of (often refl., as *trees ~ themselves in the lake*); ‖~*ing-jack*, machine used in dressing leather. [f. prec., cf. earlier GLAZE]

glass'|y̆ (-ah-), a. Having properties of, resembling, glass; (of eye etc.) lacking fire, dull, fixed; (of water) lustrous & transparent, or smooth, as glass (so ~*y calm, surface*, etc.). Hence ~ILY² adv., ~INESS n. [-Y²]

Glâswē'gian (-z-), a. & n. (Inhabitant) of Glasgow. [perh. on GALWEGIAN]

Glaub'er's salt(s) (glaw-, glow-), n. Crystalline (hydrated) sodium sulphate. [J. R. *Glauber*, German chemist (d. 1668)]

glaucōm'a, n. An eye-disease with tension of the globe & gradual loss of sight. Hence ~TOUS a. [f. L f. Gk *glaukōma* f. *glaukos* (foll.)]

glauc'ous, a. (esp. nat. hist.). Of dull greyish green or blue; (Bot.) covered with bloom as of grapes. [f. L f. Gk *glaukos* + -OUS]

glāze, v.t. & i., & n. **1.** Fit (window, picture) with glass, furnish (building) with glass windows (~ *in*, enclose thus). **2.** Cover (pottery etc.) with vitreous substance fixed by fusion (n., this substance, smooth surface resulting); fix (paint) *on* pottery thus; overlay (cloth, leather, pastry, etc.) with smooth lustrous coating (n., this coating, surface produced). **3.** Cover (eye) with a film (n., filmy look). **4.** Cover (painted surface) with thin coat of different transparent colour to modify tone (n., this coat). **5.** Give glassy surface to, e.g. by rubbing (n., polished look); become glassy (esp. of eyes); ~d *frost*,

= SILVER[1] *thaw.* Hence glāz'ER[1](1, 2) n., glāz'Y[2] a. [ME *glasen* (GLASS[1])]

glā'zier (-zher, -zier), n. One whose trade is to glaze windows etc. Hence glā'ziERY (2) n. [GLASS[1]; see -IER]

glāz'ing, n. In vbl senses also: windows; material used to produce glaze. [-ING[1]]

gleam, n., & v.i. 1. Subdued or transient light; faint, temporary, or intermittent show of some quality etc. (*an occasional ~ of humour; not a ~ of hope*); hence ~'Y[2] a. 2. v.i. Emit ~s, shine with subdued or interrupted brightness. [OE *glǣm*, cogn. w. OS *glimo*, MHG *glīmen* shine, OHG *gleimō* glow-worm, WG *glaim-]

glean, v.i. & t. Gather ears of corn left by reapers, gather (such remains); strip (field etc.) thus; collect in small quantities, scrape together, (news, facts, etc.). Hence ~'ER[1], ~'ING[1](1, 2), nn. [ME, f. OF *glener* f. LL *glennare*, of Celt. orig.]

glēbe, n. (Poet.) earth, land, a field; portion of land going with clergyman's benefice. [ME, f. L *gleba* clod, soil]

glee, n. 1. Musical composition for three or more (prop. adult male) voices, one to each part, set to words grave or gay, often with contrasted movements & prop. without accompaniment. 2. Mirth, lively & manifest delight, whence ~'FUL, ~'SOME, aa., ~'fullY[2] adv. [OE *glīw*, *glēo*, ON *glý*]

gleet, n. Thin morbid discharge from wound, ulcer, etc. (rare), or from the urethra. Hence ~'Y[2] a. [ME *glet* f. OF *glette* slime]

glen, n. Narrow valley. [f. Gael. *gleann*]

glen'doveer, n. Beautiful sprite of kind represented by Southey as occurring in Hindu myths. [altered f. *grandouver* in F travel-book perh. f. Skr. *gandharva* semi-divine spirit]

glēngā'rry (-n-g-), n. Kind of Highland cap. [place]

glen'oid, a. (anat.). ~ *cavity, fossa, surface,* shallow cavity on bone (esp. scapula & temporal bone) receiving projection of other bone to form joint. [f. Gk *glēnoeidēs* (*glēnē* socket, -OID)]

glib, a. & adv. (-bb-). 1. (Of surface etc.) smooth, offering no resistance, (of movement) unimpeded, easy, (rare) (of speaker, speech, etc.) fluent, ready, more voluble than sincere or thoughtful; hence ~'LY[2] adv., ~'NESS n. 2. adv. Volubly (now rare). [rel. to obs. *glibbery* = MLG *glibberich*, Du. *-ig*, perh. of imit. orig.]

glid|e, v.i. & t., & n. 1. Pass, change place, by smooth continuous movement (of liquid, ship, bird, carriage, snake, person skating, etc.); fly without engine (~'ER[1](2) n., engineless aeroplane); go quietly or stealthily; (of time etc.) pass gently & imperceptibly; pass gradually, shade off insensibly, *into*; cause to ~e (*light airs ~ed her on her course*); hence ~'ingLY[2] adv. 2. n. Act of ~ing (Mus.)

succession of sounds made in passing from one note to another without silencing voice or instrument; (Phon.) gradually changing sound made in passing from one position of speech organs to another. [OE, OS *glīdan*, OHG *glītan*]

glim, n. (sl.). Light, candle, lantern, (DOUSE *the~*). [in 17th c. cant perh. short. f. GLIMMER or GLIMPSE, but cf. MDu., MHG *glimmen*]

glimm'er, v.i., & n. 1. Shine faintly or intermittently. 2. n. (Also ~ING[1] n.) feeble or wavering light, faint gleam of hope etc., glimpse, half view. [ME, cogn. w. MHG, Du. *glimmeren*, (cf. Sw. *glimra*) f. WG *glim-*, *glaim-* (GLEAM)]

glimpse, n., & v.t. & i. 1. Faint & transient appearance, momentary or imperfect view of, (*the ~s of the moon,* the earth by night, sublunary affairs). 2. vb. Catch ~ of, see faintly or partly; (poet.) appear faintly, dawn. [ME *glimse*, corresp. to MHG *glimsen* f. WG *glimisōjan* (prec.)]

glint, v.i. & t., & n. Flash, glitter, sparkle, (v. & n.); make flash, reflect, (light). [n. f. vb, alt. of ME *glent* of Scand. orig., cf. Sw. *glänta, glinta*]

glissade (-ahd, -ād), n., & v.i. (mountaineering). Slide (n. & v.) down steep slope esp. of ice or snow usu. on the feet with support of ice-axe etc. [vb f. n., F (*glisser* slip, -ADE)]

glissé (glisā'), n. A sliding step in ballet in which the flat of the foot is freq. used (also *pas ~*). [F]

glis'ten (-isn), v.i., & n. Shine fitfully; glitter, sparkle, (v. & n.). [n. f. vb, OE *glisnian* (*glisian* shine, -EN[6])]

glis'ter, v.i., & n., (arch.). Sparkle, glitter. [ME, f. MLG *glistern*, MDu. *-eren*, cogn. w. prec.]

glitt'er, v.i., & n. (Shine with) brilliant tremulous light, gleam, sparkle; be showy or splendid (*with* jewels etc.). [ME, f. ON *glitra* f. Gmc *glit-*]

gloam'ing, n. Evening twilight. [OE *glōmung* (*glōm* twilight cogn. w. GLOW, -ING[1])]

gloat, v.i. Feast eyes or mind lustfully, avariciously, malignantly, etc., (*up*)*on* or *over.* Hence ~'ingLY[2] adv. [orig. unkn., but perh. cogn. w. ON *glotta* grin, MHG *glotzen* stare]

globe, n., & v.t. & i. 1. Spherical body; *the* earth; planet, star, sun; spherical chart of (*terrestrial ~*) the earth or (*celestial ~*) the constellations (*use of the ~s,* arch., teaching of geography & astronomy by these); golden orb as emblem of sovereignty; (Anat.) eyeball; approximately spherical glass vessel, esp. lampshade or fishbowl; ~*-fish,* able to inflate itself into globular form; ~*-flower,* ranunculaceous plant with round yellow flowers; ~ *lightning,* = FIRE[1]-*ball*; ~*-trotter, -trotting,* hurried traveller, travelling, through foreign countries for sightseeing; so glōb'AL (1) a. world-wide, embracing the totality of a group of items, categories, etc., **glōb′oID** a. & n., **globose′**[1] a., **globōs′ITY** n. 2. vb. Make (usu. in pass.), or become, globular. [F, f. L *globus*]

glŏb′ūlar, a. Globe-shaped, spherical; composed of globules. Hence ~ITY (-ă′r°) n., ~LY[2] adv. [foll., -AR[1], & see -UL-]

glŏb′ūle, n. Small globe or round particle, drop, pill. [f. F, or L *globulus* (GLOBE, -ULE)]

glŏb′ūlin, n. Protein found usu. associated with albumen in animal tissues. [prec., -IN]

glochid′iate (-k-), a. (bot.). Barbed at tip. [f. Gk *glōkhidion* (*glōkhis* arrowhead), -ATE[2]]

glŏck′enspiel (-pēl), n. Musical instrument consisting of a series of metal bars struck by a hammer (earlier, a kind of CARILLON). [G, = bell-play]

glŏm′erate, a. (bot., anat.). Compactly clustered. [L *glomerare* (*glomus* -*eris* ball), -ATE[2]]

glŏm′erule (-ōōl), n. Clustered flower-head; cluster of small organisms, tissues, blood-vessels, etc. [f. mod. L *glomerulus* (L *glomus* see prec., -ULE)]

glōōm[1], n. Darkness, obscurity; melancholy, despondency. [orig. f. foll.; sense 'darkness' perh. back form. f. GLOOMY]

glōōm[2], v.i. & t. Look sullen, frown, be melancholy; (of sky etc.) lour, be dull or threatening; appear darkly or obscurely; cover with gloom, make dark or dismal. [ME *gloume* of unkn. orig.; cf. GLUM]

glōōm′|y̆, a. Dark, unlighted; depressed, sullen; dismal, depressing. Hence ~ILY[2] adv., ~INESS n. [perh. f. prec. + -Y[2]]

glōr′ia, n. (Short for) G~ *Patri*, doxology *Glory be to the Father* etc., G~ *tibi*, response *Glory be to thee* etc., or G~ *in excelsis*, hymn *Glory be to God on high*; aureole. [L, = glory]

glōr′i|fy̆, v.t. Make glorious, exalt to the glory of heaven; invest with radiance; transform into something more splendid, invest (common or inferior thing) with charm or beauty (*nothing more than a* ~*fied*, or ~*fication of a, cottage*); extol, laud. Hence ~FICA′TION n. [ME, f. OF *glorifier* f. LL *glorificare* (*glorificus* f. L *gloria* glory, -FIC)]

glōr′iōle, n. Aureole, halo. [F, f. L *gloriola* dim. of *gloria* glory]

glōr′ious, a. Possessing glory, illustrious; conferring glory, honourable; splendid, magnificent, intensely delightful, (*a* ~ *view, day*; also joc., as ~ *fun*; & iron., as *the* ~ *uncertainty of cricket, a* ~ *muddle*; (colloq.) ecstatically happy with drink. Hence ~LY[2] adv. [ME, f. AF f. L *gloriosus* (foll., -OSE[1])]

glōr′y̆[1], n. Exalted renown, honourable fame; subject for boasting, special distinction, ornament, pride; adoring praise & thanksgiving (~ *be!* or ~ *!*, vulgar excl. of surprise or delight); re-

splendent majesty, beauty, or magnificence, effulgence of heavenly light, imagined unearthly beauty; bliss & splendour of heaven (*go to* ~, die; *send to* ~, joc., kill); state of exaltation, prosperity, etc. (*is in his* ~); circle of light round head or figure of deity or saint, aureole, halo; ~*hole* (sl.), untidy room, drawer, or receptacle. [ME, f. L *gloria*]

glōr′y̆[2], v.i. Exult, pride oneself, *in* thing or *doing, to* do. Hence ~INGLY[2] adv. [ME, f. L *gloriari* boast (*gloria* glory)]

glŏss[1], n., & v.t. & i. 1. Word inserted between lines or in margin to explain word in text; comment, explanation, interpretation, paraphrase; misrepresentation of another's words; glossary, interlinear translation, or set of notes. 2. vb. Insert ~es in (text etc.); write ~es; make comments esp. of unfavourable sort; read different sense into, explain away. [16th c. alt. of GLOZE after L *glossa*]

glŏss[2], n., & v.t. 1. Superficial lustre; deceptive appearance, fair outside; hence ~Y[2] a., ~ILY[2] adv., ~INESS n. 2. v.t. Make ~y; give specious appearance to (often *over*). [vb f. n.; 16th c. of unkn. orig.; cf. obs. Du. *gloos*, Icel. *glossi*, nn., glow, blaze]

glŏss′al, a. (anat.). Of the tongue, lingual. [f. Gk *glōssa* tongue + -AL]

glŏss′ar|y̆, n. Collection of glosses; list & explanations of abstruse, obsolete, dialectal, or technical terms, partial dictionary. Hence **glōssār′IAL** a., ~IST(1) n. [f. L *glossarium* (*glossa* GLOSS[1], -ARY[1])]

glŏssāt′or, n. Commentator, esp. medieval commentator on Civil & Canon Law. [med. L (*glossare* f. *glossa* GLOSS[1], -OR)]

glŏss(o)-, comb. form of Gk *glōssa* tongue, as *gloss′(o)-epiglŏtt′ic* of tongue & epiglottis, *glossIT′IS*; also of GLOSS[1], as *glossŏg′rapher* commentator, *glossŏl′ogy* terminology.

glŏtt′|is, n. Opening at upper part of windpipe & between vocal chords, affecting modulation of voice by contracting or dilating. Hence ~AL (~*al stop*, sound produced by the sudden explosive release of breath from behind the closed ~is), ~IC, aa. [Gk *glōttis* (*glōtta* var. of *glōssa* tongue)]

glove (-ŭv), n., & v.t. 1. Covering of leather, cotton, silk, wool, or formerly steel, for the hand, usu. with separated fingers (*throw down, take up, the* ~, make, accept, challenge; *fit like a* ~, exactly; HAND[1] *in or &* ~); (also *boxing-*~) padded ~ for boxing (*take off, without*, etc., *the* ~s, of arguing or contending in earnest, mercilessly, etc.); ~*fight*, fight with boxing-~s; ~*sponge*, in shape of ~; ~*stretcher*, instrument for enlarging ~*fingers*; hence ~*LESS* (-ŭvl-) a., **glo′VER**[1] (3) (-ŭv-) n. 2. v.t. Provide with ~s. [OE *glōf*, ON *glófi*, perh. f. Gmc *galōfō* (*ga-* = *y*-, cf. Goth. *lōfa* hand)]

glow (-ō), v.i., & n. 1. Be heated to

incandescence, throw out light & heat without flame; shine like thing intensely heated; show warm colour; burn with bodily heat or emotional fervour (with); ∼-worm, coleopterous insect with winged male & wingless female, the latter emitting green light at tail; hence ∼'ingLY² adv. 2. n. ∼ing state (in a ∼, all of a ∼, hot or flushed); brightness & warmth of colour, e.g. red of cheeks; ardour, passion; ∼-lamp, with carbon etc. incandescent under electric current. [OE glówan, OS glójan, OHG gluoen, ON glóa]

glower (-owr), v.i. Stare, scowl, (usu. at). Hence ∼'ingLY² adv. [orig. uncert.; perh. var. of 14th c. glore (Sc. dial.), or f. obs. (ME) glow stare +-ER⁵]

glöxin'ia, n. American tropical plant with large bell flowers of various colours. [B. P. Gloxin botanist c. 1785 +-IA¹]

glöze, v.i. & t. ‖ Comment (up)on (arch.); palliate, explain away, extenuate, (usu. over); talk speciously, use fair words, fawn. Hence glōz'ingLY² adv. [ME, f. OF gloser f. glose f. L f. Gk glōssa (foreign) tongue or word; cf. GLOSS¹]

glucin'um (-ōōs-), n. White metal obtained from beryl, beryllium. [f. Gk glukus sweet (some compds of it being sweet)]

glu'cōse (glōō-), n. (chem.). Grape-sugar or dextrose, commercially prepared from starch and other carbohydrates by hydrolysis. Hence glucōs'IC a., glu'cosIDE n., (glōō-). [F, f. Gk gleukos, see -OSE²]

glue (-ōō), n., & v.t. 1. Hard brittle brownish gelatin made by boiling hides & bones & used warm for uniting substances; adhesive or viscous substance got from other sources (fish, vegetable, casein, resin, ∼); ∼-pot, with outer coat holding water to heat ∼; hence ∼'Y² (glōō'ĭ) a. 2. v.t. (part. gluing). Fasten or join (as) with ∼; attach tightly or closely (eye, ear, ∼d to the keyhole). [ME, f. OF glu f. LL glus glutis]

glŭm, a. Sullen, looking dejected or displeased. Hence ∼'LY² adv., ∼'NESS n. [rel. to dial. glum vb frown, var. of gloume GLOOM²]

glume (-ōōm), n. (bot.). Chafflike bract in inflorescence of grasses & sedges; husk of grain. Hence glumA'CEOUS, glumOSE'¹, aa., (-ōōm-). [f. L gluma]

glŭt, v.t. (-tt-), & n. 1. Feed (person, stomach) or indulge (appetite, desire) to the full, overload with food (lit. or fig.), satiate, cloy; choke up, fill to excess; overstock (market) with goods. 2. n. Full indulgence, one's fill, surfeit; supply exceeding demand (a ∼ in the market). [n. f. vb ME f. OF gloutir swallow f. L gluttire]

glu'tĕn (glōō-), n. Sticky substance, whence ∼inIZE(3) v.t., ∼inOUS a., ∼-inOUSLY² adv.,∼inOS'ITY n., (-ōō-); viscid animal secretion; nitrogenous part of

flour remaining as viscid substance when starch is washed out. [F, or f. L, genit. -inis, glue]

glŭtt'on, n. Excessive eater, gormandizer; greedy reader of books, person with great appetite for work; voracious animal of weasel kind but larger, wolverene. Hence or cogn. ∼IZE(2) v.i., ∼ous a., ∼ousLY² adv.,∼Y¹ n. [ME, f. OF gluton, -un f. L gluttonem nom. -o (glutire swallow)]

glý'cerināte, v.t. Treat with glycerine (esp. vaccine lymph). [-ATE³]

glý'cer|ine (-ēn), -in, n. Colourless sweet liquid got from any fatty substance, liquid or solid, by saponification, used as ointment, as vehicle for drugs, in explosives, etc. Hence glýcĕ'rIC a. (chem.), ∼ATE¹ (3), ∼IDE, ∼YL, nn., ∼o- comb. form. [f. F -ine f. Gk glukeros sweet, -IN]

glý'cerŏl, n. (chem.). (Name preferred in scientific use for) glycerine. [prec., -OL(1)]

glý'co-, comb. form, irreg. for glycy-, of Gk glukus sweet, also used in names of chem. compounds containing glycerol or other substance in glyc-.

glýc'ogĕn, n., glýcogĕn'ĭc, a., (chem.). (Substance) producing glucose in animal tissues. So glýcoGEN'ESIS n. [prec., -GEN(1)]

glýc'ŏl, n. Any aliphatic dihydric alcohol, esp. ethylene glycol. Hence glýcŏl(l)'IC a. [GLYCO-, -OL(1)]

glýcŏn'ic, a. & n. (Gk & L pros.). (Line, metre) normally of the form (⁻ ᵕᵕ⁻ᵕᵕ⁻ᵛ). [Glukōn Gk poet, -IC]

glýcosūr'|ia, n. (path.). Diseased condition with sugar in the urine. Hence ∼IC a. [F glycose GLUCOSE, Gk ouron urine, -IA¹]

glýph'ograph (-ahf), glýphŏg'raphў, nn. (Plate or copy, -ph, made by) electrotype process giving raised copy of engraved plate for use in letterpress printing (-y). So glýph'ograph (-ahf) v.t. & i., glýphŏg'RAPHER n., glýphoGRAPH'IC a. [f. Gk gluphē carving (gluphō carve), -GRAPHY]

glýp'tic, a. Of carving esp. on precious stones. [f. Gk gluptikos (gluphō carve, -IC]

glýp'todŏn, n. Extinct S.-Amer. quadruped allied to armadillos with fluted teeth. [f. Gk gluptos carved (as prec.) + odous -ontos tooth]

glýptŏg'raphў, n. Art & science of gem-engraving. [as prec., -GRAPHY]

*G-man, n. (sl.). Federal criminal investigation officer. [Government]

gnarled (närld), gnärl'ў (n-), aa. (Of tree; & fig.) covered with protuberances, twisted, rugged. [var. of obs. knurled, f. knurl knob (=MLG, MDu., MHG knorre), -ED², -Y²]

gnăsh (n-), v.i. & t. (Of teeth) strike together; grind the teeth, grind (the teeth). [var. of (north.) ME gnast, rel. to ON gnastan (imit.)]

gnăt (n-), n. Small two-winged fly of

which female has blood-sucking proboscis; (as type) insignificant annoyance, tiny thing, (*strain at* ~, be scrupulous about trifles). [OE *gnætt*, cogn. w. LG *gnatte*, G dial. *gnatze*]

gnath'ic (n-), a. Of jaws. [Gk *gnathos* jaw, -IC]

gnaw (n-), v.t. & i. (p.p. ~*ed*, ~*n*). Bite persistently, wear away thus (often *away, off, in two*, etc.; also intr. with *at, into*); (of destructive agents, pain, etc.) corrode, waste away, consume, torture. Hence ~'ingLY[2] adv. [OE, OS, OHG *gnagan*, ON *gnaga*]

gneiss (gnīs, nīs), n. (geol.). Laminated rock of quartz, feldspar, & mica. Hence ~'IC, ~'OID, ~'OSE[1], ~'Y[2], aa. [G]

gnōm'ē̆[1] (n-; *also* nŏm), n. Maxim, aphorism. [f. Gk *gnōmē* (*gignōskō* know)]

gnome[2] (nŏm), n. Diminutive spirit of subterranean race guarding treasures of earth (cf. SYLPH, SALAMANDER, NYMPH), goblin, dwarf. Hence **gnōm'ISH**[1] (n-) a. [F, f. mod. L *gnomus* (Paracelsus), perh. irreg. or erron. for *genomos* (Gk *gē* earth, *-nomos* dwelling)]

gnōm'ic (n-), a. Of, consisting of, using, GNOME[1]'s, sententious; (Gram.) ~ *aorist*, used without past sense to express a general truth, e.g. *men were deceivers ever*. [also 17th c. *-ical* f. LL f. Gk *gnōmikos* (GNOME[1], -IC)]

gnōm'on (n-), n. Pillar, rod, pin or plate of sundial, showing time by its shadow on marked surface; column etc. used in observing sun's meridian altitude; (Geom.) part of parallelogram left when similar one has been taken from its corner. Hence **gnōmŏn'IC** (n-) a. [F, or L f. Gk *gnōmōn* indicator etc. (*gignōskō* know)]

gnōs'is (n-), n. Knowledge of spiritual mysteries; Gnosticism. [Gk (-ō-), = knowledge, as prec.]

gnōs'tic (n-), a. & n. **1.** Relating to knowledge, cognitive; having esoteric spiritual knowledge; of the Gnostics, occult, mystic. **2.** n. (usu. pl.; *G*~) early Christian heretic(s) claiming GNOSIS, whence ~ISM(3) n., ~IZE(2, 3, 4) v.i. & t., (n-). [f. LL f. Gk *gnōstikos* (as prec., -IC)]

gnu (nū), n. Oxlike antelope. [Hottentot]

gō[1], v.i. & t. (*went, gone* pr. gawn, gŏn; 2nd sing. *gŏest*, 3rd *goes* pr. gŏz & arch. *gŏeth*). **1.** Start, depart, move, continue moving, with self-originated or imparted motion, from some place, position, time, etc. (often not specified because obvious, whereas the goal etc. is always specified if it matters; cf. COME). **2.** Journey, travel, proceed, progress, (*going strong*, with vigour; *he will go far*, reach distinction; *go easy, straight; go west*, sl., be killed or die; *go the* PACE; *went miles round; go a walk, journey, voyage; go the same, the shortest, way*). **3.** (Of line etc.) lie, point, lie certain direction. **4.** Be guided *by*, act in harmony *with*, judge or

act *upon*, (*a good rule to go by*; *have nothing to go upon*; *always goes with his party*; *promotion goes by favour*; *go with tide* or *times*, do as others do). **5.** Be habitually in specified state (*go hungry, armed, in rags, in fear of* one's *life*; *six months* etc. *gone with child*, having spent that time in gestation). **6.** Be moving, acting, working, etc. (*Who goes there?*, sentry's challenge; *a going concern*, business in working order; *clock does not go, goes well; tongue goes nineteen to the* DOZEN). **7.** Make specified motion (*go like this with your left foot*). **8.** (Of bell, striking clock or hour, gun, etc.; also with interjections of sound as *go bang, crack*) sound (*go phut*, sl., collapse). **9.** (Of time) pass, elapse. **10.** Be current (*the sovereign went anywhere; the story goes*, it is said); be known *by, under, the name of*; be on the average (*is a good actor as actors go nowadays*). **11.** (Of document etc.) run, have specified tenor. **12.** (Of verse, song) be rhythmical, be adaptable *to* a tune. **13.** (Of events) turn out *well, ill,* HARD, etc., (of election etc.) issue *for* or *against*, (of constituency, politician, voter) take certain course or views (*Liverpool went Labour; America went dry*, adopted prohibition of intoxicants; *case goes by default*, takes its course against absent party; *dinner, play, went well*, succeeded; *goes without* SAYING). **14.** Begin motion (*Go!*, starter's word in race: HERE *goes!*). **15.** Get away *free, unpunished*, etc. **16.** Be sold (*go cheap, for 2/6*, etc.; *going!, gone!*, auctioneer's announcement that bidding is almost, quite, closed). **17.** (Of money) be spent (often *in* books etc.) **18.** Be relinquished, abolished, or lost (*Greek, the carriage, must go; my sight, our trade, is going; next wicket went for nothing*). **19.** Die (esp. in p.p.; & in many phrr., as *go the way of all the earth* or pop. *of all flesh, to a better world, to* one's *account* or *own place, aloft, off the hooks*, etc.). **20.** Fail, give way, succumb, break down, crack. **21.** Make way *to, towards, into*, etc. (*go to Jericho,* || *Bath, blazes, hell*, etc., be off out of speaker's presence; *go to Canossa*, humble oneself after recalcitrance, w. ref. to Emperor Henry IV in 1077; *go to the* DEVIL[1]; *which way goes to Bristol; go to a ball, to church, market*, etc., attend it; *go to school*, get instruction; *go to the bar, to sea*, become barrister, sailor; *go on the stage, the streets*, become actor, prostitute; *go to* STOOL). **22.** Proceed to do (*went to find him*), and do (esp. colloq. = be so foolish as to do; also vulg. *have been & gone & done it*, made a blunder etc.), (*a-*)*doing, on* pilgrimage, an errand, spree, etc. **23.** Act as bail (*for* person: also abs. in parenthesis *I'll go bail*, I assure you). **24.** Have recourse, refer, appeal, *to* (|| *go to the* COUNTRY, test opinion by general election; *go to war, work*, etc.: vulg., *would not go to* or *for to*

do it, be so inconsiderate etc. as to).
25. Carry action to certain point (*went
all lengths*; *will go so far as to say*; *will go
as high as £100*, in bidding or offering
price; *go halves* or *shares*, share equally
with, or abs.; *went to great expense,
trouble*, etc.; *go the whole* HOG; *go better* or
one better, outbid or outdo adversary).
26. Penetrate, sink, (*ship went to the
bottom*; *goes to one's heart*, grieves him);
find room, (of number) be capable of
being contained in another either without
remainder or simply, (*will not go into* or
in the basket; *6 into 12 goes twice, into 5
will not go, into 13 goes twice and one over*;
thread too thick to go through needle).
27. Belong *in* receptacle, *on* shelf etc.
28. Pass, be allotted, etc., *to* person (of
prize, victory, inheritance, office, etc.),
be applied *to* purpose, contribute to or
towards result, amount together to (*12
inches go to the foot*), tend *to show* etc.
29. Reach, extend, (*the difference goes
deep*; *as, so, far as it goes*, caution against
taking statement too widely; *goes a long
etc. way*, has great etc. effect *towards*,
also of food, money, etc., lasts long etc.,
buys much etc.). 30. Pass into certain
condition (*go brown, blind, mad, to seed*;
go hot & cold, have accesses of fever or
shame; *go to pieces*, break up). 31. v.t.
Bid, declare, as ~ NAP[3], *two spades*. 32.
Phrr.: ~ *native*, (of a white man) adopt
the uncivilized mode of life of the natives
among whom he lives; *go sick* (Mil.), enter
oneself on the sick list; (sl.) *go it*, act
vigorously, furiously, etc., indulge in
dissipation; *go it alone*, act by oneself or
without support; *going fifteen* etc., in one's
fifteenth etc. year; *going to*, about to,
intending to (used as fut. part.); *be gone*,
take oneself off; *gone*, dead (often *dead &
gone*); *gone on* (sl.), infatuated with; *far
gone*, very ill, deeply entangled; *go fetch !*
(order to dog). 33. With prepp.: *go about*,
set to work at; *go at*, attack, take in hand
energetically; *go behind* (decision etc.),
re-examine grounds of; *go for*, go to fetch,
pass or be accounted as *nothing, little*,
etc., be applicable to, strive to attain,
(sl.) attack; *go into*, enter (profession,
Parliament), frequent (society), take part
in, allow oneself to pass into (hysterics
etc.), dress oneself in (mourning etc.),
investigate; *go off* one's HEAD[1]; *go on*,
become chargeable to (parish, relief fund,
etc.); *go over*, inspect details of, rehearse,
retouch; *go through*, discuss in detail,
scrutinize, perform, (ceremony, recitation,
etc.), undergo, (of book) be sold out in (so
many editions); *go up the line* (Mil.), leave
the base for the front; *go with*, be concomitant of, take same view as, match,
follow the drift of; *go without*, not have,
put up with want of. 34. With advv.:
go about, move from place to place,
endeavour *to* do; *go ahead*, proceed without hesitation; *go along with*, = go with;

go back from or *upon* one's *word* etc., fail
to keep it; *go by*, pass; *go down*, sink (of
ship), be continued *to* specified point, fall
before conqueror, be recorded in writing,
be swallowed, find acceptance *with*, ‖ leave
university; *go in*, enter as competitor (*go
in & win !*, form of encouragement),
(Cricket) take or begin innings, (of sun
etc.) be obscured; *go in for*, take as one's
object, pursuit, style, principle, etc.; *go
off*, leave the stage, begin, explode, die,
gradually cease to be felt, deteriorate,
become unconscious in sleep, faint, etc.,
be got rid of by sale, succeed *well, badly*,
etc.; *go on*, continue, persevere, (*doing,
with, in*, or abs.), proceed as next step to
do, conduct oneself *shamefully* etc., rail *at*
(colloq.), appear on stage, begin bowling,
take one's turn to do something, (colloq.
in imperat.) don't talk nonsense; *going on
for*, approaching (a time, age, etc.); *go
out*, leave room or house, fight duel, be
extinguished, leave office (of Government), cease to be fashionable, depart
to colony etc., (esp. of girls) leave home
for employment usu. *as* governess etc.,
mix in society, (of workmen) strike, (of
heart etc.) expand with love etc. *to* person, play first 9 holes in round of golf;
go over, change one's party or religion;
go round, pay informal visit *to*, be long
enough to encompass, (of food etc.)
suffice for whole party; *go through with*,
complete, not leave unfinished; *go to*
(imperat.; arch.), interjection of remonstrance, incredulity, impatience, etc.; *go
together*, be concomitant, match; *go under*,
sink, fail, succumb. 35. Comb.: *go-ahead*,
enterprising; *go-as-you-please*, unfettered
by regulations; *go-between*, intermediary,
negotiator; *go-by*, passing (usu. in *give the
go-by to*, outstrip, leave behind, elude,
disregard, cut, slight); *go*[c]*cart*, wheeled
frame for teaching child to walk, kind of
perambulator, litter, palankeen, hand-
cart; *go-off'*, start (usu. *at the first go-off*);
go-to-meeting, (of hat, clothes, etc.) fit or
kept for going to church in. [OE, OHG
gān, OHG *gān*, *gēn* f. Gmc **gai-*, **gǣ-*]

go[2], n. (pl. *goes*). Act of going (*come-&-go*,
traffic, movement to & fro); mettle,
spirit, dash, animation; (colloq.) embarrassing turn of affairs (*here's, what,
a go !*; *a rum go*); (colloq.) success (*make a
go of it*); turn at doing something (*have a
go at*); portion of liquor or food served;
(Cribbage) player's inability to play,
counting one to opponent; (colloq.)
it's no go, nothing can be done; (colloq.)
all or *quite the go*, in fashion; (colloq.) *near
go*, close shave; (colloq.) *on the go*, in
motion, also in a state of decline; ‖ LITTLE-
-go. [f. prec.]

goad, n. & v.t. 1. Spiked stick used for
urging cattle; thing that torments, in-
cites, or stimulates. 2. v.t. Urge with ~;
irritate; instigate, drive, by annoyance
(often *on*; also *to* do, *into* doing, *to* or

into fury etc.). [OE *gād*, cogn. w. Lombard *gaida* arrowhead f. Gmc *gaidō]

goal, n. Point marking end of race; object of effort or ambition; destination; posts between which ball is to be driven in football etc., points so won (DROP³, *make, score, a* ~); (Rom. Ant.) pillar at turning-point in chariot race; ~'*keeper,* player stationed to protect~; ~-*line,* line between each pair of ~-posts produced as end-boundary of field of play (cf. TOUCH- -*line*). Hence ~'*ie* [-Y³] n. (colloq.), ~keeper. [ME *gol* (once) limit, common from 16th c., of unkn. orig.]

goat, n. Hardy lively wanton usu. horned & bearded ruminant quadruped (*sheep & ~s,* the good & the wicked, see *Matt.* xxv. 32, 33); (pl.) sub-family to which ~ belongs; zodiacal sign Capricorn (G~); licentious person; *get* one's ~ (sl.), irritate one; *play the* GIDDY ~; ~-*god,* Pan; ~'*herd,* one who tends ~s; ~'*beard,* meadowsweet, also salsify; ~'*skin,* (garment, bottle, made of) skin of ~; ~'*sucker,* nocturnal bird resembling swift; ~'*s wool,* non- -existent thing. Hence ~'ISH¹, ~'Y², aa., ~'ISHLY² adv., ~'ISHNESS n. [OE *gāt,* OS *gēt,* OHG *geiz,* ON *geit,* Goth. *gaits* f. Gmc *gaitaz cogn. w. L *haedus* kid]

goatee', n. Chin-tuft like goat's beard. [-EE]

goat'ling, n. Goat 1–2 years old. [-LING¹]

gob¹, n., & v.i. (vulg.). **1.** Clot of slimy substance, e.g. spittle; mouth. **2.** v.i. (-bb-). Spit. [f. OF *gob* mouthful]

***gob²,** n. (sl.). Sailor.

gōbăng', n. Game played on chequer- -board. [f. Jap. *goban* f. Chin. *k'i pan* chessboard]

gŏbb'ĕt, n. (arch.). Piece, lump, esp. of raw flesh or food; extract from a text set for translation or comment. [ME, f. OF *gobet* (GOB¹, -ET¹)]

gŏb'ble¹, v.t. & i. Eat hurriedly & noisily; ‖~-*stitch,* one made too long from hurry. Hence **gŏbb'ler¹** [-ER¹] n. [perh. f. GOB¹ + -LE(3)]

gŏb'ble², n. (golf). Rapid straight putt into the hole. [perh. f. prec.]

gŏb'ble³, v.i. (Of turkey-cock) make characteristic sound in throat; make such sound when speaking, from rage etc. Hence **gŏbb'ler²** n., turkey-cock. [imit.]

***gŏb'bledegōōk'** (-bĕldĭ-), -dȳ-, n. (sl.). Pompous official jargon. [imit. of turkey- -cock]

gŏb'elin, a. G~ *tapestry,* made, or imitated from that made, at the State factory in Paris called *Gobelins* after its founders. [f. F *gobe-mouches* lit. fly-catcher (*gober* swallow, *mouches* flies)]

gobe'mouche (gŏb'mōōsh), n. (pl. ~s pr. like sing.). Credulous newsmonger. [f. F *gobe-mouches* lit. fly-catcher (*gober* swallow, *mouches* flies)]

gŏb'lĕt, n. (Arch.) metal or glass drink- ing-cup, bowl-shaped & without handles, sometimes with foot & cover; (poet.) drinking-cup; (commerc.) glass with foot

& stem. [ME, f. OF *gobelet,* dim. of *gobel* of unkn. orig.]

gŏb'lin, n. Mischievous ugly demon. [ME, f. OF *gobelin,* med. L *gobelinus,* of obsc. orig.]

gŏb'ȳ, n. Small fish with ventral fins joined into a disc or sucker. [f. L *gobius, co-,* f. Gk *kōbios* GUDGEON]

gŏd¹, n. **1.** Superhuman being worshipped as having power over nature & human fortunes, deity, (~ of *heaven,* Zeus, Jupiter; ~ of *hell,* Dis, Pluto; ~ of *the sea,* Poseidon, Neptune; ~ of *day,* sun, Apollo, Phoebus; ~ of *fire,* Hephaestus, Vulcan; ~ of *war,* Ares, Mars; ~ of *love, blind ~,* Eros, Cupid; ~ of *wine,* Bacchus; ~ of *this world,* the Devil; *Ye ~s !, Ye ~s & little fishes !,* mock-heroic exclamations; *feast, sight, for the ~s,* something exquisite etc.). **2.** Image, animal, or other object, wor- shipped as symbolizing, being the visible habitation of, or itself possessing, divine power; an idol. **3.** Adored, admired, or influential person. **4.** (theatr., pl.). Occupants of gallery. **5.** (*God*). Supreme being, Creator & Ruler of universe, (*God,* often *the Lord God, Almighty God, God Almighty; God the Father, Son, Holy Ghost,* Persons of Trinity; ACT¹ *of God; with God,* dead & in heaven; *God's truth,* the absolute truth; *God's earth,* the whole earth; *God's* (*own*) *country,* alleged description of the U.S. by Americans; *oh, my, good,* etc., *God !,* exclamations of pain, grief, or anger; *God bless, damn, help, you !, him !,* etc., *God forbid !, grant ~!,* prayers or imprecations; *God bless me !, my life !, my soul !, you !,* etc., exclamations of surprise; *God willing,* if circumstances allow; *under God,* used to qualify attribution of full agency to man; *thank God !,* parenthetic expression of pleasure at turn of events etc.; *God knows,* it is beyond mortal or my knowledge, I do not know, (also) I call God to witness that; *for God's sake,* with urgent petitions; *by God,* confirmatory oath; *so* HELP¹ *me God !*). **6.** ~'*father,* ~'*mother,* ~'*parent,* ~'*papa,* ~'*mamma,* sponsor at baptism, & so of the converse relation ~'*child,* ~'*son,* ~'*daughter;* ~'*father* (fig.), person after whom person or thing is named, (vb) be responsible for, give one's name to; ~'*fearing,* sincerely religious; ~'*forsaken,* devoid of all merit, dismal (*what a* ~*forsaken hole !*); *God'man',* Christ; *God's-acre* (imit. of German), churchyard; *God's book,* Bible; ~'*send,* unexpected welcome event or acquisi- tion; *God's image,* human body; ~*speed',* utterance of words *God speed you !,* usu. in *bid* person ~*speed,* wish him success in undertaking, journey,' etc. Hence ~'HOOD, ~'SHIP, nn., ~'WARD adv. & a., ~'WARDS adv. [OE, OS, ON *god,* OHG *got,* Goth. *guth* f. Gmc *gutham]

gŏd², v.t. (rare, -dd-). Deify; ~ *it,* play the god. [f. prec.]

gŏdd'ĕss, n. Female deity in polytheism (esp., in Latin mythol.: ~ *of heaven, hell, love, wisdom, moon, corn, war,* Juno, Proserpine, Venus, Minerva, Diana, Ceres, Bellona); woman one adores. [-ESS[1]]

gŏ'det (-dā), n. Triangular piece of stuff inserted in a dress, glove, etc. (also attrib., as ~ *skirt*). [F]

godē'tia (-shạ), n. Free-flowering hardy annual plant. [*Godet* Swiss botanist, -IA[1]]

gŏd'head (-ĕd), n. Being God or a god, divine nature, deity; *the G~*, God. [-HEAD]

gŏd'lĕss, a. Without a god; not recognizing God; impious, wicked. Hence ~NESS n. [-LESS]

gŏd'like, a. Resembling God or a god in some quality; fit for, like that of, a god. [-LIKE]

gŏd'li|ў, a. Religious, pious, devout. Hence ~INESS n. [-LY[1]]

godown', n. (Anglo-Ind.). Warehouse in parts of Asia, esp. India. [f. Malay *godong*]

gŏd'wit, n. Wading bird like curlew but with slightly upcurved bill. [orig. unkn.]

gŏ'er, n. Person, thing, that goes (*good, slow,* etc., ~; *comers & ~s*). [-ER[1]]

goes, goest, goeth. See GO[1].

Goethian (gẽrt'ĭan), a. & n. (Follower of) Goethe, like Goethe, his writings, views, etc. [J. W. von *Goethe*, German poet 1749–1832, -IAN]

gŏf'er, *gau'fre (gŏf'er), n. Thin batter-cake stamped with honeycomb pattern by the irons it is baked in. [f. F *gaufre* honeycomb, gofer, see WAFER, WAFFLE]

gof(f)'er, goph'er, gauff'er (gŏ-, gŏf-), v.t., & n. **1.** Make wavy, flute, crimp, (lace edge, trimming, etc.) with heated irons; ~*ed edges* of book, embossed. **2.** n. Iron used for ~ing; ornamental plaiting used for frills etc. [f. F *gaufrer* stamp with patterned tool, f. *gaufre* (prec.)]

*gŏ'gĕtt'er, n. (colloq.). One who secures what he sets out to get; pushing person, thruster. [GO[1], GET[1], -ER[1] (1)]

gŏg'gle, v.i. & t., a., & n. **1.** Squint, roll eyes about (or with *eyes* as subj.), (of eyes) project; turn (eyes) sideways or from side to side. **2.** adj. (Of eyes) protuberant, full & rolling; so ~-EYED (-gel-ĭd) a. **3.** n. pl. Kind of spectacles for protecting eyes from glare, dust, etc., often with coloured glasses, wire gauze, etc.; (sl.) round-lensed spectacles; sheep disease, staggers. [a. & n. f. vb, 14th c. prob. f. imit. base *gog (cf. *jog*)+-LE(3)]

gŏg'lĕt, gŭgg'lĕt, n. (Anglo-Ind.). Long-necked vessel usu. of porous ware for keeping water cool. [f. Port. *gorgoleta*]

Goid'ĕl, n. Member of GADHELIC races. Hence (= GADHELIC) **Goidĕl'IC** a. & n. [f. OIr. *Góidel*]

gŏ'ing, n. In vbl senses; esp.: condition of ground for walking, riding, etc.; (for *a-going,* & now regarded as part.) in action (*set the clock ~*), existing, to be had, (*one of the best fellows ~*; *there is cold*

beef ~); ~*s-on,* (usu. *strange, such,* etc.) behaviour. [-ING[1]]

goi'tre (-ter), n. Morbid enlargement of thyroid gland, often showing as large pendulous swelling in neck, bronchocele, dewlap. Hence **goi'trED**[2] (-terd) a. [F, back formation f. *goitreux* ult. f. L *guttur* throat, -OUS]

goit'rous, a. Affected with, like, of, (of places) characterized by prevalence of, goitre. [f. F *goitreux* see prec.]

Gŏlcŏn'da, n. Mine of wealth (lit. or fig.). [old name of Hyderabad]

gŏld, n. & a. **1.** Precious yellow non-rusting malleable ductile metal of high specific gravity (*as* GOOD *as* ~; *go off* ~, abandon the ~ STANDARD); coins made of this, money in large sums, wealth; (fig.) brilliant, beautiful, or precious things, stuff, etc. (*a heart, voice, of* ~; *age of* ~, = GOLDEN *age*; *she is pure* ~; *all that glisters* or *glitters is not* ~); the metal used for coating surface or as pigment, gilding; the colour of the metal (*old* ~ n., dull brownish-golden yellow; *old-* ~ adj., thus coloured); bull's eye of archery target (usu. gilt). **2.** ~ *amalgam,* ~ combined with mercury in plastic state; ~*-beater,* one who beats ~ out into ~-leaf; ~*-beater's skin,* membrane used to separate leaves of ~ during beating, also as covering for slight wounds; ~ *bloc* (of countries with currencies tied to ~); ~ *brick* (orig. U.S. sl.), thing with only a surface appearance of value, sham, fraud; ~*'crest,* very small bird with golden crest; ~*-digger,* one who digs for ~, *(sl.) coquette who wheedles money out of men; ~*-dust,* ~ in fine particles as often found; ~*-fever,* rage for going in search of ~; ~*-field,* district in which ~ is found; ~*'finch,* bright-coloured song-bird with patch of yellow on wings; ~*'fish,* small red Chinese carp kept for ornament; ~*-foil,* ~*-leaf,* ~ beaten into thin sheet, -foil being the thicker; ~*-mine,* lit. & fig. source of wealth; ~ *plate,* vessels made of ~; ~*-rush,* a rush to some new ~-field; ~*'smith,* worker in ~ (~*-smith beetle,* with ~-coloured wing-covers); ‖ *Gold Stick,* (bearer of) gilt rod borne on State occasions by colonel of Lifeguards or captain of Gentlemen-at-arms. **3.** adj. Wholly or chiefly of, coloured like, ~; (of sums in depreciated currencies) reckoned at par (~ *francs* etc., the stated amount at the nominal undepreciated value of the franc etc.). [OE, OS, OHG *gold,* ON *gull,* Goth. *gulth* f. Gmc *gultham; cogn. w. YELLOW]

gŏl'den, a. Made, consisting, of gold (*G~ FLEECE*; ~ *key,* money used to remove obstacle); abounding in, yielding, gold; coloured, shining, like gold; precious, excellent, important, (~ *opinions,* high respect; ~*-mouthed,* eloquent; *a* ~ *remedy, opportunity, saying*; *the* ~ *rule,* that in *Matt.* vii. 12; ~ *mean,* neither too much nor too little, principle of moderation; ~ *number*, named as important in fixing Easter, year's number in Metonic lunar cycle of 19 years; ~ *age*, first of four ages, see BRAZEN[1], when men were happy & innocent, also most prosperous period of nation's condition or literature); ~ *balls*, = *three* BALL[1]s; ~*-eye*, kind of sea-duck; *G~ Horn*, curved inlet of Bosporus, the harbour of Istanbul; ||~*-knop*, ladybird; ~ *rain*, kind of firework; ~*-rod*, plant with rod-like stem & spike of bright yellow flowers; *°G~ State*, California; ||~ SYRUP;; ~ *wedding*, fiftieth anniversary. [-EN[5], replacing *gilden* f. OE *gylden*]

gŏl'dilŏcks, n. Kinds of plant, esp. a species of buttercup. [f. obs. *goldy*[2], LOCK[1]]

gŏlf (*also* gŏf), n., & v.i. 1. Game for two persons or couples in which a small hard ball is struck with clubs having wooden or metal heads into each of a series of (18 or 9) holes on smooth greens at varying distances apart and separated by fairways, rough ground, hazards, etc., the object being to hole the ball in the fewest possible strokes; ~*-club*, implement used in striking ball, (premises occupied by) association for playing ~. 2. v.i. Play ~, whence **gŏl'fER**[1] (*also* gŏf[2]) n. [15th c. Sc., of unkn. orig.]

Goli'ath, n. Giant; ~ *beetle*, large African black white-striped beetle; ~ (*crane*), powerful travelling crane. [1 *Sam.* xvii]

gŏll'iwŏg, n. Grotesque usu. black doll; bugbear. [orig. unkn.]

gŏll'y, int. (Used, esp. by Negroes, for) God, *by* God. [deformation of GOD]

|| **golosh.** See GALOSH.

golŭp'tious (-shŭs), **golŏp'**, a. (joc.). Luscious, delightful. [joc. for *voluptuous*]

|| **gŏmbeen'**, n. (Anglo-Ir.). Usury (~*-man*, money-lender). [f. Ir. *gaimbin* perh. f. same OCelt. as med. L *cambium* CHANGE]

gŏm(b)rŏŏn', n. Persian pottery, imitated in Chelsea ware. [town on Persian gulf]

Gomŏ'rrah, n. (Type of) wicked town. [*Gen.* xviii, xix]

-gon, suf. f. Gk *-gōnos* -angled, forming nn. as *hexagon, polygon, n-gon*, figure with six, several, n, angles.

gŏn'ăd, n. (biol.). Undifferentiated germ-gland, serving both as ovary & spermary. [f. Gk *gonē, gonos*, generation, seed, +-AD]

gŏn'dola, n. Light flat-bottomed boat with cabin amidships & high point at each end worked by one oar at stern, used on Venetian canals; car suspended from airship. [It.]

gŏndolier', n. Sculler of gondola. [F, f. It. *gondoliere* (prec., -IER)]

gone (gŏn, gawn), a. In vbl senses; esp.: lost, hopeless, (*a ~ man*, also gon'ER[1], n., sl.; *a ~ case*, COON); past, bygone, (usu. *past & ~*); ~ *on* (sl.), enamoured of. [p.p. of GO]

gŏn'falon, n. Banner, often with streamers, hung from cross-bar, esp. as standard of some Italian republics. [f. It. *gonfalone* f. WG **gundfano* (**gund-* war, *fano* banner)]

gŏnfalonier', n. Standard-bearer; (hist.) chief magistrate in some Italian republies. [F, or f. It. *-iere* (prec., -IER)]

gŏng, n., & v.t. 1. Metal disc with turned rim giving resonant note when struck; saucer-shaped bell; (sl.) medal. 2. v.t. (Of motoring-traffic police) direct (motorist) to stop by striking ~. [f. Malay *gong*]

gŏn'gorism (-ngg-), n. A Spanish literary style marked by inversion, antithesis, & classical allusion, corresponding to EUPHUISM in England. [*Gongora y* Argote, Sp. poet, 1561-1627, +-ISM]

gŏniom'eter, n. Instrument for measuring angles. So **gŏniom'ETRY** n., **gŏnio-mĕt'ric(AL)** aa. [F (*-mètre*), f. Gk *gōnia* angle, -METER]

gŏnorrhoe'|a (*-orēa*), n. Inflammatory discharge of mucus from urethra or vagina. Hence ~AL (*-rē'al*) a. [LL, f. Gk *gonorrhoia* (*gonos* seed, *rhoia* flux)]

gŏŏd, a. (BETTER, BEST), & n. 1. Having the right qualities, satisfactory, adequate, (*a ~ fire*, not too small or dull; *meat keeps ~*, untainted; ~ *soil*, fertile; *not ~ enough*, colloq., not worth doing, accepting, etc.; ~ *money*, genuine; as conventional epithet in *the ~ ship —, the ~ town of —*; ~ *law*, valid, sound; *is ~ eating* etc., attractive to eat etc.). 2. Commendable (esp. in ~ *men & true*; ~ *old —!*, colloq. form of approval; *that's a ~ un!*, sl., a lie worth telling; also in courteous, patronizing, ironically polite, or indignant address, as *my ~ friend, man, sir*, or in polite or indulgently contemptuous description, as *your ~ lady, the ~ man*; *the ~ people*, fairies; *of ~ family*, well-born; *in ~ spirits*, not depressed; *a ~ leg*, well shaped). 3. Right, proper, expedient, (*it is ~ to be here*; *I thought, it seemed, ~ to* do something; also abs. as excl. of approval or consent). 4. Morally excellent, virtuous. 5. Kind, benevolent, (so of God etc., esp. in prayers & exclamations, as ~ *God!*, ~ *heavens!*, ~ *gracious!*; *be so ~ as*, ~ *enough*, *to*, ~ *please to*; *how ~ of you!*; *did me a ~ turn or office*; *has always been ~ to me*; *say a ~ word for*, commend, defend). 6. (Esp. of child) well behaved, not giving trouble, (often *as ~ as gold*). 7. Gratifying, agreeable, favourable, advantageous, beneficial, wholesome, (~ *news*; *things are in ~ train*, going well; so in forms of greeting or parting, as ~ *morning*, ||~ *day*, ~ *night*; *have a ~ time*, enjoy oneself; *have a ~ night*, sleep well; *a ~ saying or story or thing*, *as ~ as a play*, amusing; *oil is ~ for burns*; *beer is not ~ for him or his health*; *are acorns ~ to eat?*; *take in ~ part*, not be annoyed at). 8. Adapted to an end, efficient, suitable, competent, (esp. with agent-nouns, as a ~ driver; ~ at describing etc.; has been a ~ wife to him). 9. Reliable, safe, sure, (a ~ man, financially sound, able to meet liabilities; ~ debts, sure to be paid; a ~ life, likely to last long, such as insurance office will accept; ~ for an amount, safely to be trusted to pay it, also of draft etc., drawn for so much; ~ for, inclined for, up to, as ~ for a ten-mile walk). 10. Valid, sound, thorough, ample, considerable, (gave her a ~ beating; did it for ~ reasons; rule holds ~; a ~ excuse; a ~ DEAL[1], FEW, MANY; have a ~ mind, be much inclined to do; often as intensive before adj., as went a ~ round pace, will take a ~ long time). 11. Not less than (played for a ~ hour; it is three miles ~ from the station). 12. As~ as, practically (he as ~ as told me so; as ~ as dead; it is as ~ as done); make ~, compensate for, pay (expense), fulfil (promise), effect (purpose), demonstrate (statement), substantiate (charge), gain & hold (position), replace or restore (thing lost or damaged), (without obj.) accomplish what one has attempted. 13. ~ breeding, correct or courteous manners; ~ fellow, virtuous man, sociable person, agreeable companion, ~-fellowship, conviviality, sociability; ~-for-nothing, ~-for-nought, aa. & nn., worthless (person); G~ FRIDAY; ~ humour, cheerful mood or disposition, amiability, whence ~-hum-oured[2] a., ~-hum'ouredly[2] (-merdl) adv.; ~-look'ing, handsome; ~-looking, of virtuous appearance; ~ looks, personal beauty; ~ luck, being fortunate, happy chance, (often ~ luck to you!, as wish); || ~'man (arch.), head of household, husband, father, etc.; ~ money (colloq.), high wages; || ~ morrow (arch.), = ~ morning; ~ nature, kindly disposition, willingness to postpone one's own interests, whence ~-na'tured[2] a., ~-na'turedly[2] adv.; ~-neighbourhood, -neighbourliness, -neighbourship, friendly conduct; ~ sense, soundness of judgement, practical wisdom; ~ temper, freedom from irritability, whence ~-tem'pered[2] a., ~-tem'pered-ly[2] adv.; ~ thing, anything one approves of, advantageous bargain or speculation, witty saying, (pl.) dainties; || ~'wife, mistress of house (esp. Sc.). 14. n. Virtuous persons (the ~; ~ & bad alike respect him). 15. What is ~ or beneficial, well-being, profit, benefit, advantage, (is a power for ~; deceive him for his ~; what ~ will it do?; much ~ may it do you!, often iron.; do ~, show kindness to, act philanthropically, be beneficial to or benefit: to the ~, as balance on right side, net profit, something extra, etc.; come to ~, yield ~ result; for ~, for ~ & all, permanently, finally, definitively; be any, some, no, much, ~, be of any etc. use; what is the ~ of it?; what ~ is it?). 16. Desirable end or object, thing worth attaining; no ~, some mischief (is up to,

after, no ~). 17. pl. Movable property; merchandise, wares, (piece of ~s, joc., person); || things for transmission by rail etc. (opp. passengers; so ~s agent, station, train, etc.; by ~s, by ~s train). Hence ~'ISH[1](2) a. [OE, OS gōd, OHG guot, ON gōthr, Goth. gōths f. Gmc *gōdhaz cogn. w. gadh- in GATHER]

good-bye', int. & n. (Saying of) farewell. [contr. of God be with you!, with good substituted on anal. of good-night etc.]

good'ly, a. Comely, handsome; of considerable size etc.; (iron.) fine, grand. Hence ~iNESS n. [OE gōdlic (GOOD, -LY[1])]

good'ness, n. Virtue; positive or comparative excellence; benevolence, kindness, generosity, (have the ~, be kind enough to; what is good in thing, its essence or strength; (in exclamations, substituted for) God (~ gracious!, excl. of surprise or indignation; ~ knows, I do not know, I appeal to Heaven to witness; I wish to ~; thank ~!; for ~' sake). [OE gōdnes (GOOD, -NESS)]

good'will', n. Kindly feeling to person, favour; cheerful acquiescence, heartiness, zeal; established custom or popularity of business etc.; privilege granted by seller of business, of trading as recognized successor.

Good'wins, n. pl. The ~, the Goodwin sands. [place]

Good'wood, n. (Used for) race-meeting on course near ~ Park, Sussex (~ cup, chief prize at this). [place]

good'y[1], n. (arch.). Elderly woman of lower class (often as prefix to surname). [for GOODwife, cf. HUSSY]

good'y[2], n. A sweet, bonbon. [-Y[3]]

good'y[3], good'y-good'y, a. Primly, pretentiously, inopportunely, obtrusively, weakly, or sentimentally virtuous (talk ~, in ~ manner). Hence good'iNESS n. [-Y[3]]

goof, n. (sl.). Silly or stupid person. Hence ~'Y[2] a. (sl.), silly. [var. of dial. goff (16th c.) f. F goffe]

goog'ly, n. (cricket). Off-break ball bowled with leg-break action. [orig. unkn.]

*goon, n. Person hired by racketeers to terrorize workers; stupid person. [orig. unkn.]

goosan'der, n. Duck with sharp serrated bill. [app. f. GOOSE after bersander]

goose, n. (pl. geese pr. gēs). 1. Kinds of web-footed bird between duck & swan in size, female of this (opp. GANDER), its flesh, (all his geese are swans, he over-estimates; kill the ~ that lays the golden eggs, sacrifice future profit to present necessities; COOK[2] person's ~; say BO to ~; sauce for ~ is sauce for GANDER). 2. Simpleton, whence goos'ey[3] n. 3. Tailor's smoothing iron (with handle like ~'s neck; pl. ~s). 4. FOX[1] & geese; || ~-club, for providing poor people with Christmas ~ paid for by small instalments; ~-flesh, rough bristling state of skin produced by cold or fright; ~-foot, kinds of plant named from shape of leaves:~-*grass*, cleavers: ~'*herd*, one who tends geese; ~-*quill*, quill- -feather of ~ esp. used as pen; ~-*skin*, = ~-*flesh*; ~-*step*, balancing-drill taught to army recruits & much used in German army. [OE *gōs*, OHG *gans*, ON *gūs* f. Gmc **gans*- cogn. w. L *anser*, Gk *khēn*]

goose'berr|y̆ (-zb-), n. (Edible berry of) any thorny species of *Ribes*; wine made of ~ies; *play~y*, act as chaperon, play propriety, for pair of lovers'; ~*y*-FOOL². [16th c., perh. f. prec., but cf. contemporary *groser* (F *groseille*)]

|| goose'gŏg (-zg-), n. (colloq.). Gooseberry. [joc.]

gopher¹. See GOFFER.

gŏph'er², n. American burrowing rodent; N.-American ground-squirrel; nocturnal burrowing land-tortoise of Southern U.S. [orig. unkn.]

gŏph'er³, n. Tree from wood of which Noah's ark was made; (*~-wood*) tree yielding yellowish timber. [Heb.]

gŏr'al, n. An Indian antelope. [native name]

gŏr'cŏck, n. Male of the red grouse. [*gor-* of unkn. orig.]

Gŏrd'ian, a. ~ *knot*, intricate knot, difficult problem or task, (*cut the ~ knot*, solve problem by force or by evading the conditions). [f. *Gordius*, who tied the knot cut by Alexander the Great, +-AN]

gōre¹, n. Blood shed & thickened or clotted. Hence gōr'y² a., gōr'ily³ adv. [OE *gor* dung, dirt, = OHG, ON *gor*, Du. *goor*]

gōre², n., & v.t. 1. Wedge-shaped piece of cloth adjusting width of a garment; triangular or lune-shaped piece in umbrella, balloon, dome, globe, etc. 2. v.t. 'Shape, narrow, with ~. [OE *gāra* triangular piece of land, = OHG *gēro*, ON *geire*, cogn. w. OE *gār* spear, w. ref. to shape of spearhead]

gōre³, v.t. Pierce with the horn or (rarely) tusk (of rocks piercing ship). [15th c. Sc. & north. *gorre*, of unkn. orig.]

gŏrge¹, n. (Rhet.) internal throat; what has been swallowed, contents of stomach, (*cast the ~ at*, reject with loathing); one's ~ *rises at*, one is sickened or disgusted by); (Fortif.) neck of bastion or other outwork, rear entrance to a work; narrow opening, usu. with stream, between hills; solid object meant to be swallowed as bait for fish. [ME, f. OF f. LL *gurga*, -*es* gullet, belly, f. L *gurges* abyss]

gŏrge², v.i. & t., & n. 1. Feed greedily; satiate, glut; swallow, devour greedily; fill full, distend, choke up. 2. n. Act of gorging, surfeit. [ME, f. OF *gorger* (prec.)]

gŏr'geous (-jus), a. Richly coloured, sumptuous, magnificent; (of diction) ornate, dazzling. Hence~LY² adv.,~NESS n., (-jus-). [earlier *gorgayse*, -*yas* f. OF *gorgias* of unkn. orig.]

gŏr'gĕt¹, n. (Hist.) piece of armour for

throat, woman's wimple; necklace; patch of colour on throat of bird etc.; ~ *patch*, distinguishing mark on collar of military uniform. [f. OF *gorgete* (GORGE¹, -ET¹)]

gŏr'gĕt², n. (surg.). Channel-shaped steel instrument used in operations for stone etc. [f. F *gorgeret* (GORGE¹, as tubular)]

Gŏr'glŏ, n. (pl. -*os*). (Gipsy for) non-gipsy. [Romany]

gŏrg'on, n. (Gk Myth.) one of three snake-haired women (esp. MEDUSA) whose looks turned any beholder to stone; terrible or ugly person, repellent woman. Hence gŏrgŏn'IAN a. [f. L *Gorgo* -*onis* f. Gk *Gorgō* (*gorgos* terrible)]

gŏrgōn'ia, n. (pl. -*iae*, -*ias*). Sea-fan, kind of polyp. [prec., as hardening in air, +-IA¹]

gŏrg'onize, -ise (-īz), v.t. Stare at like gorgon. [-IZE]

Gŏrgonzŏl'a, n. A rich veined cheese. [~ in Italy]

gorill'a, n. Large powerful ferocious arboreal anthropoid ape. [Afr. for wild man in Gk account of Hanno's voyage 5th or 6th c. B.C.]

gŏrm'andīze, -ise (-īz), n., & v.i. & t. *gourmandise* (see Ap.), n. 1. Habits of a GOURMAND, indulgence in good eating, gluttony. 2. vb. Eat, devour, voraciously, whence gŏrm'andIZER¹ n. [vb f. n., f. F *gourmandise* (GOURMAND, -ISE)]

gŏrm'lĕss, a. (colloq.). Foolish, lacking sense. [orig. *gaumless* f. dial. *gaum* understanding, +-LESS]

|| gŏrse, n. Prickly yellow-flowered shrub, whin, furze. Hence gŏrs'y² a. [OE *gorst* cogn. w. OHG *gersta*, L *hordeum*, barley]

Gŏrs'edd (-ĕdh), n. Meeting of Welsh bards & druids (esp. as daily preliminary to the eisteddfod). [W, = session]

|| gŏsh, int. (Also *by*~) by God. [for *God*]

gŏs'hawk (-s-h-), n. Kinds of large short- -winged hawk. [OE *gōs-hafoc* (GOOSE HAWK)]

Gŏsh'en, n. Place of light or plenty. [*Gen.* xlv. 10 etc., *Exod.* viii. 22, ix. 26]

gŏs'ling (-z-) n. Young goose. [-LING¹]

gŏs'pel, n. 1. Glad tidings preached by Christ; religious doctrine of Christ & his apostles, Christian revelation; protestant or evangelical doctrine (opp. *mass*); record of Christ's life in books of four evangelists; any of those books; portion from one of them read at Communion service. 2. Thing that may safely be believed (*takes his dreams for*~); principle that one acts upon, believes in, or preaches (*the ~ of efficiency, laissez faire, soap & water*). 3. ~-*book*, containing ~s read at Communion; ~ *oath*, sworn on the ~s; || ~-*shop*, Methodist chapel; ~ *side*, N side of altar, at which ~ is read; ~ *truth*, truths contained in ~, something as true as ~. [OE *godspel*, orig. *gōdspell* (GOOD tidings; SPELL¹), rendering LL *bona annuntiatio*, *bonus nuntius* = *evangelium* EVANGEL; early assoc. w. *god* GOD]

gŏs′peller, n. Reader of gospel in Communion service; *hot* ~, zealous puritan, rabid propagandist. [-ER¹]

gŏss′amer, n. & a. 1. Light filmy substance, the webs of small spiders, floating in calm air or spread over grass; *a* thread of this; something flimsy; delicate gauze; hence ~ED² (-*erd*), ~Y², aa. 2. adj. Light & flimsy as ~. [ME *gossomer* app. = goose-summer or St Martin's summer, i.e. early November when geese were eaten, ~ being most seen then]

gŏss′ip, n., & v.i. 1. ‖ (Arch.) familiar acquaintance, friend, (esp. of women); idle talker, newsmonger, tattler; idle talk, groundless rumours, tittle-tattle; easy unconstrained talk or writing esp. about persons or social incidents; hence ~RY(4, 5) n., ~Y² a. 2. v.i. Talk idly or lightly, tattle; write*in gossipy style; hence ~ER¹ n. [earlier senses, *sponsor, fellow- -sponsor, one's child's sponsor, at baptism*; OE *godsibb* person related to one in God; see SIB]

gossōōn′, n. (Anglo-Ir.). Lad. [f. F *garçon*]

gŏt, past & p.p. of GET. ~-*up*, factitious, artificially produced, adorned, etc., with a view to effect or deception.

Gŏth, n. One of a German tribe who invaded Eastern & Western Empires in 3rd–5th cc. & founded kingdoms in Italy, France, & Spain; rude, uncivilized, or ignorant person, esp. one who destroys works of art (cf. VANDAL), whence ~′ISH¹ a. [OE *Gotan* (pl.), ON *Gotar*, Goth. *°Gutos* or *°Gutans*; ME *Gothe* f. LL *Gothi*, Gk *Gotthoi*]

Gŏt′ham (-*tam*), n. Typical foolish town (*wise man of*~, fool); *°(colloq.) New York City (*usu. pr.* gŏ′tham). Hence ~ITE¹(1) n. [perh. f. the village in Notts.]

Gŏth′ic, a. & n. 1. Of the Goths or their language. 2. (archit.). In the pointed- -arch style prevalent in Western Europe in 12th–16th cc., including in England the Early English, Decorated, & Perpendicular (orig. sense *not classical*). 3. Barbarous, rude, uncouth. 4. (Print., a. & n.) German, also black-letter, (type); hence Gŏth′ICALLY adv., ~ISM(2, 3, 4) n., ~IZE(2, 3) v.i. & t. 5. n. ~ language; ~ architecture; ~ type. [f. F *gothique* or LL *gothicus* (GOTH, -IC)]

gŏtt′en, p.p. (arch., & U.S.) of GET¹.

gouache (gōō′ahsh), n. Way of painting in opaque colours ground in water & thickened with gum & honey. [F, f. It. *guazzo*]

Goud′a, n. Flat round cheese made at ~ in Holland. [place]

gouge (gowj, gōōj), n., & v.t. 1. Concave- -bladed chisel used in carpentry & surgery. 2. v.t. Cut with ~; cut *out* (a cork, a channel) (as) with ~; force (*out*, esp. person's eye with thumb) (as) with ~; force out eye of. [F, f. LL *gubia*]

goulash (gōō′lahsh), n. 1. Highly seasoned stew of steak and vegetables. 2. (Contract Bridge) re-deal of the four hands (unshuffled, but with each hand arranged in suits and order of value). [f. Magyar *gulyds-hus* f. *gulyds* herdsman + *hus* meat]

gourd (gŏrd, goord), n. (Large fleshy fruit of) kinds of trailing or climbing plant; rind of the fruit emptied, dried, & used as bottle etc., whence ~′FUL(2) n. [ME, f. F *gourde* f. L *cucurbita*]

gourmand (goorm′and, & see Ap.), a. & n. 1. Gluttonous, fond of eating. 2. n. (Usu. as F) lover of delicate fare, judge of good eating; greedy feeder, glutton. Hence ~ISM(2) (goor-) n. [15th c. f. OF, alt. f. *gormet* GOURMET]

gourmandise. See GORMANDIZE.

gourmet (goorm′ā), n. Connoisseur of table delicacies, esp. of wine. [F, see GOURMAND]

gout, n. 1. Paroxysmal disease with inflammation of smaller joints, esp. that of great toe, & chalk-stones (*rich, poor, man's* ~, ascribed to over, under, -feeding & drinking). 2. Wheat-disease caused by ~-*fly*. 3. Drop, splash, or spot. Hence ~Y² a. (~*ies* as n. pl., overshoes), ~′ILY² adv., ~′INESS n. [ME, f. OF *goute* f. L *gutta* drop w. ref. to medieval theory of flowing down of humours]

go′vern (gŭ-), v.t. & i. 1. Rule with authority, conduct the policy, actions, & affairs, of (State, subject) despotically or constitutionally; regulate proceedings of (corporation etc.; ~*ing body*, managers of hospital, school, etc.); be in military command of (fort, town). 2. Exercise function of government in person (*king reigns but does not* ~, merely selects those who are to ~). 3. Sway, rule, influence, regulate, determine, (person, his acts, course or issue of events); be the predominating influence. 4. Conduct oneself in some way; curb, bridle, (one's passions, one*self*). 5. Constitute a law, rule, standard, or principle, for; serve to decide (case). 6. (Gram., esp. of vb or prep.) have (noun, case) depending on it, require (a certain case). Hence ~ABLE a., ~ABIL′ITY n. [ME, f. OF *governer* f. L *gubernare* steer, govern, f. Gk *kubernaō* steer]

go′vernance (gŭ-), n. Act, manner, fact, or function, of governing, sway, control. [ME, f. OF *governance* (prec., -ANCE)]

go′vernėss (gŭ-), n. Female teacher, instructress, esp. of children in private household; ‖ ~-*car*(*t*), light two-wheeled vehicle with side- seats face to face. [earlier *governeress* f. OF (GOVERNOR, -ESS¹)]

go′vernment (gŭ-), n. (More modern word for) GOVERNANCE; portion of country ruled by a governor, province; system of governing, form of polity; body or successive bodies of persons governing a State, the State as an agent, an administration or ministry (‖ *form a G*~, of

Prime Minister selecting colleagues); (Gram.) relation between GOVERNING & other word; ‖ G~ *house*, official residence of governor; *G~ paper*, securities, bonds, exchequer bills, etc., issued by ~. Hence **governmĕn'taL** a., **governmĕn'talLY²** adv., (gŭ-). [OF (-*ement*), see GOVERN, -MENT]

go'vernor (gŭ-), n. **1.** One who governs, ruler; official appointed to govern province, town, etc., representative of Crown in dominion (*G~ General*) or colony; executive head of each of U.S.; officer commanding fortress or garrison; head, or one of governing body, of institution; official in charge of prison. **2.** One's employer, one's father, sir, (sl., freq. *guv'nor*). **3.** (mech.). Automatic regulator of supply of gas, steam, water, etc., to machine, ensuring even motion. **4.** Kind of fishing-fly. **5.** ~ *general*, ~ with deputy ~s under him, whence ~-gĕn'eralSHIP n. Hence ~SHIP(1, 2) n. [ME, f. OF *governeor* f. L *gubernalorem* (GOVERN, -OR)]

‖ **ğow'an**, n. (Sc.). Daisy. [prob. var. of dial. *golland* & connected w. dial. *gold*, OE *golde*, marigold, perh. f. GOLD]

gowk, n. (Dial.) cuckoo; awkward or half-witted person, fool. [ME *goke* f. ON *gaukr* = OE *gēac*, OHG *gouh* f. Gmc **gaukaz*]

gown, n., & v.t. Loose flowing upper garment, esp. woman's dress (usu. of dress with pretensions to elegance, or in comb. as *tea*, *dinner*, ~~), frock; ancient Roman toga (*arms*, *gown*, war & peace); official or uniform robe of various shapes worn by alderman, judge, lawyer, clergyman, member of university, college, or school, etc. (*town & ~*, non-members & members of university at Oxf. & Camb.); ~*s'man*, civilian, member of university; (vb, chiefly in p.p.) attire in ~. [ME, f. OF *goune* f. med. L *gunna* fur garment (cf. Byz. Gk *gouna* fur)]

goy, n. (Yiddish for) Gentile. [Heb., = nation]

Graaf'ian (-rahf-), a. ~ *follicle*, *vesicle*, one of small sacs in mammal ovary in which ova are matured. [R. de *Graaf*, Dutch anatomist d. 1673, -IAN]

grăb, v.t. & i. (-bb-), & n. **1.** Seize suddenly; appropriate rapaciously; capture, arrest; make snatch *at*; hence (-)~b'ER¹ n. **2.** n. Sudden clutch, grasp, seizure, or attempt to seize; practice of ~bing, rapacious proceedings esp. in politics or commerce; (mech.) device or implement for clutching; children's card game. [n. f. vb; f. MLG, MDu. *grabben*; cf. GRIP², GRIPE, GROPE]

grăb'ble, v.i. Grope about, feel for something; sprawl on all fours (often *for* something). [f. Du. *grabbelen* (prec., -LE(2))]

grăce, n., & v.t. **1.** Pleasing quality, attractiveness, charm, esp. that belonging to elegant proportions or ease & refinement of movement, action, expression, or

manner, whence ~'FUL a., ~'fulLY² adv., ~'fulNESS n., (-sf-). **2.** Becomingness, air with which something is done, (*cannot with any ~ ask him; have the ~ to*, do something that decency requires; *with a good ~*, as if willing; *with a bad ~*, reluctantly, ungraciously). **3.** Attractive feature, accomplishment, ornament, (*airs & ~s*, behaviour put on with a view to effect or attraction). **4.** (Mus.; also ~-*note*, -*notes*) embellishment of extra note(s) not essential to harmony or melody. **5.** (Gk Myth.) *the G~s*, three beautiful goddess sisters (Aglaia, Euphrosyne, Thalia), the bestowers of beauty & charm. **6.** Favour, benignant regard or its manifestation, on part of superior (*be in* one's *good ~s*, enjoy his favour or liking). **7.** Unconstrained goodwill as ground of concession (*act of ~*, privilege, concession, that cannot be claimed as right, & see below; *by the ~ of God*, appended to royal titles); boon. **8.** ‖ (Univv.) permission of Congregation, also of College or Hall, to take degree, dispensation from statutes. **9.** (theol.) Unmerited favour of God, divine regenerating, inspiring, & strengthening influence, condition (also *state of ~*) of being so influenced, divinely given talent etc., (*the —th year of ~*, with date = A.D.; *in this year of ~*, usu. iron., when Christianity has been so long established). **10.** Favour shown by granting delay (*give a day's*, *year's*, etc., ~; *days of ~*, time allowed by law for payment of bill of exchange—in Britain three days—or insurance premium after it falls due). **11.** Mercy, clemency, (*Act of ~*, formal, esp. general, pardon by Act of Parliament; & see above). **12.** Short thanksgiving before or after meal (~-*cup*, cup of wine etc. passed round after ~, parting draught). **13.** ‖ *His*, *Her*, *Your*, *G~*, forms of address or description for duke, duchess, or archbishop. **14.** v.t. Add ~ to, adorn, set off *with*; confer honour or dignity on, honour *with* title etc.; do credit to. [ME, f. OF *grace* f. L *gratia* (*gratus* pleasing, GRATEFUL)]

grăce'lèss (-sl-), a. Unregenerate, depraved, (arch. or joc.); wanting sense of decency, unabashed; without charm or elegance (rare); ~ *florin* (of 1849, on which the letters *D.G.* were omitted). Hence ~LY² adv., ~NESS n. [-LESS]

grā'cile, a. Slender; (erron.) gracefully slight. Hence **gracil'ITY** n., slenderness, (of literary style) unornamented simplicity. [f. L *gracilis* slender]

grā'cious (-shus), a. & int. **1.** Agreeable, pleasing, (arch.); kindly, benevolent, courteous, (chiefly poet.); condescending, indulgent & beneficent to inferiors, (of exalted persons, or sarcastic or joc.; esp. as polite epithet of royal persons or their acts; *the ~ speech from the throne*); (of God) dispensing grace, merciful, benignant; hence ~LY² adv., ~NESS n.,

(-shus-). 2. int. (Ellipt. for ~ *God*, as *good*) ~ *!*, *my* ~ *!*, excll. of surprise (also in ~ *me!*, ~ *goodness!*). [ME, f. OF, f. L *gratiosus* (GRACE, -OUS)]

grắc'kle, n. Kinds of bird allied to jackdaw. [ult. f. L *graculus* jackdaw]

gradāte', v.i. & t. (Cause to) pass by imperceptible degrees from one shade of colour to another; arrange in steps or grades. [back formation f. foll.]

gradā'tion, n. (Usu. pl.) stage(s) of transition or advance; series of degrees in rank, merit, intensity, divergence, etc., (pl.) such degrees; arrangement in such degrees; (Fine arts) insensible passing from one shade, tone, etc., to another; (Philol.) ablaut. Hence ~AL a., ~alLY² adv., (-shon-). [f. L *gradatio* (*gradus* step, -ATION)]

grāde, n., & v.t. 1. Degree in rank, proficiency, quality, value, etc., class of persons or things alike in these; *class, form, in school. 2. (Cattle-breeding) variety produced by crossing native stock with superior breed. 3. (Zool.) group supposed to have branched from parent stock at same stage of development. 4. (Philol.) relative position in ablaut-series. 5. Gradient, slope, rate of ascent or descent, (on the up, down, ~, rising or falling, lit. & fig.; *make the ~, succeed). 6. v.t. Arrange in ~s, class, sort; blend so as to affect ~ of; colour with tints passing into each other. 7. Reduce (road, canal, etc.) to easy gradients. 8. (Cattle-breeding) cross with better breed (~ up, improve thus). 9. (Philol., in pass.) be changed by ablaut. [vb f. n., F, f. L *gradus* step]

∥**grāde'ly** (-dli), a. (obs. exc. dial.). Excellent, thorough; handsome, comely; real, true, proper. [ME *greithlic* f. ON *greithligr* (*greithr* = OE *geræde* READY, -LY¹)]

grād'ient, n. ∥ Amount of slope, inclination to the horizontal, in road, railway, etc.; proportional rise or fall of thermometer or barometer in passing from one region to another. [perh. formed on GRADE after *salient*]

grād'in(e) (*also* -adēn'), n. One of series of low steps or tier of seats; ledge at back of altar. [f. It. *gradino* (*grado* GRADE)]

grād'ual¹, n. Respond sung between Epistle & Gospel in the service of the Mass. [so called as sung at steps of altar or while deacon mounted ambo; f. med. L *graduale* neut. adj. as n., see foll. & GRAIL¹]

grād'ual², a. Taking place by degrees, slowly progressive, not rapid, steep, or abrupt; ~ *psalm*, = *song* of DEGREES. Hence ~LY² adv., ~NESS n. [f. med. L *gradualis* (L *gradus* -*ūs* step, -AL)]

grād'uănd, n. (Sc.), One about to receive an academic degree. [f. med. L *graduandus* gerundive of *graduare* GRADU-ATE²]

grād'uāte¹, n. One who holds academic degree; chemist's graduated measuring-glass. [f. med. L *graduatus* (foll., -ATE²)]

grād'uḷāte², v.i. & t. Take, admit to (chiefly U.S.), academic degree, (transf.) qualify or perfect oneself *as*; mark out in degrees or portions; arrange in gradations, apportion incidence of (tax) according to a scale; pass *away* by degrees, change (intr.) gradually *into*; concentrate (solution) by evaporation. Hence ~A'TION, ~ātOR, nn. [f. med. L *graduare* (*gradus* -*ūs* step), -ATE³]

grād'us, n. Dictionary of Latin prosody used in schools to help in writing Latin verse. [for ~ *ad Parnassum* step to Parnassus]

Gr(a)e'cism (grē-), n. A Greek idiom, esp. as imitated in another language; Greek spirit, style, mode of expression, etc., imitation of these. [f. F *grécisme* or med. L *graecismus* (*Graecus* GREEK, -ISM)]

Gr(a)e'cīze (grē-), -ise (-īz), v.t. & i. Give a Greek cast, character, or form, to; favour, imitate, the Greeks. [f. L *graecizare* (prec., -IZE)]

Gr(a)e'co- (grē-), comb. form of L *Graecus* GREEK, as ~-*Roman*. Hence ~MAN'IA(c) nn., ~PHIL a. & n.

graffi'tō (-fē-), n. (pl. -*ti*, pr. -tē). Drawing or writing scratched on wall etc., esp. on ancient wall as at Pompeii; decoration by scratches through plaster showing different-coloured under-surface. [It.]

graft¹ (-ah-), n., & v.t. 1. Shoot or scion inserted in slit of another stock, from which it receives sap; (Surg.) piece of transplanted living tissue; process of ~ing; place where ~ is inserted. 2. v.t. Insert (scion) as ~ (*in*, *into*, *on*, *upon*, *together*); (fig.) insert or fix *in* or *upon* so as to produce vital or indissoluble union; insert ~(s); insert ~(s) upon (stock); (Surg.) transplant (living tissue); (Naut.) cover (ring-bolt etc.) with weaving of small cord; ~*ing-clay*, -*wax*, composition for covering united parts of ~ & stock. [15th c. for earlier *graff* n. & v. f. OF *grafe* f. L f. Gk *graphion* stilus (*graphō* write)]

∥**graft²** (-ah-), n. Depth of earth that may be thrown up at once with spade; crescent-bladed spade. [cogn. w. GRAVE²]

*graft³ (-ah-, -ǎ-), n., & v.i. (colloq.). Illicit spoils in connexion with politics or business, practices intended to secure these; (vb) seek, make, ~, whence ~'ER¹ n. [orig. unkn.]

grail¹, n. = GRADUAL¹. [ME, f. OF *grael* f. eccl. L *gradale* var. of *graduale* GRADUAL¹]

grail², n. (Also *holy* or *saint* ~, or *sangreal*) platter used by Christ at Last Supper, & in which Joseph of Arimathea received his blood at the Cross. [ME, f. OF *graal* etc. f. med. L *gradalis* dish, of unkn. orig.; cf. SANGRAIL, -GREAL]

grail³, n. Comb-maker's file. [f. F *grêle* (*grêler* make thin f. *grêle* adj. f. L *gracilis*)]

grain, n., & v.t. & i. **1.** A fruit or corn of a cereal; (collect. sing.) wheat or the allied food-grasses or their fruit, corn, a particular species of corn; ~ ELEVATOR; (pl.; also ~*s of Paradise* or *Guinea* ~*s*) capsules of W.-Afr. plant used as spice & drug; (pl.) refuse malt after brewing or distilling. **2.** Small hard particle of sand, gold, SALT, gunpowder (*large, small,* ~ *powder*), incense, etc. **3.** Smallest unit of weight, 1/480 of oz. Troy, 1/437.5 of oz. av., smallest possible quantity (*without a* ~ *of vanity, love,* etc.). **4.** (Hist.) kermes, cochineal, or dye made from either of these (*dye in* ~, dye in kermes, dye in any fast colour, dye in the fibre or thoroughly; *in* ~, thorough, genuine, by nature, down-right, indelible); (poet.) dye, colour. **5.** Granular texture, roughness of surface, mottling; texture, arrangement & size of constituent particles, in flesh, skin, wood, stone, etc.; lines of fibre in wood giving a pattern, lamination or planes of cleavage in coal, stone, etc.; (fig.) nature, temper, tendency, (*against the* ~, contrary to inclination). **6.** ~*-leather*, dressed with the ~*-side* (on which the hair was) out; ~*-sick* n., cattle-disease, distension of rumen; hence ~'LESS, ~'Y², (-)~ED³ (-nd), aa. **7.** vb. Form (t. & i.) into ~s; dye in ~; give granular surface to; remove hair from (hides); paint in imitation of ~ of wood or marble; hence ~'ER¹(1, 2) n. [ME, f. OF f. L *gronum*, & f. OF *graine* f. Rom. **grana* collect. fem., orig. neut. pl. of L *granum*]

grains (-z), n. Forked fish-spear or harpoon. [orig. pl. of obs. *grain* fork, prong, f. ON *grein* division; now used as sing.]

graip, n. (Sc.). A three- or four-pronged fork used for lifting dung or placing potatoes etc. [f. ON *greip* corresp. to OE *grāp* grasp]

grallatōr'ial, a. (zool.). Of the *Grallatores* or long-legged wading birds. [f. L *grallator* stilt-walker (*grallae* stilts)]

grāll'och (-ox, see Ap.), n., & v.t. Dead deer's viscera; (vb) disembowel (deer etc.). [f. Gael. *grealach* intestines]

grām¹, n. Chick-pea; any pulse used as horse-fodder. [f. Port. *grāo* f. L *granum* grain]

grām², **grāmme**, n. Unit of mass in metric system, the thousandth part of the international prototype 'kilogram' held in the custody of the *Bureau International des Poids et Mesures* at Sèvres near Paris; *gram-force*, unit of force, that force which when applied to a body of mass one ~ imparts thereto the standard acceleration of exactly 980·665 centimetres per second squared. [F (*-me*), f. LL f. Gk *gramma* small weight, see -GRAM]

-grām, suf. (chiefly) f. Gk *gramma -atos* (*graphō* write, -M) thing written, letter of alphabet, forming nn. (1) prepositional compds f. Gk (*anagram, diagram, epigram*), (2) n. compds (*chronogram, logo-*

gram), (3) compds of Gk numeral with *gramma* or with *grammē* line, where Gk would have *-grammon* neut. adj., (4) *telegram* (1857), violating Gk anal., suggested *cablegram*.

grām'a, **grămm'a**, n. (Also ~ *grass*) kinds of low pasture grass in W. & S.W. parts of U.S. [f. Sp. *grama*]

‖ **grām'arȳe**, n. (arch.). Magic, necromancy. [ME, f. AF *gramarie* learning, GRAMMAR]

‖ **gramēr'cȳ**, int. (arch.). Thank you. [ME, f. OF *grant merci* (God give you) great reward (GRAND, MERCY)]

grămĭnā'ceous (-shus), **gramĭn'ĕous**, aa. Of, like, grass, grassy. So **grāmĭnĭv'orous** a. [f. L *gramen -inis* grass, -ACEOUS, & L *gramineus* (-EOUS)]

grămm'alogue (-ŏg), n. (shorthand). Word represented by single sign; letter or character standing for word, logogram. [irreg. f. Gk *gramma* (-GRAM), *logos* word]

grămm'ar, n. Art & science dealing with a language's inflexions or other means of showing relation between words as used in speech or writing, & its phonetic system (usu. divided into phonology, accidence, & syntax; *general, philosophical,* or *universal* ~, science of the distinctions of thought recognized & variously expressed in the grammatical systems of actual languages; *historical* ~, study of the development of a language's inflexions & syntax; *comparative* ~, study of the relation between two or more ~s); treatise or book on ~; person's manner of using grammatical forms, speech or writing regarded as good or bad by the rules of ~, what is correct according to those rules; body of forms & usages in a language (*Latin* ~); elements, rudiments, of an art or science; ~*-school*, ‖ school founded about 16th c. for teaching Latin, of which many are now of the public-school type. Hence ~'LESS a. [ME, f. OF *gramaire* irreg. f. L f. Gk *grammatikē* (*tekhnē* art) of letters (*gramma* see -GRAM)]

grammar'ian, n. One versed in grammar, philologist. [ME, f. OF *gramarien* (prec., -IAN)]

grammăt'ic|al, a. Of grammar (~*al gender*, determined by form not sex; ~*al sense*, literal, irrespective of other considerations than the rules of grammar); conforming to the rules of grammar, or to the formal principles of an art, so (f. earlier *grammatic*)~IZE(3) v.t. Hence~al|LY² adv. [f. F, or LL *grammaticalis* (GRAMMAR, -AL)]

grămme. See GRAM².

grăm'ophône, n. Phonograph of the kind using flat discs for its reproduction of sound. [irreg. form made by inverting PHONOGRAM]

grăm'pus, n. Kinds of blowing spouting blunt-headed dolphin-like cetacean; person who breathes loud. [16th c. *graundepose* f. 14th c. *grapeys* f. OF *grapois* f. L *crassus piscis* fat fish]

gränadill'a, grĕ-, n. Kinds of passion-flower. [Sp., dim. of *granada* pomegranate]

grän'arў, n. Storehouse for threshed grain; region producing, & esp. exporting, much corn. [f. L *granarium* (*granum* grain, -ARY¹); cf. GARNER]

gränd, a. & n. **1.** (In official titles) chief over others, of highest rank, (*G~ Almoner, Falconer,* etc., holders of old offices still existing; *G~* CROSS¹; *G~ Duke, Duchess,* hist., ruler of some European States called *G~ Duchy,* also child of Tsar, whence *G~dūc'*AL a.; ~ *duke,* also, great horned owl; *G~ Master,* head of military order of knighthood, head of Freemasons or of one of their provinces, & of Oddfellows etc.; *G~ Vizier,* chief minister of a Moslem country, esp. formerly of Turkish Empire). **2.** (Law) great, principal, (opp. *petty, common;* ~ *assize, inquest, jury*). **3.** Of most or great importance (*that is the* ~ *question; made a* ~ *mistake*), final, summing up minor constituents, (~ *total;* ~ *finale; the* ~ *sum* or *result of his achievements*). **4.** (Distinguishing parts of large building) main (*the* ~ *staircase, entrance,* etc.). **5.** (In F phrases or imitations) great (~ *army, G~ Canal, G~ Hotel; G~ Fleet,* main British fleet in the war of 1914–18). **6.** Conducted with solemnity, splendour, etc.; fine, splendid, gorgeous. **7.** Belonging to high society, distinguished, (*do the* ~, put on airs); imposing, impressive, great & handsome. **8.** Dignified, lofty, in conception, treatment, or expression (~ *style,* fitted for great subjects); morally imposing, noble, admirable, (*the G~ Old Man* or *G.O.M.,* W. E. Gladstone). **9.** Very satisfactory (colloq.; *had a* ~ *run; ground was in* ~ *condition*). **10.** (In names of relationships) in the second degree of ascent or descent (~*'son,* one's child's son; ~*nephew,* one's nephew's or niece's son; ~*'mother,* ~*aunt,* one's parent's mother or aunt; so ~*'child;* ~*daughter;* ~*'father,* ~*father's clock,* worked by weights in tall wooden case; ~*mamma;* ~*'mother,* whence ~*'*motherLY¹ a., esp. of legislation etc. = excessively PATERNAL; *leach your* ~*mother to suck* EGGS; ~*mother* v.t., coddle etc.; ~*niece* ~*'papa;* ~*'parent;* ~*'sire,* esp. of animal's sire, also = ancestor, old man, & a method of ringing changes on bells; ~*uncle*). **11.** ~ *air,* distinguished appearance; ‖ ~ *committee,* one of two standing committees of House of Commons sessionally appointed to consider Law & Trade Bills; ~ LODGE; *G~ Monarch,* Louis XIV of France; ‖ *G~ National,* annual steeplechase at Liverpool; ~ *piano(forte),* large horizontal piano; ~ *stand,* principal stand for spectators at races etc.; ~ *tour* (arch.), tour of chief towns etc. of Europe completing education. **12.** n. ~ *piano (upright* ~, usu. a large upright piano with all improvements). **13.** *A

thousand dollars (sl.). Hence ~*'*LY² adv.; ~*'*NESS n. [OF, f. L *grandis* full-grown]

grän'dăm(e), n. (arch.). Grandmother; (-*m* only) animal's dam's dam; ancestress; old woman. [ME, f. AF *graund dame* (prec., DAM²)]

grän(d)'dăd, n. (Childish or affectionate for) grandfather. [GRAND, DAD]

grande (see Ap.), fem. of GRAND (~ *toilette* pr. twahlĕt', ceremonial costume; ~ *passion* pr. pås'yawn, engrossing love affair). [F]

grändee', n. Spanish or Portuguese nobleman of highest rank: person of high rank or eminence. [f. Sp. & Port. *grande* GRAND]

grän'deur (-dyer**),** n. Great power, rank, or eminence; great nobility of character; sublimity, majesty, of appearance or effect; conscious dignity, splendour of living, surroundings, etc. [F (GRAND)]

Grand Guignol (grahn gēnyŏl'**),** n. Dramatic entertainment in which short pieces often of strongly sensational type are played successively. [name (= Great Punch) of theatre in Paris; F *Guignol* name of a town character of Lyons (1795)]

grändil'oquｌent, a. Pompous in language; given to tall talk. Hence ~ENCE n., ~ently² adv. [after *eloquent* f. L *grandiloquus* (GRAND, -*loquus* -speaking f. *loqui* speak)]

grän'diōse, a. Producing, intended or trying to produce, an impression of greatness, planned on a magnificent scale, pompous. Hence *grändios'*ITY (-ŏs²) n., ~LY² (-sl-) adv. [F, f. It. *grandioso* (GRAND, -OSE¹)]

Grändisōn'ian, a. Marked by stately courtesy & chivalric magnanimity. [Sir C. *Grandison* in Richardson's novel, -IAN]

gränge (-j**),** n. ‖ Barn (arch.); country house with farm-buildings attached. [ME, f. AF *graunge* f. med. L *granica* (*granum* grain)]

grän'ger|ize (-j-**), -ise (-**īz**),** v.t. Extra-illustrate (book) by inserting prints etc. often cut from other books. Hence ~īzA²-TION, ~IZER¹, ~ISM(1), ~ITE(1), nn. [J. *Granger* published 1769 a Hist. of England with blank pages for illustrations]

granif'erous, a. Producing grain or grain-like seed. So **grän'**IFORM, **graniv'**OROUS, aa. [f. L *granifer* (GRAIN, -FEROUS)]

grän'ite, n. Granular crystalline rock of quartz, orthoclase feldspar, & mica, used for building (*bite on* ~, waste pains, persist in vain); ~*ware,* speckled pottery imitating ~, kind of enamelled ironware; *the* ~ *city,* Aberdeen. Hence **granit'**IC a., **grän'**ITOID a. & n., **granit'**IFORM a. [f. It. *granito* orig. grained (*grano* f. L *granum*)]

gränn'om, grän'am, n. Kind of water-fly; imitation of it for fly-fishing. [orig. unkn.]

gränn'ў, n. (Fam., affectionate, or derog. for) grandmother; (also ~*'s bend* or *knot*) reef-knot crossed the wrong way. [f. obs. *grannam* for GRANDAM +-Y³]

grănolith′ic, a. Of a kind of concrete. [L *granum* grain, Gk *lithos* stone, -IC]

grant (-ah-), v.t., & n. **1.** Consent to fulfil (request etc.; in p.p. formerly common, now rare, as answer to *I beg your pardon*); concede as indulgence, allow (person) to have (thing; noun, *that*, or *to* do); bestow (possession, right) formally, transfer (property) legally, whence **grantee′**, **grantor′**, (-ah-) nn.; concede (proposition) as basis for argument (noun, *this* etc., *that*-clause, or something *to be* something; *I ~ you*, I admit; *take for ~ed*, assume); hence ~'ABLE a. **2.** n. ~ing (*the ~ or refusal of*); formal conferment, legal assignment; thing, esp. sum. ~ed (often *capitation ~, ~-in-aid*); conveyance by written instrument; ~-*aided school*, one receiving some financial assistance from public funds. [ME, f. OF *greanter* f. Rom. *credentare f. part. of *credere* entrust]

Granth (grŭnt), n. Sacred scriptures of the Sikhs. [Hindi, = book, code (f. Skr. *grantha* tying, literary composition)]

grăn′ūl|ar, a. Of, like, grains; with granulated surface or structure. Hence ~ă′RITY n., ~arLY² adv., ~o- comb. form, ~ous a. [f. LL *granulum* small grain (*granum*, -ULE), -UL-, -AR¹]

grăn′ūl|āte, v.t. & i. Form (t. & i.) into grains; roughen surface of; (of wound etc.) form small prominences as beginning of healing or junction, heal, join. Hence or cogn. ~ATE² (-*at*) a., ~A′TION, ~ātor, nn. [as prec., -ATE³]

grăn′ūle, n. Small grain. [as prec.]

grāpe, n. Green or purple berry growing in clusters on vine, eaten as fruit or used in making wine (*the ~, the juice of the ~*, wine; *the ~s are sour, sour ~s*, said when person disparages what he vainly desires); ~-*shot*; diseased growth like bunch of ~s on pastern of horse etc., or on pleura in cattle; ~-*brandy*, distilled from~s, or wine, alone; ~-CURE¹; ~-*fruit*, large round yellow citrus fruit with rather acid juicy pulp; ~-*house*, vinery; ~-*scissors*, for thinning ~-bunches at early stage of growth, also for dividing bunches at table; ~-*shot* (hist.), small balls put several together in bag etc. to make scattering charge for cannon; ~-*stone*, one of seeds inside ~; ~-*sugar*, dextrose or glucose; ~-*vine*, vine, skating figure in which both feet are on ice together & form interlacing lines, rumour, (false) report. Hence **grăp′ery**(3) n., **grăp′y²** a. [ME, f. OF, bunch of ~s, prob. f. *graper* gather with vine-hook (f. *grape*, f. WG *krăppo (= OHG *krăpfo* hook))]

grăph¹ (*or* -ahf), n., & v.t. Symbolic diagram expressing system of mathematical or chemical connexion; curve (in statistical statements); (v.t.) plot or trace on a ~. [abbr. of *graphic formula*]

grăph² (-ahf), n., & v.t. Gelatine copying apparatus; (v.t.) copy; multiply, with this. [colloq. abbr. of *chromograph*, *hectograph*, etc.]

-graph (-ahf), suf. repr. F -*graphe*, L f. Gk -*graphos*, -written, -writing, -writer, denoting (1) thing written in such a way (f. Gk, as *auto~, chiro~, holo~*; on Gk st., as *litho~, photo~*; & in hybrids, as *picto~*); (2) instrument that records something or by some means (*helio~, seismo~, tele~*); (3) write in such a way (*calli~, hecto~*).

-grapher, suf. repr. Gk -*graphos* (prec.) & forming nn. denoting one versed in -GRAPHY. [-ER¹]

grăph′ic(al rare), aa. Of drawing, painting, engraving, etching, etc.; vividly descriptive, lifelike; of writing; (of minerals) showing marks like writing on surface or in fracture; of diagrams or symbolic curves. [f. L f. Gk *graphikos* (*graphē* writing, -IC)]

-grăph′ic(al), suff. = of or by -GRAPHY.

grăph′icallÿ, adv. As in a picture, vividly; by writing; by diagrams or GRAPH¹s. [-LY²]

grăph′īte, n. PLUMBAGO. Hence **graphīt′-ic**, **grăph′itoid**, aa. [f. G *graphit* (Gk *graphō* write, -ITE¹)]

grăph′iūre, n. S.-Afr. rodent with tail ending in pencil of hairs. [f. Gk *grapheion* pencil, *oura* tail]

graphŏl′ogÿ, n. Study of, art of inferring character from, handwriting; system of graphic formulae, notation for GRAPH¹s. [f. Gk *graphē* writing, -LOGY]

grăph′otýpe, n. (Process for making) relief block for surface-printing. [as prec. +TYPE]

-graphÿ, suf. = F, G -*graphie*, L-*graphia*, repr. Gk -*graphia* forming nn. denoting (1) styles of writing, drawing, etc. (*litho~, brachy~, steno~, calli~*); (2) descriptive science (*geo~, biblio~, seleno~*).

grăp′nel, n. Iron-clawed instrument thrown with rope to seize object, esp. enemy's ship; small anchor with several flukes used for boats & balloons. [ME, f. AF *grapenel f. OF *grapon* (mod. *grappin*) f. WG *krăppo see GRAPE]

grăp′ple, n., & v.t. & i. **1.** Clutching-instrument, grapnel. **2.** Hold or grip (as) of wrestlers, close contest. **3.** vb. Seize, fasten, (as) with grapnel; take hold of, grip, with the hands, come to close quarters with; contend *with, together*, or abs., in close fight, battle *with*; ~ *with*, try to overcome, accomplish, or deal with. [(1) f. OF *grapil* dim. of *grappe*, see GRAPE, GRAPNEL]

grăp′pling, n. In vbl senses; also, ~-*iron*, grapnel. [-ING¹]

grasp (-ah-), v.t. & i., & n. **1.** ~ *at*, try to seize, accept with avidity; clutch at, seize greedily, (part.) avaricious, whence ~'ingLY² adv., ~'ingNESS n.; hold firmly (~ *nettle*, tackle difficulty or danger boldly), grip; get mental hold of, comprehend; hence ~'ABLE a. **2.** n. Fast hold, grip, (*within, beyond,*) one's ~, close, not close, enough to be ~ed); control, mastery; mental hold, comprehensiveness of mind. [14th c. *grasp*, *grapse* perh. f. OE *grǽpsan* f. Gmc *graip*- GROPE, but cf. LG (G), EFris. *grapsen*]

grass (-ah-), n., & v.t. **1.** Herbage of which blades or leaves & stalks are eaten by cattle, horses, sheep, etc. (*not let ~ grow, ~ does not grow, under one's feet,* of person who wastes no time in doing something; *hear the ~ grow,* be of preternatural acuteness); any species of this (including in bot. use, excluding in pop. use, the cereals, reeds, & bamboos; usu. with defining words, as *bunch, spear, ~,* *~ of Parnassus*); (sl.) asparagus; grazing, pasture, (*be at, go, put, send, turn out, to ~; at ~,* fig., out of work, making holiday, etc.; so perh. *~ widow,* wife whose husband is absent); pasture land; *~-* -covered ground (*keep off the~*); (Mining) earth's surface, pit-head; *send, go, to ~,* knock (person), be knocked or fall, down; *~'hopper,* kinds of jumping & chirping insect (*~-hopper-beam,* working-beam in engine pivoted at end instead of in middle); *~-snake,* ‖ common ringed snake; *~-tree,* kinds of Australasian tree; hence *~'LESS, ~'Y²,* aa. **2.** v.t. Cover with turf; lay (flax etc.) on *~* to bleach; knock down, fell, (opponent); bring (fish) to bank, (bird by shot) to ground. [OE *grǽs,* OS, OHG, ON, Goth. *gras* f. Gmc *grasom,* cogn. w. GREEN, GROW]

grāte¹, n. = GRATING (rare), whence **grāt'ED²** a.; (frame of metal bars for confining fuel in) fireplace or furnace. Hence *~'LESS* (-tl-) a. [15th c., f. OF *grate* f. Rom. *grata, crata* f. L *cratis* hurdle; cf. GRIDDLE]

grāt|e², v.t. & i. Reduce to small particles by rubbing on rough surface, whence (-)*~'ER¹*(2) n.; have irritating effect (*up*)*on*; grind (teeth); rub (i. & t.) with harsh scraping noise *against* or (*up*)*on* something else; sound harshly or discordantly (*a ~ing laugh, voice*); (of hinge etc.) creak. Hence *~'ingLY²* adv. [15th c., f. OF *grater* f. Rom. *grattare* f. WG *kratton* (= OHG *krazzōn*) SCRATCH]

grāte'ful (-tf-), a. Acceptable, comforting, refreshing; thankful, feeling or showing gratitude (*to* person, *for* thing). Hence *~LY²* adv., *~NESS* n. [f. obs. *grate* adj. f. L *gratus* +-FUL]

grāt'ĭcŭle, n. Fine lines or fibres incorporated in telescope or other optical instrument as measuring scale or as aid in locating objects; (Surveying) network or lines on paper representing meridians & parallels. [F, f. med. L *graticula* for *craticula* gridiron (L *cratis* hurdle, -ULE)]

grāt'ĭfy, v.t. Remunerate, fee, make present usu. of money to; bribe; please, satisfy, oblige, delight, whence *~ING²* a.

(*to*), *~ingLY²* adv.; please by compliance, assent to wish of, give free course to or indulge (desire, feeling, impulse). So **grātĭfĭCA'TION** n. [f. F *gratifier* or L *gratificari* (*gratus* pleasing, -FY)]

grātin (see Ap.), n. Way of cooking, dish cooked, by crumbling bread or grating cheese & cooking between two fires to produce light crust; *au* (ō) *~,* so prepared. [F]

grāt'ing, n. Framework of parallel or crossed wooden or metal bars; (Opt.) set of parallel wires, or surface of glass etc. ruled with parallel lines, for producing spectra by diffraction. [GRATE¹ +-ING¹]

grāt'ĭs, adv. & a. Gratuitous(ly), (given, done) for nothing, without charge, free. [L, contracted abl. pl. of *gratia* favour]

grāt'ĭtūde, n. Being thankful, appreciation of & inclination to return kindness. [f. F, or LL *gratitudo* (*gratus* thankful, -TUDE)]

grātū'ĭtous, a. Got or given free, not earned or paid for; uncalled for, unwarranted, motiveless, done or acting without good or assignable reason (*a ~ lie* or *liar*). Hence *~LY²* adv., *~NESS* n. [f. L *gratuitus* spontaneous, cogn. w. *gratia* favour, +-OUS]

grātū'ĭty, n. Money present of amount fixed by giver in recognition of an inferior's good offices, tip; bounty to soldiers etc. on demobilization or retirement or some other occasions. [f. F *gratuité* or med. L *gratuitas* gift (*gratus* grateful, -TY)]

‖ **grāt'ŭlāte, -ā'tion.** (Arch. for) congr-.

‖ **grāt'ŭlātŏry,** a. Expressing joy at another's success etc., complimentary, congratulatory. [f. L *gratulatorius* (L *gratulari* congratulate +-ORY)]

gravām'ĕn, n. (pl. *-mina,* rare). Grievance; ‖ memorial from Lower House of Convocation to Upper on disorders or grievances of Church; essence, worst part, *of* accusation. [LL, inconvenience (*gravare* to load f. *gravis* heavy, -MEN)]

grāve¹, n. Excavation to receive corpse, mound or monument over it, (*secret as the ~,* quite; *make one turn in his ~,* of act etc. that he would have been pained by while alive; *someone walking on my ~,* said when one shivers unaccountably; *one* FOOT¹ *in the ~*), whence *~'LESS* (-vl-) a.; being dead, death, Hades, whence *~ᶜ* WARD (-vw-) adv. & a.; receptacle of for what is dead (*~ of reputations,* where many reputations have been lost); trench for earthing up potatoes etc.; *~-* -*clothes,* wrappings in which corpse is buried; *~-digger,* lit., also kinds of insect that bury bodies of insects etc. as food for their larvae; *~'stone,* stone over *~,* inscribed stone at head or foot of *~;* *~'yard,* burial ground. [OE *grǽf,* OS *graf,* OHG *grap* f. WG *grabhom*]

grāve², v.t. (p.p. *~n, ~d,* as stated). (Arch.) bury (*~d*); (arch.) carve, sculpture, engrave, (material, representation; ~n, ~d; ~n image, idol); (fig.) fix indelibly (on, in, mind etc.; ~n, ~d). [OE grafan, OHG graban, ON grafa, Goth. graban f. Gmc *grabhan (prec.; see GROOVE)]

grāve³, a. & n. 1. Important, weighty, needing serious thought; (of faults, difficulties, responsibilities, symptoms) formidable, threatening, serious; dignified, solemn, slow-moving, not gay; sombre, plain, not showy; hence ~'LY² (-vl-) adv. 2. (Of accent) low-pitched, not acute; ~ ACCENT¹. 3. n. ~ accent. [f. F, or L gravis heavy, serious]

grāve⁴, v.t. Clean (ship's bottom) by burning off accretions & tarring while aground or in graving-DOCK⁴. [perh. f. OF grave = grève shore]

grăv'el, n., & v.t. (-ll-). 1. Coarse sand & small water-worn or pounded stones, much used for laying paths & roads; (Geol., Mining) stratum of this, esp. one containing gold (pay ~, containing enough gold to yield profit); (Path.) (disease with) aggregations of visible urinary crystals; ~-blind, more than SAND-BLIND (Shaks., M. of V., II. ii. 38); hence ~lY² a. 2. v.t. Lay, strew, with ~; perplex, puzzle, nonplus, (f. obs. sense run aground). [ME, f. OF gravele f. grave (prec.)]

grăv'er, n. In vbl senses; esp., burin. [-ER¹]

Graves (grahv), n. Light white wine produced in the ~ district of France. [place]

grăv'id, a. (literary) Pregnant. [f. L gravidus (GRAVE³)]

grăv'it|āte, v.i. & t. Move or tend by force of gravity towards a body; sink (as) by gravity, tend to low level, settle down; (Diamond-digging) manipulate (gravel) so that heavy stones sink to bottom; (transf.) be strongly attracted to(wards) some centre of influence. Hence ~A'TION n., ~ā'tional (-shon-), ~ATIVE, aa. [f. mod. L gravitare (after GRAVITY), -ATE³]

grăv'itў, n. 1. Being grave, solemnity; importance, seriousness; staidness, sobriety, serious demeanour. 2. Weight (CENTRE¹ of ~; specific ~, relative weight of any kind of matter, expressed by ratio of given volume to same volume of a standard—usu. water for liquid or solid, & air for gas). 3. Attractive force by which bodies tend to centre of earth, degree of intensity of this measured by acceleration, degree of intensity with which one body is affected by the attraction of gravitation exercised by another body. [f. F gravité or L gravitas (GRAVE³, -TY)]

gravūre', n. (Short for) PHOTOGRAVURE.

grāv'ў, n. Juices that exude from flesh during & after cooking; dressing for food made from these with other materials; ~-boat, boat-shaped vessel for ~; ~ beef, part of leg of beef cooked for its~. [perh.

a misreading as grave of grane in OF cookery books; OF grane, grenon = stew]

gray. See GREY.

gray'ling, n. Silver-grey freshwater fish with long high dorsal fin; butterfly with grey under-side to wings. [GREY+-LING¹]

grāz|e¹, v.i. & t. Feed (esp. cattle, or intr. of cattle) on growing grass etc. or ~'ING¹(3) n.; feed on (grass etc., often down); tend ~ing cattle; pasture cattle. [OE grasian (GRASS n.)]

grāz|e², v.t. & i., & n. 1. Touch lightly in passing; abrade (skin etc.) in rubbing past; suffer slight abrasion of (part of body); go with passing contact against, along, through, by, past, etc. 2. n. ~ing abrasion. [orig. obsc.; perh. by transf. f. prec. 'take off the grass close to the ground' (of a bullet etc.]

grā'zier (-zher), n. One who feeds cattle for market. Hence grā'ziERY(2) (-zheri) n. [GRASS+-IER]

grease¹ (-ēs), n. Fat of deer or other game (in~, in pride or prime of ~, fit for killing, fat); melted fat of dead animals, esp. when soft; oily or fatty matter, esp. as lubricant; oily matter in wool, uncleansed wool, (wool in the ~, in fleeces); disease in horses' heels; ~-box, attached to train-wheel for lubrication; ~-paint, composition for painting actors' faces; ~-trap, appliance for catching ~ in drains. [ME, f. OF graisse f. Rom. *crassia (L crassus a. fat]

grease² (or -ēz), v.t. Anoint, soil, or lubricate, with grease (~ the wheels, make affairs go smoothly, esp. by money; ~ palm of, bribe; like~d lightning, sl., very fast); affect (horse) with grease. [f. prec.]

greas'er (or -z-), n. In vbl senses, esp.: head fireman on steamer; *(sl.) native Mexican or Spanish-American. [-ER¹]

greas'lў (or -z-), a. Smeared or covered with, containing, made of, like, with too much, grease; (of wool) uncleansed; (of horse) affected with the grease; slimy with mud or moisture; (of manners or expression) disagreeably unctuous; ~y fritillary, kind of butterfly; ~y pole, greased for climbing or working on in sports. Hence~ILY² adv.,~INESS n., (-z-). [-Y²]

great (grāt), a. & n. 1. Large, big, (usu. with implied surprise, admiration, contempt, indignation, etc., as made a ~ blot, look at that ~ wasp; often colloq. preceding other adj., a ~ big loaf or thick stick; as distinctive epithet of the larger species or individual, as ~ A, Z, the capital letters, ~ St John's wort, also ~er celandine etc., ~ titmouse, G~ BEAR¹, G~ Malvern etc., G~ Portland Street; also in a few phrases, as a ~ DEAL¹, MANY; the ~ majority, much the larger part; ~est common MEASURE, lived to a ~ age, a ~ while ago; || ~ with child, arch., pregnant). 2. Beyond the ordinary (take ~ care; of ~ popularity; shows ~ ignorance). 3. Important, elevated, distinguished, critical, the chief, pre-eminent, (*it is a ~ thing to have —*; *a ~ occasion*; *the ~ attraction*; *the G~ Powers of Europe*, chief States; *the ~ world*, high society; in excll., as *G~ God!*, *Caesar!*, *Scott!*; *the G~*, appended in sense *the best known of the name*, as *Alexander the G~*, or prefixed in titles, as *the G~ King*, of ancient Persia, *the G~ Mogul*, etc., & burlesqued in *the G~ UNPAID, UNWASHED*). **4.** Of remarkable ability, genius, intellectual or practical qualities, loftiness or integrity of character, (*a ~ judge, painter*, etc.; *the truly ~ man*; *~ thoughts*), whence *~-hearted*[2] a. **5.** pred. Having much skill *at* or information *on*; highly satisfactory (*wouldn't it be ~ if — ?*). **6.** Fully deserving the name of, (with agent-nouns) doing the act much or on a large scale, (*a ~ scoundrel, fiasco; ~ friends; is a ~ dancer, landowner*). **7.** (Prefixed once or more to *uncle, aunt, nephew, niece*, & kinship words compounded with GRAND) one degree further removed upwards or downwards. **8.** *G~ Assize, Day*, or *Inquest*, Day of Judgement; *G~ Bible*, Coverdale's Version 1539; *G~ BRITAIN, CHARTER, CIRCLE*[1]; ||*~'COAT*[1], whence *~coat'ED*[2], *~coat'LESS*, aa.; *the ~ COMMONER; G~er BRITAIN; ~est happiness of the ~est number*, test principle of Benthamism; ||*~ go*, final examination for B.A. at Cambridge, cf. *greats* below; *~ gross*, twelve gross; *~ house*, chief house in village etc.; *~ organ*, chief manual with its related pipes and mechanism in an organ having two or more manuals; *~ PRIMER; ~ toe*, now usu. BIG *toe; G~ War* (of 1914–18). Hence *~'EN*[6] v.t. & i. (arch.), *~'NESS* n., (-āt-). **9.** n. (Abs. use of adj.) *the~*, (pl.) = persons (also without *the* in *~ & small*) (sing.) what is *~*. **10.** ||*~s*, Oxford B.A. final examination, esp. that for honours in Lit. Hum. [OE *grēat*, OS *grōt*, OHG *grōz* f. WG **grautaz*]

great'ly (-rāt-), adv. Much, by much, (usu. with vbs, participles, or comparatives; *~ esteemed, superior; should ~ prefer*); nobly, loftily. [-LY[2]]

greave, n. (usu. pl.). Piece(s) of armour for shin(s). [ME, f. OF *greve* shin, greave, of unkn. orig.]

greaves (-vz), n. pl. Fibrous tallow refuse, used as food of dog etc. or fish-bait. [f. LG *greven* pl.]

grebe, n. Kinds of short-bodied lobe-footed almost tailless diving bird; its plumage as trimming. [f. F *grèbe* of unkn. orig.]

Gre'cian (-shn), a. & n. **1.** Greek (rare except of architecture & facial outline; also in ||*~ bend*, affected attitude in walking prevalent c. 1870, = GREEK *gift; ~ gift*, ||*~ knot*, way of dressing woman's hair at back of head, *~ nose*, straight & continuing forehead line without dip, *~ profile*, with *~ nose*, ||*~ slippers*, trade name

for oriental shape). **2.** n. Greek scholar; || boy of highest class at Christ's Hospital [f. L *Graecia* Greece *+ -AN*]

Grecism, Grecize, Greco-. See Grae-.

greed, n. Insatiate longing esp. for wealth. [back formation f. foll.]

greed'|y̆, a. Ravenous, voracious, gluttonous, avaricious, covetous, rapacious, (often *of*); eager, keen, intensely desirous (*to do*). Hence *~ĭLY*[2] adv., *~ĭNESS* n. [OE *grēdig*, OS *grādag*, OHG *grātac*, ON *grāthugr*, Goth. *grēdags* f. Gmc **grēdhuz* hunger]

Greek, n. & a. **1.** Native of Greece, member of *~* race, (*when ~ meets ~, then comes the tug of war*, orig. *~s joined ~s, then was*, said of equal encounter); member of *~* Church; cunning person, sharper; the *~* language (*~ to me*, beyond my comprehension), whence *~'LESS* a, **2.** adj. Of Greece or its people, Hellenic; of, according to, written or spoken in, *~* (*~ Fathers*, FATHER[1]s of the Church who wrote in *~*); *~ Church*, also *Orthodox* or *Eastern*, Church acknowledging Patriarch of Constantinople, divided from Rome in 9th c., & including esp. Christians of Greece, Russia, & Turkish Empire; *~ CALENDS, FIRE*[1], *FRET*[1] or *key; ~ CROSS*[1]; *~ gift*, one given with intent to harm (Virg. *Aen.* ii. 49). [adj. f. n.; OE *Crēcas* (pl.), OHG *Chrēch*, Goth. *Krēks* f. Gmc **Krekaz* f. L *Graecus* f. Gk *Graikoi* prehistoric name of Hellenes; sp. *G-* already in OE *Grecas* after L]

green[1], a. & n. **1.** Of the colour between blue & yellow in the spectrum, coloured like grass, sea-water, emerald, olive, etc. **2.** Covered with herbage, verdant, in leaf, (*a ~ Christmas, season, Yule*, mild, without snow). **3.** (Of complexion) pale, sickly-hued, (*~ eye*, jealousy, whence *~'eyED*[3] (-īd) a.; *~ jaundice*, kind in which patient's skin is *~*); (fig.) jealous, envious. **4.** Vegetable (*~ food*, MEAT). **5.** (Of fruit etc.) unripe, young & tender, flourishing, not dried. **6.** Full of vitality, not withered or worn out, (*in the ~, dry, tree*, under good, bad, conditions; *a ~ old age*). **7.** Immature, undeveloped, inexperienced, gullible. **8.** Not dried, seasoned, or tanned. **9.** Fresh, not healed, (*a ~ wound*). **10.** **~back*, U.S. legal-tender note, note issued by any U.S. national bank; *~-blind*, having retina insensitive to *~* rays; *~ cheese*, unripened cheese, whey cheese, cheese coloured *~* with sage; (*Board of*) *G~ Cloth*, Lord Steward's department of Royal Household; *~ crop*, used for food in *~* state (opp. *hay* etc.); ||*~ drake*, mayfly; *~ earth*, hydrous silicate of potassium, iron, & other bases; *~ fat*, of turtle, esteemed by epicures; *~'finch* or *~ linnet*, bird with yellow & *~* plumage; ||*~ fingers* (colloq.), skill in gardening; ||*~'fly*, kind of aphis; *~'gage*, roundish *~* fine-flavoured plum (Sir W. Gage c. 1725); *~ goose*, killed under four

months old and eaten without stuffing;
~'grocer(y), (business of, things sold by)
retail dealer in fruit & vegetables; ~'heart,
a British Guiana timber tree; ~'horn, ignoramus, raw hand, simpleton; ~'house, of
glass for rearing delicate plants; ‖~ light
(colloq.), permission to go ahead with
some project; ~-man, golf-course keeper;
~ manure, growing plants ploughed into
soil; ‖~-peak, ~ woodpecker (transl.
of It. picchio verde); ~-room, accommodating actors & actresses when off stage;
~'sand, = ~ earth, kind of sandstone
largely of this earth, stratum largely of
this sandstone; ~'shank, large kind of
sandpiper; ~'sick(ness), (affected with)
CHLOROSIS; ~-stick, bone-fracture, esp.
in children, in which one side of bone is
broken & one only bent; ~'stone, kinds
of ~ eruptive rock containing feldspar
& hornblende, also kind of jade; ~-
stuff, vegetation, ~ vegetables; ~'sward,
turf; ~ table, gaming table; ~'tail, gran-
nom; ~ tea, made from steam-dried
leaves; ~'weed, kind of genista used for
dyeing; ~'wood, woodlands in summer,
esp. as scene of outlaw life; ‖~'yard,
enclosure for stray beasts, pound; hence
~'ISH¹(2), & (in comb. as ~y-yellow) ~'Y²,
aa., ~'LY² adv., ~'NESS n. 11. n. What is
~, ~ part of anything, ~ colour, (do you
see any ~, i.e. sign of gullibility, in my
eye?); ~ dye (usu. with epithet, as mineral,
Paris, ~). 12. Vigour, youth, virility,
(usu. in the ~). 13. Verdure, vegetation,
also ~'ERY n. 14. ‖(pl.). ~ vegetables
before or after cooking. 15. Piece of
public or common grassy land; grass-plot
used for special purpose (esp. in comb. as
bleaching, bowling, putting, ~~). [OE
grēne, OS grōni, OHG gruoni, ON grœnn
f. Gmc *grōnjaz f. *gro- (GROW)]

green², v.i. & t. Become green, esp. with
verdure; dye green, soil etc. with green;
(sl.) hoax, take in. [OE grēnian (prec.)]

green'er, n. (sl.). Raw hand, esp. newly
arrived foreigner seeking work. [-ER¹]

green'ing, n. Kind of apple, green when
ripe. [-ING³]

green'let, n. = VIREO. [GREEN¹, -LET]

greenth, n. (rare). Verdure. [-TH¹]

Greenwich (grĭn'ĭj), n. Town in Kent,
formerly with State observatory now
moved to Herstmonceux in Sussex (~
time, mean time for meridian of ~, standard time in Britain & some other
countries); ~ Hospital, formerly used to
accommodate old and disabled navy
seamen (who are now out-pensioners),
later occupied by the Royal Naval
College for officer students.

greet¹, v.t. Accost with salutation; salute
with words or gestures, receive on meeting or arrival with speech or action
(friendly or not); (of cheers etc.) hail; (of
sight etc.) meet (eye, ear). Hence ~'ING¹
n. [OE grētan, OS grōtian, OHG gruozzen
f. WG *grōtjan cry out etc.]

‖greet², v.i. (Sc.). Weep. [OE grētan
(grēotan), OS (griotan), ON grâta, Goth.
grētan f. Gmc *grætan]

greff'ier, n. Registrar, notary, (esp. in
foreign countries & Channel Islands). [F,
f. med. L graphiarius f. L graphium
stilus; see GRAFT¹]

gregar'ious, a. Living in flocks or communities; fond of company; (Bot.) growing in clusters; of flocks, of crowds.
Hence ~LY² adv., ~NESS n. [f. L gregarius
(grex -egis flock, -ARY¹)+-OUS]

Gregŏr'ian, a. & n. 1. Of, according to,
the plain-chant or plain-song ritual music
named after Pope Gregory I (n., a ~
chant); ~ tones, eight plain-song melodies
prescribed for psalms in R.C. Ch. 2.
Established by Pope Gregory XIII (~
CALENDAR, correction 1582 of the Julian;
~ style=new STYLE¹; ~ epoch, from 1582).
[f. LL f. Gk Grēgorios Gregory+-AN]

greg'orў-powd'er, n. Compound powder
of rhubarb, used as aperient. [J. Gregory,
Scottish physician d. 1822]

grem'ial, n. Silk apron placed on bishop's
lap at some ceremonies. [f. LL gremialis
(L gremium lap, -AL)]

‖grem'lin, n. (R.A.F. sl.). Mischievous
sprite alleged to cause mishaps. [orig.
unkn.]

grenade', n. Small explosive shell thrown
by hand or (rifle-~) shot from rifle-barrel;
glass receptacle thrown to disperse
chemicals for testing drains, extinguishing fires, etc. [F, f. Sp. granada POME-
GRANATE]

grenadier', n. 1. (Orig.) soldier who
threw grenades; (now) ‖G~s or G~
Guards, first regiment of household
infantry. 2. S.-Afr. weaver-bird with red
& black plumage. [F (prec., -IER)]

gren'adine¹, n. Dish of veal or poultry
fillets, trimmed, larded, & glazed. [F -in]

gren'adine², n. Dress-fabric of open silk
or silk & wool. [F]

gren'adine³ (-ēn), n. French cordial
syrup of pomegranate. [see POMEGRANATE]

Gresham's law. See LAW¹.

grĕssōr'ial, a. (zool.). Walking, adapted
for walking. [f. L gradi gress- walk, -OR,
-IAL]

grew. See GROW.

grey (grā), (esp. U.S.) gray, a. & n., & v.i.
& t. 1. Intermediate between black &
white, coloured like ashes or lead, (~
monk, Cistercian; ~ friar, Franciscan; ~
sister, of third order of St Francis; ~
mare is better horse, wife rules husband);
between light & dark, dull, clouded,
depressing, dismal; (of person or his or
her hair) turning white with age etc.;
ancient, immemorial; belonging to old
age, experienced, mature; ~ crow or
~-back, hooded crow; ~'beard, old man,
large stoneware jug for spirit, ‖ kind of
lichen; ‖~'coat, Cumberland yeoman;
‖~ drake, kind of ephemera; ~ eminence,
= éminence grise (see EMINENCE); ~ goose,

GREYLAG; ~-*headed*, old, of long service *in*, ancient, time-worn; ~-*hen*, female of black grouse (cf. BLACK[1]-*cock*); ~ *matter*, material of active part of brain; ~'*stone*, ~volcanic rock; hence~'ISH[1](2) a., ~'LY[2] adv., ~'NESS n., (grā-). 2. n. ~ clothes; cold sunless light; ~ colour; ~ pigment; ~ horse (*the Greys* or *Scots Greys*, 2nd Dragoons). 3. vb. Become, make, ~; (Photog.) dull surface of (glass), give mezzotint effect to (photograph) by covering negative with such glass. [OE *grǣg*, OHG *grāo*, ON *grár* f. Gmc *grǣwaz*]

‖ grey'cing (grā-), n. (colloq.). Greyhound-racing. [abbr.]

grey'hound (grā-), n. Slender long-legged keen-sighted swift dog used in coursing hares etc. (*ocean* ~, swift ship); ~-*racing*, modern sport in which mechanical hare is coursed by ~s as opportunity for betting. [OE *grīghund* corresp. to ON *greyhundr* f. *grey* bitch (not rel. to GREY)]

grey'lăg (gōōse)(grā-), n. Common European wild goose. [*lag* said to refer to its staying long in England for a migrant]

grey'wacke (grā'wăke, *or* -āk), n. A conglomerate rock consisting of rounded pebbles and sand cemented together. [anglicized f. G *grauwacke* (*grau* grey + WACKE)]

grid, n. Frame of spaced parallel bars, grating, (Electr.) wire network between filament and anode of valve; system of numbered squares printed on military etc. map and forming basis of map references; network of lines, electric-power connexions, etc.; gridiron (for cooking, & docking). [back formation f. GRIDIRON]

grid'dle, n., & v.t. Circular iron plate for baking cakes on; miner's wire-bottomed screen (vb, screen with ~). [ME *gredil* f. OF *gredil* (later *grail*, *greil*) f. Rom. *graticulum* (-*ula*) f. L *craticula* dim. of *cratis* hurdle; cf. GRATE[1], GRILL[2]]

gride, v.i., & n. Cut, scrape, *along*, *through*, etc., with strident or grating sound (also ~*s its way*); (n.) grating sound. [orig. sense *pierce*, by metath. f. GIRD[2]]

grid'iron (-īrn), n. Barred metal cooking utensil for broiling; (Naut.) frame of parallel beams for supporting ship in dock; *football field (from the parallel lines marking out field of play); (Theatr.) plank structure over stage supporting mechanism for drop-scenes etc.; a naval evolution; (also ~-*pendulum*) compensation pendulum with parallel rods of different metals. [13th c. *gredire*, var. of *gredil* GRIDDLE, later assoc. w. *iron*; cf. ANDIRON]

grief, n. Deep or violent sorrow, keen regret, (*come to* ~, meet with disaster, fail, fall). [ME, f. OF (*grever* GRIEVE)]

griev'ance, n. Real or fancied ground of complaint. [f. OF *grevance* (prec., -ANCE)]

grieve[1], v.t. & i. Give deep sorrow to; feel grief (*at*, *for*, *about*, *over*). [ME, f. OF *grever* f. Rom. *grevare f. L *gravare* (*gravis* heavy)]

‖ grieve[2], n. (Sc.). Farm-bailiff, overseer. [f. OE *gerēfa*; see REEVE[1]]

griev'ous, a. Bringing serious trouble, injurious; (of pain etc.) severe; flagrant, heinous; exciting grief. Hence ~LY[2] adv. [ME, f. OF *grevos* (GRIEVE[1], -OUS)]

griff'in[1], n. (Anglo-Ind.). (Also griff) newly arrived European, novice, greenhorn. Hence ~AGE(2), ~HOOD, ~SHIP, nn., ~ISH[1] a. [orig. unkn.]

griff'in[2], griff'on[1], grȳph'on, n. Fabulous creature with eagle's head & wings & lion's body; ‖ *the Griffin*, monument on site of Temple Bar, London; (-*fon*) kind of vulture (also ~-*vulture*). [ME, f. OF *grifoun* (L *gryphus* f. Gk *grups*, -OON)]

griff'on[2], n. Kind of foreign coarse-haired terrier-like dog. [F, = prec.]

grig, n. ‖ Small eel; grasshopper or cricket (*merry*, *lively*, *as a* ~; sense *cricket* doubtful, perh. invented to account for phrase). [orig. unkn.]

grill[1], v.t. & i., & n. 1. Broil (t. & i.) on gridiron (also fig. of torture or great heat), whence ~'ER[1](1, 2) n.; *subject to severe questioning (esp. by police); scallop (oysters etc.). 2. n. ~ed food; (also ~-*room*) room where steaks etc. are ~ed & served. [f. F *griller* (foll.)]

grill[2], n. Gridiron. [F *gril* = OF *grail*, *greil* f. Rom. *graticulum (-*ula*); see GRIDDLE].

grill'age, n. Heavy framework of cross-timbering as foundation for building in treacherous soil. [F (foll., -AGE)]

grille, grill[3], n. Grating, latticed screen, esp. in door for observing callers, in convent separating nuns from visitors, formerly in front of ladies' gallery in House of Commons, etc.; (Tennis) square opening in wall; spawn-hatching frame. Hence grilleD[2] (-ld) a. [F, = OF *graille*, *greille* f. Rom. *graticula (-*ulum*); see GRIDDLE]

grilse, n. Young salmon that has been only once to the sea. [orig. unkn.]

grim, a. (-mm-). Stern, unrelenting, merciless, severe; of forbidding or harsh aspect (often of death; *hold on like* ~ *death*, tight); sinister, ghastly, unmirthful, (*has a* ~ *truth in it*; *a* ~ *smile*; ~ *laughter*, *pastime*, etc.). Hence ~LY[2] adv., ~'NESS n. [OE, OS, OHG *grim*, ON *grimmr* f. Gmc *grimmaz]

grimāce', n., & v.i. 1. Wry face expressing annoyance etc. or meant to raise a laugh; affected look; use of such looks, affectation. 2. v.i. Make wry face. Hence or cogn. grimā'CER[1], grimā'CIER, nn. [F, f. Sp. *grimazo* f. *grima* fright, f. Goth. *grimms (GRIM)]

grimal'kin (-awl-, -ăl-), n. Old she-cat; spiteful old woman. [f. *grey* + *Malkin* (*Matilda*, -KIN)]

grime, n., & v.t. **1.** Soot, dirt, ingrained in some surface, esp. the skin; hence **grim'y²** a., **grim'iness** n. **2.** v.t. Blacken, befoul. [cf. Flem. *grijm(en)*]

Grimm's law. See LAW¹.

grin, v.i. & t. (-nn-), & n. **1.** Show teeth in sign of amusement or pain or in forced or unrestrained stupid smile (often *at*; ~ *& bear it*, take pain etc. stoically; ~ *like Cheshire cat*, constantly & meaninglessly; ~ *through horse-collar*, in grimacing-match at rustic sports); express (contempt, satisfaction) by ~ning. **2.** n. Act of ~ning (often *on the* ~ or *broad* ~). [OE *grennian* (cf. OHG *grennan*, ON *grenja*) f. Gmc *gran-*; cogn. w. GROAN]

grind, v.t. & i. (*ground*), & n. **1.** Reduce to small particles or powder by crushing between mill-stones, teeth, etc. (often *down*, *small*, *to pieces*, *into dust*, etc.); (quasi-pass.) admit of being ground (*will not* ~ *fine*); oppress, harass with exactions, (often *down*; a ~*ing tyranny*; also ~ *the faces of the poor* etc.); produce (flour) by ~ing; sharpen or smooth by friction (*has an* AXE *to* ~; ~ *lenses, diamonds*, etc.); work (hand-mill); turn handle of (hurdy-gurdy; also abs.); produce, bring *out*, (music) from hurdy-gurdy; toil monotonously, study hard; teach (subject, pupil *in* it) laboriously; rub (t. & i.) gratingly on, *into*, or *against* (*ground his heel into it*; *ship was* ~*ing on rocks*), rub (teeth) hard together (~ *out an oath*, utter while ~ing teeth); ~'*stone*, thick revolving stone disc for ~ing, sharpening, & polishing (*hold, keep*, one's *nose to the* ~*stone*, make him work incessantly), kind of stone used for these. **2.** n. ~ing; hard monotonous work or task (*the daily* ~ colloq., one's usual day's work); ‖ walk for exercise; steeplechase; ‖ (at Cambridge) a ferry. [ME, f. isolated OE *grindan*]

grin'der, n. Molar tooth; grinding-machine; upper mill-stone; person who grinds (esp. in comb. as *organ-, knife-, ~*); ‖ crammer. [-ER¹]

grin'dery, n. ‖ Cobblers' material of all kinds. [GRIND, -ERY; perh. extended f. the cobbler's whetstone]

grin'go (-ngg-), n. (Spanish-America; pl. -os). Foreigner (esp. an Anglo-American). [Mex. Sp.]

grip¹, n. Firm hold, tight grasp or clasp (*at, come to*, ~s, close combat), grasping power; way of clasping hands; way of grasping or holding (*overlapping* ~); control, mastery, intellectual hold; power of arresting attention; part in machinery etc. that clips, part of weapon etc. that is held; = *GRIP²*sack*; ~*-brake*, worked by gripping with hand. [f. OE *gripe* grasp & *gripa* handful, both f. root of GRIPE]

grip², v.t. & i. (-pp-). Seize, grasp, or hold, tightly; take firm hold; compel attention of; *~'*sack*, handbag. Hence

~**p'ER¹**(2) n. [late OE *grippa*, = MHG *gripfen*, f. root of GRIPE]

‖ **grip³**, n. Small open ditch. [OE *grype* cogn. w. *grēop* burrow]

gripe, v.t. & i., & n. **1.** Clutch, grip; oppress, pinch; affect with colic pains; (Naut.) secure with ~s, (of ship) come up into wind in spite of helm. **2.** n. Act of griping, clutch; hold, control, (*in the* ~ *of*); (pl.) colic pains; handle of implement or weapon; (Naut., pl.) lashings securing boat in its place; ~*-water*, horse-medicine for colic. [OE, OS *gripan*, OHG *grifan*, ON *gripa*, Goth. *greipan*, cogn. w. GROPE]

grippe, n. Influenza. [F]

grisaille (-zāl, & see Ap.), n. Method of decorative painting, stained-glass window etc., in grey monochrome representing objects in relief. [F (*gris* grey)]

gris'eous (-z-), a. (bot., zool.). Bluish or pearl grey. [f. med. L *griseus* (prec.), -OUS]

grisette (-z-), n. French working-class girl (formerly dressed in grey). [F (*gris* grey, -ETTE)]

‖ **gris'kin**, n. Lean part of loin of bacon pig. [app. f. obs. *gris*, dial. *grice* f. ON *griss* young pig +-KIN]

gris'ly (-z-), a. Causing horror, terror, or superstitious dread. [late OE *grislic*, f. *grisan, obs. *grise* to shudder]

grist¹, n. Corn for grinding (*brings* ~ *to the mill*, is profitable; *all is* ~ *that comes to his mill*, he utilizes everything); malt crushed for brewing. [OE *grist* f. WG *grinst- f. *grindan GRIND]

grist², n. Size or thickness of yarn or rope. [perh. cogn. w. GIRD¹]

gris'tle (-sl), n. Whitish tough flexible tissue in vertebrates, cartilage, (*in the* ~, immature—infants having ~ for bone). Hence **gris'tly²** (-sl), a. [OE, = OFris. & MLG *gristel*, of unkn. orig.]

grit¹, n. Small particles of stone or sand, esp. as causing discomfort or clogging machinery etc., whence ~**t'y²** a., ~**t'iness** n.; (also ~'*stone*) coarse sandstone; grain or texture of stone; (colloq.) strength of character, pluck, endurance. [OE *grēot*, OS *griot*, OHG *grioz*, ON *grjót* f. Gmc *greut-; cf. GRITS, GROATS]

grit², v.i. & t. (-tt-). Produce, move with, grating sound; grind (teeth). [f. prec.]

grits, n. pl. Husked but unground oats; coarse oatmeal. [OE *grytt(e)*, = OHG *gruzzi* f. WG *grut-, cf. GRIT¹, GROATS]

‖ **griz'zle**, v.i. (colloq.). (Esp. of children) whimper, cry fretfully. [orig. unkn.]

griz'zled (-zeld), a. Grey(-haired). [f. *grizzle* grey f. OF *grisel* f. *gris* grey (-LE(2)) +-ED²]

grizz'ly, a. & n. **1.** Grey, greyish, grey-haired, (~ *bear*, large fierce N.-Amer. kind); ~ *king, queen*, fishing-flies. **2.** n. ~ bear. [prec., -Y²]

groan, v.i. & t., & n. (Make) deep inarticulate sound expressing pain, grief, or disapproval (~ *inwardly*, be distressed);

utter with ~s (often *out*); be oppressed or loaded *under, beneath, with,* (~ *under injustice; shelf* ~*s with books;* ~*ing board,* well-loaded table); long *for;* ~ *down,* silence (speaker) with ~s. Hence ~'ing-LY[2] adv. [OE *grānian* (cogn. w. OHG *grīnan* grin) f. Gmc **grain-* cogn. w. GRIN]

groat, n. (hist.). Silver coin = 4*d.* issued 1351–1662 (occasionally used of the fourpenny piece 1836–56); small sum (*don't care a* ~). [f. MDu. *groot* orig. great, in sense thick (penny), cf. GROSCHEN]

groats, n. pl. Hulled (sometimes also crushed) grain, esp. oats. [rel. to OE *grotan* pl., *grot* fragment, f. WG **grut-;* cf. GRIT, GRITS]

Grōb'ian, n. Clownish slovenly person. [G, f. med. L *Grobianus,* joc. f. G *grob* coarse]

grō'cer, n. Dealer in spices, dried fruits, sugar, tinned foods, & miscellaneous domestic stores (~*'s itch,* eczema caused by handling sugar). Hence grō'CERY(2, &, usu. pl., 1) n. [late ME; orig. one who sells in the gross, f. OF *grossier* f. med. L *grossarius* (GROSS, -ARY[1])]

grŏg, n., & v.i. & t. 1. Drink of spirit & water; social meeting with ~; ~*-blossom,* pimple or redness on nose from intemperance. 2. vb. Drink ~; extract spirit from (empty cask) by pouring in hot water. [reputedly f. GROGRAM, nickname (from his cloak) of Adm. Vernon, who in 1740 first had ~ served out instead of neat rum]

grŏgg'|ў (-g-), a. Drunk(en); bibulous; (of horse) weak in forelegs, tottering; unsteady, shaky. Hence ~iNESS n. [-Y[2]]

grŏg'ram, n. Coarse fabric of silk, mohair & wool, or these mixed, often stiffened with gum. [f. F *gros grain* coarse grain]

groin[1], n., & v.t. 1. Depression between belly & thigh. 2. (archit.). Edge formed by intersecting vaults, arch supporting vault, (vb, build with ~s), whence ~'ING[1](6) n. [ME (f. OE) *grynde,* later *gryne, groin;* perh. f. Gmc **grundjo-* GROUND]

*groin[2]. Var. of GROYNE.

Grōl'ier, n. ~ *binding* (in the highly ornate style introduced by Jean ~ de Servin, Vicomte d'Aiguisy (d. 1565), French book-collector).

*grŏm(m)'ĕt. See GRUMMET.

grŏm'well, n. Kinds of plant with stony seeds formerly used in medicine. [ME, f. OF *gromil,* prob. f. med. L **gruinum milium* crane's millet (*gruis* crane, MILLET)]

grōōm, n., & v.t. 1. ‖ One of certain officers of Royal Household (*G*~ *of the stole, in waiting,* etc.). 2. Servant having care of horses (vb, curry, tend, etc.; also in p.p. of persons, as *well* ~*ed,* neatly got up, esp. with well-trimmed hair, beard, etc.). 3. Bridegroom; ~*s'man,* unmarried friend officially attending bridegroom at wedding. [ME *grom,* orig. male child, of unkn. orig.]

grōōve, n., & v.t. 1. Channel or hollow, esp. one made to direct motion or receive corresponding ridge (vb, make ~ or ~s in). 2. Piece of routine, undeviating course, rut, whence grōōv'Y[2] a., grōōv'i-NESS n. [f. Du. *groeve,* OHG *gruoba,* ON *gróf,* Goth. *grōba* cogn. w. GRAVE[1]]

grōpe, v.i. Feel about as in dark (*for, after,* or abs.), search blindly (lit. & fig.); ~ *one's way,* find it by feeling, proceed tentatively. Hence grōp'ingLY[2] adv. [OE *grāpian* f. WG **graip-,* cogn. w. GRIP[2], GRIPE]

grōp'er, n. Var. of GROUPER.

grŏs'beak, n. Kinds of small bird with large strong beak. [f. F *grosbec* (GROSS[2], BEAK[1])]

gro'schen (-ōshn), n. Small bronze Austrian coin. [G]

gros de Naples (grō'denäh'pl), n. Heavy silk fabric. [F (*gros* GROSS[2], *Naples*)]

grōss[1], n. (pl. *gross*). Twelve dozen. [f. F *grosse* (*douzaine*) fem. of *gros* GROSS[2]]

grōss[2], a. Luxuriant, rank; overfed, bloated, repulsively fat; flagrant, glaring; total, without deductions, not net; dense, thick, solid; not ethereal, transparent, or impalpable; (of food) coarse, greasy, uncleanly, repulsive, (~ *feeder,* one who likes such food, also, plant avid of manure); (of senses etc.) not delicate, dull; coarse in manners or morals, unrefined, indecent; (abs.) *in (the)* ~, in a general way, apart from detail, on the whole. Hence ~'LY[2] adv., ~'NESS n. [ME, f. OF *gros grosse* big f. LL *grossus*]

grŏt, n. (poet.). Grotto. [f. F *grotte* f. It. *grotta* GROTTO]

grotĕsque' (-sk), n. & a. 1. Decorative painting or sculpture with fantastic interweaving of human & animal forms with foliage; (pop.) comically distorted figure or design. 2. adj. (Archit.) in the above style; distorted, bizarre; ludicrous from incongruity, absurd; hence ~LY[2] (-skl-) adv., ~NESS (-skn-), grotĕs'querie (-skerī) [-ERY(5)], nn. [16th c. *crot-* f. F *crotesque* f. (w. assim. to OF *crote* GROTTO) It. *grottesca* (GROTTO, -ESQUE)]

grŏtt'ō, n. (pl. ~*es,* ~*s*). Picturesque cave; artificial ornamental cave, room etc. adorned with shells etc. in imitation of cave, as cool retreat. Hence ~ED[2](-ōd) a. [f. It. *grotta* f. L f. Gk *kruptē* CRYPT]

*grouch (rhzwith ~ch), v.i. & n. (colloq.). 1. Grumble. 2. n. Discontented person; fit of the sulks. [var. of *grutch,* see GRUDGE]

ground[1], n. 1. Bottom of sea (now chiefly fig., as *touch* ~, come to something solid after vague talk etc.; of ship, *take* ~, strand); (pl.) dregs, esp. of coffee, whence ~'Y[2] a. 2. (electr.). = EARTH[2]. 3. Base, foundation, motive, valid reason, (*on the* ~ *of,* by reason or under pretext of; *on public* etc. ~*s*), whence ~'LESS a., ~'lĕssLY[2] adv., ~'lĕssNESS n. 4. Substratum, underlying part, surface worked upon in embroidery, painting, etc.

undecorated part, prevailing colour or
tone; (Etching) composition spread on
metal & cut through with needle where
acid is to act. 5. Surface of earth (*fall, be
dashed, to the* ~, be abandoned, fail, of
scheme, hope; BREAK¹ ~; *down to the* ~,
colloq., in all respects, thoroughly; *above*
~, alive; *cut the* ~ *from under one's feet*,
anticipate & stultify his arguments or
plans). 6. pl. Enclosed land for ornament
or recreation attached to house. 7. Position, area, or distance, on earth's surface
(*cover much* ~, of inquiry, report, etc., be
far-reaching; *stand, shift*, one's ~, maintain, change, one's argument or intention;
gain ~, advance; *lose, give*, ~, retreat,
decline). 8. Area of special kind or use
(*fishing-*~*s*; *forbidden* ~, subject that
must be avoided; *classic* ~, historic place;
cricket etc. -~). 9. Person's property in
land. 10. (cricket). *His* etc. ~, behind
popping-crease (*in, out of, his* ~); ‖ paid
staff of players attached to club. 11. (In
names of birds) terrestrial, (of beasts)
burrowing or lying on ~, (of plants)
dwarfish or trailing. 12. ~-*ash*, ash
sapling, walking-stick of this; ~-*bait* n.
& v.t., (prepare with) bait thrown to
bottom of intended fishing-~ to attract
fish; ~ *bass*, short passage in bass of
composition, repeated many times with
upper part of music varied; ~-*box*, small
BOX¹ used to edge garden beds; ~-*colour*,
first coat of paint, prevailing colour on
which design is done; ~-*fish*, living at
bottom; ~-*fishing*, with bait near bottom;
‖ ~ *floor*, rooms etc. on or near level of
outside~ (*get in on the* ~ *floor*, be admitted
to company etc. on same terms as pro-
moters); ‖ ~ *game*, hares, rabbits, etc.;
~-*gudgeon*, loach; ~-*hog*, Amer. marmot;
~-*ice*, formed at bottom of water, anchor-
-ice; ~ *ivy*, ale-hoof, creeping herb with
bluish-purple flower & kidney-shaped
leaf; ‖ ~ *landlord*, owner of ~ leased for
building; ~-*man* (in charge of cricket etc.
~); ~-*note*, on which a common chord is
built, fundamental bass; ~-*nut*, (edible
tuber of) N.-Amer. wild bean, also W.-
-Ind. & Afr. pea with pod ripening under
~, PEANUT; ~-*pine*, herb with resinous
smell, also clubmoss; ~-*plan*, plane
drawing of divisions of building at ~
level, also outline or general design of
anything; ~-*rent*, paid to ~-land-
lord; ~ *sea*, heavy sea without apparent
cause; ~*s'man*, = ~-*man*; ~ *speed* (Aviation), aircraft's speed relative to ~ (cf.
AIR¹ *speed*); ~ *staff*, non-flying members
of aerodrome staff; ~ *swell*, heavy sea
caused by distant or past storm or earthquake; ~ *torpedo*, fixed to bottom of sea;
~'*work*, foundation or basis (usu. fig.),
chief ingredient, general surface of thing
showing where not overlaid with embroidery or other ornament. [OE, OS
grund, OHG *grunt*, Goth. *grundus* f.
Gmc *grundus*]

ground², v.t. & i. Base, establish, (institution, principle, belief) *on* some fact
or authority (in pass. also *in*; p.p., *well,
ill*, etc., founded, also abs.=well founded,
whence~'ĕDLY² adv.); instruct thoroughly (*in* elements), whence **groun'**DING¹ n.;
prepare ground of (embroidery etc.); lay
(esp. arms) on ground; (Electr.) connect
with earth as conductor; alight on
ground; run (t. & i.) ashore, strand;
prevent (aircraft, airman) from flying.
[f. prec.]

ground³, p.p. of GRIND. ~ *glass*, made
non-transparent by grinding.

‖ **groun'dage**, n. Duty on ship lying on
beach or entering port. [-AGE]

ground'ling, n. Kinds of GROUND¹-*fish*;
creeping or dwarf plant; spectator or
reader of inferior taste (ref. to *Hamlet* III.
ii. 12). [-LING¹]

ground'sel¹, n. Kinds of weed, of which
the commonest is used as food for cage-
-birds. [OE *gundæswelgiæ* perh. f. *gund*
pus, SWALLOW¹, = pus-absorber, as being
used for poultices, later assimilated to
ground]

ground'sel², n. (arch.). Timber serving
as foundation, lowest part of wooden
framework; threshold. [SILL]

group (-ōōp), n., & v.t. & i. 1. (Fine arts)
two or more figures or objects forming
complete design or distinct part of one;
number of persons or things standing
near together, knot, cluster; number of
persons or things belonging or classed
together (in Pol., used of smaller unit
than the party, & esp. in assemblies
where the two-party system does not
prevail; in scientific classification, used
vaguely of cross-divisions outside the
regular hierarchy of class-terms); *Oxford*
G~, see BUCHMANISM; ~ *captain*, officer of
AIR¹ *Force*. 2. vb. Form (t. & rarely i.)
into a ~, place in a ~ *with*; form (t. & i.
of colours, figures, etc.) into well-arranged
& harmonious whole; classify. Hence
~'AGE(3) n. [f. F *groupe* f. It. *gruppo*
f. Gmc **krupp-* cogn. w. CROP¹]

group'er (-ōō-), n. Kinds of W.-Ind. &
Austral. fish. [f. Port. *garupa* (prob.
S.-Amer.)]

grouse¹, n. (pl. *grouse*). (Prop.) any wild
gallinaceous bird with feathered feet;
(pop.) moor fowl or game or red ~,
reddish game-bird of British Isles (*black*
~, BLACK¹ *game*; *wood* or *great* ~, caper-
caillie; *white* ~, ptarmigan), its flesh.
[orig. unkn.]

‖ **grouse**², v.i., & n. (sl.). Grumble. [orig.
unkn.]

grout¹, n., & v.t. 1. Thin fluid mortar
for filling interstices. 2. v.t. Fill up or
finish with this. [cf. F *grouter*]

‖ **grout**², v.i. & t. (Of pigs) turn up earth,
turn up (earth etc.), with snout. [18th c.,
var. of *groot* vb f. ME *groot* mud, rel. to
OE *grēot* GRIT]

grove, n. Small wood, group of trees, (in

Bible, mistransl. of Hebrew word=pillar used as idol, or name of goddess). Hence ~ED² (-vd), ~e′LESS (-vl-), ~′Y², aa. [excl. E, OE *gráf*]

gróv′el (*or* -ŭv-), v.i. (-ll-). Lie prone, humble oneself, (often *in the dirt* or *dust*); (part.) abject, low, base, whence ~ᴵngLY³ adv. Hence ~ᴵER¹ n. [back formation f. obs. *grovelling* adv. (obs. *on grufe* f. ON *á grúfu* on one's face, -LING²) taken as part. in lay ~*ling* etc.]

grow (-ō), v.i. & t. (*grew* pr. grōō, ~*n* p.p. often as act. intr. with *is*, cf. -ED¹ (2), & as adj.). 1. Develop or exist as living plant (also joc. of lifeless things etc., be found in some place; ~ *into one, together,* etc., coalesce), germinate, sprout, spring up, be produced, come naturally into existence, arise. 2. Increase in (freq. *in*) size, height (~ᴵng¹ *pains,* neuralgic pains in limbs of the young), quantity, degree, power, etc. (~ *downwards,* diminish; *habit, person, picture,* etc., ~*s on* one, becomes more influential with or admired by him), whence ~′ᴵngLY² (-ō′l-) adv. 3. Become gradually (~ *rich*); ~ *up,* advance to maturity (~*n-up* a. & n., adult); emerge from soil, reach full size; (of custom) arise, become common. 4. Produce by cultivation, bring forth, let (beard etc.) ~, whence ~′ABLE (-ō′a~) a. 5. pass. Be covered (often *up* or *over*) with some growth. [OE *grówan,* OHG *gruoen,* ON *gróa* f. Gmc *grō-* cogn. w. GRASS, GREEN]

grow′er (-ō′er), n. Plant that grows in specified way (*fast, free,* etc., ~); person growing produce (often in comb., as *fruit-*~). [-ER¹]

growl, v.i. & t., & n. (Make) guttural sound of anger (*at*); rumble; murmur angrily, angry murmur, complain(t); utter with a ~ (*out*). Hence ~′ᴵngLY² adv. [prob. imit.]

growl′er, n. In vbl senses; also: ‖ four-wheeled cab; kinds of fish; small iceberg. [-ER¹]

growl′erў, n. Growling; place to growl in, private room, den. [-ERY; cf. BOUDOIR]

grown, p.p. of GROW. ~ *man* etc., mature.

growth (-ōth), n. Growing, development, increase, (*of foreign* etc. ~, grown abroad etc.; *full* ~, size ultimately attained); cultivation *of* produce; what has grown or is growing, (Path.) morbid formation. [-ᴛʜ¹]

groyne, *groin, n., & v.t. 1. Timber framework or low broad wall run out to check drifting of beach & so stop encroachment of sea. 2. v.t. Supply (beach) with ~s. [f. (dial.) *groin* snout f. OF *groin* f. LL *grunnium* pig's snout f. L *grunnire* grunt]

grŭb¹, n. Larva of insect, caterpillar, maggot; dull drudge, literary hack, sloven, smug; ball bowled along ground at cricket; (sl.) food, a feed; *~-stake* (Mining sl.), supply (prospector) with

outfit, provisions, etc., in return for part of profits, (n.) outfit etc. so supplied. [ME; perh. f. foll.]

grŭb², v.i. & t. (-bb-). Dig (t. & i.) superficially; clear (ground) of roots & stumps, clear away (roots etc.), (often *up*); fetch up or *out* by digging (fig., discover in books etc.); search, rummage, (intr.); plod, toil, *on, along, away*; (sl.) feed, provide (boarder etc.) with food, [prob. f. prec.]; ~*-axe, -hoe, -hook,* for ~bing up stumps. Hence (~)~b′ER¹(1, 2) n. [ME; perh. repr. OE *grybba* f. Gmc *grubh-,* *grabh-* GRAVE²]

grŭbb′ў, a. Of, infested with, grubs; dirty, grimy, slovenly, whence ~ᴵNESS n. [-Y²]

Grŭb′street, n. & a. (Region inhabited by) the tribe of needy authors & literary hacks; (adj.) of these. [a London street (now Milton St) so inhabited in 17th c.]

grŭdge, v.t., & n. 1. Be unwilling to give, grant, or allow (thing, person thing, thing *to* person), or *to* do; (part.) reluctant, whence grŭdg′ᴵngLY³ adv. 2. n. Feeling of resentment or ill will (*have a* ~ *against; bear, owe,* one *a* ~). [f. ME *grutch* f. OF *grouchier* of unkn. orig.]

grŭ′el (-ōōl), n., & v.t. (-ll-). Liquid food chiefly for invalids of oatmeal etc. boiled in milk or water (*have, get,* one's ~, be punished, severely defeated, or killed; so *give* one his ~, & ~ vb sl. in same sense, whence ~ᴵng¹ (-ōōl-) n.). [ME, f. OF, f. Rom. *grutellum,* f. Gmc *grūt-* (GROATS)]

grue′some (-ōōs-), a. Grisly, disgusting. Hence ~LY² adv., ~NESS n. [f. Sc. & north. *grew* to shudder; cf. O Sw. *grua* + -SOME]

grŭff, a. Surly, laconic, rough-mannered, rough-voiced. Hence ~′LY² adv., ~′NESS n., ~′ᴵSH¹(2) a. [f. MDu., MLG *grof* coarse, = OHG *grob*]

grŭm′bl|e, v.i. & t., & n. (Utter) dull inarticulate sound, murmur, growl faintly; rumble; complain(t) (*at, about, over*); utter complainingly (often *out*). Hence ~ER¹ n., ~ᴵngLY³ adv. [f. obs. *grumme* +-LE(3); cf. MDu. *grommen,* MLG *grom-melen*]

grume (-ōōm), n. (med.). Clot of blood, viscous fluid. So grum′ous (-ō̄-) a. [f. L *grumus* small heap]

grŭmm′ĕt, *gró̄m(m)′ĕt, n. (naut.). Ring usu. of twisted rope as fastening, rowlock, wad, etc. [f. obs. F *gromette* f. *gourmer* to curb, of unkn. orig.]

grŭm′p|ў, grŭm′p|ish, aa. Ill-tempered, surly. Hence ~ᴵLY² adv., ~ᴵNESS n. [f. *grumps* ill-humour +-Y²]

Grŭn′dўism, n. Conventional propriety, prudery. [f. 'What will Mrs Grundy (a neighbour) say?' in Morton's *Speed the Plough* 1798]

grŭnt, v.i. & t., & n. (Utter) low gruff sound characteristic of pigs; express discontent, dissent, fatigue, etc., by this; utter with ~ (often *out*). Hence ~′ᴵngLY³ adv. [OE *grunnettan* = OHG, G *grunzen*, frequent. of *grunian* imit.]

grün'ter, n. In vbl senses; esp.: pig; kinds of fish. [-ER¹]

gru'yère (groō'yâr), n. Swiss pale cows'-milk cheese with many cavities. [*G*~, Swiss town]

grȳs'bŏk, n. Small grey S.-Afr. antelope. [f. Du. *grijsbok* (*grijs* grey, BUCK¹)]

guacharo (gwahchah'rō), n. The oil-bird of S. America. [S.-Amer. Sp.]

guacho, incorrect for GAUCHO.

guai'ăc, -acum, (gwī-), n. Kinds of W.-Ind. trees & shrubs (*-um* only); brownish-green wood of two kinds of these used in medicine, lignum vitae; resin from these, drug made from it. [*-um* mod. L f. Sp. *guayaco* of Haytian orig.]

guan (gwahn), n. Kinds of S.-Amer. gallinaceous bird allied to curassow. [prob. native]

gua'na (gwah-), n. Iguana; any large lizard. [var. of IGUANA]

guana'cō (gwanah-), n. (pl. *-os*). Wild llama with reddish-brown wool. [native S.-Amer. *huanaco*]

gua'nō (gwah-), n. (pl. *-os*), & v.t. Excrement of sea-fowl found esp. in islands off Peru used as manure; artificial manure esp. that made from fish; (vb) fertilize with ~. [Sp., f. native *huanu*]

guarantee' (gă-), n., & v.t. **1.** Person making guaranty or giving security; guaranty; thing given or existing as security for fulfilment of conditions or permanence etc. of something; person to whom guaranty is given [correl. to *guarantor*; prop. a separate formation with -EE]; ~ *fund*, sum pledged as contingent indemnity for loss. **2.** v.t. Be ~ for, answer for due fulfilment of (contract etc.) or genuineness etc. of (article), assure permanence etc. of; engage *that* something has happened or will happen; secure possession of *to* person; secure *against* or *from* (risk etc.), or *in* (possession etc.); hence **gua'rantOR** (gă-; *also* -ôr') n. [in first sense, orig. *guaranté*, prob. f. Sp. *garante* = F *garant* WARRANT¹; other senses of n. by confusion w. foll. or misuse of -EE]

gua'rantȳ (gă-), n., & v.t. Undertaking written or other to answer for payment of debt or performance of obligation by another person liable in first instance; ground or basis of security; (vb) guarantee (now rare). [f. AF *guarantie*, var. of *warantie*, WARRANTY]

guard¹ (gärd), n. **1.** Defensive posture or motion in fencing, boxing, etc. (in cricket, position of bat to defend wicket; *take, give,* ~, of batsman, umpire, ascertaining correct spot on ground for this). **2.** Watch, vigilant state, (*keep* ~, *be on* ~, act as sentry etc.; *on, off,* one's ~, prepared, unprepared, against attack, surprise, or one's own impulses etc.). **3.** Protector, defender, sentry; ‖ official in

general charge of stage-coach (hist.) or train; ‖ (pl.) household troops (including *Foot*-~s, *Horse*-~s, *Life*-~s, & by extension some (orig. seven) regiments of *Dragoon G*~s). **4.** Body of soldiers etc. serving as protectors of place or person, escort, separate portion of army, etc: (*advance, rear,* ~; ~ *of honour;* HOME¹ *G*~; *mount, relieve,* ~, earlier *the* ~, take up, take others' place in, sentry duty). **5.** Contrivance to prevent injury or accident (often in comb., as *fire, trigger,* -~). **6.** ~-*boat,* boat going rounds of fleet in harbour to see that good watch is kept, also official harbour boat enforcing quarantine or customs regulations; ~-*book'* (arranged for the reception of additional leaves, letters, etc.); ~-*chain,* securing watch, brooch, etc.; ~'*house,* accommodating military ~ or securing prisoners; ~-*rail,* hand or other rail to prevent falling etc.; ~-*ring,* preventing other ring from slipping off finger, keeper; ~*room,* as ~*house* above; ~-*ship,* warship protecting harbour & receiving seamen till they can join their ships; ~*s'man,* ‖ soldier, esp. officer, of *G*~s; ~-*tent,* as ~*house* above. Hence ~'LESS a. [ME, f. OF *garde* f. *garder* f. Rom. *wardare WARD]

guard² (gärd), v.t. & i. Keep safe, stand guard over, keep (door etc.) so as to control passage, protect, defend (*from, against*); secure by explanations or stipulations etc. from misunderstanding or abuse, (Med.) administer correctives with (drug); keep (thoughts, speech) in check (~*ed language* etc., cautious, measured), whence ~'ĕdLY² adv., ~'ĕdNESS n.; use a fencing guard; take precautions *against*; (Curling, Bowling) protect (stone, bowl) by placing one's own between it & later player, (Chess) protect (piece, pawn) with another. Hence ~'ANT (her.), depicted full-face. [f. prec., or OF *garder*]

guard'ian (gär-), n. Keeper, defender, protector, (‖ *G*~ *of the poor,* or *G*~, member of Board formerly elected to administer poor-laws in parish or district); (*G*~) title of newspaper; (Law) one having custody of person or property or both of infant, idiot, etc. (cf. WARD); superior of Franciscan convent; ~ *angel,* spirit watching over person or place. [late ME, f. AF *gardein,* OF *-en,* f. *garde* GUARD¹; see WARDEN]

guard'ianship (gär-), n. Office of guardian, legal tutelage; keeping, guard, (*under the* ~ *of the laws*). [-SHIP]

gua'va (gwah-), n. (Tropical myrtaceous tree yielding) acid fruit used for making jelly. [f. Sp. *guayaba* prob. f. S.-Amer. or W.-Ind. name]

guayule' (gwahyōōl'), n. Aster-like Mexican plant the sap of which furnishes a rubber substitute. [native name]

gūbernatōr'ial, a. Of a governor. [f. L *gubernator* GOVERNOR + -IAL]

‖ **gŭd′dle,** v.t. & i. (Sc.). Catch (fish) with the hands, by groping under the stones or banks of a stream, grope for fish thus. [orig. unkn.]

gŭdg′eon¹ (-jon), n. Smal! freshwater fish used as bait; credulous person.. [ME, f. F *goujon* f. L *gobionem* nom. -o GOBY]

gŭdg′eon² (-jon), n. Pivot at end of beam, axle, etc., on which bell, wheel, etc., works; ring of gate fitting on hook of post; socket in which rudder works; pin holding two blocks of stone etc. together; ~-*pin*, (esp.) that holding piston-rod & connecting-rod together. [ME, f. OF *gojon* dim. of *gouge* GOUGE]

Guebre (gē′ber, gā⁻), n. Zoroastrian, fire-worshipper, Parsee. [f. F *guèbre* f. Pers. *gabr*]

guel′der rōse (gĕ-; -z), n. Shrub with round bunches of creamy-white flowers, snowball-tree. [*Guelders* in Netherlands]

Guelph, -lf, (gwĕ-), n. Member of medieval Italian party supporting Pope against Emperor (cf. GHIBELLINE). Hence ~ɪᴄ a. [f. It. *Guelfo* f. MHG *Welf* name (of founder of princely family of Guelphs, ancestors of British Royal Family) used as war-cry at battle of Weinsberg 1140 against Conrad III]

guerd′on (gĕr-), n., & v.t. (poet.). Reward, recompense. Hence ~ʟᴇss a. [ME, f. OF f. med. L *widerdonum* f. OHG *widarlōn* (*wider* again, LOAN) w. assim. to L *donum* gift]

Guern′sey (gĕrn′zǐ), n. One of Channel Islands; (*g*~; also ~ *shirt, coat, frock*) thick knitted woollen usu. blue outer tunic or jersey; ~ *cow*; ~ *lily*, kind of amaryllis orig. from S. Africa.

guer(r)ill′a (ger-), n. (Usu. now ~ *war*) irregular war waged by small bodies acting independently; man engaged in this. [Sp. (-*rr*-) dim. of *guerra* WAR]

guess (gĕs), v.t. & i., & n. 1. Estimate without measurement or detailed calculation; think likely, think one divines nature of, form hypothesis as to, conjecture, hazard opinion about, (noun, *that, how, when, whether,* etc., thing *to be*; also intr. with *at*; often abs. in parenthesis; *I* ~, chiefly U.S., I feel sure or know well); conjecture (answer to riddle, solution of problem) rightly, divine. 2. n. Rough estimate, conjecture, hypothesis, (*by* ~, at haphazard; *by* ~ *and by God*; *anybody's* ~, a matter of individual conjecture); ~-*work*, (procedure based on) ~ing; OTHER~. [n. f. vb, ME *gesse*, of uncert. orig.; cf. OSw. *gissa*, MLG, MDu. *gissen*; f. root of GET]

guest (gĕst), n. Person entertained at another's house or table (*paying* ~, boarder); person lodging at hotel, boarding-house, etc.; animal or vegetable parasite (cf. HOST²); ~-*chamber*, kept for ~s; ~-*house*, superior boarding-house; ~-*night*, on which ~s are entertained at club, college, mess, etc. Hence ~'ꜱʜɪᴘ n.

[OE *giest*, OS, OHG *gast*, ON *gestr*, Goth. *gasts* f. Gmc **gastiz* cogn. w. L *hostis*]

guest′-rōpe, guess′, (gĕs-), n. Second rope fastened to boat in tow to steady it; rope slung outside ship to give hold for boats coming alongside. [orig. uncert.; perh. f. GUEST]

guffaw′, n., & v.i. & t. 1. Coarse or boisterous laugh. 2. vb. Make, say with, ~. [orig. Sc.; imit.]

guggle. = GURGLE.

guichet (gēsh′ā), n. Grating, hatch, ticket-office window. [F]

guide¹ (gīd), n. 1. One who shows the way; hired conductor of traveller or tourist; (esp. in Switzerland etc.) professional mountain-climber. 2. (Mil.) one of company formed for reconnoitring etc.; (Naut.) ship on which rest of fleet regulate their movements.· 3. Adviser; directing principle or standard (*the feelings are a bad* ~; *Scripture is our* ~). 4. = GIRL ~. 5. Book of rudiments, manual, (also ~-*book*) book of information on a city, cathedral, museum, etc., (*to*). 6. (mech.). Bar, rod, etc., directing motion of something, gauge etc. controlling tool. 7. Thing marking a position or guiding the eye. 8. ~-*post*, FINGER-*post*; ~-*rope*, GUY¹, small rope attached to load of crane to guide it, rope trailed along ground to guide balloon or small airship to assist in preserving altitude, one of several ropes steadying an airship before flight; ~'*way*, groove, track. Hence ~'ʟᴇss (gīd-) a. [ME, f. OF f. *guider* (foll.)]

guide² (gīd), v.t. Act as guide to, go before, lead, direct course of; arrange course of (events); be the principle, motive, or ground, of (action, judgement, etc.); conduct affairs of (State etc.); ~*d missile* (under remote control); *guiding-stick*, maulstick. Hence guid′ᴀʙʟᴇ a., guid′ᴀɴᴄᴇ n., (gī-). [ME, f. OF *guider*, older *guier* (whence ME *guy* vb) f. Rom. **widare* f. Gmc **witan* (cf. Goth. *fairweitjan* gaze intently) cogn. w. *witan* (WIT¹)]

guid′on (gī-, gĕ-), n. Pennant narrowing to point at free end (used as standard of dragoons). [F, f. It. *guidone* f. *guida* GUIDE]¹

g(u)ild (gĭ-), n. Society for mutual aid or prosecution of common object; *G*~-*hall*, in which a medieval ~ met, (freq., from being used as meeting-place of Corporation) town-hall; ‖ (*the*) *Guildhall*, hall of the Corporation of the City of London, used for State banquets, municipal meetings, etc.; ~ *socialism*, system by which the resources, methods, & profits, of each industry should be controlled by a council of its members. [f. OE *gield, gild* & ON *gildi* guild, payment, rel. to OS *geld*, OHG *gelt*, ON *gjald*, Goth. *gild* f. Gmc **geldh*-; see YIELD]

guil′der (gĭ-), n. Obsolete gold coin of Netherlands etc.; Dutch silver coin. [alt. of Du. *gulden* (GOLDEN)]

guile (gīl), n. Treachery, deceit, cunning devices. Hence ~'ꜰᴜʟ a., ~'ꜰᴜʟʟʏ² adv., ~'ꜰᴜʟɴᴇꜱꜱ n., (gilf-), ~'ʟᴇꜱꜱ a., ~'ʟèꜱꜱʟʏ² adv., ~'ʟèꜱꜱɴᴇꜱꜱ n. (gil-l-). [ME, f. OF of unkn. (presumably Gmc) orig.; cf. ᴡɪʟᴇ]

guill'emot (gī-), n. Kinds of sea-bird. [F, f. *Guillaume* William]

guilloche (gĭlōsh', & see Ap.), n. Architectural ornament imitating braided ribbons. [f. F *guillochis*, or f. F *guilloche* the tool used]

guillotine (gĭl'otēn, *or* -tēn'), n., & v.t. **1.** Machine with knife-blade sliding in grooves for beheading; surgical instrument for excising uvula etc., kinds of machine for cutting paper etc.; || (Parl.) method of preventing obstruction by fixing times at which parts of Bill must be voted on. **2.** v.t. Use the ~ upon. [F (Dr *Guillotin*, its proposer in 1789)]

guilt (gĭ-), n. The having committed a specified or implied offence; criminality, culpability. [OE *gylt*, of unkn. orig.]

guilt'less (gĭ-), a. Innocent (often *of* offence); not having knowledge or possession of (~ *of Greek, soap, moustache*, etc.). Hence ~ʟʏ² adv., ~ɴᴇꜱꜱ n. [-ʟᴇꜱꜱ]

guil'ty|ў (gĭ-), a. Criminal, culpable; conscious of, prompted by, guilt (~*y conscience, behaviour, look*); having committed a particular offence (*of*; ~*y, not* ~*y*, verdicts in criminal trials). Hence ~ɪʟʏ² adv., ~ɪɴᴇꜱꜱ n. [-ʏ²]

guimp. = ɢɪᴍᴘ.

Guinea, g-, (gĭn'ĭ), n. **1.** (*G*~). Part of W. coast of Africa. **2.** (*g*~). Former gold coin named as first coined for the African trade (1663–1717 nominally 20/- but of fluctuating value; from 1717 fixed at 21/-; last coined 1813), & now money of account 21/- used in stating professional fees, amount of subscriptions, & prices of pictures, horses, estates, etc. **3.** *g*~*-fowl*, *-hen*, gallinaceous bird with slate-coloured white-spotted plumage domesticated in Europe; *G*~ ɢʀᴀɪɴꜱ, *g*~*-pig*, S.-Amer. rodent now half-domesticated in Europe etc. as pet (origin of name doubtful), person receiving ~ fees, esp. company director or deputy clergyman, person used as subject for medical experiment; *G*~ *worm*, tropical parasite in human skin. [f. Port. *Guiné*]

guipure (gēp'oor, & see Ap.), n. Kind of lace; kind of gimp. [F]

guise (gīz), n. Style of attire, garb, (arch.); external appearance; semblance, assumed appearance, pretence, (*under, in, the* ~ *of*). [ME f. OF, f. Gmc (ᴡɪꜱᴇ²)]

guitar' (gĭ-), n., & v.i. (-rr-). **1.** Six-stringed lute played with hand with fretted finger-board; hence ~ɪꜱᴛ(3) n. **2.** v.i. Play ~. [f. Sp. *guitarra* f. Gk *kithara*; cf. ᴄɪᴛʜᴇʀ, ɢɪᴛᴛᴇʀɴ]

***gulch**; n. Ravine, esp. one with gold deposit. [perh. f. dial. *gulch* to swallow]

gul'den (gōō-), n. Dutch silver coin. [Du.

& G, = golden (orig. name of various gold coins)]

gules (-lz), n., & a. (usu. after noun), (her.). Red. [ME, f. OF *goules* pl. ermine dyed red]

gulf, n., & v.t. **1.** (Geog.) portion of sea, proportionally narrower at mouth than bay, partly surrounded by coast; deep hollow, chasm, abyss, (poet.) profound depth or the sea; whirlpool, what swallows up anything; impassable dividing line (*Luke* xvi. 26); || (Univ. sl.) degree allowed to honour-candidate who fails but deserves pass; *G*~*-stream*, oceanic warm current issuing from *G*~ of Mexico; ~*-weed*, seaweed of tropical waters with berry-like air vessels. **2.** v.t. Engulf, swallow up; || (Univ.) give ~ to. [ME, f. OF *golfe* f. It. *golfo* f. late Gk *kolphos* (Gk *kolpos*)]

gull¹, n. Kinds of long-winged web-footed mostly marine bird, usu. white with mantle varying from pearl-grey to black, & bright bill. Hence ~'ᴇʀʏ(3) n. [ME; perh. f. W *gwylan*]

gull², n., & v.t. Dupe, fool. So ~'ɪʙʟᴇ a., ~ɪʙɪʟ'ɪᴛʏ n., ~'ɪꜱʜ¹ a. [uncert. which is source of other; for the n., cf. dial. *gull* young bird (ON *gulr* yellow); for the vb, cf. obs. *gull* vb 'stuff' or 'cram']

gull'et, n. Food-passage from mouth to stomach, oesophagus; throat; water-channel, strait, defile, (arch. & dial.). [ME, f. OF dim. of *gole* (now *gueule*) f. L *gula*]

gull'y|ў¹, n., & v.t. **1.** Water-worn ravine; deep artificial channel, gutter, drain, sink; (Cricket) fielding position between point & the slips; ~*-drain*, to sewer from ~*-hole*, opening in street for drainage; ~*-trap*, anti-gas ᴛʀᴀᴘ¹ in ~*-drains*. **2.** v.t. Make gullies in, form (channels) by water action. [f. F *goulet* (prec.)]

gull'y², n. Large knife. [orig. unkn.]

gulos'ity, n. (rare). Gluttony. [f. LL *gulositas* (L *gulosus* gluttonous f. *gula* ɢᴜʟʟᴇᴛ)]

gulp, v.t. & i., & n. **1.** Swallow (usu. *down*) hastily, greedily, or with effort (~ *down sobs, tears*, suppress them); perform act of swallowing with difficulty, gasp, choke; hence ~'ɪɴɢʟʏ² adv. **2.** n. Act of ~ing (*drained it at one* ~); effort to swallow; large mouthful; hence ~'ʏ² a. [f. MDu. *gulpen* (init.)]

gum¹, n. (usu. pl.). Firm flesh in which the teeth stand; ~'*boil*, small abscess on ~*s*. [OE *gōma*, OHG *guomo*, ON *gōmr*]

gum², n., & v.t. & i. (-mm-). **1.** Viscid secretion of some trees & shrubs that hardens in drying but is soluble in water (cf. ʀᴇꜱɪɴ), used to stick paper etc. together & stiffen linen etc.; secretion collecting in inner corner of eye; hard transparent sweet made of gelatine etc.; (also ~*-tree*) any tree exuding ~, esp. kinds of eucalyptus (*up a*~*-tree*, in a fix, at end of one's resources); morbid secretion of ~ as disease of fruit-trees; *(pl.) rubber boots;

~ ARABIC; ~ *bichromate*, method of controlled photographic printing based on the CARBON process; ~ *boot*, rubber boot; ~ *dragon*, tragacanth; ~ *juniper*, sandarac; ~ *resin*, vegetable secretion of resin mixed with ~, as gamboge; ~ *senegal*, kind of ~ arabic from Senegal. **2.** vb. Stiffen, smear, with ~; fasten *down, together, up, in*, etc., with ~; exude ~. [ME, f. OF *gomme* f. L *gummi* f. Gk *kommi*]

‖ **gŭm³**, n. (vulg.). God (in oaths, as *my, by, ~ !*). [deformation of *God*]

*gŭm´bō, n. = OKRA; soup thickened with okra pods. [of Negro orig.]

gŭm´lah, n. Large Indian earthenware water-jar. [Hind. *gamla*]

gŭmm´a, n.(path.; pl.~*s*,~*ta*). Syphilitic tumour. Hence ~tous a. [mod. L, f. L *gummi* GUM², from nature of contents]

gŭmm´|ȳ, a. Viscid, sticky; abounding in, exuding, gum; (of ankles & legs) puffy, swollen. Hence ~INESS n. [-Y²]

gŭmp´tion, n. (colloq.). Resource, enterprising spirit, go, ready practical sense; (Painting) vehicle for colour. [Sc., of unkn. orig.]

gŭn, n., & v.t. & i. **1.** Metal tube for throwing missiles with gunpowder or some explosive force, piece of ordnance, cannon, musket, fowling-piece, rifle, carbine, (*sure as a* ~, certainly, beyond question; *stand, stick, to* one's ~*s*, maintain position; *big* ~, eminent person; *blow great*~*s*, violently, a gale); *revolver (~ *moll*, gangster's mistress); starting-pistol (*beat, jump, the* ~, start before the signal is given, also fig.); insecticide spray. **2.** Member of shooting-party. **3.** ~-BARREL¹; ~*boat*, small vessel of shallow draught & with relatively heavy ~ armament; ~-CARRIAGE; ~-*cotton*, explosive made by steeping cotton in nitric & sulphuric acids used for blasting; ~ *crew*, team manning ~; ~ *dog*, one trained to follow ~*s*; ~-*fire*, firing of ~, esp. (Mil., Naut.) of morning or evening ~ to show time, independent firing by each ~ of a battery; ~-*harpoon*, propelled from ~, not by hand; ~-*lock*, mechanism by which charge of ~ is exploded; ~-*man*, (esp., U.-S. sl.) armed robber; ~-*metal*, alloy of copper & tin or zinc (formerly used for ~s); ~-*pit*, to protect ~ crews & ~s from enemy's fire; ~-*powder*, explosive of saltpetre, sulphur, & charcoal, for use in ~s & blasting (~-*powder plot*, 5th Nov. 1605 to blow up Parliament), fine green tea of granular appearance, *white* ~-*powder*, kinds of modern explosive; ‖~-*room*, compartment in warship fitted up for junior officers or as lieutenants' mess-room (orig. for gunner & his mates); ~-*runner, -running*, (person engaged in) illegal introduction of fire-arms into country; ~-*shot*, range of ~ ~ (*out of, within,* ~*shot*); ~-*shy*, frightened at report of ~ (esp. of sporting dog);

~-*smith*, maker and repairer of small fire-arms; ~-*stock*, wooden mounting of ~-barrel. Hence (*heavily* etc.)~-nED³(-nd), ~-LESS, aa. **4.** vb. (-nn-). Shoot (at), go shooting. [ME; perh. f. *Gunna* pet-form of ON *Gunnhildr* woman's name used as personal name (as with ships, & cf. *Mons Meg* cannon kept at Edinburgh) for ballistae & cannon (*una magna balista de cornu quae vocatur Domina Gunilda*, 1330)]

gŭnn´el¹, n. A small eel-shaped sea-fish, the butter-fish. [orig. unkn.]

gunnel². See GUNWALE.

gŭnn´er, n. ‖ Officer or man of artillery (as official term, private); *Master G~*, R.A. warrant officer in charge of equipment etc. in a fort, or similarly employed; (Naut.) warrant officer in charge of battery, magazine, etc. (~*'s daughter*, gun to which sailors were lashed for flogging; *kiss, marry, the* ~*'s daughter*, be flogged); game-shooter. [-ER² (2)]

gŭnn´era, n. The prickly rhubarb, an ornamental foliage plant with large leaves. [f. J. E. *Gunnerus*, naturalist; see -A(1)]

gŭnn´erȳ, n. Construction & management of large guns (~-*lieutenant*, ‖ (sl.) ~ *jack*, with warrant of competence to supervise ~ from ~-*ship*, for training in ~); firing of guns. [-ERY]

gŭnn´ing, n. Shooting, esp. of game (usu. *go* ~); wildfowling in shooting-punt. [-ING¹]

gŭnn´ȳ, n. Coarse sacking, sack, usu. of jute fibre. [f. Hind. *goni* f. Skr. *goni* sack]

gŭn´ter, n. (Also *G~'s scale*) flat 2-ft rule with scales, logarithmic lines, etc., used for solving mechanically problems in surveying & navigation; topmast, or its sail, sliding up & down lower mast on rings (from resemblance to sliding G~'s scale); *G~'s chain*, 66-ft surveying CHAIN. [E. *G~*, mathematician d. 1626]

gŭn´wale (-nal), **gŭn´el**, n. Upper edge of ship's or boat's side (~ *to, under*, level with, below, water). [GUN + WALE (formerly used to support guns); cf. CHANNEL²]

gŭn´yah, n. Native Australian hut. [native]

gŭp, n. (Anglo-Ind.). Gossip. [Hind.]

gŭrgĭtā´tion, n. Surging, bubbling motion or sound. [f. LL *gurgitare* to surge (*gurges -itis* whirlpool) + -ATION]

gŭr´gle, v.i. & t., & n. (Make) bubbling sound as of water from bottle or among stones; utter with such sounds. [limit., or f. Du. *gorgelen*, G *gurgeln*, or It. *gorgogliare*, f. L (*gurgulio* gullet); cf. GARGLE, GUGGLE]

gŭr´jun, n. E.-Ind. tree yielding ~ balsam or oil, used medicinally. [native]

Gurkha (goork´a), n. Member of ruling Hindu race in Nepal (~ *regiments*, of ~s in British army). [native]

gŭrn´ard, **gŭrn´ĕt**, n. Kinds of sea-fish with large head, mailed cheeks, & three free pectoral rays. [ME, f. OF *gornart, gournart* ult. f. *gron(d)ir* (GRUNT)]

gŭ'rrah, n. Common Indian earthen jar. [native]

gŭ'rry, n. Small Indian fort. [Hind. *ɡarhī*]

guru (gōō'rōō), n. Hindu spiritual teacher. [Skr., = grave, dignified]

gush, v.i. & t., & n. (Issue in, send forth) sudden or copious stream (often fig. of speech, tenderness, etc.); emit (water) copiously; (speak, behave, with) effusiveness, sentimental affectation, whence ~'ER² n., (also) oil-well from which the oil flows without pumping, ~'inGLY² adv.,~'Y² a. [ME *gosshe* perh. imit.]

gŭss'ét, n. Triangular piece let into garment to strengthen or enlarge some part; iron bracket strengthening angle of structure. Hence ~ED² a. [ME, f. OF *gousset (gousse* pod, shell) flexible piece filling up joint in mail-coat]

gŭst¹, n., & v.i. Sudden violent rush of wind; burst of rain, fire, smoke, sound, or passion; (v.i.) blow in~s. Hence gŭs'tY² a., gŭs'tiLY² adv. [f. ON *gustr*]

gŭst², n. (arch. & poet.). Sense of taste; keen relish (*have a ~ of*, appreciate); flavour. [ME, f. L *gustus* taste]

gŭstā'tion, n. Tasting. So gŭs'tATIVE, gŭs'tatorY, aa. [f. L *gustatio (gustare* f. *gustus* taste, -ATION)]

gŭs'tō, n. Special flavour (arch.; *enjoy the full ~ of*); zest, enjoyment with which something is done. [It., as GUST²]

gŭt, n., & v.t. & i. (-tt-). 1. (Pl.) bowels or entrails (esp. of animals), contents of anything (*has no ~s in it*, is of no real value or force); particular part of lower alimentary canal, intestine, (*blind ~*, caecum). 2. (Usu. pl.) belly as seat of appetite (vulg.); (pl., sl.) pluck, force of character, staying power. 3. Material for violin strings made from intestines of animals; *surgical ~* (for suture); material for fishing-lines made from intestines of silkworm. 4. Narrow water-passage, sound, straits, ‖ (Oxf. & Camb.) bend of river in racing-course; defile, narrow lane or part of street. 5. vb. Take out ~s of, clean, (fish); remove or destroy internal fittings of (house etc.); extract essence of (book etc.); eat greedily (vulg.). [OE *guttas* pl., prob. cogn. w. *geotan* pour]

gŭtt'ae, n. pl. Drops in a row as ornament esp. in Doric architecture. [pl. of L *gutta* drop]

gŭtta-pérch'a, n. Tough greyish-black substance flexible when thin, of inspissated juice of various Malayan trees. [f. Malay *getah* gum, *percha* name of tree]

gŭtt'āte, a. (nat. hist.). Speckled. [f. L *guttatus (gutta* drop, -ATE²)]

gŭtt'er, n., & v.t. & i. 1. Track made by running water (rare); shallow trough below eaves, or channel at side of street, carrying off rain-water (~*-child*, street arab; *take child* etc. *out of~*, remove from

poor surroundings); open conduit for outflow of fluid; groove; ~*-man*, cheap street--vendor of trifles; ~ *press, journalism* (catering for depraved or vulgar tastes); ~*-snipe*, street arab. 2. vb. Furrow, channel; flow in streams; (of candle) melt away by becoming channelled so that wax etc. runs down. [ME, f. AF *gotere* f. Rom. **guttaria* (L *gutta*, -ER²)]

gŭt'tle, v.i. & t. Eat gluttonously. Hence gŭtt'lER¹ n. [prob. f. GUT after GUZZLE]

gŭtt'ural, a. & n. Of the throat; (of sounds) produced in throat or by back of tongue & palate (n., ~ sound or letter, as k, g). Hence ~IZE(3) v.t., ~ISM(1) n., ~LY² adv. [F, f. L *guttur* throat+-AL]

gŭtt'uro-, comb. form of L *guttur* throat (see -o-), as ~*maxill'ary* of throat & jaws.

guy¹ (gī), n., & v.t. 1. Rope, chain, etc., to steady load of crane etc. or hold tent etc. in place. 2. v.t. Secure with ~(s). [of LG or Du. orig.; cf. LG, Du. *gei* brail etc.]

guy² (gī), n., & v.t. & i. 1. Effigy of Guy Fawkes burnt on 5th Nov.; ‖ grotesquely dressed person, fright; *(sl.) man, fellow; ‖ (sl.) act of decamping (*give the ~ to*, escape from; *do a ~*, disappear). 2. v.t. Exhibit in effigy; ridicule; (sl.) run away. [person]

Guy's (gīz), n. (Used for) Guy's Hospital in London. [person]

gŭz'zle, v.i. & t. Drink, eat, greedily (i. & t.); consume (money etc.) in guzzling (often *away*). Hence gŭzz'lER¹ n. [imit.]

gwўn'iăd, n. White-fleshed lake fish of salmon kind. [W (*gwyn* white)]

gȳbe, *jibe, v.i. & t., & n. (Of fore-&-aft -sail or boom) swing across, make (sail) do this, in wearing or running before wind; (of ship, crew, etc.) change course so that this happens. [f. Du. *gijben*]

gȳle (g-), n. Quantity of beer brewed at once; fermenting wort; fermenting-tun. [f. MDu. *ghijl (gijlen* to ferment)]

gȳm, n. (colloq.). Gymnasium, gymnastics. [abbr.]

gȳmkha'na (-kah-), n. (orig. Anglo-Ind.). Public place with facilities for athletics; athletic-sports display. [mixture of *gym-* (*nastics*) & Hind. (*gend-)khana* ball-house, racquet court]

gȳmnā'sium (-z-), n. (pl. *-ums*, *-a*). 1. Place, room, or building, with appliances for practice in gymnastics. 2. Continental, esp. German, school of highest grade preparing for universities (*often pr.* gimnah'ziōŏm; pl. occas. *-ien*), whence gȳmnā'siAL a. [L, f. Gk *gumnasion (gumnazō* exercise f. *gumnos* naked)]

gȳm'năst, n. Expert in gymnastics. [f. Gk *gumnastēs (gumnazō* see prec.)]

gȳmnăs'tǀic, a. & n. 1. Of gymnastics, involving bodily or (rarely) mental exercise, discipline, effort, or activity; hence ~ICALLY adv. 2. n. Course of instruction regarded as discipline (*grammar is a good* ~*ic*); (pl.) exercises developing the muscles, esp. such as are performed in gymnasium (also in same sense as sing.). [f. L f. Gk *gumnastikos* (prec., -IC)]

gymno-, comb. form of Gk *gumnos* naked, bare, used in many bot., zeol., & biol. terms, as ~*sperm'ous* having seeds unprotected by seed-vessels.

gymnŏs'oph|ist, n. One of ancient Hindu philosophic sect going nearly naked & given up to contemplation; mystic, ascetic. So ~Y¹ n. [F, or f. L f. Gk *gumnosophistai* pl. (prec., SOPHIST)]

gymnŏt'us, n. The electric eel. [f. Gk *gumnos* naked + *nōton* back (from absence of dorsal fins)]

gy̆naecē'um (g-, j-), n. (Gk & Rom. Ant.) women's apartments in house; (Bot.) freq. incorrectly -*oe'cium* female organs of flower. [L, f. Gk *gunaikeion* (*gunē -aikos* woman); -*oecium* from confusion with Gk *oikion* house]

gy̆naeco- (g-, j-), comb. form of Gk *gunē -aikos* woman, as ~*logy* (-ŏl⁴), science of diseases of women. Hence ~C'RACY (-ŏk⁴) n.

gy̆năn'drous (g-, j-), a. (bot.). With stamens & pistil united in one column as in orchids. [f. Gk *gunandros* (*gunē* woman, *anēr andros* man) of doubtful sex + -OUS]

gy̆n(o)- (g-, j-), shortened form of GYNAECO-, esp. in Bot. = pistil-, ovary-, as *gyn'obāse*, enlargement of receptacle supporting gynaeceum, *gyn'ophŏre*, pedicel supporting ovary, also (Zool.) bud-bearing branch in hydrozoa; also = woman-, whence g̑y̆nŏc'RACY n.

-gy̆nous (g-, j-), suf. f. mod. L f. Gk -*gunos* (*gunē* woman) + -OUS, forming adjj. = having specified female organs or pistils, as *mono*~, *tetra*~, *andro*~.

‖ **gy̆p¹**, n. College servant at Cambridge & Durham (cf. SCOUT¹); ~*room*, ~'*s* pantry. [perh. for obs. *gippo* scullion, orig. man's short tunic, f. obs. F *jupeau*]

‖ **gy̆p²**, n. (sl.). *Give* one ~, scold or punish or defeat him unmercifully, pain one. [orig. unkn.]

*° **gy̆p³**, v.t. (sl.; -pp-). Cheat, swindle. [orig. unkn.]

gy̆ps. = GYPSUM.

gy̆psŏph'ila, n. Kinds of garden plant with profusion of small white composite flowers. [foll., -PHIL]

gy̆p's|um, n. Hydrated calcium sulphate, mineral from which plaster of Paris is made, whence ~ŎG'RAPHY n.; this used as manure, whence ~um v.t. Hence ~EOUS, ~IF'EROUS, ~OUS, aa. [L, f. Gk *gupsos*]

gy̆psy. See GIPSY.

gy̆r'ate¹, a. (bot.). Arranged in rings or convolutions. [f. L *gyratus* (GYRE, -ATE²)]

gy̆rāte'², v.i. Go in circle or spiral, revolve, whirl. Hence gy̆rA'TION n., gy̆r'ATORY a. [f. LL *gyrare* (foll.), -ATE³]

gy̆r'e, v.i., & n. (poet.). = prec.; (n.) gyration. [vb as prec.; n. f. L f. Gk *guros* ring]

gy̆r'ŏ, n. (pl. -*os*). Gyroscope (see foll.); ~-*compass*, compass giving true north & bearings from it by means of a gyroscope. [abbr. of foll.]

gy̆r'o-, comb. form of Gk *guros* ring, as ~*graph* (-ahf), instrument recording revolutions; ~*magnetic* a., of the magnetic properties of a rotating electrical particle; ~*plane*, form of aircraft deriving its lift mainly from freely rotating overhead vanes; ~*scŏpe*, ~*stăt*, instruments illustrating dynamics of rotating bodies, also (~*scope*) rapidly spinning wheel fixed in something, e.g. car on single rail, to keep it in equilibrium, & having, by the independent stability of its axis, great value in mechanics; ~-*tiller*, cultivator in which tines rotate round axis.

gy̆rōse', a. (bot.). Folded & waved, marked with wavy lines. [GYRE, -OSE¹]

gy̆ttja (gĭt'yä), n. (geol.). Late or post-glacial deposit, usu. covered over by peat of a later date, in Sweden. [Sw., = mud, ooze]

gy̆ve, n. (usu. pl.), & v.t. (poet.). Shackle, fetter. [ME *give* (*pr.* g-), of unkn. orig.]

H

H, h, (āch), letter (pl. *Hs*, H's). DROP² one's *hs*; *H-iron*, girder of H-shaped section.

ha¹ (hah), int. expr. surprise, joy, suspicion, triumph, etc. [ME]

ha² (hah). See HUM v.

haaf (hahf), n. (In Shetland & Orkney) deep-sea fishing ground. [f. ON *haf* high sea]

hāb'ĕăs cōrp'us, n. Writ requiring body of person to be brought before judge or into court, esp. to investigate lawfulness of his restraint; *Habeas Corpus Act* (of Charles II, 1679, facilitating use of this). [L, = you must have the body]

hăb'erdăsh|er, n. Dealer in small articles of dress etc. Hence ~ERY(1) n. [conn. w. obs. *haberdash* small wares, prob. f. AF *hapertas*, of unkn. orig.]

hăb'ergeon (-jon), n. (hist.). Sleeveless coat of mail. [ME, f. OF *haubergeon* (HAUBERK, -OON)]

hăb'ile, a. (literary). Skilful, dextrous. [15th c. var. of ABLE]

habil'iment, n. (Pl.) dress suited to any office or occasion (joc. of ordinary clothes); (sing.) equipment, attire, (rare). [ME, f. OF (*h*)*abillement* (*habiller* fit out f. *habile* ABLE, see -MENT)]

habil'it|āte, v.t. & i. Furnish (mine) with working capital; (intr.) qualify for office (esp. in German Univ.). So ~A'TION n. [f. med. L *habilitare* (as ABILITY), see -ATE³]

hăb'it¹, n. Settled tendency or practice, as *he is in*, *has* (*fallen into*), *the* or *a* ~ *of* contradiction; mental constitution, esp. ~ *of mind*; bodily constitution, as *a man of corpulent* ~; (Bot., Zool.) mode of growth; (arch.) dress, esp. of religious order; (also *riding-*~) lady's riding-dress. [ME, f. OF f. L *habitus -ūs* f. *habēre habit-have*, (refl.) be]

hăb′it², v.t. Clothe; ‖ (arch.) inhabit. [f. OF *habiter* f. L *habitare* inhabit, as prec.]

hăb′it|able, a. That can be inhabited. Hence ~aBIL′ITY, ~ableNESS, nn., ~aBLY² adv. [ME, f. OF f. L *habitabilis* (as prec., see -ABLE)]

hăb′itant, n. Inhabitant; (pr. ahbĕtahn′) Canadian of French descent. [F (HABIT², -ANT)]

hăb′ităt, n. Natural home of plant or animal; habitation, [L, 3rd sing pres. as HABIT²]

hăbitā′tion, n. Inhabiting, as *fit for human* ~; place of abode; branch of Primrose League. [ME, f. OF f. L *habitationem* (as HABIT², -ATION)]

habit′ūal, a. Customary; constant, continual; given to (specified) habit, as a ~ *drunkard*. Hence ~LY² adv., ~NESS n. [f. med. L *habitualis* (as HABIT¹, -AL)]

habit′ū|āte, v.t. Accustom *to* thing, *to doing*. So~A′TION n. [f. LL *habituare* (as HABIT¹), see -ATE³]

hăb′itūde, n. Mental or bodily constitution; custom, tendency. [ME, f. OF f. L *habitudinem* (*habēre* have, see -TUDE)]

habit′ué (-ā), n. Habitual visitor or resident. [F, p.p. of *habituer* (as HABITU-ATE)]

hachures (hăshūr′), n. pl. Lines used in hill-shading on maps to indicate slope. [F]

haciĕn′da (ă-, ah-), n. (Sp.-Amer.). Estate, plantation; factory, works. [Sp.]

hăck¹, n. Mattock; miner's pick; gash, wound, esp. from kick with toe of boot. [f. MLG *hakke*, & f. foll.]

hăck², v.t. & i. Cut, notch, mangle; kick shin of (opponent at football); deal cutting blows (*at*); emit short dry coughs; *a* ~*ing* (short dry frequent) *cough*; ~*-saw* (for metal-cutting). [OE *haccian*, MLG, MDu., MHG *hacken* f. WG *hakkôn*]

hăck³, n. Board on which hawk's meat is laid (of eyas hawk) *be at* ~ (not allowed to prey for itself); frame for drying bricks. [var. of HATCH¹, perh. assoc. w. HECK]

hăck⁴, n. Horse let out for hire; jade; horse for ordinary riding; common drudge (also attrib., as ~ *writer*); *⁕*~*′stand*, cabstand. [abbr. of HACKNEY]

hăck⁵, v.t. & i. Make common, hackney; ride (horse), ride on horseback, on road at ordinary pace; use hired horses. [f. prec.]

hăck′erў, n. Indian bullock-cart. [perh. f. Hindi *chhakrā*]

hăc′kle¹, n., & v.t. 1. Steel flax-comb; long feathers on neck of domestic cock & other birds; *with his* ~*s up*, (of cock, dog, man) angry, ready to fight; artificial fly dressed with~. 2. v.t. Dress (flax, fly) with ~. [ME *hechele*, *hek-*, *hakele*, f. OE *⁕hacule*, *⁕hecile* f. Gmc *⁕hak-* prick,

pierce; cf. HOOK; cogn. w. MHG *hachele*, MLG, MDu. *hekele*]

hăc′kle², v.t. Hack, mangle. [HACK²+ -LE(3)]

hăck′lў, a. Rough, jagged. [f. prec.+-Y²]

hăck′matăck, n. Amer. larch. [native]

hăck′ney, n., & v.t. 1. Horse of middle size & quality for ordinary riding; drudge, hireling; ~*-carriage*, *-coach* (kept for hire). 2. v.t. (Esp. in p.p. ~*ed*) make common or trite. [orig. much disputed; Skeat conjectures ME f. *Hackenei* in Middlesex, whence OF *haquenee* & other Rom. forms]

had. See HAVE.

hădd′ock, n. Fish allied to cod. [ME, of unkn. orig.; OF *hadot* prob. f. E]

hāde, v.i. (geol., mining). Incline from the vertical. [orig. unkn.]

Hād′ēs (-z), n. (Gk Myth.). Lower world, abode of departed spirits. [Gk, orig. a name of Pluto]

Hădj′i̇, **Hăjj′i̇**, n. (Title of) Mohammedan pilgrim who has been to MECCA. [f. Arab. *ḥaji*]

hadn′t. See HAVE.

haeccē′itў (hĕks-), n. (philos.). Thisness; individuality. [f. med. L *haecceitas* (*haec* fem. of *hic* this, see -TY)]

haem′al, a. (anat.). Of the blood; situated on same side of body as the heart & great blood-vessels. [f. Gk *haima* blood +-AL]

haemăt′ic, a. & n. Of or containing blood; (n.) medicine acting on the blood. [f. Gk *haimatikos* (as foll., see -IC)]

haem′atin, n. (chem.). Bluish-black amorphous substance, constituent of haemoglobin. [f. Gk *haima -matos* blood +-IN]

haem′atite, **hĕm²**, n. A red, brown, or blackish, iron oxide ore. [f. L f. Gk *haimatitēs* (*lithos*) blood-like stone (as prec., see -ITE)]

haem′ato-, (chiefly U.S.) **hĕm′ato-**, in comb. = Gk *haima -matos* blood, as ~*cele*, tumour containing extravasated blood.

haematūr′ia, n. (path.). Presence of blood in the urine. [f. prec.+Gk *ouron* urine]

haem′o-, **hĕm′o-**, in comb. short for H(A)EMATO-.

haemoglŏb′in, n. Oxygen-carrying pigment contained in red blood-cells of vertebrates. [f. HAEMO- +GLOBULIN]

haemophil′ia, **hĕm-**, n. (med.). (Hereditary) tendency to bleeding from even a slight injury. [f. Gk *haima* blood, -o-, *philia* affection]

haem′orrhage, **hem²**, (hĕm′orĭj), n. Escape of blood from blood-vessels, bleeding. [17th c. f. L f. Gk *haimorrhagia* (*haima* blood+st. of *rhēgnumi* burst); 16th c. also *-agy* f. OF *-agie*]

haem′orrhoids, **hem²**, (hĕm′oroidz), n. pl. Piles. [14th c. *emeraudes* (Bibl. *emerods*) f. OF *emeroyde*; later dir. f. L f. Gk *haimorrhoides* (*phlebes*) bleeding (veins) (*haima* blood +-*rhoos* -flowing)]

ha'fiz (hah-), n. Mohammedan who knows Koran by heart (used as title). [Arab.]

häf'nium, n. (chem.). Metallic element discovered in 1923. [Da. *(Kjöben)havn* Copenhagen + -IUM]

haft (hah-), n., & v.t. Wooden shaft of pick-axe, mattock, felling-axe, etc.; handle (of dagger, knife, etc.); (v.t.) furnish (knife etc.) with ~. [OE *hæft(e)*, OHG *hefti*, ON *hepti* f. Gmc **haftjom* f. **haf-* HEAVE].

häg¹, n. Ugly old woman; witch; (formerly) evil spirit in female form; (also ~*'fish*) a parasite fish allied to lamprey; ~*'ridden*, afflicted by nightmare. Hence ~**g'ISH¹** (-g-) a. [ME *hegge*, *hagge* perh. f. OE *hægtesse* (= OHG *hagazissa*, G *hexe*) of unkn. orig.]

‖ **häg²**, n. Soft place in moor; firm place in bog. [ON *högg* ravine]

hagga'dah (-gah-), n. Legendary part of the Talmud; book recited at SEDER. [Heb., = tale, f. *higgid* tell]

hägg'ard, a. & n. **1.** Wild-looking (esp. as a result of fatigue, privation, worry, etc.). **2.** (Of hawk) caught in her adult plumage, untamed; (n.) such a hawk. Hence ~NESS n. [f. F *hagard*, of unkn. orig.]

‖ **hägg'is** (-g-), n. Minced heart, lungs, & liver, of sheep etc., boiled in maw with suet, oatmeal, etc. [ME; orig. unkn.]

häg'gle, v.i., & n. Dispute, wrangle, (*about*, *over*); (v.i.) bargain. [f. dial. *hag* chop f. ON *höggva* (HEW) + -LE(3)]

häg'iarchy (-gī-; -ki), n. Rule, order, of saints. [f. foll. + Gk *arkhē* rule]

hägio- (-g-), comb. form of Gk *hagios* saint(ly), as: ~*cracy* (-ŏkᴸ), government of holy persons; ~*grapha* (-ŏgᴸ), books of the Hebrew Scriptures not included under Law & Prophets; ~*grapher* (-ŏgᴸ), ~*graph'ic*, (writer) of any of these, or of saints' lives; ~*graphy* (-ŏgᴸ), writing of saints' lives; ~*latry* (-ŏlᴸ), worship of saints; ~*logy* (-ŏlᴸ), literature treating of lives & legends of saints; ~*scope* (hägᴸ), (modern term for) squint (eccl.).

hah, int. & v.i. = HA¹,².

ha ha (hah hah), int. repr. laughter.

ha-ha (hah'hah), n. Sunk fence bounding park or garden. [F]

hai(c)k (hah'īk, hāk), n. Arabian outer wrapper for head & body. [Arab. *ḥayk* f. *ḥak* weave]

hail¹, n. Pellets of frozen rain falling in shower, as ~*'storm*; shower of missiles, curses, questions, etc.; ~*'stone*, pellet of ~. Hence ~*'*Y² a. [OE *hægl*, OS, OHG *hagel*, ON *hagl* f. Gmc **hag(a)laz*, *-am*]

hail², v.i. & t. *It* ~s, hail falls; (fig.) pour down (blows, words, etc.), come down, violently. [OE *hagalian* (prec.)]

hail³, int. of greeting; ~*-fellow*, ~*-fellow--well-met*, intimate, too intimate, *with*. [ellipt. use of obs. adj. *hail* f. ON *heill* sound, HALE, WHOLE]

hail⁴, v.t. & i., & n. **1.** Salute; greet (person etc. *as* king etc., also ~ *him king*);

call to (ship, person) to attract attention; (of ship, person) be come *from* (place). **2.** n. Salutation, esp. *within*~, near enough to be ~ed. [ME, f. prec.]

hair, n. **1.** One or (collect. sing.) all of the fine filaments growing from skin of animals, esp. from human head (pl. ~*s* in collect. sense is arch.); (of plants) elongated cell growing from epidermis; ~*-like* thing; jot, tittle; *against the* ~, against the grain; *to a* ~, exactly; *a* ~ *of the* DOG *that bit you*; (sl.) *keep your* ~ *on*, keep cool; *get* person *by the short* ~*s* (sl.), have complete control over, have at one's mercy; (of girl) *put up*, *turn up*, *her* ~, dress it in woman's fashion; *do* or *put up*, *let down her* ~; *let* one's *(back)* ~ *down* (colloq.), drop ceremony, behave in an unconventional way; *not turn a* ~, show no sign of exhaustion or discomposure; ~ *stands on end* (with fright or horror). **2.** ~*'breadth* or ~*'s breadth*, minute distance (~*breadth escape*, very narrow); ~*'brush*, toilet brush for ~; ~*'cloth* (made of ~, for various purposes); ~*'cut*, cutting of the ~; ~*-do* (colloq.), style or process of woman's ~*dressing*; ~*'dresser*, one whose business is to dress and cut ~; ~*-line*, line, rope, made of ~, (also) up-stroke in writing; ~*-net*, *-oil* (used for the ~); ~*'pin* (for fastening the ~; ~*pin bend*, doubling back of road); ~*-powder*, scented powder for ~, now used by men-servants; ~ *shirt* (of ~cloth, for ascetics); ~*-slide*, horn or tortoise-shell clip for keeping ~ in position; ~*-space* (Typ.), very thin space; ~*-splitting* a. & n., over-subtle(ty); ~*'spring*, fine spring in watch, regulating balance-wheel; ~*-stroke*, fine up-stroke in writing; ~ *trigger*, secondary trigger releasing main one by slight pressure. Hence ~*'*INESS n., (-)~ED² (-rd), ~*'*LESS, ~*'*LIKE, ~*'*Y², aa. (~*y-heeled*, sl., deficient in breeding or manners). [OE *hær*, *hēr*, OS, OHG, ON *hār*, f. Gmc **hēram*]

hāke¹, n. Fish like cod. [15th c., of unkn. orig.]

hāke², **haik**, n. Wooden framework for drying bricks & other purposes. [prob. var. of HACK³, HECK]

hakeem', **-kim'¹** (-ēm), n. (In India & Mohammedan countries) physician. [Arab. *ḥakīm* wise, physician]

ha'kīm² (hah-), n. (As prec.) judge, ruler, governor. [Arab. *ḥākim*]

halā'tion, n. (photog.). Spreading of light beyond its proper boundary in a negative (and consequent fogging) caused by internal reflection in the support of the emulsion. [irreg. f. HALO + -ATION]

häl'berd, **-rt**, n. (hist.). Combined spear & battle-axe. [f. OF *halebarde*, ult. f. MHG *helmbarte* (*helm* handle + *barte* axe)]

hälberdier' (-ēr), n. Man armed with halberd. [f. OF *hallebardier* (as prec., see -IER)]

häl'cyon, n. & a. **1.** Bird fabled by the ancients to breed in floating nest on sea at winter solstice, & to charm wind &

waves into calm for the purpose; (Zool.) Australasian kingfisher. **2.** adj. Calm, esp. ~ *days* (orig. 14 days about winter solstice). [ME, f. L *halcyon* f. Gk *alkuŏn* kingfisher]

hāle¹, a. Robust, vigorous, (esp. of old persons). Hence ~'NESS (-ln-) n. [north. repr. of OE *hǣl* WHOLE]

hāle², v.t. Drag, draw, forcibly (lit. & fig.). [ME, f. OF *haler* f. ON *hala* = OS, OHG *halōn*; cf. OE *geholian* obtain; see HAUL]

half (hahf), n. (pl. *halves* pr. hahvz), a., & adv. **1.** One of two equal or corresponding parts into which a thing is divided, as *the* ~ *of 10 is 5, cut it in* ~ (into halves), *your* ~ *is bigger than mine, two ounces & a* ~ (ounce) or *two & a* ~ *ounces, ~ of it is* (but *of them are*) *rotten*; (colloq.)=~-pint, -mile, -back, -holiday; ‖ school term (the school year being formerly divided into two portions); *better* ~, wife; *do a thing by halves* (imperfectly); *too clever by* ~ (far); *go halves*, share equally (*with* person *in* thing); *cry halves*, claim equal share. **2.** adj. Forming a ~, as *a* ~ *length, a* ~ *share*; (adj. now viewed as=*the* ~ *of*) ~ *the men*, ~ *your time*, ~ *a crown* (2/6), ~ *a pint*, ~ *a pound* (is ~ *the battle*, goes a long way towards success). **3.** adv. To the extent of ~, (loosely) to a considerable extent, as *it is* ~ *cooked, a* ~-*cooked potato*, ~ *dead, I* ~ *wish, not* ~ (nearly) *long enough*, (colloq.) *not* ~ (not at all) *bad, not* ~ *a bad fellow*; ‖ *not* ~ (sl.), to the greatest possible extent, as *he didn't* ~ *swear* (swore violently); (adv., prob. orig. adj.)~ (an hour) *past two* (o'clock); (Naut.) ~ *three*, 3½ (fathoms), *east* ~-*south* (5⅝° south of east). **4.** ~-*&*-~, (what is) ~ one thing & ~ another, esp. mixture of ale & porter; ~ *as much* or *many again*, 1½ times the amount; ~-*back*, (Footb.) position, player, immediately behind forwards; ~-*baked*, (fig.) not thorough, not earnest, ~-*witted*; ~-*ball* (Billiards etc.), with moving ball directed at edge of object ball; ~-*binding* of book, leather back & corners, cloth or paper sides (similarly ~-*bound*, ~-*calf*, ~-*morocco*, etc.); ~-*blood*, person having one parent in common with another, this relationship, (also) person of mixed nationality; ~-*blooded*, born of different races; ~-*blue*, badge or colours (see BLUE²) awarded to second string or to representative in minor sports; ~-*boot* (reaching up to the calf); ~-*bred*, of mixed breed, mongrel; ~-*breed*, ~-blooded person; ~-*brother*, -*sister* (by one parent only); ~ *butt*, cue of length between ordinary cue & long butt; ~-*caste* a. & n., ~-*bre(e)d*, esp. (child) of European father & Indian mother; ~ COCK¹(2); ‖ ~-*crown*, ‖ silver coin of 2/6, (usu. ~ *a crown*, see above) amount of 2/6, (adj.) priced at or worth 2/6; ~-*deck*, (esp.) quarters of cadets & apprentices on a merchant vessel; ~-*fifteen*, -*thirty*, -*forty*

(Lawn Tennis), handicap (in strokes allowed in certain games of each set) given to a weaker player; ~-*hearted*, lacking courage or zeal, so ~-*heartedly*, -*ness*; ~ HITCH; ~ *holiday*, day of which (the latter)~ is taken as holiday; ~-*length*, portrait of upper ~ of person; ~-*life* (Phys.), time during which radio-activity of substance falls to ~ of its original value; ~-*mast high*, (of flag) lowered to ~ height of mast as mark of respect for the dead; ~ *measures*, compromise, ~-&-~ policy etc.; ~ *moon*, moon of which only ~ is illuminated, semicircular object; ~ *mourning*, black relieved by grey etc.; ~(-)*nelson*, a hold in wrestling (*get a* ~ *nelson on*, hold in a crippling position, gain complete mastery over); ~ *pay*, reduced allowance to army etc. officer when neither retired nor in actual service; ~-*seas-over*, ~ drunk; ~-*time*, time showing that ~ of a game or contest is completed; ‖ ~-*timer*, (formerly) child attending school for ~ usual time, earning money in other ~; ~-*title*, title or short title of a book, printed on recto of leaf preceding the title-leaf; also title of section of a book printed on recto of leaf preceding it; ~-*tone*, illustration printed from a block (produced by photographic agency) in which the lights & shades of the original are represented by small or large dots (~-*tone block, process*); ~-*truth*, statement that conveys only part of the truth; ~ VOLLEY; ~-*way house*, inn midway between two towns etc., (fig.) compromise; ~-*witted*, imbecile, so ~-*wit* n.; ~-*yearly* a. & adv., (occurring) every ~ year. [OE *h(e)alf*, OS *half*, OHG *halb* ON *halfr*, Goth. *halbs* f. Gmc **halbhaz*]

‖ **halfpenny** (hāp'ni), n. (pl. as PENNY). Bronze coin worth half a penny (*turn up again like a bad* ~, persistently, unfailingly); *three halfpence* (hāp'ens), (usu. for) a penny ~, 1½*d.*; ~*worth* (usu. pron. hāp'ath), ha'p'orth, as much as a ~ will buy.

hăl'ibut, hŏl', n. Large flat fish used for food. [ME, f. *haly* HOLY + *butt* flat fish]

hăl'idom, n. (arch.). Holy thing, esp. (as oath) *by my* ~. [OE *hāligdōm* (HOLY, -DOM)]

hălieut'ic, a. & n. Of fishing; (n. pl.) art of fishing. [f. L f. Gk *halieutikos* (*halieuō* fish f. *hals* sea, see -IC)]

hălitos'is, n. (med.). Abnormally foul breath. [f. L *halitus* breath + -OSIS]

hall (hawl), n. Large public room in palace etc., *servants'* ~, room in which servants dine; ‖ mansion, large residence esp. of landed proprietor; ‖ (Univv.) building set apart for residence or instruction of students; ‖ (in Eng. colleges etc.) common dining-room, dinner in this; building of guild, as *Saddlers' H*~; large room for public business; entrance-passage of house; *Liberty H*~, place where one may do as one likes; ~'mark, mark used at Goldsmiths' H~ (& by Government assay offices) for marking standard of gold & silver, (v.t.) stamp with this (often fig.). [OE h(e)all, OS, OHG halla, ON hǫll f. Gmc *hal- cogn. w. HELL]

hallelujah, -luiah. See ALLELUIA.

halliard. See HALYARD.

hallo̅', -loa' (-lō), int., n., & v.i. Int. calling attention or expr. surprise; informal greeting; (n., & v.i.) (the) cry ~. [var. of earlier HOLLO]

halloo̅'¹, int. inciting dogs to the chase, calling attention, or expressing surprise (also as n., the cry~). [perh. var. of HOLLO]

halloo̅'², v.i. & t. Cry 'halloo!', esp. to dogs; urge on (dogs etc.) with shouts; shout (t. & i.) to attract attention; (prov.) do not ~ until you are out of the WOOD. [f. prec.; or = HALLOW³]

hǎll'ow¹ (-ō), n. Holy person, saint, (now only in all ~s, ~mas, feast of All-hallows, = ALL Saints' Day; Hall'ow̆e'en, Sc., U.S., eve of this). [OE hālga, form of hālig HOLY]

hǎll'ow² (-ō), v.t. Make holy; honour as holy. [OE hālgian, OS hē-, OHG heilagōn, ON helga f. Gmc *hailag- HOLY]

hǎll'ow³ (-ō), v.t. & i. Chase with shouts; incite with shouts; shout to incite dogs etc. [ME halowen prob. f. OF halloer]

Hallstatt (hahl'shtaht), a. (Used attrib.) relating to the civilization of a phase of the early iron age. [~, village in Upper Austria, where remains of this period were discovered]

hallu'cināte (-lōō-), v.t. Produce false impressions in the mind of (person). [f. L (h)al(l)ucinari wander in mind, see -ATE³]

hallucinā'tion (-lōō-), n. Illusion; apparent perception of external object not actually present. So hallu'cinatory (-lōō-) a. [f. L alucinatio (as prec., see -ATION)]

halm. See HAULM.

hǎl'ma, n. Game played on board of 256 squares. [Gk = leap, f. hallomai leap, see -M]

hǎl'o̅, n. (pl. ~es), & v.t. 1. Circle of light round luminous body, esp. sun or moon; circle, ring; disc of light surrounding head of saint, nimbus; (fig.) ideal glory investing person etc. 2. v.t. Surround with ~. [f. med. L halo f. L f. Gk halōs threshing-floor, disc of sun or moon]

hǎl'ogĕn, n. (chem.). Any of the group of elements fluorine, chlorine, bromine, & iodine, which form haloids by simple union with a metal (e.g. sodium chloride or common salt). [f. Gk hals salt + -GEN]

hǎl'oid, a. & n. (chem.). (Salt) having a composition like that of common salt. [f. Gk hals salt + -OID]

halt¹ (hawlt), n., & v.i. & t. 1. Temporary stoppage on march or journey; || railway stopping-place used for local services only and without regular station buildings etc.

2. v.i. Make a ~. 3. v.t. Cause (troops etc.) to ~. [(vb f. n.) orig. in phr. make halt f. G halt machen (halt hold)]

halt² (hawlt), a. (arch.). Lame; crippled. [OE h(e)alt, OS halt, OHG halz, ON haltr, Goth. halts f. Gmc *haltaz]

halt³ (hawlt), v.i., & n. Walk hesitatingly; hesitate, as ~ between two opinions; (of argument, verse, etc.) be defective; (arch.) be lame; (n., arch.) ~ing, limp. Hence ~'ingLY² adv. [OE h(e)altian, f. prec.]

hal'ter (hawl-), n., & v.t. 1. Rope, strap, with noose or headstall for horses or cattle; rope with noose for hanging person; death by hanging; ~-break v.t., accustom (horse) to ~. 2. v.t. Fasten (often up) with ~, hang (person) with ~. [OE hælftre, OLG heliftra, OHG halftra, WG f. root halbh, whence HELVE]

halve (hahv), v.t. Divide into halves; share equally; reduce to half; (Golf) ~ a hole with, reach it in same number of strokes as (other player), ~ a match, win same number of holes; fit (crossing timbers) together by cutting out half thickness of each. [ME HALFen]

hǎl'yard, hǎll'iard, haul'yard, n. (naut.). Rope, tackle, for raising or lowering sail, yard, etc. [14th c. halier (HALE², -YER)]

hǎm¹, n. Back of thigh, thigh & buttock; (formerly) bend of the knee; thigh of hog salted & dried in smoke or otherwise for food; (sl.) an amateur (radio ~, operator of an amateur radio station), an inexpert performer, (also ~ actor) an inexperienced or ineffective actor, one who rants & overacts; (sl.) ~-fisted, -handed, heavy-handed, clumsy. [OE ham(m), hom(m), OHG ham(m)a, ON hǫm f. Gmc *ham(m)- be crooked]

hǎm², n. (hist.). Town, village. [OE hām HOME; seen in Oakham etc.]

hǎmadry̆'ăd, n. (Gk Myth.) nymph living & dying with the tree she inhabited; venomous Indian serpent; Abyssinian baboon. [f. L f. Gk hạmadruas (hama with + drus tree)]

Hǎm'burgh (-bĕrg, -buru), n. Black variety of grape; small variety of domestic fowl. [Hamburg in Germany]

*hǎm'bŭrger (-ger), n. (Also Hamburg steak) chopped steak usu. cooked or eaten with onions; kind of sausage. [prec., -ER¹]

hāmes, n. pl. Two curved pieces of iron or wood forming (part of) collar of draught horse. [ME, f. MDu. hame]

Hăm'īte¹, n. (Supposed) descendant or other Ham, member of Egyptian or other African people. Hence Hămĭt'IC a. [-ITE]

hăm'īte², n. Fossil cephalopod with hook-shaped shell. [f. L hamus hook, see -ITE]

hăm'lĕt, n. Small village, esp. one without church. [f. OF hamelet dim. of hamel dim. f. OFrank. haim HOME]

hammam (hŭmahm', hŭm'ŭm), n. Turkish bath or bathing establishment. [Arab.]

hämm'er[1], n. Instrument for beating, breaking, driving nails, etc., with solid (usu. steel) head at right angles to handle; machine with metal block serving same purpose; similar contrivance, as for exploding charge in gun (whence ~LESS a.), striking string of piano, etc.; auctioneer's mallet indicating by rap that article is sold; *come under the*~, be sold by auction; *knight of the* ~, blacksmith; *throwing the* ~, athletic contest with heavy ~; ~ *and sickle*, symbol of worker and peasant, emblem on national flag of U.S.S.R.; ~ *and tongs*, with might & main; ~-*beam* (projecting from wall at foot of principal rafter); ~-*cloth* (covering driver's seat in coach; hist. unexpl.); ~-*head*, head of ~, kind of shark, African bird; ~-*lock*, hold in which a wrestler's arm is bent behind his back; ~*man*, ~-*smith*, smith who works with ~; ~-*toe* (permanently bent upwards). [OE *hamor*, OS -*ur*, OHG -*ar*, ON -*arr*]

hämm'er[2], v.t. & i. Strike, beat, drive, (as) with hammer; (colloq.) inflict heavy defeat(s) on in war or games; ~ *out*, devise; ~ (force) *idea into* person's *head*; work hard *at*; || (St. Exch.) declare (person) a defaulter with three taps of hammer. [f. prec.]

hämm'ock, n. Hanging bed of canvas or netting suspended by cords at ends, used esp. on board ship; ~ *chair* (made of canvas suspended on adjustable framework). [f. Sp. *hamaca* of Carib. orig.]

häm'per[1], n. Basketwork packing-case; consignment of eatables, wines, etc., however packed (usu. as a present; *Christmas*~). [ME, f. obs. *hanaper* f. OF *hanapier* case for goblet (*hanap* f. WG (OFrank., OS) *hnap*)]

häm'per[2], v.t. & n. 1. Obstruct movement of (person etc.) with material obstacles; (fig.) impede, hinder. 2. n. (naut.). Necessary but cumbrous part of equipment of vessel. [ME, of unkn. orig.; perh. rel. to MHG *hemmen*, Icel. *hemja* restrain]

Hämp'ton Court (kŏrt), n. (Used for) ~ Palace, now partly occupied by persons of rank in reduced circumstances, partly open to the public. [place]

häm'shäckle, v.t. Shackle (horse etc.) with rope connecting head and foreleg. [Sc. & north. dial., of unkn. orig.]

häm'ster, n. Rodent like large rat, with cheek-pouches for carrying grain to its winter store. [G]

häm'string, n., & v.t. (-*inged* or -*ung*). 1. (In man) one of five tendons at back of knee; (in quadrupeds) great tendon at back of knee in hind leg. 2. v.t. Cripple (person, animal) by cutting the~s. [HAM[1]]

häm'ulus, n. (anat., zool., bot.; pl. -*li*). Hook-like process. [L, dim. of *hamus* hook]

händ[1], n. 1. Terminal part of human arm beyond wrist; similar member of all four limbs of monkey; forefoot of quadruped. 2. Authority, disposal, as *in the* ~*s of*; agency, as *by the*~*s of*, *pass through many* ~*s*; share in action, as *have a* ~ *in it*. 3. Pledge of marriage, as *give* one's ~ *to*. 4. (Usu. pl.) manual worker(s) of factory etc. 5. Person who does something, as *a picture by the same* ~; *all* ~*s*, the whole crew; *a good* ~ (skilful) *at singlestick* or *acrostics, an old parliamentary* ~; person, source, from which thing comes, as *first*, SECOND, ~ (*at 1st* etc. ~, directly, more or less indirectly; *first* etc. -~, of hearsay); COOL ~. 6. Skill, as *a* ~ *for pastry*; style of workmanship; turn, innings, at cricket, billiards, etc. 7. Style of writing, as *a legible* ~; signature, as *witness the* ~ *of A.B.* 8. ~-like thing, esp. pointer of clock or watch (~ *of* BANANAS). 9. Fixed quantity of various commodities, e.g., bundle of tobacco leaves. 10. A lineal measure of horse's height, = 4 in. 11. (Cards) cards dealt to a player, player holding these, as *first, third*, ~. 12. (Theatr. sl.) applause. 13. *At* ~, close by, about to happen soon; *by* ~, by manual labour (*brought up by* ~, of child fed from bottle); *for* one's *own* ~, on one's own account; (*live*) *from* ~ *to mouth*, improvidently; *in* ~, held in the ~, at one's disposal, under control, receiving attention; *off* ~, without preparation, then & there; *on* ~, in one's possession; *on* one's ~*s*, resting on one as a responsibility; *on all* ~*s*, to, from, all quarters; *on the one* ~, *on the other*~, (of contrasted points of view etc.); *out of* ~, at once, extempore, (also) out of control; *to* ~, within reach; *to* one's ~, ready for one without exertion on one's own part; *bear a* ~, take part *in*; *come to* ~, turn up, be received; *do a* ~'s *turn*, make the slightest effort (usu. w. neg.); *lay* ~*s on*, touch, seize; *take in* ~, undertake; *change* ~*s*, (of property) pass from one person to another; *clean* ~*s*, (fig.) innocence; *with a heavy* ~, oppressively; *with a high* ~, boldly, arrogantly; *have, keep*, one's ~ *in*, be in practice; *his* ~ *is out*, he is out of practice; (*win*) ~*s down*, easily; ~*s off l*, do not touch; ~*s up l* (direction to persons to hold up their ~*s* as a sign of assent etc., or to preclude resistance); ~ *in* ~, with ~*s* mutually clasped; *go* ~ *in* ~ *with*, keep step with, lit. & fig.; ~ *over* ~ *or fist*, with each ~ successively passing over the other, as in climbing rope, (fig.) with steady or rapid progress (in overtaking etc.); ~ *to* ~, (of conflict etc.) at close quarters; *bind* one ~ *& foot* (completely), *serve* (person) ~ *& foot* (assiduously); *be* ~ *in* (or *&*) *glove* (intimate) *with*; ~~ (opp. *machine*-, as ~-*knitted, -sewn, -painted*), 14. ~'*bag* (small, carried by women in lieu of pocket); ~'*ball*, ball for throwing with ~, game played with this between two goals; ~-*barrow* (carried by ~); ~'*bell*, bell rung by ~, esp one of a set for musical performance; ~'*bill*, printed notice circulated by ~; ~'*book*, short treatise, manual, guide-book; ~-*canter*, gentle canter; ~'*cart* (pushed or drawn by ~); ~'*cuff* v.t., secure with ~*cuffs* (pair of metal rings joined by short chain, for securing prisoner's ~s); ‖ ~'*fast*(*ing*) (Sc.), betrothal; ~-*gallop*, easy gallop; ~'*glass*, magnifying glass held in ~, small mirror with handle; ~'*grip*, grasp, seizure with the ~ (friendly or hostile); ~'*hold*, something for the ~s to grip on (in climbing etc.); ~'*line*, fishing-line worked without rod; ~'*made*, made by ~ (esp. opp. to *machine-made*); ‖ ~'*maid*(*en*), female servant (arch., exc. fig.); ~ *of glory*, charm made from mandrake root or dried ~ of executed felon [transl. of F *main de gloire*, corrupted f. *mandragore* mandrake]; ~-*organ*, barrel-organ with crank turned by ~; ~-*picked*, (of supporters etc.) carefully chosen; ~'*rail*, railing along edge of stairs etc.; ~'*shake*, shake of person's ~ with one's own, as greeting; ~'*spike*, wooden lever shod with iron, used on shipboard & by artillery; ~'*writing*, writing with the ~ with pen or pencil, esp. of particular person. Hence (-)~'ED[2], ~'LESS, aa. [OE *hand*, *hond*, OS *hand*, OHG *hant*, ON *hönd*, Goth. *handus*]

hand[2], v.t. Help (person) with the hand (*into*, *out of*, carriage etc.); (Naut.) take in (sail); deliver, transfer, by hand or otherwise (*over to* person, *down* or *on to* succeeding generations, *in* at office, *on*, *up*, etc.); ~-*off* (Rugby football), push off opponent with hand (also as v.t. and n.); ~-*out*, information ~ed out to the press etc., *food or money given to beggar at the door. [f. prec.]

hand'ful (-ŏŏl), n. (pl. ~s). Quantity that fills the hand; small number (of men etc.); (colloq.) troublesome person or task. [OE *handfull* (HAND[1], see -FUL)]

hăn'dicăp, n. & v.t. (-pp-). 1. Race, competition, in which chances of competitors are equalized by start, difference in weight to be carried (in horse-races), etc.; extra weight or other condition imposed or advantage conferred on competitor; (fig.) hindrance. 2. v.t. Impose ~ on (competitor); (fig., of circumstances) place (person) at disadvantage. Hence ~PER[1] n. [in 17th c. app. f. phr. *hand i'* (= *in*) *cap* describing a kind of sporting lottery]

hăn'dicraft (-ahft), n. Manual skill; manual art or trade or occupation; ~*sman*, man skilled in a ~. [alt. of older (f. OE) *handcraft*, after foll.]

hăn'diwork (-wĕrk), n. Work done, thing made, by the hands or by anyone's personal agency. [OE *handgeweorc* (HAND[1] + collect. form of *weorc* WORK)]

handkerchief (hăng'kerchif), n. Square of linen, silk, etc., carried in pocket (*pocket-~*) for wiping nose etc. or worn about neck (also *neck ~*, *neckerchief*); *throw the ~ to* (person, in certain games, to invite him to pursue), also, express condescending preference for (person). [HAND[1] + KERCHIEF]

hăn'dle[1], n. That part of a thing which is made to hold it by; ~-*bar* of bicycle etc., steering-bar with ~ at each end; ~ *to* one's *name*, title; fact that may be taken advantage of (*gave a ~ to his critics*); *fly off the ~* (colloq.), lose control of oneself. [OE *handle* f. HAND[1] + -LE]

hăn'dle[2], v.t. Touch, feel, with the hands; manipulate; manage (thing, person); treat (person *roughly*, *kindly*, etc.); treat of (subject); deal in (goods). [OE *handlian* (prec.)]

hăn(**d**)'**sel** (-ns-), n., & v.t. (-ll-). 1. Gift at beginning of New Year, or on entering on new circumstances; earnest-money; foretaste. 2. v.t. Give ~ to, inaugurate, be the first to try. [ME, corresp. to OE *handselen* giving into a person's hands, ON *handsal* giving of the hand (esp. in a promise); f. HAND[1] + OE *sellan*; see SELL]

hănd'some (-ns-), a. Of fine form or figure; (of conduct etc.) generous, as *a ~ present*, *~ treatment*; (prov.) ~ *is that ~ does*; (of price, fortune, etc.) considerable. Hence ~LY[2] (-ml-) adv., ~NESS (-mn-) n. [HAND[1], -SOME]

hănd'dĭǀy̆, a. Ready to hand; convenient to handle; clever with the hands; ~*y-dandy*, child's game in which one player guesses which of other player's hands conceals some object; ~*y man* (useful for odd jobs, often of sailors). Hence ~ILY[2] adv., ~INESS n. [-Y[2]]

hăng[1], v.t. & i. (*hŭng*, exc. as below). 1. Suspend, attach loosely, (*from*, *to*, hook or other object above); suspend (meat, game) to dry (*hung beef*, so cured) or become tender or high. 2. Place (pictures) on wall (*hung on the line*, at best height for seeing; HANGING *committee* of Royal Academy etc.). 3. Attach (wall-paper); fit up (bells in belfry). 4. Rest (door on hinges, coach on springs) in free swinging position. 5. (past & p.p. ~ed). Suspend on gibbet as capital punishment; (as imprecation) ~!, ~ *it*, ~ *you*, *I'll be* ~*ed if* ~. 6. Let droop; ~ *the head* (from shame etc.). 7. Remain, be, suspended, lit. & fig., as *sword*, *punishment*, ~s *over his head*, *rogue shall* ~ *for it*; ~s *in the balance*, is undecided; *curtain* ~s *loose, in folds*, etc. 8. Decorate *with* (things suspended). 9. ~ (loiter) *about*; ~ *back*, show reluctance to act or move; ~ (lag) *behind*; ~ *fire*, (of fire-arm) be slow in going off (also fig.); ~ *heavy*, (of time) pass slowly; ~ *off*, ~ *back*; ~ *on*, depend or rely on, attend carefully to, stick closely (*to*), remain in office, stick to duty etc., (colloq., in telephoning) not ring off; ~ *out*, suspend from window etc., (intr.) protrude downwards, (sl.) reside; ~ *together*, be coherent, be associated; ~ *up*, suspend, (fig.) put aside, postpone indefinitely; ~'*dog* n. & a., base & sneaking (fellow), ashamed; ~'*man*, executioner; ~'*nail*, = AGNAIL; ~'*over* n. (sl.), unpleasant after-effects of (esp. alcoholic) dissipation. [(1) OE *hōn* trans. (Goth. *hāhan*); (2) OE *hangian* intr. (OS *hangōn*); (3) ON *hengja* causal; f. Gmc **hang-*, **hanh-*]

hăng², n. Downward droop or bend; the way a thing hangs; *get the ~ of*, get the knack of, understand; (colloq.) *not a ~*, not at all. [f. prec.]

hăng'ar (*or* -ngg-), n. Shed for housing aircraft etc. [F]

|| **hăng'er¹**, n. Wood on side of steep hill. [OE *hangra* f. *hangian* HANG¹]

hăng'er², n. In vbl senses, esp.: *bell*, *paper*, ~~; loop etc. by which thing is hung; chain, rod, to which pot is hung in fireplace by pot-hook; stroke with double curve in writing (()), cf. POT-*hook*; short sword, orig. hung from belt; ~-*on*, follower, dependent. [-ER¹]

hăng'ing, n. In vbl senses, esp.: drapery with which walls etc. are hung (usu. pl.); || ~ *committee* (deciding on ~ of pictures in exhibition); *a ~ matter* (resulting in capital punishment). [-ING¹]

hănk, n. Circular loop or coil, esp. as definite length of cotton yarn (840 yds), worsted (560 yds), etc.; (Naut.) ring of rope, iron, etc., for securing staysails to stays. [f. ON *hönk* hank, cf. Swed. *hank* string, Da. *hank* handle]

hănk'er, v.i. Crave, long, *after*. Hence ~ING¹ n. [rel. to syn. obs. *hank* (-ER⁵); cf. Du. *hunkeren*, *hank*-]

hănk'y, n. (colloq.). Handkerchief. [abbr.; see -Y³]

hănk'y-pănk'y, n. Jugglery; underhand dealing. [arbitrary, perh. on *hocus-pocus*]

Hăn'over, n. *House of ~*, British sovereigns from George I. Hence **Hănōvēr'IAN** a. & n. [place]

Hăns (-z), n. (Nickname for) German or Dutchman. [G & Du. f. L *Johannes* John]

Hăn'sard, n. Official report of proceedings in British Parliament. Hence || ~IZE v.t., confront (M.P.) with his former utterances recorded in ~. [Luke ~ (d. 1828), original compiler]

Hănse, n. (hist.). Guild of merchants; political and commercial league of Germanic towns, whence **Hănsèat'IC** a.; entrance-fee of guild. [f. MLG (=MHG) *Hanse*, =OHG, Goth. *hansa* (= OE *hōs*) company; in med. L (AL) *hansa*]

hăn'som (**căb**), n. Two-wheeled cabriolet for two inside, with driver mounted behind and reins going over roof. [*Hansom*, patentee, 1834]

hăp¹, n. (arch.). Chance, luck, lot; (w. pl.) chance occurrence. [ME, f. ON *happ*]

hăp², v.t. (arch.). (-pp-). Come about by chance; happen (*to* do). [ME *happe(n)*, f. prec.]

hăp'ăx lĕgŏm'ĕnon, n. (pl. -ena). Word of which only one use is recorded. [Gk, = once said]

hăphăz'ard (-p-h-), n., a., & adv. Mere chance, esp. *at*, *by*, ~; casual(ly). [HAP¹ +HAZARD]

hăp'lĕss, a. Unlucky. Hence ~LY² adv. [-LESS]

hăplŏg'raphў, n. The mistake of writing once what should be written twice (e.g. *philogy* for *philology*), cf. DITTOGRAPHY. [f. Gk *haplous* single + -GRAPHY]

hăp'lў, adv. (arch.). By chance; perhaps. [HAP¹ + -LY²]

|| **ha'p'orth**. See HALFPENNY.

hăpp'en, v.i. Come to pass (by chance or otherwise), whence ~ING¹ n. (usu. pl.); chance, have the fortune, *to* (do); come *upon* (person, thing) by chance; (euphem., of death) *if anything should ~ to me*, if I die. [ME (HAP¹ + -EN⁶)]

hăpp'ў, a. (Of person or circumstance) lucky, fortunate; contented with one's lot; *I shall be ~* (pleased) *to assist*; ~ FAMILY; apt, felicitous (of language or conduct); (sl.) dazed (*bomb*, *shell*, ~~); ~-*go-lucky*, haphazard (adj.). Hence **hăpp'ILY²** adv., **hăpp'INESS** n. [f. HAP¹ + -Y²]

hăra-kĭ'rĭ, n. Suicide by disembowelment, as practised by higher classes in Japan when in disgrace or sentenced to death. [Jap. (vulg.), f. *hara* belly + *kiri* cut]

harăngue' (-ng), n., & v.i. & t. Speech to an assembly; loud or vehement address; (v.i.) make ~; (v.t.) make ~ to. [ME *arang* f. OF *arenge* f. Pr. *arenga*, It. *aringa* f. Goth. **harirings* 'army-ring' as legal court]

hă'ras (*or* ahrah'), n. Breeding station for horses. [ME, f. OF *haras* of unkn. orig.]

hă'rass, v.t. Vex by repeated attacks; trouble, worry. Hence ~MENT n. [f. F *harasser*, f. OF *harer* set a dog on]

hărb'inger (-j-), n., & v.t. One who announces another's approach, forerunner; (formerly) one sent to purvey lodgings for army, royal train, etc.; (v.t.) announce approach of. [ME, f. OF *herbergere* f. *herberge* lodging f. WG **heriberga* (*heri* army + *bergan* protect); *-n-* as in messenger]

hărb'our (-ber), n., & v.t. & i. **1.** Place of shelter for ships; shelter; ~-*master*, officer in charge of ~. **2.** v.t. Give shelter to (esp. vermin, criminal, evil thoughts); (v.i.) come to anchor in ~. Hence ~LESS (-berl-) a. [(vb f. n.) ME *hereberge* f. OE **hereberg* f. WG **heriberga* (prec.)]

hărb'ourage (-ber-), n. (Place of) shelter. [-AGE]

hărd, a., n., & adv. **1.** Firm, unyielding to touch, solid; ~ *cash*, specie, as opp. to paper currency; ~ *facts* (not disputable like opinions etc.); difficult (*to* do; ~ *nut to crack*; ~ problem, person ~ to make out or influence); ~ *of hearing*, somewhat deaf; difficult to understand or explain, as ~ *words, question*; (of person or conduct) unfeeling, harsh (~ *as nails*); involving undue or unfair suffering (~ *cases make bad law*); stingy; difficult to bear, as ~ *life, times,* LINE²s; ~ (severe) *winter*; *a* ~ *bargain* (without concession); harsh, unpleasant,.to eye or ear; *(of liquor) spirituous; ~ *water* (unfit for washing owing to its mineral salts); (of markets and prices) high, unyielding; (Phonetics) *k, t, and p, are* ~ *as opposed to g, d, & b, c is* ~ *in cat, g is* ~ *in go*; strenuous, as ~ *fight,* ~ *labour* (imposed on some criminals, abolished in U.K. in 1948), ~ *row to hoe* (difficult task), ~ *worker*; ~ *swearing,* (euphem. for) unabashed perjury. 2. n. || Sloping roadway across foreshore; (sl.) = ~ labour (*got 2 years* ~). 3. adv. Strenuously, severely, as *try* ~, *raining* ~, *freezing* ~, ~ *pressed* (closely pursued); with difficulty, as ~-*earned,* ~-*baked,* -*boiled* (so as to be ~); ~-*boiled,* (also, orig. U.S. colloq.) callous, ~-*headed,* tough; *be* ~ *put to it,* be in difficulties; *die* ~ (only after ~ struggle), & cf. DIE²-~; *it will go* ~ *with him* (prove to his disadvantage); *it shall go* ~ *but* (short of overpowering difficulties) *I will find them*; ~ *by,* close by: ~ (*up*)*on,* too severe in criticism or treatment (*don't be too* ~ *on him*), (of circumstances) bearing with undue severity on; ~ *upon,* close to; *run* (person) ~, pursue him closely. 4. ~ & *fast,* (of rules) strict; || ~'*bake,* almond toffee; ~'*bitten,* tough in fight etc.; ~'*board,* sheet (usu. 8 ft by 4 ft) of compressed and processed wood-pulp fibre used for panels of doors, cupboards, partitions, etc.; || ~ *core,* heavy material forming foundation of road; ~ *court,* lawn tennis court made of asphalt, concrete, etc. (opp. *grass court*); ~ *currency,* one not likely to depreciate suddenly or fluctuate greatly in value; ~-*favoured,* -*featured,* of harsh or ugly features; ~-*fisted,* stingy; ~-*headed,* practical, not sentimental; ~-*hearted,* unfeeling, so ~-*heartedly,* -*ness* ; ~ *hit,* severely troubled; ~-*laid,* (of string, fabric, etc.) tightly twisted or woven; || ~-*lying money,* extra pay granted to officers & men while serving in torpedo boats & other small craft; ~-*mouthed,* (of horse) not easily controlled by bit (also fig.); ~ *set,* set so as to be ~, (of egg) that has been subjected to incubation, (of person) hungry; ~'*shell,* having a ~ shell, (fig.) rigid, uncompromising, esp. *Hardshell Baptists*; ~ *tack,* ship-biscuit; ~ *up,* in want (esp. of money), at a loss *for,* (Naut., adv., of tiller) as far as possible to windward; ~'*ware,* ironmongery; ~' *wareman,* dealer in this; ~'*wood,* wood of deciduous trees as opposed to pines and firs. Hence ~'NESS n. [OE *h*(*e*)*ard,* OS *hard,* OHG *hart,* ON *harthr,* Goth. *hardus* cogn. w. Gk *kratus* strong]

hård'en, v.t. & i. Make or become hard, callous (esp. in p.p.), or robust. [-EN⁶]

hård'ihŏŏd, n. Boldness, audacity. [f. HARDY a. +-HOOD]

hård'lў, adv. In a hard manner; with difficulty; harshly; scarcely. [-LY²]

hård'ship, n. Hardness of fate or circumstance; severe suffering or privation. [-SHIP]

hård'|ў¹, a. Bold, audacious, whence ~iLY² adv.; robust, capable of endurance; (Hort., of plants) able to grow in the open air all the year; *half* ~*y,* requiring shelter in winter only; ~*y annual,* one that may be sown, or sows itself, in the open, (fig., joc.) subject that comes up yearly. Hence ~iNESS n. [ME, f. OF *hardi* p.p. of *hardir* f. WG **hardjan* make HARD]

hård'ў², n. Blacksmith's bar of hard iron for cutting metal on etc. [prob. f. prec. or HARD]

håre, n. || Kinds of mammal of medium size with tawny fur, long ears, short tail, and hind legs longer than fore ones, inhabiting fields, hills, etc.; BELGIAN ~; *mad as a March* ~ (~ in breeding season); (prov.) *first catch your* ~ (*then cook him*); *hold* (or *run*) *with the* ~ *& run* (or *hunt*) *with the hounds,* keep in with both sides; ~ *& hounds,* paper-chase; ~'*bell* (-ărb-), *hairbell,* round-leaved bell-flower, also (see BLUE¹-*bell*) wild hyacinth; ~-*brained,* rash, wild; ~'*lip* (-ărl-), fissure of upper lip; ~'*s-foot,* species of clover with soft hair about flowers, (also) corkwood tree, (also) ~'s foot used for applying rouge etc. to face. [OE *hara,* OHG *haso,* ON *heri*]

hår'em, -am, hareem', -im (-ēm), n. Women's part of Mohammedan dwelling--house; its occupants; (usu. -*am*) Mohammedan sacred place. [f. Arab. *haram,* -*im,* prohibited f. *harama* prohibit]

hå'ricot (-kō), n. Ragout(usu. of mutton); ~ (*bean*), French bean. [F]

hårk, v.i. & t. Listen (usu. *to,* rarely trans.; also abs. in imper.); (as call to hounds) go *forward, away, off,* etc.; ~ *back,* (of hounds) retrace course to find scent, (fig.) revert (*to* subject), (trans.) recall (hounds). [ME *herkien,* OE *heorcian,* = MLG, MDu. *horken,* OHG *hôrechen*; cf. HEARKEN]

hårl¹, v.t. & i. (Sc.). Drag along the ground; drag oneself along; rough-cast with lime and small gravel. [ME, of unkn. orig.]

hårl(e)², n. Barb, fibre, of feather. [f. MLG *herle. harle,* fibre of flax or hemp]

Hårlei'an (-lē-), a. Of (the library of) Robert Harley, Earl of Oxford, d. 1724. [-EAN]

hårl'equin, n. 1. Character in Italian comedy; mute character in English pantomime, invisible to clown & pantaloon, usu. wearing particoloured tights; buffoon. 2. (Also ~ *duck*) northern duck with variegated plumage. [F, f. It. *arlecchino*]

harléquinäde', n. Part of pantomime in which harlequin plays chief part. [f. F *arlequinade* (as prec., see -ADE)]

Härl'ey Street, n. London street associated with fashionable physicians.

harl'ot, n., & v.i. Prostitute; (v.i.) play the ~. Hence ~RY(4) n. [ME, f. OF *har-*, *herlot* lad, knave, vagabond, of unkn. orig.]

harm, n., & v.t. Damage, hurt, (*out of* ~'*s way*, in safety). Hence ~'FUL, ~'LESS (doing no ~), aa., ~'fulLY², ~'lessLY², advv., ~'fulNESS, ~'lessNESS, nn. [OE *hearm*, OS, OHG *harm*, ON *harmr* f. Gmc *harmaz*]

harmätt'an, n. Parching land-wind on coast of Upper Guinea in Dec., Jan., & Feb. [f. W.-Afr. *haramata*]

harmön'ic, a. & n. 1. Harmonious, concordant; relating to harmony; ~ *tones* (produced by vibration of aliquot parts of strings etc.); ~ *quantities* (whose reciprocals are in arithmetical progression, as ⅓, ⅓, ⅓, or as 12, 15, 20), ~ *progression*, series of these. 2. n. ~ tone. Hence harmön'icALLY adv. [f. L f. Gk *harmonikos* (as HARMONY, see -IC)]

harmön'ica, n. Name of several musical instruments; *mouth organ. [L fem. adj. as prec.]

harmön'ious, a. Concordant, forming a consistent or agreeable whole; free from dissent; sweet-sounding; singing, playing, tunefully. Hence ~LY² adv. [f. F *harmonieux* (as HARMONY)]

harm'on|ist, n. Person skilled in harmony; musician; collator of parallel narratives, whence ~is'tic a.; harmonizer. [f. HARMONIZE, see -IST]

harmön'ium, n. Keyboard instrument in which notes are produced by air blown through reeds. [F, as HARMONY]

harm'oniz|e, -is|e (-īz), v.t. & i. Bring into, be in, harmony (*with*); make, be, agreeable in artistic effect; add notes to (melody) to form chords. Hence ~A'TION n. [f. F *harmoniser* (as HARMONY, see -IZE)]

harmonöm'eter, n. Instrument measuring harmonic relations of notes. [f. F *harmonomètre* (as foll., see -METER)]

harm'onÿ, n. Agreement; *pre-established* ~ (between body & soul before their creation); agreeable effect of apt arrangement of parts; combination of simultaneous notes to form chords (cf. MELODY); sweet or melodious sound; collation of parallel narratives etc., esp. of the four Gospels. [ME, f. OF *harmonie* f. L f. Gk *harmonia* (*harmo-* join]

harn'ess, n., & v.t. 1. Gear of draught horse or other animal; (fig.) working equipment; *in* ~, in the routine of daily work; apparatus in loom for shifting warp-threads; (hist.) defensive armour; ~-*cask* (with rimmed cover, for keeping salt meat on board ship). 2. v.t. Put~ on

(horse etc.); (fig.) utilize (river, waterfall, natural forces) for motive power. [ME; (vb f. OF *harneschier*) f. OF *harneis*, of obsc. orig.]

harp¹, n. Stringed musical instrument, roughly triangular, played with the fingers. [OE *hearpe*, OS, ON *harpa*, OHG *harfa*, f. Gmc *harpôn*]

harp², v.i. Play on harp, whence ~'ER¹, ~'IST, nn.; dwell tediously *on* (subject). [OE *hearpian* (as prec.)]

harpoon', n., & v.t. 1. Spear-like missile with rope attached, for catching whales etc.; ~-*gun* (for firing this). 2. v.t. Strike, spear, with ~. [(vb f. n.) f. F *harpon* (*harpe* clamp f. L f. Gk *harpē* sickle)]

harp'sichord (-k-), n. Keyboard instrument with strings plucked by quill or leather points, used 16th–18th c. [f. obs. F *harpechorde* (LL *harpa* harp + *chorda* string)]

harp'ÿ, n. (Gk & L Myth.) rapacious monster with woman's face & body & bird's wings & claws; rapacious person; ~-*eagle*, S.-Amer. bird of prey. [f. L f. Gk *harpuiai* pl. (cf. *harpazō* snatch)]

har'quëbus, är-, n. (hist.). Early type of portable gun, supported on tripod by hook or on forked rest. So ~IER' n. [f. F (*h*)*arquebuse*, ult. f. MLG *hakebusse* or MHG *hakenbühse* (*haken* hook + *bühse* gun)]

hä'rridan, n. Haggard old woman, vixen. [17th c. cant; perh. f. F *haridelle* old jade]

hä'rrier¹, n. One who harries. [-ER¹]

hä'rrier², n. Hound used for hunting hare; (pl.) pack of these with huntsmen (also as name of hare-&-hounds club); kinds of raptorial bird. [f. HARE + -IER, prob. assoc. w. prec.]

Hä'rris tweed, n. Kind made in Harris in the Hebrides.

Harröv'ian, a. & n. (Member) of Harrow school; (inhabitant) of Harrow. [-IAN]

hä'rrow¹ (-ō), n. Heavy frame with iron teeth for breaking clods on ploughed land, covering seed, etc.; *under the* ~, in distress. [ME *harwe*, obsc. rel. to MLG, MDu. *harke* rake, ON *hervi* harrow]

hä'rrow² (-ō), v.t. Draw harrow over (land); lacerate, wound, (lit., & fig. the feelings etc.), whence ~ING² (-ōī-) a. [f. prec.]

hä'rrow³ (-ō), v.t. Harry, spoil, (chiefly in phr. ~ *hell*, of Christ). [var. of foll.]

hä'rrÿ, v.t. Ravage, waste, spoil, (land, or abs.); despoil (person); harass, worry. [OE *hergian*, OS, OHG *heriōn*, ON *herja* f. Gmc *harjaz* army]

harsh, a. Rough to the touch, taste, eye, or ear; repugnant to feelings or judgement; cruel, unfeeling. Hence ~'LY² adv., ~'NESS n. [(1) ME *harsk* corresp. in form to OSw., Da. *harsk* rank, rancid; (2) 16th c. *harsh* f. syn. MLG *harsch* (HAIR, -ISH)]

hart, n. Male of (esp. red) deer, esp. after fifth year; ~ *of ten* (branches on horns);

~**'s-tongue**, fern with slender undivided fronds. [OE *heor(o)t*, OS *herut*, OHG *hir(u)z*, ON *hjortr* f. Gmc **herutaz*]

hart'al, n. Closing of Indian shops as political gesture or mark of sorrow. [Hindi]

hart'(é)beest, n. S.-African kind of antelope. [S.-Afr. Du.]

harts'horn (-s-h-), n. Substance got from horns of hart, formerly chief source of ammonia; *(spirit of)* ~, aqueous solution of ammonia; *salt of* ~, smelling-salts.

har'um-scar'um, a. & n. Reckless (person, conduct). [arbitrary]

harv'est, n., & v.t. 1. (Season for) reaping & gathering of grain or other products; corn-crop; season's yield of any natural product; (fig.) product of any action; ~*-bug*, mite troublesome during ~; ~ *festival*, thanksgiving service for ~; ~ *home*, close of ~ing, festival of this; ~ *moon* (full within fortnight of Sep. 22 or 23); ~ *mouse*, small species, nesting in stalks of growing grain. 2. v.t. Reap & gather in (crop, or abs.), lay up, husband. [OE *hærfest*, OS *hervist*, OHG *herbist*, ON *haust* f. Gmc **harbhistaz*]

harv'ester, n. Reaper; reaping-machine (esp. sheaf-binding); harvest-bug; ~-*thresher*, COMBINE. [-ER¹]

has. See HAVE¹.

has'-been (-z-), n. (colloq.). Person who, thing which, has lost a quality or proficiency formerly possessed, a back number. [HAVE¹]

hash¹, v.t. (Also ~ *up*) cut (meat, also fig.) in small pieces. [f. F *hacher* (*hache* HATCHET)]

hash², n. Dish of hashed meat; old matter served up in new form; medley; *make a* ~ *of*, spoil in dealing with; *settle person's* ~, make an end of, do for, him. [HASH¹]

Hash'emite, a. ~ *Kingdom of the Jordan*, country bounded by Syria, Israel, Saudi Arabia, and Iraq.

hash'ish, -eesh, n. Top leaves & tender parts of hemp, dried for smoking or chewing as a drug, in Arabia, Egypt, Turkey, etc. (cf. BHANG). [Arab. *hashish* dry herb]

has'let, hars'-, n. Piece of meat to be roasted, esp. pig's fry. [ME *hastelet* f. OF dim. of *haste* roast meat, spit, f. OLG *harst* roast]

hasn't (-z-). See HAVE¹.

hasp (bah-), n., & v.t. Fastening contrivance, esp. clasp passing over staple & secured by padlock; hank, skein, of yarn; (v.t.) fasten with ~. [OE *hæpse, hæsp;* corresp. to MLG *haspe*, OHG *haspa*, ON *hespa*]

hass'ock, n. Hard cushion for kneeling on esp. in church; tuft of matted grass etc.; ‖(in Kent) soft calcareous sandstone. [OE *hassuc*, of unkn. orig.]

hast. See HAVE¹.

has'tate, a. (chiefly bot.). Spear-shaped. [f. L *hastatus* (*hasta* spear, see -ATE²)]

haste, n., & v.i. 1. Urgency of movement; hurry, precipitancy, as *more* ~, *less speed; make* ~, be quick *(to do, and* do). 2. v.i. Make ~ *(to do*, or abs.). [ME; (vb f. OF *haster*) f. OF *haste* f. WG **haisti-* violence, cogn. w. ON *heifst*, Goth. *haifsts*]

hä'sten (-sn), v.t. & i. Cause (person) to make haste; accelerate (work etc.); make haste; come or go in haste *(to* etc.). [ME; -EN²]

has'tly̆, a. Hurried; speedy; rash, inconsiderate; quick-tempered; ‖~*y pudding* (of flour stirred to thick batter in boiling milk or water). Hence~ILY² adv.,~INESS n. [f. OF *hastif* (as HASTE¹, see -IVE²)]

hăt, n., & v.t. (-tt-). 1. Man's, woman's, outdoor head-covering, usu. with brim (cf. BONNET, CAP); *top, high, chimney-pot,* ~, cylindrical silk ~; *opera* ~ (cylindrical compressible); *cardinal's* or *red* ~, (fig.) office of cardinal; ~ *in hand*, servile(ly); *send round the* ~, solicit contributions; *talk through* one's ~ (sl.), boast or bluff or exaggerate; *as black as my* ~, quite black; ~'*band* (put round ~); ~'*block* (for moulding ~ on); ~ *trick*, (Cricket) taking 3 wickets by successive balls, (transf.) scoring of 3 goals by same player, winning of 3 races, etc.; ‖ *bad* ~ (sl.), immoral or dishonourable person. 2. v.t. Cover, furnish, with ~. Hence ~'FUL, ~'t'ER (3; *as mad as a* ~*ter*), nn., ~'LESS *a.* [OE *hætt*, ON *höttr* f. Gmc **hattuz;* cf. HOOD]

hătch¹, n. Lower half of divided door; aperture in door, wall, floor or deck; (Naut.) ~*way*, trap-door covering this; *under* ~*es*, below deck, (fig.) down out of sight, brought low, dead; floodgate; ~'*way*, opening in ship's deck for lowering cargo. [OE *hæcc*, MLG *heck*, f. WG **hak-;* cf. HACK², HAKE², HECK]

hătch², v.t. & i., & n. 1. Bring forth (young birds etc., or abs.) from egg; incubate (egg); emerge from egg; (of egg) produce young; contrive & develop (plot etc.). 2. n. ~*ing*, brood ~*ed*, (~*es, catches, matches, & dispatches*, newspaper list of births, engagements, marriages, & deaths). [ME *hacche*, rel. to MHG *hecken*, Sw. *häcka*, Da. *hække*, of unkn. orig.]

hătch³, v.t., & n. 1. Engrave (usu. parallel) lines on (surface); (Archit.) ~*ed moulding* (with two crossing sets of parallel lines). 2. n. Engraved line. [(n. f. vb) f. F *hacher* (as HATCHET)]

hătch'erў, n. Place for hatching eggs esp. of fish & poultry. [-ERY]

hătch'ĕt, n. Light short-handled axe; ~ (narrow, sharp) *face*; BURY *the* ~; *throw the helve after the* ~, add new loss to that already incurred. [ME, f. OF *hachette* dim. of *hache* f. WG **hapja* (= OHG *happa, heppa* sickle-shaped knife)]

hătch'ment, n. Large (usu. diamond-shaped) tablet with deceased person's armorial bearings, formerly affixed to house, now only on wall of church. [contr. of ACHIEVEMENT]

K

häte¹, n. (chiefly poet.). Hatred. [ME *hate* (replacing OE *hete*) partly f. vb, partly f. ON *hatr*; see foll.]

häte², v.t. Have strong dislike of; bear malice to. Hence **hāt'ABLE** a. [OE *hatian*, OS *hatōn*, OHG *hazzōn*, ON *hata*, Goth. *hatan* f. Gmc **hatōjan*]

häte'ful (-tf-), a. Exciting hatred. Hence ~**LY²** adv., ~**NESS** n. [-FUL]

häth. Arch. 3rd sing. pres. of HAVE¹.

hāt'red, n. Active dislike; enmity, ill will. [ME (HATE¹ + -red = OE *rǣden* condition)]

hättī'ī, n. Turkish edict made irrevocable by Sultan's mark. [abbr. of Pers. *khaṭṭisherif*, *-humayun*, sacred writing]

haub'erk, n. Coat of mail. [ME, f. OF *hau(s)berc* f. WG **halsberg* (*hals* neck + *bergan* protect)]

∥ **haugh** (haw, *Sc.* hahx), n. Piece of flat alluvial land by river. [ME, prob. f. OE *healh* corner]

haught'ly̆ (-awt-), a. Proud, arrogant; dignified. Hence ~**ILY²** adv., ~**INESS** n. [extension of *haught* a., (earlier *haut*) f. OF *haut* f. L *altus* high, -Y²]

haul, v.t. & i., & n. 1. Pull, drag, forcibly; transport by cart or other conveyance; pull *at, upon*, (rope etc.); (Naut.) turn ship's course; ~ *upon the wind*, bring ship round to sail closer to wind; (of wind) shift. 2. n. Act of ~ing, (fig.) amount gained, acquisition. Hence ~**'AGE(3)** n. [17th c. var. of HALE²]

∥ **haul'ier**, n. One who hauls (esp. tubs in coal-mine to bottom of shaft); jobbing carter. [f. prec., see -YER]

∥ **ha(u)lm** (hawm, hahm), n. Stalk, stem; (collect. *sing.*) stems, stalks, of peas, beans, potatoes, etc., without the pods etc. [OE *h(e)alm*, OS, OHG *halm*, ON *halmr* f. Gmc **halmaz*]

haunch (haw-, hah-), n. Part of body (esp. of sheep, deer) on side of spine between last ribs & hip-bone; leg & loin of deer etc. as food; side of arch between crown & piers. [ME, f. OF *hanche*, f. WG **hanka*; cf. LG, G *hanke* hind leg of a horse]

haunt, v.t. & i., & n. 1. Frequent (place); frequent company of (person); (of thoughts etc.) visit (person) frequently; (p.p.) visited, frequented, by ghosts; stay habitually (*in, about*, place, *with* person). 2. n. Place of frequent resort, usual feeding-place of animals, den frequented by criminals. [ME, f. OF *hanter*, of unkn. orig.]

haut'boy (hōb-), **hō'boy**, **ōb'oe** (-bō), n. Wood-wind double-reed instrument of treble pitch; reed-stop on organ imitating this; tall species of strawberry. [f. F *haulbois* (*haut* high + *bois* wood)]

haute école (ōt'ākŏl), n. The more difficult feats of horsemanship. [F, = high school]

hauteur (ōtœ̄r', & see Ap.), n. Haughtiness of manner. [F]

haut goût (hōgōō'), n. Taint, high flavour. [F, = seasoning, lit. high flavour]

Havän'a, n. Cigar made at Havana or in Cuba. [place]

hăve¹ (*or* hav), v.t. & i. & auxil. (Pres.: *I have*, arch. *thou hast*, *he has*, pr. hăz, baz, arch. *he hath*, *we*, *you*, *they*, *have*; past *had*, pr. hăd, had, arch. 2nd sing. *hădst*; p.p. *had*; abbr. *I've*, *we've*, etc., *I'd*, *we'd* etc., '*s*=has; colloq. neg. *haven't*, *hasn't*, *hadn't*). Hold in possession; experience the existence of (persons etc. in various relations), as *I* ~ *two sons, no uncle, no equals*; possess, contain, as appendage, part, quality, etc., as *June has 30 days, trees* ~ *leaves, it has its advantages*; enjoy, suffer, as *I had that pleasure, a toothache, no fear*; permit (person) to, as *I will not* ~ *you say such things*; know, as *he has no Greek*; be burdened with, as *I had my work to do*; be obliged, as *I had to do my work*; retain, as ~ *this in mind*; entertain, as ~ *no doubt*; show by action etc. that one possesses, as ~ *the impudence to say*; engage in, carry on, as *had some conversation*, ~ *a game*, ~ *a try* (make an attempt); *he will* ~ *it* (maintains) *that*; *as Plato has* (expresses) *it*; obtain, receive, take (food), as *we had news*, ~ *an egg*; *the ayes* ~ *it* (~ the advantage); *let him* ~ *it*, punish or reprimand him; *I had him there* (gained advantage over him); ∥ (sl.) *you were had* (cheated); ~ *her make* (cause her to make) *a copy*; ~ *him* (cause him to be) *shot*; ~ *him up*, cause him to be brought before court of justice; *I had my leg broken* (experienced such breakage); ~ *it your own way* (form of refusal to argue further); *he has had it* (sl.), he is a fatal casualty, he is now a back number, there's no longer any chance of his getting it, his fate is sealed; ~ *at*, make attack upon; ~ *done*, stop; ~ *on*, be wearing (clothes); ~ *it out*, settle dispute (*with* person) by discussion etc., (also) get tooth extracted; **~ nothing on* (person), ~ *no advantage over*, ~ *no incriminating evidence against*; (in past subj., ⇒ *would* ~) *had rather* (would prefer to) *go*, *had better go*, would act more wisely in going; (auxiliary) *I* ~, *had*, *shall* ~, *packed*, my packing is, was, will be, complete, *had I* (if I had) *known* etc. [OE *habban*, OS *hebbian*, OHG *habēn*, ON *hafa*, Goth. *haban* f. Gmc **habhēn* of uncert. orig.]

hăve², n. ~s & ~nots, rich & poor; ∥ (sl.) a swindle, take-in. [f. prec.]

hăv'en, n. Harbour, port; (fig., often ~ *of rest*) refuge. [OE *hæfen* f. ON *höfn* corresp. to MLG *havene*, MDu. *haven*]

haven't (hăvnt). See HAVE¹.

∥ **hăv'er**, v.i., & n. (Sc.). 1. Talk foolishly, babble. 2. n. (usu. pl.). Foolish talk, nonsense. [orig. unkn.]

hăv'ersăck, n. Stout canvas bag for provisions. [f. F *havresac* f. G *habersack* (*haber* oats + SACK²)]

hăv'ildar, n. Sepoy officer corresponding

to sergeant. [f. Pers. *ḥawāldār* (Arab. *ḥawalah* charge + Pers. *dār* holder)]

hăv′ing, n. In vbl senses; also, property, belongings, (often pl.). [-ING¹]

hăv′oc, n., & v.t. (~king, ~ked). Devastation, destruction, as *make ~ of*, *play ~ among*; *cry ~*, give signal to army to seize spoil (now fig.); (v.t.) devastate (often abs.). [f. AF *havok* f. OF *havot* of unkn. orig.]

haw¹, n. (Fruit of) hawthorn; (hist.) hedge, enclosure; ~′*buck*, country bumpkin; ~′*finch*, common grosbeak. [OE *haga*, MLG, MDu. *hage*, OHG *hac*, ON *hagi* f. Gmc *hagon*-, see HEDGE]

haw², n. Third eyelid of horse, dog, etc., cartilage within inner corner of eye. [orig. unkn.]

haw³. See HUM¹.

haw′-haw¹, int. & n. Boisterous laugh. Hence haw′-haw v.i. [imit.]

haw′-haw². = HA-HA.

hawk¹, n., & v.i. & t. 1. Bird of prey used in falconry, with rounded wings shorter than falcon's; *know a ~ from a handsaw* (perh. corrupt of HERNSHAW), have ordinary discernment (see *Haml.* II. ii. 397); rapacious person; ~*-eyed*, keen-sighted; ~*-moth*, fast-flying moth, mostly large and crepuscular; ~*-nosed*, with aquiline nose; ~*'s-bill*, kind of turtle. 2. v.i. Hunt game with ~; (v.i. & t.) ~ (*at*), attack as ~ does, (of swallows etc.) hunt insects. Hence ~′ISH¹, ~′LIKE, aa. [OE *heafoc*, OS *habuc*, OHG *habuh*, ON *haukr* f. Gmc *habhukaz*]

hawk², v.t. Carry (goods) about for sale (often fig.). [back form. f. HAWKER]

hawk³, v.i. & t. Clear the throat noisily; bring (phlegm etc.) *up* from throat. [imit.]

hawk⁴, n. Plasterer's square board with handle. [orig. unkn.]

hawk′er, n. One who hawks goods about. [16th c., prob. f. LG; cf. MLG *hoker*, LG *hōker*, Du. *heuker*; see HUCKSTER]

hawse (-z), n. Part of ship's bows in which ~*-holes* are cut for cables; space between head of anchored vessel & anchors; situation of cables before ship's stem when moored with two anchors out from forward, one on starboard, other on port bow. [15th c. *halse*, prob. f. ON *hals* neck]

haws′er (-s-, -z-), n. (naut.) Large rope, small cable, now often of steel. [ME, f. AF *haucer*, -*eour* f. OF *haucier* hoist f. Rom. *altiare* (*altus* high); cf. LL *altare* exalt]

haw′thorn, n. Thorny shrub, with white, red, or pink blossom & small dark red berry, the HAW¹. [OE *hagathorn* (as HAW¹, see THORN)]

hay¹, n., & v.t. & i. 1. Grass mown & dried for fodder; *Burgundian ~*, lucerne; *look for a needle in a* BOTTLE³ (*or bundle*) *of ~*; *make ~*, turn it over for exposure to sun; *make ~ of*, throw into confusion;

make ~ while the sun shines, seize opportunities. 2. ~′*box* (stuffed with ~, in which heated food is left to continue cooking); ~′*cock*, conical heap of ~; *~ fever*, summer disorder usu. with asthmatic symptoms, caused by pollen or dust; ~*-fork* (for turning over or loading ~); ~′*maker*, one who lifts, tosses, & spreads ~ after mowing, apparatus for shaking & drying ~, (sl.) swinging blow; ~′*rick*, ~′*stack*, regular pile of ~ with pointed or ridged top; *~′seed* (colloq.), a rustic, hick; ~′*wire*, anything tangled (*go ~ wire*, become excited or distracted). 3. v.t. Put (land) under ~, make into ~; (v.i.) make ~. [OE *hēg*, *hieg*, OS *hōi*, OHG *hewi*, ON *hey*, Goth. *hawi* f. Gmc *hauwan* HEW]

hay², hey² (hā), n. (Figure in) country dance. [orig. unkn.]

hay′ward (-ŏrd), n. Officer of parish etc. in charge of fences & enclosures. [ME, f. obs. *hay* hedge (as HAW¹) + WARD]

hăz′ard, n., & v.t. 1. Game at dice, with complicated chances; chance; danger; *at all ~s* (risks); each of winning openings in tennis-court; ‖ (Billiards) *winning ~*, striking object ball into pocket, *losing ~*, pocketing own ball off another; (Golf) obstruction in playing a shot, e.g. bunker, water, road, etc.; ‖ (in Ireland) cab-stand. 2. v.t. Expose to ~, run the ~ of; venture on (action, statement, guess). [vb f. F *hasarder*) ME, f. OF *hasard*, of Arab. orig.]

hăz′ardous, a. Risky; dependent on chance. Hence ~LY² adv., ~NESS n. [-OUS]

hāze¹, n., & v.t. 1. Obscuration of atmosphere near earth, mainly due to heat, smoke, or fine dust; (fig.) mental obscurity or confusion. 2. v.t. Make hazy. [prob. back form. f. earlier HAZY]

hāze², v.t. (naut.). Harass with overwork, *bully*. [cf. OF *haser* harass, worry]

hăz′el, n. Bush whose fruit is the ~*-nut*; (stick of) its wood; reddish-brown or greenish-brown colour (esp. of eyes). Hence ~LY² a. [OE *hæsel*, OHG *hasal*, ON *hasl* f. Gmc *hasalaz*]

hăz′lў, a. Misty; vague; indistinct; slightly drunk. Hence ~ILY² adv., ~INESS n. [17th c., naut., also *hawsey*, *heysey*, of unkn. orig.]

H-bomb (āch′bŏm), n. Hydrogen bomb. [*H* for HYDROGEN]

hē¹, pron. (obj. *him*, poss. *his*, pl. *they*, obj. *them*, poss. *their*), & n. (pl. *hes*). 1. pron. The male person in question. 2. n. Male; (attrib. esp. of animals) *he-goat* etc.; *he-man*, masterful or virile man. [OE, f. Gmc st. (3rd pers. sing.) *hi*-, as in OFris., OS *he*, *hi* (cf. Goth. *hi(ta)* etc.); var. st. *i*-repr. by OHG *ir*, *er*, Goth. *is*]

hē², int. expr. amusement or derision (often repeated, *he he*). [in many langg.]

head¹ (hĕd), n. 1. Anterior part of body of animal, upper part of man's body, containing mouth, sense-organs, and brain;

(as measure) *taller by a ~*, (Horse-racing) *won by a ~*; *cannot make ~ or tail of* (understand). **2.** Seat of intellect or imagination; natural aptitude or talent (*a good ~ for business*). **3.** *~ache*, esp. as result of overnight intoxication (colloq.). **4.** Life, as *it cost him his ~*. **5.** Image of *~*, esp. on one side of coin (opp. to *tail*), as *~s I win, tails you lose*. **6.** Antlers of deer, as *deer of the first ~* (when antlers are first developed). **7.** Person, as *crowned ~s, some hot~* (hasty person); individual, as *twopence a or per ~*, esp. of cattle, as *every ~ of.cattle, twenty ~*; *large ~* (number) *of game*; *good ~* (stock) *of shell*. **8.** Thing like *~* in form or position, e.g. cutting or striking part of tool, knobbed end of nail etc.; (of plants) compact mass of leaves or flowers at top of stem. **9.** Foam on top of liquor; || cream on top of milk. **10.** Top (of mast, staircase, page, etc.). **11.** Matured part of boil etc. **12.** Upper end; end of table occupied by host; end of bed at which river enters it; end of bed at which one's ~ rests; FOUNTAIN-~. **13.** Body of water kept at height for mill etc.; pressure (per unit of area) of confined body of steam etc. **14.** Front (of procession, army, etc.); front part of plough, holding the share; bows of ship, as *by the ~*, with ~ lower in water than stern, (fig.) slightly drunk. **15.** Promontory, as *BeachyH~*. **16.** Underground passage for working coal mine. **17.** Ruler, chief, (often attrib.); master etc. of college; *~ master of school*. **18.** Position of command, as *at the ~ of*. **19.** Main division in discourse; category. **20.** Culmination, crisis, as *come to a ~*. **21.** (naut.). Seamen's latrine in ship's bows. **22.** Phrases: *beat person's ~ off*, outdo him thoroughly; *by (the) ~ and ears*, forcibly (esp. of dragging in a story); *by (the) ~ and shoulders*, = by ~ and ears, (also) considerably (*taller*, & fig. of mental or moral stature); *from ~ to foot*, all over the person; *give (horse) his ~*, let him go freely; *~ first or foremost*, with the ~ foremost (of plunge etc.), (fig.) precipitately; *~ of hair*, the hair on the ~, esp. when copious; *over heels*, topsyturvy; *keep one's ~*, keep calm; *keep one's ~ above water*, (fig.) keep out of debt; *lay (our etc.) ~s together*, consult together; *lose one's ~*, be beheaded, (also) become confused; *make ~*, press forward; *make ~ against*, resist successfully; *off one's ~*, crazy; *old ~ on young shoulders*, wisdom in the young; *on one's ~* (of vengeance falling, guilt resting, on person); (*stand etc.*) *on one's ~*, with feet in air (*could do it on my ~*, sl., find it quite easy); *out of one's ~*, from one's own invention; *over ~ & EARS*; *over one's ~*, above one, esp. fig. of danger impending etc., (also) beyond one's comprehension, *as he talks over our ~s*, (also) *person is promoted over another's ~* (who has prior

claim); *put (thing) into person's~*, suggest it to him; *put (thing) out of one's ~*, cease to think of it, give up the idea of it; *put (thing) out of person's~*, make him forget it (*something put it out of my ~*); *talk person's ~ off*, weary him with talk; (prov.) *two ~s (minds) are better than one*. **23.** Comb.: *~'ache*, continuous pain in ~, (colloq.) troublesome problem; *~'achy* (-kI), suffering from, producing, this; *~ & front*, essence (of offence etc.; but cf. *Oth.* I. iii. 80), (pop.) leader, ringleader; *~'band*, band worn round ~; *~'borough* (hist.), petty constable; *~-dress*, covering (esp. woman's ornamental attire) for the ~; *~'fast*, rope at ~ of vessel to make her fast to wharf etc.; *~'gear*, hat, cap, ~-dress; *~-hunter*, savage who collects ~s of his enemies as trophies; *~'land*, promontory, (also) strip left unploughed at end of field; *~'light*, powerful light carried on front of locomotive, car, or aeroplane, or at mast-head of ship; *~'line*, line at top of page containing title etc., title or sub-title in newspaper, (pl., also) || summary at beginning of BBC news bulletin; *~'man*, chief man, chief of tribe etc.; || *~ master, mistress*, principal master, mistress, of school; *~-money* (paid for or by each person); *~'on* (adj.), involving the meeting ~ to ~ of two vehicles (*a ~-on collision*), or of the ~ of a vehicle with stationary object; *~-on'* (adv.), with the ~ pointed directly towards some object; *~'phone*, (in wireless and other telephony) telephone receiver fitting over ~; *~'piece*, helmet, (also) intellect, man of intellect, (also) ornamental engraving at ~ of chapter etc. in book, cf. TAIL[1]-*piece*; *~-quarters*, (Mil.) quarters of officer commanding army, corps, division, etc., (gen.) centre of operations; *~'spring*, main source of stream (also fig.); *~'stall*, part of bridle or halter that fits round ~; *~'stock*, bearings of revolving parts in machine; *~'stone*, gravestone; *~ stone*, chief stone in foundation (also fig.); *~-voice*, one of higher registers of voice in singing or speaking; *~'way*, progress, (of ship) rate of progress, (Archit.) height of arch etc.; *~ wind* (meeting one directly in front); *~-word*, word forming a heading; *~-work*, mental work. Hence (-)*~'ED*, *~'LESS*, aa., (hĕd-). [OE *hĕafod*, OS *hōbid*, OHG *houbit*, ON *haufuth*, Goth. *haubith* f. Gmc *haubhudh-*]

head[2] (hĕd), v.t. & i. Furnish with head; (also *~ down*) lop off head of (plant, tree); be, form, the head of; place name etc., (of name etc.) be placed, at the head of (chapter, list, etc.); come to a head, develop; be, put oneself, at the head of (a company etc.); lead; excel; oppose; go round the head of (lake etc.); (Footb.) strike (ball) with head; *~ back, off*, get ahead of so as to turn back, aside; (intr.) front (in named direction); (of ship) make for (place, point). [f. prec.]

-head, suf. = -HOOD, f. ME -*hēd(e)* repr. OE -*'hǣdu)*, a phonetic var. of -*hōd*, see -HOOD. Orig. an independent noun, it became a suf. in early ME & survives in *godhead, maidenhead* (distinct in meaning f. *godhood, maidenhood*); now repl. by -HOOD.

head'er (hĕd-), n. One who puts heads on casks etc.; brick, stone, laid at right angle to face of wall (cf. STRETCHER); plunge head first. [-ER¹]

head'ing (hĕd-), n. In vbl senses; also or esp.: (Footb.) striking ball with head; title etc. at head of page etc.; horizontal passage in preparation for tunnel. [-ING¹]

head'lŏng (hĕd-), adv. & a. Head foremost (in falling etc.);` precipitate(ly); impetuous(ly). [ME *headling* (HEAD¹ + -LING²), assim. to -LONG]

head'most (hĕd-), a. Foremost.

heads'man (hĕd-), n. One who beheads; man in command of whaling boat. [HEAD¹ + -ES + MAN]

head'strŏng (hĕd-), a. Violently self--willed. Hence ～NESS n. [= strong in head]

head'|y (hĕd-), a. (Of person, thing, action) impetuous, violent; (of liquor etc.) apt to intoxicate. Hence ～ĭLY² adv., ～ĭNESS n. [-Y²]

heal, v.t. & i. Restore (person, wound) to health (lit. & fig.); cure (person of disease); (of wound) become sound or whole; ～*-all*, universal remedy (pop. name of various plants). Hence ～'ER n. (*time is a great ～er*). [OE *hǣlan*, OS *hēlian*, OHG *heilen*, ON *heila*, Goth. *hailjan* f. Gmc **hailaz* WHOLE]

health (hĕl-), n. Soundness of body (also fig.); condition of body, as *good, bad,* ～; ～*-officer*, officer of ～, (charged with administering ～ laws etc.); toast drunk in person's honour; BILL⁴ of ～. [OE *hǣlth*, OHG *heilida* f. WG **hailitha* (WHOLE, -TH¹)]

health'ful (hĕl-), a. Health-giving; conducive to moral or spiritual welfare. Hence ～LY² adv., ～NESS n. [-FUL]

health'|y (hĕl-), a. Having good health (lit. & fig.); conducive to good health. Hence ～ĭLY² adv., ～ĭNESS n. [HEALTH + -Y²]

heap¹, n. Group of things lying one on another; (colloq.) large number, as *a ～ of people, ～s of times*, (adv.) *he is ～s better*; (colloq.) *struck all of a ～*, mentally prostrated. [OE *hēap*, OS *hōp*, OHG *houf, hūfo*, f. Gmc **haupaz, *hūpon-*]

heap², v.t. Pile (things *up, together,* etc.) in a heap; load (cart, person, etc. *with* goods, benefits, etc.); accumulate (insults etc. *upon*). [OE *hēapian*, as prec.]

hear, v.t. & i. (*heard* pr. hĕrd). Perceive (sound etc. or intr.) with the ear, as *I ～d a groan, I ～ him groaning, I ～d him groan* (but *he was ～d to groan*); listen, give audience, to, as ～ *him out* (to the end), ～ *him, his lesson, ～ a sermon*; listen judicially to (case, plaintiff, etc.); grant (prayer); *he will not ～* (entertain the notion) *of it*; *you will ～ of this* (be reprimanded for it); be informed (*that, of, about*); ～ *from*, receive letter or message from; ～ *tell of* (arch.), be told about; ‖ (as form of cheering, often iron.) ～ *!* ～ *!*. Hence ～'ABLE a., ～'ER¹ n. [OE *hieran*, OS *hōrian*, OHG *hōrren*, ON *heyra*, Goth. *hausjan* f. Gmc **hauzjan*]

hear'ing, n. In vbl senses, esp.: perception by ear, as *hard of ～*, deaf; *within, out of,* ～, near enough, too far off, to be heard; *give him a fair ～*, listen impartially to him; ～ *aid*, small sound amplifier worn by deaf people. [-ING¹]

heark'en (här-), här-, v.i. Listen `(*to*). [OE *he(o)rcnian* (as HARK, -EN⁵)]

hear'say, n. What one hears (but does not know to be true), gossip, (often attrib., as ～ *evidence*).

hearse (hĕrs), n. Vehicle for carrying coffin at funeral; (formerly) framework supporting pall at funeral, often adapted for carrying tapers. [ME, f. OF *herse*, f. L *hirpicem* (nom. *-ex*) rake, harrow]

heart (härt), n. **1.** Hollow organ keeping up circulation of blood by contracting & dilating; *right, left,* ～ (side of ～); *smoker's ～* (～ disorder due to smoking). **2.** Breast; mind; soul (～ *to ～*, with candour; so～*-to-*～ *talks*; *after* one's (*own*) ～ (desire). **3.** Seat of the emotions, esp. of love, as *give, lose,* one's ～ *to, win the ～ of,* (person); *union of ～s* (depending on affection, not constraint). **4.** Sensibility, as *he has no* ～; courage, as *pluck up* or *take, lose,* ～. **5.** (As term of endearment to person) *dear, sweet,* ～; (Naut.) *my ～s* (brave fellows). **6.** Central part, esp. of tree, as (fig.) ～ *of oak,* courageous man; vital part, essence, (*the ～ of the matter*). **7.** (Of land) fertility, as *out of ～*, in poor condition. **8.** ～*-shaped* thing; (Cards, pl.) suit marked with ～s, (sing.) one of these. **9.** *At ～*, in one's inmost feelings; *by ～*, in, from, memory, as *have, learn, say, by ～; from* one's ～, sincerely; *in* one's ～, secretly, in one's essential feelings; *in* ～, in good spirits; *near(est)* one's ～, *dear(est)* to one; *out of ～*, in low spirits; *with all* one's ～, sincerely, with the utmost goodwill; *find* in one's ～, (esp. w. neg.) prevail on oneself (*to do*); *have* thing *at* ～, be deeply interested in it; *lay* thing to ～, think it over seriously; *searchings of* ～, misgivings; *take* thing *to* ～, be much affected by it; *break* person's ～, overwhelm him with sorrow; *cry* one's ～ *out*, cry violently; *eat* one's ～ *out*, pine away from vexation etc.; *have a* ～ (sl.), be merciful; *have the* ～, (esp. w. neg.) be hard-hearted enough (*to do*); ～ *& hand*, enthusiastically; *in* one's ～*-of-s* (inmost feelings); ～ *& soul*, with all one's energy; *have* one's ～ *in* one's mouth, be violently alarmed or startled; *his ～ is in the right place*, he means well; *take ～ of grace,* pluck up courage; *wear* one's ~ *upon* one's *sleeve*, lack proper reserve; *it does my* ~ *good*, it rejoices me. 10. ~'*ache*, mental anguish; ~'*beat*, pulsation of ~, (fig.) emotion; ~('*s*)-*blood*, life-blood, life; ~-*break*, overwhelming distress; ~-*breaking*, -*broken*, causing, crushed by, this; ~'*burn*, burning sensation in lower part of chest; ~-*burning*, jealousy, grudge; ~-*disease* (of ~); ~'*felt*, sincere (*emotion* etc.); ~-*rending*, distressing; ~'*s*-*ease*, pansy; ~'*sick*, despondent; ~'*sore*, grieved at ~; ~-*strings*, (fig.) ~, deepest affections; ~-*whole*, undismayed, with the ~ unengaged, not in love. Hence ~~'ED² (här-) a. [OE *heorte*, OS *herta*, OHG *herza*, ON *hjarta*, Goth. *hairtō* cogn. w. L *cor* -*dis*, Gk *kardia*]

heart'en (här-), v.t. & i. Inspirit, cheer (often *up*, also *on*); (intr.) cheer *up*. [f. arch. vb *heart* (OE *hiertan*, as prec.) + -EN¹]

hearth (här-), n. Floor of fireplace; ~-*rug* (laid before fireplace); ~'*stone*, flat stone forming ~, (also) stone etc. for whitening ~s. [OE *heorth*, OS *herth*, OHG *hert* f. WG *herth*-].

heart'ily (här-), adv. With goodwill, courage, or appetite; very, as ~ *sick of it*. [HEARTY, -LY²]

heart'less (här-), a. Unfeeling, pitiless, cruel. Hence ~LY² adv., ~NESS n. [-LESS]

heart'|y (här-), a. & n. 1. Cordial, genial; (of feelings) sincere; (of meals) abundant. 2. n. (As address to sailors) *my* ~*ies*; ‖ (in English university use) outdoor man, athlete (opp. AESTHETE). Hence ~iNESS n. [-Y²]

heat¹, n. 1. Hotness; sensation, perception, of this; *red, white,* etc., ~, at which metals etc. are red, white, etc. 2. (phys.). Kinetic & potential energy of the invisible molecules of bodies, capable of transmission by conduction or radiation (formerly held an elastic material fluid); *latent* ~, ~ required to convert a solid into liquid or vapour, or a liquid into vapour; *specific* ~, ~ required to raise temperature of a given substance to given extent (usu. one degree), usu. calculated relatively to water. 3. Hot weather. 4. Inflamed state of body. 5. Pungency of flavour. 6. *Prickly* ~, skin disease common in hot climates. 7. Single effort, esp. *at a* ~; (*trial*) ~s, races, contests, the winners of which compete in *final* (~). 8. Warmth of feeling, anger; violent stage (of debate etc.). 9. Sexual excitement of animals during breeding season (*on, in, at,* ~, of females). 10. ~-*spot*, freckle, (also) point of the skin at which ~ can be felt; ~-*stroke*, prostration by excessive ~; ~-*wave*, wave of radiant ~, (also) access of great ~ in atmosphere regarded as passing from place to place. [OE *hætu*, OFris. *hête*, cogn. w. OS *hittia*, OHG *hizza*, Goth. *heitō*; f. Gmc *hait*-, *hit*-, *hit*- (see HOT)]

heat², v.t. & i. Make hot; inflame (blood etc.); inflame with passion, whence ~'ĕdLY² adv.; (intr.) become hot (lit. & fig.). Hence ~'ER¹(2) n. [OE *hǣtan*, OHG *heizan*, ON *heila* f. Gmc *haitjan* f. *haitaz* HOT]

heath, n. ‖ Bare flat waste tract of land, esp. if covered with shrubs; name of such shrubs, esp. of genus *Erica*; ~-*bell*, flower of ~ & other plants; ~-*berry*, bilberry, crowberry, & other berries; ~-*cock*, blackcock. Hence ~'Y² a. [OE *hæth*, cogn. w. OHG *heida*, ON *heithr*, Goth. *haithi* f. Gmc *haith*-]

heath'en (-dh-), a. & n. (One who is) neither Christian, Jewish, nor Mohammedan; (n. pl. collect.) *the* ~; unenlightened person; *the* ~ CHINEE. Hence ~DOM, ~ISM(2), ~ISHNESS, ~RY, nn., ~ISH¹ a., ~ISHLY² adv., ~IZE(3) v.t. & i., (-dh-). [OE *hǣthen*, OS *hêthin*, OHG *heidan*, ON *heithinn*, Goth. *haithnō* gentile, f. Gmc *haith*- HEATH, rendering LL *paganus* PAGAN]

hea'ther (hědh-), n. Various species of genus *Calluna vulgaris* (called in the North Ling); ‖ *take to the* ~ (Sc.), become an outlaw; ~-*bell*, (flower of) species of *Erica*; ~ *mixture*, (fabric) of mixed hues supposed to resemble ~. Hence ~Y² a. [14th c. Sc. & north. *hathir, haddir,* of unkn. orig.; since 18th c. assim. to *heath*]

heave¹, v.t. & i. (past & p.p. ~d or, esp. naut., *hôve*). Lift (heavy thing); (of vein or stratum) displace (another); utter (groan, sigh) with effort; (Naut. & colloq.) throw; (Naut.) haul up, haul, by rope; rise, swell up; rise with alternate falls, as waves; pant; retch; pull (*at* rope etc.); ~ *down*, turn (ship) over on one side for cleaning etc.; ~ *to*, bring (vessel, or abs.) to standstill with head to wind; ~ *in sight*, become visible; ~ *ho* (cry of sailors in heaving anchor up). [OE *hebban*, OS -*ian*, OHG *heffen*, ON *hefja*, Goth. *hafjan* f. Gmc *hafjan* cogn. w. L *capere*]

heave², n. Heaving; ~ *of the sea*, force exerted by swell of sea on ship's course; a recognized trip or throw in wrestling (*Cornwall* ~); horizontal displacement of vein or stratum; (pl.) disease of hórses, broken wind. [f. prec.]

hea'ven (hě-), n. Sky, firmament, (in prose now usu. pl.); region of the atmosphere in which clouds float, winds blow, & birds fly; (formerly) each of the heavenly SPHERES; habitation of God & his angels, usually placed beyond sky (cf. HELL); *seventh* ~, ~ *of* ~s, highest of seven ~s recognized by Jews, abode of God; *in the seventh* ~, in a state of extreme delight or exaltation; God, Providence, as *it is H*~'*s will*; (in asseverations & exclamations) *by* ~ !, *good* ~s !; place, state, of supreme bliss; ~-*born*, of divine origin; ~-*sent*. Hence ~WARD a., ~WARD(s) adv. [OE *heofon*, OS *heban*, MLG *heven*, of unkn. orig.]

hea′venlȳ (hĕ-), a. Of heaven, divine, (*the H~ City*, Paradise); of the sky, as ~ *bodies*; *the H~ Twins*, = GEMINI; ~ HOST[1]; of superhuman excellence; (colloq.) *what* ~ (excellent) *figs!*; ~*-minded*, holy, devout. Hence **hea′venliɴess** (hĕ-) n. [ME, f. OF *heofonlic* (as prec., see -LY[1])]

Hea′viside (hĕ-) lay′er, n. Layer of the atmosphere that reflects wireless waves back & causes them to follow the contour of the earth. [Oliver *Heaviside*, English physicist (d. 1925)]

hea′vȳ (hĕ-), a., n., & adv. **1.** Of great weight; of great specific gravity; weighty because abundant, as *a ~ crop*; laden *with*; (of ordnance of the larger kind) ~ *guns*, *metal*, *artillery*; (fig.) ~ *metal*, formidable opponent(s); (Mil.) carrying ~ arms. **2.** Striking, falling, with force, as ~ *storm*, *sea*. **3.** (Of ground) clinging, difficult to travel over. **4.** (Of bread etc.) dense from not having risen; (of food) hard to digest. **5.** (Of horse) ~ *in* or *on hand*, bearing or hanging on bit, (fig.) dull, hard to entertain. **6.** (Of sky) overcast, gloomy. **7.** Clumsy in appearance or effect; (of persons) intellectually slow; unwieldy; (of artistic or literary productions) dull, tedious; (Theatr.) serious, sombre, as ~ *father*. **8.** Oppressive, grievous, as *a ~ fate*; sad, as ~ *news*; despondent; doleful; drowsy; *it lies ~* (makes its weight felt); *time hangs ~* (passes slowly). **9.** n. pl. || *The Heavies*, Dragoon Guards, (also) ~ artillery. **10.** adv. Heavily (now chiefly in compounds; as ~*-buying*, *-laden*, *-pulling*). **11.** ~*-armed*, bearing ~ arms or armour; ~ CHEMICALs; ~*-hearted*, melancholy, doleful; ~ *oil*, a heavier-than-water oil obtained from coal-tar by distillation; ~ *spar*, barytes; ~ *swell* (colloq.), man who emphasizes his real or imagined importance by overdressing etc.; ~ *water*, water with a density about 10 per cent. greater than that of ordinary water, the oxide of DEUTERIUM or ~ *hydrogen*; ~*-weight*, jockey etc. of more than average weight, boxer over 12st. **7.** Hence **hea′vıly[1]** adv., **hea′viɴess** n., ~ısʜ[1] a., (hĕ-). [OE *hefig*, OS *hebig*, OHG *hebig*, ON *höfugr*, f. Gmc *hafjan* HEAVE]

hĕb′domăd, n. Week (esp. in reference to *Dan.* ix. 27). [f. L f. Gk *hebdomas -ados* (*hepta* seven, see -AD)]

hĕbdŏm′adal, a. Weekly; || (Oxf. Univ.) *H~ Council*, board meeting weekly. [f. LL *hebdomadalis* (as prec., see -AL)]

Hĕb′ê, n. (Gk Myth.) goddess of youth, cupbearer of Olympus; (joc.) waitress, barmaid. [Gk]

hĕb′ētāte, v.t. & i. Make, become, dull. [f. L *hebetare* (*hebes -etis* blunt, see -ATE[3]]

hĕb′ētūde, n. Stupidity. [f. LL *hebetudo* (*hebes*, see prec., -TUDE)]

Hĕbrā′|ic, a. Of Hebrew or the Hebrews. Hence ~ıcALLY adv. [f. LL f. Gk *Hebraïkos* (as HEBREW, see -IC)]

Hĕb′rā|ısm, n. Attribute of the Hebrews; Hebrew system of thought or religion; Hebrew idiom or expression esp. in the Greek of the Bible. So ~ıze(3) v.t. & i., ~ıs′tic a., ~ıs′tıcALLY adv. [f. late Gk *Hebraïsmos*, or as prec. +-ısm, after *Hellenism* etc.]

Hĕb′rāıst, n. Hebrew scholar; adherent of Hebrew thought or religion. [as prec. -ıst]

Hĕb′rew (-ōō), n. & a. **1.** Israelite, Jew; *Epistle to the ~s*, book in N.T.; language of the ancient ~s; *modern ~*, as now used by Jews; (colloq.) unintelligible speech (cf. GREEK). **2.** adj. Of ~, of the Jews. [ME, f. OF *Ebreu* f. med. L *Ebreus* f. L f. Gk *Hebraios* f. Aram. *'ebrai* = Heb. *'ibri* one from the other side ('*abar* cross over)]

hĕc′atomb (-ŏm, -ōōm), n. (Gk Ant.) Great public sacrifice (prop. 100 oxen). [f. L f. Gk *hekatombē* (*hekaton* hundred + *bous* ox)]

hĕck[1], n. Frame obstructing passage of fish in river. [ME, northern form of HATCH[1]]

hĕck[2], n. & int. (sl.). Euphem. for HELL esp. in imprecations.

hĕc′kle, v.t., & n. (Dress *flax*, *hemp*, with) HACKLE[1]; catechize (esp. election candidate) severely. [15th c. *hekele* etc.; see HACKLE[1]]

hĕc′tāre, n. (In metric system) superficial measure of 100 ares (2.471 acres). [f. HECTO- + ARE[1]]

hĕc′tic, a. & n. **1.** ~ *fever*, that which accompanies consumption and similar diseases, attended with flushed cheeks and hot skin; consumptive; morbidly flushed (lit. & fig.); (sl.) exciting, wild, impassioned, (*for a ~ moment*). **2.** n. ~ fever, patient, flush. [14th c. *etik*. f. OF *etique* (mod. *hectique*) f. LL f. Gk *hektikos*; hec- after F & LL]

hĕc′to-, irreg. contr. of Gk *hekaton* hundred, used as comb. form, as: ~*graph*, apparatus for multiplying copies, (v.t.) multiply with this; (metric system) ~*gram*, weight of 100 grams (3.52 oz), ~*litre*, -*liter*, (-lēter), 100 litres (3.531 cub. ft), ~*metre* (-ter), -*meter*, 100 metres (328·089 ft); cf. OENTI-.

hĕc′tor, n., & v.t. & i. Bluster(er), bully. [(vb f. n.) f. Gk *Hektōr*, son of Priam and Hecuba, Trojan hero in *Iliad*]

hĕd′dles, n. pl. Small cords or wires through which warp is passed in loom before going through the reed. [16th c. var. of syn. *heald* f. OE *hefeld* f. hef- raise (HEAVE)]

hedge[1], n. Fence of bushes or low trees, living (*quickset ~*) or dead (*dead ~*), or of turf, stone, etc. (*doesn't grow on every ~*, is rare); line of things or persons forming barrier; (fig.) barrier; (Betting) act, means, of hedging; || ~*-priest*, illiterate priest of low status; ~*'row*, row of bushes forming ~; || ~*-school*, low-class school, (formerly) open-air school esp. in Ireland;

~-*sparrow*, common British and European bird, allied to the warblers. [OE *hecg, hegg*, ME *hegge, heg*, = MDu. *hegghe*, OHG *hegga, hecka* f. Gmc *hagjō- see HAW¹]

hědge², v.t. & i. Surround with hedge (lit. & fig.); fence *off*; hem *in*; make, trim, hedges, whence **hĕdg′ER¹** n.; secure oneself against loss on (bet, speculation, or abs.) by compensating transactions on the other side; (intr.) avoid committing oneself. [f. prec.]

hědge′hŏg (-jh-), n. Small spiny, nocturnal, almost omnivorous mammal, rolling itself up into ball for defence; name of various animals armed with spines; (Mil.) small self-contained defensive position bristling with fortifications on all sides; prickly seed-vessel of some plants; person hard to get on with, whence ~**gy²** (-g-) a. [HEDGE (from its habits) + HOG (from its snout)]

hēdŏn′ic, a. & n. Of pleasure; (n. pl.) doctrine of pleasure. [f. Gk *hēdonikos* (foll., -IC)]

hēd′on|ism, n. Doctrine that pleasure is the chief good. So ~**IST** n., ~**ĭs′tic** a. [f. Gk *hēdonē* pleasure + -ISM]

heed, v.t. (Sc. & literary), & n. 1. Concern oneself about, take notice of. 2. n. Careful attention, as *take* ~, *pay* or *give* ~ *to*. Hence ~**′FUL**, ~**′LESS**, aa., ~**′fuLLY²**, ~**′lĕsslY²**, advv., ~**′fulNESS**, ~**′lĕssNESS**, nn. [OE *hēdan*, OS *hōdian*, OHG *huotan* f. WG *hōdjan*; n. f. vb]

hee′haw′, n. Ass's bray; loud laugh. [imit.]

heel¹, n. 1. Hinder part of human foot below ankle (~ *of Achilles*, only vulnerable spot, weak point); (Anat.) corresponding part of hind limb in quadruped, often raised above ground; (pop., of quadruped) hinder part of hoof, (pl.) hind feet. 2. Part of stocking that covers ~; part of boot that supports ~. 3. Thing like ~ in shape or position, as handle end of violin bow, crook in head of golf club, after end of ship's keel; (hort.) irregularly shaped piece of plant attached to a cutting. 4. *Cad, low-down person (sl.). 5. *At* ~, *at, on, upon*, one's ~*s*, close behind one; *down at* ~, (of shoes) with ~ part crushed down, (of person) wearing such shoes, slovenly; *to* ~, (of dog) close behind, under control; ~-*&-toe* WALK¹*ing*; ~*s over head*, (usu.) *head over* ~*s*, upside down, in a somersault; *kick* one's ~*s*, stand waiting; **COOL²** one's ~*s*; *lay, clap, by the* ~*s*, imprison; *show a clean pair of* ~*s, take to* one's ~*s*, run away; *have the* ~*s of*, out-run; *turn on* one's ~, turn sharply round; *be carried with the* ~*s foremost* (as a corpse); (Cribbage) *his* ~*s*, knave if turned up by dealer, scoring two (cf. **NOB**). ~′*ball*, shoemaker's polishing mixture of hard wax and lamp-black; ~′*tap*, a thickness of leather in ~, liquor left at bottom of glass. [OE *hēla, hæla*,

OFris. *hēla*, MDu. *hiele*, ON *hæll* f. Gmc *hāhil* cogn. w. HOUGH]

heel², v.i. & t. Touch ground with heel, e.g. in dancing; furnish (boot etc.) with heel; chase or follow closely; (Football) pass ball *out* at back of scrummage with the heels; (Golf) strike (ball) with heel of club. Hence ~-**ED²** (-ld) a. (colloq.), armed with revolver, supplied with money. [f. prec.]

heel³, v.i. & t. (Of ship etc.) lean over owing to pressure of wind or uneven load; cause (ship) to do this. [alt. f. 14th c. *heeld, hield* f. OE *hieldan*, OS *heldian*, OHG *heldan* f. Gmc *halthjan* incline, lean]

heel⁴, n. (naut.). Inclination of heeling ship (cf. LIST³). [f. prec.]

hĕft, n., & v.t. (dial., U.S.). Weight; (dial.) lift, push, (v.t.) lift, esp. to judge weight. [(vb prob. f. n.) 16th c., f. HEAVE vb, cf. *weave weft*]

hĕf′ty̆, a. Sturdy, stalwart, (a *battalion of* ~ *fellows*). [prec., -Y²]

Hegēl′ian (hā-, hē-), a. & n. Relating to G. W. F. Hegel (d. 1831) or his philosophy; (n.) a follower of Hegel. [-IAN]

hĕgĕm′on′ic (hēgĕ-, hĕgī-), a. Ruling, supreme. [f. Gk *hēgemonikos* (as foll., see -IC)]

hĕgĕm′on̄y (-g-, -j-; *also* hēgĕ²), n. Leadership, esp. of one State of a confederacy [f. Gk *hēgemonia* (*hēgemōn* leader)]

hĕ′jira (-jira, n. Mohammed's flight from Mecca to Medina; Mohammedan era reckoned from this (622 A.D.). [med. L, f. Arab. *hijrah* departure from one's country (*hajara* separate)]

hei′fer (hĕf-), n. Young cow esp. one that has not had calf, female calf. [OE *heahfore*, of unkn. orig.]

heigh (hā), int. expr. encouragement or inquiry; ~-*ho*, int. expr. boredom, disappointment, etc.

height (hīt), n. Measurement from base to top; elevation above ground or recognized (esp. sea) level; considerable elevation, as *situated at a* ~; high point; top; *the* ~ (utmost degree) *of folly* etc.; rising ground; *at its* ~ (highest degree). [OE *hiehth*(o), OHG *hōhida*, Goth. *hauhitha*; see HIGH, -TH¹]

height′en (hīt-), v.t. & i. Make high(er); intensify; inflate (description, story); (intr.) rise (usu. fig.). [prec. + -EN⁴]

hei′nous (hān-), a. (Of crime or criminal) odious, atrocious. Hence ~**LY²** advv., ~**NESS** n. [ME, f. OF *hainos, -eus* (*haïne* hatred f. *haïr*); see -OUS]

heir (ār), n. Person receiving or entitled to receive property or rank as legal representative of former owner; (fig.) one to whom something (joy, punishment, etc.) is morally due; ~ APPARENT; ~-*at-law* (by right of blood); ~ *in tail* (to entailed estate); ~ *male*, male ~ tracing descent wholly through males; ~ PRESUMPTIVE. Hence ~**DOM**, ~**′ESS¹**, ~**′SHIP**, nn., ~**′LESS**

a., (ār-). [ME, f. OF, f. LL *herem* = L *heredem* (nom. *heres*)]

heir′lōom (ār-), n. Chattel that follows devolution of real estate; piece of personal property that has been in family for generations (also fig. of qualities). [prec.+LOOM¹]

hejira. See HEGIRA.

held. See HOLD¹.

hēle, heal, v.t. Cover, hide, (now dial.); set (plant) in the ground and cover it *in*. [OE *helian* f. st. *hal-* of *helan*; cf. HELL]

hēl′i-, comb. form of HELICOPTER, as in ~*drōme,* ~*pŏrt,* station for helicopters.

hēli′acal, a. (astron.). Relating to, near, the sun; ~ *rising, setting,* first rising of a star after, last setting before, a period of invisibility due to conjunction with the sun. [f. LL f. Gk *hēliakos* (*hēlios* sun, see-AC)+-AL]

Hēliăn′thus, n. Genus including common sunflower. [f. Gk *hēlios* sun+*anthos* flower]

hēl′ical, a. Spiral. Hence or cogn.~ally² adv., ~oid, ~oid′al, aa. [as HELIX+-AL]

Hēl′icon, n. Boeotian mountain, sacred to Muses; source of poetic inspiration. So Hēlicōn′IAN a. [L, f. Gk *Helikōn*]

hēl′icŏpter, n. Flying-machine deriving both its lift and its propulsive power from horizontally revolving blades or rotors, and capable of ascending and descending vertically. [f. Gk *helix -ikos* screw, *pteron* wing]

hēl′iō, n. (colloq.). Abbr. of HELIOgram, -*graph*.

hēl′io-, comb. form of Gk *hēlios* sun, as: ~*cĕn′tric,* as viewed from centre of sun, taking sun as centre; ~*chrōmy,* photographic representation in natural colours; ~*gram,* message by ~graph (3); ~*graph,* n., (1) engraving obtained by exposure to light, (2) apparatus for photographing sun, (3) signalling apparatus reflecting flashes of sunlight; ~*graph,* v.t., send (message) by ~graph, photograph by ~graphy; ~*graph′ic,* or ~graphy; ~*graphy* (-ŏg²), description of the sun, engraving process, signalling by ~graph; ~*gravūre′,* photogravure; ~*meter* (-ŏm²), instrument for finding angular distance between two stars (orig. for measuring diameter of sun); ~*scope,* apparatus for observing sun without injury to eye; ~*thĕ′rapy,* use of sun-baths in treating disease; ~*trop′ic,* ~*tropism* (-ŏt²), (of plants) turning, property of turning, in particular way under influence of light; ~*type,* picture obtained from gelatine film exposed to light.

hēliolith′ic, a. Of the civilization characterized by megaliths & sun-worship. [f. HELIO-, after *eolithic* etc.]

hēliōs′is, n. (Bot.) spots on leaves caused by concentration of sun's rays through glass etc.; sunstroke. [Gk *hēliōsis* (*hēlios* sun, see -OSIS)]

hēl′iotrōpe, n. Plant with fragrant purple flowers; colour, scent, of these; bloodstone. [f. L f. Gk *hēliotropion* plant turning flowers to the sun (*hēlios* sun+-*tropos* f. *trepō* turn)]

hēl′ium, n. A colourless inodorous inert gaseous element, inferred as existing in sun's atmosphere in 1868, first obtained in 1895. [f. Gk *hēlios* sun, -IUM]

hēl′ix, n. (pl. -*icēs*). Spiral (like corkscrew, or in one plane like watch-spring); (Archit.) spiral ornament; rim of external ear; genus including common snail. [L f. Gk *helix*]

hĕll, n. Abode of the dead; abode of condemned spirits; place, state, of wickedness or misery; *a ~ of a* (considerable) *noise*; den for captives in Prisoner's Base & other games; gaming-house; (in imprecations) ~!, *what the ~ do you want?*; *give* (a person) ~, make things hot for him; *like ~,* desperately, extremely (often as mere intensive); ~-*box* (printer's sl.), receptacle for refuse type; ~-*cat,* spiteful or furious woman; ~ *for leather,* at top riding-speed (usu. *ride* ~ *for leather*); ~-*hound,* fiend; ~-*weed,* name of various plants. Hence ~′ish¹ a., ~′ishLY² adv., ~′ishness n., ~′ward adv. & a. [OE *hel*(*l*), OS *hellja,* OHG *hella,* ON *hel,* Goth. *halja* f. Gmc *hel-, hal-* to hide, HELE]

hĕll′ebōre, n. Ancient name of various plants supposed to cure madness; (Bot.) species including Christmas rose. [ME, f. OF, ult. f. L f. Gk *helleboros*]

Hĕll′ēne, n. Ancient Greek of genuine Greek race; subject of modern kingdom of Greece. So Hĕllēn′ic a. [f. Gk *Hellēn*]

Hĕll′en|ism, n. Greek idiom or construction; imitation of the Greeks; Grecian culture; Greek nationality. So ~IZE(3) v.t. & i. [f. Gk *Hellēnismos* (as prec., see -ISM)]

Hĕll′en|ist, n. One who used the Greek language but was not a Greek; Greek scholar. Hence ~is′tic a. [f. Gk *Hellēnistēs* (as prec., see -IST)]

hĕllō′, n. & v. = HALLO.

hĕlm¹, n. (Arch.) helmet; (also ~-*cloud*) cloud forming over mountain before or during storm. Hence ~ED² (-md) a. [OE, OS, OHG *helm,* ON *hjalmr,* Goth. *hilms* f. Gmc. *helmaz* f. *hel-* (HELL)]

hĕlm², n., & v.t. 1. Tiller, wheel, by which rudder is used; space through which ~ is turned, as *more, little,* ~; *down (with the)* ~, *up (with the)* ~, place ~ so as to bring rudder to leeward, to windward; *weather, lee,* ~, ~ *put up, down;* (fig.) government, guidance, (*take the* ~, assume control); ~*s′man,* steersman. 2. v.t. Steer (usu. fig.). [OE *helma* corr. to ON *hjalm*; cf. MHG *helm* handle]

hĕl′mĕt, n. Defensive head-cover of soldiers, firemen, etc.; felt or pith hat for hot climates; upper part of retort; (Bot.) arched upper part of corolla in some flowers; shell of a genus of molluscs.

Hence ~ED² a. [ME, f. OF dim. of *helme* f. WG (HELM¹)]

hĕl′minth, n. Worm (usu. intestinal). Hence ~i′ASIS n., disease characterized by presence of ~s in the body, **hĕlmin′thic**, **hĕlmin′thoid**, aa., ~ŏL′OGY n. [f. Gk *helmins -inthos* maw-worm]

hĕl′ot, n. (*H*~) one of a class of serfs in ancient Sparta; *drunken H*~ (made drunk as warning to Spartan youth); serf. Hence ~ISM(2), ~RY(1, 2), nn., ~IZE(3) v.t. [f. L *Helotes* f. Gk *Heilōtes* (pl. of *Heilōs*) taken as=inhabitant of *Helos*, Laconian town]

hĕlp¹, v.t. (~ed; arch. past *hŏlp* & p.p. *hŏlpen*). Aid, assist, as ~ *me*, ~ *me to lift it*, ~ *me to an answer*, ~ *the work on or forward*, ~ *me over the stile*, ~ *me out (of a difficulty)*; ~ *person off, off, with coat* etc., ~ *him to put it on, take it off*; ~ (person) *to*, serve him with (food); distribute (food at meal); remedy, prevent, as *it can't be* ~*ed*, *I can't* ~ *that*, *don't be longer than you can* ~ (cannot); (w. neg.) refrain from or avoid doing (*cannot* ~ *hoping that* —); (in invocation or oath) *so* ~ *me God* (as I keep my word, as I speak the truth, etc.). [OE, OS *helpan*, OHG *helfan*, ON *hjalpa*, Goth. *hilpan* f. Gmc *help-*, *halp-*, *hulp-*]

hĕlp², n. Assistance, as *we need your* ~, *she, it, is a great* ~, *by* ~ *of*; *domestic servant*, employees; || *lady* ~, assistant & companion to mistress of house; *mother's* ~, superior nursemaid; remedy or escape, as *there is no* ~ *for it*; helping (of food). [OE *help*, f. prec.]

hĕlp′ful, a. (Of person or thing) useful, serviceable. Hence ~LY² adv., ~NESS n. [-FUL]

hĕl′ping, n. In vbl senses, esp. portion of food served. [-ING¹]

hĕlp′less, a. Lacking help; unable to help oneself. Hence ~LY² adv., ~NESS n. [-LESS]

hĕlp′māte, n. Helpful companion or partner (usu. husband or wife). [HELP+MATE, prob. infl. by foll.]

hĕlp′meet, n. = prec. [formed by misunderstanding of *Gen.* ii. 18, 20, *help meet* (i.e. suitable) being taken as one word]

hĕl′ter-skĕl′ter, adv., a., & n. (In) disordered haste. [imit.]

hĕlve, n. Handle of weapon or tool; *throw the* ~ *after the* HATCHET. [OE *htelfe* (WG *halbhjo-*) f. Gmc *hal-* as in HALTER, with MLG, MDu. *helf*, OHG *halp*]

Hĕlvē′tian (-shn), a. & n. Swiss. [f. L *Helvetius*+-AN]

hĕm¹, n. Border, edge, of cloth etc., esp. border made by turning in edge & sewing it down. [OE *hem(m)* (once), perh. rel. to dial. *ham* enclosed pasture; cf. NFris. *heam* hem]

hĕm², v.t. (-mm-). Turn down & sew in edge of (cloth etc., or abs.); ~ *in, about, round*, enclose, confine. [f. prec.]

hĕm³, int., n., & v.i. 1. (Also *h'm*) int. calling attention or expressing hesitation. 2. n. Utterance of this. 3. v.t. (-mm-). Utter sound ~, clear throat, hesitate in speech. [imit.]

hemato- etc. See haemato-.

hĕmi-, pref. in wds f. Gk or on Gk elements, = half-, affecting one half, etc., as ~*anŏp′sia*, half-blindness, *hem′icycle*, half-*moon figure*, || ~*dĕmīsĕmīquăv′er*, half a demisemiquaver, ~*hĕd′ral*(Cryst.), having half proper number of planes, ~*metăb′ola*, insects undergoing incomplete metamorphosis, ~*plē′gia*, paralysis of one side. [Gk *hēmi-* = L *semi-*]

hĕm′isphēre, n. Half sphere; half the celestial sphere, esp. as divided by the equinoctial or by the ecliptic; half the earth, containing (*Eastern* ~) Europe, Asia, & Africa, or (*Western* ~) America; *Northern, Southern*, ~s, halves of the earth as divided by equator; *Magdeburg* ~s, pair of brass ~s exhausted of air to show atmospheric pressure by their cohesion. Hence **hĕmīsphĕ′rIC**(AL) aa. [ME forms f. OF *emisp(h)ere* & LL *hemisphaerium* f. Gk HEMI(*sphaira* SPHERE)]

hĕm′istich (-k), n. Half of line of verse. [f. L f. Gk HEMI(*stikhion* f. *stikhos* verse)]

hĕm′lŏck, n. Poisonous umbelliferous plant, used as powerful sedative; poisonous potion got from this. [OE *hymlic(e)*, of unkn. orig.]

hemorrhage etc. See haem-.

hĕmp, n. Herbaceous plant, native of India; its cortical fibre used for rope & stout fabrics; (joc.) rope for hanging; name of various other plants yielding fibre (*European, Manilla,* ~, with soft, hard, fibre); ~ *agrimony*, perennial plant of the daisy family with pale-purple flowers and hairy leaves. Hence **hĕm′pEN⁵** a. [OE *henep*, OHG *hanaf*, ON *hampr* f. Gmc *hanapiz* cogn. w. Gk *kannabis*]

hĕm′stitch, v.t., & n. (Hem *cloth* etc. with) kind of ornamental stitch.

hĕn, n. Female of common domestic fowl, pheasant, partridge, woodcock, etc. (~ *blackbird,* ~ *thrush*, etc., cf. COCK¹); occas. second element in name of female birds, as *guinea-*~, *pea-*~, *moor-* etc.; *like a* ~ *with one chicken*, absurdly fussy; ~ *& chickens*, name of a compound daisy & other plants; ~*'bane*, narcotic & poisonous plant, drug got from this; ~*-coop* (for keeping poultry in); ~ *crab, lobster*, female; ~*-harrier*, blue hawk, a bird of prey; ~*-hearted*, pusillanimous; ~*-party* (of women only, colloq.; cf. STAG-*party*); ~*'pecked*, domineered over by one's wife; ~*-roost*, place where fowls roost at night; ~*-run*, enclosure for fowls. [OE *henn*, OHG *henna* f. WG *hannja* dim. of *hano* (OE *hana*) cock]

hĕnce, adv. (Arch.) from here, from this, (often pleonast. *from* ~); (poet., rhet.) ~ *!*, go away, ~ *with*, away with, take away, go ~, die; ~*forth'*, ~*for'ward*, from this time forward; *five years* ~, in five years' time from now; as a result from this; from this origin; as an inference from this (~ *it appears that*), therefore. [ME *hennes* f. *henne* adv. (OE *hionan* f. root of HE) + -ES]

hĕnch'man, n. **1**. (hist.). Squire, page of honour. **2**. Chief attendant of Highland chief; trusty follower; political supporter. [14th c., f. OE *hengest* male horse (Du. & G *hengsl*) + MAN]

hĕn'dĕca- in comb. = Gk *hendeka* eleven, as *hendĕc'agon*, plane rectilineal figure of eleven sides; ~*syllăb'ic* a. & n., (verse) of eleven syllables, ~*syll'able*, such a verse (esp., in Gk & Latin: ‿‿-(or -‿) -‿‿-‿-‿-).

hĕndi'adys, n. Expression of a complex idea by two words connected with *&* (e.g. *in goblets & gold* for *in golden goblets*). [med. L, f. Gk *hen dia duoin* one thing by two]

Hĕn'ley, n. (Used for) annual regatta at ~-on-Thames. [place]

hĕnn'a, n. Egyptian privet; its shoots & leaves used as a dye for esp. the hair. [Arab. *henna'*]

hĕnn'ў, a. & n. Hen-like; (n.) hen-like cock. [HEN + -Y²]

hĕn'othĕism, n. Belief in one God without asserting that he is the only God (cf. MONOTHEISM). [f. Gk *heis henos* one + *theos* god + -ISM]

hĕpăt'ic, a. Of, good for, the liver; liver-hued. [f. LL f. Gk *hēpatikos* (HEPATO-, -IC)]

hĕpăt'ica, n. Anemone with lobed leaves resembling the liver. [med. L, fem. of *hepaticus* (prec.)]

hĕpatit'is, n. Inflammation of the liver. [HEPATO-, -ITIS]

hĕp'atĭz|e, -ise (-ĭz), v.t. Convert (lungs) into liver-substance.. Hence ~A'TION n. [as foll. + -IZE]

hĕpato-, comb. form of Gk *hēpar -atos* liver, as ~*genous* (-ŏj-), originating in the liver.

Hĕp'plewhite (-elwĭt), n. A delicate style of furniture. [G. ~, d. 1786]

hĕp'ta- in comb. = Gk *hepta* seven, as: ~*chord*, 7-stringed instrument, 7-note scale; ~*glot* a. & n., (book) in seven languages; ~*gon*, plane rectilineal figure of seven sides, so ~*gonal* (-ăg-) a.; ~*hĕd'ron* (-a-h-), solid of seven faces; ~*syllăb'ic* a., seven syllables; ~*teuch* (-k), first seven books of Bible.

hĕp'tad, n. Set, group, of seven. [f. LL f. Gk *heptas -ados* set of seven (*hepta*)]

hĕp'tarchy (-k-) n. Government by seven rulers; seven kingdoms of Angles & Saxons in Britain. So **hĕptarch'ic**(AL) (-k-) aa. [f. HEPTA- + Gk *-arkhia* government]

her¹, pron. Objective case of SHE; colloq. also subjective, as *Was that* ~ *?* [OE *hire*, dat. of *hio, heo*, SHE]

her², pron. & a. Possessive case of, & adj. corresp. to, SHE, with absolute form ~*s*, as *it is* ~ *hat, it is* ~*s*, ~*s is best, my father & ~s suffer(s) for it*, ~ (vulg. ~*s*) *& my* (common) *father*, ~ (vulg. ~*s*) *& my* (respective) *father(s)*. [OE *hi(e)re*, genitive as prec.]

hĕ'rald¹, n. **1**. Officer who made State proclamations, bore messages between princes, officiated in the tourney, arranged various State ceremonials, regulated use of armorial bearings, settled questions of precedence, & recorded names & pedigrees of those entitled to armorial bearings; ‖*H*~*s' College*, corporation (now) recording pedigrees & granting badges of arms. **2**. Messenger (often as title of newspaper); forerunner. [ME, f. OF *heraut*, f. WG *heriwald* 'army-wielder']

hĕ'rald², v.t. Proclaim the approach of; usher in. [ME, f. OF *herauder* (as prec.)]

hĕrăl'dic, a. Of heraldry. [-IC]

hĕ'raldrу̌, n. Science of a herald; CANT³-*ing* ~; armorial bearings; heraldic pomp. [-RY]

hĕrb, n. Plant whose stem is not woody or persistent; plant of which leaves etc. are used for food, medicine, scent, flavour, etc.; ~ *beer*, drink made from ~*s*; ~ *bennet*, yellow-flowered species of Avens [prob. f. OF *herbe beneite* = L *herba benedicta* blessed herb]; ~ *Robert*, kind of geranium; ~ *-tea, -water*, medicinal infusion of herbs. So ~A'CEOUS (-āshus; ~*aceous border* in gardens, one devoted to perennial flowering plants), ~iF'EROUS, iV'OROUS, ~'LESS, aa. [ME, f. OF *erbe* f. L *herba* grass]

hĕrb'age, n. Herbs collectively; succulent parts of herbs; (Law) right of pasture on another's ground. [ME, f. OF (prec., -AGE)]

hĕrb'al, a. & n. (Book with descriptions) of herbs. [f. med. L *herbalis* (as prec., see -AL)]

hĕrb'alist, n. One skilled in herbs (now of early botanical writers); dealer in medicinal herbs. [prec. + -IST]

hĕrbār'ium, n. (Book, case, room, for) collection of dried plants. [LL HERB, -ARIUM)]

hĕrb'or|ize, -ise (-ĭz), v.i. Gather herbs, botanize. So ~IZA'TION, ~IST, nn. [f. F *herboriser*, irreg. f. *herbe* HERB, after *arboriscr*]

hĕrb'у̌, a. Abounding in herbs; of the nature of a herb. [-Y²]

Hĕrcŭl'ean (*also* -ē'an), a. Of Hercules; strong as Hercules; difficult as his labours. [f. L *Herculeus* (as foll.) + -AN]

Hĕrc'ŭlēs (-z), n. (Gk & Rom. Myth.) hero of prodigious strength, who performed 12 immense labours; *Pillars of* ~, rocks on either side of Strait of Gibraltar, (fig.) ultimate limit; strong man; ~ *beetle* (S.-Amer., 5 in. long); a northern constellation. [L, f. Gk *Hēraklēs*]

herd[1], n. Company of animals, esp. cattle, feeding or travelling together; large number of people (derog.), esp. *the, the common, the vulgar,* ~; *the* ~ *instinct,* gregariousness & mutual influence as a psychological factor; ~*book,* pedigree-book of cattle or pigs; ~*s'man,* keeper of ~s. [OE *heord,* OHG *herta,* ON *hjorth,* Goth. *hairda* f. Gmc **herdō*]

herd[2], n. Keeper of herds, herdsman, esp. w. word prefixed, as *cow*~, *swine*~. [OE *hirde,* OS *hirdi,* OHG *hirti,* ON *hirthir,* Goth. *hairdeis* f. Gmc **herdjaz*]

herd[3], v.i. & t. Go in a herd (*together, with* others; esp. fig. of persons); tend (sheep, cattle). [f. HERD[1,3]]

here, adv. & n. **1.** In this place; in this country; (answering roll-call) ~ *l,* I am present; (calling attention to person's presence) *my son* ~ *will show you*; (in drinking healths) ~*'s* (a health) *to*; in this life (esp. ~ *below*); at this point (in discourse etc.); in this matter; to this place; *look* ~ (in this direction; esp. in bespeaking attention or making protest); *I don't belong* ~ (to this place); ~ *& there,* in various places; ~, *there, & everywhere,* everywhere, all about; *neither* ~ *nor there,* not to the point, of no importance; (colloq., to announce commencement of bold act) ~ *goes l* **2.** n. This place or point, as *from, to, near,* ~. **3.** ~*'about(s)',* somewhere near ~; ~*af'ter,* in future, later on, in the world to come, (n.) the future, the world to come; ~*at'* (arch.), at this; ~*by',* by this means, as a result; ~*in',* in this point, book, etc.; ~*inaf'ter,* below (in document etc.); ~*inbefore',* in a preceding part (of this document etc.); ~*of'* (arch.), of this; ~*to'* (arch.), to this matter; ~*tofore',* formerly; ~*un'der,* below (in book etc.); ~*upon',* after this, in consequence of this; ~*with',* with this (esp. of enclosure in letter etc.). [OE, OS, ON, Goth. *her,* OHG *hiar,* app. f. Gmc **hi-* (HE[1])]

her'edita|ble, a. That may be inherited. So ~BIL'ITY n. [obs. F, f. *héréditer,* f. LL *hereditare* (*heres -edis* heir), see -ABLE]

her'edit'ament (or *hrēd[2]*), n. Property that can be inherited; real property; inheritance. [f. med. L *hereditamentum* (as prec., see -MENT)]

herēditār'ian, n. One who holds the doctrine of heredity. [f. HEREDITY, see -ARIAN]

herěd'itar|y̆, a. Descending by inheritance; (of diseases, instincts, etc.) transmitted from one generation to another; like, the same as, that one's parents had, as ~*y creed, hatred*; of, holding position by, inheritance. Hence ~ILY[2] adv., ~iNESS n. [f. L *hereditarius* (as HEREDITY, see -ARY[1])]

herěd'it|y̆, n. Tendency of like to beget like. Hence ~ISM(3) n. [f. F *hérédité* or LL *hereditas* heirship (as HEIR, see -TY)]

He'reford, n. (Used for) a breed of cattle originating in Herefordshire, England.

Hèrer'o (-ār'ō), n. Name of negroid people and their language in S.W. Africa.

hĕrēs'iärch (-k), n. Leader, founder, of a heresy. [f. LL (-*cha*) f. Gk *hairesiarkhēs* (as foll. + -*arkhēs* ruler)]

hĕ'rĕsy̆, n. Opinion contrary to the orthodox doctrine of the Christian Church, or to the accepted doctrine on any subject. Hence **hĕrēsiŏl'OGIST, hĕrēsiŏl'OGY,** nn. [ME, f. OF (*h*)*eresie* f. Rom. **heresia* f. L & LL *haeresis* f. Gk *hairesis* choice, sect (*haireomai* choose)]

hĕ'rĕtic, n. Holder of an unorthodox opinion (orig. in the matter of religion). So **hĕrĕt'ICAL** a. [ME, f. OF *heretique* f. LL f. Gk *hairetikos* (as prec., see -IC)]

|| **hĕ'riot,** n. (law). Render of best live beast or dead chattel, or money payment, to lord on decease of tenant (now only of manorial tenures). [OE *heregeatwa* (*here* army + *geatwa* trappings)]

hĕ'ritab|le, a. That passes to heirs-at-law (opp. to movable property); transmissible from parent to child; capable of inheriting. Hence ~LY[2] adv. [ME, f. OF, f. *heriter* f. LL *hereditare* (see HEREDITABLE)]

hĕ'ritage, n. What is or may be inherited; (fig.) portion allotted to any one; (Bibl.) the ancient Israelites, the Church; inherited lot. [ME, f. OF (as prec., see -AGE)]

hĕ'ritor, n. One who inherits. [f. AF *heriter,* OF -*ier* (as HEREDITARY), assim. to wds in -OR]

hĕrl, n. Var. of HARL(E)[2].

hĕrmăph'rod|īte, n. & a. **1.** Human being, animal, combining characteristics of both sexes; (Zool.) animal having normally both male & female sexual organs, e.g. earth-worm; (Bot.) plant in which same flower has stamens & pistils; person, thing, combining opposite qualities; ship having characters of two kinds of craft. **2.** adj. Combining both sexes or opposite characteristics. Hence ~īt'IC(AL) aa., ~īTISM n. [f. L f. Gk *Hermaphroditos,* who became one with the nymph Salmacis]

hĕrmēneut'ic, a. & n. Of interpretation; (n. pl.) interpretation, esp. of Scripture. So ~AL a. [f. Gk *hermēneutikos* (*hermēneuō* interpret, see -IC)]

Hĕrm'ēs (-z), n. (Gk Myth.) son of Zeus & Maia, messenger of the gods, god of science, eloquence, etc.; ~ *Trismegistus* (Thrice-Great), Neo-platonist name of Egyptian god Thoth, as author of mysterious doctrines, secrets of alchemy, etc. [L f. Gk *Hermēs*]

hĕrmĕt'|ic, a. Of alchemy, as ~*ic art*; ~*ic seal,* air-tight closure by fusion etc. (also fig.), whence ~ICALLY adv. [f. mod. L *hermeticus* irreg. f. HERMES *Trismegistus*]

hĕrm'it, n. Early Christian recluse; person living in solitude; ~*crab,* kind that lives in mollusc's cast-off shell to protect its shell-less hinder parts. [ME, f. OF (*h*)*ermite* f. LL (-*ta*) f. Gk *erēmitēs* (*crēmius* desert, see -ITE[1]); cf. EREMITE]

hẽrm'itage, n. Hermit's abode; solitary abode; French wine from hill near Valence (with ruined ~ on top). [ME, f. OF (as prec., see -AGE)]

hern. See HERON.

hẽrn'i|a, n. (path.). Rupture. Hence ~AL, ~ARY[1], aa., ~ŏT'OMY n. [L]

hẽrn'shaw. [ME, f. OF heronceau, dim. of HERON]

hẽr'ō, n. (pl. ~es). (Gk Ant.) man of superhuman qualities favoured by the gods, demigod; illustrious warrior, (rhet.) one who has fought for his country (homes for ~es, housing for ex-service men); man admired for achievements & noble qualities; chief man in poem, play, or story; ~-worship(per), worship(per) of the ancient ~es or of some great man or men. [f. L f. Gk hērōs]

hẽrō'ic, a. & n. 1. (Of acts or qualities) of, fit for, a hero; (of persons) having the qualities of a hero; the ~ age (of Greece, before return from Troy); (of poetry) dealing with heroes; ~ verse, that used in ~ poetry (Gk & L hexameter, E five-foot iambic, F Alexandrine); (of language) grand, high-flown; bold, attempting great things. 2. n. ~ verse; (n. pl.) high-flown language or sentiments. Hence hẽrō'IC-ALLY adv. [f. F -ique or L f. Gk hērōikos (as prec., see -IC)]

hẽrōi-cŏm'ic, a. Combining the heroic with the comic. [HERO + -I- + COMIC]

hẽrō'ify, v.t. Make a hero of. [as prec. + -FY]

hẽ'rōin (or hīrō'īn), n. A sedative drug prepared from morphine. [P]

hẽ'rōine, n. Demigoddess; heroic woman; chief woman in poem, novel, etc. [f. L f. Gk hērōinē, fem. of hērōs HERO]

hẽ'rōism, n. Heroic conduct or qualities. [f. F héroïsme (héros HERO, see -ISM)]

hẽ'rōize, -ise (-īz), v.t. & i. Make a hero of; make heroic; play the hero. [-IZE]

hẽ'ron, hẽrn (poet. etc.), n. Long-legged wading bird. [ME, f. OF hai(g)ron f. WG (Frank.) *haigiro = OHG heigaro (G reiher), OE hrāgra heron]

hẽ'ronrỹ, n. Place where herons breed. [-RY]

hẽrp'ēs (-z), n. Skin disease, with patches of distinct vesicles. Hence hẽrpĕt'IC a. [L, f. Gk herpēs, -ētos shingles (herpō creep)]

hẽrpĕt|ŏl'ogỹ, n. Study of reptiles. So ~ŏL'OGIST n. [f. Gk herpeton reptile (herpō creep) + -LOGY]

Herr (hãr), n. (pl. Herren). German equivalent of Mr; German gentleman.

hẽ'rring, n. North Atlantic fish, much used for food, coming near coast in large shoals to spawn; kippered ~, = KIPPER; RED ~; ~-bone, stitch resembling bones of ~, (Archit.) zigzag arrangement of stones or tiles, (v.t.) work with ~-bone stitch, mark with ~-bone pattern; ~-pond, (joc.) North Atlantic. [OE hæring, hēring, MLG hēr-, hãrink, OHG hãrinc]

Herrn'huter (hãrn'hŏŏ-), n. One of the sect of Moravians. [f. Herrnhut, their first German settlement]

hers. See HER.

hẽrsĕlf', pron. Emphatic & reflexive form corr. to SHE, as she ~ told me, she said it ~, she has hurt ~, ask the woman ~; she is not ~ (in her normal state of body or mind). [OE hire self]

Hẽrt'zian, a. ~ waves, electric waves (so called from the discoveries of H. R. Hertz, German physicist, d. 1894); ~ telegraphy, wireless. [-IAN]

hĕs'it|ant (-z-), a. Hesitating; irresolute. So ~ANCE, ~ANCY, nn. [as foll., see -ANT]

hĕs'itāt|e (-z-), v.i. Show, speak with, indecision; scruple, be reluctant, to (do). Hence or cogn. ~INGLY[2] adv., hĕsitA-TION n., ~IVE a., (-z-). [f. L haesitare frequent. of haerēre haes- stick fast, see -ATE[3]]

Hĕspēr'ian, a. (poet.). Western. [f. L f. Gk Hesperios (as HESPERUS) + -AN]

Hĕs'peris, n. Genus of plants including ROCKET[1] & dame's violet. [L, f. Gk Hesperis of evening, of the West (as foll.)]

Hĕsperŏrn'is, n. American genus of fossil birds. [as foll + Gk ornis bird]

Hĕs'perus, n. Evening star. [L, f. Gk hesperos a. & n., western evening (star)]

Hĕ'ssian (-shn), a. & n. 1. Of Hesse in Germany; ~ (boot), high boot first worn by ~ troops; ~ fly, fly whose larva destroys wheat. 2. n. Strong coarse cloth of hemp or jute. [-IAN]

hĕst, n. (arch.). Behest. [OE hǣs (hãtan, see HIGHT), assim. to OE nn. in -t]

hĕt, p.p. (now dial. & U.S.). Heated; ~ up (sl.), excited. [p.p. of HEAT[2]]

hĕtaer'a (-tẽra), -air'a (-īra), n. (pl. -rae). Courtesan, mistress. [Gk hetaira, fem. of hetairos companion]

hĕtaer'ism (-ẽr-), -air'ism (-ĩr-), n. Open concubinage; communal marriage in a tribe. [f. Gk hetairismos (as prec., see -ISM)]

hĕt'ero- (before vowel heter-), comb. form of Gk heteros other, different; freq. opp. to homo-, occas. to auto-, homoeo-, iso-, ortho-, syn-: ~chrōm'ous, of different colours; ~cỹc'lic, (of chem. compounds) with mólecule of a ring composed of atoms of different kinds; ~gamous (-ŏg⁴), irregular as regards stamens & pistils; ~graphy (-ŏg⁴), incorrect or inconsistent spelling; ~morph'ic, of dissimilar forms; ~morph'ism, diversity of form; ~nomous (-ŏn⁴), subject to different laws (of growth etc.), subject to an external law (cf. AUTONOMOUS); ~nomy (-ŏn⁴), presence of a different law, subjection to external law; ~pãth'ic, = ALLOPATHIC, (also) differing in effect; ~phyll'ous, bearing leaves of different forms on same plant; ~sexual a., relating to or characterized by the normal relation of the sexes (also as n.; opp. HOMOSEXUAL); ~taxy, abnormal disposition of organs or parts.

hĕt′eroclite, a. & n. (gram.). Irregularly declined; (n.) ~ noun. [16th c. f. F *hétéroclite* or LL f. Gk HETERO(*klitos* f. *klinō* inflect)]

hĕt′erodŏx, a. (Of person or opinion) not orthodox. So ~Y¹ n. [17th c. f. LL f. Gk HETERO(*doxos* f. *doxa* opinion)]

hĕt′erodyne, n. & a. (Relating to) production of a lower (audible) frequency from the combination of two high frequencies (in radio). [HETERO-, Gk *dunamis* force]

hĕterogĕn′eous, a. Diverse in character; composed of diverse elements; (Math.) incommensurable because of different kinds. Hence or cogn. **hĕterogĕnē′ITY**, ~NESS, nn., ~LY² adv. [f. scholastic L *heterogeneus* f. Gk HETERO(*genēs* f. *genos* kind) + -OUS]

hĕterogĕn′esis, n. Birth of a living being otherwise than from parent of same kind, esp. spontaneous generation from inorganic matter. So **hĕterogĕn**ET′IC a. [HETERO-]

hĕterozyg′|ōte, n. (Mendelism). Zygote resulting from fusion of unlike gametes. So ~OUS a. [HETERO-].

hĕt′man, n. Polish military commander (retained as title among Cossacks). [Polish]

heuris′tic (hūr-), a. & n. Serving to discover; ~ method, system of education under which the pupil is trained to find out things for himself, so ~s n. pl. [irreg. f. Gk *heuriskō* find, see -IC]

hew, v.t. & i. (p.p. ~n or ~ed). Chop, cut, (thing *down, away, off, asunder, to pieces,* etc.) with axe, sword, etc.; cut into shape; ~ one's *way,* make a way for oneself by ~ing; deal cutting blows *at, among,* etc. [OE *hēawan,* OS *hauwan,* OHG *houwan,* ON *höggva* f. Gmc **hauw-*]

hew′er, n. One who hews; man who cuts coal from seam; ~s *of wood & drawers of water,* drudges (Joshua ix. 21). [-ER¹]

hĕx′a- in comb. (before vowel, & in some mod. words before consonant, *hex-*) = Gk *hex* six, as: ~*chord* (-k-), diatonic series of six notes with semitone between third & fourth; ~*gon,* ~*gonal* (-ăg⁴), (figure) having six sides; ~*gram,* figure formed by two intersecting equilateral triangles (the angular points coinciding with those of a ~*gon*), figure of six lines; ~*hĕd′ral* (-a-h-) a., ~*hĕd′ron* (-a-h-) n., (figure) having six faces; ~*pod* n. & a., (insect) with six feet; ~*pody* (-ăp⁴), line of verse of six feet; ~*style* a. & n., (portico) of six columns; ~*syllăb′ic*; ~*teuch* (-k), first six books of Bible.

hĕx′ad, n. A six (uses as PENTAD). [f. Gk *hexas -ados* (*hex* six, -AD)]

hĕxăm′eter, n. Line of six metrical feet, esp. *dactylic* ~ (five dactyls & trochee or spondee, any of first four feet, & rarely the fifth, being replaced by spondee). Hence **hĕxămĕt′ric** a., **hĕxăm′ētrist** n. [L. f. Gk HEXA(*metros* f. *metron* measure)]

hĕx′apla, n.. Six-fold text in parallel columns, esp. of Old or New Testament. [Gk, neut. pl. of HEXA(*ploos* -fold)]

hey (hā), int. calling attention, or of joy, surprise, or interrogation; ~ *for* — ! (expr. applause or exultant appreciation); ~ *presto* (conjuror's phrase of command, hence used to announce surprising transformation etc.). [ME, Du., G]

hey′day¹ (hā-), int. expr. joy, surprise, etc. [16th c., orig. obsc.; cf. LG (G) *heidi, heida,* excl. denoting gaiety]

hey′day² (hā-), n. Full bloom, flush, (of youth, vigour, prosperity, etc.). [16th c., perh. sb. use of prec.; later assoc. w. *day*]

heyduck (hī′dook), n. Hungarian of an ennobled military class; Polish liveried retainer. [f. Pol. *hajduk* brigand]

hi, int. calling attention. [parallel form to HEY]

hiāt′us, n. (pl. ~es). Break, gap, esp. in a series, account, or chain of proof; break between two vowels coming together not in the same syllable. [L, vbl n. f. *hiare* gape]

hib′ern|āte, v.i. Spend the winter (of animals) in torpid state, (of persons) in mild climate; (fig.) remain inactive. So ~ANT a., ~A′TION n. [f. L *hibernare* (*hibernus* wintry), see -ATE³]

Hibĕrn′ian, a. & n. (Native) of Ireland. [f. L *Hibernia* + -AN]

Hibĕrn′icism, n. Irish idiom, expression, or bull. [as prec., on *Anglicism* etc.]

hibis′cus, n. Cultivated malvaceous plant or shrub; rose-mallow. [L f. Gk *hibiskos* marsh mallow]

hicc′up, n., & v.i. & t. Involuntary spasm of respiratory organs, with sudden closure of glottis & characteristic sound; (v.i.) make ~; (v.t.) say, bring *out,* with ~(s). [(vb f. n.) earlier *hicket,* imit.; *hiccough* due to pop. etym.]

hĭc jā′cĕt, n. Epitaph. [L, = here lies]

*hick, H-, n. (colloq.). Countryman, farmer, provincial. [by-form of *Richard;* cf. *Dick*]

hick′ory, n. N.-Amer. tree allied to walnut, with tough heavy wood; wood, stick, of this. [f. native Virginian *pohickery*]

hid, hidden. See HIDE².

hidăl′gō, n. (pl. ~s). Spanish gentleman. [Sp., f. *hijo dalgo* son of a 'somebody']

hide¹, n., & v.t. 1. Animal's skin, raw or dressed; (joc.) human skin, as *to save his own* ~; ~′*bound,* (of cattle) with skin clinging close as result of bad feeding, (fig.) narrow-minded. 2. v.t. (colloq.). Flog. Hence (-)hĭd′ED² a. [OE *hўd,* OS *hūd,* OHG *hūt,* ON *húth* f. Gmc **hudhiz* cogn. w. L *cutis*]

hide², v.t. & i. (past hĭd, p.p. *hidden, hĭd*), & n. 1. Put, keep, out of sight (~ one's *light under a* BUSHEL); keep (fact) secret (*from*); keep (thing) from view without that intention; ~ one's *head,* keep out of sight from shame etc.; (intr.) conceal oneself; ~-*&-seek,* children's game (also fig. of dealings with evasive person or thing). **2.** n. Place of concealment used in observation of wild animals; ~-*out* (colloq.), hiding-place. [OE *hȳdan*, MLG, MDu. *hūden*, f. WG *hūdjan*]

hide[3], n. (hist.). Measure of land, as much as would support one free family & dependants (varied from 60 to 120 acres according to locality). [OE *hīd*, *hīgid*, f. *hīw-*, *hīg-* household]

hid'eous, a. Frightful, repulsive, revolting, to senses or mind, as ~ *crime*, *noise*, *pattern*. Hence ~LY[2] adv., ~NESS n. [ME, f. AF *hidous* = OF *hidos*, *-eus*, earlier *hisdos* f. *hisde* horror, of unkn. orig.; see -EOUS]

hid'ing[1], n. Thrashing. [f. HIDE[1]+-ING[1]]

hid'ing[2], n. In vbl senses of HIDE[2], esp.: *be in* ~, remain hidden; ~-*place*, place of concealment. [-ING[1]]

hie, v.i. (poet.; part. *hying*). Go quickly (*to* etc.); (with pers. pron. used reflexively, orig. dat.) ~ *thee*, *he* ~*d him*. [OE *hīgian* strive, pant, cf. MDu., MLG *higen* pant]

hi'erärch (-k), n. Chief priest; archbishop. [f. med. L (*-cha*) f. Gk *hierarkhēs* (*hieros* sacred +*-arkhēs* ruler)]

hi'erärchy (-k-), n. Each of three divisions of angels; the angels; priestly government; organized priesthood in successive grades; any graded organization. Hence hierärch'ic(AL) aa., hi'erärchism(3) n., (-k-). [ME, f. OF *ierarchie* or LL (*ier-*) f. Gk *hierarkhia* (as prec.)]

hierät'ic, a. Of the priests (esp. of ancient Egyptian writing, & of Egyptian & Greek traditional styles of art); priestly. [f. L f. Gk *hieratikos* f. *hieraomai* be a priest (*hiereus*), -IC]

hiero- in comb. = Gk *hieros* sacred, holy, as: ~*cracy* (-ŏk[2]), priestly rule; ~*gram*, ~*graph*, (hĭ[2]), sacred inscription or symbol; ~*latry* (-ŏl[2]), worship of saints; ~*logy* (-ŏl[2]), sacred literature or lore.

hi'eroglyph, n. Figure of an object standing for a word, syllable, or sound, as used in ancient Egyptian & other writing; writing of this kind; secret symbol; writing difficult to make out. [f. foll.]

hieroglyph'ic, a. & n. **1.** Of, written in, hieroglyphs; symbolical. **2.** n. pl. Hieroglyphs. Hence ~AL a., ~ALLY[2] adv. [f. F *-ique* or LL f. Gk HIERO(*gluphikos* f. *gluphē* carving, see -IC)]

hi'erophänt, n. (Gk Ant.) initiating priest; expounder of sacred mysteries. Hence **hierophän'tic** a. [f. LL f. Gk HIERO(*phantēs* f. *phainō* show)]

hï'-fï'. See HIGH-*fidelity*.

hig'gle, v.i. Dispute about terms; chaffer. [app. modification of HAGGLE]

hig'gledy-pig'gledy (-geld-), adv., a., & n. (In) utter confusion. [symbolic]

high (hï), a., n., & adv. **1.** Of great or specified upward extent, as *a* ~ *hill*, *one inch* ~; situated far above ground, sea level, etc.; upper, inland, as H~ *Asia*, H~ *Dutch*, *German*; (of physical actions) extending to or from, performed at, a

height, as ~ *jump*, ~ *flying*; of exalted rank; *the Most H*~, God; of exalted quality, as ~ *art*, ~ *minds*; ~ *spirit* (courageous, enterprising); *a* ~ (very favourable) *opinion of*; ~ *life*, that of the upper classes; ~ (luxurious) *feeding*; (of meat or game) slightly tainted; great, intense, extreme, as *in* ~ *favour*, ~ *pressure*, ~ *temperature*; *how is that for* ~ ? (sl. appeal to wonder); ~ *latitude* (far from equator); ~ *colour*, (esp.) red complexion, flush, blush; expensive, as *corn is* ~; (of time) far advanced, as ~ *noon*, *it is* ~ *time to go*; (of sounds) acute in pitch, shrill; ~ (angry) *words*; extreme in opinion, as *a* ~ *Tory*; ~ (elated, hilarious) *spirits*; ~ *& dry*, (of ship) out of the water, (fig.) out of the current of events, stranded; (of officers etc.) chief, as *H*~ *Admiral*, *Chancellor*; *with a* ~ *HAND*; *on the* ~ HORSE; ~ *& low*, (people) of all conditions, (adv.) everywhere (esp. *search* ~ *& low*); ~ *& mighty*, arrogant; *on the* ~ *ropes*, (colloq.) elated, disdainful, enraged. **2.** n. A ~ level or figure; the ~*est card* dealt or drawn; *from on* ~, from heaven or *a* ~ *place*; *on* ~, in or to heaven or *a* ~ *place*; *the H*~ (colloq.), H~ Street, esp. at Oxford. **3.** adv. Far up, aloft; in, to, *a* ~ *degree*; at *a* ~ *price*; (of sounds) at, to, *a* ~ *pitch*; *play* ~, play for ~ stakes, *play card of* ~ value; *run* ~, (of sea) have strong current with ~ *tide* (also fig. of feelings). **4.** ~ (chief) *altar*; ~*ball*, a whisky-and-soda served in a tall glass; ~*blower*, horse that flaps nostrils noisily; ~*born*, of noble birth; ~*brow*, a. & n. (colloq.), (person) of detached intellectual or cultural interests (~*browed*, of ~*brow* kind); H~ *Church* n. & a., (party, principles) giving a ~ place to authority of Episcopate and priesthood, saving grace of sacraments, etc.; H~*Churchman*, holder of these principles; ~(*er*) *command*, the commander-in-chief of an army and his staff; ‖H~ *Court* (*of Justice*), court below Court of Appeal, see JUDICATURE; ~ *day*, festal day; ~ EXPLOSIVE; ~ *falut'in*(g) (-lōō-) a. & n. [orig. unkn.], bombast(ic); ~ *farming*, extensive use of fertilizers in cultivation; ~-*fidelity* a., (of radio receiver etc.) reproducing sound faithfully (colloq. abbr. *hi-fi*); ~'-*flown*, extravagant, bombastic; ~'*flyer*, *-flier*, (fig.) ambitious person, one who has ~-*flown* notions; ~'*flying*, (fig.) ambitious; ~ FREQUENCY; ~-*handed*, overbearing, arbitrary; ~*-hat*, (n.) person affecting superiority, (v.t.) treat superciliously, (v.i.) assume a superior attitude; ~ JINKS; *High'lander*, inhabitant of (esp. the Scottish) Highlands; *Highland line*, imaginary line dividing Highlands of Scotland from Lowlands; ~*lands*, mountainous or elevated country, esp. (*Highlands*) hilly parts of N. Scotland; ~'*light*, (of paintings etc.) any of the brightest parts of the subject or its representation (often pl.), moment or detail of vivid interest, outstanding feature; ~*'light* v.t., bring into prominence; ~*lows* (arch.), boots reaching over ankles; ~ MASS[1]; ~*-mind'ed*, of morally lofty character, (arch.) proud (*Lord, I am not* ~*-minded*); ~*-mind'edness*, one of these qualities; ~*-pitched*, (of sound) acute in pitch, (of roof etc.) steep, (fig.) of lofty character; ~ *priest*, chief priest, esp. of the Jews; ~ *priori road* (joc.), resort to assumption (see A PRIORI) in preference to reasoning; ~*-ranking*, senior; ~ *road*, main road; ~ *school* (for secondary education); ~ SEAs; ~*'spirited*, of lofty or courageous spirit; ~*'stepp'er*, horse that lifts its feet ~ in walking & trotting (also fig.); ‖ H~ *Street* (often proper name of principal street in town, at Oxford usu. *the H*~); ~*'strung'*, in ~ state of vigour or sensitiveness; ‖ ~*table* (for the fellows of college, colloq. *the* ~); ~ *tea*, tea at which meat is served; ~ TIDE; ~ TREASON; ~ *water*, state of tide when water is ~est, time when tide is at the full; ~*-wa'ter mark*, level reached at ~ water, (fig.) recorded maximum in any fluctuation; ~*'way*, public road (often *the queen's, king's,* ~*way*), main route by land or water, (fig.) ordinary direct course (of action etc.); ‖*Highway Code*, an official code of directions for road users (first issued 1930); ~*'wayman*, man (usu. mounted, cf. FOOT-*pad*) who robs passengers on ~*way*; ~-WING. [OE *hēah*, OS, OHG *hōh*, ON *hár*, Goth. *hauhs* f. Gmc *hauhaz*]

high'ly (hīl-), adv. In a high degree, as ~ *amusing,* ~ *polished,* ~ *probable*; com*mend, esteem*, ~; honourably, favourably, as *think, speak,* ~ *of*; ~ *descended* (of noble parentage). [OE *hēalice* (as prec., see -LY[2])]

high'ness (hīn-), n. Title of various British and other princes etc., as *His, Her, (Royal, Serene, Imperial) H*~; (used where *height* is not idiomatic) *the*~ *of his character, of taxation, fell from sheer* ~ *of* (but *reached the height of his) ambition.* [OE *hēanes* (as HIGH, see -NESS)]

hight (hīt), p.p. (arch., poet., joc.). Called, named. [p.p. (from 14th c.) of OE *hātan*]

•hi'jacker, n. (sl.). Person who preys on bootleggers, appropriating & profiting by their illicit liquor. [orig. unkn.]

hijra, n. = HEGIRA.

hike, n., & v.i. & t. (colloq.). 1. Long tramp in the country undertaken for pleasure or exercise, walking-tour. 2. vb. Walk vigorously or laboriously; go for long tramp; HITCH[1]~; hoist, shove, force to move. Hence hik'ER[1] n. [orig. unkn.]

hilar'ious, a. Mirthful, joyous. Hence or cogn. ~LY[2] adv., ~NESS, hilā'RITY, nn. [f. L *hilaris*+-OUS]

‖ **Hil'ary,** n. ~ *term*, legal or university term beginning in Jan. [*Hilarius,* d. 367, w. festival 13 Jan.]

hill, n., & v.t. Natural elevation of earth's surface, small mountain; *the* ~*s* (Anglo-Ind.), a ~*-station* as health-resort etc.; heap, mound, however raised, as *ant-, dung-, mole-,* ~; (v.t.) form into ~, bank *up* (plants) with soil. Hence ~*'Y*[2] a., ~*'iNESS* n. [OE *hyll,* MDu. *hil(le), hul,* LG *hull;* cogn. w. L *collis*]

hillo', **-loa'** (-lō), (or hī[2]-), int. used to hail distant person or to express surprise at meeting. [cf. HALLO]

hill'ock, n. Small hill or mound. [-OCK]

hilt, n., & v.t. Handle of sword or dagger; *prove etc. up to the* ~, completely; (v.t.) furnish with ~. [OE, MDu. *hilt,* ON *hjalt;* also OS *hilta,* OHG *helza*]

hil'um, n. (bot.; pl. -la). Point of attachment of seed to seed-vessel. [L, = little thing, trifle]

him, pron. Objective case of HE; colloq. also subjective, esp. after *than,* as *that's* ~, *you are worse than* ~. [OE, dat. of HE & IT]

himself', pron. Emphatic & reflexive form corr. to HE, as *he did it* ~, *he* ~ *told me, I saw the man* ~, *he hurt* ~; *he is not* ~ (not in his normal state of body or mind). [HIM+SELF]

hind[1], n. Female of (esp. red) deer, esp. in and after third year. [OE, ON *hind,* also OHG *hinta;* f. Gmc *hindō*]

‖ **hind**[2], n. Farm servant, esp. (in Scotland & northern England) married & skilled farm-workman, formerly having charge of two horses, & provided with cottage on the farm; steward; rustic, boor. [ME *hine* f. OE *hine* pl., app. f. *hina, higna* gen. pl. of *hīgan, hīwan* 'members of a family'; cf. HIDE[3]]

hind[3], a. Situated at the back, posterior, (less usu. than *hinder* exc. of things in pairs, front & back, as ~ *leg, quarters, wheel).* [ME (cf. OE *hindan* adv.), of uncert. orig.; perh. (1) shortened f. OE *behindan* BEHIND, or (2), less likely, f. HINDER adj.; ult. extended f. *hin-* (HENCE) f. *hi-* (HE)]

hind'er[1], a. See prec.

hin'der[2], v.t. Impede, obstruct, prevent, as *you will* ~ *him,* ~ *his work,* ~ *its completion,* ~ *him from working* (or abs.). [ME *hindre* f. OE *hindrian* (= ON *hindra,* OHG *hintarōn*) f. Gmc *•hindar* HIND[3]]

Hin'di (-ē), a. & n. (Of) a major set of languages (*W. & E.*~) of N. India. [Hindi *(Hindī* India)]

hind'most, a. Furthest behind; most remote. [HIND[3]]

hin'drance, n. Obstruction, prevention; obstacle. [f. HINDER[2]+-ANCE]

hind'sight (-sīt), n. Back sight of gun; wisdom after the event (opp. *foresight).* [HIND[3], SIGHT[1]]

Hindu' (-dōō), **-doo'**, (or hī[2]-), n. & a. 1. Aryan of N. India who (also, any one who) professes Hinduism. 2. adj. Of the ~s, that is a ~; (loosely) Indian. [Pers., f. *hind* India = Skr. *Sindhu* river (esp. the Indus)]

Hin'duism (-ōō-), **-dooism**, n. Polytheistic religion of the Hindus. [-ISM]

Hin'duize (-ōō-), **-dooize**, **-ise** (-iz), v.t. Render Hindu in religion, customs, etc. [-IZE]

Hindusta'ni (-ahnē), a. & n. **1.** adj. Of Hindustan or its people; of Hindustani. **2.** n. An Indic language with large admixture of Arabic, Persian, etc., current as standard language & lingua franca in much of India & Pakistan. [Hindi, = of *Hindustan* (HINDU + *-stan* place)]

hinge (-j), n., & v.t. & i. **1.** Movable joint or mechanism like that by which door is hung on side post; natural joint doing similar work, as that of bivalve shell; small piece of gummed paper for fastening postage stamp to album or sheet; *off the ~s*, in disordered state of body or mind; (fig.) central principle, critical point, on which all turns. **2.** v.t. Attach (as) with ~. **3.** v.i. (Of door etc. or fig.) hang & turn *on* (post, principle, etc.). Hence **hinged**[2] (-jd), **~'LESS** (-jl-), aa. [ME *heng* rel. to HANG; cf. MLG *heng(e)*, Du. *henghe* hinge]

hinn'y[1], n. Offspring of she-ass by stallion, cf. MULE[1]. [f. L *hinnus*]

‖ **hinn'y**[2], **-nie.** See HONEY.

hint, n., & v.t. & i. **1.** Slight indication, covert or indirect suggestion. **2.** v.t. Suggest slightly (thing, *that*). **3.** v.i. ~ *at*, give a ~ of. [(vb f. n.) app. f. obs. *hent* (OE *hentan*) lay hold of, of uncert. orig.]

hin'terland, n. District behind coast or river's banks, occas. with suggestion of sparse population or inferior civilization. [G]

hip[1], n. Projection of pelvis & upper part of thigh-bone, in men & quadrupeds; *have* (person) *on the* ~ (at a disadvantage); *smite* ~ *& thigh* (unsparingly); (Archit.) arris of roof from ridge to eaves; ~*-bath* (in which one sits immersed to the ~s); ~*-disease* (of ~-joint, with fungous growth); ~*-roof* (with ends as well as sides inclined). Hence (-)**hipped**[2] (-pt) a. [OE *hype*, OHG *huf*, Goth. *hups* f. Gmc **hupiz*]

hip[2], **hep,** n. Fruit of (esp. wild) rose. [OE *hēope*, OS *hiopo*, OHG *hiufo* f. Gmc **heup-*]

hip[3], **hyp,** n. Morbid depression, the blues. [= *hyp*(ochondria)]

hip[4], v.t. (-pp-). Make low-spirited. [f. prec.]

hip[5], int. Introducing united cheer, as ~, ~, hurrah.

hipe, v.t., & n. Throw (antagonist in wrestling) in a particular manner; (n.) such throw. [perh. f. HIP[1]]

hipp'o, n. (colloq.; pl. ~s). Hippopotamus. [abbr.]

hippo- in comb. = Gk *hippos* horse, as: ~*cen'taur*, = CENTAUR; ~*phagy* (-ŏf²), practice of eating horse-flesh; ~PHIL (hǐ²); ~PHOB'IA.

hippocam'pus, n. (pl. *-pī*). Kinds of small fishes, sea-horse; (Anat.) ~ *major*, *minor*, eminences on floor of each lateral ventricle of brain. [f. L f. Gk HIPPO-(*kampos* sea-monster)]

hipp'ocras, n. (hist.). Wine flavoured with spices. [ME, f. OF *ipocras* f. *Hippo-kratēs* Gk physician of 5th c. B.C., prob. because strained through filter called *Hippocrates's sleeve*]

Hipp'ocrēne, n. Fountain on Mount Helicon sacred to the Muses. [L f. Gk (*hippos* horse, *krēnē* fountain, as having been produced by stroke of Pegasus's hoof)]

hipp'odrōme, n. (Gk & Rom. Ant.) course for chariot races etc.; circus; (*H~*) theatre for various stage entertainments. [F, or f. L f. Gk HIPPO(*dromos* race, course)]

hipp'ogrïph, -grȳph, n. Fabulous griffin--like creature with body of horse. [f. F *hippogriffe* f. It. *ippogrifo* (HIPPO- + *grifo* GRIFFIN)]

hippopŏt'amus, n. (pl. *-muses*, *-mī*). Large African pachydermatous quadruped inhabiting rivers etc. [ME, f. L f. Gk HIPPO(*potamos* river)]

hir'cine, a. Goat-like. [f. L *hircinus* (*hircus* goat, see -INE[1])]

hire[1], n. Payment by contract for use of thing or for personal service; engagement on these terms; (fig.) reward; ‖ ~*-pur-chase*, ~ *system* (by which hired thing becomes hirer's after certain number of payments); *on* ~, ready to be hired. [OE *hȳr*, OLG **hūria*, G *heuer* f. WG **hūrja*]

hire[2], v.t. Employ (person) for wages; procure, grant (also ~ *out*), temporary use of (thing) for stipulated payment; **borrow* (money); **~d girl*, domestic servant. Hence **hir'ABLE** a. [OE *hȳrian*, OLG **hurian* f. prec.]

hire'ling (hīrl-), n. One who serves for hire (usu. derog.). [OE *hȳrling* (as HIRE[1], see -LING[1])]

hirs'ūte, a. Hairy, shaggy; untrimmed. Hence ~NESS (-tn-) n. [f. L *hirsutus*]

his (hǐz), a. & pron. Possessive case of, & adj. corr. to, HE, also in absolute use, as ~ *hat, it is* ~. [OE, genit. of HE & IT]

his'pid, a. (bot., zool.). Shaggy; bristly. [f. L *hispidus*]

hiss, v.i. & t., & n. (Of person, snake, goose, liquid poured on fire, etc.) (make) sharp sibilant sound of *s*, esp. as sign of disapproval or derision; express disapproval of (person etc.) thus; ~ *off* (the stage), *away*, *down*, etc., drive off etc. by ~es; utter (quoted words) with angry ~. [ME; imit.]

hist, int. used to call attention, enjoin silence, or incite dog etc.

histo-, comb. form of Gk *histos* web, tissue, in biol. wds, as: ~*gen'esis*, ~*geny* (-ŏj²), production of organic tissues; ~*genĕt'ic*, concerned with this; ~*logy* (-ŏl²), science of organic tissues, whence

~lo′gical, ~logist (-ŏl̆); ~lysis (-ŏl̆), breaking down of organic tissues.

histŏr′ian, n. Writer of history (esp. in higher sense, as opp. to mere annalist or compiler); *English, ancient,* ~, writer or student of English, ancient, history. [f. F *historien* f. L as HISTORY +-AN]

histŏr′iātĕd, a. (Of ornamental letters etc.) decorated with figures of men or animals. [f. med. L *historiare* (as HISTORY), see -ATE²]

histŏ′ric, a. Noted in history; (Lat. & Gk Gram.) ~ *tenses,* those normally used of past events, imperfect, Gk aorist & Lat. perfect in same sense, pluperfect, (cf. PRIMARY), ~ *present* (used for past), ~ *infinitive* (used for indicative); = foll. [f. L f. Gk *historikos* (as HISTORY, see -IC)]

histŏ′rical, a. Of history, as ~ *evidence, principles;* belonging to history, not legend; ~ *method* (of investigation), that based on history; in connexion with history, from the historian's point of view (of *purely* ~ *interest*); belonging to the past, not of the present; (of novel, picture, etc.) dealing with ~ events; = prec. Hence~LY² adv. [-AL]

histori′citў, n. Historical character, genuineness, of alleged event etc. [-ITY]

histŏriŏg′rapher, n. Writer of history, esp. official historian of a court etc. [f. LL *historiographus* (as HISTORY, see -GRAPHER)]

histŏriŏg′raphў, n. Writing of history. Hence histŏriŏgráph′IC(AL) aa. [f. Gk *historiographia* (as foll., see -GRAPHY)]

his′torў, n. Continuous methodical record of public events; (no pl.) study of growth of nations; whole train of events connected with nation, person, thing, etc.; eventful past career, as *this knife has a* ~; (no pl.) aggregate of past events, course of human affairs; *ancient* ~ (usu. to A.D. 476), (joc.) thing that is out of date; *medieval, modern,* ~ (to, from, 15th c.); systematic account of natural phenomena etc., esp. NATURAL¹ ~; historical play. [late ME, f. L *historia*]

his′trion, n. Stage-player (usu. derog.). [16th c. f. F, or L *histrio*]

histriŏn′lic, a. & n. 1. Of actors or acting; stagy, hypocritical, whence his′trionISM, ~ĭcISM, nn. 2. n. pl. Theatricals, theatrical art, pretence. Hence ~ICALLY adv. [17th c. (16th c. *-ical*) f. prec., or as prec., +-IC; cf. LL *histrionicus,* F *-ique*]

hit¹, v.t. & v.i. 1. (*hit*). Strike with blow or missile; direct blow *at*; (of moving body) strike; (intr.) strike *against, upon*; deliver (blow, person etc. a blow); (fig.) affect sensibly, wound, as *hard* ~ (e.g. by money losses); (also ~ *upon*) light upon, get at, (thing aimed at); (also ~ *off*) imitate to a nicety; fall in with, suit; ~ *below the belt,* play foul in boxing & fig.; ~ *it,* ~ *the* (right) *nail on the head,* guess right, express the exact truth; ~ *it off,*

agree (*with, together*); ~ *out,* deal vigorous blows; ~ *up* (Cricket), score, make (runs). [late OE *hittan,* f. ON *hitta* meet with]

hit², n. Blow, stroke; stroke of sarcasm etc. (*at*); stroke of good luck; successful attempt. [f. prec.]

hitch¹, v.t. & i. Move (thing) with jerk; shift; ~ *up,* lift with jerk; contrive to bring (thing *into* story etc.); fasten with loop, hook, etc.; become so fastened (*in, on to,* etc.); ~ *one's* WAGON *to a star;* •~ *-hike* v.i., & n., travel by begging lifts from passing motor vehicles. [15th c., of obsc. orig.; partly syn. w. Sc. *hotch* move by jerks]

hitch², n. Jerk, abrupt pull or push; (Naut.) noose, knot, of various kinds, as *half* ~ (formed by passing end of rope round its standing part & then through the bight); CLOVE~; temporary stoppage; impediment. [f. prec.]

hith′er (-dh-), adv. & a. 1. To, towards, this place (now usu. *here*); ~ *& thither,* in various directions, here & there. 2. adj. Situated on this side, *the* nearer (of two). 3. ~*to′* (-tŏŏ), up to this time; ~*ward* (arch.), in this direction. [OE *hider,* corresp. to ON *hethra,* Goth. *hidrē,* f. hi-(HE) +suf. cogn. w. L (*ci*)*tra; -th-* as in FATHER]

Hit′ler|ism, n. The political system, aims, or methods of the German Fuehrer, Adolf Hitler (1889–1945). So ~ITE¹(1) a. & n. [-ISM]

Hitt′ite, n. & a. 1. Member, language, of an ancient people of Turkey & Syria. 2. adj. Of the ~s or ~. [f. Heb. *Hittim*]

hive, n. & v.t. & i. 1. (Also *bee*~) artificial habitation for bees; (fig.) busy swarming place; ~ful of bees; swarming multitude; ~-shaped thing. 2. v.t. Place (bees) in ~, house (persons etc.) snugly, hoard up; (v.i.) enter ~, live together like bees; ~ *off,* (of firm) assign production of some goods to subsidiary company. [OE *hýf* (= Gmc type **hūfiz*), not repr. elsewhere in Gmc; whence ON *húfr* hull of ship]

hives (-vz), n. pl. Skin eruption; inflammation of bowels, larynx, etc. [Sc. & north. (f. c. 1500), of unkn. orig.]

h′m. = HEM³, HUM².

hō, int. expr. surprise, admiration, triumph, derision; calling attention; added to other intt. as *heigh-ho, what ho,* or (Naut.) to name of destination etc., as *westward ho.* [ME; imit.; cf. ON *hó*]

hoar (hōr), a. & n. 1. Grey-haired with age; greyish white; ~*-frost,* frozen water vapour deposited in clear still weather on lawns etc.; (of things) grey with age; ||~*'stone,* ancient boundary stone. 2. n. Hoariness, ~*-frost.* [OE *hār,* OHG *hēr,* ON *hárr* f. Gmc **hairaz*]

hoard (hōrd), n., & v.t. & i. 1. Stock, store, (esp. of money) laid by; amassed stock of facts etc.; (Archaeol.) ancient cache of treasure etc. 2. v.t. Amass (money etc. or abs.) & put away, store *up*; treasure up in the heart; (v.i.) overstock oneself with food etc. in time of scarcity. [OE. OS *hord*, OHG *hort*, ON *hodd*, Goth. *huzd* f. Gmc *huzdom*]

‖ **hoard'ing** (hōr-), n. Fence of boards round building during erection or repairs, often used for posting bills. [f. obs. *hoard* (-ING[1]) f. AN *hurdis* f. OF *hourd*, *hourt* f. WG *hord* (= OHG *hurd*); see HURDLE]

hoarhound. See HOREHOUND.

hoarse (hōrs), a. (Of voice) rough, husky, croaking; having such a voice. Hence ~'LY[2] (-si-) adv., hoars'EN[6] v.t. & i., ~[2] NESS (-sn-) n. [late ME *hors* f. ON *hārs* f. Gmc *hairsaz*; earlier ME *hōs*, OE *hās*, OS *hēs*, OHG *heis*(i) f. Gmc *haisaz*]

hoar'|y (hōr-), a. (Of hair) grey, white, with age; having such air, venerable; (Bot., Entom.) covered with short white hairs. Hence ~iNESS n. [-Y[2]]

hoax, v.t. & n. 1. Deceive, take in, (person) by way of joke. 2. n. Humorous or mischievous deception. [c. 1800, app. contr. f. HOCUS]

hŏb, n. Side casing of fireplace, having surface level with top of grate; peg, pin, as mark in quoits etc.; ‖ shoe of sledge; = HOBNAIL. [orig. unkn.]

hŏb'ble[1], v.i. & t. Walk lamely, limp; (fig.) proceed haltingly in action or speech; (of verse) have halting rhythm; cause to ~; tie together legs of (horse etc.) to prevent it from straying etc.; tie (legs) thus. [(1) 14th c.; prob. LG; cf. Du. *hobbelen* rock from side to side, stammer; (2) see HOPPLE]

hŏb'ble[2], n. Uneven or infirm gait; awkward situation; rope, clog, etc., for hobbling horse etc.; ~ *skirt* (so narrow at foot as to impede wearer in walking). [f. prec.]

hŏb'blede|hoy' (-beldi-), hŏbbad-, hŏb-bĕd-, n. Awkward youth, between boyhood & manhood. Hence ~hoy'HOOD, ~hoy'ISM, ~hoy'ISH[1] a. (-beldi-). [16th c.; of many forms, & much disputed orig.]

hŏbb'y̆, n. Favourite subject or occupation that is not one's main business; (arch.) small horse; (hist.) early type of velocipede. [ME *hobyn, hoby*, a by-name of *Robin*; cf. DOBBIN]

hŏbb'y̆[2], n. A small falcon. [f. OF *hobe*]

hŏbb'y̆-hŏrse, n. Wicker horse used in morris-dance etc.; child's stick with horse's head; rocking-horse; horse on merry-go-round; (now rare) = HOBBY[1].

hŏb'gŏblin, n. Mischievous imp; bogy; bugbear. [f. *hob* for *Rob*(in) + GOBLIN]

hŏb'nail, n. Heavy-headed nail for boot-soles. [HOB]

hŏb'nailed (-ld), a. Furnished or set with hobnails; ~ *liver* (studded with projections like nail-heads). [-ED[2]]

hŏb'nŏb, v.i. (-bb-). Drink together; hold familiar intercourse (*with*). [f. *hob* or *nob* = give & take, earlier *hab nab*, = have or not have]

*hŏb'ō, n. (pl. ~s). Wandering workman or tramp. [orig. unkn.]

Hŏb'son's choice. See CHOICE[1]. [person]

hŏck[1], n. Joint of quadruped's hindleg between true knee & fetlock. [southern by-form of HOUGH]

hŏck[2], n. German white wine (prop. that of Hochheim). [17th c., short f. G *Hoch-heimer*]

hŏck[3], v.t. & n. (sl.). Pawn, pledge; *in* ~, in pawn, in prison, or in debt. [f. Du. *hok* in sl. sense of debt]

hŏck'ey, n. Game played with ball (or puck in *ice* ~) & curved clubs between goals. [16th c., orig. unkn.]

Hŏck'tīde, n. (hist.). Old festival kept on second Monday and Tuesday after Easter. [ME *hoke*, of unkn. orig.]

hŏc'us, v.t. (-ss-). Take in, hoax; stupefy (person) with drugs; drug (liquor). [f. obs. n. *hocus*=foll.]

hŏc'us-pŏc'us, n., & v.i. & t. (-ss-). Jugglery, deception; typical conjuring formula; (v.i.) juggle; (v.t.) play tricks on. [17th-c. sham L]

hŏd, n. Builder's light open trough on staff for carrying mortar etc.; ~'*man*, labourer who carries ~, (fig.) mechanical worker, literary hack. [prob. = dial. *hot* f. OF *hotte* pannier, of Gmc orig.]

‖ **hŏdd'en,** n. (Sc.). Coarse woollen cloth; ~ *grey*, grey ~, typical rustic garb. [orig. unkn.]

‖ **Hŏdge,** n. Typical English agricultural labourer. [pet form of *Roger*]

hŏdge'pŏdge, n. = HOTCHPOTCH. [assim. to prec.]

hŏdiĕrn'al, a. Of the present day. [f. L *hodiernus* (*hodie* today) + -AL]

hŏdŏm'ĕter, ŏd-, n. Instrument for measuring distance travelled by wheeled vehicle. [f. F *odomètre* f. Gk *hodos* way, see -METER]

hoe, n., & v.t. & i. (part. ~ing). 1. Tool for loosening soil, scraping up weeds, etc.; *Dutch* ~, kind pushed forward by user. 2. v.t. Weed (crops), loosen (ground), dig *up*, cut *down*, with ~; (v.i.) use ~. [ME, f. OF *houe* f. OFrank. *hauwa* f. Gmc *hauwan* HEW]

hŏg[1], n. Swine, esp. castrated male reared for slaughter; ‖ (dial.) young sheep before first shearing; (fig.) coarse, gluttonous, or filthy person; = ROAD[1]~; *go the whole* ~, do the thing thoroughly; ~'*back*, ~'*s-back*, crested hill-ridge; ~'*-fish*, fish with bristles on head; ~ *in armour*, stiff clumsy person; ~ *mane*, horse's mane cut short; ~'s *pudding*, ~'s entrail variously stuffed; ~'*wash*, kitchen swill etc. for ~s. Hence ~g'ISH[1] (-g-), ~g'LIKE, aa., ~g'ISH-LY[2] adv., ~g'ISHNESS, ~g'LING[1], nn. [14th c., deriv. *hoggaster* 12th c.; orig. unkn.]

hŏg[2], v.t. & i. (-gg-). Raise (back etc.), rise, archwise in the centre; cut (mane) short; (colloq.) behave like a road-hog. [f. prec.]

‖ **högg′ĕt** (-g-), n. Yearling sheep. [HOG¹ +-ET¹]

högg′ĭn (-g-), n. Mixture of sand & gravel. [19th c., of unkn. orig.]

hŏg′manay, n. (Sc.). Last day of year; gift of cake etc. demanded by children on that day. [17th c., corresp. in sense & use to OF *aguillanneuf*, of unkn. orig.; the Norman form *hoguinané* may have been the immed. source]

hŏgs′head (-z-hĕd), n. Large cask; liquid measure, 52¼ imperial gallons (abbr. *hhd*). [ME, f. HOG¹+HEAD; orig. unexpl.]

hoi(c)k, v.t. & i. Force (aeroplane) to turn abruptly upwards; ~ aeroplane. [orig. unkn.]

hoick(s), int. used to incite hounds (also *yoicks*). [orig. unkn.]

hoi polloi. See POLLOI.

hoist¹, v.t., & n. 1. Raise aloft (esp. flags); raise by means of tackle etc. 2. n. ~ing, shove up; goods elevator, lift. [16th c. alt. of *hoise* f. (15th c.) *hysse*, prob. of LG orig.; cf. LG *hissen* (16th c.), Du. *hijschen*]

hoist², p.p. ~ *with his own petard*, blown up by his own bomb, ruined by his own devices against others. [p.p. of *hoise*, see prec.]

hoit′y-toit′y, n., a., & int. 1. n. (arch.). Riotous or giddy conduct. 2. adj. Frolicsome; haughty; petulant. 3. int. expr. surprised protest at undue assumption etc. [17th c., f. obs. *hoit* indulge in riotous mirth; orig. unkn.]

hŏk′ey-pōk′ey, n. = HOCUS-POCUS; cheap ice-cream sold by street vendors. [f. HOCUS-POCUS; second sense of unkn. orig.]

hŏk′um, n. (orig. U.S., sl.). Theatrical plot or business, (now esp.) film scenario, designed to appeal to the uncritical; bunkum. [orig. unkn.]

hōld¹, v.t. & i. (*hĕld*); also arch. p.p. *~en* in formal reports of meetings etc.). 1. Keep fast, grasp (*held l* at Rugby football, claim that ball being held by opponent as well as runner must be put down); keep (oneself, one's head, etc.) in particular attitude, esp. *up*; (of vessel) contain; possess, be the owner or holder or tenant of, (property, stocks, land); (Mil.) keep possession of (place); occupy (place, person's thoughts, etc.); engross (person, his attention); keep (person etc.) in specified place, condition, etc., as ~ *him at bay, in suspense*; *detain in custody; ~ *thing over* one, threaten him constantly with it; make (person) adhere *to* (terms, promise), observe, celebrate, conduct, (festival, meeting, conversation); use (insolent etc. language); ~ *to* (bind by) *bail*; restrain, as ~ *your noise, tongue*, (~ one's *hand*, refrain from punishing or other action; *there is no ~ing* him etc., he etc. is restive or in high spirits or determined); think, believe, (thing, *that*, person etc. *to* be; ~ *it good*, think it advisable *to* do); (of judge

or court) lay down, decide (*that*); entertain specified feeling towards, as ~ *him in esteem, contempt*; ~ *thing cheap* (not value it); ~ *dear* (regard with affection). 2. intr. Remain unbroken, not give way; ~ *by, to*, adhere to (choice, purpose, etc.); ~ *with* (sl., usu. neg.), approve of; (of laws etc., also ~ *good, true*) be valid, apply; keep going, esp. ~ *on* one's *way*; (arch.) ~ *l*, stop, wait. 3. ~ one's *head high*, behave proudly; ~ *up* one's *head*, not be downcast; ~ one's *ground*, or one's *own*, not give way, (of sick person) not get worse; ~ *the* BABY; ~ *water*, (fig.) be sound, bear examination. 4. ~ *aloof*, avoid communication with persons etc.; ~ *back*, (trans.) restrain, (intr.) hesitate, refrain *from*; *~ *down*, remain in (one's situation), keep (one's job); ~ *forth*, speak publicly (usu. derog.); ~ *hard*, stop (imperative); ~ *in*, confine, keep in check; ~ *off*, (intr.) delay; ~ *on*, keep one's grasp on something, not ring off, (colloq. imper.) stop; ~ *out*, (trans.) stretch forth, offer (inducement etc.), (intr.) endure, persist, (of besieged fortress etc.) keep from yielding; ~ *over*, postpone; ~ *together* t. & i., (cause to) cohere; ~ *up*, support, sustain, (lit. & fig.), exhibit, display, (esp. *to* derision etc.), arrest progress of, obstruct, stop & rob on highway, (of horse) keep up, not fall; *~-up*, detention by force (of person, vehicle, train, etc.), for purposes of robbery (also attrib.), stoppage or delay by traffic, fog, etc. 5. *~all*, portable case for clothes etc.; *~back*, hindrance; *~fast*, firm grasp, staple or clamp securing object to wall etc. [OE *h(e)aldan*, OS *haldan*, OHG *halten*, ON *halda*, Goth. *haldan*]

hōld², n. Grasp (lit. & fig.), esp. *take, get, keep*, ~ *of*; opportunity of holding, thing to hold by; (fig.) ~ (*on*), influence (over). [f. prec.]

hōld³, n. Cavity in ship below deck, where cargo is stowed. [16th c. alt. of 15th c. *holl, hole*, f. MDu. *hol* HOLE]

hōld′er, n. In vbl senses, esp.: occupant of office etc.; contrivance for holding something, as *cigar, pen, ~*. [-ER¹]

hōld′ing, n. In vbl senses, esp.: tenure of land; land held; stocks etc. held; ~ *company*, one created to hold the shares of other companies. [-ING¹]

hōle¹, n. Hollow place in solid body; deep place in stream etc.; animal's burrow; small mean abode; cavity into which ball etc. must be got in various games; (Golf) point scored by player who gets ball from one ~ to another with fewest strokes, distance from tee to ~; perforation; (sl.) awkward situation (*am in rather, a devil of, a hole*); FOX¹~; FUNK~; *pick ~s in*, find fault with; *make a ~ in*, use large amount of; *round (square) peg in square (round) ~*, person not fitted for his place; *~-&-corner*, secret, underhand. Hence **hōl′ex²** a. [OE, OS, OHG,

ON *hol*, neut. of adj. *hol* f. Gmc *hulaz; cogn. w. HELL, HELM[1], HOLLOW]

hōle[2], v.t. & i. Make holes in; (Naut.) pierce side of (ship); make (shaft, tunnel); (Mining, intr.) dig through from one working to another; put into hole; (also ~ *out*) put (golf-ball, or abs.) into hole. [OE *holian*, as prec.]

hŏl'iday (-dĭ *or* -dǎ), n. Day of cessation from work or of recreation; (usu. pl.) period of this, vacation; || BANK[2] ~; BLIND[1] *man's* ~; *make* ~, *take a* ~, cease from work; ~ (gay) *clothes*; || ~ *task* (to be done by schoolboy during ~s); = HOLY *day*. [OE *hāligdæg*, see HOLY & DAY]

hŏl'ilÿ, adv. In a holy manner. [-LY[2]]

hōl'iness, n. Sanctity; *H*~, *his H*~, title of Pope. [OE *hāliġnes* (HOLY, -NESS)]

bŏl'ism, n. (philos.). Tendency in nature to form wholes that are more than the sum of the parts by creative evolution. [as HOLO- + -ISM]

hŏll'a, int. See HOLLO. [f. F *holà*]

Hŏll'and, n. Province of northern Netherlands, kingdom of the Netherlands, whence ~ER[1](4) n.; a linen fabric; *brown* ~, this unbleached. [Du., f. *holt* wood + *-lant* land]

Hŏll'ands (-z), n. A grain spirit. [f. Du. *hollandsch genever*, Holland gin]

hŏll'ō[1], int. calling attention; (n.) the cry ~. [conn. w. HOLLA]

hŏll'ō[2], -low[1] (-ō), -la, -loa (-ō), v.i. & t. Shout (i. & t.); call to hounds. [as prec.]

hŏll'ow[2] (-ō), a., n., & adv. Having a hole, not solid; ~ SQUARE; empty, hungry; (of sound) not full-toned; (fig.) empty, insincere, false; (n.) ~ place, hole, valley, basin; (adv.) *beaten* ~ (completely); ~-*eyed*, with eyes deep sunk; ~-*hearted*, insincere; ~ *race* etc., feebly contested; ~ *ware*, ~ articles of metal, china, etc., as pots, kettles, jugs. Hence ~LY[2] (-ŏlĭ) adv., ~NESS (-ōn-) n. [ME *holg, holu*, adj. f. OE *holh* n., cogn. w. HOLE[1]]

hŏll'ow[3] (-ō), v.t. (Also ~ *out*) excavate; bend into hollow shape. [f. prec.]

|| **Hŏll'oway** (-o-w-), n. (Used for) ~ prison (for women; formerly for debtors). [place]

hŏll'ÿ, n. Evergreen shrub with prickly leaves, small white flowers, & red berries. [f. OE *holegn* (dial. *hollin*), cogn. w. OS, OHG *hulis* (G *hulst*)]

hŏll'ÿhŏck, n. Tall plant with large flowers of many varieties of colour. [f. HOLY + obs. *hock* mallow, OE *hoc*, of unkn. orig.]

Hŏll'ÿwŏŏd, n. (Used for) moving pictures of American type, chiefly made at ~ in California. [place]

bŏlm[1], -me, (hōm), n. Islet, esp. in river or near mainland; || flat ground by river, submerged in time of flood. [f. ON *holmr*]

bŏlm[2] (hōm), n. (Usu. ~-*oak*) evergreen oak, ilex. [ME alt. of obs. *holin*; see HOLLY]

hŏl'o-, comb. form of Gk *holos*-whole, as: ~*graph* a. & n., (document) wholly in handwriting of person in whose name it appears; ~*hĕd'ral*, (of crystal) having full number of planes for perfect symmetry; ~-*metăb'ola* n. pl., insects undergoing complete metamorphosis; ~*phōte*, apparatus for making available all the light of a lamp (in lighthouse etc.).

hŏl'ocaust, n. Whole burnt-offering; wholesale sacrifice (fig.) or destruction. [ME, f. OF *holocauste* f. LL f. Gk HOLO-*kauston* burnt f. *kaiō*)]

hŏlothūr'ian, a. & n. (Animal) of the genus *Holothuria*, sea-slug. [f. mod. L *Holothuria* n. pl. f. Gk *holothourion*, a zoophyte]

holpen. See HELP[1].

hŏl'ster, n. Leather case for pistol, fixed to saddle or worn on belt. [17th-c.; syn. w. Du. *holster*; rel. & orig. unkn.]

|| **hŏlt**[1], n. (Poet.) wood, copse; wooded hill. [OE, OS, ON *holt*, OHG *holz* f. Gmc *hultaz]

hŏlt[2], n. Animal's (esp. otter's) lair. [var. of HOLD[2]]

hŏl'us-bŏl'us, adv. All in a lump, altogether. [app. sham L]

hŏl'ÿ, a. & n. 1. Consecrated, sacred; morally & spiritually perfect; belonging to, commissioned by, devoted to, God; of high moral excellence. 2. n. ~ *of holies*, inner chamber of sanctuary in Jewish temple, separated by veil from ~ *place* or outer chamber, (fig.) innermost shrine. 3. *H*~ *Alliance*, covenant formed in 1815-16 between the sovereigns of Russia, Prussia, and Austria, by which they bound themselves to be guided by Christian principles in domestic and foreign policy; *H*~ CITY; ~ *cross* (of Christ); *H*~ *Cross day*, festival of Exaltation of the Cross, Sep. 14; ~ *day*, religious festival; *H*~ FAMILY; *H*~ *Ghost*, *Spirit*, third person of the Godhead; *H*~ GRAIL; ~ *Joe* (naut. sl.), pious person; *H*~ *Land*, W. Palestine, esp. Judaea; *H*~ OFFICE; ~ ORDERS; *H*~ ROMAN *Empire*; ~ *terror* (sl.), formidable person, embarrassing child, bore; *H*~ *Thursday*, (prop.) Ascension Day, (pop.) Thursday in H~ *Week*; *H*~ *Saturday* (in H~ *Week*); ~ *water*, water dedicated to ~ uses, or blessed by a priest; *H*~ *Week* (before Easter Sunday); ~ *Willie*, a hypocritically pious person; *H*~ *Writ*, ~ writings collectively, esp. the Bible. [OE *hālig*, OS *hēlag*, OHG *heilag*, ON *heilagr*, Goth. *hailags* f. Gmc *hailagaz f. *hailaz WHOLE]

hŏl'ÿstōne, n., & v.t. (Scour with) soft sandstone used for scouring decks. [19th c.; cf. Du. *bijbel*, LG *bibel* in similar naut. use]

hŏm, n. Sacred plant of ancient Persians & Parsees; its juice. [Pers.]

hŏm'age, n. (Feud.) formal public acknowledgement of allegiance; acknowledgement of superiority, dutiful reverence, as *pay, do*, ~ *to* (person, his qualities). [ME, f. OF *omage* f. med. L *hominaticum* (*homo* -*minis* man, see -AGE)] *hombre* (ŏm'brā), n. Man. [Sp.]

Hŏm'bŭrg, n. (Used for) soft felt hat with narrow brim and dent in top of crown, trilby. [~ in Prussia, where first worn]

hŏme¹, n., a., & adv. **1.** Dwelling-place; fixed residence of family or household; native land; ~ *of lost causes,* Oxford; *long* or *last* ~, the grave; place where thing is native or most common; institution of refuge or rest for destitute or infirm persons, as *convalescent, nursing,* ~ (for the sick); (in games) goal; *a* ~ *from* ~, place where one feels at ~; *at* ~, in one's own house or native land, at one's ease, familiar *with* or *on* or *in* (subject etc.), accessible to callers (*esp. not at* ~), (n.) see ⊥T-HOME. **2.** adj. Of, connected with, ~; carried on at ~; proceeding from ~; in the neighbourhood of ~; ‖ H~ *Counties,* those nearest to London (Middlesex, Surrey, Kent, Essex, & occas. Hertford & Sussex); carried on, produced, in one's own country, as ~ *industries, products; the* ~ *trade* or *market* (inland; opp. *foreign*); treating of domestic affairs; ‖ H~ *Office,* department of Secretary of State for H~ Affairs, building used for this; that comes ~ to one, as ~ *question, truth, thrust.* **3.** adv. To one's ~ or country, as *come, go,* ~; arrived at ~, as *he is* ~; to the point aimed at, as *the thrust went* ~; as far as possible, as *drive a nail* ~; *bring charge* ~ *to* person, convict him of it; *come* ~ *to,* be realized by; *nothing to write* ~ *about* (colloq.), unexciting, trivial. **4.** ~-*born,* native; ~-*bred,* bred at ~; ~-*brewed* a. & n., (beer etc.) brewed at ~; ~-*coming,* arrival at home; ~-*felt,* felt intimately; H~ *Guard,* (member of) British citizen army formed in 1940 (orig. called *Local Defence Volunteers*); ~-*keeping* a., stay-at-home; ~-*made,* made at ~ or for ~ consumption; H~ *Rule,* government of a country by its own citizens; ~*sick*(*ness*), depressed, depression, as result of absence from ~; ~*work,* work (to be) done at ~, esp. lessons to be done by a school-child at ~. Hence ~'LESS, ~'LIKE, aa., (-ml-). [OE *hām,* OS *hēm,* OHG *heim,* ON *heimr,* Goth. *haims*]

hŏme², v.i. & t. Go home (esp. of pigeons); send or guide homewards; furnish (person etc.) with a home. [f. prec.]

hŏme'llў (-ml-), a. Simple, plain; primitive; unpretending; *(of persons or features) uncomely, plain. Hence ~INESS n. [-LY¹]

homeo-. See under *homoeo-.*

hŏm'er, n. Homing pigeon. [-ER¹]

Home'rĭc, a. Of, in the style of, Homer or the poems ascribed to him; ~ *laughter* (like that of Homer's gods as they watched lame Hephaestus hobbling); ~ *question* (of authorship of *Iliad* & *Odyssey*). [f. L f. Gk *homērikos* (*Homēros;* traditional author of *Iliad* & *Odyssey,* see -IC)]

hŏme'spŭn (-ms-), a. & n. (Cloth made of yarn) spun at home; (anything) plain, homely.

hŏme'stead (-mstĕd), n. House with outbuildings; farm. [OE *hāmstede* (HOME, STEAD)]

hŏme'ward (-mw-), adv. & a., -**wards** (-z), adv. (Going, leading) towards home; ~-BOUND⁶, (esp. of ship) preparing to go, or on the way, home. [-WARD(S)]

hŏm'ĭcĭde, n. **1.** One who kills a human being. **2.** Killing of a human being (*culpable, justifiable,*~). Hence hŏmĭcid'AL a. [ME, f. OF f. L (1) *homicida,* (2) *homicidium* (*homo* man, see -CIDE)]

hŏmĭlĕt'ĭc, a. & n. Of homilies; (n. pl.) art of preaching. [f. LL f. Gk *homilētikos* (*homileō* hold converse, consort, as foll.; see -ETIC)]

hŏm'ilǀў, n. Sermon (*Books of H~ies,* for use in parish churches of the Ch. of England, published in 1547 & 1563); tedious moralizing discourse. [ME, f. OF *omelie* f. eccl. L f. Gk *homilia* f. *homilos* crowd (*homou* together + *ilē* crowd)]

hŏm'ing, a. That goes home; (of pigeons) trained to fly home, bred for long-distance racing; ~ *device,* mechanism for automatic guiding of missiles. [part. of HOME²]

hŏm'inў, n. Coarsely ground maize boiled with water or milk. [of Amer.-Ind. orig.]

hŏm'ō, n. (zool.). Man; *H~ săp'iens* (L=wise), modern man regarded as a species. [L]

hŏm'o-, comb. form of Gk *homos* same, as: ~*cen'tric,* having same centre; ~*gamous*(-ŏg⁴),(Bot.) having all florets hermaphrodite or of same sex; ~*genĕt'ic,* having common descent or origin; ~*geny* (-ŏj'-), similarity due to common descent; ~*morph'ic,*~*morph'ous,* of same or similar form; ~*nomous* (-ŏn²), having same law of growth; ~*phone,* word having same sound as another, but of different meaning or origin (e.g. *gait, gate*), (also) symbol denoting same sound as another; ~*phŏn'ic,* (Mus.) of same pitch, characterized by the predominance of one part or melody; ~*phonous* (ŏf²), (of music) ~*phonic,* (of symbols) denoting same sound; ~*phony* (-ŏf²), unison; ~*plăs'tic,* similar in structure; ~*type,* part, organ, like another in structure; ~*zўg'ote* (Mendelism), zygote of like gametes (cf. HETEROZYGOTE), & so ~*zўg'ous* a.

hŏm'oeopăth (-mǐ-), n. One who practises homoeopathy. [f. foll.]

hŏmoeǀŏp'athў (-mǐ-), n. Hahnemann's treatment of disease by drugs (usu. in minute doses) that in healthy person would produce symptoms like those of the disease. So ~opăth'IC a. (often *joc.,* = minute), ~opăth'ICALLY adv., ~ŏp'athIST n., (-mǐ-). [f. Gk *homoios* like + *-patheia* f. *pathos* suffering; first used by Hahnemann (G *homöopathie*)]

hŏmogĕn'ēous, a. Of the same kind;

consisting of parts all of the same kind, uniform. Hence or cogn. **hŏmŏgĕnē′ITY**, ~NESS, nn., ~LY² adv., **homŏ′gĕnIZE** v.t., make ~, make (milk) more digestible by breaking up the fat droplets into smaller particles. [f. schol. L *homogeneus* f. Gk HOMO(*genēs* f. *genos* kind)+-OUS]

hŏm′ograph (-ahf), n. Word spelt like another, but with different meaning. [HOMO-+-GRAPH]

hŏmoious′ian (-ows-), a. & n. (One who held that Father & Son in the Godhead were) of like substance (cf. HOMOOUSIAN). [f. LL f. Gk *homoiousios* (*homoios* like+ *ousia* essence)+-AN]

‖**homŏl′og̈āte**, v.t. (Sc.). Acknowledge, admit; confirm. So ~A′TION n. [f. med. L *homologare* f. Gk HOMO(*logeō* f. *logos* word), see -ATE³]

homŏl′ogize, **-ise** (-Iz), v.i. & t. Be homologous, correspond; make homologous. [as foll. +-IZE]

homŏl′ogous, a. Having the same relation, relative position, etc.; corresponding. [f. med. L f. Gk HOMO(*logos* ratio)]

hŏm′ologue (-ŏg), n. Homologous thing. [F, f. Gk (neut. adj.) as prec.]

homŏl′ogy, n. Correspondence, sameness of relation. Hence **hŏmolŏ′gICAL** a., **hŏmolŏ′gicalLY²** adv. [f. med. L f. Gk *homologia* (as prec.)]

hŏm′onȳm, n. Word of same form as another but different sense (e.g. POLE¹, POLE²); namesake. So **hŏmonȳm′IC**, **homŏn′ȳmous**, aa. [f. L f. Gk *homōnumon*, neut. adj. (HOMO-+*onoma* name)]

hŏmŏous′ian, **hŏmous-**, (-ow-), a. & n. (One who held the persons of the Trinity to be) of the same substance (cf. HOMOIOUSIAN). [f. LL *homousianus* f. LL f. Gk HOMO(*ousios* f. *ousia* essence)+-AN]

hŏmosĕx′ual, a. & n. Having a sexual propensity for persons of one's own sex; (n.) ~ person. [irreg. f. HOMO-+SEXUAL]

homŭnc′ūle, **-cle**, n. Little man, manikin. [f. L *homunculus* (*homo -minis* man, see -CULE)]

hŏm′ȳ, a. Suggesting home, home-like. [-Y²]

hōne, n., & v.t. 1. Whetstone, esp. for razors; various stones as material for this. 2. v.t. Sharpen on ~. [OE *hān*, = ON *hein*]

hŏn′ĕst (ŏ-), a. Fair & upright in speech & act, not lying, cheating, or stealing; sincere; (of act or feeling) showing uprightness; (of gain etc.) gained by fair means, as *turn, earn, an ~ penny*; (of things) unadulterated, unsophisticated; (arch., of woman) chaste, virtuous; *make an ~ woman of*, marry (seduced woman); (patronizing or joc.) good, worthy; ~ *Injun* (= Indian), sl. phr. questioning (~ *Injun?*) or confirming statement. Hence ~LY² adv. [ME, f. OF *honeste* f. L *honestus* (*honos* HONOUR)]

hŏn′ĕstȳ (ŏ-), n. Uprightness; truthfulness; ~ *is the best policy* (maxim of self-interested morality); plant with purple flowers & translucent pods. [ME, f. OF *oneste* f. L *honestatem* (prec., -TY)]

ho′ney (hŭ-), n. (pl. ~s). Sweet viscid yellow fluid, the nectar of flowers collected by bees & other insects; (fig.) sweetness; (also Sc. & North. *hinnie*, -*ny*) sweetheart, darling; ~*-bee*, common hive-bee; ~*-buzzard*, bird of prey feeding on larvae of bees & wasps; ~ *dew*, sweet sticky substance found on leaves & stems, excreted by aphides, ideally sweet substance, tobacco sweetened with molasses; ~*suckle*, woodbine, climbing shrub with fragrant yellow and pink flowers; ~*-sweet*, sweet as ~. Hence ~ED², honied, (hŭn′Id), a. [OE *hunig*, OS *honig*, OHG *hona(n)g*, ON *hunang* f. Gmc *huna(n)gam*]

ho′neycomb (hŭ-; -m), n., & v.t. 1. Bees' wax structure of hexagonal cells for honey & eggs; cavernous flaw in metal, esp. guns; ornamental or other work hexagonally arranged. 2. v.t. Make full of cavities, undermine, mark with ~ pattern. [OE *hunigcamb*, see prec. & COMB]

ho′neymŏŏn (hŭ-), n., & v.t. 1. Holiday spent together by newly married couple. 2. v.i. Spend ~ (*in, at*, place). [16th c., HONEY+MOON, reference being orig. to waning affection, not to period of a month]

hŏng, n. (In China) set of buildings used as factory etc.; foreign trading establishment in China or Japan. [f. Chin. *hang* row, rank]

hŏnk, n., & v.i. 1. Wild goose's cry; sound of motor horn. 2. v.i. Emit or give ~. [imit.]

hŏnorār′ium (hŏ-, ŏ-), n. (pl. *-ums*, *-a*). (Voluntary) fee esp. for professional services nominally rendered without payment. [L as foll.]

hŏn′orarȳ (ŏ-), a. Conferred as an honour (without the usual requirements, functions, etc.); holding ~ title or position; ~ *secretary, treasurer*, etc., serving without pay (abbr. *hon*.); (of obligations) depending on honour, not legally enforceable. [f. L *honorarius* (as HONOUR¹, see -ARY¹)]

hŏnorif′ic (ŏ-), a. & n. (Expression) implying respect (esp. of Oriental forms of speech). [f. L *honorificus* (as HONOUR¹, see -FIC)]

hŏnōr′is caus′a, adv. phr. As a mark of esteem. [L, = for the sake of honour]

hŏn′our¹ (ŏ-), n. 1. High respect; glory; reputation, good name; nobleness of mind. 2. Allegiance to what is right or to conventional standard of conduct; (of woman) chastity, reputation for this. 3. Exalted position (*your, his, H~*), said to or of County-Court judge, & in rustic speech to or of any person of rank). 4. Thing conferred as distinction; (Golf) right of driving off first as having won last hole (*it is my ~*); (pl.) civilities rendered to guests etc., esp. *do the ~s of* (the table, a house, the town, etc.); *last, funeral,* ~s, observances of respect at funeral; *military* ~s, marks of respect paid by troops at burial of soldier, to royalty, etc.; ~*s of war,* privileges granted to capitulating force, as that of marching out with colours flying etc. 5. (Univv., pl.) special distinction for proficiency beyond that required to pass examination. 6. Person, thing, that reflects ~ on (*to*) another, as *he is an* ~ *to his profession.* 7. (In whist) ace, king, queen, knave, of trumps (in bridge the ten also). 8. (commerc.). *Acceptance* (of protested bill by third party) *for the* ~ *of* (to save the credit of) drawer or indorser. 9. *In* ~ (celebration) *of; bound in* ~ (as a moral duty) *to* (do); *be on* one's ~ (under moral obligation) *to* (do); (forms of asseveration) *upon my* ~, (colloq.) ~ *bright; code, law, of* ~, rules forming conventional standard of conduct; AFFAIR, DEBT, LEGION, MAID, POINT[1], WORD[1], *of* ~. [ME, f. OF (*h*)*onor* f. L *honorem* (nom. -*or*) repute, office, beauty]

hŏn′our² (ŏ-), v.t. Respect highly; **confer dignity upon;** (Co'mmerc.) accept, **pay, (**bill) when due. [ME, f. OF *honorer* f. L *honorare* (as prec.)]

hŏn′ourable (ŏner-), a. Worthy of honour; bringing honour to its possessor; consistent with honour; upright; person's *intentions* (in courting woman) *are* ~, he has marriage in view; title (abbr. *Hon.*) || of wives of younger sons of Earls and of all sons of Viscounts and Barons, Maids of Honour, Justices of High Court, Lords of Session, members of Government or Executive Councils in Dominions & Colonies; || *MostH*~, title of Marquises, Order of Bath, & Privy Council; || *Right H*~, title of peers below rank of Marquis, Privy Councillors, & others. Hence **hŏn′ourabLY²** (ŏner-) adv. [ME, f. OF *honorable* f. L *honorabilis* (as prec., see -BLE)]

hōōch, n. (sl.). Alcoholic liquor. [abbr. of Alaskan *hoochinoo*]

hōōd, n., & v.t. 1. Covering for head & neck, whether part of cloak etc. or separate; (Univv.) badge worn over gown etc. to indicate degree; leather covering for hawk's head; *bonnet of motor-car; thing like ~ in shape or use. 2. v.t. Cover with ~. Hence ~'ED² a. [(vb f. n.) OE *hōd,* OHG *huot* f. WG *hōd-,* cogn. w. HAT]

-**hōōd,** suf. forming nn. of condition or quality on nn. & aa., ME -*hōd.* Orig. an independent noun, OE *hād* (person(ality), sex, condition, quality, rank) = OS *hēd,* OHG *heit,* ON *heithr,* Goth. *haidus* f. Gmc *haiduz.* It became a suf. in ME both in new formations on aa. & nn. & to replace -HEAD in similar wds.

hōōd′ie, -dȳ, n. (Also ~ *crow, grey, hooded, Royston, crow*) piebald grey and black crow. [HOOD + -Y²]

*hōōd′lum, n. Street rowdy, young ruffian. [orig. unkn.]

|| **hŏŏd′man-blind,** n. Old name for BLIND-MAN'S-BUFF.

hōō′dōō, n., & v.t. (chiefly U.S.). Bad luck; (vb) render unlucky. [var. of VOODOO]

hōōd′wink, v.t. Deceive, humbug; blindfold. [HOOD n. + WINK v.]

*hōō′ey, n. & int. (sl.). Nonsense, humbug. [orig. unkn.]

hōōf, n. (pl. -*fs, -ves*), & v.t. & i. 1. Horny casing of foot of horse & other animals; CLOVEN ~; (joc.) human foot; ~-*pad,* pad to prevent one foot from striking the other; ~-*pick* (for removing stones from ~). 2. v.t. Strike with ~; (sl., of person) kick (another) *out* etc.; (v.i.) go on foot. Hence (-)~ED² (-ft) a. [OE, OS *hōf,* OHG *huof,* ON *hófr* f. Gmc *hófaz*]

hōōk¹, n. Piece of metal or other material bent back at an angle or with round bend, for catching hold or for hanging things upon; (sl.) anchor; (also *fish-*~) bent piece of wire, usu. barbed, for catching fish; ~, *line, & sinker,* (fig.) entire(ly); (fig.) trap, snare; stroke (see foll.) in cricket or golf; (Boxing) short swinging blow with elbow bent; curved cutting instrument, esp. *reaping-*~; ~ *& eye,* small metal ~ & loop as dress-fastening; sharp bend, e.g. in river; projecting point of land, esp. *H*~ *of Holland* = POT~; *by* ~ *or by crook,* by fair means or foul; (sl.) *on* one's *own* ~ (account); *take* one's ~ (sl.), = *hook it* (see foll.); ~-*nose*(*d*), (having) aquiline nose; ~-*worm,* kind of nematoid worm infesting men and animals, male of which has ~-like spines. [OE *hōc,* MLG *hōk,* Du. *hoek*]

hōōk², v.t. & i. Grasp with hook; secure with hook(s); ~ *on, in, up,* etc., attach with hook; ~ *on* intr., take person's arm; (sl.) steal; catch (fish) with hook (also fig., esp. husband); (Golf) drive (ball) slightly to left; (Cricket) play (ball) round from off to on side without hitting it at the pitch; (Rugby football) secure and pass (ball) backward with foot in scrummage; (Boxing) strike (opponent) with elbow bent; ~ *it* (sl.), make off, run away; ~-*up* (orig. U.S.), interconnexion of broadcasting stations for special transmissions. [f. prec.]

hŏŏk′ah (-ka), n. Smoking-pipe with long flexible tube, smoke being drawn through water in vase to which tube and bowl are attached. [f. Arab. *ḥuqqah,* casket, hookah-bottle]

hōōked (-kt), a. Hook-shaped; furnished with hook(s). [-ED[1,2]]

hōōk′er¹, n. In vbl senses, esp. (Rugby football) each of the two players in front row of scrummage who try to get the ball by hooking it. [-ER¹]

hōōk′er², n. Kinds of small Dutch & Irish sailing ship (*the old* ~, said scornfully or fondly of any ship). [17th c., f. Du. *hoeker* fishing-boat f. *hoek* HOOK¹]

hŏŏk′ey, -kӯ, n. *Play ~ (sl.), play truant; *blind*~, gambling game at cards. [f. HOOK¹′²]

hoo′lee, hō′li (-lē), n. Hindu festival in honour of Krishna & the milkmaids. [Hind. (-*i*)]

‖ **hŏŏl′ĭgan,** n. One of gang of young street roughs. Hence ~ISM(3) n. [name]

hŏŏp¹, n., & v.t. **1.** Circular band of metal, wood, etc., esp. for binding staves of casks etc.; wooden or iron circle trundled along by child; circle of elastic material for expanding woman's skirt; iron arch used in croquet; large ring with paper stretched over it through which circus-riders jump (*go through the* ~ or ~*s*, undergo an ordeal); kind of finger-ring; ~*-iron* (in long thin strips for binding purposes); ~ *petticoat* (expanded by ~*s*). **2.** v.t. Bind with ~*s*, surround as ~ does. [late OE *hōp*, MDu. *hoop*]

hŏŏp², v.i., & n. **1.** Utter the cry ~: ~*ing cough*, see WHOOP. **2.** n. The cry ~, sound heard in whooping cough. [ME, f. OF *houper* (imit.); cf. WHOOP]

hŏŏp′la (-ah), n. Game played at fairs etc., in which rings are thrown at objects that are won if encircled.

hŏŏp′oe (-ōō), n. S.-European bird with variegated plumage & large erectile crest. [17th c., alt. of 15th c. *hoop* f. OF *huppe* f. L *upupa*]

hŏŏsh, n. (sl.). Hotchpotch or stew in Arctic travel. [orig. unkn.]

***Hŏŏ′sier** (-zher), n. (Nickname for) inhabitant of State of Indiana. [orig. unkn.]

hŏŏt, v.i. & t., & n. **1.** Make loud sounds, esp. of disapproval (*at* or abs.); assail (person etc.) with derisive shouts; drive (person) *out*, *away*, etc. by ~*ing*; (of owl) utter cry; (of steam whistle or motor car or driver) sound (intr.). **2.** n. Inarticulate shout, esp. of derision or disapprobation; owl's cry; *not care, not worth, a* ~ or *two* ~*s* (sl., = anything at all). [ME *huten*, imit.]

‖ **hŏŏt(s),** int. (Sc. & north.) expr. dissatisfaction or impatience. [cf. Sw. *hut* begone, W *hwt* away, Ir. *ut* out, all in similar sense]

hŏŏt′er, n. In vbl senses, esp. siren, steam whistle, esp. as signal for work to begin or cease. [-ER¹]

hŏŏve, n. Disease of cattle, with inflation of stomach, usu. caused by green fodder. [19th c., perh. ult. rel. to *hove*, p.p. of HEAVE]

Hŏŏv′er, n., & v.t. Make of vacuum cleaner; (v.t.) clean (carpet etc.) with ~. [P]

hooves. See HOOF.

hŏp¹, n., & v.t. & i. (-pp-). **1.** Climbing perennial plant, cultivated for the cones borne by the female; (pl.) ripe cones of this, used for giving bitter flavour to malt liquor etc.; ~*-bind*, *-bine*, climbing stem of ~; ~*-fly*, aphis destructive to ~*s*;

‖ ~*-garden*, field for cultivation of ~*s*; ~*-picker*, labourer, machine, employed to pick ~*s*; ~*-pillow* (stuffed with ~*s*, to produce sleep); ~-POCKET; ~*-pole* (on which ~ plant is trained). **2.** v.t. Flavour with ~*s*; (v.i.) bear, gather, ~*s*. [ME *hoppe* f. MLG, MDu. *hoppe* = OS *hoppo*, OHG *hopfo*; orig. unkn.]

hŏp², v.i. & t. (-pp-). Spring (of person) on one foot, (of animals) with all feet at once; (trans.) ~ over (ditch etc.); (sl.) ~ (*the twig* or *stick*), depart suddenly, die, ~ (*it*), go away, ~ *off*, (of aircraft) start; *cloud-*~*ping*, (of aircraft) flying from cloud to cloud esp. to gain cover; *hedge*, *wave*, ~*-ping*, flying very low over land, over water; ‖ ~*-'o'-my-thumb*, dwarf, pygmy; ~*'scotch*, child's game of ~*ping* on one foot & with it pushing flat stone etc., over *scotches* (lines) marked on ground. [OE *hoppian*, MHG *hopfen*, ON *hoppa* f. Gmc **hoppōjan*]

hŏp³, n. Hopping (*on the* ~, colloq., bustling about); spring; (colloq.)informal dance; (Aviation) one of the stages of a long-distance flight; ~, *skip* (or *step*), & *jump*, exercise consisting of these three movements in sequence. [f. prec.]

hōpe¹, n. Expectation & desire combined (*of* thing, *of doing, that*); feeling of trust; ground of ~, probability, (*hoping against* ~, clinging to a mere possibility); person, thing, that ~ centres in; FORLORN HOPE. [OE *hopa*, *tōhopa*, OLG *tōhopa*, MLG, MDu. *hope*, MHG *hoffe*; OE-LG, OE-LG, of unkn. orig.]

hōpe², v.i. & t. Look with expectation & desire (*for* thing or abs.); expect & desire (thing, *that, to* do.). [OE *hopian*, MLG, MDu.; *hopen*; see prec.]

hōpe′ful (-pf-), a. & n. Feeling hope; inspiring hope, promising, often iron. as (n.) *young* ~ (of boy or girl). Hence ~LY³ adv., ~NESS n. [HOPE¹ + -FUL]

hōpe′less (-pl-), a. Feeling no hope; admitting no hope, as *a* ~ *case*. Hence ~LY² adv., ~NESS n. [-LESS]

hŏp′lite, n. Heavy-armed foot-soldier of ancient Greece. [f. Gk *hoplitēs* (*hoplon* weapon, see -ITE¹)]

hŏpp′er¹, n. One who hops; hopping insect, esp. flea or cheese-maggot; inverted pyramid or cone (orig. with hopping motion) through which grain passes in mill; similar contrivance in various machines; barge carrying away mud etc. from dredging-machine & discharging it; ~*-light* or *-casement* (hinged below with opening at top for ventilation). [HOP² + -ER¹]

hŏpp′er², n. Hop-picker. [HOP¹ + -ER¹]

hŏp′ple, v.t., & n. Fasten together legs of (horse etc.); (n.) apparatus for this. [16th c., prob. LG; cf. early mod. Flem. *hoppelen* = MDu. *hobelen* jump, dance; *hobble*, in same sense, a 19th c. var. infl. by earlier senses of HOBBLE]

hŏr′arӯ, a. Of the hours; occurring every

hour. [f. LL *horarius* (*hora* hour, see -ARY[1])]

Horā′tian (-shn), a. Of, like, (the poems of) Horace (Q. Horatius Flaccus, d. B.C. 8). [f. L *Horatianus* (*Horatius*, see -AN)]

hōrde, n. Troop of Tartar or other nomads; gang, troop, (usu. in contempt). [ult. f. Turki *orda*, see URDU]

hore′hound, hoar-, (hōr-), n. Herb with bitter aromatic juice used for coughs etc. (also *common*, *white*, ~); other allied herbs. [OE *hāre hūne* (*hār* hoar + *hūne*, a plant)]

hori′zon, n. Line at which earth & sky appear to meet; *apparent*, *sensible*, *visible*, ~, circle of contact with earth's surface of a cone whose vertex is at observer's eye; *celestial*, *rational*, *true*, ~, great circle of the celestial sphere, plane of which passes through centre of earth & is parallel to that of sensible ~ of a place; (fig.) limit of mental perception, experience, interest, etc.; *on the* ~ (fig., of events just imminent or becoming apparent). [ME, f. OF *orizonte* f. LL *horizontem* (nom. -*on*) f. Gk *horizōn* (*kuklos*) bounding (circle)]

hōrizōn′tal, a. & n. 1. Of, at, the horizon; parallel to the plane of this, at right angles to the vertical; level, flat; (of machinery etc.) having its parts working in ~ direction. 2. n. ~ line, bar, etc. Hence ~ITY (-ăl-) n., ~LY[2] adv. [16th c., f. F, or mod. L (as prec. +-AL)]

hŏr′mŏne, n. (physiol.). Kinds of internal secretion that pass into the blood & stimulate organs to action. [f. Gk *hormōn* part. of *hormaō* impel]

hōrn[1], n. 1. Non-deciduous excrescence, often curved & pointed, on head of cattle, sheep, goats, & other mammals, found in pairs, single, or one in front of another; *take the* BULL[1] *by the* ~*s*; each of two deciduous branched appendages on head of deer; projection on head of other animals, as snail's tentacles, insect's antennae, crest of horned owl; emblem of cuckold; *draw in* one's ~*s*, restrain one's ardour, draw back; substance of which ~*s* consist; ~-*shavings* (used as manure); thing made of ~, as SHOE-~; drinking-vessel, powder-flask, made of ~; GATE[1] *of* ~; ~ *of plenty*, = CORNUCOPIA; wind instrument (not now made of ~, but of brass), as *hunting*-~, *French* ~ (of trumpet class, used in orchestra), *English* ~ (kind of oboe); ~-shaped projection; extremity of moon or other crescent; arm, branch, of bay, river, etc.; either alternative of a dilemma; *the H*~, Cape H~. 2. ~-*bar*, cross-bar of carriage; ~′*beam*, tree of beech kind with hard tough wood; ~-*bill*, bird with ~-like excrescence on bill; ~′*book* (hist.), paper containing alphabet, Lord's Prayer, etc., mounted on wooden tablet with handle, & protected by thin plate of ~; ~-*mad* (arch.), stark mad (orig. of horned beasts); ~*rimmed* (of

spectacles or their wearers); ~′*stone*, brittle siliceous rock; ~′*work* (fortif.), outwork consisting of two demi-bastions joined by a curtain. Hence ~′FUL n., ~′LESS a. [OE, OS, OHG, ON *horn*, Goth. *haurn* f. Gmc *hornaz, -*am*, cogn. w. L *cornu*]

hōrn[2], v.t. & i. Furnish with horns (esp. in p.p.); shorten or cut off (horns of cattle); gore with the horns; adjust (frame of ship) at right angles to line of keel; ~ *in*, intrude, interfere. [f. prec.]

hōrn′blēnde, n. Dark-brown, black, or green mineral, a constituent of granite & many rocks, composed chiefly of silicates of calcium, magnesium, & iron. [G (*horn* + BLENDE)]

hōrn′er, n. Maker of horn spoons, combs, etc.; one who blows a horn. [HORN[1] +-ER[1]]

hōrn′ĕt, n. Large insect of wasp family, inflicting serious sting; *bring* ~*s*′ *nest about* one's *ears*, stir up host of enemies. [OE *hyrnet(u)* = OHG *hornuz*; ME *hernet*, *harnet*, *hornet* prob. f. MLG, MDu. *horn(e)te*; perh. rel. to HORN; cf. OS *hornobero*]

hōrn′pīpe, n. Obsolete wind instrument; (music for) lively dance, usu. of single person (esp. associated with merry-making of sailors).

hōrn′|ў, a. Of, like, horn; abounding in horns; hard as horn, callous, as ~*y* *handed*. Hence ~INESS n. [-Y[2]]

hŏ′rolŏge, n. Time-piece, dial, clock. So **horŏl′oGER[1]**(3), **horŏl′oGIST**(3), nn. [ME, f. OF *orloge* f. L f. Gk *hōrologion* (*hōra* time + -*logos* -telling)]

horŏl′ogў, n. Study of measuring time or making clocks, watches, etc. So **hŏrolŏ′GIC(AL)** aa. [f. Gk *hōra* time + -O-+-LOGY]

horŏp′ter, n. Aggregate of points seen single in any given position of eyes. [f. Gk *horos* limit + *optēr* one who looks]

hŏ′roscōpe, n. (astrol.). Observation of sky & planets at certain moment, esp. at person's birth; scheme showing disposition of the heavens at particular moment; *cast a* ~, erect such scheme by calculating degree of ecliptic on eastern horizon at person's birth etc. So **hŏroscŏp′IC(AL)** aa., **horŏs′copY[1]** n. [ME, f. OF, or L f. Gk *hōroscopos* (*hōra* time + *skopos* observer)]

hŏ′rrent, a. (poet.). Bristling. [f. L *horrēre* bristle, shudder at, see -ENT]

hŏ′rrib|le, a. Exciting, fit to excite, horror; hideous, shocking; (colloq.) excessive, unpleasant, as ~*le noise*, *bore*, *weather*. Hence ~lENESS (-beln-) n., ~LY[2] adv. [ME, f. OF f. L *horribilis* (as prec., see -BLE)]

hŏ′rrid, a. Terrible, frightful; (poet., arch.) rough, bristling; (colloq.) as prec. Hence ~LY[2] adv., ~NESS n. [f. L *horridus* (as prec., see -ID[1])]

hŏ′rrifў, v.t. Excite horror in; shock,

scandalize. So **horrif'ic** a., **hŏrrific-**
a'tion n. (joc.). [f. L *horrificare* (as
HORRENT, see -FY)]

hŏrripila'tion, n. Goose-flesh; bristling
of the skin caused by chill, fright, etc.
[f. LL *horripilatio*, ult. f. L *horrēre* to
bristle + *pilus* hair]

hŏ'rror, n. Terrified shuddering; intense
dislike (*of*); (Med.) shuddering, as
symptom of disease; *the ~s*, fit of ~ or
depression, esp. as in delirium tremens;
~-struck or *-stricken*, shocked; horrifying
thing; *Chamber of H~s*, place full of ~s
(orig. room of criminals etc. in Tussaud's
waxwork exhibition). [ME, f. OF *orror* f.
L *horrorem* (as prec., see -OR)]

hors (see Ap.), adv. & prep. Outside, as
~ *concours*, (of exhibit) not competing for
prize; ~ *de combat* pred. a., out of fight,
disabled; *~-d'œuvre* (pl. usu. *-s*), extra
dish served as relish at beginning or in
interval of meal. [F wds]

hŏrse[1], n. 1. Solid-hoofed quadruped with
flowing mane & tail, used as beast of
burden & draught, & for riding on (*you
may take a ~ to the water, but you can't
make him drink*, prov.); (esp.) adult male
~, stallion or gelding, (cf. MARE, COLT);
(collect. sing.) cavalry; *high ~*, trained
for HAUTE ÉCOLE; *light ~*, lightly armed
mounted soldiers; SEA-~. 2. Vaulting-
-block in gymnasium; frame (often with
legs) on which something is supported, as
clothes-~; (Naut.) rope, bar, in various
uses; (Mining) obstruction in vein. 3. *To
~*, (as command) mount your ~s; FLOG
a dead ~; *grin through a ~-collar*, practise
elementary humour; *look a gift-~ in the
mouth*, find fault with a gift; *mount, ride,
the high ~*, put on airs; DARK, WILLING, ~;
put the CART before the ~; *eat, work, like a
~* (much); *on ~-back*, mounted on a ~.
4. ~ *artillery* (the light mobile type);
~-block, small platform of stone or wood
for mounting ~; ‖ *~-box*, closed vehicle
for taking ~ by rail or for slinging ~ into
ship, (joc.) large pew; *~-breaker*, one who
breaks in ~s; *~-chestnut*, large tree with
conical clusters of white or pink or red
flower, fruit of this (like edible chestnut,
but of coarse bitter taste); *~-cloth* (used
to cover ~, or as part of trappings);
~-COPER; *~-flesh*, flesh of ~, esp. as food,
~s collectively; *~-fly*, insect (of various
kinds) troublesome to ~s; ‖ *H~ Guards*,
cavalry brigade of English Household
troops, esp. (*Royal H.G.*) second regiment
of it, (also) headquarters of such cavalry,
esp. a building in Whitehall, (also) military authorities at head of army; ~ *hair*,
hair from mane or tail of ~ (often attrib.);
~ *latitudes*, belt of calms at northern edge
of N.E. trade-winds; *~-laugh*, loud coarse
laugh; *~-leech*, large kind of leech, in-
satiable person, (*daughters of the ~leech*,
Prov. xxx. 15); *~-mackerel*, (kinds of) large
fish of the mackerel type, cavally, scad,
tunny, etc.; *~-man*, (skilled) rider on

~-back; *~-manship*, art of riding, skill in
riding, on *~-back*; *~-marines*, imaginary
corps of mounted marines, as type of non-
existent body, (prov.) *tell that* (nonsense)
to the ~-marines; *~-mastership*, skill in
managing ~s; *~-mushroom*, coarse but
edible variety with hollow stem; *~ opera*
(sl.), western film; *~-play*, boisterous
play; *~-pond* (for watering & washing
~s, prov. as ducking-place for obnoxious
persons); *~-power*, machine by which
work of ~ is made to drive other machinery, (Mech.) unit of rate of doing work,
= 550 foot-pounds per second (abbr.
h.p.); *~-race* (between ~s with riders);
~-radish, plant whose pungent root is
scraped or grated as condiment; ~ *sense*
(colloq.), plain rough sagacity; *~-shoe*,
iron shoe for ~, thing of this shape (often
attrib., as *~-shoe table*); *~-tail*, tail of ~
(used in Turkey as standard, or as ensign
denoting rank of pasha), genus of cryptogamous plants like *~'s tail*; *~-whip*, whip
for ~, (v.t.) chastise (person) with this;
~-woman, woman who rides on *~-back*.
Hence *~-LESS* (-sl-) a. [OE *hors*, OS, OHG
hros, ON *hross* f. Gmc *horsam*, *-az*]

hŏrse[2], v.t. & i. Provide (person, vehicle)
with horse(s); carry (person) on one's
back; place (person) on man's back to be
flogged; (intr.) mount, go, on horseback.
[f. prec.]

hŏrs'|y̆, a. Concerned with, addicted to,
horses or horse-racing; affecting dress
& language of groom or jockey. Hence
~-ILY[2] adv., *~-INESS* n. [f. HORSE[1] + -Y[2]]

hŏrt'at|ive, a. Tending, serving, to ex-
hort. So *~-ORY* a. [f. L *hortativus* (*hortari*
exhort, see -IVE)]

hŏrt'icŭlture, n. Art of garden cultivation. Hence **hŏrticŭl'tural** a., **hŏrti-**
cŭl'turist n., (-cher-). [f. L *hortus* garden
+ CULTURE]

hŏrt'us sicc'us, n. Arranged collection
of dried plants; (fig.) collection of uninteresting facts etc. [L, = dry garden]

hŏsănn'a (-z-), n. Cry of ~, shout of
adoration (*Matt.* xxi. 9, 15, etc.). [ME, f.
LL f. Gk *hōsanna* f. Heb. *hosha'na* for
hoshi'ahnna save, pray!]

hose (hōz), n., & v.t. 1. (Collect. as pl.)
stockings, *half-~*, socks, (now chiefly
shop); (w. pl. *~s*) flexible tube for watering plants etc., putting out fires, dispersing rioters, etc.; ‖ *~-tops*, footless stockings. 2. v.t. Provide with ~, drench or
water with ~. [OE, OS, OHG, ON *hosa*
f. Gmc *husōn-*]

hō'sier (-zher), n. Dealer in hose &
frame-knitted or woven underclothing.
Hence **hō'sIERY**(1) (-zher-) n. [f. HOSE +
-IER]

hŏs'pice, n. House of rest for travellers,
esp. one kept by religious order; ‖ home
for the destitute or sick. [F, f. L *hospi-
tium* (as HOST[2])]

hŏs'pitab|le, a. Giving, disposed to give,
welcome & entertainment to strangers or

guests. Hence ~LY² adv. [F, f. med. L *hospitare* entertain, as prec., -ABLE]

hŏs′pital, n. Institution for care of the sick or wounded; charitable institution (in proper names, as *Christ's H~*, public school formerly in London); (hist.) hospice, establishment of Knights Hospitallers; ~ *fever*, kind of typhus formerly prevalent in crowded ~s; *H~ Saturday, Sunday*, days for collecting money in streets etc. (*Saturday*), in churches (*Sunday*), for the local ~s. Hence ~IZE v.t., admit to, treat in, ~, ~īZA′TION n. [ME, f. OF f. med. L *hospitale* neut. adj. place for guests (as HOST², see -AL)]

hŏs′pitalism, n. (Hygienic imperfections of) the hospital system. [-ISM]

hŏspităl′ĭtў, n. Friendly & liberal reception of guests or strangers; *afford me the ~ of your columns*, print my letter. [ME, f. OF *hospitalite* f. L *hospitalitatem* (as HOSPITAL, see -TY)]

hŏs′pital(l)er, n. Member of charitable religious order; ‖ (in some London hospitals) chaplain; *Knights H~s*, order of military monks founded c. 1048. [ME, f. OF *hospitalier* f. med. L *hospitalarius* (as prec., see -ARY¹)]

hŏst¹, n. Large number (*of*; *person is a ~ in himself*, can do as much as a number of ordinary persons); (arch.) army; (Bibl.) *Lord* (*God*) *of* ~s (armies), ~(s) *of heaven*, sun, moon, & stars, (also) angels. [ME, f. OF f. L *hostis* stranger, enemy]

hŏst², n. One who lodges or entertains another; landlord of inn; *reckon without one's* ~, overlook difficulty, opposition, etc.; (Biol.) animal, plant, having parasite or commensal. [ME, f. OF *oste* f. L *hospitem* (nom. -*pes*) host, guest]

hŏst³, n. Bread consecrated in the Eucharist. [ME, f. OF *oiste* f. L *hostia* victim]

hŏs′tage, n. Person given to another as pledge; pledge, security; ~ *to fortune*, person, thing, that one may lose. Hence ~SHIP (-ĭjsh-) n. [ME, f. OF (*h*)*ostage* f. Rom. *obsidaticum* f. LL *obsidatus* f. L *obses -idis* hostage, see -AGE]

‖ hŏs′tel, n. Inn; house of residence for students or other special class; YOUTH ~. [ME, f. OF (as HOSPITAL)]

‖ hŏs′telrў, n. Inn. [ME, f. OF *ostelerie* (*ostelier* innkeeper, f. med. L as HOSPITALLER, see -ERY)]

hŏs′tĕss, n. Woman who entertains guests; mistress of inn; AIR¹ ~. [ME, f. OF *ostesse* (HOST², -ESS¹)]

hŏs′tile, a. Of an enemy; unfriendly; opposed. Hence ~LY² (-l-lĭ) adv. [f. F, or L *hostilis* (as HOST², see -IL)]

hŏstĭl′ĭtў, n. Enmity; state of warfare; (pl.) acts of warfare; opposition (in thought etc.). [f. F *hostilité* or LL *hostilitas* (as prec., see -TY)]

hostler (ŏs′ler), n. = OSTLER.

hŏt¹, a. & adv. (-tt-). 1. Of a high temperature; very warm; communicating or

feeling heat; producing the sensation of heat, as ~ *fever, blush*; (of pepper etc.) pungent, biting; ardent, passionate; angry; excited; exciting; (Hunt., of scent) strong; (fig., of news etc.) fresh, recent; ‖ (colloq., of Treasury bills) newly issued; (of a hit, return, etc., in ball-games) difficult for opponent to deal with; (of competitor in race or other sporting event) strongly fancied to win (*a ~ favourite*); (of dance music) highly elaborated & florid, fast & with great emphasis on rhythm; (sl., of stolen jewellery, bank-notes, etc.) easily identifiable & so difficult to dispose of; BLOW¹ ~ & *cold*; ~ & ~, (of food) served as soon as cooked; *give it him* ~, chastise, reprimand, him severely; *make it, the place, too* ~ (uncomfortable, by persecution) *for, to hold, him*. 2. adv. Hotly, eagerly, angrily. 3. ~ *air* (sl.), excited or boastful talk; ~ & *strong*, vehement(ly); ~′*bed*, bed of earth heated by fermenting manure, (fig.) place favourable to growth of (vice. etc.); ~ *blast* (of heated air forced into furnace); ~-*blooded*, ardent, passionate; ~-*brained, -headed*, excitable; ~ *cockles* (hist.), rustic game in which blindfolded person guessed who struck him; *°~ dog* (colloq.), ~ *sausage* sandwiched in roll of bread; ~′*foot*, in ~ haste; ~′*head*, impetuous person; ~′*house*, heated building with glass roof & sides for growing plants out of season or from warmer climate; ~-*pot*, mutton, beef, with potatoes etc. cooked in oven in tight-lidded pot; ~-*press*, press of glazed boards & ~ metal plates for smoothing paper or cloth, (v.t.) press (paper etc.) in this; ~-*short*, (of iron) brittle in its ~ state; ~′*spur*, rash person (sobriquet of Sir H. Percy, d. 1403); ~ *stuff* (sl.), person of high spirit, vigour, skill, or strong will or passions; ~ *water*, (fig.) trouble, disgrace, scrape; ~ *well*, spring of naturally ~ water, reservoir in condensing steam-engine. Hence ~′LY² adv., ~′NESS n. [OE *hāt*, OS *hēt*, OHG *heiz*, ON *heitr* f. Gmc *°haitaz*; see HEAT¹]

hŏt², v.t. (colloq.; -tt-). Heat, warm *up*. [f. prec.]

hŏtch′pŏtch, -pŏt, n. Dish of many mixed ingredients, esp. mutton broth with vegetables; (Law) blending of properties for purpose of securing equal division (esp. of property of intestate parent); mixture, medley. [ME *hochepot* f. OF (*hocher* shake + POT); -*potch* (15th c.) by assim.]

hotĕl′ (*also* hō-, ŏ-, o-), n. House for entertainment of travellers etc., (usu. large) inn. [F *hôtel*, later form of HOSTEL]

hotĕl′ier, n. Hotel-keeper. [F *hôtelier*]

Hŏtt′entŏt, n. Member of S.-Afr. people formerly occupying region near the Cape; (fig.) person of inferior intellect or culture. [Du., perh. = stammerer]

‖ **hough** (hŏk), n., & v.t. **1.** Joint of quadruped's hind leg between true knee & fetlock. **2.** v.t. Hamstring, whence ～'ER¹ (hŏk'er) n. [ME ho(u)gh = OE hōh (heel) in hōhsinu hamstring; cf. HOCK¹]

hound¹, n. Dog for chase, esp. one hunting by scent; the ～s, pack of fox-～s; MASTER of ～s; despicable man; player who follows scent in HARE & ～s; dogfish (short for ～'fish); nurse'～, smooth～, kinds of dogfish; ～'s-tongue, kinds of plants of the borage family. Hence ～'ISH¹ a. [OE, OS hund, OHG hunt, ON hundr, Goth. hunds f. Gmc *hundaz cogn. w. L canis, Gk kuōn]

hound², v.t. Chase (as) with hound; set (hound, or fig. person) at (quarry etc.); urge (person) on. [f. prec.]

hour (owr), n. Twenty-fourth part of day, 60 minutes; short indefinite period of time; the time o'clock; (pl.) fixed time for daily work etc., as office ～s are 10 to 3; at the eleventh ～, at a late stage (Matt. xx); small ～s, 1, 2, etc., a.m.; good or early, bad or late, regular, ～s, (time for getting up & going to bed); the question of the ～ (present time); in a good, evil, ～, (un)luckily; (prayers to be said at) seven stated times of day appointed for prayer; (Astron.) 15° of longitude; ～circle, meridian (24 of which are usu. marked on globe); ～-glass, sand-glass running for an ～; ～-hand (showing ～ on clock etc.). [ME ure etc. f. OF (h)ure f. L f. Gk hōra season, hour]

houri (boor'ĭ, howr'ĭ), n. Nymph of Mohammedan Paradise; voluptuously beautiful woman. [F. f. Pers. huri f. Arab. ḥaura (ḥawira have eyes like gazelle's)]

hour'ly (owr-), a. & adv. (Occurring, done, reckoned) every hour; continual(ly), frequent(ly). [HOUR + -LY¹,²]

house¹ (bows), n. (pl. pron. -zĭz). **1.** Building for human habitation or (usu. w. defining prefix) occupation, as ALMS～, BAKE～, LIGHT¹～, SUMMER～; ～ of God, church, place of worship; inn (a drink on the ～, at innkeeper's expense); bow down in the ～ of Rimmon, sacrifice one's principles for the sake of conformity (2 Kings v. 18); ALE, COFFEE, EATING, ～; PUBLIC, TIEd, ～. **2.** Building for keeping animals or goods, as hen～, STORE～, WARE¹～. **3.** (Place of abode of) religious fraternity. **4.** ‖ (Oxf. Univ.) the H～, Christ Church. **5.** = (boys in) BOARDING-～. **6.** (Building used by) an assembly, public offices, firms, & institutions, as H～ of COMMONS, LORDS, H～s of PARLIAMENT; make a H～, secure presence of 40 members in H～ of Commons; ‖ the H～, (colloq.) Stock Exchange, (euphem.) work～, (Pol.) H～ of Commons or Lords (a question was asked in the H～); CLEARING, CUSTOM, ～; ‖ COUNTING-HOUSE. **7.** (Audience in) theatre (full ～, with all seats engaged); performance in theatre etc.

(second ～ starts at 9 o'clock). **8.** Household, family, dynasty (the H～ of Windsor, British Royal family); mercantile firm. **9.** (astrol.). Twelfth part of heavens. **10.** A game of chance playable by large numbers with no apparatus but pencil & paper; (Army sl.) gambling form of lotto. **11.** attrib. (Of animals) kept in, frequenting, infesting, the ～, as ～-cat, -fly, etc. **12.** ～ of call, ～ where carriers call for commissions, where person may be heard of, etc.; ～ of cards (built by child out of playing-cards; often fig. of insecure scheme etc.); ～ of ill fame, brothel; ‖ H～ of Keys, branch of Manx legislature; ～ & ～ home, (emphatic) home; ～-to-～, carried on from ～ to ～; BRING down the ～; keep ～, maintain, provide for, a household; keep open ～, provide general hospitality; keep the ～, not go outdoors; like a ～ on fire, vigorously, fast. **13.** ‖ ～-agent (for sale & letting of ～s); ～'boat, boat fitted up for living in; ～'breaker, person entering another's ～ by day (cf. BURGLAR) with felonious intent, man employed in demolishing old ～s; ～ dinner, (at clubs) specially appointed dinner for members & guests; ～-dog (kept to guard ～); ～-flag, that flown by a firm's ship; ～'flannel (coarse, for cleaning floor etc.); ～'keeper, woman managing affairs of household, (also) person in charge of ～, office, etc.; ～'keeping, (good, bad, liberal, etc.) domestic economy; ～'leek, plant with pink flowers growing on walls & roofs; ～'maid, female servant in charge of reception & bed rooms; ～maid's knee, inflammation of knee-cap due to kneeling; ～'master (of school boarding-～); ～ party (of guests staying at country ～ etc.); ‖ ～-place, living-room in farm-～ etc.; ～-proud, preoccupied with the care & beautification of the home; ～-room, accommodation in ～ (would not give it ～-room, take it as a gift); ～-surgeon, -physician, residing in hospital; ～-to-～ collection etc., performed or conducted by calling at～ after～; ～-top, esp. proclaim from the ～-tops, publicly; ～-trained, (of domestic animals) trained to be clean in the ～; ～-warming, celebration of entrance into new ～; ～'work, cleaning, cooking, etc. Hence ～'FUL(2) (-sf-) n., ～'LESS (-sl-) a. [OE hūs, OS, OHG, ON hūs, Goth. -hūs f. Gmc *hūsam]

house² (-z), v.t. & i. Receive (person etc.), store (goods), in house or as house does; (Naut.) place (gun etc.) in secure position, lower (upper masts); take shelter (as) in house; provide houses for (population; esp. the housing problem); (Carpentry) fix in a socket, mortise, etc. [OE husian (as prec.)]

house'hold (-s-h-), n. Inmates of house; domestic establishment; (pl.) second quality of flour; ‖ ～ troops (employed nominally to guard sovereign's person); ～ gods, (Rom. Ant.) Lares & Penates, (fig.) essentials of home life; ~ *word*, familiar saying or name. [HOUSE¹+HOLD²]

house′hōlder (-s-h-), n. One who occupies house as his own dwelling (esp. formerly as entitled to franchise); head of household. [HOUSE¹+HOLDER]

housewife, n. 1. (hows′wif). Mistress of family; (*good, bad*) domestic economist. 2. (hŭz′if). Case for needles, thread, etc. Hence **house′wīfeLY¹** (-fĭl) a. [ME *hus(e)wif* (HOUSE¹, WIFE)]

house′wīfery (-swĭfrĭ), n. Domestic economy, housekeeping. [prec.+-RY]

hous′ing (-z-), n. Horse's cloth covering, for protection or ornament. [f. obs. *house* f. OF *houce* f. OFrank. *hulfti (cf. MHG *hulft, hulst* covering)]

Houyhnhnm (hwĭ′nĭm), n. Horse with human characteristics (*Gulliver's Travels*). [imit. of horse's neigh; made by Swift]

Hōv′a, n. One of ruling tribe in Madagascar. [native]

hove. See HEAVE.

hŏv′el (*or* hŭ-), n. Open shed, out-house; miserable dwelling; conical building enclosing kiln. [15th c., of unkn. orig.]

hŏv′eller (*or* hŭ-), n. Unlicensed pilot or boatman, esp. one who goes out to wrecks. [18th c., of unkn. orig.]

hŏv′er (*or* hŭ-), v.i. & n. (Of bird etc., esp. of hawk) hang in the air (*over, about,* spot); loiter *about* (person, place); (n.) ~ing, state of suspense. [frequent. of & replacing ME *hove*, of unkn. orig.; -ER⁶]

how, ădv. & n. 1. (In direct or indirect question) in what way, as ~ *does he do it?*, ask him ~ *he does it, tell him ~ to do it,* (with intensive addition) ~ *the deuce, devil, dickens,* ~ *ever,* ~ *on earth;* ~ *are you?,* ~ *do you do?,* what is your state of health? ; ~ *is that for high, queer,* etc.? (colloq. invitation to wonder); (colloq.)~-*d′ye-do*, embarrassing situation; (Crick.) ~'*s that?*, is he out or not? ; ~ *now?,* what is the meaning of this? ; ~ (can you show that to be) *so?;* ~ (at what price) *is corn?;* (in indirect statement, rhet. for) that (*told us* ~ *God was almighty*); (in question or exclamation) to what extent, as ~ *far is it?,* ~ *far it is!,* ~ *many are there?,* ~ *many there are!,* ~ *would you like it?,* ~ *he snores!;* (in relative clause) in whatever way, as, (*do it* ~ *you can*); *•&~!* (sl.), = & a good deal more (chiefly used ironically or intensively); *here's* ~! = here's your good health (drinking formula). 2. n. *The* way a thing is done (*the* ~ *of it*). 3. ~*bē′it* (arch.), nevertheless; ~*ev′er,* in whatever way, to whatever extent, nevertheless, (arch.) in any case; ~ EVER; ~*soev′er, how — soever,* in whatsoever manner, to what extent soever; ~ *much?,* (sl.) what? (as request to person to repeat his remark or a particular word; *he plays the saxtuba. Plays the* ~ *much?*). [OE *hū*, OS *hwō*, OHG *wuo*, f. Gmc *hwō f. stem **hwa-* WHO]

howd′ah (-*a*), n. Seat for two or more, usu. with canopy, on elephant's back. [f. Pers. *haudah* f. Arab. *haudaj* litter]

how′itzer, n. Short piece of ordnance for high-angle firing of shells at lower velocities than a gun. [17/18th c. *howitts, haubitz, hauwitzer,*. *haubitzer,* combining the forms of Du. *houwitser,* (f.) G *haubitze* f. Czech *houfnice* catapult]

howl¹, v.i. & t. (Of animals) utter long loud doleful cry; (of persons) utter long cry of pain, derision, etc., freq. of (esp. child's) loud weeping; utter (words) with ~ing. [ME *houle,* = MLG, MDu. *hūlen,* MHG *hūlen, hiulen* (imit.)]

howl², n. Long doleful cry of dog, wolf, etc.; loud cry of pain; yell of derision; (Wireless) whining noise in receiver during tuning-in, often affecting other listeners. [f. prec.]

howl′er, n. In vbl senses; esp. : S.-Amer. monkey; (sl.) glaring blunder. [-ER¹]

‖ **howl′ĕt**, n. (dial.). Owl. [late ME, f. OF *hulotte* f. OFrank. *hūwila* OWL]

howl′ing, a. That howls; ~ DERVISH; (Bibl.)~ (dreary) *wilderness;* (sl.) extreme, glaring, as *a* ~ *shame.* [-ING²]

hoy¹, n. Small vessel, usu. rigged as sloop, carrying passengers & goods esp. for short distances. [f. MDu. *hoei,* of unkn. orig.]

hoy², int. used to call attention, drive beasts, & (Naut.) hail or call aloft. [natural cry]

hoy′a, n. Kinds of climbing plants with pink, white, or yellow flowers, known as *wax-flowers.* [T. *Hoy,* gardener, d. 1821]

hoyd′en, n. Boisterous girl. Hence ~-HOOD, ~ISM, ~ISH, ~ISH¹ a. [prob. f. MDu. *heyden* (=HEATHEN) rude fellow]

hŭb¹, n. Central part of wheel, rotating on or with axle, & from which spokes radiate; nave; (fig.) central point of interest etc. (esp. ~ *of the universe*). [orig. unkn.]

hŭb², **hŭbb′ÿ**, n. (colloq.) Husband. [abbr.]

hŭb′ble-bŭbble, n. Form of hookah; bubbling noise; confused talk. [imit.]

hŭbb′ŭb, n. Confused din; disturbance, riot; confused yelling of war-cry. [of Ir. orig.; cf. Gael. *ubub* int. of contempt, Ir. *abu,* a war-cry]

hŭb′rĭs, n. Insolent pride or security; (Gk tragedy) overweening pride leading to NEMESIS. So **hubris′tic** a. [Gk; prop. *hy-*]

hŭck′abăck, n. Stout linen fabric with rough surface, for towels etc. [orig. unkn.]

hŭc′kle, n. Hip; haunch; ~-*back(ed),* hump-back(ed); ~-*bone,* hip, haunch, -bone, (also) knuckle-bone of quadruped. [f. obs. *huck* hip (cf. earlier *huck(le)bone*), of unkn. orig.]

hŭc′kleberry (-kelb-), n. (Fruit of) low berry-bearing shrub common in N. Amer. [prob. alt. of *hurtleberry* WHORTLEBERRY] hŭck′st|er[1], n. Pedlar, hawker; merce- nary person. Hence ~ERY(2) n. [c. 1200, of uncert. orig.; cf. dial. *huck* vb, *hucker* n. & vb, *huckle* vb (all later); MDu. *hoek- ster, hoeker*; MHG *hucker* etc.; cf. HAWKER]

hŭck′ster[2], v.i. & t. Bargain, haggle; carry on petty traffic in (lit. & fig.); adulterate. Hence ~ER[1], ~ESS[1], nn. [f. prec.]

hŭd′dle, v.t. & i., & n. 1. Heap together confusedly; crowd (things etc.) promiscu- ously *together, up, into, out of*, etc.; coil one*self up*; hurry *over, through*, botch *up*, (work etc.); (intr.) nestle closely *together*. 2. n. Confused mass; confusion, bustle; *(secret) conference, esp. *go into* a ~ (with)* (sl.). [16th c., of obsc. orig.; perh. ult. rel. to root *hŭd-* HIDE[2]]

Hŭdĭbrăs′tic, a. In the metre or manner of Butler's *Hudibras*, mock-heroic poem 1663-78, esp. of comical compound rhymes. [after *fantastic* etc.]

hūe[1], n. Colour, tint; variety of colour caused by admixture of another. Hence -huED[2] (hŭd) a. [OE *hīew, hīw* form etc., Goth. *hiwi* f. Gmc *hewja*]

hūe[2], n. ~ & *cry*: loud cry raised for pursuit of wrongdoer; outcry (*against*); proclamation for capture of criminal. [f. OF *hu, heu*, outcry, f. *huer* (imit.)]

hŭff[1], v.t. & i. Bully, storm at; bully (person *into, out of*, thing or do*ing*); offend; take offence; (Draughts) remove (opponent's man) from board as forfeit (orig. after blowing on the piece). [imit. f. sound of blowing; v. & n. f. 16th c.]

hŭff, n. Fit of petulance, pique. *in a ~, take ~*; (Draughts) act of huffing. Hence ~′ISH[1], ~′Y[2], aa., ~′ILY[2], ~′ishLY[2], advv., ~′INESS, ~′ishNESS, nn. [see prec.]

hŭg, v.t. (-gg-), & n. 1. Squeeze tightly in one's arms, usu. with affection; (of bear) squeeze (man etc.) between its forelegs; delight in, cling to, (prejudices etc.); ex- hibit fondness for (person); congratulate one*self (on, for)*; keep close to (shore, kerb, etc.); ~*-me-tight*, woollen wrap. 2. n. Strong clasp; grip in wrestling, esp. *Cornish ~*. [late 16th c., of unkn. orig.]

hūge, a. Very large; enormous; (of im- material things) great. Hence ~′NESS (-jn·) n. [ME *huge, hoge* f. OF *ahuge, ahoge* of unkn. orig.]

hūge′lÿ (-jll), adv. Enormously, very much. [prec. + -LY[2]]

hū′geous (-jus), a. (usu. joc.). Huge. Hence ~LY[2] adv., ~NESS n., (-jus-). [-OUS]

hŭgg′er-mŭgg′er (-g·), n., a., adv., & v.t. & i. Secrecy; secret(ly); confusion; con- fused(ly); (v.t.) conceal, hush *up*; (v.i.) proceed in secret or muddled fashion. [prob. rel. to ME *hoder* huddle, *moker* conceal; cf. syn. 15th c. *hoder moder*, 16th c. *hucker mucker*]

‖ hŭgg′ery (-g·), n. Practice (on part of barrister etc.) of courting attorney etc. for employment. [f. HUG[1] + -ERY]

Hŭg′uenŏt (-ge·; *or* -nŏ), n. (hist.). French Protestant. [F, assim. of G *eidgenoss* confederate to F pers. name *Hugues*]

•huh (hŭ), int. expr. interrogation, con- tempt, etc.

hul′a (-ŏŏ-), n. Hawaiian woman's dance (also *hula-hula*). [native word]

hŭlk, n. Body of dismantled ship, used as store vessel etc. or (pl., hist.) as prison; unwieldy vessel; (fig.) big person or mass. [ME, f. OE *hulc* (= OHG *holcho*, G *hulk*) & MLG, MDu. *hulk(e)*, ult. f. med. L *hulcus* f. Gk *holkas* ship of burden]

hŭl′king, a. Bulky; clumsy. [prec. + -ING[2]]

hŭll[1], n., & v.t. 1. Outer covering of fruit, esp. pod of peas & beans; (fig.) covering. 2. v.t. Remove ~ of. [OE *hulu* f. st. *hul* rel. to *helan* cover; see HELL]

hŭll[2], n., & v.t. 1. Frame of ship, airship, flying-boat, etc.; ~ *down, far away*, so that ~ is invisible. 2. v.t. Strike (ship) in ~ with shot, torpedo, etc. [15th c., of obsc. orig.; perh. spec. use of prec.]

hŭllabalŏŏ′, n. Uproar. [18th c, redupl. of *hallo, hullo*, etc.]

hŭllŏ′, -loa (-lŏ), int. used to call atten- tion, express surprise, or answer call, esp. on telephone. [cf. HALLO]

hŭm[1], v.i. & t. (-mm-). Make continuous murmuring sound, as of bee, spinning top, etc.; make low inarticulate vocal sound, esp. (usu. ~ & *haw* or *ha*) of hesitation; sing with closed lips; (colloq.) be in state of activity, as *make things ~*; (sl.) smell unpleasantly; (v.t.) utter, sing, with closed lips. [ME, imit.; so MHG *hum- men*]

hŭm[2], n. Humming sound esp. of hesita- tion (usu. ~*s & ha's*), applause, surprise, etc.; (sl.) bad smell. [imit.]

hum[3] (hem), int. expr. hesitation, dissent, etc.

hŭm[4], n. (sl.). Sham, hoax. [= HUMBUG]

hūm′an, a. & n. Of, belonging to, man, as ~ *nature*; that is a man or consists of men, as ~ *race, creature*; of man as opp. to God, as *to err is ~, to forgive divine*; having, showing, the qualities distinctive of man, as *more, less, than ~*; (n.) ~ being. Hence ~NESS (-n ·n-) n. [ME *humain(e)* f. OF, f. L *humanus* (*homo* man, see -AN)]

hūmāne′, a. Benevolent, compassionate; ‖ H~ *Society* (for rescue of drowning per- sons); ~ *killer*, instrument for painless slaughter of cattle; (of branches of study) tending to refinement, elegant, cf. LITERAE HUMANIORES. Hence ~LY[2] (-nl·) adv., ~NESS (-n·n-) n. [differentiated f. prec. after 1700]

hūm′anism, n. Devotion to human in- terests; system concerned with human (not divine) interests, or with the human race (not the individual); Religion of HUMANITY; literary culture, esp. that of the humanists. [f. after foll.; -ISM]

hūm′anist, n. Student of human nature or human affairs; student (esp. in 14th- 16th cc.) of Roman & Greek literature &

antiquities, whence **hūmanĭs′tĭc** a. [16th c. f. F -*iste* f. It. *umanista* (as HUMAN, see -IST)]

hūmănĭtār′ian, n. & a. **1.** One who professes humanism (Religion of Humanity); visionary philanthropist. **2.** adj. Holding, concerned with, the views of ∼s. Hence ∼ISM n. [f. foll. + -ARIAN]

hūmăn′ĭt|y̆, n. Human nature; (pl.) human attributes; the human race; humaneness, benevolence; (pl.) benevolent acts; *Religion of H*∼*y* (rejecting the supernatural & concerned chiefly or wholly with the advancement of man's welfare); *the* ∼*ies*, polite scholarship, esp. of Latin & Greek classics; *H*∼*y* study of Latin. [ME, f. OF -*ité* f. L *humanitatem* (as HUMAN, -TY)]

hūm′anĭz|e, -is|e (-īz), v.t. & f. Make human, give human character to (∼*ed milk*, cow's milk prepared to resemble human milk); make, become, humane. Hence ∼A′TION n. [f. F *humaniser* (as HUMAN, see -IZE)]

hūm′ankind′, n. Mankind.

hūm′anly̆, adv. In a human manner; by human means; from human point of view; with human feeling. [-LY²]

hŭm′ble, a. (*comp. & sup. pron.* -bler, -blĭst), & v.t. **1.** Having, showing, low estimate of one's importance; (formerly, esp. in subscribing letter) *your* ∼ *servant*; of lowly condition; (of things) of modest pretensions, dimensions, etc.; *eat* ∼ *pie*, make ∼ apology, submit to humiliation; ∼ *plant*, common SENSITIVE plant. **2.** v.t. Make ∼, bring low, abase (one*self* etc.). Hence ∼NESS (-bel-) n., **hŭm′bly̆²** adv. [ME (*h*)*umble* f. OF f. L *humilis* lowly (*humus* ground, -IL)]

hŭm′ble-bee (-bel-), n. Bumble-bee. [15th c., prob. f. obs. (14th c.) *humble* hum, as BUMBLE-BEE f. *bumble*; but cf. MLG *hummelbē*, MDu. *hommel*, OHG *humbal*]

hŭm′bŭg, n., & v.t. & f. (-gg-). **1.** Fraud, sham; deception; (as int.) nonsense!; impostor; kind of hard boiled sweet usu. flavoured with peppermint. **2.** v.t. Delude (person *into*, *out of*, thing or do*ing*); (v.i.) be, behave like, a ∼. Hence **hŭmbŭg̃′ERY** (-g-) n. [f. c. 1750, sl., of unkn. orig.]

*****hŭm′ding′er**, n. (sl.). Excellent person or thing. [orig. unkn.]

hŭm′drŭm, a. & n., & v.i. (-mm-). Commonplace(ness), dull(ness); (v.i.) proceed in ∼ way. Hence ∼NESS n. [f. 1550; prob. redupl. f. HUM v.]

hŭm′er|**us**, n. (anat.). Bone of the upper arm in man; corresponding bone in other vertebrates. Hence ∼AL a., (also n., ∼al veil, oblong silk scarf worn round priest's shoulders during parts of the Mass etc.). [L, = shoulder]

hŭm′id, a. Moist, damp. So **hūmid′IFY** v.t., **hūmid′ITY** n. (*relative* ∼*ity*, amount

of moisture in atmosphere as compared with that of complete saturation at the given temperature). [f. F *humide* or L *humidus* (*umēre* be moist, see -ID¹)]

hūmĭl′i|**āte**, v.t. Lower the dignity or self-respect of; mortify. Hence or cogn. ∼ātĭNG² a., ∼A′TION n. [f. LL *humiliare* (as HUMBLE, see -ATE³)]

hūmĭl′ĭty̆, n. Humbleness, meekness; humble condition. [ME, f. OF *humilite* f. L *humilitatem* (as HUMBLE, see -TY)]

‖ **hŭmm′el**, a. (Sc.). (Of cattle and stags) hornless. [cf. LG *hommel* hornless beast]

hŭmm′ing, a. In vbl senses; ∼*-bird*, several species that make ∼ sound by vibration of wings); ∼*-top* (∼ when it spins). [f. HUM v. + -ING¹]

hŭmm′ock, n. Hillock, knoll; rising ground, esp. in marsh; hump or ridge in icefield. Hence ∼Y² a. [orig. naut.; 16th c. ham-, hom-; orig. unkn.]

hūm′oral, a. (med.). Of the bodily humours; ∼ *pathology*, doctrine referring all disease to state of the humours, whence ∼ISM, ∼IST, nn., ∼is′tĭc a. [f. F, or med. L **humoralis* as HUMOUR, see -AL]

hūm′orist, n. Facetious person; humorous talker, actor, or writer. Hence **hūmoris′tĭc** a. [16th c., f. F *humoriste* (as prec., see -IST)]

hūm′orous, a. Full of humour; facetious, funny. Hence ∼LY² adv., ∼NESS n. [-OUS]

hūm′our¹ (-mer; also ū-), n. State of mind, mood; inclination, as *in the* ∼ *for fighting*; facetiousness, comicality; faculty of perceiving this; jocose imagination (less intellectual & more sympathetic than wit), whence ∼LESS a.; *out of* ∼, displeased; *good*, *ill*, ∼ (temper), whence ∼∼ED² (-erd) a.; *cardinal* ∼s (hist.), four chief fluids of the body (blood, phlegm, choler, melancholy), determining person's physical & mental qualities; *aqueous*, *vitreous*, ∼, transparent fluid parts of the eye. [ME, f. AF f. L (*h*)*umorem* moisture (as HUMID, see -OR)]

hūm′our² (-mer; also ū-), v.t. Gratify, indulge, (person, taste, temper, etc.); adapt oneself to, make concessions to. [f. prec.]

hūm′oursome (-mer-), a. Capricious; peevish. Hence ∼NESS n. [-SOME]

hŭmp, n., & v.t. **1.** Protuberance, esp. on the back, as deformity or (in camel etc.) as normal feature; rounded boss of earth etc.; (fig.) critical point (of undertaking, ordeal, etc.), esp. in phr. *over the* ∼, over the worst, well begun; ‖ (sl.) fit of depression or vexation, as *it gives me the* ∼; ∼*′back*, (person having) back with a ∼; ∼*′backed*, having such a back. **2.** v.t. Make ∼-shaped; annoy, depress; (Austral.) hoist up, shoulder, (one's pack, swag, or *bluey*). Hence ∼ED²(-pt), ∼′LESS, ∼′Y², aa. [f. 1680, ∼*-backed* replacing *crump-backed*; perh. rel. to LG *hümpel* hump, LG *humpe*, Du. *homp* lump, hunk (of bread)]

humph (hmf), int., & v.i. Int. expr. doubt or dissatisfaction; (v.i.) utter this.

hŭmp'tў-dŭmp'tў, n. Short dumpy person; (from nursery rhyme in which *H*~ is taken to mean an egg) person, thing, that once thrown down cannot be restored; person who makes words mean what he chooses. [app. f. *hump(y)* & *dump(y)*; *-ty* unexpl.]

hŭm'pў, n. Australian hut. [native *oompi*]

hŭm'us, n. Vegetable mould. [L, = ground]

Hŭn, n. One of an Asiatic nomad race who invaded & ravaged Europe in 4th & 5th cc.; (derog.) German (esp. Prussian). Hence ~n'ISH[1] a. [OE *Hūne* f. med. L *Hunni*]

hŭnch[1], v.t. Bend, arch, convexly; thrust *out, up*, to form a hump. [orig. unkn.]

hŭnch[2], n. Hump; thick piece; ~'*back(ed)*, hump-back(ed); *presentiment, intuition. Hence ~'Y[2] a. [orig. unkn.]

hŭn'dred, n. & a. (Cardinal number) ten times ten (100, C), as *a, one, six, several, ~ men, a, one, six ~ of them or of my friends, ~s of men, ~s of them, some, several, ~s of* etc.; (in compds) the ~*-&-first, six-~-&-ninth*; (also ~ *& one*) large number; *not a ~ miles from* (joc.), at or close to; *a ~ per cent efficient*, doing the utmost in practice that it theoretically should; ~ *pounds* (of money); || (chiefly hist.) subdivision of county or shire, having its own court; CHILTERN HUN-DREDS; *great, long, ~, 120; ~ of* BRICK[1]*s; ~weight*, 112lb. avoirdupois (abbr. *cwt*), *100lb.; ~s & thousands*, sweets like small shot used chiefly for decorating cakes etc. Hence ~FOLD n., ~TH[2] a. & n. (*Old Hundredth*, hymn 'All people that . . .', version of Ps. C, or its tune). [OE, f. *hund* (cogn. w. L *centum*) + Gmc *rath* number (cf. Goth. *rathjō* number]

hung. See HANG v.

Hŭngār'ian (-ngg-), a. & n. **1.** Of Hungary or its inhabitants. **2.** n. Native, language, of Hungary. [f. med. L *Hungaria* + -AN]

hŭng'er[1] (-ngg-), n. Uneasy sensation, exhausted condition, caused by want of food; (fig.) strong desire (*for, after*, etc.); ~*march* (undertaken by body of unemployed to call attention to their condition; so ~*marcher*); ~*strike*, prisoner's refusal to take food in order to procure release. [OE *hungor*, OS, OHG *-ar*, ON *hungr*, (Goth. *huggrjan* vb), f. Gmc *hungruz*]

hŭng'er[2] (-ngg-), v.i. & t. Feel hunger; have craving (*for, after*): (p.p., arch.) hungry; (trans.) starve (*into* submission, *out of* place etc.). [OE *hyngran*, assim. to prec.]

hŭn'grў (-ngg-), a. Feeling hunger (~ *as a hunter*); showing hunger, as *a ~ look*; inducing hunger, as *a ~ air*; ~ *rice*, W.-African grain allied to millet; (fig.) eager, greedy; (of soil) poor, barren; || *H~ Forties* (hist.), the decade 1840-9 in England, a period of great distress among

the poor. Hence hŭn'grILY[2] adv., hŭn'grINESS n. [OE *hungrig* (as HUNGER[1], see -Y[2])]

hŭnk, n. Large piece cut off; clumsy piece; hunch. [19th c.; cf. WFlem. *hunke*]

|| **hŭnk'ers**, n. pl. The hams (esp. in phr. *on* one's ~, in a squatting position). [Sc., f. *hunker* to squat]

hŭnks, n. Close-fisted man, miser. [orig. unkn.]

***hŭnkў-dōr'ў**, a. (sl.). Excellent, top-hole.

Hunnish. See HUN.

hŭnt[1], v.i. & t. Pursue wild animals, go fox-~ing; (trans.) chase (these) for food or sport; seek *after, for*; drive *away, out*; scour (district) in pursuit of game; use (horse, hounds) in ~ing; *shoot (game); ~ *down*, bring to bay; ~ *out*, track out, find by search; ~ *up*, search for; ~ *in* COUPLES; ~ *the hare, slipper, squirrel*, games. [OE *huntian* f. *hunta* hunter, cogn. w. OE *hentan*, Goth. *hinthan* seize]

hŭnt[2], n. Hunting (lit. & fig.); persons hunting with a pack; hunting district; ~ *ball* (given by members of ~, men wearing pink). [f. prec.]

hŭn'ter, n. One who hunts; (fig.) *fortune, place*, etc., ~; horse for hunting; watch with hinged cover protecting glass or (*half-*~) outer part of it; ~'s *moon*, next full moon after harvest moon. Hence **hŭn'trESS**[1] n. [-ER[1]]

hŭn'ting, n. In vbl senses; ~*box*, small house for use during ~*season*; ~ COG[1]; ~*crop*; ~*ground*, place where one hunts (often fig.); *happy ~ground(s)*, the future state (prop. as expected by Amer. Indians), good place for ~ (fig.); ~*horn*, horn used in ~, second pommel on near side of side-saddle. [-ING[1]]

hŭnts'man, n. Hunter; man in charge of (esp. fox-) hounds.

hŭr'dle, n., & v.t. Portable rectangular frame strengthened with withes or wooden bars, for temporary fence etc.; wooden frame to be jumped over in ~*-race*; (hist.) frame on which traitors were dragged to execution; (v.t.) fence *off* etc. with ~s. [OE *hyrdel* (-LE 1), f. Gmc *hurdiz* (= Goth. *haurds*, ON *hurth* door, OHG *hurt* hurdle), cogn. w. L *cratis*]

hŭrd'ler, n. One who makes hurdles, or runs in hurdle-races. [-ER[1]]

hŭrd'ў-gŭrdў, n. Musical instrument with droning sound, played by turning handle, orig. one with rosined wheel turned by right hand & played by left; (colloq.) barrel organ & street piano. [prob. imit.]

hŭrl, v.t., & n. **1.** Throw violently from some position (lit. & fig.); throw (missile etc., also fig.); || (Sc.) convey in a wheeled vehicle. **2.** n. ~ing, violent throw; || (Sc.) a ride in a wheeled vehicle. [ME, prob. imit., but corresp. in form & partly sense w. LG *hurreln*]

hŭrl'ey, n. (Ir.). Kind of hockey. [as prec.]

Hŭrl'ingham (-ngam), n. (Used for) ~ Park, Fulham, headquarters of ~ Polo Club.

hŭrl'y, n. (arch.). Commotion. [as HURL]

hŭrl'y-bŭrl'y, n. Commotion, tumult. [f. 1540; redupl. f. HURL v.]

hurrah' (hu-, hŏŏ-), **-ray'**, int., n., & v.i. Int. expr. exultation or approbation; (n.) this cry; (v.i.) shout ~. [replaces *huzza*; cf. Swed. & Da. *hurra*, Du. *hoera*]

hŭ'rricane, n. Storm with violent wind with velocity of 75 miles an hour or over, esp. W.-Indian cyclone (also fig.); ~-*bird*, frigate-bird; ~ *deck*, light upper deck; ~ *lamp* (designed to resist wind). [f. Sp. *huracan*, of Carib orig.]

hŭ'rry¹, n. Undue haste; eagerness to get a thing done quickly; eagerness (*to do*, *for* thing); (w. neg. or interrog.) need for haste; (colloq.) *you will not beat that in a* ~ (easily), *shall not ask again in a* ~ (willingly); ~-*scurry* adv., adj., & n., (in) disorderly haste, (v.i.) proceed thus. [16th c., rel. to HURL, HURLY, HURLY-BURLY, etc.]

hŭ'rr|y², v.t. & i. Carry, drive, (person etc. *away*, *along*, *into*, *into doing*, etc.) with undue haste; move, act, with great or undue haste; ~*y up*, make haste. Hence ~**iedLY²** adv., ~**iedNESS** n., (-id-). [as prec.]

hŭrst, n. Hillock; sandbank in sea or river; wooded eminence; wood. [OE *hyrst*, rel. to OS, OHG *hurst*]

hŭrt¹, n. Wound, material injury; harm, wrong. Hence ~**'FUL**, ~**'LESS**, aa., ~**'fulLY²** adv., ~**'fulNESS** n. [ME, f. OF *hurte* f. *hurter* (foll.)]

hŭrt², v.t. & i. (*hurt*). Cause bodily injury or pain to; damage; inflict injury upon; distress, wound, (person, his feelings etc.; (colloq.) suffer injury or pain (*does your hand* ~?). [ME, f. OF *hurter* (mod. *heurter*) f. Gallo-rom. **hurtare*]

hŭr'tle, v.t. & i., & n. Strike against; hurl swiftly; strike *against*; move with clattering sound; come with a crash; (n.) hurtling, clashing sound. [f. HURT² + -LE(3)]

hŭs'band¹ (-z-), n. Man joined to woman by marriage; ‖ (arch.) *good*, *bad*, ~ (economist). Hence ~**HOOD**, ~**SHIP**, nn., ~**LIKE** a. [late OE *húsbonda* f. ON *húsbóndi*; see HOUSE & BOND⁴]

hŭs'band² (-z-), v.t. Manage thriftily, economize; ‖ (arch.) till (ground), cultivate (plants); (poet., joc.) provide with husband; (rare) marry (woman). [f. prec.]

hŭs'bandman (-z-), n. Farmer.

hŭs'bandry (-z-), n. Farming; (*good*, *bad*) economy; careful management. [-RY]

hŭsh¹, n. Stillness; silence; ~-*money*, paid to prevent exposure. [f. foll.]

hŭsh², v.t. & i. Silence, quiet; ~ *up*, suppress (affair); be silent, esp. (as int.) ~!; ~-*aby̆*, int. used to lull child; ~!-~ adj. phr., to be kept specially secret; ~-*ship* (of great length, speed, & gun-power,

secretly built; cf. Q-*ship*). [back formation f. obs. adj. *husht* f. *husht*, *hust*, intt. (imit.)]

hŭsk, n., & v.t. **1.** Dry outer covering of some fruits or seeds; (fig.) worthless outside part of anything; disease of cattle. **2.** v.t. Remove ~ from. [late ME, of unkn. orig.]

hŭs'k|y¹, a. & n. Of, full of, husks; dry as a husk; (of voice or person) dry, hoarse, whence ~**iLY²** adv., ~**iNESS** n.; (colloq.) tough, strong, hefty (& as n., ~*y* person). [-Y²]

hŭs'ky², n. Eskimo dog; (*H*~) Eskimo person or language. [? contr. f. ESKIMO]

‖ **hussar'** (-z-), n. Soldier of light cavalry regiment (orig. Hungarian light horseman of 15th c.). [f. Hung. *huszár* f. OSerb. *husar* f. It. *corsaro* CORSAIR]

Hŭss'ite, n. Follower of John Huss, Bohemian religious reformer of 15th c. [-ITE¹]

hŭss'y, -zzy̆, n. Woman of light or worthless character; pert girl. [f. HOUSEWIFE]

hŭs'tings (-z), n. Platform from which (before 1872) candidates for Parliament were nominated; election proceedings; court (now rarely) held in Guildhall of London. [OE *hústing* f. ON *hústhing* house-assembly]

hŭs'tl|e (-sl), v.t. & i., & n. **1.** Push roughly, jostle; thrust (person etc. *into*, *out of*, etc.); impel unceremoniously (*into* thing or *doing*); (v.i.) push roughly *against*; push one's way; hurry, bustle. **2.** n. ~*ing*. [17th c., f. MDu. *husselen* shake, toss]

hŭt, n., & v.t. & i. (-tt-). **1.** Small mean house of rude construction; (Mil.) temporary wooden house for troops; ~-*circle* (Archaeol.), ring of stones or earth indicating site of prehistoric ~. **2.** v.t. Place (troops etc.) in ~*s*; (v.i.) lodge in ~. Hence ~**'MENT** n., ~ *encampment*. [17th c., f. F *hutte* f. MHG *hütte*]

hŭtch, n. Box-like pen for rabbits etc.; hut, cabin, small house; truck used in mining etc. [ME, f. OF *huche* f. med. L *hutica* of unkn. orig.]

Huzoor', n. Title of respect used by Indians in addressing superiors. [Arab. *ḥaḍūr* the presence]

huzza' (-ah), int., n., & v.i. & t. (arch.). Int. of exultation, encouragement, or applause; (make, greet with) the cry ~. [16th c., imit.]

hy'acinth, n. Kinds of bulbous plants with bell-shaped flowers of various colours, esp. purplish blue, so (esp. as Homeric epithet of doubtful sense for *locks*, *hair*) ~**INE²** (-in¹) a.; this colour; precious stone, orange variety of zircon. [in 16th c. replacing JACINTH; f. F *hyacinthe* f. L f. Gk *huakinthos*, flower & gem, also name of youth loved by Apollo]

Hy'adēs (-z), n. pl. Group of stars near Pleiades. [f. Gk *Huades* (acc. to pop. etym., f. *huō* rain, but perh. f. *hus* swine)] hyaena. See HYENA.

hy'aline, a. & n. Glass-like, vitreous (chiefly techn.); (n., poet.) smooth sea, clear sky, etc. [f. LL f. Gk hualinos (hualos glass, see -INE²)]

hy'alite, n. Colourless variety of opal. [f. Gk hualos glass, see -ITE]

hy'aloid, a. & n. (anat.). Glassy; ~ (membrane), thin transparent membrane enveloping vitreous humour of eye. [f. F hyaloïde f. LL f. Gk hualoeidēs (as prec., see -OID)]

hy̆b'rid, n. & a. 1. Offspring of two animals or plants of different species or varieties; person of mixed nationality; (fig.) thing, word, composed of incongruous elements, esp. of different languages. 2. adj. Cross-bred, mongrel; heterogeneous; ‖~ bill in Parliament, one combining characteristics of public & private bill, & referred to a~ committee. Hence~ITY (-ĭd²) n. [f. L hybrida, hibrida offspring of tame sow & wild boar]

hy̆b'ridism, n. Fact, condition, of being hybrid; cross-breeding. [prec. +-ISM]

hy̆b'ridiz|e, -is|e (-ĭz), v.t. & i. Subject (species etc.) to cross-breeding; produce hybrids; (of animal or plant) interbreed. Hence ~ABLE a., ~A'TION n. [HYBRID + -IZE]

hy̆d'atid, n. (path.). Cyst containing watery fluid, morbid formation (esp. one formed by, & containing, a tape-worm larva). [f. Gk hudatis -idos watery vesicle (hudōr -atos water, -ID²)]

Hy̆de Pa̍rk, n. A London park, a fashionable resort, & the scene of many political and other demonstrations.

hy̆d'ra, n. (Gk Myth.) snake whose many heads grew again when cut off; (fig.) thing hard to extirpate; water-snake; a fresh-water polyp. [L, f. Gk hudra water-snake]

hy̆dră̍n'gea (-ja), n. Kinds of shrubs with globular clusters of white, blue, or pink flowers. [f. Gk hudōr water + aggos vessel]

hy̆d'rant, n. Pipe (esp. in street) with nozzle to which hose can be attached, for drawing water from main. [U.S., f. Gk hudōr water + -ANT]

hy̆d'rate¹, n. (chem.). Compound of water with another compound or an element. [f. F hydrate f. Gk hudōr water, see -ATE¹]

hy̆d'r|āte², v.t. (chem.). Combine with water. Hence ~A'TION n. [f. prec.]

hy̆draul'ic, a. & n. 1. Of water conveyed through pipes or channels; operated by water-power, as ~ lift; ~ ram, automatic pump in which kinetic energy of descending column of water raises some of the water above its original level; hardening under water, as ~ cement; ~ press, hydrostatic press. 2. n. pl. Science of conveyance of liquids through pipes etc., esp. as motive power. Hence or cogn. hy̆draul'ICALLY adv., hy̆drauli'-

CIAN (-ĭshn) n. [f. L f. Gk hudraulikos (hudōr water + aulos pipe, see -IC)]

hy̆d'r|ic, a. (chem.). Of, containing, hydrogen. So ~IDE n. [f. HYDROGEN + -IC]

hy̆d'rō, n. (pl. ~s). = HYDROPATHIC. [colloq. abbr.]

hy̆dro-, comb. form of Gk hudōr water, (1) in miscell. terms, w. sense ' having to do with water ', (2) in names of diseases, w. sense ' dropsical ' or ' affected with accumulation of serous fluid ', (3) in chem. terms, usu. w. sense ' combined with hydrogen '; as: ~carb'on, compound of hydrogen & carbon; ~cĕph'alus, water on the brain; ~cephăl'ic, ~cĕph'alous, affected with this; ~chlor'ic, containing hydrogen & chlorine; ~cyăn'ic, containing hydrogen & cyanogen, esp. ~cyanic acid, prussic acid; ~dȳnăm'ic(al), of the forces acting on or- exerted by liquids; ~dȳnăm'ics, science of these forces; ~elĕc'tric, developing electricity by utilization of water power, (of electricity) produced by utilization of water-power; ~grapher (-ŏg²), person skilled in, ~graph'ic(al) having to do with, ~graphy; ~graphy (-ŏg²), scientific description of the waters of the earth; ~kinĕt'ic(s), (science) of the motion of liquids; ~logy (-ŏl²), science of the properties, laws, etc., of water; ~lysis (-ŏl²), decomposition of a compound by reaction with water, the water also being decomposed; ~măn'ia, craving for water; ~mechăn'ics (of liquids); ~meter (-ŏm²), instrument for finding specific gravity of liquids (occas. also of solids); ~mĕt'ric, ~metry (-ŏm²), concerned with, determination of, specific gravity of liquids; hȳd'rophane, opal that absorbs water & becomes transparent on immersion; hȳd'rophone, instrument for detection of sound-waves in water; hȳd'rophȳte, aquatic plant; hȳd'roplane, fin-like device enabling submarine to rise or fall, light fast motor-boat designed to skim over surface, seaplane; ~pneumăt'ic, involving combined action of water & air; ~quin'one, preparation from quinone, used (Phot.) as developer; hȳd'rosphere, waters of the earth's surface; hȳd'rostat, electrical device for detecting presence of water; ~therapeut'ic, ~thĕ'rapy, hydropathic, hydropathy; ~therm'al, of the action of heated water on earth's crust; ~thor'ax, dropsy of the chest; ~tropism (-ŏt²), (of plants) tendency to turn to or from moisture; ~zō'a n. pl., class of coelenterate animals chiefly marine, including jelly-fish & fresh-water hydra.

hy̆d'rogĕn, n. Colourless invisible odourless gas, an element, the lightest substance known, combining with oxygen to form water; ~ bomb, (also fusion or thermo-nuclear bomb) immensely powerful bomb utilizing fusion of ~ atomic nuclei. Hence hȳdrŏ'gĕnous a. [f. F HYDRO(gène -GEN)]

hy̆drŏ'gĕn|āte, v.t. Charge, cause to combine, with hydrogen. So ~IZE v.t. [prec. +-ATE³]

hy̆d'roid, a. & n. (zool.). (Animal) like, allied to, the hydra (polyp). [-OID]

hy̆d'romĕl, n. Mixture of honey & water; *vinous* ~ (also *mead*), this fermented. [L, f. Gk *hudromeli* (*meli* honey, see HYDRO-)]

hy̆dropăth'ĭc, a. & n. **1.** Of, concerned with, hydropathy. **2.** n. Hotel where ~ treatment may be had. [f. foll. +-IC]

hy̆drŏp'ath|y̆, n. Medical treatment by external & internal application of water. So ~IST n. [f. G *hydropathie* (HYDRO-, -PATHY)]

hy̆drophōb'|ia, n. Aversion to water, esp. as symptom of rabies in man; rabies, esp. in man; (joc.) dread of water. So ~IC a. [16th c., f. LL f. Gk *hudroPHOBIA*, see HYDRO-]

hy̆drŏp'ĭc, a. Dropsical. [ME, f. OF *ydropique* f. L f. Gk *hudrōpikos* (as HYDROPSY, see -IC)]

hy̆dropŏn'ĭcs, n. Soilless culture, art of growing plants without soil, in water impregnated with chemicals. [HYDRO-, Gk *ponos* labour]

hy̆d'rŏpsy̆, n. (arch. or med.). Dropsy. [ME, f. OF *ydropisie* f. med. L *hydropisia* (for L -sis) f. Gk *hudrōps* (*hudōr* water)]

hy̆drostăt'ĭc, a. & n. **1.** Of the equilibrium of liquids & the pressure exerted by liquids at rest; ~ *paradox*, principle that any quantity of a perfect liquid, however small, may be made to balance any other quantity; ~ *press* (also *hydraulic, Bramah's, press*), machine in which pressure of a body of water is multiplied by transmission from small to larger cylinder. **2.** n. pl. Branch of mechanics concerned with the pressure & equilibrium of liquids at rest. Hence ~AL a., ~alLY² adv. [17th c., f. Gk *hudrostatēs* ~ balance (HYDRO-, STATIC)]

hy̆d'rous, a. (chem., mineral.). Containing water. [f. Gk *hudōr* water +-OUS]

hy̆drŏx'īde, n. (chem.). Compound of element or radical with hydrogen & oxygen, not with water. [HYDRO- +OXIDE]

hy̆ēn'a, hy̆aen'a, n. Carnivorous quadruped allied to dog tribe; *striped* ~, variety whose howl is compared to fiendish laughter; cruel, treacherous, or rapacious person; Tasmanian tiger; ~ *-dog*, S.-African canine quadruped like ~. [L (-ae-) f. Gk *huaina* fem. f. *hus* pig]

hy̆eto-, comb. form of Gk *huetos* rain, as ~*graphy* (-ŏg²), mapping of rainfall; ~*meter* (-ŏm²), rain-gauge.

Hȳgei'a (-jē'a), n. Goddess of health; health personified. Hence **hȳgēi'AN** (-jē'an) a. [f. Gk *Hugeia* late for *Hugieia* (*hugiēs* healthy)]

hȳ'gi|ēne (or -jēn), n. Principles of health; sanitary science. Hence ~ĕn'IC(AL) aa., ~ĕn'icalLY² adv., ~ĕn'ICS, ~enIST, DD., (or -jēn²). [f. F *hygiène* f. Gk *hugieinē* (*tekhnē* art) of health, f. *hugiēs* healthy]

hȳgro-, comb. form of Gk *hugros* wet, fluid, as: *hȳg'rodeik* (-dīk), form of ~*meter*; ~*logy* (-ŏl²), study of the humidity of atmosphere etc.; ~*meter* (-ŏm²), instrument for measuring humidity of air or gas; ~*mĕl'ric*, ~*metry* (-ŏm²), concerned with, measurement of, humidity; *hȳg'roscōpe*, instrument indicating but not measuring humidity of air; ~*scop'ic*, of the ~*scope*, (of bodies) tending to absorb moisture.

Hy̆k'sōs (-z), n. pl. The shepherd kings of Egypt (about 2000 B.C.). [Gk *Huksōs*]

hȳl'ic, a. Of matter, material. [f. LL f. Gk *hulikos* (*hulē* matter, see -IC)]

hȳlo-, comb. form of Gk *hulē* matter, as: ~*morph'ism*, doctrine that primordial matter is first cause of the universe; *hȳl'otheism*, doctrine that God & matter are identical; *hȳl'otheist*, ~*theïs'tic*, holder of, concerned with, this doctrine; ~*zō'ism*, ~*zoist(ic)*, ~*zō'ic*, materialism, -ist(ic).

Hy̆m'ĕn¹, n. (Gk & Rom. Myth.). God of marriage. So **hy̆mēnē'AL** a., **hy̆mēnē'alLY²** adv. [L, f. Gk *Humēn*]

hy̆m'ĕn², n. (anat.). Virginal membrane, stretched across external orifice of vagina. [f. LL f. Gk *humēn* membrane]

hy̆mĕn|o-, comb. form of Gk *humēn* membrane, as ~*ŏp'tera* n. pl., large order of insects with four membranous wings, so ~*ŏp'teral*, ~*ŏp'terous*, aa.

hymn (hĭm), n., & v.t. & i. **1.** Song of praise to God, esp. metrical composition sung in religious service; song of praise in honour of a god or other exalted being; ~*-book* (of ~s). **2.** v.t. Praise (God etc.) in ~s, express (praise etc.) in ~; (v.i.) sing ~s. Hence **hy̆m'nIC** a., **hy̆m'nIST** n. [ME *ymne* etc. f. OF *ymne* f. L f. Gk *humnos*; OE dir. f. L]

hy̆m'n|al, a. & n. Of hymns; (n.) hymn-book, so ~ARY¹ n. [n. 15th c. f. med. L *hymnale* (prec. +-AL)]

hy̆m'nod|y̆, n. Singing of hymns; composition of hymns, whence ~IST n.; hymns collectively. [f. med. L f. Gk *humnōdia* (*humnos* hymn + *ōdē* song, ODE)]

hy̆mnŏg'rapher, n. Composer of hymns. [f. LL f. Gk *humnographos* (as prec., see -GRAPHER)]

hy̆mnŏl'og|y̆, n. Composition, study of, hymns; hymns collectively. So **hy̆mnolŏ'gic** a., ~IST n. [HYMN +-O- +-LOGY]

hy̆'oid a. & n. (anat.). **1.** ~ *bone*, tongue--bone between chin & thyroid cartilage; pertaining to this. **2.** n. ~ bone. [f. F *hyoïde* f. Gk *huoeidēs* shaped like letter U]

hy̆oscy̆'amine, hy̆'oscine, nn. Alkaloids contained in henbane & used in medicine. [L, f. Gk *huoskuamos* henbane (*hus huos* pig, *kuamos* bean), -INE⁵]

hy̆p. See HIP³.

hy̆paeth'ral, -pēth'ral, a. Open to the sky, roofless (orig. of Gk temples); open--air. [f. L f. Gk *hupaithros* (*aithēr* air, see HYPO-)]

hўpăll'agė, n. (gram.). Reversal of natural relations of two elements in a proposition (e.g. *apply the wound to water* for *apply water to the wound*). [LL, f. Gk *hupallagē* (*allassō* exchange, see HYPO-)]

hўper-, pref. = Gk *huper* in senses 'over', 'above', 'exceeding', 'excessive'.

hўperaesth|ēs'ia, n. (Path.) morbid sensitiveness of nerves; excessive sensibility. So ~ET'IC (-ĕt'-) a. [HYPER- + Gk -*aisthēsia* f. *aisthanomai* perceive]

hўpẽrb'atŏn, n. Inversion of normal order of words, esp. for sake of emphasis. [L, f. Gk *huperbaton* (*bainō* step, see HYPER-)]

hўpẽrb'ola, n. (geom.). Curve produced when cone is cut by plane making larger angle with base than side of cone makes (cf. ELLIPSE). Hence hўperbŏl'IC a. [mod. L, f. Gk *huperbolē* f. *huperballō* exceed (*ballō* throw, see HYPER-)]

hўpẽrb'ol|ė, n. (rhet.). Exaggerated statement not meant to be taken literally. Hence hўperbŏl'ICAL a., hўperbŏl'icAL-LY[2] adv., ~ISM, ~IST, nn. [L, as prec.]

hўperbŏr'ėan, a. & n. (Inhabitant) of the extreme north of the earth or (colloq.) of a country; (Gk Myth.) one of a race living in land of sunshine & plenty beyond north wind. [f. LL *hyperboreanus* (L -*boreus*) f. Gk *huperboreos* (*Boreas* north wind, see HYPER-)]

hўpercătalĕc'tic, a. (pros.). (Of verse) having extra syllable after last complete dipody. [f. LL HYPER(*catalecticus* CATA-LECTIC)]

hўpercrit'ic|al, a. Too critical, esp. of small faults. Hence ~alLY[2] adv., ~ISM n., ~IZE v.t. & i. [f. mod. L *hypercriticus* (HYPER-, CRITICAL)]

hўpermĕt'ric(al), aa. (Of verse) having a redundant syllable; (of syllable) redundant. [f. Gk *hypermetros* (*metron* metre, HYPER-)]

hўpermĕtr|ōp'ia, n. Morbidly long sight. Hence ~ōp'IC a. [as prec. + Gk *ōps* eye + -*ia* -Y[1]]

hўperphўs'ical (-z-), a. Supernatural. [HYPER-]

hўp'ersthēne, n. Orthorhombic rock--forming mineral of the pyroxene group. [f. F HYPER(*stène* f. Gk *sthenos* strength, from its hardness)]

hўpertĕn's|ion (-shn), n. Abnormally high blood pressure. So ~IVE a. [HYPER- + TENSION]

hўpẽrt'roph|ў, n. Enlargement (*of* organ etc.) due to excessive nutrition. Hence or cogn. hўpertrŏph'IC, ~iED[2] (-Id), aa. [HYPER- + Gk -*trophia* nourishment f. *trephō*]

hypethral. See HYPAETHRAL.

hўph'en, n., & v.t. 1. Sign (-) used to join two words together, to join separated syllables of word broken at end of line, or to divide word into parts; short pause between syllables in speaking. 2. v.t. Join (words) with ~, write (compound word) with ~. [LL, f. Gk *huphen* together (*hupo* under + *hen* one)] ·

hўph'enāte, v.t. = prec. vb (~*d Ameri-cans*, German-Americans, Irish-Ameri-cans, etc.). [prec., -ATE[3]]

hўpno- (bef. vowel *hypn*-), comb. form of Gk *hupnos* sleep, as : ~*gen'esis*, ~*genĕt'ic*, induction of, inducing, the hypnotic state; ~*logy* (-ŏl[2]), science of the pheno-mena of sleep.

hўpnōs'is, n. (pl. -*ōsēs*). Artificially pro-duced sleep; hypnotic state. [f. Gk *hupnoō* make sleep, -OSIS]

hўpnŏt'ic, a. & n. 1. Of, producing, hyp-notism. 2. n. Thing that produces sleep; person under influence of hypnotism. [f. F *hypnotique* f. LL f. Gk *hupnōtikos* (as prec., see -OTIC)]

hўp'not|ism, n. (Artificial production of) a state resembling deep sleep, in which the subject acts only on external sug-gestion. So ~IST n., ~IZE v.t. [f. prec. + -ISM]

hўp'ō, n. (photog.). The salt formerly called hyposulphite, now thiosulphate, of soda, used in fixing. [abbr.]

hўpo-, pref. (bef. vowel *hyp*-) = Gk *hupo* under, below, slightly; (Chem.) form-ing names of oxygen compounds lower in the series than those with the simple name. Exx.: *hŷp'oblast*, inner layer of cells in blastoderm; ~*brăn'chial* (-ngk-), situated under the gills; ~*cŷc'loid*, curve traced by point in circumference of circle rolling round interior circumference of another circle; ~*găs'trium*, lowest region of abdomen; ~*gĕ'al*, ~*gē'an*, aa., under-ground; *hŷp'ogēne*, (of rocks) formed under the surface; ~*ge'um*, pl. ~*gea*, underground chamber; ~*gloss'al* (nerve), motor nerve of tongue; ~*gynous* (-ŏj[2]) (Bot.), situated below pistils or ovary; *hŷp'onăsty* (Bot.), tendency in plant--organs to grow more rapidly on under side; ~*phŏs'phite*, salt of hypophosphor-ous acid; *hŷp'ostŷle*, (hall etc.) with roof supported on pillars; ~*trachel'ium* (-kē-), lower part of capital of column.

hўp'ocaust, n. (Rom. Ant.). Hollow space under floor in which heat from furnace was accumulated for heating house or bath. [f. L f. Gk *hupokausion* place heated from below (*kaiō*, *kau*-, burn, see prec.)]

hўpochŏn'dr|ia (-k-), n. Morbid depres-sion either apparently causeless or due to (unnecessary) anxiety about health. So ~i'ASIS n. [f. LL f. Gk (*ta*) *hupokhondria* soft parts of body below costal cartilages (*khondros* cartilage, see HYPO-)]

hўpochŏn'dr|iăc (-k-), a. & n. 1. Of, affected by, hypochondria. 2. n. ~iac person. Hence ~i'ACAL a., ~i'acalLY[2] adv. [f. F *hypochondriaque* f. med. L f. Gk *hupokhondriakos* (as prec., see -AC)]

hўpocoris'tic, a. (gram.). Of the nature of a pet-name. [f. Gk *hupokoristikos* (*hupokorizomai* play the child)]

hўpŏc′risў, n. Simulation of virtue or goodness; dissimulation, pretence. [ME, f. OF *ypocrisie* f. eccl. L f. Gk *hupokrisis* lit. acting of a part f. *hupokrinomai* (*hupo-* HYPO- + *krinō* decide, judge)]

hўp′ocrite, n. Person guilty of hypocrisy; dissembler, pretender. So **hўpocrit′ICAL** a., **hўpocrit′icaLLY**[2] adv. [ME, f. OF *ypocrile* f. eccl. L (-*ta*) f. Gk *hupokrilēs* actor (as prec.)]

hўpoderm′|ic, a. & n. 1. (Med., of drugs etc.) introduced beneath the skin, as ~*ic injection*; ~*ic needle*, *syringe*, for ~ic injection; (Anat.) lying under the skin. 2. n. ~ic injection, syringe. Hence ~ICALLY adv. [f. HYPO- + Gk *derma* skin +-IC]

hўpŏs′tas|is, n. (pl.~*es*, pr. -ēz). 1.(med.). Excess of blood in organs of body. 2. (metaphys.). Underlying substance, opp. to attributes or to what is unsubstantial. 3. (theol.). Personality (of Christ), person (of the Godhead). So **hўpostāt′IC(AL) aa.**, **hўpostāt′icaLLY**[2] adv., ~IZE(3), **hў-pŏs′tatIZE(3)**, vv.t. (metaphys.). [f. LL f. Gk *hupostasis* (*hupo-* HYPO- + *stasis* standing, state)]

hўpoten′s|ion (-shn), n. Low blood pressure. So ~IVE a. [HYPO- + TENSION]

hўpŏt′ĕnūse, n. Side opposite right angle of triangle. [f. L f. Gk *hupoteinousa* (*grammē*) subtending line (*hupo-* HYPO- + *teinō* stretch); also (improp.) -*thenuse*]

hўp′othĕc, n. (Rom. & Sc. Law). Security established by law over thing belonging to debtor. So **hўpŏth′ĕcaRY**[1] a. [f. F *hypothèque* or LL f. Gk *hupothēkē*]

hўpŏth′ĕc|āte, v.t. Pledge, mortgage. Hence ~A′TION n. [f. med. L *hypothecare* (as prec.), see -ATE[3]]

hўpŏth′ĕsis, n. (pl. -*thesēs*). Supposition made as basis for reasoning, without assumption of its truth, or as starting-point for investigation; groundless assumption. So **hўpothĕt′IC(AL) aa.**, **hўpothĕt′icaLLY**[2] adv. [f. LL f. Gk *hupothesis* foundation]

hўpŏth′ĕsize, -ise (-īz), v.i. & t. Frame a hypothesis; (trans.) assume. [f. prec. +-IZE]

hўpso-, comb. form of Gk *hupsos* height, as: ~*graphy* (-ŏg[2]), department of geography dealing with altitudes; ~*meter* (-ŏm[2]), ~*mĕt′ric(al)*, ~*metry* (-ŏm[2]), instrument for, concerned with, science of, measuring altitudes.

Hўr′āx, n. Genus of small rabbit-like mammals, including Syrian rock-rabbit and S.-Afr. rock-badger. [f. Gk *hurax* shrew-mouse]

hўs′on, n. Kind of green tea from China. [f. Chin. *hsi-ch′un* lit. bright spring]

|| **hў[2]-spў**, I **spў**, n. Kind of hide-&-seek.

hўss′op, n. Small bushy aromatic herb, formerly used medicinally; (Bibl.) plant whose twigs were used for sprinkling in Jewish rites, bunch of this used in purification. [ME *ysope* f. OF f. L f. Gk

hyssōpos, of Semitic orig.; *h-* f. 16th c.; OE dir. f. L]

hўsterēs′is, n. (phys.). Lagging of magnetic induction behind the magnetizing force. [f. Gk *husterēsis* (*husteros* coming after)]

hўstēr′ia, n. Functional disturbance of nervous system (esp. of women), characterized by anaesthesia, convulsions, etc., & usu. attended with disturbance of moral & intellectual faculties (formerly thought to be due to disturbance of womb); morbid excitement. [mod. medical L, on foll.]

hўstē′ric, a. & n. 1. = foll. 2. n. pl. Hysterical fits or convulsions. [f. L f. Gk *husterikos* of the womb (*hustera*, see -IC)]

hўstĕ′rical, a. Of, affected with, hysteria; morbidly emotional. Hence ~LY[2] adv. [as prec. +-AL]

hўstero-, comb. form of Gk *hustera* womb, as: ~*gĕn′ic*, ~*geny* (-ŏj[2]), productive, production, of HYSTERIA; ~*logy* (-ŏl[2]), treatise on the uterus; ~*tomy* (-ŏt[2]), operation of cutting into the uterus.

hўs′terŏn prŏt′erŏn, n. (Gram.) figure of speech in which what should come last is put first; inversion of natural order. [LL, f. Gk *husteron proteron* latter (put in place of) former]

I

I[1], **i**, (I), letter (pl. *I*s, I′s). As Roman numeral I or i = 1, as i 1, ii 2, iii 3, iv (rarely iiii) 4, vi 6, viii 8, ix (rarely viiii) 9, xi 11, xiv 14, li 51, cii 102, miv 1,004.

I[2] (ī), pron. & n. Subjective case of 1st pers. pron. (objective *me*, poss. *my*; pl. *we*, obj. *us*, poss. *our*); (n., metaphys.) *the I*, the ego, subject or object of self-consciousness. [OE *ic*, OS *ik*, OHG *ih*, ON *ek*, Goth. *ik*, cogn. w. L, Gk *egō*]

-i, suf. forming pl. of L nn. in -*us* & -*er* of 2nd decl. & of Ital. wds in -*o*, -*e*; retained in E in wds of scientific or learned use, as *cirri*, *foci*, *dilettanti*, *literati*; also freq. in mod. L names of groups or orders in Nat. Hist., as *acanthopterygii*, *acrocarpi*.

-i-, connecting vowel in L, being stem-vowel, as in *omnivorus*, weakened representative of this, as in *herbivorus* (*herba-*), *granivorus* (*grano-*), or merely connective, as in *graminivorus* (*gramin-*); so in E wds f. L or thr. F, & in mod. wds formed on L models, as *hydriform*, *setiform*. Cf. -O-.

-ia[1], suf., f. L & Gk -*ia*, forming abstract nn. etc., as *hydrophobia*, *mania*, *militia*; freq. in mod. L terms of pathology (*cephalalgia*, *hysteria*); of bot. (classes, as *Cryptogamia*, & personal names, as *dahlia*, *fuchsia*; in name of countries, as *Australia*; & in names of alkaloids, as *morphia*, *strychnia*, (in more recent nomenclature -*ine*). F -*ie* f. -*ia* gives -Y[1].

-ia², suf. forming pl. of Gk nn. in *-ion* & L nn. in *-ium*, as *paraphernalia, regalia*; freq. in mod. L names of classes etc. in zool., as *mammalia, reptilia*.

-ial, suf. repr. L *-ialis*, in adjj. f. n. -stems in *-io-, -ia-*, as *curialis, tibialis*; much used in med. L, F, & E, to form adjj. f. L adjj. in *-is* & *-ius*, as *celestial, dictatorial* (L *-tis, -rius*). Cf. -AL.

i'amb, n. = IAMBUS. [Anglicized f. IAMBUS]

iăm'bic, a. & n. (pros.). Of, containing, based on, iambuses; (n.) ~ verse. [f. F *iambique* or LL f. Gk *iambikos* (as foll., see -IC)]

iăm'bus, n. (pl. *-buses, -bī*). The metrical foot ‿‑. [L, f. Gk *iambos* iambus, lampoon (*iaptō* assail)]

-ian, suf. of aa. & nn. = L *-anus* -AN added to stems in *-i-*, as *Italian, Virgilian*, or w. connective *-i-*, as *Christian*; esp. forming aa. on proper names, as *Addisonian, Bostonian*, (varying in place-names with *-er*, as *Londoner*, & often added to Latinized stems, as *Mancunian, Glaswegian, Oxonian, Liverpudlian*).

Ibēr'ian (ī-), a. & n. 1. Of ancient Iberia; of Spain & Portugal as one country. 2. n. Inhabitant, language, of ancient Iberia. [f. L *Iberia* f. Gk *Ibēres* Spaniards + -AN]

ĭb'ĕx, n. (pl. ~es). Wild goat of Alps & Apennines, with large recurved horns. [L]

ĭbid'ĕm, adv. In the same book, chapter, passage, etc. (abbr. *ib., ibid.*). [L]

ĭb'ĭs, n. (pl. ~es). Stork-like bird with long curved bill found in lakes & swamps of warm climates; *Sacred I~*, kind venerated by ancient Egyptians. [L f. Gk]

-ible, suf. f. L *-ibilis*, i.e. *-bilis* -BLE as appended to p.p. stems, 3rd conj. vbs, & some 2nd conj. (*terrible*), or f. L *-ibilis* (*-bilis* with 4th conj.); also in mod. formations, as *avertible*. Displaced by *-able* in many wds taken thr. F or formed really or apparently on E vbs. Meaning: ‘that can be —d’.

-ic, suf. 1. In adjj., immed. repr. F *-ique*, f. L *-icus* (= Gk *-ikos*) in wds of L formation as *classicus, publicus*, or in L adoptives f. Gk, as *grammaticus, poeticus*. Later E adjj. in *-ic* are direct f. Gk, or on Gk elements, or (esp. scientific terms) on wds f. L or other langg., as *carbonic, Byronic*. (Chem.) *-ic* in names of oxygen acids etc. indicates higher degree of oxidation than *-ous*, as in *chloric, sulphuric*. 2. Gk adjj. in *-ikos* were used as nn. in 3 ways: in masc. sing., as *kritikos* man able to discern, critic; in fem. sing., as *mousikē (tekhnē)* art of the muses, music; in neut. pl., as *ta oikonomika* things pertaining to management, economics. In L the last two both became *-ica*, whence much fluctuation in med. L as to grammatical treatment. The Rom. langg. usu. had fem. sing. for names of arts & sciences, but F occas. had pl., as *les mathématiques*. E wds before 1500 were sing., as still *arithmetic, music, magic, logic, rhetoric*;

later, *-ics* became usu. form for names of sciences, as *acoustics, conics, dynamics*, (treated as sing.), & of practical matters, as *athletics, politics, tactics*, (pl.). Besides this spec. use, other adjj. in *-ic* become nn., as *epic, emetic, cosmetic, rustic, mechanic*.

-ical, suf. (*-ic* + *-al*) forming adjj. f. nn., as *musical*, or more commonly secondary adjj. f. adjj. as *comical, historical*. Many adjj. have both the *-ic* & *-ical* form, often with distinction in meaning (see -AL).

-ically, suf. (*-ical* + *-LY²*) forming advv. corr. to adjj. in *-ic, -ical*, advv. in *-icly* as *publicly, politicly*, being rare.

ice¹, n. 1. Frozen water; *dry* ~, frozen carbon dioxide; *break the* ~, (fig.) make a beginning, break through reserve or stiffness; CUT² *no* ~; *on thin* ~ (fig.), on dangerous ground; (w. pl.) frozen confection, ~-cream, water-~. 2. ~-*age*, glacial period; ~-*axe* (used by Alpine climbers for cutting steps); ~'*blink*, luminous appearance on horizon, caused by reflexion from ~; ~-*boat*, boat mounted on runners for travelling on ~, (also ~-*breaker*) boat used for breaking ~ on river etc.; *~-box*, refrigerator; ~-*cream*, flavoured cream or custard congealed in freezing-mixture; *coconut* etc. ~, slabs of sugar flavoured with coconut etc.; ~-*fall*, steep part of glacier like frozen waterfall; ~-*field*, expanse of ~, esp. in Polar regions; ~-*foot*, belt of ~ along coast in Arctic regions; ~-*hockey* (played on skates); ~-*house*, building often partly or wholly underground for storing ~; ~'*man*, man skilled in traversing ~, (also) maker of ~s; (~-)PACK¹; ~-*pick*, stiletto for splitting up table ~; ~-*plant* (with leaves covered with watery vesicles looking like ~-specks); ~-*pudding*, a frozen confection; ~-*run*, artificial tobogganing track of ~; ~-*wool* (glossy kind used in crochet etc.). [OE *is*, OLG, OHG *is*, ON *iss* f. Gmc **isa-*]

ice², v.t. & i. Freeze; cover (as) with ice; cool (wine) in ice; cover (cake etc.) with concretion of sugar; become covered with ice, freeze *up*. [f. prec.]

-ice, suf., OF, f. L *-itia* in abstract nn. (*justice, avarice, malice, notice*, & F formations *cowardice, jaundice*) & f. L *-itius, -itium*, (*novice, precipice, service*). But E *-ice* has freq. diff. orig., as in *apprentice, bodice, practice*, where *-ice* is partly due to assim. See -ISE².

ice'bĕrg (īs'b-), n. Huge floating mass of ice, detached portion of glacier carried out to sea; (fig.) unemotional or cold-blooded person. [prob. f. Du. *ijsberg* (*ijs* ice + *berg* hill)]

Ice'land (īs'l-), n. Large island between Norway and Greenland; ~ *lichen, moss*, edible species; ~ *poppy*, yellow Arctic poppy; ~ *spar*, transparent variety of calcite. Hence ~ER¹(4) n. [ME, f. ON *Island* (*iss* ice + LAND¹)]

Icelăn'dic (īsl-), a. & n. (Language) of Iceland. [-IC]

Ich'abŏd (ĭk-), n. (As exclamation of regret =) the glory has departed. [Heb., see 1 *Sam*. iv. 21]

ĭchneum'on (-k-), n. **1.** Small brown weasel-like quadruped allied to mongoose, noted for destroying crocodiles' eggs. **2.** (Also ~*fly*) small parasitic hymenopterous insect depositing eggs in or on larva of another insect. [L, f. Gk *ikhneumōn* spider-hunting wasp f. *ikhneuō* track (*ikhnos*)]

ĭchnc· (ĭk-) in comb. = Gk *ikhnos* track, trace, as: ~*graph'ic(al)*, ~*graphy* (-ŏg²), (of) the drawing of ground-plans; ~*lite* (ĭk²), fossil footprint (also *ichnite*, pr. ĭk'nĭt); ~*logy* (-ŏl²), study of fossil footprints.

ĭch'ōr (ĭk-), n. (Gk Myth.) fluid flowing like blood in veins of gods; (Path.) watery acrid discharge from wounds etc. Hence ~OUS (ĭk'or-) a. [Gk *ikhōr*]

ĭchthyo· (ĭk-) in comb. (bef. vowel *ichthy·*) = Gk *ikhthus* fish, as: ~*grapher*, ~*graphy*, (-ŏg²), writer on, description of, fishes; ~*latry* (-ŏl²), worship of a fish-god; ~*lite* (ĭk²), fossil fish; ~*logy* (-ŏl²), study of fishes, whence ~*lo'gical*, ~*logist* (-ŏl²); ~*phagi*, ~*phagist*, (-ŏf²), fish-eater(s); ~*phagous* (-ŏf²), fish-eating; *ichthyor'nis*, extinct genus of toothed birds.

ĭch'thyoid (-k-), a. & n. Fish-like; (n.) vertebrate of fish type. [prec. + -OID]

ĭchthyosaur'us (-k-), n. Extinct marine animal with large head, tapering body, four paddles, & long tail. [ICHTHYO- + Gk *sauros* lizard]

ĭchthÿlōs'ĭs (-k-), n. Disease in which epidermis becomes dry & horny. So ~OT'IC (-ŏt²) a. [f. Gk *ikhthus* fish + -OSIS]

-ician (-ĭshn), suf. (= F *-icien*), spec. form of -IAN (ME & F *-ien*) added to names of arts or sciences in *-ic(s)* to form personal designations (= one skilled in or concerned with), as *arithmetician*, *logician*, *optician*, *politician*; occas. used when there is no corresp. n. (& even no adj.) in *-ic*, as *algebrician*, *mortician*.

ĭ'cicle, n. Tapering ice-formation, produced by freezing of successive drops trickling from the point of attachment. [ME (f. Scand., cf. MSw. *isikil*) f. ICE + (dial.) *ickle* (= OE *gicel*, ON *jǫkull* ~); repl. OE *isgicel (cf. MLG *isjokel*)]

ĭ'cing, n. In vbl senses of ICE², esp.: sugar etc. coating of cake etc.; formation of ice on aircraft. [-ING¹]

ĭc'kle, a. (nursery). Little.

ĭc'ŏn, n. Image, statue; (Eastern Church) painting, mosaic, etc., of sacred personage, itself regarded as sacred. [L, f. Gk *eikōn* image]

ĭcŏn'ĭc, a. Of (the nature of) an image or portrait; (of statues) following a conventional type. [f. L f. Gk *eikonikos* (as prec., see -IC)]

ĭcono· in comb. = Gk *eikōn* image, as: ~*graphy* (-ŏg²), illustration of subject by drawings or figures, book whose essence is pictures, treatise on pictures or statuary, study of portraits esp. of an individual; so ~*grapher* (-ŏg²), ~*graph'ic*; ~*later*, ~*latry*, (-ŏl²), worshipper, worship, of images; ~*logy* (-ol²), study of icons (in any sense); ~*machy* (-ŏm'akĬ), war against use of images in connexion with worship; ~*stasis* (-ŏs²), (Eastern Church) screen separating sanctuary from main body of church, & on which icons are placed.

ĭcŏn'oclăsm, n. Breaking of images (lit. & fig.). [prec. + Gk *klasma* (*klaō* break, -M)]

ĭcŏn'oclăst, n. Breaker of images, esp. one who took part in movement in 8th & 9th cc. against use of images in religious worship in churches of the East; (fig.) one who assails cherished beliefs. Hence ~IC (-ăs²) a. [f. med. L f. Gk *eikonoklastēs* (*eikōn* ICON + *klastēs* f. *klaō* break)]

ĭcŏnŏm'ēter, n. (Photog.) direct-vision view-finder (either fixed to camera, or detached & adjustable for various lenses & sizes of plate); (Surv.) optical instrument for ascertaining size or distance of an object. [ICONO- + -METER]

ĭc'osahĕd'ron (-a-h-), n. Solid contained by twenty plane faces. [f. Gk *eikosaedron* (*eikosi* twenty + *hedra* base)]

-ics. See -IC(2).

ĭc'tus, n. (pros.). Rhythmical or metrical stress. [L, = blow, f. *icere* strike]

ĭ'cȳ, a. Abounding in, covered with, ice; very cold (lit., & fig. as ~*manners*). Hence **ĭ'cĭLY²** adv., **ĭ'cĭNESS** n. [-Y²]

ĭd, n. (Biol.) a unit of germ-plasm or idioplasm; (Psycho-anal.) *the* instinctive impulses of the individual. [first sense, abbr. IDIOPLASM; second, f. L *id* that]

-id¹, suf. repr. F *-ide* f. L *-idus*, which forms adjj. chiefly f. vbs w. *-ē-* stems, as *timidus* timid f. *timēre*, but also f. vbs w. *-i-* or consonant stem, as *rapidus* rapid f. *rapēre*, & f. nn., as *morbidus* morbid f. *morbus*. Earlier E wds come thr. F, others f. L direct.

-id², suf. of nn. (= F *-ide*) f. L f. Gk *-id-* (nom. *-is*), as *chrysalid*, *pyramid*. In bot., *amaryllid*, *orchid*, etc., should denote plants amaryllis, orchis, etc., but in fact denote members of the family of which these are typical genera (*Amaryllideae*, *Orchidaceae*).

-id³, suf. of nn. & aa. (zool.). **1.** f. L names of families in *-idae* pl. of *-ides* f. Gk *-ĭdēs* son of, as *Seleucid*, member of the dynasty founded by Seleucus. **2.** f. L names of classes in *-ida* taken as neut. pl. of *-ides* (= Gk *-idēs*), as *Arachnid*, member of the class *Arachnida*. **3.** (Astron.) applied to groups or showers of meteors radiating from a constellation, after which they are named, as *Leonid*.

-id⁴, suf. Early spelling of -IDE, now chiefly U.S.

ide, n. Fish allied to carp. [f. Swed. *id*]

-ide, suf. (chem.) forming names of simple compounds of an element with another element or radical, the suf. *-ide* being added to the name (usu. abbrev.) of the more electro-negative element, as *sodium chloride, carbon sulphide, calcium carbide*; first used in *oxide* from *oxygen*.

idē′a (or *-ĭa*), n. **1.** Archetype, pattern, as distinguished from its realization in individuals; (Platonic) eternally existing pattern of which individual things in any class are imperfect copies. **2.** Conception, plan, of thing to be aimed at, created, etc.; plan of action. **3.** Notion conceived by the mind; way of thinking (*the young ~*, the child's mind); vague belief, fancy, as *the ~ of his doing such a thing, I had no ~ you were there*. **4.** (Descartes, Locke) immediate object of thought or mental perception; (Kant) conception of reason transcending all experience. **5.** Man of *~s*, resourceful person; **the big ~*, scheme, proposal (usu. ironical: *what's the big ~?*, what folly have you in mind?). Hence *~′d*, *~ED²*, (-ĭ′ad), *~LESS* (-ĭ′al-), aa. [L f. Gk, = form, kind, f. *id-* see]

idē′al, a. & n. **1.** Answering to one's highest conception; embodying an idea; existing only in idea; visionary; relating to, consisting of, (Platonic) ideas. **2.** n. Perfect type; actual thing as standard for imitation. Hence *~LY²* adv. [f. F *idéal* f. LL *idealis* (as prec., see -AL)]

idē′al|ism, n. Representation of things in ideal form, imaginative treatment, practice of forming or following after ideals, (cf. REALISM), so *~ĬZA′TION* n., *~IZE* v.t. & i.; (Philos.) system of thought in which the object of external perception is held to consist of ideas (cf. REALISM). So *~IST* n., *~ĬS′TIC* a. [-ISM]

idēăl′itȳ, n. Quality of being ideal; (Phrenol.) imaginative faculty. [-ITY]

idē′āte, v.t. & i. Imagine, conceive; form ideas. Hence **idēA′TION** n., **idēā′tionAL** (-shon-) a. [f. IDEA + -ATE³]

idée fixe (ēdāfēks′), n. Idea that dominates the mind, monomania. [F, lit. fixed idea]

id′ĕm, n. or adv. (abbr. *id.*). (In) the same author (ĭ-); the same word (ĭ-); *idem quod* (abbr. *i.q.*), the same as. [L]

idĕn′tic, a. (Diplom.) *~ note*, simultaneous & uniformly worded expression of opinion from several powers to another; = foll. [f. med. L *identicus* (cf. IDENTITY)]

idĕn′tical, a. (Of one thing viewed at different times) the very same; (of different things) agreeing in every detail (*with*); (of twins) developed from a single fertilized ovum; (Logic, Math.) expressing an identity (*~ proposition*, of the type *Man is man*). Hence *~LY²* adv. [-AL]

idĕn′ti|fȳ, v.t. Treat (thing) as identical (*with*); associate one*self* inseparably *with* (party, policy, etc.); establish identity of. Hence *~FIABLE* a., *~FICA′TION* n. (*~fication* or *~ty disc*, of rubber or metal worn by

soldier etc. **on active service** & bearing his name etc.). [f. med. L *identificare* (as foll., see -FY)]

idĕn′titȳ, n. Absolute sameness; individuality, personality, (*~ disc*, see prec.); (Alg.) equality of two expressions for all values of the literal quantities, expression of this, e.g. $(x+1)^2 = x^2 + 2x + 1$. [f. LL *identitas*, irreg. f. *idem* same (see -TY)]

id′ĕo-, comb. form of Gk *idea* IDEA, as: *~gram, ~graph*, character symbolizing the idea of a thing without expressing its name (e.g. Chinese characters), whence *~graph′ic(al), ~graphy* (-ŏg′-).

idĕŏl′ogȳ, n. Science of ideas; visionary speculation; manner of thinking characteristic of a class or individual, ideas at the basis of some economic or political theory or system, as *Fascist, Nazi, ~*. So **idĕolō′gICAL** a., **idĕŏl′ogIST** n., **id′ĕo-LOGUE** (-lŏg) n., theorist, visionary. [f. F *idéologie* (prec., -LOGY)]

ides (īdz), n. pl. (Rom. Ant.). Eighth day after nones (15th of March, May, July, October, 13th of other months). [OF, f. L *Idūs*]

id ēst (abbr. *i.e.*). That is to say. [L]

id′iocȳ, n. Extreme mental imbecility. [16th c., irreg. f. IDIOT + -CY, after *hypocrite, -isy* etc.]

id′iom, n. Language of a people or country; specific character of this; form of expression peculiar to a language, peculiarity. [f. F *idiome* or LL f. Gk *idiōma -matos* (*idioomai* make one's own f. *idios*, see -M)]

idiomăt′|ic, a. Characteristic of a particular language; relating to or conforming to idiom. Hence *~ICALLY* adv. [f. F (prec., -IC)]

idiŏp′athȳ, n. (path.). Disease not preceded or occasioned by another. Hence **idiopăth′ĭc** a., **idiopăth′ICALLY** adv. [f. Gk *idiopatheia* (*idios* own, see -PATHY)]

id′ioplăsm, n. (biol.). Portion of PLASM that determines an organism's nature. [Gk *idios* own, PLASM]

idiosync′rasȳ, n. Mental constitution, view, feeling, peculiar to a person; mode of expression peculiar to an author; (Med.) physical constitution peculiar to a person. So **idiosyncrăt′ĭc** a. [f. Gk *idiosugkrasia* (*idios* own + *sun* together + *krasis* mixture f. *kerannumi* mix)]

id′iot, n. Person so deficient in mind as to be permanently incapable of rational conduct; utter fool; *~-stitch*, TRICOT-stitch (the easiest in crochet work). So **idiŏt′ĭc** a., **idiŏt′ICALLY** adv. [ME, f. OF f. L (-ta) f. Gk *idiōtēs* private person, 'layman', ignorant person, f. *idios* own, private]

ī′dle, a. (-er, -est), & v.i. & t. **1.** (Of action, thought, word) ineffective, meaningless, vain; groundless; useless; unoccupied; lazy, indolent; *~ wheel* or *~r*, safety wheel coming into operation in case of breakdown, (also) intermediate wheel between two geared wheels. **2. v.i.** Be ~; (of motor-car, aero, etc., engine) revolve slowly with throttle nearly closed; (v.t.) pass (time etc.) *away* in ~ness. Hence ~NESS (ĭ'dln-), ĭd'lER[1], nn., ĭd'LY[2] adv. [OE *idel*, OS *idal*, OHG *ītal*]

ĭd'lésse, n. Idleness. [pseudo-arch.. -ESS[2]]

Ido (ēd'ō), n. An artificial universal language based on Esperanto. [= offspring (in Ido)]

ĭd'ol, n. Image of deity used as object of worship; false god; person, thing, that is the object of excessive devotion; phantom; (Logic) false mental conception, ~*s* of the tribe, cave, market, theatre, (L *idola tribus, specus, fori, theatri*), four classes of fallacies (Bacon, *Nov. Org.* I. xxxix) referable respectively to limitations of human mind, prejudices of idiosyncrasy, influence of words, philosophical & logical prepossessions. [ME *ydele, ydole* f. OF f. L f. Gk *eidōlon* phantom (*eidos* form)]

ĭdŏl'at|er, n. Worshipper of idols; devoted admirer (*of*). So ~RESS[1], ~RY[2] (*honour* one *on this side* ~*ry*, short of making a god of him), nn., ~ROUS a., ~ROUSLY[2] adv. [(1) ME *idolatrer* f. OF+ -ER[1], or f. IDOLATRY + -ER[1]; (2) 16th c. *idolater* alt. f. (1), or f. OF *idolatre* (-*astre*) f. Rom. **idolatra* f. LL f. Gk *eidōlolatrēs* (IDOL, -LATRY)]

ĭd'oliz|e, -is|e (-ĭz), v.t. & i. Make an idol of; venerate, love, to excess; practise idolatry. Hence ~A'TION n. [-IZE]

ĭdŏl'um, n. (pl. -*la*). Mental image, idea; (Logic) fallacy (see IDOL). [L, as IDOL]

ĭd'yll, -ўl, n. Description in verse or (*prose* ~) in prose of picturesque scene or incident, esp. in rustic life; episode suitable for such treatment, freq. a love-story. Hence ĭdўll'ıc a., ĭdўll'ICALLY adv., ~IST n., ~IZE(1) v.t. [f. L f. Gk *eidullion* (*eidos* form)]

-ie, earlier form of -Y[3], & usu. in Sc.; also in E'use, cf. *birdie, doggie.*

-ier, suf. forming personal nn. denoting occupation etc. (1) in wds of ME age, in wh. the suf., of obsc. & app. diverse orig., is unstressed, & varies, or has varied, w. -*yer*, as *collier, grazier, hosier, bowyer, lawyer*; (2) in later wds f. 16th c. the suf., normally accented, is F -*ier* f. L -*arius* (-ARY[1]), as *bombardier, cavalier*; many of these occur w. anglicized sp., as *muleteer*; see -EER.

if, conj. & n. **1.** On the condition or supposition that, as *if you are* (now) *tired we will sit down, if you* (hereafter) *see him give him the message, if he has found it he will send it, if he had fair warning he has nothing to complain of, if he had been warned he has* (or *had*) *nothing to complain of*, (w. past tense implying that condition is not fulfilled) *if I knew what to do I should do it, if he had been warned he would have* (or *would have had*) *nothing to complain of;*

whenever, as *if I feel any doubt I inquire, if I felt any doubt I inquired, if I had been badly treated I complained;* whether, as *ask, see, try, if you can turn the handle;* (when *if* is omitted, order of verb & subject is inverted, as) *were I* (if I were) *in your place, would, could, should, might, had, he* (if he would, could, etc.), (poet.) *loved I not honour more;* (without apodosis) *if I only knew!*, I wish I knew, *if I haven't lost my watch!* (I have, to my surprise or disgust); *as if*, as the case would be if, as *it seems as if he meant* (vulg. *means*) *to compromise, he talks as* (he would) *if he were drunk; as if you didn't know*, you know quite well. **2.** n. Condition, supposition, as *if ifs & ans were pots & pans.* [OE *gif*, OS *ef* (*of*), OHG *ibu, oba*, ON *ef*, Goth. *ibai*]

ĭg'lōo, n. Eskimo dome-shaped hut, esp. one built of snow. [native, = house]

ĭg'nèous, a. Of fire, fiery; produced by volcanic agency. [f. L *igneus* (*ignis* fire) + -OUS]

ĭg'nĭs fǎt'ŭus, n. Will-o'-the-wisp, phosphorescent light (now rarely) seen on marshy ground, supposed due to spontaneous combustion of gas from decaying organic matter; delusive hope or gain. [med. or mod. L, = foolish fire]

ĭgnĭt|e, v.t. & i. Make intensely hot; (Chem.) heat to the point of combustion or chemical change; set fire to; take fire. Hence or cogn. ~'ABLE a., **ĭgnĭ'**TION n., (also) mechanism for, act of, starting combustion of the mixture in cylinder of internal-combustion engine. [f. L *ignire* -*t*- (*ignis* fire)]

ĭgnō'b|le, a. (-er, -est). Of low birth, position, or reputation; mean, base, dishonourable. Hence ~leNESS (-ln-) n., ~LY[2] adv. [F, or f. L *ignobilis* (*in*- not + (*g*)*nobilis* NOBLE)]

ĭg'nominÿ, n. Dishonour, infamy; infamous conduct. So **ĭgnomin'ious** a. (now usu. in less damnatory sense, = humiliating), **ĭgnomin'iousLY**[2] adv. [f. F *ignominie* or L *ignominia* (*in*- not + (*g*)*nomen* name)]

ĭgnorām'us, n. (pl.~*es*). Ignorant person. [L, = we do not know, (legal) we take no notice of (bill); mod. sense perh. f. Ruggle's *Ignoramus* (1615) exposing lawyers' ignorance]

ĭg'norance, n. Want of knowledge (*of* thing, or in general; *where ~ is bliss, 'tis folly to be wise*). [ME, f. OF f. L *ignorantia* (as foll., see -ANCE)]

ĭg'norant, a. Lacking knowledge; uninformed (*of, in, subject, of* fact). Hence ~LY[2] adv. [ME, f. OF f. L, as IGNORE, see -ANT]

ĭgnorā'tio (-shĭō) **ēlěn'chi** (-kĭ), n. (logic). Argument that appears to refute opponent while actually disproving something not advanced by him. [L]

ĭgnore, v.t. Refuse to take notice of; (of Grand Jury) reject (bill) as unfounded. [f.

F *ignorer* or L *ignorare* not know, ignore (*in-* not +*gno-* know)]

ignōt′um pēr ignōt′ius, n. Explanation obscurer than the thing it is meant to explain. [L, = the unknown by the still less known]

igua′na (-gwah-), n. Large W.-Ind. & S.-Amer. arboreal lizard. [Sp., f. Carib *iwana*]

iguăn′odŏn (-gw-), n. Large herbivorous lizard, found fossil. [f. prec.+Gk *odous odontos* tooth, after *mastodon* etc.]

IHS, abbr. repr. Gk *Iēsous* Jesus (Gk cap. *ē* being like H); often taken to mean *Jesus Hominum Salvator* (Saviour of men), *In Hoc Signo* (*vinces*) in this sign (thou shalt conquer), *In Hac* (*cruce*) *Salus* in this (cross) is salvation.

il-, pref. = IN¹, ² before *l*.

ik′on, n. Var. of ICON.

-il, -ile, suf. of adjj. & sometimes nn., repr. L *-ilis* or when added to *-i-* stems *-ilis* (*civilis*). In OF *-ilis* appeared as *-il*, but *-ilis* lost *i*, tonic accent falling on prec. syllable (*humble* L *humilem, frêle* L *fragilem*). L wds adopted early in OF took *-il* masc., *-ile* fem. (*civil, -ile*); later wds have *-ile* for both genders (*agile, facile*). Few E wds have *-il* (*civil, fossil, utensil*); & the tendency (not in U.S.) is to pronounce *-ile* of either origin with *i*.

îl′ex, n. (pl. ~es). Holm-oak; (Bot.) genus including common holly. [L]

îl′iăc, a. Of the flank(-bone), as ~ *artery*; ~ *passion*, painful affection due to intestinal obstruction. [f. LL *iliacus*, in form f. L *ilia* flanks (see -AC); in sense f. L *ileus* f. Gk *eileos* colic]

Il′iad (I-), n. Epic poem attributed to Homer & describing siege of Troy; (fig.) ~ (long series) *of woes*. [f. L f. Gk *Ilias -ados* (*poiēsis*) (poer ι) of Ilium or Troy]

îl′ium, n. (pl. *-ia*). Hip-bone. [L, see ILIAC]

‖ **ilk,** a. (Sc.). *Of that* ~, of the same, as *Guthrie of that* ~, Guthrie of Guthrie; (vulg.) *that* ~, that family, class, or set. [OE *ilca* same, f. *i-, i-* (st. of HE, cf. Goth. *is*) +*lik-* (LIKE¹, -LY¹)]

ill, a., n., & adv. **1.** Out of health, sick, as *he is* ~, *was taken* ~, (*of or with* disease, *with* anxiety etc.); (of health) unsound, disordered; morally bad, as ~ *fame*, disrepute, ~ *blood*, ~ *will*, animosity, strife, ~ *nature*, churlishness, ~ (morose) *humour, temper*; harmful, as (prov.) ~ *weeds grow apace*; *do an* ~ *turn to person*, harm him or his interests; wretched, disastrous, as (prov.) *it's an* ~ *wind that blows nobody good*; (arch.) difficult, as ~ *to please*; faulty, unskilful, as ~ *management*; (of manners or conduct) improper; ~ (imperfect) *success*. **2.** n. Evil, the opposite of good; harm, injury; *speak* ~ (something unfavourable) *of*; (pl.) misfortunes. **3.** adv. Badly, as *behaved* ~; *take* (thing) ~, take offence at it; unfavourably, as *it would have gone* ~ *with him*; imperfectly,

scarcely, as ~ *provided, it* ~ *became him to speak*; ~ *at ease*, embarrassed, uneasy. **4.** ~*-advised′, -advis′ĕdly*, imprudent(ly); ~*-affec′ted*, not well disposed; ~*-bred*, badly brought up, rude; ~ *breed′ing*, bad manners; ~*-condi′tioned*, of evil disposition, (also) in bad condition; ~*-disposed′*, disposed to evil, malevolent, (also) unfavourably disposed (*towards*); ~*-fat′ed*, destined to, bringing, bad fortune; ~*-fav′oured*, uncomely, (also) displeasing, objectionable; ~*-gott′en*, gained by evil means; ~*-hum′oured*, bad-tempered; ~*-judged′*, unwise; ~*-mann′ered*, unmannerly, rude; ~*-na′tured*(*ly*), churlish(ly); ~*-om′ened*, attended by bad omens; ~*-starred′*, born under an evil star, unlucky; ~*-lem′pered*, morose, peevish; ~*-timed′*, unseasonable; ~*-treat′, -use′*, treat badly. [ME *ill* f. ON *illr* of unkn. orig.]

illā′tion, n. Deduction, conclusion; thing deduced. [f. L *illatio* (as INFER, see -ION)]

illāt′ive, a. (Of words) stating, introducing, an inference, as ~ *particles*; inferential. Hence ~LY² (-vl-) adv. [f. L *illativus* (as prec., see -IVE)]

illēg′al, a. Not legal; contrary to law. Hence or cogn. **illēgăl′ity** n., ~LY² adv. [f. F, or med. L IL(*legalis* LEGAL)]

illē′g|ible, a. Not legible. Hence ~IBIL²-ITY n., ~IBLY² adv. [IL-]

illēgit′im|ate¹, a. & n. Not authorized by law; improper; not born in lawful wedlock, bastard; wrongly inferred; abnormal; (n.) one whose position is ~ate, esp. bastard. Hence ~ACY n., ~ateLY² adv. [f. LL *illegitimus*, after LEGITIMATE]

illēgit′im|āte², v.t. Declare illegitimate. Hence ~A′TION n. [f. prec.]

illib′eral, a. Not befitting a free man; without liberal culture; vulgar, sordid; narrow-minded; stingy. Hence or cogn. ~ITY (-ăl-) n., ~LY² adv. [f. F, or L IL(*liberalis* LIBERAL)]

illi′cit, a. Unlawful, forbidden, esp. ~ *still*. Hence ~LY² adv. [f. L *illicitus* (IL-, LICIT)]

illim′it|able, a. Boundless. Hence ~ABIL′ITY, ~ableNESS, nn., ~abLY² adv. [IL-]

illit′er|ate, a. & n. Ignorant of letters; unlearned; unable to read; (n.) ~ate person. Hence ~ACY, ~ateNESS, nn. [f. L IL(*litteratus* LITERATE)]

ill′nĕss, n. Unhealthy condition of body, sickness. [-NESS]

illō′gical, a. Devoid of, contrary to, logic. Hence ~ITY (-ăl-) n., ~LY² adv. [IL-]

illume′ (-lōō-, -lū-), v.t. (poet.). Light up, make bright, (lit. & fig.). [poet. shortening of ILLUMINE]

illum′in|āte (-ōō-, -ū-), v.t. Light up, whence ~ANT a. & n.; give spiritual or intellectual light to; throw light upon (subject); shed lustre upon; decorate (buildings etc.) profusely with lights as sign of festivity; decorate (initial letter in manuscript etc.) with gold, silver, &

brilliant colours. So ~A'TION, ~ātoR, nn., ~ātive a., (-ōō-, -ū-). [f. L IL(*luminare* f. *lumen -minis* light), see -ATE³]

illumināt'i (-ōō-, -ū-; *also* -ah'tē), n. pl. Secret society founded by Weishaupt in 1776, holding deistic & republican principles, & organized like freemasons; persons claiming to possess special enlightenment. So illum'inISM(3), illum²inIST(2), nn., (-ōō-, -ū-). [L (as prec., see -ATE²) or It., whence occasional sing. -*ato*]

illum'ine (-ōō-, -ū-), v.t. Light up; enlighten spiritually; brighten. [ME, f. OF *illuminer* (as ILLUMINATE)]

illu'sion (-lōōzhn), n. Deception, delusion; sensuous perception of an external object involving a false belief; a transparent tulle. [ME, f. F f. L *illusionem* f. IL(*ludere lus-* play), see -ION]

illu'sion|ist (-lōōzhon-), n. One who disbelieves in objective existence, so ~ISM n.; one who produces illusions, esp. conjurer. [-IST]

illus'|ive (-lōō-), a. Deceptive. Hence or cogn. ~iveLY², ~oriLY², advv., ~iveNESS, ~oriNESS, nn., ~orY a. [as ILLUSION, see -IVE]

ill'ustrāt|e, v.t. Make clear, explain; make clear by examples; elucidate (description etc.) by drawings; ornament (book, newspaper, etc.) with designs. Hence ~OR n. [f. L IL(*lustrare* light up, f. st. of *lumen* light)]

illustrā'tion, n. Illustrating; example; drawing etc. illustrating book or article in paper. [ME, f. OF, f. L *illustrationem* (prec., -ATION)]

illūs'trative, a. Serving as explanation or example (*of*). Hence ~LY² (-vl-) adv. [as ILLUSTRATE, see -IVE]

illūs'trious, a. Distinguished, renowned. Hence ~LY² adv., ~NESS n. [f. L IL(*lustris* see ILLUSTRATE) +-OUS]

im-¹, ², pref. = IN-¹, ² before *b, m, p*.

im'age¹, n. Artificial imitation of the external form of an object, e.g. statue (esp. of saint etc. as object of veneration); optical counterpart produced by rays of light reflected from mirror, refracted through lens, etc.; form, semblance; counterpart, as *he is the very ~ of his father*; type; simile, metaphor; idea, conception. Hence ~LESS (-ijl-) a. [ME, f. OF f. L *imaginem* (nom. -*go*)]

im'age², v.t. Make an image of, portray; reflect, mirror; picture (thing *to* oneself); describe vividly; typify. Hence ~ABLE (-ija-) a. [f. prec.]

im'agerỹ (-ij-), n. Images; statuary, carving; figurative illustration. [ME, f. OF *imagerie* (as IMAGE¹, see -ERY)]

imā'ginab|le, a. That can be imagined, *as the greatest difficulty ~le, took all the trouble ~le*. Hence ~LY² adv. [ME, f. LL *imaginabilis* (as IMAGINE, see -BLE)]

imā'ginal, a. (entom.). Of an insect imago. [f. L as IMAGE¹ +-AL]

imā'ginar|ỹ, a. Existing only in imagina-

tion; (Math.) having no real existence, but assumed to exist for a special purpose (e.g. square root of negative quantity). Hence ~iLY² adv. [ME, f. L *imaginarius* (as prec., see -ARY¹)]

imāginā'tion, n. Imagining; mental faculty forming images of external objects not present to the senses; fancy; creative faculty of the mind. [ME, f. OF f. L *imaginationem* (as IMAGINE, see -ATION)]

imā'ginative (*or* -ātĭv), a. Of, given to using, having or showing in a high degree, the faculty of imagination. Hence ~LY² (-vl-) adv., ~NESS (-vn-) n. [OF (-*if*, -*ive*), as prec., see -ATIVE]

imā'gine, v.t. Form mental image of; conceive (thing, thing *to* be or do, *that* it is, *how, what*, etc.); guess, as *cannot ~ what he is doing*; suppose, be of opinion, (*that*); take into one's head (idea, *that*). [ME, f. OF *imaginer* f. L *imaginari* (as IMAGE¹)]

im'agist, n. One of a group of early 20th--c. poets who, in revolt against romanticism, seek clarity of expression through the use of precise images. [IMAGE¹ + -IST(2)]

imāg'ō, n. (pl. -*gines* pr. -jĭnēz, -*gos*). Final & perfect stage of insect after all metamorphoses, e.g. butterfly. [mod. L sense of *imago* IMAGE¹]

imam', imaum', (-ahm), n. Officiating priest of mosque; title of various Mohammedan leaders. Hence imam'ATE¹ (-ahm-) n. [Arab. (*am*) f. *amma* go before]

imbal'ance, n. Lack of balance. [IM-²]

im'bécile (-ēl, -ĭl), a. & n. 1. Mentally weak, stupid, idiotic; physically weak. 2. n. Person of weak intellect. Hence or cogn. ~LY² (-l-l-) adv., imbēcil'ITY n. [f. F *imbécille* (now -*ile*) f. L *imbecillus*]

imbibe', v.t. Drink in, assimilate, (ideas etc.); drink (liquid); inhale (air etc.); absorb (moisture etc.). So imbibi'tion n. [(1) f. OF *imbiber*; (2) f. L IM¹(*bibere* drink)]

im'bric|āte, v.t. & i. Arrange (leaves, scales of fish, etc.), be arranged, so as to overlap like tiles. So ~ATE² (-at), ~ātive, aa., ~A'TION n. [f. L *imbricare* form like a tile (*imbrex -icis* f. *imber* shower), -ATE³]

imbro'glio (-ōlyō), n. (pl. ~*s*). Confused heap; complicated (esp. political or dramatic) situation. [It., f. *broglio*, cf. BROIL¹]

imbrue' (-ōō), v.t. Stain (one's hand, sword, etc., *in, with*, blood, slaughter, etc.). [f. OF *embrouer* bedabble f. *en* IM- +*breu* f. Rom. *•brodum*; see BROTH]

imbrute', èm-, (-ōōt), v.t. Brutalize. [IM-¹]

imbue', v.t. Saturate (*with*); dye (*with*); permeate, inspire, (*with* feelings etc.); = IMBRUE. [16th c., f. F *imbu* or its source L *imbuere* moisten]

im'it|āte, v.t. Follow example of; mimic; be (consciously or not) like. So ~ABIL-

ITY, ~ātoR, nn., ~ABLE a. [f. L *imitari*, see -ATE³]

imitā'tion, n. Imitating (~ *is the sincerest flattery*); copy; counterfeit (often attrib., as ~ *leather*); (Mus.) repetition of melody etc., usu. at different pitch, in another part or voice. [f. F, or L *imitatio* (prec., -ATION)]

im'itātive, a. Following model or example (*of*); ~ *arts*, painting & sculpture; ~ *word*, one that reproduces a natural sound (e.g. *fizz*) or whose sound is thought to correspond to appearances etc. of object described; counterfeit. Hence ~LY² adv., ~NESS n. [f. LL *imitativus* (as IMITATE, see -ATIVE)]

immāc'ulate, a. Pure, spotless; faultless (often iron.); I~ *Conception* (of Virgin Mary, as conceived free from taint of original sin); (Nat. Hist.) not spotted. Hence immāc'ulACY, ~NESS, nn., ~LY² adv. [f. L IM²(*maculatus* f. *macula* spot)]

imm'an|ent, a. Indwelling, inherent, (*in*); (of God) permanently pervading the universe. Hence ~ENCE, ~ENCY, nn. [f. LL IM¹(*manēre* remain), see -ENT]

immatēr'ial, a. Not material, incorporeal; unimportant. Hence ~ITY (-āl²) n., ~IZE(3) v.t. [f. LL IM²(*materialis* MATERIAL)]

immatēr'ial|ism, n. Doctrine that matter does not exist in itself apart from perception. So ~IST n. [-ISM]

immatūr|e', a. Not mature. So ~'ITY n. [f. L IM²(*maturus* MATURE)]

immea'sur|able (-mězher-), a. Not measurable, immense. Hence ~ABIL'ITY, ~ableNESS, nn., ~ablY² adv. [IM-²]

immēd'iate, a. (Of person or thing in its relation to another) not separated by any intervening medium; (of relation or action) direct, without intervening medium; (Logic) ~ *inference* (from single premiss, without intervention of middle term); nearest, next, as *my* ~ *neighbour*, *predecessor*; occurring at once, without delay, as *an~ reply*. Hence immēd'iACY, ~NESS (-tn-), nn., ~LY² (-tl-) adv. [f. F -*at*, or LL IM²(*mediatus* MEDIATE)]

immēmōr'ial, a. Ancient beyond memory; very old. Hence ~LY² adv. [f. med. L IM²(*memorialis* MEMORIAL)]

immēnse', a. Vast, huge; (sl.) very good. Hence or cogn. ~NESS (-sn-), immēns'ITY, nn. [F, f. L IM²(*mensus* p.p. of *metiri* measure) immeasurable]

immēnse'ly (-slī), adv. In an immense degree; (colloq.) very much. [-LY²]

immērse', v.t. Dip, plunge, (*in* liquid); put overhead in water, esp. baptize thus; bury, imbed, (*in*); involve deeply, absorb, (*in* debt, difficulties, thought, etc.). [f. L IM¹(*mergere mers-* dip)]

immēr'sion (-shn), n. Immersing; baptism by plunging whole person in water (cf. AFFUSION); (fig.) absorption (*in* thought etc.); (Astron.) disappearance of celestial body behind another or in its

shadow; ~ *heater*, electric heater designed for direct ~ in a liquid. [f. LL *immersio* (prec., -ION)]

imm'igr|āte, v.i. & t. Come as settler (*into* foreign country); bring in (person) as settler. So ~ANT a. & n., ~A'TION n. [f. L IM¹(*migrare* MIGRATE)]

imm'in|ent, a. (Of events, esp. dangers) impending, soon to happen. Hence or cogn. ~ENCE n., ~entLY² adv. [f. L IM¹(*minēre*, see EMINENT) overhang, see -ENT]

immis'c|ible, a. That cannot be mixed. Hence ~IBIL'ITY n., ~ibLY² adv. [f. LL *immiscibilis* f. IM-²+L *miscēre* mix, see -BLE]

immit'igab|le, a. That cannot be softened or toned down. Hence ~LY² adv. [f. LL IM²(*mitigabilis*, see MITIGATE)]

immix'ture, n. Mixing up; being involved (*in*). [f. L IM¹(*miscēre mixt-* mix) +-URE]

immōb'ile, a. Immovable; not mobile; motionless. So immōBIL'ITY n. [OF, f. L IM²(*mobilis* MOBILE)]

immōb'iliz|e, -is|e (-īz), v.t. Fix immovably; make (troops, vehicle) incapable of being shifted; withdraw (specie) from circulation. Hence ~A'TION n. [f. F *immobiliser* (as prec., see -IZE)]

immōd'erate, a. Excessive, wanting in moderation. Hence ~LY² (-tl-) adv. [ME, f. L IM²(*moderatus* MODERATE)]

immōd'est, a. Indecent, indelicate; forward, impudent. Hence ~LY² adv., ~Y¹ n. [f. L IM²(*modestus* MODEST)]

imm'ol|āte, v.t. Kill (victim) as sacrifice; (fig.) sacrifice (thing etc. *to* another). So ~A'TION, ~ātoR, nn. [f. L IM¹*molare* sprinkle with meal (*mola*), sacrifice, -ATE³]

immō'ral, a. Opposed to morality; morally evil; vicious, dissolute. Hence immoral'ITY n., ~LY² adv. [IM-²]

immōrt'al, a. & n. 1. Undying; divine; unfading, incorruptible; famous for all time; (colloq.) constant, long-lasting. 2. n. ~ being, esp. (pl.) gods of antiquity; person esp. author of enduring fame, member of French Academy; (pl.) royal bodyguard of ancient Persia. So ~ITY (-āl²) n. [f. L IM²(*mortalis* MORTAL)]

immōrt'aliz|e, -is|e (-īz), v.t. Confer enduring fame upon; endow with endless life; perpetuate. Hence ~A'TION n. [-IZE]

immōrt'allУ, adv. Eternally; (colloq.) infinitely, very. [-LY²]

immōrtëlle', n. Composite flower of papery texture retaining colour after being dried, often used to adorn graves. [F, fem. of *immortel* IMMORTAL]

immo'v|able (-mōō-), a. & n. That cannot be moved; motionless; not subject to change; ~*able* FEAST; steadfast, unyielding; emotionless; (Law, of property) consisting of land, houses, etc. (also as n. pl.). Hence ~ABIL'ITY, ~ableNESS, nn., ~ablY² adv. [IM-²]

immūne', a. & n. Having immunity (*from*, *against*, *to*, poison, contagion, etc.);

(n.) ~ person. [f. L IM²*munis* exempt from public burden (*munus*); med. use f. F]

immūn'itў, n. (Law) exemption (*from* taxation, jurisdiction, etc.); freedom (*from*); being proof against contagion etc. (*from*). [f. L *immunitas* (as prec., see -TY); med. use f. F]

imm'ūnizǀe, -isǀe (-īz), v.t. Render immune (*against* contagion). Hence ~A'TION n. [-IZE]

immūre', v.t. Imprison; shut one*self* up. Hence ~MENT (-ūrm-) n. [f. F *emmurer* or med. L IM¹(*murare* f. *murus* wall)]

immūt'ǀable, a. Unchangeable; not subject to variation in different cases. Hence ~ABIL'ITY n., ~abLY² adv. [f. L IM²(*mutabilis* MUTABLE)]

imp¹, n. Child of the devil; little devil; mischievous child; ‖ (arch.) child. [OE *impa* young shoot, scion, conn. w. foll.]

imp², v.t. Mend broken pinion feather of falcon by inserting new feather in stump of broken one and binding with silk; (rare) enlarge, eke *out*. [OE *impian* = OHG *impfōn, impitōn* f. Rom. *impotare* f. med. L *impotus* graft f. Gk *emphuein* implant]

im'pǎct¹, n. Striking (*on, against*), collision; effect, influence. [f. L *impingere* -*pact*- IMPINGE]

impǎct'¹², v.t. Press, fix, firmly (*into, in*). So impǎc'tIon n. [back formation f. *impacted* f. L p.p. as prec.+-ED¹]

impair', v.t. Damage; weaken. So ~MENT n. [ME *empeir* f. OF *empeirer* f. Rom. *impejorare* (*pejor* worse)]

impa'la (-ah-), n. Small African antelope. [Zulu]

impāle', v.t. Transfix (body etc. *upon, with,* stake etc., esp. as form of capital punishment); (Her.) combine (two coats of arms) by placing side by side on one shield separated by vertical line down middle; ‖ (rare) fence in with stakes. So ~MENT (-lm-) n. [f. F *empaler* or med. L IM¹(*palare* f. *palus* stake)]

impǎl'pǀable, a. Imperceptible to the touch; not easily grasped by the mind, intangible. Hence ~ABIL'ITY n., ~abLY² adv. [f. F, or LL IM²(*palpabilis* PALPABLE)]

impǎl'ūdism, n. Morbid state, with tendency to intermittent fevers & enlargement of spleen, found in dwellers in marshes. [f. IM-¹+L *palus -udis* marsh + -ISM]

impǎn'ate (or Im'pa-), a. (Of the body of Christ) contained in the bread after consecration. So impana'TION n. [f. med. L IM¹(*panare* f. *panis* bread), see -ATE²]

impanel. See EMPANEL.

impa'radise, èm-, v.t. Bring into state of supreme happiness; ravish; make a paradise of (place, state). [16th c.; cf. contemporary *paradise* vb, It. *imparadisare*, F *emparadiser*]

impǎrisўllǎb'ic, a. & n. (Gk & Lat. Gram.). (Noun) that has fewer syllables

in nominative than in other cases. [f. L IM²(*par* equal) + SYLLABIC]

impǎrk', v.t. Enclose (beasts) in park; enclose (land) for park. Hence ~A'TION n. [ME, f. OF EM(*parquer* f. *parc* PARK)]

impǎrt', v.t. Give share of (thing *to* person etc.); communicate (news etc. *to*). Hence ~A'TION, ~MENT, nn. [15c., f. OF *impartir* f. L IM¹(*partire* PART²)]

impǎr'tial (-shal), a. Not partial, unprejudiced, fair. Hence ~ITY (-shiǎl⁴) n., ~LY² (-shal-) adv. [IM-²]

impǎrt'ible, a. (Of estate) not divisible. [f. LL IM²(*partibilis* PARTIBLE)]

impass'ǀable (-pah-), a. That cannot be traversed. Hence ~ABIL'ITY, ~ableNESS, nn. [IM-²]

impasse' (-ahs; *or* ǎnpahs'), n. Blind alley; position from which there is no escape. [F (IM-² + *passer* PASS¹)]

impǎss'ǀible, a. Incapable of feeling or emotion; incapable of suffering injury; not subject to suffering. Hence ~IBIL'ITY, ~ibleNESS, nn., ~ibLY² adv. [ME, f. OF, or LL IM²(*passibilis* PASSIBLE)]

impǎ'ssion (-shn), v.t. Stir the passions of, excite strongly, (chiefly in p.p.). [f. It. IM¹(*passionare* f. *passione* PASSION)]

impǎss'ive, a. Deficient in feeling or emotion; serene; without sensation; not subject to suffering. Hence ~LY² adv., ~NESS, impǎssiv'ITY, nn. [IM-²]

impǎste', v.t. Enclose (as) with paste; make into a paste; paint by laying on colours thickly. [f. It. IM¹(*pastare* f. *pasta* PASTE)]

impǎs'tō, n. (paint.). Laying on of paint thickly. [It., as prec.]

impǎ'tiǀent (-shent), a. Not enduring with composure; intolerant *of*; restlessly desirous (*for* thing, *to* do). Hence or cogn. ~ENCE (-shens) n., ~entLY² (-shent-) adv. [ME, f. OF f. L IM²(*patientem* part. of *pati* suffer)]

impawn', v.t. Put in pawn; (fig.) pledge, plight. [IM-¹]

impay'able (*or* ǎnpǎyah'bl), a. Beyond price; (colloq.) going beyond ordinary limits. [F (IM-²)]

impeach', v.t. Call in question, disparage, (character etc.); accuse (person) *of*, charge (*with*); find fault with (thing); accuse of treason or other high crime before competent tribunal. Hence ~ABLE a. [ME, f. OF *empechier* impede f. LL IM¹-(*pedicare* f. *pedica* fetter, f. *pes pedis* foot) entangle]

impeach'ment, n. Calling in question; accusation, esp. (joc.) *the soft* ~ (Sheridan, *Rivals* v. iii); accusation & prosecution for treason etc. [f. OF *empechement* (as prec., see -MENT)]

impěc'ǀable, a. Not liable to sin; (of things) faultless. Hence or cogn. ~ABIL'ITY n., ~abLY² adv., ~ANT a. [f. L IM²(*peccabilis* f. *peccare* sin, see -BLE)]

impecūn'iǀous, a. Having little or no money. Hence ~os'ITY n. [f. IM-² +obs.

pecunious t. L *pecuniosus* (*pecunia* money t. *pecu* cattle, see -OUS)]

imped'ance, n. (electr.). Total virtual resistance of electric circuit to alternating current, arising from the resistance & the reactance of the circuit. [f. foll. +-ANCE]

impēde', v.t. Retard, hinder. [f. L IM¹· (*pedire* f. *pes* foot) lit. shackle the feet of]

impĕd'iment, n. Hindrance, obstruction, esp. *just cause or* ~; ~ (*in one's speech*), stammer; (pl., also L *impedimen'ta*) baggage, esp. of army. Hence ~AL (-ĕn⁴) a. [f. L *impedimentum* (as prec., see -MENT)]

impĕl', v.t. (-ll-). Drive, force, (person etc. *to* action, *to* do); drive forward, propel. So ~l'ENT a. & n. [f. L IM¹(*pellere puls-* drive)]

impĕnd', v.i. Hang, be suspended, (*over*); (fig., of danger) hang threateningly (*over*); be imminent. So **impĕn'**DENCE, -ENCY, nn., **impĕn'**DENT a. [f. L IM¹(*pendēre* hang)]

impĕn'ĕtr|able, a. That cannot be penetrated; inscrutable, unfathomable; impervious (*to, by* ideas etc.); (Nat. Phil.) having that property in virtue of which two bodies cannot occupy same place at same time. So ~ABIL'ITY, ~ableNESS, nn., ~ABLY² adv. [f. F *impénétrable* f. L IM²(*penetrabilis* PENETRABLE)]

impĕn'ĕtrāte, v.t. Penetrate deeply. [IM-¹]

impĕn'it|ent, a. Not penitent. Hence or cogn. ~ENCE, ~ENCY, nn., ~entLY² adv. [f. LL IM²(*paenitens* PENITENT)]

impĕ'rative, a. & n. 1. (Gram.) expressing command; commanding, peremptory; urgent; obligatory. 2. n. ~ mood, whence **imperativ'**AL a.; CATEGORICAL ~. Hence ~LY² (-yĭ-) adv., ~NESS (-vn-) n. [f. LL *imperativus* f. IM¹(*perare* = *parare* make ready) command, -IVE]

imperāt'or, n. (Rom. Hist.). Commander (title conferred by salutation of soldiers on victorious general, under the Republic); emperor. So **imperatōr'**IAL a. [L (as prec., see -OR)]

impercĕp'tib|le, a. That cannot be perceived; very slight, gradual, or subtle. Hence ~LY² adv. [f. F, or med. L IM²(*perceptibilis* PERCEPTIBLE)]

impercip'ient, a. Lacking perception. [IM-¹]

im'perence, n. (Form, ascribed to illiterate speakers, of) impudence.

imperfĕct, a. & n. 1. Not fully formed or done, incomplete; faulty; (Gram.) ~ *tenses*, those that denote action going on but not completed (e.g. *he is, he will be, singing*, but usu. of past time, as *he was singing*). 2. n. ~ tense. Hence ~LY² adv. [ME *imparfit* etc., f. OF; see IM-², PERFECT]

imperfĕc'tion, n. Incompleteness; faultiness, fault, blemish. [ME, f. OF f. LL *imperfectionem* (as prec., see -ION)]

impĕr'forate, a. Not perforated, esp. (Anat.) lacking the normal opening (also of sheet of postage-stamps or single stamp). [IM-²]

impĕr'ial, a. & n. 1. Of an empire or sovereign state ranking with an empire. 2. *I~ Institute*, former name of COMMONWEALTH *Institute*; ~ *preference*, taxing of imports from parts of the Empire at lower rates than those from foreign countries. 3. Of an emperor; supreme in authority; majestic, august; magnificent. 4. (Of weights & measures used by statute in U.K.) ~ *gallon, acre*, etc.; (of paper) 22×32 in. 5. n. Small part of beard left growing beneath lower lip (from Napoleon III); trunk for luggage, adapted for roof of coach; Russian tsarist gold coin= 15 silver roubles. Hence ~LY² adv. [ME, f. OF, f. L *imperialis* (IMPERIUM, see -AL)]

impĕr'ial|ism, n. Rule of an emperor; (hist.) extension of British Empire where trade required protection of the flag; (hist.) union of different parts of British Empire for purposes of warlike defence, internal commerce, etc.; belief in value of colonies & dependencies (cf. LITTLE *Englandism*). So ~ĭs'TIC a., ~IZE(3) v.t. [-ISM]

impĕr'ialist, n. Adherent of an emperor, esp. (1600-1800) of German Emperor; advocate of imperial rule, esp. adherent of Bonaparte family; advocate of (British) imperialism. [17th c., f. F *impérialiste* (as prec., -IST]

impĕ'ril, v.t. (-ll-). Bring into danger. [IM-¹]

impĕr'ious, a. Overbearing, domineering; urgent, imperative. Hence ~LY² adv., ~NESS n. [f. L *imperiosus* (as IMPERIUM, see -OUS)]

impĕ'rish|able, a. That cannot perish. Hence ~ABIL'ITY, ~ableNESS, nn., ~ABLY³ adv. [IM-²]

impĕr'ium, n. Absolute power; empire; ~ *in imperio*, supreme authority within jurisdiction of another authority. [L, = command, dominion]

impĕrm'an|ent, a. Not permanent. Hence ~ENCE, ~ENCY, nn. [IM-²]

impĕrm'ĕ|able, a. That cannot be passed through; (Phys.) that does not permit passage of fluids. Hence ~ABIL'ITY n. [f. LL IM²(*permeabilis* PERMEABLE)]

impermiss'ible, a. Not permissible. [IM-²]

imperscrip'tible, a. Not backed by written authority. [f. IM-²+L PER-(*scribere script-* write) register, see -BLE]

impĕrs'onal, a. (Gram.) ~ *verb*, verb when used only in 3rd sing. (e.g. *it rains, methinks*); having no personality or personal reference or tone. Hence ~ITY (-ăl⁴) n., ~LY² adv. [f. LL IM²(*personalis* PERSONAL)]

impĕrs'on|āte, v.t. Represent in bodily form, personify; play the part of; PERSONATE²; act (character). Hence ~A'TION, ~ātoR, nn., ~ātive a. [f. IM-¹+L *persona* PERSON+-ATE³]

imperson'ifў, v.t. Personify. [IM-[1]]

impert'in|ent, a. Not to the point; intrusive; out of place, absurd; insolent, saucy. Hence or cogn. ~ENCE n., ~entlу[2] adv. [f. F, or L IM[2](pertinens PERTINENT)]

imperturb'|able, a. Not excitable, calm. Hence ~ABIL'ITY, ~ableNESS, nn., ~ablу[3] adv. [late ME, f. LL IM[2] (perturbabilis PERTURBABLE)]

imperv'ious, a. Not affording passage (to); (fig.) ~ (deaf) to argument etc. Hence ~LУ[2] adv., ~NESS n. [f. L IM[2](pervius PERVIOUS)]

impĕtīg'ō, n. Contagious pustular disease of skin. So impĕtī'ginous a. [L, gen. -ginis, f. IM[1](petere seek) assail]

im'pĕtr|āte, v.t. (Theol.) obtain by request; (rare) ask for. So ~A'TION n., ~ātory a. [f. L IM[1](petrare = patrare bring to pass), see -ATE[3]]

impĕt'ūous, a. Moving violently or rapidly; acting with rash or sudden energy. Hence or cogn. impĕtūos'ITY, ~NESS, nn., ~LУ[2] adv. [ME, f. OF impetuous f. L impetuosus (as foll., see -OUS)]

im'pĕtus, n. (pl. ~es). Force with which a body moves; (fig.) moving force, impulse. [L, = assault, force, f. IM[1](petere seek) assail]

im'peyan (-pĭan), a. ~ pheasant, E.-Indian pheasant, with crested head & brilliant plumage. [Sir Elijah Impey, 1787]

im'pī, n. Body of Kaffir warriors. [Zulu]

impī'etў, n. Ungodliness; want of dutifulness or reverence. [ME, f. OF impiete or L IM[2](pietas PIETY)]

impinge' (-j), v.i. & t. Make impact (on, upon); (trans.; arch.) make (thing) do this. Hence ~MENT (-jm-) n. [f. L IM[1](pingere = pangere fix, drive) drive (thing) at]

im'pious, a. Not pious, wicked, profane. Hence ~LУ[2] adv. [f. L IM[2](pius PIOUS)]

im'pish, a. Of, like, an imp. Hence ~LУ[2] adv., ~NESS n. [-ISH[1]]

impit'ēous, a. (poet.). Pitiless. [IM-[2]]

implăc'|able (or -lāk[2]), a. That cannot be appeased. Hence or cogn. ~ABIL'ITY n., ~ablу[2] adv. [f. F, or L IM[2](placabilis PLACABLE)]

implacĕn'tal, a. With no placenta. [IM-[2]]

implant' (-ahnt), v.t. Insert, infix, (in); instil (principle, idea, etc., in mind etc.); plant. Hence ~A'TION (-ahn-) n. [f. F implanter or LL IM[1](plantare PLANT)]

implaus'|ible (-z-), a. Not plausible. Hence or cogn. ~IBIL'ITY n., ~IBLУ adv. [IM-[2]]

implead', v.t. (law). Prosecute or take proceedings against (person). [IM-[1]]

implĕdge', v.t. Put in pledge, pawn. [IM-[1]]

im'plĕmĕnt[1], n. Article of furniture, dress, etc., (pl.) equipment of these; tool, instrument, (esp. in pl.); || (Sc. Law) full performance. [ult. f. LL implementum f. L IM[1](plēre fill), see -MENT]

im'plĕmĕnt[2] (or -mĕnt'), v.t. Complete

(contract etc.); fulfil (engagement); fill up, supplement. [f. prec.]

implē'tion, n. Filling; fullness. [f. LL impletio f. IM[1](plēre plet- fill), see -ION]

im'plicate[1], n. Thing implied. [f. L IM[1](plicare plicat- or plicit- fold), see -ATE[2]]

im'plic|āte[2], v.t. Entwine, entangle; involve, imply, as inference, so ~ātive a.; involve (person in charge, crime, etc.); (pass.) be affected in (a thing's operation). So ~A'TION n. [as prec., see -ATE[3]]

impli'cit, a. Implied though not plainly expressed; virtually contained (in); ~ faith (not independently reached by the individual, but involved in general belief of Church, absolute, unreserved, cf. EXPLICIT). Hence ~LУ[2] adv., ~NESS n. [EX-ite, or L implicit- as IMPLICATE[1]]

implōr|e', v.t. Beg earnestly for; entreat (person to do). Hence ~ingLУ[2] adv., ~ingNESS n. [f. F implorer or L IM[1](plorare weep)]

impluv'ium (-plŏŏ-), n. (Rom. Ant.). Square basin in middle of atrium receiving rain-water from open space in roof. [L, f. IM[1](pluere rain)]

implӯ', v.t. Involve the truth of (thing not expressly asserted, that); mean; insinuate, hint. Hence impli'ĕdLУ[2] adv. [ME en-, em-, im- f. OF emplier f. L implicare (IMPLICATE[1]); cf. doublet EMPLOY]

|| impōld'er, v.t. Make a POLDER of; reclaim from sea. [f. Du. inpolderen, see IM-[1], POLDER]

impŏl'icў, n. Bad policy; inexpediency. [IM-[2]]

impolīte', a. (-est). Uncivil, rude. Hence ~LУ[2] (-tl-) adv., ~NESS (-tn-) n. [f. L IM[2](politus POLITE)]

impŏl'itic, a. Not politic; inexpedient. Hence ~LУ[2] adv. [IM-[2]]

impŏnderabil'ia, n. pl. Imponderables. [L]

impŏn'derable, a. & n. 1.(Phys.) having no weight; very light; (fig.) that cannot be estimated. 2. n. ~ thing (esp. fig., pl., of qualities, emotions, etc.). [IM-[2]]

impōn'ent, a. & n. (Person) that imposes a duty etc. [f. L IM[1](ponere place) lay on, see -ENT]

impōrt'[1], v.t. Bring, introduce, (thing, esp. goods from foreign country, into), whence ~ABLE a., ~ABIL'ITY, ~A'TION, ~ER[1], nn.; imply, indicate, mean, (thing, (that); express, make known, (that); be of consequence to, as questions that ~ us nearly, it ~s us to know. [f. L IM[1](portare carry) bring in, in med. L = be of consequence]

im'pōrt[2], n. What is implied, meaning; importance; (usu. pl.) commodity imported; importation. [f. prec.]

impōrt'ance, n. Being important; weight, significance; personal consequence, dignity; pompousness (usu. self-~). [F, f. med. L importantia (as IMPORT[1], see -ANCE)]

impŏrt'ant, a. Carrying with it great consequence (*to* person concerned or purpose etc.), weighty, momentous; consequential, pompous. Hence ~LY² adv. [F, f. med. L as IMPORT¹, see -ANT]

impŏrt'ūnate, a. Persistent, pressing, in solicitation; (of affairs) urgent.· Hence or cogn. ~LY² adv., impŏrtūn'ITY n. [f. L IM²(*portunus* f. *portus* port) inconvenient, -ATE²]

impŏrtūne' (*or* impŏr⁴), v.t. Solicit pressingly (person or abs.). [f. F *importuner* f. med. L *importunari* (as prec.)]

impōs|e' (-z), v.t. & i. (Arch.) place (thing) *upon*; (Print.) lay (pages of type) in proper order & secure them in a chase; lay (tax, duty, charge, obligation, *upon*); palm off (thing *upon* person); exert influence (*on* person) by striking character or appearance, whence ~'ɪnGLY² adv., ~'ɪnGNESS n., (-z-); ~e *upon*, take advantage of (person); practise deception (*upon*). [f. F IM¹(*poser*, cf. COMPOSE)]

imposi'tion (-z-), n. In vbl senses of IMPOSE; also or esp.: laying on *of hands* (in ordination etc.); impost, tax, duty; piece of deception or overcharge; ‖ work set as punishment at school (colloq. abbr. *impo, impot*). [ME, f. OF, or L *impositio* f. IM¹(*ponere posit-* place), -ION]

impŏss'|ible, a. Not possible (often w. *it* as subj., as *it is ~ible to alter them*); (loosely) not easy, not convenient; (colloq.) outrageous, intolerable, as *an ~ible hat, person.* Hence or cogn. ~IBIL'ITY n., ~IBLY² adv. [ME, f. OF f. L IM² (*possibilis* POSSIBLE)]

im'pōst¹, n. (Hist.) tax, duty, tribute; (Racing sl.) weight horse carries in handicap. [f. F *impost* f. med. L *impostus, -um* (as IMPOSITION)]

im'pōst², n. Upper course of pillar, bearing arch. [f. F *imposte* or It. *imposta* (as prec.)]

impŏs't|or, n. One who assumes a false character or passes himself off for someone else; swindler. Hence ~ROUS a. [f. F *imposteur* f. LL *impostor* (as IMPOST¹, see -OR)]

impŏs'tūme, -thume (-tūm), n. (arch.). Purulent swelling, abscess, (lit. & fig.). [ME, f. OF *empostume* f. L f. Gk APO(*stēma* f. *sta-* stand, -M)]

impŏs'ture, n. Fraudulent deception. [F, f. LL *impostura* (IMPOST¹, -URE)]

‖ **im'pŏt.** See IMPOSITION.

im'pot|ent, a. Powerless; helpless, decrepit; (of males) wholly lacking in sexual power. Hence or cogn. ~ENCE, ~ENCY, nn., ~entLY² adv. [ME, f. OF, f. L IM²(*potens* POTENT)]

impound', v.t. Shut up (cattle) in pound; shut up (person, thing) as in pound; take legal possession of; confiscate. [IM-¹]

impŏv'erish, v.t. Make poor; exhaust strength of. So ~MENT n. [ME, f. OF EM(*poverir* f. *povre* POOR), see -ISH²]

imprăc'tic|able, a. Impossible in prac-

tice; (of persons or things) unmanageable; (of roads etc.) impassable. Hence ~ABIL¹ ITY, ~ableNESS, nn., ~ablY² adv. [IM-²]

im'prec|āte, v.t. Invoke, call down, (evil *upon* person etc.). So ~A'TION n. (esp. spoken curse), ~ātorY a. [f. L IM¹(*precari* pray)]

imprĕg'n|able, a. (Of fortress etc.) that cannot be taken by arms; (fig.) proof against attack. Hence ~ABIL'ITY n., ~ablY² adv. [late ME & OF *imprenable* (IM-², *prendre* take); -g- f. 16th c.]

imprĕg'nate¹, a. Pregnant (lit. & fig.); permeated (*with*). [f. LL IM¹(*praegnare* be pregnant), see -ATE²]

imprĕg'n|āte², v.t. Make (female) pregnant; (Biol.) fecundate (female reproductive cell or ovum); fill, saturate, (*with*); imbue, fill, (*with* feelings, moral qualities, etc.). Hence ~A'TION n. [as prec., see ATE³]

imprĕsā'riō, n. (pl. ~s). Organizer of public entertainments, esp. manager of operatic or concert company. [It. (*impresa* undertaking, as EMPRISE, see -ARY¹)]

imprescrip'tible, a. Not subject to prescription, that cannot be legally taken away, esp. ~ *right.* [F (IM-²)]

im'press¹, n. Stamping; mark made by seal, stamp, etc.; (fig.) characteristic mark. [f. foll.]

imprĕss'², v.t. Apply (mark etc.) with pressure, imprint, stamp, (*on*); imprint, enforce, (idea etc., *that, what,* etc., *on* person, his mind); mark (thing *with* stamp etc. lit. & fig.); affect, influence, deeply, whence ~IBLE a., ~IBIL'ITY n.; affect (person) strongly (*with* idea etc.). [ME, f. OF *empresser* & L IM¹(*primere=premere* PRESS²)]

imprĕss'³, v.t. Force (men) to serve in army or navy (hist.); seize (goods etc.) for public service; enlist, make use of, (thing) in argument etc. Hence ~MENT n. [IM-¹ +PRESS³]

imprĕs'sion (-shn), n. Impressing (of mark); mark impressed; print taken from type or engraving; (printing of) number of copies forming one issue of book, edition, (also, unaltered reprint from standing type or plates, as opp. to *edition*); effect produced (esp. on mind or feelings); notion, (vague) belief, impressed on the mind, as *that is my ~, I was under the ~ that.* [ME, f. OF f. L *impressio* (as IMPRESS², see -ION)]

imprĕs'sion|able (-shon-), a. Susceptible of impressions, easily influenced. Hence ~ABIL'ITY n. [F (*impressionner*, as prec., see -ABLE)]

imprĕs'sion|ism (-shon-), n. Method of painting or writing so as to give general tone & effect without elaborate detail, or (in painting, opp. *pre-Raphaelitism*) with details so treated as to be apprehended simultaneously, & not successively with changes of focus, cf. POST-~*ism.* So ~ARY¹, ~ĭs'tɪc, aa., ~ɪsT n. [-ISM]

impress'ive, a. (Of language, scenes, etc.) able to excite deep feeling. Hence ~LY² (-vl-) adv., ~NESS (-vn-) n. [-IVE]

im'prest, n. Money advanced to person to be used in State business. [f. phr. *in prest* (15th c., f. OF *prest* loan) on account, in advance]

imprǐmāt'ur̆, n. Official licence to print (now usu. of works sanctioned by R.-C. Church); (fig.) sanction. [mod. L. = let it be printed]

imprǐm'ǐs, adv. In the first place. [assim. f. L *in primis* among the first things]

im'print¹, n. Impression, stamp, (lit. & fig.); *publisher's, printer's,* ~ (name, place etc., on title-page or at end of book). [f. F *empreinte* stamp (as foll.)]

imprint'², v.t. Stamp (figure etc. *on*); impress (idea etc. *on, in,* mind etc.); impress (quality etc. *on, in*); stamp (thing *with* figure). [ME, f. OF *empreinter* f. *empreindre, -preint* f. L IM¹(*primere = premere* press)]

impris'on (-z-), v.t. Put into prison; (fig.) confine, shut up. So ~MENT (-z-) n. [ME, f. OF EM²(*prisoner* f. PRISON)]

improb'|able, a. Not likely to be true or to happen. Hence ~ABIL'ITY n., ~ABLY² adv. [f. F, or L IM²(*probabilis* PROBABLE)]

improb'ǐt̆y, n. Wickedness; dishonesty. [f. L *improbitas* f. IM²(*probus* honest), see -TY]

imprŏmp'tū, adv., n., & a. Extempore (performance, composition, speech); musical composition having character of improvisation. [17th c., f. F, = L *in promptu* in readiness (*promere,* see PROMPT)]

improp'er, a. Inaccurate, wrong; ~ *fraction* (greater than 1, with numerator greater than denominator); unseemly, indecent. Hence ~LY² adv. [f. F *impropre* or L *improprius* (IM-², PROPER)]

‖improp'ri|āte, v.t. Annex (ecclesiastical benefice) to corporation or person as property; place (tithes, ecclesiastical property) in lay hands. So ~ATE² (-at) a., ~A'TION n. [f. med. L IM¹(*propriare* f. *proprius* own), see -ATE³]

‖improp'riātor, n. One to whom benefice is impropriated. [as prec., see -OR]

impropri'ĕt̆y, n. Incorrectness; unfitness; indecency. [f. F *-été* or L IM²(*proprietas* PROPRIETY)]

improv'|able (-ōōv-), a. That can be improved; adapted for cultivation. Hence ~ABIL'ITY, ~ableness, nn. [-ABLE]

improve' (-ōōv), v.t. & i. Make, become, better; ~ *away,* get rid of by improvements; make good use of (*the occasion, the opportunity*); ~ *upon,* produce something better than; preach on (*the occasion*) with a view to edification. So ~MENT (-ōōvm-) n., (also) addition, alteration, etc., that adds to the value (of lands, houses, etc.). [16th c. *em-, improw(e)* f. AF f. OF *em-* EM-+*prou* profit]

improv'er (-ōōv-), n. In vbl senses; also

or esp.: one who works at trade for low wage or none to improve his skill; = DRESS-~. [-ER¹]

improv'id|ent, a. Unforeseeing; heedless; thriftless. Hence or cogn. ~ENCE n., ~ently² adv. [IM-²]

improv'isātŏr (-z-), **improv(v)isatōr'e** (-vĕzahtōrĕ), n. (It. pl. *-ori,* pron. *-ōrē*). One who improvises or composes extempore. So **improv(v)isatric'e** (-vĕzah-trēch'ā) [-TRIX] n. [It. (*-e,*) as IMPROVISE, see -OR]

improvise' (-z; *also* Im'-), v.t. Compose, utter, (verse, music, etc., or abs.) extempore; provide, get up, extempore. Hence **improvisā'TION** n., **improvisātŏr'IAL, improvis'atŏry**, aa., (-z-). [f. F *improviser* (f. It. *improv(v)isare*) f. L IM-² (*provisus* p.p. as PROVIDE) or on the earlier E *improvisation*]

imprud'|ent (-rōō-), a. Rash, indiscreet. Hence or cogn. ~ENCE n., ~ently² adv. [f. L IM²(*prudens* PRUDENT)]

im'pud|ent, a. Shamelessly forward; unblushing; insolently disrespectful. Hence or cogn. ~ENCE n., ~ently² adv. [ME, f. L IM²*pudens* (*pudēre* be ashamed, -ENT)]

impudi'cit̆y, n. Shamelessness, immodesty. [f. F *impudicité* f. L IM²(*pudicus* as prec.), -TY]

impugn' (-ūn), v.t. Assail by word, call in question, (statement, action). Hence ~ABLE a., ~MENT n., (-ūn-). [f. L IM-¹ (*pugnare* fight) assail]

impu'iss|ant, a. Impotent, weak. So ~ANCE n. [F (IM-²+PUISSANT)]

im'pulse, n. Impelling, push; (Dynam.) indefinitely large force enduring inappreciably short time but producing finite momentum, e.g. blow of hammer, (also) product of average value of force multiplied by time during which it acts; mental incitement; sudden tendency to act without reflection; impetus. [f. L *impulsus -ūs* (as IMPEL)]

impul'sion (-shn), n. Impelling push; mental impulse; impetus. [ME, f. OF, f. L *impulsionem* (as IMPEL, see -ION)]

impul'sive, a. Tending to impel; (of persons, conduct, etc.) apt to be moved, prompted, by sudden impulse. Hence ~LY² (-vl-) adv.; ~NESS (-vn-) n. [f. F (*-if, -ive*) or LL *impulsivus* (as prec., see -IVE)]

impūn'ǐt̆y, n. Exemption from punishment, esp. *with* ~; exemption from injury as consequence of act. [f. L *impunitas* f. IM²(*punis* f. *poena* penalty), see -TY]

impūre', a. Dirty; unchaste; mixed with foreign matter, adulterated, (lit. & fig.); (of colour) mixed with another colour. Hence or cogn. ~LY² (-rl-) adv., **impūr'ITY** n. [f. L IM²(*purus* PURE)]

impūt'e|e', v.t. Attribute, ascribe, (fault etc., rarely good quality etc., *to* person etc.); (Theol.) ascribe (righteousness, guilt, *to* person) by vicarious substitution. So ~ABIL'ITY, ~A'TION, nn., ~'ABLE,

~'atⁱᵥᴇ, aa., ~'atⁱᵥᴇʟʏ² adv. [ME, f. OF *imputer* f. L IM¹(*putare* reckon) enter in the account]

in¹, prep. expr. inclusion or position within limits of space, time, circumstance, etc., as: *in Europe, England, London* (so of any large city or of town etc. in which speaker lives, cf. AT), *in the house, a box, a car, a pond, a crowd*; (of dress etc.) *in muslin, mourning, white, brown boots*; *in* (the works of) *Thackeray*; (of part affected) *blind in one eye*; (of ratio) *not one in a hundred*; (of body etc. to which one belongs etc.) *in the army, shares in a company*; (of non-physical regions) *in politics, fancy, my opinion*; (of situation, often idiomatic) *in* CLOVER, HOT *water, fetters, leading-strings, the* DARK², *health, hope* (of), *sorrow,* CALF, *in* (supplied with) *cash, in* (under influence of) *liquor*; (of occupation) *in search of, in pursuance of, in* (while) *crossing the river*; (of form or arrangement) *packed in dozens, sold in building-plots, falling in folds, in* ORDER¹ (2) *to* or *that*; (of instrument or material) *drank his health in a glass of whisky, the coat was in green velvet*; (of purpose) *in reply to, in quest of, in honour of*; (of time) *in* (during) *the day, in* (within the space of) *three months, in* (at the end of) *five minutes*; *in itself*, apart from all else, absolutely; (colloq.) *the latest thing in* (within the sphere of) *radios*; (of person's capacity etc.) *as far as in me lies, did not think he had it in him* (was capable of it); *not in it*, not in the running, not a serious competitor; *nothing, little, not much, in it,* (Racing) no decided advantage as yet gained by any competitor, no guessing who will win; (with vbs of motion or change) *put it in your pocket, cut it in half, throw it in the fire*; (expr. relation of vb to indirect object), *believe in, trust in, share in, engage in, rejoice in*; (so with adjj. & nn.) *weak in* (as regards) *algebra, wanting in courage, your trust in him, a change in the constitution*; (of number or dimension) *seven in number, four feet in width*; (forming adv. phr.) *in fact, in truth, in honour, in any case; in so* (or *as*) *far as,* in such measure as; *in that*, since, because. [OE, OS, OHG, Goth. *in*, ON *í*, cogn. w. L *in*, Gk *en*]

in², adv. expr. position bounded by certain limits or motion to a point enclosed by them, as: *come in, send him in, walk in,* (into house, enclosed ground, etc.), *put a notice in* (into a paper), *lock him in, he is in* (the house etc., esp. = at home); *in with it*, put, take, it in; *throw in the harness* (to the bargain, in addition); *a coat with the woolly side in* (nearest the body); *the Liberals were in* (office); *short skirts, oysters, are in* (in fashion or season); (Crick.) *before he had been in* (batting) *five minutes; keep the fire in* (burning); *train, boat, summer, is in* (arrived); (with trans. vbs) *burn, cut, rub,* (thing) *in* (so as to

penetrate into another), *hem, cover, wall,* (thing) *in* (so as to enclose it); *in for,* involved in, committed to, (usu. something unpleasant, esp. *it*), also, engaged in competition for (race, prize, etc.); *be, keep, in* (on friendly terms) *with*; *breed in & in* (repeatedly within same stock); *in & out,* now in, now out, to & fro, with alternation or oscillation; *in on it* (colloq.), in the know. [OE *in*(n), OS, OHG *in* (G *ein*), ON, Goth. *inn,* also OE *inne,* OS, OHG, Goth. *inna,* ON *inni,* derivatives f. prec.]

in³, a. Internal, living etc. inside, as *in patient, in-patient,* one who remains in hospital while under treatment. [prec. used attrib.]

in⁴, n. (Pl.) political party in office; *ins & outs,* turnings to & fro (usu. fig.), details (of procedure etc.). [f. IN²]

in⁵, prep. (L). *In absĕn'tĭa,* in (his or her) absence; *in artĭc'ŭlō mŏr'tĭs,* in the instant of death; *in* CAMERA; *in căp'ĭtĕ,* in chief, holding or held immediately of the crown; *in commĕn'dam,* as a charge or trust of benefice pending appointment of regular incumbent, or of its revenue enjoyed by layman etc.); *in cŏntŭmā'cĭam* (-shĭ-), in contempt of court; *in ĕss'ĕ,* in actual existence, cf. *in posse; in extĕn'sō,* at full length; *in extrēm'ĭs,* at the point of death; *in flagrăn'tĕ dĕlĭc'tō,* in the very act of committing an offence; *in fŏrm'a paup'erĭs,* as poor person not liable to costs; *in lŏc'ō parĕn'tĭs,* in place of a parent; *in mĕd'ĭăs rēs,* into the thick of it; *in mĕmōr'ĭăm,* in memory of; *in nŭb'ĭbus,* in the clouds, vague, speculative; *in pärt'ĭbus (infĭdēl'ĭum),* (of Rom. Cath. titular bishop) in a heretical country; *in pŏss'ĕ,* potentially, opp. to *in esse; in prŏp'rĭa pĕrsŏn'a,* in his (her) own person; *in pur'ĭs nătŭrāl'ĭbus,* stark naked; *in* RE²; *in sĭt'ū,* in its (original) place; *in stăt'ū pŭpĭllār'ī,*under guardianship; *in stăt'ū quō,* in the same state (as formerly); *in tĕrrōr'ĕm,* as a warning; *in tōt'ō,* completely; *in vĭt'rō,* (in laboratory use) in a test-tube etc. (lit. in glass).

in-¹, pref. = L *in* in, on, into, towards, against (becoming *il-* before *l, im-* before *b, m, p, ir-* before *r*). In OF *in-, im-,* became *en-, em-*; E has usu. *in-, im-,* in wds obviously of L orig., to which the wds adopted from OF were, from the 14th c., made to conform (see EN-¹). Words that still retain both forms are given in this dictionary under the more usual form.

in-², pref. = L *in-* (*il-* etc. as prec.), cogn. w. Gk *a-, an-,* Gmc *un-,* prefixed to adjj. & their derivatives to express negation. As living E pref., *in-* often interchanges with *un-,* which is preferred in wds not obviously answering to L types (*unavailing, uncertain, undevout*).

-in, a modification of the chem. suf. -INE³ forming names of neutral substances such as glycerides, glucosides, proteins, etc.

(*albumin, casein, fibrin, gelatin*) to distinguish them from names of alkaloids & basic substances. Some wds of this class were formerly spelt *-ine*, & are still so spelt in pop. use (*margarine, gelatine*).

-ina[1], L fem. suf. found in *regina*, extended in It. or Sp. & used in E to form fem. titles (*czarina*) & proper names (*Georgina*); occurring also in names of musical instruments (*concertina, seraphina*). Cf. -INE[4].

-ina[2], suf., neut. pl. of (often mod.) L adjj., used, in agreement with *animalia* animals understood, to form names of groups of animals related to some typical genus, as *Bombycina* (genus *Bombyx*).

inabil'ity̆, n. Being unable; lack of power or means. [IN-[2]]

inaccess'|ible (-ks-), a. That cannot be reached; (of persons) not open to advances, unapproachable. Hence ~IBIL'ITY n., ~IBLY[2] adv. [F, or f. LL IN[2](*accessibilis* ACCESSIBLE)]

inacc'ūr|ate, a. Not accurate. Hence ~ACY n., ~ately[2] adv. [IN-[2]]

inăc't|ion, n. Absence of action; sluggishness, inertness. So ~IVE a., ~IVELY[2] adv., ~iv'ITY n. [IN-[2]]

inadaptabil'ity̆, n. Want of adaptability. [IN-[2]]

inăd'équ|ate, a. Not adequate (*to* purpose, *to* do); insufficient. Hence ~ACY n., ~ately[2] adv. [IN-[2]]

inadhēs'ive (-h-), a. Not adhesive. [IN-[2]]

inadmiss'|ible, a. That cannot be admitted or allowed. Hence ~IBIL'ITY n. [IN-[2]]

inadvert'|ent, a. Not properly attentive; negligent; (of actions) unintentional. Hence or cogn. ~ENCE, ~ENCY, nn., ~entLY[2] adv. [f. earlier *inadvertence*, *-ency* (IN-[2], ADVERT, -ENT)]

inadvīs'able (-z-), a. Not advisable. [IN-[2]]

ināl'ien|able, a. Not alienable. Hence ~ABIL'ITY n., ~ABLY[2] adv. [IN-[2]]

inal'ter|able (-awl-), a. Unalterable. Hence ~ABIL'ITY n., ~ABLY[2] adv. [IN-[2]]

inămora'tŏ (-rah-), n. (fem. *-ta*). Lover. [It. (now *inn-*) f. IN [1](*amorare* f. *amore* f. L *amor* love) enamour]

ināne', a. & n. Empty, void, silly; senseless; (n.) *the* ~, vacuity, infinite space. Hence or cogn. ~LY[2] (-nl-) adv., inăn'ITY n. [f. L *inanis* empty, vain]

inăn'imate, a. Destitute of life; not endowed with animal life, as ~ *nature* (outside the animal world); spiritless, dull. Hence or cogn. ~LY[2] adv., inănima̱[2̲]TION n. [f. LL IN[2](*animatus* ANIMATE[1])]

inani'tion, n. Emptiness, esp. from want of nourishment. [f. LL *inanitio* f. *inanire* make empty (as INANE), see -ION]

inappeas'able (-z-), a. Not appeasable. [IN-[2]]

inappell'able, n. Not to be appealed against. [f. IN-[2]+L *appellare* APPEAL+-BLE]

inăpp'ětence, n. Want of appetence. [F (IN-[2], APPETENCE)]

inăpp'lic|able, a. Not applicable, unsuitable, (*to* case, purpose). Hence ~ABIL'ITY n., ~ABLY[2] adv. [IN-[2]]

inăpp'osite, a. Not apposite, out of place. Hence ~LY[2] adv. [IN-[2]]

inapprē'ciab|le (-sha-), a. Imperceptible, not worth reckoning; that cannot be appreciated. Hence ~LY[2] adv. [IN-[2]]

inapprēcia'tion, n. Failure to appreciate. So inapprē'ciative (-sha-) a. [IN-[2]]

inăpprehĕn'sible, a. That cannot be grasped by senses or intellect. [f. LL *-ibilis* (IN-[2], APPREHENSIBLE)]

inapproach'able, a. Unapproachable. [IN-[2]]

inapprŏp'rĭate, a. Not appropriate. Hence ~LY[2] adv., ~NESS n. [IN-[2]]

inăpt', a. Unfit, unskilful. Hence inăp'tiTUDE, ~NESS, nn., ~LY[2] adv. [IN-[2]]

inarch', v.t. Graft by connecting growing branch without separation from parent stock. [IN-[1]+ARCH v.]

inărm', v.t. (poet.). Embrace. [IN[1]+ARM[1]]

inartic'ulate, a. Not jointed; (of speech) not articulate; unable to speak distinctly; dumb. Hence ~LY[2] adv., ~NESS n. [f. LL IN[2](*articulatus* ARTICULATE)]

inărtifi'cial (-shal), a. Lacking in art, inartistic; artless, natural. Hence ~LY[2] adv. [f. L IN[2](*artificialis* ARTIFICIAL)]

inărtis't|ic, a. Not following the principles of art; unskilled in art. Hence ~ICALLY adv. [IN-[2]]

inasmŭch' (-az-), adv. ~ *as*, since, because; (arch.) in so far *as*. [ME; orig. three wds]

inatten't|ion, n. Want of attention, heedlessness; neglect to show courtesy. So ~IVE a., ~IVELY[2] adv., ~IVENESS n. [IN-[2], or f. F]

inaud'|ible, a. That cannot be heard. Hence ~IBIL'ITY n., ~IBLY[2] adv. [f. LL IN[2](*audibilis* AUDIBLE)]

inaug'ūral, a. & n. Of inauguration; *(n.)* ~ speech or address. [F, f. *inaugurer* (as foll.)]

inaug'ūr|āte, v.t. Admit (person) to office etc. with ceremony; enter with ceremony upon (undertaking etc.); initiate public use of (building etc.). Hence or cogn. ~A'TION, ~ātoR, nn., ~ātorY a. [f. L IN[2](*augurare* take omens, f. *augur*), see -ATE[3]]

inauspi'cious (-shus), a. Not of good omen; unlucky. Hence ~LY[2] adv., ~NESS n. [IN-[2]]

in'board (-ōrd), adv. & a. (naut.). (Situated) within sides of or towards centre of ship. [IN[1]]

in'bŏrn, a. Implanted by nature. [IN[2]]

inbreathe' (-dh), v.t. Breathe (thing) in (lit. & fig.). [IN[2]]

in'brĕd, a. Innate, inherent by nature; bred in and in. [IN[2]]

in′breeding, n. Breeding in & in, breeding from animals closely related. [IN²]

Inc′a (ĭ-), n. Emperor or king of Peru before Spanish conquest; one of royal race of Peru. [Peruv.]

incăl′cŭl|able, a. Too great for calculation; that cannot be reckoned beforehand; (of person, character, etc.) uncertain. Hence ~ABIL′ITY n., ~ABLY² adv. [IN-²]

incăndĕsce′, v.i. & t. Glow, cause to glow, with heat. [f. after foll.]

incăndĕs′c|ent, a. Glowing with heat; shining brightly; (of electric & other light) produced by glowing of filament etc. Hence ~ENCE n. [F, f. L IN¹(candescere incept. of candēre be white), see -ENT]

incăntā′tion, n. (Use of) magical formula; spell, charm. [ME, f. OF f. LL incantationem f. IN¹(cantare chant) bewitch, see -ION]

incăp′|able, a. Not capable (of conduct etc., of doing; often in good sense, = too honest etc. to do); not susceptible (of improvement etc.); lacking in ordinary powers, as drunk & ~able. Hence ~ABIL′ITY n., ~ABLY² adv. [f. F, or LL IN²(capabilis CAPABLE)]

incăpă′cit|āte, v.t. Render incapable or unfit (for work etc., for, from, doing). Hence ~A′TION n. [f. foll. +-ATE³]

incăpă′cĭty, n. Inability (for doing, for work etc., to do, or abs.); legal disqualification. [f. F IN²(capacité CAPACITY)]

incăr′cer|āte, v.t. Imprison (lit. & fig.). Hence or cogn. ~A′TION, ~ātor, nn. [f. med. L IN¹(carcerare f. carcer prison), see -ATE³]

incăr′nadǐne, a., & v.t. (poet.). (Dye) flesh-coloured, crimson. [(vb f. a.) F (-in, -ine) f. It. incarnadino (for -tino) f. incarnato INCARNATE¹]

incăr′nāte¹, a. (Of person, spirit, quality, etc.) embodied in flesh, esp. in human form, as he is an ~ fiend, Liberty ~; (as p.p., of Christ) was ~ by the Holy Ghost. [ME, f. LL IN¹(carnare f. caro carnis flesh), see -ATE²]

incăr′nāte² (or ĭn′k-), v.t. Embody in flesh; put (idea etc.) into concrete form, realize; (of person etc.) be living embodiment of (quality). [as prec., see -ATE³]

incărnā′tion, n. Embodiment in (esp. human) flesh, esp. the I~ (of Christ); impersonation, living type, (of quality etc.). [ME, f. OF f. LL incarnationem (as prec. see -ION)]

incau′tious (-shus), a. Rash. Hence~LY² adv., ~NESS n. [IN-²]

incĕn′diar|y̆, a. & n. 1. Of, guilty of, the malicious setting on fire of property (~y bomb), filled with inflammatory substance(s) for causing fires; (fig.) tending to stir up strife, inflammatory. 2. n. ~y person (lit. & fig.); ~y bomb. Hence

~ISM n. [f. L incendiarius f. incendium conflagration f. IN(cendere cens- set fire to), see -ARY¹]

incĕnse¹, n. Gum, spice, producing sweet smell when burned; smoke of this, esp. in religious ceremonial; (fig.) praise, flattery. [ME, f. OF encens f. LL incensum thing burnt, incense, neut. p.p. as prec.]

incĕns|e², v.t. Fumigate (person, thing) with incense; burn incense to (deity etc.); suffuse with fragrance. Hence ~A′TION n. [ME, f. OF encenser (as prec.)]

incĕnse′³, v.t. Enrage, make angry (~d against, with, at, by). [ME, f. OF incenser f. L incendere (see INCENDIARY)]

incĕn′sory, n. Vessel for burning incense, censer. [f. med. L incensorium (INCENSE¹, -ORY)]

incĕn′tive, a. & n. 1. Tending to incite. 2. n. Incitement (to action, to do, to doing), provocation, motive. [f. L incentivus setting the tune f. IN¹(cinere cent- = canere sing) sing to; -IVE]

incĕpt′, v.i. & t. ∥ (Formerly at Camb. Univ.) commence the taking of Master's or Doctor's degree, so **incĕp′tor** n.; (Biol.) take in. [f. L IN¹(cipere cept- = capere take) begin]

incĕp′tion, n. Beginning; ∥ (Camb. Univ.) incepting. [ME, f. OF, or L inceptio (as prec., see -ION)]

incĕp′tive, a. & n. Beginning; initial; (Gram.) ~ verb, one that denotes the beginning of an action; (n.) ~ verb. [f. LL inceptivus (as INCEPT, see -IVE)]

incert′itude, n. Uncertainty. [f. F, or LL incertitudo (IN-², CERTITUDE)]

incĕss′ant, a. Unceasing, continual, repeated. Hence **incĕss′ANCY**, ~NESS, nn., ~LY² adv. [f. F, or LL IN²(cessans -antpart. of cessare CEASE)]

in′cĕst, n. Sexual commerce of near kindred. [ME, f. L incestus -ūs or IN²(cestum neut. adj. = castum chaste)]

incĕs′tŭous, a. Involving, guilty of, incest. Hence~LY² adv. [f. LL incestuosus (as prec., see -OUS)]

inch¹, n., & v.t. & i. 1. Twelfth part of (linear) foot; square, cubic, ~, area equal to square, content equal to cube, whose side is an ~; (as unit of rainfall) quantity that would cover surface to depth of an ~; (of atmospheric or other pressure) amount that balances weight of column of mercury 1 in. high in mercurial barometer; small amount; by ~es, bit by bit; every ~, entirely; (pl.) stature (a man of your ~es); give him an ~ & he'll take an ELL; flog person within an ~ of his life, almost to death; an ~ of cold iron, stab with a dagger etc. 2. v.t. & i. Move by ~es, edge in, forward, etc. [OE ynce = OHG unza, Goth. unkja f. L uncia twelfth part, see OUNCE¹]

∥ **inch²**, n. Small (esp. Scottish) island (freq. in place names). [f. Gael. innis]

In wds from incalculable to incautious pronounce ĭn-k-, not ĭngk-.

in'chŏate[1] (ĭn-kō-), a. Just begun; undeveloped. [f. L IN[1](*cohare, choare*), see -ATE[2]]

in'chŏ|āte[2] (ĭn-kō-), v.t. Begin; originate. So~A'TION n., ~ātive (*or* -kō'a-) a. [prec., -ATE[3]]

in'cidence, n. Falling on, contact with, a thing; *what is the~ of the tax?*, on whom will it fall?; (Phys.) falling of line, or of thing, moving in a line, upon a surface; *angle of ~*, that which the incident line, ray, etc., makes with the perpendicular to the surface at point of ~; range, scope, extent, of influence. [ME, f. OF (as INCIDENT[2], see -ENCE)]

in'cident[1], n. Subordinate or accessory event; event, occurrence; hostile clash of e.g. troops of countries not at war, as *frontier ~*; detached event attracting general attention; distinct piece of action in play or poem; (Law) privilege, burden, etc., attaching to estate etc. [ME, f. OF (as foll.)]

in'cident[2], a. Apt to occur, naturally attaching, (*to*); (Law) attaching *to* (cf. prec.); (of light etc.) falling, striking, (*upon*). [ME, f. OF, or L IN[1](*cĭdere = cadere* fall), see -ENT]

incidĕn'tal, a. Casual, not essential; liable to happen *to*; *~ images, colours* (perceived as consequence of impressions no longer present); *~ music* (introduced during the action of a play). Hence~LY[2] adv. (also, loosely, by the way, parenthetically).

incin'er|āte, v.t. Reduce to ashes; consume (body etc.) by fire. Hence or cogn. ~A'TION, ~ātor, nn. [INCIDENT[1]+-AL] [f. med. L IN[1](*cinerare* f. *cinis -eris* ashes), see -ATE[3]]

incip'i|ent, a. Beginning; in an initial stage. Hence ~ENCE, ~ENCY, nn., ~ent-LY[2] adv. [f. L as INCEPT, see -ENT]

in'cipit, sent. n. (Here) begins (book etc.), cf. EXPLICIT[1]. [L]

incise' (-z), v.t. Make a cut in; engrave. [f. F *inciser* f. L IN[1](*cĭdere cis- = caedere* cut)]

inci'sion (-zhn), n. Cutting into a thing; cut, division produced by cutting, notch. [ME, f. OF f. L *incisionem* (prec., -ION)]

incis'ive, a. Cutting, penetrating; (fig.) mentally sharp; acute, trenchant. Hence ~LY[2] (-vl-) adv., ~NESS (-vn-) n. [F (-if, -ive), or f. med. L *incisivus* (as INCISE, see -IVE)]

incis'or (-z-), n. Any tooth between the canine teeth in either jaw. [med. L, = cutter (as INCISE, see -OR)]

incite', v.t. Urge, stir up, (person etc. *to* action, *to* do). Hence or cogn. incitA'TION, ~MENT (-tm-), nn. [late ME, f. F *inciter* f. L IN[1](*citare* rouse frequent. of *ciēre cit-*)]

incivil'ity, n. Rudeness, discourtesy. [f. F *incivilité* or LL IN[2](*civilitas* CIVILITY)]

in'civism, n. Want of good citizenship,

esp. of loyalty to French Revolution principles. [f. F IN[2](*civisme* f. L *civis* citizen)]

|| **in'-clearing**, n. The cheques etc. collectively payable by a bank & received through clearing-house for settlement. [IN adv.]

inclĕm'|ent, a. (Of weather or climate) severe, esp. cold or stormy. So~ENCY n. [f. F, or L IN[1](*clemens* CLEMENT)]

inclin'able, a. Inclined, disposed; (*to* thing, *to* do); favourable (*to*). [ME, f. OF *enclinable* (as INCLINE[1], see -ABLE)]

inclinā'tion, n. Leaning, slope, slant; difference of direction of two lines, esp. as measured by angle between them; disposition, propensity, (*to, for, towards,* thing, *to* do); liking, affection, (*for*). [ME, f. OF, or f. L *inclinatio* (foll., ;ATION)]

incline'[1], v.t. & i. Bend (head, body, one-*self*) forward or downward; *~ one's ear,* listen favourably (*to* person, prayer, etc.); dispose (mind, heart, person, *to* do), as *~ our hearts to keep this law, I am ~d to think*; be disposed, as *I ~ to think*; lean, cause to lean, from the vertical etc.; *~d* (sloping) *plane,* one of the MECHANICAL *powers*; tend (*to* corpulence etc.). [ME *en-* f. OF *encliner* f. L IN[1](*clinare* bend)]

in'cline[2] (*or* -īn'), n. Inclined plane; slope. [f. prec.]

inclinŏm'ēter, n. Instrument measuring vertical intensity of earth's magnetic force as shown by dip of magnetic needle, or for measuring slope. [INCLINE+-0-+ -METER]

includ|e (-lōō-), v.t. Comprise, embrace, (thing etc.) as part of a whole; (part. in abs. constr.) if we ~e, as *seven were killed, ~ing the guard*; treat, regard, as so comprised; *~e out,* (specifically) exclude; (p.p.) shut in. [ME, f. L IN[1](*cludere clus- = claudere* shut)]

inclus'ive (-lōō-), a. Including, comprising, (*of,* or abs.); (abbr. *incl.*) *pages 7 to 26* ~ (including pages 7 & 26); including much or all, as *~ terms* (at hotel etc.). Hence or cogn. inclu'SION (-lōōzhn) n., ~LY[2] adv., ~NESS n. [f. med. L *inclusivus* (as prec., see -IVE)]

incŏg', a., n., & adv. Colloq. abbr. of foll.

incŏg'nitō, a. & n. (pl. *-ti* pron. -tē; fem. *-ta* pron. -ta, pl. *-te* pron. -tā), & adv. (Person) concealed under disguised character; (adv.) with one's name, character, etc., concealed, as *travel, do good,~*. [It., =unknown, f. L IN[2](*cognitus* p.p. of *cognoscere* get to know)]

incŏg'nizable (-kŏgn-, -kŏn-), a. That cannot be apprehended by senses or intellect. [IN-[2]]

incŏg'niz|ant (as prec.), a. Unaware, unconscious *of*. So ~ANCE n. [IN-[2]]

incohēr'|ent, a. Not coherent (lit. & fig.). So ~ENCE n., ~entLY[2] adv. [IN-[2]]

incohēs'ive, a. Not cohesive. [IN-[2]]

In wds from *in-clearing* to *incurve*, pronounce'ĭn-k-, not ĭngk-.

incombŭs′t|ible, a. That cannot be consumed by fire. Hence ~ɪBIL′ɪTY n. [f. med. L ɪN²(*combustibilis* COMBUSTIBLE)]

in′come, n. Periodical (usu. annual) receipts from one's business, lands, work, investments, etc.; ~ *tax* (levied on this). [ɪN adv.]

in′com′er (-kŭ-), n. One who comes in; immigrant; intruder; successor. [ɪN adv.]

in′com′ing¹ (-kŭ-), n. Entrance, arrival; (usu. pl.) revenue, income. [ɪN adv.]

in′coming² (-kŭ-), a. Succeeding; immigrant; (of profit) accruing. [ɪN adv.]

incommen′sur|able (-sher-), a. (Of magnitudes) having no common measure integral or fractional (*with* another); irrational, surd; not comparable in respect of magnitude; not worthy to be measured *with*. Hence ~ABIL′ɪTY n., ~ABLY² adv. [f. LL ɪN²(*commensurabilis* COMMENSURABLE)]

incommen′surate (-sher-), a. Out of proportion, inadequate, (*with, to*); = prec. Hence ~NESS n. [ɪN²]

incommōde′, v.t. Trouble, annoy; hinder. [f. F *incommoder* or L ɪN²(*commodare* f. *commodus* COMMODIOUS)]

incommōd′ious, a. Not affording good accommodation, uncomfortable. Hence ~NESS n. [ɪN²]

incommūn′ic|able, a. That cannot be shared; that cannot be told. Hence ~ABIL′ɪTY, ~ableness, nn., ~ABLY² adv. [f. F, or LL ɪN²(*communicabilis* COMMUNICABLE)]

incommūnica′dō (-ah-), a. Without means of communication, (of prisoner) in solitary confinement. [Sp. (-*omu*-)]

incommūn′icātive, a. Not communicative. Hence ~LY² adv., ~NESS n. [ɪN²]

incommūt′ab|le, a. Unchangeable; not commutable. Hence ~LY² adv. [ME, f. OF, or L ɪN²(*commutabilis* COMMUTABLE)]

incompăct′, a. Not compact (esp. fig.). [ɪN²]

incŏm′parab|le, a. Matchless; not to be compared (*with, to*). Hence ~leNESS n., ~LY² adv. [ME, f. OF f. L ɪN²(*comparabilis* COMPARABLE)]

incompăt′|ible, a. Opposed in character, discordant; inconsistent (*with*). So ~ɪBIL′ɪTY n. [f. OF, or med. L ɪN²(*compatibilis* COMPATIBLE)]

incŏm′pět|ent, a. Not qualified or able (*to* do); not legally qualified. Hence or cogn. ~ENCE, ~ENCY, nn., ~entLY² adv. [f. F, or LL ɪN²(*competens* COMPETENT)]

incomplēte′, a. Not complete. Hence ~LY² (-tl-) adv., ~NESS (-tn-) n. [ME, f. OF, or LL ɪN²(*completus* COMPLETE)]

incŏmprĕhĕn′s|ible, a. That cannot be understood; (Athanas. Creed) boundless (also as n., *three* ~*ibles*). Hence ~ɪBIL′ɪTY, ~ɪbleNESS, nn., ~ɪbLY² adv. [ME, f. L ɪN²(*comprehensibilis* COMPREHENSIBLE)]

incŏmprĕhĕn′sion (-shn), n. Failure to understand. [ɪN²]

incompress′|ible, a. That cannot be compressed. Hence ~ɪBIL′ɪTY n. [ɪN²]

incompūt′able, a. That cannot be computed. [ɪN²]

inconceiv′|able (-sĕv-), a. That cannot be imagined; (pop.) very remarkable. Hence ~ABIL′ɪTY n., ~ABLY² adv. [ɪN²]

inconclus′ive (-kloo-), a. (Of argument, evidence, action) not decisive or convincing. Hence ~LY² adv., ~NESS n. [ɪN²]

incondĕn′sable, a. That cannot be condensed, esp. that cannot be reduced to liquid or solid condition. [ɪN²]

incŏn′dīte, a. (Of literary composition etc.) ill constructed; crude, unpolished. [f. L ɪN²(*conditus* p.p. of *condere* put together)]

inconfŏrm′itў, n. Dissimilarity, want of conformity, (*to, with*); = NONCONFORMITY. [ɪN²]

incŏng′ruous (-kŏnggrŏŏ-), a. Disagreeing, out of keeping, (*with*); out of place, absurd. Hence or cogn. **incongru′ɪTY** (-grŏŏ-), ~NESS, nn., ~LY² adv. [f. L ɪN²(*congruus* CONGRUOUS)]

inconsĕc′ūtive, a. Wanting in sequence, inconsequent. Hence ~LY² adv., ~NESS n. [ɪN²]

incŏn′sĕqu|ent, a. Not following naturally, irrelevant; wanting in logical sequence; disconnected. Hence or cogn. ~ENCE n., ~ĕn′tɪAL (-shal) a., ~ĕn′tiaLY² (-shal-), ~entLY² adv. [f. L ɪN²(*consequens* CONSEQUENT)]

inconsid′erable, a. Not worth considering; of small size, value, etc. [f. F, or ɪN²+CONSIDERABLE]

inconsid′er|ate, a. (Of person or action) thoughtless, rash; lacking in regard for feelings etc. of others. Hence or cogn. ~ateLY² adv., ~ateNESS, ~A′TION, nn. [f. L ɪN²(*consideratus* CONSIDERATE)]

inconsis′t|ent, a. Not in keeping, discordant, incompatible, (*with*); (of single thing) having ~ent parts; acting at variance with one's own principles or former conduct. Hence ~ENCY n., ~entLY² adv. [ɪN²]

inconsōl′ab|le, a. (Of person, his grief, etc.) that cannot be consoled. Hence ~LY² adv. [f. F, or L ɪN²(*consolabilis* CONSOLABLE)]

incŏn′son|ant, a. Not harmonizing (*with, to*). Hence ~ANCE n. [ɪN²]

inconspic′ūous, a. Not conspicuous; (Bot., of flowers) small, pale, or green. Hence ~NESS n. [f. LL ɪN²(*conspicuus* CONSPICUOUS)]

incŏn′st|ant, a. (Of person) fickle, changeable; variable, irregular. Hence or cogn. ~ANCY n., ~antLY² adv. [ME, f. OF f. L ɪN²(*constantem* CONSTANT)]

inconsūm′able, a. That cannot be consumed by fire etc.; (Pol. Econ.) not meant to be consumed in use. [ɪN²]

incontĕs′tab|le, a. That cannot be disputed. Hence ~LY² adv. [F (ɪN²)]

Incŏn'tin|ent, a. Wanting in self-restraint (esp. in regard to sexual appetite); unable to hold in something (of secrets, tongue, urine, etc.). So ~ENCE n. [ME, f. OF, or L IN²(continens CONTINENT)]

Incŏn'tinentlў, adv. (literary). At once, immediately. [arch. *incontinent* adv. (thr. F) f. LL *in continenti (tempore)* in continuous time, +-LY²]

Incŏntrovert'ib|le, a. Not to be disputed. Hence ~LY² adv. [IN-²]

Inconvēn'ience, n., & v.t. Want of adaptation to personal requirement or ease; instance of this; (v.t.) put (person etc.) to~, incommode. [ME, f. OF, f. LL *inconvenientia* (as foll., see -ENCE)]

Inconvēn'ient, a. Unfavourable to ease or comfort, awkward, troublesome. Hence~LY² adv. [ME, f. OF *inconvenient* f. L IN²(convenientem CONVENIENT)]

Inconvert'|ible, a. Not convertible (esp. of currency). Hence ~ĬBIL'ITY n., ~ĬBLY² adv. [f. LL IN²(convertibilis CONVERT-IBLE)]

Inconvin'cĭble, a. Not to be convinced. [IN-²]

Incoŏrdĭnā'tion, n. Want of coordination. [IN-²]

Incŏrp'orate¹, a. (Of company etc.) formed into a corporation; (of persons) united in a corporation. [as foll., see -ATE²]

Incŏrp'or|āte², v.t. & i. Unite (*in* one body, *with* another thing); combine (ingredients) into one substance; constitute as a legal corporation; become ~ated (*with*); ~ated, abbr. *inc.* (esp. U.S.), forming a legal corporation. Hence or cogn. ~A'TION, ~ātor, nn. [ME, f. LL IN¹(corporare f. corpus -oris body), -ATE³]

Incŏrpŏr'éal, a. Not composed of matter; of immaterial beings; (Law) having no material existence, esp.~*hereditament*. Hence ~LY² adv., incŏrporē'ity n. [f. L IN²(corporeus f. corpus -oris body)+-AL]

Incorrect', a. Not in accordance with fact; (of style etc.) improper, faulty; (of book) not properly corrected for press. Hence ~LY² adv., ~NESS n. [ME, f. OF, or L IN²(correctus CORRECT)]

Incŏr'rig|ible, a. (Of person or habit) incurably bad or depraved. Hence ~ĬBIL'ITY n., ~ĬBLY² adv. [ME, f. OF, or L IN²(corrigibilis CORRIGIBLE)]

Incorrŭp't|ible, a. That cannot decay, or ~ION n. (bibl.); eternal; that cannot be corrupted, esp. bribed. Hence or cogn. ~ĬBIL'ITY n., ~ĬBLY² adv. [ME, f. LL IN²(corruptibilis CORRUPTIBLE)]

Incrăss'ate, a. (bot., zool.). Of thick or swollen form. [f. LL IN¹(crassare f. crassus thick), see -ATE²]

Increas|e'¹, v.i. & t. Become greater; grow in numbers, esp. by propagation; advance (*in* quality, attainment, etc.); make greater or more numerous; in-

tensify (quality). Hence ~'ingLY² adv. [ME, f. OF *encreistre* (st. *-eiss-*) f. L IN¹(crescere grow)]

in'crease², n. Growth, enlargement; growth in numbers, multiplication (of men, animals, or plants); *on the* ~, increasing; increased amount; (arch.) crops. [f. prec.]

incred'|ible, a. That cannot be believed; (colloq.) hard to believe, surprising. So ~ĬBIL'ITY n., ~ĬBLY² adv. [ME, f. L IN²(credibilis CREDIBLE)]

incred'ulous, a. Unbelieving (*of* or abs.). Hence or cogn. incrēdŭl'ITY n., ~LY² adv. [f. L IN²(credulus CREDULOUS)]

in'crèment, n. Increase; amount of this; profit; UNEARNED ~, see UN-²(1); (Math.) small amount by which variable quantity increases. [ME, f. L *incrementum* (as INCREASE, see -MENT)]

incrim'in|āte, v.t. Charge with crime; involve in accusation. Hence ~atORY a. [f. LL IN¹(criminare CRIMINATE)]

incrŭstā'tion, n. Encrusting; crust, hard coating; facing of marble etc. on building; (fig.) accretion of habit; scab. [f. F, or LL *incrustatio* (as ENCRUST, see -ATION)]

in'cūbāte, v.t. & i. Hatch (eggs) by sitting on them or otherwise; sit on eggs, brood. [f. L IN¹(cubare cubit- or cubatlie), see -ATE³]

incūbā'tion, n. Hatching; *artificial* ~ (by artificial heat); (of the Holy Ghost) brooding; (Path.) phase through which germs of disease pass before development of first symptoms. So in'cūbātive, in'cūbātory, aa. [f. L *incubatio* (as prec., see -ATION)]

in'cūbātor, n. Apparatus for hatching birds, rearing children born prematurely, or developing bacteria. [f. INCUBATE +-OR]

in'cūbus, n. (pl. *-bī, -buses*). Evil spirit supposed to descend on sleeping persons; nightmare; person, thing, that oppresses like nightmare. [ME; LL, = L *incubo* nightmare (as INCUBATE)]

in'culc|āte, v.t. Urge, impress, (fact, habit, idea) persistently (*upon* or *in* person, mind). So ~A'TION, ~ātor, nn. [f. L IN¹(culcare = calcare tread f. calx -lcis heel), -ATE³]

in'culpāte, v.t. Accuse, blame; involve in charge. Hence inculpA'TION n., in-cŭl'patORY a. [f. LL IN¹(culpare f. culpa fault), -ATE³]

incŭlt', a. (rare). Untilled; unpolished, rude; (of person or manners) coarse. [f. L IN²(cultus p.p. of colere till)]

incŭm'bencў, n. Office, tenure, sphere, of an incumbent. [f. foll., see -ENCY]

incŭm'bent¹, n. Holder of ecclesiastical benefice or (rare, exc. U.S.) of any office. [as foll.]

incŭm'bent², a. Lying, pressing, (*on*); resting (*up*)*on* (person) as duty, *as it is* ~

on you to warn them. [f. L IN¹(*cumbere* lie), -ENT]

Incŭnăb′ula, n. pl. Early stages of thing; (w. sing. *-um*) books printed early, esp. before 1501. [L, = swaddling-clothes, f. *cunae* cradle]

incŭr′, v.t. (-rr-). Fall into, bring on oneself, (danger, blame, punishment, etc.). [f. L IN¹(*currere curs-* run)]

incŭr′|able, a. & n. (Person) that cannot be cured. Hence ~ABIL′ITY, ~ableNESS, nn., ~ably² adv. [ME, f. OF f. LL IN²(*curabilis* CURABLE)]

incŭr′ious, a. Devoid of curiosity; heedless, careless; uninteresting (usu. *not* ~). Hence incŭri̇̄os′ITY n., ~LY² adv. [f. L IN²(*curiosus* CURIOUS)]

incŭr′s|ion (-shn), n. Hostile invasion; sudden attack. So ~IVE a. [ME, f. L *incursio* (as INCUR, see -ION)]

incŭrv|e′, v.t. Bend into a curve; curve inwards (esp. in p.p.). So ~A′TION n. [f. L IN¹(*curvare* CURVE)]

in′cus, n. Bone of ear receiving vibrations from MALLEUS. [L = anvil (as foll.)]

incŭse′¹ (ĭnkūz′), a. & n. (Of impression on coin etc.) hammered or stamped in; (n.) such impression. [f. L IN¹(*cudere cus-* forge)]

incŭse′² (ĭnkūz′), v.t. (esp. in p.p.). Impress (figure etc.) by stamping; mark (coin etc.) with such figure. [as prec.]

Ind (Ĭ-), n. (arch. or poet.). India. [ME, f. OF *Inde*]

inda′ba (-ah-), n. A conference between or with S.-African natives. [Zulu, = business]

indĕbt′ĕd (-dĕt-), a. Owing money (*to*); owing gratitude (*to* person, or fig. *to* thing, *for* benefit etc.). Hence ~NESS n. [ME, f. OF *endette* p.p. of EN(*detter* f. *dette* DEBT)]

indĕ′cent, a. Unbecoming; immodest, obscene. Hence or cogn. indĕ′cENCY n., ~LY² adv. [f. F, or L IN²(*decens* DECENT)]

indĕcid′uous, a. Not deciduous. [IN-²]

indĕciph′erable, a. That cannot be deciphered. [IN-²]

indĕci′sion (-zhn), n. Want of decision, hesitation. [f. F IN²(*décision* DECISION)]

indĕcis′ive, a. Not decisive; undecided, irresolute. Hence ~LY² adv., ~NESS n. [IN-²]

indĕclin′able, a. That cannot be declined; having no inflexions. [ME, f. OF & L (LL) IN² (*declinabilis* DECLINABLE)]

indĕcompos′able (-z-), a. That cannot be decomposed or resolved into constituents. [IN-²]

indĕcŏr′ous (*or* -dĕk′o-), a. Improper; in bad taste. Hence ~LY² adv., ~NESS n. [f. L IN²(*decorus* DECOROUS)]

indĕcŏr′um, n. Lack of decorum; improper proceeding. [L, neut. adj. as prec.]

indeed′, adv. In truth, really, as *he was,* ~, *a remarkable man*; (intensifying) *I shall be very glad* ~, *this is quick work* ~, yes,

~ *!, no,* ~ *!*; (echoing last speaker's words with approval or iron.) *who is this Mr Smith?—who is he,* ~ *!* (= you may well ask, or, can you ask?); (concessive) *there are* ~ *exceptions*; (interrog.) really? is it so?; as int., expr. irony, contempt, incredulity, etc. [ME; IN prep.+DEED]

indĕfăt′ig|able, a. (Of persons, qualities, etc.) that cannot be tired out, unremitting. Hence ~ABIL′ITY n., ~abLY² adv. [f. obs. F *indéfatigable* or L IN²(*defatigabilis* f. DE*fatigare* wear out, see -BLE)]

indĕfeas′|ible (-z-), a. That cannot be forfeited or done away with, esp. ~*ible right.* Hence ~iBIL′ITY n., ~iBLY² adv. [IN-²]

indĕfĕc′tible, a. Unfailing, not liable to defect or decay; faultless. [f. F, or LL IN²(*defectibilis* DEFECTIBLE)]

indĕfĕn′s|ible, a. Admitting of no defence (by force of arms or by argument). Hence ~iBIL′ITY n., ~iBLY² adv. [IN-²]

indĕfin′ab|le, a. That cannot be defined. Hence ~LY² adv. [IN-²]

indĕf′inite, a. Vague, undefined; unlimited; (Gram., of adjj., pronouns, etc.) not determining the person, thing, time, etc., to which they refer, esp. ~ *article* (a, an); (of tenses) denoting an action without specifying whether it is continuous or complete (e.g. Greek aorist, English past). Hence ~LY² (-tl-) adv., ~NESS (-tn-), indĕfin′ĬTUDE, nn. [f. L IN²(*definitus* DEFINITE)]

indĕhis′cent, a. (bot.). Not dehiscent. [IN-²]

indĕl′|ible, a. (Of mark, stain, ink, etc., & fig. of disgrace etc.) that cannot be blotted out. Hence ~iBIL′ITY n., ~iBLY² adv. [f. F *indélébile* or L IN²(*delebilis* f. *delēre* DELETE, see -BLE)]

indĕl′ic|ate, a. Coarse, unrefined; immodest; tactless. Hence ~ACY n., ~ateLY² adv. [IN-²]

indĕm′ni|fy, v.t. Protect, secure, (person *from, against,* harm or loss); secure (person against legal responsibility (*for* actions); compensate (person *for* loss, expenses incurred, etc.). Hence ~FICA′TION n. [f. L IN²(*demnis* f. *damnum* loss), see -FY]

indĕm′nity, n. Security against damage or loss; legal exemption from penalties etc. incurred; compensation for loss incurred; sum paid for this, esp. sum exacted by victorious belligerent as one condition of peace. [f. F *indemnité* f. LL *indemnitas* (as prec., see -TY)]

indĕmŏn′strable, a. That cannot be proved (esp. of primary truths). [f. F, or L IN²(*demonstrabilis* DEMONSTRABLE)]

indĕnt′¹, v.t. & i. 1. Make tooth-like notches in; form deep recesses in (coast-line etc.). 2. Divide (document drawn up in duplicate) into two halves with zig-zag line, draw up (document) in exact duplicate. 3.(print.). Set back (beginning of line) farther from margin to mark new paragraph etc. **4.** Make requisition (prop. written order with duplicate) *upon* (person *for* thing); order (goods) by an indent. [ME, f. AF *endenter* f. med. L IN¹ (*dentare* f. *dens -ntis* tooth)]

Indent'² (*or* ĭnⁿ), n. Indentation; indenture; ‖ official requisition for stores; order (esp. from abroad) for goods. [f. prec.]

Indĕnt'³, v.t. Make a dent in; impress (mark etc.). [IN⁻¹]

in'dĕnt⁴, n. Dent, depression. [f. prec.]

in'dĕntā'tion, n. Indenting; cut, notch; zigzag; deep recess in coastline etc. [INDENT¹,³ +-ATION]

Indĕn'tion, n. Indenting of line in printing; = prec. [irreg. f. INDENT¹ +-ION]

Indĕn'ture, n., & v.t. **1.** Indented document (see INDENT¹); any sealed agreement or contract, esp. that which binds apprentice to master; *take up* one's ∼s, receive them back on completion of service; formal list, certificate, etc.; indentation. **2.** v.t. Bind (person) by ∼s esp. as apprentice. [ME, f. AF *endenture* (as INDENT¹, see -URE)]

Indĕpĕn'den|ce, -en|cy̆, nn. 1. (∼*ce*). Being independent (*on, of,* or abs.); independent income; *I∼ce Day,* July 4 (on which, in 1776, the DECLARATION of I∼ce was made). **2.** (∼*cy*). = CONGREGATIONALISM (hist.); independent State. [f. foll., see -ENCE, -ENCY]

Indĕpĕn'dent, a. & n. **1.** Not depending on authority (*of,* or abs.); (*I∼*)=CONGREGATIONAL (hist.); not depending on something else for its validity, efficiency, etc., as ∼ *proof, research, observer*; not needing to earn one's livelihood; ∼ *income* (dispensing one from earning livelihood); unwilling to be under obligation to others. **2.** n. Person who acts (in politics etc.)∼ly of any party; Congregationalist (hist.). [IN⁻²; partly f. F]

Indĕscrib'|able, a. Vague, indefinite; too great, beautiful, bad, etc., to be described. Hence ∼ABIL'ITY n., ∼abLY² adv. [IN⁻²]

Indĕstrŭc't|ible, a. That cannot be destroyed. Hence ∼ĭBIL'ITY n., ∼ĭbLY² adv. [IN⁻²]

Indĕtĕrm'inable, a. That cannot be ascertained; (of disputes etc.) that cannot be settled. [ME, f. LL IN²(*determinabilis* DETERMINABLE)]

Indĕtĕrm'inate, a. Not fixed in extent, character, etc.; vague; left doubtful; ∼ *sentence,* one that leaves prisoner's release dependent on his conduct & on probability of amendment; ∼ *vowel,* sound in *ago,* moment, cousin, opine, support, certain; (Math., of quantity) not limited to fixed value(s). Hence ∼LY² (-tl-) adv., ∼NESS (-tn-) n. [ME, f. LL IN²(*determinatus* DETERMINATE)]

Indĕtĕrminā'tion, n. Want of determination; being indeterminate. [IN⁻²]

Indĕtĕrm'in|ism, n. Theory that human

action is not wholly determined by motives. So ∼IST n. [IN⁻²]

In'dĕx, n. (pl. ∼*es, ĭn'dĭcēs*), & v.t. **1.** Forefinger; (on instruments) pointer showing measurements etc.; ∼ *number* (indicating the relative level of prices or wages at a particular date compared with the figure (100) ruling at a period taken as standard); guiding principle; alphabetical list, usu. at end of book, of names, subjects, etc. with references; (R.C.) *the I∼*, list of books forbidden to Roman Catholics, or to be read only in expurgated editions (in full, *I∼ librōr'um prohĭbĭtōr'um*); ∼ *∼ expurgatōr'ius,* list of passages to be expunged in books otherwise permitted (in fig. use often confused with last); (Alg.) exponent (pl. *indices*). **2.** v.t. Furnish (book) with∼ (esp. in p.p.), enter (word etc.) in∼. Hence ∼LESS a. [L (gen. *-icis*), = forefinger, informer, sign, f. IN⁻¹+*dic-* INDICATE]

In'dia (ĭ-), n. Country of S. Asia east of river Indus & south of Himalayas; *Republic of ∼,* (since 1947) this country excluding Pakistan; ∼*man,* ship engaged in Indian trade; ∼ *Office,* former department of British Government dealing with Indian affairs; ∼ *paper,* soft absorbent kind imported from China, used for proofs of engravings (*Oxford ∼ paper,* thin tough opaque printing-paper); ∼ *proof* (on ∼ paper); ∼*rubber, india-rubber,* coagulated juice of certain plants, used for rubbing out pencil marks etc. [L, f. Gk (*Indos* Indus, f. Pers. *hind* = Skr. *sindhu* river, -IA¹)]

In'dian (ĭ-), a. & n. (Native) of India; (one) of the original inhabitants of America & W. Indies; European, esp. Englishman, formerly resident in India; *Red ∼,* one of aboriginal race of N. America; ‖∼ *civilian,* member of former ∼ Civil Service; ∼ *club* (bottle-shaped, for use in gymnastics); ‖∼ *corn,* maize, N. American graminaceous plant; ∼ *cress, -*TROPAEOLUM; ∼ *file,* single file; *India(n) ink,* black pigment made in China & Japan; ∼ *meal* (made from ∼ corn); ∼ *summer,* period of calm dry hazy weather in late autumn in North. U.S., also transf. in other countries; ∼ *weed,* tobacco. Hence ∼IZE(3) v.t., ∼ĪZA'TION n., process or policy of making ∼ in character or composition. [-AN]

in'dic|āte, v.t. Point out, make known, show; suggest, call for; state briefly; be a sign of, betoken, (thing, *that,* etc.); ∼*ated horse-power* (shown by∼ator; abbr. *i.h.p.*). So ∼A'TION n. [f. L IN¹(*dicare* make known), see -ATE³]

indic'ative, a. & n. **1.** (Gram.) stating a thing as a fact, not as conception, wish, etc., of speaker; (*also* ĭn'dĭkātĭv) suggestive, giving indications, *of.* **2.** n. ∼ mood. Hence ∼LY² (-vl-). [f. F (-*if, -ive*) or LL *indicativus* (prec., -IVE)]

in'dicāt|or, n. Person, thing, that points

out, esp. recording instrument attached to apparatus etc. Hence ~ORY a. [LL (as prec., see -OR)]

indi′cium (-shǐ-), n. (pl. -*ia*). Indication, sign, (now rare). [L (as INDEX)]

indict′ (-īt), v.t. Accuse (person *for* riot etc., *as* a rioter, *on* charge), esp. by legal process. [ME, f. AF *enditer* indict f. OF *enditer* make known f. Rom. *°IN*¹(*dictare* DICTATE); see INDITE]

indict′able (-īt-), a. Liable, (of action) rendering one liable, to be indicted. [-ABLE]

indic′tion, n. Fiscal period of 15 years instituted by Constantine & reckoned from Sep. 1st, 312; assessment of property-tax by Roman Emperors at beginning of each 15 years; this tax; proclamation. [ME, f. L *indictio* f. IN¹(*dicere dict*- say), see -ION]

indict′ment (-īt-), n. Formal accusation; legal process in which this is preferred to & presented by Grand Jury; document containing charge; *bill of* ~, written accusation as preferred to Grand Jury. [ME, f. AF *enditement* (as INDICT, see -MENT)]

indiff′er|ence, n. Absence of interest or attention (*to, towards*, or abs.); neutrality; unimportance, esp. *a matter of* ~*ence*, so ~ENCY n. [f. L *indifferentia* (as foll., see -ENCE)]

indiff′erent, a. Having no inclination for or against (*to*); neither good nor bad; rather bad, esp. *very* ~; neutral in chemical, electrical, or magnetic quality. Hence ~LY² adv. [ME, f. OF f. L IN²-(*differens* DIFFERENT)]

indiff′erent|ism, n. Spirit of indifference, professed or practised, esp. in religious matters. So ~IST n. [-ISM]

in′digène, n. Native. [f. F *indigène* f. L *indigena* (*indi*- = IN-¹+*gen*- be born)]

indi′genous, a. Native (esp. of flora & fauna), belonging naturally, (*to* soil etc., also fig.). Hence ~LY² adv. [f. L *indigenus* (as prec.)+-OUS]

in′dig|ent, a. Needy, poor. So ~ENCE n. [ME, f. OF f. LL *indigēre* (*indi*- = IN-¹ +*egēre* want), see -ENT]

indigĕs′tĕd, a. Shapeless; not thought out; not digested in stomach. [f. obs. *indigest* a. f. L IN²(*digestus* p.p. as DIGEST²) +-ED¹; or f. IN-²+DIGESTED]

indigĕs′t|ible, a. Not digestible (lit. & fig.). Hence ~IBIL′ITY n. [f. LL IN²-(*digestibilis* DIGESTIBLE)]

indigĕs′tion (-schon), n. Difficulty in digesting food, dyspepsia; undigested condition (lit. & fig.). [ME, f. OF f. LL IN²(*digestionem* DIGESTION)]

indigĕs′tive, a. Suffering from, tending to, indigestion. [IN-²]

‖**indign′** (-īn), a. (arch.). Unworthy. [ME, f. OF *indigne* or f. L IN²(*dignus* worthy)]

indig′nant, a. Moved by mingled anger & scorn or feeling of injured innocence (*at* thing, *with* person, or abs.). Hence ~LY² adv. [f. L *indignari* (as prec.), see -ANT]

indignā′tion, n. Anger excited by supposed meanness, injustice, wickedness, or misconduct (*at* thing, *against, with*, person), freq. *righteous* ~; ~-*meeting* (to express public ~). [ME, f. OF, or L *indignatio* (prec., -ATION)]

indig′nity, n. Unworthy treatment; slight, insult. [f. F, or L *indignitas* (as INDIGN, see -TY)]

in′digō, n. (pl. ~s). (Orig.) blue powder from plants of genus *Indigofera*, used as dye, now chiefly synthetic; ~ *blue*, blue-violet (often attrib.); ~-*bird*, N.-Amer. species of painted finch; ~ *white*, reduced ~, a white crystalline powder. Hence **indigŏt′ic** [-*t*- euphon.] a. [16th c. *indico* (f. Sp.), *indigo* (f. Pg.) f. L f. Gk *indikon* Indian (dye)]

indirect′, a. 1. (Of road etc.) not straight; not going straight to the point. 2. (Pol. Econ., of taxes) not direct, paid by consumer in the form of increased price for the taxed goods. 3. (gram.). ~ *speech*, reported speech, with necessary changes of pronouns, tenses, etc. (e.g. *I will help you*, he said *he would help me*); ~ *object*, person, thing, affected by verbal action but not primarily acted on (e.g. *him* in *give him the book*); ~ *passive*, passive having for subject the ~ object of the active (e.g. *I* in *I was told it*). 4. Not directly aimed at, as *an* ~ *result*. Hence ~LY² adv., ~NESS n. [ME, f. OF, or LL IN²(*directus* DIRECT²)]

indirec′tion, n. Roundabout means, esp. *by* ~ (after Shak. *Ham.* II. i. 66); deceit, trickery. [prec.+-ION]

indiscern′ib|le, a. & n. (Thing) that cannot be discerned or distinguished from another; *identity of* ~*les*, doctrine that things cannot exist together as separate entities unless they have different attributes. Hence ~LY² adv. [f. LL IN²(*discernibilis* DISCERNIBLE)]

indiscerp′t|ible, a. Incapable of, not destructible by, dissolution of parts. Hence ~IBIL′ITY n. [IN-²]

indis′ciplin|e, n. Want of discipline. So ~ABLE a. [f. F, or IN-²]

indiscreet′, a. Injudicious, unwary. Hence ~LY² adv. [ME, f. LL IN²(*discretus* DISCREET)]

indis′crēte, a. Not divided into distinct parts. [IN-², or f. L; see DISCRETE]

indiscrē′tion, n. Injudicious conduct; accidental or (*calculated* ~) supposed accidental revelation of official secret etc.; imprudence; transgression of social morality. [ME, f. OF, or LL IN²(*discretio* DISCRETION)]

indiscrim′in|ate, a. Confused, promiscuous; making no distinctions. Hence ~ately² adv., ~ateness, ~a′tion, nn., ~ative a. [IN-²]

indispen′s|able, a. That cannot be dispensed with, necessary; (of law, duty, etc.) that cannot be set aside. Hence ~abil′ity, ~ableness, nn., ~ably² adv. [f. med. L IN²(*dispensabilis* DISPENSABLE)]

indispose' (-z), v.t. Render unfit or unable (*for* thing, *to* do); make averse (*towards*, *from*, thing, *to* do); (esp. in p.p.) put out of health. [back form. f. *indisposed*, f. F -*sé* or L *indispositus*, partly f. IN-² + DISPOSED]

indisposi'tion (-zǐ-), n. Ill health, ailment, (esp. of passing kind); disinclination (*to* thing, *to* do); aversion (*to*, *towards*). [f. F, or IN-² + DISPOSITION]

indis'put|able, a. That cannot be disputed. Hence ~ABIL'ITY, ~ableNESS, nn., ~ably² adv. [f. LL IN²(*disputabilis* DISPUTABLE)]

indiss'ol|uble (-lŏŏ-; *or* Indǐsŏl'), a. Lasting, stable, as *an* ~*uble bond*; that cannot be dissolved or decomposed. Hence ~UBIL'ITY n., ~ubLY² adv. [f. L IN²(*dissolubilis* DISSOLUBLE)]

indistinct', a. Not distinct; confused, obscure. Hence ~LY² adv., ~NESS n. [f. L IN²(*distinctus* DISTINCT)]

indistinc'tive, a. Not distinctive. Hence ~LY² adv. [IN-²]

indisting'uishab|le (-nggw-), a. Not distinguishable. Hence ~LY² adv. [IN-²]

indistrib'utable, a. That cannot be distributed. [IN-²]

indite', v.t. Put into words, compose, (poem, speech, etc.); (usu. joc.) write (letter etc.). [ME, f. OF EN(*diter* f. L *dictare* DICTATE); see INDICT]

indivert'ib|le, a. That cannot be turned aside. Hence ~LY² adv. [IN-² + DIVERT + -IBLE]

individ'ual, a. & n. 1. Single; particular, special, opp. to *general*; having distinct character; characteristic of particular person. 2. n. Single member of class; single human being, opp. to *society*, *family*, etc.; (vulg.) person, as *an* ~ *of somewhat prepossessing appearance*. [f. med. L *individualis* f. IN²(*dividuus* f. *dividere* DIVIDE), see -AL]

individ'ual|ism, n. Self-centred feeling or conduct, egoism; social theory favouring free action of individuals (cf. SOCIALISM). So ~IST n. (freq., U.S., or of U.S., *rugged* ~*ist*), ~IS'TIC a. [f. F -*isme* (as prec., -ISM)]

individŭāl'itỹ, n. Separate existence; individual character, esp. when strongly marked; (pl.) individual tastes etc. [-ITY]

individ'ŭalīz|e, -is|e (-īz), v.t. Give individual character to; specify. Hence ~A'TION n. [-IZE]

individ'ŭally, adv. Personally, in an individual capacity; in a distinctive manner; one by one, not collectively; ~ *different*, different as individuals though perhaps identical in species. [-LY²]

individ'ŭ|āte, v.t. Individualize, form into an individual. So ~A'TION n. [f. obs. F -*er*, or med. L *individuare* (as INDIVIDUAL), see -ATE³]

indivis'|ible (-z-), a. & n. Not divisible; (n.) infinitely small particle or quantity.

Hence ~ĭBIL'ITY n., ~ĭbLY² adv. [f. LL IN²(*divisibilis* DIVISIBLE)]

In'dō- (I-) in comb. = Indian, as: ~-*Ar'yan*, Aryan of or in India; ~-*Chinese'*, of the region between India & China; ~-*Europe'an*, ~-*German'ic*, of the family of languages spoken over greater part of Europe & Asia as far as N. India; ~-*Irān'ian*, of the subfamily of ~-European languages spoken chiefly in India & Persia; ~-*nēs'ian*, of the East Indian Islands. [f. L f. Gk *Indos*]

indō'cile (*or* -dōsǐl), a. Not docile. Hence **indocil'ity** n. [f. F, or L IN²(*docilis* DOCILE)]

indŏc'trin|āte, v.t. Teach, instruct; imbue with a doctrine, idea, or opinion. Hence ~A'TION n. [IN-¹, DOCTRINE, -ATE³]

in'dol|ent, a. Slothful, lazy; (Med.) causing no pain, as ~*ent tumour*. Hence or cogn. ~ENCE n., ~entLY² adv. [f. LL *indolens* (IN-² + *dolēre* grieve, see -ENT]

indŏm'itab|le, a. Unyielding; stubbornly persistent. Hence ~LY² adv. [f. LL IN²(*domitabilis* f. *domitare* tame, see -BLE]

in'door (-dôr), a. Situated, carried on, within doors or under cover, as ~ *games*; within workhouse, as ~ *relief* (hist.). [IN prep.]

indoors' (-ôrz), adv. Within a house; under cover. [earlier *within doors*]

indōrsa'tion, n. Endorsement. [f. *indorse* var. of ENDORSE + -ATION]

indōrsee', n. One in whose favour note or bill is endorsed. [as prec., see -EE]

in'draught (-ahft), -**draft** (-ah-), n. Drawing in; inward flow or current. [IN adv.]

in'dri, n. Babacoote, lemurine animal of Madagascar. [f. Malagasy *indry* behold, mistaken for its name]

indub'itab|le, a. That cannot be doubted. Hence ~LY² adv. [f. F, or L IN²(*dubitabilis* f. *dubitare* doubt, see -BLE]

indūce', v.t. Prevail on, persuade, (*to* do, now rarely *to* action etc.; *nothing shall* ~ *me to*, I will never); bring about, give rise to; (Electr.) produce (current) by induction; infer, derive as an induction. [ME, f. L IN¹(*ducere duct*- lead)]

indūce'ment (-sm-), n. What induces; attraction that leads one on (*to*). [-MENT]

indŭct', v.t. Introduce formally into possession (*to* benefice); install (*into* seat, room, etc.); introduce, initiate, (*to*, *into*). [ME; as INDUCE]

indŭc'tile, a. Not ductile. [IN-²]

indŭc'tion, n. Inducting; ‖ (arch.) preamble, prologue, introduction; production (*of* facts) to prove general statement; inferring of general law from particular instances (cf. DEDUCTION); *mathematical* ~, proving universal truth of theorem by showing (1) that if true of any particular case it is true of the next case in a series, (2) that it is true of a particular case; (Electr., Magnet.) bringing about of electric or magnetic state in a body by proximity (without contact) of electrified or magnetized body; ~-*coil* (for converting direct current to alternating by ~). So **indŭc'**TANCE n., capacity for magnetic ~, coefficient of self-~ in magnetic circuits. [ME, f. OF, or L *inductio* (as INDUCE, see -ION)]

indŭc'tive, a. (Of reasoning etc.) of, based on, induction; of electric or magnetic induction. Hence ~LY² (-vl-) adv., ~NESS (-vn-) n. [f. LL *inductivus* (as INDUCE, see -IVE)]

indŭc'tor, n. One who inducts clergyman; any part of electric induction apparatus. [L, as INDUCE, see -OR]

indŭlge' (-j), v.t. & i. Gratify (person, oneself, in wish, matter, etc.); gratify (person *with* thing given); give free course to, entertain, (desire etc.); (intr.) take one's pleasure freely in (strong language, cycling, a cigar); (colloq.) partake (too freely) of intoxicants. Hence **indŭl'gENT** a., **indŭl'gENT**LY² adv. [f. L *indulgēre*, -*dult*-]

indŭl'gence, n. Indulging (*in*, t. & i.); (also *self-*~) habitual indulging of one's desires; privilege granted; *Declaration of I*~, proclamation of religious liberties, esp. those of Charles II in 1672 & of James II in 1687; (R.-C. Ch.) remission of punishment still due to sin after sacramental absolution. [ME, f. OF, or L *indulgentia* (as prec., see -ENCE)]

indŭl'genced (-nst), a. (R.-C. Ch.). (Of prayers, material objects, etc.) procuring indulgence to the user. [-ED²]

indŭlt', n. Pope's licence for thing not sanctioned by common law of Church. [F, f. LL *indultum*, neut. p.p. as INDULGE]

indun'a (-ōō-), n. (S. Afr.). Native headman. [Zulu]

in'dūr|āte, v.t. & i. Make, become, hard; make callous or unfeeling; become inveterate. Hence or cogn. ~A'TION n., ~ātive a. [f. L IN¹(*durare* f. *durus* hard), see -ATE³]

indŭs'ium (-z-), n. (pl. -*ia*). Membranous shield covering fruit-cluster of fern; collection of hairs enclosing stigma of some flowers; case of larva. [L, = tunic, f. *induere* ENDUE]

indŭs'trial, a. & n. **1.** Of industries (~ *maintenance,* system by which each industry should provide for its own unemployed; *the* ~ *revolution,* changes in the relation between employers & employed brought about in the late 18th & early 19th cc. esp. by mechanical inventions); designed, or only fit, for ~ use (~ *alcohol*); ~ *school* (hist.), one where neglected children were taught a trade besides ordinary subjects.). **2.** n. One engaged in ~ pursuits; (pl.) shares in joint-stock ~ enterprise. Hence ~ISM(3), ~IST(3), nn., ~IZE(3) v.t., ~LY² adv. [as INDUSTRY, see -AL; in 19th c. partly f. F -*el*]

indŭs'trĭous, a. Diligent, hard-working. Hence ~LY² adv. [f. F -*ieux* or LL *industriosus* (as foll., see -OUS)]

in'dustry̆, n. Diligence; habitual employment in useful work; branch of trade or manufacture. [f. F (-*ie*) or L *industria*]

indwell', v.t. & i. (*indwelt*). (Usu. fig., of spirit, principle, etc.) inhabit, occupy; (intr.) be permanently present *in*. Hence ~ER¹ n. [IN prep.]

-ine¹, suf. of adjj., repr. L -*inus*, w. sense 'pertaining to, of the nature of'; appearing in F as -*in* masc., -*ine* fem., in E formerly as -*in*, now usu. as -*ine* (*asinine, divine, marine, supine*). On model of proper names f. L, adjj. like *Florentine, Caroline*, are formed in E. Nat. Hist. forms adjj. on names of genera (*equine, caprine, feline*); these have (-īn) unstressed; others have (-īn) stressed or not (*divine', Al'pine*), (-ĭn) unstressed (*fem'inine*), or (-ōn) stressed (*marine'*).

-ine², suf. of adjj., repr. L -*inus* f. Gk -*inos* in names of minerals, plants, etc. (*adamantine, hyacinthine*); also repr. orig. L -*inus* (*pristine*). Norman pronunc. (-ĭn) is giving place to (-īn).

-ine³, suf. forming fem. nn., repr. F -*ine* f. L -*ina* f. Gk -*inē* (*heroine*). E represents in same way -*in* in G *markgräfin* etc. (*margravine*).

-ine⁴, suf. of nn., repr. F -*ine* f. L -*ina* (-*inus*), orig. = -INE¹ used in L to form abstract nn. f. vbs (*rapina rapine, ruina* ruin), f. agent nouns (*disciplina, doctrina, medicina*), & f. other sources (*resina, urina*). L adjj. in -*inus, -ina*, were also used as nn. (*concubina, lupinus*), esp. in prop. names (*Antoninus, Agrippina*). For -*ina*, E has -*ine*, sometimes -*in* (*resin*); for -*inus*, E has -*in* (*Crispin, Justin*) or -*ine* (*lupine, Constantine*). E further forms names of derivative products (*dentine, brilliantine, nectarine*). Fem. names of Rom. orig. also often take -*ine* (-ĭn), as *Caroline, Catharine*.

-ine⁵, suf. (chem.), offshoot of prec. in names of derived substances, orig. used unsystematically, & interchangeable with -IN; now confined to alkaloids & basic substances (*aconitine, cocaine, nicotine*) & (less freq.) Hofmann's names of hydrocarbons; also retained in the four elements *chlorine, fluorine, iodine, bromine*; formerly denoting mineral species now ending in -ITE¹ (*erythrine, -ite*).

inēb'riate¹, a. & n. **1.** Drunken. **2.** n. ~ person, esp. habitual drunkard. [f. L IN¹(*ebriare* f. *ebrius* drunk), see -ATE²]

inēb'ri|āte², v.t. Make drunk, intoxicate (lit. & fig.). So ~A'TION n. [as prec., -ATE³]

inēbri'ety̆, n. (Habit of) drunkenness. [f. INEBRIATE, after EBRIETY]

ined'|ible, a. Not edible. Hence ~IBIL'ITY n. [IN-²]

inĕd'itĕd, a. Not published; published without editorial alterations or additions. [IN-²]

inĕff'ab|le, a. Unutterable, too great for words. Hence ~LY² adv. [ME, f. OF, or L IN²(*effabilis* f. EF*fari* speak, utter, see -BLE)]

inĕffäce'|able (-sabl), a. That cannot be effaced. Hence~ABIL'ITY n.,~abLY² adv. [IN-²]

inĕffĕc'tive, a. Not producing the desired effect; (of person) inefficient; lacking artistic effect. Hence ~LY² adv., ~NESS n. [IN-²]

inĕffĕc'tual, a. Without effect, fruitless. Hence~LY² adv., ~NESS n. [IN-²]

inĕfficā'cious (-shŭs), a. (Of remedy etc.) not efficacious. [IN-²]

inĕffi'ci|ent (-shent), a. (Of person) not fully capable, not well qualified; ineffective. Hence ~ENCY n., ~entLY² adv., (-shen-). [IN-²]

inĕlăs'tic, a. Not elastic; unadaptable, unyielding. Hence **inĕlăsti'**CITY n. [IN-²]

inĕl'ĕg|ant, a. Ungraceful; unrefined; (of style) unpolished. Hence ~ANCE n., ~antLY² adv. [f. F IN²(*élégant* ELEGANT)]

inĕl'ig|ible, a. Not eligible (esp. of men unfit for military service). Hence ~i-BIL'ITY n., ~ibLY² adv. [IN-²]

inĕlŭc'table, a. That cannot be escaped from. [f. L IN²(*eluctabilis* f. E*luctari* struggle out, see -BLE)]

inĕpt', a. Out of place; absurd, silly. Hence or cogn. **inĕp'ti**TUDE, ~NESS, nn., ~LY² adv. [f. L IN²(*eptus = aptus* APT)]

inĕ'quable, a. Not uniform; of unequal incidence. [f. L *inaequabilis* uneven]

inĕqual'itÿ (-ŏl-), n. Want of equality in magnitude, quality, rank, circumstances, etc.; variableness; (of surface) irregularity; (Astron.) deviation from uniformity in motion of heavenly body. [f. obs. F *inéqualité* or L IN²(*aequalitas* EQUALITY)]

inĕquilăt'eral, a. Of unequal sides. [IN-²]

inĕ'quitab|le, a. Unfair, unjust. Hence ~LY² adv. [IN-²]

inĕ'quitÿ, n. Unfairness. [IN-²]

inĕrăd'icab|le, a. That cannot be rooted out. Hence~LY² adv. [IN-²]

inĕ'rr|able, a. Not liable to err. Hence or cogn. ~ABIL'ITY, ~ANCY, nn., ~abLY² adv., ~ANT a. [f. L IN²(*errabilis* f. *errare* ERR, see -BLE)]

inĕrt', a. Without inherent power of action, motion, or resistance; without active chemical or other properties; sluggish, slow. Hence ~LY² adv., ~NESS n. [f. L IN²(*ers -ertis* f. *ars* ART)]

inĕr'tia (-shĭa), n. (Phys.) property of matter by which it continues in its existing state of rest or uniform motion in straight line, unless that state is changed by external force (also *vis inertiae* force of~); inertness, sloth. [L, as prec.]

inĕscăp'able, a. Not to be escaped. [IN-²]

inĕssĕn'tial (-shal), a. Not indispensable. [IN-²]

inĕs'timab|le, a. Too great, intense, precious, etc., to be estimated. Hence

~LY² adv. [ME, f. OF f. L IN²(*aestimabilis* ESTIMABLE)]

inĕv'it|able, a. Unavoidable, sure to happen, esp. *the ~able*; (colloq.) tiresomely familiar (*the ~able Derby dog*); (of character-drawing, development of plot, etc.) so true to nature etc. as to preclude alternative treatment or solution, convincing. Hence ~aBIL'ITY, ~ableNESS, nn., ~abLY² adv. [f. L IN-²(*evitabilis* f. E*vitare* avoid, see -BLE)]

inĕxăct' (-gz-), a. Not exact. Hence **inĕxăc'ti**TUDE, ~NESS, nn.,~LY² adv. [IN-²]

inĕxcūs'ab|le (-za-), a. (Of person, action, etc.) that cannot be justified. Hence ~LY² adv. [f. F, or L IN²(*excusabilis* EXCUSABLE)]

inĕxĕc'ūtable (-gz-), a. That cannot be carried out. [IN-²]

inexhaus't|ible (-igzaw-), a. That cannot be exhausted. Hence~iBIL'ITY n.,~ibLY² adv. [IN-²]

inĕx'or|able, a. Relentless. Hence ~a-BIL'ITY n., ~abLY² adv. [f. F, or L IN²(*exorabilis* f. Exorare entreat, -ABLE)]

inexpĕc'tant, a. Not expectant. [IN-²]

inexped'i|ent, a. Not expedient. Hence ~ENCY n. [IN-²]

inexpĕn'sive, a. Cheap. Hence ~LY² adv., ~NESS n. [IN-²]

inexper'ienc|e, n. Want of experience. So ~ED² (-st) a. [f. F, or LL IN²(*experientia* EXPERIENCE)]

inexpĕrt', a. Unskilled. Hence ~LY² adv. [f. OF, or L IN²(*expertus* EXPERT)]

inĕx'piab|le, a. (Of offence) that cannot be expiated; (of resentment etc.) implacable. Hence ~LY² adv. [f. L IN²(*expiabilis* EXPIABLE)]

inĕx'plic|able, a. That cannot be explained or accounted for. Hence~aBIL'ITY n.,~abLY² adv. [f. F, or L IN²(*explicabilis* EXPLICABLE)]

inexpli'cit, a. Not definitely or clearly expressed. Hence ~LY² adv., ~NESS n. [IN-²]

inexplōs'ive, a. Not explosive. [IN-²]

inexprĕss'ib|le, a. & n. That cannot be expressed in words; (n. pl., joc. & arch.) trousers. Hence ~LY² adv. [IN-²]

inexprĕss'ive, a. Not expressive; (arch.) inexpressible. Hence~LY² adv.,~NESS n. [IN-²]

inexpŭg'nable, a. Impregnable, invincible, (lit. & fig.). [f. F, or L IN²(*expugnabilis* f. Expugnare storm, see -BLE)]

inextĕn'sible, a. Not extensible. [IN-²]

inexting'uishable (-nggw-), a. Unquenchable (lit. & fig.). [IN-²]

inĕx'tricab|le, a. (Of place, state, etc.) that cannot be escaped from; (of knot, problem, etc.) that cannot be unravelled or solved. Hence ~LY² adv. [f. F, or L IN²(*extricabilis* EXTRICABLE)]

infăll'ibil|ism, n. Principle of the Pope's infallibility. So ~IST n. [-ISM]

infăll'|ible, a. Incapable of erring; (of method, test, proof, etc.) unfailing. Hence

~iBIL'ITY n. (esp. as attribute of the Pope speaking *ex cathedrâ*, defined 1870 by the Vatican Council), ~iBLY² adv. [f. med. L IN²(*fallibilis* FALLIBLE)]

in'famize, -ise (-iz), v.t. Render infamous. [f. L IN²(*famis* f. *fama* fame) infamous, see -IZE]

in'famous, a. Of ill fame, notoriously vile; abominable; (Law) deprived of all or some rights of citizen on account of ~ crime. Hence or cogn. ~LY² adv., in'famy¹ n. [ME, f. med. L *infamosus* = L *infamis* (see prec.)]

in'fancy, n. Early childhood, babyhood; (Law) minority (to end of one's 21st year); early state of development. [f. L *infantia* (foll., -ANCY)]

in'fant, n. Babe; child under 7 years of age; minor (under 21); ~school (for children, usu. under 7). [ME, f. OF *enfant* f. L IN²(*fans -ntis* part. of *fari* speak)]

infàn'ta, n. (hist.). Daughter of king & queen of Spain or Portugal (usu. eldest daughter who is not heir to throne). So infàn'te (-tā) n. (second son). [Sp., Port., f. L as prec.]

infàn'ti|cide, n. Murder of infant after birth, esp. with mother's consent; custom of killing new-born infants. Hence or cogn. ~CIDE(1) n., ~cid'AL a. [f. LL *infanticidium* (as INFANT, see -CIDE(2))]

in'fant|ile, a. Of, as of, infants (~*ile paralysis*, POLIOMYELITIS); in its infancy. So ~INE¹ a. [f. LL *infantilis* (INFANT, -IL)]

infàn'tilism, n. (med.). State of being mentally or physically undeveloped. [prec., -ISM]

in'fantry, n. Foot-soldiers; ~*man* (-an), soldier of ~ regiment. [f. F *infanterie* f. It. *infanteria* (*infante* youth, foot-soldier, as INFANT, see -ERY)]

infàt'u|āte, v.t. Affect (person) with extreme folly; inspire with extravagant passion. Hence ~ātèdLY² adv., ~A'TION n. [f. L IN¹(*fatuare* f. *fatuus* foolish), see -ATE³]

infèct', v.t. Fill (air etc.) with noxious corruption or germs; affect (person, body, mind, *with* disease etc. lit. & fig.); imbue (person *with* opinion etc.). So infèc'tIVE a., infèc'tiveNESS, infèctiv'ITY, nn. [ME, f. L IN¹(*ficere fect-* = *facere* make) taint]

infèc'tion, n. Communication of disease, esp. by agency of atmosphere or water etc. (cf. CONTAGION); moral contamination; diffusive influence of example, sympathy, etc. [ME, f. OF, or LL *infectio* (as INFECT, see -ION)]

infèc'tious (-shus), a. Infecting with disease, pestilential; (of disease) liable to be transmitted by air or water (cf. CONTAGIOUS); (of emotions etc.) apt to spread, catching. Hence ~LY² adv., ~NESS n. [prec., -IOUS]

infèlicif'ic, a. Producing unhappiness. [IN-²]

infèli'citous, a. Not felicitous. [IN-²]

infèli'city, n. Unhappiness; misfortune;

inaptness of expression etc. [ME, f. L IN²(*felicitas* FELICITY)]

infèr', v.t. (-rr-). Deduce, conclude, (thing, *that*, *when*, etc.; *from* fact etc.); (of fact or statement) imply. Hence in'ferABLE a. [f. L IN¹(*ferre* bring)]

in'ference, n. Inferring; thing inferred. Hence inferèn'tIAL (-shal) a., inferèn'tiaLLY² adv. [f. med. L *inferentia* (as prec., see -ENCE)]

infèr'ior, a. & n. 1. Situated below (~ LIMIT¹); lower in rank, quality, etc. (*to*, or abs.); (of poor quality; (of planets) whose orbit lies within that of the earth; (Bot., of calyx) below ovary, (of ovary) below calyx; (Print.) placed at bottom of ordinary letters (e.g. H₂, Cₙ). 2. n. Person ~ to another esp. in rank (*kind to* ~*s*). Hence inferiö'rITY n. (~*ity complex*, abnormal reactions, such as assertiveness or megalomania, from suppressed sense of ~ity, (pop.) sense of ~ity), ~LY² adv. [L, comp. of *inferus* low]

infèrn'al, a. Of hell; hellish, fiendish; (colloq.) abominable, confounded; ~ *machine* (now usu. joc.), apparatus (usu. disguised) for producing explosion destructive of life or property. Hence ~ITY (-ál²) n., ~LY² adv. [ME, f. OF, f. LL *infernalis* (*infernus* situated below, see -AL)]

infèrn'ō, n. (pl. ~s). Hell (esp. w. reference to Dante's *Divine Comedy*); scene of horror. [It., f. L *infernus*, see prec.]

infèr'rable, a. = INFERABLE.

infèrt'ile, a. Not fertile. So infèrtil'ITY n. [F, f. LL IN²(*fertilis* FERTILE)]

infèst', v.t. (Of vermin, pirates, diseases, etc.) haunt, swarm in or about, (place). So ~A'TION n. [f. F *infester* or L *infestare* assail (*infestus* hostile)]

|| infeudā'tion, n. Enfeoffment; ~ *of tithes*, granting of tithes to laymen. [f. med. L *infeudatio* f. IN¹(*feudare* f. *feudum* fee), see -ATION]

in'fidel, n. & a. 1. Disbeliever in religion; (hist.) adherent of religion opposed to Christianity; (from Jewish or Mohammedan point of view) disbeliever in the true religion; (gen.) unbeliever. 2. adj. Unbelieving, of unbelievers. Hence ~IZE(3) v.t. & i. [late ME, f. OF *infidele* or L IN²(*fidelis* faithful f. *fides* faith)]

infidèl'ity, n. Disbelief in Christianity; disloyalty, esp. (also *conjugal* ~) to husband or wife. [f. F *-té* or L *infidelitas* (as prec., see -TY)]

in'field, n. Farm land around or near homestead; arable land; land regularly manured & cropped; (Cricket) part of the ground near the wicket, or fieldsmen stationed there (opp. OUTFIELD). [IN³]

in'fight|ing (-fīt-), n. Boxing at closer quarters than arm's length. [IN²]

infil'tr|āte (*or* in'fil-), v.t. & i. Introduce (fluid) by filtration (*into*, *through*); permeate (t. & i.) by filtration. Hence ~A'TION n. (esp. Mil. & Pol., gradual unobserved occupation of ground or territory by detached parties or settlers). [IN-¹, after F *infiltrer*]

In'finite, a. & n. Boundless, endless; very great; (w. pl. noun) innumerable, very many; (Gram., of verb parts) not limited by person or number, e.g. infinitive, gerund, supine (cf. FINITE); (n.) *the I~*, God; *the ~, ~* space. Hence ~LY² (-tl-) adv. [ME, f. L IN¹(*finitus* FINITE)]

Infinites'imal, a. & n. Infinitely or very small (amount); *~ calculus*, the differential & integral calculuses conceived as one. Hence ~LY² adv. [as prec. on CENTESIMAL etc.]

Infin'itive, a. & n. (gram.). (Verb-form) that expresses the verbal notion without predicating it of any subject (e.g. *ask*, *to ask*). Hence **infinitiv'AL** a. [f. L IN-² (*finitivus* f. *finire -it-* define, see -IVE)]

Infin'itude, n. Boundlessness; boundless number or extent (*of*). [as INFINITE, -TUDE]

Infin'ity, n. — prec.; (Math.) infinite quantity (symbol: ∞). [ME, f. OF *infinite* f. L *infinitas* (as INFINITE, see -TY)]

Infirm', a. Physically weak, esp. through age; (of person, mind, judgement, etc.) weak, irresolute (often *~ of purpose*). Hence or cogn. ~ITY n., ~LY² adv. [ME, f. L IN²(*firmus* FIRM²)]

Infirm'ary, n. Hospital; sick-quarters in school, workhouse, etc. [f. med. L *infirmaria* (as prec., see -ARY¹)]

Infix'¹, v.t. Fix (thing *in* another); impress (fact etc. *in* mind); (Gram.) insert (formative element) in body of word. [IN adv.]

In'fix², n. (gram.). Modifying element infixed in word, esp. *nasal ~*, as *n* in Latin *fingo* from stem *fig~*. [IN-¹, after *prefix*, *suffix*]

Inflame', v.t. & i. Set ablaze; light up (as) with flame; excite passionately (*~d with*, *by*); raise (body, blood, etc.) to morbid heat; aggravate; catch fire; become excited; become morbidly ~d. [ME, f. OF *enflammer* f. L IN¹(*flammare* f. *flamma* flame)]

Inflamm'|able, a. & n. Easily set on fire; easily excited; (n.) ~able substance. Hence~aBIL'ITY, ~ableNESS, nn. [f. prec., see -BLE; cf. F *inflammable*]

Inflammā'tion, n. Inflaming (lit. & fig.); morbid process affecting a part of the body with heat, swelling, pain, & redness. [f. L *inflammatio* (as prec., see -ATION)]

Inflämm'atory, a. Tending to inflame with desire or passion (usu. in bad sense); of, tending to, inflammation of the body. [f. L as INFLAME, see -ORY]

Inflate', v.t. Distend with air or gas; puff up (person *with* pride etc.); (Finance) resort to inflation of (the currency, or abs.); raise (price) artificially; (p.p., of language) bombastic. So **inflā'tion** n. (in vbl senses, & esp.) undue increase in the quantity of money in relation to goods available for purchase (cf. DEFLATION), **inflāt'or** n. [f. L IN¹(*flare* blow), see -ATE³]

Inflĕct', v.t. Bend inwards, curve; (Gram.) vary form of (word) to express grammatical relation; (Mus.) flatten, sharpen, (note). [ME, f. L IN¹(*flectere flex-* bend)]

Inflĕc'tion, = INFLEXION.

Inflĕc'tive, a. (gram.). Of inflexion. [-IVE]

Inflĕx'|ible, a. Unbendable; (fig.) unbending, rigid. Hence ~ɪBIL'ITY n., ~ɪBLY² adv. [f. L IN²(*flexibilis* FLEXIBLE)]

Inflĕ'xion (-kshon), n. Inflecting; inflected form of word; suffix etc. used to inflect; modulation of voice; (Geom.) change of curve from convex to concave. Hence ~AL, ~LESS, aa., (-kshon-). [f. F, or L *inflexio* (as INFLECT, see -ION)]

Inflict', v.t. Lay on (stroke, wound, *upon*); impose (suffering, penalty, one*self*, one's company, etc., *upon*). Hence or cogn. ~ABLE a., **inflic'tion** n. (esp., troublesome or boring experience), ~OR n. [f. L IN¹(*fligere flict-* dash)]

Inflores'cence n. (bot.). Arrangement of flowers of plant in relation to axis & to each other; collective flower of plant; flowering (also fig.). [f. LL IN¹(*florescere* come into flower f. *flos floris*), see -ESCENT, -ENCE]

In'flow (-ō), n. Flowing in. So ~ING¹, ² (-ōing) n. & a. [IN adv.]

In'fluence (-lōō-), n., & v.t. 1. (Astrol.) flowing from stars of ethereal fluid affecting character & destiny of man (also fig. of personal power); action insensibly exercised (*upon*); UNDUE ~; ascendancy, moral power, (*over*, *with*, person etc.); thing, person, exercising (usu. non-material) power; (colloq., ellipt.) *under the ~* (sc. of alcohol, of drink); (Electr.) = INDUCTION. 2. v.t. Exert ~ upon, have effect upon. [ME, f. OF, or LL *influentia* f. L IN¹(*fluere* flow), see -ENCE]

In'fluent (-lōō-), a. & n. Flowing in (lit. & fig.); (n.) tributary stream. [ME, f. L as prec., see -ENT]

Influen'tial (-lōŏĕnshal), a. Having great influence. Hence ~LY² adv. [f. med. L *influentialis* (INFLUENCE, -AL)]

Influen'za (-lōō-), n. Infectious febrile disorder, usu. with rapid prostration & severe catarrh; (also *~ cold*) severe catarrh; (fig.) mental or commercial epidemic. [It., as INFLUENCE]

In'flux, n. Flowing in, esp. of stream etc. (*into* river etc.), or of persons or things (*into* place etc.). [f. F, or LL IN¹(*fluxus* FLUX)]

Inform', v.t. & i. Inspire, imbue, (person, heart, thing, *with* feeling, principle, quality, etc.), tell (person *of* thing, *that*, *how*, etc.), so ~ANT n.; bring charge (*against* person). [ME, f. OF *enformer* f. L IN¹(*formare* f. *forma* form) give shape to, fashion]

Inform'al, a. Not according to due form; without formality. Hence ~ITY (-ăl⁴) n., ~LY² adv. [IN-²]

informā'tion, n. Informing, telling; thing told, knowledge, items of knowledge, news, (*on, about*); (Law) charge, complaint, lodged with court or magistrate (*against*). Hence ~AL a. [ME, f. OF *enformacion* f. L *informationem* (as INFORM, see -ATION)]

inform'at|ive, a. Giving information, instructive. So ~ORY a. [-ATIVE]

informed' (-md), a. Instructed, knowing the facts, educated, intelligent, esp. *well, ill,* -~. [-ED¹]

inform'er, n. One who informs against another, esp. (also *common* ~) one who makes it his business to detect offenders & lay information against them. [-ER¹]

in'fra, adv. (abbr. *inf.*). Below, lower down, further on, (in book), as *vide* ~, see below. [L, = below]

infra- in comb.= L *infra* below; used esp. in anat. terms in sense 'below, under, some part', as ~ren'al, ~scap'ular, ~stern'al, beneath the kidneys, shoulder-blade, breast-bone; ~-red', of invisible rays beyond red end of spectrum; ~-structure, system of airfields, telecommunications, and public services forming a basis for defence.

infrăc'tion, n. Violation, infringement. [f. L *infractio* (as INFRINGE, see -ION)]

in'fra dig., pred. a. Beneath one's dignity, unbecoming. [abbr. L *infra dignitatem*]

infralăpsār'ian, n. & a. Calvinist who held that God's election of some was consequent to his prescience of the Fall, or that it contemplated man as already fallen (cf. SUBLAPSARIAN, SUPRALAPSARIAN); (adj.) of these views. [f. INFRA- +L *lapsus* fall + -ARIAN]

infrē'quent, a. Not frequent. Hence or cogn. ~ENCY n., ~entLY² adv. [f. L IN²(*frequens* FREQUENT¹)]

infringe' (-j), v.t. Transgress, violate, (law, oath, etc.). Hence ~MENT (-jm-) n. [f. L IN²(*fringere fract-=frangere* break)]

infrŭc'tuous, a. Unfruitful; (fig.) fruitless. [f. L IN²(*fructuosus* FRUCTUOUS, see -OUS]

infŭndib'ūlar, a. Funnel-shaped. [f. L *infundibulum* funnel (used in E of parts of body) f. IN¹(*fundere* pour)]

infūr'iāte, v.t. Fill with fury, enrage. [f. med. L IN¹(*furiare* f. *furia* FURY, see -ATE³]

infūs|e' (-z), v.t. & i. Pour (thing *into*); (fig.) instil (grace, spirit, life, etc., *into*); steep (herb. tea, etc.) in liquid to extract its soluble constituents, whence ~'ER¹(2) (-z-) n.; (v.i.) undergo infusion (*let it* ~*e for five minutes*). [f. L IN¹(*fundere fus-* pour)]

infūs'|ible (-z-), a. That cannot be fused or melted. Hence ~iBIL'ITY n. [IN-²]

infū'sion (-zhn), n. Infusing (lit. & fig.); liquid extract thus obtained; infused element, admixture. [t. F, or L *infusio* (as INFUSE, see -ION)]

infūsōr'|ia, n. pl. Class of protozoa

found in infusions of decaying animal or vegetable matter. Hence ~IAL a., ~iAN, infūs'ORY, aa. & nn. [mod. L (INFUSE, -ORY, -IA²)]

-ing¹, suf. forming vbl nn., OE *-ung, -ing,* f. Gmc *-ungō, -ingō. -ing* orig. formed mere nn. of action (*asking*), but came in ME to acquire partly vbl (gerundial) character, being qualified by adv. (*the habit of speaking loosely*) or governing an object (*the idea of building him a house*). This use, peculiar to E, led to introduction of perf., fut., & pass. forms (*having killed, being killed*). The substantival nature of *-ing* is marked by the possess. case or adj. that often precedes it (*after John's behaving so badly, upon my granting the request*); but mod. tendency is to drop the possess. sign exc. with pronn. or single nn. Meanings: (1) vbl action (*bicycling, forebodings*), esp. as occupation (*banking*) or as inflicted (*thrashing*), or formed f. nn. (*soldiering*); (2) thing produced by vbl action (*carving, filings, building*); (3) material for (*sacking*), whether f. n. or vb (*fencing* = what fences or serves as fence); (4) what is used to do vbl action (*binding, dentist's filling*); (5) what is to be operated on (*washing, darning*); (6) set or arrangement of (*colouring, feathering*).

-ing², suf. of pres. part. (often used as adj., as *charming*, occas. as prep. or adv., as *during*). OE *-ende* (= OHG *-anti,* L *-ent-,* Gk *-ont-,* Skr. *-ant-*) was weakened to *-inde* & thus confused with *-inge* -ING¹, which became the regular form in 14th c. As result of the confusion, some constructions gerundial in orig. now appear participial, as *he went hunting* (i.e. on hunting, vbl n.), *the ark was building* (on building). On the other hand, some wds in *-ing* that might be explained as attrib. nouns in -ING¹ are perh. better regarded as quasi-pass. participles (*washing* tie, *cooking* apple, *breech-loading* gun). Compds are formed with advv. & adjj. (*well-meaning, fair-seeming*; for stress cf. -ED²), & with objective nn. (*cheese-paring, heart-breaking*; stressed on first component).

-ing³, suf. (OE *-ing,* Gmc *-inga*; cf. -LING¹) forming nn. w. sense 'one belonging to', 'one having the quality of'; also used as patronymic & dim. Exx.: *Atheling, king, shilling, farthing, Riding, gelding, herring, whiting.*

in'gathering (in-gădh-), n. Gathering in, harvest.

ingĕm'ināte (-j-), v.t. Repeat, reiterate, (esp. ~ *peace,* constantly urge it). [f. L IN¹(*geminare* GEMINATE)]

ingēn'ious (-j-), a. Clever at contriving; cleverly contrived (~ *machine, explanation, theory*). Hence ~LY² adv. [f. F *ingénieux* or L *ingeniosus* (*ingenium* cleverness, see -OUS)]

ingénue (see Ap.), n. Artless girl, esp. a stage type. [F]

ingĕnū′itў (-j-), n. Skill in contriving. [f. L *ingenuitas* ingenuousness (as foll., see -TY); E meaning by confusion of IN-GENIOUS w. foll.]

ingĕn′uous (-j-), a. Open, frank; innocent, artless. Hence ~LY² adv., ~NESS n. [f. L IN¹(*genuus* f. *gen-* beget) free-born, frank]

ingĕst′ (-j-), v.t. Take in (food) to the stomach. So **ingĕs′tion** (-schon) n., **ingĕs′tive** a. [f. L IN¹(*gerere gest-* carry)]

ingle (ĭng′gl), n. Fire burning on hearth; ~-nook, chimney-corner. [Sc., perh. f. Gael. *aingeal* fire, light]

inglŏr′ious (ĭn-g-), a. Shameful, ignominious; obscure. Hence ~LY² adv. [f. F -*eux* or L IN²(*gloriosus* GLORIOUS)]

in′gŏing (ĭn-g-), a. & n. Going in; sum paid for fixtures, improvements, etc., by incoming tenant of business or other premises.

ĭng′ot (-ngg-), n. Mass (usu. oblong) of cast metal, esp. of gold, silver, or steel. [ME; perh. f. IN adv.+*goten* p.p. of OE *geotan* cast]

ingrain (ĭn⸣grān *before noun*, ĭn-grān′ *after n. or in pred.*), a. Dyed in grain; inherent, inveterate, ingrained. [orig. two wds]

ingrained (ĭn′-grānd *before noun*, -ānd′ *elsewhere*), a. Deeply rooted, inveterate; thorough. Hence **ingrain′ĕdLY²** (ĭn-g-) adv. [var. of ENGRAINED]

‖ **ingrāte′** (ĭn-g-, *or* ĭn⸣), a. & n. (arch.). Ungrateful; (n.) ungrateful person. [f. OF, or L IN²(*gratus* grateful)]

ingrā′tiāt|e (ĭn-grāshĭ-), v.t. Bring oneself into favour *with*. Hence ~**inglY³** adv. [f. It. *ingratiare* f. L *in gratiam* into favour, see -ATE³]

ingrăt′itūde (ĭn-g-), n. Want of gratitude. [ME, f. OF, f. LL *ingratitudo* (as INGRATE, see -TUDE)]

ingravĕs′c|ent (ĭn-g-), a. (med.). (Of disease etc.) growing worse. So ~ENCE n. [f. L IN¹(*gravescere* f. *gravis* heavy), see -ENT]

ingrēd′ient (ĭn-g-), n. Component part, element, in a mixture. [f. L IN¹(*gredi gress-* = *gradi* step) enter, see -ENT]

in′grĕss (ĭn-g-), n. Going in; right of entrance. [f. L *ingressus -ūs* (as prec.)]

ĭn′group (-ōŏp), n. (sociol.). Group of people sharing common interests. [IN a.]

in′growing (-n-grōi-), a. Growing inwards, esp. (of nail) growing into the flesh, also of branches of tree. So **ĭn′growth** (ĭn-grōth) n. [IN adv.]

ĭng′uinal (-nggw-), a. Of the groin. [f. L *inguinalis* (*inguen -inis* groin, see -AL)]

ĭngŭr′git|āte (-n-g-), v.t. Swallow greedily; (fig.) engulf. So ~A′TION n. [f. L IN¹(*gurgitare* f. *gurges -itis* whirlpool), see -ATE³]

inhăb′it, v.t. (Of men or animals) dwell in, occupy, (region, town, house; also fig.). Hence or cogn. ~ANT, ~A′TION, nn. [ME *en-, in-,* f. OF *enhabiter* or L IN¹(*habitare* dwell, see HABIT)]

inhăb′itancў, n. Residence as inhabitant, esp. during specified period, so as to acquire rights etc. [-ANCY]

inhāle′, v.t. Breathe in (air, gas, etc., or abs.), take (esp. tobacco-smoke or abs. of this) into the lungs (also fig.). So **inhalA′TION**, **inhāl′ER**¹(2), nn. [f. L IN¹(*halare* breathe)]

inhărmŏn′ic, a. Not harmonic. [IN-²]

inhărmŏn′ious, a. Not harmonious. Hence ~LY² adv. [IN-²]

inhēr|e′, v.i. (Of qualities etc.) exist, abide, *in*; (of rights etc.) be vested *in* (person etc.). So ~ENCE n., ~ENT a., ~′entLY² adv. [f. L IN¹(*haerēre haes-* stick)]

inhĕ′rit, v.t. Receive (property, rank, title)·by legal descent or succession; derive (quality, character) from one's progenitors; (abs.) succeed as heir. Hence ~OR, ~RESS¹, **inhĕ′riTRIX**, nn. [ME, f. OF *enheriter* f. LL *inhereditare* f. *heres hered-* HEIR]

inhĕ′rit|able, a. Capable of inheriting or of being inherited (lit. & fig.). Hence ~ABIL′ITY n. [AF (as prec., see -ABLE)]

inhĕ′ritance, n. Inheriting; what is inherited (lit. & fig.). [f. AF *enheritance* (as prec., see -ANCE)]

inhē′sion (-zhn), n. Inhering. [f. LL *inhaesio* (as INHERE, see -ION)]

inhĭb′it, v.t. Forbid, prohibit, (person etc. *from* doing; esp. in Eccl. Law); forbid (ecclesiastic) to exercise clerical functions; hinder, restrain, (action, process). So **inhibi′tion** n., (in vbl senses, & esp. Psych.) instinctive or induced habitual shrinking from some impulse or action as a thing forbidden, ~ORY a. [f. L IN¹(*hibēre hibit-* = *habere* hold)]

inhŏmogēn′eous, a. Not homogeneous. Hence **inhomogēnē′ITY** n. [IN-²]

inhŏs′pitab|le, a. Not hospitable; (of region, coast, etc.) not affording shelter etc. Hence ~leNESS n., ~LY² adv. [f. F, or med. L -*abilis*]

inhŏspităl′itў, n. Being inhospitable. [f. F -*té*, or L -*itas* (IN-², HOSPITALITY)]

inhūm′an, a. (Of person or conduct) brutal, unfeeling, barbarous, so ~ITY (-ăn′) n., ~LY² adv.; not of the ordinary human type. [f. F(-*ain*), or L IN²(*humanus* HUMAN)]

inhūm|e′, v.t. Bury. Hence ~A′TION n. [f. L IN¹(*humare* f. *humus* ground)]

inĭm′ical, a. Hostile (*to*); harmful (*to*). Hence ~LY² adv. [f. LL *inimicalis* f. IN²(*imicus* = *amicus* friend), see -AL]

inĭm′itab|le, a. That defies imitation. Hence ~leNESS n., ~LY² adv. [f. F, or L IN²(*imitabilis* IMITABLE)]

inĭ′quit|ў, n. Unrighteousness, wickedness; gross injustice. Hence ~OUS a., ~OUSLY² adv. [ME, f. OF *iniquite* f. L *iniquitatem* f. IN²(*iquus* = *aequus* just), see -TY]

inĭ′tial (-shal), a. & n., & v.t. (-ll-, -l-). **1.** Of, existing or occurring at, the beginning, as ~ *stage, expenses, difficulties*; ~ *letter* (standing at beginning of word). **2.** n. ~ letter, esp. (pl.) first letters of person's name & surname. Hence ~**s.** Hence ~LY² adv. [f. L *initialis* f. *initium* f. IN¹(*ire it-* go), see -AL]

Ini'ti|āte¹ (-shI-), v.t. Begin, set going, originate; admit (person), esp. with introductory rites or forms, (*into* society, office, secret, in mysteries, science, etc.). So ~A'TION, ~ātor, ~ātrix, nn., ~atory (-shya-) a. [f. L *initiare* (as INITIAL), see -ATE³]

Ini'tiate² (-shI-), a. & n. (Person) who has been initiated. [as prec., see -ATE³]

Ini'tiative (-shya-), n. & a. **1.** First step, origination; *take the* ~, take the lead (*in* doing); *have the* (power, right, to take the) ~, (Mil.) be able to make enemy conform to one's movements; ability to initiate things, enterprise (esp. with negative or virtual negative as *he lacks, has little or no*, ~); right of citizen(s) outside legislature to originate legislation (as in Switzerland). **2.** adj. Beginning, originating. [f. F (as prec., see -ive)]

Ini'tio (-shiō), adv. At the beginning (in reference to passage in book etc.; abbr. *init.*); AB~. [L]

Inject', v.t. Drive, force, (fluid, medicine, *into* cavity etc.) as by syringe; fill (cavity etc. *with*) by ~ing. Hence **injĕc'tor** n. [f. L IN¹(*jicĕre ject-* = *jacĕre* throw)]

Injĕc'tion, n. Injecting; liquid or solution injected. [f. F, or L *injectio* (as prec., see -ION)]

Injudi'cious (-jŏōdĭshus), a. Unwise, ill-judged. Hence ~LY² adv., ~NESS n. [IN-³]

In'jun (I-), n. (colloq. & dial.). American Indian, esp. in HONEST ~.

Injunc'tion, n. Authoritative admonition or order; judicial process restraining person from wrongful act or compelling restitution etc. to injured party, whence **injunct'** v.t. (colloq.). [f. LL *injunctio* f. *injungere* ENJOIN, see -ION]

In'jure (-jer), v.t. Do wrong to; hurt, harm, impair. [back formation f. INJURY]

In'jured (-jerd), a. Wronged; showing sense of wrong, offended, as *in an* ~ *voice*. [p.p. of prec.]

Injur'ious (-oor-), a. Wrongful; (of language) insulting, calumnious; hurtful. Hence ~LY² adv., ~NESS n. [f. F *injurieux* or L *injuriosus* (as foll., see -OUS)]

In'jury, n. Wrongful action or treatment; harm, damage. [ME, f. L IN²(*juria* f. *jus juris* right) wrong]

Injus'tice, n. Want of equity, unfairness; unjust act; *you do him an* ~ (judge him unfairly). [ME, f. OF f. L IN²(*justitia* JUSTICE)]

Ink, n., & v.t. **1.** Fluid (black, red, etc.) for writing with pen; MARKING-~; (*printer's* ~) viscous paste similarly used in printing; black liquid ejected by cuttle-fish etc. from bladder (~*-bag*) to assist its escape; ~*-bottle, -pot* (for holding ~);

~*-horn*, small vessel of horn formerly used for holding ~; ~*-pad* (for ~ing rubber stamp etc.); ~*stand*, stand for one or more ~-bottles, often with pen-tray etc.; ~*-well* (pot fitted into hole in desk). **2.** v.t. Mark (*in, over*, etc.) with ~; cover (types etc.) with ~ so as to print from them. Hence ~'iNESS n., ~'LESS, ~'Y², aa. [ME *enke, inke* f. OF *enque* f. LL *encau(s)tum* f. Gk *egkauston* (as ENCAUSTIC) purple ~ used by Roman emperors for signature]

ink'er, n. Telegraph instrument recording message in ink; (Print. etc.) inking-roller. [-ER¹]

ink'ling, n. Hint, slight knowledge or suspicion, (*of*). [f. ME *inkle* utter in an undertone; orig. unkn.]

in'land (-and, -ănd), n., a., & adv. **1.** Interior of country. **2.** adj. Placed in this, remote from sea or border; carried on within limits of a country, as ~ *trade*, ~ *duty* (on ~ trade), ‖ ~ *revenue* (consisting of taxes & ~ duties). **3.** adv. In, towards, the interior. Hence ~ER¹(4) n., ~ISH¹ a. [IN³]

in'-law, n. (colloq.). (Usu. pl.) relative by marriage. [IN prep.]

inlay'¹, v.t. (*inlaid*). Embed (thing *in* another) so that their surfaces are even; ornament (thing with another inlaid); insert (page, plate, cut) in space cut in larger stouter page. [IN²]

in'lay² (or Inlā'), n. Inlaid work. [f. prec.]

in'let, n. Small arm of sea, creek; piece inserted. [IN adv. + LET² v.]

in'lier, n. (geol.). Space occupied by one formation & completely surrounded by later formation. [IN adv.]

in'ly, adv. (poet.). Inwardly, in the heart; intimately. [OE *innlīce* (IN¹, see -LY²)]

in'lying, a. Lying inside. [IN adv.]

in'māte, n. Occupant (*of* house etc.), esp. one of several; now usu. occupant of institution, asylum, etc. [IN adv.]

in'mōst (or -ost), a. Most inward; (fig.) deepest, most intimate. [OE *innemest* (IN adv., see -MOST)]

inn, n. Public house for lodging etc. of travellers, smaller & less pretentious than hotel & usu. in country or small town; ~'*keeper*, one who keeps an ~; ‖ *Inns of Court*, (buildings in London belonging to) four legal societies having exclusive right of admitting persons to practise at bar (*Inner Temple, Middle Temple, Lincoln's Inn, Gray's Inn*); ‖ *Inns of Chancery* (hist.), buildings in London formerly used as hostels for law students. [OE, f. IN adv.]

inn'ards (-dz), n. pl. (colloq.). Entrails. [INWARD n.]

innāte' (or Inⁱ), a. Inborn, natural. Hence ~LY² (-tl-) adv., ~NESS (-tn-) n. [f. L IN¹ (*natus* p.p. of *nasci* be born)]

innāv'igable, a. Not navigable. [f. F, or L IN²(*navigabilis* NAVIGABLE)]

inn'er, a. & n. **1.** Interior, internal; ~ *tube*, separate inflatable tube inside cover of pneumatic tire; *the ~ man*, man's soul or mind, (joc.) stomach, as *refreshed his ~ man*. 2. n. Division of target next outside bull's-eye, shot that strikes this. Hence ~MOST a. [OE *innera* a., compar. of IN²]

innerv'|āte, v.t. Supply (organ etc.) with nerve-force or nerves. Hence ~A'TION n. [f. IN-¹+NERVE+-ATE³]

inn'ings (-z), n. (pl. same, colloq. ~es). 1. (crick. etc.) Portion of game played by either side while in or batting, play of one batsman during his turn. 2. (fig.) Tenure of office, dominance, of political party, cause, etc. [orig. pl.; in sense 1 sing. *inning* is usu. in U.S.; f. IN adv. + -ING¹]

inn'ocent, a. & n. 1. Free from moral wrong, sinless; ignorant of evil (without implication of virtue); not guilty (*of* crime etc.); (colloq.) *windows ~ of* (without) *glass*, simple, guileless; harmless. 2. n. ~ person, esp. young child; *I ~s' Day*, Dec. 28, festival of the slaughter of children by Herod (*Matt.* ii. 16); ‖ (Parl. sl.) *massacre* or *slaughter of the ~ s*, sacrifice of measures at end of session for want of time; simple person; idiot. Hence or cogn. inn'OCENCE, -ENCY (rare), nn.,~LY² adv. [ME, f. OF, or L IN²(*nocens -ent*-part. of *nocēre* hurt)]

innoc'uous, a. Not injurious, harmless (esp. of snakes). Hence innocu'ITY, ~NESS, nn., ~LY² adv. [f. L IN²(*nocuus* as prec.)+-OUS]

innom'inate, a. Unnamed; (Anat.) ~ *bone*, hip-bone (made up of three original bones). [f. LL IN²(*nominatus*, as NOMIN-ATE)]

inn'ov|āte, v.i. Bring in novelties; make changes *in*. Hence or cogn. ~A'TION, ~ātor, nn.,~ātorY a. [f. L IN¹(*novare* make new f. *novus*), see -ATE³]

innox'ious (-kshus), a. Harmless. Hence ~LY² adv., ~NESS n. [f. L IN²(*noxius* NOXIOUS)]

innuen'do, n. (pl. ~es), & v.i. Oblique hint, allusive remark (usu. depreciatory); (v.i.) make ~es. [L, gerund of IN¹(*nuere* nod), = by nodding, i.e. by way of explanation, as ‘he, innuendo the plaintiff ’, i.e., to wit]

innum'erable, a. Countless. [ME f. L IN²(*numerabilis* NUMERABLE)]

innutri'tion, n. Lack of nutrition. [IN-²]

innutri'tious (-shus), a. Not nourishing. [IN-²]

inobserv'ance (-z-), n. Inattention; non-observance (*of* law etc.). [f. F, or L IN²(*observantia* OBSERVANCE)]

inoccupā'tion, n. Want of occupation. [IN-²]

inoc'ul|āte, v.t. Impregnate (person, animal, *with* virus or germs of disease) to induce milder form of it & so safeguard person against its attacks (cf. VACCINATE); implant (disease etc.) thus (*on, into*, person etc.); insert (bud, scion) in plant,

treat (plant) thus. Hence or cogn. ~A'TION, ~ātor, nn.,~ātive a. [f. L IN¹(*oculare* f. *oculus* eye, bud) engraft, see -ATE³]

inod'orous, a. Having no odour. [f. L IN²(*odorus* ODOROUS)]

inoffen'sive, a. Unoffending; not objectionable. Hence ~LY² adv., ~NESS n. [IN-²]

inoffi'cious (-shus), a. Without office or function; (Law) not in accordance with moral duty. [f. L IN²(*officiosus* dutiful, see OFFICIOUS)]

inop'erable, a. (Of tumours etc.) that cannot be operated on. [IN-²]

inop'erative, a. Not working or taking effect. [IN-²]

inopp'ortune, a. Unseasonable. Hence ~LY² adv.,~NESS n. [f. LL IN²(*opportunus* OPPORTUNE)]

inord'inate, a. Immoderate, excessive; intemperate; disorderly. Hence ~LY² adv. [ME, f. L IN²(*ordinatus* p.p. of *ordinare* f. *ordo -dinis* order)]

inorgan'ic, a. Having no organized physical structure; (Chem., of compounds etc.) of mineral origin, not ORGANIC; ~ *chemistry*, that of ~ substances; not arising by natural growth, extraneous. [IN-²]

inorganizā'tion, n. Lack of organization. [IN-²]

inornāte', a. Not ornate. [IN-²]

inos'cul|āte, v.i. & t. (Of blood-vessels etc.) join, have terminal connexion, (*with*); (of fibres etc.) unite closely, be interwoven; (trans.) unite (fibres etc.) closely. Hence ~A'TION n. [f. IN-¹+LL *osculare* furnish with mouth (*osculum* dim. of *os* mouth), -ATE³]

in'pouring (-pōr-), a. & n. Pouring in.

in'quest (in-kw-), n. Legal or judicial inquiry to ascertain matter of fact; inquisition; = CORONER'S ~; *great, last, ~*, last Judgement; coroner's jury; *grand ~* (hist.), grand jury (*grand ~ of the nation*, House of Commons). [ME, f. OF *enqueste* f. Rom.* *inquesta* as INQUIRE]

inqui'etude (in-kw-), n. Uneasiness of mind or body. [ME, f. OF, or LL (-*do*) f. IN²(*quietus* QUIET), -TUDE]

in'quiline (in-kw-), n. Animal living in the home of another, commensal. [f. L *inquilinus* (IN-¹, *colere* dwell)]

inquir|e', en-, (in-kw-), v.i. & t. Make search (*into* matter); seek information (*of* person, *about, after*, thing etc.); ~*e after, for, him* (how he is); ask *for* (goods in shop etc.); ask to be told (person's name, business, etc., *whether, how*, etc.). Hence ~'ingLY² adv. [ME *enquere* f. OF *enquerre* f. Rom. **inquaerere* f. L IN¹-(*quirere quisit*- = *quaerere* seek)]

inquir'|y, en-, (in-kw-), n. Asking; question; investigation; *make ~ies*, ask (*about* etc.); *court of ~y* (investigating circumstances of mishap etc.). [f. prec. +-Y⁴]

inquisi'tion (in-kwiz-), n. Search, investigation; judicial or official inquiry; (Rom. Cath.) *the I~* (hist.), ecclesiastical tribunal for suppression of heresy, the Holy Office. Hence ~AL (in-kwĭzĭsh-) a. [ME, f. OF f. L *inquisitionem* (as INQUIRE, see -ION)]

inquis'itive (ĭn-kwĭz'-), a. Inquiring, curious; prying. Hence ~LY² adv., ~NESS n. [ME, f. OF (-*if*, -*ive*), f. LL *inquisitivus* (as prec., see -IVE)]

inquis'itor (ĭn-kwĭz'-), n. Official investigator; officer of the Inquisition (hist.); *Grand I~*, director of court of Inquisition in some countries; *I~ General*, head of this in Spain. [f. OF *inquisiteur* f. L *inquisitorem* (as INQUIRE, see -OR)]

inquisitŏr'ial (ĭn-kwĭz'-), a. Of, like, an inquisitor; offensively prying. Hence ~LY² adv. [f. med. L *inquisitorius* (as prec., see -ORY) + -AL]

in'road, n. Hostile incursion, raid; (fig.) forcible encroachment. [IN adv. + ROAD [²] n. in sense ' riding ']

in'rŭsh, n. Rushing in. [IN adv.]

insăl'iv|āte, v.t. Mix (food) with saliva. Hence ~A'TION n. [f. IN- ¹ + SALIVA + -ATE³]

insalŭb'r|ious (-lōō-), a. (Of climate or place) unhealthy. So ~ITY n. [f. L IN²(*salubris* SALUBRIOUS)]

insāne', a. Mad; senseless; ~ *asylum* (for ~ persons). Hence or cogn. ~LY² (-nl-) adv., insăn'ITY n. [f. L IN²(*sanus* SANE)]

insān'itary, a. Not sanitary. [IN-²]

insā'ti|able (-sha-), a. That cannot be satisfied; inordinately greedy (*of*). Hence ~ABIL'ITY n., ~abLY² adv., (-sha-). [ME, f. OF, or L IN²(*satiabilis*, as SATIATE, see -BLE)]

insā'tiate (-shyat), a. Never satisfied. [f. L IN²(*satiatus*, as prec.)]

inscrīb|e', v.t. Write (words etc. *in*, *on*, stone, metal, paper, etc.); enter name of (person) on list, in book (esp. for presentation); || (esp. in p.p.) issue (loan) in form of shares with registered holders, as ~*ed stock*; mark (sheet, tablet, etc., *with* characters); (Geom.) trace (figure) within another so that some particular points (or all angular points) of it lie in the boundary of that other (cf. CIRCUMSCRIBE), whence ~'ABLE a. [f. L IN¹(*scribere* script-write)]

inscrip'tion, n. Words inscribed, esp. on monument, coin, stone, etc., so ~AL (-shon-), inscrip'tIVE, aa.; inscribing (*of* loan). [ME, f. L *inscriptio* (as prec., -ION)]

inscrŭt|able (-rōō-), a. That cannot be penetrated (fig.), wholly mysterious. Hence ~ABIL'ITY, ~ableNESS, nn., ~abLY² adv. [ME, f. LL IN²(*scrutabilis* f. *scrutari* search, see -BLE)]

in'sĕct, n. Small invertebrate segmented animal having head, thorax, abdomen, and three pairs of thoracic legs, usu. with one or two pairs of thoracic wings; (fig.) insignificant person or creature; ~*powder* (for killing or driving away ~). Hence ~ĭv'ORA n. pl., ĭnsĕc'tivorE n., ~ĭv'OROUS

a. [f. L *insectum* (*animal*) notched animal, f. IN¹(*secare sect-* cut)]

insĕctār'ium, n. Place for keeping insects. [-ARIUM]

insĕc'ti|cīde, n. Insect-killer, esp. preparation used for killing insects. Hence ~cīd'AL a. [-CIDE]

insĕc'tŏl'ogy̆, n. Science of insects, esp. in their economic relations to man. [f. F *insectologie* (as INSECT, see -O- & -LOGY)]

insĕcūr|e', a. Unsafe; (of ice, ground, etc.) liable to give way. Hence or cogn. ~e'LY² (-rl-) adv., ~'ITY n. [f. med. L IN²(*securus* SECURE)]

insĕm'in|āte, v.t. Sow (seed etc., lit. & fig., *in*). Hence ~A'TION n., esp. artificial ~ation of animals. [f. L IN¹(*seminare* f. *semen -minis* seed), see -ATE³]

insĕn'sate, a. Without sensibility, unfeeling; stupid; mad; without physical sensation. Hence ~LY² (-tl-) adv. [f. LL IN²(*sensatus* f. *sensus* SENSE, see -ATE³)]

insĕnsibil'ity̆, n. Lack of mental feeling or emotion; indifference (*to*); unconsciousness, swoon. [f. LL *insensibilitas* (as foll., see -TY)]

insĕn'sib|le, a. Too small or gradual to be perceived, inappreciable, whence ~LY² adv.; unconscious, as *he fell down & was long ~le*; unaware (*of*, *to*, *how*, etc.); emotionless, callous. [ME, f. OF, or L IN²(*sensibilis* SENSIBLE)]

insĕn'sitive, a. Not sensitive (*to* touch, sight, light, mental or moral impressions). Hence ~NESS n. [IN-²]

insĕn'tient (-shĭ-), a. Inanimate. [IN-²]

insĕp'ar|able, a. & n. That cannot be separated; (Gram.) ~*able prefix*, one that cannot be used as separate word (e.g. *dis-, mis-, un-*); (n., usu. pl.) ~able person or thing, esp. friend. Hence ~ABIL'ITY n., ~abLY² adv. [ME, f. L IN²(*separabilis* SEPARABLE)]

insĕrt', v.t. Place, fit, thrust, (thing *in*, *into*, another, *between* edges etc.); introduce (letter, word, article, *in*, *into*, written matter, newspaper, etc.). [f. L IN¹(*serere sert-* join)]

insĕr'tion, n. Inserting; thing inserted, esp. in writing or print; each appearance of an advertisement in newspaper etc.; ornamental needlework etc. inserted into plain material, as *lace~*; (Anat.) mode of attachment of muscle, organ, etc. [f. F, or LL *insertio* (as prec., see -ION)]

in'sĕt¹, n. Extra page(s) inserted in sheet or book; small map etc. inserted within border of larger; piece let into dress; pair of white slips worn as edging to waistcoat opening. [IN adv. + SET n.]

insĕt'², v.t. (~ or ~*ted*). Put in as an inset. [IN adv. + SET v. or f. prec.]

in'shŏre', adv. & a. Close to shore; ~ *of*, nearer to shore than. [IN¹]

inside, n., a., adv., & prep. **1.** n. (ĭn'sīd'). Inner side or surface, (of path) side next to wall or away from road; inner part, interior; (ĭnsĭd'), stomach & bowels (colloq.); ‖ *the in'side'* (middle part) *of a week*; (insĭd') passenger travelling ~ coach etc. (hist.); *turned in'side out*, so that inner side becomes outer. 2. adj. (in'sĭd). Situated on or in, derived from, the ~ (~ *information*, not accessible to outsiders; *an ~ job*, burglary by a resident). 3. adv. (insĭd'). On or in the ~; (colloq.) ~ *of* (in less than) *a week*. 4. prep. (insĭd'). On the inner side of, within. [IN a. + SIDE]

Insid'er, n. One who is in some society, organization, etc. (cf. OUTSIDER); one who is in the secret. [f. prec. + -ER¹]

Insid'ious, a. Treacherous, crafty; proceeding secretly or subtly, as ~ *disease*. Hence~LY² adv.,~NESS n. [f. L *insidiosus* cunning f. IN¹(*sidiae* f. *sedēre* sit) ambush, see -OUS]

In'sight (-īt), n. Penetration (*into* character, circumstances, etc.) with the understanding. [IN adv. + SIGHT]

Insig'nia, n. pl. Badges, distinguishing marks, (*of* office, honour, etc.). [L, neut. pl. of IN¹(*signis* f. *signum* SIGN¹) distinguished]

Insignif'ic|ant, a. Unimportant, trifling; contemptible; meaningless. Hence ~ANCE, ~ANCY, nn., ~antly² adv. [IN-²]

Insincēre', a. Not sincere, disingenuous. Hence ~LY² (-rl-) adv. **insincē'rity** n. [f. L IN²(*sincerus* SINCERE)]

Insin'ū|āte, v.t. Introduce (thing, one*self*, *into* place; one*self*, person, *into* favour, office, etc.) gradually or subtly; convey indirectly, hint obliquely, (idea, *that*). Hence ~ātingly² adv., ~ā'TION, ~ātor, nn., ~ātive a. [f. L IN¹(*sinuare* f. *sinus* -*ūs* curve), see -ATE³]

Insip'id, a. Tasteless; wanting in flavour; lifeless, dull, uninteresting. Hence ~ITY (-ĭd⁴), ~NESS, nn., ~LY² adv. [f. LL IN²(*sipidus* = *sapidus* well-tasting, f. *sapere* taste, be wise, see -ID¹)]

Insist', v.i. & t. Dwell long or emphatically (on), as ~ *on this point, on his unpunctuality*; maintain positively, as ~ *on his innocence*, ~ (*on it*) *that he is innocent*; make a stand on as essential (*I ~ on being present, on your being present, on your presence, on it that you shall be present*). Hence ~ENCE, ~ENCY, nn., ~ENT a., ~ently² adv. [f. F *insister*, or L IN¹(*sistere* stand)]

Insobri'ety, n. Intemperance, esp. in drinking. [IN-²]

Insolā'tion, n. Exposure to sun's rays, for purposes of bleaching etc., as medical treatment, or as cause of disease. [f. L *insolatio* f. IN¹(*solare* f. *sol* sun), see -ATION]

In'sol|ent, a. Offensively contemptuous, insulting. Hence or cogn. ~ENCE n., ~ently² adv. [f. L IN²(*solens* part. of *solēre* be accustomed), see -ENT]

Insōl'ū|ble, a. That cannot be solved; that cannot be dissolved. Hence ~ūbIL² ITY, ~ūbleNESS, nn., ~ūbLY² adv. [ME, f. L IN²(*solubilis* SOLUBLE)]

insōl'vent, a. & n. (Debtor) unable to pay debts; relating to ~s, as ~ *laws*. Hence **insōl'vency** n. [IN-²]

insŏm'nia, n. Habitual sleeplessness. [L, f. IN²(*somnis* f. *somnus* sleep) sleepless]

insomŭch', adv. To such an extent *that*.

insouci|ant (see Ap.), a. Careless, unconcerned. So ~ANCE n. [F (*soucier* care)]

inspān', v.t. (S.-Afr.; -nn-). Yoke (oxen etc.) in team to vehicle; harness (wagon). [f. Du. IN¹(*spannen* SPAN²)]

inspect', v.t. Look closely into; examine officially. So **inspěc'TION**, **inspec'TOR** (esp., police officer below superintendent & above sergeant, also official appointed to ~ & send in reports, e.g. ~*or of schools, of mines, of weights & measures*), **inspěc'**torSHIP, nn., **inspěc'tor**AL, ~ōr'IAL, aa. [f. L IN¹(*spicere spect*- look), & *inspectare*]

inspěc'torate, n. Office of inspector; body of inspectors; district under inspector. [-ATE¹]

inspirā'tion, n. Drawing in of breath; inspiring; divine influence, esp. that which is thought to visit poets etc. & that under which books of Scripture are held to have been written, whether *verbal* ~ (dictating every word), *plenary* ~ (covering all subjects treated), or *moral* ~ (confined to moral & religious teaching), whence ~ISM(3), ~IST(2), nn.; thought etc. inspired, prompting; sudden happy idea; inspiring principle. Hence ~AL a. [ME, f. OF f. LL *inspirationem* (as INSPIRE, see -ATION)]

in'spirātor, n. Apparatus for drawing in air or vapour. [L as foll., see -OR)]

inspīr|e', v.t. Breathe in, inhale, (air etc. or abs.), whence ~'atORY a.; infuse thought or feeling into (person; esp. of divine or supernatural agency; often in p.p.); animate (person etc. *with* feeling); infuse (feeling *into* person etc.), create (feeling *in* person); *an ~ed article* (in journal), one secretly suggested by or emanating from influential person etc. [ME, f. OF *enspirer* f. L IN¹(*spirāre* breathe)]

inspi'rit, v.t. Put life into, animate, encourage (person *to* action, *to* do). Hence ~ING² a. [IN-¹ + SPIRIT n.]

inspiss'|āte (or IN²), v.t. Thicken, condense. So ~A'TION n. [f. LL IN¹(*spissare* f. *spissus* thick), see -ATE³]

instabil'ity, n. Lack of stability (usu. fig. of moral qualities etc.). [ME, f. OF *instabilite* f. L *instabilitatem* f. IN²(*stabilis* STABLE¹), see -TY]

install' (-awl), v.t. Place (person *in* office or dignity) with ceremonies, whence ~ANT (-awl-) a. & n.; establish (person, one*self*, *in* place, condition, etc.); place (heating or lighting apparatus etc.) in position for use. So ~A'TION n. (also, usu. pl., buildings etc. for technical operation). [f. med. L IN¹(*stallare* f. *stallum* STALL¹)]

instal'ment (-awl-). n. Each of several parts. successively falling due, of a sum payable; each of several parts supplied etc. at different times. [f. obs. IN¹(*stall* v. arrange, fix)+-MENT]

in′stance¹, n. Fact illustrating a general truth, example; particular case (*in your, this*,~); *for*~, as an example; *at the*~ (request, suggestion) *of*; (Law) process, suit, as *court of first*~ (primary jurisdiction); *in the first*~, in the first place, at the first stage of a proceeding. [ME, f. OF f. L *inslantia* (as INSTANT¹, see -ANCE)]

in′stance², v.t. Cite (fact, case) as an instance; (usu. pass.) exemplify. [f. prec.]

in′stancy, n. Urgency. [as prec., -ANCY]

in′stant¹, a. Urgent, pressing; (abbr. *inst.*) of the current month, as *the 6th inst.* (cf. PROXIMO, ULTIMO); immediate. [F, f. L IN¹(*stare* stand) be present, press upon, see -ANT]

in′stant², n. Precise (esp. the present) point of time, moment, as *come this*~, *I went that*~ *or on the*~; *I told you the*~ (as soon as) *I knew*; short space of time, moment. [after med. L *instans* (prec.)]

instantané (see Ap.), n. Snapshot, (fig.) short sketch in a few sentences. [F]

instantan′eous, a. Occurring, done, in an instant; (Dynam.) existing at a particular instant. Hence ~LY² adv., ~NESS n. [f. med. L *-eus* (INSTANT², -ANEOUS), after LL *momentaneus*]

instan′ter, adv. Immediately, at once, (now usu. joc.). [L, f. *instans* INSTANT¹]

in′stantly, adv. At once. [INSTANT¹ + -LY²]

in′star, n. Form assumed by insect at particular stage of development. [L]

instaura′tion, n. Restoration, renewal. So **in′staurator** n. [f. L *instauratio* f. IN¹(*staurare*, see RESTORE & -ATION)]

instead′ (-ĕd), adv. As a substitute or alternative; in place *of*, as ~ *of this*, ~ *of going, you should be out*~ *of* (*sitting*) *in on this fine day*, (also *in his, my, our*, STEAD). [ME; IN prep.+STEAD n.]

in′step, n. Upper surface of foot between toes & ankle; part of shoe etc. fitting this; ~-shaped thing. [16th c., ult. f. IN+STEP, but immed. orig. obsc.]

in′stigate, v.t. Urge on, incite, (person *to* action, *to* do freq. something evil); bring about (revolt, murder, etc.) by persuasion. So ~A′TION, ~ator, nn. [f. L *instigare* urge, incite; see -ATE³]

instil(l)′, v.t. (-ll-). Put in (liquid *into* thing) by drops; infuse (feeling, ideas, etc. *into* person, mind, etc.) gradually. Hence or cogn. **instilla′TION**, **instil′MENT**, nn. [f. L IN¹(*stillare* drop); cf. DISTIL]

in′stinct¹, n. Innate propensity, esp. in lower animals, to certain seemingly rational acts performed without conscious design; HERD¹~; innate impulse; intuition, unconscious skill. Hence **instinc′tive** a., **instinc′tively²** (-vl-) adv. [f. L *instinctus -ūs* f. IN¹(*stinguere* stinct- prick) incite]

instinct′², pred. a. Imbued, charged,

(*with* life, beauty, force, etc.). [f. L p.p. as prec.]

in′stitute¹, n. 1. Society, organization, for promotion of scientific or other object; building used by this. 2. pl. Digest of elements of a subject, esp. of jurisprudence, as *I*~*s of Justinian*. [f. L neut. p.p. as foll.]

in′stitute², v.t. Establish, found; set on foot (inquiry etc.); appoint (person *to, into*, benefice). [ME, f. L IN¹(*stituere -tut- = statuere* set up)]

institu′tion, n. Instituting; establishment (*of* person) in cure of souls; established law, custom, or practice; (colloq.) of person etc.) familiar object; organization for promotion of some public object; building used by this. Hence ~AL (-shon-) a., (also, of religion) organized into or finding expression through ~s (churches, priests, ritual, etc.). [ME, f. OF f. L *institutionem* (as prec., see -ION)]

instruct′, v.t. Teach (person etc. *in* subject); inform (person *that, when*, etc.); (of client, solicitor) give information to (solicitor, counsel); direct, command, (person *to* do). Hence or cogn. **instruc′tor, instruc′tress**¹, nn. [ME, f. L IN¹(*struere struct-* pile up) build, teach]

instruc′tion, n. Teaching; (pl.) directions, orders; (pl.) directions to solicitor or counsel. Hence ~AL (-shon-) a. [ME, f. OF, f. L (in sense LL) *instructionem* (as prec., see -ION)]

instruc′tive, a. Tending to instruct, conveying a lesson. Hence ~LY² adv., ~NESS n. [-IVE]

in′strument (-rŏŏ-), n., & v.t. 1. Thing used in performing an action; person so made use of; tool, implement, esp. for delicate or scientific work; (also *musical* ~) contrivance for producing musical sounds by vibration of strings etc. (*stringed* etc. ~*s*) or of body of air in pipe etc. (*wind* ~*s*); formal, esp. legal, document. 2. v.t. Arrange (music) for ~s. [ME, f. OF, or L *instrumentum* (as IN-STRUCT, see -MENT)]

instrumen′tal (-rŏŏ-), a. Serving as instrument or means (*to* purpose, *in* work, *in* doing); of, arising from, an instrument, as ~ *errors*; (of music) performed on instruments (cf. VOCAL), whence ~IST(3) n.; (Gram.) ~ *case* (denoting the instrument). Hence ~LY² adv. [f. F, or med. L *instrumentalis* (as INSTRUMENT, see -AL)]

instrumen′tality (-rŏŏ-), n. Agency, means, esp. *by the*~ *of*. [-ITY]

instrumenta′tion (-rŏŏ-), n. Arrangement of music for instruments; study of character, power, pitch, etc., of musical instruments; operation with surgical or other instrument; instrumentality. [F, (as INSTRUMENT, see -ATION)]

insubord′in|ate, a. Disobedient, rebellious. Hence ~A′TION n. [IN-³]

insubstan′tial (-shl), a. Not real; lacking solidity or substance. Hence ~ITY

(-shĭăl⁴) n. [f. LL IN²(*substantialis* SUBSTANTIAL)]

insuff'erab|le, a. Unbearable, unbearably arrogant, corceited, etc. Hence ~LY² adv. [IN-²]

insuffi'ci|ent (-shent), a. Not sufficient, inadequate. Hence or cogn. ~ENCY n., ~ently² adv., (-shen-). [f. OF, or LL IN²(*sufficiens* SUFFICIENT)]

in'sufflāt|e, v.t. Blow, breathe, (air, gas, etc.) into cavity of the body etc.; treat (nose etc.) thus. Hence ~OR n., (also) device for blowing powder on to surface of object in order to make latent finger-prints visible. [f. LL IN¹(SUF*flare* blow upon), see -ATE³]

insufflā'tion, n. Blowing on or into; breathing on person as rite of exorcism. [f. LL *insufflatio* (as prec., see -ION)]

in'sular, a. Of (the nature of) an island; applied to a development of Latin handwriting current in the British Isles in the early Middle Ages; of, like, islanders, esp. ignorant of or indifferent to other countries & their culture, narrow-minded, whence ~ISM n. Hence **insŭlă'rity** n., ~LY² adv. [f. LL *insularis* (as foll., see -AR¹)]

in'sul|āte, v.t. Make (land) into an island; detach (person, thing) from surroundings, isolate; isolate (thing) by interposition of non-conductors, to prevent passage of electricity or heat. Hence ~A'TION, ~ātoR, nn. [f. L *insula* island + -ATE³]

in'sulin, n. A specific for diabetes extracted from the islets of Langerhans in the pancreas of animals. [f. L *insula* island + -IN]

in'sult¹, n. Insulting speech or action, affront. [f. F, or LL IN¹(*sultus = saltus* leap, as foll.)]

insult'², v.t. Treat with scornful abuse, offer indignity to; (of person or thing) affront. Hence ~ingLY² adv. [f. F *insulter*, or L IN¹(*sultare = saltare*, frequent. of *salire* salt- leap)]

insŭp'er|able, a. (Of barriers etc. & fig. of difficulties etc.) that cannot be surmounted or overcome; ‖ (rare) unsurpassable. Hence ~abIL'ITY n., ~abLY² adv. [ME, f. OF, or L IN²(*superabilis* f. *superare* overcome, -BLE)]

insupport'ab|le, a. Unbearable. Hence ~LY² adv. [f. F, or LL IN²(*supportabilis* SUPPORT, -ABLE)]

insur'ance (-shoor-), n. Insuring; sum paid for this, premium; *National I~ Act*, one requiring wage-earners to make weekly payments supplemented by their employers in return for which they receive State assistance in sickness, unemployment, etc. [earlier *en-*, f. OF *enseurance* (as ENSURE, see -ANCE)]

insur'ant (-shoor-), n. Person to whom insurance policy is issued. [f. foll. + -ANT]

insur|e' (-shoor), v.t. Secure payment of sum of money in event of loss of or damage to (property, life; cf. ASSURANCE)

by payment of premium; secure payment of (sum of money) thus (said of owner of the property or of insurance company); *the ~ed*, the person to whom such payment is secured; make certain. Hence ~'ABLE (-shoor-) a. [ME, earlier ENSURE]

insur'er (-shoor-), n. One who insures property in consideration of premium, underwriter. [-ER¹]

insur'g|ent, a. & n. 1. Rising in active revolt; (of sea etc.) rushing in. 2. n. Rebel. Hence ~ENCY n. [f. L IN¹(*surgere surrect-* rise), see -ENT]

insurmoun'tab|le (-ser-), a. Not to be surmounted. Hence ~LY² adv. [IN-²]

insurrec'tion (-su-), n. Rising in open resistance to established authority; incipient rebellion. Hence ~AL, ~ARY¹, aa., ~IST(3) n., (-*u*rĕksho-). [ME, f. OF f. LL *insurrectionem* (as INSURGENT, see -ION)]

insuscep't|ible, a. Not susceptible (*of* treatment, *to* agency etc.). Hence ~IBIL'ITY n. [IN-²]

intact', a. Untouched; entire; unimpaired. [ME, f. L IN²(*tactus* p.p. of *tangere* touch)]

inta'gliāted (-tăl-), a. Carved on the surface. [f. It. *intagliato* p.p. of IN¹(*tagliare* cut), as ENTAIL²]

inta'gliō (-tăl-), n. (pl. ~s), & v.t. Engraved design; carving in hard material; gem with incised design (cf. CAMEO); (v.t.) engrave (material, design) thus. [(vb f. n.) It. (as prec.)]

in'tāke, n. Place where water is taken into channel or pipe from river etc.; airway in mine; abrupt narrowing in pipe, stocking, etc.; person(s) or thing(s) taken in or received; land reclaimed from moor. [IN adv. + TAKE v.]

intăn'g|ible (-j-), a. & n. 1. That cannot be touched; impalpable; that cannot be grasped mentally. 2. n. ~ible thing. Hence ~IBIL'ITY n., ~IBLY² adv. [f. med. L IN²(*tangibilis* TANGIBLE)]

in'tĕger, n. Whole number, undivided quantity, (cf. FRACTION); thing complete in itself. [L, adj. = untouched, whole; see ENTIRE]

in'tĕgral, a. & n. 1. Of, necessary to the completeness of, a whole; whole, complete; (Math.) of, denoted by, an integer, involving only integers; ~ *calculus* (dealing with finding & properties of ~s of functions, cf. DIFFERENTIAL). 2. n. Quantity of which a given function is the differential coefficient. Hence or cogn. ~ITY (-ăl⁴) n., ~LY² adv. [f. LL *integralis* (as prec., see -AL)]

in'tĕgrant, a. (Of parts) component, making up a whole. [as foll., see -ANT]

in'tĕgrate¹, a. Made up of parts; whole, complete. [as foll., see -ATE²]

in'tĕgr|āte², v.t. Complete (imperfect thing) by addition of parts; combine (parts) into a whole; (Math.) find the integral of; indicate mean value or total sum of (area, temperature, etc.), whence

~**ātor** n. Hence or cogn. ~**A'TION** n., ~**ātive** a. [f. L *integrare* make whole (INTEGER), see -ATE³]

integ'rity, n. Wholeness; soundness; up-rightness, honesty. [ME, f. OF -*te*, or L *integritas* (INTEGER, see -TY)]

integ'ument, n. Skin, husk, rind, or other (usu. natural) covering. Hence ~**ARY**¹ (-ĕn²) a. [f. L *integumentum* f. IN¹(*legere* cover), see -MENT]

in'tellect, n. Faculty of knowing & reasoning; understanding; person, persons collectively, of good understanding. [ME, f. L *intellectus -ūs* (as INTELLIGENT)]

intellec't|ion, n. Action, process, of understanding, esp. as opp. to *imagina-tion*. So ~**IVE** a. [f. med. L *intellectio* (as INTELLIGENT, see -ION)]

intellec'tual, a. & n. **1.** Of, appealing to, requiring the exercise of, intellect. **2.** (Person) possessing a good understanding, enlightened person, esp. *the* ~*s* (*of a country etc.*). Hence or cogn. ~**ITY** (-ăl²), ~**IZA'TION,** nn., ~**IZE**(3) v.t. & i., ~**LY²** adv. [ME, f. L *intellectualis* (as INTELLECT, see -AL)]

intellec'tual|ism, n. Doctrine that know-ledge is wholly or mainly derived from pure reason. So ~**IST**(2) n. [-ISM]

intelli'gence, n. Intellect, understanding, whence **intelligen'TIAL** (-shal) a.; quick-ness of understanding, sagacity, (of person or animal; ~ *test*; ~ *quotient*, abbr. *I.Q.*, a number denoting the ratio of a given person's ~ to the normal or aver-age) rational being; information, news, (*I~ Department*, engaged in collecting information esp. for mil. purposes). [ME, f. OF, f. L *intelligentia* (as INTELLIGENT)]

intelli'gencer, n. Bringer of news, in-formant; secret agent, spy. [f. prec. + -ER¹]

intelli'gent, a. Having or showing (usu. a high degree of) understanding; clever, quick of mind. Hence ~**LY²** adv. [f. L *intelligere* understand (INTER- + *legere* gather, pick out, read), -ENT]

intelligent'sia, -zia, n. The part of a nation that aspires to independent think-ing. [Russ. *intelligentsiya*]

intelli'gible, a. That can be understood, comprehensible *to*; (Philos.) that can be apprehended only by the intellect, not by the senses. Hence ~**IBIL'ITY** n., ~**ibLY²** adv. [f. L *intelligibilis* (as prec., see -BLE)]

intem'per|ate, a. (Of person or conduct or speech) immoderate, unbridled, vio-lent; excessive in the indulgence of an appetite; addicted to drinking. Hence or cogn. ~**ANCE** n., ~**ateLY²** adv. [f. L IN²-(*temperatus,* as TEMPER v.)]

intend', v.t. Purpose, design, as *we* ~ *to go, we* ~ *no harm, we* ~ *that it shall be done today, was this* ~*ed* (done on purpose)?; design, destine, (person, thing) for a pur-pose, as *we* ~ *our son for the bar,* ~ *him to go,* ~ *it as a stopgap, this bun is* ~*ed for*

you (to eat), *this daub is* ~*ed for* (meant to represent) *me* ; mean, as *what exactly do you* ~ *by the word?*. [ME en-, in- f. OF *entendre* & IN¹(*tendere tent-* or *tens-* stretch, tend) strain, direct, purpose]

inten'dan|t, n. Superintendent, manager, of public business etc. (chiefly as foreign title). Hence ~**CY** n. [F, f. L as prec., -ANT]

inten'ded, n. (colloq.). Affianced lover, as *your his, her,* ~. [p.p. of INTEND as n.]

intend'ment, n. True meaning as fixed by law. [ME en- f. OF *entendement* mean-ing (as INTEND, see -MENT)]

intense', a. (-er, -est). (Of quality etc.) existing in a high degree, violent, ve-hement; having some quality in high degree; (of feeling or action) eager, ardent; feeling, apt to feel, ~ *emotion*. Hence ~**LY²** (-sl-) adv., ~**NESS** (-sn-), **intensifica'TION, inten'SITY,** nn., **inten'-sify** v.t. & i., (also, Photog.) increase the opacity of the deposit in a negative by chemical or other means. [ME, f. OF as INTENT²]

inten'sion (-shn), n. Intensity, high degree, of a quality; strenuous exertion of mind or will. [f. L *intensio* (INTEND, -ION)]

inten'sive, a. Of, relating to, intensity as opp. to extent; producing intensity; (Gram.) expressing intensity, giving force; concentrated, directed to a single point or area or subject, (~ *bombardment, study*); (Econ.) serving to increase pro-duction of given area, as ~ *methods, agriculture*; (Med.) ~ *inoculation* (in which intensity of matter introduced is increased in successive operations). Hence ~**LY²** (-vl-) adv. [F (-*if, -ive*), f. med. L as INTEND, see -IVE]

intent'¹, n. Intention, purpose, esp. *with* ~ *to* (defraud etc.), *with malicious, good,* etc., ~; (pl.) *to all* ~*s & purposes,* practi-cally, virtually. [ME & OF (1) *entent* f. L *intentus -ūs,* (2) *entente* f. Rom. **intenta* fem. p.p., both as INTEND]

intent'², a. Resolved, bent, (*on doing, on* object); sedulously occupied (*on*); (of faculties, looks, etc.) earnest, eager. Hence ~**LY²** adv., ~**NESS** n. [f. L as INTEND]

inten'tion, n. Intending; thing intended, purpose, whence (-)~**ED²** (-shond) a.; ultimate aim; (pl., colloq.) purposes in respect of proposal of marriage; (Med.) *second* ~, healing of wound by granula-tion, *first* ~, healing without this by immediate re-union of parts; (Logic) con-ception, as *first* ~*s,* primary conceptions of things (e.g. a tree, an oak), *second* ~*s,* secondary conceptions (e.g. difference, identity, species); (Theol.) *special, parti-cular,* ~, special object for which mass is celebrated etc. [ME, f. OF, f. L *inten-tionem* (as INTEND, see -ION)]

inten'tional (-shon-), a. Done on purpose. Hence ~**LY²** adv. [f. med. L *intentionalis* (as prec., see -AL)] inter'¹, v.t. (-rr-). Deposit (corpse etc.) in earth, tomb, etc.; bury. [ME en- f. OF *enterrer* f. Rom. *IN*(*terrare* f. *terra* earth)]

in'ter², prep. (L). Between, among, as ~ *āl'ia*, amongst other things; ~ *nōs, sē*, between ourselves, themselves; ~ *viv'ōs*, between the living (esp. of gift as opp. legacy).

inter-, pref. = prec. *Inter-* is used freely to form (1) vbs, nn., & aa., expr. mutual or reciprocal action or relation, or with sense 'among', 'between', as: ~*bed'*, embed (thing) between others; ~*cen'sal*, between two censuses; ~*collē'giate*, carried on etc. between colleges; ~*colum'nar*, placed, existing, between two columns; ~*columnia'tion*, placing of columns at intervals, such interval; ~*connect'*, connect by reciprocal links; ~*convert'ible*, interchangeable; ~*cross'*, t. & i., lay, lie, across each other, (cause to) propagate with each other; ~*flow*, n. & v.i., flow into each other; ~*grada'tion*, gradual approximation; ~*grade*, (v.i.) pass into another form by intervening grades, (n.) such grade; ~*growth'*, growing of things into each other; ~*jac'ulatory*, expressed in parenthetical ejaculations; ~*knit'*, intertwine; ~*lap'*, overlap; ~*link'*, link together (things, one *with* another); ~*ocean'ic*, between, connecting, two oceans; ~*plait'*, plait together; ~*plan'etary* a., between planets; ~*provin'cial*, situated, carried on, between provinces; ~*punc'tion*, punctuation; ~*punc'tuate*, punctuate; ~*ra'cial*, existing between different races; ~*shoot'*, shoot or glance (t. & i.) at intervals, variegate (thing *with* colours etc., esp. in p.p. ~*shot*); *in'terspace*, interval of space or time; ~*tan'gle*, tangle together, whence ~*tan'glement* n.; ~*tex'ture*, interweaving; ~*trib'al*, existing between different tribes; ~*twist'*, twist together; ~*vein'*, intersect (ás) with veins; ~*work'*, (trans.) interweave lit. & fig., (intr.) work upon each other; ~*wreathe'*, wreathe together. (2) Scientific, esp. anat., wds w. sense 'between', chiefly adjj., as: ~*artic'ular*, between contiguous surfaces of a joint; ~*cos'tal*, between the ribs (of body or ship), (n. pl.) ~costal parts; ~*di'gital*, between fingers or toes; ~*di'gitate*, interlock like fingers of clasped hands, so~*digita'tion* n.; ~*fa'cial*, included between two faces of crystal or other solid; ~*fem'oral*, between the thighs; ~*folia'ceous*, placed alternately between a pair of opposite leaves; ~*gla'cial*, between glacial periods; ~*lob'ular*, between lobes; *in'ternode*, (Bot.) part of stem between two of the knots from which leaves arise, (Anat.) slender part between two joints, esp. bone of finger or toe; ~*oss'eous* between bones; ~*pari'etal*, between right & left parietal bones of skull; ~*sep'tal*, between partitions; ~*spin'al*, ~*spin'ous*,

between spines or spinous processes; ~*stell'ar*, between stars; ~*stratifica'tion*, ~*strat'ified*, interspersion, interspersed, (*with* strata).

in'teract¹, n. Interval between two acts of play; interlude. [INTER-, after F ENTR'ACTE]

interact'² , v.t. Act reciprocally, act on each other. Hence interác'tion n., interāc'tive a. [INTER-]

interblend', v.t. & i. Mingle (things, one *with* another); (intr.) blend with each other. [INTER-]

interbreed', v.t. & i. Cross-breed; (intr., of animals of different race or species) breed with each other. [INTER-]

intérc'alary, a. (Of day or month) inserted in calendar to harmonize calendar with solar year, e.g. Feb. 29 in leap years; (of year) having such additions; interpolated, intervening. [f. L *intercalarius* (as foll., see -ARY¹)]

intérc'alāte, v.t. Insert (intercalary day etc., or abs.); interpose (anything out of ordinary course, esp. in p.p. of strata). So~A'TION n. [f. L INTER(*calare* proclaim), see -ATE³]

intercēde', v.i. Interpose on behalf of another, plead (*with* one person *for* another). [f. L INTER(*cedere cess-* go) intervene]

inter|cépt', v.t. Seize, catch, (person etc.) on the way from place to place; cut off (light etc. *from*); check, stop; (Math.) mark off (space) between two points etc. Hence or cogn. ~*cép'tion*, ~*cép'tor*, nn., ~*cép'tive* a. [f. L INTER(*cipere cept-* = *capere* take)]

inter|cé'ssion (-shn), n. Interceding, esp. by prayer. So~*céss'or* n., ~*céssor'ial*, ~*céss'ory*, aa. [f. L *intercessio* (as INTERCEDE, see -ION)]

in'terchänge¹ (-j), n. Reciprocal exchange (*of* things) between two persons etc.; alternation. [f. OF *entrechange* (as foll.)]

interchänge'² (-j), v.t. (Of two persons) exchange (things) with each other; put each of (two things) in the other's place; alternate. Hence or cogn. ~ABIL'ITY, ~ableness, nn., ~ABLE a., ~abLY² adv., (-jab-). [ME, f. OF *entrechangier* (*entre-* INTER- + *changier* CHANGE)]

intercolōn'ial, a. Existing, carried on, between different colonies. [INTER-]

in'tercŏm, n. System of intercommunication esp. in aircraft. [abbr.]

intercommūn'ic|āte, v.i. Have mutual intercourse; have free passage to each other. So~A'TION n. [INTER-]

intercommūn'ion (-yon), n. Intimate intercourse; mutual action or relation. [INTER-]

intercommūn'itÿ, n. Being common to various parties; having things in common. [INTER-]

For other words in *inter-* see INTER-.

in'tercourse (-ōrs), n. Social communication, dealings, between individuals; communion between man & God; communication for trade purposes etc. between different countries etc.; sexual connexion. [ME, f. OF *entrecours* f. *entrecorre* run between f. L INTER(*currere curs-* run)]

intercŭ'rr|ent, a. (Of time or event) intervening; (of disease) occurring during progress of another, (also) recurring at intervals. Hence ~ENCE n. [f. L as prec., -ENT]

interdè|pend', v.i. Depend on each other. So ~**pĕn'dence**, -ENCY, nn., ~**pĕn'dent** a., ~**pĕn'dent**LY[2] adv. [INTER-]

in'terdict[1], n. Authoritative prohibition; (Sc. Law)=INJUNCTION; (R.-C. Ch.) sentence debarring person or place from ecclesiastical functions etc. [ME & OF *entredit* f. L *interdictum* p.p. of INTER(*dicere dict-* say)]

interdict'[2], v.t. Prohibit (action); forbid use of; restrain (person *from* doing); forbid (thing *to* person). So **interdic'**TION n., **interdic'**TORY a. [ME, as prec.]

in'terest[1], n. 1. Legal concern, title, right, (*in* property); pecuniary stake (*in* commercial undertaking etc.); VESTED ~s. 2. Advantage, profit, *as it is (to) your ~ to go, I do it in your ~, in the ~* (or ~s) *of truth*. 3. Thing in which one is concerned; principle in which a party is concerned; party having a common ~, as *the brewing ~*. 4. Selfish pursuit of one's own welfare; *make ~*, bring personal ~ to bear (*with* person). 5. Concern, curiosity, or quality exciting them (*take an ~, no ~, in; this has no ~ for me*). 6. Money paid for use of money lent or for forbearance of debt (*with*~, transf., with increased force etc., as *returned the blow, his kindness, with ~*); *simple ~* (reckoned on principal only, & paid at fixed intervals); *compound ~* (reckoned on principal & on accumulations of ~). [ME *interesse*, f. AF, alt. app. after OF *interest* f. L INTER(*esse* be), & *interest*, 3rd sing. pres. = it matters]

in'terest[2], v.t. Cause (person) to take personal interest or share (*in*); (p.p.) having a private interest, not impartial or disinterested, as ~*ed parties, motives*; excite curiosity or attention of, whence ~ING[2] a. (|| *in an ~ing condition*, pregnant), ~ing**LY**[2] adv. Hence ~èd**LY**[2] adv. [alt. f. earlier *interess* vb after prec.]

inter|fere', v.t. (Of things) come into collision or opposition (*with*); (of person) meddle (*with* or abs.), whence ~**fer'**ING[2] a.; intervene, take part, (*in*); (Physics, of waves of light etc.) strike against each other; (of horse) knock one leg against another. Hence ~**fer'**ENCE n. [f. obs. Fr *s'entreférir* strike each other (*entre*-INTER-+*férir* f. L *ferire* strike)]

interferō̆m'eter, n. Instrument for measuring the length of light-waves by means of interference phenomena. [prec.+-METER]

interf'luent (-ōō-), a. Flowing into each other. [f. L INTER(*fluere* flow), see -ENT]

interfūse' (-z), v.t. & i. Intersperse, mix, (thing *with*); blend (things) together; (of two things) blend with each other. So **interfū'**SION (-zhn) n. [f. L INTER(*fundere fus-* pour)]

in'terim, adv., n., & a. 1. adv. (arch.). Meanwhile. 2. n. Intervening time; *the I*~ (Eccl.), truce pending a General Council between German Protestants & the Papacy in 16th c. 3. adj. Intervening; provisional, temporary; ~ *dividend* (paid between two annual etc. balances & not in pursuance of a published balance-sheet). [L (*inter*+adv. suf. -*im*)]

inter'ior, a. & n. 1. Situated within; inland, remote from coast or frontier; internal, domestic, opp. to *foreign*; existing in mind or soul, inward. 2. n. ~ part, inside; inland region; inside of building or room (also attrib., as ~ *decorator, decoration*), picture of this; inner nature, soul; (department dealing with) home affairs of a country, as *Minister of the I*~. Hence ~LY[2] adv. [L, compar. adj. f. INTER[2]]

interjā'cent, a. Lying between, intermediate. [f. L INTER(*jacēre* lie), see -ENT]

interject', v.t. Throw in, interpose, (remark etc.) abruptly; remark parenthetically. [f. L INTER(*jicēre ject-* = *jacēre* throw)]

interjec'tion, n. Ejaculation, exclamation; natural ejaculation viewed as part of speech (e.g: *ah!, whew!*). Hence or cogn. ~AL (-shon-), **interjec'**TORY, aa., ~al**LY**[2] adv. [ME, f. OF f. L *interjectionem* (prec., -ION)]

interlāce', v.t. & i. Bind together intricately, entangle; interweave (often fig.); mingle (two things, one *with* another); (intr.) cross each other intricately. Hence ~MENT (-sm-) n. [ME *entre*-, f. OF *entrelacier* (*entre*-INTER-+*lacier* LACE[2])]

interlārd', v.t. Mix (writing, speech, *with* foreign words etc.). [f. F *entrelarder* (*entre*-INTER-+*larder* LARD[2])]

in'terleaf, n. (pl. -*ves*). Extra leaf (usu. blank) between leaves of book. [INTER-]

interleave', v.t. Insert (usu. blank) leaves between leaves of (book), (also fig.). [f. as prec.]

interline', v.t. Insert words between lines of (document etc.); insert (words) thus. So **interlinēā'**TION n. [ME, f. med. L INTER(*lineare* f. *linea* LINE[3])]

interlin'ear, a. Written, printed, between the lines. [ME, f. med. L INTER(*linearis* LINEAR)]

interlŏck', v.i. & t. (Intr.) engage with each other by overlapping etc.; (trans., usu. pass.) lock, clasp, within each other; (Railways) connect (levers for signals etc.) by bolts etc. to ensure uniformity of movement. [INTER-]

interlŏc'ū|tor, n. One who takes part in dialogue or conversation; compère of negro minstrel troupe; *my* ~*tor*, the person in conversation with me. Hence or cogn. **interlocu′**TION, ~TRESS¹, ~TRIX, nn., ~TORY a., (also) pronounced during course of a legal action (*an* ~*tory decree*). [f. L INTER(*loqui locut*- talk), see -OR]

in′terlöper, n. Intruder, one who (esp. for profit) thrusts himself into others' affairs; (hist.) unauthorized trader. So **interlöpe′** v.i. [INTER- + *loper* f. *lope* dial. form of LEAP]

in′terlude (-lōōd), n. Pause between acts of play; what fills this up; (Mus.) instrumental piece played between verses of psalm or hymn etc.; intervening time or space of different character; event, amusing incident, etc., interposed; (hist.) dramatic or mimic representation between acts of mystery-plays or moralities. [f. med. L INTER(*ludium* f. *ludus* play)]

intermă′rriage (-rij), n. Marriage between members of different families, castes, tribes, etc., or (loosely) between near relations. [INTER-]

intermă′rry̆, v.i. (Of tribes, nations, families, etc.) become connected by marriage (*with* other tribes etc.). [INTER-]

intermĕd′dle, v.i. Concern oneself (*with, in*, esp. what is not one's business). [ME, f. AF *entremedler* (*entre*- INTER- + *medler* MEDDLE)]

intermĕd′iary̆, a. & n. 1. Acting between parties, mediatory; intermediate. 2. n. ~ person, thing, esp. mediator. [f. INTER-MEDIUM + -ARY¹, or f. F *intermédiaire*]

intermĕd′iate¹, a. & n. Coming *between* two things, as regards time, place, or order; (n.) ~ thing. Hence ~LY² (-tl-) adv. [f. med. L *intermediatus* (as INTER-MEDIUM, see -ATE²)]

intermĕd′ĭăte², v.i. Act between others, mediate, (*between*). Hence ~A′TION, ~ă-TOR, nn. [f. prec., after MEDIATE]

intermĕd′ium, n. (pl. -*ia*, -*iums*). Intermediate thing, medium, esp. one serving to transmit energy through space. [LL, neut. of L adj. INTER(*medius* middle)]

intĕrm′ent, n. Burial. [ME; INTER¹ + -MENT]

intermĕ′zzo (-dzō), n. (pl. -*zi*, -*zos*). Short light dramatic or other performance between acts of drama or opera, short movement connecting main divisions of large musical work. [It., pop. form of *intermedio* (as INTERMEDIATE¹)]

intermĭgră′tion, n. Reciprocal migration. [INTER-]

intĕrm′inab|le, a. Endless; tediously long. Hence ~leNESS n., ~LY² adv. [ME, f. LL IN²(*terminabilis* f. *terminare* TERMIN-ATE, see -BLE)]

intermingle (-mĭng′gl), v.t. & i. Mix together (two things, one *with* another); (intr.) mingle (*with*). [INTER-]

intermi′ssion (-shn), n. Pause, cessation, esp. *without* ~; (musical selection during)

interval in theatre etc. [f. F, or L *inter-missio* (as foll., see -ION)]

intermit′, v.t. & i. (-tt-). Suspend, discontinue; stop for a time (esp. of fever, pain, etc., or of pulse). Hence or cogn. ~t′ENCE n., ~t′ENT a., ~t′entLY² adv. [f. L INTER(*mittere miss*- send)]

intermix′, v.t. & i. Mix together. So ~TURE n. [first in p.p., see MIX]

intĕrn′¹, v.t. Oblige to reside within limits of country etc. Hence ~EE′ n., ~MENT n. (~*ment camp*, for prisoners of war & aliens). [f. F *interner* f. L *internus* internal (*in* + suf. -*ternus*)]

•in′tĕrn², n. Advanced student or recent graduate residing in hospital & acting as assistant physician or surgeon. [after F *interne*]

intĕrn′al, a. & n. 1. Of, situated in, the inside of a thing; of the inner nature of a thing, intrinsic; ~ *evidence*, derived from what is contained in the thing itself (cf. EXTERNAL); ~*combustion engine* (in which motive power is derived from explosion of mixture of gas, or vaporized oil or petrol, & air in the cylinder); of the domestic affairs of a country; •~ (inland) *revenue*; of the mind or soul, inward, subjective. 2. n. pl. Intrinsic qualities. Hence ~ITY (-ăl⁴) n., ~LY² adv. [f. late med. L *internalis* (as INTERN¹, see -AL)]

intĕrna′tional (-shon-), a. & n. 1. Existing, carried on, between different nations; of the I~ Working Men's Associations (for promoting joint political action of working classes in all countries). 2. n. One who takes part in ~ (usu. athletic) contests; ~ *contest*; *first, second, third*, I~, three Associations as above (1st, Marxist, 1862–73; 2nd, French socialist, 1889 —; 3rd, Russian communist, abbr. *Comintern*, 1919–43); member of any of these. Hence ~ITY (-shonăl⁴) n., ~LY² adv. [INTER-]

internationale′ (-shonahl), n. *The* ~, (orig. French) communist song sung at demonstrations; = *International Associa-tion* (see prec.). [F]

intĕrna′tional|ist (-shon-), n. One who advocates community of interests between nations, esp. supporter of Association named in prec., so ~ISM n.; one versed in international law. [-IST]

intĕrna′tionaliz|e (-shon-), -is|e (-īz), v.t. Make international, esp. bring (territory etc.) under combined protection etc. of different nations. Hence ~A′TION n. [-IZE]

interne′cine, a. Mutually destructive; (orig.) deadly, as ~ *war*. [f. L *internecinus* f. INTER(*necare* kill) destroy, see -INE¹]

internŭn′cial (-shal), a. (Of nerves) communicating between different parts of the system. [f. foll. + -AL]

internŭn′cio (-shĭō), n. Ambassador of Pope when or where no nuncio is employed; (hist.) minister representing (esp.

Austrian) government at Ottoman Porte. [f. It. *internunzio* f. L INTER(*nuntius* messenger)]

interŏs′cŭl|āte, v.i. Intermingle with each other; form connecting link. Hence ~A′TION n. [INTER-]

interpāge′, v.t. Print, insert, on intermediate pages. [INTER-]

intĕrp′ĕll|āte, v.t. (In foreign, esp. French, Chamber) interrupt order of day by demanding explanation from (Minister concerned). So ~A′TION, ~āt′OR, nn. [f. L INTER(*pellare* var. of *pellere* drive), see -ATE³]

interpĕn′ĕtr|āte, v.t. & i. Penetrate thoroughly, pervade; penetrate reciprocally; (intr., of two) penetrate each other. So ~A′TION n., ~ātĪVE a. [INTER-]

in′terplay, n. Reciprocal play; operation of two things on each other. [INTER-]

interplead′, v.i. Litigate with each other in order to settle a point in which a third party is concerned. [INTER-]

intĕrp′ol|āte, v.t. Make insertions in (book etc.), esp. so as to give false impressions as to date etc.; introduce (words) thus; (Math.) insert (intermediate term) in series. So ~A′TION, ~ātOR, nn. [f. L INTER(*polare* cogn. w. *polire* POLISH¹) furbish up, -ATE³]

interpŏs|e′ (-z), v.t. & i. Insert, make intervene, (*between*); put forth, introduce, (veto, objection, authority, etc.) by way of interference; intervene (*between* disputants etc.); say (quoted words) as an interruption; make an interruption. Hence ~AL (-z-) n. [f. F INTER(*poser*, see COMPOSE)]

intĕrposi′tion (-z-), n. Interposing; thing interposed; interference. [ME, f. OF, f. L *interpositionem* f. INTER(*ponere posit*-place)]

intĕrp′rĕt, v.t. & i. Expound the meaning of (abstruse words, writings, dreams, etc.); make out the meaning of; bring out the meaning of, render, by artistic representation or performance; explain, understand, in specified manner, as *this we ~ as a threat*; act as interpreter. Hence or cogn. ~ABLE, ~ATIVE (-ātĭv) aa., ~A′TION n. [ME, f. OF *interpreter* or L *interpretari* f. *interpres-pretis* explainer]

intĕrp′rĕt|er, n. One who interprets; one whose office it is to translate orally in their presence the words of persons speaking different languages. Hence ~ership, ~RESS¹, nn. [ME, f. OF *interpreteur* f. LL *interpretatorem* (as prec., see -OR)]

interrĕg′num, n. (pl. -*na*, -*nums*). Period during which State has no normal ruler, esp. between end of king's reign & accession of successor; interval, pause. [L INTER(*regnum* REIGN)]

interrĕlā′tion, n. Mutual relation. [INTER-]

interrĕlā′tionship (-shon-), n. Mutual relationship. [INTER-]

intĕr′rogāt|e, v.t. Ask questions of (person etc.), esp. closely or formally. So ~OR n. [f. L INTER(*rogare* ask), see -ATE³]

intĕrrogā′tion, n. Asking questions; question; *point, mark, note, of* (used to express) ~ (?), in Greek (;). [f. F, or L *interrogatio* (as prec., see -ATION)]

interrŏg′ative, a. & n. 1. Of, having the form or force of, a question; of inquiry, as *an ~ tone*; (Gram., of words) used in asking question, as ~ *pronouns* (*who?, which?*, etc.). 2. n. ~ word, esp. pronoun. Hence ~LY² (-vl-) adv. [f. LL *interrogativus* (as prec., see -IVE)]

interrŏg′atory, a. & n. 1. Of inquiry, as *an ~ tone*. 2. n. Question, set of questions, esp. (Law) one formally put to accused person etc. [f. LL *interrogatorius* (as prec., see -ORY)]

inter|rŭpt′, v.t. Break in upon (action, process, speech, person speaking, etc., or abs.); obstruct (view etc.); break the continuity of. Hence or cogn. ~rŭp′tĕdLY² adv., ~rŭp′tER¹, ~rŭp′tION, nn., ~rŭp′tory a. [ME, f. L INTER(*rumpers rupt*- break)]

intersĕct′, v.t. & i. Divide (thing) by passing or lying across it; (of lines etc.) cross, cut, each other. [f. L INTER-(*secare sect*- cut)]

intersĕc′tion, n. Intersecting; point, line, common to intersecting lines, planes; place where two roads intersect. Hence ~AL (-shon-) a. [f. L *intersectio* (as prec., see -ION)]

interspĕrse′, v.t. Scatter, place here & there (*between, among*); diversify (thing) *with* (others so scattered). So **interspĕr′sion** (-shn) n. [f. L INTER(*spergere spers*- = *spargere* scatter)]

•**in′terstate**, a. Existing, carried on, between States. [INTER-]

intĕrs′tice (*or* in′ter-), n. Intervening space; chink, crevice. [f. LL *interstitium* f. INTER(*sistere stit*- stand)]

intersti′tial (-shl), a. Of, forming, occupying, interstice(s). (as prec. + -AL]

intertwine′, v.t. & i. Entwine (things, one *with* another); become entwined. Hence ~MENT (-nm-) n. [INTER-]

in′terval, n. Intervening time or space; pause; break, gap, esp. in theatre etc.; *at ~s*, here & there, now & then; (Mus.) difference of pitch between two sounds, in melody or harmony; distance between persons or things in respect of qualities. Hence **intervăll′ic** a. [ME, f. OF -*valle* & L INTER(*vallum* rampart) space between ramparts, interval]

intervĕn|e′, v.i. Come in as something extraneous; occur in the meantime; (of person or thing) come between, interfere, so as to prevent or modify result etc. (*between* persons, *in* affair); (Law) interpose in lawsuit to which one was not an original party (‖ esp. of Queen's Proctor in divorce cases), whence ~′ER¹ n.; lie, be situated, *between*. So ~′IENT a., **intervĕn′tion** n. [f. L INTER(*venire vent*- come)]

In'terview (-vū); n., & v.t. **1.** Meeting of persons face to face, esp. for purpose of conference; oral examination of candidate; meeting between person employed by newspaper & someone from whom he seeks to get statements for publication. **2.** v.t. Have an ~ with (person), esp. with a view to publication of his statements. Hence ~ER¹ (-vŭer) n. [(vb f. n.) f. F *entrevue* f. *s'entrevoir* (*entre*- INTER- + *voir* f. L *vidēre* see)]

Intervŏlve', v.t. Wind, roll up, (things) within each other. [f. INTER- + L *volvere* roll]

Interweave', v.t. Weave together, interlace, (things, one *with* another); blend (things) intimately. [INTER-]

Interwind', v.t. & i. Wind together. [INTER-]

Intĕs'tate, a. & n. **1.** (Of person) not having made a will, as *he died* ~. **2.** n. ~ person. Hence **intĕs'tacy** n. [f. L IN²(*testatus* p.p. of *testari* make will f. *testis* witness)]

Intĕs'tin|e¹, n. (Usu. pl.) lower part of alimentary canal from pyloric end of stomach to anus; *small*, *large*, ~*e*, parts of this. So ~AL (or -in²) a. [f. L neut. adj. as foll.]

Intĕs'tine², a. (Of wars etc.) internal, domestic, civil; ~ *motion* (entirely within a body). [f. L *intestinus* internal (*intus* within)]

In'timate¹, a. & n. **1.** Close in acquaintance, familiar, as ~ *friend*(*ship*); ~ (close) *connexion*; ~ *knowledge* (resulting from familiarity); essential, intrinsic; (of diary) recording emotions etc. **2.** n. ~ friend. Hence **in'timacy** n., (also, euphem.) illicit sexual relations, ~LY² (-ti-l) adv. [foll., -ATE²]

In'tim|āte², v.t. Make known, state, announce, (fact, wish, *that*); imply, hint. So ~A'TION n. [f. LL *intimare* (*intimus* inmost), -ATE³]

Intim'idāte, v.t. Inspire with fear, cow, esp. in order to influence conduct. Hence ~A'TION, ~ātOR, nn. [f. med. L IN¹(*timidare* f. *timidus* TIMID), see -ATE³]

Intim'itÿ, n. Inwardness; privacy. [f. F *intimité* (as INTIMATE¹, -ITY)]

Intinc'tion, n. Dipping of the Eucharistic bread in the wine, to enable the communicant to receive both kinds. [f. LL *intinctio* f. IN¹(*tingere tinct*- TINGE)]

Intit'ūle, v.t. Entitle (Act of Parliament, usu. p.p.). [f. OF *intituler* f. LL IN¹(*titulare* f. *titulus* TITLE)]

In'to (-tōō), prep. **1.** Expr. motion or direction to a point within a thing, lit. & fig., as *come* ~ *the garden*, *throw it* ~ *the fire*, *look* ~ *the box*, *the matter*, *inquire* ~ *it*, *get* ~ *trouble*, *'come* ~ (acquire) *properly*, *watching far on* ~ *the night*. **2.** Expr. change, condition, result, as *turn stones* ~ *gold*, *collect them* ~ *heaps*, *divide them* ~

three classes, *flogged* ~ *submission*. [OE; IN + TO]

In'toed (-ōd), a. Having the toes turned inwards. [IN adv. + TOE + -ED²]

Intŏl'erab|le, a. That cannot be endured. Hence ~leNESS n., ~LY² adv. [ME, f. L IN²(*tolerabilis* TOLERABLE)]

Intŏl'er|ant, a. Not tolerant (*of*, esp. religious opinions differing from one's own). Hence or cogn. ~ANCE n., ~antLY² adv. [f. L IN²(*tolerans* TOLERANT)]

In'tonāte, v.t. = INTONE. [-ATE³]

intonā'tion, n. Reciting in singing voice; (Church Mus.) opening phrase of plainsong melody; utterance, production, of musical tones; modulation of voice, accent. [as foll., see -ATION]

intōne', v.t. Recite (psalm, prayer, etc., or abs.) in singing voice; utter with particular tone. [f. OF *entoner* & med. L IN¹(*tonare* f. *tonus* TONE)]

Intŏx'icant, a. & n. Intoxicating (liquor). [as foll., see -ANT]

Intŏx'ic|āte, v.t. Make drunk; excite, exhilarate, beyond self-control (~*ated with*, *by*). Hence ~ātING² a., ~A'TION n. [f. med. L IN¹(*toxicare* poison f. L f. Gk *toxikon*), see -ATE³]

Intra- in comb. = L *intra* on the inside, within, as: ~*crān'ial*, within the skull; ~*mūr'al*, existing, done, within walls; ~*na'tional*, (not inter)national; ~*vēn'ous*, in(to) a vein or veins.

Intrac't|able, a. Not docile, refractory; (of things) not easily dealt with. Hence ~ABIL'ITY, ~ableNESS, nn., ~abLY² adv. [f. F, or L IN²(*tractabilis* TRACTABLE)]

Intrad'ŏs, n. (archit.). Lower or interior curve of arch (cf. EXTRADOS). [F (INTRA- + *dos* back)]

Intrăn'sig|ent (-z-), a. & n. **1.** Uncompromising in politics. **2.** n. An irreconcilable (in politics). So ~ENCE n. [f. F *intransigeant* f. Sp. *los intransigentes* extreme republicans f. IN-² + L TRANS-(*igere = agere* act) come to an understanding, see -ENT]

Intran'sitive (-ahns-), a. & n. (Verb) that does not take a direct object (cf. TRANSITIVE). Hence ~LY² adv. [f. LL IN²(*transitivus* TRANSITIVE)]

In'trant, n. One who enters a college, association, etc. [f. L *intrare* enter, see -ANT]

Intrĕp'id, a. Fearless, brave. Hence **intrĕpid'ity** n., ~LY² adv. [f. L IN²(*trepidus* alarmed)]

In'tric|ate, a. Perplexingly entangled; involved; obscure. Hence ~ACY n., ~āteLY² adv. [f. L IN¹(*tricare* f. *tricae* tricks), see -ATE³]

In'trig(u)ant (-gant; *or* ăntrēgahň'), n. (fem., ~*e*, pr. ăntrēgahňt'). Intriguer. [F (-*guant*), part. as foll.]

Intrigue'¹ (-ēg), v.i. & t. Carry on underhand plot; employ secret influence (*with*);

have a liaison (*with*); (as gallicism, v.t.) rouse the interest or curiosity of. [f. F *intriguer* f. It. *intrigare* (as INTRICATE)]

intrigue'² (-ēg), n. Underhand plotting or plot; secret amour, liaison. [F, f. It. *intrigo* f. *intrigare* (as INTRICATE)]

intrin's|ic, a. Belonging naturally, inherent, essential, esp. ~*ic value* (cf. EXTRINSIC). Hence ~ICALLY adv. [f. F *intrinsèque* f. LL *intrinsecus* (adj. f. L adv.); cf. EXTRINSIC]

intro- in comb. = L *intro* to the inside, as: ~*fle'xion*, inward bending; ~*gre'ssion*, going or coming in; ~*suscep'tion*, (Physiol., Biol.) = INTUSSUSCEPTION.

introduce', v.t. Bring in; place in, insert, bring into use (custom, idea, improvement, etc., *into* place, system, etc.); usher in, bring forward, (matter etc.); (of conjunctions etc.) open (sentence); make known, esp. in formal manner (person *to* another); bring (young lady) out, into society; draw attention of (person *to* subject etc.); bring (bill etc.) before Parliament. So **introduc'tory** a. [f. L INTRO(*ducere duct-* lead)]

introduc'tion, n. Introducing; preliminary matter prefixed to book (usu. longer & less personal than a PREFACE, which it freq. follows); (as title) introductory treatise; formal presentation of one person to another; *letter of* ~ (given by one person to another & introducing him to a third). [ME, f. OF, or L *introductio* (as prec., see -ION)]

intro'it, n. (eccl.). Psalm, antiphon, sung while priest approaches altar to celebrate Mass or Holy Communion. [ME, f. OF or f. L *introitus -ūs* f. INTRO(*ire it-* go)]

intromit', v.t. (arch.; -tt-). Let in, admit, (*into*); insert. So **intromi'ssion** (-shn) n., esp., in Sc. Law, intermeddling with the effects of another, ~t'ENT a. [f. L INTRO(*mittere miss-* send)]

intro|spect', v.t. Examine one's own thoughts & feelings. Hence ~spec'TION n., examination or observation of one's own mental processes, ~spec'tionist, ~spec'tiveness, nn., ~-spec'tive a., ~spec'tively² adv. [f. L INTRO(*spicere spect-* look)]

intro|vert', v.t. Turn (mind, thought) inwards upon itself; (esp. Zool.) withdraw (organ etc.) within its own tube or base, as finger of glove, whence ~vers'ible a. Hence ~ver'sion (-shn) n., in'trovert n., person given to ~version (opp. EXTROVERT), ~vers'ive, ~vert'ive, aa. [17th c., f. INTRO- +L *vertere vers-* turn]

intrude' (-rōōd), v.t. & i. Thrust, force, (thing *into*); force (thing *upon* person); come uninvited, thrust oneself in, (*into* place, company, etc., *upon* person, his privacy, etc.). Hence ~ER¹ (-ōō-) n. (also, raiding aircraft). [f. L IN¹(*trudere trus-* thrust)]

intru'sion (-rōōzhn), n. Intruding; forcing in; forcing oneself in (*into*, *upon*);

(Geol.) influx of rock in state of fusion between strata etc.; settlement of minister of Church of Scotland without consent of congregation (hist.), whence ~IST(2) n. So intrus'IVE a., intrus'IVELY² adv., intrus'IVENESS n., (-rōōs-). [ME, f. OF or f. med. L *intrusio* (as prec., see -ION)]

intub'|ate, v.t. (med.). Insert tube into (larynx etc.) to keep it open. Hence ~A'TION n. [f. IN-¹ +L *tuba* tube +-ATE³]

intu'it, v.t. & i. Know by intuition; receive knowledge by direct perception. [f. L IN¹(*tuēri tuit-* look)]

intui'tion, n. Immediate apprehension by the mind without reasoning; immediate apprehension by sense; immediate insight. Hence ~AL (-shon-) a. [f. F, or LL *intuitio* (as prec., see -ION)]

intui'tional|ism (-shon-), n. Doctrine that the perception of truth is by intuition. So ~IST n. [-ISM]

intui'tion|ism (-shon-), n. Doctrine that in perception external objects are known immediately by intuition; = prec. So ~IST n. [-ISM]

intu'itive, a. Of, possessing, perceived by, intuition. Hence ~LY² (-vl-) adv., ~NESS (-vn-) n. [f. med. L *intuitivus* (INTUIT, -IVE)]

intu'itiv|ism, n. Doctrine that ethical principles are matters of intuition. So ~IST n. [-ISM]

intumes'c|ent, a. Swelling up. So ~ENCE n. [f. L IN¹(*tumescere* incept. of *tumēre* swell), see -ENT]

intussuscep'tion, n. (Physiol.) taking in of foreign matter by living organism, & its conversion into organic tissue; taking in (*of* ideas etc.); withdrawal of one portion of intestine within another. [f. F, or L *intus* within +*susceptio* f. SUS(*cipere = capere* take) take up, see -ION]

inunc'tion, n. Smearing, rubbing, with oil. [ME, f. OF *en-* or L IN¹(*unctio* UNCTION)]

in'und|ate, v.t. Overflow, flood, (land etc. *with* water, also fig.). So ~A'TION n. [f. L IN¹(*undare* flow f. *unda* wave), see -ATE³]

inurbane', a. Not urbane, discourteous. Hence inurbān'ITY n. [f. L IN¹(*urbanus* URBANE)]

inure', -en-, v.t. & i. Accustom, habituate, (person etc. *to* thing, *to* do), whence ~MENT (-ūrm-) n.; (intr., chiefly Law; often *en-*) come into operation, take effect. [IN-¹ +obs. *ure* work (cf. MANURE) f. OF *uevre* f. L *opera*]

inurn', v.t. Put (ashes of cremated body) in an urn. [IN-¹]

inut'ile, a. Useless. So inutil'ITY n. [F, f. L IN²(*utilis* useful)]

invad|e', v.t. Make hostile inroad into (country etc.); swarm into; (fig. of sounds, diseases, feelings, etc.) assail; encroach upon (rights etc.). Hence ~ER¹ n. [f. L IN¹(*vadere vas-* go)]

invag'in|ate, v.t. Put in a sheath; introvert (tubular sheath). Hence ~A'TION n. [f. IN-¹ +L *vagina* sheath +-ATE³]

ĭn'valid[1] (-ēd), a. & n. (Person) enfeebled or disabled by illness or injury. Hence ~HOOD, ~ISM(3), nn., (-ēd-). [f. L IN[2](*validus* VALID), pronunc. after F *invalide*]

ĭnvalid'[2] (-ēd; *also* ĭn[2]), v.t. & i. Lay up, disable, (person) by illness (usu. pass.); treat as an invalid; remove from active service, send *home* etc., as an invalid; (intr.) become an invalid, go on the sick-list. [f. prec.]

ĭnvăl'id[3], a. Not valid, esp. having no legal force. Hence ~LY[2] adv. [as IN-VALID[1]]

ĭnvăl'id|āte, v.t. Make (esp. argument etc.) INVALID[3]. Hence ~A'TION n. [prec. + -ATE[3]]

ĭnvalid'itỹ, n. Want of validity; bodily infirmity. [INVALID[3,1] + -ITY]

ĭnvăl'ūable, a. Above price, priceless. [IN-[2]]

ĭn'văr, n. An iron-nickel alloy with negligible coefficient of expansion, used in manufacture of clocks and scientific instruments. [abbr. of foll.; P]

ĭnvăr'i|able, a. Unchangeable; always the same; (Math.) constant, fixed. Hence ~ABIL'ITY, ~ableNESS, nn., ~abLY[2] adv. [f. F, or LL IN[2] (*variabilis* VARIABLE)]

ĭnvā'sion (-zhn), n. Invading; encroachment. So **ĭnvās'IVE** a. [f. F, or LL *invasio* (as INVADE, see -ION)]

ĭnvĕc'tive, n. Violent attack in words; abusive oratory. [ME, f. OF, & LL *invectivus* adj., *-iva* n. (as foll., see -IVE)]

ĭnveigh' (-vā), v.i. Speak violently, rail loudly, *against*. [f. L IN[1](*vehi* pass. of *vehere vect-* carry) go into, assail]

ĭnvei'gle (-vē-, -vā-), v.t. Entice, seduce, (*into* place, conduct, etc., *into* do*ing*). Hence ~MENT.(-vĕgelm-, -vā-) n. [c. 1500 *en-*, *in-* f. F *aveugler* f. *aveugle* blind]

ĭnvĕn'ĭt, ĭnvēnē̆r'unt (abbr. *inv.*), v. sing. & pl. 3rd pers. (So-&-so) designed this work (used with artist's signature). [L, perf. of *invenio*, see foll.]

ĭnvĕnt', v.t. Devise, originate, (new method, instrument, etc.); fabricate (false story etc.). Hence or cogn. **ĭnvĕn'tIVE** a., **ĭnvĕn'tIVELY**[2] adv., **ĭnvĕn'tIVENESS**, **ĭnvĕn'tOR**(esp. in Law, patentee of INVENTION), **ĭnvĕn'tRESS**[1], nn. [f. L IN[1](*venire vent-* come) find, contrive]

ĭnvĕn'tion, n. Inventing; thing invented, contrivance, (Law) any new manufacture the subject of letters patent; fictitious story; inventiveness; *I~ of the Cross*, (festival, May 3, commemorating) finding of the Cross by Helena mother of Constantine, A.D. 326. [ME, f. OF, f. L *inventionem* (as prec., see -ION)]

ĭn'ventorỹ, n., & v.t. **1**. Detailed list (of goods, furniture, etc.); stock of goods in this; *trader's stock. **2**. v.t. Enter goods etc.) in ~, make ~ of. [f. med. L *inventorium* f. LL *-arium* (whence obs. *-ary*); as INVENT, see -ORY]

ĭnverā'cĭtỹ, n. Untruthfulness. [IN-[2]]

Invernĕss' (I-), n. Town in Scotland; ~

cloak, coat, or *i~* as n., man's sleeveless cloak with removable cape.

ĭnverse' (*or* ĭn[2]), a. & n. **1**. Inverted in position, order, or relations; ~ *ratio*, *proportion* (between two quantities one of which increases in proportion as the other decreases). **2**. n. Inverted state, thing that is the direct opposite (*of* another). Hence **ĭnverse'LY**[2] (-sl-) adv. [f. L as INVERT]

ĭnver'sion (-shn), n. Turning upside down; reversal of normal position, order, or relation, esp. (Gram.) of order of words; reversal of a ratio; (Mus.) process or result of inverting (see foll.). So **ĭnvers'IVE** a. [f. L *inversio* (as foll., see -ION)]

ĭnvert'[1], v.t. Turn upside down (~*ed commas*, those above the line before & after quotations, the first single or double comma being ~*ed*, as *what is a ' German peace '* or *" German peace "?*); reverse position, order, or relation, of; (Mus.) change relative position of notes of (chord, interval) by placing lowest note higher. [f. L IN[1](*vertere vers-* turn)]

ĭn'vert[2], n. Inverted arch, as at bottom of sewer; (Psych.) person whose sex instincts are inverted; ~ *sugar*, mixture of dextrose & laevulose. [f. prec.]

ĭnvert'ebrate, a. & n. **1**. Not having backbone or spinal column; (fig.) wanting in firmness. **2**. n.~ animal or (fig.) person. [f. IN-[2]+L *vertebra* joint of spine+-ATE[2]]

ĭnvĕst', v.t. & i. **1**. Clothe (person etc. *in*, *with*); cover as garment; clothe, endue, (person etc. *with* qualities, insignia of office, rank, etc.). **2**. Lay siege to. **3**. Employ (money *in* stocks etc.); (intr.) ~ *in*, put money into (stocks), lay out money on, as ~ *in a car*. Hence **ĭnvĕs'tOR** n. [f. F *investir* or L IN[1](*vestire* clothe); sense 3 f. It. *investire*]

ĭnvĕs'tig|āte, v.t. Examine, inquire into. Hence or cogn. ~A'TION, ~ātOR, nn., ~ātIVE, ~ātORY, aa. [f. L IN[1](*vestigare* track), see -ATE[3]]

ĭnvĕs'titure, n. Formal investing of person (*with* office); enduing (*with* attributes). [f. med. L *investitura* (as INVEST, see -URE)]

ĭnvĕst'ment, n. Investing of money; money invested; property in which money is invested; investiture; clothing; (Mil.) act of besieging, blockade. [-MENT]

ĭnvĕt'er|ate, a. Long-established; (of disease, habit, prejudice, etc.) deep-rooted, obstinate. Hence ~ACY n., ~ateLY[2] (-tl-) adv. [f. L IN[1](*veterare* make old f. *vetus -eris* old), see -ATE[2]]

ĭnvid'ious, a. (Of conduct etc.) giving offence, esp. by real or seeming injustice etc.; (of thing) likely to excite ill feeling against the possessor. Hence ~LY[2] adv., ~NESS n. [f. L *invidiosus* (*invidia* ENVY, see -OUS)]

ĭnvi'gil|āte, v.i. || Watch over students at examination. Hence ~A'TION, ~ātOR, nn. [f. L IN[1](*vigilare* watch), -ATE[3]]

ĭnvig'or|āte, v.t. Make vigorous; animate. Hence ~**ātɪᴠᴇ** a., ~**āᴛoʀ** n. [f. ɪɴ-¹+L *vigor* ᴠɪɢouʀ+-ᴀᴛᴇ³]

invin'c|ible, a. Unconquerable (lit. & fig.). Hence ~**ɪʙɪʟ'ɪᴛʏ** n., ~**ɪʙʟʏ²** adv. [ME, f. OF, f. L ɪɴ²(*vincibilis* f. *vincere* conquer, -ʙʟᴇ)]

invi'ol|able, a. Not to be violated; (of laws, persons, places, etc.) to be kept sacred from infraction, profanation, etc. Hence ~**ᴀʙɪʟ'ɪᴛʏ** n., ~**ᴀʙʟʏ²** adv. [f. F, or L ɪɴ²(*violabilis*, as foll., see -ʙʟᴇ)]

invi'olate, a. (Of laws, places, etc.) not violated; unbroken; unprofaned. Hence **invi'ol**ᴀᴄʏ, ~ɴᴇss, nn., ~ʟʏ² adv. [ME, f. L ɪɴ²(*violatus* p.p. as ᴠɪoʟᴀᴛᴇ)]

invis'ib|le (-z-), a. & n. That cannot be seen; not to be seen at particular time, as *when I called she was* ~*le*; too small to be seen; ~*le exports*, shipping services, insurance, & similar items that account for the apparent excess of a. country's imports over exports; ~*le ink* (visible only after heating etc.); (n.) *the* ~*le*, the unseen world, God. Hence or cogn. **invisɪʙɪʟ'ɪᴛʏ**, ~**ʟᴇɴᴇss**, nn., ~**ʟʏ²** adv., (-z-). [ME, f. OF, f. L ɪɴ²(*visibilis* ᴠɪsɪʙʟᴇ)]

invit|e', v.t., & n. 1. Request courteously to come (*to* dinner, *to* one's house, *in*, etc.); request courteously (*to* do what is presumably agreeable); solicit courteously (suggestions, opinion, confidences); bring on, tend to bring on, (thing) unintentionally; (of thing) present inducements, attract, whence ~'**ɪɴɢʟʏ²** adv., ~'**ɪɴɢɴᴇss** n. 2. n. (colloq. or vulg.). Invitation. So **invita'ᴛɪoɴ** n., ~'**ᴀᴛoʀʏ** a. [f. F *inviter* or L *invitare*]

invocā'tion, n. Invoking, calling upon God etc. in prayer; *the* ~, (esp.) the words ' In the name of the Father ' etc. as used by preacher before sermon (cf. ᴀsᴄʀɪᴘ-ᴛɪoɴ); appeal to Muse for inspiration or assistance in poem. So **invŏc'atoʀʏ** (or **in'vokā-**) a. [ME, f. OF, f. L *invocationem* (as ɪɴᴠoᴋᴇ, see -ᴀᴛɪoɴ)]

in'voice, n., & v.t. 1. List of goods shipped or sent, with prices & charges. 2. v.t. Make an ~ of (goods). [app. orig. *invoyes* pl. of *invoy* as ᴇɴᴠoʏ¹; -ce as in ᴛʀuᴄᴇ]

invōke', v.t. Call on (God etc.) in prayer or as witness; appeal to (person's authority etc.); summon (spirit) by charms; ask earnestly for (vengeance, help, etc.). [f. F *invoquer* f. L ɪɴ¹(*vocare* call)]

in'volucre (-lŏŏker), n. Covering, envelope, (esp. Anat.); (Bot.) whorl of bracts surrounding inflorescence. [f. F, or L *involucrum* (as ɪɴᴠoʟᴠᴇ)]

invŏl'untar|y, a. Done without exercise of the will, unintentional. Hence ~**ɪʟʏ²** adv., ~**ɪɴᴇss** n. [f. LL ɪɴ²(*voluntarius* ᴠoʟuɴᴛᴀʀʏ)]

in'volute (-lŏŏt), a. & n. 1. Involved, intricate; curled spirally; (Bot.) rolled inwards at edges. 2. n. (geom.). Locus of point in a straight line that rolls without sliding on a curve in the plane of that curve (cf. ᴇᴠoʟuᴛᴇ). [as ɪɴᴠoʟᴠᴇ]

involu'tion (-lŏŏ-), n. Involving; entanglement; intricacy; curling inwards; part so curled; (Math.) raising of quantity to any power. [f. L *involutio* (as foll., see -ɪoɴ)]

involve', v.t. Wrap (thing *in* another); wind spirally; entangle (person, thing, *in* difficulties, mystery, etc.); implicate (person *in* charge, crime); include (*in*); imply, entail; (p.p.) complicated in thought or form (*an* ~*d sentence*). [ME, f. L ɪɴ¹(*volvere volut-* roll)]

involve'ment (-vm-), n. Involving; financial embarrassment; complicated affair. [-ᴍᴇɴᴛ]

invŭl'ner|able, a. That cannot be wounded or hurt (esp. fig.). Hence ~**ᴀʙɪʟ'ɪᴛʏ** n., ~**ᴀʙʟʏ²** adv. [f. L ɪɴ²(*vulnerabilis* ᴠuʟɴᴇʀᴀʙʟᴇ)]

in'ward, a. & n. 1. Situated within; mental, spiritual; directed towards the inside. 2. n. pl. Entrails (freq. colloq. *innards*). [OE *innanweard* (*innan* in adv., see -ᴡᴀʀᴅ)]

in'wardly, adv. On the inside; (of speaking) not aloud; in mind or spirit. [-ʟʏ²]

in'wardnèss, n. Inner nature, essence; quality of being inward; spirituality. [-ɴᴇss]

in'ward(s) (-z), adv. (Of motion or position) towards the inside; within mind or soul. [prec.]

inweave', èn-, v.t. Weave in (thing *with* another, lit. & fig.). [ɪɴ-¹]

inwrought (ɪnrawt', *before noun* ɪnⁿ), a. (Of fabric) decorated (*with* pattern); (of pattern) wrought (*in*, *on*, fabric); (fig.) intimately blended (*with*). [ɪɴ+*wrought* p.p. of ᴡoʀᴋ]

inya'la (-ah-), n. S. Afr. antelope. [native]

i'od|ine (-ēn), n. Non-metallic element resembling chlorine & bromine in chemical properties, used in medicine & photography. Hence **iŏd'ɪᴄ** a., ~**ɪᴅᴇ** n., compound of ~*ine* with another element or radical, ~**ɪsᴍ(5)** n., ~**ɪᴢᴇ(5)** v.t. [f. F *iode* f. Gk *iōdēs* violet-like (*ion* violet, see -oɪᴅ), from colour of its vapour, +-ɪɴᴇ⁵]

iō'dofórm (or ī'o-), n. Compound of iodine chemically analogous to chloroform, a pale yellow solid with antiseptic properties. [f. prec.+-o-, after ᴄʜʟoʀo-ᴏʀᴍ]

i'olite, n. Silicate of aluminium, iron, & magnesium, of blue or violet colour. [f. Gk *ion* violet, see -ʟɪᴛᴇ]

i'on, n. One of the electrically charged particles into which the atoms or molecules of certain chemicals (esp. salts, acids, & bases) are dissociated by solution in water, and which make such a solution a conductor of electricity; a similarly charged molecule of gas occurring e.g. in air. Hence ~ɪᴢᴇ v.t., convert into ~, ~ɪᴢᴀ'ᴛɪoɴ n. [Gk *ion* neut. part. of *eimi* go]

-ion, suf., mainly thr. F -*ion* (also direct) f. L -*ionem* (nom. -*io*) forming nouns of condition or action, rarely f. adjj. & nn. (*communio*), occas. f. vb stems (*legio*), but chiefly f. p.p. stems in *t, s, x*, producing the compd suff. -TION, -SION (-*xion*), -ITION, -ATION.

Iōn′ian (Ī-), a. & n. 1. Of Ionia; (Mus.) ~ *mode*: ancient Greek MODE; eleventh of eccl. modes, with C as final & G as dominant, corresp. to modern major key of C. 2. n. Member of part of the Hellenic race which occupied Attica, western Asia Minor, ~ Islands, etc. [f. L f. Gk *Iōnios* + -AN]

Iŏn′ic (Ī-), a. Of Ionia, as ~ *dialect*, that of which Attic was a development; ~ ORDER (characterized by two lateral volutes of the capital); (Pros.) *i*~ *ā̆ majŏr′ĕ*, metrical foot --‿‿, *i*~ *ā̆ minŏr′ĕ*, ‿‿--. [f. L f. Gk *Iōnikos*]

iŏn′ium, n. Radio-active element obtained from uranium. [f. ION + -IUM]

iŏn′osphēre, n. = HEAVISIDE LAYER. [f. ION, -O-, SPHERE]

-**ior**[1], suf., later spelling of -IOUR, as in *warrior*.

-**ior**[2], suf. = L -*ior* of comparatives, as in *senior, ulterior*. See also -OR.

iōt′a, n. Greek letter (*I, ι,* = I); atom, jot, (after *Matt.* v. 18). [Gk *iōta*]

iōt′acism, n. Excessive use of iota; pronunciation of other Greek vowels like iota (ē), cf. ITACISM. [f. LL f. Gk *iōtakismos*]

I O U (ī ō ū′), n. Signed document bearing these letters followed by specified sum, constituting formal acknowledgement of debt. [= I owe you]

-**iour**, suf. = -*i*- representing some formative or stem element + -*our* -OR, as *saviour*, ME & AF *sauveor* f. LL *salvatorem*.

-**ious**, suf. repr. L -*iosus*, F -*ieux*, = -*i*- (part of another suf.) + -OUS, w. sense ' characterized by, full of '. L has -*iosus* (1) in adjj. f. derivative nn. in -*ia*, -*ies*, -*ius*, -*ium*, (*invidiosus, perniciosus, odiosus*, & by false anal. *curiosus* f. *cura*), (2) in adjj. f. nn. in -*ion*- (nom. -*io*), as *ambitiosus, captiosus, religiosus*. E tends to use -*ious* for any noun in -*ion* (*rebellious, cautious, contradictious*). E also forms adjj. in -*ious* by adding -OUS to stem of L adjj. in -*ius* (*various*); see also -ITIOUS & -OUS.

ĭpĕcăcŭăn′ha (-na), n. Root of a S.-Amer. shrub, used as emetic & purgative. [Port., f. native *ipekaaguene*]

ĭp′sĕ dīx′ĭt, n. Dogmatic statement resting on bare authority. [L, = he himself (the master) said it]

ĭpsĭss′ĭma vēr′b′a, n. pl. The precise words [L]

ĭp′sŏ făc′tō, adv. By that very fact. [L]

ir-[1,2] (Ĭ-r), preff. = IN-[1,2] before *r*.

ira′dè (-ah-), n. (hist.) Written decree of Sultan of Turkey. [Turk., f. Arab. *iradah* will]

Irak′, Iraq′ (īrahk′). n. Arab kingdom including Mesopotamia, formerly ad-

ministered by British Empire as mandatary. So **Ira′ki, -qi,** (-ahkī) a.

Irăn′ian (ī-), a. & n. 1. Persian ; (of languages) of the Asiatic family comprising Zend, Old Persian, & their modern descendants. 2. n. Member of ~ race. [Pers. *iran* Persia, -IAN]

irăs′cible (*or* ī-), a. Irritable, hot-tempered. Hence ~IBIL′ITY n. [f. F, or LL *irascibilis* (*irasci* grow angry, see -BLE)]

irāte′, a. Angry. [f. L *iratus* p.p. as prec.]

īre, n. (poet.). Anger. Hence ~′FUL a., ~′fulLY[2] adv., (Ĭr-). [ME, f. OF, f L *ira*]

irĕn′ic(al), aa. Aiming or aimed at peace. [f. Gk *eirēnikos* (*eirēnē* peace) + -AL]

irenicon. See EIRENICON.

iridā′ceous (-shus), a. Of the iris kind. [-ACEOUS]

irĭdes′c|ent, a. Showing colours like those of rainbow; changing colour with position. Hence ~ENCE n. [as IRIS + -ESCENT]

irĭd′ium, n. White metallic element of the platinum group. [as IRIS + -IUM]

irĭdŏs′mine (*or* īr-), n. Native alloy or mixture of osmium & iridium, used in pointing gold pens. [IRID(IUM) + OSM-(IUM) + -INE[2]]

īr′is, n. 1. Flat circular coloured membrane behind cornea of eye, with circular opening (PUPIL) in centre. 2. Kinds of plants, chiefly with tuberous roots, sword-shaped leaves, & showy flowers; FLORENTINE ~. 3. Kind of rock-crystal reflecting prismatic colours. 4. ~ *diaphragm* (Opt.), contractile diaphragm of thin overlapping plates for regulating the admission of light to a lens or lens system. [ME, f. L, f. Gk *iris* -*idos* (goddess of) rainbow, iris]

Ir′ish (Ī-), a. & n. 1. Of Ireland; ‖~ *bridge*, open stone drain carrying water across road ; ~ BULL[4] ; ~ STEW. 2. n. ~ language; (as pl.) *the* ~ (people); ~*man*, ~*woman*, native of Ireland. Hence ~ISM(4) n., ~IZE(3) v.t. [f. *Ir-* st. of OE *Iras* n. pl. + -ISH[1]]

īrīt′is, n. Inflammation of the iris. [-ITIS]

īrk, v.t. (arch.). Disgust, tire, bore, esp. *it* ~*s* (*me, him,* etc.). [ME *irken,* of unkn. orig.]

īrk′some, a. Tedious, tiresome. Hence ~LY[2] (-ml-) adv., ~NESS (-mn-) n. [-SOME]

iron[1] (Ī′ern), n. & a. 1. Metal largely used for tools etc. (*wrought* ~, *cast* ~, STEEL), often fig. as type of hardness, as *a man of* ~, *rod of* ~; preparation of ~ as tonic; tool made of ~, as *curling, grappling,* ~ ; branding tool; golf-club with ~ head ; ~ tool for smoothing out linen etc. ; (usu. pl.) fetters (esp. *in* ~*s*, handcuffed); (esp. in pl.) stirrup ; (pl.) leg-supports to correct malformations etc.; *the* ~ *entered into his soul* (*Ps.* cv. 18, L mistranslation of Heb. ' his person entered into the iron ', i.e. fetters); (Provv.) *strike while the* ~ *is hot* (at a good opportunity), *have* (*too*) *many*

~*s in the fire* (many undertakings, also,
many expedients). **2.** adj. Of ~, very
robust, firm, unyielding, merciless. **3.** ~
age, age of cruelty, oppression, etc. (cf.
BRAZEN[1]), (also, cf. BRONZE, STONE, *age*)
era of ~ implements; ~*bark,* species of
eucalyptus with solid bark; ~*-bound,*
bound with ~, (of coast) rock-bound,
(fig.) rigorous, hard & fast; ~*clad,* clad in,
protected with, ~, (n., hist.) ship cased
with plates of ~; *I*~ *Cross,* German war
decoration; ~ *curtain* (fig.,) barrier to
passage of information at (esp. Western)
limit of Soviet sphere of influence; *I*~
Duke, Duke of Wellington; ~*-grey* a. & n.,
(of) the colour of freshly broken ~; ~
horse, locomotive steam-engine, also,
bicycle or tricycle; ~ *lung,* ~ case fitted
over patient's body, used for administering artificial respiration by means of
mechanical pumps; ~*master,* manufacturer of ~; ~*-mould,* spot caused by ~-
-rust or ink-stain, (v.t. & i.) stain, be
stained, with this; ~ *rations,* soldier's
modicum of food to be touched only
in emergency; *I*~*sides,* man of great
bravery, esp. (pl.) Cromwell's troopers;
~*-stone,* name of various hard ~-ores;
~*work,* work in ~, things made of ~;
~*works* (sing. or pl.), place where ~ is
smelted or ~ goods are made. [(1) OE
īsern, īsen = OS, OHG, ON *isarn,* Goth.
eisarn f. Gmc **isarnam;* (2) OE *iren,*
whence mod. E form, not paralleled in
other langg.]

iron²(ī'ern), v.t. Furnish, cover, with iron;
shackle with irons; smooth (linen etc.)
with flat-iron etc.; smooth *out* (difficulties
etc.). [f. prec.]

īrŏn'ic|(al), aa. Of, using, said in, addicted
to, irony. Hence ~alLY² adv. [f. LL f.
Gk *eirōnikos* (as IRONY¹, see -IC)]

ĭr'onist, n. One who uses irony. [f. Gk
eirōn dissembler + -IST]

∥ **ir'onmong|er** (ī'ernmŭngg-), n. Dealer
in hardware etc. Hence ~ERY(1, 2,
3) n.

ĭr'onў¹, n. Expression of one's meaning
by language of opposite or different
tendency, esp. simulated adoption of
another's point of view for purpose of
ridicule; ill-timed or perverse arrival of
event or circumstance in itself desirable,
due to the feigned good will & actual
malice *of* (Fate, circumstance, etc.); use of
language that has an inner meaning for a
privileged audience & an outer meaning
for the persons addressed or concerned
(occas. including speaker, cf. TRAGIC ~);
Socratic ~, simulation of ignorance as
means of confuting adversary. [f. L f.
Gk *eirōneia* simulated ignorance]

irony² (īrn'ĭ), a. Of like, iron. [-Y²]

irrād'i|ant, a. Shining brightly. So
~ANCE n. [as foll., see -ANT]

irrād'iāt|e, v.t. Shine upon; (fig.) throw
light on (subject); light up (face etc. *with*
joy etc.); subject to sunlight or ultra-

-violet rays. Hence ~IVE a. [f. L
IR¹(*radiare* f. *radius* RAY¹), see -ATE³]

irrādiā'tion, n. Shining, illumination,
(lit. & fig.); apparent extension of edges
of illuminated object seen against dark
ground. [F, or f. prec., see -ATION]

irra'tional (-shon-), a. & n. **1.** Unreasonable, illogical, absurd; not endowed with
reason; (Math., of roots etc.) not rational,
not commensurable with the natural
numbers (e.g. non-terminating decimal).
2. n. ~ number, surd. Hence ~ITY
(-shŏnălⁱ) n., ~IZE(3) v.t., ~LY² adv. [f.
L IR²(*rationalis* RATIONAL)]

irrĕclaim'ab|le, a. Not to be reclaimed
or reformed. Hence ~LY² adv. [IR-²]

irrĕcŏg'nizable, a. Unrecognizable. [IR-²]

irrĕc'oncīl|able, a. & n. **1.** Implacably
hostile; (of ideas etc.) incompatible. **2.** n.
Implacable opponent of political measure
etc. Hence ~ABIL'ITY, ~ableNESS, nn.,
~abLY² adv. [IR-²]

irrĕco'verab|le (-kŭ-), a. That cannot be
recovered or remedied. Hence ~LY² adv.
[IR-²]

irrĕcūs'able (-z-), a. That must be accepted. [f. LL IR²(*recusabilis* f. *recusare*
refuse, see -BLE)]

irrĕdeem'ab|le, a. (Of government an-
nuities) not terminable by repayment;
(of paper currency) for which issuing
authority does not undertake to pay
coin; irreclaimable, hopeless, whence
~LY² adv. [IR-²]

irrĕdĕn't|ist, n. (It. politics) advocate of
recovery to Italy of all Italian-speaking
districts; Greek, Pole, etc., of similar
views. So ~ISM n. [f. It. *irredentista* f.
(*Italia*) *irredenta* unredeemed (Italy)]

irrĕdū'c|ible, a. That cannot be brought
(*to* desired condition); that cannot be reduced, as ~*ible minimum;* that cannot be
simplified. Hence ~IBIL'ITY n. [IR-²]

irrĕf'ragab|le, a. (Of statement, argu-
ment, person) indisputable, unanswerable.
Hence ~LY² adv. [f. LL IR²(*refragabilis* f.
EF*ragari,* see -BLE)]

irrĕfrăn'gible, a. Inviolable; (Opt.) incapable of being refracted. [IR-²]

irrĕf'ūt|able (*or* -ūt²), a. Not to be refuted.
Hence ~ABIL'ITY n., ~abLY² adv. [f. LL
IR²(*refutabilis* REFUTABLE)]

irrĕg'ūlar, a. & n. **1.** Not regular, contrary to rule; abnormal; not of symmetrical form; (of surface) uneven; disorderly; uneven in duration, order, etc.;
(Gram., of part of speech) not normally
inflected; (of troops) not in regular
service. **2.** n. pl. ~ troops. Hence *or*
cogn. ~ITY (-ă'r-) n., ~LY² adv. [ME, f.
OF *irreguler* f. LL IR²(*regularis* REGULAR)]

irrĕl'ative, a. Unconnected, unrelated,
(*to*); having no relations, absolute. Hence
~LY² adv. [IR-²]

irrĕl'ĕv|ant, a. Not to the point; that
does not apply (*to* matter in hand).
Hence ~ANCE, ~ANCY, nn., ~antLY² adv.
[IR-²]

irrĕli'g|ion (-jn), n. Hostility to, disregard of, religion. Hence or cogn. ~ionɪsᴛ(2) (-jon-) n., ~ious (-jus) a., ~iousʟʏ² adv. [f. F, or L ɪʀ²(*religio* RELIGION).

irrĕmēd'iab|le, a. That cannot be remedied. Hence ~ʟʏ² adv. [f. L ɪʀ²-(*remediabilis* REMEDIABLE).]

irrĕmiss'ib|le, a. Unpardonable; unalterably binding. Hence~ʟʏ² adv. [ME, f. OF *irremissible* f. LL ɪʀ²(*remissibilis*, as REMIT, see -BLE)]

irrĕmo'v|able (-moo-), a. That cannot be removed, esp. from office. Hence ~ᴀʙɪʟ-ɪᴛʏ n., ~ᴀʙʟʏ² adv. [ɪʀ-²]

irrĕp'arab|le, a. (Of injury, loss, etc.) that cannot be rectified or made good. Hence~leɴᴇss n., ~ʟʏ² adv. [ME, f. OF *irreparable* f. L ɪʀ²(*reparabilis* REPARABLE).]

irrĕplāce'able (-sa-), a. Of which the loss cannot be made good. [ɪʀ-²]

irrĕprĕss'ib|le, a. & n. Not to be repressed or restrained; (n., colloq.) ~le person. Hence ~ʟʏ² adv. [ɪʀ-², REPRESS, -ɪBLE]

irrĕproach'|able, a. Free from blame, faultless. Hence ~ᴀʙɪʟ'ɪᴛʏ n., ~ᴀʙʟʏ² adv. [f. F ɪʀ²(*réprochable*, as REPROACH v., see -ABLE)]

irrĕsis't|ible (-zĭs-), a. Too strong, convincing, charming, etc., to be resisted. Hence ~ĪBɪʟ'ɪᴛʏ n., ~ɪʙʟʏ² adv. [f. LL ɪʀ²(*resistibilis*, as RESIST, see -BLE)]

irrĕs'olute (-zolōōt), a. Undecided, hesitating; wanting in resolution. Hence or cogn. ~ʟʏ² adv., ~ɴᴇss, **irrĕsolu'tion** (-zolōō-), nn. [ɪʀ-²]

irrĕsol'vable (-zŏl-), a. That cannot be resolved into parts; (of problem) that cannot be solved. [ɪʀ-²]

irrĕspĕc'tive, a. ~ *of*, not taking into account, without reference to, (often quasi-adv., as *the posts were filled ~ of nationality*). Hence ~ʟʏ² adv. [ɪʀ-²]

irrĕspŏn's|ible, a. Not responsible for conduct; acting, done, without due sense of responsibility. Hence ~ĪBɪʟ'ɪᴛʏ n., ~ɪʙʟʏ² adv. [ɪʀ-²]

irrĕspŏn'sive, a. Not responsive (*to*). Hence ~ɴᴇss n. [ɪʀ-²]

irrĕtĕn'tion, n. Failure to retain (esp. the urine). [ɪʀ-²]

irrĕtĕn'tive, a. Not retentive. Hence ~ɴᴇss n. [ɪʀ-²]

irrĕtriev'|able, a. That cannot be retrieved. Hence ~ᴀʙɪʟ'ɪᴛʏ n., ~ᴀʙʟʏ² adv. [ɪʀ-²]

irrĕv'er|ent, a. Wanting in reverence. Hence or cogn. ~ᴇɴᴄᴇ n., ~ĕn'ᴛɪᴀʟ (-shl) a., ~entʟʏ² adv. [f. L ɪʀ²(*reverens* REVERENT)]

irrĕvĕr's|ible, a. Unalterable; not reversible. Hence~ĪBɪʟ'ɪᴛʏ n., ~ɪʙʟʏ² adv. [ɪʀ-²]

irrĕv'oc|able, a. Unalterable; gone beyond recall. Hence~ᴀʙɪʟ'ɪᴛʏ n., ~ᴀʙʟʏ² adv. [f. L ɪʀ²(*revocabilis* REVOCABLE)]

i'rrig|āte, v.t. (Of streams etc.) supply (land) with water; water (land) with

channels etc.; (Med.) supply (wound etc.) with constant flow of liquid; (fig.) refresh as with moisture. Hence or cogn. ~ABLE, ~āᴛɪᴠᴇ, aa., ~ᴀ'ᴛɪᴏɴ, ~āᴛᴏʀ, nn. [f. L ɪʀ²(*rigare* moisten), see -ᴀᴛᴇ³]

i'rrit|able, a. Quick to anger, touchy, whence~abʟʏ² adv.; (of organ etc.) very sensitive to contact etc.; (Physiol., of muscles & nerves) capable of being excited to vital action by physical stimulus. So ~ABɪʟ'ɪᴛʏ n. [f. L *irritabilis* (as IRRITATE¹, see -BLE)]

i'rritancy¹, n. Irritation, annoyance. [as IRRITANT, see -ANCY]

i'rritancy², n. (law). Making, being, null & void. [as IRRITATE², see -ANCY]

i'rritant, a. & n. 1. Causing (usu. physical) irritation. 2. n. = substance or agency (also fig.). [as foll., see -ANT]

i'rritāt|e¹, v.t. Excite to anger, annoy, vex, (~*ed at, by, with, against*), whence ~ingʟʏ² adv.; excite, produce uneasy sensation in, (bodily organ etc.); (Physiol.) stimulate (organ) to vital action. Hence or cogn. irrita'ᴛɪᴏɴ n., ~ɪᴠᴇ a. [f. L *irritare*, see -ᴀᴛᴇ³]

i'rritāte², v.t. (law). Make null & void. [f. L *irritare* f. ɪʀ²(*ritus* = *ratus* established) invalid, see -ᴀᴛᴇ³]

irrŭp'tion, n. Invasion; violent entry. [f. L *irruptio* f. ɪʀ¹(*rumpere rupt-* break), see -ɪᴏɴ]

Irv'ing|ite (ĕrv-), n. Member of a religious body called by its members the Catholic Apostolic Church. [E. *Irving*, minister of Ch. of Scotland, d. 1834]

is. See BE.

Isabĕll'a, Is'abĕl, (ĭz-), a. & n. Greyish yellow. Hence **isabĕll'ɪɴᴇ** (-ᴢ-) a. [Sp. *Isabella*, F *Isabelle*, = *Elisabeth*]

isagŏ'gic, a. & n. Introductory; (n. pl.) study of literary & external history of Bible. [f. L f. Gk *eisagōgikos* f. *eisagōgē* introduction (*eis* into + *agōgē* leading f. *agō*), see -ɪᴄ]

is'atin, n. (chem.). Crystalline reddish substance got from indigo by oxidation. [f. L f. Gk *isatis* woad + -ɪɴ].

ischiăt'ic, -dic, (-k-), a. Of the hip, sciatic. [f. LL *ischiaticus*, alt. f. L f. Gk *iskhiadikos* f. *iskhias -ados* pain in hip (*iskhion*), see -ɪᴄ]

-ise¹. See -ɪᴢᴇ.

-ise², suf. of nn., = OF -*ise*, prop. f. L -*itia*, but also (in learned formations) f. L -*icia*, -*itia*, -*icium*, -*itium* (OF *justise*, *juise*, *servise*, f. L *justitia*, *judicium*, *servitium*). In wds f. L, later F changed -*ise* to -*ice*, which E adopted; but in native wds F & E retain -*ise* (*franchise*, *merchandise*; E also has *exercise*, F -*ice*). See -ɪᴄᴇ.

-ish¹, suf. of adjj., = OE, OS, OHG -*isc*, Goth. -*isks*, ON -*iskr*, cogn. w. Gk -*iskos* dim. suf. of nn. In old formations, prec. vowel was modified, as still in *English*, *French*, *Welsh*. 1. OE chiefly formed aa. f. national names (*British*, *Danish*), with a few in sense ' belonging to, of the nature of ' (*heathenish*, *outlandish*); later aa. have usu. not the neutral sense (*boyish*, *girlish*), but that of ' having the bad qualities of ' (*foppish*, *monkish*, *swinish*; f. names of things *bookish*, *hellish*; f. vbs & advv. *snappish*, *stand-offish*, *uppish*). **2.** Sense peculiar to E is ' somewhat ' (*stiffish*). **3.** Colloq. added to names of hours of the day or numbers of years to denote ' round about, somewhere near ' (*eightish*, *fortyish*).

-ish², suf. of vbs repr. F *-iss-* seen in some parts of vbs in *-ir* (*périssant*, *finissais*), f. L inceptive suf. *-isc-*, used in It. & F to form vbs without incept. sense to correspond to L vbs in *-ire*, *-ere*. In a few wds F *-iss-* became in E *-ise* (*chastise*, *advertise*); on the other hand, other F endings have become *-ish* (ADMONISH, LAVISH, RELISH).

Ish'mäĕl (ĭ-), n. Outcast, one at war with society. Hence ~ITE¹ n. [*Gen.* xvi. 12]

is'inglass (ĭzĭngglahs), n. Whitish semi-transparent substance, a form of gelatin, got from some freshwater fish, esp. sturgeon, & used in making jellies, glue, etc. [corrupt. of obs. Du. *huisenblas* sturgeon's bladder]

Is'lam (ĭz-; *or* -ahm'), n. Mohammedanism; the Mohammedan world. Hence **Islām'ĭc**, ~ĭt'ĭc, aa., ~ĭsm(3), ~ĭte¹(1), nn., (ĭz-). [Arab., = surrender, n. f. *aslama* he surrendered f. *salama* he became safe, whence also *salaam*, *Moslem*, *Mussulman*]

isl'and (ĭl-), n., & v.t. **1.** Piece of land surrounded by water; (fig.) anything detached or isolated, esp. woodland surrounded by prairie, street REFUGE; (Naut.) ship's superstructure, bridge, etc.; (Physiol.) detached portion of tissue or group of cells. **2.** v.t. Make into an ~, isolate; dot as with ~s. Hence ~ER¹(4) n. [ME *iland* f. OE *īgland* (f. *īeg* = ON, OFris. *ey* isle +LAND); *-s-* by assoc. w. *isle*]

isle (ĭl), n. Island (in prose usu. only with proper name, as *Isle of Wight*, *British Isles*, & usu. of small islands); *Isles of the* BLEST. [ME, f. OF *īle* f. L *insula*; later ME & OF *isle* after L]

isl'ĕt (ĭl-), n. Little island; isolated tract or spot. [f. F *islette* (as prec., see -ET¹)]

ism (ĭ'zm), n. Any distinctive doctrine or practice (~s & ologies). [foll. used as n.]

-ism, suf. forming abstract nn.: (1) of action on vbs in -IZE, as *baptism*; (2) of typical conduct or condition on class nouns, as *heroism*, *barbarism*; (3) of system or principle on name of subject or founder or connected catchword, as *conservatism*, *Arianism*, *jingoism*; (4) of peculiarity in language, as *gallicism*, *archaism*; (5) of morbid condition induced by excessive use of drug, as *alcoholism*. [= F *-isme* f. L f. Gk *-ismos* or *-isma* f. *-izō* -IZE]

isn't. See BE.

iso- in comb. = Gk *īsos* equal, as: **ĭs'obär**

n., ~bä'ric a., (line on map) connecting places at which atmospheric pressure is the same (at given time or on the average); *ĭs'ocheim* (-kĭm) n., ~cheim'al, ~chĭm'enal, (-k-), aa. & nn., (line on map) connecting places of same mean winter temperature; ~chromät'ic, of same colour; ~chronous (-ŏk²), occupying equal time, vibrating uniformly, as pendulum; ~clĭn'al, ~clĭn'ĭc, showing equal magnetic inclination (~clinic lines, lines joining, on a map or chart, points at which the magnetic dip is the same); ~cracy (-ŏk²) n., ~cröt'ĭc a., (polity) in which all have equal political power; ~dynäm'ĭc, indicating equal magnetic force; ~gē'otherm, line connecting points in interior of earth having same temperature; ~gŏn'ĭc, indicating equal angles (of magnetic variation); ~mĕ'ric, composed of same elements in same proportions, & having same molecular weight, but with atoms differently grouped; ~mĕt'rĭc(al), of equal measure; ~mŏrph'ĭsm, ~mŏrph'ous, (property of) crystallizing in same or closely related geometric forms; ~nomy (-ŏn²), equality of political rights; ~perimĕt'rĭcal, having equal perimeters; ~seis'mal (-sĭz-), connecting points at which earthquake-shock is of same intensity; ~theral (-ŏth²) a. & n., (line) connecting places of same mean summer temperature; *ĭs'othĕrm* n., ~thĕrm'al a. & n., (line) connecting places of same mean annual temperature.

ĭs'olät|e, v.t. Place apart or alone; (Chem.) free (substance) from its combinations; (Electr.) = INSULATE; subject (person etc.) to quarantine. Hence ~OR n. [orig. in p.p., f. F *isolé* f. It. *isolato* (as INSULATE)]

ĭsolä'tion, n. Isolating or being isolated; ~ *hospital* or *ward* (for patients with infectious diseases). Hence ~ISM(3) n., policy of holding aloof from affairs of other countries, ~IST n., advocate of this policy (also attrib.). [prec., -ATION]

-ison, suf. of nn., f. OF *-aison*, *-eison*, *-ison*, f. L *-ationem*, *-etionem*, *-itionem*; later formations took -ATION, -ITION.

ĭs'opŏd, n. Kinds of crustacea comprising wood-lice and allied marine and fresh-water species. [f. F *isopode* (ISO-, Gk *pous podos* foot]

ĭsŏs'celēs (-selēz), a. (Of triangle) having two sides equal. [LL, f. Gk ISO(*skelēs* f. *skelos* leg)]

ĭs'otōpe, n. One of two or more forms of an element differing from each other in weight of atoms. Hence **ĭsotŏp'ĭc** a., **ĭsŏt'opy** n. [f. ISO- + Gk *topos* place]

Is'raĕl (ĭz-), n. The Jewish people, whence ~ITE¹(1) n., ~ĭtĭsh¹ a.; (fig.) God's elect; the Jewish State established in Palestine in 1948, also attrib. Hence ~i (Izrā'ĭ) a. & n., (inhabitant) of this State. [LL (earlier *istrahel*, *israhel*), f. Gk *Israēl* f. Heb. *yisrael* striver with God (*Gen.* xxxii. 28)]

iss'ūe¹, n. **1.** Outgoing, outflow; termination (*of* matter etc.); discharge of blood etc., incision to procure this. **2.** Way out, outlet; mouth of river. **3.** Progeny, children, as *without male* ~. **4.** Result, outcome; *in the* ~, as things turn out. **5.** Point in question, esp. (Law) between contending parties in action, as ~ *of fact* (when fact is denied), ~ *of law* (when application of the law is contested). **6.** *At* ~, (of persons) at variance, (of things) in dispute; *join* ~, proceed to argue (*with* person *on* point agreed upon as basis of dispute), (Law) submit an ~ jointly for decision, (of one party) accept the ~ tendered by the other. **7.** Giving out, issuing, (of bills of exchange, notes, stamps, etc.); number of coins, notes, copies of newspaper, etc., issued at one time; (of book) part of EDITION with special features issued at certain period. Hence ~LESS (-ūl-) a. [ME, f. OF *issue* fem. of *issu*, p.p. of OF *issir* f. L *exire*]

iss'ūe², v.i. & t. Go or come out (often *out*, *forth*); emerge from a condition; be derived, spring, (*from*); result (*from*); end, result, (*in*); come out, be published; send forth; publish, put into circulation, (notes, newspaper), whence **iss'ūABLE** a., **iss'ūANCE** n.; (Mil.) supply (soldier) *with* article of equipment. [f. prec.]

-ist, suf. forming personal nn.: (1) of agent, corresp. to Gk vbs in -*izō* or possible E vbs in -IZE, as *antagonist*, *plagiarist*; (2) of adherent of creed etc. in -ISM, as *atheist*, *ventriloquist*, *Darwinist*, *fatalist*; (3) of one concerned with any subject (apart from -*ism*, -*ize*), as *dentist*, *tobacconist*, *balloonist*, esp. as player of musical instrument (*violinist*). [= F -*iste*, It. & Sp. -*ista*, f. L -*ista* f. Gk -*istēs* (-*izō* -IZE + -*tēs* agent-suf.); *tobacconist*, *accompanist* are formed irreg.]

-ister, suf. of nn., f. OF -*istre*, by-form of -*iste* -IST, perh. by false anal. f. *ministre* (L *minister*) etc.; in E prob. associated with -ER¹. Exx.: *chorister*, *palmister*, *sophister*.

isth'm|us (or Is'mus), (pl. ~uses). Neck of land; (Anat., Bot.) narrow part connecting two larger parts. Hence ~IAN a. [L, f. Gk *isthmos*]

is'tle (-tli), n. Fibre used for cord, nets, etc., got from species of agave etc. [f. Mex. *ixtli*]

it¹, pron. (poss. *its*; pl. *they*, obj. *them*, poss. *their*). **1.** The thing in question; the person in question, as *who is it* (that knocks)?, *it* (the person that knocks) *is I*, (arch. poet.) *it* (what occupies my mind) *is the miller's daughter*, *& she is grown so dear*, (nursery sympathetic) *has it lost its rattle then?* (have you, your). **2.** (As subjects of impers. vb) *it rains, it is cold; it* (the season) *is winter, it* (the day) *is Ash Wednesday, it is Ash Wednesday today, it* (the distance) *is 6 miles to Oxford; it says in the Bible* (the Bible says) *that all men*

are liars; *I would go if it were not* (would go but) *for the expense*. **3.** (As subject, anticipating deferred virtual subject in more or less conscious apposition) *it is absurd talking* (or *to talk*) *like that, it is incredible that he should refuse, it is a dirty business, this meat-canning*. **4.** (Anticipating deferred subject introduced by *that* conj., separated from *it* by adv. predicate) *it is seldom that he fails, it is in vain that you quibble, it is to him that you must apply*. **5.** (As antecedent to relative of either number & any gender, separated by predicate) *it was a purse that he dropped, it was the Russians that began it*. **6.** (As indef. obj. w. trans. or intr. vb) *face it out, carry it with a high hand, deuce take it, run for it, lord it over him, cab it* (go habitually or on the particular occasion in cab), *give it him* (hot), *have done it* (blundered). **7.** The ne plus ultra (colloq.; *for barefaced lying you really are it*). **8.** Sex appeal (colloq.). [OE *hit* (neut. nom. & acc.) f. (orig. demonstr.) stem *hi-* (see HE), = (in form & sense) OFris., OLFrank. *hit*, (in form) Goth. *hita* (demonstr.); the neut. pronn. OS *it*, OHG *iz*, Goth *ita* are from the parallel stem *i-* see HE)]

‖ **it²**, n. (colloq.). Short for *Italian vermouth* (in *gin & ~*). [abbr.]

it'acism (ē-), n. Pronunciation of Greek *ē* like English *ē*, cf. ETACISM; substitution in MS. of Greek iota for other vowels. [f. Gk *ēta* the letter *ē*, spelt *ita* to indicate the pronunc. (ēta)]

Ital'ian (itǎl'yan), a. & n. **1.** Of Italy; ~ *cloth*, satin-faced linen cloth for linings; ~ *handwriting*, that now current in Britain, Italy, France, etc., opp. to Gothic; ~ *iron* (cylindrical, with rounded end, for crimping lace etc.); ‖ ~ *warehouse(man)*, for supply of ~ groceries, fruits, olive oil, etc. **2.** n. Language, native, of Italy. Hence ~ATE² a., having ~ style or appearance, ~ISM (2, 4) n., ~IZE(3) v.t. & i. [15th c., f. It. *Italiano* f. Rom. *Italianus* f. L *Italia* Italy, see -AN]

itǎl'ic, a. & n. **1.** (*I*~) of ancient Italy, esp. as apart from Rome; ~ *type*, sloping type introduced by Aldus Manutius of Venice (c. 1500). **2.** n. pl. Letters thus sloping, now used for emphasis or distinction, e.g. to indicate foreign word (cf. ROMAN). [f. L f. Gk *Italikos* (*Italia* Italy, see -IC)]

itǎl'icize, -ise (-īz), v.t. Print (words) in italics, usu. for emphasis or distinction. [-IZE]

Itǎl'iot (I-), **-ōte**, n. & a. (Inhabitant) of ancient-Greek colonies in S. Italy. [f. Gk *Italiōtēs* (*Italia* Italy, see -OT²)]

itch¹, n. Irritation in the skin; contagious disease accompanied by this & caused by the ~-*mite*, which burrows in the skin; restless desire, hankering, (*for* thing, *to* do). Hence ~'NESS n., ~'Y² a. [OE *gicce*, as foll.]

itch², v.i. Feel irritation in skin; *scratch where it ~es* (where there is an ~ing); (of person or his *fingers*) crave uneasily (*for* thing, *to* do). [OE *gicc(e)an*, OS *jukkian*, OHG *jucchen* f. WG *jukkjan*]

-ite¹, suf. of adjj. & nn., = F *-ite* f. L *-ita* f. Gk *-itēs* (also used in E, as *pyrites*), w. sense '(one) belonging to or connected with'; (1) in names of persons, in mod. formation often derog. (*Stagirite, Sybarite, Parnellite, Shelleyite, Israelite, Pre-raphaelite*); (2) in names of fossil organisms (*ammonite, belemnite*); of mineral species, often superseding *-ane, -in, -ine*, etc. (*anthracite, haematite, graphite, darwinite*); of constituent parts of body or organ (*somite, cerite, segment of body, of horn*); of some saccharine substances, glucoses, etc. (*dulcite, pinite*); of explosives (*cordite, dynamite*); of commercial products (*ebonite, vulcanite*); of salts of acids denominated in *-ous* (*nitrite, sulphite*).

-ite², suf. formed in adjj. f. L p.p. in *-ītus* (*erudite, composite*) & similar vbl nn. (*appetite*), & in vbs formed on L p:p. stem in *-it-* (*expedite, unite*); but vbs f. L p.p. st. *-īt-* end in *-it* (*deposit, merit*).

it'em, n. & adv. 1. Article, unit, included in enumeration (properly not the first); entry of this in account etc.; detail of news etc. in newspaper etc.; hence *~-IZE(3)* v.t., state by *~s.* 2. adv. Likewise, also, (introducing mention of *~).* [L, adv., = in like manner, also]

it'er|āte, v.t. Repeat (quoted words etc.); make (charge, assertion, objection, etc.) repeatedly. Hence or cogn. *~ANCE, ~ANCY, ~A'TION*, nn., *~ative* a. [f. L *iterare* (*iterum* again), see *-ATE³*]

-ites. See *-ITE¹*.

Ithŭr'iel's spear (I-), n. Infallible test of genuineness. [Milt. *Par. Lost*, iv. 810]

ithўphäll'ĭc, a. & n. Of the phallus carried in Bacchic festivals; lewd; in the metre used for Bacchic hymns; (n.) poem in this metre, licentious poem. [f. LL f. Gk *ithuphallikos* (*ithus* straight + *phallos* PHALLUS, see *-IC*)]

ĭtin'er|ant, a. Travelling from place to place; (of justices) travelling on circuit; (of Methodist ministry) removing from circuit to circuit. Hence *~ACY, ~ANCY*, nn. [as ITINERATE, see *-ANT*]

ĭtin'erarў, n. & a. Route; record of travel; guide-book; (adj.) of travelling, of roads. [f. LL *itinerarius* a., *-um* n. (also used in E), f. *iter itineris* journey, see *-ARY¹*]

ĭtin'er|āte, v.i. Travel from place to place; (of Methodist minister) remove from circuit to circuit. Hence *~A'TION* n. [f. L *itinerari* (as prec.), see *-ATE³*]

-ition, suf., thr. F *-ition* (or dir.) f. L *-itionem* (nom. *-itio*) = *-ION* appended to L 2nd or 3rd or 4th conj. p.p. stems in *-ŭt-, -it-* (*admonition, perdition, sortition*).

-itious¹, suf. of adjj., f. L *-icius* + *-ous* (*-t-*

by confus. of *c* & *t* in LL MSS.), formed usu. on L p.p. stems (*factitious*).

-itious², suf. in which *-IOUS* is appended to L stems in *-it-* chiefly nn. in *-itio* (*ambitious, nutritious*, cf. *supposit-*ITIOUS¹).

-itis, suf. forming esp. names of inflammatory diseases (*appendicitis, bronchitis*), f. Gk *-itis*, forming the fem. of adjj. in *-itēs*, w. *nosos* disease understood.

-itous, suf. of adjj., = *-IT(Y)* + *-OUS*, corresp. to F *-iteux*, L *-itosus* for *-itatosus* (*calamitosus* calamitous).

ĭts, poss. a. See IT. [replaces HIS *c.* 1600]

ĭtsĕlf', pron. Emphatic & reflexive form corresp. to IT; *by* ~, automatically, apart from its surroundings; *in* ~, apart from its surroundings, viewed in its essential qualities etc. [IT + SELF, but often treated as ITS + *self*, cf. *its own self*]

-ity [ME & OF *-ite* (mod. F *-ité*) f. L *-itatem*], the usu. form in wh. the suf. (L *-tas, -tatem*, expr. state or condition) appears in E, either f. learned F adoptives or dir. f. L. In L the *-i-* is usu. either the stem-vowel (*suavitas* suavity) or its weakened repr. (*puritas* (*puro-*) purity), rarely a mere connective, as in *majoritas* majority. The phonetic resultant in OF of L *-itatem* was *-te* (*-cte*): see *-TY¹*.

-ium, suf. forming names of metallic elements, but some (esp. later) metals have names in *-um*, the L termination for metals.

-ive, suf. forming adjj. w. sense 'tending to, having the nature of', f. F *-if* (fem. *-ive*) f. L *-ivus* added to p.p. stem (*activus, passivus*), pres. stem (*cadivus*), or noun (*tempestivus*). Most E wds are of mod. formation, chiefly in *-sive, -tive*, & esp. *-ative*, which tends to become living suf. (*talkative*). Some are formed immed. on vb stems (esp. in *-s, -c, -t*), as *amusive, coercive*. As in L these adjj. are freely used as nn., e.g. *adjective, captive*.

ĭv'orў, n. Hard white substance composing main part of tusks of elephant, hippopotamus, walrus, narwhal, & (*fossil* ~) mammoth; *vegetable* ~, hard albumen of seed of S.-Amer. palm (*~-nut*); *black~* (hist.), African Negro slaves; colour of ~; (sl., pl.) dice, billiard-balls, piano-keys; (sl., sing. or pl.) teeth; (pl.) articles made of ~; ~ *black*, black pigment from calcined ~; ~ TOWER. [ME, f. OF *yvoire* f. L *eboreus* a. (*ebur -oris*)]

ĭv'ў, n. Climbing evergreen shrub, with dark-green shining leaves, usu. five-angled; ~ *geranium*, ~-leaved pelargonium. Hence **ĭv'ɪED²** (-Id) a. [OE *ifig*, rel. to MLG *if(löf)*, OHG *ebah, ebahewi* (G *epheu, efeu*)]

ĭx'ĭa, n. Kinds of S.-Afr. iridaceous plants, with large showy flowers. [Gk]

Ixī'on's wheel (I-), n. (Gk Myth.). Wheel on which Ixion was condemned to revolve eternally in Hades.

ĭz'ard, n. Goatlike antelope of Pyrenees, allied to chamois. [f. F *isara*, orig. unkn.]

-ize, -ise, suf. of vbs, = F -iser f. LL -izare f. Gk -izō; in Gk either intr., ' act like ', as hellenizō speak, act as a, Greek, or trans., as katharizō clean; Christian Gk vbs, as euaggelizō evangelize, were first Latinized, & -izare so established as L for Gk vbs (cf. G -iren for Rom. vbs); F extended -iser to form vbs from names etc., whence the mod. use. -ize is the better spelling for all wds, mod. or f. Gk, that contain the Gk suf. & is here uniformly so written (advertise, surprise, etc., do not). Meanings: (1) trans., treat in such a way (catechize); (2) intr., follow, have, such a practice or feeling (apostatize, sympathize); (3) t. & i., bring, come into such a state (pulverize, anglicize, cicatrize); (4) t. & i., act like, treat on system of, (Calvinize, Bowdlerize); (5) trans., impregnate etc. with (oxidize). Nn. are formed in -izer, -ization, as well as -IST, -ISM.

Izz'ard, n. (arch.). The letter z (from A to I~). [var. of ZED]

Izz'at, n. (Anglo-Ind. and Eastern). Honour, reputation, self-respect (occas. self-importance). [Arab.]

J

J, j, (jā), letter (pl. Js, J's).

jā'al-goat (or yah-), n. Wild goat of Sinai, Upper Egypt, etc. [f. Heb. yā'ēl wild goat]

jāb, v.t. (-bb-), & n. 1. Poke roughly; stab; thrust (thing) abruptly (into). 2. n. Abrupt blow with pointed thing or fist. [var., orig. Sc., of JOB³]

jābb'er, v.i. & t., & n. 1. Speak volubly & with little sense; utter (words) rapidly & indistinctly; chatter, as monkeys etc. 2. n. ~ing, gabble, gibberish. [imit., see -ER⁵]

jāb'iru (-ōō), n. Tropical American bird of stork family. [native]

jāborān'di, n. Dried leaflets of Brazilian plant with diuretic & sudorific properties. [f. native jaburandi]

jābot (zhǎbō'), n. Ornamental frill on woman's bodice; (hist.) frill on man's shirt-front. [F, orig. unkn.]

jāc'ana (-ah), n. Small tropical wading bird with disproportionately large straight claws (enabling it to walk on floating leaves). [native jasand]

jācaran'da, n. Kinds of tropical American hardwood tree with scented wood & trumpet-shaped blue flowers. [Braz.]

jā'cinth, n. Reddish-orange gem, variety of zircon. [ME iacynt f. OF iacinte or med. L iacint(h)us f. L hyacinthus HYACINTH]

jāck¹, n. (J~) familiar form of name John, esp. as type of the common people, as J~ & Jill, lad & lass; every man ~, every individual; = ~ tar; ‖ labourer, man who does odd jobs, etc.; CHEAP J~; STEEPLE-~;

(Cards) knave; machine for turning spit in roasting meat; machine for lifting heavy weights; (also carriage-~) machine for lifting axle off ground while cleaning wheel; BOOT¹-~; parts of various machines etc.; pike, esp. young or small one; (Bowls) ball for players to aim at; J~ Frost, frost personified; before you could say J~ Robinson, very quickly or suddenly; J~-a-dandy, dandy; ~'ass, male ass, dolt, blockhead; laughing-~ass, giant kingfisher of Australia; ~'boot, large boot coming above knee; ~'daw, thievish small crow haunting church towers; J~ in office, self-important official; ~-in-the-box, toy figure that springs out of box when opened, (also) kind of firework; J~-in-the-green, man or boy enclosed in framework covered with leaves in May-day sports; J~ Ketch, common hangman; ~-knife, large clasp-knife for the pocket; J~ of all trades, one who can turn his hand to anything; ~-o'-lantern, will-o'-the-wisp (often fig.); ~-plane (for coarse work); ~'pot (Poker), accumulating pool that can only be opened by player holding two ~s or better, (transf.) prize in lottery etc.; ~ pudding, buffoon, clown; ~-rafter, short rafter in hip-roof; ~-snipe (small species); ~ tar, common sailor; ~-towel (endless, hung from roller). [ME Jakke, by-name for John (erron. assoc. w. F Jaques)]

jāck², v.t. Hoist with jack; ~ up, abandon (attempt etc., or abs.). [first sense f. prec.; second prob. imit.; cf. chuck]

jāck³, n. Ship's flag, smaller than ensign, esp. one flown from ~-staff at bow, indicating nationality, as British, French, ~; single flag flown on foremast as signal for pilot (Brit. pilot's ~, union ~ with white border); UNION J~; ~-staff, (also) stick on which flag is bent that is to show above mast-head. [prob. = JACK¹]

jāck⁴, n. (arch.). Foot-soldier's sleeveless tunic; (also black ~) vessel for liquor, usu. of waxed leather coated with tar etc. [ME, f. OF jaque (whence G jacke), of unkn. orig.]

jāck⁵, n. E.-Ind. fruit, like bread-fruit but coarser. [f. Port. jaca f. Malayalam chakka]

jāck'al (-awl), n., & v.i. (-ll-). Animal of dog kind, of size of fox, formerly supposed to hunt up lion's prey for him; (fig.) person who does preparatory drudgery etc.; (vb) act as ~ (for). [f. Turk. chakal f. Pers. shagal, cogn. w. Skr. s'rgala]

jāck'anāpes (-ps), n. ‖ (Arch.) monkey; pert fellow; coxcomb; pert child. [earliest form Jack Napes (1450), supposed to refer to Duke of Suffolk, whose badge was an ape's clog & chain]

jāck'arōō, n. (Austral. sl.). New chum, novice. [perh. portmanteau of Jack and kangaroo]

jāck'ĕt, n., & v.t. 1. Sleeved outer garment for man or woman; NORFOLK, ETON, ‖ DINNER, ~; *dust his* ~, beat him; outer covering round boiler etc. for protection, keeping in heat, etc.; paper wrapper, freq. coloured & artistically designed, in which a bound book is issued; animal's coat; *potatoes boiled in their* ~*s* (skins). 2. v.t. Cover with~. [15 c., f. OF *jaquet*, dim. as JACK⁴]

Jăc'ob, n. ~*'s ladder*, plant with corymbs of blue or white flowers, & leaves suggest-ing ladder, (Naut.) rope ladder with wooden rungs, esp. one slung from a boom to the water; ~*'s staff*, surveyor's iron-shod rod used instead of tripod, (also) instrument for measuring distances & heights. [f. LL f. Gk *Iakōbos* f. Heb. *ya'aqob*]

Jăcobē'an, a. Of the reign of James I; of St James the Less; (in furniture trade) of the colour of dark oak. [f. mod. L *Jacobaeus*, as prec. +-EAN]

Jăc'obin¹, n. Dominican friar [from con-vent near to church of S. Jacques]; member of extreme democratic club established in Paris in old ~ convent (1789), sympathizer with its principles, extreme radical, whence **Jăcobin'ic**(AL) aa., ~ISM(3) n., ~IZE(3) v.t. [F, f. med. L *Jacobinus* (JACOB, -INE¹)]

jăc'obin², n. Pigeon with reversed feathers on back of neck, suggesting cowl. [f. F *jacobine*, fem. as prec.]

Jăc'ob|ite, n. Adherent of James II after his abdication, or of his descendants. Hence ~it'ICAL a., ~ĭTISM(3) n. [f. L *Jacobus* James +-ITE¹]

jacōb'ŭs, n. (pl. ~*es*). English gold coin struck in reign of James I, worth 20–24*s*. [as prec.]

jăc'onĕt, n. Cotton cloth of medium thickness, esp. dyed waterproofed kind for poulticing etc. [f. Hind. f. place-name; see JUGGERNAUT]

Jacquard (jăk'ǎrd) lōŏm, n. Loom fitted with apparatus invented by J. M. Jac-quard of Lyons (d. 1834) to facilitate the weaving of figured fabrics.

jacquerie (zhăkerē'), n. Rising of peasantry, esp. that of 1357–8 in France. [F *Jacques* James, peasant, see -ERY]

jăctita'tion, n. ‖ (Law) ~ *of marriage*, offence of falsely claiming to be a person's wife or husband; (Med.) restless tossing of body in illness; twitching of limb or muscle. [f. med. L *jactitatio* f. L *jactitare* toss, boast, (*jacĕre jact-* throw), see -ATION]

jāde¹, n., & v.t. Inferior, wearied, or worn-out horse; (in reprobation, usu. playful) woman; (v.t., esp. in p.p.) wear out with hard work. [ME; orig. unkn.]

jāde², A silicate of lime & magnesia, a hard green, blue, or white stone, a variant of hornblende; (also ~*'īte*, pr. -dīt) sili-cate of sodium & aluminium like this in appearance. [f. F *le jade* for *l'ejade* f. Sp. (*piedra de) ijada* (stone of) the colic, f. L *ilia* pl. flank]

j'adoube (zhahdōŏb'), phr. Expression used by a chess-player touching a piece he does not propose to move (= I adjust). [F]

Jaeg'er (yāg-), n. Kind of woollen clothing-material from which vegetable fibres are excluded as unwholesome. [person; P]

‖ **Jăff'a**, n. (Used for) kind of dessert orange. [~ in Israel, the bibl. *Joppa*]

jăg¹, n. Sharp projection, e.g. point of rock. Hence ~g'y² (-g-) a. [c. 1400, prob. imit.]

jăg², v.t. (-gg-). Cut, tear, in uneven manner; make indentations in, whence ~g'ER¹(2) n. Hence ~g'ĕDLY² adv., ~g'ĕDNESS n., (-g-). [f. prec.]

jăg³, n. (sl.). Drinking bout. [16th c. (dial.), = load for one horse; orig. unkn.]

jäger = YAGER.

jăgg'erў (-g-), n. Coarse brown Indian sugar made from palm-sap; other crude sugar. [f. Indo-Port. *jāgara* SUGAR]

jaghir|(e)' (jagēr'), n. (India). Assignment by the State of a district & its revenue to an individual or body, with power to administer; tract so assigned. Hence ~'dār (-ērd-) n., holder of a ~e [Pers. *ddr* holder]. [f. Pers. *jā* place +*gir* hold-ing]

jăg'uar (-war, -ūar), n. Large carnivorous spotted mammal of cat kind, in some wooded parts of America. [f. native *yaguara*]

Jah, n. Jehovah. [repr. Heb. *Yah* short-ened form of *Yahweh* JEHOVAH]

jail etc. See GAOL etc.

Jain (jīn), n. & a. (Member) of a non--Brahminical E.-Ind. sect, with doctrines like those of Buddhism. Hence ~'ISM n. [f. Hind. f. Skr. *jaina* of a Buddha (*jina* f. root *ji* conquer)]

jăl'ap, n. Purgative drug got esp. from tuberous roots of a Mexican climbing plant. [F, f. Sp. *jalapa* f. *Xalapa, Ja-*Mexican city, f. Aztec *Xalapan* (*xalli* sand +*atl* water +*pan* upon)]

*****jalōp(p)'ў**, n. Dilapidated motor-car. [orig. unkn.]

jalousie (zhăl'ōōzĕ), n. Slatted shutter on outside of window, Venetian blind. [F, as JEALOUSY]

jăm¹, v.t. & i. (-mm-), & n. 1. Squeeze (thing) between two surfaces; cause (part of machine) to be fixed so that it cannot work; squeeze (things) together in com-pact mass; thrust (thing) violently (*into* space); block, fill up, (passage etc.) by crowding into it; become tightly wedged; (Radio) make (message, instrument) unintelligible by operating elsewhere. 2. n. Crush, squeeze, stoppage (of machine etc.) due to this; crowded mass; (colloq.) fix, awkward position; ~*-stroke*, = PENDULUM *stroke*. [imit.]

jăm², n. Conserve of fruit, made by boil-ing it with sugar to a thick consistency; (sl.) *real* ~, a real treat. [f. prec.]

Jamaic′a, n. ~ (*rum*), rum made in ~.

Jamb (jăm), n. Side post of doorway, window, etc., esp. (pl.) stone sides or cheeks of fireplace. [ME, f. OF *jambe* f. LL *gamba* leg]

jămboree′, n. Celebration, merry-making; large rally of boy scouts. [U.S. sl.]

∥ **Jān(e)′ite** (-nī-), n. Admirer of Jane Austen's novels. [-ITE¹(1)]

jangle (jăng′gl), v.i. & t., & n. (Make) harsh noise; cause (bell etc.) to do this; speak, utter, in discordant or noisy way; (arch.) dispute, wrangle, (n. & vb). [ME, f. OF *jangler*, of unkn. orig.]

jăn′itor, n. Doorkeeper, caretaker. [L, f. *janua* door]

jăn′izarỹ, -nissarỹ, (jă-, yă-), n. (Hist.) one of body of Turkish infantry forming Sultan's guard (abolished in 1826); Turkish soldier; (fig.) personal instrument of tyranny. [ult. f. Turk. *yeñi-tsheri* (*yeñi* new + *tsheri* soldiery)]

jănn′ock, a. (dial., esp. Lancs. & Yorks.). Straightforward, honest, genuine. [orig. unkn.]

Jăn′sen⸱is̄t, n. Member of party in Rom. Cath. Church esp. in France holding with Cornelius Jansen (d. 1638) the perverseness & inability for good of the natural human will. So ~ISM n., ~is̄′tic a. [-IST]

Jăn′uarỹ, n. (abbr. *Jan.*). First month of year. [ME & ONF *Jenever*, f. L *Januarius* (*mensis* month) of JANUS, see -ARY¹]

Jăn′us, n. Ancient Italian god, whose temple was closed in time of peace, guardian of doors & gates, represented with faces on front & back of head. [L]

Jăp, a. & n. (colloq.). Japanese. [abbr.]

japăn′¹, n. 1. (*J~*) island group on east of Asia, whence JAPANESE′ (-ēz) a. & n., **JăpanESQUE′** (-ĕsk) a. 2. Hard varnish, esp. kind brought orig. from J~; work in Japanese style. [app. f. Malay *Japung* f. Chin. *Jih-pun* sunrise (*jih* (Jap. *ni*, see NIPPON) sun + *pun* origin)]

japăn′², v.t. (-nn-). Lacquer with japan; make black & glossy as with japan. [f. prec.]

jăpe, v.i., & n. (literary). Jest. [f. 14th c., of unkn. orig.]

Japhĕt′ic, a. Of, descended from, Japheth son of Noah; Indo-European. [-IC]

japŏn′ic, a. Japanese. [f. *japon* = JAPAN + -IC]

japŏn′ica, n. Kinds of Japanese plant, esp. ornamental variety of pear or quince. [mod. L fem. adj. as prec.]

jăr′¹, n. Sound, vibration, esp. harsh one; thrill of nerves or feelings, shock; want of harmony, disagreement; quarrel. [as foll.]

jăr′², v.i. & t. (-rr-). Sound discordantly, make grating impression (*upon* person, his ear, nerves, etc.); strike with grating sound (*upon*, *against*, object); (of body affected) vibrate, resound, discordantly; (of opinion, statement, action) be at variance, disagree, (*with*); dispute,

wrangle; cause (thing) to ~; send shock through (nerves). Hence ~r′ingLY² adv [prob. imit.]

jăr′³, n. Earthenware, stoneware, or glass vessel with or without handle(s), usu. cylindrical; LEYDEN ~. Hence ~′FUL(2) n. [f. F *jarre* f. Arab. *jarrah*]

jăr′⁴, n. (colloq.). On the, on a, on, ~, ajar. [later form of obs. *char*; see AJAR¹]

jardinière (zhărdīnyăr′), n. Ornamental pot or stand for display of growing flowers in room, on window-sill, etc. [F]

jăr′gon′¹, n. Unintelligible words, gibberish; barbarous or debased language; mode of speech full of unfamiliar terms, as *critics′* ~, *metaphysical* ~; twittering of birds. Hence ~IZE(2, 3) v.t. & i. [ME, f. OF, of unkn. orig.]

jăr′gon′², jărgōon′, n. Translucent, colourless, or smoky variety of zircon found in Ceylon. [F, perh. ult. f. ZIRCON]

jărgonĕlle′, n. Kind of pear that ripens early. [F, dim. of prec.]

jărl (y-), n. (hist.). Old Norse or Danish chief. [ON, orig. man of noble birth; = EARL]

jă′rrah, n. (Durable timber of) W.--Austral. mahogany gum-tree. [f. native *jerrhyl*]

∥ **jărv′ey**, n. (pl.~s). Hackney-coachman; driver of Irish car. [by-form of surname *Jarvis*]

∥ **jăs′ey**, n. (old sl.). Wig, esp. of worsted. [said to be = Jersey]

jăs′min(e), jĕss′amin(e), n. Kinds of shrubs with white or yellow flowers, esp. *common* or *white* ~, climbing shrub with fragrant flowers; *winter* ~, with yellow flowers. [16th c., with F *jasmin, jessemin* f. Arab. f. Pers. *yasmin*]

jas′per (-ah-), n. Opaque variety of quartz, usu. red, yellow, or brown. [ME, f. OF *jaspre* f. L f. Gk *iaspis*, of oriental orig., = any bright chalcedony except carnelian; cf. Heb. *yashpeh*]

Jat (jaht), n. Member of a people widely distributed in N.W. India & varying in religion & occupation.

jaun′dice, n., & v.t. 1. Morbid state caused by obstruction of bile, & marked by yellowness of skin, fluids, & tissues, constipation, & loss of appetite; disordered vision (usu. fig.), as characteristic of this. 2. v.t. Affect with ~; (fig. esp. in p.p.) affect (person, his judgement etc.) with envy or jealousy. [ME *iaunes, iaund-,* f. OF *jaunice* f. *jaune* yellow, -ICE]

jaunt, v.i., & n. (Take) excursion, journey, esp. for pleasure; ~*ing-car*, light two-wheeled vehicle popular in Ireland. [16th c., orig. unkn.]

jaun′t⸲y̌, a. & n. 1. Having or affecting easy sprightliness, airy self-satisfaction. 2. n. (naut. sl.). ∥ Head of ship's police. Hence ~ilY² adv., ~iness n. [17th c. *jentee* repr. F pron. of F *gentil*; cf. GENTEEL]

Ja′van, Javanese′ (-ēz), (jah-), aa. & nn.

(Native) of Java; (-ese) language of central Java. [-AN; later -ESE after *Japanese*]

jäv′elin (-vl-), n. Light spear, dart. [f. F *javeline*, prob. of Celt. orig.]

jaw, n., & v.i. & t. **1.** *Lower, upper,* ~, two bones or sets of bones forming framework of mouth & masticating apparatus in vertebrates : ~-*bone*, each of the two bones forming lower ~ in most mammals, these two combined into one in others; (pl.) bones of mouth including teeth, mouth; (pl.) narrow mouth of valley, channel, etc.; (pl.) seizing members of machine, e.g. vice; (colloq.) loquacity, as *hold your* ~, stop talking, (also) sermonizing talk, lecture (esp. PI ²~); ~-*breaker* (colloq.), word hard to pronounce. **2.** vb. (sl.). Speak esp. at tedious length : lecture (person). [ME *jow(e)*, later *jaw(e)*, w. collateral *chaw(e)* (1530–1675); orig. unexpl.]

jay, n. Noisy chattering European bird of brilliant plumage; genus to which this belongs; (fig.) impertinent chatterer, simpleton; *~-walker*, pedestrian who crosses, or walks in, a street or road without due care or regard for traffic regulations. [ME, f. OF (mod. F *geai*), f. LL *gaius, gaia*]

jäzz, n., a., & v.i. & t. **1.** Music & dance of U.-S. Negro origin with characteristic harmony & ragtime rhythm; noisy or grotesque proceedings. **2.** adj. Discordant, loud in colour etc., rude, burlesque; ~ *band* (of such combinations as piano, trumpet, saxophone, banjo, & drums). **3.** vb. Play, dance, indulge in, ~; transform into, arrange as, ~. [orig. unkn.]

jea′lous (jĕl-), a. Solicitous for preservation *of* (rights etc.); resentful towards another on account of known or suspected rivalry; envious (*of* person, his advantages, etc.); (Bibl., of God) intolerant of unfaithfulness; (of inquiry, supervision, etc.) suspiciously vigilant. Hence ~LY² adv. [ME, f. OF *gelos* f. med. L *zelosus* (as ZEAL, see -OUS)]

jea′lousy (jĕlu-), n. Quality, state, of being jealous. [ME, f. OF *gelosie* (as prec., see -Y¹)]

jean (jān *or* jēn), n. Twilled cotton cloth; (pl.) garment of this, tight-fitting rather short slacks. [16th c., attrib. use of ME *Gene, Jane,* &c., = OF *Janne(s)*, mod. F *Gênes*, Genoa]

*jeep, n. Small utility motor vehicle. [f. *g p*, pr. jē pē, initials of *general purposes*]

jeer¹, n. (naut.). (Usu. pl.) tackle for hoisting & lowering lower yards. [orig. unkn.]

jeer², v.i. & t., & n. **1.** Scoff derisively (*at*); deride. **2.** n. Gibe, taunt. [orig. unkn.]

jehad. See JIHAD.

Jĕhō′vah (-*a*), n. Principal name of God in O.T. [repr. Heb. *Yahwe(h)*]

Jĕhō′vist, n. Author(s) of those parts of the Hexateuch in which God is called

Jehovah (cf. ELOHIST). Hence **Jĕhōvĭs′tĭc** a. [-IST]

Jĕ′hū, n. (joc.). Furious driver; driver. [*2 Kings* ix. 20]

jejune′ (-ōōn), a. Meagre, scanty; (of land) barren; unsatisfying to the mind. Hence ~LY² adv., ~NESS n. [f. L *jejunus* fasting]

Jĕk′yll and Hyde, n. Single person in whom two personalities alternate. [*Dr J. & Mr H.,* by Stevenson]

*jĕll, n. & v.i. (colloq.). Jelly. [f. foll.]

jĕll′y, n., & v.t. & i. **1.** Soft stiff semitransparent food, consisting chiefly of gelatin, got from skin, bones, etc., by boiling & cooling; similar preparation of juice of fruit etc.; ~-*bag* (for straining ~); ~-*fish*, pop. name of medusa or sea-nettle; ||~-*graph*, copying apparatus employing sheet of ~ in tray. **2.** vb. (Cause to) set as ~, congeal. [ME, f. OF *gelee* frost, jelly, f. Rom. *gelata* (L *gelare* freeze, see -Y⁴)]

jĕm′adār, n. Junior native officer of Indian army; Indian police-officer; head servant; (Anglo-Ind. colloq.) sweeper (domestic scavenger). [Urdu, f. Pers. (Arab.) *jama′* collection (of men)+Pers. *ddr* holder]

||**jĕmĭm′as** (-z), n. pl. (colloq.). Elastic-sided boots; goloshed cloth over-boots. [f. female personal name]

jĕmm′y, n. Crowbar used by burglars, usu. made in sections; || sheep's head as a dish. [fam. form of *James*]

je ne sais quoi (zhenesăkwah′), n. An indescribable something. [F, = I know not what]

jĕnn′ĕt, n. Small Spanish horse. [f. F *genet* f. Sp. *jinete* light horseman]

jĕnn′ĕtĭng, n. Kind of early apple. [f. F name *Jeannet*+-ING³]

jĕnn′y, n. Locomotive crane; = SPINNING-~; a stroke at billiards; she-ass; ~ *wren*, (pop. & nursery name for) wren. [fam. form of *Janet*]

jeo′pardize (jĕp-), -**ise** (-īz), v.t. Endanger. [foll., -IZE]

jeo′pardy (jĕp-), n. Danger. [ME *iuparti* f. OF *iu* (*ieu*) *parti* divided (i.e. even) game, f. L *jocus* game+*partitus* p.p. of *partiri* divide f. *pars -rtis* part]

jĕqui′rĭty, n. Indian twining shrub with parti-coloured seeds used for ornament & in medicine. [f. F *jéquirity* f. Tupi-Guaraní *jekiriti*]

jĕrbō′a (*or* jērb⁴), n. Small rodent of African deserts, with long hind legs & great jumping powers. [f. Arab. *yarbu′* flesh of loins, jerboa]

jĕrĕmi′ad, n. Lamentation, doleful complaint. [f. F *jérémiade* f. *Jérémie* f. LL *Jeremias* Jeremiah, see -AD]

Jĕrĕmi′ah, n. Doleful prophet or denouncer of the times. [*Lamentations of* ~, O.-T. bk]

Jĕ′richo (-kō), n. Town in Palestine; *go to* ~ (to the devil).

jerid' (-ĕd), **-eed**, n. Javelin used by Persian, Turkish, & Arabian horsemen; game in which this is used. [f. Arab. *jarīd*]

jĕrk¹, n. Sharp sudden pull, twist, etc.; involuntary spasmodic contraction of muscle; (pl.) spasmodic movements of limbs or face, esp. in religious excitement; PHYSICAL ~s. Hence ~'ĭLY² adv., ~'ĭNESS n., ~'Y² a. [16th c., imit.]

jĕrk², v.t. & i. Pull, thrust, twist, etc., with a jerk; throw with suddenly arrested motion; (intr.) move with a jerk. [as prec.]

jĕrk³, v.t. Cure (esp. beef) by cutting in long slices & drying in sun. [f. Amer. Sp. *charquear* (*charque* f. Peruv. *ccharqui* dried flesh)]

jĕrk'in, n. (hist.). Man's close-fitting jacket, often of leather. [c. 1500, of unkn. orig.]

Jĕrobo'ăm, n. Wine-bottle of 8–12 times ordinary size. ['A mighty man of valour' who made Israel to sin '—1 *Kings* xi. 28, xiv. 16]

jĕ'rry, n. ~-builder, -building, builder, building, of unsubstantial houses with bad materials; ~-built, so built; ‖ (also ~-shop) low beer-shop; ‖ (sl.) chamber-pot; (army sl., J~) German soldier, the Germans; jĕ'rrican, ~can, kind of (orig. German) petrol-can. [variously derived]

jĕrrymander. Erron. var. of GERRY-MANDER.

jĕrs'ey (-zĭ), n. (pl. ~s). 1. (J~). One of the Channel Islands (often attrib.); J~ cow. 2. Close-fitting woollen knitted tunic, esp. as worn in athletic exercises; similar garment worn as undervest; woman's close-fitting knitted jacket.

Jerus'alem (-rōō-), n. City in Israel; ~ (*pony*), donkey; ~ ARTICHOKE.

jĕss, n., & v.t. 1. Short strap of leather, silk, etc., round legs of hawk used in falconry. 2. v.t. Put ~es on (hawk). [ME *ges* f. OF *ges* nom. of *get* (mod. F *jet*) f. L *jactus* -*ūs* throw f. *jacĕre jact*-]

jessamine. See JASMINE.

Jĕss'e, n. ~ *window* (with Christ's descent from ~ represented). [*Is.* xi. 1, *Matt.* i. 6, 16]

jĕst¹, n. Piece of raillery or banter; taunt, ·jeer; joke; fun, esp. *in* ~, not seriously; object of derision, as *a standing* ~; ~-*book*, book of ~s. [orig. = exploit, f. OF *gĕste* f. L *gesta*, neut. pl. p.p. of *gerere* do]

jĕst², v.i. Joke; jeer; speak, act, in trifling manner, whence ~'ĭngLY² adv. [f. prec.]

jĕs'ter, n. One who jests, esp. professed maker of amusement maintained in court or noble household. [-ER¹]

Jĕs'ūit (-z-), n. Member of Society of Jesus, R.-C. order founded by Ignatius Loyola (1533); (derog., hist.) dissembling person, equivocator; ~s' (Peruvian) *bark*. Hence Jĕsūit'ICAL a., Jĕsūit'icalLY² adv., ~ISM(2), ~RY(4), nn., ~IZE(3) v.t. & i., (-z-). [f. mod. L *Jesuita* (*Jesus*, see -ITE¹)]

jĕt¹, n. & a. Hard black lignite taking brilliant polish; (of) colour of this, deep glossy black, (also ~-*black*). [ME *gete*, *ieet*, f. OF *jaiet* f. L f. Gk *gagātēs*]

jĕt², n. Stream of water, steam, gas, etc., shot forward or upwards esp. from small opening; spout, nozzle, for emitting water etc. thus; (colloq.) ~-propelled plane; ~-*propelled*, (esp. of aircraft) deriving propulsive power from the backward thrust of high-velocity ~s of gas discharged through nozzles in the rear of the wings, fuselage, etc.; so *jet* attrib., as ~ *engine*, *plane*. [f. foll. & f. F *jet* as foll.]

jĕt³, v.t. & i. (-tt-). Spurt forth in jets. [f. F *jeter* throw f. LL *jectare* = L *jactare* frequent. of *jacĕre jact*- throw]

jĕt'sam, n. Goods thrown overboard from ship to lighten it, & (in mod. use) washed ashore (cf. FLOTSAM). [contr. of foll.]

jĕtt'ison, n., & v.t. 1. Throwing of goods overboard, esp. to lighten ship in distress. 2. Throw (goods) overboard thus. [f. AF *getteson* (OF *getaison*) f. L *jactationem* (*jactare* throw, see JET³ & -ATION)]

jĕtt'on, n. Counter with stamped or engraved device. [F *jeton* (*jeter*, see JET³)]

jĕtt'y¹, n. Mole running out to defend harbour or coast; landing-pier. [f. OF *jetee* (mole) thrown out, fem. p.p. as JET³]

jĕtt'y², a. Jet-black. [JET¹, -Y²]

jeu (zher), n. (pl. ~x, pr. zher). ~ *de mots* (demō), play on words, pun; ~ *d'esprit* (děsprē'), witty or humorous (usu. literary) trifle. [F]

jeune fille (zhern fē'ye), n. Young girl, miss. [F]

jeune premier (zhern premyā'), n. (theatr.). Juvenile lead. [F]

jeunesse dorée (see Ap.), n. The gilded youth, young swells. [F]

Jew (jōō), n. One of the Hebrew or Jewish people, or one who professes Judaism; (transf., derog., vulg.) usurer, trader who drives hard bargains; ~-*baiting*, persecution of ~s; ~'s-*ear*, edible cup-shaped fungus; ~'s-*harp*, small lyre-shaped musical instrument, played by holding frame between teeth & striking metal tongue. Hence ~'ESS¹ n., ~'ISH¹ a., (jōō-). [ME, f. OF *giu* f. L f. Gk *Ioudaios* f. Aramaic *y'hudai* = Heb. *y'hudi* f. *y'hudah* Judah]

jew'ĕl (jōō-), n., & v.t. (-ll-). 1. Ornament containing precious stone(s), worn for personal adornment; precious stone; highly prized person or thing; *the* ~-*house*, room in Tower of London in which crown ~s are kept; hence or cogn. ~IER¹, ~IERY(1), ~RY, nn., ~IY² a. 2. v.t. Adorn, furnish, with ~s; fit (watch) with ~s for the pivot-holes. [ME, f. AF *juel* = OF *joel*, *jouel*, *joiel*, of disputed orig.]

jew'ing (jōō-), n. Wattles at base of beak in some domestic pigeons. [*Jew* (from resemblance to hooked nose) + -ING¹]

Jewry (joor'ĭ), n. The Jews; (hist.) Jews' quarter in town etc. [ME, f. AF *juerie* (JEW, -ERY)]

Jezail' (-zīl), n. Long Afghan musket. [Pers. *jazā'il*]

Jěz'ěbel, n. Impudent or abandoned woman; woman who paints her face. [~, wife of Ahab]

jib[1], n. Triangular stay-sail from outer end of ~-boom to fore-topmast head in large ships, from bowsprit to masthead in smaller ones; *cut of his* ~, his personal appearance; ~-*boom*, spar run out from end of bowsprit; projecting arm of crane. [17th c., goes w. foll.]

jib[2], v.t. & i. (naut.: -bb-). Pull (sail, yard) round from one side of ship to the other; (intr., of sail etc.) swing round thus. [17th c., shortened f. *jibe*, GYBE]

jib[3], v.i. (-bb-). (Of horse etc.) stop & refuse to go on, move backwards or sideways instead of going on, whence ~b'ER[1] n.; (fig.) refuse to proceed in some action; ~ *at*, show repugnance to (course, person). [19th c., of unkn. orig.]

jibb'a(h) (-ba), jŭ- (*or* jŏŏ-), dj-, n. Mohammedan's long cloth coat. [var. of Arab. *jubbah*]

jib door (dōr), n. Door flush with wall in which it stands, usu. painted etc. so as to be indistinguishable. [orig. unkn.]

jibe. See GIBE.

jiff' (y̆), n. (colloq.). Very short time, as *in a* ~, (*wait*) *half a* ~. [18th c., of unkn. orig.]

jig[1], n. Lively dance; music for this, usu. in three-four or six-eight time; appliance that holds a piece of work & guides the tools operating upon it. [16th c., orig. unkn.; perh. ult. imit.]

jig[2], v.i. & t. (-gg-). Dance a jig; move (t. & i.) up & down rapidly & jerkily; separate coarser & finer portions of (ore) by shaking it under water in box with perforated bottom; work upon with a ~, equip with ~s; ~*saw*, machine fretsaw (~*saw puzzle*, picture pasted on board & cut in irregular pieces with ~saw). [goes w. prec.]

jigg'er[1] (-g-), n. (Naut.) small tackle consisting of a double & single block with rope; small sail, small smack with this; (Billiards) rest for cue (sl.); (Golf) iron club with narrow face; one who jigs ore; ~*mast*, aftermost mast in four-master. [partly f. prec. +-ER[1]]

jigg'er[2] (-g-), n. = CHIGOE. [corrupt.]

jigg'ered (-gerd), a. (colloq.). (As mild oath) confounded (*I'm* ~). [euphem.]

‖**jigg'ery-pōk'ery** (-g-), n. (colloq.). Underhand scheming; hocus-pocus, humbug. [cf. Sc. *joukery-pawkery*]

jig'gle, v.t. Rock or jerk lightly. [f. JIG[2] +-LE(3)]

jihad', jē-, (-ahd), n. Religious war of Mohammedans against unbelievers; (fig.) crusade for or against a doctrine etc. [Arab. *jihad*]

Jill. Var. of GILL[3], as in JACK *&* ~.

jilt, n., & v.t. 1. One esp. a woman who capriciously casts off lover after encouragement. 2. v.t. Play the ~ towards, be faithless to. [' a new canting word ' in 1674, of unkn. orig.]

Jim Crow (-ō), n. Negro (~ *car*, to which Negroes in some southern States of U.S. are restricted on railroads); implement for straightening iron bars or rails by screw pressure. [nickname]

jim'-jăms', n. pl. (sl.). Delirium tremens; fit of the creeps. [whimsical reduplication]

‖**jimp**, a. (Sc.). Slender, graceful; scanty. [*c.* 1500, of unkn. orig.]

jingl|e (jĭng'gl), n., & v.i. & t. 1. Mingled noise like that of small bells, links of chain, etc.; repetition of same or similar sounds in words, esp. if designed to catch the attention; ~*ing* verse; Irish & Australian covered two-wheeled car. 2. vb. Make, cause (keys etc.) to make, a ~e; (of writing) be full of alliterations, rhymes, etc. [ME; imit.]

jing'ō (-ngg-), int., n. (pl. ~es), & a. 1. (In asseverations) *by* (*the living*) ~ *!*; supporter of bellicose policy, blustering patriot (orig. supporter of Disraeli's policy in 1878, f. use of *by* ~ in popular song). 2. adj. Vulgarly dashing. Hence ~ISM(2), ~IST(2), nn., ~ĭs'tĭc a. [17th c.; orig. conjurer's gibberish]

jink, v.i. & t., & n. 1. Move elusively, dodge, elude by dodging; (sl.) manœuvre aircraft, be manœuvred, jerkily to avoid anti-aircraft fire etc. 2. n. Act of ~ing; *high* ~s, boisterous sport, merrymaking. [orig. Sc.; prob. imit. of nimble motion]

jinnee', n. (pl. *jinn*, often used as sing.; fem. ~*yeh* pr. -yä). (In Mohammedan demonology) spirit, lower than angels, able to appear in human & animal forms, & having supernatural power over men (also GENIE). [f. Arab. *jinni*; cf. GENIE]

jinrick'sha, -rik'isha, n. Light two-wheeled hooded vehicle drawn by man or men, first used in Japan *c.* 1870. [Jap. (-*kisha*), f. *jin* man + *riki* power + *sha* vehicle]

***jinx**, n. (sl.). Person or thing that brings bad luck. [orig. unkn.]

jĭr'g'a, n. Assembly of Afghan headmen. [Pushtu]

***jit'ney**, n. (sl.). Five cents; motor-bus carrying passengers at low rates. [orig. unkn.]

jĭtt'er, v.i., & n. (sl., orig. U.S.). 1. Be nervous, act nervously; ~*bug* n., person addicted to dancing to ' hot ' music, nervous person. 2. n. pl. Extreme nervousness, ' nerves ', (*have the* ~s, be in a blue funk). Hence ~Y[2] a. (sl.), nervy, jumpy. [imit.; cf. dial. *chitter*]

jiu-jitsu. See JU-JUTSU.

jive, n., & v.i. 1. Kind of jazz music. 2. v.i. Play ~, dance to ~. [orig. unkn.]

Job¹, n. Piece of work, esp. one done for hire or profit; (colloq.) employment, post; transaction in which duty is sacrificed to private advantage; anything one has to do (*on the ~*, sl., in action, alert); *do person's ~*, ruin him; *bad ~*, thing on which labour is wasted, failure; *good, bad, ~* (state of affairs); *~ lot*, lot of goods bought as speculation; ||*~'master*, one who lets out horses & carriages by the *~*; *~-work*, done & paid for by the *~*. [16th c., of unkn. orig.]

Job², v.i. & t. (-bb-). Do jobs; ||hire (horse, carriage) for definite time or job, let out on hire thus; buy & sell (stock, goods) as broker; deal in stocks; turn position of trust to private advantage; deal corruptly with (matter), whence *~b'ERY*(4)n. Hence *~b'ER¹* n. [f. prec.]

Job³, v.t. & i. (-bb-). n. 1. Prod, stab slightly; hurt (horse) with bit; (intr.) thrust *at* (thing). 2. n. Prod, thrust, jerk at bit. [15th c., app. imit.; cf. JAB]

Job⁴, n. Patriarch whose story forms *Book of Job* in O.T. (*would try the patience of ~*, is vexatious); *~'s comforter*, one who under guise of comforter aggravates distress; *~'s tears*, seeds of a grass used as beads.

jobā'tion, n. (colloq.). Reprimand, esp. lengthy one. [17th c., f. obs. *jobe* reprove f. prec. +-ATION]

||**jobb'ernowl** (-ōl), n. (colloq.). Stupid head; stupid person. [f. obs. *jobard* fool (f. F, f. *jobe* silly) +NOLL]

||**Jock**, n. (army sl.). Scottish esp. Highland soldier. [= Jack]

jock'ey¹, n. (pl. *~s*). Professional rider in horse-races (also colloq. jock); *J~ Club*, club established at Newmarket, the body controlling horse-racing; ||lad, understrapper. Hence *~DOM*, *~SHIP*(3), nn. [f. Sc. *Jock* Jack +-Y³]

jock'ey², v.t. & i. Outwit, cheat; get (person etc.) *away, out, in*, etc., by trickery; cheat (person *into, out of, doing*); (intr.) cheat; *~ for position*, try to gain an advantageous position esp. by skilful manœuvring in yacht-racing, try to gain an unfair advantage. [f. prec.]

jock'o, n. (pl. *~s*). Chimpanzee. [F, made by Buffon f. Gaboon *engeco* (prop. *ncheko*)]

jocōse', a. Playful; waggish. Hence *~LY³* adv., *~NESS*, jocōs'ITY, nn. [f. L *jocosus* (*jocus* jest, see -OSE¹)]

joc'ular, a. Mirthful; humorous. Hence or cogn. *~ITY* (-ă'r-) n., *~LY²* adv. [f. L *jocularis* (*joculus* dim. of *jocus* jest, -AR¹)]

joc'und, a. Merry, sprightly; pleasant. Hence or cogn. jocŭn'dITY n., *~LY²* adv. [ME, f. OF, f. LL *jocundus* f. L *jucundus*, influenced by assoc. w. *jocus* jest]

jodh'purs (jŏdpĕrz), n. pl. Long breeches for riding etc., tight from knee to ankle. [*Jodhpur* in India]

||**Jōe**, n. *Not for ~* (i.e. me) *!*, sl. refusal.

Jōe Mill'er, n. Stale joke, chestnut. [f. *Joseph Miller*, comedian, d. 1738]

jō'ey¹, n. (pl. *~s*). Young kangaroo; young animal. [f. native Austral. *joë*]

||**jō'ey²**, n. (sl.). A threepenny (orig. in 1836 a fourpenny) bit. [f. *Joseph Hume*]

jŏg, v.t. & i. (-gg-), & n. 1. Shake with push or jerk; nudge (person), esp. to arouse attention; stimulate (person's, one's own, memory); move up & down with unsteady motion; proceed laboriously, trudge, (often *on, along*); go on one's way, depart, as *we must be ~ging*; proceed, get through the time, as *we must ~ on somehow, matters ~ along*; *~'trot*, slow regular trot, (fig.) monotonous progression (often attrib.). 2. n. Shake, push, nudge, slow walk or trot. [16th c., app. imit.]

jŏg'gle¹, v.t. & i., & n. 1. Shake, move, (as) by repeated jerks. 2. n. Slight shake. [f. prec. +-LE(3)]

jŏg'gle², n., & v.t. 1. Joint of two pieces of stone or timber, contrived to prevent their sliding on one another; notch in one of two pieces, projection in the other, or small piece let in between both, for this purpose. 2. v.t. Join by means of a *~*. [(vb f.n.) perh. f. *jog* =JAG¹]

Jŏhänn'ine, a. Of the apostle John. [f. L as JOHN, see -INE¹]

Jŏhänn'isbërger (-g-), n. Fine white wine from Johannisberg in the Rheingau. [G]

John (jŏn), n. Masculine Christian name; *~ BARLEYcorn*; *~ Bull*, English nation, typical Englishman; *~ Chinaman*, typical Chinese; *~ COMPANY*; *~ Doe*, fictitious character in law (cf. RICHARD *Roe*); *~ DORY¹*; *~-o'-Groat's* (-*House*), north of Scotland (*from ~-o'-Groat's to Land's End*, through Gt Britain). [f. LL *Jo(h)annes* f. Gk *Iōánnēs* f. Heb. *Yokhanan*]

John'ian (jŏn-), a. & n. (Member) of St John's College, Cambridge. [-IAN]

johnn'y (jŏn-), n. ||Fellow, esp. fashionable idler; ||*J~ Armstrong* (naut. sl.), hand-power; *J~ Raw*, novice; *~-cake*, cake of (U.S.) maize-meal or (Austral.) wheat-meal. [f. JOHN, -Y³]

Johnsōn'ian (jŏn-), a. Of, like, Samuel Johnson, man of letters & lexicographer (d. 1784), esp., abounding in Latin-derived polysyllables. So **JohnsonESE'** (jŏnsŏnēz') n. [-IAN]

joie de vivre (zhwah de vē'vr), n. Feeling of healthy enjoyment of life. [F, = joy of living]

join, v.t. & i., & n. 1. Put together, fasten, unite, (things, one *to* another); connect (two points) by straight line; unite (persons, one *with* or *to* another) in marriage, friendship, alliance, etc.; (intr.) come together, be united, (*with, to*, or abs.); take part with others (*in doing*); come into the company of (person); become member of (club etc.); take, resume, one's place in (regiment, ship, company, etc.); come into connexion with, as *the Cherwell ~s the Thames below Oxford*; *~ battle*, begin fighting; *~ hands*, clasp one's hands together, clasp each other's hands, (fig.) combine in action or enterprise; ~ ISSUE¹; ~ *up* (intr.), enlist in the army etc. 2. n. Point, line, of junction. [ME, f. OF *joindre* (st. *joign-*) f. L *jungere junct-* join]

join′der, n. (rare exc. law). Joining, union. [f. F *joindre* JOIN taken as noun, cf. -ER¹]

join′|er, n. In vbl senses, esp. one who makes furniture, house fittings, & other woodwork lighter than carpenter's, whence ~ERY(1, 2) n. [ME, f. AF *joignour* (JOIN, -ER¹, -OR)]

joint¹, n. Place at which two things are joined together; structure in animal body by which two bones are fitted together; *out of* ~, (of bone) dislocated, (fig.) out of order; *put* (person's) NOSE *out of* ~; part of stem from which leaf or branch grows; point at which, contrivance by which, two parts of artificial structure are joined, rigidly or so as to allow of movement; (Geol.) fissure in mass of rock; one of the parts of which a body is made up; ‖ one of the parts into which butcher divides carcass, esp. as served at table; (sl., esp. U.S.) a place of meeting or resort; ~*-stool* (orig. *joined*), one made of parts fitted by a joiner, night-stool, commode. Hence ~LESS a. [ME, f. OF, p.p. as JOIN]

joint², a. Held or done by, belonging to, two or more persons etc. in conjunction, as ~ *action, opinion, estate*; (of persons) sharing (*with* others in possession, action, state, etc.), as ~ *owners*; *during their* ~ *lives*, while they are all alive; ~ *stock*, capital held ~ly, common fund, (attrib.) holding, formed on basis of, a ~ stock, as ~*-stock bank, company*. Hence ~LY² adv. [ME, f. OF, as prec.]

joint³, v.t. Connect by joints; fill up joints of (masonry etc.) with mortar etc., point; prepare (board etc.) for being joined to another by planing its edge; divide (body, member) at a joint or into joints. [f. JOINT¹]

join′ter, n. In vbl senses, esp.: plane for jointing; mason's tool for pointing; workman employed in jointing esp. electric wire. [-ER¹]

join′tress, n. Widow who holds a jointure. [f. obs. *jointer* joint possessor + -ESS¹]

join′ture, n., & v.t. 1. Estate settled on a wife, to be enjoyed by her after her husband's death. 2. v.t. Provide (wife) with ~. [ME, f. OF, f. L *junctura* (as JOIN, see -URE)]

joist, n. One of parallel timbers stretched on edge from wall to wall for ceiling laths or floor boards to be nailed to. Hence **jois′ted²** a. [ME *giste* f. OF *giste* (*gesir* lie f. L *jacēre*)]

joke¹, n. Thing said or done to excite laughter; witticism, jest; ridiculous circumstance; *practical* ~, trick played on person in order to have laugh at his expense; *it is no* ~ (a serious matter). Hence **jŏk′Y²** a. [f. 17th c., prob. f. L *jocus* jest]

joke², v.i. & t. Make jokes; poke fun at, banter. Hence **jŏk′ingLY²** adv. [f. prec. or f. L *jocari* as prec.]

jŏk′er, n. One who jokes; (sl.) fellow, chap; (Cards) odd (often blank) card in some games, counting as (highest) trump; *a clause unobtrusively inserted in a bill or document & affecting its operation in a way not immediately apparent. [-ER¹]

jokul, jökull (yō′kool̄, yĕr̄-), n. Snow-mountain in Iceland. [Icel. *jökull*; see ICICLE]

jŏll′i|fy, v.i. & t. Make merry, esp. tipple; make jolly. Hence ~FICA′TION n. [-FY]

jŏll′ity, n. Merrymaking, festivity. [ME, f. OF *jolivete* (as JOLLY, see -TY)]

jŏll′y, a., adv., n., & v.t. 1. Joyful; slightly drunk; festive, jovial; *the* ~ *god*, Bacchus; (colloq., of person or thing) very pleasant, delightful, (often iron., as *he must be a* ~ *fool to do it*), whence **jŏll′ILY²** adv. 2. adv. (colloq.). Very, as *he will be* ~ *savage, you will* ~ *well have to*. 3. n. (sl.). ‖ Royal Marine. 4. v.t. (colloq.). Flatter, cajole (usu. ~ *along*); chaff, banter. [ME & OF *joli(f)* gay, pretty; ult. orig. unkn.]

jŏll′y-boat, n. (Also *jolly*) clinker-built ship's boat, smaller than cutter. [18th c., of unkn. orig.; cf. 16-17th c. *jolywat*, *gellyvatte*; cf. YAWL²]

jŏlt, v.t. & i., & n. 1. Shake (person etc.) with jerk from seat etc., esp. in locomotion; (of vehicle) move along with jerks, as on rough road. 2. n. Such jerk. Hence **jŏl′tY²** a. [c. 1600, of unkn. orig.]

jŏl′terhead (-hĕd), n. Clumsy head; stupid person. [extension of obs. *jolthead*, of unkn. orig.]

Jŏn′ah (-a), n. Person who brings, or is sacrificed lest he bring, ill luck. [see *Jonah*, O.T. book]

Jŏn′athan, n. 1. (*Brother*) ~, personified people of, typical citizen of, United States. 2. Kind of dessert apple. [perh. f. ~ Trumbull, governor of Connecticut]

jongleur (see Ap.), n. (hist.). Itinerant minstrel. [F, var. of *jougleur* JUGGLER]

jŏn′quil (or jŭ-), n. Species of narcissus, daffodil with rushlike leaves; ~ colour, pale yellow. [f. mod. L *jonquilla* = F *jonquille*, Sp. *junquillo*, f. L dim. of *juncus* reed]

jŏrd′an, n. (not in polite use). Chamber-pot. [ME also *jurdan(e)* vessel used by alchemists; orig. unascert.]

Jŏrd′an almond (ahm-), n. Fine almond esp. from Malaga. [ME *jardyne*, app. f. OF or Sp. *jardin* garden]

jŏr′um, n. Large drinking-bowl; its contents, esp. punch. [orig. unkn.; conject. = *Joram* (2 *Sam.* viii. 10); cf. JEROBOAM]

jŏs′eph (-z-), n. (*J*~) chaste man; woman's long riding-cloak of 18th c. [see *Gen.* xxxix, xxxvii. 3]

*jŏsh, n., & v.t. & i. (sl.). **1.** Good-natured joke, leg-pull. **2.** vb. Hoax, banter; indulge in ridicule. Hence ~'ER¹ n. [U.S.]

jŏs'kin, n. (sl.). Country bumpkin, dolt. [cf. *bumpkin*, & *joss* dial. to bump]

jŏss, n. Chinese idol; ~-*house*, Chinese temple; ~-*stick* (of fragrant tinder mixed with clay, as incense). [app. f. Port. *deos* f. L *deus* god]

‖ **jŏss'er,** n. (sl.). Fool; fellow. [-ER¹]

jŏ'stle (-sl), v.i. & t., & n. **1.** Knock, push, *against*; struggle *with* (person *for* thing); push against, elbow; push (person *away*, *from*, etc.). **2.** n. Jostling, encounter. [earlier *justle*, f. *just* JOUST + -LE(3)]

jŏt¹, n. (Usu. w. negative expressed or implied) small amount, whit; ~ *or* TITTLE. [f. L f. Gk *iōta* letter *i*]

jŏt², v.t. (-tt-). Write (usu. *down*) briefly or hastily. [prob. f. prec.]

joule (jŏŏl), n. (electr.). Unit of work or energy, amount of work done or heat generated by a current of one ampere acting for one second against a resistance of one ohm. [Dr. J. P. *Joule*, Eng. physicist (d. 1889)]

jounce, v.t. & i. Bump, bounce, jolt. [15th c., of unkn. orig.]

journ'al (jĕr-), n. **1.** (In bookkeeping by double entry) book in which each transaction is entered, with statement of accounts to which it is to be debited & credited. **2.** Daily record of events; (Parl.) *the J*~s, record of daily proceedings; (Naut.) log-book; daily newspaper, other periodical. **3.** Part of shaft or axle that rests on bearings (hist. unexpl.); ~-*box* (enclosing ~ & bearings). [ME, f. OF f. LL *diurnalis* DIURNAL]

journ'al|ist (jĕr-), n. One whose business it is to edit or write for a public journal. Hence or cogn. ~ESE' (-ēz) n., style of language characteristic of (hasty or inferior) newspaper writing, ~ISM n., ~is'TIC a. [-IST]

journ'alīze (jĕr-), -ise (-īz), v.t. & i. (Bookk.) enter in journal; record in, keep, private journal. [-IZE]

journ'ey (jĕr-), n. (pl. ~s), & v.i. **1.** Distance travelled in specified time, as *a day's*, *4 days'*, ~; expedition to some distance, round of travel (usu. by land, cf. VOYAGE), as *take*, *undertake*, *perform*, *a* ~; ~*man*, qualified (dist. *apprentice*) mechanic or artisan who works for another, (fig.) mere hireling; (Astron.) ~*man* (*clock*), secondary clock in observatory; ~-*work*, work of a ~man (esp. fig.). **2.** v.i. Make a ~. [ME; (v̆b f. AF *journeyer*) f. OF *jornee* day, day's work or journey, f. Rom. **diurnata* day (LL *diurnum* day f. L -*us* daily); see -Y¹]

joust (jŏŏst), jŭst, v.i., & n. (Engage in) combat between two knights etc. on horseback with lances. [(n. f. OF *juste*) ME *just(e)* f. OF *juster* f. Rom. **juxtare* approach (*juxta* near)]

Jōve, n. Jupiter, esp. ‖ *by* ~ *!* [f. L *Jovem* (nom. *Jupiter*)]

jŏv'ial, a. Merry; convivial. Hence or cogn. ~ITY (-ăl⁴) n., ~LY² adv. [f. F f. It. *gioviale* f. LL *jovialis* of Jupiter (*Jupiter Jovis*, see -AL)]

jōv'ian, a. Of, like, Jove; of the planet Jupiter. [f. F *jovien* or LL *Jovianus* (as prec., -AN)]

jowl, n. Jawbone, jaw; cheek, esp. *cheek by* ~; external throat or neck when prominent, dewlap of cattle, crop of bird; head & shoulders of salmon & other fish. [(1) ME *chauel* jaw (f. OE *ceafl*); (2) ME *cholle* neck (cf. OE *ceolur*); (3) ME *cholle* head of man, beast, fish; f. 16th c. all levelled out into unexplained *joule*, *jowl*]

joy¹, n. Vivid emotion of pleasure, gladness; thing that causes delight; ~-*bells* (rung on festive occasions); ~-*ride* (sl.), stolen or other pleasure-ride in motor etc.; ~-*stick* (sl.), control lever of aeroplane. Hence or cogn. ~'FUL, ~'LESS, ~'OUS, aa., ~'fulLY², ~'lessLY², ~'ousLY², advv., ~'fulNESS, ~'lessNESS, ~'ousNESS, nn. [ME, f. OF *joie* f. Rom. **gaudia* fem. f. L *gaudia* pl. of *gaudium*]

joy², v.i. & t. (chiefly poet.). Rejoice; gladden. [ME, f. OF *joir* rejoice ult. f. L *gaudēre* rejoice]

jub'il|āte¹ (jŏŏ-), v.i. Exult, make demonstrations of joy. Hence or cogn. ~ANCE, ~A'TION, nn., ~ANT a., ~antLY² adv. [f. L *jubilare* (*jubilum* shout), see -ATE³]

Jubilāt'e² (jŏŏ-; *or* yŏŏblaht'I), n. Hundredth psalm as canticle in Anglican service; outburst of triumph. [L, = shout ye (its first word)]

jub'ilee (jŏŏ-), n. **1.** (Jewish hist.) year of emancipation & restoration, kept every 50 years, acc. to *Lev.* xxv; (R.-C. Ch.) year of remission from penal consequences of sin, granted formerly at various intervals, now at any time. **2.** Fiftieth anniversary; *silver* ~, twenty-fifth anniversary; *Diamond J*~, 1897, sixtieth year of reign of Queen Victoria. **3.** Season of rejoicing; exultant joy. [ME, f. OF *jubile* f. LL *jubilaeus* (*annus* year) of jubilee f. Gk *iōbēlaios* (*iōbēlos* f. Heb. *yobel* ram, ram's-horn trumpet, jubilee) by assoc. w. L *jubilare* shout]

Judā'ic (jŏŏ-), a. Jewish. [f. L f. Gk *Ioudaikos* (*Ioudaios* JEW¹, see -IC)]

Jud'ā|ize (jŏŏ-), -ise (-īz), v.i. & t. Follow Jewish customs or rites; make Jewish. So ~ISM, ~IST, nn. [f. LL *judaizare* f. Gk *ioudaïzō* (as prec., see -IZE)]

jud'as (jŏŏ-), n. (*J*~) disciple who betrayed Christ, infamous traitor; peephole in door; (of beard etc.) *J*~-*colour(ed)*, red. *J*~ *kiss* (see *Matt.* xxvi. 48); *J*~-*tree* (with purple flowers appearing before the leaves).

jŭdd'er, v.i. & n. **1.** Shake, wobble. **2.** n. Shaking, wobbling. [imit.]

Jud'enhetze (yŏŏdenhĕtze), n. Systematic persecution of Jews. [G]

judge¹, n. Public officer appointed to hear & try causes in court of justice; (of God) supreme arbiter; (Heb. hist.) officer having temporary authority in Israel in period between Joshua & the kings; (pl., abbr. *Judg.*) book of O.T.; person appointed to decide dispute or contest; person who decides a question; person who is qualified to decide on merits of thing or question, as *am no ~ of that, good~ of claret*; *J~ Advocate General*, civil officer in supreme control of courts martial in army and R.A.F.; *~made law*, principles based on ~s' decisions. Hence ~'SHIP(1, 2) n. [ME, f. OF *juge* f. L *judicem* (nom. *-dex*) f. *jus* right + *-dicus* speaking]

judge², v.t. & i. Pronounce sentence on (person) in court of justice; try (cause); decide (question); decide, decree, *(that* etc.); form opinion about, estimate, (person etc. *by* his deeds etc.); (arch.) criticize, censure (*~ not that ye be not~d*); conclude, consider, suppose, (thing *to be, that*, etc., *from...or by* data); act as judge; form a judgement (*of* thing etc.). [ME, f. OF *jugier* f. L *judicare* (as prec.)]

judgemăt´ic|(al) (-jm-), aa. (colloq.). Judicious, discerning. Hence~aLLY² adv. [f. JUDGE, on *dogmatic* etc.]

judge´ment (-jm-), **-gment** (-jm-), n. Sentence of court of justice; *the last ~* (by God at end of world); misfortune viewed as sign of divine displeasure, as *it is a ~ on you for getting up late*; criticism; opinion, estimate, as *in my ~*; critical faculty, discernment; good sense; *~day* (of God's final *~*); *~ debt* (for payment of which a *~* has been given); *~ creditor, debtor* (for, against, whom *~* has been given); ǁ*~ summons* (for failure to pay *~* debt); *~-seat*, judge's seat, tribunal. [ME, f. OF *jugement* (as prec., see -MENT)]

jud´icature (joo-; *also* -kā-), n. Administration of justice; *Supreme Court of J~ in England* (consisting of the Court of Appeal & the High Court of Justice; the latter is composed of the Queen's Bench, the Chancery, & the Probate, Divorce, & Admiralty divisions, & the Court of Criminal Appeal); judge's (term of) office; body of judges; court of justice. [f. F, or med. L *judicatura* (as JUDGE, -URE)]

judicial (jŏodĭsh´al), a. Of, done by, proper to, a court of law; *~ murder*, legal but unjust death sentence; inflicted as a divine judgement (esp. *~ blindness*, punitive infatuation); having the function of judgement, as *a ~ assembly*; of, proper to, a judge; expressing a judgement, critical; impartial. Hence ~LY² adv. [ME, f. OF, or L *judicialis* (as foll., -AL)]

judiciary (jŏodĭsh´arĭ), n. The judges of a State collectively. [f. L *judiciarius* (*judicium*, see foll.)]

judicious (jŏodĭsh´us), a. Sensible, pru-

dent; sound in discernment and judgement. Hence ~LY² adv., ~NESS n. [f. F *judicieux* f. L *judicium* judgement (as JUDGE¹), see -OUS]

ju´dō (jōō-), n. (Now usu. name for) JU-JUTSU.

jŭg¹, n. Deep vessel for holding liquids, with handle & often with spout, whence *~'FUL(2)* n.; (sl., also *stone~*) prison. [perh. f. *Jug*, pet form of *Joan* &c.]

jŭg², v.t. (-gg-). Stew, boil, (hare, rabbit) in jug or jar (usu. in p.p.); (sl.) imprison. [f. prec.]

jŭg³, v.i. (-gg-). (Of nightingale or other bird) utter sound *jug*. So *~, ~·~*, nn. [imit.]

jug´ate (jōō-), a. (bot.). Having leaflets in pairs. [f. L *jugare* join (*jugum* yoke), see -ATE²]

Jŭgg´ernaut (-g-), n. (Hind. myth.) Krishna, eighth avatar of Vishnu, his idol at Puri, annually dragged in procession on huge car, under wheels of which devotees are said to have formerly thrown themselves; (fig., also *~ car*) institution, notion, to which persons blindly sacrifice themselves or others. [f. Hind. *Jagannath* f. Skr. *-natha* (*jagat* world + *natha* lord)]

jŭgg´ins (-gĭnz), n. (sl.). Simpleton. [perh. f. proper name *Juggins* (as JUG¹); cf. MUGGINS]

jŭg´gle, v.i. & t., & n. **1.** Play conjuring tricks; *~ with*, deceive (person), misrepresent (facts); cheat (person etc. *out of* thing); bring, get, change, (*away, into*, etc.) by trickery. **2.** n. Piece of juggling, fraud. [ME, f. OF *jogler* f. L *joculari* jest (*joculus* dim. of *jocus* jest)]

jŭgg´l|er, n. Conjurer; trickster, impostor. So ~ERY(2, 4) n. [ME, f. OF *jo(u)glere*, acc. *-eor*, f. L *joculator, -orem* (as prec., see -OR)]

Jugoslav (ūg´oslahv), a. & n. (Inhabitant) of the State, including Serbia, Montenegro, & parts of the former Austrian Empire, called *Jugoslavia*. [Serb., = south Slav]

jŭg´ular (*or* jōō-), a. & n. **1.** Of the neck or throat; *~ veins*, great veins of neck, conveying blood (*external ~*) from superficial parts of head, (*internal ~*) from inside of skull; (of fish) having the ventral fins in front of the pectoral. **2.** n. *~* vein. [f. LL *jugularis* f. L *jugulum* collar-bone, throat]

jŭg´ulāte (*or* jōō-), v.t. Kill, esp. (fig.) arrest course of (disease etc.) by powerful remedy etc. [f. L *jugulare* (as prec.), see -ATE³]

juice (jōōs), n. Liquid part of vegetables or fruits; fluid part of animal body or substance, esp. *the ~s*, the bodily humours, *gastric ~*; (fig.) essence, spirit, of anything; (sl.) petrol or electricity used in engine etc. Hence ~´LESS (-sl-) a. [ME, f. OF *jus* f. L *jus* broth, juice]

jui´c|y̆ (jōō-), a. Full of juice, succulent;

(of weather) wet; (colloq.) of rich intellectual quality, interesting; (art sl.) of rich colouring suggestive of moisture. Hence ~ɪ̄NESS n. [-Y²]

ju-ju (jōō'jōōb), n. (W.-Afr.). Charm or fetish; ban effected by this. [perh. f. F *jou-jou* toy]

ju'jube (jōō'jōōb), n. Edible berry-like drupe of certain plants; lozenge of gelatin etc. flavoured with or imitating this. [F, or med. L *jujuba* f. Gk *zizuphon*]

ju-jutsu, jiu-jitsu, (jōōjutsōō'), n. Japanese art of wrestling etc. (now usu. *judo*). [Jap. (*ju-*)]

•**juke'box** (jōōk-), n. Machine that automatically plays selected gramophone records when coin is inserted. [*juke* app. of W.-Afr. orig.]

jul'ep (jōō-), n. Sweet drink, esp. as vehicle for medicine; medicated drink as stimulant etc.; •iced & spiced spirit & water, esp. *mint* ~. [ME, f. OF, f. Arab. *julab* f. Pers. *gulab* (*gul* rose + *ab* water)]

Jul'ian (jōō-), a. Of Julius Caesar; ~ *calendar* (introduced by him, in which the year consisted of 365 days, every fourth year having 366, cf. GREGORIAN). [f. L *Julianus* (*Julius*, see -AN)]

julienne (see Ap.), n. Soup of vegetables cooked in meat broth. [F]

July' (jōō-), n. Seventh month of year, called after Julius Caesar. [ME & OF *Jule*, *Juil* f. L *Julius*; also *Julie* f. AF f. L; 18th-c. pron. jōō'lı̌, mod. pron. irreg. & unexpl.]

jŭm'bal, -ble¹, n. Kinds of crisp thin sweet cake. [perh. orig. a use of GIMBAL]

jŭm'ble², v.i. & t. Move (t. & i.) about in disorder; mix *up*, confuse. [prob. imit.]

jŭm'ble³, n. Confused assemblage; muddle; jolting; ‖ ~-*sale* (of miscellaneous cheap articles at bazaar etc.); ~-*shop* (where miscellaneous goods are sold). Hence **jŭmb'lȳ²** a. [f. prec.]

jŭm'bō, n. (pl. ~s). Big clumsy person, animal, or thing, esp. (*J*~) famous elephant in London Zool. Gardens; notably successful person. [perh. = second element in MUMBO-JUMBO]

jŭmp¹, n. Leap, bound, spring from ground; *long*, *high*, ~, athletic competitions; start caused by shock or excitement, esp. (sl.) *the* ~*s*, delirium tremens; abrupt rise in amount, price, value, etc.; sudden transition, gap in series, argument, etc. Hence **jŭm'pĭNESS** n., **jŭm'pȳ²** a. [f. foll.]

jŭmp², v.i. & t. **1.** Spring from ground etc. by flexion & sudden muscular extension of legs or (of fish) tail; move suddenly with leap or bound (*up* from seat etc., *out*, etc.); ~ *in*, get quickly into carriage etc.; start with sudden jerk from excitement, shock, etc., esp. ~ *for joy*. **2.** Rise suddenly in price etc. **3.** Come *to*, arrive *at*, (conclusion) hastily. **4.** ~ *at*, (fig.) accept (offer, bargain) eagerly; ~ (*up*)*on*, attack (offender etc.) crushingly

with word or act. **5.** Agree, coincide, (*together*, one *with* another). **6.** Pass over (gate etc.) by leap; (of railway carriage) leave (line). **7.** Help (child etc.) to ~ *down* etc.; cause (thing) to ~; startle (person, nerves). **8.** Cook (potatoes etc.) in frying--pan, occasionally shaking them (usu. in p.p.). **9.** Pounce upon (thing); steal a march upon (~ *the queue*); take summary possession of (claim abandoned or forfeited by former occupant). **10.** Skip over (subject, part of book, etc.). **11.** Drill (rock, hole in rock) with jumper. **12.** ~ *down* person's *throat*, answer, interrupt, him violently; ~ *out of one's skin*, ~ with surprise; ~ *over the* BROOMstick. Hence ~'ABLE a. [f. 1500; prob. imit.]

jŭm'per¹, n. In vbl senses, esp.: member of Welsh Methodist body (or later sects) who jump(ed) as part of worship; jumping insect, e.g. flea; rope made fast to keep yard, mast, etc., from jumping; heavy chisel-ended iron bar for drilling blasting-holes. [-ER¹]

jŭm'per², n. Loose outer jacket of canvas etc. worn by sailors etc.; woman's loose outer garment of any material slipped on over head & reaching hips. [prob. f. (17th c., now dial.) *jump* short coat perh. f. F *juppe*]

jŭm'ping, a. In vbl senses, esp. in names of ~ animals, as ~-*deer*, N.-Amer. black--tailed deer; ~-*bean*, seed of Mexican plant ~ owing to movements of enclosed larva; ~ CAT¹. [-ING²]

jŭnc'tion, n. Joining; joint, meeting--place; station where railway lines meet & unite (often in proper names, as *Clapham J*~). [f. L *junctio* (as JOIN, see -ION)]

jŭnc'ture, n. Joining; place where things join; concurrence of events, state of affairs, as *at this* ~. [ME, f. L *junctura* (JOIN, -URE)]

June (jōōn), n. Sixth month of year. [ME *Juyn* f. OF *Juin* f. L *Junius*; also ME *June*, after L]

jungle (jŭng'gl), n. Land overgrown with underwood or tangled vegetation, esp. in India (often attrib. of animals inhabiting ~, as ~-*bear*, -*cat*, -*fowl*); wild tangled mass; ~ *fever*, kind of severe malaria. Hence **jŭng'lED²**, **jŭng'lȳ²**, (-ngg-), aa. [f. Hind. *jangal* desert, forest]

jun'ior (jōō-), a. & n. **1.** The younger (esp. of son having same name as father, as *John Smith* ~, or of younger of two boys of same surname in school; abbr. *jun.*, *jr*); of less standing, of lower position, as ~ *partner*. **2.** n. person, as *the* ~*s*, *is my* ~. Cf. SENIOR. Hence ~ITY (-ŏ'r-) n. [L, compar. of *juvenis* young]

jun'iorate (jōō-), n. (In Society of Jesus) two-years' course attended by junior members before entering priesthood. [-ATE¹]

jun'iper (jōō-), n. Kinds of coniferous evergreen shrubs, esp. *common* ~, shrub with prickly leaves & dark berries yielding *oil of* ~ used in medicine & in making gin. [ME, f. L *juniperus*]

Junk¹, n., & v.t. Old cable cut up for oakum etc.; discarded material, rubbish; lump, chunk; (naut.) salt meat; lump of tissue in sperm-whale, containing spermaceti; ~*-shop*, marine store, (derog.) antique dealer's shop; (v.t.) divide into ~s. [f. 1485, of unkn. orig.]

Junk², n. Flat-bottomed sailing vessel used in Chinese seas. [16th c., app. ult. f. Javanese *djong*]

Junker (yŏong'ker), n. Young German noble; member of exclusive aristocratic party in Prussia. [G, earlier *junkher* (YOUNG, HERR); see YOUNKER]

Junk'ĕt, n., & v.i. 1. Dish of sweetened curds & whey, usu. with scalded cream on top; feast. 2. v.i. Feast, picnic. Hence ~ING¹ n. [ME *jonket*, app. f. ONF *jonquette* rush-basket (for making ~) f. *jonc* rush f. L *juncus*]

Jun'o (jōō-), n. (pl. ~s). Wife of Jupiter; woman of stately beauty; third of the asteroids. [L]

Jŭn'ta, n. Deliberative or administrative council in Spain or Italy; = foll. [Sp., f. L *juncta*, fem. p.p. as JOIN]

Jŭn'tŏ, n. (pl. ~s). Clique, faction, political or other combination of persons. [erroneous f. prec.]

Jupe (jōōp), n. Woman's skirt. [F]

Ju'piter (jōō-), n. (Rom. myth.) king of gods; ~ *Plu'vĭus* (plōō-), god of rain (joc.); largest planet of solar system. [L]

Jur'al (joor-), a. Of law, of (moral) rights & obligations. [f. L *jus juris* right + -AL]

Jurăss'ic (joor-), a. Of the Jura mountains between France & Switzerland; marked like these by prevalence of oolitic limestone. [f. F *jurassique* after *liassic, triassic*]

‖ **jur'at** (joor-), n. Municipal officer like alderman; life magistrate in Channel Is. [f. med. L *juratus* (*jurare* swear)]

jurid'ical (joor-), a. Of judicial proceedings; legal. [f. L *juridicus* (*jus juris* right + -dicus f. *dicere* say) + -AL]

jur'isconsŭlt' (joor-), n. One learned in law, jurist. [f. L *jurisconsultus* (*jus juris* law + p.p. as CONSULT)]

jurisdic'tion (joor-), n. Administration of justice; legal or other authority; extent of this, territory it extends over. Hence ~AL (joorĭsdĭk'shon-) a. [ME *jure-, juri-, juris-* f. OF *jure-, juridiction* & L *jurisdictio* (as prec., see DICTION)]

jurisprud'|ence (joorĭsprōō-), n. Science, philosophy, of human law, whence ~en'tIAL (joorĭsprōōděn'shal) a.; skill in law, so ~ENT (joorĭsprōō-)'a. & n. [f. LL *jurisprudentia* (as prec., see PRUDENCE)]

jur'ist (joor-), n. One versed in law; legal writer; student of, graduate in, law. Hence **juris'tIC(AL)** aa., **juris'ticalLY²** adv., (joor-). [f. F *juriste* or med. L *jurista* (*jus juris* law, see -IST)]

jur'or (joor-), n. Member of jury; one who takes an oath (cf. NON-*juror*). [ME, f. AF *jurour* (OF *jureor*) f. L *juratorem* (*jurare* swear, see -OR)]

jur'ȳ (joor-), n. Body of persons sworn to render verdict on question submitted to them in court of justice; *grand* ~ (of persons formerly appointed to inquire into indictments before they were submitted to trial~); *trial, common, petty,* ~ (of 12 persons who try final issue of fact in civil or criminal cases & pronounce verdict; *special* ~ (of persons of certain station in society); CORONER'S ~; ~ *of matrons* (in case where pregnancy is pleaded in stay of execution); body of persons selected to award prizes in competition; ~*-box*, enclosure for ~ in court; ~*-man,* ~*-woman,* member of ~. [ME, f. AF (OF) *juree* oath, inquiry, f. med. L *jurata* (*jurare* swear, cf. -Y⁴)]

jur'y-mast (joor'Imahst), n. Temporary mast in place of broken or lost one. [orig. unkn.]

jŭss'ive, a. (gram.). Expressing a command. [f. L *jubēre juss-* command]

jŭst¹, a. (Of person or conduct) equitable, fair, (*to* person etc.); (of treatment etc.) deserved, as *a* ~ *reward*; (of feelings, opinions, etc.) well-grounded, as ~ *resentment, fear*; right in amount etc., proper. Hence ~'LY² adv., ~'NESS n. [ME, f. OF *juste* or L *justus* (*jus* right)]

jŭst², adv. Exactly, as ~ *at that spot,* ~ *there,* ~ *then,* ~ *three o'clock,* ~ *as you say,* ~ *so, that is* ~ *it* (precisely the point in question), ~ *how many there are remains to be seen*; barely, as *I* ~ *managed it*; exactly at that moment, (loosely) not long before, as *I have* ~ (a moment, or not long, ago) *seen him pass*; ~ *now,* at this moment, (also) a little time ago; (colloq.) positively, quite, as *it is* ~ *splendid, not* ~ *yet*; (as sl. emphasizer) *Won't I* ~ *give it him!, ' Did he swear? Didn't he,* ~*!* ' [ME, f. prec.]

jŭst³. See JOUST.

jŭs'tice n. Just conduct; fairness; exercise of authority in maintenance of right; *poetic(al)* ~, reward of virtue & punishment of vice; judicial proceedings, as *Court of J~*; magistrate; judge, esp. (in England) of Supreme Court of Judicature, whence ~SHIP n.; *J~ of the Peace,* lay magistrate appointed to preserve peace in county, town, etc.; *do* ~ *to,* treat fairly, show due appreciation of; *do oneself* ~, perform worthily of one's abilities. [ME, f. OF (*-ice, -ise*), f. L *justitia* (as JUST¹, see -ICE)]

jŭsti'ciable (-shya-), a. Subject to jurisdiction; (n.) person subject to jurisdiction (*of* another). [OF, f. *justicier* bring to trial f. med. L *justitiare* (as prec.), see -ABLE]

jŭsti'ciar (-shya*r*), n. Chief political & judicial officer under Norman & early Plantagenet kings. [as foll., see -AR²]

justi'ciary (-shya-), n. & a. **1.** Administrator of justice; = prec. **2.** adj. Of the administration of justice. [f. med. L *justitiarius* (JUSTICE, -ARY¹)]

jus'ti|fy̆, v.t. Show the justice or rightness of (person, act, etc.); vindicate, (of circumstances) be such as to ~fy; (theol.) declare (person) free from penalty of sin on ground of Christ's righteousness or (Rom. Cath.) of the infusion of grace; (print.) adjust (line of type) to fill a space neatly; make good (statement etc.); adduce adequate grounds for (conduct, claim, etc.); ~fy̆ bail, show by oath of person furnishing bail that he is pecuniarily qualified. Hence or cogn. ~fiABIL'ITY, ~fiCA'TION, nn., ~fiABLE, ~fic̆ative, ~fic̆atory, aa., ~fiabLY² adv. [f. F *justifier* f. LL *justificare* (as JUST¹, see -FY)]

jŭt, n., & v.i. (-tt-). **1.** Projection; protruding point. **2.** v.i. Project (often *out*, *forth*). [var. of JET², ³]

jute¹ (jōōt), n. Fibre from certain plants, chiefly imported from Bengal, used for sacking, mats, etc. [f. Bengali *jhoṭo* f. Skr. *juṭa* = *jaṭa* braid of hair]

Jute² (jōōt), n. One of Low German tribe invading Britain in 5th & 6th cc. [rendering Baeda's *Jutae*, *Juti*, in OE *Eotas*, *Iōtas* = Icel. *Iótar* people of Jutland]

juveněs'c|ence (jōō-), n. (Transition from infancy to) youth. So ~ent a. [f. L *juvenescere* reach age of youth (*juvenis* young), see -ENCE]

juv'ĕnile (jōō-), a. & n. **1.** Young, youthful; suited to, characteristic of, youth. **2.** n. Young person; (pl., trade term for) books meant for children. Hence or cogn. ~ly² (-l-li) adv.; juvenil'ity (jōō-) n. [f. L *juvenilis* (as prec., -IL)]

juvenil'ia (jōō-), n. pl. Works produced in author's youth (often as title of collection of such writings). [L, neut. pl. of *juvenilis* JUVENILE]

jŭxtapōse' (-z), v.t. Place (things) side by side. [f. F *juxtaposer* (L *juxta* next + *poser*, see COMPOSE)]

jŭxtaposi'tion (-zi-), n. Placing, being placed, side by side. [F (L *juxta* next, POSITION)]

K

K, k, (kā), letter (pl. Ks, K's).

kaama (kah'ma), n. Hartebeest. [S. Afr.]

Kaba'ka (-bah'-), n. (Title of) ruler of Buganda. [native]

kabbalah. = CABBALA.

Kabȳle', n. A Berber of Algeria or Tunis; Berber dialect spoken by the ~s. [f. Arab. *qabā'il* tribes]

ḱădd'īsh, n. Jewish mourner's prayer; the *Magnificat* in the synagogue service. [f. Aram. *qaddish* holy]

kadi. See CADI.

Kăff'ir (-fer), (obs.) **Căf'fre** (-fer), n. Member of a S.-Afr. people of Bantu

family; (pl.) S.-Afr. mine shares. [as foll.]

Kăf'ir (-er), n. Native of Kafiristan in Asia. [Arab. *kāfir* infidel]

ka'gŏ (kah-), n. Japanese basket-work palanquin slung on pole. [f. Jap. *kango* of Chin. orig.]

kail(yard). See KALE.

kain'ĭt(e) (kīn-), n. Hydrated double salt of magnesium chloride & sulphate & potassium sulphate, used as fertilizer. [G (-*it*), f. Gk *kainos* new, see -ITE¹]

kai'ser (kīz-), n. (hist.). Emperor; German Emperor; Emperor of Austria; head of Holy Roman Empire. Hence ~SHIP n. [in mod. E f. G *kaiser* & Du. *keizer*; in ME f. OE *cāsere* f. Gmc adoption (thr. Gk (whence Goth.) *kaisar*) of L CAESAR]

kajă'wah (-jahwa), n. Camel-litter for women. [Hind. & Pers.]

ka'ka (kah-), n. New Zealand parrot. So ~pō n., New Zealand owl-like nocturnal parrot. [Maori (*po* = night)]

kăkemōn'ŏ, n. Japanese wall-picture (usu. painted on silk & mounted on rollers). [f. Jap. *kake-* hang +*mono* thing]

kala-azar (kahlah-ahzär'), n. Virulent infectious malarial disease of oriental tropics. [Assamese, = black disease]

kāle, kail n. Kinds of cole or cabbage, esp. borecole, kind with wrinkled leaves; *Scotch* ~, kind with purplish leaves; broth made of this or other vegetables; SEA ~; ~'yard, kitchen-garden; ~yard school, writers of fiction describing, with much use of the vernacular, common life in Scotland. [ME; northern form of COLE]

kaleid'o|scope (-lid-), n. Tube through which are seen symmetrical figures, produced by reflections of pieces of coloured glass, & varied by rotation of the tube; (fig.) constantly changing group of bright objects. Hence ~scŏp'ic(AL) aa., ~scŏp'icalLY² adv. [f. Gk *kalos* beautiful +*eidos* form +-SCOPE]

kalends. See CALENDS.

kăl'ĭ, n. Prickly saltwort, from which soda-ash was obtained. [f. Arab. *qali* ALKALI]

kalian, -lioun, (kahlyahn', -yōōn), n. Persian form of hookah. [Pers. (-*an*), f. Arab. *qalyan, -un*]

Kăl'mŭck, -mȳk, a. & n. (Member, language) of a Mongolian people living on the Caspian.

ka'lŏng (kah-), n. Malay frugivorous fox-bat, largest known bat. [Malay]

kăl'pa, n. Great age of the world, day of Brahma, (4,320,000,000 years). [Skr.]

kămerad' (-ahd), int. of German soldier offering to surrender. [G, f. F as COMRADE]

ka'mĭ (kah-), n. Japanese title of governors etc.; divinity, god, in Japanese native religion.

kămpŏng', n. Enclosed space, village. [Malay; see COMPOUND³]

kăn'aka, n. South Sea Islander, esp. one formerly employed in Queensland on sugar plantations. [Polynesian, = man]

Kănarēse' (-z), n. (Member of) Dravidian people living in western India; language of the ~. [f. N. & S. *Kanara* in India]

kăngaroō' (-ngg-), n. Marsupial mammal with strongly developed hindquarters & great leaping-power, native of Australia, Tasmania, etc.; ~ *rat*, small Australian marsupial; (sl., pl.) W.-Australian mining shares, dealers in these; ~ *bicycle*, one with sloping back, early form of safety; ‖ ~ *closure* (when chairman in committee selects some amendments for discussion and excludes others). [perh. native Austral.]

kanoōn', n. Kind of harp with fifty to sixty strings. [f. Pers. or Arab. *qanun*]

Kǎn't|ĭan, a. Of Immanuel Kant, German philosopher, d. 1804. So ~ISM n. [-IAN]

ka'olĭn (kah-, kā-), n. Fine white clay produced by decomposition of feldspar, used in making porcelain. Hence ~IZE(3) v.t. [F, f. Chin. *kao-ling*, name of mountain (*kao* high + *ling* hill)]

kăpěll'meister (-mī-), n. Conductor of orchestra, opera, choir, etc.; ~ *music*, uninspired music in routine style. [G]

kăp'ŏk, n. Fine cotton wool surrounding seeds of certain tree, used for stuffing cushions etc. [f. Malay *kapoq*]

kăpp'a, n. Greek letter k (*K, κ*).

kăput' (-ŏŏt), a. (sl.). Done for, smashed (in pred. use only). [G]

Kǎr'aïte, n. Member of Jewish sect that rejects Rabbinical tradition & interprets scriptures literally, found chiefly in Crimea. [f. Heb. *q'raïm* (*qara* read) + -ITE[1]]

kǎrm'a, n. (Buddh.). Sum of person's actions in one of his successive states of existence, viewed as deciding his fate in the next; destiny. [Skr., = action, fate]

kar(r)oō', n. Elevated plateau of clayey soil in S. Africa, waterless in dry season; *the Great K~* (in Cape Province). [of Hottentot orig.]

karŏss', n. Mantle of animals' skins with the hair on, used by S.-African natives. [f. Afrikaans *karos*, of unkn. orig.]

kǎrt'el, n. Wooden bed in S.-African ox--wagon. [Afrikaans, prob. f. Port. *catel* f. Tamil *kaṭṭil* bedstead]

kartěll'. See CARTEL.

kătabăt'ĭc, a. (meteorol.). (Of winds) caused by air flowing downward (cf. ANABATIC). [f. Gk *katabatikos* f. *katabainō* go down]

kătăb'olism, cata-, n. (biol.). Breaking down of animal tissues (cf. METABOLISM). [f. Gk *katabolē* throwing down (*kataballō* throw down) +-ISM]

kathode. Var. of CATHODE.

kation. Var. of CATION.

kăt'ўdid, n. Large green orthopterous insect abounding in America. [imit. of the sound the insect produces]

kauri (kowr'ĭ), n. Coniferous tree of New Zealand, furnishing valuable timber & a resin, ~-*gum*. [Maori]

ka'va (kah-), n. (Diuretic beverage from roots of) a Polynesian shrub. [native]

kavăss', n. Armed constable, servant, or courier, in Turkey. [f. Turk. *qawwas* bow-maker (*qaws* bow)]

kay'ak (kī-), n. Eskimo canoe of light wooden framework covered with seal-skins. [Eskimo]

kea (kā'a), n. Green alpine parrot of New Zealand which destroys sheep for their kidney-fat. [Maori, imit.]

kĕck, v.i. Make sound as if about to vomit; ~ *at*, reject (food etc.) with loathing. [imit.]

keddah. See KHEDA.

kĕdge, v.i. & t., & n. **1.** Warp ship by means of hawser attached to small anchor; (of ship) move thus; move (ship) thus. **2.** n. (Also ~-*anchor*) small anchor for this purpose. [perh. spec. use of obs. *cagge*, dial. *cadge* bind, tie]

kĕdg'eree, n. Indian dish of rice, split pulse, onions, eggs, etc.; European dish of fish, rice, eggs, etc. [f. Hind. *khichri*, Skr. *k'ṛsara*]

‖ **keek**, v.i., & n. (Sc.). Peep. [ME *kike*; cf. MDu., MLG *kiken*]

keel[1], n., & v.t. **1.** Lowest longitudinal timber of vessel, on which framework of the whole is built up; combination of iron plates serving same purpose in iron vessel; (poet.) ship; *false* ~ (attached to bottom of true ~ to protect it); ~-*blocks* (on which ~ rests in building etc.); ~-*haul*, haul (person) under ~ as punishment. **2.** v.t. Turn (ship) ~ upwards; ~ *over*, upset, capsize, (person etc.). Hence ~'LESS (-l-l-) a. [ME *kele*, f. ON *kjölr* f. Gmc **keluz*]

keel[2], n. Flat-bottomed vessel, esp. of kind used on Tyne etc. for loading colliers; amount carried by this. [ME *kele* f. MLG *kēl, kil*, MDu. *kiel*, ship, boat, = OE *cēol* &c. f. Gmc **keulaz*]

keelson. See KELSON.

keen[1], n. Irish funeral song accompanied with wailing. [f. Ir. *caoine*, as foll.]

keen[2], v.i. & t. Utter the keen; bewail (person) thus; utter in wailing tone. [f. Ir. *caoinim* wail]

keen[3], a. Having sharp edge or point; (of edge etc.) sharp; (of sound, light, etc.) penetrating, vivid, strong; (of frost) moderately hard; (of pain etc.) acute, bitter; (of person, desire, interest) eager, ardent, (colloq. *on* thing, *on* doing; ~ *as mustard*, enthusiastic, w. pun on *Keen's* mustard); (of eyes, sight, smell) sharp, highly sensitive; intellectually acute; ~-*set*, hungry, eager, (*for*). Hence ~'LY[2] adv., ~'NESS n. [OE *cēne*, OHG *kuoni*, ON *kœnn* f. Gmc **kōnjaz*]

keep, v.t. & i. (*kĕpt*). **1.** Pay due regard to, observe, stand by, (law, promise, faith, treaty, appointment; ~ *the* PEACE). **2.** Celebrate (feast, ceremony, etc.). **3.** Guard, protect, (person, as *God* ~ *you!*

fortress, town, etc., goal at football etc.).
4. Have charge of; retain possession of, not lose or destroy. **5.** Maintain (house etc.) in proper order (~ *open house*, entertain all comers), carry on (shop etc.); maintain (diary, accounts, books) by making requisite entries. **6.** Provide for sustenance of (family, one*self*, etc.); own & manage (cows, bees, etc.); maintain (woman) as mistress. **7.** Have (commodity) habitually on sale. **8.** ~ COMPANY[1], PACE, STEP, LOOK[1] *out*, TIME, WATCH[1], WICKET (also abs., act as wicket-keeper). **9.** Maintain in proper or specified condition (often in spec. senses, as ~ *the* BALL[1] *rolling*, *pot boiling*, one's HAIR *on*, one's HEAD[1]; ~ one's *balance*, not lose it, lit. & fig.). **10.** Detain (person *in prison*, *in custody*, etc.); restrain (person, thing, one*self*, *from doing*, *from* thing); refrain *from*. **11.** Reserve (thing *for* future time etc.). **12.** Conceal, as ~ one's COUNSEL[1], *a secret*. **13.** Continue to follow (way, course; ~ *track of*, follow the course or development of). **14.** Remain in (one's bed, room, house); retain one's place in (the saddle, the field, the stage, one's ground, etc.) against opposition; ~ one's *feet*, not fall; ~ HOUSE; remain (indoors etc.); ‖ (colloq., esp. Camb. Univ.) reside, as *where do you* ~ ? **15.** Remain in specified condition, as ~ *in good health*, ~ *in* TOUCH *with*, ~ *cool*, (colloq.) ~ *friends*. **16.** Continue in specified direction, course, or action, as ~ *straight on for two miles, she* ~*s giggling*. **17.** (Of food etc.) remain in good condition; (fig., of news etc.) admit of being reserved for later occasion. **18.** ~ (work, cause to work, persistently) *at*; ~ (abstain) *from*; ~ *to*, adhere to (course, promise), confine oneself to; ~ (thing etc.) *to* one*self*, refuse to share it with others; ~ one*self to* one*self*, avoid society. **19.** ~ *away*, avoid coming, prevent from coming; ~ *back*, hold back, retard progress of, conceal; ~ *down*, hold in subjection, ~ low in amount, (mil.) lie low in skirmishing; ~ *in*, continue, restrain, (feelings etc.), confine (schoolboy) after hours, ~ (fire) burning, (intr.) remain indoors, remain on good terms *with*; ~ one's HAND *in*; ~ *off*, ward off, avert, (intr.) stay at a distance; ~ *on*, continue to hold, use, show, etc., (intr.) continue (*doing*); ~ *out*, not let enter; ~ *together*, remain, cause to remain, together; ~ *under*, hold in subjection; ~ *up*, prevent (one's spirits, prices, etc.) from sinking, maintain (~ one's END[1] *up*; ~ *it up*, not slacken), ~ in repair, in efficient or proper state, etc., (~ *up appearances*; ~ *up your Greek*), carry on (correspondence etc.), cause (person) to sit up at night, (intr.) bear up, not break down, proceed at equal pace *with* (~ *up with the Joneses*, ~ on terms of equality with one's neighbours). [late OE *cēpan* of unkn. orig.]

keep², n. (Hist.) tower, stronghold; maintenance, food required for this, as *you don't earn your* ~; *for* ~*s* (colloq.), in permanence. [f. prec.]

keep'er, n. In vbl senses, esp.: ‖=GAME[1]-~; custodian of museum, art gallery, etc.; lunatic's attendant; ring that keeps another, esp. wedding-ring, on the finger. [-ER[1]]

keep'ing, n. In vbl senses, also or esp.: custody, charge, as *in safe* ~, *in his* ~; agreement, harmony, (orig. esp. of painting) as *in*, *out of*, ~ (*with*); (attrib., or intr. part.) fit for ~, as ~ *apples*; *~-room*, sitting-room usually occupied. [-ING[1]]

keep'sāke, n. Thing kept for sake, or in remembrance, of giver; (attrib.) namby-pamby, like certain literary annuals of 19th c. called ~s. [KEEP[1]+SAKE]

keeshond (kās'hŏnd), n. Breed of Dutch dogs resembling the chow. [Du.]

kĕf, **keif** (kĭf), **kief** n. Drowsy state produced by bhang etc.; enjoyment of idleness; Indian hemp etc. smoked to produce ~. [f. Arab. *kaif*, colloq. *kef*, well-being]

kĕffi'yeh (-fēyǎ), n. Bedouin Arab's kerchief worn as head-dress. [f. Arab. *kaffiyah*, *kuffiyeh*, perh. f. LL *cofea* COIF]

kĕf'ir (-er), n. Effervescent liquor like koumiss, used for invalids. [Caucas.]

kĕg, n. Small barrel, usu. of less than 10 gals. [f. 15th c. *cag*, f. ON *kaggi*, of unkn. orig.]

kĕlp, n. Large kinds of seaweed; calcined ashes of seaweed used for the sake of carbonate of soda, iodine, etc. contained, formerly used in making soap & glass. [ME *cŭlp(e)*, of unkn. orig.]

kĕl'pie, **-pȳ**, n. (Sc.). Water-spirit, usu. in form of horse, reputed to delight in the drowning of travellers etc. [orig. unkn.]

kĕl'son, **keel'son**, n. Line of timber fastening ship's floor-timbers to keel. [ME *kelswayn*, -*sweyn*, -*swyn(e)*, -*syng* f. MDu. *kelswijn*, MLG *kelswin* (as KEEL, SWINE); *kelson* as *bosun* f. *boatswain*]

kelt[1] etc. See CELT etc.

kĕlt², n. Salmon or sea trout after spawning. [ME; orig. unkn.]

kĕmp, n. Coarse hair in wool. Hence **kĕm'pY²**a. [f. ON *kampr* beard, whisker]

kĕn[1], n. Range of sight or knowledge, esp. *in*, *out of*, *beyond*, one's ~. [f. foll.]

‖ **kĕn²**, v.t. (now Sc. or north.; *kĕnt*). Recognize at sight; know (person, thing, fact, *that* etc.). [OE *cennan*, OS *kennian*, OHG *chennan*, ON *kenna*, Goth. *kannjan* f. Gmc *kann-* CAN²]

kĕnn'el[1], n., & v.i. & t. (-ll-). **1.** House for shelter of house-dog or hounds; mean dwelling. **2.** v.i. Live in, go to, ~; (v.t.) put into, keep in, ~ [ME, f. ONF *kenil* (F *chenil*) f. med. L *canile* (*canis* dog)]

kĕnn'el², n. Gutter. [earlier *cannel* f. OF *canel* CHANNEL]

kĕnōs'ĭs, n. (theol.). Renunciation of divine nature, at least in part, by Christ in the incarnation. So **kĕnŏT'ĬC** (-ŏt-) a., **kĕnŏt'ĬCISM**(3) n. [Gk *kenōsis* (*kenoō* vb empty f. *kenos*, see -OSIS)]

Kĕn'tish, a. Of Kent; ‖ ~ *fire*, prolonged volley of applause or demonstration of dissent; ~ *man* (born W. of Medway, opp. *man of Kent* born E.); ~ *rag*, hard limestone found in Kent. [OE *Centisc* (*Cent* f. L *Cantium*, see -ISH[1])]

kĕnt'lĕdge, n. (naut.). Pig-iron used as permanent ballast. [f. F *quintelage* ballast, w. assim. to *kentle* QUINTAL; see -AGE]

kĕp'ĭ, n. French military cap with horizontal peak. [f. F *képi* f. G-Swiss *käppi* dim. of *kappe* cap]

Kepler's laws. See LAW[1].

kept. See KEEP[1].

kĕ'ratin, n. Nitrogenous substance forming the basis of horns, claws, nails, etc. [as foll. +-IN]

kĕ'ratōse, a. & n. **1.** Of horny substance. **2.** n. Horn-like substance forming part of some sponges. [f. Gk *keras -atos* horn + -OSE[1]]

‖ **kĕrb, ⋆cŭrb**, n. **1.** Stone edging to pavement or raised path; ~*stone*, one of stones forming this. **2.** (St. Exch. sl.). The STREET; ~*stone broker* (not a member of the Stock Exchange); ~ *market*, (place for) sale of securities after hours or of shares not dealt with on the Stock Exchange). [var. of CURB n.]

kĕrch'ief (-ĭf), n. Cloth used to cover head; (poet.) handkerchief. Hence ~ED[2] (-ĭft) a. [ME *curchef, ker-*, f. OF *couvrechief, cuevre-*, (*covrir* COVER + *chief* head f. L *caput*)]

kĕrf, n. Slit made by cutting, esp. with saw; cut end of felled tree. [OE *cyrf*, f. st. of CARVE]

kĕrm'es (-ĭz), n. Pregnant female of an insect, formerly taken for a berry, feeding on ~ *oak*, an evergreen oak of S. Europe & N. Africa; red dye-stuff consisting of dried bodies of these; amorphous trisulphide of antimony, of brilliant red. [also 16th c. *chermez*, f. F *kermes* & It. *chermes* f. Arab. & Pers. *qirmiz*]

kĕrm'ĭs n. Periodical·fair in Holland etc., with much noisy merrymaking. [Du., orig.=mass on anniversary of dedication of church, when yearly fair was held. (*kerk* KIRK +*miss* MASS[1])]

kĕrn(e), n. (hist.). Light-armed Irish foot-soldier; peasant, boor. [f. Ir. *ceithern*]

kĕrn'el, n. Softer (usu. edible) part within hard shell of nut or stone-fruit; body of seed within husk etc., e.g. grain of wheat; nucleus, centre of formation (often fig.). [OE *cyrnel*, dim. of CORN]

kĕ'rosēne, -ine (-ēn), n. Lamp-oil obtained by distillation of petroleum & from coal & bituminous shale, paraffin. [irreg. f. Gk *kēros* wax + -ENE]

Kĕ'rrў, n. attrib. ~ *blue*, a breed of terrier. [place]

kĕrs'ey (-zĭ), n. Kind of coarse narrow cloth woven from long wool, usu. ribbed. [ME, prob. f. K~ in Suffolk]

kĕrs'eymēre (-zĭ-), n. Twilled fine woollen cloth; (pl.) trousers of this. [alt. of *cassimere*, var. of CASHMERE, assim. to prec.]

kĕs'trel, n. Species of small hawk. [16th c. *cast-, kist-, kest-*, perh. f. OF *cresserelle* of unkn. orig.]

kĕtch, n. Two-masted vessel with mizzen-mast stepped forward of rudder. [in 15th c. *cache, catch*, f. CATCH[1, 2]]

kĕtch'up, n. Sauce made from juice of mushrooms, tomatoes, etc. [prob. f. Chin. *kôe-chiap* brine of pickled fish]

kĕt'ōne, n. One of a class of organic compounds allied to the aldehydes of which acetone is the simplest. [f. G *keton* alt. of *acetone*]

kĕt'tle, n. Vessel, usu. of metal with spout & handle, for boiling water; FISH[1]·~; *a pretty ~ of fish*, awkward state of affairs; ~*drum(mer)*, (player of) hollow brass or copper hemisphere, over edge of which parchment is stretched & tuned to definite note; ~*drum*, (also) large afternoon tea-party; ~*holder*, piece of cloth etc. to protect hand from heat of ~ handle. Hence ~FUL(2) n. [f. ON *ketill* = OE *cetel, cietel* (ME *chetel*), OS *ketel*, CHG *kezzil*, Goth. ⋆*katils* f. L *catillus, catinus*]

kĕv'el, n. (naut.). Peg, cleat, ısu. fixed in pairs, to which certain ropes are belayed. [ME, f. ONF *keville* (F *cheville*) f. L *clavicula* dim. of *clavis* key]

Kew Gárdens, n. pl. National botanical gardens at Kew, London.

key[1] (kē), n. **1.** Instrument, usu. of iron, for moving bolt of lock forwards or backwards; *get, have, the~ of the street*, be shut out for the night, homeless; MASTER[1] ~. **2.** *House of Keys*, elective branch of legislature of I. of Man; *St Peter's* ~*s*, cross ~s borne in Papal arms. **3.** What gives or precludes opportunity for or access to something; *golden, silver, ~*, money used as bribe. **4.** (pl.). Ecclesiastical authority as transmitted to the Pope, esp. *power of the* ~*s*. **5.** Place that from its position gives control of sea, territory, etc. **6.** Solution, explanation, literal translation of foreign book; book of solutions of mathematical problems etc.; word or system for solving cipher or code (also ~*word*). **7.** (Mus.) system of notes definitely related to each other & based on particular note; (fig.) tone, style, of thought or expression; ~*note*, note on which a ~ is based, (fig.) prevailing tone or idea. **8.** Piece of wood or metal inserted between others to secure them. **9.** Part of first coat of wall plaster passing between laths & so securing the rest. **10.** Lever pressed by finger in playing organ, piano, flute, concertina, etc.; similar lever in typewriter etc. **11.** Instrument for grasping screws, pegs, nuts, etc., esp. one for winding. **12.** ~'*board*, set of ~s on piano etc.; ~-*bugle* (fitted with ~s to increase number of sounds); ~'*hole* (by which ~ is put into lock); ~ *industry*, one essential to the carrying on of others, e.g. coal-mining, dyeing; ~ *map* (in bare outline, to simplify use of full map); ~ (*move*), (chess) first move in solution of a problem; ~-*ring* (for keeping ~s on); ~*stone*, voussoir at summit of arch locking the whole together, (fig.) central principle etc. on which all depends. Hence ~'LESS (kē-) a. [OE *cǣg*(*e*), OFris *kei*, *kay*, of unkn. orig.]

key[2] (kē), v.t. Fasten (often *in*, *on*, etc.) with pin, wedge, bolt, etc.; regulate pitch of strings of (piano etc.); word (an advertisement in a particular periodical) so that answers to it can be identified (usu. by varying the form of address given); (fig.)~ *up*, stimulate (person *to do*, *to* condition etc.), raise the tone or standard of, brace up, raise (offer, demand, endeavour). [f. prec.]

key[3] (kē), n. Low island or reef. [f. Sp. *cayo*, see CAY, QUAY]

khadd'ar (kă-), n. Indian homespun cloth. [Hindi]

khakan (kahkahn'), n. = KHAN[1]. [f. Turk. *khaqan* king, emperor]

kha'ki (kah-), a. & n. **1.** Dust-coloured, dull-yellow. **2.** n. ~ fabric of twilled cotton or wool, used in Brit. army since S.-African war. [Hmd., = dusty (*khak* dust)]

khal'ifa, khal'ifăt, (kă-), nn. = CALIPH-(ATE).

kham'sin (kă-), n. Hot S. or S.E. wind in Egypt for about 50 days in March, April, & May. [Arab. (*khamsun* fifty)]

khan[1] (kăn, kahn), n. Title of rulers & officials in Central Asia, Afghanistan, etc.; (hist.) supreme ruler of Turkish, Tartar, & Mongol tribes, & emperor of China, in Middle Ages. Hence ~'ATE[1](1) n. [Turk., alt. f. KHAKAN]

khan[2] (kăn, kahn), n. Caravanserai. [Arab., = inn]

khe'da (kă-), *kĕdd'ah*, n. Enclosure used in Bengal etc. to catch elephants. [Hind. (-*da*)]

Khedive' (kĭdēv'), n. (hist.). Title of viceroy of Egypt, accorded to Ismail Pasha by Turkish Government in 1867; abolished in 1914. Hence Khedi'v(I)AL (kĭdē-) aa. [f. F *khédive* ult. f. Pers.]

khi (kī), n. Greek letter (*X*, *χ*)=ch. [Gk]

khid'mutgar (kĭ-), n. Male servant who waits at table (in India). [f. Urdu *khidmatgar* (*khidmat* service + -*gar* suf.)]

khil'afăt, n. = KHALIFAT; (hist.). ~ *agitation*, anti-British movement in India based on Moslem resentment of the loss of power by Islam in & after the 1914–18 war, & contemporary Hindu discontents.

|| kib'ble[1], n. Iron hoisting-bucket used in mines. [17th c., f. G *kübel*]

|| kib'ble[2], v.t. Grind coarsely. [orig. unkn.]

kibbutz' (-ŏŏts), n. (pl. ~*zĭm*). Communal farming centre in Israel. [mod. Heb.]

kībe, n. Ulcerated chilblain, esp. on heel; *tread on* one's ~*s*, hurt his feelings. [ME; prob. f. W *cibi* (also *cibwst*)]

kĭbĭt'ka, n. Tartar's circular tent covered with felt; Tartar household; Russian hooded sledge. [Russ.]

kib'itzer, n. (colloq.). Meddlesome person, one who gives advice gratuitously, one who watches a game of cards from behind the players. [Yiddish, f. G *kiebitz* looker-on]

kib'lah, n. Point to which Mohammedans turn at prayer, i.e. temple at Mecca. [f. Arab. *qiblah* (*qabala* be opposite)]

kib'ōsh (*or* kĭbŏsh'), n. (sl.). Nonsense, humbug; *put the* ~ *on*, do for, knock on the head. [orig. unkn.]

kick[1], n. Act of kicking; (colloq.) reacting-power, resilience, (*has no* ~ *left*); (colloq.) sharp stimulant effect, pleasurable thrill (*has some* ~ *in it*); DROP[1]-, PLACE-, ~; *more* ~s (harshness) *than half-pence* (kindness); recoil of gun when discharged; (footb.) *good*, *bad*, etc., ~ (kicker), ~-*off*, ~ with which game is started; ~-*starter*, lever on motor-cycle by kicking which it can be started. [f. foll.]

kick[2], v.i. & t. **1.** Strike out with the foot; ~ *against the pricks*, resist to one's own hurt. **2.** Show annoyance, dislike, etc. (*against*, *at*, proposal, treatment). **3.** Strike with foot; (sl.)~ *the bucket*, die; ~ one's HEELS. **4.** Drive, move, (thing) by ~ing. **5.** (footb.) Score (goal) by a kick. **6.** Drive forcibly & contemptuously (*out*, *downstairs*, etc.; ~ one *upstairs*, fig., shelve him by giving him peerage or titular promotion). **7.** ~ *off*, throw off (shoes) by ~ing, (footb.) begin game; ~ *up*, raise (dust), create (fuss, noise), ~ *up* its *heels* (of horse in play); ~*ing-strap* (arranged to prevent carriage-horse from ~ing). [ME *kike*, of unkn. orig.]

kick[3], n. Indentation in bottom of glass bottle. [orig. unkn.]

kick'er, n. In vbl senses, esp. horse given to kicking. [-ER[1]]

kick'shaw, n. Fancy dish in cookery (usu. derog.); toy, trifle. [f. F *quelque chose* something]

kid[1], n., & v.t. & i. (-dd-). **1.** Young of goat; leather from skin of this, used for gloves & boots; *the Kids* or *Kid*, three small stars in Auriga; (sl.) child, whence ~d'y[3] n.; ~-*glove* (adj.), over-dainty, avoiding everyday work etc. **2.** v.t. Give birth to (~); (v.i.) give birth to ~. [ME *kide* f. ON *kith* f. Gmc *kithjam*, rel. to OHG *chizzi*, -*in*]

kid[2], v.t. (-dd-), & n. (sl.). Hoax, humbug, (vb often abs.). [perh. f. prec.]

kid[3], n. Small wooden tub, esp. (formerly) sailor's mess-tub. [perh. var. of KIT[1]]

Kidd′erminster, n. Town in Worcestershire; ~ *carpet* (with pattern formed by intersection of two cloths of different colours).

kid′dle, n. Barrier in river with opening fitted with nets etc. to catch fish; arrangement of stake-nets on sea-beach. [ME, f. AF *kidel,* = OF *quidel, guidel,* mod. *-eau*]

kid′năp, v.t. (-pp-). Steal (child); carry off (person) by illegal force. Hence~PER¹ n. [KID¹+*nap* = NAB]

kid′ney, n. (pl. ~*s*). One of pair of glandular organs in abdominal cavity of mammals, birds, & reptiles, serving to excrete urine & so remove effete nitrogenous matter from blood; ~ of sheep, cattle, & pigs, as food; temperament, nature, as *a man of that* ~, *of the right* ~; (also ~ *potato*) oval kind of potato; ‖~ *bean,* (1) dwarf French bean, (2) scarlet-runner. [ME *kidnei,* pl. *kidneiren,* of obsc. formation]

kief, See KEF.

kie-kie (kē′kē), n. New Zealand climbing plant with leaves used for baskets etc. [Maori]

kier, n. Vat in which cloth is boiled for bleaching etc. [f. ON *ker,* = OHG *char,* Goth. *kas*]

kieselguhr (kē′zlgoor), n. Diatomaceous earth used for polishing & as absorbent of nitro-glycerine in manufacture of dynamite. [G *kiesel* gravel+dial. *guhr* earthy deposit]

Kikuyu′ (-ōoyōō), n. (Member, language, of) a Bantu-speaking people of E. Africa; (used for) the controversy in the Anglican Church on the admissibility to Holy Communion of members of other Christian Churches. [~ in Brit. E. Africa (now Kenya), a conference at which in 1913 gave rise to the controversy]

kil′derkin, n. Cask for liquids etc., containing 16 or 18 gal.; this as measure. [alt. of ME *kinderkin* f. MDu. *kinde(r)kin, kinneken,* dim. of *kintal* QUINTAL; see -KIN]

kill¹ v.t. & i. 1. Put to death, slay (~ *two birds with one stone,* effect two purposes at once); (of disease, grief, shock, drink, poison, etc.) cause the death of; ~ *off,* get rid of (number of persons etc.) by ~ing. 2. (Abs., esp. sport.) perform act of ~ing, do execution. 3. (Intr., quasi-pass.) yield good or much meat when ~ed, as *pigs do not* ~ *well at that age.* 4. Represent in fiction etc. as dead, as ~ *your villain in the last chapter.* 5. Destroy vitality of (plant, disease, etc.); destroy, put an end to, (feelings etc.). 6. Neutralize (colour etc.) by contrast. 7. Consume (time) for the sake of doing so. 8. Overwhelm (person) with admiration, amusement, etc. (*got up to* ~, fascinatingly dressed), whence ~′ING² a., ~′ingLY² adv. 9. (lawn tennis) strike (ball) so that it cannot be returned; (footb.) stop (ball) dead. 10. Contrive defeat of (bill in Parliament). 11. ~ (fatally harm) *with* (mistaken) *kindness;* ~*-devil,* artificial bait made to spin in water; ~*′joy,* one who throws gloom over social enjoyment; ~*-time* n. & a., (occupation) intended to ~ time. [ME *cülle, kille,* of unkn. orig.]

kill², n. Act of killing; animal killed, esp. by sportsman. [f. prec.]

kill′er, n. One who, that which, kills; murderous ruffian; HUMANE ~; ~ *whale,* voracious cetacean (esp. the grampus). [-ER¹]

kill′ick, -ock, n. Heavy stone used by small craft as anchor; small anchor; ‖ (nav. sl.) leading rating. [17th c., of unkn. orig.]

kiln (or kil), n. Furnace, oven, for burning, baking, or drying, esp. (*lime-*~) for calcining lime, or (*brick-*~) baking bricks; ~*-dry* v.t.; dry in ~. [OE *cylene* f. L *culina* kitchen]

kil′ō (or kē-), n. (pl. ~*s*). Abbr. for KILOGRAM(ME), KILOMETRE. [F]

kil′o- in comb., arbitrary representative (f. F) of Gk *khilioi* 1,000, as: ~*cycle,* unit of frequency of vibration (1,000 oscillations per second) used esp. of wireless waves; ~*gram(me),* weight of 1,000 grammes (2·205 lb. avoird.); ~*gramme′tre* (-ter), energy that will raise one kilogram to the height of one metre; ~*litre,* ~*liter,* (-lēter), measure of 1,000 litres (35·31 cub. ft); ~*mètre,* ~*mēter,* measure of 1,000 metres (3280.89 ft), whence ~*mēt′ric(al)* aa.; ~*ton,* unit of explosive power equivalent to 1,000 tons of T.N.T.; ~*watt,* 1,000 watts.

kilt¹, v.t. Tuck up (skirts) round body; gather in vertical pleats (esp. in p.p.). [of Scand. orig.; cf. Da. *kilte* (op) tuck (up), Sw. dial. *kilta* swathe, ON *kilting, kjalta* skirt, lap]

kilt², n. Skirt, usu. of tartan cloth, reaching from waist to knee, part of Highland male dress; similar garment worn by children & young women. Hence **kil′tie** [-Y³] n., wearer of a ~, esp. kilted Highland soldier. [f. prec.]

•kil′ter, kĕ-, n. Good working order (*out of* ~, not working properly). [Eng. dial.]

kimōn′ō, n. (pl. ~*s*). Long loose Japanese robe with wide short sleeves, held together by a sash; European dressing--gown or wrap modelled on this. [Jap.]

kin, n. & a. Ancestral stock, family, as *comes of good* ~; one's relatives; KITH & ~; (pred. adj.) related, as *we are* ~, *he is* ~ *to me; of* ~, akin, related by blood ties or (fig.) in character; *near of* ~, closely related; NEXT *of* ~. Hence ~′LESS a. [OE *cynn,* OS *kunni,* OHG *chunni,* ON *kyn,* Goth. *kuni* f. Gmc **kunjam* f. root **kin, *kan, *kun* cogn. w. L *genus*]

-kin, suf. form. dimm., corresp. to MDu. *-kijn, -ken,* MLG *-kin* = OHG *-chin,* G *-chen;* chiefly in wds f. Du., incl. early proper names, as *Malkin, Perkin, Simkin;* some wds in *-kin* are of doubtful orig.

Lambkin is the only E formation of real currency.

kin'chin, n. (cant). Child; ~ *lay*, practice of stealing money from children sent on errands. [16th c. cant, prob. f. G *kindchen* (*kind* child, see prec.)]

kin'cŏb (-ngk-), n. Rich Indian stuff embroidered with gold or silver. [f. Urdu *kimkhab*]

kind¹, n. **1.** Race, natural group, of animals, plants, etc., as *human* ~, the *rabbit* ~. **2.** Class, sort, variety, as *of what* ~ *is it?*, *of a different* ~; *something of the* ~, something like the thing in question; *nothing of the* ~, not at all like it; (derog.) *we had coffee of a* ~ (that scarcely deserved the name). **3.** (eccl.). Each of the two elements in the Eucharist. **4.** (In transposed constr.) *what* ~ *of tree is this?*, of what ~ is this tree?, *this is the* ~ *of thing I meant* (a thing of the ~ I meant); (colloq.) *these* ~ *of men* (men of this ~) *annoy me.* **5.** (Implying looseness, vagueness, exaggeration, etc., in the term used) *he is a* ~ *of stockbroker, of millionaire, felt a* ~ *of compunction*; (colloq.) *I* ~ *of* (to some extent) *expected it.* ‖ **6.** (arch.). Nature in general, as *the law of* ~; way, fashion, natural to person etc., as *they act after their* ~. **7.** Character, quality, as *they differ in* ~ (not merely in degree). **8.** *In* ~, (of payment) in goods or natural produce, not in money, (of repayment, esp. fig.) *repay his insolence in* ~ (with insolence). [OE *gecynde* (*ge*- Y- + **cynde* f. root *kun*- see KIN]

kind², a. Of gentle or benevolent nature; friendly in one's conduct *to* (person etc.); affectionate; ~*-hearted*, having a ~ heart. Hence ~*'lȳ¹* [-LY²] adv. (often politely in requests, or ironically in commands), ~*'NESS* n. [OE *gecynde* (as prec.); orig. = natural, native]

kin'dergärten, n. School for developing minds of children by object-lessons, toys, games, etc. Hence ~*ISM* n. [G, = children's garden]

kin'dle, v.t. & i. Set on fire, light, (flame, fire, substance); (fig.) inflame, inspire, (passion etc.), stir up (person *to* emotion etc., *to* do); (intr.) catch fire, burst into flame; (fig.) become animated, glow with passion etc.; make, become, bright, (cause to) glow (often *up*); hence kind-*LING¹* n., (esp., sing. or pl.) small wood for lighting fires. [ME, f. ON *kynda* kindle + -LE(3); cf. ON *kyndill* candle, torch]

kind'l|y̆² (for ~*y¹* see KIND²), a. Kind; (of climate etc.) pleasant, genial; ‖ (arch.) native-born, as *a* ~*y Scot*. Hence ~*ilY¹* adv., ~*ĭNESS* n. [OE *gecyndelic* (as KIND², see -LY¹)]

kin'drĕd, n. & a. **1.** Blood relationship; (fig.) resemblance in character; one's relatives. **2.** adj. Related by blood; (fig.) allied, connected, similar, as *frost & ~ phenomena, ~ spirit*. [ME, f. KIN + *-red*, OE *ræden* condition, reckoning]

kine. See cow¹.

kĭnēm'a, n. orig. form of CINEMA.

kĭnĕmăt'ĭc, a. & n. **1.** Of motion considered abstractly without reference to force or mass. **2.** n. pl. Science of this. Hence ~*AL* a. [f. Gk *kinēma -matos* motion (*kineō* move, see -M) + -IC]

kĭnĕm'atograph, -ĭc, -y. = CINEMATO-GRAPH etc.

kĭnĕt'ĭc, a. & n. **1.** Of, due to, motion; ~ ENERGY; ~ *theory of heat*, of gases (that heat, the gaseous state, is due to motion of particles). **2.** n. pl. Science of the relations between the motions of bodies & the forces acting on them. [f. Gk *kinētikos* (*kineō* move, see -ETIC]

kĭng¹, n. **1.** Male sovereign (esp. hereditary) ruler of independent state. **2.** (Hist.) *K~ Emperor* (of U.K. & India; also of Austria-Hungary); *K~ Log, K~ Stork*, rulers going to extremes of laissez-faire, oppression (w. ref. to fable of the frogs); *K~ of ~s*, God, (also) title assumed by many Eastern ~s; *K~ of Terrors*, Death; *K~ Charles's* SPANIEL; ‖ *K~'s* BENCH, BOUNTY, COLOUR¹, COUNSEL¹, ENGLISH, EVIDENCE, HEAD¹, HIGHWAY, PIPE¹, SHILLING, WEATHER; *K~ of the Castle*, child's game. **3.** Great merchant etc., as *fur, railway*, ~. **4.** ~ *of beasts, birds*, lion, eagle. **5.** Best kind (of fruits, plants, etc.). **6.** (Chess) piece that has to be protected from checkmate, ~*'s bishop, knight, rook, pawn* (placed on ~'s side of board at beginning); (draughts) piece that, having traversed the board & reached opponent's base-line, is crowned; (cards) card bearing representation of ~, & usu. ranking next below ace. **7.** ~*'bird*, kind of bird of paradise, (also) American tyrant fly-catcher; ~ *'bolt*, main or large bolt; ~*-crab*, kinds of marine arachnid with crustacean affinities having horseshoe-shaped carapace; ~*'craft*, skilful exercise of royalty; ~*'cup*, buttercup, ‖ (also) marsh marigold; ~*'fisher*, small bird with dagger-shaped bill & brilliant plumage, feeding on fish it captures by diving; ~*'maker*, one who sets up ~s, esp. Earl of Warwick in reign of Henry VI; ‖ *K~ of Arms*, any of five chief heralds of College of Arms, *Garter, Clarenc(i)eux, Norroy*, (Scotland) *Lyon*, (Ireland, formerly) *Ulster*; ~*'pin*, = ~*bolt*, also fig.; ~*'post*, upright post from tie-beam to rafter-top; ~*'s evil*, scrofula, formerly held to be curable by ~'s touch; ~*'s peg*, drink of champagne & brandy; ‖ *K~'s Roll* (of employers pledged to employ at least a fixed proportion of ex-service men). Hence ~*'LESS, ~'LIKE, ~'LY¹*, aa., ~*'liNESS*, ~*'SHIP*(1), nn. [OE *cyning*, OS, OHG *kuning*, ON *kuningr* f. Gmc **kuningaz* (KIN, -ING²)]

kĭng², v.i. & t. Act the king, govern, esp. ~ *it*; make (person) a king. [f. prec.]

kĭng'dom, n. Monarchical State; *United K~*, Great Britain & Northern Ireland;

territory subject to king; spiritual reign of God, sphere of this, esp. *the ~ of heaven*; domain; province of nature, esp. *animal, vegetable, mineral, ~*; (sl.) *~-come*, the next world (echo of *thy ~ come* in Lord's Prayer). Hence ~ED² (·omd) a. [OE *cyningdōm* (as KING¹, see ·DOM)]

king'|let, n. Petty king (usu. derog.), so ~LING¹ n.; golden-crested wren. [·LET]

kink, n., & v.i. & t. 1. Back twist in wire or chain or rope such as may cause obstruction or a break; (fig.) mental twist, crotchet. 2. v.i. (Of rope etc.) form a ~; (v.t.) cause (rope) to do this. Hence ~ʏ³ a. [f. MLG *kinke*, Du. *kink* f. root *kink, *kik* twist; cf. Icel. *kikna* bend at the knees; vb f. Du. *kinken*]

kink'ajou (·ōō), n. Arboreal animal with prehensile tail allied to racoon. [f. F *quincajou* f. N. Amer. Ind.]

kinn'īkinic', n. Mixture of dried sumach-leaves, bark of willow, etc., as substitute for tobacco, or mixed with it; any plant used for this. [Algonquin]

ki'nō (kē-), n. Gum of various trees, resembling catechu, & used in medicine & tanning as astringent. [W.·Afr.]

kins'|folk (·ōk), n. pl. Relations by blood. So ~MAN, ~WOMAN, nn. [f. KIN + FOLK]

kin'ship, n. Blood relationship; similarity, alliance, in character. [·SHIP]

kin'tal, early form of QUINTAL.

ki'ŏsk (kē-), n. Light open pavilion in Turkey & Persia; *Yildiz K~*, Turkish Sultan's palace; light out-of-door structure for sale of newspapers, bandstand, etc.; structure for public telephone. [f. F *kiosque* f. Turk. *kiushk*]

kip¹, n. Hide of young or small beast as used for leather. [in E sense 'set or bundle of hides' f. MDu. *kip, kijp*]

kip², n., & v.i. (·pp·; sl.). Common lodging-house; lodging; bed; (v.i.) sleep. [cf. Da. *kippe* mean hut or alehouse]

kipp'er¹, n. Male salmon in spawning season; kippered fish, esp. herring. [of obsc. orig.; formally = OE *cypera* (once)]

kipp'er², v.t. Cure (salmon, herring, etc.) by splitting open, cleaning, rubbing with salt, pepper, etc., & drying in open air or smoke. [f. prec.]

Kirghiz (kērgēz'), a. & n. (Member, language) of a Mongolian people living on the Caspian, N.E. of the Kalmucks.

|| **kirk**, n. (Sc. & north.) church; (in E use) *K~ of Scotland*, Church of Scotland as opp. to Church of England or to Episcopal Church in Scotland; ~'man, member of K~ of Scotland; ~ *session*, lowest court in K~ of Scotland & (hist.) other Presbyterian Churches, composed of ministers & elders. [ME, f. ON *kirkja*, itself f. OE *circe* CHURCH]

kirsch(wasser) (kērsh'vahser), n. Spirit distilled from fermented liquor of wild cherries. [G (*kirsche* cherry + *wasser* water)]

|| **kir'tle**, n. (arch.). Woman's gown or

outer petticoat; man's tunic or coat. [OE *cyrtel*, = ON *kyrtill*, ult. perh. f. L *curtus* short]

kis'met, n. Destiny. [Turk., f. Arab. *qisma(t)* f. *qasama* divide]

kiss¹, n. Caress given with lips; (billiards) impact between moving balls; kind of sugar-plum. [OE *coss* (ME *cos(s), cus(s), kisse*) f. Gmc. *kussaz* (foll.); form *kiss* f. the vb]

kiss², v.t. Touch with the lips, esp. as sign of love, affection, greeting, or reverence; (abs., of two persons) ~ *& be friends*, become reconciled; (billiards, of ball) touch (ball) with KISS¹ (also abs. of two balls); ~ *away*, remove (tears etc.) with kisses; ~ *the book* (Bible, in taking oath); ~ *the dust*, yield abject submission, (also) be slain; ~ *the ground*, prostrate oneself in token of homage, (fig.) be brought low; ~ *one's hand to*, wave a kiss to; ~ *hands* or *the hand* (of sovereign etc. as ceremonial salutation or on appointment to office); ~ *the rod*, accept chastisement submissively; ~*·in-the-ring*, game for young people in which one pursues & ~es another of opposite sex; ~*·me-quick*, small bonnet standing far back on head, curl worn on forehead. Hence ~'ABLE a., ~'abʟʏ² adv. [OE *cyssan*, OS *cussian*, OHG *chussen*, ON *kyssa* (Goth. *kukjan*) f. Gmc *kussjan* f. *kussaz*]

kiss'ing¹, a. In vbl senses; ~*·crust*, soft crust where loaf has touched another in baking. [·ING²]

kiss'ing², n. In vbl senses; || ~*·gate* (hung in U or V shaped enclosure); ~ *kind*, on affectionate terms. [·ING¹]

kit¹, n., & v.t. & i. (·tt·). 1. || Wooden tub for various purposes; (articles carried in) soldier's etc. pack etc.; personal equipment, esp. as packed for travelling; workman's outfit; ~*·bag* (for carrying soldier's or traveller's ~). 2. vb. Fit out, be fitted out, with ~ (freq. *up*). [f. MDu. *kitte* wooden vessel; orig. unkn.]

kit², n. Abbr. of KITTEN.

kit³, n. (now rare). Small fiddle used by dancing-master. [perh. ult. as CITHERN]

kit'·căt, n. *K~ Club*, club of Whig politicians founded under James II; member of this; ~ (*portrait*), portrait of less than half-length, but including hands. [f. *Christopher* (or *Kit*) *Cat*, keeper of pie-house where club met]

kitch'en, n. Part of house where food is cooked; ~ *garden* (for fruit & vegetables); ~*·maid*, servant employed in ~, usu. under cook; ~ MIDDEN; ~ *physic*, good & plentiful food; ~*·stuff*, ~ requisites, esp. vegetables. [OE *cycene*, OS *kukina*, OHG *chuhhina* f. *cocina* var. of LL *coquina* (*coquere* cook)]

kitch'ener, n. || Cooking-range; person in charge of monastery kitchen. [·ER¹]

kitchenette', n. Small room, alcove, etc., fitted up as miniature kitchen & scullery (esp. in modern flat). [·ETTE]

kīte, n., v.i. & t. **1.** Bird of prey of same family as falcon, with long wings, usu. forked tail, & no tooth in bill; rapacious person, sharper; toy consisting of light wooden frame, usu. in form of isosceles triangle with circular arc as base, with paper stretched over it, flown in strong wind by string; BOX²~; *fly a* ~, (fig.) make experiment to gauge public opinion etc.; (commerc. sl.) accommodation bill *(fly a*~, raise money by this); (pl.) highest sails of ship, set only in light wind; ~ *balloon*, sausage-shaped captive balloon for military observation; *K~'mark*, trade mark (representing a ~) on goods approved by the British Standards Institution. **2.** v.i. Soar like ~; (v.t.) cause to do this, (commerc.) convert into ~. [OE *cȳta*, of unkn. orig.]

kith, n. ~ *& kin*, friends & relations. [OE *cȳthth* f. Gmc *kunthitha* f. *kunth-* known (see UNCOUTH, -TH¹)]

kitsch n. Worthless pretentiousness in (esp. dramatic) art. [G]

kitt'en, n., v. & v.t. **1.** Young of cat; skittish young girl. **2.** v.t. Bring forth (~s, or abs.). Hence ~ISH¹ a. [ME *kito(u)n*, *ketoun* f. AF **kitoun*, **ket-* = OF *chitoun*, *chetoun* dim. of *chat* CAT]

kitt'iwāke, n. Kind of sea-gull. [imit.]

kit'tle, a. Ticklish, difficult to deal with, esp. ~ *cattle* (usu. fig. of persons or things). [f. ME (now Sc. & dial.) *kittle*, prob. f. ON *killa* = OS *kitilōn*, OHG *chizzilōn*]

kittul' (-ōōl), **kitōōl'**, n. Kind of palm; strong black fibre from leaf-stalks of this. [f. Sinhalese *kitul*]

kitt'ȳ¹, n. Pet name for kitten. [f. KIT²+ -Y³]

kitt'ȳ², n. Pool in some card games; joint fund; (bowls) jack. [orig. unkn.]

ki'wi, n. (kē'wē), n. = APTERYX; ‖ (sl.) non-flying member of Air Force; (colloq., *K~*) a New Zealander. [Maori]

Klǎx'on, n. Powerful electric motor-horn. [P; f. Gk *klazō* shriek]

klěpht, n. One of the Greeks who after Turkish conquest of Greece in 15th c. maintained independence in mountains; brigand. [f. mod. Gk *klephtēs* f. Gk *kleptēs* thief]

klěpt|omān'ia, n. Irresistible tendency to theft in persons not tempted to it by needy circumstances. Hence ~MAN'IAC n. [f. Gk *kleptēs* thief +-o-+-MANIA]

klip'springer, n. Small S.-Afr. antelope. [Afrikaans (*klip* rock + *springer* springer)]

klōof, n. Ravine, valley, in S. Africa. [Du., = cleft]

kn-. In all words beginning thus k is silent.

knǎck, n. Acquired faculty of doing a thing adroitly; ingenious device; trick, habit, of action, speech, etc. Hence ~'Y² a. [prob. = ME *knack* sharp blow or sound, of LG orig.; cf. Du., LG *knak* &c.; ult. imit.]

knǎck'|er, n. ‖ One who buys & slaughters useless horses, whence ~ERY(3) n.; one who buys old houses, ships, etc., for the materials. [orig. unkn.]

knǎg, n. Knot in wood, base of a branch. Hence ~g'Y² (-g-) a. [ME, perh. f. LG *knagge*]

knǎp¹, n. (dial.). Crest of hill, rising ground. [OE *cnæp(p)*, cogn. w. ON *knappr* knob]

knǎp², v.t. (-pp-). Break (flints for roads or building) with hammer, whence ~p'ER¹(1, 2) n.; (Bibl., dial.) knock, rap, snap asunder. [goes w. 15th c. *knap* smart blow, of imit. orig.; cf. KNACK]

knǎp'sǎck, n. Soldier's or traveller's canvas or leather bag, strapped to back & used for carrying necessaries, cf. RUCKSACK. [LG, prob. f. *knappen* bite +SACK¹]

knǎp'weed, n. Common weed with hard stem & light purple flowers on dark globular head. [earlier *knopweed* (KNOP+WEED)]

knǎr, n. Knot in wood, esp. protuberance covered with bark on trunk or at root of tree. [ME *knarre*, rel. to LG *knarre(n)*, Du. *knar* stump of tree, knot, knob; cf. KNUR(R)]

knǎv|e, n. Unprincipled man, rogue, whence ~'ERY(4), ~'ĭshNESS, nn., ~'ISH¹ a., ~'ĭshLY² adv.; (cards) lowest court-card of each suit. [OE *cnafa* boy, servant, = OHG *knabo* f. WG **knabhon-*]

knead, v.t. Work up (moist flour or clay) into dough or paste; make (bread, pottery) thus; (fig.) blend, weld together; operate on (muscles etc.) as if ~ing, massage. Hence ~'ABLE a., ~'ER¹(1, 2) n. [OE *cnedan*, OS *knedan*, OHG *knetan*, ON *knotha* f. Gmc **kned-*, **knud-*]

knead'ing, n. In vbl senses; ~*-trough*, wooden trough in which dough is kneaded. [-ING¹]

knee¹, n. **1.** Joint between thigh & lower leg in man, corresponding joint in animals; *give a* ~ *to*, support (pugilist) on one's ~ between rounds, act as second to; *on* one's ~s, kneeling, esp. in supplication, worship, or submission; *bring* (person) *to his* ~s, reduce him to submission; *is on the* ~s *of the gods*, is yet uncertain (after Homer). **2.** Part of garment covering the ~. **3.** Thing like ~ in shape or position, esp. piece of wood or iron with angular bend. **4.** ~*-breeches* (reaching down to or just below ~); ~*-cap*, convex bone in front of ~-joint, (also) protective covering for ~; ~*-deep*, so deep as to reach the ~s; ~*-hole* (*table*), (writing-table with) hole between drawer pedestals to admit ~s; ~ *holly*, butcher's broom; ~*-joint*, joint of ~, joint of two pieces hinged together; ~*-pan*, ~*-cap*; ~*-swell*, (in Amer. organ etc.) lever worked by ~, for producing crescendo & diminuendo effects. [OE *cnēo(w)*, OS *knio*, OHG *kneo*, ON *knē*, Goth. *kniu* f. Gmc **knewam*, cogn. w. L *genu*]

knee², v.t. Touch with the knee; fasten (framework etc.) with knees; (colloq.) cause (trousers) to bulge at knees. [f. prec.]

kneel, v.i. (*knĕlt*). Fall, rest, on the knee(s) esp. in prayer or reverence (*to* person). [ME *cneolen* f. OE *cnēowlian* (as KNEE¹)]

knĕll¹, n. Sound of bell, esp. of one rung solemnly after death or at funeral; (fig.) announcement, event, etc., regarded as an omen of death or extinction. [OE *cnyll* (as foll.)]

knĕll², v.i. & t. (arch.). (Of bell) ring, esp. at death or funeral; give forth doleful sound; (fig.) sound ominously; (v.t.) proclaim as by a knell. [ME *knylle* f. OE *cnyllan*; ME *knell* prob. imit. alt. (cf. *bell*)]

knelt. See KNEEL.

Knĕss′et, n. Israeli parliament. [Heb.]

knew. See KNOW¹.

knick′erböcker, n. (*K*∼) New Yorker; (pl.) loose-fitting breeches gathered in at knee. [*K*∼, pretended author of W. Irving's *History of New York*]

knick′ers, n. pl. Knickerbockers (colloq.); woman's drawers of knickerbocker shape. [abbr. of prec.]

knick′-knăck, nick′-năck, n. Light dainty article of furniture, dress, or food; trinket, gimcrack. Hence ∼ERY(2, 5) n., ∼ISH¹ a. [redupl. of KNACK in obs. sense 'trinket']

knife, n. (pl. *knives* pr. nīvz), & v.t. (*-fed*). 1. Blade with sharpened longitudinal edge fixed in handle either rigidly, as in *table*, *carving*, ∼, or with hinge, as in *pocket-*∼ or PEN³∼, used as cutting instrument or as weapon; (of malicious or vindictive person) *get a* ∼ *into* (person); *war to the*∼, relentless war; blade forming part of machine, as in turnip-cutter etc.; *the* ∼, surgical operations, as *have a horror of the*∼; *before you can say* ∼, very quickly or suddenly; *play a good* ∼ & *fork*, eat heartily. 2. ∼*-board* (on which knives are cleaned), (transf.) ‖ double bench placed lengthways on the top of omnibus; ∼*-boy* (formerly employed to clean table-knives); ∼*-edge*, edge of ∼, steel wedge on which pendulum etc. oscillates, = ARÊTE; ∼*-grinder*, itinerant sharpener of knives etc., one who grinds knives etc. in process of making; ∼*-machine* (for cleaning knives); ∼*-rest*, metal or glass support for carving ∼ or fork at table. 3. v.t. Cut, stab, with ∼. [late OE *cnīf* f. ON *knīfr*, = MLG *knīf*, MDu. *cnijf*, f. Gmc **knībhaz*]

knight (nīt), n., & v.t. 1. Military follower, esp. one devoted to service *of* (lady) as attendant or champion in war or tournament. 2. Person, usu. one of noble birth who had served as page & squire, raised to honourable military rank by king or qualified person. 3. One on whom corresponding rank is conferred as reward for personal merit or services to crown or country. 4. (hist.). (Also, ∼ *of the shire*) person representing shire or county in parliament. 5. (Rom. Ant.) one of the class of equites, orig. the cavalry of Roman army; (Gk Ant.) citizen of second class at Athens. 6. Piece in game of chess, usu. with horse's head. 7. ∼ BACHELOR, COMMANDER, COMPANION¹, HOSPITALLER, TEMPLAR; ∼ *errant*, medieval ∼ wandering in search of chivalrous adventures, (fig.) person of chivalrous or of quixotic spirit; ∼*-errantry*, practice, conduct, of a ∼ errant (lit. & fig.); ∼*-heads*, two vertical timbers supporting bowsprit; ∼ *of the post*, one who got his living by giving false evidence; ∼*-service* (hist.), tenure of land by military service. 8. v.t. Confer ∼hood on. Hence ∼′HOOD n., ∼′LIKE, ∼′LY¹, ∼′LY² adv. (poet.), (nit-). [OE *cniht*, OS, OHG *kneht* f. WG **knehta*]

knight′age (nīt-), n. Whole body of knights; list & account of knights. [-AGE]

knit, v.t. & i. (∼*ted* or *knit*). Form (close texture, garments etc. of this) of interlooping yarn or thread; contract (brow) in wrinkles; make, become, close or compact (esp. in p.p., as *a well-*∼*frame*); (fig.) unite (t. & i.) intimately by means of common interests, marriage, etc., (often *together*); ∼ *up*, repair by ∼ting, (fig.) close up, conclude, (argument etc.). [OE *cnyttan*, MDu., MLG *knutten* (G dial. *knütten*) f. WG **knuttjan* f. **knutt-*KNOT¹]

knitt′ing, n. In vbl senses, esp. work in process of ∼; ∼*-needle*, slender rod of steel, wood, ivory, etc., two or more of which are used together in ∼. [f. prec. + -ING¹]

knit′tle, n. (naut.). Small line made of yarn. [f. KNIT + -LE]

knŏb, n., & v.t. & i. (-bb-). 1. Rounded protuberance, esp. at end or on surface of thing; handle of door (often *door-*∼) or drawer; small lump (of sugar, coal, etc.); (sl.) head (usu. nob); ∼′*kerrie* [after Afrikaans *knopkierie*], short stick with ∼bed head as weapon of S.-Afr. tribes; ∼′*stick*, ∼bed stick, esp. as weapon, ‖ (also) workman who works during strike; *with* ∼*s on* (sl.), = that, & more (phr. indicating ironic or emphatic agreement). 2. v.t. Furnish with ∼s; (v.i.) bulge *out*. Hence ∼b′Y² a., ∼b′INESS n. [ME *knobbe* f. MLG *knobbe*; cf. Flem. *knobbe(n)* lump of bread]

knŏb′bl|e, n. Small knob. Hence ∼Y² a. [15th c., f. Du. & LG *knobbel* dim. of prec.]

knŏck¹, v.t. & i. 1. Strike with hard blow; strike door, strike *at the door*, to gain admittance; (of motor or other engine) make thumping or rattling noise as result of loose bearing or other mechanical defect; *(sl.) criticize; ‖ (sl.) make strong impression on, as *what* ∼*s me is his impudence*; ∼ (person etc.) *on the head*, stun, kill, him by blow on head, (fig.) put an end to (scheme etc.); ∼ *one's head against*, (fig.) come into unpleasant collision with (unfavourable facts or conditions); ~ *head* vb, kotow; drive (thing) *in*, *out*, *off*, etc., by striking (see also below); ~ *into a* COCK[2]*ed hat*; ~ one *into the middle of next week*, send him flying; ~ *the bottom out of*, render (argument etc.) invalid. 2.~ *about*, strike repeatedly, treat roughly, (intr.) wander, lead irregular life; ~ *against*, collide with, come across casually; ~ *back* (sl.), drink; ~ *down*, strike (person etc.) to ground with blow, (fig.) cause to succumb, (at auction) dispose of (article *to* bidder) by knock with hammer, (colloq.) call upon (person *for* a song etc.), (colloq.) lower (prices), (commerc.) take (machinery etc.) to pieces to save space in transport; ~ *off*, strike off with blow, leave off work, leave off (work), (colloq.) dispatch (business) or rapidly compose (verses etc.), deduct (sum from price, bill, etc.), ~ person's *head off*, (fig.) surpass him easily; ~ *out*, empty (one's pipe) by tapping, disable (pugilist) so that he cannot respond to call of ' Time ', (fig.) vanquish, (colloq.) make (plan etc.) hastily; ~ *together*, put hastily together; ~ *under*, submit, knuckle under; ~ *up*, drive upwards with blow, make or arrange hastily, score (runs) rapidly at cricket, arouse (person) by ~ing at door, exhaust, become exhausted, *(sl.) make pregnant. 3. ~ *about* n. & a., boisterous, noisy (performance in music-hall etc.), wandering irregularly, (of clothes) suitable for rough use; ~*down* a. & n., (of blow, lit. & fig.) overwhelming, (of price at auction) reserve, minimum, (n.) free fight; ~*knees* (that ~ together in walking); ~*kneed*, having ~*knees*; ~*out*, (blow) that ~s boxer out, (n.) ‖ one of gang who join at auction to buy goods at low price, afterwards reselling among themselves, this practice, such sale, (sl.) outstanding person or thing. [late OE *cnocian*, = ON *knoka*, prob. imit.]

knŏck², n. Blow; rap esp. at door; sound of knocking in motor etc. engine (see prec.); (sl.) innings at cricket; ~*up*, practice or casual game at cricket, fives, etc.; *take the*~ (sl.), be hard hit financially. [f. prec.]

knŏck'er, n. In vbl senses, esp.: appendage, usu. of iron or brass, so hinged to door that it may be struck against metal plate to call attention (*up to the* ~, sl., to perfection); goblin held to dwell in mines & indicate presence of ore by knocking. [-ER¹]

knŏll¹, n. Small hill, mound. [OE *cnoll* hill-top, rel. to MDu., MHG *knolle* clod, ON *knollr* hill-top]

‖ **knŏll²**, v.t. & i. (arch.). Ring (bell); (of bell) sound; toll out (hours); summon by sound of bell. [var. of KNELL]

knŏp, n. (arch.). Knob; bud of flower. [ME, f. MLG, MDu. *knoppe*, = OHG *chnopf*]

knopkierie, n. Afrikaans sp. of KNOB*kerrie*.

knŏt¹, n. 1. Intertwining of parts of one or more ropes, strings, etc., to fasten them together; GRANNY'S, REEF¹-, SLIP-, WEAVER'S, ~; ribbon etc. so tied as ornament or adjunct to dress, as SHOULDER, SWORD, TOP, TRUE-*love*, ~. 2. (naut.). Division marked by ~s on log-line, as measure of speed; unit of speed equivalent to a nautical mile per hour; (loosely) nautical mile (6,080 ft). 3. Difficulty, problem; GORDIAN ~; central point in problem or plot of story etc., cf. DENOUEMENT; *marriage*, *wedding*, ~ (bond). 4. Hard lump in animal body; excrescence in stem, branch, or root, of plant; (hard mass formed in trunk at insertion of branch, causing) round cross-grained piece in board; node on stem of plant. 5. Group, cluster, of persons or things. 6. ‖ (Usu. *porter's*~) double shoulder-pad used for carrying loads. 7. ~-*grass*, common weed with intricate creeping stems & pale pink flowers; ~*work*, ornamental work representing or consisting of intertwined cords, (also) kind of fancy needlework. Hence ~*LESS* a. [OE *cnotta*, = Du. *knot*, LG *knütte*, MHG *knotze* f. WG *knutton*-; cogn. w. OHG *chnodo*, *chnoto* (G *knoten*)]

knŏt², v.t. & i. (-tt-). Tie (string etc.) in knot; make knots for fringes, (trans.) make (fringe) thus, whence ~t'ING¹ n.; knit (one's brows); unite closely or intricately; entangle. [f. prec.]

knŏt³, n. Small wading bird of sandpiper family. [orig. unkn.]

knŏtt'|y̆, a. Full of knots; (fig.) puzzling, hard to explain, as ~*y subject*, *question*, *point*. Hence ~*iNESS* n. [f. KNOT¹ + -Y²]

knout (or nŏŏt), n., & v.t. (F'log with) scourge formerly used in Russia, often fatal in its effects. [F, f. Russ. *knut*]

know¹ (nō), v.t. & i. (*knew* pron. nū, ~*n*). 1. Recognize, identify, as *I knew him at once*, *knew him for an American*, *shall you* ~ *him again?*; be able to distinguish (*don't* ~ *him from Adam*; ~ *one from another*, a HAWK¹ *from a handsaw*). 2. Be acquainted with (thing, place, person) *by sight*, *to speak to*, etc. (~ *by name*, have heard the name of, be able to give the name of); have personal experience of (fear, pain, etc.); be on intimate terms with; (bibl.) have sexual intercourse with. 3. Be aware of (fact), be aware (*that*, *how*, *what*, etc.); ~ (person etc.) *to be* (that he is). 4. Be versed in (language etc.). 5. *He would do it if he knew how* (knew the way); *all one* ~*s*, all one can, (adv.) to the utmost of one's power; ~ *about*, have information about; *I* ~ *better* (*than that*), I am too well informed of the facts to believe that; ~ *better than*, be too well-mannered *to* do; ~ *of*, be aware of; *not that I* ~ *of*, not so far as I ~; ~ one's *own mind*, not vacillate; ~ *what's what*, have proper knowledge of the world & of things in general; *don't you* ~ (esp. as parenthetic expletive in various contexts; *it's such a bore, don't you* ~); ~ *the* ROPES. **6.** ~*-all*, one who ~s or professes to ~ everything; ~*-how*, faculty of ~ing how, technical expertness; ~*-nothing*, ignorant person, (also) agnostic, whence ~*-nothingism*. Hence ~ABIL'ITY, ~'ableNESS, nn., ~'ABLE a., (nōa-). [OE (*ge*)*cnāwan*, OHG -*cnāhan*, ON *knd*, cogn. w. L (*g*)*nosco*, Gk *gignōskō*]

know² (nō), n. (colloq.). *In the~*, knowing (about) the thing in question or what is not generally known. [f. prec.]

know'ing (nōī-), a. In vbl senses, esp.: cunning, wide-awake (freq. rather derog.); (colloq.) stylish, smart, as *a* ~ *hat.* Hence ~NESS n. [-ING²]

know'ingly (nōī-), adv. In a knowing manner; consciously, intentionally, as *I have never* ~ *injured him.* [-LY²]

knowl'edge (nōl-), n. Knowing, familiarity gained by experience, (of person, thing, fact); person's range of information, as *it came to my* ~ (became known to me), *not to my* ~, not so far as I know, *he had to my* (*certain*) ~ *been bribed* (I know he had); theoretical or practical understanding (*of* subject, language, etc.); the sum of what is known, as *every branch of* ~; (philos.) certain understanding, dist. from opinion. Hence ~ABLE (nōlija-) a., (colloq.), well-informed, intelligent. [ME *knaulege*, w. earlier vb *knawlechen*, f. KNOW; second element obsc., perh. f. OE -*lǣcan* f. *lāc*, as in *wedlock*]

knuc'kle, n., & v.t. & i. **1.** Bone at finger--joint, esp. at root of finger; projection of carpal or tarsal joint of quadruped; joint of meat consisting of this with parts above & below it; *a* RAP¹ *on the* ~s; *near the* ~ (colloq.), verging on the indecent; ~*bone*, bone forming ~, esp. of sheep or the like, (pl.) game played with such bones; ||~*duster*, metal instrument protecting ~s from injury in striking. **2.** v.t. Strike, press, rub, with ~s; (v.i.) place ~s on ground in playing at marbles; ~ *down, under,* give in, submit (to). [ME *knokel* f. MLG, MDu. *knōkel*, dim. of *knoke* bone; cf. G *knöchel, knochen*]

knur(r), n. Hard excrescence on trunk of tree; hard concretion; wooden ball in north-country game like trap-ball. [ME *knorre*, rel. to MLG, MDu., MHG *knorre*; cf. KNAR]

knurl, n. Knot, knob (esp., that by which typewriter platen is turned); bead or ridge in metal work, whence ~ED² (-ld) a. [prob. f. prec.]

knut, *joc,* spelling of NUT used of youths.

kō'a, n. An acacia in Sandwich Is. [native]

koa'la (-ah-), n. Native bear of Australia, a tailless arboreal marsupial. [native]

kōb'öld, n. (Germ. myth.). Familiar spirit, brownie; underground spirit in mines etc. [G, of obsc. orig.]

kŏd'äk, n. Kind of photographic camera with continuous roll of sensitized film. [P]

koedoe, n. Afrikaans sp. of KOODOO.

kō'ĕl, n. Indian & Australian kinds of cuckoo. [f. Hind. *kŏīl* f. Skr. *kokila*]

koh'i-noor, (kōĭ-), n. Famous Indian diamond, property of British Crown since 1849; anything superb (*of* its class). [f. Pers. *kohi nur* (*koh* mountain + *nur* light)]

kohl (kōl), n. Powder, usu. antimony, used in East to darken eyelids etc. [f. Arab. *koh'l*, see ALCOHOL]

kohlra'bi (kōlrah-), n. Cabbage with turnip-shaped stem. [G, f. It. *cavoli rape* pl. (see COLE & RAPE³)]

Koin'ē, n. The common literary language of the Greeks from the close of classical Attic to the Byzantine era. [f. Gk *koinē* (*dialektos*) common (language)]

kola. See COLA.

Kōlār'ian, a. & n. Of various primitive non-Aryan tribes in the forests & hill districts of Bengal; (n.) ~ native. [f. *Kolar* = Canarese *kallar* thieves +-IAN]

kolin'skȳ, n. Fur of the Siberian mink. [Russ. (-*ski*) f. *Kola*, district in N.-W. Russia]

kŏlkhoz' (-kōz), n. Collective farm in U.S.S.R. [Russ. *kol(lektivnoe) khoz-(yaistvo)* collective farm]

komita(d)ji. Var. of COMITADJI.

kōō'dōō, kudu (kōō'dōō), n. Large white--striped spiral-horned S.-Afr. antelope. [native]

kōōkabūr'a, n.(Austral.). Laughing jackass. [native]

koolah. Obs. form of KOALA.

kopec(k), -peek, -pek, = COPECK.

kŏp'je (-pī), n. (S.-Afr.). Small hill. [Du., dim. of *kop* head]

koppie, n. S.Afr. sp. of KOPJE.

Kŏr'an (*or* Korahn'), n. Sacred book of the Mohammedans, collection of Mohammed's oral revelations, written in Arabic. Hence **korän'IC** a. [f. Arab. *quran* recitation (*qara'a* read)]

kōsh'er, a. & n. **1.** (Of food or shop where food is sold or used) fulfilling requirements of Jewish law. **2.** n. ~ food or shop. [f. Heb. *kasher* right]

kōtow', n., & v.i. **1.** Chinese custom of touching ground with forehead as sign of worship or absolute submission. **2.** v.i. Perform the ~, act obsequiously (to person etc.). [(vb f. n.) f. Chin. *k'o-t'ou* (*k'o* knock +*t'ou* head)]

kŏt'wal (-ahl), n. Chief constable of Indian town; magistrate. [Hind.]

koum'iss (kōō-), n. Fermented liquor prepared from mare's milk. [f. Tartar *kumiz*]

kourb'äsh (koor-), **koor-**, n. Hide whip as instrument of punishment in Turkey & Egypt. [f. Arab. *qurbash* f. Turk. *qirbash*]

kowtow. Var. of KOTOW.

kraal (krahl), n. S.-African village of huts enclosed by fence; enclosure for cattle or sheep. [Afrikaans, f. Port. CORRAL]

krait (krīt), n. Peculiarly venomous snake common in Bengal. [Hind. *karait*]

kra'ken (-ah-, -ä-), n. Mythical sea--monster appearing off coast of Norway. [Norw.]

krans (-ah-), n. (S.-Afr.). Precipitous or overhanging wall of rocks. [Du. *krans* coronet]

krĕm'lin, n. Citadel within Russian town, esp. that of Moscow; the K~, (used for) the Russian Government. [F, f. Russ. *kreml*]

kreu'tzer (kroit-), n. Small silver & copper coins formerly current in Germany & Austria. [f. G *kreuzer* (*kreuz* cross)]

krieg'spiel, n. War-game in which blocks representing troops etc. are moved about on maps. [G]

kris. See CREESE.

Krish'naism, n. Worship of Krishnā, great deity of later Hinduism, worshipped as incarnation of Vishnu. [-ISM]

kromĕs'kў, n. Minced chicken etc. rolled in bacon & fried. [f. Russ.]

krōn'e (-e), n. Silver coin of Denmark, Norway, & Sweden; former Austrian silver coin; former German 10-mark gold piece. [G & Da. *krone*, Sw. *krona*, crown]

Krōō, Krou, Kru (-ōō), n. & a. (Member) of Negro race on coast of Liberia, skilful as seamen (often, for the n., ~-boy, ~--man). [W.-Afr.]

krŷp'tŏn, n. (chem.). A rare inert gaseous element discovered by Ramsay in 1898. [f. Gk *krupton* hidden, neut. adj. f. *kruptō* hide]

Ksha'trĭya (-ah-), n. Member of the second or military caste of the Hindus. [Skr., f. *kshatra* rule]

kūd'ŏs, n. (sl.). Glory, renown. [Gk]

Kufic. See CUFIC.

*•**Kū'Klŭx(-Klän'),** n. Secret society hostile to Negroes & R. Catholics formed in southern States after civil war; similar organization in U.S. to combat alien influences after 1914–18 war. [arbitrary]

***kuk'rĭ** (kōō-), n. Curved knife broadening towards point, used by Gurkhas of Nepal. [Hind.]

kul'äk (kōō-), n. (Russ. pl. ~i). Well-to-do Russian peasant (-proprietor). [Russ., = tight-fisted person]

***kultur** (kōōltoor'), n. Civilization as conceived by the Germans. [G, = culture]

***kultur'kampf** (kōōltoor'kahmpf), n. Conflict between German imperial government and Pope for control of schools and church appointments (1872–87). [G]

kümm'el (see Ap.), n. Cumin-flavoured liqueur. [G]

Kuomĭntäng' (kōōō-), n. Nationalist party in China (founded in 1912). [Chin., lit. ' people's national party ']

Kurd (koord), n. Native of Kurdistan.

***kursaal** (koor'zahl), n. Building for use of visitors esp. at German health resort. [G, = cure-room]

kväss, n. Russian rye-beer. [f. Russ. *kvas*]

kў'anīze, -ise (-īz), v.t. Treat (wood) with solution of corrosive sublimate to prevent decay. [f. J. H. *Kyan*, inventor, +-IZE]

kyl'in (kē-), n. Fabulous composite animal figured on Chinese & Japanese pottery. [f. Chin. *ch'i-lin* (*ch'i* male +*lin* female)]

|| **kyl'ōe,** n. One of small breed of long--horned Scotch cattle. [K~, place-name]

kўm'ograph(-ahf),n. Instrument recording variations in pressure, e.g. in sound--waves. [Gk *kuma* wave + -o- + -GRAPH(2)]

***kyrie eleison** (kēr'iĭ ĭlā'ison, ki'riĕ), n. Words of short petition used in Eastern & Roman Churches, esp. at beginning of Mass, musical setting of these; response to commandments in Communion Service in Anglican Church. [f. Gk *Kurie eleēson*, Lord, have mercy]

L

L (ĕl), letter (pl. Ls, L's). Thing shaped like L (*L-iron*, = ANGLE[1]*-iron*); rectangular joint of pipes etc.; Roman numeral = 50, as CL 150, XL 40, lx 60, lv 55, (LXX, the Septuagint).

la (lah), lah, n. (mus.). Sixth note of octave. [first syl. of L *labii*, see GAMUT]

laag'er (lahg-), n., & v.t. & i. **1.** Camp, encampment, esp. in circle of wagons; (mil.) park for armoured vehicles. **2. vb.** Form (vehicles) into ~; encamp (persons) in ~; encamp. [S.-Afr. Du., & G, *lager*, Du. *leger*, see LEAGUER[1]]

lăb, n. (colloq.). Laboratory. [abbr.]

lăb'arum, n. Constantine the Great's imperial standard with Christian added to Roman-military symbols; symbolic banner. [LL *labarum*, of unkn. orig.]

labdacism. See LAMBDACISM.

lăbĕfăc'tion, n. Shaking, weakening, downfall. [f. L *labefacere* (*labare* totter, *facere* make), see -FACTION]

lăb'el, n., & v.t. (-ll-). **1.** Slip of paper, card, linen, metal, etc., for attaching to object & indicating its nature, owner, name, destination, etc.; (fig.) short classifying phrase or name applied to persons etc. (freq. derog. in literary or artistic criticism); adhesive stamp; (archit.) dripstone. **2. v.t.** Attach ~ to; assign to a category (as, obj. & compl., or abs.). [ME, f. OF, prob. f. OFrank. *labba* (= OHG *lappa* LAP[1]) + dim. *-el*]

lăb'ial, a. & n. Of the lips; (anat., zool.) of, like, serving as, a lip, lip-like part, or labium; (mus.) ~ pipe, in organ, one furnished with lips, flue-pipe; (phonet.) (sound) requiring closure or approximation of lips (*p, b, f, v,* also *m, w,* & vowels in which lips are rounded, as *o*), whence

~ISM(1), ~ĪZA'TION, nn., ~IZE(3) v.t. [f. med. L *labialis* (LABIUM, -AL)]

lāb'iate, a. & n. (Bot.) with corolla or calyx divided into two parts suggesting lips (n., such plant); (bot., zool.) like lip or labium. [LABIUM+-ATE²]

lăb'ile, a. (phys., chem.). Unstable, liable to displacement or change. [f. LL *labilis* (*labi* to LAPSE², -IL)]

lăb'io-, comb. form of foll. = of the lip(s) & —, as ~*dental*, made with lip & teeth.

lāb'ĭum, n. (pl. *-ia*). (Anat.; usu. pl.) lip(s) of female pudendum; floor of mouth of insects, crustaceans, etc.; inner lip of univalve shell; lip, esp. the lower, of labiate corolla. [L, = lip]

lăb'oratorў (or *labŏ²-*), n. Room or building used for experiments in natural science, esp. chemistry, or for research (also fig., ~ *of the mind, of ideas,* etc.). Hence **lăboratŏr'IAL** a. [f. med. L *laboratorium* (*laborare* LABOUR², -ORY)]

labŏr'ious, a. Hard-working; toilsome; (of style etc.) showing signs of toil, not facile or fluent. Hence ~LY² adv., ~NESS n. [ME, f. OF *laborieus* f. L *laboriosus* (foll., -IOUS)]

lāb'our¹ (-ber), n. **1.** Bodily or mental toil, exertion, (HARD ~; *lost* ~, fruitless efforts; ~ *of love*, task one delights in); toil tending to supply wants of community; body of those who contribute by toil to production, labourers; (opp. CAPITAL², usu. *L~*) the working classes as a political force. **2.** Task (~ *of Hercules, Herculean* ~, one needing enormous strength etc.). **3.** Pains of childbirth, travail, (*in* ~). **4.** ‖ *L~ Exchange*, local office under State for finding employment for those seeking it; ~*market*, supply of ~ with reference to demand on it; *L~ Party*, that claiming to represent wage--earners, M.P.s elected by it. [ME, f. OF *labor* f. L *laborem* nom. *-or*]

lāb'our² (-ber), v.i. & t. Use labour, exert oneself, work hard; strive *for* end or *to* do; advance with difficulty (*wheels* ~ *in the sand*); be troubled (*her* ~*ing heart*) or impeded, suffer *under* mistake etc.; (of ship) roll or pitch heavily; (arch. or poet.) till (ground); elaborate, work out in detail, treat at length, (*I will not* ~ *the point*; ~*ed*, much elaborated, showing signs of labour, not spontaneous); ~*ing man*, labourer. [ME, f. OF *labourer* f. L *laborare* (*labor* LABOUR¹)]

lāb'ourer (-ber-), n. In vbl senses; esp., man doing for wages work that requires strength or patience rather than skill or training. [ME, f. OF *laboureur* (as prec., -ER¹)]

lāb'ourite (-ber-), n. Member, adherent, of Labour Party. [-ITE¹(1)]

Lăb'radŏr, n. attrib. ~ *dog, retriever*, breed of retriever. [place]

lăb'rĕt, n. Piece of shell, bone, etc., inserted in lip as ornament. [L *labrum* lip, -ET¹]

labŭr'num, n. Small tree with racemes of bright yellow flowers. [L]

lăb'yrinth, n. Complicated irregular structure with many passages hard to find way through or about without guidance, maze; intricate or tortuous arrangement; (anat.) complex cavity of internal ear; entangled state of affairs. Hence ~INE² (-In'thin) a. [f. F *labyrinthe* or L f. Gk *laburinthos*]

lăbyrin'thodŏn, n.-dŏnt, n. & a. (Kinds of large fossil amphibian) with labyrinthine teeth. [*-dont* f. *-don* mod. L, f. Gk as prec.+*odous -ontos* tooth]

lăc¹, n. A resinous substance secreted by the lac insect as a protective covering. [f. Hind. *lakh* f. Skr. *laksha*]

lăc², lăkh(-k), n. (Anglo-Ind.). A hundred thousand (usu. ~ *of rupees*). [Hind. *-kh*] f. Skr. *laksha*]

lāce¹, n. Cord or leather strip for fastening or tightening opposite edges of shoes, corsets, etc., by help of eyelets or hooks; braid for trimming men's coats etc. (usu. *gold* or *silver* ~); fine open fabric of linen, cotton, silk, woollen, or metal threads usu. with inwrought or applied patterns; ~*glass*, Venetian with ~-like designs; ~*pillow*, laid on lap of woman making ~. Hence lā'cY² a. [ME, f. OF *laz, las,* f. Rom. **lacium* f. L *laqueus* noose]

lāce², v.t. & i. Fasten or tighten (shoe, corsets, etc.) with lace(s) (freq. ~ *up*); compress waist of by drawing stay-laces tight, (intr.) compress one's waist; interlace or embroider (fabric) *with* thread etc.; pass (cord etc.) *through*; trim with lace; diversify (flower *with* streaks of colour); lash, beat, (also intr. as ~ *into* person); flavour, fortify, (milk, beer, etc.) *with* spirit. Hence lā'cING¹(1, 3, 6) n. [ME, f. OF *lacier* f. Rom. **laciare* as prec.]

lă'cer|āte, v.t. Mangle, tear, (esp. flesh or tissues); afflict, distress, (heart, feelings). Hence or cogn.~ABLE,~ATE²(-at),~ATIVE, aa.,~A'TION n. [f. L *lacerare* (*lacer* torn), -ATE³]

lacĕrt'ian, -tīne, aa. Of lizards; lizard--like. [f. L *lacerta* lizard+-IAN, -INE¹]

lācĕt', n. Work made of braid or tape shaped into a design with lace stitches. [-ET¹]

lăch'es (-Iz), n. (Law) negligence in performing a legal duty, delay in asserting right, claiming privilege, etc.; culpable negligence. [ME, f. OF *laschesse* (*lasche* f. Rom. **lascus* f. L *laxus* LAX)]

lach'rŷma Chris'tĭ (lăk-; krĭ-), n. Strong sweet red S.-Ital. wine. [L, = Christ's tear]

lăch'rŷmal (-k-), a. & n. Of, for, tears (~ *vase,* or ~ as n., to hold tears; ~ *canal, duct, gland, sac,* in anat.; also ~*s* as n., these organs). [med. L (*-alis*), f. L *lacrima* tear]

lăchrŷmā'tion (-k-), n. Flow of tears. [f. L *lacrimatio* (*lacrimare* as prec., -ATION)]

lăch'rŷmatorу(-k-), a. & n. **1.** Of, causing, tears (~ *bomb*, emitting gas that disables by making eyes water). **2.** n. Phial of kind found in anc.-Roman tombs & conjectured to be tear-bottles. [f. *lacrimare* see prec. +-ORY]

lăch′rÿmōse (-k-), a. Tearful, given to weeping. Hence ~LY² adv. [f. L *lacrimosus* (*lacrima* tear, -OSE¹)]

lacin′iate, -āted, aa. (bot., zool.). Cut into deep irregular segments, slashed, jagged, fringed. [f. L *lacinia* lappet, -ATE²]

lăck, n., & v.i. & t. **1.** Deficiency, want, need, *of* (*no* ~, plenty *of*; *for* ~, owing to want or absence *of*). **2.** vb. Be wanting (only in part. forms, as *money was* ~*ing*, *is* ~*ing in courage*); be without, not have, be deficient in; ~′*land*, (person) having no land; ~′*lustre*, (of eye etc.) dull. [early ME *lac*, *lacen*, corresp. to MLG *lak*, MDu. *lac* deficiency, MDu. *laken* to lack]

lăckadais′ical (-z-), a. Languishing, affected, given to airs & graces, feebly sentimental; listless. Hence ~LY² adv., ~NESS n. [f. arch. *lackaday*, *-daisy*, int. (ALACK) +-ICAL]

lacker. See LACQUER.

lăck′ey, lăc′quey (-kĭ), n. (pl. ~s), & v.t. **1.** Footman, man-servant (usu. liveried); obsequious person, parasite. **2.** v.t. Dance attendance on, behave servilely to. [f. F *laquais* (obs. *alaquais*) f. Sp. *lacayo*]

Lacōn′ian, a. & n. (Inhabitant) of Laconia, Spartan. [f. L *Laconia* +-AN]

lacŏn′|ic, a. Brief, concise, sententious; given to such speech or style. Hence ~ICALLY adv., ~ICISM(2) n. [f. L f. Gk *lakōnikos* (*Lakōn* Spartan, -IC)]

lăc′onism, n. Brevity of speech; short pithy saying. [f. Gk *lakōnismos* (*lakōnizō* behave like Spartan or *Lakōn*, -ISM)]

lăc′quer (-ker), **lăck′er,** n., & v.t. **1.** Gold-coloured varnish of shellac dissolved in alcohol used esp. as coating for brass; kinds of resinous varnish (esp. *Japanese* ~) taking hard polish & used for wood etc., articles so coated. **2.** v.t. Coat with ~. [f. obs. F *lacre* sealing-wax, f. unexpl. var. of Port. *lacca* LAC¹]

lacquey. See LACKEY.

lacrim-, lacrym-. See lachrymi-.

lacrosse (lahkraws′, -ŏs), n. Game like hockey, but with ball driven by & carried in CROSSE, orig. N.-Amer. [F *la* the + CROSSE]

lăctā′tion, n. Suckling; secreting of milk. [f. L *lactare* suckle (*lac -tis* milk) +-ATION]

lăc′tĕal, a. & n. **1.** Of milk; conveying chyle or other milky fluid. **2.** n. pl. Vessels of mesentery doing this. [f. L *lacteus* (*lac* see prec.) +-AL]

lăctĕs′cence, n., **lăctĕs′cent,** a. Milky (appearance); (yielding) milky juice. [f. L *lactescere* (*lactēre* be milky, see prec.), -ENCE, -ENT]

lăc′tĭc, a. (chem.). Of milk; ~*ic acid*, formed in sour milk, whence ~ATE¹(3) n. [f. L *lac -tis* milk +-IO]

lăctif′erous, a. Yielding milk or milky fluid. [f. LL *lactifer* (prec., -FEROUS)]

lăc′to-, comb. form (-I-, -O-) of L as prec.; ~*prot′ein,* albuminous constituent of milk; ~METER (-ŏm²), ~SCOPE, instruments for testing purity of milk.

lăctōse′, n. Milk sugar, less sweet than cane sugar. [as prec. +-OSE²]

lacūn′|a, n. (pl. ~*ae*, ~*as*). Hiatus, blank, missing portion (esp. in ancient MS, book, etc.), empty part; cavity in bone, tissue etc. Hence ~AL, ~AR, ~ARY, ~OSE¹, aa. [L (*lacus* LAKE¹)]

lacŭs′trine, a. Of, dwelling or growing in, lake(s); ~ *age*, of LAKE¹-dwellings. [f. L *lacus* LAKE¹ (after *paluster* marshy) +-INE¹]

lacy. See LACE¹.

lăd, n. Boy, youth, young fellow; fellow; stable-man (of any age). Hence ~d′ie [-Y³] n. [ME *ladde*, of unkn. orig.]

lădd′er, n., & v.i. Set of steps (called *rungs*) inserted usu. in two uprights of wood or metal or in two cords to serve as (usu. portable) means of ascending building etc.; STEP²-~; || (transf.) vertical flaw in stocking caused by stitch(es) becoming undone through several rows (v.i., develop ~), whence ~PROOF² a.; (fig.) means of rising in the world or attaining object (*kick down* ~, abandon friends or occupation that have helped one to rise), & see RUNG¹; ~*dredge*, with buckets carried round on ~-like chain; ~*stitch*, crossbar stitch in embroidery. [OE *hlǣd(d)er* = MDu. *lēdere*, OHG *leitara* f. Gmc *hli-*, *hlai-* (LEAN²)]

lāde, v.t. (p.p. ~*n*). Put cargo on board (ship); ship (goods) as cargo (BILL⁴ *of lading*), whence lād′ING¹(3) n.; (p.p., of vehicle, beast of burden, person, tree, branch, table, etc.) loaded (*with*); (p.p.) painfully burdened *with* sin, sorrow, etc. [OE, OS, OHG *hladan*, ON *hlatha*, Goth. *-hlathan*; cf. LAST²]

la-di-da′ (lah-, -ah), a. & n. (Person given to) swagger or pretension in manners & pronunciation; pretentious in this way. [imit. of pronunciation used]

Ladin′ (-ēn), n. RHAETO-ROMANIC of the Engadine. [f. It *Ladino* f. L LATINUS]

lā′dle, n., & v.t. **1.** Large spoon with cup bowl & long handle for transferring liquids; hence ~FUL(2) (-dlfŏŏl) n. **2.** v.t. Transfer (liquid) with ~ from one receptacle to another. [OE *hlǣdel* f. *hladan* LADE +-LE(1)]

lād′ÿ, n. **1.** Ruling woman (poet. exc. in ~ *of the manor, our sovereign* ~). **2.** Woman to whom man is devoted, mistress, love. **3.** *Our L-*~, Virgin Mary. **4.** Woman belonging to, or fitted by manners, habits, & sentiments, for the upper classes (corresp. to GENTLEMAN; || ~ *of bedchamber*, ~*in-waiting*, ~ attending sovereign; FINE³ ~). **5.** (Courteously for) woman (as voc., only poet. or vulg. in sing., but usu. form of address in pl.). **6.** || (Title used as less formal prefix for) Marchioness (of), Countess (of), Viscountess, Baroness, (also prefixed to Christian name of) daughter of duke, marquis, or earl, (or to husband's Christian name of) wife of holder of courtesy title *lord* William etc., (or to surname of) wife of baronet or knight, (also in the compound title) *L~ Mayoress*, wife of Lord Mayor. 7. *My ~*, form of address used chiefly by servants etc. to holders of title ~; *my dear* or *good ~* (address in ord. use). 8. Wife (arch. or vulg., exc. of those who hold the title ~); *your good ~*, your wife, 9. *Ladies & gentlemen* (voc. in addressing company of both sexes). 10. (With *clerk*, *doctor*, *president*, *dog*, etc.) female; || (with *cook*, *parlourmaid*, *help*, etc.) claiming to be treated as ~. 11. *Ladies* (as sing. n.), women's public lavatory etc.; *Ladies' chain*, figure in quadrille; *Ladies' gallery*, in House of Commons reserved for ladies. 12. *~ of EASY virtue*; *painted ~*, kind of butterfly. 13. *L~-altar* (in L~-chapel); *~bird*, coleopterous insect, usu. reddish-brown with black spots; *L~-Bountiful, ~* playing the part of Providence in a village etc. (character in Farquhar's *Beaux's Stratagem*); *~chair*, made by two persons' interlaced hands to carry wounded man etc.; *L~-chapel*, in large church usu. east of high altar, dedicated to Virgin; *~clock, -cow, ~bird; L~ Day*, Feast of the Annunciation, 25th March, || one of the quarter-days; *~-fern*, tall slender kind; || *~ help, ~* employed as domestic; *~-killer*, man devoting himself to making conquests of ladies; *~-love*, sweetheart; *L~'s* BED¹*-straw*; *~'s companion*, roll containing cottons etc.; || *L~'s cushion*, mossy saxifrage; || *L~'s finger*, kidney vetch; *L~'s laces*, kind of striped grass; *~'s-maid*, in charge of ~'s toilet; *~'s man*, *ladies' man*, (fond of female society); *L~'s mantle*, rosaceous plant with yellowish-green flowers; *L~-smock*, cuckoo-flower; *L~'s slipper*, orchidaceous wild & garden plant with usu. yellow bag- or slipper-shaped flowers, calceolaria; *L~'s tresses*, kind of orchis. Hence *~HOOD* n. [OE *hlæfdīge* (*hlāf* LOAF, *dig-* knead cf. DOUGH); in *~-altar, -bird, -chapel, -clock, -cow, -day, -smock, ~* is old genit. = (Our) Lady's]

lād'y̆fy̆, -ify̆, v.t. Make lady of; call lady; (p.p.) having the airs of a fine lady. [-FY]

lād'y̆like, a. With manners etc. of a lady; (of man) effeminate; befitting a lady. [-LIKE]

lād'y̆ship, n. Being a lady; *her, your, ~, their ~s*, she, you, they (in respectful mention of or address to titular lady). [-SHIP]

laer, n. Afrikaans sp. of LAAGER.

l(a)evo- (lēv'o), comb. form of L *laevus* left, esp. in terms concerned with chem. property of causing plane of polarized light ray to rotate to left (opp. DEXTRO-); so *~gȳr'ous, ~rot'atory*, of substances having this; *~com'pound*, chemical compound having it.

l(a)ev'ŭlōse (lēv-), n. (chem.). Laevorotatory sugar of fruit & honey, fruit-sugar. [prec., -UL-, -OSE²]

lăg¹, v.i. (-gg-), & n. 1. Go too slow, not keep pace, fall behind (often *behind* adv. & prep.). 2. n. (phys.). (Amount of) retardation in current or movement (*~ of tide*, interval by which it falls behind mean time in 1st & 3rd quarters of moon, cf. PRIMING²); TIME¹ *~*. Hence *~g'ARD* n. & a., *~g'ER¹* n., *~g'ING²* a., (-g-). [16th c. 'hindmost person', 'hang back'; perh. f. a fanciful distortion of *last* in children's games (*fog, seg, ~, = 1st, 2nd, last, in diall.*)]

lăg², v.t. (-gg-), & n. (sl.). 1. Send to penal servitude; apprehend, arrest. 2. n. Convict, esp. *old~*. [orig. unkn.]

lăg³, n., & v.t. (-gg-). 1. (Piece of the) non-conducting cover of boiler etc. 2. v.t. Case with *~s*, whence *~g'ING¹*(3) (g-) n. [f. ON *logg* barrel-rim]

lăg'an, lĭg'an, n. (legal). Goods or wreckage lying on bed of sea. [OF, perh. of Scand. orig. f. root of LIE³, LAY³]

la'ger (beer) (lahg-), n. Light kind of (orig. German or Bohemian) beer. [f. G *lager-bier* (*lager* store)]

lagōōn', -une (-ōōn), n. Stretch of salt water parted from sea by low sandbank; enclosed water of atoll. [f. F *lagune*, f. It. & Sp. *laguna* f. L LACUNA]

lah. See LA.

lā'ic, a. & n. Non-cleric(al), lay(man), secular, temporal. So *~AL* a., *~alLY²* adv. [f. LL f. Gk *laikos* (*laos* people, -IC)]

lā'iciz|e, -is|e (-īz), v.t. Make lay; commit (school etc.), throw open (office), to laymen. Hence *~A'TION* n. [prec., -IZE]

laid. See LAY³.

lain. See LIE³.

lair, n., & v.i. & t. 1. Place where animals lie down; || shed or enclosure for cattle on way to market, whence *~'AGE*(1, 3) n.; wild beast's lying-place. 2. vb. Go to, rest or place in, *~*. [OE *leger*, OS *-ar*, OHG *-er*, ON *legr*, Goth. *ligrs* bed f. Gmo **leg-* LIE³]

|| laird, n. (Sc.). Landed proprietor in Scotland. Hence *~'SHIP* n. [Sc. form of LORD w. changed sense]

Lā'is, n. Accomplished or beautiful courtesan. [name of two celebrated Greek hetaerae]

laissez-aller (lās'ā āl'ā), n. Unconstrained freedom, absence of constraint. [F, = let go]

laiss'ez-faire (-sā-), n. Government abstention from interference with individual action esp. in commerce. [F, = let act]

lā'ity, n. Being a layman; laymen. [f. LAY² +-ITY]

lāke¹, n. Large body of water entirely surrounded by land; *the Great L~*, Atlantic ocean; *the Great L~s*, Superior, Huron, Michigan, Erie, & Ontario, forming boundary of U.S. & Canada; *~-country, ~land, the L~s*, region of

English ~s in Westmorland, Cumberland, & Lancs.; ~-*dweller*, prehistoric inhabitant of ~ *dwelling*, built on piles driven into bed of ~; ~ *poets*, Coleridge, Southey, & Wordsworth, who lived in ~land. Hence ~'LESS a., ~'LET n., (-kl-). [ME, f. OF *lac* f. L *lacus*]

lake², n. Pigment, orig. made from lac, now formed by dye & mordant. [var. of LAC¹]

lakh. See LAC².

Lǎll'an, a. & n. (Sc.). 1. Of the Lowlands of Scotland. 2. n. (Also ~s) Lowland Scots dialect. [var. of LOW'*land*]

lǎllā'tion, n. LAMBDACISM. [f. L *lallare* sing lullaby +-ATION]

lǎm, v.t. & i. (sl.; -mm-). Thrash, hit (t., & i. with *into*) hard with cane etc. [perh. f. Scand.; cf. ON *lemja* beat so as to LAME]

la'ma¹ (lah-), n. Tibetan or Mongolian Buddhist monk; (*Dalai* (pr. dǎl'ĭ) L~, (obs.) *Grand L*~, head of ~ist church & ruler of Tibet. Hence ~ISM n., ~IST n. & a. [Tibetan *blama* (silent *b*)]

lama². See LLAMA.

Lamārck'ian, a. & n. (Follower) of Lamarck or his theory of organic evolution by the inheritance of acquired characters. [*Lamarck*, F botanist & zoologist, d. 1829, +-IAN]

lama'serȳ (-mah-), n. Monastery of lamas. [f. F *lamaserie* irreg. f. LAMA¹]

lǎmb (-m), n., & v.t. & i. 1. Young of sheep (*as well be hanged for a sheep as for a* ~, sin boldly, go the whole hog; *like a* ~, unresistingly; *wolf, fox, in* ~'*s skin*, hypocrite); its flesh as food; young member of church flock; innocent, weak, or dear person; *The L*~ (*of God*), Christ; ~'*s-fry*, product of ~'s castration; ~ᴸ-*skin*, with wool on, or as leather; ~'*s-tails*, ‖ hazel catkins; ~'*s-wool*, used in hosiery; hence ~'HOOD (-mh-), ~'KIN (-mk-), nn., ~'LIKE (-ml-) a. 2. vb. (Pass.; of ~s) be brought forth; bring forth ~, yean; tend (~ing ewes), whence ~'ER¹ (-mer) n. [OE (= OS, OHG, ON, Goth.) *lamb* f. Gmc *lambaz*]

lǎmbāste', v.t. (dial.). Thrash, beat. [perh. = LAM +BASTE³]

lǎmb'da, n. Greek letter L (*Λ λ*); ~*moth*, with ~ on wings. [Gk, also *labda*]

lǎ(m)b'dacism, n. Pronunciation of *r* as *l*. [prec., -ISM]

lǎmb'doid, lǎmbdoid'al, aa. *Λ* -shaped (~ *suture*, connecting two parietal bones with occipital. [f. F *lambdoïde* f. Gk *lambdoeidēs* (LAMBDA, -OID) +-AL]

lǎm'b|ent, a. (Of flame or light) playing on surface without burning it, with soft radiance; (of eyes, sky, etc.) softly radiant; (of wit etc.) gently brilliant. Hence ~ENCY n., ~entLY² adv. [f. L *lambere* lick, -ENT]

Lǎm'bĕth, n. (Used for) Archbishop of Canterbury's palace at ~, the Archbishop as representing the Church, etc.;

~ *degree*, honorary degree conferred by the Archbishop of Canterbury.

lǎm'brequin (-kĭn), n. Short piece of drapery over top of door or window, or hung from mantelpiece. [F, f. Du. *lamperkin*, dim. of *lamper* veil; see -KIN]

lāme, a., & v.t. 1. Crippled by injury or defect in a limb, esp. foot or leg, limping or unable to walk, (of person, limb, steps, etc.; ~ *of* or *in a leg* etc.); (of argument, story, excuse) imperfect, unsatisfactory; (of metre) halting; ~ DUCK¹; hence lǎm'ISH¹(2) a., ~'LY² (-ml-) adv., ~'NESS (-mn-) n. 2. v.t. Make ~, cripple, (lit. & fig.). [OE *lama*, OS *lamo*, OHG *lam*, ON *lami* f. Gmc *lamon*]

lamé (lahmā'), a. & n. (Material) with gold or silver thread inwoven. [F]

lamĕll'|a, n. (pl. ~ae). Thin plate, scale, layer, or film, esp. of bone or tissue. Hence ~AR¹, lǎm'ĕllATE², -āted, ~OSE¹, aa., ~I- comb. form. [L, dim. of LAMINA]

lamĕnt', n., & v.t. & i. 1. Passionate expression of grief; elegy, dirge. 2. vb. Express or feel grief for or about, be distressed at, regret, (also intr. with *for* or *over*, or abs.); (p.p.) mourned for (esp. conventionally of the dead, as *the late* ~*ed* —). [vb f. F *lamenter* or L -*ari*; n. f. vb, or L *lamentum*]

lǎm'entab|le, a. Mournful (arch.); (of events, fate, condition, character, etc.) deplorable, regrettable. Hence ~LY² adv. [ME, f. OF, or L *lamentabilis* (prec., -ABLE)]

lǎmĕntā'tion, n. Lamenting, lament; *L*~s (*of Jeremiah*), O.-T. book (abbr. *Lam.*). [ME, f. OF, or L *lamentatio* (LAMENT, -ATION)]

lǎm'ia, n. Monster in woman's shape preying on human beings & sucking children's blood. [L f. Gk]

lǎm'in|a, n. (pl. ~ae). Thin plate, scale, layer, or flake, of metal, bone, membrane, stratified rock, vegetable tissue, etc. Hence ~AR¹, ~OSE¹, aa., ~I- comb. form. [L]

lǎm'in|āte, v.t. & i. Beat or roll (metal) into thin plates; split (t. & i.) into layers or leaves; overlay with metal plates; manufacture by placing layer on layer. Hence or cogn. ~ATE² (-at) pa., ~A'TION n. [prec. +-ATE³]

Lǎmm'as, n. First of August, formerly observed as harvest festival (*later* ~, non-existent date, day that will never come, cf. *Greek* CALENDS). [OE *hlāfmæsse* (LOAF¹, MASS¹)]

lǎmm'ergeyer (-gī-), n. Bearded vulture, largest European bird of prey. [f. G *lämmergeier* (*lämmer* lambs, *geier* vulture)]

lǎmp, n., & v.i. & t. 1. Vessel with oil & wick for giving light; glass vessel enclosing candle, gas-jet, incandescent wire, or other illuminant (*smell of the* ~, betray nocturnal study, be laborious in style etc.); SAFETY ~; SPIRIT¹~; (fig.) sun, moon, star; source of spiritual or intellectual light, hope, etc.; ~*black*, pigment made from soot; ~*chimney*, glass cylinder making draught for ~-flame; ~*light*, given by ~ or ~s; ~*lighter*, man who formerly lighted street ~s (*like a* ~*lighter*, with speed); ~*post*, usu. of iron supporting street ~; hence ~*LESS a.* 2. *vb.* Shine; supply with ~s; illuminate; *(sl.) look at. [ME, f. OF *lampe* f. LL *lampada* = L f. Gk *lampas*]

lăm′pas[1], *n.* Horse-disease with swelling in roof of mouth. [F, of obsc. orig.; cf. F dial. *lampas* throat]

lăm′pas[2], *n.* Kind of flowered silk orig. from China. [F]

lăm′pion, *n.* Pot of usu. coloured glass with oil & wick used in illuminations. [F, f. It. *lampione* (*lampa* LAMP, -OON)]

lămpoon′, *n.*, & *v.t.* 1. Virulent or scurrilous piece of satire; hence ~IST (1) *n.* 2. *v.t.* Write ~ or ~s against, whence ~ER[1] *n.* [f. F *lampon* conjectured to be f. *lampons* let us drink]

lăm′prey, *n.* (pl. ~s). Eel-like pseudo-fish with sucker mouth, pouch gills, & seven spiracles on each side, & fistula on top, of head. [ME, f. OF *lampreie* f. med. L *lampreda*, (whence OE *lampreda*, OHG *lampreta*) ; cf. *lampetra* (as f. L *lambere* lick + *petra* stone); see LIMPET]

Lăncăs′trian, *a.* & *n.* (Inhabitant) of Lancashire or Lancaster; (adherent) of family descended from John of Gaunt Duke of Lancaster, or of the Red-rose party fighting for it in Wars of the Roses. [*Lancaster*, -IAN]

lance[1] (-ah-), *n.* Weapon with long wooden shaft & pointed steel head used by horseman in charging; similar implement for spearing fish or killing harpooned whale; FREE′~; (pl., w. numbers) = lancers; ~-*corporal* (&, sl., ~*jack*) N.C.O. below corporal; ~*sergeant*, corporal acting as sergeant; ~*fish*, launce; ~*snake*, venomous Amer. kind; ~*wood*, tough elastic W.-Ind. kind used for carriage-shafts, fishing-rods, etc. [ME, f. OF, f. L *lancea*; ~*corporal* on anal. of obs. *lancepesade* lowest grade of N.C.O.]

lance[2] (-ah-), *v.t.* Fling, launch, (poet.); (surg.) prick or cut open with lancet; pierce with lance. [ME; poet. sense f. OF *lancier* f. LL *lanceare* (*lancea* LANCE[1]); other senses f. prec.]

lance′lĕt (-ahnsl-), *n.* Small fish-like animal. [LANCE[1], -LET]

lăn′ceolate, *a.* Shaped like spear-head, tapering to each end. [f...LL *lanceolatus* (*lanceola* dim. of *lancea* lance, -ATE[2])]

la′ncer (-ah-), *n.* Soldier of cavalry regiment orig. armed with lances; (pl.) kind of quadrille, music for it. [f. F *lancier* (LANCE[1], -IER)]

la′ncĕt (-ah-), *n.* 1. Surgical instrument usu. with two edges & point for bleeding or lancing. 2. (Also ~ *arch, light, window,* etc.) narrow arch or window with pointed

head, whence ~ED[2] *a.* [ME, f. OF *lancette* (LANCE[1], -ETTE)]

la′ncinating (lah-), *a.* (Of pain) acute, shooting. [part. of rare *lancinate* f. L *lancinare* rend]

lănd[1], *n.* 1. Solid part of earth's surface (opp. *sea, water; travel by* ~; *how the* ~ *lies,* what is the state of affairs); ground, soil, expanse of country; country, nation, State, (~ *of promise,* Canaan; ~ *of hope & glory;* ~ *of* CAKE[1]s; ~ *of the leal,* heaven; ~ *of the living,* present life); landed property, (pl.) estates; (S. Afr.) ground fenced off for tillage; strip of plough or pasture ~ parted from others by water furrows. 2. Any of the divisions between the rifling-grooves in guns. 3. ~*agent,* -*agency,* ‖ steward(ship) of estate, agent, agency, for sale etc. of estates; ~*bank,* ‖ issuing notes on security of landed property; ~*breeze,* blowing seaward from ~; ~*carriage,* transport by ~; ~*crab,* kinds that live on ~ but breed in sea; ~*fall* (naut.), approach to ~ esp. for first time on voyage (*good, bad,* ~*fall,* according, not according, to calculation); ~ *force(s),* military, not naval; ‖~*girl* (doing farmwork, esp. in wartime); ~*grabber,* (esp.) man who took Irish farm after eviction of tenant; ~*holder,* proprietor or (usu.) tenant of ~; ~*hunger,* -*hungry,* eager(ness) to acquire ~; ‖~*jobber,* speculator in ~; ~*lady,* woman keeping inn, boarding-house, or lodgings, also woman having tenants; ~*law* (usu. pl.), law(s) of landed property; *L*~ *League,* Irish association 1879–81 for reducing rents, introducing peasant-proprietorship, etc.; ~*locked,* almost or quite enclosed by ~; ~*lord,* person of whom another holds any tenement (opp. *tenant*), keeper of inn, lodgings, etc.; ~*lubber* (naut.), person ignorant of the sea & ships; ~*mark,* object marking boundary of country, estate, etc., conspicuous object in district etc., object or event or change marking stage in process or turning-point in history; ~*mine,* explosive mine laid in or on ground, parachute mine; ~*owner,* owner of ~; ~*rail,* corncrake; *L*~*'s End,* western point of Cornwall (see JOHN-o'-*Groat's*); ~*service,* military; ~*shark,* one who lives by preying on seamen ashore; ~*sick* (naut.; of ship), impeded in movement by nearness of ~; ~*slide* (orig. U.S.), overwhelming majority of votes for one side, esp. in an election; ‖~*slip,* sliding down of mass of ~ on cliff or mountain; ~*s′man,* non-sailor; ~*swell,* roll of water near shore; ~*tax,* assessed on landed property; ~*tie,* rod, beam, or piece of masonry, securing or supporting wall etc. by connecting some part of it with the ground; ~*wind,* = ~*breeze.* Hence ~*LESS a.,* ~*WARD a.* & *adv.,* ~*WARDS adv.* [OE, OS *land,* OHG *lant,* ON, Goth. *land* f. Gmc *landam*]

land², v.t. & i. Set or go ashore (p.p. = having come ashore, see -ED¹(2), esp. in comb. as *newly-~ed*), disembark (*at*); (of aircraft) come down to ground or surface of water; set down from vehicle; bring to, reach or find oneself in, a certain place, stage, or position; deal (person blow etc.; *~ed him one in the eye*); bring (fish) to land, (fig.) win (prize etc.); (trans. of jockey, intr. of horse) bring or come in (*first* etc., or abs. = first); alight after jump etc. [f. prec.]

Land³ (lahnt), n. (pl. *Länder*, pr. lĕn⁴). Land, country. [G]

lan'dau, n. Four-wheeled carriage with top of which front & back halves can be independently raised & lowered. [*L~* in Germany]

landaulĕt(te)', n. Coupé with landau top. [-LET]

lǎnd'drŏst n. (hist.). Magistrate in S. Africa. [Du., = sheriff]

lǎn'dĕd, a. Possessed of land (*the ~ interest*, owners & holders of land); consisting of land (*~ estate, property*). [LAND¹ +-ED²]

lǎnd'grāve, n. (fem. *-gravine*, pr. -avēn). (Former) German title of nobility. [f. MHG *lantgrāve* (LAND¹, G *graf* count)]

lǎn'ding, n. In vbl senses; also: (also *~-place*) place for disembarking; platform between two flights of stairs; *~-craft*, any of numerous types of naval craft esp. designed for putting ashore troops and equipment; *~-net*, for landing large fish when hooked; *~-stage*, platform, often floating, on which passengers & goods are disembarked. [-ING¹]

lǎnd'lŏrdism, n. System by which land is owned by landlords receiving fixed rents from tenants (esp. derog. of former Irish system); advocacy of this. [-ISM]

lǎndŏc'racÿ, n. (joc.). The landed class. So **lǎnd'ocrat** n. [-CRACY]

lǎnd'scăpe (*or* -ns-; earlier **-skip**), n. (Picture representing, art reproducing, or actual piece of) inland scenery; ‖ *~-gardening, -gardener*, laying, layer, out of grounds in imitation of natural scenery; *~-marble*, kind with treelike markings; *~-painter*, who paints*~s*, also **lǎnd'scăp-ist**(1) n. [c. 1600 f. MDu. *landscap* (LAND¹, -SHIP)]

land'sturm (lah-, -oorm), n. (Hist., in Germany etc.) general levy in war, of men outside army, navy, & Landwehr. [G]

land'tag (lah-, -ahx), n. Legislative body, diet, of a German State. [G]

land'wehr (lah-, -vār), n. (In Germany etc.) militia serving continuously only during war. [G]

lāne, n. Narrow road usu. between hedges (*it is a long ~ that has no turning*, change is sure to come), narrow street; passage made or left between rows of persons; strip of road for single line of traffic; course prescribed for ocean steamers; *red ~*, throat; ‖ *the ˙L~*, Drury L~

(theatre). [OE *lane*, = OFris. *lana, laen*, Du. *laan*, of unkn. orig.]

lǎng'rage, -idge, (-ngg-), n. Case-shot with irregular pieces of iron formerly used to damage rigging. [orig. unkn.]

‖ **lǎng sÿne**, adv. & n. (In) the old days. [Sc., = long since]

lǎng'uage (-nggw-), n. A vocabulary & way of using it prevalent in one or more countries (DEAD *~*); (transf.) method of expression (*finger ~*, talk by conventional signs with fingers; *~ of flowers*, symbolic meanings attached to various kinds); words & their use; faculty of speech; person's style of expressing himself (*bad ~*, or ‖ vulg. *~*, oaths & abusive talk; *strong ~*, expressing vehement feelings); professional or sectional vocabulary; literary style, wording; *~-master*, teacher of (usu. mod. foreign)*~* or*~s*. [ME, f. OF *langage* (L *lingua* tongue, -AGE)]

langue d'oc, langue d'oïl, nn. (see Ap.). Medieval French as spoken south, north, of the Loire, the latter the staple of modern French. [OF *langue* LANGUAGE, & *oc* (= L *hoc*), *oïl* (= L *hoc ille*), these being the respective forms for *yes*]

lǎng'uid (-nggw-), a. Inert, lacking vigour, indisposed to exertion, spiritless, apathetic, not vivid, dull, uninteresting, sluggish, slow-moving, faint, weak. Hence *~LY²* adv., *~NESS* n. [f. F *languide*, or L *languidus* (foll., -ID¹)]

lǎng'uish (-nggw-), v.i. Grow or be feeble, lose or lack vitality; live *under* enfeebling or depressing conditions; grow slack, lose intensity; droop, pine (*for*); put on languid look, affect sentimental tenderness, whence *~ingLY²* adv. Hence *~MENT* n. [ME, f. OF *languir* (-ISH²) f. L *languēre*]

lǎng'uor (-ngger), n. Faintness, fatigue; lassitude, inertia, want of alertness; soft or tender mood or effect; slackness, dullness, drooping state; (of sky etc.) oppressive stillness. So *~OUS* a., *~OUSLY²* adv., (-nggo-). [ME, f. OF f. L *languorem* nom. *-or* (prec., -OR)]

langur (lŭnggoor), n. (Kinds of) common Indian long-tailed monkey. [Hind.]

lǎn'iarÿ, a. & n. (Tooth) adapted for tearing, canine. [f. L *laniarius* (*lanius* butcher f. *laniare* tear, -ARY¹)]

lǎnif'erous, -i'gerous, aa. Wool-bearing. [f. L (*-fer, -ger*) f. *lana* wool, -FEROUS, -GEROUS]

lǎnk, a. Shrunken, spare; tall & lean; (of grass etc.) long & flaccid; (of hair) straight & limp, not wavy. [OE *hlanc* f.·Gmc **hlank-* (cf. MHG *lenken* bend); cf. FLANK, LINK¹]

lǎnk'|ÿ, a. Ungracefully lean & long or tall (of limbs, person). Hence *~iNESS* n. [-Y²]

lǎnn'er, lǎnn'erĕt, nn. Kind of falcon, female of it, (-*er*); (-*et*) male of it. [ME, f. OF *lanier* prob. f. OF *lanier* cowardly]

lǎn'olin, n. Fat which permeates sheep's

wool as basis of ointments. [G, f. L *lana* wool+-OL(2)+-IN]

läns'quenēt (-kĭ-), n. Card-game of German origin. [F, f. G *landsknecht* 17th-c. mercenary]

län'tern, n. Transparent case protecting flame of candle etc. (BULL[1]'s-*eye*, CHINESE, DARK[1], HURRICANE, MAGIC, ~); the moon; = magic~, whence ~IST(3) n.; light-chamber of lighthouse; erection on top of dome or room with glazed sides to admit light; luminous proboscis of ~-*fly*; ~ *jaws*, long & thin, giving hollow look to face, whence ~-jawED[2] a. [ME, f. OF *lanterne* f. L *lanterna*]

län'thanum, n. (chem.). Rare element belonging to aluminium group, discovered 1839–41. [f. Gk *lanthanō* escape notice,+-UM]

‖ **län'thorn** (-tern), n. Lantern. [pop. assim. of *lantern* to *horn*, common former material]

län'yard, n. (Naut.) short rope or line attached to something to secure it; cord attached to breech mechanism for firing gun; cord hanging round the neck or looped round the shoulder, to which may be attached a knife, whistle, or the like. [15th c. *lanyer*, earlier *layner*, f. OF *laniere* (-*yard* f. 17th c.)]

Lãodīcē'an, a. & n. (Person) lukewarm esp. in religion or politics. [*Rev.* iii. 15, 16]

lăp[1], n. Hanging part or flap of garment, saddle, etc.; lobe of ear; front part of skirt held up to contain something; waist to knees of one sitting, with dress, as place on which child is nursed or object held (*in Fortune's* ~, *in the* ~ *of luxury*, etc.), whence ~'FUL(2) n.; hollow among hills; ~-*dog*, small pet dog; ~'*stone*, shoemaker's stone held in ~ to beat leather on. [OE *lappa*, *læppa*, OS *lappo*, OHG *lappa*; cf. ON *leppr* rag]

lăp[2], v.t. & i. (-pp-). Coil, fold, wrap, (garment etc. *about*, *round*, advv. or prepp.); enfold, swathe, *in* wraps etc.; (of influences etc.) surround, encircle, (often *round*), enfold caressingly (esp. pass., ~*ped in luxury*); make (valve, roof-*slate*, etc.) overlap; project *over* something (also ~ *over* adv. = *overlap* intr.); (racing) pass (competitor) by one or more laps. [ME, prob. f. prec.]

lăp[3], n. Amount of overlapping, overlapping part (*half-*~, joining of rails, shafts, etc., by halving thickness of each at end); layer or sheet (of cotton etc. being made) wound on roller; single turn of rope, silk, thread, etc., round drum or reel; one circuit of race-track; ~-*joint*, = *half-*~ above; ~-*streak*, clinker-built boat. [f. prec.]

lăp[4], n., & v.t. (-pp-). 1. Rotating disc for polishing gem or metal. 2. v.t. Polish with~. [perh. f. prec.]

lăp[5], v.i. & t. (-pp-), & n. 1. Take up liquid, drink (*up* liquid), by scooping with tongue; consume (liquid) greedily (usu. up or *down*), also fig.; (of water) move, beat upon (shore), with sound of ~ping. 2. n. Liquid food for dogs; single act of ~ping, amount taken up by it; sound of wavelets on beach etc. [ME *lape* f. OE *lapian* = MLG, MDu. *lapen*, OHG *laffan* f. Gmc **lap-*; ME *lap* prob. f. OF *laper* (f. WG)]

lăpar(o)-, comb. form of Gk *lapara* flank, in anat. & surg. terms; *lap'arocele*, lumbar hernia; ~*ĕc'tomy*, excision of part of intestine at side; ~*ŏt'omy*, cutting of abdominal walls.

lapĕl', n. Part of coat-breast folded back. Hence ~lED[2] (-ld') a. [LAP[1], -EL]

lăp'icīde, n. Cutter of stones or inscriptions on stone. [f. L *lapicida* irreg. f. *lapis* -*idis* stone; see -CIDE]

lăp'idary, a. & n. 1. Concerned with stones (esp. ~ *bee*, building in stone walls etc.); engraved on stone, (of style) suitable for inscriptions, monumental. 2. n. Cutter, polisher, or engraver, of gems. [f. L *lapidarius* (*lapis* -*idis* stone, -ARY[1])]

lăp'idāte, v.t. Stone, stone to death. So ~A'TION n. [f. L *lapidare* (prec.), -ATE[3]]

lapĭd'i‖fỹ, v.t. Make into stone. Hence ~FICA'TION n. [f. F *lapidifier* f. med. L *lapidificare* (prec., -FY)]

lăp'is lăz'ūlī, n. A sodium aluminium silicate containing combined sulphur, bright blue pigment from it; its colour. [L *lapis*+med. L *lazuli* gen. of *lazulum*; see AZURE]

Lăpp, n. & a. 1. One of dwarfish race of northern Scandinavia; (also ~'ISH[1] n.) their language; *Lăp'land*, their country, whence **Lăp'land**ER[1] (4) n. 2. adj. (Also ~*ISH[1]* a.) of the ~s or their language. [f. Sw. *Lapp*, perh. term of contempt, cf. MHG *lappe* simpleton]

lăpp'ĕt, n. Flap, fold, loose or overlapping piece of garment, flesh, membrane, etc.; lobe of ear etc.; = lapel; streamer of lady's head-dress; (also ~-*moth*) kind of large moth. Hence ~ED[2] a. [LAP[1]+-ET[1]]

Lappōn'ian, a. & n. = LAPP. [f. med. L *Lappo* -*onis*+-IAN]

lăpse[1], n. Slip of memory, tongue, or pen, slight mistake; weak or careless deviation from right, moral slip; falling away *from* faith or *into* heresy; decline to lower state; termination of right or privilege through disuse; (of water) gentle flow; passage or interval *of* time; ~ *rate* (meteor.), rate of fall of temperature with height. [f. L *lapsus* -*ūs* (*labi laps-* glide)]

lăpse[2], v.i. Fail to maintain position or state for want of effort or vigour; fall *back* or *away* (often *into* inferior or previous state); (of benefice, estate, right, etc.) fall in, pass away, become void, revert *to* someone, by failure of conditions, heirs, etc.; glide, flow, subside, pass *away*; (p.p.) that has lapsed, see -ED[2](2). [f. L *lapsare* (prec.); partly f. the n.]

lăp'sus, n. (pl. -*ūs*). Slip (usu. in ~

ling'uae, pr. -gwē, of the tongue,~ *căl'amī* of the pen). [L]

Lapūt'an, a. & n. (Inhabitant) of Laputa; chimerical, visionary, absurd. [*Laputa* in *Gulliver's Travels* +-AN]

lăp'wing, n. Bird of plover family, peewit. [OE *hlēapewince* (*hlēapan* LEAP[1], WINK, w. ref. to manner of flight) assim. to LAP[2], WING]

lăr, n. 1. (pl. *lăr'es*, pr. -ēz). Ancient-Roman household deity (usu. pl.: *Lares*, *Lares & Penates*, the home). 2. (pl. ~s, pr. -z). White-handed Burmese gibbon. [L]

‖ **lărb'oard** (-berd), n. & a. (naut.). (Older term now replaced, to save confusion with *starboard*, by) PORT[5]. [ME *lad*(*d*)*e*-, *lathe*- (perh. = LADE), in 16th c. alt. after *starboard*]

lăr'cĕn|y̆, n. (Law) felonious taking away of another's personal goods with intent to convert them to one's own use (*grand*, *petty*, ~*y*, formerly, of property above, below, value of 12*d*.); theft. Hence ~ER[1], ~IST(1), nn., ~OUS a., ~OUSLY[2] adv. [f. AF *larcin* f. L *latrocinium* (*latro* robber) + -Y[1]]

lărch, n. Bright-foliaged & deciduous coniferous tree yielding Venice turpentine, tough timber, & bark used in tanning; its wood. [f. G *lärche* f. L *larix-icis*]

lărd[1], n. Internal fat of abdomen of pigs esp. when rendered & clarified for use in cooking & pharmacy. Hence ~Y[2] a. [ME, f. OF, = bacon, f. L *lar*(*i*)*dum* cogn. w. Gk *larinos* fat]

lărd[2], v.t. Insert strips of bacon in (meat etc.) before cooking (~*ing-needle*, -*pin*, instrument for doing this); garnish (talk, writing) *with* metaphors, technical terms, foreign words, etc. [ME, f. OF *larder* (prec.)]

lărdā'ceous (-shus), a. (med.). Lardlike (esp. of degeneration of tissue or of patient suffering from it). [-ACEOUS]

lărd'er, n. Room or closet for meat etc. [ME, f. OF *lardier* f. med. L *lardarium* (LARD[1], -ARY[1])]

lărd'on, **lărdoon'**, n. Strip of bacon or pork used to lard meat. [F (-*on*); LARD[1], -OON]

lărd'y̆-dărd'y̆, a. (sl.). Affected, languidly foppish. [cf. LA-DI-DA]

lares. See LAR.

lărge, a., n., & adv. 1. (Arch.) liberal, generous, kindly, munificent, unprejudiced, (still in ~ *views*, *charity*, *tolerance*, ~-*minded*, whence ~-*mind'* ed NESS n., ~-*hearted*, whence ~-*heart'*ĕd NESS (-hăr-) n., etc.); of wide range, comprehensive, (~ *powers*, *discretion*); (of artistic treatment) free, sweeping, broad; of considerable or relatively great magnitude (less colloq. than *big*, & without emotional implications of *great*; seldom used of persons except as in ~ *of limb*=with~ limbs etc.); (with agent nouns) on a ~ *scale* (~ & *small farmers*); hence **lăr'**GISH[1](2) a., ~*NESS* (-jn-) n., **lăr'**gEN[6] v.i. & t. (poet.).

2. n. (now only with *at*, *in*). *At* ~: at liberty, free; (of narration etc.) at full length, with details; as a body or whole (*popular with the people at* ~); *represent*-ing a whole State etc. & not merely a part of it; without particularizing, without definite aim, (*scatters imputations at* ~; *gentleman at* ~, gentleman attached to the court without special duties, person who has no occupation); *in* ~, on ~ scale (opp. *in little*). 3. adv. BY[1] & ~. [ME, f. OF f. fem. of L *largus* copious]

lărge'ly̆ (-jl-), adv. In adj. senses; also, to a great or preponderating extent (*is* ~ *due to*). [-LY[2]]

lăr'gĕss(e), n. (arch.). Money or gifts freely bestowed esp. by great person on occasion of rejoicing; generous or plentiful bestowal. [ME, f. OF (-*e*), f. L *largus* copious, -ESS[2]]

lărg'ō, adv. & n. (mus.). (Movement) in slow time with broad dignified treatment. [It., = broad]

lă'riat, n. Rope for picketing horses etc.; lasso. [f. Sp. *la reata* f. *reatar* tie again (RE-, L *aptare* fit)]

lărk[1], **lăv'erock** (-vr-; poet.), n. Kinds of small bird with sandy-brown plumage & long hind-claws, esp. the SKY*lark* (*crested*, *horned*, *red*, *shore*, ~, other kinds); *rise with the* ~, get up early; *if the sky fall*, *we shall catch* ~*s* (comfort for alarmists); ~-*heel*, ~*spur*, also Indian cress or garden nasturtium; ~'*spur*, plant of genus Delphinium with spur-shaped calyx. [OE *lāferce*, = MLG, MDu. *lēwer*(*i*)*ke*, OHG *lērahha*, ON *lǣvirki*]

lărk[2], n., & v.t. 1. Frolic, spree, amusing incident (*what a* ~ *!*, how amusing!); hence ~Y[2] a. 2. v.i. Play tricks, frolic. [orig. unkn.]

lărn, v.t. & i. (Joc. & vulg. for) LEARN.

lă'rrikin, n. (Usu. young) street rowdy, hooligan. [c. 1870, Australian; perh. f. name *Larry*]

lă'rrup, v.t. (colloq.). Thrash. [dial.]

lă'rum, n. (Now rare for) ALARUM.

lărv'|a, n. (pl. ~*ae*). Insect from time of leaving egg till transformation into pupa, grub; immature form of other animals that undergo some metamorphosis. Hence ~AL a., ~I- comb. form. [L, = ghost, mask]

laryng'oscope (-ngg-), n. Mirror apparatus for examining larynx. [LARYNX, -SCOPE]

lăr̆yngŏt'omy̆ (-ngg-), n. Cutting into larynx from without, esp. to provide breathing-channel. [foll., -TOMY]

lă'rynx, n. Cavity in throat holding vocal cords. Hence **laryn'**gĕAL a. (also n., hypothetical phonetic element of a laryngeal quality supposed to have existed in Proto-Indo-European), **laryn'**gic, a., **lăr̆yngīt'**IS n., (-j-), **laryn'go**-comb. form, **lăr̆yngŏL'**OGY n., (-ngg-). [f. Gk *larugx-ggos*]

Lăs'car, n. (E.-) Indian sailor. [erron. f.

Hind. LASHKAR army, or f. *lashkari* military]

lasciv′ious, a. Lustful, wanton; inciting to lust. Hence ~LY² adv., ~NESS n. [ME, f. LL *lasciviosus* (L *lascivia* f. *lascivus* sportive, -OSE¹)]

lash¹, v.i. & t. **1.** Make sudden movement of limb, tail, etc.; pour, rush, vehemently, whence ~**ings** [-ING¹(2)] n. pl. (sl.), plenty (*of*); strike violently *at*; hit or (of horse) kick *out*; break *out* into excess, strong language, etc. **2.** Beat with lash, flog; (of waves) beat upon; castigate in words, rebuke, satirize; urge as with lashes (~ one*self into a fury*, work up a rage); hence~′ING¹(1) n. **3.** Fasten (*down, on, together, to* something) with cord, twine, etc., whence ~′ING¹(4) n.; ~*up* a. & n., makeshift. [sense 1 perh. imit.; sense 2 f. foll.; sense 3 prob. separate wd, of unkn. orig.]

lash², n. Stroke with thong, whip, etc.; flexible part of whip (*the* ~, punishment of flogging); = EYE-~, whence ~′LESS a.; goading influence. [f. prec. in sense 1]

lash′er, n. In vbl senses; ‖ esp. (water rushing over) weir, pool below weir. [-ER¹]

lash′kar, n. Body of armed Indian tribesmen. [Hind., = army]

‖ **läs′pring**, n. Young salmon. [perh. alt. of obs. *lax-pink* (LAX², PINK⁵)]

lasque (lahsk), n. Flat, ill-formed, or veiny diamond. [perh. f. Pers. *lashk* piece]

läss, n. Girl (north., poet., etc.); sweetheart. Hence ~′ie [-Y³] n. [ME *lasce*, cf. MSw. *lösk* (*kona*) unmarried (woman)]

läss′itŭde, n. Weariness, languor, disinclination to exert or interest oneself. [f. F, or L *lassitudo* (*lassus* tired, -TUDE)]

läss′ō (or *lasōō′*), n. (pl. ~*s*), & v.t. **1.** Sp.-Amer. noosed rope of untanned hide for catching cattle etc. **2.** v.t. Catch with~. [f. Sp. *lazo* LACE¹]

last¹ (-ah-), n. Shoemaker's wooden model for shaping shoe etc. on (*stick to* one's ~, not meddle with things one does not understand, w. ref. to L prov. *ne sutor supra crepidam*). [OE *læste* last; cf. OHG *leist* last, Goth. *laists* track, OHG -*leisa* track, f. Gmc *lais-*; cf. LAST⁴]

last² (-ah-), n. Commercial measure of weight, capacity, or quantity, varying with place & goods (~ *of wool*, 12 sacks or 4,368 lb.; ~ *of malt*, 10 qrs or 80 bushels). [OE *hlæst*, MLG, MDu. *last*, OHG (*h*)*last*, f. Gmc *hlath-* LADE + n. suff. -*sti-*]

last³ (-ah-), a., n., & adv. **1.** After all others, coming at the end, (*the* ~ *two* etc. = the ~ & ~ but one etc., *the two* etc. ~ being now usu. held incorrect in this sense; ~ *but not least*, ~ in order of mention or occurrence but not of importance); belonging to the end, esp. of life or the world (*the four* ~ *things*, death, judgement, heaven, hell; ~ *day*, Day of Judgement; *on* one's ~ LEGS); next before expressed or implied point of time, latest up to date, most recent, (*in the* ~ *fortnight*, ~ *Christmas*, ~ *Tuesday* or *Tuesday* ~; ~ *evening* or *night* or *week* or *month* or *year* used as adverbs, but not ~ *morning, day*, or *afternoon*; also ellipt, as n. (or ~ *letter, joke, baby*, etc., *as I said in my* ~, *have you heard* —'*s* ~ ?, *Mrs* —'*s* ~); lowest, of least rank or estimation; only remaining (~ *crust, resource*); latest *to be* (*was the* ~ *to be consulted*); least likely, willing, suitable, etc. *to* or *to be* (*should be the* ~ *to do it*; *is the* ~ *thing to try*); conclusive, definitive, (*has said the* ~ *word on the matter*); most up-to-date (*the* ~ *thing in hats*); utmost, extreme, (*is of the* ~ *importance*). **2.** n. ~-mentioned person or thing (*the, this, which*, ~); ~ day or moments, death, (*the* or *his* etc. ~); ~ performance of certain acts (*breathe, look*, one's ~); ~ mention (*shall never hear the* ~ *of it*); *at* ~, (also) *at long* ~, in the end, after much delay; *to, till, the* ~, to the end, esp. till death. **3.** adv. After all others (~ *came & ~ did go*; freq. in comb. as ~-*made*, -*mentioned*); on the ~ occasion before the present (*when did you see him* ~ ?); (in enumerations) in the ~ place, finally, also ~′LY² adv. [OE *latost* superl. of *læt* a., *late* adv.; see LATE¹, -EST; loss of *-t-* as in BEST]

last⁴ (-ah-), v.i. & t., & n. **1.** Go on, remain unexhausted or adequate or alive; suffice (*will* ~ *me eight months; will* ~ *my time*); ~ *out*, continue esp. in vigour or use at least as long as. **2.** n. Staying power, stamina. [OE *læstan*, OS *lēstian*, OHG *leisten*, Goth. *laistjan* f. Gmc **laist-* LAST¹]

last′ing (-ah-), a. & n. **1.** Enduring, permanent (*no* ~ *benefit*); durable; hence ~LY² adv., ~NESS n. **2.** n. Kind of durable cloth. [-ING²]

Lătaki′a (-ēa), n. Kind of Turkish tobacco chiefly used in mixtures. [~ (anc. *Laodicea*), a Syrian port]

lätch, n., & v.t. **1.** Door or gate fastening made of small bar falling into catch & lifted by lever etc. from outside; small spring-lock of outer door catching when door is closed & worked by ~key; ~′*key*, any outer-door key, (fig.) symbol of emancipation; *on the* ~, fastened by ~ only. **2.** v.t. Fasten with~. [(1) prob. f. obs. (exc. dial.) *latch* vb f. OE *læccan* grasp; (2) f. sense 1]

‖ **lätch′ět**, n. (arch.). Thong for fastening shoe. [f. OF *lachet*, var. of *lacet* dim. of *laz, las* LACE¹]

lāte¹, a. (comp. ~*r*, LATTER; superl. ~*st*, LAST³), & n. After the due or usual time (*was* ~ *for dinner*; *it is too* ~ *to go*); with agent nouns, as ~-*comer* = one who comes ~); backward in flowering, ripening, etc.; far on in day or night (~ *dinner*, in evening; ~ *hours*, after usual time for rising or going to bed), or in time (*on Wednesday at* ~*st*, then if not before); far on in a period, development, etc. (~ *stained glass*, ~ LATIN); no longer alive, no longer having specified status etc., that was recently so-&-so, (*the ~ prime minister*, dead or resigned; *my ~ husband, residence*); of recent date (*the ~ floods, war; of ~ years*, in the last few; also as n. in *of~*, recently); ‖ *~ fee*, on letter posted after ordinary collection time. Hence lāt'ᴇɴ⁶ v.t. & i., ~'ɴᴇss (-tn-) n., lāt'ɪsʜ¹ (2) a. & adv. [OE *læt*, OS *lat*, OHG *laz*, ON *latr*, Goth. *lats* f. Gmc *ᵃlataz* slow, cogn. w. L *lassus*]

lāte², adv. (*~r, ~st*, ʟᴀsᴛ³). After proper time (*better ~ than never*), far on in time (*this happened ~r on*; *sooner or ~r, early or ~, soon or ~*, some time or other); at or till late hour (*we sat ~*); (poet.) recently, lately, (*I sent thee ~ a rosy wreath*); formerly but not now (*his own room, ~ the chaplain's*); at late stage of development etc. (*traces remained as ~ as the Stuart times*); *~ in the day*, (colloq.) at a late stage, esp. unreasonably *~ in* the proceedings etc. [OE *late*, adv. form of prec.]

lateen', a. *~ sail*, triangular on long yard at angle of 45° to mast; (of ship etc.) so rigged. [f. F (*voile*) *latine* Latin (sail), named as common in Mediterranean]

lāte'ly (-tl-), adv. Not long ago, recently, in recent times. [OE *lætlīce* (ʟᴀᴛᴇ¹, -ʟɪᴋᴇ)]

lāt'ent, a. Hidden, concealed; existing but not developed or manifest; dormant; *~ ʜᴇᴀᴛ*. Hence lāt'ᴇɴᴄʏ n., ~ʟʏ² adv. [f. L *latēre* be hidden, -ᴇɴᴛ]

-later, suf. See -ʟᴀᴛʀʏ.

lāt'eral, a. & n. 1. Of, at, towards, from, the side, side-, (*~ branch* of family, descended from brother or sister of person in direct line). 2. n. Side part, member, or object, esp. *~ shoot* or branch. Hence ~ʟʏ² adv. [f. L *lateralis* (*latus -eris* side, -ᴀʟ)]

Lāt'eran, n. & a. *The ~, St John ~*, cathedral church of St John *~* (*Sancti Joannis in~*o) in Rome; *~ Council*, one of five general councils of Western Church there held. [f. L *~a, ~um*, named f. ancient-Roman family of Plautii ~i]

lāt'erīte, n. Red friable ferruginous surface clay much used for roadmaking in tropics. [f. L *later* brick + -ɪᴛᴇ¹(2)]

lāt'ex, n. (bot.). Milky fluid of (esp. rubber) plant. [L, = liquid]

lath (-ah-), n. (pl. pr. -dhz), & v.t. 1. Piece of sawn or riven timber ³⁄₁₆ in. to ⅜ in. thick & 1 in. to 1¼ in. wide esp. for use as support for slates or plaster or as material for trellis or Venetian blind (*as thin as a ~*, of persons, when la'thy² (-ah-) a.; *~ & plaster*, material for interior wall--faces, ceilings, partitions, etc.). 2. v.t. Provide (wall, ceiling) with *~s*, whence la'thing¹(3) (-ah-) n. [ME *laththe*, repr. OE *ᵃlæththᵃ*, = OS, OHG *latta*; ult. rel. obsc.]

‖ lāthe¹ (-dh), n. One of the administrative districts of Kent. [OE *lǣth* estate]

lāthe² (-dh), n. (Also *turning~*) machine for turning wood, metal, ivory, etc., by rotating article against tools used; (also *potter's ~*) machine with horizontal revolving disc for throwing & turning pottery; *~-bearer, -carrier, -dog*, appliance connecting object with *~* centres or holders; *~-bed*, lower framework of *~* with slot from end to end for adjustment. [prob. rel. to Da. *-lad* structure, frame, as in *drejelad* turning-lathe, f. ON *hlath*, rel. to *hlatha* ʟᴀᴅᴇ]

lāth'er (-dh-), n., & v.t. & i. 1. Froth of soap & water; frothy sweat esp. of horse; (fig.) state of agitation; hence *~ʏ²* a. 2. vb. Cover (esp. chin etc. for shaving) with *~*; (of horse) become covered with *~*; (of soap) form *~*; beat, thrash, whence *~ɪɴɢ¹*(1) n. [OE *lēathor* = ON *lauthr* washing-soda, f. Gmc *ᵃlauthram* cogn. w. L *lavare* wash]

lathi (laht'ī), n. Long heavy iron-bound stick used as weapon by Indian natives & police. [Hind.]

lātifūn'dia, n. pl. Large estates, esp. as characterizing a country's social system. [L (sing. *-um*), f. *latus* broad, *fundus* farm]

Lat'in, a. & n. 1. Of Latium or ancient *~s* or Romans; of, like, in, the language of the ancient Romans, whence *~ɪsᴍ*(4) n.; of the Roman Catholic Church; *~* (see ᴡᴇsᴛᴇʀɴ) *Church*; (of peoples) inheriting Roman customs etc., speaking one of the languages descended from *~*, Romance, (*the ~ peoples*, France, Spain, Portugal, Italy, etc.); *~ Quarter* (F *Quartier Latin*), educational centre of Paris, where *~* was spoken in the Middle Ages, noted for its unconventional mode of life. Hence *~ᴀᴛᴇ²* a., having a *~* character. 2. n. The *~* language (*old ~*, before about 75 ʙ.ᴄ., preclassical; *classical ~*, that of great writers of late republican & early imperial Rome, about 75 ʙ.ᴄ. to ᴀ.ᴅ. 175; *late ~*, about ᴀ.ᴅ. 175 to 600; *medieval ~*, about ᴀ.ᴅ. 600 to 1500; *modern ~*, since ᴀ.ᴅ. 1500; *low ~*, = medieval, or late & medieval; sɪʟᴠᴇʀ¹ *~*; *thieves' ~*, secret language of thieves etc.; ᴅᴏɢ *~*), whence *~ʟᴇss* a., *~ɪsᴛ*(3) n.; inhabitant of Latium, (Rom. ant.) Italian with special franchise. [ME, f. OF, or L *Latinus* (*Latium* Roman district, -ɪɴᴇ¹)]

Latin'ē, adv. In Latin (giving Latin equivalent of word etc.). [L]

Latin'itў, n. Way person writes Latin, quality of Latin style or grammar. [f. L *Latinitas* (prec., -ᴛʏ)]

lāt'inīz|e, -is|e (-īz), v.t. & i. Give Latin form to (word), put into Latin; make conformable to ideas, customs, etc., of the ancient Romans, Latin peoples, or Latin Church; use Latin forms, idioms, etc. Hence *~ᴀ'ᴛɪᴏɴ*, *~ᴇʀ¹* a., nn. [f. LL *latinizare* (ʟᴀᴛɪɴ, -ɪᴢᴇ)]

lāt'itūd|e, n. 1. (Joc.) breadth (*hat with great ~e of brim*); (rare) scope, full extent, (*understood, taken, in its proper ~e*). 2. Freedom from narrowness, liberality of interpretation, tolerated variety of action or opinion, whence (esp. of religious matters) ~inar'ian a. & n., ~inar'ianism(3) n. 3. (geog.). Angular distance on a meridian (degree, minute, etc., of ~e); place's angular distance on its meridian N. or S. of equator (in ~e 40° N. etc.); (usu. pl.) regions, climes, esp. w. ref. to temperature (high ~es, far N. or S.; low ~es, near equator). 4. (astron.). Angular distance of heavenly body from ecliptic. So ~inAL (-ŭd⁴) a. (geog.). [ME, f. L latitudo -inis (latus broad, -TUDE)]

latrine' (-ēn), n. Place for evacuation of bowels or bladder, esp. in camp, barracks, hospital, etc. [F, f. L latrina for lavatrina (lavare wash, -INE)⁴]

-latry, suf. f. Gk latreia worship, in wds f. an existing Gk original (idolatry), & mod. formations on same model (angelolatry, Mariolatry). In (humorous) hybrid formations -o- is added to the initial component as lordolatry, babyolatry. Corresponding personal nn. (-worshipper) are formed in -(o)later f. Gk -latrēs.

lätt'en, n. Alloy of copper, zinc, lead, & tin, formerly used for monumental brasses; sheet tin; metal in thin plates. [ME latoun f. OF laton, leiton]

lätt'er, a. (Arch.) later, second, (~ grass, aftermath); belonging to end of period, world, etc. (in these ~ days, at this late period of the world's history; ~ end, death); second-mentioned (opp. former; also the ~ ellipt. = second-mentioned thing or person); ~-day, modern (~-day saints, Mormons). [OE lætra comp. of læt LATE¹, later being a new formation]

lätt'erly, adv. Towards the end of life or some period; nowadays, of late. [f. prec.]

lätt'ice, n. Structure of cross laths with interstices serving as screen, door, etc.; (also ~-work) laths so arranged; ~ bridge, made with ~ girders; ~ frame or girder, girder made of two flanges connected by iron ~-work; ~ window, one having ~, also one with small panes set in diagonal lead-work. Hence lätt'icED² (-st) a., lätt'icING¹(6) n. [ME, f. OF lattis f. latte (f. WG *latta LATH), + -is -ICE]

Lät'vian, a. & n. (Inhabitant) of the Socialist Soviet Republic of Latvia, the country of the Letts, on the Gulf of Riga in the Baltic. [f. Latvi see LETTISH + -AN]

laud, n., & v.t. 1. Praise (rare exc. in hymns); (pl.) first of day-hours of church; hymn of praise. 2. v.t. Praise, celebrate; so ~A'TION, ~ät'OR, nn., ~'ATIVE, ~'atORY, aa. [ME; n. f. OF laude, vb f. L laudare, f. L laudem nom. laus praise]

laud'|able, a. Commendable, praiseworthy; (med., of secretions) healthy, sound. Hence or cogn. ~abil'ITY n., ~ablY² adv. [f. L laudabilis (prec., -ABLE)]

laudanum (lŏd'num), n. Tincture of opium. [name given by Paracelsus to a costly panacea or elixir, later transferred to preparations containing opium; perh. var. of L f. Gk lādanon, lē-, a gum-resin, f. lēdon mastic]

laudat'or tem'poris ǎc'tī (sē pū'erō), phr. One who prefers the good old days (when he was a boy). [L, = praiser of time past]

laugh (-ahf, -ǎf), v.i. & t., & n. 1. Make the sounds & movements of face & sides by which lively amusement, sense of the ludicrous, exultation, & scorn, are instinctively expressed, have these emotions, (~ in one's sleeve, be secretly amused; ~ing HYENA, JACKASS; ~ on wrong side of mouth, have revulsion from joy or amusement to tears or vexation; he ~s best who ~s last, warning against premature exultation); (of water, landscape, corn, etc.) be lively with play of movement or light; utter ~ingly; hold up to scorn; ~ at, make fun of, ridicule, also look pleasantly or smile at; get (person) out of habit, belief, etc., by ridicule (~ person, opinion, etc., out of court, deprive of a hearing by ridicule); ~ away, dismiss (subject) with a ~, while away (time) with jests; ~ down, silence with laughter; ~ off (embarrassment etc.), get rid of with a jest; ~ over, discuss with laughter; hence ~'ER¹ n., ~'ING² a., ~'ingLY² adv., (-ahf-, -ǎf-). 2. n. Sound made in, act of, ~ing (join in the ~, esp. of person taking banter good-humouredly; have, get, the ~ of, turn the tables on assailant, also have the ~ on one's side); person's manner of ~ing. [OE hliehhan, OS *hlahhian, OHG hlahhan, ON hlǽja, Goth. hlahjan f. Gmc *hlah-]

laugh'ab|le (-ahf-, -ǎf-), a. Exciting laughter, amusing. Hence ~LY² adv. [prec. n. or v. + -ABLE]

laugh'ing (-ahf-, -ǎf-), n. In vbl senses; esp.: no ~ matter, serious thing, not a fit subject for ~; ~-gas, nitrous oxide, with intoxicating effect when inhaled, used as anaesthetic; ~-stock, person or thing generally ridiculed. [-ING¹]

laugh'ter (-ahf-, -ǎf-), n. Laughing; HOMERIC ~. [OE hleahtor, OHG hlahtar, ON hlátr f. Gmc *hlahtraz]

launce (lahns, lǎns), n. Sand-eel. [perh. f. LANCE¹, cf. garfish]

launch¹ (law-, lah-), v.t. & i., & n. 1. Hurl, discharge, send forth, (missile, blow, censure, threat, decree); burst (usu. out) into expense, strong language, etc. (also ~ out, abs., spend money freely, expatiate in words); set (vessel) afloat; send off, start, (person, enterprise) on a course; go forth, out, on an enterprise; ~ing pad, site, etc., pad etc. from which rockets are ~ed. 2. n. Process of ~ing ship. [ME, f. AF launcher = OF lancier LANCE²]

launch² (law-, lah-), n. Man-of-war's largest boat, used for shore-going, visiting other ships, etc. (admiral's ~, canopied or cabined ~ for use of admiral); engined pleasure-boat on rivers etc. [f. Sp. *lancha* pinnace perh. f. Malay *lancharan* (*lanchar* swift)]

laun'der (lawn-, lahn-), v.t. & i. (Chiefly as p.p.) wash & get up (linen); (of fabric, with adv.) admit of being ~ed. Hence ~ETTE' (-ĕt) n., establishment with automatic washing machines available for public use. [f. ME *launder* n., washer of linen, contr. of *lavander* f. OF *-ier* f. Rom. *lavandarius (*lavanda* neut. pl. gerundive of L *lavare* wash, -ARY[1])]

laun'dress (lawn-, lahn-), n. Woman who washes & gets up linen; ‖ caretaker of chambers in Inns of Court. [f. *launder* n. (prec.) + -ESS[1]]

laun'dry (lawn-, lahn-), n. Establishment for washing linen; batch of clothes sent to or from ~. [contr. f. *lavendry* (f. OF *lavanderie*) after *launder*; see -RY]

laur'éate (or lŏ-), a. & n. Wreathed with, (of wreath) consisting of, laurel; worthy of laurels as poet (*poet* ~, or ~ as n., poet receiving stipend as writer of Court odes, whence ~SHIP (-t-sh-) n.), or for eloquence etc. [f. L *laureatus* (*laurea* laurel-wreath f. *laurus* laurel, -ATE[2])]

lau'rel (lŏ-), n., & v.t. (-ll-). 1. Kinds of garden shrub (*Portugal* ~, with large glossy leaves); foliage of bay-tree as emblem of victory or distinction in poetry (collect. sing. or pl.; *reap, win,* ~*s*; *rest on* one's ~*s*, cease to strive for further glory; *look to* one's ~*s*, beware of losing pre-eminence); ~*-bottle*, filled with ~*-leaves* for killing insects. 2. v.t. Wreathe with ~. [ME *lorer* f. OF *lorier* f. *lor* f. L *laurus*; *-l* by dissim.]

laurustin'us, -res-, (lŏ-), n. Evergreen flowering shrub. [mod. L f. L *laurus* laurel + *tinus* a plant]

la'va (lah-), n. Matter flowing from volcano, solid substance it cools into; (w. pl.) kind, bed, of ~. [It. (*lavare* It. & L wash)]

lavāb'ō, n. (pl. ~*s*). Ritual washing of celebrant's hands at offertory, towel or basin used for this; monastery washing-trough; wash-basin, (pl.) lavatory, (after F). [L, = I will wash, first wd of *Ps.* xxvi. 6]

lavā'tion, n. Washing. [f. L *lavatio* (*lavare* wash, -ATION)]

lăv'atorў, n. Vessel for washing (arch.); room etc. for washing hands & face; (euphem.) water-closet(s) and urinal. [f. LL *lavatorium* f. *lavare* wash, -ORY(2)]

lāve, v.t. (poet.). Wash, bathe; (of stream etc.) wash against, flow along. [ME *lave* f. OF *laver* f. L *lavare* wash; coalescing w. OE *lafian* wash by affusion, rel. to MDu. *laven*, OHG *labōn* refresh]

lāve'ment (-vm-), n. (med.). Injection, enema. [F (prec., -MENT)]

lăv'ĕnder, n., & v.t. 1. Small lilac-flowered narrow-leaved shrub cultivated for perfume; its flowers & stalks laid among linen etc. (*lay up in* ~, often fig., preserve piously for future use); pale blue colour with trace of red; ~*-water*, perfume of distilled ~, alcohol, & ambergris. 2. v.t. Put ~ among (linen). [ME, f. AF *lavendre*, ult. dissimilated f. med. L *lavandula* etc.; further history obsc.]

lāv'er[1], n. Kinds of marine algae, esp. the edible species. [L]

lāv'er[2], n. (Bibl.) large brazen vessel for Jewish priests' ablutions; (arch.) washing or fountain basin, font. [ME *lavo(u)r* f. OF *laveor, -eoir* LAVATORY]

laverock. See LARK[1].

lăv'ish, a., & v.t. 1. Giving or producing without stint, profuse, prodigal, (of money etc., *in* giving); very or over abundant; hence ~LY adv., ~NESS n. 2. v.t. Bestow or spend (money, effort, blood, admiration, etc.) profusely; hence ~MENT n. [15th c. *lavas,* f. obs. n. *lavas* (later *-ish*) profusion, f. OF *lavasse* (*-ache*) deluge of rain; see -ISH[2]]

law[1], n. 1. Body of enacted or customary rules recognized by a community as binding, this personified, (the ~ *forbids, allows;* often *the* ~ *of the land; the* ~ *of the Medes & Persians,* unalterable ~, see *Dan.* vi. 12; *lay down the* ~, talk authoritatively, hector). 2. One of these rules. 3. Their controlling influence, ~*-abiding* state of society, (often ~ *& order; necessity knows no* ~, over-rides its sanctity; *be a* ~ *unto* oneself, take one's own line, disregard convention); *the* ~*s* as a system (COURT *of* ~; so SON-*in*-~ etc.) or science (*learned in the* ~; *read* ~, study the ~s), jurisprudence. 4. Binding injunctions (*give the* ~ *to,* impose one's will upon; *his word is* ~). 5. (With defining word) one of the branches of the study of ~, *the* ~*s* concerning specified department, (*commercial* ~; *the* ~ *of evidence;* CANON, CIVIL, COMMON[1], MARTIAL, ~; *international* ~, ~ *of nations,* regulating relations between States). 6. The statute & common ~ (opp. EQUITY). 7. (In pred. use, of decisions, opinions, etc.; also *good, bad,* etc., ~) borne out, or not, by the relevant ~*s* (*it may be common sense, but it is not* ~). 8. The legal profession (usu. *the* ~; *bred to the* ~); legal knowledge. 9. Judicial remedy, ~ courts as providing it, litigation, (*go to* ~; *have, take, the* ~ *of* person; *take the* ~ *into* one's *own* hands, redress one's wrong by force); *the Law, Courts,* ‖ (esp.) the ROYAL *Courts of Justice.* 10. (Also ~ *of Moses*) precepts of Pentateuch, Mosaic dispensation. 11. Rule of action or procedure, esp. in an art, department of life, or game. 12. (Also ~ *of nature* or *natural* ~) correct statement of invariable sequence between specified conditions & specified phenomenon (~*s of motion,* three propositions formulated by Newton; *Gresham's* ~, that bad money drives out good; *Kepler's* ~*s*, three propositions on planetary motions; *Grimm's, Verner's,* ~, on consonant changes in Germanic languages; *Parkinson's* ~, that work expands so as to fill the time available for its completion, and that subordinates multiply at a fixed rate regardless of the amount of work produced). **13.** ~s of nature, regularity in nature (*where they saw chance, we see* ~); *Law of Nature* (see also above) or *Reason*, principles of conduct recognized as pleasing to God or as intrinsically reasonable. **14.** (Sport) allowance, start, given to hunted animal or competitor in race, (whence gen.) time of grace, respite. **15.** ~-*abiding*(*ness*), obedient, obedience, to ~; ~ *calf*, unstained used for binding ~-books; ~ COURT[1]; ~ *French*, the Anglo-Norman terms used in ~-books & ~; ~*giver*, one who makes (esp. code of) ~s; ∥ ~-*hand*, handwriting used in legal documents; ~ *Latin*, barbarous Latin of early English statutes; ∥ *Law Lord*, Lord of Appeal in Ordinary, member of House of Lords qualified to perform its legal work; ~'*maker*, legislator; ~ *merchant*, mercantile ~, ~s regulating trade & commerce, differing in some respects from Common Law; ~ *officer*, legal functionary, ∥ esp. Attorney-General or Solicitor-General or Lord Advocate; ~-*stationer*, selling stationery needed by lawyers ∥ & taking in documents to be engrossed; ~'*suit*, prosecution of claim in ~-court; ~-*term*, word or expression used in ~, also period appointed for sitting of ~ courts; ~-*writer*, writer on ~, ∥ also engrosser of legal documents. [late OE *lagu* f. ON *lagu pl. of *lag* something 'laid down' or fixed, cogn. w. LAY[3]]

∥ **law²**, laws, int. (vulg.) expressing astonishment. [var. of LO, or earlier *la*, or *lor'* for *Lord*]

law'ful, a. Permitted, appointed, qualified, or recognized, by law, not illegal or (of child) illegitimate. Hence ~LY[2] adv., ~NESS n. [-FUL]

lawk(s), int. (vulg.) expressing astonishment; *lawk-a-mussy* (vulg.), = Lord have mercy. [for ALACK or *Lord*]

law'less, a. (Of country etc.) where law is non-existent or inoperative; regardless of, disobedient to, uncontrolled by, law, unbridled, licentious. Hence ~NESS n. [-LESS]

lawn¹, n. Kind of fine linen used esp. for bishop's sleeves; ~ *sieve*, fine sieve of ~ or silk. Hence ~'Y² a. [prob. f. *Laon* in France]

lawn², n. ∥ Glade (arch.); (extent of) grass-covered land; close-mown turf-covered piece of pleasure-ground or garden, whence ~'Y² a.; ~-*mower*, machine with revolving spiral knives for mowing ~s; ~-*sprinkler*, machine for watering ~s etc.; ~ *tennis*, modification of tennis played by two persons (*single*) or four (*double*) on a level court ('grass' or 'hard') without walls. [16th c., f. ME *laund(e)* f. OF *launde* (mod. *lande*) f. Gaulish *landā LAND¹]

law'yer (or *loi'er*), n. Member of legal profession, esp. attorney, solicitor; person versed in law (*good, no*, etc., ~); *Penang* ~, walking-stick of Penang palm (perh. f. native tree name); SEA ~. [-YER]

lăx¹, a. Loose, relaxed, not compact, porous, (rare) negligent, careless, not strict, vague. Hence or cogn. ~'ITY n., ~'LY² adv. [ME, f. L *laxus* cogn. w. *languĕre* LANGUISH]

lăx², n. Swedish or Norwegian salmon. [OE *leax*, OS, OHG *lahs*, ON (Sw., Da.) *lax* f. Gmc *lahs-]

lăx'ative, a. & n. (Medicine) tending to loosen the bowels. [F (-*if*, -*ive*), f. LL *laxativus* (*laxare*, see LAX¹, -ATIVE)]

lay¹, n. Short lyric or narrative poem meant to be sung; (poet.) song, poem, song of birds. [ME, f. OF *lai*, of unkn. orig.]

lay², a. Non-clerical, not in orders; of, done by,~man or laity; non-professional, not expert, (esp. w. ref. to law or medicine); ~ *brother, sister*, person who has taken habit & vows of religious order but is employed in manual labour & excused other duties; ~ *clerk*, singing man in cathedral or collegiate church, parish clerk; ~ *communion*, membership of church as ~man, also communicating of laity in eucharist; ~ *deacon*, man in deacon's order but also following secular employment; ∥ ~ *lord*, peer who is not LAW¹ lord; ~'*man*, one of the laity, non-expert in regard to some profession, art, or science (esp. law or medicine); ~ *reader*, ~man licensed to conduct religious services. [ME, f. OF *lai* f. LL f. Gk *laïkos* LAIC]

lay³, v.t. & i. (*laid*), & n. **1.** Prostrate (~ *low*, bring down, humble); (of wind or rain) beat down (crops); cause (sea, wind, dust, misgivings, ghost) to subside. **2.** Deposit; place in recumbent posture (~ *to sleep* or *rest*, lit., & fig. = bury; ~ *one's bones*, be buried in specified place); (of hen) produce (egg, or abs.); put down (amount, one's head or life, etc.) as wager, stake, (abs.) announce readiness to bet (*that* ―). **3.** Place, set, apply, (~ *to* HEART; ~ *heads together*, confer; *laid a spark to the train*; ~ *hounds on scent*; ~ *hold on* or *of*, seize, grasp, & fig. make capital *of* opponent's weak point etc.; ~ *one's hopes on*; ~ *great store upon*, value highly; ~ *snare, trap, ambush*; ~ WAIT; ~ *siege to*, besiege, importune); locate (scene; *scene of tale is laid in London*); put (limb etc.) in certain position (*horse laid his ears back*; ~ *hands on*, seize, appropriate, also do violence to, esp. *oneself* = commit suicide, also find, as *cannot* ~ *my hands upon it*, also confirm or ordain by imposition of hands); aim (big gun) for direction; (with compl.) put into specified state (~ *land fallow, under water*; ~ person *under obligation*, oblige him, *under necessity*, compel him, *under contribution*, make him contribute; ~

bare, denude, reveal; ~ *waste*, ravage; ~ *open*, reveal, explain, also break skin of; ~ *fast, by the heels*, confine or imprison; ~ ABOARD). 4. Present, put forward, (esp. *claim to* something; ~ *an information*, bring indictment in legal form); place (facts, question) for consideration *before* person; (Parl.) *Foreign Secretary* etc. *will* ~ *papers* (i.e. on the table, to give information to the House of Commons); (of suitor) fix (damages) *at* certain sum; (arch.) impute (fault) *to* person or (mod.) to his *charge, at* or *to* his *door*; represent (evil) as consequent on some cause. 5. Impose (penalty, command, obligation, burden, tax), cast (blame), (*up*)*on* (~ *stress, weight, emphasis, on*, emphasize, treat as important); bring (stick etc.) down *on* (also ~ *blows* or *it on* adv.; & abs. ~ *into*, sl., belabour, ~ *about* one, hit out on all sides). 6. Dispose, arrange, esp. horizontally (foundation, floor, bricks, submarine cable; ~ *table, cloth*, or *breakfast* etc., prepare table for meal; ~ *the fire*, put fuel ready for lighting); make (strand, rope) by twisting yarn or strands; fix outlines of, devise (plan, plot; ~ one's ACCOUNT²) put (colour etc.) on a surface in layers; cover, coat, strew, (surface) *with* carpet, metal, straw, etc.; *laid paper* (having ribbed surface owing to wires used in making). 7. v.i. (vulg., also naut.). = LIE³; ~ *on your oars*, stop rowing but keep oars out; ~*about* n., habitual loafer or tramp. 8. ~ *aside* or *by*, put away, cease to use or practise or think of, abandon, save (money etc.) for future needs; ~ *down*, put on the ground etc. (~ *down* one's *arms*, surrender), relinquish (office, hopes), pay or wager (money), sacrifice (one's life), (begin to) construct (ship, railway), formulate (rule, principle, course; ~ *down the* LAW¹), set down (chart etc.) on paper, convert (land) into pasture (*in, to, under, with*, grass, clover, etc.), store (wine) in cellar; ~ *in*, provide oneself with stock of, (also, colloq.) shower blows; ~ *off*, discharge (temporarily) for lack of work, (colloq.) desist; ~ *on*, impose (tax, command, penalty), deal blows, inflict (blows), ply (lash etc.), apply coat of (paint etc.; ~ *it on thick* or *with a trowel*, use obvious flattery), provide pipes etc. supplying (gas, water, electricity), provide (entertainment, means of transport, etc.); ~ *out*, spread, expose to view etc., prepare (body) for burial, (sl.) kill, (colloq.) put (person) out of action temporarily at football etc., expend (money), (refl.) take pains *to* do, dispose (grounds, garden) according to a plan; ~ *up*, store, put by, put (ship) out of commission, save (money, or abs.), (pass.) be confined to bed or house. 9. n. Line of business, job, pursuit, (sl.); direction or amount of twist in rope-strands; way, position, or direction, in which something (esp. country) lies, lie;

~*-by*, portion of road widened to permit a vehicle to stop there without interfering with traffic; ~*'out*, disposing or arrangement of ground etc., (of plans etc.) drawing showing arrangement, make-up of book, newspaper, advertisement, etc.; ~ *shaft*, secondary shaft of a machine, not forming part of main system of power-transmission. [OE *lecgan*, OS *leggian*, OHG *legen*, *lecken*, ON *leggja*, Goth. *lagjan* f. Gmc **leg-*, **lag-* LIE³]

lay⁴. See LIE³.

lay'er, n., & v.t. & i. In vbl senses; also: stratum, thickness of matter (esp. one of several) spread over surface; (gardening) shoot fastened into earth to strike root while attached to parent plant (v.t., propagate thus); (pl.) patches of laid corn (v.i., of corn, be laid flat by weakness of growth); oyster-bed; *good, bad*, etc., ~ (of fowls); ~*s & backers*, persons betting against, on, individual horse etc.; ~*-stool*, root from which ~s are produced. Hence ~ED² (*-erd*) a. [LAY³, -ER¹]

layétte', n. Clothes, toilet articles, & bedding, needed for newborn child. [F]

lay fig'ure (*-ger*), n. Jointed wooden figure of human body used by artists for arranging drapery on etc.; unimportant person, nonentity; unreal character in novel etc. [*lay* f. obs. *layman* lay figure f. Du. *leeman* (*led* joint)]

lay'lock, n. (Dial. for) LILAC.

lay'-off (*-awf*) n. Period during which a workman is temporarily discharged; slack season. [LAY³]

|| **lay'stall** (*-awl*), n. Refuse heap. [LAY³, STALL]

lǎz'ar, n. (arch.). Poor & diseased person, esp. leper; ~*-house*, = foll. [ME, f. med. L *lazarus* f. proper name (*Luke* xvi. 20)]

lǎzarét', *-étt'ō* (pl. *-os*), n. Hospital (chiefly in foreign countries) for diseased poor, esp. lepers; building or ship for performing quarantine in; after part of ship's hold used for stores. [F (*-et*), f. It. *lazzaretto* (*lazzaro* LAZAR)]

Lǎz'arus, n. Beggar, poor man, (esp. in contrasts, ~ *& Dives* etc.). [see LAZAR]

lāze, v.i. & t., & n. (colloq.). 1. Be lazy; pass (time) *away* in laziness. 2. n. Lazy time. [back formation f. LAZY]

lǎz'ūlī, n. = LAPIS LAZULI.

lā'zy, a., & v.i. & t. 1. Averse to labour, indolent, slothful; appropriate to or inducing indolence; ~*-bed*, bed for potato-growing about 6 ft wide with trench on each side; ~*-bones*, ~ person; ~ *pinion*, serving as transmitter of motion between other pinions or wheels; ~*-tongs*, arrangement of zigzag levers for picking up distant objects; hence lāz'ILY² adv., lāz'INESS n. 2. vb. = LAZE. [16th c. *laysie, lasie, laesy*, of LG orig.; cf. LG *lasich, läsig*, lazy]

lǎzzarōn'e, n. (pl. *-ni*, pr. *-nē*). Neapolitan street-lounger living by odd jobs & begging. [It. (LAZAR, -OON)] 'ld, abbr. of *would* (now rare, cf. 'D).

-le, -el, suf. 1. f. ME *-el*, *-le*, f. OE *-el*, *-ela*, *-(e)le* in nn. (Gmc *-ila-*), *-ol*, *-ul*, *-el*, in adjj.; after *ch*, soft *g*, *n*, *r*, *sh*, *th*, *v*, *-el* is retained, & after *m* the suf. becomes *-ble*. Nn. formed on n. stems have dim. sense (*bramble*), or that of tool, appliance, (*thimble, handle*); nn. formed on vb stems express agent (*beadle*), instrument (*bridle, girdle*), or less definite relations (*bundle*); adjj. formed on vb stems have the sense *apt or liable to the vbl action* (*brittle, nimble*). 2. Occas. repr. ME *-el*, *-elle*, in nn. f. OF *-el* (mod. F usu. *-eau*) f. L *-ellus*, *-ellum* (*bowel, tunnel, castle, mantle*), OF *-ele* (mod. *-elle*) f. L *-ella* (*chapel, novel*); also f. other sources, as L *-ale* (*cattle*); f. F *-aille* f. L *-alia* see *-AL* (*battle*), or F *-eille* f. L *-icula* (*bottle*); f. L *-ulus, -ula, -ulum*, (*angle*); *-el* in some mod. scientific wds on L anal. (*carpel*). 3. Verbal, f. ME *-(e)len* f. OE *-lian* f. Gmc *-ilōjan*, w. frequent. or dim. sense (*nestle, twinkle, wrestle, crumple, dazzle*).

lea¹, n. (poet.). Tract of open ground, esp. grass land. [OE *lēa(h)*, cogn. w. OHG *lōh* grove, f. Gmc *lauh-*, cogn. w. L *lucus*]

lea², n. Measure of yarn (300, 200, 120, & 80 yds in different districts etc.). [ME *lee*, perh. rel. to F *lier* f. L *ligare* to bind]

leach, v.t. Make (liquid) percolate through some material; subject (bark, ore) to action of percolating fluid; purge (soluble matter) *away* etc. by such means. [prob. repr. OE *leccan* to water]

lead¹ (lĕd), n., & v.t. & i. 1. Heavy easily fusible soft malleable base metal of dull pale bluish-grey colour (*red ~*, red oxide of *~* used as pigment, minium; *while ~*, mixture of *~* carbonate & hydrated *~* oxide used as pigment, ceruse; = BLACK¹-*-~*, whence = is used, w. pl., for the small stick of graphite in pencil or pencil-case; *ounce of ~*, bullet). 2. Lump of *~* used in sounding water (*cast, heave, the ~*; *arm the ~*, fill hollow in it with tallow, to learn nature of bottom; ‖ *swing the ~*, sl., malinger or scrimshank). 3. ‖ pl. Strips of *~* used to cover roof, piece of (esp. horizontal) *~*-covered roof; *~* frames or cames holding glass of lattice or painted window. 4. (print.). Metal strip to give space between lines. 5. *~ comb*, made of *~* & used to darken hair; *~ pencil*, of graphite usu. enclosed in cedar; *~*-*poisoning*, acute or chronic poisoning by taking of *~* into system; *~'s man*, sailor who heaves the *~*; *~ wool*, *~* in a fibrous state, used for jointing water-pipes; *~*-*work*, plumber's or glazier's work; *~*-*works*, place where *~*-ore is smelted; *~'wort*, plumbago; hence *~'LESS a.* 6. vb. Cover, weight, frame, (panes) with *~*, (print.) separate lines of (printed matter) with *~s*: (of gun-barrel) become foul with coating of *~*. [OE *lēad*, MLG *lôd*, MHG *lôt*]

lead² (lĕd), v.t. & i. (*lĕd*). 1. Force to go with one (*~ captive*, take away as prison-

er). 2. Conduct, guide, esp. by going in front (of person, also of motive, circumstance, etc.; *curiosity, chance, led him to Rome*; *~* one a DANCE²; *~* one *a life*, worry him constantly; *~ the way*, go first, take the lead in course lit. or fig.). 3. (Of commander) direct movements of. 4. Conduct (person) by the hand or contact, (animal) by halter etc., (*led horse*, spare horse led by groom etc.; *led captain*, hanger-on, toady, parasite; *~* woman *to altar*, marry); (Sc.) cart (corn etc.); guide by persuasion (*is easier led than driven*; *~ astray*, esp. tempt to sin etc.; *~ by the nose*, induce to do unconsciously all one wishes). 5. Guide actions or opinions of, bring by argument etc. *to* conclusion, induce *to* do (*~* one *to suppose* etc., deceive him into thinking); ply (witness) with leading questions. 6. (Of road etc.) conduct (person, or usu. abs.) *to* place (*all roads ~ to Rome*; also fig. = have as result, *this led to confusion*). 7. Make (rope, water, etc.) go through pulley, channel, etc. 8. Pass, go through, spend, (life etc., esp. w. epithet as *~ a miserable existence, a double life*). 9. Have first place in (*~ the dance, van*; (abs.) go first (*~ off*, begin intr.), be first at some point in race, be ahead in game (*Kent led on the first innings*). 10. Direct by example (*~ orchestra, band, chorus*, etc.), set (fashion); be official director or spokesman of (party), ‖ act as leading counsel in (case, or usu. abs.). 11. (cards). Play as first card, be first player, in trick (*~ up to*, play so as to elicit higher card in later player's hand), play one of (suit) when *~ing*. 12. *~ away*, (usu. in pass.) induce to follow unthinkingly; *~ off*, begin (dance, conversation, or abs.); *~ on*, entice into going farther than was intended; *~ up the* GARDEN (*path*); *~ up to*, form preparation for, serve to introduce, direct conversation towards, (subject). Hence *~'ABLE a.* [OE *lǣdan*, OS *lēdian*, OHG *leiten*, ON *leitha*, f. Gmc *-laidhjan* f. *-laidhō* LOAD¹]

lead³ (lĕd), n. Direction given by going in front, example, (*follow the ~ of*; *give* one *a ~*, encourage him by doing thing, esp. leaping fence in hunting, first); leading place, leadership, (*take the ~*); artificial water-course, esp. leading to mill; (electr.) conductor conveying current from source to place of use, (*~-in*, conducting wire joining wireless receiver with external aerial); channel in ice-field; string etc. for leading dog; (cards) act or right of playing first (*return ~*, lead from suit already led by partner); (theatr.) (player of) chief part; *~-off*, commencement. [f. prec.]

lea'den (lĕd-n), a. (As) of lead (*sleep's ~ sceptre*, stupefying power; *~ sword*, useless); heavy, slow, burdensome, (*~ limbs*); inert, deadening, (*~ rule*); lead-coloured. [-EN¹]

Leadenhall (lĕd'enhawl'), n. (Used for) ~ meat and poultry market in London.

lead'er (lēd²), n. In vbl senses of LEAD² (FOLLOW *my* ~); also or esp. : ~ *of House of Commons & House of Lords*, member of Government with official initiative in business; ‖ counsel who leads in case, also Q.C., also senior counsel of circuit; front horse(s) in team or tandem (opp. WHEEL-ER); leading performer in orchestra; shoot growing at apex of stem or principal branch; tendon; ‖ = LEADING² *article*; (print.) line of dots or dashes to guide eye. Hence ~LESS a., ~SHIP(1, 3) n. [-ER¹]

‖ **leaderĕtte'** (lēd-), n. Short editorial paragraph after leading article. [prec., -ETTE]

lead'ing¹ (lēd²), n. In vbl senses; esp.: *men of light & ~*, of deserved influence; ~*-business*, parts usu. taken by ~ actor; ~*-rein*, to lead horse with; ~*-staff*, attached to ring in bull's nose; ~*-strings*, with which children were formerly taught to walk (*in* ~*-strings*, in state of pupilage). [-ING¹]

lead'ing² (lēd²), a. In vbl senses; ‖ ~ *article*, editorial expression of opinion at full length in newspaper, (commerc). article of trade sold at low price to attract custom for other things; ~ *case* (law), serving as precedent for deciding others; ~ *edge*, foremost edge of aircraft's wing, opp. *trailing edge*; ~ *lady*, *man*, taking chief part in play; ~ *motive*, transl. of LEITMOTIV; ~ *note*, seventh of diatonic scale, semitone below keynote; ~ *question*, prompting desired answer. [-ING²]

leaf, n. (pl. *leaves*), & v.i. & t. **1.** Expanded organ (usu. green) of plant springing from side of stem or branch or direct from root; (pop.) petal (esp. *rose-*~); foliage (*fall of the* ~, autumn; *in* ~, with leaves out), leaves of tobacco or tea. **2.** Single thickness of folded paper, esp. (= 2 pages) in book (*take a* ~ *out of* person's BOOK¹; *turn over a new* ~, mend one's ways). **3.** Very thin sheet of metal, esp. gold or silver, or horn, marble, talc, etc. **4.** Hinged part or flap of door, shutter, table (also used of extra section inserted in expansible table), bridge (= bascule), or rifle-sight. **5.** Tooth of pinion. **6.** ~ *brass*, brass foil; ~ *insect* (having wings resembling ~ of plant); ~*-lard* (made from layers of fat round pig's kidneys); ~*-mould*, soil composed chiefly of decaying leaves; hence ~'AGE(1) n., (-)~ED² (-ft), ~'LESS, aa., ~'lèssNESS n., ~'Y² a., ~'ïNESS n. **7.** vb. Put forth leaves; turn over leaves or pages of (book etc.). [OE *lēaf*, OS *lōf*, OHG *loup*, ON *lauf*, Goth. *laufs* f. Gmc *laubhaz*, *-am*]

leaf'lĕt, n. (Bot.) one division of compound leaf; young leaf; small leaf of paper, or sheet or leaves folded but not stitched, with printed matter, esp. for gratuitous distribution. [-LET]

league¹ (-g), n. Varying measure of road-distance, usu. about three miles. [ME; ult. f. LL *leuga*, *leuca*, of Gaulish orig.]

league² (-g), n., & v.t. & i. **1.** Compact for mutual protection & assistance or prosecution of common interests, parties (whether States or individuals) to such compact, (*Solemn L~ & COVENANT*; PRIM-ROSE *L~*; *in* ~ *with*, allied with); ‖ *L~ football* (in which clubs forming a ~ play each other for championship); *L~ of Nations* (established by the treaty of peace 1919 to try to prevent war), now replaced by UNITED *Nations*. **2.** vb. Join (t. & i.) in ~ (esp. in p.p. ~*d together* or *with*). [f. F *ligue* f. It. *liga*, var. of *lega* f. *legare* (L *ligare* bind)]

‖ **leag'uer¹** (-ger), n., & v.t. & i. = LAAGER. [f. Du. *leger* camp, cogn. w. LAIR]

leag'uer² (-ger), n. Member of LEAGUE². [-ER¹]

leak, n., & v.i. & t. **1.** Hole caused by injury, wear, etc., through which fluid makes way into or out of vessel that is immersed in or contains it or through a DIKE (*spring a* ~, develop one). **2.** vb. Let fluid, (of fluid) pass, out or in through ~; (of secrets etc.) transpire, come out gradually; hence ~'AGE(3) n., what ~s out or in, transpiring of secrets, unexplained disappearance of money pointing to embezzlement etc.; divulge (secret etc.). [of LG orig.; MDu. *lek*, *lēk-* n. (cogn. w. ON *leki*), *lekan* vb (ON *leka*, cf. OHG *zelechen*, (G *leck*) leaky), f. Gmc *lek-*, *lak-*]

leak'|y̆, a. Having leak(s); incontinent of urine; given to letting out secrets. Hence ~ïNESS n. [-Y²]

‖ **leal**, a. (Sc. & literary). Loyal, honest, (LAND¹ *of the* ~). [ME, f. OF *leel*, *leal*, *loial* LOYAL]

lean¹, a. & n. **1.** (Of persons) thin, not plump; meagre, of poor quality, innutritious, (~ *crops*, *diet*; ~ *years*, of scarcity); unremunerative; (of meat) consisting chiefly of muscular tissue, not of fat. **2.** n. ~ part of meat. Hence ~'NESS n. [OE *hlǣne*, f. Gmc **hlainjaz*]

lean², v.i. & t. (past & p.p. ~*ed*, or ~*t* pr. lĕnt), & n. **1.** Incline one's body against something for support, support oneself (of thing, be supported in sloping position) *against* or *on* (mil., ~ *upon*, have as protection on flank); rely or depend (*up*)*on*; incline body *back*, *forward*, *over*, *towards*, etc. (~ *over backwards*, go to the other extreme, go to the limit of eagerness to agree); stand obliquely, out of the perpendicular (~*ing tower*); have tendency *to* mercy etc., be partial *to* cause, opinion, or person, whence ~'ING¹(1) n.; place (thing) in ~ing position; ~*'to'*, building with rafters resting against side of another, pent-house. **2.** n. Inclination, slope, (*has a decided* ~ *to the right*). [OE *hleonian*, *hlinian*, OS *hlinōn*, OHG (*h*)*linēn*, f. Gmc **hli-*, **hlai-*; cogn. w. LADDER, CLIMAX]

leap[1], v.i. & t. (past & p.p. ~t pr. lĕpt, or ~ed). = JUMP (LOOK[1] *before you* ~); ~t ·frog, (n.) game in which players vault with parted legs over others bending down, (vb) perform such vault (*over*). Hence ~'ER[1] n. [OE *hléapan*, OS ·*hlōpan*, OHG *hlauffan*, ON *hlaupa*, Goth. ·*hlaupan* f. Gmc **hlaupan*]

leap[2], n. Jump (~ *in the dark*, hazardous attempt of doubtful issue; *by ~s & bounds*, with startlingly rapid progress); thing to be jumped; ~·*day*, 29th Feb.; ~·*year*, with intercalary day (perh. because fixed festivals after February in ~·year fall two weekdays, instead of as usual one, later than in the preceding year), ~·*year proposal* (joc., of woman to man, allowable only in ~·year). [OE *hlȳp* f. root of prec.]

learn (lẽrn), v.t. & i. (past & p.p. ~t, ~ed pr. -nd). Get knowledge of (subject) or skill in (art etc.) by study, experience, or being taught (*from*, *of*); commit to memory (esp. ~ *by heart* or *rote*); become aware by information or from observation *that*, *how*, etc. (*I am* or *have yet to* ~, do not know, usu. with implication of disbelief), be informed of, ascertain; receive instruction; (arch., joc., or vulg.) teach. Hence ~'ABLE a., ~'ER[1] n., (lẽr·). [OE *leornian*, OS *linōn*, OHG *lirnēn*, *lernēn* f. Gmc **lis-*, **lais-*; see LORE[1]]

learn'ed (lẽr·), a. Deeply read, erudite; showing profound knowledge; ‖ (in conventionally courteous mention of lawyer in House of Commons, law courts, etc.) ~ in the law (esp. *my* ~ *friend* or *brother*); (of language, profession, etc.) pursued or studied by, (of words in a language) introduced by, ~ men. Hence ~LY[2] adv. [f. prec. in obs. sense (still in vulg. use) *teach*, +·ED[1]]

learn'ing (lẽr·), n. In vbl senses; esp. (possession of) knowledge got by study, esp. of language or literary or historical science (*the new* ~, studies, esp. of Greek, introduced into England in 16th c., renaissance). [-ING[1]]

lease[1], n., & v.t. 1. Contract by which lessor, usu. in consideration of rent, conveys land or tenement to lessee for specified time (*put out to* ~; *by* or *on* ~; *a new* ~ *of life*, prospect of living due to recovered health or removal of anxiety etc.); ~'*hold(er)*, (person having) tenure, real property held, by ~; *L~-Lend* (later *Lend-L~*), applied orig. in 1941 to an arrangement whereby sitts in British oversea possessions were ~d to the United States as bases in exchange for the loan of destroyers, later extended to the pooling of the resources & output of the United Nations, also attrib. & as v.t. 2. v.t. Grant or take ~ of. [f. AF *les* = OF *lais*, *leis*, f. *lesser*, *laissier* f. L *laxare* (LAX) to loose]

lease[2], n. Crossing of warp-threads in loom; . = foll. (weaving). [app. var. of

LEASH, perh. by confusion w. F *lisse*, *lice*]

leash, n., & v.t. 1. Thong in which hounds or coursing-dogs are held (*hold in* ~, control); set of three hounds, hares, etc.; (weaving) cord with eye to receive warp-thread extending between parallel laths of loom-heddle. 2. v.t. Connect, hold in, with ~. [ME, f. OF *lesse* f. spec. use of *lesser*, *laissier*; see LEASE[1]]

leas'ing (-z-), n. (bibl.). Lying, lie. [OE *léasung* f. *léasian* f. *léas* false, f. Gmc **laus-*; see LOOSE[1], -LESS]

least, a., n., & adv. 1. Smallest, slightest, (*the* ~, esp. after neg., any however small; ~ *common* MULTIPLE; *line of* ~ RESISTANCE). 2. n. ~ amount (*to say the* ~ *of it*, to put the case moderately; ~ *said soonest mended*, discussion will only make things worse); *at* ~, at all events, even if a wider statement is disputable, (also *at the* ~) at the lowest computation; (*in*) *the* ~, in the smallest degree, at all. 3. adv. In the ~ degree. [OE *lǽst*, *lǽsest* f. Gmc **laisistaz*, superl. of **laisiz* (LESS, -EST)]

least'ways (-z; vulg.), **least'wise** (-z; rare), advv. Or at least, or rather, [-WAYS, -WISE]

‖ **leat**, n. Open water-course conducting water to mill etc. [OE ·*gelǣt* (Y·+root of LET[2])]

lea'ther (lĕdh-), n., & v.t. 1. Skin prepared for use by tanning or similar process (*patent* ~, with fine black varnished surface; ‖ *American* ~, kind of oilcloth; ~ *& (prop. or) prunella*, a difference in clothes only, see Pope, *Essay*, iv. 204; *nothing like* ~, one's own goods will serve all purposes; vb, cover or arm with ~). 2. Article, or part of one, made of ~, piece of ~ for polishing; thong (esp. *stirrup-*~; vb, beat with strap, whence ~ING[1](1) n.); (sl.) cricket-ball (~*-hunting*, fielding) or football; (pl.) leggings or breeches. 3. ~*-back*, kind of turtle; ~*-head*, blockhead; ~*-jacket*, kinds of fish, ‖ crane-fly grub; ~*-neck*, (sailor's name, w. ref. to ~ stock formerly worn, for) soldier; ~*-wood*, kinds of tough-barked tree. Hence ~ETTE'(2) n., ~n [-EN[5]], ~Y[2] (esp. of meat etc., tough), aa. [OE *lether*, OS ·*ar*, OHG *ledar*, ON *lethr* f. Gmc **lethram*]

lea'theroid (lĕdh-), n. Cotton paper chemically treated & resembling raw hide. [-OID]

leave[1], n. Permission (*to do*; *by your* ~, apology, often iron., for taking liberty, making unwelcome statement, etc., esp. as porter's formula for asking person to make way for him & his load; *without a ' with your* ~ *' or ' by your* ~ *'*, colloq., without even asking ~); (in Services, offices, schools) ~ (*of absence*), permission to be absent from duty, period for which this lasts (*on* ~, absent thus; ~*-breaker*, person remaining away beyond the period; ‖ TICKET *of* ~); *take (one's)* ~ (*of*), bid farewell (to; *take ~ of* one's *senses*, go mad), whence ~'*taking*¹(1) n.; FRENCH~; WAY ~. [OE *léaf*, OHG **louba* (cf. *irlouben*, Goth. *uslaubjan* to permit), f. WG **laubhā*; cogn. w. BELIEF, LIEF, LOVE]

leave², v.t. (*léft*), & n. **1.** Cause to or let remain, depart without taking, (~*s a wife & three sons*; *six from seven* ~*s one*; ~*s much etc. to be desired*, is unsatisfactory; *left his gloves*); bequeath. **2.** Abstain from consuming or dealing with; (pass.) remain over. **3.** Let remain in specified state (*this* ~*s me cool, cold*, does not excite me; ~ *it at that*, colloq., abstain from comment or further action; *be well etc. left*, provided for by legacy etc.; ~ *undone, unsaid,* etc.). **4.** Commit, refer, *to* another agent etc. than oneself (~ *it to you, sir*, fix my pay yourself; *nothing was left to accident*; ~ *him to himself*, do not try to control). **5.** Allow (person, thing) *to* do something without interference. **6.** Deposit, entrust, (thing, instructions, message), station (person), to be seen to, delivered, etc., or to discharge function, in one's absence (~ *card on* person, as equivalent of formal call). **7.** Quit, go away from, (*left him quite well an hour ago*; ~ *this* or *here*; ~ *the track, room*); (abs.) depart (*we* ~ *tomorrow*, often *for* destination). **8.** Pass (object) so as to put it in specified relative direction (~ *the church on the left*). **9.** Cease to reside at (place), belong to (school, society), or serve (employer), (also abs., as *I am leaving at Christmas*). **10.** Abandon, forsake (esp. ~ *in the lurch*; *get left*, colloq., be deserted or worsted). **11.** ~ *alone*, not interfere with; ~ *behind*, go away without, ~ *as* consequence or trace, pass; ~ *go* (vulg.), relax one's hold; ~ *hold of*, cease holding; ~ *off*, cease to wear, discontinue (habit, *doing, work*), (intr.) come to or make an end; ~ *out*, omit; ~ *over*, let stand over for the time. **12.** n. (billiards). Position in which player ~s the balls. Hence (usu. pl.) leav'ING¹(2) n. [OE *léafan*, OS *-lêbian*, OHG *leiben*, ON *leifa*, Goth. *-laibjan* f. Gmc **laibhjan* f. **libh-*, **laibh-* (LIFE, LIVE)]

(-)leaved (-vd), a. Having leaves (rare); having — leaves (*one*~ *table*; *red-*~). [f. LEAF + -ED²]

lea'ven (lĕ-), n., & v.t. **1.** Substance added to dough to produce fermentation, esp. fermenting dough reserved for purpose; (fig.) spreading & transforming influence (*Matt.* xiii. 33), tinge or admixture *of* some quality; *the old* ~, traces of unregenerate state (1 *Cor.* v. 6, 7). **2.** v.t. Ferment (dough) with ~; permeate & transform, modify *with* tempering element. [ME *levain(e)* f. OF *levain* f. Rom. spec. use of L *levamen* (*levare* lift, -MEN)]

leaves. See LEAF.

lebensraum (lāb'ensrowm), n. Territory which the Germans believed was needed for their natural development. [G, = living-space]

lěch'er, n. (arch.). Fornicator, debauchee. So ~OUS a., ~OUSLY² adv., lěch'ERY(4) n. [ME, f. OF *lecheor* etc., f. *lechier* to live in debauchery or gluttony, f. Frank. **likkōn* LICK]

lěc'tern, n. Reading or singing desk in church, esp. that for the lessons. [ME *lettorne* f. OF *lettrun, leitrun* f. LL *lectrum* (*legere lect-* read)]

lěc'tionary (-sho-), n. Book containing, list of, portions of Scripture appointed to be read at divine service. [f. med. L *lectionarium* (*lectio* reading, see prec., -ARY¹)]

lěc'tur|e, n., & v.i. & t. **1.** Discourse before audience or class on given subject, usu. by way of instruction; admonition, reproof, (*read one a* ~*e*, reprove him). **2.** vb. Deliver ~e or ~es (*on* subject); instruct or entertain (class etc.) by ~e; admonish, reprimand; hence ~ER¹ (-kche)- n. [ME, f. OF, or med. L *lectura* (*legere lect-* read, -URE)]

lěc'tureship (-kcher-), (rare) -urership, n. Office of lecturer. [prec. + -SHIP (unusual formation)]

led. See LEAD².

lědge, n. Narrow horizontal surface projecting from wall etc.; shelf-like projection on side of rock or mountain; ridge of rocks, esp. below water; (mining) stratum of metal-bearing rock. Hence lědg'Y², lědgED² (-jd), aa. [poss. f. ME *legge* LAY³]

lědg'er, n. & a. **1.** Principal book of the set used for recording trade transactions, containing debtor-&-creditor accounts; horizontal timber in scaffolding, parallel to face of building; flat grave-stone; ~-blade, stationary blade in cloth-shearing machine acting with revolving spiral blade; ~-tackle, kind of fishing-tackle in which lead bullet keeps bait on bottom. **2.** adj. (mus.). ~ (or *leger*) *line*, short line added above or below stave for. outside notes (perh. attrib. use of n. in scaffolding sense). [f. the senses of Du. *ligger & legger*, the forms being conformed to the dial. (ME) *ligge, legge* of LIE³, LAY³ (cf. LEDGE)]

lee, n. Shelter given by neighbouring object (*under the* ~ *of*); (also ~ *side*) sheltered side, side away from wind, (opp. *windward, weather side*; often attrib., ~ or ~-, = belonging to ship's ~ side, or to leeward of other object, whence ~'MOST a.); ~-*board*, plank frame fixed to side of flat-bottomed vessel & let down into water to diminish ~way; ~ *shore*, shore to leeward of ship; ~'*way*, lateral drift of ship to leeward of course (*make up* ~*way*, fig., struggle out of bad position, often *much* ~*way to make up*). [OE *hlēo*, OS *hlēo*, ON *hlē* f. Gmc **hlew-*]

‖ **leech¹**, n. (arch., poet., or joc.). Physician, healer; ~'*craft*, art of healing. [OE *lǽce*, OS *lâki*, OHG *lâhhi*, Goth. *lēkeis* f. Gmc **lǣkjaz*]

leech², n. Kinds of aquatic bloodsucking worm, esp. that used medicinally for bleeding (*stick like a* ~, persistently); person who sucks profit out of others. [OE *lǣce*, cf. MDu. *lake*]

‖ **leech³**, n. Perpendicular or sloping side of sail. [15th c., orig. unkn.; rel. to ON *lik* (cf. Sw. *lik*, Da. *lig* bolt-rope), Du. *lijk*, G *liek* leech-line]

leek, n. Culinary herb like onion, but with cylindrical bulb; this as Welsh national emblem (cf. ROSE; *eat the*~, pocket affront, see Shak. *Hen. V*, v. 1.). [OE *lēac*, OHG *louh*, ON *laukr* f. Gmc *laukaz*]

leer¹, v.i., & n. Glance (esp. sideways) with sly, lascivious, or malign expression. Hence ~ingLY² adv. [16th c., perh. f. obs. *leer* cheek, as though ' to glance over one's cheek ']

leer², n. Annealing-furnace for glass. [orig. unkn.]

leer'y̆, a. (sl.). Knowing, sly. [perh. f. LEER¹ n. + -Y²]

lees (-z), n. pl. Sediment of wine etc. (*drink, drain, to the* ~, lit. & fig.); basest part, refuse. [ME *lie*, pl. *lies*, f. OF *lie*, f. med. L *lia* (pl. *liae*) f. Gaulish *liga*]

leet¹, n. (hist.). Yearly or half-yearly court of record (also *court* ~) holdable by lords of certain manors; its jurisdiction, its district. [ME, f. AF *lete* (= AL *leta*) of unkn. orig.]

‖ **leet²**, n. (Sc.). Selected list of candidates for some office; *short* ~, select list for final choice. [15th c. *lite*, prob. f. AF, OF *lit(t)e*, var. of *liste* LIST¹]

lee'ward (or, esp. *naut.*, lū'ard), a., adv., & n. On, towards, the sheltered side (opp. *windward*); (n.) this direction (*to* ~, *on the* ~ *of*). Hence ~MOST a. [LEE + -WARD]

lee'wardly̆ (see prec.), a. (Of ship) apt to fall to leeward (opp. *weatherly*). [-LY¹]

left¹, a., adv., & n. **1.** Belonging to the side of a person's body that is westward when he faces N. or that has normally the less-used hand, having corresponding relation to front of any object (~ *wing* or *flank* of army; ~ *bank* of river, assuming it to face the way it flows); situated nearer to or more directly in front of observer's or speaker's ~ hand than his right; ~ *hand*, lit., &=region or direction nearer the ~ hand, (*on the* ~ *hand of*, in that direction relatively to; *marry with the* ~ *hand*, morganatically; ~-*hand blow*, delivered with it; ~-*hand man*, standing next one on ~; ~-*hand rope*, twisted counter-clockwise); *over the* ~ (*shoulder* now rare), sl. phr. denoting that what is said is to be interpreted by contraries; ~ *turn*, that brings one's front to face as one's ~ side did before; hence ~MOST a., ~'WARD a. & adv., ~'WARDS adv. **2.** adv. On or to the ~ side. **3.** n. ~ hand (lit. in pugilism, as *got in one with his*~; *cannon to* ~ *of them*); ~ *wing* of army; (pol., L~, orig. of continental legislatures) more radical section of legislative chamber

seated on president's ~, political radicals collectively; advanced or innovating section of philosophical school, religious sect, etc. Hence (colloq.) ~'ISM(3) n., principles or policy of the political ~, ~'IST(2) n. & a. [ME *lüft*, *lift*, *left*; orig. sense 'weak, worthless' in OE *lyft-ādl* paralysis, also EFris. *luf*, Du. *loof*; sense 'left' in MDu., LG *luchter*, *lucht*, *luft*, NFris. *leeft*, *leefter*]

left². See LEAVE².

left'-hand'ĕd, a. Having left hand more serviceable than right, using it by preference; awkward, clumsy; ambiguous, double-edged, of doubtful sincerity or validity, (esp. ~ *compliment*; also occas. of marriage = fictitious, cf. correct sense below); (arch.) ill-omened, sinister; (of marriage) morganatic (from German custom by which bridegroom gave left hand in such marriages); adapted for use of, (of blow) delivered with, left hand. Hence ~LY² adv., ~NESS n. [-ED²]

left'-hand'er, n. Left-handed person (esp. in games) or blow. [-ER¹]

lĕg, n., & v.i. & t. (-gg-). **1.** Organ of support & locomotion in animal, esp. human, body, part of this from hip to ankle, (*all* ~*s*, overgrown; BOOT² *is on other* ~; *pull* one's ~, colloq., befool him; *give* one *a* ~ *up*, help him to mount or get over obstacle material or other; BONE *in* one's ~; *have the* ~ *of*, be able to go faster than; *put* one's BEST¹~ *foremost*; *shake a* ~, dance; *show a* ~, get out of bed; *stretch* one's ~*s*, take walking exercise; *take* to one's ~*s*, run away; *on* one's ~*s*, also joc. *hind* ~*s*, standing esp. to make speech, also well enough to go about, also in prosperous or established state, esp. *set* one *on his* ~*s*; *stand on* one's *own* ~*s*, be self-reliant or independent; FALL¹ *on* one's ~*s*; *has not a* ~ *to stand on*, cannot support thesis by any facts or sound reasons; *on* one's *last* ~*s*, near death or end; *walk* etc. one *off his* ~*s*, tire him out in walking etc.; *feel*, *find*, one's ~*s*, get power of standing or walking; *keep* one's ~*s*, not fall; ~ *before wicket*, abbr. *l.b.w.*, illegal stopping of cricket ball by batsman's ~; SEA-~*s*). **2.** ~ of animal as food (~ *of mutton*; ~-*of-mutton sail, sleeve*, so shaped). **3.** Obeisance made by drawing back one ~ (usu. *make a* ~; arch.). **4.** ‖ Swindler (for BLACK¹~). **5.** (crick.). Part of field to left rear of batsman in position (~ *stump*, stump nearest this; *long, short, square*, ~, fielders variously posted in it; *hit to* ~). **6.** Artificial ~ (*cork, wooden*, etc., ~). **7.** Part of garment covering ~. **8.** Support, pole, prop. of machine etc.; support of chair, table, bed, etc.; one branch of forked object; side of triangle other than base. **9.** (naut.). Run made on single tack (usu. *long, short*, ~). **10.** (colloq.). One of two games constituting a round; hop or stage of long-distance flight or journey. **11.** *Give* ~-*bail*,

decamp; ~-BYE; ~-*guard*, pad for ankle, shin, & knee, in cricket; ~-*pull* (colloq.), an attempt to befool a person; ~-*rest*, support for seated invalid's ~; ~ *theory* (cricket), bowling to ~ with fieldsmen massed on that side. Hence (-)~GED[2] (-gd), ~'LESS, aa. 12. v.i. ~ *it*, walk or run hard; (v.t.) propel (boat) through canal-tunnel by pushing with ~s against tunnel-sides, whence ~g'ER[1] (-g-)n. [ME, f. ON *leggr*, f. *lagjaz*]

lĕg'acў, n. Sum of money or article given by will; material or immaterial thing handed down by predecessor; ~-*hunter*, person who pays court to another to secure ~. [ME, f. OF *legacie* legateship, f. med. L *legatia* (LEGATE, -ACY)]

lĕg'al, a. Of, based on, falling within province of, occupied with, law (~ *aid*, official assistance allowed under certain conditions towards the expense of litigation); required or appointed by law (~ *tender*, money that creditor is bound to accept in payment); *~(bank) *holiday*; recognized by law as distinguished from equity; lawful, whence ~IZE(3) v.t., ~ĪZA'TION n.; (theol.) of the Mosaic law, of salvation by works not faith. Hence ~LY[2] adv. [f. F, or L *legalis* (*lex legis* law, ·AL), cf. LEAL, LOYAL]

lĕg'al|ism, n. (Theol.) preference of the Law to the Gospel, doctrine of justification by works; exaltation of law or formula, red tape. So ~IST(2) n. [-ISM]

lēgăl'itў, n. Legalism; lawfulness. [f. F *légalité* or med. L -*itas* (LEGAL, -ITY)]

lĕg'ate[1], n. Ecclesiastic deputed to represent Pope (~ *ā lāt'ĕrĕ*, one of highest class & full powers), whence **lĕg'atINE[1]** (-ĭn) a.; (arch.) ambassador, delegate. Hence ~SHIP (-tship) n. [ME, f. OF *legat* f. L *legatus* p.p. of *legare* commission]

lĕgāt|e'[2], v.t. Bequeath (often *give & ~e*). So ~OR n. [f. L *legare* (prec.), -ATE[3]]

lĕgatee', n. Recipient of legacy. [prec., -EE]

lēgā'tion, n. Sending of legate or deputy; body of deputies; diplomatic minister & his suite (esp. when he does not rank as ambassador), his official residence; legateship. [ME, f. L *legatio* (LEGATE[1], -ION)]

lĕgā'tō (-ah-), mus. direction. Smoothly, without breaks. [It., = bound (L *ligare* bind)]

lĕ'gend, n. Collection of lives of saints or similar stories, esp. *the* (*Golden*) *L~*, particular 13th-c. collection (hist.); traditional story popularly regarded as historical, myth, such literature or tradition (so *in* ~), whence ~ARY[1] a.; inscription or motto, esp. on coin or medal; (print.) title on illustration. Hence ~RY(5) n. [ME, f. OF *legende* f. med. L *legenda* what is read (L *legere* read)]

lĕ'ger. Var. of LEDGER a.

lĕ'gerdémain', n. Sleight of hand, conjuring tricks, juggling; trickery, sophistry. [f. F *léger de main* light of hand]

lĕgg'ing (-g-), n. (usu. pl.). Outer covering of leather etc. for leg from knee to ankle. [-ING[1]]

lĕgg'|ў (-g-), a. Lanky-legged (esp. of boy, colt, puppy). Hence ~iNESS n. [-Y[2]]

lĕghorn' (-gŏrn), n. Kind of straw plaiting for hats etc.; kind of domestic fowl. [imported f. *L~* (now *Livorno*) in Italy]

lĕ'g|ible, a. (Of handwriting or print) clear, capable of being read. Hence ~iBIL'ITY n., ~iBLY[2] adv. [f. LL *legibilis* (*legere* read, -IBLE)]

lē'gion (-jn), n. Division of 3,000–6,000 men, including complement of cavalry, in ancient Roman army; || *British L~*, national association of ex-service men formed 1921 & incorporated 1925 by Royal Charter; *foreign ~*, body of foreign volunteers in modern, esp. French, army; vast host, multitude, or number (*their name is L~*, they are numberless, see *Mark* v. 9); *L~ of Honour*, French order of distinction. [ME, f. OF f. L *legionem* nom. -*o* (*legere* choose)]

lē'gionarў (-jo-), a. & n. (Soldier) of (a) legion(s). [f. L *legionarius* (prec., -ARY[1])]

lē'gioned (-jond), a. (poet.). In legions. [-ED[1]]

lĕgislā'tion, n. (Enacting of) laws. Hence **lĕ'gislATIVE** a., **lĕ'gislātIVElў**[2] adv. [f. LL *legislatio* (*lex legis* law, *latio* proposing f. *lat-* part. st. of *ferre* bring, -ION)]

lĕ'gisl|ātor, n. Lawgiver, member of legislative body. Hence ~āte (by back formation) v.i., ~atŏr'IAL a. (rare), ~ātress[1] n. [L (as prec., -OR)]

lĕ'gislāture n. Legislative body of a State. [after prec., -URE]

lĕ'gist, n. Person versed in law. [f. F '*légiste* f. med. L *legista* (L *lex legis* law, -IST)]

lĕgĭt'im|ate[1], a. Born in lawful wedlock (also said of parent, birth, descent, etc.); lawful, proper, regular, conforming to standard type (*the ~ate drama*, body of plays, Shakespearian or other, of recognized merit, normal comedy & tragedy as dist. from musical comedy, farce, revue, etc., also ellipt., sl., *the ~ate*); (of sovereign's title) based on strict hereditary right; logically admissible. Hence ~ACY n., ~atElў[2] (-tl-) adv., ~atIZE(3) v.t. [as foll., -ATE[2]]

lĕgĭt'im|āte[2], v.t. Make legitimate by decree, enactment, or proof; justify, serve as justification for. Hence ~A'TION n. [f. med. L *legitimare* (L *legitimus* lawful f. *lex legis* law), -ATE[3]]

lĕgĭt'im|ism, n. Adherence to sovereign or pretender whose claim is based on direct descent (esp. in Spanish & French politics). So ~IST(2) n. & a. [f. F *légitimisme* (*légitime* f. L see prec., -ISM)]

lĕgĭt'imiz|e, -is|e (-īz), v.t. Legitimatize (see LEGITIMATE[1]). Hence ~A'TION n. [as LEGITIMATE[2], -IZE]

lĕg'um, n. genit. pl. (*abbr.* LL.). Of laws

(in titles of academic degrees). [L (*lex* law)]

leg'ūme, legūm'en, n. Fruit, edible part, pod, of leguminous plant; vegetable used for food. [F(*légume*), f. L(-*en*)f. *legere* pick]

legūm'inous, a. Of, like, of the botanical family of, pulse. [LEGUMEN -*inis*, -OUS]

lei (lāi', lā), n. Garland of flowers. [Hawaiian]

Leibnīt'zian (līb-), a. & n. (Follower) of G. W. Leibnitz (d. 1716) or his philosophy. [-IAN]

leis'ter (lēs-), n., & v.t. Pronged salmon-spear; (vb) spear with this. [f. ON *líóstr* (*líósta* to strike)]

leisur|e (lĕzh'er), n. (Opportunity *to do, for,* afforded by) free time, time at one's own disposal (*wait* etc. one's ~*e*, wait till he has ~*e; at* ~*e,* not occupied, also deliberately, without hurry; *at* one's ~*e,* when one has time). Hence ~ED² (lezh'erd), ~ELESS (-*erl*-), aa. [ME, f. OF *leisir* n. use of infin. f. L *licēre* be allowed; see -URE]

lei'surel|ȳ (lĕzh'er-), a. & adv. Having, acting or done at, leisure, deliberate; hence ~ĪNESS n.; (adv.) deliberately, without haste. [-LY¹, ³]

leit-motiv, -if (līt'mōtēf'), n. (mus.). Theme associated throughout piece with some person, situation, or sentiment. [G (LEAD², MOTIVE]]

‖ **lĕm'an, n.** (arch.). Lover, sweetheart; unlawful lover or (usu., in mod. archaistic use) mistress. [ME *leofmon* (LIEF, MAN)]

lĕmm'a, n. (pl. ~*ta,* ~*s*). Assumed or demonstrated proposition used in argument or proof; argument or subject of literary composition, dictionary article, annotation, etc., prefixed as heading; motto appended to picture etc. [L, f. Gk (-*ē*-) f. root of *lambanō* take]

lĕmm'ing, n. Small arctic rodent resembling vole. [Norw.]

lĕm'on¹, n. Pale-yellow oval acid-juiced fruit used for flavouring & for making the beverage ~ADE(1) (-ād') n.; SALT of ~, an oxalate used in removing ink-stains; tree bearing ~s; pale-yellow colour; (sl.) unattractive girl (cf. PEACH¹); ~*-drop,* sugar-plum flavoured with ~; ~ *kāli,* effervescing drink of tartaric acid, soda bicarbonate, & water; ~*-plant,* ~-scented verbena; ~ *pudding* (flavoured with ~); ‖ ~ *squash,* drink of ~-juice & soda-water; ~*-squeezer,* instrument for pressing juice out. Hence ~Y² a. [ME, f. OF *limon* f. Oriental source (Arab. *laimun,* Pers. *limun*), cf. LIME²]

lĕm'on², n. (Usu. ~ *dab,* ~ *sole*) kind of plaice resembling sole. [f. F *limande*]

lĕm'ūr, n. Kinds of nocturnal mammal esp. of Madagascar, allied to monkeys but with pointed muzzle. Hence **lĕm'ūrINE¹** a., **lĕm'ūroID** a. & n. [f. L *lemures* pl. spirits of the dead]

lĕnd, v.t. (*lĕnt*). Grant (person) use of (thing) on understanding that it or its equivalent shall be returned; let out (money) at interest, (books etc.; so ~*ing--library*) for hire; bestow, contribute, (something of temporary service or effect, as *enchantment, dignity,* ~ *ear, an ear,* one's ears, listen; ~ *a hand* or *helping hand,* help; arch., ~ *person a box on the ear*); accommodate oneself *to* some policy or purpose (thing ~*s itself to,* is serviceable for); *Lend-Lease,* (later form of) LEASE¹-*Lend.* Hence ~'ABLE a., **lĕn'DER¹,** lĕn'DING¹(1, 4), nn. [ME *lend,* for *len* f. OE *lǣnan* f. (past & p.p.) *lǣn* LOAN; cf. Du. *leenen,* OHG *lēhanōn*]

lĕngth, n. 1. Thing's measurement from end to end, greatest of body's three dimensions (*know* ~ *of* person's FOOT). **2.** Extent in, of, or with regard to, time (*a stay of some* ~; *the* ~ *of a speech*). **3.** Distance thing extends (*at arm's* ~, as far away as an arm can reach; *keep* one *at arm's* ~, avoid intimacy with him; *ships a cable's* ~ *apart; horse, boat, wins by three* etc. ~*s,* i.e. of itself). **4.** (With *go*) degree of thoroughness in action (*prepared to go all* ~*s, went to great* ~*s, will not go the* ~ *of asserting*). **5.** (pros.). Vowel's or syllable's quantity. **6.** (crick.). Distance from wicket at which ball pitches (*bowler keeps a good* ~; ~ *or good-* ~ *ball,* that pitches at right~). **7.** Long stretch or extent; piece of cloth etc. of certain ~. **8.** *At* ~, in detail or without curtailment (also *at full, great, some,* ~), at last or after a long time; *at full* ~ (see above; also) lying with body fully extended. Hence ~'WAYS (-āz) adv., ~'WISE (-īz) adv. & a. [OE *lengthu* = Du. *lengte,* ON *lengd* f. Gmc **langithō* (LONG, -TH¹)]

lĕng'then, v.t. & i. Make or become longer; (pros.) make (vowel) long. [-EN⁶]

lĕng'th|ȳ, a. (Of speech, writing, style, speaker, etc.) of unusual length, prolix, tedious. Hence ~ILY² adv., ~INESS n. [-Y²; orig. an Americanism]

lēn'i|ent (-nye-), a. Emollient (arch.); tolerant, gentle, indisposed to severity; (of punishment etc.) mild. Hence ~ENCE, ~ENCY, nn., ~entLY² adv., (-nye-). [f. L *lenire* soothe (*lenis* gentle), -ENT]

Lĕn'in|ism, n. Policy & economic principles of Lenin (assumed name of V. I. Ulianov (d. 1924), leader of the Russian Revolution of 1917). So ~IST n. & a., ~ITE¹ n. & a. [-ISM]

lēn'itive, a. & n. Soothing (drug, appliance), palliative. [f. med. L *lenitivus* LENIENT, -IVE]

lĕn'itȳ, n. Mercifulness; mercy shown. f. L *lenitas* (*lenis* gentle, -TY)]

lĕns (-z), n. (pl. ~*es*). Piece of glass or other transparent surface with both sides (or one only) curved for concentrating or dispersing light-rays; combination of ~es in photography; (anat.) = CRYSTALLINE ~, one facet of compound eye. Hence ~ED² (-zd), ~'LESS (-z-), aa. [L *lens lentis* lentil]

Lĕnt¹, n. Period from Ash Wednesday to Easter Eve of which the 40 week-days are devoted to fasting & penitence in commemoration of Christ in the wilderness; || (pl., at Cambridge) ~-term boat--races; ||~ *lily*, daffodil; ||~ *term*, university term in which ~ falls (called HILARY in some univv.). [f. LENTEN]

lent², n. See LEND.

-lent, suf. in adjj. f. L-*lentus*, approx. = -FUL; the L suf. is normally preceded by -*u*- (*turbulentus*); but *pestilentus, violentus*.

Lĕn'ten, 1-, a. Of, in, or appropriate to Lent (~ *fare*, without meat; ~ *face*, dismal look). [prop. n., of which the attrib. use is now regarded as adj. = LENT¹ +-EN⁵; orig. sense *spring*, now obs. in E, but the only sense in cogn. Gmc wds; OE *lenċten*, = MDu. *lentin*, OHG *lengizin, lenzin*, f. WG *lang*- LONG, perh. w. ref. to lengthening of day in spring]

lĕntĭc'ŭlar, a. Shaped like lentil or lens, double-convex; of the lens of the eye. [f. LL *lenticularis* (foll., -AR¹)]

lĕn'tĭl, n. (Double-convex seed of) leguminous plant grown for food. [F (-*lle*), f. Rom. *lenticula* f. L -*icula* (LENS, -CULE)]

lĕn'tĭsk, n. The mastic tree. [f. L *lentiscus*]

lĕn'tĭtūde, n. Sluggishness. [f. L *lentitudo* (*lentus* slow, -TUDE)]

lĕn'tŏ, mus. direction. Slow(ly). [It.]

lĕn'toid, a. Lens-shaped. [LENS, -OID]

Lē'ō, n. Zodiacal constellation the Lion; fifth sign of the zodiac. [L, = LION]

Lē'onĭd, n. One of the meteors that seem to radiate from Leo. [f. L *leo -onis*, -ID³]

lē'onīne¹, a. Lionlike, of lions. [ME, f. OF *leonin* or L *leoninus* (prec., -INE¹)]

Lē'onīne², a. & n. Of, made or invented by, person (esp. one of the Popes) called Leo; ~ *City*, part of Rome round Vatican fortified by Leo IV; ~ *verse*, line (also ~ as n.) or lines of medieval Latin verse in hexameter or elegiac metre with internal rhyme (e.g. *Daemon languebat, monachus tunc esse volebat*). [as prec.; inventor of ~ verse unknown]

leo'pard (lĕp-), n. Large African & S.--Asian carnivorous quadruped with dark--spotted yellowish-fawn coat, panther, (*black* ~, black-coated kind; *American* ~, jaguar; *hunting* ~, cheetah; *snow* ~, ounce; *can the* ~ *change his spots?*, character persists); (her.) lion passant guardant as in arms of England; (in names of animals etc.) ~-, spotted like ~; ~'*s bane*, kinds of composite plant of thistle family. Hence ~ESS¹ n. [ME, f. OF f. LL f. late Gk *leopardos* (LION, PARD)]

lē'otārd, n. Short close-fitting garment worn with tights by acrobats, ballet--dancers, etc. [J. *Léotard*, 19th-c. French trapeze performer]

Lĕp'cha, n. One of a race of people inhabiting Sikkim & parts of Tibet.

lĕp'er, n. Person with leprosy. [14th c. attrib. use of ME *leper* leprosy f. OF *lepre*

f. L f. Gk *lepra* fem. of *lepros* scaly (*lepos* scale)]

lĕpĭdŏp'ter|ous, a. Of the *Lepidoptera*, order of insects with four membranous scale-covered wings including butterflies & moths. So ~IST(3) n. [f. Gk *lepis -idos* scale, *pteron* wing, -OUS]

lĕp'orĭne, a. Of the hare kind. [f. L *leporinus* (*lepus -oris* hare, -INE¹)]

lĕprechaun' (-χ-; see Ap.), n. (Irish). Sprite. [f. OIr. *luchorpán* (*lu* small, *corp* body)]

lĕp'rosỹ, n. Chronic infectious disease affecting skin and nerves, resulting in mutilations and deformities; (arch.) any loathsome disease; (fig.) moral corruption or contagion. [foll., -Y¹]

lĕp'rous, a. Having, like, (as) of, leprosy. [ME, f. OF, f. LL *leprosus* (*lepra* see LEPER, -OSE¹)]

lĕpto-, comb. form of Gk *leptos* fine, small, thin, delicate, in zool. & bot. terms, as ~*cephăl'ic* narrow-skulled, ~*dac'tyl* n. & a., (bird) with long slender toes.

Lĕs'bĭan (-z-), a. & n. Of Lesbos (~ *vice*, SAPPHISM); (n.) female homosexual. Hence ~ISM n. [L f. Gk *Lesbios* (*Lesbos*), -AN]

lèse-majesté (läz mäzh'ĕstā), n. = foll. (in frequent use about foreign States, & joc. of presumptuous conduct on the part of inferiors etc.). [F]

lese-mǎj'ĕstỹ (lēz-), n. (civil law). Treason. [f. F *lèse-majesté* f. L *laesa majestas* injured majesty (of the sovereign people)]

lē'sion (-zhn), n. Damage, injury, esp. (path.) morbid change in functioning or texture of organs. [f. OF f. L *laesionem* nom. -*o* (*laedere laes*- injure, -ION)]

lĕss, a., prep., n., & adv. 1. adj. (Of abstracts expressing measurement, as *size, degree, duration, number*) smaller (opp. *greater*; *in a* ~ *degree*, *of* ~ *magnitude* or *importance*); of smaller quantity, not so much, not so much of, (opp. *more*; *find* ~ *difficulty*; *eat* ~ *meat*; *of two evils choose the* ~; *may your shadow never be* ~, may you not grow thin); of lower rank etc. (rare; *no* ~ *a person than*; *James, Ajax, the L*~). **2. prep.** Minus, deducting, (*a year* ~ *three days*). **3. n.** Smaller amount, quantity, or number (*cannot take* ~; *in* ~ *than no time*, joc., very quickly or soon; (colloq.) ~ *of your lip!*; often *far, little, much, nothing, something*, ~; *expected nothing* ~ *than an attack*, expected an attack & nothing ~ than an attack, but see under the adv.). **4. adv.** To smaller extent, in lower degree, (often *none the, no, not the*, ~; ~ *known* etc. or ~-*known* etc.; *do not suspect him of equivocation, still* ~ *or much* ~ *of lying*; *nothing* ~, anything rather; *expected nothing* ~ *than an attack*, did not expect attack at all, but see the now usu. sense under n.). [OE. *læs* adv. = OFris. *lēs* f. Gmc *laisiz* f. *laisa*-; OE *lǣssa* adj. = OFris. *lǣssa* f. Gmc *laisizon*-]

-less, suf. f. OE *lēas* (used both as separate adj. in sense *free from, devoid of,* & as suf.) forming adjj. (*guileless, homeless*) & advv. (*doubtless*) f. nn. On anal. of compds in which the component n. was of same form as the corr. vb (*countless, dauntless, numberless*) & the sense was *unable, -less* has been appended to vbs (*resistless, describeless, tireless*).

lessee′, n. Holder of, tenant (*of* house, theatre, etc.) under, lease. Hence ~SHIP n. [AF, = OF *laissee* (LEASE[1], -EE)]

less′en, v.i. & t. Decrease, diminish. [-EN[6]]

less′er, a. (attrib. only). Not so great as the other or the rest, minor, (*the L~ Bear; the ~ evils of life*). [double comparat.; LESS + -ER[3]]

less′on, n., & v.t. **1.** One of two readings from O.T. (*first* ~) & N.T. (*second* ~) at morning & evening prayer (PROPER ~); thing to be learnt by pupil; amount of teaching given at one time, time assigned to it, (pl.) systematic instruction *in* subject (*give, take,* ~s *in*); occurrence, example, rebuke, or punishment, that serves as encouragement or warning. **2.** v.t. Admonish, rebuke, discipline. [ME, f. OF *lecon* f. L *lectionem* (*legere lect-* read, -ION)]

less′or, n. Person who lets on lease. [AF (LEASE[1], -OR)]

lest, conj. In order that — not, for fear that; (after *fear* vb or n., & similar words) that. [OE *thȳ lǣs* whereby less; *thȳ* was dropped in ME, & *les the* became *leste* by normal change]

let,[1] v.t. (arch.; *letted* or *let*), & n. **1.** Hinder, obstruct. **2.** n. Stoppage, hindrance, (arch.); (rackets, lawn tennis, etc.) obstruction of ball or player in certain ways, requiring round to be played again. [OE *lettan*, OS *-ian*, OHG *lezzan*, ON *letja*, Goth. *latjan* hinder f. Gmc **lata-* LATE]

let,[2] v.t. & aux. (*let*), & n. **1.** v.t. Allow or cause (liquid, air) to escape (~ BLOOD); grant use of for rent or hire (also intr. in pass. sense, as *the rooms* ~ *well;* *to* ~, offered for rent; ‖ n., ~ting, as *cannot get a* ~ *for the rooms*); allow to, suffer to, (*we* ~ *them go; I was* ~ *see him;* pass. now rare, & occas. followed by *to*); cause to (only in ~ one *know* etc., inform him). **2.** ~ *alone*, not interfere with, attend to, or do (~ WELL[3] *alone;* ~ one *alone to* do, he may be trusted to; ~ *alone* imperat., not to mention, far less or more); ~ *be*, not interfere with, attend to, or do; ~ *down*, lower, fail (friend) at need, disappoint (~ *him down gently*, avoid humiliating abruptly), (n., ~*down*) disappointment; ~ DRIVE[1]; ~ *fall*, drop (lit., & fig. hint, significant word) intentionally or by accident, (geom.) draw (perpendicular) from outside point (*up*)*on* line; ~ FLY[2]; ~ *go*, release, set at liberty, lose hold of, lose or relinquish hold *of*, dismiss from

thought, cease to restrain (~ one*self go*, give way to enthusiasm, impulse, etc.); ~ *in*, admit or open door to (~ *in a flood of light; this would* ~ *in all sorts of evils;* ~ one*self in*, with latchkey etc.), insert into surface of something, involve in loss or difficulty (often *for*); ~ (trans.) *into*, admit to, insert into surface of, make acquainted with (secret etc.); ~ (intr. or abs.) *into*, assail with blows or words; ~ *loose*, release or unchain (dog, fury, maniac, etc.); ~ *off* adv., discharge (gun, & fig. joke etc.), not punish or compel, punish *with* light penalty, allow or cause (fluid, steam, etc.) to pass away, (n., ~*off*) being allowed to escape something (esp. in cricket, not being caught etc. when there is a chance); ~ *off* prep., excuse (person penalty); ~ *on*, sl., peach, reveal secret, betray fact; ~ (trans.) *out*, open door for exit to, exculpate, allow (person etc., secret) to escape (~ *the cat out of the* BAG[1]), make (garment) looser, put out to hire esp. to several tenants, divulge (often *that*); ~ (intr. or abs.) *out*, strike out with fist, lash out with heels, use strong language; ~ *slip*, loose from leash, miss (opportunity); ~ *up* (colloq.), become less severe, diminish; ~*up* n., cessation, diminution. **3.** v. aux. supplying 1st & 3rd persons of imperat. in exhortations (~ *us pray;* ~ *you* & *me try now*), commands (~ *it be done,* ~ *him do it, at once*), assumptions (~ *AB be equal to CD*), & permissions (~ *him do his worst*). [OE *lǣtan*, OS *lātan*, OHG *lāzan*, ON *lāta*, Goth. *lētan* f. Gmc **lǣt-* rel. to *lat-* LATE]

-let, suf. forming nn. usu. dim. (*ringlet, streamlet*), but occas. denoting articles of attire or ornament (*armlet, frontlet*); *-let* appears to come f. wrong division of wds taken f. OF diminutives in which *-el(e)* (see -ET[1]) is added to nn. in *-el* (L *-ellus, -ella, -ellum*, dim. suff., or L *-ale* neut. adj. used as n.), as *chaplet, hamlet,* f. OF *chapelet, hamelet,* dimm. of *chapel, hamel,* mod. F *chapeau, hameau.*

leth′al, a. Causing, sufficient or designed to cause, death (~ *chamber,* for killing animals painlessly). Hence **lethăl′ITY** n. [f. L *let(h)alis* (*letum* death, -AL)]

leth′arg|y, n. Morbid drowsiness, prolonged & unnatural sleep; torpid, inert, or apathetic state, want of interest & energy. So **lethăr′gic** a., **lethăr′gically** adv., ~IZE(3) v.t. [f. LL f. Gk *lēthargia* (*lēthargos* forgetful f. *lēth-, lanthanō* forget), -Y[1]]

Leth′e, n. (River in Hades producing) forgetfulness of the past. So **Lēthē′an** a. [L, use of Gk *lēthē* forgetfulness, see prec.]

Lett, n. Member of a people living about the Baltic; = LETTISH n. [see LETTISH]

lett′er, n. & v.t. **1.** Character representing one or more of the simple or compound sounds used in speech, one of the alphabetic symbols, (*capital* ~, of the large form A, B, etc., opp. *small*, a, b, etc.; ROMAN, ITALIC, ~); (print. type,) fount of type (now chiefly in *return of* ~ for DISTRIBUTION; (pl.) ~ing, inscription, (now only in PROOF[1] *before* ~s). 2. Missive, epistle, (~ *of advice*, notifying dispatch of goods, drawing of bill, etc.; ~ *of attorney*, = POWER *of attorney*); (pl.) epistle of legal or formal kind for various purposes (~s PATENT, *of* ADMINISTRATION, etc.; ‖ ~s of business, royal authority to Convocation to deal with a matter). 3. Precise terms of statement (*to the* ~, with adherence to every detail), strict verbal interpretation (opp. SPIRIT; esp. *in* ~ *& in spirit*, in form & substance). 4. pl. Literature, acquaintance with books, erudition, (*man of* ~s, scholar, author; *commonwealth* or *republic of* ~s, authors as a body; *the profession of* ~s, authorship, whence ~ED[2] (-erd) a. 5. ~*-balance*, for ascertaining postage of ~s; ~*-book*, in which copies of correspondence are kept; ‖ ~*-box*, into which ~s are delivered; ‖ ~*-card*, folded card with gummed edge for use as postal missive; ~*-case*, pocket-book for holding ~s; ~*-lock*, kind of padlock opened by making out of certain ~s on it a word known to owner; ~*-paper*, paper for ~s; ~*-perfect* (theatr.), knowing one's part perfectly; ~*-press*, contents of illustrated book other than the illustrations, printed matter relating to illustration; ~*-weight*, = ~*--balance*, occas. = paper-weight; ~*-worship*, undue devotion to the ~; ~*-writer*, lit., also as title for manuals of ~*-writing*; hence ~LESS *a*. 6. v.t. Impress title etc. on (book-cover); classify with ~s of the alphabet. Hence ~ING[1](1, 6) n. [ME, f. OF *lettre* f. L *littera* ~ of alphabet, (pl.) epistle]

Lĕtt'ĭc, a. & n. = foll.; (of) the group of languages comprising Lettish, Lithuanian, & Old Prussian; of these peoples. [as foll., -IC]

Lĕtt'ish, a. & n. (Language) of the Letts. [*Lett* f. G *Lette* f. native *Latvi* + -ISH[1]]

lĕtt'uce (-tĭs), n. Garden herb with crisp leaves much used as salad (*cabbage*, COS, ~, kinds of it). [ME *letuse*, rel. to OF *laitue* (f. L *lactuca*) poss. thr. a var. *letuse* f. Rom. *lactucea*, *lattucea*]

leuc'o-, comb. form of Gk *leukos* white, as ~*cyte*, colourless corpuscle of blood or found in lymph etc.; ~*pathy* (-ŏp²), albinism; ~*rrhoe'a*, mucous discharge from female genitals, the whites; ~*tomy* (-ŏt²), incision by kind of needle (~*tōme*) into frontal lobe of brain to relieve some cases of mental disorder.

leukaem'ĭa, n. (med.). Disease in which there is usu. an excess of white corpuscles in the blood. [f. Gk *leukos* white, *haima* blood; see -IA[1]]

lĕv, n. (pl. ~*a*). Bulgarian monetary unit. [Bulg., = lion]

Lĕvănt'[1], n. Eastern part of Mediterranean with its islands & neighbouring countries; ~ MOROCCO. [F, part. of *lever* rise, used as n. = east, f. L *levare* lift]

‖ **lĕvănt'**[2], v.i. Abscond, bolt, esp. with betting or gaming losses unpaid. Hence **lĕvăn'ter**[1] [-ER[1]] n. [perh. f. Sp. *levantar el campo* break up camp (*levar* f. L *levare* lift)]

lĕvăn'ter[2], n. (*L*~) inhabitant of Levant; strong Mediterranean easterly wind. [LEVANT[1], -ER[1]]

Lĕvăn'tine (or lĕv'an-), a. & n. Of, trading to, inhabitant of, the Levant. [-INE[1]]

lĕvāt'or, n. (Also ~*-muscle*) muscle that raises structure or organ. [mod. L, agent- n. f. L *levare* raise]

lĕv'ee[1] (-vĭ), n. (Formerly) reception of visitors on rising from bed; assembly held by sovereign or his representative at which men only are received; assembly of visitors. [f. F *levé* var. of *lever*, see LEVY, -EE]

*lĕvee[2] (lĭvē', lĕv'ĭ), n. Embankment against river floods. [f. F *levée* fem. p.p. of *lever* [L *levare* raise]

lĕv'el, n., a., & v.t. (-ll-). 1. Instrument giving line parallel to plane of horizon for testing whether things are horizontal; horizontal line or plane (*on a* ~ *with*, in same horizontal plane as; *find one's* ~, reach right place with regard to others; *water finds its* ~, its surface in communicating receptacles will be at same ~ unless they have no common ~); plane or standard in social, moral, or intellectual matters; more or less ~ surface; flat country; *on the* ~ (colloq.), truthful(ly), honest(ly). 2. adj. Horizontal, perpendicular to the plumb-line; on a ~ or equality (*with*, or abs.; ~ *race*, in which leading competitors are close together; ‖ ~ CROSSING); even, equable, uniform, well-balanced, in quality, style, temper, judgement, etc. (~*-headed*; *do one's* ~ *best*, not be remiss, take all possible pains); hence ~LY[2] adv. (rare), ~NESS n. 3. v.t. Make ~, even, or uniform; place on same ~, bring *up* or *down* to a standard; raze, lay low, (*to* or *with the ground*, *in the dust*, or abs.); (rarely) knock (person) down; abolish (distinctions); aim (missile, or abs.), lay (gun), direct (satire, accusation, or abs.), (*at* or *against*); ~*ling--screw*, for adjusting parts of machine etc. to exact ~. [ME, f. OF *livel* (mod. *niveau*) f. Rom. *libellum* f. L *libella* dim. of *libra* balance]

lĕv'eller, n. In vbl senses; esp., person who would abolish social distinctions, advocate of equality. [-ER[1]]

lĕv'er, n., & v.i. & t. 1. Bar used to prize up heavy or fixed object; (mech.) straight bar or other rigid structure of which one point (*fulcrum*) is fixed, another is connected with the force (*weight*) to be resisted or acted upon, & a third is connected with the force (*power*) applied (~ *of first order* with fulcrum, *of second order* with weight, *of third order* with power, between the other two); piece by which barrel of breechloader is opened; = ~ watch; ~-, acting as or worked by ~; ~ *escapement*, with connexion between pallet & balance made by two ~s; ~ *watch*, with ~ escapement. 2. vb. Use~; lift, move, act on, with ~ (often *along*, *away*, *out*, *over*, *up*, etc.). [ME, f. OF *leveour* f. lever (L *levare*), see -OR]

lěv'erage, n. Action of, way of applying, lever; set or system of levers; power, mechanical advantage gained by use, of lever; means of accomplishing a purpose, power, influence. [-AGE]

lěv'erět, n. Young (esp. first-year) hare. [f. AF *leveret* (= OF *levreteau*), dim. of OF *lievre* f. L *leporem* nom. *-us* hare, -ET¹]

levī'athan, n. Sea monster (bibl.); huge ship; anything very large of its kind; person of formidable ability, power, or wealth; (in allusion to Hobbes) autocratic monarch or state. [LL, i. Heb. *livyathan*]

lěv'ig|āte, v.t. Reduce to fine smooth powder; make smooth paste of. Hence ~A'TION n. [f. L *levigare* (*lēvis* smooth), -ATE³]

lěv'in, n. (poet.). (Flash of) lightning. [ME *leven(e)*, of unkn. orig.]

lěv'ir|āte, n. Jewish etc. custom by which dead man's brother or next of kin had to marry his widow. Hence ~āt'IC(AL) aa. [f. LL *levir* brother-in-law +-ATE¹]

lěv'it|āte, v.i. & t. (Make) rise & float in air (w. ref. to spiritualism). Hence ~A'TION n. [f. L *lēvis* light, after GRAVITATION]

Lěv'īte, n. One of tribe of Levi, esp. of that part of it which provided assistants to priests in worship of Jewish temple. [ME, f. LL f. Gk *leuitēs* (*Leui* f. Heb. *Levi*)]

Lěvit'ic|al, a. Of Levites or the tribe of Levi; of Levites' ritual; of Leviticus. So ~ISM(3) n. [f. LL f. Gk *leuitikos* (prec., -IC) +-AL]

Lěvit'icus, n. (abb. *Lev.*). Third book of Pentateuch with Levitical law & ritual. [prec.]

lěv'ity, n. Lightness of weight (rare); want of thought, frivolity, unseasonable jocularity, inconstancy; light behaviour. [f. F *levité* or L *levitas* (*lēvis* light, -TY)]

levulose. See LAEVULOSE.

lěv'ȳ, n., & v.t. 1. Collecting of assessment, tax, etc. (*capital ~*, appropriation by the State of a fixed proportion of all or some of the wealth in the country); enrolling of men for war etc. (*~ in mass*, of all able-bodied men); amount or number levied, body of men enrolled (also pl.). 2. v.t. Raise (contribution, taxes), impose (rate, toll), whence lěv'IABLE a.; raise (sum) by legal execution or process on person's goods; extort (*~ blackmail*); enlist, enrol, (soldiers, army); collect men & munitions for, proceed to make, (war; usu. *upon*, *against*). [ME, f. OF *levee* (*lever* f. L *levare* raise), see -Y⁴]

lewd, a. Base, worthless, (bibl.); lascivious, unchaste, indecent, whence ~LY² adv., ~'NESS n. [OE *lǽwede* lay, not clerical; orig. unkn.]

lew'is (loo-), n. Iron contrivance for gripping heavy blocks of stone for lifting; son of a freemason. [orig. unkn.]

Lew'is gŭn (loo-), n. Kind of light machine-gun. [I. N. *Lewis*, inventor]

lew'isite (loo-), n. A blister gas used in chemical warfare. [W. L. *Lewis*, -ITE¹(2)]

lěx'ical, a. Of the words of a language (opp. *grammatical*); (as) of a lexicon. Hence ~LY² adv. [f. Gk *lexikos*, & LEXI-CON, +-AL]

lěxicŏg'raphȳ, n. Dictionary-making. So lěxicŏg'RAPHER n., lěxicoGRAPH'ICAL a. [foll., -GRAPHY]

lěx'icon, n. Dictionary, esp. of Greek, Hebrew, Syriac, or Arabic. [Gk·(·*kon*), neut. of *lexikos* (*lexis* word f. *legō* speak, -IC)]

lěxig'raphȳ, n. System of writing in which each character represents a word. [*lexis*, see prec., -GRAPHY]

lěx tāliōn'is, n. The law of retaliation, an eye for an eye. [L]

ley (lā), n. Land temporarily under grass. [var. of LEA¹]

Ley'den (lī-), n. Dutch city (*~ jar*, kind of electrical condenser invented 1745 at ~; *~ battery*, of several *~* jars).

li (lē), n. Chinese mile (about 633 yds); Chinese weight (about ⅔ gr.). [Chin.]

liabil'itȳ, n. Being liable (‖ *limited ~*, being responsible only to limited amount for debts of trading company; so *limited-~ company*, or ellipt. *limited company*) ; what one is liable for, (pl.) debts or pecuniary obligations. [foll., -BILITY]

li'able, a. Legally bound, answerable *for*, subject or amenable *to* tax or penalty, under obligation *to* do; exposed or open *to*, apt *to* do or suffer, something undesirable (*difficulties are ~ to occur*). [of obsc. orig.; conjectured to be AF *liable* that may be bound, f. *lier* f. L *ligare* bind]

liais'on (-zn), n. 1. Illicit intimacy between a man & a woman. 2. Sounding of ordinarily silent final consonant before vowel or mute *h* in French. 3. (mil. etc.). Connexion, touch, (*~ officer*, acting as go-between for allied forces or units of the same force). So **liaise'** (-āz) v.i., establish or maintain *~ with*. [F, f. *lier* (L *ligare* bind, -ATION)]

lia'na (-ah-), **liane'** (-ahn), n. Kinds of climbing & twining tropical-forest plant. [f. F *liane*, of obsc. orig.]

li'ar, n. Teller (esp. habitual) of lie(s). [OE *lēogere* (LIE², -AR²)]

li'as, n. Blue limestone rock of some S.-W. counties; (geol.) lower strata of Jurassic series, blue argillaceous limestone rich in fossils. Hence **liäss'IC** a. [c. 1400, f. OF *liois* (mod. *liais*)]

libā'tion, n. (Pouring of) drink-offering

to god; (joc.) potation. [f. L *libatio* (*libare* pour a little of, -ATION)]

lib'el, n., & v.t. (-ll-). 1. (Civil & eccl. law) plaintiff's written declaration; (law) published statement damaging to person's reputation, act of publishing it (*the greater the truth, the greater the* ~); (pop.) false & defamatory statement, (transf.) thing that brings discredit *on* by unsuccessful portrayal etc. (*the portrait is a* ~ *on him*; *the book, play, is a* ~ *on human nature*); hence ~IST(1) n., ~lOUS a., ~lOUSLY[2] adv. 2. v.t. Defame by ~lous statements, accuse falsely & maliciously, (law) publish~ against, whence ~IER[1] n.; (eccl. & Admiralty law) bring suit against, whence ~IANT(1), ~IEE', nn. [ME, f. OF, or L *libellus* dim. of *liber* book]

lib'eral, a. & n. 1. Fit for a gentleman (now rare exc. in~ *education*, i.e. directed to general enlargement of mind, not professional or technical); *~ arts* (dist. from science & technology); generous, open-handed, not sparing *of*; ample, abundant; not rigorous or literal; open-minded, candid, unprejudiced; (pol.) favourable to democratic reforms & abolition of privilege (esp. *L~ party*; cf. CONSERVATIVE; *L~ Conservative*, member of Conservative party not ill disposed to reforms; *L~ Unionist*, member of section that seceded from L~ party in 1886 on Home Rule), whence ~ISM(3) n., ~IST(2) n. & a., ~is'tic a., ~IZE(3) v.t. & (rarely) i., ~īZA'TION n.; hence ~LY[2] adv. 2. n. (*L~*) member of (esp. the British) L~ party. [ME, f. OF f. L *liberalis* (*liber* free (man), -AL)]

liberăl'ĭtў, n. Free giving, munificence; freedom from prejudice, breadth of mind. [ME, f. OF *liberalite* f. L *liberalitatem* (prec., -TY)]

lib'erāt|e, v.t. Set at liberty, release *from* (in chem., from combination). Hence ~OR n. [f. L *liberare* (*liber* free), -ATE[3]]

liberā'tion, n. Releasing, release; ‖ *L~ Society*, advocating church disestablishment, whence ~ISM(3) n., ~IST(2) n. & a., (-sho-). [ME, f. OF, or L *liberatio* (prec., -ATION)]

libertār'ian, n. & a. Believer, believing, in free will (opp. *necessitarian*); advocate of liberty. Hence ~ISM(3) n. [·ARIAN]

libĕrt'icide, n. & a. Destroyer, destructive, of liberty. [F (LIBERTY, -CIDE)]

lib'ertin|e, n. & a. Free-thinker on religion; licentious (man); free-thinking, antinomian; *chartered~e*, person allowed to do as he pleases (Shak. *Hen. V*, I. i. 48). Hence ~ISM(2) & (in same sense) ~AGE, nn. [f. L *libertinus* freedman (*libertus* made free, cogn. w. *liber* free)]

lib'ertў, n. 1. Being free from captivity, imprisonment, slavery, or despotic control (CAP[1] *of* ~; *natural* ~, state in which there are no laws; *civil* ~, natural ~ limited only by laws established on behalf of community; ~ *of conscience*,

system allowing all members of State to follow what form of religion seems good to them; ~ *of the press*, system by which anyone may print & publish what he pleases without previous permission, but not without liability to penalties for publishing libellous or criminal matter). 2. Right or power to do as one pleases or to do something; (philos.) freedom from control of fate or necessity. 3. A setting aside of rules, licence, (*take the* ~ *to do*, *of doing*, presume or venture to; *take liberties*, be unduly familiar *with* person or abs., deal freely *with* rules or facts). 4. Freedom from despotic rule personified. 5. pl. Privileges, immunities, or rights, enjoyed by prescription or grant. 6. *At* ~, free (*set at* ~, liberate), having the right *to do*, disengaged; *to* HALL; ~ *man*, sailor with leave to go ashore. [ME, f. OF *liberte* f. L *libertatem* (*liber* free, -TY[1])]

libĭd'inous, a. Lustful. Hence ~LY[2] adv. [ME, f. L *libidinosus* (*libido* -*inis* lust, -OUS)]

libĭd'ō, n. (psych.). Emotional craving prompting any specific human (esp. sexual) activity. [L, = lust]

lī'bra, n. (pl. -*ae*). 1. Pound weight (used only in abbr. *lb.*, as 1 lb., 10 lb.); pound sterling (used only in abbr. *£. s. d.*, & *l.* placed after figure as 50*l.*). 2. (astron.; *L~*) zodiacal constellation the Scales, seventh sign of zodiac. [L]

librār'ian, n. Custodian of library. Hence ~SHIP(1) n. [f. L as foll. + -AN]

lib'rarў, n. Room or building containing books for reading or reference; room in large house devoted to books; collection of books for use by the public, some part of it, or members of some society, public institution charged with care of such collection, (*lending* ~, from which books may be taken away with or without payment; *reference* ~, in which books may be consulted; *free* ~, *public* ~, used by public without payment & usu. supported by rates; *circulating* ~, letting out use of books for profit); person's book-collection; series of books issued by publisher in similar bindings as connected in some way; *walking* ~, person of erudition; ~ *edition*, of good size & print. [ME, f. OF *librairie* f. *libraire* f. L *librarius*, -*a* (a. & n.) f. *liber* book; see -ARY[1], -Y[1]]

lībrāte', v.t. Oscillate, be poised, balance, sway, quiver. Hence **lī'brATORY** a. [f. L *librare* (*libra* balance), -ATE[3]]

lībrā'tion, n. Librating (~ *of moon*, apparent oscillation by which parts near edge of disc are alternately visible & invisible). [f. L *libratio* (prec., -ATION)]

librĕtt'|ō, n. (pl. -*ti*, pr. -*tē*). Book or words of an opera or long musical work. Hence ~IST(1) n. [It., dim. of *libro* book f. L *liber* -*bri*]

Lib'ўan, a. & n. (Inhabitant) of ancient Libya; (poet.) N. African; (of) the Berber language or the group of mod. Hamitic languages to which it belongs. [f. L f. Gk *Libuē* + -AN]

lice. See LOUSE.

li′cence¹, n. **1.** Leave, permission, (*have I your~ to remove the fence?*); permit from government etc. to marry, print something, preach, carry on some trade (esp. that in alcoholic liquor), etc. **2.** University certificate of competence in some faculty. **3.** Liberty of action esp. when excessive, abuse of freedom, disregard of law or propriety; licentiousness. **4.** Writer's or artist's irregularity in grammar, metre, perspective, etc. (usu. *poetic* ~). [ME, f. OF, f. L *licentia* (*licēre* be lawful, -ENCE)]

li′cense, -ce², v.t. Allow (person *to* do, thing to be done; rare); (in p.p.) allow complete freedom to (*a~d satirist*); grant permit (see prec.) to (person; ‖ *~d* VICTU-ALLER); authorize use of (premises) for certain purpose; authorize publication of (book etc.) or performance of (play). Hence license*ee′* n. [ME, f. prec.; -*se* on anal. of *practise, prophesy,* vv., cf. *practice, prophecy,* nn.; the distinction perh. comes by imit. of spelling in pairs like *advise, advice,* where the sound differs]

li′censer, n. In vbl senses; esp. ~ *of the press* (hist.), ~ *of plays,* officials licensing publication or performance when satisfied that law, morals, & decency are not outraged. [-ER¹]

licen′tiate (-shĭat), n. Holder of university licence or attestation of competence from collegiate or examining body (chiefly in abbr. L. as part of title); licensed preacher not yet having appointment esp. in Presbyterian Church. [f. med. L *licentiare* (LICENCE¹), -ATE²]

licen′tious (-shŭs), a. Disregarding accepted rules esp. of grammar or style (rare); lascivious, libertine, lewd. Hence ~LY² adv., ~NESS n. [f. L *licentiosus* (LICENCE¹, -OSE¹)]

lich, lych, lyke, n. (obs.). ‖ Corpse; -*ch-gate,* roofed gateway of churchyard where coffin awaits clergyman's arrival; -*ch-house,* mortuary; ‖ -*ch-owl,* screech-owl (boding death); -*ch-stone,* to place coffin on at ~-gate; ‖ *lyke-wake,* watch kept at night over corpse. [OE, OS *līk,* OHG *līh,* ON *lík,* Goth. *leik* f. Gmc *līkam* body; cf. LIKE]

li′chen (-k-), n. Kinds of cellular cryptogamic plant (prob. fungus parasitic on alga) usu. of green, grey, or yellow tint growing on & colouring rocks, tree-trunks, roofs, walls, etc., whence ~ED² (-kend) a., ~ŏL′OGY n.; skin-disease with reddish eruption. Hence ~OUS a. [f. L f. Gk *leikhēn*]

li′cit, a. Not illicit. Hence ~LY² adv. [f. L *licitus* (*licēre* be lawful)]

lick, v.t. & i., & n. **1.** Pass tongue over to taste, moisten, clean, etc. (~ one's *chops*

or *lips,* in relish or anticipation of food; ~ *into shape,* mould, make presentable or efficient; ~ one's *shoes,* show servility to him; ~ *the dust,* fall, be vanquished); take *up* or *off,* make *clean,* by ~ing; (of waves, flame, etc.) play lightly over, (of flame) swallow *up* in passing; (sl.) thrash (person, fault *out of* person), beat in fight or competition, excel, (*~s creation,* is beyond everything), whence ~ING¹(1) n.; (sl.) surpass comprehension of (*this ~s me*); (sl.) go, hasten, (*as hard as he could* ~); ~′*spittle,* toady. **2.** n. Act of ~ing with tongue; (also *salt-~*) spot to which animals resort for salt; smart blow with stick etc.; (sl.) pace (*at a great ~; full* or *at full* ~). [OE *liccian,* OS *liccōn,* OHG *leckōn* f. WG **likkōn*]

lick′erish, li′quorish (-ker-), a. Fond of dainty fare; greedy, longing; lecherous [alt. f. ME *lickerous* f. AF var. of OF *lecheros*; see LECHER]

licorice. See LIQUORICE.

licor′us. Var. of *lickerous,* LICKERISH.

lic′tor, n. Officer attending ancient Roman consul (12 ~s) & dictator (24 ~s), bearing fasces, & executing sentence on offenders. [L, perh. f. st. of *ligare* bind]

lid, n. Hinged or detached cover for aperture, esp. for opening at top of vessel; *with the* ~ *off,* with all horrors etc. exposed to view; ‖ *put the* ~ *on* (sl.), be the culmination (of), surpass all; = EYE¹-~*lid*; (bot., conch.) operculum. Hence (-)~d′ED², ~′LESS, aa. [OE *hlid,* OHG *hlit* (G *lid*), ON *hlith* f. Gmc **hlidham*]

‖ **Lid′ō** (lē-), n. Public open-air swimming pool. [bathing beach in Venice]

lie¹, n. Intentional false statement (*tell a* ~, make this; *act a* ~, deceive without verbal lying; *white* ~, excused or justified by its motive; *give one the* ~, accuse him of lying; *give the* ~ *to* supposition etc., serve to show its falsity, belie it); imposture, false belief, mistaken convention, (*worship, maintain,* a ~). [OE *lyge* (cf. OHG *lugi,* ON *lygi*) f. Gmc **lug-,* see foll.]

lie², v.i. & t. (*lў′ing*). Speak falsely, tell lie(s), (*you* ~ *in your teeth, throat,* arch. or joc. forms of accusation); take *away* (reputation etc.), get (*oneself,* person) *into, out of,* by lying; (of things) deceive (part., deceptive). [OE *lēogan,* OS, OHG *liogan,* ON *ljúga,* Goth. *liugan* f. Gmc **leug-, *lug-*]

lie³, v.i. (*lў′ing*; past *lay;* p.p. *lain* & bibl. *li′en*). **1.** Of persons or animals: Have one's body in more or less horizontal position along ground or surface (often *asleep, sick,* etc.; ~ DOGGO; *let sleeping dogs* ~, avoid mooting debatable questions; ~ *on the bed* one *has made,* endure consequences of past acts); have sexual intercourse *with;* (of the dead) be in the grave *at* or *in,* ~ *in* STATE; assume lying position (usu. *down, back,* etc.); be kept or remain in specified state (~ *in prison,* *at the mercy of, helpless, idle,* CLOSE[1], LOW[1], PERDU, *in ambush, in* WAIT[2]; (of *of* one's *money,* remain unpaid); (of game-birds) not rise; (of troops) be encamped *at, in, near,* a place. **2.** Of things: Be at rest, usu. more or less horizontally, on surface (~ *in ruins* or *the dust,* be fallen); ~ *heavy,* be a weight on one's *stomach* or *conscience*); be stored up in specified place (*money lying at the bank*); remain in specified state esp. *idle, hid, barren*; be situated (*land lying high, to the east, round*; *find out how the land* ~s, fig., how affairs stand); be spread out to view (~s *on the surface, before us, open*); (of road) lead *through, by, along, among,* etc.; (of ship) float in berth or at anchor; (of abstracts) exist, be to be found, reside, be arranged or related, in some position or manner (*the choice* ~s *between* —; *his acquaintance lay among* —; *knows where his interest* ~s; *how do they* ~ *to each other?*; *as far as in me* ~s, to best of my power; ~s *with you to do,* is your business or right; *the remedy* ~s *in education*; *her strength lay in her weakness*; ~s *in a* NUT*shell*); (law) be admissible or sustainable (*action, appeal, objection, will not* ~). **3.** With advv.: ~ *by,* be unused, keep quiet or retired; ~ *down* in part., behaving in abject manner, not standing up to opponent etc., (*take defeat, chastisement,* & esp. *it, lying down*); ~ *in,* be brought to bed in childbirth (*lying-in hospital*); ~ *off* (naut.), stand some distance from shore or other ship; ~ *over,* be deferred; ~ *to* (naut.), come almost to a stop with head near wind by backing or shortening sail; ~ *up,* go into or be in retirement, take to one's bed or room, (of ship) go into dock or be out of commission. **4.**~'*-abed,* late riser. [OE *licgan,* OS *liggian,* OHG *liggen,* ON *liggja,* (Goth. *ligan*), f. Gmo **ligjan* f. **leg-, *lag-, *læg-,* cogn. w. L *lectus* bed]

lie[4], n. Way, direction, or position, in which thing lies; ~ *of the land,* (fig.) posture of affairs; place where beast, bird, or fish, is accustomed to lie. [f. prec.]

Lie′big('s extract of beef) (lē-), n. Concentrated preparation of beef without albumen, gelatin, or fat. [Baron von *Liebig,* d. 1873, inventor]

lied (lēd), n. (pl. ~*er*). German song or poem of ballad kind. [G]

lief, adv. (comp. ~*er,* rare). Gladly, willingly, (usu. *I would as* ~ do something out of the question *as*). [OE *lēof* dear (cogn. w. LOVE); ME *I had as* ~ (adj.) i.e. should find it as pleasant, early altered to *I would as* ~ (adv.)]

liege, a. & n. **1.** (Of superior) entitled to receive, (of vassal) bound to give, feudal service or allegiance (~ *lord,* feudal superior, sovereign; ~'*man,* sworn vassal, faithful follower). **2.** n. ~ lord (esp. *my* ~ voc.); vassal, subject, (usu. *the* ~s).

[ME, f. OF *lige, liege* f. med. L *laeticus* f. *laetus,* of WG orig.]

li′en[1] (lē'en), n. Right to keep possession of property till debt due in respect of it is discharged (usu. *a* ~ *on* or *upon*). [F, f. L *ligamen* (*ligare* bind, -MEN)]

lien[2]. See LIE[3].

lierne′, n. Short rib connecting bosses & intersections of vaulting-ribs. [15th c. *leyrn,* f. F *lierne*]

lieu (lū), n. *In* ~, in the place, instead, *of.* [F, f. L *locus* place]

lieuten′ant (lĕft-, lĕft-, *in navy* let-; **lōō-*), n. (abbr. Lieut. & *in comb.* Lt-). Deputy, substitute, vicegerent, acting for a superior (still as formal title in *L*~ *of the Tower,* acting commandant of Tower of London; & see LORD *L*~, DEPUTY *L*~); ~, ~*-colonel,* ~*-commander,* ~*-general,* OFFICERS of navy & army; ~*-governor-*(*ship*), (position of) actual governor of district etc. in subordination to governor general. Hence **lieutĕn′ANCY** n. [ME, f. OF (prec., TENANT)]

life, n. (pl. **lives**). **1.** State of functional activity peculiar to organized matter, & esp. to the portion of it constituting an animal or plant before death, animate existence, being alive, (*a matter of* ~ & *death,* something on which it depends whether one shall live or die; NECESSARY, STAFF, *of* ~; *come, bring, to* ~, recover (i. & t.) from swoon; *lose, save, lay down,* one's ~; *safe in, escape with,* ~ & *limb*; SELL one's ~ *dear(ly)*; *great sacrifice of* ~, many killed; *have no regard for human* ~, kill men or let them die recklessly; *for* one's, *for dear,* ~, to escape death; *cannot for the* ~ *of me* etc. by exag., could not if my ~ depended on it; '*pon my* ~, asseveration). **2.** Energy, liveliness, vivacity, animation; vivifying influence (*was the* ~, or ~ & *soul, of the party*; *my* ~, voc. of affection). **3.** Living things & their motions (*very little* ~ *to be seen*); the living form or model, ~-size figure etc., (*taken from the* ~; *as large as* ~, ~-size, also joc. as *here he is as large as* ~, i.e. in person; *portray* etc. *to the* ~, with fidelity to the original; whence ~'LIKE (-fī-) a. **4.** Period from birth to death, birth to present time, or present time to death (*have done it all my* ~; *have the time of* one's ~, sl., enjoy oneself as never before; ~ *sentence, rent, annuity,* to continue for rest of person's ~; ‖ *lease for three* etc. *lives,* to terminate with last of three etc. named persons' lives; ~ ASSURANCE, INSURE one's ~; *expectation of* ~, average period that person at specified age may expect to live; *a good, bad,* ~, person likely to pass, fall short of, this average; *new* LEASE[1] *of* ~). **5.** Fresh start after narrowly escaped lit. or metaph. death (*cat has nine lives,* is hard to kill; *batsman was given a* ~, not put out on giving a chance; *pool-player has three lives,* successive chances). **6.** Individual's actions & fortunes, manner of existence, *(with all the pleasure in ~,* greatest possible; *nothing in~,* at all; *this ~,* that on earth; *the other, future, eternal, everlasting, ~,* state of existence after death; *the* SIMPLE *~; has led a good* etc. *~*); written story of these, biography. 7. Active part of existence, business & pleasures of the world, *(see ~,* mix freely with others; *high, low, ~,* social customs of upper, lower, classes). 8. (theol.). Salvation, regenerate condition, (also *eternal, everlasting, ~,* see above also). 9. *~'belt,* of buoyant material to support body in water; *~-blood,* blood necessary to *~,* vitalizing influence, involuntary twitching of lip or eyelid; *~'boat,* of special construction for saving *~* in storms; *~-breath,* inspiring influence, sustaining principle; *~'*BUOY[1]*; ~ estate,* property that one holds for *~* but cannot dispose of further; *~-giving,* that gives, sustains, or restores, physical or spiritual *~* ; *~-guard,* body-guard of soldiers; || *L~ Guards,* regiment of household cavalry; || *L~-Guardsman,* soldier of *L~* Guards; *~ interest,* right to *~* estate; *~-jacket,* as *~belt; ~'line,* rope used for *~-saving,* e.g. that attached to *~*buoy, diver's signalling line, (palmistry) = line of *~; ~'long,* continued for a *~*time; *~-office,* for *~-assurance; ~ peer(age),* with title lapsing at death; *~-preserver,* short stick with heavily loaded end; *~-spring,* source of *~;~-strings,* hold on *~ (~-strings are cut* or *broken,* person dies); *~-table,* statistics of expectation of *~; ~'time,* duration of person's *~;~-work,* task pursued through *~.* Hence *~'*LESS a., *~'*lèssLY[2] adv., *~'*lèssNESS n., (-fl-), (-)līvED[2] (-vd)'a. (esp. *long-, short-).* [OE, OS *līf,* ON *līf,* OHG *līb* life, body, f. Gmc **lībham* f. **lībh-* (LIVE[2]), **laibh-* (LEAVE[2])]

lif′er, n. (sl.). One sentenced to, sentence of, imprisonment for life. [-ER[1]]

lift, v.t. & i., & n. 1. Raise to higher position, take up, hoist, (often *up, off, out*), elevate to higher plane of thought or feeling, give upward direction to (eyes, face), *(~ up* or *~* one's *hands* or *heart,* in prayer etc.; *~* one's *hand,* to take oath; *~ a hand,* make the slightest effort, usu. *to do; never ~ed a hand against* one, struck him; *~ up* one's *head,* recover vigour after prostration, *~ up* another's *head,* bibl., restore to liberty or dignity; *~ up* one's *heel,* kick; *~ up* one's *horn,* be ambitious or proud; *~ up a cry,* one's *voice,* cry out); hold or have on high *(church ~s its spire);* steal (esp. cattle), take (passage, information) in the way of plagiarism; remove (tents etc.); dig up (potatoes); hit (cricket-ball) into air; (of ship afloat) rise on wave; yield to a *~ (window will not ~);* (of cloud, fog, darkness) rise, disperse; (of floor) swell upwards, bulge. 2. n. *~*ing (DEAD *~; give* one a *~,* take him up into vehicle for part of way, also fig. give him helping hand);

AIR[1]*~;* one layer of leather in boot-heel; apparatus for raising & lowering people or things to other floor of house, elevator, hoist; rise in the ground; upward pressure which the air exerts on an aircraft, counteracting the force of gravity. [ME, f. ON *lypta* f. Gmc **luftjan* f. **luftuz* air (whence OE *lyft* (obs. E *lift*), ON *loft* LOFT)]

lig′ament, n. Tie, bond of union, (rare); (anat.) short band of tough flexible fibrous tissue binding bones together, (loosely) any membranous fold keeping organ in position, similar part in lower organisms. Hence *~*AL, *~*ARY[1], *~*OUS, aa., (-mĕn[2]). [ME, f. L *ligamentum* (*ligare* bind, -MENT)]

lig|āte′, v.t. (surg.). Tie up (bleeding artery etc.). Hence *~*A′TION n. [f. L *ligare,* -ATE[3]]

lig′ature, n., & v.t. Thing used in tying, esp. band or cord used to tie up bleeding artery, strangulate tumour, etc. (vb, bind with *~*); thing that unites, bond; tying, ligation; (mus.) slur, tie; (print.) two or more letters joined (fi etc.). [ME, f. LL *ligatura* (prec., -URE)]

lig′er (-g-), n. Offspring of lion and tigress. [portmanteau wd]

light[1] (līt), n. 1. The natural agent that stimulates the sense of sight. 2. Medium or condition of space in which sight is possible (opp. *darkness*). 3. Appearance of brightness (NORTHERN *~s;* ZODIACAL *~; saw a distant ~*). 4. Sensation peculiar to optic nerve. 5. Amount of illumination in place (*in a good ~,* easily visible); one's fair or ordinary share of this (*stand in* one's *~,* deprive him of this, (fig.) prejudice his chances). 6. Vivacity in person's eyes. 7. Favouring aspect (*~ of* one's *countenance,* his favour, approving presence, or sanction, often iron.). 8. Sun's direct or diffused or reflected rays, daylight, (*see the ~,* be born). 9. Being visible or exposed (*come, bring, to ~,* be revealed, reveal). 10. (Poet.) eyesight; (sl., pl.) eyes. 11. Object from which brightness emanates (*~ of* one's *eyes,* beloved person), sun or other heavenly body, ignited candle or lamp or the like (*see the* RED *~*); (collect.) lamps etc. illuminating place; beacon lamp esp. of ship or *~*house. *~*house; (fig.) eminent person or luminary (often *shining ~*). 12. Mental illumination, elucidation (*throw, shed, ~ upon,* help to explain), enlightenment (*by the ~ of nature,* without aid of revelation or teaching; *men of ~ &* LEADING[1]); (pl.) facts or discoveries serving to explain subject (*we have many new ~s upon it since then*); (pl.) one's natural or acquired mental powers (usu. *do one's best* etc. *according to* one's *~s*); (sing.) aspect in which thing is viewed (*in the ~ of these facts,* with the help given by them; *appeared in the ~ of a scoundrel,* seemed to be one; *place thing in a good ~,* represent it favourably); (in acrostic puzzles) one of the words whose initial & final letters make up the answer. **13.** (theol.). Brightness of heaven, illumination of soul by divine truth. **14.** Window or opening in wall for admission of ~, perpendicular division of mullioned window, glazed compartment of side or roof in greenhouse. **15.** (paint.). Illuminated surface, part of picture represented as lighted up. **16.** (law). ~ falling on windows, the obstruction of which by neighbour is illegal (*Ancient L~s*, inscription giving notice of this). **17.** Flame or spark serving to ignite (*strike a ~*, produce this with match etc.); thing used for igniting, spill, taper, match. **18.** ~ *due, duty*, toll on ships for maintenance of ~'*houses* (tower or other structure) & ~'*ships* (moored or anchored) containing beacon ~s for warning or guiding ships at sea. Hence ~'LESS a. [OE *lēoht*, OS, OHG *lioht*, f. Gmc *leuh-tam, cogn. w. Goth. *liuhath*, L *lux*]

light² (līt), a. Well provided with light, not dark; pale-coloured (often prefixed to adjj. & nn. of colour, as *a ~-blue ribbon, I prefer ~ blue*; *the ~*, BLUE²s). [as prec.]

light³ (līt), v.t. & i. (*lĭt* or ~*ed*; as attrib. adj., ~*ed* is usu.). Set (lamp etc., fire, combustible) burning (often *up*; ~ *up*, abs., begin to smoke pipe etc., also kindle the lights in street or room at dusk), (of fuel, lamp, etc.) take fire, begin to burn; give light to (room, street, etc.; ~ *up*, ~ brightly or make conspicuous by light); brighten (t. & i., with *eyes, face*, etc., as obj. or subj.) with animation; show (person his) way or surroundings with a light. Hence (-)~'er¹ (lĭt-), see -ER¹(1, 2), n., (esp.) automatic device for ~ing cigarette etc. [OE *lĭhtan*, OS *liuhtian*, OHG -*en*, Goth. *liuhtjan* f. Gmc **leuht-*LIGHT¹]

light⁴ (līt), a. & adv. **1.** Of little weight, not heavy, (~-*armed*, with ~ equipment & weapons); deficient in weight (~ *coin, gold*, etc.). **2.** Of small specific gravity. **3.** Having or intended for a small load (~ *ship*, unladen; ~ *waterline* etc., that of ship when ~; ~ *engine*, with no train attached; ~ *railway*, for ~ traffic; ~ *porter*; ~ *horse*, ~-armed cavalry, & so ~ *horseman*, ~ *infantry*; ~ *marching order*, in which only arms & ammunition are taken); (of ship, cart, etc.) made ~ly for small loads & quick movement. **4.** (Of building) not looking heavy, graceful, elegant. **5.** Acting gently, applied delicately, not violent, (~ *hand*, lit., & fig. = tactful management, whence ~'-hand'ED² a., ~'hand'edLY² adv., ~'-hand'edNESS n.; ~ *touch, blow, wind, step*, etc.). **6.** Not dense or tenacious; porous, friable, (~ *soil, pastry*). **7.** Easy of digestion; (of wine or beer) not strong. **8.** (Of syllable) unemphatic. **9.** Not important (*make ~ of*, treat as of no

consequence), slight, trivial, venial, not grave, jesting, thoughtless, frivolous (whence ~'mind'ED² a., ~'mind'edNESS n.). **10.** Wanton, unchaste, (esp. of women or their conduct). **11.** Nimble, quick-moving, (~ *of foot*; ~ *heels*, whence ~'heelED'² a.; ~ *movements*; ~ *rhythm*; ~ *fingers*, good at stealing, whence ~'-fing'erED² a.). **12.** Fickle, inconstant. **13.** Easily borne (~ *punishment, taxation, rule, expense*) or done (~ *work, task*). **14.** Aimed or aiming at entertainment merely (~ *literature, writer, comedy, comedian, programme*). **15.** (Of sleep) easily disturbed, not profound, (so ~ *sleeper*). **16.** Free from sorrow, cheerful, sanguine, (~ *heart*; *did it with a ~ heart*, sanguinely, rashly; so ~'heart'ED² a., ~'heart'edLY² adv., ~'heart'edNESS n.). **17.** Delirious (now only in ~'head'ED² a., ~'head'ed-NESS n.). **18.** || ~-BOB⁵; ~'*foot*, springy, nimble; ~ *heavy* (BOX⁵); ~-o'-*love*, fickle woman, harlot; ~-*weight* a., ~ *weight* n., (man or animal) below average weight, esp. in boxing 9 st. 9 to 9 st., (person) of little importance; hence ~'LY² adv., ~'NESS n., (lit-). **19.** adv. In ~ manner (esp. *tread, sleep*, ~; ~ *come* ~ *go*, what is easily gained is soon lost). [OE *lēoht*, OS *lĭht*, OHG *lĭht*(i), ON *lĕttr*, Goth. *leihts* f. Gmc **lĭnh-*, **lung-*, cogn. w. LUNG]

light⁵ (līt), v.t. & i. (*lĭt* or ~*ed*). (Naut.) lift (rope etc.) along, lend a hand in hauling ropes etc.; (arch.) alight, descend, come down; chance, come by chance, (*up*)*on*. [OE *lĭhtan*, OHG (*gi*)*lĭhten*, ON *lĕtta* fr. Gmc *lĭhtjan f. **lĭnht-*LIGHT⁴; sense ' alight ' f. idea of relieving horse etc. of weight]

light'en¹ (līt-), v.t. & i. Reduce load of (ship etc.), (of ship) have her load reduced; relieve (heart etc.), (of heart etc.) feel relief; reduce weight of, (fig.) mitigate; grow lighter. [LIGHT⁴ + -EN⁶]

light'en² (līt-), v.t. & i. Shed light upon, make bright, (also fig., as ~ *our darkness*); (of face, eyes, sky, etc.) grow bright, shine, flash; (of sky, clouds, or *it*) emit lightning (also fig. of scorn etc.). [LIGHT² + -EN⁶]

light'er² (līt-; for *lighter¹* see LIGHT³), n., & v.t. **1.** Boat, usu. flat-bottomed, for unloading & loading ships not brought to wharf & for transporting goods in harbour. **2.** v.t. Remove (goods) in ~. Hence ~AGE (4) n. [15th c., f. MDu. *lichter* (as LIGHT⁵, -ER¹]

light'ish¹, ² (līt-), aa. Somewhat LIGHT²; somewhat LIGHT⁴. [-ISH¹(2)]

light'ning (līt-), n. Visible electric discharge between clouds or cloud & ground (*forked, chain*, or *chained* ~, ~-flash in form of zigzag or divided line; *sheet* ~, ~ flash of diffused brightness; *summer, heat*, ~, sheet ~ without audible thunder, result of distant storm; *like* ~, with greatest conceivable speed; *with* ~ *speed*); ~-*rod* or -*conductor*, metal rod or wire fixed to exposed part of building or to mast to divert ~ into earth or sea; ~ *strike*, labour strike at short notice by way of surprise. [14th c., differentiated form of *lightening* vbl n. of LIGHTEN²]

lights (līts), n. pl. Lungs of sheep, pigs, bullocks, etc., used as a food esp. for cats & dogs. [n. use of LIGHT⁴, cf. LUNG]

light′some¹ (līt-), a. (rare & poet.). Light, graceful, elegant, in appearance; light-hearted, merry; nimble. Hence ~LY² adv., ~NESS n. [ME, f. LIGHT¹, -SOME]

light′some² (līt-), a. (rare). Light-giving, luminous; well lighted, bright. [ME, f. LIGHT¹, -SOME]

light′wŏŏd (līt-), n. Kinds of tree with light wood; kinds of tree with wood that burns with bright flame. [LIGHT⁴, ¹]

lign-aloes (līnǎl′ōz), n. The drug aloes; aloes-wood, an aromatic Mexican wood. [ME, f. LL *lignum aloes* wood of the ALOE]

lig′neous, a. (Of plants) woody (opp. *herbaceous*). [f. L *ligneus* (foll.) + -OUS]

lig′ni-, comb. form of L *lignum* wood. Hence ~F′EROUS, ~FORM, aa., ~FY v.t. & i., ~FICA′TION n.

lig′nite, n. Brown coal showing traces of ligneous structure. [F, see prec., -ITE²(2)]

lig′num vīt′ae, n. Guaiacum. [L, = wood of life]

lig′ulate, a. (bot.). With strap-shaped fillet(s). [L *ligula* strap + -ATE²]

like¹, a. (often governing noun like trans. part.; *more*, *most*, rarely or poet. ~*r*, ~*st*), prep., adv. (arch.), conj. (colloq.), & n. **1**. adj. Similar, resembling something or each other or the original, (*in ~ manner* or *wise*; *on this & the ~ subjects*; *the two letters are very ~*; *as ~ as two peas*; ~ *father ~ son*, ~ *master ~ man*, as the one is so will the other be; *the picture is not~*; in alg., ~ *signs*, both positive or both negative, ~ *quantities*, expressed by same letters; occas. with *with*, as *beings of ~ passions with us*; now rarely, & chiefly in comp. ~*r*, with *to*, as ~*r to God than man*); resembling, such as, (*nothing ~* LEATHER, as good as; *what is he, it, ~?*, what sort of person or thing is he or it?; *look~*, have appearance of; ~ *that*, of the kind just seen or referred to; *a critic ~ you*, of the class that you exemplify; *something ~ £1,000*, nearly, about; *something ~ a day*, with stress on ~, remarkably fine or otherwise satisfactory; so abs., *this is something ~*; *nothing ~ as good*, not nearly); characteristic of (*that is ~ your impudence*; *it was ~ him to think of himself last*); in promising state or right mood for doing (*looks ~ lasting*; *feel ~ working* or *stopping work*; also *looks ~ with n.* = promises the finding or suggests the agency of, as *looks ~ rabbits*); (arch.) likely, (arch. & colloq.) likely *to* (*had*, = *was*, ~ *to have* done, narrowly escaped doing); ~*-minded*, having same tastes, views, etc. **2**. prep. In the manner of, to the same degree as, (*cannot do it ~*

you; *do not talk ~ that*; ~ *a shot*, without demur, willingly, regardless of consequences; ~ *fun*, *blazes*, *one o'clock*, *anything*, MAD, etc., vigorously); (in proverbial or joc. pseudo-proverbial phrr.; emphasizing vbs) *blush ~ a peony*, *drink ~ a fish*, *fit ~ a glove*, *get on ~ a house on fire*, *smoke* i.e. tobacco ~ *a chimney*, *spread ~ wildfire*, *swear ~ a trooper*, *swim ~ a duck*; less usu. w. noun in objective relation, *hate* person etc. ~ *poison*, *scatter them~ chaff*). **3**. adv. In the same manner as (arch.); probably (now only in *very ~*, ~ *enough*, usu. parenthetic); (illit.) so to speak (*by way of argument ~*). **4**. conj. (for arch. ~ *as*; colloq.). As (*cannot do it ~ you do*; *snow is falling ~ in January*). **5**. n. Counterpart, equal, ~ thing or person, (*mix with your~s*; *shall not see his ~ again*; *did you ever see the ~ of it?*; ~*cures~*; *the~s of me*, colloq., persons so humble as I; *the ~s of you*, colloq., persons so distinguished as you); (golf) stroke that equalizes number of strokes played by each side; (ellipt. use of adj. with pl. ~) thing(s) of the same kind (*will never do the ~ again*; *& the ~* often as pl. = etcetera, as *music*, *painting*, *& the ~*; *or the ~*, or other thing(s) of the kind). [ME *lich*, *lik*, shortened form (= ON *līkr*) of OE *gelíc* = OS *gilīk*, OHG *gilīh*, ON *glíkr*, Goth. *galeiks* f. Gmc *galik-*, see Y-, LICH]

like², v.t. & i., & n. **1**. Be pleasing to (arch. or joc.; chiefly impers., *it ~s me not*, *well*, etc.); thrive (obs. exc. in *well--liking*); find agreeable, congenial, or satisfactory, feel attracted by, wish for, (*I ~ you*, *the offer*, *his visits*, (iron.) *his impudence*, *her to be within reach*, *to see them now & then*; *do not ~ such subjects discussed*; *should much~ to come*; *should ~ to know* or *see* (iron.), think you will find it hard to tell me, am not likely to see; *should ~ time to consider it*; *how do you ~ it?*, do you ~ it much or little or dislike it?, whence **lik′ABLE** a., **lik′ableNESS** n.; *if you ~* (expr. consent to request, as *you will come if you ~*, or limited assent, as *I am shy if you~*, i.e. but not misanthropic, or emphatic selection, as *I am shy if you ~*, i.e. but someone else is not); suit (only in *I ~ it*, i.e. kind of food, *but it does not ~ me*). **2**. n. (Usu. pl.) liking(s), predilection(s) (esp. ~*s & dislikes*). [OE *lícian*, OS *líkōn*, OHG *líhhēn*, ON *líka*, Goth. *leikan* f. Gmc *līkam* (prec., LICH)]

-like, suf. (i.e. LIKE a. & adv. in comp.) **1**. Appended to nn. ~ forms adjj. (*god~*, *woman~*, *plumbago~*); advv of similar form are perh. arch., & in mod. use possible advv. can usu. be explained as adjj. (*he*, *coward~*, *refused*). **2**. Appended to adjj. it forms adjj. chiefly Sc. (*human-~*, *auld~*) & Sc. advv.

like′lihŏŏd (-kl-), n. Being likely, probability, (esp. *in all ~*, probably). [-HOOD]

like′ly (-kl-), a. & adv. (*more*, *most*, *-er*

-*iest*). **1.** Probable, such as might well happen, or be or prove true, or turn out to be the thing specified, (*a ~ story*, often iron.; *it is not ~ he will come*; *his most ~ halting-place is —*); to be expected to (*he, this, is* or *was not ~ to come, happen*); promising, apparently suitable *for* purpose or *to* do or be, capable-looking, (*called at every ~ house*; *six ~ young fellows*; *the likeliest place for smugglers* or *to find him in*). **2.** adv. Probably (usu. *most* or *very ~*). [f. ON *likligr* (LIKE[1], -LY[1])]

lik′en, v.t. Find or point out resemblance in (thing) *to*; (rare) make like to (*its arbitrary character ~s it to a despotism*). [-EN[6]]

like′ness (-kn-), n. Being like, resemblance (*between, to*); semblance (*enemy in ~ of friend*); representation, copy, portrait (*take* one's ~, portray him); person or thing having the exact appearance *of* another. [-NESS]

like′wise (-kwīz), adv. & conj. Similarly (bibl.); also, moreover, too. [for *in like wise*]

likin (lē′kĕn′), n. Provincial transit duty in China. [Chin.]

lik′ing, n. What one likes, one's taste (*is it to your ~?*); regard, fondness, taste, fancy, *for* (*have a ~ for him, for precise statement; no ~ for flattery*). [OE *lícung* (LIKE[2], -ING[1])]

*lil. Dial. var. of LITTLE.

lil′ac, n. & a. Shrub with fragrant pale pinkish-violet, or white, blossoms; (of) pale pinkish-violet colour. [17th c., f. F *lilac* (mod. *lilas*) f. Sp. f. Arab. f. Pers. *lilak*]

liliā′ceous (-shŭs), a. Of the lily kind. [f. LL *liliaceus* (LILY, -ACEOUS)]

Lillibullēr′ō, n. Song popular at end of 17th c., often referred to by writers. [part of refrain]

Lilliput′ian (-shn), a. & n. Native of Lilliput, diminutive (person or thing). [*Lilliput* in *Gulliver's Travels*, -IAN]

lilt, v.t. & i., & n. **1.** Sing melodiously or rhythmically. **2.** n. (Song with) marked rhythmical cadence or swing. [ME *lulte* (cf. 1450 *lilt-pipe*), of unkn. orig.]

lil′y, n. (Flower of) kinds of bulbous plant bearing large showy white or reddish or purplish flowers on tall slender stem, esp. the white or madonna ~ (*orange, tiger, turk's cap*, etc., ~); kinds of plant allied to these (*belladonna, calla, Guernsey, Lent, water*, etc., ~); ~ *of the valley*, spring herb with two large leaves & racemes of white bell-shaped fragrant flowers; person or thing of special whiteness or purity (*lilies & roses*, fair complexion); heraldic fleur-de-lis (*the lilies*, arms of old French monarchy, Bourbon dynasty); (attrib.) delicately white (~ *maid, hand*, etc.), pallid; ~-*iron*, harpoon with detachable head for killing swordfish; ~-*liv′ered*, cowardly; ~-*white*, as a ~,

Hence **lil′ied**[2] (-lĭd) a. [OE *lilie* f. L *lilium*]

limb[1] (-m), n., & v.t. **1.** Leg, arm, or wing (*escape with life & ~*, without grave injury); (orig. ~ *of the devil* or *Satan*) mischievous child, so ~ *of the law*, lawyer, policeman, etc.; main branch of tree (*out on a ~*, isolated, stranded), one of four branches of cross, clause of sentence, spur of mountain; hence (-)~ED[2] (-md), ~′LESS (-ml-), aa. **2.** v.t. Disable ~ of (person or animal), dismember (body). [OE *lim*, = ON *limr*, f. Gmc **li-* as in dial. *lith*]

limb[2] (-m), n. (scient.). Edge of surface; graduated edge of quadrant etc.; edge (*eastern, lower*, etc., ~) of sun, moon, etc.; expanded part of petal, sepal, or leaf. [f. F *limbe* or L *limbus* hem; see LIMBO]

lim′bate, a. (biol., bot.). Having distinct or different-coloured border. [f. LL *limbatus* (prec., -ATE[2])]

lim′bĕc, n. (arch.). = ALEMBIC.

lim′ber[1], n., & v.t. **1.** Detachable front of gun-carriage (two wheels, axle, pole, & ammunition-box). **2.** v.t. Attach ~ to (gun), fasten together two parts of (gun-carriage; also abs.), (usu. *up*). [15th c. *limo(u)r*, 16th c. *lymnar*, app. rel. to med. L *limonarius* (F -*ier*), f. *limo* shaft (F *limon*)]

lim′ber[2], n. (naut.). One of the holes cut in floor-timbers for drainage to pump-well. [perh. f. F *lumière* light, so used]

lim′ber[3], a., & v.t. **1.** Flexible; lithe, nimble. **2.** v.t. Make ~; also abs. [16th c., of unkn. orig.]

lim′bō, n. (pl. ~s). Region on border of hell where pre-Christian just men & unbaptized infants are confined; prison, durance; condition of neglect or oblivion. [ME, f. med. L phr. *in limbo* (LIMB[2])]

lime[1], n., & v.t. **1.** Sticky substance made from holly bark for catching small birds (usu. *bird~*). **2.** White caustic alkaline earth (calcium oxide) got by burning ~ *stone*, kinds of rock chiefly carbonate of calcium, & used for making mortar, as fertilizer, etc. (also *quick-~*; *slaked~*, this after combination with water, hydrate of calcium), whence ~′LESS (-ml-), **lim′y**[2], aa. **3.** ~-*burner*, maker of ~; ~-*cast*, outer layer of ~ on building; ~-*kiln*, for burning ~stone; ~-*light*, intense white light got by heating cylinder of ~ in oxyhydrogen flame (*the ~light*, fig., w. ref. to use in theatre, full glare of publicity); ~-*pit*, for steeping hides to remove hair; ~-*twig*, smeared with bird~. **4.** v.t. Smear (twigs), catch (bird), with bird~ (also fig.); treat, dress (land), with ~; steep (skins) in ~ & water. [OE *lím*, = MDu., OHG *lím*, ON *lím* f. Gmc **lim-* cogn. w. L *limus* mud, & LOAM]

lime[2], n. Round fruit smaller & more acid than lemon; ~-*juice*, used as drink & esp. as antiscorbutic; *~-*juicer* (naut. sl.), British sailor (also *lim′ey) or ship (because use of ~-juice was enforced on board); *limey, (also, sl.) any British person. [F, f. Arab, limaʰ; cf. LEMON]

lime³, n. Ornamental tree with heart--shaped leaves & small fragrant yellowish blossom (often ~-tree). [alt. of line = lind; see LINDEN]

lim'en, n. (psych.). Limit below which given stimulus ceases to be perceptible, minimum of nerve-excitation required to produce sensation. Hence lim'inal a. [L (genit. -inis), = threshold, representing G schwelle]

lim'erick, n. Kind of nonsense verse (now usu. applied to the five-line form based on Lear's nursery rhymes). [said to be f. chorus 'Will you come up to ~? ' sung after extempore verses contributed each by member of party]

‖ lime-wort (-ert), limp-, n. = BROOK¹-lime. [f. *lime, *lempe, OE hleomece]

lim'it¹, n. Bounding line, terminal point (superior, inferior, ~, earliest & latest possible date, largest & smallest possible or permissible amount), bound that may not or cannot be passed, (without ~, unlimited; is the ~, sl., is the last straw, intolerable etc.; ~ man, receiving longest start allowed in handicap, opp. scratch). Hence ~LESS a. [ME, f. OF limite f. L limitem nom. -mes]

lim'it², v.t. Confine within limits, set (usu. immaterial) bounds to, restrict to; serve as limit to; (p.p.) scanty; ‖ ~ed company, see LIABILITY; ~ed mail, taking only ~ed number of passengers; ~ed monarchy etc., subject to constitutional restrictions (opp. absolute). So ~ATIVE a. [ME, f. OF limiter, or f. L limitare (prec.)]

limitār'ian, n. & a. (Holder) of doctrine that only a limited part of mankind is to be saved. [LIMIT¹, -ARIAN]

lim'itary, a. Subject to restriction; of, on, serving as, limit. [f. L limitaris (LIMIT¹, -ARY²)]

limitā'tion, n. Limiting; limited condition, disability or inability, (has his ~s, is not talented in all directions); limiting rule or circumstance; legally specified period beyond which action cannot be brought, estate or law is not to continue, etc. (statute of ~s, any that fixes such period). [f. L limitatio (LIMIT², -ATION)]

lim'itrophe (-ōf), a. (Of district etc.) on frontier, adjacent to. [F, f. LL -us (L limes LIMIT¹, Gk -trophos -feeding), orig. of lands set apart for support of frontier troops]

‖ limn (-m), v.t. (arch.). Paint (picture); depict, portray. Hence lim'nER¹ n. [f. obs. lumine illuminate (MSS.) f. OF luminer f. med. L luminare (L lumen -inis light)]

limnöl'ogy, n. Study of physical phenomena of lakes; study of pond-life. [Gk limnē lake, -o-, -LOGY]

lim'ousine (-ōozēn), n. Motor-car with permanently enclosed body (cf. cabriolet). [F, fem. adj. = of Limoges]

limp¹, v.i., & n. 1. Walk lamely, (of verse) halt; (of damaged ship, aircraft, etc.) proceed slowly or with difficulty. 2. n. Lame walk. Hence ~'ingLY² adv. [cogn. w. OE lemp-healt lame, MHG limpfen limp, f. WG *limp-, *lamp-]

limp², a. Not stiff, flexible, (of book-bindings) not stiffened with mill-board; (fig.) wanting in energy. Hence ~'LY² adv., ~'NESS n. [18th c., of unkn. orig.; cf. MHG lampen hang limp]

lim'pet, n. Gasteropod mollusc with tent-shaped shell sticking tightly to rocks; (fig.) person, esp. State employee, who clings to office; ~ mine (attached to ship's bottom). [late OE lempedu f. med. L lampreda limpet, LAMPREY]

lim'pid, a. Pellucid, clear, not turbid, (of liquids, atmosphere, eyes, literary style). Hence or cogn. ~LY² adv., ~ITY (-id'-), ~NESS, nn. [f. F -ide or L limpidus]

limp'kin, n. Kinds of bird between cranes & rails. [LIMP¹, -KIN, from their movements]

‖ limp-wort. See LIME-WORT.

lin'age, n. Number of lines in printed matter; payment according to this. [-AGE]

linch'pin, n. Pin passed through axle-end to keep wheel on. [OE lynis, OS lunisa (G lünse) + PIN]

Lin'coln green (-ngkon), n. Bright green stuff made at Lincoln.

linc'tus (-ngk-), n. Medicine to be licked up; soothing cough mixture. [L, f. lingere lick]

lin'den, n. Lime-tree. [sb. use of obs. adj. linden f. OE lind lime-tree (= OHG linda, ON lind) + -EN⁵; cf. LIME³]

line¹, n. Fine long flax separated from the tow. [OE lin, = OS, OHG, ON lin, Goth. lein f. Gmc *linam, cogn. w. or f. L linum]

line², n. (Order of main senses) 1. Cord; 2. Long narrow mark; 3. Row; 4. Series; 5. Direction. 1. Piece of rope (esp. naut., e.g. for sounding; so prob. hard ~s, bad luck, hardship; also = CLOTHES-~); wire or cable for telegraph or telephone (hold the ~; the ~ is bad; ~'man, charged with keeping wire etc. in repair), route traversed by this; cord bearing fish-hook(s) (~-fishing, opp. net-fishing; HOOK¹, ~, & sinker; give one ~ enough, let him go his own way for a time in order to secure or detect him later); cord for measuring, levelling, etc. (PLUMB-~; by rule & ~, with precision); (pl.) one's lot in life (Ps. xvi. 6, w. ref. to marking out land); rule or canon (obs. exc. in ~ upon ~, see Is. xxviii. 10, with slow & regular progress). 2. Long narrow mark traced on surface; use of these in draughtsmanship (boldness, purity, of ~; translate life etc. into ~ & colour; ~-drawing, done with pen or pencil; ~-engraving, done with incised ~s, as opp. etching & mezzotint; ~-work, with pen or pencil not wash etc.; ~ of beauty, ~ with two opposite curves like elongated S); one of the very narrow vertical sections in which televised scenes are photographed and reproduced; (games) mark limiting court or ground or special parts of them; thing resembling traced mark, band of colour, seam, furrow, wrinkle (~ *of life, fortune*, etc., folds in palm of hand significant in palmistry); (math.) straight or curved continuous extent ·of length without breadth, track of moving point, (with defining word, as *isothermal*~) curve connecting all points having specified common property; *the L*~, equator; straight ~ (~ *of* FIRE[1], *force*, etc.; *picture hung on the*~, exhibited with its centre about level of spectator's eye; *go as straight as a* ~); contour, outline, lineament (*the savage*~*s of his mouth*), (pl.) plan or draft (esp. of ship in horizontal, vertical, & oblique sections) or manner of procedure (*on conservative, political, the same*, etc., ~*s; on the* ~*s laid down by* someone); (as measure) 1/12 inch; limit, boundary, (DRAW[1] *the* ~; so *dividing* ~; *on the* ~, not clearly one thing or the other). **3.** Row of persons or ·things (*come, bring, into* ~, agree or co-operate, induce to do so; *toe the* ~, fig., accept party programme etc.); (mil.) connected series of field-works (GO[1] *up the* ~); ‖ also row of tents or huts in camp; (naut.) ~ *abreast*, number of parallel ships ranged on ~ crossing keels at right angles, ~ *ahead*, ships following in a string, ~ *of* BATTLE[1], *ship of the* ~ or ~*-of-*BATTLE[1] *ship*; (mil.) double row (front & rear ranks) of men ranged side by side, also arrangement of companies side by side (opp. COLUMN; *drawn up in, form, wheel into,* ~; *all along the* ~, at every point, often fig. of success etc.); (army) *the* ~; regular & numbered regiments (not Guards, Engineers, or Artillery, & occas. understood to exclude Cavalry; row of words in page or newspaper column (*read between the* ~*s*, detect hidden meaning in document, speech, etc.; ~*-filling*, flourish or ornament in blank space at end of~ in MS.); (by exag.) short letter (*just a* ~ *to tell you that* —); single verse of poetry; (pl.) piece of poetry (often *upon* subject or *to* person); ‖ (pl.) specified amount (*100* etc. ~*s*) of usu. Latin verse to be written out as school punishment; (pl., also *marriage* ~*s*) certificate of marriage; (pl.) words of actor's part. **4.** Series or regular succession of steamers, buses, aircraft, etc., plying between certain places; connected series of persons or things following one another in time (*can show a long* ~ *of heroes*), esp. several generations of family (*male, female, direct,* etc., ~), family, lineage, stock (*comes of a good*~). **5.** Direction, course, track, (~ *of march, communication,* etc.); (Railways) single track of rails (*up, down,* ~, to, from, chief terminus esp. London), one branch of system (*main, branch, loop,*

~) or whole system under one management (*Southern* etc. ~); course followed in riding to hounds (*take, keep to,* one's *own,* ~, often also fig.); course of procedure, conduct, thought, etc.; department of activity, province, branch of business, (*something in, out of,* one's ~, that interests or concerns one, or not; *in the banking, oil-&-colour,* etc., ~); (commerc.) class of goods, order for or stock of this. [(1) ME *li(g)ne* f. OF *ligne* f. L *linea* f. *linum* LINE[1]; (2) OE *line* = OHG, ON *lina,* f. Gmc **linam* (prec.)]

line³, v.t. & i. Mark *in, off, out,* with lines on paper etc.; cover with lines (*a face* ~*d with pain*); ~ *through,* cross out; draw (men or objects) *up* in line; come *up* or spread (t. & i.) *out* in line; post troops etc. along (road, hedge, etc.) (of troops) form open or close line along (pass etc.), (of things) stand at intervals along (wall etc.). [f. prec.]

line⁴, v.t. Apply layer of (usu. different) material to inside of (garment, box, vessel, bag, etc.); fill (purse, pocket, stomach, etc.); serve as lining for. Hence **lin′er¹** [-ER¹] n., (esp.) removable metal lining saving wear & tear (in heavy guns & machinery), **lin′ING**[1](4) n. (*every cloud has a silver lining,* there is good in every evil). [f. LINE[1], w. ref. to use of linen for linings]

line⁵, v.t. Copulate with, cover, (bitch). [ME, f. OF *lignier*]

lin′eage, n. Lineal descent, ancestry, pedigree. [ME, f. OF *lignage* (L *linea* LINE[2], -AGE)]

lin′eal, a. In the direct line of descent or ancestry (opp. *collateral*); (rare) of, in, line(s), linear. Hence ~LY² adv. [ME, f. OF *lineal* f. LL *linealis* (LINE[2], -AL)]

lin′eament, n. (Usu. pl.) distinctive feature(s), or characteristic(s) esp. feature(s) of face, (sing. chiefly in *every* ~). [ME, f. L *lineamentum* f. *lineare* (f. *linea* LINE[2]), -MENT]

lin′ear, a. Of, in, line(s) (~ PERSPECTIVE); (math., physics) involving measurement in one dimension only (~ *equation,* of first degree); long, narrow, & of uniform breadth. Hence ~LY² adv. [f. L *linearis* (LINE[2], -AR[1])]

lineā′tion, n. Drawing of, marking with, arrangement of, lines. [ME, f. L *lineatio* (LINEAMENT, -ATION)]

lin′en, a. & n. **1.** Made of flax (~ *cloth*). **2.** n. Cloth woven from flax, (with pl.) particular kind of this; (collect.) shirts, sheets, cloths, etc., of~, calico, etc. (*wash one's dirty* ~ *at home, in public,* keep, not keep, quiet about domestic quarrels etc.); ‖ ~*-draper,* dealer in ~, calico, etc.; ~*-fold,* carved or moulded ornament representing a fold or scroll of ~; hence ~ETTE′(2) n. [OE *linen,* OS, OHG *linin* f. WG (LINE[1], -EN[5])]

lin′er² (for *liner*[1] see LINE[4]), n. Ship, usu. steamer, belonging to line of passenger ships; aircraft belonging to a regular line, used esp. for passenger transport. [-ER¹]

lines'man (-nz-), n. ‖ Soldier of line regiment; (lawn tennis, football) official assisting umpire or referee by deciding whether or where ball touches or crosses line. [*line's* (LINE²)]

ling¹, n. Long slender N.-Europ. sea-fish used (usu. cured) for food. [ME *lenge*, *linge*, f. MDu.; cf. early mod. Du. *lenghe*, *linghe*, = ON *langa*; perh. cogn. w. LONG¹]

ling², n. Kinds of heather. Hence **lin'gy²** (-ngi) a. [ME *lyng* f. ON *lyng*]

-ling¹, suf. forming nn.: OE, OS, OHG *-ling*, ON *-lingr*, Goth. *-liggs* f. Gmc *-ingaz* -ING³ appended to *-ila-* -LE(1). **1.** In OE, ME, & mod. E, ~ is added to nn. to form nn. denoting person or thing connected w. primary n. (*hire~*, *nurs~*, *sap~*), & to adjj. to form nn. (*gray~*, *dar~*, *young~*); so also, f. adv., *under~*. On anal. of *nurs~* etc., where first component is ambiguous, *shave~*, *starve~*, are formed on vv. **2.** In ON ~ had dim. force; instances of this appear in E in 14th & 15th cc. (*cod~*, *duck~*); in this use alone (esp. in formation of contemptuous dimm., as *lord~*, *prince~*) the suf. is a living one.

-ling², **-lings**, suf. forming advv.; Gmc *-ling*, *-lang*, *-lung*, (+-ES) used in OE added to nn. to form advv. of direction, as *bæcling* back, *andlang* ALONG, *grundlunga* to ground; in other wds the suf. forms advv. of condition or situation (*darkling*), usu. now dial. only; see -LONG.

ling'a(m) (-ngg-), n. The phallus (esp. as symbol of Siva). [Skr. *linga*]

ling'er (-ngg-), v.i. & t. Put off departure esp. from reluctance to go; stay about, not depart or arrive at expected or right time; dally *round* place or *over* or (*up*)*on* subject; drag *on* a feeble existence (of invalids & moribund customs); be protracted (*~ing disease*, *agonies*); be tardy, delay; throw (time) *away* in delays. Hence ~ER¹ n., ~ingLY² adv. [f. obs. *leng* (OE *lengan* (f. LONG¹), = OHG *langēn* lengthen)+-ER²]

lingerie (see Ap.), n. (Stock of) linen articles, women's underwear. [F]

ling'ō (-ngg-), n. (pl. ~es). (Derog. for) foreign language, vocabulary of special subject or class of people. [alt. f. *lingua* (It., Pg., LINGUA FRANCA), *-o* being a common ending of 'foreign' wds]

-lings. See -LING².

ling'ua frānc'a (-nggwa), n. Mixture of Italian, French, Greek, & Spanish, used in the Levant; any language serving as medium between different peoples (also fig. of common ideas etc.). [It., =Frankish tongue]

ling'ual (-nggw-), a. & n. (Anat.) of the tongue; (phonet.) formed by the tongue (n., ~ sound; both a. & n. now rare),

whence ~IZE(3) v.t.; of speech or languages (~ *studies*). [f. med. L *lingualis* (L *lingua* tongue, -AL)]

ling'uifōrm (-nggw-), a. (bot., anat., zool.). Tongue-shaped. [prec., -I-, -FORM]

ling'uist (-nggw-), n. Person skilled in foreign languages (*good*, *bad*, *no*, ~). [f. L *lingua* language+-IST]

linguis't|ic (-nggw-), a. & n. **1.** Of the study of languages; of language, lingual. **2.** n. pl. ~ic science. Hence ~ICALLY adv. [prec.+-IC; sense 2 f. F *-ique*, G *-ik*]

ling'ūlate (-ngg-), a. Tongue-shaped. [f. L *lingula* dim. of *lingua* tongue, -ATE²]

ling'uo- (-nggw-), comb. form of L *lingua* tongue (*-o-*), as *~den'tal* made with tongue & teeth (of sounds).

‖ **lin'hay**, **linn'(e)y**, (lĭn'ĭ), n. (S.-W. Eng. dial.). Farm-shed or outbuilding open along front. [orig. unkn.; first element perh. f. LEAN²]

lin'iment, n. Liquid usu. made with oil used in rubbing body for rheumatism etc., embrocation. [f. LL *linimentum* (*linire* smear, -MENT)]

lin'ing. See LINE³.

link¹, n., & v.t. & i. **1.** One ring or loop of chain (as measure, 1/100 of surveying chain or 7·92 in.); = SLEEVE-~; loop in knitting etc.; connecting part, thing or person that unites others, filler of gap, member of series (MISSING ~). **2.** vb. Connect, join, (things, persons) *together* or (thing, person) *to*; clasp (hands); hook (arm *in* or *through* another's, or arms); attach oneself *on* or *in* to system, company, etc. Hence ~AGE(1, 3) n. [ME, f. ON **hlenkr*, cogn. w. OE *hlanc* LANK, OHG *hlanca* FLANK, f. Gmc **hlank-*]

link², n. Torch of pitch & tow formerly used for lighting people along streets; *~boy*, *~man*, employed to carry *~s*. [16th c., orig. unkn.]

links, n. pl. Level or undulating sandy ground near sea-shore, with turf & coarse grass (Sc.); ground on which golf is played, often resembling that of prec. sense (also *a ~* as sing.). [OE *hlinc* perh. cogn. w. LEAN²]

‖ **linn**, n. (chiefly Sc.). Waterfall; pool below this; precipice, ravine. [perh. mixture of OE *hlynn* torrent & Gael. *linne*]

Linn(a)e'an (-nēan), a. & n. (Follower) of Linnaeus or his system of classifying plants & animals. [*Linnaeus* latinized name of C. Linné, Swedish naturalist (d. 1778), +-AN]

linn'ĕt, n. Common brown or warm-grey song-bird. [f. OF *linette* (*lin* flax, f. its food)]

linn(e)y. See LINHAY.

lin'ocut, n. Design cut in relief on block of linoleum; print obtained from this. [LINO]

linōl'ĕum, n. (also·lin'ō abbr.). Floorcloth of canvas with thick coat of oxidized linseed oil etc. Hence ~ED² (-md) a. [L *linum* flax, *oleum* oil]

lin'otȳpe, n. Machine for producing

lines of words as substitute for type-setting by hand, much used in printing newspapers. [= *line o' type*]

lin'săng, n. Civet cat of Borneo & Java. [Javanese]

lin'seed, n. Seed of flax; ~ *cake*, ~ (with the ~ *oil* pressed out) as cattle-food; ~ *meal*, ground ~; ~ *poultice*, of ~ or ~ meal. [late OE *linsæd* (LINE[1], SEED)]

lin'sey-woŏl'sey (-z-, -z-), n. Dress material of coarse inferior wool woven on cotton warp (orig. of wool & flax); (fig.) strange medley, nonsense. [15th c., f. *linsey* (poss. f. LINE[1] + obs. *say* silk) + WOOL, w. jingling termination]

lin'stŏck, n. (hist.). Match-holder used in old gunnery. [16th c. *lint*-, *linestocke*, f. Du. *lontstok* (*lont* match, *stok* stick), w. assim. to LINT & LINE[1]]

lint, n. Soft material for dressing wounds made by scraping linen cloth on one side. [14th c. northern *lint*, obsc. rel. to LINE[1]; ult. orig. unkn.]

lin'tel, n. Horizontal timber or stone over door or window. Hence ~LED[2] (-ld) a. [ME, f. OF *lintel* threshold, f. Rom. **limitale* (cf. var. OF *lintier* f. **limitare*) by conf. w. LL *liminare* (L *limen* threshold); see LIMIT[1], -LE(2)]

lin'ȳ, a. Marked with lines; wrinkled; (art) using line too much. Hence **lin'i-**NESS. [-Y[2]]

li'on, n. 1. Large powerful tawny African & S.-Asian (formerly also European) carnivorous mammal with tufted tail & (in the male) flowing shaggy mane (~ *in the way* or *path*, obstacle, esp. imaginary; ~*'s mouth*, perilous position; ~*'s share*, largest or best part; ~ *& unicorn*, supporters of royal arms; ~*'s skin*, false assumption of courage; *twist* ~*'s tail*, of foreign, esp. U.-S., journalists or orators defying or insulting Great Britain). 2. Courageous person, so ~-heartED[2] a. 3. pl. ‖ Sights worth seeing in town etc. (from custom of showing country visitors the ~s formerly kept in Tower of London; *see, show, the* ~s). 4. Person of literary or other celebrity sought after to be shown off at social gatherings (~-*hunter*, host or hostess depending much on ~s), whence ~HOOD, ~SHIP, nn. 5. National emblem of Great Britain (*the British L*~, the nation personified). 6. (*L*~) constellation & zodiacal sign LEO. Hence ~LIKE a., ~ESS[1], ~ET[1], nn. [ME, f. AF *liun* f. L *leonem* nom. *leo* f. Gk *leōn leontos*]

li'on|ize, -|ise (-ĭz), v.t. & i. See or show the sights (see prec.) of (place); show these to (visitor); see the sights; treat (person) as celebrity, make a lion (see prec.) of, whence ~ISM(1) n. [-IZE]

lip, n., & v.t. (-pp-). 1. One of the fleshy edges of the opening of the mouth (*upper*, *lower* or *under*, ~; *bite* one's ~, in vexation or to repress emotion, stifle laugh, etc.; *stiff upper* ~, fortitude or obstinacy; *curl* one's ~, in scorn; *hang* one's ~, in

humiliation; *lick, smack*, one's ~s, in enjoyment or anticipation of food or fig.; *hang on* one's ~s, listen to his every word in reverence; *word* etc. *escapes* one's ~s, is uttered thoughtlessly). 2. Saucy talk, impudence, (sl., esp. *none of your* ~ *!*). 3. Edge of cup, vessel, cavity, wound, etc. 4. ~, from the ~s only, professed, not heartfelt or sincere, (~-*homage*, -*religion*, -*Christian*, -*service*, -*worship*); ~-*deep*, superficial, insincere; ~-*language*, -*reading*, -*speaking*, use & interpretation of motions of ~s to & by the deaf or dumb; ~'*salve*, ointment for sore ~s, (fig.) flattery; ~'*stick*, stick of cosmetic for colouring ~s; hence (-)~PED[2] (-pt). ~'LESS, aa. 5. v.t. Touch with ~s, apply ~s to; (of water) just touch, lap; (golf) hit ball just to edge of (hole), (of ball) reach edge of (hole) but fail to drop in; murmur, utter softly. [OE *lippa*, MLG, MDu., (G) *lippe*, MSw. *lippe* f. Gmc **lipjon*- cogn. w. L *labrum*]

lipŏg'raphy̆, n. Omission of letter(s) or word(s) in writing. [f. Gk *lip*- st. of *leipō* omit, -GRAPHY]

lipp'er, n. (naut.). Rippling or ruffled motion, surface roughness, of sea. [16th c. n. & vb, prob. frequent. f. LAP[5]]

liquăte, v.t. Separate or purify (metals) by liquefying. Hence **liqua'TION** n. [f. L *liquare* melt, cogn. w. LIQUOR, -ATE[3]]

li'que|fy̆, v.t. & i. Bring (solid or gas) or come into liquid condition. Hence or cogn. ~FA'CIENT (-āshe̥nt) a. & n., ~FAC-TION n., ~făctive, ~fiABLE, aa., ~fiER[1](1, 2) n. [f. F *liquéfier* f. L *liquefacere* (*liquēre* be LIQUID, -FY)]

liquĕs'cent, a. Becoming, apt to become, liquid. [f. L *liquescere* (prec., -ESCENT)]

liqueur' (-kūr), n. Strong alcoholic liquor sweetened & flavoured with aromatic substances & usu. drunk in small quantities; mixture of sugar & alcohol or wines used to flavour champagne, whence ~ v.t.; ~ *brandy*, of special quality for drinking as ~; ~-*glass*, very small for ~s; ~-*frame*, -*stand*, for holding ~-bottles. [F, = LIQUOR]

li'quid, a. & n. 1. (Substance that is) incompressible but offering no resistance to change of shape, neither solid nor gaseous, resembling water or oil in normal state, in fluid but not gaseous condition (~ *air*, reduced to ~ state by intense cold; ~ *fire*, projected from flame-thrower); watery. 2. Having the transparence, translucence, or brightness, of water or wine (~ *lustre, eyes, sky, air, blue*). 3. (Of sounds) flowing clear, fluent, pure, not grating or discordant, not guttural, vowel-like, (*blackbird's* ~ *notes*; *in his* ~ *Italian*; n., one of the letters *l, r*, & occas. *m, n*). 4. Not fixed, unstable, (*has very* ~ *convictions* or *principles*). 5. (Of assets, securities, etc.) easily convertible into cash. Hence or cogn. ~ITY (-ĭd[i]), ~NESS, nn., ~IZE(3) v.t., ~LY[2] adv.

li'quidate, [ME, f. L *liquidus* (*liquēre* be liquid cf. LIQUATE, LIQUOR)]

li'quid|āte, v.t. & i. Pay, clear off, (debt); put an end to, suppress, get rid of, (often by violent means); wind up, ascertain liabilities & apportion assets of, (company, firm), whence ~**ātor** n.; (intr., of company) have this done. Hence ~**A'TION** n. (*go into* ~*ation*, of company, have its affairs wound up, become bankrupt). [f. med. L *liquidare* make clear (LIQUID, -ATE³)]

li'quor (-ker), n., & v.t. & i. **1.** Liquid part of secretion or product of operation; liquid used as wash etc.; water used in brewing; liquid (usu. fermented or distilled) for drinking. (*malt* ~, ale, beer, porter, etc.; *spirituous* ~, spirits; DISGUISED *with* ~; *in* ~, *the worse for* ~, more or less drunk; *a* ~ or ~-*up*, sl., taking of ~ as refreshment); water in which food has been boiled; (pharmacy, pr. lik'wōr) solution of specified drug in water (~ *ammoniae* etc.). **2.** vb. Dress (leather, shoes) with grease or oil; steep (malt etc.) in water; (sl.) ~ *up* or ~, have a drink of alcoholic ~. [ME *licour(e)* f. OF *licour* f. L *liquorem* (*liquēre* see LIQUID, -OR)]

li'quorice (-ko-), **lic'orice**, n. (Black substance used in medicine & as sweetmeat made from) root of *Glycyrrhiza glabra*; the plant. [ME, f. AF *lycorys* f. LL *liquiritia* f. Gk *glukurrhiza* (*glukus* sweet, *rhiza* root)]

li'quorish (-ko-), a. Fond of, indicating fondness for, liquor. Hence ~**LY²** adv., ~**NESS** n. [misuse of LICKERISH]

lira (lēr'a), n. (pl. *lire* pr. -ā, ~*s*; abbr. *L.*). Italian & Turkish monetary unit. [It., f. L LIBRA]

lisle thread (līl thrĕd), n. Fine hard-twisted thread made orig. at Lisle (now Lille) in France.

lisp, v.i. & t., & n. **1.** Substitute one of the sounds of *th* for sibilants in speaking; (of child) speak with imperfect pronunciation; say with a ~ (often *out*); hence ~**'ing**LY² adv. **2.** n. ~*ing* pronunciation; rippling of waters, rustling of leaves. [OE *-wlispian* (f. *wlisp* adj., = OHG *lisp*), = MLG *wlispen*, LG, Du., OHG *lispen*]

liss'om(e), a. Lithe, supple, agile. Hence ~**NESS** n. [contr. of LITHE*some*]

list¹, n., & v.t. & i. **1.** Selvage or edge of cloth, usu. of different material, whence ~**'ING¹**(3) n.; such edges torn off & used as a material (~ *slippers*; *line edges of door with* ~, to keep out draughts; vb, fasten ~ round edges of, as *have* ~*ed my doors*). **2.** pl. Palisades enclosing tilting-ground; (fig.) scene of contest (*enter the* ~*s against*, challenge or accept challenge of, usu. to controversy). **3.** Roll or catalogue of names, of persons or things belonging to a class, of articles with prices, of things to be done, etc. (*active* ~, of officers in army or navy or air force liable to be called on for service; *free* ~, of persons to be admitted free to theatre etc., also of duty-free articles; ARMY, CIVIL, SICK, ~~); (vb) enter in a ~, (now rare or vulg.) go as soldier, enlist. [senses 1 & 2: OE *liste*, = MDu. *lijste*, OHG *līsta* (sense 2 infl. by OF *lisse*, of obsc. orig.); sense 3 f. F *liste* f. Gmc as in 1]

∥ **list²**, v.t. (arch.; 3 sing. pres. ~ or ~*eth*, past ~ or ~*ed*). Be pleasing to (*shall do what him* ~*eth*; *did as him* ~); desire, choose, (*to* do or abs.; *ye who* ~ *to hear*; *wind bloweth where it* ~*eth*). [OE *lystan*, OS *lustian*, OHG *lusten*, ON *lysta* f. Gmc *lustjan* f. *lustuz* LUST]

list³, n., & v.i. Lean(ing) over to one side (of ship, owing to leak, shifting cargo, subsidence, etc., cf. HEEL³; also of building, fence, etc.). [17th–18th c. also *lust*, of obsc. orig.; perh. transf. use of obs. *list* pleasure, inclination, f. prec.]

∥ **list⁴**, v.i. & t. (arch.). Listen, listen to. [OE *hlystan*, f. *hlyst* sense of hearing, = OS, ON *hlust* f. Gmc *hlustiz* f. *hlus-*; cogn. w. LOUD]

li'sten (-sn), v.i. & t. Make effort to hear something, hear person speaking with attention; give ear to or now usu. *to* (person or sound or story); yield *to* temptation or request; ~ *in*, tap telephonic communication, use wireless receiving set; ~*ing-post*, point near enemy's lines for detecting his movements by sound. Hence ~**ER¹** (-sn-) n. (*good* ~*er*, one who habitually ~s with interest or sympathy; (also) person receiving broadcast wireless programmes. [O Northumb. *lysna*, *hlysna*, MHG *lüsenen* f. Gmc *hlus-* (prec.)]

lis'terine, n. An antiseptic solution. [Lord *Lister* (d. 1912), -INE⁴; P]

lis'terīze, **-ise** (-īz), v.t. Treat (wound) on the antiseptic methods introduced by Lord Lister. So **listēr'IAN** a. [-IZE]

list'lĕss, a. Languid, indifferent, uninterested, disinclined for exertion. Hence ~**LY²** adv., ~**NESS** n. [ME, f. obs. *list* inclination (LIST²) + -LESS]

lit. See LIGHT³·⁵; ~ *up* (sl.), drunk.

lit'any, n. Series of petitions for use in church services or processions recited by clergy & responded to usu. in repeated formula(s) by people (*the L-*~, that contained in the Book of Common Prayer); ~*-desk*, *-stool*, at which reciter of ~ kneels. [ME, f. OF f. LL f. Gk *litaneia* prayer]

litchi (lēchē'), n. Fruit(-tree) orig. from China grown in Bengal. [f. Chin. *li-chi*]

-lite, suf. forming names of minerals; F, f. Gk *lithos* stone; usu. preceded by -o-.

lit'eracy, n. Ability to read & write. [LITERATE, -CY, after *illiteracy*]

∥ **līt'erae hūmānĭōr'ēs** (-z), n. (abbr. *Lit. Hūm.*). Polite letters, esp. as name of classical school or examination for B.A. degree at Oxford. [L]

lit'eral, a. & n. **1.** Of, in, expressed by, letter(s) of alphabet (~ *error*, also ~ as n., misprint.) **2.** Following the letter, text, or exact or original words (~ *translation*, *transcript*, etc.), whence ~ISM(4) n. **3.** Taking words in their usual or primary sense & applying the ordinary rules of grammar, without mysticism or allegory or metaphor; (~ *interpretation*; *I hear nothing in the* ~ *sense of the word*, with the ears as opp. other means of getting news), whence ~ISM(3), ~IST (2), nn.; (of persons) prosaic, matter-of-fact. **4.** So called without exaggeration (~ *decimation*; often incorrectly used, as *a* ~ *flood of pamphlets*). Hence ~ITY (-ăl²), ~NESS, nn., ~LY² adv. [ME, f. OF, or LL *litteralis* (LETTER, -AL)]

lit'eralize, -ise (-īz), v.t. Take (metaphor etc.) in literal sense. [-IZE]

literār'um dŏc'tŏr, n. Doctor of literature (as University degree). [L]

lit'erar|y, a. Of, constituting, occupied with, literature, polite learning, or books & written composition esp. of the kind valued for form (~*y history of a thing*, of its treatment in literature; ~*y property*, exclusive right of publication, books etc. subject to this; ~*y man*, man of LETTERS); (of word or idiom) uncolloquial, affected by writers. Hence ~iLY² adv., ~iNESS n. [f. L *litterarius* (LETTER, -ARY¹)]

lit'erate, a. & n. (Person) having some acquaintance with literature or (now usu.) able to read & write; ‖ man admitted to Anglican orders without university degree. [ME, f. L *litteratus* (LETTER, -ATE²)]

literāt'ī, n. pl. Men of letters, the learned class. [L, as prec.]

literāt'im, adv. Letter for letter, textually, literally. [med. L]

lit'erātor, n. Literary man. [L (LITERATE, -OR) elementary teacher, grammarian, sciolist]

lit'erature, n. Literary culture (arch.); literary production (*engaged in* ~), the literary profession (~ *was represented by* —); realm of letters, writings of country or period; writings whose value lies in beauty of form or emotional effect (LIGHT⁴ ~); *the* books treating *of* a subject; (colloq.)'printed matter. [ME, f. OF, or L *litteratura* (LITERATE, -URE)]

-lith, suf. repr. Gk *lithos* stone (*aerolith*, *monolith*); cf. -LITE.

lith'ārge (-j), n. Lead monoxide. [ME, f. OF *litarge* f. L f. Gk *litharguros* (*lithos* stone, *arguros* silver)]

lithe (-dh), a. Flexible, supple. Hence ~'NESS (-dhn-) n., ~'SOME (-dhs-) a. [OE *lithe*, OS *līthi*, OHG *lindi* f. Gmc **lin-*, cogn. w. L *lentus*]

lith'ia, n. Oxide of lithium; ~*-water*, used for gout. [changed f. earlier *lithion* f. Gk neut. of *litheios* (*lithos* stone) after *soda* etc.]

lith'ic, a. Of the stone or calculus; of stone. [f. Gk *lithikos* (prec., -IC)]

lith'ium, n. Metallic element resembling sodium. [LITHIA, -IUM]

lith(o)-, comb. form of Gk *lithos* stone, esp. in wds having ref. either to the treatment of stone in the bladder or kidneys, or to the use of stone in printing.

lith'ograph (-ahf), n., & v.t. **1.** Lithographic print. **2.** v.t. Print by lithography; write or engrave on stone. [prec., -GRAPH]

lithŏg'raphy, n. Drawing or writing on kind of yellow slaty limestone (*lithographic stone*) so that impressions in ink can be taken. So **lithŏg'RAPHER** n., **litho-GRAPH'IC** a. [LITHO-, -GRAPHY]

lithŏl'ogy, n. Science of the nature & composition of stones & rocks, whence **litholŏg'ical** a.; department of medical science dealing with calculus. [LITHO-, -LOGY]

lithŏntrip'tic, a. & n. (Medicine) that breaks up stone in bladder. [f. F *lithontriptique* f. Gk *lithōn thruptika* (drugs) comminutive of stones]

lith'ophyte, n. (Zool.) polyp whose substance is calcareous, as some corals; (bot.) plant that grows on stone. [LITHO-, Gk *phuton* plant (*phuō* grow)]

lithŏt'om|y, n. Operation of cutting for stone in bladder. Hence or cogn. **lithotŏm'IC(AL)** aa., ~IST(1) n., ~IZE(1) v.t. [f. LL f. Gk *lithotomia* (LITHO-, -TOMY)]

lithŏt'rit|y, n. Operation of crushing stone in bladder into small particles that can be passed through urethra. Hence ~IST(1) n., ~IZE(1) v.t. [f. LITHO- + L *terere trit-* rub, replacing LITHONTRIPTIC etc.]

Lithūān'ian, a. & n. (Language or native) of Lithuania. [-AN]

lit'ig|āte, v.i. & t. Go to law, be party to lawsuit; contest (point) at law, whence ~ABLE a. Hence ~ANT(1) n. & a., ~A'TION n. [f. L *litigare* (*lis litis* lawsuit), -ATE³]

liti'gious (-jus), a. Given to litigation, fond of going to law; disputable at law, offering matter for lawsuit; of lawsuits. Hence ~LY² adv., ~NESS n. [ME, f. OF *litigieux* or L *litigiosus* (*litigium* litigation, cf. prec.)]

lit'mus, n. Blue colouring-matter got from lichens that is turned red by acid & restored to blue by alkali; ~*-paper*, unsized & stained with ~ as test for acids. [ME, f. ONorw. *litmosi* f. ON *litr* (whence E dial. *lit*) dye +*mosi* moss]

līt'otēs (-z), n. Understatement often ironical (as ' *scoundrel* ' *is* rather *a rude word*), esp. the expressing of an affirmative by the negative of its contrary, as *no small* for *great*. [Gk (-ēs) f. *litos* plain, meagre]

litre (lēt'er), n. Unit of capacity in metric system, = cube of 1/10 metre, about 1¾ pints. [F, from 1793, f. *litron*, an obs. measure of capacity, f. med. L f. Gk *litra* pound]

litt'er, n., & v.t. & i. **1.** Vehicle containing couch shut in by curtains & carried on men's shoulders or by beasts; framework with couch for transporting sick &

wounded; straw, rushes, etc., as bedding esp. for animals; straw & dung of farm-yard; odds & ends, leavings, state of untidiness, disorderly accumulation of papers etc., whence ~Y² a.; the young brought forth at a birth. **2. vb.** Provide (horse etc.) with ~ as bed (usu. *down*); spread ~ or straw on (floor, stable; usu. *down*); make (place) untidy (of objects lying about, or of person *with* these or simply); scatter & leave lying; bring forth (whelps etc., or abs.). [ME, f. AF *litere* (OF *-iere*) f. Rom. **lectaria* (L *lectus* bed, *-ARY*¹)]

litterae, -rarum. See lite-.

littérateur (see Ap.), n. Literary man. [F]

lit′tle, a. (LESS, LESSER, LEAST; also *smaller, smallest*), n., & adv. (LESS, LEAST). **1.** Small (often with emotional implications not given by *small*, cf. GREAT), not great or big (the idiomatic antitheses are *great & ~, big & ~, great & small, large & small*, not *large & ~* nor *big & small*); (as distinctive epithet) of smaller or smallest size etc. (*the L~ Auk, L~ Malvern, the L~* BEAR¹, *the ~ finger* or *toe*). **2.** Young (*the ~ Joneses*, Jones's children; ~ *man* or *woman*, boy or girl, esp. as voc.; *his, her, its, our, ~ ones*, children or cubs etc.). **3.** As of a child, evoking tenderness, patronage, amusement, etc., (*her poor ~ efforts to please; we know his ~ ways; so that is your ~ game*, what you are hoping to do undetected). **4.** Short in stature, distance, or time (*a ~ man; the ~ people*, fairies; *will go a ~ way with you; wait a ~ while*). **5.** Trivial, unimportant, (*every ~ difficulty*); mean, paltry, contemptible, (*with the ~ cunning of ~ minds*). **6.** Not much (*gained ~ advantage from it*; often *but* or *very ~*). **7.** *A ~*, some though not much, even a small amount of, (prob. f. the n. use with ellipse of *of; give me a ~ butter; a ~ care would have prevented it*); (abs.) *the ~*, persons of ~ power or importance, what is ~; *in ~*, on a small scale; ~*-ease* (hist.), prison-cell too small to stand or lie full-length in; ~*-Englander, -dism*, (hist.; holder of) principle that Great Britain should contract her responsibilities for colonies & dependencies (opp. IMPERIALIST, *-ISM*); ‖ ~*-go* (rare), first examination for B.A. degree at Cambridge; ‖ ~ *Mary* (colloq.), the stomach; *L~ Masters*, group of 16th-c. German engravers, followers of Dürer, named from size of their prints. Hence ~NESS (*-ln-*) n. **8. n.** Not much, only a small amount, a mere trifle, (~ *or nothing*, hardly anything; *did not a ~ for the cause*, much; *got but, very, rather, ~ out of it; a ~ makes us laugh; gives me ~ of his company; did what ~ he could; the ~ of his work that remains*); a certain but no great amount (*knows a ~ of everything; a ~*, rather, somewhat; *not a ~*, extremely); (for a) short time or distance (*after, for,*

a ~; leave me here a ~; ~ by ~, by ~ & ~, by degrees). **9. adv.** To a small extent only (*I like him ~; ~ -known authors; is ~ more than a cento*); not at all (*he ~ knows, dreams*, etc.). [OE *lŷtel*, = OS *luttil*, OHG *luzzil* f. WG **luttil* f. Gmo **lut-*]

litt′oral, a. & n. **1.** Of, on, the shore. **2. n.** Region lying along the shore. [(1) f. L *litoralis* (*litus -oris* shore, *-AL*); (2) f. It. *-ale*, F *-al*]

lit′urgỹ (*-ter-*), n. Communion office of Eastern Church; form of public worship, set of formularies for this; *the* Book of Common Prayer; (Gk ant.) public office or duty performed gratuitously by rich Athenian. Hence litŭr′gICAL a., litŭr′giCALLY² adv. [f. LL f. Gk *leitourgia* public worship]

liv′able, a. (Of house, room, climate, etc.) fit to live in; (of life) worth living; companionable, easy to live with. Hence ~NESS n. [LIVE², *-ABLE*; cf. RELIABLE]

live¹, a. (attrib.). That is alive, living; (joc.) actual, not pretended or pictured or toy (*a real ~ burglar, steam-engine, mountain*); (of broadcast) heard or seen during the occurrence of an event, not a recording; full of power, energy, or importance, not obsolete or exhausted, (*make the question a ~ issue*); glowing (~ *embers*); (of shell, match, wire) unexploded, unkindled, charged with electricity; (of rock) not detached, seeming to form part of the earth's frame; (of wheels etc. in machinery) moving or imparting motion; ~*-bait*, living fish or worm as fishing-bait; ~ *load*, stress resulting from transverse motion of weights (as of locomotive crossing bridge); ~*-oak*, Amer. evergreen tree; ~*stock*, animals kept or dealt in for use or profit; ~ *wire* (fig.), highly energetic forceful person. [aphetic f. ALIVE]

live², v.i. & t. **1.** Be alive, have animal or vegetable life. **2.** Subsist (*up*)*on* (~ *on fruit*), depend (*up*)*on* for subsistence (~*s upon his wife, wife's earnings*, etc.; *living* WAGE¹); (fig.) sustain one's position or repute (*up*)*on* (~*s on his name*), get livelihood *by* one's wits etc. or *by doing*, (~ *& let ~*, condone others' failings to secure the same treatment for oneself; ~ *from* HAND¹ *to mouth*). **3.** Conduct oneself *honestly, viciously, like a saint*, etc. (~ *up to* one's *principles, faith*, etc., put them in practice). **4.** Arrange one's habits, expenditure, feeding, etc. (~ FAST⁴, *in* CLOVER; ~ *well*, on dainty food; ~ *on air*, (appear to) take no food; ~ *in a small way*, cheaply & quietly; ~ *a double life*, (esp.) sustain two different characters, act two different parts, in life; ~ *to* one-*self*, in isolation). **5.** (With cogn. obj.) spend, pass, experience, (~ *a virtuous life; he ~d what he narrated*). **6.** Wear down (scandal, prejudice, effect of past guilt) by blameless course of life. **7.** Express in one's life (~ *a lie*). **8.** Enjoy life intensely. **9.** Continue alive, have one's life prolonged, (*patient cannot* ~; ~*d to see his children's children*; ~ *& learn!*, way of greeting new fact; ~ *out the night*, remain alive through it); (of things) survive (*his memory* ~s), (of ship) escape destruction (*nothing could* ~ *afloat*); dwell (|| ~ *in, out*, of shop-assistants or domestic servants residing on premises or not), spend daytime in room (*room does not seem to be* ~*d in*). [OE *libban, lifian*, OS *libbian*, OHG *lebēn*, ON *lifa*, Goth. *liban* f. Gmc **libhǣ-* f. **libh-* LIFE]

live′lihōod (-vl-), n. Means of living, sustenance. [OE *liflād* (LIFE, *lād* course) assim. to obs. *livelihood* liveliness]

live′lŏng (-vl-), a. (poet., rhet.). Whole length of (*the* ~ *day, night, summer*, with implication of weariness or delight). [c. 1400 *lefe* (= LIEF) *longe*; in 16th c. assim. to LIVE[2]]

live′l|y̆ (-vl-), a. Lifelike, realistic, (*a* ~*y description*; *give a* ~*y idea of*); full of life, vigorous, energetic, brisk, vivid, interesting; (joc.) exciting, dangerous, difficult, (*police had a* ~*y time*; *press is making it* or *things* ~*y for* —); (of colour) bright; gay, vivacious; (of boat etc.) rising lightly to waves. Hence ~iLY[2] adv., ~iNESS n. (*a certain* ~*iness*, sl., some heavy gunfire). [OE *liflic* (LIFE, -LY[1])]

liv′en, v.t. & i. Brighten, cheer, (usu. *up*), [LIFE, -EN[6]]

liv′er[1], n. Large glandular organ in vertebrates secreting bile & purifying venous blood; (also ~*-complaint*) diseased state of ~, whence ~ISH[1] a.; (also ~*-colour*) dark reddish brown; flesh of some animals' ~ used as food; (arch.) ~ as seat of emotion (*hot* ~, passionate or amorous temperament; *white* or *lily* ~, cowardice, whence ~ED[2] a.); ~*-line*, one of lines of palm significant in palmistry; ~ *wing*, right wing of cooked fowl, under which ~ is tucked; ~*wort*, kinds of plant with ~-shaped parts or used in ~ disease. Hence ~LESS a. [OE *lifer* MDu. *lever*, OHG *lebara*, ON *lifr* f. Gmc **libh-*]

liv′er[2], n. One who lives in specified way (*clean, loose*, ~; *good* ~, virtuous person, also one given to *good* LIVING[1]). [-ER[1]]

Liverpŭd′lian, a. & n. (Inhabitant) of Liverpool. [joc. formation]

liv′er̄y̆[1], n. **1.** Provision of food or clothing served out to retainers etc. (hist.); allowance of provender for horses (*at* ~, of horse, kept for owner & fed & groomed for fixed charge). **2.** Distinctive clothes worn by member of city company or person's servant (*in, out of*, ~, of servant, so attired or in plain clothes; also fig., *birds in their winter* ~, *the* ~ *of grief, of other men's opinions*, etc.), whence **liv′eriED[1]** (-rĭd) a. **3.** Membership of city company (*take up* one's ~, become ~*man*). **4.** (law). Legal delivery of property (|| *sue* one's ~, bring suit as heir in court of wards to get possession), writ allowing

this. **5.** || ~ *company*, one of London City companies that had formerly distinctive costume; || ~ *fine*, payment for becoming member of ~ company; ~*man*, member of ~ company, keeper of or attendant in ~ stable; ~ *servant*, wearing ~; ~ *stable*, where horses are kept at ~ or let out for hire. [ME, f. AF *livere*, OF *livree* (*livrer* see DELIVER, -Y[4])]

liv′er̄y̆[2], a. Of the consistence or colour of liver; || (of soil) tenacious; having a disordered liver, feeling out of sorts, irritable. [-Y[2]]

liv′id, a. Of bluish leaden colour; discoloured as by bruise; || (colloq.) furiously angry. Hence or cogn. **livid′ITY** n., ~LY[2] adv. [f. F *livide* or L *lividus*]

liv′ing[1], n. In vbl senses; also or esp.: livelihood, maintenance, (*make* one's ~); || (eccl.) benefice; *good* ~, luxurious feeding; *plain* ~ *& high thinking*, frugal & philosophic life; ~*-room* (for general day use); ~*-space*, transl. of LEBENSRAUM; ~ *wage*, on which it is possible for worker to live in more comfort than on *subsistence wage*. [-ING[1]]

liv′ing[2], a. In vbl senses; esp.: contemporary, now existent, (*no man* ~ *could do better*; *the greatest* ~ *master of irony*; *the first of* ~ *artists*; *the* ~, those now alive; *in the land of the* ~, alive); (of likeness) exact, whence ~LY[2] adv.; ~ *water*, perennially flowing; ~ *rock, coal*, = LIVE[1]; ~ *language*, still in vernacular use; ~ *death*, state of hopeless misery; *within* ~ *memory*, that of persons still ~. [-ING[2]]

livre (lē′vr), n. Old French money of account (20 sous). [F, f. L LIBRA]

lixiv′i|āte, v.t. Separate (substance) into soluble & insoluble constituents by percolation of water. Hence ~A′TION n. [f. L *lixivius* made into lye (*lix*), -ATE[3]]

liz′ard, n. Kinds of reptile having usu. long body & tail, four legs, & scaly or granulated hide; fancy variety of canary. [ME, f. OF *lesard* f. L *lacertus* w. assim. to -ARD]

'll, contr. of WILL in *I'll, he'll, that'll*, etc.

lla′ma (lah-, lyah-), n. S.-Amer. ruminant allied to camel but smaller, humpless, & woolly-haired, used as beast of burden; (material made of) its wool. [Sp., prob. f. Peruvian]

lla′nō (lah-, lyah-), n. S.-Amer. treeless plain or steppe. Hence **llanero** (lyah-nār̄′ō) n., inhabitant of the ~s. [Sp., f. L *planus -num* PLAIN[1]]

Lloyd's (loidz), n. Incorporated society of underwriters in London; ~ *list*, newspaper devoted to maritime intelligence; ~ *register*, annual alphabetical list of ships assigned to various classes. [orig. 17th-c. coffee-house established by Edward *Lloyd*]

lō, int. (arch.). Look!, see!, behold! (freq. *lo and behold!*, as joc. introduction of surprising fact). [combining OE *lā* int. & ME *lo* = *loke*, LOOK[1]]

loach, n. Small edible freshwater fish. [ME, f. OF *loche*, of unkn. orig.]

load[1], n. What is (to be) carried, burden; amount usu. carried (*cart-*~ etc.) recognized unit in measure or weight of certain substances; material object or force acting as weight or clog, resistance of machinery worked to motive power, pressure of superstructure on arch etc.; (electr.) amount of current supplied by a dynamo or generating station at any given time (see PEAK[1]); burden of responsibility, care, grief, etc. (*take a ~ off* one's *mind*, relieve him of anxiety); (pl., colloq.) plenty, superabundance, heaps, lots, *of*; ~-*displacement*, -*draught*, of ship when laden; ~-*shedding*, temporary curtailment of supply of electricity to a specific area to prevent excessive ~ on generating plant; ~'*stone, lodestone,* magnetic oxide of iron, piece of it used as magnet, thing that attracts, (= way stone, see etym.); ~-(*water*)*line,* ship's flotation line when laden, Plimsoll's mark. [OE *lād* way, journey, conveyance, corresp. to OHG *leita,* ON *leith* way, course, f. Gmc **laidhō* (LEAD[2]); cf. LODE]

load[2], v.t. & i. Put load on or aboard (person, vehicle, ship, etc.), (of ship, vehicle, person responsible for these, or person) take load aboard etc. (often *up*); place (load, cargo) aboard ship, on vehicle, etc.; add weight to, be burden upon, oppress *with* (*stomach ~ed with food*), weight with lead (*a ~ed cane; ~ed dice,* so weighted as to fall with a certain face up), strain bearing-capacity of (*table ~ed with food*); adulterate with something to increase weight or (of wines) strength; supply or assail overwhelmingly *with* (*~ed her with gifts, praise, abuse; air ~ed with carbon*); charge (fire-arms; *am ~ed,* have my gun etc. charged); insert film in (camera); charge with some hidden implication (esp. in p.p., as *a ~ed question*); (Stock-Exch.) buy heavily of stock (*~ed up with,* having large amounts of in hand as security); (life-insurance) add extra charge or ~'ING[1] n. to (premium) for special reasons. [f. prec.]

load'er, n. In vbl senses; esp.: attendant loading sportsman's guns; loading- -machine; ~, gun loaded in specified way (*breech, muzzle, single, ~*), so -**load'ing**[2] a. [-ER[1]]

loaf[1], n. (pl. *loaves* pr. lōvz). Piece of bread baked alone or as separate or separable part of batch, usu. of some standard weight as 1lb., 2lb., or 4lb. (COTTAGE, *household, tinned,* ~, various shapes; QUARTERN ~; *brown* ~, of BROWN bread; *white* ~, of FIRSTS; *loaves & fishes,* personal profit as inducement to religious profession or public service, see *John* vi. 26; *half a* ~ *is better than no bread,* motto of compromise, opp. *all or nothing*); (sl.) head (*use* one's ~, use one's common sense); (also *sugar-*~) conical moulded mass of sugar (~ *sugar,* this as whole or cut into lumps); || solid roundish head of cabbage or lettuce, whence **loaved**[2] (-vd) a. [OE *hlāf,* OHG *leip* (G *laib*), ON *hleifr,* Goth. *hlaifs* f. Gmc **hlaibhaz*]

|| **loaf**[2], **loave,** v.t. (Of cabbage etc.) form a loaf or head. [f. prec.]

loaf[3], v.i. & t., & n. 1. Spend time idly; saunter; ~ (time) *away,* spend in ~ing; hence ~'ER[1] n. 2. n. ~ing (*going to have a, on the,* ~). [orig. unkn.]

loam, n. Paste of clay & water, composition of moistened clay & sand with chopped straw etc. used in making bricks, plastering, etc.; fertile soil chiefly of clay & sand with admixture of decayed vegetable matter, whence ~'Y[2] a. [OE *lām,* MDu. *leem,* OHG *leimo* f. Gmc **laim-,* f. **lai-, *li-* (LIME[1])]

loan, n., & v.t. 1. Thing, esp. sum of money, lent to be returned with or without interest; word, custom, etc., adopted by one people from another (so ~-*god,* -*myth, -word*); lending or being lent (*on* ~; *may I have the* ~ *of* —?, may I borrow it?); money contribution from individuals or public bodies to State expenses acknowledged as debt; arrangement or contract by which a government receives advances of money usu. for stipulated interest. 2. ~ *collection,* of pictures etc. lent by owners for exhibition; ~-*holder,* person holding debentures or other acknowledgements of ~, mortgagee; ~-*office,* for lending money to private borrowers, also for receiving subscriptions to government ~; ~-*society,* of periodical subscribers to fund from which members may have ~s; ~-*translation,* expression adopted by one language from another in more or less literally translated form (e.g. *reason of State* f. F *raison d'état, marriage of convenience* f. F *mariage de convenance*). 3. v.t. (now chiefly U.S.). Grant ~ of, whence ~'ABLE a., ~EE', ~'ER[1], nn. [ME *lan*(*e*) f. ON *lán,* = OE *lǣn* (see LEND), M.Du. *lēne,* OHG *lēhan,* f. Gmc **laihwn-,* cogn. w. Goth. *leihwan* lend]

loan[2], **loan'ing,** nn. (Sc.). Lane; open place where cows are milked. [ME by- -form of LANE; -ING[1]]

loath, lōth, a. (pred. only). Disinclined, reluctant, unwilling, (usu. *to* do or abs.; also *for* person *to* do, or *that*; *nothing* ~, quite willing or willingly); ~-*to-depart,* tune played as farewell. [OE *lāth,* OS *lēth,* OHG *leid,* ON *leithr* f. Gmc **laithaz*]

loathe (-dh), v.t. Regard with disgust, abominate, detest. Hence ~'ING[1](1) n., ~'ingLY[2] adv., (-dh-). [OE *lāthian* f. Gmc **laithjan* (prec.)]

loath'ly (-dh-), a. (Arch. & literary for) loathsome. Hence ~iNESS n. [OE *lāthlic* (LOATH, -LY[1])]

loath'some (-th-, -dh-), a. Exciting nausea or disgust, offensive to the senses, sickening, repulsive, odious. Hence ~LY[2] adv., ~NESS n. [ME, f. LOATH, -SOME]

loaves. See LOAF¹.

lob, v.i. & t. (-bb-), & n. **1.** Walk, run, or move, heavily or clumsily or slowly (often *along*); toss, bowl, or send, (ball) with slow or high-pitched motion. **2.** n. Ball bowled underhand at cricket or sent high in air at lawn tennis. [earlier: pendulous object; bumpkin; prob. of LG, Du. orig. (MLG *lobbe, lubbe,* Du. *lob, lobbe* seed-lobe, Du. *lobbes* bumpkin); cf. LUBBER]

lŏb'|āte, a. (nat. hist.). Having lobe(s). Hence ∼A'TION n. [LOBE, -ATE²]

lŏbb'ў, n., & v.t. & i. **1.** Porch, anteroom, entrance-hall, corridor; (in House of Commons etc.) large hall open to public used esp. for interviews between members & outsiders, (also *division* ∼) one of two corridors to which members retire to vote; *body of ∼ists. **2.** vb (chiefly U.S.). Influence (members of legislature), get (bill etc.) *through,* by ∼ interviews etc.; frequent ∼ of legislature, solicit members' votes, whence ∼IST(1) n. [f. med. L *lobia, 'lobium,* LODGE¹]

lōbe, n. Roundish & flattish projecting or pendulous part, often one of two or more such parts divided by fissure (so ∼ *of liver* or *lungs;* ∼s *of brain;* ∼ *of ear,* lower soft pendulous external part). Hence lŏb'AR¹ a. (esp. of the lungs, as *lobar pneumonia*). lŏbED²(-bd), ∼'LESS(-bl-), aa. [f. LL f. Gk *lobos* lobe, pod]

lŏbĕc'tomў, n. (med.). Excision of lobe of an organ, as of a lung, thyroid gland, etc. [-ECTOMY]

lobĕl'ia, n. Kinds of herbaceous plant with blue, scarlet, or purple flowers having deeply cleft corolla without spur. [M. de *Lobel* (d. 1616), -IA¹]

lŏblŏll'ў măn, boy, nn.(naut.). Surgeon's mate, attendant. [perh. f. dial. *lob* eat up noisily + dial. *lolly* soup]

lŏbŏt'omў, n. (med.). = LEUCOtomy. [f. LOBE, -O-, -TOMY]

lŏb'scouse (-ows), n. Sailor's dish of meat stewed with vegetables & ship's biscuit. [cf. LOBLOLLY; LG(G) *labskaus* said to be f. E]

lŏb'ster, n. Large marine stalk-eyed ten-tailed long-tailed edible crustacean with large claws formed by first pair of feet, bluish black before & scarlet after boiling; its flesh as food; ∼-*eyed,* with protruding eyes; ∼ *joint* (adaptable kind in pipe or tube); ∼-*pot,* basket in which ∼s are trapped. [OE *lopustre* corrupt. of L *locusta* crustacean, LOCUST]

lŏb'ūl|e, n. Small lobe. Hence ∼AR¹ a. [LOBE, -ULE]

lŏb'worm (-wẽrm), n. ·Large earthworm used as fishing-bait; marine worm (also *lug*) similarly used. [f. obs. *lob* n., see LOB]

lōcal'¹, lŏcale', (-ahl), n. Scene or locality of operations or events. [F (-*l*), abs. use of adj. = foll.; -*e* is E respelling to indicate stress, cf. MORALE]

lōc'al², a. & n. **1.** In regard to place (∼ *habitation,* position in space as test of thing's material existence; *London is a* ∼ *name;* ∼ *adverb*). **2.** Belonging to, existing in, or peculiar to certain place(s) (∼ *time,* reckoned from sun's transit over place's meridian; *the* ∼ *lawyer;* globe-*flower is very* ∼, not generally distributed; ∼ *government,* administration of town etc. by inhabitants' representatives, ‖ *L*∼ *Government Board,* State department later absorbed by MINISTRY *of Health;* ‖∼ *examination,* held in various places under university board & giving certificates to boys & girls; ∼ *preacher,* Methodist layman authorized to preach in his own circuit; ∼ *option, veto,* system by which inhabitants of district may prohibit sale of liquor in it; ∼ *colour,* details characteristic of the scene or time represented in novel or other literary work inserted to give actuality, & see below). **3.** Affecting, of, a part & not the whole (∼ *disease, pain, remedy;* ∼ *colour* in picture, that of separate objects apart from general colour-scheme, & see above). **4.** (math.). Of a locus. **5.** ‖ (Post.; written on cover of letter as warning to P.O. officials) for delivery in this town or district. Hence ∼LY² adv. **6.** n. Inhabitant of, professional man practising in, particular district; ∼ *preacher;* (item of) ∼ *news* in newspaper; postage-stamp current in limited district; train serving stations of district; ‖ (colloq.) the ∼ public house; ‖ (pl.) ∼ *examination*(s). [ME, f. OF, f. LL *localis* (*locus* place, -AL)]

lōc'alism, n. Attachment to a place; limitation of ideas etc. resulting; favouring of what is local; a local idiom, custom, etc. [-ISM]

local'itў, n. Thing's position, place where it is; site or scene of something; faculty of remembering & recognizing places, finding one's way, etc. [f. F *localité* or LL *localitas* (LOCAL², -TY)]

lōc'alīz|e, -is|e (-īz), v.t. Invest with the characteristics of a particular place; restrict to particular place; attach to districts, decentralize; concentrate (attention) *upon;* (rare) = LOCATE. Hence ∼ABLE a., ∼A'TION n. [-IZE]

locāte', v.t. *Establish in a place, (pass.) *be situated; state locality of; discover exact place of (∼ *the enemy's camp*). Hence loca'TION n., (also, cinemat.) place outside studio where (part of) picture is filmed (esp. *on location*). [f. L *locare* (*locus* place), -ATE³]

lōc'ative, a. & n. (gram.). (Case) denoting place where. [prec., -IVE, after *vocative*]

‖ **loch** (lŏχ), n. Scottish lake; an arm of the sea, esp. when narrow or partially landlocked. [Gael.]

lŏck¹, n. Portion of fairly long hair that hangs together, tress, (pl.) hair of head; tuft of wool or cotton. Hence ∼ED²(kt)

a. [OE *loc*, OS *lok*, OHG *loc*, ON *lokkr*, f. Gmc **lokkaz*]

lŏck², n. 1. Appliance for fastening door, lid, etc., with bolt that requires key of particular shape to work (*under ~ & key*, locked up); appliance to keep wheel from revolving or slewing. **2.** Mechanism for exploding charge of gun (*~, stock, & barrel*, whole of thing, completely). **3.** Confined section of canal at point where level changes for raising & lowering boats by use of sluiced gates. **4.** Ante-chamber to chamber in which engineering work is done in compressed air. **5.** Interlocking, e.g. block or jam of vehicles in street. **6.** Extent to which fore-wheel's can be made to cross hind-wheel's plane. **7.** (Also *L~Hospital*) hospital for venereal disease. **8.** *~'fast*, secured with ~; *~-keeper*, **•** *~sman*; *~'man*, coroner's summoner in I. of Man; *~s'man*, keeper of canal ~; *~'smith*, maker & mender of ~s. *~'LESS a.* [OE *loc*, corresp. to OS *lok*, OHG *loh* hole, ON *lok* lid, f. Gmc **lokam*]

lŏck³, v.t. & i. 1. Fasten (door, box, etc.) with lock, shut *up* (house etc.) by fastening doors thus, (of door etc.) admit of being so fastened, have a lock; shut (person, thing) *up, in,* or *into*; *~ the stable door after the horse has been stolen*, take precautions too late. **2.** (Of land, hills, etc.) hem in (usu. in pass.). **3.** (fig.) Store (*up* or *away*) inaccessibly (*facts ~ed up in hieroglyphics*; *capital ~ed up in land*); imprison (*senses ~ed in sleep*). **4.** Keep (person) *out* by *~*ing door (esp. of employer coercing workmen by refusing them work; *~-out n.*, this procedure, cf. STRIKE). **5.** Bring or come into rigidly fixed position, engage, (make) catch, fasten by interlacing or fitting of corresponding parts, entangle; (p.p.) joined in hostile or other embrace. **6.** (mil.). (Of rear rank) march so close to front rank that feet overlap. **7.** (Of vehicle or wheels) (have fore-wheels that) admit of being slewed into different planes from those of hind-wheels. **8.** Provide (canal etc.) with locks; convey (boat) *up* or *down* through lock; go through lock. **9.** *~-chain*, for *~*ing wheels of vehicle; *~-jaw, ~ed-jaw*, (pop. name for) trismus, variety of tetanus, tonic spasm of muscles of mastication causing jaws to remain rigidly closed; *~-nut*, extra nut screwed over another to prevent its starting; *~-spring*, closing watch-case; *~-stitch*, sewing-machine stitch by which two threads are firmly *~*ed together; *~-up*, (time of) *~*ing up school etc. for night, unrealizable state of invested capital or amount of capital *~*ed up, house or room for temporary detention of prisoners, (attrib.) that can be *~*ed up (*~-up garage*). [ME, f. prec.]

lŏck'age, n. Amount of rise or fall effected by canal locks; toll for use of lock; use or number of locks. [-AGE]

lŏck'er, n. In vbl senses; also; small cup-board, esp. one of many reserved each for individual's use in public room, e.g. cricket pavilion or schoolroom; (naut.) chest or compartment for clothes, stores, ammunition, etc. (*not a shot in the ~*, no money in one's pocket; DAVY JONES'S LOCKER). [-ER¹]

lŏck'et, n. Metal plate or band on scabbard; small gold or silver case holding portrait, lock of hair, etc., & usu. hung from neck. [f. OF *loquet* dim. of *loc* latch f. WG **lok* LOCK², -ET¹]

Lŏck'|ian, a. Of John Locke (d. 1704) or his philosophy or followers. So *~*IST(2) n. [-IAN]

lŏc'ō¹, n. Locomotive engine. [abbr.]

lŏc'ō², n. Poisonous leguminous plant found in U.S. (*~-disease*, brain disease affecting cattle eating ~). Hence *•~, •~-*ED²(-ŏd), aa. (sl.), crazy. [Sp., = insane]

lŏc'ō citāt'ō, adv. (abbr. *loc. cit.* or *l.c.*), In the passage already quoted. [L]

lōcomō'tion, n. (Power of) motion from place to place; travel, way (esp. artificial) of travelling. [17th c., f. L *loco* abl. of *locus* place + *motio* MOTION; suggested by the scholastic phr. *in loco moveri* move in space]

lŏc'omōtive, a. & n. 1. Of locomotion (*~ faculty, power*), (joc.) of travel (*in these ~ days*); having power of or given to locomotion, not stationary, (*the ~ bivalves*; *a ~ person*, joc., constantly travelling; *~ engine*, that goes from place to place by its own power, esp. steam-engine for drawing train along rails); effecting locomotion (*the ~ organs*). **2. n. ~** engine; *~* animal. [(1) 17th c. as prec.; see -IVE; (2) n.f. adj., short for *~ engine*]

lŏc'omōtor, n. & a. 1. Locomotive person or thing. **2.** adj. Of locomotion (*~* ATAXY). [as prec., MOTOR]

lŏc'omōtorỹ, a. Of, having, locomotion. [as prec., MOTORY]

lŏc'ŭl|us, n. (zool., anat., bot.; pl. *~i*). One of a number of small separate cavities. Hence *~*AR¹ **a.** [L, dim. of LOCUS]

lŏc'um tĕn'ĕns (-z; also colloq. **lŏc'um**), **n.** Deputy acting esp. for clergyman or doctor. Hence **lŏc'um-tĕn'ency** n. [med. L, (one) holding place TENANT, (foll.)]

lŏc'us, n. (pl. *-ci* pr. *-sī*). Locality or exact place of something; (math.) curve etc. made by all points satisfying particular equation of relation between co-ordinates, or by point, line, or surface, moving according to mathematically defined conditions; *~ class'icus*, best known or most authoritative passage on a subject; *~ in quō*, scene of event; *~ poenitĕn'tiae* (-shiē), opportunity allowed for receding until decisive step has been taken; *~ stăn'dī*, recognized position, right to intervene, appear in court, etc. [L, = place]

lŏc'ust, n. Kinds of African & Asian winged edible insect migrating in swarms

& consuming vegetation of districts; person of devouring or destructive propensities; fruit of carob-tree; cassia pod; (also ~-*tree*) kinds of tree, esp. carob & false acacia; ~-*bird*, -*eater*, kinds of bird feeding on ~s. [ME, f. L *locusta* lobster, locust]

locu″tion, n. Style of speech; word or phrase considered in regard to style, idiom, (*a barbarous* ~; *to use the Greek* ~). [ME, f. L *locutio* (*loqui locut*- speak, -ION)]

lŏc′utŏrў, n. Parlour or conversation--room in monastery; grille for interviews between inmates of monastery & outsiders. [f. LL *locutorium* (prec., -ORY)]

lŏde, n. ‖ Watercourse, open drain in fens; vein of metal ore; ~'*star, loadstar,* star that is steered by, esp. the pole-star, (fig.) guiding principle, object of pursuit; ~'*stone* see LOAD[1] *stone*. [var. of LOAD[1]]

lŏdge[1], n. 1. Small house (arch.). 2. Cottage at gates of park or grounds of large house, occupied by gardener or other servant; house (e.g. in Scottish Highlands) occupied in the hunting or shooting season. 3. Porter's room at gate of college, factory, or house of chambers or flats. 4. (Freemasonry etc.) (place of meeting for) members of branch; *grand* ~, governing body of freemasons & societies imitating them. 5. Residence of head of college at Cambridge, cf. LODGINGS. 6. Beaver's or otter's lair. 7. N.-Amer. Indian's tent or wigwam. [ME *log(g)e* f. OF *loge* f. Rom. *lobia, med. L *laubia*, *lobia* (LOBBY), f. Gmc *laubja f. *laubam LEAF]

lŏdge[2], v.t. & i. 1. Provide with sleeping--quarters; receive as guest or inmate; establish as resident *in* house or room(s), (pass.) be *well, ill*, etc., accommodated in regard to house-room. 2. Serve as habitation for, contain, (pass.) be contained *in*. 3. Leave *in* place or *with* person for security. 4. Deposit in court or with official a formal statement of (complaint, information); (pop.) allege (objection etc.). 5. Place (power etc.) *in, with, in the hands of,* (person). 6. (Of wind) lay (crops) flat. 7. (Make, let) stick or remain in place without falling or going further (~*d bullet, bullet* ~*d, in his brain; tide* ~*s mud in the cavities*). 8. Reside, be situated; ‖ be inmate paying for accommodation in another's house, whence **lŏdg′ER**[1] n. (~*r franchise,* right to vote at election of M.P. enjoyed by a class of ~rs before the 1918 extension). [ME, f. OF *logier* (prec.)]

lŏdg′ing, n. In vbl senses; esp.: accommodation in hired rooms; dwelling-place, abode, (pl.) room(s) hired elsewhere than in hotel for residing in, residence of head of college at Oxford (cf. LODGE[1]); ~-*house,* in which ~s are let (‖ *common* ~ -*house,* usu. one with dormitory in which bed can be had for the night); ~ *turn,* spell of

duty in railway service during which a train crew sleeps away from home for a night. [ME; -ING[1]]

lŏdge′ment, -gment, (-jm-), n. (Mil.) temporary defensive work on captured part of enemy's works; stable position gained, foothold, (*make, effect, a* ~); (law) deposit(ing) of money; accumulation of matter intercepted in fall or transit. [f. F *logement* (prec., -MENT)]

lŏ′ĕss, n. Deposit of fine yellowish-grey loam in Rhine & other river valleys. [G *löss*]

loft (law-, lŏ-), n., & v.t. 1. Attic; room over stable; pigeon-house; flock of pigeons; gallery in church or hall; (golf) backward slope in club-head,~ing stroke. 2. v.t. Hit (golf-ball) high up, clear (obstacle) thus; keep (pigeons) in ~. [late OE *loft* f. ON *loft* air, sky, upper room, cogn. w. OE *lyft*; see LIFT]

lof′ter (law-, lŏ-), n. Golf-club for lofting. [-ER[1]]

lof′t|y̆ (law-, lŏ-), a. Of imposing height, towering, soaring, (~*y mountain, flight, stature;* not of persons); haughty, consciously superior or dignified, (~*y contempt, good humour*); exalted, distinguished, high-flying, high-flown, elevated, sublime, grandiose. Hence ~ĭLY² adv., ~ĭNESS n. [-Y²]

lŏg[1], n., & v.t. (-gg-). 1. Unhewn piece of felled tree or similar rough mass of wood (*in the* ~, unhewn; *float, lie, fall, like a* ~, in helpless or stunned state; *roll my* ~ *& I'll roll yours,* applied to mutual help, esp. to unprincipled political combinations & puffing of each other's works by author--reviewers, whence ~'*röll* v.i., ~'*röll*-ING[1, 2] n. & a.; *King Log.* fainéant ruler, w. ref. to fable of Jupiter & the frogs, cf. STORK). 2. Float attached to line wound on reel for gauging speed of ship, other apparatus for same purpose, (*heave, throw, the* ~, use this; *sail by the* ~, calculate ship's position by it); = ~-book. 3. ‖ Table by which journeyman-tailor's work-time is assessed. 4. ~-*board,* on which entries are made for transcription into ~-*book,* book with permanent record daily made of all events occurring in ship's voyage including rate of progress shown by ~, (also) traveller's diary etc.; ~ *cabin,* hut built of ~s; ~-*line,* to which float of ship's ~ is attached; ~'*wood,* (wood of) Amer. tree used in dyeing. 5. v.t. Cut into ~s; enter (distance made etc.) in ship's ~-*book,* (of ship) make (distance); enter (seaman's name with offence committed) in ~-*book,* fine (offender). [ME *logge,* of obsc. orig.; cf. contemporary CLOG]

lŏg[2], = LOGARITHM of (prefixed to number or algebraic symbol).

lŏg′anbĕrrў, n. Fruit got by cross between raspberry & blackberry. [J. H. *Logan,* of California]

lŏg′an(-stōne), n. Poised heavy stone

rocking at a touch. [= *logging* (dial. *log* to rock)]

logaoed'ic (-aŏ-), a. & n. (Line) in metre composed of dactyls & trochees. [f. LL f. Gk *logaoidikos* combining prose & poetry (*logos* speech, *aoidē* song, -IC)]

log'arithm, n. One of a class of arithmetical functions tabulated for use in abridging calculation & enabling computer to substitute addition & subtraction for multiplication & division, & the latter two for involution & evolution; index of power to which fixed number (the *base*) must be raised to produce given number (*the ~ of 1,000 is 3*; *common ~s*, whose base is 10). Hence lŏgarith'mic a., lŏgarith'mIcALLY adv. [f. Gk *logos* reckoning, ratio, *arithmos* number]

loge (lōzh), n. Box in theatre etc. [F]

-loger, suf. repr. L *-logus* or Gk *-logos*. *Astrologer*, the oldest wd of the type, may be either f. L *astrologus* + -ER¹ (afterwards a common type of formation) or f. *astro-logy* + -ER¹ (cf. -GRAPHER). As living suf., ~ was used to form personal nn. corresp. to wds in -LOGY, but is now superseded by -LOGIST.

logg'erhead (-gerhĕd), n. 1. Blockhead, fool, (arch.; *We three ~s be*, inscription under two wooden heads on inn-sign). 2. Iron instrument with ball at end heated for melting pitch etc.; post built into boat for catching turn of rope to; kinds of large-headed turtle & bird. 3. *At ~s* (*with*), disagreeing or disputing (with), (prob. f. notion of trying whose head is harder). [prob. f. dial. *logger* block of wood for hobbling horse]

logg'ia (-jya), n. (pl. ~s or *loggie* pr. -ă). Open-sided gallery or arcade. [It., = LODGE]

lo'gic, n. Science of reasoning, proof, thinking, or inference; particular scheme of or treatise on this; chain of reasoning, correct or incorrect use of argument, ability in argument, arguments (CHOP⁶ ~; *argues with great learning & ~*; *is not governed by ~*); (with purposely perverted sense) converting-power, compulsion, (*the ~ of events, facts, necessity, war*, etc.). So logi'CIAN (-ĭshn) n. [ME, f. OF *logique* f. LL *logica*, -e sing. (also L (Cic.) *logica* pl. = Gk *ta logika*) f. Gk *logikē* (*tekhnē* art) of reason f. LOGOS, -IC(2)]

-logic, -logical, suff. orig. repr. Gk adjj. in *-logikos* (thr. F & L), derived f. adjj. & nn. in *-logos*, *-logon*, wh. have derivative nn. in *-logia* -LOGY. Such adjj. are commonly apprehended as if f. *-logy* + -IC. Hence mod. formations in *-logy* may always have correl. adjj. in *-logical* (rarely *-logic*), & nn. in *-logist* (occas. -LOGER).

lo'gical, a. Of logic or formal argument; not contravening the laws of thought, correctly reasoned; deducible, defensible on ground of consistency, reasonably to be believed or done; capable of correct reasoning. Hence ~ITY (-ăl⁴) n., ~LY³ adv. [f. obs. F, or med. L *logicalis* (prec., -AL)]

lo'gie (-gĭ), n. Zinc ornament looking like jewel used in theatres. [D. *Logie*, inventor]

lŏg'iŏn (-g-), n. (pl. -*ia*). Saying of Christ, not recorded in Gospels but preserved elsewhere. [Gk, = oracle (LOGOS)]

-logist, suf. forming nn. meaning *one versed in -logy*, f. -LOGY, -IST.

logis'tics, n. pl. Art of moving & quartering troops (cf. STRATEGY, TACTICS), & supplying & maintaining a fleet. So logis'tic a. [f. F *logistique* (*loger* LODGE², -IC)]

lŏg'ogram, n. Sign or character representing a word in shorthand. [LOGOS, -GRAM]

lŏg'ograph (-ahf), n. = prec.; = LOGOTYPE. [LOGOS, -GRAPH]

logŏg'rapher, n. (Gk ant.). One of the Greek prose historians before Herodotus; ancient-Greek professional speech-writer for law courts. [f. LL f. Gk *logographos* (LOGOS, -GRAPHER)]

lŏg'ogriph, n. Kind of anagrammatic word-puzzle. [f. F *logogriphe* (LOGOS, Gk *griphos* riddle)]

logŏm'achy (-k-), n. (literary). Dispute about words, controversy turning on merely verbal points. [f. Gk *logomakhia* (LOGOS, *-makhia* -fighting)]

lŏg'ŏs, n. (no pl.). The Word or Second Person of the Trinity. [Gk, = word, reason, f. *legō* speak, used in mystic sense by Hellenistic & Neo-Platonist philosophers & in St John]

lŏg'otype, n. Word, or more letters than one, cast in one piece but not as ligature, for use in printing. [prec., TYPE]

-logue (lŏg), suf. repr. Gk *-logos*, *-logon*, chiefly in wds f. F (*cata~*, *dia~*). Personal nn. = *one skilled in* -LOGY (*ideo~*) are now rare, -LOGER or -LOGIST being usu. preferred.

-logy, suf. f. Gk *-logia* (in early instances, thr. F *-logie* f. med. L *-logia*). 1. In most wds *-log-* is the *o* form of Gk *leg-* speak, *-logia* indicating the character, action, or branch of knowledge, of a person (Gk *-logos* n. or a.) who speaks in a certain way (*brachy~*, *tauto~*, *eu~*) or treats of a certain subject (*theo~*, *astro~*). E compounds of the latter kind, in which first component is alw. n., take *-o-* with some exceptions (*genea~*, *minera~*). *Socio~*, *termino~*, are hybrids. 2. In a few wds *-log-* is the Gk *logos* discourse (*tri~*, *tetra~*).

loin, n. (Pl.) part of body on both sides of spine between false ribs & hip-bones (*gird up one's ~s*, prepare for journey or effort; *fruit, child,* etc., *of, sprung from,* etc., one's *~s*, one's begotten offspring); joint of meat that includes the ~ vertebrae; *~-cloth*, worn for decency & fastened round *~s*. Hence ~ED² (-nd) a. [ME, f. OF *loigne* f. Rom. *lumbea (fem. of **-eus* adj.) f. L *lumbus*]

loir (loi*'er*), n. The fat dormouse. [F. f. pop. L *lere, f. L *glirem* nom. *glis*]

loit'er, v.i. & t. Linger on the way, hang about; travel indolently & with frequent pauses; pass (time etc.) *away* in ~ing. Hence ~ER⁴ n., ~ING̅LY³ adv. [ME, f. MDu. *loteren* wag about]

lŏll, v.t. & i. Hang (one's tongue) *out*, (of tongue) hang (usu. *out*); stand, sit, or recline, in lazy attitude; let (one's head or limbs) rest lazily on something. Hence ~'ING̅LY² adv. [14th c.; prob. imit.]

Lŏll'ard, n. One of the 14th-c. heretics who followed Wyclif or held opinions like his. Hence ~ISM(3) n. [f. MDu. *lollaerd* (*lollen* mumble, -ARD)]

lŏllipŏp, n. (usu. pl.). Sweetmeat(s), sugar-plum(s). [orig. unkn.; cf. *lolly* (north. dial.) tongue]

lŏll'op, v.i. (colloq.). Flop about; move or proceed in a lounging or ungainly way. [extension of LOLL]

lŏll'y̆, n. (Colloq.) lollipop; (sl.) money. [abbr.]

Lom'bard (lŭ-, lŏ-), n. & a. **1.** One of the Germanic 6th-c. conquerors of Italy; native of Lombardy. **2.** adj. Of the ~s or Lombardy, Lombardic; ~ *street*, a London street formerly occupied by ~ bankers, & still containing many of chief London banks, (transf.) the money market, financiers as a body (~ *Street to a china orange*, virtual certainty, long odds). [ME, f. OF *lombard* or MDu. *-baerl*, f. It. *Lombardo* f. LL *Longobardus*, L *Lango-*, f. Gmc *Langobardhaz (LONG¹, L *Bardi* name of the people)]

Lŏmba̅rd'ic, a. Of the Lombards or Lombardy (esp. of N.-Ital. 7th–13th-c. architecture & 15th–16th-c. painting). [f. med. L *Lombardicus* (prec., -IC)]

lŏm'ĕnt, n. (bot.). Kind of pod that breaks up when mature into one-seeded joints. Hence ~A'CEOUS (-āshᵘs) a. [f. L *lomentum* bean-meal (orig. cosmetic) f. *lo-*, *lavare*, wash, -MENT]

Lo'ndon (lŭ-), attrib. a. ~ *clay*, geological formation in lower division of eocene tertiary in S.-E. England; ~ *ivy*, fog or smoke of ~; ~ *particular*, colloq., kind of fog peculiar to ~: ~ *pride*, kind of saxifrage; ~ *smoke*, dull grey colour. So ~ER¹(4), ~ISM(4), nn., ~IZE(3) v.t.

lo̅ne, attrib. a. Solitary, companionless, unfrequented, uninhabited, lonely, (poet. or rhet., exc. in ~ *hand*, hand played or player playing against the rest at quadrille & euchre, also fig.); feeling or making feel lonely, whence ~'SOME (-ns-) a., ~'somELY² adv., ~'someNESS n.; (of woman) single or widowed. [ME; aphetic f. ALONE]

lo̅ne'l|y̆ (-nl-), a. Solitary, companionless, isolated; unfrequented. Hence ~INESS n. [-LY¹]

lo̅ng¹, a. & n. **1.** Measuring much from end to end in space or time (~ *line*, *distance*; *journey*; ~ *life*, whence ~'lIVED²

(-vd') a.; *make a ~ arm*, reach out for something esp. at table; *has a ~ arm*, can make his power felt far; ~ *face*, dismal; ~ *head*, of more than average length, (fig.) shrewdness or foresight, whence ~'-head'ED² a., ~'head'ĕdNESS n., (-hĕd-), lit. & fig.; *make a ~ nose*, cock a SNOOK; ~ *tongue*, loquacity; *two* etc. ~ *miles* etc., more than that; *by a ~* CHALK¹; *grievance* etc. *of ~ standing*, not recent); ¦(prefixed to name; colloq.) tall (*L~ Tom*, gun of great length & range). **2.** Far-reaching, acting at a distance, involving great interval or difference, (~ *sight*, that sees distant but not near objects, (fig.) penetration, whence ~'sight'ED² a., ~'sight'ĕdNESS n., (-sit-), lit. & fig.; *little* PITCHERS *have ~ ears*; *take ~ views*, consider remote effects; ~ *odds* in betting, very uneven; ~ *bowls*, fighting at ~ range, opp. *close quarters*; ~ *date*, distant date for maturing of bill etc.; ~ *waist* in dress, made far down). **3.** (Usu. appended to measurement) having specified length or duration (*tail 6 in. ~*; *vacation is two months ~*; *as* BROAD *as it is ~*). **4.** Of elongated shape; remarkable for or distinguished by or concerned with length or duration (~ *clay*, churchwarden pipe; ~ DIVISION; ~ *drink*, one served in tall glass; ~ *ears*, stupidity as of ass, whence ~'earED² (-ērd') a.; ~ *finger*, the second; ~ *jump*, measured along ground, opp. *high jump*; ~ *measure*, miles, yards, inches, etc.; ~ *metre*, hymn-stanza of four eight-syllable lines; *L~ Parliament*, that elected 1640 & dissolved 1660; ~ PRIMER; ~ *robe*, legal attire, esp. *gentlemen of the ~ robe*, lawyers; *in the ~ run*, in the end after vicissitudes; ‖ ~ *service*, system of military etc. enlistment for many e.g. 12 years; ‖ ~ *vacation*, summer vacation of law-courts & universities; ~ *wind*, capacity for running far without rest, or fig. for talking or writing at tedious length, whence ~'wind'ED² a., ~-wind'ĕdNESS n.). **5.** Expressed by many ciphers or consisting of many individuals (~ *figure* or *price*, heavy cost; ~ *family*, of many children; ~ *bill*, of many items; ~ *suit*, many cards of one suit in a hand, also, colloq., thing at which one excels). **6.** Lengthy, prolix, tedious. **7.** Of more than the usual numerical amount (~ DOZEN, HUNDRED). **8.** Lasting, going far back or forward, (*a ~ custom, memory, farewell*). **9.** (phonet., pros.). (Of vowel or syllable) having the greater of the two recognized durations, (also, of vowel) having the pronunciation shown in its name (e.g., *pale* & *lucre* have ~, *pat* & *put* or *but* short a & u). **10.** ~-*bill*, kinds of bird, esp. snipe; ~'*boat*, sailing-ship's largest boat (cf. LAUNCH²); ~-*bow*, drawn by hand & discharging ~ feathered arrow (cf. CROSS-BOW), *draw the ~-bow*, tell exaggerated or invented stories; ~-*butt*, cue for reaching billiard-ball beyond range of half-butt; ~ *cloth*, kind of calico made in ~ pieces; ~-*clothes*, & arch. -*coats*, clothes of baby in arms; ~-*distance*, (of weather forecast) made several days in advance; ~ *field*, ~ off or on (see below), also part of ground behind bowler; ‖~ FIRM¹; ~'*hand*, ordinary writing (opp. SHORTHAND; ~ *hop*, short-pitched ball in cricket; (*daddy*-) ~-*legs*, crane-fly; ~ *off, on*, man fielding at bowler's left, right, rear; ~ *pig*, sailors' transl. of cannibals' name for human flesh; ‖~ *pull*, over-measure given by public-houses to attract custom; ~'*shanks*, stilt or ~-*legged* plover; ~'*stop*, man fielding straight behind wicket-keeper, (vb) field there; ~ *wave* (radio), having a wave-length of (about) 800 metres or more; hence ~'ISH¹(2) a., ~'WAYS, ~'WISE, (-z), advv. 11. n. ~ Interval or period (*shall see you before* ~; *shall not be away for* ~; *will not take* ~; *it is* ~ *since I saw him*; so al ~*est*, to mention the most distant date possible); recital at length (*the* ~ *& the short of it*, all that can or need be said, the total upshot); ~ syllable (~*s & shorts*, verse esp. classical); (archit.) ~*s & shorts*, ~ & short blocks placed alternately; ‖~ vacation. [OE, OS, OHG *lang*, ON *langr*, Goth. *laggs* f. Gmc *langaz* cogn. w. L *longus*]

long³, adv. (~*er*, ~*est*, pr. -ngg-). For a long time (*have* ~ *thought so*; *nor wants that little* ~; *so* or *as* ~ *as*, transf., provided that, if only; *be* ~ *doing*, &, prob. by confusion of the adv. w. the adj., *in doing*, take a long time, be slow, to do, as *he was* ~ *finding it out*, *the chance was* ~ *in coming*; *not be* ~ *for this world*, have short time to live; ~-*liver*, one who lives ~); by a long time (~ *before, after, since, ago*); (appended to nn. of duration) throughout specified time (*all day* ~, *his life* ~); (comp., with *no, any, much*, etc.) after implied point of time (*shall not wait any* ~*er*; *no* ~*er*, not henceforth as formerly); ~-*ago* a. & n., (belonging to) the distant past; ~-*drawn*(-*out*), unduly prolonged; ~-*standing*, that has ~ existed; ~-*suffering* n. & a., bearing provocation patiently. [OE *lange* (prec.)]

long³, v.i. Yearn, wish vehemently, *for* thing or *to* do. Hence ~'ING¹(1)n., ~'INGLY² adv. [OE *langian* seem LONG¹ to]

-**long**, suf., f. LONG¹, has ousted -LING² in *side*~, *head*~. *End*~ f. ON *endlangr* adj. orig. meaning *extending from end to end* was used in E as adv. meaning *endwise*, & ~ thus came to be regarded as var. of -*ling*.

longanim'ity (-ngg-), n. (rare). Long-suffering, forbearance. [ME, f. LL *longanimitas* (LL *longanimus*, -*is* f. L *longus* long, *animus* spirit, -TY)]

lon'geron (-j-), n. (usu. in pl.). Longitudinal member of aeroplane's fuselage or nacelle. [F, = girder]

longev'al, -gae-, (-j-), a. Long-lived. [f. L *longaevus* (*longus* long, *aevum* age, -AL)]

longev'ity (-j-), n. Long life. [f. LL *longaevitas* (prec., -TY)]

lon'gi- (-ji-), comb. form of L *longus* long in scientific terms, as ~*caud'ate* long-tailed, ~*corn* kinds of beetle with long threadlike antennae.

lon'gitude (-j-), n. Length (now joc.); (geog.) angular distance east or west from a standard meridian, as that of Greenwich, to the meridian of any place, reckoned to 180° E. or W. (*abbr.* long.); (astron.) angular distance eastward on ecliptic from vernal equinoctial point to foot of body's or point's circle of latitude. [ME, f. L *longitudo* -*inis* (prec., -TUDE)]

longitud'inal (-ji-), a. Of or in length; running lengthwise; of longitude. Hence ~LY² adv. [-AL]

Long'obard, n. = LOMBARD (1st sense).

long'shore, a. Existing or found or employed on, frequenting, the shore; ~-*man*, landsman employed in loading ships, shore-fishing, etc. [for *along shore*]

longue haleine (lawnggahlän'), n. *Work* etc. of (or *de*) ~ (requiring long persistent effort; esp. of books). [F, = long-winded]

longueur (lawnggör'), n. Tedious passage in book, film, or play (usu. pl.). [F]

loo, n., & v.t. Round card-game with penalties paid to the pool; (having to pay) this penalty; *unlimited* ~, in which penalty is=amount already in pool; (vb) subject to the penalty. [abbr. of obs. *lanterloo* f. F *lanturelu* refrain of a song]

loo'by, n. Silly fellow. [cf. LOB, LUBBER]

loo'fah (-*a*), n. Pod of *Luffa aegyptiaca* used as flesh-brush. [f. Arab. *lufah* the plant]

look, v.i. & t., & n. 1. Use one's sight, turn eyes in some direction, direct eyes *at*, (*fair* etc. *to* ~ *at*, in outward appearance; ~ *before you leap*, avoid precipitate action; *to* ~ *at him* etc., judging by his etc. ~*s*; *will not* ~ *at*, refuses to take, rejects, scorns). 2. Contemplate, examine, (~*ed me through & through*; ~ *a gift* HORSE¹ *in the mouth*; ~ *one, death*, etc., *in the face*, face him etc. boldly or at close quarters). 3. Express, threaten, show, by one's ~s (~ *compassion, death, daggers*, etc.). 4. Ascertain or observe by sight *who, how, whether*, etc. 5. (fig.). Make mental search (*let him* ~ *at home*), inquire (*when one* ~*s deeper*), aim one's attention *at* & consider (*way of* ~*ing at things*; *what I* ~ *at is the comfort of it*), take care or make sure *that*, expect to do; (~ *you!*, observe, mind; ~ *here!*, formula for demanding attention or expostulating; ~ *sharp*, orig., keep strict watch, now, lose no time, bestir oneself). 6. (Of things) face, be turned, have or afford outlook, in some direction (*towards, on to, into, down*, etc.). 7. Have certain appearance, seem, (~ *grave* etc., whence ~'ING² a.; ~ *a fool*, *every inch a king*, BLACK¹, BLUE¹; ~ *small*, be exposed as mean etc.; ~ *alive!*, make haste; ~ *well* or *ill*, in good or bad health, also of things, seem to be going so; ~*s to be*, seems; ~ *as if*, suggest by appearance the belief that; ~ *like*, seem to be, also threaten or promise, as *it* ~*s like rain, he* ~*s like biting* or *winning*); seem to be (~*s his age*, seems as old as he really is; ~ one*self again*, seem recovered). 8. ~-*-in'*, informal call or visit, (sport) *will have a* ~*-in*, come near winning & perhaps win; ~*ing-glass*, mirror, quicksilvered glass for mirrors; ~*-out'*, watch, ~ing out, (*keep a good* ~*-out*; *on the* ~*-out for* or *to do*), post of observation, man or party or boat stationed to ~ out, view over landscape, prospect of luck (*it's a bad* ~*--out for him*), person's own concern (*that is his* ~*-out*, he must see to that himself); ||~*-see* (sl.), a survey, inspection. 9. (With prepp.): ~ *about* one, examine one's surroundings, take time to form plans; ~ *after*, follow with the eye, seek for, attend to, take care of; ~ *down* one's *nose at* (colloq.), regard with covert displeasure; ~ *for*, expect, hope or be on the watch for, search for (~ *for* TROUBLE); ~ *into*, examine the inside of (box etc.), dip into (book), investigate; ~ *on*, regard *as*, regard *with* distrust etc.; ~ *over*, inspect, overlook or pardon; ~ *through*, direct eyes through (window etc.), penetrate (veil etc.) with sight or (pretence or pretender) with insight, be visible through (*his greed* ~*s through his eyes*), glance through (book etc.); ~ *to*, consider, take care of, be careful about (~ *to your manners*; ~ *to it that*), keep watch over, rely on (person or thing) *for*, expect, count upon, aim at; ~ *towards* (colloq.), drink health of; ~ *upon*, regard *with* specified feeling (also with adv., as *favourably*), regard *as*. 10. (With advv.): ~ *about*, be on the watch, be in search *for*, let one's eyes rove; ~ *ahead*, (of rower) turn round to see where he is going (esp. imperat.); ~ *back*, be half-hearted about enterprise one has begun (usu. w. neg.), turn one's thoughts *upon* or *to* something past, cease to progress (usu. w. neg.), ~ in again, call back; ~ *down*, subdue with a ~, (commerc.) sink in price, ~ *down* (*up*)*on*, consider oneself superior to; ~ *forward to*, anticipate (usu. with pleasure, also *with apprehension* etc.); ~ *in*, make short visit or call; ~ *on*, be mere spectator, whence ~ER¹-ŏn' n.; ~ *on with*, read from book etc. at same time as (another person); ~ *out*, direct eyes or put head out of window etc., be vigilant, keep one's eyes open *for* expected person, be prepared for squalls etc., have or afford outlook *on, over,* etc., select by inspection; ~ *over*, inspect one by one or part by part; ~ *round*, esp. examine the possibilities etc, with a view to deciding on a course; ~ *through*, survey with searching glance (~*ed him through*), inspect exhaustively or successively; ~

up, (esp. commerc.) improve in price or prosperity, search for (esp. word in dictionary or facts in book of reference), call on (person), raise eyes (~ *up to*, respect, venerate), ~ one *up & down*, scrutinize him keenly or contemptuously; hence ~ER¹ n., (esp.) *handsome person (colloq.; also *good*~*er*). 11. n. Act of ~ing, direction of eyes, glance (*a kind, scornful,* ~); (sing. or pl.) appearance of face, expression, personal aspect, (*good* ~*s*, beauty); (of things) appearance (*the place has a European* ~). [OE *lōcian*, OS *lōcon*, f. WG **lōk-, *lōg-* (OHG *luogēn*]

loom¹, n. Machine for weaving yarn or thread into fabric; (inboard part of) shaft of oar. [ME *lome* f. OE *gelōma* tool, of unkn. orig.]

loom², v.i., & n. 1. Appear indistinctly, be seen in vague & often magnified or threatening shape, (lit. & fig.; often ~ *large* etc.). 2. n. Vague first appearance of land at sea etc. [cf. EFris. *lōmen* move slowly, MHG *lüemen* be weary]

loom³, n. Kinds of guillemot & diver. Hence ~'ERY(3) n. [f. ON *lómr*]

loon¹, n. (Sc. & arch.). Scamp, idler, boor; lad. [15th c. *loun*, of obsc. orig.]

loon², n. Kinds of water-bird, esp. of diver & grebe. [app. = LOOM³ w. assim. to prec.]

loon'y̆, lu-, n. & a. (sl.). Lunatic, esp. ~*-bin*, mental home. [-Y³]

loop¹, n., & v.t. & i. 1. Figure produced by a curve, or bent string or withe, that crosses itself; attachment or ornament formed of cord, thread, etc., so crossed & fastened at crossing; ring or curved piece of metal as handle etc.; (also ~*-line*) railway or telegraph line that diverges from main line & joins it again; circuit in centrifugal railway along top of which passenger travels head downwards (~*ing the* ~, bicyclist's or airman's similar feat); (skating) curve crossing itself made on single edge; hence ||~*-y²* a. (sl.), crazy. 2. vb. Form (string etc.) into ~(s); form ~ (esp. of LOOPER larvae); enclose (as) with ~; fasten (*up, back*) or join (*together*) with ~(s). [c. 1400, of unkn. orig.]

loop², n. (rare). = LOOP-HOLE. [ME, prob. conn. w. MDu. *lūpen* to peer]

loop'er, n. Caterpillar of geometer moths, progressing by arching itself into loops; contrivance in sewing-machine etc. for making loops. [-ER¹]

loop'-hŏle, n., & v.t. 1. Narrow vertical slit in wall for shooting or looking through or to admit light or air; outlet, means of evading rule etc. 2. v.t. Make ~s in (wall etc.). [LOOP²]

loose¹, a. 1. Released from bonds or restraint. 2. Detached or detachable from its place (*come, get,* ~; *play* FAST² *&* ~); (chem.) free, uncombined; hanging partly free (esp. ~ *at* a ~ *end*, without definite occupation); not rigidly

fixed, apt to shift, (*have a* SCREW ~).
3. Slack, relaxed, not tense or tight, (*with
a* ~ *rein*, lit. of riding, & fig. indulgently;
~ *tongue*, given to blabbing; ~ *bowels*,
tending to diarrhoea; ~ *clothes*; ~ *build*
or *make*, ungainly figure). **4.** Not compact, dense, or serried (~ *soil, fabric*; ~
order, military arrangement with wide
intervals; ~ *handwriting*, straggling; ||~
play or *game* in football, in which players
do not lock together). **5.** (Of statements,
ideas, etc.) inexact, indefinite, vague,
incorrect; (of translation) not close or
faithful; (of style) ungrammatical; (of
agent) doing the act ~ly (~ *thinker*).
6.(crick.).~ *bowling*, inaccurately pitched,
~ *fielding*, careless or bungling. **7.** Morally
lax, dissolute, wanton in speech or act,
(~ *fish*, dissolute person; *on the* ~, having
a spree). **8.** ~ BOX²; ~*-leaf* (of ledgers,
notebooks, etc.) with each leaf separate
& detachable;· ~-, ~ly, as ~*-flowing*,
-fitting. Hence.~'LY² (-sl-) adv., ~'NESS
(-sn-) n., lōōs'ISH¹(²) a. [ME *lōs* f. ON
louss, lauss (= OE *lēas*, OS, OHG *lōs*,
Goth. *laus*), f. Gmc **laus-*; cf. LOSE]
lōōse², v.t., & n. **1.** Release, set free,
free from constraint (*wine~d his tongue*);
untie, undo, (knot, fetters, seal, hair of
head); detach from moorings; discharge
(arrow), (abs.) discharge gun (*at*); relax
(now only in ~ *hold*). **2.** n. Vent, free expression, (give ~ or *a* ~ *to* one's *feelings*
etc.); || loose play (see prec.). [ME; f.
prec.]
lōōs'en, v.t. & f. Loose (person's tongue);
make or become less tight or compact or
firm; relieve (bowels) from costiveness or
(cough) from dryness; relax (discipline
etc.). [-EN⁶]
lōōse'strife (-s-s-), n. Two kinds of
herbaceous plant (*golden* or *yellow*, & *red*
or *purple* or *spiked*, ~). [mistransl. of
LL f. Gk *lusimakhion* (Gk pers. name
Lusimakhos) as if directly f. *luō* undo,
makhē battle]
lōōt, n., & v.t. & f. **1.** Goods taken from
enemy, spoil; booty, illicit gains made by
official. **2.** vb. Plunder, sack, (city etc., or
abs.); carry off as booty. Hence ~'ER¹
n. [f. Hind. *luṭ*]
lŏp¹, n., & v.t. & f. (-pp-). **1.** Smaller
branches & twigs of trees (~ *& top*, ~ *&
crop*, trimmings of tree). **2.** vb. Cut off
branches & twigs & rarely top of (tree);
strip tree of (branches etc.; often *off*,
away), whence ~'p'ings [-ING¹(²)] n. pl.;
cut off (person's limb or head); make
~ping strokes *at*. [(1) 15th c., orig. unkn.;
(2) prob. f. (1)]
lŏp², v.i. & t. (-pp-), & n. **1.** Hang limply;
let (ears) hang; slouch, dawdle, hang
about; = LOPE; ~*-ears*, drooping ears,
whence ~'earED² (-ērd) a.; ~*-ear*, kind of
rabbit; hence ~p'Y² a. **2.** n. ~*-eared*
rabbit. [(1) imit., cf. LOB; (2) short for
~*-rabbit*]
lŏp³, v.i. (-pp-), & n. **1.** (Of water) break

in short lumpy waves. **2.** n. Such motion
of water. [imit.]
lōpe, v.i., & n. (Run with) long bounding
stride (esp. of animals). [ME, var. of Sc.
loup f. ON *hloupa* LEAP¹]
lŏph'o-, comb. form of Gk *lophos* crest, in
scientific wds as: ~*dŏnt*, (animal) with
transverse ridges on crowns of molars;
~*brăn'chiate*, (fish) with gills disposed in
tufts.
lŏp-sĭd'ĕd, a. With one side lower or
smaller than the other, unevenly
balanced. Hence ~LY² adv., ~NESS n.
[f. LOP²]
loquā'cious (-shus), a. Talkative; (of
birds, water) chattering, babbling. Hence
or cogn. ~LY² adv., ~NESS, loquA'CITY
(-ăs-), nn. [L *loquax* (*loqui* talk), -ACIOUS]
lō'quat (-ŏt), n. Chinese & Japanese fruit
(-tree) naturalized in S. Europe, Australia,
etc. [f. Chin. *luh kwat* rush orange]
lŏ'quĭtŭr, v.i. 3 sing. pres. (abbr. *loq*.).
Speaks (with speaker's name added, as
stage-direction or notice to reader). [L]
|| lōr, lŏr, form of LORD used (vulg.) as int.
lōr'al, a. Of the LORE². [-AL]
lŏr'cha, n. Ship with hull of European
shape but Chinese rig. [Port.]
lŏrd, n. & int., & v.i. & t. **1.** Master, ruler,
chief, prince, sovereign, (*our sovereign* ~
the King; ~*s of creation*, mankind, also
joc. men as opp. women); (poet.) owner
(~ *of few acres*; cf. *landlord*); magnate in
some trade (*the cotton* ~*s*; cf. *king*). **2.**
Feudal superior (MESNE ~; ~ *of the* MANOR;
~ PARAMOUNT). **3.** (poet. & joc.). Husband
(also ~ *& master*). **4.** (astrol.). Dominant
planet. **5.** (Usu. *the L*~ exc. in voc.; also
with *God*) God (*L*~ *knows who, how,* etc.,
I cannot guess who etc., some one etc. or
other; *L*~ *have mercy, L*~ *bless me* or *us* or
my soul or *you*, excll. of surprise etc.;
also *L*~ *!* alone as excl.); Christ (*the* or
more usu. *our L*~; *in the year of our L*~,
anno domini; *L*~*'s day*, Sunday); *L*~*'s
prayer*, the *Our Father*; *L*~*'s supper*,
Eucharist; *L*~*'s table*, Christian altar,
Eucharist. **6.** Nobleman, peer of the
realm or person entitled by courtesy to
the prefix *L*~ (see below) as part of his
ordinary style (*live, treat, like a* ~, fare,
entertain, sumptuously; *drunk as, swear
like, a* ~, excessively; *L*~ *in waiting,
of the Bedchamber*, nobleman attending
sovereign, called by former title if queen
is reigning, by latter if king); (pl., *the
L*~*s*) temporal & spiritual peers of Parliament (*House of L*~*s*, upper legislative
chamber of United Kingdom, also committee of specially qualified members of
this appointed as ultimate judicial appeal
court). **7.** pl. (Also in full *L*~*s Commissioners*) members of board performing
duties of high State office put in commission (*L*~*s of the Admiralty, Treasury,*
etc.; *First L*~, president of such board;
Civil L~, civilian member of Admiralty
board, opp. *Sea L*~*s*); *L*~*s of Session,*

judges of Scottish *Court of* SESSION. **8.** First word of many official titles (L~ CHAMBERLAIN, CHANCELLOR, *Chief Justice, High Commissioner*; L~ *Justice General*, L~ *Justice Clerk*, president, vice-president, of Scottish Court of Justiciary; L~ *Lieutenant*, viceroy of Ireland till 1922, chief executive authority & head of magistracy in each county; L~ *Rector*, triennially elected honorary head of a Scottish university court; L~ MAYOR; L~ *Bishop*, any bishop in ceremonious mention). **9.** (Prefixed as part of personal designation) marquis, earl, viscount, or baron (whether peer, or peer's eldest son holding his second title by courtesy) with suppression of *of*, e.g. *Earl of*, or L~, *Derby*; ~ is invariable instead of *baron*, which is used as prefix only in foreign titles); (followed by Christian & family name) younger son of duke or marquis. **10.** *My* ~ (voc.), respectful or polite formula for addressing nobleman below duke, bishop, ~ mayor, or judge of supreme court; ~*s & ladies*, wild arum; hence ~'LESS a., ~'LING[1](2), ~ÖL'ATRY, nn. **11.** vb. Play the ~ *over* (usu. in pass., *will not be ~ed over*; or with *it*, as ~*ing it over his household*); ennoble, confer title of ~ upon. [OE *hlāford* f. *hlāfweard* = bread--keeper (LOAF[1], WARD)]

lōrd'lȳ, a. Haughty, imperious, lofty, disdainful; grand, magnificent, fit for or belonging to a lord. Hence ~ÌNESS n. [OE *hlāfordlic* (prec., -LY[1])]

lōrdōs'ĭs, n. (med.). Forward curvature of spine. [Gk, f. *lordos* bent back, -OSIS]

Lōrd's (-z), n. (Used for) ~ cricket ground in London, headquarters of the M.C.C. and English cricket. [Thomas Lord (d. 1832), maker of successive grounds named after him]

lōrd'ship, n. Dominion, rule, ownership *of* or *over*; domain, estate, manor; lord's personality (*your* ~, *his* ~, you, he, in speaking deferentially to or of a lord, also joc. to or of other persons or animals). [-SHIP]

lōre[1], n. **1.** (arch.). Doctrine; erudition, scholarship. **2.** Body of traditions & facts on a subject (*ghost, bird, animal, fairy*, etc., ~). [OE *lār*, OS, OHG *lēra* f. Gmc *laizō* f. *lais*- LEARN]

lōre[2], n. (nat. hist.). Strap-like surface, in birds between eye & upper mandible, in snakes between eye & nostril. [f. L *lorum* strap]

lorgnette (lŏrnyĕt'), n. Pair of eye-glasses usu. held by long handle; opera-glass. [F]

lō'ricate, a. (zool.). Having defensive armour of bone, plates, scales, etc. [f. L *loricatus* (*lorica* cuirass f. *lorum* strap, -ATE[2])]

lō'rikeet (or -eet'), n. Small brightly--coloured Polynesian parrot allied to the lory. [dim. of LORY, after *parakeet*]

lō'rimer, -iner, n. (hist.). Bit-maker,

spurrier, (now only in title of a livery company). [ME, f. OF *loremier, -nier* (*lorain* harness-strap f. L *lorum* thong)]

lŏr'is, n. Small slender tailless nocturnal climbing quadrumanous Sinhalese mammal; kinds of lemur. [F]

lōrn, a. (poet. & joc.). Desolate, forlorn, (often *lone* ~). [p.p. of obs. *leese* OE *lēosan* LOSE]

‖ **lŏ'rrȳ**, n. Long low flat wagon; truck used on railways & tramways; motor truck for transporting goods, troops etc. [orig. unkn.; cf. RULLEY]

lŏr'ȳ, n. Kinds of bright-plumaged parrot--like bird. [f. Malay *luri*]

lose (lŏōz), v.t. & i. (*lost* pr. law- *or* lŏ-). **1.** Be deprived of, cease by negligence, misadventure, separation, death, etc., to possess or have (property, life, quality, limb, father, friend, etc.; *doctor~s patient*, fails to keep him alive, also is left by him for another doctor; ~ *patience*, one's *temper*, become impatient, angry; ~ one's HEAD[1]; ~ one's HEART; ~ HEART; ~ *ground*, fail to keep position, recede, decline; *have lost my cold*, got rid of it; ~ *interest*, of person, cease to be interested, of thing, cease to interest); (pass.) disappear, perish, die or be dead, (*letter--writing is a lost art*; *the ship & all hands were lost*; *lost to sense of duty, shame*, etc., no longer affected by them; *lost soul*, damned). **2.** Suffer loss or detriment, incur disadvantage, be the worse off in money or otherwise *by* transaction etc., (*the publisher lost by it*; *the army lost heavily*; *story does not* ~ *in the telling*, is if anything exaggerated). **3.** Become unable to find, fail to keep in sight or follow or mentally grasp, (~ *a document*, one's *way*, *the thread of a discourse, a person* etc. *under observation*). **4.** Spend (time, opportunities, pains) to no purpose, waste, (pass., *be lost upon*, fail to influence or draw the attention of). **5.** Fail to obtain, catch, see, or hear (~ one's *train*, *a legacy*, *a word* or *remark*, *a fox*). **6.** Forfeit (stake), be defeated in (*game, battle, lawsuit*, or abs.; *losing battle, game*, in which defeat seems inevitable; *cannot play a losing game*, ~*s* heart or temper in it); fail to carry (motion). **7.** Cause person the loss of, cost, (*will* ~ *you your place*); (refl. & pass.) go astray, become merged or engrossed (*in*), be obscured (*in*); ‖ *losing* HAZARD. Hence los'ABLE (-ŏōz-) a. [OE *losian* perish, destroy (*los* LOSS); later sense-development infl. by obs. (cogn.) *leese*, wh. it superseded]

‖ **lŏs'el** (-z-), n. (arch.). Profligate, rake, ne'er-do-well. [ME, app. f. *los*-, stem of LOSE]

los'er (-ŏōz-), n. In vbl senses: esp.: *be a* ~ *by*, suffer loss by; *good* ~, person not dejected or angered by losing game etc.; person, horse, etc., that loses race etc.; ‖ (billiards) losing HAZARD. [-ER[1]]

loss (laws, lŏs), n. Losing or being lost

(see LOSE); person, thing, or amount lost (CUT² a or the~); detriment, disadvantage, resulting from ~ (person etc. *is a great, no little*, etc., ~, the ~ of him is a serious etc. blow); PROFIT¹ *& ~; at a ~ (for, to discover*, etc.), puzzled, at fault; *~ leader*, article sold at a ~ to attract custom. [ME *los, loss(e)* poss. back form. f. *lost*, p.p. of LOSE; not continuous w. OE & ME *los* in phr. *to lose* (= ON *los* dispersion, rout) f. Gmc *lus-* cogn. w. LOOSE¹]

löss (G), n. = LOESS.

lost. See LOSE.

löt, n., & v.t. (-tt-). **1.** One of a set of objects used to secure a chance decision in dividing goods, selecting officials, etc. (now only in *draw, cast, ~s*, usu. *between, for, who*, etc., & in *throw* or *cast in* one's *~ with*, share fortunes of); this method of deciding (*the ~; by ~*); choice resulting from it (*the ~ fell upon me*). **2.** What falls to person by ~, share (*have no part nor ~ in*); person's destiny, fortune, condition, (*the ~ falls to me, it falls to my ~, it falls to me as my ~, to do*). **3.** ‖ Tax, due, (SCOT¹ *& ~*). **4.** Plot or allotment of land. **5.** Article or set of articles offered separately at sale, item at auction, (*bad ~*, disreputable or vicious person). **6.** Number or quantity of persons or things of same kind or somehow associated (*the ~*, the whole number or quantity); (colloq.) considerable number or amount, *a good or great deal* (also in pl., as *has ~s of friends*). **7.** v.t. Divide (land, usu. *out*, or goods for sale) into *~s*. [OE *hlot*, w. var. cognates in Gmc, f. Gmc *hleut-*, *hlaut-*, *hlut-*]

loth. See LOATH.

Lothär'iö, n. (pl. ~s). Libertine, rake. [character in Rowe's *Fair Penitent*]

lö'tion, n. Liquid preparation used externally to heal wound, cure skin-disease, clear complexion, etc. [f. L *lotio* (*lavare lot-* wash, -ION)]

lött'ery, n. Arrangement for distributing prizes by chance among purchasers of tickets; *~-wheel*, wheel with box used for shuffling numbers corresponding to those on tickets; (fig.) thing that defies calculation (*life, marriage, is a ~*). [f. It. *lotteria* (LOT, LOTTO)]

lött'ö, n. Game of chance with drawing of numbers as in lottery. [It.]

löt'us, n. Plant represented in ancient Greek legend as inducing luxurious dreaminess & distaste for active life (*~-eater*, person given to indolent enjoyment; so *~-eating* a. & n.); Egyptian & Asian water-lily; kinds of plant, esp. bird's-foot trefoil; *~-land*, place of indolent enjoyment. [L, f. Gk *lōtos*]

loud, a. & adv. **1.** Strongly audible, sonorous (*~ speaker*, naut. *~ hailer*, apparatus that converts electrical impulses into sounds ~ enough to be heard at some distance); clamorous, noisy; (of colour, dress, pattern, manners) obtrusive, conspicuous, flashy; hence ~'EN⁶

v.i., ~'ISH(2) a., ~'LY² adv., ~'NESS n. **2.** adv. ~ly (*don't talk so ~; laughed ~ & long*); ~-SPOKEN. [OE, OS *hlūd*, OHG *hlūt*, f. WG **hlūth-*, cogn. w. Gk *klutos* renowned]

lough (see Ap.), n. (Anglo-Ir.). Lake, arm of sea. [ME, perh. repr. O Northumb. *luh* (= *fretum, stagnum*), f. Ir. *loch* LOCH]

Louis (lōō'i), n. (pl. *Louis* pr. -z). Name of many French kings; *louis* or *louis-d'or* (-dôr'), French gold coin of about 20 fr. from ~ XIII to ~ XVI; ~ *Treize* (trāz), *Quatorze* (kătörz'), *Quinze* (kănz), *Seize* (sāz), used adj. of furniture etc. in styles prevalent in those reigns.

loung|e (-j), v.i. & t., & n. **1.** Go lazily, saunter; loll, recline; idle (intr., & *~e away* time etc.); hence ~'ER¹ n., ~'ingLY² adv., (-j-). **2.** n. Spell of ~ing, saunter, stroll; place where one can ~e, esp. entrance-hall or gallery furnished for the purpose (*~e-lizard*, sl., professional dance-partner at hotel~e-dances); sitting-room in house; sofa or deep chair; ‖ *~e suit*, man's suit for day wear, with tailless jacket. [*c.* 1500, of unkn. orig.]

lour, lower, (lowr), v.i., & n. **1.** Frown, scowl, look sullen, (*on, upon, at*); (of clouds, sky, storm) look dark & threatening; hence ~'ingLY² adv. **2.** n. Scowl; gloominess of sky etc., whence ~'Y² a. [ME *loure*, of obsc. orig.; cf. Du. *loeren* frown, MHG *lūren*; see LURK]

louse, n. (pl. *lice*). Parasitic insect infesting human hair & skin; kinds of parasite of mammals, birds, fish, & plants; *~wort*, kind of plant with purple-pink flowers found in marshes and wet fields. Hence **lous'y¹** (-z-) a., (also, sl.), disgusting, abundantly supplied *with money* etc., **lous'iNESS** (-z-) n. [OE *lūs*, MLG, OHG *lūs*, ON *lús*]

lout¹, n. Awkward fellow, bumpkin, clown. Hence ~'ISH¹ a., ~'ishLY² adv., ~'ishNESS n. [16th c., perh. of dial. orig., conn. w. foll.]

lout², v.i. (arch.). Bow, make obeisance. [OE *lūtan*, = ON *lúta*]

louver, -vre, (lōō'ver), n. Domed turret-like erection on hall-roof etc. with side openings to let smoke out or air in; (pl., also *~-boards*) arrangement of overlapping boards or slips of glass to admit air but exclude rain. Hence **louv'erED²** (-erd) a. [ME, f. OF *lover*, repr. by med. L *lodium*; orig. unkn.]

Louvre (lōōvr), n. *The ~*, former royal palace, now art museum, in Paris. [F]

lo'vable (lŭ-), a. Deserving love, amiable. Hence ~LY² adv., ~leNESS n. [LOVE², -ABLE]

lo'vage (lŭ-), n. Kinds of herb. [ME *loveache* alt. f. OF *levesche* f. LL *levisticum* f. L *ligusticum*]

love¹ (lŭv), n. **1.** Warm affection, attachment, liking, or fondness, paternal benevolence, affectionate devotion, (*of, for, to*, or *towards* person, *for* or *to* thing;

give ~ *to*, convey affectionate message to, *send* one's ~ *to*, get this done; *for the* ~ *of*, for sake or in name of, esp. in adjurations; *for* ~ *or money*, by any means, esp. *cannot get it* etc. *for* ~ *or money*; *labour of* ~, that one delights in, or that one does for ~ of someone; *there's no* ~ *lost between them*, they dislike each other; *play for* ~, for the pleasure of it, not for stakes). **2.** Sexual affection or passion or desire, relation between sweethearts, this feeling as a literary subject, a personified influence, or a god (also representation of Cupid, or of naked winged child, or in pl. children, symbolizing ~), (*in* ~, possessed by this; *in* ~ *with*, enamoured of, also transf. fond of a pursuit, thing, etc.; *fall in* ~, become enamoured; *all's* FAIR[2] *in* ~ *& war*; ~ *in a cottage*, marriage on insufficient means; *make* ~, pay amorous attentions *to* or *abs.*, whence ~'makING[1] n.). **3.** Beloved one, sweetheart, (esp. of woman, cf. LOVER; hence ~'Y[3] n.; *my* ~, common form of address between husband & wife); (colloq.) delightful person or pretty thing (*he is an old* ~; *what* ~*s of teacups!*). **4.** (In games) no score, nothing, nil, (~ *all*, neither side has yet scored; ~ *game*, in which loser has not scored). **5.** ~-*affair*, affair between lovers, amour; ~-*apple*, (old name for) tomato; ~-*begotten*, illegitimate; ~-*bird*, small bird of parrot kind said to pine away at death of its mate; ~-*child*, illegitimate; ~-*feast*, meal in token of brotherly ~ among early Christians, religious service among Methodists etc. imitating this; ~-*in-a--mist*, fennel-flower; ~-*in-idleness*, heart's--ease; ~-*knot*, peculiarly interlaced bow of ribbon; ~-*letter*, between sweethearts & concerned with ~; ~-*lies-bleeding*, garden plant with long drooping spike of purple--red bloom; ~'*lock*, tress or curl worn on temple or forehead; ~-*lorn*, pining with ~, deserted by one's love(r); ~-*match*, marriage made for ~'s sake only; ~-*philtre*, philtre; ~-*seat*, armchair or sofa for two persons; ~'*sick*, languishing with ~; ~-*song*, about or expressing ~; ~-*story*, novel etc. of which main theme is ~, facts of a wooing etc.; ~-*token*, thing given in sign of ~. Hence ~'WORTHY a., ~'WORTHINESS n. [OE *lufu*, OHG *luba*, cogn. w. Goth. *lubains* f. Gmc *leubh-*, *laubh-*, *lubh-*; see LIEF, LEAVE[1], BELIEVE]

love[2] (lŭv), v.t. & i. Hold dear, bear love to, be in love with, be fond of, (~ *me*, ~ *my* DOG[1]; *Lord* ~ *you!*, excl. of surprise at person's mistake etc.; ~ *one's love with an A, a B,* etc., formula in game of forfeits); be in love; cling to, delight in, enjoy having, be addicted to, admire or be glad of the existence of, (life, honour, comfort, golf, *doing*, 'virtue, man who knows his own mind, etc.); (w. inf.) be (habitually) inclined (*children* ~ *to ape their elders*); (colloq.) like, be delighted,

(*he simply* ~*s to find mistakes*; *Will you come?* — *I should* ~ *to*). [OE *lufian* (prec.)]

Love'lace (lŭvl-), n. Libertine, accomplished rake. [character in Richardson's *Clarissa Harlowe* (1747–48)]

love'less (lŭvl-), a. Unloving; unloved, Hence ~LY[2] adv., ~NESS n. [-LESS]

love'l|y (lŭvl-), a. & n. Attractively or admirably beautiful; *beautiful in moral quality; (colloq.) delightful, very pleasing, intensely amusing; (n., sl.) a ~ young woman. Hence ~ILY[2] adv. (rare), ~iNESS n. [OE *luflic* (LOVE[1], -LY[1])]

lo'ver (lŭ-), n. Woman's sweetheart or suitor (*it was a* ~ *and his lass*), (pl.) pair in love; paramour, gallant; admirer, devotee, *of* thing, action, or idea; ~*s' knot*, LOVE[1]-knot. Hence ~LESS a., ~LIKE, ~LY[1,2], aa. & adv. [-ER[1]]

lo'ving (lŭ-), a. That loves, affectionate, (*our* ~ *subjects*, formula in royal proclamation; *your* ~ *friend* etc., formula in concluding letter); manifesting or proceeding from love (~-*cup*, large drinking-vessel passed round at banquet; ~-*kindness*, tender consideration). Hence ~LY[2] adv., ~NESS n. [-ING[2]]

low[1] (lō), a. & adv. (~*er*, ~*est*, as aa. & advv.), & n. **1.** Not reaching far up, not high or tall, (~ *house*, *forehead*, *stature*; not used of persons; ~ *dress*, leaving neck & part of shoulders & breast exposed, so ~ *neck*; ~ *relief*, bas-relief). **2.** Not elevated in geographical etc. position (*Low Countries*, Netherlands; *Low* GERMAN[2], DUTCH; *Lower Egypt* etc.; ~ *moon* etc., near horizon; ~ *tide* or *water*, level of ebbed sea, time of extreme ebb; ~-*water mark*, ~*est* point reached by ebb--tide, & fig.; *in* ~ *water*, out of funds etc.). **3.** Of or in humble rank or position (*the* ~*er orders* or *classes*; ~ *birth*; *high & ~*, every one). **4.** Not exalted or sublime, commonplace, undignified, little civilized, not highly organized; abject, mean, degraded, coarse, vulgar, (~ *cunning*). **5.** Ill-nourished, not nourishing, indicative of ill nutrition, wanting in vigour, depressed, not intense, (~ *condition*, *diet*, *fever*; ~ *spirits*, whence ~-*spi'ritED a.). **6.** Of small amount as measured by a scale or degrees (~ *price*, *wages*, *rates*, *temperature*; *have* ~ *opinion of*, do not estimate highly; *at* ~*est*, to mention the least possible amount etc.; ~ *latitudes*, near equator). **7.** (Of sounds) not shrill or high up, produced by slow vibrations, (also) not loud. **8.** (Of liquid, receptacle, supply of anything) esp. fig. of purse or money) nearly exhausted or empty (often *run* ~). **9.** Recent (chiefly in compar. & superl.; *belongs to a* ~*er date*). **10.** (Also ~-*church*) giving ~ place to authority of bishops & priests, inherent grace of sacraments, ecclesiastical organization, & ritual, not sacerdotal, approximating to protestant nonconformity, (*Low Church*, party in Church of England thus minded; *Low Churchman*, member of it). **11.** *Bring ~*, depress, reduce, in health, wealth, or position; *lay ~*, overthrow; *lie ~*, crouch, be prostrate or dead or abased, keep quiet or out of the way, say nothing, bide one's time; BURN² *~*. **12.** *~'brow* (colloq.), (one who is) not highly intellectual or cultured (opp. HIGH*brow*); *~'browed*, lit., also (of rocks) beetling, (of building etc.) with *~* entrance, gloomy; *~ celebration* of Eucharist, without choir or assistant ministers; *~ comedian*, actor in *~ comedy*, in which subject & treatment border on farce; *~-down*, abject, mean, dishonourable; *•~-down* n. (sl.), true facts, inside information; ‖*~er boy*, in *~er* school at public schools; *~er* CASE²; *~er chamber*, = *~er House*; *~er critic(ism)*, of the verbal or textual kind; *~er deck*, immediately over hold (‖ *the ~er deck*, petty officers & men of the Navy or of a ship); *~er Empire*, later Roman Empire, usu. from Constantine; *~er House*, *~er* branch of legislative assembly, e.g. House of Commons; *~er school* in public schools, usu. forms below fifth; *~er world*, the earth, (also) hell; *~'land*, (usu. pl.) *~lying* country, (adj.) of or in this; *Low'lands* (-andz), part of Scotland lying S. & E. of Highlands, whence **Low'lander**¹(4) n.; *Low'land* (adj.), of or in this; *~* LATIN²; *~* life, that of the *~er* classes, whence *~'*ll**IVED**² (-vd'), a. ; *~* MASS¹; *~ pitch*, *~* key or note, also slight angular elevation of roof, whence *~-pitch*ED² a. ; *~* PRESSURE; *Low Sunday*, *Week*, after Easter Day & Week ; *~¹*WING; hence *~'er*MOST (lō'er-), *~'*ISH¹(2) (lō'ĭ-), aa., *~'*NESS (lō'n-) n. **13.** adv. In or to *~* or mean position (*hangs ~*; *aim* or *shoot ~* or *~er*; *tackle ~* in football, catch at or below waist; *bowed ~*; *never fell so ~ as that*); on poor diet (*live ~ for a time*); for small stakes (*play ~*); in *~* tone, on or to *~* note, (*talk ~*; *cannot get so ~*); (of date) late (*find it as ~ as the 18th century*); *~-born*, of humble birth; *~-bred*, of vulgar manners; *~ down*, far down, also in mean or ungenerous way (esp. *play it ~ down*, or *~, upon*, treat scurvily). **14.** n. What is *~*; an area of *~* barometric pressure; *•a ~* level or figure. [ME *lāh* (*lāg*-) f. ON *lágr*, = MDu. *lage*, MHG *læge* f. Gmc *•læg*- (LIE³)]

low² (lō), v.i. & t., & n. **1.** Utter cry (as) of cow, moo; say, utter *forth*, with *~ing* sound. **2.** n. Cow's cry. [OE *hlōwan*, = OHG *hluojen*, f. Gmc *•hlō·* cogn. w. L *clamare*]

low'er¹ (lō'er), v.t. & i. Let or haul down; (naut., abs.) let down boat, haul down sail, etc. (freq. *~ away*); diminish height of; sink, descend, slope downwards; diminish (price etc.), (of price etc.) come down; diminish (t. & i.) in intensity or pitch; degrade, disgrace; reduce bodily condition of (*a ~ing diet*). [f. *lower* comp. of LOW¹]

lower². See LOUR.

low'l‖**y̆** (lō-), a. & adv. **1.** Humble in feeling, behaviour, or condition, modest, unpretending. **2.** adv. In *~y* manner. Hence *~*ĬLY² adv., *~*ĬNESS n. [LOW¹, -LY¹, ²]

lŏxŏdrŏm'‖ic, a. & n. Of oblique sailing or sailing by the RHUMB; (n.) *~ic* line or table. Hence *~*ICS n. [f. Gk *loxos* oblique, *dromos* course, -IC]

loy'al, a. & n. **1.** True, faithful, to duty, love, or obligation (*to*); faithful in allegiance to sovereign, government, or mother-country; enthusiastically devoted to sovereign's person & family; exhibiting loyalty; hence *~*ISM(3), *~*IST(2), nn., *~*IZE(3) v.t., *~*LY² adv. **2.** n. Person who remains *~* in time of disaffection. [16th c., f. *Loyal*, OF *loial* etc. (see LEAL) f. L *legalis* LEGAL]

loy'alty̆, n. Loyal temper or conduct. [c. 1400, f. OF *loialte* (prec., -TY)]

lŏz'enge (-j), n. RHOMB, diamond figure, esp. as bearing in heraldry; *~-shaped* shield for spinster's or widow's arms; *~--shaped* facet of cut gem; small tablet (orig. *~-shaped*) of flavoured sugar, medicine, meat essence, etc., to be dissolved in mouth; *~-shaped* pane in casement. [ME, f. OF *losenge*, perh. deriv. of Iber.--Rom. *•lausa*, cf. Pr. *lausa* tombstone]

lŏz'enged (-jd), a. With lozenges of alternate colours; with lozenge panes. [-ED²]

£.s.d. (ĕl'ĕsdĕ'), n. Pounds, shillings, & pence; money, riches; *L. S.Dĕ'ism* (joc.), money-worship. [L *librae, solidi, denarii*, pounds, shillings, pence]

'lt. See WILL¹.

lŭbb'er, n. Big clumsy stupid fellow, lout; clumsy seaman; *~'s hole* (naut.), hole in platform of ship's top (saving climbing by FUTTOCK shrouds); *~'s line* (naut.), line marked on compass showing direction of ship's head. Hence *~*LIKE a., *~*LY¹, ² a. & adv., *~*liNESS n. [14th c., of obsc. orig.; cf. 16th c. (now dial.) *lob* bumpkin; dial. Sw. *lubber*; Da. *lobbes* clown; see LOB]

lub'ric‖āte (lōō-, lū-), v.t. Make slippery or smooth by applying fluid or unguent; minimize friction of (machinery) with grease etc. (also fig.). Hence *~*ANT (2) a. & n., *~*āTOR, *~*A'TION, nn. [f. L *lubricare* (*lubricus* slippery), -ATE³]

lubri'ci‖ty̆ (lōō-, lū-), n. Slipperiness, smoothness, oiliness, (lit. & fig.); lewdness, wantonness. So *~*OUS (-shus), *lub'ricous*, aa. [f. F *lubricité* or LL *lubricitas* (prec., -TY)]

Luc'an (lōō-, lū-), a. Of St Luke. [f. LL *Lucas* Lᵛke, -AN]

Lucca (lōōk'a, lŭk'a), n. *~ oil*, superior quality of olive oil. [*~*, in N. Italy]

luce (lōōs, lūs), n. Pike fish, esp. when full-grown. [ME, f. OF *lus* f. LL *lucius*]

lu'cent (lōō-, lū-), a. Shining, luminous; translucent. Hence **lu'**CENCY n. [f. L *lucĕre* shine (*lux lucis* light), -ENT]

‖ **lucĕrn(e)'** (lōō-, lū-), n. Cloverlike plant

used for fodder. [f. F *luzerne*, f. Prov. *luzerno* glow-worm, w. ref. to the shiny seeds]

Lucian´ic (lōōsǐ-), a. After the manner of Lucian, witty & scoffing. [f. Gk *Loukianos* + -IC]

lu´cid (lōō-, lū-), a. Bright (poet.); (entom., bot.) with smooth shining surface; clear, pellucid, (usu. fig. of reasoning, literary style, etc.); ~ *interval*, period of sanity between attacks of madness, or of quiet between disturbances. Hence or cogn. **lucíd´ITY** n., **~LY²** adv. [f. F *lucide*, or L *lucidus* (LUCENT)]

Lu´cifer (lōō-, lū-), n. **1.** (Planet Venus as) morning star. **2.** (Supposed name, see A.V. & R.V. of *Isa.* xiv. 12, of) the chief, rebel angel, Satan, the devil, (as *proud as* ~). **3.** *l*~ (*match*), friction match (now rare). [L, light-bringing, morning star, (*lux lucis* light, *-fer* f. *ferre* bring)]

lucif´ūgous (lōō-, lū-), a. (nat. hist.). Shunning daylight. [f. L *lucifugus* (prec., *fugere* flee), -OUS]

lŭck, n. **1.** (Chance as bestower of) good or ill fortune, fortuitous events affecting one's interests, person's apparent tendency to be (un)fortunate, supposed tendency of chance to bring a succession of (un)favourable events, (*bad* ~ *to him* etc.!, form of imprecation; *as* ~ *would have it*, fortunately or unfortunately; *down on* one's ~, dispirited by misfortune, temporarily unfortunate; *try* one's ~, make a venture at gaming-table or in anything; *just my* ~, usu. = I am unlucky as usual; *worse* ~, parenth., more's the pity, unfortunately for me or us). **2.** Good fortune, success due to chance, (*have the* ~, be fortunate enough *to*; *for* ~, to bring good ~; *in, out of,* ~; *have no* ~), whence **~´LESS** a., **~´léssNESS** n. **3.** ~-*money*, -*penny*, piece of money kept for ~, also sum returned by seller to buyer esp. in livestock sale. [ME, f. LG *luk*, f. MLG *geluke*, = MDu. *ghelucke*, MHG *gelücke*]

lŭck´ilў, adv. (As ordinary adv.) by luck (rare); (as qualification of sentence or clause) which is etc. a fortunate thing, thank goodness, (~ *for me I was wrong*; *on a snow-slope which was* ~ *in good order*). [foll., -LY²]

lŭck´ў¹, a. Constantly attended by good luck, enjoying it on a particular occasion, having as much success or happiness as one deserves & more, (*you're a* ~ *dog*, form of congratulation esp. to accepted lover; ~ *beggar !*, ~ *bargee !*, of or to person in luck); right by luck, of the nature of a fluke, (~ *guess, hit, shot*); coming in the nick of time; presaging bringing, worn etc. for, good luck, well-omened, (~ *penny, stone, day*); ~-*bag*, -*tub*, at bazaars etc. containing articles of more or less value for one of which payer of small sum may dip. Hence **lŭck´iNESS** n. [-Y²]

lŭck´ў², n. (sl.). *Cut* one's ~, decamp, make off. [orig. unkn.]

luc´rative (lōō-, lū-), a. Yielding gain, profitable. 'Hence **~LY²** adv., **~NESS** n. [ME, f. L *lucrativus* (*lucrari* to gain, see foll., -ATIVE)]

lucre (lōōk´er, lū-), n. Pecuniary profit or gain (derog.); FILTHY ~. [ME, f. OF, or L *lucrum*]

Lucretia (lōōkrěsh´a), n. Model of chastity, woman preferring honour to life. [see Livy i. 57–8]

luc´ūbrāt|e (lōō-, lū-), v.i. Express one's meditations in writing; produce lucubrations, Hence ~OR n. [f. L *lucubrare* work by lamplight (*lux lucis* light), -ATE³]

lucūbrā´tion (lōō-, lū-), n. Nocturnal study or meditation; literary work esp. of pedantic or elaborate character. [f. L *lucubratio* (prec., -ATION)]

luc´ulent (lōō-, lū-), a. (rare). Clear, convincing, lucid, (~ *proof, instance, explanation*). Hence **~LY²** adv. [f. L *luculentus* (*lux lucis* light, -LENT)]

luc´us ā nōn lucěn´dō (lōō-, lū-), n. Paradoxical derivation; (transf.) reference of effect to paradoxical cause, explanation by contraries. [L, = *lucus* (grove) is derived from *lucēre* (shine) because it does not shine there]

∥ **lŭd.** *My* ~, = my lord in representations of counsel's pronunciation in addressing judge.

Lŭdd´īte, n. & a. (Member) of band of mechanics (1811–16) who raised riots for destruction of machinery. [orig. doubtful; leaders were called *Captain Ludd*]

lud´icrous (lōō-, lū-), a. Absurd, ridiculous, exciting or deserving derision. Hence **~LY²** adv., **~NESS** n., **lud´icro-** comb. form. [f. L *ludicrus* prob. f. *ludicrum* stage-play (*ludere* play)]

lŭd´ō (or lōō-), n. Simple game played with dice & counters on special board. [L, = I play]

lues (lōō´ēz), n. Plague, contagious disease, contagion, (~ *Boswellian´a*, biographer's tendency to magnify his subject, see BOSWELL); (also ~ *vener´ea*) syphilis, whence (irreg.) **luET´IC** (lōōět²-) a. [L, genit. *luis*]

lŭff, n., & v.i. & t. (naut.). **1.** Side of fore- -&-aft sail next mast or stay; ∥ broadest part of ship's bow where sides begin to curve in. **2.** vb. Bring ship's head, bring head of (ship), nearer wind; turn (helm) so as to secure this; (yacht- -racing) get windward side of (opponent; -*ing-match*, struggle for this). [ME *lof(e)*, *loof*, = MLG *lôf*, LG, Da. *luv*, Du. *loef*; in ME app. a contrivance (e.g. an auxiliary rudder) for altering ship's course; poss. rel. to ON *lófi*, Goth. *lôfa* flat hand]

Luftwaffe (lōōft´vahfe), n. German Air Force. [G]

lŭg¹, n. Large marine worm used as bait. [orig. unkn.]

lŭg², n. = LUG-SAIL.

lŭg³, v.t. & i. (-gg-), & n. **1.** Drag or tug (heavy object) with effort or violence;

(intr.) pull hard *at*; bring (subject etc.) irrelevantly *in* or *into*; force (person) *along*. **2.** n. Hard or rough pull. [ME; cf. Sw. *lugga* pull person's hair (*lugg* fore-lock)]

lŭg[4], n. ‖ (Sc.) ear; (mech.) projection from a casting etc. by which it may be fixed in place. [prob. of Scand. orig.; cf. prec.]

luge (lōōzh), n., & v.i. **1.** Short raised toboggan used in Switzerland. **2.** v.i. Toboggan in this. [Swiss dial. wd]

lŭgg′age, n. ‖ Traveller's baggage, port-manteaus, boxes, etc. [LUG[3], -AGE]

lŭgg′er (-g-), n. Small ship with four--cornered sails set fore & aft. [18th c., f. foll.]

lŭg′sail (-sl), n. Four-cornered sail bent on yard slung at a third or quarter of its length from one end. [17th c., of unkn. orig.]

lugŭb′rious (lōō-, lū-), a. Doleful, dismal, mournful. Hence ~LY[2] adv., ~NESS n. [f. L *lugubris* (*lugēre* mourn), -OUS]

lukewarm (lōōk′wŏrm, lū-), a. & n. Moderately warm, tepid; not zealous, indifferent, (n., ~ person). Hence ~LY[2] adv., ~NESS n. [ME, f. (dial.) *luke*, rel. to (dial.) *lew* (OE *hleow*, OHG *lāo*, ON *hlýr*)]

lŭll, v.t. & i., & n. **1.** Soothe or send to sleep by sounds or caresses, quiet (sus-picion etc.) usu. by deception; (usu. pass.) quiet (sea, storm); (of storm or noise) lessen, fall quiet; hence ~′ingLY[2] adv. **2.** n. Intermission in storm lit. or fig. [ME, imit.; cf. Sw. *lulla*, Du. *lullen*]

lŭll′aby̆, n., & v.t. Soothing refrain or song to put child to sleep; (vb) sing to sleep. [prec., -*by* as in BYE-BYE]

lŭmbāg′o̅, n. (pl. ~s). Rheumatic affec-tion in loins. Hence **lŭmbā′gı̆nous** a. [LL; f. L *lumbus* loin]

lŭm′bar, a. & n. (Artery, vein, nerve, or vertebra) of or in loin. [prec., -AR[1]]

lŭm′ber[1], v.i. Move in clumsy blunder-ing noisy way (*along*, *past*, *by*, etc.). Hence ~ING[2] a., ~ingLY[2] adv., ~SOME a. [ME *lomere*, perh. f. *lome* LAME]

lŭm′ber[2], n., & v.t. & i. **1.** Disused articles of furniture etc. taking up room (~*room*, in which such things are kept), useless or cumbrous material; superfluous fat; roughly prepared timber (~*carrier*, *boat* in ~*trade*; ~*jack*, ~*man*; ~*mill*, for sawing ~; ~*man*, feller, dresser, or conveyer of ~; ~*scaler*, one who measures ~). **2.** vb. Fill up inconve-niently, obstruct, (room, place; often *up*, *over*); heap together, treat, as ~; cut & prepare forest timber, whence ~ER[1] n. [poss. f. prec.; later assoc. w. obs. *lumber* pawnbroker's shop]

lŭm′bo-, comb. form of L *lumbus* loin, as ~*abdom′inal* of loins & abdomen.

lŭm′brical, a. & n. ~ *muscle* or ~, one of the muscles flexing fingers or toes. [f. L *lumbricus* earthworm, w. ref. to the shape]

lum′ĭnary̆ (lōō-, lū-), n. Natural light--giving body, esp. sun or moon; person of intellectual, moral, or spiritual eminence, person of light & leading. [ME, f. OF *luminaire* or LL *luminarium*, -*are* (L *lumen -inis* light, -ARY[1])]

luminif′erous (lōō-, lū-), a. Producing or transmitting light. [prec., -FEROUS]

lum′inous (lōō-, lū-), a. Emitting or full of light, bright, shining, (~ *paint*, phos-phorescent kind making thing conspicu-ous at night), whence **luminŏs′ITY** n.; (of writers etc.) throwing light upon sub-ject. Hence ~NESS n., ~LY[2] adv. [ME, f. L *luminosus* (*lumen -inis* light, -OUS)]

lŭmm′e̅, int. (vulg.) of surprise or em-phasis. [= (Lord) love me]

lŭmp[1], n., & v.t. & i. **1.** Compact shape-less or unshapely mass (~ *in throat*, feeling of pressure caused by emotion; *is a ~ of selfishness*, is selfish through & through); great quantity, lot, heap; mass of clay or dough ready for moulding or bak-ing; protuberance, excrescence, swelling, bruise; heavy dull person; *in the* ~, taking things as a whole, in gross, whole-sale; ~ *sugar*, loaf sugar broken or cut into ~s or cubes; ~ *sum*, covering number of items, also paid down at once (opp. *instalments*). **2.** vb. Put together in one ~, mass together, treat as all alike, disregard differences between or among, (*together*, *with*, *in with*, *under* title etc.); lay whole of (sum) *on* horse, event, etc.; rise or collect (intr.) into ~s; go heavily *along*, sit heavily *down*. [ME *lump*, of Scand. orig.; cf. Norw. & Sw. dial. *lump* block, stump, log, Da. *lump(e)* lump]

lŭmp[2], n. Uncouth spiny-finned leaden--blue fish clinging tightly to objects by sucking-disc on belly. [16th c. f. MDu. *lompe*, MLG *lumpen* (G *lumpfisch*); cf. Du. *lomp* heavy, clumsy]

lŭmp[3], v.t. Be displeased at, put up with ungraciously, (now only in *if you don't like it you may* ~ *it*). [imit.; cf. *dump*, *grump*, etc.]

lŭm′per, n. Labourer employed in (un)-'loading cargoes; ‖small contractor taking work in the lump & giving it out in the piece; classifier who avoids minute sub-division. [LUMP[1], -ER[1]]

lŭm′ping, a. (colloq.). Big, plentiful, (~ *weight*, good weight). [LUMP[1], -ING[2]]

lŭm′pish, a. Heavy & clumsy; stupid, lethargic. Hence ~LY[2] adv., ~NESS n. [LUMP[1], -ISH[1]]

lŭm′ply̆, a. Full of or covered with lumps; (of water) cut up by wind into small waves. Hence ~ILY[2] adv., ~iNESS n. [-Y[2]]

lun′acy̆ (lōō-, lū-), n. Being a lunatic, in-sanity (formerly of the intermittent kind attributed to changes of moon), (law) such mental unsoundness as interferes with civil rights or transactions ‖ (*Com-mission of* ~, authorization of inquiry into person's sanity; *Commissioner in* ~, mem-ber of board of ten for inspecting asylums etc.; *Master in* ~, officer investigating cases of alleged ~); great folly. [LUNATIC, -ACY]

lun'ar (lōō-, lū-), a. & n. **1.** Of, in, as of, the moon (~ CYCLE; ~ *distance*, of moon from sun, planet, or star, used in finding longitude at sea; ~ *month*, interval between new moons, about 29½ days, (pop.) period of four weeks; ~ *nodes*, at which moon's orbit cuts ecliptic; ~ *observation*, finding of longitude by ~ distance; ~ *politics*, unpractical questions; ~ *rainbow*, made by moon's rays); (of light, glory, etc.) pale, feeble; crescent-shaped, lunate, (esp. ~ *bone* in wrist); of or containing silver (from alchemists' use of *luna* moon for silver; ~ *caustic*, nitrate of silver fused). **2.** n. ~ distance or observation; ~ bone. [f. L *lunaris* (*luna* moon, -AR¹)]

lunār'ian (lōō-, lū-), n. Inhabitant of moon; astronomer or navigator with special knowledge of the moon. [prec., -IAN]

lun'āte (lōō-, lū-), a. (nat. hist.). Crescent--shaped. [f. L *lunatus* (*luna* moon, -ATE²)]

lun'atic (lōō-, lū-), a. & n. Insane (person; see LUNACY), mad(man); (of actions etc.) outrageously foolish, frantic, mad; eccentric, foolish, (person); ~ *asylum*, hospital for reception & treatment of ~s (now *mental home* or *hospital*); ~ *fringe*, the more eccentric or visionary adherents of a political or other movement. [ME, f. LL *lunaticus* (*luna* moon, -ATIC)]

lunā'tion (lōō-, lū-), n. Time from one new moon to next. [ME, f. med. L *lunatio* (prec., -ATION)]

lunch, n., & v.i. & t., **lŭn'cheon** (-chn), n., (-*ch* now usu. exc. in formal or ceremonious use). **1.** (With late diners) midday meal; (with midday diners) light refreshment taken between breakfast & dinner. **2.** vb (-*ch*). Take ~; provide ~ for. [(1) *lunch*, *luncheon* (in 16th c., a thick piece or hunk), app. f. LUMP, after *hump*, *hunch*, etc., w. *luncheon* as an extension (cf. *punch*, *puncheon*, etc.); (2) *luncheon* (17th c.) slight repast between meals; (3) *lunch* (19th c.) abbr. f. *luncheon*]

lune (lōōn, lūn), n. (geom.). Figure formed on sphere or plane by two arcs enclosing space. [F, f. L *luna* moon]

lunette' (lōō-, lū-), n. Arched aperture in concave ceiling to admit light; crescent--shaped or semicircular space in dome or ceiling decorated with painting etc.; (fortif.) work larger than redan, with two faces & two flanks; watch-glass of flattened shape; hole for neck in guillotine. [F (prec., -ETTE)]

lŭng, n. Either of the pair of breathing--organs in man & most vertebrates (*good* ~s, strong voice); IRON¹~; ~*s of London* etc., open spaces in or close to great city; ~*s of oak*, ~*wort*; ~*-fish*, having ~s as well as gills; ~*-power*, power of voice; ~*'wort*, plant of borage kind with white--spotted leaves likened to diseased ~,

(‖ also ~*s of oak*) kind of lichen supposed to be good for ~-disease. Hence ~-ED² (-gd), ~'LESS, aa. [OE *lungen*, MLG *lunge*, OHG *lungun*, ON *lunga* f. Gmc *lung-*, cogn. w. LIGHT¹]

lünge¹ (-j), **longe** (-ŭnj), n., & v.t. **1.** Long rope with which horse-breaker holds horse while he makes it canter in circle; circular exercise-ground for training horses. **2.** v.t. Exercise (horse) with or in ~. [f. F *longe*, ult. f. L *longus* long]

lünge² (-j), n., & v.i. & t. **1.** Thrust with sword etc. esp. in fencing; sudden forward movement, plunge, rush. **2.** vb. Make ~ in fencing, deliver blow from shoulder in boxing, (*at*, *out*); (of horse) kick *out*; drive (weapon, sting, etc.) violently in some direction; rush, make sudden start in some direction. [18th c. *longe*, aphetic f. earlier *allonge*, F, f. *allonger* lunge (à *long* LONG¹)]

lunisōl'ar (lōō-, lū-), a. Of sun & moon (~ *period*, of 532 years between agreements of solar & lunar cycles; ~ *year*, with divisions regulated by changes of moon, & average length made to agree with sun's revolution). [f. L *luna* moon, -I-, L *sol* sun, -AR¹]

lŭnk'ah (-a), n. Kind of strong Indian cheroot. [f. Hind. *lanka* islands (of delta where the tobacco is grown)]

luny. See LOONY.

lup'in(e¹) (lōō-, lū-), n. Kinds of garden & fodder plant with long tapering spikes of blue, purple, white, or yellow flowers; (usu. pl.) seed of these. [ME, f. L *lupinus*]

lup'ine² (lōō-, lū-), a. Of wolf or wolves, wolf-like. [f. L *lupinus* (*lupus* wolf, -INE¹)]

lup'|us (lōō-, lū-), n. Ulcerous disease of skin. Hence ~OID, ~OUS, aa. [L, = wolf]

lurch¹, n. *Leave in the* ~, desert (friend, ally) in difficulties. [16th c. = state of score in some games in which winner was far ahead of loser, f. F *lourche* game like backgammon, also bad defeat in this]

lurch², n., & v.i. **1.** Sudden lean to one side, stagger. **2.** v.i. Make ~(es), stagger. [18th c., naut., of unkn. orig.]

lurch'er, n. Petty thief, swindler; spy; ‖ cross-bred dog between collie or sheep-dog & greyhound, used esp. by poachers. [f. obs. *lurch* vb var. of LURK]

lūre, n., & v.t. **1.** Falconer's apparatus for recalling hawk (bunch of feathers, within which it finds its food while being trained, attached to thong); something used to entice, decoy; enticing quality of a pursuit etc. **2.** v.t. Recall (hawk) with ~; entice (person, animal; usu. *away* or *into*). [ME, f. OF *luerre*, f. WG *löder* = MHG *luoder* bait]

lūr'id, a. Ghastly, wan, glaring, unnatural, stormy, terrible, in colour or combination of colours or lights (of complexion, landscape, sky, lightning, thunder-clouds, smoky flame, glance, etc.; *casts a* ~ *light on* facts or character, explains or reveals them in a tragic or terrible way); (bot. etc.) of dingy yellowish brown. Hence ~LY³ adv., ~NESS n. [f. L *luridus* pale--yellow]

lurk, v.i., & n. Be hidden *in, under, about,* etc.; escape notice, exist unobserved, be latent; (n.) *on the* ~, spying; ~*ing-place,* hiding-place. [northern ME, f. LOUR w. frequent. -*k* as in *talk*; cf. Norw. *lurka* sneak forth]

lu′scious (-shus), a. Richly sweet in taste or smell; sickly sweet, cloying; (of language or literary style) over-rich in sound, imagery, or voluptuous suggestion. Hence ~LY² adv., ~NESS n. [orig. obsc.; perh. alt. of obs. *licious,* aphetic f. DELICIOUS]

lush¹, a. Luxuriant & succulent (of plants, esp. grass). [var. of obs. *lash* (15th c.), f. OF *lasche* LAX]

lush², n., & v.t. & i. (sl.). 1. Liquor, drink. 2. vb. Ply with liquor; drink. [18th c. cant, of unkn. orig.]

lush′y̆, a. (sl.). Drunk. [-Y²]

lust, n., & v.i. 1. (Bibl., theol.) sensuous appetite regarded as sinful; animal desire for sexual indulgence, lascivious passion, whence ~′FUL a., ~′fulNESS n.; passionate enjoyment or desire of (~ *of battle, conquest, accumulation, applause*). 2. v.i. Have strong or excessive desire (usu. *after* or *for*). [OE, OS, OHG *lust,* Goth. *lustus* f. Gmc **lustuz*]

lus′tral, a. Of, used in, ceremonial purification. [f. L *lustralis* (LUSTRUM, -AL)]

lus′tr|āte, v.t. Purify by expiatory sacrifice, ceremonial washing, or other such rite. So ~A′TION n. [f. L *lustrare* (LUSTRUM), -ATE³]

lus′tre¹ (-ter), n., & v.t. 1. Gloss, refulgence, shining surface, brilliance, bright light, radiant beauty, whence ~LESS (-terl-), lus′trous, aa., lus′trousLY² adv.; splendour, glory, distinction, (*add* ~ *to, throw* or *shed* ~ *on*). 2. (Prismatic glass pendant of) chandelier. 3. Thin dress--material with cotton warp, woollen woof, & lustrous surface. 4. v.t. Put ~ on (cloth, pottery, etc.). [F (L *lustrare* illumine)]

lus′tre² (-ter), n. = LUSTRUM.

lus′trine, *lus′tring, nn. Glossy silk fabric. [LUSTRE¹]

lus′trum, n. (pl. -*a, -ums*). Period of five years. [L, orig. purificatory sacrifice after quinquennial census]

lus′t|y̆, a. Healthy & strong; vigorous, lively. Hence ~iHOOD, ~iNESS, nn., ~iLY² adv. [-Y²]

lu′sus naturae (loō-, lū-). n. Sport or freak of nature, strikingly abnormal natural production. [L]

lu′tanist (loō-, lū-), n. Lute-player. [f. med. L *lutanista* (*lutana* LUTE¹, -IST)]

lute¹ (loōt, lūt), n. Guitar-like instrument used in 14th–17th centuries (RIFT *within the* ~). [ME, f. OF *luth* f. Arab. *al′ud*]

lute² (loōt, lūt), n., & v.t. 1. Clay or

cement used to stop hole, make joint airtight, coat crucible, protect graft, etc. 2. v.t. Apply ~ to. Hence lu′tING¹(3) n. [ME, f. OF *lut* n., *luter* vb, or L *lutum* mud, clay, *lutare*]

lu′tĕo- (loō-, lū-), comb. form of L *luteus* orange-coloured (*lutum* weld), as ~*ful′vous* orange-tawny.

lu′tĕous (loō-, lū-), a. (nat. hist.). Of deep orange yellow. [prec., -OUS]

lute′string (loōts-, lū-), n. Glossy silk fabric. [app. assim. of *lustring* var. of LUSTRINE to *lute, string*]

Lutetian (loōtē′shn, lū-), a. Parisian. [f. L *Lutetia* ancient name of Paris, -AN]

Lu′theran (loō-, lū-), a. & n. (Follower) of Martin Luther (d. 1546), (member) of Church accepting the Augsburg confession. Hence ~ISM(3) n., ~IZE(2) v.i., (3) v.t. [-AN]

lux′|āte, v.t. Dislocate (joint etc.). So ~A′TION n. [f. L *luxare* (*luxus* dislocated, -ATE³]

luxūr′i|ant, a. Prolific (lit., & of imagination etc.); profuse of growth, exuberant, rank; (of literary or artistic style) florid, richly ornamented. Hence ~ANCE n., ~antLY² adv. [f. L *luxuriare* grow rank (*luxuria* LUXURY), -ANT]

luxūr′iāte, v.i. Revel, enjoy oneself, *in* or *on*; take one′s ease, be luxurious. [prec., -ATE³]

luxūr′ious, a. Given, contributing, to luxury, self-indulgent, voluptuous, very comfortable. Hence ~LY² adv., ~NESS n. [ME, f. OF f. L *luxuriosus* (foll., -OUS)]

lux′ury (-ksheri), n. (Habitual use of) choice or costly food, dress, furniture, etc.; thing that one enjoys; thing desirable but not indispensable; luxuriousness. [ME, f. OF *luxurie* f. L *luxuria* (*luxus* abundance)]

-ly¹, suf. f. OE *-lic,* = OS *-lik,* OHG *-lich,* ON *-ligr,* Goth. *-leiks* f. Gmc **-liko-* (*likam* form). The suf. forms adjj. f. nn. w. sense *having the qualities of* (*kingly, scholarly, soldierly*), or w. sense of recurrence (*daily, hourly*).

-ly², suf. forming advv., f. OE *-lice,* = OS *-liko,* OHG *-licho,* ON *-liga, -lega,* Goth. *-leiko* f. Gmc **-liko-* (prec.) + adv. suf. *-ō.* In Gmc an adv. in *-ly* implies the existence of an adj. in *-ly¹*; but even in OE the suf. (in the form *-lice*) was added to other adjj., & later became the usu. ending for advv. Down to 17th c. adv. *-ly* was added even to adjj. in *-ly,* the orig. *-likō* being thus doubly represented; these advv. in *-lily* are now avoided as awkward, & as the adv. use of the adj. (*to live godly*) is also avoided, adjj. in *-ly* have in ordinary use no corr. adv. *Partly* is a solitary formation on n. Wds in *-le* have *-ly* for *-lely* (*feebly, supply,* not *feeblely, supplely*).

lỹcăn′thropy̆, n. Transformation of witch into a wolf; form of madness in which patient imagines himself some beast &

exhibits depraved appetites, change of voice, etc. [f. Gk *lukanthrōpia* (*lukos* wolf, *anthrōpos* man, -Y¹)]

lycée (lēs'ā), n. State secondary school in France. [F; see foll.]

Lȳcē'um, n. Garden at Athens in which Aristotle taught, his philosophy & followers (cf. ACADEMY, GARDEN, PORCH); literary institution, lecture-hall, teaching- -place. [L, f. Gk *Lukeion* neut. of *Lukeios* epithet of Apollo (from whose neighbouring temple the ∼ was named)]

lych. See LICH.

Lȳch'nis (-k-), n. Genus of plants including campion & ragged robin. [L, f. Gk *lukhnis* red flower (*lukhnos* lamp)]

lȳc'opŏd, -pŏd'ium, n. Clubmoss; (*-ium* only) fine powder from kind of ∼ used as absorbent in surgery, & in making stage- -lightning. [*-d* anglicized f. *-ium* mod. L (Gk *lukos* wolf, *pous podos* foot)]

lȳdd'ite, n. High explosive chiefly of picric acid used in shells. [*Lydd* in Kent, -ITE¹]

Lȳd'ian, a. & n. (Language, inhabitant) of Lydia, ancient division of Asia Minor; ∼ *mode*: ancient Greek MODE, reputedly effeminate in character; fifth of eccl. modes, with F as final & C as dominant. [f. L f. Gk *Ludios*, -AN]

lȳe, n. Water alkalized by lixiviation of vegetable ashes, any strong alkaline solution esp. for washing, any detergent. [OE *lēag*, MDu. *loghe*, OHG *louga*, ON *laug* f. Gmc **laugō* f. **lau-* (cf. LATHER)]

lȳ'ing¹, n. In vbl senses of LIE²,³; also: place to lie (*soft, dry,* ∼); ∼ *in*, being in childbirth (also attrib., as ∼*-in hospital*). [-ING¹]

lȳ'ing², a. In vbl senses of LIE²,³; esp.: deceitful, false, whence ∼LY² adv.; ∼, placed, as *low-∼ land.* [-ING²]

‖ **lȳke-wāke,** n. Watch kept at night over dead body. [LICH, WAKE²]

lȳme-grass (-ahs), n. Kind of grass planted on sand to keep it from shifting. [perh. f. LIME¹ w. ref. to its binding effect]

lȳmph, n. Pure water (poet.); (physiol.) colourless alkaline fluid from tissues or organs of body, like blood but without red corpuscles; exudation from sore etc., (also *vaccine* ∼) matter taken from cow- pox vesicles & used in vaccination, other morbid matter used for similar purposes. Hence ∼OUS a. [f. L *lympha* water]

lȳmphăt'ic, a. & n. 1. Of, secreting, conveying, lymph, (∼ *gland, vessel*; ∼ *system*, these glands & vessels); (of persons or temperament) flabby-muscled, pale-skinned, sluggish, (qualities formerly attributed to excess of lymph). 2. n. Veinlike vessel conveying lymph. [in 17th c. also 'frenzied', f. L *lymphaticus* mad (*lympha*, see prec.); now assoc. w. *lymph* (on anal. of *spermatic* etc.)]

lȳncē'an a. Lynx-eyed, keen-sighted. [f. L f. Gk *lugkeios* (*lugx* lynx), -AN]; often

also w. ref. to *Lynceus* the keen-sighted Argonaut]

lȳnch, n., & v.t. 1. ∼ (or *L*∼) *law*, procedure of self-constituted illegal court that summarily executes person charged with flagrant offence; *Judge L*∼, imaginary authority to whom sentences are attributed. 2. v.t. Execute (person) thus. [orig. U.S., earlier *Lynch's law*, named after Captain William *L*∼ of Virginia, indemnified 1782 for illegally punishing persons]

lynchpin. Var. of LINCHPIN.

lȳnx, n. Kinds of animal of the cat tribe with tufted ear-tips, short tail, spotted fur, & proverbially keen sight; ∼ *fur*; ∼- *-eyed*, sharp-sighted. [L, f. Gk *lugx*]

Lȳ'on, n. (Also ∼ *King of Arms*) chief herald of Scotland. [arch. for *lion*; named f. lion on royal shield]

Lȳr'a, n. Northern constellation. [L, f. Gk *lura* LYRE]

Lȳr'aid, Lȳr'id, n. (usu. pl.). Meteor(s) radiating from Lyra about 20 Apr. [-ID²]

lȳr'ate, a. (nat. hist.). Lyre-shaped. [-ATE²]

lyre (līr), n. Obsolete instrument of harp kind but of size fit for holding up in left hand, & with strings supported by two symmetrically curved horns, chiefly used for accompanying voice; ∼*-bird*, Australian bird with ∼-shaped tail. So **lȳr'ist**(3) n., player on ∼, (*pr.* lī'r-) lyric poet. [ME, f. L f. Gk *lura*]

lȳr'ic, a. & n. 1. Of or for the lyre, meant to be sung; of the nature of, expressed or fit to be expressed in, song (∼ *drama,* opera); (of poem) expressing writer's own thoughts & sentiments usu. at no great length & in stanzas or strophes, (of poet), writing in this manner. 2. n. ∼ poem, (pl.) ∼ verses. Hence ∼o- comb. form. [f. L f. Gk *lurikos* (prec., -IC)]

lȳr'ical, a. = prec.; resembling, couched in or using language appropriate to, lyric poetry. Hence ∼LY² adv. [-AL]

lȳr'icism, n. Lyric character or (w. pl.) expression; high-flown sentiments. [-ISM]

lȳs'ol, n. Saponified mixture of cresol (see CREOSOTE) & oil, soluble in water, used as disinfectant. [P; f. Gk *lusis* (*luō* loosen) + -OL]

M

M, m, (ĕm), letter (pl. *Ms*, M's). (As numeral) 1,000, as MMCI 2,101, MCMLI 1,951; (Print., m), = EM.

-m, -ma, -me, suf. in nn. taken f. Gk (*-ma -matos*), usu. expr. result of verbal action; as *phlegm, poem, comma, coma, scheme, theme.* Adjj. formed on these show the *-at-* of the Gk stem (*phlegmatic, comatose*).

ma (mah), n. (vulg.). = MAMMA².

ma'am (mahm, măm, m'm), n. Madam (esp. used at Court in addressing Queen

or royal princess, *pr.* măm, or by servants, *pr.* m'm).

maca'bre (-ahbr), a. *Danse ~*, dance of
death; grim, gruesome. [15th c. *-bree* f. F
macabré (mod. F, erron., *macabre*), conject. referred to *Macabé* Maccabee]

macāc'ō¹, n. Monkey of genus Macacus.
[Port., = monkey]

macāc'ō², n. Kinds of lemur. [f. F
(Buffon) *mococo*, of unkn. orig.]

macăd'am, a. & n. 1. (Of roads) made in
the manner & with the materials advocated by J. L. McAdam (d. 1836), i.e.
with successive layers of broken stone of
nearly uniform size, each subjected to
pressure before next is laid. 2. n. Such
material; TAR~; TARMAC. Hence~IZE v.t.,
~ĪZA'TION n.

macarōn'|i, n. 1. Wheaten paste formed
into long tubes, used as food; *~i cheese*,
savoury pudding of ~i & cheese baked.
2. (hist.). 18th-c. exquisite affecting continental tastes, whence ~ISM n. [f. It.
maccaroni, f. late Gk *makaria* barley food]

macarōn'ic, a. & n. pl. (Verses) of
burlesque form containing Latin (or
other foreign) words & vernacular words
with Latin etc. terminations; medley. [f.
prec. +-IC]

macarōōn', n. Small cake or biscuit of
ground almonds, white of egg, sugar, etc.
[f. F *macaron* (as MACARONI)]

macāss'ar, a. & n. ~ (*oil*), kind of hair
oil. [f. *Mangkasara*, in island of Celebes]

macaw'¹, n. Kinds of parrot. [f. Port.
macao; cf. Tupi *macavuana*]

macaw'², n. Kinds of palm. [prob. Carib]

Maccabē'an, a. Of the *Maccabees*, Jewish
princes who freed Judaea from tyranny
of Antiochus Epiphanes, *c.* 166 B.C. [f.
LL f. Gk *Makkabaios* +-AN]

macc'aboy, -baw, n. Kind of snuff, usu.
scented with attar of roses. [f. *Macouba*,
district in Martinique]

mace¹, n. (Hist.) heavy usu. metal-
-headed & spiked club; staff of office resembling this; *~-bearer*, official carrying
this staff; stick used in bagatelle. [ME,
f. OF *masse* f. Rom. **mattea*]

mace², n. Dried outer covering of nutmeg, as spice. [ME *macis* (taken as pl.,
whence *mace*), f. OF *macis*, f. L *macir*]

mā'cĕdoine (-ĕdwahn), n. Fruit or vegetables in jelly as a dish or as cook's
material. [F]

mā'cer|āte, v.t. & i. Soften by soaking;
waste away by fasting. So ~A'TION n. [f.
L *macerare*, see -ATE³]

mach. See MACH (NUMBER).

machan' (-ahn), n. (Anglo-Ind.). Elevated platform used in tiger-shooting
etc. [Hind.]

machete (-āt'ă), n. See MATCHET.

Machiavĕll'|i (-kĭ-), n. Unscrupulous
schemer; one who practises duplicity in
statecraft, whence ~IAN a., ~ISM n. [f.
Niccolò *Machiavelli* (d. 1527), Florentine
statesman, author of work *del Principe*, in

which unscrupulous statecraft is thought
to be advocated]

machic'ol|āte, v.t. Furnish (parapet etc.)
with openings between supporting corbels for dropping stones etc. on assailants.
Hence ~A'TION n. [18th c., f. OF *mache-*,
machicoler]

machicoulis (mahshĭkōōl'ĭ), n. Machico-
lation. [f. F *māchicoulis*]

măch'in|āte (-k-), v.i. Lay plots,.intrigue.
So ~A'TION, ~ātoR,' nn. [f. F *machiner* or
L *machinari* contrive (foll., -ATE³)]

machine' (-shēn), n., & v.t. & i. 1. Apparatus for applying mechanical power,
having several parts each with definite
function (the kind often being specified,
as *sewing, printing, ~*); bicycle, tricycle;
bathing-~ (see BATHE¹); person who acts
mechanically & without intelligence, or
with unfailing regularity; (mech.) instrument that transmits force or directs its
application, as *simple ~*, one without
parts, e.g. lever; controlling political
organization; *~-gun*, mounted gun
mechanically loaded & fired, delivering
continuous fire, (v.t.) shoot at with *~-
-gun*; *~-made*, made by~ (occas. derog.);
~ tool, mechanically operated tool for
working on metal, wood, and plastics.
2. vb. Make or operate on with ~ (esp. of
sewing & printing); use ~. [F, f. L
machina f. Gk *mēkhanē* f. *mēkhos* contrivance, cogn. w. MAY¹]

machi'nery (-shē-), n. Machines; work of
a machine, mechanism; contrivances,
esp. supernatural persons & incidents,
used in literary work. [f. prec. +-ERY]

machi'nist (-shē-), n. One who makes or
controls machinery; one who works (esp.
sewing-) machine. [f. as prec. +-IST]

mach (nŭm'ber) (mahx), n. Ratio of the
speed of a body to the speed of sound in
the surrounding atmosphere. [E. *Mach*,
Austrian physicist (d. 1916)]

măc(k), n. (colloq.). Mackintosh. [abbr.]

măck'erel, n. Sea-fish used as food &
approaching shore in shoals in summer
to spawn; ~ *breeze, gale* (strong, &
so favourable to ~-catching); ~ *sky*
(dappled with small white fleecy clouds).
[ME, f. AF *nakerel*, OF *maquerel*]

măc(k)'intŏsh, n. Waterproof material of
rubber & cloth for garments, esp. that
patented by C. Macintosh (d. 1843);
cloak, coat, of this.

mā'cle, n. Twin crystal; dark spot in
mineral. [F, f. MACULA]

Mâcon (mahkawn'), n. Wine produced in
the neighbourhood of~ in France. [place]

macra'mé (-rahmĭ), n. Fringe, trimming,
of knotted thread or cord. [prob. f.
Turk. *maqrama* towel]

măc'ro-, comb. form of Gk *makros* long,
large, as; *~cephal'ic*, long, large, -headed;
~cosm, the great world, the universe, (cf.
MICROCOSM), any great whole; *~meter*
(-ŏm²), instrument for measuring distant
objects; *~scop'ic*, visible to naked eye.

măc′rŏn, n. Mark placed over vowel (ā) to show that it is long. [Gk, neut. adj. as prec.]

măc′ūl|a, n. (pl. ~ae). Dark spot in sun; spot in mineral; spot, esp. permanent one, in skin, whence ~AR¹ a., ~A′TION n. [L]

măd¹, a. (-dd-). Out of one's mind, insane; (of person or conduct) wildly foolish; *like* ~, furiously, violently, as *I ran like* ~; wildly excited, infatuated, (*after, about, for, on*, thing, subject, etc.); (colloq.) annoyed, as *I was rather* ~ *at missing my train*; (of animals) rabid; (prov.) ~ *as a March* HARE, *as a hatter*; extravagant, wild, in gaiety; ~′*cap*, wildly impulsive person; ~*-doctor* (treating the ~); ~′*house*, lunatic asylum; ~′*man*, ~′*woman*, ~ person. Hence ~′LY² adv., ~′NESS n. [f. OE *gemǣd(e)d* p.p. of **gemǣden* f. *gemǣd* mad, corresp. to OS *gimēd*, OHG *gameit*, Goth. *gamaiths* (crippled) f. Gmc **maidh-*]

măd², v.t. & i. (-dd-; rare). Make mad; be mad, act madly, as *the ~ding crowd* (as quot. from Gray's *Elegy*, now often taken as = distracting). [f. prec.]

măd′am, n. Polite formal address to woman; (euphem.) brothel-keeper. [ME, f. OF *ma* DAME my lady]

madame (madahm′, măd′am; pl. *mesdames* pr. mādahm′). F form of prec. as title or form of address; *M*~ *Tussaud's* (tōōsōz′), show in London of waxwork figures of celebrated & notorious persons (often w. ref. to the chamber of HORRORS in it). [as prec.]

măd′d|en, v.t. & i. Make, become, mad; irritate. Hence ~ingLY².adv. [f. MAD¹+ -EN⁶]

măd′d′er, n. Herbaceous climbing plant with yellowish flowers; dye got from this. [OE *mǣdere*, rel. to ON *mathra* (Sw. *madra*, Norw. *modra*), MLG, MDu. *mēde*]

māde, a. P.p. of MAKE. Special uses: ~ *dish* (of several ingredients); ~ *gravy* (artificially compounded); *a* ~ *man*, one whose success in life is assured; (of person etc.) *well, stoutly, loosely, powerfully,* ~ (built, formed).

Madeir′a (-ēra), n. Island in Atlantic Ocean; white wine there produced; ~ *cake*, kind of sponge-cake. [Port., f. L *materia* MATTER, timber from its thick woods]

mademoiselle (mădamazĕl′, & see Ap.), n. (pl. *mesdemoiselles*, pr. mādmwazĕl′). Unmarried Frenchwoman; French governess. [F]

măd′ia, n. Plant allied to sunflower; ~ *oil* (got from its seed, & made into cake for cattle). [f. Chil. *madi*]

madŏnn′a, n. (Picture, statue, of) Virgin Mary; ~ *lily* (white, as in pictures of M~). [It. (*ma* = *mia* my + *donna* lady f. L *domina*)]

maCrăs′ah (-a), **mĕdrĕss′ek** (-ă), n.

Mohammedan college. [Arab. (-*sah*) f. *darasa* v. study]

măd′re|pōre, n. Kinds of perforate corals; animal producing these. Hence ~pŏ′ric, ~pŏr′iFORM, aa. [F, f. It. *madrepora* (*madre* mother + *poro*, coral-like but porous substance)]

măd′rig|al, n. Short amatory poem; part-song for several voices, prop. with elaborate contrapuntal imitation & without instrumental accompaniment. Hence ~ăl′IAN a. [f. It. *-gale*, of unkn. orig.]

maduro (mahdoor′ō), a. (Of cigars) full-flavoured. [Sp., = matured]

Maecēn′äs, n. Generous patron of literature or art. [~, patron of Horace & Virgil]

mael′strom (māl-), n. Whirlpool on W. coast of Norway; great whirlpool (lit. & fig.). [early mod. Du., f. *malen* grind, whirl, +*stroom* STREAM]

maen′ad, n. Bacchante. [f. L f. Gk *mainas -ados* f. *mainomai* rave]

maĕstŏs′ō (mah-), adv. (mus.). Majestically. [It.]

maĕs′trŏ (mah-), n. (pl. *-ri*, pr. *-ē*). Great musical composer, teacher, or conductor. [It.]

Mae′ Wĕst (mā), n. (sl.). Airman's life-jacket. [person]

măff′ick, v.i. Exult riotously. [back formation f. *Mafeking* (relief of which in 1900 was celebrated extravagantly in London etc.), treated as gerund]

mafia (mah′fia), n. Hostility to law & its minⁱʰters among Sicilian population, often shown in crimes; those who share in this. [Sicil.]

‖ **măg¹, n.** (sl.). Halfpenny. [orig. unkn.]

măg², n. (Short for) MAGNETO (esp. in comb., as ~*-generator*).

măgazine′ (-zēn), n. **1.** Store for arms, ammunition, & provisions, in time of war; store for gunpowder or other explosives; ~ *gun* (with chamber containing supply of cartridges fed automatically to the breech). **2.** Periodical publication (now usu. illustrated) containing articles by various writers. [f. F *magasin* f. Arab. *makhazin* pl. of *makhzan* storehouse (*khazana* store up)]

Măg′dalén, -lēne, n. Reformed prostitute. [Mary *Magdalene* of Magdala (*Luke* viii. 2) identified with the sinner of *Luke* vii. 37. *Magdalen* College, Oxford, & *Magdalene* College, Cambridge, are pr. mawd′lin]

Măgdalēn′ian, a. (archaeol.). Of the (latest) palaeolithic period represented by remains found at La Madeleine, Dordogne, France. [-IAN]

māge, n. (arch.). Magician; learned person. [f. OF *mage* MAGUS]

magĕn′ta, n. & a. **1.** Brilliant crimson aniline dye, discovered soon after battle at *M*~ in N. Italy (1859). **2.** adj. Coloured with or like ~.

mě′gg′ot, n. Larva, esp. of cheese-fly & bluebottle; *red* ~, larva of wheat-midge] whimsical fancy, esp. ~ *in* one's *head*. Hence ~Y² a. [ME; app. alt. form of *maddock*, early ME *mathek* f. ON *mathkr*, see MAWKISH]

Ma'gi. See MAGUS.

Ma'gian, a. & n. (One) of the Magi; magician. Hence ~ISM(3) n. [-IAN]

ma'gic, a. & n. (Of) the pretended art of influencing course of events by occult control of nature or of spirits, witchcraft; *black*, *white*, *natural*, ~ (involving invocation of devils, angels, no personal spirit); inexplicable or remarkable influence producing surprising results; ~ *square*, one divided into smaller squares containing each a number, so arranged that sum of a row, vertical, horizontal, or diagonal, is always same; ~ *lantern*, optical instrument throwing magnified image of glass picture on white screen in dark room; ~ *mirror* (in which future or distant scenes are presented to spectator). Hence ~AL a., ~alLY² adv. [ME, f. OF *magique* a. & n. f. L *magicus* a., LL *magica* n. f. Gk *magikos* (as MAGUS, see -IC)]

magi'cian (-shn), n. One skilled in magic, wizard, conjuror. [ME, f. OF *magicien* (as prec., see -ICIAN)]

magilp'. See MEGILP.

Maginot line (mah'zhēnō), n. French fortified line on Franco-German frontier before the 1939–45 war. [person]

măgister'ial, a. Of, conducted by, a magistrate; invested with authority; dictatorial; (of opinions) authoritative. Hence ~LY² adv. [f. LL *magisterialis* f. LL *magisterius* (as MASTER)]

magis'tral, a. Of a master or masters, as *the* ~ *staff* (of a school); (pharm., of remedy etc.) devised by physician for particular case, not included in the pharmacopoeia (cf. OFFICINAL). [F, or f. L *magistralis* (as MASTER, see -AL)]

mä'gistr|ate, n. Civil officer administering law; JUSTICE of the peace. Hence or cogn. ~ACY, ~ateship, ~atURE, nn. [ME, f. L *magistratus -ūs* (orig. office of) magistrate (as prec., see -ATE¹)]

Măglemōs'ian (-z-), a.. Of the early European culture illustrated by articles found at Maglemose in Denmark. [-IAN]

măg'ma, n. (pl. ~*ta*, ~*s*). Crude pasty mixture of mineral or organic matters; one of supposed fluid strata under solid crust of earth. [L f. Gk (*massō* knead, root *mag-*, see -M)]

Măg'na C(h)ärt'a (k-), n. Great charter of English personal & political liberty obtained from John in 1215. [med. L]

măgnāl'ium, n. Light tough alloy of aluminium & magnesium. [MAGN(ESIUM) +AL(UMINIUM) +-IUM]

măgnăn'imous, a. High-souled, above petty feelings. Hence or cogn. măgnanim'ITY n., ~LY² adv. [f. L *magnanimus* (*magnus* great +*animus* soul) +-OUS]

măg'nāte, n. Great man; wealthy or

eminent man. [f. LL *magnas -atis* (*magnus* great)]

măgnē'si|a (-sha), n. Oxide of magnesium; (pop.) hydrated magnesium carbonate, white powder used as antacid & cathartic. Hence ~AN (-shn) a. [ME, f. med. L, f. Gk *magnēsia* (*lithos* stone) of Magnesia, (1) loadstone, (2) perh. talc]

măgnēs'ium (*or* -shyum), n. Metallic element, present in magnesia; ~ *flare*, *light*, blinding light got by burning ~ wire. [f. prec., see -IUM]

măg'nět, n. Piece of iron or ore having the properties of attracting iron & of pointing north & south when suspended, natural (as in loadstone) or induced by contact with a ~, by induction, or by electric current; *horse-shoe* ~ (in shape of bar bent till ends nearly meet); = LOAD¹*stone*; (fig.) thing that attracts. [ME, f. OF *magnete* or L f. Gk *Magnēs -ētos* (*lithos* stone) of Magnesia]

măgnět'ic, a. & n. 1. Having properties of magnet; producing, produced by, acting by, magnetism; ~ *equator*, ACLINIC line; ~ *mine*, submarine mine detonated by approach of large mass of ~ material, e.g. ship; ~ NEEDLE, NORTH; capable of receiving properties of, or being attracted by, loadstone; (fig.) very attractive; mesmeric. 2. n. pl. Science of magnetism. Hence măgnět'ICALLY adv. [f. F *-ique* or LL *magneticus* (prec., -IC)]

măg'nětism, n. Magnetic phenomena; natural agency producing these; *terrestrial* ~, magnetic properties of the earth as a whole; *animal*~, = MESMERISM; (fig.) attraction, personal charm. So **măg'nět**IST(3) n. [-ISM]

măg'nětite, n. Magnetic iron oxide. [-ITE]

măg'nětiz|e,-is|e (-īz), v.t. Give magnetic properties to; attract (lit. & fig.) as magnet does; mesmerize. Hence ~A'TION n. [-IZE]

măgnět'ō, n. (pl.~*s*). An electric generator using magnets which are independent of the current produced (esp. type of igniting-apparatus of internal-combustion engines producing the required intermittent high-tension current independently of a battery). [abbr. of *magneto-electric*].

măgnět'o'-, comb. form of Gk *magnēs magnēt-* MAGNET, as: ~*elec'tric*, (of electric generators) using magnets which are independent of the current produced, so ~*electri'city*; ~*graph*, instrument recording movements of ~*meter* (-ŏm'-) (instrument measuring magnetic forces, esp. terrestrial magnetism).

măg'nětrŏn, n. (phys.). Thermionic tube for generating very high frequency oscillations. [f. MAGNET +(ELEC)TRON]

măgnif'ic(al), aa. (arch.). Magnificent, sublime. [f. F *magnifique* or L *magnificus* (*magnus* great, see -FIC) +-AL]

măgnif'icăt, n. Hymn of Virgin Mary in *Luke* i. 46–55, used as canticle, &

beginning thus. [L, 3rd sing. of *magnificare* MAGNIFY]

magnif´ic|ent, a. Splendid, stately; sumptuously constructed or adorned; splendidly lavish; (colloq.) fine, excellent. Hence or cogn. ~ENCE n., ~entLY[2] adv. [OF, f. L *magnificent-* stem seen in comp. & sup. of *magnificus* MAGNIFIC]

magnif´icō, n. (pl. ~*es*). Venetian magnate; grandee. [It., as MAGNIFIC]

mag´ni|fy, v.t. Increase apparent size of (thing), as with lens or microscope; exaggerate; (rare) increase; (arch.) extol. Hence or cogn. ~FICA´TION, ~FIER[1](2), nn. [ME, f. L *magnificare* (*magnus* great, see -FY), partly thr. OF]

magnil´oqu|ent, a. Lofty in expression; boastful. Hence ~ENCE n., ~entLY[2] adv. [f. L *magniloquus* (*magnus* great + -*loquus* -speaking) + -ENT]

mag´nitūde, n. Largeness; size; importance; *first, seventh, etc.,* ~, classes of fixed stars arranged according to degree of brilliancy, (fig.) *of the first* ~ (importance). [ME, f. L *magnitudo* (*magnus* great, see -TUDE)]

Magnōl´ia, n. Genus of trees or shrubs cultivated for foliage & flower. [f. P. *Magnol*, botanist (d. 1715), -IA[1]]

mag´num, n. (Bottle containing) two quarts (of wine or spirits). [L, neut. of *magnus* great]

mag´num-bon´um, n. Large yellow cooking plum; kind of potato. [L wds = large good]

magnum opus. See OPUS.

mag´pie, n. 1. European bird with long pointed tail & black-&-white plumage; idle chatterer; variety of pigeon. **2.** (Rifle shot that strikes) outermost division but one of target. [f. *mag* abbr. of *Margaret* + PIE[1]]

mag´us, n. (pl. -*gi*, pr. -jī). Member of ancient Persian priestly caste; sorcerer; *the (three) Magi,* the 'wise men' from the East who brought offerings to the infant Christ. [L, f. Gk *magos* f. OPers. *magus*]

Magyar, n. & a. 1. (mŏd´yar). (Member, language) of the people now predominant in Hungary. **2.** (măg´yar). ~ (*blouse*), blouse with sleeves cut in one piece with main part of garment. [native]

Mahabharata (mahhahbah´rata), n. An ancient Hindu epic. [Skr.]

Maharaja(h) (mah-harahj´a), n. Title of some Indian princes. [Hind. (*maha* great + RAJAH)]

Maharanee (mah-harahn´ī), n. Maharajah's wife. [Hind. (*maha* great, *rani* queen)]

Mahăt´ma (ma-h-), n., (esoteric Buddhism). One of a class of persons with preternatural powers, supposed to exist in India & Tibet; pop. prefixed as title in India to names of exalted personages, esp. Gandhi. [f. Skr. *mahatman* (*maha* great + *atman* soul)]

Mahd´i, n. Spiritual & temporal leader expected by Mohammedans (often applied to leaders of insurrection in Sudan), whence **Mahd´(i)ism(3)** n. [f. Arab. *mahdiy* he who is guided right, p.p. of *hada* guide]

mah-jŏng(g)´, n. A Chinese game for four played with 144 pieces called tiles, adopted in Europe & America *c.* 1923. [Chin., = sparrows]

mahlstick. See MAULSTICK.

mahŏg´any (ma-h-), n. Wood of a tropical American tree, much used for furniture, & taking high polish; the tree; dining-table (*have one's knees under* person's ~, be dining with him); the colour of ~, reddish-brown, (often attrib.). [orig. unkn.]

Mahŏm´étan (ma-h-). See MOHAMMEDAN.

Mahound´ (ma-hoönd), n. (arch., joc.). Mohammed. [f. OF *Mahun* short for *Mahomet*]

mahout´ (ma-howt), n. Elephant-driver. [f. Hind. *mahaut*]

Mahrătt´a (mară-), n. Member of a warlike Indian race. [Hind. *Marhatta*]

mah´seer, n. Large Indian freshwater game fish. [Hind. *mahāsir*]

maid, n. Girl; young unmarried woman; spinster; *old* ~, elderly spinster, (also) round game at cards; (also ~´*servant*) female servant, as *house-, nurse-, lady's-,* ~, ~ *of all work;* ~ *of honour,* unmarried lady attending on queen or princess, (also) kind of cheesecake. Hence ~´ISH[1] a., ~´Y[3] n. [early ME, shortened f. MAIDEN]

maidan (mīdahn´), n. (Anglo-Ind.). Open space in town; parade-ground. [Pers.]

maid´en, n. & a. 1. Girl; spinster; (hist.) kind of guillotine used at Edinburgh; = ~ *over.* **2. adj.** Unmarried; ~ *name* (before marriage); (of female animals) uncoupled; (of horse) that has never won prize, (of race) open to such horses; (of plant) grown from seed; (of soldier, sword, etc.) untried; ‖~ *assize,* one at which there are no cases for trial; (crick.) ~ *over* (in which no runs are scored); ~ *speech,* M.P.'s first speech in the House; ~*hair,* kinds of fern with fine hairlike stalks & delicate fronds; ~*head* (-hĕd), virginity. Hence ~HOOD n., ~ISH[1], ~LIKE, ~LY[1], aa. [OE *mægden,* dim. (-EN[2]) f. *mægeth* = OS *magath,* OHG *magad,* Goth. *magaths,* Gmc **magathiz*]

maieut´ic (māū-), a. (Of Socratic mode of inquiry) obstetric, serving to bring out a person's latent ideas into clear consciousness, pertaining to intellectual midwifery. [f. Gk *maieutikos* f. *maieuomai* act as midwife (*maia*), see -IC]

mail[1], n. Armour composed of rings or chain-work, defensive armour for the body, as *chain, plate, ring,* ~. [ME, f. OF *maille* f. L *macula* spot, mesh]

mail[2], v.t. Clothe (as) with mail; *the* ~*ed fist,* (fig.) physical force. [f. prec.]

mail[3], n., & v.t. 1. Bag of letters for con-

veyance by post; this system of conveyance, the post, (esp. for foreign letters);
the ~, all that is so conveyed on one
occasion; ~ (*train*), train carrying this;
‖ *~-cart*, cart for carrying ~ by road,
(also) light vehicle for carrying children;
~-coach, (now) = *~-cart*, (formerly) stage-
-coach for entire conveyance of ~; ~
order, order for goods sent by post (*~-
-order firm*, firm doing business on this
system); FAN³*~*. 2. v.t. Send (letters etc.)
by post. [ME & OF *male* wallet f. WG
(= OHG) *malha*]

maim, v.t. Mutilate, cripple, (lit. & fig.).
[ME *maynhe* &c. f. OF *mahaignier* &c., of
unkn. orig.]

main¹, n. (In game of hazard) number
(5, 6, 7, 8, or 9) called by caster before
dice are thrown; match between cocks.
[16th c., app. spec. application of MAIN³]

main², n. Physical force (only in *with
might & ~*); SPANISH ~; (poet.) high sea;
in the ~, for the most part; principal
channel, duct, etc., for water, sewage,
etc. [OE *mægen*, OS *megin*, OHG *magan*,
ON *magn*, *megin* f. Gmc **mag-* MAY v.]

main³, a. 1. Exerted to the full, as *by ~
force*; chief in size or extent, as *the ~
body* (of army etc.); principal, most important, as *the ~ point* (in argument), ‖ *~
line* (of railway), whence *~'LY²* adv.; *~
have an eye to the ~ chance* (one's own
interests). 2. (naut.). *~ brace* (attached
to ~ yard, esp. *splice the ~ brace*, serve
extra rum ration); *~ deck*, (in man-of-
-war) deck next below spar deck, (in
merchantman) upper deck between poop
& forecastle; *~'mast*, principal mast;
~'sail (-sāl, -sl), (in square-rigged vessel)
sail that is bent to the ~ yard, (in fore-&-
-aft rigged vessel) sail set on after part of
~mast; *~'stay*, stay from ~top to foot
of foremast, (fig.) chief support; *~'top*,
platform above head of lower ~ mast;
~ yard, yard on which ~sail is extended.
3. *~'land*, extent of land excluding the
neighbouring islands; *~'spring*, principal
spring of watch, clock, etc., (fig.) chief
motive power or incentive; **M~ Street*,
principal street of a town (esp. allus., as
M~-street ideals). [ME, f. ON *meginn,
megn* adj.; partly f. OE *mægen-* (prec.) in
compp.]

maintain' (*or* měn-), v.t. Carry on, keep
up, (war, contest, action at law, condition,
position, attitude, relations, correspondence); cause (person etc.) to continue
in (condition, possession of thing, etc.);
support (life, one's state in life) by nourishment, expenditure, etc.; furnish (one-
self, children) with means of subsistence;
keep (road etc.) in repair; back up (cause,
party); assert as true (opinion, statement,
that). Hence *~ABLE* a. [ME, f. OF *main-
tenir* f. Rom. **manutenere* f. L*manu tenēre*
hold in the hand]

main'tènance, n. Maintaining; enough
to support life; *cap of ~*, cap, hat, worn

as symbol of official dignity or carried
before sovereign etc.; (law) offence of
aiding a party in litigation without lawful cause. [ME, f. OF (as prec., see -ANCE)]

maison(n)ětte' (-z-), n. Small house;
part of a house let separately (not necessarily all on one floor). [F (-*nn-*), dim. of
maison house]

maître d'hôtel (mātr dōtěl'), n. Major-
-domo; hotel manager. [F, = house-
master]

‖ **maize**, n. Indian corn, its grain. [f. Sp.
maiz, of Cuban orig.]

majěs't|ic, a. Possessing grandeur, impos-
ing. Hence *~ICALLY* adv. [f. foll. + -IC]

māj'ěstў, n. Impressive stateliness of
aspect, bearing, language, etc.; sovereign
power; (in speaking to or of sovereign)
(*Your, His, Her, M~*, you, he, she, as
*Your M~ forgets that with the best of in-
tentions it is scarcely in your M~'s* (or
your) *power to miss your train*); representation of God (the Father or Son)
enthroned within aureole. [ME, f. OF
majeste f. L *majestatem* (as MAJOR², see -TY)]

Mājlis', n. Persian parliament. [Pers.]

majŏl'ica, maio- (-yŏ-), n. Kinds of
glazed & ornamented Italian ware;
modern imitation of these. [f. It.
maiolica, f. former name of *Majorca*]

māj'or¹, n. Officer next below lieutenant-
-colonel & above captain (also in army
sl. for *sergeant-~*). Hence *~SHIP* n. [F,
short for *sergent-major*]

māj'or², a. & n., & v.i. 1. Greater (not
foll. by *than*) of two things, classes, etc.;
~ PROPHETS; *~ epilepsy*, epilepsy proper;
~ suit (bridge), spades or hearts; (log.)
~ term (that enters into predicate of
conclusion of syllogism); *~ premiss* (containing *~* term); *~ axis* of conic section
(passing through the foci); (mus., of
intervals) greater by chromatic semitone than minor intervals, as *~ third*, (of
keys) in which scale has a *~ third*; *~
part*, majority (*of*); (mil.) *~-general* (see
OFFICER), SERGEANT-*~*; *bugle, drum, pipe,
trumpet, ~* (head bugler etc. of unit);
‖ (in schools) *Brown, Smith, ~* (the elder
or first to enter school); of full age. 2. n.
Person of full age; (log., ellipt. for) *~
term* or *premiss* (*I deny your ~*); **student's special subject or course (v.i., take,
or qualify, *in* a *~*); *~-dŏm'ō* (pl. -os), chief
official of Italian or Spanish princely
household, house-steward. [L, compar.
of *magnus* great]

majŏ'ritў, n. 1. Greater number or part
(*of*); *the* (*great*) *~*, the dead, esp. *join the
(great) ~*, die; *absolute ~* of votes, more
than half number of electors or actual
voters; number by which votes cast on
one side exceed those on other. 2. Full
age, as *attained his~*. 3. Office of MAJOR¹.
[f. F *majorité* f. med. L *majoritatem* (as
prec., see -TY)]

majŭs'cūl|e, a. & n. (palaeogr.). Large
(letter), whether capital or uncial. Hence

~AR¹ a. [F, f. L *majuscula* (*littera* letter, dim. of MAJOR)]

māke¹, v.t. & i. (*măde*).. **1.** Construct, frame, as *God made man* (*a rational creature*), *bees ~ cells of wax, you were made for this work*; *pipes are made* (consist) *of clay*. **2.** ~ GOOD, SURE. **3.** Compose, draw up, (book, will). **4.** Prepare (tea, coffee, beds); ~ HAY; ~ (arrange & light materials for) *a fire*. **5.** Cause to exist, bring about, (disturbance, sport, noise, one's mark in the world, a corner in wheat); ~ *no* BONES; ~ *fun, game, of,* trifle with, treat with ridicule; ~ (conclude treaty of) *peace*; ~ (give) *place, room, way* (*for* others); ~ one's *way*, progress. **6.** Result in, as *it ~s a difference*; '*find* ' ~s (becomes) *in the past tense* '*found* '. **7.** Establish, enact, (distinctions, rules, laws); ~ FRIENDS. **8.** Get together (a HOUSE¹, quorum); ~ *a bag,* kill number of game; ~ *a book*, arrange series of bets on some event; ~ WATER¹. **9.** ~ *a habit of it*, cause it to become one, so ~ *an* EXAMPLE¹, *exhibition, fool, beast* (of oneself, person); ~ *a night of it*, carry it (festivity etc.) on through the night. **10.** ~ *of*, conclude to be the meaning or character of (*can you ~ anything of it* ?; *what am I to ~ of your behaviour* ?); ~ *much, little, the best*, etc., *of*, derive much etc. advantage from, (also) attach much etc. importance to, so ~ LIGHT⁴ *of*; ~ *a* HASH² *of*. **11.** Entertain, feel, (doubt, scruple, *of, about*); ~ HEAD *or tail of*. **12.** (Naut.) discern, come in sight of, (also) arrive at; (sl.) catch (a train etc.); *~ *it*, succeed in traversing ·a certain distance, (fig.) be successful. **13.** Amount to, as *2 & 2 ~ 4*; constitute, as *one swallow does not ~ a summer*; form, be counted as, (*this ~s the tenth time*; *will you ~ one of the party* ?); serve for, as *this ~s pleasant reading*. **14.** Become, turn out to be, ·as *she will ~ a good wife*. **15.** Gain, acquire, (money, a living, one's fortune); (cards) win (trick), play (card) to advantage, (also) shuffle (cards, or abs.). **16.** Proceed (*towards* etc.), also w. *for* (~ *for home*). **17.** ~ *sail*, set sail, (also) spread additional sail. **18.** Secure the advancement of, cf. MADE; ~ *or mar*, cause success or ruin of. **19.** Cause to be, as ~ *it* HOT, ~ *oneself a martyr*, ~ *oneself* SCARCE, ~ *him a duke*; convert *into*. **20.** Consider to be, (*what do you ~ the time* ?; *I ~ it 5 miles*). **21.** Cause, compel, (without *to* in act.), as ~ *him repeat it*, but *he was made to repeat it*. **22.** ~ *believe*, pretend (*to* do, *that*); ~ *do*, manage *with* (something) as an inferior or temporary substitute; *what bird do you ~* (consider) *that to be* ?; *he ~s Richard die* (represents him as having died) *in 1026*. **23.** Wage (war). **24.** Execute (bodily movement, bow, FACE¹, LEG). **25.** Perform (journey etc., & with many nn. expr. vbl action, as *acquisition, attempt, blunder, start, venture*); ~ (eat) *a good breakfast*; ~ HEAD¹,

LOVE. **26.** Accomplish (distance, knots, etc.). **27.** ~ *as if one had*, pretend one has; ~ BOLD, FREE¹, MERRY. **28.** (Of flood or ebb tide) begin to flow or ebb. **29.** ~ *after*, pursue; ~ *against*, be unfavourable to; ~ (hasten) *away*; ~ *away with*, get rid of, kill, squander; ~ *for*, conduce to (happiness etc.), confirm (view), proceed towards, assail; ~ *off*, run away, decamp, (often *with* stolen goods etc.); ~ *out*, draw up, write out, (list, document, cheque), get together with difficulty, as *articles put in to ~ out a volume*, (try to) prove, as *how do you ~ that out* ?, *you ~ me out* (*to be*) *a hypocrite*, understand, as *I can't ~ him out, can't ~ out what he wants*, decipher (handwriting etc.), distinguish by sight, as *I made out a figure in the distance*; ~ *over*, transfer possession of (thing *to* person), esp. by assignment; ~ *up*, supply (deficiency), complete (amount, party), compensate, as ~ *up lost ground*, ~ *up for lost time, we must ~ it up to* (compensate) *him somehow*, compound, put together, (medicine, hay *into* bundles, butter, etc.), sew together (coat etc.), get together (company, sum of money), arrange (type) in pages, compile (list, account, document), concoct (story), (of parts) compose (whole), prepare (actor) for his part by dressing, false hair, etc., apply cosmetics (to), arrange (marriage etc.), settle (dispute), ~ *it up*, be reconciled, ~ *up* one's *mind to*, decide to (do), resolve upon (course); ~ *up to*, court, curry favour with. **30.** ‖ ~ *bate* (arch.), breeder of strife; ~ *-believe*, pretence; ~ *peace*, peacemaker; ~ *shift*, temporary substitute or device; ~ *up*, disguise of actor, cosmetics etc. used for this, making up of type, type made up; (cosmetics for) woman's facial decoration; person's character & temperament; ~ *weight*, small quantity added to ~ up weight, (also fig. of persons), (fig.) unimportant point added to ~ case seem stronger. (OE *macian*, OS *makon*, OHG *mahhōn* f. WG **makōjan* f. **mak-* fit, suitable, cogn. w. MATCH¹]

māke², n. (Of natural or manufactured thing) style of structure or composition; mental or moral disposition; *American* ~, made in America; *is this your own* ~ (made by you) ?; *on the* ~ (sl.), intent on gain; (electr.) making of contact, position in which this is made, esp. *at* ~; ‖ ~ *& mend* (naut.), a period of leisure or no fixed duties for the hands (orig. for work on their clothes). [f. prec.]

māk'er, n. In vbl senses, esp. *the, our*, etc., *M~*, the Creator; (arch.) poet. [-ER¹]

māk'ing, n. In vbl senses, esp.: *be the ~ of*, ensure success or favourable development of; (pl.) earnings, profits; (pl.) essential qualities, as *he has the ~s of a general*; ***(pl.) paper & tobacco for rolling a cigarette. [-ING¹]

măl- pref. ▪ F *mal* f. L *male* badly, in

sense (1) bad(ly), as *maltreal*, (2) un-, as *maladroit*.

Malăcc'a, n. Town & district on Malay peninsula; ~ *cane*; rich-brown walking-cane, from stem of a palm.

măl'achite (-kĭt), n. Hydrous carbonate of copper, green mineral taking high polish. [f. OF *melochite* (Gk *malakhḗ* mallow, see -ITE¹)]

măl'aco-, comb. form of Gk *malakos* soft, as: ~*derm*, soft-skinned animal (esp. of sea-anemones & of one division of reptiles); ~*logist*, ~*logy*, (-ŏ̆l̆), student, science, of molluscs; ~*ptery'gian* a. & n., soft-finned (fish).

măladjŭst'ment, n. Faulty adjustment. [MAL-]

măladministrā'tion, n. Faulty administration. [MAL-]

măl'adroit, a. Clumsy, bungling. Hence ~LY² adv., ~NESS n. [F (MAL-+ADROIT)]

măl'adў, n. Ailment, disease, (lit. & fig.). [ME, f. OF *maladie* f. *malade* sick f. pop. L *male habitus* (*male* ill+*habitus* p.p. of *habēre* have)]

măl'a fĭd'ē, adv. & a. (Acting, done) in bad faith. [L]

Măl'aga, n. Seaport in S. Spain; white wine from this.

Mălagăs'ў, a. & n. (Language, inhabitant) of Madagascar. [used in native lang., but prob. of foreign orig.]

măl'aise (-z), n. Bodily discomfort, esp. without development of specific disease; also fig. [F (OF *mal* bad+*aise* EASE)]

măl'amūte, **măl'e-**, n. An Eskimo dog. [name of Alaskan Eskimo tribe]

măl'anders, **măll'en-**, n. pl. Scabby eruption behind knee in horses. [ME, f. OF *malandre* f. L *malandria*]

măl'apĕrt, a. & n. (arch.). Impudent, saucy, (person). [ME, f. OF (MAL-+*apert* = *espert* EXPERT)]

măl'apröp(ism), n. Ludicrous misuse of word, esp. in mistake for one resembling it (e.g. *a nice derangement of epitaphs* for *arrangement of epithets*). Hence **mălaprŏp'IAN** a. [f. Mrs. *Malaprop* in Sheridan's *Rivals*]

mălăpropos' (-pō), adv., a., & n. (Thing) inopportunely (said, done, or happening). [f. F *mal à propos* (mal ill, see APROPOS)]

măl'ar, a. & n. (Bone) of the cheek. [f. L *mala* jaw, see -AR¹]

mălār'|ia, n. Kinds of intermittent & remittent fever caused by bite of mosquito, which conveys the germs; unwholesome atmosphere caused by exhalations of marshes, to which these fevers were formerly referred. Hence ~IAL, ~IAN, ~IOUS, aa. [f. It. *mal' aria* bad air]

Malay', a. & n. (Language, member) of a people predominating in Malaya & Eastern Archipelago; ~ *fowl*, large domestic variety. Hence ~AN a. & n. [f. native *malayu*]

Mălaya'lam (-yah-), n. Language of Malabar. [native]

măl'contĕnt, a. & n. Discontented (person), (one) inclined to rebellion. [F(MAL-)]

măl de mer' (mār), n. Seasickness. [F]

māle, a. & n. **1.** Of the sex that begets offspring or performs the fecundating function (used of persons or animals, & of plants whose flowers contain only fecundating organs, also of plants to which sex was once attributed on account of colour etc., as ~ *fern*, commonest lowland fern); of men or ~ animals; (of parts of machinery etc.) designed to enter or fill the corresponding FEMALE part, as ~ *screw*; ~ (MASCULINE) *rhyme*. **2.** n. ~ person or animal. [ME, f. OF, f. L *masculus* (*mas* male, see -CULE)]

māle- in comb. = L *male* ill.

mălēdic't|ion, n. Curse. So ~ORY a. [ME, f. L *maledictio* f. MALE(*dicere* *dict*-speak), see -ION, MALISON]

măl'efactor, n. Criminal: evil-doer. So **mălēfăc'tion** n. [ME, f. L, f. MALE(*facere* *fact*- do), see -OR]

malēf'ic, a. (Of magical arts etc.) harmful, baleful. [f. L MALE(*ficus* -FIC)]

malēf'ic|ent, a. Hurtful (to); criminal. So ~ENCE n. [f. L altered stem of *maleficus* MALEFIC; cf. MAGNIFICENT]

malēv'ol|ent, a. Desirous of evil to others. Hence or cogn. ~ENCE n., ~entLY² adv. [16th c. *mali*- f. (obs.) F *mali*- f. L *mali*-MALE(*volens* part. of *velle* wish)]

mălfeas'|ance (-ēz-), n. (law). Evil-doing, esp. official misconduct. So ~ANT a. & n. [AF, f. OF MAL(*faisant* part. of *faire* do f. L *facere*), see -ANCE]

mălförm|ā'tion, n. Faulty formation. So ~ED¹ (-md') a. [MAL-]

măl'ic, a. (chem.). ~ *acid* (derived from apple & other fruits). [f. F *malique* f. L *malum* apple, see -IC]

măl'ice, n. Active ill-will; desire to tease; *bear* ~ (to), cherish vindictive feelings (against); (law) wrongful intention, esp. as increasing guilt of certain offences, esp. murder; ~ PREPENSE. So **mali'cious** (-shus) a., **mali'ciousLY²** (-shus-) adv. [ME, f. OF, f. L *malitia* (*malus* bad, see -ICE)]

malign'¹ (-īn), a. (Of things) injurious; (of diseases) = MALIGNANT; malevolent. Hence ~LY² adv. [ME, f. OF *maligne* or L *malignus* (*malus* bad, cf. BENIGN)]

malign'² (-īn), v.t. Speak ill of, slander. [ME, f. OF *maligner* or LL *malignare* contrive maliciously, as prec.]

malig'n|ant, a. & n. **1.** (Of disease) very virulent or infectious (now usu. denoting definite variety of disease, as ~*ant cholera*); harmful; feeling or showing intense ill-will. **2.** (hist.). Supporter of, supporting, Charles I against Parliament. Hence ~ANCY n., ~antLY² adv. [f. LL part. as prec.]

malig'nitў, n. Deep-rooted ill-will; (of diseases) malignant character. [ME, f. OF *malignite* or L *malignitas* (as MALIGN¹, see -TY)]

maling'er (-ngg-), v.i. Pretend, produce, or protract, illness in order to escape duty (esp. of soldiers, sailors, etc.). Hence ~ER¹ n. [f. F malingre sickly, of obsc. orig.]

māl'ism, n. Doctrine that it is a bad world. [f. L malus bad +-ISM]

māl'ison (-sn, -zn), n.(arch.). Curse. [ME, f. OF maleison MALEDICTION]

mall (mawl, măl), n. Sheltered walk as promenade, ‖ esp. the M~ (măl) in St James's Park, London, orig. alley for game of PALL-MALL; (hist.) this game, alley for it, mallet for it. [special use of MAUL¹]

măll'ard, n. Wild drake or duck; its flesh. [ME, f. OF mal(l)art, of obsc. orig.]

māll'éable, a. (Of metals etc.) that can be hammered or pressed out of form without tendency to return to it or to fracture; (fig.) adaptable, pliable. Hence māllêaBIL'ITY n. [ME, f. OF, f. L malleare hammer (malleus, see -BLE]

māll'ĕmŭck, mŏll'ỹmawk, n. Fulmar, petrel, or similar bird. [f. Du. mallemok (mal foolish +mok gull)]

māll'ĕt, n. Hammer, usu. of wood; implement for striking croquet or polo ball. [ME, f. OF maillet, dim. as MAUL¹]

mäll'ĕus, n. Bone of ear transmitting vibrations of tympanum to incus. [L, = hammer]

māll'ow (-ō), n. Wild plant with hairy stems & leaves & purple flowers; garden varieties of this. [OE mealuwe f. L malva]

malm (mahm), n. Soft chalky rock; loamy soil from disintegration of this; fine-quality brick made originally from~, marl, or similar chalky clay. [OE mealm, cogn. w. OS, OHG melm dust, ON malmr ore, Goth. malma sand f. mel- grind (MEAL¹)]

mälmais'on (-z-), n. Kind of carnation. [M~, palace of empress Josephine]

malmsey (mahm'zi), n. Strong sweet wine from Greece, Spain, etc. [ME, f. med. L malmasia (in MDu., MLG malmesie, -cye, MHG malmasier), f. later var. of Gk Monemvasia in the Morea; see MALVOISIE]

mälnūtri'tion, n. Insufficient nutrition. [MAL-]

mālŏd'orous, a. Evil-smelling. [MAL-]

mālprăc'tice, n. Wrongdoing; (law) physician's improper or negligent treatment of patient; (law) illegal action for one's own benefit while in position of trust. [MAL-]

malt¹ (mawlt), n. Barley or other grain prepared for brewing or distilling; extract of ~ (as food for invalids); ~ liquor (made from ~ by fermentation, not distillation, e.g. beer, stout); ~-house (for preparing & storing ~); ~-worm, (fig.) toper. [OE mealt, OS malt, OHG malz, ON malt f. Gmc *malt- cogn. w. MELT]

malt² (mawlt), v.t. & i. Convert (grain)

into malt; (of seeds) come to condition of malt from germination's being checked by drought. [f. prec.]

Mal'ta(maw-), n. Island in Mediterranean; ~ fever, complicated fever common in ~.

Maltese' (mawltēz), a. & n. (pl. same). (Language, native) of Malta; ~ cat, dog, fancy kind; ~ CROSS¹. [-ESE]

māl'tha, n. Cement of pitch & wax or other ingredients. [L f. Gk]

Mălthūs'ian (-z-), a. & n. (Follower) of T. R. Malthus (d. 1834) who advocated moral restraint (pop. understood as abstention from marriage) as means of checking increase of population. Hence ~ISM (-zhan-) n. [-IAN]

mal'ting (maw-), n. In vbl senses; also, malt-house. [-ING¹]

mal'tōse (maw-), n. (chem.), Sugar produced from starch-paste by action of malt. [F (MALT +-OSE²)]

māltreat', v.t. Ill-treat. So ~MENT n. [f. F MAL(trailer TREAT)]

maltster (mawl(t)'ster), n. One who makes malt. [-STER]

mălvā'ceous (-shus), a. Of the genus Mallow. [f. L malvaceus (as MALLOW, -ACEOUS)]

mălversā'tion, n. Corrupt behaviour in position of trust; corrupt administration (of public money etc.). [F, f. malverser f. L male badly +versari behave frequent. of vertere vers- turn, see -ATION]

mălvoisie' (-vwazē'), n. = MALMSEY. [ME, f. OF malvesie (mod. -voi-) f. med. L malvasîa, var. of malmasia; see MALMSEY]

măm'ba, n. (Kinds of) venomous African snake. [f. Kaffir m'namba]

măm'elon, n. Rounded eminence. [F, = nipple f. mamelle breast f. MAMILLA]

Măm'ĕluke (-ook), n. (hist.). Member of military body (orig. Caucasian slaves) that seized throne of Egypt in 1254; (in Mohammedan countries) slave. [ult. f. Arab. mamluk slave (malaka possess)]

mamill'|a, n. Nipple of female breast; nipple-shaped organ etc. So măm'illARY¹, măm'illATE²(2), măm'illātED¹, ~iFORM, aa. [L, dim. of MAMMA²]

mam(m)a'¹ (-ah), n. Mother (used esp. by children). [instinctive]

mămm'|a², n. (pl. ~ae). Milk-secreting organ of female in mammals; corresponding structure in males. Hence ~ARY¹, mammiF'EROUS, ~iFORM, aa. [L]

mămm'al, n. One of foll. class. [f. foll.]

Mammāl'ia, n. pl. Class of animals having mammae for nourishment of young. Hence mammāl'IAN a. & n., mammăl'OGIST, mammăl'OGY, nn. [neut. pl. of LL mammalis (as MAMMA², see -AL)]

mămmalif'erous, a. (geol.). Containing mammalian remains. [f. prec. +-FEROUS]

mămmee', n. Tropical American tree with large yellow-pulped fruit. [f. Sp. mamey f. Haytian]

mămm'on, n. Wealth regarded as idol or evil influence; the worldly rich; the ~

of unrighteousness, wealth ill used or ill gotten. Hence ~ISH¹ a., ~ISM, ~IST, ~ITE nn. [f. LL *mam(m)ona* f. Gk *mamōnas* f. Aram. *mamon* riches; see *Matt.* vi. 24, *Luke* xvi. 9–13]

mămm'oth, n. & a. **1.** Large extinct elephant. **2.** adj. Huge. [f. Russ. *mammot*]

mămm'y̆, n. Child's word for mother; *coloured woman in charge of white children. [f. *mam* (instinctive)+-Y³]

măn¹, n. (pl. *měn*). **1.** Human being (*a ~ & a brother,* fellow ~); (in indefinite or general application) person, as *any, no, ~, some, few, men;* (all) to *a ~,* all without exception. **2.** The human race (~ *is born unto trouble; ~ is a political animal).* **3.** *Inner, outer, ~,* spiritual, material, parts of ~, (joc.) interior, esp. stomach, exterior, of ~; NEW, OLD, ~. **4.** Adult male, opp. to *woman, boy,* or both; *~ & boy* (adv.), from boyhood upwards. **5.** (As impatient or lively vocative) *nonsense, ~ ! hurry up,~ (alive) !* ; (joc. or endearing) *little ~,* young boy. **6.** One, as *what can a ~ do in such a case?* **7.** Individual (male) person, as *~ for ~, between ~ & ~, 5/- per ~* ; *as a ~,* viewed simply in regard to his personal character; *if you want noise, he is your ~* (can supply you); *I'm your ~* (accept your offer etc.); *be one's own ~,* be free to act, (also) be in full possession of one's faculties, senses, etc.; *every ~* JACK¹. **8.** (In comb., denoting one who follows profession, uses implement, trades in article, etc.) *clergy~, post~, brake~, pen~, rag-&-bone- ~* ; BEST¹, HANDY, ~. **9.** ~ eminently endowed with manly qualities, as *be a, play the, ~.* **10.** Husband, in *~ & wife.* **11.** (Hist.) vassal; ~servant, valet; workman, as *the employers locked out the men.* **12.** (Usu. pl.) soldiers, esp. common soldiers. **13.** Piece in game of chess, draughts, etc. **14.** *~ of* STRAW. **15.** (In comb.) ship, as *~-of-war,* armed ship belonging to a country's navy, INDIA~, MERCHANT~. **16.** *~ of the* WORLD; *~ Friday,* servile follower, factotum, (name given by Robinson Crusoe to his servant); *~ about town,* || London society idler; *~-at-arms,* soldier, esp. heavy-armed & mounted; *~-(male) child; ~eater,* cannibal, biting horse, *~-eating* shark or tiger; *~'handle,* move by force of *~* alone, (sl.) handle roughly; *~'hole,* opening in floor, sewer, etc., for *~* to pass through; *~-hour,* work done by one *~* in one hour; *~ in the moon,* semblance of *~* in moon, esp. as type of imaginary person; *the ~ in* (*or on) *the street,* the ordinary *~* (esp. as opp. experts on the matter in question); *~-MILLINER; ~ of Kent* (see KENTISH); *~ of LETTERS; ~'power,* amount of men available for military or other service; *~'servant,* male servant; *~'slaughter,* slaughter of human beings, (Law) criminal homicide without malice aforethought; *~'trap* (for catching men, esp. trespassers). Hence *~'LESS a.* [OE

man(n), OS, OHG *man,* ON *mathr,* Goth. *manna,* f. Gmc **mann-, *mannon-*]

măn², v.t. (-nn-). Furnish (fort, ship, etc.) with men for service or defence; (naut.) place men at (part of ship); fill (post); fortify spirits or courage of (esp. one*self*). [OE *mannian,* as prec.]

măn'acle, n. (usu. pl.), & v.t. **1.** Fetter (prop. for the hand; also fig.). **2.** v.t. Fetter with *~s.* [ME, f. OF *manicle* handcuff f. L *manicula* dim. of *manus* hand]

măn'age¹, n. (arch.). Training of horse; trained movements of horse; riding-school. [f. It. *maneggio,* as foll.]

măn'age², v.t. & i. Handle, wield, (tool etc.); conduct (undertaking etc.); control (household, institution, State); take charge of (cattle etc.); subject (person, animal) to one's control; gain one's ends with (person etc.) by flattery, dictation, etc., whence **măn'agĭng²** (-nij-) a.; contrive (to do, often iron., as *he ~d to muddle it);* succeed in one's aim (often *with* inadequate material etc.); (with *can* or *be able to)* cope with, make proper use of, as *can you ~ another slice?* Hence ~ABIL'ITY, ~ableness, nn., ~ABLE a., ~ablY² adv., (-Ija-). [f. It. *maneggiare* f. Rom. **manidiare (manus* hand)]

măn'agement (-ijm-), n. In vbl senses; also or esp.: trickery, deceitful contrivance; *the ~,* governing body, board of directors, etc. [-MENT]

măn'ager (-nij-), n. Person conducting a business, institution, etc. (esp. *general ~);* || member of either House of Parliament appointed with others for some duty in which both Houses are concerned; *good, bad,* etc., *~* (of money, household affairs, etc.); || (law) person appointed, usu. by Court of Chancery, to manage a business for benefit of creditors etc. Hence ~ESS¹, ~SHIP, nn., **mănagē̆r'IAL a.** [-ER¹]

măn'akin, n. (Kinds of) brightly-coloured small tropical American bird. [var. of MANIKIN]

mănatee', n. Large aquatic herbivorous mammal, sea-cow. [f. Sp. *manati* f. Carib *manattoui*]

Măn'chester, n. || *~ goods,* cotton textiles (sold in *~ department* of a shop); *~ School,* adherents of the doctrines of free trade & *laissez-faire* (name given by Disraeli to Cobden & Bright & their followers). [place]

mănchineel', n. W.-Ind. tree with poisonous milky sap & acrid fruit. [f. F *mancenille* f. Sp. *manzan(ill)a* f. L *matiana* kind of apple f. Roman gens *Matia*]

măn'ciple, n. Officer who buys provisions for college, inn of court, etc. [ME, f. OF, f. L *mancipium* = (in med. L) office of *manceps* buyer (*manus* hand+*capere* take)]

Măncūn'ian, a. & n. (Inhabitant) of Manchester. [f. L *Mancunium* Manchester, -AN]

-mancy, suf. f. OF *-mancie* f. LL f. Gk *manteia* divination, = divination by —; see -CY.

Măndae′an, a. & n. (Member, language) of a Gnostic sect surviving in Iraq. [f. Aram. *mandā* knowledge]

mǎndǎm′us, n. ‖ Judicial writ issued from Queen's Bench Division as command to inferior court. [L, = we command]

mǎn′darin[1], n. Chinese official in any of 9 grades (hist.); standard spoken Chinese; party leader who lags behind the times; nodding toy figure in Chinese costume; ~ *duck*, small Chinese duck noted for its bright plumage. [f. Port. *mandarim* f. Malay f. Hind. *mantri* f. Skr. *mantrin* counsellor]

mǎn′darin[2], **-ine** (-ēn), n. Small flat deep-coloured orange; colour of this (got from coal-tar); a liqueur. [F (*-ine*); perh. f. prec. w. ref. to his yellow robes]

mǎn′datǎrÿ, n. (law). One to whom a mandate is given (for spec. sense see foll.). [f. LL *mandatarius* (foll., -ARY[1])]

mǎn′date[1], n. Judicial or legal command from superior; commission to act for another, esp. one from League of Nations to a State (the *mandatary*) to govern a people not qualified for independence; (poet.) command; papal rescript; (law) contract by which mandatary undertakes to perform gratuitously some service in respect of thing committed to him; (after F *mandat*) political authority supposed to be given by electors to (party in) parliament. [f. L *mandatum*, neut. p.p. of *mandare* command (*manus* hand +*dare* give)]

mǎndāte′[2], v.t. Commit (territory etc. *to* mandatary). [f. prec.]

mǎn′datorÿ, a. & n. 1. Of, conveying, a command, compulsory. 2. n. = MANDATARY. [f. LL *mandatorius* (as prec., see -ORY)]

mǎn′dible, n. Jaw, esp. lower jaw in mammals & fishes; upper or lower part of bird's beak; (in insects) either half of upper pair of jaws. So **mǎndǐb′ŭlAR**[1], **mǎndǐb′ŭlATE**[2](2), aa. [f. F or LL *mandibula* (*mandere* masticate)]

mǎndōl′a, **-ōr′a**, n. Kind of mandolin or lute. [It., var. of PANDORA]

mǎn′dolǐn(e), n. Musical instrument of lute kind with paired metal strings, played with plectrum. [F (*-ine*), f. It. *mandolino* dim. of prec.]

mǎndrǎg′ora, n. = foll. esp. as type of narcotic (Shak. *Othello* III. iii. 330). [ME also *-oras*, f. L (LL *-ora*) f. Gk *mandragoras*]

mǎn′drāke, n. Poisonous plant with emetic & narcotic properties, with root thought to resemble human form & to shriek when plucked. [ME *mandrag(g)e*, shortened f. prec., assoc. w. *drake* dragon]

mǎn′drel, **-il**, n. (In lathe) axis to which work is fixed while turned; cylindrical rod round which metal or other material

is forged or shaped; (dial.) miner's pick. [orig. unkn., cf. F *mandrin*]

mǎn′drill, n. Large, hideous, & ferocious baboon. [prob. MAN[1]+DRILL[3]]

mǎn′dūc|āte, v.t. Chew, eat. So ~A′TION n., ~ātORY a. [f. L *manducare* (*mandere* chew), see -ATE[3]]

māne, n. Long hair on neck of horse, lion, etc. (also fig. of person). Hence (-)mānED[2] (-nd), ~′LESS (-nl-), aa. [OE *manu*, OHG *mana*, ON *mǫn* f. Gmc *manō*]

manège, -ege, (manäzh′), n. Riding-school; movements of trained horse; horsemanship. [F (*-ège*), as MANAGE[1]]

mǎn′ēs (-z), n. pl. Deified souls of departed ancestors; shade of departed person, as object of reverence. [L]

mǎn′ful, a. Brave, resolute. Hence ~LY[2] adv., ~NESS n. [MAN[1]+-FUL]

mǎn′gabey (-ā), n. African species of monkey. [M~, region of Madagascar]

mǎng′anese (-ngganēz), n. Black mineral used in glass-making etc.; metallic element of which this is the oxide. Hence **mǎngane′sIAN** ·(-ngganēz-), **mǎngǎn′IC** (-ngg-), aa. [f. F *manganèse*, f. It. *-ese*, alt. f. MAGNESIA]

mǎnge (-j), n. Skin disease in hairy & woolly animals, caused by an arachnidan parasite; (loosely) dirty condition of skin. [ME *manjewe* f. OF *manjue* itch f. *mangier* (mod. *manger*) eat (as MANDUCATE)]

‖ **mǎng′el** (-wūrz′el), **mǎng′old** (-wūrz′el), (-ngg-), n. Large kind of beet, used as cattle food. [G *-gold-* (*-gel-*), f. *mangold* beet +*wurzel* root]

mǎn′ger (-j-), n. Box, trough, in stable etc. for horses or cattle to eat from; DOG *in the* ~. [ME, f. OF *mangeoire* f. Rom. *manducatoria* (as MANDUCATE, see -ORY)]

mangle[1] (mǎng′gl), n., & v.t. 1. Machine of two or more cylinders for rolling & pressing washed clothes. 2. v.t. Press (clothes) in ~. [f. Du. *mangel* (*-eln* vb), ult. f. Gk as MANGONEL]

mangle[2] (mǎng′gl), v.t. Hack, lacerate, by blows; cut roughly so as to disfigure; spoil (quotation, text, etc.) by gross blunders, disguise (words) by mispronouncing. [f. AF *ma(ha)ngler*, app. frequent. of *mahaignier* MAIM]

mǎng′o (-nggō), n. (pl. ~es). (Indian tree bearing) fleshy fruit yellowish-red in colour, eaten ripe or used green for pickles etc.; ~*-fish*, golden-coloured Indian fish; ~ *trick* (in which ~*-tree* appears to spring up & bear fruit in few hours). [f. Port. *manga* f. Tamil *mankay* (*man*~-tree +*kay* fruit)]

mangold (-wurzel). See MANGEL.

mǎng′onel (-ngg-), n. (hist.). Military engine for casting stones etc. [ME, f. OF *mangonel(le)*, dim. f. LL *manganum*, *-gonum*, *-gona* f. Gk *magganon*]

mǎng′osteen (-ngg-), n. (E.-Indian tree bearing) fruit with thick red rind & white juicy pulp. [f. Malay *mangustan*]

mǎng′rōve (-ngg-), n. Tropical tree or

shrub, bark of which is used in medicine & tanning. [17th c., of unkn. orig.]

măn´g|y (-jĭ), a. Having the mange; squalid, shabby. Hence ~ĭLY² adv., ~ĭNESS n. [f. MANGE + -Y²]

mănhătt´an, n. Cocktail made of vermouth, whisky, etc. [M~, in N. York]

măn´hŏŏd, n. State of being a man (in any sense); ~ suffrage (granted to all male citizens of lawful age not disqualified by crime, insanity, etc.); manliness, courage; the men of a country. [MAN¹ + -HOOD]

măn´ia, n. Mental derangement marked by excitement, hallucination, & violence; great enthusiasm (for thing, doing). Hence **măn´ic** a., of or affected by ~ (manic-depressive psychosis, kind of mental disorder alternating between periods of elation and depression, occas. with intermediate periods of sanity). [LL f. Gk, = madness]

-mānia, suf. denoting scientifically a special type of madness (klepto~, megalo~, nympho~); also (pop.) eager pursuit (biblio~) or admiration (Anglo~). Hence personal suf. -maniac (cf. -PHOBE, -PHOBIA). [as prec.]

măn´iăc, a. & n. (Person) affected with mania, raving mad(man). Hence **mani´acAL** a., **mani´acalLY²** adv. [f. LL maniacus (as MANIA, see -AC)]

-māniac, suf. See -MANIA.

Mănichee´ (-k-), n. Adherent of religious system (3rd to 5th c.) that represented Satan as coeternal with God. Hence **Mănich(a)e´AN** a. & n., **Măn´ich(a)eISM** n., (-kē-). [f. LL f. Gk Manikhaios, founder of sect, living in Persia]

măn´icŭr|e, n., & v.t. 1. (One who undertakes) treatment of hands & finger-nails as profession. 2. v.t. Apply ~e treatment to (hands, person). Hence ~IST n. [(vb f. n.) F (L manus hand + cura care)]

măn´ifĕst¹, n. List of cargo for use. of Customs officers. [f. F manifeste (as MANIFEST³)]

măn´ifĕst², a. Clear, obvious, to eye or mind. Hence ~LY² adv. [ME, f. L manifestus]

măn´ifĕst³, v.t. & i. Show plainly to eye or mind; be evidence of, prove; display, evince, (quality, feeling) by one's acts etc.; (of thing) reveal itself; record in ship's manifest; (of ghost) appear. So ~A´TION n., ~atIVE (-ĕs⸳) a. [ME, f. OF manifester or L manifestare (as prec.)]

mănifĕs´tō, n. (pl. ~s). Public declaration of policy by sovereign, State, or body of individuals. [It., as MANIFEST²]

măn´ifōld¹, a. & n. 1. Having various forms, applications, etc.; performing several functions at once; many & various, as ~⸳vexations; ~⸳writer, carbon copying-apparatus. 2. n. (mech.). Pipe or chamber with several openings. Hence ~LY² adv., ~NESS n. [OE manigfeald, repr. in OS, OHG, ON, Goth.; f. MANY + -FOLD]

măn´ifōld², v.t. Multiply copies of (letters etc.) as by MANIFOLD¹ writer. [OE & ME (obs.) f. prec.; in mod. use formed anew]

măn´ikin, n. Little man, dwarf; artist's lay figure; anatomical model of the body; small tropical American bird. [f. Du. manneken, dim. of MAN¹]

manill´a¹, n. Metal bracelet used by African tribes as medium of exchange. [Sp.; prob. dim. of L manus hand]

Manill´a², -il´a, n. (-ila) capital of Philippine islands; (also ~ hemp) fibrous material for ropes, matting, etc.; cheroot made in ~; ~ paper, brown wrapping-paper made from ~ hemp etc. [native (-ila)]

manille´, n. Second best trump or honour in quadrille & ombre. [corrupt. of Sp. malilla dim. mala bad f L malus]

măn´iŏc, n. Cassava; meal made from it. [f. Tupi mandioca]

măn´iple, n. 1. (Rom. ant.) subdivision of legion, containing 120 or 60 men. 2. Eucharistic vestment, strip hanging from left arm. [OF, f. L manipulus (manus hand)]

manip´ŭl|āte, v.t. Handle, treat, esp. with skill (material thing, question); manage (person) by dextrous (esp. unfair) use of influence etc. Hence or cogn. ~A´TION, ~ātOR nn., ~ātIVE, ~ātORY, aa. [back formation f. manipulation, after F manipuler (f. L as prec.)]

măn´itou (-ōō), n. (Amer. Ind.). Good or evil spirit; thing having supernatural power. [f. Algonquin manito, -tu]

mănkind, n. 1. (-kīnd´). Human species. 2. (măn⸳). Male sex. [MAN¹ + KIND n.]

măn´like, a. Having good or bad qualities of a man; (of woman) mannish. [-LIKE]

măn´l|ȳ, a. Having a man's virtues, courage, frankness, etc.; (of woman) having a man's qualities; (of things, qualities, etc.) befitting a man. Hence ~ĭNESS n. [-LY¹]

măn´n´a, n. Substance supplied as food to Israelites (Exod. xvi); spiritual nourishment, esp. the Eucharistic; sweet juice from ~-ash & other plants, used as gentle laxative (~ in tears, in sorts, superior, inferior, kinds of this); ~-croup, coarse granular wheat meal [Russ. krupa groats]. [ME f. LL f. Gk, f. Heb. man, explained as = man hu? what is it?, but perh. = Arab. mann exudation of Tamarix gallica]

mănn´equin (or -kĭn), n. Person, usu. woman, employed by dressmakers etc. to wear & show off costumes. [F, = lay figure, f. Du. as MANIKIN]

mănn´er, n. Way a thing is done or happens, as in, after, this ~; (arch.) in α ~ of speaking, so to speak; (gram.) adverb of ~, one that asks or tells how; to the ~ born, (Shak. Ham. I. iv. 15) destined by birth to be subject to the custom, (pop.) naturally fitted for the position etc.; (pl.) modes of life, conditions of society; outward bearing; *the grand ~·*, old-fashioned dignity; (pl.) *good, bad,* etc. behaviour in social intercourse, habits indicating good breeding, as *he has no ~s*, whence ~LESS a.; style in literature or art; mannerism; (arch.) kind, sort, as *what ~ of man is he?*; *all ~ of*, every kind of; *no ~ of right*, no right at all; *in a ~*, in some sense, to some extent. [ME, f. AF *manere* = OF *maniere* f. Rom. *manuaria mode of handling, fem. of L *manuarius* of the hand (*manus*), -ARY¹]

mann′ered (-ĕrd), a. *Ill, well, rough, ~*, having bad etc. manners; (of style, artist writer) showing mannerism. [-ED²]

mann′er|ism, n. Excessive addiction to a distinctive manner in art or literature; trick of style; trick of gesture or speech (esp. of an actor). Hence ~IST n., ~ĭs′tIC(AL) aa. [-ISM]

mann′erl|y̆, a. Well-mannered, polite. Hence ~INESS n. [-LY¹]

mann′ish, a. (Of woman) masculine; characteristic of man as opp. to woman, as *what a ~ way to thread a needle!* Hence ~NESS n. [-ISH¹]

mann′ite, n. (Also *~sugar*) substance obtained from manna. Hence **mann′itose²** n. [f. MANNA + -ITE¹]

manœu′vre|¹, *-euver, (-nōōver, -nū-), n. Planned movement of troops or ships of war; deceptive or elusive movement; skilful plan; MASS² of ~. [F, f. med. L *man(u)opera*, as foll.; cf. MANURE¹]

manœu′vr|e², *-euver, (as prec.), v.i. & t. Perform, cause (troops) to perform, manœuvres; employ artifice; force, drive, (person, thing, *into, out, away,* etc.) by contrivance; manipulate adroitly. Hence ~ER¹ n. [f. F *manoeuvrer* f. med. L *man(u)operare* (*manus* hand, *operari* to work); cf. MANURE²]

manŏm′eter, n. Pressure gauge for gases & vapours. Hence **mănomĕt′rĭc** a. [f. F *manomètre* (Gk *manos* thin, see -METER)]

ma nŏn trŏp′pō, mus. direction appended to another. But not to excess. [It.]

măn′or, n. English territorial unit, orig. of nature of feudal lordship, now consisting of lord's demesne & of lands from whose holders he can exact certain fees etc.; *lord of the ~*, person, corporation, having rights of this; *~-house*, his mansion. Hence manŏr′IAL a. [ME, f. AF *maner*, OF *manoir*, f. L *manēre* remain]

manqué (see Ap.), a. (after its n.) That might have been but is not, that has missed being, (*a Napoleon, comic actor, ~*). [F]

măn′sard, n. (Usu: *~ roof*) curb roof in which each face has two slopes, lower one steeper than upper. [f. F *mansarde* (F. *M~*, architect, d. 1666)]

mănse, n. Ecclesiastical residence, esp. Scottish Presbyterian minister's house. [ME, f. med. L *mansus, -sa, -sum,* house (*manēre mans-* remain)]

măn′sion (-shn), n. Large residence (∥ in pl. often of large buildings divided into flats); ∥*~-house*, house of lord of manor or landed proprietor, official residence, esp. (*the M~-house*) of Lord Mayor of London. [ME, f. OF, f. L *mansionem* (as prec., see -ION)]

măn′suetude (-swĭ-), n. (rare). Meekness, docility. [ME, f. L *mansuetudo* (*mansuetus* tame f. *manus* hand, *suesco* be used)]

măn′tel, n. (Now usu. *~piece*) structure of wood, marble, etc., above & around fireplace; (usu. *~shelf*) shelf projecting from wall above fireplace; *~-board*, wooden shelf (usu. draped) fixed upon this; *~-tree*, beam across opening of fireplace. [var. of MANTLE¹]

mănt(e)′lĕt, n. Kinds of short mantle; bullet-proof screen for gunners. [ME, f. OF (*-el-*), dim. of *mantel* MANTLE¹]

măn′tic, a. Of divination. [f. Gk *mantikos* (*mantis* prophet, see -IC)]

măntill′a, n. Large veil covering woman's hair & shoulders; small cape. [Sp., dim. of *manta* MANTLE¹]

măn′tis, n. Orthopterous insect; *praying ~*, kind that holds forelegs in position suggesting hands folded in prayer. [Gk, = prophet]

măntiss′a, n. Decimal part of logarithm. [L, = makeweight]

măn′tle¹, n. Woman's loose sleeveless cloak; (fig.) covering; fragile lace-like tube fixed round gas-jet to give incandescent light; outer fold of skin enclosing mollusc's viscera. [(1) OE *mentel*, (2) f. OF *mantel*, both f. L *mantellum* cloak]

măn′tle², v.t. & i. Clothe (as) in mantle; cover, conceal, envelop; (of liquids) become covered with coating or scum; (of blood) suffuse cheeks, (of face) glow, with blush. [f. prec.]

mantlet. See MANTELET.

măn′tŭa, n. Woman's loose gown in 17th--18th cc.; *~-maker*, dressmaker. [corrupt. of *manteau* (F, as MANTLE¹)]

măn′ŭal, a. & n. 1. Of, done with, the hands, as *~ labour*; (mil.) *~ (exercise)*, drill in handling rifle; *~ fire-engine* (worked by hand, not steam); *~ (finger) alphabet*; SIGN¹ *~*. 2. n. Small book for handy use, handbook; organ keyboard played with hands; (hist.) book of the forms to be used by priests in the administration of the Sacraments. Hence ~LY² adv. [ME, f. OF *manuel*, later assim. to L *manualis* (*manus* hand, see -AL)]

mănŭfăc′torў, n. Factory, workshop. [f. L as foll., see -ORY]

mănŭfăc′ture¹, n. Making of articles by physical labour or machinery, esp. on large scale; branch of such industry, as *woollen ~*; *of home, English,* etc., *~*, made at home etc.; (derog.) mechanical production (of literature etc.). [c. 1600 f. F, f. L *manu* by hand + *facture* (whence E *facture* 15th c.) f. L *factura* (*facere* facimake, see -URE)]

mănūfăc'tur|e², v.t. Work up (material) for use; produce (articles) by labour, esp. on large scale (derog. of literary work etc.); invent, fabricate, (story). Hence ~ER¹ n. [f. prec.]

mănūmǐt', v.t. (hist.; -tt-). Set (slave) free. So **mănūmǐ'ssion** n. [f. L *manumittere* (*manus* hand + *mittere* miss- send)]

manūre'¹, n. Any substance, esp. dung and compost, spread over or mixed with soil to fertilize it. Hence **manūr'IAL** a. [f. foll.]

manūre'², v.t. Apply manure to (land, or abs., also fig.). [ME, f. AF *maynoverer*, = OF *manouvrer* MANŒUVRE²]

măn'ūscript, a. & n. (abbr. *MS*. pr. ĕmĕs', pl. *MSS.* pr. ĕmĕs'ĭz). (Book, document) written by hand, not printed; author's copy for printer. [f. med. L *manuscriptus* (*manu* by hand + *scriptus* p.p. of *scribere* write)]

măn'ward, a. Tending, directed, towards man. [-WARD]

Mănx, a. & n. **1.** Of the Isle of Man, as ~ *cat*, tailless variety; ~*man*, inhabitant of I. of Man. **2.** n. ~ cat, language; (as pl., *Manx*) ~ people. [f. ON *manskr f. *Man-* (OIr. *Manu*)]

ma'nў (mĕ-), a. & n. Numerous, as ~ *times*, (poet., rhet.) ~ *a time* (& *oft*), ~ & ~ *a time*, ~ *people wish*, ~ *wish*, ~ *of us wish how* ~ (*of them*) *can I have?*, *as* ~ *as you like*, (pred., rare) *his reasons were* ~ *and good*, *six mistakes in as* ~ (six) *lines*; ~ '*s the*, there are ~ *that* (~ '*s the tale he has told us*); ~ '*s the time*, often (~ '*s the time I have seen you do it*); *the* ~, the multitude; *the one & the* ~ (philos.), unity & plurality; *one too* ~, not wanted, in the way; *he was* (*one*) *too* ~ *for us* (out-witted, baffled, us); *a good, great*, ~, fair, large, number; ~*-headed beast*, *monster*, the populace; ~*plies* (mĕn'ĭplĭz), (dial. for) *third* STOMACH; ~*-sided*, having ~ sides, aspects, capabilities, etc., so ~*-sidedness*. [OE *manig*, OS, OHG *manag*, Goth. *manags* f. Gmc *managaz]

Maori (mowr'ĭ), n. Member, language, of brown race in New Zealand. [native]

măp¹, n. Representation (usu. on plane surface, cf. GLOBE) of (part of) earth's surface, showing physical & political features etc., or of the heavens; *off the* ~ (colloq.), of no account, obsolete; *on the* ~ (colloq.), to be reckoned with, of importance. Hence ~'LESS a. [f. L *mappa* napkin; in med. L *mappa mundi* map of world]

măp², v.t. (-pp-). Represent on map; ~ *out*, plan out, arrange in detail (course of conduct, one's time, etc.). [f. prec.]

mā'ple, n. Kinds of trees & shrubs grown for shade, ornament, wood, or sugar; wood of these; ~*-leaf*, emblem of Canada. [ME *mapul* etc., OE *mapeltrēow*; cf. OE, OS *mapulder*, MLG *mapeldorn*]

Maquis (mahkē'), n. Secret force of

patriots in France in 1939–45 war. [F. = brushwood, f. Corsican It. *macchia*]

mâr, v.t. (-rr-). Impair fatally, ruin, esp. *make* (or *mend*) *or* ~; spoil, disfigure; ~*plot*, one who hinders undertaking by officiousness. [OE *merran*, OS *merrian*, OHG *merren*, ON *merja*, Goth. *marzjan* f. Gmc **marz-*]

mă'rabou (-bōō), n. Large W.-Afr. stork; tuft of down from its wings or tail as trimming for hat etc. [F, prob. f. vulg. Arab. use of foll.]

mă'rabout (-bōōt), n. Mohammedan her-mit or monk, esp. in N. Africa; shrine marking ~'s burial-place. [F, f. Arab. *murabit*]

măraschi'nō (-kē-), n. (pl. ~s). Liqueur from a small black cherry. [It. (*marasca* small black cherry, for *amarasca* f. *amaro* bitter f. L *amarus*)]

marăs'm|us (-z-), n. Wasting away of body. Hence ~IC a. [f. Gk *marasmos* (*marainō* wither)] ·

Mă'rathon, n. ~ (*race*), a race of ab-normal length (w. ref. to Phidippides, who ran 150 miles to secure Spartan aid for the Athenians in the battle of ~ in 490 B.C.); (attrib.) requiring extreme endurance (applied to competitions of various kinds).

maraud', v.i. & t. Make plundering raid (*on*); go about pilfering: (trans.) plunder. Hence ~ER¹ n. [f. F *marauder* (*maraud* rogue)]

mărave'dï (-vă-), n. (hist.). Gold & silver Spanish coins. [Sp. f. Arab. *Murabitin*, MARABOUTS, Moorish dynasty at Cordova]

mâr'ble, n., & v.t. **1.** Limestone in crystalline (also, in granular) state & capable of taking polish, used in sculpture & architecture; this as type of hardness or durability or smoothness (often attrib.); (pl.) collection of sculptures, as *Elgin* ~*s*; small ball or ~, clay, glass, etc., as toy. **2.** v.t. Stain, colour, (paper, edges of book, soap) to look like variegated ~ (esp. in p.p.). Hence **mârb'lY² a. [ME, f. OF *marbre, marble*, f. L *marmor*]

mârc, n. Refuse from pressed fruit. [F, f. *marcher* tread, MARCH⁵]

Mârc'an, a. Of St Mark. [f. L *Marcus* Mark, -AN]

mâr'casite, n. (Usu. white iron) pyrites. [15th c., f. med. L *marcasita*, f. Arab. *marqashita*]

mârcĕl', n., & v.t. (-ll-). **1.** ~ (*wave*), kind of artificial wave in hair. **2.** v.t. Wave (hair) thus. [*M*~, inventor of method]

mârcĕs'c|ent, a. (Of parts of plant) withering but not falling. Hence ~ENCE n. [f. L *marcescere* incept. of *marcēre* wither, see -ESCENT]

Mârch¹, n. (abbr. *Mar.*). Third month of year; ~ *brown*, fly used in angling; ~ HARE. [ME, f. OF *march(e)*, dial. var. of *marz, mars*, f. L *Martius* (*mensis* month) of Mars]

mârch², n. (hist.). Boundary, frontiers,

(often pl., esp. of borderland between England & Scotland or Wales); tract of (often debatable) land between two countries. [ME, f. OF *marche* f. Gmc *marko* MARK[1]]

march[3], v.i. (Of countries, estates, etc.) border *upon*, have common frontier *with*. [ME, f. OF *marchir* (as prec.)]

march[4], n. (Mil.) marching of troops; *line* (route) *of* ~; long toilsome walk; progress (*of events, time, intellect, mind*); distance covered by troops in a day; FORCED ~; uniform step of troops etc., as QUICK, SLOW, ~; ~ *past*, ~ of troops in line past saluting-point at review; (mus.) composition meant to accompany ~, as DEAD ~. [f. F *marche* (as foll.)]

march[5], v.i. & t. Walk *away, forth, past* (reviewing officer or sovereign), *out*, etc., in military manner with regular and measured tread; walk, proceed, steadily; ~*ing orders*, direction for troops to depart for war etc.; (as gallicism) make progress; (trans.) cause to go *on, off*, etc. [f. F *marcher*, f. Gallo-Rom. *marcare* f. LL *marcus* hammer]

mar'chioness (-sho-), n. Wife, widow, of marquis; lady holding in her own right position equal to that of marquis. [f. med. L *marchionissa* f. *marchio* -onis (MARCH[2]) captain of the marches]

march'pāne, marz'ipăn, n. Paste of pounded almonds, sugar, etc., made up into small cakes etc.; such cake. [c. 1500 *marchpayne*, later *marzepaine* (cf. F *marcepain*, It. *marzapane*), *mazapane* (cf. F *massepain*),*marzipan* (f. G); orig. unkn.]

marcōn'i, n., & v.i. & t. (hist.). **1.** = foll. **2.** vb. Send ~, send (message) thus. [see foll.]

marcōn'igrăm, n. (hist.). Message sent by Marconi's system of wireless telegraphy. [*Marconi* (d. 1937) inventor, -GRAM]

Mardi gras (mård'ēgrah), n. Shrove Tuesday; last day of carnival. [F, = fat Tuesday]

mar'e[1], n. = *claus'um*, sea under jurisdiction of particular country; ~ *lib'erum*, sea open to all nations. [L]

mare[2], n. Female of equine animal, esp. horse; GREY[1] ~; SHANKS'S ~; ~*'s-nest*, illusory discovery; ~*'s-tail*, kinds of aquatic plant, long straight streaks of cirrus. [OE *mere*, MDu., MLG *mer(r)ie*, OHG *mar(i)ha*, ON *merr* f. Gmc *marhjōn*, f. *marhaz* horse; see MARSHAL]

Maréchal Niel (*usu. pr.* mårsh'al nĕl), n. Kind of climbing rose. [after Adolphe *Niel*, Marshal of France (d. 1869)]

maremm'a, n. Low marshy unhealthy country by seashore. [It.]

mårg'arine (-g-, -j-; *also* -ēn), n. Substance made from edible oils and meat fats with water or skimmed milk, used as a spread on bread etc. and as a cooking fat. [F, misapplication of a chem. term, f. Gk *margaron* pearl, see -IN]

mårg'ay, n. S.-Amer. tiger-cat. [F, f. native *mbaracaia*]

marge[1], n. (poet.). Margin. [F, as MARGIN]

marge[2], n. (colloq.). Margarine. [abbr.]

mar'gin, n., & v.t. **1.** Edge, border, of surface, whence ~ATE[2](2), ~āted, aa.; condition near the limit below or beyond which a thing ceases to be possible etc.; extra amount (of time, money, etc.) over & above the necessary; (commerc.) sum deposited with stockbroker to cover risk of loss on transaction of account; space round main body of matter on page. **2.** v.t. Furnish with ~ or marginal notes; deposit ~ on (stock). [ME, f. L *margo -ginis*]

mar'ginal, a. Of, written in, the margin; having ~ notes; of, at, the edge; (of land) difficult & expensive to cultivate; close to the limit. Hence ~LY[2] adv. [-AL]

marginäl'ia, n. pl. Marginal notes. [mod. L neut. pl., as MARGIN, see -AL]

mårg'rāve, n. (hist.). German title of some princes of Holy Roman Empire, orig. of military governor of border province. [f. MDu. *markgrave* border count (MARK[1] + *grave* count)]

mårg'ravine, n. Margrave's wife. [f. Du. *markgravin* (as prec., see -INE[3])]

mårg'uerite (-gerēt), n. Ox-eye daisy. [F, f. L (-*ta*) f. Gk *margarītēs* (*margaron* pearl, see -ITE[1])]

mariage de convenance (see Ap.), n. Marriage contracted from prudential motives. [F]

Mār'ian, a. & n. **1.** Of the Virgin Mary, Mary Queen of England (orig. of Mary Tudor), or Mary Queen of Scots. **2.** n. Adherent of the last. [f. LL *Maria* Mary + -AN]

mä'rĭd, n. Jinn of most powerful class. [Arab., part. of *marada* rebel]

mä'rigöld, n. Kinds of plant with golden or yellow flowers; CORN ~; MARSH ~. [ME, f. *Mary* (prob. the Virgin) + *gold*]

marijuana, -huana, (mahrīhwah'nah), n. Dried leaves of Indian hemp, used to make narcotic cigarettes (called *reefers*). [Sp. -*hu*-]

marim'ba, n. Primitive African xylophone; modern orchestral instrument evolved from this. [native name]

mărinäde', n., & (also -te) v.t. Pickle of wine, vinegar, & spices; fish, meat, thus pickled; (v.t.) pickle with ~. [F, f. Sp. *marinada* (*marinar* pickle in brine, as foll., -ADE]

marine' (-ēn), a. & n. **1.** Of, found in, produced by, the sea; of shipping or naval matters, as ~ *insurance*; || ~ *stores*, old ships' materials & similar odds & ends as merchandise; for use at sea; (of soldiers) serving on board ship. **2.** n. Country's shipping, fleet, or navy, esp. *mercantile, merchant*, ~; soldier on warship (*blue, red*, ~s, hist., artillery, light infantry); specialist in Commando &

mariner, amphibious warfare; *tell that to the* (HORSE[1])*~s*. [ME, f. OF *marin* (fem. *-ine*) f. L *marinus* (*mare* sea, *-INE*[1])]

mā'riner, n. Sailor, seaman; *master ~*, captain of merchant ship. [ME, f. AF (OF *-ier*), f. Rom. **marinarius* (as prec., see *-ARY*[1])]

Marin'|ism (-ēn-), n. Affected style of It. poet Marini (d. 1625). So *~IST* n. [*-ISM*]

Mā'riŏl'atrȳ, n. (derog.). Worship of the Virgin Mary. [f. Gk *Maria* Mary + *-LATRY*]

mă'rionĕtte', n. Puppet worked by strings, representing person etc. [f. F *marionnette* (*Marion* dim. of *Marie* Mary, *-ETTE*)]

mă'rish, n. & a. (poet.). Marsh(y). [ME & OF *mareis* f. WG **marisk* MARSH]

Mā'rist, n. Member of Rom. Cath. Society of Mary. [f. F *Mariste* (*Marie* Mary, see *-IST*)]

mă'rital (*or* marīt[2]), a. Of a husband; of marriage. Hence *~LY*[2] adv. [f. L *maritalis* (*maritus* husband, see *-AL*)]

mă'ritime, a. Living, found, near the sea; connected with the sea, as *~ insurance*. [f. L *maritimus* (*mare* sea)]

mȧ'rj'oram, n. Aromatic herb used in cookery. [ME, f. OF *majorane* f. Rom. **majorana*, of unkn. orig.]

mȧrk'[1], n. **1.** Target or other object to be aimed at; *beside, wide of, the ~*, not hitting it, (fig.) not to the point. **2.** (boxing). Pit of stomach. **3.** Desired object, as *hit, miss, the ~*. **4.** Sign indication, (*of* quality, character, etc.), esp. *~ of mouth*, depression in horse's tooth indicating age. **5.** Affixed or impressed sign, seal, etc.; EAR[1], HALL, TRADE, *-~*. **6.** Cross etc. made in place of signature by illiterate person. **7.** Written symbol; this as sign of *good* or *bad* conduct. **8.** Unit of numerical award of merit in examination, as *he gained 46 ~s*. **9.** Line etc. serving to indicate position; *Plimsoll's ~*, line showing how far ship may legally be submerged when loaded; *below, up to*, etc., *the ~* (standard). **10.** (footb.). Heel-*~* on ground made by player who has caught the ball direct from kick or knock on or throw forward by opponent. **11.** Stain, scar, etc., esp. BIRTH-*~*. **12.** *Make* one's *~*, attain distinction; *of ~*, noteworthy. **13.** (As apology for mentioning anything horrible etc.) (*God*) *save the ~* (freq. sarcastic). **14.** (hist.). Tract of land held by Teutonic village community. **15.** (athletics). Line indicating the starting-point (*get off the ~*, start). **16.** *Easy ~* (orig. U.S., sl.), person easily gulled. [OE *mearc*, OS *marka*, OHG *marcha*, ON *mǫrk*, Goth. *marka* f. Gmc **markō* boundary]

mȧrk'[2], v.t. **1.** Make a mark on (thing) by stamping, cutting, writing, etc.; put identifying mark or name on (linen); attach figures indicating prices to (goods); (pass.) have natural marks, as *~ed with silver spots*. **2.** *~ out*, trace out boundaries for (ground), plan (course), destine, as *~ed out for slaughter*; *~ off*, separate (thing *from* another, lit. & fig.) by boundary. **3.** Name or indicate (place on map, length of syllable) by signs or marks. **4.** Record (points gained in games). **5.** Manifest (one's displeasure etc. *by*); (pass.) *this tendency is strongly ~ed* (noticeable), *a ~ed difference*, whence *~'ĕdLY*[2] adv., *~'ĕdNESS* n. **6.** Accompany, be a feature of, as *no triumph ~s her manner*. **7.** *~ time*, move feet as in marching, but without advancing (often fig.). **8.** See, notice; observe mentally, as *~ my words*; *a ~ed man*, one whose conduct is watched with suspicion or hostility; (also *~* one expected to reach eminence. **9.** (Also *~ down*) note & remember spot to which (grouse etc.) has retired. **10.** || (footb.). Keep close to (opponent) so as to hamper him if he receives ball. **11.** *~ down*, (also) *~ at* a lower price; *~ up*, *~ at* a higher price; *~-'up* n., amount added by shopkeepers to cost price of goods to cover overhead charges & profit. [OE *mearcian*, OS *markōn*, OHG *marchōn*, ON *marka* f. Gmc **markōjan* (as prec.)]

mȧrk'[3], n. Denomination of weight for gold & silver, usu. 8 oz (now only for continental weights); German coin (formerly about 1/-); (hist.) English money of account. [late OE *marc*, MDu. *marc*, MHG *mark*, ON *mǫrk*, obsc. rel. to med. L *marca, marcus*]

mȧrk'er, n. In vbl senses, esp.: one who marks down game; one who records score, esp. in billiards; flare etc. to assist bombers in air-raid; = BOOK[1]*-~*. [MARK[2] + *-ER*[1]]

mȧrk'ĕt[1], n. Gathering of people for purchase & sale of provisions, livestock, etc.; time of this; *bring one's eggs or hogs to a bad ~*, fail in one's schemes; open space or covered building in which cattle etc. are exposed for sale; *make a ~ of*, (fig.) barter away; demand (*for* commodity); *the corn ~*, the trade in corn; *come into the ~*, be offered for sale; *put on the ~*, offer for sale; BLACK[1] *~*; (*European*) *Common M~*, economic and political association of certain (European) countries as a unit with internal free trade and common external tariffs; MONEY-*~*; STOCK-*~*; rate of purchase & sale, *~ value*, as *the ~ fell*; seat of trade; *~ cross* (erected in *~-place*); *~-day* (on which *~* is held); || *~ garden* (in which vegetables are grown for *~*); *~-place*, square, open space, where *~* is held; || *~-town* (where *~* is held); *~ value*, saleable value (dist. from cost & from BOOK[1] *value*). [late OE *market* = OS *-at*, OHG *-ât*, f. pop. L *marcatus* f. L *mercatus*; see MERCHANT]

mȧrk'ĕt[2], v.i. & t. Buy or sell in market; sell (goods) in market or elsewhere; whence *~ABLE* a., *~abLY*[2] adv. [f. prec.]

mȧr'khor (-kōr), n. Large spiral-horned

wild goat of N. India. [Pers., = snake-eater]

mȧrk'ing, n. In vbl senses, esp. colouring of feathers, skin. etc.; ~-*ink* (indelible, for marking linen). [MARK² + -ING¹]

mȧrks'man, n. (pl. -*men*). One skilled or practised in aiming at mark, esp. one who attains certain standard of proficiency in rifle practice. Hence ~SHIP (1, 3) n. [MARK¹ + -ES + MAN]

Mȧrk Tăp'ley, n. Invincibly cheery person. [character in Dickens's *Martin Chuzzlewit*]

mȧrl, n., & v.t. 1. Soil consisting of clay and carbonate of lime, a valuable fertilizer. 2. v.t. Apply ~ to (ground). Hence ~'Y² a. [ME, f. OF *marle* f. med. L *margila* f. L *marga*]

Marl'borough House (mawl'bro), n. Royal Palace used as a London residence.

mȧrl'ine, n. (naut.). Small line of two strands; ~-*spike*, *marlinspike*, pointed hard-wood or iron tool for separating strands of rope in splicing. [(a) 15th c., f. Du. *marlijn*, -*ing* (*marren*, *marlen* bind, +LINE², -ING¹); (b) *marlin-spike* f. *marling*- f. (15th c.) *marl* f. LG, Du. *marlen*, frequent. of *marren*; so LG *marl-spieker*]

mȧrl'ite, n. Kind of marl that resists action of air. [-ITE¹]

mȧrm'alāde, n. Preserve of oranges or specified fruit. [f. F *marmelade* f. Port. -*lada* f. *marmelo* quince f. L f. Gk *melimēlon* (*meli* honey +*mēlon* apple) see -ADE]

mȧrm'ite, n. Extract made from fresh brewer's yeast. [P; F, = cooking-pot]

mȧrm'olite, n. Laminated serpentine of pale green colour. [irreg. f. Gk *marmairō* shine, see -LITE]

mȧrmŏr'ēal, a. (poet.). Of, like, marble. [f. L *marmoreus* (as MARBLE) + -AL]

mȧrm'osĕt (-z-), n. Small tropical American monkey with bushy tail. [f. OF *marmouset* grotesque image]

mȧrm'ot, n. Rodent of squirrel family. [f. F *marmotte* prob. f. Roumansch *murmont* f. L *murem* (nom. *mus*) *montis* mountain mouse]

mȧ'rocain, n. A dress-fabric made in silk (or other materials). [F, = Moroccan]

Mȧ'ronīte, n. One of a sect of Syrian Christians dwelling in Lebanon. [f. med. L *Maronīta* (*Maron* founder, see -ITE¹)]

marōōn'¹, n. & a. 1. (Of) brownish-crimson colour. 2. Firework exploding with loud report. [f. F *marron* chestnut f. It. *marrone*]

marōōn'², n. One of class of Negroes, orig. fugitive slaves, in mountains & forests of Dutch Guiana & W. Indies; marooned person. [f. F *marron*, f. Sp. *cimarron* wild]

marōōn'³, v.t. & i. Put (person) ashore & leave him on desolate island or coast as punishment; idle, hang about. [f. prec.]

mȧrque (-k), n. (hist.). *Letter(s) of* ~ (& *reprisal*), licence to fit out armed vessel & employ it in capture of enemy's merchant shipping; (sing.) ship carrying licence. [f. AF, OF *marque* f. Prov. *marca* f. *marcar* seize as a pledge]

mȧrquee' (-kē), n. Large tent. [f. MARQUISE taken as pl. n.]

mȧr'quetry̆, -terie, (-kǐ-), n. Inlaid work. [F (-*erie*), f. *marqueter* variegate (MARK¹)]

mȧr'quis, -quĕss, n. Noble ranking between duke & earl or (in foreign countries) count. Hence **mȧr'quiSATE¹**(1) n. [ME, f. OF *marchis* f. Rom. *marchensis* (MARCH², -ESE)]

mȧrquise' (-kēz), n. 1. (Of foreign nobility) marchioness. 2. Finger-ring set with oval pointed cluster of gems. 3. (arch.). Tent. [F, fem. of *marquis*]

mȧr'quois (-kwoiz), n. ~ *scale*, apparatus for drawing equidistant parallel lines. [app. blunder for F *marquoir* marker (MARK¹)]

mȧ'rram, n. A shore grass that binds sand. [f. ON *marálmr* (*marr* sea, HAULM)]

mȧ'rriage (-rǐj), n. Relation between married persons, wedlock; *give*, *take*, *in* ~ (as husband or wife); *communal* ~, system by which all the men in small community are married to all the women; *companionate* ~, see COMPANION¹; act, ceremony, of marrying; *civil* ~ (performed by civil official without religious ceremony); (fig.) intimate union (*the* ~ *of true minds*); (cards) union of king & queen of same suit; ~ *articles*, antenuptial agreement respecting rights of property & succession; ~-*bed*, (fig.) marital intercourse; ~ LICENCE¹; ‖ ~ *lines*, certificate of marriage; ~ *market*, supply & demand of eligible partners for ~; ~ *settlement*, arrangement securing property to wife & sometimes to children. [ME, f. OF *mariage* f. *marier* MARRY¹; see -AGE]

mȧ'rriageable (-rǐja-), a. Of an age to marry; (of age) fit for marriage. [-ABLE]

mȧ'rried (-ǐd), a. United in wedlock; of person(s) so united, as ~ *life*. [p.p. of MARRY¹]

marron glacé (see Ap.), n. Chestnut iced with sugar as sweetmeat. [F]

mȧ'rrow¹ (-ō), n. Soft fatty substance in cavities of bones, often a type of rich food or of vitality (*chilled to the* ~, right through); *spinal* ~, substance forming spinal cord; essential part, as *pith* & ~; *vegetable* ~, kind of pumpkin; ~*bone*, bone containing edible ~, (pl., joc.) knees; ~(*fat*), kind of large pea; ~-*spoon* (for getting ~ from bones). Hence ~LESS (-ōl-), ~'Y² (-ōi), aa. [OE *mearg*, OS, OHG *marg*, ON *mergr* f. Gmc *mazg*-]

‖ **mȧ'rrow²** (-ō), n. (dial.). Mate, consort, match, very image *of*. [15th c., prob. f. ON *margr* friendly, communicative]

mȧ'rry¹, v.t. & i. (Of priest etc.) join (persons, one *to* another) in wedlock; (of parent or guardian) give (son, daughter, etc.) in marriage (also ~ *off*, implying activity on parents' part); (of either contracting party) take in marriage; (fig.)

unite intimately; (naut.) splice (rope-
-ends) together without increasing girth;
(intr.) take husband or wife. [ME, f. OF
marier f. L *maritare* f. *maritus* husband]

măˈrrў², int. (arch.) expr. surprise, asseveration, indignation, etc.; ~ *come up*
(expr. indignant or contemptuous surprise). [ME, = (the Virgin) *Mary*]

Mäˈrs (-z), Roman god of war; warfare;
planet fourth in order of distance from
sun. [L]

Marsa'la (-sah-), n. White wine like light
sherry, from ~ in Sicily.

Marseillaise' (-seläz, & see Ap.), n.
National song of French Republic, first
sung by Marseilles patriots. [F, fem. adj.
f. *Marseille*, -ESE]

Marseilles' (-sälz), n. Seaport in S.
France; stiff cotton fabric like piqué.
[E name for *Marseille*]

märsh, n. Low land flooded in winter &
usu. watery at all times; ~ *gas*, light
carburetted hydrogen; ~ *mallow*, (confection made from root of) shrubby herb
growing near salt~es; ~ *marigold*, gold-
-flowered ranunculaceous plant growing
in moist meadows. Hence ~'iNESS n., ~'Y²
a. [OE *mersc, merisc*, MLG, MDu.
mersch, f. WG *marisk* (MARISH), f. Gmc
mari- sea, MERE¹]

märsh'al¹, n. ‖ EARL ~; officer of highest
rank in some foreign armies; PROVOST ~;
FIELD ~, ~ *of the Royal* AIR¹ *Force*, AIR¹~;
(hist.) *knight* ~, officer of royal household
with judicial functions; ‖ (*judge's*) ~,
official accompanying judge on circuit,
with secretarial duties; officer arranging
ceremonies etc. Hence ~SHIP n. [ME, f.
OF *mareschal, -cal* f. LL *mariscalcus* (Lex
Salica) f. OFrank. *marhskalk* f. *marh*
horse (cf. MARE) + *skalk* servant]

märsh'al², v.t. & i. (-ll-). Arrange in due
order (persons at feast etc., soldiers, facts,
etc.); (her.) combine (coat of arms);
conduct (person) ceremoniously (*into* etc.);
~*ling yard*, railway yard in which goods
trains etc. are assembled. [f. prec.]

märsh'alsea, n. (hist.). Court held,
prison in Southwark controlled, by
knight marshal. [alt. f. *marshalcy* (MAR-
SHAL¹ + -CY)]

märsūp'ial, a. & n. (anat., zool.). 1. Of,
like, a pouch, as ~ *muscle*. 2. (Animal) of
the class of mammals characterized by
having a pouch in which to carry their
young, born imperfect. [f. L f. Gk *mar-
supion* pouch dim. of *marsipos* purse + -AL]

märt, n. Market-place; auction room;
trade centre. [ME, f. Du. (obs.) *mart,
markt*, f. L as MARKET]

märtěll'ō, n. (hist.; pl. ~s). ~ (*tower*),
small circular fort, usu. on coast to
prevent hostile landing. [alt. f. Cape
Mortella in Corsica]

märt'ěn, n. Animal like weasel, with
valuable fur. [ME, f. Du. *martren* f. OF
(*peau* skin) *martrine*, adj. f. *martre* (whence
obs. E *marter*) + -ine —INE¹]

mär'tial (-shl), a. Of, suitable for, appropriate to, warfare, whence ~IZE (-sha-)
v.t.; ~ *law*, military government, by
which ordinary law is suspended; brave;
fond of fighting; (*M*~) of the planet Mars.
Hence ~LY² adv. [ME, f. OF, or L
martialis of MARS, see -AL]

Mär'tian (-shn), a. & n. (Inhabitant) of
Mars. [f. L *Martius* of MARS + -AN]

märt'in, n. 1. *St M*~, bishop of Tours in
4th c.; *M*~*mas, St M*~'*s day*, Nov. 11;
‖ *St M*~'*s summer*, fine season about this
time. 2. Birds of swallow family esp.
house~, which builds mud nest on house
walls etc.; SAND-~. [F, f. L *Martinus*]

märtinět', n. Strict (esp. military or
naval) disciplinarian. Hence ~'ISM n.,
~t'ISH¹ a. [*M*~, French drill-master in
reign of Louis XIV]

märt'ingäle (-ngg-), n. 1. Strap, set of
straps, fastened at one end to nose-band,
at other end to girth, of horse to prevent
rearing etc.; (naut.) rope for guying
down jibboom. 2. Gambling system of
doubling stakes in hope of eventual turn
of luck. [F, of unkn. orig.]

märti'ni¹ (-ēnī), n. The M~-Henry rifle.
[*M*~, inventor of its breech action]

märti'ni² (-ēnī), n. Cocktail made of gin,
vermouth, orange bitters, etc. [*M*~,
inventor]

märt'lět, n. Swift; (her.) footless bird.
[f. F *martelet* alt. f. *martinet* dim. f.
MARTIN]

märt'yr (-er), n., & v.t. 1. One who
undergoes penalty of death for persistence
in Christian faith or obedience to law of
Church, or undergoes death or suffering
for any great cause; ~ *to* (constant
sufferer from) *gout* etc.; *make a* ~ *of* one-
self, (pretend to) sacrifice one's inclinations, for sake of credit thus gained.
2. v.t. Put to death as ~, torment. [OE,
f. LL f. late Gk *martur* = Gk *martus -uros*
witness]

märt'yrdom (-ter-), n. Sufferings & death
of martyr; torment. [-DOM]

märt'yrize, -ise (-īz), v.t. Make a martyr
of (oneself, person). [ME, f. OF, or LL
martyrizare (MARTYR, -IZE)]

märtyr|o-, comb. form of Gk *martur -uros*,
as : ~*ol'atry*, worship of martyrs; ~*ol'ogy*,
list, register, history, of martyrs, whence
~*olō'gical*.

märt'yrў, n. Shrine, church, erected in
honour of martyr. [ME, f. OF -*ie* or LL
f. Gk *marturion* (as MARTYR)]

mär'vel¹, n. Wonderful thing; wonderful
example of (quality); (arch.) astonishment; ~ *of Peru*, showy garden plant
with flowers opening in afternoon. [ME, f.
OF *merveille* f. LL *mirabilia* neut. pl. of L
mirabilis (*mirari* wonder at, see -BLE)]

mär'vel², v.i. (-ll-). Be surprised (*at, that*);
wonder (*how, why*, etc.). [ME, f. OF
merveillier (as prec.)]

mär'vellous, a. Astonishing; extravagantly improbable, esp. *the* ~. Hence

~LY² adv., ~NESS n. [ME, f. OF *merveillos* (as prec., -OUS)]

Marx'|ian, a. & n. (Adherent) of the doctrines of the German socialist Karl Marx (1818–83). So ~ISM(3) n., ~IST(2) n. & à. [-IAN]

marzipan. See MARCHPANE.

mas̆căr'a, n. Preparation for darkening eyelashes etc.[It. *mascara, maschera* MASK¹]

mas̆'cot, n. Person, thing, that brings luck. [f. F *mascotte*, f. Prov. *mascotto* dim. of *masco* witch]

ma'scūline (mah-, mă-), a. & n. 1. Of the gender to which names of males normally belong; ~ *rhyme* (in French verse, between words ending in stressed syllables, not *e* mute), ~ *ending*, ending of line with stressed syllable; of the male sex; manly, vigorous; (of woman) having qualities appropriate to man. 2. n. ~ gender, word. Hence ~NESS, masculin'ITY, nn., (mah-, mă-). [ME, f. OF *masculin* (fem. -*ine*) f. L *masculinus* (as MALE, see -INE¹)]

mash¹, n.. Malt mixed with hot water to form wort; (also *bran* ~) mixture of boiled grain, bran, etc., given warm to horses etc.; soft pulp made by crushing, mixing with water, etc.; (sl.) mashed potatoes (*sausage & ~*); confused mixture; ~-*tub* (in which malt is mashed). [OE *māsc, māx-*, = MLG *mēsch*, MHG *meisch* f. WG **maisk-*, perh. cogn. w. MIX]

mash², v.t. Mix (malt) with hot water; crush, pound, to pulp; reduce (potatoes etc.) to uniform mass by crushing. [ME, f. prec.]

mash³, v.t., & n. (obsolesc. sl.). 1. Excite sentimental admiration in (one of opposite sex); *be ~ed on*, have such admiration for. 2. n. Person on whom one of opposite sex is ~ed. [orig. unkn.]

mash'er, n. (obsolesc. sl.). Fop posing as lady-killer. [prec.]

mash'ie, -y̆, n. Iron golf club used for lofting or for medium distances; ~ *niblick*, club intermediate between ~ & niblick. [orig. unkn.]

ma'sjid (mŭ-), n. Mosque. [Arab.]

mask¹ (mah-), n. Covering, usu. of velvet or silk, for concealing face at balls etc., or of wire, gauze, etc., for protection; hollow figure of human head worn by ancient Greek & Roman actors; clay or wax likeness of person's face, esp. (also *death-~*) one made by taking mould from face; (fig.) disguise, as *throw off the ~*; masked person; face, head, of fox. [f. F *masque*, f. It. *maschera* f. Arab. *maskhara*¹]

mask² (mah-), v.t. Cover (face) with mask; (pass.) be disguised with mask; (mil.) conceal (battery etc.) from enemy's view, hinder (army etc.) from action by watching with adequate force, hinder (friendly force) by standing in line of its fire; disguise (feelings etc.); ~*ed ball* (at which masks are worn). [f. prec.]

ma'sker, -quer, (mah-), n. One who takes part in masquerade or masque. [prec. +-ER¹]

măskinŏn'ge (-j, -ji), n. Large pike in great lakes of N. America. [Odjibwa]

masochism (măz'okizm), n. Form of (esp. sexual) perversion in which a sufferer derives pleasure from pain or humiliation (opp. SADISM). [f. L. von Sacher-*Masoch* (d. 1895), Austrian novelist who described a case of ~]

mās'on, n., & v.t. 1. Worker in stone; (~*'s mark*, device carved on stone by ~); freemason, whence masŏn'IC a. 2. v.t. Build, strengthen, with masonry. [ME, f. OF *masson*, mod. *maçon*, f. Rom. **mation-, *macion-*; ult. orig. obsc.]

mās'onry, n. Mason's work, stonework. [ME, f. OF *maçonnerie* (as MASON, see -ERY)]

Măs(s)ōr'a(h) (-ra), n. Body of traditional information on text of Hebrew Bible. [f. Heb. *masoreth* perh. = bond]

Măs(s)'orēte, -īte, n. Jewish scholar contributing to the Masora. Hence **măs(s)orēt'IC** a. [(-*ete*) corrupt. of Heb. as prec.; (-*ite*) prec. +-ITE¹]

masque (mahsk), n. Amateur histrionic & musical entertainment, orig. in dumb show, later with metrical dialogue; dramatic composition for this. [as MASK¹]

masquerāde'¹(mahske-), n. Masked ball; false show, pretence. [f. Sp. *mascarada* (*máscara* mask, see -ADE)]

masquerāde'² (mahske-), v.i. Appear in disguise; assume false appearance. [f. prec.]

mäss¹ (*or* mahs), n. (A) celebration (usu. Rom. or Anglo-Cath.) of the Eucharist, as ~ *was said, we attend, go to, hear,* ~, ~*es were said for his soul*; liturgy used in this; musical setting of parts of this; *high* ~ (with incense, music, & assistance of deacon & subdeacon); *low* ~ (with no music & minimum of ceremony). [OE *mæsse* f. Rom. **messa* f. eccl. L *missa*, app. f. *mittere miss-* dismiss]

mäss², n., & v.t. & i. 1. Coherent body of matter of indefinite shape; dense aggregation of objects, as *a* ~ *of fibres*; large number (*of*); *he is a* ~ *of* (covered with) *bruises*; unbroken expanse (*of* light etc.); *the* (*great*)·~, the majority (*of*); *the* ~*es*, the lower orders, cf. CLASSES; *in the* ~, in the aggregate; (phys.) quantity of matter a body contains; ~ ENERGY; ~ *meeting*, large (usu. political) assembly of people; ~ *observation*, study & reporting of social customs etc. of ordinary people; ~ *of manœuvre*, body of troops kept free for strategic needs; ~ *production* (of large quantities of a standardized article by standardized mechanical processes); ~ *spectrograph*, apparatus separating isotopes by atomic discharge through electric & magnetic fields. 2. vb. Gather (t. & i.) into ~; (mil.) concentrate (troops). [ME; (vb f. OF *masser*) f. OF *masse* f. L *massa* prob. f. Gk *maza* barley-cake (*massō* knead)]

măss'acre (-ker), n., & v.t. **1.** General slaughter, carnage, (of persons, occas. of animals). **2.** v.t. Make a ~ of, murder cruelly or violently (a number of persons). [F; in OF *maçacre, macecle*, &c. shambles, whence *maceclier* butcher, executioner, ult. orig. unkn.; vb f. F *massacrer*]

măssage' (-ahzh; *or* măs⁴), n., & v.t. **1.** Rubbing, kneading, etc., of muscles & joints of the body with the hands, to stimulate their action, etc. **2.** v.t. Treat (part, person) thus. [F, f. *masser* treat with massage, perh. f. Port. *amassar* knead, f. *massa* dough (MASS²), see -AGE]

măssé (măs'ā), n. (billiards). Stroke made with cue held perpendicular. [F, p.p. of *masser* make such stroke (as MACE¹)]

măsseur', măsseuse', (-êr, -êrz, & see Ap.), nn. Man, woman, who practises massage. So **măss'ER¹, măss'OR**, nn. [F (as MASSAGE, see -OR)]

măss'if (*or* mahsêf'), n. Mountain heights forming a compact group. [F (see MASSIVE) in n. use]

măss'ive, a. Large & heavy or solid; (of features, head, etc.) largely moulded; (fig.) solid, substantial; impressive, imposing; (psych.; of sensation etc.) having large volume or magnitude. Hence ~LY² adv., ~NESS n. [ME, f. OF (-*if, -ive*), as MASS², see -IVE]

măss'|ỹ, a. Solid; weighty. Hence~ĬNESS n. [MASS²+-Y²]

mast¹ (-ah-), n. **1.** Long pole of timber, iron, etc., set up on ship's keel to support sails; BEFORE *the*~; HALF-~ *high*; hence (of ship) ~'ED² a., ~'ER¹ n.; ~-*head*, highest part of ~, esp. of lower ~ as place of observation or punishment, (v.t.) send (sailor) to this, raise (sail) to its position. **2.** Post, or lattice-work upright, for supporting a wireless aerial; (also *mooring*-~) strong steel tower to top of which an airship can be moored. [OE *mæst*, OHG *mast*, ON *mastr* f. Gmc **mastaz*]

mast² (-ah-), n. Fruit of beech, oak, & other forest-trees, esp. as food for swine. [OE *mæst*, MDu., OHG *mast*, WG corresp. to Gmc **mast-*]

măs'taba, n. (archaeol.). Ancient Egyptian tomb with sloping sides & flat roof. [Arab. *maṣṭaba* bench]

ma'ster¹ (mah-), n. **1.** Person having control; (naut.) captain of merchant vessel; employer; owner of dog, horse, etc.; male head of household, as ~ *of the house*; *be* ~ *of*, have at one's disposal; *be* one's *own* ~, be independent or free to do as one will; *make oneself* ~ *of*, acquire thorough knowledge of or facility in using; one who has or gets the upper hand, as *we will see which of us is* ~. **2.** Teacher, tutor, esp. (also *school*~) in school; HOUSE¹-~; teacher in philosophy etc. **3.** *The M*~, Christ; *M*~ *of Arts* (abbr. *M.A.*), holder of university degree

orig. giving authority to teach in university. **4.** Skilled workman, or one in business on his own account, as ~ *carpenter*. **5.** Great artist, esp. *old* ~ (esp. of painters of 13th–17th cc.), picture etc. by a ~. **6.** Head of some colleges. **7.** ‖ (As title of legal functionaries) *M*~ *in Chancery* etc.; *M*~ *of Ceremonies* (see CEREMONY), MISRULE, *the* ROLLS; *M*~ (organizer, leader, esp. in Royal Household & Inns of Court) *of the revels*; *M*~ *of the Horse*, official in English royal household; *M*~ (one who has control) *of foxhounds* (abbr. *M.F.H.*), *beagles*, etc. **8.** (Prefixed, esp. by servants & in address of letter, to name of young gentleman) *M*~ *Tom, M*~ *Jones*. **9.** attrib. Commanding, superior, (*a* ~ *mind*). **10.** ~-*at-arms*, police officer on man-of-war; ~-*key* (opening many locks, each also opened by separate key); ~ *mason*, (as above, also) freemason who has passed third degree; ~*piece*, consummate piece of workmanship; ~-*stroke*, surpassingly skilful act (of policy etc.). Hence ~DOM, ~HOOD, nn., ~LESS a. [OE *mægester* (later also f. OF *maistre*) f. L *magister* cogn. w. *magis* more]

ma'ster² (mah-), v.t. Overcome, defeat; reduce to subjection; acquire complete knowledge of (subject) or facility in using (instrument etc.); rule as a master. [ME, f. prec.]

ma'sterful (mah-), a. Self-willed, imperious. Hence ~LY² adv., ~NESS n. [-FUL]

ma'sterl|ỹ (mah-), a. Worthy of a master, very skilful. Hence~ĬNESS n. [-LY¹]

ma'stership (mah-), n. Dominion, control; office, function, of master, esp. in school. [-SHIP]

ma'sterỹ (mah-), n. Sway, dominion; *the* upper hand; masterly skill; masterly use or knowledge (of instrument, subject). [ME, f. OF *maistrie* (as MASTER¹, see -Y¹)]

măs'tic, n. Gum or resin exuding from bark of certain trees, used in making varnish; trees yielding this; kinds of cement; liquor flavoured with ~, used in Turkey & Greece; ~ colour, pale yellow. Hence **măsti'cIC** a. (chem.). [ME, f. OF, f. LL *mastichum* f. L f. Gk *mastikhē*]

măs'tic|ate, v.t. Grind (food) with teeth, chew. Hence or cogn. ~ABIL'ITY, ~A'TION, ~ātOR, nn., ~ātORY a. [f. LL *masticare*, -ATE³]

ma'stiff (mah-), n. Large strong dog with drooping ears & pendulous lips. [ME; obsc. f. OF *mastin* f. Rom. **mansuetinus* f. *mansuetus* tame, see -INE¹]

măsti'tis, n. Inflammation of female breast. [f. Gk *mastos* breast, see -ITIS]

măs'todŏn, n. Large extinct mammal like elephant, with nipple-shaped tubercles on crowns of molar teeth. Hence **măstodŏn'tic** a. [f. Gk *mastos* breast + *odous odontos* tooth]

măs'toid, a. & n. (anat.). **1.** Shaped like

female breast; ~ *operation*, surgical procedure for relief of disease of tympanum or ear-drum; ~ *process*, conical prominence in the temporal bone to which muscles are attached. 2. n. ~ process; (colloq.) abscess on ~ process. [f. Gk *mastos* breast, see -OID]

mäs'turb|āte (-ter-), v.i. Produce an orgasm by exciting one's own genitals. Hence ~Ā'TION n. [f. L *masturbari*, see -ATE³]

mät¹, n. Coarse fabric of plaited rushes, straw, etc., for lying upon, packing furniture, etc.; piece of this for wiping shoes upon, esp. *door*-~; *on the* ~ (army sl.), in trouble (i.e. on the orderly room ~ before the C.O.). [OE *matt(e)*, OHG *matta* f. LL *matta*]

mät², v.t. & i. (-tt-). Cover, furnish, with mats; entangle (often *together*) in thick mass (esp. in p.p., as ~*ted hair*); become ~ted. [f. prec.]

mät³, mätt, a., n., & v.t. (-tt-). 1. (Of colours, surfaces, etc.) dull, without lustre. 2. n. Border of dead gold round framed picture; appearance of unburnished gold; roughened or frosted groundwork. 3. v.t. Make (gilding etc.) dull; frost (glass). [(vb f. F *mater*) F, identical w. *mat* MATE¹; see CHECKMATE]

mät'adōr, n. Man appointed to kill bull in bull-fight; principal card in some games. [Sp., f. *matar* kill f. Arab. *mat* (prec.) + -OR]

mätch¹, n. 1. Person able to contend with another as an equal, as *find, meet*, one's ~, *be* (*more than*) *a* ~ *for*; person equal to another in some quality, as *we shall never see his* ~; person, thing, exactly like or corresponding to another. 2. Contest of skill etc. in which persons are matched against each other, as *cricket*-~. 3. Matrimonial alliance; *make a* ~, bring this about; person viewed in regard to his or her eligibility for marriage, esp. as to rank or fortune, as *he is an excellent* ~. 4. ~*board*, one with tongue cut along one edge & groove along another, so as to fit into similar boards; ~*'maker*, one fond of scheming to bring about marriages; ~ *play* (golf), in which the score is reckoned by counting the holes won by each side; ~ *point(s)*, state of a game when one side needs only one more point to win the ~ (occas. ~ *ball*). [OE *gemæcca* mate, companion, f. Gmc **mako-* fit, suitable; see MAKE¹; later senses infl. by foll.]

mätch², v.t. & i. Join (person *with* another) in marriage; prove a match for; place (person etc.) in conflict *against* another; *well* ~*ed*, fit to contend with each other, live together, etc., on equal terms; place (person, thing) in competition *with*; be equal, correspond in quantity, quality, colour, etc., to (thing etc.; also intr. *with*) as *the carpets* ~ *the wallpaper, these ribbons do not* ~, *do not* ~ *with your hat, trimmed with velvet to* ~;

find material etc. that ~es with (another), as *can you* ~ *me this silk?* [ME, f. prec.]

mätch³, n. Short piece of wood, wax taper, etc., tipped with composition that bursts into flame when rubbed on rough or (*safety* ~) specially prepared surface; piece of wick, cord, etc., designed to burn at uniform rate, for firing cannon etc.; ~*-box* (for holding ~es); ~*'lock*, (gun with) lock in which ~ is placed for igniting powder; ~*'wood*, wood suitable for ~es, minute splinters, (*make* ~*wood of*, utterly smash). [ME, f. OF *mesche*, of obsc. orig.]

mätch'ĕt (*or* -ĕt'), n. Broad heavy knife used in America etc. as tool & weapon. [f. Sp. *machete*]

mätch'lĕss, a. Without an equal, peerless. Hence ~LY² adv. [MATCH¹ + -LESS]

māte¹, n., & v.t. (chess). = CHECKMATE; *fool's* ~ (in which first player is ~d at opponent's second move); STALE¹~. [see CHECKMATE]

māte², n. 1. (In working-classes) companion, fellow worker, (also as general form of address). 2. One of a pair, esp. of birds; fitting partner in marriage. 3. (naut.). Officer on merchant ship who sees to execution of master's commands & takes command in his absence, (also) assistant to some functionary, as *cook's, gunner's, surgeon's,* ~. Hence ~'LESS (-tl-) a., māt'(e)y² a., sociable, familiar (*with*). [ME, f. MLG *mate* f. *gemate* (cf. OHG *gimazzo*) f. WG **gimato* messmate (*ga*- Y- + *mat* MEAT)]

māte³, v.t. & i. Join (two persons, one *with* another) in marriage; marry (*with*, or abs.); pair (birds), (of birds) pair; keep company (*with*). [f. prec.]

mä'tĕ (-ā), n. (Vessel for) infusion of leaves of a shrub, Paraguay tea; the shrub. [f. Sp. *mate* f. native *mati*]

matelot, ‖ **mät'lŏ(w)**, (mät'lō), n. (naut. sl.). Sailor. [F (-*elot*)]

mät'elote (-ot), n. Dish of fish etc. with sauce of wine, onions, etc. [F, f. *matelot* sailor]

mät'er, n. ‖ Mother (sl.); DURA MATER, PIA MATER; ~*famil'ĭās*, mother of household. [L]

matēr'ĭal, a. & n. 1. Concerned with the matter, not the form, of reasoning; of matter, corporeal; ~ *theory* of heat (that it is a ~ substance); (of conduct, point of view, etc.) unspiritual; concerned with bodily comfort etc., as ~ *well-being*, important, essential, (*to*, or abs.; *at the* ~ *dates*). 2. n. Matter from which thing is made, as *raw* (unmanufactured) ~; elements, constituent parts, (*of* substance, *for* historical composition etc.); stuff, fabric; *writing*-~s (requisites). Hence ~ITY (-ăl²) n., ~LY² adv. [ME, f. OF *materiel, -al*, f. LL *materialis* (as MATTER, see-AL)]

matēr'ĭal|ĭsm, n. Opinion that nothing exists but matter & its movements & modifications, also, that consciousness &

will are wholly due to material agency; (Art) tendency to lay stress on material aspect of objects. So ~IST n., ~IS'TIC a., ~IS'TICALLY adv. [-ISM]

matēr'ializ|e, **-is|e** (-īz), v.t. & i. Make, represent as, material; cause (spirit) to appear, (of spirit) appear, in bodily form; become actual fact; make materialistic. Hence ~A'TION n. [-IZE]

matēr'ia mĕd'ĭca, n. Remedial substances used in practice of medicine. [med. L]

matériel (matārĭĕl'), n. Stock-in-trade, available means (opp. *personnel*). [F, as MATERIAL]

matern'al, a. Of mothers; motherly; related on the mother's side, as ~ *uncle*, mother's brother; (joc.) one's mother's. Hence ~LY² adv. [ME, f. OF *maternel* or L *maternus* (*mater* mother), see -AL]

matern'ity, n. Motherhood; motherliness; ~ *hospital*, *nurse*, *ward*, (for women during confinement); ~ *robe*, *skirt*, (suitable for wear by pregnant woman). [f. F *maternité* or med. L *maternitas* (prec., -TY)]

māthĕmāt'ical, a. Of mathematics; (of proofs etc.) rigorously precise. Hence ~LY² adv. [f. F -*ique* or L f. Gk *mathēmatikos* (*mathēma* science f. *manthanō*, root *math*-, learn, see -IC)]

māthĕmāt'ics, n. pl. (usu. treated as sing.). (Also *pure* ~) abstract science of space & quantity; (also *mixed*, *applied*, ~) this applied to branches of physical research, e.g. astronomy. So **māthĕmati'CIAN** (-ĭshn) n. [as prec., see -ICS]

mati'cō (-tē-), n. Peruvian shrub; its leaves used as styptic. [Sp., dim of *Mateo* Matthew]

māt'ĭn, n. (Pl.) one of canonical hours of breviary, prop. a midnight office, but also recited at daybreak; (pl.) morning prayer in Church of England (often *mattins*); (poet., sing. or pl.) morning song of birds. [ME, f. OF *matines* f. eccl. L *matutinas*, acc. fem. pl. adj. as n. f. L *matutinus* of the morning, see -INE¹]

matinée (măt'ĭnā), n. Afternoon theatrical or musical performance (*the ~ hat*, lady's hat obstructing, also hat designed not to obstruct, view of stage). [F, = what occupies a morning (*matin* morning)]

māt'lō, **-low** (-lō). See MATELOT.

māt'rāss, n. Long-necked glass vessel with round or oval body, used for distilling etc. [f. F *matras*, of unkn. orig.]

māt'riärch (-k), n. Woman corresponding in status to patriarch (usu. joc.). [f. L *mater* mother on false anal. of *patriarch*]

māt'riärchy (-k-), n. Social organization in which mother is head of family. So **mātriärch'al** (-k-) a. [prec. + -Y¹]

māt'ricid|e, n. One who kills his, killing of one's, own mother. So ~AL a. [f. L *matricida* (MATER, see -CIDE)]

matric'ul|āte, v.t. & i. Admit (student) to privileges of university; (intr.) be thus admitted. Hence ~A'TION n., ~ātORY a. [f. med. L *matriculare* (L *matricula* register, dim. of MATRIX, + -ATE³]

māt'rimony, n. 1. Rite of marriage; state of being married. 2. A card game; combination of king & queen of trumps in some card games. So **mātrimōn'ial** a., **mātrimōn'ialLY²** adv. [ME, f. OF *matremoine* f. L *matrimonium* (*mater* -*tris* mother, see -MONY)]

māt'rix, n. (pl. *-ices* pr. -ĭsēz, *-ixes*). Womb; place in which thing is developed; formative part of animal organ; mass of rock etc. enclosing gems etc.; (biol.) substance between cells; mould in which type etc. is cast or shaped. [L, f. *mater* mother]

māt'ron, n. Married woman; woman managing domestic affairs of hospital, school, etc. Hence ~AGE(1, 2), ~HOOD, ~SHIP, nn., ~AL, ~LY¹, aa. [ME, f. OF *matrone* f. L *matrona* (*mater* mother)]

mātt. Var. of MAT³ (esp. photogr.).

mătt'amōre, n. Subterranean dwelling or storehouse. [f. F *matamore* f. Arab *maṭmūrah* (*tamara* store up)]

mătt'er¹, n. 1. Substance(s) of which a physical thing is made. 2. Purulent discharge, whence ~Y² a., purulent, festering. 3. Physical substance in general, as opp. to spirit, mind, etc. 4. (log.). Particular content of proposition, distinguished from its form. 5. Material for thought or expression; substance of book, speech, etc. (often opp. to *manner* or *form*). 6. Occasion (*of*, *for*, complaint, regret, etc.). 7. Thing(s), as *printed* ~; *postal* ~, all that may be sent by post; *no* ~, it is of no importance (*when*, *how*, etc., or abs.); *what* ~?, that need not disquiet us. 8. Affair; thing (of a kind specified esp. by vbl n.), as *a hanging* ~, *no laughing* ~, *money* ~s; *that is* a ~ (*case*, question) *of habit* etc.; *for that* ~, so far as that is concerned; *a* ~ *of* (about) *40 years*; *what is the* ~?, what is amiss (*with*)? (*what is the* ~ *with* —?, sl., surely — will do); *in the* ~ *of*, as regards. 9. ~ *of course* (also as adj., w. hyphens), thing to be expected in natural course; ~ *of fact*, what pertains to the sphere of fact (opp. to *opinion* etc.), esp. *as a* ~ *of fact*, (law) part of judicial inquiry concerned with truth of alleged facts (opp. to ~ *of law*), (adj., with hyphens) unimaginative, prosaic. [ME, f. AF *materie*, *-ere*, OF *-iere* f. L *materia* timber, stuff]

mătt'er², v.i. 1. Be of importance, signify, (*to* person etc. *how*, *when*, etc.,; esp. w. neg.). 2. Secrete or discharge pus. [f. prec.]

mătt'ing, n. In vbl senses (MAT²), esp. fabric of hemp, bast, grass, etc. as covering etc., as *coco-nut* ~. [-ING¹]

mattins. See MATIN.

mătt'ock, n. Tool of PICK¹ shape, with an adze & a chisel edge as ends of head. [OE *mattuc*, of unkn. orig.]

mǎtt'oid, n. Person of erratic mind, compound of genius & fool. [f. It. *mattoide* (*matto* mad)]

mǎtt'rèss, n. Canvas case stuffed with hair, straw, feathers, etc., as bed or support for bed; (usu. *spring* ~) similar appliance of springs stretched in frame. [ME, f. OF *materas* f. It. *materasso* prob. f. Arab. *almaṭraḥ* place, cushion (*ṭaraḥa* throw)]

mǎt'ūrāte, v.i. (med.). (Of pustule etc.) come to maturation. [as MATURE², -ATE³]

mātūrā'tion, n. Ripening of morbific matter esp. of cataract; causing of this, whence **matur'ative** a.; ripening of fruit; maturing, development. [f. F, or L *maturatio* (as MATURE², see -ATION)]

matūre'¹, a. Complete in natural development; with fully developed powers of body & mind; ~ (careful) *deliberation*, ~ *plans* (formed after this); (of bill) due. So ~**LY²** (-rl-) adv., ~**NESS** (-rn-), **matūr'ITY**, nn. [ME, f. L *maturus* ripe]

matūre'², v.t. & i. Develop fully; ripen; perfect (plan etc.); come to maturity; (of bill) become due. [f. obs. F *maturer* or L *maturare* (as prec.); & f. prec.]

matūtin'al (or matŭt'inal), a. Of, occurring in, the morning; early. So **mǎt'ūtine** a. [f. LL *matutinalis* (*matutinus* f. *Matuta* goddess of dawn)]

maud, n. Scots shepherd's grey striped plaid; travelling-rug like this. [orig. unkn.]

maud'lin, a. & n. Mawkishly sentimental, esp. of tearful stage of drunkenness; (n.) mawkish sentiment. [(adj. f. n.) f. OF *Madelaine* MAGDALEN]

∥ **mau'gre** (-ger), prep. (arch.). In spite of. [ME, f. OF *maugre* (*mal* bad f. L *malus* + *gré* f. L *gratus* pleasing)]

maul'¹, mall (mawl), n. Kinds of special hammer, commonly of wood. [ME, f. OF *mail* f. L *malleus* hammer]

maul'², v.t. Beat & bruise; handle (material thing, subject, quotation) roughly or carelessly; damage by criticism. [f. prec.]

maul'stick, mahl-, n. Light stick held by painter in left hand as support for right, with padded leather ball at one end. [f. Du. *maalstok* (*malen* paint + *stok* stick)]

maund, n. Asian measure of weight of varying value (Indian standard ~ = 82⅔ lb.). [Hind. & Pers. *man*]

maun'der, v.i. Move, act, listlessly; talk in dreamy or rambling manner. [perh. imit.; cf. dial. *daunder*]

maun'dy̆, n. (In R.-C. countries) ceremony of washing the feet of poor people (*John* xiii. 14); (in English use) distribution of ~ *money* (specially minted silver coins) by royal almoner to the poor on *M*~ *Thursday* (next before Easter). [ME, f. OF *mande* f. L *mandatum* (*novum*) MANDATE]

Mau'ser (mowz-), n. Kind of magazine rifle or pistol. [W. ~, inventor (d. 1882)]

mausolē'um, n. Magnificent tomb, orig. that of Mausolus king of Caria erected by his queen Artemisia in 4th c. B.C. [L, f. Gk *Mausōleion* (*Mausōlos*)]

mauvais (mō'vä,, & see Ap.), a. ~ *sujet* (see Ap.), black sheep, rogue; ~ *quart d'heure* (kärdér', & see Ap.), short but unpleasant experience, interview, etc. [F]

mauvaise honte (mōväz'awnt, & see Ap.), n. False shame; painful diffidence. [F, = ill shame]

mauve (mōv), n. & a. **1.** Bright but delicate purple dye from coal-tar aniline. **2.** adj. Of the colour of this. [F, f. L *malva* MALLOW]

*****mǎv'erick**, n., & v.i. Unbranded calf or yearling; (transf.) masterless person, rover; (v.i.) stray. [f. S. A. *M*~, Texas engineer who owned unbranded cattle c. 1850]

māv'is, n. (poet.). Song-thrush. [ME, f. OF *mauvis*, of unkn. orig.]

mavour'neen (-oor-), n. & int. My darling. [Ir. *mo mhuirnin*]

maw, n. Stomach (only joc. of men), esp. last of ruminant's four stomachs; ~'**worm**, intestinal worm. [OE *maga*, MDu. *maghe*, OHG *mago*, ON *magi* f. Gmc *magon*-]

mawk'ish, a. Of faint sickly flavour; feebly sentimental. Hence ~**LY²** adv., ~**NESS** n. [f. obs. *mawk* maggot f. ON *mathkr* + -ISH¹]

maw'seed, n. Seed of opium poppy. [f. G (dial.) *mohsamen* (G *mohn* poppy)]

mǎxill'∥a, n. (pl. *-ae*). Jaw(bone), esp. upper jaw in animals & most vertebrates. Hence ~**ARY¹**, ~**IFORM**, aa. [L]

mǎx'im'¹, n. A general truth drawn from science or experience; principle, rule of conduct. [ME, f. OF *maxime* or med. L *maxima* (*propositio*), fem. adj., greatest]

Mǎx'im'², n. Single-barrelled quick-firing machine gun, with water-casing to keep parts cool. [H. ~, inventor (d. 1916)]

mǎx'imalist, n. Person who holds out for the maximum of his demands & rejects compromises. [MAXIMUM, -AL, -IST]

mǎx'imĭz∣e, -is∣e (-īz), v.t. Increase, magnify, to the utmost; interpret (doctrine etc.) vigorously. Hence ~**A'TION** n. [f. L *maximus* greatest + -IZE]

mǎx'imum, n. (pl. usu. *-ima*), & a. Highest possible magnitude or quantity (often attrib.); ~ *price* (that may not be exceeded); ~ *thermometer* (recording highest temperature within given period); (adj.) largest or largest possible. [L, neut. as prec.]

∥ **mǎx'imus**, a. (In schools) eldest of the name, as *Jones* ~. [see MAXIMIZE]

may'¹, v. auxil. (3rd sing. *may*; past *might*, pr. mīt; no infin. or part. or gerund). **1.** Expr. possibility, as *it* ~ *be true* (neg. *it cannot be*), *it* ~ *not be* (perhaps is not) *true*, *you* ~ *walk miles without seeing one*, *he* ~ *or might* (perhaps will) *lose his way*, *I was afraid he might* (perhaps would) lose his way, I ~ have been (perhaps was) wrong, afraid he might have (perhaps had) lost it. **2.** Expr. permission, as you ~ (neg. MUST[4] not or cannot) go, I wish I might; you might (I request you to) call at the baker's; you might (ought to, yet do not) offer to help, you might (ought to) have offered. **3.** (In final clauses, & after wish, fear, etc.) take, took, such a course as ~, might, avert the danger; I hope he ~, hoped he might, succeed. **4.** (Expr. wish) ~ you live to repent it ! **5.** (In questions, emphasizing uncertainty) who ~ you be? **6.** ~'be (also arch. ~hăp'), perhaps; might-have-been, a past possibility. [OE mæg (1st sing.) = OS, OHG, Goth. mag, ON má, f. Gmc *mag- be strong; cf. MAIN[2], MIGHT]

may[2], n. (poet.). Maiden. [ME, perh. f. ON møy, mey = Goth. mawi]

May[3], n. **1.** Fifth month of year; (fig.) bloom, prime; Queen of (the) ~, girl chosen to be queen of games on ~ Day. **2.** (may). Hawthorn (blossom). **3.** ‖(Camb. Univ., pl.) ~ examination, ~ boat-races held during ~ Week (late in ~ or early in June). **4.**~Day, May 1 (mayING[1], keeping this, picking may); ‖ May'fair, district in West End of London (named from fair formerly held in~); may'fly, an ephemeral insect; ~ games, on ~ Day; may'pole, pole painted & decked with flowers, for dancing round on ~ Day; ‖~meetings (of religious & philanthropic societies held during ~ in London). [ME, f. OF mai f. L Maius]

ma'ya (mah-), n. (Hind. philos.). Illusion. [Skr.]

Ma'yan (mah-), a. Of the ancient culture of the Mayas before their conquest by the TOLTECS.

may'day, n. International radio-telephonic distress signal used by ships & aircraft. [pron. of F m'aider help me]

may'hěm, n. (hist.). Crime of maiming a person so as to render him partly or wholly defenceless. [f. AF mahaym MAIM]

mayonnaise' (-āz), n. (Salmon, chicken, etc., ~, dish with) dressing of eggs, oil, cream, vinegar, etc. [F]

mayor (mār), n. Head of municipal corporation of city or borough (in London & some other cities Lord M~); ~ of the palace, nominal subordinate to whom the power of his titular superior has passed (see ROI fainéant). Hence may'orAL a. [ME, f. OF maire, as MAJOR[2]]

may'oralty, n. Mayor's (period of) office. [f. OF mairalte (as prec., see -AL & -TY)]

may'oress, n. Mayor's wife; female mayor; lady fulfilling ceremonial duties of ~. [-ESS[1]]

măz'ard, -zz-, n. (Arch.) head, face; wild sweet cherry of Europe. [alt. of MAZER]

măzarine' (-ēn), n. & a. Deep rich blue. [perh. f. name of Cardinal Mazarin (d. 1661), or Duchesse de Mazarin (d. 1699)]

Măz'daïsm, n. Zoroastrianism. [f. Avestic mazda, good principle in Persian theology]

māze, n., & v.t. **1.** Complex network of paths, labyrinth; confused mass etc. **2.** v.t. Bewilder, confuse, (esp. in p.p.). Hence māz'ILY[2] adv., māz'iNESS n., māz'y[2] a. [ME; cf. AMAZE, rel. to which is uncert.]

māz'er, n. (hist.). Hard-wood drinking-bowl, usu. silver-mounted. [ME, f. OF masere, masdre maple-wood, f. WG *maser; cf. OS masur, OHG masar excrescence on tree, maple (cf. māsa spot), ON mǫsurr, see MEASLES]

mazûrk'a, n. Lively Polish dance; music for this in triple time. [Polish, = woman of province Mazovia]

mazz'ard, n. Var. of MAZARD.

'McCar'thȳ|ism (makär-), n. Policy of hunting out (suspected) Communists & removing them esp. from Government departments. Hence ~ITE[1] a. & n. [f. Joseph McCarthy, U.S. senator (d. 1957), -ISM]

me[1] (mē, mǐ), pron., objective case of I (& colloq. subjective, as it's only me); (arch. & poet., reflexive) myself, I laid me down; (arch.) corresp. to ETHIC dative (but me no buts); (in intt.) ah me!, dear me! [repr. OE acc. (1) mē, (2) mec, & dat. (3) mē; (1) = OS mī, mē f. Aryan *me, *eme, cf. L mē, Gk (e)me: (2) = OS, ON, Goth. mik, OHG mih f. Aryan *me-gé, cf. Gk emege (3) = OS mī, OHG mir, ON mér, Goth. miz f. Aryan *mes]

mē[2]. See MI.

mead[1], n. Alcoholic liquor of fermented honey & water. [OE meodu, MLG mede, OHG metu, ON mjǫthr f. Gmc *meduz, cogn. w. Gk methu wine]

mead[2], n. (poet.). = foll. [see foll.]

meadow (měd'ō), n. Piece of grass land, esp. one used for hay; low well-watered ground, esp. near river;~ brown, common brown butterfly; ~ pipit, titlark; ~ saffron, perennial plant abundant in ~s, with lilac flowers; ~sweet, rosaceous plant common in moist ~s, with creamy-white fragrant flowers. Hence ~Y[2] (měd'ŏī) a. [OE mædwe obl. case of mæd (whence prec.) f. Gmc *mædwō f. *mæ-MOW[3]]

mea'gre (-ger), a. (Of persons etc.) lean, thin; poor, scanty, (esp. of meals, as ~ fare); (of literary composition, ideas, etc.) wanting in fullness. Hence ~LY[2] adv., ~NESS n., (-ger-). [ME, f. OF megre f. L macer]

meal[1], n. Edible part of any grain or pulse (usu. exc. FLOUR) ground to powder; WHOLE ~. [OE meolu, OS, OHG melo, ON mjǫl f. Gmc *mel-, cogn. w. L molere grind]

meal[2], n., & v.i. Customary (also, any) occasion of taking food; food so taken (make a ~ of, consume); ‖ quantity of milk given by cow at a milking; ~time, usual time of eating; (v.i.) eat a ~. [OE *mǣl* mark, fixed time, meal, = OS, OHG, ON *māl*, Goth *mēl* f. Gmc *mǣlam*]

meal'ie, n. (S.-Afr.). Maize (usu. pl.). [f. Afrikaans *milje* f. Port. *milho* MILLET]

meal'y, a. Of, like, containing, meal; (of boiled potatoes) dry & powdery; ~-bug, insect infesting vines etc.; ~ primrose (mauve-flowered with powdery stem); (of horses) spotty; (of complexion) pale; (usu. ~-mouthed) apt to mince matters, soft-spoken. Hence meal'iNESS n. [MEAL¹+-Y²]

mean¹, n. 1. Condition, quality, virtue, course, equally removed from two opposite (usu. blamable) extremes, esp. *the golden, happy, ~*. 2. (math.). Term between first & last terms of arithmetical, geometrical, etc., progression. 3. pl. (Often treated as sing., as *a ~s*) that by which a result is brought about, as *it has been the ~s of extending our trade, by fair ~s*, WAYS *& ~s*, *~s of grace* (sacraments etc.). 4. Pecuniary resources, as *he lives beyond his, on his own, ~s* (also attrib., as *~s test*, principle of requiring some proof of need as condition of assistance); wealth, as *a man of ~s*. *By all (manner of)~s*, in every possible way, at any cost, certainly; *by no (manner of)~s*, not at all, certainly not; *by~s* (the instrumentality) of (person, thing, do*ing*). [f. foll., partly thr. F]

mean², a. (Math.) equally far from two extremes, as *5 is the ~ quantity between 2 & 8*; *~ sea level* (half-way between those of high and low water); *~ sun*, fictitious sun moving in celestial equator at ~ rate of real sun; *~ proportional*, second of three quantities of which first is to it as it is to third; *in the~* (inter-, vening) *time, while*; *~'time, ~'while*, advv., in the ~ time. [ME, f. OF *men, meien*, f. L *medianus* MEDIAN]

mean³, a. (Of capacity, understanding, etc.) inferior, poor; (hist.) ~ *white*, landless white man in S. United States; not imposing in appearance, shabby; *he is no ~* (a good) *scholar*; ignoble, smallminded; stingy; uncomfortable, malicious, ill tempered; *(colloq.) secretly ashamed (feel ~)*. Hence ~'LY² adv., ~'NESS n. [ME, repr. OE *gemǣne*, OS *gimēni*, OHG *gimeini*, Goth. *gamains*, cogn. w. L *communis*]

mean⁴, v.t. (~*t*, pr. mĕnt). Purpose, have in mind, (*mischief, business*, to do); design, destine, for an object etc., as ~ *it to be used, ~ it for a stopgap, he was~t* (by parents etc., also, by Providence) *for a soldier; I ~ you to* (am determined that you shall) *go*; ~ *well to, by*, be kindly disposed towards; intend to convey (specified sense) or indicate (object), as *I ~ that he is stingy, I ~ his father*; (of a person) be of (specified) importance *to* (another); (of words or person) signify, import, (thing, *that*); *what do you ~ by*

(how do you justify) *it?* [OE *mǣnan, mēnian*, OHG *meinen* f. WG *mainjan*]

mëan'der, n., & v.i. 1. (Pl.) sinuous windings of river; (pl.) winding paths; (usu. pl.) circuitous journey; ornamental pattern of lines winding in & out. 2. v.i. Wander at random, (of stream) wind about. [(vb f. n.) L, f. Gk *Maiandros*, river in Phrygia]

mëan'drine, a. Full of windings (esp. of genus of corals with surface like human brain). [MEANDER+-INE¹]

mean'ing¹, n. What is meant; *with ~*, significantly. Hence ~LESS a. [-ING¹]

mean'ing², a. Expressive, significant, whence ~LY² adv.; *well~*, having good intention. [-ING²]

mea'sles (-zlz), n. pl. Infectious disease of man, marked by red spots on skin; such spots; disease in swine; GERMAN² ~. [ME *masele(s)* (pl.), f. MLG *masele*, = M.Du. *masel*, Du. *mazelen*; cf. OHG *masala* pustule, cogn. w. *masar* MAZER]

meas'ly (-z-), a. Of, affected with, measles; (sl.) contemptible, worthless. [f. prec.+-Y²]

measure¹ (mĕzh'er), n. 1. Size, quantity, found by measuring, whence ~LESS a., *beyond ~, infinite; short, full, ~*, less, not less, than professed amount; || *clothes made to ~* (in accordance with measurements taken); *take* (person's) ~, measure him for clothes etc., (fig.) gauge his character, abilities, etc. 2. Degree or extent or amount (esp. *in a or some ~*, partly). 3. Vessel of standard capacity for dealing out liquids etc., as *pint ~*. 4. Rod, tape, etc., for measuring, as *tape-~, yard-~*. 5. Unit of capacity, e.g. bushel, as *20 ~s of wheat*. 6. System of measuring, as *liquid, linear, ~*, dist. *weight*. 7. That by which a thing is computed, as *a chain's weakest link is the ~ of its strength*. 8. Quantity contained in another an exact number of times; *greatest common ~* (greatest that divides each of given quantities). 9. Prescribed extent or quantity, as *set ~s to*, limit, *beyond ~*, excessively. 10. Poetical rhythm, metre; time of piece of music; (mus.) bar; (arch.) dance, as *tread a ~*. 11. Suitable action, as *take ~s*. 12. Legislative enactment. [ME, f. OF *mesure* f. L *mensura* (*metiri mens-* measure, -URE)]

measur|e² (mĕzh'er), v.t. &1. 1. Ascertain extent or quantity of (thing) by comparison with fixed unit or with object of known size; ascertain size & proportions of (person) for clothes. 2. Look (person) up & down *with one's eye*. 3. Mark off or off (line etc. of given length). 4. ~*e one's length*, fall prostrate; *~e swords*, (of duellists) see that swords are of equal length, (fig.) try one's strength *with* (person). 5. Estimate (immaterial thing, person's character, etc.) by some standard or rule. 6. Deal *out* (thing to person). 7. Bring (one's strength etc.) into competition *with* (another's). 8. (poet.). Traverse (distance). 9. v.i. Take measurements; be of specified size (*it ~es six inches*); *~e up to*, have necessary qualifications for. Hence ~ABLE (mězh'er-) a. (*within ~able distance of* ruin etc., getting near it), ~ABLY² adv., ~EMENT (mězh'erm-) n. (esp., pl., detailed dimensions). [ME, f. OF *mesurer* (as prec.)]

mea'sured (mězh'erd),·a. In vbl senses, also: rhythmical, regular in movement, as ~ *tread*; (of language) carefully weighed. [p.p. of prec.]

meat, n. Animal flesh as food, usu. (also *butcher's* ~) excluding fish & poultry; *green* ~, grass, green vegetables, as food; (arch.) food of any kind (*as full as an egg is of* ~, quite full; *one man's* ~ *is another man's poison*); *this was~ & drink* (a great pleasure) *to him*; (arch.) meal, as *before, after,* ~; *~·safe*, cupboard for storing ~, usu. of wire gauze etc.; (bibl.) *~-offering* (R.V. *meal*-), sacrifice of flour & oil. Hence~'LESS a. [OE *mete* food, OS *meti, mat*, OHG *maz*, ON. *matr*, Goth. *mats*]

meāt'us, n. (anat.; pl. *-ūs*, *-uses*). Channel, passage, in the body, as *auditory* ~, channel of the ear. [L, f. *meare* flow, run]

meat'ў, a. Full of meat, fleshy; (fig.) full of substance; or of like meat. [-Y²]

Mĕcc'a, n. Mohammed's birthplace; (fig.) place one aspires to visit, (also) birthplace of a faith, policy, pursuit, etc. [f. Arab. *makkah*]

mĕcca'nō (-ah-), n. Set of miniature parts from which engineering models can be constructed. [P]

mĕchăn'ic (-k-), n. 1. Handicraftsman; skilled workman, esp. one who makes or uses machinery. 2. pl. Branch of applied mathematics treating of motion & tendencies to motion, (also) science of machinery. [ME, f. OF *-ique* or L f. Gk *mēkhanikos* adj. (as MACHINE, see -IC)]

mĕchăn'ical (-k-), a. Of machines or mechanism; *the* ~ *powers*, lever, wheel & axle, pulley, inclined plane, wedge, screw; of the nature of handicraft; working, produced, by machinery; ~ *drawing* (done with compasses etc.); ~ *transport* (abbr. M.T.), motor branch of R.A.S.C.; (of persons or actions)like machines, automatic, lacking originality; (of agencies, principles, etc.) belonging to mechanics; (of theories etc.) explaining phenomena by assumption of ~ action, whence~ ISM n.; of mechanics as a science. Hence~LY² adv.,~NESS a. [ME, as prec., see -AL]

mĕchani'cian (-kănĭshn), n. One skilled in constructing machinery. [MECHANIC + -IAN]

mĕch'anĭsm (-k-), n. Structure, adaptation of parts, of machine (lit. & fig.); system of mutually adapted parts working together (as) in machine; (art) mechanical execution, technique. [f. mod. L *mechanismus* (as MACHINE, -ISM)]

mĕch'an|ĭst (-k-), n. Machinist (now rare); mechanician, expert in mechanics; (philos.) one who holds that all natural phenomena admit of mechanical explanation (opp. VITALIST), whence ~ĭs'tĭc a. [f. MECHANIC + -IST]

mĕch'anĭz|e (-k-), -**ĭs|e** (-ĭz), v.t. Give mechanical character to. Hence ~A'TION n., (esp.) substitution of motor transport for horse-drawn vehicles, replacement of cavalry by tanks & armoured cars, etc. [-IZE]

Mĕch'lĭn (-k-), n. (Also ~ *lace*) lace made at ~ (now *Mechelen* or *Malines*) in Belgium.

mĕd'al, n. Piece of metal, usu. in form of coin, struck or cast with inscription & device to commemorate event etc., also awarded as distinction to soldier, scholar, etc., for services rendered, proficiency, etc.; *the reverse of the* ~, other side of question; ~ *play* (golf), play in which the score is reckoned by counting the number of strokes taken for the round, opp. *match play*. Hence~lED² (-ld), **mĕdăl'ĭc**, aa. [f. F *médaille* f. It. *medaglia* f. Rom. *medallia* f. *metallea* f. *metallum* METAL]

mĕdăl'ion (-yon), n. Large medal; thing so shaped, e.g. decorative panel or tablet, portrait, etc. [f. F *médaillon* (as prec., see -OON)]

mĕd'allist, n. Engraver, designer, of medals; recipient of medal, as *gold* ~. [-IST]

mĕd'dl|e, v.i. Busy oneself unduly *with*, interfere *in*. Hence ~ER¹, ~esomeNESS, nn., ~**esome** (-dls-) a. [ME, f. OF *medler*, var. of *mesler* f. Rom. *misculare* f. L *miscēre* mix]

mĕd'ĭa n. (pl. *-ae*). Voiced or soft mute (*b, d, g*), cf. TENUIS; middle membrane of artery or vessel. [L, fem. of *medius* middle]

mĕdiaev'al, -diēv'al, a. Of, imitating, the Middle Ages. Hence ~ISM(2,3), ~IST(3), nn., ~IZE(2, 3) v.t. & i., ~LY² adv. [f. L *medius* middle + *aevum* age + -AL]

mĕd'ial, a. Situated in the middle; of average dimensions. Hence ~LY² adv. [f. LL *medialis* (as prec., see -AL)]

mĕd'ian, a. & n. 1. Situated in the middle. 2. n. (Anat.) ~ artery, vein, nerve, etc.; (math.) straight line drawn from angular point of triangle to middle of opposite side. [f. F *médian* or L *medianus* (as prec., see -AN)]

mĕd'iant, n. (mus.). Third of any scale. [f. It. *mediante* (as MEDIATE², see -ANT)]

mĕdiāstin'|um, n. (anat.). Membranous middle septum, esp. between lungs. Hence ~AL a. [med. L, neut. adj., = middle, f. L *medius*]

mĕd'iate¹, a. Connected not directly but through some other person or thing; involving intermediate agency. Hence ~LY² adv. [as foll., see -ATE²]

mĕd'i|āte², v.i. & t. Form connecting link between; intervene (*between* two persons) for purpose of reconciling them; be the medium for bringing about (result) or conveying (gift etc.). So ~A'TION n. [f. LL mediare (medius middle), see -ATE³]

med'iatiz|e, -is|e (-iz), v.t. Annex (principality) to another State, leaving former sovereign his title & some rights of government. Hence ~A'TION n. [f. F médiatiser (médiat, as MEDIATE¹, see -IZE)]

med'iator, n. One who mediates, esp. Christ. Hence or cogn. mediato'r'IAL, med'iatORY, aa., med'iaTRIX n. [ME, f. OF mediatour f. LL mediatorem (as MEDIATE², see -OR)]

med'icable, a. Admitting of remedial treatment. [f. L medicabilis (as MEDICATE, see -BLE)]

med'ical, a. & n. 1. Of the healing art; ~ man, physician or surgeon; of medicine as opp. to surgery, obstetrics, etc.; requiring ~, not surgical, treatment; ~ jurisprudence, the legal knowledge required of a doctor. 2. n. (colloq.). ~ student. Hence ~LY² adv. [f. F médical or LL medicalis (medicus physician, see -AL)]

medic'ament (or mĕd²), n. Substance used in curative treatment. [F, or f. L medicamentum (as MEDICATE, see -MENT)]

med'icaster, n. Quack. [f. L medicus physician, see -ASTER]

med'ic|ate, v.t. Treat medically; impregnate with medicinal substance. Hence or cogn. ~A'TION n., ~ātIVE a. [f. L medicari (as prec.), see -ATE³]

Medicē'an, a. Of the Medici family, rulers of Florence in 15th c. [f. mod. L Mediceus + -AN]

medi'cinal, a. Of medicine; having healing properties. Hence ~LY² adv. [ME, f. OF f. L medicinalis (as foll., see -AL)]

medicine (mĕd'sn, mĕd'isin), n., & v.t. 1. Art of restoring & preserving health, esp. by means of remedial substances & regulation of diet etc., as opp. to surgery & obstetrics; substance, esp. one taken internally, used in this; (among savages) spell, charm, fetish, as ~-man, magician; take one's ~, submit to the disagreeable; ~ ball, stuffed leather ball thrown & caught as means of exercise. 2. v.t. (arch.). Give ~ to, cure with ~. [ME; (vb f. OF medeciner) f. OF medecine f. L medicina (medicus physician)]

med'icō, n. (colloq.; pl.~s). Doctor. [It.]

med'ico-, irreg. comb. form of L medicus physician, medical-, as ~botan'ical, ~galvan'ic, ~judi'cial.

medieval. See MEDIAEVAL.

med'iōcre (-ker), a. Of middling quality, indifferent, neither good nor bad. So mediōc'rITY n. (in adj. senses, & esp. ~ person). [f. F médiocre or L mediocris of middle degree (medius middle)]

med'itat|e, v.t. & i. Plan mentally, design; (intr.) exercise the mind in (esp. religious) contemplation (on, upon, subject). Hence or cogn. meditA'TION, ~OR,

~ĪVENESS, nn., ~IVE a., ~ĪVELY² adv. [f. L meditari, see -ATE³]

mĕditerrān'ēan, a. & n. (Of land) remote from coast (rare); (of water surfaces) landlocked; M~ (Sea), that which separates Europe from Africa. [f. L mediterraneus (medius middle + terra land) + -AN]

mēd'ium, n. & a. (pl. -a, -ums). 1. Middle quality, degree, etc. (between extremes, or abs.); intervening substance through which impressions are conveyed to senses etc., e.g. air; (fig.) environment, conditions of life; agency, means, as by, through, the ~ of; ~ of circulation, that serves as instrument of commercial transactions, e.g. coin; liquid vehicle with which pigments are mixed, e.g. oil, water; person claiming ultraphysical perception and revealing its results to others, whence ~ISM n., ~is'tic a., ~IZE(3) v.t. 2. adj. Intermediate between two degrees or amounts, average, moderate; ~ bowler (neither fast nor slow); ~ wave (radio), having a wave-length between 100 & 800 metres. [L, neut. of medius middle]

mēd'lar, n. (Tree with) fruit like small brown apple, eaten when decayed. [ME, f. OF medler f. *medle (whence obs. E medle) f. mesle f. L f. Gk mespilē, -on]

med'ley, n. (pl. ~s), a., & v.t. Heterogeneous mixture; mixed company; literary miscellany; (adj.) mixed, motley; (v.t.) make a ~ of, intermix. [ME, f. OF medlee var. of meslee (as MEDDLE)]

Mēdoc' (mā-), n. Red wine from ~, district in S.W. France.

mĕdŭll'a, n. Marrow of bones; spinal marrow; ~ (oblongāt'a prolonged) hindmost segment of brain; central parts of some organs, esp. kidney; pith of mammalian hair; soft internal tissue of plants. So mĕdŭll'ARY² a. [L, = pith, marrow, prob. cogn. w. medius middle]

mĕdūs'|a, n. (pl.~ae, ~as). 1. (Gk myth.; M~a) one of the three GORGONS, with snakes for hair. 2. (zool.). Jelly-fish, whence ~AL, ~AN, aa., ~OID a. & n. [L, f. Gk Medousa]

meed, n. (poet.). Reward; merited portion (of praise etc.). [OE mēd, OS mēda, OHG mēta f. WG *mēda cogn. w. Goth. mizdō, Gk misthos reward]

meek, a. Piously humble & submissive; submitting tamely to injury etc.; (provv.) as ~ as a lamb, as Moses. Hence ~'LY² adv., ~'NESS n. [ME meoc f. ON miukr soft, gentle]

meer'kāt, n. Small S.-Afr. mammal like an ichneumon. [Du., = sea-cat]

meer'schaum (-shm), n. Hydrous silicate of magnesium, found in soft white masses; tobacco-pipe with ~ bowl. [G, = sea-foam (meer sea + schaum foam)]

meet¹, n. Meeting of hounds & men for hunt or of cyclists etc. [f. foll.]

meet², v.t. & i. (met). 1. Come face to face with (person coming from opposite direction); go to place to receive (person, train, etc.) on arrival; make the acquaintance of (imperat., U.-S. form of introduction, as ~ *Dr Smith*); ~ (person) *half-way*, respond to friendly advances of, come to compromise with. 2. (Of line, road, etc.) reach point of contact with (another line etc.). 3. ~ *the eye, ear*, be visible, audible; ~ person's *eye*, see he is looking at one, (also) return his gaze. 4. Oppose in battle or duel; grapple with (evils etc.). 5. Come by accident or design into the company of. 6. Come into conformity with (person, his wishes). 7. Satisfy (demand; ~ *the case*, be adequate); pay (bill) at maturity. 8. (Of two or more persons) come face to face; come *together*, as *they had* or *were met together*; assemble for purpose of conference, business, etc. 9. Come into contact (*waistcoat won't* ~, is too small); (of qualities) unite in same person. 10. ~ *with*, come across (person, obstacle, etc.), experience (treatment etc.). [OE *mētan*, OS *mōtian*, ON *mǣta*, Goth. *gamōtjan* f. Gmc **mōt-* MOOT]

meet[3], a. (arch.). Suitable, fit, proper, (*for* thing, *to do*, *to be* done); *it is* ~ (proper) *that*. Hence ~'LY[2] adv., ~'NESS n. [ME *mēte* repr. OE *gemǣte* f. Gmc **gamǣtja-* (**ga-* Y- + **mǣt-* METE[2])]

meet'ing, n. In vbl senses, esp.: duel; race-~; assembly of people for entertainment etc.; assembly for worship; persons assembled, as *address the* ~; ~-*house*, place of worship (usu. disparaging; exc. of Quakers); ~-*place* (appointed for ~). [MEET[2] + -ING[1]]

meg'a-, comb. form of Gk *megas* great, as: ~*cephāl'ic*, large-headed; ~*lith*, large stone, esp. as monument; ~*lith'ic*, made of, marked by use of, large stones; ~*phōne*, instrument for carrying sound a long distance, large speaking-trumpet (v.t., announce with ~phone); ~*pōde*, ~*pŏd*, kinds of mound-building birds (lit. large-footed); ~*scope*, kind of magic lantern; ~*scŏp'ic*, visible to naked eye; ~*thēr'ium*, extinct kind of huge herbivorous sloth-like animals; ~*ton* 1,000,000 tons; ~*watt*, 1,000 kilowatts.

meg'alo-, comb. form of Gk *megas megal-* great, as: ~*mān'ia*, insanity of self-exaltation, passion for big things; ~*saur'us*, extinct kind of huge carnivorous lizards.

mēgāss(e)', n. Fibrous residue after expression of sugar from cane. [orig. unkn.; cf. BAGASSE]

mĕgg'er (-g-), n. (electr.). Apparatus for measuring insulation resistance. [P; cf. MEGOHM]

mégilp' (-g-), n. Vehicle (usu. linseed oil & turpentine) for oil colours. [orig. unkn.]

mĕg'ohm (-ōm), n. (electr.). Unit of resistance (one million ohms). [MEGA- + OHM]

mĕg'rim[1], n. Severe headache usu. on one side only; whim, fancy; (pl.) low spirits, vapours; (pl.) staggers, vertigo,

in horses etc. [ME *mygrane* f. OF *migraine* f. LL f. Gk HEMI(*krania* CRANIUM)]

mĕg'rim[2], n. (Local name for) the smooth sole or similar flat fish. [orig. unkn.]

meios'is (mīŏ-), n. = LITOTES; (biol.) phase of nuclear change in germ cells. [Gk *meiōsis* (*meioō* lessen, f. *meiōn* less, see -OSIS)]

meis'tersĭnger (mīs-), n. pl. & sing. German lyric poets & musicians of 14th--16th cc. organized in guilds & having elaborate technique; (sing.) member of such guild. [G (*master*)]

mēkŏm'ēter, n. Portable military range-finder. [f. Gk *mēkos* length + -METER]

mĕlanchŏl'ia (-k-), n. Emotional mental disease marked by depression & ill-grounded fears. [LL, see MELANCHOLY]

mĕlanchŏl'ic (-k-), a. Melancholy; liable to melancholy. [f. L f. Gk *melagkholikos* (as foll., see -IC)]

mĕl'anchŏly (-k-), n. & a. 1. (Habitual or constitutional tendency to) sadness & depression; pensive sadness. 2. adj. (Of persons) sad, gloomy; (of things) saddening, depressing. [ME; (adj. f. n.) f. OF (-*lie*), f. LL f. Gk *melagkholia* (*melas* black + *kholē* bile)]

Mĕlānē's|ia (-sha), n. Group of islands N.E. of Australia, in which the dominant race is dark-skinned & frizzly-haired. Hence ~IAN a. & n., (native, language) of these islands. [f. Gk *melas* black + *nēsos* island + -IA[1]]

mélange (see Ap.), n. Mixture, medley. [F (*méler* mix, see MEDDLE)]

mĕl'anism, n. Darkness of colour resulting from abnormal development of black pigment in epidermis, hair, etc. [f. Gk *melas -anos* black + -ISM]

mĕlanŏch'rōi (-k-), n. pl. (anthrop.). Smooth-haired class of men with dark hair & pale complexion. [f. Gk *melanokhroos* (*melas* black + *khroa* skin)]

mĕlan|ōs'is, n. Morbid deposit, abnormal development, of black pigment in tissue; black cancer. Hence ~OT'IC (-ŏt-) a. [Gk *melanōsis* f. *melanoō* blacken (*melas* black), see -OSIS]

Mĕl'ba, n. ~ *toast* (also *toast* ~), thin crisp toast; PÊCHE ~. [Dame Nellie ~, Australian prima donna (d. 1931)]

*mĕld[1], v.t. & i. Merge. [perh. f. *melt* + *weld*]

mĕld[2], v.t. & i., & n. (In some card games) declare for a score; (n.) act of ~ing, group of cards (to be) ~ed. [f. G *melden* announce]

mêlée (mĕl'ā), n. Mixed fight, skirmish; lively debate. [F, as MEDLEY]

mĕl'ic, a. (Of poem, esp. Gk lyric) meant to be sung. [f. Gk *melikos* (*melos* song, -IC)]

mĕl'inite, n. An explosive of French invention. [f. F *mélinite* f. Gk *mēlinos* (*mēlon* apple), see -ITE[2]]

mĕl'ior|āte, v.t. & i. Improve. Hence ~A'TION n. [f. LL *meliorare* (as foll.), -ATE[3]] měl'ior|ism, n. Doctrine that the world may be made better by human effort. So ~IST n. [L *melior* better + -ISM]

měll'ay, n. (arch.). = MÊLÉE.

mellif'erous, a. Yielding, producing, honey. [f. L *mellifer* (*mel* honey, see -FEROUS)]

mellif'lu|ous (-lŏŏ-), a. (Of voice, words) sweet as honey. So ~ENCE n., ~ENT a., (-lŏŏ-). [f. LL *mellifluus* (*mel* honey, *fluere* flow) + -OUS]

měll'ow (-ō), a. (~er, ~est), & v.t. & i. 1. (Of fruit) soft, sweet, & juicy; (of wine) well-matured; (of earth) rich, loamy; (of character) softened by age or experience; (of sound, colour, light) full & free without harshness; genial, jovial; partly intoxicated. 2. vb. Make, become, ~. Hence ~LY² (-ōlī) adv., ~NESS (-ŏn-) n. [15th c., formally corresp. to OE *melu melw-* MEAL¹, of wh. *mellow* may be an attrib. use]

mělōd'ĕon, -dion, -dium, n. Small organ with suction-operated reeds; kind of accordion. [f. MELODY]

mělōd'ic, a. Of or relating to melody. [f. F *mélodique* (as MELODY, see -IC)]

mělōd'ious, a. Of, producing, melody; sweet-sounding. Hence ~LY² adv., ~NESS n. [ME, f. OF *-icus* (as MELODY, see -OUS)]

měl'odist, n. Singer; composer of melodies. [f. MELODY + -IST]

měl'odize, -ise (-īz), v.i. & t. Make melody; make melodious. [f. MELODY + -IZE]

měl'odrama (-rah-), n. Sensational dramatic piece with violent appeals to emotions & happy ending; language, behaviour, suggestive of this; (formerly) play with songs interspersed & with orchestral music accompanying the action. Hence mělodramăt'ic a., mělodramăt'ICALLY adv., mělodrăm'atist n., mělodrăm'atIZE v.t. [earlier -*drame* f. F *mélodrame* (Gk *melos* music + F *drame* DRAMA)]

měl'odў, n. Sweet music; musical arrangement of words; arrangement of single notes in musically expressive succession; principal part in harmonized music, air. [ME, f. OF *melodie* f. LL f. Gk *melōidia* (*melos* song, see ODE)]

měl'on, n. Kinds of gourd, esp. WATER~; ~-*cutting* (sl.), sharing of spoils or profits. [ME, f. OF, f. LL *melonem* (nom. -*lo*), shortened f. L (-*po*) f. Gk *mēlopepōn* (*mēlon* apple + *pepōn* gourd)]

Mělpŏm'ěnē, n. The MUSE¹ of tragedy. [Gk]

mělt¹, n. Melted metal; amount melted at a time. [f. foll.]

mělt², n., v.i. & t. (p.p. ~*ed* &, as adj. of metal, *mŏlten*). Become liquefied by heat; ~ *away*, disappear thus: (colloq., of person) suffer extreme heat; (of tender food) *it* ~*s* (is easily dissolved) *in the mouth*; (of clouds) break *into rain*; (of person, heart, feelings) be softened by or

with pity or love, dissolve *into tears*, esp. *the* ~*ing mood*, whence měl'tingLY² adv.; dwindle *away*; (of sound) be soft & liquid; pass imperceptibly *into* (another form); reduce (metal etc.) to liquid condition by heat; ~ *down* (plate etc., to use the metal as raw material); *go into the* ~*ing-pot* (fig.), be revolutionized; soften (person, feelings). [OE *meltan, mieltan*, corresp. to ON *melta* digest, Goth. *maltjan* dissolve, f. Gmc **melt-*; cogn. w. MALT]

měl'ton, n. Kind of cloth for men's clothes;∥ *M~ Mowbray* (mŏb-) *pie*, kind of pasty. [*M~ Mowbray*, in Leics.]

měm'ber, n. Part, organ, of body, esp. limb; *inruly* ~, tongue; (fig.) ~ *of Christ*, Christian; constituent portion of complex structure; person belonging to a society etc.; *M~* (one formally elected to take part in proceedings) *of Parliament* (abbr. M.P., pl. M.M.P. or M.P.s); person admitted to Order of the British Empire, 5th class (M.B.E.), or to Royal Victorian Order, 4th or 5th class (M.V.O.); part, branch, of political body; division, clause, of sentence; group of figures, part of numerical expression. Hence (-)~ED² (-erd), ~LESS, aa. [ME, f. OF *membre* f. L *membrum* limb]

měm'bership, n. Being a member; number of members. [-SHIP]

měm'brāne, n. Pliable sheet-like connective tissue or lining in animal or vegetable body; morbid formation in some diseases; skin of parchment, forming part of a roll. So měmbrana'CEOUS (-āshŭs), měmbrān'EOUS, měm'branOUS, aa. [f. L *membrana~*, parchment, as MEMBER]

měm'brumvĭrīl'ě, n. = PENIS. [L, = male member]

měmen'tō, n. (pl. ~*es*, ~*s*). Object serving as reminder or warning, or kept as memorial of person or event; ~ *mŏ'rī* (= remember you must die), warning or reminder of death (e.g. skull). [L, imperat. of *meminisse* remember]

měm'oir (-wǎr), n. Record of events, history written from personal knowledge or special sources of information; (auto)biography; essay on learned subject specially studied by the writer. [f. F *mémoire* masc., spec. use of *mémoire* fem. MEMORY]

měm'orabĭl'ĭa, n. pl. Memorable things. [L, neut. pl. as foll.]

měm'or|able, a. Worth remembering, not to be forgotten, easily remembered. Hence ~abIL'ITY n., ~abLY² adv. [ME, f. OF, or L *memorabilis* (*memorare* bring to mind f. *memor* mindful, -BLE)]

měmorăn'dum, n. (pl. -*da*, -*dums*; abbr. *mem.*, *memo.*). Note to help the memory; record of events etc. for future use; (law) document recording terms of contract etc.; informal letter without signature etc., usu. on paper headed *M~*. [ME, f. L, neut. sing. gerundive as prec.]

memōr′ial, a. & n. **1.** (Of statue, festival, etc.) serving to commemorate; of memory. **2.** n. ~ object, custom, etc.; record, chronicle, (usu. pl.); informal State paper of various kinds; statement of facts as basis of petition etc. Hence~IST n. [ME, f. OF, f. L *memorialis* (as MEMORY, see -AL)]

memōr′ialize, **-ise** (-ĭz), v.t. Commemorate; address memorial to (person). [prec. +-IZE]

memōr′ia tech′nica (těk-), n. System, contrivance, used to assist memory. [L, = artificial memory]

mem′orize, **-ise** (-ĭz), v.t. Put on record; commit to memory. [f. foll. + -IZE]

mem′orÿ, n. Faculty of remembering; this in an individual, as a *good, bad,* ~ (*convenient* or *accommodating* ~, that retains only what it is to one's interest to remember); recollection; information storage device in electronic computer; *in* ~ *of*, as a record of, to keep alive the ~ of; posthumous repute, as *his* ~ *has been censured, of blessed, happy,* etc., ~ (used esp. of deceased princes etc.); length of time over which ~ extends, as *beyond, within, the* ~ *of men, within living* ~. [ME, f. OF *memorie, memoire* f. L *memoria* f. *memor* mindful]

mem′sah′ib, n. (In India) European married lady. [f. MA′AM+SAHIB]

-men, suf. in L wds, often side by side with L -*mentum* -MENT & w. same meaning, as *fundamen-tum*. Many wds of slightly technical or learned use, as *acumen, stamen, gravamen, albumen, cognomen, regimen, specimen*.

men′ace[1], n. (literary). Threat. [ME, OF f. Rom. *minacia = L -*iae* (L *minax* f. *minari* threaten)]

men′ac|e[2], v.t. Threaten. Hence~ingLY[2] adv. [ME, f. OF *menacer* f. Rom. *minaciare (as prec.)]

ménage (mānahzh′), n. Household management; domestic establishment; ~ *à trois* (trwah), household consisting of husband, wife, & lover of one of these. [f. OF *manaige* f. Rom. *mansionaticum (as MANSION, see -AGE)]

ména′gerie, n. Collection of wild animals in cages etc. [f. F *ménagerie* (as prec., see -ERY)]

mend[1], n. Repaired hole in material etc.; *on the* ~, improving in health or (of affairs etc.) condition. [f. foll.]

mend[2], v.t. & i. Restore to sound condition, repair, (broken articles, clothes, roads, etc.); ~ (correct) one's *ways*; *least said soonest* ~*ed* (rectified); ~ (add fuel to) *fire*; cut to required shape (quill pen); (intr.) regain health; ~ (improve state of) *matters*; ~ (quicken) one's *pace*; ~ *or end*, improve or abolish. Hence ~′ABLE a. [ME, aphetic f. AMEND]

mendā′cious (-shŭs), a. Lying, untruthful. Hence or cogn. ~LY[2] adv., mendā′cITY n. [f. L *mendax* f. root of *mentiri* lie, see -ACIOUS]

Men′delism, n. A proven theory of heredity which reduces to numerical law the recurrence of inherited characters. So **Mendĕl′ian** a. & n. [G. *J. Mendel*, 1822–84]

men′dic|ant, a. & n. **1.** Begging; ~*ant friars* (living solely on alms). **2.** n. Beggar. Hence or cogn. ~ANCY, mĕndi′cITY, nn. [f. L *mendicare* (*mendicus* beggar), see -ANT]

menhād′en, n. Fish of herring family, used for manure, & yielding valuable oil. [Amer. Ind. *munnawhatteaug*]

men′hir (-ĕr), n. (archaeol.). Tall upright monumental stone found in Europe, Africa, & Asia. [f. Breton *men hir* long stone]

men′ial, a. & n. **1.** (Of service) servile; (of servant, usu. derog.) domestic. **2.** n. ~ servant. Hence ~LY[2] adv. [AF, f. OF *mesnie* household (obs. E *meinie*) f. Rom. *mansionata (as MANSION, see -ADE)]

men′inx, n. (usu. in pl. *menin′gēs*). Any of three membranes enveloping brain & spinal cord (*dura mater, arachnoid, pia mater*). Hence **menin′gēAL** a., **menin**-**ġit′is** (-jit-), **menin′goCELE**, nn. [Gk *mēninx*]

menis′cus, n. (pl. -*cī*). Lens convex on one side, concave on the other; (math.) figure of crescent form; (phys.) curved upper surface of liquid in tube. [f. Gk *mēniskos* crescent (*mēnē* moon)]

Menn′onite, n. Member of a Protestant sect that arose in Friesland in 16th c. with tenets resembling those of Quakers & Baptists. [f. *Menno Simons*, founder]

men′o-, comb. form of Gk *mēn mēno-* month, as: ~*pause*, final cessation, ~*rrhä′gia* excessive flow, ~*rrhœe′a*, ordinary flow, of the menses.

menŏl′ogÿ, n. Calendar, esp. that of Greek Church, with biographies of saints. [f. late Gk *mēnologion* (*mēn* month +*logos* account)]

mēns (-nz) *cŏn′scia* (-shǐa) *rěc′tĭ*, L phr. = a clear conscience.

men′sēs (-z), n. pl. Flow of blood from mucous coat of uterus of female, occurring on the average at intervals of lunar month. [L, pl. of *mensis* month]

Men′shevik, n. Russian socialist of the more moderate party (cf. BOLSHEVIK). [Russ., = minority within the party, cf. BOLSHEVIK]

mēns (-nz) *sān′a in cŏrp′ore sān′ō*, L phr. = sound mind in sound body, used esp. as expressing the ideal of education. [Juvenal X. 356]

men′stru|al (-ŏŏ-), a. Of the menses, so ~ous a.; (astron.) monthly. [f. L *menstrualis* (as MENSTRUUM), see -AL)]

men′stru|āte (-ŏŏ-), v.i. Discharge the menses. Hence ~A′TION n. [f. LL *menstruare* (as foll.), see -ATE)]

men′struum (-ŏŏ-), n. (pl. -*rua*). Solvent (lit. & fig.). [neut. of L *menstruus* monthly (*mensis* month)]

měn′sŭrable, a. Measurable, having fixed limits; (mus.) having fixed rhythm. [F, or LL *mensurabilis* (LL *mensurare* f. L *mensura* MEASURE, see -BLE)]

měn′sŭral, a. Of measure; (mus.)=prec. [f. LL *mensuralis* (as MEASURE, see -AL)]

měnsŭrā′tion, n. Measuring; (math.) rules for finding lengths, areas, & volumes. [f. LL *mensuratio* (as MENSURABLE, see -ATION)]

-ment, suf., f. F *-ment* (or direct) f. L *-mentum*, forming nn. expr. result or means of vbl action, as *fragmentum*, *alimentum*, *ornamentum*; f. F are *habili~*, *abridge~*; E formations, freq. *hybrid*, are *amaze~*, *better~*, *embank~*, *bereave~*; a few are on adjj., as *odd~*, *funni~*.

měn′tal¹, a. & n. Of the mind; done by the mind, as ~ *arithmetic* (performed without use of written figures); (colloq.) affected with ~ disorder; ~ *patient* (under care for disordered mind); ~ RESERVATION; ~ *home*, *hospital*, ASYLUM; (n., colloq.) ~ case or patient. Hence~LY² adv. [ME, f. OF, or LL *mentalis* (*mens -ntis* mind, see -AL)]

měn′tal², a.. Of the chin. [F, f. L *mentum* chin, see -AL]

měntǎl′itў, n. The being mental or in or of the mind; (degree of) intellectual power; (loosely) mind, disposition, character. [f. MENTAL¹+-ITY]

měntā′tion, n. Mental action; state of mind. [f. L *mens -ntis* mind, see -ATION]

měn′thŏl, n. Camphor-like substance got from oil of peppermint etc., used to relieve neuralgia etc. [G, f. L *mentha* mint, see -OL(2)]

měn′tion¹, n. Mentioning, naming, (of thing); = ~ in dispatches; *honourable ~*, award of merit to candidate in examination, work of art, etc., not entitled to prize. [ME, f. OF, f. L *mentionem* (*men-* root of *mens* mind, see -ION)]

měn′tion², v.t. Refer to, remark upon, specify by name (esp. thing not obviously essential to context, as *this was expressly ~ed*; *that*); (in deprecation of apology or thanks) *don't ~ it*; (introducing fact or thing of secondary or, as rhet. artifice, of primary importance) *not to ~*. [f. F *mentionner* (as prec.)]

měn′tŏr, n. Experienced & trusted adviser. [F, f. Gk *Mentōr* adviser of Telemachus (root *men-* think)]

měn′ū (& see Ap.), n. Bill of fare. [F adj. = small, n. = detailed list]

měp′acrine (-ēn), n. Odourless yellow anti-malarial chemical. [f. *methoxyacridine* w. inorganic -P-]

Měphist|ŏph′elēs (-z), n. Evil Spirit to whom Faust, in German legend, sold his soul; fiendish person. Hence ~ŏphělē′AN, ~ophēl′IAN, aa. [G, of unkn. orig.]

měphit′is, n. Noxious emanation, esp. from the earth; noisome or poisonous stench. So **měphit′ic** a. [L]

měrc′antil|e, a. Of trade, commercial; ~*e theory* (that money is the only wealth); ~*e marine*, shipping employed in commerce; mercenary, ·fond of bargaining. Hence ~ISM, ~IST, nn. [F, f. It. *mercantil* (as MERCHANT)]

Měrcāt′or. See PROJECTION.

měr′cénar|ў, a. & n. 1. Working merely for money or other reward; hired. 2. n. Hired soldier in foreign service. Hence ~INESS n. [ME, f. L *mercenarius* (*merces -edis* reward, see -ARY¹)]

‖ **měr′c|er**, n. Dealer in textile fabrics, esp. silks & other costly materials. Hence ~ERY(1) n. [ME, f. AF *mercer* (OF *-ier*) f. Rom. **merciarius* (*merx mercis* goods, -ARY¹)]

měr′cerize, -ise (-īz), v.t. Treat (cotton fabrics & thread) with caustic alkali under tension to give greater strength and impart lustre. [J. *Mercer* (d. 1866), patentee, +-IZE]

měrch′andise (-z), n. Commodities of commerce, goods for sale. [ME, f. OF *marchandise* (as foll., see -ISE)]

měrch′ant, n. & a. Wholesale trader, esp. with foreign countries; ~ *prince*, wealthy ~; LAW¹ ~; ~ *ship*, ~*man*, (ship conveying merchandise); ~ (mercantile marine) *service*; ~ (sl.), one given to — (*speed-~*, speed-loving motorist; *lob-~*, slow bowler). [ME, f. OF *marchant* f. Rom. **mercatare* frequent. of *mercari* trade (*merx mercis* merchandise), see -ANT]

měrch′antable, a. Salable, marketable. [ME, f. *merchant* v. (now rare) f. OF *marcheander* (as prec.) +-ABLE]

měr′ciful, a. Having, showing, or feeling mercy. Hence~LY² adv.,~NESS n. [-FUL]

měr′cilěss, a. Pitiless, showing no mercy. Hence ~LY² adv.,~NESS n. [-LESS]

mercūr′ial, a. & n. 1. Sprightly, ready-witted, & volatile, whence ~ITY (-ǎl⁴) n.; of, containing, mercury; (*M~*) of the planet Mercury. 2. n. ~ drug, whence ~ISM(5) n., ~IZE(5) v.t. Hence ~LY² adv. [ME, f. OF *mercuriel* or L *mercurialis* (MERCURY, -AL)]

měrc′ūrў, n. 1. (*M~*) Roman god of eloquence, skill, thieving, etc., & messenger of gods, messenger (joc., & often in newspaper titles). 2. (*M~*) planet nearest to sun. 3. A white normally liquid metal usu. got from cinnabar & used in barometers, thermometers, amalgams, & mirrors (*the~ is rising*, weather or temper is improving), quicksilver, whence mer-cūr′IC, měrc′ūrous, aa. (chem.); (fig.) liveliness (*has no ~ in him*). [ME, f. L *Mercurius*, prob. f.*merx -rcis* merchandise]

měr′cў, n. Compassion shown by one to another who is in his power & has no claim to kindness (*have ~ on* or *upon*, *show ~ to*; ~ *!*, ~ *on* or *upon us !*, appeals, or excll. usu. playful of terror or surprise); compassionateness; *at the ~ of*, wholly in the power of, liable to danger or harm from; *that is a ~* (blessing, thing to be thankful for); (joc.) *left to the* *tender mercies of*, exposed to probable rough handling by; ~*-seat*, golden covering of Ark of Covenant, throne of God; (attrib., passing into adj.) administered or performed out of ~ or pity for suffering person (~ *killing*). [ME, f. OF *merci* f. L *mercedem* (nom. *-ces*) reward, (Christian L) pity]

mere[1], n. Lake, pond, (poet., exc. in place names). [OE *mere*, OS, OHG *meri*, ON *marr*, Goth. *mari* cogn. w. L *mare* sea]

mere[2], a. That is solely what the noun implies, as *a* ~ *swindler*, *the* ~*st buffoonery* (law) ~ *right* (without possession). Hence ~LY[2] (mēr'lǐ) adv. [f. L *merus* unmixed]

mere[3] (mě'rǐ), n. Maori war-club, esp. one made of greenstone. [Maori]

měrĕtrī'cious (-shŭs), a. Of, befitting, a harlot; (of ornament, literary style, etc.) showily attractive. Hence ~LY[2] adv., ~NESS n. [f. L *meretricius* f. *meretrix* harlot (*mereri* earn, see -TRIX) +-OUS]

mĕrgăn'ser, n. Diving fish-eating duck. [f. L *mergus* diver +*anser* goose]

mĕrge, v.t. & i. Lose, cause (thing) to lose, character or identity *in* (another), esp. sink (title, estate, *in* greater one). Hence mĕr'GENCE n. [f. law F *merger* f. L *mergere mers-* dip]

mĕr'ger, n. Merging; combination. [-ER[4]]

mĕrid'ian, n. & a. 1. Circle passing through celestial poles & zenith of any place on earth's surface; circle lying in the plane of this & passing through the place & the poles, as ~ *of Greenwich* (of longitude 0° in British maps); point at which sun or star attains highest altitude; prime, full splendour; *calculated for the* ~ (to suit the tastes etc.) *of* (place, people). 2. adj. Of noon; (fig.) of the period of greatest splendour, vigour,· etc. [ME; n. f. adj.) f. OF *meridien* or L *meridianus* (*meridies* midday f. *medius* middle +*dies* day, see -AN)]

mĕrid'ional, a. & n. Of (the inhabitants of) the south of Europe; of a meridian (n.) inhabitant of the south (esp. of France). [f. OF *meridional* f. LL *meridionalis* (irreg. as prec., -AL)]

meringue' (-ăng), n. Confection of sugar, white of eggs, etc., small cake of this. [F]

meri'nō (-rē-), n. (pl. ~s). (Also ~ *sheep*) kind of sheep with fine wool; soft woollen or wool-&-cotton material like French cashmere, orig. of ~ wool; fine woollen yarn. [Sp., prob. f. L *majorinus* of a larger kind (*major* greater, see -INE[1])]

mě'rit, n., & v.t. 1. Quality of deserving well; excellence, worth; (usu. pl.) thing that entitles to reward or gratitude; *make a* ~ *of*, view, represent, (one's own conduct) as meritorious; *the* ~*s*, intrinsic rights & wrongs (of case etc., esp. law); *judge* (proposal etc.) *on its* ~*s* (with only its intrinsic excellences etc. in view). 2. v.t. Deserve (reward, punishment). [ME; (vb f. F *mériter*) f. OF *merite* f. L *meritum* neut. p.p. of *mereri* earn, deserve]

mĕritōr'ious, a. (Of person or act) deserving reward, praise, or gratitude (often as term of limited praise, = well-meant, well-meaning). Hence ~LY[2] adv., ~NESS n. [ME, f. L *meritorius* (*merēri* merit-earn, see -ORY) +-OUS]

mĕrle, n. (arch., Sc.). Blackbird. [F, f. L *merulus*, *-la*]

mĕrl'in, n. Kind of falcon. [ME, f. AF *merilun* f. OF *esmerillon* augm. (*-oon*) f. *esmeril* f. Rom. *smerillo* f. WG *smiril*; cf. OHG *smiril* (G *schmerl*)]

mĕrl'on, n. Part of embattled parapet between two embrasures. [F, f. It. *merlone* (*merlo* battlement, perh. f. *mergola* dim. f. L *mergae* pitchfork; see -OON)]

mĕrm'aid, n. Half-human being, with head & trunk of woman & tail of fish. So mĕrm'AN n. [ME, f. MERE[1] +MAID]

mě'ro-, comb. form of Gk *meros* part, in senses 'partly', 'partial', as: ~*blast*, ovum that is only partly germinal; ~*hēd'ral*, (of crystal) having less than full number of faces admissible.

-merous, suf. (bot.) = having so many parts, as *dimerous*, *5-merous*. [f. Gk as prec. +-OUS]

Měrovin'gian (-j-), a. & n. (King) of the Frankish line founded by Clovis & reigning in Gaul & Germany *c.* 500–750. [f. F *Mérovingien* f. med. L *Merovingi* of Germanic orig.]

mě'rriment, n. Hilarious enjoyment, mirth, fun. [f. obs. vb *merry* be merry + -MENT]

mě'rry[1], n. Kind of black cherry. [f. F *merise* taken as pl. (cf. CHERRY)]

mě'rry[2], a. Joyous, mirthful; ~ (pleasant) *England*; *the* ~ *monarch*, Charles II; slightly tipsy; *make* ~, be festive; *make* ~ *over*, make fun of; ~ *andrew*, mountebank's assistant, clown, buffoon, (also fig.); ~ *DANCERS*; ~*-go-round*, revolving machine with wooden horses or cars; ~*-making*, festivity; ~*thought*, forked bone between neck & breast of bird. Hence mě'rrILY[2] adv., mě'rrINESS n. (rare). [OE *myr(i)ge*, corresp. to MDu. *merch* (whence *merchle* mirth, *mergen* obs. vb *merry*); f. Gmc *murgi*, whence OHG *murgi* short, Goth. *gamaurgjan* shorten]

***me'sa** (mā-), n. High rocky tableland with precipitous sides. [Sp., = table, f. L *mensa*]

mésalliance (see Ap.), n. Marriage with person of inferior social position. [F]

mesdames, mesdemoiselles. See MADAME, MADEMOISELLE.

méseems' (-z), v.i. (arch.). It seems to me. [*me* dat. +SEEMS]

mĕsĕmbriǎn'thĕmum, -brў-, n. Kinds of succulent plant with bright flowers. [f. Gk *mesĕmbria* noon +*anthemon* flower]

mĕs'entery, n. Fold of peritoneum attaching some part of intestinal canal to posterior wall of abdomen. Hence mĕsĕntē'rıc a., mĕsĕnterıT'ıs n. [f. med. L

f. Gk *mesenterion* (MESO-+*enteron* intestine)]

mĕsh[1], n. Open space, interstice, of net; (pl.) network, (fig.) snare; (physiol., pl.) interlaced structure; (of teeth of wheels) *in* ~, engaged. [16th c. *meash, mash* f. MDu. *maesche, masche* = OHG *māsca*; cogn. w. OE *max*, ON *møskvi* net]

mĕsh[2], v.t. & i. Catch in net (lit. & fig.); (of teeth of wheel) be engaged (*with* others). [f. prec.]

mes'ial (mēz-, mĕs-), a. Of, in, directed towards, middle line of a body. Hence ~LY[2] adv. [irreg. f. Gk *mesos* middle+ -IAL]

mes'mer|ism (mĕz-), n. Hypnotic state, usu. involving insensibility to pain & muscular rigidity, produced on patient by operator's influence over will & nervous system; doctrine concerning, influence producing, this. Hence **mĕs-mĕr'ic** a., ~IST, ~IZA'TION, nn., ~IZE(4) v.t., (mĕz-). [F. A. *Mesmer*, Austrian physician, d. 1815, +-ISM]

mesne (mēn), a. Intermediate, as ~ *profits* (received from estate by wrongful tenant between two dates); ~ *process*, proceedings in suit intervening between primary & final process; (feud.) ~ *lord* (holding of superior lord). [ME, altered sp. of AF *meen* MEAN[2]]

mĕs'o-, comb. form of Gk *mesos* middle, intermediate, as; ~*cephăl'ic*, (of skull) intermediate between BRACHYCEPHALIC and DOLICHOCEPHALIC; ~*gas'ter*, membrane attaching stomach to dorsal wall of abdomen; ~*lith'ic*, of stone age between palaeolithic & neolithic; ~*phyll*, inner tissue of leaf; ~*tron*, sub-atomic positive or negative particle having a mass about 200 times that of an electron; *M*~*zō'ic*,of second geological period (cf. CAINOZOIC, PALAEOZOIC).

mĕs'ŏn, n. (phys.). Fundamental particle intermediate in mass between proton & electron, found in cosmic rays & atomic nuclei. [f. Gk *mesos* middle]

Mĕs'pot, n. (sl.). Mesopotamia. [abbr.]

mĕs'quit(e) (-kēt), n. N.-Amer. leguminous tree; (also ~*-grass*) kinds of grass growing near this. [f. Mex. Sp. *mezquite*]

mĕss[1], n. **1.** Portion of liquid or pulpy food (freq. *savoury* ~); ~ *of pottage*, material comfort etc. for which something higher is sacrificed (*Gen.* xxv. 29–34); liquid or mixed food for hounds etc.; concoction, medley. **2.** Dirty or untidy state of things; *make a* ~ *of*, bungle (undertaking). **3.** Company of persons who take meals together, esp. in the fighting services; meal so taken, as *at* ~, *go to* ~ (often attrib., as ~*-jacket*, coat worn at ~); ~*mate*, one of the same (usu. ship's) ~. Hence ~'Y[2] a. (~*y floor, food, job*), ~'iLY[2] adv., ~'iNESS n. [ME, f. OF *mes* f. LL *missus* course at dinner p.p. of *mittere* send]

mĕss[2], v.t. & i. Make a mess of, dirty,

(thing), freq. ~ *up*; muddle (business); potter *about*; take one's meals (*with* or abs.). [f. prec.]

mĕss'age[1], n. Oral or written communication sent by one person to another; prophet's, writer's, preacher's, inspired communication. [ME, f. OF, f. Rom. *missaticum* (*mittere* miss- send, see -AGE)]

mĕss'age[2], v.t. Send as a message; transmit (plan etc.) by signalling etc. [f. prec.]

mĕss'enger, n. One who carries a message; paper sent up string from flier to kite; endless rope passing from capstan to cable to haul it in. [ME & OF *messagier* (prec., -ER[1]); -*n*- as in *passenger*]

Mĕssi'ah (-*a*), n. Promised deliverer of Jews; Christ as this; liberator of oppressed people or country. Hence ~SHIP n. [ME *Messie* f. OF, *Messias* f. LL f. Gk *Messias* f. Heb. *mashiah* anointed; *Messiah* alt. sp. to give the wd a more Hebraic aspect]

Mĕssiän'ic, a. Of the, inspired by hope or belief in a, Messiah. [prec., -AN, -IC]

messieurs' (mĕsyĕr'), n. pl. Pl. of MONSIEUR or (in abbr. form *Messrs*, pron. mĕss'erz) of Mr, used esp. as prefix to name of firm, or introducing list of gentlemen.

mĕss'uage (-swij), n. (law). Dwelling-house with outbuildings & land assigned to its use. [ME, f. AF *messuage*, perh. alt. sp. f. OF *mesnage* dwelling f. Rom. *mansionaticum* (MANSION, -AGE)]

mĕsti'zō (-tē-), n. (pl. ~s). Spanish or Portuguese half-caste, esp. child of Spaniard & Amer.-Indian. [Sp.]

mĕt[1]. See MEET[2].

mĕt[2], a. (colloq.). Meteorological etc. [abbr.]

mĕta- in comb. (before vowel *met-*, before aspirate *meth-*) = Gk *meta* with, after; occas. w. sense ' change '.

mĕtăb'olism, n. Process, in organism or single cell, by which nutritive material is built up into living matter (*constructive* ~) or protoplasm is broken down into simpler substances (*destructive* ~). So **mĕtăbŏl'ic** a., **mĕtăb'olIZE(3)** v.t. [f. Gk *metabolē* change f. META(*ballō* throw) change +-ISM]

mĕtacărp'us, n. Part of hand between wrist & fingers. [f. META-+Gk *karpos* wrist]

mĕt'age, n. Official measuring of load of coal etc.; duty paid for this. [f. METE[2] +-AGE]

mĕtagĕn'ĕsis, n. Alternation between sexual & asexual reproduction. So **mĕtagĕnET'IC** a. [META-+GENESIS]

mĕt'al, n., & v.t. (-ll-). **1.** Any of a class of substances represented by gold, silver, copper, iron, lead, tin, etc., all of which are crystalline when solid and many of which are opaque, ductile, malleable, of high specific gravity, good conductors of heat & electricity, and characterized by a peculiar lustre; BELL[1], BRITANNIA, GUN,

WHITE, YELLOW, ~; HEAVY ~; (mil.) tanks, armoured vehicles, etc.; material used for making glass, in molten state; (also *road*-~) broken stone for macadam roads or railway; ‖ (pl.) rails of a railway line (*train leaves the* ~s, is derailed). 2. v.t. Furnish, fit, with ~; mend (road) with ~. [ME, f. OF, or L f. Gk *metallon* mine]

metăll′ic, a. Of metal(s); ~ *currency*, gold, silver, copper, etc., cf. PAPER; characteristic of metals as ~ *lustre* (peculiar sheen of metals), ~ *sound*. So **mĕt′alline¹** a. [f. F (-*ique*), or L f. Gk *metallikos* (as METAL, see -IC)]

mĕt′alliz|e, -is|e (-īz), v.t. Render metallic; coat with thin layer of metal; vulcanize (rubber). Hence ~A′TION n. [-IZE]

mĕtăllŏg′raphў, n. Descriptive science of internal structure of metals. [f. METAL + -GRAPHY]

mĕt′alloid, a. & n. 1. Having form or appearance of metal. 2. n. Element with characteristics both of metals and non--metals. [-OID]

mĕtăll′urgў (-ler-; or mĕt′al-), n. Art of working metals, esp. of extracting metals from their ores. Hence **mĕtallŭr′gic(AL) aa.**, **mĕtăll′urgist** (-ler-) n. [f. Gk *metallourgos* metal-worker (*metallon* METAL + -*ergos* -worker), see -Y¹]

mĕt′amēre, n. (zool.). One of several similar segments of a body. [f. META- + Gk *meros* part]

mĕtamĕ′ric, a. (Chem.) having same composition & molecular weight, but different chemical properties; (zool.) of metameres. So **mĕtăm′erism** n. (chem., zool.). [as prec. + -IC]

mĕtamŏrph′|ic, a. Of, marked by, metamorphosis; (geol., of rock) that has undergone transformation by natural agencies, whence ~ISM n. [f. META- + Gk *morphē* form + -IC]

mĕtamŏrph′ose (-z), v.t. Change in form, turn (*to, into*, new form); change nature of. [f. foll.; cf. *anchylose, diagnose*]

mĕtamŏrph′osis, n. (pl. -*oses*, pr. -ēz). Change of form (by magic or by natural development etc.); changed form; change of character, conditions, etc. [L, f. Gk *metamorphōsis* f. META(*morphoō* f. *morphē* form)]

mĕt′aphor, n. Application of name or descriptive term to an object to which it is not literally applicable (e.g. *a glaring error*); instance of this; *mixed* ~, combination of inconsistent ~. Hence **mĕtaphŏ′rical** a., **mĕtaphŏ′rically²** adv. [f. F *métaphore* or L f. Gk *metaphora* f. META(*pherō* bear) transfer]

mĕt′aphrāse (-z), n. & v.t. Translation, esp. word-for-word; (v.t.) put into other words. So **mĕtaphrăs′tic** a. [f. Gk *metaphrasis* f. META*phrazō* translate]

mĕtaphȳs′ical (-z-), a. & n. 1. Of metaphysics; based on abstract general

reasoning; over-subtle; incorporeal; supernatural; visionary; (of some 17th c. poets, esp. Donne) addicted to fanciful conceits and far-fetched imagery. 2. n. (esp. pl.). *The M*~*s*, ~ poets. Hence~LY² adv. [-AL]

mĕtaphȳs′|ics (-z-), n. pl. (often treated as sing.). Theoretical philosophy of being & knowing; philosophy of mind; (pop.) abstract or subtle talk, mere theory. So ~I′CIAN (-ïshn) n., ~ICIZE(2) v.i. [ME -*ic*, later -*ics* (see -IC 2) f. med. L *metaphysica* fem. sing. & neut. pl., f. med. Gk *phusika* f. Gk *ta meta ta phusika* the works *meta*-(of Aristotle) placed after the PHYSICS]

mĕt′aplăsm (-z-), n. (biol.). Part of protoplasm that contains formative material. [META- + -*plasm* as in PROTOPLASM]

mĕtapŏl′itics, n. pl. Abstract political science (often derog.). Hence **mĕtapŏlit′ical** a., **mĕtapŏliti′cian** (-ïshn) n. [META-, after METAPHYSICS]

mĕtapsych′ics (-sīk-), n. pl. Psychical research. [META- + PSYCHICS, after *metaphysics*]

mĕtăs′tasis, n. (pl. -*ses*, pr. -sēz). Transference of bodily function, disease, etc., from one part or organ to another; transformation of chemical compounds into others in process of assimilation by an organism. So **mĕtastăt′ic** a. [LL f. Gk, f. *methistēmi* change]

mĕtatărs′|us, n. (anat.). Group of five long bones of foot between tarsus & toes. Hence ~AL a. [META-]

mĕtăth′esis, n. (pl. -*ses*, pr. -sēz). (Gram.) transposition of sounds or letters in word; (chem.) interchange of atoms between two molecules. [LL f. Gk, f. META(*tithēmi* place) transpose]

métayage (mĕt′āyahzh), n. Land tenure in which farmer pays part (usu. half) of produce as rent to owner, who furnishes stock & seed. [F, see foll., -AGE]

metayer (mĕt′āyā), n. Holder of land on prec. system. [F, f. med. L *medietarius* (*medietas* MOIETY, see -ARY¹)]

mēte¹, n. Boundary, boundary stone, esp. (law) ~s & bounds. [ME, f. OF, f. L *meta* goal]

mēte², v.t. (literary) (Poet.) measure; portion out, allot, (punishment; reward); ‖~-*wand*, -*yard*, (fig.) standard of estimation. [OE, OS *metan*, OHG *mezzan*, ON *meta*, Goth. *mitan* f. Gmc *met-, *mǣt- MEET³]

mĕtĕmpī′ric, n. (Also ~*s*) philosophy of things outside the sphere of experience; believer in this. Hence~AL a.,~IST n. [f. META- + EMPIRIC, after *metaphysics*]

mĕtĕmpsўchōs′|is (-k-), n. (pl. -*es*, pr. -ēz). Transmigration of soul of human being or animal at death into new body of same or different species. Hence ~IST(2) n. [LL f. Gk (META- + *en* in + *psukhē* soul + -OSIS)]

mēt′eor, n. (Any atmospheric phenomenon, esp.) shooting star, small mass of matter from celestial space rendered luminous by collision with earth's atmosphere. [ME, f. med. L *meteorum* f. Gk *meteōros* lofty, (neut. pl.) atmospheric phenomena (META- + *aeirō* raise)]

mĕtèŏ'ric, a. Of the atmosphere; dependent on atmospheric conditions; of meteors; (fig.) dazzling, rapid. [prec. + -IC, partly f. med. L *-icus*]

mĕt'èor|ite, n. Fallen meteor, meteoric stone. So **~OLITE** n. [METEOR + -ITE[1]]

mĕt'èorograph (-ahf), n. Apparatus recording meteorological phenomena. [METEOR, -GRAPH]

mĕt'èor|oid, n. Body moving through space, of same nature as those which by passing through atmosphere become visible as meteors. Hence **~oid'AL** a. [-OID]

mĕtèor|ŏl'ŏgÿ, n. Study of motions & phenomena of atmosphere, esp. for weather forecast; atmospheric character (*of region*). Hence or cogn. **~olŏ'ġıc**(AL) aa., **~olŏ'ġicalLY[2]** adv., **~ŏl'ŏġıst** n. [f. Gk *meteōrologia* (as METEOR, -LOGY)]

mĕt'er, n. Person, thing, that measures, esp. *gas, water*, etc., **~**, instruments for recording volume of gas etc. supplied. [(1) person: 14th c. f. METE[2] + -ER[1]; (2) instrument: 19th c., prob. application of (1) suggested by *gasometer* & other wds w. foll. suf.]

-mĕter, suf. in names of measuring instruments on Gk nn. (but not on Gk anal.), as *barometer*, L nn., as *calorimeter*, mod. wds as if Gk or L, as *gasometer*, or without assim. to Gk or L, as *ammeter*. [f. Gk *metron* measure]

mĕth'āne, n. (chem.). Odourless colourless inflammable gaseous hydrocarbon, marsh gas, fire-damp. [f. METH(YL) + -ANE]

mĕthĕg'lin, n. (hist., dial.). Spiced kind of mead. [f. W *meddyglyn* (*meddyg* healing f. L *medicus* + *llyn* liquor)]

mĕthinks', v.i. (arch.; past *methought* pr. -awt). It seems to me. [ME dat. + THINKS]

mĕth'od, n. Special form of procedure esp. in any branch of mental activity, whence **~ŏl'OGY** n.; orderly arrangement of ideas; orderliness, regular habits; *there's* **~** *in his* etc. *madness*, (joc.) his conduct or proposal is not so mad as it seems; (nat. hist.) scheme of classification. Hence or cogn. **mĕthŏd'ICAL** a., **mĕthŏd'icalLY[2]** adv. [f. F (-*ode*), or L f. Gk *methodos* (META- + *hodos* way)]

mĕth'odist, n. 1. (*M~*) member of any of several religious bodies (now united) originating in the evangelistic movement of Charles & John Wesley & George Whitefield, whence **mĕthodis'tIC**(AL) aa., **mĕthodis'ticalLY[2]** adv. 2. (derog.). Person of strict religious views. 3. One who follows a method, esp. in nat. hist. Hence **Mĕth'odISM** n. [-IST]

mĕth'odize, -ise (-īz), v.t. Reduce to order, arrange in orderly manner. [-IZE]

methought. See METHINKS.

Mĕthus'elah (-ōozela), n. A pre-Noachian patriarch who is stated to have lived 969 years (hence as type of longevity). [Heb.]

mĕth'ÿl, n. Radical of **~** alcohol (wood spirit) present in many organic compounds. Hence **mĕthÿl'IC** a. [F (& G) *méthyl*, back form. f. F *méthylene* (Gk *methu* wine + *hulē* wood)]

mĕth'ÿlāte, v.t. Mix, impregnate, (esp. spirit of wine, to make it unfit for drinking, so as to exempt it from duties) with methyl alcohol, as **~d** *spirit*. [-ATE[3]]

mĕtic'ŭlous, a. Over-scrupulous about minute details; (pop.) very careful, accurate. Hence **~LY[2]** adv. [f. L *meticulosus*, (or F -*eux*), f. *metus* fear, see -CULE, -OUS]

mĕtier (mĕt'yā), n. One's trade, profession, or line. [F]

mĕt'is, n. Offspring of white & American Indian, esp. in Canada. [f. F *métis* f. LL *misticius* (*miscēre* mix), whence MESTIZO]

Mĕtŏn'ic, a. **~** *cycle*, period of 19 years (235 lunar months) covering all the changes of the moon. [*Melon*, Athenian astronomer of 5th c. B.C.]

mĕtŏn'ÿmÿ, n. Substitution of the name of an attribute for that of the thing meant (e.g. *crown* for *king*). Hence **mĕtonÿm'ICAL** a., **mĕtonÿm'icalLY[2]** adv. [f. LL f. Gk *metōnumia* (META- + *onoma* name)]

mĕt'ope (-opI, -ōp), n. (archit.). Square space between triglyphs in Doric frieze. [f. L f. Gk *metopē* (META- + *opē* hole for beam)]

mē'tre[1] (-ter), n. Any form of poetic rhythm, determined by character & number of feet. Hence **mĕtrı'CIAN** (-ĭshn), **mĕt'rICS**, **mĕt'rIST**, nn. [ME, f. OF, f. L f. Gk *metron* measure; OE *meter* dir. f. L]

mē'tre[2] (-ter), n. Unit of length in metric system (39·37 in.). [f. F *mètre* (as prec.)]

mĕt'ric, a. Of the METRE[2]; **~** *system*, decimal measuring-system with the metre, & the litre & gram determined by it, as units of length, capacity, & weight (the prefixing to *metre* etc. of the Greek-derived *deca-, hecto-, kilo-*, denotes multiplication by 10, 100, 1,000, as *kilometre* 1,000 metres; that of the Latin-derived *deci-, centi-, milli-*, division by 10, 100, 1,000, as *decilitre* tenth of a litre). [f. F *métrique* (prec., -IC)]

mĕt'rical, a. Of, composed in, metre, esp. **~** *psalms*; of, involving, measurement, as **~** *geometry*. Hence **~LY[2]** adv. [ME, f. OF, or L f. Gk *metrikos* (METRE[1], -ICAL)]

mĕtrŏl'ogÿ, n. Science, system, of weights & measures. Hence **mĕtrolŏ'ġıcAL** a. [as METRE[1] + -LOGY]

mĕt'ronōme, n. (mus.). Instrument marking time by means of pendulum, beating rod, etc. Hence **mĕtronŏm'IC** a. [as METRE[1] + Gk *nomos* law]

mĕtrŏp'olis, n. Chief city of a country; capital; || *the* **~**, London; metropolitan bishop's see; centre of activity. [LL, f. Gk *metropolis* parent State (*mētēr -tros* mother + *polis* city)]

mĕtropŏl'itan, a. & n. Of a or the metropolis; belonging to, forming (part of), mother country as dist. from its colonies etc.; of an ecclesiastical metropolis; ~ (*bishop*), bishop having authority over bishops of a province, in the West equivalent to archbishop, in Greek church ranking above archbishop & below patriarch, whence ~ATE[1] (-*at*) n.; ~ *magistrate*, paid London magistrate, cf. STIPENDIARY; inhabitant of a metropolis. [f. LL *metropolitanus* f. Gk *mētropolitēs* (as prec., -ITE[1]), see -AN]

-mĕtrў, suf. in names of systems corresp. to instruments in -METER on anal. of Gk *geōmetria* GEOMETRY, but also in hybrids, as *alkalimetry*. [f. Gk -*metria* (-*mètrès* measurer, as METRE[1])]

mĕt'tl|e, n. Quality of disposition; natural ardour; spirit, courage; *be on* one's ~e (incited to do one's best). Hence (-)~ED[2] (-ld), ~ESOME (-tls-), aa. [var. of METAL n.]

mē'um, n. ~ *& tū'um,* mine & thine (used to express rights of property). [L, neut. of *meus*]

mew[1], n. (Also *sea*-~) gull, esp. common gull. [OE *māw*, OS *mēu*, MDu., MLG *mēwe* (whence G *mōwe*)]

mew[2], n., & v.t. **1.** Cage for hawks, esp. while moulting. **2.** v.t. Put (hawk) in ~; (fig.) shut *up*, confine. [ME, f. OF *mue*, f. *muer* (foll.)]

mew[3], v.t. (arch.). (Of hawk) moult, shed, (feathers). [ME, f. OF *muer* f. L *mutare* change]

mew[4], v.i., & n. **1.** (Of cat, sea-birds) utter sound *mew*. **2.** n. This sound, esp. of cat. [ME; imit.]

mewl, mūle, v.i. Cry feebly, whimper; mew like cat. [imit., cf. MIAUL]

∥ **mews,** n. Set of stabling round open yard. [pl. (now used as sing.) of MEW[2]; orig. of royal stables on site of hawks' mews]

mĕ'zzanine (-ēn), n. Low storey between two others (usu. between ground & first floors); (theatr.) floor beneath stage. [F, f. It. *mezzanino* dim. of *mezzano* f. L *medianus* MEDIAN]

mĕ'zzo (-dzō), adv. (Mus.) half, moderately, as ~ FORTE[2], PIANO[1]; ~-*rilie'vo* (-lyăvō), half-relief, in which figures project half their true proportions; ~-*sopra'no*, (person with, part for) voice between soprano & contralto. [It., f. L *medius* middle]

mĕ'zzotint (-dz-), n., & v.t. **1.** Method of engraving in which plate is roughened uniformly, lights & half-lights being given by scraping away the roughness thus produced, deep shadows by leaving it; print produced by this. **2.** v.t. Engrave in ~. [f. It. *mezzotinto* (also used in E) f. *mezzo* half + *tinto* TINT]

mi (mē), mē, n. (mus.). Third note of octave. [first syllable of L *mira*, see GAMUT]

miaow (mīow'), n., & v.i. (Make) cry of cat. [imit.]

miäs'm|a (-z-), n. (pl. ~*ata*, ~*as*). Infectious or noxious emanation. Hence ~AL, ~ăt'IC, aa., (-z-). [Gk, f. *miainō* pollute, see -M)]

miaul', v.i. Cry like cat. [f. F *miauler*, imit.]

mĭc'a, n. Any of several minerals composed of silicate of aluminium with other silicates, found in small glittering scales in granite etc., or in crystals, used as an (electrical) insulator; ~*schist*, -*slate*, slaty rock of quartz & ~. Hence **mĭcA'CEOUS** (-āshus) a. [L, = crumb]

Micaw'ber, n. ~, *Mr* ~, *Wilkins* ~, sanguine idler trusting that something good will turn up. Hence ~ISM(3) n. [person in Dickens's *David Copperfield*].

mice. See MOUSE[1].

Mich'ael (-kel), n. An archangel; *Order of St* ~ *& St George*, English civil & military order of knighthood, now esp. awarded for distinguished services abroad; ~*mas* (mĭk'el-), feast of St ~, Sep. 29, ∥ a quarter-day. [f. Heb. *mikhael* who is like God?]

∥ **mĭc'kle,** mŭc', a. & n. (arch., Sc.). Much, great; (n.) a large amount (in prov. *many a little,* or *pickle, makes a* ~). [OE *micel*, OS *mikil,* OHG *mihhil,* ON *mikell,* Goth. *mikils* f. Gmc **mikilaz,* cogn. w. Gk *megalo*-]

mĭc'ro-[1], comb. form of Gk *mikros* small, as: ~*cephăl'ic* a. & n., (person) with abnormally small head, so ~*cĕph'alous* a.; ~*film* n. P, (photographic reproduction on) a very small film; (v.t. & i.) photograph on ~*film*; ~*lith'ic,* constructed of small stones, marked by monuments so constructed; ~*logy* (-ōl[2]-), hair-splitting; ~*meter* (-ŏm[2]), instrument for measuring small objects or (astron.) distances, so ~*met'rical,* ~*metry* (-ŏm[2]); ~-*organism,* organism of (ultra) microscopic size; ~*phŏt'ograph* (of microscopic object on magnified scale), microscopic plant, esp. bacterium; ~*seism* (-sĭzm), faint earthquake tremor, whence ~*seismic,* ~*seis'mograph,* ~*seismol'ogy;* ~*spore,* parasitic fungus with small spores, small spore; ~*tōme,* instrument for cutting thin sections for microscope; ~*tōne,* mus. interval smaller than semitone; ~*wave,* Hertzian wave of length between 50 cms & 1 cm; ~*zȳme,* zymotic microbe.

mĭc'ro-[2] (etym. as prec.) prefixed in physics to unit-names = the millionth part of the unit; ~*ampere,* ~*coulomb,* ~*farad,* ~*gram,* ~*litre,* ~*metre,* ~*milli-metre, mĭc'rŏhm,* ~*volt.*

mĭc'rŏbe, n. Minute living being, plant or animal (esp. of bacteria causing diseases & fermentation). Hence **mĭcrŏb'IAL** a.,

microbiōl′ogy n. [F (MICRO-¹ + Gk *bios* life)]

mic′rocŏsm (-zm), n. Man viewed as epitome of the universe; any community or complex unity so viewed; miniature representation (*of*). Hence **mīcrocŏs′mic** (-z-) a. [ME, f. med. L MICRO¹(*cosmus* f. Gk *kosmos* world); partly thr. F *microcosme*]

mic′rŏn, n. The millionth of a metre. [f. Gk neut. of *mikros* small]

mic′rophōne, n. Instrument for intensifying small sounds or converting sound waves into electrical energy which may be reconverted into sound after transmission by wire or wireless, as the transmitter of a telephone or (colloq. abbr. *mike*) the mouthpiece for broadcasting. [f. MICRO-¹ + Gk *phōnē* sound]

mic′roscōpe, n. Instrument magnifying objects by means of lens(es) so as to reveal details invisible to naked eye. [MICRO-¹ + -SCOPE]

microscŏp′ic, a. Of the microscope, whence ~AL a.;.too small to be visible (in detail) without microscope. Hence ~alLY² adv. [-IC]

micrŏs′cop|y̆, n. Use of the microscope. So ~IST n. [-Y¹]

mictūri′tion, n. Morbidly frequent desire to make water; (improp.) making water. [f. L *micturire* -*it*-, desiderative f. *mingere mict*- make water, see -ION]

mid¹, a. (sup. ~*most*). The middle of (usu. after *in*, as *in* ~ *air*, *career*, *Channel*, *course*, *stream*, *winter*; also with *from*, *to*, etc., as *from* ~ *June* to ~ *August*; & in attrib. compounds, as *a* ~*winter day*); that is in the middle, medium, half, (~ *iron*, golf iron with medium loft; ~ *off*, ~ *on*, = ~*wicket off*, on; ~*rib*, central rib of leaf; ~*way* adv., in middle of distance between places; ~*wicket off* or *on*, fielder near bowler on off, on, side). ~*WING*. [OE *midd*, OS *middi*, OHG *mitti*, ON *mithr*,. Goth. *midjis* f. Gmc *midhja*- cogn. w. L *medius*]

mid², prep. (poet.). = AMID.

mid′day, n. Noon (often attrib.). [OE *middæg*, see MID¹ & DAY]

midd′en, n. Dunghill; *kitchen* ~, prehistoric refuse-heap, chiefly of shells & bones. [ME *myddyng*, of Scand. orig.; cf. Da. *mødding*]

mid′dle¹, a. (not pred.; rare sup. ~*most*) & n. **1.** (Of member of group) so placed as to have same number of members on each side; equidistant from extremities; intermediate in rank, quality, etc.; ~ *course*, *way*, compromise between two extremes; (gram.) applied to a voice in (esp. Greek) verbs that developed passive senses but retained active or quasi--reflexive senses; *M*~ ENGLISH; ~ *age*, between youth & old age; ~*aged*, of such age; *the M*~ *Ages* (about 1000–1400, or in a wider sense 600–1500); ‖ ~ *article*, brief essay of literary kind in weekly or other

journal often placed between political articles & book-reviews; ~ *class*, class of society between upper & lower (often attrib., ~-*class*); *M*~ EAST; ~ (second) *finger*; *M*~ *Kingdom*, China (orig. of Honan as central & sovereign State); ~ *life*, the ~ part of life, ~ *age*; *in the* ~ *of*, while (*doing*), during (progress); (log.) ~ (*term*), term common to both premisses, *principle of excluded* ~ (that anything must be included either under a given term or under its negative); ~*man*, any of the traders through whose hands commodity passes from producer to consumer; ~ *passage*, sea journey between W. Africa & W. Indies (with ref. to the slave trade); ~ *watch* (from midnight to 4 a.m.); ~-*weight* (boxing), from 11 st. 11 to 11st. **2.** n. ~ point or position or part (*of*), waist; ~ voice; ‖ ~ article. [OE *middel*, OS -*il*, OHG *mittil* f. WG *middil*- f. Gmc *midhja*- MID]

mid′dle², v.t. (Footb.) return (ball or abs.) from wing to mid field in front of goal; (crick.) strike (ball) with middle of bat; (techn.) place in the middle; (naut.) fold in the middle. [f. prec.]

midd′ling, a. & adv. **1.** (Commerc., of goods) of the second of three grades, so ~s n. pl. (also in spec. senses, flour of medium fineness, & comminuted bran); moderately good; second-rate; (colloq.) fairly well (in health), as *I am only* ~. **2.** adv. Fairly or moderately, as ~ *good*, *fast*. Hence ~LY² adv. [of Sc. orig., f. MID¹ + -LING² & ² (confused)]

midd′y̆, n. See MIDSHIP.

midge, n. Kinds of gnat-like insect; small person. [OE *mycg(e)*, OS *muggia*, OHG *mucca*, f. Gmc *mugj*-]

midg′ét, n. Extremely small person, esp. when exhibited as curiosity; very small thing (also attrib.). [f. prec. + -ET¹]

midinĕtte′ (mēdē-), n. Parisian shop-girl (esp. milliner's assistant). [F]

mid′land, n. & a. **1.** Middle part of country; (pl.) *the* middle inland counties of England. **2.** adj. Of, in, the ~ or ~s, [MID + LAND]

mid′night (-nīt), n. The middle of the night, 12 o'clock; intense darkness (often attrib.). [OE *midniht* (MID + NIGHT)]

mid′răsh n. (pl. ~*im*, pr. -ăsh′ĕm). Ancient Jewish commentary on part of Hebrew Scriptures. [Heb.]

mid′riff, n. Diaphragm. [OE *midhrif* (*midd* MID + *hrif* belly)]

mid′ship, n. Middle part of ship or boat; ~*man* (abbr. *middy*—not used by Royal Navy), rank between naval cadet & sub--lieutenant; ~*s*, = AMIDSHIPS. [MID + SHIP]

midst, n., adv., & prep. *In the* ~ *of*, among, during the continuance of; *in our*, *your*, ~, among us, you; (adv., only in phr.) *first*, ~, *& last*; (prep., poet.) in the ~ of. [prob. comb. (1) MID + -*st*, see -ES, & (2) sup. of MID]

mid′sŭmmer, n. Period of summer solstice, about June 21; M~ *day*, June 24, ‖ a quarter-day; ~ (the height of) *madness*. [MID]

mid′wife, n. (pl. *-wives*). Woman who assists other women in childbirth. Hence **mid′wif**ERY(2) (-wĭfrĭ, *-wī-) n., obstetrics. [ME, f. MID¹, or obs prep. *mid* with (cf. G *mit*), +WIFE]

mien (mēn), n. (literary). Air, bearing, of person, as showing character or mood. [prob. aphetic f. obs. *demean* n., assim. to F *mine* expression]

miff, n., & v.i. & t. (colloq.). Petty quarrel; huff; (v.i.) take offence *with* or *at*; (v.t.) put out of humour. [perh. imit.; cf. G *muff*, exclamation of disgust]

might¹ (mit), n. Great (bodily or mental) strength; power to enforce one's will (opp. *right*); *with* ~ *& MAIN*². [OE *miht*, OS, OHG *maht*, Goth. *mahts* f. Gmc *mahtiz* f. *mag-* MAY¹]

might². See MAY¹.

might′|ly̆ (-ĭt-), a. & adv. 1. Powerful, strong, in body or mind; (bibl.) ~*y works*, miracles; massive, bulky; (colloq.) great, considerable; HIGH *& ~y*. 2. adv. (colloq.). Very, as *that is ~y easy*. Hence ~iLY² adv., ~iNESS n. (esp. in *your* etc. high ~*iness* as burlesque title). [OE *mihtig* (MIGHT¹ +-Y²)]

mignon (see Ap.), a. Small & delicately formed. [F]

mignonette′ (mĭnyo-), n. 1. Plant with fragrant flowers; colour of these, greyish green. 2. Kinds of lace & fine net. [f. F (-*onn*-), dim. of prec.]

migraine′ (mē-), n. = MEGRIM (first sense). [as MEGRIM]

migrāte′ (or mī²), v.i. Move from one place (country, town, college, house) to another; (of birds & fishes) come & go with the seasons. Hence or cogn. **mīg′r**ANT & n., **migrā′**TION, **migrāt′**OR, nn., **mig′rat**ORY a. [f. L *migrare*, see -ATE³]

mika′dŏ, (-kah-), n. (pl. ~s). Emperor of Japan. [Jap. *mi* august +*kado* door]

‖ **mike**¹, v.i., & n. (sl.). Shirk work, idle; (n.) idling (*on the ~*). [orig. unkn.]

mike², n. (colloq.). Microphone. [abbr.]

mil, n. A thousand (*per ~*, as *per cent*); (pharm., short for) MILLIlitre; unit measure for diameter of wire etc., = $\frac{1}{1000}$ in. [f. L *mille* thousand, *millesimum* thousandth]

mil′age, n. Var. of MILEAGE.

Milanēse′ (-z), a. & n. (pl. same). (Native) of Milan, chief city of Lombardy; *the ~*, territory of old duchy of Milan. [It. (*Milano* Milan), -ESE]

milch, a. (Of domestic mammals) giving, kept for, milk; ~ *cow*, (fig.) source of profit, esp. person from whom money is easily drawn. [ME *mielch*, rel. to OE *meolc*, OHG *melch* (G *melk*), ON *mjolkr*; see MILK]

mild, a. Gentle & conciliatory; (of rule, punishment, etc.) not severe; (of weather) moderately warm; (of medicine) operating gently; (of food, tobacco, etc.) not sharp or strong in taste etc.; (of beer) not strongly flavoured with hops, opp. to *bitter*; tame, feeble, lacking in energy or vivacity; ~ *steel*, containing small percentage of carbon, strong & tough, but not readily tempered. Hence ~′EN⁶ v.t. & i., ~′LY² adv., ~′NESS n. [OE *milde*, OS *mildi*, OHG *milti*, ON *mildr*, Goth. *milds* f. Gmc *mildh*-]

mil′dew, n., & v.t. & i. 1. Destructive growth of minute fungi on plants; similar growth on paper, leather, etc., exposed to damp. 2. vb. Taint, be tainted, with ~. Hence ~Y² a. [OE *meledēaw* (= OHG *militou*) f. Gmc *melith* honey + *dawwa*-DEW]

mile, n. Unit of lineal measure, in Britain now 1,760 yards (orig. Roman measure of 1,000 paces, about 1,618 yards); *geographical, nautical*, ~, one minute of great circle of earth, fixed by British Admiralty at 6,080 feet; race extending over a ~; *not 100 ~s from*, in or at or close to (as sham-mysterious indication); ~*stone*, pillar set up on road to mark~s, (fig.) stage, event, in life. Hence ~′AGE (-lĭj) n., ~s travelled, used, etc.; expenses per ~. [OE *mīl*, OHG *mīla*, f. WG *mīlja* f. L *mīl(l)ia* pl. of *mille* thousand]

mil′er, n. (colloq.). Man, horse, qualified or trained specially to run a mile; also in comb., as *three-~*. [-ER¹]

Milē′sian (-shn), a. & n. (joc.). Irish(man). [f. *Milesius* fabulous Spanish king whose sons are said to have conquered Ireland *c.* 1300 B.C., +-AN]

mil′foil, n. Common yarrow & other plants. [ME & OF, f. L *millefolium* (*mille* thousand +*folium* leaf)]

mil′iary, a. (path.). Like millet-seed in size or form, as ~ *gland, tubercle*; ~ *fever* (marked by rash like measles, with vesicles of form of millet-seed). [f. L *miliarius* (as MILLET, -ARY¹)]

milieu (see Ap.), n. Environment, state of life, social surroundings. [F]

mil′itant, a. Engaged in warfare, as *the Church ~*; combative. Hence **mil′it**ANCY n., ~LY² adv. [ME, f. OF f. L, as MILITATE, see -ANT]

mil′itar|**ism**, n. Spirit, tendencies, of the professional soldier; undue prevalence of military spirit or ideals. So ~IZA′TION n., ~IZE(3) v.t. [f. F *militarisme* (as MILITARY, see -ISM)]

mil′itarist, n. Student of military science; one dominated by military ideas. [-IST]

mil′itary̆, a. & n. 1. Of, done by, befitting, soldiers; ~ *band*, wood-wind, brass, & percussion combination; ~ *chest*, treasury of army; ~ *fever*, enteric; ~ *testament*, soldier's nuncupative will.

2. n. (Usu. *the* ~) soldiery, troops, the army. Hence **mil′itarily** adv. [f. F *militaire* or L *militaris* (*miles -itis* soldier, see -ARY²)]

mil′itate, v.i. Take part in warfare (usu. fig.); (of facts, evidence) have force, tell, (*against*, rarely *in favour of*, conclusion etc.). [f. L *militare* (*miles -itis* soldier) see -ATE³]

mili′tia (-sha), n. Military force, esp. citizen army; branch of British military service formerly raised by the several counties, usu. by voluntary enlistment; ‖ British conscript army formed 1939; ~*man*, member of the ~. [L (prec., -IA¹)]

milk¹, n. **1.** Opaque white fluid secreted by female mammals for nourishment of their young; (fig.) ~ *for babes*, simple forms of literature, doctrine, etc., opp. to *strong meat*; CONDENSED ~; ~ *& honey*, abundant means of enjoyment; ~ *of human kindness*, kindness natural to humanity; *no use crying over spill* ~ (irremediable loss or error); ~-like juice of plants; ~-like preparation of herbs, drugs, etc., as ~ *of almonds.* **2.** ~ *& water*, feeble or mawkish discourse or sentiment (attrib. ~-*&-water*); ~-*bar* (for sale of beverages made from ~, other non--alcoholic drinks, ice cream, etc.); ~-*crust*, skin-eruption in infants; ~-*fever* (occurring to women shortly after childbirth); ~-*leg*, swelling, esp. of legs, after childbirth; ‖ ~-*float*, light low vehicle used in delivering ~; ~-*maid*, woman who milks or works in dairy; ~-*man*, man who sells or delivers ~; ~-*powder*, ~ dehydrated by evaporation; ~ *pudding* (of rice, sago, tapioca, etc., baked with ~ in dish); ~-*punch*, drink made of spirits & ~; ~--SHAKE²; ~-*sop*, spiritless man or youth; ~-*tooth*, temporary tooth in young mammals; ~-*walk*, ~-man's round; ~-*weed*, kinds of wild plant with milky juice; ~-*white* (as ~); ~-*wort*, kinds of heath or pasture plant formerly supposed to increase production of ~. [OE *meoluc*, OS *miluk*, OHG -*uh*, ON *mjolk*, Goth. *miluks* f. Gmc *melk*- to milk, cogn. w. L *mulgēre*]

milk², v.t. Draw milk from (cow, ewe, goat); ~ *the ram* or *bull*, engage in hopeless enterprise; get money out of, exploit, (person); (sl.) steal message from (telegraph or telephone wire); extract juice, virus, etc., from (snake etc.). [OE *milcian, meolcian* (as prec.)]

mil′k|y̆, a. Of, like, mixed with, milk; (of liquid) cloudy, not clear; effeminate, weakly amiable; *M~y Way*, luminous band of countless stars encircling the heavens. Hence ~**INESS** n. [-Y²]

mill¹, n. **1.** Building fitted with machinery for grinding corn (often *water~*, *wind~*; *put, go, through the* ~, subject to, undergo, training or experience; *the* ~*s of God grind slowly,* retribution is often delayed).

2. Any mechanical apparatus for grinding corn; apparatus for grinding any solid substance to powder or pulp, as *coffee*, *pepper*, *paper*, ~.. **3.** Any machine, or building fitted with machinery, for manufacturing processes etc., as *saw*, *cotton*, *silk*, ~ (~-*hand*, factory worker). **4.** Pugilistic encounter. **5.** ~-*board*, stout pasteboard for bookbinding etc.; ~-*dam*, dam put across stream to make it available for ~; ~-*pond*, water retained by this (*like a* ~-*pond*, said of calm sea), (joc.) = HERRING-*pond*; ~-*race*, current of water that drives ~-wheel; ~-*stone*, one of pair of circular stones for grinding corn, as NETHER ~*stone*, *see far into a* ~*stone*, (usu. iron.) be extraordinarily acute, *between upper & nether* ~*stone*, subject to irresistible pressure; ~*stone grit*, a hard siliceous rock; ~-*wheel*, one (esp. water-wheel) used to drive ~; ~-*wright*, one who designs or erects ~s. [OE *mylen*, OS *mulin*, OHG *muli*(*n*), f. LL *molinum*, -*na* (*mola* mill f. *molere* grind)]

mill², v.t. & i. Thicken (cloth etc.) by fulling; grind (corn), produce (flour), in mill; produce regular markings on edge of (coin, esp. in p.p.); beat (chocolate) to froth; beat, strike, fight, (person); (of cattle or persons) move round & round in a mass; ~*ing machine*, machine tool for cutting grooves or slots in metal sheets. [f. prec.]

*****mill³**, n. One-thousandth of a dollar, money of account. [f. L *millesimum* thousandth part, on anal. of CENT]

millenār′ian, a. & n. (Of the millennium; (person) believing in this. Hence ~ISM n. [as foll. +-AN]

mill′enary, a. & n. (Period) of 1,000 years; of, (person) believing in, the millennium. [f. LL *millenarius* consisting of a thousand (*milleni* a thousand each f. *mille* thousand, -ARY¹)]

millĕnn′i̇|um, n. Period of a thousand years, esp. that of Christ's reign in person on earth (*Rev.* xx. 1–5); (fig.) period of good government, great happiness, & prosperity. Hence ~AL a. [f. L *mille* thousand+*annus* year, on anal. of *biennium* two years' space]

mill′epēde, mill′i-, n. Kinds of myriapods, with numerous legs usu. placed on each segment in double pairs; kinds of terrestrial crustacean, esp. common woodlouse & armadillo. [f. L *millepeda* woodlouse (*mille* thousand + *pes pedis* foot)]

mill′er, n. Proprietor, tenant, of corn--mill; one who works any mill; kinds of white or white-powdered insect; cockchafer; ~'*s thumb*, bull-head & other fishes. [MILL¹+-ER¹]

millĕs′imal, a. & n. Thousandth (part); consisting of thousandths. [f. L *millesimus* (*mille* thousand+-AL)]

mill′et, n. Gramineous plant, native of India, bearing large crop of small nutritious seeds; its seed; ~-*grass*, a tall hand-some grass. [F, dim. of *mil* f. L *milium*]

mill'i-, comb. form of L *mille* thousand, = one thousandth of a — (in metric system), as: ~*gram* ('0154 of English grain); ~*litre* (-ēter; '061 cub. in.); ~*mètre* (-ter; '0394 in.).

‖ **mill'iard** (-yard), n. A thousand millions. [F (*mille* thousand)]

mill'in|er, n. Person (usu. woman) who makes up hats & other female head-gear; *man~er*, (fig.) man busied in trifling occupations. Hence ~ERY(1) n. [f. *Milan* +-ER[1]; orig.=vendor of Milan goods]

mill'ion (-yon), n. & a. A thousand thousand (things, *of* things, or abs.); a ~ pounds or *dollars; the ~*, bulk of the population. Hence ~FOLD a. & adv., ~TH[2] a. & n., (-yon-). [ME, f. OF f. It. *millione* (*mille* thousand +-*one* -OON)]

millionaire' (-yon-), n. Person possessing a million pounds, dollars, francs, etc.; person of great wealth. [f. F *millionnaire* (prec., -ARY[1])]

millipede. See MILLEPEDE.

Mills bŏmb (-z; -m), n. Oval hand-grenade. [inventor (d. 1932)]

milŏr(d)', n. French word for English lord or wealthy Englishman. [f. E *my lord*]

mil'reis (-āis), n. Former Portuguese gold coin. [Port. (*mil* thousand +REIS)]

milt, n., & v.t. 1. Spleen in mammals; analogous organ in other vertebrates; roe of male fish. 2. v.t. Impregnate (roe of female). [OE *milte*, corresp. to MDu. *milte*, OHG *milzi*, ON *milti*, f. Gmc *milt*-prob. cogn. w. MELT]

mil'ter, n. Male fish in spawning time. [-ER[1]]

Miltŏn'ic, a. Of, in the style of, Milton. So **Miltŏn'IAN** a. [-IC]

mime, n., & v.i. 1. (Gk or Rom. ant.) simple farcical drama marked by mimicry; performer in this; pantomimist, buffoon. 2. v.i. Act with mimic gesture, usu. without words. [f. L f. Gk *mimos*]

mim'ěograph (-ahf), n., & v.t. Apparatus for holding stencils of written pages, from which many copies may be taken; (v.t.) reproduce by means of ~. [irreg. f. Gk *mimeomai* imitate, see -GRAPH]

mimēs'is, n. (biol.). Close external resemblance between animal & another animal or inanimate object. [Gk, = imitation (as prec.)]

mimět'|ic, a. Of, addicted to, imitation, mimicry, or mimesis. Hence ~ICALLY adv. [f. Gk *mimētikos* (as prec., see -ETIC)]

mim'ic[1], a. & n. 1. Apt to imitate; imitative as opp. to *real*. 2. n. Person skilled in ludicrous imitation. [f. F -*ique*, or L f. Gk *mimikos* (as MIME, see -IC)]

mim'ic[2], v.t. (~ked, ~king). Ridicule by imitating (person, manner, etc.); copy minutely or servilely; (of things) resemble closely. [f. prec.]

mim'icry̆, n. Mimicking; thing that mimics another; (zool.) = MIMESIS. [MIMIC[1] +-RY]

mim'iny̆-pim'iny̆, a. Over-refined, finicking. [imit.]

mimōs'a (or -z-), n. Kinds of leguminous shrubs, including common sensitive plant. [f. L as MIME +-*osa* fem. suf., see -OSE[1]]

mim'ūlus, n. Kinds of flowering plants, incl. monkey-flower. [app. dim. as prec.]

min'a[1], n. (pl. -*ae*). Ancient-Greek denomination of money; ancient unit of weight in Greece, Egypt, etc., about 1 lb. [L, f. Gk *mna*]

min'a[2], n. Kinds of eastern passerine bird. [f. Hind. *maina*]

minā'cious (-shus), a. Threatening. Hence ~LY[2] adv., minā'CITY n. [f. L *minax* (*minari* threaten), see -ACIOUS]

‖ **minār'**, n. Lighthouse; turret. [f. Arab. *manar* f. root of *nar* fire]

min'arĕt, n. Slender turret connected with mosque, from which muezzin calls people to prayer. [f. Arab. *manarat* (as prec.)]

min'atory̆, a. Threatening. [f. LL *minatorius* (*minari* threaten, -ORY)]

mince[1], n. Minced meat; ~'*meat*, mixture of currants, raisins, sugar, apples, candied-peel, etc., for ~ *pie* (small round pie containing this); *make* ~*meat of*, destroy (person, argument, etc.). [f. foll.]

mince[2], v.t. & i. Cut (meat etc.) small; (usu. w. negative) ~ *matters*, express oneself politely in condemnation; restrain (one's words) within bounds of politeness; utter (words), walk, with affected delicacy, whence min'cingLY[2] adv. [ME, f. OF *mincier* f. Rom. *minutiare*, as MINUTIA; cf. MINISH]

‖ **Min'cing Lāne**, n. (Used for) the wholesale trade in tea & similar imports. [London street]

mind[1], n. 1. Remembrance, as *have* or *keep in* ~, *bring* or *call to* ~, remember, *go* or *pass out of* ~, be forgotten; TIME[1] *out of* ~. 2. Candid opinion, as *speak* one's ~, *tell* (person) one's ~, *give* him *a piece of* one's ~. 3. *Be of* (person's) ~, agree in opinion with him; *to my* ~, as I think; *be of a* or *one* ~, agree; *know* one's *own* ~, form & adhere to decision; *make up* one's ~, resolve (*to do, to* a course etc., or abs.), reconcile oneself to fact as inevitable (*the crop is ruined, we must make up our* ~s *to that*); *change* one's ~, alter one's purpose; *have a good* or *great* ~, *half a* ~, be strongly, somewhat, disposed (*to do*); *be in two* ~s, vacillate, be irresolute; MONTH's ~. 4. Direction of thoughts or desires, as *set* one's ~ *on*, desire to attain, *give* one's ~ (attention) *to; to* one's ~, as one would have it. 5. Way of thinking & feeling, as *frame, state, of* ~.' 6. Seat of consciousness, thought, volition, & feeling. 7. Soul, opp. to *body*; ~'*s eye*, mental view. 8. Person, as embodying mental qualities. 9. Intellectual powers, opp. to will & emotions, whence ~LESS a. **10.** ABSENCE, PRESENCE, of ~; ~-*stuff* (philos.), supposed rudimentary form of psychical existence regarded as the reality of which matter is an aspect. [ME *mynd* f. OE *gemynd*, = OHG *gimunt*, Goth. *gamunds* f. Gmc **gamundhiz* f. root **men-, *man-, *mun-*, cogn. w. L *mens*]

mind², v.t. & i. **1.** Bear in mind (chiefly in imperat.); give heed to, as *never ~ the expense.* **2.** Concern oneself (*never ~* imperat., take comfort, also as refusal to answer question). **3.** Apply oneself to (business etc.; ~ *your own business*, leave other people's alone). 4. (Chiefly in neg. or quasi-neg. sentences) object to, as *would you ~ ringing?*, *I should not ~* (should like) *a cup of tea, if you don't ~* (have no objection). **5.** Remember & take care (*that* thing is done, or omit *that*). **6.** ~ *you* or ~ (parenth. imperat.), please to observe (*but I have no objection*, ~ *you*; *now ~, not a word till I give the signal*); (sl.) ~ *your eye*, be on the lookout; ~ one's *P's & Q's*, be careful as to one's words or behaviour. **7.** Be on one's guard against or about, as ~ *the step* (remember there is one). **8.** Have charge of. Hence ~'ER¹ n., one whose business it is to attend to something, (now esp.) machine-~er. [f. prec.]

mind′ed, a. Disposed (*to* do); having (specified) mind, as *high*, *small*, -~. [-ED²]

mind′ful, a. Taking thought or care (*of*, or abs.). Hence ~LY² adv., ~NESS n. [MIND¹+-FUL]

mine¹, n. **1.** Excavation in earth for metal, coal, salt, etc.; (fig.) abundant source (*of* information etc.); iron ore. **2.** (Mil. etc.) subterranean gallery in which explosive is placed to blow up fortifications, (formerly) subterranean passage under wall of besieged fortress; receptacle filled with explosive placed in or on ground for destroying enemy personnel or material, or moored beneath or floating on or near surface of water for destroying or impeding enemy ships; ACOUSTIC, MAGNETIC, ~; ~′*field*, area of land or sea beset with ~s; ~′*layer*, ship or aircraft for laying ~s; ~′*sweeper*, ship for clearing away floating or submarine ~s; ~′*thrower* [tr. of G *minenwerfer*], trench mortar. [ME, f. OF *mine*, f. Gallo--Rom. **mina*, of Celt. orig.]

mine², v.t. & i. Burrow in (earth); make (hole) underground; make subterranean passages under; (fig.) undermine; (mil. etc.) lay mines under or in; obtain (metal etc.) from mine; dig in (earth etc.) for ore etc. Hence mīn′ING¹(1) n. (freq. in comb., as *coal*, *gold*, -*mining*; also attrib., as *mining engineer*). [ME, f. OF *miner*, rel. to prec.; cf. MINERAL]

mine³, poss. pron. & a. corresponding in pred. & elliptical uses to MY, as *it is* ~, *I have lost* ~, *me & ~* (my relations), *is a friend of* ~; also used (arch., poet.) before

noun beginning with vowel or *h*, as ~ *eyes.* [OE *mīn*, OS, OHG *mīn*, ON *minn*, Goth. *meins* f. Gmc **mīn-* f. **me-* ME]

mīn′er, n. One who works in a mine; soldier whose duty it is to lay mines; SAPPERS *& ~s.* [ME, f. OF *minour* (as MINE², see -OR)]

min′eral, a. & n. (Substance) obtained by mining; (belonging to) any of the species into which inorganic substances are classified; ~ KINGDOM; ~ *water*, water found in nature impregnated with ~ substance, artificial imitation of this, esp. soda-water, also, other effervescent drink, e.g. ginger-beer; ‖ (esp. in pl.) artificial ~ water; ~ WOOL. Hence ~IZA′TION n., ~IZE(3) v.t. & i. [ME, f. OF *mineral* f. med. L *mineralis* f. *minera* f. OF *miniere* f. **mina* MINE¹]

miner‖ăl′ogy, n. Science of minerals. Hence~alŏ′gICAL a.,~alŏ′gICALLY² adv., ~ăl′ogIST n. [f. prec.+-LOGY]

Minerv′a, n. Roman goddess of wisdom; ~ *press*, printing-press in London, ultra-sentimental novels issued from it *c.* 1800. [L]

min′ever, -iver, n. Kind of fur used in ceremonial costume. [ME, f. OF *menu vair* (*menu* small, as MINUTE³; VAIR)]

mingle (mǐng′gl), v.t. & i. Mix, blend; ~ *their* etc. *tears*, weep together; ~ *with*, go about among. [late ME *mengel* f. obs. *meng* (OE *mengan*, cogn. w. AMONG) +-LE(3); cf. MDu. *mengelen*]

‖ **min′gy** (-jǐ), a. (colloq.). Mean, stingy. [prob. portmanteau of MEAN³ and STINGY]

min′iāte, v.t. Paint with vermilion; illuminate (manuscript). [f. L *miniare* f. MINIUM, see -ATE³]

min′iature, n. & a. & v.t. **1.** Picture in illuminated manuscript; small-scale minutely finished portrait, usu. on ivory or vellum; this branch of painting, as *portrait in* ~; reduced image; *in* ~, on a small scale, small-scale. **3.** v.t. Represent in ~. Hence min′iatūrIST (-ya-) n. [f. It. f. L *miniare* (as prec., -URE)]

min′icăb, n. Small taxi. [MINI(ATURE) CAB]

min′ifȳ, v.t. Represent as smaller or less important than it is; lessen in size or importance. [irreg. f. L *minor* less, see -FY]

min′ikin, n. & a. Diminutive (creature); affected, mincing. [f. Du. *minneken* (*minne* love+-*kijn* -KIN)]

min′im, n. (Mus.) note half the value of SEMIbreve; single down-stroke of pen; creature of the smallest size or importance; sixtieth part of fluid drachm. [f. L *minimus* smallest]

min′imal, a. Very minute; the least possible, of minimum. [as prec., see -AL]

min′imalist, n. Person ready to accept a minimum provisionally (opp. MAXIMALIST). [prec., -IST]

min′imiz‖e, -is‖e (-ĭz), v.t. Reduce to, estimate at, smallest possible amount or degree. Hence ~A'TION n. [as prec., see -IZE]

min'imum, n. (pl. *-ima*), & a. Least amount attainable, usual, etc.; ~ *thermometer* (automatically recording lowest temperature within period); ~ *wage* (than which, by law or agreement, less is not to be offered); (adj.) smallest (possible). [L, neut. as foll.]

‖ **min'imus,** a. (In schools) youngest of the name, as *Jones* ~. [L, = least]

min'ion (-yon), n. Favourite child, servant, animal, etc. (derog.); royal favourite; slave; ~*s of the law*, gaolers, police, etc.; (print.) size of TYPE. [f. F *mignon*, of Gaulish orig.]

min'ish, v.t. & i. (arch.). Diminish (t. & i.); reduce in power etc. [ME, f. OF *menusier*, var. of *mincier*: see MINCE[2]]

min'ister[1], n. Person employed in execution *of* (purpose, will, etc.); person administering department of State; PRIME ~; political agent accredited by one State to another, cf. AMBASSADOR; clergyman esp. in Presbyterian and Nonconformist Churches; (also ~ *general*) superior of some religious orders; ‖ *M~ of State*, departmental senior ~ intermediate between head of department and junior ~. [ME, f. OF *ministre* f. L *minister* servant (*minus* less)]

min'ister[2], v.i. & t. Render aid or service (*to* person, cause, etc.; ~*ing angel*, w. ref. to *Mark* l. 13, esp. of sick-nurse etc.); be helpful, contribute, (*to* result); (arch.) furnish, supply, (help etc.). [ME, f. OF *ministrer* f. L *ministrare* (prec.)]

ministēr'ial, a. Concerned with the execution of law; subsidiary, instrumental; of a minister of religion or his office; of a minister of State; siding with the Ministry against Opposition, whence ~IST(2) n. Hence ~LY[2] adv. [f. obs. F -*ial* (now -*iel*), or LL *ministerialis* (as MINISTRY, see -AL)]

ministrā'tion, n. Ministering, esp. in religious matters; supplying (*of*). So **min'istrant** a. & n., **min'istrative** a. [ME, f. L *ministratio* (as MINISTER[2], see -ATION)]

min'istry, n. Ministering; *the body of* ministers of the government or of religion; *the* clerical profession; State department, as *M~ of Agriculture, Fisheries, and Food, of Aviation, of Defence, of Education, of Health, of Housing and Local Government, of Labour, of Pensions and National Insurance, of Power, of Public Building and Works, of Transport.* [ME, f. L *ministerium* (as MINISTER[1])]

min'ium, n. Red·lead; cinnabar. [L]

min'iver. See MINEVER.

mink, n. Small semi-aquatic stoat-like animal; its fur. [cf. Sw. *mänk, menk*]

minn'esinger, n. German lyrical poet & singer in 12–14th cc. [G (*minne* love)]

Minn'ie, n. (army sl.). Trench mortar. [abbr. of G *minenwerfer* minethrower]

minn'ow (-ō), n. Small freshwater fish (loosely used of several kinds, esp. stickleback); *Triton among the ~s*, one who seems great from insignificance of others. [late ME *menow*, repr. OE **mynwe, myne,* = OHG *mun(i)wa* (G *münne*)]

Minō'an, a. (archaeol.). Of the Cretan civilization (3000–1500 B.C.) named from king Minos. [f. Gk *Minōs* + -AN]

min'or, a. & n. 1. Lesser (not followed by *than*), as ~ PROPHETS; ~ *canon*, clergyman assisting in daily cathedral service, not member of chapter; comparatively unimportant, as ~ *poet*; (log.) ~ *term*, subject of conclusion of categorical syllogism, ~ *premiss* (containing this); (mus.) ~ *interval*, see MAJOR[2], ~ *key* (in which scale has ~ third), (fig.) *conversation in a* ~ *key* (doleful); ~ *suit* (bridge), diamonds or clubs; (in schools) *Jones* ~ (the younger). 2. n. Franciscan friar; ~ term or premiss; person under age. [L, = less]

Minōrc'a, n. One of the Balearic Isles; ~ (*fowl*), black variety brought from Spain. [f. Sp. *Menorca*]

minō'rity, n. State of being under age, period of this; smaller number or part, esp. smaller party voting together against majority; number of votes cast for this. [f. F *minorité* or med. L *minoritas* (as MINOR, see -TY)]

Min'otaur (-tŏr), n. *The* ~, fabulous monster, half bull half man, fed with human flesh. [f. Gk *Minōtauros* (*Minōs*, king of Crete, husband of ~'s mother, + *tauros* bull)]

min'ster, n. Church of a monastery; name given to some large or important churches. [OE *mynster* = OHG *munist(i)ri* f. Rom. *monisterium* f. LL f. Gk *monastērion* MONASTERY]

min'strel, n. Mediaeval singer or musician, who sang or recited (often his own) poetry; (hist.) person who entertained his patrons with singing, buffoonery, etc.; (pl.) band of public entertainers, with blacked faces etc., performing songs & music ostensibly of Negro origin. [ME, f. OF *menestral* (as MINISTERIAL)]

min'strelsy, n. Minstrel's art; minstrels; minstrel poetry. [ME, f. OF *menestralsie,* as prec.]

mint[1], n. Place where money is coined, usu. under State authority; (fig.) source of invention etc.; (transf.) ~ *state, condition,* (of books, prints, postage-stamps, etc.) fresh, unsoiled, perfect; vast sum *of money*; ~*·mark*, mark placed on coin to show at what ~ it was struck (also fig.); ~·*master*, superintendent of coinage at ~. [OE *mynet*, OS *munita*, OHG *munizza* f. WG **munita* f. L *moneta* MONEY]

mint[2], v.t. Make (coin) by stamping metal; invent, coin, (word, phrase, etc.). Hence **min'tAGE**(3, 4) n. [f. prec.]

mint[3], n. Aromatic plant, much used in cookery; ~ *sauce* (of finely chopped

~ with vinegar & sugar, eaten with roast lamb), || also, with pun on *mint*[1], money. [OE *minte*, OHG *minza* f. WG **minta* f. L *ment(h)a* f. Gk *minthē*]

minüet', n. Slow stately dance for two in triple measure; music for this, music in same rhythm & style. [f. F *menuet*, dim. of *menu* (as MINUTE a.)]

min'us, quasi-prep. & a. With the deduction of (symbol −), as 7 ~ 4 *is equal to 3*; (colloq.) deprived of, as *he came back* ~ *an arm*; *a* ~ (negative) *quantity*. [L, neut. of MINOR]

minūs'cūle, a. & n. (Of kind of cursive script developed in 7th c.) small; (n.) small letter. [F, f. L *minuscula* (*littera* letter, dim. of MINOR); cf. MAJUSCULE]

min'ute[1] (-It), n. 1. Sixtieth part of hour; short time, instant; exact point of time, as *the* ~ (*that*), as soon as. 2. Sixtieth part of degree (in angles). 3. Rough draft, memorandum; (pl.) brief summary of proceedings of assembly, committee, etc.; official memorandum authorizing or recommending a course, as *a Treasury* ~. 4. ~*-book* (for writing ~s in); ~*-gun* (fired at intervals of a ~); ~*-hand* (indicating ~s on watch or clock); **~-man* (hist.), American militiaman of revolutionary period (because ready to march at a ~'s notice); ~*-mark* (', cf. SECOND-*mark*). [ME, f. OF, f. L *minuta* fem. as MINUTE[2]; ~ of time etc., f. med. L (*pars*) *minuta* (*prima*); see SECOND]

min'ute[2] (-It), v.t. Find the exact tin.e of; draft (document, scheme); record in minutes; ~ *down*, make a note of. [f. prec.]

minūte'[3], a. Very small; trifling, petty; (of inquiry, inquirer, etc.) accurate, precise. Hence ~ly[1] (-ūt'll) [-LY[2]] adv., ~NESS (-ūt'n-) n. [ME, f. L *minutus*, p.p. of *minuere* lessen]

min'ute|ly[2] (-nĭtlĭ), a. Occurring every minute. So ~LY[2] (-nĭtlĭ) adv. [MINUTE[1] +-LY[1]]

minū'tia (-shĭa), n. (usu. in pl. *-ae*). Precise or trivial detail. [L (as MINUTE[3])]

minx, n. Pert girl, hussy, flirt. [16th c., poss. orig. f. MINIKIN +-ES]

Mī'ocēne, a. & n. (geol.). (Of) a division of the Tertiary preceding the Pliocene. [irreg. f. Gk *meiōn* less + *kainos* new]

mir (mēr), n. Russian village community. [Russ.]

mi'racle, n. Marvellous event due to some supernatural agency; remarkable occurrence; remarkable specimen (*of* ingenuity, impudence, etc.); *to a* ~, surprisingly well; (also ~ *play*) dramatic representation in Middle Ages, based on life of Christ or saints. [ME, f. OF f. L *miraculum* (*mirari* wonder f. *mirus* wonderful)]

mirăc'ūlous, a. Supernatural; surprising. Hence ~LY[2] adv., ~NESS n. [f. F *miracu-*

leux f. med. L *miraculosus* (as prec., see -OUS)]

mirage' (-ahzh), n. Optical illusion, esp. illusive appearance of sheet of water in desert etc. (also fig.). [F, f. *se mirer* be reflected; see MIRROR]

mire[1], n. Swampy ground, bog; *stick, find oneself in* ~; mud, dirt. [ME, f. ON *mýrr* f. Gmc **meus-*, **mus-*: see MOSS]

mire[2], v.t. Plunge in mire; (fig.) involve in difficulties; defile, bespatter. [f. prec.]

mi'rror, n., & v.t. 1. Polished usu. glass surface reflecting image, looking-glass; (fig.) what gives faithful reflection or true description of thing. 2. v.t. Reflect as in ~. [ME, f. OF *mirour* f. Rom. **miratorium* (**mirare* look at, f. L *mirari* wonder at, see -ORY)]

mĭrth, n. Merriment, laughter. Hence ~'FUL, ~'LESS, aa., ~'fulLY[2] adv., ~'fulNESS n. [OE *myrgth* (MERRY[2], -TH[1])]

mĭr'ÿ, a. Muddy; vile. [f. MIRE[1] +-Y[2]]

mĭr'za (mēr'zah), n. (In Persia) title added to name of prince or prefixed to that of official or man of learning. [Pers.]

mis-[1], pref. added freely to vbs & vbl nn. w. sense 'amiss', 'badly', 'wrongly', 'unfavourably', or intensifying unfavourable meaning contained in vb (*misdoubt*). [OE, OS, ON *mis-*, OHG, Goth. *missa-*, f. Gmc **missa-* (1) divergent (2) mutual]

mis-[2], pref. to vbs, adjj., & nn., derived f. F, in same sense as prec. [f. OF *mes-* f. MINUS, used in com.-Rom. as pref.]

misadvĕn'ture, n. (Piece of) bad luck; (law) *homicide by* ~ (accident). [ME, f. OF *mesaventure* (see MIS-[2] & ADVENTURE)]

misalli'ance, n. Unsuitable alliance, esp. marriage. [MIS-[1], after MÉSALLIANCE]

mis'anthrōpe, n. Hater of mankind; one who avoids human society. Hence or cogn. **misanthrŏp'IC(AL)** aa., **misăn'thropIST, misăn'thropy**[1], nn., **misăn'thropIZE**(2) v.i. [f. Gk *misanthrōpos* (*miseō* hate + *anthrōpos* man)]

misăpplica'tion, n. Wrong application, wrong use (esp. of funds). [MIS-[1]]

misapplȳ', v.t. Apply wrongly. [MIS-[1]]

misăpprĕhĕnd', v.t. Misunderstand (words, person). So ~ĕn'sion (-shn) n., ~ĕn'sive a. [MIS-[1]]

misapprōp'ri|āte, v.t. Apply (usu. another's money) to wrong (esp. one's own) use. So ~A'TION n. [MIS-[1]]

misbêcome' (-ŭm), v.t. Suit ill, be unbecoming to. [MIS-[1]]

misbêgŏtt'en, a. Illegitimate, bastard, (often as general term of opprobrium). [MIS-[1] + *begotten* p.p. of BEGET]

misbêhāve', v.t. Behave (oneself, or abs.) improperly. So **misbêhāv'iour** (-yer) n. [ME; MIS-[1]]

misbĕl|ief', n. Wrong religious belief;

For words in *mis-* not given see MIS-[1].

false opinion. So~iev′er n., ~iev′ing a. [ME; MIS-¹]

misbèseem′, v.t. Misbecome. [MIS-¹]

miscǎl′cŭl|āte, v.t. & i. Calculate (amount, results, etc., or abs.) wrongly. So~A′TION n. [MIS-¹]

miscall′ (-awl), v.t. Call by a wrong name; || (dial.) call (person) names. [ME; MIS-¹]

miscǎ′rriage (-rǐj), n. Failure (of letter) to reach destination; ~ (failure of court to attain the ends) of justice; untimely delivery (of woman), abortion; failure (of scheme etc.). [MIS-¹]

miscǎ′rry, v.i. (Of person or business) fail, be unsuccessful; (of woman) be delivered prematurely (of child); (of letter) fail to reach destination. [ME; MIS-¹]

miscas′ting (-ah-), n. Wrong addition (of accounts); unsuitable casting (of actors). [MIS-¹]

miscêgénā′tion, n. Mixture of races, esp. sexual union of whites with Negroes. [irreg. f. L miscēre mix+genus race+ -ATION]

miscellān′éa, n. Literary miscellany. [L, neut. pl. as foll.]

miscellān′éous, a. Of mixed composition or character; (w. pl. noun) of various kinds; (of persons) many-sided. Hence ~LY² adv., ~NESS n. [f. L miscellaneus (miscellus mixed f. miscēre mix, see -ANEOUS]

mis′cellanў (or mǐsĕl²), n. Mixture, medley; collection of treatises etc., in one volume; such volume. Hence miscĕll′anIST(3) n. [app. f. F miscellanées fem. pl. or MISCELLANEA]

mischance′ (-ahns), n. (Piece of) bad luck, esp. by ~. [ME, f. OF mesch(e)ance (MIS-², CHANCE n.)]

mischief (-chǐf), n. Harm, injury, wrought by person or other agent (do one a ~, vulg., wound or kill him); make ~, create discord, so ~-maker, -making; the ~ (annoying part) of it is that etc.; worker, source, of harm or annoyance; vexatious conduct, esp. of children; pranks, scrapes, (get into, keep out of, ~); playful malice, archness, satire, (eyes full of ~); where the ~ (devil) have you been? [ME, f. OF meschief (MIS-², chief end, CHIEF)]

mis′chievous (-chǐv-), a. (Of things) having harmful effects; (of persons, conduct, etc.) disposed to acts of playful malice or annoyance. Hence ~LY² adv., ~NESS n. [ME, f. AF meschevous (prec., -OUS)]

mis′ci|ble (-sǐ-), a. That can be mixed (with). Hence ~BIL′ITY n. [f. med. L miscibilis, f. L miscēre mix, -IBLE]

misconceive′ (-sēv), v.i. & t. Have a wrong conception (of, or abs.); misunderstand (word, person). So misconcĕp′tion n. [ME; MIS-¹]

miscon′duct, n. Improper conduct, esp. adultery; bad management. So miscondŭct′ v.t. & refl. [MIS-¹]

miscǒn′strue (-ōō; or -konstrōō′), v.t. Put wrong construction on (word, action); mistake meaning of (person). So misconstrŭc′tion n. [ME; MIS-¹]

miscount′, n., & v.t. & i. (Make) wrong count, esp. of votes; count (things) wrongly. [MIS-¹]

mis′crèant, a. & n. 1. (Arch.) heretical; depraved. 2. n. (arch.). Heretic; vile wretch. [ME, f. OF mescreant (MIS-² + creant f. L credere believe, see -ANT)]

miscrè|āt′éd, a. Ill-formed (often as abusive epithet). So ~A′TION n. [MIS-¹]

mis-cue′, n., & v.i. (billiards). 1. Failure to strike ball properly with cue. 2. v.i. Make a ~. [MIS-¹ or MISS v.)]

misdāte′, v.t. Date wrong. [MIS-¹]

misdeal′, v.t. & i., & n. 1. Make mistake in dealing (cards, but usu. abs.). 2. n. Such mistake. [MIS-¹]

misdeed′, n. Evil deed; crime. [OE misdǣd (see MIS-¹ & DEED)]

misdeem′, v.t. & i. (arch., poet.). Have wrong opinion of; mistake (person, thing for another); form wrong judgement (of). [ME, f. ON misdéma (MIS-¹, DEEM)]

misdèmean′ant, n. Person convicted of misdemeanour or guilty of misconduct; first, second, -class ~ (to be treated with more, less, indulgence). [f. arch. misdemean, f. foll. (-ANT)]

misdèmean′our (-nor), n. (Law) indictable offence less heinous than felony; offence, misdeed. [ME; MIS-¹]

misdirĕct′, v.t. Direct (person, blow, etc.) wrongly. So misdirĕc′tion n. [MIS-¹]

misdo′ing (-dōō-), n. Misdeed. [MIS-¹]

misdoubt′ (-owt), v.t. (arch.). Have doubts as to the truth or existence of; have misgivings, be suspicious, about; suspect (that). [MIS-¹]

mise (mēz, mīz), n. (Hist.) settlement by agreement, as M~ of Lewes (between Henry III & barons, 1264); ~ en scène (F, see Ap.), scenery & properties of acted play, (fig.) surroundings of an event. [ME, f. OF fem. p.p. of mettre put f. L mittere miss- send, used as n.]

mis′er¹ (-z-), n. One who hoards wealth & lives miserably; avaricious person. [L, = wretched]

mīs′er² (-z-), n. Boring instrument for well-sinking. [orig. unkn.]

mis′erab|le (-z-), a. Wretchedly unhappy; (of events etc.) causing wretchedness; contemptible, mean, as a ~le hovel. Hence ~LY² adv. [f. F misérable or L miserabilis (miserari pity f. miser wretched, -BLE)]

mǐserēr′é (-z-), n. Fifty-first psalm (M~ mei Deus); cry for mercy; (improp.) = foll. (last sense). [ME, f. L, = have mercy (miserēri as MISER¹)]

misĕ′ricord (-z-), n. 1. Apartment in monastery in which some indulgences were permitted. 2. Dagger for giving the *coup de grâce.* **3.** Shelving projection on under side of hinged seat in choir stall, serving when seat was turned up to support person standing. [ME, f. OF *misericorde* f. L *misericordia* f. *misericors* compassionate (stem of *miserēri* pity + *cors -rdis* heart)]

mis´erl|y (-z-), a. Like a miser, stingy. Hence ~**iness** a. [-LY[1]]

mis´ery (-z-), n. Wretched state of mind or of outward circumstances; (cards, colloq. for F *misère*) declaration by which caller undertakes not to take any tricks. [ME, f. AF **miserie* f. L *miseria* (as MISER[1])]

misfeas´ance (-z-), n. (Law) transgression, esp. wrongful exercise of lawful authority (also gen., esp. joc.). [ME, f. OF *mesfaisance* f. *mesfaire* misdo (MIS-[2], *faire* do f. L *facere*), -ANCE; cf. MALFEASANCE]

misfire´, v.i. & n. (Of gun, motor engine, etc.) fail(ing) to go off or start action. [for phr. *to miss fire*]

misfit´, n. Garment etc. that does not fit the person it is meant for; badly adjusted person. [MIS-[1]]

misfort´une (-chn, -tyŏon), n. Bad luck (*more his ~ than his fault*). [MIS-[1]]

misgive´, v.t. (Person's) *mind ~s him*, fills him with suspicion or foreboding (*about* thing, *that*). [MIS-[1]]

misgiv´ing, n. Feeling of mistrust or apprehension. [f. prec. + -ING[1]]

misgo´vern (-gŭ-), v.t. Govern (State etc.) badly. So ~MENT n. [ME; MIS-[1]]

misguid|e´ (-gīd), v.t. (chiefly in p.p.), Mislead, cause to err in thought or action. Hence ~´**edLY**[2] adv. [MIS-[1]]

mishan´dle (-s-h-), v.t. Handle (person, thing) roughly or rudely, ill-treat. [MIS-[1]]

mishap´ (-s-h-), n. Unlucky accident. [ME; MIS-[1]]

mishear´ (-s-h-), v.t. Hear amiss or imperfectly. [OE *mishīeran*; MIS-[1]]

mis´hit, n., & v.t. **1.** Faulty or bad hit. **2.** v.t. (*pr.* mis-hit´). Hit (a ball) faultily. [MIS-[1]]

mish´mash, n. Confused mixture. [ME; redupl. f. MASH n.]

mish´n|a(h) (-na), n. Collection of precepts forming basis of Talmud. Hence ~**IC** a. [post-bibl. Heb., = repetition, instruction, (*shanah* repeat)]

misin|form´, v.t. Give wrong information to, mislead. So ~**forma´tion** n. [ME; MIS-[1]]

misinterp´ret, v.t. Give wrong interpretation to, make wrong inference from. So ~A´TION n. [MIS-[1]]

misjudge´, v.t. & i. Judge wrongly (person etc., or abs.); have wrong opinion of. [MIS-[1]]

mislay´, v.t. Put (thing) by accident where it cannot readily be found. [MIS-[1]]

mislead´ (-lēd), v.t. Lead astray, cause to

go wrong, in conduct; give wrong impression to. [OE *mislǣdan*; MIS-[1]]

mislike´, v.t. (arch.). Dislike. [OE; MIS-[1]]

misman´age, v.t. Manage badly or wrongly. So ~MENT (-ijm-) n. [MIS-[1]]

misname´, v.t. Call by wrong name. [MIS-[1]]

misnom´er, n. Use of wrong name, wrong use of term. [ME, f. AF, f. OF *mesnommer* (mes- MIS-[2] + *nommer* name f. L *nominare*)]

miso-, comb. form (irreg.) of Gk *misē̌o* hate, = 'hater, hatred, of ', as: ~*logist*, ~*logy*, (-ŏl[2]), hater, hatred, of reason or of learning; ~*nē´ism*, ~*nē´ist*, hatred, hater, of novelty.

misŏg´am|y̆, n. Hatred of marriage. So ~**IST** n. [MISO-, Gk *gamos* marriage, -Y[1]]

misŏg´ynist (-j-, -g-), n. Hater of women. So **misogȳn´ic** a. [f. Gk MISO(*gunēs* f. *gunē̌* woman) + -IST]

mis´pickel, n. (min.). Arsenical pyrites. [G]

misplace´, v.t. Put in wrong place or hands; set (affections) on wrong object; place (confidence) amiss; time (words, action) badly. So ~MENT (-sm-) n. [MIS-[1]]

misprint´, v.t. **1.** Mistake in printing. **2.** v.t. Print wrongly. [MIS[1].]

mispri´sion[1] (-zhn), n. (law). Wrong action or omission, esp. ~ *of treason* or *felony*, (now restricted to) concealment of one's knowledge of treasonable designs etc. [ME, f. AF, f. OF *mesprision* f. *mesprendre* mistake (MIS-[2], PRISON)]

‖**mispri´sion**[2] (-zhn), n. (arch.). Contempt; failure to appreciate the value (*of*). [f. foll., after prec.]

misprize´, v.t. Despise; fail to appreciate. [ME, f. OF *mespriser* (see MIS-[2] & PRIZE[1])]

mispro|nounce´, v.t. Pronounce wrongly. So ~**nuncia´tion** n. [MIS-[1]]

misquote´, v.t. Quote wrongly. So **misquota´tion** n. [MIS-[1]]

misread´, v.t. (*-read*, pr. -rĕd). Read or interpret wrongly. [MIS-[1]]

misrĕpresĕnt´ (-z-), v.t. Represent wrongly, give false account of. So ~ā´tion n. [MIS-[1]]

misrule´ (-ŏol), n. Bad government; *Lord, Abbot, Master, of M~* (hist.), person presiding over Christmas revels. [ME; MIS-[1]]

miss[1], n. Failure to hit or attain; *a ~ is as good as a mile*, failure or escape is what it is, however narrow the margin; *miscarriage*; NEAR[2]~; (billiards) *give a ~*, avoid hitting object ball so as to leave one's own in safe position; *give* (something) *a ~*, (also, transf.) avoid, leave alone (*I shall give the party, the prunes, a ~*). [f. foll.]

miss[2], v.t. & i. (Of person or missile) fail to hit (mark etc., or abs.); fail to find, get, or meet; let slip (opportunity); fail to catch (train); ~ *the* BUS; fail to hear or understand (remark etc.); (also ~ *out*) leave out (words etc. in reading, writing, etc.); fail to keep (appointment) or perform; notice esp. with regret the absence of, feel the want of; (ellipt., of internal--combustion engines) misfire; ~ *fire*, (of gun) fail to go off, (fig.) fail in one's object; *~ *out* (*on*), fail to get (something), be unsuccessful; (naut.) ~ *stays*, fail in attempt to go about from one tack to another. [OE, OHG *missan*, MLG, MDu. *missen*, ON *missa* f. Gmc *missjan* f. *missa-* MIS-[1]]

miss[3], n. (As title of unmarried woman or girl) M~ *Smith*, (pl. *the* M~ *Smiths*, *the Misses Smith*; M~ 1963 or current year, the modern girl, also, chosen beauty of that year, so M~ *Great Britain* etc.); (usu. derog. or playful) girl, esp. school-girl, as *a pert* ~, whence ~'ISH[1] a., ~'ish-NESS n.; (voc., in servants' or trade use) young lady. [abbr. of MISTRESS]

miss'al, n. Book containing service of Mass for whole year; (loosely) Rom. Cath. service-book, esp. illuminated one. [ME, f. med. L *missale* (MASS[1], -AL)]

miss'el, n. (Usu. ~-*thrush*) kind of thrush that feeds on mistletoe etc. berries. [OE *mistel* basil, mistletoe, = OHG, ON *mistil*; orig. unkn.]

mis-shāp'en, a. Ill-shaped, deformed. [ME, f. MIS-[1] + *shapen* p.p. of SHAPE]

miss'ile, a. & n. (Object, weapon) suitable for throwing or for discharge from machine or engine (or, rarely, gun); = GUIDE[2]*d* ~. [f. L *missilis* (*mittere miss-* send, see -IL)]

miss'ing, a. In vbl senses; also: wanting, not in its place, as *there is a page* ~, *a page is* ~; *the* ~, soldiers neither present after battle etc. nor known to have been killed or wounded; ~ *link*, thing lacking to complete series, (zool.) hypothetical intermediate type, esp. between man & anthropoid apes. [MISS[2] + -ING[2]]

mi'ssion (-shn), n. 1. Body of persons sent to foreign country to conduct negotiations etc. 2. Body sent by religious community to convert heathen; field of missionary activity; missionary post; organization in a district for conversion of the people; course of religious services etc. for this purpose. 3. Errand of political or other ~; operational sortie. 4. Person's vocation or divinely appointed work in life. [F, or f. L *missio* (*mittere miss-* send, -ION)]

mi'ssionary̆ (-sho-), a. & n. 1. Of, concerned with, religious missions; ~-*box* (for contributions to ~ work). 2. n. Person who goes on ~ work; ‖ person attached to magistrates' court to influence or help offenders or applicants. [-ARY[1]]

mi'ssioner (-sho-), n. Missionary; person in charge of parochial mission. [-ER[1]]

miss'ĭs, -us, n. (As used by servants) the mistress; (vulg., joc.) *the* ~, one's own or another's wife; see also MRS. [corrupt. of MISTRESS]

miss'ive, a. & n. 1. *Letter(s)* ~, letter from sovereign to dean & chapter nominating person to be elected bishop. 2. n. Letter, esp. official one. [ME, f. OF or f. med. L *missivus* (as MISSION, -IVE)]

mis-spell', v.t. (-*spelt*). Spell wrongly. [MIS-[1]]

mis-spend', v.t. (-*spent*). Spend amiss or wastefully (esp. in p.p.). [ME; MIS-[1]]

mis-stāte', v.t. State wrongly. Hence ~MENT (-tm-) n. [MIS-[1]]

miss'y̆, n. (Affectionate, playful, or derog.) = MISS[3] (not followed by name). [-Y[3]]

mist, n., & v.i. & t. 1. Water vapour descending in fine drops smaller than raindrops & causing obscuration of the atmosphere; *Scotch* ~, ~ like fine rain frequent on Scottish hills; filmy appearance before eyes caused by disorders of body or by tears; ~-*net*, fine-threaded net used to catch birds. 2. vb. Cover, be covered, as with ~. Hence ~'FUL a., ~'LIKE a. & adv. [OE (= MLG, MDu.) *mist*, Icel. *mistur*]

mistāke'[1], n. Misunderstanding of a thing's meaning; error, fault, in thought or action; (emphasizing preceding statement) *and*, or *make*, *no* ~, undoubtedly. [f. foll.]

mistāke|e'[2], v.t. & i. Misunderstand meaning or intention of (person, statement, purpose); err in opinion; (p.p.) wrong in opinion, (of action etc.) ill--judged, as *you are* ~*en*, ~*en kindness*, whence ~'enLY[2] adv., ~'enNESS (-n-n-) n.; ~*e A for* (think he is) *B*; *there is no* ~*ing*, no one can help recognizing (person, fact). Hence ~'ABLE a. [ME, f. ON *mistaka* (MIS-[1] + *taka* TAKE)]

mis'ter, n. (pl. *Messrs*, pr. mĕs'erz), & v.t. 1. Title prefixed to man's name or to designation of office etc. (written *Mr*), as *Mr Jones*, *Mr Secretary*, *Mr Speaker*; *Mr Right* (joc.), destined husband; (alone as voc., vulg.) = *sir*; the word ~ as title, as *please don't call me* ~; untitled person, as *be he prince or mere* ~. 2. v.t. Address as Mr, as *don't* ~ *me*. [weakened form of MASTER]

mis'tĭgris, n. (cards). (Blank card in) a variety of poker. [f. F *mistigri* knave of clubs]

mistime', v.t. Say, do, (thing) out of season (esp. in p.p.). [ME; MIS-[1]]

mis'tletoe (-zltō, -sltō), n. Parasitic plant growing on apple & other trees, & bearing glutinous fruit used in making birdlime; *kiss under the* ~ (w. ref. to the custom permitting a girl standing below ~ used as Christmas decoration to be kissed by the finder). [OE *mistiltān*, = ON *mistil-teinn* (as MISSEL + *tán* twig)]

mis'tral (*or* -trahl'), n. Cold NW. wind

in Mediterranean provinces of France etc. [F & Pr., f. L as MAGISTRAL]

mistrans|lāte' (-z-), v.t. Translate incorrectly. So ~lā'TION n. [MIS-¹]

mistreat', v.t. Treat badly. Hence ~'MENT n. [ME; MIS-¹]

mis'tress, n. Woman in authority over servants; female head of household. **2.** Woman who has power to control or dispose *of*, as *you are* ~ *of the situation, you are your own* ~, (fig. of countries) ~ *of the world* etc. **3.** Woman who has thorough knowledge (*of* subject). **4.** Woman loved & courted by a man; woman illicitly occupying place of wife or having habitual illicit intercourse with man. **5.** Female teacher in school or of special subject, as *music*-~. **6.** ‖ *M*~ *of the Robes*, lady charged with care of Queen's wardrobe. **7.** (As title) see MRS. Hence ~-SHIP n. [ME, f. OF *maistresse* (*maistre* MASTER¹, see -ESS¹)]

mistri'al, n. Trial vitiated by error. [MIS-¹]

mistrust', v.t., v.i., n. **1.** Feel no confidence in (person, one*self*, one's powers etc.). **2.** n. Lack of confidence, whence ~FUL a., ~FULLY² adv., ~FULNESS n. [ME; MIS-¹]

mis't|y̆, a. Of, covered with, mist; indistinct in form; (fig.) obscure, vague, as *a* ~*y idea*. Hence ~ĭLY² adv., ~ĭNESS n. [OE *mistig* (as MIST, see -Y²)]

misünderständ', v.t. (-stŏŏd). Take (words etc., or abs.) in wrong sense; misinterpret words or actions of (person, esp. in p.p.). So ~ĭng n. [ME; MIS-¹]

misüse' (-z), v.t. Use wrongly, apply to wrong purpose; ill-treat. So **misüse'** (-s) n. [ME; MIS-¹]

mite, n. Kinds of arachnid, esp. *cheese*-~ (found in cheese), whence **mit'y̆**² a.; (orig.) Flemish copper coin of small value, (pop.) half-farthing (as in *Mark* xii. 42); modest contribution, the best one can do, as *let me offer my* ~ *of comfort*; (colloq.) *not a* ~, not at all; small object, esp. child; *a* ~ *of a* (a tiny) child etc. [(1) OE *mīte*, MLG. MDu. *mīte*, OHG *mīza* gnat f. Gmc *mītŏn*-; (2) ME, f. MLG. MDu. *mīte* (prob. same as (1)]

Mith'r|ăs, -ra, n. Persian god identified with sun. Hence ~rā'ic a., ~raISM, ~raIST(2), nn. [L f. Gk (-*as*) f. OPers. (-*a*)]

mithrid'at|īze, -|ise (-īz), v.t. Render proof against poison by gradually increasing doses of it. So **mithrid̆āt'ic** a., ~ISM n. [f. *Mithridates VI*, king of Pontus, +-IZE]

mit'ig|āte, v.t. Appease (anger etc.); alleviate (pain, grief); reduce severity of (punishment); moderate (heat, cold, severity, etc.). So ~ā'TION n., ~ātorY a. [ME, f. L *mitigare* (*mitis* mild), see -ATE³]

mitŏs'is, n. (biol.; pl. -*oses* pr. -ōs'ēz). Process of division of a cell into minute threads. Hence **mitŏt'ic** a. [f. Gk *mitos* thread +-OSIS]

mitrailleuse' (-trahyĕrz, & see Ap.), n. Many-barrelled breech-loading machine gun discharging small missiles simultaneously or in rapid succession. [F, fem. agent-n. f. *mitrailler* (*mitraille* small missiles, OF small money, f. *mite* MITE)]

mit'ral, a. & n. Of, like, a mitre; ~ (*valve*), a valve of the heart. [f. mod. L *mitralis* (as foll., see -AL)]

mi'tre¹ (-ter), n. Bishop's & abbot's tall cap, deeply cleft at top, esp. as symbol of episcopal office, whence **mi'trED²** (-terd) a.; [perh. different wd] joint of two pieces of wood etc. at angle of 90°, such that line of junction bisects this angle; ~-*block*, -*board*, -*box*, guide for saw in cutting ~-*joints*; ~-*wheels*, pair of bevelled cog-wheels with teeth set at 45° & axes at right angles. [ME, f. OF, f. L f. Gk *mitra* girdle, turban]

mi'tre² (-ter), v.t. Bestow mitre on; join with mitre; shape off (end of wood etc.) to a mitre; *mitring-machine* (for doing this). [ME, f. prec.]

mitt'en, mitt, n. (*Mitten*) kind of glove with thumb but no fingers, for warmth or protection in hedgers' work etc.; (pl., sl.) boxing-gloves; (now usu. *mitt*) woman's lace or knitted glove covering forearm & part of hand, but not fingers; *frozen* ~ (sl.), chilly reception; *give, get, the mitten* (sl.), dismiss (lover), be dismissed, (gen.) be dismissed from office etc. Hence **mitt'enED²** (-nd) a. [ME, f. OF *mitaine*, f. Rom. *medietana (sc. *muffula* MUFFLE²)]

mitt'imus, n. Warrant committing person to prison; (colloq.) dismissal from office, as *get one's* ~. [L, = we send]

mix, v.t. & i. Put together (two or more substances or groups, one *with* another) so that the particles or members of each are diffused among those of the others (also of immaterial things); prepare (compound) by ~ing ingredients; (intr.) join, be ~ed, as *oil will not* ~ *with water, they* (persons) *do not* ~ *well* (get on together); have intercourse *with*; ~ *up*, ~ thoroughly, also, confuse esp. in thought, so ~-*up* n.; *be* ~*ed up*, be involved (*in, with*, shady dealings etc.). Hence ~'ER¹ n.: one who, that which, ~es (esp. apparatus controlling the combination of various sounds in preparation of talking films & in dramatic broadcasting); (orig. U.S., colloq.) *good, bad*, ~*er*, one who gets on well, badly, with other people (esp. those of a different social class). [back formation f. foll., taken as E p.p.]

mixed (-kst), a. In vbl senses, esp.: of diverse qualities or elements; (of company) not select, containing persons of doubtful status; (colloq.) mentally confused, muddled; ill-adjusted, so ~-*up* adj.; for persons of both sexes, as ~

school, bathing; ~ MATHEMATICS. Hence **mix′éd**NESS n. [15th c. *mixt* f. OF *mixte* f. L *mixtus* p.p. of *miscēre* mix]

‖ **mix′en**, n. (dial.). Dung-hill. [OE, f. *meox* dung + -EN³; cogn. w. OS *mehs*, OHG *mist*, Goth. *maihstus*]

mix′ture, n. Mixing; what is mixed, esp, medical preparation (*the ~ as before*, also transf.); HEATHER ~; mechanical mixing of two substances, involving no change in their character, opp. to *chemical combination*; gas or vaporized oil mixed with air, forming explosive charge in internal-combustion engine. [F, or f. L *mixtura* (as MIXED, see -URE)]

Miz′pah, n. ~ *ring*, one inscribed ~ w. ref. to *Gen.* xxxi. 49 & given as love-token.

miz(z)′en, n. (naut.). (Also ~*-sail*) lowest fore-&-aft sail (rarely set, SPANKER being usual) of full-rigged ship's ~*-mast* (aftermost mast of three-masted ship); ~ *yard* (on which ~ is extended). [15th c., f. OF *misaine* f. It. *mezzana* ~-sail, fem. of *mezzano*; see MEZZANINE]

‖ **miz′zle**¹, v. impers., & n. Drizzle. Hence **miz′zly**² a. [15th c., of LG orig.; cf. MDu. *miezelen*, LG *miseln*, & *misig* drizzly]

miz′zle², v.i. (sl.). Go, decamp. [orig. unkn.]

mnēmŏn′ic (n-), a. & n. **1.** Of, designed to aid, the memory. **2.** n. pl. Art of, system for, improving memory. Hence **mnēm′o**-NIST (n-) n. [f. LL f. Gk *mnēmonikos* (*mnēmōn* mindful f. *mna* -remember, see -IC)]

mnēmotech′n|y̆ (n-, -tĕk-), n. = prec. (n. pl.). Hence ~IC a. [f. Gk *mnēmē* memory + *tekhnē* art]

mō, abbr. (colloq.) for *moment* (esp. *wait, in, half a mo*).

mō′a, n. = DINORNIS. [Maori]

moan¹, n. Long low murmur of physical or mental suffering; (arch.) *make* (one's) ~, complain. Hence ~FUL a. [ME, f. OE *mān*, whence *mǣnan*, obs. *mean*, vb, replaced by foll.]

moan², v.i. & t. Make moan(s); utter (specified words) with moans; lament (misfortune etc.); lament for (dead person etc.). [f. prec.]

moat, n., & v.t. Deep wide ditch surrounding house, castle, etc., usu. filled with water; (v.t.) surround (as) with ~. [ME *mot*(e) f. OF *mot*(*l*)e mound]

mŏb¹, n. The lower orders; rabble, tumultuous crowd; promiscuous assemblage of persons; ~ *law* (imposed, enforced, by ~); ~*s′man*, swell pickpocket; *swell* ~, class of stylishly dressed pickpockets. Hence ~**b′ISH**¹ a., ~**ŏc′RACY** n. [abbr. of *mobile*, n. (17th c.), short for *mobile vulgus*, L, = excitable crowd (MOBILE)]

mŏb², v.t. & i. (-bb-). (Of mob) attack, molest; assemble in a mob. [f. prec.]

mŏb′căp, n. Woman's indoor cap cover-

ing whole head, worn in 18th & early 19th cc. [f. obs. (18th c.) *mob*; cf. obs. vb (17th c.) *mob* muffle the head]

mōb′ile, a. Movable, not fixed, free to move; (of person or mind) easily, too easily, changing; (of troops) that may be easily moved from place to place. So **mobil′ITY** n. [f. F, or L *mobilis* (*movēre* move, see -BLE)]

mōb′iliz|e, -is|e (-iz), v.t. Render movable, bring into circulation; prepare (forces) for active service (also quasi-pass. of forces). So ~ABLE a., ~A′TION n. [f. F *mobiliser*, as prec.]

mŏcc′asin, n. Foot-gear of deerskin etc. worn by N.-Amer. Indians, trappers, etc. [f. native *mockasin*]

mō′cha¹ (-k-), n. Kind of chalcedony. [perh. same as foll.]

mō′cha² (-k-), n. (Also *M*~ *coffee*) fine quality of coffee, orig. from *M*~, Arabian port at entrance of Red Sea.

mŏck¹, n. (arch.). Derision; thing deserving scorn; imitation, counterfeit. [ME, f. MOCK³]

mŏck², a. (not pred.). Sham; ~ *sun, moon*, = PARHELION, PARASELENE; ~ *duck, goose*, pork with duck stuffing; ~*-turtle soup* (usu. of calf's head, to imitate turtle); ~*-heroic* a. & n., burlesquely imitating, burlesque imitation of, heroic style. [prec. & foll.]

mŏck³, v.t. & i. Hold up to ridicule; defy contemptuously; impose upon; ridicule by imitation; mimic, counterfeit; scoff *at*; ~*ing-bird*, American song-bird that mimics notes of other birds, other birds that do this; ~*-up* n., special model showing appearance of (part of) proposed machine. Hence ~**′ingLY**² adv. [ME *mokke, mocque*, f. OF *mocquer*]

mŏck′erY, n. Derision; subject, occasion, of this; counterfeit representation (*of*); ludicrously or insultingly futile action etc. [ME, f. OF *moquerie* (as prec., see -ERY)]

mōd′al, a. Of mode or form as opp. to substance; ~ *legacy* (with directions as to mode in which it is to be applied); (gram.) of the mood of a verb, (of particle) denoting manner; (log.) ~ *proposition*, one in which predicate is affirmed of subject under some qualification, (also) one that involves affirmation of possibility, impossibility, necessity, or contingency. Hence or cogn. **modăl′ITY** n. (esp. in pl. = method laid down for discharge of obligation etc.), ~LY² adv. [f. med. L *modalis* (as foll., see -AL)]

mōde, n. **1.** Way, manner, in which thing is done; prevailing fashion or custom; (arch.) *the* ~, the fashion in dress etc. **2.** (mus.). Ancient Greek scale system, as DORIAN, LYDIAN, PHRYGIAN, ~; used similarly in mediaeval music; in modern music, each of the two chief scale systems (MAJOR², MINOR, ~). **3.** (log.). Character of modal proposition. [(1) F; (2) & (3) f. L *modus* measure, manner]

mŏd′el¹, n. Representation in three dimensions of proposed structure etc.; *working* ~ (imitating movements of machine it represents); figure in clay, wax, etc., to be reproduced in other material; design, style of structure; person, thing, proposed for imitation; person who poses for artists; woman in draper's shop wearing clothes etc. to show their effect to customers; *The New M~*, plan for reorganization of Parliamentary army 1644–5; (attrib.) exemplary, ideally perfect. [f. F *modèle* (earlier *-elle*) f. It. *modello* dim. of *modo* (as MODE)]

mŏd′el², v.t. & i. (-ll-). Fashion, shape, (figure) in clay, wax, etc.; give shape to (document, argument, etc.); form (thing) *after, on, upon*, a model; (of mannequin) display (garment) by wearing it; (v.i.) act or pose as artist's model or mannequin. [f. prec.]

mŏd′ena, n. Deep purple. [*M~*, Italian city]

mŏd′erat|e¹, a. & n. **1.** Avoiding extremes, temperate in conduct or expression; (of wind) of medium strength; fairly large or good; *~e prices*, low (in advertisements etc., as *prices strictly ~e*). **2.** n. One who holds *~e* opinions in politics etc., whence *~*ISM n. Hence *~*LY² adv., *~*ENESS n. [ME, f. L *moderare* (*modus* MODE) +-ATE²]

mŏd′erate², v.t. & i. Render less violent, intense, vigorous, etc.; (of fury, storm, etc.) become less vehement; act as moderator. [as prec., see -ATE³]

mŏdera′tion, n. Moderating; moderateness; *in ~*, in a moderate manner or degree; || (Oxf. Univ., pl.) *M~s* first public examination for degree of B.A. (abbr. *Mods*). [ME, f. OF *moderation* or L *moderatio* (as MODERATE², see -ATION)]

mŏd′erātor, n. Arbitrator; mediator; presiding officer; || one of two officers presiding over mathematical tripos at Cambridge; || examiner for moderations; Presbyterian minister presiding over any ecclesiastical body; ~ *lamp* (with contrivance for regulating flow of oil). Hence *~*SHIP n. [ME, f. OF *moderateur* or f. L *moderator* (as prec., see -OR)]

mŏd′ern, a. & n. **1.** Of the present & recent times; ~ *English* (from 1500 onwards); ~ *history* (subsequent to Middle Ages); ||~ *school*, ~ *side*, in school (in which ~ subjects are chiefly or exclusively taught); new-fashioned, not antiquated. **2.** n. Person living in ~ times. Hence or cogn. **modĕrn′**ITY, *~*NESS, *~*IZA′TION, nn., *~*IZE(3) v.t. & i., *~*LY² adv. [f. LL *modernus* (*modo* just now)]

mŏd′ern|ism, n. Modern view(s) or method(s), esp. tendency in matters of religious belief to subordinate tradition to harmony with modern thought; so *~*IST(2) n.; modern term or expression. [-ISM]

mŏd′est, a. Having a humble estimate of one's own merits; retiring, bashful; (esp. of women) decorous in manner & conduct, scrupulously chaste; (of demands, statements, etc.) not excessive (freq. iron.); (of things) unpretentious in appearance, amount, etc. Hence or cogn. *~*LY² adv., *~*Y¹ n. (*~y* or *~y vest*, lace slip worn above point of corsage). [f. F *modeste* or L *modestus* (*modus* MODE)]

mŏd′icum, n. Small quantity (*of* food etc.). [L, neut. of *modicus* moderate (*modus* measure)]

mŏd′i|fy̆, v.t. Make less severe or decided, tone down; make partial changes in; (gram.) qualify sense of (word etc.); change (vowel) by umlaut. Hence or cogn. *~*fiaBIL′ITY, *~*FICA′TION, nn., *~*fī-ABLE, *~*ficātory, aa. [ME, f. OF *modifier* f. L *modificare* (as MODE, see -FY)]

modill′ion (-yon), n. (archit.). Projecting bracket under corona of cornice in Corinthian & other orders. [f. It. *modiglione*]

mŏd′ish, a. Fashionable. Hence *~*LY² adv., *~*NESS n. [f. MODE +-ISH¹]

mōdiste′ (-ēst), n. Milliner, dressmaker. [F (as MODE, see -IST)]

mŏd′ul|āte, v.t. & i. Regulate, adjust; vary (thing) conformably *to*; adjust or vary tone or pitch of (speaking voice); (mus.) pass (*from* one key *to* another). So *~*A′TION n. (also, radio) alteration in amplitude or frequency of a wave by a frequency of a different order, *~*ātOR n., chart used in tonic sol-fa system for exercise in sight-singing. [f. L *modulari* measure, adjust, (as foll.), see -ATE³]

mŏd′ule, n. Standard, unit, for measuring; (archit.) unit of length for expressing proportions, usu. semidiameter of column at base. [F, or f. L (as foll.)]

mŏd′ulus, n. (pl. *-lī*). Constant multiplier or coefficient; constant indicating relation between amount of physical effect & that of force producing it. [L, =measure, dim. of foll.]

mōd′us, n. ~ *ŏperăn′dī*, way a person goes to work, way a thing operates; ~ *vivĕn′dī*, mode of living, i.e. arrangement between disputants pending settlement of debate, arrangement between people(s) who agree to differ; money payment in lieu of tithe (orig. ~ *decimăn′dī*). [L, = MODE]

mofĕtte′, n. (Fissure in earth from which issues) exhalation of mephitic gas. [F, or f. It. (Naples) *mofetta*]

mofŭss′il, n. (Anglo-Ind.). Rural localities as opp. to chief station. [f. Hind. *mufaççil* f. Arab. *mufaççal*]

Mogŭl′, n. & a. Mongolian; *the* (*Great* or *Grand*)*~*, emperor of Delhi; (*m~*) tycoon. [f. Pers. *mugul* f. MONGOL]

mō′hair, n. (Fine camlet, yarn, from) hair of Angora goat. [ult. f. Arab. *mukhayyar* lit. = choice, select, (*khayyara* choose)]

Mohămm′edan, n. & a. (Follower) of Mohammed, founder of the Moslem religion. Hence ~ISM(3) n., ~IZE(3) v.t. [*Mohammed* f. Arab. *Muḥammad* + -AN]

Moha′rram (-hŭr-), **Mu-**, n. First month of Mohammedan year; great Shiite fast during first ten days of this month. [Arab. (*Mu-*), = sacred]

Mō′hawk, n. One of a tribe of N.-Amer. Indians; their language; (skating) step from either edge in one direction to same edge on other foot in opposite direction (cf. CHOCTAW). [native]

Mō′hŏck, n. (hist.). One of a class of aristocratic ruffians infesting London streets at night in 18th c. [f. prec.]

mŏ′hūr, n. (Also *gold* ~) former gold coin of India, worth 15 rupees. [f. Pers. *muhr* seal]

‖ **moid′er**, v.t. (dial.). To perplex, confuse, worry (esp. in p.p.). [orig. unkn.]

moid′ōre, n. Former Portuguese gold coin. [f. Port. *moeda d'ouro* (*moeda* MONEY + *ouro* gold)]

moi′etȳ, n. Half, esp. in legal use; (loosely) one of two parts into which thing is divided. [ME, f. OF *moit(i)e* f. L *medietatem* middle point (as MEDIUM, see -TY)]

moil, v.i. Drudge, esp. *toil & ~*. [ME, f. OF *moillier* moisten, paddle in mud, f. Rom. *molliare* f. L *mollis* soft]

moire (mwahr), n. (Also ~ *antique*, see Ap.) watered fabric, usu. silk, orig. mohair. [F, earlier *mouaire*, f. MOHAIR]

moiré (mwah′rā), a. & n. (Of silk) watered; (of metals) having clouded appearance like watered silk; (n.) this appearance. [F, p.p. of *moirer* f. prec.]

moist, a. Slightly wet, damp; (of season etc.) rainy; (of disease) marked by discharge of matter etc. Hence ~′NESS n. [ME, f. OF *moiste*]

moi′sten (-sn), v.t. & i. Make moist; become moist. [-EN²]

mois′ture, n. Water or other liquid diffused in small quantity as vapour, condensed on surface, etc. Hence ~LESS a. [ME, f. OF *moistour* (as MOIST, see -OR)]

mōke, n. (sl.). Donkey. [orig. unkn.]

mōk′ō, n. Maori system of tattooing. [Maori]

mōl′ar¹, a. & n. 1. (Usu. of mammal's back teeth) serving to grind. 2. n. ~ tooth. [f. L *molaris* (*mola* millstone, see -AR¹)]

mōl′ar², a. Of mass; acting on or by means of large masses; freq. opp. MOLE-CULAR. [f. L *moles* mass, see -AR¹]

molăss′ĕs (-z), n. pl. (treated as sing.). Uncrystallized syrup drained from raw sugar; syrup got from sugar in process of refining, treacle. [f. Port. *melaço* f. LL *mellaceum* must (*mel* honey, see -ACEOUS)]

mōle¹, n. Spot, blemish, small lump on human skin. [OE *māl*, corresp. to OHG *meil*, Goth. *mail*]

mōle², n. Small burrowing animal with (usu. blackish) velvety fur & very small eyes; other mammals of same family;

blind as a ~ (quite); ~*-cricket*, nocturnal burrowing insect; ~*′hill*, small mound thrown up by ~ in burrowing (*make mountains out of ~hills*, exaggerate obstacles etc.); ~*′skin*, skin of ~ as fur, kind of cotton fustian with surface shaved before dyeing, (pl.) clothes, esp. trousers, of this. [ME *molle* f. MDu. *moll(e)*, *mol*, MLG *mol*, *mul*]

mōle³, n. Massive structure, usu. of stone, as pier, breakwater, or junction between places separated by water; artificial harbour. [f. F *môle* f. med. Gk *mōlos* f. L *moles* mass]

molĕc′ūlar, a. Of, relating to, consisting of, molecules; ~ *weight* of substance (of one of its molecules relatively to the weight of one atom of hydrogen). Hence ~ITY (-ă′r-) n., ~LY² adv. [-AR¹]

mŏl′ĕcule, n. (Physics, chem.) one of the minute groups of atoms (in some elements, esp. the inert gases, one of the single atoms) of which material substances consist, the smallest portion to which a substance can be reduced by subdivision without losing its chemical identity; (loosely) small particle. [f. F *molécule* f. L *moles* mass; see -CULE]

molĕst′, v.t. Meddle hostilely or injuriously with (person). So mŏlĕsta′TION n. [f. OF *molester* f. L *molestare* (*molestus* troublesome)]

Mŏl′in|ism, n. Doctrine of Luis Molina (d. 1600), that efficacy of grace depends on the will that freely accepts it; doctrine of Miguel de Molinos (d. 1696), quietism. Hence ~IST n. [f. *Molina*, *Molinos*, + -ISM]

mŏll, n. Prostitute; gangster's mistress. [pet form of *Mary*]

mŏll′i|fȳ, v.t. Appease, soften. So ~FICA′TION n. [ME, f. OF *mollifier* or L *mollificare* (*mollis* soft, see -FY)]

mŏll′usc, n. Animal belonging to the *Mollusca*, sub-kingdom of soft-bodied & usu. hard-shelled animals, including limpets, snails, cuttle-fish, oyster, mussel, etc. Hence **mollŭs′cAN**, **mollŭs′cous**, aa., **mollŭs′coID** a. & n. [f. F *mollusque* f. L *molluscus* (*mollis* soft)]

mŏll′ȳ, n. Effeminate man or boy, milksop; ~*-coddle*, (n.) milksop, (v.t.) coddle, cocker up. [pet form of *Mary*]

Mŏl′och (-k), n. Canaanite idol to whom children were sacrificed (often fig.); thorn-lizard, a hideous Australian reptile. [LL f. Gk, f. Heb. *molek*]

molŏss′us, n. Metrical foot – – –. [Gk]

Mŏl′otŏv. Name of Soviet commissar used attrib.; ~ *cocktail* (sl.), anti-tank inflammatory hand-grenade used in 1939–45 war.

mōl′ten. See MELT.

mŏl′tō, adv. Very (preceding mus. direction, as ~ *espressivo*). [It., f. L *multus* much]

mōl′ȳ, n. Fabulous herb with white flower & black root, endowed with magic properties; wild garlic & other plants. [L, f. Gk *mōlu*]

molyb′denum, n. Silvery-white brittle metallic element with which steel is alloyed for making high-speed tools. [earlier *-dena*, f. L f. Gk *molubdaina* f. *molubdos* lead]

mōm′ent, n. 1. Minute point of time, instant; *one* ~, *half a* ~, (colloq.) *half a mō̆*, (ellipt.) wait a ~; *come here this* ~ (at once); *came the very* ~ (as soon as) *I heard of it*; *timed to the* ~ (with absolute accuracy); *the* ~ (time that affords an opportunity); *am, was, busy at the* ~ (just now, then), so *men of* (important at) *the* ~; PSYCHOLOGICAL ~. 2. (mech.). ~ *of a force about a point*, measure of its power in causing rotation. 3. Importance, as *of great, little, no,* ~, whence **momĕn′t**ous a., momĕn′tous**LY**[2] adv., momĕn′tous-NESS n. [ME, f. OF, or L *momentum*]

mōm′entar|y̆, a. Lasting only a moment; short-lived, transitory. Hence ~**ILY**[2] adv., ~**INESS** n. [f. L *momentarius* (as prec., see -ARY[1])]

mōm′ently̆, adv. From moment to moment; every moment; for a moment. [-LY[2]]

momĕn′tum, n. (pl. *-ta*). (Mech.) quantity of motion of moving body, product of its mass by its velocity; (pop.) impetus gained by movement (lit. & fig.). [L (as MOVE, see -MENT)]

Mōm′us, n. Greek god of ridicule; fault-finder. [f. Gk *Mōmos*]

mŏn′ac(h)al (-k-), a. Monastic. So **mŏn′achism** (-k-) n. [f. LL *monachalis* (MONK, -AL)]

mŏn′ad, n. The number one, unit; ultimate unit of being (e.g. a soul, an atom, a person, God), esp. in philosophy of Leibnitz, whence ~**ISM**(3), ~**ŏl′ogy**, nn.; (biol.) simple organism assumed as first term in genealogy of living beings; (chem.) element, radical, with combining power of one atom of hydrogen. Hence **monăd′ic** a. [f. LL f. Gk *monas -ados* unit]

mŏnadĕlph′ous, a. (bot.). (Of stamens) having filaments united into one bundle; (of plants) with ~ stamens. [f. Gk *monos* one + *adelphos*, brother + -OUS]

monăn′drous, a. (bot.). Having a single stamen. [f. Gk *monandros* (*monos* one + *anĕr andros* male) + -OUS]

monăn′dry̆, n. Custom of having only one husband at a time. [as prec. + -Y[1]]

mŏn′arch (-k), n. 1. Sovereign with title of king, queen, emperor, empress, or equivalent; supreme ruler (often fig.). 2. Large orange & black butterfly. Hence **monărch′al**, **monărch′ic(al)**, aa., **monărch′ally**[2], **monărch′ically**, advv. (-k-). [f. F (*-arque*) or L (*-cha*) f. Gk *monarkhēs* (*monos* alone + *arkhō* rule)]

mŏn′arch|ism (-k-), n. Principles of, attachment to, monarchy. So ~**IST** (-k-) n. [-ISM]

mŏn′archy̆ (-k-), n. (State under)

monarchical government; *constitutional, limited,* ~ (subject to constitutional restrictions). [ME, f. OF *monarchie* or L f. Gk *monarkhia* (MONARCH, -Y[1])]

mŏn′astery̆, n. Residence of community (usu. of monks) living secluded under religious vows. [ME, f. eccl. L f. late Gk *monastērion* (*monazō* live alone f. *monos*)]

monăs′t|ic, a. Of monks or monasteries; (bookbind.) finished by tooling without gold (also *antique*). So ~**ICALLY** adv., ~**ICISM**(3) n., ~**ICIZE**(3) v.t. [f. F (*-ique*) or LL f. Gk *monastikos* (as prec., see -IC)]

mondaine (mawⁿdǎn′), n. Woman of the fashionable world; worldly woman. [F]

Mon′day (mŭn′dǐ), n. Second day of week; *Black* ~ (school sl.), first day of term; ‖ *St* ~, ~ as day of little work (w. ref. to saint's-day holidays). [OE *Mōnan dæg* (= moon's day), rendering LL *lunae dies*]

Mon′dayish (mŭn′dǐ-), a. (Of clergy) indisposed as result of Sunday work; (of others) slack as result of Sunday holiday. [-ISH[1]]

monde (mawⁿd), n. The fashionable world, society; the set in which one moves. [F]

mŏn′dial, a. World-wide. [F, f. LL *mundialis* f. L *mundus* world]

mo′netary̆ (mŭ-, mŏ-), a. Of the coinage; of money. [f. F *monétaire* or LL *monetarius* (as MONEY, see -ARY[1])]

mo′netiz|e (mŭ-, mŏ-), -is|e (-īz), v.t. Put (metal) into circulation as money. Hence ~**A′TION** n. [f. L *moneta* MONEY + -IZE]

mo′ney (mŭ-), n. (pl. ~s). 1. Current coin; coin & promissory documents representing it (*paper* ~), esp. government & bank notes; (w. pl.) particular coin; (pl.) sums of ~; ~ *of* ACCOUNT[2]; CONSCIENCE ~; property viewed as convertible into ~; coin in reference to its purchasing power, as (prov.) ~ *makes the mare to go, time is* ~, *for* LOVE[1] *or* ~; *make* ~, acquire wealth, *coin* ~, do this rapidly; ‖~ *for jam or for old rope* (sl.), a profitable return for little or no trouble; *not every man's* ~, not worth its price to every one. 2.~*-bag*, bag for ~, (pl.) wealth; ~*-bags*, wealthy or avaricious person; ~*-box*, closed box into which savings or contributions are dropped through slit; ~*-changer*, one whose business it is to change ~ at fixed rate; ~*-grubber*, person sordidly intent on amassing ~, ~*-grubbing* a. & n., (given to) this practice; ~*-lender* (derog.), one whose business it is to lend ~ at interest; ~*-market*, sphere of operation of dealers in stocks etc.; ~ ORDER[1](3); ~*-spinner*, small spider thought to bring good luck, something that brings in much ~, e.g. book, film, play, etc.; ~*-wort*, plant with round glossy leaves; ~*'s-worth*, anything recognized as equivalent to ~. Hence ~**LESS** (mŭn′ǐl-) a. [ME, f. OF *moneie* f. L *moneta* mint, money, orig. goddess in whose temple at Rome ~ was coined]

moneyed (mŭn'īd), a. Rich; consisting of money, as ~ *resources, assistance;* ~ *interest,* the class concerned in money as a possession. [-ED²]

mo'nger (mŭng-), n. Dealer, trader, (chiefly in comb., as *cheese~, fish~, iron~, coster~,* & fig. *scandal~* etc.). [OE *mangere* (*mangian* to traffic f. L *mango* dealer)]

Mŏng'ol (-ngg-), n. & a. (Member) of Asian people now inhabiting Mongolia, between China & Siberia. Hence ~OID a., of Mongolian type (also, n. = MONGO-LIAN). [native, perh. f. *mong* brave]

Mŏngŏl'ian (-ngg-), a. & n. = prec.; (anthrop.) of the yellow-skinned straight--haired type of mankind; of a class of idiots like ~s. [-IAN]

mŏng'ōose, mŭng'ōose, (-ngg-), n. (pl. ~s). An ichneumon, common in India, & able to kill venomous snakes unharmed; kind of lemur. [f. native *mangus*]

mo'ngrel (mŭngg-), n. & a. 1. Dog of no definable breed; animal, plant, resulting from crossing of different breeds or kinds; person not of pure race. 2. adj. Of mixed origin, nature, or character. Hence ~ISM(2) n., ~IZE(3) v.t., ~LY¹ a. [app. f. root *mang-, mong-,* mix, +-REL]

‖ mŏn'ial, n. Mullion. [ME, f. OF *moinel* middle f. *moien* MEAN² (-AL)]

mŏnil'ifŏrm, a. Suggesting necklace or string of beads. [F, or mod. L *moniliformis* (*monile* necklace, -FORM)]

mŏn'‖ism, n. Doctrine that only one being exists; any of the theories that deny the duality of matter & mind. Hence ~IST n., **monis'tıc** a. [f. Gk *monos* one, -ISM]

moni'tion, n. Warning (*of* danger); formal notice from bishop or ecclesiastical court admonishing person to refrain from some offence; (in courts that use civil law process) summons. [ME, f. OF, or L *monitio* (*monēre monit-* warn, -ION)]

mŏn'itor, n., & v.t. & i. 1. (arch.). One who admonishes. 2. Senior pupil in school with duties of keeping order etc., whence **mŏnitŏr'IAL** a., ~SHIP n. 3. Lizard supposed to give warning of approach of crocodiles. 4. Shallow-draught warship of heavy gunpower. 5. One who listens to & reports on foreign broadcasts, misuse of official telephones, etc. 6. Detector of induced radio-activity, esp. in workers in an atomic plant. 7. vb. Act as ~ (sense 5), act as ~ of. Hence **mŏn'itress¹** n. [L (as prec., -OR)]

mŏn'itory, a. & n. 1. Warning, admonitory. 2. n. Bishop's or pope's letter of admonition. [f. L *monitorius* (as prec., see -ORY)]

monk (mŭ-), n. Member of community of men living apart under vows of poverty, chastity, & obedience; ~*'s-hood,* plant with hood-shaped flowers. Hence ~ᴸ HOOD, ~SHIP, nn. [OE *munuc,* = OS *munik,* OHG *munih,* ON *munkr,* f.

*monicus var. of LL f. Gk *monachos* solitary (*monos* alone)]

monk'‖ery (mŭ-), n. (colloq.). Monastic life; monastery; monks; monkish practices. So ~DOM n. [-ERY]

mo'nkey (mŭ-), n. (pl. ~s), & v.t. & i. 1. Mammal of a group closely allied to & resembling man, ranging from anthropoid apes to marmosets; (as term of playful contempt, to or of person) *young* ~ etc. 2. Machine hammer for pile-driving etc.; globular earthenware water-vessel with straight upright neck. 3. (sl.). ‖ *Put his* ~ *up,* enrage him; *get one's* ~ *up,* become angry. 4. ‖ £500 (sl.). 5. ~*-bread,* fruit of baobab tree; ~*-cup,* pitcher-plant; ~*-flower,* kind of mimulus with bright yellow flowers; ~*-jacket,* short close-fitting one worn by sailors etc.; ‖~*-nut,* peanut; ~*-puzzle, puzzle-~,* Chile pine, prickly tree of genus *Araucaria;* ~*-wrench,* one with adjustable jaws. 6. v.t. Mimic, mock; (v.i.) play mischievous tricks (*with*), fool *about.* Hence ~ISH¹ a., ~ishNESS n., (mŭng'kǐ-). [16th c., of unkn. (poss. LG) orig.]

monk'ish (mŭ-), a. Of monks, monastic; characteristic of monks (usu. in bad sense). [-ISH¹]

mŏn'o-, comb. form (bef. vowels *mon-*) of Gk *monos* alone, sole, single; as: (1) ~*bās'ic* (chem.), having one base or atom of a base; ~*carp'ic,* ~*carp'ous,* bearing fruit only once; ~*cēph'alous* (bot.), having only one head; ~*clīn'al,* (of strata) dipping in one & the same direction; ~*cŏtȳlēd'on*(ous), (plant with) single cotyledon; *monŏc'racy,* government by single person; *monŏc'ūlar,* with, adapted to, one eye; ~*cycle,* velocipede with one wheel; ~*dac-tylous,* having one finger, toe, or claw; ~*drama,* piece for one performer; *mo-noe'cious* (-nēshŭs), (bot.) with male & female organs on same plant, (zool.) hermaphrodite; ~*gen'esis,* development of all beings from single cell, so ~*genĕt'ic* a.; *monŏ'geny,* descent of mankind from one pair of ancestors; ~*glot* a. & n., (one) who uses only one language; *monŏ'gȳnous,* with only one pistil or stigma; *monŏ'gȳny,* usage of mating with only one female; ~*īdē'ism,* concentration on single idea, esp. as form of monomania; *monŏlᴸ atry,* worship of one god without denying that others may exist; ~*mān'ia,* insanity on one subject only, so ~*mān'iăc* n., ~*mani'acal* a.; ~*mer,* one of the units forming a polymer molecule, (also) a compound which can undergo polymerization; ~*mĕt'allism,* standard of currency based on one metal, so ~*metăll'ic* a.; ~*morph'ic,* ~*morph'ous,* not changing form during development; ~*pĕt'alous,* having corolla in one piece, or petals united into tube; ~*phthong,* single vowel sound; ~*plane,* aeroplane with one plane; ~*psy'chism* (-sĭk-), theory that all souls are one; ~*rail,* railway of one rail;

~*rhyme*, poem in which all lines have same rhyme; ~*sperm'ous* (bot.), having one seed; *monŏs'tichous* (-k-) (bot., zool.), arranged in, consisting of, one layer or row; ~*strŏph'ic*, consisting of repetitions of one strophic arrangement; ~*tint*, representation, picture, in only one colour; ~*trēme*, member of lowest order of mammals with one vent for urinary, genital, & digestive organs; ~*type*, composing-machine that casts & sets up single types P; ~*tyˇp'ic*, represented by only one type. (2) chem. wds denoting presence of a single atom or combining equivalent, as ~*brŏm'ide*, ~*carb'on*, ~*chlor'ide*, *monŏv'alent*, *monŏx'ide*.

mŏn'ochŏrd (-k-), n. Instrument for determination of musical intervals. [ME, f. OF *monocorde* or LL f. Gk MONO(*khordon* f. *chordē* CHORD)]

mŏnochromăt'ic (-k-), a. (Of light) presenting one colour only; executed in monochrome. [MONO- + CHROMATIC]

mŏn'ochrōme (-k-), n. & a. 1. Painting executed in different tints of one colour; representation in one colour. 2. adj. Having only one colour. [ult. f. Gk MONO-(*khrōmatos* f. *khrōma* colour)]

mŏn'ocle, n. Single eye-glass. [F, f. LL *monoculus* one-eyed (MONO- + *oculus* eye)]

mŏn'od|ý, n. Ode sung by single actor in Greek tragedy; poem in which mourner bewails someone's death. Hence or cogn. **monŏd'ic** a., ~**IST** n. [f. LL f. Gk *monōidia* f. *monōidos* singing alone (MONO- + *ŏid-*, *aoid-*, f. *aeidō* sing)]

monŏg'am|ý, n. Practice, circumstance, of being married to one at a time; (rare) practice of marrying only once; (zool.) habit of having only one mate. Hence or cogn. ~**IST** n., ~**OUS** a. [f. F *monogamie* f. LL f. Gk MONO(*gamia* f. *gamos* marriage)]

mŏn'ogrăm, n. Two or more letters, esp. person's initials, interwoven. So **mŏnogrammăt'ic** a. [f. LL *monogramma* f. Gk MONO(*grammon*, neut. adj. as -GRAM)]

mŏn'ograph (-ahf), n., & v.t. Separate treatise on single object or class of objects; (v.t.) write a ~ on. Hence **monŏg'raphER¹**, **monŏg'raphIST**, nn., **mŏnogrăph'IC** a., **mŏnogrăph'ICALLY** adv. [MONO- + -GRAPH]

mŏn'olith, n. Single block of stone, esp. shaped into pillar or monument. Hence **mŏnolith'IC** a., (also) solidly uniform throughout, showing or allowing no variation. [f. F -*lithe*, or L f. Gk MONO-(*lithos* stone)]

mŏn'ologue (-ŏg), n. Scene in drama in which one person speaks by himself; dramatic composition for single performer; long speech by one person in a company; soliloquy. Hence **mŏnolŏ'gICAL** a., **monŏl'ogIST**, **mŏn'olŏguIST** (-gĭst), nn., **monŏl'ogIZE(2)** v.i. [F, = one who loves to hear himself talk, f. Gk MONO(*logos* -LOGUE)]

‖ **mŏn'omărk**, n. Combination of letters and/or figures registered as identification mark for goods, articles, addresses, etc. [MONO-]

monŏm'ial, n. & a. (alg.). (Expression) consisting of one term. [MONO-, on *binomial*]

Monŏph'yˇsīte, n. One who holds there is only one nature in the person of Christ. [f. eccl. L (-*ta*) f. eccl. Gk MONO(*phusitēs* f. *phusis* nature, see -ITE¹)]

monŏp'olist, n. One who favours monopoly; one who assumes monopoly (*of*). [-IST]

monŏp'olizǀe, -**isǀe** (-īz), v.t. Obtain exclusive possession or control of (trade, commodity, the conversation, person's attention, etc.). Hence ~**A'TION** n. [f. foll. + -IZE]

monŏp'olý, n. Exclusive possession of the trade in some commodity; this conferred as privilege by State; exclusive possession, control, or exercise (*of*); thing that is monopolized. [f. L f. Gk MONO-(*pōlion* f. *pōleō* sell)]

mŏnosyˇll'|able, n. Word of one syllable; *speak in* ~*ables*, answer little but Yes or No, with intentional curtness. Hence or cogn. ~**ăb'IC** a., ~**ăb'ICALLY** adv., ~**abISM(2)** n., ~**abIZE(3)** v.t. [f. L MONO-(*syllabus* SYLLABLE)]

mŏn'othēǀism, n. Doctrine that there is only one God. Hence ~**IST** n., ~**is'tIC** a. [f. MONO- + Gk *theos* god +-ISM]

mŏn'otōne, a. & n., & v.t. 1. (Utterance of successive syllables) without change of pitch, whence **mŏnotŏn'IC** a. (mus.); sameness of style in writing. 2. v.t. Recite, speak, sing, in unvaried tone. [f. late Gk MONO(*tonos* TONE)]

monŏt'on|ous, a. (Of sound or utterance) without variation in tone or cadence; lacking in variety, wearisome through sameness. Hence or cogn. ~**IZE(3)** v.t., ~**OUSLY²** adv., ~**OUSNESS**, ~**Y¹**, nn. [as prec. + -OUS]

Monrōe'|ism (-ōī-), n. Monroe DOCTRINE. So ~**IST** n. [-ISM]

monseigneur (see Ap.), n. (pl. *nosseigneurs* pr. nosănyér'). French title given to eminent persons, esp. princes, cardinals, archbishops, & bishops. [F]

monsieur (musyér', & see Ap.), n. (pl. *messieurs* pr. mĕsyér'). French equivalent of MR, but also used by itself as substitute for name, as *did M~ring?*; Frenchman; (hist.) title of second son or next younger brother of French king. [F]

monsignor(e) (mŏnsēnyŏr', -ī; pl. -*ori*), n. Title of some R.-C. prelates, officers of Papal court, & others. [It., after MONSEIGNEUR]

monsōon', n. Wind in S. Asia, esp. in Indian Ocean, blowing from SW. in summer (*wet* ~) & NE. in winter (*dry* ~); rainy season; other winds with periodic alternations. [f. Du. *monssoen* f. Port. *monção* perh. f. Arab. *mausim*, lit. season, (*wasama* mark)]

mŏn'ster, n. & a. 1. Mis-shapen animal or plant, abortion; imaginary animal compounded of incongruous elements, e.g. centaur, sphinx, griffin; inhumanly wicked person, inhuman example *of* (cruelty etc.); animal, thing, of huge size. 2. adj. Huge. [ME, f. OF *monstre* f. L *monstrum* portent, monster (*monēre* warn)]

mŏn'strance, n. (R.-C. Ch.). Open or transparent vessel of gold or silver in which the host is exposed. [f. OF, f. med. L *monstrantia* (*monstrare* show, see -ANCE)]

mŏnstrŏs'itў, n. Monstrousness; abortion, imaginary monster, outrageous thing. [f. LL *monstrositas* (as foll., see -TY)]

mŏn'strous, a. & adv. 1. Abnormally formed, of the nature of a monster; huge; outrageously wrong or absurd; atrocious. 2. adv. (arch.). Extremely, as ~ *good friends*. Hence ~LY[2] adv., ~NESS n. [ME, f. OF *monstreux* f. LL *monstrosus* (MON-STER, -OUS)]

mŏn'tage (-ahzh), n. (cinemat.). Selection, cutting, & piecing together as a consecutive whole of the separate shots taken in the making of a film. [F, f. *monter* to mount]

mŏn'tāne, a. Of, inhabiting, mountainous country. [f. L *montanus* (as MOUNT, see -ANE)]

mŏntbrē'tia (-sha), n. Iridaceous plant with bright orange-coloured flowers. [after A. F. E. D. de *Montbret*, French botanist (d. 1801), -IA[1]]

mŏn'tė, n. Spanish game of chance, played with 45 cards; *three-card* ~, game of Mexican origin. [Sp., = mountain, heap of cards]

Mŏntĕnĕg'rĭn, n. & a. (Inhabitant) of Montenegro (now in Jugoslavia). [-INE[1]]

Montĕssōr'ĭ sȳs'tĕm, n. Method of educating very young children, both normal & defective, initiated c. 1900 by Dr Maria Montessori of Rome (by direction of natural activities rather than strict control).

month (mŭ-), n. Any of the twelve portions into which the year is divided (also *calendar* ~); *lunar* ~, period in which moon makes complete revolution; space of time from a day in one ~ to corresponding day in next; space of 28 days; ~ *of Sundays*, indefinite period; *this day* ~, a ~ from today; ~'s *mind*, mass etc. in commemoration of deceased person a ~ after death, ‖ (also) inclination, liking. [OE *mōnath*, OS *mānoth*, OHG *mānōd*, ON *mānathr*, Goth. *mēnōths* f. Gmc **mǣnōth-* cogn. w. MOON]

mo'nthlў (mŭn-), a. & n. 1. Done, recurring, payable, etc., once a month; ~ *nurse* (attending woman during first month after childbirth); ~ *rose*, a rose, supposed to flower monthly. 2. n. Magazine etc. published each month; (pl.) menses. So mo'nthLY[2] (mŭn-) adv. [-LY[1]]

mŏn'tĭcŭle, n. Small hill; small mound caused by volcanic eruption; minute eminence on surface of animal etc. [F, f. LL *monticulus* (mons MOUNT, see -CULE)]

mŏn'ūment, n. Written record; anything that serves to commemorate, esp. structure, building; ‖ *the M~*, column in London commemorating fire of London in 1666; stone or other structure placed over grave or in church etc. in memory of the dead. [ME, f. L *monu-*, *monimentum* (*monēre* remind, see -MENT)]

mŏnūmĕn'tal, a. Of, serving as, a monument; ~ *mason*, tombstone maker; (of literary works) massive & permanent; stupendous, as ~ *ignorance*. Hence ~LY[2] adv. [f. LL *monumentalis* (as prec., see -AL)]

mŏnūmĕn'talize, -ise (-īz), v.t. Record, commemorate, as by monument. [prec. +-IZE]

-mony, suf. repr. L *-monia*, *-monium* (occas. thr. F *-moine*, *-monie*, as *matri~*, *patri~*, *cere~*), wh. formed nn. f. aa. (*acrimonia*), nn. (*patrimonium*), & vbs (*alimonium*).

mōō, v.i., & n. (Of cow or ox) low, make the sound *moo*; (n.) this sound. [imit.]

mōōch, mouch (mōō-), v.i. & t. (sl.). Loiter *about*, slouch *along*; (trans.) steal. [15th c. *mouche*, identified w. ME (now dial.) *miche*, app. f. OF *muchier* hide, skulk]

mōōd[1], n. State of mind or feeling; *in the* ~, *in no* ~, inclined, disinclined, (*for* thing, *to* do). [OE, OS *mōd*, OHG *muot*, ON *mōthr*, Goth. *mōths* f. Gmc **mōda-*]

mōōd[2], n. (Gram.) any of the groups of forms in conjugation of verb that serve to indicate its function, as *indicative*, *imperative*, *subjunctive*, ~; (mus.) = MODE; (log.) any of the classes into which each of the figures of valid categorical syllogism is subdivided. [var. of MODE, by assoc. w. prec.]

mōōd'ў, a. Gloomy, sullen. Hence ~ĭLY[2] adv., ~ĭNESS n. [OE *mōdig* (see MOOD[1] & -Y[2]]

moollah. See MULLAH.

mōōl'vĭ(e), mou~, n. Mohammedan doctor of the law; learned person, teacher (esp. as term of respect among Indian Moslems). [Hind. *mulvī* f. Arab. *maulawiyy* = judicial]

mōōn[1], n. 1. Satellite of the earth, revolving round it monthly, & deriving light from sun & reflecting it to earth; this in particular month, regarded as a distinct object from that visible in other months, as *age of the* ~, *new* ~ (at beginning of revolution), *full* ~ (with disc entirely illuminated); HARVEST, HUNTER'S, ~; (poet.) month (*where summer is but three* ~s *long*); *once in a* BLUE[1] ~; *old* ~ *in new* ~'s *arms*, ~ *during first quarter*, when dark part of orb is made faintly luminous by earth-light. 2. ~'*beam*, ray of ~*light*; ~'*calf*, born fool; ~'*flower*, oxeye daisy; ~*light*, light of ~ (often attrib.); ~*light flitting*, removal of household goods by night to avoid paying rent; ~*lighter* (hist.), one who in Ireland perpetrated outrages by night on tenants who incurred hostility of Land League; ~*lit*, lit up by ~; ~*raker*, ‖ native of Wiltshire, sail above the horizon; ~*raking* (fig.), daydreaming, woolgathering; ~*shine*, visionary tale or ideas, (also) smuggled spirits; *~*shiner* (sl.), illicit distiller, spirit-smuggler; ~*shiny*, lighted by ~, (also) visionary; ~*stone*, feldspar of pearly appearance; ~*struck*, deranged in mind. Hence ~*LESS* a. [OE *mōna*, OS, OHG *māno*, ON *māni*, Goth *mēna* f. Gmc *mænon-*; cogn. w. L *mensis* month]

moon[2], v.i. & t. Move, look, listlessly (*about, around*, etc.); pass *away* (time) in listless manner. [f. prec.]

moon'shee, munshi (mōōn'shē), n. Secretary or language-teacher in India. [f. Hind. *munshi* f. Arab. *munshi'* (*ansha'a* compose)]

moon'y, a. Of, like, the moon; listless, stupidly dreamy. [MOON[1,2]+-Y[2]]

moor[1], n. Tract of open waste ground, esp. if covered·with heather; (in Cornwall)· waste land where tin is found; ~ *game*, red (rarely, black) grouse; ~*cock*, male of this; ~*hen*, female of this, (also) water-hen; ~*land*, country abounding in heather; ~*stone*, kind of granite. Hence ~*ISH*[1], ~*Y*[2], aa. [OE, OS *mōr*, OHG *muor*, f. Gmc *mōr*-]

Moor[2], n. One of a Mohammedan people, mixed Berber & Arab, inhabiting NW. Africa. Hence ~*ISH*[1] a. [ME, f. OF *More* f. L f. Gk *Mauros* inhabitant of Mauretania, region of N. Africa]

moor[3], v.t. Attach (boat or other floating thing) to moorings; ~*ing*-MAST[1]. Hence ~*AGE*(3, 4) n. [15th c. *more*, prob. f. (M)LG *mōren*, rel. to MDu. *māren*]

moor'ing, n.(Usu. pl.) permanent anchors & chains laid down for ships to be moored to, what a floating object is moored to; (pl.) place where vessel is moored. [-ING[1]]

moose, n. (pl.~). N.-Amer. animal closely allied to or same as European elk. [f. native *moos*]

moot, n., a., & v.t. **1.** (Hist.) assembly; (law) students' discussion of hypothetical case for practice. **2.** adj. Debatable (freq. ~ *point*). **3.** v.t. Raise (question) for discussion. [(1) OE (*ge*)*mōt* f. Gmc *mōt*-, whence MEET[1]; (2) f. (1); (3) OE *mōtian* f. (1)]

mop[1], n. Bundle of coarse yarn or cloth fastened at end of stick, for cleaning floors etc.; similar instruments for various purposes; ~*head*, (fig.) thick head of hair like ~, person with this. Hence ~*p'y*[2] a. [15th c. *mappe* perh. ult. conn. w. L *mappa* napkin]

mop[2], v.t. (-pp-). Wipe, clean, (as) with mop; wipe tears, sweat, etc., from (brow etc.); (sl.) ~ *the floor with*, have & use over-

whelming advantage of (combatant); ~ *up*, wipe up (as) with mop, (sl.) absorb (profits etc.), dispatch, make an end of, (mil.) complete the occupation of (district etc.) by capturing or killing troops left there, capture or kill (stragglers). [f. prec.]

mop[3], v.i. (-pp-), & n. ~ & *mow*, make grimaces; ~*s* & *mows*, grimaces. [perh. imit.; cf. Du. *moppen* pout]

‖ **mop**[4], n. A fair or gathering in the autumn at which farm hands & servants were hired. [perh. = *mop-fair* (MOP[1])]

mope, v.i. & t., & n. **1.** Abandon oneself to listless condition; (refl. or pass.) make one*self*, be, the victim of ennui. **2.** n. One who ~*s*; *the* ~*s*, depression of spirits. Hence **mop'ISH**[1] a., **mop'ishLY**[2] adv., **mop'ishNESS** n. [orig. unkn.]

mop'ed, n. Motorized pedal cycle. [f. *mo*(*torized*) *ped*(*al*)]

mo'poke, **more'pork** (mōrp-), n. In New Zealand, an owl; in Tasmania, nightjar; in Australia, various birds. [imit. of bird's note]

moquette' (-kĕt), n. Material of wool & hemp or linen, used for carpets & upholstery. [F]

mo'ra, -*rra*, n. Italian game in which player guesses number of fingers held up simultaneously by another. [It. *mora*]

moraine', n. Debris carried down & deposited by glacier. [F]

mo'ral, a. & n. **1.** Concerned with character or disposition, or with the distinction between right & wrong; ~ *sense*, power of distinguishing right & wrong; (of literary work etc.) dealing with regulation of conduct, as ~ *science*; ~ *philosophy*, ethics; ~ *law*, the requirements to which right action must conform; (of rights .etc.) founded on ~ law; capable of ~ action; ~ *victory*, defeat, indecisive result, that eventually produces the ~ effects of victory; ~ *courage*, courage to encounter odium, contempt, etc., rather than abandon right course; ~*ly* good, conforming to rules of morality; virtuous as regards general conduct; ~ *certainty*, probability so great as to admit of no reasonable doubt. **2.** n. The ~ teaching of a fable, story, event, etc. (*draw the* ~, show what it is); ~ maxim or principle (*point a* ~, illustrate or apply it); (pl.)~ habits, esp. sexual conduct; =foll. Hence ~*LY*[2] adv. [ME, f. L *moralis* (*mos moris* custom, pl. *mores* morals, -AL)]

morale' (-ah-), n. Moral condition, esp. (of troops) as regards discipline & confidence. [f. F *moral* respelt to preserve pronunciation, cf. LOCAL(E), CHORAL(E)]

mo'ralism, n. Natural system of morality, religion reduced to moral practice. [-ISM]

mo'ral|ist, n. One who practises or teaches morality; man who is merely moral. Hence ~*is'TIC* a. [MORAL+-IST]

moral'ity, n. Moral science; (pl.) moral

principles, points of ethics; particular system of morals, as *commercial* ~; moral conduct (esp. good); moralizing; (hist.) kind of drama inculcating moral lesson, popular in 16th c. [ME, f. OF *moralite* or LL *moralitas* (MORAL, -TY)]

mŏ′ralīz|e, -is|e (-īz), v.i. & t. Indulge in moral reflection or talk (*on* subject); interpret morally, point the moral of; improve the morals of. So ~A′TION n. [f. F *moraliser* or med. L *moralizare* (as MORAL, see -IZE)]

morāss′, n. (literary). Bog, marsh. [f. Du. *moeras* f. MDu. *marasch* f. OF as MARISH]

mŏr′ăt, n. (hist.). Drink made of honey flavoured with mulberries. [f. med. L *moratum* (*morus* mulberry, see -ATE¹)]

mŏrātŏr′ium, n. (Period of) legal authorization to debtors to postpone payment. [neut. of LL *moratorius* (L *morari* delay, -TORY)]

Morăv′ian, a. & n. (Inhabitant) of Moravia; (one) of Protestant sect holding Hussite doctrines, founded in Saxony by ~ emigrants. [f. *Moravia*, now part of Czechoslovakia, -AN]

mŏrb′id, a. (Of mind, ideas, etc.) unwholesome, sickly; given to ~ feelings; (med.) of the nature, or indicative, of disease; ~ *anatomy* (of diseased organs etc.). Hence ~LY² adv., ~NESS n. [f. L *morbidus* f. *morbus* disease (*mori* die)]

mŏrbĭde′zza (-ětsa), n. (painting). Lifelike delicacy in flesh-tints. [It. (as prec.)]

mŏrbĭd′ĭtў, n. Morbidness; prevalence of disease (in a district). [-ITY]

mŏrbĭf′ĭc, a. Causing disease. [f. F *morbifique* (L *morbus* disease, see -FIC)]

mŏrceau′ (-ō), n. Short literary or musical composition. [F (as MORSEL)]

mŏrd′|ant, a. & n. 1. (Of sarcasm etc.) caustic, biting, so ~A′CIOUS (-āshŭs) a., ~A′CITY, ~ANCY, nn.; pungent, smarting. 2. (Of acids) corrosive or cleansing (n., such acid). 3. (Substance) serving to fix colouring-matter or gold-leaf. [F, part. of *mordre* bite f. L *mordēre*]

mŏrd′ent, n. (mus.). Grace consisting in rapid alternation of written note with one immediately below it. [G, f. It. *mordente* part. of *mordere* bite, as prec.]

mōre, a. & adv. 1. Existing in greater quantity, amount, or degree, as *there is* ~ *truth in it than you think, 10 is 2* ~ *than 8, bring some* ~ *water*; (abs.) greater quantity, as ~ *is meant than meets the ear, hope to see* ~ *of you; what is* ~ (~ important); ~ *than one person has* (not *have*) *found it so*. 2. adv. In greater degree, as *you must attend* ~ *to details,* ~ *in sorrow than in anger,* ~ *frightened than hurt*; (forming compar. of most adjj. of more than one syllable & most advv.) ~ *absurd(ly),* ~ *curious,* ~ *easily,* ~ *truly*; ~ *& ~*, in an increasing degree; ~ *or less*, in greater or less degree, or thereabouts; THE ~; *be no* ~, be dead; again, as *once, twice, never,*

~; *neither* ~ *nor less than* (simply, literally) *absurd* etc. [OE *māra*, OS, OHG *mēro*, ON *meire*, Goth. *maiza* f. Gmc **maizon-* f. *mais adv.]

moreen′, n. Stout woollen or woollen & cotton material for curtains etc. [perh. fanciful f. MOIRE]

morĕl′¹, n. Kinds of nightshade, esp. black nightshade. [ME, f. OF *morele*, fem. of adj. (-*el*) as n., f. med. L *maur-*, *morellus* f. *maurus* MOOR²]

morĕl′², n. An edible fungus. [f. F *morille*, f. Du. *morilje*; cf. OHG *morhila* (G *morchel*)]

morĕll′ō, n. Bitter kind of cherry. [f. It. *morello* (as MOREL¹)]

moreov′er (mŏrōv-), adv. Further, besides, (introducing new statement). [MORE+OVER]

morepork. See MOPOKE.

mōr′es (-ēz), n. pl. Customs or conventions regarded as essential or vital to a social group. [L]

Morĕsque′ (-k), a. Moorish in style or design. [F, f. It. *moresco* (*Moro* Moor, see -ESQUE)]

mŏrgănăt′|ĭc, a. ~*ic marriage*, one between man of exalted rank & woman of lower rank, who remains in her former station, the issue having no claim to succeed to possessions or title of father; ~*ic wife* (so married). Hence ~ICALLY adv. [f. med. L phr. *matrimonium ad morganaticam*, prob. f. *morganaticum* f. OHG *morgangeba morning gift from husband to wife the morning after consummation of marriage (the ~ic wife's only claim on husband's possessions)]

mŏrgue¹ (-g), n. Building (esp. one formerly in Paris) in which bodies of persons found dead are exposed for identification; (journalism) repository where miscellaneous material for reference is kept. [F, app. same wd as foll.]

mŏrgue² (-g), n. Haughty demeanour. esp. (~ *anglaise*, see Ap.) as English characteristic. [16th c., F, of unkn. orig.]

mŏ′rĭbŭnd, a. At the point of death (lit. & fig.). [f. L *moribundus* (*mori* die)]

mŏ′rion, n. (hist.). Helmet without beaver or visor. [F, f. Sp. *morrion* f. *morra* skull]

Moris′cō, a. & n. 1. Moorish. 2. n. Moor, esp. in Spain; morris dance. [Sp. (*Moro* MOOR²)]

Mŏrm′on, n. Member of religious body founded in 1830 by Joseph Smith in New York on basis of supposed Divine revelations in *Book of* ~ (imaginary author); (loosely) person who practises polygamy (once regarded as chief feature of the sect). Hence ~ISM r.

mŏrn, n. (poet.). Morning. [OE *morgen*, *myrgen*, *margen*, OS, OHG *morgan*, ON *myrginn*, *merginn*, Goth *maurgins* f. Gmc **murgan-*, **murgin-*, **margan-*]

mŏrn′ing, n. Early part of day-time, ending at noon, or at hour of midday

meal; *good* ~, form of salutation; (poet.) dawn; (attrib. of clothes) meant to be worn in the ~, as ~ *coat*, tail-coat with front sloped away; ~ *draught*, liquor taken before breakfast; ~ *gift* (see MOR-GANATIC, etym.); ~ *glory*, kind of convolvulus; ~ *performance*, matinée; ~ *prayer*, Anglican service of matins; ~ -*room*, sitting-room for the ~; ~ *star*, Venus (or other planet or bright star) seen in E. before sunrise; ~ *watch* (naut.), 4–8 A.M. [ME *mor(we)ning* f. *morwen* MORN +-ING], after *evening*]

morŏcc'ō, n. (pl.~s). Leather made (orig. in Morocco, now also in Europe) from goatskins tanned with sumac; *French* ~, inferior small-grained kind; *Levant* ~, high-grade large-grained kind. [f. It. *Marocco* f. name of chief city *Marrakesh*]

mŏr'on, n. Adult whose mental development is arrested at the stage normal in a child of 9–12 years; (pop.) degenerate brute, fool. Hence **moron'ic** a. [neut. of Gk *mōros* dull]

morŏse', a. Sullen, gloomy, & unsocial. Hence ~LY[2] adv., ~NESS n. [f. L *morosus* (*mos moris* manner, see -OSE[1])]

mŏrph'ēme, n. (philol.). A morphological element considered in respect of its functional relations in a linguistic system. [F (-*ème*), f. Gk *morphē* form]

Mŏrph'eus, n. God of dreams or sleep; *in the arms of* ~, asleep. [L]

mŏrph'ine, morph'ia, nn. Alkaloid narcotic principle of opium, largely used to alleviate pain. Hence **mŏrph'inism**(5) n. [f. G *morphin* (prec., -INE[5] (-IA[1]))]

mŏrphŏl'og|y̆, n. (Biol.) study of the form of animals & plants; (philol.) study of the form of words. Hence **mŏrpho-lō'gical** a., **mŏrpholō'gically**[2] adv., ~IST n. (biol.). [f. Gk *morphē* form +-LOGY]

mŏ'rris, a. & n. ~ (*dance*), grotesque dance by persons in fancy costume, usu. as characters in Robin Hood legend (medieval, & as modern revival); ~-*pike* (hist.), form of pike supposed to be of Moorish origin. [f. *morys*, var. of MOORISH]

mŏ'rris tūbe, n. Small-bore rifle barrel insertable in rifle for practice on miniature range. [R. *Morris* (d. 1891), inventor]

mŏ'rrow (-ō), n. (literary). *The* ~, the following day; (fig.) *on the* ~ *of* (time following on) *a long war* etc. [ME *morwe, moru*, shortened var. of *morwen* MORN]

mŏrse[1], n. Walrus. [f. Lapp *morsa*]

Mŏrse[2], n. & a. (Of) the recording telegraph invented by S. F. B. Morse (d. 1872), as ~ *alphabet, code* (in which letters are represented by variations on two signs, e.g. dot & dash, long & short flash, etc.).

mŏrse[3], n. Clasp, often jewelled etc., of cope. [ME, f. OF *mors* f. L *morsus* bite, catch]

mŏrs'el, n. Mouthful, small piece, (*of* food etc.); fragment. [ME, f. OF, dim. of *mors* a bite f. L *mordēre mors-* bite]

mŏrt[1], n. Note sounded on horn at death of deer, wild boar, etc. [16th c., alt. f. ME *mote* f. OF *mot* note of horn]

mŏrt[2], n. Salmon in third year. [orig. unkn.]

mŏrt[3], n. (dial.). A great amount or number of (*a* ~ *of*). [orig. unkn.]

mŏrt'al, a. & n. 1. Subject to death; causing death, fatal, (*to*, often fig.); (of battle) fought to the death; (of enemy) implacable; (of pain, fear, etc.) deadly; (of sin) entailing spiritual death, deadly; accompanying death, as ~ *agony*; (sl.) very great, as *in a* ~ *hurry*; (sl.) long & tedious, as *for two* ~ *hours*. 2. n. ~, esp. human, being; (joc.) person, as *a thirsty* ~. Hence ~LY[2] adv. [ME. f. OF *mortel*, or L *mortalis* (*mors -rtis* death, see -AL)]

mŏrtăl'it̆y, n. Mortal nature; loss of life on large scale; number of deaths in given period etc.; death-rate; BILL[4]s *of* ~; ~ *tables* (showing expectation of life at various ages etc.). [ME, f. OF *mortalite* f. L *mortalitatem* (as prec., see -TY)]

mŏrt'ar, n., & v.t. 1. Vessel of hard material, e.g. marble, in which ingredients are pounded with pestle. 2. Short piece of ordnance for throwing shells at high angles; contrivance for firing shells in pyrotechnic displays. 3. Mixture of lime, sand, & water, for joining stones or bricks. whence ~LESS, ~Y[2], aa.; ~-*board*, board for holding ~, (pop.) square college cap. 4. v.t. Plaster, join, with ~; attack, bombard, with ~s. [ME, f. OF *mortier* f. L *mortarium*]

mortgage[1] (môrg'ij), n. Conveyance of property by debtor (*mortgager*, -*or*) to creditor (*mortgagee*) as security for debt, with proviso that it shall be reconveyed on payment of debt within certain period; deed effecting this. [ME, f. OF, = dead pledge (*mort* f. L *mortuus* dead + GAGE[1])]

mortgage[2] (môrg'ij), v.t. Make over (property) by mortgage; pledge (one*self*, one's powers etc., *to* object etc.). Hence **mortgagEE'** (môrg-), **mortgagER**[1] (môrg-), **mortgagOR'** (môrgajôr'), nn. (see prec.). [f. obs. F *mor(t)gager*, or prec.]

**mŏrti'cian (-shn), n. Undertaker. [f. L *mors -rtis* death +-ICIAN]

mŏrt'i|fy̆, v.t. & i. Bring (body, passions, etc.) into subjection by self-denial or discipline; cause (person) to feel humiliated, wound (feelings), whence ~fyING[2] a.; (intr., of flesh) be affected by gangrene or necrosis. So ~FICA'TION n. [ME, f. OF *mortifier* f. LL *mortificare* (*mors -rtis* death, see -FY)]

mŏrt'ise, -ĭce, n., & v.t. 1. Hole in a framework designed to receive the end of some other part esp. a TENON; ~ *chisel* (with stout blade, for cutting ~s); ~ *lock* (recessed in frame cf door etc.). 2. v.t. Join (things *together*, one *to* or *into* another) securely, esp. by tenon & ~. [ME, f. OF *morteise*, f. Arab. *murtazz* fixed in]

mórt'main, n. (law). (Condition of) lands or tenements held inalienably by ecclesiastical or other corporation; (fig.) *in* ~, under posthumous control. [ME, f. OF *mortemain* f. med. L *mortua manus* dead hand, prob. in allusion to impersonal ownership]

mórt'ūarў, a. & n. **1.** Of death or burial. **2.** n. Building in which dead bodies are kept for a time. [ME, f. AF *mortuarie* f. L *mortuarius* (*mortuus* dead, see -ARY[1])]

mosā'ic[1] (-z-), a., n., & v.t. (~*king*, ~*ked*). **1.** (Form or work of art) in which pictures etc. are produced by joining together minute pieces of glass, stone, etc., of different colours (also fig. of any diversified whole); ~ *disease* in plants, esp. tobacco, maize, & sugar-cane); ~ *woolwork* (producing effect like that of ~); ~ *gold*, a disulphide of tin, also alloy of copper & zinc used in cheap jewellery etc. **2.** v.t. Adorn with ~s; combine (as) into ~. Hence ~IST(3) n. [f. F *mosaïque* f. It. *mosaico* f. med. L *mo-*, *musaicus* f. Gk *mouseion* mosaic work, f. *mousa* MUSE[1]]

Mosā'ic[2] (-z-), a. Of Moses, esp. ~ *Law* (in Pentateuch). [f. LL *Moses* +-IC]

mōsasaur'us (-ōr-), n. (pl. *-rī*). Large extinct marine reptile, first found near Maestricht on Meuse. [L *Mosa* Meuse + Gk *sauros* lizard]

mōschatěl' (-k-), n. Small plant with pale-green flowers & musky smell. [f. F *moscatelle* f. It. *moscatella* (*moscato* MUSK)]

mosělle' (-z-), n. Dry white wine produced near the river M~ in Germany.

Mǒs'lěm, Mǔs'lim, (or -z-), a. & n. (pl. *-ms*, *-min*). Mohammedan. Hence **Mǒs'lěmISM** n. [Arab. (*-im*), part. of *aslama*; see ISLAM]

mǒsque (-k), n. Mohammedan place of worship. [f. F *mosquée* f. It. *moschea* f. Arab. *masgid* (*sagada* vb worship)]

mosqui'tō (-kē-), n. (pl. ~*es*). Kinds of gnat, female of which punctures skins of animals with long proboscis & sucks their blood; ~*net*, *-curtain* (to keep off ~es); ~*craft*, small light vessels for rapid manoeuvring. [Sp. dim. of *mosca* f. L *musca* fly]

mǒss, n., & v.t. **1.** Wet spongy soil; peat-bog; kinds of small herbaceous cryptogamous plant, some growing in bogs, others on surface of ground, trees, stones etc., in crowded masses, whence ~'iNESS n., ~'Y[2] a.; *rolling stone gathers no* ~, one who constantly changes his place or employment will not grow rich. **2.** ~*bunker*, ◼ MENHADEN; ~*-grown*, overgrown with ~; ‖ ~*-hag*, broken ground from which peat has been taken; ~*-rose*, garden variety of cabbage rose, with ~*-like growth on calyx & stalk; ~*'trooper*, border freebooter of 17th c. **3.** v.t. Cover with ~. [OE (MDu., OHG) *mos* bog, (cf. ON *mosi*), f. Gmc **mos-*; cogn. w. OE *mēos*, OHG *mios* moss, ON *myrr* MIRE]

mōst, a. & adv. **1.** Existing in greatest quantity or degree, as *you have made* ~ *mistakes*, *see who can make* ~ *noise*, (abs., quasi-noun) *this is the* ~ *I can do*; *make the* ~ *of it*, employ it to the best advantage, (also) represent it at the best or worst; the majority, as ~ *people think so*, (quasi-n.) ~ *of them are broken*; *for the* ~ *part*, in the main, usually, whence ~'LY[2] adv. **2.** adv. In the highest degree, as *what* ~ *annoys me*, (forming superl. of most adjj. of more than one syllable & most advv.) ~ *ludicrous(ly)*, ~ *certain(ly)*, ~ *callous(ly)*; *ten at* ~, not more than ten; *this is at* ~ (is no more than) *a makeshift*. [OE *mǣst*, OS *mēst*, OHG *meist*, ON *mestr*, Goth. *maists* f. Gmc **maist-* (**mais* MORE, -EST)]

-most, suf. forming superl. adjj. formed not on adjj. but on prep. stems (*after*~, *fore*~, *in*~, *ut*~) & later on wds indicating position in place, time, or order, (*back*~, *top*~, *centre*~, & the compar. *upper*~, *utter*~, *further*~, etc.); also in *better*~; altered form of OE *-mest*, combining two superl. suff., *-mo-* & *-isto-* -EST, cf. L *optimus*, Gk *bellistos*; in late OE *-mest* was confused with MOST (see prec.), whence usu. mod. pronunc. (mōst) for the unstressed (most).

mot (mō), n. (pl. ~*s*, pr. mōz) Witty saying; BON MOT; ~ *juste* (see Ap.), the expression that conveys a desired shade of meaning with more precision than any other. [F, = word, f. Rom. **mottum* = L *muttum* (*muttire* murmur)]

mōte, n. Particle of dust; ~ *in* (another's) *eye*, trifling fault if compared to one's own (see *Matt.* vii. 3). [OE *mot*, corresp. to Du. *mot* dust, sawdust]

mōtěl', n. Hotel or group of furnished cabins by the roadside where motorists may stay for the night. [f. *motorists'* hotel]

motět', n. (mus.). Anthem (usu. unaccompanied) in R.C. or Lutheran Church; non-ecclesiastical work on similar lines. [ME, f. OF, dim. of MOT]

mǒth, n. (Also *clothes-*~) small nocturnal lepidopterous insect breeding in cloth etc., on which its larva feeds (~, *the* ~, collect., ~s), whence ~'Y[2] a.; insect of the order *Lepidoptera* excluding butterflies, apt to scorch itself by fluttering about light; (fig.) person hovering around temptation; ~*-ball* (of chemical preventive for keeping ~s from clothes), (also) airtight plastic cover sprayed on & enclosing working parts of gun-mountings, machinery, etc. of ship, (v.t.) enclose thus; ~*-eaten*, destroyed by ~s, (fig.) antiquated, time-worn. [OE *moththe*, corresp. to M Du., MLG, MHG, ON *motte*]

mo'ther[1] (mŭdh-), n. **1.** Female parent. **2.** Quality, condition, etc., that gives rise to another, as *necessity is the* ~ *of invention*. **3.** Head of female religious community (often M~ *Superior*). **4.** (Term of address for) elderly woman of lower class. **5.** (Also *artificial* ~) apparatus for rearing chickens. **6.** (Arch., f. obs. sense *womb*) hysteria. **7.** *M*~ *Carey's* CHICKEN; *M*~ *Church* (as of maternal authority); *M*~*Church* (whence others have sprung); ~ *country*, country in relation to its colonies; ~*craft*, skill in treatment of offspring; ~ *earth*, earth as ~ of its inhabitants etc., (joc.) the ground; *M*~ *Hubbard*, person in nursery rhyme, kind of cloak or overall; ~*in-law*, one's wife's or husband's ~; ~*land*, one's native land; ~ *lodge* (freemasonry), masonic lodge in which one was initiated; ~ *of pearl*, smooth shining iridescent substance forming inner layer of some shells (often attrib., w. hyphens); ~ *of thousands* or *millions*, ivy-leaved toadflax; || ~ *ship* (in charge of torpedo-boats, submarines, etc.); ~'s *son*, man, esp. *every* ~'s *son of* (*you* etc.); ~ *tongue*, one's native tongue, (also) tongue from which others spring; ~ *wit*, native wit, common sense. Hence ~HOOD n., ~LESS, ~LIKE, aa. [OE *mōdor*, OS *mōdar*, OHG *muotar*, ON *mōthir* f. Gmc *mōthar- cōgn. w. L *mater*]

mo'ther² (mŭdh-), v.t. Give birth to (usu. fig.); protect as a mother; acknowledge or profess oneself the mother of (child, lit. & fig.); ||~*ing Sunday*, 4th Sunday in Lent, with old custom of visiting parents with gifts. [f. prec.]

mo'ther³ (mŭdh-), n. (Also ~ *of vinegar*) mucilaginous substance produced in vinegar during fermentation by mould-fungus. Hence ~Y² a. [prob.=MOTHER¹; cf. MDu. *moeder*, G *mutter* in same sense]

mo'therl|ȳ (mŭdh-), a. Having, showing, the good qualities of a mother. Hence ~INESS n. [OE *mōdorlic* (MOTHER¹, -LY¹)]

mōtif' (-ēf), n. Constituent feature, dominant idea, in artistic composition; ornament of lace etc. sewn separately on dress. [F, as MOTIVE a.]

mōt'ile, a. (zool., bot.). Capable of motion. Hence **motil'ITY** n. [as MOVE, see -IL]

mō'tion¹, n. **1.** Moving, change of place; manner of moving the body in walking etc.; change of posture; gesture; *in* ~, moving, not at rest; *put in* ~, set going or working; ~ *picture*, cinematographic film. **2.** Formal proposal in deliberative assembly; (law) application by party etc. for rule or order of court. **3.** Evacuation of bowels. **4.** Piece of moving mechanism. Hence ~AL, ~LESS, aa., (-shon-). [ME, f. OF, f. L *motionem* (as MOVE, -ION)]

mō'tion², v.t. & i. Direct (person *to*, *towards*, *away*, etc., to do) by sign or gesture; make gesture (*to* person) directing him (*to* do). [f. prec.]

mōt'ive¹, a. & n. **1.** Tending to initiate movement, whence **mōtiv'ITY** n.; ~ *power*, moving or impelling power, esp. form of mechanical energy used to drive machinery, e.g. steam, electricity; con-

cerned with movement. **2.** n. What induces a person to act, e.g. desire, fear, circumstance, whence ~LESS a.; = MOTIF. [ME, f. OF *motif* f. LL *motivus* (MOVE, -IVE)]

mōt'ive², **mōt'ivāte**, vv.t. Supply a motive to, be the motive or motif of. Hence **mōtivā'TION** n. [f. prec. n.]

mōt'ley, a. & n. **1.** Diversified in colour; of varied character, as ~ *assembly*. **2.** n. Incongruous mixture; (hist.) fool's parti-coloured dress, esp. *wear* ~, play the fool. [ME; orig. obsc.; poss. f. AF *motelé, f. MOTE+-LE]

mōt'or, n., a., & v.i. & t. **1.** What imparts motion; machine supplying motive power for carriage or vessel, esp. internal-combustion engine, as (attrib.) ~ (*bi*)*cycle*, *cab*, (*omni*)*bus*, *boat*, *mower*, *ship*; || ~*-car*; ~, *bandit*, thief who uses a ~*-car* in his depredations; || ~*-car*, car propelled by ~ for use on ordinary roads, whence ~IST(3) n.; ~ *cycle*, bicycle etc. worked by ~ engine; ~*way*, arterial road specially made for fast-moving ~ traffic. **2.** (anat.). Muscle designed to move a part of the body; (nerve) designed to excite muscular activity, whence **motōr'IAL**, **mōt'ORY**, aa. **3.** vb. Go or convey in ~*-car*. [L (MOVE, -OR)]

***mōt'orcāde**, n. Procession or parade of motor-cars. [f. MOTOR(-*car*)+(CAVAL-)CADE]

mōt'orīz|e, -is|e (-īz), v.t. Equip (troops etc.) with motor transport. Hence ~A'TION n. [-IZE]

mōt'tle, n., & v.t. **1.** Arrangement of spots or confluent blotches of colour; such spot; variegated woollen yarn. **2.** v.t. Mark (esp. soap) with ~s (esp. in p.p.). [prob. f. MOTLEY]

mōtt'ō, n. (pl. ~*es*). Sentence inscribed on some object & expressing appropriate sentiment; word or sentence accompanying coat of arms or crest; maxim adopted as rule of conduct; verses etc. in paper cracker; quotation prefixed to book or chapter; (mus.) recurrent phrase having some symbolical significance. [It., as MOT]

moue (moō), n. POUT². [F; see MOW²]

mouff'lon (moō-), n. Wild mountain sheep of S. Europe. [f. F *mouflon* f. LL *mufronem*]

moujik, muzhik (moō'zhĭk), n. Russian peasant; lady's loose fur cape. [f. Russ. *muzhik* peasant]

mould¹ (mōld), n. Loose earth; upper soil of cultivated land; *man of* ~, mere mortal; ~*-board*, board in plough that turns over the furrow-slice. [OE *molde*, MDu. *moude*, OHG *molta*, ON *mold*, Goth. *mulda* f. Gmc *moldō* f. *mul-*, *mel-* (MEAL¹)]

mould² (mōld), n. Pattern, templet, used by masons, bricklayers, etc., as guide in shaping mouldings; hollow form into which molten metal etc. is cast to cool into required shape; metal or earthenware vessel used to give shape to puddings etc., pudding etc. so shaped; (fig.) *cast in heroic* etc. ~, of such character; form, shape, esp. of animal body; (archit.) group of mouldings; ~ *candle* (made in a ~); ~*loft*, room on floor of which plans of ship are drawn full size. [ME *mold(e)* app. f. OF *modle* f. MODULUS]

mould[3] (mōld), v.t. Produce (object) in certain shape, *out of* (elements), or *upon* (pattern), lit. & fig.; bring into certain shape; shape (bread) into loaves. [f. prec.]

mould[4] (mōld), n. Woolly or furry growth of minute fungi on things that lie for some time in moist warm air. [prob. f. obs *mould* a., p.p. of *moul* grow mouldy]

moul'der[1] (mōl-), n. One who moulds, esp. workman making moulds for casting. [-ER[1]]

moul'der[2] (mōl-), v.i. Decay to dust, rot *away*, (often fig.). [perh. MOULD[1] + -ER[5]; but cf. Norw. dial. *muldra* crumble]

moul'ding (mōl-), n. In vbl senses, esp. moulded object, esp. ornamental variety of outline in cornices etc. of building, woodwork, etc.; ~-*board* (on which dough is kneaded); *picture-*~ (for framing pictures). [MOULD[3] + -ING[1]]

moul'd|y[1] (mōl-), a. Overgrown with mould; (fig.) stale, out-of-date; (sl.) dull, tiresome, boring. Hence ~INESS n. [MOULD[4] + -Y[2]]

moul'dy[2] (mōl-), n. (nav. sl.). Torpedo.

moulin (mōōlǎn'), n. Nearly vertical shaft in glacier, formed by surface water falling through crack in ice. [F, lit. = mill]

moult (mōlt), v.t. & i., & n. 1. (Of birds) shed (feathers), shed feathers, in changing plumage (also fig.); (loosely, of animals) shed hair etc. 2. n. ~ing. [ME *moulten* f. OE **mūtian*, = OLG *-mūtōn*, OHG *mūzzōn*, WG f. L *mutare* change; *-l-* after *fault* &c.]

mound[1], n. Ball of gold etc. representing earth, surmounting crown etc., & used in heraldry. [ME, f. OF *monde* f. L *mundus* world]

mound[2], n., & v.t. Elevation of earth or stones, esp. of earth heaped on grave; hillock; ~-*builder*, one of prehistoric Indian race in N. America who erected ~s, (also) kinds of bird depositing eggs in a ~; (v.t.) enclose with, heap up in, ~s. [in 16th c. (1) hedge or fence: orig. unkn.; (2) embankment &c., perh. after MOUNT[1]]

mount[1], n. Mountain, hill, (abbr. *Mt,* preceding name, as *Mt Ephraim*); (palmistry) fleshy prominence on palm of hand. [OE *munt* f. L *mons -ntis*; in ME reinforced by OF *mont*]

mount[2], v.i. & t. 1. Ascend (hill etc. or abs.); proceed upwards; (of blood) rise into cheeks. 2. Rise to higher level of rank, power, intensity, etc.; (also ~ *up*) rise in amount. 3. Get *on* horse etc. for purpose of riding; get on (horse etc. or abs.); put (person) on horse etc.; furnish (person) with horse. 4. Raise (guns) into position on a fixed ~ING[3]; put (loom etc.) in working order; put (picture etc.) in a MOUNT[3]; fit (gems etc.) in gold etc.; fix (object) on microscope slide. 5. Put (play) on stage; display (article of costume). 6. ~ *an offensive* (mil.), act on, take, the offensive; ~ (go on duty as) *guard* (*over* thing or abs.). [ME, f. OF *munter* f. Rom. **montare* f. *mons* (prec.)]

mount[3], n. Margin surrounding picture, card on which drawing is mounted; ornamental metal parts of thing; horse for person's riding; chance of riding, esp. as jockey. [f. prec.]

moun'tain (-tǐn), n. Natural elevation of earth's surface, large or high & steep hill; *waves ran* ~s (very) *high,* ~*-high*; large heap or pile; (also ~ *wine*) Malaga wine from ~ grapes; *the M*~, extreme party in first French Revolution, occupying elevated position in chamber of assembly; ~ *ash,* tree with delicate pinnate leaves & scarlet berries, rowan; ~ *chain,* series of ~s; ~ *dew* (colloq.), Scotch whisky; ~ *sickness,* malady caused by rarefied ~ air; ~ *tobacco,* species of arnica. [ME, f. OF *montaigne* f. Rom. **montania,* = LL *montana* mountain (MOUNT[1], -AN)]

mountaineer' (-tǐn-), n. Dweller amongst mountains; one skilled in mountain climbing, whence ~ING[1] n. [-EER]

moun'tainous (-tǐn-), a. Abounding in mountains; huge. [ME, f. OF *montagnous* f. LL *montaniosus* MOUNTAIN, -OUS]

moun'tebank, n. Itinerant quack who held forth to audience from platform; charlatan. Hence ~ERY(4) n. [f. It. *montambanco* = *monta in banco* mount on bench]

mourn (môrn), v.i. & t. Feel sorrow or regret (*for, over,* dead person, lost thing, loss, misfortune, etc.); show conventional signs of grief for period after person's death; sorrow for (dead person, thing). [OE *murnan,* OS *mornon,* OHG *mornēn,* ON *morna,* Goth. *maurnan* be anxious]

mourn'er (môr-), n. One who mourns; esp. who attends funeral of friend or relation; person hired to attend funeral. [-ER[1]]

mourn'ful (môr-), a. Doleful, sad, sorrowful. Hence ~LY[2] adv., ~NESS n. [MOURN + -FUL]

mourn'ing (môr-), n. In vbl senses, also or esp.: (wearing of) black clothes as sign of ~; DEEP[1], HALF, ~; *complimentary* ~ (worn as tribute to unrelated dead); *in* ~, wearing such garments, (sl., of the eye) blacked in fighting etc., (sl., of finger-nails) dirty; ~-*coach* (attending funeral); ~-*paper,* notepaper with black edge; ~-*ring* (worn as memorial of deceased person). [-ING[1]]

mouse[1] (mows), n. (pl. *mice*). Animal of any of the smaller species of a genus of rodents, esp. *house*, *field-*, *harvest-*, ~; timid, shy, retiring person; weight & cord for passing sash-lines over pulleys etc.; (sl.) black eye; ~*-colour*, dark grey with yellow tinge; ~*-ear*, hawkweed & other plants; ~*'trap* (for catching mice; ~*trap cheese*, of poor quality). Hence mous'y² a. [OE *mūs* (= OS, OHG, ON *mús*), f. Gmc *mūs-* cogn. w. L *mus*]

mouse² (-z), v.i. & t. (Of cat or owl) hunt for or catch mice, whence mous'ER¹ (-z-) n.; search industriously, prowl *about* in search of something; (naut.) put some turns of spunyarn round (point & shank of a hook). [ME, f. prec.]

mousse (mōōs), n. Dish of flavoured cream whipped & frozen (*chestnut*, *chocolate*, etc., ~). [F, = froth]

mousseline (mōōslēn'), n. French muslin; ~*-de-laine*, dress material of wool & cotton; ~*-de-soie* (swah), thin silk fabric of muslin-like texture. [F, see MUSLIN]

moustache, *mus-, (mŭstahsh'), n. Hair on either side (usu. in pl.) or both sides of a man's upper lip; similar hair round mouths of some animals; ~*-cup* (with partial cover to protect~ when drinking). [F, f. It. *mostaccio* f. Gk *mustax -akos*]

Moustēr'ian (mōō-), a. (archaeol.). Of the palaeolithic epoch represented by remains found in the Moustier cave in France. [-IAN]

mouth¹ (mowth), n. (*pl. pr. -dhz*). **1.** External orifice in head, with cavity behind it containing apparatus of mastication & organs of vocal utterance; (sl.) impudent talk, cheek; (of horse, with reference to his readiness to feel & obey pressure of bit) *good*, *bad*, *hard*, ~; ~ *waters at* (food; referring to flow of saliva caused by anticipation); *useless* ~, one who does no work but must be fed; *this sounds strange in your* ~ (when said by you); *put words into his* ~, tell him what to say; *put* (speech) *into* person's ~, represent him as having made it; *take the words out of* person's ~, say what he was about to say; (of dog) *give* ~, bark, bay; *down in the* ~, dejected; *laugh on wrong side of* one's ~, show chagrin; *make a wry* ~, grimace in sign of disapproval etc. **2.** Opening of bag, sack, cave, furnace, etc.; outfall of river. **3.** ~*-filling*, bombastic, inflated; ~*-organ*, thin rectangular box containing metal reeds, each tuned to a note, moved before ~ to play tunes; ~*'piece*, part of pipe, musical instrument, etc., placed between lips, (also) one who speaks for another or others. Hence (~)~ED² (-dhd), ~'LESS, aa., ~'FUL n. [OE, OS *mūth*, *mund*, OHG *mund*, ON *munnr*, *muthr*, Goth *munths* f. Gmc *munthaz* cogn. w. L *mentum* chin]

mouth² (mowdh), v.t. & i. Utter (words or abs.) pompously or very distinctly, rant, declaim; take (food) in, touch with, the mouth; train mouth of (horse); grimace. [f. prec.]

mouth'y (-dhǐ), a. Railing, ranting; bombastic. [MOUTH¹ + -Y²]

mo'vable (mōō-), a. & n. **1.** That can be moved; (of property) that can be removed, personal as opp. to *real*; ~ *feast*, one that varies its date, (joc.) meal taken at no regular time. **2.** n. Article of furniture that may be removed from the house, opp. to *fixture*; (pl.) personal property. Hence movaBIL'ITY, ~NESS, nn. (mōō-). [ME, f. OF (as MOVE², see -ABLE)]

move¹ (mōōv), n. Moving of a piece in chess & other games; player's turn to do this; change of residence, business premises, etc.; device, step taken to secure object; *on the* ~, moving about; *make a* ~, go, esp. rise & go from dinner-table etc.; *get a* ~ *on* (sl.), hurry up, bestir oneself. [f. foll.]

move² (mōōv), v.t. & i. **1.** Change position of; change position of (piece) in chess etc.; put, keep, in motion, shake, stir; ~ *heaven & earth*, make every effort (*to* do); change posture of (one's body, limbs, etc.). **2.** Cause (bowels) to act. **3.** Provoke (laughter, anger, etc., *in* person, person *to* these); affect (person) with (usu. tender or sympathetic) emotion, whence mo'VING² a., mo'vingLY² adv., (mōō-). **4.** Prompt, incline, (person *to* action, *to* do); *the spirit* (orig. in Quaker use, = Holy Spirit) ~s *me*, I feel inclined (*to* do). **5.** Make formal application to court etc. *for*; propose (question, resolution, *that* thing be done) in deliberative assembly. **6.** Go, pass, (*about*, *away*, etc.) from place to place; make progress, as *the work* ~s *slowly*; make a move at chess etc. **7.** Change one's abode; ~ *about*, do this often; ~ *in*, take possession of new abode. **8.** ~ *on* (policeman's order to person who stands too long in one place), (trans.) cause person to ~ on by giving this order. **9.** (Of person or part of body) change posture; (of inanimate things) suffer change of position; *moving staircase*, one made on principle of endless chain, with steps moving up or down continuously, escalator. **10.** (Of bowels) be ~d. **11.** Make request or application (*for*); take action, proceed, (*in* matter). Hence ~'LESS a. (rare). [ME, f. AF *mover*, OF *movoir* f. L *movēre mot-*]

move'ment (mōōvm-), n. Moving; military evolution; moving parts of mechanism (esp. of clock or watch), particular group of these; mental impulse; development of poem, story, etc.; (mus.) principal division of a musical work (e.g. suite, sonata, symphony), having a distinctive structure of its own; series of actions & endeavours of a body of persons for special object, as *the* OXFORD ~, *the Labour* ~; activity in market for some commodity. [ME, f. OF f. med. L *movimentum* (as prec., see -MENT)]

mo'ver (mōō-), n. In vbl senses, esp.: one who moves proposal; *prime* ~, initial source (natural or mechanical) of motive power, (also) author of fruitful idea. [-ER¹]

mo′vies (mōōvĭz), n. pl. (sl.). Cinema pictures. [= *moving pictures*]

mow¹ (mō), n. Stack of hay, corn, peas, etc.; place in barn where hay etc. is heaped; ~*burnt*, spoilt by becoming overheated in the ~. [OE *mūga*, = ON *mûgi* swath, crowd]

mow² (mō, mow), n., & v.i. See MOP³. [ME, f. OF *moue* mouth, lip, pout, or f. MDu. *mouwe*, in same sense]

mow³ (mō), v.t. (~*ed* pr. mōd, ~n). Cut down (grass etc. or abs.) with scythe or machine; cut down produce of (field) thus; destroy sweepingly, cut *off* or *down* in great numbers. Hence ~′ER¹(1, 2) (mō′er) n. [OE *māwan*, OHG *māen*, f. Gmc **mǣ-* as in MEADOW]

mox′a, n. Down from dried leaves of a plant, used for burning on skin as counter-irritant for gout; anything so used. [f. Jap. *mokusa* (*moe kusa* burning herb)]

moy′a, n. Volcanic mud. [S.-Amer. Sp.]

Mŏză′rab, n. (hist.). Christian owning allegiance to Moorish king but allowed his own religion. Hence ~IC a. [f. Sp. *Mozárabe* f. Arab. *musta′rib* would-be Arab (*′arab*)]

Mprĕt, n. Albanian ruler. [f. L *imperator* emperor]

Mr (mĭs′ter). See MISTER.

Mrs (mĭs′ĭz), n. Title prefixed to surname of married woman who has no superior title; *Mrs Grundy* (see GRUNDYISM). [abbr. of MISTRESS]

mū, n. Greek letter M (*M, μ*). [Gk]

much, a. & adv. **1.** Existing in great quantity, as ~ *trouble, too* ~ *noise, not* ~ *rain*, (abs., quasi-n.) *I have stood* ~, ~ *of what you say is true; too* ~ (more than a match) *for*; THINK, MAKE, ~ *of; he is not* ~ *of a* (not a good) *scholar; how* ~ (what price) *is it? how* ~ (what amount) *do I owe you?* **2.** adv. In a great degree (qualifying vb or p.p., cf. VERY), as *I* ~ *regret the mistake, was* ~ *annoyed*; (qualifying compar. or superl. adj.) ~ *better,* ~ *the most likely*; pretty nearly, as ~ *of a size*, about the same size. Hence ~′LY² adv. (joc.). [ME, f. *muchel* MICKLE]

much′ness, n. Greatness in quantity or degree; *much of a* ~, very nearly the same or alike. [prec. + -NESS]

mū′cilage, n. Viscous substance from various plants; gum; viscous fluid in animal bodies, e.g. mucus. So **mūcilā′ginous** a. [F, f. LL *mucilago* -*ginis* (MUCUS)]

mŭck¹, n. Farmyard manure; dirt; (colloq.) anything disgusting; (colloq.) untidy state; ~′*rake* (for collecting ~, usu. fig.); ~′*worm*, worm that lives in ~, (fig.) money-grubber, street arab. Hence ~Y² a. [ME *muk* f. ON *myki* dung]

mŭck², v.t. & i. Make dirty; remove muck from; manure with muck; (sl.)

bungle (job); (sl.) go aimlessly *about*. [ME, f. prec.; cf. ON *moka* shovel dung]

‖ **mŭck′er**, n. (sl.). Heavy fall (lit. & fig.); *come a* ~, experience this; *go a* ~, plunge into extravagance (*on, over*, purchase). [-ER¹]

mŭc′kle. See MICKLE.

mū′cous, a. Of, covered with, mucus, as ~ *membrane*, internal prolongation of the skin so covered. So **mūcŏs′ITY** n. [f. L *mucosus* (as MUCUS, see -OUS)]

mū′crō, n. (bot., zool.; pl. ~*nes* pr. -ōn′ēz). Pointed part or organ. Hence **mū′cronATE²**(2) a. [L, = point]

mū′cus, n. Slimy substance secreted by mucous membrane; gummy substance found in all plants; slimy substance exuded by some animals, esp. fishes. [L, cogn. w. *emungere* blow the nose]

mŭd, n. Wet soft earthy matter, mire; (fig.) what is worthless or polluting (*his name is* ~); *fling, throw,* ~, make disgraceful imputations; *here′s* ~ *in your eye!*, sl. drinking toast; STICK *in the* ~; ~′*bath* (in ~ of mineral springs, for rheumatism etc.); ~′*guard*, (metal) hood covering wheel of cycle etc. to protect rider from ~; ~′*lark*, one who dabbles, works, or lives, in ~, esp. street arab; ~ *pie,* ~ shaped like pie by child; ~ *volcano* (discharging ~). [ME *mode, mudde*, f. MLG *mudde*; cf. MHG *mot* bog]

mudâr′, ma-, n. E.-Ind. shrub, of which root-bark is used in medicine & inner bark yields silky fibre (yercum). [Hind. (*ma-*)]

mŭd′dle¹, n. Disorder; *make a* ~ *of,* bungle; ~-*headed*(*ness*), stupid(ity). [f. foll.]

mŭd′dle², v.t. & i. Bewilder, esp. with drink; mix (things *up, together*) blunderingly; bungle (affair); busy oneself in confused & ineffective way; ~ *on,* get on in haphazard way; ~ *through,* attain one's end by tenacity not skill. [f. MUD + -LE(3); cf. MDu. *moddelen*, f. *modden* dabble in mud]

mŭdd′l̮y, a., & v.t. **1.** Like, abounding in, covered with, mud; (of liquid) turbid; (of light) dull; (of voice) thick; mentally confused; obscure. **2.** v.t. Make ~y. Hence ~ILY² adv., ~INESS n. [(vb f. adj.) f. MUD + -Y²]

mudir (mōōdēr′), n. Governor of Turkish village or of Egyptian province. [Turk. f. Arab., part. of *adara* govern]

muĕzz′in (mōō-), n. Mohammedan crier who proclaims hours of prayer usu. from minaret. [f. Arab. *mu′adhdhin* (*adhana* proclaim)]

mŭff¹, n. Woman's fur or other covering (usu. cylindrical) into which both hands are thrust from opposite ends to keep them warm; *foot*-~, contrivance serving same purpose for feet. [f. Du. *mof*, MDu. *moffel*, f. F *moufle*, as MUFFLE²]

mŭff², n., & v.t. **1.** Person who is awkward or stupid, orig. in some athletic sport;

failure, esp. to catch ball at cricket etc. 2. v.t. Bungle, miss (catch, ball, etc.). Hence ~ISH¹ a. [orig. unkn.]

‖ **müffétee'**, n. Worsted cuff worn on wrist. [app. irreg. f. MUFF¹]

müff'în, n. ‖ Light flat round spongy cake, eaten toasted & buttered; ‖ ~-*bell* (rung by ~-*man*, seller of ~s). [orig. unkn.; cf. OF *mouflet* soft (bread)]

müffineer', n. Small castor for sprinkling salt or sugar on muffins. [-EER]

müf'fle¹, n. Thick part of upper lip & nose of ruminants & rodents. [f. F *mufle*, of unkn. orig.]

müf'fle², n. 1. Leather glove for lunatics who tear clothes etc.; mitten. 2. Receptacle placed within furnace, in which substances may be heated without contact with products of combustion; chamber in kiln for baking pottery. [f. F *moufle* mitten f. med. L *muffula*; cf. MDu. *moffel* MUFF]

müf'fle³, v.t. Wrap, cover *up*, (oneself, one's throat etc., or abs.) for warmth; wrap up head of (person) to prevent his speaking; wrap up (oars, bell, drum, horse's hoofs) to deaden sound; repress, deaden, sound of (curse etc., usu. in p.p.). [ME, perh. f. OF *enmoufler* f. *moufle* MUFFLE²]

müff'ler, n. Wrap, scarf, worn for warmth; boxing-glove; thick glove; thing used to deaden sound, esp. felt pad between hammer & string of piano. [f. prec. + -ER¹]

müf'ti, n. 1. Mohammedan priest or expounder of law. 2. ‖ Plain clothes worn by one who has right to wear uniform, esp. *in* ~. [Arab., part. of *afta* decide point of law]

müg¹, n. Drinking-vessel, usu. cylindrical, with or without handle; its contents; a cooling drink; [perh. diff. wd] (sl.) face, mouth. [perh. of Scand. orig.; cf. Norw. *mugga*, *mugge*, Sw. *mugg*, LG *mukke*]

‖ **müg²**, n. (sl.). Simpleton, muff.

‖ **müg³**, v.i. & t. (-gg-), & n. (sl.). 1. Study hard (*at* subject or abs.); (also ~ *up*) get up (subject). 2. n. One who studies hard; examination. [orig. unkn.]

mügg'er (-g-), n. Broad-nosed Indian crocodile. [f. Hind. *magar*]

mügg'ins (-g-), n. Simpleton; children's game of cards; game of dominoes. [perh. the surname *M*~, w. allusion to MUG²]

Müggletŏn'ian (-gel-), a. & n. (Member) of sect founded by, & believing in personal inspiration of, L. Muggleton & John Reeve, c. 1650. [-IAN]

mügg'ly (-g-), a. (Of weather, day, etc.) damp & warm. Hence ~iNESS n. [f. dial. *mug* drizzle, cf. ON *mugga*, + -Y²]

***müg'wümp**, n. Great man, boss; one who holds aloof from party politics; one who sits on the fence. [f. native *mugquomp* great chief]

Muhammadan. See MOHAMMEDAN.

mülätt'ō, n. (pl. ~s), & a. 1. Offspring of

European & Negro. 2. adj. Of ~ colour, tawny. [f. Sp. *mulato* young mule, mulatto, irreg. f. *mulo* MULE¹]

mül'berry, n. 1. Kinds of tree, leaves of which are much used for feeding silkworms: its fruit; ~ *bush*, children's game with ditty *Here we go round the* ~ *bush*. 2. (*M*~) code name of prefabricated harbour used in the invasion on D-DAY and subsequently. [ME *mol-*, *mool-*, *mulberry*, by dissim. f. OE *mōr*, ME *moor*, f. L *morum* mulberry; thus MHG *mūlber* (G *maulbeere*) f. OHG *mūrberi*]

mülch, n., & v.t. 1. Mixture of wet straw, leaves, etc., spread to protect roots of newly planted trees etc. 2. v.t. Treat with ~. [prob. subst. use of ME *molsh* soft; cf. dial. *melsh*, *melch* (= OE *melsc*)]

mülct, n., & v.t. 1. Fine imposed for offence. 2. v.t. Punish (person) by fine (*in* amount, or with amount as second object), deprive (person etc. *of*). [f. obs. F *mul(c)te*, *mul(c)ter*, or L *mul(c)ta*, *mul(c)tare*]

müle¹, n. 1. Offspring of he-ass & mare, or (pop.) of she-ass & stallion (prop. *hinny*), used as beast of draught & burden & noted for obstinacy; stupid or obstinate person; hybrid plant or animal; ~ *canary*, cross between canary & other finch. 2. Kind of spinning-machine. Hence **mül'ısh¹** a., **mül'ishLY²** adv., **mül'ishNESS** n. [ME, f. OF *mul(e)*, f. L *mulus*, *-la*; OE *mūl* f. L]

müle², v.i. = MEWL.

müle³, n. Heelless slipper. [F]

müléteer', n. Mule-driver. [f. F *muletier* (*mulet* dim. of OF *mul* mule, see -EER)]

mülĭěb'rity, n. Womanhood; the normal characteristics of a woman (opp. VIRILITY); softness, effeminacy. [f. LL *muliebritas* (*mulier* woman)]

müll¹, n. Thin variety of plain muslin. [shortened f. *mulmull* f. Hind. *malmal*]

‖ **müll²**, n. & v.t. 1. Muddle, mess, esp. *make a* ~ *of*. 2. v.t. Make a ~ of (catch etc.); ponder *over*. [n. perh. f. ME *mul* dust, ashes, f. MDu. *mol*, *mul* (MULLOCK)]

müll³, v.t. Make (wine, beer) into a hot drink with sugar, spices, yolk of egg, etc. [orig. unkn.]

‖ **müll⁴**, n. (Sc.). Promontory (*M*~ *of Kintyre*). [Icelandic *múli*]

‖ **müll⁵**, n. (Sc.). Snuffbox. [var. of MILL¹, box orig. having a grinder]

müll'ah, **mooll'ah**, n. Mohammedan learned in theology & sacred law. [f. Pers., Turk., Hind., *mulla* f. Arab. *maula*]

müll'ein (-lin), n. Kinds of herbaceous plant with woolly leaves & yellow flowers. [ME, f. AF *moleine*, f. Gaulish *melena]

müll'er, n. Tool used for grinding powders etc. on slab. [ME *mol-*, *mulour* f. *mul* grind (MULL² v.) + -ER; cf. MULLOCK]

müll'ět, n. Two genera of fishes of which *red* & *grey* ~ are the types. [ME, f. OF *mulet* dim. f. L *mullus* red ~]

mŭl̄ligatawn′y̆, n. (Also ~ *soup*) E.-Ind. highly seasoned soup; ~ *paste*, curry paste used for this. [f. Tamil *milagu-tannir* pepper-water]

mŭll′ĭgrŭbs (-z), n. pſ. Depression of spirits; stomach-ache. [arbitrary]

mŭll′ion (-yon), n. Vertical bar dividing lights in window. Hence ~ED² (-yond) a. [prob. metathetic f. MONIAL]

mŭll′ock, n. .(Austral.) rock containing no gold, also, refuse from which gold has been extracted; (dial.) rubbish. [f. dial. *mull* dust, rubbish, rel. to OE *myl* dust, MDu. *mul, mol* f. Gmc root *mul- grind, +-OCK]

mŭltăng′ūlar (-ngg-), a. Many-angled. [f. MULTI-+ANGULAR]

mŭlte′it̆y̆, n. Manifoldness. [f. L *multus* many; cf. *variety*]

mŭl′ti-, comb. form (bef. vowel occas. *mult-*) of L *multus* many, as : ~*colour*(ed), of many colours; ~*fid* (bot., zool.), cleft into many parts; ~*flor′ous*, (of stalk) bearing more than three flowers; ~*foil* (archit.), ornament consisting of more than 5 foils; ~*form*, having many forms, of many kinds, so ~*form′ity* n.; ~*lăt′eral*, having many sides, (of an agreement, treaty, etc.) in which three or more parties participate; ~*ling′ual* (-nggw-), in many languages; ~*millionaire′* (-yon-), person with fortune of several millions; ~*nŏm′ial* a. & n. (alg.), (expression) of more than two terms; *mullip′arous*, bringing forth many young at a birth, (of woman) who has borne more than one child; ~*părt′ite*, divided into many parts;~*ra′cial*,(composed)of many races; ~*valve* a. & n., (shell, animal with shell) of many valves; *multiv′ocal* a. & n., (word) susceptible of many meanings; *multŏc′ular*, having many eyes; *multăng′ūlate* a. & n., (animal) with more than two functional hoofs.

mŭltifăr′ious, a. Having great variety; (w. pl. n.) many & various. Hence ~LY² adv.,~NESS n. [f. L MULTI(*farius* f. *-fariam* adv.)+-OUS]

mŭl′tiple, a. & n. 1. Of many parts, elements, or individual components (~ *shop*, with branches in various places); (w. pl. n.) many & various;~ PERSONALITY, 2. n. Quantity that contains another some number of times without remainder, as *14 is a ~ of 7* ; *least common ~*, (abbr. L.C.M.) least quantity that contains two or more given quantities exactly; ~ *shop* or store. [F, f. LL *multiplus* = foll.]

mŭl′tiplĕx, a. Manifold, of many elements. [L (MULTI- +-*plex* -*plicis* -fold)]

mŭl′tiplicable, a. Multipliable. [f. L *multiplicabilis* (as MULTIPLY, see -ABLE)]

mŭltiplic′ănd, n. Quantity to be multiplied, cf. MULTIPLIER. [f. L as MULTIPLY]

mŭltiplicā′tion, n. Multiplying, esp. the arithmetical process (*symbol of* ~, ×, as in 2 × 3); ~ *table*, table of products of factors taken in pairs. So mŭl′tiplica-

tive a. [ME, f. OF, or f. L *multiplicatio* (as MULTIPLY, see -ATION)]

mŭltipli′cit̆y̆, n. Manifold variety; *a, the,* ~ (great number) *of*. [f. F (-*ité*), or LL *multiplicitas* (as MULTIPLEX, see -TY)]

mŭl′tiplier, n. In vbl senses, esp. : quantity by which MULTIPLICAND is multiplied; (econ.) factor by which an increment of income exceeds the resulting increment of saving or investment; (electr., magn.) instrument for multiplying intensity of force, current, etc., so as to make it appreciable. [f. null.+-ER¹]

mŭl′tipl̄y̆, v.t. & i. Produce large number of (instances etc.); breed (animals), propagate (plants); (intr.) increase in number by procreation; (math.) substitute for (given number, the ~*icand*) a number (the *product*) equal to a given number (the ~*ier*) of times its value, as ~*y 6 by 4 & the product is 24*, or *6* ~ *ied by 4 is 24*. Hence ~IABLE a. [ME, f. OF *multiplier* f. L *multiplicare* (MULTIPLEX)]

mŭl′ti|tūde, n. Numerousness; great number (*of*); large gathering of people, crowd; *the ~tude*, the common people. Hence ~tūd′inous a., ~tūd′inously² adv.,~tūd′inousNESS n. [ME, f. OF, or L *multitudo* -*dinis* (*multus* many, see -TUDE)]

mŭltitūd′in|ĭsm, n. Principle that prefers interests of multitudes to those of individuals. So ~IST n. [as prec. +-ISM]

mŭl′tum ĭn părv′ō, n. Much in small compass; (attrib., w. hyphens) small but comprehensive. [L]

‖ **mŭl′ture**, n. Toll of grain or flour paid to miller. [ME, f. OF *molture* f. med. L *molitura* (*molere* -*it*- grind, see -URE)]

mŭm¹, int. & a. 1. Silence!, esp. ~'s *the word*. 2. adj. Silent. [ME *mom*(*me*) n. & v., imit.; cf. MLG *mummen*, Du. *mommen*]

mŭm², v.i. (-mm-). Act in dumb show. [16th c., f. OF *momer* f. *momon* mask]

mŭm³, n. (hist.). Kind of beer orig. brewed in Brunswick. [f. G *mumme*]

‖ **mŭm⁴**, n. (nursery). = MUMMY².

mŭm′ble, v.i. & t., & n. 1. Speak indistinctly; utter indistinctly; bite, chew, (as) with toothless gums. 2. n. Indistinct utterance. [ME *momele*, as MUM¹, -LE(3); cf. MDu. *mom-, mummelen*]

Mŭm′bō Jŭm′bō, n. (pl. ~s). Grotesque idol said to have been worshipped by some tribes; (fig.) object of senseless veneration: meaningless ritual. [orig. unkn.]

mŭmm′er, n. Play-actor; actor in folk--play. [ME, f. OF *momeur* (*momer* MUM²)]

mŭmm′er̆y̆, n. Performance of mummers; ridiculous (esp. religious) ceremonial. [f. OF *momerie* (as prec., see -ERY), whence Du. *mommerij*, G *mummerei*]

mŭmm′i|f̄y̆, v.t. Preserve (body) by embalming & drying; shrivel, dry up,

(tissues etc., esp. in p.p.). Hence ~FICA²-
TION n. [f. F momifier (as foll., see -FY)]

mŭmm′y¹, n. 1. Body of human being or
animal embalmed for burial; dried-up
body. 2. Pulpy substance or mass, esp.
beat (thing) *to a* ~. 3. Rich brown pigment. [f. F *momie* f. med. L *mumia* f.
Arab. *mumiya* (*mum* wax)]

‖ **mŭmm′y²**, n. Mother. [nursery form of
MAMMA¹]

mŭmp¹, v.i. Be silent & sullen; assume
demure expression, whence ~ING² a.
[17th c.; also 16th c. as n.= grimace,
‘ mouth ’; imit.]

mŭmp², v.i. Beg, go about begging.
[17th c., f. Du. *mompen* cheat]

mŭmps, n. pl. (treated as sing.). Contagious disease with swelling of parotid
& salivary glands; sulks, whence **mŭm′-
PISH¹** a. [16th c., f. MUMP¹]

mŭnch, v.t. & i. Eat (food, or abs.) with
much action of jaws, as cattle chew
fodder. [ME, imit.; cf. *crunch*]

Munchaus′en (-zn), n. *Baron* ~, hero of
extravagant book of adventures written
in English by R. E. Raspe, a German
(1785); extravagantly mendacious story.

mŭn′dāne, a. Of this world; of the universe. Hence ~LY² adv., ~NESS n. [ME,
f. OF *mondain* f. L *mundanus* f. *mundus*
world, see -AN]

mŭng′ō (-ngg-), n. Substance used in
making cloth of poorer quality than
SHODDY. [poss. f. dial. *mong* mixture; cf.
stingo]

Mün′ich (-ĭk), n. An act of appeasement
between nations. [f. the agreement to
dismember Czechoslovakia made with
Hitler in 1938 at ~ in S. Germany]

mŭni′cipal, a. Of, under, local self-
-government or corporate government of
city or town, whence ~ISM(2), ~IST(2, 3),
nn., ~IZE(3) v.t.; carried on etc. by a
municipality (~ *debt, kitchen, trading,
undertaking*); ~ *law*, that of particular
State, opp. to law of nations. Hence
~LY² adv. [f. L *municipalis* f. *municeps
-cipis* citizen of city that had privileges of
Roman citizens (*munia* civic offices +
root of *capere* take), see -AL]

mŭnicipăl′ity, n. Town, district, having
local self-government; governing body of
this. [f. F *municipalité* (as prec., see
-TY)]

mŭnif′ic|ent, a. Splendidly generous,
bountiful. Hence or cogn. ~ENCE n.,
~entLY² adv. [f. L *munificent-*, var. stem
of *munificus* (*munus* gift, see -FIC)]

mŭn′iment, n. (usu. pl.). Document kept
as evidence of rights or privileges; archives (esp. in ~-*room*) [ME, f. OF, f. L
munimentum defence (*munire* fortify,
-MENT)]

mŭni′tion, n., & v.t. 1. (Pl. exc. in comb.)
military weapons, ammunition, equipment, & stores (*Ministry* etc. *of* ~s; ~-
-*factory*) (arch.) ~, or ~s, *of war*; hence
~ER¹ (-sho-) n. (esp. worker in ~-factory).

2. v.t. Supply with ~s. [F, f. L *munitio-
nem* fortification (as prec., see -ION)]

munnion. = MULLION.

munshi. See MOONSHEE.

mŭnt′jak, n. Small Asian deer. [f. native
minchek]

Mŭntz, n. (Also ~ *metal*), alloy (60% copper, 40% zinc) used for sheathing ships
etc. [G. F. ~, inventor]

mŭr′age, n. (hist.). Tax levied for build-
ing or repairing walls of town. [ME, f.
OF, in med. L *muragium* (*murus* wall, see
-AGE)]

mŭr′al, a. & n. 1. Of, like, on, a wall, as ~
paintings; (Rom. ant.) ~ *crown*, garland
(given to soldiers who first scaled wall of
besieged town). 2. n. ~ painting etc. [f.
F, or L *muralis* (*murus* wall, see -AL)]

Mŭratŏr′ian, a. Of Muratori, Italian
scholar, d. 1750; ~ *fragment* or *canon*,
earliest Western canon of N.T. [-AN]

mŭrd′er¹, n. Unlawful killing of human
being with malice aforethought (freq.
wilful ~); JUDICIAL ~; (prov.) ~ *will out*
(cannot be hidden); *the* ~ *is out*, the secret
is revealed or mystery explained; (as int.
of alarm) ~!; *cry blue* ~, make extravagant outcry. [OE *morthor*, Goth *maurthr*
f. Gmc *murthram*, cogn. w. L *mori* die]

mŭrd′er², v.t. Kill (human being) unlawfully with malice aforethought; kill
wickedly or inhumanly; spoil by bad
execution, mispronunciation, etc. Hence
~ER¹, ~ESS¹, nn. [OE *myrthrian*, OHG
murdran, Goth. *maurthrjan* (prec.)]

mŭrd′erous, a. (Of person, weapon,
action, etc.) capable of, bent on, involving, murder. Hence ~LY² adv. [-OUS]

mŭre, v.t. Confine as in prison; shut *up*.
[ME, f. OF *murer* f. LL *murare*, see IM-
MURE]

mŭr′ĕx, n. (pl. *-icēs*, *-exes*). Shellfish
yielding purple dye. [L]

mŭr′iate, n. (now commerc.). Chloride.
[F, f. *muriatique*, as foll.]

mūriăt′ic, a. (now commerc.). ~ (hydrochloric) *acid*. [f. L *muriaticus* (*muria*
brine, see -ATIC)]

mŭrk, mĭrk, a. (Of night, day, place,
etc.) dark; misty, dense. [OE *mirce*, OS
mirki, ON *myrkr* f. Gmc **merkw-*]

mŭrk′|y̆, a. Dark, gloomy; (of darkness)
thick. Hence ~ĭLY² adv., ~ĭNESS n. [f.
murk n. darkness, rel. to prec., + -Y²]

mŭrm′ur¹ (-er), n. Subdued continuous
sound, as of waves, brook, etc.; subdued
expression of discontent; softly spoken
word or speech. Hence ~OUS a., ~OUSLY²
adv. [ME, f. OF *murmure* or L *murmur*]

mŭrm′ur² (-er), v.i. & t. Make low continuous sound; complain in low tones,
grumble, (*at, against*) utter (words) in low
voice. [ME, f. OF *murmurer* f. L *mur-
murare* (*murmur*)]

mŭrph′y̆, n. (sl.). Potato. [Irish sur-
name]

mŭ′rrain (-rĭn), n. Infectious disease in
.cattle; (arch.) *a* ~ (plague) *on you!* [ME,

f. OF *morine* f. Rom. ***morire** f. L *mori* die]

mŭ'rrey, a. & n. (arch.). (Ot) the colour of a mulberry, purple-red. [ME, f. OF *more* f. med. L *moratum* (*morum* mulberry)]

mŭ'rrhine (-rĭn, -rīn), a. ~ *glass*, modern delicate ware from the East, made of fluor-spar. [f. L *murr(h)inus* (*murra*, substance of which precious vases etc. were made, see -INE[1])]

mŭs'cadine, n. Musk-flavoured kinds of grape. [prob. Engl. form. as MUSCAT]

mŭs'cardine, n. Disease of silkworms caused by vegetable parasite. [F]

mŭs'cāt, mŭscatěl', -děl', nn. Muscadine ; strong sweet wine from muscadines; (-*tel*) raisin from muscadine. [(-*at*) F, f. Pr. *muscat* adj. f. LL *muscatus* (MUSK, -ATE); (-*tel, -del*) OF dim.]

mŭ'scle (-sl), n., & v.i. 1. Any of the contractile fibrous bands or bundles that produce movement in animal body; *not move a* ~, be perfectly motionless; that part of the animal body which is composed of ~s, the chief constituent of flesh ; ~-*bound*, with ~s stiff & inelastic through over-exercise or over-training; hence ~LESS a. 2. v.i. *(sl.). ~ *in*, intrude by violent means (as of one racketeer poaching on another's preserves). [f. F, or L *musculus* dim. of *mus* mouse]

mŭsc|öl'ogў, n. Study of mosses. So ~öL'OGIST n. [f. L *muscus* moss, -LOGY]

mŭscova'dŏ (-vah-), n. Unrefined sugar got from juice of sugar-cane by evaporation & draining off molasses. [f. Sp. *mascabado* (sugar) of lowest quality]

mŭs'covīte[1], n. Common mica (earlier *Muscovy glass*). [as foll.]

Mŭs'covīte[2], n. & a. Russian; citizen of Moscow. [f. foll. +-ITE[1]]

Mŭs'covў, n. (Arch.) Russia; ~ *duck*, MUSK-duck. [f. F *Muscovie* f. Russ. *Moskova* Moscow]

mŭs'cūlar, a. Of, affecting, the muscles; having well-developed muscles; ~ *Christianity*, ideal of religious character exhibited in writings of C. Kingsley. Hence **mŭscūlā'rITY** n. [as MUSCLE, see -AR[1]]

mŭs'cūlature n. Muscular system of body or organ. [F, as MUSCLE, see -URE]

mūse[1] (-z), n. *The Muses*, nine goddesses, daughters of Zeus & Mnemosyne, inspirers of poetry, music, etc. (*Calliope, Clio, Erato, Euterpe, Melpomene, Polyhymnia, Terpsichore, Thalia, Urania,* Muse of epic poetry, history, lyric poetry, music, tragedy, sacred song, dancing, comedy, astronomy); *the* ~, poet's inspiring goddess, poet's genius; (poet.) poet. [ME, f. OF, or f. L f. Gk *Mousa*]

mūse[2] (-z), v.i., & n. 1. Ponder, reflect, (*on, upon*): gaze meditatively (*on* scene etc.). 2. n. (arch.). Fit of abstraction. [ME, f. OF *muser* to waste time]

mūsětte' (-z-), n. Kind of bagpipe; soft pastoral air imitating bagpipe's sound; dance for which this served; reed stop on organ. [OF, dim. of *muse* bagpipe]

mūsē'um (-z-), n. Building used for storing & exhibition of objects illustrating antiquities, natural history, art, etc.; ~ *piece*, specimen of art, manufacture, etc., fit for a ~ (also derog. of old--fashioned person, machine, etc.). [L, f. Gk *mouseion* seat of the Muses (*Mousa*)]

mŭsh[1], n. Soft pulp; (N.-Amer.) kind of porridge. Hence ~'INESS n., ~'Y[2] a. (also sl., weakly sentimental, soppy). [app. var. of MASH[1]]

mŭsh[2], v.i., & n. (U.S. & Canada). (Go on) journey across snow with dog-sledge. [prob. corrupt. f. F *marchons* imper. of *marcher* advance]

mŭsh'rōŏm, n., & v.i. 1. Edible kind of fungus, proverbial for rapid growth (~ *growth* etc., sudden development or thing suddenly developed); (fig.) upstart; (colloq.) lady's hat with down-curved brim. 2. v.i. Gather ~s; spring up rapidly, expand like a ~ cap. [ME, f. OF *mousseron*, f. LL *mussirionem*]

mŭs'ic (-z-), n. Art of combining sounds with a view to beauty of form & expression of emotion; sounds so produced; pleasant sound, e.g. song of bird, murmur of brook, cry of hounds; *set* (poem etc.) *to* ~, provide it with ~ to which it may be sung; written or printed score of musical composition; *face the* ~, face one's critics etc., not shirk; *rough* ~, noisy uproar, esp. with vexatious intention; *~ *box*, = MUSICAL *box*; ~-*hall* || (used for singing, dancing, & other entertainments); ~-*stool* (with adjustable seat, for piano-playing). [ME, f. OF *musique* f. L f. Gk *mousikē* (*tekhnē* art) of the Muses (*Mousa* Muse, see -IC)]

mŭs'ical (-z-), a. & n. 1. Of music; (of sounds, voice, etc.) melodious, harmonious; fond of, skilled in, music; set to, accompanied by, music; ~ *box*, mechanical ~ instrument played by causing toothed cylinder to work in comb-like metal plate; ~ *chairs*, drawing-room game in which *n* players circulate round *n*−1 chairs till music ceases, when the one who finds no seat is eliminated, and a chair is removed before the next round; ~ *comedy*, light dramatic entertainment of songs, dialogue, & dancing connected by a slender plot; ~ *film* (in which music is an important feature); ~ *glasses*, kinds of ~ instrument in which notes are produced by graduated glass bowls or tubes; ~ *ride*, military equestrian dance-like exercise performed to ~ accompaniment. 2. n. (colloq.). ~ film or comedy; *MUSIC-ALE. Hence **mŭsicā'lITY**, ~NESS, nn., ~LY[2] adv., (-z-). [ME, f. OF f. med. L *musicalis* (*musica* MUSIC, see -AL)]

***mūsicale'** (-zikahl), n. Musical party. [F, for *soirée* or *matinée* ~]

mūsi'cian (-zishn), n. Person skilled in

science or practice of music. [ME, f. OF *musicien* (MUSIC, -ICIAN); cf. *physician*]

mŭsĭcŏl'og|y̆ (-z-), n. All study of music except that directed to proficiency in performance or composition. Hence **~IST** n., **mŭsĭcŏlŏ'GICAL** a., (-z-). [f. MUSIC + -OLOGY]

mŭsk, n. Odoriferous reddish-brown substance secreted in gland by male ~-deer, used for perfumes & as stimulant etc.; kinds of plant with ~y smell; ~-deer, small hornless ruminant of Central Asia; ~-duck (also *Muscovy* duck), tropical American variety, (also) Australian variety male of which has ~y smell; ~ melon, common melon; ~-ox, ruminant with curved horns found in Arctic America; ~-rat (also *musquash*), large N.-Amer. aquatic rodent, its fur; ~-rose, rambling rose with large fragrant white flowers; ~-tree, -wood, trees with ~y smell. Hence **mŭs'kY̆²** a. [ME, f. OF *musc* f. LL *muscus* f. late Gk *mosk(h)os* f. Pers. *mušk*]

mŭs'kĕt, n. Infantry soldier's hand-gun (now usu. of obsolete kinds, cf. RIFLE); ~-shot, shot fired from ~, range of ~. [f. F *mousquet* f. It. *moschetto* sparrow-hawk]

mŭskĕteer', n. (hist.). Soldier armed with musket. [-EER]

mŭs'kĕtry̆, n. Muskets; art of using, troops armed with, muskets. [f. F *mousqueterie* (as MUSKET, see -ERY)]

Muslim. See MOSLEM.

mŭs'lĭn (-z-), n. Kinds of delicately woven cotton fabric for ladies' dresses, curtains, etc.; (sl.) *bit of ~*, woman, girl; ~-de-laine, see MOUSSELINE. Hence ~ED² (-nd) a. [f. F *mousseline* f. It. *mussolina* (*Mussolo*, = Mosul in Iraq whence ~ came, see -INE¹)]

mŭslĭnĕt' (-z-), n. Thick kind of muslin. [-ET¹]

mŭs'mon, n. = MOUFFLON. [f. L *mus(i)mo* f. late Gk *mousmōn*]

mŭs'quash (-ŏsh), n. (Fur of) MUSK-rat. [f. Algonkin *muskwessu*]

*****mŭss**, v.t., & n. (colloq.). **1.** Disarrange, throw into disorder (*up*). **2.** n. State of confusion, untidiness, mess. Hence ~'Y³ a. [app. var. of MESS]

mŭssal' (-ahl), n. (Anglo-Ind.). Torch; (also ~chee) torch-bearer. [f. Arab. *mas'al*]

mŭss'el, n. Kinds (sea, freshwater, ~) of bivalve mollusc; ~ *plum*, dark purple plum. [OE *muscle* = OS, OHG *muscula*, f. Rom. **muscula* bivalve, fem. corresp. to L *musculus* (as MUSCLE); ME *mussel* f. MDu., MLG *mussel*]

mŭss'uck, n. (Anglo-Ind.). Leather water-bag. [Hind. *masak*]

Mŭss'ulman, n. & a. (pl. ~s). Mohammedan. [f. Pers. *musulmān* (as MOSLEM)]

mŭst¹, n. New wine; grape-juice before fermentation is complete. [OE, ME, f. L *mustum* neut. of *mustus* new]

mŭst², n. Mustiness, mould. [back formation f. MUSTY]

mŭst³, a. & n. **1.** (Of male elephants & camels) in state of frenzy. **2.** n. This state. [f. Hind. f. Pers. *mast* intoxicated]

mŭst⁴, v. auxil. (3rd sing. *must*; past *must*, only as below; no infin. or part. or gerund), & n. **1.** Be obliged to (do), as *you ~* (neg. *need not*, see below & cf. MAY¹) *find it, it ~ be found*, (w. necessity less emphasized) *we ~ see what can be done, I ~ ask you to retract that, you ~ know* (I now tell you); be certain to (do), as *you ~ lose, whichever happens; you ~ be* (surely are) *aware of this; he ~ be* (clearly is) *mad*; (as past tense, reporting reflection made at the time) *it was too late now to retreat, he ~ make good his word or incur lasting disgrace*; (past or historic present, w. reference to perverse destiny) *just as I was getting better, what ~ I do but break my leg?, just as I was busiest, he ~ come worrying*; ~ *have* done, (1) surely did, as *you ~ have known quite well what I meant*, (2) necessarily would have done, as *you ~ have caught it if you had run*; (w. negative belonging in sense to dependent vb, cf. MAY¹) *you ~ not infer* (~ avoid the inference), *you ~ never contradict*. **2.** n. *A ~*, a thing that cannot or should not be missed. [OE *mōste* (= OHG *muosa*, Goth *musste*) f. pret. pres. *mōt* (= Goth. *gamōt*, OHG *muoz*, G *muss*), ME & arch. *mote* may, be permitted to]

*****mustache.** See MOUSTACHE.

mŭsta'chio (-ahshō), n. (arch.; pl. ~s). Moustache. [(partly f. Sp. *mostacho*) f. It. as MOUSTACHE]

mŭs'täng, n. Wild horse of Mexico & California; ~ (small red Texas) grape. [f. Sp. *mestengo* (now *mesteño*), app. f. *mesta* company of graziers]

mŭs'tard, n. Kinds of plant, esp. *black* & *white* ~, seeds of which are ground, made into paste, & used as condiment or for poultice or ~ *plaster*; (fig.) **zestful thing or person (sl.); *grain of ~ seed*, small thing capable of vast development (*Matt.* xiii. 31); ||~ *& cress* (used in seed-leaf for salad); *field ~*, charlock; *French ~* (mixed with vinegar); ~ *gas*, kind of liquid poison gas, a powerful irritant & vesicant; ~-pot (for table ~). [ME, f. OF *mostarde*, f. Rom. **mosto* MUST¹; orig. of the condiment as prepared w. must]

mŭs'ter¹, n. Assembling of men for inspection etc. (*pass ~*, be accepted as adequate), assembly, collection; ~-book, (for registering military forces); ~-roll, official list of officers & men in army or ship's company (also fig.). [ME, f. OF *mo(u)stre* f. L *monstrare* show]

mŭs'ter², v.t. & i. Collect (orig. soldiers) for inspection, to check numbers, etc.; collect, get together, (t. & i.); summon (courage, strength, etc.; often *up*). [ME, f. OF *mostrer* f. L as prec.]

mŭs't|y̆, a. Mouldy; of mouldy or stale

smell or taste; (fig.) stale, antiquated. Hence ~iNESS n. [16th c., of obsc. orig.; perh. alt. f. *moisty* (MOIST)]

mūt'able, a. Liable to change; fickle. Hence mūtaBIL'ITY n. [f. L *mutabilis* (*mutare* change, see -BLE)]

mūtā'tion, n. Change, alteration; (biol.) genetic change which when transmitted to offspring gives rise to heritable variation; (mus.) ~ *stop*, organ stop in which notes produced are not at normal pitch but at that of some harmonic (other than mere octaves). Hence [ME, f. OF, or f. L *mutatio* (as prec., see -ATION)]

mūtăt'ĭs mūtăn'dĭs, adv. With due alteration of details (in comparing cases). [L]

‖ **mŭtch**, n. (Sc.). Woman's or child's linen cap. [ME, f. MDu. *mutse*, = G *mütze*]

mūte¹, a. & n. **1.** Silent; not emitting articulate sound; (law) *stand* ~ *of malice*, refuse deliberately to plead; (of person or animal) dumb; (of hounds) not giving tongue; not expressed in speech, as ~ *appeal, adoration*; temporarily bereft of speech; (of consonant) produced by entire interruption of passage of breath or complete closure of organs of mouth, stopped, (usu. applied to *b p f d t th k g*); (of letter) not pronounced, as *the* e *in* late *or in French* aime *is*~. **2.** n.~consonant; dumb person; actor whose part is in dumb show; dumb servant in Oriental countries; hired mourner; clip for deadening resonance of strings of violin etc., pad for deadening sound of wind instrument. Hence ~'LY² adv., ~'NESS n. [ME & OF *muet*, dim. of *mu* f. L *mutus*]

mūte², v.t. Deaden, muffle, the sound of (esp. musical instrument). [f. prec.]

mūte³, v.i. & t. (Of birds) void the faeces, discharge thus. [f. OF *mutir*]

mūt'il|āte, v.t. Deprive (person etc.) of limb or organ; cut off, destroy the use of, (limb etc.); render (book etc.) imperfect by excision etc. So ~A'TION, ~ātor, n. [f. L *mutilare* (*mutilus* maimed), see -ATE³]

mūtineer', n. One who mutinies. [f. F *mutinier* (*mutin* rebellious, ult. f. L *movēre* mōt- MOVE)]

mūt'inous, a. Rebellious. Hence ~LY² adv. [f. obs. *mutine* rebellion f. F *mutin* (see prec.) +-OUS]

mūt'iny̆, n., & v.i. **1.** Open revolt against constituted authority, esp. of soldiers etc. against officers; *Indian M~*, revolt of Bengal native troops, 1857-8; *M~ Act* (dealing with offences against military & naval discipline, now embodied in Army Act, 1881). **2.** v.i. Revolt (*against* or abs.). [n. f. obs. *mutine* (vb or n.) as prec. +-Y¹; vb f. n.]

mūt'ism, n. Muteness; silence; dumbness. [f. F *mutisme* f. L as MUTE¹, see -ISM]

mūt'o-, comb. form (irreg.) of L *mutare* change, as:~*graph*, apparatus for taking series of photographs of moving objects,

(v.t.) portray with this;~*scope*, apparatus for exhibiting scene recorded by~*graph*, so ~*scōp'ic a.*

mŭtt, n. (sl.). Ignorant blunderer, dunderhead; small dog (derog.). [perh. abbr. of *mutton-head*]

mŭtt'er, v.i. & t., & n. **1.** Speak low in barely audible manner; murmur, grumble, (*against, at*): utter (words etc.) in low tone; (fig.) say in secret. **2.** n. ~ing, ~ed words. [ME, imit., w. suf. -ER⁵]

mŭtt'on, n. Flesh of sheep as food; (joc.) sheep (*to our* ~*s*, gallicism = let us come back to our subject); *dead as* ~, quite dead; *eat one's* ~, dine *with*; ~ *chop*, piece of ~ (usu. rib & half vertebra to which it is attached) for frying etc., side whisker shaped like this; ~ *dressed like lamb* (colloq.), elderly woman got up to look young; ~-*head* (colloq.), dull, stupid person. Hence ~Y² a. [ME, f. OF *moton* f. med. L *multonem* f. Gaul. **multo*, cf. OIr. *molt* ram]

mūt'ual, a. (Of feelings, actions, etc.) felt, done, by each to(wards) the other, as ~ *affection, benefit, suspicion*; standing in (specified) ~ relation, as ~ *well-wishers*; ~ *admiration society*, set of persons who overestimate each other's merits; ~ *insurance company* (in which some or all of the profits are divided among the policy-holders); (commerc.) ~ *terms* (by which exchange of services takes the place of money payments); (improp.) common to two or more persons, as *our* ~ *friend*. Hence mūtuăl'ITY n., ~LY² adv. [ME, f. OF *mutuel* f. L *mutuus* borrowed (cf. *mutare* change), see -AL]

mūt'ual|ism, n. Doctrine that mutual dependence is necessary to well-being. So ~IST n. [-ISM]

mūt'ule, n. (archit.). Modillion proper to cornice in Doric order. [F, or L *mutulus*]

muzhik. See MOUJIK.

‖ **mŭzz**, v.t. (sl.). Make muzzy. [orig. obsc.]

mŭz'zle¹, n. Projecting part of animal's head including nose & mouth; open end of fire-arm; contrivance of strap or wire put over animal's head to prevent its biting, eating, etc.; ~-*loader*, gun that is loaded at the~. [ME, f. OF *musel* f. med. L *musellum* dim. of *musum*]

mŭz'zle², v.t. Put muzzle on (animal, its mouth, &, fig., a person); impose silence upon; take in (sail). [f. prec.]

mŭzz'|y̆, a. Dull, spiritless; stupid from drinking. Hence ~iLY² adv., ~iNESS n. [cf. earlier *mussy, nosy*]

my, poss. adj. of 1st pers. sing. (with abs. form MINE). (prefixed to some terms of address) *my boy, friend, man, son, daughter*, (not colloq. w. other terms of relationship), *dear, darling, love; my* (vulg. *mine*) *& her* (common) *father, my* (vulg. *mine*) *& her* (respective) *father(s)*; (in ejaculations) *my! my eye!*, etc. [ME *mĭ*, reduced f. OE *mīn* MINE³]

myăl′gia (-ja), n. (path.). Muscular rheumatism. [Gk *mus* muscle, *algos* pain, -IA¹]

my′alism, n. Kind of sorcery practised esp. in W. Indies. [prob. of W.-Afr. orig.]

my′all, n. Austral. acacia, with scented wood used for pipes. [f. native *maial*]

mycēl′i|um, n. (bot.). Spawn of fungi. Hence ∼AL a. [f. Gk *mukēs* mushroom + Latin ending]

Mȳcēnae′an, a. (archaeol.). Of the prehellenic or Achaean culture illustrated by remains at Mycenae in Greece, & by Homer. [f. L f. Gk *Mukēnaios* + -AN]

mycētōm′a, n. Fungoid disease of foot or hand. [f. Gk *mukēs mukēt-* mushroom, see -M]

mȳcŏl′og|ỹ, n. Study of fungi. So ∼IST n. [irreg. f. Gk as prec., see -LOGY]

mycōs′is, n. Presence of, disease caused by, parasitic fungi. [as prec., see -OSIS]

myelit′is, n. Inflammation of spinal cord. [f. Gk *muelos* marrow, see -ITIS]

Mȳl′odŏn, n. Extinct genus of gigantic sloths with cylindrical teeth. [f. Gk *mulē* mill + *odous -ontos* tooth]

myna(h). = MINA².

mȳnheer′, n. Dutchman. [f. Du. *mijnheer* Mr, sir, (*mijn* my + *heer* master)]

mȳo-, comb. form of Gk *mus muos* muscle, as: ∼*card′ium*, muscular substance of heart, whence ∼*cardIT′IS*; *mȳŏl′ogy*, science of muscles.

my′ōpe, n. Short-sighted person. Hence or cogn. **mȳŏp′IA¹**, **mȳ′opY¹**, nn., **mȳŏp′-ic** a. [F, f. LL f. Gk *muōps* (*muŏ* shut + *ōps* eye)]

mȳōs′is, n. Contraction of pupil of eye. So **mȳŏt′IC** a. [f. Gk *muŏ* shut, see -OSIS]

my′osŏte, n. Forget-me-not. [f. foll.]

Mȳosŏt′is, n. Genus of small plants with blue, pink, or white flowers. [L, f. Gk *muosōtis* (*mus muos* mouse + *ous ōtos* ear)]

mȳ′riad, a. & n. (poet., rhet.). Ten thousand; (of) indefinitely great number. [f. LL f. Gk *murias -ados* (*muriŏi* 10,000)]

mȳ′riapŏd, a. & n. (Animal) with many legs, of the class comprising centipedes & millepedes. [as prec. + Gk *pous podos* foot]

mȳriora′ma (-rah-, -rä-), n. Entertainment consisting of series of views. [f. Gk *murios* countless + *horama* view (*horaŏ* see)]

myrm′idon (mẽr-), n. (*M*∼) any of a warlike Thessalian people who followed Achilles; hired ruffian; base servant, as ∼ *of the law*, policeman, bailiff, etc. [f. L f. Gk *Murmidones* pl.]

mȳrŏb′alan, n. Astringent plum-like fruit used in dyeing, tanning, etc. [f. F (-*bol*-) or L *myrobalanum* f. Gk *myrobalanos* (*muron* unguent + *balanos* acorn)]

myrrh¹ (mẽr), n. Gum resin used in perfumery & medicine, & in incense. Hence ∼′IC, ∼′Y², aa. [OE *myrra*, f. L *murra, myrr(h)a* f. Gk *murra*]

myrrh² (mẽr), n. Sweet cicely, an aromatic plant. [f. L *myrrhis*, f. Gk]

Myr′tle (mẽr-), n. Genus of plants, esp. *common* ∼, shrub with shiny evergreen leaves & white scented flowers, sacred to Venus. So **myrta′CEOUS** (mẽrtā′shus) a., of family *Myrtaceae* (∼ etc.). [ME, f. med. L *myrtilla, -us*, dim. f. L f. Gk *murtos*]

mȳsĕlf′, pron. Emphatic & poetical & reflexive form corresp. to *I*, as *I saw it* ∼, *I* ∼ (for my part) *am doubtful, I have hurt* ∼; *I am not* ∼ (in my normal state of body or mind). [f. ME + SELF; *my-* partly on anal. of *herself*]

mȳs′tagogue (-ŏg), n. Teacher of mystical doctrines, esp. (Gk ant.) to candidates for initiation in Eleusinian & other mysteries; freq. derog. So **mȳstagŏ′gic(AL)** aa. [F, or f. L f. Gk *mustagōgos* (*mustēs* one initiated into mysteries + *-agōgos* -leading)]

mȳstēr′ious, a. Full of, wrapt in, mystery; (of persons) delighting in mystery. Hence ∼LY² adv., ∼NESS n. [f. foll. + -OUS]

mȳs′terȳ¹, n. Hidden or inexplicable matter; *make a* ∼ *of*, treat as a secret; secrecy, obscurity, as *is wrapped in* ∼; (practice of) making a secret of (unimportant) things; religious truth divinely revealed, esp. one beyond human reason; religious rite, esp. (pl.) Eucharist; (pl.) secret religious rites of Greeks, Romans, etc.; miracle-play; ∼*-ship*, warship disguised as tramp steamer etc. to decoy submarines in the 1914-18 war. [ME, f. AF *misterie*, = OF *mistere* f. or f. L Gk *mustērion* (*muo* close lips or eyes)]

‖ **mȳs′terȳ²**, n. (arch.). Handicraft, trade, esp. (in indentures) *art & ∼*. [ME, f. med. L *mi(ni)sterium* (MINISTER), confused w. prec.]

mȳs′tic, a. & n. **1.** Spiritually allegorical; occult, esoteric; of hidden meaning, mysterious; mysterious & awe-inspiring. **2.** n. One who seeks by contemplation & self-surrender to obtain union with or absorption into the Deity, or who believes in spiritual apprehension of truths beyond the understanding, whence ∼ISM n. (often derog.). Hence ∼AL a., ∼alLY² adv., ∼IZE(3) v.t. [ME, f. OF *mystique* or L f. Gk *mustikos* (as MYSTERY¹, -IC)]

mȳs′ti|fỹ, v.t. Hoax, play on credulity of; bewilder; wrap up in mystery. So ∼FICA-TION n. [f. F *mystifier* (irreg. as prec., -FY)]

mȳstique′ (-tēk), n. The atmosphere of mystery & veneration investing some creeds, doctrines, arts, professions, etc., or personages; any professional skill or technique which mystifies & impresses the layman. [F, as MYSTIC]

mȳth (or mĭ-), n. Purely fictitious narrative usu. involving supernatural persons etc. & embodying popular ideas on natural phenomena etc.; allegory, as *Platonic* ∼; fictitious person or thing. So **mȳth′-ic(AL)** aa., **mȳth′icalLY²** adv. [f. Gk *muthos*]

mȳth′ic|ize, -|ise (-īz), v.t. Treat (story etc.) as a myth, interpret mythically. So **~ISM, ~IST, nn.** [MYTHIC + -IZE]

mȳtho-, comb. form of Gk *muthos* myth, as: **~grapher** (-ŏg²), writer of myths; **~graphy** (-ŏg²), representation of myths in plastic art; **~pœic** (-pē′ĭk), **~poët′ic**, making, productive of, myths; **~pō′et**, **~pō′etry**, poetical writer, writing, of myths.

mȳthŏl′og|ȳ (or mĭ-), n. Body of myths, esp. relating to particular person or subject; study of myths. Hence or cogn. **~ER¹, ~IST**, nn., **mȳtholŏ′gic(al) aa., mȳtholŏ′gically²** adv., **~IZE**(2, 3) v.t. & i. [ME, f. OF *mythologie* or LL f. Gk *muthologia* (see prec., & -LOGY)]

mȳth′us, n. Myth. [mod. L, as MYTH]

mȳxoedēm′a (-ed-), n. A metabolic disease caused by sluggish working or atrophy of the thyroid gland, & characterized by thickening of the subcutaneous tissues & loss of physical & mental energy. [f. Gk *muxa* mucus + OEDEMA]

mȳxōm′a, n. (path.; pl. *-ta*). Tumour of mucous or gelatinous tissue. Hence **~TOS′IS** n., virus disease in rabbits. [mod. L, f. Gk *muxa* mucus; see -OMA]

N

N (ĕn), letter (pl. *Ns*, N's). (Print.) *n* (also *en*) unit of measurement; (math.) indefinite number (*to the nth*, to any required power, also fig. to any extent, to the utmost); *N-rays*, *N¹-rays*, forms of radiation.

năb, v.t. (sl.; -bb-). Apprehend, arrest; catch in wrong-doing. [17th c., also *nap*, as in KIDNAP; orig. unkn.]

nāb′ŏb, n. (Hist.) Mohammedan official or governor under Mogul empire; (arch.) wealthy luxurious person, esp. one returned from India with fortune. [f. Port. or Sp. *nabab*, NAWAB]

Nāb′ŏth's vine′yard (-ny-), n. Possession that one will stick at nothing to secure. [see 1 *Kings* xxi]

năc′arăt, n. Bright orange-red colour. [F, f. Sp. & Port. *nacarado* (NACRE)]

nacĕlle′, n. Outer casing of aeroplane's engine; car of airship. [F, f. LL *navicella* dim. of L *navis* ship]

nā′cre (-ker), n. (Shellfish yielding) mother of pearl. Hence **năc′rēous, năc′rous**, aa. [F, = Sp. & Port. *nacar*, med. L *nac-(ch)ara*]

nād′ir, n. Point of heavens directly under observer (opp. ZENITH); (transf.) lowest point, place or time of greatest depression etc. [ME, f. OF, f. Arab. *naḍīr (es-scmt)* opposite to (zenith)]

năg¹, n. Small riding horse or pony; horse (colloq.). [c. 1400, of unkn. orig.; cf. MDu. *negghe*]

năg², v.i. & t. (-gg-). Find fault or scold (intr.) persistently (*at* person); annoy

thus. Hence **~g′ING¹** (-g-) n. [of dial., prob. Scand., orig.; cf. Norw. & Sw. *nagga* gnaw, irritate]

naga′na (-ahna), n. (S. Africa). Disease of livestock transmitted by tsetse fly. [Zulu *nakane*]

năg′ŏr, n. Senegal antelope. [wd made by Buffon]

nai′ad (nī-), n. (pl. ~s, ~es pr. -ēz). Water--nymph. [f. L f. Gk *naias -ados (naō* flow)]

naif (nah-ēf′), a. (rare, exc. of males). = NAÏVE. [F]

nail¹, n. **1.** Horny covering of outer tip of finger & upper tip of toe (~-*brush*, -*scissors*, for cleaning & paring ~s; TOOTH *& ~*), whence *-~*ED² (-ld) a.; claw, talon; hard excrescence on some soft-billed birds' upper mandible. **2.** Small metal spike usu. with point & broadened head driven in with hammer to hold things together or as peg or ornament (*hit ~*, or *right ~*, *on head*, give true explanation, propose or do right thing, hit the mark; *~ in* one's COFFIN; *on the ~*, without delay, esp. of payment; *hard as ~s*, in fine training, (also, of character) hard-boiled; *right as ~s*, quite right); ~-*head*, architectural ornament. **3.** An old measure of length (2¼ in.). Hence *~′LESS* a. [OE *nægel*, OS, OHG *nagal*, ON *nagl*, Goth. **nagls* f. Gmc **naglaz*]

nail², v.t. Fasten with nails (*on, to, together, down, in*, etc.; ~ *colours to mast*, persist in course of action; ~ (usu. *lie*) *to counter, barndoor*, expose as spurious, vile; ~ *up*, close, affix at height, with nails); fix or keep fixed (person, attention, etc.); secure, catch, engage, succeed in getting hold of, (person or thing). Hence *~′ING²* a. [OE *næglan* f. prec.]

nail′er, n. Nail-maker, whence **nail′ERY**(3) n. [-ER¹]

nain′sŏŏk, n. Fine cotton fabric, orig. Indian. [f. Hind. *nainsukh (nain* eye, *sukh* pleasure)]

naïve (nah-ēv′), **naive** (nāv), a. Artless, unaffected; amusingly simple. Hence **naïve′LY²**, **naive′lȳ** (-vl-), adv., **naïveté** (nah-ēv′tā), **naïveTY**(nah-ēv′tĭ), **naiv′etȳ**, n. [F, fem. of *naif* f. L *nativus* NATIVE]

nāk′ed, a. Unclothed, nude, (*as ~ as my mother bore me*); defenceless; unsheathed; plain, undisguised, (*the ~ truth*; ~ *facts*; *in its ~ absurdity*), exposed for examination (*his ~ heart*); devoid of; treeless, leafless, barren; (of rock) exposed, without vegetation; (of rooms) unfurnished; without ornament; (of candles etc.) exposed to air; without leaves, hairs, scales, shell, etc.; without addition, comment, support, evidence, etc. (~ *faith, quotations, word, assertion*); unassisted (~ *eye*, without telescope etc.); ~ *lady*, ~ *boys*, meadow saffron. Hence **~LY²** adv., **~NESS** n. (*the ~ness of the land*, person's or institution's or State's lack of resources or openness to attack, see *Gen.* xlii. 9). [OE *nacod*, OHG *nakot*, ON *nǫkkvithr*, Goth. *naqaḍ-* f. Gmc *naq-*, cogn. w. L *nudus*]

nāk′er, n. (hist.). Kettledrum. [ME, f. OF *nacre*, f. Arab. & Pers. *naqāra(h)*]

năm′bў-păm′bў, a. & n. 1. Insipidly pretty, mildly sentimental. 2. n. Talk of this kind. [formed on name of Ambrose Philips, pastoral writer, d. 1749]

nāme¹, n. 1. Word by which individual person, animal, place, or thing, is spoken of or to (*mention person by* ~; *Tom by* ~, *by* ~ *Tom*, called; *know by* ~, individually, also by hearsay only; *of* or *by the* ~ *of*, called; *put one's* ~ *down for*, apply as candidate etc., promise to subscribe; *keep one's* ~ *on*, *take one's* ~ *off*, the books, remain, cease to be, member of college, club, etc.). 2. Word denoting any object of thought, esp. one applicable to many individuals (*call person* ~*s*, describe him by uncomplimentary ~*s*; *give it a* ~, colloq., mention the drink, present, etc., that you wish); PROPER ~. 3. Person as known, famed, or spoken of (*adore the* ~ *of God; Nelson himself & many great* ~*s were there*). 4. All who go under one ~, family, clan, people. 5. Reputation (*has an ill, a good*, ~; *has a* ~ *for honesty, the* ~ *of being honest; win oneself a* ~; *bequeath a great* ~; *persons of* ~; *one's good* ~). 6. Merely nominal existence, practically non-existent thing, (opp. *fact, reality, deed; virtuous in* ~; *honour had become a* ~). 7. In person's ~, *in the* ~ *of*, invoking, relying upon, calling to witness, (*in God's* ~; *in the* ~ *of goodness, fortune, common sense*), acting as deputy for or in the interest of (*in one's own* ~, independently, without authority); ~-*child*, one named after another (*my* etc. ~-*child*); ~-*day*, day of saint after whom person is named (esp. of continental sovereigns); ~-*part*, that after which play is named, title-role; ~'*sāke* (-ms-), person or thing with same ~ as another (*his* etc. ~*sake*) [prob. f. phr. *for the* ~'*s sake*). [OE *nama*, OS, OHG *namo*, ON *nafn*, Goth. *namō* f. Gmc *namon*, cogn. w. L *nomen*]

nāme², v.t. Give name to (*after, from*), call so-&-so; call (person, thing) by right name; nominate, appoint (*to office* etc.); mention, specify, (*not to be* ~*d on* or *in same day with*, quite inferior to; ~ *your price*); || (of Speaker) mention (M.P.) as disobedient to Chair (~!, vb or n., appeal to do this, or to give name of some person alluded to in speech); cite as instance; specify as something desired (~ *the day*, of woman fixing date for wedding). Hence **nām′ABLE** a. [OE (*ge*)*namian* as prec.]

nāme′less (-ml-), a. Obscure, inglorious; not mentioned by name, left unnamed on purpose (esp. *who shall be* ~); anonymous, unknown; having no name, bearing no name-inscription; inexpressible, indefinable; too bad to be named, abominable, loathsome, (esp. ~ *vices*). [-LESS]

nāme′lў (-ml-), adv. That is to say, viz. [NAME¹, -LY²]

|| **nammet**. Var. of NUMMET.

năn′cў, n. & a. (sl.). Effeminate (man or boy); homosexual. [pet-form of female name *Ann*]

nānkeen′, n. Kind of cotton cloth orig. made of naturally yellow cotton; (pl.) trousers of this; yellow or pale buff colour. [f. *Nankin(g)* in China]

nănn′ў, n. ~ (-*goat*), she-goat (cf. BILLY); child's nurse. [f. the female name]

năp¹, v.i. (-pp-), & n. 1. Sleep lightly or briefly (*catch* ~*ping*, find asleep, take unawares, detect in negligence or error). 2. n. Short sleep, doze, esp. by day (often *take a* ~). [OE *hnappian*, app. rel. to OHG (*h*)*naffezan* (MHG *nafezen*) to slumber]

năp², n., & v.t. (-pp-). 1. Surface given to cloth by raising & then cutting & smoothing the short fibres, pile, whence ~'LESS a.; soft or downy surface. 2. v.t. Raise ~ on (cloth). [ME *noppe* f. MDu. or MLG *noppe(n)*]

năp³, n., & v.t. 1. A card-game (~ *hand*, fig., position that justifies confident expectation of winning if one takes a risk; *go* ~, risk attempting highest form of win in ~, also fig.); (betting) the putting of all one's money on one chance, a tipster's choice for this. 2. v.t. Name (horse) as probable winner. [abbr. of *Napoleon*]

năp′alm (-ahm), n. Product of naphthalene & coconut oil (~ *bomb*, one containing jellied petrol). [f. NA(PHTHALENE), PALM¹]

nāpe, n. Back of or usu. *of* neck. [ME, of unkn. orig.]

nāp′erў, n. (Sc. & arch.). Household, esp. table, linen. [ME, f. OF *naperie* f. *nape* (as NAPKIN), see -ERY]

năph′tha, n. Kinds of inflammable oil got by dry distillation of organic substances, as coal, shale, or petroleum. [L, f. Gk, = inflammable volatile liquid issuing from earth]

năph′thal|ēne, -īne, n. White crystalline substance got in distilling coal-tar & used in manufacture of dyes etc. Hence ~IZE(5) v.t. [prec. + -l- + -ENE, -INE⁵]

năp′kin, n. (Also *table-*~) square piece of linen for wiping lips or fingers with at meals, or serving fish etc. on; small towel esp. for nursery purposes, baby's diaper; *lay up* etc. *in a* ~, make no use of (*Luke* xix. 20); ~-*ring*, to distinguish person's table-~. [ME, f. OF *nappe* f. L *mappa* (MAP¹), +-KIN]

Nāp′les yĕll′ow (-lz, -ō), n. Bright yellow pigment used by artists. [f. *Naples* in Italy]

napol′éon, n. French gold twenty-franc piece of Napoleon I (*double* ~, forty-franc piece); kind of top-boot; the game NAP³. [f. name of French emperor]

Napōlĕŏn′|ic, a. Of, like, etc., Napoleon I or the Napoleon family. Hence or cogn. ~ICALLY² adv., Napōl′éonISM(3), Napōl′-éonIST(2), nn., Napōl′éonIZE(4) v.t. & i. [as prec., -IC]

‖ **napoo'** (nah-), int. (obs. army sl.). Vanished!, lost!, done!, finished!, no go! [f. F dial. *n'a pu* (= *il n'y en a plus*) there isn't any more]

näpp′ÿ[1], a. (arch.). (Of ale etc.) foaming, heady, strong. [app. f. NAP[2], -Y[2]]

‖ **näpp′ÿ**[2], n. (colloq.). Baby's napkin. [abbr.; see -Y[3]]

napu (nah′pŏŏ), n. Musk-deer of Java & Sumatra. [Malay]

när′cėïne, n. Alkaloid got from opium occas. used instead of morphine. [F, f. Gk *narkē* numbness + -INE[5]]

narciss′|ism, n. (psycho-anal.). Tendency to self-worship, absorption in one's own personal perfections. Hence ~**is′tic** a. [Gk *Narkissos* youth who fell in love with his reflection in water, -ISM]

narciss′|us, n. (pl. ~*uses*, ~*i*). Kinds of bulbous plant, esp. one bearing heavily scented single white flower with un-divided corona edged with crimson & yellow. [L, f. Gk *narkissos*]

nārc′olėpsÿ, n. Disease with fits of somnolence. [f. Gk *narkē* numbness + (EPI)LEPSY]

narcōs′is, n. Operation or effects of narcotics; state of insensibility. [f. Gk *narkōsis* (*narkoō* benumb); see -OSIS]

narcōt′|ic, a. & n. (Substance) inducing drowsiness, sleep, stupor, or insensibility; (fig.) soporific (a. & n.); of narcosis. Hence ~**ICALLY** adv., **nārc′otize**(3, 5) v.t., **nārcotiza′tion**, **nārc′otism**(5), **nārc′ot-ist**(2), nn. [ME, f. OF *narcotique* or med. L f. Gk *narkōtikos* (prec., -IC)]

nārd, n. (Plant yielding) aromatic balsam of ancients. [ME, f. L f. Gk *nardos* f. Oriental wd]

nārg′hile (-gĭlĕ), n. Oriental tobacco-pipe with smoke passed through water, hookah. [f. Pers. *nargileh* (*nargil* coco-nut)]

nārk, n. (sl.). Police decoy or spy. [Romany *nak* nose]

narr|āte′, v.t. Relate, recount, give continuous account of, (abs.) utter or write narrative. Hence or cogn. ~**A′TION**, ~**āt′OR**, ~**āt′ress**[1], nn. [f. L *narrare*, see -ATE[3]]

nä′rrative, n. & a. **1.** Tale, story, recital of facts, esp., in fiction, story told in first person; kind of composition or talk that confines itself to these. **2.** adj. In the form of, concerned with, narration, whence ~**LY**[2] adv. [f. F *narratif* (-*ive*) f. LL *narrativus* (prec., -IVE)]

nä′rrow (-ō), a. (~*er*, ~*est*) & n., & v.i. & t. **1.** Of small width in proportion to length, wanting in breadth, constricted, (*the* ~ *way*, righteousness, see *Matt*. vii. 14; ~ *vowels*, made with tongue & uvula tense); of small size, confined or confining, (*the* ~ *bed, cell, house*, grave; *within* ~ *bounds* etc.); of limited scope, restricted, (*in the* ~*est sense*; ~ *circumstances*, poverty); with little margin (*a* ~ *majority, escape*); lacking in breadth of view or

sympathy, illiberal, prejudiced, exclusive, self-centred, whence ~**-mīnd′ED**[2] a., ~**-mīnd′ėdLY**[2] adv., ~**-mīnd′ėdNESS** n.; searching, precise, exact, (*after a* ~ *examination*); ~ *cloth*, under 52 in., of single width usu. about a yard; ~ *goods*, ribbons, braid, etc.; ~ GAUGE on railway, any of less than 4 ft 8½ in. (formerly, the gauge of 4ft 8½ in.); ‖ ~ *seas*, English & Irish channels; hence ~**ISH**[1] (-ŏĭ-) a., ~**LY**[2] (-ŏl-) adv., ~**NESS** (-ŏn-) n. **2.** n. (usu. pl.). ~ part of a sound, strait, river, pass, or street. **3.** vb. Make or become ~er, diminish, lessen, contract. [OE *nearu*, OS *naru*; cf. MDu. *nare* dismal; ult. orig. unkn.]

när′thėx, n. Railed-off western portico or ante-nave in early Christian churches for women, penitents, & catechumens. [Gk (-*ēx*), orig. name of a plant = FERULA]

när′whal (-wal), n. Arctic delphinoid cetacean with straight horn(s) developed from one or both of its two teeth. [f. Da. or Sw. *narhval* (*hval* WHALE); ON *náhval* (perh. f. *nár* corpse)]

nās′al (-z-), a. & n. **1.** Of the nose (~ *organ*, joc., nose). **2.** (Of letters or sounds) requiring the nose passage to be open (n., such a letter etc., e.g. *m, n, ng*), of voice or speech) having the twang described as speaking through the nose, whence ~**IZE**(2, 3) v.i. & t., ~**IZA′TION** n., (-z-). Hence **nasäl′ITY** n., ~**LY**[2] adv., (-z-). [f. med. L **nasalis* (L *nasus* nose, -AL)]

nās′cent, a. In the act of being born, just beginning to be, not yet mature. So **nās′CENCY** n. [f. L *nasci* be born, -ENT]

nāse′berry (-zb-), n. Tree yielding Sapodilla plum. [f. Sp., Port., *néspera* medlar]

nās′o- (-z-), comb. form of L *nasus* nose, as ~*fron′tal* of nose & forehead.

nastū′rtium (-shm), n. (Bot.) kinds of pungent-tasting cruciferous plants including watercress; (improp.) trailing garden plant with bright yellow or red flowers. [L]

nas′t|ÿ (nah-), a. Disgustingly dirty, filthy; obscene, delighting in obscenity; disagreeable to smell or taste, unpalatable lit. & fig., annoying, objectionable (also colloq. of a person, as *a* ~*y bit* or *piece of work*); (of weather etc.) foul, wet, stormy; hard to deal with or get rid of, serious, (*a* ~*y sea, fence, blow, illness*; *a* ~*y one*, rebuff, snub, disabling blow, etc.); ill-natured, spiteful *to*. Hence ~**ILY**[2] adv., ~**iNESS** n. [ME, of unkn. orig.; cf. Du. *nestig* dirty]

nāt′al, a. Of, from, one's birth. [ME, f. L *natalis* (NATION, -AL)]

natäl′itÿ, n. Birth-rate. [F (-*té*), as prec., -TY]

natā′tion, n. Swimming. [f. L *natatio* (*natare* swim, -ATION)]

natätōr′ial, nāt′atorÿ, aa. Swimming, of swimming. [LL *natatorius* (prec.), -ORY, -AL]

nāt′ēs (-z), n. pl. (anat.). Buttocks; anterior pair of optic lobes in brain. [L]

nāth(e)′lĕss (-thl-), adv. (arch.). Nevertheless. [f. OE *nā* (*ne* not, *ā* ever) +THE (2) +LESS]

nā′tion, n. Congeries of people, either of diverse races or of common descent, language, history, etc., inhabiting a territory bounded by defined limits (*most favoured* ~, to which State accords lowest scale of import duties); || (in medieval & some Scots univv.) body of students from particular country or district; LAW *of* ~s; LEAGUE² *of N*~s; UNITED *N*~s. Hence ~HOOD n. [ME, f. OF f. L *nationem* nom. *-o* (*nasci nat-* be born, -ION)]

nā′tional (-sho-), a. & n. **1.** Of a or the nation, common to the whole nation; peculiar to or characteristic of a particular nation; ~ *anthem,* ' God save the Queen ' & corresponding hymns of other peoples; ~ DEBT; ||*N*~ *Gallery,* ||*N*~ *Portrait Gallery,* buildings in London in which pictures, portraits, owned by the nation are permanently exhibited; *N*~ *Government,* coalition of parties; *N*~ INSURANCE; ~ *newspapers* (circulating throughout the country); *N*~ *Socialist,* NAZI; ||*N*~ *Society,* founded 1811 to promote education of the poor; ||*Grand N*~ (*Steeplechase*), chief steeplechase of year, at Aintree in March. **2.** n. pl. One's fellow countrymen (*consul's powers over his own* ~s); citizens of a specified country. Hence ~LY² adv. [F (prec., -AL)]

nā′tional|ĭsm (-sho-), n. Patriotic feeling, principles, or efforts; policy of national independence. So ~IST(2) n. [-ISM]

nătionăl′itў (-sho-), n. Being national, national quality; patriotic sentiment; one's nation (*what is his* ~*y?*); a nation (*men of all* ~*ies*); existence as a nation; race forming part of one or more political nations. [-ITY]

nā′tionaliz|e (-sho-), **-is|e** (-ĭz), v.t. Make national; make into a nation; naturalize (foreigner); convert (land, railways, coal--mines, etc.) into national property or undertakings. Hence ~A′TION n. [-IZE]

nāt′ive¹, n. **1.** One born, or whose parents are domiciled, in a place (*of*); local inhabitant; (Austral.) white born in Australia. **2.** Member of non-European or uncivilized people. **3.** Indigenous animal or plant; oyster reared wholly or partly in British waters, esp. in artificial beds. [ME, f. med. L *nativus* n. (L *nativus* a., see foll.)]

nāt′ive², a. **1.** Belonging to a person or thing by nature, innate, inherent, natural *to,* whence ~LY² adv. **2.** Unadorned, simple, artless. **3.** Of one's birth, where one was born; belonging to one by right of birth. **4.** (Of metals etc.) found in pure or uncombined state (~ *rock,* in its original place). **5.** Born in a place (esp. of non-Europeans), indigenous, not exotic; of the natives of a place. [ME,

f. OF *natif* (*-ive*) or L *nativus* (NATION, -IVE)]

nāt′iv|ĭsm, n. (philos.). Doctrine of innate ideas. So ~IST(2) n. [-ISM]

nativ′itў, n. Birth of Christ, the Virgin, or St John Baptist; picture of the N~ of Christ; festival of Christ's N~, Christmas, or of birth of Virgin (8 Sept.) or St John (24 June); birth; (astrol.) horoscope. [ME, f. OF *nativite* f. LL *nativitatem* (NATIVE, -TY)]

nāt′ron, n. Native SESQUIcarbonate of soda. [F, f. Sp., f. Arab. *natrun* f. Gk *nitron* NITRE]

nătt′er, v.i. (colloq.). Chatter idly; grumble, talk fretfully. Hence ~ed (*-erd*), ~ў, aa., peevish. [var. of dial. *gnatter* be peevish]

||**nătt′erjăck,** n. British species of toad with yellow stripe down back. [perh. f. prec., from its loud croak]

nătt′ier blue (*-ōō*), n. Soft shade of blue, much used by the French painter J. M. Nattier (d. 1766).

nătt′|ў, a. Spruce, trim, daintily tidy; deft-handed; showing deftness. Hence ~ILY² adv., ~INESS n. [of unkn. (sl.) orig.]

nătural (-cher-), a. & n. **1.** Based on the innate moral sense, instinctive, (~ *law, justice*). **2.** Constituted by nature (~ DAY, *year*). **3.** (mus.). ~ *note* or *key,* not sharp or flat, so *B* ~, *F* ~, etc.; ~ *scale,* having no sharps or flats, i.e. C major. **4.** (sci.). ~ *classification,* (now obs.) *orders* with abbr. N.O., etc., esp. in bot. of Jussieu's arrangement of species according to likeness as opp. Linnaeus's sexual system. **5.** Normal, conformable to the ordinary course of nature, not exceptional or miraculous or irregular, (~ MAGIC; ~ *death,* by age or disease, not accident, poison, or violence). **6.** Not enlightened or communicated by revelation (*the* ~ *man;* ~ *religion, theology*). **7.** Physically existing, not spiritual or intellectual or fictitious, concerned with physical things, (*the* ~ *world;* one's ~ *life,* duration of one's life on earth; ~ *law*). **8.** Existing in or by nature, not artificial, innate, inherent, self-sown, uncultivated. **9.** Lifelike; unaffected, easy-mannered, not disfigured or disguised. **10.** Not surprising, to be expected. **11.** Consonant or easy *to* (*comes* ~*to him*). **12.** Destined to be such by nature (~ *enemies, antithesis*). **13.** So related by nature only, illegitimate, (~ *son, child, brother,* etc.). **14.** Dealing with nature as a study (~ *history,* study of animal or vegetable life, esp. as set forth for popular use, also aggregate of facts about the ~ objects or the characteristics *of* a place or class; ~ *historian,* writer on ~ history; ~ *philosophy,* physics; ~ *philosopher,* physicist; ~ SCIENCE). **15.** ~-*born,* having the character or position by birth. Hence ~NESS n. **16.** n. Person half-witted from birth; person who is naturally expert in some respect; thing that is by nature successful, a certainty. **17.** (mus.). ~ note, white key in piano. **18.** Hand making 21 as first dealt in vingt-et-un. [adj. (ME) f. OF -*al* or L *naturalis* (NATURE, -AL); n. (16th c.) f. adj. & F *naturel*]

nā′turalism (-cher-), n. Action based on natural instincts; moral or religious system on purely natural basis; (philos.) view of the world that excludes the supernatural or spiritual; realistic method, adherence to nature, in literature & art; indifference to conventions. [prec. +-ISM, partly thr. F *naturalisme*]

nā′turalist (-cher-), n. & a. **1.** One who believes in or practises naturalism; student of animals or plants; ‖ (shop) dealer in cage animals, dogs, etc.; ‖ (shop) taxidermist. **2.** adj. = foll. [f. F -*iste* (as prec., -IST)]

nāturalis′t|ic (-cher-), a. Of, according to, naturalism; of natural history. Hence ~ICALLY adv. [-IC]

nā′turaliz|e (-cher-), -**is|e** (-ĭz), v.t. & i. Admit (alien) to citizenship; adopt (foreign word, custom, etc.); introduce (animal, plant) into another country; become ~ed; free from conventions, make natural; free from the miraculous, place on naturalistic basis; pursue natural history. Hence ~A′TION n. [f. F *naturaliser* (NATURAL, -IZE)]

nā′turally (-cher-), adv. In adj. senses; esp. as might be expected, of course. [-LY²]

nā′ture, n. **1.** Thing's essential qualities, (*in* or *by* or *from the* ~ *of the case* or *of things*, inevitably considering these qualities); person's or animal's innate character (whence **-nā′tur**ED² (-cherd) a.; *by* ~, innately; GOOD, ILL, SECOND, ~); general characteristics & feelings of mankind (often *human*~; TOUCH² *of*~); specified element of human character (*the rational, animal, moral,* ~); person of specified character (*sanguine* ~*s do not feel this*; *there are* ~*s who can never*—). **2.** Kind, sort, class, (*things of this* ~; *is in* or *of the* ~ *of a command*). **3.** Inherent impulses determining character or action (*against* ~, unnatural, immoral). **4.** Vital force or functions or needs (~ *is exhausted*; *such a diet will not support* ~; *ease* ~, evacuate bowels or bladder). **5.** Resin or sap in wood (esp. *full of* ~, still resinous). **6.** Physical power causing phenomena of material world, these phenomena as a whole, (*N*~, these personified; *N*~'s *engineering*; *all* ~ *looks gay*; *N*~ *is the best physician*; LAW¹ *of* ~; *in the course of* ~, in the ordinary course; *debt of* ~, death; *in* ~, actually existing, also anywhere, at all; *against* or *contrary to* ~, miraculous, miraculously). **7.** Naturalness or fidelity in art. **8.** *State of* ~, unregenerate condition (opp. *state of* GRACE¹), condition of man before society is organized, uncultivated or undomesti-

cated state of plants or animals, bodily nakedness. **9.** ~-*printing*, method of producing print of leaves etc. by pressing them on prepared plate; ~ *study* (as school subject), practical study of plant & animal life, physical phenomena, etc. [ME, f. OF, f. L *natura* (*nasci nat*- be born, -URE)]

naught (nawt), n. & pred. a. (arch.). **1.** Nothing, nought, (*set at* ~, or NOUGHT); (arith.) cipher, nought. **2.** adj. Worthless, useless. [OE *nāwiht, -wuht* (*nā* see NATHLESS, WIGHT)]

naught′|y̆ (nawt-), a. (used of, to, or by children, or in imit. of childish speech). Wayward, disobedient, badly behaved; wicked, blameworthy, indecent. Hence ~ILY² adv., ~INESS n. [prec., -Y²]

naus′ĕa, n. Feeling of sickness; sea-sickness; loathing. [L, f. Gk *nausia* (*naus* ship)]

naus′ĕāt|e, v.t. & i. Reject (food, or fig.) with loathing; affect with nausea, whence ~ING² a.; feel sick (*at*), loathe food, occupation, etc. [f. L *nauseare* (prec.), -ATE³]

naus′ĕous, a. Causing nausea; offensive to taste or smell, nasty; disgusting, loathsome. Hence ~LY² adv., ~NESS n. [f. NAUSEA +-OUS or f. L *nauseosus*]

nautch, n. E.-Indian exhibition of professional dancing-girls (~-*girl,* one of these). [f. Hind. *nach*]

naut′ical, a. Of sailors or navigation, naval, maritime; ~ *almanac,* year-book containing astronomical & tidal information for navigators etc. Hence ~LY² adv. [f. F *nautique* or L f. Gk *nautikos* (*nautēs* sailor f. *naus* ship), see -ICAL]

naut′ilus, n. (pl. -*luses, -lī*). *Paper* ~, small cephalopod of which the female has very thin shell & webbed sail-like arms; *pearly* ~, cephalopod with chambered shell having nacreous septa. [f. L f. Gk *nautilos* sailor (prec.)]

nāv′al, a. Of, in, for, etc., ships or (usu.) the or a navy (~ *stores,* all materials used in shipping; ~ *officer,* in navy); fought, won, etc., by or consisting of or based on ships of war. Hence ~LY² adv. [ME, f. L *navalis* (*navis* ship, -AL)]

nāve¹, n. Central block of wheel holding axle & spokes, hub. [OE *nafu,* OS, OHG *naba,* ON *nǫf,* f. Gmc **nabhō,* see NAVEL]

nāve², n. Body of church from West door to chancel, usu. separated by pillars from aisles. [f. L *navis* (in med. L); cf. It. *nave*]

nāv′el, n. Depression in front of belly left by abruption of umbilical cord; central point of anything; ~ *orange,* large orange with ~-like formation at top; ~-*string,* structure connecting foetus & placenta, umbilical cord; ~-*wort,* pennywort. [OE *nafela,* OHG *nabalo,* ON *nafli,* f. Gmc **nabhalan-* f. **nabh-* NAVE¹; cogn. w. L UMBILICUS]

nāv′icĕrt, n. Certificate that ship's cargo does not contravene war contraband regulations; commercial passport for a particular consignment. [f. L *navis* ship + CERT(IFICATE)]

navic′ular, a. & n. Boat-shaped (of shrines, & of parts of plants or body; esp. ~ *bone* in hand or usu. foot; ~ *disease*, or ~ as noun, disease in horse's ~ bone). [f. F *-aire* or LL *navicularis* (L *navicula* dim. of *navis* ship, -AR¹)]

năv′iga|ble, a. (Of river, sea, etc.) afford-ing passage for ships; seaworthy (*in ~ble condition*); (of balloon) steerable, diri-gible. Hence ~BIL′ITY n. [f. F, or L *navigabilis* (foll., -ABLE)]

năv′igate, v.i. & t. Voyage, sail ship; sail over or up or down (sea, river); manage, direct course of, (ship or aircraft). [f. L *navigare* (*navis* ship, *agere* drive), -ATE³]

năviga′tion, n. Navigating (*inland* ~, communication by canals & rivers; *aerial* ~, of airship or aeroplane); methods of determining ship's or aircraft's posi-tion & course by geometry & nautical astronomy, seamanship; voyage; ~*-coal*, steam-coal. [f. F, or L *navigatio* (prec., -ATION)]

năv′igātor, n. One charged with or skilled in navigation; sea explorer; ‖ (now rare) navvy. [L (NAVIGATE, -OR)]

năvv′ў, n. ‖ Labourer employed in ex-cavating etc. for canals, railways, roads, etc.; (also *steam-*~) mechanical excavator. [c. 1830, abbr. of prec.]

năv′ў, n. Fleet (poet.); whole of State's ships of war with their crews & all the organization for their maintenance; offi-cers & men of ~; ‖ ~ *bill*, issued by Ad-miralty in lieu of cash payment; ~ *blue* n., ~*-blue* a., (of) the dark blue used in naval uniform; ‖ ~ *cut*, cake tobacco finely sliced; ~ *league*, association founded to rouse national interest in ~; ~ *list*, official book with all naval officers' names & other information. [ME, f. OF *navie* ship, fleet f. L *navia* ship, pop. var. of cl. L *navis*]

nawab′ (-wawb), n. Title of governor or nobleman in India; (rare) rich retired Anglo-Indian, nabob. [f. Hind. *nawwab*, pl. f. Arab. *nā′ib* deputy: cf. NABOB]

nay, particle equivalent to negative sentence, & n. **1.** = NO⁴ (arch.), why, well, (vaguely introducing comment on another's statement etc.; arch.); or rather, & even, & more than that, (*weighty*, ~ *unanswerable*). **2.** n. The word ~ (*will not take* ~, disregards re-fusals; *yea & *~, shilly-shally; *say* ~, utter denial or usu. refusal, = refuse or contradict, as *cannot say him* ~). [ME, f. ON *nei* (*ne* not, *ei* AYE)]

Năzarēne′, n. & a. Native of Nazareth; (in Jewish, Moham., use) Christian; mem-ber of early Jewish-Christian sect (adj., of this sect). [ME, f. LL f. Gk *Nazarēnos* (*Nazaret* Nazareth)]

Năz′arīte¹, n. Native of Nazareth. [f. LL *Nazaraeus* f. Gk *Nazōraios* + -ITE¹(1)]

Năz′arīte², -zir-, n. Hebrew who had taken certain vows of abstinence (*Numb.* vi). [f. LL *Nazaraeus* f. Heb. *nazir* (*nazar* separate oneself) + -ITE¹(2)]

năze, n. Promontory, headland, ness. [= NESS]

Nazi (naht′sĭ, nah′zĭ), n. & a. (Member) of the German National Socialist party. Hence ~DOM, **Na′z(ĭ)ISM**, nn., ~FY v.t. [repr. pronunc. of *Nati-* in G *Nationalsozialist*]

Něăn′derthal (-tahl), a. Of or belonging to the primeval type of man widely dis-tributed in palaeolithic Europe. [f. the ~ *valley* in the Rhine province where parts of a skeleton were found in 1857]

neap, a. & n., & v.t. & i. **1.** ~*-tide′* or ~, tide soon after moon's first & third quarters in which high-water level is at lowest, cf. SPRING²*tide*. **2.** vb. (Of tides) tend towards ~; (of tide) reach highest point of ~-tide; (pass., of ship) be pre-vented from getting off by ~ing of tides. [OE *nēpflōd*, of unkn. orig.]

Něăpŏl′itan, a. & n. (Inhabitant) of Naples (~ *ice*, ice-cream made in strata of different colours & flavours, sweetmeat of similar appearance; ~ *violet*, double sweet-scented kind of viola). [f. L *Neapo-litanus* (*Neapolites* f. L f. Gk *Neapolis* f. *neos* new, *polis* city, -AN)]

near¹, adv. & prep. (~*er*, ~*est*, also as advv. & prepp.). **1.** To, at, a short distance, in(to) proximity in space or time, (*far & *~, everywhere; ~ *at hand*, within easy reach, not far in the future; ~ *by*, not far off; ~ *upon*, not far in time from); almost, nearly, *not* nearly or any-thing like, (now usu. *nearly*; *was* ~ *dead with fright*; *lasted* ~ *a century*; so ~ *upon*; *not* ~ *so numerous*); closely (*as* ~ *as one can guess*; *the* ~*er it resembles him the less I like it*); parsimoniously (*lives very* ~); *go* ~ *to do*, *come* or *go* ~ *doing*, nearly do etc. **2.** prep.~ in space, time, condi-tion, or resemblance, to (*comes no* ~*er the end*; *lies* ~ *his heart*, affects him deeply; *the time draws* ~ *Christmas*; *sun is* ~ *setting*; *hope came* ~ *fulfilment*; *who comes* ~*est him in wit?*); (in comb.) resembling, intended as a substitute for, as ~*-beer*. [ME, f. ON *nǽr* orig. comp. of *nd-* = OE *nēah* NIGH]

near², a. (often governing n. in pred. use; so also in comb. & superl.). Closely re-lated (~ *relation*; *is* ~ *akin to*; *is* ~ *me in blood*; ~ *& dear*), intimate (*a* ~ *friend*); (of parts of animals or vehicles, or horses etc. in team) left (opp. *off*; *the* ~ *fore leg*, *wheel*; *the* ~ *wheeler*); close at hand, close to, in place or time (also, esp. U.S., ~*by*; *the* ~*est man*; *on a* ~ *day*; *the man* ~ or ~*est you*; *is* ~*er to*, or ~*er*, *us*; ~ *work*, that must be done with the eye close to it; *the* ~ *distance*, part of scene between background & foreground; *the* ~ *prospect of reward*); (of road or way) direct; close, narrow, (*a* ~ *guess*, *resemblance*, *transla-*

tion, race, escape); niggardly ; ~ *miss*, not a hit, but ~ enough to damage target, esp. in bombing ; ~*-sighted*, short-sighted. Hence ~'ISH¹(2) a., ~'NESS n. [ME, f. prec.]

near³, v.i. & t. Draw near (*to*), approach. [f. NEAR¹,²]

Nearc'tic, a. (zool.). Of arctic & temperate parts of N. America. [f. Gk *neos* new (w. ref. to the New World), ARCTIC]

near'ly, adv. Closely (*examine it* ~; ~ *related*; *concerns me* ~; *approached the place* ~; *correspond, resemble,* ~); almost; *not* ~, nothing like, far from. [NEAR², -LY²]

neat¹, n. (sing. & collect. as pl.). Any animal of ox kind; (collect.) cattle; ~ *herd*, cowherd; ~*-house*, cattle-shed; ~*'s-foot*, ~*'s-tongue*, used as food; ~*'s--leather*, ox-hide. [OE *nēat*, OS *nōt*, OHG *nōz*, ON *naut* f. Gmc *nautam*; cogn. w. OE *nēotan* possess]

neat², a. (Of liquor, esp. alcoholic) un-diluted ; of elegant simplicity in form or arrangement, nicely made or propor-tioned; (of language, style, sayings) brief, clear, & pointed, cleverly phrased, epigrammatic; deft, dextrous, cleverly done; tidy, methodical; ~*-handed*, dex-trous. Hence ~'LY² adv., ~'NESS n. [f. F *net* f. L *nitidus* shining (*nitēre* shine)]

neath, prep. (poet.). Beneath. [f. BE-NEATH]

neb, n. (Sc.). Beak or bill; nose; snout; tip, spout, point. [OE *nebb* = ON *nef*, rel. to MDu., MLG *nebbe*; cf. NIB]

neb'ula, n. (pl. *-lae*). Clouded speck on cornea causing defective sight; (astron.) luminous patch made by cluster of distant stars or by gaseous or stellar matter outside solar system. [L, =mist, rel. to Gk *nephelē* cloud]

neb'ular, a. Of nebula(e); ~ *theory* or *hypothesis*, that solar & stellar systems were developed from nebulae. [-AR¹]

nebûl'ium, n. Element formerly assumed to exist in gaseous nebulae as cause of bright lines in green part of spectrum. (These lines are now believed to be due to one of the known terrestrial elements in a more rarefied gaseous state than has yet been produced on earth.) [-IUM]

neb'ûlous, a. (Astron.) of, like, nebula(e); ~ *star*, small cluster of indistinct stars, or star in luminous haze; cloud-like; hazy, vague, indistinct, formless; clouded, tur-bid. So **nēbûlos'ITY** n. [f. F (*-eux*) or L *nebulosus* (NEBULA, -OUS)]

nĕcĕssār'ian, n. & a. = NECESSITARIAN. Hence ~ISM(3) n. [NECESSARY, -ARIAN]

nĕ'cĕssarily, adv. As a necessary result, inevitably. [-LY²]

nĕ'cĕssar|y̆, a. & n. 1. Indispensable, requisite, (*to* or *for* person etc.; *it is* ~*y that, to* do); requiring to, that must, be done; determined by predestination or natural laws, not by free will, happening or existing by necessity; (of concept or mental process) inevitably resulting from nature of things or the mind, inevitably produced by previous state of things; (of agent) having no independent volition. 2. n. Thing without which life cannot be maintained (often *the*~*ies of life*); (loosely) desirable thing not generally regarded as a luxury; (abs. use of adj.) *the* ~*y* (sl.), money or action needed for a purpose (*provide, find, do, the* ~*y*). [ME, f. AF *necessarie* (OF *-aire*) f. L *necessarius* (*necesse* needful, -ARY¹)]

nĕcĕssitār'ian, n. & a. (Person) denying free will & maintaining that all action is determined by antecedent causes. Hence ~ISM(3) n. [NECESSITY, -ARIAN]

nĕcĕss'itāte, v.t. Force, compel, (person) *to* do (now rare); render necessary, in-volve as condition or accompaniment or result. [f. med. L *necessitare* (NECESSITY), -ATE³]

nĕcĕss'itous, a. Poor, needy. [foll., -OUS]

nĕcĕss'ity, n. Constraint or compulsion regarded as a law prevailing through the material universe & governing all human action (often *physical* ~; *logical* ~, com-pulsion to believe that of which the oppo-site is inconceivable; *absolute, moral, natural,* etc., ~); constraining power of circumstances, state of things compelling to certain course, (*of* ~, unavoidably; *make a virtue of* ~, claim credit for doing what one cannot help doing, do thing with a good grace; *am under the* ~ *of doing*; ~ *knows no law*, absolves from any offence); imperative need (*for*; ~ *is the mother of invention*); indispensability (*the* ~ *of protecting life & property*); indis-pensable thing, necessary; (usu. pl.) want, poverty, hardship, pressing need. [ME, f. OF *necessite* f. L *necessitatem* (*necesse* needful, -TY)]

neck¹, n., & v.i. & t. 1. Part of body that connects head with shoulders (*break* one's ~, dislocate vertebrae of this, be killed so; *break* ~ *of* task etc., get hardest part of it over; *save* one's ~, escape hanging; ~ *& crop*, headlong, bodily; *get it in the* ~, sl., suffer fatal or severe blow; *stick* or *shoot* one's ~ *out*, sl., invite attack; *talk through* (*the back of*) one's ~, sl., talk foolishly or wildly; ~ *or nothing*, desper-ately, staking all on success, *it is* a case for desperate attempts; ~ *& ~*, running even in race); (sl.) impudence; flesh of animal's ~ as food (esp. ~ *of mutton*); part of shirt etc. that touches ~. 2. Narrow part of vessel, esp. of bottle near mouth, or *of* passage, pass, or channel; pass, narrow channel, isthmus; narrow connecting part between two parts of thing; (archit.) lower part of capital. 3. ~*'band*, part of garment round ~; ~*'cloth*, cravat; ~*'erchief* (*-chĭf*), kerchief worn round ~; ~*'lace* (*-lĭs*), ornament of precious stones or metal, or beads etc., worn round ~; ~*'tie*, band of silk etc. securing or seeming to secure shirt-collar;

~-verse, Latin verse (usu. beginning of *Ps.* li) printed in black letter by reading which person claiming benefit of clergy might save his ~; *~'wear* (shop), collars & ties; hence (-)~ED² (-kt) a. 4. vb. *(sl.), (Of couples) clasp one another round the ~; hug, embrace, (person); *~ing* (petting) party. [OE *hnecca,* MDu., MLG *necke,* cogn. w. OHG *hnacch,* ON *hnakki*]

∥ **nĕck²,** n. Last sheaf of corn cut. [orig. unkn.]

nĕck'ing, n. (archit.). Part of column between shaft & capital. [NECK¹, -ING¹]

nĕck'lĕt, n. Ornament or fur protector for neck. [-LET]

nĕc'ro-, comb. form of Gk *nekros* corpse, dead body, as *~gĕn'ic* produced by contact with dead bodies, *~*PHIL(E), *~phŏre* burying beetle, *~biōs'is* decay in tissues of body, *~*LATRY (-ŏl⁴), *~logy* (-ŏl⁴) death--roll or obituary notice, *~phagous* (-ŏf⁴) feeding on carrion, *~polis* (-ŏp⁴) cemetery, *nĕc'ropsy* or *~scopy* (-ŏs⁴), post-mortem examination.

nĕc'romǎnc|ў, n. Art of predicting by means of communication with the dead; magic, enchantment. So~ER¹ n., **nĕcromǎn'TIC** a. [ME, f. OF *nigromancie* f. med. L *nigromantia* changed by assoc. w. L *niger* black f. LL f. Gk *nekromanteia* (prec.,-MANCY)]

nĕcrōs'is, n. (path.; pl. *-ōsēs*). Death of circumscribed piece of tissue, esp. mortification of bones. Hence **nĕcrŏt'ic** a., **nĕc'rotize(3)** v.i. [f. Gk *nekrōsis* (*nekroŏ* kill, see NECRO-, -OSIS)]

nĕc'tar, n. (Gk myth.) drink of the gods (cf. AMBROSIA); any delicious drink; sweet fluid or honey produced by plants; kind of aerated water. Hence or cogn. **nĕctār'EAN, nĕctār'EOUS, ~ED²(-ard),~ĬF'ER-OUS, ~OUS,** aa. [f. L f. Gk *nektar*]

nĕc'tarine, n. Kind of peach with thin downless skin & firm flesh. [n. use of obs. or rare adj. (NECTAR, -INE¹)]

nĕc'tarў, n. Flower's or plant's honey--secreting organ. [irreg. f. NECTAR + -ARY¹]

Nĕdd'ў, n. Donkey. [dim. of Edward; -Y³]

née (nā), a. Born (used in adding woman's maiden name as *Mrs Smith, ~ Jones*). [F]

need¹, n. Circumstances requiring some course (*if ~ be* or *were, there is no etc. ~, to do* or abs.; *have ~,* require *to; had ~,* ought to, as *had ~ remember*); necessity for presence or possession of (*the ~ of further securities; have ~ of,* require, want); emergency, crisis, time of difficulty, (*a friend in ~ is a friend indeed; good at ~; failed him in his ~*); destitution, lack of necessaries, poverty, whence *~'Y² a., ~'INESS* n.; thing wanted, respect in which want is felt, requirement, (*my ~s are few*); (pl.) offices of nature (*do one's ~s*); *~'fire,* fire got from dry wood by friction, beacon, bonfire. [OE *nīed,* OS·*nŏd,* OHG *nŏt,* ON *nauth,* Goth. *nauths* f. Gmc *nauthiz, *nauthiz*]

need², v.i. & t. (3 sing. pres. ~s, & ~

as specified below). Be necessary (arch.; *it ~s not,* it is needless; *there ~s, so-&-so* is required; *more than ~s,* than is necessary; *what ~* or *~s?,* why should one?); stand in need of, require, (intr.) be needy; be under necessity or obligation to (do etc.) or *to* do (3 sing. ~ , & *to* omitted, in neg. & interrog. forms; *he ~ not trouble himself; it ~s to be done with care; why ~ he have come tonight?; ~ not have done etc.,* usu. form = did not ~ to do etc.; often ellipt., as *don't be longer away than you ~*). [OE *nēodian* (prec.)]

need'ful, a. Requisite, necessary, indispensable, (*to, for,* or abs.; *it is ~ to* do, or *that; the ~,* what is necessary, esp. sl., the money or action required, also *do the ~* in football, convert try into goal). Hence *~*NESS n. [-FUL]

nee'dle, n., & v.t. & i. 1. Thin round long piece of steel pointed at one end & with eye for thread at other used in sewing (*knitting, darning, packing, crochet, etc., ~*, shapes or modifications of it for different purposes; *sharp as a ~,* lit., & fig. acute, observant; *look for ~* in BOTTLE³ etc. *of hay;* PINS & *~s; ~'s eye,* least possible aperture, esp. w. ref. to *Matt.* xix. 24). 2. Piece of magnetized steel used as indicator on dial of compass & magnetic & electric apparatus, esp. in telegraphy; strip of standard gold or silver used for comparison in assaying with touchstone. 3. Pointed etching instrument; pointed surgical instrument used in soft cataract; end of hypodermic syringe; thin pointed piece of metal, wood, or fibre, or long thorn, that receives & transmits the vibrations set up by a revolving gramophone record; steel pin exploding cartridge of breechloader. 4. Obelisk; sharp rock, peak. 5. Beam used as temporary support during under--pinning. 6. *~*-shaped crystal. 7. Leaf of fir or pine. 8. ∥ *The ~* (sl.), fit of nervousness. 9. *~-bath,* shower-bath with fine spray discharged horizontally from vertical pipes surrounding bather; *~-book,* book-shaped case for *~s; ~-fish,* kinds of fish, esp. garfish; *~ful,* length of thread etc. put into ~ at once; *~ game, match,* etc., one closely contested & arousing personal feeling or animosity; *~-lace,* made with *~s* not bobbins; *~-point,* fine sharp point, also point-lace made with *~s; ~-woman,* sempstress, also *good* or *bad* user of *~; ~-work,* sewing or embroidery. 10. vb. Sew, pierce, or operate on, with *~;* thread (one's way) between or through things; under-pin with *~-beams;* form *~-shaped crystals;* thread one's way; incite, irritate, prod into action. [OE *nǣdl,* OS *nādla,* OHG *nādala,* ON *nál,* Goth. *nēthla* f. Gmc *·nē-* sew, cogn. w. L *nēre* spin]

need'less, a. Unnecessary, uncalled for, (*~ to say* used parenth., as I need not tell you). Hence *~*LY² adv., *~*NESS n. [·LESS]

‖ **need'ments,** n. pl. Things needed, esp. personal necessaries carried on journey. [NEED n. or v., -MENT]

needs (-z), adv. Of necessity (now only after or before *must*; ~ *must* do, cannot help or avoid or get out of doing; *must* ~ do, occas. = ~ *must* do, usu. foolishly insists or insisted on doing). [OE *nēdes, nȳdes* (NEED[1], -ES)]

ne'er (nār), adv. (Poet.) never (not used elliptt for sentence like *never*); ~ *a,* not a single; ~*-do-well,* ~*-do-weel,* good-for-nothing (person). [contr. of NEVER]

nefār'ious, a. Wicked, iniquitous. Hence ~LY[2] adv., ~NESS n. [f. L *nefarius* (*nefas* wrong), -OUS]

negāte', v.t. Nullify, deny existence of, imply or involve non-existence of, be the negation of. [f. L *negare* deny, -ATE[3]]

negā'tion, n. Denying; negative statement or doctrine; refusal, contradiction, denial *of*; (log.) affirmation of difference or exclusion; absence or opposite of something actual or positive; negative or unreal thing, nonentity. So **nĕg'atory** a. [f. F, or L *negatio* (prec., -ATION)]

negā'tionist (-sho-), n. One who denies accepted beliefs without proposing substitutes. [-IST]

nĕg'ative[1], a. 1. Expressing or implying denial, prohibition, or refusal (~ *proposition* in logic, asserting difference or discrepancy; ~ *statute, vote, answer*; ~ *voice,* right of veto). 2. Wanting, consisting in the want of, positive attributes (~ *virtue,* abstention from wrongdoing; ~ *instance, evidence,* of non-occurrence of something). 3. (Alg.) denoting quantities to be subtracted from others or from zero (~ *sign,* —); (colloq., joc.) ~ *quantity,* nothing. 4. (electr.). Of the kind produced by friction on resin etc. (opp. *positive,* on glass), containing or producing such electricity. 5. Of opposite nature to thing regarded as positive (*debt* is ~ *capital, & capital* ~ *debt*). 6. (photog.). Having lights & shadows of the actual object or scene reversed. Hence ~LY[2] adv., ~NESS, nĕgativ'ITY, nn. [f. OF (*-if, -ive*), or LL *negativus* (NEGATE, -IVE)]

nĕg'ative[2], n. 1. Negative statement, reply, or word (*it is hard to prove a* ~; *he returned a* ~, answered 'no' etc.; *two* ~s *make an affirmative*; right of veto; *in the* ~, negative(ly) (esp. in ministerial answers in Parliament, *the answer is in the* ~, no; *it was decided in the* ~, proposal was rejected). 2. Negative quality, want of something, (*his character is made up of* ~s). 3. (alg.). Negative or minus quantity. 4. (photog.). Image on glass etc. with reversed lights & shadows from which positive pictures are taken. 5. Negative plate or metal in voltaic battery. [f. prec., or F *negative* or LL *negativa*]

nĕg'ative[3], v.t. Veto, reject, refuse to accept or countenance; disprove (infer-

ence, hypothesis); contradict (statement); neutralize (effect). [f. prec. adj.]

nĕg'ativism, n. Attitude of NEGATIONIST. So ~IST(2) n. [-ISM]

nĕglĕct', v.t., & n. 1. Slight, not pay attentions to; leave uncared-for; leave undone, be remiss about; omit *to* do or doing; hence ~ABLE a. (rare). 2. n. ~ing or being ~ed; disregard *of*; negligence; hence ~FUL a., ~FULLY[2] adv., ~FULNESS n. [(n. f. L *neglectus -ūs*) f. L *neglegere -lect-* (*neg-* not, *legere* pick up)]

négligé (nĕg'lizhā), n. Free & easy or unceremonious attire. [F, p.p. of *négliger* (prec.)]

nĕg'ligeable, a. (rare). Negligible. [f. F *négligeable* (prec., -ABLE)]

nĕg'ligence, n. Want of proper care or attention, (piece of) carelessness; *contributory* ~*ence,* ~ence on a person's part that has helped to bring about the injury that he has suffered; freedom from restraint or artificiality in literature or art. So ~ENT a.' (*of* duty etc.), ~entLY[2] adv. [ME, f. OF, or L *neglegentia* (NEGLECT, -ENCE)]

nĕg'ligible, a. That need not be regarded (esp. ~ *quantity*). [as prec., -IBLE]

negō'tiāte (-shi-), v.i. & t. 1. Confer (*with* another) with view to compromise or agreement. 2. Arrange (affair), bring about (desired object), by ~ating. 3. Transfer (bill) to another for a consideration, convert into cash or notes, get or give value for (bill, cheque) in money. 4. Clear, get over, dispose of, (fence, obstacle, difficulty). Hence or cogn. ~ABLE (-sha-) a., ~ANT(1) (-shi-) n., ~A'TION (-sī-, -shi-), ~ātOR (-shi-), ~atrESS[1] (-sha-), ~atRIX (-sha-), nn. [f. L *negotiari* (*negotium* business), -ATE[3]]

Nĕg'rĕss. See NEGRO.

nĕgrill'ō, n. (pl. ~s). Small Negro; one of dwarf Negro people in Central & S. Africa. [Sp., dim. of NEGRO]

nĕgri'tō (-rē-), n. (pl. ~s). One of small negroid people in the Malayo-Polynesian region. [as prec.]

Nĕg'rŏ, n. (pl. ~*es*; fem. *Negress*) & a. 1. Member, esp. male, of black-skinned woolly-haired flat-nosed thick-lipped African people. 2. adj. Of this race, black-skinned, (n~ *minstrels,* troupe of real or sham ~es performing ~ songs & dances); occupied by, connected with, ~es; black or dark (n~ *ant, bat, monkey,* dark species). 3. n~*-head,* strong black plug tobacco, also inferior indiarubber. Hence **nĕg'roID** a. & n., **nĕgroid'**AL a., **nĕg'ro-**PHIL a. & n., **nĕgrŏph'ilISM** n., **nĕgro-**PHOB'IA n. [Sp., f. L *nigrum* nom. *niger* black]

Nĕg'us[1], n. Ruler of Abyssinia. [native]

nĕg'us[2], n. Hot sweetened wine & water. [Col. F. N~, d. 1732]

neigh (nā), v.i., & n. (Utter) cry (as) of horse. [OE *hnǣgan,* = MDu. *neyen,* MHG *nēgen* of imit. orig.]

neighbour (nāb'er), n., & v.t. & i. **1.**
Dweller next door, near, in same street
or village or district, or in adjacent
country (*my ~ Jones; are next-door ~s;
his nearest ~ is 12 miles off; our ~s across
the Channel*), esp. regarded as one who
should be friendly (*good, bad, ~s; ~LY*[1]
a., ~**LINESS** n.) or as having claim on
others' friendliness (*duty to one's~, to any
fellow man*); person or thing near or next
another (*my ~ at dinner; falling tree
brought down its ~*); (attrib.) ~ing; hence
~**LESS** a., ~**SHIP** n. **2.** vb. Adjoin, border
upon, border *upon*, (chiefly now in ~**ING**[2]
a.). [OE *nēahgebūr* (NIGH, BOOR)]
neighboured (nāb'erd), a. Having neighbours or surroundings of specified kind
(*ill ~; a beautifully ~ town*). [-ED[2,1]]
neighbourhood (nāb'er-), n. Neighbourly
feeling or conduct (usu. *good~*); nearness,
vicinity *of* (*in the ~ of £100*, about); neighbours, people of a district, district. [-HOOD]
neith'er (nidh-, nēdh-), adv., conj., a., &
pron. **1.** adv. (Introducing word, clause,
etc., that is to be negatived equally with
a following one attached to it by *nor*) not
either, not on the one hand, (*~ knowing
nor caring; ~ you nor I know, ~ he nor I
know, ~ I nor he knows*; also often vulg.,
*~ he nor she know; ~ does cowardice en-
sure nor courage preclude defeat; ~ HERE
nor there*); (colloq.; placed at end to
emphasize preceding negative) either,
any more than something else, (*I don't
know that ~*); (in apodosis after negative
protasis) not either (*if you do not go, ~
shall I*); (bibl.) not even (*but ~ so did
their witness agree*). **2.** conj. (arch.). Nor,
nor yet, (*I know not, ~ can I guess*).
3. adj. & pron. Not either, not the one
nor the other, (*~ accusation, ~ of the
accusations, is true; ~ of them knows,
often also irreg. know*); (loosely) none of
any number of specified things. [ME
naither, neyther, assim. of OE *nauther*
contr. of *nāhwæther* (*nā* not, WHETHER) to
EITHER]
nek, n. (S.-Afr.). = COL. [Du., = NECK[1]]
nek'ton, n. (biol.). The forms of free-
-swimming organic life found at various
depths in the ocean & in lakes, taken
collectively. [G, f. Gk *nēktos* swimming
(*nēkhō* swim)]
nell'y, n. Largest kind of petrel. [perh.
the feminine name]
nem'at|o-, comb. form of Gk *nēma -atos*
thread in scientific terms (= filamentous,
having filament, thread-like), as ~*ocўst*,
cell in jelly-fish etc. containing coiled
thread that can be projected as sting,
~*ōde* & ~*oid*, aa. & nn., (worm) of slender
cylindrical shape.
Nem'esis, n. Goddess of retribution; retributive justice, downfall that satisfies
this. [Gk (*nemō* give what is due)]
nĕm'ĭnĕ, abl. of L *nemo* no one; ~ *contradicente* or *dissentiente* (pr. kŏntradīsĕn'tĬ,
dĬsĕntĬĕn'tĬ; abbr. *nĕm. con.* or *diss.*),

unanimously (or without a dissenting
vote).
nēm'ō mē ĭmpūn'ē lăcĕss'ĭt, sent. No
one attacks me with impunity. [L]
nĕn'uphar, n. Water-lily. [med. L, f.
Arab.-Pers. *ninufar*]
ne'o-, comb. form of Gk *neos* new, used as
living pref. to adjj. & nn., & adding the
notions *new, modern, later, recast, lately
found* or *invented* (~*-Cath'olic*, ~*-pāg'anism*; ~*-Cām'brian*, geol., of the later
Cambrian period; ~*-clăss'ic*(*ism*)); ~*-
-Hĕll'enism*, revival of Greek ideals; ~*-
-Malthu'sianism* (-zha-), use of preven-
tives against conception; ~*-Plăt'onism*,
3rd-cent. mixture of Platonic ideas with
Oriental mysticism; *ne'odoxy*, new doctrine or view; *nĕōntŏl'ogy*, study of extant
animals; ~*zō'ic*, geol., of later period of
geological history, post-palaeozoic.
neolith'ic, a. Of the later stone age, when
ground or polished stone weapons & implements prevailed. [prec., Gk *lithos*
stone, -IC]
neolo'gian, a. & n. **1.** Of, inclined to,
marked by, neologism in theology. **2.** n.
Neologist in theology. [NEOLOGY, -AN]
neŏl'og|ism, neŏl'og|ў, nn. Coining or
using of new words, new-coined word;
tendency to or adoption of novel or
rationalistic religious views. So ~**IST**[2]
n., ~**IZE**(2) v.i. [f. F *néologie, néologisme*
(NEO-, -LOGY)]
ne'on, n. (chem.). Inert gaseous element
occurring in the atmosphere; used in
illuminated signs (~ *lights*), giving a
coloured glow when electricity is passed
through it in a sealed low-pressure tube.
[neut. of Gk *neos* new]
ne'ophrŏn, n. White Egyptian vulture &
allied birds. [name of man turned to
vulture in *Metamorphoses* of Antoninus
Liberalis]
ne'ophўte, n. New convert esp. among
primitive Christians or Roman Catholics;
newly ordained R.-C. priest; novice of
religious order; beginner, novice, tiro.
[f. eccl. L f. Gk *neophutos* newly planted
(NEO-, *phuō* plant)]
neotē'ric, a. Recent, newfangled, modern. [f. LL f. Gk *neōterikos* (*neōteros* comp.
of *neos* new, -IC)]
neotrŏp'ical, a. Of, found in, tropical &
S. America. [NEO-, TROPICAL]
nepĕn'the(s) (-ĭ, -ēz), n. Drug producing
forgetfulness of grief (poet.); (-s) kinds of
plants with pitcher-shaped leaves, pitcher-
-plant. [(-s) L f. Gk, neut. of *nēpenthes*
griefless (*nē-* not, *penthos* grief)]
ne'phew (-v-), n. Brother's or sister's son.
[ME, f. OF *neveu* f. L *nepotem* nom. *-pos*
grandson, nephew]
nephŏl'ogў, n. Study of the clouds. [f.
Gk *nephos* cloud, -LOGY]
nephrit'ic, a. Of or in the kidneys, renal.
[f. LL f. Gk *nephritikos* (foll., -IC)]
nephrit'is, n. Inflammation of the kidneys. [LL f. Gk (*nephros* kidney, -ITIS)]

nĕphr|(o)-, comb. form of Gk *nephros* kidney, as *~ĕc'tomy* excision of kidney, *~ŏl'ogy*, *~ŏt'omy*.

nĕ plŭs ŭl'tra, n. Prohibition of advance, impassable obstacle; furthest point attained or attainable: highest pitch or form *of*, acme, culmination. [L, = not more beyond, supposed inscription on Pillars of Hercules]

nĕp'otism, n. Undue favour from holder of patronage to relatives (orig. from Pope to illegitimate sons called nephews). So *~ist*(1) n. [f. F *-isme*, or It. *nepotismo* (as NEPHEW, -ISM)]

Nĕp'tūne, n. 1. (God of) the sea (*~'s cup*, kinds of coral). 2. One of the farthest planets of solar system. [f. L *Neptunus*]

Nĕptūn'ian, a. & n. (Geol.) produced by water action; (person) maintaining aqueous origin of certain rocks, so **Nĕp'tūn-ist**(2) n. (opp. *Vulcanist*); of planet Neptune. [f. L *Neptunius* (prec.), -AN]

nĕptūn'ium n. Unstable element produced when uranium atoms absorb bombarding neutrons, & changing to plutonium. [as NEPTUNE, -IUM]

nēr'ĕïd, n. Sea-nymph; (zool.) long sea--worm or centipede. [f. L f. Gk *Nērēis -idos* daughter of sea-god Nereus]

ner'ō ánti'cō (nār̄-, -tē-), n. Kind of black marble found in Roman ruins. [It.]

nēr'olī, n. Essential oil from orange--flowers used in perfumery. [F (*né-*), f. It., f. name of Italian princess]

Nĕrōn'ian, a. Of, as of, the emperor Nero or his times, cruel, licentious, tyrannical. [f. L *Neronianus* (*Nero -onis*, -IAN)]

nĕrv'āte, a. (bot.). (Of leaves) having ribs. So **nērva'tion** n. [foll., -ATE²]

nĕrve, n., & v.t. 1. Sinew, tendon, (now poet., exc. in *strain every ~*, make all possible efforts; also in pl. fig., as *good laws are the ~s of a State*). 2. Vigour, energy, well-strung state. 3. (bot.). Rib, esp. midrib, of leaf. 4. (anat.). Fibre or bundle of fibres connecting & conveying impulses of sensation & motion between brain or spinal cord or ganglionic organ & some part of body. 5. pl. Bodily state in regard to physical sensitiveness & interaction between brain & other parts, disordered state in these respects, exaggerated sensitiveness, nervousness, (*does not know what~s are*, of equable temperament; *a fit of ~s*, nervous state; *get on one's ~s*, be a worry or annoyance to him; *has iron ~s*, *~s of steel*, etc., is not easily upset or frightened; WAR¹ *of ~s*). 6. Nervous fibre. 7. Coolness in danger, boldness, assurance, (*lose one's ~*, become timid or irresolute; (colloq.) audacity, impudence. 8. *~-centre*, group of closely connected ganglion-cells; *~-knot*, ganglion; hence (-)nĕrved² (-vd) a., nĕrv'o- comb. form. 9. v.t. Give strength, vigour, or courage, to; collect *oneself* to face danger or suffering. [f. L *nervus*, rel. to Gk *neuron*]

nērve'lèss (-vl-), a. Inert, wanting in vigour or spirit, listless; (of style) flabby, diffuse; (bot., entom.) without nervures; (anat., zool.) without nerves. Hence *~LY²* adv., *~NESS* n. [-LESS]

nērv'ine, a. & n. (med.). (Medicine) relieving nerve-disorders. [NERVE, -INE¹]

nērv'ous, a. Sinewy, muscular, (arch.); (of literary style) vigorous, terse; full of nerves; of the nerves (*~ system*, nerves & nerve-centres as a whole); acting on the nerves; having disordered or delicate nerves, excitable, highly strung, easily agitated, timid. Hence *~LY²* adv., *~NESS* n. [f. L *nervosus* (NERVE, -OSE¹)]

nērv'ure (-yer), n. One of the tubes forming framework of insect's wing, vein; principal vein of leaf. [F (NERVE, -URE)]

nērv'y̆, a. Sinewy, strong, (poet.); (sl.) cool, confident, impudent; jerky, nervous; (sl.) trying to the nerves. [-Y²]

nescience (nĕsh'yens), n. Not knowing, absence of knowledge *of*. [f. LL *nescien-tia* f. L *nescire* not know (*ne-* not, *scire* know), -ENCE]

nescient (nĕsh'yent), a. & n. Ignorant (*of*); agnostic (a. & n.). [prec., -ENT]

nĕss, n. Promontory, headland, cape. [OE *næs*, = ON *nes*, LG *nesse*, rel. to OE *nasu* NOSE]

-ness, suf. appended freely to adjj. (*bitter~*), participles (*loving~*, *tired~*), compd adjj. (*tongue-tied~*), & adj. phrr. (*up-to--date~*) to form nn. expressing state or condition. [OE *-nes(s)* &c., OS *-nesse* &c., OHG *-nessi* &c., Goth. (*-in*)*assus*; the *n* is not orig. part of suf. but an accretion f. stem]

nĕst, n., & v.t. & i. 1. Structure or place made or chosen by bird for laying eggs & sheltering young (*it's an ill bird that fouls its own ~*, one should not speak ill of home etc.; FEATHER² one's *~*); animal's or insect's abode or spawning or breeding place; snug or secluded retreat, lodging, shelter, bed, receptacle; haunt *of* robbers etc.; fostering-place *of* vice etc.; brood, swarm; collection, series, *of* similar objects; small chest *of drawers*; *~-egg*, real or imitation egg left in *~* to induce hen to go on laying there, sum of money kept as reserve or nucleus; hence *~'FUL*(2) n., *~'LIKE* a. 2. vb. Make or have *~* in specified place, take to *~-building* (p.p.) established (as) in *~*, (of boxes etc.) packed one inside another; take bird's *~s* or eggs. [OE, OHG *nest* cogn. w. L *nidus*]

nĕ'stle (-sl), v.i. & t. = prec. vb (first sense; now rare); settle oneself, be settled, comfortably *down*, or *in*, *into*, *among*, etc., leaves, wraps, chair, etc.; press oneself affectionately *close to*, *to*, person; lie half--hidden or embedded; push (head, face, shoulder, etc.) affectionately or snugly *in*; hold embraced (usu. in p.p.). [OE *nest-lian*, = MDu., MLG *nestelen*, see NEST, -LE(3)]

nĕ'stling (-sl-, -stl-), n. Bird too young to leave nest. [ME, f. NEST n. +-LING¹, or prec +-ING³]

Nĕs'tŏr, n. Wise old man, senior *of* company etc. [name of character in Homer's *Iliad*]

Nĕstŏr'ian, a. & n. (Adherent) of doctrine of Nestorius patriarch of Constantinople A.D. 428 asserting that Christ had distinct divine & human persons. Hence ~ISM(3) n. [f. LL *Nestorianus* (-AN)]

nĕt¹, n., & v.t. & i. (-tt-). 1. Meshed fabric of twine, cord, hair, etc.; piece of this used for catching fish etc. (*beach, casting, trawl, herring, lark, clap*, etc., -~), or for covering, confining, protecting, carrying, etc. (*fruit, hair, tennis, cricket*, etc., -~); moral or mental snare; spider's web; reticulation, ~work; ~'*ball*, girls' game in which a ball has to be thrown so as to fall through an elevated horizontal ring from which a ~ hangs; ~'*work*, arrangement with intersecting lines & interstices recalling those of ~, complex system *of* railways, rivers, canals, etc., ramification, number of broadcasting stations connected for simultaneous broadcast of same programme; hence ~'FUL(2) n. 2. vb. Cover, confine, catch, with ~(s); fish (river etc.) with ~s, set ~s in (river); make netting; make (purse, hammock, etc.) by ~ting; (usu. in p.p.) mark with ~like pattern, reticulate. [OE *net(t)*, OS *net(ti)*, OHG *nezzi*, ON *net*, Goth. *nati* f. Gmc *natja-*]

nĕt², a., & v.t. (-tt-). 1. Free from deduction, remaining after necessary deductions, (~ *profit*, true profit, actual gain after working expenses have been paid, opp. GROSS; ~ *price*, real price off which discount is not allowed, opp. *nominal, publisher's, price*). 2. v.t. Gain or yield (sum) as ~ profit. [F, see NEAT²]

nĕ tĕm'erĕ, n. The papal decree of 1907 under which marriages between Roman Catholics and others are not valid unless solemnized by R.-C. bishop or his deputy. [initial L words, = lest rashly]

nĕth'er (-dh-), a. (arch. or joc.). Lower (~ *lip* or *jaw*; ~ *garments* etc., trousers; ~ *man* or *person*, legs etc.; ~ *millstone*, simile for hard heart etc.; ~ *world*, rarely the earth, usu. hell, also ~ *regions*). Hence ~MOST a. [OE *nithera* &c., f. OE (ME) advv. *nithor, nither* lower, downwards, f. Gmc *nithar*; see -THER]

Nĕth'erlander, n., **Nĕth'erlandish**, a., **Nĕth'erlands**, attrib., (-dh-). (Native) of the Netherlands. [f. Du. *Nederlander*, -*landsch*, (*Nederland*, -ER¹, -ISH¹)]

nĕt'suke (-sŏŏkǎ), n. Carved buttonlike ornament worn by Japanese. [Jap.]

nĕtt'ing, n. In vbl senses; also: netted string, thread, or wire; piece of this used for various purposes. [-ING¹]

nĕt'tle, n., & v.t. 1. Kinds of plants including *great* or *common* ~ & *small* ~, two species growing profusely on

waste land & covered with stinging hairs; other plants resembling these, esp. DEAD-~; GRASP *the* ~; ~*rash*, eruption on skin in patches like those made by ~ stings. 2. v.t. Beat with ~s; get one*self* stung with ~s; irritate, provoke, annoy. [OE *netele*, MDu. *netele*, MLG *net(t)ele*, OHG *nezzila*, f. Gmc *nat-* (OHG *nazza*) + dim. suf. -LE(1)]

neum(e) (nūm), n. (mus.). Sign in plainsong indicating note or group of notes to be sung to a syllable. [ME, f. OF *neume*, f. med. L *neuma* f. Gk *pneuma* breath]

neur'al (nūr-), a. Of the nerves, of the central nervous system. [f. Gk *neuron* nerve, -AL]

neurā'tion (nūr-), n. Distribution of nervures, venation. [irreg. f. foll., -ATION]

neur|(o)- (nūr-), comb. form of Gk *neuron* nerve; ~*ǎl'gia* (-ja), affection of nerve(s) usu. of head or face causing intense intermittent pain, so ~*ǎl'gic* a.; ~*ǎsthĕn'ia*, nervous debility, so ~*ǎsthĕn'ic* a.; ~*ĕc'tomy*, excision of nerve; ~'*īne*, nerve-tissue; ~IT'IS n.; ~*ŏl'OGY*, ~*ŏl'ogIST*, ~*olŏ-gICAL*; ~o-*mŭs'cular*, of nerves & muscles; ~'*opǎth*, person of abnormal nervous sensibility or affected by nervous disease, so ~*opǎth'*IC a., ~*opathŏl'*OGY, ~*ŏp'athY*; ~*ŏp'athist*, specialist in ~opathy; ~o-*physiŏl'ogy*, physiology of nervous system; ~o-*psych'ic* (-sīk-), of nervous & psychic functions; ~*ŏp'terous*, of the *Neuroptera*, order of insects having four naked membranous transparent wings with reticulate neuration; ~*ŏt'omy*, cutting of nerve to produce sensory paralysis; ~*ўpnŏl'ogy*, science of hypnotism. [f. prec.]

neurōm'a (nūr-), n. (pl. ~*ta*). Tumour on nerve or in nerve-tissue. [f. Gk *neuron* nerve, -OMA]

neurōs'is (nūr-), n. (pl. -*ōsēs*). Functional derangement due to disorders of nervous system; change in nerve-cells of brain prior to psychic activity. [as prec., -OSIS]

neurŏt'ic (nūr-), a. & n. (Drug) affecting nervous system; (person) affected with nervous disorder, of abnormal sensibility. [as prec., -OTIC]

neut'er, a. & n. 1. (Gram.) neither masculine nor feminine (cf. COMMON¹, EPICENE), (of verb) intransitive; neutral, not taking or assisting either side, in war, argument, opinion, etc. (esp. *stand* ~, remain neutral, declare neutrality); (bot.) without pistils & stamens, asexual; (entom.) sexually undeveloped, sterile. 2. n. ~ noun, adjective, verb, or gender; person standing ~; sexually undeveloped female insect, esp. bee or ant; castrated animal. [L, = neither (*ne-* not, *uter* either)]

neut'ral, a. & n. 1. Not assisting either of two belligerent States, belonging to a State that thus stands aloof, exempted or excluded from active or passive hostilities, taking neither side in dispute or difference of opinion, indifferent,

impartial. **2.** Not distinctly marked or
coloured, indefinite, vague, indeterminate, (~ *tint*, grey or slate-colour, whence
~-tint'ED² a. lit. & fig.). **3.** (Chem.)
neither acid nor alkaline; (electr.) neither
positive nor negative; (entom., bot.)
sexually undeveloped, asexual; hence or
cogn. neutrāl'ITY n., ~LY² adv. **4.** n. ~
State or person; subject of ~ State. **5.**
Position of the parts in a gear mechanism
in which no power is transmitted. [f.
obs. F, or L *neutralis* of neuter gender
(prec., -AL)]

neut'raliz|e, -is|e (-īz), v.t. Counter-
balance, render ineffective by opposite
force or effect; exempt or exclude (place)
from sphere of hostilities. Hence ~A'TION
n. [f. F -*iser* or med. L *neutralisare* (prec.,
-IZE)]

neut'rŏn, n. Electrically neutral particle
of about the same mass as a proton and
probably consisting of an electron & a
proton in close association. [f. NEUTRAL
after *electron*]

névé (nĕv'ā), n. Expanse of granular snow
not yet compressed into ice at head of
glacier. [F (L *nix nivis* snŏw, -ATE²)]

nĕv'er, adv. At no time, on no occasion,
not ever, (often ~ *before, since, after, yet*;
also repeated for emphasis; NOW *or* ~;
~ *is a long word* or *day*, comment on rash
renunciation or despair or negative prophecy; *it is* ~ *too late to mend*, reformation
is always possible); (colloq. expressing
surprise or incredulity in sentence or ellipt.) surely not, you do not mean it, (*you*
~ *left the key in the lock!*; '*He ate the
whole turkey.*'—'*Never!*'; *I* ~ *did!*,
Well, I ~ *l*, i.e. heard of such a thing
etc.); not at all (~ *fear*; ~ *mind*, do not
be troubled); ~ *a*, not a, no — at all; ~
a one, none; (in condit. clauses) ~ *so*, to
unlimited extent, ever so; (with compar.)
~ *the*, none the; (with particles etc.)
~-*enough-to-be-regretted*, ~-*to-be-forgotten*,
~-*ceasing*, -*dying*, -*ending*, -*fading*, -*failing*; ~*more'*, at no future time; *Never
Never* (*Land*), north Queensland; (joc.)
~-~ (hire-purchase) *plan, system*; ~*the-
less'* adv. & conj., for all that, but for all
that, notwithstanding, all the same. [OE
nǣfre (ne not, *ǣfre* EVER)]

new¹, a. **1.** Not existing before, now first
made, brought into existence, invented,
introduced, known or heard of, experienced, or discovered, (*New* TESTAMENT);
unfamiliar *to*. **2.** Renewed, fresh, further,
additional; different, changed, (*a* ~ *morality*; ~ *man*, theol., one converted to
Christianity, *put on the* ~ *man*, show conversion by amendment; *a* ~ *fashion*,
whence ~-fă'shionED² (-shond) a.; *my* ~
tailor; *lead a* ~ *life*; ~ STYLE; *turn over a* ~
LEAF). **3.** (With *the*, as distinctive epithet
implying difference of character) later,
modern, ~fangled, (*the* ~ LEARNING,
MODEL, COMEDY; *the* ~ *diplomacy, journalism, theology*, etc., advanced in method or

doctrine, usu. derog.; *the* ~ *poor, rich*,
classes recently impoverished, enriched;
the ~ *woman*, women who aspire to freedom & independence & reject convention;
the New World, America). **4.** Of recent
origin, growth, arrival, or manufacture,
now first used, not worn or exhausted,
(~ *red sandstone*; ~ *potatoes, wine, cheese*;
~ *furniture, clothes*; ~ *countries, soil*; *a
heart, pleasures, ever* ~; ~ CHUM; ~
members of Parliament etc.; ~ *look*, recent
(1947) fashion in women's dress marked
esp. by longer & fuller skirt, (colloq.) up-
-to-date appearance); not yet accustomed
to, fresh *from*. **5.** (Of family or person)
lately risen in position. **6.** ~ *comer*,
person lately arrived; ~ DEAL²; *New
Englander*, inhabitant of *New England*,
six NE. States of U.S.A.; ~*fāng'led*
[-nggled; f. obs. ~*fangle* a. in same sense
(-*fangel* inclined to take f. OE st. *fang*-,
infin. *fōn* take)], fond of novelty (now
rare), different from the good old fashion,
objectionably novel; ~ *moon*, moon when
first seen as crescent after conjunction
with sun, time of such appearance, (bibl.)
Hebrew festival; ~ *year*, coming or lately
begun year, first few days of year (~-
-*year's gift, wishes*, etc.; ~-*year's day*,
1 Jan.; ~-*year's eve*, 31 Dec.); *New Zealander*, Maori, also European inhabitant
in New Zealand. Hence ~'ISH¹ a., ~'NESS
n. [OE *niwe*, OS *niwi*, OHG *niuwi*, ON
nȳr, Goth. *niujis* f. Gmc **neujaz*, cogn. w.
L *novus*]

new², adv. (preceding, & now usu. hyphened with, qualified word). **1.** Newly,
recently, just, (~-*blown*, having just
come into bloom, lit. & fig.; ~-*born*, &
see below; ~-*built*, & see below; ~-
-*coined*, esp. of words; ~-*come*, lately arrived; ~'-*comer*, one who has lately
come; ~-*fallen snow*; ~-*fledged*; ~-*found*;
~-*laid eggs*; ~-*made*; ~-*mown hay* or
lawn). **2.** Anew, afresh, re-, (~-*born*, re-
generated, & see above; ~-*build*, rebuild,
& see above; ~-*create*; ~-*front*, put new
front to; ~-*furnish*; ~-*model*, recast). [f.
prec.]

new'el, n. Centre pillar of winding stair
(open or hollow ~, central well of winding
stair); post supporting stair-handrail at
top or bottom. [ME, f. OF *nouel* f. Rom.
*nucale f. LL *nucalis* like a nut (L *nux
nucis* nut, -AL)]

Newfound'land (*or* -fŭndlănd'), n. Island
at mouth of St Lawrence (~ *dog* or ~,
also ~*er*, large breed of spaniel kind
noted for swimming powers). Hence
~ER¹(4) n.

Newg'ate, n. Celebrated London prison
(~ *Calendar*, publication with accounts of
~ prisoners; ~ *fringe, frill*, beard grown
below chin while face is shaven; ||~
knocker, curl worn by costermongers etc.).
[place]

new'l'y, adv. Recently (usu. with p.p.
= NEW² in sense 1 & often now preferred;

hyphened w. attrib. part.; *the ~-dis-
covered country* (~-*wed* a. & n.; *a guest ~
arrived*): in new manner. [-LY²]

Newm′árkĕt, n. Town noted for horse-
-races (~ *coat* or ~, close-fitting overcoat
for men or women); a card-game.

news (-z), n. pl. (usu. followed by sing. vb).
1. Tidings, new information, fresh events
reported, (*have you heard the, this,* or
rarely *these*, ~?; *ill ~ flies apace*; *no ~ is
good ~*; *that is no ~,* already well known;
is there any, what is the, ~?); interesting
information; (*N~*) part of newspaper
title, as *Evening N~.* **2.** ‖ ~-*agent,* dealer
in ~papers etc., ~-*boy, -man,* selling ~-
papers in streets; ~′*cast*(*er*), radio broad-
cast(er) of news reports; ~-*letter,* letter
sent out periodically with the ~ to country towns etc.; ~′*monger,* gossip; ~′*paper,*
printed publication usu. daily or weekly
containing the ~, advertisements, &
literary matter; ~′*print,* paper for printing ~papers on; ~-*reel,* cinema film giving
the ~ of the day; ~-*room,* ‖ reserved for
~paper-reading; ~-*sheet,* simple form of
~paper; ~-*stand,* stall for sale of ~papers;
~-*vendor,* ~paper-seller. Hence ~′LESS,
~′Y², aa., ~′INESS n., (-z-). [ME, pl. of
NEW¹ after OF *noveles* (F *nouvelles*) or
med. L *nova* neut. pl. of L *novus* new]

newt, n. Small tailed amphibian allied to
salamander, eft. [ME, for *ewt* (*a newt =
an ewt,* cf. NICKNAME) var. of *ewet* EFT]

Newtŏn′ian, a. & n. **1.** Of Newton or his
theory of the universe; devised etc. by
Newton. **2.** n. Follower of Newton; ~
telescope or reflector. [Sir Isaac *Newton*
(1642–1727), -IAN]

nĕxt, a. (occas. governing noun), adv.,
prep., & n. **1.** adj. Lying, living, being,
nearest or nearest *to* or nearest to (*in the
~ house*; *my ~ neighbour*; *lives ~ door,* in
the ~ house; ~-*door neighbours*; ~-*door
to felony, to blasphemous,* almost; ~ *to
nothing, none, impossible,* almost; *the
chair ~ the fire*; *the skin with the flesh ~
it*; *the shop ~ to the corner*); soonest come
to, first ensuing, immediately following,
coming nearest in order etc. *to,* immediately *before,* (*will ask the ~ man I see,
the ~ policeman*; *shall return ~ year,* ~
Friday, on *Friday* ~; *what is the ~
article?,* shopman's formula; *the Sunday
~ before Easter*; *what is true one day may
be false the ~*; *not till ~ time,* joc. addition to promise of abstention; *the ~
town to London in size*; ~-*best,* second-
-best; *the person ~ him,* or ~ *to him,* in
rank). **2.** adv. (Often indistinguishable f.
pred. use of adj.) in the ~ place or degree,
on the ~ occasion, (*in the week ~ ensuing*;
~ *came a strange figure*; *what* ~?, can
anything follow to beat this for absurdity
etc.?; *placed his chair ~ to hers*; *New York
was the largest city ~ to London*; *when I ~
saw him he was lame*). **3.** prep. (Often
indistinguishable f. pred. adj. governing
noun) in or into the ~ place, on the ~

occasion, in the ~ degree, to (*I was
standing ~ him*; *placed his chair ~ hers*;
loves him ~ her own child; *wear flannel ~
your skin*). **4.** n. (or ellipt. use of adj.).~
person or thing (~ *of kin,* person nearest
of kin to someone; *will tell you in my* ~,
i.e. letter; *to be continued in our* ~, i.e.
issue of magazine etc.; *her* ~, i.e. husband,
was a greengrocer, i.e. child, *was a girl*; ~
please, ask your ~ question, let the ~
man come, etc.). [OE *nēahst* (NIGH, -EST)]

nĕx′us, n. Bond, link, connexion, (fig.);
the cash ~ (consisting in money payments). [L (*nectere nex-* bind)]

Niăg′ara, n. Cataract, torrent, din, (*shoot
~,* run fearful risks). [N.-Amer. water-
fall]

nib, n., & v.t. (-bb-). **1.** Point of quill pen;
metal or quill pen-point; point of tool etc.
2. pl. Fragments of crushed cocoa-beans.
3. v.t. Make, mend, insert ~ of, (pen). [f.
MDu.*nib,* or MLG *nibbe,* var. f. *nebbe* NEB]

nib′ble, v.t. & i., & n. **1.** Take small bites
at; bite (t. & i.) gently or cautiously or
playfully (esp. of fish with bait, or rabbits;
often ~ *at,* lit., & fig. of dallying with
temptation, bargain, etc.); carp *at,* make
trifling criticisms. **2.** n. Act of nibbling,
esp. of fish at bait; enough (grass etc.) to
~ at. [f. LG *nibbelen,* also *gnibbelen,
knabbelen,* whence obs. *knabble*]

nib′lick, n. Golf-club with large round
heavy head, used esp. for playing out of
bunkers. [orig. unkn.]

nibs (-z), n. (sl.). *His* etc. ~, burlesque
title after *His Grace* etc. [cf. earlier (cant)
nabs]

nice, a. & adv. **1.** Fastidious, dainty, hard
to please, of refined or critical tastes; precise, punctilious, scrupulous, particular,
(*must not be too ~ about the means*). **2.** Requiring precision, care, tact, or discrimination (*a ~ experiment, question, point,
negotiation*). **3.** Minute, subtle, (*a ~ distinction, shade of meaning*). **4.** Attentive,
close, (*a ~ inquiry, observer*). **5.** Delicately sensitive, discriminative, or deft (*a ~
ear, judgement, hand*; *weighed in the ~st
scales,* lit. or fig.). **6.** (colloq.). Agreeable,
attractive, delightful, well-flavoured,
satisfactory, kind, friendly, considerate,
generally commendable (often iron., as
here is a ~ mess). **7.** ~ (*and*), satisfactorily, as *the house stands ~ & high, car
is going ~ & fast, this is a ~ long one*; ~-
-*looking,* pretty or of engaging appearance. Hence ~′LY², (-sl-) adv., ~′NESS
(-sn-) n., ní′CISH¹(2) a. [ME senses, *stupid,
wanton*; OF, f. L *nescius* ignorant
(NESCIENCE)]

Nicēne′ (or nī⁻), a. Of Nicaea (*first &
second ~ councils,* held A.D. 325, 787, to
settle the Arian controversy & the question of images; ~ *Creed,* formal statement of Christian belief based on that
adopted at first ~ council). [f. LL *Nicae-
nus, Nicenus* (L f. Gk *Nikaia*)]

ni′cĕtў, n. Punctiliousness; precision,

accuracy, (*to a* ~, exactly); **intricate or subtle quality** (*a point of great* ~); **minute distinction, subtle or unimportant detail,** (pl.) **minutiae.** [ME, f. OF *nicete* (NICE, -TY)]

niche, n., & v.t. **1. Vertical recess in wall to contain statue, vase, etc.; (fig.) place destined for person's occupation, esp.** ~ *in the temple of fame,* **right to be remembered for one's achievements. 2.** v.t. **Place** (statue etc.) **in** ~ (usu. in p.p.); **ensconce, settle,** (esp. one*self,* or in p.p.) **in some hollow or corner.** [F, f. *nicher* make a nest, f. Rom. **nidicare* f. *nidus* nest]

nick[1], n. **Notch serving as catch, guide, mark,** etc.; (print.) **groove on side of type-letter; certain throws in hazard;** *in the* ~ (*of time*), **just at the right moment.** [orig. unkn.]

nick[2], v.t. & i. **Make nick(s) in, indent; make incision at root of** (horse's tail; also with *horse* etc. as obj.) **to make him carry it higher; hit upon, guess rightly,** (~ *it, the truth,* etc.); **just catch** (the time, a train, etc.); **catch, nab,** (criminals etc.); **make** (certain winning throws at hazard; **cut** *in* by short cut, at corner, etc., in hunting or racing; (of breeding stocks) **mingle** *well* etc. with others. [orig. unkn.]

nick'el, n., & v.t. (-ll-). **1. Hard silvery- -white lustrous ductile metallic element** much used esp. in alloys; U.S. **five-cent piece or kinds of Continental coin corresponding to English & French coppers;** ~ *brass,* alloy of copper, ~, & zinc; ~ *silver,* alloy like German silver; ~ *steel,* alloy of iron with ~. **2.** v.t. **Coat with** ~. [abbr. of G *kupfernickel* copper-coloured ore f. which ~ was first got (*kupfer* copper, *nickel* demon, w. ref. to disappointing nature of ore, which yielded no copper); cf. COBALT]

nick'nack. See KNICK-KNACK.

nick'name, n., & v.t. **1. Name added to or substituted for person's, place's, or thing's proper name; abbreviation or familiar form of Christian name. 2.** v.t. **Call** (person or thing *a* ~, give ~ to, (*some people are never* ~*d*; *they* ~ *patience cowardice*; *Cumberland,* ~*d Butcher*). [15th c. *neke-,* orig. *an* EKE[1]*-name,* cf. NEWT]

nico'tian (-shĭ-), a. & n. **Of tobacco;** (n.) smoker. [foll., -IAN]

nic'otin|e (-tēn), n. **Poisonous alkaloid extracted as oily liquid from tobacco.** Hence ~ISM(5) n., ~IZE(5) v.t. [F (*Nicot,* introducer of tobacco into France, -INE[5])]

nic'tāte, nic'titāte, vv.i. **Close & open the** eyes, wink, chiefly in *nict(it)ating membrane,* third or inner eyelid of many animals. Hence NICTA'TION, nictita'TION, nn. [f. (med. L *nictitare* frequent. of) L *nictare,* -ATE[3]]

ni'cy, n. (nursery). **Sweet, lollipop.** [NICE, -Y[3]]

nidamen'tal, a. **Serving as receptacle for** ova in molluscs etc. (~ *gland, capsule, ribbon*). [f. L *nidamentum* (NIDUS, -MENT)]

nid(d)'ering, n. & a. (pseudo-arch.). **Base or cowardly** (person). [misreading of obs. *nithing* f. ON *nithingr;* given currency by Scott]

nid'dle-nŏd'dle, a., & v.i. & t. **1. Nodding, quivering, unsteady. 2.** vb. **Keep nodding** (head, or intr.), **totter, sway.** [redupl. f. NOD, -LE(3)]

|| **nīde,** n. **Brood of pheasants.** [f. L NIDUS]

nid'ificāte, nid'ify, vv.i. **Build nest(s).** So **nidifica'TION** n. [f. L *nidificare* (NIDUS, -FY), -ATE[3]]

nid'nŏd, v.i. & t. (-dd-). **Keep nodding.** [reduplicated f. NOD]

nid'us, n. (pl. *-dī, -duses*). **Place in which insects etc. deposit eggs; place in which spores or seeds develop; place of origin or development for disease, or for some quality, doctrine, etc.; natural receptacle; collection of eggs, tubercles, etc.** [L, see NEST]

niece, n. **One's brother's or sister's daughter.** [ME & OF *nece, nice* f. LL *neptia* (also *nepta, neptis*) niece f. L *neptis* granddaughter]

niĕll'ō, n. (pl. *-li* pr. *-lē, -lōs*). **Black composition for filling engraved lines in silver or other metal; (specimen of) such ornamental work.** Hence ~ED[2] (-ōd) a. [It., f. neut. of L *nigellus* dim. of *niger* black]

Nier'steiner (nērstī-), n. **Rhenish wine from Nierstein.** [G]

Nietzsch'ean (nēch[4]-), a. & n. (Admirer, follower) of the German philosopher F. Nietzsche (d. 1900); (supporter) of his principles (see OVERMAN). [-AN]

*nif'ty̆, a. (sl.). **Spruce, smart, stylish; smelly.**

nigg'ard, n. & a. **Stingy person, grudging giver** *of;* (adj., rhet. & poet.) = foll. [ME, alt., by suf. substitution, f. earlier (obs.) *nigon,* perh. of Scand. orig.; cf. NIGGLE]

nigg'ardl|y̆, a. & adv. **Parsimonious, stingy, sparing, scanty, giving or given grudgingly or in small amounts;** hence ~ÎNESS n.; (adv.) in ~y manner. [-LY[1, 2]]

nigg'er (-g-), n. **Negro** (usu. derog.; *****~ *in the woodpile* or *fence,* sl., suspicious circumstance, something that spoils a good thing; *work like a* ~, toil very hard; (loosely) **member of any dark-skinned people,** e.g. E.-Indian, native Australian; ~(*-brown*), **dark shade of brown;** ~ *minstrel,* see NEGRO; ~ *melody, song,* etc., such as prevail among American Negroes; ~*head,* = NEGRO-*head.* Hence ~DOM n. [18th c. alt. f. *neger* (16th c.) f. F *nègre* f. Sp. *negro* NEGRO]

|| **nig'gle,** v.i. **Spend time, be over-elaborate, on petty details.** [app. of Scand. orig.; cf. Norw. *nigla*]

nigg'ling, a. **Trifling, petty, lacking in breadth, largeness, or boldness of effect;** (of handwriting) **cramped.** [-ING[2]]

nigh (nī), adv., prep., & a., (comp. & sup. formerly *near*, *next*, now ~*er*, ~*est*, also as advv., prepp., & aa., cf. NEAR[1], [2]). = NEAR[1], [2] (arch., poet., or dial.). [OE *nēah*, OS, OHG *nāh*, ON *ná-*, Goth. *nēhwa*; the orig. comp. & superl. are repr. by NEAR, NEXT; the forms ~*er*, ~*est* date f. 16th c.]

night (nīt), n. **1.** Dark period between day & day, time from 6 p.m. to 6 a.m. or from sunset to sunrise, darkness then prevailing, the dark, (also ~'*fall*) end of daylight, weather or experiences or occupation of a~, (*black, dark, as* ~; *went forth into the* ~; *the* ~ *of ignorance* or *barbarism*; *stayed three* ~*s with them*; *a dirty* ~, stormy or rainy; *have a good, bad,* ~, sleep well or ill, be comfortable or in pain, cf. GOOD~; *make a* ~ *of it*, spend ~ in festivity; ~ *out*, festive evening, also evening on which servant is allowed out; ~ *& day*, always, without cessation; *all* ~, *all* ~ *long*, for the whole ~; *by* ~, during, under cover of, the ~; *at* ~, at ~*fall*, in the evening, also added to the hours from 6 p.m. to midnight, cf. *in the morning* of hours 1–6 a.m.; *cannot sleep o'* ~*s for thinking of*); ~-, by, like, during, appropriate to, employed for, active in, the ~ (-*veiled*, -*black*, -*walking*, -*haunted*, *brawl*, -*attire*, *lamp*, -*porter*, -*moth*). **2.** ~-*bird*, esp. owl or nightingale, also person esp. of disreputable character who goes about by ~; ~-*blindness*, nyctalopia; ~-*boat*, passenger-boat crossing by ~; ~'*cap*, worn in bed, also alcoholic drink taken before going to bed; ‖ ~-*cellar*, underground drinkshop of low class; ~-*chair*, = ~-*stool*; ~-*clothes*, worn in bed; ~-*club* (open to members for dancing, supper, etc.); ~-*dress*, ~-*gown* (also ~'Y[3] n., pr. nīt'ī), woman's or child's ~ attire; ~-*flower*, that opens at ~ & closes in the day; ~-*glass*, short telescope for ~ use at sea; ~-*hag*, female demon riding the air at~, ~*mare*; ~-*hawk*, thieving or other nocturnal prowler; ~-*jar*, the GOAT*sucker*; ~-*light*, short thick candle giving dim light through ~ for invalids etc.; ~-*line*, left with baited hooks to catch fish by ~; ~-*long*, lasting through the ~; ~'*man*, employed to remove ~-soil; ~'*mare*, female monster sitting upon & seeming to suffocate sleeper, incubus, oppressive or paralysing or terrifying or fantastically horrible dream (whence ~'MĀRISH[1] a.), also haunting fear or thing vaguely dreaded; ~-*piece*, (painting of) ~ scene or landscape; ~-*school*, providing instruction for workmen after day's work; ~ *season*, = ~-time (poet., rhet.); ~-*shirt*, boy's or man's long shirt for sleeping in; ~-*soil*, contents of cesspools etc. removed at ~; ~-*stool*, close-stool or commode for use at ~; ~-*suit*, set of pyjamas; ~-*time*, = ~ as a state of things or opportunity (*in the* ~-*time*, by ~); ~-*watch*, (person or party keeping) watch by

~, Hebrew or Roman division (one of three or four) of the ~ (*in the* ~-*watches*, during the anxious, wearisome, wakeful, etc., ~-*work*, done, that must be done, by ~). Hence ~'LESS (nīt-) a. [OE *neaht*, *niht*, OS, OHG *naht*, ON *nátt*, Goth. *nahts* f. Gmc *naht- cogn. w. L *nox* -*ctis*]

night'ingāle (nītingg-), n. Small reddish-brown migratory bird singing melodiously & powerfully both by night & in the day. [OE *nihtegale* (obs. *nightgale*), OS, OHG *nahta-*, *nahtigala* (NIGHT, *galan* sing); forms -*in*- f. 13th c.]

night'lÿ[1] (nīt-), a. Happening, done, existing, etc., in the night; happening every night; (poet.) of or suiting night. [OE *nihtlīc* (NIGHT, -LY[1])]

night'lÿ[2] (nīt-), adv. Every night. [-LY[2]]

night'shāde (nīt-), n. Kinds of plants, esp. *black* ~ with white flowers & black poisonous berries, *woody* ~ with purple flowers & bright red berries (also *bitter-sweet*), & *deadly* ~ or BELLADONNA. [OE *nihtscada*, OHG *nahtscato*, app. f. NIGHT + SHADE]

nigrĕs'c|ent, a. Blackish. So ~ENCE n. [f. L *nigrescere* (*niger* black), -ENT]

nig'ritūde, n. Blackness (lit. & fig.). [f. L *nigritudo* (prec., -TUDE)]

nī'hĭl ăd rĕm, pred. a. Irrelevant. [L]

nī'hil|ism (nī'il-, ni'hil-), n. Negative doctrines, total rejection of current beliefs, in religion or morals; (philos.) scepticism that denies all existence; doctrines of extreme revolutionary party in 19th-c. Russia finding nothing to approve of in the constituted order of things. Hence ~IST(2) n., ~is'tIC a. [f. L *nihil* nothing, -ISM]

nihil'itÿ, n. Non-existence, nothingness; mere nothing, trifle, nullity. [f. med. L *nihilitas* (prec., -TY)]

nil, n. Nothing, no number or amount, (esp. in scoring at games etc., as *three goals to* ~); ~ *admirari* (ădmīrār'ī), attitude of being surprised at, or admiring, nothing, nonchalance. [L]

nil'gai (-gī), n. Var. of NYLGHAU.

‖ **nill**, v.i., 3rd sing. pres. condit. *Will he* ~ *he*, whether he likes it or not (now usu. *willy-nilly*). [OE; obs. *ne* not, WILL[1]]

Nīlŏm'ēter, n. Graduated pillar etc. showing height to which Nile rises. [f. Gk *Neilometrion* (-METER)]

Nīlŏt'ic, a. Of the Nile or Nile region or its inhabitants. [f. L f. Gk *Neilōtikos* (*Neilos* Nile, -OT[2], -IC)]

nim'ble, a. Quick in movement, agile, swift, (*the* ~ *shilling*, or *ninepence* arch., circulating quickly); (of the mind etc.) versatile, clever, quick to apprehend, dextrous. Hence ~NESS n., nim'bLY[1] adv. [f. OE *numol* f. *niman* take, -LE (1)]

nim'bus, n. (pl. -*bī*, -*buses*). Bright cloud or halo investing deity or person or thing; bright disc or aureole round or over head of saint etc. in picture; (meteorol.) rain-cloud. Hence ~ED[2] (-st) a. [L, = cloud]

nĭmĭ'ĕtў, n. (rare). Excess, too much. [f. LL *nimietas* f. *nimis* too much, -TY]

nĭm'ĭnÿ-pĭm'ĭnÿ, a. Affected, mincing, prim. [imit.]

Nĭm'rŏd, n. Great hunter or sportsman. [see *Gen.* x. 8, 9]

nĭnc'ompŏŏp, n. Simpleton, person without sense or character, ninny. [17th c. *nicom-*, of unkn. orig.]

nine, a. & n. **1.** One more than eight, 9, ix, IX, (often agreeing with understood noun, as ~ *of the men*, ~ *of them*, ~ *o'clock* or ~, *cost* ~ & *six*, *will be* ~ *next birthday*; ~*o'clock wind*, blowing from rifleman's left hand; *twenty*-~ etc. or, not beyond ~ & *ninety*, ~ & *twenty* etc.; *the N*~, the Muses; ~ *days' wonder*, novelty that attracts much attention but is soon forgotten; ~ *times out of ten*, generally; *possession is* ~ POINTS *of the law*; *cat has* ~ *lives*, see LIFE); || ~*'pins*, kinds of skittles; ~ *tenths*, nearly the whole; hence ~'FOLD (-nf-) a. & adv. **2.** n. The number ~; *card of* ~ pips; *to the* ~s, to perfection (esp. *dressed up to the* ~s, elaborately). [OE, OS *nigon* &c., f. Gmc *nigun*, var. of *niwun* (whence OHG, Goth. *niun*, ON *nīu*); cogn. w. L *novem*]

nine'teen' (-nt-), a. & n. One more than eighteen, 19, xix, XIX, (*is nearly* ~, years old; *twice* ~ *is* 38; *a* ~-&-*sixpenny pair of shoes*; ~ *to the* DOZEN). Hence ~TH[2] a. (~*th hole*, joc., golf-club's bar) & n. [-TEEN]

nine't|ÿ (-nt-), a. & n. **1.** Nine times ten, 90, xc, XC, (~*y-one* etc., or *one* etc. & ~*y*; ~*y-first* etc.; ~*y-nine out of a hundred*, nearly all); hence ~iĕTH[2] a. & n. **2.** n. The number ~*y*; (pl.) *the* ~*ies*, degrees on thermometer etc., years of century or life, between 89 & 100. [-TY[2]]

Nĭn'ĕvīte, n. Inhabitant of Nineveh. [f. LL *Ninevita* (*Niniveh*, -ITE[1])]

nĭnn'ÿ, n. Simpleton, fool, person of weak character or mind. [perh. for INNOCENT]

nīnon (nē'nawn), n. Light-weight silk dress fabric. [F]

ninth, a. & n. **1.** Next after eighth (*on the* ~, day of month; ~ *part*, one of nine equal parts into which thing may be divided; ~ *part of a man*, tailor). **2.** n. ~ part; (mus.) interval of octave & second. [NINE, -TH[2]]

ninth'lÿ, adv. In the ninth place (in enumerations). [-LY[2]]

Nī'obè, n. Inconsolable bereaved woman. Hence **Nīobē'AN** a. [Gk (-ē̆), woman turned to stone while weeping for slain children]

nīŏb'|ĭum, n. (chem.). A rare metallic element usu. found associated with tantalum. Hence ~IC (chem.), ~OUS (chem.), aa. [prec., -IUM; named 1845]

nĭp[1], v.t. & i. (-pp-), & n. **1.** Pinch, squeeze sharply, bite; pinch *off* (bud etc.); check growth of (esp. ~ *in the* BUD[1]; lit. & fig.); (of cold) affect injuriously, pain, whence ~p'ING[2] a., ~p'ingLУ[2] adv.; take *up*, *out*, etc., hurriedly or unob-

served; (sl.) step etc. nimbly *in(to)*, *out*, *up*, whence ~p'У[2] a., || (also as n., colloq. P, waitress in a restaurant of Messrs J. Lyons & Co., Ltd). **2.** n. Pinch, sharp squeeze, bite; sharp saying, sarcasm; (check to vegetation caused by) coldness of air. [14th c., rel. to obs. *nipe* f. MDu. *nipen* (Du. *nijpen*)]

nĭp[2], n., & v.i. & t. (-pp-). Small quantity of spirits etc. as pick-me-up; (vb) take ~s, take ~s of. [app. short f. 17th c. (obs.) *nipperkin* small measure, prob. of LG orig.; cf. LG, Du. *nippen* to sip]

nī'pa (nē-, nī-), n. Kind of E.-Indian palm. [f. Malay *nipah*]

nĭpp'er, n. In vbl senses of NIP[1], [2]; also or esp.: kinds of fish; || boy, lad, esp. costermonger's assistant or street arab; (pl.) implement with jaws for gripping or cutting, forceps, pincers, pliers, (often *pair of* ~s); (pl.) pince-nez; horse's incisor tooth; crustacean's claw. [-ER[1]]

nĭp'ple, n. Small projection in which mammary ducts terminate in mammal of either sex, teat, esp. on woman's breast; cover for protecting woman's teat while child sucks; teat of nursing-bottle; ~-like protuberance on skin, glass, metal, etc.; small rounded elevation on mountain; perforated projection of musket-lock on which percussion-cap was placed; || ~*wort*, yellow-flowered weed. [16th c. also *neble*, *nible*, perh. dim. f. NEB + -LE(1)]

Nĭpp'on, n. Japan. Hence **Nĭppŏn'IAN** a. [f. Dai ~, native name of Japan (lit. 'Great land of the rising sun')]

nĭrva'na (-vah-), n. Buddhist beatitude, i.e. extinction of individuality & absorption into the supreme spirit. [Skr., f. *nirvā* (*nir*, *nis* out + *vā* to blow)]

nĭs'ĭ, conj. (legal). Unless (*decree*, *order*, *rule*, etc., ~, decree etc. valid unless cause is shown for rescinding it before appointed time at which it is 'made absolute'; || ~ *pri'us*, hearing of civil causes by judges of assize, court-business of this kind). [L; ~ *prius*, unless previously, words from writ directing sheriff to provide jury on certain day unless judges come sooner]

Nĭss'en hŭt, n. Tunnel-shaped hut of corrugated iron with cement floor. [P. N. *Nissen* (d. 1930)]

nĭt, n. Egg of louse or other parasitic insect. [OE *hnitu*, = MDu., MLG *nēte*, OHG (*h*)*niz*]

nĭt'on, n. (Orig. name of) RADON. [f. L *nitēre* to shine, after *argon* etc.]

nĭt'rate[1], n. Salt given by combination of nitric acid with base, or compound made by interaction of nitric acid & alcohol; (short for) *potassium* or *sodium* ~. [f. F, or NITRE + -ATE[1](3)]

nĭtr|āte'[2], v.t. Treat, combine, or impregnate, with nitric acid. Hence ~A'TION n. [foll., -ATE[3]]

nī'tre (-er), n. Saltpetre, potassium nitrate; *cubic* ~, sodium nitrate. [ME, f.

OF, f. L f. Gk *nitron* perh. of Oriental orig.]

nit′ric, a. Of, containing, nitrogen; ~ *acid*, clear colourless pungent highly corrosive & caustic liquid, aquafortis. [f. F *nitrique* (prec., -IC)]

nit′rify, v.t. Impregnate with nitrogen, turn into nitrous or nitric acid. So ~FICA-TION n. [f. F *nitrifier* (NITRE, -FY)]

nit′rite, n. Compound of base or alcohol with nitrous acid. [NITRE, -ITE¹(2)]

nitro-, comb. form of Gk *nitron* NITRE, = of, containing, made with or by use of, nitric acid or nitroxyl or nitre or nitrogen; ~*-a′cid*, compound of nitric with organic acid; ~*-com′pound* (made by action of nitric acid); ~*-explōs′ive* (prepared by means of nitric acid); ~*-gly′cerin(e)*, yellowish oily violently explosive liquid made by adding glycerine to mixture of nitric & sulphuric acids; ~*-powd′er*, gunpowder made with nitric acid; ~*-sulphur′ic*, formed by mixture of nitric & sulphuric acids; *nitrŏx′yl*, chemical grouping of nitrogen & oxygen.

nit′rogĕn, n. Colourless tasteless scentless gas forming four-fifths of atmosphere. Hence **nitrŏ′gĕnous** a. [f. F *nitrogène*, see NITRE, -GEN(1)]

nit′rous, a. Of, like, impregnated with, nitre (~ *acid*, containing less oxygen than nitric acid; ~ *oxide*, gas used as anaesthetic, laughing-gas). [f. L *nitrosus* (NITRE, -OUS); later f. F *nitreux*]

nit′wit, n. A person of little intelligence. Hence ~TED² a. [cf. U.S. sl. *nit* none]

‖**nix¹**, int. (sl.) giving warning to confederates etc. that master etc. is approaching. [orig. unkn.]

nix², n. (fem. ~*ie*). Water-elf. [G (fem. *nixe*), cogn. w. obs. *nicker* (OE *nicor*)]

nix³, n. (sl.). Nothing. [f. colloq. Du. *niks*, G *nix*, (for *nichts*)]

Nizam′ (-ahm), n. Former title of ruler of Hyderabad; (man, men, of) Turkish regular army. [Hind. & Turk., f. Arab. *niḍām* order, arrangement]

nō¹, a. **1.** Not any (*no circumstances could justify it*; *no date*, abbr. n.d., = undated, in library lists etc. (of books, letters, etc.); *no song no supper*, you must sing first; *no* END¹; *by no* MEAN¹s). **2.** Not a, quite other than a, (*service of no honourable kind*; *is no part of my plan*; *is no genius*); hardly any (*is no distance*; *did it in no time*; *there is* etc. *no —ing*, none is etc. possible (*there's no accounting for tastes*; *there was no mistaking what he meant*). **3.** Imperfect substitute for, absence of, (often *no-*; *these opinions or rather no opinions*; *his faith or no-faith*). **4.** (In ellipt. sentences) we will not have any, let there not be any, there is not any, (*no Popery, surrender*, etc., whence *no--Popery riots*, a *no-confidence vote*, etc.; *now no mistake*, understand me clearly; *& no* MISTAKE¹; *no cards, no flowers*, invitations to funeral are not being sent

out, floral tributes are not desired; *no* DOUBT¹; *no* FEAR¹; *no* WONDER¹). **5.** *No ball*, unlawfully delivered ball in cricket, umpire's pronounce of this, (vb, *no-ball*) pronounce (bowler) to have bowled no ball; *no-being*, non-existence; *no′body*, no person (*everybody's* BUSINESS *is nobody's business*; *nobody ever did his*, or irreg. *their, work better*), (w. pl.) person of no importance, authority, or position; *no bon* (army sl.), no good; *no* GO²; *no′how*, in no way, by no means, (now chiefly dial.), *be, feel, look*, etc., *nohow*, out of order, out of sorts; *no man*, no person (*no man's land*, piece of waste, unowned, or debatable ground, esp. mil. the space between opposed trenches); *no meaning*, nonsense; *no one*, no person, (also, as adj.) no single (*no one man could lift it*); *no side* (football), (referee's announcement of the) end of the game; *no thoroughfare*, notice that path, street, etc., is closed at other end, or that entrance is not permitted, (also) such path; *no trump(s)* (bridge), declaration, bid, involving playing without a trump suit; *no--trumper*, hand on which a no-trump bid can be, or has been, made; *no′way(s)*, *no′wise*, in no manner, not at all; *no²-whence, no′whither*, from, to, no place; *no whit*, not at all (usu. w. compar.). [for NONE, orig. only before consonants]

nō², adv. (Alw. as alternative after *or*) not (usu. *whether or no*, in either case, also *tell me whether or no*; *pleasant or no, it is true*). [prob. f. prec. by extension of adj. use as in *whether there be any church or no (church)*]

nō³, adv. **1.** (Alw. with compar.) by no amount, not at all, (*no better than before*; *is no better than she should be*, is not quite respectable; *no sooner had he said it than*, as soon as he had said it; *no sooner said than done*; *no* LONG¹er). **2.** *No less (than)*, as much (n., a., adv.) or many (as) (*gave me £50, no less, no less than £50*; *no less than ten people have told me*; *did it no less for my warning*; *is no less than a scandal*; *a no less fatal victory*). **3.** *No more*, (n.) nothing further (*have no more to say*; *want no more of it*; often ellipt. for *say no more* or *let us have no more of it*); (adj.) not any more (*no more wine?*); (adv.) no longer (*is no more*, is dead or passed away), never again, to no greater extent (*is no more a lord than I am*; *could no more help laughing than I could fly*), just as little, neither, (*you did not come, no more did he*). [OE *nā*, see NATHLESS]

nō⁴, particle equivalent to negative sentence, & n. (pl. *noes*). **1.** The answer to your question is negative, your request or command will not be complied with, the statement made or course intended or conclusion arrived at is not correct or satisfactory, (*no, nor*, form for substituting stronger phrase, as *a man could not lift it, no, nor half a dozen*). **2.** n. The word *no*, a denial or refusal, (*two noes make a yes*; *will not take no for an answer*, persists in spite of refusals); (pl.) voters against a motion (*the noes have it*, are in a majority). [as prec.]

nō⁵, noh, n. Kind of (orig. religious) Japanese drama with dance & song. [Jap.]

Nōach′ian, Nōach′ic, (-k-), aa. Of Noah or his time. [*Noach* = Noah, -IAN]

Nō′ah (-*a*), n. Hebrew patriarch; ~*'s ark*, in which ~, his family, & animals were saved (*Gen.* vi), imitation of it as child's plaything, large or cumbrous or old--fashioned trunk or vehicle, small bivalve, detached fragment of flying cloud; ~*'s nightcap*, the plant eschscholtzia (w. ref. to conical bud-sheaths).

nŏb¹, n., & v.t. (sl.; -bb-). Head; (cribbage) knave of same suit as turn-up (*one for his* ~, point scored by holder of this); (vb, boxing) hit on the head. [perh. var. of KNOB]

nŏb², n. (sl.). Member of upper classes. [Sc. form (f. 18th c.) *knabb, nab,* orig. unkn.]

∥**nŏb′ble,** v.t. (sl.). Tamper with (racehorse) to prevent its winning; secure partiality of by underhand means; get hold of (money etc.) dishonestly; catch (criminal). [orig. unkn.]

nŏbb′y, a. (sl.). Suitable for a NOB², smart, elegant. [-Y²]

Nōbĕl′ prize, n. One of the annual prizes (for physics, chemistry, medicine, literature, & the promotion of peace) awarded from the bequest of Alfred Nobel (d. 1896), Swedish inventor of dynamite.

nobil′iary (-lya-), a. Of (the) nobility (~ *particle*, preposition, as French *de*, German *von*, prefixed to title; ~ *pride, rank,* etc.). [f. F *nobiliaire* (NOBLE, -ARY)]

nobil′ity, n. Noble character, mind, birth, or rank; *the* or *a* class of nobles. [ME, f. OF *-ite* or L *nobilitas* (foll., -TY)]

nō′ble, a. & n. 1. Illustrious by rank, title, or birth, belonging to the nobility; of lofty character or ideals (so ~-**mind**′ED² a., ~-**mind**′ed**NESS** n.); showing greatness of character, magnanimous, morally elevated; splendid, magnificent, stately, imposing, impressive, in appearance; excellent, admirable, (*a* ~ *horse, cellar,* etc.); (of metals such as gold, silver, platinum) resisting chemical action, not corroding or tarnishing in air or water, not easily attacked by acids; ~*man,* peer; ~*woman,* woman of ~ birth or rank; hence ~NESS n., **nōb′LY²** adv. 2. n. ~man; obsolete coin, usu. 6/8. [ME, f. OF, f. L *nobilis* (*noscere* KNOW, -BLE)]

noblĕsse′, n. The class of nobles (esp. of a foreign country); ~ *oblige* (ŏblĕzh′), privilege entails responsibility. [F]

nŏck¹, n., & v.t. 1. Notch at ends of bow for holding string; notch(ed horn tip) of arrow for receiving bowstring. 2. v.t. Set

(arrow) on string. [14th c., prob. rel. to foll.]

nŏck², n. Forward upper corner of some sails. [f. MLG *nock,* MDu. *nocke*]

nŏct|(ĭ)-, comb. form of L *nox noctis* night = by night, as ~*ăm′bŭlant* night-walking, ~*ĭflōr′ous* night-flowering, ~*ĭlūc′a* phosphorescent animalcule, ~*ĭv′agant,* ~*ĭv′a-gous,* night-wandering.

nŏc′tūle, n. Largest British species of bat. [F, f. It. *nottola* bat]

nŏctūrn′al, a. Of, in, done by, active in, the night. [f. LL (-*alis*) f. L *nocturnus* (NOCT-), -AL]

nŏc′tūrne, n. Dreamy musical piece; (paint.) night-scene. [F, cf. prec.]

nŏd, v.i. & t. (-dd-), & n. 1. Incline head slightly & quickly in salutation (~*ding acquaintance,* very slight one *with* person or subject), assent, or command; let head fall forward in drowsiness, be drowsy, make sleepy mistake (*Homer sometimes* ~*s,* the best of us may be dull or make a slip); (of buildings etc., also fig.) incline from perpendicular (esp. ~*s to its fall*); (of plumes) dance up & down; incline (head); signify (assent etc.) by ~. 2. n. ~ding of the head; this as sign of absolute power (*the empire was at* or *dependent on his* ~); *land of Nod,* sleep (with ref. to phr. in *Gen.* iv 16). [ME *nodde,* orig. unkn.]

nŏd′dle¹, n. (colloq.). Head, pate. [15th c. *nodle,* orig. unkn.]

nŏd′dle², v.t. Nod or wag (head). [NOD, -LE(3)]

nŏdd′y, n. Simpleton, noodle; tropical sea-bird. [16th c., goes w. obs. *noddy* adj. silly, of unkn. orig.]

nōde, n. Knob on root or branch; point at which leaves spring; hard tumour esp. on gouty or rheumatic joint; intersecting point of planet's orbit & ecliptic or of two great circles of celestial sphere, whence **nōd′ICAL** a.; point or line of rest in vibrating body; central point in system; point at which curve crosses itself. Hence **nōd′AL** a. [f. L NODUS]

nodōse′, a. Knotty, knobbed. [f. L *nodosus* (NODUS, -OSE¹)]

nodŏs′itў, n. Knottiness; knot, protuberance. [f. LL *nodositas* (prec., -TY)]

nŏd′ūl|e, n. Small rounded lump of anything; small node in plant; small knotty tumour, ganglion. Hence ~AR¹, ~**ātĕd** [-ATE²], ~OSE¹, ~OUS, aa., ~A′TION n. [f. L *nodulus* (foll., -ULE)]

nōd′us, n. (pl. *-dī*). Knotty point, difficulty, complication in plot of story etc. [L, = knot]

Nōĕl′. = NOWEL.

noĕt′ic, a. & n. 1. Of the intellect; purely intellectual or abstract; given to intellectual speculation. 2. n. (Sing. or pl.) science of the intellect. [f. Gk *noētikos* (*noētos* f. *noeō* apprehend, -IC)]

nŏg¹, n., & v.t. (-gg-). 1. Pin, peg, small block, of wood; snag or stump on tree. 2. v.t. Secure with ~s; build in form of (*brick-, concrete, stone-*) ~ǵ'ING¹ (-g-) n., i.e. brickwork etc. in timber frame. [orig. unkn.]

|| nŏǵ², n. Kind of strong beer brewed in E. Anglia. [orig. unkn.]

nŏǵǵ'in (-g-), n. Small mug; small measure, usu. ¼ pint, of liquor. [orig. unkn.]

noil, n. (Sing. or pl.) short wool-combings. [orig. unkn.]

noise (-z), n., & v.t. & i. **1.** Loud outcry, clamour, shouting, din of voices & movements; any sound, esp. loud or harsh or undesired one, whence ~'LESS a., ~'lèss-LY² adv., ~'lèssNESS n., (-zl-); *big* ~ (colloq., orig. U.S.), person of importance; *make a* ~, lit., also talk or complain much *about*, also be much talked of, attain notoriety *in the world*. **2.** vb. Make public, spread *abroad*, (person's fame, fact ; *it was* ~*d abroad that*—); (rare) make ~. [ME, f. OF *noise*, = Prov. *nausa*, f. L *nausea*]

noisette¹ (nwahzĕt'), n. Kind of rose, cross between China & musk. [N~, grower, 1817]

*noisette*² (as prec.), n. (Usu. pl.) small piece(s) of meat cooked in certain way. [F]

nois'ome, a. Harmful, noxious; ill-smelling; objectionable, offensive. Hence ~NESS n. [ME; obs. *noy* for ANNOY n., -SOME]

nois'|ў (-z-), a. Clamorous, turbulent; full of, making much, noise; (of colour, costume, literary style) loud, conspicuous, violent, glaring. Hence ~iLY² adv., ~iNESS n. [-Y²]

nŏl'ēns vŏl'ēns (-z), adv. Willy-nilly, perforce. [L part. = unwilling, willing]

nŏl'i mē tăn'gerĕ (-j-), n. Erosive ulcer(s), lupus; warning against meddling or approach (*carries a* ~ *in his face; a* ~ *manner*); picture of Christ as he appeared to Magdalen at sepulchre (*John* xx. 17). [L, = touch me not]

¶ nŏll, n. (now dial.). (Crown of) head. [OE *knoll*, corresp. to MDu. *nolle*, OHG (*h*)*nol*, *nollo* point, summit, hill, obsc. rel. to KNOLL]

nŏll'ĕ prŏs'equī, n. (legal). Relinquishment by plaintiff or prosecutor of (part of) his suit, stay of proceedings, entry of it on record. [L, = to refuse to pursue]

nŏl'ŏ ĕpĭscopār'ī, n. (Formula expressing) avoidance of responsible office. [LL, = I do not wish to be a bishop]

nŏm'ad (*also* nō-), n. & a. (Member of tribe) roaming from place to place for pasture; wanderer, wandering. Hence or cogn. nomăd'IC a., nomăd'ICALLY adv., ~ISM(2) n., ~IZE(2) v.i. [f. L f. Gk *nomas* -*ados* (*nemō* to pasture)]

nŏm'āde. Var. (now rare) of prec.

nom de guerre (see Ap.), n. Pseudonym, sobriquet, assumed name under which person fights, plays, writes, etc. [F, = war-name]

nom de plume (see Ap.), n. Writer's pseudonym, title or initials or borrowed name under which he writes. [formed in E of F words = pen-name on anal. of prec.]

nŏm'enclātor, n. Slave or client in ancient Rome charged with naming persons met, usher assigning places at banquet, (also in mod. use with ref. to these senses); giver or inventor of names, esp. in nat.-hist. classification. [L (*nomen* name, *calare* call, -OR)]

nŏm'encl|āture, n. Catalogue, register, (now rare); person's or community's system of names for things; terminology of a science etc.; systematic naming. So ~ATIVE a. [f. L *nomenclatura* (prec., -URE)]

nŏm'inal, a. Of, as, like, a noun (~ *& verbal roots*); of, in, names (~ *& essential distinctions*); ~ *definition*, statement of all marks connoted in name of concept); existing in name only, not real or actual, (~ *& real price, ruler*; ~ *sum, rent,* etc., virtually nothing), whence ~LY² adv.; consisting of, giving, the names (~ *list of officers* etc.; ~ *roll*). [f. L *nominalis* f. *nomen* -*inis* name; see -AL]

nŏm'inal|ism, n. (philos.). Doctrine that universals or abstract concepts are mere names (opp. *realism*). So ~IST(2) n., ~is-TIC a. [f. F *nominalisme* (prec., -ISM]

nŏm'ināt|e, v.t. Call by the name of, mention by name, name or appoint (date, place), (now rare); appoint, propose for election, to office (*a board of six* ~*ed & six elected members; the candidates were* ~*ed today*), whence or cogn. ~OR, nŏmĭnEE', nn. [f. L *nominare* (NOMINAL), -ATE³]

nŏmĭnā'tion, n. In vbl senses; also, right of nominating for appointment (*have a* ~ *at your service*). [ME, f. OF, or L *nominatio* (prec., -ATION)]

nŏm'inative, a. & n. **1.** (Case) used as or in agreement with subject of verb, (~ *absolute*, construction like Latin ablative absolute, as *this being so, I did nothing*); of this case (~ *ending, form*); word in this case, (loosely) subject (*of* verb); hence nŏminatĭv'AL a. **2.** (*pr.* -ātĭv). Of, appointed by, nomination (*the* ~ *& the elective principles, members*). [ME, f. OF (-*if*, -*ive*) or L *nominativus* (NOMINATE, -IVE)]

nŏn, Latin adv. = not, forming part of phrases : ~ *assump'sĭt* (he did not undertake), plea that defendant made no promise ; ~ *cŏm'pŏs* (*měn'tĭs*), (not master of his mind), lunatic, mad, (legal, & in gen. use); ~ *ĕss'ĕ* (not to be), non-existence; ~ *ĕst ĭnven'tus* (he has not been found), ~ *ĕst*, or ~ *ĭnvĕn'tus*, sheriff's statement, in returning writ, that defendant is not to be found in his bailiwick (legal, & transf. in gen. use); ~ *li'quĕt* (it is not clear), jury's verdict in doubtful case deferring matter to another day; ~ *nōb'īs* (not unto us; *Ps.* cxv), formula attributing victory etc. not to oneself but to God, song of rejoicing; ~ *plā'cĕt* (it does not please), negative vote in ecclesiastical or university assemblies (also as v.t., throw out); ~ *plus ul'tra*, = NE PLUS ULTRA; ~ *pôss'ŭmus* (we cannot), statement of inability, refusal to act or move; ~ *sē'quitur* (it does not follow), illogical inference, paradoxical result.

nŏn-, pref. (AF *noun-* = OF *non-*, *nom-* (mod. F *non-*), f. prec.) now freely prefixed: **1.** Usu. to vbl n. giving neg. vbl n. corresp. to *not* w. parent vb, = failure to do, abstention from doing, or rarely to other n. giving neg. abstract n. corresp. to *not* w. connected adj.; ~*accep'tance*; ~*ac'cess*, impossibility of access for sexual intercourse (in questions of paternity); ~*acquain'tance*; ~*appear'ance* (esp. in court as party or witness); ~*atten'dance*; ~*claim*, failure to make claim within legal time; ~*committ'al*, avoidance of committing oneself to definite course or either side (usu. attrib., as ~*committal answer*); ~*compli'ance*; ~*co-opera'tion* (Indian pol.), refusal or failure to co-operate (with the British); ~*feas'ance* (-z-; legal), omission of act that ought to have been done; ~*interfer'ence*, -*interven'tion*, principle or practice, esp. in politics & international affairs, of keeping aloof from others' disputes; ~*intru'sion* (Church of Scotland), principle that patron shall not thrust unacceptable minister on congregation; ~*join'der* (legal), omission of partner etc. to join another as party to suit; ~*pay'ment*; ~*percep'tion*; ~*perform'ance*; ~*resis'tance* (hist.), 17th-c. principle that authority must not be resisted even if unjustly exercised; ~*success'*; ~*us'age*; ~*use'*; ~*us'er* (legal), neglect to use a right, by which it may become void. **2.** To n. of designation, giving n. (occas. w. derivatives) = person, thing, or all, that is not the thing specified; ~*abstain'er*, one who does not abstain (esp. from liquor); ~*eg'o* (metaphys.), all that is not the conscious self, the object as opposed to the subject; ~*mem'ber* (so ~*mem'bership*); ~*met'al* (esp. chem. = element that is not a metal; so ~*metall'ic*). **3.** To attrib. n., giving adj. (occas. w. derivatives) that can only be used attributively, = unconnected with, not involving; ~*jur'y*, tried without jury; ~*part'y*, that may be dealt with [irrespective of political partisanship; ~*skid'*, (of tires) safe against skidding; ~*soci'ety*, -*ŭn'ion* (also ~*ŭn'ionist*), not belonging to a workman's society or trade union; ~*stop'*, (of trains, buses, etc.) not stopping at intermediate stations, halts, etc., (of journey) made without a stop, (n.) ~-stop train, bus, or run, (adv.) without a stop. **4.** To adj. (usu. participial in -*ant*, -*ent*, -*ing*, -*ate*, -*ed*), giving adj. (& occas. n. or derivatives) = not-; ~*belli'gerent* a. & n., (country) taking no active part in war; ~*colle'giate*, (student) not belonging to a college, (of universities)

without colleges; ~*com'batant*, (person, esp. in the fighting services, e.g. surgeon, chaplain, ambulance man) who has not to fight, civilian; ~*commi'ssioned*, not holding commission (esp. of army officers such as *sergeant, corporal*, abbr. N.C.O. or *non--com.*); ~*commŭn'icant*, (person) who does not attend the communion service; ~*conduc'ting*, that will not conduct heat or electricity (so ~*conduc'tor*, ~*conducting medium or substance*; ~*conductibil'ity*); ‖~*content*, voter against motion in House of Lords; ~*essen'tial* a. & n.; ~*Euclid'éan*, denying or dispensing with any of the assumptions of Euclid's geometry; ~*exis'tent*, -*exis'tence*; ~*flamm'able*, (of flannelette etc.) not inflammable; ~*jur'ing*, -*jur'or*, (joor-; hist.), (beneficed clergyman) who refused oath of allegiance to William & Mary; ~*nuclear*, (of warfare, weapons, etc.) conventional; ~*off'ice-holding* etc.; ‖~*provid'ed*, (of schools) other than PROVIDED. **5.** To adj. requiring a neutral negative form free from some special sense, usu. of condemnation, attached to the compd in *in-*, *un-*, = not coming under the description of, not; ~*effec'tive*, (soldier, sailor) not qualified for active service (cf. INEFFECTIVE); ~*hŭm'an*, not belonging to human race (cf. INHUMAN); ~*lo'gical*, proceeding by other means than logic (cf. ILLOGICAL); ~*mo'ral*, unconcerned with morality (cf. IMMORAL); ~*na'tural*, deviating from the natural order (cf. UNNATURAL). **6.** To adv., as ~-*conten'tiously*.

nŏn'age, n. Being under age, minority; immaturity, early stage. [ME, f. OF (prec., AGE)]

nŏnagénār'ian, a. & n. (Person) between 89 & 100 years old. [f. L *nonagenarius* (*nonageni* 90 each, -ARY[1]), -IAN]

nŏn'arў, a. & n. (Arith., of SCALE[3] of notation) having nine as basis; (n.) group of nine. [f. L *nonarius* (*nonus* ninth, -ARY[1])]

nŏnce, n. Time being, present occasion, (only *in for the* ~); ~*word*, coined for one occasion. [ME *to*, *for, then anes* = (for) the ONCE, cf. NEWT]

nŏn'chal|ant (-sh-), a. Unexcited, unmoved, cool, indifferent. Hence ~ANCE n., ~antLY[2] adv. [F, part. of *nonchaloir* (NON-, L *calēre* be warm)]

nŏnconfôrm'ist, n. One who does not conform to doctrine or discipline of an established Church, esp. member of sect dissenting from Anglican Church (usu. not including Roman-Catholics), protestant dissenter (*the* ~ *conscience*, opinions as to right & wrong prevalent among ~s esp. as affecting their political attitude). [NON-(2)]

nŏnconfôrm'itў, n. Principles, practice, the body, of nonconformists, protestant dissent; failure to conform (*to* rule etc.); want of correspondence between things. [NON-(2)]

nŏn'dèscript, a. & n. (Person, thing) not easily classified, neither one thing nor another, hybrid. [NON-(4), L *descriptus* (DESCRIBE)]

none (nŭn), pron., a., & adv. **1.** Not any of (~ *of them came*; ~ *of them is*, or *are*, acc. to sense required; ~ *of this concerns me*; ~ *of your impudence !*); no person, no one, (now rare; ~ *can tell*); no persons (~ *but fools have ever believed it*). **2.** adj. (rarely with noun; usu. ellipt. = *no* with reference defined by noun previously used or shortly to follow). No, not any, not to be counted in specified class, (*make of* ~ *effect*, arch.; *you have money & I have* ~; *he is* ~ *of my friends*, ~ *of your canting hypocrites*; *his understanding is* ~ *of the clearest*; *this is* ~ *other but the house of God*; *seeking rest & finding* ~; *if a linguist is wanted, I am* ~; *would rather have a bad reputation than* ~ *at all*; *poetry we have almost* ~). **3.** adv. By no amount, not at all, (w. *the* & comparat., *so*, or *too*; *am* ~ *the better for it*; ~ *the less*, = NEVERTHE-*less*; *are* ~ *so fond of him*; *the pay is* ~ *too high*). [OE *nān* (*ne* not, ONE)]

nonĕn'tity, n. **1.** (nŏn-). Non-existence, non-existent thing, figment. **2.** (non-). Person or thing of no importance, cipher. [NON-(2)]

nŏnes, n. pl. **1.** (Rom. ant.). Ninth day by inclusive reckoning before IDES, i.e. 7th of Mar., May, July, Oct., & 5th of other months. **2.** (eccl.). Daily office orig. said at ninth hour or 3 p.m. [sense 1 f. OF *nones* or L *nonae*, sense 2 pl. of rare *none* f. L *nona*, (*nonus* ninth); cf. NOON]

nonesuch. See NONSUCH.

nŏnĕt', n. (mus.). Composition for nine instruments or voices. [f. It. *nonetto* (*nono* ninth f. L *nonus*)]

nonill'ion (-yon), n. ‖ Ninth power of million, 1 with 54 ciphers. [see NONARY, BILLION]

nŏn'ius, n. Contrivance for graduating mathematical instruments, of which the VERNIER is an improved form. [latinized from *Nuñes*, Portuguese inventor]

nŏnpareil' (-rĕl), a. & n. Unrivalled or unique (person, thing); (print.) size of TYPE; kinds of comfit, apple, bird, wheat, moth, etc. [F (NON-, *pareil* equal, f. L PAR]

nŏnplŭs', n., & v.t. (-ss-). **1.** State of perplexity, standstill, (usu. *at a* ~), perplexed, *reduce* etc. *to a* ~). **2.** v.t. Reduce to hopeless perplexity. [f. L *non plus* not more]

nŏn-rĕs'id|ent (-z-), a. & n. (Clergyman) not residing where his duties require him, absentee (incumbent); (person) sojourn-ing in place only for short time or residing elsewhere. So ~ENCE n. [NON-(2)]

nŏn'sense, n. & int. **1.** Absurd or meaningless words or ideas, foolish or extravagant conduct; arrangement etc. that one disapproves of. **2.** int. You are talking or proposing ~, it surely cannot be true, etc. **3.** ~-*book*, meant to amuse by absurdity; ~ *verses*, having no sense or an

absurd one. Hence **nŏnsen'sICAL** a., **nŏnsĕn'sicaLLY** adv. [NON-(2)]

nŏn'sŭch, none'sŭch (nŭns-), n. Person or thing that is unrivalled, paragon; kind of lucerne. [NONE, SUCH, usu. now assim. to NON-]

nŏn'suit (-ūt), n., & v.t. **1.** Stoppage of suit by judge when plaintiff fails to make out legal case or bring sufficient evidence. **2.** v.t. Subject (plaintiff) to ~. [ME, f. AF *no(u)nsuit* (NON-(1), SUIT)]

nŏn'us. See PRIMUS[1].

no͞o'dle[1], n. Simpleton. Hence ~DOM n. [orig. unkn.]

no͞o'dle[2], n. Strip of dough made of flour & eggs, dried & used in soups. [f. G *nudel*]

no͞ok, n. Out-of-the-way corner, recess, secluded place. [ME, of unkn., prob. Scand., orig.]

no͞on, n. Twelve o'clock in the day, mid-day; ~'*day*, ~'*tide*, midday. [OE *nōn*, = ON *nón*; cf. OS, OHG, ON *nōna*, f. L *nona* (*hora*) ninth hour; orig. = 3 p.m.]

no͞ose, n., & v.t. **1.** Loop with running knot, tightening as rope or wire is pulled, esp. in snare, lasso, or hangman's halter; the marriage tie; snare or bond. **2.** v.t. Capture with ~, ensnare; make ~ on (cord); arrange (cord) in ~ *round* neck etc. [late ME *nose*, perh. f. OF *nous* f. L *nodus* knot]

nŏp'al, n. American cactus grown in plantations for breeding cochineal. Hence ~RY(3) n. [Sp., f. Mex. *nopalli* cactus]

nor (nôr, nor), adv. & conj. **1.** (arch.). Neither (as the first *nor* in ~ *gold* ~ *silver*). **2.** conj. And not, & no more, neither, & not either, (*had neither arms* ~ *provisions*; *not a man* ~ *a child was to be seen*; *I said I had not seen it*, ~ *had I* ; *all that is true*, ~ *must we forget*; also poet. & arch. w. omission of preceding *neither* or ~, as *thou* ~ *I have made the world*). [contr. f. obs. *nother* (OE *nā* see NATHLESS, WHETHER)]

nor'-. Shortened form of NORTH.

Nôrd'ic, a. (ethnol.). Of the tall blond dolichocephalic people found in northern Europe esp. in Scandinavia (of more limited application than *Teutonic*). [f. F *nordique*, f. *nord* NORTH, see -IC]

Nôr'folk (-ok), n. English county (‖ ~ *capon*, red herring; ‖ ~ *dumpling, turkey*, inhabitant or native of ~; ~ *jacket*, man's loose jacket with waistband; ~ *plover*, stone-curlew).

‖nôrl'and, n. Northern region. [for *northland*]

nôrm, n. Standard, pattern, type. [f. L *norma* carpenter's square]

nôrm'al, a. & n. **1.** (Geom.) standing at right angles, perpendicular; conforming to standard, regular, usual, typical; ~ *school*, for training teachers; hence **nôr-māl'**ITY (also irreg. ~CY) n., ~IZE(3) v.t., ~iZA'TION n., ~LY[2] adv. **2.** n. (Geom.) ~ line; (phys.) average or mean of observed quantities; usual state, level, etc.,

~ **temperature** (98·4° F.) of human body. [f. L *normalis* (prec., -AL)]

Nŏrm'an, n. & a. **1.** Inhabitant or native of Normandy, descendant of mixed Scandinavian & Frankish race there established; = ~ *French* below; = ~ *style* below. **2.** adj. Of the ~s (~ *Conquest*, of England by ~s 1066; ~ *English*, English as spoken or influenced by ~s; ~ *French*, French as spoken by ~s or later in English law-courts; ~ STYLE in architecture, whence ~ESQUE', pr. -čsk, a.); hence ~ISM(2, 4) n., ~IZE(3, 4) v.t. & i., ~IZA'TION n. [f. OF *Normans* pl. f. Gmc *NORTHman*]

Nŏrn, n. One of the female fates of Scandinavian mythology. [ON, orig. unkn.]

‖ **Nŏ'rroy**, n. Third KING of Arms, with jurisdiction north of the Trent. [ME, f. AF *nor*- NORTH +*rey, roy* king]

Nŏrse, n. & a. **1.** The Norwegian language (*Old*~, language of Norway & its colonies down to 14th c.). **2.** adj. Norwegian, of Norway, so ~'*land*, ~'*man*. [f. Du. *noorsch* (*noord* NORTH, -ISH¹)]

Nŏrsk, n. & a. = prec. [Scand.]

nŏrth, adv., n., & a., (abbr. N.; in compp. & derivv. often shortened to *nor*'-). **1.** Towards or in the region lying to right of observer on equator at equinox who faces setting sun (~ BY *east* etc.; ~ *of*, further ~ than; DUE¹ ~; *lies* etc. ~ & *south*, lengthwise along line running between ~ & south); ~-*east'*, ~-*west'*, (abbr. NE., NW.), advv., nn., & aa., (regions) midway between ~ & east, west, ~-~-*east'*, ~-~-*west'*, (abbr. NNE., NNW.), advv., nn., & aa., (regions) midway between ~ & ~-east, ~-west, (with uses & derivatives corresponding to those of *north*; so esp. ~-*east'erly*, -*west'erly*, -*east'ern*, -*west'ern*, -*east'ward*, -*west'ward*, -*east'wardly*, -*west'-wardly*, see NORTHERLY etc.; ~-*east*, ~-*west*, *passage*, passages for ships along northern coasts of Europe & Asia, northern coast of America, formerly thought of as possible routes to E., & from Atlantic to Pacific; *the* N~-*west*, = NW. territories of Canada); hence ~'WARD adv., n., & a., ~'WARDS adv. & n. **2.** n. Cardinal point lying ~ (*magnetic* ~, point indicated by ~ end of compass-needle); northern part of England (beyond Humber), Great Britain, Scotland, Ireland, or Europe; *northern States in which slavery did not exist; northern part *of* any country; ~ wind. **3.** adj. Situated, dwelling, in or more towards the ~ (N~ *Germany, Wales, America*; ~ *latitude*; ~ POLE²), whence ~-pŏl'AR a.; ~ *transept*); facing ~ (~ *window, aspect*); coming from the ~ (~ *wind*; ~ *light*, esp. as desired by painters & factory designers); N~ *Britain*, Scotland (abbr. N.B. in addresses); N~ *Briton*, Scot; ‖~ *country*, ~ part of England or Great Britain (~-*coun'tryman*, native of northern England; ~-*coun'try*, from or characteristic of ~ country); N~'*land* (poet.), northern lands, northern part of

a country; ~ *light*, Aurora Borealis; N~'*man*, native of Norway or Scandinavia; N~ *Sea*, between Britain, Netherlands, Germany, & Scandinavia; N~ *star*, POLE²-*star*. [OE, OS *north*, OHG *nort*, ON *northr*]

north-east'er, nŏr'-, n. NE. wind. [-ER¹]

***nŏrth'er**, n. Strong cold north wind blowing in autumn & winter over Texas, Florida, & Gulf of Mexico. [-ER¹]

nŏrth'erly (-dh-), a. & adv. = foll. (rare): (of direction) towards the north; (of wind) blowing from the north or thereabouts. [f. NORTH as EASTERLY]

nŏrth'ern (-dh-), a. & n. **1.** Living or situated in, coming from, the north esp. of England or Europe; *of the NORTH; (of wind) northerly (rare); characteristic of the north (a *pallid* ~ *day*); ~ *lights*, Aurora Borealis; hence ~ER¹(4) n., ~MOST a. **2.** n. ~er. [-ERN]

nŏrth'ing, n. Northward progress or deviation in sailing or travelling (*two miles* ~; *have made very little* ~). [-ING¹]

Nŏrthŭm'brian, a. & n. (Native, dialect) of ancient Northumbria (England N. of Humber) or modern Northumberland. [obs. *Northumber*, person living beyond Humber, +-IAN]

nŏrth'wardly, adv. & a. Northwards; (of wind) northerly. [-LY²]

nŏrth-wěst'er, nŏr'-, n. NW. wind. [-ER¹]

nŏr'ward(s) (-z). = NORTHward(s).

Nŏrwē'gian (-jn), a. & n. (Native, language) of Norway. [f. med. L *Norvegia* + -AN, w. assim. to *Norway*]

nŏr'-wěst'er, n. North-wester: glass of strong liquor; oilskin hat, sou'-wester. [NOR'-]

nōse (nōz), n., & v.t. & i. **1.** Member of face or head placed above mouth containing nostrils & serving as organ of smell (*as plain as the* ~ *in your face*, easily seen; *bite* or *snap* one's ~ *off*, answer him snappishly; *count* or *tell* ~s, count supporters etc., decide question by mere numbers; *cut off* one's ~ *to spite* one's *face*, indulge pique at one's own expense; *follow* one's ~, go straight forward, be guided by instinct; *keep* one's ~ *to the* GRINDstone; LEAD¹ *by the* ~; *look down* one's ~ (with disdain) *at*; *make a* LONG¹ ~; ~ *of wax*, person or thing easily influenced or moulded; *parson's or pope's* ~, rump of cooked fowl; *pay through the* ~, be overcharged, have to pay exorbitant prices; *poke, thrust*, etc., one's ~, pry or intrude *into* something; *put* one's ~ *out of joint*, supplant or disconcert or frustrate him; *speak through* one's ~, pronounce with nasal twang; *turn up* one's ~ *at*, show disdain for; *under* one's~, straight before him, regardless of his displeasure). **2.** Sense of smell (*has a good* ~, esp. of dogs, & fig. of detectives etc.). **3.** ‖ Odour, perfume, of hay, tea, etc. **4.** Open end or nozzle of pipe, tube, bellows, retort, etc. **5.** Prow; projecting part. **6.** ~-*ape*, proboscis-monkey; ~'*bag*, containing fodder for hanging to horse's head; ~'*band*, lower band of bridle passing over ~ & attached to cheek-straps; ~'*dive*, aeroplane's downward plunge (v.i., make this); ~-*flute*, musical instrument blown with ~ among Siamese, Fijians, etc.; ~'*gay* [GAY in obs. n. use = toy], bunch of (esp. sweet-scented) flowers; ~-*monkey*, proboscis-monkey; ~-*piece*, = ~band, also part of microscope to which object--glass is attached; ~'*pipe*, piece of piping used as nozzle; ~'*rag* (sl.), pocket-hand-kerchief; ~'*ring*, fixed in ~ of bull etc. for leading, also ornament worn by savages; ~'*warmer* (sl.), short pipe; hence (-)nōsED² (-zd), ~'LESS (-zl-), aa. **7. vb.** Perceive smell of, discover by smell, (fig.) detect (~*s a job in everything*), smell *out*; rub with the ~, thrust ~ against or into; sniff (*at, about* adv. & prep.), pry or search (*after, for*); push one's way, push (one's *way*), with the ~ (esp. of ship); (of strata etc.) dip *in*, basset *out*. [OE *nosu*, MDu., MLG *nose*, obsc. rel. to OE *nasu*, MDu. *nase*, OHG *nasa* (G *nase*), ON *nǫs*; cogn. w. L *nasus*; see NAZE, NESS]

nōs'er (-z-), n. Strong head wind (esp. *dead*~). [prec., -ER¹]

nōs'ing (-z-), n. Rounded edge of step, moulding, etc., or metal shield for it. [NOSE, -ING¹]

noso-, comb. form of Gk *nosos* disease, as *nosŏG'RAPHY*, systematic description of diseases; *nosŏL'OGY*, (branch of medical science dealing with) classification of diseases (so *nŏsoLO'GICAL*, *nosŏL'OGIST*).

nŏstăl'g|ia, n. Home-sickness as a disease; sentimental yearning for (some period of) the past. Hence ~IC a. [f. Gk *nostos* return home, Gk *algos* pain, -IA¹]

nŏs'tŏc, n. Kinds of gelatinous blue-green algae. [name invented by Paracelsus]

Nŏstradām'us, n. Prediction-monger, professed seer. [latinized f. M. de *Nostredame*, French physician who made prophecies 1555]

nŏs'tril, n. Either opening in nose admitting air to lungs & smells to olfactory nerves (*stink in* one's ~*s*, be offensive to him). Hence (-)~lED² (-ld) a. [OE *nosthyrl* (NOSE, obs. *thirl* f. OE *thȳrel* hole, cf. THRILL)]

nŏs'trum, n. Medicine prepared by person recommending it, quack remedy, patent medicine; pet scheme for political or social reform, special device. [L, neut. of *noster* our, my]

nōs'ȳ (-z-), a. & n. Large-nosed (person; esp. of Duke of Wellington); ill-smelling (esp. of heated corn, mouldy hay, etc.); fragrant (of tea); sensitive to bad smells; (sl.) inquisitive (‖ esp. *N~ Parker*, busy--body). [-Y²]

nŏt, n't (see below), adv. **1.** Negativing & following ordinary verbs (arch. for usu. neg. form with *do*; *I know* ~; *I doubt* ~;

say ~ *so*; *fear* ~; *saidst thou* ~?). **2.** (Often *n't* joined to word) negativing auxiliaries & vb *be*, & following them or (in questions having *not* in full) their subjects (*I cannot* or *can't say*; *he will* ~ or *won't*, or arch. *he'll* ~, *come*; *she is* ~, *isn't*, or vulg. *ain't*, *here*; *do* ~, or usu. *don't*, *stir*; *didn't you*, or formally *did you* ~, *tell me*?; *am I* ~, or *ain't I, aren't we, smart*?). **3.** Negativing & preceding particles & infinitives (~ *knowing, I cannot say*; *begged him* ~ *to move*). **4.** Used elliptically for negative sentence or verb or phrase (*Are you ill? Not at all. Not so. If it clears we will go out*; *if* ~, ~. *Popular or* ~, *it is right. I would as soon do it as* ~); preceding *that* with sense *it is* ~ *to be inferred, however, that*, or *but what* or (formal) *but that* or (arch.) *but* with sense *all the same* or *nevertheless* (*If he said so* —— *that he ever did*—*he lied. I cannot do it*; ~ *but what* etc. *a stronger man might*). **5.** Preceding word etc. that is to be rejected for one that follows with *but* or to emphasize by contrast one already used (*He is* ~ *my son, but yours*, or *but my nephew. He is your son*, ~ or *& ~ mine*). **6.** Preceding emphatic appended pronoun (*they will* ~ be ‘*had*’, ~ *they*). **7.** Preceding *a* with sense ~ *one* (~ *a hair of your head shall be touched*). **8.** Preceding in litotes or periphrasis a word of opposite sense to that required (~ *a few*, ~ *seldom*; ~ *once or nor twice*, many times; ~ *too well*, rather ill, rather badly; ~ *unconnected with*; ~ *reluctant*, only too glad). **9.** ~ *at* HOME; ~-*being*, non-existence; ‖ ~ *half* (adv. sl.), very, very much, (‘*Was he annoyed?*’ ‘*Not half*’, i.e. yes, exceedingly); ~ *out*; ~-*self*, = NON-*ego*; ~ *sufficient*, or usu. *N.S.*, banker's mark on dishonoured cheque. [ME; contr. of NOUGHT]

nŏt'a bĕn'e, vb imperat. (abbr. N.B.). Observe what follows, take notice, (usu. drawing attention to a qualification of what has preceded). [L, = note well]

nŏtabil'ity, n. Prominent person, (rare) notable object or thing worth seeing; worthiness of notice (*names of no historical* ~); ‖ (arch.) housewifely skill. [ME, f. OF *notabilite* or LL (med. L) *notabilitas* (foll., -ITY)]

nŏt'able, a. & n. **1.** Worthy of note, remarkable, striking, eminent, (chem.) perceptible (*a* ~ *quantity of*); (of women) occas. pr. nŏt-) capable, bustling, housewifely; hence **nŏt'ABLY²** adv. **2.** n. Eminent person (esp. *Assembly of N~s*, irregular council serving as temporary parliament in emergencies). [ME, f. OF, f. L *notabilis* (NOTE², -ABLE)]

nŏt'arȳ, n. Person publicly authorized to draw up or attest contracts etc., protest bills of exchange etc., & perform other formalities (also ~ *public*). Hence **notār'iAL** a., **notār'iALLY²** adv. [ME, f. L *notarius* secretary (NOTE¹, ², -ARY¹)]

notā'tion, n. Representing of numbers,

quantities, pitch and duration of sound, etc., by symbols; any set of symbols used for this, esp. in arith., alg., & mus.; *note, annotation; SCALE³ *of* ~. [f. L *notatio* (NOTE², -ATION)]

notch, n., & v.t. **1.** V-shaped indentation in edge or on convex surface; nick made on stick etc. by way of keeping count; *defile, pass; ~-*wing*, kinds of moth; hence ~'Y², ~ED² (-cht; bot., zool.), aa. **2.** v.t. Make ~es in; make *into* saw etc. by ~ing; score (items etc.; often *up, down*) by ~es; secure or insert (steps in staircase etc.) by ~es. [16th c., f. obs. F *oche* (mod. *hoche*) with (*a*)*n* prefixed, cf. NEWT]

note¹, n. **1.** Written sign representing pitch & duration of a musical sound; key of pianoforte etc.; single tone of definite pitch made by musical instrument, voice, etc.; (single tone in) bird's song or call; significant sound or way of expressing oneself (there is a ~ *of self-complacency in his voice; sound the ~ of war*). **2.** Sign, token, characteristic, distinguishing feature, proof of genuineness, guarantee consisting of, (these are the ~s *of Neopaganism; catholicity is one ~ of the true Church; has the ~ of catholicity*); stigma, mark of censure, (*on which the law has set a ~ of infamy*); mark *of exclamation* or *admiration, interrogation*. **3.** Brief record of facts, impressions, or topics for speech or article (usu. pl.; *make* or *take a ~ of*,~s; COMPARE~s; *preaches from*~s; *spoke for an hour without a ~*); annotation appended to passage in book etc.; short or informal letter; formal diplomatic communication; (usu. ~ *of hand*) written promise to pay sum by certain time; ‖ BANK³~; CIRCULAR ~. **4.** Eminence (*critic, philosopher, person, of* ~, distinguished); notice, attention, (*worthy of* ~; *take ~ of*), whence ~'WORTHY (-twêrdhl) a. **5.** ~'book, for entering memoranda in; ~'case, pocket wallet for holding bank-~s; ~'paper, kinds used for (esp. private) correspondence. Hence ~'LESS a., ~'LET n., (-tl-). [ME, f. OF, f. L *nota* mark]

note², v.t. Observe, notice, give attention to; set down, set *down*, as thing to be remembered or observed; annotate (book etc.); (p.p.) celebrated, well known *for*. [ME, f. OF *noter* f. L *notare* (prec.)]

nothing (nŭ-), n. & adv. **1.** No thing (with adj. following, as ~ *great is easy*). **2.** Not anything, nought, (*has* ~ *in him*, is insignificant or without individuality; *there is* ~ *in it*, it is untrue or unimportant, & see IN¹; ~ *doing*, sl. announcement of failure or refusal of request; ~ *venture* ~ *have*, excuse for or encouragement to bold action; ~ *like* LEATHER; NECK *or* ~; *dance on* ~, be hanged; *fade away* etc. *to* ~, disappear gradually; *no* ~, colloq., conclusion of negative list, as *no bread, no butter, no cheese, no* ~; ~ *else than* or *but*, ~ *but, force* etc., merely force etc.,

force etc. alone, unmistakable force etc.; *there is* ~ *for it but* to, no alternative; ~ *if not critical* etc., critical as leading characteristic; *get thing for* ~, gratis; *have endured it for* ~, to no purpose; *so it was not for* ~ *that he read Plato; that is* ~ *to you*, not your concern; *make* ~ *of*, treat as trifle; *make* ~ *of doing*, do without hesitation or as ordinary matter; *can make* ~ *of*, cannot understand, find solution of, use, develop, or deal with; *come to* ~, turn out useless, fail, not amount to anything; *have* ~ *to do with*, not be concerned with, avoid dealing with or society of; *all to* ~, longest odds). **3.** Trifle, very inferior thing, (*that is*~, i.e. in comparison with what I am going to tell you; *he is* ~ *without his money; learning is* ~ *to*, i.e. compared with, *genius*). **4.** (arith.). No amount, nought, (*multiply 6 by* ~, *& the result is* ~). **5.** Non-existence, what does not exist. **6.** (With *a* & pl.) trifling thing, event, remark, or person (*the little* ~s *of life; whisper soft* ~s; *the new commander-in-chief was a* ~). **7.** (Of religious belief) *be* ~, belong to no denomination, be an atheist or agnostic. **8.** adv. Not at all, in no way, (*differs* ~ *from; is* ~ *less than monstrous*, positively; *helps us* ~; *avails* ~; *is* ~ *like as* or *so good* etc.; *is* ~ *near so extensive*; ~ LO(A)TH); *(as int., colloq.) not at all (Is it gold? Gold* ~; *it's pinchbeck*). [OE *nān thing*, NO¹, THING]

nothingness (nŭ-), n. Non-existence, the non-existent; worthlessness, triviality, unimportance, insignificance, trifles. [-NESS]

notice, n., & v.t. **1.** Intimation, intelligence, warning, (*give, have,* ~; *at short, ten minutes'*, etc., ~, with such time for preparation); information or directions pasted on ~-board. **2.** Formal intimation of something or instructions *to do* something (~ *to* QUIT; *till* FURTHER¹ ~); announcement by party to agreement that it is to terminate at specified time (esp. between landlord & tenant or employer & employed; *give a week's* etc. ~; *take my* ~). **3.** Heed, attention, cognizance, observation, (*come into* ~, attract attention; *takes no* ~ *of it*, does not observe it, or takes no action in consequence of it; *brought it to his* ~; *take* ~ *that*, I warn you that; *baby takes* ~, shows signs of intelligence). **4.** Paragraph or article upon something in newspaper, esp. review of book, play, etc. **5.** ~-*board*, bearing ~ or provided for ~s to be posted on. **6.** v.t. Remark upon, speak of. **7.** Perceive, take ~ *of*; treat with politeness or condescension. **8.** Serve with ~, give ~ to, (*was* ~d *to quit*); hence ~ABLE a., ~ably² adv. [ME, f. OF, f. L *notitia* (*notus* p.p. of *noscere* know, -ICE)]

notifiable, a. (Of diseases) that must be notified to public-health authorities. [-ABLE]

notify, v.t. Make known, announce, report; inform, give notice to, (person *of*, *that*, or abs.). So **nōtifica′tion** n. [ME, f. OF *notifier* f. L *notificare* (NOTICE, -FY)]

nō′tion, n. **1.** General concept under which particular thing may be classed (in philos., *first, second,* ~, = *first, second,* INTENTION). **2.** Idea, conception, (*the ~ of my doing it is absurd*; *what he means I have not the haziest ~*); view, opinion, theory, vaguely held or insecurely based, (*has a ~ that*; *such is the common ~*). **3.** Faculty, capability, or intention of (*has no ~ of obeying, obedience, discipline, letting himself be made a fool of*). **4.** *Something in the way of miscellaneous wares, esp. cheap useful ingenious article. **5.** pl. ‖ Traditional special vocabulary of Winchester College. [f. L *notio* (NOTICE, -ION)]

nō′tional (-sho-), a. (Of knowledge etc.) speculative, not based on experiment or demonstration, whence ~IST(2) n., ~LY² adv.; (of things, relations, etc.) existing only in thought, imaginary; (of persons) fanciful. [f. med. L *notionalis* (prec., -AL)]

nōto-, comb. form of Gk *nōton* back, in scientific terms, as ~*branch′iate* (-ngk-), having dorsal gills; *nōt′ochord*, cartilaginous band forming basis of spinal column; ~*nec′ta* [Gk *nēktēs* swimmer], water--beetle swimming on back, the boat-fly.

Nōtogae′a (-jēa), n. Zoological region comprising Australian, New-Zealand, & neotropical regions. [f. Gk *notos* south, *gaia* land]

notōr′ious, a. (Of facts) well or commonly known (esp. *it is ~ that*); (with designations of persons, conduct, etc., that imply condemnation) undisguised, talked of, generally known to deserve the name, (~ *smuggler, offender, vice*); unfavourably known (*for* some quality or conduct, or abs.; *a ship ~ for ill-luck*; *the ~ Titus Oates*). Hence or cogn. **nōtorī′ety** n., ~LY² adv. [f. med. L *notorius* (NOTICE, -ORY), -OUS]

Notōr′nis, n. (zool.). Genus of rare flightless birds, chiefly of New Zealand. [f. Gk *notos* south, *ornis* bird]

Notre-Dame (nôtre dahm′), n. The Cathedral of Paris. [F, = Our Lady]

nōtwithstánd′ing, prep., adv., & conj. **1.** In spite of, not the less for, (~ *his resistance*; *this ~*. The second order is the orig., the prep. having been developed f. a part. abs.). **2.** adv. Nevertheless, all the same. **3.** conj. (arch.) (Developed from prep. or part. abs. with *that*, still occas. retained) although, in spite of the fact (*that*). [ME, f. NOT, WITHSTAND, -ING²]

nougat (nōōg′ah), n. Sweetmeat of sugar, nuts, etc. [F (L *nux nucis* nut, -ATE¹)]

nought (nawt), n. Nothing (poet., arch., & arith.; *come, bring to,* ~, be ruined or fail, ruin or baffle; *set at* ~, disregard, ridicule); figure 0, cipher, (~*s & crosses,* child's game). [OE *nōwiht* f. *ne* not +*ōwiht*, var. of *āwiht* AUGHT]

noum′en|ŏn, n. (pl. ~*a*). Object of intellectual intuition devoid of all phenomenal attributes. Hence ~AL a., ~alLY² adv. [f. Gk *nooumenon* neut. pres. part. pass. of *noeō* apprehend, taken by Kant as antithesis to *phenomenon*]

noun, n. (gram.). Word used as name of person or thing, substantive; (formerly) substantive or adjective. Hence ~′AL a. (rare). [ME, f. AF, = OF *nun, nom,* f. L *nomen* name]

nou′rish (nŭ-), v.t. Sustain with food (lit. & fig.), whence ~ING² a.; foster, cherish, nurse, (feeling, hope, etc.) in one's heart. [ME, f. OF *norir* (-ISH²) f. L *nutrire*]

nou′rishment (nŭ-), n. Sustenance, food; nourishing. [ME, f. OF *norissement* (prec., -MENT)]

nous, n. (Gk philos.) mind, intellect; (colloq.) common sense, gumption. [Gk]

nouveau riche (nōōv′ō rēsh′), n. Wealthy parvenu. [F, = new rich]

nouv′elle (nōō-), n. Short novel. [F]

nŏv′el¹, n. **1.** One of the tales in such a collection as Boccaccio's *Decameron*. **2.** Fictitious prose narrative of volume length portraying characters & actions representative of real life in continuous plot; *the~*, this type of literature; whence ~ESE′ (-ēz) n. **3.** (Rom. law). New decree supplementary to the Codex. [f. It. *novella* f. L neut. pl. as foll.]

rŏv′el², a. Of new kind or nature, strange, hitherto unknown. [ME, f. OF, f. L *novellus* dim. of *novus* new]

nŏvelětte′, n. Short novel, story of moderate length, (freq. derog.); (mus.) piano piece of free form with several themes. [-ETTE]

nŏv′el|ist, n. Novel-writer. Hence ~is′tic a. [-IST]

nŏv′eliz|e, -is|e (-iz), v.t. Convert (drama, facts) into a novel. Hence ~A′TION n. [-IZE]

nŏv′eltý, n. New or unusual thing or occurrence; novel character of something. [ME, f. OF *novelte* (NOVEL², -TY)]

Nověm′ber, n. Eleventh month. [ME; L (*novem* nine); cf. DECEMBER]

novēn′a, n. (R.-C. Church). Devotion consisting of special prayers or service on nine successive days. [med. L, f. L *novem* nine]

ncverc′al, a. Stepmotherly. [f. L *novercalis* (*noverca* stepmother, -AL)]

nŏv′ice, n. Person received in religious house on probation before taking the vows; new convert; inexperienced person, beginner, tiro. [ME, f. OF, f. L *novicius* (*novus* new, -ITIOUS¹)]

novi′ciate, -tiate, (-shi-), n. Novice's probationary period or initiation or apprenticeship; novice; quarters assigned to novices. [f. F *noviciat* or med. L *novitiatus* (prec., -ATE¹)]

nŏv′ocaine, n. (pharm.). A regional anaesthetic. [P; f. L *novus* new +(CO)-CAINE]

now, adv., conj., & n. **1.** adv. At the present time; by this time; under the present circumstances (*I cannot ~ ever* believe you again; ~ that I know you, it is different); immediately (must go ~); in the immediate past (just ~, & arch. even, but, ~); (in narrative) then, next, by that time, (Caesar ~ marched east; it was ~ clear); (every) ~ & then or again, from time to time, intermittently; ~ . . . ~, ~ . . . then, ~ . . . & again, at one moment — at another; ~ or never !, this is the nick of time. **2.** (Without temporal force, giving various tones, soothing, reproving, explanatory, threatening, etc., to sentence) pray, I beg, I insist, I warn you, & yet, you must know, it must be admitted, surely, (Now what do you mean by it ?. Oh, come ~ !. No nonsense ~ !. You have revealed the secret ; ~ you were paid to keep it. Now Barabbas was a robber. Now this was bad enough, but —. Now then, what mischief are you at ?. You don't mean it, ~). **3.** conj. (Orig., as often still, now adv. followed by that) consequently upon or simultaneously with the fact that (Now I am a man I think otherwise. Now you mention it, I do remember). **4.** n. This time, the present (chiefly after prepp. ; is there by, ere, till, ~, from ~ till, etc. ; read the future in the ~). [OE nū, also in all older Gmc langg., corresp. to L nunc, Gk nun, Skr. nú]

now'aday, a. Of nowadays. [f. foll.]

now'adays (-z), adv. & n. (At) the present day, (in) these advanced or newfangled times. [ME, f. NOW adv., A², DAY, -ES]

Nowel (nōĕl'), int. expr. joy in Christmas carols. [ME, f. OF noel f. L NATALIS]

no'where (-hwār, -wār), adv. In, at, to, no place (~ near, not nearly ; be, come in, ~, not be placed in race or competition). [OE nā-, later nōhwǣr ; NO¹, WHERE]

no'xious (-kshus), a. Harmful, unwholesome. Hence ~LY² adv., ~NESS n. [f. L noxius (noxa harm), -OUS]

noyade (nwahyahd'), n. Execution by drowning, esp. wholesale as in France in 1794. [F]

noyau (nwahyō'), n. Liqueur of brandy flavoured with fruit-kernels. [F (L nux nucis nut, -AL)]

nŏz'zle, n. Spout, mouthpiece, end fitted to hose etc. [NOSE, -LE(1)]

n't. See NOT.

nū, n. Greek letter (N, ν) = n. [Gk]

nuance (see Ap.), n. Delicate difference in or shade of meaning, feeling, opinion, colour, etc. [F, f. nuer to shade, ult. f. L nubes cloud]

nŭb, nŭb'ble, nn. Small knob or lump, esp. of coal; (nub) point or gist (of matter or story). Hence **nŭbb'ly²** a. [app. var. of knub, f. MLG knubbe, knobbe KNOB]

nūb'ile, a. Marriageable (esp. of women). Hence **nūbil'ITY** n. [f. L nubilis (nubere become wife)]

nū'chal (-kl), a. Of nape of neck. [f. nucha nape, f. med. L nucha spinal cord]

nūci-, comb. form of L nux nucis nut, as nūciF'EROUS, nū'civ'OROUS.

nūc'lĕar, a. Of, relating to, constituting, a nucleus; = ~-powered; ~ (= ATOMIC) bomb; ~ energy (released or absorbed during reactions taking place in atomic nuclei); ~ fission, splitting up of a heavy atom, e.g. of uranium, into two or more new atoms, with an enormous release of energy; ~ fuel, source of atomic energy; ~ physics (dealing with the atomic nucleus); ~ power (derived from ~ energy); ~-powered a., (of ship) using ~ power; ~ reactor, atomic PILE²; ~ (= ATOMIC) war. [f. NUCLEUS, -AR¹]

nūc'lĕ|ōle, n. (biol.). Nucleus of or within a nucleus. Hence ~olAR¹, ~olāt'ĕd [-ATE²], aa., ~olo- comb. form. [f. L nucleolus dim. of foll.]

nūc'lĕ|us, n. (pl. ~ī). (Astron.) condensed part of comet's head; (phys.) positively charged central portion constituting main mass of atom; central part or thing round which others are collected, kernel of aggregate or mass, beginning meant to receive additions, central part of ovule, seed, plant-cell, animal cell, etc., portion of medullary matter from which nerves spring, (the ~us of a sun-spot, community, library, story, empire, etc.). Hence ~AL, ~ARY, aa., ~o- comb. form. [L, dim. of nux nucis nut]

nūde, a. & n. **1.** Naked, bare, unclothed, undraped, (~ contract in law, lacking a consideration & therefore void unless under seal); so **nūd'I-** comb. form (zool.), **nūd'ITY** n.; (as colour adj., esp. of stockings) flesh-coloured. **2.** n. ~ figure in painting or sculpture; the ~, the undraped figure, undraped state. Hence **nūd'IST** n., adherent of the cult of the ~ (also attrib., as nudist colony). [f. L nudus]

nŭdge, v.t., & n. **1.** Push slightly with elbow to draw attention privately, (fig.) draw attention of. **2.** n. Such push. [orig. unkn.; cf. Norw. dial. nugga, nyggja to push, rub]

nu'gae (-gē, -jē), n. pl. Trifles, learned triflings, profitless minutiae. [L]

nūg'atory, a. Trifling, worthless, futile; inoperative, not valid. [f. L nugatorius (nugari trifle f. prec., -ORY)]

nŭgg'ar, n. Large broad-beamed boat used on upper Nile. [native]

nŭgg'ĕt (-g-), n. Rough lump of native gold. [app. f. dial. nug lump &c.]

nuis'ance (nūs-), n. Anything injurious or obnoxious to the community or member of it for which legal remedy may be had (|| commit no ~, notice to public not to defile place); obnoxious person, offensive object, annoying action, anything disagreeable (also attrib., as ~ value). [ME, f. OF, f. nuire nuis- f. L nocēre hurt, -ANCE)]

nŭll, a. & n. Not binding, invalid, (often ~ & void); without character or expression; non-existent, amounting to nothing, (rare); || (n.) dummy letter in a cipher. [f. F nul or L nullus (ne not, ullus any)] *nŭll'a bōn'a*, n. Sheriff's return stating that party has no goods to be distrained upon. [L, = no goods]

nŭll'ah (-*a*), n. (Anglo-Ind.). Stream, watercourse, ravine. [f. Hind. *nala*]

nŭll'ĭfy, v.t. Cancel, neutralize. So ~-FICA'TION n. [f. F *nullifier* (as NULL, -FY), or med. L *nullificare* annul]

nŭll'ipōre, n. Kind of marine vegetation. [f. L *nullus* no +PORE[1]]

nŭll'itỹ, n. Being null, invalidity, (esp. ~ *of marriage*; ~ *suit*, for this); act, document, etc., that is null; nothingness; a mere nothing; a nonentity. [f. F *nullité* or med. L *nullitas* (NULL, -ITY)]

nŭmb (-m), a., & v.t. 1. Deprived of feeling or power of motion (~ *with cold* etc.); ~-*fish*, the electric ray or TORPEDO; ~'*skull*, hence ~LY[2] (-mll) adv., ~'NESS (-mn-) n. 2. v.t. Make ~, (fig.) stupefy, paralyse. [15th c. *nome*, p.p. of obs. *nim* take (OE, OS, Goth. *niman*)]

nŭm'ber[1], n. (written N°, for *numero*=in ~, with pl. N°ˢ, before distinguishing figure, as *bedroom* N° *15*, N°ˢ *1–10*). 1. Tale, count, sum, company, or aggregate, or persons (also *of*) or things (also *of*) or abstract units, symbol or figure representing such aggregate, ticket etc. bearing such figure, person or thing (esp. single issue of magazine, or part of opera etc.) whose place in series is indicated by such figure, (*the ~ of fools is infinite*; *N~s*, abbr. *Num.*, O.T. book containing census; *the greatest ~ on record is 59 persons*; *to the ~ of 80*, as many as; GOLDEN ~; *science of ~s*, arithmetic; *took the driver's ~*; *sleeps in N° 5*; *N° 9 (pill)*, army doctor's reputed panacea; *N° 10 Downing Street*, *N° 10*, (used for) Prime Minister's official residence (when he is also First Lord of the Treasury); *one's ~ goes up*, he dies; ~ *one*, oneself, esp. in *take care of ~ one*, also ‖ (nav. sl.) first lieutenant; *story issued in ~s*, in parts successively published bearing ~s; *back ~*, earlier issue of magazine, (fig.) anything out of date; *is not of our ~*, included among us; *is now added to the ~ of my enemies*); (sing. or pl.) *large, small*, etc., or large, collection or company of or abs. (*were present in great, only in small*, or *in*, ~s; *saw a great*, or *a*, ~ *of birds*; *a small ~ came*; *there are ~s who live by begging*). 2. pl. Numerical preponderance (*won by ~s* or *force of ~s*). 3. Numerical reckoning (*the laws of ~ & proportion pervade Nature*; *without ~*, innumerable, also ~LESS a.; *in ~*, when counted or estimated, numerically, as *one people exceeds another in ~*). 4. (gram.). Class of word-forms including all singular, all plural, or all dual etc. words (*Greek has three ~s*; '*things*' *is of the plural ~*). 5. Rhythm; (pl.) groups of musical notes, metrical feet, verses. [ME, f. OF *nombre* f. L *numerus*]

nŭm'ber[2], v.t. Count, ascertain number of; (pass.) be restricted in number (*his years are ~ed*, he has not long to live); include, regard as, *among, in*, or *with* some class; assign a number to, distinguish with a number; have lived, live, (so many years); be able to show (so many inhabitants etc.); amount to (specified number). [ME, f. OF *nombrer* f. L *numerare* (prec.)]

‖ **nŭm'bles** (-blz), n. pl. (arch.). Deer's entrails. [ME, f. OF *num-, nombles* loin &c., app. f. **lomble(s)* f. L *lumbulus* dim. of *lumbus* loin; later *umbles*, whence HUMBLE pie]

nŭm'erable, a. That can be numbered. [f. L *numerabilis* (NUMBER[2], -ABLE)]

nŭm'eral, a. & n. (Word, figure, group of figures) denoting a number; of number. [f. LL *numeralis* (NUMBER[1], -AL)]

nŭmerā'tion, n. Method or process of numbering or computing; calculation; assigning of numbers; (arith.) expression in words of number written in figures; ~ *table*, showing value of figures according to their place in system of notation. [ME, f. OF, or L *numeratio* (NUMBER[2], -ATION)]

nŭm'erātor, n. Number above line in vulgar fraction showing how many of the parts indicated by the denominator are taken; person who numbers. [LL (NUMBER[2], -OR)]

nŭmĕ'ric, n. What is either a number, a proper or improper fraction, or an incommensurable ratio. [f. L *numerus* number, -IC]

nŭmĕ'rical, a. Of, in, denoting, etc. number. Hence ~LY[2] adv. [-AL]

nŭm'erous, a. Comprising many units (*a ~ acquaintance, library, family, army, class*); coming from many individuals (*the ~ voice of the people*; *a ~ hum*); (arch.) thronged (*a ~ country*); (with pl. noun) many (*received ~ gifts*); (of verse or prose) rhythmic, harmonious. Hence ~LY[2] adv. [f. L *numerosus* (NUMBER[1], -OUS)]

nŭm'inous, n. The ~, the combined feeling of attraction & awe characteristic of man's sense of communion with God & religion. [f. L *numen -inis* divine will, divinity +-OUS]

nūmismăt'ĭc (-z-), a. Of coins or coinage. So ~ICALLY adv., ~ICS, **nūmis'matĭst**(3), **nūmismatŏl'OGY**, nn. [F (-*ique*), f. L (*num-*) f. Gk *nomisma -atos* coin (*nomizō* use currently f. *nomos* custom, -IC]

nŭmm'arỹ, nŭmm'ūlarỹ, aa. Of, in, coin. [f. L *nummarius* (*nummus* coin, -ARY[1]), & *nummulus* dim. +-ARY[1]]

‖ **nŭmm'ĕt**, n. (dial.). Lunch. [= *noon meat*]

nŭmm'ūlite, n. Disc-like fossil shell of Tertiary strata. [*nummulus* (see NUMMARY), -ITE[1](2)]

nŭm'nah (-*a*), n. Saddle-cloth, pad placed under saddle. [Anglo-Ind. *numdah* felt f. Hind. *namda* f. Pers. *namad* carpet]

nŭm'skŭll, n. Dolt or his head. [NUMB]

nŭn, ŋ. Woman living in convent usu.

under vow of poverty, chastity, & obedience; kinds of bird & moth; ~'s *cloth*, thin woollen stuff; ~'s *thread*, fine white sewing cotton; ~'s *veiling*, thin dress-stuff. Hence~'HOOD, ~'SHIP, nn., ~'LIKE, ~n'ISH[1], aa. [OE *nunne*, OHG, ON *nunna*, f. LL *nonna* fem. of *nonnus* monk, orig. title given to elderly persons; in ME reinforced f. OF *nonne*]

nun'atăk (-ōōn-), n. Isolated peak of rock projecting above surface of land ice or snow e.g. in Greenland. [Eskimo]

nŭn'-buoy (-boi), n. Buoy circular in middle & tapering to each end. [f. obs. *nun* spinning-top]

nŭnc dĭmĭt'tĭs. n. The canticle *Lord, now lettest thou* (sing ~, be willing to depart from life etc.). [L, = now lettest thou go]

nŭn'ciature (-shatūr), n. (Tenure of) office of papal nuncio. [f. It. *nunziatura* (foll.)]

nŭn'cio (-shiō), n. (pl. ~s). Pope's ambassador at foreign court. [It., f. L *nuncius* messenger]

nŭnc'ŭp|āte, v.t. Declare (will, testament) orally, not in writing. So ~A'TION n., ~ATIVE a. [f. L *nuncupare* name, (*nomen* name, *capere* take), -ATE[3]]

nŭnnā'tion, n. Addition of final *n* in declension of (orig. Arabic) nouns. [f. Arab. *nun* the letter n+-ATION]

nŭnn'erў, n. Religious house for nuns, convent. [ME, f. AF *nonnerie* (NUN, -ERY(3)]

nŭph'ăr, n. Yellow water-lily. [for NENUPHAR]

nŭp'tial (-shl), a. & n. 1. Of marriage or wedding. 2. n. (usu. pl.). Wedding. [f. F, or L *nuptialis* (*nuptiae* wedding f. *nubere* nupt- become wife)]

nûrse[1], n. 1. Woman employed to suckle & take charge of infant (usu. *wet-*~), or having charge of young children (also *dry-*~). 2. Country etc. that fosters some quality etc. (*the ~ of liberty*). 3. Nursing or being nursed (*at* ~, *put out* or *put to* ~, of child, & fig. of estate). 4. Person, usu. woman, charged with or trained for care of the sick or decrepit. 5. (Forestry) tree planted as shelter to others; (entom.) sexually imperfect bee, ant, etc., caring for the young brood, worker; (zool.) individual in asexual stage of metagenesis. 6. ~*-child*, foster-child; ~*-frog*, kind of which male carries eggs till hatched; ~*-maid*, girl having charge of child(ren); ‖ ~ *ship*, (nav.), = MOTHER[1] ship. Hence **nûrs'eў[3]** n. [reduced f. ME & OF *norice* f. LL *nutricia* fem. of *nutricius*, *-itius* f. L *nutrix -icis* (*nutrire* nourish)]

nûrse[2], v.t. & i. 1. Suckle (child), give suck, act as wet-nurse; act as nursemaid to, have charge of; (pass.) be brought up (*in* luxury, certain place, etc.). 2. Foster, tend, promote development of, (the arts, hatred, etc.); manage (plants, estate) with solicitude; cherish (grievance etc.). 3. Wait upon (sick person), try to cure

(sickness), be sick-nurse. 4. Hold or clasp (baby, one's knees or foot) caressingly; sit close over (fire). 5. ‖ Keep (constituency) in good humour by attentions. 6. (billiards). Keep (balls) together for series of cannons. 7. ‖ *Nursing home*, private hospital, house for surgical operations, reception of invalids, etc.; *nursing father, mother*, foster-. [later form of ME *nursh* f. NOURISH, assim. to NURSE[1]]

nûrse[3], n. Kinds of dogfish or shark. [15th c. *nusse*, perh. f. obs. *huss* dogfish, of obsc. orig. w. adherent (a)n, cf. NEWT]

nûrs'erў, n. 1. Room assigned to children & their nurses (~ *governess*, one combining duties of nurse & governess). 2. Practice, institution, sphere, place, in or by which qualities or classes of people are fostered or bred. 3. Plot of ground in which young plants are reared for transplantation (~*man*, owner of this); fish-rearing pond; place where animal life is developed. 4. (billiards). Grouped balls (see NURSE[2]; esp. in ~ *cannon*). [14th c., prob. f. AF *noricerie* (NURSE[1], -ERY)]

nûrs(e)'ling (-sl-), n. Infant, esp. in relation to its nurse; ~ *of*, person or thing bred in or fostered by. [NURSE[1], -LING[1]]

nûr'ture, n., & v.t. 1. Bringing up, training, fostering care; nourishment. 2. v.t. Nourish, rear, foster, train, educate. [ME, f. OF *nurture*, var. of *noureture*, f. Rom. *nutritura* (L *nutrire* nourish, -URE)]

nŭt, n., & v.i. (-tt-). 1. Fruit consisting of hard or leathery shell enclosing edible kernel (see also EARTH-~, PEA-~; DEAF-~; *can't shoot* etc. *for* ~s, sl., do thing even tolerably well; *hard* ~ *to crack*, difficult problem, person or thing hard to deal with or get the better of; *be* ~s or *dead* ~s *on*, sl., delight in, be skilful at). 2. (sl.). Showy young man (now rare); *head* (*off* one's ~, insane, mad); (pl.) crazy (also *'nerts*). 3. Small toothed projection on spindle engaging with cog-wheel, small spur-wheel. 4. Small usu. hexagonal metal block pierced with screw-thread to accommodate screw on bolt etc. and operated by spanner. 5. Holder that tightens or relaxes horse-hair of fiddle-bow etc. 6. pl. Small lumps of coal. 7. ~*-brown*, coloured like ripe hazel-~ (esp. of girl's complexion, & of ale); ~*-butter*, food like butter made from ~s; ~*'cracker*, (usu. pl.) instrument for cracking ~s, prominent chin & nose with points naturally, or by loss of teeth, near each other (also used attrib. in sing., as *a ~-cracker face*), (sing.) common European but rare British bird; ~*-gall*, gall found on dyer's oak used as dye-stuff; ~*'hatch*, small climbing bird feeding on ~s, insects, &c. [HATCH[3]]; ~*-oil*, got esp. from hazel-~s & walnuts, & used in paints & varnishes; ~*-palm*, Australian palm bearing ~s; ~*'shell*, hard exterior covering of ~, tiny receptacle or dwelling, briefest possible way of expressing, epitome, (*can give it you in a ~shell*); ~-*tree*, bearing ~s, esp. hazel; ~-*weevil*, beetle laying eggs in green hazel & filbert ~s. **8. v.i.** Seek or gather ~s (usu. in gerund, *went ~ting* etc.). [OE *hnutu*, MLG, MDu. *note*, OHG (*h*)*nuz*, ON *hnot* f. Gmc. *hnut-]

nūt'|āte, v.i. (bot.). Nod, droop. So ~ANT a. [f. L *nutare* frequent. of *nuere* nod, -ATE[3]]

nūtā'tion, n. Nodding; (astron.) oscillation of earth's axis making motion of pole of equator round pole of ecliptic wavy; oscillation of spinning top; curvature in stem of growing plant. [f. L *nutatio* (prec., -ION)]

nŭt'mĕg, n. Hard aromatic spheroidal seed got from fruit of evergreen E.-Indian tree (~-*tree*), used as spice & in medicine; ~-*apple*, fruit of ~-tree yielding mace & ~s; ~-*liver*, diseased state of liver, red atrophy. [ME; partial transl. of OF *nois mugede*, = med. L *nux muscata* musky nut]

nŭt'ria, n. Skin or fur of the S.-Amer. coypu, an aquatic rodent. [Sp., = otter f. L *lutra*]

nŭt'rient, a. Serving as or providing nourishment. [f. L *nutrire* nourish, -ENT]

nŭt'riment, n. Nourishing food (lit. & fig.). Hence **nūtrimĕn'tAL** a. (rare). [f. L *nutrimentum* (prec., -MENT)]

nŭtri'tion, n. (Supplying or receiving of) nourishment, food. Hence ~AL (-shon-) a., of or relating to ~. [f. F, or LL *nutritio* (as NUTRIENT, -ION)]

nŭtri'tious (-shus), a. Nourishing, efficient as food. Hence ~LY[2] adv., ~NESS n. [f. L *nutritius* (NURSE[1], -ITIOUS[2])]

nŭt'ritive, a. & n. Serving as food; concerned in nutrition; (n.) article of food. [ME, f. OF (-*if*, -*ive*) f. med. L *nutritivus* (NUTRIENT, -IVE)]

nŭtt'ў, a. Abounding in nuts; tasting like nuts, of rich mellow flavour; (sl.) amorous or enthusiastic (*upon*); *(sl.) crazy. [-Y[2]]

nŭx vŏm'ica, n. Seed of E.-Ind. tree yielding the poison strychnine. [med. L (L *nux* nut, *vomere* vomit, -IC)]

nŭz'zle, v.i. & t. Nose, burrow or press or rub or sniff with the nose, press nose or press (nose) *into* or *against*; nestle, lie snug, (also refl.). [NOSE[1], -LE(3)]

nўctalōp'ia, n. Night-blindness or recurrent loss of vision after sunset; inability to see clearly except at night. [LL (Gk *nuktalōps* f. *nukt*- night, *alaos* blind, *ōps* eye, -IA[1]); incorrect second sense due to overlooking of -*al*-]

nўctitrŏp'ic, a. (bot.). Turning in certain direction at night. [f. combining form of Gk *nux nuktos* night + *tropos* turn, -IC]

nўl'ghau (-gaw), n. Short-horned Indian antelope. [f. Pers. *nilgaw* (*nil* blue, *gaw* ox)]

nўl'ŏn, n. Synthetic plastic material of great toughness, tensile strength, & elas-ticity, widely used in industry & as a dress fabric; (pl., colloq.) garments, esp. women's stockings, made of ~. [P]

nўmph, n. 1. One of class of mythological semi-divine maidens inhabiting sea, rivers, fountains, hills, woods, or trees, or attending superior deities, whence or cogn. ~ē'AN, ~'ISH[1], ~'LIKE, aa. **2.** (poet.). Young & beautiful woman. **3.** Immature form of insect which has incomplete metamorphosis. [ME, f. OF *nimphe* f. L f. Gk *numphē*]

nўm'pholepsy, n. Ecstasy or frenzy caused by desire of the unattainable. [foll., after *epilepsy*]

nўm'pholĕpt, n. Person inspired by violent enthusiasm esp. for an ideal. Hence ~ĕp'TIC a. [f. Gk *numpholēptos* nymph-caught (NYMPH, *lambanō* take)]

nўmpho|mān'ia, n. (path.). Morbid & uncontrollable sexual desire in women. Hence ~MAN'IAC n. [f. Gk *numphē* bride, -o-, -MANIA]

nўstăg'mus, n. Eye-disease common among miners, with continual oscillation of eyeballs. [f. Gk *nustagmos* nodding (*nustazō* nod)]

O

O[1] (ō), letter (pl. *Os*, *O*'s, *Oes*). O-shaped mark, circle, (esp. *round O*).

O[2], oh, (ō), int. prefixed to vocative name (*O*), or expressing various emotions (usu. *oh* if separated by punctuation, otherwise *O. O dear me!*; *O for a breathing-space!*; *Oh, what a lie!*; *Oh, is that so?*); *O yes!*, = OYES. [ME. prob. f. L]

O'[1] (*o*), pref. of Irish names, as *O'Connor*. [Ir. *ó*, *ua*, descendant]

o'[2] (*o*), prep. short for *of*, *on*, still in some phrases, as (= *of*) *o'clock*, *Jack-o'-lantern*, *Will-o'-the-wisp*, *man-o'-war*, (colloq.) *cup o' tea*, (= *on*) *cannot sleep o' nights.*

-o-, terminal vowel of combining forms of wds; prop. used in Gk compounds, (-*i*- being usu. in L), but now extended to many scientific & other terms made of non-Gk wds (*occipito-frontal*, *joco-serious*), &, in meaning, expressing not merely modification of second element by first (*Franco - German* = essentially German with some French characteristics), but equal or any other relations (*Franco--German war*); used also in forming true derivatives w. Gk endings as -*cracy*, -*logy*, & perh. taken for part of the suf., whence ' ologies ' etc.

oaf, n. (pl. ~s, *oaves*). Elf's child, changeling, (arch.); misbegotten, deformed, or idiot child; awkward lout. Hence ~'ISH[1] a. [var. of obs. *auf* f. ON *álfr* ELF]

oak, n. 1. Kinds of tree & shrub, of which the best known is a forest tree yielding hard timber & acorns & having jagged leaves (*dyer's*, *holm*, *scarlet*, etc., ~, other species; *dwarf*, *ground*, etc., ~, plants named from some resemblance to ~); wood of the ~ (HEART *of* ~), (poet.) wooden ships; ‖ (Univv.) outer door of set of rooms (*sport* one's ~, shut this to exclude visitors); leaves of ~ (~ *is still worn on 29th May*); colour of young ~ leaves; *the Oaks*, race at Epsom for three--year-old fillies [f. name of estate]; (attrib., =, but now more usual than)~en. **2.** ~*apple*, -*fig*, -*gall*, -*plum*, -*potato*, -*spangle*, -*wart*, kinds of excrescence produced on ~s by gall-flies; ‖~*-apple day*, 29th May (Charles II restored 1660) on which ~-apples are worn in memory of the ROYAL-~ incident; ~*-beauty*, -*egger*, -*hook-tip*, kinds of moth bred on or resembling leaf etc. of ~ ; ~*-fern*, smooth three-branched polypody; ~*-tree*, ~ ; ~*-wood*, forest, copse, etc., of ~s, also ~ timber. Hence~'EN⁵ a., ~'LET, ~'LING¹(2), nn. [OE *āc*, OHG *eih*, ON *eik* f. Gmc *aiks*]

oak'um, n. Loose fibre got by picking old rope to pieces & used esp. in caulking (*pick* ~, make this, esp. as formerly common task of convicts & paupers). [OE *ǣ-*, *ācumbe*, OHG *āchambi*, f. *ǣ-* away, off +*camb-* st. of COMB]

oar (ōr), n., & v.t. & i. **1.** Pole with blade used (usu. in even numbers) to propel boat by leverage, esp. one worked by single rower (cf. SWEEP) with both hands (cf. SCULL), or to steer (*chained to the ~*, constrained to work hard & long, with allusion to galley-slaves; *pair*-~, *four*-~, etc., boat with two, four, etc., ~s; *pulls a good* ~, is good ~sman; *put in one's* ~, interfere; *have an* ~ *in every man's boat*, be a meddler; *rest on one's* ~s, cease work for a time); *good, bad, young, practised*, etc., ~sman; (fig.) wing, fin, arm used in swimming, etc.; ~*s'man*, ~*s'woman*, rower, whence ~s'manship(3) n.; hence ~'AGE(1) n. (poet.), (-)ED² (ōrd), ~'LESS, ~'Y² (poet.), aa., (ōr-). **2.** vb. Row (t. & i.; poet.; ~ *boat, water, air,* one's *way*; ~ one's *arms* or *hands*, move them as in swimming). [OE *ār*, cogn. w. ON *ár*, *ǫr*, f. Gmc *airō*, perh. cogn. w. Gk *eretmos* oar, *eretēs* rower]

ōā'sis, n. (pl. *oasēs*). Fertile spot in desert (lit. & fig.). [LL f. Gk, app. of Egypt. orig.]

oast, n. Hop-drying kiln; ~*-house*, building containing this. [OE *āst*, = MLG, MDu. *eist*, f. Gmc. *aistaz*, cogn. w. L *aestus* heat]

oat, n. (Pl.) (grain yielded by) hardy cereal grown in cool climates as food for men & horses; (sing., rare exc. in comb.) ~*-plant*, variety of ~s; *wild* ~, tall grass resembling ~s (*sow* one's *wild* ~s, indulge in youthful follies before becoming steady); (poet.) ~*-stem* used as musical pipe by shepherds etc., pastoral or bucolic poetry; ~*'cake*, thin unleavened cake made of ~meal, esp. in Scot-

land & N.; ~*'meal*, meal from ~s used esp. in ~cake & porridge; **feel* one's ~ (colloq.), feel important, display self--importance. Hence ~'EN⁵ a. [OE *āte*, pl. *ātan*, excl. E, of unkn. orig.]

oath, n. (*pl. pr.* ōdhz). **1.** Solemn appeal to God or revered or dreaded person or object in witness that statement is true or promise shall be kept (*take an*, *make*, *swear an*, ~, bind oneself thus; *on* ~, having thus sworn, made or stated or given by sworn person; BIBLE, CORPORAL¹, ~); (form of words containing) statement or promise so corroborated (~ *of allegiance, office, supremacy*, etc.). **2.** Name of God etc. used as expletive to give emphasis or express anger etc., piece of profanity in speech, curse. [OE *āth*, OS *ēth*, OHG *eid*, ON *eithr*, Goth *aiths* f. Gmc **aithaz*]

ob- (before *c*-) **oc-**, (before *f*-) **of-**, (before *p*-) **op-**, pref. f. L *ob* in the way of, occurring chiefly in wds already compounded in L, w. senses: **1.** Exposure, openness, (*object, obnoxious, obtrude, obverse*). **2.** Meeting (*occasion, occur, offend*), facing (*observe, obstetric, obviate, obvious, opportune*), direction (*oblation, oblique, oblong, obsecrate, obtest, offer*), spontaneity or friendliness (*obey, obsequious, office*). **3.** Opposition or hostility (*objurgate, obloquy, obstreperous, oppose, oppress, opprobrium, oppugn*) or resistance (*obdurate, obmutescent, obstinate, obtuse*). **4.** Hindrance, blocking, veiling, (*obbligato, obese, obfuscate, oblige, obliterate, obscure, obsess, obstacle, obstruct, obturate, occlude, occult, oppilate*). **5.** Finality or completeness (*obiit, oblivion, obsolete, obtain, obtruncate, occident, occupy*). **6.** (In mod. sci. wds) inversely, in direction or manner contrary to the usual (*obconical, obcordate, oblanceolate, obovate*, shaped like cone, heart, spike, egg, tapering downwards).

ŏbblïga'tō (-ah-), a. & n. (mus.). **1.** (Of accompaniment or part) inseparable, forming integral part of the composition, (opp. *ad libitum*). **2.** n. (pl. ~s). Such part or accompaniment. [It., f. L *obligatus* (OBLIGE)]

ŏb'dūrate (or -ūr⁴-), a. Hardened, impenitent, stubborn. Hence **ŏb'dūrACY** n., ~LY² adv., (or -ūr⁴-). [ME, f. L OB(*durare* harden f. *durus* hard), -ATE²]

ōb'èah (-a), **ōb'ï**¹, n. Kind of sorcery practised by Negroes. [W. Afr.]

obēd'ience, n. Obeying as act or practice or quality, submission to another's rule, compliance with law or command, (*in* ~ *to*, actuated by or in accordance with; *passive* ~, surrender of one's will to another's without co-operation, also compliance with commands irrespective of their nature); (eccl., esp. R.-C.) being obeyed, (sphere of) authority, district or body of persons bound to ~, (*return to the* ~ *of the Pope*; *not belonging to either the*

Roman or the Byzantine ~). [ME, f. OF *obedience* f. L *obedientia* (OBEY, -ENCE)]

obēd′ient, a. Submissive to or complying with superior's will, dutiful, (‖ *your* ~ *servant*, phrase spoken formerly in courtesy, now only ironically, in taking leave, & written as concluding formula in letters of official or public character). Hence ~LY[2] adv. [ME, f. OF *obedient* (OBEY, -ENT)]

obēdiĕn′tiary̆ (-sha-), n. Holder of any office under superior in monastery or convent. [ME, f. med. L *obedientiarius* (OBEDIENCE, -ARY[1])]

obeis′ance (-bās-), n. Gesture, esp. bow or curtsy, expressing submission, respect, or salutation (arch.; *make an, do, pay*, ~); deference, homage, submission, (*do, make, pay*, ~). [ME, f. OF *obeisance* (OBEY, -ANCE)]

ŏb′ĕlisk, n. 1. Tapering usu. monolithic shaft of stone square or rectangular in section with pyramidal apex; ~-shaped mountain, tree, etc. 2. (Also *obelus*) mark used in ancient MSS. to indicate that word or passage is spurious etc. (—, ÷); (also *obelus*) mark of reference to note in margin etc. (†; *double* ~, ‡). [f. L f. Gk *obeliskos* dim. of *obelos* spit]

ŏb′ĕlīze, -ise (-īz), v.t. Mark with the obelisk as spurious etc. [f. Gk *obelizō* (*obelos* see prec., -IZE)]

ŏb′ĕlus, n. (pl. *-li*). See OBELISK.

obēse′, a. Corpulent. So obēs′ITY n. [f. L OB(*esus* p.p., = having eaten, of *ĕdere* eat)]

obey′ (′-bā), v.t. & i. Perform bidding of, be obedient to; execute (command); be actuated by (force, impulse); do what one is bidden. [ME, f. OF *obeir* f. L OB(*edire* = *audire* hear)]

ŏb′fuscāte, v.t. Darken, obscure, (mind etc.); stupefy, bewilder. So ~A′TION n. [f. LL OB(*fuscare* f. *fuscus* dark), -ATE[3]]

obi[1]. See OBEAH.

ŏb′i[2], n. Bright broad sash worn by Japanese women & children. [Jap.]

ŏb′ĭit, v.i. 3rd sing. past (abbr. *ob.*). Died (with date of death). [L, f. OB(*ire it-* go) die]

ŏb′it, n. (arch.). Memorial service esp. in institution on anniversary of founder's or benefactor's death. [ME, f. OF *obit*, f. L *obitus* death, as prec.]

ŏb′iter, adv. By the way, in passing, (usu. ~ *dic′tum*, pl. *-ta*, judge's expression of opinion uttered in arguing point or giving judgement but not essential to his decision & therefore without binding authority; also gen., incidental remark). [L, = *ob iter* by the way]

obit′ūar|y̆, n. & a. 1. Notice of death(s) esp. in newspaper, brief biography of deceased person; hence ~IST(1) n. 2. adj. Recording a death, concerning deceased person. [f. med. L *obituarius* (L *obitus* death, see OBIT, -ARY[1])]

ŏb′jĕct[1], n. 1. Thing placed before eyes or presented to sense, material thing, thing observed with optical instrument or represented in picture. 2. Person or thing of pitiable or ridiculous aspect. 3. Person or thing to which action or feeling is directed, subject of or for, (*the Bible had been the* ~ *of his study*; *he is a proper* ~ *of* or *for charity*). 4. Thing aimed at, end, purpose; *no* ~, formula in advertisements etc. announcing that the other party may make his own terms in the specified respect (*money, time, distance*, etc., *no* ~). 5. (philos.). Thing thought of or apprehended as correlative to the thinking mind or subject, external thing, *the* non--ego. 6.(gram.). Noun or noun-equivalent governed by active transitive verb or by preposition (*direct, indirect*, ~, that primarily, secondarily, affected by action, as *shilling, him*, in *I gave him a shilling*). 7. ~-*ball*, at which player aims his in billiards etc.; ~-*finder*, contrivance for registering position of ~ on mounted microscopic slide so as to find it again; ~-*glass* or -*lens*, lens in telescope etc. nearest the ~; ~-*lesson*, instruction about a material ~ that is present for inspection, (fig.) striking practical illustration of some principle; ~-*plate*, on which ~ is placed for microscopic examination: ~-*staff*, surveyor's levelling staff. Hence ~LESS a. [ME, f. med. L *objectum* thing presented to the mind, p.p. of L OB(*jicere* reject- throw)]

objĕct′[2], v.t. & i. Adduce (quality, fact) as objection (*to* theory etc.); state (usu. *that*-clause) as damaging fact *to* or *against* person etc.; state objection, feel or express disapproval, have objection or dislike *to* (*I* ~ *to being*, & incorrectly *to be, treated like this*; ‖ *I* ~, words used in House of Commons in announcing intention to oppose a motion etc. & so shelve it as not unopposed business). Hence objĕc′tOR n. (*conscientious* ~*or*, excused compulsory service, vaccination, etc. on pleading conscience). [ME, f. L *object*-(prec.)]

objĕc′tif̆y, v.t. Present as object of sense, make objective, express in concrete form, embody. Hence ~FICA′TION n. [OBJECT[1], -I-, -FY]

objĕc′tion, n. Objecting, thing objected, adverse reason or statement; expression or feeling of disapproval or dislike. [ME, f. OF, or LL *objectio* (OBJECT[1], -ION)]

objĕc′tionab|le (-sho-), a. Open to objection; undesirable, unpleasant, offensive, disapproved of. Hence ~LY[2] adv. [prec., -ABLE]

objĕc′tive, a. & n. 1. (philos.). Belonging not to the consciousness or the perceiving or thinking SUBJECT[2], but to what is presented to this, external to the mind, real. 2. (Of person, writing, picture, etc.) dealing with outward things, exhibiting actual facts uncoloured by exhibitor's feelings or opinions; (med., of symptoms) observed by another & not only felt by patient, whence ~NESS, ŏbjĕctiv'ITY, nn. 3. (gram.) Constructed as, appropriate to, the object (~ *case* in English, that governed by transitive verb or preposition, distinguished in form from the subjective only in some personal pronouns, as *him*, cf. *he*; ~ *genitive*, as in ' the fear *of God* ', cf. SUBJECTIVE *genitive*). 4. (Mil.) ~ *point*, towards which advance of troops is directed, (transf.) point aimed at; hence ~LY[2] adv. 5. n.=OBJECT[1]-*glass*; (gram.) ~ *case*; (mil. & transf.) ~ point. [f. med. L *objectivus* (OBJECT[1], -IVE)]

objĕc'tivism, n. Tendency to lay stress on the objective; doctrine that knowledge of non-ego is prior & superior to that of ego. [-ISM]

ŏb'jŭrg|āte, v.t. Chide, scold. So ~A'TION n., ~ātory (or -ĕrg'a-) a. [f. L OB(*jurgare* quarrel), -ATE[3]]

ŏb'lāte[1], n. Person dedicated to monastic or religious life or work. [f. (med. L sense of) L OB(*latus* p.p. of *ferre* bring)]

oblāte'[2] (or ŏb⊙), a. (geom.). (Of spheroid) flattened at poles (cf. PROLATE). [as prec., sense of *ob*- doubtful]

oblā'tion, n. (Presenting of bread & wine to God in) Eucharist; thing offered to God, sacrifice, victim; donation for pious uses. Hence ~AL (-sho-), ŏb'latORY, aa. [ME, f. OF or LL *oblatio* (OBLATE[1], -ION)]

ŏb'lĭgāte, v.t. Bind (person legally or morally) *to* do (chiefly in p.p.). [f. L (OBLIGE, -ATE[3])]

ŏblĭgā'tion, n. Binding agreement esp. one enforceable under legal penalty, written contract or bond; constraining power of a law, precept, duty, contract, etc. (of ~, obligatory); one's bounden duty, a duty, burdensome task; (indebtedness for) service or benefit (*be, put, under an* ~; *repay an* ~). [ME, f. OF f. L *obligationem* (OBLIGE, -ATION)]

oblĭg'atory (or ŏb'lĭgā-), a. Legally or morally binding, imperative & not merely permissive; constituting an obligation. [ME, f. LL *obligatorius* (foll., -TORY)]

oblīge', v.t. Bind (person, one*self*) by oath, promise, contract, etc.; to person or *to* do (arch., legal; also with *oath* etc. as subj.); be binding on; make indebted by conferring favour, gratify *by doing* or *with*; (colloq.) make contribution to entertainment (*with* song etc., or abs.); (pass.) be bound (*to* person) by gratitude (*for* small service); constrain, compel, *to* do. [ME, f. OF *obliger* f. L OB(*ligare* bind)]

ŏblĭgee', n. (Law) person to whom another is bound by contract or to whom bond is given (cf. OBLIGOR); (rare) person who has received a favour. [prec., -EE]

oblī'ging, a. Courteous, accommodating, ready to do kindness, complaisant. Hence ~LY[2] adv., ~NESS n. [-ING[2]]

ŏb'lĭgŏr, n. (legal). One who binds him-

self to another or gives bond. [OBLIGE, -OR]

oblique' (-ēk), a., & v.i. 1. Slanting, declining from the vertical or horizontal, diverging from straight line or course. 2. (Geom.) (of line, plane figure, surface) inclined at other than right angle, (of angle) acute or obtuse, (of cone, cylinder, etc.) with axis not perpendicular to plane of base; (anat.) neither parallel nor perpendicular to body's or limb's long axis; (bot., of leaf) with unequal sides. 3. Not going straight to the point, roundabout, indirect. 4. (gram.) ~ *case*, other than nominative or vocative; ~ *oration* or *narration* or *speech*, speaker's words with the changes of person, tense, etc., usual in reports, indirect speech; hence or cogn. ~LY[2] (-ēkl-) adv., oblī'quITY n. 5. v.i. (esp. mil.). Advance ~ly. [f. L *obliquus*]

oblĭt'er|āte, v.t. Blot out, efface, erase, destroy, leave no clear traces of. So ~A'TION n. [f. L *oblitterare*, see -ATE[3]]

oblĭv'ion, n. Having or being forgotten, disregard, unregarded state, (*Act, Bill, of O*~, amnesty; *fall into* ~, be forgotten or disused). [ME, f. OF, f. L *oblivionem* f. *oblivisci* forget, -ION]

oblĭv'ious, a. Forgetful, unmindful, (*of*); (poet.) of, inducing, oblivion. Hence ~LY[2] adv., ~NESS n. [ME, f. L *obliviosus* (*oblivium* forgetfulness as prec., -OSE[1])]

ŏb'lŏng, a. & n. 1. Deviating from square or circular form by having one long axis, (of spheroid) prolate; (geom.) rectangular with adjacent sides unequal; (of paper, book, rectangular postage stamp or panel, etc.) greater in breadth than height; hence oblŏng'o- (-nggŏ) comb. form (bot.). 2. n. ~ figure or object. [f. L OB(*longus* long)]

ŏb'loquў, n. Abuse, detraction; being generally ill spoken of. [ME, f. LL *obloquium* f. L OB(*loqui* speak) gainsay]

ŏbmūtĕs'c|ence, n. Obstinate silence. So ~ENT a. [f. L OB(*mutescere* f. *mutus* dumb, -ESCENT, -ENCE)]

obnŏ'xious (-kshŭs), a. Liable *to* harm or evil or attack (now rare); offensive, objectionable, disliked, whence ~LY[2] adv. Hence ~NESS n. [f. L *obnoxiosus*, or *obnoxius* +-OUS]

ŏb'ōe, n. Wood-wind double-reed instrument of treble pitch & plaintive incisive tone; organ reed-stop imitating this. Hence ŏb'ōIST(3) n. [It., f. F as HAUTBOY]

ŏb'ol, n. Ancient-Greek silver coin. [f. L f. Gk *obolos*]

obscēne', a. Repulsive, filthy, loathsome, (arch.); grossly indecent, lewd. Hence or cogn. ~LY[2] adv., obscēn'ITY n. [f. F *obscène* or L *obscenus*]

obscūr'ant, n. Opponent of inquiry, enlightenment, & reform. Hence ~ISM(3) n., ~IST(2) n. & a. [= G *obscurant*, f. L (OBSCURE, -ANT)]

obscūre', a. & n., & v.t. 1. Dark, dim, (~ *rays*, invisible heat-rays of solar spectrum); (of colour) dingy, dull, indefinite;

indistinct, not clear; hidden, remote from observation; unnoticed; unknown to fame, humble; unexplained, doubtful; not perspicuous or clearly expressed; hence or cogn. ~LY² adv., **obscūr′ITY** n. 2. n. Obscurity, indistinctness. 3. v.t. Make ~, dark, indistinct, or unintelligible; dim glory of, outshine; conceal from sight; so **ŏbscūrA′TION** n. [ME; adj. f. OF *obscur* f. L *obscurus*; vb f. adj. or f. L *obscurare*]

ŏbscūr′um pēr ŏbscūr′ĭus, n.=IGNOTUM PER IGNOTIUS. [L, = the obscure by the still more obscure]

ŏbsĕcrā′tion, n. Earnest entreaty; Litany petition beginning with *By*. [ME, f. L *obsecratio* f. OB(*secrare* = *sacrare* f. *sacer* sacred) entreat]

ŏb′sĕquies (-ĭz), n. pl. Funeral rites, a funeral. Hence **obsē′quiAL** a. [ME; pl. of obs. *obsequy* f. OF *obseque* f. med. L *obsequiae* mixture of L *exsequiae* funeral with *obsequium* see foll.]

ŏbsē′quious, a. Obedient, dutiful, (arch.); servile, fawning. Hence ~LY² adv., ~NESS n. [ME, f. L *obsequiosus* f. OB(*sequium* f. *sequi* follow) compliance]

ŏbsĕrv′|ance (-z-), n. Keeping or performance of (also *of*) law, duty, custom, ritual, etc.; act of religious or ceremonial character, customary rite; the rule of a religious order; ‖ paying of deference or respect (arch.), also ~ANCY n. [ME, f. OF, f. L *observantia* (OBSERVE, -ANCE)]

ŏbsĕrv′ant (-z-), a. & n. 1. Attentive in observance; acute or diligent in taking notice; hence ~LY² adv. 2. n. Member of branch of Franciscan order that observes the strict rule. [F (OBSERVE, -ANT)]

ŏbsĕrvā′tion (-z-), n. 1. Noticing or being noticed, perception, faculty of taking notice; *post, attitude, of ~*, favourable for watching from or in; ~ *car*, in train esp. in U.S., so built as to afford good views. 2. (mil.). Watching of fortress or hostile position or movements (*army* etc. *of ~*, so engaged; ~ *post*, abbr. *O. P.* or *O. Pip*, esp. for watching effect of artillery fire). 3. Accurate watching & noting of phenomena as they occur in nature (cf. *experiment*) with regard to cause & effect or mutual relations. 4. Taking of sun's or other heavenly body's altitude to find latitude or longitude. 5. Remark or statement, esp. one of the nature of comment. Hence ~AL a., ~alLY² adv., (-zervǎsho-). [ME, f. L *observatio* (OBSERVE, -ATION)]

ŏbsĕrv′atorỹ (-z-), n. Building etc. whence natural, esp. astronomical, phenomena may be observed. [f. F *observatoire*, f. L *observare* see foll., -TORY]

ŏbsĕrv′|e′ (-z-), v.t. & i. 1. Keep, follow, adhere to, perform duly, (law, command, appointed time, method, principle, silence,

rite, anniversary, etc.). 2. Perceive, mark, watch, take notice of, become conscious of, (*the ~ed of all ~ers*, person etc. on whom etc. attention is concentrated). 3. Examine & note (phenomena) without aid of experiment. 4. Say, esp. by way of comment; make remark(s) *on*. Hence ~′ABLE a., ~′ER¹ n. (esp., interested spectator, person carried in aeroplane to note enemy's position etc., person trained to watch for & identify aircraft; *O~er*, esp. newspaper title), ~′ingLY² adv. [ME, f. OF *observer* f. L OB(*servare* keep)]

ŏbsĕss′, v.t. (Of evil spirit, delusion, or fixed idea) haunt, harass, preoccupy, fill mind of, (*~ed by, with*). So **obsĕ′ssION** (-shn) n. [f. L OB(*sidēre sess-*=*sedēre* sit) besiege]

ŏbsid′ian, n. Dark vitreous lava or volcanic rock like bottle-glass. [f. L *obsidianus*, false reading for *Obsianus* (*Obsius* personal name, -AN)]

ŏbsolĕs′c|ent, a. Becoming obsolete, going out of use or date; (biol., of organ once developed more fully) gradually disappearing. So ~ENCE n. [f. L OB(*solescere* f. *solēre* be accustomed, see -ESCENT), -ENT]

ŏb′solēte, a. & n. 1. Disused, discarded, antiquated; (biol.) less developed than formerly or in cognate species, rudimentary; hence ~NESS, **ŏb′solētISM**(3, 4), nn. 2. n. ~ person or thing. [f. L *obsoletus* p.p. as prec.]

ŏb′stacle, n. Hindrance, impediment, (*~-race*, in which artificial or natural ~s have to be passed). [ME, f. OF, f. L *obstaculum* f. OB(*stare* stand) impede]

obstĕt′ric(al), aa. Of midwifery, of childbirth & its antecedents & sequels, as branch of medicine & surgery. Hence **obstĕt′rics**, **ŏbstĕtri′cIAN** (-ĭshn), nn. [irreg. f. L *obstetricius* f. *obstetrix* midwife f. OB(*stare* or *sistere* stand), -TRIX]

ŏb′stin|ate, a. Stubborn, inflexible, self-willed, refractory. Hence or cogn. ~ACY n., ~ateLY² adv. [ME, f. L *obstinatus* p.p. of OB(*stinare* deriv. form of *stare* stand) persist]

obstrĕp′erous, a. Noisy, vociferous; turbulent, unruly, noisily resisting control. Hence ~LY² adv., ~NESS n. [f. L *obstreperus* f. OB(*strepere* make noise), -OUS]

obstrŭct′, v.t. & i. Block up, fill with impediments, make impassable or difficult of passage; prevent or retard progress of, impede; practise (esp. Parliamentary) obstruction. [f. L OB(*struere struct-* build)]

obstrŭc′tion, n. Blocking or being blocked, making or becoming more or less impassable; hindering, esp. of Parliamentary business by talking against time, whence ~ISM(3), ~IST(2), (-sho-), nn.; obstacle (*~-guard*, bar fixed before locomotive to remove ~s from rails). [f. L *obstructio* (prec., -ION)]

obstrŭc′tive, a. & n. 1. Causing, intended

to produce, obstruction; hence ~LY² adv., ~NESS n. 2. n. ~ person, esp. in House of Commons. [as OBSTRUCT, -IVE]

obtain', v.t. & i. Acquire, have granted one, get, whence ~MENT n. (rare), ~ABLE a.; be prevalent or established or in vogue. [ME, f. OF *obtenir* f. L OB(*tinēre* = *tenēre* hold) keep]

obtěct', a. (entom.). (Of the pupae of certain insects) enclosed in an outer chitinous case. [f. L OB(*tegere tect-* cover)]

obtěst', v.t. & i. (arch.). Adjure, supplicate, call to witness; protest. So ŏbtěsTA'TION n. [f. L OB(*testari* f. *testis* witness)]

obtrude' (-ōōd), v.t. Thrust forward (*upon* or *on* person or his attention) importunately. So obtru'SION (-ōōzhn) n., obtrus'IVE a., obtrus'IVELY² adv., obtrus'IVENESS n., (-ōō-). [f. L OB(*trudere trus-* push)]

obtrŭnc'āte, v.t. Cut off head of, top. [f. L OB(*truncare* f. *truncus* maimed), -ATE³]

obtŭnd', v.t. (med.). Blunt, deaden, (sense or faculty). [ME, f. L OB(*tundere tus-* beat)]

ŏb'tŭr|āte, v.t. Stop up, close, seal, (orifice in body, breech of gun, etc.). Hence or cogn. ~A'TION, ~ātOR, nn. [f. L *obturare*, -ATE³]

obtūse', a. Of blunt form, not sharp-pointed or sharp-edged; (geom., of angle) greater than one & less than two right angles; (of pain, the senses) dull, not acute; stupid, slow of perception. Hence ~LY² adv., ~NESS n., obtūs'I· comb.form. [f. L p.p. of OBTUND*ere*]

ŏb'vērse, a. & n. 1. Narrower at base or point of attachment than at apex (esp. in nat. hist., including as general term OB*ovate*, OB*lanceolate*, etc.); answering as counterpart to something else; hence ~LY² adv. 2. n. Side of coin or medal bearing the head or principal design (cf. REVERSE); face of anything meant to be presented, front; counterpart of a fact or truth. [f. L *obversus* p.p. (foll.)]

obvērt', v.t. (log.). Infer another proposition with contradictory predicate by changing quality of (proposition). So obvēr'SION (-shn) n. [f. L OB(*vertere vers-* turn)]

ŏb'viāte, v.t. Clear away, get rid of, get round, neutralize (danger, inconvenience, etc.). [f. LL OB(*viare* f. *via* way) withstand]

ŏb'vious, a. Open to eye or mind, clearly perceptible, palpable, indubitable. Hence ~LY² adv., ~NESS n. [f. L *obvius* (*ob viam* in the way), -OUS]

oc-, pref. See OB-.

ŏcari'na (-rē-), n. Small egg-shaped porcelain or metal musical wind-instrument. [It. (*oca* goose, -INA¹)]

occa'sion (-zhn), n., & v.t. 1. Juncture suitable for doing something, opportunity, (*take* ~, avail oneself of opportunity *to* do; *take* ~ *by the* FORELOCK¹). 2. Reason,

ground, justification, incitement, need, (*there is no* ~ *to be angry*; *avoid all* ~*s of quarrel*; *Queen has no* ~ *for services of officer, formula of dismissal*; *gave* ~ *to a burst of laughter*). 3. Subsidiary, incidental, or immediate cause (*the cause of a revolution may be obscure while its* ~ *is obvious*). 4. pl. Affairs, business, (esp. *go about one's lawful* ~*s*). 5. (Particular time marked by) special occurrence (*on this festive* ~; *on the* ~ *of his marriage*; *celebrate the* ~; *rise to the* ~, show requisite energy etc.; *this is a great* ~); (*up*)*on* ~, whenever need arises, now & then. 6. v.t. Be the ~ or cause of, bring about esp. incidentally, cause (action etc., or person or thing *to* do). Hence, f. OF, or L *occasio* f. OC(*cidere cas-* = *cadere* fall), -ION]

occa'sional (-zho-), a. Arising out of, made or meant for, adapted for use on, acting on, special occasion(s); happening irregularly as occasion presents itself; coming now & then, not regular or frequent; ~ *cause*, secondary cause, occasion, also apparent cause (see foll.); ‖~ *licence* (to sell liquor only at specified times & places). Hence ~ITY (-ǎl⁴) n., ~LY² adv. [-AL]

occa'sional|ism (-zho-), n. Doctrine of some Cartesians that volition & sensation are connected with the following & preceding material phenomena not causally but as separate productions of God on the same occasion. So ~IST(2) n. [-ISM]

Oc'cident (ŏks-), n. ·The west; western Europe; Europe; Europe & America; America; European as opposed to Oriental civilization, whence ŏccidĕn'talISM(3) n., ŏccidĕn'talIZE(3) v.t., ŏccidĕn'talIST (2, 3) n., (-ks-). So ŏccidĕn'tAL a., ŏccidĕn'talLY² adv., (-ks-). [ME, f. OF, or f. L *occident-* setting (OCCASION, -ENT)]

oc'ciput (ŏks-), n. Back of head. So ŏccip'itAL a., ŏccip'itO- comb. form, (-ks-). [L OC(*ciput -itis* = *caput* head)]

occlude' (-lōō-), v.t. (sci.). Stop up, close, obstruct, (pores, orifice); (chem.) absorb & retain (gases). So occlu'SION (-lōōzhn) n., (also, meteor.) closing of the cold front on to the warm front in a depression, occlus'OR (-lōō-) n. [f. L OC(*cludere -clus-* = *claudere* shut)]

occŭlt'¹, a. Kept secret, esoteric; recondite, mysterious, beyond the range of ordinary knowledge; involving the supernatural, mystical, magical, whence ~·ISM(3), ~IST(2, 3), nn.; *the* ~, that which is ~. Hence ~LY² adv., ~NESS n. [f. L OC(*culere -cult-* cf. *celare* hide)]

occŭlt'·², v.t. & i. Conceal, cut off from view by passing in front, (usu. astron., & applied only when concealing body is of much greater apparent size than concealed); ~*ing light* in lighthouses, one that is cut off at regular intervals. So ŏccultA'TION n. [f. L *occultare* frequent. as prec.]

ŏcc'ŭp|ant, n. Person holding property,

esp. land, in actual possession; one who occupies, or resides or is in, a place; one who establishes title to unowned thing by taking possession. Hence ~ANCY n. [F, or f. L as OCCUPY, -ANT]

ŏccŭpā'tion, n. Occupying or being occupied; taking or holding possession, esp. of country or district by military force (*army of* ~, left to hold occupied region till regular government is set up), tenure, occupancy; what occupies one, means of filling one's time, temporary or regular employment, business, calling, pursuit; || ~ *franchise,* right to vote as tenant; ~ *bridge, road,* etc., private for use of occupiers of land. Hence ~AL (-sho) a., (esp.) incident to or arising from a person's ~ (~*al disease,* based on or utilizing esp. light employment (~*al therapy*). [ME, f. OF, f. L *occupationem* (OCCUPY, -ATION)]

ŏcc'ŭpier, n. Person in (esp. temporary or subordinate) possession esp. of land or house, holder, occupant. [ME, f. foll., -ER[1]]

ŏcc'ŭpy̆, v.t. Take possession of (country, region, town, strategic position) by military force or settlement; hold (office), reside in, tenant; take up or fill (space, time), reside or be in (place, position); busy, keep engaged, (esp. in pass. & refl.) *occupied,* ~ *oneself, with* or *in*). [ME, irreg. f. OF *occuper* f. L oc(*cupare* cf. *capere* take) seize]

ŏccŭr', v.i. (-rr-). Be met with, be found, exist, in some place or conditions; come into one's mind (esp. *it* ~s or ~*red to me that* —); take place, befall, happen. [f. L oc(*currere* run) go to meet]

ŏccŭ'rrence, n. Happening (*is of frequent* ~, often occurs); incident, event. [F, = med. L *occurrentia* (prec., -ENT), -ENCE]

ocean (ō'shn), n. Great body of water surrounding the land of the globe; one of the main areas into which geographers divide this (usu. reckoned as five, the *Atlantic, Pacific, Indian, Arctic,* & *Antarctic,* O~s; *German* ~, = NORTH *Sea*); the sea (also poet, without *the,* as *the dark unfathomed caves of* ~); immense expanse or quantity of anything (often ~*s of*); ~ *greyhound,* swift ship, esp. passenger liner; ~ *lane,* track prescribed for steamers; ~ *tramp,* cargo-carrying steamer not engaged in single trade. Hence ~OG'RAPHY (ōsha-) n., ~OGRAPH'IC(AL) (oséa-, ōsha-) aa., ~WARD(S) adv. [ME, f. L f. Gk *ōkeanos* stream encircling earth's disc, Atlantic]

Oceăn'ia (ōshi-, ōsi-), n. Islands of Pacific & adjacent seas. [f. F *Océanie* (prec., -IA[1])]

Ocean'ian (ōshiăn'yan, ōsi-), a. & n. (Native) of Oceania. [-AN]

oceăn'ic, O-, (ōshi-, ōsi-) a. Of, like, etc., the ocean; of Oceania. [-IC]

Ocĕ'anid (os-), n. (pl. ~s, ~es pr. -ăn'Idēz). Ocean nymph of Greek mythology. [f. Gk *Ōkeanis -idos* daughter of Ocean]

ocĕll'us, n. (pl. -lī). One of simple as

opposed to compound eyes of insects; facet of compound eye; spot of colour surrounded by ring of other colour, whence o'cĕllATE[2], -ātĕd, aa. [L, dim. of *oculus* eye]

o'cĕlot, n. Animal of cat tribe of S. & Central America, resembling leopard. [F, abridged by Buffon f. Mex. *tlal*(*ocelotl* jaguar) of the field, & applied to different animal]

|| **och** (see Ap.), int. = *oh, ah,* used in Scotland & Ireland.

ŏchlŏc'racy̆ (-kl-), n. Mob-rule. Hence **ŏch'loc**RAT n., **ŏchloc**RAT'IC a., (-kl-). [f. F *ochlocratie* f. Gk *okhlokratia* (*okhlos* mob, -CRACY)]

ochre (ōk'er), n. Kinds of native earth consisting of clay & hydrated oxide of iron used as pigments varying from light yellow to brown; pale brownish yellow. Hence ~ISH (ōk'er-), **ochra**'CEOUS (-krā-shus), ~OUS (ōk'rĭ-), **ŏch'r**OUS, **ŏch'r**Y[2], (-kr-), aa., ~O- (ōk'rĭ-) comb. form. [ME, f. OF *ocre* f. L f. Gk *ōkhra* yellow ochre f. *ōkhros* yellow]

-ock, suf. forming nn. orig. w. dim. sense (*hill*~, *bitt*~, *bull*~, *padd*~), which many of them have lost (*padd*~, *bull*~, *poll*~); *hass*~, *bann*~, *matt*~, are prob. of different orig.

o'clock. See CLOCK[1].

oct-. = OCTA-, OCTO-, before vowel.

ŏc'ta-, comb. form of Gk *oktō* eight. Hence **ŏctăm**'EROUS a.

ŏc'tachŏrd (-k-), a. & n. Eight-stringed (musical instrument); series of eight notes, e.g. the diatonic scale. Hence ~AL (-kŏrd[2]) a. [f. L f. Gk *oktakhordos* (prec., CHORD)]

ŏc'tad, n. Group of eight. [f. LL f. Gk *oktas* f. *oktō* eight, -AD(1)]

ŏc'tagon, n. & a. Plane figure with eight angles & sides, object or building of such section; so **ŏctăg'on**AL a., **ŏctăg'onal**LY[2] adv.; (adj.) ~al. [f. L f. Gk *oktagōnos* (OCTA-, *gōnia* angle)]

ŏctahēd'r|on, n. Solid figure contained by eight plane faces, & usu. by eight triangles (*regular*~on, by equal & equilateral triangles); body, esp. crystal, of regular ~al form. So ~AL a. [f. Gk *oktaedron* (OCTA-, *hedra* seat)]

ŏc'tāne, n. Hydrocarbon of the paraffin series; *high*-~, (of fuels used in internal--combustion engines) having good anti--knock properties, not detonating readily during the power stroke. [OCT-, -ANE(2)]

ŏc'tant, n. 1. Arc of circle=1/8 of circumference; 1/8 of circular area contained within two radii & arc; one of eight parts into which three planes intersecting (esp. at right angles) at point divide space round it. 2. (astron.). Point in planet's apparent course 45° distant from given point, esp. point at which moon is 45° from conjunction or opposition with sun. 3. Instrument in form of graduated eighth of circle used in astronomy &

navigation. [f. L *octans* (L *octo* eight, cf. QUADRANT)]

ŏc'tarchy (-kĭ), n. Aggregate of eight petty kingdoms (substituted by some historians for HEPTARCHY). [OCTA-, cf. HEPTARCHY]

octaroon. See OCTOROON.

ŏc'tastȳle, a. & n. (Portico or building) with eight columns at end or in front. [f. L f. Gk *oktastulos* (OCTA-, *stulos* pillar)]

ŏc'tateuch (-k), n. First 8 O.-T. books. [f. LL f. Gk OCTA*teukhos*, cf. PENTATEUCH]

ŏc'tave (-ĭv), n. 1. The day week of a festival, eight days including festival & its day week. 2. Group or stanza of eight lines, octet. 3. (mus.). Note produced by twice or half the vibration rate of given note & eight diatonic degrees above·or below it (*second* ~, ~ of the ~ in same direction; so *third* etc. ~); interval between note & its ~; series of notes filling this; note & its ~ sounding together. 4. Group of eight. 5. A fencing position. 6. ‖ Wine-cask holding 13¼ gal. 7. ~- -*coupler*, device connecting organ-keys an ~ apart; ~-*flute*, piccolo, also organ flute- -stop an ~ higher than the ordinary. [(1) ME, f. OF, f. L *octava dies* eighth day by inclusive reckoning (*octavus* f. *octo* eight); (2) repr. OTTAVA RIMA; (3) F, f. med. L *octava* (*vox*)]

ŏctāv'ō, n. (abbr. *8vo*, *oct.*; pl. ~s). (Size of) book or page given by folding sheet three times to form quire of eight leaves. [f. L IN⁵ *octavo* (prec.)]

ŏctāv'us. See PRIMUS¹.

ŏctěnn'ial, a. Lasting, recurring every, eight years. [f. LL OCT(*ennium* f. *annus* year) period of eight years, -AL]

ŏctět(te)', n. (Composition for) eight singers or players; group of eight lines, esp. the first eight of sonnet. [f. L *octo* eight, after DUET, QUARTET(TE)]

ŏctill'ion (-lyon), n. ‖ Eighth power of million (1 followed by 48 ciphers). Hence ~TH² a. & n. [F (now = ninth power of thousand) as prec. after MILLION]

‖ **ŏctingēntēn'arȳ** (-j-), n. 800th anniversary. [f. L *octingenti* 800, after CENTENARY]

octo-, oct-, comb. form of L *octo*, & occas. (= OCTA-) of Gk *oktō*, eight.

Octōb'er (ō-), n. Tenth month; beer brewed in ~ (arch.). [OE, f. L (prec.), cf. DECEMBER; ME *Octobre* f. OF]

Octōb'rist (ō-), n. & a. (Member) of moderate party in Russian Duma. [*Oct.* 30, 1905, date of Imperial Constitutional Manifesto]

ŏctōcēntēn'arȳ (*or* -sěn'tĭn-), **ŏctōcēntēnn'ial**, nn. (Irreg. for) OCTINGENTENARY.

ŏctōdě'cimō, n. (abbr. *18mo*; pl.~s). (Size of) book or page given by folding sheets into eighteen leaves. [for IN⁵ ~ f. L OCTO- (*decimus* tenth) eighteenth, cf. OCTAVO]

ŏctōgēnār'ian, a. & n. (Person) between 79 & 90 years old. [f. L *octogenarius* (*octogeni* eighty each, -ARY¹), -AN]

ŏc'tonal, a. Proceeding by eights (of coinage, numeral system, etc.). [f. L *octoni*, see foll., -AL]

ŏctonār'ian, a. & n. (pros.). Eight-foot (line). [f. L *octonarius versus* eight-foot line (*octoni* eight each f. *octo* eight, -ARY¹), -AN]

ŏc'tonarȳ, a.. & n. = OCTONAL; (n.) group of eight, eight-line stanza (esp. of divisions of *Ps.* 119). [see prec.]

ŏc'topus, n. (pl. ~*es*). (Kinds of) cephalopod mollusc with eight suckered arms round mouth; organized & usu. harmful ramified power or influence. [f. Gk *oktopous* eight-footed (OCTO-, *pous* foot)]

ŏctoroōn', -ta-, n. Offspring of quadroon & white, person of one-eighth Negro blood. [irreg. f. OCTO- after QUADROON]

ŏctosyllāb'ic, a. & n. Eight-syllable (verse). [f. LL OCTO(*syllabus* f. *syllaba* SYLLABLE), -IC]

ŏctosyll'able, n. & a. = prec.; word of eight syllables. [see prec.]

ŏc'troi (-rwah), n. Duty levied in some continental countries on goods entering town; place where, officials by whom, it is levied. [F (*octroyer* grant, as AUTHOR-IZE)]

ŏc'tuple, a., n., & v.t. Eightfold; (n.) product after multiplication by eight *of*; (vb) multiply by eight. [f. L *octuplus* a. (*octo* eight, cf. DOUBLE)]

ŏc'ular, a. & n. Of, for, by, with, etc., the eye(s) or sight, visual, (~ *demonstration*, proof appealing to the eyes; (n.) eye- -piece of optical instrument. Hence ~LY² adv. [f. LL *ocularis* (*oculus* eye, -AR¹)]

ŏc'ularist, n. Maker of artificial eyes. [f. F *oculariste* (prec., -IST)]

ŏc'ulate, -ātěd, aa. = OCELLATE. [f. L *oculus* eye, -ATE²]

ŏc'ul|ist, n. Specialist in eye-diseases. Hence ~is'tic a. [f. F *oculiste* (L *oculus* eye, -IST)]

ŏc'ulo-, comb. form of L *oculus* eye, (-o-), as ~*nās'al* of eye & nose.

ŏd, n. Power assumed to pervade nature & account for magnetism, crystallization, chemical action, mesmerism, etc. [arbitrary formation of Baron v. Reichenbach 1788–1869]

ŏd'alisque (-k), n. Eastern female slave or concubine, esp. in Turkish Sultan's seraglio. [F, f. Turk. *odaliq* (*odah* chamber, -*liq* function)]

ŏdd, a. & n.. 1. Left over when the rest have been divided into two numerically equal sets (*the* ~ *man*, to whom casting- -vote falls in uneven-numbered committee etc.; *the* ~ *trick* in whist, thirteenth when each side has won six; ~ *man out*, way of selecting one of three persons by tossing coins till only two agree). 2. (Of number) not divisible by two (~ & *even*, a game of chance); (of things or persons numbered consecutively) bearing such number. 3. (Appended to number, sum, weight, etc.) with something over of lower denomination etc. (*forty* ~, between 40 & 50; *sixty thousand* ~, with some extra hundreds, tens, or units; *sixty* ~ *thousand*, between 60 & 70 thousand; *twelve pounds* ~, with some shillings or pence). **4.** By which round number, given sum, etc., is exceeded (*Here is a pound note; pay the bill & keep the* ~ *money. There are 1006*; *what shall we do with the* ~ *six?*). **5.** Additional, casual, beside the reckoning, unconnected, unoccupied, incalculable, (*picks up* ~ *jobs*; *do it at* ~ *moments*; *in some corner*; ~ *numbers, volumes*, belonging to incomplete sets of magazines etc.). **6.** Extraordinary, strange, queer, remarkable, eccentric, whence ~'ISH¹(2) a., ~'LY² adv. **7.** ~'*fellow*, member of friendly society of Oddfellows with rites imitative of freemasonry; hence ~'NESS n. **8.** n. (golf). *The* ~, the stroke which one player has played more than his opponent (opp. *the like*). [ME, f. ON *odda-* in *odda-mathr* third man, odd man, *odda-tala* odd number, f. *oddi* angle, triangle, cogn. w. OE *ord* tip]

ŏdd'ĭtў, n. Strangeness; peculiar trait; queer person; fantastic object, strange event. [-ITY]

ŏdd'ments, n. pl. Odds & ends. [-MENT]

ŏdds, n. pl. (formerly always, & still in phrases as below, treated as sing.). Inequalities (*make* ~ *even*, do away with these); difference (*what's the* ~?, what does it matter?); variance, strife, (*are at* ~ *with fate*); balance of advantage (*the* ~ *are in our favour*; *have fought against longer* ~); equalizing allowance to weaker competitor (*give, receive,* ~); ratio between amounts staked by parties to bet (*lay, give,* ~ *of three to one*, said of party offering the advantage; *take* ~, accept the advantage; ~-*on*, state of betting when ~ are laid); chances or balance of probability in favour of some result (*it is* ~ *or long* ~ *that* or *but, the* ~ *are that, he will do it*); ~ *& ends*, remnants, stray articles, (perh. alteration of earlier *odd ends*. [app. pl. of ODD used as n.; cf. *news*]

ōde, n. (Orig.) poem meant to be sung (*choral* ~, song of chorus in Greek play etc.); (mod.) rhymed or rarely unrhymed lyric often in form of address, usu. of exalted style and enthusiastic tone, often in varied or irregular metre, & usu. between 50 & 200 lines in length. [f. F, f. LL *oda* f. Gk *ōidē* contr. of *aoidē* (*aeidō* sing)]

-ode, suf. forming nn. w. sense *thing of the nature of* (*geode, phyllode*); *anode, cathode, electrode*, are not examples. [f. Gk -*ōdēs* adj. ending (-o-, -*eidēs* -like)]

ōdē'um, n. (pl. -s, -*ĕa*). Building for musical performances, esp. among ancient Greeks & Romans. [f. L f. Gk *ōideion*]

ŏd'ic, a. Of OD. [-IC]

ō̆d'ious, a. Hateful, repulsive. Hence ~LY² adv., ~NESS n. [ME, f. OF *odieus* f. L *odiosus* (ODIUM, -OSE¹)]

ō̆d'ium, n. General or widespread dislike or reprobation incurred by person or attaching to action (*exposed me to* ~; *the* ~ *of the transaction*); ~ *thĕolo'gĭcum*, bitterness notoriously characterizing theologians who disagree. [L, = hatred]

odometer. See hod-.

odŏn't|(o)-, comb. form of Gk *odous odontos* tooth, as ~*orhync'ous*, having toothlike serrations in the bill; ~*oglŏss'um*, kinds of orchids with large beautifully coloured flowers with tongue-shaped lips; ~OID; *ŏdontŏl'*OGY.

ōdorif'erous, a. Diffusing (usu. agreeable) scent, fragrant. Hence ~LY² adv. [ME, f. L *odorifer* (ODOUR, -FEROUS)]

ō̆d'orous, a. (chiefly poet.).=prec. Hence ~LY² adv. [foll., -OUS]

ō̆d'our (-*der*), n. Pleasant or unpleasant smell, whence ~LESS a.; fragrance (arch., usu. pl.) substance(s) emitting sweet scent, perfume(s); (fig.) savour, trace, (*no* ~ *of intolerance attaches to it*); *good* or *bad* or *ill* repute or favour (*is in bad* ~ *with the nonconformists*); ~ *of sanctity*, reputation for holiness (orig. lit., sweet ~ exhaled by dying or exhumed saint). [ME, f. AF *odour*, OF *odor* f. L *odorem* -OR)]

ō̆d'ўl, n. = OD. [-YL]

Ŏd'ўssey (ŏ-), n. (pl. ~*s*). One of two great ancient-Greek national epics (cf. ILIAD) describing adventures of Odysseus or Ulysses returning from siege of Troy; any of the 24 books of this (*in the fourth* etc. ~); series of wanderings, long adventurous journey. [f. L f. Gk *Odusseia* (*Odusseus*, -IA¹)]

oe'cist (ēs-), n. Founder of (esp. ancient--Greek) colony. [f. Gk *oikistēs* (*oikizō* settle f. *oikos* house, -IST)]

oecŏl'ogў (ēk-), n. Var. of ECOLOGY.

oecūmĕn'ical (ēk-), a. Of or representing the whole Christian world or universal church, general, universal, catholic, (of general councils of early, & of mod. R.-C., Church); world-wide. So **oecūmĕni'CITY** (ēk-) n. [f. LL f. Gk *oikoumenikos* f. *hē oikoumenē* the inhabited (earth) f. *oikeō* inhabit, -AL]

oedēm'a (ēd-), n. (path.; no pl.). Swollen state of tissue etc. with serous fluid, local dropsy. Hence ~toSE¹, ~tous, aa., ~tousLY² adv., (*ĕdēm'* or *ēdēm'*). [f. Gk *oidēma -atos* (*oideō* swell)]

Oed'ipus (ēd-), n. Solver of riddles; ~ *complex*, a sexual complex held by psycho--analysts of the Freudian school to influence the child in regard to the parent of opposite sex. [f. Gk *Oidipous*, who guessed the Sphinx's riddle, & in ignorance married his mother]

o'er (ōr), adv. & prep. = OVER (poet.).

oer'stĕd (ēr-), n. Unit of magnetic force. [O~, Danish physicist (d. 1851)]

oesŏph'ag|us (ēs-), n. (pl.~*i* pr. -jī, ~*uses*). Canal from mouth to stomach, gullet. Hence **oesophā'gĕAL** (-j-) a., ~o- comb. form. [f. Gk *oisophagos*]

oes'trogen (ēs-), n. Female sex-hormone. [foll., -GEN]

oes'trum, -us, (ēs-), n. Gadfly; stimulus, vehement impulse, frenzy; sexual heat of animals, rut. [f. Gk *oistros*]

of (ŏv, ov), prep. connecting its noun with preceding n., adj., adv., or vb, & indicating the relations roughly classified as follows: **1.** Removal, separation, point of departure, privation, (*north, within a mile, upwards,* have the advantage, *of*; •*back of,* behind; *wide of the mark*; *heal, rid, ease, brought to* BED[1], *of*; *destitute, empty, free, bare, of*; *take* LEAVE[1] *of*; *balk, cheat, defraud, deprive, disappoint, of*; *independently, guiltless, irrespective, of*). **2.** Origin, derivation, cause, agency, authorship, (*be, come, descend, spring, of*; *borrow, buy, win, receive, hire, of*; TAKE *it ill of*; *have comfort, wish* one *joy, of*; *ask, demand, learn, expect, of*; of one's own ACCORD[2]; *of* COURSE[1], *of* RIGHT, *of* NECESSITY; *of oneself,* spontaneously; *die of*; *smell, savour, smack, of*; *tired, ashamed, afraid, glad, proud, of*; *sick of measles,* laid up with, *sick of delays,* disgusted by; *warned of God, forsaken of God & man,* by; *it was kind, foolish, naughty, clever, cruel, well done, of you to say so*; *has the approval of his master*; *the works of Shakespeare, Iliad of Homer*). **3.** Material, substance, closer definition, identity, (*house of cards; built of brick; make a* FOOL[1], *the* BEST[1], *of*; MAKE[1] *much of*; *a family of eight*; *the name of Jones*; *the class of idiots*; *city of Rome, vice of drunkenness*; *a fool of a man, her scamp of a husband, the worst liar of any man I know*; *had a bad time, troublesome journey, of it*). **4.** Concern, reference, direction, respect, (*think well of him*; *never heard of it*; *was informed of the fact*; *is true of every case*; *repent, beware, of*; *cannot conceive, accept, approve,* THINK, *of*; *does not admit or allow of*; *accuse, convict, suspect, of*; *avail, bethink,* oneself *of*; SHORT, *guilty, certain, sure, confident, fond, of*; *swift of foot, blind of an eye, hard of heart,* HARD *of hearing*; *at 30 years of age*). **5.** Objective relation (*the levying of taxes*; *love of virtue*; *in search of knowledge*; *great eaters of pork*; *redolent, productive, fruitful, lavish, prodigal, sparing, capable, sensible, careful, observant, desirous, impatient, characteristic, destructive, indicative, of*). **6.** Description, quality, condition, (*man of tact, person of consequence, farm of 100 acres, the hour of prayer, potatoes of our own growing*; *girl of ten years,* or, with mixed construction, *of ten years old*). **7.** Partition, classification, inclusion, selection, (*no more of that*; *some, five, of us,* = (a) a portion, or five, of us who are more numerous, or by extention, (b) we, being several or five persons; so *any* part, or *the whole, of it*; *the most dangerous of enemies*; *he of all men, he most or least of all*; *is the one thing of all others that,* illog. for *of all that*; *song of*

songs, *holy of holies, those best deserving the name*; *is one of a, ten, thousand,* such as occurs only in one among 1,000, 10,000, cases; *a friend of mine, of the vicar's,* i.e. orig. in the number of my, the vicar's, friends, but extended to illog. contexts, as *that long nose of his, this only son of the vicar's*; *drink deep of flattery, partake of food*; *was sworn of the Council,* admitted as member; *his temper is of the quickest,* belongs to the quickest class; *a sort of thud*; *comes in of an evening,* at some time in the evenings; *of old, yore, late years, late,* somewhere in the specified periods). **8.** Belonging, connexion, possession, (*we of the middle class*; *companions of his exile*; *articles of clothing*; *the manners of today*; *a thing of the past*; *the master of the house*; *the widow of the man who was killed*; *a topic of conversation*; esp. with words that naturally require supplementing, as *the cause, result, counterpart, opposite, image, of*). **9.** BECAUSE, *by* MEAN[1]s, *for* FEAR[1], *for the* SAKE, *in* BEHALF, *in* CASE[1], *in* FACE[1], *in* RESPECT, *in* SPITE, INSTEAD, *on* ACCOUNT[2], *on* BEHALF, *on the* POINT, *of*. [OE *of,* unaccented form of *æf,* orig. *af,* = OS, ON, Goth *af,* OHG *ab(a)* f. Gmc *•abh(a),* cogn. w. L *ab,* Gk *apo*]

of-, pref. See OB-.

off (awf, ŏf), adv., prep., a., n., & v.t. **1.** adv. Away, at or to a distance, (*rode ~*; *beat ~ the attack*; *keep assailant ~*; *ward ~ disaster*; *take* oneself, *be, make, ~,* depart; *~ with you!,* go; *~ with his head!,* behead him; *fall, go, ~,* deteriorate; of ship, *fall ~,* become less close to wind; *the bullet glanced ~*; *go ~,* fall asleep; *is far, three miles, two years, ~*; (so as to be) out of position, not on or touching or dependent or attached, loose, separate, gone, (*my hat is ~*; *take his clothes ~*; *cut, break, shake,* etc., *~*; *throw ~ reserve,* become open or candid; *be ~ with the old love,* have severed connexion; *get* one's *daughters, stock, ~,* disposed of by marriage, sale; *the gilt is ~,* disillusionment has come; *we are ~ now,* just started, starting, or about to start); so as to break continuity or continuance, discontinued, stopped, not obtainable, (*broke ~,* ceased to speak; *leave ~ work*; *the engagement, bargain, negotiation, is ~*; *declare ~,* refuse or rescind engagement; *cut ~ supplies*; *the gas, asparagus, is ~,* no longer to be got); to the end, entirely, so as to be clear, (*clear, drink, pay, polish, work, ~*); BUY, COME, DASH[1], GET, MARK[2], PALM, PASS, RATTLE, SHOW, TAKE, ~; RIGHT, STRAIGHT, ~; *well, badly, comfortably,* etc., *~,* so circumstanced or supplied with money; *~ & on,* intermittently, waveringly, now & again; *~-load, ~-saddle,* S.-Afr. for *un-.* **2.** prep. From, away or down or up from, disengaged or distant from, (so as to be) no longer on, (*drove them ~ the seas*; *is ~ the beaten track*; *fell ~ a ladder*; *take cover ~ dish*; *eats ~ silver plate*; *take thing,* matter, ~ one's *hands*, relieve him of it; *had borrowed £20 ~ plaintiff* vulg.; ~ one's HEAD[1], FEED[2]; ~-*beat*, unusual or unconventional; ~. *colour*, out of condition, indisposed; ~ one's *game*, not playing as well as usual; ~ *smoking*, not indulging in it, disinclined for it; *took something ~ the price*; *is ~ duty* or *work*; *cut a slice ~*, *dine ~*, *the joint*; *was only a yard ~ me*; *keep ship two points ~ the wind*; ~ *the point*, irrelevant(ly); ~ *the map*, sl., vanished, no longer existing; *in a street ~ the Strand*, turning out of it; *from ~*, arch., poet., or vulg., = ~; ~-*hand*, extempore, without premeditation, unceremoniously, whence ~**hănd'**, ~**hănd'ED**[2] aa., ~**hănd'ĕdLY**[2] adv., ~**hănd'ĕdNESS** n.; ~ *shore*, a short way out to sea; so ~-*shore fisheries*; *~-*shore purchases*, goods and services purchased by one country in another country; ~-*shore wind*, blowing seawards; *anchored ~ the point, cape*, etc., opposite & a short way from it; ~ *side* in football, between ball & opponents' goal, so ~-*side play, rule*; ~-*white*, not quite white); with a handicap of (*he plays ~* 5). 3. adj. Farther, far, (*on the ~ side of the wall*); (of horses etc. or vehicles) right (opp. NEAR[2], w. ref. to side at which rider usu. mounts; *the ~ leader, front wheel, hind leg, side*); (crick.) towards, in, or coming from, that half of the field as divided by line through two middle stumps in which playing batsman does not stand (opp. ON[2], LEG; *an ~ drive*, whence ~**drive'** v.t.; ~ *stump*; LONG[1] ~; *an ~ break*); subordinate, divergent, (*in an ~ street*; fig. of argument etc., *that is an ~ issue*); contingent, improbable, (*there is an ~ chance that*); disengaged (*will do it on my next ~ day*); ‖ ~-*licence*, to sell beer etc. for consumption ~ the premises; ~-*print*, a separate, printed copy of article etc. that was orig. part of larger publication. 4. n. (crick.). The ~ side. 5. v.t. (colloq.). Announce intention of abandoning or annulling (negotiation, agreement, undertaking); withdraw from negotiation or engagement with (person). [different. sp. of OF, since 15/16th c.]

ŏff'al, n. Refuse, waste stuff, scraps, garbage; parts cut off as waste from carcass meant for food, esp. entrails, also head, tail, kidneys, heart, tongue, liver, etc.; carrion, putrid flesh; low-priced fish (e.g. plaice as opp. sole or other prime fish); bran or other by-product of grain (often pl.); offscourings, dregs; ~ *milk, wheat, wood*, etc., inferior. [ME, f. MDu. *afval* f. *af* OF+*vallen* FALL[1]]

offence', ***offense'**, n. Stumbling-block, occasion of unbelief etc., (now rare); attacking, aggressive action, taking the offensive, (*the most effective defence is ~*); wounding of the feelings, wounded feeling, annoyance, umbrage, (*no ~ was meant; too quick to take ~; give ~ to*;

cannot be done without ~); transgression, misdemeanour, illegal act, (esp. *commit an ~ against*). Hence ~**LESS** (sl-) a. [ME & OF *offens* f. L *offensus*, -*ūs* annoyance, & ME & F *offense* f. L *offensa* a striking against, both f. OF(*fendere fens*- strike)]

offĕnd', v.i. & t. Stumble morally, do amiss, transgress, (*against* law, decency, person, etc.), whence ~**ER**[1] n. (esp. FIRST ~*er*), ~**ING**[2] a.; wound feelings of, anger, cause resentment or disgust in, outrage, (*am sorry you are ~ed; ~ed at* or *by* thing, *with* or *by* person; ~ *her delicacy, my sense of justice*), whence ~**ĕdLY**[2] adv. [ME, f. OF *offendre* f. L as prec.]

offĕn'sive, a. & n. 1. Aggressive, intended for or used in attack, (~ *arms, movement*; opp. DEFENSIVE); meant to give offence, insulting, (~ *language*); disgusting, ill-smelling, nauseous, repulsive; hence ~**LY**[2] adv., ~**NESS** n. 2. n. Attitude of assailant, aggressive action, (*take, act on, abandon, the ~*); an attack; ~ campaign or stroke, (*the long-expected German ~*); movement, as *peace ~*. [f. F (-*if*, -*ive*) or f. med. L *offensivus* (OFFENCE, -IVE)]

ŏff'er[1], v.t. & i. 1. Present (victim, first-fruits, prayer) to deity, revered person, etc., by way of sacrifice, give in worship or devotion, whence ~**ING**[1](4) n. 2. Hold out in hand, or tender in words or otherwise, for acceptance or refusal (~*ed me his hymn-book to look over*; TAKEN & ~*ed*; *was ~ed a free pardon*; ~ *an opinion, a few remarks*, etc.; ~ *no apology*). 3. Make proposal of marriage. 4. Show for sale. 5. Give opportunity to enemy for *battle*. 6. Express readiness *to* do if desired; essay, try to show, (violence, resistance, etc., often *to*); show an intention *to* do (~*ed to strike me*). 7. (Of things) present to sight or notice (*each age ~s its characteristic riddles*); present itself, occur, (*as opportunity ~s; the first path that ~ed*). [OE *offrian* in religious sense f. L OF(*ferre* bring); other senses f. OF *offrir* of same orig.]

ŏff'er[2], n. Expression of readiness to give or do if desired, or to sell on terms (*on ~*, for sale at certain price), proposal esp. of marriage; bid. [ME, f. OF *offre* (prec.)]

ŏff'ertory̌, n. Part of mass or communion preceding canon, at which alms of congregation are usu. collected; (improp., by confusion of offertory & offerings) the alms collected; collection of money at religious service. [ME, f. eccl. L *offertorium* (LL *offert*- for L *oblat*- p.p. st. of *offerre* OFFER[1], -ORY) offering]

ŏff'ice, n. 1. Piece of kindness, attention, service, (*ill ~*) disservice, (*owing to, by, the good* or *ill ~s of*). 2. Duty attaching to one's position, task, function, (*it is my ~, the ~ of the arteries, to*). 3. Position with duties attached to it, place of authority or trust or service esp. of public kind (*was given an ~ under Government*), tenure of official position esp. that of minister of

State (*take, enter upon, hold, leave, resign,* ~; JACK[1] *in* ~). 4. Ceremonial duty (esp. *perform the last* ~*s to*, rites due to the dead). 5. (eccl.). Authorized form of worship, daily service of R.-C. breviary (also *divine* ~; *say* ~, recite this), Anglican morning & evening prayer, (introit at beginning of) mass or communion service, any occasional service such as the *O*~ *for the Dead*. 6. Place for transacting business (*goes down to the* ~ *at 9 a.m.*); room etc. in which the clerks of an establishment work, counting-house; (with qualification) room etc. set apart for business of particular department of large concern (|| *booking, inquiry, goods, lost-property,* ~ in railway station) or local branch of dispersed organization (*our Manchester* ~; *a post, telegraph,* ~) or company for specified purpose (*insurance, fire* or *fire-insurance,* ~). 7. (*O*~) quarters or staff or collective authority of a Government department (*the* FOREIGN, WAR[1], POST[2], *O*~). 8. pl. Parts of house devoted to household work, storage, etc. 9. || (sl.). Hint, signal, as *give, take, the* ~. 10. *Holy O*~, the inquisition; ~-*bearer*, official or officer. [ME, f. OF f. L OF(*ficium* f. *facere* do) service]

öff'icer, n., & v.t. 1. Holder of public, civil, or ecclesiastical office, queen's servant or minister, appointed or elected functionary, (usu. with qualification, as ~ *of* HEALTH, *of the Household*, or *public, medical,* ~; || *relieving* ~, see RELIEVE). 2. President, treasurer, secretary, etc., of society. 3. Bailiff, constable. 4. Person holding authority in navy, army, air force, or mercantile marine, esp. with commission in army or navy (GENERAL, STAFF, COMMISSION[1]*ed*, FIELD[1], COMPANY[1], BREVET, WARRANT[1], NON-*commissioned*, ~ in army; FLAG[1], COMMISSION[1]*ed*, WARRANT[1], PETTY, ~ in navy; *Naval* ~*s*: Admiral of the Fleet, Admiral, Vice-Adm., Rear--Adm., Commodore, Captain, Commander, Lieut.-Commander, Lieutenant, Sublieut., Midshipman; *Army* ~*s*: Field Marshal, General, Lieut.-Gen., Major--Gen., BRIGADIER (formerly *Brigadier--Gen.*), Colonel, Lieut.-Col., Major, Captain, Lieutenant, Second Lieut.; AIR[1] *Force* ~*s*); || *Officers' Training Corps* (abbr. O.T.C.; orig. for the Territorial Force, & multiplied for the 1914–18 war); member of 4th class of Order of the British Empire (O.B.E.). 5. v.t. (usu. in p.p.). Provide with ~s, act as commander of. [ME, f. AF *officer*, = OF -*ier*, f. med. L *officiarius* (prec., -ARY[1])]

offi'cial (-shl), a. & n. 1. Of an office, the discharge of duties, or the tenure of an office; holding office, employed in public capacity; derived from or vouched for by person(s) in office, properly authorized; (med.) according to the pharmacopoeia, officinal; usual with persons in office (~ *solemnity, red tape,* etc.); hence ~LY[2]

adv. ~IZE(3) v.t., (-sha-). 2. n. Presiding officer or judge of archbishop's, bishop's, or esp. archdeacon's court (usu. ~ *principal*); person holding public office or engaged in ~ duties, whence ~DOM, ~ESE' (-ēz), ~ jargon, ~ISM(2), nn., (-sha-). [adj. 16th c. f. F f. LL *officialis* (OFFICE, -AL); n. ME f. AF, OF (as prec.)]

offi'ci|āte (-shī-), v.i. Discharge priestly office, perform divine service, so ~ANT(1) n.; act in some official capacity, esp. on particular occasion (usu. *as* host, best man, etc.). [f. med. L *officiare* perform divine service (OFFICE, -ATE[3])]

offi'cinal, a. (Of herb or drug) used in medicine or the arts; (of medical preparation) kept ready at druggists', made from pharmacopoeia recipe (now usu. OFFICIAL), (of name) adopted in pharmacopoeia. Hence ~LY[2] adv. [f. med. L *officinalis* f. L *officina*, -AL]

offi'cious (-shus), a. (Given to) offering service that is not wanted, doing or undertaking more than is required, intrusive, meddlesome, whence ~NESS n.; (diplom., opp. *official*) informal, unofficially friendly or candid, not binding. Hence ~LY[2] adv. [f. L *officiosus* obliging (OFFICE, -OUS)]

öff'ing (or aw-), n. Part of visible sea distant from shore or beyond anchoring ground (*was seen in the* ~); position at distance from shore (*gain, keep*, etc., *an* ~); freq. fig., cf. horizon. [OFF, -ING[1]]

off'ish (aw-, ŏ-), a. (colloq.). Inclined to aloofness, distant or stiff in manner. Hence ~NESS n. [OFF, -ISH[1]; cf. UPPISH]

off'scourings (awfskowr-, ŏ-), n. pl. Refuse, filth, dregs, (usu. *of*; lit., & fig. of persons, as *the* ~ *of humanity*). [OFF, SCOUR, -ING[1](2)]

off'sět (aw-, ŏ-), n., & v.t. 1. Start, set-off, outset, (rare); short side shoot from stem or root serving for propagation, (transf. & fig.) offshoot, scion, mountain-spur; compensation, set-off, consideration or amount diminishing or neutralizing effect of contrary one; (surv.) short distance measured perpendicularly from main line of measurement; (archit.) sloping ledge in wall etc. where thickness of part above is diminished; bend made in pipe to carry it past obstacle; (typ.) smudging of clean sheet through being laid on freshly--printed surface; ~ *process*, method of printing in which ink is first transferred from a plate to a uniform rubber surface and then to the paper etc. 2. v.t. Counterbalance, compensate. [OFF, SET[1]]

off'shoot (aw-, ŏ-), n. Side shoot or branch (lit. & fig.), derivative. [OFF, SHOOT]

öff'spring (or aw-), n. Progeny, issue, (fig.) result. [OE (OF, OFF, SPRING)]

Of'lăg (ŏ-), n. German prison camp for officers. [G, = *Offizierslager*]

oft (aw-, ŏ-), adv. Often (arch. except in comb. with p.p. or part., as ~-*told*, ~--*recurring; many a time &* ~, often);

~*times*, often (arch.). [OE *oft*, OS *oft*(*o*), OHG *ofto*, ON *oft*, Goth. *ufta*]

often (aw'fn, ŏ'fn; *occas*. -ten), adv. & a. (~*er*, ~*est*). Frequently, many times, at short intervals, (with singular generalized subject) in a considerable proportion of the instances (*the victim ~ dies of it*); ~ & ~, emphatic form; ~*times*, ~ (arch.); (adj.; arch.) frequent (*by ~ study of it*). [ME, extended f. prec.]

ŏg'doăd, n. The number, a set of, eight. [f. LL f. Gk *ogdoas* (*oktō* eight, -AD)]

ōgee', n. & a. (Moulding) showing in section a double continuous curve, concave below passing into convex above; S-shaped (line); ~ *arch, doorway, window*, with two ~ curves meeting at apex. Hence ~'**d** [-ED²] a. [app. f. F OGIVE, being the usu. moulding in groin-ribs]

og(h)am (ŏg'am), n. Ancient British and Irish alphabet of twenty characters; inscription in this; ŏne of the characters. [OIr. *ogam*, referred to *Ogma* supposed inventor]

ogive (ōj'ĭv, ojĭv'), n. Diagonal groin or rib of vault; pointed or Gothic arch, whence **ogīv'AL** a. [F, of unkn. orig.]

ō'gle, v.i. & t., & n. 1. Cast amorous glances; eye amorously; hence **ōg'lER¹** n. 2. n. Amorous glance. [late 17th c. cant, of LG orig.; cf. LG *oegeln* (= G *äugeln*) to eye or ogle]

Og'pu (ŏg'pōō), n. Former (1922–35) organization for combating counter-revolutionary activities in Soviet Russia. [initial letters of *Obedinennoe Gosudarstvennoe Politicheskoe Upravlenie*, United State Political Administration]

ō'gre (-ger), n. Man-eating giant. Hence or cogn. ~**ISH¹** (-ger-), **ōg'rISH¹**, aa., **ōg'rESS¹** n. [F, first used by Perrault 1697, of unkn. orig.]

Ogy'gian (o-), a. Of obscure antiquity, prehistoric. [f. L f. Gk *Ōgugios* of *Ōgugēs* mythical king of Attica or Boeotia]

oh (ō), int. See o².

ohm (ōm), n. Unit of electrical resistance; ~-*ammeter*, instrument measuring electrical current & resistance. Hence ~'AGE n., electrical resistance measured in ~s, ~'METER n. [G. S. *Ohm*, German physicist 1787–1854]

ohō', int. expressing surprise or exultation. [O², HO]

oh yes. See OYEZ.

-oid, suf. forming adjj. & nn. w. sense (*something*) *having the form of, resembling*; chiefly on Gk (*rhomboid*), rarely L (*fucoid*) or other (*alkaloid*) stems; adjj. as *thyroid, simioid*, nn. as *asteroid, amygdaloid*; from the nn. an adj. in -*oidal* is formed as *cycloidal*. [f. mod. L -*oïdēs* f. Gk -*oeidēs* (-o-+-*eidēs* like) f. which also -ODE]

oil¹, n. 1. (Kinds of) liquid viscid unctuous inflammable chemically neutral substance lighter than & insoluble in water & soluble in alcohol & ether (there are three classes : *fatty* or *fixed* ~s of animal

or vegetable origin, greasy & non-distillable, subdivided into *drying* ~s, which by exposure harden into varnish, & *non-drying* ~s, which by exposure ferment, the latter used as lubricants, illuminants, soap constituents, etc. ; *essential* or *volatile* ~s chiefly of vegetable origin. acrid, limpid, & distillable, giving plants etc. their scent, used in medicine & perfumery; *mineral* ~s used as illuminants. Particular kinds are named from source with *of*, as ~ *of almonds*, or with source or use preceding, as *cod-liver, olive, salad, hair, ~*); *pour ~ on the flame* etc., aggravate passion etc. ; *pour ~ on the waters*, smooth matters over; *smell of* ~, bear marks of study; *burn the midnight* ~, read or work far into the night; *strike* ~, lit., find petroleum by sinking shaft, fig., attain prosperity or success; ~ & *vinegar*, type of dissimilar or irreconcilable things; *strap* etc. ~, flogging with strap etc. 2. = ~-colour (often pl.). 3. = ~skin (usu. pl.). 4. ~-*bird, -nut, -palm, -plant, -seed, -tree*, kinds of bird etc. from which ~ is got; ~-*bush*, ~-filled socket for upright spindle [BUSH³]; ~'*cake*, mass of compressed linseed etc. left when ~ has been expressed, used as cattle food or manure; ~'*can*, containing ~, esp. long-nozzled for oiling machinery; ~'*cloth*, fabric waterproofed with ~, ~-*skin*, canvas coated with drying ~ & used to cover table or floor; ~-*coat*, of ~skin; ~-*colour*, paint made by grinding pigment in ~ (usu. pl.); ~-(-)*engine* (driven by the explosion of vaporized ~ mixed with air); ~'*field*, district yielding mineral ~; ~-*gauge*, hydrometer measuring specific gravity of ~s; ~-*gilding, -gold*, goldleaf laid on linseed-~ mixed with yellow pigment; ~-*gland*, secreting ~; ~-*hole*, in machinery to receive lubricating ~; ~'*man*, maker or seller of ~s; ~-*meal*, ground linseed cake; ~-*paint*, = ~-colour; ~-*painting*, art of painting, picture painted, in ~-colours; ~-*paper*, made transparent or waterproof by soaking in ~; ~-*press*, apparatus for pressing ~ from seeds etc.; ~'*skin*, cloth waterproofed with ~, garment or (pl.) suit of this; ~-*spring*, yielding mineral ~; ~-*stone*, (fine-grained stone used with ~ as) whetstone; Hence ~'LESS a. [ME *oli, oile* f. ONF *olie* = OF *oile* &c. f. L *oleum* (*olea* olive); OE *ele* dir. f. L]

oil², v.t. & i. Apply oil to, lubricate, (~ *the wheels*, lit., & fig. make things go smoothly by courtesy, bribery, etc. ; ~ *one's hand* or ~ *one*, bribe him; ~ *one's tongue*, say smooth things, flatter); (with *butter, grease*, etc., as subj. or obj.) turn (t. & i.) into oily liquid; impregnate or treat with oil (~*ed sardines*; ~*ed silk*, waterproofed with oil); ~*ed* (sl.), slightly drunk. [f. prec.]

oil'er, n. In vbl senses; esp. oilcan for oiling machinery. [-ER¹]

oil'| y̆, a. Of, like, covered or soaked with, oil; (of manner etc.) fawning, insinuating, unctuous. Hence ~**ILY**[2] adv., ~**INESS** n. [-Y[2]]

oint'ment, n. Unctuous preparation applied to skin to heal or beautify, unguent. [ME *oigne-, ointment* f. OF *oignement* f. *oindre* (ANOINT, -MENT); forms *oint-* after obs. vb *oint* ANOINT]

Oireachtas (ŏī´ax̌thăs), **n.** Legislature of Eire, the President & two Houses, Dail Eireann (Chamber of Deputies) & Seanad Eireann (Senate). [Ir.]

oka'pi (-ah-), **n.** Bright-coloured partially striped Central-Afr. ruminant discovered 1900 with likeness to giraffe, deer, & zebra. [native]

ŏk'ra, n. Tall malvaceous plant bearing mucilaginous seed-pods used as a vegetable & for thickening soups. [W.-Afr. native name]

-ol, chem. suf. **1.** Termination of *alcohol* used in names of alcohols in the wider sense or analogous compounds (*methol, phenol*). **2.** = L *oleum* oil (*benzol*).

ŏld, a. (ELDER[1], *eldest*, in particular uses: ordinarily ~*er*, ~*est*), & n. **1.** Advanced in age, far on in natural period of existence, not young or near its beginning, (*the* ~, aged people; *young & ~,* every one; ~*age*, later part of life; ~*-age pensions,* || weekly payments to ~ persons on account of their age; || *Old Lady of Threadneedle Street,* Bank of England; ~ *man of the sea,* person who cannot be shaken off; ~ *man, woman, party,* etc.; ~ *man,* also as name for southernwood, & naut. sl. for ship's captain; *my* etc. ~ *man,* colloq., husband; ~ *man's beard,* kind of moss, also wild clematis; *my* etc. ~ *woman,* colloq., wife; ~ *woman,* fussy or timid man, whence ~**wo'manISH**[1], ~**wo'manLY**[1], aa., ~**wo'manISHNESS,** ~**wo'-manLINESS,** nn., (-wŏŏ-); *my* etc. ~ *bones,* I or me etc. who am ~; *the century grows* ~). **2.** Having characteristics, experience, feebleness, etc., of age (~ *head on young shoulders,* wisdom beyond one's years; *child has an* ~ *face;* ~ *buffer, fogy,* etc.; *a man is as* ~ *as he feels*); worn, dilapidated, shabby, (~ *clothes* etc.). **3.** (Appended to period of time) of age (*is ten years* ~*, a ten-year-* ~ *boy, a boy* OF *ten years* ~*, could read Greek at ten years* ~; also ellipt. *four* etc. *-year-* ~, person or animal, esp. racehorse, of that age, w. pl. ~*s*). **4.** Practised or inveterate *in action* or quality or as agent etc. (~ *in crime, folly, cunning, diplomacy; an* ~ *campaigner, offender;* ~ *bird,* person on his guard against snares; ~ *hand,* practised workman, person of experience in something, *at doing;* ~ STAGER; ~ *bachelor,* man confirmed in bachelorhood; ~ *maid,* elderly spinster, whence ~**maid'ISH**[1] a., also precise & tidy & fidgety man, also a round card game). **5.** Dating from far back, made long ago, long established

or known or familiar or dear, ancient, not new or recent, primeval, (~ *Ocean, Night,* etc.; ~ *red* SAND*stone;* of ~ *standing,* long established; so ~*-established;* ~ *as the hills;* ~ *countries,* long inhabited or civilized; ~ *friends; an* ~ *debt, grudge,* ~ SCORES; *an* ~ *name, family;* ~ *wine,* matured with keeping; ~ *gold,* colour of tarnished gold; ~ CATHOLIC; *the* ~, what is not new; ~ TESTAMENT; ~ *boy, chap, fellow, man,* esp. in voc., intimate or person treated as such, also in mod.*sl.* ~ *bean, egg, fruit, thing, top; Old England; Old Glory,* the Stars & Stripes; *the* ~ *one* or *gentleman, Old Harry, Nick, Scratch,* etc., the devil; *good* ~ with name, sl. exclamation in real or ironical commendation of person's or thing's performance; *have a fine, good, high,* etc., ~ *time* etc., sl., be well amused or entertained; *any* ~ *thing,* sl., anything no matter what). **6.** Belonging only or chiefly to the past, obsolete or obsolescent, out of date, antiquated, antique, concerned with antiquity, not modern, bygone, only lingering on, former, quondam, (*the good* ~ *times,* customs etc. of earlier generations; ~ *annals;* ~ *fashions,* that have gone or are going out, whence ~**-fā'shionED**[2] a., ~**-fā'shionedNESS** n., (-shond-), opp. *newfangled* etc.; *am* ~*-fashioned enough to think,* used in ironical self-depreciation; *of the* ~ *school,* ~*-fashioned; the* ~ *country, home,* etc., used by colonists or colonials of mother-country; *call up* ~ *memories; the* ~ *order changeth; have lost my* ~ *beliefs;* ~ *boy,* former member of school; so ~ *Etonian* etc.; ~ *guard,* original or past or right-wing member(s) of party etc.; ~ SCHOOL[1] *tie; the Old* COMEDY, HUNDREDTH; ~ *masters,* great painters of earlier times, pictures by these; ~ *London, Paris, England,* etc., London etc. as it once was, or the extant relics of its former state; *the* ~ *man,* one's unregenerate self; *the Old World,* Eastern hemisphere; ~*-world,* not American, also belonging to ~ times, & so ~*-time* attrib.; *Old* STYLE, abbr. O.S.; *the* ~ *year,* just ended or about to end; ~ *clothes,* discarded; ~*-clothesman,* dealer in these); hence ~*-*ISH[1](2) a., ~*'*NESS n. (rare). **7.** n. ~ *time* (only in *of* ~ adj. & adv., as *the men of* ~, *of* ~ *there were giants; have heard it of* ~, from long ago). [OE, OS *ald,* OHG *alt,* f. Gmc **aldhaz* (cf. Goth. *altheis*) f. **al-* grow, nourish, cogn. w. L *alere* feed]

|| **ōl'den**[1], **a.** (arch. & literary). Old-time, of a former age, (esp. *the* ~ *time*). [-EN[5]]

|| **ōl'den**[2], **v.t. & i.** Make or grow feeble etc. as with age. [-EN[6]]

ōld'ster, n. One who is no longer a youngster (usu. antithetically to *youngster*). [-STER]

ōlĕā'ginous, a. Having properties of or producing oil, oily, fatty, greasy. [f. F *oléagineux* f. L *oleaginus* (*olea* olive)]

ōlĕăn′der, n. Evergreen poisonous Levantine shrub with leathery lanceolate leaves & fine red & white flowers. [med. L]

ōlĕăs′ter, n. The wild olive; small yellow-flowered tree like it. [L (*olea* olive, -ASTER)]

ōl′ĕo-, comb. form of L *oleum* oil, (-o-), as ~*graph*, picture printed in oils, also ~GRAPHY (-ŏg²); ~*marg′arine*, fatty substance extracted from beef fat & serving as constituent of margarine, °margarine made from vegetable oils; ~*meter* (-ŏm²), instrument determining density & purity of oils; ~*res′in*, natural mixture of volatile oil & resin, balsam, also artificial mixture of fixed or volatile oil & resin etc.

ōlfăc′t|ion, n. Smelling, sense of smell. So ~IVE a. [f. L *olfacere* v.t. smell, *facere fact-* make); see -TION]

ōlfăc′tory, a. & n. Concerned with smelling (~ *organ*, nose; ~ *nerves*); (n., usu. pl.) ~ organ. [prec., -ORY]

olib′anum, n. Aromatic gum resin used as incense. [ME, f. med. L, f. LL f. Gk *libanos* frankincense]

ōl′id, a. Rank-smelling, fetid. [f. L *olidus* (*olēre* smell, -ID¹)]

ōl′igărch (-k), n. Member of oligarchy. [f. Gk *oligarkhēs* (*oligoi* few, *arkhō* rule)]

ōl′igărchy (-kǐ), n. Government, State governed, by the few; members of such government. So **ōlĭgărch′ic**(AL) aa., **ōlĭgărch′icaly²** adv., (-kǐ-). [f. Gk *oligarkhia* (prec., -Y¹)]

ōl′ig|(o)-, comb. form of Gk *oligos* small, *oligoi* few, as ~*ocarp′ous*, having few fruits; ~*ocēne*, geol., between MIOCENE & EOCENE.

ōl′iō, n. (pl. ~s). Mixed dish, hotchpotch, stew of various meats & vegetables; medley, farrago, miscellany. [f. Sp. *olla* stew f. L *olla* jar]

ōlivā′ceous (-shŭs), a. (nat. hist.). Olive-green, of dusky yellowish green. [L *oliva* olive, -ACEOUS]

ōl′ivary, a. (anat.). Olive-shaped, oval. [f. L *olivarius* (foll., -ARY¹)]

ōl′ive, n. & a. 1. (Also ~*-tree*, evergreen tree with narrow leaves hoary below & axillary clusters of small white flowers, bearing) small oval drupe with hard stone & bitter pulp, of dusky yellowish green when unripe & bluish black when ripe, yielding oil, & pickled unripe for eating as relish; leaf, branch, or wreath of ~ as emblem of peace (also ~*-branch*, often fig.; *hold out the* ~*-branch*, make overtures, show disposition, for reconciliation); wood of the ~ (also ~*-wood*). 2. ~-shaped kinds of gasteropod mollusc. 3. pl. Slices of beef or veal rolled up with herbs & stewed (usu. *beef*, *veal*, ~*s*). 4. ~-shaped bar or button for fastening garment by insertion in corresponding loop, whence **ōl′ivet¹** or **ōlivette′** n. 5. ~ colour. 6. ~ *crown*, garland of ~ as sign of victory; ~*-branch*, see above, also (usu.

pl., w. ref. to *Ps.* cxxviii. 3) child(ren); ~ *oil*, extracted from ~s. 7. adj. Coloured like the unripe ~ (also ~*-green*); (of complexion) yellowish-brown. [ME, f. OF, f. L *oliva*]

ōl′iver¹, n. Tilt-hammer attached to axle & worked by treadle for shaping nails etc. [orig. unkn.]

Ol′iver² (ŏ-), n. See ROLAND.

ōl′ivine, -in, n. Kind of chrysolite, chiefly olive-green. [L *oliva* olive, -INE⁴]

ōll′a podri′da (-rē-), rarely ōll′a, n. = OLIO. [Sp., = lit. rotten pot (OLIO, L PUTRIDᵤₛ)]

(-)ōl′ogȳ, suf. f. -O-+-LOGY; as quasi- n. used joc. = any science, w. pl. = the sciences, mere theory.

olym′piăd, n. Period of four years between celebrations of Olympic games, used by ancient Greeks in dating events (abb. Ol.), 776 B.C. being first year of first O~; celebration of modern Olympic games. [f. F (-*ade*), or L f. Gk *olumpias* -*ad-* (*Olumpios* see foll., -AD)]

Olym′pian, a. & n. 1. Of Olympus, celestial; (of manners etc.) magnificent, condescending, superior; = foll. 2. n. Dweller in Olympus, one of the greater ancient-Greek gods; person of superhuman calmness & detachment. [f. L f. Gk *Olumpios* + -AN]

Olym′pic, a. Of or at Olympia in Elis in the Peloponnese (~ *games*, held there every four years by ancient Greeks with athletic, literary, & musical competitions; also, modern quadrennial international athletic meeting at various places, the first at Athens 1896). [f. L f. Gk *Olumpikos* of Olympus (*Olumpia* being named from the games in honour of Zeus of Olympus)]

Olym′pus, n. Thessalian mountain on which dwelt the chief Greek gods, divine abode, heaven. [L, f. Gk *Olumpos*]

-oma, **-ome**, suf. f. Gk -*ōma*, denoting result, f. vbs in -*ousthai* (as *rhizōma* f. *rhizousthai* take root); (1) nn. denoting some formation or member of the nature of that denoted by the radical part, in this use now superseded by -*ome*, as *rhizome*, *trichome*; (2) names of tumours or other abnormal growths, as *carcinoma*, *sarcoma*; cf. -MA, -ME.

ŏm′bre (-ber, & see Ap.), n. Card-game popular in 17th-18th cc. [f. Sp. *hombre* f. L *hominem* nom. *homo* man, perh. thr. F (*h*)*ombre*]

ŏmbro-, comb. form of Gk *ombros* rain, as ~LOGY (-ŏl²), ~METER (-ŏm²).

ōm′ĕga, n. Last letter (Ω, ω) of Greek alphabet, long o; last of series; final development etc. (ALPHA *&* ~). [Gk, = great o]

ŏm′elĕt(te) (-ml-), n. Beaten eggs fried in melted butter & folded & often flavoured with or containing herbs, cheese, chopped ham, jam, etc. (*savoury* ~, with herbs etc., *sweet* ~, with sugar or jam; *cannot make* *an* ~ *without breaking eggs*, end necessitates means). [F (-*te*), earlier *amelette* by metath. f. *alumette* var. of *alumelle* thin plate prob. f. L LAMELLA]

ŏm′ĕn, n., & v.t. Occurrence or object portending good or evil, prognostic, presage; prophetic signification (*is of good* etc. ~); (vb) foreshow, give presage of. [L]

omen′t|um, n. (anat.; pl. ~*a*). Fold of peritoneum connecting stomach with other viscera, caul. Hence ~AL a. [L]

omic′ron, n. Greek letter (*O, o*) = ŏ. [Gk, = small o]

ŏm′inous, a. Giving or being an omen (*of good or evil, or abs.*), portentous, (rare); of evil omen, inauspicious, foreshowing disaster, threatening. Hence ~LY² adv. [f. L *ominosus* (OMEN -*inis*, -OUS)]

omi′ssion (-shn), n. Omitting, non-inclusion; non-performance, neglect, duty not done, (*sins of* ~ *& commission*, negative & positive). So **omiss′IVE** a. [ME, f. OF, or LL *omissio* (foll., -ION)]

omit′, v.t. (-tt-). Leave out, not insert or include; leave undone, neglect *doing*, fail *to* do. So **omiss′IBLE** a. [f. L *omittere* -*iss*- (o- for OB-, *mittere* send)]

ŏmni-, comb. form of L *omnis* all, in compounds taken f. L or formed chiefly w. L elements, w. sense *all-, of all things, in all ways* or *places*, as ~*com′petent*, having jurisdiction in all cases; ~*far′ious*, of all sorts; *ŏmnĭf′ic*, all-creating; *ŏmnĭg′enous*, of all kinds; *ŏmnĭp′otence*, infinite power, also God, also great influence; so *ŏmnĭp′otent* a. (*the* Omnipotent, God), ~*p′otentLY²* adv.; ~*pres′ence*, ubiquity, also being widespread or constantly met with; so ~*pres′ent* a.; *ŏmnĭ′science* (-shens), infinite knowledge, also God, also wide information or the affectation of it; so *ŏmnĭ′scient* (-shyent) a. (*the* Omniscient, God), ~*scientLY²* adv.; *ŏmnĭv′orous*, feeding on anything that offers (esp. fig. of reading); so ~*v′orousLY²* adv., ~*v′orousNESS* n.

ŏm′nibus, n. (pl. ~*es*) & a. **1.** (Now usu. *būs*) large wheeled public vehicle plying on fixed route & taking up & setting down passengers at fixed, or at any, points in this; (also *hotel* ~) vehicle conveying guests between hotel & railway station; (also *private* or *family* ~) vehicle provided by railway company for conveying party & luggage to or from station; ~ *book*. **2.** adj. Serving several objects at once, comprising several items, (*an* ~ *bill, resolution, clause,* etc.; ~ *book*, volume containing several stories, plays, etc. (freq. by a single author), published at a low price to be within the reach of all; ~ *box* in theatre, box on pit tier appropriated to number of subscribers; ||~ *train*, stopping at all stations; ~ *bar, wire,* etc. in electricity, through which whole current passes). [f. F (1828), f. L dat. pl. of *omnis* = for all].

ŏm′nium găth′erum (-dh-), n. Miscellaneous assemblage of persons or things, queer mixture, party to which everyone is invited. [mock L (L *omnium* of all, GATHER)]

ŏm′oplăte, n. Shoulder-blade, scapula. [in 16th c. f. F f. Gk *ōmoplatē* (*ōmos* shoulder, *platē* blade)]

ŏm′phalo-, comb. form of Gk *omphalos* NAVEL, chiefly in surg. & med. wds as ~CELE; ~TOMY (-ŏt²), dividing of umbilical cord.

ŏm′phalŏs, n. (Gk ant.) boss on shield, conical stone at Delphi supposed to be central point of earth; centre, hub, (*the centre & ~ of a world-wide empire*). [see prec.]

on¹ (ŏn, on), prep. (See UPON for idiomatic preference.) **1.** (So as to be) supported by or attached to or covering or enclosing (*sat on the table*; *floats on the water*; *is on the horns of a dilemma*; *lives on the continent, on an annuity*; *have you a match on you?*, about your person; *is, gets, falls, on his* LEGS, *knees,* etc.; *travels on foot, wheels, the wing, the wings of the wind*; *tread on air,* one's *toes*; *dropped it, threw him, on the floor*; *had, put, a ring, gloves on his finger, hands*; *put a notice on the board*; *hangs on the wall*; *walks on the ceiling*; *has a blister on the sole of his foot*; *a scholar on the foundation*; *a colonel on half-pay*; *went on board*; *is on the jury, committee, general staff*; *a writer on the press*; *dog is on the chain*; *on the* BENCH, BOARD¹s, CARD²s, FENCE¹, MARKET¹, NAIL¹, PARISH, RACK³, SHELF, SPOT¹, STREETS, STUMP, TURF, WAY; *on* CHANGE¹, HAND¹, one's HAND¹s, one's *own* HOOK¹, one's KNEE¹s, TENTERhooks; *on a* LEVEL¹, *an* EQUALITY, *a* PAR). **2.** With axis, pivot, basis, motive, standard, confirmation, or guarantee, consisting in (*turn on* one's *heel*; *works on a peg*; *based on fact*; *imprisonment on suspicion*; *on my conscience*; *swear on the Bible*; *had it on good authority*; *decided on no evidence*; *did it on purpose, deliberation*; *got it on good terms*; *on account of*; *on the average, whole*; *on penalty of death*; *charged him on his life to do it*; *a tax on paper*; *borrowed money on his jewels*; *interest on* one's *capital*; *profit on sales*). **3.** (So as to be) close to, in the direction of, touching, arrived at, against, *just at,* (*house is on the shore, road*; •*on Fifth Avenue*; *on the right, North, far side, both sides, of*; *Clacton-on-Sea*; *marched on London*; *hit him on the head*; *a box on the ear*; *left a card on him*; *serve a notice, writ, on*; *lay hold, seize, on*; *bowling is on the wicket,* straight; *drew his knife on me*; *smile, frown, turn* one's *back, on*; *make an attack on*; *put* one *on inquiring* or *inquiry*, induce him to inquire; *curse, plague,* etc., *on him, it!*; *rose on their oppressors*; *on* HIGH; *on side* in football, not OFF *side*; *ship is driving on shore*; *an on-shore wind*). **4.** (Of time) during, exactly at, contemporaneously with, immediately after, as a result of, (*happened on the morning* etc. *of 29 Feb.*, *on Christmas eve*, *on the next day*; *on the instant*, immediately; *on time*, *the minute*, etc., punctually; *on arriving*, *my return*, *analysis*, *examination*, *I found*). **5.** In manner specified by adj. (*on the cheap*, *sly*, SQUARE) or state or action specified by noun (*on fire*, TAP, *loan*, *lease*, *sale*, *strike*, *guard*; *on the look-out*, *move*, *run*, *wane*, *watch*; *on one's best behaviour*). **6.** Concerning, about, while engaged with, so as to affect, (*keen*, *mad*, *bent*, *determined*, *set*, *on*; *gone on*, sl., enamoured of; *court martial was held on him*; *my opinion on free trade*; *writes*, *speaks*, *lectures*, *on finance*; *a book*, *an essay*, *on grammar*; *meditating on vanity*; *take vengeance on person*; *have something on* (against, to the disadvantage of) *person*; *the drinks are on* (to be paid for by) *me*; *did it on my way*; *was*, *went*, *on an errand*; *is not binding on us*; *work tells severely on him*; *title was conferred on him*; *draw cheque on bank*; *condoled with him on his loss*). **7.** Added to (*ruin on ruin*, *heaps on heaps*). [OE *an*, *on*, OS, OHG *an*, *ana*, ON *ă*, Goth. *ana* f. Gmc, cogn. w. Gk *ana*; hence A²]

ŏn², adv., a., & n. **1.** (So as to be) supported by, attached to, covering, enclosing, or touching, something (*has*, *drew*, *his boots on*; *put the tablecloth on*; *keep your* HAIR *on*; *on with your coat*, put it on). **2.** In some direction, towards something, farther forward, towards point of contact, in advanced position or state, with continued movement or action, in operation or activity, (LOOK¹, LOOK¹*er-*, *on*; *getting on for two o'clock*; *broadside*, *stem*, *end*, *on*, with that part forward; ellipt. for imperat. of *go* or *come on*, as on, *Stanley*, *on!*; *send on*, in front of oneself; MOVE² *on*; *happened later on*; *from that day on*; *was well on in the day*; *is rather on*, sl., half-drunk; *speak*, *work*, *wait*, etc., on, continue to do; so *struggle on to the end*, cf. *on to* below; *slow bowler is*, *went*, *on*, is, began, bowling; *Macbeth is on*, being performed; *gas*, *water*, *is on*, lit. running, or procurable by turning tap; *get*, *be*, *on*, make, have made, bet; *drove Jones on for 4* in cricket, to the on). **3.** CARRY¹, CATCH¹, COME,¹ GET¹, GO¹, HOLD¹, KEEP¹, PUT¹, TAKE¹, TRY, *on*. **4.** *Be on* (colloq.), be in favour of, willing to be a party to, something (*There's a show tonight*; *are you on?*); *be on to* (person), be aware of his intentions etc., find fault with, nag (*he's always on to me*); *on & off*, = OFF *& on*; *on to*, compound prep. (corresponding to *on* as *into* to *in*, but usu. written as two words, & avoided in writing though common in speech; to be distinguished from the use in which each word has independent force as in *went on to the next*), to a position on (*jumped on to the landing-stage*). **5.** adj. Towards or in part of field to left front of playing batsman's wicket (cf. OFF, LEG,

MID¹ *on*; *an on drive*, whence **ŏn-drive′** v.t.); ‖ *on licence*, for selling beer etc. to be drunk on premises. **6.** n. The on side in cricket (*a fine drive to the on*). [f. prec.]

on-, pref. used with attrib. participles, gerunds, verbal nouns, agent-nouns in -ER¹, & other derivative nn., f. vv. followed idiomatically by ON² (occas. alternatively with the reverse order): *on^coming* n. & a., approach(ing); *on′fall* n., assault; *on′flow*, onward flow; *on′goings* or *goings-on′*, (usu. strange or improper) proceedings; *on′hanger*, HANGER²-*on*; *on′looker* or LOOK¹*er-on′*; *on′rush* n., *on^rushing* a.; ONSET.

ŏn′ager, n. (pl. -*s*, -*gī*). Kinds of wild ass. [ME, f. L, f. Gk *onagros* (*onos* ass, *agrios* wild)]

ŏn′anism, n. Interrupted coïtion; masturbation. [*Onan* (*Gen.* xxxviii. 9) -ISM]

once (wŭns), adv., conj., & n. **1.** For one time or on one occasion only, multiplied by one, by one degree, (*have read it more than~*; *shall die~*; *~ or twice*, *~ & again*, a few times; *~more*, again, another time; *~ for all*, in final manner, definitively; *~ in a while* or *way*, very rarely; *~ & away*, = *~ for all*, *~ in a way*; *~ bit(ten) twice shy*, pain, loss, etc., teaches caution; *~ nought is nought*; *second cousin ~* RE-MOVED). **2.** (In negative or conditional or indefinite clause etc.) ever, at all, even for one or the first time, (*if we ~ lose sight of him*; *when ~ he understands*; *have not seen him ~*; *~ within call*, *we are safe*). **3.** On a certain but unspecified past occasion (also *~ upon a time*), at some period in the past, former(ly), (*~ there was a giant*; *a ~-famous doctrine*, *~-loved friend*; *my ~ master*, *ally*). **4.** *At ~*, immediately, without delay, at the same time, (*do it at ~*, *please*; *don't all speak at ~*, lit., & as iron. deprecation inviting offers etc. from reluctant party; *at ~ stern & tender*); *for this*, or *that*, *~*, on one occasion by way of exception; *•~-over* n. (colloq.), preliminary inspection (often with additional sense of cursoriness). **5.** conj. As soon as, if *~*, when *~*. (*~ he hesitates*, *we have him*). **6.** n. One time, performance, etc. (*~ is enough for me*). [ME *ānes*, *ōnes*, (ONE, -ES)]

‖ **oncer** (wŭn′ser), n. (colloq.). One who attends church only once on a Sunday. [ONCE + -ER¹]

on dit (see Ap.), n. Piece of hearsay. [F]

one (wŭn), a., n., & pron. **1.** numeral adj. Single & integral, neither none nor fractional nor plural, numbered by the first or lowest integer, half of two, a, (*~ man ~ vote*, opp. PLURAL *vote*; *~ vote ~ value*, principle of equal constituencies; *~-&-twenty* etc., or usu. *twenty* etc. *~*; *~-&-twentieth* etc., twenty etc. -first; *~ dozen*, *hundred*, etc., precise or formal for *a*; *~ man in ten*, *a thousand*, etc., relatively few; *some ~ man must direct*; *for ~ thing*, *he drinks; ~ or two people*, a few; *God is ~*). **2.** adj. with secondary senses developed from the numeral. *The only, single, forming a unity, united, identical, the same, unchanging, a particular but undefined, to be contrasted with another,* (*the ~ way to do it; no ~ man is equal to it; is ~ & undivided; cried out with ~ voice; were made ~,* married; *become ~,* coalesce; *remains for ever ~,* always the same; *all in ~ direction; met him ~ night; will take you there ~ day; ~ man's meat is another man's poison*). **3.** numeral noun. (With *a* & pl.; often used as substitute for repetition of previously expressed or implied noun) the number ~, thing numbered with it, written symbol for it, a unit, unity, a single thing or person or example, (~ *is half of two; in the year ~,* long ago; *Aeneid, book ~,* first book of; *number ~,* oneself. esp. as centre of selfish care; *write down a, three ~s; came by ~s & twos; sell scores where they sold ~s; never a ~,* none; *will you make ~?,* arch., join the party; *ten etc. to ~,* long odds, high probability; *all in ~,* combined; *the all & the ~,* totality & unity; *at ~,* reconciled, in agreement; *I lose a neighbour & you gain ~; pick me out a good ~, some good ~s; which, what kind of, ~ or ~s do you like?; that ~, the ~ in the window, will do*). **4.** adj. used ellipt. for itself or *a* with noun elsewhere expressed or customarily omitted & to be supplied with more or less of certainty. Single person or thing of the kind implied (~ *of them lost his* or *her hat; ~ of the richest men in England; shall see you again ~ of these fine days; at ~ o'clock* or ~, i.e. hour; ~ *& sixpence,* i.e. shilling; *gave him ~ in the eye, owe him ~, that was a nasty ~,* blow lit. or fig.; *at ~-&-twenty,* years of age; *I for ~ do not believe it; go ~ better,* bid, offer, risk, more by ~ point; *is ~ too many for him,* too hard etc. for him to deal with by ~ degree; *it is all ~ to me,* the same thing, indifferent; ~ *& all,* all jointly & severally; ~ *by ~,* ~ *after another,* singly, successively; ~ *with another,* on the average; ~ *or the ~ —, the other,* formula distinguishing members of pair, as ~ *is immoral, the other non-moral,* also with pl. constr., as *sheep & goats, of which the ~ are the good* etc.; ~ *another,* formula of reciprocity with ~ orig. subjective & *another* objective or possessive, as *struck ~ another, write to ~ another, buy ~ another's goods*). **5.** pron. A particular but unspecified person (arch.; ~ *came running; ~ said it pleased him not*); a person of specified kind (ANY, EVERY, SOME, NO[1], SUCH *a,* ~; *many a ~,* rhet., many people; LITTLE, *dear, loved, ~s; the Holy One, One above,* God; *the Evil One,* the devil; *behaves like ~ frenzied; what a ~ he is to make excuses! colloq.; bought it from ~ Stephens*); any person, esp. the speaker, spoken of as representing people in general (possessive *~'s,*

objective ~, reference-form ~, refl. *~self,* formerly *his, him, he* & *him, himself,* or ungrammatically *their, them, they* & *them, themselves; if ~ cuts off ~'s nose,* ~ *hurts only ~self; it offends ~ to be told ~ is not wanted;* also incorrectly for *I,* as ~ *let it pass, for ~ did not want to seem mean*). **6.** *~-armed bandit* (sl.), FRUIT machine; *~-eyed,* having only, blind of, ~ eye; *~-handed,* having, done etc. with, ~ hand only; *~-horse,* drawn or worked by single horse, (fig., sl.) petty, poorly equipped; *~-idea'd, -ideaed,* possessed by single idea, narrow-minded; *~-legged,* having only ~ leg, (fig.) *~-sided,* unequal; *~-man,* requiring, consisting of, done or managed by, ~ man; *~-pair,* ∥ room or set of rooms on first floor (above ~ pair or flight of stairs; *~-pair back, front,* ∥ such room in back or front of house); *~self',* reflexive, & emphatic appositional, form of ~ as generalizing pronoun (*to starve ~self is suicide; to do right ~self is the great thing*); *~-sided,* having, occurring on, ~ side only (*a ~-sided street,* with houses on ~ side only; *a ~-sided plant,* with leaves or flowers all on ~ side of stem), larger etc. on ~ side, partial, unfair, prejudiced; so *~-sid'edLY*[2] adv., *~-sid'edNESS* n.; *~-step,* vigorous kind of foxtrot in duple time; *~-way street* (in which traffic may pass in ~ direction only). Hence ~FOLD a. [OE *ān,* OS *ēn,* OHG *ein,* ON *einn,* Goth. *ains* f. Gmc **ainaz,* cogn. w. L *unus*]

-ōne, chem. suf. (1) used unsystematically as in OZONE; (2) in names of hydrocarbons (see -ANE). [f. Gk -*ōnē* fem. patronymic]

oneir'o- (-nī̆r-), comb. form of Gk *oneiros* dream; *~MANCY; ~crit'ic,* interpreter of dreams; so *~crit'icAL* a., *~crit'icISM* n.

one'ness (wŭn-n-), n. Being one, single-ness; singularity, uniqueness; wholeness, unity, union, agreement, concord; identity, sameness, changelessness. [-NESS]

on'er (wŭ-), n. Remarkable or pre-eminent person or thing (sl.; *a ~ at,* expert in; *gave him a ~,* severe blow); (colloq.) stroke etc. counting one, esp. one-run hit at cricket; ∥ (sl.) thumping lie. [-ER[1]]

ŏn'erous, a. Burdensome, causing or requiring trouble, (~ *property* in law, accompanied with obligations). Hence *~LY*[2] adv., *~NESS* n. [ME, f. OF *onerous* f. L *onerosus* (*onus oneris* burden, -OUS)]

onion (ŭn'yon), n., & v.t. **1.** (Plant with) edible rounded bulb of many concentric coats & pungent smell & flavour, much used in cooking or eaten pickled; FLAMING *~s; know* one's *~s* (sl.), be good at one's job; *off* one's *~* (sl.), off one's head; *~-couch* or *-grass* or *twitch,* kind of wild oat; *~-shell,* kinds of mollusc; hence *~Y*[2] (ŭn'yo-) a. **2.** v.t. Rub (eyes) with ~ to make them water. [ME, f. OF *oignon* f. L *unionem* nom. -o large pearl, onion]

ŏn'ly[1], a. That is (or are) the one (or all the) specimen(s) of the class, sole, (*the ~*

way is to die; the ~ child of his parents; the ~ instances known; was an ~ son; one ~ object was visible; my one & ~ hope; motley's the ~ wear, best or ~ one worth considering). [OE *ānlic* (ONE, -LY¹)]

ŏn'lÿ, adv. & conj. **1.** Solely, merely, exclusively, & no one or nothing more or besides or else, & that is all, (*is right because it is customary ~, is right ~ because it is customary, is ~ right because it is customary; ~ you* or *you ~ can guess,* no one else can; *you can ~ guess* or *guess ~,* can do no more; *I ~ thought I would do it,* formed the design & did not execute it, or did it without external instigation; *I not ~ heard it, but saw it; if ~,* assuming merely that, also as wishing formula, as *if ~ someone would leave me a legacy!; ~ not,* all but; *has ~ just come, came ~ yesterday,* no longer ago; *~ too glad, true,* etc., glad etc. & not, as might be expected, the opposite). **2.** conj. It must however be added that, but then, (*he makes good resolutions, ~ he never keeps them*); with the exception, were it not, *that* (*he does well, ~ that he is nervous at the start; ~ that you would be bored, I should —*). [ME *ŏnliche,* f. *ŏnlich* (ONLY¹); see ONE, -LY²]

ŏn'omatŏp, -ōpe, n. Onomatopoeic word. [shortened f. foll.]

onŏmato|poe'ia (-pĕa, -pēya), n. Formation of names or words from sounds that resemble those associated with the object or action to be named, or that seem naturally suggestive of its qualities; word so formed (e.g. *cuckoo*). So **~poe'ic** (-pē-), **~pŏĕt'ic,** aa., **~poe'ically** (-pē-), **~pŏĕt'ically,** advv. [f. LL f. Gk *onomatopoiia* word-making (*onoma -atos* name, *poieō* make)]

ŏn'sĕt, n. Attack, assault, impetuous beginning, (esp. *at the first ~*). [f. *to* SET ON]

ŏn'slaught (-awt), n. Onset, fierce attack. [early 17th c., f. Du. *aanslag* (*aan* on, *slag* blow) w. assim. to obs. *slaught*]

ŏn'to, prep. See ON² *to.*

ŏnto-, comb. form of *on, ont-,* neut. part. of Gk *eimi* am: *~gĕn'esis,* origin & development of the individual being (cf. PHYLOGENESIS), whence *~genĕt'ic* a., *~genĕt'ically* adv.; *onto'geny, ~* genesis, also embryology; *ŏntŏl'ogy,* department of metaphysics concerned with the essence of things or being in the abstract, so *~lo'gical* a., *~lo'gically* adv., *ŏntŏl'ogist* n.

ŏn'us, n. (no pl.). Burden, duty, responsibility; *~ probăn'dī, =* BURDEN¹ *of proof.* [L]

ŏn'ward, adv. & a., **ŏn'wards** (-z), adv. Further on, towards the front, with advancing motion; (adj.) directed *~.* [ON², -WARD(S)]

ŏn'ÿmous, a. Not anonymous. [f. Gk *onuma* name +-OUS after *anonymous*]

ŏn'ÿx, n. Kind of quartz allied to agate with different colours in layers; (path.) opacity of lower part of cornea; *~ marble,*

of banded *~*-like structure. [ME *oniche* f. OF *oniche, onix* f. L f. Gk *onux* finger-nail, onyx]

ōo-, ō-, comb. form of Gk *ōion* egg, ovum, in scientific usu. biol. wds, as *ōogĕn'esis,* production or development of ovum; *ooe'cium* (ōē-), budlike sac for receiving & fertilizing ova in polyzoa; *ōōg'amous,* reproducing by union of male & female cells; *ōŏl'ogy,* study, collecting, of birds' eggs, so *ōoLO'GICAL, ōŏL'OGIST;* *ō'osperm,* fertilized ovum or female cell.

ōo'dle, n. (colloq.). (Always in pl.) superabundance (*~s of money*). [orig. unkn.]

ōof, n. (sl.). Money, pelf, cash; *~-bird,* source of money, rich person. Hence *~'Y² a.* [for *oof-tish* Yiddish = G *auf dem tische* on the table]

ō'olite, n. Granular limestone, each grain being a calcareous particle in carbonate of lime, roe-stone; (geol.) series of fossiliferous rocks of this formation lying between Chalk, or Wealden, & Lias. Hence **ōolit'IC** a. [f. F *oölithe* (OO-, -LITE)]

ōōl'ŏng, n. A dark kind of cured Chinese tea. [Chin. *wulung,* = black dragon]

ōŏm, n. (S.-Afr.). Uncle (esp. *Oom Paul =* President Kruger). [Du.]

-ōōn, suf. formerly used in borrowing F wds in *-on* (*drag~*) except when the final syl. was not accented (*baron*); esp. for F *-on* f. It. *-one* f. L *-onem* nom. *-o* (*ball~, buff~, cart~*); rarely in native wds (*spit-~*); F wds now taken have *-on* in E (*chignon*); the L expresses humorous or contemptuous description (*Naso* Nosey), the It. bigness or coarseness, the F (exc. in It. borrowings) small size; in E the suf. has no definite meaning.

ōŏnt, n. (Anglo-Ind.). Camel. [Hind.]

ōōze¹, n. **1.** Wet mud, slime, esp. in river-bed or estuary or on ocean bottom. **2.** Tanning liquor, infusion of oak-bark etc.; *~-calf,* calf-skin through which dye has been forced. **3.** Exudation, sluggish flow, something that oozes. Hence **ōōz'Y² a., ōōz'ILY² adv., ōōz'INESS n.** [1 f. OE *wāse* cogn. w. ON *veisa* puddle; 2 f. OE *wōs* juice, sap; 3 f. foll.]

ōōze², v.i. & t. (Of moisture) pass slowly through the pores of a body, exude, percolate; (of substance) exude moisture, (fig.) leak *out* or *away* (*the secret ~d out; my courage is oozing away*); emit (moisture, information, encouragement). [ME *wōsen,* f. prec. 2]

ŏp., n. (colloq.). Operation. [abbr.]

op-. See OB-.

opă'cĭtÿ, n. Being opaque, quality of not allowing passage to or (rarely) of not reflecting light, non-transparency, obscurity; obscurity of meaning, obtuseness of understanding. [f. F *opacité* f. L *opacitatem* (OPAQUE, -TY)]

ŏp'ah (-*a*), n. Rare brilliant-coloured large N.-Atlantic fish of mackerel family, king-fish, moon-fish. [W.-Afr. name]

ŏp'al, n. Amorphous quartz-like form of

hydrous silica some kinds of which show changing colours (e.g. *common* ~, milk-white or bluish with green, yellow, & red reflexions), whence ~ES'CENT, ~ESQUE' (-ĕsk), aa., ~ES'CENCE n.; (commerc.) semi--translucent white glass. [f. F *opale*, or L *opalus*]

ōp'al|ine, a. & n. **1.** Opal-like, opalescent, iridescent. **2.** n. Semi-translucent white glass. So ~IZE(3) v.t. [prec., -INE¹]

opāque' (-k), a. (~r, ~st), & n. Not re-flecting (rare) or transmitting light, not shining (rare), impenetrable to sight; not lucid, obscure; obtuse, dull-witted; (n.) *the ~,* darkness. Hence ~LY² (-kl-) adv., ~NESS (-kn-) n. [15th c. *opak,* f. L *opacus*; sp. now assim. to F]

ōpe, v.t. & i. (Poet. for) OPEN². [ME, after obs. adj. *ope* reduced f. *open* on anal. of p.p. (cf. *awake, wove,* f. *awaken, woven*)]

ōp'en¹, a. (~er, ~est), & n. **1.** Not closed or blocked up, allowing of entrance or passage or access, having gate or door or lid or part of boundary withdrawn, unenclosed, unconfined, uncovered, bare, exposed, undisguised, public, manifest, not exclusive or limited, (~ *gate, passage, church, drawer, box, field, grave, carriage, hostilities, scandal, contempt;* ~ *air,* out-doors; *door flew* ~; ~ *boat,* undecked; *lay* ~, expose esp. by cutting skin etc. of; ~ *ears,* eagerly attentive, whence ~--earED² a.; ~ *mouth,* in voracity, frank-ness, etc., & esp. in gaping stupidity or surprise, whence ~-mouthED², pr. -dhd, a.; ~ *mind,* accessibility to new ideas, unprejudiced or undecided state, whence ~-mindED² a., ~-mind'edLY² adv., ~--mind'edNESS n.; *is~ to conviction, offers,* etc.; *keep* ~ *doors* or *house,* entertain all comers, be hospitable; *the* ~ *door,* free admission of foreign nations to country for trade; *force an* ~ *door,* demand from willing giver; *the exhibition is now* ~, admitting visitors; *shop, show, court, is* ~ *at such hours;* ~ *heart,* frankness, un-suspiciousness, kindliness, cordiality, whence ~-heartED² a., ~-heart'edLY² adv., ~-heart'edNESS n.; ~ *champion,* ‖ *scholarship,* successful, won, after un-restricted competition; *race is* ~ *to all; position is* ~ *to attack; O*~ *Brethren,* less exclusive section of the Plymouth Brethren; ~*cast* (surface) *coal;* ~ *hearth process* (of steel-making in shallow rever-beratory furnace); ~ *time,* what is not CLOSE¹ time; *river, harbour, is* ~, free of ice; ~ *weather, winter,* not frosty; *bowels are*~, not constipated; ~ *country,* without houses, free of fences; *there are three courses* ~ *to us;* ~ *question,* matter on which differences of opinion are legiti-mate; ~ VERDICT). **2.** Expanded, un-folded, outspread, spread out, not close, with intervals, porous, communicative, frank, (~ *book, flower;* ~ *letter,* esp. protest etc. printed in newspaper etc. but addressing individual; ~ *country,*

affording wide views; ~ *order,* mil. & nav., formation with wide spaces between men or ships; ~ *harmony,* of chord with wide intervals; ~ *ice,* through which navigation is possible; *receive with* ~ *arms,* heartily, whence ~-armED a.; *with* ~ *eyes,* not unconsciously or under misapprehension, also in eager attention or surprise, whence ~-eyED² (-īd) a.; *has an* ~ *hand,* gives freely, whence ~-hand-ED² a., ~-hand'edLY² adv., ~-hand'ed-NESS n.; ~ *face,* ingenuous-looking, whence ~-facED² a.; ~ *work* or ~*work,* pattern with interstices in metal, lace, etc.; *will be* ~ *with you,* speak frankly). **3.** (mus.). (Of note) produced from un-stopped pipe or string or without slide, key, or piston. **4.** (phonet.). (Of vowel) produced with relatively wide opening of mouth (cf. CLOSE¹); (of syllable) ending in vowel; hence ~NESS n. **5.** n. *The* ~, ~ space or country or air, public view. [OE *open,* OS *opan,* OHG *offan,* ON *opinn;* f. root of UP]

ōp'en², v.t. & i. **1.** Make or become OPEN¹ or more open (~ SESAME; *shops* ~ *at 9 a.m.;* ~ *a business, shop, account, campaign,* etc., start or establish it or set it going; ~ *fire,* begin shooting; abs. for ~ *book,* as ~*ed at p. 12;* ~ *ground,* break up with plough etc.; ~ *bowels,* cause evacuation; ~*s a prospect* lit. or fig., brings it to view; ~ *the door to,* give opportunity for; ~ *one's designs,* reveal or communicate them; ~ *one's eyes,* show surprise; ~ *another's eyes,* undeceive or enlighten him; ~ *the mind, heart,* etc., expand or enlarge it; *not* ~ *lips,* remain silent; ~ *the* BALL²; ~ PARLIAMENT; ~ *the case,* (of counsel in lawcourt) make preliminary statement before calling witnesses; ~ *the debate,* begin it, be first speaker; *door, room,* ~*s into passage, on to lawn,* etc.; *the wonders of astronomy were* ~*ing to him,* becoming known; ~ *one's shoulders* in cricket, of batsman's attitude in driving). **2.** Commence speaking (~*ed upon the fiscal question, with a compliment,* etc.). **3.** Make a start (*lard* ~*ed active,* was in demand at once; *session* ~*ed yesterday*). **4.** (Of hounds, & derog. of men) begin to give tongue. **5.** (naut.). Get view of by change of position, come into full view, (*take care not to* ~ *the obelisk; the harbour light* ~*ed*). **6.** ~ *out,* unfold, develop, ex-pand, (t. & i.), accelerate, become com-municative; ~ *up,* make accessible, bring to notice, reveal. Hence ~ABLE a., (-)~ER¹ (1, 2) n. [OE *openian,* f. prec.]

ōp'ening (-pn-), n. In vbl senses; also or esp.: gap, passage, aperture; commence-ment, initial part; counsel's preliminary statement of case; (chess) recognized se-quence of moves for beginning game; opportunity, favourable conjuncture *for.* [ME; -ING¹]

ōp'ening (-pn-), a. In vbl senses; esp., initial, first, (*his* ~ *remarks*). [ME; -ING²]

op'enlỹ, adv. Without concealment, publicly, frankly. [ME; -LY²]

op'era¹, n. Dramatic performance or composition of which music is an essential part, branch of art concerned with these, (*grand* ~, without spoken dialogue; *comic* ~, of humorous character; *opéra comique* F, with spoken dialogue, not necessarily humorous; ~ *bouffe* pr. bŏŏf, of farcical character); ~-*cloak*, -*hood*, lady's for wearing at ~ or going to evening parties; ~-*glass(es)*, small binocular for use at ~ or theatre; ~-*hat*, man's tall collapsible hat; ~-*house*, theatre for performance of ~. [It. f. L, = labour, work]

op'era², See OPUS.

op'erāt|e, v.i. & t. 1. Be in action, produce an effect, exercise influence, (*the tax ~es to our disadvantage*); play (up)on person's fears etc., try to act (up)on; (of medicines etc.) have desired effect, act. 2. Perform surgical or other operation (whence, of cases, **op'erable** a.); (try to) execute purpose; (mil.) carry on strategic movements; (of stockbroker etc.) buy & sell esp. with view of influencing prices. 3. Bring about, accomplish, (*energy ~es changes*); manage, work, conduct, (chiefly U.S.). 4. ~*ing-room*, -*table*, for use in surgery; ~*ing-theatre*, room for surgical operations done before students. So ~OR n. [f. L *operari* work (*opus -eris* work), -ATE³]

op'erāt|ic, a. Of, like, opera. Hence ~ICALLY adv. [irreg. f. OPERA, after *dramatic*]

opera'tion, n. 1. Working, action, way thing works, efficacy, validity, scope, (*is in, comes into*, ~; *its* ~ *is easily explained*; *must extend its* ~, make it valid for longer time or in wider sphere). 2. Active process, activity, performance, discharge of function, (*the ~ of breathing, thinking, pruning*, etc.). 3. Financial transaction. 4. (surg.). Thing done with hand or instrument to some part of body to remedy deformity, injury, disease, pain, etc. (colloq. abbr. *op.*). 5. Strategic movement of troops, ships, etc. (COMBINED ~). 6. (math.). Subjection of number or quantity to process affecting its value or form, e.g. multiplication. Hence ~AL (-sho-) a., (esp.) engaged in or on, used for, (warlike) ~s. [ME, f. OF, f. L *operationem* (OPERATE, -ION)]

op'erative, a. & n. 1. Having effect, in operation, efficacious; practical, not theoretical or contemplative, (*the ~ part of the work*); of surgical operations; hence ~LY² adv. 2. n. Worker, artisan, mechanic, workman, mill-hand. [f. F (-*if*, -*ive*) or LL *operativus* (OPERATE, -IVE)]

op'eratize, -**ise** (-īz), v.t. Put into operatic form. [irreg. after *dramatize*, cf. OPERATIC]

operc'ŭl|um, n. (pl. ~a). Fish's gill-cover; lid or valve closing aperture of shell when tenant is retracted; similar lidlike struc-ture in plants, eggs of some insects, etc. Hence ~AR¹, ~ATE², ~āted, aa., ~I-comb. form. [L (*operire* cover, -CULE)]

operětt'a, n. One-act or short light opera. [It. (OPERA, -ETTE)]

op'erōse, a. (pedant.). Requiring or showing or taking great pains, laborious. Hence ~LY² adv., ~NESS n. [f. L *operosus* (*opus -eris* work, -OSE¹)]

oph'icleide (-līd), n. Keyed wind-instrument consisting of tapering brass tube bent double serving as bass or alto to key-bugle; (also *tuba*) powerful organ reed-pipe. [f. F *ophicléide* (Gk *ophis* serpent, *kleis -dos* key)]

ophid'ian, a. & n. (Member) of the *Ophidia* or order of reptiles including snakes. [mod. L *ophidia* (-IA²), irreg. f. Gk *ophis* snake, -AN]

ophio-, comb. form of Gk *ophis* snake, as ~LATER, ~LATRY, (-ŏl⁴), serpent-worship(per), ~LOGY (-ŏl⁴).

oph'ite, n. Serpentine, serpentine marble. Hence ophit'ic a. [f. L f. Gk *ophitēs* f. *ophis* snake, -ITE¹(2)]

ophthăl'mia, n. Inflammation of the eye. [LL f. Gk (*ophthalmos* eye)]

ophthăl'mic, a. & n. Of the eye; affected with ophthalmia; (remedy) good for eye-disease. [f. L f. Gk *ophthalmikos* (prec., -IC)]

ophthălm|(o)-, comb. form of Gk *ophthalmos* eye, as ~IT'IS, ~ŏL'OGY, ~ŏL'OGIST, ~ŏT'OMY; *ophthăl'mo*SCOPE, instrument for inspecting retina.

op'iate¹, a. (arch.). & n. 1. Containing opium, narcotic, soporific. 2. n. Drug containing opium & easing pain or inducing sleep. [f. med. L *opiatus* (OPIUM, -ATE²)]

op'iāte², v.t. Mix with opium. [app. f. med. L *opiare* (OPIUM, -ATE³]

opīne', v.t. Express or hold the opinion (*that*, or abs. in parenthesis). [f. L *opinari*]

opin'ion (-yon), n. 1. Judgement or belief based on grounds short of proof, provisional conviction, view held as probable, (*in my* ~, as it seems to me; *am of* ~ *that*, believe; *a matter of* ~, disputable point); (also *public* ~) views or sentiment, esp. on moral questions, prevalent among people in general. 2. What one thinks on or *on a* particular question, a belief, a conviction, (*the* COURAGE *of*, *act up to*, one's ~s). 3. Formal statement by expert when consulted of what he holds to be the fact or the right course, professional advice, (*you had better have another* ~). 4. Estimate (*have, formed, a very high, low, favourable,* ~ *of him*); (with neg.) favourable estimate (*have no* ~ *of Frenchmen*). [ME, f. OF, f. L *opinionem* (OPINE, -ION)]

opin'ionātĕd (-nyo-), a. Obstinate in opinion, dogmatic; self-willed. Hence ~NESS n. [f. obs. *opinionate* in same sense, perh. latinized form of obs. *opinion*ED²]

opin'ionātive (-nyo-), a. = prec. [OPINION +-ATIVE, cf. TALKATIVE]

O. Pip. See OBSERVATION, PIP⁵.

ŏpisŏm'ĕter, n. Instrument for measuring curved lines as on map, made of wheel running on screw. [f. Gk *opisō* backwards, -METER]

opĭs'thograph (-ahf), n. (Gk & Rom. ant.). Parchment or slab with writing on both sides. [f. Gk *opisthographos* f. *opisthen* behind + -GRAPH]

ŏp'ĭum, n., & v.t. **1.** Reddish-brown heavy-scented bitter drug prepared from juice of kind of poppy, smoked or eaten as stimulant, intoxicant, or narcotic, & used as sedative (LAUDANUM) in medicine; ~ *den,* haunt of ~-smokers; ~ *habit,* of taking ~; hence ~ISM(5) n., ~IZE(5) v.t. **2.** v.t. Drug or treat with ~. [ME, f. L f. Gk *opion* poppy-juice (*opos* juice)]

ŏpodĕl'dŏc, n. Kinds of soap liniment. [wd used & prob. made by Paracelsus for kinds of medical plaster]

opŏp'anăx, n. A fetid gum resin formerly used in medicine; a gum resin used in perfumery. [ME, f. L f. Gk, f. *opos* juice, *panax* (*pas pantos* all, *akos* cure) name of plant]

opŏss'um, n. Kinds of American small arboreal or aquatic nocturnal marsupial with thumbed hind-foot (see also POSSUM); (Austral.) = PHALANGER. [Amer.-Ind.]

‖ **ŏpp'idan,** a. & n. (Inhabitant) of a town (now rare); (at Eton) non-colleger, boy in boarding-house in town. [f. L *oppidanus* (*oppidum* town, -AN)]

ŏpp'il|āte, v.t. (med.). Block up, obstruct. So ~A'TION n. [f. L OP(*pilare* ram)]

oppŏn'encў, n. (rare). Antagonism, opposition. [foll., -ENCY]

oppŏn'ent, a. & n. **1.** Opposing, contrary, opposed, (now rare; ~ *muscle,* opposing thumb or lateral digit to other digit). **2.** n. Adversary, antagonist. [f. L OP(*ponere* place), -ENT]

ŏpp'ortūne (*also* -ŭn'), a. (Of time) suitable, well-selected or as favourable as if chosen; (of action or event) well-timed, done or occurring by design or chance at favourable conjuncture. Hence ~LY² adv., ~NESS n., (*also* -ŭn⁴). [ME, f. OF *opportun* f. L OP(*portunus* f. *portus* -*ūs* harbour)]

ŏpportūn'|ism, n. Allowing of due or undue weight to circumstances of the moment in determining policy; preference of what can to what should be done, compromise, practical politics, adaptation to circumstances; putting of expediency before principle or place before power, political time-serving. So ~IST (2) n. [f. prec. after It. (-*ismo*) & F (-*isme*)]

ŏpportūn'itў, n. Opportuneness (rare); favourable juncture, good chance, opening, (of *doing,* to *do, for* action, or abs.; *find, make, get, seize, give, afford, an* ~; *take the* ~ of). [ME, f. OF *opportunite* f. L *opportunitatem* (OPPORTUNE, -TY)]

oppōs|e' (-z), v.t. **1.** Place or produce or cite (thing, person) as obstacle, antagon-

1st, counterpoise, or contrast, *to,* represent (things) as antithetical, (*to fury let us* ~*e patience; you are* ~*ing things that are practically identical; to Plato I* ~*e Aristotle;* ~*ed himself to it with all his power; the thumb can be* ~*ed to any of the fingers,* placed against it front to front, whence ~'ABLE (-z-) a., ~ABIL'ITY n.). **2.** Set oneself against (person, thing); withstand, resist, obstruct, propose the rejection of (resolution, motion, etc.); (abs.) act as opponent or check (*it is the duty of an opposition to* ~*e*). **3.** p.p. Contrary, opposite, contrasted, (*characters strongly* ~*ed; black is* ~*ed to white*); (of persons) hostile, adverse, (*is firmly* ~*ed to protection*). [ME, f. OF OP(*poser* POSE¹)]

oppōse'lèss (-zĭ-), a. (poet.). Irresistible. [-LESS]

ŏpp'osite (-z-), a. (often governing n. by ellipse of *to*), n., adv., & prep. **1.** Contrary in position (to), facing, front to front or back to back (with), (*on* ~ *sides of the square; came from, went in,* ~ *directions; the tree* ~ *to* or ~ *the house;* ~ *leaves* etc. in bot., placed at same height on ~ sides of stem, or placed straight in front of other organ, opp. *alternate;* ~ *number,* person or thing similarly placed in another set etc. to the given one); of contrary kind, diametrically different to or *from, the* other of a contrasted pair, (*of an* ~ *kind to, from, what I expected; much liked by the* ~ *sex*); hence ~LY² adv. (chiefly bot.), ~NESS n., (-z-). **2.** n. ~ thing or term (*you are cold-blooded, she is the* ~; *the most extreme* ~*s have some qualities in common*). **3.** adv. & prep. In ~ place, position, or direction (to) (*there was an explosion* ~, in the house across the street; ~ *prompter* in theatre, abbr. *o.p.,* usu. to actor's right; *happened* ~ *the Mansion House); play* ~, (of leads in stage-play or film) háve (specified actor or actress) as one's leading man, lady. [ME, f. OF, f. L OP(*positus* p.p. of *ponere* place)]

oppōs'iti- (-z-), comb. form of L *oppositus* (prec.) in bot. wds, as ~*fol'ious,* opposite-leaved; ~*sep'alous,* (of stamen) placed straight in front of sepal.

ŏpposi'tion (-z-), n. **1.** Placing opposite (~ *of the thumb,* cf. OPPOSE): diametrically opposite position (esp. astron., of two heavenly bodies when their longitude differs by 180°, opp. CONJUNCTION; *planet is in* ~, opposite sun); contrast, antithesis. **2.** (log.). Relation between two propositions with same subject & predicate but differing in quantity or quality or both. **3.** Antagonism, resistance, being hostile, (*offer a determined* ~; *did it in* ~ *to public opinion; was in* ~ *at the time,* belonging to the ~ in next sense). **4.** ‖ *The* O~, *Her Majesty's* O~, chief parliamentary party opposed to that in office (*the leader of the* O~; *the* O~ *whips, benches,* etc.). **5.** Any party opposed to some proposal. Hence ~AL a. (rare), ~IST(2) n. & a. (rare), (-zĭsho-). [ME, f. OF, f. L OP(*positionem* POSITION)]

oppŏs′itive (-z-), a. (rare). Adversative, antithetic; fond of opposing. [prec., -IVE]

opprĕss′, v.t. Overwhelm with superior weight or numbers or irresistible power; lie heavy on, weigh down, (spirits, imagination, etc.); govern tyrannically, keep under by coercion, subject to continual cruelty or injustice. So **opprĕ′ssion** (-shn), ~OR, nn., ~IVE a., ~IVELY² adv., ~IVENESS n. [ME, f. OF *oppresser* f. med. L OP(*pressare* frequent. of L *premere* press)]

opprŏb′rious, a. Conveying reproach, abusive, vituperative. Hence ~LY² adv. [ME, f. OF -*eux*, or LL *opprobriosus* (foll., -OUS)]

opprŏb′rium, n. Disgrace attaching to some act or conduct, infamy, crying of shame. [L, f. OP(*probrare* f. *probrum* disgraceful act)]

oppugn′ (-ūn), v.t. Controvert, call in question, whence ~ER¹ (-ŭn²) n.; (rare) attack, resist, be in conflict with, (so **oppŭg′nant** a. & n., **oppŭg′nance**, oppŭg′nancy, **ŏppugnA′tion**, nn., all rare). [ME, f. L OP(*pugnare* fight) attack, besiege]

ŏp′simăth, n. (rare). One who learns late in life. So **ŏpsim′athy¹** n. [f. Gk *opsimathēs* (*opse* late, *math*-learn)]

ŏpsŏn′ic, a. Having the effect on bacteria of making them easier of consumption by phagocytes (~ *action*, *power*; ~ *index*, numerical expression of the phagocytic power of the serum of a patient under anti-bacterial injections as below). So **ŏp′sonin** n., the substance produced in patient's blood by injection of dead cultures of the bacteria of his disease. [f. Gk *opson* cooked meat, +-IC]

ŏpt, v.i. Exercise an option, make choice, (*between* alternatives or *for* alternative or *out*). Hence ~′ANT n. [f. F *opter* f. L *optare* choose, wish]

ŏp′tative (or ŏptā⁴), a. & n. (gram.). 1. Expressing wish (~ *mood*, set of verbal forms of this kind, distinct chiefly in Sanskrit and Greek; ~ *use of subjunctive*); hence ~LY² adv. 2. n. ~ mood, verbal form belonging to it. [F (-*if*, -*ive*), f. LL *optativus* (prec., -ATIVE)]

ŏp′tic, a. & n. 1. (anat.). Of the eye or sense of sight (~ *nerve*, *neuritis*, etc.; ~ *angle*, between lines from extremities of object to eye, or from two eyes to one point). 2. n. Eye (now usu. joc.); ‖ device fastened to neck of bottle for measuring out spirits; (pl., with sing. constr.) science of sight & esp. of the laws of its medium, light. [f. F *optique* or med. L f. Gk *optikos* (*optos* seen f. *op*- see); *optics* renders med. L *optica*; see -IC]

ŏp′tical, a. Visual, ocular, (~ *illusion*, produced by too implicit confidence in the evidence of sight); of sight or light

in relation to each other, belonging to optics, constructed to assist sight or on the principles of optics. Hence ~LY² adv. [as prec., see -ICAL]

ŏpti′cian (-shn), n. Maker or seller of optical instruments esp. spectacles. [f. F *opticien* (OPTIC, -ICIAN)]

‖ **optime**. See WRANGLER.

ŏp′tim|ism, n. Doctrine, esp. as set forth by Leibnitz, that the actual world is the best of all possible worlds; view that good must ultimately prevail over evil in the universe; sanguine disposition, inclination to take bright views. So ~IST(2) n. & a., ~is′tic a., ~is′tically adv., ~IZE(2) v.i. [f. F *optimisme* (L *optimus* best, -ISM)]

ŏp′timum, n. (chiefly biol.). Most favourable (natural) conditions (for growth, reproduction, etc.); (attrib.) best or most favourable (~ *temperature*). [L, neut. of *optimus* best]

ŏp′tion, n. Choice, choosing, thing that is or may be chosen, (*make one's* ~; *none of the* ~*s is satisfactory*); liberty of choosing, freedom of choice, (LOCAL² ~; *imprisonment without the* ~ *of a fine*; *have no* ~ *but to*, must); (St. Exch. etc.) purchased right to call for or make delivery within specified time of specified stocks etc. at specified rate. [F, or f. L *optio* (st. of *optare* choose, -TION)]

ŏp′tional (-sho-), a. Not obligatory. [prec., -AL]

ŏptŏ|m′eter, n. Instrument for testing the refractive power & visual range of the eye. Hence ~m′etrIST n., sight-tester, ~m′etry n. [f. Gk *optos* seen +-METER]

ŏp′tophone, n. Instrument converting light into sound, & so enabling the blind to read print etc. by ear. [f. as prec., + Gk *phōnē* sound]

ŏp′ulent, a. Rich, wealthy; abounding, well stored. Hence or cogn. **ŏp′ulence** n., ~LY² adv. [f. L *opulentus* (*opes* wealth, -ULENT)]

ŏp′us, n. (pl. rare *ŏp′era*). Musician's separate composition of any kind (used esp. in citing it from among his works by number; abbr. *op.*; *Beethoven op. 15*); *măg′num* ~, ~ *măg′num*, or ~, great literary undertaking, writer's or other artist's chief production. [L, = work]

opŭs′cūle, **opŭs′cŭlum** (pl. -*la*), n. Minor musical or literary composition. [(-*ule* F) f. L (-*um*) dim. of prec. (-CULE)]

ŏr¹, n. (her.). Gold or yellow in armorial bearings. [F, f. L *aurum* gold]

‖ **ŏr²**, prep. & conj. (arch.). Before, ere, (chiefly now in *or ever*, or *e′er*, poet.). [OE *ār* f. ON *ár* (= Goth. *air*) early, assim. in sense to OE *ǣr* ERE]

or³ (ôr, or), conj. introducing second of two alternatives (*white or black*), all but the first (*white or grey or black*) or only the last (*white, grey, or black*) of any number, the second of each of several pairs (*white or black*, *red or yellow*, *blue or green*), or (poet.) each of two (*or in the heart or in the head*). An alternative introduced by *or* may be (1) on equal footing with preceding (*shall you be there or not?; any Tom, Dick, or Harry*); (2) as true as the preceding (*ripe tomatoes are red or yellow*); (3) mere synonym (*common or garden*); (4) indication that preceding is doubtfully accurate (*one or two, five or six*, etc., a few); (5) explanation of preceding (*saw a dug-out or hollowed-tree boat*); (6) statement of only remaining possibility *or choice given (often after either; a thing must surely be or not be; for goodness' sake either take it or leave it*); (7) statement of result of rejection etc. of preceding (often with *else; she must weep or she must die; make haste, or else you will be late*); (8) second etc. member of indirect question or conditional protasis after WHETHER (*ask him whether he was there or not; must do it whether I like or dislike it*). In syntax, a set of alternatives with *or* is sing. if each member is sing. (*man or woman, boy or girl, goes unmolested*; not *go*); if the members differ in number etc., the nearest prevails (*were you or he, was he or you, there? either he or you were, either you or he was*), but some forms (e.g., *was I or you on duty?*) are avoided; forms in which difference of gender in the members causes difficulty with pronouns (*a landlord or landlady expects their, his or her, his, rent*) are usually avoided, *their rent or the rent due to them* being ungrammatical, *his or her rent or the rent due to him or her* clumsy, & *his rent or the rent due to him* slovenly. [reduced form of obs. *other* conj. which superseded OE *ohthe* or]

-or, a term. of wds, & form of var. suff., of L orig. **1.** (a) L *-or, -orem*, OF *-or, -ur* (F *-eur*), in ME first *-or, -ur*, later *-our*, which was subsequently largely refash. after L *-or*. In Gt. Britain many early spellings *-our* have survived, but Amer. usage favours *-or* in all. Generally, the sp. *-or* repr. either (i) older wds in *-our* refash. after L *-or*, or (ii) later adoptives taken f. F or direct f. L; (b) L nn. in *-ator, -etor, -itor* developed regularly in OF as *-ëor, -ëur* (F *-eur*), in AF *-eour*, ME *-our*, which thus fell together w. wds f. simple L *-or, -orem* (see (a), above). **2.** In E wds, this term. appears in the foll. suff.: (a) *-or* (formerly freq. *-our*), ult. repr. L *-or, -orem* in nn. of condition f. intr. vbs, as *error, horror*; (b) *-or* (formerly freq. *-our*), repr. L *-or, -orem* of agent- nn. f. p.p. or supine stems, as (i) *actor, confessor, doctor*; (ii) repr. L *-ator* etc. (see 1(b)), as *donor, emperor, vendor*, & anal. formations in OF or AF on the vb, as *tailor, warrior*; (iii) f. L wds in *-ator* &c. (see 1 (b)) in later adoptives (f. OF, or AF, or L) retaining the L *-t-*, as *administrator, creditor*; (c) *-or* is occas. an alt. of another suf., as in *bachelor, chancellor* (earlier *-er*), or of E *-er*, as in *sailor*

(earlier *-er*). When *-or* & *-er* coexist, *-or* has occas. a more legal or professional sense; conversely, *-or* has been altered to *-er*, as in *barber* (ME & AF *barbour*); (d) *-or (-our)* occas. repr. F *-oir* (*manor, mirror*); (e) *-or* repr. ME, AF *-our* f. L *-or*, var. of *-ior* suf. of compar. degree: see *-IOR²*.

ŏ′rach(e), n. Kinds of wild and kitchen-garden plants of goosefoot family. [15/16th c. *arage, arache* f. AF *arasche* (= F *arroche*), ult. f. L *atriplex* f. Gk *atraphaxus*]

ŏ′racle, n. **1.** Place at which ancient Greeks etc. were accustomed to consult their deities for advice or prophecy (*work the ~*, secure desired answer by tampering with priests etc., also fig. bring secret influence to bear in one's favour); response, often ambiguous or obscure, given at such place. **2.** Holy of holies or mercy-seat in Jewish temple. **3.** (Vehicle, personal or other, of) divine inspiration or revelation. **4.** Person or thing serving as infallible guide, test, or indicator (*I am Sir O~*); authoritative, profoundly wise, or mysterious adviser or advice, judge or judgement, prophet or prophecy. Hence (esp. w. ref. to obscurity) **orăc′ŭlAR¹**, a., **orăc′ŭlarLY²** adv., **orăcŭlă′rITY** n. [ME, f. OF, f. L *oraculum* f. *orare* speak]

ŏr′al, a. & n. **1.** Spoken, verbal, by word of mouth; (anat.) of the mouth. **2.** n. (colloq.). ~ examination etc. Hence **~LY²** adv. [f. LL *oralis* (L *os* oris mouth, *-AL*)]

ŏ′range¹ (*-inj*), n. & a. **1.** (Evergreen tree bearing) large roundish many-celled juicy acid or sweet fruit enclosed in bright reddish-yellow tough rind (*squeeze the ~*, take all the good from anything; *squeezed ~*, thing from which no more good can be got; BLOOD¹ *~; China ~*, former name of common *~*; MANDARIN² *~; mock ~*, the shrub *syringa*; TANGERINE *~; ~s & lemons*, nursery game, also kind of toadflax; *Blenheim ~*, kind of apple); (also *~-colour*) reddish-yellow; *~-blossom*, flowers of *~*, worn by brides at wedding; *~-fin*, kind of trout; *~* MARMALADE; *~ stick*, thin pointed stick for finger-nails; *~-tip*, kind of butterfly. **2.** adj. *~*-coloured, reddish-yellow. Hence **ŏ′rangERY(3)** (*-inj-*) n. [ME. f. OF, ult. f. Arab. *nāranj*]

Orange² (*ŏ′rinj*), n. Town on Rhône from which *Princes of ~* took title (*William of ~* in Eng. hist., King William III); (attrib. & comb.) connected with Irish ultra-protestant party (prob. f. the *~men*, political society formed 1795 for protestant ascendancy in Ireland, prob. named after *~* lodge of freemasons in Belfast, prob. named after William), whence **ŏ′rangISM(3)** (*-inj-*) n. [F.= L *Arausio*]

ŏrangeade′ (*-injād*), n. Effervescent or still drink of orange juice etc. [*-ADE*]

orăng′-outăng′ (*-ŏŏt-*), **ŏr′ang-ut′an** (*-ŏŏt-*), n. Large long-armed arboreal anthropoid ape of Borneo & Sumatra. [Malay (-*utan*) = man of the woods]

** orāte'**, v.i. (joc.). Make speech, hold forth, play the orator. [back form. f. foll.]

orā'tion, n. Formal address or harangue or discourse esp. of ceremonial kind; (gram.) language, way of speaking (*direct*, *indirect* or *oblique*, ~, person's words as actually spoken, or with the changes of person, tense, etc., usual in reporting). [ME, f. L *oratio* (*orare* speak, -ATION)]

ŏ'rator, n. Maker of a speech; eloquent public speaker; ‖ *Public O~*. official at Oxford & Cambridge speaking for university on State occasions. Hence **ŏ'ratress**[1] n. [ME, f. OF *orateur* f. L *oratorem* (prec., -OR)]

ŏratŏr'iō, n. (pl. ~s). Semi-dramatic musical composition usu. on sacred theme performed by soloists, chorus, & orchestra, without action, scenery, or costume. [It., orig. of musical services at oratory of St Philip Neri]

ŏ'ratorize, -ise (-īz), v.i. = ORATE. [-IZE]

ŏ'ratory[1], n. Small chapel, place for private worship; (*O~*) R.-C. religious society of simple priests without vows founded in Rome 1564 to give plain preaching & popular services, also any branch of this in England etc., whence **ŏratŏr'IAN** a. & n. [ME, f. LL *oratorium* neut. of L *oratorius* (*orare* pray, speak, -TORY)]

ŏ'ratory[2], n. (Art of making) speeches, rhetoric; highly coloured presentment of facts, eloquent or exaggerating language. Hence **ŏratŏ'rICAL** a., **ŏratŏ'rically**[2] adv. [f. L *oratoria* (*ars* art) of speaking, fem. as prec.]

ŏrb, n., & v.t. & i. 1. Circle, circular disc, ring, (now rare); sphere, globe; heavenly body; eyeball, eye, (poet.); globe surmounted by cross as part of regalia; organized or collective whole; hence ~'LESS a. 2. vb. Enclose in, gather (t. & i.) into, ~. [f. L *orbis* ring]

ŏrbic'ŭl|ar, a. Circular, discoid, ring-shaped (~*armuscle*, sphincter); spherical, globular, rounded, (fig.) forming complete whole. Hence or cogn. ~ā'rITY n., ~arLY[2] adv., ~ATE[2] a. (nat. hist.). [ME, f. L *orbicularis* (*orbiculus* dim. as prec., -AR[1])]

ŏrb'it, n., & v.i. 1. Eye-socket, whence ~o- comb. form; border round eye of bird or insect; curved course of planet, comet, satellite, etc.; (fig.) range, sphere of action. 2. v.i. (Of satellite etc.) move in an~. Hence ~AL a. [f. L *orbita* track of wheel or moon (*orbis* ring)]

ŏrc, **ŏrc'a**, n. Kinds of cetacean; sea or other monster. [f. F *orque*, or f. L *orca* kind of whale]

Orcād'ian (ôr-), a. & n. (Native) of Orkney. [f. L *Orcades* Orkney Islands, -IAN]

ŏrch'ard, n. Enclosure with fruit-trees; ~*man*, fruit-grower, also ~IST(3) n. [OE *ortgeard* f. L *hortus* garden, YARD[2]; cf. Goth. *aurtigards*]

ŏrchĕs't|ĭc (-k-), a. Of dancing. Hence ~ICS n. [f. Gk *orkhēstikos* (*orkhēstēs* dancer, see foll.)]

ŏr'chĕstra (-k-), n. 1. Semicircular space in front of ancient-Greek theatre-stage where chorus danced & sang. 2. Part of modern theatre or concert-room assigned to band or chorus. 3. Body of instrumental performers, or combination of bowed, wood-wind, brass, & percussion instruments, in theatre or concert-room, whence **ŏrchĕs'trAL** (-k-) a. [L, f. Gk *orkhēstra* (*orkheomai* dance)]

ŏr'chĕstr|āte (-k-), v.t. & i. Compose (t. & i.), arrange, or score, for orchestral performance. Hence ~A'TION n. [-ATE[3]]

ŏrchestri'na (-kĭstrē-), ***ŏrchĕs'trion** (-k-), nn. Elaborate kind of barrel-organ meant to give orchestra-like effect. [-INA[1]]

ŏr'chid, **ŏr'chis**, (-k-), n. Member of large family of monocotyledonous plants (-*is* is usu. of wild English kinds, -*id* of exotics or in bot. use), of which English kinds are terrestrial with tuberous root & erect fleshy stem with spike of usu. red or purple flowers, & many exotic kinds have flowers of fantastic shapes & brilliant colours. Hence **ŏrchidA'CEOUS** (-kĭdāshus) a., **ŏr'chid**IST(3) (-k-) n. [(-*id* made 1845 by Lindley, see -ID[2]) f. L f. Gk *orkhis -ios* testicle, orchis, (w. ref. to shape of tuber)]

ŏr'chido- (-k-), assumed comb. form of Gk *orkhis* (prec.), correctly *orchio-*, as ~MAN'IA, ~LOGY (-ŏl[2]-).

ŏr'chil, n. Red or violet dye from lichen. [ME, f. OF *orchel*, of unkn. orig.]

ŏrchit'is (-k-), n. Inflammation of the testicles. [f. Gk *orkhis* testicle + -ITIS]

ŏr'cĭn, n. (chem.). Colourless crystalline substance extracted from lichens & yielding various dyes when compounded. [f. mod. L *orcina* (ORCHIL, -IN)]

ŏrdain', v.t. (Eccl.) appoint ceremonially to Christian ministry, confer holy orders (esp. those of deacon or priest) on (*was* ~*ed priest, elder*, etc., or abs.); (of God, fate, etc.) destine, appoint, (*has* ~*ed the time, death as our lot, us mortal, us to die, that we should live*); appoint authoritatively, decree, enact, (*what the laws* ~; ~ *that* —). [ME, f. OF *ordener* f. L *ordinare* (*ordo -inis* order)]

ŏrdain'ment, n. (rare). Decree(ing). [-MENT]

ŏrdeal' (or ôrd'ēl), n. Ancient Teutonic mode of deciding suspected person's guilt or innocence by subjecting him to physical test such as plunging of hand in boiling water, safe endurance of which was taken as divine acquittal; experience that tests character or endurance, severe trial. [in 16th c. repr. med. L *ordalium* or OE *ordāl*, -*dēl* (= OS *urdēli*, OHG *urteili*) judgement; corresp. to vb *ādǣlan* deal out (= OHG *irteilen*)]

ŏrd'er[1], n. (Main senses) 1. Rank, row, class. 2. Sequence, arrangement. 3. Mandate. 1. Tier (now rare; ~ *on* ~ *of* *sculptured figures*); social class or rank, separate & homogeneous set of persons, (*esp. the higher, lower, ~s; all ~s & degrees of men; the ~ of baronets; the clerical, military, ~*); kind, sort, (*talents of a high, considerations of quite another, ~*); any of the nine grades of angels (seraphim, cherubim, thrones, dominations, principalities, powers, virtues, archangels, angels); grade of Christian ministry (*holy ~s* in Anglican church, those of bishop, priest, & deacon, in R.-C., these & subdeacon; *minor ~s* in R.-C. Church, those of acolyte, exorcist, reader, & doorkeeper); (pl.) status of clergyman (*take ~s*, be ordained; *in ~s*, ordained; often in these phrr., & always elsewhere, *holy ~s*); fraternity of monks or friars, or formerly of knights, bound by common rule of life (*the Franciscan ~; the Teutonic ~; the ~ of Templars*); ‖ company usu. instituted by sovereign to which distinguished persons are admitted by way of honour or reward (*~ of the Garter, the Bath, Merit*, etc.), insignia worn by members of this (*sent him, wears, the ~ of the Golden Fleece*); (archit.) mode of treatment with established proportions between parts, esp. one of the *five* (*classical*) *~s*, Doric, Ionic, Corinthian, Tuscan, & Composite, of column and entablature, the first three being Greek in origin, the others Roman; (math.) degree of complexity (*line, equation, fluxion, of the first* etc. *~*), (also *~ of magnitude*) class in a system of classification determined by size (*measurements of the ~ of one in a million*); (nat. hist.) classification-group below CLASS¹ & above family (*natural ~* in bot., abbr. N.O., of plants allied in general structure, not merely agreeing in single characteristic as in Linnaean system). **2.** Sequence, succession, manner of following, (*in alphabetical, chronological*, etc., *~*; *out of ~*, not systematically arranged; *follow the ~ of events*; inverts the natural *~*; *take them in ~*, one after another according to some principle); regular array, condition in which every part or unit is in its right place, tidiness, normal or healthy or efficient state, (*drew them up in ~*; *are scattered without any ~*; *love of ~*; *is in bad, out of, ~*, not working rightly; *is in ~ or good ~*, fit for use); ‖ (arch.) suitable action, measures, (*take ~ to do*; *take ~ with*, arrange, dispose of); constitution of the world, way things normally happen, collective manifestations of natural forces or laws, natural or moral or spiritual system with definite tendencies, (esp. *the ~ of nature or things or the world*; *the old ~ changeth*; *whether there is a moral ~ or not*); stated form of divine service (*the ~ of confirmation*); principles of decorum & rules of procedure accepted by legislative assembly or public meeting, or enforced by its president (*Speaker called him to ~*; *O~! O~!*, protest against in-

fringement of it; *rise to ~* or *a point of ~*, interrupt debate etc. with inquiry whether something being said or done is in or out of *~*; *~ of the day*, programme, business set down for treatment, whence, in gen. use, prevailing state of things, as *industry, thunder, cricket, is the ~ of the day*; ‖ *~-paper*, written or printed *~* of the day; ‖ *~-book*, in which motions to be submitted to the House of Commons must be entered); prevalence of constituted authority, law-abiding state, absence of riot, turbulence, & violent crime, (often *law & ~*; *~ was restored*; *keep ~*, enforce it); *close, open, ~* (mil. etc.), formation with narrow, wide, spaces between men or ships; *marching, review*, etc., *~* (mil.), the regulation uniform & equipment carried by the soldier in marching, at review, etc. (cf. MARCH⁵*ing ~s*); (mil.) *the ~*, position of company etc. with arms ordered (see foll.); *in ~ to do*, with a view to, for the purpose of, doing; *in ~ that*, with the intention or to the end that. **3.** Mandate, injunction, authoritative direction or instruction, (often pl.; *gave ~s, an ~, the ~, for* something *to be done, that it should be done*, etc.; *is obedient to ~s*; ‖ *O~ in Council*, sovereign *~* on some administrative matter given by advice of Privy Council; *by ~*, according to direction of the proper authority; *judge gave, made, refused, an ~* or *the ~*); (banking etc.) instruction to pay money or deliver property signed by owner or responsible agent (*~ cheque, cheque to* person's *~*, one requiring payee's endorsement before being cashed; *postal, money* or pop. *post-office, ~*, kinds of Post-Office cheque for remitting money, the latter non-transferable); (commerc.) direction to manufacturer, tradesman, etc., to supply something (*made to ~*, according to special directions, to suit individual measurements, etc., opp. *ready-made*; *grocer has sent for ~s*; *is on ~*, has been ordered but not yet supplied; *a large ~*, colloq., difficult job; *~-book*, in which tradesman enters *~s*; *~-clerk*, with duty of entering *~s*; *~-form*, skeleton *~* to be filled in by customer); pass admitting bearer gratis, cheap, or as privilege, to theatre, museum, private house, etc. [ME, f. OF *ordre* f. L *ordinem* nom. *-o*]

o̅rd´er², *v.t.* Put in order, array, regulate, (arch.; *~ed his troops*; *~* one's *affairs*; *has ~ed his life well*); (mil.) *~ arms*, stand rifles butt on ground & hold them close to right side; (of God, fate, etc.) ordain (*so we hoped, but it was otherwise ~ed*); command, bid, prescribe, (*~ a retreat*, thing *to be* done, person *to do, that* person or thing *should*; *~ed him a mustard plaster*); command or direct (person etc.) to go *to, away, home*, etc. (*was ~ed to Egypt*; *~ about*, send hither & thither, domineer over); direct tradesman, servant, etc., to supply (~ *dinner*, settle what it shall consist of). [ME, f. prec.]

ōrd′erl‖ў, a. & n. **1.** Methodically arranged or inclined, regular, obedient to discipline, not unruly, well-behaved, whence ~ĪNESS n.; (mil.) of, charged with conveyance or execution of, orders ‖ (~*y book*, regimental or company book for entry of orders; ~*y officer*, officer of the day; ~*y room*, in barracks for company's business); ‖~*y bin*, street box for refuse. **2.** n. Soldier in attendance on officer to carry orders etc.; attendant in (esp. military) hospital; street cleaner. [-LY¹]

ōrd′inal, a. & n. **1.** (Number) defining thing's position in series (*first, twentieth,* etc., *are* ~s or ~ *numbers*; cf. CARDINAL). **2.** Of a nat.-hist. order. **3.** n. Service-·book used at ordinations. [ME, f. LL *ordinalis* (ORDER¹, -AL)]

ōrd′inance, n. Authoritative direction, decree (SELF-*denying* ~); religious rite; (rare) collocation of parts in literary work or architecture. [ME, f. OF *ordenance* f. med. L *ordinancia* (ORDAIN, -ANCE)]

ōrd′inănd, n. Candidate for ordination. [f. L *ordinandus* (*ordinare* ORDAIN)]

ōrd′inarў, a. & n. **1.** Regular, normal, customary, usual, not exceptional, not above the usual, commonplace, (‖ *in* ~ appended to *physician* etc., by permanent appointment, not temporary or extraordinary; *in the* ~ *way I should refuse*, if the circumstances were not exceptional; *something out of the* ~; ~ *seaman*, abbr. O.S., lower rating than *able*; *in* ~, of ships laid up, not in commission), whence **ōrd′inariLY²** adv., **ōrd′inariNESS** n. **2.** ‖ (Authority) having immediate or *ex officio* & not deputed jurisdiction (*the O*~, archbishop in province, bishop in diocese; *O*~ or *Lord O*~ in Scotland, one of five judges of Court of Session constituting Outer House). **3.** Rule or book laying down order of divine service. **4.** ‖ Public meal provided at fixed time & price in inn etc. **5.** (her.) Charge of earliest, simplest, & commonest kind (esp. chief, pale, bend, fesse, bar, chevron, cross, saltire). **6.** Early type of bicycle, with one large & one very small wheel (opp. *safety*). [f. L *ordinarius* (ORDER¹, -ARY¹); partly thr. OF -*arie*, F -*aire*]

ōrd′inate, n. (geom.). Any of series of parallel chords of conic section in relation to bisecting diameter (esp. used of half the chord, from curve to diameter); straight line from any point drawn parallel to one co-ordinate axis & meeting the other. [16th c., f. L (*linea*) *ordinate* (*applicata*) line applied parallel]

ōrdinā′tion, n. Arrangement in ranks, classification; conferring of holy orders, admission to church ministry; decreeing, ordainment. [ME, f. OF, or L *ordinatio* (ORDAIN, -ATION)]

ōrdinee′, n. Newly ordained deacon. [ORDAIN, -EE]

ōrd′nance, n. Mounted guns, cannon, ‖ branch of public service dealing esp. with military stores & materials (*Royal Army O*~ *Corps*, formerly with wider powers *Board of O*~; ‖~ *survey*, Government survey of Great Britain & Ireland; ‖~ *datum*, mean sea level as defined for ~ survey). [var. of ORDINANCE]

ōrd′ūre (or -dyer), n. Excrement, dung; obscenity, foul language. [ME, f. OF (*ord* foul f. L HORRIBILIS, -URE)]

ōre, n. Solid native mineral aggregate from which valuable constituent(s) not necessarily metal may be usefully extracted; (poet.) metal, esp. gold. [in form repr. OE *ār* brass (= OS, OHG *ēr*, ON *eir*, Goth. *aiz*, cogn. w. L *aes aeris*); in sense repr. OE *ōra* (= Du. *oer*, LG *ür*, ore, of unkn. orig.]

ōr′eăd, n. (L & Gk myth.). Mountain nymph. [f. L *oreas -ados* f. Gk *oreias* f. *oros* mountain, -AD(1)]

ōrĕc′tic, a. (philos., med.). Of desire or appetite, appetitive. [f. Gk *orektikos* (*oregō* stretch out, -IC)]

ōr′eïde, n. Kind of brass resembling gold used in imitation jewellery. [f. F *oréide* (or f. L *aurum* gold); see -IDE, OROIDE]

ōrfe, n. Kind of goldfish. [G & F, f. L f. Gk *orphos* sea perch]

ōrg′an, n. **1.** Musical instrument of pipes supplied with wind by bellows, sounded by keys, & distributed into sets or stops having special tone, which in turn form groups or partial ~s (*great, choir, swell, solo, pedal,* ~) each with separate keyboard, whence ~IST(3) n.; = BARREL¹-~ (~-*grinder*, player of this); keyboard wind-instrument with metal reeds, harmonium; AMERICAN ~; *mouth* ~, child's toy reed-instrument. **2.** Part of animal or vegetable body adapted for special vital function (~*s of speech, perception, digestion, generation,* etc.; NASAL ~). **3.** Person's voice with reference to its quality or power (*has a magnificent* ~). **4.** Medium of communication, mouthpiece of opinion, esp. newspaper or magazine or review representing a party, cause, sect, pursuit, etc. **5.** ~-*blower*, person or mechanism working~ bellows; ~-*builder*, of musical ~s; ~-*loft*, gallery in church or concert-room for ~; ~ *piano*, with mechanism giving sustained tones as in ~; ~-*screen*, ornamental screen often between choir & nave on which ~ is placed in cathedral etc.; ~-*stop*, set of pipes of similar tone in ~, handle of mechanism that brings it into action. Hence ~LESS a. [ME, f. OF *organe*, f. L f. Gk *organon* tool (*erg*- WORK)]

ōrg′andie, n. Kind of very fine translucent muslin. [F (-*di*), of unkn. orig.]

ōrgăn′ic, a. **1.** (Physiol.) of the bodily organs, vital; (path., of disease) affecting structure of an organ (opp. *functional*). **2.** Having organs or organized physical structure, of animals or plants, (opp. *in-*

organic). **3.** (chem.). (Of compound substances etc.) existing as constituent of organized bodies or formed from bodies so existing, containing carbon in its molecule (~ *chemistry*, that of carbon compounds). **4.** Constitutional, inherent, fundamental, structural. **5.** Organized or systematic or co-ordinated (~ *unity*; *an* ~ *whole*). Hence **ŏrgăn′**ICALLY adv. [f. F (-*ique*) or L f. Gk *organikos* (ORGAN, -IC)]

ŏrg′anĭsm, n. Organized body with connected interdependent parts sharing common life, (material structure of) individual animal or plant; whole with interdependent parts compared to living being. [f. F (-*isme*); see ORGANIZE, -ISM]

ŏrganizā′tion, n. In vbl senses of foll.; also, organized body or system or society. [ME, f. med. L *organizatio* (foll., -ATION)]

ŏrg′anĭz|e, -ĭs|e (-īz), v.t. & i. Furnish with organs, make organic, make into living being or tissue, (usu. in p.p.), (intr.) become organic; form into an organic whole (with constituents or resulting whole as obj.); give orderly structure to, frame & put into working order, make arrangements for or get up (undertaking involving co-operation). Hence ~ABLE a., ~ER¹ n. [ME, f. med. L *organizare* (ORGAN, -IZE)]

ŏrg′anŏn, -anum, n. Instrument of thought, system of or treatise on logic. [Gk (-*on*), & L (-*um*), see ORGAN; -*on* was title of Aristotle's logical writings, & *novum* (new) *organum* that of Bacon's]

ŏrg′anothĕ′rapў, n. Treatment of disease with organic extracts. [f. *organo*- comb. form of Gk *organon* ORGAN, +-THERAPY]

ŏrg′anzine (-ēn), n. Silk thread in which the main twist is in contrary direction to that of the strands. [f. F *organsin* f. It. *organzino*, of unkn. orig.]

ŏrg′ăsm, n. Violent excitement, rage, paroxysm; height of venereal excitement in coition. So **ŏrgăs′**TIC a. [f. mod. L *orgasmus*, f. Gk *orgaō* swell]

ŏr′gĕăt (or -zhah), n. Cooling drink made from barley or almonds & orange-flower water. [F, f. Pr. *orjat* (*orge* barley, -ADE)]

ŏrgiăs′tic, a. Of the nature of an orgy. [f. Gk *orgiastikos* (*orgiastēs* agent n. f. *orgiazō* celebrate ORGY)]

ŏr′gў, n. (Gk & Rom. ant.; usu. pl.) secret rites in worship of various gods, esp. in that of Bacchus celebrated with wild dancing, drinking, and singing; drunken or licentious revel, (pl.) revelry or debauchery. [earlier pl. only, f. F *orgies* f. L f. Gk *orgia* pl.]

-orial. See -ORY.

ŏr′iel, n. Large windowed polygonal recess projecting usu. from upper storey & supported from ground or on corbels; (also ~ *window*) window of ~, projecting window of upper storey. [ME, f. OF *oriol*, of undetermined orig.]

ŏr′ient¹, n. & a. **1.** *The* eastward part of sky or earth (poet.); *the* East or countries E. of Mediterranean; ~ pearl; peculiar lustre of pearl of best quality. **.2.** adj. Oriental (poet.); (of precious stones and pearls, of finest kinds, as coming anciently from the East) lustrous, sparkling, precious; (of sun, daylight, etc., or fig.) rising, nascent. [ME, f. OF f. L *orientem* nom. -*ens* rising sun, east, (*oriri* rise, -ENT)]

ŏriĕnt′², ŏ′rientāte, (or ŏr′-), vv.t. & i. Place (building etc.) so as to face E., build (church) with chancel end due E., bury with feet eastward; place or exactly determine position of with regard to points of compass, settle or find bearings of, (fig.) bring into clearly understood relations (~ one*self*, determine how one stands); (intr.) turn eastward or in specified direction. Hence **ŏrienta′**TION n. [f. F *orienter* (prec.)]

ŏriĕn′tal (or ŏr′-), a. & n. Easterly (arch.); (inhabitant) of the East or countries E. of Mediterranean, esp. Asian, occurring in or coming from or characteristic of the civilization etc. of the East, whence ~ISM(2, 4), ~IST(3), nn., ~IZE(2, 3) v.i. & t.; (of pearls etc.) orient; ~ *stitch*, close kind of herringbone stitch. Hence ~LY² adv. [ME, f. OF, or L *orientalis* (ORIENT¹, -AL)]

ŏ′rifice, n. Aperture, mouth of cavity, perforation, vent. [F, f. LL *orificium* (*os oris* mouth, -*ficere* = *facere* make)]

ŏ′riflămme, n. Sacred banner of St Denis, banderole of red silk on lance received by early French kings from abbot of St Denis on starting for war; (fig.) anything material or ideal serving as rallying-point in struggle; bright conspicuous object, blaze of colour, etc. [ME, f. OF (L *aurum* gold, *flamma* flame)]

ŏ′rigan, orig′anum, n. Wild marjoram, & kinds of allied plant. [ME, f. OF *origan* & L (-*um*), f. Gk *origanon*]

ŏ′rigin, n. Derivation, beginning or rising from something, person's extraction, source, starting-point, (*a word of Latin, a man of humble,* ~). [f. F *origine*, or L *origo* -*in*- (*oriri* rise)]

ori′ginal, a. & n. **1.** Existent from the first, primitive, innate, initial, earliest, (~ *sin*, innate depravity common to all human beings in consequence of the fall); that has served as pattern, of which copy or translation has been made, not derivative or dependent, first-hand, not imitative, novel in character or style, inventive, creative, thinking or acting for oneself, (*where is the* ~ *picture?*; *what does the* ~ *Greek say?*; *where whooping-cough is* ~; *is it an* ~ *drawing or a woodcut?*; *made a very* ~ *remark*; *has an* ~ *mind*; ~ *people do* ~ *things*); hence or cogn. **origĭnăl′**ITY n., ~LY² adv. **2.** n. Pattern, archetype, thing from which another is copied or translated, (*several transcripts from the* same ~, reads Don Quixote in the ~); eccentric person. [ME, f. OF, f. L originalis (prec., -AL)]

ori′gin|āte, v.t. & i. Give origin to, initiate, cause to begin, whence ~ATIVE a.;. have origin, take rise, (usu. from or in thing or place, with or from person). So ~A′TION, ~ātor, nn. [f. med. L originari (ORIGIN, -ATE³)]

ŏrināš′al (-zl), a. & n. Of, sounded with, both mouth & nose (esp. of French nasalized vowels); (n.) ~ vowel. [L os oris mouth, -I-, L nasus nose, -AL]

ŏr′iŏle, n. (Also golden ~) bird with black & yellow plumage visiting British Isles in summer; other old-world birds of same genus; kinds of bird of similarly coloured American genus. [f. med. L oriolus f. L aureolus dim. of aureus golden (aurum gold)]

Ori′on, n. (astron.). Brilliant constellation S. of zodiac, figured as hunter with belt & sword (~'s belt, three bright stars in short line across ~; ~'s hound, Sirius). [L, f. Gk Ōriōn]

Ori′onid, n. (astron.). One of meteor--system with radiant point in Orion. [prec., see -ID³]

-orious. See -ORY.

ŏ′rison (-zn), n. A prayer (usu. in pl.). [ME, f. OF, f. L orationem speech (orare speak, pray, -ATION)]

Orl′éans (ŏr-), n. Kind of plum; fabric of cotton warp & worsted weft. [name of French city]

ŏrl′op, n. Lowest deck of ship with three or more decks. [ME, f. MDu. overloop covering (overloopen run over, see OVER, LEAP¹)]

ŏrm′er, n. Edible univalve mollusc, the sea-ear. [Channel-I. F, f. F ormier contr. of oreille de mer ear of sea]

ŏrm′olu (-lōō), n. Gilded bronze used in decorating furniture; gold-coloured alloy of copper, zinc, & tin; articles made of or decorated with these. [f. F or moulu ground gold (for use in gilding)]

ŏrn′ament¹, n. (Eccl., usu. pl.) what is necessary for worship (e.g. altar, chalice, sacred vessels, service books); ~ rubric, that immediately before Order for Morning & Evening Prayer in prayer-book; thing used or serving to adorn, quality or person whose existence or presence confers grace or honour, (mantelpiece crowded with ~s; the ~ of a quiet spirit; was an ~ to his country or age); (pl., mus.) grace notes; (sing. only) adorning, being adorned, embellishment, features or work added for decorative purposes, (a lower rich in ~; by way of ~). Hence ~AL a., ~alLY² adv., ~alIST(3), ~alISM(3), nn., (all -ĕn⁴). [ME, f. OF ornement f. L ornamentum equipment (ornare equip,-MENT)]

ŏrn′ament² (or -ĕnt′), v.t. Adorn, beautify. Hence ~A′TION n. [f. prec.]

ŏrnāte′, a. Elaborately adorned; (of literary style) embellished with flowers of

rhetoric etc. Hence ~LY² adv., ~NESS n. [ME, f. L ornatus p.p. (prec.)]

ŏrnith|(o)-, comb. form of Gk ornis -ithos bird, in many scientific wds, as orn′ithOID, approaching birds in structure (of some reptiles); ~ŏL′OGY, ~ŏlO′GICAL, ~ŏL′OGIST; ornith′omANCY; ~orhync′us (-rĭ-), Australian duck-billed platypus, an aquatic mammal with dark-brown fur, webbed feet, & duck's bill, & laying eggs; ~ŏs̆copy, augury.

ŏrogĕn′esis, n. (geol.). Process of making mountains. So ŏrogĕnET′IC a. [f. Gk oros mountain, GENESIS]

ŏrŏg′raphy̆, ŏrĕŏ-, n. Branch of physical geography dealing with mountains; hence ŏrOGRAPH′IC(AL) aa. So ŏr(ĕ)ŏL′OGY n., ŏr(ĕ)olO′GICAL a., ŏr(ĕ)ŏL′OGIST n. [Gk oros -eos mountain, -GRAPHY]

ŏrohipp′us, n. Fossil quadruped held to be ancestral form of horse. [Gk oros mountain, hippos horse]

ŏr′oide, n. Gold-coloured alloy of copper & zinc. [F or gold f. L aurum, Gk eidos form; cf. -OID, OREIDE]

ŏr′otŭnd, a. (Of utterance or phrasing) swelling, mouth-filling, imposing, dignified, pompous, magniloquent, pretentious. [f. L ore rotundo (Hor. A.P. 323) with round mouth]

ŏrph′an, n. & a., & v.t. 1. (Child) bereaved of parent(s); hence ~HOOD n., ~IZE(3) v.t. 2. v.t. Bereave of parent(s). [ME, f. LL f. Gk orphanos bereaved]

ŏrph′anage, n. Orphanhood; institution for orphans' education etc. [-AGE]

Orph′ic, Orphē′an, (ŏr-), aa. Of Orpheus or the mysteries or doctrines associated with his name, oracular, mysterious, (usu. -ic); like Orpheus's music, melodious, entrancing, (usu. -ean). [f. Gk Orphikos (Orpheus, -IC)]

ŏrph′rey, ŏrf′ray, n. Ornamental often richly embroidered stripes and borders of ecclesiastical vestment. [ME orfreis (gold) embroidery, f. OF f. med. L aurifrisium etc. f. L aurum gold + Phrygius Phrygian, also 'embroidered'; loss of -s as in PEA]

ŏrp′iment, n. A mineral, trisulphide of arsenic, formerly used as yellow dye and as artists' pigment. [ME, f. OF f. L auripigmentum (aurum gold, PIGMENT)]

ŏrp′in(e), n. Succulent herbaceous fleshy--leaved purple-flowered plant. [ME, f. OF (-n), prob. alt. of prec., orig. of yellow--flowered species of same genus]

Orp′ington (ŏr-), n. A breed of poultry. [town in Kent]

ŏ′rra, a. (Sc.). Odd, not matched, occasional, extra. [orig. unkn.]

ŏ′rrery, n. Clockwork model of the planetary system. [named after Earl of O~ c. 1700]

ŏ′rris¹, n. Kind of iris, flower-de-luce, (now rare); ~root, fragrant root of three species of iris used in perfumery & medicine; ∼-*powder*, powdered ∼-*root*. [16th c., app. an unexpl. alt. of IRIS]

ŏ′rris², n. Kinds of gold or silver lace or embroidery. [c. 1700, app. alt. of *orfreis* ORPHREY]

ŏrt, n. (dial. & arch.; usu. pl.). Refuse scrap(s), leavings. [15th-c. *ortys* pl., f. MLG *orte*, cf. Du. *oor-aete* remains of food]

ŏrth|(o)-, comb. form of Gk *orthos* straight, in many scientific wds w. senses *straight, rectangular, upright, right, correct*: ∼o*cephăl′ic*, with breadth of skull from ¾ to ⅘ of length, between brachycephalic & dolichocephalic; ∼*ochromăt′ic*, giving correct relative intensity to colours in photography; *orth′oclase*, common feldspar in crystals with two cleavages at right angles; ∼*odŏn′tia* (-shĭa), ∼*odŏn′tics*, nn., correction of irregularities in teeth, ∼*dŏn′tic* a., ∼*odŏn′tIST*; ∼*ŏ′epy*, science of correct pronunciation, whence ∼*ŏĕp′IC*, ∼*ŏ′epIST*(3); ∼*ogĕn′esis*, a view of evolution according to which variations follow a defined direction & are not merely sporadic & fortuitous; ∼*ŏg′nathous*, upright-jawed, not prognathous; ∼*ŏg′onal*, of or involving right angles; ∼*ŏp′terous*, of the insect order *Orthoptera* with straight narrow forewings including cockroaches, crickets, grasshoppers, etc.; ∼*ŏp′tic*, of straight or correct seeing, esp. used as n. or a. of opaque perforated eyeglass assisting aim in rifle-shooting; ∼*orhŏm′bic* a. (cryst.), having three unequal axes at right angles to each other; *orth′otone*, (word) having independent accent, not enclitic or proclitic.

ŏrth′odŏx, a. Holding correct or the currently accepted opinions esp. on religious doctrine, not heretical or independent-minded or original; generally accepted as right or true esp. in theology, in harmony with what is authoritatively established, approved, conventional; *the O∼ Church*, the Eastern or Greek recognizing Patriarch of Constantinople as head & the national Churches of Russia, Romania, etc., in communion with it. Hence ∼LY² adv. [f. F -*doxe* or LL -*doxus*, ult. f. Gk ORTHO(*doxos* f. *doxa* opinion)]

ŏrth′odŏxy̆, n. Being orthodox. [f. LL f. Gk *orthodoxia* (prec., -Y¹)]

ŏrthŏg′raphy̆, n. 1. Correct or conventional spelling; spelling with reference to its correctness (*his ∼ is shocking*). 2. Perspective projection used in maps & elevations in which the point of sight is supposed infinitely distant so that the rays are parallel, map etc. so projected. So ŏrthogrăph′IC(AL) aa., ŏrthogrăph′i-calLY² adv. [ME, f. OF *ortografie* f. L f. Gk ORTHO(*graphia* -GRAPHY)]

ŏrth′opaedy̆, n. The curing of deformities in children or others, surgery directed to this. So ŏrthopaed′IC a. [f. F ORTHO-(*pédie* f. Gk *paideia* rearing of children)]

ŏrt′olan, n. The garden bunting, small bird esteemed as table delicacy. [F, f. Pr.

ortolan orig. gardener f. L *hortulanus* (*hortulus* dim. of *hortus* garden, -AN)]

-ory, suf. (1) of nn., originating in ONF & AF -*orie* = OF -*oire* (*glorie, gloire*), whence ME -*oric*, later -*ory*, wh. came to be the normal E repr. of L -*oria*, -*orium*, F -*oire*, most numerous being adaptations of L wds in -*orium* (*dormit∼, laborat∼*). In some tech. wds L -*orium* is preserved, as *auditorium, crematorium*. (2) of adjj., (whence also nn.), originating in AF -*ori*, -*orie*, & repr. (occas. thr. OF -*oir*, -*oire*) L -*orius*, -*a*, -*um*. As every L vb could form agent n. in -*or*, E has adjj. in -*ory* corresp. to L vbs even when L has neither adj. in -*orius* nor agent n. in -*or* (*compuls∼, dispensal∼, illus∼*), or when the L vb is not itself repr. in E (*amat∼, perfunct∼*). As alternatives to -*ory*, E has often -*orial* (∼+-AL), less often -*orious* (∼+-OUS).

O′ry̆x (ŏ-), n. (Genus of) large straight-horned African antelope. [ME, f. L, f. Gk *orux*]

Ŏs′can (ŏ-), a. & n. (Of, in) the language, allied to Latin, of the Osci, Opsci, or Opici, a primitive people of Campania. [L *Osci*, -AN]

°Ŏs′car (ŏs-), n. One of the statuettes awarded by the Motion Picture Academy for excellence in acting, directing, etc. [man's name]

ŏs′cill|āte, v.i. & t. Swing (i., rarely t.) like pendulum, move to & fro between two points; vacillate, vary between extremes of opinion, action, condition, etc.; (electr., of current) undergo high-frequency alternations as across spark-gap or in valve-transmitter circuit; (of radio receivers) radiate electromagnetic waves owing to faulty operation. Hence or cogn. ∼A′TION, ∼ātOR, nn., ∼ātORY a. [f. L *oscillare*, -ATE³]

oscitā′tion (ŏsĭ-), n. (rare). Yawning, inattention, negligence. [f. L *oscitatio* (*oscitare* gape f. *os* mouth, *citare* move, -ATION)]

ŏs′cular, a. Of the mouth, of kissing (joc.); (math.) that osculates. [f. L *osculum* mouth, kiss, (*os* mouth, -CULE), -AR¹]

ŏs′cul|āte, v.i. & t. 1. Kiss (i. & t., rare, usu. joc.). 2. (Nat. hist., of species etc.) have contact through intermediate species etc., have common characters *with* another or with each other; (math., of curve or surface) have contact of higher order with, coincide in three or more points. Hence or cogn. ∼ANT a. (esp. nat. hist.), ∼A′TION n., ∼ātORY a. (esp. math.). [f. L *osculari* kiss (prec.), -ATE³]

-ose¹, suf. f. L -*osus* abounding in; chiefly in adjj. of a technical kind, in ordinary use having -OUS; but there are *bellicose, jocose, grandiose*, & a few others. Nn. are formed from them usu. in -*osity*, also in -*oseness*.

-ose², suf. in chem. wds formed on *glucose*

(mod. F adoption of Gk *gleukos* must) giving names for the related carbo--hydrates *saccharose* & *cellulose* & isomeric substances, as *dextrose, laevulose*.

ō'sier (-zher), n. (Shoot of) species of willow used in basket-work; ∼-BED[1]; (attrib.) of ∼s. [ME, f. OF, cf. med. L *auseria, os-*, willow-bed]

-ōsis, suf. forming nn. of process or condition on Gk & occas. L stems; names of diseases or pathological states (*amaur∼, trichin∼*); a few rhetorical terms (*mei∼*); & some in gen. use (*metamorph∼, apothe∼*). [f. Gk *-ōsis* n. suf. usu. f. vbs in *-oō*]

-ōsity, suf. See -OSE[1], -OUS.

Osmǎn'li (ŏs-), a. & n. = OTTOMAN[1]. [Turk., native wd for which *Ottoman* is the use. E form]

ŏs'mium (ŏs-, ŏz-), n. A metal of the platinum group, having the greatest density of any known substance. [f. Gk *osmē* smell, -IUM]

ŏs'mōse, ŏsmŏs'is, (ŏs-, ŏz-), n. (phys.). (Tendency to) percolation & intermixture of fluids separated by porous septa. Hence **ōsmŏt'ic** a., **ōsmŏt'ically** adv. [irreg. f. Gk *ōsmos* push (*ōtheō* push) +-OSIS]

ŏs'mund (ŏz-, ŏs-), n. The flowering or royal fern; any fern of genus *Osmunda*. [ME, f. AF *osmunde*, OF *osmonde*, of unkn. orig.]

ŏs'prey (-ā, -ĭ), n. (pl. ∼s). **1.** Large bird preying on fish, the fishing-eagle, or sea--hawk. **2.** (Milliner's name for) egret--plume on hat or bonnet. [ME, app. ult. repr. L *ossifraga* sea-eagle, osprey, whence also F *orfraie*]

ŏss'ēous, a. Consisting of bone, ossified; having bony skeleton (∼ *& cartilaginous fishes*); abounding in fossil bones. [f. L *osseus* (*os ossis* bone) +-OUS]

ŏss'icle, n. (anat.). Small bone, small piece of bony or chitinous or calcareous substance in animal framework. [f. L *ossiculum* (prec., -CULE)]

ŏss'ifrage, n. = OSPREY. [OSPREY]

ŏss'ifȳ, v.i. & t. Turn (i. & t.) into bone, harden, make or become rigid or callous or unprogressive. So **ŏssif'ic** a., **ŏssi-FICA'TION** n. [L *os ossis* bone, -FY]

ŏss'ūary̆, n. Receptacle for bones of dead, charnel-house, bone-urn; cave in which ancient bones are found. [f. LL *ossu-arium* (irreg. f. *os* see prec., -ARY[1])]

ŏstĕn'sib|le, a. Professed, for show, put forward to conceal the real, (*his∼le errand was to —*). Hence ∼LY[2] adv. [F, f. med. L *ostensibilis* (L *ostendere -ens-*, -IBLE)]

ŏstĕn'sory̆, n. Receptacle for displaying Host to congregation, monstrance. [f. med. L *ostensorium* as prec., +-ORY(2)]

ŏstentā't|ion, n. Pretentious display esp. of wealth or luxury, showing off, attempt or intention to attract notice. Hence ∼IOUS (-shŭs) a., ∼IOUSLY[2] adv. [ME, f. OF, f. L *ostentationem* (*ostentare* frequent. of *ostendere -ent-* show, -ATION)]

ŏstĕ|(o)-, comb. form of Gk *osteon* bone in many med. & anat. terms, as ∼IT'IS; ∼*ogen'esis*, formation of bone; ∼*ŏg'raphy*, scientific description of the bones; *ŏs'te-*OID a.; ∼*ōl'ogy*, anatomy dealing with bones, animal's bony structure; ∼*oma-lā'cia*, softening of bone by loss of earthy salts; ∼*omȳelīt'is*, inflammation of the marrow of a bone; ∼*ŏp'athy*, manipulative surgery as a profession, *ŏs'teopath*, practitioner of it.

ŏs'tler (-sl-), n. Stableman at inn. [earlier *hostler* (HOSTEL, -ER[1])]

ŏs'trac|ize, -|ise (-īz), v.t. **1.** (Gk ant.; at Athens) banish (dangerously powerful or unpopular citizen) for ten or five years by peculiar voting-system, name of person to be ∼ized being written on potsherd. **2.** Exclude from society, favour or common privileges, send to Coventry, etc. So ∼ISM(1) n. [f. Gk *ostrakizō* (*ostrakon* potsherd)]

ŏs'treï-, ŏs'treo-, comb. forms of L *ostrea, ostreum*, & Gk *ostreon*, oyster, as *os'treiculture*, oyster-breeding; *ostreŏph'a-gous*, eating oysters.

ŏs'trich, n. Large swift-running African & Arabian bird with wing & tail feathers valued as ornaments, swallowing hard substances to assist working of gizzard, & reputed to bury its head in sand when pursued in the belief that it cannot be seen (*has the digestion of an∼*; ∼ *policy, belief*, etc., depending on self-delusion); ∼*-farm*, breeding ∼es for feathers; ∼*-plume*, feather, or bunched feathers, of ∼; ∼*-tip*, tip of ∼-feather. [ME, f. OF *ostrice, -iche* (mod. *autruche*) f. Rom. **avis* *struthio* (*avis* bird, LL f. Gk *strouthiōn* ostrich f. *strouthos* sparrow, ostrich)]

-ot[1], suf. = F *-ot*, orig. dim., but often not so now; *ballot, chariot, parrot*.

-ot[2], -ote, suf. expressing nativity in ancient Gk names, as *Epirot*, & in mod. names from places near Greece, as *Cypriot*; also in a few Gk derivatives of other meanings (*idiot, helot, patriot, zealot*). [repr. F *-ote*, L *-ota*, Gk *-ōtēs*]

o'ther (ŭdh-), a., n. or pron., & adv. **1.** Not the same as one or more or some already mentioned or implied, separate in identity, distinct in kind, alternative or further or additional, *the* etc. only remaining, *every* second, different than or from, (for sing. use with *an*, see ANOTHER; *we have* ∼ *evidence*; ∼ *people think otherwise*; *it must be decided by quite* ∼ *considerations*; *have no* ∼ *place to go to*; ∼ *things being equal*, if the conditions are or were, in everything but the point in question, alike, as ∼ *things being equal, I should prefer you to him, but he is rich & you are poor*; *a few* ∼ *examples would be useful*; *give me some* ∼ *ones*; *now open the, your,* ∼ *eye*; *happens every* ∼ *day*, on alternate days, as often as not; *any person* ∼ *than your-self, do not wish him, them,* ∼ *than he is, they are*; *a world far* ∼ *from ours*; *on the*

~ *hand*, used to introduce fact or argument making against or contrasted with previous one; *the* ~ *day* adv., a few days ago; *some time or* ~ adv., one day etc.; *someone or* ~, a person unknown; *some idiots or* ~ *have been shouting all night*; *it was none* ~ *than Jones*, = no ~ one or person; *the* ~ *world*, future life, ~ -*world*, concerned with or thinking of this only, whence ~-**wor'ldlY**[1] (-wêr-) a., ~-**wor'ldliNESS** n.; often ellipt. with numerals, as *another, the* ~ *two*, i.e. person or persons, thing or things, of kind not needing specification; ~*guess* a. [corrupt. of ~*gates* adv. (GATE[2], -ES) in another way], of very different kind (arch. & colloq.); ~*whence*, from elsewhere; ~*where*(s), elsewhere (poet.); ~*while*(s),. at ~ times. **2.** n. or pron. (orig. elliptic use of adj., & often indistinguishable from this in sing., but now distinguished in pl. by -*s*, cf. *the* ~ *six, the six* ~*s*). ~ person, thing, specimen, etc. (*give me another, some* ~*s*; *do good to* ~*s*; *if this soap is, these candles are, too soft, have you any* ~*s ?*; *one or* ~ *of us will be there*; *let* ~*s talk, I act*; *I can do no* ~, arch., nothing else; *you are the man of all* ~*s for the work*; *one neutralizes the* ~; *they neutralize* EACH ~ or ONE *another*; *in* ~*s of his sermons*). **3.** adv. Otherwise (~ *than cursorily*). [OE *ōther*, OS *ōdar, andar*, OHG *ander*, ON *annarr*, Goth. *anthar*, cogn. w. Skr. *antaras*; see -THER]

o'ther**nèss** (ŭdh-), n. (rare). Being other, diversity, difference; thing or existence that is not the thing mentioned or the thinking subject. [-NESS]

o'ther**wise** (ŭdh'erwĭz), adv. In a different way (*could not have acted* ~; *Judas,* ~ *called, or* ~, *Iscariot*; occas. preceded by *any, no,* with reminiscence of its etym., as *could do it no* ~, *does not influence him any* ~ *than by example*); if circumstances are or were different, else, or (*seize the chance,* ~ *you will regret it*); in other respects (*he is unruly, but not* ~ *blameworthy*; also qualifying the adj. sense in n., as *his* ~ *dullness*); in different state (*how can it be* ~ *than fatal ?*; *should not wish it* ~); *& ~, or* ~, ungrammatical substitute for *&* or followed by the negation or opposite of a noun or adj. or by *other* (*the merits or* ~ *of the Bill*, i.e. *or demerits* usu. omissible; *additions automatic & ~*, i.e. *& other*); ~*-minded*, having different, or jarring, inclinations or views, averse to current opinions. [OE *on othre wisan* (OTHER, WISE[2])]

ŏt'ic (or ō-), a. Of or relating to the ear. [f. Gk *ous ōtos* ear, -IC]

-otic, suf. forming aa. corresp. to nn. in -OSIS, in sense *affected with* or *producing* or *resembling* -*osis*, so *neur*~, *hypn*~, *narc*~; *Quix*~, *ex*~, *er*~, are not exx. [f. Gk -*ōtikos* f. nn. in -*ōtēs* formed on same stems as -OSIS]

otiose (ōshĭŏs', *also* ō-), a. At leisure, lazy,

unoccupied, (rare); sterile, futile, (rare); not required, serving no practical purpose, functionless. Hence ~LY[2] adv., ~NESS n. [f. L *otiosus* (*otium* leisure, -OSE[1])]

o'tium **cŭm dĭgnĭtāt'ė** (ōshĭ-), n. Dignified ease. [L]

ōt(o)-, comb. form of Gk *ous ōtos* ear, as *ōtŏL'OGY*, science of ear diseases, anatomy, etc.; *ōt'oSCOPE*, instrument for examining cavity of ear, or for auscultation of sounds in it.

otta'va ri'ma (-tah-, rē-), n. Stanza of eight lines, 11-syllabled in Italian, 10--syllabled in English, with rhymes as abababcc (as in Byron's *Don Juan*). [It.]

ŏtt'er, n. Furred aquatic fish-eating mammal with short legs, round feet, and webbed toes; its fur; kinds of fishing--tackle (also as name for the paravane when used on non-naval craft); ~*dog*, -*hound*, breed used in ~-hunting; ~--*spear*, used in ~-hunting. [OE *otr*, MDu., MLG *otter*, OHG *ottar*, ON *otr* f. Gmc *ⁱotraz*, cogn. w. Skr. *udras* otter, & WATER]

ŏtt'o, n. ~ *of roses*, = ATTAR. [f. ATTAR]

Ott'oman[1] (ŏ-), a. & n. **1.** Of the dynasty of Othman I, his branch of the Turks, or the empire ruled by his descendants, Turkish. **2.** n. (pl. ~*s*). ~ person, Turk. [F, f. Arab. name of *Othman* (pronounced in Turk. *osman*, whence OSMANLI)]

ŏtt'oman[2], n. Cushioned seat like sofa or chair without back or arms, often a box with cushioned top. [f. prec. (cf. DIVAN)]

ou'bit (ōō-), n. = WOOBUT.

oubliètte' (ōō-), n. Secret dungeon with entrance only by trapdoor. [F (*oublier* forget)]

‖ ouch, n. (arch.). Clasp or buckle often jewelled; setting of precious stone. [ME *ouche* f. *nouche*, OF *nouche, nosche*, etc. f. WG *ⁱnuskja* clasp; loss of *n-* as in *adder*]

ought[1] (awt), n. (vulg.). Figure denoting nothing, nought. [perh. f. *an ought* for *a nought*, cf. ADDER]

ought[2] (awt), v. aux. (the only form in use, except arch. ~*est* or ~*st*, is ~ serving as present or past finite) expressing duty, rightness, shortcoming, advisability, or strong probability; the past sense (except when merely due to sequence of tenses in reporting etc.) is indicated by a following perf. infin. Exx.: *we* ~ *to love our neighbours*; *it* ~ *not to be allowed*; *you* ~ *to know better*; *you* ~ *to go to Pinafore*; *Eclipse* ~ *to win*; *it* ~ *to be done at once, have been done long ago*; *I told you it* ~ *to be, have been, done*; *I said it, & still think I* ~ *to have said it*. [OE *āhte* past of *āgan* OWE; the mod. uses represent the imperf. subj. = would owe]

ought[3], var. of AUGHT.

ouija (wē'jah, -yah), n. (Also ~-*board*) board lettered with alphabet & other signs, used with movable pointer to obtain messages in spiritualistic séances. [f. F *oui* and G *ja*, = yes]

ounce[1], n. (abbr. *oz*). Unit of weight, 1/12 **lb.** in Troy weight, 1/16 lb. in avoirdupois (also fig., as *an ~ of practice* etc. *is worth a pound of theory* etc.); (pharm.) 1/20 pint, *1/16 pint. [ME, f. OF *unce* f. L *uncia* twelfth of pound or foot (cf. INCH[1])

ounce[2], n. (Poet. etc.) lynx or other vaguely identified medium-sized feline beast; (zool.) the mountain panther or snow leopard smaller than leopard but marked like it. [ME, f. OF *once* for earlier *lonce* (*l* mistaken for def. art.), = It. *lonza* f. Rom. **luncea* f. L *lynx* LYNX]

our (owr), a. Of or belonging to us (see WE), that we are concerned with or speaking or thinking of, (*is in ~ midst*; *acting on ~ behalf*; *have done ~ share*; *Our Father*, the creator of us men; *Our Saviour, Lady*, of us Christians, Christ, the Virgin; *given under Our seal*, of Us the king or queen, emperor or empress; *a worthless book in ~ opinion*, of us the present spokesman of a newspaper etc.). [OE *ūre* orig. genit. pl. of first pers. pron. = of us (thus OS *ūser*, OHG *unsĕr*, ON *vár*, Goth *unsara*); then inflected as adj. to form poss. adj. (= OS *ūsa*, OHG *unser-*, ON *várr*, Goth. *unsar*)]

-our, suf. in *colour* etc.; see -OR.

ours (owrz), pron. & pred. a. **1.** The one(s) belonging to us (*~ is a large family*; *I like ~ better*; *let me give you one of ~*; *look at this garden of ~*, this our garden); ǁ our regiment or corps (*Jones of ~*). **2.** pred. adj. Belonging to us (*became ~ by purchase*). [OUR, -ES; double possessive for the emphatic abs. use]

oursĕl|**f'** (owr-), pron. (pl. *~ves*, which is the usu. form, the sing. being used similarly when *We* represents a sovereign, & alternatively with the pl. when *we* represents a newspaper writer or the average man). **1.** (emphat.; usu. pl.). We or us in person, in particular, in our normal condition, & not others, or alone, (usu. in apposition with *we*, & either next after it or later, rarely substituted for it; usu. substituted for *us*, rarely after it in apposition; *we ~ves will see to it*; *we will see to it ~ves*; *~ves are first to be thought of*; *it was good for the others, if not for ~ves*; *let us do it ~ves*; *we were not ~ves for some time*; *what touches us~f shall be last served*; *can we imagine a world in which ~f does not exist ?*). **2.** (refl.; usu. pl., always in objective case). The person(s) previously described as *we* (*we shall only harm, do harm to, ~ves*; *we cannot persuade ~f or ~ves that the Government is in earnest*; *we shall give~ves the pleasure of calling*. [OUR, SELF]

ous, suf. forming adjj. meaning 'abounding in, characterized by', ult. f. L *-osus* (see -OSE[1]). AF, OF, & early ME *-os, -us*, later ME *-ous*, which form has been retained, & has now become the established anglicizer for many L adjj., esp. in *-eus, -tus, -er, -ax -acis, -ox -ocis, -endus, -ulus*, & *-vorus* (*igne~, dubi~, adulter~, capaci~, feroci~, tremend~, bibul~, herbivor~*); for *righte~, courte~, gorge~*, etc., see -EOUS; (chem. of acids etc.) with larger proportion of the element indicated by the stem than those in -IC (*chlor~ acid*). Nn. f. adjj. in ~ have usu. *-ousness*, sometimes *-osily* (*curiosity*), cf. -OSE[1].

ousel. See OUZEL.

oust, v.t. Put out of possession, eject, deprive *of*, expel *from*, drive out, force oneself or be put into the place of. Hence **oust'**ER[4] n. (legal), ejection. [f. AF *ouster*, OF *oster* (now *ôter*) take away, f. L OB(*stare* stand) oppose, hinder]

out, adv., prep., n., a., int., & v.t., (for spec. uses of the adv. in comb. with vbs see the vbs). **1.** adv. Away from or not in or at a place, the right or normal state, the fashion, etc., (*is ~*, not at home; *keep him ~*; *go ~ for a walk*; *has her Sundays ~*; *arm is ~*, dislocated; *Tories are ~*, not in office; *her son is ~ in Canada*; *anchored some way ~*; *on the voyage ~*; *batsman is ~*, no longer in possession of wicket; *all ~*, side's innings over; *~, not ~*, umpire's decision against, for, batsman in answer to claim of opponents; *miners are ~*, not at work, on strike; *candle, fire, is ~*, not burning; *crinolines are ~*, not in fashion; *was ~ in my calculations*, incorrect; *~ with*, no longer on friendly terms with; also as interj., *~ with him* etc., turn him ~); in(to) the open, publicity, existence, notice, hearing, sight, clearness, etc. (*book, rose, chicken, secret, girl, is ~*, published, open, hatched, revealed, introduced to society; *is the best game ~*; *tell him right ~*; *the eruption is ~ all over him*; *~ for,~ to do*, colloq., engaged in seeking, as *is ~ for kudos, to capture the market*; *all ~*, sl., showing one's utmost pace or effort; *~ at* ELBOW[1]*s*; *~ & about*, able to leave bed or house & appear; also ellipt. for *come ~*, as *murder will ~*); to or at an end, completely, (*she had her cry ~*; *tired ~*; *before the week is ~*; *~ & away*, by far; *~ & ~*, thorough, -ly, surpassing, -ly, whence **out-&-out'**ER[1] n. sl.); *~ of* compd prep., from within, not within, from among, beyond range of, (so as to be) without, from, owing to, by use of (material), at specified distance from (town etc.), beyond, transgressing rules of, (*come ~ of the house*; *happened ~ of England*; *~ of doors*, in or into the open air, so *~-of-door* as adj.; *must choose ~ of these*; *is ~ of sight*; *was swindled ~ of his money*; *is ~ of breath, his mind, work, brown sugar*, etc.; *get money ~ of him*; *a filly got by Persimmon ~ of Lutetia*; *asked ~ of curiosity*; *what did you make it ~ of ?*; *is seven miles ~ of Liverpool*; *~ of wedlock*, without marriage; *times ~ of number*, beyond counting; *~ of doubt*, undoubtedly; *is ~ of drawing*, incorrectly drawn; *~ of it*, not included, forlorn, at a loss, wrongly informed or mistaken; ~ *of* DATE[2], CHARACTER[1], HAND[1], one's *own* HEAD[1], KEEPING, TEMPER, *the* WOOD, SORTS, *the* WAY). **2.** prep. = ~ of (only now in *from* ~, as *from* ~ *the dungeon came a groan).* **3.** n. *The*~*s*, the party ~ of office; *the* IN*'s* & ~*s*. **4.** adj. *An* ~ *match,* played away from home ground; ~ *size,* beyond the ordinary; ~*'size* n. & a., (of) exceptionally large size (in garments etc.). **5.** int. (arch.). Expr. abhorrence, reproach, etc. (*Out upon you!*). **6.** v.t. (sl. or colloq.). Eject forcibly; (boxing) knock ~. [OE (= OS, ON, Goth.) *ūt,* OHG *uz,* cogn. w. Skr. *ud-*]

out-, pref. = prec. prefixed adverbially or adjectively or prepositionally to vbs or nn.

1. To any vb, making equivalent of same vb followed by *out;* chiefly in poet. & rhet. use. So~*'blaze',*~*'branch',*~*'speak', ~'spread'.*

2. Vbs that are followed in other parts by *out* often form partt. & gerunds with prefixed *out;* the meaning is often a specialized one. So ~*'cast* a. & n., (person) cast out from home & friends, homeless & friendless (vagabond); ||~*ᴸclearing* n., sending out of bills & cheques to Clearing-house for settlement; ~*'fighting,* boxing at arm's length, opp. *infighting;* ~*'lying* a., situated far from a centre, remote; ~*mŏd'ed,* a., out of fashion; ~*'spoken* (or -ōk*ᴸ*) a., frank, given to plain speaking, whence ~*spok'enℒY*[2] adv., ~*spok'en*NESS n. ; ~*'spread;* ~*'standing* a., prominent, still unsettled; ~*'stretched;* ~*'worn',* worn out (poet.), (fig.) out of date, obsolete, exhausted.

3. Nn. are formed f. vbs that can be followed by *out,* either with the simple vb form or with a derivative n.; the meaning, which is often specialized, may be:—

a. the verbal action or its occurrence. So ~*'break,* a breaking out of emotion esp. anger, hostilities, disease, volcanic energy, etc., ~crop, an insurrection; ~*'burst,* explosion of feeling esp. expressed by vehement words, volcanic eruption, ~crop; ~*'crop,* emergence of stratum, vein, or rock, at surface (also b.); ~*'cry* (also c.); ~*'flow;* ~*'going* (also b.); ~*'look* (also c.); ~*'rush* (also b.); ~*'sight,* perception of external things (only as antithesis to *insight*); ~*ᴸthrust,* outward pressure of some part in architecture.

b. that which does the action. So ~*ᴸ come,* issue, result; ~*'crop* (also a.); ~*'fit,* complete equipment material or mental, (colloq.) group of persons regarded as a unit, gang, (v.t.; -tt-) provide (person) *with*; ~*'fitter,* supplier of equipment; ~*ᴸ flow* (also a.); ~*'go,* ~*'goings* (also a. in sing.), expenditure, ~lay; ~*'growth,* offshoot, natural product; ~*'lier,* ~lying part or member, (geol.) minor part of

formation separated from main body by denudation; ~*'pour;* ~*'rush* (also a.).

c. that which is made or done by or suffers the action. So ~*'cry* (also a.), clamour, uproar; ~*'lay,* what one spends, expenses; ~*'look,* what one sees on looking out, view, prospect, esp. fig. of what seems likely to happen, mental attitude; ~*'pouring,* effusion, verbal or literary expression of emotion; ~*'put,* ~*ᴸturn,* amount produced by manufacture, mining, labour, etc.; ~*ᴸthrow,* amount ejected.

d. the place or time of occurrence. So ~*'fall,* ~let of river etc.; ~*'let,* means of exit or escape, vent, way out; ~*'set,* start, commencement, (usu. *at* or *from the* ~ *set*).

4. *out-* is prefixed w. adj. force to nn., meaning : —

a. external. So ~*'back* a. & n. (Austral.), (of) the more remote settlements; OUTLINE, OUTSIDE.

b. connected but separate, subordinate & detached, not at the centre, some way off. So ~*'building,* ~house; ~*'field,* ~lying land of farm, ~lying region of thought etc., (crick.) part remote from wickets; ~*'house,* house or building or shed belonging to & near or built against main house; ~*land'ish* a. [f. obs. ~*'land* foreign countries], foreign looking or sounding, unfamiliar, bizarre, uncouth; ~*ᴸpatient, -pensioner,* receiving aid from institution etc. without being lodged in it; ~*'post,* detachment on guard at some distance from army to prevent surprise; ||~*ᴸrelief,* ~door relief (5); ~*'rider,* mounted attendant riding before, behind, or with carriage, also commercial traveller; OUTRIGGER; ~*'runner,* running attendant on carriage, horse in traces outside shafts, dog acting as guide to sledge--team; ~*'sentry,* man stationed as ~-post; ~*'skirts,* outer border, fringe, of city, district, etc., or subject; ~*'station,* at distance from headquarters; ||~*'voter,* non-resident parliamentary elector; ~*ᴸ work,* advanced or detached part of fortification, also work done outside shop or house; ~*'worker,* one who does ~work.

5. *out-* is prefixed to & governs nn. with the force of *out of,* forming adjj. or advv. f. which vbs or nn. may be secondary formations. So~*'board* a. & adv., (naut.) on or towards or nearer than something else to ship's outside, (of a motor-boat) having the engine & driving apparatus attached outside the boat; ~*'caste* a. & n., (person) having lost or been expelled from his or not belonging to a caste; ~*- caste'* v.t., expel from caste; ||~*'college* a., not residing in or not belonging to a or the college; ~*'door* a., done or existing or used ~doors ||(~*door relief,* given to person not resident in workhouse or institution; ~*door agitation* etc., conducted outside

Parliament); ~*doors'* adv., in the open air; ~*law* n. & v.t. [OE *ūtlaga* n. f. *ūtlag* a. outlawed], person deprived of the protection of the law, banished or exiled person, (vb) proscribe, declare ~law, whence ~*'law*RY, condition of or condemnation a. ~law.

6. *out-* with general sense of excess is prefixed

a. to simple vbs capable of taking the same object, adding the idea of more than, or successfully, doing the action. So ~*bal'ance*, weigh down; ~*brave'*, defy; ~*face'*, look out of countenance; ~*fight'*; ~*-hec'tor*; ~*last'* (*will not* ~ *last six months*) also b.); ~*match'*; ~*meas'ure*; ~*riv'al*; ~*scold'*; ~*'trump'*, at cards.

b. to any vb, or n. such as *general* used for the nonce as vb, enabling it to take as obj. a person or thing that the subj. surpasses or defeats by doing the action more, better, or longer. So ~*-act'*, *-arg'ue*, *-bell'ow*; ~*bid'*, bid higher than at auction, promise more than, surpass in exaggeration or anecdote; ~*-blaze'*, *-brag'*, *-dance'*, *-dare'*; ~*do'*, surpass; ~*-eat'*; ~*fight'*, fight better than (also a.); ~*fly'*; ~*gen'eral*, defeat by superior generalship; ~*go'*, go faster than, (fig.) surpass; ~*grow'*, grow faster or get taller than (also c.); ~*-hec'tor*, be more formidable at hectoring than (also a.); ~*jock'ey*, overreach; ~*jug'gle*; ~*-jump'*; ~*lab'our*; ~*last'*, last longer than (another; also a.); ~*live'* (also c.); ~*manœu'vre*, *-march'*, *-paint'*, *-preach'*, *-reach'*, *-reas'on*, *-ride'*, *-row'* (-ō); ~*run'* (~*run the* CONSTABLE; also c.); ~*sail'*; ~*scold'* (also a.); ~*shine'* lit. & fig.; ~*shoot'*; ~*sing'*; ~*sit'*, stay longer than (other guests); ~*spar'kle*, *-spend'*, *-stare'*; ~*stay'* (also c.); ~*stink'*, *-swim'*, *-talk'*, *-think'*, *-thun'der*, *-toil'*, *-trade'*, *-trav'el*; ~*vie'*, surpass in competition; ~*vote'*, *-walk'*; ~*watch'*, keep awake longer than (also c.); ~*weep'*; ~*weigh'*, exceed in weight, value, importance, or influence; ~*work'*; ~*yell'*.

c. to vb, enabling it to take as obj. something in the nature of a limit or amount that is exceeded. So ~*grow'*, get too big for (clothes), get rid of (childish habit or ailment or taste) with advancing age, (also b.); ~*live'*, live beyond (a century, the ordinary span, etc.), come safely through (accident etc.), get over effect of (disrepute etc.), (also b.); ~*ride'*, (of ship) keep afloat through (storm; also b.); ~*run'*, pass the limit of (*his imagination* ~*runs the facts*; also b.); ~*stay'* (*never* ~*stay your welcome*; also b.); ~*step'*, pass limit of (~*steps the truth*); ~*watch'*, keep awake beyond the end of (the night etc.; also b.); ~*wear'*, pass away (time) by endurance.

d. to n. or rarely adj., forming vb expressing that subj. surpasses obj. in this respect. ~*class'*, belong to higher class

than; ~*-dis'tance*, get far ahead of; ~*flank'*, have flank overlapping that of (enemy); ~*num'ber*; ~*pace'*, go faster than; ~*-range'*, (of gun or its user) have longer range than; •~*-smart'* v.t. (colloq.), be too clever for, ~*wit'*; ~*speed'*; ~*val'ue*; ~*voice'*, speak louder or more effectively or persuasively than; ~*wit'*, prove too clever for, overreach, take in.

e. to name of person noted for some quality, forming vb (w. the name usu. repeated as obj.) indicating that subj. surpasses even him in it. So ~*-he'rod* Herod, ~*-zol'a* Zola, be more blustering, realistic, than Herod or Zola.

out'back, a. & n., see OUT-4 a; **outbal'ance** v.t., OUT- 6 a; **outbid'** v.t. (-dd-), OUT- 6 b; **out'board** a. & adv., OUT- 5; **outbrave'** v.t., OUT- 6 a; **out'break** n., OUT- 3 a; **out'building** n., OUT- 4 b; **out'burst** n., OUT- 3 a; **out'cast** a. & n., OUT- 2; **out'caste** a. & n., outcaste' v.t., OUT- 5; **outclass'** v.t., OUT- 6 d; || **out'clearing** n., OUT- 2; || **out'college** a., OUT- 5; **out'come** n., OUT- 3 b; **out'crop** n., OUT- 3 a b; **out'cry** n., OUT- 3 a c; **outdis'tance** v.t., OUT- 6 d; **outdo'** v.t., OUT- 6 b; **out'door** a., **outdoors'** adv., OUT- 5.

out'er, a. & n. 1. Farther from centre or inside, relatively far out, external, of the outside; objective, physical, not subjective or psychical; ~ *space*, immense expanse beyond the earth; *the* ~ *man*, personal appearance, dress; *the* ~ *world*, people outside one's own circle; hence ~MOST a. 2. n. Circle of rifle-target farthest from the bull's-eye, hit on this. [14th-c. formation substituted for & differentiated f. UTTER as compar. of OUT]

outface', v.t., see OUT- 6 a; **out'fall** n., OUT- 3 d; **out'field** n., OUT- 4 b; **out'fighting**, OUT- 2; **out'fit**, **out'fitter**, nn., OUT- b; **outflank'** v.t., OUT- 6 d; **out'flow** n., OUT- 3 a; **outgen'eral** v.t. OUT- 6 b; **outgo** n., OUT- 3 b, vb, OUT- 6 b; **out'going(s)** n., OUT- 3 a b; **outgrow'** v.t., OUT- 6 b c; **out'growth** n., OUT- 3 b; **out-he'rod** v.t., OUT- 6 e; **out'house** n., OUT- 4 b.

out'ing, n. Pleasure-trip, holiday away from home. [f. obs. *out* vb put or go out, *-*ING[1]]

out-jock'ey, v.t., see OUT- 6 b; **outland'ish** a., OUT- 4 b; **outlast'** v.t., OUT- 6 a b; **out'law** n. & v.t., **out'lawry** n., OUT- 5; **out'lay** n., OUT- 3 c; **out'let** n., OUT- 3 d; **out'lier** n., OUT- 3 b.

out'line, n., & v.t. 1. (Sing. or pl.) lines enclosing the apparently plane figure presented by any object to sight, contour, external boundary; sketch containing only contour lines & no shading (*in* ~, so sketched); rough draught, verbal description of essential parts only, summary, (pl.) main features, general principles. **2.** v.t. Draw or describe in ~; mark ~ of in decorating etc. [OUT- 4 a]

outlive', v.t., see OUT- 6 b c; **out′look** n., OUT- 3 c; **out′lying** a., OUT- 2; **outmanœu′vre** v.t., OUT- 6 b; **outmarch′** v.t., OUT- 6 b; **outmatch′** v.t., OUT- 6 a; **outmod′ed** a., OUT- 2.

out′most, a. = OUTERMost.

out′ness, n. Externality, objectivity. [-NESS]

outnum′ber, v.t., see OUT- 6 d; **outpace′** v.t., OUT- 6 d; **out′patient** n., OUT- 4 b; **out′post** n., OUT- 4 b; **out′pouring** n., OUT- 3 c; **out′put** n., OUT- 3 c.

out′rage, n. (-ij), & v.t. (-āj). **1.** Forcible violation of others' rights, sentiments, etc. (*never safe from* ~); deed of violence, gross or wanton offence or indignity (*an* ~ *upon decency, justice,* etc.). **2.** v.t: Do violence to, subject to ~, injure, insult, violate, ravish; infringe (law, morality, etc.) flagrantly. [ME, f. OF *ultrage outrage*, f. *outrer* exceed (L *ultra* beyond, -AGE)]

outrā′geous (-jus), a. Immoderate, extravagant, extraordinary; violent, furious; grossly cruel, immoral, offensive, or abusive. Hence ~LY² adv., ~NESS n. [ME, f. OF *outrageus* (prec., -OUS)]

outrange′, v.t. See OUT- 6 d.

outré (ōŏt′rā), a. Outside the bounds of propriety, eccentric, outraging decorum. [F]

|| **out′-relief**, n., see OUT- 4 b; **outride′** v.t., OUT- 6 b c; **out′rider** n., OUT- 4 b.

out′rigged (-gd), a. (Of boat etc.) having outriggers. [f. OUT-, RIG, -ED¹ after foll.]

out′rigger (-g-), n. Beam, spar, framework, rigged out & projecting from or over ship's side for various purposes; similar projecting beam etc. in building; extension of splinter-bar enabling extra horse to be harnessed outside shafts, such horse; iron bracket bearing rowlock attached horizontally to boat's side to increase leverage of oar, boat with these. [OUT-, RIG, -ER¹; perh. partly after obs. (naut.) *outligger*]

outright′ (-rīt), adv. & a. **1.** Altogether, entirely, once for all, not by degrees or instalments or half & half, (*kill, buy,* ~); without reservation, openly. **2.** adj. Downright, direct, thorough, whence ~NESS (-rīt-) n. [OUT, RIGHT]

outriv′al, v.t. (-ll-), see OUT- 6 a; **outrun′** v.t., OUT- 6 b c; **out′runner** n., OUT- 4 b; **out′set** n., OUT- 3 d; **outshine′** v.t. OUT- 6 b.

outside′, n., adj., adv., & prep. **1.** External surface, outer parts, (*knows only the* ~s *of books; ride on the* ~ *of an omnibus*); external appearance, outward aspect; all that is without, *the* world as distinguished from the thinking subject, (*impressions from the* ~); position without (*open the door from* ~); highest computation (*there were a hundred, it is a mile, at the* ~); (pl.) outer sheets of ream of paper;

|| ~ *passenger on coach* etc.; ~ *in,* = IN-SIDE *out.* **2.** adj. Of, on, nearer, the ~, outer, (~ *edge* in skating, progression on outer edge of one skate; ~ *seat,* nearer the end; ~ *work,* done off the premises; || ~ *porter,* conveying luggage from station); (of a chance) remote, very unlikely; not belonging to some circle or institution (~ *opinion,* esp. of people not in Parliament; ~ *broker,* not member of Stock Exchange); greatest existent or possible or probable (*quote the* ~ *prices*). **3.** adv. On or to the ~, the open air, open sea, etc., not within or enclosed or included, (*come* ~, out from room or house, esp. as challenge to fight; *is black* ~ *& in*; ~ *of,* = ~ prep.; *get* ~ *of,* sl., eat or drink; ~ *of his own family no one will speak to him*). **4.** prep. External to, not included in, beyond the limits of, not in, to the ~ *of,* at or to the exterior of, (*natural forces are* ~ *morality; cannot go* ~ *the evidence*). [OUT- 4 a, SIDE¹]

outsid′er, n. Non-member of some circle, party, profession, etc., uninitiated person, layman; person without special knowledge, breeding, etc., or not fit to mix with good society (freq. *rank* ~); competitor not known to have a chance in race or competition. [-ER¹]

out′sight, n., see OUT- 3 a; **outsit′** v.t., OUT- 6 b; **out′skirts** n. pl., OUT- 4 b; **outsmart′** v.t., OUT- 6d.

out′span, v.i. & t. (-nn-), n. (S. Afr.). **1.** Unyoke, unharness. **2.** n. Act, time, or place of ~ning. [f. Du. *uitspannen* (OUT, SPAN²); cf. INSPAN]

out′spoken, a., see OUT- 2; **out′spread** a., OUT- 2; **out′standing** a., OUT- 2; **outstay′** v.t., OUT- 6 b c; **outstep′** v.t., OUT- 6 c; **out′stretched** a., OUT- 2.

outstrip′, v.t. (-pp-). Pass in running etc.; surpass in competition or relative progress or ability. [OUT- 6 b, obs. *strip* run fast]

out′thrust, n., see OUT- 3 a; **out′turn** n., OUT- 3 c; **outval′ue** v.t., OUT- 6 d; **outvie′** v.t., OUT- 6b; **outvoice′** v.t., OUT- 6 d; **outvote′** v.t., OUT- 6 b; **out′voter** n., OUT- 4 b.

out′ward, a., adv., & n. **1.** Outer (arch.); directed towards the outside; bodily, external, material, visible, apparent, superficial, (*the* ~ *eye,* ~ opp. *mind's eye*; ~ *form,* appearance; ~ *man* in theol., body, opp. *soul,* also joc. = clothing etc.; *to* ~ *seeming,* apparently; ~ *things,* the world around us); hence ~LY² adv. **2.** adv. = OUTWARDS (~*bound,* of ship or passenger, going away from home). **3.** n. ~ appearance; (pl.) ~ things, externals. [OE *ūtweard* (OUT, -WARD)]

out′wardness, n. External existence, objectivity; interest or belief in outward things, objective-mindedness. [-NESS]

out′wards (-z), adv. In an outward direction, towards what is outside. [-WARDS]

outwatch', v.t., see OUT- 6 b c; **outwear'** v.t., OUT- 6 c; **outweigh'** v.t., OUT- 6 b; **outwit'** v.t. (-tt-), OUT- 6 d.

‖ **out'with** (-dh), prep. (Sc.). Outside of. [f. OUT adv. + WITH]

out'work, n., see OUT- 4 b; **outwork'** v.t., OUT- 6 b; **out'worker** n., OUT- 4 b; **out'worn'** a., OUT- 2.

ouzel, -sel, (ōō'zl), n. Kinds of small bird (ring, water, brook, ~). [OE *ōsle*, = OHG *amsala*; orig. unkn.]

ova. See OVUM.

ōv'al, a. & n. 1. Egg-shaped or ellipsoidal; having the outline of an egg or elliptical; hence ~LY² adv., ~NESS n. 2. n. Closed curve with one axis considerably longer than the other, like ellipse or outline of egg; thing with ~ outline; ‖ the O~, the Surrey County cricket ground, Kennington O~ in S. London. [ME, f. med. L *ovalis* (OVUM, -AL)]

ōv'arȳ, n. Either of two reproductive organs in which ova are produced in female animals, whence **ovārīŏr'OMY**, **ōvārīt'IS**, nn.; lower part of pistil, consisting of one or more carpels, seed-vessel, germen. Hence **ovār'IAN** a., **ovārīo-** comb. form. [f. mod. L *ovarium* (OVUM, -ARY¹)]

ōv'āte, a. (nat. hist.). Egg-shaped as solid or in outline, oval. Hence **ovāt'o-** comb. form. [f. L *ovatus* (OVUM, -ATE²)]

ova'tion, n. (Rom. ant.) lesser TRIUMPH; enthusiastic reception, spontaneous applause. [f. L *ovatio* (*ovare* exult, -ATION)]

o'ven (ŭ-), n. Brick or stone or iron receptacle for baking bread or other food in (*Dutch* ~, metal box of which open side is turned towards ordinary fire); small furnace or kiln used in chemistry, metallurgy, etc.; ~-bird, kinds making domed or ~-shaped nests. [OE *ofen*, OHG *ovan*, ON *ofn*, Goth. *auhns*]

ōv'er, adv., n., a., & prep., **o'er** (ōr), adv. & prep. (poet.). 1. Outward & downward from brink or from erect position (*lean, fall, jump, knock*, etc., ~). 2. So as to cover or touch whole surface (*brush, paint, it* ~). 3. With motion above something, so as to pass across something, (*climb, look, boil*, ~). 4. So as to produce fold or reverse position, upside down, (*bend it* ~; *turn* ~, turn other side of leaf up; *turn him* ~ *on his face; roll* ~ *& ~*, so that same point comes uppermost repeatedly); (crick., as umpire's direction) change ends for bowling etc. 5. Across a street or other space or distance (*take this* ~ *to the post-office; asked him* ~, to come as visitor from some place not far off; *is* ~ *in, am going* ~ *to, America*; ~ *against*, in opposite situation to, in contrast with). 6. With transference or change from one hand, party, etc., to another (*malcontents went* ~ *to the enemy; handed* ~ *the seals; made* ~ *the balance to a charity*; GIVE¹~). 7. Too, in excess, in addition, besides, more, apart, (~ *anxious*

etc. more than is right, see OVER-; *not* ~ *well* etc., rather badly etc.; *shall have something* ~; *20 lb. &* ~; *that can stand* ~, not be dealt with now; ~ *& above*, moreover, into the bargain). 8. From beginning to end, with repetition, with detailed consideration, (*read, count*, ~; *did it six times* ~, ~ *& ~*, ~ *again*, ~ *& ~ again; talk, think, the matter* ~). 9. At an end, done with, settled, (*the struggle is* ~). 10. *All* ~, in characteristic attitude, behaviour, etc. (*that is Jones all* ~, that is what one would expect of Jones). 11. n. (crick.). Number of balls (orig. 4 or 5, later 6 or 8) allowed between two calls of ~ (sense 4); the play that results; MAIDEN ~. 12. adj. Upper, outer, superior, excessive, (usu. written as one word with n., see OVER-). 13. prep. Above, on, at all or various points upon, to & fro upon, all through, round about, concerning, engaged with, (*a* ~ *b*, i.e. *a/b*, = *c*; *an umbrella* ~ *his head; projects* ~ *the street; doubt hangs* ~ *the question*; ~ *our heads*, beyond our comprehension, also without consulting us; HAND¹ ~ *hand; writing* ~ *the signature X.*; ~ *head & ears*, completely immersed lit. & fig.; ~ *shoes* ~ *boots*, no half measures; *with his hat* ~ *his eyes; draw a veil* ~ *it; a change came* ~ *him; blush spread* ~ *his face; rice is grown all* ~ *India; you may travel* ~ *Europe or Europe* ~; *all the world* ~, in all countries etc.; *went* ~ *his notes; sitting* ~ *the fire, a cheerful glass*, etc.; *pause* ~ *the details; laugh* ~ *the absurdity of it; go to sleep* ~ *one's work); all* ~ (sl.), infatuated with (a person); ~ *all*, from end to end (in attrib. use ~-*all; an* ~-*all length of 200 ft*); see also OVERALL. 14. With or so as to get or give superiority to, beyond, more than, (*is king, reigns, has jurisdiction*, ~ *twenty millions; was victor, won the victory, was victorious*, ~; *set him* ~ *the rest; has no command* ~ *herself; give me the preference* ~ *him; cost* = £50; ~ *& above*, besides, not to mention). 15. Out & down from, down from edge of, so as to clear, across, on or to the other side of, throughout, through duration of, till end of, (*fell* ~ *the edge, precipice; stumble* ~, be tripped up by; *jumped* ~ *the brook*; ~ *the bags or top*, of troops emerging from trench to attack; *looking* ~ *the hedge; spoke* ~ *her shoulder; coursing* ~ *the plain; a pass* ~ *the company's line; the house* ~ *the way*, opposite; *the King* ~ *the water*, Jacobite phr. for exiled king; *if we can tide* ~ *the next month; payments spread* ~ *a series of years; will not live* ~ *today; can you stay* ~ *Wednesday?*). Hence ~LY² adv. (chiefly U.S. & Sc.), excessively, too. [OE *ofer*, OS *obar*, OHG *ubar*, ON *yfir*, Goth. *ufar*, cogn. w. Gk *huper*, Skr. *upari* f. *up-* (whence Gmc *°uf-* in ABOVE) with compar. term.]

ōv'er-, pref. = prec. Unless otherwise shown stress is on first part of compound.

1. Used as adj. in agreement with second part of compound, = upper, outer, of higher kind, upside down, extra, to or in higher position. So ~*arm* a. & adv., = ~*hand*; ~*coat*, worn outside another; ~*dress*, outer part of gown made to resemble one dress worn over & showing parts of another of different colour etc.; ~*fault* (geol.), reverse fault with inclination towards upthrow side; ~*fold* (geol.), fold of strata so complete that middle part is upside down; ~*hand* a. & adv., with hand above object held, with hand above shoulder (~*hand bowling*; *bowls* ~*hand*), out of water (~*hand stroke* in swimming), etc.; ~*lord*, supreme lord, suzerain, whence ~*lord's*SHIP n.; ~*man*, mining ~*seer*, an underground foreman, (philos., also *superman*) the ideal man, beyond good & evil, or superior to moral restrictions, of Nietzsche's philosophy; ~*plus*, surplus, superabundance; ‖ ~*shoe*, of rubber or felt worn outside another; ~*sleeve*, *for* pulling on over sleeve to protect it; ~*soul*, God as animating the universe & including all human souls; ~*thrust* (geol.), thrust of strata on one side over those of other side of fault; ~*time*, during which workman works beyond regular hours; ~*tone* n. (mus.), upper PARTIALS; ~*weight*, preponderance, excessive weight.

2. As prep. governing second component & making with it n., a., or adv. So ~*all* n., woman's loose work-garment, (pl.) outer trousers or leggings or combination suit for dirty work, ‖ (mil., pl.) officer's full-dress tight trousers; ~*board* adv., from within ship into water (usu. *fall*, *throw*, ~*board*; throw ~*board*, fig., abandon, discard); ~*door* n., ornamental woodwork above door; ~*front* n., armflap of Inverness cape etc.; ~*ground* a., raised above ground, not underground; ~*head'* adv., on high, in the sky, in the storey above; ~*head* a., placed ~head (esp. ~*head wires*; ~*head charges* etc., commerc., those due to office expenses, management, interest on capital, & other general needs of a business); ~*house* a., (of wires) supported on housetops instead of poles; ~*knee* a., reaching above knee; ~*land'* adv., by land & not sea; ~*land* a., entirely or partly by land (esp. of route by Mediterranean to India, or from Atlantic to Pacific across continent); ~*leaf'* adv., on other side of leaf (of book); ~*mantel* n., ornamental shelves etc. over mantelpiece; ~*night'* adv., on the preceding evening with a view to, or as regarded from, the next day; ~*night* a., done etc. ~night; ~*proof* a., containing more alcohol than proof spirit; ~*sea(s)'* adv., ~*sea(s)* a., across or beyond sea; ~*side'* adv., ~*side* a., (of loading & unloading ship) over the side into or out of lighters; ~*time'* adv., beyond regular hours of work; ~*weigh'* a., beyond weight allowed (esp. ~*weight luggage*).

3. As prep. prefixed to vbs, but itself governing case independently, often with specialized sense; also in abs. uses of, or in derivatives from, such vbs. So ~*brim'* v.t. & i. (*water* ~*brimmed the cup*; also said of the vessel); ~*come'* v.t. & i., prevail over, master, get the better of, be victorious, (p.p.) exhausted, made helpless, deprived of self-possession, (*with* or *by* emotion etc.; ~*come with liquor*, drunk); ~*crow'* v.t., exult or triumph over (rival), outswagger; ~*flow* n., what ~flows or is superfluous (~*flow meeting*, of those who have not found room at a demonstration etc. & ˙meet elsewhere); ~*flow'* v.t. & i., flow over (brim etc.), flood (surface), (fig., of crowd etc.) extend beyond limits of (room etc.), (of receptacle etc.) be so full that contents~flow, (of kindness, harvest, etc.) be very abundant, whence ~*flow*ING[1,2] a. & n. (esp. *full to* ~*flowing*), ~*flow'ing*LY[2] adv.; ~*grow'* v.t. (of creeping plants); ~*growth* n., plants that have grown over anything, (fig.) accretion; ~*hang'* v.t. & i. (-*hung*), jut out over, jut out, (fig.) impend over, impend; so ~*hang* n., fact or amount of ~hanging; ~*lap'* v.t., partly cover, cover & extend beyond, (reciprocally of pl. subj.) partly coincide (*the great difficulty in classification is the* ~*lapping of species*); ~*lap* n., fact or process of ~lapping, ~lapping part; ~*leap'* v.t., leap over, surmount, omit, ignore; ~*lie'* v.t., lie on top of, smother (child) thus; ~*look'* v.t., have prospect of or over from above, be higher than, fail to observe, take no notice of, condone, superintend, ~see, bewitch with the evil eye; ~*pass'* v.t. & i., pass over, across, beyond, etc., get to the end of, surmount, surpass; ~*ride'* v.t., ride over (enemy's country) with armed force, trample (person) under one's horse's hoofs, (fig.) trample under foot, set aside, refuse to comply with, have or claim superior authority to (~*riding clause*, *authority*), (surg., of fractured bone) ~lap; ~*run*, v.t., flood, harry & spoil (enemy's country), (of vermin, weeds, etc.) swarm or spread over, exceed (limit); ~*sail'ing*, (of masonry course etc.) projecting beyond the one below; ~*see'* v.t. look at from above (rare), superintend or look after (workmen, execution of work, etc.), whence ~*seer* (-sēr) n. (‖ ~*seer of the poor*, hist., parish officer charged with poor-relief & other duties); ~*shoot'* v.t., send missile, go, beyond (mark etc. lit. & fig.; ~*shoot the mark*, also ~*shoot oneself*, go too far, exaggerate, ~do something; ~*shot wheel*, turned by water flowing above it); ~*sight* n., supervision, omission to notice, mistake of inadvertence; ~*spread'* v.t., become diffused over, cover or occupy surface of; ~*step'* v.t., pass beyond (boundary lit. or fig.).

4. As adverb in local senses (*above, by way of cover, down from above or from* *erectness, past, beyond, in addition*) modifying vb or derived n. without itself governing object. So ~*arch'* v.t. & i.; ~*bal'ance* v.i. & t., lose balance & fall, cause to do this; ~*bear'* v.t., bear down or upset by weight or force, put down or repress by power or authority, surpass in importance etc., outweigh; ~*bear'ing* a., domineering, masterful, whence ~*bear‑ingly*[2] adv., ~*bear'ing*NESS n.; ~*blown'* p.p., (of storm etc.) passed; ~*can'opy* v.t.; ~*cloud'* v.t.; ~*crust'* v.t.; ~*fall* n., turbulent stretch of sea etc. caused by set of tide or current over submarine ledge or meeting of currents, ~*flow* opening to keep water of lock or canal up or down to required level; ~*film'* v.t.; ~*gild'* v.t.; ~*haul'* v.t., pull to pieces for purposes of examining, examine condition of, (esp. naut.) catch up, come up with; ~*haul* n., thorough examination, esp. with a view to repairs; ~*hear'* v t., hear as an eavesdropper or as an unperceived or unintentional listener; ~*lay'* v.t., cover surface of *with* coating etc., (incorrectly) ~*lie*; ~*lay* n., thing laid over something, coverlet, small tablecloth, etc.; ~*passed'*, -*past'*, a., gone by, past; ~*sew* v.t., sew (two edges) with every stitch passing in same direction through both, the inter-stitch parts of thread lying across & outside united edge; ~*shad'ow* v.t., shelter from sun, protect from attack (rare), cast into the shade, diminish conspicuousness of by outshining; ~*spill* n., what is spilt, surplus population etc.; ~*spread'* v.t., cover *with* (chiefly Pass.; *heaven was* ~*spread with clouds*); ~*strung* a., (of piano) with strings in sets crossing each other obliquely; ~*take'* v.t., come up with, catch up, catch up and pass, (person etc. who has start, or arrears of work), (of storm, misfortune, etc.) come suddenly upon (~*taken in drink*, drunk); ~*throw'* v.t., upset, knock down, cast out from power, vanquish, subvert, put an end to (institution etc.); ~*throw* n., defeat, subversion, (crick.) fielder's return not stopped near wicket & so allowing further run(s); ~*turn'* v.t. & i., upset, (cause to) fall down or over. ~*throw*, subvert, abolish; ~*turn* n., upsetting, revolution; ~*whelm'* v.t., bury beneath superincumbent mass, submerge utterly, crush, bring to sudden ruin, overpower with emotion etc., deluge *with* inquiries etc.; ~*whel'ming* a., irresistible by numbers, amount, etc., whence ~*whel'mingly*[2] adv.

5. As adv. with trans. vb, adding sense of *effectually, completely, into submission.* So ~*awe'* v.t.; ~*cloy'* v.t.; ~*joyed'* p.p., transported with joy (*at*); ~*mas'ter* v.t.; ~*persuade'* v.t., persuade in spite of reluctance or better judgement.

6. As adv. or adj. prefixed to vb, adj., adv., or n., adding notion of excess over the desirable, the truth, or a definite

limit. So ~-*abound'* v.i.; ~-*abun'dant* a.; ~-*abun'dantly* adv.; ~-*abun'dance* n.; ~*act'* v.t. & i., act (part, emotion, etc.), act part, with exaggeration; ~-*ac'tive* a.; ~*activ'ity* n.; ~-*anx'ious* a.; ~-*anx'iously* adv.; ~-*anxi'ety* n.; ~*bid'* v.t. (bridge), make a higher bid than (one's partner), bid more on (one's hand) than it is worth, so ~*bid* n.; ~*blow'* v.t. (mus.), blow (pipe etc.) with such force as to produce harmonic instead of fundamental note; ~*blown'* a., (of flowers) too fully open, past prime, also fig. of female beauty; ~*bold'* a.; ~*burd'en* v.t., & n.; ~*burd'ensome* a.; ~*bu'sy* a., too much occupied, officious; ~*buy'* v.i., buy more than enough to meet demand; ~*call'* v.t. (bridge), = ~*bid*; ~*call* n.; ~-*cap'italize* v.t., fix or estimate capital of (company etc.) too high; ~-*care'* n.; ~-*care'ful* a.; ~-*cau'tion* n.; ~-*cau'tious* a.; ~-*cau'tiously* adv.; ~*charge'* v.t., put too much explosive or electricity or the like into, put exaggerated details or too much detail into (description, picture, etc.), charge too high a price for (thing) or to (person), charge (specified sum) beyond right price; ~*charge* n. excessive charge (of explosive, or in money, see prec.); ~-*col'our* v.t., exaggerate (details of description etc.); ~-*con'fident* a.; ~-*con'fidently* adv.; ~-*con'fidence* n.; ~-*cred'ulous* a.; ~-*credul'ity* n.; ~*crop'* v.t., exhaust (land) by continuous cropping; ~*crowd'* v.t.; ~-*cunn'ing* n., cunning that ~ reaches itself; ~-*cur'ious* a., too inquisitive, too careful or precise or fastidious; ~-*cur'iously* adv.; ~-*curios'ity* n.; ~-*del'icacy* n.; ~-*del'icate* a.; ~-*devel'op* v.t. (photog.); ~*do'* v.t., carry to excess, go too far in, cook too much (esp. in p.p.), overtax strength of; ~*dose'* v.t.; ~*dose* n.; ~*draft* n.; ~drawing of bank account, amount by which draft exceeds balance; ~*draw'* v.t. & i., draw cheque in excess of (one's account) or in excess of one's account, exaggerate in describing; ~*dress'* v.t. & i.; ~*drive'* v.t., drive (horse etc.), work (person), to exhaustion; ~-*eag'er* a.; ~-*eag'erly* adv.; ~-*eag'erness* n.; ~-*earn'est* a.; ~-*es'timāte* v.t., put value or amount of too high; ~-*es'timate* (-at) n.; ~-*excite'* v.t.; ~-*exer'tion* n.; ~-*expose'* v.t., ~-*expo'sure* n. (photog.); ~-*fatigue'* v.t., & n.; ~*fish,'* v.t., fish (stream etc.) to depletion; ~*fond'* a.; ~-*fulfil'ment* n., completion of a Soviet five-year plan before the appointed time; ~-*go'vern* v.t., subject to needless restrictions &• regulations; ~-*go'vernment* n.; ~*growth'* n., growth too great for health etc., ~-*haste'* n., ~-*has'ty* a., ~-*has'tily* adv.; ~-*heat'* v.t., ~*housed'* (-zd) a., living in too large a house, ~-*indulge'* v.t. & i., ~-*indul'gence* n. ~-*iss'ue* v.t., issue (notes, shares, etc.) beyond authorized amount or ability to pay ~-*iss'ue* n. things or amount so issued; ~*lab'our* v.t., elaborate to excess; ~*lad'en* a.; ~*large'* a.; ~*load'* v.t.; ~*load* n.; ~*long'* a.; ~*ma'ny* a.; ~*mast'ed* a., with too tall or heavy masts; ~*mea'sure* n., amount beyond the due or sufficient; ~*mod'est* a.; ~*much'* a., n., & adv. (*be not righteous* ~*much*); ~*nice'* a., too fastidious; ~*nice'ness*, ~*ni'cety*, nn.; ~*pay'* v.t., recompense (person, service) too highly; ~*peo'pled* a., ~stocked with people; ~*pitch'* v.t., bowl (cricket ball) so that it pitches too near wicket; ~*pop'ulated* a., too thickly populated; ~*popula'tion* n., ~populated condition; ~*pot'* v.t., plant in too large a pot; ~*praise'* v.t., & n.; ~*pre'ssure* n., pressing or being pressed too hard, esp. ~work; ~*print'* v.t. (photog.), also, print additional matter on (an already printed surface, esp. of postage stamps); ~:*produce'* v.i. & t., produce too much of (commodity, or usu. abs.) for the demand; ~*produc'tion* n.; ~*pun'ish* v.t.; ~*rate'* v.t., have too high an opinion of, assess too high for rating purposes; ~*read'* v.i., do too much reading; ~*refine'* v.i., make too subtle distinctions; ~*ride'* v.t., exhaust (horse) by riding; ~*ripe* a.; ~*scrup'ulous* a.; ~*sell'* v.t. & i., sell more of (commodity, stock, or abs.) than one can deliver; ~*sen'sitive* a.; ~*sen'sitiveness* n.; ~*soli'citous* a.; ~*soli'citude* n.; ~*stale'* v.t., state too strongly, exaggerate; ~*state'ment* n.; ~*stock'* v.t.; ~*stock* n.; ~*strain'* v.t., damage by exertion, make too much of (scruples etc.; esp. in p.p.); ~*strain* n., ~straining or being ~strained; ~*strung'* a., (of person, his nerves, etc.) intensely strained or wound up; ~*stud'y* v.i., & n.; ~*su'btle* a.; ~*supply'* n.; ~*swoll'en* a.; ~*task'* v.t., give or be too heavy a task to or for; ~*tax'* v.t., make excessive demand on (person's strength etc.), burden with excessive taxes; ~*tire'* v.t.; ~*toil'* n.; ~*tone'* v.t. (photog.); ~*train'* v.t. & i., subject to or undergo too much athletic training, with injury to condition; ~*use'* v.t.; ~*use* n.; ~*val'ue* v.t.; ~*ween'ing* a., arrogant, presumptuous, conceited, self-confident; ~*weight'ed* a., unduly loaded *with*; ~*wind'* v.t., wind (watch etc.) beyond proper stopping-point; ~*work'* v.t. & i., (cause to) work too hard, weary or exhaust with work; ~*work'* n., excessive work; ~*wrought'* a., ~excited, suffering reaction from excitement, too elaborate; ~*zeal'* n.; ~*zea'lous* a.; ~*zea'lously* adv.

7. Prefixed to vb & enabling it to take *self* as obj., or be used in p.p., with sense *damage oneself by doing action to excess*; many of these compounds can also be used abs. in same sense. So ~*drink'*, ~*eat'*, ~*feed'* (also trans.), ~*grow'* (in p.p., that has ~grown himself etc.); ~*jump'* oneself, strain sinew etc. in jumping; ~*preach'*; ~*reach'* oneself, strain oneself

by reaching too far, defeat one's object by going too far, (of horse) injure forefoot by striking it with hind-hoof; ~*run'*; ~*sleep'* oneself, miss intended hour of rising by sleeping too long, also v.i.; ~*smoke'*; ~*spend'* (oneself or abs.), spend money beyond one's means; ~*toiled'* p.p.; ~*walk'*; ~*watched'* p.p., exhausted by keeping awake; ~*write'* oneself, damage one's work by writing too much.

8. Prefixed to vb or deriv., or adj., with added sense of *more than*. So ~*bal'ance* v.t., outweigh lit. & fig.; ~*balance* n., (amount of) excess; ~*due'* a.; ~*fill'* v.t.; ~*full'* a.; ~*match'* v.t., be too strong etc. for, defeat; ~*match* n.; ~*poise'* v.t., outweigh; ~*subscribe'* v.t., subscribe more than amount of (loan etc.; usu. in p.p.).

9. As prefix making trans. vb out of intr. vb, or vb not taking same obj., or n, usu. with sense of *exceeding*. So ~*build'*, build too closely on (land); ~*cast'*, cover (sky etc.) with clouds or darkness (usu. p.p.), stitch over (edge) to prevent unravelling, esp. with blanket or button-hole stitch; ~*live'*, live beyond (other person, specified age, etc.); ~*pow'er*, reduce to submission, subdue, master, make (thing) ineffective or imperceptible by greater intensity, (of heat, emotion, etc.) be too intense for, ~whelm; ~*pow'ering*, a., irresistible; ~*pow'eringly* adv.; ~*reach'*, circumvent, outwit, get the better of by cunning or artifice; ~*rent'*, charge too high a rent for (land etc.) or to (farmer etc.); ~*rule'*, set aside (decision, argument, proposed course) by superior authority, annul decision or reject proposal of (person); ~*stay'*, stay beyond (one's welcome etc.); ~*top'*, be or become higher than; ~*trump'*. play higher trump than.

overact, v.t. & i., see OVER- 6; **overall** n., OVER- 2; **overarch** /.t. & i., OVER- 4; **overarm** a. & adv., OVER- 1; **overawe** v.t., OVER- 5; **overbalance** v.i. & t., & n., OVER- 4, 8; **overbear** v.t., **overbearing** a., OVER- 4; **overbid** v.t. & n., **overblow** v.t., OVER- 6; **overblown** a., OVER- 4, 6; **overboard** adv., OVER- 2; **overbrim** v.t. & i., OVER- 3; **overbuild** v.t., OVER- 9; **overburden** v.t., **overbusy** a., **overbuy** v.i., **overcall** v.t., & ɔ., OVER- 6; **over-canopy** v.t., OVER- 4; **over-capitalize** v.t., **overcare** n., OVER- 6; **overcast** v.t., OVER- 9; **over-caution** n., **overcharge** v.t., & n., OVER- 6; **overcloud** v.t., **overcloy** v.t., OVER- 5; **overcoat** n., OVER- 1; **over-colour** v.t., OVER- 6; **overcome** v.t., OVER- 3; **over-confidence** n., **over-credulity** n., **overcrop** v.t., OVER- 6; **overcrow** v.t., OVER- 3; **overcrowd** v.t., OVER- 6; **overcrust** v.t., OVER- 4; **overcunning** n., **over-curious** a., **over-delicacy** n., **over-develop** v.t., **overdo** v.t., OVER- 6; **overdoor** n., OVER- 2; **overdose** v.t. & n., **overdraft** n.,

overdraw v.t. & i., OVER- 6; **overdress** n. OVER- 1, v.i. OVER- 6; **overdrink** v. refl. & i., OVER- 7; **overdrive** v.t., OVER- 6; **overdue** a., OVER- 8; **overeat** v. refl. & i., OVER- 7; **over-estimate** v.t., & n., over--expose v.t., over-exposure n., OVER- 6; **overfall** n., OVER- 4; **over-fatigue** v.t., & n., OVER- 6; **overfault** n., OVER- 1; **overfeed** v.t. & i., OVER- 7; **overfill** v.t., OVER- 8; **overfilm** v.t., OVER- 4; **overfish** v.t., OVER- 6; **overflow** v.t. & i., & n., **overflowing** n. & a., OVER- 3; **overfold** n., OVER- 1; **overfront** n., OVER- 2; **over--fulfilment** n., OVER- 6; **overfull** a., OVER- 8; **overgild** v.t., OVER- 4; **over-govern** v.t., **over-government** n., OVER- 6; **overground** a., OVER- 2; **overgrow** v.t. OVER- 3, v. refl. & i. OVER- 7; **overgrowth** n., OVER- 3, 6; **overhand** adv. & a., OVER- 1; **overhang** v.t. & i., & n., OVER- 3; **overhaul** v.t., & n., OVER- 4; **overhead** adv. & a., OVER- 2; **overhear** v.t., OVER- 4; **overhouse** a., OVER- 2; **overhoused** a., **over-indulgence** n., **over-issue** v.t., & n., OVER- 6; **overjoyed** a., OVER- 5; **overjump** v. refl., OVER- 7; **overknee** a., OVER- 2; **overlabour** v.t., **overladen** a., OVER- 6; **overland** adv. & a., OVER- 2; **overlap** v.t. & i., & n., OVER- 3; **overlay** v.t., & n., OVER- 4; **overleaf** adv., OVER- 2; **overleap** v.t., **overlie** v.t., OVER- 3; **overlive** v.t., OVER- 9; **overload** v.t., & n., OVER- 6; **overlook** v.t., OVER- 3; **overlord, overlordship, overman, nn.**, OVER- 1; **overmantel** n., OVER- 2; **over-many, overmasted, aa.**, OVER- 6; **over-master** v.t., OVER- 5; **over-match** v.t., & n., OVER- 8; **over-measure** n., **overmuch** a., adv., & n., **over-nice** a., **over-niceness, over-nicety, nn.**, OVER- 6; **overnight** adv. & a., OVER- 2; **over-pass** v.t., OVER- 3; **overpassed, -past, a.**, OVER- 4; **overpay** v.t., **overpeopled** a., OVER- 6; **over-persuade** v.t., OVER- 5; **overpitch** v.t., OVER- 6; **overplus** n., OVER- 1; **overpoise** v.t., OVER- 8; **over-population** n., **overpot** v.t., OVER- 6; **overpower** v.t., **overpowering** a., OVER- 9; **overpraise** v.t., & n., OVER- 6; **over-preach** v. refl. & i., OVER- 7; **overpressure** n., **overprint** v.t., **over-produce** v.t. & i., **over-production** n., OVER- 6; **overproof** a., OVER- 2; **overrate** v.t., OVER- 6; **overreach** v. refl. & i. OVER- 7, v.t. OVER- 9; **over-read** v.i., **over-refine** v.i., OVER- 6; **over-rent** v.t., OVER- 9; **override** v.t., OVER- 3, 6; **overripe** a., OVER- 6; **overrule** v.t., OVER- 9; **overrun** v.t., OVER- 3, 7; **oversailing** a., OVER- 3; **oversea** a., & adv., **overseas** a. & adv., OVER- 2; **oversee** v.t., **overseer** n., OVER- 3; **oversell** v.i. & t., OVER- 6; **oversew** v.t., OVER- 4; **overshadow** v.t., OVER- 4; **overshoe** n., OVER- 1; **overshoot** v.t., **overshot** a., OVER- 3; **overside** adv. & a., OVER- 2; **oversight** n., OVER- 3.

‖ **ŏv′erslaugh** (-aw), n. (mil.). Passing over of one's turn of duty in consideration of another duty that takes precedence of it. [f. Du. *overslag* (*overslaan* omit f. OVER, *slaan* strike)]

oversleep, v. refl. & i., see OVER- 7; **oversleeve** n., OVER- 1; **oversmoke** v. refl. & i., OVER- 7; **oversoul** n., OVER- 1; **overspend** v. refl. & i., OVER- 7; **overspill** n., OVER- 4; **overspread** v.t., OVER- 3, 4; **overstate** v.t., **overstatement** n., OVER- 6; **overstay** v.t., OVER- 9; **overstep** v.t., OVER- 3; **overstock** v.t., & n., **overstrain** v.t., & n., OVER- 6; **overstrung** a., OVER- 4, 6; **overstudy** v. i., & n., OVER- 6; **oversubscribe** v.t., OVER- 8; **over-supply** n., **overswollen** a., OVER- 6.

ōv′ert, a. Openly done, unconcealed, patent; *market ~*, open displaying of goods for sale to all comers. Hence **~LY²** adv. [ME, f. OF, p.p. of *ovrir* (now *ouvrir*)]

overtake, v.t., see OVER- 4; **overtask** v.t., **overtax** v.t., OVER- 6; **overthrow** v.t., & n., OVER- 4; **overthrust** n., OVER- 1; **overtime** adv. OVER- 2, n. OVER- 1; **overtire** v.t., OVER- 6; **overtoil** n., OVER- 6; **overtoiled** a., OVER- 7; **overtone** v.t., OVER- 6; **overtone** n., OVER- 1; **overtop** v.t., OVER- 6; **overtrain** v.t. & i., OVER- 6; **overtrump** v.t., OVER- 9.

ōv′erture, n. Opening of negotiations with another, formal proposal or offer, (usu. pl., esp. *make ~s to*); (mus.) orchestral piece opening opera, oratorio, etc. (*concert ~*, one-movement composition in same style); beginning of poem etc. [ME, f. OF, f. L *apertura* APERTURE]

overturn, v.t. & i., & n., see OVER- 4; **over-use** v.t., & n., **overvalue** v.t., OVER- 6; **overwalk** v. refl. & i., **over-watched** a., OVER- 7; **overweening** a., OVER- 6; **overweight** n. OVER- 1, adj. OVER- 2; **overweighted** a., OVER- 6; **overwhelm** v.t., **overwhelming** a., OVER- 4; **overwind** v.t., **overwork** v.t. & i., & n., OVER- 6; **overwrite** v. refl. & i., OVER- 7; **overwrought** a., OVER- 6.

ōvi-¹, comb. form of OVUM; **ov′iduct** n., canal through which ova pass from ovary esp. in oviparous animals; **ov′iform** a., egg-shaped; **ovip′arous** a., producing young by means of eggs expelled from body before being hatched (opp. VIVIPAROUS); **ovipŏs′it** (-z-) v.i., lay egg(s), esp. with *ovipŏs′itor* n., pointed tubular organ with which female insect deposits eggs; **ovorhomboid′al** etc., between rhomboid etc. & oval; **ovŏl′ogy** n., science of the formation of animals' ova; **ovovivip′arous** a., producing young by eggs hatched within body.

ōvi-², comb. form of L *ovis* sheep; **~bōv′ine** a. & n., (animal) having characters intermediate between sheep & ox, musk-ox; **ov′icide** n. (joc.), sheep-killing.

Ovid′ian, a. (As) of Ovid or his poetry. [L *Ovidius* Ovid, -IAN]

ōv′ine, a. Of, like, sheep. [f. LL *ovinus* (*ovis* sheep, -INE¹)]

ōvo-, irreg. f. OVI-[1] (see -O-).

ōv′oid, a. & n. **1.** Solidly or superficially egg-shaped, oval with one end more pointed. **2.** n. ~ body or surface. [f. F *ovoïde* (OVUM, -OID)]

ōv′olō, n. (pl. *-li* pr. -lē). Convex moulding of quarter-circle or quarter-ellipse section, receding downwards. [It. (now *uovolo*), dim. of *uovo* egg f. L OVUM]

ōv′ūle, n. Rudimentary seed, female germ-cell, unfertilized ovum. Hence **ōv′ūlAR**[1] a. [F (foll., -ULE)]

ōv′um, n. (pl. *ova*). Female germ in animals, capable of developing into new individual when fertilized by male sperm, egg esp. of mammals, fish, or insects. [L, = egg]

ow, int. expr. sudden pain.

owe (ō), v.t. & i. (*owing*). Be under obligation to (re)pay (person money, money *to* person, money) or render (person honour etc., gratitude etc. *to* person), be in debt (*for* thing, with creditor in dat.; *he ~s not any man*; *I ~ you for your services*, *~d for all my clothes*); ~ one a grudge, cherish resentment against him; be indebted for *to* person (or with dat.; *we ~ to Newton the principle of gravitation*; *I ~ him much*). [a preterite-present vb like CAN, DARE, MAY: OE *āgan* (see OUGHT[2]), OS *ēgan*, OHG *eigan*, ON *eiga*, Goth. *aigan* f. Gmc *aig-*]

Ow′enism (ō-), n. Communistic co-operation advocated by Robert Owen (d. 1858). [-ISM]

ow′ing (ōī-), pred. a. Yet to be paid, owed, due, (*paid all that was ~*); ~ *to*, attributable to, caused by, (*all this was ~ merely to ill luck*), (as prep.) on account of (*~ to the drought, crops are short*). [OWE, -ING[2]]

owl, n. Kinds of large-headed hook-beaked large-eyed soft-plumaged nocturnal bird of prey (esp. *barn ~*, *tawny ~*, & *long-eared* or *horned ~*, each with other names, as *church*, *screech*, *hooting*, etc., ~; *fly with the ~*, have nocturnal habits; *~s to Athens*, = COAL[1]*s to Newcastle*); solemn person, wise-looking dullard, whence ~′ISH[1] a., ~′ISHLY[2] adv.; (also ~ *pigeon*) fancy variety of pigeon; ~-*light*, dusk, twilight. Hence ~′ERY(3) n. [OE *ūle*, OLG *ūla*, ON *ugla*, f. Gmc *ūwwalōn*, cf. OHG *ūwila*; ult. imit., cf. L *ulula*]

owl′et, n. Owl, young owl. [earlier HOWLET]

own[1] (ōn), a. **1.** (Appended to possessive adj. or case) in full ownership, proper, peculiar, individual, & not another's, (*saw it with my ~ eyes*; *has a value all its ~*; *let them STEW*[2] *in their ~ juice*; *loves truth for its ~ sake*; *be one's ~ man*, independent, free; *God's ~ heaven*; *may I have it for my ~* or *my very ~?*; *my ~ sweetheart* etc., or abs. *my ~*, esp. in voc. expressing affection; often also used to emphasize not the ownership; but the personality of the subject etc., as *cooks*

her ~ meals, every man his ~ lawyer, am my ~ master; also used abs. = private property, kindred, etc., as *may I not do what I will with my ~?*, the DEVIL[1]*'s ~*; *of one's ~*, belonging to one, as *I have nothing of my ~*, *will give you one of my ~*; *get one's ~ back*, colloq., get even with, revenge oneself (*on*); *hold one's ~*, maintain position, not be defeated; *on one's ~*, independently, on one's ~ account or responsibility or resources). **2.** (Without preceding possessive) ~ *brother*, *sister*, with both parents the same; ~ *cousin*, first. [OE *ǣgen*, *āgen*, OS *ēgan*, OHG *eigan*, ON *eiginn* f. Gmc *aiganaz* f. p.p. of *aigan* possess; see OWE]

own[2] (ōn), v.t. & i. Have as property, possess, whence **ow′nER**[1], **ow′ner**SHIP(1), nn., **ow′ner**LESS a., (ōn-); acknowledge authorship, paternity, or possession, of (*child, pamphlet, hat, that nobody will ~*); admit as existent, valid, true, etc. (*~s his deficiencies, himself indebted, he or that he did not know*); confess to (*~s to a sense of shame, to having done*); ~ *up*, colloq., make frank confession; submit to (person's sway etc.) without protest; *the ~er* (nav. sl.), captain of the ship. [OE *āgnian* f. *āgen* OWN[1])]

ox, n. (pl. *oxen*). **1.** Any bovine animal, individual of kinds of large usu. horned cloven-footed ruminant used when domesticated for draught, for supplying milk, and for eating as meat, (esp.) castrated male of domestic species, (*the black ox has trod on one's foot*, misfortune or old age has come upon him); *ox-bird*, kinds of small bird, esp. the dunlin. **2.** *Ox-eye*, large human eye, whence **ox-eyED**[2] (-īd) a., kinds of plant esp. (*yellow ox-eye*) corn marigold, (*white ox-eye*) ox-eyed daisy; *ox-fence* or **ox′ER**[1] n., strong cattle-fence of railing & hedge & occas. ditch; *ox-gall* (used for cleansing, & in painting & pharmacy); *ox′herd*, cowherd; *ox′hide*; *ox′lip*, prinula, (pop.) hybrid of primrose & cowslip; *ox′tail*, tail of ox, much used for soup-making. [OE *oxa*, OS, OHG *ohso*, ON *uxi*, *oxi*, Goth. *auhsa* f. Gmc *ohsan-*, cogn. w. Skr. *ukshan*]

ox-, comb. form (chem.) = OXY-, as *oxacet′ic* or *oxyacet′ic*, or = OXAL-, as *oxam′ic*.

ōxal(o)-, comb. form of *oxalic acid*, whence **ōx′al**ATE[1](3) n.; *oxalo-nit′rate* etc.

ōxal′ic, a. (chem.). Derived from wood-sorrel (*~ acid*, a highly poisonous & sour acid found in wood-sorrel & other plants). [f. F *oxalique* (L f. Gk *oxalis* kinds of plant including wood-sorrel, -IC)]

Ox′bridge (ō-), n. Name for a university of ancient foundation. [*Ox(ford)*, (*Cam*)*bridge*]

Ox′ford (ō-), n. University town in England; ||~ *bags*, very wide trousers; ~ *blue* (dark with purple tinge); ~ *clay*, deposit of stiff blue clay underlying coral rag in midland counties; ||~ *frame*, picture-frame of which sides cross each other at corners & project ;~ *Group* (*Movement*), see BUCHMANISM; ~ *movement*, for revival of Catholic doctrine & observance in Church of England begun *c.* 1833; ~ *shirting*, kind of shirt or dress material; ~ *shoes*, low shoes lacing over instep; ~ *Tracts*, the ' TRACT²s for the Times '.

ŏx′idāte, v.t. & i. Oxidize. Hence **ŏxidA′TION** n., oxidizing or being oxidized. [f. F *oxider*, -ATE³]

ŏx′ide, n. Compound of oxygen with another element or with organic radical. [F, f. *oxygène* + -*ide*, after *acide*; see OXY-, -IDE]

ŏx′idiz|e, -is|e (-ĭz), v.t. & i. Cause to combine with oxygen; cover (metal) with coating of oxide, make rusty; take up or enter into combination with oxygen, rust; ~*ed silver*, (incorrect name for) silver with dark coat of silver sulphide. Hence ~ABLE a., ~A′TION, ~ER¹(2), nn. [prec., -IZE]

Oxōn′ian (ŏ-), a. & n. (Member) of University of Oxford; (citizen) of Oxford. [*Oxonia* latinized name of *Ox*(*en*)*ford*,-AN] || **ŏx′ter**, n., & v.t. (Sc.). 1. Armpit; inner side of upper arm. 2. v.t. Support with or by taking the arm, put under the arm; hug. [f. OE *ōhsta*, *ōxta*]

ŏxy-, comb. form of Gk *oxus* sharp: (1) in gen. senses, as ~*carp′ous*, with pointed fruit; ~*ŏp′ia*, abnormal keenness of vision; OXYGEN; OXYMORON; OXYTONE; (2) in chem. wds as comb. form of *oxygen*, (a) denoting presence or admixture of oxygen; ~-*acet′ylene*, consisting of, involving use of, a mixture of oxygen & acetylene (~-*acetylene blowpipe*, for producing intensely hot flame for welding etc.); ~-*house²gas*, ~-*pa′raffin*, etc., used attrib. of flame produced by mixing the vapour of the gas etc. with oxygen; ~-*cal′cium light*, limelight; ~-*hyd′rogen blowpipe, flame, light*, etc.; ~*a′cid* (& see b.); *ox′ysalt*, containing oxygen; (b) loosely used for *hydroxy-*, denoting compound of organic substance having atom of hydroxyl substituted for one of hydrogen, as ~*a′cid* (& see a.).

ŏx′ȳgĕn, n. Colourless tasteless scentless gas, one of the non-metallic elements, existing in air & combined in water & most minerals & organic substances, & being essential to animal & vegetable life. Hence **ŏxȳ′gĕnous** a. [f. F *oxygène* acidifying principle, see OXY-(2), -GEN; it was at first held to be the essential principle in formation of acids]

ŏx′ȳgĕn|āte (or ŏksĭ²), v.t. Supply, treat, or mix, with oxygen, oxidize; charge (blood) with oxygen by respiration. So ~ANT(2), ~A′TION, nn. [f. F *oxygéner* (prec.), -ATE³]

ŏx′ȳgĕnīze (or ŏksĭ²), -ise (-ĭz), v.t. = prec. [-IZE]

ŏx′ȳmĕl, n. Syrup of honey & vinegar. [L f. Gk *oxumeli* (OXY-, *meli* honey)]

ŏxȳmŏr′on, n. (rhet.). Figure of speech

with pointed conjunction of seeming contradictories (e.g. *faith unfaithful kept him falsely true*). [Gk (-*mō-*) f. OXY-(1), *mōros* foolish]

ŏx′ȳtone, a. & n. (Gk gram.). (Word) with acute accent on last syllable. [f. Gk *oxutonos* f. OXY-(1), *tonos* TONE]

oy′er, n. Criminal trial under the writ of ~ & *terminer* or commission to judges on circuit to hold courts. [ME, f. AF *oyer et terminer* (L *audire* hear, *terminare* determine), -ER⁴]

oyez, oyes, o yes (ŏyĕs′), int. uttered, usu. thrice, by public crier or court officer to bespeak silence & attention. [ME, f. AF, OF (-*z*), imperat. pl. of *oïr* hear = L *audiatis* (*audire* hear)]

oys′ter, n. Kinds of edible bivalve mollusc usu. eaten alive; ~-shaped morsel of meat in fowl's back; ~-*bank*, -*bed*, part of sea-bottom where ~s breed or are bred; ~-*bar*, counter in restaurant etc. where ~s are served; ~-*catcher*, coastal wading bird; ~-*farm*, sea bottom used for breeding ~s; ~-*knife*, of shape adapted for opening ~s; ~ *patty*, piece of pastry containing cooked ~s. [ME, f. OF *oistre* (now *huître*) f. L *ostrea* (-*eum*) f. Gk *ostreon*]

ozō′cerite, ozŏk′erit, n. Wax-like fossil resin used for candles, insulating, etc. [G (-*kerit*), f. Gk *ozō* smell, *kēros* wax, -ITE¹]

ŏz′ōn|e, n. Condensed form of oxygen with three atoms to molecule having pungent refreshing odour, (fig.) exhilarating influence. Hence **ozōn′IC**, ~*iF′ER*-*OUS*, aa., ~IZE(3, 5) v.t., ~īZER¹(2), ~ŏm′ETER, nn. [f. G *ozon* (Gk *ozō* smell, -ONE)]

P

P, p, (pē), letter (pl. *Ps*, **P's**). *Mind* one's *P's & Q's*, be careful of propriety.

pa¹ (pah), n. (colloq.). = PAPA. [abbr.]

pa² (pah), pah, n. (hist.). Native fort in New Zealand; (now) Maori village. [Maori]

păb′ulum, n. Food (often fig., as *mental* ~). [L (*pascere* feed)]

păc′a, n. Kinds of large rodents in Central & South America. [native]

pāce¹, n. Single step in walking or running; space traversed in this (about 30 in.); space between successive stationary positions of same foot in walking (about 60 in.); mode of walking or running, gait; any of various gaits of (esp. trained) horse, mule, etc.; = AMBLE; (fig.) *put person through his* ~*s*, test his qualities in action etc.; speed in walking or running; rate of progression (often fig.); *keep* ~, advance at equal rate *with*; *go the* ~, go at great speed, (fig.) indulge in dissipation; ~-*maker*, rider, runner, etc., who sets ~ for another in race etc.; || ~-*stick*, drill-sergeant's adjustable two-legged appliance for measuring length of ~.

Hence **-pāced²** (-st) a. [ME, f. OF *pas* f. L *passus* (*pandere pass-* stretch)]

pāce², v.t. & t. Walk with slow or regular pace; traverse thus; measure (distance) by pacing; (of horse) amble; set pace for (rider, runner, etc.). [f. prec.]

pā'ce³, prep. ~ *tū'ā*, ~ *Smith*, (in announcing contrary opinion) with all deference to you, to Smith. [L, abl. of PAX]

pā'cer, n. In vbl senses, esp. horse that paces. [-ER¹]

pacha etc. See PASHA etc.

pachi'sĭ (-chē²), n. Four-handed Indian game with cowries for dice. [Hind., = of 25]

păch'ydĕrm (-k-), n. Thick-skinned quadruped, esp. one of Cuvier's (now discarded) group *Pachydermata* (hoofed quadrupeds that do not chew cud, e.g. elephant, horse, etc.); (fig.) thick-skinned person. So **păchydĕrm'atous** (-k-) a. [f. F *pachyderme* f. Gk *pakhudermos* (*pakhus* thick + *derma -matos* skin)]

pacif'ĭc, a. & n. Tending to peace; of peaceful disposition; *the* P~ (*Ocean*), that between America & Asia. Hence **pacif'Ically** adv. [f. F *-ique*, or L *pacificus* (*pax pacis* peace, see -FIC)]

păcifica'tion, n. Pacifying; treaty of peace. So **pacif'icātory** a. [F, f. L *pacificationem* (as PACIFY, see -FICATION)]

pacif'icism, pā'cifism, n. The doctrine that the abolition of war is both desirable & possible. Hence **pacif'icist, pā'cifist**, n. [f. F *pacifisme, -iste*; shorter forms earlier & preferred to pedantically correct longer forms]

pā'cifȳ, v.t. Appease (person, anger, excitement, etc.); reduce (country etc.) to state of peace. [ME, f. OF *pacifier* f. L *pacificare* (as PACIFIC, see -FY)]

păck¹, n. 1. Bundle of things wrapped up or tied together for carrying, parcel, esp. pedlar's bundle or soldier's knapsack. 2. A measure of various goods. 3. Lot, set, (~ *of fools, lies, nonsense*, etc.). 4. Number of hounds kept together for hunting, or of beasts (esp. wolves) or birds (esp. grouse) naturally associating; organized group of U-boats. 5. (In rugby footb.) a side's forwards. 6. Set of playing-cards. 7. Large area of large pieces of floating ice in sea. 8. Quantity of fish, fruit, etc., packed in a season etc.; (commerc.) method of packing for the market. 9. ~*drill*, military punishment of walking up and down in full *marching* ORDER¹(2); ~*horse* (for carrying ~s); ~*'man*, pedlar; ~*saddle* (adapted for supporting ~s); ~*'thread*, stout thread for sewing or tying up ~s. [ME, f. MDu. *pak*, MLG *pak, packe*, of unkn. orig.]

păck², v.t. & i. 1. Put (things) together into bundle, box, bag, etc., for transport or storing (often ~ *up*, esp. abs.); (of things) admit of being ~ed *well, easily*, etc. 2. Prepare & put up (meat, fruit, etc.) in tins etc. for preservation. 3. Put

closely together; (naut.) ~ (put) *on all sail*; form (hounds) into pack; place (cards) together in pack; (intr.) crowd together, (of animals) form into pack. 4. Cover (thing) with something pressed tightly round; (med.) wrap (body etc.) in wet cloth. 5. (boxing sl.). Be capable of delivering (a punch) with skill or force. 6. Fill (bag, box, etc.) with clothes etc.; cram (space etc. *with*); load (beast) with pack. 7. Depart with one's belongings; *send* (person) ~*ing*, dismiss him summarily; ~ (person) *off*, send him away. 8. [prob. diff. wd]. Select (jury etc.) so as to secure partial decision. 9. (sl.). ~ *it in*, end it, finish; ~ *it up*, desist; ~ *up*, (of an engine) peter out, go out of action. [ME, f. prec.]

păck'age, n., & v.t. 1. Bundle of things packed, parcel; box etc. in which goods are packed; ~ *deal*, transaction agreed to as a whole, the less favourable items as well as the more favourable. 2. v.t. Make up into, enclose in, a ~. [-AGE]

păck'er, n. In vbl senses, esp.: one who packs meat, fruit, etc., for market; machine for packing. [-ER¹]

păck'ĕt, n. Small package; ||(sl.) considerable sum won or lost in betting, speculation, etc.; || *catch, stop, a* ~ (sl.), be (severely) wounded by bullet etc.; ~(-*boat*), mail-boat. [PACK¹ + -ET¹]

păck'ing, n. In vbl senses; also (oil-absorbing) material closing a joint or assisting in lubrication of a journal; ~*box*, = STUFFING-*box*; ~*needle*, large needle for sewing up packages; ~*sheet*, (1) sheet for packing goods in, (2) wet sheet used in hydropathy. [-ING¹]

păct, n. Compact; PEACE P~. [ME, f. OF, f. L *pactum*, neut. p.p. of *paciscere* agree]

păd¹, n. 1. (sl.). Road, esp. *gentleman, knight, squire, of the* ~, highwayman; FOOT'~. 2. (Also ~*nag*) easy-paced horse. [16th c. cant, f. Du., LG *pad* PATH]

păd², v.t. & i. (-dd-). Tramp along (road etc.) on foot; travel on foot; ~ *it*, ~ *the hoof*, (sl.), go on foot. [f. prec., or LG *padden, pedden* tread]

păd³, n. 1. Soft stuffed saddle without tree; part of double harness to which girths are attached. 2. Cushion, stuffing, used to diminish jarring, fill out hollows, etc.; guard for parts of body in cricket etc. 3. Number of sheets of blotting-, writing-, or drawing-paper fastened together at edge. 4. Fleshy cushion forming sole of foot in some quadrupeds; paw of fox, hare, etc. 5. Socket of brace, tool-handle. [16th c., of unkn. orig.]

păd⁴, v.t, (-dd-). Furnish with a pad, stuff; fill out (sentence etc.) with superfluous words; ~*ded cell*, room in lunatic asylum with ~ded walls. Hence ~*d'ING¹* (4) n. [19th c., f. prec.]

păd⁵, n. Open pannier used as measure of fruit etc. [16th c., var. of *ped* (14th c.), of unkn. orig.]

păd′dle[1], n. Small spade-like implement with long handle; short broad-bladed oar used without rowlock; *double* ~ (with blade at each end); one of the boards fitted round circumference of ~-wheel; ~-shaped instrument; (zool.) fin or flipper; ~-*wheel*, wheel for propelling ship, with boards round circumference so as to press backward against water; ~-*box*, casing over upper part of this. [c. 1400, of unkn. orig.; cf. syn. (Sc. & north.) *pattle*]

păd′dle[2], v.i. & t., & n. **1.** Move on water, propel canoe, by means of paddles; ~ *one's own canoe*, (fig.) depend on oneself alone; row gently. **2.** n. Action, spell, of paddling. [f. prec.]

păd′dle[3], v.i. Dabble with the feet in shallow water; toy with the fingers (*in*, *on*, *about*, thing); (of child) toddle. [cf. PUDDLE[2] & LG *pudeln* (POODLE)]

pădd′ock[1], n. Small field, esp. as part of stud farm; turf enclosure near race-course, where horses are assembled before race; (Austral.) field, plot of land. [app. var. of (now dial.) *parrock* (OE *pearroc*): see PARK]

‖ **pădd′ock**[2], n. (arch., dial.). Frog or toad. [f. ME *padde* (= ON *padda*, MDu., MLG *padde*) toad, +-OCK]

Pădd′y[1], n. (Nickname for) Irishman. [pet-form of *Padraig*, *Patrick*]

pădd′y[2], n. Rice in the straw or in the husk. [f. Malay *padi*]

‖ **pădd′y**[3], **pădd′ywhăck**, nn. (colloq.). A rage, fit of temper. [PADDY[1]]

Pa′dishah, **Pa′dshah**, (pah-), n. Title in Persia of Shah, in Europe formerly of Sultan of Turkey, and in India of British sovereign. [Pers. (*pati* master + *shah* SHAH)]

păd′lock, n., & v.t. **1.** Detachable lock hanging by pivoted hook on object fastened; ~ *law*, one providing for closing & locking up premises. **2.** v.t. Secure with ~. [ME; first elem. unexpl.]

padouk (pahdowk′), n. Burmese timber-tree; its wood, resembling rosewood. [native name]

padre (pahd′rā), n. (colloq.). Chaplain. [f. It., Sp., Pg. *padre* father, priest]

padrōn′e, n. Master of Mediterranean trading-vessel; Italian employer of street musicians, begging-children, etc.; proprietor of Italian inn. [It.]

păd′ūasoy, n. Strong corded silk fabric much worn in 18th c. (cf. POULT-DE-SOIE). [18th c. *poudesoy* f. F *pou-de-soie*, of unkn. orig.; assoc. w. *Padua*]

pae′an, n. Chant of thanksgiving for deliverance (orig.) addressed to Apollo or Artemis; song of praise or triumph. [L, f. Gk *paian* hymn to Apollo under name of Paian]

paed′er|ăstў, pēd′-, n. Sodomy with a boy. So ~**ăst** n., sodomite. [f. Gk *paiderastia* (*pais paidos* boy +*erastēs* lover)]

paed|(o)-, pēd|(o)-, comb. form of Gk

pais paidos; ~*o-băp′tism*, infant baptism, ~*o-băp′tist*, adherent of this; ~*o-gĕn′esis*, reproduction by immature insect; ~*i-ăt′ric* a., relating to ~*iăt′rics* n. pl., branch of medical science dealing with the study of childhood & the diseases of children, so ~*iatri′cian* (-shn), ~*iăt′rist*, nn. [Gk *iatros* physician]

pae′on, n. Metrical foot of one long syllable placed first, second, third, or fourth (*first* etc. ~) & three short. Hence **paeŏn′ic** a. [L, f. Gk *paiōn*, Attic form of *paian* PAEAN]

păg′an, n. & a. Heathen; unenlightened (person). Hence ~**DOM**, ~**ISM**(2), nn., ~**ISH**[1] a., ~**IZE**(3) v.t. & i. [ME, f. L *paganus* (*pagus* country district, -AN); sense 'heathen' in Christian L]

păge[1], n., & v.t. **1.** Boy, usu. in livery, employed to attend to door, go on errands, etc.; ‖ ~ *of honour*, *of the presence*, etc., titles of various officers of royal household; boy employed as personal attendant of person of rank; boy in training for knighthood & attached to knight's service (hist.); hence ~′**HOOD**, ~′**SHIP**, nn. **2.** v.t. *Summon by means of a ~ (who calls out the name of person wanted until found). [ME, f. OF, f. It. *paggio* f. Gk *paidion*, dim. of *pais* boy (PAEDO-)]

păge[2], n. One side of leaf of book etc.; (fig.) episode fit to fill a ~ in history etc. [F, f. L *pagina* (*pangere* fasten)]

păge[3], v.t. Put consecutive numbers on pages of (book etc.). [f. prec.]

pă′geant (-jnt; *also* pā-), n. Brilliant spectacle, esp. procession, arranged for effect; spectacular procession, or play performed in the open, illustrating the history of a place; tableau, allegorical device, etc., on fixed stage or moving car; (fig.) empty or specious show. [14th c. *pagyn* (in contemporary AL *pagina*), of unkn. orig.; later -*t* as in *ancient*]

pă′geantry (-jn-), n. Splendid display; empty show. [prec. +-RY]

‖ **Pă′gĕtt, M.P.**, n. Traveller who expects to know all there is to know of a country in a few months. [character in Kipling]

pă′gin|al, a. Of pages; page for page. So ~**ARY**[1] a. [f. LL *paginalis* (PAGE[2], -AL)]

pă′gin|āte, v.t. Page (book etc.). Hence ~**A′TION** n. [f. L *pagina* PAGE[2] +-ATE[3]]

pagŏd′a, n. **1.** Sacred building, esp. tower usu. of pyramidal form, in India, China, etc.; ornamental imitation of this. **2.** Gold coin once current in S. India; ~*tree*, kinds of Indian & Chinese tree, (fig.) tree fabled to produce ~s (coin), esp. *shake the ~-tree*, make rapid fortune in India. [f. Port. *pagode* of Ind. orig.]

pagŭr′ian, a. & n. (Of) the hermit-crab. [f. L f. Gk *pagouros*, kind of crab, +-IAN]

pah[1], int. expr. disgust. [natural]

pah[2], n. Var. of PA[2].

paid. See PAY[2].

pail, n. Vessel, usu. round, of wood or metal for carrying liquids etc.; amount

contained in this, as *half a ~ of milk.*
Hence *~'FUL* n. [ME *payle*, of uncert.
orig.; cf. OE *pægel* gill, OF *paelle* frying-
-pan, wine-measure, etc. f. L *patella* dim.
of *patina* dish]

paillasse, palliasse, (păl'yăs' *or* păl'yas),
n. Straw mattress. [F (*pai*-), f. *paille*
straw f. L *palea*]

paillette (păl'yĕt'), n. Piece of bright
metal used in enamel painting; spangle.
[F (dim. as prec.)]

pain[1], n. Suffering, distress, of body or
mind, whence *~'FUL, ~'LESS,* aa., *~'fuLLY*[2],
~'lĕssLY[2], advv., *~'fulNESS, ~'lĕssNESS,*
nn.; (pl.) throes of childbirth; (pl.) trouble
taken, esp. *take~s, be at the ~s of* (doing),
get (a thrashing etc.) *for* one's *~s*; punishment, now only in *~s & penalties, on* or
under ~ of (death or other punishment
to be incurred); *~-killer,* medicine for
alleviating *~*; *~s'taking,* careful, industrious. [ME, f. OF *peine* f. L *poena*
penalty]

pain[2], v.t. & i. Inflict pain upon; give
rise to pain, ache (*my arm is ~ing*). [ME,
f. OF *pener* f. LL *poenare* (as prec.)]

paint[1], n. Colouring-matter, suspended in
liquid vehicle so as to impart colour to a
surface; LUMINOUS *~*; colouring-matter
for face etc., rouge etc.; *~'brush,* house-
-painter's, artist's brush. [f. foll.]

paint[2], v.t. Portray, represent, (object, or
abs.) in colours; adorn (wall etc.) with
~ing; (fig.) represent (incident etc.) in
words vividly as by *~ing*; *not so black
as he is ~ed* (represented); cover surface
of (object) with paint; apply paint of
specified colour to, as *~ the door green*;
(sl.) *~ the town red,* cause commotion by
riotous spree etc.; apply rouge to (face,
often abs.); *~ out,* efface with paint;
~ed lady, butterfly of orange-red colour
with black & white spots. Hence *~'ING*[1]
(1, 2) n. [ME, f. *peint,* p.p. of OF *peindre*
f. L *pingere pict-* paint]

paint'er[1], n. One who paints pictures;
workman who colours woodwork etc.
with paint; *~'s colic,* form of colic to
which *~s* who work with lead are liable.
So **paint'RESS**[1] n. [ME, f. AF, OF *pein-
tour* f. Rom. **pinctorem* f. L *pictor* (as
prec., see -OR)]

paint'er[2], n. Rope attached to bow of
boat for making it fast to ship, stake,
etc.; *cut the ~,* (fig.) effect a separation.
[c. 1400 *paynter* (also obs. vb *paynt*) rope
or chain to secure anchor when carried at
cathead; orig. obsc.; cf. OF *penteur* rope
passing over mast-head]

paint'y, a. Of paint; (of picture) overcharged with paint. [-Y[2]]

pair[1], n. Set of two, couple, (esp. *of* things
that usu. exist or are used in couples, as
gloves, shoes, sculls, heels, eyes); *~
royal,* set of three cards of same denomination or of three dice turning up same
number; article consisting of two corresponding parts not used separately, as

~ of scissors, tongs, trousers; engaged or
married couple; mated couple of animals;
~ (of horses), two horses harnessed together; (Parl.) two voters on opposite
sides absenting themselves from division
by mutual agreement, person willing to
act thus (*cannot find a ~*); the other member of a *~ (where is the ~ to this sock ?)*;
*~ (flight) of stairs, of steps (one, two, three,
~ front or back,* room on the first etc.
floor or its occupant; *another ~ of* SHOES;
~-horse a., for a *~ of* horses; *~-oar,* boat
rowed by *~ of* oars. [ME, f. OF *paire* f. L
paria neut. pl. of *par* equal]

pair[2], v.t. & i. Arrange (persons, things),
be arranged, in couples (unite (t. & i.) in
love or marriage; (of animals) mate;
unite (*with* one of opposite sex); *~ off,*
put two by two, (intr.) go off in pairs,
(Parl.) make a pair, (colloq.) marry (*with*).
[f. prec.]

pajamas. See PYJAMAS.

Pakistan' (pah-, -ahn), n. Moslem autonomy; proposed separate Moslem State
(established as a separate Dominion in
1947; since 1956 an independent republic
in Asia. [f. Punjab, *A*fghan Frontier,
*K*ashmir, Baluchi*s*tan, lands where
Moslems predominated]

păl, n., & v.i. (sl.; -ll-). **1.** Comrade, mate.
2. v.i. (Usu. *~ up*) associate (*with*). [E
Gipsy]

păl'ace, n. Official residence of sovereign, archbishop, or bishop; stately mansion; spacious building for entertainment,
refreshment, etc.; ‖ GIN[2]*~*; ‖*~ car,*
luxurious railway-carriage. [ME, f. OF
palais f. L *Palatium,* hill in Rome,
house of Augustus built on this]

păl'adin, n. Any of the Twelve Peers of
Charlemagne's court, of whom the Count
Palatine was the chief; knight errant,
champion. [F, as PALATINE[1]]

pălae|(o)-, pălĕ|(o)-, comb. form of Gk
palaios ancient (cf. NEO-), as: *~ocrys'tic,* of
ancient ice, frozen from remote ages;
~ŏg'raphy, study of ancient writing, so
~ŏg'rapher, ~ograph'ic; ~olith'ic, marked
by use of primitive stone implements;
~ŏntŏl'ogy, study of extinct organized
beings, so *~ŏntolo'gical, ~ŏntŏl'ogist;
păl'aeolhēre,* extinct genus of tapir-like
mammal; *~ozo'ic,* of, containing, ancient
forms of life, of the first geological period
(cf. CAINOZOIC, MESOZOIC).

palaes'tra, palĕs', n. Wrestling-school,
gymnasium. [L, f. Gk *palaistra* (*palaiō*
wrestle)]

păl'afitte, n. Prehistoric hut on piles
over lake in Switzerland or N. Italy. [F,
f. It. *palafitta* pile-fence (*palo* stake+*fitto*
fixed)]

pălanquin', -nkeen', (-kĕn), n. Covered
litter for one, in India & the East, carried
usu. by four or six men; (loosely) closed
carriage in the East. [f. Port. *palanquim,*
cf. Malay *palangki,* Hind. *palki*]

păl'atab|le, a. Pleasant to the taste; (fig.)

agreeable to the mind. Hence ~LY² adv. [f. PALATE +-ABLE]

pǎl'atal, a. & n. Of the palate; (sound) made by placing tongue against (usu. hard) palate, whence~IZE(3) v.t. [F (foll. -AL)]

pǎl'ate, n. 1. Roof of the mouth in vertebrates; *bony* or *hard*, *soft*, ~, its front, back part; *cleft* ~ (see CLEAVE¹). 2. Sense of taste; mental taste, liking. [f. L *palatum*]

palā'tial (-shl), a. Like a palace; splendid. [f. L as PALACE +-AL]

palăt'inate, n. 1. Territory under a count palatine; *the (Rhine) P*~, State of old German Empire, under rule of the Count Palatine of the Rhine. 2. ‖ (In Durham Univ.) light shade of purple or lavender, blazer of this colour as sports distinction. [f. foll. +-ATE¹]

pǎl'atíne¹, a. & n. 1. (*Count) P*~, count having within the territory jurisdiction such as elsewhere belongs only to sovereign (in Eng. Hist. also *Earl P*~); *County P*~, his territory (still in England of Lancashire and Durham). 2. n. Woman's fur tippet. [F (-*in*, -*ine*), f. L *palatinus* of the PALACE, see -INE¹]

pǎl'atíne², a. & n. Of the palate; (n. pl., also ~ *bones*) two bones forming hard palate. [F (-*in*, -*ine*), as PALATE, see -INE¹]

pǎl'atogrăm, n. Record of the use made of the palate in producing a sound. [f. L *palatum* palate +-GRAM]

pala'ver (-lah-), n., & v.i. & t. 1. Conference, (prolonged) discussion, esp. between African or other natives & traders etc.; profuse or idle talk; cajolery; (sl.) affair, business. 2. vb. Talk profusely; flatter, wheedle. [vb f. n. f. Port. *palavra* word f. L as PARABLE]

pāle¹, n. Pointed piece of wood for fence etc., stake; boundary, esp. (fig.) *within*, *beyond*, etc., *the* ~; (hist.) *the (English) P*~, part of Ireland under English rule; (her.) vertical stripe in middle of shield. [ME, f. OF *pal* f. L *pālus* stake; cf. PEEL¹]

pāle², a. (Of person or complexion) of whitish or ashen appearance; (of colours) faint; faintly coloured; of faint lustre, dim; ~-*face*, supposed N.-Amer.-Ind. name for white man. Hence ~'LY² adv., ~'NESS n. [ME, f. OF *pal*(*l*)*e* f. L *pallidus* (*pallēre* be pale)]

pāle³, v.i. & t. Grow pale; (fig.) become pale in comparison (usu. *before* or *beside*); make pale. [ME, f. OF *palir* (as prec.)]

pāled(-ld), a. Having palings. [PALE¹, -ED²]

palēs'tra. See PALAESTRA.

pǎl'etot (-etō), n. Loose cloak for man or woman. [F]

pǎl'ette, n. Artist's thin wooden slab carried in hand and used for holding and mixing colours when painting; colours used by particular artist or on particular occasion; ~-*knife*, thin steel blade with handle for mixing colours. [F, dim. of *pale* shovel; cf. PEEL²]

pa'lfrey (-paw-, -pǎ-), n. (arch., poet.). Saddle-horse for ordinary riding, esp. for ladies. [ME, f. OF *palefrei* f. med. L *palafredus*, LL *paraveredus* (Gk *para* beside, extra, + *veredus* light horse, whence G *pferd*)]

Pa'li (pah-), n. Language used in canonical books of Buddhists. [for *pali-bhasa* (*pali* canon +*bhasa* language)]

pǎl'ikar, n. Member of band of Greek or Albanian military chief, esp. during War of Independence. [f. mod. Gk *palikari* lad (Gk *pallax -akos* youth)]

pǎl'impsĕst, n. & a. Writing-material, manuscript, the original writing on which has been effaced to make room for a second; (improp.) monumental brass turned & re-engraved on reverse side; (adj.) so treated. [f. L f. Gk *palimpsestos* (*palin* again +*psaō* rub smooth)]

pǎl'indrōme, n. & a. (Word, verse, etc.) that reads the same backwards as forwards (e.g. *madam, radar*). Hence pǎlindrŏm'IC a. [f. Gk *palindromos* running back again (*palin* again +*drom-* run)]

pǎl'ing, n. (Fence of) pales. [PALE¹, -ING¹]

pǎlin|gĕn'esis (-nj-), n. Regeneration (lit. & fig.); revival; (biol.) exact reproduction of ancestral character, whence ~gĕnĕt'IC a. [f. Gk *palin* again +GENESIS]

pǎl'inōde, n. Poem in which author retracts thing said in former poem; recantation. [F, or f. LL f. Gk *palinōidia* (*palin* again +*ōidē* song)]

pǎlisāde, n., & v.t. 1. Fence of pales or of iron railings; (mil.) strong wooden stake. 2. v.t. Furnish, enclose, with ~. [f. F *palissade* f. Prov. -*ada*, as PALE¹, see -ADE]

pǎl'ish, a. Somewhat pale. [-ISH¹]

pall¹ (pawl), n. Cloth, usu. of black or purple or white velvet, spread over coffin, hearse, or tomb; woollen vestment worn by Pope & some metropolitans or archbishops; (fig.) mantle, cloak; ~'*bearer*, person holding up corner of ~ at funeral. [OE *pæll*, f. L *pallium* cloak]

pall² (pawl), v.i. & t. Become insipid (now only fig.), esp. ~ *on* (person, mind, taste); satiate, cloy. [ME, aphetic f. APPAL]

Pallād'ian, a. (archit.). In the neoclassical style of the 16th-c. Italian Palladio. [-AN]

pallād'ium¹, n. (pl. -*ia*). Image of Pallas on which safety of Troy was held to depend; safeguard. [ME, f. L f. Gk *palladion*]

pallād'ium², n. Rare hard white metallic element of platinum group. [f. *Pallas*, an asteroid +-IUM]

pǎll'et¹, n. Straw bed; mattress. [ME *paillet* f. AF *paillette* straw, f. OF *paille* f. L *palea*]

pǎll'et², n. Flat wooden blade with handle, used by potters etc.; artist's PALETTE; projection on a part of a machine, serving to change mode of motion of wheel; valve under each pipe in wind-chest of organ. [f. F *palette* PALETTE]

palliasse. See PAILLASSE.

păll′i|āte, v.t. Alleviate (disease) without curing; extenuate, excuse. So ~A′TION n. [f. LL *palliare* cloak (PALLIUM), see -ATE³]

păll′iative, a. & n. (Thing) that serves to palliate. [F *-if, -ive*), as prec., see -IVE]

păll′id, a. Pale. Hence ~LY² adv., ~NESS n. [f. L *pallidus*, as PALE²]

păll′i|um, n. Man's large rectangular cloak, esp. among the Greeks; archbishop's PALL¹; integumental fold of mollusc, whence ~AL a. [L]

pall-mall (pĕl′mĕl′), n. Game in which ball was driven through iron ring suspended in long alley; || *Pall-Mall*, street in London developed from such an alley, & noted for clubs. [f. obs. F *pallemaille* f. It.*pallamaglio*(*palla* ball +*maglio* MALLET)]

păll′or, n. Paleness. [L (*pallēre* be pale, see -OR)]

păll′y, a. (colloq.). Friendly. [PAL, -Y²]

palm (pahm), n. Large family of trees, chiefly tropical, usu. with upright unbranched stem & head of large pinnate or fan-shaped leaves; branch of ~-tree as symbol of victory; supreme excellence, prize for this, esp. *bear, yield, the* ~; branch of various trees substituted for ~ in northern countries, esp. in celebrating *P~ Sunday*; ~*-honey*, refined sap of coquito ~; ~*-oil* (got from various ~s; also, with pun on *palm²*, bribe-money); *P~ Sunday*, Sunday before Easter, on which Christ's entry into Jerusalem is celebrated by processions, in which branches of ~ are carried. Hence **pălmā′CEOUS** (-āshus) a. [OE *palm(a)* f. L *palma* (foll.); ME *palme* reinforced by OF *palme*]

palm² (pahm), n. Part of hand between wrist & fingers, esp. its inner surface; part of glove that covers this; breadth (about 4 in.), length (about 8 in.), of hand as measure; *grease* person's ~, bribe him; *sailmaker's* ~, lead boss mounted in leather straps fastened round ~, used as thimble. Hence (-)~ED² (pahmd) a., ~′FUL n. [ME, f. OF *paume* f. L *palma*; later assim. to L]

palm³ (pahm), v.t. Impose fraudulently, pass *off* (thing *on* person); conceal (cards, dice, etc.) *in* hand; touch with palm; bribe. [prec.]

Păl′ma Chris′ti (k-), n. Castor-oil plant. [med. L, = palm of Christ, from handlike shape of leaves]

păl′mar, a. Of, in, the palm of the hand. [f. L *palmaris* (as PALM², see -AR¹)]

păl′mary, a. Bearing the palm, pre-eminent, esp. ~ *emendation*, a certain textual correction. [f. L *palmarius* (as PALM¹, see -ARY¹)]

păl′mate, -ĕd, aa. PALM²-shaped. [f. L *palmatus* (as PALM¹, see -ATE²)]

pa′lmer (pahm-), n. 1. Pilgrim returning

from Holy Land with palm branch or leaf; itinerant monk under vow of poverty. 2. (Also ~*-worm*) destructive hairy caterpillar. 3. Hairy artificial fly in angling. [ME, f. AF, = OF *palmier* f. med. L *palmarius* pilgrim (PALMARY)]

pălmĕtt′ō, n. (pl. ~s). Kinds of small palm, esp. dwarf fan-palm. [f. Sp. *palmito* dim. of *palma* PALM¹, refash. on It. wds in *-etto*]

păl′miped, -pĕde, a. & a. Web-footed (bird). [f. L *palmipes -pedis* (as PALM² + *pes pedis* foot)]

pa′lmistry (pahm-), n. Divination from palm of hand. So **pa′lmist**(3) (pahm-) n. [15th c., f. PALM² + (orig. *-estry*) second element unexpl.; *-ist* is a 19th c. back form.]

pa′lmy (pahm-), a. Of, like, abounding in, palms; triumphant, flourishing, esp. ~ *days*. [PALM¹ + -Y²]

pălmȳr′a, n. Kind of palm grown in India & Ceylon, with fan-shaped leaves used for matting etc. [f. Port. *palmeira*]

pălp, păl′pus (pl. *-pī*), nn. Jointed sense-organ in insects etc., feeler. Hence **păl′pAL** a. [L (*-pus*)]

păl′p|able, a. That can be touched or felt; readily perceived by senses or mind. Hence ~ABIL′ITY n., ~ABLY² adv. [ME, f. LL *palpabilis* (as foll., see -BLE)]

păl′p|āte, v.t. Handle, esp. in medical examination. So ~A′TION n. [f. L *palpare*, -ATE³]

păl′pebral, a. Of the eyelids. [f. LL *palpebralis* (*palpebra* eyelid, see -AL)]

păl′pitate, v.i. Pulsate, throb; tremble (*with* fear, pleasure, etc.). [f. L *palpitare* frequent. as PALPATE, see -ATE³]

pălpitā′tion, n. Throbbing; increased activity of heart due to exertion, agitation, or disease. [f. L *palpitatio* (as prec., see -ATION)]

pa′lsgrāve (pawl-), n. Count palatine. [16th c. *paltsgrave* f. Du., (= G *pfalzgraf*) f. *palts* PALATINATE +*grave* count]

pa′lstāve (pawl-), n. Celt of bronze etc. shaped to fit into split handle. [f. Da. *paalstav* f. Icel. *pálstafr* (*páll* hoe)].

palsy (pawl′zi), n., & v.t. 1. Paralysis; (fig.) cause, condition, of utter helplessness. 2. v.t. Paralyse (usu. fig.). [ME *pa(r)lesie* f. OF *paralisie* as PARALYSIS]

pa′lter (pawl-), v.i. Shuffle, equivocate, (*with* person); haggle (*with* person *about* thing); trifle (*with* subject). [orig. unkn.]

pa′ltr|ȳ (pawl-), a. Worthless, petty, contemptible. Hence ~ĭNESS n. [16th c., app. attrib. use of (now dial.) *palt, pelt* rubbish +-RY (cf. *trumpery*); cf. EFris., LG *palte* rag, MDu. *palt*; LG *paltrig* ragged]

pălūd′al (or păl-), a. Of a marsh; malarial. [f. L *pălūs -udis* marsh + -AL]

păl′ȳ, a. (poet.). Somewhat pale. [-Y²]

păm, n. Knave of clubs, esp. in five-card loo. [F *Pamphile*, cf. Sc. *Pamphie*, prob. f. Gk name *Pamphilos*]

păm′pa, n. (usu. pl., pr. *-az, -as*). Large treeless plain in S. America south of the Amazon; ~*(s)-grass*, large ornamental grass introduced into Europe from S. America. [Sp., f. Peruv. *pampa* steppe, flat]

păm′per, v.t. Over-indulge (person, tastes, etc.); ~*ed* menial, flunkey. [ME, in form f. obs. *pamp* cram + -ER[3]; cf. WFlem. *pamperen*, G dial. *pampen* in same sense]

pămper′o (-ār′ō), n. (pl. ~*s*). Strong cold S.W. wind blowing from Andes to Atlantic. [Sp., as PAMPA]

pămph′lĕt, n. Small usu. unbound treatise, esp. in prose on subject of current interest. [ME, f. *Pamphilet*, familiar name of 12th-c. Latin amatory poem *Pamphilus seu de Amore*, see -ET[1]]

pămphlĕteer′, n., & v.i. 1. Writer of pamphlets. 2. v.i. Write pamphlets. [-EER]

păn[1], n. Metal or earthenware vessel, usu. shallow, for domestic purposes; STEW, WARM[2]*ing,* ~; ~like vessel in which substances are heated etc.; part of lock that held the priming in obsolete types of gun; hollow in ground, as SALT-~; (also *hard-*~) substratum of soil; BRAIN-~; ~′*cake*, thin flat batter-cake fried in ~, esp. *flat as a* ~*cake,* quite flat (v.i., sl., of aeroplane, descend vertically in level position). Hence ~′FUL n. [OE *panne*, OS *panna*, OHG *pfanna*, of uncert. orig.]

păn[2], v.t. & i. (-nn-). Criticize severely (colloq.); ~ *off*, *out*, wash (gold-bearing gravel) in pan; (intr.) ~ *out*, yield gold, (fig.) succeed, work, (*well* etc.). [f. prec.]

Păn[3], n. Greek rural god; the spirit of nature, paganism, the pre-Christian or the non-moral world. [Gk]

pan[4] (pahn), n. Leaf of the BETEL; (used for) the mixture of ~, lime, & areca-nut parings chewed by Asians as a masticatory. [Hind.]

păn-, comb. form of Gk *pas*, neut. *pan* all, as ~*Af′rican,* of, for, all Africans; ~*-Ang′lican,* of the Anglican Church & its branches (~*-Anglican conference*); ~*-cos′mism,* doctrine that material universe is all that exists; ~*-gen′esis,* theory that each unit of an organism reproduces itself; ~*-Germ′an,* of all the Germans in political union; ~*-Hell′enism,* political union of all Greeks, so ~*-Hellēn′ic* a.; ~*-Is′lam,* union of Mohammedan world, so ~*-Islăm′ic* a.; ~*logis′tic,* (of Hegel's philosophy) treating only the rational as real, so ~′*logism*; ~*-Sla′vism* (-lah-), movement for political union of all Slavs; ~*sperm′atism,* ~*sperm′y,* theory that the atmosphere is full of minute germs that develop in favourable environment.

pănacē′a, n. Universal remedy. [L, f. Gk *panakeia* f. PAN(*akēs* remedy)]

panache′ (-ahsh, -āsh), n. Tuft, plume, of feathers esp. as head-dress or on helmet;

(fig.) display, swagger. [F, f. It. *pennachio* (*penna* feather)]

pana′da (-nah-), n. Bread boiled to pulp & flavoured. [Sp. (*pan* bread f. L *panis*, see -ADE)]

Pănama′ (-ah), n. ~ (*hat*), hat of fine pliant strawlike material made (orig. in Ecuador) from leaves of the screw-pine. [place]

panchayat (pŭnchī′at), n. (India). Village council. [Tamil *panchāyattu* f. Skr. *pancha* five]

pănchromăt′ic(-k-),a.(photog.). Equally sensitive to all spectrum colours. [PAN-]

păncrăt′ic, a. Of the pancratium; (opt., of eyepiece) extensively adjustable. [f. foll. + -IC]

păncrā′ti|**um** (-shǐ-), n. (Gk ant.). Athletic contest combining wrestling & boxing. So ~AST, **pănc′ratist,** nn. [L, f. Gk *pagkration* (PAN- + *kratos* strength)]

pănc′rĕ|**ăs,** n. Gland near stomach discharging a digestive secretion (~atic juice) into duodenum, sweetbread. So ~ăt′ic a., ~atIN n., one of the active principles of ~atic juice, digestive extract prepared from the ~ases of animals. [f. Gk *pagkreas* (PAN- + *kreas -atos* flesh)]

păn′da, n. Indian racoon-like animal, red bear-cat; *giant* ~, Tibetan black-and-white bear-like mammal. [native]

Pănde′an, -aean, a. Of PAN[3]; ~ *pipe*, ▬ PAN-PIPE. [irreg. f. Gk *Pan*]

păn′dĕct, n. (usu. pl.). Compendium in 50 books of Roman civil law made by order of Justinian in 6th c.; -complete body of laws. [f. F *pandecle*, or L f. Gk PAN(*dektēs* f. *dekhomai* receive) all-receiver]

păndĕm′ic, a. & n. (Disease) prevalent over the whole of a country or over the world; ~, or *păndēm′ian,* VENUS. [f. Gk PAN(*dēmos* people) + -IC]

păndĕmōn′ium, n. Abode of all demons; place of lawless violence or uproar; utter confusion. [mod. L (Milton) f. PAN- + DEMON]

păn′der, n., & v.i. & t. 1. Go-between in clandestine amours, procurer; one who ministers to evil designs. 2. v.i. Minister (*to* base passions, evil designs); (v.t.) act as ~ to (person's lust). [vb f. n. f. *Pandare,* character in Chaucer's *Troilus & Criseyde* & in Boccaccio, f. L f. Gk *Pandaros*]

pandit. See PUNDIT.

păndōr′a, -dōre′, n. Stringed instrument of cither type. [It., f. LL f. Gk *pandoura*]

Păndōr′a's bŏx, n. The box in which Hope alone remained when by its rash opening all objects of desire were dispersed to play havoc among mankind. [Gk myth., see Hesiod, *Op.* 50–105]

păn′dour (-oor), -oor, n. (Pl.) force of rapacious & brutal soldiers raised by Baron Trenck in 1741 & afterwards enrolled in Austrian army. [f. Serbo-

For words in *pan-* not given see PAN-.

-Croatian *pàndur* f. med. L *banderius* follower of a BANNER]

pāne[1], n. Single sheet of glass in compartment of window; rectangular division of chequered pattern etc. Hence ~'LESS (-nl-) a. [ME, f. OF *pan* f. L *pannus* piece of cloth]

pāne[2], v.t. Make up (garment etc.) of strips of different colours (chiefly in p.p.). [f. prec.]

pănĕgy̆'ric, n. & a. Laudatory discourse (*upon*); (adj.) laudatory. Hence ~AL a. [f. F *panégyrique* f. L f. Gk *panēgurikos* f. PAN(*ēguris* = *agora* assembly), see -IC]

păn'ĕgy̆rize, -ise (-īz), v.t. Speak, write, in praise of, eulogize. So **pănĕgy̆'rIST** n. [f. Gk *panēgurizō* (as prec., see -IZE)]

păn'el[1], n. 1. Stuffed lining of saddle; kind of saddle. 2. Slip of parchment; list of jury; jury; || (Sc. law) person(s) on trial, the accused; || list of the doctors registered in a district as accepting Insurance-Act patients (*on the* ~, so registered); team in some radio quiz programmes, whence ~LIST n., member of this. 3. Distinct compartment of surface, esp. of wainscot, door, etc., often sunk below or raised above general level. 4. Piece of stuff of different kind or colour inserted in woman's dress. 5. Large size of photograph, with height much greater than width. [ME & OF, f. Rom. **pannellus* dim. as PANE[1]]

păn'el[2], v.t. (-ll-). Saddle (beast) with panel; fit (wall, door, etc.) with panels; ornament (dress etc.) with panel(s). Hence ~LING[1](2) n. [f. prec.]

păng, n. Shooting pain; sudden sharp mental pain. [orig. unkn.]

păn'ga (-ngg-), n. African MATCHET. [native]

pāngōl'in (-ngg-), n. Scaly ant-eater. [f. Malay *peng-goling* roller (from habit of rolling itself up)]

*păn'handle, n., & v.t. & i. 1. Narrow strip of one political division of a country extending between two others. 2. v.t. & i. (sl.) Beg (from). [PAN[1]]

păn'ic[1], n. Kinds of grasses including Italian millet. [f. L *panicum*]

păn'ic[2], a., n., & v.t. & i. 1. (Of terror) unreasoning, excessive. 2. n. Infectious fright, sudden alarm (e.g., in commerce) leading to hasty measures; ~*-monger*, one who fosters a ~. 3. vb. Affect, be affected, with ~. Hence ~KY[2] a. (colloq.). [f. F *panique* f. Gk *panikos* of god Pan, reputed to cause ~]

păn'icle, n. (bot.). Loose irregular type of compound inflorescence, as in oats. [f. L *panicula*, dim. of *panus* ear of millet]

pănifica'tion, n. Bread-making. [F, f. L *panis* bread, see -FICATION]

pănjăn'drum, n. Mock title of exalted personage; pompous official or pretender. [arbitrary]

|| **pănn'age**, n. (Right of, payment for) pasturage of swine; acorns, beech-mast,

etc., as food for swine. [ME, f. OF *pasnage, panage* f. med. L *pastionaticum* (L *pastio* pasture f. *pascere past-*, -AGE)]

pănne, n. A soft long-napped cloth used as dress-material. [F]

pănn'ier[1] (-nyer), n. 1. Basket, esp. one of those carried, usu. in pairs, by beast of burden or on the shoulders; covered basket for surgical instruments & medicines for ambulance. 2. Part of skirt looped up round hips. [ME, f. OF *panier* f. L *panarium* bread-basket (*panis* bread, see -ARY[1])]

|| **pănn'ier**[2] (-nyer), n. (colloq.). Robed waiter in Inner Temple. [orig. unkn.]

pănn'ikin, n. Small metal drinking-vessel; its contents. [f. PAN[1]+-KIN]

păn'opl|y̆, n. Complete suit of armour (often fig.). Hence ~iED[2] (-lĭd) a. [f. Gk PAN(*oplia* f. *hopla* arms)]

pănŏp'ticon, n. Bentham's proposed circular prison with cells round warders' well in centre. [f. PAN-+Gk *optikos* of sight (*op-* see)]

pănora'ma (-rah-, -rä-), n. Picture of landscape etc. arranged on inside of cylindrical surface or successively rolled out before spectator; continuous passing scene; unbroken view of surrounding region (often fig.). Hence **pănorăm'IC** a., **pănorăm'ICALLY** adv. [f. PAN-+Gk *horama* view (*horaō* see)]

păn'-pīpe(s), n. Musical instrument made of series of reeds. [*Pan*, Greek rural god, +PIPE]

păn'sy (-zĭ), n. 1. Wild & garden plant with flowers of various colours, heartsease. 2. (colloq.). (Also ~ *boy*) effeminate youth, homosexual. [f. F *pensée* thought, pansy, f. *penser* think f. L *pensare* frequent. of *pendere pens-* weigh]

pănt, v.i. & t., & n. 1. Gasp for breath; (fig.) yearn (*for, after*, thing, *to* do); throb violently; utter gaspingly. 2. n. Gasp, throb. [ME, shortened f. OF *pantaisier* pant, f. Rom. **pantasiare* for **ph-* be oppressed with nightmare (as PHANTASY)]

pant- in comb. = PANTO- before vowels.

păntagru'el|ism (-ōŏl-), n. Extravagant coarse humour like that of Pantagruel, a character in Rabelais. So **pănta-gruěl'IAN** (-ōŏ-) a., ~IST n. [-ISM]

păntalēt(te)s' (-ts), n. pl. Woman's drawers, cycling knickerbockers, etc. [f. foll., see -ETTE]

păntaloōn', n. 1. (*P*~). Character in Italian comedy wearing ~s; (now) clown's butt & abettor in pantomime. 2. (hist.; pl. or sing.). Garment of breeches & stockings in one piece, close-fitting breeches down to ankle as transition from knee-breeches to trousers. 3. (pl.; chiefly U.S., & now usu. *pants*). Trousers. [f. F *pantalon* f. It. *pantalone*, Venetian character in Italian comedy, perh. f. *San Pantaleone*, favourite Venetian saint]

|| **păntěch'nicon** (-kn-), n. Furniture warehouse (orig. name of a bazaar); ~ *van*

(for removing furniture). [f. PAN-+Gk *tekhnikon* of art (*tekhnē*, see -IC)]

păn'the|ism, n. Doctrine that God is everything & everything God; heathen worship of all gods. So ~IST n., ~ĭs'tĭc(AL) aa. [f. PAN-+Gk *theos* god +-ISM]

păn'theon (*or* -ē'on), n. Temple dedicated to all the gods, esp. circular one at Rome; deities of a people collectively; building in which illustrious dead are buried or have memorials; building in London opened for public entertainment in 1772. [ME, f. L f. Gk PAN(*theion* holy f. *theos* god)]

păn'ther, n. Leopard; *American* ~, puma or cougar. Hence ~ESS[1] n. [ME, f. OF *pantere* f. L *panthera* f. Gk *panthēr*]

păn'ties (-tĕz), n. pl. (colloq.). Pants worn by children; close-fitting knickers worn by women. [dim. of PANTS; see -Y[3]]

păn'tile, n. Roof tile transversely curved to ogee shape, one curve being much larger than the other. [PAN[1]+TILE]

păntisŏc'racÿ, n. Community in which all are equal & all rule. [PANT-+Gk *isocratia* isocracy]

panto-, comb. form of Gk *pas pantos* all, as: ~*lo'gic*, (of) universal knowledge; ~*morph'ic*, taking all shapes; ~*pragmat'ic* a. & n., (person) meddling in everything; ~*scŏp'ic*, with wide range of vision.

păn'to|graph (-ahf), n. Instrument for copying plan etc. on any scale. Hence ~**grăph'ic** a. [f. F (-*graphe*), f. PANTO-+Gk -*graphos* writing]

păn'tomim|e, n., & v.t. & i. 1. (hist.). Roman actor performing in dumb show, mimic actor. 2. ‖ Dramatic entertainment usu. produced about Christmas & based on a fairy tale, with singing, dancing, clowning, topical jokes, a TRANSFORMATION scene, & certain stock roles. 3. Dumb show. 4. vb. Express (thing), express oneself, by dumb show. Hence or cogn. **păntomim'ic** a., ~IST(3) n. [f. F, or L f. Gk PANTO(*mimos* MIME)]

păn'trÿ, n. Room in which bread & other provisions. or (*butler's, housemaid's*, ~) plate, table-linen, etc., are kept; ~*man*, butler or his assistant. [ME, f. OF *paneterie* f. *panetier* baker f. med. L *panetarius* (*panis* bread, -ER[1]); see -ERY]

pănts, n. pl. (colloq.). (Chiefly U.S.) trousers; ‖ (shop) long tight drawers. [abbr. of PANTALOON]

păn'zer (-tser), a. & n. Armoured (~ *division, troops*); (n. pl., colloq.) ~ troops. [G, = armour]

păp[1], n. (arch.). Nipple of woman's breast; corresponding part of man; (pl.) conical hilltops side by side. [ME, of Scand. orig.; cf. Sw. dial. *pappe, papp*; ult. imit.]

păp[2], n. Soft or semi-liquid food for infants br invalids; mash, pulp. Hence

~**p'y[2]** a. [ME, prob. f. MLG, MDu. *pappe*]

papa' (-ah), n. Father (used chiefly by children). [F f. L; imit.]

păp'acÿ, n. Pope's (tenure of) office; papal system. [ME, f. med. L *papatia* (*papa* pope, -ACY)]

păp'al, a. Of the pope or his office. Hence ~ISM(3), ~IST(2), nn., ~IZE(3) v.t. & i., ~LY[2] adv. [ME, f. OF *papal* f. med. L *papalis* (as prec., see -AL)]

papāv'erous, a. Like, allied to, the poppy. So **papāvera'CEOUS** (-ăshus) a. [f. L *papaver* poppy +-OUS]

papaw', pawpaw', n. (Fruit of) palmlike S.-Amer. tree of which stem, leaves, & fruit contain a milky juice that makes meat tender; *N.-Amer. tree with purple flowers & oblong edible fruit. [16th c. *papayo* &c., f. Sp., Port. *papaya*, of Carib. orig.]

păp'er[1], n. 1. Substance used for writing, printing, drawing, wrapping up parcels, etc., made of interlaced fibres of rags, straw. wood, etc.; *commit to* ~, write down; *put pen to* ~, begin writing; negotiable documents, e.g. bills of exchange; (also ~ *money*) bank-notes etc. used as currency, opp. to coin, so ~ *currency* (cf. METALLIC); (sl.) free passes to theatre etc.; (pl.) documents proving person's or ship's identity, standing, etc.; *send in* one's ~s, resign; set of questions in examination; ~ NEWS~; essay, dissertation, esp. one read to learned society; ~ *war(fare)* (carried on in books or news~s); *on* ~, hypothetically, to judge from statistics, etc., as *on* ~ *he is the better man*, so (attrib.) ~ *profits* (hypothetical). 2. ~-*bag* cookery, method of cooking food of various kinds by enclosing it in buttered ~-bag before putting it in moderately hot oven; ~-*chase*, cross-country run in which a trail of torn-up ~ is laid by one or more runners to set a course for the rest; ~-*hangings, wall-*~, ~ for covering walls of room etc.; ~-*hanger*, one who covers walls with these; ~-*knife* (of ivory, wood, etc., for cutting open leaves of book etc.); ~-*mill* (in which ~ is made); ~-*stainer*, one who stains ~ or makes ~-hangings; ~-*weight*, small heavy object for securing loose ~s from being displaced. Hence ~Y[2] a. [ME, f. AF *papir*, = OF *papier* f. PAPYRUS]

păp'er[2], v.t. Enclose in paper; decorate (wall etc.) with paper; furnish with paper; (sl.) fill (theatre etc.) by means of free passes. [f. prec.]

papier mâché (păp'yă măsh'ā), n. Moulded paper pulp used for boxes, trays, etc. [F, = chewed paper]

papiliona'ceous (-yonăshus), a. (bot.). With corolla like a butterfly. [f. L *papilio* -*onis* butterfly, see -ACEOUS]

papill'a, n. (pl. -*ae*). Small nipple-like

protuberance in a part or organ of the body; (bot.) small fleshy projection on plant. Hence or cogn. **păp'illARY**[1], **păp'illATE**[2](2), **păp'illOSE**[1], aa. [L, = nipple, dim. of PAPULA]

păp'ist, n. Advocate of papal supremacy; Roman Catholic (usu. in hostile or joc. sense). Hence **papis'tic**(AL) aa., **papis'**ticALLY[2] adv., **~RY** n. [f. F *papiste*, or 16th-c. L *papista* (*papa* POPE, see -IST)]

papoōse', n. N.-Amer.-Indian young child. [native]

papoōsh', -ouche' (-ōōsh), n.=BABOUCHE. [f. Pers. *paposh* (*pa* foot+*posh* covering)]

păpp'us, n. (bot.). Downy appendage on fruit of thistles, dandelions, etc. So **păpPOSE'**[1] a. [mod. L, f. Gk *pappos*]

păp'rika (-ē-), n. Hungarian red pepper. [Hungarian]

păp'ūl|a, -ūl|e, nn. (pl.~ae, ~es). Pimple; small fleshy projection on plant. Hence **~AR**[1], **~OSE'**[1], **~OUS**, aa. [L (-*la*)]

păpy̆rā'ceous (-shus), a. (nat. hist.). Of the nature of, thin as, paper. [f. PAPYRUS, see -ACEOUS]

papy̆ro-, comb. form of Gk *papuros* usu. in sense ' paper ', as : ~*graph*, apparatus for copying documents by means of paper-stencil ; ~*graphy* (-ŏg²-), ~*type*, copying processes in which picture etc. is transferred from paper to zinc plate etc. ; ~*logist*, ~*logy*, (-ŏl²), student, study, of ancient papyri.

papy̆r'us, n. (pl. **-rī**). Aquatic plant of sedge family, paper reed ; ancient writing-material prepared by Egyptians etc. from stem of this ; (with pl.) MS. written on this. [ME, f. L, f. Gk *papuros*]

păr[1], n. Equality, equal footing, esp. *on a ~* (*with*); ~ *of exchange*, recognized value of one country's currency in terms of another's: (of stocks, shares, etc.) *at ~*, at face value, *above ~*, at a premium, *below ~*, at a discount; average or normal amount, degree, or condition, *as on a~*, on an average, *above, below, up to, ~*; (golf) the number of strokes a scratch player should require for a hole or course (calculated according to a formula & usu. less than the BOGEY figures). [L, a. & n., = equal(ity)]

păr[2], n. (colloq.). Paragraph (also *pă'ra*).

para-[1] (bef. vowel or *h* usu. *par-*), comb. form of Gk *para*, used in wds adopted from Gk or formed on Gk models, in senses ' beside ', ' beyond '. ' wrong, irregular ', esp. in scientific terms; ~*mil'itary* a., having a status or function ancillary to that of military forces; (chem., before a vowel *par-*) denoting modification of substance to whose name prefix is attached (*parăl'dehyde*, polymer of ALDEHYDE, used as narcotic & remedy against insomnia.

para-[2], f. F f. It. *para-* imperat. of *parare* ward off, shelter, as *parachute, parasol*.

parăb'asis, n. (pl. -*basēs*). Part sung by chorus in Greek comedy, addressed to

audience usu. in the poet's name. [Gk, f. PARA¹(*bainō* gō) go aside, step forward]

pă'rable, n. Fictitious narrative used to typify moral or spiritual relations (*the ~s of Christ in the Gospels*); allegory; (arch.) enigmatical saying, proverb; (arch.) *take up* one's ~, begin to discourse. [ME, f. OF *parabole*, f. LL sense ' parable ' of L *parabola* comparison (foll.)]

parăb'ola, n. Plane curve formed by intersection of cone with plane parallel to its side. [f. mod. L f. Gk PARA¹ (*bolē* throw, f. *ballō*) placing side by side, comparison]

parăbŏl'|ic(al), aa. 1. (Usu. ~*ical*) of, expressed in, a parable, whence ~ICALLY adv. 2. (Usu.~*ic*) of, like, a parabola. [f. LL f. late Gk *parabolikos* (as prec., -IC)]

parăb'oloid, n. Solid some of whose plane sections are parabolas, esp. (also ~ *of revolution*) that generated by revolution of parabola about its axis. [-OID]

parăch'ronism (-k-), n. Error in chronology. [f. PARA-¹+Gk *khronos* time+-ISM]

pă'rachute (-shōōt), n., & v.t. & i. 1. Umbrella-like apparatus for descending safely from a height, esp. from aircraft, (~ *flare*, one dropped by ~ to illuminate target area; ~ *mine*, large case containing explosive dropped from aircraft by ~; ~ *troops*, (airborne troops landing by ~); natural or artificial contrivance serving this purpose. 2. vb. Convey, descend, (as if) by means of ~. Hence **pă'rachut**IST (-shōōt-) n., user of ~, (pl.) ~ troops. [F (PARA-²+*chute* fall)]

pă'raclete, n. Advocate (as title of the Holy Spirit, see *John* xiv. 16, 26, etc.). [ME, f. LL f. Gk PARA¹(*klētos* f. *kaleō* call)]

parāde'[1], n. 1. Display, ostentation, esp. *make a ~ of* (one's virtue etc.); *programme ~* (radio), list of items to be seen or heard. 2. Muster of troops for inspection, *~p*. one held regularly at set hours; ground used for this. 3. Public square or promenade (often as name of street). [F, = show, f. Sp. *parada* & It. *parata* f. L *parare* prepare, furnish, see -ADE]

parāde'[2] v.t. & i. Assemble (troops) for review or other purpose; display ostentatiously: march through (streets etc.) with display; (intr.) march in procession with display. [f. prec.]

pă'_adigm (-im), n. Example, pattern, esp. of inflexion of noun, verb, etc. So **parădigmăt'ic** (-ig-) a. [f. LL f. Gk *paradeigma* f. PARA¹(*deiknumi* show)]

pă'radise, n. (Also *earthly ~*) garden of Eden; heaven; region, state, of supreme bliss; FOOL'S ~; park in which animals are kept; BIRD *of ~*. Hence or cogn. **parădisa'ic**(AL) [irreg. on *Mosaic* etc.], **păradis'éan**, **păradis'iac**(AL), **paradis'iAL**, **păradis'iAN**, **părádis'ic**(AL), aa. [ME, f. OF *paradis* f. LL f. Gk *paradeisos* f. OPers. *pairidaeza* park (*pairi* around+*diz* mould); cf. PARVIS]

păr'adŏs (*or* -dō), n. Elevation of earth

behind fortified place to secure from reverse attack or fire, esp. the mound along back of trench. [F (PARA-[2]+*dos* back f. L *dorsum*)]

pă′radŏx, n. Statement contrary to received opinion; seemingly absurd though perhaps really well-founded statement; self-contradictory, essentially absurd, statement; person, thing, conflicting with preconceived notions of what is reasonable or possible; HYDROSTATIC ~. Hence or cogn. ~ER[1](3), ~IST(3), ~ĭcăl-ĭTY,~Y[1], nn., pă′radŏx′ĭcăl a., pă′radŏx-ĭcălĭY[2] adv. [f. LL f. Gk *paradoxon* neut. adj. (PARA-[1]+*doxa* opinion)]

pără′dŏx′ūre, n. Palm-cat, animal with remarkably long curving tail. [f. Gk *paradoxos* (see prec.)+*oura* tail]

pă′raffĭn, n., & v.t. Colourless tasteless inodorous oily & waxy substance got by distillation from petroleum & shale & used for making candles etc. (~ *wax*, solid ~ obtained by distillation from petroleum; *liquid* ~, odourless tasteless mild laxative; ‖ (also ~ *oil*) oil so obtained & used as illuminant or lubricant; (v.t.) treat with ~. [G (1830), f. L *parum* little + *affinis*, from small AFFINITY it has for other bodies]

păragŏ′ge (-jĭ), n. (gram.). Addition of letter or syllable to a word. Hence **păragŏ′gĭc** a. [LL, f. Gk *paragōgē* leading past (PARA-[1]+*agōgē* f. *agō* lead)]

pă′ragon, n., & v.t. Model of excellence; supremely excellent person or thing, model (*of* virtue etc.); perfect diamond of more than 100 carats; (v.t., poet.) compare (thing *with*). [obs. F (mod. *parangone*) f. It. *paragone*, f, med. Gk *parakone* whetstone]

pă′ragraph (-ahf, -ăf), n., & v.t. **1.** Distinct passage or section in book etc., marked by indentation of first line; symbol (usu. ¶) formerly used to mark new ~, now as REFERENCE mark; detached item of news etc. in newspaper, freq. without heading, whence ~ER[1](3), ~IST(3), ~Y[1], nn. **2.** v.t. Write ~ about (person, thing), arrange (article etc.) in ~s. Hence **păragrăph′ĭc** a., **păragrăph′ĭcălĭY** adv. [f. F *paragraphe* f. med. L f. Gk PARA-[1] (*graphos* f. *graphō* write) short stroke marking break in sense]

pă′raguay (-gwä, -gwĭ), n.=MATÉ. [name of S.-Amer. river & republic]

părahēlĭ|ŏt′ropĭsm, n. Tendency in plants to turn leaves parallel to incidence of light-rays. So ~otrŏp′ĭc a. [PARA-[1]+ HELIOTROPISM]

pă′rakeet, **pă′roquet** (-kĕt), n. Small (esp. long-tailed) kinds of parrot. [f. obs. F *paroquet* (mod. *perro*-), = It. *parro-, perrochetto*; perh. ult. f. *Pierrot* dim. of *Pierre* Peter; see PARROT]

pă′rakīte, n. **1.** Kite acting like parachute. **2.** Tailless kite for scientific purposes. [1. f. PARACHUTE + KITE. 2. PARA-[1]]

păralĭp′sĭs, -leĭp′sĭs (-lĭ-), n. Trick of

securing emphasis by professing to omit all mention of subject, e.g. *I say nothing of his antecedents, how from youth upwards etc.* [f. LL f. Gk PARA[1](*leipsis* f. *leipō* leave) passing over]

pă′rall|ăx, n. (Angular amount of) apparent displacement of object, caused by actual change of point of observation. So ~ăc′tĭc a. [f. F *parallaxe* f. Gk *parallaxis* change f. *parallassō* (PARA-[1]+*allassō*)]

pă′rallel[1], a. & n. **1.** (Of lines etc.) continuously equidistant, (of line) having this relation *to*; ~ *bars*, pair of ~ bars supported on posts for gymnastic exercises; ~ *ruler*, twc rulers connected by pivoted cross-pieces, for drawing ~ lines; (fig.) precisely similar, analogous, or corresponding. **2.** n. ~ (*of latitude*), each of the ~ circles marking degrees of latitude on earth's surface in map, as *the 49th* ~; (mil.) trench ~ to general face of works attacked; person, thing, precisely analogous to another; ~ position; comparison, as *draw a* ~ *between* (two things); two ~ lines (‖) as REFERENCE mark. [f. F *parallèle* f. L f. Gk *parallēlos* (PARA-[1]+*allēlous* one another)]

pă′rallel[2], v.t. (-l-). Represent as similar, compare, (things, one *with* another); find, mention, something parallel or corresponding to; be parallel, correspond, to. [f. prec.]

părallelĕp′ĭpĕd (*or* -epĭp′ĭd), n. Solid contained by parallelograms. [f. Gk *parallēlepipedon*, as PARALLEL[1]+EPI(*pedon* ground) plane surface]

pă′rallelĭsm, n. Being parallel (lit. or fig.); comparison or correspondence of successive passages, esp. in Hebrew poetry. [f. Gk *parallēlismos* f. *parallēlizō* place side by side (as PARALLEL[1], see -IZE]

părallĕl′ŏgrăm, n. Four-sided rectilineal figure whose opposite sides are parallel; ~ *of forces*, (~ illustrating) theorem that if two forces acting at a point be represented in magnitude & direction by two sides of a ~, their resultant is represented by a diagonal drawn from that point. [f. F *parallélogramme* f. LL f. Gk *parallēlogrammon* (as PARALLEL[1]+*grammē* line)]

păral′og|ĭsm, n. Illogical reasoning (esp. of which reasoner is unconscious, cf. SOPHISM); fallacy. So ~IZE(2) v.i. [f. F *paralogisme* f. LL f. Gk *paralogismos* f. *paralogizomai* f. PARA[1](*logos* reason) contrary to reason]

pă′ralўs|e (-z), v.t. Affect with paralysis; (fig.) render powerless, cripple. Hence ~A′TION n. [app. f. F *paralyser*, as foll.; cf. ANALYSE]

păral′ўsĭs, n. Nervous affection marked by impairment or loss of motor or sensory function of nerves; (fig.) state of utter powerlessness. [L, f. Gk *paralusis* f. PARA[1](*luō* loose) disable]

păralўt′|ĭc, a. & n. (Person) affected with paralysis (lit. or fig.); (sl.) very drunk. Hence ~ĭcălĭY adv. [ME, f. OF *para-

lytique f. L f. Gk *paralutikos* (as prec., see -IC)]

păra|măgnĕt'ĭc, a. Capable of being attracted by poles of magnet (cf. DIAMAGNETIC). So ~**măg'nĕtĭsm** n. [PARA-¹+MAGNETIC]

păramătt'a, n. Light dress fabric of merino wool & silk or cotton. [f. *Par(r)amatta*, town in New S. Wales]

părăm'ĕter, n. (math.). Quantity constant in case considered, but varying in different cases. [f. PARA-¹+Gk *metron* measure]

pă'ramō, n. (pl.~*s*). High treeless plateau in tropical parts of S. America. [f. Sp. & Pg. *páramo* f. L *paramus*]

pă'ramount, a. Supreme; *lord, lady, ~* (in supreme authority); pre-eminent, as *of ~ importance*; superior (*to*). Hence ~**OY** n., ~**LY²** adv. [f. AF *paramont* f. OF *par* by + *amont* above f. L *ad montem* to the hill]

pă'ramour (-oor), **n.** (rhet.). Illicit partner of married man or woman. [ME, f. OF *par amour* by love]

par'ăng (pahr-), **n.** Malay heavy sheath-knife. [Malay]

păranoi'a, -noe'a (-nēa), **n.** Mental derangement, esp. when marked by delusions of grandeur, persecution, etc. Hence **păranoi'ĂC** a. & n. [Gk (-*noia*) f. PARA¹(*noos* mind) distracted]

pă'rapĕt, n. Low wall at edge of balcony, roof, etc., or along sides of bridge etc.; (mil.) defence of earth or stone to conceal & protect troops, esp. mound along front of trench (cf. *parados*). Hence ~**ED²** a. [f. F, or It. PARA²(*petto* breast f. L *pectus*)]

pă'răph, n. Flourish after a signature, orig. as precaution against forgery. [f. OF *paraphe* f. med. L *paraphus* for *paragraphus* PARAGRAPH]

păraphĕrnāl'ia, n. pl. Personal belongings; mechanical accessories, appointments, etc.; (formerly) articles of personal property that law allowed married woman to keep & treat as her own. [med. L, neut. pl. adj. f. LL f. Gk PARA¹(*pherna* f. *phernē* dower), see -AL]

pă'raphrāse (-z), **n.**, & **v.t. 1.** Free rendering or amplification of a passage, expression of its sense in other words; any of a collection of metrical ~*s* of passages of Scripture used in Church of Scotland etc. **2. v.t.** Express meaning of (passage) in other words. So **păraphrăs'TIC** a., **păraphrăs'TICALLY** adv. [(n.) F, or f. L f. Gk *paraphrasis* f. PARA¹(*phrazō* tell); (vb) f. F *paraphraser*]

păraplĕ'g|ia, n. Paralysis of lower limbs & part or whole of trunk. So ~**IC** a. [Gk (-ē-) f. PARA¹(*plēg-* strike)]

pă'rasăng, n. Ancient-Persian measure of length, about 3½ miles. [f. L (-*ga*) f. Gk *parasaggēs*, of Pers. orig.]

păraselēn'ė, n. (pl. -ae). Bright spot on lunar halo, mock-moon. [PARA-¹+Gk *selēnē* moon]

pă'rasĭt|e, n. Interested hanger-on, toady; animal, plant, living in or upon another & drawing nutriment directly from it (cf. COMMENSAL, SYM*biosis*); (loosely) plant that climbs about another plant, wall, etc. Hence or cogn. **părasĭt'ĬC(AL)** aa., ~**ĬSM**(2), ~**ŎL'OGY**, nn. [f. L f. Gk PARA¹(*sitos* food)]

părasĭt'ĭcĭde, n. Agent that destroys parasites. [as prec.+-CIDE]

pă'rasĭtĭze, -ise (-īz), **v.t.** Infest as a parasite (chiefly in p.p.). [as prec.+-IZE]

părasŏl' (*or* păr'-), **n.** Sunshade. [F, f. It. PARA²(*sole* sun f. L *sol*)]

părasўn'thĕsis, n. (philol.). Derivation from a compound. So **părasўnthĕt'ĬC** a. [PARA-¹+SYNTHESIS]

păratăx'ĭs, n. (gram.). Placing of clauses etc. one after another, without words to indicate co-ordination or subordination. So **păratăc'TIC** a., **păratăc'TICALLY** adv. [f. Gk PARA¹(*taxis* arrangement f. *tassō*)]

pă'ratrōōp|s, n. pl. Airborne troops landing by parachute (~*er*, one of these). [PARA(CHUTE) TROOP]

păratŷph'oid, n. Kinds of fever resembling typhoid, but caused by different bacteria. [PARA-¹]

pă'ravāne, n. Torpedo-shaped device towed at a depth regulated by its vanes or planes to cut the moorings of submerged mines. [PARA-²]

păr avion (ăvyawn'), **phr.** By airmail. [F, = by aeroplane]

parb'oil, v.t. Boil partially; (fig.) overheat. [ME, f. OF *parboillir* f. LL PER-(*bullire* boil) boil thoroughly, by confus. w. *part*]

parb'ŭckle, n., & **v.t. 1.** Rope for raising or lowering casks & cylindrical objects, the middle being secured at the upper level, & both ends passed under & round the object & then hauled or let slowly out. **2. v.t.** Raise (*up*) or lower (*down*) thus. [17th c. -*unkle*, orig. unkn.]

păr'cel¹, n. & **adv. 1.** (Arch.) part, esp. PART¹ *& ~*; piece of land, esp. as part of estate; goods etc. wrapped up in single package; *~ post*, branch of postal service concerned with ~*s*; (commerc.) quantity dealt with in one transaction. **2. adv.** (arch.). Partly, as *~ blind, drunk*; *~ gilt*, partly gilded, esp. (of cup etc.) with inner surface gilt. [ME, f. OF *parcelle* f. Rom. **particella*, dim. as PARTICLE]

păr'cel², v.t. (-ll-). Divide (usu. *out*) into portions; (naut.) cover (caulked seam) with canvas strips & pitch, wrap (rope) with canvas strips. [f. prec.]

păr'celling, n. In vbl senses, esp. (naut.) strip of canvas, usu. tarred, for binding round rope. [-ING¹]

păr'cenarŷ, n. Joint heirship. [f. AF *parcenarie* = OF *parçonerie* (as foll., see -ERY)]

păr'cėner, n. Coheir. [ME, f. AF, = OF *parconier* f. med. L *parti(ti)onarius* (PARTITION, -ER²)]

P

parch, v.t. & i. Roast (pease etc.) slightly; (of sun, thirst, etc.) make (earth, person, etc.) hot & dry; become hot & dry. [ME *perch, parche*, of unkn. orig.]

parch′ment, n. Skin, esp. of sheep or goat, prepared for writing, painting, etc.; manuscript on this; ~-like skin, esp. husk of coffee-bean. Hence ~Y² a. [ME, f. OF *parchemin* f. Rom. **particaminum*, blending LL *pergamina* of Pergamum w. *Parthica pelles* Parthian skin]

‖ **pard¹**, n. (arch.). Leopard. [ME, f. OF, f. L f. Gk *pardos*]

*****pard²**, n. (sl.). Partner. [abbr.]

pard′on¹, n. Forgiveness; (eccl.) = IN-DULGENCE, festival at which this is granted; (law) remission of legal consequences of crime; *general* ~ (for offences generally, or to number of persons not named individually); courteous forbearance, esp. *I beg your* ~ (apology for thing done, for dissent or contradiction, or for not hearing or understanding what was said). [ME & OF *perdun, pardon* f. *perduner*, see foll.]

pard′on², v.t. Forgive (person, offence, person his offence); make allowance for, excuse, (person, fault, person *for doing*). So ~ABLE a., ~ableNESS n., ~abLY² adv. [ME, f. OF *pardoner* f. med. L PER(*donare* give) concede, remit]

pard′oner, n. (hist.). Person licensed to sell papal pardons or indulgences. [PARDON¹+-ER²]

pare, v.t. Trim (thing) by cutting away irregular parts etc.; cut away skin, rind, etc. of (fruit etc.); ~ (nails etc.) *to the quick* (so deep as to reach sensitive parts); (fig.) diminish little by little (often *away, down*); shave, cut, *off, away*, (edges etc.). Hence **par′ER¹**(2), **par′ING¹**(1, 2), nn. [ME, f. OF *parer* f. L *parare* prepare]

parego′ric, a. & n. ~ (*elixir*), camphorated tincture of opium flavoured with aniseed & benzoic acid. [f. LL f. Gk *paregorikos* soothing (PARA-¹+-*agoros* speaking f. *agora* assembly)]

pareir′a (-āra), n. Drug from root of Brazilian shrub, used in urinary disorders. [f. Port. *parreira* vine trained against wall]

paren′chym|a (-ngk-), n. (Anat.) proper substance of gland, organ, etc., as distinguished from flesh & connective tissue; (bot.) tissue of cells of about equal length & breadth placed side by side (cf. PROS-ENCHYMA), usu. soft & succulent, found esp. in softer parts of leaves, pulp of fruits, etc. Hence ~AL, **parĕnchym′a-**tous, aa., (-ngk-). [f. Gk *paregkhuma* something poured in beside (PARA-¹ + *egkhuma* f. *egkheō* pour in f. *en* in + *kheō* pour)]

par′ent, n. Father or mother; forefather, esp. *our first* ~s, Adam & Eve; animal, plant, from which others are derived, (often attrib., as the ~ *bird, tree*); (fig.) source, origin, (*of* evils etc.). So **paren′-tAL** a., **paren′talLY²** adv., ~HOOD (-t-h-)

n. [ME, f. OF f. L *parens* (*parĕre* beget, see -ENT)

par′entage, n. Descent from parents, lineage, as *his* ~ *is unknown*. [F, as prec., see -AGE]

paren′thesis, n. (pl. *-thesēs*). Word, clause, sentence, inserted into a passage to which it is not grammatically essential, and usu. marked off by brackets, dashes, or commas; (sing. or pl.) round brackets ( ) used for this; (fig.) interlude, interval. [LL, f. Gk *parenthesis* f. *parentithĕmi* put in beside (PARA-¹+EN-(2) +*tithĕmi* place)]

paren′thesize, -ise (-īz), v.t. Insert (words etc., or abs.) as parenthesis; put between marks of parenthesis. [f. prec., see -IZE]

parenthĕt′ic, a. Of, inserted as a, parenthesis; (fig.) interposed. So ~AL a., ~alLY² adv. [f. med. L *parentheticus* (as PARENTHESIS, see -ETIC)]

parerg′on, n. (pl. *-erga*). By-work, work apart from one's main employment. [L, f. Gk *parergon* (PARA-¹+*ergon* work)]

pă′resis, n. (med.). Partial paralysis, affecting muscular motion but not sensation. So paret′IC a. [Gk *paresis* f. *pariĕmi* let go (PARA-¹+*hiĕmi* let go)]

par excellence (see Ap.), adv. By virtue of special excellence, above all others that may be so called, as *Mayfair was the fashionable quarter* ~. [F]

par′gět (-j-), v.t., & n. 1. Plaster (wall etc.). 2. n. Plaster. [ME, f. OF, f. (w. confus. of pref.) OF *porgeter* (*porget*) in same sense, f. *pour-* PRO-+*jeter* throw]

parhel′|ion (-lyon), n. (pl. ~*ia*). Spot on solar halo at which light is intensified, mock sun. Hence ~i′ACAL, ~IC, aa. [f. L f. Gk *parēlion* (PARA-¹+*hēlios* sun)]

păr′iah (or pă²), n. Member of a low caste in S. India; member of low or no caste; (fig.) social outcast; ~-*dog*, vagabond dog of low breed in India etc. [f. Tamil *paṛai-yar* pl. of *paraiyan* drummer (*parai* drum)]

Pā′rian, a. & n. 1. Of the island of Paros, famed for white marble. 2. n. Fine white kind of porcelain. [f. L *Parius* of Paros +-AN]

pari′ĕtal, a. Of the wall of the body or of any of its cavities; ~ *bones*, pair forming part of sides & top of skull; (bot.) of the wall of a hollow structure etc. [f. F, or LL *parietalis* (*paries -etis* wall, see -AL)]

pari mut′uĕl (pahrē), n. Form of betting in which winners divide losers' stakes (less a percentage for management). [F, = mutual stake]

pār′i păss′ū, adv. With equal pace; simultaneously & equally. [L]

Pă′ris, n. Capital of France; ~ *blue*, kinds of pigment; ~ *doll*, dressmaker's lay figure; ~ *green*, poisonous chemical used as pigment & insecticide; ~ *white*, fine whiting used in polishing.

pă′rish, n. Subdivision of county, having its own church & clergyman; ‖ (also *civil*

~) district constituted for administration of Poor law etc., as *go on the* ~, receive parochial relief; the inhabitants of a ~; ~ *clerk*, official performing various duties connected with the church, esp. (formerly) leading responses; ‖ ~ *council*, local administrative body in rural civil ~; ~ LANTERN; ~ *register*, book recording christenings, marriages, & burials, at ~ church. [ME *paroche*, *-osse*, f. OF *paroche*, *-oisse* f. LL *parochia*, *-ocia*, f. Gk *paroikia* district round (a church) f. *paroikos* (PARA-[1]+*-oikos* -dwelling f. *oikeō* dwell)]

parish'ioner (-sho-), n. Inhabitant of parish. [f. ME (obs.) *parishen* (f. OF *paroissien*, as prec.+*-ien* = -IAN)+-ER[1]]

Pari'sian (-zhyan), a. & n. (Native, inhabitant) of Paris. [f. F *parisien* f. med. L *parisianus* (*Parisii* Paris, see -AN)]

părisÿlläb'ic, a. (Of Gk & L nouns) having same number of syllables in nominative as in oblique cases of singular. [f. L *par* equal+SYLLABIC]

pă'rity, n. Equality, esp. among members or ministers of church; parallelism, analogy, as ~ *of reasoning*; (commerc.) equivalence in another currency, being *at* PAR[1]. [f. F *parité* or LL *paritas* (PAR[1], -TY)]

părk[1], n. **1.** Large enclosed piece of ground, usu. with woodland & pasture, attached to country house etc.; enclosure in town ornamentally laid out for public recreation; large tract of land kept in natural state for public benefit. **2.** (Space occupied by) artillery, stores, etc., in encampment; area assigned for motor--cars etc. to wait in. **3.** *Oyster-~*, enclosed area for oyster-breeding, overflowed by sea at high tide. Hence ~'ISH[1] a. [ME, f. OF *parc* f. Rom. **parricus*, whence OHG *pferrih*, OE *pearroc* (see PADDOCK[1])]

părk[2], v.t. Enclose (ground) in or as park; (mil.) arrange (artillery etc.) compactly in a park; leave (car etc.) in park; (colloq.) deposit and leave; *~ing-meter*, coin--operated meter that charges for car ~ed at side of street. [f. prec.]

părk'a, n. Skin jacket with hood attached, worn by Eskimos. [Aleutian]

‖ **Părk'hŭrst,** n. ~ (*prison*), a convict prison. [place]

‖ **părk'in,** n. (dial.). Cake of oatmeal & treacle. [perh. f. name *P~*]

Parkinson's law. See LAW[1].

‖ **părk'ў,** a. (sl.). Chilly (of air, morning, etc.). [orig. unkn.]

părl'ance, n. Way of speaking, as *in common*, *legal*, etc., ~. [f. AF & OF, f. *parler* speak f. Rom. **paraulare* f. **parabolare* f. L PARABOLA (in LL speech, whence Rom. **paraula* word, F PAROLE); see -ANCE]

Parl'ement (-mahn), n. (hist.). French judicial court (abolished 1792). [F]

Parlementaire' (-mahntär), n. Bearer of a flag of truce. [F]

părl'ey[1], n. (pl. ~s). Conference for debating of points in dispute, esp. (mil.) discussion of terms, as *beat*, *sound*, *a* ~, call for it by drum or trumpet. [f. foll., or obs. F *parlée* (p.p.), or F *parler*; see PARLANCE]

părl'ey[2], v.i. & t. Discuss terms (*with* enemy etc.); speak (esp. foreign language). [f. prec., or F *parler* (prec.)]

părleyvoo' (-lĭv-), n., & v.i. (joc.). **1.** French; Frenchman. **2.** v.i. Speak French. [f. F *parlez-vous (français)?* do you speak (French)?]

părl'iament (-lam-), n. **1.** Council forming with the Sovereign the supreme legislature of United Kingdom, consisting of House of Lords (Spiritual & Temporal) & House of Commons (representatives of counties, cities, etc.); (of Sovereign) *open P~*, declare it open with ceremonial; corresponding legislative assembly in other countries; *the P~ Act*, that of 1911 depriving the Lords of their veto on money bills & making their veto on other bills merely suspensory; LONG[1] *P~* (met Nov. 3rd, 1640, dissolved March 1660); *Short P~* (sat from Apr. 13 to May 5, 1640). **2.** (Also *~-cake*) thin crisp cake of gingerbread. [ME, f. OF *parlement* speaking (as PARLANCE, see -MENT)]

părliamentär'ian (-lam-), n. & a. **1.** Skilled debater in parliament; adherent of Parliament in Civil War of 17th c. **2.** adj. = foll. [foll., -AN]

părliamĕn'tarў (-lam-), a. Of parliament (*old* ~ HAND[1]); ‖ ~ *agent* (charged with interests of party concerned in private legislation of Parliament); enacted, established, by Parliament; ‖ ~ *train* (formerly carrying passengers at rate not above 1*d.* per mile); (of language) admissible in Parliament, (colloq.) civil. [-ARY[1]]

părl'our (-ler), n. Ordinary sitting-room of family in private house; room in inn for private conversation; ~ *boarder*, boarding-school pupil living in principal's family; **~ car*, luxuriously fitted railway coach; ‖*~maid*, maid who waits at table. [ME & AF *parlur*, OF *parleor*, f. *parler* (see PARLANCE, -ORY)]

părl'ous, a. & adv. (arch., joc.). Perilous; hard to deal with; surprisingly clever etc.; (adv.) extremely. [ME, = PERILOUS]

Parmĕsän' (-z-), a. & n. ~ (*cheese*), kind of cheese made at Parma & elsewhere. [F, f. It. *parmegiano* of Parma]

Parnăss'us, n. Mountain in central Greece, anciently sacred to Muses; *grass of* ~, white-flowered plant found in bogs. So ~IAN a. & n., (esp., member) of a later 19th-c. school of French poets. [L, f. Gk *Parna(s)sos*]

Părn'ellⁱsm, n. Policy of Irish Home--Rule party led by C. S. Parnell from 1880 to 1891. So ~ITE[1] n. [-ISM]

parŏch'ial (-k-), a. Of a parish; (fig., of affairs etc.) confined to narrow area. Hence ~ISM, parŏchĭăl'ITY, nn., ~IZE(3) v.t., ~LY² adv., (-k-). [ME, f. AF & OF, f. LL *parochialis* (as PARISH, see -AL)]

pă′rod|ў, n., & v.t. **1.** Composition in which an author's characteristics are ridiculed by imitation; feeble imitation, travesty. **2.** v.t. Make (literary work, manner, etc.) ridiculous by imitation. So ~IST(3) n. [f. F *parodie* or L f. Gk *parōidia* (PARA-¹ + *ōidē* ODE)]

parôle′, n., & v.t. **1.** (Also ~ *of honour*, F ~ *d'honneur* pr. dŏnĕr′) word of honour, esp. (mil.) prisoner's promise that he will not attempt escape, or will return to custody if liberated, or will refrain from taking up arms against captors for stated period; *on* ~, (liberated) on this understanding; (mil.) password used only by officers or inspectors of guard (cf. COUNTERSIGN). **2.** v.t. Put (prisoner) on ~. [F, = word; see PARLANCE]

păronomăs′ia (-*zy*a, -sĭa), n. Word-play, pun. [L, f. Gk *paronomasia* (PARA-¹ + *onomasia* f. *onomazō* f. *onoma* name)]

paroquet. See PARAKEET.

parŏt′id, a. & n. **1.** Situated near the ear, esp., ~ *gland* (in front of ear, with ~ *duct*, opening into mouth). **2.** n. ~ gland. [f. F *parotide* or L f. Gk *parōtis*, *-idos* (PARA-¹ + *ous ōtos* ear)]

părotīt′is, n. Mumps. [f. prec. + -ITIS]

pă′roxўsm, n. Fit of disease; fit (*of* rage, laughter, etc.). Hence **păroxўs-măl** (-zm-) a. [f. F *paroxysme* or med. L f. Gk *paroxusmos* f. *paroxunō* exasperate (PARA-¹ + *oxunō* sharpen f. *oxus* sharp)]

parŏx′ўtone, a. & n. (Gk gram.). (Word) with acute accent on last syllable but one. [f. Gk *paroxutonos* (PARA-¹ + OXY-TONE)]

părp′en, n. Stone passing through wall from side to side, with two smooth vertical faces. [ME, f. OF *parpain* of unkn. orig.]

păr′quet (-kĭt), n., & v.t. **1.** Wooden flooring of pieces of wood, often of different kinds, arranged in pattern. **2.** v.t. Floor (room) thus. So ~RY(1) n. [F, = small compartment, floor, dim. of *parc* PARK]

părr, păr, n. Young salmon. [Sc., orig. unkn.]

pă′rri|cīde, n. **1.** One who murders his father or near relative or one whose person is held sacred; person guilty of treason against his country. **2.** Any of these crimes. So ~cīd′AL a. [F, or f. L (1) *parricida* (2) *-cidium*, see -CIDE]

pă′rrot, n., & v.t. Kinds of birds, of which many species have beautiful plumage, & some can be taught to repeat words; person who repeats another's words or imitates his actions unintelligently; (v.t.) repeat (words, or abs.) mechanically, drill (person etc.) to do this, whence ~RY(4) n.; ~*-fish*, kinds with brilliant colouring or mouth like ~'s bill. [prob. f. obs. & dial. F *perrot* parrot, dim. of *Pierre* Peter; cf. PARAKEET]

pă′rrў, v.t., & n. **1.** Ward off, avert, (weapon, blow, awkward question). **2.** n. Warding off. [repr. F *parez*, imper. of *parer* f. It. *parare* ward off]

părse (-z, -s), v.t. Describe (word) grammatically, stating inflexion, relation to sentence, etc.; resolve (sentence) into its component parts & describe them. [f. ME (obs.) f. OF *pars*, pl. of *part* PART¹, or f. L *pars*]

părs′ĕc, n. Unit of stellar distances, the distance at which a star would have a parallax of one second of arc, i.e. at which the mean radius of the earth's orbit subtends this angle. [f. PAR(ALLAX) + SEC(OND)]

Părsee′, n. **1.** Adherent of ZOROASTRIAN-ism, descendant of Persians who fled to India from Mohammedan persecution in 7th & 8th cc., whence ~ISM(3) n. **2.** Language of Persia under Sassanian kings. [f. Pers. *Parsi* Persian (*Pars* Persia)]

părs′im|onў, n. Carefulness in employment of money etc. or (fig.) of immaterial things; stinginess; *law of* ~*ony* (that no more causes or forces should be assumed than are necessary to account for the facts). So ~ōn′IOUS a., ~ōn′IOUSLУ² adv. ~ōn′IOUSNESS n. [f. L *parsimonia*, *parci-* (*parcere* pars- spare, see -MONY)]

părs′ley, n. Biennial umbelliferous plant with white flowers & aromatic leaves, used for seasoning & garnishing dishes; ~ *fern* (with leaves like ~). [ME *persil* etc. f. OF *peresil* f. Rom. *petrosilium* f. L f. Gk *petroselinon* (*petra* rock + *selinon* parsley); OE *petersilie*, ME *petrosilye* dir. f. Rom.]

părs′nip, n. (Plant with yellow flowers &) pale yellow root used as culinary vegetable; *fine words* BUTTER² *no* ~s. [ME *passenep* (w. assim. to *nep* turnip) f. OF *pasnaie* f. L *pastinaca*]

părs′on, n. Rector; vicar or any beneficed clergyman; (colloq.) any clergyman; ~*-bird*, New Zealand bird with dark plumage & white neck; ~'s *nose*, rump of fowl etc. Hence **părsŏn′IC** a. [ME *person(e)*, *parson* f. OF *persone* f. L *persona* PERSON, (med. L) rector]

părs′onage, n. Rector's or other incumbent's house. [ME *personage*, *parsonage*, f. OF (prec. + -AGE)]

părt¹, n. & adv. **1.** Some but not all of a thing or number of things, as (*a*) ~ *of it was spoilt*, (*a*) ~ *of them have arrived*, (*a*) *great part of this is true, most* ~ (the majority) *of them failed*. **2.** Division of books etc., esp. as much as is issued at one time. **3.** Portion of animal body; *the* (privy) ~s. **4.** Each of several equal portions of a whole, as *three* ~s (quarters), *19* ~s (twentieths), *take 3* ~s *of sugar, 5 of flour, 2 of ground rice*, etc. **5.** Portion allotted, share, esp. *have neither* ~ *nor lot* (no concern) *in*; ART² & ~; person's share in action, his duty, as *I have done my* ~, *it was not my* ~ *to interfere*. **6.** Character assigned to actor on stage; words spoken by actor on stage; copy of these; (fig.) *play a noble, an unworthy, ~, behave nobly* etc.; *play a ~,* act deceitfully. **7.** (mus.). Melody assigned to particular voice or instrument. **8.** pl. (arch.). Abilities, as *a man of (good) ~s.* **9.** pl. Region (*a stranger in these ~s*). **10.** Side in dispute. **11.** *~ & parcel,* essential ~; *~ of speech,* each of the grammatical classes of words (noun, adjective, pronoun, verb, adverb, preposition, conjunction, interjection); *for the most ~,* in most cases, mostly; *take ~,* assist (*in doing, in* discussion etc.); *take the ~ of,* support, back up; *for my ~,* as far as I am concerned; *in ~,* partly; *take* (words, action) *in good ~,* not be offended at; *on the ~ of,* proceeding from, done etc. by, as *there was no objection on my ~;* *~-owner,* one who owns in common with others; *~-song,* song with three or more voice-~s, freq. without accompaniment, & harmonic rather than contrapuntal in character; *~ time,* less than full time; *~-timer* (colloq.), ~-time worker. **12.** adv. In ~, partly (*made ~ of iron & ~ of wood; a lie that is ~ truth*). [ME, f. OF *part* f. L *pars partis;* in OE dir. f. L]

part², v.t. & i. **1.** Divide (t. & i.) into parts, as *the crowd ~ed & let him through, an islet ~s the stream, the cord ~ed* (broke). **2.** Separate (hair of head) with comb; separate (combatants, friends, etc.); *~ company,* dissolve companionship (*with*); *~* BRASS *rags with.* **3.** Quit one another's company, as *let us ~ friends, the best of friends must ~;* *~ from* or *with,* say goodbye to; *~ with,* give up, surrender (property etc.). **4.** (colloq.). ~ with one's money, pay, (*if I know him, he won't ~*). **5.** (arch.). Distribute (thing) in shares. [ME, f. OF *partir* f. L *partiri* (prec.)]

pártake′, v.t. & i. (*-took, -taken*). Take a share in; take a share (*in* or *of* thing, *with* person); take, esp. eat or drink some or (colloq.) all *of,* as *he partook of our lowly fare, partook of a bun;* have some (*of* quality etc.), as *his manner~s of insolence.* [16th c., back form. f. *partaker, partaking* = part-taker etc.]

|| **párt′an** (-Sc.). Crab. [Celt.]

párterre′ (-târ), n. Level space in garden occupied by flower-beds; part of ground-floor of auditorium of theatre, behind orchestra. [F, = *par terre* on the ground]

pártheno|gĕn′esis, n. (biol.). Reproduction without sexual union. So ~**gĕnĕT′IC** a. [f. Gk *parthenos* virgin]

Párth′ian, a. Of Parthia, ancient kingdom of W. Asia; *~ shaft, glance,* etc., remark, glance, etc., reserved for the moment of departure, like missile shot backwards by flying ~ horseman. [-AN]

parti (pártĕ), n. Person regarded as eligible etc. in the marriage market (*is quite a, a desirable, an unsuitable, ~*); *~ pris* (prē), preconceived view, bias. [F]

pār′tial (-shl), a. & n. **1.** Biased, unfair; *~ to,* having a liking for (person, thing); forming only a part, not complete, as *a ~ success;* *~ eclipse* (in which part only of the luminary is covered or darkened). **2.** n. (mus.). A ~ note; *upper ~s,* higher notes more faintly heard than main note produced from string, pipe, etc. Hence ~**LY²** (-sha-) adv. [ME, f. OF *parcial* f. LL *partialis* (as PART¹, see -AL)]

pártiāl′itў (-shi-), n. Bias, favouritism; fondness (*for*). [ME, f. OF *parcialite* f. med. L *partialitas* (as prec., see -TY)]

pārt′ible, a. That can or must be divided (*among;* esp. of heritable property). [f. LL *partibilis* f. L as PART², -IBLE]

parti′cip|āte, v.t. & i. **1.** Have share in (thing *with* person); have share (*in* thing *with* person); have something *of,* as *his poems ~ate of the nature of satire.* So~**ANT,** **părticipA′TION,** **~ātor,** nn. [f. L *participare* (as PART¹ + *cip-* = *cap-* st. of *capere* take)]

pārt′iciple, n. Verbal adjective qualifying noun but retaining some properties of verb, e.g. tense & government of object. So ~**d** (-ld), **părticip′iAL,** aa., **părticip′iaLLY²** adv. [ME, f. OF, by-form of *participe* f. L *participium* (as prec.)]

pārt′icle, n. Minute portion of matter; smallest possible amount, as *has not a ~ of sense;* minor part of speech, esp. short indeclinable one; common prefix or suffix such as *un-, out-, -ness, -ship.* [ME, f. L *particula* (PART¹, -CULE)]

pārt′icoloured, párt′ў-, (-ŭlerd), a. Partly of one colour, partly of another. [f. PARTY²]

partic′ular, a. & n. **1.** Relating to one as distinguished from others, special; *P~ Baptists,* body holding doctrines of *~ election & ~ redemption* (i.e. of only some of the human race); (log., of a proposition) in which something is predicated of some, not all, of a class (opp. *universal*); one considered apart from others, individual, as *this ~ tax is no worse than others;* worth notice, special, as *took ~ trouble, for no ~ reason;* minute, as *full & ~ account;* scrupulously exact; fastidious (*about, what* or *as to what* one eats etc.); *in ~,* especially, as *mentioned one case in ~.* **2.** n. Detail, item; (pl.) detailed account. Hence or cogn. ~**ITY** (-ă′r) n., ~**LY²** adv. [ME, f. OF *particuler* f. L *particularis* (as PARTICLE, see -AR¹)]

partic′ular|ism, n. Doctrine of PARTICULAR election or redemption; exclusive devotion to a party, sect, etc.; principle of leaving political independence to each State in an empire etc. So ~**IST** n. [f. F *-isme* or G *-ismus:* see -ISM]

partic′ulariz|e, -is|e (-īz), v.t. Name specially or one by one, specify, (often abs.). Hence ~**A′TION** n. [f. F *particulariser* (as PARTICULAR, see -IZE)]

părt′ing, n. In vbl senses, esp.: leave-taking (often attrib., as *~ injunctions*);

dividing line of combed hair; ~ *of the ways*, point at which road divides into two or more (often fig. of choice between courses). [-ING¹]

pártisăn¹ (-z-), **-zăn**, (or pårt²), n. **1.** Adherent of party, cause, etc., esp. unreasoning one (often attrib., as *in a ~ spirit*). **2.** (mil.). Member of light irregular troops employed in special enterprises (hist.); (in recent use) a guerrilla (applied orig. to Russians resisting in parts of their country occupied by the enemy). Hence ~SHIP n. [F, f. It. *partigiano* (*parte* PART¹, see -AN)]

pårt'isan² (-zn), **-zan**, n. (hist.). Long-handled spear like halberd. [f. 16th c. F *partizane* f. It. *partesana, partigiana*]

pårt'ite, a. (bot., entom.). Divided (nearly) to the base. [f. L *partiri -it-* PART²]

pårti'tion, n., & v.t. **1.** Division into parts; such part; structure separating two such parts, esp. slight wall, whence ~ED² (-shond) a.; division of a country; (law) division of real property between joint tenants etc. **2.** v.t. Divide into parts; ~ *off*, separate (part of room etc.) by a ~. [ME, f. OF, f. L *partitionem* (as prec., see -ION)]

pårt'itive, a. & n. (Word) denoting part of a collective whole (e.g. *some, any*); ~ *genitive*, that used to indicate a whole divided into parts, expressed in English by *of*, as in *most of us*. Hence ~LY² adv. [f. F, or med. L *partitivus* (PARTITE, -IVE)]

Pårt'lét, n. (arch.). Used as proper name for a hen, esp. *Dame ~*, also applied to women. [f. OF *Pertelote*, proper name]

pårt'lý, adv. With respect to a part; in some degree. [-LY²]

pårt'ner, n., & v.t. **1.** Sharer (*with* person, *in* or *of* thing); person associated with others in business of which he shares risks & profits; || SLEEP²*ing* ~; · || *pre-dominant* ~, England (among constituents of United Kingdom); wife, husband, companion in dance, esp. *dancing* ~; player associated with another in many games; (naut., pl.) timber framework round hole in deck through which mast, pump, etc., passes. **2.** v.t. Associate (persons, one *with* another) as ~s, (also) be ~ of. Hence ~LESS a., ~SHIP n. (1) ME alt. of PARCENER, after PART¹; (2) (naut.) ME *pauteneres* pl. f. OF *pautonier* servant (= F *valet*); cf. similar use of *carlings* f. ON *karl* CARL, CHURL]

pårt'ridge, n. Kinds of game-bird, esp. *common* or *grey* ~; ~*-wood*, hard red wood used for cabinet work etc., (also) speckled effect produced on wood by certain fungus. [ME *pertrich* etc. f. OF *perdriz* etc. f. L f. Gk *perdix -dikos*; -*rich* for -*riz* unexpl.]

pårtůr'ient, a. About to give birth (often fig. of the mind etc.). [f. L *parturire* in labour (*parĕre part-* bear), see -ENT]

pårtůri'tion, n. Act of bringing forth young, childbirth (also fig.). [f. LL *parturitio*, as prec., see -ION]

pårtůr'iunt mŏn'tēs (-z), (, *născět'ur ridĭc'ulŭs mŭs*), sent. (As comment on fiasco) the mountains are in labour (, the product a poor mouse). [Hor., *A.P.* 139]

pårt'ý¹, n. Body of persons united in a cause, opinion, etc.; system of taking sides on public questions; ~ *spirit*, zeal for a ~ (freq. derog.); body of persons travelling or engaged together, as *fishing, reading, -*~; social gathering, esp. of invited guests at private house, as *dinner, tea, -*~. **2.** Each of the two or more persons making the two sides in legal action, contract, marriage, etc.; accessory (*to* action); (now vulg. or joc.) person, as *an old ~ with spectacles*. **3.** ~*-coloured*, see PARTI-COLOURED; ~*-wall*, wall shared by each of the occupiers of the two buildings etc. that it separates. [ME, f. OF *partie*, p.p. of *partir* f. L as PART²]

pårt'ý², a. (her.). Divided into parts of different tinctures. [f. OF *parti*, as prec.]

pårv'enu (-ŏō, & see Ap.), n. Person of obscure origin who has gained wealth or position, upstart, (often attrib.). [F, p.p. of *parvenir* arrive f. L PER(*venire* come)]

pårv'is, n. Enclosed area in front of cathedral, church, etc. [ME, f. OF *pare-(v)is*, f. *pareīs*, f. Rom. **paravisus* f. LL *paradisus* PARADISE, court in front of St Peter's, Rome]

pas (pah), n. Precedence, esp. *dispute, give, take, the* ~; step in dancing, as ~ *seul* (sŭl, & see Ap.), ~ *de deux* (dedū', & see Ap.), dance for one, two. [F, = step]

păsch'al (-k-), a. Of the Jewish Passover; of Easter. [ME, f. OF *pascal* f. LL *paschalis* (*pascha* f. Gk *paskha* f. Heb. *pesakh* Passover f. *pasakh* pass over, see -AL)]

păsh, n. (sl.). Passion. [abbr.]

pasha, -cha, (pah'sha, pá'sha, pashah'), n. (hist.). Turkish officer of high rank, e.g. military commander, governor of province, etc.; ~ *of three, two, tails, of one tail*, (of first, second, third, grade; from number of horse-tails displayed as symbol in war). [Turk. *pasha*; cf. BASHAW]

pa'shalic, -ch-, (pah-; *also* pashah²), n. (hist.). Jurisdiction of pasha. [f. Turk. *pashalik*]

pă'shm, n. Under-fur of hairy quadrupeds in Tibet etc., esp. that of goats as used for Cashmere shawls. [Pers., = wool]

păsque'-flower (-skf-), n. Anemone with bell-shaped purple flowers. [16th c. *passe-flower*, f. F *passe-fleur*; assim. to *pasque* = obs. *pasch* (as PASCHAL), Easter]

păsquinăde', n. Lampoon, satire, orig. one affixed to public place. [f. It. *pasquinata* (*Pasquino*, statue at Rome on which Latin verses were annually posted, see -ADE)]

pass¹ (-ah-), v.i. & t. (p.p. ~*ed* or as adj. *past*). **1.** intr. Move onward, proceed, (*along, down, over, on*, etc.); circulate, be current; ~ *for*, be accepted as; ~ (be currently known) *by the name of*; be transported from place to place; change (*into* something, *from* one state to another); die (now usu. ~ *hence*, ~ *from among us*, etc.); go by, as *saw the procession* ~, *time* ~*es rapidly*, *remarks* ~ *unnoticed*; come to an end, as *kingdoms & nations* ~; get through, effect a passage; go uncensored, be accepted as adequate; (of bill in Parliament, proposal, etc.) be sanctioned; (of candidate) satisfy examiner; happen, be done or said, as *I saw or heard what was* ~*ing*; adjudicate (*upon*); (of judgement) be given (*for* plaintiff etc.); (cards) forgo one's opportunity, e.g. of making a bid, (also) throw up one's hand; ~*ed pawn* (chess), pawn with no opposing pawn on its own or adjoining files. **2.** trans. Leave (thing etc.) on one side or behind as one goes (*has* ~*ed the chair*, been chairman, president, mayor, etc.); ~ *a dividend*, not declare it; go across (sea, frontier, mountain range); (of bill) be examined & approved by (House of Commons etc.); reach standard required by (examiner, examination); ~ MUSTER[1]; outstrip; surpass; be too great for, as *it* ~*es my comprehension*; transport (usu. w. prep. or adv.); move, cause to go, as ~*ed his hand across his forehead*, ~ *your eye* (glance) *over this letter*, ~ *a rope round it*, ~ (= *hand*) *in* one's CHECK[1]*s*; (football, hockey, etc.) kick or hand or hit (ball) to player of one's own side (also abs.); cause to go by, as ~ (troops) *in review*; cause, allow, (measure in Parliament, candidate for examination, etc.) to proceed after scrutiny; spend (*time, the winter*, etc.); hand round, transfer, as *read this & ~ it on*; give currency to (coin, esp. base coin); plédge (one's word, oath, etc.); utter (criticism, judicial sentence, *upon*); ~ *the* TIME[1] *of day*; ~ *water*, void urine. **3.** Spec. senses w. advv. & prepp.: ~ *away*, die, come to an end; ~ *by* (adv. or prep.), omit, disregard, walk etc. past; ~ *off*, (of sensations etc.) fade away, (of proceedings) be carried through (*without a hitch* etc.), (trans.) palm off (thing *upon* person *for or as* what it is not), distract attention from (awkward situation or allusion); ~ *out* (colloq.), die, become insensible as a result of drinking; ~ *over* (adv. or prep.), omit, make no remark upon, as ~ *over his subsequent conduct*, ~ *it over in silence*; ~ *through*, experience; *~ up*, refuse to have further dealings with, renounce. [ME, f. OF *passer* f. Rom. *passare* f. L *passus* PACE[1]]

pass[2] (-ah-), n. **1.** Passing, esp. of examination; || (Univv.) attainment of standard that satisfies examiners but does not entitle to honours. **2.** *Bring to* ~, accomplish, carry out; *come to* ~, happen. **3.** Critical position, as *things have come to a*

(*strange*) ~. **4.** Written permission to pass into or out of a place, or to be absent from quarters (*on* ~, *away* thus); disc etc. given to person leaving a place of entertainment temporarily so that on presenting this he will be re-admitted without payment; (usu. *free* ~) ticket authorizing holder to travel free on railway etc. **5.** Thrust in fencing; juggling trick; passing of hands over anything, esp. in mesmerism; *make a* ~ *at* (sl.), make amatory advances to. **6.** (football etc.). Transference of ball to another player of one's own side. **7.** ~'*book*, book supplied by bank to person having current or deposit account, showing all sums deposited & drawn; ~'*key*, private key to gate etc. for special purposes, (also) master-key; || ~'*man*, one who takes ~ degree at university; ~'*word*, selected word or phrase distinguishing friend from enemy. [partly f. prec., partly f. F *passe*, f. *passer* as prec.]

pass[3] (-ah-), n. Narrow passage through mountains; (mil.) such passage viewed as key to a country (*sell the* ~, fig., betray a cause); navigable channel, esp. at river's mouth; passage for fish over weir. [ME, f. OF *pas* f. L *passus* PACE[1]]

pa'ssab|le (-ah-), a. In vbl senses, esp. that can pass muster, fairly good, whence ~LY[2] adv. [ME, f. OF as PASS[1], see -ABLE]

pǎss'age[1], n. Passing, transit (BIRD *of* ~); transition from one state to another; liberty, right, to pass through; voyage, crossing, from port to port; right of conveyance as passenger by sea; passing of a measure into law; way by which one passes; corridor etc. giving communication between different rooms in house; (pl.) what passes between two persons mutually, interchange of confidences etc.; ~ (*of* or *at arms*), fight (often fig.); short part of book etc., as *famous, difficult, corrupt*, ~; particular phrase in a piece of music. [ME, f. OF (as PASS[1], see -AGE)]

pǎss'age[2], v.i. & t. (Of horse or rider) move sideways, by pressure of rein on horse's neck & of rider's leg on opposite side; make (horse) do this. [f. F *passager*, earlier *passéger* f. It. *passeggiare* (*passeggio* walk f. L *passus* PACE[1])]

pǎss'ant, a. (her.). Walking, & looking to dexter side, with three paws on ground & dexter fore-paw raised. [ME, f. OF, part. as PASS[1]]

passé (pǎs'ā, & see Ap.), a. (fem. ~e). Past the prime, esp. (of woman) past the period of greatest beauty; behind the times. [F, p.p. as PASS[1]]

pǎsse'menterie (-smentrĭ, & see Ap.), n. Trimming of gold or silver lace, braid, beads, etc. [F (*passement* gold lace etc. as PASS[1] see -MENT & -ERY)]

pǎss'ėnger (-j-), n. Traveller in public conveyance by land or water or air; (colloq.) member of team, crew, etc., who does, or can do, no effective work; *foot*~, traveller on foot; ~*-pigeon*, wild pigeon of N. America, capable of long flight (now rare or extinct). [ME *passager* f. OF *-ier* (PASSAGE, see *-ER²(2)*); *-n-* as in *messenger* etc.]

passe-partout (pahspártŏŏ'), n. Master-key; mount for photograph etc.; picture-frame (esp. for mounted photographs) consisting of two pieces of glass fastened together at edges with adhesive tape. [F, = pass everywhere]

pa'sser (-ah-), n. In vbl senses; ~*-by*, one who passes, esp. casually. [-ER¹]

păss'erīne, a. & n. (Bird) of the order of *Passeres* or perchers; of the size of a sparrow. [f. L *passer* sparrow +-INE¹]

păss'|ible, a. (theol.). Capable of feeling or suffering. So ~ĪBIL'ITY n. [ME, f. LL *passibilis* (*pati pass-* suffer, see -BLE]

păss'ĭm, adv. (Of allusions, phrases, etc., to be found in specified author or book) in every part, as *this occurs in Milton* ~. [L, = scatteredly (*pandere pass-* spread)]

pa'ssĭng¹ (-ah-), n. In vbl senses; ~*-bell* (rung in moment of person's death); ~ *-note* (not belonging to the harmony but interposed to secure smooth transition). [-ING¹]

pa'ssĭng² (-ah-), a. & adv. In vbl senses, esp.: transient, fleeting; cursory, incidental; (adv., arch.) very (~ *strange, rich*). [-ING²]

pă'ssĭon (-shn), n. **1.** Strong emotion; outburst of anger; sexual love; strong enthusiasm (*for thing, for doing*). **2.** (*The P~*) sufferings of Christ on cross, (musical setting of) narrative of this from Gospels; ~*-play*, mystery-play representing Christ's P~; ~*-flower*, kinds of (chiefly climbing) plants, flower of which was supposed to suggest instruments of Christ's P~; *P~ Sunday*, fifth Sunday in Lent; *P~ Week*, week between *P~ Sunday* and PALM *Sunday*, (also)=HOLY *Week*. Hence ~LESS a., -lĕss'LY² adv., ~lĕssNESS n., (-sho-). [ME, f. OF f. L *passionem* (*pati pass-* suffer, see -ION)]

pă'ssĭon² (-shn), v.i. (poet.). Feel or express passion. [f. OF *passionner*, as prec.]

pă'ssĭonal¹ (-sho-), n. Book of the sufferings of saints & martyrs. [f. med. L *passionale* neut. adj. as n. (as foll.)]

pă'ssĭonal² (-sho-), a. Of, marked by, passion. [f. LL *passionalis* (as PASSION¹, see -AL)]

pă'ssĭonate (-sho-), a. Dominated by, easily moved to, strong feeling, esp. love or anger; due to, (of language etc.) showing, passion. Hence ~LY² adv., ~NESS n. [ME, f. med. L *passionatus* (as PASSION¹, see -ATE²)]

Pă'ssĭonist (-sho-), n. Member of an R.-C. order pledged to do their utmost to keep alive the memory of Christ's Passion. [-IST]

păss'ive, a. & n. **1.** Suffering action, acted upon; (gram.) ~ *voice* (comprising those forms of transitive verbs that attribute the verbal action to the person etc. to whom it is directed, cf. ACTIVE); offering

no opposition, submissive; ~ RESISTANCE; not active, inert; ~ *debt* (on which no interest is paid). **2.** n. (gram.). ~ voice or form of verb. Hence~LY² adv.,~NESS, passiv'ITY, nn. [ME, f. OF, or L *passivus* (*pati pass-* suffer, see -IVE)]

pa'ssōver (-ah-), n. (*P~*) Jewish festival commemorating liberation of Israelites from Egyptian bondage (*Exod.* xii), held from 14th to 21st day of month Nisan; Paschal lamb, (fig.) Christ (1 *Cor.* v, 7). [f. *pass over*]

pa'ssport (-ah-), n. Document issued by competent authority permitting person specified in it to travel in the country & entitling him to protection; (fig.) thing that ensures admission, as *flattery is the sole* ~ *to his favour*. [f. F *passeport* (*passer* PASS¹ +PORT¹)]

past¹ (-ah-), a. & n. **1.** As p.p. or adj. in vbl senses of PASS¹, esp.: gone by in time, as *his prime is* ~, *our* ~ *years* ; just gone by, as *the* ~ *month, for some time* ~ ; (gram.) expressing ~ action or state, as ~ *tense*, ~ *participle*; ~ *master*, one who has been master in guild, freemasons' lodge, etc., (also) thorough master (*in, of*, a subject). **2.** n. ~ time, esp. *the* ~ ; what has happened in ~ time, as *cannot undo the* ~ ; person's ~ life or career, esp. one that will not bear inquiry, as *a woman with a* ~.

past² (-ah-), prep. & adv. **1.** Beyond in time or place, as *stayed till* ~ *two o'clock, half* ~ *three, old man* ~ *seventy, ran* ~ *the house*; beyond the range or compass of, as ~ *endurance, bearing, praying for*. **2.** adv. So as to pass by, as *hastens* ~. [prob. f. misuse of *am past* with object, *past* being then mistaken for prep., e.g. *I was now* ~ *the house*]

pāste¹, n. Flour moistened & kneaded, with butter, suet, etc., as cooking material; kinds of sweet confection; relish of pounded fish, as *anchovy* ~; cement of flour & water; any soft plastic mixture; hard vitreous composition used in making imitation gems; ~*board*, stiff substance made by pasting together sheets of paper, (attrib., fig.) unsubstantial, flimsy, (sl.) visiting-card, railway-ticket. [ME, f. OF f. LL *pasta*, perh. f. Gk *pastē* (*pastos* sprinkled)]

pāste², v.t. Fasten with paste; stick *up* (playbill etc.) on wall with paste; cover (thing *with* paper etc.) by pasting; (sl.) beat, thrash. [f. prec.]

păs'tel, n. Woad; blue dye from this; artists' crayon made of dried paste compounded of pigments with gum-water; drawing in ~, whence ~(l)IST n. [F, f. It. *pastello*, dim. of *pasta* PASTE¹]

păs'tern, n. Part of horse's foot between fetlock & hoof. [ME *pastron* f. OF *pasturon* f. *pasture* hobble]

păs'teurism (-ter-), n. Prevention or cure of diseases esp. hydrophobia by successive inoculations. [f. L. *Pasteur*, French scientist (1822–1895) +-ISM]

păs'teurĭz|e (-ter-), -ĭs|e (-ĭz), v.t. Subject (milk etc.) to Pasteur's method of partial sterilization; treat by pasteurism. Hence ~A'TION n. [-ĪZE]

păsti'ccio (-ĭchō), **păstiche'** (-ēsh), nn. Medley, esp. musical composition, picture, made up from various sources; (usu. *-iche*) literary or other work of art composed in the style of a known author. [F (*-iche*) f. It. (*-iccio*), f. *pasta* PASTE[1]]

păs'til, păstille' (-tĕl), n. Small roll of aromatic paste burnt as fumigator etc.; lozenge. [F (*-le*), f. L *pastillus*]

pa'stime (-ah-), n. Recreation; game, sport. [f. PASS[1]+TIME]

pa'stor (-ah-), n. 1. Minister in charge of church or congregation, whence ~SHIP n.; person exercising spiritual guidance. 2. Kind of starling. [ME & AF *-our*, OF *-or*, f. L *pastorem* shepherd (*pascere pastfeed*, see -OR)]

pa'storal (-ah-), a. & n. 1. Of shepherds; (of land) used for pasture; (of poems etc.) portraying country life, whence ~ISM n.; of a pastor, as ~ *epistles* (of Paul to Timothy & Titus, dealing with pastor's work). 2. n. ~ play, poem, poetry, or picture; letter from pastor, esp. bishop, to clergy or people. Hence ~ITY (-ăl⁴) n., ~LY[2] adv. [f. L *pastoralis* (as prec.,. see -AL)]

pastora'lĕ (pahstorah-), n. (pl. *-ali* pr. -lĕ, or *-ales*). Simple opera etc. with rural subject; slow quiet instrumental composition with notes flowing in groups of three & usu. with drone notes in bass suggesting bagpipes. [It., as prec.]

pa'storate (-ah-), n. Pastor's (tenure of) office; body of pastors. [f. med. L *pastoratus* (as PASTOR, see -ATE[1])]

păs'trў, n. Baked flour-paste; articles of food made wholly or partly of this; ∥~-*cook*, one who makes ~, esp. for public sale. [app. f. PASTE[1]+-RY]

pa'sturage (-ahscher-), n. Pasturing; herbage for cattle etc.; pasture-land. [f. OF, f. *pasturer* (as foll., see -AGE)]

pa'sture (-ah-), n. & v.t. & i. 1. Herbage for cattle; (piece of) land covered with this. 2. v.t. Lead, put, (cattle) to ~; (of sheep etc.) eat down (grass-land); (of person) put sheep etc. on (land) to graze, whence **pa'sturABLE** (-ahscher-) a. 3. v.i. Graze. [ME, f. OF f. LL *pastura* (as PASTOR, see -URE)]

pa'stў[1] (pah-, pǎ-), n. Pie of meat, fruit, jam, etc. enclosed in paste & baked without dish. [ME & OF *pastee* f. LL *pasta* PASTE[1]+p.p. ending *-ee*, see -Y[1]]

păs'tў[2], a. Of, like, paste; (also ~*-faced*) of pale complexion. [-Y[2]]

păt[1], n. Stroke, tap, esp. with hand as caress etc.; small mass (esp. of butter) formed by patting; sound made by striking lightly with something flat. [ME, prob. imit.]

păt[2], v.t. & i. (-tt-). Strike (thing) gently with flat surface (~*'ball*, ∥ poor or feeble

lawn tennis); flatten thus; ~*-a-cake*, first words of nursery rhyme, connected child's game; strike gently with inner surface of fingers, esp. to mark sympathy, approbation, etc.; (fig.) ~ (person, one*self*) *on the back*, express approbation of; beat lightly *upon*. [16th c., goes w. prec.]

păt[3], adv. & a. Apposite(ly), opportune-(ly), as *story came ~ to his purpose*; ready for any occasion, as *have the story ~*; *stand ~*, (poker) abide by hand dealt to one, not draw other cards, (fig.) refuse to change, stick to one's decision etc. [16th c., goes w. PAT[1, 2]]

Păt[4], n. (Nickname for) Irishman. [abbr. of *Patrick*]

pătagĭ'um, n. (zool.; pl. *-ia*). Wing-membrane of bat or similar animal; scale covering wing-joint in *Lepidoptera*. [L, f. Gk *patageion* gold edging on gown]

pătavĭn'ĭtў, n. Dialectal characteristics of Patavium (Padua) as seen in Livy's Latin; provincialism. [f. L *patavinitas* (*Patavinus* of Padua, see -INE[1] & -ITY)]

pătch[1], n. 1. Piece of cloth, metal, etc. put on to mend hole or rent; piece of plaster etc. put over wound; pad worn to protect injured eye; *not a ~ on*, not comparable to, nothing to. 2. Small disc etc. of black silk stuck on either side of face, worn in 17th & 18th cc. for adornment. 3. Large or irregular spot on surface. 4. Piece of ground; number of plants growing on this, as *brier-~*. 5. Scrap, remnant. 6. *Strike a bad ~*, go through a period of bad luck; ~*-pocket* (consisting of a piece of cloth sewn on garment); ~*-work*, work made up of fragments of different kinds & colours (often fig. & attrib.). Hence ~'ERY(1), ~'INESS, nn., ~'ĬLY[2] adv., ~'Y[2] a. [ME *pacche*, perh. var. of *peche* (see PIECE]

pătch[2], v.t. Put patch(es) on; ~ *up*, repair with patches; (of material) serve as patch to; (fig., usu. ~ *up*) repair, set to rights (matter, trouble, quarrel), freq. temporarily or imperfectly; (usu. ~ *up*) put together hastily; (piece (things) together (lit. or fig.); appear as patches on (surface). [f. prec.]

pătch'oulĭ (-ōōl-; *also* pachŏō⁴), n. Odoriferous Indian plant; perfume got from ~. [native]

pāte, n. (now colloq.). Head, often as seat of intellect. Hence -pāt'ED[2] a. [ME, of unkn. orig.]

pâté (pǎt'ā, & see Ap.), n. Pie, patty; ~ *de foie gras* (de fwah grah), pie etc. of fatted goose liver. [F, f. OF *paste*, cf. PASTY]

pătěll'a, n. (pl. *-ae*). Knee-cap, whence **pătěll'AR**[1], **pătěll'ATE**(2), aa.; (Rom. ant.) small pan. [L, dim. as foll.]

păt'en, n. Shallow dish used for bread at eucharist; thin circular plate of metal. [ME, f. OF *patene* or L *patena, -ina*]

păt'ent[1] (*or* pā-), a. ∥ *Letters ~* (OF *lettres patentes*, L *litterae patentes*), open letter from sovereign etc. conferring right, title, etc., esp. sole right for a term to make, use, or sell, some invention; conferred, protected, by this; ~ LEATHER; ~ log, elaborated rotary form of ship's log, recording speed on dial fixed on taffrail; (fig.) to which one has proprietary claim; (colloq.) such as might be patented, ingenious, well-contrived; (of door etc.) open, (fig.) plain, obvious, whence **pāt′-ENCY** n., **~LY**² adv. [ME, f. OF, & L *patēre* lie open, see -ENT]

pāt′ent² (*or* pǎ-), n. ‖ = *letters* PATENT¹; government grant of exclusive privilege of making or selling new invention; invention, process, so protected; (fig.) sign that one is entitled to something, possesses a quality, etc., as a ~ *of gentility*; ~ *office* (from which ~s are issued); ‖~-*roll* (containing ~s issued in Great Britain in a year). [short for *letters patent*]

pāt′ent³ (*or* pǎ-), v.t. Obtain patent for (invention). [f. prec.]

pǎtentee′, n. Taker-out or holder of a patent, person for the time being entitled to the benefit of a patent. [-EE]

pāt′er, n. Father (sl.). [L, = father]

pǎterfamil′iǎs, n. (Rom. law & joc.) 'head of family. [L]

patern′al, a. Of a father; fatherly; related through the father, as ~ *grandmother*, father's mother; ~ *government*, *legislation*, etc. (that limits the freedom of the subject by well-meant regulations). Hence ~**LY**² adv. [f. LL *paternalis* (*paternus* f. *pater* father), see -AL]

patern′ity, n. Fatherhood; one's paternal origin; (fig.) authorship, source. [ME, f. OF *paternite* or LL *paternitas* (as prec., see -TY)]

pǎt′ernŏs′ter, n. The Lord's Prayer, esp. in Latin; *black, white,* ~, forms of words said as charms etc.; *devil's* ~, muttered imprecation; bead in rosary indicating that ~ is to be said; ~ *line*, weighted fishing-tackle with hooks at intervals. [OE, ME, f. L *pater noster* our father]

path, n. (pahth, *pl. pr.* pahdhz). Footway, esp. one merely beaten by feet, not specially constructed (also ~′*way*); track laid for foot or cycle racing, esp. *cinder* ~; line along which person or thing moves; ~′*finder*, explorer, aircraft (or its pilot) sent ahead of bombers to guide them to their objective & mark out their targets. Hence ~**LESS** (-ah-) a. [OE *pæth*, OLG *pad*, OHG *pfad* f. WG **patha*]

Pathan′ (-tahn), n. Member of a people inhabiting N.W. Pakistan and S.E. Afghanistan. [Hindi]

pathět′|ic, a. & n. Exciting pity or sadness; of the emotions (~*ic fallacy*, crediting nature with human emotion); (n. pl.) study of, indulgence in, demonstration of, these. Hence ~**ICALLY** adv. [f. F *pathétique*, f. LL f. Gk *pathētikos* (*path-*, root of *paskhō* suffer, see -ETIC)]

pǎth′|ic, n. = CATAMITE. [f. L f. Gk *pathikos* passive (PATHOS, -IC)]

pǎtho-, comb. form of Gk *pathos* suffering, disease, passion, as: ~*gen′esis*, ~*geny* (-ǒj′-), production of disease, so ~*genět′ic*, ~*gěn′ic*, ~*genous* (-ǒj′-), aa.; ~*gnomŏn′ic*, characteristic of particular disease; ~*gnomy* (-ǒg′-), study of the emotions, so ~*gnŏm′ic* a.; *pathŏl′ogy*, science of (usu. bodily) diseases, so ~*lo′gical* a., ~*lo′gically* adv., *pathŏl′ogist* n.

pǎth′ŏs, n. Quality in speech, writing, events, etc., that excites pity or sadness. [f. Gk *pathos* suffering, see PATHETIC]

-pathy̌, suf. repr. Gk *-patheia* suffering, feeling, the second element of the word HOMOEOPATHY, extended to ALLOPATHY & (w. sense curative treatment) to other compds, as *hydro*~, *kinesi*~, *electro*~.

pā′tience (-shns), n. 1. Calm endurance of pain or any provocation; perseverance; *have no* ~ *with*, be irritated by, be unable to endure, (person, his conduct, etc.); *out of* ~ *with*, no longer able to endure; *the* ~ *of Job*, the utmost limits of ~ (*would try the* ~ *of Job*). 2. Game of cards, usu. for one. 3. ~-*dock*, kinds of plant. [ME, f. OF, f. L *patientia* (as foll., see -ENCE)]

pā′tient (-shnt), a. & n. 1. Having, showing, patience; ~ *of*, enduring with patience, (also) admitting of or compatible with (*the facts are* ~ *of two interpretations*). 2. n. Person under medical treatment. Hence ~**LY**² adv. [ME, f. OF, f. L *pati* suffer, see -ENT]

pǎt′in|a, n. Incrustation, usu. green, on surface of old bronze, esteemed as ornament; gloss produced by age on woodwork. Hence ~**ātěd** [-ATE²], ~**OUS**, aa. ~**A′TION** n. [f. It. *patina*, whence F *patine*, f. L *patina* dish]

pa′tǐŏ (pah-), n. (pl. ~s). Inner court open to sky in Spanish or Span.-Amer. house. [Sp.]

pǎt′ois (-twah, & see Ap.), n. Dialect of common people in a district, differing materially from the literary language. [F, of unkn. orig.]

pāt′riarch (-k), n. 1. Father & ruler of family or tribe; (pl.) sons of Jacob, (also) Abraham, Isaac, & Jacob, & their forefathers. 2. (In early & Eastern Churches) bishop, esp. of Antioch, Alexandria, Constantinople, Jerusalem, or Rome; (in R.-C. Church) bishop ranking next above primates & metropolitans. 3. Founder of an order, science, etc.; venerable old man; *the* oldest living representative (*of* a class etc.). Hence **pātriärch′AL** (-k-) a. [ME, f. OF *patriarche* f. LL (-*cha*) f. Gk *patriarkhēs* (*patria* family f. *patēr* father + -*arkhēs* ruler)]

pāt′riarchate (-k-), n. Office, see, residence, of ecclesiastical patriarch; rank of tribal patriarch. [f. med. L PATRIARCH-*atus* (-ATE²)]

pāt′riarch|y̌ (-k-), n. Patriarchal system of society, government, etc. So ~**ISM** n. [f. med. L f. Gk *patriarkhia* (as PATRIARCH, see -Y¹)]

patri'cian (-shn), n. & a. **1.** Ancient Roman noble (cf. PLEBEIAN); member of a noble order in later Roman Empire; officer representing Roman Emperor in provinces of Italy & Africa; nobleman (cf. PLEBEIAN), esp. (hist.) in some Italian republics. **2.** adj. Noble, aristocratic, esp. of the ancient Roman nobility. Hence ~SHIP n. [f. L *patricius* (*pater* -*tris* father, pl. senators, nobles) +-AN]

patri'ciate (-shI-), n. Patrician order, aristocracy; rank of patrician. [f. L *patriciatus* (as prec., see -ATE¹)]

păt'ricīde, n. Parricide (less correct & less usual than *parricide*, but occas. preferred in the narrower sense of murder(er) of one's father). Hence **pătricīd'al** n. [PATER, -CIDE]

păt'rimony̆, n. Property inherited from one's father or ancestors, heritage (often fig.); endowment of church etc. So **pătrimōn'IAL** a. [ME -*moigne* f. OF *patrimoine* f. L *patrimonium* (*pater* -*tris* father, see -MONY)]

păt'riot, n. One who defends or is zealous for his country's freedom or rights. Hence or cogn. **pătriŏt'IC** a., **pătriŏt'ICALLY** adv., ~ISM n. [f. F *patriote* f. LL (-*ta*) f. Gk *patriōtēs* (*patrios* of one's fathers f. *pater* -*tros* father, see -OT²)]

patris'tic, a. Of (the study of the writings of) the Fathers of the Church. [f. G *patristisch* f. L *pater*-*tris* father +-IST +-IC]

patrŏl', n., & v.i. & t. (-ll-). **1.** Going the rounds of garrison, camp, etc.; perambulation of town etc. by police (*~man*, policeman; *~ wagon*, prison van); detachment of guard, police constable(s), told off for this; detachment of troops sent out to reconnoitre; routine operational flight of aircraft. **2.** vb. Act as ~; go round (camp, town, etc.) as ~. [n. (thr. F *patrouille*) & vb. f. F *patrouiller*, orig. = paddle in mud, earlier *patouiller*, cf. OF *patoueil* puddle, mire]

păt'ron, n. One who countenances, protects, or gives influential support to (person, cause, art, etc.); (shop) regular customer; (also ~ *saint*) tutelary saint; (Rom. ant.) former owner of manumitted slave, (also) protector of a CLIENT; ‖ one who has right of presentation to benefice. So **păt'roNESS¹** n. [ME, f. OF, = patron PATTERN, f. L *patronus* (*pater* -*tris* father]

păt'ronage, n. Support, encouragement, given by patron; ‖ right of presentation to benefice or office, as *has a great deal of* ~ *in his hands*; patronizing airs; customer's support. [ME, f. OF (as prec., see -AGE)]

păt'ronal, a. Of a patron saint (*the* ~ *festival* etc.). [F, or f. LL *patronalis* (as prec., -AL)]

păt'roniz|e, -is|e (-Iz), v.t. Act as patron towards, support, encourage, (person, practice, etc.); treat condescendingly, whence ~**inGLY²** adv. [f. F, or med. L; see -IZE]

pătrony̆m'ic, a. & n. (Name) derived from that of a father or ancestor. [f. LL f. Gk *patrōnumikos* f. *patrōnumos* (*pater* -*tros* father +*onoma* name), see -IC]

‡patrōōn', n. (hist.). Possessor of landed estate with manorial privileges (abolished *c.* 1850) under Dutch governments of New York & New Jersey. [Du. *patroon* PATRON]

pătt'en, n. Overshoe with wooden sole on iron ring etc., for raising wearer's shoes out of mud etc. [ME, f. OF *patin*, f. *patte* paw +-*in* -INE¹]

pătt'er¹, n. Lingo of a profession or class; speechifying; rapid speech introduced into song; words of song, comedy, etc. [18th c. cant, f. foll.]

pătt'er², v.t. & i. Repeat (prayers etc.) in rapid mechanical way; talk glibly. [14th c., f. *pater* = PATERNOSTER]

pătt'er³, v.i. & t., & n. **1.** Make rapid succession of taps, as rain on window-pane; run with short quick steps; cause (water etc.) to ~. **2.** n. Succession of taps. [f. PAT³ +-ER⁵]

pătt'ern, n., & v.t. **1.** Excellent example, as *she is a ~ of domestic virtues*; (attrib.) perfect, ideal, model, (esp. of persons, as ~ *wife, father*); model from which thing is to be made; sample (of tailor's cloth etc.); decorative design as executed on carpet, wallpaper, cloth, etc.; marks made by shot from gun on target; ~ *room, -shop*, part of foundry etc. in which ~*s* are prepared. **2.** v.t. Model (thing *after, upon*, design etc.), decorate with ~. [ME *patron* (see PATRON); different. in sense & sp. since.16/17th c.]

pătt'y̆, n. Little pie or pasty; ~*pan* (for baking ~ in). [f. F *pâté* PASTY¹]

păt'ūlous, a. Open, expanded; (of boughs etc.) spreading. Hence ~LY² adv., ~NESS n. [f. L *patulus* (*patēre* be open) +-OUS]

pau'city̆, n. Smallness of number or quantity. [ME, f. OF *paucité* or L *paucitas* (*paucus* few, see -TY)]

Paul, n. *Rob* PETER¹ *to pay* ~; ~ *Pry*, inquisitive person (character in comedy by J. Poole 1825).

Paul'ine, a. & n. **1.** Of St Paul, as *the* ~ *epistles*. **2.** n. ‖ Member of St Paul's School in London. [-INE¹]

paulo-pŏst-fū'ture, n. (Gk gram.) tense expressing state resulting from future act, future-perfect; (joc.) immediate future. [f. med. L, = future a little after]

paunch, n., & v.t. **1.** Belly, stomach; ruminant's first stomach; (naut.) thick strong mat, (*rubbing* ~) wooden shield on mast, to prevent chafing. **2.** v.t. Disembowel. [ME, f. ONF *panche* f. Rom. *‡pantica* f. L *pantex* -*icis*]

paup'er, n. Person without means of livelihood, beggar; recipient of poor-law relief; person who may sue IN⁵ *forma pauperis*. Hence ~DOM, ~ISM(2). ~**IZA'TION**, nn., ~IZE(3) v.t. [L, = poor]

pause (-z), n., & v.i. **1.** Interval of inaction or silence, esp. from hesitation; temporary stop; *give* ~ *to*, cause (person) to hesitate; break made in speaking or reading; (mus.) mark (⌢ or ⌣) over or under note or rest that is to be lengthened indefinitely. **2.** v.i. Make a ~, wait; linger *upon* (word etc.). [ME, f. OF, f. L *pausa* f. Gk *pausis* (*pauō* stop)]

pāv′age, n. Paving; tax, toll, towards paving of streets. [AF, OF (PAVE, -AGE)]

pǎv′an, n. Stately dance in which dancers were elaborately dressed. [f. F *pavane* f. Sp. *pavana*, poss. f. *pavo* PEACOCK]

pāve, v.t. Cover (street, floor, etc.) with or as with pavement (often fig., as ~*d with flowers, with good intentions*); (fig.) ~ (prepare) *the way* (*for, to,* reform etc.). Hence **pāv′ER¹**, **pāv′IOUR** (-*vyer*), nn. [ME, f. OF *paver* f. L *pavire* beat, ram, or back form. f. *pavement*]

pavé (pǎv′ā), n. Pavement; setting of jewels placed close together. [F, p.p. as prec.]

pāve′ment (-vm-), n. Covering of street, floor, etc., made of stones, tiles, wooden blocks, asphalt, etc., ‖ esp. paved footway at side of road (*crazy* ~, of irregular flat stones for garden paths etc.); ‖~-*artist*, one who draws coloured figures on ~ to get money from passers-by; (zool.) ~-*like* formation of close-set teeth etc. [ME, f. OF f. L *pavimentum* (as PAVE, see -MENT)]

pavil′ion (-lyon), n., & v.t. **1.** Tent, esp. large peaked one; light ornamental building, esp. one attached to cricket or other ground for players and distinguished spectators; projecting (usu. highly decorated) sub-division of building; part of cut gem-stone below girdle. **2.** v.t. Enclose in, furnish with, ~. [ME, f. OF *pavillon* f. L *papilionem* (nom. *-io*) butterfly, in LL, tent]

pavona′zzo (pah-, -ătsō), a. & n. (Marble) with peacock-coloured markings. [It.]

pāv′onine, a. Of, like, a peacock. [f. L *pavoninus* (*pavo -onis* peacock, see -INE¹)]

paw¹, n. Foot of beast having claws or nails, opp. to HOOF; (colloq.) hand, person's handwriting. [ME *pawe, powe* f. OF *poue* f. WG (Frank.) *pauta = MDu., MLG *pōte*]

paw², v.t. & i. Strike with paw; (of horse) strike (ground), strike ground, with hoofs; (colloq.) handle awkwardly or rudely. [f. prec.]

‖ **pawk′ |ȳ**, a. (Sc., dial.). Drily humorous. Hence ~ILY² adv., ~INESS n. [f. Sc. & north. dial. *pawk* trick, of unkn. orig., +-Y²]

pawl, n., & v.t. **1.** Lever with catch for teeth of wheel or bar; (naut.) short bar used to prevent capstan, windlass, etc., from recoiling. **2.** v.t. Secure (capstan etc.) with ~. [f. LG, Du. *pal*]

pawn¹, n. Piece of smallest size & value in chess (often fig. of persons). [ME, f. AF *poun*, OF *peon* f. L *pedonem* (nom. *-o*), in med. L foot-soldier (*pes pedis* foot)]

pawn², n. Thing, person, left in another's keeping as security, pledge, (now chiefly fig.); state of being pledged, esp. *in, at,* ~; ~'*broker*, one who lends money upon interest on security of personal property pawned; ~'*broking*, his occupation; ~'*shop*, his place of business. [ME, f. OF *pan*, obsc. rel. to OFris., OS *pand*, OHG *pfant*]

pawn³, v.t. Deposit (thing) as security for payment of money or performance of action; (fig.) pledge (one's life, honour, word). [f. prec.]

pawnee′, n. Person with whom pawn is deposited. [-EE]

pawpaw′. Var. of PAPAW.

pǎx, n. **1.** Tablet with representation of Crucifixion etc. kissed at Mass by priests & congregation, osculatory; the kiss of peace as liturgical form at High Mass. **2.** ~ *Rōmăn′a, Brĭtănn′ĭca*, peace imposed by Roman, British, rule; ~ *vōb′ĭs, vōbĭs′cum*, peace be to, with, you (esp. as priestly blessing). **3.** ‖ (school sl., as int.). Peace!, truce! [ME, f. L, = peace]

pǎx′wǎx, n. (dial., colloq.). Stout tendon extending from dorsal vertebrae to occiput in man & other mammals. [ME *faxwax*, app. f. OE *feax* hair + *weax growth (WAX²)]

pay¹, n. Payment: *in the* ~ (employment) *of*; wages; ~-*day*, day on which payment is (to be) made, ‖ (Stock Exch.) day on which transfer of stock has to be paid for; ~ *load*, part of aircraft's load which produces revenue; ~'*master*, official who pays troops, workmen, etc. (often fig.); ~-*master general*, ‖ minister at head of a department of Treasury. [ME, f. OF *paie*, f. *payer* (foll.)]

pay², v.t. & i. (paid). **1.** Give (person) what is due in discharge of debt or *for* services done or goods received; ~ *off*, ~ in full & discharge or be quit of (ship's crew, creditor, etc.); (fig.) reward, recompense; ~ (person) *out*, punish him; ~ *him in his own* COIN; (colloq.) *that has put paid to* (settled) *him*. **2.** Recompense (work). **3.** Hand over (money owed *to* person, or w. double object); hand over the amount of (debt, wages, ransom, tithes). **4.** ~ *in,* ~ to one's own or another's banking account; ~ one's *way*, not get into debt; ~ *through the* NOSE, ~ *the* PIPER; ~ *up,* ~ full amount of (arrears, or abs.). **5.** Render, bestow, (attention, respect, court, compliment, *to*). **6.** (Of business etc.) yield adequate return, yield adequate return to (person). **7.** ~ *for,* hand over the price of, bear the cost of (~ *for* one's WHISTLE), (fig.) be punished for (fault etc.); ~ *off,* yield results, succeed, (of ship) fall off to leeward when helm is put up; (naut.) ~ *out, away,* let out (rope) by slackening it. **8.** ‖~-*as-you-earn* (abbr. *P.A.Y.E.*), method of collecting income-tax by deducting at source as income is earned. Hence ~EE′, ~′ER¹, nn. [ME, f.

OF *paier* f. L *pacare* appease (*pax pacis* peace))

‖ pay², v.t. (naut.). Smear with pitch, tar, etc., as defence against wet. [f. OF *peier* f. L *picare* (*pix picis* pitch)]

pay'able, a. That must be paid, due; that may be paid; (of mine etc.) profitable. [-ABLE]

pay'ment, n. Paying; amount paid; (fig.) recompense. [ME, f. OF *paiement* (PAY²)]

payn'im, n. (arch.). Pagan, esp. Mohammedan (often attrib.). [ME, f. OF *paienime* f. LL *paganismus* (PAGAN, see -ISM)]

paysage' (-zahzh), n. Rural scene, landscape; landscape painting, so pays'agIST n. [F]

pea, n. 1. Leguminous plant whose seeds are used for food; its seed, as *green* ~s (gathered unripe for food), SPLIT ~s; SWEET ~; *as like as two* ~s, undistinguishable. 2. ~'*nut*, (plant whose fruit is a pod containing) seed used as food & yielding oil; ~'*shooter*, tube from which dried ~s are shot; ~ *soup* (made from esp. dried ~s); ~'*souper* (colloq.), thick yellow fog; ~*soupy*, (of fog) thick & yellow. [back formation f. PEASE taken as pl.]

peace, n. 1. Freedom from, cessation of, war, as ~ *with honour*, ~ *at any price*, *make* (bring about) ~; *a treaty of* ~ between two powers at war. 2. Freedom from civil disorder; BREACH¹ *of the* ~; *the* (*queen's*) ~, general ~ of the realm as secured by law, as *commission*, JUSTICE, *of the* ~, *be sworn of the* ~ (made a magistrate). 3. Quiet, tranquillity; (in & after bibl. use) ~ *be with you*, ~ *to his ashes!*; mental calm, as ~ *of mind, conscience.* 4. *At* ~, in state of friendliness, not at strife (*with*); *hold* one's ~, keep silence; *keep the* ~, prevent, refrain from, strife; *make* (person's, one's) ~, bring person, oneself, back into friendly relations (*with*); ~'*maker*, one who brings about ~; ~ OFFENSIVE; ~-*offering*, propitiatory gift, (bibl.) offering presented as thanksgiving to God; ~- *pipe*, CALUMET, tobacco- -pipe as token of ~ among N.-Amer. Indians. [ME & OF *pais* f. L *pacem* (nom. *pax*)]

peace'ab|le (-sa-), a. Disposed, tending, to peace; free from disturbance, peaceful. Hence ~leNESS n., ~LY² adv. [ME & OF *peisible* &c. (as prec., see -BLE)]

peace'ful (-sf-), a. Characterized by, belonging to a state of, peace; ~ CO-EXISTENCE. Hence ~LY² adv., ~NESS n. [ME; -FUL]

peach¹, n. Large fruit, usu. round, with downy white or yellow skin flushed with red, highly flavoured sweet pulp, & rough stone; (also ~-*tree*) tree bearing this; (sl.) person or thing of superlative merit, specially attractive girl; ~-*blow*, (glaze of) delicate purplish-pink colour; ~ *brandy*, spirituous liquor from ~ juice; ~-

-*colour(ed)*, (of) soft pale red; ~ *Melba*, = PÊCHE MELBA. [ME, f. OF *pesche* f. Rom. **persica* f. L *persicum* (*malum*), lit. Persian apple]

peach², v.i. (now sl.). Turn informer; inform (*against, upon*, accomplice). [ME, aphetic f. *appeach* f. OF *empechier* IM-PEACH]

pea'chick, n. Young pea-fowl.

peach'|y̆, a. Like a peach, esp. (of cheeks) in colour & softness. Hence ~iNESS n. [-Y²]

pea'cŏck, n., & v.t. & i. 1. Bird with splendid plumage & tail that can be expanded erect like fan (often as type of ostentatious display; *proud as a* ~); ~ *blue*, lustrous blue of ~'s neck; ~ *butterfly*, maroon butterfly with ocellated wings; ‖ ~ *coal* (iridescent); ~-*fish*, fish with brilliant green, blue, red, & white colouring. 2. vb. Plume one*self*, make display; strut about ostentatiously, whence ~ERY (4) n. Hence ~ISH¹, ~LIKE, aa. [ME *pecock* f. OE *pēa* (also *pāwa* whence ME *pocock*) f. L *pavo*, +COCK¹]

pea'fowl, n. Peacock or peahen. [see prec.]

pea'hĕn, n. Female of the peacock. [ME, see PEACOCK]

pea'jăckĕt, n. Sailor's short overcoat of coarse woollen cloth. [f. obs. *pee* f. MDu. *pie* (now *pij*) pea-jacket+JACKET, or dir. f. Du. *pij-jekker*]

peak¹, n. 1. Projecting part of brim of cap. 2. (naut.). Narrow part of ship's hold esp. (also *fore*~, *after*~) at bow or stern; upper outer corner of sail extended by gaff. 3. Pointed top, esp. of mountain; point e.g. of beard. 4. Highest point in curve or record of fluctuations (~-*load*, maximum of electric power, traffic, etc.). Hence ~ED² (-kt), ~'Y², aa. [16th c. equivalent of PIKE¹ (as 15th c. *peaked* for ME *piked*), of obsc. form.; w. sense 2 cf. LG *piek*]

peak², v.i. Waste away, esp. (Shakespeare) ~ *& pine*; (p.p.) sharp-featured, pinched. So ~'Y² a., sickly, puny. [16th c., of obsc. orig.]

peak³, v.t. & i. (naut.). Tilt (yard) vertically; place (oars) APEAK; (of whale) raise (tail, flukes), raise tail or flukes, straight up in diving vertically. [f. APEAK]

peaky. See PEAK¹, PEAK².

peal¹, n., & v.i. & t. 1. Loud ringing of bell(s), esp. series of changes on set of bells; set of bells; loud volley of sound, esp. of thunder or laughter. 2. v.i. Sound forth in a ~. 3. v.t. Utter sonorously; ~ *bells*, ring them in ~s. [ME *pele*, aphetic f. *apele* APPEAL]

peal², peel, n. (In Ireland) salmon grilse; (in England) sea-trout. [orig. unkn.]

pear (pâr), n. A fleshy fruit, tapering towards stalk; ~-*shaped*; ~-*tree*; PRICKLY ~. [OE *pere*, MDu., MLG *pere* f. WG **pera* f. Rom. **pira* f. L *pirum*]

pearl¹ (pêrl), I. n. Concretion, usu. white

or bluish-grey, formed within shell of ~-*oyster* & other bivalve mollusc, having beautiful lustre & highly prized as gem; MOTHER[1]-*of*-~; SEED ~. 2. Precious thing, finest example (*of* its kind); *cast* ~*s before swine*, offer good thing to one incapable of appreciating it. 3. ~-like thing, e.g. dewdrop, tear, tooth. 4. Size of TYPE. 5. Small fragment of various substances. 6. ~-*ash*, potassium carbonate; ~-*barley*, -*sago*, etc. (reduced by attrition to small rounded grains); ~-*diver*, one who dives for ~-oysters; ~-*fisher*, one who fishes for~-*s*; ~-*fishery*, his occupation, place of this; ~-*powder*, -*white*, cosmetic used to whiten skin; ~-*shell*, mother-of-~ as naturally found. Hence ~ED[2] (-ld), ~'Y[2], aa., ~'INESS n., (pẽr-). [ME, f. OF *perle* f. Rom. *perla*, of obsc. orig.]

pearl[2] (pẽrl), v.t. & i. Sprinkle with pearly drops; make pearly in colour etc.; reduce (barley etc.) to small pearls; form pearl-like drops; fish for pearls. [f. prec.]

pearl[3] (pẽrl), n. One of a row of fine loops forming decorative edging on pillow-lace etc. [app. var. of PURL[1]]

‖ **pear'lies** (pẽr'liz), n. pl. Costermongers' dress with mother-of-pearl buttons.

pear'main (pãr-), n. Kind of apple. [f. OF *permain* prob. f. Rom. *parmanus* of Parma]

pea'sant (pĕz-), n. Countryman, rustic, worker on the land. [ME, f. AF *paisant*, OF *païsent* f. *païs* country f. LL *pagensis* (*pagus* canton)]

pea'santry (pĕz-), n. (Body of) peasants. [-RY]

pease (-z), n. Peas, esp. in ~-*pudding*; (arch.) ~'*cod*, pea-pod. [OE *pise* pea, pl. *pisan*, f. LL *pisa* f. L *pisum* f. Gk *pison*; cf. PEA]

peat[1], n. (Cut piece of) vegetable matter decomposed by water & partly carbonized, used for fuel; ~'*bog*, ~'*moss*, bog composed of ~; ~'*reek*, smoke of, whisky distilled over, ~-fire. Hence ~'ERY(3) n., ~'Y[2] a. [ME *pete* f. Celt. *pett*-; see PIECE]

peat[2], n. (arch.). Girl, belle, (esp. *proud* ~). [16th c., of unkn. orig.]

peb'ble, n. Small stone worn & rounded by action of water; colourless transparent rock-crystal used for spectacles, lens of this; kinds of agate or other gem. Hence **pĕbb'lY**[2] a. [OE *papol-stān*; ME *pobble*, *puble*; 16th c. *pebble*; orig. unkn.]

pébrine (pābrēn'), n. Epidemic disease of silkworms characterized by black spots. [F, f. Pr. *pebrino* (*pebre* PEPPER)]

pecan', n. Kind of hickory of the Mississippi region; its nut. [Algonkin *pakan*]

pĕcc'|able, a. Liable to sin. Hence ~**ABIL'ITY** n. [f. F, or med. L *peccabilis* (*peccare* sin, see -BLE)]

pĕccadill'o, n. (pl. ~*es*). Trifling offence. [f. Sp. *pecadillo*, dim. of *pecado* sin, as foll., or It. *peccadiglio*]

pĕcc'|ant, a. Sinning; (med.) morbid, inducing disease. So ~**ANCY** n. [f. L *peccare* sin, see -ANT]

pĕcc'arÿ, n. American gregarious quadruped allied to swine. [f. native *pakira*]

pĕccāv'ī, sent. & n. I have sinned, esp. *cry* ~; (n.) this confession. [L]

pêche Mĕl'ba (pāsh), n. (Also *peach Melba*) confection of ice-cream & peaches flavoured with liqueurs etc. [F, after Dame Nellie *Melba*, Australian prima donna (d. 1931)]

peck[1], n. Measure of capacity for dry goods, = 2 gallons; vessel used for this; *a* ~ (large number, amount) *of troubles*, *of dirt*. [ME, AF *pek*, of unkn. orig.; cf. OF *pek* (once), *picote*, *picotin* peck]

peck[2], v.t. & i., & n. 1. Strike (thing) with beak; ~ *out*, pluck out thus; make (hole etc.) thus; kiss (person's cheek etc.) perfunctorily; aim *at* (thing) with beak, (fig.) carp *at*; (colloq.) eat (food, or abs.), esp. in nibbling fashion; mark with short strokes; break (ground, wall, etc. *up*, *down*, etc.) with pointed tool. 2. n. Stroke with beak, mark made with this; hasty kiss; (sl.) victuals. [prob. f. MLG *pekken*, of unkn. orig.]

peck[3], v.t. & i. (sl.). Throw (stone), throw stones (*at*). [dial. var. of PITCH[2]]

peck'er, n. Bird that pecks (chiefly in comb., esp. WOOD~); kind of hoe; ‖ (sl.) *keep your* ~ (spirits, perh. orig. = beak) *up*. [-ER[1]]

peck'ish, a. (colloq.). Hungry. [-ISH[1]]

Peck'sniff, n. Unctuous hypocrite prating of benevolence etc. [in Dickens' *Martin Chuzzlewit*]

pec't|ĕn, n. (zool.; pl. ~*ines* pr. -ēz). Comb-like structure of various kinds in animal bodies, so ~**inATE**[2], ~**inātĕd**, aa., ~**inA'TION** n.; scallop. [L, gen. -*tinis*, comb]

pec't|in, n. (chem.). Soluble gum-like carbohydrate, the setting agent in jams & jellies, formed in fruits from pectose by ripening or (in fruits & fruit-juice) by heating. So ~**IC** a. [f. Gk *pēktos* congealed (*pēgnumi* make solid) +-IN]

pec'toral, n. & a. 1. Ornamental breast-plate, esp. that of Jewish high priest; ~ fin, muscle, etc. 2. adj. Of, for, good for diseases of, the breast or chest; worn on the breast (~ *cross*, by bishops). [ME, f. OF, or L *pectoralis* a., -*le* n. (*pectus -oris* breast, see -AL]

pec'tōse, n. (chem.). Insoluble substance related to cellulose & found with it in unripe fruits etc. [as PECTIN, see -OSE[2]]

pec'ŭl|āte (pĕk-), v.t. & i. Embezzle (money, or abs.). So ~**A'TION**, ~**ātor**, nn. [f. L *peculari* (as foll.), see -ATE[3]]

pecūl'iar, a. & n. 1. Belonging exclusively *to*; belonging to the individual, esp. one's *own* ~ (character etc.); particular, special, as *a point of* ~ *interest*; strange, odd, as *a* ~ *flavour*, *he has always been a little* ~; ~ *people*, the Jews, (in wider sense) God's elect, (P~ *People*) evangelical Christian denomination founded 1838 relying on divine healing for cure of disease. **2.** n. ~ property, privilege, etc.; parish, church, exempt from jurisdiction of diocese in which it lies; (P~) one of the P~ People. [ME, f. OF *peculier*, or L *peculiaris* of private property (*peculium* f. *pecu* cattle, see -AR[1])]

pĕcūliă'rĭtў, n. Being peculiar; characteristic; oddity. [-ITY]

pĕcūl'iarlў, adv. As regards oneself alone, individually, as *does not affect him* ~; especially, more than usually, as ~ *annoying*; oddly, as *they dress* ~. [-LY[2]]

pĕcūn'iar|ў, a. (Consisting) of money, as ~*y aid*, *consiaerations*; (of offence) having ~*y* penalty. Hence ~ILY[2] adv. [f. L *pecuniarius* (*pecunia* money f. *pecu* cattle, see -ARY[1])]

pĕd'agŏgue (-g), n. Schoolmaster, teacher, (usu. derog. implying pedantry). Hence or cogn. **pĕdăgŏg'IC(AL)** (-ŏg-, -ŏj-) aa., **pĕdăgŏg'icalLY**[2] adv., **pĕd'agŏg(u)-** ISM(1) (-gizm) n. [ME, f. OF f. L f. Gk *paidagōgos* (*pais paidos* boy + -*agōgos* f. *agō* lead)]

pĕd'agŏg|ў (-gĭ, -jĭ), n. Science of teaching. So ~ICS (-gŏg[2], -gŏj[2]) n. [f. F *pédagogie* f. Gk *paidagōgia*, as prec.]

pĕd'al[1]**, n., & v.i. & t.** (-ll-). **1.** (In organ) each of the wooden keys played upon by the feet, (also) foot-lever for drawing out several stops at once or other purposes; (in piano) foot-lever for making the tone fuller (*loud* ~) or softer (*soft* ~); foot-lever in various machines, esp. bicycle (~ *cycle*) or tricycle; (mus.) note sustained in one part, usu. bass, through successive harmonies some of which are independent of it. **2.** vb. Play on organ ~s, work bicycle ~s; work (bicycle) thus. [f. F *pédale* f. It. *pedale* f. L as foll.]

pĕd'al[2]**, a.** (zool.). Of the feet or foot (esp. of mollusc). [f. L *pedalis* (*pes pedis* foot, see -AL)]

pĕd'ant, n. One who overrates or parades book-learning or technical knowledge or insists on strict adherence to formal rules; one who is possessed by a theory, doctrinaire. Hence or cogn. **pĕdăn'tIC** a., **pĕdăn'tICALLY** adv., ~IZE(2, 3) v.t. & i., ~ŏc'RACY, ~RY(1, 4, 5), nn. [f. F, f. It. *pedante*; app. f. *pedagogue* + -*ant* -ANT]

pĕd'ate, a. (Zool.) footed; (bot., of leaf) having divisions like toes or bird's claws. [f. L *pedatus* (*pes pedis* foot, see -ATE[2])]

pĕd'dle, v.i. & t. Follow occupation of pedlar; busy oneself with trifles; deal out in small quantities, retail, (usu. fig.). [(1)16th c., app. back form. f. PEDLAR; (2)16th c., var. of PIDDLE]

pederasty. See PAEDERASTY.

pĕd'ĕstal, n., & v.t. (-ll-). Base supporting column or pillar; base of statue etc.; each of two supports of knee-hole table; foundation (lit. & fig.); movable cupboard for chamber-pots; (v.t.) set, support, on

~. [f. F *piédestal* f. It. *piedestallo* (*piè* foot f. L *pes pedis* + *di* of + *stallo* STALL[1])]

pĕdĕs'trian, a. & n. 1. Going, performed, on foot; of walking; prosaic, dull, uninspired. **2.** n. One who walks, esp. as athletic performance, whence ~ISM(2) n., ~IZE(2) v.i. [f. F (-*tre*) or L *pedester* -*tris* + -IAN]

pĕd'icel, pĕd'icle, nn. (bot., zool.). Small (esp. subordinate, cf. PEDUNCLE) stalk-like structure in plant or animal. Hence **pĕd'icellATE**[2]**, pĕdic'ūlATE**[2]**, aa.** [f. mod. L *pedicellus* dim. of L *pediculus* dim. of *pes pedis* foot, see -CULE]

pĕdic'ūlar, -lous, aa. Lousy. So **pĕdĭcūlos'IS** n. [f. L *pedicularis, -losus* (*pediculus* louse, see -AR[1], -OUS)]

pĕd'icūre, n., & v.t. 1. Chiropody; chiropodist. **2.** v.t. Cure or treat (feet) by removing corns etc. [f. F *pédicure* f. L *pes pedis* foot + *cura* care]

pĕd'igree, n. Genealogical table; ancestral line (of man or animal); derivation (of word); ancient descent; (attrib.) having known line of descent, as ~ *cattle*. Hence **pĕd'igreED**[2] a. [15th c. *pedegru* etc., f. AF = OF *pie de grue* crane's foot, mark denoting succession in ~s]

pĕd'iment, n. Triangular part crowning front of building in Grecian style, esp. over portico; similarly placed member of same or other form in Roman & Renaissance styles. Hence **pĕdimĕn'tAL, ~ED**[2]**, aa.** [c. 1600 *periment*, perh. corrupt. of PYRAMID]

pĕd'lar, n. Travelling vendor of small wares usu. carried in pack; (fig.) retailer (*of gossip* etc.); ~*'s French*, thieves' cant. Hence **pĕd'larY n.** [14th c. *pedlere*, alt. of *pedder* (13th c.), f. *ped* pannier (14th c.), of unkn. orig.]

pedo-. See PAEDO-.

pĕdŏl'ogў, n. Science of soils. Hence ~L'OGIST n. [f. Gk *pedon* ground, -LOGY]

pĕdŏmĕt'er, n. Instrument for estimating distance travelled on foot by recording number of steps taken. [f. F *pédomètre* f. L *pes pedis* foot + -o- + -METER]

pĕd'rail, n. Device for facilitating progress of heavy vehicles over rough ground by attachment of broad footlike supporting surfaces to wheel-rims. [f. L *pes pedis* foot + RAIL[1]]

pĕdŭnc'|le (-ŭng'kl), n. (Bot.) stalk of flower, fruit, or cluster, esp. main stalk bearing solitary flower or subordinate stalks (*pedicels*); (zool.) stalklike process in animal body. Hence ~ūlAR[1], ~ūlATE[2] (-at), aa. [f. mod. L *pedunculus* f. L *pes pedis* foot + -UNCLE]

pee, v.i., & n. (colloq.). Urinate; urination. [f. PISS, cf. F *pipi*]

peek, v.i. Peep, peer, (*in, out,* etc.); ~*a-boo* (now U.S.), = BO-PEEP. [ME *pike, pyke*, of unkn. orig.]

peel[1]**, n.** (hist.). Small square tower built in 16th c. in border counties of England

& Scotland. [ME *pel* stake, palisade, f. AF *pel*, = OF *piel* f. L *palus* stake; cf. PALE[1]]

peel[2], n. Shovel, esp. baker's for thrusting loaves etc. into oven. [ME & OF *pele* f. L *pala*; cf. PALETTE]

peel[3], v.t. & i., & n. **1.** Strip the ~, rind, bark, etc., from (orange, potato, tree, etc.); take *off* (skin, ~, etc.); (arch., from *Isa.* xviii. 2, perh. mistransl.) *scattered & ~ed* (pillaged); (intr., of tree, animal body, etc.) become bare of bark, skin, etc., (of bark, surface, etc.) come off or *off* like ~, (of person, now sl.) strip for exercise etc. **2.** n. Rind, outer coating, of fruit; *candied ~* (usu. of citron). Hence ~'*er*[1] [-ER[1](1, 2)] n., ~'ING[1](2) n. (esp. *potato ~ings*). [in 17th c. different. f. PILL[2]]

peel[4], n. See PEAL[2].

peel'*er*[2], n. ‖ Policeman (sl.); member of Irish constabulary, founded under Peel's secretaryship (hist.). [Robert *Peel* (d. 1850), cf. BOBBY, +-ER[1]]

Peel'ite, n. Conservative siding with Sir R. Peel when he introduced measure for repeal of Corn-laws in 1846. [-ITE[1]]

peen, n. Wedge-shaped or thin end of a hammer-head (opp. *face*). [also *pane*, of uncert. orig.; cf. Norw. *pen*, *pænn* in same sense]

peep[1], v.i., & n. (Make) feeble shrill sound of young birds, mice, etc., chirp, squeak. [late ME var. of PIPE[2]]

peep[2], v.i. Look through narrow aperture (*at*, *into*, etc.); look furtively (~*ing Tom*, type of prurient curiosity, in tale of Godiva); (of daylight, flower, distant object) come cautiously or partly into view, emerge, (often *out*), (fig., of qualities etc.) show itself unconsciously. [late 15th c.; cf. earlier *pike* (= PEEK), *kike*, *keke*]

peep[3], n. Furtive or peering glance; first appearance, esp. *of dawn*, *of day*; ~*-of--day boys*, Protestant organization in Ireland (1784–95) searching opponents' houses at daybreak for arms; ~*-hole*, small hole to peep through; ~*-show*, small exhibition of pictures etc. viewed through lens in small orifice (also fig.); ~ *sight*, aperture sight of some rifles. [f. prec.]

peep'er, n. One who peeps; (sl.) eye. [PEEP[2]+-ER[1]]

peep'ul, pi'pal (pē-), n. Large Indian fig-tree allied to banyan, bo-tree. [Hind. *pīpal*]

peer[1], n. **1.** An equal in civil standing or rank; equal in any respect, as *you will not easily find his ~*, whence ~'LESS a., ~'lèssLY[2] adv., ~'lèssNESS n. **2.** Member of one of the degrees (duke, marquis, earl, viscount, baron) of nobility in United Kingdom, whence ~'ESS[1] n.; ~*s of the realm* or *United Kingdom* (all of whom may sit in House of Lords), ~*s of Scotland, of Ireland*, (represented in H. of Lords by 16 elected to each parliament,

by 28 elected for life); noble (of any country). [ME & OF *per* f. L *par* equal]

peer[2], v.t. & i. Rank with, equal; rank as equal *with*; make (man) a peer. [ME, f. OF *perer* f. LL *pariare* (*par* equal)]

peer[3], v.i. Look narrowly (*into*, *at*, etc.); appear, peep out; come in sight. [16th c., of obsc. orig.; cf. syn. (14th c., now dial.) *pire*, of LG orig.]

peer'age, n. The peers; nobility, aristocracy; rank of peer; book containing list of peers with genealogy etc. [-AGE]

peeved (-vd), a. (sl.). Irritated. [PEEV(ISH), -ED[1]]

peev'ish, a. Querulous, irritable. Hence ~LY[2] adv., ~NESS n. [ME, of unkn. orig.]

peewit. See PEWIT.

pĕg[1], n. Pin, bolt, of wood, metal, etc., usu. round & slightly tapering, for holding together parts of framework etc., stopping up vent of cask, hanging hats etc. on, holding ropes of tent, tightening or loosening strings of violin etc., marking cribbage score, etc.; *round ~ in square* HOLE[1]; CLOTHES-~; (fig.) *a ~ to hang* (discourse etc.) *on*, (occasion, pretext, theme); ‖ a drink, esp. of spirits; *off the ~*, (of clothes) ready-made; ‖ *put* (a man) *on the ~* (army sl.), bring before the C.O. for an offence; *take* (person) *down a ~ or two*, humble him; ~'*top*, pear-shaped spinning-top with métal ~, ~*top trousers* (wide at hips, narrow at ankles). [ME, of LG orig.; cf. MDu. *pegge*, dial. Du. *peg*, LG *pigge*]

pĕg[2], v.t. & i. (-gg-). Fix (thing *down*, *in*, *out*, etc.) with peg; ~ *down*, restrict (*to* rules etc.); (Stock Exch.) prevent price of (stock etc.) from falling (rising) by freely buying (selling) at given price; stabilize (prices, wages, etc.); strike, pierce, aim *at*, with peg; (sl.) throw (stone), throw stones etc., (*at*); mark (score) with pegs on cribbage-board; mark *out* boundaries of (mining claim etc.); ~ (*away*), work persistently (*at*); drive pegs into (cricket--bat); ~ *out*, (croquet) hit peg with ball as final stroke in game, (sl.) die, be ruined. [f. prec.]

Pĕg'asus, n. Winged horse that with stroke of hoof caused fountain Hippocrene to flow on Mt Helicon, (fig.) poetic genius. [L, f. Gk *Pēgasos* (*pēgē* fount)]

peignoir (pān'wahr, & see Ap.), n. Woman's loose dressing-gown. [F (*peigner* comb)]

peine forte et dure (pān fôrtā dūr'), n. Severe & hard punishment, i.e. pressing to death, inflicted on person charged with felony who refused to plead. [F]

pĕj'or'ative (*or* pĭjŏ'r-), a. & n. Depreciatory (word), as *the ~ suffix -aster*. [f. LL *pejorare* make worse (*pejor*), see -ATIVE]

pĕk'an, n. N.-Amer. carnivorous beast of weasel family, valued for fur. [f. native *pékané*]

pēke, n. PEKIN(G)ESE dog. [abbr.]

pĕk'in' (*or* -īng'), n. Kind of silk stuff; [f. F *pékin* as used by Napoleon I's soldiers] civilian. [f. F *pékin* f. Chin. *Pe-king* northern capital]

Pěkin(g)ēse' ('-z), n. & a. (Inhabitant) of Pekin(g); small short-legged snub-nosed dog with long silky hair. [-ESE]

Pěk'ing măn, n. Prehistoric type of man represented by remains first found in 1929 at Peking.

pěk'ŏe, n. Superior kind of black tea. [f. Chin. *pek-ho* (*pek* white + *ho* down), leaves being picked young with down on them]

pěl'age, n. Fur, hair, wool, etc., of quadruped. [F *poil* hair + -AGE]

Pělā'gian¹, a. & n. (Follower) of the monk Pelagius (4th–5th c.), who denied doctrine of original sin. Hence ~ISM n. [-AN]

pělā'gian², a. & n. Of, inhabiting, inhabitant of, the open sea. [f. L *pelagius* (*pelagus* sea f. Gk *pelagos*) + -AN]

pělā'gic, a. Of, performed on, the open sea, esp. ~ *sealing, whaling*. [f. L *pelagicus* (as prec., -IC)]

Pělargōn'ium, n. Genus of plants with showy flowers & fragrant leaves (pop. called *geranium*). [f. Gk *pelargos* stork]

Pělăs'gic (-zj- or -zg-), a. Of the Pelasgians, an ancient people, on coasts & islands of Eastern Mediterranean & Aegean; ~ *architecture*, oldest form of masonry found in Greece. [f. L *Pelasgus* (*Pelasgi* f. Gk *Pelasgoi*, see -IC)]

pěl'erine (or -ēn'), n. Woman's long narrow cape or tippet. [f. F *pèlerine*, fem. of *pèlerin* PILGRIM]

pělf, n. Money, wealth, (usu. derog. or joc.). [ME, f. ONF *pelfe*, var. of OF *pelfre*, of unkn. orig.; see PILFER]

pěl'ican, n. Large water-fowl with pouch for storing fish, fabled to feed its young with its own blood. [OE, in ME reinforced by OF *pelican* f. LL *pelicanus* f. Gk *pelekan*]

pělisse' (-ēs), n. Woman's mantle with armholes or sleeves, reaching to ankles; child's outdoor garment worn over other clothes; hussar officer's fur-trimmed undress jacket. [F, f. med. L *pellicia* (*vestis* garment) of fur (*pellis* skin)]

pěllǎg'r|a, n. Deficiency disease characterized by cracking of skin & often ending in insanity. So ~OUS a. [It., f. *pelle agra* rough skin]

pěll'ět, n., & v.t. Small ball of paper, bread, etc.; pill; small shot; circular boss in coins etc.; (vb) hit with (esp. paper) ~s. [ME, f. OF *pelote* f. Rom. *pelota* f. L *pila* ball]

pěll'icle, n. Thin skin; membrane; film. Hence **pěllic'ŭlAR¹** a. [f. L *pellicula*, dim. of *pellis* skin]

pěll'itorỹ, n. **1.** (~ *of Spain*) plant with pungent-flavoured root, used as local irritant etc. **2.** (~ *of the wall*) low bushy plant with greenish flowers growing on or at foot of walls. [1. alt. f. ME *pelletre* f. OF, f. L f. Gk *purethron* PYRETHRUM; 2. f. LL *parietaria* (*paries -etis* wall)]

pěll'-měll', adv., a., & n. **1.** In disorder, promiscuously; headlong, recklessly. **2.** adj. Confused, tumultuous. **3.** n. Confusion, medley, mêlée. [f. F *pêle-mêle* (*pêle* orig. uncert. +*mêle* f. *mêler* mix)]

pěllū'cid, a. Transparent, clear; clear in style or expression; mentally clear. Hence or cogn. **pěllūcid'ITY** n., ~LY² adv. [f. L *pellucidus* f. PER(*lucēre* shine), see -ID¹]

Pěl'manism, n. A 20th-c. mind-training system. [P]

pěl'mět, n. Valance or narrow pendant border (esp. over window or door to conceal curtain rods). [prob. f. F *palmette* conventional palm-leaf design used on cornices]

pělōr'us, n. Sighting device on ship's compass for taking bearings. [f. P~, reputed name of Hannibal's pilot]

pělōt'a, n. Basque game played with ball & wicker racket. [Sp., = ball, see PELLET]

pělt¹, n. Skin of sheep or goat with short wool on; undressed skin of fur-bearing animal; raw skin of sheep etc. stripped of wool or fur, so **pělt'ry**(1) n. [ME, obsc. rel. to obs. *pell* or *pellet* skin, or back form. f. *peltry*; ult. f. L *pellis* skin]

pělt², v.t. & i., & n. **1.** Assail with missiles (also fig.); (intr., of rain etc.) beat with violence; strike repeatedly with missiles, go on firing *at*. **2.** n. ~ing; (*at*) *full* ~ (speed). [c. 1500, of unkn. orig.]

pěl't|a, n. (pl. ~*ae*). Small light shield of ancient Greeks, Romans, etc.; (bot.) shield-like structure, so ~ATE²(2) a. [L, f. Gk *peltē*]

pěl'v|is, n. (anat.). Basin-shaped cavity formed in most vertebrates by haunch-bones with sacrum & other vertebrae, whence ~IC a.; basin-like cavity of kidney. [L, = basin]

Pěm'broke, n. Town in Wales: ~ *table*, *p~*, table on four fixed legs with hinged flaps that can be spread out & supported.

pěmm'ican, n. N.-Amer.-Ind. cake of dried & pounded meat mixed with melted fat; beef so treated & flavoured with currants etc. for travellers; (fig.) condensed literary matter. [f. native *pimecan* (*pime* fat)]

pěm'phig|us, n. (path.). Formation of watery vesicles or eruptions on skin of body. Hence ~OID, ~OUS, aa. [f. Gk *pemphix -igos* bubble]

pěn¹, n. Small enclosure for cows, sheep, poultry, etc., or for other purposes; (W.-Ind.) farm, plantation; *submarine* ~, enclosure (often with concrete roof) for sheltering submarines. [OE *penn*, of unkn. orig.]

pěn², v.t. (-nn-). Enclose, shut *up*, shut *in*; shut up (cattle etc.) in pen. [ME *pennen*, app. f. prec.]

pěn³, n., & v.t. (-nn-). **1.** Quill-feather with quill pointed & split into two sections, for writing with ink; similar instrument of steel, gold, etc., fitted into rod of wood etc. (~'*holder*); writing, style of this, **as** *made a living with his* ~, *wields a formidable* ~; FOUNTAIN-~. **2.** ~ *& ink*, instruments of writing, writing; ~-*&-ink* a., drawn, written, with these; ~-*feather*, quill-feather of bird's wing; ~'*knife*, small knife usu. carried in pocket; ~'*man* (*-an*), one who writes a (*good, bad*, etc.) hand, author; ~'*manship*, skill in writing, style of handwriting, action or style of literary composition; ~-*name*, literary pseudonym; ~'*wiper*, appliance usu. of small pieces of cloth for wiping ~ after use. **3.** v.t. Write, compose & write, (letter etc.). Hence ~-FUL¹ n. [ME, f. OF *penne* f. L *per.na* feather]

pĕn⁴, n. Female swan. [orig. unkn.]

pēn'al, a. Of punishment; concerned with inflicting this, as ~ *laws*; (of offence) punishable, esp. by law; inflicted as punishment, as ~ *servitude*, imprisonment with hard labour (abolished 1948); used as place of punishment, as *a* ~ *colony*. Hence ~LY² adv. [ME, f. OF, or L *poenalis* f. *poena* (PAIN¹), see -AL]

pē'nalize, -ise (*-īz*), v.t. Make, declare, (action) penal; (sport.) subject (competitor, also fig.) to penalty or comparative disadvantage. [-IZE]

pĕn'alty, n. Punishment, esp. (payment of) sum of money, for breach of law, rule, or contract; *the* ~ *of*, disadvantage resulting from (quality etc.); (sport.) disadvantage imposed on competitor for breaking rule or winning previous contest; (bridge) points added to player's score under the laws of the game; (football) ~ *area*, part of ground in front of goal in which a breach of the rules by defenders involves award of a ~ *kick* (at goal). [ult. f. med. L *poenalitas* (as PENAL, see -TY)]

pĕn'ance, n., & v.t. (In theological use) a sacrament including contrition, confession, satisfaction, & absolution; act of self-mortification as expression of penitence, esp. one imposed by priest; *do* ~, perform such act; (v.t.) impose ~ on. [ME, f. OF *peneance* f. L *paenitentia* (as PENITENT, see -ANCE)]

pĕnänn'ular, a. Almost ring-like. [f. L *paene* almost, ANNULAR]

Pĕnāt'ēs (-z), n. pl. (Rom. myth.). Household gods. [L]

pence. See PENNY.

penchant (see Ap.), n. Inclination, liking, (*for*). [F, part. of *pencher* incline]

pĕn'cil¹, n. (Arch.) artist's paint-brush (still tech. of small brushes, esp. in comb., as *sable-, camelhair,* ~); (fig.) draughtsman's art or style; instrument for drawing or writing, esp. of graphite enclosed in cylinder of wood or in metal case with tapering end; (optics) set of rays meeting at a point; (geom.) figure formed by set of straight lines meeting at a point; ~-*shaped object*; ~-*case*, holder, usu. of metal, for ~ or ~-lead. [ME, f. OF *pincel* ult. f. L *penicillum* paint-brush]

pĕn'cil², v.t. (-ll-). Tint or mark (as) with lead pencil; jot down with pencil; enter (horse's name) in betting-book, whence ~IER¹ n. (racing sl.), bookmaker or his clerk; (esp. in p.p.) mark delicately with thin concentric lines of colour or shading. [f. prec.]

pĕn'dant¹, -ent¹, n. **1.** Hanging ornament, esp. one attached to necklace, bracelet, etc. **2.** (naut.). (Also *pennant*) short rope hanging from head of mast etc. with eye at lower end for receiving hooks of tackles, (also) tapering flag, esp. that flown at mast-head of vessel in commission; *broad* ~, short swallow-tailed ~ distinguishing commodore's ship in squadron; ebank & ring of watch by which it is suspended. **3.** (*Also pr.* pahn'dahṅ) match, parallel, companion, complement, (*to*). [ME, f. OF (*-ant*), f. *pendre* hang f. L *pendēre*, see -ANT]

pĕn'dent², -ant², a. Hanging; overhanging; undecided, pending, whence pĕn'dENCY n.; (gram.) of which the construction is incomplete, esp. ~*nominative* (with no verb). [ME, as prec.]

pĕndĕn'tĕ līt'ĕ, adv. Pending the suit. [L]

pĕndĕn'tive, n. (archit.). Each of spherical triangles formed by intersection of dome by two pairs of opposite arches springing from the four supporting columns. [F (*-if, -ive*), adj., as PENDANT¹ +-IVE]

pĕnd'ing, a. & prep. **1.** Undecided, awaiting decision or settlement, as *a suit, a treaty, was then* ~. **2.** prep. During, as ~ *these negotiations* (orig. = while these negotiations are ~); until, as ~ *his return*. [after F PENDANT², -ING²]

pĕndrăg'on, n. Ancient British or Welsh prince. [W, = chief leader (*pen* head + DRAGON standard)]

pĕn'dūlāte, v.i. Swing like a pendulum; (fig.) be undecided. [as foll. +-ATE³]

pĕn'dūline, a. (Of nest) suspended; (of bird) building such nest. [F (as foll. +-INE¹)]

pĕn'dūlous, a. Suspended, hanging down, (esp. of bird's nest, flower, etc.); oscillating. Hence ~LY² adv. [f. L *pendulus* (*pendēre* hang) +-OUS]

pĕn'dūlum, n. Body suspended so as to be free to swing, esp. rod with weighted end regulating movement of clock's works; *swing of the* ~, alternation of power between political parties; COMPENSATION ~; person, thing, that oscillates (lit. & fig.). [f. L neut. adj. as prec.]

Pĕnĕl'opē, n. Chaste wife. [f. Gk *Penelopē*, wife of Odysseus]

pĕn'ēplain, n. (geol.). A region that is almost a plain. [f. L *paene* almost, PLAIN¹]

pĕnĕträl'ia, n. pl. Innermost shrine or recesses. [L, neut. pl. of *penetralis* interior, as foll., -AL(2)]

pĕn'ĕträte, v.t. & i. Find access into or through, pass through; (of sight) pierce through (darkness, thicket, etc.); permeate; imbue (person, thing, *with*); (fig.) see into, find out, discern, (person's mind, meaning, design, the truth); (intr.) make a way (*into, through, to*); (part.) gifted with or suggestive of insight, (of voice etc.) easily heard through or above other sounds. Hence or cogn. ~ABIL′ITY, ~A′-TION, ~ātor, nn., ~ABLE, ~ātive, aa., ~ātingLY², ~ātiveLY², advv. [f. L *penetrare* f. root of *penitus* interior, see -ATE³]

pĕng′uin (-nggw-), n. Sea-fowl of southern hemisphere with wings represented by scaly paddles with which it swims under water. [orig. obsc.]

pēn′ĭal, a. Of the penis. [-AL]

pĕn′ĭcillate, a. (nat. hist.). Furnished with, forming, small tuft(s); marked with streaks as of pencil or brush. [as PENCIL, -ATE²]

pĕnĭcill′in, n. Therapeutic drug (first discovered in mould) for preventing the growth of certain disease bacteria. [f. mod. L *penicillium* mould (L *penicillum* PENCIL¹) +-IN]

pĕnin′sŭla, n. Piece of land almost surrounded by water or projecting far into the sea; *the P~*, (in the Peninsular war) Spain & Portugal, (in 1914–18 war) Gallipoli. [f. L *paeninsula* (*paene* almost +*insula* island)]

pĕnin′sŭlar, a. & n. **1.** Of (the nature of) a peninsula; of the Peninsula or of the war there carried on between French & English etc. (1808–14). **2.** n. Inhabitant of a peninsula; (*P~*) soldier of the P~ war. [-AR¹]

pĕnin′sŭlāte, v.t. Make (land) into a peninsula. [-ATE³]

pēn′ĭs, n. (pl. -*nēs*). Copulatory organ of male animal. [L, = tail, penis]

pĕn′ĭt|ent, a. & n. **1.** That repents, contrite. **2.** n. Repentant sinner, person doing penance under direction of confessor; (pl.) various R.-C. orders associated for mutual discipline etc. Hence or cogn. ~ENCE n., ~entLY² adv. [ME, f. OF *penitent* f. L *paenitēre* repent, -ENT]

pĕnĭtĕn′tial (-nshl), a. Of penitence or penance; *the ~ psalms* (vi, xxxii, xxxviii, li, cii, cxxx, cxliii). Hence ~LY² adv. [f. LL *paenitentialis* (*paenitentia* penitence, as prec., see -ENCE & -AL)]

pĕnĭtĕn′tiarў (-shⱥ-), n. & a. **1.** Office in papal court deciding questions of penance, dispensations, etc.; *Grand P~*, cardinal presiding over this; ‖ asylum for prostitutes resolving on amendment; reformatory prison. **2.** adj. Of penance, of reformatory treatment. [ult. f. med. L *penitentarius* adj. & n. (PENITENCE, -ARY)]

pĕnn′ant, n. = PENDANT¹ (naut.); = PEN-NON. [compromise between *pendant* & *pennon*]

pĕnn′ĭfŏrm, a. (nat. hist.). Having the form or appearance of a feather. So **pĕnnĭf′erous** a. [f. L *penna* feather, see -FORM]

pĕnn′īless, a. Having no money; poor, destitute. [f. PENNY +-LESS]

pĕnn′ill, n. (pl. ~*ion* pr. -ĭl′yon). (Stanza of) improvised verse sung to harp at Eisteddfod etc. [Welsh, f. *penn* head]

pĕnn′on, n. Long narrow flag, triangular or swallow-tailed, esp. as military ensign of lancer regiments; long pointed streamer of ship; flag. Hence ~ED² (-nd) a. [ME, f. OF *penon* f. L *penna* feather, see -OON]

pĕnn′ў, n. (pl. *pĕnce* exc. as below). **1.** English bronze coin worth 1/12 of shilling (in pl. *pence* combined with numbers from 2 to 11 & 20, pr. without stress, as *six‵pence* but *eight′een pence′*; after numeral written *d*. = DENARIUS, as 6*d.*; pl. *pennies* of individual coins as such, as *gave me my change in pennies, doled it out in single pennies*); *(colloq.) a cent; (bibl.)* = DENARIUS. **2.** *A pretty ~*, a good sum of money; PETER′s ~, *pence; a ~ for your thoughts* (said to person absorbed in thought); *in for a ~, in for a pound*, thing once begun must be concluded at all costs; *take care of the pence*, be sparing in small outlays; *turn an honest ~*, make something by an odd job; *a ~ plain & twopence coloured* (jeer at cheap showiness). **3.** ~-*a-line* a., (of writing) cheap, superficial, hack writer; ‖ ~*blood* (sl.), = ~ DREADFUL; ‖ ~ *farthing* (colloq.), old type of high bicycle; ~-*in--the-SLOT*; ‖ ~ *post* (for conveyance of letters at former ordinary charge of 1*d.* irrespective of distance); ~-*weight* (abbr. *dwt*), measure of weight, 24 grains, 1/20 of an ounce Troy; ~ *wise*, (over-)careful in small expenditures, esp. ~ *wise & pound foolish*, careful in small, wasteful in large matters; ~*wort* (-wĕrt), (also *wall* ~*wort*) plant with rounded concave leaves growing in crevices of rocks & walls, (*marsh* or *water* ~*wort*) small herb with rounded leaves growing in marshy places; ~*worth*, *penn′orth*, (pĕn′lwĕrth, pĕn′erth), as much as can be bought for a ~, *not a* ~*worth*, not the least bit, *a good, bad*, ~*worth* (bargain); ‖ *five~, ten~*, etc., nail, sizes of nail orig. costing 5*d.* etc. per 100. [OE, OS *penning*, OHG *pfenning*, ON *penningr*, of unkn. orig.]

pĕnnўroy′al, n. Kind of mint cultivated for supposed medicinal virtues. [app. f. earlier *pulyole ryale* f. OF *poliol* thyme (dim. f. L *pulegium*) +ROYAL]

pēnŏl′og|ў, n. Study of punishment & of prison management. Hence **pēnŏlŏ′gĭ-CAL** a., ~IST n. [f. L *poena* penalty +-o- +-LOGY]

pĕn′sĭle, a. Hanging down, pendulous; (of bird etc.) that constructs ~ nest. [f. L *pensilis* (*pendēre pens-* hang, see -IL)]

pĕn′sion (-shn), n., & v.t. **1.** Periodical payment made esp. by government, company, or employer, in consideration of past services or of relinquishment of rights etc. (‖ *Ministry of P~s*, department instituted in 1914–18 war); such payment to person who is not a professed servant for good will, secret service, etc., or to artists, scientists, etc., to enable them to carry on work of public interest; *old-age* ~, weekly payment by government to poor persons, or every one, after specified age. 2. ‖ Consultative assembly of members of Gray's Inn. 3. (*pr.* pahn'si-awn). Boarding-house at fixed rate; *live* ~ (= as boarder). 4. v.t. Grant ~ to, buy over with ~ ; ~ *off*, dismiss with ~. Hence ~LESS (-sho-) a. [ME, f. OF f. L *pensionem* payment (*pendĕre* pens-pay, -ION)]

pĕn'sionable (-sho-), a. Entitled, (of services etc.) entitling person, to pension. [-ABLE]

pĕn'sionarў (-sho-), a. & n. (Recipient of) a pension; creature, hireling; *Grand P~* (hist.), first minister of Holland & Zealand (1619–1794). [f. med. L *pensionarius* (as PENSION, see -ARY[1])]

pĕn'sioner (-sho-), n. Recipient of pension; hireling, creature (obs.); ‖ (Camb. Univ.) undergraduate who is not a scholar on the foundation or a sizar but pays for his own commons etc. (= COMMONER at Oxf. Univ.). [ME, f. AF *pensionner* (OF -*ier*) (as prec.)]

pĕn'sive, a. Plunged in thought; melancholy. Hence ~LY[2] adv., ~NESS n. [ME, f. OF (-*if*, -*ive*), f. *penser* think f. L *pensare* frequent. of *pendēre* pens- weigh]

pĕn'stŏck, n. Sluice, flood-gate. [PEN[1] in sense 'mill-dam' + STOCK]

pĕnt, a. Closely confined, shut *in* or *up*. [p.p. of *pend* var. of PEN[2]]

pĕnt|a- (bef. vowel *pent*-), comb. form of Gk *pente* five, as: *pen'tachord* (-k-), musical instrument of 5 strings, series of 5 notes; ~*adac'tyl* a. & n., (person, animal) with 5 toes or fingers on each limb, so ~*adactyl'ic* a., ~*adac'tylism* n.; ~*ā'gynous*, with 5 pistils; ~*ahĕd'ron* (-a-h-), solid figure of 5 faces, so ~*ahĕd'ral* a.; ~*ăm'erous*, (bot., also written 5-*merous*) having parts of flower-whorl 5 in number, (zool.) consisting of 5 joints; ~*ăn'drous*, with 5 free stamens; ~*apet'alous*, with 5 petals; ~*ăp'ody*, verse, sequence in verse, of 5 feet; *pen'tastich* (-k), group of 5 lines in verse; ~*atŏm'ic*, having 5 atoms of some substance in the molecule; ~*atŏn'ic*, of 5 notes; ~*āv'alent*, with combining power of 5 atoms of hydrogen etc.

pĕn'tacle, n. Figure used as symbol, esp. in magic, prob. = PENTAGRAM. [F, or f. med. L*pentaculum*, app. f. PENTA-+-CULE]

pĕn'tăd, n. The number, group of, five; five-day period; (chem.) element, radical, with combining power of five. [f. LL f. Gk *pentas* -*ados* (*pente* five, -AD)]

pĕn'tagon, n. Five-sided (usu. plane rectilineal) figure; *the P~*, headquarters of U.S. defence forces. Hence pĕntăg'onAL a. [f. F (-*gone*) or LL f. Gk PENTA(*gōnon* f. *gōnia* angle)]

pĕn'tagrăm, n. Five-pointed star formed by producing sides of pentagon both ways till they intersect, formerly used as mystic symbol. [f. Gk PENTA(*grammon* f. *grammē* line)]

pĕntăm'éter, n. (Gk & Lat. pros.) form of dactylic verse composed of two halves each of two feet (dactyls in second half, dactyls or spondees in first) & long syllable, chiefly used alternately with hexameters to form elegiac verse; English iambic verse of ten syllables. [L, f. Gk PENTA(*metros* f. *metron* measure)]

pĕn'tāne, n. Paraffin hydrocarbon having five carbon atoms in the molecule occurring as a colourless fluid in petroleum etc. [f. Gk *pente* five + -ANE(2)]

Pĕn'tateuch (-k), n. First five books of O.T., traditionally ascribed to Moses. Hence pĕntateuch'AL (-kl) a. [f. LL f. Gk PENTA(*teukhos* implement, in late Gk, book) of five books]

pĕntăth'lŏn, n. (Gk ant.) athletic contest of five events in each of which all competitors took part; similar contest (in riding, fencing, pistol-shooting, swimming, cross-country running) in modern Olympic Games. [Gk, f. PENTA- + *athlon* contest]

Pĕn'tĕcŏst, n. Jewish harvest festival, on fiftieth day after the second day of Passover (*Levit.* xxiii. 15, 16), (later) synagogue anniversary of giving of Law on Sinai; (arch.) Whit Sunday. Hence pĕntĕcŏs'tAL a. [OE, ME, f. LL f. Gk *pentēcostē* (*hēmera*) fiftieth (day)]

pĕnt'house (-t-h-), (arch.) **pĕn'tĭce**, n. Sloping roof, esp. as subsidiary structure attached to wall of main building; *apartment or flat built on roof; awning, canopy, or the like. [ME *pentis*, aphetic f. OF *apentis*, -*dis*, = med. L *appendicium*, in LL = appendage]

pĕn'tōde, a. (Of wireless valves) having five electrodes. [f. Gk *pente* five + *hodos* way]

Pĕn'tonville, n. Prison in Islington, London.

pĕntstĕm'on (*or* pĕnt'-), n. Genus of American herbaceous plants allied to foxglove with showy flowers, usu. tubular & two-lipped. [irreg. f. PENTA- + Gk *stēmōn* warp (cf. STAMEN)]

pĕnŭlt (*or* pĕ-), (n.) last syllable but one. Last but one; (n.) last syllable but one. [(-*ult* abbr.) f. L *paene* almost + ULTIMATE after L *paenultimus*]

pĕnŭm'br|a, n. Partly shaded region around shadow of opaque body, esp. round total shadow of moon or earth in eclipse; lighter outer part of sun-spot; partial shadow. Hence ~AL a. [f. L *paene* almost + *umbra* shadow]

pĕnŭr'ious, a. Poor, scanty; stingy, grudging, whence ~LY[2] adv., ~NESS n. [f. med. L *penuriosus* (foll., -OUS)]

pĕn'urў, n. Destitution, poverty; lack, scarcity, (of). [ME, f. L *penuria*]

pē'on (*or* **pŭn**), n. (In India) office--messenger, attendant, orderly; (Span. Amer.) day-labourer; (Mex.) enslaved debtor (hist.). [(1) f. Port. *peão*, F *pion*; (2) f. Sp. *peon*; f. L as PAWN[1]]

pē'onage, n. Employment, service, of peons. [-AGE]

pē'onȳ, n. Plant with large globular red or white flowers, in cultivation often double. [ME & ONF *pione* f. L f. Gk *paiōnia* (*Paiōn*, physician of the gods); later *peony* assim. to L, whence dir. OE *peonie*]

people (pē'pl), n., & v.t. **1.** Persons composing community, race, or nation, as *the English* ~, *English-speaking* ~s, *a warlike* ~, (treated as sing.); the persons belonging to a place or forming a company or class etc. (*the* ~ *of the western counties were in revolt, the* ~ *here are furious*), subjects of king etc., congregation of parish priest etc., (as pl.); armed followers, retinue, workpeople, etc., (as pl.); CHOSEN, PECULIAR, ~; one's parents or other relatives, as *his* ~ *are sure to hear of it*; *the* commonalty (as pl); *the* body of enfranchised or qualified citizens (as sing. or pl.); persons in general, as ~ *don't like to be kept waiting.* **2.** v.t. Fill with ~, populate, fill (place *with* animals etc.); (of persons, animals, etc.) inhabit, occupy, fill, esp. in p.p., as *a thickly* ~*d country.* [ME, f. OF *pople, poeple, peuple,* etc., f. L *populus*]

*pĕp, n. (sl.). Vigour, go, spirit; ~ *pill* (for inducing ~); ~ *talk,* exhortation to activity. Hence ***~p'Y²** a. (sl.), full of ~. [abbr. *pepper*]

pĕperi'nō (-rē-), n. Light porous (usu. brown) volcanic rock formed of sand, cinders, etc. [It., f. *pepere* PEPPER, see -INE[1]]

pĕpp'er¹, n. **1.** Pungent aromatic condiment got from dried berries of certain plants used whole (~*corns*) or ground into powder; *black* ~, plant chiefly used for this; *black, white,* ~ (from unripe, ripe, berries); CAYENNE ~; (fig.) anything pungent. **2.** ~*-&-salt,* cloth of dark & light wools woven together, showing small dots of dark & light intermingled; ~*box,* small usu. round box with perforated lid for sprinkling ~, || irregular buttress in Eton fives-court; ~*-castor,* *-er,* = ~*box* (1st sense); ~*corn,* dried berry of black ~, esp. as nominal rent; ~*mint,* kind of mint grown for its essential oil, this oil, lozenge flavoured with ~mint; ~*-pot,* = ~*-castor,·* (also) W.-Ind. dish of meat etc. stewed with red ~ etc., (also, as nickname) Jamaican. [OE *pipor,* OHG *pfeffar,* ON *piparr* f. L *piper* = Gk *peperi* of oriental orig.]

pĕpp'er², v.t. Sprinkle, treat, with pepper; besprinkle as with pepper; pelt with missiles (lit. or fig.); punish severely. [f. prec.]

pĕpp'erȳ, a. Of, like, abounding in,

pepper; (fig.) pungent, stinging, hot--tempered. [-Y²]

pĕp'sin, n. A ferment contained in gastric juice, converting proteins into peptones in presence of weak acid. [f. Gk *pepsis* digestion (*pep-* cook) +-IN]

pĕp'tic, a. & n. Digestive; ~ *glands* (secreting gastric juice); (n. pl., joc.) digestive organs. [f. Gk *peptikos* (as prec., see -IC)]

pĕp'tōne, n. Class of albuminoid substances soluble in water & non-coagulable by heat into which proteins are converted by the action of pepsin in the process of digestion. Hence **~onIZE(3)** v.t. [f. G *pepton* f. Gk *pepton* cooked]

pĕr, prep. Through, by, by means of. **1.** In L phrr. (usu. ital.); ~ *ănn'um,* (so much) by the year, yearly; ~ *căp'ut* (& erron. ~ *căp'ǐta*), a head, each; ~ *cŏn'tra* adv. & n., (on) the opposite side (of an account etc.); ~ *dǐ'ĕm,mĕn'sĕm,*(so much) by the day, month; ~ *mǐll'e,* in or to the thousand; ~ *prōcūrātiŏn'ĕm* (abbr. ~ *proc.,* ~ *pro., p.p.*), by proxy, by the action of (person signing document); ~ *săl'tum,* without intermediate steps, all at once; ~ *sē,* by or in itself, intrinsically. **2.** As E prep.; by, by means or instrumentality of, as ~ *post, rail, steamer, bearer;* (joc.) as ~ *usual,* as usual; for each, as *a shilling* ~ *man, 5* ~ *cent*; ~ *second* ~ *second,* ~ second every second (of rate of acceleration over indefinite period). [L]

per-, pref. = L prep. *per* (prec.). **1.** In L senses; through, all over, (~*forate,*~*vade*); completely, very (~*turb*); to destruction, to the bad, (~*vert,* ~*dition*). **2.** Chem. denoting maximum of some element in combination; in names of binary compounds in *-ide* (formerly *-uret*), as ~*chloride,* ~*iodide,* ~*oxide,* ~*sulphide*; in adjj. in *-ic* naming oxides, acids, etc., as ~*chloric,* ~*iodic,* ~*manganic*; in names of salts of these etc., as ~*chlorate,* ~*iodate,* ~*manganate,* ~*sulphate.*

pĕradvĕn'ture, adv. & n. (arch. or joc.). **1.** Perhaps; *if, lest,* ~, if, lest, it chance that. **2.** n. Uncertainty, chance, conjecture; *beyond, without,* (*all*) ~ (doubt). [ME, f. OF *per* or *par aventure* by chance (PER +*aventure* ADVENTURE)]

pĕrai' (-rahī, -rī), **pira'ya** (-rahya), n. Voracious Amer. freshwater fish. [native (-*ya*)]

pĕram'būl|āte, v.t. Walk through, over, or about; travel through & inspect (territory); formally establish boundaries of (parish etc.) by walking round them. Hence or cogn. ~A'TION n., ~ātORY a. [f. L PER(*ambulare* walk), see -ATE³]

|| pĕram'būlātor, n. Hand carriage for one or two children, with three or four wheels, pushed from behind (colloq. abbr. *prăm*). [f. prec. +-OR]

percāle' (*or* -ahl), n. A closely woven cotton fabric. [F, of unkn. orig.]

perceive' (-sēv), v.t. Apprehend with the mind, observe, understand, (circumstance, *that*, *how*, etc.); apprehend through one of the senses, esp. sight. [ME, f. **perceivre*, north. form of OF *percoivre*, f. L PER(*cipere cept-* = *capere* take)]

percen'tage, n. Rate, proportion, per cent; (loosely) proportion, as *only a small ~ of books are worth reading*. [-AGE]

per'cept, n. (philos.). Object of perception; mental product, as opp. to action, of perceiving. [as PERCEIVE]

percep'tible, a. That can be perceived by senses or intellect. Hence ~IBIL'ITY n., ~IBLY² adv. [f. LL *perceptibilis* (as prec., see -BLE)]

percep'tion, n. Act, faculty, of perceiving; intuitive recognition (*of* truth, aesthetic quality, etc.); (philos.) action by which the mind refers its sensations to external object as cause; (law) collection (of rents etc.). Hence or cogn. ~ional (-shŏ-), ~IVE, aa., ~IVELY² adv., ~IVENESS n., **percep'tiv**'ITY, nn. [ME, f. OF, or L *perceptio* (as PERCEIVE, see -ION)]

perch¹, n. European spiny-finned freshwater fish, used as food. [ME, f. OF *perche* f. L f. Gk *perkē*]

perch², n. 1. Horizontal bar for bird to rest upon; anything serving for this, as *bird takes its ~* (alights); (fig.) elevated or secure position; *hop the ~*, die, *knock* (person) *off* his *~*, vanquish, destroy, him; centre pole of some four-wheeled vehicles. 2. (Also *pole*, *rod*) measure of length esp. for land, 5½ yds; *square ~*, 30¼ sq. yds. [ME, f. OF *perche* f. L *pertica* pole]

perch³, v.i. & t. Alight, rest, as bird (*upon* bough etc.); (of person etc.) settle, alight, (*upon*); place (as) upon perch (esp. in p.p., as *town ~ed on a hill*). Hence ~'ER¹ n., (one of) a large class of passerine birds with feet adapted for ~ing. [ME, f. OF *percher*, as prec.]

perchance' (-ah-), adv. (arch.). By chance; possibly, maybe. [ME, f. AF *par chance* (*par* by +CHANCE)]

percheron (pār'sherawn), n. Strong & swift horse bred in le Perche, district of France. [F]

percip'ient, a. & n. 1. Perceiving, conscious. 2. n. One who perceives esp. (telepathy) something outside range of senses. Hence ~ENCE n. [f. L as PERCEIVE, see -ENT]

perc'olate, v.i. & t. (Of liquid) filter, ooze, through (also fig.); (trans.) ooze through, permeate; (of person or strainer) strain (liquid, powder) through pores etc. Hence or cogn. ~A'TION, ~ātor, nn. [f. L PER(*colare* strain f. *colum* strainer), -ATE³]

percuss', v.t. (med.). Tap gently with finger or instrument for purposes of diagnosis etc. [f. L PER(*cutere cuss-* = *quatere* shake) strike]

percu'ssion (-shn), n. Forcible striking of one (usu. solid) body against another;

(med.) percussing; (mus.) *instrument of* (played by) ~; ~ *cap*, small copper cap or cylinder in fire-arm, containing fulminating powder and exploded by ~ of a hammer. So **percu**'ssIVE a. [f. F, or L *percussio* (as prec., see -ION)]

percutān'eous, a. Made, done, through the skin. [PER-+CUTANEOUS]

perdi'tion, n. Eternal death, damnation. [ME, f. OF *perdiciun* f. LL *perditionem* f. PER(*dere dit-* = *dare* give) destroy, see -ION]

perdu(e)', a. (Mil.) placed as an outpost in hiding, esp. *lie ~*; (often as F, with fem. *-due*) hidden. [F, p.p. of *perdre* lose, as prec.]

perdur'able, a. Permanent; eternal; durable. Hence or cogn. ~ABIL'ITY n., ~ABLY² adv. [ME, f. OF f. LL PER(*durabilis* DURABLE)]

père (pār, & see Ap.), n. Father (appended to surname to distinguish father from son, cf. FILS). [F]

pe'regrin|āte, v.i. (now joc.). Travel, journey. So ~A'TION, ~ātor, nn. [f. L *peregrinari* (as foll.), see -ATE³]

pe'regrin(e), a. & n. 1. (arch.). Foreign, imported from abroad, outlandish. 2. ~ (falcon), kind esteemed for hawking. [f. L *peregrinus* (*peregre* abroad, f. PER + *ager* field, see -INE¹)]

pe'remptor|y (or perěmp²), a. Final, esp. (law) ~*y mandamus* (in which the command is absolute), ~*y writ* (enforcing defendant's appearance without option); (of statement or command) admitting no denial or refusal; absolutely fixed, essential; (of person etc.) dogmatic, imperious, dictatorial. Hence ~ILY² adv., ~INESS n. [f. L *peremptorius* destructive f. PER(*imere empt-* = *emere* take, buy) destroy, cut off, see -ORY: in legal use f. LL]

perenn'ial (-nyal), a. & n. 1. Lasting through, (of stream) flowing through all seasons of, the year; lasting long or for ever; (of plant) living several years (cf. ANNUAL). 2. n. ~ plant. Hence **perenn**'iāl'ITY n., ~LY² adv. [f. L PER(*ennis* f. *annus* year)+-AL]

perf'ect¹, a. & n. 1. Complete, not deficient; faultless; (of lesson) thoroughly learned; thoroughly trained or skilled (*in* duties etc.); exact, precise, as *a ~ square, circle*; entire, unqualified, as *a ~ stranger, ~ nonsense*; (gram., of tense) denoting completed event or action viewed in relation to the present (*future ~*, giving sense *will have done*); (bot.) having all four whorls of the flower; (mus.) ~ *interval*, fourth & fifth as they would occur in the major or minor scale starting upon the lower note of the interval, also the octave. 2. n. ~ tense. Hence ~LY² adv., (esp.) quite, quite well, completely, ~NESS n. [ME & OF *parfit*, *-fet* f. L PER(*ficere fect-* = *facere* do) complete]

perfect'² (or pērf'ĭkt), v.t. Complete, carry through; make perfect; improve.

Hence ~ĭBĬL'ĬTY n., perfĕc'tĬBLE a. [f. prec.]

perfĕc'tion, n. Completion; making perfect; full development; faultlessness; (loosely) comparative excellence; perfect person or thing; highest pitch, extreme, perfect specimen or manifestation, (of quality etc.); (w. pl.) accomplishment. [ME, f. OF, f. L *perfectionem* (as PERFECT[1], see -ION)]

perfĕc'tion|ĭst (-sho-), n. One who holds that religious or moral perfection may be attained; one who aims at perfection in his work (freq. derog.); (P~ĭst) member of communistic community of Oneida Creek, N.Y. So ~ĭSM n. [-ĭST]

perfĕrv'ĭd, a. Very fervid. [PER-]

pĕrf'ĭdy̆, n. Breach of faith, treachery. Hence or cogn. perfĭd'ĭOUS a., perfĭd'ĭOUSLY[2] adv., perfĭd'ĭOUSNESS n. [f. L *perfidia* f. PER(*fidus* f. *fides* faith) treacherous]

perfŏl'ĭate, a. (bot.). Having the stalk apparently passing through the leaf. [f. PER-+L *folium* leaf+-ATE[2]]

pĕrf'or|āte, v.t. & i. Make hole(s) through, pierce, esp. make rows of holes in (sheet) to separate stamps, coupons, etc., make an opening into; pass, extend, through; (intr.) penetrate (*into*, *through*, etc.). Hence or cogn. ~A'TION, ~ātŏR, nn., ~ātIVE a. [f. L PER(*forare* bore), see -ATE[3]]

perfŏrce', adv. & n. Of necessity; (n., rare) necessity, as *of*, *by*, ~. [ME, f. OF *par force* by FORCE]

perfŏrm', v.t. & i. Carry into effect (command, promise, task, operation, etc.); go through, execute, (public function, play, piece of music, etc.); (intr.) act in play, play, sing, etc.; (of trained animals) execute tricks etc. at public show etc., whence ~ING[2] a. Hence ~ABLE a., ~ER[1] n. [ME *performe* (alt., thr. AF, to -*forme* (FORM)) f. OF *parfo(u)rnir* (whence 14th c. (obs.) *perFURNISH* perform, furnish)]

perfŏrm'ance, n. Execution (*of* command etc.); carrying out, doing; notable feat; performing of play or public exhibition, as *there are two* ~s *a day, the afternoon* ~. [-ANCE, perh. thr. AF]

pĕrf'ūme[1], n. Odorous fumes of burning substance; sweet smell; smell; fluid containing essence of flowers etc., scent. Hence ~LESS a. [f. F *parfum*, as foll.]

perfūme'[2], v.t. Impart sweet scent to, impregnate with sweet smell, (esp. in p.p.). [f. F *parfumer* (PER-+L *fumare* smoke)]

perfūm'er, n. Maker, seller, of perfumes. Hence ~ERY(1, 2, 3) n. [-ER[1]]

perfŭnc'tor|y̆, a. Done merely for sake of getting through a duty, acting thus, superficial, mechanical, as *a* ~*y inspection, inquirer, in a* ~*y manner.* Hence ~ĭLY[2] adv., ~ĭNESS n. [f. LL *perfunctorius* f. PER(*fungi funct*- perform), see -ORY]

perfūse' (-z), v.t. Besprinkle (*with* water etc.); cover, suffuse, (*with* radiance etc.); pour (water etc.) through or over. Hence or cogn. perfū'SION (-zhn) n., perfūs'ĬVE a. [f. L PER(*fundere fus*- pour)]

pergamēn'ĕous, a. Of or like parchment. [f. L *pergamena* PARCHMENT+-EOUS]

pérg'ŏla, n. Arbour, covered walk, formed of growing plants trained over trellis-work. [It., f. L *pergula* projecting roof (*pergere* proceed)]

pergŭnn'ah (-*a*), -ga'na (-gŭ-), n. Division of territory in India, group of villages. [f. Pers. & Hind. *parganah* district]

perhăps' (*colloq.* präps), adv. It may be, possibly, as ~ *he has lost it, he has* ~ *lost it,* ~ *you would like to see it?* [PER+HAPS (pl.)]

pĕr'ĭ, n. (Pers. myth.) fairy, good (orig. evil) genius; beautiful or graceful being. [Pers.]

pĕri-, pref. ~ Gk *peri* round, about, as: *pē'rianth*, floral envelope; ~*cardī'ĭs* n., inflammation of the ~cardium; ~*card'ĭum*, membranous sac enclosing the heart, so ~*card'ĭac*, ~*card'ĭal*, aa.; *pē'ricarp*, seed-vessel, wall of ripened ovary of plant; ~*chon'drium* (-k-), membrane enveloping cartilages (except at joints); ~*clin'al* (geol.), sloping in all directions from central point; ~*gy̆nous* (perij[2]), (of stamen) situated around pistil or ovary; ~*ŏs'tĕum*, membrane enveloping the bones, so ~*ŏs'tĕal* a., ~*osītī'ĭs* n.; ~* pteral* (perīp[2]), (of temple) surrounded by single row of pillars; *pē'risperm*, mass of albumen outside embryo-sac in some seeds; *pē'ristōme*, (bot.) fringe of small teeth around mouth of capsule in mosses, (zool.) parts around mouth in various invertebrates; ~*ty̆phlīt'is*, inflammation of some part around the caecum, e.g. appendicitis.

pē'rĭăpt, n. Thing worn about the person as charm, amulet. [f. F *périapte* f. Gk PERI(*apton* f. *haptō* fasten)]

pē'riclāse, n. Mineral consisting of magnesia & protoxide of iron, found esp. on Vesuvius. [f. PERI-(= 'very')+Gk *klasis* breaking, from its perfect cleavage]

peric'opē, n. Short passage, paragraph; portion of Scripture read in public worship. [f. LL f. Gk PERI(*kopē* cutting f. *koptō* cut)]

pēricrān'ium, n. Membrane enveloping skull; (joc.) skull, brain, intellect. [f. Gk PERI(*kranion* CRANIUM)]

pē'ridŏt, n. (Jeweller's name for) olivine, kind of chrysolite. [ME *peritot(e)* f. OF *peritot* (mod. *péridot*), of unkn. orig.]

pē'rigee, n. That point in planet's (esp. moon's) orbit at which it is nearest to earth (cf. APOGEE). Hence pērigē'AN a. [16th c. *perige(e), perigeum*, f. F *périgée* & mod. L f. late Gk PERI(*geion* f. *gē* earth)]

For other words in *peri*- see PERI-.

pĕrihēl'ion (-lyon), n. That point in planet's orbit at which it is nearest to sun (cf. APHELION). [Graecized f. mod. L *perihelium* (PERI-+Gk *hēlios* sun), after *perigeum* (prec.)]

pĕ'ril, n., & v.t. (-ll-). 1. Danger; *in ~ of* (in danger of losing) one's *life* etc.; *you do it at your ~*, you take the risk; *keep off at your ~* (take the risk if you do not). 2. v.t. Expose to danger, imperil. Hence or cogn. ~OUS a., ~OUSLY² adv., ~OUSNESS n. [ME, f. OF *peril* f. L *periculum*]

perim'eter, n. Circumference, outline, of closed figure; length of this; outer boundary of camp or fortification; instrument for measuring the field of vision. [f. L f. Gk PERI(*metros* f. *metron* measure)]

pĕrinē'|um, n. (anat.). Region of the body between anus & scrotum or vulva. Hence ~AL a. [LL, f. Gk *pĕrinaios*, cf. *pĕris -inos* scrotum]

pēr'iod, n. & a. 1. Round of time marked by recurrence of astronomical coincidences; time of planet's revolution. 2. Time during which disease runs its course; (usu. pl.) menses. 3. Indefinite portion of history, life, etc.; any portion of time; *the ~*, the present day (*the girl, costume, catchwords*, etc., *of the ~*). 4. Complete sentence, esp. one of several clauses; (pl.) rhetorical language. 5. Full pause at end of sentence, full stop (.) marking this, (*put a ~ to*, bring to an end). 6. Set of figures marked off in large number, as in numeration, recurring decimals, etc. 7. adj. Belonging to, characteristic of, a particular (past) ~ (esp. of furniture, dress, & architecture). [ME, f. OF *periode* f. L f. Gk PERI(ODOS *hodos* way)]

pēriŏd'ic, a. Of revolution of heavenly body, as ~ *motion*; recurring at regular intervals, so **pēriodi'city** n.; recurring at intervals; ~ *table* (chem.), arrangement of elements in order of atomic numbers & in which elements of similar chemical properties appear periodically & fall into definite groups; expressed in periods. [f. F *périodique* or L f. Gk *periodikos* (as prec., see -IC)]

pēriŏd'ical, a. & n. 1. = prec. (not in last sense). 2. (Magazine, miscellany) published at regular intervals, e.g. monthly. Hence ~LY² adv. [-AL]

pĕripatĕt'|ic, a. & n. 1. (*P~ic*). Aristotelian (a. & n.; so called from Aristotle's custom of walking in Lyceum while teaching). 2. Walking from place to place on one's business, itinerant, whence ~ICALLY adv. 3. n. (chiefly joc.). Itinerant dealer. Hence ~ICISM(2, 3) n. [f. F *péripatétique* or L f. Gk *peripatētikos* f. PERI(*pateō* walk), see -IC]

pĕripĕtei'a (-ia), -tia, n. Sudden change of fortune in drama or in life. [Gk PERI(*peteia* f. *pet-* fall)]

periph'er|ȳ, n. Bounding line esp. of round surface; external boundary or surface. Hence ~AL a., ~aLY² adv. [f. LL f. Gk PERI(*phereia* f. *pherō* bear) circumference]

periph'ras|is, n. (pl. ~ēs). Roundabout way of speaking, circumlocution; roundabout phrase. Hence or cogn. **pĕriphrăs'tic** a. (~*tic conjugation, genitive*, one formed ANALYTICALLY w; aux. vb, w. preposition, instead of by inflexion, as *did go*=went, *of Caesar*=Caesar's), **pĕriphrăs'tically** adv. [L f. Gk, f. PERI(*phrazō* declare, vbl adj. *-phrastos*)]

perique' (-ēk), n. Dark Louisiana tobacco of a choice kind. [Louisiana F]

pĕ'riscōpe, n. Kinds of tube-&-mirror apparatus by which an observer in a trench or in a submarine submerged to a small depth can see things above the parapet or water; kind of photographic object-glass. Hence **pĕriscŏp'ic** a., enabling one to see distinctly for some distance round axis of vision. [PERI-, -SCOPE]

pĕ'rish, v.i. & t. Suffer destruction, lose life, come to untimely end (by the sword etc.); (of cold or exposure) reduce to distress or inefficiency (usu. in pass.; *we were ~ed with cold*; *in ~ing cold*; *the heat had ~ed all vegetation*), whence ~ingLY² adv.; *we were ~ed* (much incommoded) *with cold, hunger*, etc. Hence ~ER¹ n. (sl.), blighter, ||~ING² a. (sl.), beastly, bloody. [ME, f. OF *perir* (see -ISH²) f. L PER(*ire* go)]

pĕ'rishable, a. & n. 1. Liable to perish; subject to speedy decay. 2. n. pl. Things (esp. foodstuffs in transit) subject to this. Hence ~NESS n. [-ABLE]

pĕrispōm'ĕnon (pl. *-ena*), a. & n. (Gk gram.). (Word) with circumflex accent on last syllable. [Gk neut. part. of PERI(*spaō* draw) draw round, mark with circumflex]

periss'o- in comb. = Gk *perissos*, uneven, odd, redundant, as ~*dac'tylate* (zool.), having an odd number of toes on each foot.

peris'talith, n. (archaeol.). Ring of standing stones round burial-mound etc. [irreg. f. Gk PERI(*statos* standing)+-LITH]

pĕristăl'|tic, a. (physiol.). Applied to the automatic muscular movement consisting of wave-like contractions in successive circles, by which contents of alimentary canal etc. are propelled along it. So ~sis n., ~tic movement, ~ticALLY adv. [f. Gk *peristaltikos* (PERI-, *stellō* send)]

pĕ'ristyle, n. Row of columns surrounding temple, court, cloister, etc.; space so surrounded. [f. F *péristyle* f. L f. Gk PERI(*stulon* f. *stulos* pillar)]

pĕriton|ē'um, -n|ae'um, n. (anat.). Double serous membrane lining cavity of abdomen. Hence ~ē'AL a., ~IT'IS n. [LL, f. Gk PERI(*tonaion* f. *ton-* stem of *teinō* stretch)]

For other words in *peri-* see PERI-.

pĕ´riwig, n. Wig. Hence ~ged² (-gd) a. [16th c. *perwyke* etc., f. F *perruque* PERUKE]

pĕ´riwinkle¹, n. Kinds of plants, esp. *lesser & greater*~, evergreen trailing plants with light-blue flowers; ~ (*blue*), colour of ~s. [ME, f. AF *pervenke* = OF *pervenche* f. LL *pervinca*, w. assim. to foll.]

pĕ´riwinkle², n. Edible gastropod mollusc, winkle. [f. 1530, of unkn. orig.; cf. syn. OE *pinewinclan* (? *wine-*)]

pērj´ur|e (-jer), v. refl. ~*e* one*self*, forswear oneself; (p.p.) guilty of perjury. So ~er¹ (-er-) n. [ME, f. AF *parjurer* f. L PER(*jurare* swear)]

pērj´ury (-eri), n. Swearing to statement known to be false; wilful utterance of false evidence while on oath; breach of oath. So perjur´ious (-joor-) a., perjur´iously² adv. [ME, f. AF *perjurie* f. L *perjurium* as prec.]

pĕrk¹, v.i. & t., & a. (Also ~ *up*) lift one's head, thrust oneself forward, briskly or impudently; (trans.) smarten *up*; hold *up* (head, tail) self-assertively; (adj., rare) perky. [ME, of unkn. orig.]

pĕrk², n. (sl.). (Usu. pl.) perquisite. [abbr.]

pĕrk´|y̆, a. Self-assertive, saucy, pert. Hence ~ily² adv., ~iness n. [PERK¹+-y²]

pērl´ite, n. Obsidian or other vitreous rock in form of enamel-like globules. [= F *-ite*, G *-it*, as PEARL, see -ite¹]

pĕrm, n. (colloq.). Permanent wave; permutation. [abbr.]

pĕrm´alloy, n. Alloy of nickel & iron of great sensitiveness to magnetic forces, used for cores of telegraphic cables. [f. PERM(EABLE)+ALLOY]

pĕrm´anent, a. Lasting, intended to last, indefinitely (cf. TEMPORARY); ~ *set*, condition of metal after being subjected to the strain of use; ~ *wave*, artificial wave in the hair intended to last for some time produced by one of several processes (colloq. abbr. .*perm*); ||~ *way*, finished road-bed of railway. Hence or cogn. pĕrm´anence, pĕrm´anency (esp. = ~thing or arrangement), nn., ~ly² adv. [ME, f. OF, or L PER(*manēre* remain), -ENT]

permăng´anate (-ngg-), n. (chem.). Salt of permanganic acid, esp. *potassium* ~ or ~ *.of potash*, used as disinfectant & oxidizer when dissolved in water. [f. foll., -ate¹(3)]

pĕrmăngăn´ĭc (-ngg-), a. (chem.). ~ *acid*, acid obtained from manganese. [PER-, MANGANIC]

pĕrm´e|āte, v.t. & i. Penetrate, pervade, saturate; diffuse itself *through*, *among*, etc. Hence or cogn. ~abil´ity, ~ance, ~a´tion, nn., ~able, ~ant, aa. [f. L PER(*meare* pass, go), see -ate³]

Pĕrm´ian, a. Of the uppermost division of the Palaeozoic series of strata, consisting chiefly of red sandstone & magnesian limestone. [*Perm*, E.-Russian province, +-ian]

permiss´ib|le, a. Allowable. Hence ~ly² adv. [ME, f. OF, f. med. L *permissibilis* (as PERMIT¹, see -BLE)]

permi´ssion (-shn) n. Leave, licence, (*to* do). [ME, f. OF, or L *permissio* (as PERMIT¹, see -ION)]

permiss´ive, a. Giving permission; ~ *legislation* (giving powers, but not enjoining their use). Hence ~ly² adv., ~ness n. [ME, f. OF (-*if*, -*ive*), as foll., see -IVE]

permit´¹, v.t. & i. (-tt-). Allow, as ~ *me to remark*, *appeals are* ~*ted*, ~ *it to be altered*, *weather* ~*ting*; (intr.) admit of (alteration etc.). [f. L PER(*mittere miss-* let go)]

pĕrm´it², n. Written order giving permission esp. for landing or removal of dutiable goods etc.; (*also* permit´) permission. [f. prec.]

pĕrmūtā´tion, n. (Math.) variation of the order of a set of things lineally arranged, any one such arrangement, colloq. abbr. *perm*; (rare) alteration. [ME, f. OF *permutacion* or L *permutatio* (foll., -ION)]

permūte´, v.t. Alter the order of. [ME, f. OF *permuter* or L PER(*mutare* change)]

pĕrn, n. HONEY-buzzard. [irreg. f. Gk *pternis*, kind of hawk]

perni´cious (-shus), a. Destructive, ruinous, fatal; ~ *anaemia*, severe freq. fatal kind. Hence ~ly² adv., ~ness n. [f. L *perniciosus* (*pernicies* ruin f. *nex necis* death, see -OUS)]

pernick´ety̆, a. (colloq.). Fastidious; ticklish, requiring careful handling. [orig. Sc., of unkn. orig.]

pĕrnŏctā´tion, n. Passing the night; (eccl.) all-night vigil. [f. LL *pernoctatio* f. PER(*noctare* f. *nox noctis* night), see -ATION]

pĕr´ror|āte, v.i. Sum up & conclude speech, so ~a´tion n.; speak at length. [f. L PER(*orare* speak)]

perŏx´ide, n., & v.t. 1. (Chem.) compound of oxygen with another element containing the greatest possible proportion of oxygen; (pop.) = ~ *of hydrogen*, a colourless viscid liquid used as an antiseptic, and (esp.) to bleach hair. 2. v.t. Bleach (hair) with this. [PER-2+OXIDE]

perpĕnd´¹, v.t. (arch.). Ponder, consider, (matter, or abs.). [f. L PER(*pendĕre* weigh)]

pĕr´pend², n. Var. of PARPEN.

pĕrpendic´ular, a. & n. 1. At right angles to plane of horizon; (loosely, of ascent etc.) very steep; erect, upright; (joc.) in standing position; (geom.) at right angles (*to* given line, plane, or surface); ~ STYLE. 2. n. Plumb-rule or other instrument for showing ~ line; (pl.) two datum-lines used in designing ship & fixing its nominal length (*between* ~s); ~ line; *the* ~, ~ line or direction (*is out of* ~ or *the* ~, not straight up and down); ||(sl.) meal etc. at which guests stand. Hence ~ity (-ă´r-) n., ~ly² adv. [16th c., f. L *perpendicularis* or *perpendiculum* plumb-line, see -AR¹); in 14th c. f. OF *-er*]

pĕrp´etr|āte, v.t. Perform, commit,

(crime, blunder, pun or other thing viewed as outrageous). So ~A'TION, ~-āToR, nn. [f. L PER(*petrare* = *patrare* effect), -ATE³]

perpet'ual, a. Eternal; permanent during life; applicable, valid, for ever or for indefinite time; ~ *motion* (of machine that should go on for ever unless stopped by external force or worn out); continuous; (colloq.) frequent, repeated, as *this* ~ *nagging*; ~ *calendar*, that can be used ~ly or over a long period of time; ~ *curate* (hist.), clergyman appointed at instance of lay rector of benefice to execute spiritual duties of benefice (now known as VICAR). Hence ~LY² adv. [ME -el f. OF *perpetuel* f. L *perpetualis* f. *perpetuus*, see -AL]

perpet'ū|āte, v.t. Make perpetual; preserve from oblivion. Hence or cogn. ~ANCE, ~A'TION, ~āToR, nn. [f. L *perpetuare* (as prec.), see -ATE³]

perpetū'ity, n. Quality of being perpetual; *in, to, for*, ~, for ever; perpetual possession or position; perpetual annuity. [ME, f. OF *perpetuite* f. L *perpetuitatem* (as PERPETUAL, see -TY)]

perplex', v.t. Bewilder, puzzle, (person, his mind); complicate, confuse, (matter); entangle, intertwine, (esp. in p.p.). Hence ~ēdLY², ~ĭngLY², advv. [f. obs. *perplex* a. f. L PER(*plexus* p.p. of *plectere* plait)]

perplex'ity, n. Bewilderment; what causes this; entangled state. [ME, f. OF -*ite*, or LL *perplexitas* (as prec., see -TY)]

per'quisite (-z-), n. (sl. abbr. *perk*). Casual profit, esp. ‖ (law) that coming to lord of manor beyond regular revenue; thing that has served its primary use and to which subordinate or servant has then a customary right, as *remains of the daily commons are among the* ~*s of college scouts*; customary gratuity. [ME, f. L PER(*quirere quisit-*, = *quaerere* seek) search for]

per'ron, n. Platform in front of door of church or other large building, ascended by steps. [F, f. L *petra* stone, see -OON]

per'rry, n. Drink from juice of pears fermented. [ME *pereye* f. OF *pere* f. Rom. **piratum* f. L *pirum* PEAR, see -Y⁴]

perse, a. & n. (arch.). Bluish-grey, bluish grey. [ME, f. OF *pers*, -e f. med. L *persus*, perh. f. *Persia*; cf. obs. *inde* INDIGO]

pers'ēc|ūte, v.t. Pursue with enmity and injury (esp. holder of opinion held to be heretical); harass, worry; importune (person *with* questions etc.). So ~ū'TION n. (~*ution mania*, insane delusion that one is ~uted), ~ūToR n. [ME, f. OF *perseculer* f. L PER(*sequi secut-* follow) pursue]

persevēr'|ance, n. Steadfast pursuit of an aim, constant persistence, so ~ANT a. (rare); (theol.) continuance in state of grace. [ME, f. OF f. L *perseverantia* (foll., -ANCE)]

persēvēr|e', v.i. Continue steadfastly, persist, (*in* course, *in* doing, *with* task, or abs.). Hence ~'ĭngLY² adv. [ME, f. OF

perseverer f. L *perseverare* f. PER(*severus* SEVERE)]

Pér'sian (-shn), a. & n. (Inhabitant, language) of Persia, as ~ *carpet, cat* (with long silky hair & thick tail). [-AN]

persiēnnes' (-nz), n. pl. Outside window blinds of light horizontal laths. [F, ■ Persian (fem. pl. adj.)]

pers'iflage (-ahzh), n. Light raillery, banter. [F, f. *persifler* banter, see -AGE]

persimm'on, n. American date-plum, yellow fruit becoming sweet when softened by frost. [corrupt. of native name]

persist', v.i. Continue firmly or obstinately (*in* opinion, course, doing) esp. against remonstrance etc.; (of institutions, customs, etc.) continue in existence, survive. Hence or cogn. ~ENCE, ~ENCY, nn., ~ENT a. (esp., in zool. & bot., of horns, hair, leaves, etc.) permanent (opp. DECIDUOUS), ~entLY² adv. [f. L PER(*sistere* stand)]

pers'on, n. **1.** Individual human being; (derog.) *who is this* ~?; *young* ~, young man or (usu.) woman; living body of human being, as *he had a fine* ~, *attracted by her fortune not her* ~; *acting, appearing, in his own* (*proper*) ~ or *in* ~ (himself, personally); *found a friend in (the* ~ *of) his landlord*; (law) human being (*natural* ~) or body corporate (*artificial* ~) with recognized rights & duties; character in play or story. **2.** *The three* ~s (modes of being) *of the Godhead*, Father, Son, Holy Spirit. **3.** (gram.). Each of the three classes of personal pronouns etc. denoting respectively the ~ etc. speaking (*first* ~), spoken to (*second* ~), & spoken of (*third* ~). **4.** (zool.). Individual of a compound or colonial organism. [ME, f. OF *persone* f. L *persona* player's mask, character in play, (LL) human being]

persōn'a, n. Person, as: ~ *grāt'a, nŏn grāt'a*, acceptable, unacceptable, person; IN⁵ *prŏp'rĭa* ~. [L]

pers'onable, a. Handsome, comely. [ME, f. OF, see PERSON, -ABLE]

pers'onage, n. Person of rank or importance; person; character in play etc. [ME, f. OF, see PERSON, -AGE]

pers'onal, a. & n. **1.** One's own, individual, private, as *to suit his* ~ *convenience, this is* ~ *to myself*; done, made, etc., in person, as ~ *service, acquaintance, interview*; directed, referring, (esp. hostilely) to an individual, as ~ *abuse, remarks*; ~ (also AGONY) *column*, part of a newspaper devoted to short advertisements of a ~ or semi-~ nature; making, given to making, ~ remarks, as *do not let us become* ~; (law) ~ *property, estate*, chattels or chattel interests in land, all property except land and those interests in land that pass to one's heir, (cf. REAL); (gram.) of, denoting, one of the three persons, esp. ~ *pronouns*. **2.** n. (usu. pl.). **Newspaper paragraph relating to individual person(s). [ME, f. OF f. L *personalis* (PERSON, -AL)]

pérsonăl'it|y̆, n. Being a person; personal existence or identity; distinctive personal character; person; (of remarks) fact of being aimed .at an individual, (usu. pl.) such remark(s); (rare) = PERSONALTY; *multiple ~y* (psych.), the apparent existence of two or more distinct and alternating ~ies in a single individual; *~y cult,* extreme adulation of the individual. [ME, f. OF *personalte* f. LL *personalitatem* (as prec., see -TY)]

pérs'onaliz|e, -is|e (-īz), v.t. Personify. Hence ~A'TION n. [PERSONAL + -IZE]

pérs'onall̆y̆, adv. In person, in one's own person, as *he conducted them ~, a ~--conducted tour* (conducted by guide), *writ was served on them ~; a God existing ~* (as a person); for one's own part, as *~ I see no objection.* [-LY²]

pérs'onalt̆y̆, n. Personal estate. [f. AF *personalte* PERSONALITY]

pérs'onate¹, a. (bot.). Having the opening of the lips closed by upward projection of the lower, as in snapdragon. [f. L *personatus* masked (as foll., see -ATE²)]

pérs'on|āte², v.t. Play the part of (character in drama, also fig.); pretend to be (person) esp. for fraudulent purpose. Hence ~A'TION, ~ātor, nn. [f. LL *personare* (as PERSON), see -ATE³]

personifica'tion, n. Personifying; person, thing, viewed as striking example or embodiment *of* (quality etc.). [f. foll., see -FICATION]

persön'if̆y̆, v.t. Attribute personal nature to (abstraction); symbolize (quality) by figure in human form; embody (quality) in one's own person, exemplify typically, (esp. in p.p.). [f. F *personnifier,* see PERSON & -FY]

pérsonnĕl', n. Body of persons engaged in some public service or in a factory, office, etc. (opp. MATÉRIEL). [F,= PERSONAL, adj. as n.]

perspĕc'tive, n. & a. 1. Art of delineating solid objects on plane surface so as to give same impression of relative positions, magnitudes, etc., as the actual objects do when viewed from particular point; picture so drawn; apparent relation between visible objects as to position, distance, etc.; *linear ~* (concerned with apparent form, magnitude, & position, of objects); (fig.) relation in which parts of subject are viewed by the mind; view, prospect, (lit. & fig.); *in* (drawn according to rules of) ~. 2. adj. Of, in, ~, whence ~LY² adv. [ME, f. med. L *perspectiva* (*ars* art) f. PER(*spicere spect*- look), see -IVE]

pérs'pĕx, n. Tough unsplinterable plastic material, much lighter than glass, used for transparent parts of aircraft etc. [P; f. L PER(*spicere spect*- look)]

pérspicā'cious (-shŭs), a. Having mental penetration or discernment. Hence or cogn. ~LY² adv., pérspicā'city n. [f. L *perspicax* (as prec., see -ACIOUS)]

perspĭc'ūous, a. Easily understood, clearly expressed; (of person) clear in expression. Hence or cogn. pérspicū'ITY, ~NESS, nn., ~LY² adv. [f. L *perspicuus* (as prec.), +-OUS]

perspir'able, a. Allowing the passage of perspiration; that can be thrown off in perspiration. [c. 1600, F (as foll., -ABLE)]

pérspirā'tion, n. Sweating; sweat. So **perspir'atory a.** [F (as foll., -ATION)]

perspire', v.i. & t. Sweat; (trans.) give off (liquid) through pores in form of vapour or moisture. [f. L PER(*spirare* breathe) breathe, (of wind) blow]

persuād|e' (-sw-), v.t. Convince (person, one*self,* of fact, *that* thing is so); induce (person *to* do, *into* action); (p.p.) convinced (*of* thing, *that*). Hence or cogn. ~'ABLE a., ~'ER¹ n., persuā'siBLE a., persuāsiBIL'ITY n., (-sw-). [f. L PER(*suadēre suas*- advise)]

persua'sion (-swāzhn), n. Persuading; persuasiveness; conviction, as *it is my private ~ that he is mad*; religious belief; sect holding this, as *he is of the Roman Catholic ~*; (joc.) race, kind, sort, as *a man of the Jewish ~* (Jew), *no one of the male ~ was there.* [ME, f. OF, or L *persuasio* (as prec. see -ION)]

persuā'sive (-sw-), a. & n. Able to persuade, winning; (n.) motive, inducement. Hence~LY² adv.,~NESS n. [f. med. L *persuasivus* (as PERSUADE, see -IVE)]

pért, a. Forward, saucy, in speech or conduct. Hence ~'LY² adv:, ~'NESS n. [ME, aphetic f. *apert* f. OF f. L (1) *apertus* p.p. of *aperire* open (2) *expertus* EXPERT]

pertain', v.i. Belong as part, appendage, or accessory, *to*; be appropriate *to*; have reference, relate, *to.* [ME, f. OF *partenir* f. L PER(*tinēre = tenēre* hold)]

pértinā'cious (-shŭs), a. Stubborn, persistent, obstinate. Hence or cogn. ~LY² adv:, ~NESS, pértinā'city, nn. [f. L PER(*tinax = tenax* TENACIOUS)]

pért'in|ent, a. & n. Pertaining, relevant, apposite, (*to* matter in hand etc.); to the point; ‖ (n., usu. pl.) appurtenance(s). Hence or cogn. ~ENCE, ~ENCY, nn., ~entLY² adv. [ME, f. OF, or L as PERTAIN, see -ENT]

pertúrb', v.t. Throw into (physical) confusion; disturb mentally, agitate. So **pérturbā'TION** (-ter-) n., ~atIVE (or pért'erbāt-) a. [ME, f. OF, or L PER(*turbare* disturb)]

peruke' (-ōōk), n. Wig. [f. F *perruque* f. It. *perruca, parrucca,* of unkn. orig.]

peruse' (-ōōz), v.t. Read thoroughly or carefully; read; (fig.) examine (person's face etc.) carefully. Hence peru'sAL (-ōōzl) n. [late 15th c. (1) ‘ use up ’, f. PER- + USE; (2) ‘ go through ’, of obsc. hist.]

Peru'vian (-ōō-), a. & n. 1. Of Peru; *~ bark* (of CINCHONA tree). 2. n. Native of Peru. [f. mod. L *Peruvia* Peru +-AN]

pervāde', v.t. Spread through, permeate, saturate, (often fig. of influences etc.),

Hence or cogn. **pervā′sion** (-zhn), **pervās′iveness**, nn., **pervās′ive** a., **pervās′ively**[2] adv. [f. L PER(*vadere vas*- go)]

perverse′, a. Persistent in error; different from what is reasonable or required; wayward; peevish; perverted, wicked; (of verdict) against weight of evidence or judge's direction. Hence or cogn. ~LY[2] adv., ~NESS, **pervers′ity**, nn. [ME, f. OF *pervers*, -*e*, f. L *perversus* as foll.]

pervert′[1], v.t. Turn aside (thing) from its proper use; misconstrue, misapply, (words etc.); lead astray (person, mind) from right opinion or conduct or esp. religious belief. Hence or cogn. **perver′-sion** (-shn) n., **pervert′sive** a. [ME, f. OF *pervertir* or L PER(*vertere vers*- turn)]

pērv′ert[2], n. Perverted person, apostate; (psych.) person showing sexual perversion. [f. prec., cf. CONVERT[2]]

pērv′ious, a. Affording passage (*to*); permeable; (fig.) accessible (*to* reason etc.). Hence ~NESS n. [f. L PER(*vius* f. *via* way) +-OUS]

pēse′ta (-sā-), n. Spanish silver coin and monetary unit. [Sp.]

Peshi′tō, -tta, (-shē-), n. Principal ancient Syriac version of O. & N.T. [f. Syriac *p'shit(t)â*, -*ô*, simple]

peshwa (pāsh′wah), n. (hist.). Hereditary sovereign (earlier, chief minister) of the Mahratta State. [Pers., = chief]

*pēs′kў, a. (colloq.). Troublesome, confounded, annoying, plaguy. [orig. unkn.]

pe′sō (pā-), n. Silver coin used in most S.-Amer. republics. [Sp.]

pēss′arў, n. (med.). Instrument worn in the vagina to prevent uterine displacements; vaginal suppository. [ME, f. LL *pessarium* f. LL *pessum*, -*us* f. Gk *pessos* oval stone]

pēss′im|ism, n. Tendency to look at the worst aspect of things (cf. OPTIMISM); doctrine that this world is the worst possible, or that all things tend to evil. So ~IST n., ~is′tic a., ~is′tically adv. [f. L *pessimus* worst +-ISM]

pēst, n. Troublesome or destructive person, animal, or thing; (now rare) pestilence; ~-*house*, hospital for plague etc. [f. F *peste* or L *pestis* plague]

pēs′ter, v.t. Trouble, plague. [hist. obsc.; 16th c. ' entangle ', ' crowd '; cf. later *em*-, *impester* f. F *empester*; mod. sense infl. by *pest*]

pēstif′erous, a. Noxious, pestilential; (fig.) bearing moral contagion, pernicious. [f. L *pestifer*, -*ferus* (PEST, -FEROUS)]

pēs′tilence, n. Any fatal epidemic disease, esp. bubonic plague. So **pēstilěn′tial** (-shl) a. [ME, f. OF, f. L *pestilentia* (as foll., see -ENCE)]

pēs′tilent, a. Destructive to life, deadly; (fig.) injurious to morals etc.; (colloq.) troublesome, plaguy. Hence ~LY[2] adv. [f. L *pestilens* (also -*lentus*) f. *pestis* plague]

pē′stle (-sl), n., & v.t. & i. Club-shaped instrument for pounding substances in a mortar; kinds of appliance for pounding etc.; (v.t.) pound (as with ~; (v.i.) use ~. [ME, f. OF *pestel* f. L *pistillum* (*pinsere pist*- pound)]

pēstol′ogў, n. Scientific study of pests (esp. harmful insects) & the methods of dealing with them. [f. L *pestis* PEST +-O-+-LOGY]

pět[1], n., & v.t. (-tt-). 1: Animal tamed & kept as favourite or treated with fondness; darling, favourite, (often attrib.); one's ~ *aversion*, what one specially dislikes; ~-*cock*, small stop-cock for draining, letting out steam, etc.; ~ *name*, one expressing fondness or familiarity. 2. v.t. Treat as a ~, fondle; *~*ting party* (colloq.), social gathering of young people at which hugging, kissing, etc., are indulged in. [16th c. Sc. & north., orig. unkn.]

pět[2], n. Offence at being slighted, ill-humour, esp. *take* (usu. *the*) ~, *be in a* ~. [c. 1600, of unkn. orig.]

pět′al, n. Each of the divisions of the corolla of a flower. Hence ~INE (-īn), (-)~(l)ED[2] (-ld), ~OID, aa. [f. mod. L *petalum*; LL in sense thin plate, leaf, f. Gk (*pet*-spread)]

pět′alŏn, n. Gold plate on mitre of Jewish high priest. [as PETAL]

pětard′, n. Small engine of war formerly used to blow in door etc.; kind of firework, cracker; HOIST[2] *with his own* ~. [f. F *pétard* (*péter* break wind ult. f. L *pedere*, see -ARD)]

pět′asus, n. Ancient Greek low-crowned broad-brimmed hat, esp. as worn by Hermes; winged hat of Hermes. [L, f. Gk *petasos*]

pětaur′ist (-tŏr-), n. Marsupial of the genus *Petaurista* with a patagium enabling it to take flying leaps. [f. L (-*ta*) f. Gk *petauristēs* performer on spring-board (*petauron*)]

Pět′er[1], n. A male Christian name; *St* ~, one of Christ's disciples; *rob* ~ *to pay Paul*, take away from one to give to another, discharge one debt by incurring another; BLUE ~; ~'*s fish*, haddock or other fish with marks supposed to have been made by St ~'s thumb & finger; ~-*penny*, ~'*s-penny* or *pence*, (hist.) annual tax of penny paid to papal see, (since 1860) voluntary payments to papal treasury. [f. L f. Gk *Petros* stone]

pět′er[2], v.i. (sl.). (Of stream, vein of ore, & fig.) ~ *out*, give out, come to an end. [orig. unkn.]

pět′ersham, n. Thick ribbed or corded silk ribbon; heavy overcoat or breeches formerly worn; cloth for these. [Viscount P~, c. 1812]

pět′iŏl|e, n. (bot.). Leaf-stalk. Hence ~AR[1], ~ATE[2](2), aa. [f. L *petiolus* little foot, stalk]

petit (petē′), a. (pl. ~s pr. petē′). ~ *four* (foor), small fancy biscuit; ~s-*chevaux* (shevō′), a gambling game; ~-*maître* (mā′tr), dandy, coxcomb; ~ *mal* (mäl), mild form of epilepsy; ~ *souper* (sōōp′ā), informal supper for a few intimates; ~*s soins* (see Ap.), small attentions; ~ *verre* (vār), glass of liqueur. [F, = little]

petite (petēt′), a. (Of woman) of small dainty make. [F, fem. of prec.]

pĕti′tio (-tīshiō, -tītiō), n. ~ **prĭncĭp′ĭi**, begging the question. [L, as foll.]

pĕti′tion, n., & v.t. & i. 1. Asking, supplication, request; formal written supplication from one or more persons to sovereign etc.; *P~ & Advice* (hist.), Parliament's remonstrance to Cromwell 1657; *P~ of Right* (hist.), parliamentary declaration of rights & liberties of the people assented to by Charles I in 1628; (law) kinds of formal written application to a court. 2. v.t. Make ~ to (sovereign etc. *for* thing, *to* do). 3. v.i. Ask humbly (*for* thing, *to* be allowed to do etc.). So ~ARY[1] (-sho-) a., ~ER[1] (-sho-) n. (esp., plaintiff in divorce suit). [ME, f. OF *petition* f. L *petitionem* (*petere* -*tit*- seek, see -ION)]

pĕt′rel, n. Kinds of oceanic bird spending nearly all their lives at sea; (also *storm-~*, *stormy* ~) small sea-bird with black & white plumage & long wings. [17th c. also *pitteral*, of uncert. orig.; later assoc. w. St *Peter* (-REL)]

pĕtrifăc′tion, n. Petrifying; petrified substance or mass. [irreg. f. foll., see -FACTION; reg. *petrification* is now rare]

pĕt′rif|ȳ, v.t. & i. Convert into stone; (fig.) paralyse, stupefy, with astonishment, terror, etc. (~*ied with fear* etc.); deprive (mind, doctrine, etc.) of vitality, stiffen; (intr.) turn into stone (lit. & fig.). [f. F *pétrifier* f. L f. Gk *petra* rock, see -FY]

pĕt′ro-, comb. form of Gk *petra* rock, as: ~*glyph*, rock-carving; ~*graph*, rock-inscription; ~*graphy* (pĭtrŏg′-), scientific description of formation & composition of rocks, so ~*grapher* (pĭtrŏg′-) n., ~*graph-ic(al)* aa.; ~*logy* (pĭtrŏl′-), study of origin, structure, etc., of rocks, so ~*lo′gic(al)* aa., ~*lo′gically* adv., ~*logist* (pĭtrŏl′-) n.

‖ **pĕt′rol**, n. Refined petroleum as used in motor-cars, aircraft, etc. [f. F *pétrole* f. foll.]

pĕtrōl′éum, n. Mineral oil found in upper strata of earth, used as fuel for heating & in internal-combustion engines. [med. L (L & Gk *petra* rock + L *oleum* oil)]

pétroleur (pātrölēr′), n. (fem. -*euse* pr. -ērz). Incendiary who uses petroleum. [F]

pĕtrōl′ic, a. Of petrol or petroleum. [-IC]

pĕt′ronel, n. (hist.). Large pistol used esp. by horse-soldiers in 16–17th cc. [f. F *petrinal*, dial. form of *poitrinal* (*poitrine* chest, ult. f. L *pectus -oris*, see -AL); the butt end rested against chest in firing]

pĕt′rous, a. Of, like, rock, esp. (anat.) applied to hard part of the temporal bone. [f. L *petrosus* (L & Gk *petra* rock, see -OUS)]

pĕtt′icoat, n. Woman's (under-)garment fastened round waist & hanging loose usu. inside a skirt (*have known him since he was in ~s*, a small child); *she is a Cromwell in ~s* (in all but sex); woman, girl, (pl.) female sex; (attrib.) feminine, esp. ~ *government*, predominance of woman in the home or in politics. Hence ~ED[2], ~LESS, aa.· [orig. (15th c.) *petty coat*]

pĕtt′ifŏg, v.i. (-gg-). Practise legal chicanery; quibble, wrangle, about petty points. [app. back formation f. foll.]

pĕtt′ifŏgg|er (-g-), n. Inferior legal practitioner; rascally attorney; petty practitioner in any department. Hence ~ERY(4) n., ~ING[2] a., (-g-). [f. PETTY; -*fogger* unexpl.]

pĕtt′ish, a. Peevish, petulant, easily put out. Hence ~LY[2] adv., ~NESS n. [f. PET[2] + -ISH[1]]

pĕtt′itoes (-ōz), n.pl. Pig's trotters. [orig. giblets, f. *petite oie* giblets of a goose, w. assim. to *petty*, *toes*]

pĕtt′ō, n. *In* ~, in one's own breast, in secret. [It., f. L *pectus*]

pĕtt′|ȳ, a. Unimportant, trivial; little-minded; minor, inferior, on a small scale, as ~*y princes*, *farmers*; ~*y cash*, small cash items of receipt or expenditure; ~*y officer*, in navy corresponding in rank to N.C.O.; ~*y* JURY, LARCENY, ‖ SESSION. Hence ~ĭLY[2] adv., ~ĭNESS n. [late ME phonetic sp., after F pronunc., of orig. *petit* (f. OF)]

pĕt′ūl|ant, a. Peevishly impatient or irritable. Hence or cogn. ~ANCE n., ~antLY[2] adv. [f. F *pétulant* f. L *petulan-tem* ult. f. *petere* seek, see -ANT]

pĕtūn′ia, n. Plant with white, purple, or violet flowers of funnel shape; dark violet, purple, (esp. attrib.). [f. F *petun* f. S.-Amer. Guarani *pety* tobacco]

pétun′tsè (-ŏōn-, -ŭn-), n. White earth used in China for making porcelain. [f. Chin. *pai-tun-tze* (*pai* white + *tun* stone + suf. -*ize*)]

pew, n., & v.t. Enclosed compartment or fixed bench with back in church; (colloq.) seat, as *find*, *take*, *a* ~; ~-*rent* (for ~ or seats in church); (v.t.) furnish with ~s, enclose in ~. Hence ~AGE(4) n., ~′LESS a. [ME *puwe* f. OF *puye* balcony f. L *podia* pl. of *podium* f. Gk *podion* pedestal]

pewit, **peewit** (pē′wĭt, pū′ĭt), n. Lapwing; its cry; ~ (*gull*), black-headed gull. [imit.]

pewt′er, n. Grey alloy of tin & lead or other metal; utensils of this; ~ pot; ‖ (sl.) prize-money. [ME & OF *peutre*, = It. *peltro*; orig. unkn.]

pfĕnn′ig, -**ing**, n. Small German copper coin 1/100 of a mark. [G, cogn. w. PENNY]

phā′éton (or fā′tn), n. Light four-wheeled open carriage usu. drawn by pair of horses. [F, f. Gk *Phaethōn*, son of Helios (Sun-god) and famous for bad driving of sun chariot]

phăgĕd|aen′a, -**d|ēn′a** (-j-, -g-), n.

Spreading ulcer. So ~aen'ic, ~ĕn'ic, a. [L, f. Gk *phagedaina* (*phag*- eat)]

phăg'ocyte, n. Leucocyte capable of guarding the system against infection by absorbing microbes. [f. Gk *phag*- eat + -o- + -CYTE]

-phagous in comb. = Gk -*phagos* -eating + -ous. So -*phagy* (Gk -*phagia*).

phăl'änge (-j), n. See PHALANX.

phalăn'géal (-j-), a. (anat.). Of a phalanx. [-AL]

phalăn'ger (-j-), n. Kinds of Australian marsupial of arboreal habits, e.g. flying squirrel or opossum. [mod. L (Buffon), f. Gk *phalaggion* spider's web (PHALANX), from webbed toes of hind feet]

phăl'anst|erў, n. (Buildings of) socialistic PHALANX. Hence ~ĕr'ian a. & n. [f. F *phalanstère* f. foll. after *monastère*]

phăl'ăn|x, n. (pl. ~xes, ~ges pr. -jēz.) 1. (Gk ant.) line of battle, esp. body of Macedonian infantry drawn up in close order. 2. Set of persons banded together for common purpose; socialistic community of about 1800 persons as proposed by Fourier. 3. (Anat., also ~ge) each bone of finger or toe; (bot.) bundle of stamens united by filaments. [L, f. Gk *phalagx* -*ggos*]

phăl'arōpe, n. Kinds of small wading and swimming bird noted for their tameness. [F, irreg. f. Gk *phalaris* coot + *pous* foot]

phăll'|us, n. (pl. ~ī). Image of the penis, venerated in religious systems as symbolizing generative power in nature. Hence or cogn. ~ic a., ~(ĭc)ism(3) nn. [LL, f. Gk *phallos*]

phană'rĭŏt, n. Resident in the Phanar quarter of Constantinople; member of the Greek official class under the Turks. [f. mod. Gk *phanariōtēs* (*phanari* lighthouse f. Gk *phanarion*, see -OT²)]

phăn'er|ogăm, n. (bot.). Plant that has stamens & pistils, flowering plant, (cf. CRYPTOGAM). So ~ogăm'ic, ~ŏg'amous, aa. [f. F -*phanérogame* f. Gk *phaneros* visible + *gamos* marriage]

phăn'sĭgar, n. Thug. [Hind. (*phansi* noose)]

phăn'tăsm, n. Illusion, phantom; illusive likeness (*of*); (psychics) supposed vision of absent (living or dead) person. Hence **phăntăs'mal**, **phăntăs'mic**, aa., **phăntăs'mally²** adv., (-z-). [ME *fan*- f. OF *fantasme* f. L f. Gk *phantasma* (*phantazō* make visible f. *phainō* show)]

phăntăsmag|ŏr'ia (-z-), n. Exhibition of optical illusions in London in 1802; shifting scene of real or imagined figures. Hence ~ŏr'ric a. [f. prec. + (?) Gk *agora* assembly]

phăn'tasў. See FANTASY (the *ph*- form is used esp. for the first sense there given).

phăn'tom, n. Apparition, spectre; image (*of*); vain show, form without substance or reality; mental illusion; (attrib.) apparent, illusive, as ~ *tumour*, temporary swelling. [ME & OF *fantosme* PHANTASM]

Phăr'aoh (-rō), n. Generic name of ancient Egyptian kings; ~'s *serpent*, chemical toy fusing in serpentine form. [f. LL f. Gk *Pharaō* ult. f. Egypt. *pr'o* great house]

Phă'risee, n. One of ancient Jewish sect distinguished by strict observance of traditional & written law & pretensions to sanctity; self-righteous person, formalist, hypocrite. Hence or cogn. **Phărĭsā'ic(al)** aa., **Phărĭsā'ically²** adv., **Phă'risāism** n. [(a) OE *fari-*, *phariseus*, ME -*sew*; (b) ME, f. OF *pharise*; f. LL f. Gk *Pharisaios* ult. f. Heb. *parush* separated]

phārmaceut'|ical (-sū-, -kū-), a. Of, engaged in, pharmacy; of the use or sale of medicinal drugs. Hence or cogn. ~**ically²** adv., ~ics n. [f. LL f. Gk *pharmakeutikos* (*pharmakeutēs* druggist f. *pharmakon* drug) + -AL]

phārmacŏl'og|ў, n. Science of action of drugs on body. Hence ~ist n. [f. Gk *pharmakon* drug + -LOGY]

phārmacopœ'|ia (-pēa), n. Book (esp. one officially published) containing list of drugs with directions for use; stock of drugs. Hence ~ial (-pēal) a. [f. Gk *pharmakopoiia* (as prec. + -*poiia* making f. *poieō* make)]

phārm'acў, n. Preparation & (esp. medicinal) dispensing of drugs; drug-store, dispensary. [ME, f. OF *farmacie* f. med. L f. Gk *pharmakeia* practice of the druggist (*pharmakeus* f. *pharmakon* drug)]

phār'os, n. Lighthouse or beacon to guide mariners. [L f. Gk *Pharos*, island off Alexandria, lighthouse on this]

pharÿng'o- (-ngg-) in comb. = foll., as: ~*cele*, abnormal enlargement at base of pharynx; ~*tomy* (-ŏt-), incision into pharynx.

phă'rÿnx, n. Cavity, with enclosing muscles & mucous membrane, behind & communicating with nose, mouth, & larynx. Hence **pharÿng'al** (-ngg-), **pharÿn'géal** (-j-), aa., **pharÿngit'is** (-j-) n. [f. Gk *pharugx* -*ggos*]

phāse (-z), n., & v.t. 1. Aspect of moon or planet, according to amount of illumination (esp. applied to new moon, first quarter, full moon, last quarter); stage of change or development; aspect (of situation or question); (phys.) particular stage in recurring sequence of movements or changes (esp. of alternating electric currents), usu. expressed in degrees, the complete sequence or period being 360°; *three*-~, (of electric generators, motors, etc.) designed to supply or use simultaneously three separate alternating currents of the same voltage, but having their periods 120° apart. 2. v.t. Carry out (programme etc.) in ~s or stages. Hence **phās'ic** (-z-) a. [f. Gk *phasis* appearance (*phan*- show), also in E w. pl. pron. -sēz]

phea'sant (fēz-), n. A game-bird naturalized in Britain & other parts of Europe;

~-eyed, (of flowers) marked like ~'s eye. [ME, f. AF *fesant* f. OF *fesan* f. L f. Gk *phasianus* (bird) of the river *Phasis* in Asia Minor]

phen(o)-, formative element f. Gk *phainein* to shine, in chem. names of substances derived from coal-tar (orig. in manufacture of illuminating gas), as: *phenā'cetin*, an antipyretic; *phēn'ol*, carbolic acid; *phēn'ŷl*, radical found in benzene, phenol, etc.

phĕnŏl'ogȳ, n. Study of the times of recurring natural phenomena esp. in relation to climatic conditions. So **phēnolŏ'gıcal** a. [f. PHENOMENON + -LOGY]

phĕnŏm'ĕnal, a. Of the nature of a phenomenon; cognizable by, evidenced only by, the senses; concerned with phenomena; remarkable, prodigious. Hence ~LY[2] adv., ~IZE v.t., make, or represent as, ~. [-AL]

phĕnŏm'ĕn(al)|ism, n. Doctrine that phenomena are the only objects of knowledge. So ~IST n., ~is'tıc a. [prec. + -ISM]

phĕnŏm'ĕnon, n. (pl. -*ena*). Thing that appears or is perceived, esp. thing the cause of which is in question; (philos.) that of which a sense or the mind directly takes note, immediate object of perception; remarkable person, thing, occurrence, etc. [f. LL f. Gk *phainomenon* neut. part. of *phainomai* appear]

phew, int. expr. impatience or disgust.

phi, n. Greek letter (Φ, φ) = ph. [Gk]

phi'al, n. Small glass bottle, esp. for liquid medicine. [ME, f. OF *fiole* f. LL *fiola* f. L f. Gk *phialē* broad flat vessel]

phil- in comb. = PHILO- before vowel or *h*. **-phil**, **-phile**, suf. forming nn. w. sense ' lover of ' & adjj. = ' -loving ', as *biblio-phil(e)*, *Russophil(e)*, *gastrophil(e)*; repr. Gk *philos* dear, in Gk found as suf. only in personal names w. sense ' dear to ' (*Diphilos* dear to Zeus), the sense ' loving ' being given in Gk by PHILO-. Hence **-philous** adj. suf.

philän'der, v.i. Make love esp. in trifling manner, dangle after woman. Hence ~ER[1] n. [f. *philander* n. f. Gk PHIL(*andros* f. *anēr* man) prop.=fond of men, taken in sense ' lover ']

phil'anthrōpe, n. = PHILANTHROPIST. [f. Gk PHIL(*anthrōpos* man)]

philanthrŏp'|ic, a. Loving one's fellow men, benevolent, humane. Hence ~ICALLY adv. [f. F *philanthropique* (as prec., see -IC)]

philän'throp|ist, n. Lover of mankind; one who exerts himself for the well-being of his fellow men. So ~ISM n. [f. PHILAN-THROPY + -IST]

philän'thropize, **-ise** (-īz), v.i. & t. Practise philanthropy; make (persons) objects of this; make philanthropic. [-IZE]

philän'thropy̆, n. Love, practical benevolence, towards mankind. [f. LL f. Gk *philanthrōpia* (as PHILANTHROPE)]

philät'el|y̆, n. Stamp-collecting. Hence

philätĕl'ıc a., ~IST n. [f. F PHIL(*atélie* f. Gk *ateleia* exemption from payment f. *a-* not + *telos* toll, tax)]

philharmŏn'ic (-lär-), a. & n. (Person) fond of music. [f. F PHIL(*harmonique* HARMONIC)]

phil'hellēne (-lel-), a. & n. (Person) loving or friendly to the Greeks or supporting the cause of Greek independence. So **philhellēn'ıc** (-lel-) a., **philhĕll'ĕnısm**, **philhĕll'ĕnıst**, nn. [f. Gk PHIL(*ellēn* = *Hellēn* Greek)]

Philip'|ı. *Thou shalt see me at ~, meet at ~*, phrases threatening retribution (w. ref. to Shakesp., *J.C.*, IV. iii. 283). [battle at ~, 42 B.C.]

philipp'ic, n. (Pl.) orations of Demosthenes against Philip of Macedon, Cicero's orations against Antony; bitter invective. [f. L f. Gk *philippikos* (*Philippos* Philip, see -IC)]

philippi'na (-pē-), **-pine'** (-ēn), **philopoen'a** (-pē-), ***-open'a**, n. Almond or other nut with double kernel, the finding of which at dessert etc. & sharing it with another person involves the giving or receiving of a present at next meeting; the present; the custom. [perh. f. G *vielliebchen* darling (*viel* much + *liebchen* dim. of *lieb* dear)]

Phil'istine, n. & a. **1.** One of an alien warlike people in S. Palestine who harassed the Israelites; (joc.) enemy into whose hands one may fall, e.g. bailiff, critic, etc.; (in German univv., after G *philister*) non--student, outsider; uncultured person, one whose interests are material & commonplace, whence **phil'istinısm** n. **2.** adj. Uncultured, commonplace, prosaic. [f. F *Philistin* or LL f. Gk *Philistinos* = *Palaistinos* f. Assyr. *Palastu*, *Pilistu*]

phillum'ĕnist (-lōō-, -lū-), n. Student or collector of match-box labels. [f. PHIL-, L *lumen* light, -IST]

philo-, comb. form (bef. vowel or *h*, *phil-*) of root *phil-* in Gk *philein* to love, *philos* friend, in wds f. Gk & mod. formations, as : ~*bıb'lic*, fond of books ; ~*gȳnist* (-ōj²), lover of women ; *phil'omath*, lover of learning, esp. of mathematics ; ~*progen²itive*, prolific, (phrenol.) loving one's offspring, whence ~*progen'itiveness* ; ~*tech'nic* (-tĕk-), fond of (esp. the industrial) arts.

philŏl'og|y̆, n. Science of language; (now rare) love of learning & literature. Hence ~ER[1], **philolŏ'gıan**, ~IST, nn., **philolŏ'gıcal** a., **philolŏ'gıcalLY**[2] adv., ~IZE(2) v.i. [f. F (-*ie*), & L f. Gk PHILO-(*logia* = -LOGY fond or love of learning]

Phil'omĕl, **Philomēl'a**, nn. (poet.). The nightingale. [f. F *philomèle* or L f. Gk PHILO(*mēla* f. *melos* song or *mēlon* apple), cap. *P* in reference to myth of ~ transformed into nightingale]

philop(o)en'a. See PHILIPPINA.

philŏs'opher, n. Lover of wisdom; *natural*, *moral*, ~, student of natural, moral, philosophy; one who regulates his life by the light of philosophy; one who shows philosophic calmness in trying circumstances; ~s' (not ~'s) *stone*, supreme object of alchemy, substance supposed to change other metals into gold or silver. [ME, f. AF var. of OF *philo-*, *filosofe* f. L f. Gk *philosophos* (as PHILOSOPHY)]

philosóph'ic|(al), aa. Of, consonant with, philosophy; skilled in, devoted to, philosophy (often in titles of societies); wise; calm; temperate. Hence ~ally² adv. [f. LL *philosophicus* f. Gk as prec., see -IC]

philōs'oph|ism, n. Philosophizing system (usu. derog., esp. of the French Encyclopaedists). So ~IST n. [f. F *philosophisme* (as PHILOSOPHER, see -ISM)]

philōs'ophize, -ise (-ĭz), v.i. & t. Play the philosopher; speculate, theorize; moralize; render philosophical. [as PHILOSOPHER + -IZE]

philōs'ophў, n. Love of wisdom or knowledge, esp. that which deals with ultimate reality, or with the most general causes & principles of things; *natural* ~, study of natural objects & phenomena; *moral* ~, study of principles of human action or conduct; (w. pl.) philosophical system; system for conduct of life; serenity, resignation. [ME, f. OF *filosofie* f. L f. Gk PHILO(*sophia* wisdom f. *sophos* wise)]

phil'tre (-ter), -ter, n. Love-potion. [F (-*tre*), f. L f. Gk *philtron* f. *phileō* love]

phiz, n. (colloq.). Face; expression of face. [abbr. of PHYSIOGNOMY]

phlĕb|ĭt'ĭs, n. Inflammation of walls of vein. Hence ~ĭt'IC a. [f. Gk as foll. + -ITIS]

phlĕb'o-, comb. form of Gk *phleps phlebos* vein, as: ~*lite*, ~*lith*, morbid calcareous concretion in vein, so ~*lŭt(h)'ĭç* a.

phlĕbŏt'om|ize, -ise (-ĭz), v.i. & t. Practise phlebotomy; bleed (person, part of body). So ~IST n. [f. F *phlébotomiser* (foll., -IZE)]

phlĕbŏt'omў, n. Blood-letting as medical operation. [ME, f. OF *flebotomie* f. LL f. Gk *phlebotomia* f. PHLEBO(*tomos* -cutter f. *temnō* cut)]

phlegm (flĕm), n. 1. Thick viscid (semi-)fluid substance secreted by mucous membranes (formerly regarded as one of the four HUMOURS) esp. when morbid or excessive & discharged by cough etc., whence ~Y² (flĕm'ĭ) a. 2. Coolness, sluggishness, apathy, (supposed to result from predominance of ~ in constitution), so phlĕgmät'ĭc a., phlĕgmät'ICALLY adv. [ME & OF *fleume*, *fleme* f. LL f. Gk *phlegma* -*atos* heat, phlegm (*phlegō* burn)]

phlĕg'mon, n. Inflammatory tumour, boil. Hence phlĕgmŏn'IC, ~OUS, aa. [f. L, f. Gk *phlegmonē* (*phlegō* burn)]

phlō'ĕm, n. (bot.). Bast with associated tissues. [f. Gk *phloos* bark + -*ēma*]

phlogĭs'tic (-j-, -g-), a. Of phlogiston; (med.) inflammatory. [-IC]

phlogĭs'ton (-j-, -g-), n. Principle of inflammability formerly supposed to exist in combustible bodies. [Gk, f. *phlogizō* set on fire (*phlox phlogos* flame, see -IZE)]

phloriz'in (or flō'rĭ-), n. (chem.). Bitter substance got from bark of root of apple & other trees. [f. Gk *phloos* bark + *rhiza* root + -IN]

Phlŏx, n. Genus of plants with clusters of flowers of various colours. [L f. Gk *phlox* (lit. flame), a plant]

-phōbe, suf. forming aa. & nn., = -fearing, -fearer, f. F -*phobe* f. L f. Gk -*phobos*, adj. suf. f. *phobos* fear, as in *hydro*~, *Anglo*~, *Russo*~.

phōb'ia, n. (Morbid) fear or aversion. [foll. used as a separate wd]

-phōb'ia, suf. f. L f. Gk -*phobia*, forming abstract nn. f. adjj. in -PHOBE, as *hydro*~, *Anglo*~, *xeno*~.

Phoeb'us (fēb-), n. The Greek sun-god; (poet.) the sun. [L, f. Gk *Phoibos*]

Phoenician (fēnĭsh'n), a. & n. (Inhabitant) of Phoenicia (ancient name for part of coast of Syria) or its colonies; Carthaginian. [ME, f. OF *phenicien* f. LL *Phoenicia* f. L f. Gk *Phoinikē* + -AN]

phoen'ix (fē-), phē-, n. (Myth.) bird, the only one of its kind, that after living five or six centuries in Arabian desert burnt itself on funeral pile & rose from the ashes with renewed youth to live through another cycle; paragon. [ME & OF *fenix* f. L f. Gk *phoinix* Phoenician, purple, phoenix; OE dir. f. L]

phŏn, n. (phys.). Unit of loudness used in measuring intensity of sounds. [f. Gk *phōnē* voice]

phōn'|āte, v.i. Utter vocal sound (usu. opp. to *articulate*). Hence phonA'TION n., ~atORY a. [f. Gk *phōnē* voice + -ATE³]

phonaut'ŏgraph (-ahf), n. Apparatus for automatically recording vibrations of sound. [as prec. + AUTO- + -GRAPH]

phōne¹, n., & v.i. & t. (colloq.). Telephone.

phōne², n. Simple vowel or consonant sound. [f. Gk *phōnē* voice]

phŏn'ēme, n. (philol.). A unit of significant sound in a given language. Hence phŏnēm'IC a. [f. F -*ème* f. Gk *phōnēma* sound]

phonĕn'doscōpe, n. Apparatus for making small sounds (esp. in human body) distinctly audible. [as PHONE² + Gk *endon* within + -SCOPE]

phonĕt'ic, a. & n. 1. Representing vocal sounds, esp. (of systems of spelling) using always same symbol for same sound, whence ~ISM, ~IST, nn., ~IZE(3) v.t.; (of vocal sounds. 2. n. pl. (Study of) ~ phenomena of a language. Hence phonĕt'ICALLY adv., phŏnēt'CIAN (-ĭshn) n. [f. Gk *phōnētikos* (*phōneō* speak, see -ETIC]

phŏn'ĕtist, n. Person versed in phonetics; advocate of phonetic spelling. [-IST]

*phŏn'ey, -nў, a. (sl.). Sham, counterfeit, fictitious. [orig. unkn.]

phŏn'ĭc, a. Of sound, acoustic; of vocal sounds. [f. Gk *phōnē* voice + -IC]

phŏn'o-, comb. form of Gk *phōnē* sound, used in many modern technical terms, as: ~*lite,* kinds of volcanic rock ringing when struck; *phonŏl'ogy,* science of vocal sounds, system of sounds in a language, so ~*lo'gic(al)* aa., ~*lo'gically* adv., *phonŏl'ogist* n.; *phonŏm'eter,* instrument recording number or force of sound-waves; ~*pōre,* apparatus for transmitting telephone messages along telegraph wire without interfering with the current transmitting telegraph messages [Gk *poros* passage], so ~*pŏ'ric* a.; ~*scope,* apparatus for testing musical strings, (also) instrument for representing sound-vibrations in visible form; ~*type,* phonetic print, character used in this, so ~*tȳp'ic(al)* aa., ~*tȳpist,* ~*tȳpy,* nn.

phŏn'ogrăm, n. Symbol representing spoken sound, esp. in Pitman's phonography; sound-record made by phonograph. [PHONO- + -GRAM]

phŏn'ograph (-ahf), n., & v.t. ‖ Earlier form of gramophone using cylinders; *gramophone;* (v.t.) record, reproduce, by ~. [PHONO- + -GRAPH]

phonŏg'raph|ȳ, n. Pitman's phonetic shorthand, whence ~ER[1], ~IST, nn.; automatic recording of sounds, as by phonograph. Hence **phŏnográph'IC** a., **phŏnográph'ICALLY** adv. [PHONO- + -GRAPHY]

-phōre, suf. = bearer, f. Gk *-phoros (pherō* bear), used to form technical wds, as *carpophore, semaphore.* Hence **-phorous,** adj. suf., = *-phore* + -OUS, synonymous w. -FEROUS, but prop. used only in wds f. Gk as *carpophorous.*

phŏrm'ium, n. (Kinds of) liliaceous plant whose fibre is used commercially; New Zealand flax. [f. Gk *phormion* a species of plant]

phŏs'gēne, n. A poison gas, carbon oxychloride, used in the 1914–18 war. [f. Gk *phōs* light + -GEN(1), w. ref. to its orig. production by action of sunlight on chlorine & carbonic oxide]

phŏs'phate, n. A salt of phosphoric acid, esp. (pl.) of lime or iron & alumina as constituents of cereals etc. Hence **phŏsphăt'IC** a. [F (PHOSPHO- + -ATE[1])]

phŏs'phene, n. Appearance of rings of light produced by pressure on eyeball, due to irritation of retina. [irreg. f. Gk *phōs* light + *phainō* show]

phŏs'phide, n. (chem.). Combination of phosphorus with other element or radical. [f. PHOSPHO- + -IDE]

phŏs'phine (-ēn), n. A colourless ill-smelling gas, a hydride of phosphorus, a compound having the structure of an amine, with phosphorus in place of nitrogen. Hence **phŏsphin'IC** a. [f. PHOSPHO- + -INE[5]]

phŏs'phite, n. (chem.). A salt of phosphorous acid. [F (PHOSPHO- + -ITE[1])]

phosph(o)- in comb. = PHOSPHORUS.

phŏs'phorāte, v.t. Combine, impregnate, with phosphorus. [-ATE[3]]

phŏs'phor-brŏnze, n. Tough hard bronze alloy containing a small proportion of phosphorus, used (esp.) for bearings. [PHOSPHORUS]

phŏsphor|ĕsce', v.i. Emit luminosity without combustion, or by gentle combustion without sensible heat. So ~ĕs'CENCE n., ~ĕs'CENT a. [f. PHOSPHORUS + L *-escere* of inceptive vbs]

phŏs'phorite, n. A non-crystallized variety of phosphate of lime. [f. PHOSPHORUS + -ITE[1]]

phŏs'phor|o- in comb. = phosphorus, as: ~*ogĕn'ic,* causing ~escence; ~*ograph,* evanescent picture on ~escent surface, so ~*ograph'ic* a., ~*ŏg'raphy* n.; ~*oscŏpe,* apparatus for measuring duration of ~escence, (also) toy containing various ~escent substances glowing with different coloured lights.

phŏs'phor|us, n. A non-metallic element, a yellowish wax-like substance undergoing slow combustion at ordinary temperatures & hence appearing luminous in the dark; ~*us necrōs'is* (colloq. *phossy jaw*), gangrene of jawbone due to ~us fumes esp. in match-making. Hence or cogn. **phŏsphŏ'rIC,** ~OUS, aa., ~ISM(5) n. (path.). [L, = morning star, f. Gk *phōsphoros* (phōs* light + *-phoros* -bringing)]

phŏss'ȳ. See PHOSPHORUS.

phŏt'ism, n. Hallucinatory sensation or vision of light. [f. Gk *phōtismos* (phōlizō* shine f. *phōs phōtos* light, see -ISM)]

phŏt'ō, n. (pl. ~s), & v.t. = PHOTOGRAPH; ~ *finish,* close finish of horse-race photographed to enable judge to decide winner or placed horses.

phŏt'o-, comb. form of Gk *phōs phōtos* light (occas. = photographic), as: ~*chromy* (-krō-), colour-photography; ~*-electric* a., marked by or utilizing emission of electrons from solid, liquid, or gaseous bodies when exposed to light of suitable wave-lengths; ~*-electric cell,* cell or vacuum-tube that uses the ~-electric effect to produce an electric current; ~*-electricity* n.; ~*gen,* kind of paraffin oil; ~*gĕn'ic,* producing or emitting light, (also) suitable for being photographed; ~*glyph,* ~*glyphy,* engraved plate produced by action of light, art of producing such plates; *photŏm'eter,* instrument for measuring intensity of light, so ~*met'ric, photŏm'etry;* ~*mĭc'rograph,* photograph of object as enlarged under the microscope; ~*phŏb'ia* (path.), dread of light; ~*phone,* apparatus in which sounds are transmitted by light; ~*sphere,* luminous envelope of sun or star from which its light & heat radiate, so ~*sphĕ'ric* a.; ~*stăt* (P), apparatus for making direct facsimile reproductions of documents, drawings, etc., a reproduction so made; ~SYN'THESIS, process by which the energy of sunlight is trapped by the chlorophyll of green plants and used to build up complex materials from carbon dioxide and water; ~*teleg'raphy*, electric reproduction of pictures, writing, etc., at a distance (cf. TELEPHOTOGRAPHY); ~*type*, plate for printing from produced by photographic process, picture etc. printed from this; ~*zincog'raphy*, photographic production of design on zinc plate.

phŏt'ograph (-ahf), n., & v.t. **1.** Picture, likeness, taken by means of chemical action of light on sensitive film on basis of glass, paper, metal, etc. **2.** v.t. Take~ of (person etc., or abs.); (quasi-pass.) *I always ~ badly* (come out badly in ~). Hence**photŏg'rapheR**[1], **photŏg'raphy**[1], nn., **phŏtŏgráph'ic** a., **phŏtŏgráph'ically** adv. [PHOTO-+-GRAPH]

phŏtogravūre', n., & v.t. **1.** Picture produced from photographic negative transferred to metal plate & etched in; this process. **2.** v.t. Reproduce thus. [F (PHOTO-+*gravure* engraving)]

phrāse (-z), n., & v.t. **1.** Mode of expression, diction, as *in simple* ~, *felicity of* ~; an idiomatic expression; small group of words usu. without predicate, esp. preposition with the word(s) it governs, equivalent to adjective, adverb, or noun (e.g. the house *on the hill*, I refuse *to do it*); short pithy expression; (pl.) mere words, as *we have had enough of* ~*s*; (mus.) short & more or less independent passage forming part of longer passage or of whole piece; ~*-monger*, person addicted to fine-sounding~*s*. **2.** v.t. Express in words, as *thus he* ~*d it*. [f. L f. Gk *phrasis* (*phrazō* declare, tell)]

phras'eogram, n. Written symbol representing a phrase esp. in shorthand. [as prec.+-o-+-GRAM]

phrās'eograph (-ahf), n. Phrase for which there is a phraseogram. [as PHRASE+-o-+-GRAPH]

phrāse͟|ŏl'ogy̆, n. Choice or arrangement of words; mode of expression. Hence ~**olŏg'ical** a., ~**olŏ'gicalLY**[2] adv. [as PHRASE+-o-+-LOGY]

phrāt'ry̆, n. (Gk hist.) a kinship unit, esp. (in Athens) each of three sub-divisions of the (*phyle* or) tribe; tribal division among primitive races. [ME, f. Gk *phratria* (*phratēr*, -*tōr*, clansman, cogn. w. BROTHER)]

phrĕnĕt'ic, a. Frantic; fanatic. [ME, f. OF *frenetike* f. L f. Gk *phrenitikos* (*phrenitis* delirium, as foll., see -ITIS & -IC)]

phrĕn'ic, a. (anat.). Of the diaphragm. [f. mod. L *phrenicus* or F *phrénique* f. Gk *phrēn phrenos* diaphragm, mind, see -IC]

phrĕnŏl'oğ|y̆, n. Study of external conformation of cranium as index to development & position of organs belonging to the various mental faculties. Hence **phrĕnŏlŏ'gical** a., **phrĕnŏlŏ'gicalLY**[2] adv., ~IST n. [as prec.+-LOGY]

phrŏn'tistery̆, n. (joc.). Place for thinking in, thinkery. [f. Gk *phrontistērion* (*phrontizō* think f. *phrontis* thought)]

Phry̆'gian, a. Of Phrygia, ancient country in Asia Minor; (mus.) ~ *mode*, ancient Greek MODE reputedly warlike in character, third of eccl. modes with E as final & C as dominant; ~ *cap*, ancient conical peaked cap now identified with cap of liberty. [f. L *Phrygianus* (*Phrygia*, see -AN)]

phthis'is (th-, fth-), n. Progressive wasting disease, esp. pulmonary consumption. So (through OF *tisike*) **phthis'ical** (tiz-, fthiz-) a., of, having, ~. [L f. Gk (*phthinō* decay)]

phŭt, n. & adv. The sound of a bladder collapsing, a bullet passing, etc.; (adv., esp.) *go* ~, collapse (also fig. of scheme etc.). [f. Hind. *phatna* to burst]

phy̆lăc'ter|y̆, n. Small leather box containing Hebrew texts on vellum, worn by Jews to remind them to keep the law (*make broad* one's ~*y* or ~*ies*, make a display of righteousness); (usu. ostentatious) religious observance; amulet, charm. [ME, f. LL f. Gk *phulaktērion* amulet (*phulassō* guard)]

phy̆lĕt'ic, a. (biol.). Of a phylum, racial. [f. Gk *phuletikos* (*phuletēs* tribesman f. *phulē* tribe, see -IC)]

phy̆l|o-, comb. form of Gk *phullon* leaf, as: ~*ŏph'agan*, animal that feeds on leaves, so ~*ŏph'agous* a.; ~*'opŏd* a. & n., leaf-footed (crustacean); ~*ostŏme*, leaf-nosed bat; ~*otax'is*, arrangement of leaves on axis or stem; ~*oxēr'a* [f. Gk *xēros* dry], kinds of plant-lice, vine-pest.

phy̆lo-, comb. form of Gk *phulon* race, tribe, in biol. wds, as: ~*gĕn'esis*, ~*geny* (ŏj²), racial evolution of animal or plant type, history of this, so ~*genĕt'ic*, ~*gĕn'ic*, aa., ~*genĕt'ically* adv.

phy̆l'um, n. (biol.; pl. -*la*). Division of animal kingdom containing classes of animals. [mod. L f. Gk *phulon* race]

phy̆s'ic (-z-), n., & v.t. (-ck-). **1.** Art of healing; medical profession; (colloq.) medicine, as *a dose of* ~. **2.** pl. (usu. treated as sing.). Sciences treating of properties of matter & energy or of action of different forms of energy on matter in general (excluding chemistry & biology). **3.** v.t. Dose with ~ (lit. & fig.). [ME, f. OF *fisique* f. L f. Gk *phusikē* (*epistēmē* knowledge) of nature (*phusis*, see -IC)]

phy̆s'ical (-z-), a. Of matter, material, as ~ *force* (opp. to *moral*); of, according to laws of, natural philosophy, as ~ *explanations of miracles, a* ~ *impossibility*; belonging to physics; bodily, as ~ *exercise, strength, beauty, training* (also sl. ~ *jerks*); ~ *geography* (dealing with natural features). Hence ~LY² adv., **phy̆s'ico-** comb. form. [f. med. L *physicalis* (as prec., see -AL)]

phy̆si'cian (-zishn), n. One who practises

the healing art including medicine & surgery; one legally qualified in medicine as well as in surgery; (fig.) healer. [ME & OF *fisicien* (as PHYSIC, see -ICIAN)]

phȳs′ic|ist (-z-), n. Person skilled in physics or natural science in general; believer in the material origin of vital phenomena (cf. VITALIST), so ~ISM n. [PHYSIO +-IST]

phȳs′icky (-z-), a. Suggestive of physic. [-Y²]

physi|o- (-z-), comb. form of Gk *phusis* nature, as: ~ŏc′racy, government according to natural order; *phys′iocrat*, advocate of this, esp. member of Quesnay's school in France in 18th c.; ~ŏ′geny, genesis of vital functions; ~ŏl′atry, nature-worship; ~othĕ′rapy, treatment of disease by physical agencies, not by drugs; ~othĕ′rapist, person skilled in this.

physiogn′om|y̆ (-zĭŏn-, -zĭŏgn-), n. Art of judging character from features of face or form of body, whence ~IST(3) n.; cast of features, type of face; (vulg.) face; external features of country etc.; characteristic (moral or other) aspect. Hence or cogn. **physiognŏm′IC(AL)** aa., **physiognŏm′ical**LY² adv., ~IST(3) n. [ME *fisnomie* etc. f. OF *fiz-*, *phisnomie* f. med. L *phisionomia* f. Gk *phusiognōmonia* judging of a man's nature (by his features) f. *phusis* nature +*gnōmōn* judge f. *gnō-* know]

physiŏg′raph|y̆ (-z-), n. Description of nature, of natural phenomena, or of a class of objects; physical geography. Hence ~ER¹ n., **physiŏgrăph′IC(AL)** aa. [PHYSIO- + -GRAPHY]

physiŏl′og|y̆ (-z-), n. Science of normal functions & phenomena of living things (comprising *animal* & *vegetable* ~y). Hence or cogn. **physiolŏ′gIC(AL)** aa., **physiolŏ′gically** adv., ~IST n. [f. F (-*ie*), or L f. Gk *phusiologia*, see PHYSIO- -LOGY]

physique′ (-zēk), n. Bodily structure, organization, & development. [F, n. f. adj. (as PHYSIC)]

-phy̆te, suf. repr. Gk *phuton* plant, denoting a vegetable organism, as *proto*~, *sapro*~. See also ZOOPHYTE.

phy̆t|o-, comb. form of Gk *phuton* plant, as: ~ogen′esis, ~ŏ′geny, generation or evolution of plants; ~ŏg′raphy, descriptive botany; *phyt′omer*, plant unit; ~ŏph′agous, feeding on plants; ~ŏt′omy, dissection of plants; ~ozō′on (pl. -*zo′a*), plant-like animal or zoophyte.

pī¹, n. Greek letter p (*Π*, *π*), esp. (math., *π*) as symbol of ratio of circumference of circle to diameter (approx. 3·14159). [f. Gk *p(eripherēia)* PERIPHERY]

∥**pī²**, a. (school sl.). = PIOUS; *pi jaw*, sermonizing, moral lecture. [abbr.]

piăc′ular, a. Expiatory. [f. L *piacularis* (*piaculum* expiation f. *piare* appease, see -AR¹)]

piăffe′, v.i. (Of horse etc.) move as in trot, but slower. [f. F *piaffer*, to strut]

piăff′er, n. Movement of piaffing. [as prec.]

pī′a māt′er, n. (anat.). Innermost MENINX. [med. L transl. of Arab. *umm raqiqah* tender mother]

pianĕtte′ (pēa-), n. Low pianino. [PIANO², -ETTE]

piani′nō (pēanĕ-), n. (pl. ~s). Small upright piano. [It., dim. of PIANO²]

pīanĭss′īmō, adv. & n. (mus.). (Passage to be played) very softly. [It., superl. of PIANO¹]

pi′anist (pēa-), n. Player on piano. [f. F *pianiste* (also in E, usu. as fem.), see -IST]

pīa′nō¹ (-ah-), adv. & n. (mus.). (Passage to be played) softly; (fig.) subdued(ly). [It., f. L *planus* flat]

piăn′ō², n. (pl. ~s). Musical instrument with metal strings struck by hammers worked by levers from a keyboard (vibration being stopped by dampers), & with pedals regulating character of tone; *grand* ~, large horizontal ~ of full tone; *upright* ~, vertical ~; *cottage* ~, small upright ~; ~ *organ*, mechanical ~ constructed like barrel-organ; ~*-player*, contrivance for playing~ mechanically. [It., earlier *piano e forte* soft & strong]

piănofŏrt′e (or piăn′ofŏrt), n. (Full name, now in formal use only, for) PIANO².

pianŏl′a (pēa-), n. Kind of mechanical piano-player. [P]

piăs′tre (-ter), -ter, n. Spanish silver coin; small Turkish & Egyptian coin. [F (-*tre*), f. It. *piastra*, ult. as PLASTER]

piăzz′a (-tza), n. Public square or market-place esp. in Italian town; *veranda of house. [It., ult. f. L *platea* f. Gk *plateia* (*hodos*) broad (street)]

pibroch (pē′brŏx), n. Series of variations on a theme for bagpipe, chiefly martial. [f. Gael. *piobaireachd* (*piobair* piper f. *piob* f. E PIPE)]

pic′a, n. Size of TYPE¹. [hist. obsc.; in late 15th c., a collection of rules about Easter & other movable feasts, in med. (Anglo-) L *pica*, in ME *pie*, *pye*, then identified w. L *pica* PIE¹]

pic′adŏr, n. Mounted man with lance in bull-fight. [Sp. (*picar* prick)]

pic′amar, n. Bitter oil got from wood-tar. [f. L *pix picis* pitch +*amarus* bitter]

picarĕsque′ (-k), a. (Of a style of fiction) dealing with adventures of rogues. [F, f. Sp. *picaresco* (*picaro* rogue, -ESQUE)]

picarōōn′, n., & v.i. Rogue; thief; pirate; pirate ship; (v.i.) play the pirate or brigand. [f. Sp. *picaron* (as prec., see -OON)]

***picayune′** (-yōōn), n. & a. 1. Small coin, esp. 5-cent piece; (colloq.) insignificant person or thing. 2. adj. Mean, contemptible. [in Louisiana, f. F *picaillon* f. Pr. *picaioun*]

picc′alĭll, n. Pickle of chopped vegetables & hot spices. [18th c., orig. unkn.]

picc′aninny, pick′-, n. & a. Child, esp. of Negroes or S.-African or Australian

piccolo, natives; (adj.) very small, baby. [f. Sp. *pequeño* or Port. *pequeno*, dim. *-nino*, small]

picc'olō, n. (pl. ~s). Small flute, octave higher than the ordinary. [It., = small (flute)]

pice, n. Pakistani coin. [f. Hind. *paisa*]

pichiciāg'ō, n. Small burrowing animal of Chile etc., allied to armadillos. [f. Sp. *pichiciego* perh. f. native *pichey* + Sp. *ciego* blind f. L *caecus*]

pick[1], n. Tool consisting of iron bar usu. curved with point at one end & point or chisel-edge at other, with wooden handle passing through middle perpendicularly, used for breaking up hard ground etc., and for getting coal; instrument for picking; TOOTH~. [ME *pic*, *pykk*, app. collateral form of PIKE[1]]

pick[2], v.t. & i. **1**. Break surface of (ground etc.) with or as with pick; make (hole etc.) thus; (fig.) ~ HOLES *in*. **2**. Probe (teeth etc.) with pointed instrument to remove extraneous matter. **3**. Clear (bone, carcass) of adherent flesh; pluck, gather, (flower, fruit, etc.) from stalk etc. **4**. (Of birds) take up (grains etc.) in bill; (of persons) eat (food, or meal, or abs.) in small bits, (colloq.) eat (t. & i.). **5**. Select carefully, as ~ one's *words*, *way*, *steps*; ~ *& choose*, select fastidiously; ~ (contrive) *a quarrel with*. **6**. ~ (person's) *brains*, extract his ideas for one's own use; ~ (person's) *pocket*, steal its contents; (intr.) ~ *& steal*, pilfer; ~ *a lock*, open it (esp. with intent to rob) with pointed instrument, skeleton key, etc. **7**. Pull asunder, esp. ~ *oakum*; ~ *to pieces*, pull asunder, (fig.) criticize (person etc.) hostilely. **8**. *~ at*, nag at, gird at; ~ *off*, pluck off, (also) shoot (persons etc.) deliberately one by one; *~ on*, = ~ *at*; ~ *out*, select, distinguish from surrounding objects, relieve (ground colour *with* another), make out (meaning of passage etc.), play (tune) by ear on piano etc.; ~ *up*, break up (ground etc.) with pick, lay hold of & take up, (golf, ellipt.) ~ up one's ball, raise one*self* from a fall etc., gain, acquire (livelihood, profit, tricks, information), succeed in seeing or hearing with searchlight, radio, etc., take (person, or thing overtaken) along with one, esp. *train stops to ~ up passengers*, make acquaintance of (person) casually (~*-up* n., such person), regain (lost path etc., *flesh*, *spirit*), (intr.) recover health, make acquaintance *with*, (of motor engine) accelerate *quickly* etc., (games) select sides by alternate choosing (~*-up* n., game between such sides). **9**. ~*'lock*, person who ~s locks, instrument used for this; ~*-me-up*, stimulating drink after previous depression (also fig.); ~*'pocket*, one who steals from pockets; || ~*'thank* (arch.), sycophant; ~*-up*, ~ing up (esp. of ball in cricket), device replacing sound- -box in a gramophone & enabling a record to be heard through a loud-speaker. [hist.

obsc.; ME *piken*, *pikken* (rel. to OE *pīc(i)an* prob. infl. by MLG, MDu. *pikken* to pick, peck; cf. PICK[1], PIKE[1]]

pick[3], n. Picking; selection; *the* best part *of* (*the* ~ *of the bunch*, best of the lot). [f. prec.]

pick'a-băck, adv. On shoulders or back like a bundle (of the way person or thing is carried). [orig. & form uncert.]

pick'ăx(e), n., & v.t. & i. = PICK[1]; (v.t.) break (ground etc.) with ~; (v.i.) work with ~. [ME & OF *picois* rel. to OF *pic* PIKE[1], assim. to AXE]

pick'elhaube (-howbe), n. German spiked helmet. [G, = spike cap]

pick'er, n. One who picks, gathers, or collects, as *hop*, *rag*, ~; kinds of in- strument for picking (in var. senses). [-ER[1]]

pick'erel, n. Young pike. [PIKE[1], -REL]

pick'ĕt, n., & v.t. & i. **1**. Pointed stake or peg driven into ground to form palisade, tether horse, etc.; (stake with pointed top on which person stood as) form of mili- tary punishment (hist.). **2**. (mil.). (Also *piquet*, *picquet*) small body of troops sent out (*outlying* ~) to watch for enemy, or (*inlying* ~) held ready in quarters, party of sentries, outpost; (in mod. use, chiefly camp-guard doing police duty in garrison town etc. **3**. (Usu. pl.) men stationed in a body or singly by trade union to dissuade men from work during strike etc. **4**. vb. Secure (place) with stakes, tether; post (men) as ~; beset (workmen) with ~s; act as ~. [f. F *piquet* pointed stake f. *piquer* prick, see -ET[1]]

pick'ing, n. In vbl senses, esp.: ~ *& steal- ing*; (pl.) gleanings, remaining scraps; (pl.) perquisites, pilferings. [-ING[1]]

pic'kle, n., & v.t. **1**. Brine, vinegar, or similar liquor in which flesh, vegetables, etc., are preserved; ROD *in* ~; food, esp. (pl.) vegetables preserved in ~; acid solution for cleaning purposes etc.; *sad*, *sorry*, *nice*, etc. ~ (plight); mischievous child. **2**. v.t. Preserve in ~ (esp. in p.p.), treat with ~; (naut.) rub salt or vinegar on (person's back) after flogging; ~*d* (sl.), drunk. [ME *pekille*, *pykyl*, f. MDu., MLG *pekel*; so MDu., MLG *pekelen* vb]

Pickwick'ian, a. (joc.). (Of words) *used in a* ~ (technical, constructive, or eso- teric) *sense*. [see Dickens *Pickwick* ch. i]

pic'nic, n., & v.i. (-ck-). **1**. Pleasure party including meal out of doors; (colloq.) something specially agreeable or easily accomplished (*no* ~, not an easy job). **2**. v.i. Take part in ~. Hence ~KER[1] n., ~KY[2] a. (colloq.). [18th c., f. F *piquenique*]

picot' (-kō), n. Small loop of twisted thread in edging to lace etc. [F, dim. of *pic* peak, point]

picotee', n. Carnation of which flowers have light ground with darker edging to petals. [f. F *picoté* p.p. of *picoter* prick, as prec.]

picquet. See PICKET.

pic′ric, a. ~ *acid*, yellow very bitter substance used in dyeing & surgery; & in explosives. [f. Gk *pikros* bitter + -IC]

Pict, n. One of an ancient people in N. Britain. Hence **Pict′ISH** [1] a. [ME, f. LL *Picti* perh. f. *pingere pict-* paint]

pic′tograph (-ahf), n. Pictorial symbol; primitive record consisting of these. Hence **pictogräph′IC** a., **pictŏg′raphy** [1] n. [f. L *pingere pict-* paint + -GRAPH]

pictor′ial, a. & n. 1. Of, expressed in, picture(s); illustrated; picturesque. 2. n. Journal of which pictures are main feature. Hence ~LY [2] adv. [f. LL *pictorius* (*pictor* painter, as foll.) + -AL]

pic′ture, n., & v.t. 1. Painting, drawing, of objects esp. as work of art; portrait; cinematograph film; beautiful object, as *her hat is a* ~; scene, total visual impression produced, (fig.) conjuncture or affair (*out of, come into, the* ~, irrelevant, become interesting etc.); *she looks the very* ~ (a perfect type) *of health*. 2. ~*-book* (consisting chiefly or wholly of ~s); ~*-card*, court-card; ~*-gallery*, (hall etc. containing) collection of ~s; ~*-hat*, lady′s wide-brimmed & highly decorated hat as in ~s of Reynolds & Gainsborough; ~ *postcard* (with ~ on back); ~*-writing*, mode of recording events etc. by ~s, as in early hieroglyphs etc.; ‖ *moving* ~s or ellipt. *the* ~s (cinematographic); ‖ ~*-palace*, *-theatre*, *-drome*, building etc. in which moving ~s are shown. 3. v.t. Represent in ~, describe graphically, imagine (*to oneself*). Hence **pic′turize** (-kcher-) v.t., = FILM v. [ME, f. L *pictura* (*pingere pict-* paint, see -URE)]

picturesque′ (-kcherĕsk), a. Like, fit to be the subject of, a striking picture; (of language etc.) graphically graphic, vivid. Hence ~LY [2] adv., ~NESS n. [f. F *pittoresque* f. It. *pittoresco* (*pittore* painter, as PICTORIAL, see -ESQUE)]

pic′ul, n. Chinese weight (133⅓ lb.); ~*-stick* (for carrying weights across shoulders). [Malay]

pid′dle, v.i. (Arch.) work, act, in trifling way; (colloq. or childish) make water. [(1) cf. PEDDLE (2); (2) prob. imit.]

pidd′ock, n. Bivalve mollusc used for bait. [orig. unkn.]

pidg′in, **pi′geon** (-jn), a. & n. 1. ~ *English*, jargon chiefly of English words used between Chinese & Europeans. 2. n. ‖ (colloq.). (A person′s) business, job. [corrupt. of *business*]

pie [1], n. = MAGPIE; French-, rain-, wood-, ~, kinds of woodpecker; SEA-~. [ME, f. OF, f. L *pica*]

pie [2], n. Dish of meat, fruit, etc., enclosed in or covered with paste & baked; APPLE-~ (fig.); *have a finger in the* ~, be (esp. officiously) concerned in the matter; *bran* ~, tub of bran with toys etc. hidden in it to be drawn at random at Christmas festivities etc.; MUD ~; ~*crust*, baked paste of ~, (prov.) *promises are like* ~*crust, made to be broken*; ~*man* (-an),

vendor of ~s. [ME, perh. = prec., f. miscellaneous contents compared to piebald appearance of magpie]

pie [3], n., & v.t. (print.). (Also *printers′* ~) confused mass of type; (fig.) chaos; (v.t.) mix (type). [17th c., of obsc. orig.; perh. as prec.]

pie [4], n. Pakistani coin. [f. Hind. *pa′i* f. Skr. *pad* quarter, prob. orig. same as PICE]

piebald (pīb′awld), a. Of two colours irregularly arranged, esp. black & white (usu. of animal, esp. horse), cf. SKEWBALD; (fig.) motley, mongrel. [PIE [1] + BALD]

piece [1], n. 1. One of the distinct portions of which thing is composed; *in* ~s, broken; *break to* ~s (fragments); *go to* ~s (fig.), collapse; *pick up the* ~s (said to fallen child etc.). 2. Enclosed portion *of* (land). 3. Detached portion (*of a* substance); *a* ~ *of* one′s *mind*, one′s candid opinion, rebuke. 4. Definite quantity (*of* wallpaper = 12 yds, *of* muslin = 10 yds, etc.) in which thing is made up. 5. Cask (*of* wine etc.) varying in capacity. 6. ~ (product) *of work*; example, specimen, as *a* ~ *of impudence*, *fine* ~ *of painting*, *cricket*, etc.; ~ *of* GOODS. 7. Fire-arm, (barrel of) artillery weapon. 8. Man at chess, draughts, etc. 9. Coin, as *crown*, *penny*, ~; ~ *of eight* (i.e. REAL [1]s), Spanish dollar. 10. Picture; literary or musical composition, usu. short; drama. 11. *Paid by the* ~ (according to amount done); *of a* ~, uniform, consistent, in keeping (*with*); ~*-goods*, textile fabrics (esp. Lancashire cotton goods) woven in recognized lengths; ~*-work* (paid for by the ~). [ME & OF *pece* = It. *pezza*, -*zo*, med. L *pecia*, *petia* (*-ium*) fragment, prob. of Gaulish orig.; cf. PEAT [1]]

piece [2], v.t. Put together, form into a whole; join threads in spinning, whence **pie′cER** [1] n.; fit *on* (thing *to* another); eke *out*; make *out* (story, theory, chain of evidence) by combination of parts; join *together*; patch *up*. [f. prec.]

pièce de résistance (see Ap.), n. Most substantial dish at meal (also fig.). [F]

piece′meal (-sm-), adv., a., & n. (Also *by* ~) piece by piece, part at a time; (adj.) done etc. ~. [ME (PIECE, OE *-mǣlum* suf. f. instr. pl. of *mǣl* MEAL [2])]

pied (pīd), a. Particoloured. [PIE [1], -ED [2]]

pied à terre (pyäd′ahtār′), n. Rest for the sole of one′s foot, somewhere to stay. [F]

pi(e)-dog. See PYEDOG.

pier, n. Breakwater, mole; structure of iron or wood open below running out into sea & used as promenade & landing-stage, whence ~′AGE(4) n.; support of spans of bridge; pillar; solid masonry between windows etc.; ~*-glass*, large mirror orig. used to fill up this. [12th c. *per*, rendering med. L *pera*, of unkn. orig.]

pierce, v.t. & i. (Of sharp instrument etc., also fig. of cold, pain, grief, glance, discernment, discerning person, shriek, etc.) penetrate; prick (substance *with* pin etc.); make hole in (cask etc.); force one's way through or into; penetrate *through*, *into*, etc. Hence pier′cing LY² adv. [f. OF *percer*, f. Rom. **pertusiare* f. L PER- (*tundere tus-* pound)]

Piēr′ian (*or -ĕ′rĭ-*), a. Of Pieria in N. Thessaly, reputed home of Muses. [f. L *Pierius* +-AN]

pierrot (pē′ĕrō, pyĕ′rō), n. (fem. *pierrette*). French pantomime character; itinerant minstrel with whitened face & loose white dress. [F, dim. of *Pierre* PETER¹]

pietà (pyăt′ah), n. Picture, sculpture, of Virgin Mary holding dead body of Christ on her lap. [It., f. L as PIETY]

pi′ét|ism, n. Spener's movement for revival of piety in Lutheran Church in 17th c.; pious sentiment, exaggeration or affectation of this. So ~IST n., ~is′TIC(AL) aa. [f. G *pietismus* (as PIETY, see -ISM)]

pi′ĕtў, n. Quality of being pious. [ME, f. OF *piete* f. L *pietatem* (as PIOUS, see -TY)]

piĕzŏm′ĕter, n. Kinds of instrument for measuring pressure or the sense of it. [f. Gk *piezō* press +-o- +-METER]

pif′fl|e, v.i., & n. (sl.). 1. Talk or act feebly, trifle. 2. n. Twaddle. Hence ~ER¹ n., ~ing a., trivial, worthless. [imit.]

pig, n., & v.i. & t. (-gg-). 1. Swine, hog; flesh of (usu. young or sucking)~ as meat, esp. *roast* ~; GUINEA-~ (lit. & fig.). 2. (colloq.). Greedy, dirty, sulky, obstinate, or annoying person, whence ~g′ISH¹ a., ~g′ishLY² adv., ~g′ishNESS n., (-g-). 3. Oblong mass of metal (usu. iron) from smelting-furnace, esp. ~*-iron*. 4. Segment of orange. 5. *Buy a* ~ *in a poke*, buy thing without seeing it or knowing its value; *bring one's* ~s *to a fine, a pretty, the wrong, market*, fail in a venture; ~s *might fly*, wonders might happen; *please the* ~s, joc. substitute for *please God*. 6. ~′*headed*, obstinate, stupid, whence ~′-*headedly* adv., ~′*headedness* n.; ~-*jump*, (of horse) jump sportively from all four legs not brought together as in buck-jumping; ~′*nut*, a tuber, kind of EARTH--*nut*; ~′*skin*, (leather made of) ~'s skin, (sl.) saddle; ~′*sticking*, hunting of wild boar with spear, butchering of swine, so ~′sticker n. (also, long-bladed pocket--knife); ~′*sty*, sty for~s, (fig.) dirty hovel; ~'s *wash*, ~′*wash*, swill of brewery or kitchen given to ~s; ~′*weed*, kinds of herb eaten by ~s. 7. v.t. & i. Bring forth (~s, or abs.). 8. v.i. Herd together like ~s (also ~ *it*). Hence ~′LET, ~′LING¹, nn., ~′LIKE a. [ME *pigge*, f. OE **picga*, **pigga*; cf. DOG, FROG]

pi′geon (-jn), n., & v.t. 1. Bird with many varieties, wild, domesticated, produced by fancy breeding, trained to carry missives, etc., the dove, (now preferred to *dove* exc. in poet. & rhet. contexts, or of the turtle-dove); *carrier*-~, *homing* ~, (trained to carry home messages tied to its neck etc.). 2. Simpleton, gull, as

PLUCK² *a* ~. 3. *Clay* ~, clay saucer thrown into air from trap as mark for shooting; ~-*breast*, deformed human chest laterally constricted, so ~-*breasted*; ~ *English*, see PIDGIN; ~-*hole*, small recess for ~ to nest in, one of a set of compartments for papers etc. in cabinet etc., (v.t.) deposit (document) in this, put aside (matter) for future consideration or neglect, assign (thing) to definite place in memory; ~ *pair*, boy & girl twins, or boy & girl as sole children; ~'s *milk*, partly-digested food with which ~s feed their young, ‖ imaginary article for which children are sent on fool's errand; ~-*toed*, having the toes turned inwards. 4. v.t. Cheat (person of thing). [ME, f. OF *pijon* f. LL *pipionem* (nom. *-io*) young cheeping bird (*pipire* cheep)]

pi′geonrў (-jn-), n. Pigeon-house. [-RY]

pigg′erў (-g-), n. Pig-breeding establishment; pigsty; dirty place; piggishness. [-ERY]

pigg′ў (-g-), n. Little pig; (nursery) ~-*wiggy*, little pig, dirty child; ‖ game of tip-cat. [-Y³]

pig′ment, n. Colouring-matter used as paint or dye; natural colouring-matter of a tissue. Hence ~AL (-ĕn²), ~ARY¹, aa., ~A′TION n., a colouring of tissue by deposition of ~. [ME, f. L. *pigmentum* (*pig-* root of *pingere* paint, -MENT)]

pigmy. See PYGMY.

pig′tail, n. Tobacco twisted into thin roll; plait of hair hanging from back of head, esp. as worn by Chinese under the Manchus, by young girls, & formerly by soldiers & sailors. Hence ~ED² (-ld) a.

pike¹, n., & v.t. 1. Long wooden shaft with pointed steel or iron head, infantry weapon superseded by the bayonet; ‖ (dial.) pickaxe, spike; ‖ ~′*man*, miner who uses pickaxe. 2. [perh. diff. wd of Norse orig.]. ‖ Peaked top of hill (in names of hills in Lake district). 3. [prob. abbr. of ~-*fish*, from its pointed snout]. Large voracious freshwater fish, jack. 4. v.t. Thrust through, kill, with ~. ⸀[in first sense (16th c.) f. F *pique*, in OF *pic* pickaxe, obsc. rel. to OE *pic*, ME *pik*, *pikk* (whence PICK¹) pickaxe; see PEAK¹]

pike², n. Toll-bar; toll; turnpike road; ~′*man*, keeper of turnpike. [abbr. of TURNPIKE]

pike′lĕt (-kl-), n. Kind of teacake. [f. W (*bara*) *pyglyd* pitchy (bread)]

*pik′er, n. (colloq.). Cautious or timid gambler, a poor sport. [U.S., orig. unkn.]

pike′staff (-kstahf), n. Wooden shaft of pike; *plain as a* ~ [orig. *packstaff*, smooth staff used by pedlar], quite plain. [PIKE¹ +STAFF¹]

pilăs′ter, n. Rectangular column, esp. one engaged in wall. [f. F *pilastre* f. It. *pilastro* f. med. L *pilastrum* (L *pila* pillar, see -ASTER)]

pilau, -aw, -äff, n. Oriental dish of rice with meat, spices, etc. [Pers. (*-aw*)]

pilch, n. Infant's wrapper worn over diaper. [OE *pylece*, ME *pilche* outer garment, as PELISSE]

pil'chard, n. Small sea-fish allied to herring. [16th c. *pilcher*, of unkn. orig.]

pil'corn, n. Kind of oat in which husk does not adhere to grain. [= *pilled corn*]

pile[1], n., & v.t. 1. Pointed stake or post; heavy beam driven vertically into bed of river, soft ground, etc. as support for bridge etc.; ~*-driver*, machine for driving ~s. 2. v.t. Furnish with ~s, drive ~s into. [OE *pīl*, OHG *pfīl*, f. L *pīlum* javelin]

pile[2], n. 1. Heap of things laid more or less regularly upon one another; (*funeral*) ~, heap of combustibles on which corpse is burnt; (colloq.) heap of money, fortune, as *make a* ~, *make one's* ~ (as much as one wants). 2. Lofty mass of buildings. 3. Series of plates of dissimilar metals laid one upon another alternately for producing electric current; (also *atomic* ~) apparatus designed to contain uranium & a moderating agent for the study or utilization of atomic energy. [ME, f. OF f. L *pīla* pillar, pier, mole]

pile[3], v.t. Heap up (often *up, on*); ~ *arms*, place (usu. four) rifles with butts on ground & muzzles interlocked; ~ *up* (naut.), run (ship) on rocks or aground; (colloq.) ~ *up* (or *on*) *the agony*, intensify painful description etc., ~ *it on*, exaggerate; load (table etc. *with*). [f. prec.]

‖ **pile**[4], n. (arch.). Reverse of coin; *cross or* ~, heads or tails. [ME, as PILE[2], orig. = under iron of minting apparatus]

pile[5], n. Soft hair, down, wool of sheep; nap on cloth, esp. on velvet, plush, etc., or on carpet, as *two, three*, ~ *carpet*. Hence **pil'y**[2] a. [ME, f. AF *pile* = OF *peil* f. L *pilus* hair]

pile[6], n. (Pl.) haemorrhoids, disease marked by tumours of veins of lower rectum; (sing.) such tumour; ~*wort*, lesser celandine (from reputed efficacy against ~s). [ME, prob. f. L *pila* ball]

pil'fer, v.t. & i. Steal (thing, or abs.) esp. in small quantities. Hence ~AGE(3), ~ER[1], nn. [ME, f. OF *pelfre* PELF]

pilgar'lic, n. (arch.). Bald head; bald-headed man; poor creature. [= *pilled or peeled garlic*]

pil'grim, n., & v.i. One who journeys to sacred place as act of religious devotion; person regarded as journeying to a future life (*The P~'s Progress*); traveller; *The P~s of Gt Britain, of the U.S.*, societies fostering Anglo-American friendship by mutual hospitality etc.; *P~ Fathers*, English Puritans who founded colony of Plymouth, Massachusetts, in 1620; (v.i.) wander like a ~. Hence ~IZE(2) v.i. [ME *pele-*, *pilegrim*, *-grin*, f. OF *pelegrin* f. L *peregrinus* stranger f. PER (*egre* f. *ager* field) abroad, -INE[1]]

pil'grimage, n., & v.i. Pilgrim's journey, esp. *go on* (*a*) ~; (fig.) mortal life viewed as a journey; (v.i.) go on a ~. [ME, f. OF

pelerinage f. *peleriner* go as a pilgrim (as prec.)]

pilif'erous, a. Having hair (esp. in bot.). So **pil'iform** a. [f. L *pilus* hair, see -FEROUS]

pill[1], n., & v.t. 1. Small ball of medicinal substance for swallowing whole (*a* ~ *to cure an earthquake*, half measures); (fig.) something that has to be done, a humiliation etc., (*swallow the* ~, *a bitter* ~, etc.); ~*box*, shallow cylindrical box for holding ~s, (joc.) small vehicle or building, (mil.) small isolated chiefly underground concrete fort; GILD[1] *the* ~; (sl. or joc.) ball, e.g. cannon-ball, tennis-ball, ‖ (pl.) billiards; ~*wort*, kinds of plant with small globular involucres. 2. v.t. (sl.). Blackball, defeat. [f. MDu., MLG *pille* f. L *pilula* dim. of *pila* ball]

‖ **pill**[2], v.t. (arch.). Pillage, plunder; (dial.) = PEEL[3]. [OE *pylian*, ME *pile*, later *pille*, ult. f. Rom. **piliare*, perh. f. *pilum* javelin; from 17th c., in sense 'remove the bark etc. from', different. as PEEL[3]]

pill'age, n., & v.t. 1. Plunder, esp. as practised in war. 2. v.t. Sack, plunder, (place, person, or abs.). Hence ~ER[1] n. [ME, f. OF, as prec., see -AGE]

pill'ar, n., & v.t. 1. Vertical structure of stone, wood, metal, etc., slender in proportion to height, used as support or ornament; post, pedestal; (fig.) person who is a main supporter, as *a* ~ *of the faith*; upright mass of air, water, etc.; (mining) solid mass of coal etc. left to support roof of the working; *driven from* ~ *to post* (to & fro, from one resource to another); ‖ ~*-box*, hollow ~ about 5 ft high in which letters may be posted. 2. v.t. Support (as) with ~s. Hence ~ET[1] n. [ME & OF *piler*, f. Rom. **pilare* (*pila* pillar, see -AR[1])]

pill'ion (-lyon), n. (Hist.) Woman's light saddle, cushion attached to hinder part of saddle for second rider, usu. woman; (mod.) seating for passenger behind motor-cyclist etc. [f. Gael. *pillean*, *-in* f. L *pellis* skin]

pill'iwinks, n. (hist.). Instrument of torture for squeezing fingers. [ME *pyrwykes*, *pyrewinkes*, of unkn. orig.]

pill'ory, n., & v.t. 1. Wooden framework with holes for head & hands of offender exposed to public ridicule etc. 2. v.t. Put in the ~, (fig.) expose to ridicule. [ME, f. OF *pilori*, of unkn. orig.]

pill'ow (-ō), n., & v.t. & i. 1. Cushion of linen etc. stuffed with feathers etc. as support for head in reclining esp. in bed; *take counsel of* one's ~, take a night to reflect; (techn.) ~*-shaped* block or support; ~*-case*, *-slip*, washable case of linen etc. for ~; ~*-fight*, = BOLSTER[2]*-fight*. 2. vb. Rest, prop up, on ~; rest on ~. Hence ~Y[2] (-ōī) a. [OE *pyle*, *pylu*, = MDu. *pōluwe*, OHG *pfuliwi*, *pfulwo*, f. WG **pulwi(n)* f. L *pulvinus* cushion]

pil′ōse, -ous, aa. Covered with hair. So **pilōs′ITY** n. [f. L *pilosus* (*pilus* hair, -OSE¹)]

pil′ot, n., & v.t. **1.** Person qualified to take charge of ships entering or leaving a harbour (*drop the* ~, abandon trusted adviser); steersman (arch.); (aeronaut.) person navigating aircraft or qualified.to do so, (now) one who operates the flying controls of an aircraft (P~ *Officer*, rank in AIR¹ Force); (fig.) guide, esp. in hunting-field. **2.** ~ *balloon*, small balloon whose movements are observed as it rises in the air, used to ascertain direction and velocity of currents at various heights; ~-*cloth*, blue woollen windproof cloth for overcoat used by mariners; ~ *engine* (clearing the way for another and testing the safety. of the permanent way); ~-*jacket*, = PEA-JACKET; ~-*fish*, small fish said to act as ~ to shark; ~-*light*, small gas-burner kept alight to light another (also ~-*jet*), electric indicator light or control light; ~ *scheme*, preliminary experimental trial of project on small scale. **3.** v.t. Conduct as ~ (lit. & fig.); act as ~ on (way, piece of water); act as ~ of (aircraft). Hence or cogn. ~AGE(3, 4) n., ~LESS a. [f. F *pilote* f. It. *pilota*, -*to*, f. Gk *pēdon* oar]

Pilt′down, n. A Sussex hamlet; ~ *skull* (found in 1913 at ~, & until 1953 believed to belong to a prehistoric type of man).

pil′ule, pill-, n. Pill; small pill. Hence **pil′ulAR¹, pil′ulous,** aa. [F, as PILL¹]

‖ **pim′elōde,** n. Catfish. [f. Gk *pimelōdēs* fatty (*pimelē* fat, see -ODE)]

pimèn′tō, n. Dried aromatic berries of a certain tree, Jamaica pepper; the tree. [f. Sp. *pimiento* f. L *pigmentum* PIGMENT, (med. L) spice]

pimp, n., & v.i. Pander. [c. 1600, of unkn. orig.]

pim′pernĕl, n. Small annual found in cornfields & waste ground, with scarlet (also blue or white) flowers closing in cloudy or rainy weather. [ME, f. OF *pimprenele*, f. Rom. **piperinella* f. L *piper* PEPPER]

pim′ping, a. Small, mean; sickly. [17th c., of unkn. orig.; cf. dial. *pimpy*]

pim′pl|e, n. Small solid round tumour of the skin, usu. inflammatory. Hence ~ED² (-ld), ~Y², aa. [ME, of unkn. orig.]

pin¹, n. **1.** Thin piece of (usu. tinned brass or iron) wire with sharp point & round flattened head for fastening together parts of dress, papers, etc. **2.** Peg of wood or metal for various purposes (*split* ~, metal cotter to be passed through hole & held there by the gaping of its split end); each of the pegs round which strings of musical instrument are fastened; THOLE², BELAYing, DRAWING, -~, HAIR~, ‖ NINEPIN; *don′t care a* ~ (at all). **3.** pl. (colloq.). Legs, as *quick on his* ~s. **4.** ~s *& needles*, tingling sensation in limb recovering from numbness. **5.** Small

cask of 4½ gal. **6.** ~′*cushion*, small cushion for sticking ~s in to keep them ready for use; ~-*feather*, ungrown feather; ~-*fire cartridge* (exploded by means of ~); ~-*head*, (fig.) minute thing; ~-*hole* (made by ~ or into which peg fits); ~-*money*, annual allowance to woman for dress expenses etc., allowance settled on wife for private expenditure; ~-*point*, point of ~,·(fig.) something very small, (attrib., of targets) small & requiring very accurate & precise bombing & shelling, (v.t.) locate or bomb (such target) with the requisite accuracy & precision, designate precisely; ~′*prick*, (fig.) trifling irritation; ~-*table*, kinds of mechanical amusement & gambling device; ~′*tail*, kinds of duck & grouse with pointed tail; ~-*tuck*, very narrow ornamental tuck; ~-*wheel*, small Catherine-wheel. [late OE *pinn*, MDu., MLG *pinne*, G *pinne*, ult. f. L *pinna* point etc.; cf. PINNACLE]

pin², v.t. (-nn-). Fasten (thing *to* another, *up*, etc., things *together*) with pin(s); ~ *up* (archit.), = UNDERPIN; transfix with pin, lance, etc.; ~ one′s *faith* (rely implicitly) *on* (person etc.); seize & hold fast (*against* wall etc.); bind (person etc., often *down*) *to* (promise, arrangement); enclose by bars etc.; ~-*up* n., picture of some favourite or famous person ~ned up on wall etc. (also attrib., esp. ~-*up girl*). [f. prec.]

pin′afor|e, n. Child′s washable covering worn over frock to protect it from dirt, apron. Hence~ED²(-ōrd) a. [PIN²+AFORE]

pinās′ter, n. A pine indigenous to SW. Europe. [L, = wild pine (*pinus*, -ASTER)]

pince-nez (see Ap.), n. Pair of eyeglasses with spring to clip nose. [F, lit. = pinch-nose]

pin′cers (-z), n. pl. (Also *a pair of* ~) gripping tool made of two limbs pivoted together forming pair of jaws with pair of handles to press them together with; similar· organ of crustaceans etc.; ~ *movement*, (mil.) converging movement (also *pincer movement, attack*, etc.). [ME *pinsour(s)*, f. AF f. OF *pincier* PINCH²]

pincette (pănsĕt′), n. Small pincers, tweezers. [F]

pinch¹, n. Nip, squeeze; (fig.) stress (*of* poverty etc.); *at a* ~ (critical juncture); as much as can be taken up with tips of finger and thumb, as *a* ~ *of snuff, salt*. [f. foll.]

pinch², v.t. & i. Nip, squeeze, esp. between tips of finger & thumb (also fig. of cold, hunger, etc., esp. ~*ed with cold*); *that is where the shoe* ~*es*, that is the difficulty or trouble; extort (money etc. *from, out of*, person etc.); stint (person etc. *in, of, for*, food etc.); be niggardly; ‖ urge (horse esp. in race); sail (purposely or not) too close to wind; (sl.) steal (thing), rob (person), arrest, take into custody. [ME, f. ONF **pinchier* = OF *pincier*, f. Rom. **pinctiare*]

pinch′bĕck, n. & a. **1.** Gold-like alloy of copper & zinc used in cheap jewellery etc. **2.** adj. Counterfeit, sham. [f. C. P~, watchmaker, d. 1732]

Pinda′ri (-ahrē), n. Mounted marauder in India in 17th & 18th cc. [f. Hind. *pindari*]

Pindā′ric, a. & n. **1.** Of, supposedly like, the Greek poet Pindar. **2.** n. (usu. pl.). ~ ode(s), metre, verse(s). [f. L f. Gk *Pindarikos* (*Pindaros*, see -IC)]

pine¹, n. Kinds of trees with evergreen needle-shaped leaves growing in sheathed clusters of two or more (cf. FIR), many species of which afford timber, tar, & turpentine; *Chile* ~, MONKEY-puzzle; ~*apple;* ~*apple,* large collective fruit of the ananas, so called from resemblance to ~*cone,* (sl.) hand-grenade; ~*beauty,* ~*carpet,* moths whose larvae feed on ~*trees;* ~*cone,* fruit of the ~; ~ *marten,* dark-brown British marten. [ME, f. OF *pin* f. L *pinus;* OE *pin* dir. f. L]

pine², v.i. Languish, waste away, from grief, disease, etc.; long eagerly [*for, after, to* do). [OE *pinian* f. **pin* pain (ME *pine*) f. L *poena* punishment, pain]

pin′eal, a. (anat.). Shaped like a pine-cone; ~ *gland,* gland of unknown function behind third ventricle of brain. [f. F *pinéal* f. L *pinea* PINE¹-cone, see -AL]

pin′erў, n. Place in which pineapples are grown; plantation of pines. [-ERY]

pin′fōld, n., & v.t. Pound for stray cattle etc.; (v.t.) confine in this. [OE *pundfald* (*pund POUND² *+fald* FOLD¹)]

ping, n., & v.i. **1.** Abrupt ringing sound as of rifle bullet flying through air. **2.** v.i. Make, fly with, this. [imit.]

ping′pŏng′, n. Table-tennis, game like lawn-tennis played on table with celluloid balls & parchment or wooden bats. [imit. f. sound of bat]

ping′uid (-nggw-), a. (usu. joc.). Fat, oily, greasy. [f. L *pinguis* fat +-ID¹]

ping′uin (-nggw-), n. W.-Ind. plant allied to pineapple; its fruit. [orig. unkn.]

pin′ion¹ (-nyon), n. Terminal segment of bird's wing; (poet.) wing; any flight-feather of wing; (in carving) part of wing corresponding to forearm. [ME, f. OF *pignon* f. L *pinna* PIN¹, -OON]

pin′ion² (-nyon), v.t. Cut off pinion of (wing, bird) to prevent flight; bind the arms of (person), bind (arms); bind (person etc.) fast *to* (thing). [f. prec.]

pin′ion³ (-nyon), n. Small cog-wheel engaging with larger one; cogged spindle engaging with wheel. [f. F *pignon* alt. f. obs. *pignol* f. Rom. *pineolus f. L *pinea* pine-cone]

pink¹, n. & a. **1.** Garden plant with sweet-smelling white, ~, crimson, or variegated flowers. **2.** The ~ (embodied perfection) *of elegance* etc.; *the* ~ (most perfect condition) *of health* etc. (also sl., *in the* ~, abs., quite well). **3.** (Of a) pale red slightly inclining to purple. **4.** Fox-hunter's red coat, cloth of this; fox-hunter. **5.** adj. Of pale red colour of various kinds, as *rose, salmon,* -~, whence ~′ISH¹, ~′Y² aa., ~′NESS n.; (pol.) verging on red; ~*eye,* contagious fever of horse, contagious ophthalmia in man. [orig. unkn.]

pink², n. Yellowish pigment made by combining vegetable colouring matter with some white base (*brown, French, Dutch,* etc. ~). [orig. unkn.]

pink³, n. (hist.). Sailing-vessel esp. with narrow stern (orig. small & flat-bottomed). [15th c., f. MDu. *pincke, pinke,* of unkn. orig.]

pink⁴, v.t. Pierce slightly with sword etc.; (also ~ *out*) ornament (leather etc.) with perforations; adorn, deck. [ME; cf. LG *pinken* strike, peck, perh. var. of *picken* PICK²]

‖ **pink⁵,** n. Young salmon; (dial.) minnow. [15th c. *penk,* of unkn. orig.; cf. G dial. *pink(e)* in same senses]

pink⁶, v.i. (Of a motor-engine) emit series of high-pitched explosive sounds caused by detonation of mixture following partial combustion. [imit.]

*Pink′ster, n. Whitsuntide; *p~ flower,* pink azalea. [Du., = Pentecost]

pĭnn′a, n. (pl. -ae). Broad upper part of external ear; primary division of pinnate leaf; fin, fin-like structure. [L, = *penna*]

pinn′ace, n. Warship's double-banked (usu. eight-oared) boat now usu. driven by steam or petrol. [16th c., f. F *pinasse* (but cf. ME *spinace* = AF *espynasse*)]

pinn′acle, n., & v.t. Small ornamental turret usu. ending in pyramid or cone, crowning a buttress, roof, etc.; natural peak; (fig.) culmination, climax; (v.t.) set (as) on ~, form the ~ of, furnish with ~s. [ME & OF *pinacle* f. LL *pinnaculum* (*pinna* wing, point, see PIN¹, -CULE)]

pinn′ate, a. (Bot., of compound leaf) with series of leaflets on each side of common petiole; (zool.) with branches, tentacles, etc., on each side of an axis. Hence **pinn′ātĕd** [-ATE²] a., ~LY² adv. [f. L *pinnatus* feathered (PINNA, see -ATE²)]

pinn′er, n. In vbl senses; also, coif with two long side-flaps pinned on. [f. PIN v. + -ER¹]

pinn′i-, comb. form of L *pinna, penna* wing, fin, as: ~*grade,* ~*ped,* aa. & nn., fin-footed (animal).

pinn′othēre, -tēre, n. Kinds of small crabs commensally inhabiting shells of oyster, mussel, etc. [f. L f. Gk *pinnotērēs* (*pinna* bivalve mollusc, + -*tērĕō* guard)]

pinn′ŭl|e, n. (Bot.) secondary division of pinnate leaf; (zool.) part, organ, like small wing or fin; sight at end of index of astrolabe etc. Hence ~AR¹ a. [f. L *pinnula* dim. of PINNA]

pinn′ў, n. Colloq. abbr. of PINAFORE.

*pin′oc(h)le (-ŏkl; *or* pē-), n. Game like bezique. [orig. unkn.]

*pinōl′e, n. Meal made from parched

cornflour mixed with sweet flour, sugar, etc. [Amer.-Sp., f. Aztec *pinolli*]

pint, n. Measure of capacity for liquids etc., ⅛th of gallon. [ME, f. OF *pinte*, of unkn. orig.]

pinta'dō (-ah-), n. (pl. ~s). (Now usu. ~ *bird*, *petrel*) kind of petrel; guinea-fowl. [f. Port. *pintado* painted, p.p. of *pintar* f. L *pingere* **pinct-* for *pict-*]

pin'tle, n. Kinds of pin or bolt, esp. one on which some other part turns. [OE *pintel* penis, of unkn. orig.; cf. OFris., LG, Du., G *pint*]

*pin'tō (or pē-), a. & n. Piebald (horse). [Sp.]

pīnx'ĭt, pīnxer'ŭnt, v.t. (So-&-so) painted it (in signature to picture, as FECIT). [L]

pīn'ў, a. Of, like, abounding in, pines. [-Y²]

piolet (pyŏlā'), n. Alpinist's ice-axe. [F]

pioneer', n., & v.i. & t. 1. (Mil.) one of body of foot-soldiers marching in advance with spades etc. to prepare road for main body; beginner of enterprise, original explorer, etc. 2. v.i. Act as ~. 3. v.t. Open up (road etc.) as ~; act as ~ to, conduct. [f. F *pionnier* foot-soldier, pioneer, (*pion*, f. L as PAWN¹, -IER)]

piou-piou (pyōō-pyōō'), n. (Pop.) typical French private soldier, cf. *poilu*. [F]

pi'ous, a. Devout, religious; ~ *founder* (of college etc. for glory of God & good of man); (arch.) dutiful; ~ FRAUD. Hence ~LY² adv. [f. L *pius* dutiful, pious, -OUS]

pip¹, n. Disease of poultry, hawks, etc., marked by thick mucus in throat & often by white scale on tip of tongue; ‖ (sl.) fit of depression, bad temper, (*he has, gives me, the*~). [ME, f. MDu. *pippe*, MLG *pip* f. WG *pipit f. Rom. *pipita corrupt. of L *pituita* phlegm]

pip², n. Each spot on playing-cards, dice, or dominoes; star (1-3 acc. to rank) on army officer's shoulder; single blossom of clustered inflorescence; rhomboidal segment of surface of pineapple. [late 16th c. *peep*, of unkn. orig.]

‖ **pip³**, v.t. (colloq.; -pp-). Blackball; defeat; hit with shot. [f. prec. or foll.]

pip⁴, n. Seed of apple, pear, orange, etc. Hence ~LESS a. [app. abbr. of PIPPIN]

‖ **pip⁵**, signallers' letter P, as in ~ *emma*, *o.*~.

‖ **pip⁶**, n. Short high-pitched sound, usu. mechanically produced (*the six* ~s *of the time-signal*). [imit.]

pipal. See PEEPUL.

pipe¹, n. 1. Tube of wood, metal, etc., esp. for conveying water, gas, etc. 2. Musical wind-instrument consisting of single tube; each of the tubes by which sound is produced in organ; (pl.) = BAG¹~s; boatswain's whistle, sounding of this. 3. Voice, esp. in singing; song, note, of bird. 4. Tubular organ, vessel, etc. in animal body. 5. Cylindrical vein of ore. 6. Channel of decoy for wild fowl. 7. (Also *tobacco-*~) narrow tube of clay, wood, etc.,

with bowl at one end for drawing in smoke of tobacco, quantity of tobacco held by this, as *light, smoke, a* ~; PEACE-~; ‖ *King's* or *Queen's* ~, furnace at London Docks used formerly for burning contraband tobacco; *put that in your* ~ *& smoke it*, digest that fact etc. if you can. 8. Cask for wine, esp. as measure usu. = 105 gal. 9. ~'*clay*, fine white clay used for tobacco-~s & (esp. by soldiers) for cleaning white breeches, belts, etc., (fig.) excessive attention to minutiae of dress etc. in regiment, (v.t.) whiten with ~*clay*; *~ *dream*, a notion as fantastic as a dream produced by opium-smoking; ~*-fish*, (kinds of) long slender fish with elongated snout; ~*-light*, spill for lighting ~; ~'*line* (esp. for conveying petroleum to a distance), (fig.) continuous flow of goods in transit from producer to retailer or (industrial) consumer etc.; ~ *major*, N.C.O. commanding regimental pipers; ~*-rack* (for tobacco-~s); ~*-rolls* (hist.), records of the old national Exchequer offices (prob. because subsidiary documents were rolled in ~ form); ~*-stone*, hard red clay used by Amer. Indians for tobacco-~s. Hence ~'FUL (-pfŏŏl) n., ~'LESS (-pl-), pīp'Y², aa. [OE *pipe*, OHG *pfifa*, ON *pipa*, f. Rom. *pipa f. L *pipare*, *-iare* peep, chirp]

pipe², v.i. & t. 1. Play (tune etc., or abs.) on pipe; lead, bring, (person etc.) by sound of pipe; summon (crew *up, to* meal, work, etc.) by sounding whistle (~ *away*, give signal for boat to start); whistle; utter in shrill voice; ~ *down*, (naut.) dismiss from duty, (sl.) be less noisy or cocksure; ~ *up*, begin to play or sing; ~ one's *eye*(s), weep. 2. Propagate (pinks etc.) by cuttings taken off at joint of stem. 3. Trim (dress), ornament (cake etc.), with PIPING¹. 4. Furnish with pipes; convey (oil, water, gas, etc.) by pipes. [OE *pipian* f. as prec.]

‖ **pip ĕmm'a**, adv. (colloq.). Post meridiem. [signallers' former names for letters P, M]

pip'er, n. One who plays on pipe, esp. strolling musician; bagpipe-player; *pay the* ~ (*& call the tune*), bear the cost (& have control) of a proceeding etc.; kinds of fish; broken-winded horse; ‖ decoy-dog. [OE *pipere* (PIPE¹ + -ER¹)]

pipètte', n. Slender tube for transferring etc. small quantities of liquids, esp. in chemistry. [F, dim. of PIPE¹]

pip'ing¹, n. In vbl senses, also : ornamentation of dress by means of cord enclosed in pipe-like fold; ornamental cord-like lines of sugar on cake. [f. PIPE² + -ING¹]

pip'ing², a. In vbl senses; *the* ~ *time*(s) *of peace* (marked by piping as opp. to martial music); ~ (hissing) *hot*. [f. PIPE² + -ING²]

pipistrĕl(le)', n. Small kind of bat. [F (-le), f. It. *pipistrello, vip-*, f. L *vespertilio* bat (*vesper* evening)]

pip′it, n. Bird like lark. [prob. imit.]

pip′kin, n. Small earthenware pot or pan. [orig. unkn.]

pipp′in, n. Kinds of apple. [ME & OF *pepin* seed, of unkn. orig.]

pip′-squeak, n. (sl.). Shell that emits sound so described; insignificant or contemptible person or thing. [imit.]

piquant (pēk′ant), a. Agreeably pungent, sharp, appetizing; (fig.) pleasantly stimulating or disturbing to the mind. Hence **piquancy** (pēk′an-) n., **~LY²** adv. [F (as foll., see -ANT); F fem. -*e* also as E fem.]

pique¹ (pēk), v.t., & n. 1. Irritate, wound the pride of; arouse (curiosity, interest); plume one*self on*. 2. n. Ill-feeling, enmity, resentment, as *in a fit of ~, took a ~ against me*. [f. F *piquer* vb prick, irritate, *pique* n.]

pique² (pēk), n., & v.t. & i. Winning of 30 points in cards and play at piquet before opponent begins to count; (v.t.) score a *~ against*; (v.i.) score a *~*. [f. F *pic*, of unkn. orig.]

piqué (pēk′ā), n. Stiff ribbed cotton fabric. [F, p.p. of *piquer*, see PIQUE¹]

piquet′¹ (-kĕt; or pĭk²), n. Card game for two players with pack of 32 cards (omitting 2–6). [F, of unkn. orig.]

piquet². See PICKET.

pira′gua, perïä′gua, (-gwa), n. Long narrow canoe made from single tree-trunk; two-masted sailing-barge. [Sp., f. Carib, = dug-out]

pir′ate, n., & v.t. & i. 1. (Ship used by) sea-robber; marauder; one who infringes another's copyright; one who broadcasts without official authorization. (freq. attrib., as *a ~ broadcast*); ‖ bus that encroaches on recognized routes or overcharges or preys on passengers. 2. v.t. Plunder; reproduce (book etc.) without leave for one's own profit. 3. v.i. Play the *~*. Hence or cogn. **pir′ACY** n., **pīrăt′IC(AL)** aa., **pīrăt′icalLY²** adv. [ME, f. L (-*ta*) f. Gk *peiratēs* (*peiraō* attempt, assault)]

pirogue′ (-ōg), n. = PIRAGUA. [F]

pirouette′ (-rŏŏ-), n., & v.i. 1. Ballet-dancer's spin round on one foot or on point of toe. 2. v.i. Dance thus. [F, = spinning top]

pis aller (pēzălā′, & see Ap.), n. Course etc. taken for want of a better. [F (*pis* worse + *aller* go)]

pis′carў, n. *Common of ~*, right of fishing in another's water in common with owner (& others). [ME, f. med. L *piscaria* neut. pl. of L *piscarius* (*piscis* fish, see -ARY¹)]

pis′catorў, a. Of fishers or fishing, whence **piscatōr′IAL** a.; addicted to fishing. [f. L *piscatorius* (*piscator* fisher f. *piscis* fish)]

Pis′cēs (-z), n. pl. The Fishes, 12th zodiacal constellation; 12th sign of zodiac. [L, pl. of *piscis* fish]

pis′cĭcŭlture, n. Artificial rearing of fish. Hence **pĭscĭcŭl′turAL** a., **pĭscĭcŭl**-

turIST n., (-cher-). [f. L *piscis* fish + CULTURE]

pisci′na (-sĭ-, -sē-), n. (pl. -*ae*, -*as*). Fish-pond; ancient-Roman bathing-pond; (eccl.) perforated stone basin in church for carrying away water used in rinsing chalice etc. [L, f. *piscis* fish]

pis′cine¹ (*or* -ēn), n. Bathing-pool. [F, f. prec.]

pis′cine², a. Of fish. [f. L *piscis* fish, -INE¹]

pisciv′orous, a. Fish-eating. [as prec. + -VOROUS]

pisé (pēz′ā), n. Rammed clay or earth (& gravel) as building-material. [F, p.p. of *piser* pound f. L *pi(n)sare* pound]

Pis′gah (-zga), n. Mountain whence Moses viewed the Promised Land (*Deut.* iii. 27); (fig.) ~ *glance, prospect, sight*, etc. [Heb.]

pish, int. expr. contempt, impatience, or disgust; (v.i.) say *~*. [natural]

‖ **pishogue′** (-ōg), n. (Ir.). Sorcery; charm, spell. [f. Ir. *pis(r)eog*]

pis′iform (pīs-, pĭz-), a. Pea-shaped; *~ bone*, small bone of upper row of carpus. [f. L *pisum* pea + -FORM]

pis′mire, n. Ant. [ME, f. foll. (from smell of anthill) + obs. *mire* ant]

piss, v.i. & t., & n. (not now in polite use). 1. Make water; discharge (blood etc.) with the urine; wet with ~rine; (p.p., sl.) drunk. 2. n. Urine. [ME, f. OF *pissier* f. Rom. **pišare* (imit.)]

pista′chio (-ashĭŏ, -ashō, -achō), n. (pl. ~*s*). (Tree yielding) nut with greenish edible kernel; colour of this. [f. It. *pistacchio* & Sp. *pistacho* f. L f. Gk *pistakion*; 15th c. *pistace* f. OF]

pis′til, n. Female organ of flower, comprising ovary, style, & stigma. Hence **~lARY¹, ~lATE²(2), ~lIF′EROUS, ~lINE¹,** aa. [f. F *pistile* f. L *pistillum* PESTLE]

pis′tol, n., & v.t. (-ll-). 1. Small fire-arm held & fired by one hand; *within, beyond, ~-shot* (range of ~); *~-grip*, handhold of *~-butt* shape behind trigger-guard on gunstock. 2. v.t. Shoot with ~. [f. obs. F *pistole* (mod. -*let*) f. G *pistole* f. Czech *pišt′al*]

pistōle′, n. (hist.). Foreign gold coin, esp. Spanish coin. [f. F *pistole* (as prec.)]

pis′ton, n. Disc or short cylinder of wood, metal, etc., fitting closely within tube in which it moves up & down, used in cylinder of steam or petrol engine to impart motion by means of ~-*rod*; sliding valve in cornet etc. [F, f. It. *pistone* var. of *pestone* PESTLE]

pit¹, n. 1. Natural hole in ground; hole made in digging for mineral etc. or for industrial purposes, as *chalk, clay, gravel, coal, saw, tan, ~*; covered hole as trap for wild beasts or (esp. bibl.) for enemies (*dig a ~ for*, fig., try to ensnare); *the ~ (of hell)*, hell; COCKPIT. 2. Hollow in animal or plant body or on any surface; *~ of the stomach*, depression between cartilages of false ribs; depressed scar, as after smallpox. **3.** ‖ That part of auditorium of theatre which is on floor of house, now usu. the part of this behind stalls; ‖ people occupying this. **4.** (In motor-racing) place at which cars are refuelled, re-tired, etc. **5.** *Part of floor of an exchange allotted to special trading (*wheat-~*). **6.** ~'*fall*, covered ~ as trap for animals etc., (fig.) unsuspected snare or danger; ~'*man*, collier, *connecting rod in machinery; ‖ ~ *pony* (kept underground in coal-mines). [OE *pytt*, OS *putti*, OHG *pfuzzi*, f. L *puteus* well]

pit², v.t. & i. (-tt-). Put into a pit (esp. vegetables etc. for storage); set (cock, dog, etc.) to fight in pit (*against* another), (fig.) match (person *against*); make pits, esp. scars, in (esp. in p.p.); (path., of flesh etc.) retain impression of finger etc. when touched. [f. prec.]

pit'(a-)pặt, adv. & n. With the sound ~, palpitatingly, faltering, as *his heart, feet, went* ~; (n.) the sound ~. [imit.]

pitch¹, n., & v.t. **1.** Black or dark-brown tenacious resinous substance, semi-liquid when hot, hard when cold, got from distillation of tar or turpentine, used for caulking seams of ships etc. (~-*black*, ~-*darkness*, with no light at all); ~'*blende*, native oxide of uranium, found in ~-like masses, important source of radium; ~-*cap*, cap lined with ~, used as instrument of torture; ~-*pine*, specially resinous kinds of pine; ~'*stone*, old volcanic rock looking like ~. **2.** v.t. Cover, coat, smear, with ~. [OE *pic* (whence vb *pician*), OS *pik*, OHG *peh*, ON *bik*, f. L *pix picis*]

pitch², v.t. & i. **1.** Fix & erect (tent, camp); (abs.) encamp. **2.** (Crick.) ~ *wickets*, fix stumps in ground & place bails; fix, plant, (thing) in definite position; expose (wares) for sale in market etc. **3.** Pave (road) with set stones. **4.** ~*ed battle* (c² set kind, not casual). **5.** (Mus.) set at particular pitch, (fig.) express in particular style. **6.** Throw, fling; (in games) throw (flat object) towards a mark; (sl.) tell (tale, yarn). **7.** (golf). Play (ball) with pitch shot (see foll.). **8.** Fall heavily (*on* one's head, *into*, etc.); (of ship) plunge in longitudinal direction (cf. ROLL²). **9.** ~ *in* (colloq.), set to work vigorously; ~ *into* (colloq.), assail forcibly with blows, words, etc., make vigorous attack on, (person, food, etc.); ~ *upon*, happen to select; ~-*&-toss*, game of skill & chance in which coins are ~ed at a mark; ~-*farthing*, = CHUCK³-*farthing*. [ME *pic(c)he* (also north. *pikke*, whence (now dial.) *pick*), of obsc. hist. & orig.]

pitch³, n. **1.** Pitching (e.g. of ship). **2.** Mode of delivering cricket-ball in bowling; (golf, also ~ *shot*) lofted approach shot with little run to ball after alighting. **3.** Quantity of commodity pitched in market. **4.** ‖ Place at which one (e.g. street performer, bookmaker) is sta-

tioned; (crick.) place between & about wickets. **5.** Height to which falcon etc. soars before swooping on prey, as *fly a high* etc. ~ (also fig.). **6.** Height, degree, intensity, (of quality etc.); (mus.) degree of acuteness or graveness of tone. **7.** Degree of slope; steepness of roof's slope; (mech.) distance between successive points or lines, e.g. between successive teeth of cog-wheel. **8.** ~-*pipe*, small pipe blown by mouth to set ~ for singing or tuning; ~-*wheel*, toothed wheel engaging with another. [f. prec.]

pitch'er¹, n. Large usu. earthenware vessel with handle or two ears & usu. a lip, for holding liquids; jug; *little ~s have long ears*, children are apt to overhear; (bot.) modified leaf in ~ form, ~-*plant* (with such leaves). Hence ~FUL(2) n. [ME, f. OF *pichier* f. Rom. *picarium, var. of *bicarium*, BEAKER]

pitch'er², n. In vbl senses of PITCH², esp.: player who delivers ball, esp. in baseball; ‖ street vendor who pitches stall in fixed place; stone used for paving. [-ER¹]

pitch'fork, n., & v.t. **1.** Long-handled fork with two prongs for pitching hay etc.; tuning-fork. **2.** v.t. Cast (as) with ~, (fig.) thrust (person) forcibly (*into* position, office, etc.). [in ME *pickfork*, prob. f. PICK¹ + FORK, assoc. w. PITCH²]

pitch'ỹ, a. Of, like, dark etc. as, pitch. [-Y²]

pit'eous, a. Calling for pity, deplorable. Hence ~LY² adv., ~NESS n. [ME *pitous* f. OF *pitos* f. Rom. *pietosus (as PIETY, see -ITOUS)]

pith, n., & v.t. Spongy cellular tissue in stems & branches of dicotyledonous plants; similar tissue lining rind of orange etc.; spinal cord; (fig.) essential part, quintessence, (often ~ *& marrow of*); physical strength, vigour; force, energy; *of* ~ (importance) & *moment* (Shakes. *Ham.* III. i. 86); (v.t.) slaughter or immobilize (animal) by severing spinal cord. Hence ~'LESS a. [OE *pitha*, = MDu., MLG *pitte*, *pit*; ult. orig. unkn.]

pithēcǎn'thrōpe, n. Ape-man, hypothetical link between ape & man. [f. Gk *pithēkos* ape + *anthrōpos* man]

pithēc'oid, a. Ape-like. [as prec., see -OID]

pith'lỹ, a. Of, like, abounding in, pith; condensed & forcible, terse. Hence ~ILY² adv., ~INESS n. [-Y²]

pit'iab|le, a. Calling for pity or contempt. Hence ~leNESS n., ~LY² adv. [ME, f. OF (as PITY, see -ABLE)]

pit'iful, a. Compassionate; (of things) calling for pity; contemptible. Hence ~LY² adv., ~NESS n. [ME; -FUL]

pit'iless, a. Showing no pity. Hence ~LY² adv., ~NESS n. [ME; -LESS]

pit'pǎn, n. Central American dug-out boat. [perh. native]

pitt'ance, n. Pious bequest to religious house for extra food etc. (hist.); allowance, remuneration, esp. scanty one, as *a mere* ~; small number or amount. [ME, f. OF *pitance*, app. same wd as *pitance* pity (as PIETY +-ANCE)]

‖ pitt′ite, n. Person occupying seat in pit of theatre. [-ITE[1]]

pitū′itary, a. Of or secreting phlegm, mucous; ~ *gland, body,* a small ductless gland at the base of the brain which has an important influence over the growth of the body. So pitū′itous a., pitū′itRIN n., hormone produced by ~ body, solution containing this used medicinally. [f. L *pituitarius* (*pituita* phlegm, see -ARY[1])]

pit′y, n., & v.t. 1. Feeling of tenderness aroused by person's distress or suffering, as *cannot help feeling ~ for him, felt no ~ for him, in ~ of his fate*; take ~ on, feel or act compassionately towards; (as form of entreaty) *for ~'s sake*; regrettable fact, ground for regret, as *what a ~ !, more's the ~* (so much the worse), *it is a thousand pities you did not mention it*; (arch.) *it is or was ~ of them,* one feels sorry for them. 2. v.t. Feel (often contemptuous) ~ for, as *he is much to be pitied, I ~ you if you think that.* Hence ~ingLY[2] adv. [ME, f. OF *pite* f. L as PIETY]

pityri′asis, n. (path.). Skin disease characterized by the shedding of bran-like scales. [f. Gk *pituriasis* (*pituron* bran, -ASIS)]

piv′ot, n., & v.t. & i. 1. Short shaft or pin on which something turns or oscillates; (fig.) cardinal or crucial point. 2. vb. Furnish with, attach by, ~; turn as on ~, hinge (*upon,* often fig.). Hence ~AL a. [F]

pix′y, -xie, n. Being akin to fairy. Hence *pix′ilāted* a. (dial.), slightly crazy. [orig. unkn.]

pizzicato (pitsĭkah′tō), adv., a., & n. (mus.). (Played) by plucking string of violin etc. with finger instead of using bow; (n.) passage, note, so played. [It.]

piz′zle, n. (now vulg.). Penis of animal esp. that of bull formerly used as flogging instrument. [16th c., f. LG *pēsel,* dim. of MLG *pēse* (Du. *pees*)]

plăc′|able, a. Easily appeased, mild, forgiving. Hence or cogn. ~aBIL′ITY n., ~aBLY[2] adv. [ME, f. OF, f. L *placabilis* (*placare* appease, see -BLE)]

plăc′ărd, n., & v.t. 1. Document printed on one side of single sheet for posting up, poster. 2. v.t. (*also* plakărd′). Set up ~s on (wall etc.) advertise (wares etc.) by ~s, display (poster etc.) as ~. [ME, f. OF, f. *plaquier* vb plaster f. MDu. *plakken,* see -ARD]

placāte′ (*or* plăc′āt), v.t. Pacify, conciliate. Hence plăc′atORY a., propitiatory. [f. L *placare,* see -ATE[3]]

plăce[1], n. 1. Particular part of space; part of space occupied by person or thing, as *it has changed its* ~. 2. City, town, village, etc.; (in names of groups of buildings) *Ely* etc. P~; residence, dwell-

ing; country-house with surroundings. 3. Building, spot, devoted to specified purpose, as ~ *of amusement, worship, bathing*~; ‖ (H. of Commons) *another* ~, H. of Lords; also joc. in Cambridge with ref. to Oxford, and *vice-versa*. 4. Particular spot on surface etc., as *a sore ~ on his wrist.* 5. Passage of book etc. 6. Rank, station, as *servants must know their* ~, *keep him in his* ~. 7. (In racing) position among placed competitors. 8. Position of figure in series as indicating its value in decimal or similar notation, as *calculated to 50 decimal*~s. 9. Step in progression of argument, statement, etc., as *in the first, second,* ~. 10. Proper or natural position, as *take your* ~s, *there is no* ~ *for doubt, is in or out of* (*its, his*) ~; space, seat, accommodation, for person etc..at table, in conveyance, etc., as *take two* ~s *in the coach, always a* ~ *for you at our table; in* ~ *of,* instead of; *take the* ~ *of,* be substituted for. 11. Office, employment, esp. government appointment; duties of office etc., as *it is not my* ~ *to inquire into that.* 12. *In, out of,* ~, (un)suitable, (in)appropriate; *give* ~ *to,* make room for, be succeeded by; *take* ~, happen. 13. ~-*brick* (imperfectly burnt from being on windward side of kiln); ~ (-*kick*) (footb.), kick made when ball is previously placed for that purpose on ground; ~*man,* holder of public office, esp. one appointed from motives of interest. [ME, f. OF, f. Rom. **plattia* f. L f. Gk *plateia* (*hodos*) broad (way)]

plāce[2], v.t. 1. Put (thing etc.) in particular place; arrange (set of things) in their proper places. 2. Appoint (person, esp. clergyman) to post; find situation, living, etc., for. 3. Invest (money); dispose of (goods) to customer; put (order for goods etc.) into hands of firm etc. 4. Repose (confidence etc. *in, on*). 5. Assign rank to; locate; fully identify, remember circumstances of previous meeting with, assign to a class (*I know that man's face but I can't* ~ *him*). 6. State position of (usu. any of first 3 horses or runners) in race; *be* ~d, be among first three. 7. Get (goal) by PLACE[1]-*kick.* [prec.]

placēb′ō, n. (pl. ~s, ~es). (Eccl.) opening antiphon of the vespers for the dead; (med.) medicine given to humour, rather than cure, the patient. [L, = I shall be acceptable (*placēre* please), first word of Ps. cxvi. 9 (Vulg.)]

placĕn′t|a, n. (pl. ~ae). Flattened circular spongy vascular organ in higher mammals, expelled after parturition and helping to nourish foetus, which is attached to it by umbilical cord; (bot.) part of carpel to which ovules are attached. Hence ~AL a. [f. L *placenta* = Gk *plakoeis* -*entos* flat cake f. root of *plax plakos* flat plate]

plā′cer, n. Deposit of sand, gravel, etc., in bed of stream etc. containing valuable minerals in particles. [Amer. Sp., cogn. w. *placel* sandbank f. *plaza* PLACE¹]

‖ plā′cĕt, sentence & n. (Univv.). ~, *non* ~, it pleases me (not) (forms used in voting for or against measure); (n.) such vote. [L]

plā′cid, a. Mild; peaceful; serene. Hence or cogn. placid′ITY n., ~LY² adv. [f. L *placidus* (*placēre* please, see -ID¹)]

plăck′ĕt, n. Pocket, esp. in woman's skirt; ~-*hole*, opening in outer skirt giving access to this. [var. of PLACARD]

plăc′oid, a. (Of scales) plate-shaped; (of fish) with ~ scales. [f. Gk *plax plakos* plate, -OID]

plafond (plăfawn′), n. Ceiling, esp. one enriched with paintings; such painting. [F]

plā′gal, a. (mus.). (Of ecclesiastical modes) having their sounds comprised between the dominant & its octave; ~ *cadence* (in which chord of subdominant immediately precedes that of the tonic). Cf. AUTHENTIC. [f. med. L *plagalis* f. *plaga* ~ mode, prob. f. med. L f. Gk *plagios* oblique, (med. Gk) plagal, f. *plagos* side]

plage (plahzh), n. Sea beach (esp. at fashionable resort). [F]

plā′giar|ize, -ise (-īz), v.t. Take and use another person's (thoughts, writings, inventions, or abs.) as one's own. So ~ISM, ~IST, nn. [f. foll. +-IZE]

plā′giary, n. (arch.). = PLAGIARISM; = PLAGIARIST. [f. L *plagiarius* kidnapper (*plagiare* kidnap)]

plā′gio-, comb. form of Gk *plagios* oblique, as: ~*cephăl′ic*, having anterior part of skull more developed on one side, posterior on other; ~*clas′tic* (min.), having oblique cleavage; ~*stŏme*, fish with mouth placed transversely beneath snout, as sharks & rays.

plāgue (-g), n., & v.t. 1. Affliction, esp. as divine punishment; (colloq.) nuisance, trouble; pestilence, esp. *the* (oriental or bubonic) ~; (as imprecation) ~ *on it!* etc.; ~-*spot*, spot on skin characteristic of ~, locality infected with ~, (fig.) source of symptom of moral corruption. 2. v.t. Afflict with ~; (colloq.) annoy, bother, whence ~′SOME (-gs-) a. (colloq.). [ME, f. L *plaga* stroke (*plag-* root of *plangere* beat breast)]

plāg′u|y (-gĭ), a. & adv. (arch.). Annoying(ly); exceeding(ly), as *was* ~*y glad to get back again*. Hence ~ILY² (-gĭ-) adv. [f. prec. +-Y²]

plaice, n. European flat-fish much used as food. [ME, f. OF *plaïz* f. LL *platessa* app. f. Gk *platus* broad, or *plat-* flat]

plaid (plăd, *Sc.* plād), n. Long piece of twilled woollen cloth, usu. with chequered or tartan pattern, outer article of Highland costume; cloth used for this. Hence ~′ED² a. [Gael. *plaide*, of unkn. orig.]

plain¹, a., adv., & n. 1. Clear, evident; simple, readily understood, as ~ *words, English*; not in code; not intricate, as ~ *sewing*; unembellished, (of drawings etc.)

not coloured; (of food) not rich or highly seasoned; not luxurious, as ~ *living*; outspoken, straightforward, (esp. *be* ~ *with*, tell home truths to); unsophisticated, as *I am a* ~ *man*; of homely manners, dress, or appearance; ugly, as *a pity the poor girl is so* ~; ~ *as a* PIKESTAFF. 2. adv. Clearly, as *learn to speak* ~. 3. ~ *cards* (not court-cards); ~-*chant*, = ~-*song*; ~ *clothes*, unofficial dress; ~ *dealing*, candour, straightforwardness; ~ *sailing*, sailing in a ~ course, (fig.) simple course of action; ~-*song*, vocal music composed in medieval modes & in free rhythm depending on accentuation of the words, and sung in unison; ~-*spoken*, outspoken; ~ *suit* (not trumps); ~ *tile*, flat roofing-tile. 4. n. Level tract of country; ~*s′man*, inhabitant of a ~. Hence ~′LY² adv., ~′NESS (-n-n-) n. [ME, f. OF *plain* adj. & n., f. L *planus* adj., -*num* n.]

‖ plain², v.i. (arch., poet.). Mourn; complain; emit plaintive sound. [ME, f. OF *plaindre* (st. *plaign-*) f. L *plangere planct*-beat breast]

plaint, n. ‖ (Law) accusation, charge; (poet.) lamentation, complaint. [ME & OF (1) *plaint* f. L *planctus -ūs*, (2) *plainte* f. med. L *plancta* fem. p.p. as n.; both as prec.]

plain′tiff, n. Party who brings suit into court of law (opp. *defendant*). [ME, f. OF, as foll.]

plain′tive, a. Expressive of sorrow; mournful. Hence ~LY² adv., ~NESS n. [ME, f. OF (-*if*, -*ive*) f. *plaint*-, p.p. of *plaindre* PLAIN², see -IVE]

plait (plăt), n., & v.t. 1. (Now usu. PLEAT) fold, crease, esp. flattened fold in cloth made by doubling it upon itself; (v.t.) fold (cloth etc.) thus. 2. (Now rarely PLAT²) contexture of three or more interlaced strands of hair, ribbon, straw, etc.; (v.t.) form (hair, straw, etc.) into ~. [ME, f. OF *pleit*, *plait* f. OF *pleit* f. Rom. **plic(i)tum* p.p. of *plicare* fold; see PLEAT, PLIGHT]

plăn, n., & v.t. & i. (-nn-). 1. Drawing, diagram, made by projection on flat surface (cf. ELEVATION), esp. one showing relative position of parts of (one floor of) a building; large-scale detailed map of town or district; table indicating times, places, etc., of intended proceedings etc.; scheme of arrangement; project, design; way of proceeding, as *the better* ~ *is to peel them after boiling*; ~ *of* CAMPAIGN; (perspective) any of the imaginary planes, perpendicular to line of vision, passing through objects shown in picture. 2. vb. Make a ~ of (ground, existing building); design (building to be constructed etc.); scheme, arrange beforehand, (procedure etc.), as ~*ned economy*; make ~s. Hence ~′LESS a. [F, f. earlier *plant*, f. It. *pianta* plan; see PLANT¹]

‖ plănch (-sh), n. Slab of metal, stone, etc., esp. of baked fire-clay used in enamelling. [late ME & OF *planche* PLANK¹]

plăn′chĕt (-sh-), n. Plain disc of metal of which coin is made. [prec. + -ET¹]

plănchĕtte′ (-sh-, & see Ap.), n. Small usu. heart-shaped board supported by two castors & pencil, which when person's fingers rest lightly on board is said to trace letters etc. without conscious direction. [F, dim. of planche PLANK¹]

plāne¹, n. Tall spreading tree of genus *Platanus* with broad angular palmately-lobed leaves; ~-tree (of this genus). [ME & OF plane f. L f. Gk platanos (platus broad)]

plāne², n., & v.t. 1. Tool for smoothing surface of woodwork by paring shavings from it, consisting of wooden or metal stock from smooth bottom of which projects a steel blade; similar tool for smoothing metal; smoothing-~ (used to finish surface, cf. JACK¹- & TRYing-~); moulding-~ (for making mouldings). 2. v.t. Smooth (wood, metal) with ~, pare away or down (irregularities) with ~; (arch.) level, esp. ~ the way. [(n.) ME & OF plane f. LL plana; (vb) ME f. OF planer; both f. L planare (as PLANE⁴)]

plāne³, n., & v.i. 1. Surface such that the straight line joining any two points in it lies wholly in it; imaginary surface of this kind in which points or lines in material bodies lie; level surface; flat thin object such as table-top, supporting part of aeroplane; (also ′plane) aeroplane; INCLINE¹d~; each of the natural faces of a crystal. 2. Main road in mine. 3. (fig.). Level (of thought, knowledge, etc.), as his superstition places him on the same ~ as the savage. 4. ~ sailing, art of determining ship's position on the theory that she is moving on a ~, (fig., now usu. PLAIN¹ sailing) simple course. 5. v.i. Travel, glide (down etc.), in aeroplane. [17th c., different. from PLAIN¹ (n.), after L planum, in certain senses]

plāne⁴, a. Perfectly level, as a PLANE³; (of angle, figure, etc.) lying in a plane; ~ chart (on which meridians & parallels of latitude are represented by equidistant straight lines, used in PLANE³ sailing); ~-table, surveying instrument used for direct plotting in the field. [late 17th c., different. from PLAIN¹ (adj.), after L planus, in certain senses]

plăn′ĕt¹, n. (Hist.) heavenly body distinguished from fixed stars by having apparent motion of its own (Moon, Mercury, Venus, Sun, Mars, Jupiter, Saturn), esp. (astrol.) with reference to its supposed influence on persons & events; (astron.) primary ~s, heavenly bodies revolving in approximately circular orbits round sun (major ~s, Mercury, Venus, Earth, Mars, Jupiter, Saturn, Uranus, Neptune, Pluto; minor ~s, the asteroids, whose orbits lie between those of Mars & Jupiter); secondary ~s (also satellites), those that revolve round primary; SUN & ~; ~-struck, -stricken, bewildered, terrified.

[ME & OF planete f. LL f. Gk planētēs wanderer, planet, f. planaomai wander]

plăn′ĕt², n. Chasuble. [f. med. L planeta, also LL planetica (vestis), f. Gk planētēs wanderer (prec.)]

plănĕtār′ium, n. Orrery, model of planetary system. [mod. L, see foll.]

plăn′ĕtarȳ̆, a. Of planets, as ~ influence, motions; ~ hour, twelfth part of natural day or night; ~ (solar) system; terrestrial, mundane; wandering, erratic. [f. LL planetarius (as PLANET¹, see -ARY¹)]

plănĕtēs′imal, n. One of a vast number of minute planetoids which, according to the ~ hypothesis, formed the bodies of the planets by accretion in a cold state. [f. PLANET¹ after infinitesimal]

plăn′ĕtoid, n. Minor PLANET¹. [-OID]

plăn′g|ent (-j-), a. (Of sound) thrilling, vibrating, moaning, insistent. Hence ~ENCY n. [f. L plangere beat the breast, see -ENT]

plani-, comb. form of L planus level, smooth, plane, as: ~im′ĕter, instrument for mechanically measuring area of irregular plane figure; ~im′ĕtry, measurement of plane surfaces, so plănĭmĕt′ric(al) aa.; plănĭpĕt′alous, with flat petals; plăn′isphere, map formed by projection of (part of) sphere or plane, (revolving ~isphere, device for showing the part of the heavens visible at given time & place), so plănĭsphē′ric a.

plăn′ish, v.t. Flatten (sheet metal etc.) with smooth-faced hammer or otherwise; flatten out (coining-metal) between rollers; polish (photograph etc.) with roller etc. Hence ~ER¹ (1, 2) n. [f. obs. F planir smooth (plan a. as PLANE⁴), see -ISH²]

plănk¹, n. Long flat piece of timber, 2 to 6 in. thick, 9 or more in. wide (cf. BOARD¹); item of political or other programme (cf. PLATFORM); walk the ~, (of pirates' captive etc.) walk blindfold into sea along ~ laid over side of ship; ~ bed (of boards, without mattress, used as prison discipline etc.). [ME, f. ONF planke = OF planche f. LL planca board (plancus flat-footed)]

plănk², v.t. Furnish, cover, floor, with planks, whence ~ING¹ (2, 3) n.; (colloq.) put down roughly or violently, esp. pay (money, or abs.) down on the spot. [f. prec.]

plănk′tŏn, n. (biol.). The (chiefly microscopic) forms of drifting or floating organic life found at various depths in seas, lakes, rivers, etc., taken collectively (cf. BENTHOS & NEKTON). [G, f. Gk plagktos wandering (plazomai)]

plăno-, comb. form of L planus level, flat, as: ~con′cave, ~con′vex, (of lens etc.) with one surface plane & the other concave, convex; plănŏm′ĕter, flat plate, usu. of cast iron, as gauge for plane surfaces.

plant¹ (-ah-), n. 1. Living organism capable of living wholly on inorganic substances & having neither power of locomotion nor special organs of sensation or digestion, member of the vegetable kingdom (often restricted to the smaller ~s, excluding trees and shrubs). 2. Crop; growth, as *in* ~, growing, *lose* ~, die off, *miss* ~, fail to spring from seed. 3. Mode of planting oneself, pose. 4. Fixtures, implements, machinery, etc., used in industrial process; factory; (fig.) machinery of intellectual work etc. 5. (sl.). Planned swindle or burglary, hoax. 6. ~-*louse*, kinds of insect that infest ~s, esp. aphis. Hence ~'LET n., ~'LIKE a. [OE *plante* (= OHG *pflanza*, ON *planta*), in ME reinforced by OF *plante*; f. L *planta* slip, cutting; partly also f. foll.]

plant² (-ah-), v.t. 1. Place (tree, shoot, bulb, seed, crop, etc.) in ground that it may take root & grow; deposit (young fish, spawn, oysters) in river etc.; ~ *out*, transfer (plant) from pot or frame to open ground, set out (seedlings) at intervals. 2. Fix firmly (*in, on*, ground etc.); station (person), esp. as spy; ~ one*self*, take up a position. 3. Establish, found, (community, city, church); settle (person) in a place as colonist etc.; cause (idea etc.) to take root *in* (mind); furnish (land *with* plants, district *with* settlers, etc.). 4. Deliver (blow, thrust) with definite aim. 5. (sl.). Conceal (stolen goods etc.); bury; place (gold-dust, ore) in mining claim to encourage prospective buyer, cf. SALT v.; devise (fraudulent scheme). 6. Abandon, as *there I was, fairly* ~*ed*. Hence ~'ABLE a. [OE *plantian* f. L *plantare*, as prec.]

Plantă'genet, n. & a. (Member) of the family founded by Geoffrey of Anjou, esp. any of the English kings from Henry II to Richard II. [surname, f. sprig of broom (L *planta* plant, *genesta* broom) worn as cognizance]

plăn'tain¹ (-tin), n. Kinds of plants, esp. *greater* ~, low herb with broad flat leaves spread out close to ground & seeds much used for cage-birds. [ME & OF, f. L *plantaginem* (nom. *-go*) prob. f. *planta* sole of foot, from its prostrate leaves]

plăn'tain² (-tin), n. Tree-like tropical herbaceous plant allied to banana and bearing similar fruit; its fruit. [16th c. *pla(n)tan* f. Sp. *plá(n)tano* in same sense, identical in form w. *plá(n)tano* (obs. E *plantain*) PLANE¹-tree]

plăn'tar, a. (anat.). Of the sole of the foot. [f. L *plantaris* (*planta* sole, see -AR¹)]

plăntă'tion, n. Assemblage of planted growing plants, esp. trees; estate on which cotton, tobacco, etc., are cultivated (formerly by servile labour); ~ *song* (of the kind sung by Negroes on American ~s); (hist.) colonization, colony. [ME, f. OF or f. L *plantatio* (as PLANT², see -ATION)]

pla'nter (-ah-), n. Cultivator of soil; (in Ireland) English settler on forfeited lands in 17th c., (19th c.) person settled in evicted tenant's holding; occupier of

plantation, esp. in (sub-)tropical countries, as *coffee, cotton, sugar, tobacco*, ~; machine for planting, as *corn, potato*, ~. Hence ~SHIP n. [PLANT² + -ER¹]

plănt'igrăde, a. & n. (Animal) that walks on its soles (cf. DIGITIGRADE). [F, f. L *planta* sole + -*gradus* -walking]

plănx'tў, n. (Ir. mus.). Animated harp-tune moving in triplets. [orig. unkn.]

plaque (plahk), n. Ornamental tablet of metal, porcelain, etc., plain or decorated; small tablet as badge of rank in honorary order; (path.) patch of eruption etc. So **plaquETTE'** (-ăkĕt) n. [F, f. Du. *plak* tablet]

plăsh¹, n. Marshy pool; puddle. Hence ~'Y² a. [OE *plæsc*, MDu. *plasch, plas*, prob. imit., cf. foll.]

plăsh², v.t. & i., & n. 1. Strike surface of (water) so as to break it up; splash (t. & i.). 2. n. Splash, plunge. Hence ~'Y² a. [cf. Du. *plassen*, G *platschen*, prob. imit.]

plăsh³, v.t. Bend down and interweave (branches, twigs) to form hedge; make, renew, (hedge) thus. [f. OF *plaissier* ult. f. L *plectere* plait; cf. PLEACH]

plăsm, n. Living matter of a cell, protoplasm, esp. general body of this as distinct from nucleus. [f. foll.]

plăs'm|a (-z-), n. 1. Green variety of quartz. 2. Colourless coagulable part of blood, lymph, or milk, in which the corpuscles or oil-globules **float**, so ~ăt'ıc a. 3. = prec., whence ~ıc (-z-) a. [LL & Gk (gen. *-matos*), = thing moulded (*plassō* mould)]

plăsmōd'ium (-z-), n. (biol.); pl. *-ia*). Mass of naked protoplasm formed by fusion or aggregation of amoeboid bodies without fusion of their nuclei; generic name of microscopic parasitic organism whose presence & rapid multiplication in the blood of man constitute malaria. [mod. L, f. PLASMA + -*odium*, see -ODE]

plăsmŏl'ÿsis (-zm-), n. Loss of water from, & consequent contraction of, protoplasm of vegetable cell due to immersion in a solution stronger than the cell fluid. So **plăs'molÿse** (-zm-) v.t., subject to ~. [f. PLASM, -O-, Gk *lusis* loosing f. *luō* to loose]

pla'ster¹ (-ah-), n. 1. Curative application consisting of some substance spread upon muslin etc. & capable of adhering at the temperature of the body, as COURT¹, MUSTARD, *sticking-*, ~. 2. Soft plastic mixture, esp. of lime, sand, & hair, for spreading on walls etc. to form smooth surface; ~ *of Paris*, fine white ~ of gypsum used for making moulds & as cement etc. [prepared from gypsums of Montmartre, Paris]. Hence ~Y² a. [(1) OE, f. med. L *plastrum* f. L f. Gk *emplastron*; (2) f. OF *plastre* f. same source]

pla'ster² (-ah-), v.t. 1. Cover (wall etc.) with plaster or the like, whence ~ER¹ n.; coat, bedaub; (fig.) load to excess (*with* praise etc.). 2. Apply medical plaster to, (joc.) give compensation for (blow, wound); stick, fix, (thing) like plaster upon surface. 3. Treat (wine) with gypsum etc. to neutralize acidity. [ME, f. prec.]

plăs′tic, a. Moulding, giving form to clay, wax, etc.; ~ *arts*, those concerned with modelling, e.g. sculpture, ceramics; ~ *surgery* (repairing deficiency of structure); causing growth of natural forms, formative of immaterial things; produced by moulding; capable of being (easily) moulded; ~ *bomb*, one containing ~ explosive of putty-like or dough-like consistency capable of being moulded by hand; ~ *clay* (geol.), middle group of Eocene beds; (fig.) pliant, supple; (biol.) capable of forming living tissue, (also) accompanied by this process, as ~ *bronchitis*. Hence **plăs′tiCALLY** adv., **plăsti′CITY** n., ~IZE(3) v.t., make ~, **plăs′tics** n. pl., group of synthetic resinous or other substances that can be moulded into any form. [f. L f. Gk *plastikos* (*plassō* mould, see -IC)]

plăs′ticine, n. Plastic substance used as substitute for modelling clay. [P; -INE⁴]

plăs′tron, n. Fencer's leather-covered breast-plate; breast-covering of facings--cloth worn by lancers; ornamental front to woman's bodice; man's starched shirt--front; ventral part of shell of tortoise or turtle, corresponding part in other animals; (hist.) steel breast-plate. [F, f. It. *piastrone* (*piastra* breast-plate, as PLASTER; see -OON)]

plăt¹, n. (arch.). Patch, plot, of ground, as *grass*-~. [16th c., collat. form of PLOT]

plăt², n., & v.t. (-tt-). = PLAIT (2nd sense). *plat³* (plah), n. Dish of food. [F, see PLATE¹]

plăt′an, n. Plane-tree. [ME, f. L *platanus* plane-tree]

plāte¹, n. 1. Flat thin usu. rigid sheet of metal etc. of even surface and more or less uniform thickness; this as part of mechanism. 2. Smooth piece of metal etc. for engraving; impression from this; = BOOK¹-~. 3. Piece of metal with name or inscription for affixing to something, as *coffin, door, name*, -~. 4. Thin sheet of metal, glass, etc., coated with sensitive film for photograph (*whole*-~, 8¼ × 6½ in., *half*-~, 6½ × 4¾, *quarter*-~, 4¼ × 3¼). 5. Stereotype or electrotype cast of page of composed movable types, from which sheets are printed. 6. Horizontal timber laid along top of wall to support ends of joists or rafters, or at top or bottom of a framing, as *roof, wall, window*, ~. 7. (Also ~*-rail*) early form of railroad. 8. (collect. sing.). ‖ Table & domestic utensils of silver, gold, or other metal, as *pewter* ~, *electro*~. 9. Silver or gold cup as prize for (orig. horse-) race, such race; *selling* ~, horse-race winner of which must be sold at fixed price. 10. Shallow usu. circular vessel, now usu. of earthenware or china, from which food is eaten, as *dessert, dinner, soup*, -~; contents of this, as *a* ~ *of strawberries*; similar vessel used for collection in churches etc., as *put a shilling in the* ~. 11. Thin piece of plastic material, moulded to shape of gums etc., to which artificial teeth are attached. 12. *Home, pitcher's*, ~, stations of batter, pitcher, in baseball. 13. Light shoe for racehorse. 14. ‖ ~--*basket* (for spoons, forks, etc.); ~ *glass*, thick glass of fine quality cast in ~s for shop windows etc.; ‖ ~*′layer*, man employed in fixing & repairing railway; ~*-mark*, = HALL-*mark*, (also) impression left on margin of engraving by pressure of the ~ (hence ~*-marked mount* for photographs); ~*-powder* (for cleaning silver); ‖ ~*-rack* (in which ~s are kept or placed to drain). Hence ~FUL(2) (-tŏŏl) n., ~LESS a. [ME & OF *plate*, fem. of *plat* flat, f. Rom. **plattus*, perh. f. Gk *platus* broad; sense 10 is f. OF *plat* n.]

plāte², v.t. Cover (esp. ship) with plates of metal for protection, ornament, etc.; cover (other metal) with thin coat of silver, gold, or tin; make a plate of (type) for printing. [f. prec.]

plateau′ (-tō), n. (pl. ~*x*, ~*s*, pr. -z). Tableland; ornamented tray or dish; decorative plaque; woman's hat with level top. [F, f. OF *platel* dim. of PLAT³]

plăt′en, -tt-, n. Plate in printing-press by which paper is pressed against type; corresponding part in typewriters etc. [f. OF *platine* flat piece (*plat*, see PLATE¹)]

plăt′er, n. One who plates with silver etc.; one who makes or applies plates in shipbuilding; inferior racehorse, competing chiefly for plates. [-ER¹]

plăt′fŏrm, n., & v.t. & i. 1. Raised level surface, natural or artificial terrace; ‖ raised surface of planks etc. along side of line at railway station; raised flooring in hall or open air from which speaker addresses audience, (fig.) *the* ~, ~ *oratory*; (fig.) political basis of party etc., declared policy of political party. 2. vb. Place (as) on ~; speak on ~. [f. F *plateforme* ground-plan, lit. flat form (as PLATE¹+*forme* FORM)]

plăt′ing, n. In vbl senses; also or esp.: coating of gold, silver, etc.; plate-racing. [f. PLATE¹,²+-ING¹]

plăt′inize, -ise (-īz), v.t. Coat with platinum. [-IZE]

plăt′inoid, n. Alloy of copper, zinc, nickel, & tungsten; kind(s) of metal found associated with platinum. [-OID]

plăt′inotÿpe, n. Process of photographic printing in platinum black. [f. foll. +-O- +-TYPE]

plăt′in|um, n. White heavy ductile malleable metallic element unaffected by simple acids & fusible only at very high temperature; ~*um black*, ~um in form of powder like lamp-black; ~*um blonde* (colloq., orig. U.S.), woman with gold-

-grey hair; ~*um metals*, platinoids. Hence platin'ic, ~if'erous, aa. [mod. L (see -ium) f. earlier *platina* f. Sp. dim. of *plata* silver, see -ine⁵]

plăt'it|ŭde, n. Commonplaceness; commonplace remark, esp. one solemnly delivered. Hence ~ŭd'inize(2) v.i., ~ŭd'inous a., ~ŭd'inously² adv. [F, f. *plat* (see plate¹) after *latit*ude etc.]

plătitŭdinăr'ian, n. & a. Dealer in platitudes; (adj.) of the nature of platitude. [-arian]

Platŏn'ic, a. Of Plato the Greek philosopher (died *c.* 347 b.c.) or his doctrines; ~ *love*, purely spiritual love for one of opposite sex (*p~s*, ~ *lovers' talk* or relation); (pop.) confined to words or theory, not issuing in action, harmless; ~ *year*, cycle in which heavenly bodies were supposed to go through all their possible movements & return to original positions. So Platŏn'ically adv., Plăt'onism, Plăt'onist, nn., Plăt'onize(2, 3) v.i. & t. [f. L f. Gk *Platōnikos* (*Platōn* Plato, see -ic)]

platoon', n. (Hist.) small infantry detachment, esp. a unit for volley-firing etc., volley fired by it; (in mod. use) subdivision of a company, a tactical unit commanded by a lieutenant & usu. divided into three sections. [f. F *peloton* small ball (as pellet, see -oon)]

plătt'er, n. (chiefly arch. exc. U.S.). Flat dish or plate, often of wood. [ME & AF *plater*, f. *plat* plate¹]

plăt'ў-, comb. form of Gk *platus* broad, flat, as: ~*pus*, Australian duck-mole, ornithorhynchus; ~(*r*)*rhine* (-rin), (of monkeys) with nostrils far apart & directed forwards or sideways.

plaud'it, n. (usu. in pl.). Round of applause; emphatic expression of approval. [shortened f. L *plaudite* applaud (also as E noun) pl. imperat. of *plaudere plaus*-applaud, said by Roman actors at end of play]

plaus'|ible (-z-), a. (Of arguments, statements, etc.) specious, seeming reasonable or probable; (of persons) fair-spoken (freq. implying deceit). Hence or cogn. ~ibil'ity n., ~ibly² adv. [f. L *plausibilis* (as prec., see -ble)]

play¹, v.i. & t. 1. Move about in lively or capricious manner, frisk, flit, flutter, pass gently (*around, about*, etc.), strike lightly (*upon* etc.), alternate rapidly, as *bees ~ about flowers, tresses ~ on her neck, smile ~ed on his lips, wind ~s on water, his fancy ~ed round the idea*. 2. (Of part of mechanism etc.) have free movement. 3. Wield freely, as ~ *a good knife & fork*, eat heartily; ~ *a good stick*, fence well. 4. Allow (fish) to exhaust itself by pulling against line. 5. Discharge (guns etc. on), discharge guns (*on*), (intr., of guns) be fired (*on*). 6. Direct (light *on, over, along*, etc.), (intr., of light) pass (*over, along*, etc.). 7. Perform, execute, (trick, prank,

joke, *on* person, or with double object). 8. Amuse oneself, sport, frolic; ~*'boy*, one living for pleasure; ~ *with*, amuse oneself with, trifle with, treat lightly; ~ *upon words*, pun. 9. (dial.). (Esp. of workmen on strike) abstain from work. 10. Employ oneself in the game of (cricket, whist, etc., or abs.). 11. ~*ed out*, exhausted of energy or vitality or usefulness (*our horses were, I felt, Free Trade is, ~ed out*); ~ *up*, put all one's energy into the game etc.; ~ duck¹*s & drakes*; ~ fast³ *& loose*. 12. (In cricket, lawn tennis, etc., as bowler's warning to batsman etc.) ~ *!* 13. Pretend for fun (*that we are gipsies* etc.). 14. (crick.). (Of ground) ~ *well* etc., be in good etc. condition for play. 15. ~*-or-pay bet* (holding good whether horse runs or not). 16. Game, gamble; *'*~ *the market*, gamble in stocks etc. 17. ~ booty; ~ *fair, foul*, ~ or (fig.) act (un)fairly; ~ (observe the rules of) *the game* (also fig. of keeping to code of honour); ~ *into the hands of*, act so as to give advantage to (opponent or partner); (sl.) ~ *it on*, ~ *it low on*, ~ (*low*) *down on*, take mean advantage of (person); ~ *upon the* square; ~ *at*, engage in (game), (fig.) engage in (fight*ing* etc.) in trivial or half-hearted way. 18. Contend against (person) in game; employ (person) to ~ in game, include in team. 19. Move (piece in chess etc.); take (playing-card) from one's hand & lay it face upwards on table in one's turn; (fig.) ~ *one's cards well*, make good use of opportunities. 20. (crick. etc.) Strike (ball) in specified esp. defensive manner; (crick.) ~ *on* (abs.), ~ the ball on to one's own wicket and so put oneself out. 21. ~ *off*, oppose (person *against* another) esp. for one's own advantage; cause (person) to exhibit himself disadvantageously; pass (thing) off as something else; ~*-off* n., additional match to decide a draw or tie. 22. Perform on (musical instrument, or abs.); perform (*on* instrument); ~*back*, reproduction of sound or picture from magnetic tape etc.; ~ *by ear*, perform on an instrument without technical knowledge of music; perform (music *on* instrument). 23. ~ (congregation etc.) *in, out*, ~ on organ etc. as they come in, go out; ~ (*up*)*on*, make use of (person's fears, credulity, etc.); ~ *first, second*, fiddle. 24. Perform (drama, or abs.) on stage; act (*in* drama); act (part) in drama, as ~ Shylock, (fig.) act in real life the part of (*the* deuce² or *devil* (*with*), *the fool, the man, truant*, etc., also ~ one's *part well* etc.); ~ *up to*, act in drama so as to support (another actor), (fig.) back up, flatter, toady. Hence ~'able a. [OE *plegan* exercise oneself, move briskly, play, corresp. to MDu. *pleyen* dance]

play², n. 1. Brisk, light, or fitful movement. 2. Activity, operation, as *lively ~ of fancy, other forces come into ~, are in *full* ~, *are brought* or *called into* ~; *make* ~, act effectively, esp. (racing, hunting) exercise pursuers or followers. **3.** Freedom of movement, space for this, scope for activity, as *bolts should have half an inch of* ~, *allow full* ~ *to curiosity.* **4.** Amusement, as *at* ~, engaged in playing; *said it only in* ~ (not seriously); ~ *of words,* trifling with words; ~ *on words,* pun. **5.** Playing of game; manner, style, of this; (crick., footb., etc.) *ball is in* ~ (being used in ordinary course of ~), *is out of* ~ (temporarily removed from ~ according to rules); so ~, part of ground within definite boundaries. **6.** CHILD'S~; FAIR[2], FOUL, ~. **7.** Cessation from work (of workmen on strike etc.). **8.** Dramatic piece, drama. **9.** Gaming, gambling. **10.** ~-*actor* (usu. derog.); ~'*bill,* bill, placard, announcing theatrical ~; ~-*day,* school holiday, ‖ week-day on which miners etc. do not work; ~-*debt* (incurred in gaming); ~'*fellow,* companion in (usu. children's) ~; ~'*game,* experience that falls short of another (*is a* ~*game in comparison*) or of grim reality (e.g. sham fight); ~'*goer,* frequenter of theatre; ~'*ground,* piece of ground used for ~, esp. at school (*the* ~*ground of Europe,* Switzerland); ~'*house,* theatre; ~'*mate,* ~fellow; ~'*thing,* toy, (fig.) person etc. treated as mere toy; ~'*time;* ~'*wright,* dramatist. [OE *plega* as prec.]

play'er, n. In vbl senses, esp.: person engaged at the time, person skilful, in a game; performer on musical instrument; ‖ professional ~ at cricket etc.; actor; (pool, croquet) ball that after present ~ has finished break etc. will play on him; ~-*piano* (fitted with apparatus enabling it to be played automatically). [-ER[1]]

play'ful, a. Frolicsome, sportive; humorous, jocular. Hence ~LY[2] adv., ~NESS n. [ME; -FUL]

play'ing, n. In vbl senses; ~-*cards,* set or pack of cards used in games. [-ING[1]]

pla'za (-ah-), n. Market-place, open square (esp. in Spanish town). [Sp., = place]

plea, n. Pleading, argument, excuse; (law) formal statement by or on behalf of defendant, defence, *special* ~ (alleging new fact); (hist.) action at law. [ME & OF *plaid, plait* f. L *placitum* decree, neut. p.p. of *placēre* please; *plea* = ME *plai, ple* f. AF]

pleach, v.t. Entwine, interlace; esp. = PLASH[3]. [ME *pleche* f. OF **plechier* var. of *plessier* PLASH[3]]

plead, v.i. & t. (~'*ed;* U.S., Sc., dial. *plĕd*). Address court as advocate on behalf of either party, so ~'ER[1] n.; maintain (cause) in court; allege formally as plea, (fig.) allege as excuse etc., as *I can only* ~ *inexperience,* so ~'ABLE a.; ~ (*not*) *guilty,* deny, confess, liability or guilt; ~ *with,* make earnest appeal to (person *for* person, *for, against,* thing, decision, etc.) whence

~'ingLY[2] adv. [ME, f. OF *plaidier* (PLEA)]

plead'ing, n. In vbl senses, esp.: (usu. pl.) formal (now usu. written) statement of cause of action or defence; SPECIAL ~. [-ING[1]]

plea'sance (-lĕz-), n. (arch.). Pleasure, enjoyment; pleasure-ground, esp. one attached to mansion (now chiefly surviving in proper names). [ME, f. OF *plaisance* (as foll., see -ANCE)]

plea'sant (-lĕz-), a. Agreeable to mind, feelings, or senses, as *a* ~ *breeze, flavour, discovery, companion,* has *a* ~ *manner, spent a* ~ *evening;* ‖ (arch.) jocular, facetious. Hence ~LY[2] adv., ~NESS n. [ME, f. OF *plaisant* (as PLEASE, see -ANT)]

plea'santry (-lĕz-), n. Jocularity; humorous speech, jest. [f. F *plaisanterie* (prec., -ERY)]

please (-z), v.t. & i. **1.** Be agreeable to, as *meant only to* ~ *the eye, his last book will* ~ *you;* ~ *yourself,* do as you like; *be* ~*d with,* derive pleasure from; *I shall* (or *will*) *be* ~*d* (glad) *to* (do, esp. as polite form of consent or offer). **2.** Think fit, as *take as many as you* ~. **3.** (In formal or iron. deference) *Her Majesty has been graciously* ~*d to confer* etc., *your lordship was* ~*d to doubt my veracity.* **4.** (With *it* as subject, expressed or omitted, representing a prec. or foll. infinitive, clause, or sentence, now chiefly as in last use) *it has never* ~*d him to explain;* (*may it*) ~ *your honour, there was no moon that night; the matter will be cleared up some day,* ~ *God* (or, joc., ~ *the pigs*). **5.** Give pleasure, as *he was anxious to* ~. **6.** (As polite form of request esp. for trifling services) *if you* ~, *with your permission,* as *I will take another cup, if you* ~; (with iron. implication that nothing could be more reasonable) *& now, if you* ~, *he expects me to pay for it!;* (imperat., orig. = may it ~ you) *ring the bell,* ~, *may I come in,* ~*?, coffee for two,* ~, ~ (*to*) *return it soon,* ~ *don't* (or ~ *not to*) *forget the key.* Hence pleasED[1] (-ĕzd), pleas'ING[2], aa., pleas'ingLY[2] adv., (-z-). [ME *plaise* f. OF *plaisir* (F *plaire*) f. L *placēre*]

plea'surab|le (plĕzher-), a. Affording pleasure. Hence ~leNESS n., ~LY[2] adv. [f. foll. + -ABLE]

pleasure (plĕzh'er), n., & v.t. & i. **1.** Enjoyment, delight; sensuous enjoyment as chief object of life, as *a life given up to* ~, *man of* ~, profligate; will, desire, as *shall not consult his* ~, *can be postponed during our* ~, *can be altered at* ~; (royal formula) *it is our* ~ *to,* we are graciously pleased to; *to converse with him is a* (source of) ~; *do me the* ~ *of* (gratify me by) *dining with me; he takes* (*a*) ~ *in* (likes) *contradicting* or *contradiction;* (arch.) *are now taking their* ~ (enjoying themselves) *at Bath;* ~-*boat* etc. (used for ~, not business); ~-*ground* (laid out for ~). **2.** v.b. (arch.). Give ~ to; take ~ (*in* thing, *in* doing). [ME & OF *plesir, plaisir,* PLEASE used as n.; see -URE]

pleat, n., & v.t. = PLAIT (1st sense). [collateral form of PLAIT]

pleb, n. (sl.). Plebeian, person of lower classes. [abbr.]

*plebe, n. (colloq.). Member of lowest class at U.S. Naval or Military Academy. [shortened f. PLEBEIAN]

plebei'an (-bēan), n. & a. 1. Commoner in ancient Rome (cf. PATRICIAN); commoner. 2. adj. Of low birth, of the common people, coarse, base, ignoble. Hence ~NESS n., ~IZE(3) v.t. [f. L *plebeius (plebs* common people)+-AN]

pleb'iscite (-sĭt), n. (Rom. hist.) law enacted by commonalty in *comitia tributa;* (mod.) direct vote of all electors of State on important public question; public expression of community's opinion, with or without binding force. So plébis'citary[1] a. [f. F *plébiscite* f. L *plebiscitum (plebs plebis* commons+*scitum* decree f. *sciscere* vote for)]

plec'trum, n. (pl. -ra). Small instrument of ivory, quill, etc., for plucking strings of zither etc. [L, f. Gk *plēktron (plēssō* strike)]

pled. See PLEAD.

pledge[1], n. Thing handed over to person as security (cf. REPLEVIN) for fulfilment of contract, payment of debt, etc., & liable to forfeiture in case of failure; thing put in pawn; (fig.) one's child; thing given as token of favour etc. or of something to come; drinking of a health, toast; promise, as *under ~ of secrecy;* solemn engagement to abstain from intoxicants, as *take, sign, keep, the ~;* (pol.) leader's public promise (not) to adopt some course; state of being pledged, as *goods lying in ~, taken out of ~.* [ME & OF *plege* (mod. *pleige*) f. Frankish L *plevium, plibium* (whence med. L *plevire*) f. Frank. **pligi* surety, poss. rel. to PLIGHT]

pledge[2], v.t. Deposit as security, pawn; (fig.) plight (one's honour, word, etc.); drink to the health of. Hence ~'ABLE a. [f. prec.]

pledgee', n. One with whom pledge is deposited, pawnee. So pledg'ER[1] n. [-EE]

pledg'et, n. Small wad of lint etc. [16th c., of unkn. orig.]

Plei'ad (plī-), n. (pl. ~s pr. -dz, ~es pr. -dēz). (Pl.) cluster of small stars in Taurus, usu. spoken of as 7; (fig., sing.) brilliant group of (usu. 7) persons or things, esp. the French poets of the latter part of 16th c. [f. L *Plēias* f. Gk *Pleias* -*ados*]

Pleis'tocene (-lis-), a. & n. (geol.). (Of) the division immediately following the Pliocene formation. [f. Gk *pleistos* most+*kainos* new]

plen'arily, a. Entire, absolute, unqualified; (of assembly) fully attended; ~*y* INSPIRATION. Hence ~iLY[2] adv. [f. LL *plenarius (plenus* full, see -ARY[1])]

plenipoten'tiary (-sha-), a. & n. (Person) invested with full power, esp. a diplomatic agent having such power; (of power) absolute. [f. med. L *plenipotentiarius (plenus* full+*potens* POTENT), see -ARY[1]]

plen'itude, n. Fullness, completeness; abundance. [ME, f. OF f. L *plenitudo (plenus* full, see -TUDE)]

plen'teous, a. (chiefly poet.). Plentiful. Hence ~LY[2] adv., ~NESS n. [ME & OF *plentivous* f. *plentif* f. *plente* PLENTY; see -IVE, -EOUS; cf. BOUNTEOUS]

plen'tiful, a. Abundant, copious. Hence ~LY[2] adv., ~NESS n. [ME, f. foll.+-FUL]

plen'ty, n. & adv. 1. Abundance, as much as one could desire, (of thing, or abs.), as *~ of cake, here is cake in ~, we are in ~ of time; horn of ~,* cornucopia. 2. adv. (colloq.). Quite, as *it is ~ large enough.* [ME *plenteth, plente* f. OF *plentet, -te* f. L *plenitatem (plenus* full, see -TY)]

plen'um, n. Space filled with matter (~ *system,* of ventilation by forcing air in); full assembly. [L, neut. of *plenus* full]

ple'on|asm, n. Redundancy of expression, e.g. *hear with* one's ears, *a false lie.* So ~as'tic a., ~as'tically adv. [f. LL f. Gk *pleonasmos (pleonazō* add superfluously f. *pleon* more)]

plesiosaur'us, n. (pl. -rī, -ruses). Extinct marine reptile with long neck, short tail, & four large paddles. [f. Gk *plēsios* near + *sauros* lizard]

pleth'ora (or plēthŏr'a), n. Morbid condition marked by excess of red corpuscles in the blood; (fig.) unhealthy repletion. Hence or cogn. plethō'ric a., plethō'rically adv. [LL, f. Gk *plēthōrē (plēthō* become full)]

pleur'|a (ploor'a), n. Either of the two serous membranes lining the thorax & enveloping the lungs in mammals; part of the body-wall in invertebrates. Hence ~AL a. [med. L f. Gk, = side of body, rib]

pleur'|isy (ploor-), n. Inflammation of the pleura, usu. caused by chill, & marked by pain in chest or side, fever, etc. So ~it'ic (ploor-) a. [ME, f. OF *pleurisie* f. LL *pleurisis* altered f. L f. Gk *pleuritis* (as prec., see -ITIS), also used in E]

pleuro- (ploor-), comb. form (bef. vowel *pleur-*) of Gk *pleura,* side, pleura, rib, as: ~*dyn'ia,* pain in side caused by rheumatism in muscles of chest; ~*pneumōn'ia,* pneumonia complicated with pleurisy.

plexim'eter, n. (med.). Thin plate of ivory etc. placed on part of the body & struck with plexor in medical percussion. [f. Gk *plēxis* stroke (*plēssō* strike) + -METER]

plex'or, n. (med.). Small hammer used with pleximeter. [irreg. as prec.+-OR]

plex'us, n. (Anat.) network of nerves or vessels in animal body, as *gastric, pulmonary,* SOLAR, ~; network, complication. Hence plex'iFORM a. [L, gen. -*ūs,* f. *plectere plex-* plait]

pli'able, a. = foll. Hence pliABIL'ITY n., **pli'ablY²** adv. [F(*plier* bend f. L *plicare*)]

pli'ant, a. Bending, supple; (fig.) yielding, compliant. Hence pli'ANCY n., ~LY² adv. [ME, f. OF (as prec., see -ANT)]

plic'a, n. (pl. *-ae*). Fold, as of skin or membrane; ~ (*polōn'ica* Polish), matted filthy condition of hair due to disease. [med. L, as foll.]

plic'ate, a. (bot., zool., geol.). Folded. So plicāt'ED¹ a. [f. L *plicare* fold, -ATE²]

plicā'tion, n. Folding; fold, folded condition. [ME, f. OF (as prec., see -ATION)]

pli'ers (-z), n. pl. Pincers having long jaws with parallel surfaces, for bending wire etc. [f. (dial.) *ply* bend (see PLIABLE) +-ER¹]

plight¹ (plīt), v.t., & n. **1.** Pledge (one's troth, faith, promise, esp. in p.p.); engage *oneself* (*to* person, esp. in p.p., as *~ed lovers*). **2.** n. Engagement. [OE *pliht* danger, corresp. to MDu. *plicht*, OHG *pfliht* duty, f. *pleh-*, *pleg-*, WG *plegan*, perh. rel. to PLEDGE]

plight² (plīt), n. Condition, state, esp. *a sorry, evil, hopeless*, etc. ~. [ME & AF *plit* = OF *pleit* fold, see PLAIT; -gh- by confus. w. prec.]

|| **plim, v.t. & i.** (dial.; -mm-). Swell, fill *out*, make or grow plump. [also *plum*, perh. cogn. w. PLUMP¹]

Plim'soll, a. & n. ~ *line*, ~'*s* MARK¹; || (n. pl.; *p~s*) cheap rubber-soled canvas shoes. [S. ~, agitator for Merchant Shipping Act of 1876]

plinth, n. Lower square member of base of column; projecting part of wall immediately above ground. [f. F *plinthe* or L (= plinth) f. Gk *plinthos* tile, brick]

plin'thite, n. Kind of brick-red clay. [as prec. +-ITE²]

Pli'ocène, a. & n. (geol.). (Of) the newest division of Tertiary formation. [f. Gk *pleiōn* more +*kainos* new]

plŏd, v.i. & t. (-dd-), & n. **1.** Walk laboriously, trudge, (*on, along*, etc.); drudge, slave, (*at* etc.); make (one's way) laboriously. **2.** n. Laborious walk or work. Hence ~d'ER¹ n., ~d'inglY² adv. [16th c., app. imit.]

plom'bé (-awmbā), a. Officially lead-sealed. [F]

plŏp, n., adv., & v.t. & i. (-pp-). **1.** Sound as of smooth object dropping into water without splash; act of falling with this. **2.** adv. With a ~. **3.** vb. (Cause to) fall thus. [imit.]

plŏt¹, n. Piece (usu. small) of ground; plan of play, poem, novel, etc., whence ~'LESS a.; conspiracy (GUNpowder ~); sly plan (earlier *complot*). [(?OE) ME *plotte*, of unkn. orig.; cf. PLAT¹]

plŏt², v.t. (-tt-). Make plan or map of (existing object, place or thing to be laid out, constructed, etc.); make (a curve) by marking out a number of points; plan,

contrive, (evil object, **or abs.**). Hence ~t'ER¹ n. [f. prec.]

plough¹ (plow), **n. 1.** Implement for cutting furrows in soil & turning it up, consisting of cutting blade (~'*share*) fixed in frame drawn by horses etc. & guided by man (~'*man*); *put* one's *hand to the* ~, undertake task (*Luke* ix. 62); ploughed land; kinds of instrument resembling ~, as *ice-*~ (for cutting up blocks of ice), *snow-*~ (for clearing away snow); *the P~*, CHARLES'S WAIN; || [f. foll.] rejection of candidate in examination. **2.** ~-*beam*, central beam of ~; ~-*boy*, boy who leads ~-horses etc.; ~-*land* (hist.), as much land as could be ploughed by one team of 8 oxen in the year, unit of assessment in N. & E. counties of England (cf. HIDE³); *P~ Monday* (first after Epiphany), ~-*shoe*, appliance for protecting or supporting ~share; ~-*staff* (ending in small spade, used to clear coulter etc. from earth etc.); ~-*tail*, rear of ~, (fig.) farm-labour, *as at the* ~-*tail*. [late OE *plōh* f. ON *plógr*, = OFris. *plōch*, MLG *plōh*, *plūh*, OHG *pfluoc*, f. Gmc. *plōg-*, *plōh-*]

plough² (plow), v.t. & i. 1. Turn up (earth, or abs.) with plough, esp. before sowing (~ *the sand* or *sands*, labour uselessly); ~ *back*, ~ (grass, clover, etc.) into soil to enrich it, (fig.) reinvest (profits) in business etc.; root *out*, cast *up*, thrust *down*, (roots, weeds) with plough; furrow, scratch, (surface) as with plough; produce (furrow, line) thus (~ *a lonely furrow*, fig., take one's own solitary course); produce wrinkles in (brow etc.); advance laboriously (*through* snow etc., *through* book etc.); (of ship etc.) cleave (surface of water, its way, etc.); || (sl.) reject (candidate) in examination. [f. prec.]

plo'ver (plŭ-), n. Kinds of gregarious grallatorial bird, esp. *golden, grey*, ~, & (pop.) lapwing; ~-*page*, ~'*s-page*, dunlin & other birds said to follow golden-~. [ME & AF *plover*, OF -*ier*, f. pop. L *plovarius* (L *pluvia* rain)]

|| **ploy, n.** (colloq.). Expedition, undertaking, occupation, job. [orig. unkn.]

pluck¹, n. Plucking, twitch; || rejection, failure, in examination; heart, liver, & lungs, of beast as food; courage, spirit, whence (·)~ED² (-kt), ~'LESS, ~'Y² aa., ~'ilY² adv., ~'iNESS n.; (photog. sl.) boldness of effect. [ME, f. foll.]

pluck², v.t. & i. Pull off, pick, (flower, feather, hair); (arch.) pull, drag, snatch, (*away, off*, etc.); pull at, twitch; tug, snatch, *at*; strip (bird) of feathers; CROW¹ *to* ~; plunder, swindle, as ~ *a* PIGEON; || reject (candidate) in examination; ~ *up* one's *heart, spirits, courage*, take courage. [late OE *plocc-*, *pluccian*, cogn. w. MLG *plucken*, MDu. *plocken*, ON *plokka*, *plukka*, f. Gmc *plokkōn*, ult. f. Rom. *piluccare* f. *pilus* hair]

plug¹, n. Piece of wood etc. fitting tightly into hole, used to fill gap or act as wedge (in various techn. uses); natural or morbid concretion acting thus; kinds of stopper for vessel or pipe; pin or other fitting for making electrical contacts; (pop.) release-mechanism of water-closet flushing apparatus; FIRE¹-~; SPARK²ing-~; tobacco pressed into cake or stick, piece of this cut off for chewing; *~-ugly (sl.), street rowdy. [f. MDu. (MLG) plugge, of unkn. orig.]

plug², v.t. & i. (-gg-). Stop (hole etc., often up) with plug; (sl.) shoot; (sl.) strike with fist; (colloq.) plod (away at work etc.); (colloq.) endeavour to popularize (a song, theory, policy, etc.) by dinning it into the public ear; ~ in, establish electrical contact by inserting a plug. [f. prec., or early Du. (MLG) pluggen]

plum, n. 1. Roundish fleshy fruit with sweet pulp & flattish pointed stone; (also ~-tree) tree bearing this; dried grape or raisin as used for cakes etc., SUGAR-~; ‖ French ~, fine kind of prune; (fig.) good thing, best of a collection, prize in life etc. 2. ~ cake (containing raisins, currants, etc.); ~ duff, plain flour pudding with raisins or currants; ~ pudding, boiled pudding of flour, bread-crumbs, suet, raisins, currants, eggs, spices, etc., eaten at Christmas, (also) ordinary suet-pudding with raisins; ~-pudding (Dalmatian or spotted coach) dog; ~-pudding stone (geol.), conglomerate of flint or other pebbles. [OE plūme, MLG plūme, MHG pflūme, ON plóma, f. Rom. *pruna (whence OHG pfruma, MLG prūme, Du. pruim) f. L prunum PRUNE¹]

plu'mag|e (-ōo-), n. A bird's feathers. Hence (-)~ED²(-Ijd) a. [ME, f. OF (PLUME, -AGE)]

plumassier (plōomaser'), n. One who trades or works in ornamental feathers. [F (plumasse augment. of PLUME, see -IER)]

plumb¹ (-m), n., a., & adv. 1. Ball of lead, esp. that attached to mason's ~-line (string for testing perpendicularity of wall etc., also fig.); out of ~, not vertical; sounding-lead, plummet; ~-rule, mason's ~-line attached to board. 2. adj. Vertical; (fig.) downright, sheer, as ~ nonsense; (crick., of wicket) level, true. 3. adv. Vertically; (fig.) exactly, as points ~ in the same direction; *(sl.) quite, utterly, (~ crazy, clean mad). [ME; (adj. & adv. f. n.) f. OF plomb f. L plumbum lead]

plumb² (-m), v.t. & i. Sound (sea), measure (depth, lit. & fig.), with plummet, whence ~'LESS (-ml-) a.; make vertical; (intr.) work as plumber. [f. prec.]

plumbāg'o, n. Black lead, graphite, a form of carbon used for pencils etc. & mixed with clay for making crucibles; leadwort, plant with greyish-blue flowers. Hence plumbā'ginous a. [L, gen. -ginis, f. plumbum lead]

plum'beous, a. Of, like, lead; lead-glazed. [f. L plumbeus (as prec.) +-ous]

plumb'|er (-mer), n. Artisan who fits &

repairs pipes, cisterns, etc., with lead, copper, zinc, or tin. So ~ERY(2, 3) (-mer-) n. [ME plummer etc., f. OF plummier f. L plumbarius (as prec., see -ARY)¹]

plum'b|ic a. (Chem.) combined with lead, so ~IF'EROUS a.; (path.) due to presence of lead, so ~ISM(5) n. [f. L plumbum lead +-IC]

plume¹ (-ōo-), n. Feather, esp. large one used for ornament; (fig.) borrowed ~s (referring to fable of jackdaw in peacock's ~s); ornamental feather or bunch of feathers or horsehair, esp. as attached to helmet or hat, or worn in hair, as court ~ (of ostrich feathers); (zool.) feather-like part, or formation. Hence ~'LESS, ~'LIKE, aa., ~'LET n., (-ōoml-). [ME, f. OF, f. L pluma down]

plume² (-ōo-), v.t. Furnish with plume(s); dress oneself with borrowed plumes; pride oneself (on esp. something trivial or to which one has no claim); (of bird) trim, dress, (feathers). [f. prec.]

plumm'er-block, n. (mech.). Metal case for supporting revolving shaft, with movable cover giving access to bearings. [perh. f. surname +BLOCK]

plumm'et, n., & v.i. (Weight attached to) plumb-line; sounding-lead; weight attached to fishing-line to keep float upright; (v.i.) plunge. [ME & OF plommet dim. as PLUMB¹]

plumm'y, a. Of, abounding in, plums; (colloq.) rich, good, desirable. [-Y²]

plumōse' (-ōo-), a. Feathered; feather-like. [f. L plumosus (as PLUME¹, see -OSE¹)]

plump¹, a., & v.t. & i. 1. (Esp. of person or parts of body) full, rounded, fleshy, filled out. 2. vb. Make ~, fatten up; become ~, swell out or up. Hence ~'LY² adv., ~'NESS n., ~'Y² a. [late 15th c. plompe, f. MDu. plomp blunt, MLG plump, plomp unshapen etc.]

plump², v.i. & t., n., adv., & a. 1. Drop or plunge (t. & i.) with abrupt descent (down upon etc.); ‖ vote for (one candidate alone, when one might vote for two); (fig.) go wholeheartedly for one of alternative choices. 2. n. Abrupt plunge, heavy fall. 3. adv. With sudden or heavy fall, as came ~ into the river; flatly, bluntly, as I told him ~, I lied ~. 4. adj. Direct, unqualified, as answer with a ~ No. [ME, of imit. orig.; f. MLG plumpen, MDu. plompen]

‖ plump³, n. (arch.). Company, troop, esp. ~ of spears (spearmen); cluster. [ME, of unkn. orig.; cf. clump (of trees)]

plum'per¹, n. Ball, disc, carried in mouth to fill out hollow cheeks. [PLUMP¹ +-ER¹]

plum'per², n. In vbl senses, esp.: ‖ (vote of) one who plumps for candidate; (sl.) downright lie. [PLUMP² +-ER¹]

plu'mūl|e (plōo-), n. Rudimentary stem of embryo plant, whence ~AR¹ a.; little feather of down, whence ~A'CEOUS (-āshus) a. [f. L plumula, dim. as PLUME¹]

plu'mȳ (-ŏŏ-), a. Plume-like; feathery; adorned with plumes. [-Y²]

plŭn'der, v.t., & n. 1. Rob (place, person) forcibly of goods, esp. as in war; rob systematically; steal, embezzle, (goods, or abs.). 2. n. Violent or dishonest acquisition of property; property so acquired; (sl.) profit, gain. Hence ~ER¹ n. [c. 1630, f. G *plündern*, lit., rob of household effects (MG, MHG *plunder* clothing &c.), a wd from the Thirty Years' War]

plŭn'derage, n. Plundering, esp. embezzling of goods on shipboard; spoil thus obtained. [-AGE]

plŭnge (-j), v.t. & i., & n. 1. Thrust violently (*into* liquid, cavity, etc.); (fig.) thrust (person etc. *into*, *in*, condition, action, etc.; esp. in p.p., as ~*d in gloom*); sink entirely (pot containing plant) in ground; throw oneself, dive, (*into* water, difficulty, discussion, etc.); enter impetuously (*into* room, *up*, *down*, stairs, etc.); (of horse) throw itself violently forward; (of ship) pitch; (sl.) gamble deeply, run into debt; *plunging fire* (from guns at higher level); *plunging neckline* (cut low). 2. n. Plunging, dive, (~*bath*, large enough to dive into); (fig.) critical step, as *take the* ~. [ME, f. OF *plungier* f. *plumbicare* sound with plummet (*plumbum*)]

plŭn'ger (-j-), n. In vbl senses, esp.: parts of mechanism that work with plunging motion; (sl.) reckless gambler, speculator. [-ER¹]

plŭnk, v.t. & i., & n. 1. Throw or fall heavily or suddenly; *hit unexpectedly. 2. n. Sound made by plucking strings of musical instrument (v.i., make such sound). 3. *(colloq.). Heavy blow; dollar. [imit.]

plu'pĕrf'ĕct (-ŏŏ-), a. & n. (Tense) expressing action completed prior to some past point of time specified or implied (expr. in E by *had* with p.p., as *he had called*). [contr. f. L *plus quam perfectum* more than perfect]

plur'al (-oor-), a. & n. (Form of noun, verb, etc.) denoting more than one (or, in languages with dual, more than two); more than one in number; ~ *vote, voter, voting* (of one person in more than one constituency). Hence ~LY² adv. [ME, f. OF *plurel* or L *pluralis* (*plus pluris* more, see -AL)]

plur'al|ism (-oor-), n. Holding of more than one office, esp. benefice, at a time; (philos.) system that recognizes more than one ultimate principle (cf. MONISM). So ~IST n., ~is'tic a. [-ISM]

plurăl'itȳ (-oor-), n. State of being plural; large number, multitude; holding of two or more benefices or offices; benefice, office, held with another; majority (*of* votes etc.). [ME, f. OF *pluralite* f. LL *pluralitas* (as PLURAL, see -TY)]

plur'alize (-oor-), -**ise** (-īz), v.t. & i. Make

plural, express in the plural; hold more than one benefice. [f. F *pluraliser* (as PLURAL, see -IZE)]

pluri- (-oor-), comb. form of L *plus pluris* more, as: ~*lit'eral* (Heb. gram.), having more than 3 letters in the root; ~*pres'ence*, presence in more than one place at same time; ~*sēr'ial*, ~*sēr'iate*, consisting of several series.

plŭs, prep., a., & n. 1. With the addition of (symbol+), as *3* ~ *4* (cf. MINUS); ~ *1* etc., golfer's handicap; ~*fours*, long wide knickerbockers (so named because, to produce the overhang, the length is normally increased by four inches). 2. adj. Additional, extra; (math.) positive; (electr.) positive, positively electrified. 3. n. The symbol (+); additional quantity, positive quantity. [L, = more]

plŭsh, n. & a. Kind of cloth of silk, cotton, etc., with nap longer & softer than that of velvet; (pl.) footman's ~ breeches; (adj.) of ~, sumptuous. Hence ~'Y² a. [f. obs. F *pluche* contr. f. *peluche* f. Rom. *piluceus f. *pilus* hair; see PLUCK²]

plu'tărchy (plŏŏ-, -kĭ), n. Plutocracy. [f. Gk *ploutos* wealth +*arkhia* -rule]

Plu'tō (-ŏŏ-), n. A more remote planet than Neptune (discovered 1930). [f. Gk *Ploutōn* ~, god of infernal regions]

plutŏc'racȳ (-ŏŏ-), n. Rule of the wealthy; ruling class of wealthy persons. So **plu'tocrat** n. **plutocrăt'ic** a., (-ŏŏ-). [f. Gk *ploutokratia* (as foll., see -CRACY)]

plutŏl'atrȳ (-ŏŏ-), n. Worship of wealth. [f. Gk *ploutos* wealth, see -LATRY]

Plutŏn'ic (-ŏŏ-), a. & n. Of Pluto, infernal; (geol.) igneous, as ~ *rocks*, ~ *theory* (attributing most geological phenomena to action of internal heat, whence **Plu'ton**-ISM(3), **Plu'ton**IST(2), nn.); (n.) ~ rock. So **Plutōn'IAN** (-ŏŏ-) a. [as PLUTO, -IC]

plutōn'ium (-ŏŏ-), n. Element arising from NEPTUNIUM. [f. PLUTO +-IUM]

plutōn'om|ȳ (-ŏŏ-), n. Political economy. Hence **plutonōm'ic** a., ~IST n., (-ŏŏ-). [f. Gk *ploutos* wealth +-*nomia* arrangement]

plu'vi|al (-ŏŏ-), a. & n. Of rain, rainy, so ~OUS a.; (geol.) caused by rain; (n., eccl. hist.) long cloak as ceremonial vestment. [(adj.) f. L *pluvialis* (*pluvia* rain, see -AL); (n.) f. med. L *pluviale* rain-cloak]

pluvi|ŏm'ēter (-ŏŏ-), n. Rain-gauge. Hence ~**omĕt'ric**(AL) aa. [f. L *pluvia* rain +-o- +-METER]

plȳ¹, n. Fold, thickness, layer, of cloth etc.; strand of rope etc.; *two, 2, 3,* ~, having 2 etc. thicknesses or strands; (fig.) turn, tendency, esp. *take a* ~; ~'*wood*, strong thin board made by gluing layers with the grains crosswise. [f. F *pli* f. *plier* f. L *plicare* fold]

plȳ², v.t. & i. Use, wield vigorously, (tool, weapon); work at (one's business, task); supply (person etc.) persistently *with* (food etc.); assail vigorously (person *with* questions, arguments); (naut.) work to windward; (of vessel or its master, bus, etc.) go to & fro *between* (places); ‖ (of boatman, porter, cabman) attend regularly for custom (*at* place). [ME *plye*, aphetic f. APPLY]

Plym'outh (-muth), n. ~ *Brethren*, religious body that arose at ~ *c.* 1830, with no formal creed & no official order of ministers, whence ~ISM(3), ~IST(2), ~ITE¹, (-muth-), nn.; ~ *Rock*, large breed of domestic fowl of Amer. origin. [port in England]

pneumät'ic (n-), a. & n. **1.** Of, acting by means of, wind or air; ~ *tire* (inflated with air); ~ *dispatch*, conveyance of parcels etc. along tubes by compression or exhaustion of air; ~ *trough* (for collecting gases in jars over surface of water or mercury); containing, connected with, air-cavities esp. in bones of birds; spiritual. **2.** n. ~ *tire*, cycle with such tires; (pl.) science of mechanical properties of air or other elastic fluids or gases. Hence **pneumät'ICALLY** adv., **pneumati'CITY** n., (n-). [f. F (-*ique*) or L f. Gk *pneumatikos* (*pneuma* wind f. *pneō* breathe, see -IC)]

pneum'at|o- (n-), comb. form of Gk *pneuma -matos* air, breath, spirit, as: ~*ocyst*, air-sac in body of bird etc.; ~*ŏl'ogy*, theory of spiritual beings, doctrine of the Holy Spirit, psychology, so ~*olo'gical* a.; ~*ŏm'eter*, instrument for measuring amount of air breathed at each inspiration; ~*ophore*, part of some compound hydrozoa containing air-cavity.

pneumogãs'tric (n-), a. Of lungs & stomach, esp. ~ *nerves*, tenth pair of cerebral nerves. [irreg. f. Gk *pneumōn -monos* lung + GASTRIC]

pneumōn'ia (n-), n. Inflammation of the substance of one (*single* ~) or both (*double* ~) lungs. So **pneumōn'IC** a., **pneumon**IT'IS n., (n-). [f. Gk *pneumonia* f. *pneumōn* (as prec.); see -IA¹]

pō, n. (pl. *pos*). See POT¹.

poach¹, v.t. Cook (egg) by dropping it without shell into boiling water. Hence ~'ER¹(2) n. [ME, f. OF *pochier* (*poche* POKE¹)]

poach², v.t. & i. Thrust (stick, finger, etc. *into* etc.); trample, cut *up* (turf etc.) with hoofs; (of land) become sodden by being trampled; encroach, trespass, (*on* person's *preserves* often fig., lands, etc.), whence ~'ER¹ n.; trespass on (land etc.), capture (game, fish) by illicit or unsportsmanlike methods; obtain (advantage, start, in race) by unfair means; (lawn tennis) strike (ball, or abs.) in partner's court. [16th c. *poche*, prob. f. F *pocher* in POACH¹, POKE²]

pŏch'ard (*also* -k-), n. European diving-duck with bright reddish-brown head & neck. [orig. unkn.]

pŏck, n. Eruptive spot esp. in smallpox. [OE *poc*, = MDu., MLG *pocke*; see also POX]

pŏck'ĕt¹, n. **1.** Bag, sack, esp. as measure

of hops (168 lb.) or wool (= half sack); small bag inserted in (usu. male) garment for carrying small articles, as *coat*, *waist-coat*, *trouser*, *watch*, *ticket*, ~~; (fig.) pecuniary resources, as *he will suffer in his* ~; *empty* ~, person without money; *be prepared to put your hand in your* ~ (spend some money); *put* one's *pride in* one's ~, submit to doing something that mortifies it; *out-of-*~*-expenses*, actual outlay incurred; *am 5s. in* ~, have 5s. available; *am 5s. in* ~, *out of* ~, *by the transaction* (have gained, lost); *has him in her* ~ (completely under control); pouch at each corner & on each side of billiard-table into which balls are driven; cavity in earth filled with gold or other ore, whence ~Y² a.; cavity in rock esp. (geol.) filled with foreign matter; (mil.) isolated area occupied by enemy, forces occupying this, (*mopping up enemy* ~*s* or ~*s of resistance*); = AIR¹-; (attrib.) of suitable size or shape for carrying in ~. **2.** ~ *battleship*, a ship armoured & equipped like, but smaller than, a battleship; ~-*book*, notebook, book-like case for papers etc. carried in ~; ‖~*borough* (under control of one person or family); ~ (small personal) *expenses*; ~ *handkerchief* (carried in ~); ~-*money* (for occasional expenses, esp. that allowed to children); ~-*piece*, lucky coin carried in ~ as charm; ~-*pistol*, (joc.) ~ *spirit-flask*. Hence ~FUL n., ~LESS a. [ME *poket* f. AN *pokele* dim. f. ONF *poke* POKE¹]

pŏck'ĕt², v.t. Put into one's pocket; confine as in pocket; hem in (competitor) in race; appropriate, usu. dishonestly; submit to (affront, injury); conceal, suppress, (feelings); (bill.) drive (ball) into pocket. Hence ~ABLE a. [f. prec.]

pock-pudding. See POKE¹.

pōcōcuran'e|e (-koorahntă, -kūrăntĭ), a. & n. Indifferent (person). Hence ~(ĕ)*ism* n. [It., = caring little]

pōd¹, n. Socket of brace & bit. [earlier form of PAD³(5)]

pōd², n., & v.i. & t. (-dd-). **1.** Long seed-vessel esp. of leguminous plants; cocoon of silkworm; case of locust's eggs; narrow-necked eel-net. **2.** vb. Bear ~s; shell (peas etc.). [late 17th c., of unkn. orig.]

pōd³, n., & v.t. (-dd-). Small herd of seals or whales; (v.t.) drive (seals) into a ~. [of unkn. (U.S.) orig.]

pŏd'agra (*or* pōdǎg²), n. (med.). Gout, esp. in feet. Hence or cogn. **pŏd'agRAL**, **podǎg'rIC**, **pŏd'agrOUS**, aa. [L, f. Gk *podagra* (*pous podos* foot + *agra* catching)]

pŏdd'ĕd, a. Bearing pods; growing in pod, (fig.) well-off, snug. [-ED²]

pŏdĕstà (-tah²), n. Magistrate in Italian municipalities; (hist.) chief magistrate in medieval Italian towns. [It., f. L *potestatem* power (*potis* able, see -TY)]

pŏdge, n. (colloq.). Short fat person. Hence **pŏdg'Y**² a. [var. of PUDGE]

pŏd′ium, n. (pl. *-ia*). Continuous projecting base or pedestal; raised platform round arena of amphitheatre; continuous bench round room. [L, f. Gk *podion* (*pous podos* foot)]

pŏdophyll′in, n. (chem.). Yellow bitter resin of cathartic properties got from root of wild mandrake. [f. bot. L *podophyllum*, may-apple, wild mandrake, (Gk *pous podos* foot + *phullon* leaf) + -IN]

pō′e-bîrd, n. = PARSON-bird. [f. Otaheitan wd for 'ear-rings', from tufts under throat]

pō′ĕm, n. A metrical composition, esp. of elevated character; elevated composition in prose or verse, as *prose ~*; (fig.) something (other than a composition of words) akin or compared to a *~*, *as their lives are a ~*. [f. F *poème* or L f. Gk *poēma = poiēma* (*poieō* make)]

pō′ĕsў, n. (arch.). Art, composition, of poetry; poems collectively. [ME, f. OF *poesie* f. Rom. **poesia* f. L f. Gk *poēsis = poiēsis* making, poetry, (as prec.)]

pō′ĕt, n. Writer of poems; writer in verse, esp. one possessing high powers of imagination, expression, etc.; *Poets' Corner*, part of Westminster Abbey containing graves & monuments of several *~s*, (joc.) part of newspaper devoted to poetry. Hence *~*ESS[1] n. [ME, f. OF *poete* f. L (*-ta*) f. Gk *poētēs = poiētēs* maker, poet, (as prec.)]

pōetăs′ter, n. Paltry poet. So **pōĕt′ICULE** n. [-ASTER]

pōĕt′|ic(al), aa. Of, proper to, poets or poetry; (usu. *~ic*) having the good qualities of poetry; (usu. *~ical*) written in verse, as *~ical works*; *~ic* JUSTICE, LICENCE[1]. Hence *~*ICALLY adv., *~*ICS n. [f. F *poétique* f. L f. Gk *po(i)ētikos* (as POET, see -IC & -AL)]

pōĕt′icīze, **-ise** (-īz), v.t. Make (theme) poetic. [-IZE]

pō′ĕtīze, **-ise** (-īz), v.i. & t. Play the poet, compose poetry; treat poetically; celebrate in poetry. [f. F *poétiser* (as POET, see -IZE)]

pō′ĕtrў, n. Art, work, of the poet; elevated expression of elevated thought or feeling in metrical form; poems; quality (in any thing) that calls for poetical expression; *prose ~*, prose having all the qualities of poetry except metre. [ME, f. OF *poetrie* f. med. L *poetria* (as POET)]

pŏg′ō, n. (pl. *~s*). Toy like stilt with spring, used to jump on. [app. fanciful]

pogrŏm′, n. Organized massacre orig. or esp. of Jews in Russia. [Russ.]

poign′ant (poin-), a. Sharp, pungent, in taste or smell; painfully sharp, as *~ hunger, regret, sarcasm*; pleasantly piquant; moving, touching. Hence **poign′**ANCY n., *~*LY[2] adv., (poin-). [ME, f. OF part. of *poindre* prick f. L *pungere*]

poilu (see AP.), n. (sl.). French soldier (nickname, cf. TOMMY). [F, lit. hairy, unshaven]

‖ **poind** (pĕnd, pĭnd), v.t., & n. (Sc.). Distrain upon, impound; (n.) act of *~ing*, beast or chattel *~ed*. [late ME f. OE *pyndan* impound; cf. PINFOLD]

poinsĕtt′ia, n. Plant with large scarlet leaves & small yellowish flowers. [f. J. R. *Poinsett* (d. 1851), discoverer, -IA[1]]

point[1], n. **1.** Small dot on a surface. **2.** Stop or punctuation-mark (chiefly now in *full ~*, full stop); dot, small stroke, used in Semitic languages to indicate vowels or distinguish consonants; dot separating integral from fractional parts in decimals, as *four ~ six* (4·6). **3.** Single item, detail, particular, as *we differ on these ~s, it is a ~ of conscience*, STRETCH *a ~*. **4.** *Possession is nine ~s of the law* (nine-tenths, almost the whole); *give ~s* (odds) *to* (opponent in game), (fig.) be superior to. **5.** Unit in appraising qualities of exhibit in show; unit of value in rationing (*on ~s*, rationed on a basis of such units); unit (of varying value) in quoting price of stocks etc. **6.** (print.). Unit of measurement for type bodies (British & U.S.A. 0·0138 in.). **7.** (geom.). That which has position but not magnitude, e.g. *~ of intersection of two lines*. **8.** Precise place or spot, as *~ of contact*; *~ of no return*, *~* in a long-distance flight over the ocean at which an aircraft has not enough fuel to return to its starting-place and must continue onwards; also fig.; (hunt.) spot to which straight run is made, such run, *~-to-~ race* (over course defined only by certain landmarks); (her.) any of nine particular spots on shield used for determining position. **9.** Stage, degree, in progress or increase, esp. of temperature, as *boiling, freezing, ~* (at which thing boils etc.). **10.** Precise moment for action etc., as *when it came to the ~, he declined*; *exact moment* (*of* death etc.). **11.** Distinctive trait, characteristic, as *singing is not his strong ~*; *the* essential thing, *the* thing under discussion, as *that is just the ~, come to the ~*; *to the ~*, relevant(ly) to the purpose; *make a ~ of*, regard, treat, as essential; *carry* one's *~*, secure one's object; *make a ~*, establish proposition, prove contention. **12.** (Also *~ lace*) thread lace made wholly with needle; (improp.) pillow lace imitating this. **13.** Sharp end of tool, weapon, pin, pen, etc. (*not to put too fine a ~ upon it*, to speak bluntly). **14.** Tip (*the ~ of the jaw* or *the ~*, in boxing, tip of chin as spot for knock-out blow); promontory, esp. in names, as *Start P~*; (mil.) small leading party of advanced guard; (pl.) extremities of horse, as *bay with black ~s*. **15.** Sharp-pointed tool, e.g. etching-needle; tine of deer's horn. **16.** ‖ (On railway) tapering movable rail by which train is directed from one line to another; tapered division on backgammon board. **17.** (hist.). Tagged lace for lacing bodice, attaching hose to doublet, etc. **18.** (naut.). Short piece of cord at lower edge of sail for tying up a reef. **19.** ~s *of* the compass, **32** equidistant ~s on compass (N, N by E, NNE, NE by N, NE, NE by E, ENE, E by N, E, E by S, ESE, SE by E, SE, SE by S, SSE, S by E, S, S by W, SSW, SW by S, SW, SW by W, WSW, W by S, W, W by N, WNW, NW by W, NW, NW by N, NNW, N by W), at angular intervals of 11° 15'. **20.** Salient feature of story, joke, etc., as *don't see the* ~; pungency, effectiveness, as *his remarks lack* ~. **21.** (crick.). (Position of) fieldsman placed more or less in line with popping-crease a short distance on off-side of batsman. **22.** (Of dog) act of pointing, esp. *make, come to, a* ~; *potatoes & * ~, potatoes to eat & bacon etc. to look at. **23.** *At all* ~s, in every part; *at the* ~ (on the verge) *of death* etc.; *in* ~, apposite, as *the case you take is not in* ~; *in* ~ (as a matter) *of fact*; (*up*)*on the* ~ *of*, on the very verge of (action, do*ing*); ~ *of* (thing that vitally affects one's) *honour*, esp. *the* ~ *of honour* (obligation to demand satisfaction, esp. by duel); ~ *of view*, position from which thing is viewed, (fig.) way of looking at a matter; ‖~*-duty* (of constable stationed at particular ~ to regulate traffic etc.); ‖~*s'man*, man in charge of railway ~s, constable on ~-duty. [ME (partly thr. F *point, pointe*, & f. foll.) f. L *punctum*, neut. p.p. of *pungere* prick]

point², v.t. & i. **1.** Sharpen (pencil etc.). **2.** Punctuate; mark (Psalms etc.) with signs for chanting. **3.** Give point to (words, actions), as ~*ing his remarks with apt illustrations, to* ~ *a moral.* **4.** Fill in joints of (brickwork etc.) with mortar or cement smoothed with trowel. **5.** Prick *in* (manure), turn *over* (soil), with point of spade. **6.** Direct attention (*to, at*, lit. & fig.); ~ *out*, indicate, show, (thing, fact, *that* etc.); (of hound) indicate presence of (game, or abs.) by acting as a POINTER; direct (finger, weapon, etc., *at*); direct attention of (person *to*); aim *at*, tend *towards.* [ME, f. OF *pointer*, as prec.]

point'blank', a. & adv. **1.** (Of shot) fired horizontally, level, at very close range; ~ *distance* (within which gun may be fired horizontally). **2.** adv. With direct aim, horizontally, in direct line; (fig.) directly, flatly, as *told him* ~ *it would not do;* offhand, as *refused it* ~. [prob. f. prec. +BLANK, i.e. white spot in centre of target]

point d'appui (pwăn dăpwē'), n. (mil.). Point of support, base, rallying-place. [F]

point-dĕvice', a. & adv. (arch.). Perfectly correct, extremely neat or precise; (adv.) in ~ manner. [ME *at point devis* app. f. OF *à point devis* to the point arranged, or arranged to the proper point (see POINT¹ & DEVICE)]

point'ĕd, a. Having, sharpened to, a point; (of remark etc.) having point, penetrating, cutting; emphasized, made evident. Hence ~**LY²** adv., ~**NESS** n. [-ED¹,²]

point'er, n. In vbl senses, esp.: index hand of clock, balance, etc.; rod used for pointing to words etc. on blackboard, map, etc.; (colloq.) hint; dog that on scenting game stands rigidly, with muzzle stretched towards it & usu. one foot raised; (pl.) two stars in Great Bear, straight line through which points nearly to pole-star. [-ER¹]

poin'till|ism (pwăn-), n. (Art). Method of producing light effects by crowding a surface with small spots of various colours, which are blended by the eye. So ~**IST** n. [f. F ~*isme* f. *pointiller* mark with dots f. *point* POINT¹, -ISM]

point'ing, n. In vbl senses, esp.: punctuation; filling up joints of brickwork etc. with cement, facing thus given to the joints; (Psalms etc.) system of signs for Anglican chanting. [-ING¹]

point'less, a. Without a point, blunt; without point, meaningless; not having scored a point. Hence ~**LY²** adv., ~**NESS** n. [-LESS]

poise (-z), v.t. & i., & n. **1.** Balance; hold suspended or supported; carry (one's head etc. in specified way); be balanced; hover in air etc. **2.** n. Equilibrium (lit. & fig.), carriage (*of* head etc.). [(vb) f. OF *peser* (st. *pois*-) f. L *pensare* frequent. of *pendĕre pens-* weigh; (n.) f. OF *pois* f. L *pensum* weight]

pois'on (-zn), n., & v.t. **1.** Substance that when introduced into or absorbed by a living organism destroys life or injures health, esp. (pop.) one that destroys life by rapid action & when taken in small quantity; *slow* ~ (of which repeated doses are injurious); *hate each other like* ~ (bitterly); *what's your* ~? (colloq.), what will you have to drink?; (fig.) baneful principle, doctrine, etc.; ~ GAS; ~ *ivy*, kinds of N.-Amer. sumac with leaves ~ous to touch; ~ *pen*, anonymous writer of libellous or scurrilous letter(s) to a private individual; ~*-tree, -wood*, kinds of tree or plant with ~ous properties. **2.** v.t. Administer ~ to (man, animal), kill or injure thus, whence ~**ER¹** (-z-) n.; produce morbid effects in (blood etc.), whence (-)~**ING¹** (-z-) n.; infect (air, water, etc.) with ~, smear (weapon) with ~ (esp. in p.p.); corrupt, pervert, (person, mind); destroy, spoil, (person's pleasure etc.); render (land, furnace, etc.) foul & unfit for its purpose by noxious application etc. Hence ~**OUS** a., ~**OUSLY²** adv., (-z-). [(n.) ME & OF *puison* (as POTION); (vb) f. OF *poisonner* f. the n.]

poissa͞rde' (pwŏs-), n. Parisian market-woman leading riots during first revolution; French fishwife. [F]

pōke¹, n. Bag, sack, (now dial. exc. *buy a PIG in a* ~). [ME, corresp. in form w. ONF *poke, poque*, = OF *poche*; see POUCH]

pōke², v.t. & i. Thrust, push, (thing, *in*,

up, down, etc.) with hand, arm, point of stick, etc.; stir (fire) with poker; (colloq.) shut (one*self* etc.) *up* in poky place; produce (hole etc. *in* thing) by poking; make thrusts with stick etc. (*at* etc.); thrust forward, esp. obtrusively, as (fig.) *don't ~ your nose into my affairs; ~ about, ~ & pry,* be inquisitive; *~ one in the ribs,* nudge him with finger or elbows; *~ fun at,* assail with ridicule; pry (*into*); *~ one's head,* carry head thrust forward, stoop. [ME, = MDu., MLG *pōken* poke, thrust, whence OF *poquer, pocher*; cf. POACH²]

pōke³, n. Poking; thrust, nudge; device fastened on cattle etc. to prevent their breaking through fences; projecting brim or front of woman's bonnet or hat; *~ (-bonnet),* bonnet with this, esp. as worn by Salvation Army women. [f. prec.]

pōk′er¹, n., & v.t. **1.** Stiff metal rod with handle, for poking fire; (of person's carriage or manner) *as stiff as a ~;* ‖ (Oxf. & Camb. sl.) bedell carrying mace or stave before Vice-Chancellor; kinds of instrument used in *~-work; red-hot ~,* plant with spikes of scarlet or yellow flowers; (joc. asseveration) *by the holy ~; ~-work,* burning of designs on white wood with heated implement. **2.** v.t. Execute (design) in, adorn (thing) with, *~-work.* [-ER¹]

pōk′er², n. (Orig. Amer.) card-game for two or more persons, each of whom if not bluffed into declaring his hand bets on its value; *~-face,* impassive countenance appropriate to a *~-player;* so *~-faced.* [orig. unkn.; cf. G *pochen* to brag, *pochspiel*]

pōk′y̆, a. (Of place, room, etc.) confined, mean, shabby; (of occupation etc.) pottering, petty. [f. POKE² + -Y²]

pola′cre (-ahker), **-ǎcc′a,** n. Three-masted Mediterranean merchant vessel. [f. F *polacre -aque*, Polish, Pole, hist. unexpl.]

pōl′ar, a. & n. **1.** Of, near, either pole of the earth or of the celestial sphere; *~ (white) bear, hare; ~ circles* (parallel to equator at distance of 23° 28′ from the poles); *~ distance,* angular distance of point on sphere from nearer pole. **2.** Having polarity, magnetic; having positive & negative electricity; (of molecules) symmetrically arranged in definite direction. **3.** (geom.). Relating to a POLE²; *~ curve* (related in particular way to given curve & to fixed point called pole). **4.** (fig.). Analogous to the pole of the earth or to the pole-star; directly opposite in character. **5.** n. *~ curve.* Hence *~LY²* adv. [f. F *polaire* or med. L *polaris* (as POLE², see -AR¹)]

polari-, comb. form of prec., as: *pōlarĭm̆′eter, polă′riscope,* instruments for showing polarization of light, so *polărĭmĕt′ric, polăriscŏp′ic,* aa., *pōlarĭm′etry* n.

polă′rity, n. Tendency of lodestone, magnetized bar, etc., to point with its ex-

tremities to the magnetic poles of earth; tendency of a body to place its mathematical axis in particular direction; possession of two poles having contrary qualities (also fig.); electrical condition of body as positive or negative; (fig.) magnetic attraction towards an object. [-ITY]

pōl′arize, -ise (-īz), v.t. & i. Modify the vibrations of (light, radiant heat, etc.) so that the ray exhibits different properties on different sides, opposite sides being alike & those at right angles showing maximum difference; (magn., electr.) give polarity to (bar, coil); (fig.) give to arbitrary direction, special meaning, etc., to (word etc.), (also) give unity of direction to. Hence or cogn. *~ABLE* a., *~A′TION, ~ER¹(2),* nn. [(partly thr. F) f. POLAR, see -IZE]

pōlatouche′ (-ōōch), n. Small flying squirrel. [F, f. Russ. *poletuchii* flying]

pōl′der, n. Piece of low-lying land reclaimed from sea or river in Netherlands. [Du.]

pōle¹, n., & v.t. **1.** Long slender rounded tapering piece of wood or (rarely) metal esp. as support for tent, telegraph wires, etc.; wooden shaft fitted to fore-carriage of vehicle & attached to yokes or collars of the horses etc.; *under bare ~s* (naut.), with no sail set; *up the ~* (sl.), in a fix; (as measure) rod, perch, 5½ yds; *~-jumping* (with help of *~* held in hands). **2.** v.t. Furnish with *~s;* push, move, (*off* etc.) with *~.* [OE *pāl*, MDu. *pael*, OHG *pfāl*, ON *páll,* f. L *palus* stake]

pōle², n. North, South, *~,* the two points in the celestial sphere about which the stars appear to revolve, (also) N. & S. extremities of earth's axis; *magnetic ~,* points, N. & S., in these extremities where the magnetic needle dips vertically; (geom.) *~s of a circle of a sphere,* the two points in which axis of that circle cuts surface of sphere; (geom.) fixed point to which others are referred; each of the two opposite points on surface of magnet at which magnetic forces are manifested; each of two terminal points (*positive, negative, ~*) of electric cell, battery, etc.; (biol.) extremity of main axis of any spherical or oval organ; (fig.) each of two opposed principles etc.; *~-star,* a star of Ursa Minor, now about 1° distant from N. *~* of heavens, (fig.) thing serving as guide, lodestar, centre of attraction. Hence *~′WARD* a., *~′WARD(S)* adv. [ME, f. L f. Gk *polos* pivot, axis, sky]

Pōle³, n. Native of Poland. [G, f. Pol. *Poljane* lit. field-dwellers (*pole* field)]

pōle′ax(e) (-lă-), n., & v.t. Battle-axe; axe formerly used in naval warfare as weapon & for cutting ropes etc.; halbert; butcher's axe for slaughtering, (vb) slaughter (beast) with this. [ME *pol(l)ax, -ex* f. MDu. *pol(l)aex,* MLG *-exe,* as POLL¹ + AXE]

pōle′cat (-lk-), n. ‖ Small brownish-black carnivorous mammal of weasel family, native of Europe. [ME *pol-*, *pulcat*, f. *pol-* (poss. = OF *po(u)le* fowl)+CAT]

pŏl'ĕmárch (-k), n. (Gk hist.). Military commander-in-chief with varying civil functions; (in Athens) third archon orig. with military functions. [f. Gk *polemarkhos* (*polemos* war+*-arkhos* -ruler)]

polĕm'ic, a. & n. 1. Controversial, disputatious. 2. n. Controversial discussion, (pl.) practice of this, esp. in theology; controversialist. Hence ~AL a., ~alLY² adv., pŏl'ĕmIZE(2) v.i. [f. Gk *polemikos* (*polemos* war, see -IC)]

polĕn'ta, n. Italian porridge made of barley, chestnut meal, etc. [It., f. L]

police' (-ēs), n., & v.t. 1. Civil administration, public order, (arch.); department of government concerned with this (arch.); civil force responsible for maintaining public order; (as pl.) members of this, as *the ~ are on his track*; ~*-court* (of summary jurisdiction, dealing with charges preferred by the ~); ~*-magistrate* (presiding in ~-court); ~*man*, member of ~ force; ‖~*-office*, headquarters of ~ in city or town; ~*-officer*, ~man; ~ *State*, totalitarian one controlled by political ~; ~*-station*, office of local ~ force. 2. v.t. Control (country etc.) by means of ~, furnish with~; (fig.) keep order in, control. [F., f. med. L *politia* = L *politīa* POLICY¹]

pŏliclin'ic, n. Clinic in private houses, not in hospital; out-patients' department of hospital. [f. G *poliklinik* (Gk *polis* city, CLINIC)]

pŏl'icy¹, n. Political sagacity; statecraft; prudent conduct, sagacity; craftiness; course of action adopted by government, party, etc.; ‖(Sc.) park round country seat etc.; *Court of P~*, legislative council in British Guiana. [ME, f. OF *policie* f. L f. Gk *politeia* citizenship, polity (*politēs* citizen f. *polis* city); in Sc. sense (earlier=improvement of estate) confused w. L *politus* polished]

pŏl'icy², n. (In full, ~ *of assurance*, *insurance* ~) document containing contract of assurance or insurance. [f. F *police* bill of lading, contract of insurance, f. Pr. *polissa* f. med. L *apodissa* f. L f. Gk *apodeixis* evidence, proof, f. APO(*deiknumi* show)]

pŏl'iŏ, n. (colloq.). (Person suffering from) poliomyelitis. [abbr.]

pŏl'iŏmyĕlit'is, n. (path.). Inflammation of the grey matter of the spinal cord; infantile paralysis. [f. Gk *polios* grey+MYELITIS]

pŏl'ish¹, v.t. & i. Make, become, smooth & glossy by friction; (fig.) make elegant or cultured, refine, (esp. in p.p.); smarten *up*; ~ *off*, finish off quickly. Hence ~ABLE a., ~ER¹ (1, 2) n. [ME, f. OF *polir* (see -ISH²) f. L *polīre -it-*]

pŏl'ish², n. Smoothness, glossiness, produced by friction; such friction; substance used to produce smooth surface; (fig.) refinement. [f. prec.]

Pŏl'ish³, a. & n. 1. Of Poland or the Poles. 2. n. The language of Poland. [-ISH¹]

pŏl'itárch (-k), n. (hist.). Governor of some Oriental cities, e.g. Thessalonica, under Romans. [f. Gk *politarkhēs* (*politēs* citizen+*-arkhēs* ruler)]

polite', a. Of refined manners, courteous; cultivated, cultured; well-bred; (of literature etc.) refined, elegant, as ~ *letters*. Hence ~LY² (-tl-) adv., ~NESS (-tn-) n. [f. L *politus* (POLISH¹)]

pŏl'itic, a. & n. 1. (Of person) sagacious, prudent, (of actions etc.) judicious, expedient; scheming, crafty; BODY¹ ~. 2. n. pl. Science & art of government, political affairs or life, political principles, as *what are his~s?*, *talk~s*, *is not practical* ~*s* (is too remote to be worth discussing). Hence ~LY² adv. [ME, f. OF *politique* f. L f. Gk *politikos* (as POLICY¹, see -IC)]

polit'ical, a. & n. 1. Of the State or its government; of public affairs; of politics; (of person) engaged in civil administration, as ~ *agent*, *resident*, (hist., in India) government official advising ruler of native State; having an organized polity; belonging to, taking, a side in politics; ~ ECONOMY; ~ *geography* (dealing with boundaries & possessions of States); ~ *verse*, modern Greek verse composed by accent, not quantity. 2. n. ~ agent. Hence ~LY² adv. [-AL]

pŏliti'cian (-shn), n. One skilled in politics, statesman; one interested or engaged in politics, esp. as profession; one who makes a trade of politics. [f. POLITIC, see -ICIAN]

polit'icize, -ise (-īz), v.i. & t. Act the politician; engage in, talk, politics; give political character to. [-IZE]

polit'ico- in comb. = politically, political & —, as ~*-economical*, ~*-geographical*, ~*-moral*, ~*-social*; ~*-religious*, (usu.) pertaining to politics as influenced by religion. [as POLITIC]

pŏl'ity, n. Condition of civil order; form, process, of civil government; organized society, state. [f. obs. F *politie* or L *politīa* POLICY¹]

pŏlk, v.i. Dance polka. [f. F *polker* as foll.]

pŏl'ka, n. 1. Lively dance of Bohemian origin in binary time; music for this. 2. Woman's tight-fitting jacket, usu. knitted. [F & G, f. Czech]

pŏll¹, n. (Now dial. or joc.) human head; part of this on which hair grows, as *grey*, *flaxen*, ~; counting of voters esp. at parliamentary or other election; voting at election, as *exclusion of Negroes from the~*; number of votes recorded, as *heavy*, *light*, ~; questioning of a sample of the population in order to estimate trend of popular opinion, whence ~'STER n. (colloq.); ~*-tax* (levied on every person). [ME, = obs. Du. *polle*, LG *polle*; cf. Da. *puld*, Sw. dial. *pull*]

pŏll², v.t. & i. (Arch.) crop the hair of;

cut off top of (tree, plant), esp. make a pollard of ; cut off horns of (cattle, esp. in p.p.) ; cut evenly edge of (sheet) ; take the votes of, (pass.) have one's vote taken ; (of candidate) receive (so many votes) ; give (vote) ; give one's vote. Hence ~'ABLE a. [ME, f. prec.]

pŏll³, a. & n. Polled, cut evenly; (in comb.) hornless, as ~-*beast*, -*ox*; (n.) ~ -*beast*, esp. one of a breed of hornless oxen. [short for p.p of prec.]

pŏll⁴, n. (*P~*) conventional proper name of parrot ; ~ *parrot*, parrot, user of conventional phrases & arguments. [altered f. *Moll* familiar equivalent of *Mary*]

∥ **pŏll⁵**, n. (Camb. Univ. sl.). *The P~*, the passmen; *go out in the P~*, take pass degree; (attrib.) ~ *degree*, *man*. [perh. f. POLLOI]

pŏll'ack, -ock, n. Sea-fish allied to cod. [17th c.; 16th c. (Sc.) *podlock*; orig. unkn.]

pŏll'an, n. Irish freshwater fish. [cf. Gael. *pollag*, Ir. *pollóg*, perh. f. Ir. *poll* inland lake]

pŏll'ard, n., & v.t. **1.** Animal that has cast or lost its horns; ox, sheep, goat, of hornless variety; tree polled so as to produce close rounded head of young branches; bran sifted from flour, (techn.) fine bran containing some flour. **2.** v.t. Make a ~ of (tree). [POLL² + -ARD]

pŏll'ĕn, n., & v.t. **1.** Fine powdery substance discharged from anther of flower, male element that fertilizes ovules. **2.** v.t. Convey ~ to, cover with ~. Hence ~LESS, pollin'IC, pŏlliniF'EROUS, aa. [L, gen. -*inis* = fine flour, dust]

pollicitā'tion, n. (civil law). Promise not yet formally accepted, & therefore revocable. [f. L *pollicitatio* (*pollicitari* frequent. of *polliceri* promise, see -ATION)]

pŏll'in|āte, v.t. Besprinkle with pollen, shed pollen upon. Hence ~A'TION n. [-ATE²]

pŏll'oi, n. pl. *Hoi ~*, most people, the majority, the rabble. [Gk, lit. the many]

pollute' (-ōot), v.t. Destroy the purity or sanctity of ; make (water etc.) foul or filthy. So **pollu**TION (-ōō-) n. [ME, f. L *polluere* -*lut*-]

pŏl'ō, n. Game of Eastern origin like hockey played on horseback; ~-*stick*, long-handled mallet used; WATER-~. [native]

pŏlonaise' (-āz), n. **1.** Woman's dress consisting of bodice with skirt open from waist downwards. **2.** (Music for) slow processional dance of Polish origin with three beats in bar. [F, fem. (as n.) of *polonais* Polish]

polōn'ium, n. A radio-active metallic element forming the last stage before lead in the radio-active disintegration of radium. [f. med. L *Polonia* Poland, discoverer's country, -IUM]

polŏn'ÿ, n. (Also *P~ sausage*) sausage of partly cooked pork. [app. replacing *Bologna*, -*ian sausage*]

pŏl'tergeist (-gīst), n. (Folklore & spiritualism) noisy mischievous spirit. [G]

pŏlt-'fŏŏt, n. & a. (arch.). Club-foot(ed). [obs. *poll* pestle, club, orig. unkn., +FOOT]

pŏltrōōn', n. Spiritless coward. So ~ERY(4) n. [f. F *poltron* f. It. *poltrone* f. *poltro* sluggard, see -OON]

pŏlÿ-, comb. form of Gk *polus* many, as: ~*adĕl'phous*, with stamens united in 3 or more bundles; ~*ăn'drist*, woman with several husbands or paramours; ~*ăn'drous*, of, practising, ~andry, (bot.) with numerous stamens; *pol'yandry*, plurality of husbands or paramours; *pol'yarchy* (-kĭ), government by many; ~*atŏm'ic*, containing many (esp. replaceable hydrogen) atoms; ~*autography*, lithography; ~*bās'ic* (chem.), having more than two bases or atoms of a base; ~*carp'ellary*, ~*carp'ous*, having several carpels; ~*chaete* (-kēt) a. & n., ~*chaet'an*, ~*chaet'ous*, (-kēt-), aa., (worm) with many bristles on the foot-stumps; ~*chrō'ite* (-kr-), colouring-matter of saffron, exhibiting various colours under various reagents; ~*dac'tyl* a. & n., (animal) with more than normal number of fingers or toes; ~*daem'onism*, belief in many supernatural powers; ~*gas'tric*, with many stomachs; ~*gen'esis*, origination of a race or species from several independent ancestors or germs, so ~*genēs'ic*, ~*genĕt'ic*, aa.; ~*gen'ic*, (chem.) forming more than one compound with hydrogen etc., (geol.) = ~*genous*; *polÿ'genism*, theory of ~geny; *polÿ'genist*, holder of this, so ~*genis'tic* a.; *polÿ'genous*, (geol.) composed of various kinds of rock, (chem.) = ~*genic*; *polÿ'geny*, origination of mankind from several independent pairs of ancestors; *pol'ygram*, many-lined figure or design; *pol'ygraph*, kinds of copying apparatus, (also) writer of many or various works, so ~*graph'ic* a., *polÿg'raphy* n.; *polÿg'ÿnous* (-g-), of, practising, ~gyny, (bot.) with many pistils, styles, or stigmas; *polÿg'ÿny* (-g-), plurality of wives; ~*hĕd'ron*, many (usu. more than six)-sided solid, so ~*hĕd'ral*, ~*hĕd'ric*, aa.; *pol'ymer*, compound formed by simple chemical addition from a number of identical molecules each of which consists of a number of identical units; ~*mĕ'ric*, (of compounds) composed of same elements in same proportions, but differing in molecular weight; *polÿm'erism*, condition of being ~meric or ~merous; ~*meriza'tion*, formation of a ~mer by simple chemical addition of a number of identical smaller molecules; *pol'ymerize*, render ~meric or ~merous; *polÿm'erous* (nat. hist.), composed of many parts; ~*morph'ic*, ~*morph'ous*,

For other words in *poly-* see POLY-.

multiform, esp. (nat. hist., biol.) varying in individuals, passing through successive variations, so ~*morph'ism* n.; ~*nōm'ial* a. & n. (alg.), = MULTI*nomial*; ~*ōn'ymous*, called by several different names; ~*ŏn'ymy*, use of different names for same thing; ~*ōp'ia*, affection of the eyes in which one object appears as two or more; ~*pet'alous*, having separate petals; *polyph'agous*, (zool.) feeding on various kinds of food or foodplants; *pol'yphone*, letter, symbol, standing for different sounds; ~*phŏn'ic*, *polȳph'onous*, many-voiced, (philol.) standing for different sounds, (mus.) contrapuntal; *polȳph'ony*, quality of being ~phonic, (mus.) counterpoint; ~*phylĕt'ic*, = ~*genetic*; ~*phȳll'ous*, ~*sĕp'alous*, having separate perianth-leaves, sepals; *pol'ystome* a. & n. (animal) with many mouths or suckers; ~*synthĕt'ic*, (of languages) combining several words of a sentence (e.g. verb & object) into one; ~*thăl'amous* (nat. hist.), many-chambered; *pol'ytype*, kind of stereotype, copy of engraving etc. made from this; ~*zō'a*, class of compound invertebrates, so ~*zō'ic* a.; ~*zōn'al*, (of lighthouse lens) composed of several annular segments.

pŏlȳăn'thus, n. Kinds of cultivated primula. [f. POLY-+Gk *anthos* flower]

pŏlȳchrŏmăt'ic (-kr-), a. Many-coloured. [POLY-]

pŏl'ȳchrōme (-kr-), a. & n. 1. Painted, printed, decorated, in many colours. 2. n. Work of art in several colours, esp. coloured statue; varied colouring. Hence **pŏlȳchrōm'ıc, pŏl'ȳchrōmous,** aa. [F, f. Gk *polukhrōmos* (POLY-, *khrōma* colour)]

pŏl'ȳchrŏmȳ (-kr-), n. Art of painting in several colours, esp. as applied to ancient pottery etc. [f. F *polychromie* (as prec., see -Y¹)]

pŏlȳclin'ic, n. Clinic devoted to various diseases, general hospital. [POLY-; altered in sense & form f. POLICLINIC]

pŏlȳg'amous, a. Having more than one wife or (less usu.) husband at once, so **pŏlȳgăm'ıc** a., ~IST, ~Y¹, nn.; (zool.) having more than one mate; (bot.) bearing some flowers with stamens only, some with pistils only, some with both, on same or on different plants. [f. late Gk *polugamos* (polu- POLY-+-*gamos* marrying)]

pŏl'ȳglŏt, a. & n. Of many languages; (person) speaking or writing several languages; (book, esp. Bible) with text and translation into several languages. Hence **polȳglŏtt'al, polȳglŏtt'ıc,** aa., ~TISM n. [f. Gk *poluglōttos* (polu- POLY- + *glōtta* tongue)]

pŏl'ȳgon, n. Figure (usu. plane rectilineal) with many (usu. more than four) angles or sides; ~ *of forces*, ~ illustrating theorem relating to number of forces act-

ing at a point. Hence **polȳg'onAL** a., **polȳg'onAL**LY² adv. [f. LL f. Gk *polugōnon* neut. adj. as n. (*polu*- POLY-+-*gōnos* -angled)]

Polȳg'onum, n. Genus of plants including knotgrass, snakeweed, etc. [f. Gk *polugonon* (polu- POLY-+*gonu* knee)]

pŏlȳhis'tor, n. Man of varied learning, great scholar. [f. Gk *poluistōr* (polu POLY-+*histōr*, see HISTORY)]

Polȳhym'nia, n. The MUSE¹ of sacred song. [L, f. Gk *Polumnia* (POLY-, HYMN)]

pŏl'ȳmăth, n. = POLYHISTOR. So **polȳm'athy¹** n. [f. Gk *polumathēs* (polu- POLY-+*math*- st. of *manthanō* learn)]

Polȳnē's|ia (-sha), n. Small islands in Pacific Ocean east of Australia. Hence ~IAN (-shn) a. [f. POLY- + Gk *nēsos* island]

polȳn'ia, n. Space of open water in midst of ice, esp. in arctic seas. [f. Russ. *poluinya* (*pole* field)]

pŏl'ȳp(e), n. Kinds of animal of low organization, e.g. hydra; individual of some compound organisms. [F (-pe), as POLYPUS]

pŏl'ȳparȳ, n. Common stem or supporting structure of a colony of polyps. [-*ary* = -ARIUM]

polȳp'idom (or pŏl²), n. = prec. [f. POLYPUS+L *domus* house]

pŏl'ȳpīte, n. Individual polyp. [-ITE¹]

pŏl'ȳpŏd, a. & n. (Animal) with many feet. [f. F *polypode* f. Gk as POLYPUS]

pŏl'ȳpŏdȳ, n. Kinds of ferns, esp. (common ~) species growing on moist rocks, walls, trees, etc. [f. L f. Gk *polupodion*, as POLYPUS]

pŏl'ȳp|oid, a. Of, like, a polyp or a polypus. So ~OUS a. [-OID]

pŏl'ȳpus, n. (pl. -*pī*). Kinds of tumour, usu. with ramifications like tentacles. [L, f. Gk *polupous* cuttle-fish, polypus in nose (polu-POLY+-*pous* -*podos* footed)]

pŏlȳsyllăb'|ic, a. (Of word) having many syllables; marked by polysyllables. Hence ~ICALLY adv. [f. LL f. Gk *polusullabos* (as foll.)+-IC]

pŏlȳsyll'able, n. Polysyllabic word. [f. med. L *polysyllaba* (*vox* word), see POLY- & SYLLABLE]

pŏlȳtěch'nic (-k-), a. & n. Dealing with, devoted to, various arts, as ~ *school*; *P*~ (*Institution*), technical school, ‖ esp. one in London orig. opened 1838. [f. F *polytechnique* f. Gk *polutekhnos* (*polu*- POLY-+ *tekhnē* art), see -IC]

pŏl'ȳthe|ism, n. Belief in, worship of, many gods or more than one god. So ~IST n., ~*is'*TIC a. [f. F *polythéisme* f. Gk *polutheos* of many gods (*polu*- POLY-+ *theos* god), see -ISM]

pŏm, n. POMERANIAN dog; POMMY. [abbr.]

pomace (pŭm'ĭs), n. Mass of crushed apples in cider-making before or after juice is pressed out; any pulp; refuse of fish etc. after oil has been extracted, used as fertilizer. [f. med. L *pomacium* cider f. L *pomum* apple]

pomade' (-ahd, -ād), n., & v.t. **1.** Scented ointment (perh. orig. from apples) for hair & skin of head. **2.** v.t. Anoint with ~. [f. F *pommade* f. It. *pomata* f. med. L (L *pomum* apple, -ADE)]

pŏm'ander (*or* pomăn²), n. (hist.). Ball of mixed aromatic substances carried in box, bag, etc., as preservative against infection; ball of gold, silver, etc., in which ~ was carried. [alt. f. 16th c. *pomamber* f. AF *pome ambre f. OF *pome d'ambre* (*pome* apple + *ambre* AMBER)]

Pomard', **Pomm-**, (-ahr), n. A red Burgundy wine. [~, village in France]

pomăt'um, n., & v.t. = POMADE. [f. L *pomum* apple + -*atum* -ATE¹]

pŏm'bĕ, n. Intoxicating drink from various kinds of grain & fruit in Africa. [native]

pōme, n. (Bot.) succulent INFERIOR fruit with firm fleshy body enclosing carpels forming the core, e.g., apple, pear, quince, so pomIF'EROUS a.; (poet.) apple; metal ball. [ME, f. OF, f. Rom. *poma pl. of *pomum* fruit, apple]

pōme'grănate (-mg-; *also* pŭm-), n. Fruit of a tree native to N. Africa & W. Asia, a large red berry about size of orange with tough golden or orange rind & acid reddish pulp enveloping seeds; the tree. [ME, f. OF POME *grenate* = L (*malum*) *granatum* (GRAIN, -ATE²); cf. GRENADE]

pom'elō (pŭm-), n. (pl. ~s). Small shaddock or grape-fruit. [orig. unkn.]

Pŏmerăn'ian, a. & n. Of Pomerania on S. coast of Baltic; ~ (*dog*), small dog with long silky hair, pointed muzzle, & pricked ears. [-AN]

pŏm'frĕt, n. Fish found in Indian & Pacific Oceans, used as food. [prob. ult. f. Port. *pampo*; cf. PAMPANO]

‖ **pŏm'frĕt-cāke**, n. Liquorice sweetmeat made at Pontefract (earlier Pomfret) in Yorks.

pōm'iculture, n. Fruit-growing. [f. L *pomum* fruit + CULTURE]

Pommard. See POMARD.

pomm'el (pŭm-), n., & v.t. (-ll-). **1.** Rounded knob esp. at end of sword-hilt; upward projecting front part of saddle. **2.** v.t. Strike or beat (as) with ~; beat with fists. [ME, f. OF *pomel* f. Rom. *pomellum dim. as POME]

pŏmm'ў, n. (sl.). British immigrant to Australia or New Zealand. [orig. uncert.]

pomŏl'og|ў, n. Science of fruit-growing. Hence **pōmolŏ'ɡICAL** a., **~IST** n. [as POME + -LOGY]

Pomōn'a, n. (Rom. myth.) goddess of fruits; ~ *green* (in which yellow predominates). [L]

pŏmp, n. Splendid display, splendour; (pl.) *the* ~*s & vanity of this wicked world.* [ME, f. OF *pompe* f. L f. Gk *pompē* procession, pomp, (*pempō* send)]

Pŏm'padour (-ōōr), n. Marquise de ~,

mistress of Louis XV; (attrib., designating) style of hair-dressing, cut of bodice, etc.

pŏm'panō, n. (pl. ~s). Kinds of W.-Ind. & N.-Amer. fish esteemed for food. [f. Sp. *pámpano*]

‖ **Pŏm'pey**, n. (sl.). Portsmouth.

pŏm'pier, a. ~ *ladder*, fireman's scaling ladder. [F, = fireman (as PUMP, see -IER)]

pŏm'-pŏm, n. Long-range Maxim automatic quick-firing gun. [imit.]

pŏm'pŏn (& see Ap.), n. Ornamental tuft or bunch of ribbon, flowers, etc., on women's & children's hats & shoes; round tuft on soldier's cap, front of shako, etc. [F, of unkn. orig.]

pŏm'pous, a. Magnificent, splendid; self--important, consequential, (of language) inflated, so pŏmpos'ITY n. Hence ~LY² adv., ~NESS n. [ME, f. LL *pomposus* (as POMP, see -OUS)]

pōnce (-ns), n. (sl.). Souteneur. [orig. unkn.]

pŏn'ceau (-sō), n. Poppy colour, bright red. [F]

pŏn'chō, n. (pl. ~s). S.-Amer. cloak, oblong piece of cloth with slit in middle for head; cape for cycling etc. on same plan. [native]

pŏnd, n., & v.t. & i. **1.** Small body of still water artificially formed by hollowing or embanking; (joc.) the sea; cf. HERRING-~; ~*life*, animals esp. invertebrates that live in ~s; ~*weed*, kinds of aquatic herb growing in still water. **2.** v.t. Hold *back*, dam *up*, (stream); (v.i., of water) form a pool or ~. [ME, app. var. of POUND²]

pŏn'dage, n. Capacity of pond; storage of water. [-AGE]

pŏn'der, v.t. & i. Weigh mentally, think over, (matter, *how*, etc.); think *on*, muse *over*. Hence ~inGLY² adv. [ME, f. OF *ponderer* f. L *ponderare* (*pondus -eris* weight)]

pŏn'der|able, a. Having appreciable weight (lit. & fig.). Hence ~ABIL'ITY n. [f. LL *ponderabilis* (as prec., see -BLE)]

pŏnderā'tion, n. Weighing, balancing, (lit. & fig.). [f. L *ponderatio* (as prec., see -ATION)]

pŏn'derous, a. Heavy; unwieldy; laborious; (of style) dull, tedious. Hence or cogn. pŏnderos'ITY, ~NESS, nn., ~LY² adv. [ME, f. OF *ponderous* f. L *ponderosus* (*pondus -eris* weight, see -OUS)]

pŏn'e¹, n. Leader('s partner) in some card games. [L, 2nd sing. imperat. of *ponere* place]

pōne², n. Maize bread, esp. as made by N.-Amer. Indians; fine light bread made with milk, eggs, etc.; cake, loaf, of this. [native]

pongee (pŭnjē'), n. Soft unbleached kind of Chinese silk. [perh. f. Chin. *pun-chi* own loom]

pŏn'gō (-ngg-), n. (Early name for) a large anthropoid African ape; (improp.) orang--outang. [native]

pŏn'iard (-yard), n., & v.t. Dagger; (v.t.) stab with ~. [f. F *poignard* (*poing* fist f. L *pugnus*, -ARD)]

pŏns (-nz), n. ~ *ăsĭnor'um*, bridge of asses, i.e. 5th proposition of 1st book of Euclid (' the angles at the base of an isosceles triangle are equal to one another '), hence, anything found difficult by beginners; ~ (*Varōl'ĭi*), band of nerve-fibres in brain [f. *Varoli*, Italian anatomist]. [L, = bridge]

pŏn'tĭfĕx, n. (pl. *-ĭf'ĭces* pr. -ēz). (Rom. ant.) member of principal college of priests in Rome, P~ *maximus*, head of this; = foll. [L]

pŏn'tĭff, n. (Also *sovereign* ~) the Pope; bishop; chief priest. [f. F *pontife* f. prec.]

pŏntĭf'ical, a. & n. 1. Of, befitting, a pontiff; assuming infallibility, pompously dogmatic. 2. n. Office-book of Western Church containing forms for rites to be performed by bishops; (pl.) vestments & insignia of bishop. Hence~LY² adv. [ME, f. L *pontificalis* (as PONTIFEX, see -AL)]

pŏntĭfĭcăl'ĭa, n. pl. Pontificals. [L, neut. pl. as prec.]

pŏntĭf'icate, n., & v.i. Office of pontifex, bishop, or pope; period of this; (v.i., *pr.* -āt) = foll. [f. L *pontificatus* (as PONTIFEX, see -ATE¹)]

pŏn'tĭfў, v.i. Play the pontiff, assume airs of infallibility. [f. F *pontifier* f. med. L *pontificare* (as PONTIFEX), see -FY]

pŏnt-lĕv'ĭs (or pawn levē'), n. Drawbridge. [F]

pŏntoneer', -nier (-nēr), n. One who has charge of pontoons or of construction of a pontoon-bridge. [f. F *pontonnier*, see foll. & -EER]

pŏntoon'¹, n., & v.t. Flat-bottomed boat used as ferry-boat etc.; one of several boats, hollow metal cylinders, etc. used to support temporary bridge; = CAISSON (not in first sense); (v.t.) cross (river) by means of ~s. [f. F *ponton* f. L *ponto -onis* (*pons -ntis* bridge, see -OON)]

‖ pŏntoon'², n.=VINGT(-ET)-UN. [prob. corruption]

pŏn'y̆, n. Horse of any small breed, esp. not more than 13 or (pop.) 14 hands; ‖ (sl.) £25. [f. Sc. *powney* prob. f. OF *poulenet* little foal dim. of *poulain* f. LL *pullamen* (*pullus* foal)]

pŏŏd, n. Russian weight, 36 lb. avoirdupois. [f. Russ. *pudu* f. LG or Norse *pund* POUND]

pŏŏ'dle, n., & v.t. Kinds of pet dog with long curling hair often clipped & shaved fantastically; (v.t.) clip & shave (dog) thus. [f. G *pudel*(*hund*) f. *pudeln* splash in water, see PUDDLE²]

pŏŏ'dle-fāk|er, n. (sl.). Youth too much given to tea-parties and ladies' society generally. So ~ing vbl n.

pooh (pŏŏ, pŏŏh), int. expr. impatience or contempt. [imit.]

Pooh-Bah' (pŏŏb-), n. Holder of many offices at once. [person in W. S. Gilbert's *The Mikado*]

pooh-pooh' (pŏŏpŏŏ'), v.t. Express contempt for, make light of, as *he ~ed the idea*. [see POOH]

pŏŏ'ja. Var. of PUJA.

‖ pŏŏ'ka, n. Hobgoblin. [Ir. *pūca*]

pŏŏ'kŏŏ, puku (pŏŏ'kŏŏ), n. Red antelope of S. Central Africa. [f. Zulu *mpuku*]

pŏŏl¹, n., & v.t. 1. Small body of still water, usu. of natural formation; puddle of any liquid; deep still place in river. 2. v.t. Make (hole) for insertion of wedge in quarrying, undermine (coal). [OE *pōl*, MLG *pōl*, f. WG *pōlo-]

pŏŏl², n., & v.t. 1. (In cards) collective amount of players' stake & fines; receptacle for these. 2. ‖ Game on billiard-table in which each player has ball of different colour with which he tries to pocket the others in fixed order, winner taking the whole stakes. 3. (Collective stakes in) a joint gambling venture (*football* ~, form of gambling in which a proportion of the entry money for the competition is awarded in prizes to those who correctly forecast the results of certain football matches). 4. Arrangement between competing parties by which prices are fixed & business divided to do away with competition. 5. Common fund, e.g. of the profits of separate firms; common supply of persons, commodities, etc. (also attrib., as ~ *petrol*). 6. v.t. Throw into common fund, share in common; (of transport organizations etc.) share (traffic, receipts). [f. F *poule* (= hen) in same sense, in E early assoc. w. prec.]

pŏŏn, n. E.-Indian tree; ~-*oil*, oil from seeds of this, used in medicine & for lamps. [f. Sinhalese *puna*]

pŏŏn'ah (-*a*), a. ~ *painting* (on rice or other thin paper in imitation of oriental work); ~ *brush*, *paper* (used for this). [*Poona*, Indian city]

pŏŏp¹, n., & v.t. 1. Stern of ship; aftermost & highest deck. 2. v.t. (Of wave) break over stern of (ship); (of ship) receive (wave) over stern. Hence (-)~ED²(-pt) a. [ME, f. OF *pupe* f. Rom. *puppa f. L *puppis*]

pŏŏp². See POPE³.

‖ pŏŏp³, n. (sl.). Foolish insignificant person. [abbr. NINCOMPOOP]

poor, a. 1. Wanting means to procure comforts or necessaries of life, needy, indigent; ill supplied, deficient, (*in a possession or quality*); (of soil) unproductive; scanty, inadequate, less than is expected, as *the crop was* ~, a ~ *three weeks' holiday*; (of visibility) bad; paltry, sorry, as *that is a* ~ *consolation*; spiritless, despicable, as *he is a* ~ *creature*; humble, insignificant, (often iron. or joc., as *in my* ~ *opinion*); (expr. pity or sympathy) unfortunate, hapless, as ~ *fellow!*, *the* ~ *child is inconsolable*; *the* ~, (esp.) those dependent on charitable or parochial relief. **2.** ~*-box*, money-box esp. in church for relief of the ~; ~*-house*, workhouse; ~*-law* (relating to support of paupers; hist.); ~ *man's weather-glass*, pimpernel; ‖ ~*-rate*, rate, assessment, for relief or support of the ~; ~*-spirited*, timid, cowardly. [ME & OF *pov(e)re*, *poure*, f. L *pauper*]

poor′ly, adv. & pred. a. **1.** Scantily, defectively; with no great success; meanly, contemptibly. **2.** adj. Unwell, as *he is (looking) very* ~. [prec. + -LY[2]; pred. a. prob. orig. adv.]

poor′ness, n. Defectiveness; lack of some good quality or constituent. [POOR + -NESS]

‖ *poort* (pōrt), n. (S. Afr.). Pass, narrower than a nek. [Du., = gate(way)]

pŏp[1], v.i. & t. (-pp-). Make small quick explosive sound as of cork when drawn; let off (fire-arm etc.); fire gun (*at* bird etc.); put (thing *in*, *out*, *down*, etc.) quickly or suddenly; move, go, come, (*in* etc.) thus; put (question) abruptly, esp. (colloq.)~ *the question*, propose marriage; ‖ (sl.) pawn; *parch (maize) till it bursts open, ~*corn*, maize so parched; ~*gun*, child's toy gun shooting pellets by compression of air with piston, (derog.) inefficient fire-arm; ‖ ~*shop*, pawnbroker's shop. [imit.]

pŏp[2], n., adv., & int. **1.** Abrupt explosive sound; dot, spot, esp. in marking sheep etc.; (colloq.) effervescing drink, esp. ginger-beer or champagne; ‖ (sl.) pawning, esp. *in* ~, in pawn. **2.** int. or adv. *Heard it go* (make the sound) ~ *!*; ~ *goes the weasel*, country dance in which dancer darted under arms of others to his partner. [as prec.]

pŏp[3], n. (colloq.). Popular concert, as *Saturday* ~*s*; popular disc, record, etc. [abbr.]

‖ **Pŏp**[4], n. Social & debating club at Eton. [said to be so called f. L *popina* cookshop, or E *lollipop shop* (orig. meeting-place)]

pop[5]. See POPPA.

pōpe[1], n. **1.** Bishop of Rome as head of Roman Catholic Church; (fig.) person assuming or credited with infallibility etc. **2.** P~ *Joan*, fabulous female ~, a card-game; ~*'s eye*, lymphatic gland surrounded with fat in middle of leg of mutton; ~*'s head*, round long-handled broom; ~*'s nose*, = PARSON's *nose*. Hence ~*'DOM (-pd-) n., ~*'LESS (-pl-) a. [OE *pāpa* f. eccl. L *papa* f. late Gk *papas* = Gk *pappas* father, cf. PAPA]

pōpe[2], n. Parish priest of Greek Church in Russia etc. [f. Russ. *popu* app. f. WG *papo* as prec.]

pōpe[3], **pōōp**, n., & v.t. Place in thigh on which blow is painful or paralysing, esp. *take* person's ~, strike this; (v.t.) take the ~ of. [orig. unkn.]

pōp′ery, n. Papal system, Roman Catholic religion, (in hostile use, esp. *no* ~*!*). [f. POPE[1] + -ERY]

pŏp′-eyed (-īd), a. (colloq.). Having bulging eyes; open-eyed (with surprise etc.). [POP[1]]

pŏp′injay, n. (Arch.) parrot; (hist.) figure of parrot on pole as mark to shoot at; conceited person; ‖ (dial.)green woodpecker. [f. OF *papingay* etc., cf. med. Gk *papagas*, Arab. *babagha*, prob. imit. & of Afr. orig.]

pōp′ish, a. Of popery, papistical. Hence ~LY[2] adv. [f. POPE[1] + -ISH[1]]

pŏp′lar, n. Kinds of large trees of rapid growth (often w. allusion to straightness of trunk); *trembling* ~, aspen. [ME, f. OF *poplier* f. L *pōpulus* + -IER]

‖ **Pōp′larism**, n. Policy of giving extravagant out-relief (as practised by the Poplar Board of Guardians *c.* 1920); any similar policy tending to raise the rates. [-ISM]

pŏp′lin, n. (Formerly) woven fabric of silk warp & worsted weft with corded surface; (now usu.) fabric of mercerized cotton. [f. F *popeline* f. It. *papalina* PAPAL, from the papal town Avignon where it was made]

pōplit′eal, a. Of the ham, of the hollow at back of knee, as ~ *artery*, ~ *tendons* (hamstrings). [f. L *poples -itis* ham, see -AL]

*pŏpp′a, *pŏp, n. Papa. [f. *papa*]

pŏpp′et, n. ‖ (Colloq.) small person, esp. as term of endearment; lathe-head; (naut.) short piece of wood for various purposes; ~*-head*, lathe-head, ‖ (mining) frame at top of shaft supporting pulleys for ropes used in hoisting; ~*-valve*, = PUPPET-*valve*. [ME *popet*, *-ette*, corresp. to F (16th c.) *poupette* doll, dim. f. Rom. *puppa* f. L *pupa* girl; see PUPPET]

pŏpp′ing, n. In vbl senses; (crick.) ~*-crease* [perh. = striking-crease], line **4** feet in front of & parallel to wicket within which batsman must keep one foot grounded. [-ING[1]]

pŏp′ple, v.i., & n. (Of water) tumble about, toss to & fro; (n.) rolling, tossing, ripple. Hence **pŏpp′lY**[2] a. [ME, prob. f. MDu. *popelen*, of imit. orig.]

pŏpp′y, n. Kinds of herbs having milky juice with narcotic properties & showy flowers of scarlet or other colour; *opium* ~, species from which opium is obtained; *Flanders poppies* (sacred to dead of 1914– –18 war; also as name of those made for & sold on *P~ Day*, Saturday nearest 11 Nov.); ~*-head*, seed capsule of ~, (archit.) ornamental top to end of church seat; *Shirley* ~, cultivated variety of common corn ~ [f. Shirley Vicarage, Croydon, where first produced]. Hence **pŏpp′iED**[2] (-pĭd) a. [OE *popig*, ult. f. L *papaver*]

*pŏpp′ycŏck, n. (sl.). Nonsense.

pŏp′sy(-wŏpsy), n. An endearing appellation for a girl. [extension of *pop* abbr. of POPPET, with dim. suf.]

pŏp′ūlace, n. The common people; the rabble. [F, f. It. *popolaccio* (*popolo* PEOPLE + -*accio* pejorative suf.)]

Q

pŏp′ūlar, a. Of, carried on by, the people, as ~ *election, meetings, tumult*; adapted to the understanding, taste, or means, of the people, as *in* ~ *language,* ~ *science, at* ~ (low) *prices*; liked, admired, by the people or by people generally or *with* specified class, as ~ *teachers, the* ~ *hero, is* ~ *with his men,* so **pŏpūlă′rity** n.; prevalent among the people, as ~ *falla-cies;* ~ *front* (pol.), party representing Left elements. Hence ~**LY²** adv. [ME, f. AF *populer* or L *popularis* (cf. foll.), as PEOPLE]

pŏp′ūlariz|e, -is|e (-ĭz), v.t. Make popu-lar, cause (person, principle, etc.) to be generally known or liked; extend (suffrage etc.) to the common people; present (technical subject etc.) in popular form. Hence ~**A′TION** n. [-IZE]

pŏp′ūlāte, v.t. Inhabit, form the popula-tion of, (country, town, etc.); supply with inhabitants, as *a densely* ~*d district.* [f. med. L *populare* (as PEOPLE)]

pŏpūlā′tion, n. Degree in which place is populated; total number of inhabitants, the people of a country etc.; *the* in-habitants of a place (*the* ~ *turned out to welcome him*). [f. LL *populatio* (as prec., see -ATION)]

pŏp′ūl|ist, n. Adherent of U.S. political party aiming at public control of rail-ways, graduated income-tax, etc., formed 1892; adherent of Russian political party advocating collectivism. So ~**ISM** n., ~**is′tic** a. [f. L *populus* PEOPLE + -IST]

pŏp′ūlous, a. Thickly inhabited. Hence ~**NESS** n. [ME, f. L *populosus* (as PEOPLE, see -OUS)]

pŏrb′eagle, n. Mackerel-shark. [Cornish dial., of unkn. orig.]

pŏrce′lain (-slĭn), n. Fine kind of earthen-ware with translucent body & transparent glaze; thing made of this; (fig., attrib.) delicate, fragile; ~*-shell,* cowrie; ~ *clay,* kaolin. Hence or cogn. ~**OUS** (-slĭn-), **pŏrcĕllăn′EOUS**, **pŏrcĕllăn′IC**, **pŏrcĕl′lanous**, aa. [f. F *porcelaine* Venus shell, porcelain, f. It. *porcellana* (*porcella* dim. of *porco* hog f. L *porcus*)]

pŏrce′lainize (-slĭn-), **-ise** (-ĭz), v.t. Con-vert (clay, shale, etc.) into porcelain or similar substance. [-IZE]

pŏrch, n. Covered approach to entrance of building; *the P~,* colonnade at Athens to which Zeno & his disciples resorted, (hence) Stoic school or philosophy (cf. ACADEMY, GARDEN, LYCEUM). Hence ~**ED²** (-cht), ~′**LESS**, aa. [ME, f. OF *porche* f. L *porticus*]

pŏr′cine, a. Of or like swine. [F (-*in,* -*ine*), f. L *porcinus* (*porcus* hog, see -INE¹)]

pŏrc′ūpin|e, n. ‖ Rodent quadruped with body & tail covered with erectile spines; kinds of machine with many spikes or teeth, e.g. for heckling flax etc.; (attrib., applied to animals with spines etc.) ~*e ant-eater, crab, fish, grass.* Hence ~**ISH¹**,

~**Y²**, aa. [ME, f. OF *porc espin* ult. f. L *porcus* hog + *spina* thorn; earlier also *porkenpick* f. F *porc-épic* (L *spicus*=*spica* spike) & *porpentine*]

pōre¹, n. Minute opening (esp. in skin of animal body) through which fluids may pass. [ME, f. OF f. L f. Gk *poros* passage, pore]

pōre², v.i. & t. ~ *over,* be absorbed in studying (book etc.), (fig.) meditate, think intently upon, (subject); (arch.) look intently *at, on, over;* ~ *one's eyes out,* tire them by close reading. [ME *puren, pouren,* of unkn. orig.]

pōrge, v.t. (Jew. ritual). Make (slaugh-tered beast) ceremonially clean by re-moving sinews etc. Hence **pōr′gER¹** n. [app. f. L as PURGE]

*pōrg′y (-g-), n. Perch-like salt-water fish; sea-bream (applied also, esp. locally, to many other fish). [of var. orig.; cf. *porgo, pargo* (Sp.), *paugie* (Amer.-Ind.)]

pōr′ism (or pŏ′r-), n. (math.). Proposition concerned with the conditions that will render a given problem capable of in-numerable solutions; corollary. So **pōr-ismăt′IC, pŏris′tIC**, aa. [f. LL f. Gk *porisma -matos* (*porizō* deduce)]

pŏrk, n. Flesh (esp. fresh) of swine used as food; ~*-butcher,* one who slaughters pigs for sale; ~ *pie* (of minced etc. ~); ‖ ~*-pie hat* (with flat crown & brim turned up all round). [ME & OF *porc* f. L *porcus* hog]

pŏrk′er, n. Pig raised for food; young fattened hog, so **pŏrk′ET¹** n. [-ER¹]

pŏrk′ling, n. Young or small pig. [-LING¹]

pŏrk′y, a. Of, like, pork, esp. (colloq.) fleshy, fat. [-Y²]

pŏrn|o-, comb. form of Gk *pornē* harlot, as: ~*ŏc′racy,* dominant influence of harlots, esp. in government of Rome in 10th c.; ~*ŏg′raphy,* description of manners etc. of harlots, treatment of obscene subjects in literature, inflammatory literature, so ~*ŏg′rapher* n., ~*ograph′ic* a.

pōr′oplăs′tic (or pŏ′r-), a. (surg.). (Of felt) both porous & plastic. [as PORE¹ + PLASTIC]

pōr′ous, a. Full of pores (lit. & fig.). Hence or cogn. **pōros′ITY, ~NESS**, nn. [ME; -OUS]

pŏrph′yrў, n. Hard rock anciently quar-ried in Egypt, composed of crystals of white or red feldspar in red ground-mass; (geol.) unstratified or igneous rock hav-ing homogeneous base in which crystals of one or more minerals are disseminated. [ME; ult. f. Gk *porphuros* purple]

pŏr′poise (-pus), n. Sea animal of the whale order about five feet long with blunt rounded snout. [ME *porpays, -peys, -poys,* f. OF *porpeis* f. L *porcus* hog + *piscis* fish]

pŏrrā′ceous (-shus), a. Leek-green. [f. L *porraceus* (*porrum* leek, see -ACEOUS)]

pŏrrĕct′, v.t. (Nat. hist.) stretch out (part of body); (eccl. law) tender, submit, (document). [f. L *porrigere* *-rect-* (*por-* PRO- + *regere* direct)]

|| **pŏ′rridge**, n. Soft food made by stirring oatmeal or other meal or cereal in boiling water or milk; *keep* one's *breath to cool* one's ∼, keep one's advice etc. for one's own use. [16th c., alt. f. POTTAGE]

pŏrrĭg′ō, n. (path.). Scaly eruption of scalp. So **pŏrri′ginous** a. [L, gen. *-ginis*]

pŏ′rringer (-j-), n. Small basin from which soup etc. is eaten esp. by children. [earlier *potager*, *pottinger* (as PORRIDGE, see -ER[1]); for *-n-* cf. *passenger*]

pŏrt[1], n. Harbour (lit. & fig.); town, place, possessing harbour, esp. one where customs officers are stationed; (in proper names) *P∼ Arthur, Said*, etc.; *P∼ of London Authority*, corporate body set up by P∼-of-London Act 1908 for control of ∼ & docks; *free*∼, one open for merchants of all nations to load & unload in, (also) exemption for imports or exports; *close* ∼ (lying up river); CINQUE PORTS; ∼ *admiral* (in command of naval ∼). [OE, f. L *portus*; ME reinforced f. OF *port*]

pŏrt[2], n. || Gate, gateway, esp. of walled town (chiefly Sc.); (naut.) opening in side of ship for entrance, loading, etc., (also) = ∼*hole*; (mech.) aperture for passage of steam, water, etc.; *curved mouthpiece of some bridle-bits*; ∼*hole*, aperture in ship's side for admission of light & air, or (formerly) for pointing cannon through. [ME & OF *porte* f. L *porta*; OE *port* dir. f. L]

pŏrt[3], n. External deportment, carriage, bearing; (mil.) position taken in porting arms. [ME & OF *port*, as foll.]

pŏrt[4], v.t. (mil.). Carry (rifle, or other weapon) diagonally across & close to the body, with barrel etc. opposite middle of left shoulder, esp. ∼ *arms!* [f. F *porter* f. L *portare* carry]

pŏrt[5], n., adj. v.t. & i. (naut.). 1. (Also formerly *larboard*) left-hand side of ship looking forward (cf. STARBOARD), as *put the helm to* ∼ or *a-*∼; (attrib.) *on your* ∼ (left) *bow* etc. 2. v.t. Turn (helm, or abs.) to left side of ship; (v.i., of ship) turn to her ∼ side. [orig. obsc.; poss. f. PORT[1] or PORT[2] (naut.), describing the side on which the 'port' was]

pŏrt[6], n. Strong sweet dark-red (occas. white) wine of Portugal. [shortened f. *Oporto*, city of Portugal]

pŏrt′able, a. & n. Movable (article), convenient for carrying, as ∼ *furnace, radio*. Hence **pŏrtabil′ity** n. [ME, f. OF, f. LL *portabilis* (*portare* carry, -BLE)]

pŏrt′age, n. & v.t. 1. Carrying, carriage; cost of this; *mariner's* ∼, space allowed to mariner for own venture or to be let by him for freight in lieu of wages; carrying of boats or goods between two navigable waters, place at which this is necessary. 2. v.t. Convey (boat, goods) over a ∼. [ME & OF *portage*, = med. L *portaticum*, *-agium*, as PORT[4], -AGE]

pŏrt′al[1], n. Door(way), gate(way), esp. elaborate one. [ME, f. OF, f. med. L *portale* neut. adj. as n. (*porta* gate, see -AL]

pŏrt′al[2], a. (anat.). Of the *porta* or transverse fissure of the liver, as ∼ *vein* (conveying blood to liver). [f. med. L *portalis* as prec.]

portămĕn′tō, n. (mus.). Gliding continuously from one pitch to another; (to be played) in a manner intermediate between LEGATO and STACCATO (erron.). [It.]

pŏrt′ative, a. Serving to carry or support. [OF (*-if, -ive*), f. L *portare* carry, see -IVE]

pŏrtcŭll′is, n. Strong heavy grating sliding up & down in vertical grooves at sides of gateway in fortress etc. Hence ∼ED[2] (-st) a. [ME, f. OF *porte coleice* sliding door (*porte* door f. L *porta*, see COULISSE)]

Pŏrte, n. *The* (*Sublime* or *Ottoman*) ∼ (hist.), Ottoman court at Constantinople, Turkish government to 1923. [F (*la Sublime* ∼), transl. of Turk. title of central office of Ottoman government]

porte-, comb. form of F *porte-* imperat. of *porter* carry in wds meaning '-case', '-holder', as: *port(e)-cray′on*, metal tube or other holder for crayon; ∼*feuille* (-fü′ye), portfolio; ∼*-monnaie* (-monē′), flat leathern purse or pocket-book.

porte-cochère (pŏrtkoshār′), n. Gateway & passage for vehicles through house into courtyard. [F]

pŏrtĕnd′, v.t. Foreshow, foreshadow, as an omen; give warning of, as *this* ∼*s a renewal of the conflict*. [ME, f. L *portendere -tent-* (*por-* PRO- + *tendere* stretch)]

pŏrt′ĕnt, n. Omen, significant sign; prodigy, marvellous thing. So **pŏrtĕn′tous** a., **pŏrtĕn′tously**[2] adv. [f. L *portentum* as prec.]

|| **pŏrt′er**[1], n. Gate-keeper, door-keeper. [ME & AF, f. LL *portarius* (*porta* door, see -ER[2])]

pŏrt′er[2], n. 1. Person employed to carry burdens, esp. railway servant who handles luggage, whence ∼AGE (4) n. 2. Dark-brown bitter beer brewed from charred or browned malt [perh. orig. made esp. for ∼8]. 3. *∼-house*, house at which ∼ etc. were retailed, (also) one where steaks, chops, etc., were served (∼*-house steak*, choice cut of beef from region of undercut); || ∼*'s knot*, pad resting on shoulders & secured to forehead used by ∼s in carrying loads. [ME, f. OF *porteour* f. LL *portatorem* (*portare* carry, see -OR)]

pŏrt′fire, n. Device for firing rockets, igniting explosives in mining, etc. [after F *porte-feu* (PORTE-, FIRE)]

pŏrtfŏl′iō, n. (pl. ∼s). Case for keeping loose sheets of paper, drawings, etc.; list of investments held by company etc.; (fig.) office of Minister of State; *Minister without* ∼, Cabinet Minister who is not in charge of any Department of State. [18th c., f. It. *portafogli* (*porta* imperat. of *portare* carry + *foglio* leaf f. L *folium*)]

port'ico̅, n. (pl. ~s). Colonnade, roof supported by columns at regular intervals, usu. attached as porch to a building. [It., f. L *porticus* PORCH]

portière (pòrtyār'), n. Curtain hung over door(way). [F]

por'tion, n., & v.t. **1.** Part, share; (in restaurants) amount of a dish served to a customer; dowry, whence ~LESS (-sho-) a.; one's destiny, one's lot; *a* ~, some (*of* anything). **2.** v.t. Divide (thing) into shares, distribute *out*, assign (thing *to* person) as share; give dowry to. [ME, f. OF, f. L *portionem*; vb f. OF *portionner*]

Port'land, n. (Used for) ~ *prison*; ~ *cement*, artificial cement manufactured from chalk and clay, in colour rather like ~ *stone*, a valuable building limestone obtained from the Isle of ~. [Dorset peninsula]

port'l|y̆, a. Bulky, corpulent; of stately appearance. Hence ~iNESS n. [PORT³, -LY¹]

portmän'teau (-to̅), n. (pl. ~s, ~x, pr. -z). ‖ Leather trunk for clothes etc. opening into two equal parts; (fig.) factitious word blending the sounds & combining the meanings of two others (e.g. *slithy* = lithe & slimy). [f. F PORTE-(*manteau* MANTLE)]

por'tola'no̅ (-lah-), n. (hist.). Book of sailing directions with description of harbours etc. [f. It. (*porto* PORT¹)]

por'trait (-rĭt), n. Likeness of person or animal made by drawing, painting, photography, etc.; (fig.) type, similitude; verbal picture, graphic description. [F, p.p. as PORTRAY]

por'raitist (-rĭt-), n. One who paints or takes portraits. [-IST]

por'traiture (-richer), n. Portraying; portrait; graphic description. [ME, f. OF (PORTRAIT + -URE)]

portray', v.t. Make likeness of; describe graphically. Hence ~AL(2) n. [ME, f. OF *portraire* f. L PRO(*trahere tract-* draw)]

por'reeve, n. (Hist.) chief officer of town or borough; (now) officer inferior to mayor in some towns. [OE *port-gerēfa* (*port* town (now obs.), = PORT¹ or ²+ REEVE¹)]

por'ress, n. Female PORTER¹. [-ESS¹]

Portu̅guese' (-gēz), a. & n. (pl. same). (Native, language) of Portugal; ~ *man-of--war*, dangerous (sub-)tropical jellyfish with sail-shaped crest and poisonous sting, travelling rarely to Britain. [f. Port. *portuguez* f. med. L *portugalensis* (see -ESE)]

po̅se¹ (-z), v.t. & i., & n. **1.** Lay down (assertion, claim, etc.); propound (question); place (artist's model etc.) in certain attitude; assume an attitude, esp. for artistic purposes; set up, give oneself out, *as* (connoisseur etc.); (in dominoes) place first domino on table. **2.** n. Attitude of body or mind, esp. one assumed for effect, as *his philanthropy is a mere* ~; (dominoes) posing, right to ~. [(n. f. F *pose*)

f. F *poser* f. L *pausare* PAUSE; some senses by confus. w. L *ponere* place, cf. COMPOSE]

po̅se² (-z), v.t. Puzzle (person) with question or problem. [aphetic f. obs. *oppose* or OPPOSE]

po̅s'er (-z-), n. In vbl senses of prec., esp. puzzling question or problem. [-ER¹]

po̅seur' (-zēr', & see Ap.), n. Affected person. [F]

‖ **po̅sh**, a. (sl.). Smart, tiptop.

po̅s'it (-z-) v.t. Assume as fact, postulate; put in position, place, as ~*ed by natural agency*. [f. L *ponere posit-* place]

posi'tion (-z-), n., & v.t. **1.** Proposition, laying down of this. **2.** Bodily posture; *eastward* ~ (of priest at eucharist standing in front of altar & facing east). **3.** Mental attitude, way of looking at question. **4.** Place occupied by a thing; *in, out of*, ~ (proper place); (mil.) place where troops are posted for strategical purposes (*the* ~ *was stormed*), the being advantageously placed (*manœuvring for* ~); *in a* ~ *to do, state*, etc., enabled by circumstances or resources or information to. **5.** Situation of vowel in syllable, esp. (Gk & L pros.) of short vowel before two consonants, making the syllable metrically long. **6.** (fig.). Situation in relation to other persons or things, as *difficult for a person in my* ~. **7.** Rank, status, (*people of* ~, esp. upper & upper-middle classes); official employment. **8.** v.t. Place in ~, determine ~ of; (mil.) place or post (troops). Hence ~AL (-zĭsho-) a. [ME, f. OF, f. L *positionem* (as prec., see -ION]

po̅s'itive (-z-), a. & n. **1.** Formally laid down, artificially instituted, (opp. to *natural*), as ~ *laws*. **2.** Explicitly laid down, definite, admitting no question, as ~ *assertion, have no* ~ *proof, here is proof* ~. **3.** (Of person) convinced, confident in opinion, cocksure. **4.** (gram.). ~ (*degree of*) *adjective, adverb*, primary form expressing simple quality without comparison (cf. COMPARATIVE, SUPERLATIVE). **5.** Absolute, not relative; (colloq.) downright, out-&--out, as *he is a* ~ *nuisance*. **6.** Dealing only with matters of fact, practical, as ~ *philosophy*. **7.** Marked by presence, not absence, of qualities (cf. NEGATIVE). **8.** (Alg., of quantity) greater than zero (cf. NEGATIVE), ~ *sign* (+); tending in the direction naturally or arbitrarily taken as that of increase or progress, as *clockwise rotation is* ~. **9.** ~ *electricity* (of the kind produced by rubbing glass with silk, vitreous); ~ *pole*, (of magnet) north--seeking pole, (of earth) south pole. **10.** (photog.). Showing lights & shades as seen in nature (opp. NEGATIVE¹). **11.** ~ *organ*, small (orig. portable) organ used to supplement large one in church. **12.** n. ~ *degree*, adjective, quantity, etc. Hence ~LY² adv., ~NESS, po̅sitiv'ITY, nn., (-z-). [ME & OF *positif* f. L *positivus* (as POSIT, see -IVE]

po̅s'itiv|ism (-z-), n. Philosophical system

of Auguste Comte, recognizing only positive facts & observable phenomena; religious system founded on this. So ~ist n., ~is'tic a. [f. F *positivisme* (as prec., see -ISM)]

pŏs'itrŏn (-z-), n. A positive electron. [POSI(TIVE ELEC)TRON]

posŏl'ogў, n. Study of the quantities in which drugs should be administered; (Bentham's word for) mathematics. Hence **pŏsŏlŏ'ġICAL** a. [f. F *posologie* f. Gk *posos* how great, see -LOGY]

pŏss'ė, n. Body (*of* constables); strong force or company; ~ *cōmĭtāt'us*, body of men above age of 15 in a county, whom sheriff may summon to repress riot etc.; IN ³~. [L, = to be able, (med. L) power]

possĕss' (-z-), v.t. Hold as property, own; have (faculty, quality, etc.), as *they ~ a special value for us*; maintain (oneself, one's mind, soul, *in* patience etc.); (of demon or spirit) occupy, dominate, (person etc.), as ~*ed by a devil, you are surely* ~*ed*, (fig.) *he is* ~*ed by or with this idea, what*~*es you to think of such a thing?*; *like all* ~*ed*, with the utmost vehemence or energy; ~ *oneself of*, take, get for one's own; *be* ~*ed of*, own, have. So ~OR n., ~ORY a., (-zĕs-). [f. OF *possess(i)er* f. L *possidēre* -*sess*-]

posse'ssion (-zĕshn), n. Possessing; actual holding or occupancy; (law) visible power of exercising such control as attaches to (but may exist apart from) lawful ownership; *in* ~, (of thing) possessed, (of person) possessing; ~ *is nine* POINTS *of the law*; *in* ~ *of*, having in one's ~ (*am in* ~ *of a fine specimen*); *in the* ~ *of*, held by (*the specimen is in the* ~ *of the present writer*); *rejoice in the* ~ *of*, be so fortunate as to possess; thing possessed; (pl.) property, wealth; subject territory, esp. foreign dominions; DEMONIAC ~; SELF-~. [ME, f. OF f. L *possessionem* (as prec., see -ION)]

possĕss'ive (poz-), a. & n. 1. Of possession; showing a desire to possess; (gram.) indicating possession, as ~ *pronoun* (e.g. *my, mine, his, ours*), ~ *case* (e.g. *John's, the baker's*). 2. n.~ case or word. Hence ~LY² adv., ~NESS n. [f. L *possessivus* (as POSSESS, see -IVE)]

pŏss'ĕt, n. Drink made of hot milk curdled with ale, wine, etc., often flavoured with spices etc., formerly much used as remedy for colds etc. [ME *poshote*, orig. unkn.]

pŏssib'ilist, n. Member of (esp. Spanish republican or French socialist) political party aiming at those reforms only that are immediately practicable. [f. F *possibiliste* or Sp.-*ista* (as POSSIBLE, see -IST)]

pŏssibil'itў, n. State, fact, of being possible, as *the* ~*y of miracles, cannot by any* ~*y be in time, there is no* ~*y of his coming, it is within the range of* ~*y*; capability of being used, improved, etc.; thing that may exist or happen, as *what are the* ~*ies?, there are three* ~*ies*. [ME, f. OF

possibilite f. L *possibilitatem* (POSSIBLE, -TY)]

pŏss'ible, a. & n. 1. That can exist, be done, or happen, as *that is quite* ~, *it is scarcely* ~ *to say, it is* ~ (*that*) *he knows* or *may know, there are three* ~ *excuses* (that may be made), *provide against a* ~ *loss of men* (that may occur), *get all the assistance* ~; *come if* (it is) ~, *come as early as* ~ (as you can); tolerable to deal with, reasonable, intelligible, etc., as *only one* ~ *man among them*, cf. IMPOSSIBLE. 2. n. Highest ~ score esp. in rifle practice, as *scored a* ~ *at 800 yds*; ~ candidate, member of team, etc. (as in P~s v. *Probables*, teams for football etc. trial match); *do one's* ~, do all one can (imit. of F *faire son* ~). [ME, f. OF, or f. LL *possibilis* (posse be able, -BLE)]

pŏss'iblў, adv. In accordance with possibility, as *cannot* ~ *do it, how can I* ~?; perhaps, maybe, for all one knows to the contrary. [f. prec. +-LY³]

pŏss'um, n. (colloq.). = OPOSSUM; *play* ~, pretend to be unconscious (from ~'s habit of feigning death when attacked). [abbr.]

pŏst¹, n., & v.t. 1. Stout piece of timber usu. cylindrical or square & of considerable length placed vertically as support in building; stake, stout pole, for various purposes; BED¹, DOOR, GOAL, KING¹, LAMP, SIGN¹, ~; *starting, winning*, ~, ~ that marks starting, finishing, point in race. 2. Thick compact stratum of sandstone etc.; vertical mass of coal left as support in mine. 3. v.t. Stick (paper etc., usu. *up*) to ~ or in prominent place, advertise (fact, thing, person) by placard; ‖ (in colleges) place in list that is ~ed up the names of (unsuccessful students); publish name of (ship) as overdue or missing; placard (wall etc.) with bills. [OE *post* f. L *postis*; in ME reinforced by OF *post*]

pŏst², n. & adv. 1. (hist.). One of a series of men stationed with horses along roads at intervals, the duty of each being to ride forward with letters to next stage; courier, letter-carrier, mail-cart. 2. ‖ A single dispatch of letters, letters so dispatched; letters taken from ~-office or pillar-box on one occasion, as *I missed the morning* ~; ‖ letters delivered at one house on one occasion, as *the* ~ *has come, had a heavy* ~ *today*; ‖ official conveyance of letters, parcels, etc., as *send it by* ~; GENERAL, PARCEL, PENNY, ~; ~-office or postal letter-box, as *take it to the* ~; *by return of* ~, (orig.) by same courier who brought the dispatch, (now) by next mail in opposite direction. 3. (As title of newspaper) *Evening P*~ etc. 4. Sizes (about 20 × 16 in.) & kinds of writing--paper. 5. adv. With ~-horses, express, with haste, as *ride* ~. 6. ‖ ~-*bag*, mail-bag; ‖ ~-*boat*, mail-boat, (also) boat conveying travellers between certain points; ‖ ~-*boy*, letter-carrier, (also) postilion; ‖ ~'*card*, card for conveyance by ~ at lower rate than closed letter; ∼-*chaise* (-sh-), (hist.) travelling carriage hired from stage to stage or drawn by horses or hired; ‖ ∼-*free*, carried free of charge by ∼, or with postage prepaid; ∼-*haste'*, n. (arch.) & adv., (with) great expedition; ∼-*horse* (kept at inns etc. for use of ∼ or travellers); ∼'*man*, one who delivers or collects letters etc.; ∼'*mark*, (n.) official mark stamped on letter, esp. one giving place, date, & hour, of dispatch or arrival, & serving to cancel stamp, (v.t.) mark (envelope etc.) with this; ∼'*master*[1], official in charge of a ∼-office, P∼*master General*, minister at head of the postal service; ∼'*mastership*, office of ∼master; ∼'*mistress*, woman in charge of ∼-office; ∼-*office*, public department responsible for postal & telecommunication services, house or shop where postal business is carried on (GENERAL P∼-*Office*; ∼-*office* ORDER, *savings-bank*, see SAVE[1]); ∼-*paid*, on which postage has been paid; ∼-*town* (with ∼-office, esp. one that is not sub- -office of another). [c. 1500, f. F *poste* fem. f. It. f. Rom. (= med. L) *posta* = *posita* fem. p.p. of *ponere posit-* place]

pŏst[3], v.i. & t. ‖ Travel with relays of horses; travel with haste, hurry; ‖ put (letter etc.) into post-office or letter-box for transmission; *∼ (stick) no bills; (book-keep.) carry (entry) from auxiliary book to more formal one, esp. from day- -book or journal to ledger, (also ∼ *up*) complete (ledger etc.) thus, (fig., esp. in p.p., also ∼ *up*) supply (person) with full information. [f. prec.]

pŏst[4], n., & v.t. **1.** Place where soldier is stationed, (fig.) place of duty; position taken by body of soldiers, force occupy- ing this; fort. **2.** (Also *trading-*∼) place occupied for purposes of trade esp. in un- civilized country. **3.** Situation, employ- ment. **4.** (Naval, hist.) commission as officer in command of vessel of 20 guns or more; ‖ ∼ *captain*, holder of such com- mission (not of courtesy title or inferior command). **5.** (mil.). *First, last, ∼*, bugle- -call giving notice of hour of retiring for night (*last* ∼ also blown at mil. funerals). **6.** v.t. Place, station, (soldiers etc.); ‖ (mil., nav.) appoint to a ∼ or command. [f. F *poste* masc. f. It. *posto* f. L neut. p.p. as POST[2]]

pŏst-, comb. form of L *post* after, behind, in wds f. L; & as living E prefix, as: ∼-*class'ical*, occurring later than the classical period of (esp. Greek & Roman) language, literature, or art; ∼-*com- mun'ion*, part of eucharistic office follow- ing act of communion; ∼-*cŏs'tal*, behind a rib; ∼-*date'*, (v.t.) affix, assign, a later than the actual date to (document, event, etc.), (n., ∼-*date*) such date; ∼-*diluv'ian*, a. & n., (person) existing, occurring, after the Flood; ∼-*en'try*, late or subsequent entry (for race, in book-keeping, etc.); ∼-*exil'ian*, ∼-*exil'ic*, subsequent to the

Babylonian exile; ∼-*fix'*, (v.t.) append (letters) at end of word, (n., ∼-*fix*) suffix; ∼-*glā'cial*, subsequent to the glacial period; ∼-*grăd'uate*, (of course of study) carried on after taking first degree; ∼-*impre'ssionism*, artistic aims & methods (so named as a reaction from IMPRESSION- ISM) directed to expressing rather the individual artist's than the ordinary observer's presumable conception of the objects represented; ∼-*lŭde*, concluding voluntary [after PRELUDE]; ∼-*millenn'ial*, of the period following the millennium; ∼-*millenn'ialism*, doctrine that second Advent will follow the millennium, so ∼-*millenn'ialist* n.; ∼-*nāt'al*, occurring after birth; ∼-*nup'tial*, subsequent to marriage; ∼-*or'al*, situated behind the mouth; ∼-*Pli'ocene*, of the formation immediately overlying the Pliocene; ∼- -*post'script* (abbr. P.P.S.), a second POST- SCRIPT; ∼-*Ter'tiary*, of the formations subsequent to the Tertiary.

pŏs'tage, n. Amount charged for carriage of letter etc. by post, now usu. prepaid by ∼ *stamp*, adhesive label to be affixed, or stamp embossed or impressed on envelope etc., having specified value. [-AGE]

pŏs'tal, a. & n. Of the POST[2]; ∼ ORDER[1](3); ∼ *union*, union of governments of various countries for regulation of international postage; *(n., also ∼ card)*, postcard with printed stamp sold by the post-office. [F (*poste* POST[2], see -AL)]

pŏsteen', n. Afghan sheepskin greatcoat. [Pers. *postīn*]

pŏs'ter, n. (Also *bill-*∼) one who posts bills; placard displayed in public place; (rugby football) attempt at goal that passes straight over a post. [POST[1], -ER[1]]

pŏste rĕstante' (-tah-, & see Ap.), n. Department in post-office in which letters are kept till applied for. [F, = letter(s) remaining (i.e., at the post-office)]

pŏstēr'ior, a. & n. **1.** Later, coming after in series, order, or time, so ∼ITY (-ŏ'r-) n.; hinder, whence ∼LY[2] adv., as viewed from behind. **2.** n. (in sing., or arch. in pl.). The buttocks. [L, compar. of *posterus* (*post* after)]

pŏstĕ'rĭtў, n. The descendants of any person; all succeeding generations, as *deserves the gratitude of* ∼. [ME, f. OF *posterite* f. L *posteritatem* (as prec., see -TY)]

pŏs'tern, n. (arch.). Back door; side way or entrance; (attrib.) ∼ *door, gate*. [ME, f. OF *posterne, -rle*, f. LL *posterula* dim. f. *posterus* coming after (*post*)]

pŏst hŏc ĕrg'ō prŏp'ter hŏc, L phr. (after this, therefore on account of this) ridiculing the tendency to confuse se- quence with consequence.

pŏst'humous (-tū-), a. (Of child) born after death of its father; (of book etc.) published after author's death; occurring after death. Hence ∼LY[1] adv. [f. L *postumus* last (*post* after), in LL *posth-* by assoc. w. *humus* ground, +-OUS]

postiche' (-ēsh), n. & a. **1.** Something added after the completion of a work (esp. a superfluous or unsuitable addition to sculpture or architectural work); (shop) coil of false hair, false front. **2.** adj. Counterfeit, artificial. [F, = false f. It. *posticcio*]

postic'ous, a. (bot.). Posterior, hinder. [f. L *posticus* (*post* behind)+-OUS]

pos'til, n. (hist.). Marginal note, comment, esp. on text of Scripture; commentary. [ME, f. OF *postille* f. med. L *postilla* of unkn. orig.]

postil'ion, -lion, (-lyon), n. One who rides the near horse of the leaders, or near horse when one pair only is used & there is no driver on box. [f. F *postillon* f. It. *postiglione* (*posta* POST²)]

postlim'iny, n. (Rom. law) right of banished person or captive to resume civic privileges on return; (internat. law) restoration to their former state of persons & things taken in war, when they come again into the power of the nation they belonged to. [f. L POST(*liminium* f. *limen -minis* threshold)]

post'master¹ (-mah-), n. See POST².

‖ **post'master**² (-mah-), n. Scholar of Merton College, Oxford. Hence ~SHIP n.

post merid'iem, adv. (usu. abbr. p.m., pr. pē ĕm). After midday, as *3.30 p.m.* [L]

post mort'em, adv., *post-mort'em,* a. & n. After death; (examination) made after death; (colloq.) subsequent discussion of (esp. card) game. [L]

post-ŏb'it, a. & n. **1.** Taking effect after death. **2.** n. Bond securing to lender a sum to be paid on death of specified person from whom borrower has expectations. [f. L *post* after+*obitus -ūs* decease f. OB(*ire* go) die]

postpone' (or po-), v.t. & i. Put off, defer; treat (thing) as inferior in importance (*to* another); (intr., path., of ague etc.) be later in coming on. Hence ~MENT (-nm-) n. [f. L POST (*ponere posit-* place)]

postposi'tion (-z-), n. Particle, word, placed after another, usu. as enclitic, (e.g. *-wards*). Hence ~AL, **postpos'itive,** aa., (-z-). [as prec., see -ION]

postprän'dial, a. (usu. joc.). After-lunch or -dinner, as ~ *nap, oratory, eloquence.* [f. POST- +L *prandium* lunch+-AL]

post'script (or pōsk-), n. (abbr. P.S.). Additional paragraph esp. at end of letter after signature; ‖ talk at the end of some B.B.C. news bulletins. [f. L *postscriptum* neut. p.p. of POST(*scribere* write)]

pos'tulant, n. Candidate esp. for admission into religious order. [F (as foll., see -ANT)]

pos'tulate¹, n. Thing claimed or assumed as basis of reasoning, fundamental condition; prerequisite; (geom.) claim to take for granted the possibility of simple operation, e.g. of drawing straight line between any two points. [as foll., see -ATE²]

pos'tulāte², v.t. & i. Demand, require as a necessary condition, claim, take for granted (thing, *that, to* do); stipulate *for*; (eccl. law) nominate or elect subject to superior sanction. So ~A'TION, ~ātor, nn. [f. L *postulare* demand, -ATE³]

pos'tur|e, n., & v.t. & i. **1.** Carriage, attitude of body or mind; condition, state, (*of* affairs etc.); ~e-maker, acrobat, contortionist; ~e-master, teacher of callisthenics. **2.** vb. Dispose the limbs of (person) in particular way; assume ~e (lit. & fig.). Hence ~AL a., ~ER¹ n. [F, f. It. *-ura* f. L *positura* (*ponere posit-* place), see -URE)]

pos'ý (-z-), n. (arch.). Short motto, line of verse etc., inscribed within ring (~*-ring*) etc.; nosegay. [= POESY]

pot¹, n. **1.** Rounded vessel of earthenware, metal, or glass, for holding liquids or solids, as *flower,* GLUE, *ink, jam,* WATER²*ing,* ~~; such vessel for cooking; drinking-vessel of pewter etc.; contents of ~, as a ~ *of porter, honey;* COFFEE-~; TEA-~; (also, childish, pŏ) = CHAMBER-~; = FLOWER-~; vessel, usu. of silver, as prize in athletic sports, (sl.) any prize in these. **2.** ~ *paper* or~ (also *pott*), writing or printing paper 15¼ in. × 12½, named from the orig. watermark of a ~. **3.** LOBSTER-~; CHIMNEY-~. **4.** Large sum, as *made a* ~ or ~*s of money;* (racing sl.) large sum staked or betted, as *put the* ~ *on,* ‖ (also) favourite. **5.** Big ~, important person; *the* ~ *calls the kettle black,* person blames another for fault he too has; *go to* ~ (vulg.), be ruined or destroyed; *make the* ~ *boil,* make a living; *keep the* ~ *boiling,* make a living, keep anything going briskly; *watched* ~ *never boils* (proverb against worrying). **6.** ~*-ale,* completely fermented wash in distillation; ~*-belly,* (person with) protuberant belly; ~*-boiler,* work of literature or art done merely to make a living, writer or artist who does this; ~*-bound,* (of plant) whose roots fill flower-~ & want room to expand (also fig.); ~*-boy,* ~*man,* publican's assistant; ~ *hat,* bowler; ~*-herb,* any of those grown in kitchen-garden; ~*-hole,* (geol.) deep cylindrical hole worn in rock, depression in road surface caused by traffic etc.; ~*-hook,* over fireplace for hanging ~ etc. on or for lifting hot ~, curved stroke in handwriting esp. as made in learning to write (cf. HANGER²); ~*-house,* (derog.) public house; ~*-hunter,* sportsman who shoots anything he comes across, ‖ person who takes part in contest merely for sake of prize, so ~*-hunting* n. & a.; ~ *lead,* black-lead esp. as used for hull of racing-yacht; ~ *luck,* whatever is to be had for a meal, as *come & take~ luck with us;* ~*-metal,* stained glass coloured in melting~~ so that the colour pervades the whole; ~*-roast,* (n.) piece of meat cooked by braising, (v.t.) braise; ~*-shot,*

shot taken at game merely to provide a meal, shot aimed at animal etc. within easy reach, random shot; ~-*still*, kind of STILL² (opp. *patent still*) in which heat is applied directly & not by steam-jacket; ~'*stone*, granular variety of soapstone; ~-*valiant*, valiant because drunk, so ~ *valour*; ~*wall(op)er*, householder voter (before 1832), (naut., ~-*walloper*) cook's assistant [f. *wall(op)* boil]. Hence ~'FUL n. [late OE *pott*, corresp. to OFris., MDu., MLG *pot*, Icel. *pottr*; in ME reinforced by OF *pot* f. Rom. **pottus*]

pŏt², v.t. & i. (-tt-). Place (butter, fish, minced meat, etc., usu. salted or seasoned) in pot or other vessel to preserve it (esp. in p.p., as ~*ted ham*); plant (plant) in pot; (billiards) pocket; abridge, epitomize; bag (game), kill (animal) by pot-shot; (intr.) shoot (*at*, or abs.); seize, secure. [f. prec.]

pŏt'able, a. & n. (usu. joc.). Drinkable; (n. pl.) drinkables. [F, f. LL *potabilis* (*potare* drink, see -BLE)]

potăm'ĭc, a. Of rivers. So **pŏtamŏL'OGY** n. [f. Gk *potamos* river +-IC]

pŏt'ăsh, (arch.) **potăss'** (*or* pŏt⁴), n. An alkaline substance, crude form of potassium carbonate, orig. got by lixiviating vegetable ashes & evaporating the solution in iron pots; *caustic* ~, hydroxide or hydrate of potassium; PERMANGANATE *of* ~; ~*water*, an aerated drink. [17th c. *pot-ashes*, f. Du. *pot-asschen*]

potăss'ium, n. Soft white metallic element, one of the alkali metals, used mainly in compounds; ~ *cyanide*, white soluble crystalline salt, extremely poisonous; ~ PERMANGANATE. Hence **potăss'ĭC** a. [-IUM]

potā'tion, n. Drinking; (usu. pl.) tippling; draught. So **pŏt'atORY** a. [ME, f. OF, f. L *potationem* (*potare* drink, see -ATION)]

potāt'ō, n. (pl. ~*es*). Plant with farinaceous tubers used for food; its tuber; *sweet*, *Spanish*, ~, tropical plant with tuberous roots used for food; ~*es & POINT¹; ~*-ring*, Irish (usu. silver) ring used as stand for bowl etc. [f. Sp. *patata* var. of native Amer. BATATA]

poteen', -**theen'**, n. Irish whiskey from illicit still. [f. Ir. *poitin* dim. of *pota* pot]

pŏt'|ent, a. (Chiefly poet. or rhet.) powerful, mighty; (of reasons etc.) cogent; (of drugs etc.) strong. Hence or cogn. ~ENCE, ~ENCY, nn., ~entLY² adv. [f. L *potens* part. of *posse* be able]

pŏt'entāte, n. Monarch, ruler. [ME, f. L *potentatus -ūs* (as prec., see -ATE¹)]

potĕn'tial (-shl), a. & n. **1.** Capable of coming into being or action, latent; (med.) ~ *cautery*, *corrosive* (agent producing same effect on skin as an actual one); (gram.) ~ *mood*, subjunctive expressing possibility; (clectr.) ~ *difference*, difference in electric ~, usu. expressed in volts, between two separate bodies or points on a conductor, being properly the work

done when a unit charge is moved from one to the other; ~ *energy* (existing in ~ form, not as motion); (rare) powerful. **2.** n. ~ mood; (electr.) degree of electrification, electrical pressure; possibility, as *reached its highest* ~; possible resources. Hence or cogn. ~ITY (-shiăl⁴) n., ~LY² (-sha-) adv. [f. LL *potentialis* (*potentia*, as POTENT, see -AL)]

potĕn'tialize (-sha-), -**ise** (-īz), v.t. Make potential; convert (energy) into potential condition. [-IZE]

potĕn'tiāte (-shī-), v.t. Endow with power; make possible. [f. L as foll. + -ATE³]

potĕntiŏm'ĕter (-shī-), n. Instrument for measuring or adjusting electrical potential. [f. L *potentia* power (POTENT) + -0- + -METER]

potheen. See POTEEN.

poth'er (pŏdh-, pŭdh-), n., & v.t. & i. Choking smoke or cloud of dust; noise, din; verbal commotion, as *made a* ~ *about it*; display of sorrow; (v.t.) fluster, worry; (v.i.) make a fuss. [orig. obsc.; 17th c. also *pudder*; alleged identity w. POWDER is phonetically untenable]

pō'tion, n. Dose, draught, of liquid medicine or of poison. [ME, f. OF, f. L *potionem* (*potus* drunk, see -ION)]

pŏt'lătch, -lach(e), n. Tribal feast of N.-Amer. Indians given by aspirant to chiefship. [native]

pot-pourri (pōpŏorē'), n. Mixture of dried petals & spices kept in jar for its perfume; musical or literary medley. [F, lit. rotten pot]

‖ **pŏt'shĕrd**, n. Broken piece of earthenware. [POT¹ + SHERD]

pŏtt, n. Var. of POT¹ as applied to paper.

‖ **pŏtt'age**, n. (arch.). Soup, stew; (fig.) MESS¹ *of* ~. [ME, f. OF *potage* (POT¹ + -AGE)]

pŏtt'er¹, n. Maker of earthenware vessels; ~*'s wheel*, horizontal revolving disc in ~*'s lathe* (machine for moulding clay); ~*'s asthma, bronchitis*, etc. (caused by dust in the pottery industry). [late OE *pottere* (POT¹ + -ER¹)]

pŏtt'er², v.i. & t. Work in feeble or desultory manner (*at, in*, subject or occupation); dawdle, loiter, (*about* etc.); trifle *away* (one's time etc.). Hence ~ER¹ n. [f. dial. *pote* push, OE *potian*, + -ER⁵]

pŏtt'er|y̆, n. Earthenware; potter's work or workshop; ‖ *the P~ies*, district in N. Staffordshire, seat of ~y industry. [15th c., f. OF *poterie* (POT¹, -ERY)]

pŏt'tle, n. ‖ (Arch.) measure for liquids, half gallon, pot etc. containing this; small wicker or chip basket for strawberries etc. [ME & OF *potel* (POT¹, see -LE)]

pŏtt'ō, n. (pl. ~s). W.-Afr. lemur; kinkajou. [native]

pŏtt'y̆, a. (sl.). Insignificant, trivial, (often ~ *little*; ~ *little State*, *details*; ~ *questions* in examination paper, easy to answer); foolish, crazy, mad *about* (someone or something). [orig. unkn.]

pouch[1], n. Small bag or detachable outside pocket; (arch.) purse; soldier's leathern ammunition bag; bag-like receptacle of marsupials etc.; bag-like cavity, esp. seed-vessel, in plant. Hence ~ED[2] (-cht), ~'Y[2], aa. [ME, f. ONF *pouche* = OF *poche* POKE[1]]

pouch[2], v.t. & i. Put into pouch; take possession of, pocket; ‖ (sl.) give money to, tip; make (part of dress) hang like pouch, (intr., of such part) hang thus. [f. prec.]

poudrette' (pŏo-), n. Manure of night--soil mixed with charcoal etc. [F, dim. of *poudre* POWDER]

pouf(fe) (pŏof), n. Woman's high roll or pad of hair; large cushion used as low seat; soft stuffed couch. [F]

poulp(e) (pŏo-), n. Octopus or other cephalopod. [F (*-pe*), as POLYPUS]

poult (pōlt), n. Young of domestic fowl, turkey, pheasant, etc. [ME, contr. f. PULLET]

poult-de-soie (pŏodeswah'), n. Fine corded (now usu. coloured) silk. [F]

poul'terer (pōl-), n. Dealer in poultry. [f. ME *poulter* (still in City Company's name) f. OF *pouletier* (as PULLET, see -ER[2]) +-ER[1]]

poul'tice (pōl-), n., & v.t. **1.** Soft mass of bread, linseed, etc., usu. made with boiling water & spread on muslin etc. & applied to sore or inflamed part. **2.** v.t. Apply ~ to. [ult. f. L *puls -ltis* thick pap etc.]

poul'try (pōl-), n. Domestic fowls, e.g. barn-door fowls, ducks, geese, turkeys. [ME, f. OF *pouleirie* (as PULLET, see -ERY)]

pounce[1], n., & v.t. & i. **1.** Claw, talon, of bird of prey; pouncing, sudden swoop, esp. *make a* ~. **2.** v.t. Swoop down upon & seize; (v.i.) make sudden attack *upon*, (fig.) seize eagerly *upon* (blunder etc.). [*pounce* & *punch* app. shortened f. *ponson, ponchon*; see PUNCH[1], PUNCHEON[1]]

pounce[2], n., & v.t. **1.** Fine powder used to prevent ink from spreading on unsized paper etc.; powdered charcoal etc. dusted over perforated pattern to transfer design to object beneath. **2.** v.t. Smooth (paper, surface of hat, etc.) with pumice or ~, transfer (design) by use of ~, dust (pattern) with ~. [(vb f. F *poncer*) f. F *ponce* PUMICE]

poun'cet-box, n. (arch.). Small box with perforated lid for perfumes. [in Shakespeare; f. prec., hist. unexpl.]

pound[1], n., & v.i. **1.** (Abbr. *lb.* = L *libra*) measure of weight, 16 oz avoirdupois, 12 oz Troy; ~ *of flesh* (see Shak. *Merchant of Venice*, IV. i), (fig.) any legal but unconscionable demand; (also ~*sterling*) a money of account, 20 shillings, formerly represented by gold sovereign, as *five* ~s (written £5 or 5*l.*), *five* ~ *ten* (*shillings*), (hist.) ~ *Scots*, 1s. 8*d.*; *pay* 5s. *in the* ~ (for each ~ owing); PENNY *wise & ~ foolish*; ~, *five-*~, *note*, bank-note for one ~, five ~s; ~*-cake*, rich cake containing a ~ (or equal weight) of each of chief ingredients; ~*-day* (on which a charity etc. receives contributions from all comers of a ~ of anything, e.g. £1, 1lb. of tea, etc.). **2.** v.i. ‖ Test the weight of coins by weighing the number that ought to weigh a ~. [OE *pund*, = OS, ON, Goth. *pund*, OHG *pfunt* f. WG f. L *pondo*, orig. instr. abl. of L *pondus -eris* weight]

pound[2], n., & v.t. **1.** Enclosure for detention of stray cattle or of distrained cattle or goods till redeemed; enclosure for animals; (fig.) place of confinement, (hunt.) difficult position; ~*-lock* (with two gates, opp. *flash-lock* with one). **2.** v.t. Shut (cattle etc., often *up*) in ~; (hunt.) ~ *the field*, (of barrier) be impassable, (of rider) clear fence that others cannot. [ME, f. OE **pund* (in *pundfald*, cf. PINFOLD); cf. POND]

pound[3], v.t. & i. Crush, bruise, as with pestle; thump, pummel, with fists etc.; knock, beat, (thing *to pieces, into a jelly*, etc.); deliver heavy blows, fire heavy shot, (*at, on, away at*); walk, run, ride, make one's way, heavily (*along* etc.). [OE *pūnian* f. WG **pūn-* whence Du. *puin* rubbish, LG *pün* chips of stone]

poun'dage, n. Commission, fee, of so much per pound sterling; percentage of total earnings of a business, paid as wages; payment of so much per pound weight; charge on postal order etc.; TONNAGE *& ~*. [-AGE]

poun'der[1], n. In vbl senses, esp. instrument for pounding with or in, pestle, mortar. [POUND[3]+-ER[1]]

poun'der[2], n. Thing that, gun carrying shell that, weighs a pound or (-~) so many pounds, as *a three-*~; (-~) thing worth, person possessing, so many pounds sterling. [POUND[1], -ER[1]]

pour (pōr), v.t. & i., & n. **1.** Cause (liquid, granular substance, light, etc.) to flow, discharge copiously, as ~ *hot water over it*, ~ *out the tea, river* ~s *itself into the sea*; ~ *oil upon troubled waters*, (fig.) calm disturbance with soothing words etc.; ~ *cold water on*, (fig.) discourage (person, zeal, plan); discharge (missiles, crowd from building, etc., often *forth, out*) copiously or in rapid succession; send *forth* or *out* (words, music, etc.); (intr., of liquids etc.) flow (usu. *forth, out, down*) in stream, (of rain) descend heavily, whence ~'ING[2] (pōr-) a.; *it never rains but it* ~s, (fig.) events esp. misfortunes always come together; (fig.) come *in, out*, etc., abundantly, as *letters* ~ *in from all quarters*. **2.** n. Heavy fall of rain, downpour; (found.) amount of molten metal etc. ~ed at a time. [ME *poure*, of unkn. orig.]

pourboire (poorbwahr'), n. Gratuity, tip. [F, =*pour boire* (money) for drinking]

pourparler (poor'pärlā'), n. (usu. in pl.). Informal discussion preliminary to negotiation. [F]

pour'point (poor-), **pūr-**, n. (hist.).

Stuffed & quilted doublet. [ME, f. OF p.p. of *pourpoindre* perforate (*pour* PRO- for *par* PER- + *poindre* prick f. L *pungere*)]

poussette' (poo-), v.i., & n. Dance round one another with hands joined, as two couples in country dance; (n.) this action. [F, dim. of *pousse* PUSH]

pou stŏ (poo), n. Standing-place, basis of operation, FULCRUM. [Gk *pou stŏ* where I may stand]

pout[1], n. Kinds of fish, as *whiting, eel, horn, ~*. [OE **pūta* in *ælepūta*, = MDu. *puyt(e)*, Du. *puitaal*, G *aalputte*, app. f. WG **pūt-* inflate]

pout[2], v.t. & i., & n. **1.** Protrude (lips), protrude lips, (of lips) protrude, esp. as sign of (mock) displeasure, whence ~'ING LY[2] adv. **2.** n. Such protrusion; *in the ~s*, sulky. [ME, of obsc. hist.; perh. cogn. w. WG **pūt-* (prec.)]

pout'er, n. In vbl senses, esp.: kind of pigeon with great power of inflating crop; (also *whiting-pout*) kind of fish. [-ER[1]]

pŏv'erty, n. Indigence, want; scarcity, deficiency, (*of*); deficiency *in* (a property); inferiority, poorness, meanness; ~ *-stricken*, poor, esp. fig., as *a ~-stricken language*. [ME, f. OF *poverte* f. L *paupertatem* (as PAUPER, see -TY)]

powd'er, n., & v.t. **1.** Mass of dry particles or granules, dust; medicine in the form of ~; cosmetic ~ applied to face, skin, or hair; = GUN~, as *smell of ~*, experience of fighting, FOOD *for ~*; *not worth ~ and shot*, not worth shooting, or fighting or striving for. **2.** v.t. Sprinkle ~ upon, cover (*with ~* etc.); apply ~ to (nose, hair, or abs. in same sense); decorate (surface) with spots or small figures; (esp. in p.p.) reduce to ~ (~*ed sugar*). **3.** ~ *blue*, ~ed smalt esp. for use in laundry, deep blue colour of this (also attrib.); ~*-down*, down-feathers found in definite patches on some birds; ~*-flask* (hist.), case for carrying gun~; ~*-horn* (hist.), ~-flask orig. & esp. of horn; ~*-magazine*, place where gun~ is stored; ~*-monkey* (hist.), boy employed on board ship to carry ~ to guns; ~*-puff*, soft pad usu. of down for applying ~ to skin; ~*(ing)-room*, ladies' cloakroom. Hence ~iNESS n., ~Y[2] a. [ME & OF *poudre*, ult. f. L *pulvis -eris*]

pow'er, n., & v.t. **1.** Ability to do or act, as *will do all in my ~, has the ~ of changing its colour*; particular faculty of body or mind, as *taxes his ~s to the utmost, man of varied ~s*. **2.** Vigour, energy, as *more ~ to your elbow!* (formula of encouragement or approval). **3.** Active property, as *has a high heating ~*. **4.** Government, influence, authority, (*over*); *in one's ~*, under one's control; personal ascendancy (*over*); political ascendancy, as *the party now in ~*. **5.** Authorization, delegated authority, as *a bill to extend & define their ~s*; ~ *of* ATTORNEY[2]. **6.** Influential person, body, or thing, as *the press had not become a ~ in the State*; *the ~s that be*, constituted

authorities; State having international influence. **7.** Deity, as *merciful ~s!*; sixth ORDER[1] of angels. **8.** (vulg.). Large number or amount, as *saw a ~ of people, did a ~ of work*. **9.** (math.). *Third, tenth*, etc., ~ of a number, product obtained by multiplying the number into itself three, ten, etc., times, as *the third ~ of 2 is 8*. **10.** Instrument for applying energy to mechanical purposes, esp. *the* MECHANICAL ~s, the simple MACHINES. **11.** Mechanical energy as opp. to hand-labour, esp. attrib., as ~*-lathe, -loom, -mill*; ~*-station* (in which electric ~ is generated for distribution). **12.** Capacity for exerting mechanical force,' esp. HORSE[1]~, whence (-)~ED[2] (*-erd*) a. **13.** Magnifying capacity of lens. **14.** ~*-dive* n. & v.i., (of aircraft) dive without shutting off engine(s); ~ *politics*, diplomacy backed by (the threat of) force. **15.** v.t. Supply (vehicle, vessel, etc.) with ~ (esp. of engine). [ME & AF *poër* (vb inf. as n.) f. Rom. **potere* = L *posse* be able (*potis*)]

pow'erful, a. Having great (physical or other) power or influence as ~ *grasp, horse, mind, ally, book, speech, odour*. Hence ~LY[2] adv. [ME; -FUL]

pow'erless, a. Without power; wholly unable (*to* help etc.). Hence ~LY[2] adv., ~NESS n. [-LESS]

pow'wow, pawaw', n., powwow', v.i. & t. 1. N.-Amer.-Indian medicine-man or sorcerer; magic ceremonial, conference, of N.-Amer. Indians; *political or other meeting; || (sl.) conference of officers during army manœuvres etc. **2.** v.i. Practise medicine or sorcery, hold a ~, *confer, discuss, (*about* etc.); (v.t.) doctor, treat with magic. [f. native *powwaw, powah*]

pŏx, n. Syphilis (colloq.); CHICKEN~; COWPOX; SMALL-~. [alt. sp. of POCKs]

pozz(u)olana (pŏtsolah'na, -tswo-), n. Volcanic ash found near Pozzuoli, much used for hydraulic cement. [It.]

praam. See PRAM[1].

prăc'tic|able, a. That can be done, feasible; (of road, passage, ford) that can be used or traversed; (theatr., of windows etc.) real, that can be used as such. Hence ~ABIL'ITY, ~ableNESS, nn., ~ABLY[2] adv. [f. F *praticable* (*pratiquer* PRACTISE, -ABLE)]

prăc'tical, a. Of, concerned with, shown in, practice (cf. THEORETICAL), as ~ *agriculture, philosophy*; ~ JOKE[1]; available, useful, in practice; engaged in practice, practising; inclined to action rather than speculation, as *does not appeal to ~ minds*; (derog.) unimaginative; that is such in effect though not nominally, virtual, as *a ~ atheist, has ~ control*; feasible (~ *politics*). Hence ~ITY (-ăl[2]), ~NESS, nn. [f. arch. *practic* n. & a. f. obs. F *practique* f. LL f. Gk *praktikos* + -AL]

prăc'tically, adv. In a practical manner; virtually, almost, (~ *nothing*). [-LY[2]]

prăc'tice, n. **1.** Habitual action or carrying on, as *the ~ of advertising, makes a ~ of* *saving*; method of legal procedure; habit, custom, (*has been the regular* ~). **2.** Repeated exercise in an art, handicraft, etc., as ~ *makes perfect*; *in, out of*, ~ (lately, not lately, practised in thing); *is good* ~ (improves skill); spell of this (*ball, target*, ~). **3.** Professional work, business, or connexion, of lawyer or doctor, as *has a large* ~, *sold his* ~. **4.** (arch.). Scheming, (usu. underhand) contrivance, artifice, (esp. in pl., & cf. SHARP¹ ~). **5.** (arith.). Mode of finding value of given number of articles, or of quantity of commodity at given price, when quantity or price or both are in several denominations. **6.** *In* ~, in the realm of action, as *quite useless, would never work, in* ~ ; *put* (plan, method) *in(to)* ~, carry it out. [ME, earlier *practize* app. f. PRACTISE, replacing earlier *practic* (as PRACTICAL)]

practi′cian (-shn), n. Worker, practitioner. [f. obs. F *practicien* f. med. L *practica* (as PRACTICAL) see -ICIAN)]

prăc′tis|e, v.t. & i. Perform habitually, carry out in action, 'as ~*e the same method*, ~*e what you preach*; exercise, pursue, (profession; ~*ing doctor, barrister*, etc., engaged in actual practice, not retired nor merely qualified); exercise oneself in or on (art, instrument, or abs.), as ~*e the flute, the piano, music, running*; exercise (person, oneself, in action or subject), whence ~ED¹ (-st) a.; (arch.) scheme, contrive, as *when first we* ~*e to deceive*; ~*e* (*up*)*on*, impose upon, take advantage of, (person, his credulity etc.). [ME, f. OF *pra(c)tiser, -tiquer*, or med. L *pra(e)tizare* alt. f. *-care* (as PRACTICAL)]

practi′tioner (-sho-), n. Professional or practical worker, esp. in medicine; *general* ~ (in both medicine & surgery; abbr. G.P.), opp. *consultant, specialist*, etc.). [irreg. f. PRACTICIAN + -ER¹]

prae-, pref., the L form of PRE-, kept only in a few wds.

praecō′cial (-shal), a. (Of birds) whose young can feed themselves as soon as hatched. [as PRECOCIOUS, see -AL]

praemŭnīr′e, n. (law). Writ charging sheriff to summon person accused of asserting or maintaining papal jurisdiction in England; *Statute of* ~ (of 16th Richard II, on which the writ is based). [med. L, for L PRAE(*monēre* warn), the wds ~ *facias* warn (so-&-so to appear) occurring in the writ]

praenōm′ĕn, n. (Rom. ant.). First or personal name (e.g. *Marcus Tullius* Cicero). [PRAE-, cf. COGNOMEN]

|| **praepŏs′tor**, pre-, (prīp-), n. (pub. school). = PREFECT, MONITOR. [syncop. f. *praepositor* f. L PRAE(*ponere posit*- place) set over, see -OR; irreg. altered f. L p.p. *-tus*]

praet′or, n. (Rom. hist.). (Orig.) Roman consul as leader of army; (later) annually elected magistrate performing some duties of consul. Hence **praetŏr′IAL** a., ~SHIP n. [L,f. PRAE(*ire it*- go)]

praetōr′ian, pre-, (prīt-), a. & n. **1.** Of a praetor; of the bodyguard of Roman general or emperor. **2.** n. Man of ~ rank, soldier of ~ guard. [f. L *praetorianus* (as prec., see -AN)]

prăgmăt′|ic(al), aa. Meddlesome; dogmatic; of pragmatism; (~*ic*) treating facts of history with reference to their practical lessons; (~*ic*) of the affairs of a State (~*ic sanction*, imperial or royal ordinance issued as fundamental law, esp. that of Charles VI in 1724 settling Austrian succession). Hence ~**icăl′ITY** n., ~**icalLY²** adv. [f. L f. Gk *pragmatikos* (*pragma -matos* deed), -IC, -AL]

prăg′mat|ism, n. Officiousness; pedantry; matter-of-fact treatment of things; (philos.) doctrine that estimates any assertion solely by its practical bearing upon human interests. So ~IST n., ~**is′tIC** a. [f. Gk *pragma*, see prec. & -ISM]

prăg′matize, -ise (-īz), v.t. Represent as real; rationalize (myth). [as prec., see -IZE]

prair′ie, n. Large treeless tract of level or undulating grass-land; ~*-chicken, -hen*, N.-Amer. kind of grouse; ~*-dog*, N.--Amer. rodent with bark like dog's; ~ *oyster*, raw egg swallowed whole; *~*--*schooner*, early emigrant's white-tilted wagon used in crossing the ~s. [F, f. Rom. **prataria* (L *pratum* meadow, see -ARY¹)]

praise (-z), v.t., & n. **1.** Express warm approbation of, commend the merits of, (person, thing); glorify, extol the attributes of, (God etc.). **2.** n. Praising, commendation, as *won high* ~, *was loud in his* ~*s*. Hence ~′**FUL** a., ~′**fulNESS** n., (-zf-). [ME, f. OF *preisier* price, prize, praise, f. LL *preciare, pret*-, f. L *pretium* PRICE; see PRIZE]

praise′worth|y (prāz′wĕrdhĭ), a. Worthy of praise, commendable, (often patronizing). Hence ~**iLY²** adv., ~**iNESS** n.

Pra′krit (prah-), n. Any of the dialects of N. & Central India existing alongside of or growing out of Sanskrit. [f. Skr. *prakṛta* unrefined]

pra′line (prah-), n. Sweet made by browning nuts in boiling sugar. [F (*Praslin*, surname)]

pram¹,praam,(prahm),n. Flat-bottomed boat used in Baltic etc. for shipping cargo etc.; flat-bottomed boat mounted with guns; Scandinavian ship's boat corresp. to dinghy. [f. MDu., MLG *prame*, f. Slav.]

prăm², n. (colloq.). || Perambulator; milkman's handcart. [abbr. of PERAMBULATOR]

pranc|e (-ah-), v.i. & t., & n. **1.** (Of horse) rise by springing from hind legs; cause (horse) to do this; (fig.) walk, behave, in elated or arrogant manner. **2.** n. ~*ing*, ~*ing* movement. [ME, of obsc. orig.; cf. syn. (obs.) *prank* (c. 1500)]

prăn′dial, a. (joc.). Of dinner. [f. L *prandium* lunch, see -AL]

‖ **prăng**, v.t. (R.A.F. sl.). Bomb (target) successfully; crash (aircraft). [imit.]

prănk[1], n. Mad frolic, practical joke; (fig., of machinery etc.) erratic action. Hence ~'FUL, ~'ISH[1] aa., ~'ish̄NESS n. [c. 1525; goes w. obs. *prank* vb play tricks; orig. unkn.]

prănk[2], v.t. & i. Dress, deck, (person, one*self*, thing, often *out*); adorn, spangle, (field *with* flowers etc.); (v.i.) show oneself off. [c. 1550; cogn. w. Du. *pronken* strut, parade, G *prunken*, & obs. E adj. *prank* smart, showy; cf. PRINK]

präse (-z), n. Kind of leek-green translucent quartz. [F, f. L f. Gk *prasios* leek--green (*prason* leek); earlier also as L]

prät|e, v.i. & t., & n. **1.** Chatter; talk too much; blab; tell, say, (thing) in ~ing manner. **2.** n. ~ing, idle talk. Hence ~'ER[1] n., ~'ING[2] a. [ME, f. MDu., MLG *praten*]

‖ **prät'ies** (-tiz), n. (Anglo-Ir. colloq.). Potatoes. [corrupt.]

prät'incŏle (-ngk-), n. Bird like swallow in appearance & habits, & allied to plover. [f. L *pratum* meadow + *incola* inhabitant]

prăt'ique (-ĭk, *or* prætĕk'), n. Licence to hold intercourse with port, granted to ship after quarantine or on showing clean bill of health. [F, = PRACTICE, intercourse]

prăt'tle, v.i. & t., & n. **1.** Talk in childish or artless fashion; say (thing) thus. **2.** n. Childish chatter, small talk. Hence **prătt'lER**[1] n., **prătt'lING**[2] a. [f. MLG *pratelen*; see PRATE, -LE(3)]

präv'itў, n. (rare). Depravity; ‖ badness, corruptness, (of food etc.). [f. L *pravitas* (*pravus* crooked, bad, see -TY)]

prawn, n., & v.i. Marine crustacean like large shrimp; (v.i.) fish for ~s, so ~'ING[1] n. [ME *pra(y)ne*, of unkn. orig.]

präx'is, n. Accepted practice, custom; (gram.) set of examples for practice. [Gk, = doing, f. *prassō* do]

pray, v.t. & i. Make devout supplication to (God, object of worship); beseech earnestly (God, person, *for* thing, *to* do, *that*); ask earnestly for (permission etc.); engage in prayer, make entreaty, (*to* God, *to* person, *for* thing, *for or on behalf of* person, *to* do, *that*); ~ (I beg you to) *consider* etc.; *what is the use of that*, ~ (tell me)?; ~ *in aid of* (arch.; *in* adv., not prep.), summon to one's support. [ME, f. OF *preier* f. LL *precare* (L -*ri*)]

prayer[1] (prār), n. Solemn request to God or object of worship; formula used in praying, e.g. LORD's ~; form of divine service consisting largely of ~s, as *morning*~, *evening*~, *family*~s; action, practice, of praying; entreaty to a person; thing prayed for; ~-*book*, book of forms of ~, esp. Book of Common P~, public liturgy of Church of England; ~-*meeting*, religious meeting at which several persons offer ~; ~-*wheel*, revolving cylindrical

box inscribed with or containing ~s, used esp. by Buddhists of Tibet. Hence ~'FUL (-ãr̃f-), ~'LESS (-ãr̃l-), aa., ~'fulLY[2], ~'lèssLY[2], advv., ~'fulNESS, ~'lèssNESS, nn. [ME & OF *preiere* f. med. L *precaria* fem. sing. (orig. neut. pl.) adj. as n. (as PRECARIOUS)]

pray'er[2], n. One who prays. [-ER[1]]

prē-, pref., = med. L *pre-*, L *prae-*, before (in time, place, order, degree, or importance). Occurs not only in wds of L orig., but is (freely) used as a living prefix with E wds, only the more important of which are given in their alphabetical place. In secondary wds such as those here classified, the pron. is (prē-) & the hyphen is usu. written. **1.** Vbs & vbl nn. w. sense ' do, doing, thing done, beforehand', as: ~-*acquaint'*; ~-*admi'ssion*; ~-*admon'ish*, ~-*admoni'tion*; ~-*advise'*; ~-*announce'*(*ment*), ~-*appoint'*(*ment*); ~-*arrange*(*ment*); ‖~-*aud'ience*, right (of lawyer at Bar) to be heard before another; ~-*cal'culable*, ~-*cal'culate*, ~-*calcula'tion*; ~--*compose'*; ~-*concert'*; ~-*condemn'*; ~--*condi'tion*, prior condition, one that must be fulfilled beforehand; ~-*consid'er*, ~-*considera'tion*; ~-*contract'* v.i., ~--*con'tract* n.; ~-*decease'*, (v.t.) die before (person), (n.) such death; ~*define'*; ~-*digest'*, render food easily digestible before introduction into stomach (also fig.), ~-*dige'stion*, this process; ~-*doom'* v.t. ~-*elect'*. ~-*elec'tion* (see also in 2); ~--*engage'*(*ment*); ~-*estab'lish*; ~-*es'timate* v.t., ~-*es'timate* n.; ~-*exist'* v.i., ~-*exis'tence* n., so ~-*exis'tent* a.; ~-*in'dicate*; ~-*in'timate* v.t.; ~*lim'it* v.t.; ~*mo'tion*, motion given beforehand, esp. divine act as determining the will of the creature; ~-*ordain'*, appoint beforehand, foreordain; ~*percep'tion*. **2.** Adjj. & nn. w. sense ' (person etc.) existing, dating from, before the time of ...', as: ~-*adăm'ic* a., ~*ad'amite* n. & a., (one of supposed race) existing before the time of Adam; ~-*Chris'tian*, before Christ(ianity); ~--*class'ical*, before the classical age (usu. of Greek & Roman literature); ~-*con'queror*, ~-*con'quest*, before the Norman conquest; ~-*con'scious*, antecedent to consciousness; ~-*elec'tion*, (of acts, promises) done, given, before election; ~-*exĭl'ian*, ~-*exĭl'ic*, before (usu. the Babylonian) exile; ~*glā'cial*, before the glacial period; ~-*hum'an*, existing before man existed; ~-*millenn'ial*(*ism*), (belief that Christ's Second Advent will occur) before the millennium, so ~-*millenar'ian*, ~-*millenn'ialist*; ~-*nat'al*, existing, occurring, before birth; ~-*pran'dial*, before-dinner; ~-*scientif'ic*, before the rise of modern science; ~-*war'* adj. (as ~-*war prices*) & (vulg.) adv. (as *that happened* ~-*war*), before the war. **3.** Adjj., chiefly anat. & zool. w. sense 'situated in front of', as: ~-*cord'ial*, in front of or about the heart; ~-*cos'tal*, in front of the ribs; ~-*dors'al*, anterior to the dorsal region; ~-*frŏn'tal*, in front of frontal bone of skull, in fore part of frontal lobe of brain; ~-*maxill'ary*, in front of the upper jaw; ~-*oc'ular*, in front of the eye.

preach, v.i. & n. Deliver sermon or religious address, deliver (sermon); give moral advice in obtrusive way; proclaim, expound, (the Gospel, Christ, *that*, etc.) in public discourse; advocate, inculcate, (quality, conduct, principle, etc.) thus; ~ *up*, extol, commend; ~ *down*, disparage, put down by ~ing or speaking; (n., colloq.) ~ing, sermon, lecture. Hence or cogn. ~'ABLE a., ~'ER¹, ~'ership, ~'MENT (usu. derog.), nn. [ME, f. OF *prechier* f. L PRAE(*dicare* proclaim); in eccl. L 'preach']

preach'ify, v.i. Preach, moralize, hold forth, tediously. [-FY]

preach'|y, a. (colloq.). Fond of preaching or holding forth. Hence ~iness n. [-Y²]

preăm'ble, n., & v.i. Preliminary statement in speech or writing; introductory part of statute, deed, etc.; (v.i.) make ~. [ME, f. OF *preambule* f. med. L *preambulum* f. LL *praeambulus* going before f. LL PRAE(*ambulare* walk)]

prĕb'end, n. Part of revenue of cathedral or collegiate church granted to canon or member of chapter as stipend; portion of land or tithe from which this stipend is drawn; = foll. So ~AL a. [ME, f. OF *prebende* f. LL *praebenda* pension, neut. pl. gerund. of L *praebēre* grant]

prĕb'endary, n. Holder of prebend, honorary canon; ~*stall*, ~'s stall in cathedral. Hence ~ship n. [ME, f. med. L *praebendarius* (as prec., see -ARY¹)]

precăr'ious, a. Held during the pleasure of another, as ~ *tenure*; question-begging, taken for granted, as *a* ~ *assumption*; dependent on chance, uncertain, as *makes a* ~ *living*; perilous, as *the* ~ *life of a fisherman*. Hence ~LY² adv., ~NESS n. [f. L *precarius* obtained by entreaty (*prex, prec-* prayer, see -ARY¹)+-OUS]

prĕc'atory, a. (Gram., of word or form) expressing entreaty; (in wills) ~ *words* (requesting that a thing be done), ~ *trust*, ~ words that are held to be binding. So **prĕc'ative** a. [f. LL *precatorius* (*precari* pray, see -ORY)]

precau'tion, n. Prudent foresight, measure taken beforehand to ward off evil or ensure good result. Hence ~ARY¹ (-sho-) a. [f. F *précaution* f. LL *praecautionem* f. L PRAE(*cavēre caut-* beware of), see -ION]

precēde', v.t. & i. (Of person or thing) go before in rank or importance, as *such duties* ~ *all others, sons of barons* ~ *baronets*; come before (thing etc., or abs.) in order, as *the words that* ~ (*this paragraph*); walk in front of, as ~*d by our guide*; come before in time, as *in the years preceding his accession*; cause (thing) to be ~d by, as *must* ~ *this*

measure by milder ones. [f. OF *preceder* f. L PRAE(*cedere cess-* go)]

prē'cédence (or prisēd⁴), (rarely) **-cў**, nn. Priority in time or succession; superiority, higher position, as *takes* ~ *of* (is recognized as superior to) *all others*; right of preceding others in ceremonies & social formalities. [ME, f. PRECEDENT², see -ENCE, -ENCY]

prē'cédent¹, n. Previous case taken as example for subsequent cases or as justification, as *there is no* ~ *for this, it is without* ~, *do not take this as a* ~; (law) decision, procedure, etc., serving as rule or pattern. [ME, f. OF n., as foll.]

precēd'ent² (or prĕs'ĭ-), a. (now rare). Preceding in time, order, rank, etc., as *condition*~. Hence ~LY² adv. [ME, f. OF a. & n. f. L as PRECEDE, see -ENT]

prē'cédentĕd, a. Having, supported by, precedent. [-ED²]

precĕnt', v.i. & t. Act as precentor; lead (psalm etc.) in singing. [back form. f. foll.]

precĕn'tor, n. (In some Presbyterian churches etc.) one who leads singing of congregation; (in English cathedrals) member of clergy in general control of musical arrangements, in old foundations ranking next to dean and having succentor as his deputy, and in new foundations being a minor canon. Hence or cogn. ~SHIP, **precĕn'trix**, nn. [f. L *praecentor* f. PRAE(*cinere cent-* = *canere* sing)]

prē'cĕpt, n. Command, maxim, so **precĕp'tive** a.; moral instruction, as *example is better than* ~; divine command; writ, warrant; written order to arrange for & hold election; order for collection or payment of money under a rate. [ME, f. L *praeceptum* neut. p.p. of PRAE(*cipere cept-* = *capere* take) instruct]

precĕp't|or, n. Teacher, instructor. Hence or cogn. **precĕptōr'ial** a., ~orship, ~ress¹, nn. [f. L *praeceptor* (as prec., see -OR)]

precĕp'tory, n. (hist.). Subordinate community of Knights Templars; estate, buildings, of this. [f. med. L *praeceptoria* fem. adj. as n. (as prec., see -ORY)]

precĕ'ssion (-shn), n. (astron.). ~ *of the equinoxes*, (earlier occurrence in each successive sidereal year, due to) retrograde motion of equinoctial points along ecliptic. Hence ~AL (-sho-) a. [f. LL *praecessio* (as PRECEDE, see -ION)]

prē'cinct, n. Space enclosed by walls or other boundaries of a place or building, esp. of place of worship; (pl.) *the* environs *of*; boundary; *subdivision of county or city or ward for election and police purposes. [f. med. L *praecinctum* neut. p.p. of PRAE(*cingere cinct*)]

prē'cious (-shus), a. & adv. **1.** Of great price, costly; ~ *metals*, gold, silver, (occas.) platinum; ~ *stone*, gem; of great non-material worth, as ~ *words, privilege, knowledge, blood of Christ*; affectedly refined in language, workmanship, etc., so **prĕcī**os'ITY (-shĭŏs⁴) n.; (colloq., as intensive) *made a ~ mess of it, a ~ sight more than you think*; (ellipt.) *my ~* (dear etc.). **2.** adv. (colloq.). Uncommonly, as *took ~ good care of that, ~ little of it.* Hence ~LY² adv., ~NESS n. [ME, f. OF *precios* f. L *pretiosus* (*pretium* price, see -OUS)]

prĕ'cipice, n. Vertical or steep face of rock, cliff, mountain, etc. [f. F *précipice* or L *praecipitium* falling headlong, precipice (as PRECIPITOUS)]

precip'it|ate¹, n. (Chem.) body precipitated from solution, so ~ABIL'ITY, ~ANT(2), nn., ~ABLE a.; (phys.) moisture condensed from vapour by cooling & deposited, e.g. rain, dew. [as foll.]

precip'it|ate², a. Headlong, violently hurried, as ~*ate flight*; (of person or act) hasty, rash, inconsiderate. Hence or cogn. ~ANCE, ~ANCY, ~ateNESS, nn., ~ateLY² adv. [as foll., see -ATE²]

precip'itāt|e³, v.t. Throw down headlong; (fig.) hurl, fling, (person etc. *into* condition etc.); hurry, urge on, (course of events etc.); hasten the occurrence of, as *served to ~e his ruin*; (chem.) cause (substance in solution) to be deposited in solid form; condense (vapour) into drops & so deposit. So **precipitā'TION** (esp., meteorol., fall of rain, sleet, snow, or hail), ~OR, nn. [f. L *praecipitare* (as foll.), -ATE³]

precip'itous, a. Of, like, a precipice; dangerously steep; (rare) = PRECIPITATE². Hence ~LY² adv., ~NESS n. [f. obs. F *precipiteux* f. L PRAE(*ceps -cipitis* f. *caput* head) headlong, see -OUS]

précis (prās'ē), n., & v.t. **1.** Summary, abstract. **2.** v.t. Make a~ of. [F, = foll.]

precīse', a. Accurately expressed, definite, exact; punctilious, scrupulous in observance of rules etc.; *the ~* (exact, identical) *moment* etc. Hence ~NESS (-sn-) n. [f. F *précis, -ise*, f. L PRAE(*cīdere cis-* = *caedere* cut) cut short]

precīse'ly (-sl-), adv. In precise manner; (in emphatic or formal assent) quite so. [-LY²]

precī'sian (-zhn), n. One who is rigidly precise or punctilious, esp. in religious observance. Hence ~ISM (-zha-) n. [-IAN]

precī'sion (-zhn), n. Accuracy; *arm of ~*, fire-arm fitted with sights or other mechanical aids; (attrib.) marked by, adapted for, ~ (~ *bombing, instruments, tools*). Hence ~IST(-zho-)n. [f. F *précision* or L *praecisio* (as PRECISE, see -ION)]

preclude' (-ōōd), v.t. Exclude, prevent, make impracticable, as *so as to ~ all doubt.* So **preclūs'IVE** (-lōō-) a. [f. L PRAE(*cludere clus-* = *claudere* shut)]

precō'cious (-shus), a. (Of plant) flower-

ing or fruiting early; (of person) prematurely developed in some faculty; (of actions etc.) indicating such development. Hence or cogn. ~LY² adv., ~NESS, **prĕcō'city** f. [f. L *praecox -cocis* f. PRAE-(*coquere* cook) + -OUS]

prĕcŏgni'tion, n. Antecedent knowledge; || (Sc. law) preliminary examination of witnesses etc., esp. in order to know whether there is ground for trial. [f. LL *praecognitio* f. L PRAE(*cognoscere*, cf. RECOGNIZE), see -ION]

prĕconceive' (-sēv), v.t. Conceive beforehand, anticipate in thought. So **prĕconcĕp'tion** n. (esp. = *prejudice*). [PRE-]

prĕc'onīz|e, -is|e (-īz), v.t. Proclaim publicly; commend publicly; summon by name; (Rom. Cath., of pope) approve publicly the appointment of (bishop). So ~A'TION n. [f. med. L *praeconizare* (L *praeco -onis* herald, see -IZE)]

prĕcŭrs'or, n. Forerunner, harbinger, esp. John the Baptist; one who precedes in office etc. [f. L *praecursor* f. PRAE-(*currere curs-* run), see -OR]

prĕcŭrs'|ory, a. Preliminary, introductory, serving as harbinger (*of*). So ~IVE a. [f. L *praecursorius* (as prec.; see -ORY)]

prĕdā'cious (-shus), a. (Of animals) naturally preying on others, predatory; pertaining to such animals, as ~ *instincts.* So **prĕdā'city** n. [as f. L **praedax*: see PREDATORY, -ACIOUS]

prēdāte', v.t. Antedate. [PRE-]

prĕd'ator, n. Predatory animal. [f. L *praedator* (foll.)]

prĕd'atory, a. Of, addicted to, plunder or robbery; (of animals) preying upon others. [f. L *praedatorius* (*praedari* plunder f. *praeda* booty, see -ORY)]

prĕd'ecĕssor, n. Former holder of any office or position, as *my, William's, ~s, his immediate ~*; thing to which another has succeeded, as *will share the fate of its ~*; forefather. [ME, f. AF, OF *-our* & LL PRAE(*decessor*, see DECEASE, -OR)]

prĕdĕll'a, n. (Painting on vertical face of) altar-step; (painting, sculpture, on) raised shelf at back of altar. [It., = stool]

prĕdĕstinār'ian, n. & a. (Holder of the doctrine) of predestination. [-ARIAN]

prĕdĕs'tin|āte, v.t. (Of God) foreordain (person) to salvation or to (any fate), *to* (do); determine beforehand. So ~ATE² (-at) a. [f. L PRAE(*destinare* DESTINE), see -ATE³]

prĕdĕstinā'tion, n. God's appointment from eternity of some of mankind to salvation & eternal life; God's foreordaining of all that comes to pass; fate, destiny. [ME, f. LL *praedestinatio* (as prec., see -ION)]

prĕdĕs'tine, v.t. Determine beforehand, appoint as if by fate; (theol.) = PRE-DESTINATE. [ME, f. OF *-iner* or L *praedestinare* PREDESTINATE]

prĕdĕtẽr'min|e, v.t. Decree beforehand, predestine, so ~ATE² (-*at*) a.; (of motive etc.) impel (person etc. *to* thing, *to* do) beforehand. Hence ~A'TION n. [f. LL PRAE(*determinare* DETERMINE)]

prēd'ial, a. & n. 1. Of land or farms; rural, agrarian; (of slaves) attached to the land. **2.** n. ~ slave. [f. med. L *praedialis* (L *praedium* farm, see -AL)]

prĕd'ic|able, a. & n. 1. That may be predicated or affirmed, so ~ABIL'ITY n. **2.** n. ~able thing, esp. (pl.) Aristotle's classes of predicates viewed relatively to their subjects (viz. genus, species, difference, property, accident. [f. F, or L *praedicabilis* in med. L sense ' that may be affirmed ' (as PREDICATE², see -BLE)]

prĕdic'ament, n. Thing predicated, esp. (pl.) Aristotle's ten categories, whence **prĕdicamĕn'tal** a.; unpleasant, trying, or dangerous situation. [ME, f. LL *praedicamentum* (as foll., see -MENT)]

prĕd'icant, a. & n. 1. (Of religious order, esp. Dominicans) engaged in preaching. **2.** n. = PREDIKANT. [as foll., see -ANT]

prĕd'icate¹, n. (Log.) what is predicated, what is affirmed or denied of the subject by means of the copula (e.g. *a fool in he is a fool*): (gram.) what is said of the subject, including the copula (e.g. *is a fool* in prec. ex.); quality, attribute. [as foll. see -ATE³]

prĕd'icate², v.t. Assert, affirm, as true or existent, as *many truths may be ~d about humanity*, we ~ *goodness or badness of a motive*, ~ *of a motive that it is good or bad*; (log.) assert (thing) about subject. So **prĕdica'TION** n. [f. L PRAE(*dicare* declare) proclaim, see -ATE³]

prĕdic'ative, a. Making a predication; (gram., of adj. or n., opp. *attributive*) forming part or the whole of the predicate, as in ' This is *absurd* ', cf. ' an *absurd* notion '. Hence ~LY² adv. [f. L *praedicativus*, as prec., see -IVE]

prĕd'icatorў, a. Of, given to, marked by, preaching. [f. LL *praedicatorius* (prec., -ORY)]

prĕdict', v.t. Forecast, prophesy, (thing, *that*, *who*, etc.). Hence or cogn. ~ABILITY, prĕdic'TION, nn., ~ABLE, ~IVE, aa., ~ively² adv. [f. L PRAE(*dicere dict*- say)]

prĕdic'tor, n. In vbl senses; also instrument for determining the height, direction, speed, and range of aircraft and the fuse-setting etc. required in engaging hostile aircraft with anti-aircraft fire. [-OR]

prĕdĭkant' (-ahnt), n. Minister of Dutch Protestant church, esp. in S. Africa. [Du., as PREDICANT]

prĕdilĕc'tion, n. Mental preference, partiality, (*for*). [f. F *prédilection* f. med. L PRAE(*diligere*), see DILIGENT & -ION]

prēdispōse' (-z), v.t. Render liable, subject, or inclined (*to* feeling, disease, etc., *to* do). [PRE-]

prēdisposi'tion (-zĭ-), n. State of mind

or body favourable *to* (mercy, malaria, etc.). [PRE-]

prēdŏm'in|āte, v.i. Have or exert control (*over* person etc.), be superior; be the stronger or main element, preponderate; as *garden in which dahlias* ~*ate*. Hence or cogn. ~ANCE n., ~ANT a., ~antLY², ~ātingLY² advv. [f. med. L *PRAE(dominare* DOMINATE)]

prē-ĕm'in|ent, a. Excelling others; distinguished beyond others in some quality. Hence or cogn. ~ENCE n., ~entLY² adv. [f. L PRAE(*eminens* EMINENT)]

prē-ĕmpt', v.t. & i. Obtain by preemption; *occupy (public land) so as to have right of pre-emption; (fig.) appropriate beforehand; (bridge) make preemptive bid. [back formation f. foll.]

prē-ĕmp'tion, n. Purchase by one person etc. before opportunity is offered to others; right so to purchase. So ~IVE a. (~*ive bid*, bid at bridge intended to be high enough to prevent further bidding). [f. med. L *PRE(emere empt*- buy), -ION]

preen, v.t. Trim (feathers) with beak; (of person) trim one*self*. [ME, app. var. of PRUNE³, assoc. w. Sc. & dial. *preen* pierce, pin]

prĕf'ăb, n. (colloq.). Prefabricated house. [abbr.]

prēfăb'ric|āte, v.t. Manufacture component parts of (building etc.) prior to their assembly on a site. So ~A'TION n. [PRE-]

prĕf'ace, n., & v.t. & i. **1.** Introduction to book stating subject, scope, etc.; preliminary part of a speech; introduction to central part of eucharistic service. **2.** v.t. Furnish (book etc.) with ~; introduce (act, speech, *with*), as ~*d his remarks with a snort*; (of event etc.) lead up to (another); (v.i.) make preliminary remarks. So **prēfatŏr'ial, prĕf'atory**, aa. [ME, f. OF, app. f. med. L *prefatia* for L *praefatio* f. *praefari*, see -ION]

prĕf'ĕct, n. (Rom. ant.) title of various officers, civil & military; chief administrative officer of French department; ~ *of police*, head of Paris police; (in some public schools) senior pupil authorized to maintain discipline. So **prĕfĕc'torAL**, ~ŏr'IAL, aa. [ME, f. OF, f. L *praefectus* f. PRAE(*ficere fect*- = *facere* make) set over]

prĕf'ĕctūre, n. (Period of) office, official residence, district under government, of a prefect. Hence **prĕfĕc'turAL** (-cher-) a. [F, or f. L *praefectura* (as prec., see -URE)]

prĕfẽr', v.t. (-rr-). Promote (person *to* office, whence ~MENT n.; bring forward, submit, (statement, information, etc., *to* person in authority etc., *against* offender etc.); choose rather, like better, as *gentlemen* ~ *blondes*, ~ *water to wine*, ~ *to leave it alone*, ~ *that it should be left* (*than* is unidiomatic after ~ unless *rather* is inserted, as ~*red to die rather than pay*), so **prĕf'erABLE, prĕf'erablУ²** adv. [ME, f. OF *preferer* f. L PRAE(*ferre latbear*)]

prĕf'erence, n. Liking of one thing better than another (*of A to* or *over* B); thing one prefers; prior right esp. to payment of debts; ‖ ~ *bond, share, stock,* (on which dividend is paid before any is paid on ordinary stock; favouring of one person or country before others in business relations, esp. favouring of a country by admitting its products at lower import duty. [f. F *préférence* f. med. L *praeferentia* (prec., -ENCE)]

prĕferĕn'tial (-shl), a. Of, giving, receiving, preference; (of duties etc.) favouring particular countries, whence ~ISM, ~IST, nn., (-sha-). Hence ~LY² adv. [as prec. +-AL]

prĕferred' (-ẽrd), a. In vbl senses; ~ *shares, stock,* etc., preference shares etc. [-ED¹]

prĕfĭg'ure (-ger), v.t. Represent beforehand by figure or type, picture to oneself beforehand. Hence or cogn. **prĕfĭgūr**A'TION, ~MENT (-germ-), nn., **prĕfĭg'ūra**tIVE a. [ME, f. LL PRAE (*figurare* FIGURE)]

prĕf'ĭx¹, n. Verbal element placed at beginning of word to qualify meaning or (in some languages) as inflexional formative; title placed before name, e.g. *Mr, Mrs, Sir, Dr.* [f. mod. L *praefixum,* p.p. of L PRAE(*figere* FIX)]

prĕfĭx'², v.t. Add (chapter, paragraph, etc., *to* book etc.) as introduction; join (word, verbal element) as prefix (*to* word), so **prĕfĭ'xION, prĕfĭx'TURE,** nn. [ME, f. OF PRE(*fixer* FIX¹)]

prĕfōrm', v.t. Form beforehand. [f. L PRAE(*formare* FORM²)]

prĕfōrmā'tion, n. Previous formation; (biol.) *theory of* ~ (that all parts of the perfect organism exist in the germ & are merely developed). [PRE-]

prĕfōrm'ative, a. & n. Forming beforehand; (syllable, letter) prefixed as formative element. [PRE-]

prĕg'nable, a. Not impregnable. [late ME & OF *prenable,* see IMPREGNABLE]

prĕg'nant, a. (Of woman or female animal) with child, gravid; teeming with ideas, imaginative, inventive; fruitful in results, big *with* (consequences etc.); (of words or acts) having a hidden meaning, significant, suggestive, whence ~LY² adv.; (gram.) ~ *construction* (in which more is implied than the words express). Hence **prĕg'n**ANCY n. [ME, f. L *praegnans -ntis*)]

prēhĕn'sile, a. (zool.). (Of tail or limb) capable of grasping. Hence **prēhĕnsil**ITY n. [f. F *préhensile* f. L PRAE(*hendere hens-* grasp), see -ILE]

prēhĕn'sion (-shn), n. Grasping, seizing; mental apprehension. [f. L *prehensio* (prec., -ION)]

prēhĭstŏ'r|ĭc, a. Of the period antecedent to history; (colloq.) antediluvian. Hence ~ICALLY adv. [PRE-]

prēhĭs'torў, n. Prehistoric matters or times. [PRE-, after prec.]

prē-ĭgnĭ'tion, n. Premature firing of explosive mixture in internal-combustion engine. [PRE-]

prējŭdge', v.t. Pass judgement on (person) before trial or proper inquiry; form premature judgement upon (person, cause, action, etc.). So ~MENT (-jm-), **prējudĭca'TION** (-jōō-), nn. [f. F *préjuger* or L PRAE(*judicare* JUDGE)]

prĕj'udĭce (-jōō-), n., & v.t. **1.** Preconceived opinion, bias, (*against, in favour of,* person or thing), as *divest your mind of* ~, *has a* ~ *against foreigners, has a* ~ *in our favour, this is mere* ~; injury that results or may result from some action or judgement, as *to the* ~ *of; without* ~, without detriment to existing right or claim. **2.** v.t. Impair the validity of (right, claim, statement, etc.); cause (person) to have a ~ (*against, in favour of*), esp. in p.p. [ME, f. OF *prejudice* f. L PRAE(*judicium* judgement); vb f. OF *prejudicier*]

prĕjudĭ'cial (-jōōdĭshl), a. Causing prejudice, detrimental, (*to* rights, interests, etc.). Hence ~LY² adv. [ME, f. prec. (n.) +-AL (as to sense); corresp. in form to OF *prejudicial, -el,* f. LL *-alis*]

prĕl'acў, n. Office, rank, see, of a prelate; *the* prelates; church government by prelates (usu. hostile for EPISCOPACY). [ME, f. AF *prelacie* f. med. L *praelatia* (as foll. see -ACY)]

prĕl'ate, n. High ecclesiastical dignitary, e.g. (arch)bishop, metropolitan, patriarch, (hist.) abbot or prior. Hence **prĕlāt**IC(AL) aa., **prĕlăt'ĭcaLLY²** adv. [ME, f. OF *prelat* f. L *praelatus* (as PREFER)]

prĕl'atéss, n. Abbess, prioress; (joc.) prelate's wife. [-ESS¹]

prĕl'atĭze, -ise (-īz), v.t. Bring (church) under prelatical government. [f. PRELATE +-IZE]

prĕl'ature, n. Office of prelate; *the* prelates. [f. F *prélature* f. med. L *praelatura* (as PRELATE, see -URE)]

prēlĕct', v.i. Discourse, lecture, (*to* audience *on* subject, esp. in univv.). So **prēlĕc'tION, prēlĕc'tor,** nn. [f. L PRAE(*legere lect-* read)]

prēlĭbā'tion, n. Foretaste (usu. fig.). [f. LL PRAE(*libatio* LIBATION)]

prēlĭm', n. (colloq.). Preliminary examination; (pl.; print.) pages preceding text. [abbr.]

prēlĭm'ĭnar|ў, a. & n. 1. Introductory, preparatory. **2.** n. ~y arrangement (usu. in pl.). Hence ~ĭLY² adv. [f. mod. L *praeliminaris,* pl. *-ia,* or F *préliminaire(s)* (both 1648); f. L *limen -minis* threshold, see -ARY¹]

prĕl'ūde¹, n. Performance, action, event, condition, serving as introduction (*to* another); introductory part of poem etc.;

(mus.) introductory movement esp. one preceding fugue or forming first piece of suite. Hence **prĕlŭd′**ıᴀʟ a., **prĕl′ŭd**ıᴢᴇ(2) v.i. [f. F *prélude* or med. L *praeludium*, as foll.]

prĕl′ŭde² (*or* prīlŭd′), v.t. & i. Serve as prelude to, introduce, foreshadow; introduce with a prelude; be, give, a prelude *to*; (mus.) play a prelude. So **prĕlŭ′sıon** (-zhn) n., **prĕlŭs′ıve** a. [f. L ᴘʀᴀᴇ(*ludere* *lus*- play)]

prĕmatŭre′ (*also* prĕm′), a. & n. Occurring, done, before the usual or proper time, too early, hasty, as ~ *decision*, *decay*; (n.) ~ explosion of shell. Hence or cogn. ~ʟʏ² adv., ~ɴᴇss, **prĕmatŭr′ıᴛʏ**, nn. [f. L ᴘʀᴀᴇ(*maturus* ᴍᴀᴛᴜʀᴇ)]

prĕmĕd′it|āte, v.t. Think out, design, (action etc.) beforehand (esp. in p.p.). Hence or cogn. ~ātᴇdʟʏ² adv., ~ᴀ′ᴛɪoɴ n. [f. L ᴘʀᴀᴇ(*meditari* ᴍᴇᴅɪᴛᴀᴛᴇ)]

prĕm′ier (*or* prē-), a. & n. 1. (Now chiefly sl.) first in position, importance, order, or time, as *secured* ~ *place* (in race). 2. n. Prime Minister in Great Britain or some British dominions. Hence ~sʜɪᴘ n. [ME, f. OF = first, f. L as ᴘʀɪᴍᴀʀʏ]

premìère′ (prŭmyâr′), n. First performance of play. [F, fem. adj. as prec.]

prĕm′ise¹, -ss (as below), n. 1. (log.). (Often -ss) previous statement from which another is inferred, esp. ᴍᴀᴊoʀ², ᴍɪɴoʀ, ~ in syllogism. 2. (pl.). The aforesaid, the foregoing, esp. (law) the aforesaid houses, lands, or tenements. 3. (pl.). House, building, with grounds & appurtenances, as *to be drunk on the* ~*s*. [ME, f. OF *premisse* f. med. L *praemissa* (*propositio* proposition) set in front f. L ᴘʀᴀᴇ(*mittere* *miss*-send)]

prĕmise′² (-z), v.t. Say, write, (thing, *that*) by way of introduction. [f. prec.]

prĕm′ium, n. Reward, prize, (chiefly now in *put a* ~ *on*, provide or act as incentive to, as *you, this, will put a* ~ *on fraud*); *P*~ (*Savings*) *Bond*, government security with cash prizes drawn monthly in place of regular interest; amount to be paid in consideration of contract of insurance; sum additional to interest, wages, etc., bonus; fee for instruction in profession etc.; charge for changing one currency into another of greater value, agio; *at a* ~, at more than nominal value (cf. ᴅɪsᴄoᴜɴᴛ¹), (fig.) in high esteem. [f. L *praemium* booty, reward, f. ᴘʀᴀᴇ- +*emere* buy, take]

prĕmōl′ar, n. Tooth in front of true molars (in man, ʙɪᴄᴜsᴘɪᴅ). [ᴘʀᴇ-]

prĕmoni′tion, n. Forewarning. So **prĕmŏn′ıᴛoʀ** n., **prĕmŏn′ıᴛoʀɪ**ʟʏ² adv., **prĕmŏn′ıᴛoʀʏ** a. [f. obs. F *premonicion* or LL *praemonitio* f. L ᴘʀᴀᴇ(*monēre* -*it*-warn), -ɪoɴ]

Prĕmŏnstratĕn′sian, a. & n. (Member) of order of regular canons founded at Prémontré in 1119, or of corresponding order of nuns. [f. med. L *Praemonstra-*

tensis (*Praemonstratus* Prémontré, see -ᴇssᴇ) +-ᴀɴ]

prĕmōrse′, a. (bot., entom.). With the end abruptly truncate. [f. L ᴘʀᴀᴇ-(*mordēre mors*- bite) bite off in front]

prĕn′tice, n., & v.t.(arch.). = ᴀᴘᴘʀᴇɴᴛɪᴄᴇ, esp. ~ (tiro's) *hand*. Hence ~sʜɪᴘ n. (arch.). [aphetic]

prĕŏccŭpā′tion, n. Prepossession, prejudice; occupation of a place beforehand; occupation, business, that takes precedence of all others; mental absorption. [F, or f. L *praeoccupatio* (foll., -ᴀᴛɪoɴ)]

prĕŏcc′ŭp|ȳ, v.t. Engage beforehand, engross (mind etc.); (p.p., esp.) distrait, with thoughts elsewhere, whence ~iedʟʏ² (-pīd-) adv.; appropriate beforehand. [f. ᴘʀᴇ- +occᴜᴘʏ, after L *praeoccupare*]

prĕp, n. (school sl.). ‖ Preparation. [abbr.]

prĕparā′tion, n. Preparing; (usu. pl.) thing(s) done to make ready (*for*); *make* ~*s*, prepare (*for*); ‖ (abbr. *prep*) ~ of lessons as part of school routine; substance, e.g. food or medicine, specially prepared; (mus.) preparing of a discord. [ME, f. OF f. L *praeparationem* (as ᴘʀᴇ-ᴘᴀʀᴇ, see -ɪoɴ)]

prĕpă′rative, a. & n. Preparatory; (n.) ~ act, (mil., naut.) signal on drum, bugle, etc., as order to make ready. Hence ~ʟʏ² adv. [ME, f. OF (-*if*, -*ive*), f. med. L *praeparativus* (as ᴘʀᴇᴘᴀʀᴇ, see -ɪvᴇ)]

prĕpă′rator|ȳ, a. & n. Serving to prepare, introductory (*to*); ~*y* (*school*), ‖ where pupils are prepared for higher school; (quasi-adv.) *am packing it up* ~*y to sending it by post*. Hence ~ɪʟʏ² adv. [ME, f. LL *praeparatorius* (as foll., see -oʀʏ)]

prĕpāre′, v.t. & i. Make (person, thing) ready (*for*); make ready (food, meal) for eating; make (person) mentally ready or fit (*for* news, *to* hear, etc.); get (lesson, speech, sermon) ready by previous study, get (person) ready by teaching (*for* college, examination, the army, etc.); make preparations (*for, to* do, etc.); *be* ~*d*, be ready or willing (*to* do); make (chemical product etc.) by regular process; (mus.) lead up to (discord) by sounding the dissonant note in it as consonant note in preceding chord. Hence **prĕpār′ed**ɴᴇss n., readiness (esp. of nav. and mil. preparations for possible hostilities). [ME, f. OF *preparer* or L ᴘʀᴀᴇ(*parare* make ready)]

prĕpay′, v.t. Pay (charge) beforehand; pay (postage), pay postage of (parcel, &c.) beforehand, e.g. by affixing stamp. Hence ~ᴀʙʟᴇ a., ~ᴍᴇɴᴛ n. [ᴘʀᴇ-]

prĕpĕnse′, a. Deliberate, intentional, chiefly in *malice* ~, intention to injure, *of malice* ~, with intent to injure. Hence ~ʟʏ² adv. [earlier *prepensed* p.p. of obs. *prepense* altered f. earlier *purpense* f. OF ᴘᴜʀ(*penser*, see ᴘᴇɴsɪvᴇ)]

prĕpŏn′der|āte, v.i. Weigh more, be heavier; ~*ate over*, exceed in number, quantity, etc.; be of greater moral or intellectual weight; be the chief element, predominate; (of scale of balance) sink. So ~ANCE n., ~ANT a., ~antLY[2] adv. [f. L PRAE(*ponderare* PONDER), -ATE[3]]

prĕposi'tion (-z-), n. Word serving to mark relation between the noun or pronoun it governs & normally precedes & another word (e.g. the italic wds in: found him *at* home, wait *in* the hall, what did you do it *for*? the bed (that) he slept *on*, won *by* waiting, came *through* the roof, that is what I was thinking *of*). Hence ~AL a., ~alLY[2] adv., (-zĭsho-). [ME, f. L *praepositio* f. PRAE(*ponere posit*- place)]

prĕpŏs'itive (-z-), a. (gram.). (Of word, particle, etc.) proper to be placed before or prefixed. [f. LL *praepositivus* (as prec., see -IVE)]

prĕpŏs'itor (-z-). See PRAEPOSTOR.

prĕpossĕss' (-z-), v.t. Imbue, inspire, (person *with* notion, feeling, etc.); (of idea etc.) take possession of (person, usu. pass.); prejudice, usu. favourably, whence ~ING[2] a., ~ingLY[2] adv., ~ingNESS, prĕposse'ssion (-zĕshn), nn. [PRE-]

prĕpŏs'terous, a. Contrary to nature, reason, or common sense; perverse, foolish; absurd. Hence ~LY[2] adv., ~NESS n. [f. L PRAE(*posterus* coming after) reversed, absurd, + -OUS]

prĕpŏt'|ent, a. Very powerful; more powerful than others; (biol.) having stronger fertilizing influence or power of transmitting hereditary qualities. So ~ENCE, ~ENCY, nn. [ME, f. L *praepotens* part. of PRAE(*posse* be able)]

|| **prĕ-prĕf'erence**, a. (Of shares, claims, etc.) ranking before preference shares etc. [PRE-]

prĕp'ūce, n. Foreskin, loose integument covering end of penis. So **prĕpū'tIAL** (-shl) a. [ME, f. OF, f. L *praeputium*]

Prē-Răph'āĕlite, n. Artist who aims at producing work in the spirit that prevailed before the time of Raphael; ~ Brotherhood (abbr. *P.R.B.*), group of English artists including Holman Hunt, Millais, D. G. Rossetti. So **prē-Răph'āĕl** a., **Prē-Răph'āĕl(ĭt)**ISM n. [PRE- +*Raphael* + -ITE[1]]

prĕrē'quisite (-z-), a. & n. (Thing) required as previous condition. [PRE-]

prĕrŏg'ative, n. & a. **1.** (Also *royal* ~) right of the sovereign, theoretically subject to no restriction; peculiar right or privilege, as *it is our* ~ *to* (do), *we have the* ~ *of* (doing), *the* ~ *of* (right to show) *mercy*; natural or divinely-given advantage, privilege, or faculty, as *it is the* ~ *of man to drink without thirst*; ||(pedantic) right of giving first vote and thus influencing those that follow; (hist.) ~ *court*, archbishop's court for probate of wills etc. **2.** adj. Privileged, enjoyed by privilege; (Rom. hist.) having the right to vote first. [adj. f. L PRAE(*rogativus* f.

rogare ask, see -IVE) asked first; n. f. AF, OF, f. L *praerogativa* previous choice, prognostic, privilege, fem. adj. as n.]

prĕs'age[1], n. Omen, portent; presentiment, foreboding. Hence **prĕsāge'FUL** (-jf-) a. [ME & OF *presage* f. L *praesagium* f. PRAE(*sagus* predicting)]

prĕsāge'[2], v.t. Portend, foreshadow; give warning of (event etc.) by natural means, as *such ideas are held to* ~ *insanity*; (of person) predict, (also) have presentiment of. [f. F *présager*, as prec.]

prĕsbў̆|ōp'ia (-s-, -z-), n. Form of long-sightedness incident to old age. Hence ~ŏp'IC a. [f. Gk *presbus* old man +*ōps ōpos* eye, see -IA[1]]

prĕs'bўter (-s-, -z-), n. (In early Church) one of several officers managing affairs of local church; (in Episcopal church) minister of second order, priest; (in Presbyterian church) elder. Hence or cogn. **prĕsbўt'er**AL, **prĕsbўtēr'IAL**, aa., **prĕsbўt'erATE**[1] (-ăt), ~SHIP, nn. [LL, f. Gk *presbuteros* elder]

Prĕsbўtēr'ian (-s-, -z-), a. & n. **1.** ~ *Church*, one governed by elders, all (including ministers) of equal rank; *United* ~ *Church*, that formed in 1847 by union of United Secession & Relief churches, later embodied in the United Free Church of Scotland & from 1929 in the Church of Scotland. **2.** n. Adherent of ~ system, member of ~ Church. Hence ~ISM n., ~IZE(3) v.t. [f. LL as foll. + -AN]

prĕs'bўterў (-s-, -z-), n. Eastern part of chancel beyond choir, sanctuary; body of presbyters, esp. court next above KIRK-session, district represented by this; (R.-C. Ch.) priest's house. [ME, f. OF -*terie* f. LL f. Gk *presbuterion* (as PRESBYTER)]

prĕ'scient (-shĭent), a. Having foreknowledge or foresight. Hence or cogn. **prĕ'sciENCE** (-shyens) n., ~LY[2] adv. [F. f. L PRAE(*scire* know), see -ENT]

prĕscind', v.t. & i. Cut off (part *from* whole) esp. prematurely or abruptly; ~ *from*, leave out of consideration. [f. L PRAE(*scindere* cut)]

prĕscrībe', v.t. & i. Lay down or impose authoritatively, as *do not* ~ *to me what I am to do or how to do it, the statutes* ~ *the practice*; (med.) advise use of (medicine etc., or abs.; *to or for* patient, *for* complaint; also fig.); assert prescriptive right or claim (*to, for*, thing). [f. L PRAE-(*scribere script*- write) direct in writing]

prĕs'cript, n. Ordinance, law, command. [as prec.]

prĕscrip'tion, n. Prescribing; physician's (usu. written) direction for composition & use of medicine; (law) (*positive*) ~, uninterrupted use or possession from time immemorial or for period fixed by law as giving title or right, such title or right, *negative* ~, limitation of the time within which action or claim can be

For other words in *pre-* see PRE-.

raised; (fig.) ancient custom viewed as authoritative, claim founded on long use. [ME, f. OF or L *praescriptio* (as prec., see -ION)]

prescrip′tive, a. Prescribing; based on prescription, as ~ *right*; prescribed by custom. Hence ~LY[2] adv. [f. LL *praescriptivus* (as PRESCRIBE, see -IVE)]

preselec′tive, a. (Of motor-car gears) that can be selected and set in advance. [PRE-]

pres′ence (-z-), n. Being present, as *your* ~ *is requested, in the* ~ *of a large company*; REAL[2] ~; place where person is, as *admitted to, banished from, his* ~, *in this* (*august* etc.) ~, *in the* ~ *of this* (etc.) person; ‖ *the* ~, ceremonial attendance on person of high esp. royal rank, as *remained in, retired from, the* ~; carriage, bearing, as *a man of* (*a*) *noble* ~; ~ *of mind*, calmness & self-command in sudden emergencies; ~*-chamber* (in which great personage receives guests etc.). [ME, f. OF, f. L *praesentia* (as foll., see -ENCE)]

pres′ent[1] (-z-), a. Being in the place in question (chiefly pred.), as *no one else was* ~ (*in* place, *at* proceedings etc.); being dealt with, discussed, etc., as *no excuse in the* ~ *case, the* ~ *volume* (the book you are reading or I am reviewing, *the* ~ *writer* (I) *could not verify this*; ~ *to* (felt, remembered, by) *the mind, the imagination*; ‖ (arch.) ready at hand, ready with assistance, as *a very* ~ *help in trouble*; existing, occurring, being such, now, as *the* ~ *Duke of York, in the* ~ *fashion; the* ~ *worth of* (sum that with compound interest dating from now will amount to) *£100 in 12 years*; (gram.) ~ *tense* (denoting action etc. now going on). [ME, f. OF, f. L *praesens -ntis* part. of PRAE(*esse* be) be at hand]

pres′ent[2] (-z-), n. *The* present time, the time now passing; *at* ~, now, as *do not want any more at* ~, *is at* ~ *in Egypt; for the* ~, just now, as far as the ~ is concerned, as *that will do for the* ~; = ~ *tense*; (*know all men* etc.) *by these* ~*s*, by this document (now legal or joc.). [ME, as prec.]

pres′ent[3] (-z-), n. Gift; *make a* ~ *of*, present (thing *to* person). [ME, f. OF (as prec.), orig. in phr. *mettre une chose en* ~ *à quelqu'un*, put a thing into the presence of a person]

present′[4] (-z-), v.t. & i., & n. **1.** Introduce (person *to* another); introduce (person) to sovereign at court; ~ one*self*, appear esp. as candidate for examination etc. **2.** (Of theatr. manager) cause (actor) to take part in play, produce (play). **3.** Recommend (clergyman) to bishop for institution (*to* benefice). **4.** Exhibit (thing *to* person etc.), as ~ *a ragged appearance*, ~*ed its front to me*; show (quality etc.), as *cases that* ~ *some difficulty*. **5.** (mil.). Hold (fire-arm) in position for taking aim; (also ~ *arms*) hold fire-arm etc. in deferential

position in saluting. **6.** (Of idea etc.) offer, suggest it*self*. **7.** (law). Bring formally under notice, submit, (complaint, offence, *to* authority). **8.** Aim (weapon *at*), hold out (weapon) in position for aiming (also abs. ~ *!* as word of command). **9.** Offer, give, (thing *to* person) as present; offer (compliments, regards, *to*); deliver (bill etc. *to* person etc.) for acceptance etc.; ~ *person with* thing, ~ it to him. **10.** n. Act of aiming weapon esp. fire-arm, position of weapon when aimed, position of 'P~ arms' in salute. [ME, f. OF *presenter* f. L *praesentare* (as PRESENT[1])]

presen′t|able (-z-), a. Of decent appearance, fit to be introduced or go into company; suitable for presentation as a gift etc. Hence ~ABIL′ITY n., ~ABLY[2] adv. [-ABLE]

presenta′tion (-z-), n. Presenting; ~ (gratis) *copy* of book etc.; exhibition, theatrical representation, etc.; formal introduction esp. at court; (philos.) all the modification of consciousness directly involved in the knowing or being aware of an object in a single moment of thought, whence ~AL (-sho-) a. [ME, f. OF or LL *praesentatio* (PRESENT[4], -ATION)]

presenta′tion|ism (-z-, -sho-), n. (philos.). Doctrine that in perception the mind has immediate cognition of the object. So ~(al)IST nn. [prec. + -ISM]

presen′tative (-z-), a. (Of benefice) to which patron has right of presentation; serving to present an idea to the mind; (philos.) of (the nature of) presentation. [-ATIVE]

presentee′ (-z-), n. Clergyman presented to benefice; person recommended for office; person presented at court; recipient of present. [ME, f. AF (PRESENT[4], -EE)]

presen′tient (-shi-), a. Having a presentiment (*of* event etc., or abs.). [f. L PRAE-(*sentiens* SENTIENT)]

presen′timent (-z-, -s-), n. Vague expectation, foreboding, (*of* coming event esp. evil). [f. obs. F PRE(SENTIMENT)]

presen′tive (-z-), a. (Of word) presenting an object or conception directly to the mind (opp. to *symbolic*). [-IVE]

pres′ently (-z-), adv. Soon, after a short time; (chiefly Sc.) at the present time, now. [PRESENT[1] + -LY[2]]

present′ment (-z-), n. (Law) statement on oath by jury of fact within their knowledge; formal complaint of offence made by parish authorities to bishop or archdeacon at his visitation; theatrical representation; delineation, portrait; statement, description, (*of*); act, mode, of presenting to the mind. [ME, f. OF *presentement* (as PRESENT[3], see -MENT)]

preserva′tion (-z-), n. Preserving, being preserved, from injury or destruction; state of being well or ill preserved, as *in an excellent state of* ~, (*in* (a state of) *fair* ~.

[late ME, f. OF *preservation* or med. L *praeservatio* (as PRESERVE, see -ATION)]

prĕsĕrv'at|ive (-z-), a. & n. (Drug, measure, etc.) tending to preserve; chemical substance for preserving perishable foodstuffs, whence ~IZE(5)v.t. [ME, f. OF *preservatif* or med. L *praeservativus* (as prec., see -ATIVE)]

prĕsĕrve'[1] (-z-), n. Jam; ground set apart for protection of game (often fig.); piece of water for fish; (pl.) goggles used as protection from dust etc. [f. foll.]

prĕsĕrv|e'[2] (-z-), v.t. Keep safe (*from* harm etc.); keep alive (name, memory, etc.); maintain (state of things); retain (quality, condition); prepare (fruit, meat, etc.) by boiling with sugar, pickling, etc., to prevent decomposition or fermentation; keep from decomposition by chemical treatment etc.; keep (game, game-run, river, or abs.) undisturbed for private use; *well ~ed*, (of elderly person) showing little sign of age. Hence ~'ABLE a., ~'ER[1] n., (-z-). [ME, f. OF *preserver* f. LL PRAE-(*servare* keep)]

prĕside' (-z-), v.i. Occupy chair of authority at meeting of society or company (often *over*), sit at head of table; exercise control, sit or reign supreme, (often fig.); ~ *at the organ, piano*, etc., act as organist etc. [f. F *présider* f. L PRAE(*sidēre* = *sedēre* sit)]

prĕs'idency̆ (-z-), n. Office of president; period of this; district administered by president, esp. (formerly) division of E. India Company's territory (*Bengal, Madras, Bombay, P~*). [f. Sp., Pg. *presidencia* f. med. L *praesidentia* (prec., -ENCY)]

prĕs'ident (-z-), n. Head of temporary or permanent body of persons, presiding over their meetings & proceedings; head of some colleges & U.S. universities; person presiding over meetings of academy, literary or scientific society, etc.; *person presiding over proceedings of bank or company; head of advisory council, board, etc., as *P~ of the Board of Trade*; *Lord P~ of the Council*, Cabinet Minister presiding at meetings of Privy Council; elected head of government in U.S. & other modern republics; (hist.) governor of province, colony, etc. Hence or cogn. **prĕsĭdĕn'tIAL** (-z-, -shl) a., **prĕsĭdĕn'tIaLLY**[2] adv., ~SHIP n. [ME, f. OF f. L as PRESIDE, see -ENT]

prĕs'identĕss (-z-), n. Female president; wife of president. [-ESS[1]]

prĕsĭd'iary̆, a. Of, having, serving as, a garrison. [f. L *praesidiarius* (*praesidium* garrison, as PRESIDE, see -ARY[1])]

prĕsĭd'ĭō, n. (pl. ~s). (In Spain & Sp. America) fort, garrison town. [Sp., as foll.]

prĕsĭd'ium, n. Standing committee in various Communistic organizations. [L (*praesidium*), = garrison]

prĕss[1], n. **1.** Crowding; crowd (*of* people etc.); throng, crush, in battle; pressure, hurry, of affairs, as *the ~ of modern life*. **2.** Pressing, as *give it a slight ~*. **3.** (naut.). ~ *of sail, canvas* (as much as wind etc. will allow). **4.** Kinds of instrument for compressing, flattening, or shaping, or for extracting juice etc. **5.** (Also *printing~*) machine for printing; printing-house or establishment; publishing firm etc., esp. *University P~*; the art, practice, of printing; *in the ~*, being printed, *send, go, come, to* (*the*) *~* (to be printed), *correct the ~* (errors in printing); *freedom of the ~*, right to print & publish anything without censorship; *the* newspapers generally, as *favourably noticed by the ~* (*have a good* etc. *~*, receive such notice); *the* GUTTER, YELLOW, *~* ; *~ campaign* or *stunt*, prosecution of political or other aims by newspaper letters & articles; (as name of newspaper) *Aberdeen P~ and Journal*. **6.** Large usu. shelved cupboard for clothes, books, etc., esp. in recess in wall. **7.** ~ *agent*, person employed by theatre, actor, etc., to attend to advertising and ~ *publicity*; ~-*box*, shelter for newspaper reporter at cricket match etc.; ~ *conference*, interview given to the ~ by some person to make announcement or answer questions; ‖~ CUTTING; ~-*gallery* (for reporters esp. in House of Commons); ~'*man*, journalist, operator of printing~; ~'*mark*, mark, number in book showing its place in library (now usu. *shelf-mark*). [ME & OF *presse* f. *presser* (foll.); also ME *prĕs*, later *preace*, of obsc. form.]

prĕss[2], v.t. & i. **1.** Exert steady force against (thing in contact), as *let a heavy weight ~ it, ~ it under* or *with a stone, ~ the two plates together; ~ the button*, set electric machinery in motion, (fig.) take decisive initial step; ~-*button warfare* (carried on by means of guided missiles whose flight is controlled by ~ing a button); (as sign of affection etc.) *he ~ed my hand, ~ed her to his side*; move (thing *up, down, against*, etc.) by ~ing. **2.** Exert pressure, bear with weight or force, (*on, against*, etc.). **3.** Squeeze (juice etc. *out of, from*, etc.); compress, squeeze, (thing) to flatten or shape or smooth it, or to extract juice etc., as ~*ed beef*. **4.** (Of enemy, attacking force, etc.) bear heavily on, esp. in p.p. *hard ~ed*; weigh down, oppress, (feelings, mind, spirits); (pass.) *am ~ed for* (have barely enough) *space, time, funds*, etc. **5.** Produce strong mental or moral impression, esp. weigh heavily, (*up*)*on* (mind, person). **6.** Be urgent, demand immediate action, as *time ~es, nothing remains that ~es*. **7.** Urge, entreat, (person *to do*, person or without object *for* answer etc.). **8.** Insist on strict interpretation of (words, metaphor). **9.** Urge (course, opinion,

upon person); force (offer, gift, etc. *upon*).
10. Crowd, throng, (*up, round,* etc.);
hasten, urge one's way, *on, forward,* etc.
[ME *presse* f. OF *presser* f. L *pressare*
frequent. of *premere press-*; also ME
prêse (cf. prec.)]

prĕss³, v.t., & n. (hist., exc. fig.). Force
(man, or abs.) to serve in army or navy
(also fig., esp. ~ thing *into the service of*);
take (horses, boats, etc.) for royal or
public use; (n., hist.) compulsory enlistment in navy or (less usu.) army ; ~*-gang,*
body of men employed to ~ men. [alt.
f. 16th c. (obs.) *prest* (by assoc. w. PRESS²)
f. OF *prest* loan, advance, f. *prester* f. L
PRAE(*stare* stand) vouch for, furnish]

prĕss′ing, a. (In vbl senses, esp.: urgent,
as ~ *need, danger*; importunate, persistent, as *a ~ invitation, since you are so ~.*
Hence ~LY² adv. [PRESS² + -ING²]

prĕs′sure (-sher), n. **1.** Exertion of continuous force, force so exerted, upon or
against a body by another in contact
with it; amount of this, expressed by the
weight upon a unit area. **2.** *Atmospheric ~*
(of the ATMOSPHERE; *high, low, ~,* local
atmospheric condition sending barometer
up, down); *blood-~,* varying tension, now
measured for diagnosis etc., of blood-
-vessels. **3.** Affliction, oppression; trouble,
embarrassment, as *financial ~.* **4.** Urgency, as *wrote hastily & under ~*; constraining influence, as ~ *must be brought
to bear upon him.* **5.** *High ~,* (orig.) ~
higher than atmospheric (now indefinite,
used esp. of compound engines in which
steam is used at different ~s in different
cylinders, so *low ~*), (fig.) high degree of
activity, speed, etc., as *working at high ~,
high-~ work*; ~*-cooker,* apparatus for
cooking under high ~ at high temperature, so ~*-cooking*; ~ *group,* group exerting ~ on a government for their own
special purpose. Hence **prĕs′surize**
(-sher) v.t., (esp. in p.p.) construct (aircraft, cabin) so that air-~, temperature,
etc. can be controlled in such a way that
high-altitude flying is possible without
discomfort and without the use of oxygen
apparatus. [ME, f. OF, f. L *pressura* (as
PRESS², see -URE)]

Prĕs′ter John (jŏn), n. Alleged Christian
priest & king in Abyssinia or some eastern
country in Middle Ages. [ME, f. OF
prestre (as PRESBYTER) *Jehan* priest John]

prĕstidi′gitātor, n. Juggler, conjurer.
So **prĕstidigitA′TION** n. [f. F *prestidigi-
tateur* (*preste* nimble, as PRESTO + L *digitus*
finger, see -OR); earlier *prestigiator* f. L]

prĕstige′ (-ēzh), n. Influence, reputation,
derived from past achievements, associations, etc. [F, = illusion, glamour, f. LL
prestigium (= L *-ia* fem.) f. PRAE(*stringere*
bind) blindfold, dazzle]

prĕstĭss′ĭmō, a., adv., & n. (mus.). Very
quick (piece, movement). [It., superl. as
foll.]

prĕs′tō¹, a., adv., & n. (mus.). Quick

(piece, movement). [It., f. LL *praestus*
f. L *praesto* ready]

prĕs′tō², adv. & a. (In conjurer's formulae) quickly, as *hey ~, pass!* ; (adj.) rapid,
juggling. [= prec.]

prĕsūm|e′ (-z-), v.t. & i. Take the
liberty, venture, (*to* do); assume, take for
granted, as *I ~e that he has seen them,
I ~e this decision to be final, you had better
~e no such thing,* whence ~′ABLE a.,
~′ABLY², ~′ĕdLY², advv., (-z-); ~*e* (*up*)*on,*
take advantage of, make unscrupulous
use of, (person's good nature, one's acquaintance with him, etc.), whence
~′ingLY² (-z-) adv. [ME, f. OF *presumer*
or L PRAE(*sumere sumpt-* take)]

prĕsūmp′tion (-z-), n. Arrogance, assurance; taking for granted, thing taken for
granted, as *this was a mere ~; the* (only
natural) ~ *is that he had lost it*; ground
for presuming, as *there is a strong ~
against its truth*; (law) ~ *of fact,* inference of fact from known facts, ~ *of law,*
(1) assumption of truth of thing until the
contrary is proved, (2) inference established by law as universally applicable
to certain circumstances. [ME, f. OF *pre-
sumpcion* f. L *praesumptionem* (as prec.,
see -ION)]

prĕsūmp′tive (-z-), a. Giving grounds for
presumption, as ~ *evidence,* whence ~LY²
adv.; *heir* ~ (whose right of inheritance
is liable to be defeated by birth of nearer
heir, cf. APPARENT). [f. F *présomptif* f. LL
praesumptivus (as PRESUME, see -IVE)]

prĕsūmp′tŭous (-z-), a. Unduly confident, arrogant, forward. Hence ~LY²
adv., ~NESS n. [ME, f. OF *presuntueus* f.
LL *praesumptiosus* (-*uosus*) (as PRESUME,
see -IOUS)]

prĕsuppōse′ (-z), v.t. Assume beforehand
(thing, *that*); involve, imply, as *effects ~
causes.* [ME, f. OF *presupposer,* after
med. L *praesupponere* (PRE-, SUPPOSE)]

prĕsŭpposi′tion (-zĭ-), n. Presupposing;
thing assumed beforehand as basis of
argument etc. [f. med. L PRAE(*suppositio*
SUPPOSITION)]

prĕtĕnce′, n. Claim (*to* merit etc.);
ostentation, display, as *devoid of all ~*;
false profession of purpose, pretext, as
under the ~ of helping, on the slightest ~;
pretending, make-believe. [ME, f. late
AF *pretense,* as foll.]

prĕtĕnd′, v.t. & i. Feign, give oneself out,
(*to* be or do), as *does not ~ to be a scholar*;
make believe (*to* do, *that*) in play; profess
falsely to have, as *you should ~ illness*;
allege falsely (*that*); venture, aspire, presume, (*to* do); lay claim to (right, title,
etc.); ~ *to* (arch.), try to win (person,
person's hand) in marriage; ~ *to,* profess
to have (quality etc.). Hence~ĕdLY² adv.
[ME, f. OF *pretendre* or f. L PRAE(*tendere
tent-* later *tens-* stretch)]

prĕtĕn′der, n. One who makes baseless
pretensions (*to* title etc., or abs.); *Old,
Young, P~,* son, grandson, of James II as

claimants to British throne. Hence ~SHIP n. [-ER¹].

prĕtĕn'sion (-shn), n. Assertion of a claim (*to* thing, or abs.); justifiable claim (*to* thing, *to* be or do), as *he has no ~s to the name, has some ~s to be chosen as the site, what ~ has he?*; pretentiousness. [f. med. L *praetensio*, *-tio*, (as PRETEND, see -ION)]

prĕtĕn'tious (-shus), a. (Of person, book, speech, etc.) making claim to great merit or importance; ostentatious. Hence ~LY² adv., ~NESS n. [f. F *prétentieux* (as prec., see -IOUS)]

prēter-, pref. = L *praeter* past, beyond, in senses ' beyond, outside the range of, more than ', as : *~can'ine*, more than canine; *~hum'an*, beyond what is human, superhuman; *~na'tural*, outside the ordinary course of nature, (also) supernatural, whence *~na'turally* adv.; *~na'turalism*, system, doctrine, of the ~natural; *~sen'sual*, beyond the domain of the senses.

prĕt'erite, **-ĭt**, a. & n. (Gram.) ~ (*tense*), one expressing past action or state, *~-present* (*tense*), one originally ~ but now used as present (e.g. *can*, *may*, *shall*); (joc.) past, bygone, whence~NESS n. [ME, f. OF or f. L *praeteritus* p.p. of *praeterire* pass (*ire it-* go, see prec.)]

prēteri'tion (-shn), n. Omission, disregard, (*of*); (theol.) passing over of the non-elect. [f. LL *praeteritio* (as prec., see -ION)]

prēter|mit', v.t. (-tt-). Omit to mention (fact etc.); omit to do or perform, neglect; leave off (custom, continuous action) for a time; (improp.) leave off. So~mi'ssion (-shn) n. [f. L *praetermittere* (*mittere misslet* go, see PRETER-)]

prĕt'ĕxt¹, n. Ostensible reason, excuse; *on* or *under*, or *upon*, *the ~ of* or *that*, professing as one's object etc. [f. L PRAE(*texere text-* weave)]

prĕtĕxt'², v.t. Allege (thing, *that*) as pretext. [f. F *prétexter*, as prec.]

prĕt'ōne, n. Syllable, vowel, preceding the stressed syllable. So **prĕtŏn'ic** a. [PRE-]

pretor etc. See PRAETOR etc.

pre'ttĭfy (prĭ-), v.t. Make pretty, represent with finicking prettiness. [-FY]

pre'ttĭly (prĭ-), adv. In a way that pleases the eye, ear, or aesthetic sense, as ~ *dressed*; (nursery) *eat, ask, behave, ~* (in the approved manner). [f. PRETTY + LY²]

pre'ttĭnĕss (prĭ-), n. Beauty of a dainty or childish kind; pretty thing, ornament, etc.; affected or trivial beauty of style in literature or art, so **pre'ttyism** (prĭ-) n. [-NESS]

pre'ttў (prĭ-), a., adv., & n. 1. (Of woman or child) beautiful in dainty or diminutive way; attractive to eye, ear, or aesthetic sense, as ~ *cottage, song, scene, story*; fine,

good of its kind, as *has a ~ wit, very ~ sport*, (iron.) *a ~ mess you have made* ; || (arch.) fine, stout, as *a ~ fellow* ; || (arch.) considerable in amount or extent, as *earned a ~ sum* ; (ellipt.) *my ~* (one, child). **2.** adv. Fairly, moderately, as *am ~ well, find it ~ difficult, that is ~ much* (very nearly) *the same thing* ; *sitting ~* (colloq.), comfortably placed. **3.** n. || Fluted or cut part of wine-glass or tumbler, as *fill it up to the ~* ; (golf) fairway (colloq.). **4.** ~~, overdoing the ~, aiming too much at prettiness, (n. pl.) ~-*pretties*, ornaments, knick-knacks. Hence ~ISH¹ a. [late OE *præ ttig* f. *præt* (obs. *prat*) trick, wile, +-Y² ; cf. Icel. *pretti(ug)r*, Du. *pret(tig)* in similar senses]

prĕt'zel, **b-**, n. Crisp knot-shaped biscuit flavoured with salt, used esp. by Germans as relish with beer. [G]

preux chevalier (prĕr shĕvályă'), n. Gallant knight. [F]

prĕvail', v.i. Gain the mastery, be victorious, (*against, over*); *~* (*up*)*on*, persuade (*to* do); be the more usual or prominent, predominate; exist, occur, in general use or experience, be current, whence or cogn. *~ingLY²*, **prĕv'alentLY²**, advv., **prĕv'alence** n., **prĕv'alent** a. [ME, f. L PRAE(*valere* have power), infl. by obs. *vail* = AVAIL]

prĕvă'ric|āte, v.i. Speak, act, evasively ; quibble, equivocate. So ~A'TION, ~ātOR, nn. [f. L PRAE(*varicari* straddle f. *varus* bent, knock-kneed) walk crookedly, practise collusion, (eccl. L) transgress]

prĕvĕn'ient, a. Preceding, previous ; having in view the prevention (*of*) ; (theol.) ~ *grace* (preceding repentance & predisposing the heart to seek God). [as foll., see -ENT]

prĕvĕnt', v.t. Hinder, stop, as *this may ~ him from writing, ~ his* (pop. *him*) *writing, wish to ~ all dispute* ; || (arch.) meet, deal with, (wish, question, etc.) before it is expressed etc. ; (theol.) *God ~s* (goes before, guides) *us with His grace*. Hence or cogn. ~ABLE ,~IBLE, aa. **prĕvĕn'tion** n. [f. L PRAE(*venire vent-* come) come before, hinder]

prĕvĕn'ter, n. In vbl senses, also ; (naut.) rope, chain, bolt, etc., used to supplement another. [-ER¹]

prĕvĕn'tive, a. & n. **1.** Serving to prevent, esp. (med.) to keep off disease ; || ~ *detention* (to which a persistent offender may be sentenced for not less than 5 nor more than 14 years) ; || *P~* (Coastguard) *Service*. **2.** n. ~ agent, measure, drug, etc. Hence or cogn. **prĕvĕn'tative** a. & n., ~LY² adv. [-IVE]

prĕv'iew (-vū), n., & v.t. View or examination of a film, play, book, etc., before it is submitted to the general public; (v.t.) view in advance of public presentation. [PRE-]

For other words in *pre-* see PRE-.

prĕv′ious, a. & adv. **1.** Coming before in time or order; prior *to*; done or acting hastily, as *you have been a little too ~*, whence ~NESS n.; (Parl.) *~ question*, question whether vote shall be taken on main question (put to avoid putting of main question); ‖ *P~ Examination*, = LITTLE-*go*. **2.** adv. *~ to*, before, as *had called ~ to writing*. Hence ~LY² adv. [f. L PRAE(*vius* f. *via* way)+-OUS]

prĕvise′ (-z), v.t. Foresee, forecast, (event etc., or abs.). So **prĕvi′sion** (-zhn) n., **prĕvi′sional** a., **prĕvi′sionally²** adv., (-zho-). [f. L PRAE(*vidēre vis-* see)]

prey¹ (prā), n. Animal hunted or killed by other animal for food (also fig.); *beast, bird, fish, of ~*, kinds that kill & devour other animals; (bibl.) what one brings away safe from contest etc. (*Jer.* xxi. 9); person, thing, that falls a victim (*to* enemy, disease, fear, etc.). [ME, f. OF *preie, proie*, f. L *praeda*]

prey² (prā), v.i. *~ upon*, seek, take, (animal etc.) as prey, plunder (persons); (of disease, emotion, etc.) exert baneful or wasteful influence *upon*. [ME, f. OF *preer* f. LL *praedare* (L *-ari*) as prec.]

pri′apism, n. Licentiousness; (path.) persistent erection of penis. [f. LL f. Gk *priapismos* (*Priapos*, god of procreation, see -ISM)]

price, n., & v.t. **1.** Money for which thing is bought or sold, as *what is the ~ of this?*, *try our superb tea, ~ 10/- per lb.*, *offered at reduced ~s*; *~ current*, *~-list*, list of current ~s of commodities; LONG¹, COST¹, ~; *above, beyond, without, ~*, so valuable that no ~ can be stated; *at a ~*, at a relatively high ~; *set a ~ on* person's *head*, offer reward for his capture or death; (betting) odds, as *the starting ~ of a horse*; (fig.) what must be given, done, sacrificed, etc., to obtain a thing, as *must be done at any ~*; *peace at any ~*; *every man has his ~* (can be won over by some inducement); *would not have it, do it,* etc., *at any ~*, on any terms, for any consideration; ‖ *what ~ the Concert of Europe* etc.? (sl.), taunting allusion to the failure of something vaunted; ‖ (arch.) preciousness, value, as *a pearl of (great) ~.* **2.** v.t. Fix, inquire, the ~ of (thing for sale); (fig.) estimate the value of; *~ oneself out of the market*, charge a prohibitive ~. [(n.) f. OF *pris* f. L *pretium*; ME *pris* became *prise* to secure ī, and *price* to avoid z sound of *s* between vowels; (vb) earlier *prise* PRIZE¹ assim. to *price* n.; *price, prize, praise*, are all variants of same wd]

priced (-ĭst), a. To which a price is assigned, esp. in comb., as *high, low, -~*; *~ catalogue* etc. (in which prices are named). [-ED¹,²]

price′less (-sl-), a. Invaluable; (sl.) most amusing, incredibly absurd. Hence ~NESS n. [-LESS]

prick¹, n. Pricking, puncture; (fig.) ~*s* (stinging reflections) *of conscience*; mark made by pricking; ‖ (arch.) goad for oxen, esp. (fig.) *kick against the ~s*, hurt oneself by useless resistance (*Acts* ix. 5); (vulg.) penis; *~-ears*, erect pointed ears of some dogs etc., conspicuous ears of person, esp. of Roundheads, *~-eared*, having such ears. [OE *prica, -ce*, = MLG *pricke*; goes w. foll.]

prick², v.t. & i. **1.** Pierce slightly, make minute hole in; *~ a* or *the bladder* or *bubble*, show the emptiness of a person or thing that has passed for important; (fig.) cause sharp pain to, as *my conscience ~ed me*. **2.** Make a thrust (*at, into*, etc.). **3.** (arch.) Spur, urge on, (horse); (intr.) advance on horseback. **4.** Mark off (name etc. in list) with a prick, ‖ select (sheriff) thus; mark (pattern *off, out*) with dots. **5.** *~ in, out, off*, plant (seedlings etc.) in small holes ~ed in earth; *~ up* one's *ears*, (of dog) erect the ears when on the alert, (fig., of person) become suddenly attentive. [late OE *prician*, = MDu., MLG *prikken* f. WG **prik(k)-*, perh. imit.]

prick′er, n. In vbl senses, esp., pricking instrument, e.g. awl. [-ER¹]

prick′et, n. ‖ Buck in second year, with straight unbranched horns; ‖ *~'s sister*, female fallow deer in second year; spike to stick candle on. [ME, f. AL *prikettus, -um* f. PRICK, see -ET]

prick′le¹, n., & v.t. & i. **1.** Thorn-like process developed from, & capable of being peeled off with, epidermis of plant; (pop.) small thorn; hard-pointed spine of hedgehog etc. **2.** vb. Affect, be affected, with sensation as of pricks, whence **prick′ling¹** n., **prick′ling²** a. [(n.) OE *pricel*, = MDu., MLG *prickel*; (vb) 16th c. f. prec. & PRICK, = MDu., MLG *prikkeln*]

‖ **pric′kle²**, n. Kinds of wicker basket or measure. [orig. unkn.]

prick′ly̆, a. Armed with prickles (esp. in names of plants & animals); (fig., of person) ready to give or take offence; tingling; *~ heat*, inflammation of sweat glands with eruption of vesicles & *~* sensation, common in hot countries; *~ pear*, (*~* plant bearing) pear-shaped edible fruit. Hence **prick′liness** n. [-Y²]

pride, n., & v. refl. **1.** Overweening opinion of one's own qualities, merits, etc., a deadly SIN, often personified, as *P~ will have a fall*; arrogant bearing or conduct; *~ of place*, exalted position, consciousness of this, arrogance; (also *proper ~*) sense of what befits one's position, preventing one from doing unworthy thing, *false ~*, mistaken feeling of this kind; feeling of elation & pleasure, as *take a ~ in*, be proud of (person, thing, do*ing*); object of this feeling, as *he is his mother's ~*, esp. in names of plants, as LONDON *~*; (her.) *peacock in his ~* (with tail expanded and wings drooping); company (of lions); best condition, esp. *~ of* GREASE¹; *~ of the morning*, mist or shower at sunrise. **2.** v. refl. *~ oneself (up)on*, be

proud of (thing, quality, do*ing*). Hence
~'FUL (chiefly Sc.), ~'LESS, aa., ~'fullY²
adv. [late OE *prȳtu, prȳde* f. *prūt, prūd*
PROUD; hence vb, ME *priden*]

prie-dieu (prēdyêr', & see Ap.), n. Kneel-
ing-desk; (also ~ *chair*) chair with tall
sloping back for use in praying. [F, lit.
pray God]

priest, n., & v.t. **1.** Ordained minister of
R.C. and Anglican churches; in Established church one above deacon & below
bishop with authority to administer
sacraments & pronounce absolution;
(fig.) ~ *of nature, science,* etc.; minister
of the altar, esp. officiant at Eucharist;
HIGH ~; official minister of non-Christian
religion, whence ~'ESS¹ n. **2.** ‖ Mallet
used to kill fish when spent (chiefly in
Ireland). **3.** ~'*craft,* ambitious or worldly
policy of ~s; ~'*s hood,* ~-*in-the-pulpit,*
wild arum; ~-*ridden,* held in subjection
by ~s; ‖ ~ *vicar,* minor canon in some
cathedrals. **4.** v.t. Make (person) a ~.
Hence ~'HOOD (-t-h-), ~'LING¹, nn., ~'LESS,
~'LIKE, aa. [OE *prēost,* = OHG *prēst,* ON
prestr, ult. f. L PRESBYTER]

priest'l|ȳ, a. Of, like, befitting, a priest;
(O. T. criticism) ~*y code,* one of the constituent elements in the He=ateuch, ~*y
writer* (of this). Hence ~INESS n. [-LY¹]

prig, n., & v.t. (-gg-). **1.** Precisian in
speech or morals or manners, conceited
or didactic person, whence ~g'ERY(2),
~g'ishNESS, ~g'ISM, nn., ~g'ISH¹ a.,
~g'ishLY² adv., (-g-); (sl.) thief. **2.** v.t.
(sl.). Steal. [16th c. cant, of unkn. orig.]

prim, a., & v.t. & i. (-mm-). (Of persons,
manner, speech, etc.) formal, demure;
(esp. of women) prudish; (v.i.) assume ~
air; (v.t.) form (face, lips, etc.) into ~
expression. Hence ~'LY² adv., ~'NESS n.
[f. 17th c., orig. cant]

pri'ma (prē-), a. First, chief; as: ~ *buff'a*
(bŏŏ-), chief female comic singer or actress; ~ *dŏnn'a,* (pl. ~ *donnas,* prime
donne pr. prēm'ā dŏn'ā), chief female
singer in opera, (transf.) temperamental
person. [It., fem. adj.]

prim'acȳ, n. Office of a primate; pre-
-eminence. [ME, f. OF *primacie* f. med. L
primatia (as PRIMATE, see -ACY)]

pri'ma fā'cie (-shiē), adv. & a. (Arising)
at first sight, (based) on the first impression, as *has* ~ *a good case, see a* ~
reason for it. [L]

prim'age¹, n. Percentage addition to
freight, paid to owners or freighters of
vessels. [AL *primagium,* of obsc. orig.]

prim'age², n. Amount of water carried
off suspended in steam from boiler. [f.
PRIME v. + -AGE]

prim'al, a. Primitive, primeval; chief,
fundamental. Hence ~LY² adv. [f. med.
L *primalis* (as PRIME, see -AL)]

prim'arȳ, a. & n. **1.** Earliest, original; of
the first rank in a series, not derived, as
the ~ *vowel sounds,* ~ *meaning of a word*;
of the first importance, chief; (geol.) of

the lowest series of strata; (biol.) belonging to first stage of development; ~ *amputation* (performed before inflammation
supervenes); ~ *education,* that which begins with the rudiments of knowledge,
elementary, so ~ *school, scholar* (cf.
SECONDARY); (Lat. & Gk gram.) ~ *tenses,*
present, future, perfect, & future perfect,
(cf. HISTORIC); ~ *assembly, meeting* (for
selection of candidates for election); ~
COLOUR; ~ *planets* (revolving directly
round sun as centre); ~ *battery* (in which
current is produced). **2.** n. ~ planet,
meeting, etc. Hence **prim'arILY²** adv.
[ME, f. L *primarius* (as PRIME a., -ARY¹)]

prim'ate, n. Archbishop; *P~ of England,*
Archbishop of York, *P~ of all England,*
Archbishop of Canterbury; (zool.) sing.
of foll. Hence **prima'TIAL** (-āshl) a. [ME,
f. OF *primat,* f. L *primas -atis* adj. (as
PRIME a.); in med. L = primate]

primāt'ēs (-z), n. pl. (zool.; for sing., see
prec.). Highest order of mammals, including man, monkeys, apes, & lemurs.
[as prec.]

prime¹, n. State of highest perfection, as
in the ~ *of life, manhood,* etc.; *the* best
part (*of* thing); beginning, first age, of
anything; a canonical hour of monastic
rule, appointed for first hour of day (i.e.
6 a.m.), (arch.) this time; (arch.) GOLDEN
number; prime number; (chem.) single
atom as unit in combination; a position
in fencing. [OE *prim* f. L *prima* (*hora*)
first (hour); in ME reinforced by OF
prime (as foll.)]

prime², a. Chief, most important, as ~
agent, motive; first-rate (esp. of cattle
& provisions), excellent, whence ~'LY²
adv., ~'NESS n.; primary, fundamental;
(arith., of a number) having no integral
factors except itself and unity (e.g. 2, 3,
5, 7, 11), (of numbers) having no common
measure but unity; ~ COST¹, MOVER; ~
vertical (*circle*), great circle of the heavens
passing through E. & W. points of
horizon & through zenith, where it cuts
meridian at right angles; ~ *minister,*
principal minister of any sovereign or
State (now official title of first minister &
head of Government in Great Britain).
[ME, f. OF *prime* or L *primus* first]

prime³, v.t. & i. (Hist.) supply (fire-arm,
or abs.) with gunpowder for firing charge;
wet (pump) to make it start working;
inject petrol into (cylinder or carburettor
of internal-combustion engine); equip
(person *with* information etc.); fill (person
with liquor); cover (wood etc.) with first
coat of paint or with oil etc. to prevent
paint from being absorbed; (of engine
boiler) let water pass with steam into
cylinder in form of spray. [orig. unkn.]

prim'er¹, n. **1.** (*usu.* prī-). Elementary
school-book for teaching children to
read; small introductory book, as *P~ of
Evolution, Latin P~*; (hist.) prayer-book
for use of laity esp. before Reformation

(prĭ-). **2.** (prī-). *Great, long,* ~, sizes of TYPE. [ME, AL, f. med. L *primarius, -arium*, f. L *primus* first, see -ER²(2)]

prim'er², n. In vbl senses of PRIME³, esp. cap, cylinder, etc., used to ignite powder of cartridge etc. [-ER¹]

prĭmēr'ō, n. (hist.). Gambling card-game fashionable in 16th & 17th cc. [f. Sp. *primera* fem. of *primero*, as PRIMARY]

primēv'al, -**aeval,** a. Of the first age of the world; ancient, primitive. Hence ~LY² adv. [f. L *primaevus* (*primus* first + *aevum* age) + -AL]

prim'ing¹, n. In vbl senses of PRIME³; also or esp.: gunpowder placed in pan of fire-arm; train of powder connecting fuse with charge in blasting etc.; mixture used by painters for preparatory coat; preparation of sugar added to beer; imparting of information. [-ING¹]

prim'ing², n. Acceleration of the tides taking place from neap to spring tides (cf. LAG¹). [f. *prime* vb f. PRIME¹,²]

primip'arous, a. Bearing child for the first time. [f. L *primipara* ~ woman (also used in E) f. *primus* first + *parĕre* bring forth; see -OUS]

prim'itive, a. & n. **1.** Early, ancient, as *the P~ Church* (Christian Church in its earliest times); old-fashioned, simple, rude; uncivilized or of rudimentary civilization; original, primary; (gram., of words) radical, not derivative; (math., of line, figure, etc.) from which another is derived, from which some construction begins, etc.; (of colours) primary; (geol.) of the earliest period; (biol.) appearing in earliest or very early stage of growth etc.; *P~ Methodist Connexion*, society of Methodists founded 1810 by Hugh Bourne by secession from main body, *P~ Methodist, Methodism,* member, principles, of this. **2.** n. Painter of period before Renascence, picture by such painter; ~ *word,* line, etc.; P~ Methodist. Hence ~LY² adv., ~NESS n. [ME & OF *primitif* f. L *primitivus* (as PRIME²)]

prī'mō¹ (prē-), n. (mus.). Upper part in duet etc. [It.]

prim'ō², adv. ~, *sĕcŭn'dŏ, tĕr'tiŏ* (-shĭ-), in the first, second, third, place (written 1°, 2°, 3°). [L]

primogĕn'itor, n. Earliest ancestor; (loosely) ancestor. [med. L, f. L *primo* (at) first + *genitor* begetter (*gignere* genit-bring forth, see -OR), after L *primogenitus* first-born]

primogĕn'it|ure, n. Fact of being the first-born of the children of the same parents; (*right of*) ~*ure,* right of succession belonging to the first-born, esp. feudal rule by which whole real estate of intestate passes to eldest son. So ~AL, ~ARY¹, aa. [f. med. L *primogenitura* (as prec., see -URE)]

primōrd'ial, a. Existing at or from the beginning, primeval; original, fundamental. Hence ~ITY (-ăl²) n., ~LY² adv.

[ME, f. LL *primordialis* (L *primordium* f. *primus* first + *ordiri* begin, see -AL)]

prim'rōse (-z), n. Plant bearing pale yellow flowers in early spring; flower of this; (attrib.) of the colour of this flower; *the ~ path,* the pursuit of pleasure (w. ref. to *Haml.* I. iii. 50); ‖ *P~ Day, League,* anniversary of the death (Apr. 19th, 1881) of, Conservative association formed in memory of, Benjamin Disraeli Earl of Beaconsfield; *P~ dame, knight, habitation,* (of the P~ League); ~ *peerless,* two--flowered narcissus. Hence **prim'rōsY²** (-z-) a. [ME *primerose,* corresp. to OF *primerose* & med. L *prima* rose lit. first rose, sense unexpl.]

prim'ūla, n. Kind of herbaceous perennial with flowers of various colours. [med. L, fem. adj. as n., dim. as PRIME², see -ULE]

prīm'um mŏb'ĭlĕ, n. Outermost sphere added in Middle Ages to Ptolemaic system, supposed to revolve round earth in 24 hours carrying with it the contained spheres; (fig.) prime source of motion or action. [med. L, lit. first moving thing]

prim'us¹, a. & n. **1.** ‖ (In boys' school) eldest (or of longest standing) of the name, as *Jones* ~ (usu. written *Jones* i.; similarly *secundus* ii., *tertius* iii., *quartus* iv., *quintus* v., *sextus* vi., *septimus* vii., *octāv'us* viii., *nōnus* ix., *dē'cimus* x.); (L) ~ *in'ter pār'ēs* (-z), first among equals, senior or spokesman of a board of colleagues. **2.** n. ‖ Presiding bishop in Scottish Episcopal Church. [L, = first]

prim'us², n. Brand of stove burning vaporized oil for cooking etc. [P]

prince, n. **1.** (Now rhet.) sovereign ruler; *P~ of Peace,* Christ; ~ *of darkness, the air, the world,* etc., Satan. **2.** Ruler of small State, actually or nominally feudatory to king or emperor. **3.** Male member of royal family, esp. (in Great Britain) son or grandson of king or queen (also ~ *of the blood*). **4.** *P~ of Wales,* (title conferred on) heir apparent to British throne (*P~ of Wales's feathers,* triple ostrich plume); *P~ Consort,* (title conferred on) husband of reigning female sovereign being himself a ~; *P~ of Denmark,* Hamlet. (*Hamlet without the P~ of Denmark,* thing robbed of its essence). **5.** (As English rendering of foreign titles) noble usu. ranking next below duke; (as courtesy title in some connexions) duke, marquis, earl; (title of cardinal) ~ *of the (Holy Roman) Church.* **6.** (fig.). Chief, greatest, (of novelists, liars, etc.). **7.** **P~ Albert* (colloq.), frock--coat; ~ *bishop,* bishop who is also a ~; *P~ Regent,* ~ who acts as regent, e.g. George (afterwards IV); ~ *royal,* eldest son of reigning monarch; *P~ Rupert's drops,* pear-shaped lumps of glass bursting to pieces when thin ends are broken off; ~*'s feather,* kinds of plant, esp. tall plant with feathery spikes of small red flowers; ~*'s metal,* alloy of copper & zinc. Hence

~′DOM (-sd-), ~′KIN (-sk-), ~′LET, ~′LING¹ (2), (-sl-), nn., ~′LIKE (-sl-), a. [ME, f. OF, f. L *princeps -cipis* first, prince, (*primus* first + *-cipere* = *capere* take)]

prince′l‖ў (-sl-), a. (Worthy) of a prince; sumptuous, splendid. Hence ~ɪNESS n. [-LY¹]

prin′cĕss (*or -ĕs′ exc. when followed by name*), n. (Arch.) queen; wife of prince; (also ~ *of the blood*) daughter, granddaughter, of sovereign; ~ *royal*, (title conferrable on) sovereign's eldest daughter; *P~ Regent*, ~ acting as regent, (also) wife of prince regent; ~ *dress, petticoat, slip*, (made without a seam at the waist). [ME & OF *princesse* (as PRINCE, see -ESS¹)]

prin′cipal, a. & n. 1. First in rank or importance, chief, as *their ~ food is potatoes*, *the ~ town of the district*, *the ~ persons concerned*; ~ *boy, girl*, actress who takes leading male, female, part in pantomime; main, leading, as *a ~ cause of his failure*. 2. (Of money) constituting the original sum invested or lent. 3. (gram.). ~ *sentence, clause*, one to which another is subordinate; ~ *parts* of verb, those from which the others can be derived. 4. n. Head, ruler, superior; head of some colleges & universities, whence ~SHIP n. 5. Person for whom another acts as agent etc., as *I must consult my ~*; person directly responsible for crime, either (~ *in the first degree*) as actual perpetrator or (~ *in the second degree*) as aiding; person for whom another is surety; combatant in duel (opp. *second*). 6. Any of the main rafters on which rest the purlins that support the common rafters. 7. Capital sum as distinguished from interest or from income. 8. Organ diapason stop sounding octave above normal. [ME, f. OF, or L *principalis* adj. (as PRINCE, see -AL)]

principal′itў, n. Government of a prince; State ruled by a prince; ‖ *the P~*, Wales; (pl.) an ORDER¹ 1 of angels. [ME, f. OF *principalite* f. LL *principalitatem* (as prec., see -TY)]

prin′cipallў, adv. For the most part, chiefly. [-LY²]

prin′cipate, n. (Rom. hist.) rule of early emperors while some republican forms were retained; State ruled by a prince. [ME, f. L *principatus* (as PRINCE, see -ATE¹)]

prin′ciple, n. 1. Fundamental source, primary element, as *held water to be the first ~ of all things*. 2. Fundamental truth as basis of reasoning etc., as (*first*) ~*s of political economy*; (phys.) general law (often with discoverer's name, as *Pascal's ~*); general law as guide to action, as *moral, conservative, ~s, a dangerous ~*, whence -**prin′cipl**ED² (-ld) a.; *in ~*, dist. from *in detail*; (pl. & collect. sing.) personal code of right conduct, as *a man of high ~*, *has ability but no ~s*, ~ *is everything*; *on ~*, from settled moral motive, as *I refuse on*

~ (not from selfish motive etc.). 3. Law of nature seen in working of machine etc., as *in all these instruments the ~ is the same*. 4. (chem.). Constituent of a substance, esp. one giving rise to some quality etc., as *bitter, colouring, ~*. [ME, f. OF *principe* f. L *principium*, after *manciple, participle*]

prink, v.t. & i. Make (oneself etc.) spruce; dress one*self up*; (of bird) trim (feathers); dress oneself up. [16th c., cf. PRANK²]

print¹, n. 1. Indentation in surface preserving the form left by pressure of some body, as *finger-~, foot′~*, whence ~′LESS a. 2. Printed cotton fabric, as (attrib.) ~ *dress*. 3. Language embodied in printed form, printed lettering, as *large, small, clear, ~*; state of being printed; *book is in ~*, (1) in printed form, (2) on sale, not *out of ~* (sold out); (of writer) *rush into ~*, publish book, write to newspaper etc., on insufficient grounds; (chiefly U.S.) printed publication, esp. newspaper; picture, design, printed from block or plate; (photog.) picture produced from negative. 4. ~ *hand, letters* (imitating ~); ~*-seller*, dealer in engravings etc.; ~*-shop*, his shop; ~*-works*, factory where cotton fabrics are printed. [ME, f. OF *priente, preinte*, f. p.p. of *preindre* press f. L *premere*]

print², v.t. 1. Impress, stamp, (surface, e.g. pat of butter, *with* seal, die, etc.; a mark or figure *on, in*, yielding or other surface); (fig.) impress (idea, scene, etc., *on* mind, memory). 2. Produce (book, picture, etc., or abs.) by applying inked types, blocks, or plates, to paper, vellum, etc.; (of author or editor) cause (book, MS.) to be so ~ed; express, publish, in print, as *not bound to ~ every opinion you hold*; write (words, or abs.) in imitation of typography. 3. Mark (textile fabric) with decorative design in colours; transfer (coloured design) from paper etc. to unglazed surface of pottery. 4. (photog.). (Also ~ *out, off*) produce (picture) by transmission of light through negative. Hence ~′ABLE a. [ME *prente, printe*, app. f. prec.]

prin′ter, n. In vbl senses, esp.: one who prints books; owner of printing business; printing instrument; *P~s′ Bible* (with *P~s* for *Princes*, Ps. cxix. 161); ~*'s* DEVIL¹; ~*'s mark* (device, trade-mark); ~*'s pie*, = PIE³ n. [-ER¹]

prin′ting, n. In vbl senses; ~*-ink*, ~*-press*, (for ~ on paper etc. from types etc.). [-ING¹]

pri′or¹, n. Superior officer of religious house or order, (in abbey) officer next under abbot, so ~ESS¹ n. Hence or cogn. ~ATE¹(1), ~SHIP, nn. [late OE *prior* f. L *prior* (foll.); in ME also f. OF *pri(o)ur*]

pri′or², a. & adv. 1. Earlier; antecedent in time, order, or importance, (*to*). 2. adv. ~ *to*, before, as *existing ~ to his appointment*. So **priŏ′**RITY n. (also, an interest having a ~ claim to consideration; in recent use freq. with qualification, as *a first, top, ~ity*). [L, f. OL *pri* before]

pri′or·y, n. Monastery, nunnery, governed by prior(ess); *alien ~, ~ alien*, (dependent on abbey in foreign country). [ME, f. AF *priorie*, med. L *prioria* (as prec., see -Y¹)]

|| **prise**. See PRIZE³.

pri′sm, n. Solid figure whose two ends are similar, equal, & parallel rectilineal figures, & whose sides are parallelograms; transparent body of this form, usu. triangular, with refracting surfaces at acute angle with each other; (loosely) spectrum produced by refraction through ~, (pl.) prismatic colours; *~-glasses, binoculars* (in which triangular ~s are used to shorten the instrument); PRUNE¹s *& ~*. Hence **pris′mAL** (-z-) a. [f. LL f. Gk *prisma -matos* thing sawn (*prizō* saw)]

prismăt′ic (-z-), a. Of, like, a prism; *~ compass*, hand-compass used in survey work, with attached prism enabling the dial to be read while the sight is taken; *~ powder*, gunpowder whose grains are hexagonal prisms; (of colours) formed, distributed, etc., by transparent prism, (also) brilliant, so **pris′mY²** (-z-) a.; *the ~ colours*, seven into which ray of light is separated by prism. Hence **prismăt′·ICALLY** (-z-) adv. [as prec., see -IC]

pris′moid (-z-), n. Body like prism, with similar but unequal parallel polygonal ends. Hence **prismoid′AL** (-z-) a. [-OID]

pris′on (-zn), n., & v.t. 1. Place in which person is kept in captivity, esp. building to which person is legally committed while awaiting trial or for punishment; custody, confinement, as *lie, put* (person), *in ~; ~-bird,* = GAOL-bird; *~-breaking,* breaking out of lawfully confined person from ~, so *~-breaker; ~ editor* (hist.), editor of newspaper taking legal responsibility for its contents & serving terms of imprisonment entailed by conviction; *~-house* (usu. rhet.), ~. 2. v.t. (poet.). Imprison. [ME & OF *prisun, -on*, f. L *prensionem* (*pre(he)ndere prens-* seize, see -ION)]

pris′oner (-zn-), n. Person kept in prison; *~ (at the bar)*, person in custody on criminal charge & on trial; *~ of State, State ~*, (confined for political reasons); (also *~ of war*, abbr. *P.O.W.*) one who has been captured in war; *take* (person) ~, seize & hold as ~; (fig.) *am a ~* (confined by illness etc.) *to my room* or *chair, made her hand a ~* (secured it); *~s' bars, base*, game played by two parties of boys etc., each occupying distinct base or home. [ME, f. OF *prisonier*, as prec., see -ER²(2)]

pris′tine, a. Ancient, primitive, good old. [f. L *pristinus* former]

|| **prith′ee** (-dhǐ), int. (arch.). Pray, please, as *tell me*, ~. [= (I) pray thee]

prīv′acy̆ (*also* prĭ-), n. Being withdrawn from society or public interest, as *lived in absolute ~, must disturb your~;* avoidance

of publicity, as *in such matters ~ is impossible*. [ME; PRIVATE, -ACY]

privat-docent, -ӕent, (prěvaht′ dŏtsěnt′), n. (In German univv.) private teacher or lecturer recognized by university but not on salaried staff. [G]

priv′ate, a. & n. 1. (Of person) not holding public office or official position; || ~ (*soldier*), ordinary soldier without rank, one below non-commissioned officers (freq. prefixed, as *P~ Smith*); *~ member* of House of Commons (not member of Government). 2. Kept, removed, from public knowledge, as *the matter was kept ~, had ~ reasons*. 3. Not open to the public, as *~ door, news, came through ~ channels, ~ boarding-house, carriage, hotel, theatricals; ~ view* (of exhibition of pictures esp. before it is opened to the public). 4. *~ eye, ~ detective; ~ house*, dwelling-house of ~ person (opp. to his shop or office, to public house, or to public building); *~ parts*, genitals (*~-protector*, guard worn at cricket etc.); *~ school* (|| carried on for owner's profit, cf. PUBLIC; *~ schoolmaster*, of or in this). 5. One's own, as *my ~ goods, property*; individual, personal, not affecting the community, as *motives of ~ malice*; (Parl.) *~ bill, act* (affecting individual or corporation only). 6. Confidential, as *asked for some ~ conversation; this is for your ~ ear* (confidential). 7. (Of place) retired, secluded; (arch., of person) given to retirement. 8. *In ~, ~ly*, in ~ company or life. 9. n. pl. ~ parts. Hence *~LY²* adv. [ME, f. L *privatus*, orig. p.p. of *privare* deprive]

privateer′, n. Armed vessel owned & officered by private persons holding commission from government (*letters of* MARQUE) & authorized to use it against hostile nation esp. in capture of merchant shipping, whence *~ING¹*(1) n.; commander, (pl.) crew, of this. [f. prec. +-EER, prob. after *volunteer*]

privā′tion, n. Loss, absence, (of quality), as *cold is the ~ of heat*; want of the comforts or necessaries of life, as *died of ~, suffered many ~s*. [ME, f. L *privatio* (PRIVATE, -ATION)]

prĭv′ative, a. Consisting in, marked by, the loss or removal or absence of some quality or attribute, as *cold is merely ~* (cf. prec.); (of terms) denoting privation or absence of quality etc.; (gram., of particles etc.) expressing privation, as (Gk gram.) *alpha ~* (*a-* = not-). Hence *~LY²* adv. [f. F (*-if, -ive*) or L *privativus* (as PRIVATE, see -IVE)]

prĭv′ĕt, n. Bushy evergreen shrub with small white flowers & small shining black berries, much used for hedges; *~-hawk*, large species of moth depositing eggs on ~. [16th c., of unkn. orig.]

prĭv′ilĕge, n., & v.t. 1. Right, advantage, immunity, belonging to person, class, or office (*~ of Parliament*, those of either House or its members; *breach of ~*,

esp., infringement of any of these);
special advantage or benefit, as *to converse with him was a* ~; ~ (BENEFIT[1]) *of
clergy*; *bill of* ~, petition of peer demanding to be tried by his peers; *writ of* ~,
writ to deliver ~d person from custody
when arrested in civil suit; monopoly,
patent, granted to individual, corporation, etc.; || ~ *cab* (admitted to stand
for hire in private places esp. railway
station). **2.** v.t. Invest with ~, allow
(person *to* do) as ~; exempt (person *from*
burden etc.). Hence priv′ilegED[1] (-ijd)
a. [ME; (n.) f. L *privilegium* bill, law,
affecting an individual (*privus* private +
lex legis law), & OF *privilege*; (vb) f.
med. L *privilegiare* & OF *privilegier*]

priv′ity, n. (Law) any relation between
two parties that is recognized by law, e.g.
that of blood, lease, service; being privy
(*to* designs etc.). [ME, f. OF *privite* f. L
privus private, see -TY]

priv′y, a. & n. **1.** (Of things, places, etc.)
hidden, secluded; ~ *parts*, genitals; (of
action) secret, whence priv′ILY[2] adv.; ~
to, in the secret of (person's designs etc.).
2. || P~ *Council*, sovereign's private
counsellors, (in Great Britain) body of
advisers chosen by sovereign (now chiefly
as personal dignity, most functions being
performed by Cabinet, committees, etc.)
together with princes of blood, archbishops, etc.; || ~ *counsellor*, *-cillor*,
private adviser, esp. (abbr. *P.C.*) member
of P~ Council; || ~ *purse*, allowance from
public revenue for monarch's private
expenses, keeper of this; || ~ *seal*, seal
affixed to documents that are afterwards
to pass, or that do not require, the Great
Seal; *Lord* (keeper of the) *P~ Seal*. **3.**
n. Latrine (arch., exc. U.S.); (law) person
having a part or interest in any action,
matter, or thing. [ME & OF *prive*
PRIVATE]

prize[1], n., & v.t. **1.** Reward given as
symbol of victory or superiority to
student in school or college who excels in
attainments; to competitor in athletic
contest, to exhibitor of best specimen of
manufactured products, works of art,
etc., in exhibition; (fig.) anything striven
for or worth striving for, as *many* ~*s in
the Church, missed all the great* ~*s of life*;
money or money's worth offered for competition in lottery etc. **2.** (attrib.). ~ *ox*,
poem, etc. (to which ~ is adjudged in show,
competition, etc.). **3.** || ~ *fellowship* (given
as reward for eminence in examination),
~ *fellow*, holder of this; ~*-fight*, boxing-match for money, so ~*-fighter*, ~*-fighting*,
nn.; ~′*man*, winner of (often specified) ~,
as *Smith's* ~*man*, winner of Smith's P~;
~*-ring*, enclosed area (now usu. square)
for, (fig.) practice of, ~*-fighting*. **4.** v.t.
Value highly, as *we* ~ *liberty more than life*.
Hence ~′LESS a. [(n.) diff. sp. of PRICE;

(vb) ME, f. OF *prisier*, var. of *preisier*
PRAISE]

prize[2], n., & v.t. Ship, property, captured
at sea in virtue of rights of war; || ~*-court*,
department of admiralty court concerned
with ~*s*; || ~*-money* (realized by sale of
~, esp. hist., such money as awarded to
crew of capturing ship); *make* ~ of (cargo,
ship, etc.), seize thus; *become* (*lawful* etc.)
~, be thus seized; (fig.) find or windfall
(*see what a* ~ *I have found!*); (v.t.) make ~
of. [ME & OF *prise* taking, fem. p.p. of
prendre f. L *prehendere* -*hens*- seize; 16th
c. sp. *prize* & later identified w. PRIZE[1]]

|| **prize**[3], **-se**, v.t., & n. Force (lid etc. *up*,
out, box etc. *open*) by leverage; (n.) leverage, purchase. [ME & OF *prise* levering
instrument, as prec.; 17th c. vb f. n.]

prō[1], prep. ~ *bŏn′ō pŭb′lĭcō*, for the public
good; ~ *form′a* adv. & æ., (done) for
form's sake; ~ *hăc vĭ′ce*, for this occasion
only; ~ *rāt′a* adv. & a., proportional(ly);
~ *rĕ nāt′a* adv. & a., for an occasion as it
arises, as *a meeting held* ~ *re nata, a* ~ *re
nata meeting*; ~ *tăn′tō*, so far, to that
extent; ~ *tĕm′porĕ* adv. & a. (abbr. *pro
tem.*), for the time, as *made secretary pro
tem., the pro tem. secretary*. [L]

prō[2], n. (colloq.; pl. ~*s*). A PROFESSIONAL.
[abbr.]

prō-[1], pref. (before vowel) = L *pro* in front
of, for, on behalf of, instead of, on account of. As living E pref. **1.** In sense
' substitute(d) for ', as ~*-cathed′ral* a. &
n., (church) used as substitute for cathedral, || ~*-proc′tor*, assistant or deputy
proctor in univv., ~*-rec′tor*, vice-rector in
univv. etc.; ~*-leg*, fleshy abdominal limb
of larvae of some insects, e.g. caterpillars. **2.** In sense ' (person) favouring or
siding with ' (cf. ANTI-), as ~*-Bo′er* a. & n.,
~*-Brit′ish*, ~*-educational*, ~*-Neg′ro* a. &
n., ~*-pap′ist* a. & n., ~*-slav′ery*, ~*-ta′riff
reform*.

pro-[2], pref. = Gk *pro* before (in time,
place, order, etc.) in wds f. Gk & in mod.
scientific wds.

prō′a, n. Malay boat, esp. a type of sailing-boat. [f. Malay *pra(h)u*, also used in E]

prō and cŏn, adv. & n. **1.** (Of arguments
or reasons) for & against, on both sides.
2. n. pl. *Pros & cons*, reasons for & against.
[f. L *pro* et *contra*]

prŏbabil′ior|ism, n. (R.-C. casuistry).
Doctrine that the side on which evidence
preponderates ought to be followed (cf.
foll.). So ~IST n. [f. L *probabilior* more
PROBABLE + -ISM]

prŏb′abil|ism, n. Doctrine that where
authorities differ any course may be followed for which recognized doctor of the
Church can be cited (cf. prec.); theory
that there is no certain knowledge, but
may be grounds of belief sufficient for
practical life. So ~IST n. [as PROBABLE
+ -ISM]

For other words in *pro-* see PRO-[1].

pròbabil'it|ў, n. Quality of being probable; *in all* ~*y*, most likely; *there is no* ~*y* (likelihood) *of his coming*; (most) probable event, as *what are the* ~*ies, the* ~*y is that he will come*; (math.) likelihood of an event, measured by the ratio of the favourable cases to the whole number of cases possible, as *from a bag containing 3 red balls & 7 white the* ~*y of a red ball's being drawn first is* 3|10. [f. F *probabilité* or L *probabilitas* (as foll., see -TY)]

pròb'able, a. & n. 1. That may be expected to happen or prove true, likely, as *reckon the* ~ *cost, it is* ~ *that he forgot, gives a* ~ *account of the matter*. **2.** n. A ~ candidate, member, selection, etc. Hence **pròb'ablⱬ² adv.** [ME, f. OF, or f. L *probabilis* (*probare* PROVE, see -BLE)]

pròb'ăng, n. Surgeon's strip of whalebone with sponge, button, etc., at end for introducing into throat. [altered f. inventor's wd *provang* (orig. unkn.), perh. on *probe*]

pròb'ate, n. Official proving of will; verified copy of will with certificate as handed to executors; ~ *duty*, tax on personal property of deceased testator. [ME, f. L *probatum* neut. p.p. of *probare* PROVE]

probā'tion, n. Testing of conduct or character of person esp. of candidate for membership in religious body etc. (*on* ~, undergoing it before full admission etc.); moral trial or discipline; system of releasing young criminals esp. first offenders on suspended sentence during good behaviour under supervision of person (~ *officer*) acting as friend & adviser. [ME, f. OF *probacion* or L *probatio* (as PROVE, see -ATION)]

probā'tion|arў (-sho-), a. Of, serving for, done in the way of, probation, so ~AL a.; undergoing probation. [-ARY¹]

probā'tioner (-sho-), n. Person on probation, e.g. hospital nurse at early stage of training; offender under PROBATION. Hence ~SHIP n. [-ER¹]

pròb'ative, a. Affording proof, evidential. [f. L *probativus* (as PROVE, see -IVE)]

pròbe, n., & v.t. 1. Blunt-ended surgical instrument usu. of silver for exploring wound etc.; *(fig.; f. vb) investigation. **2.** v.t. Explore (wound, part of body) with ~, penetrate (thing) with sharp instrument; (fig.) examine closely, sound, (person, motive, report, etc.). [(vb f. n.) f. LL *proba* PROOF, med. L examination]

pròb'itⱬ, n. Uprightness, honesty. [f. L *probitas* (*probus* good, see -TY)]

pròb'lèm, n. 1. Doubtful or difficult question, as *how to prevent it is a* ~, *the* ~ *of ventilation*; (attrib.) ~ *child* (difficult to control, unruly); ~ *play, novel* (in which social or other ~ is treated). **2.** Thing hard to understand, as *his whole conduct is a* ~ *to me*. **3.** (Geom.) proposition in which something has to be constructed (cf. THEOREM); (phys., math.) inquiry starting from given conditions to

investigate a fact, result or law, as *Kepler's* ~; (chess) arrangement of pieces on the board in which player is challenged to accomplish specified result, often under prescribed conditions. [f. ME & OF *probleme* f. L f. Gk *problēma -matos* f. PRO²(*ballō* throw)]

pròblèmăt'ic(al), aa. Doubtful, questionable, as *its success is* ~, *the whole question is* ~; (log.) enunciating or supporting what is possible but not necessarily true. Hence **pròblèmăt'icallⱬ² adv.** [f. F *problématique* or LL f. Gk *problēmatikos* (as prec., see -IC)]

pròb'lèm(at)ist, nn. One who studies or composes (esp. chess) problems. [-IST]

pròbòscid'ĕan, -ian, aa. & nn. Having a proboscis; of, like, a proboscis; (mammal) of the order *Proboscidea*, containing elephant & extinct allies. [f. mod. L *Proboscidea* + -AN]

probòs'cis, n. Elephant's trunk; long flexible snout of tapir etc.; elongated part of mouth of some insects; sucking organ in some worms; (joc.) human nose; ~-*monkey* (with nose projecting far beyond mouth). So **probòscidif'EROUS, pròbòscid'IFORM, aa.** [L, gen. *-cidis*, f. Gk *proboskis* f. PRO²(*boskō* feed)]

procéd'ur|e (-dyer), n. Proceeding; mode of conducting business (esp. in parliament) or legal action. Hence ~AL (-dyer-) a., of or relating to ~e. [f. F *procédure* (as foll., see -URE)]

proceed', v.i. Go on, make one's way, (*to* place); go on (*with, in*, action, investigation, remarks, etc., *to* another subject, *to* do); adopt course of action, as *how shall we* ~?; take legal proceedings *against* person; (abs.) go on to say, as '*in either case* ' *he* ~*ed* ' *our course is clear* '; || ~ *to* (take) *the degree of M.A.*, ~ (take degree of) *M.A.*; (of action) be carried on, take place, as *the case, the play, will now* ~; come forth, issue, originate, as *sobs heard to* ~ *from next room, volumes* ~ *from the Pitt Press, exertions* ~ *from a false hope*. [ME, f. OF *proceder* f. L PRO¹(*cedere* cessgo)]

proceed'ing, n. In vbl senses, esp.: action, piece of conduct, as *a high-handed* ~; *legal* ~*s*, (steps taken in) legal action, as *shall institute legal* ~*s* (go to law); (as title) *P*~*s of Royal Society* etc. [-ING¹]

prō'ceeds, n. pl. Produce, outcome, profit, as *the* ~ *will be devoted to charity*. [f. PROCEED v.; sing. now obs.]

prŏcĕleusmăt'ic, a. & n. (prosody). ~ (*foot*), metrical foot of four short syllables. [f. LL f. Gk *prokeleusmatikos* f. *prokeleusma* exhortation f. PRO² (*keleuō* command), see -IC]

prŏcĕllār'ian, a. & n. (Bird) of the genus or family to which petrels belong. [f. L *procella* storm, see -ARIAN]

prō'cĕss¹, n., & v.t. 1. Progress, course, esp. *in* ~ *of construction* etc., being constructed etc., *in* ~ *of time*, as time goes on; course of action, proceeding, esp. method of operation in manufacture, printing, photography, etc.; natural or involuntary operation, series of changes. **2.** (Print from block produced by) method other than simple engraving by hand. **3.** Action at law, formal commencement of this, summons or writ (~-*server*, sheriff's officer). **4.** (anat., zool., bot.). Outgrowth, protuberance. **5.** v.t. Institute legal ~ against (person); treat (material), subject (food) to special ~, reproduce (drawing), by a~. Hence~ER¹, ~OR, nn. [ME & OF *proces* f. L *processus* -*ūs*, as PROCEED; vb f. n., exc. legal use f. OF *processer*]

procéss'², v.i. (colloq.). Walk in procession. [back formation f. foll.]

procé'ssion (-shn), n., & v.i. & t. Proceeding of body of persons (or of boats etc.) in orderly succession, esp. as religious ceremony or on festive etc. occasion, as *go, walk, in* ~; body of persons doing this; (fig.) ill-contested race; (theol.) emanation of the Holy Ghost; ~ *caterpillars*, kinds that go in ~, so ~ *moth*, whence ~ARY¹ (-shŏ) a.; (v.i.) go in ~; (v.t.) walk along (street) in~. [ME, f. OF f. L *processionem* (as PROCEED, see -ION)]

procé'ssional (-sho-), a. & n. **1.** Of processions; used, carried, sung, in processions. **2.** n. ~ hymn; (eccl.) office-book of ~ hymns etc. [f. med. L *processionalis* a., -*le* n., (as prec., see -AL)]

procé'ssion|ist (-sho-), n. One who goes in procession. So ~IZE v.i. [-IST]

procès verbal (prŏsā'věrbahl'), n. (pl. -*baux* pr. -bō). Written report of proceedings, minutes; (Fr. law) written statement of facts in support of charge. [F]

prō'chronism (-k-), n. Referring of event etc. to an earlier than the true date, as *races held in June & called by a* ~ *the Mays*. [f. PRO-² on ANACHRONISM]

proclaim', v.t. Announce publicly & officially (thing, *that*); declare (war, peace); announce officially the accession of (sovereign); declare (person, thing) officially to be a (traitor etc.); declare publicly or openly (thing, *that*); place (district etc.) under legal restrictions, prohibit (meeting etc.), by declaration, as *the whole county is* ~*ed.* So **prŏclamᴀ'TION** n., **proclăm'atory** a. [ME -*clame* f. L PRO¹(*clamare* cry out), sp. after CLAIM]

proclit'ic, a. & n. (gram.). (Monosyllable) closely attached in pronunciation to following word & having itself no accent, as *at home'*. [f. PRO-² on ENCLITIC]

procliv'ity, n. Tendency (*to, towards,* action or habit, esp. bad one, *to* do). [f. L *proclivitas* f. PRO¹(*clivis* f. *clivus* slope), see -TY]

prōcŏn'sul, n. (Rom. hist.) governor of Roman province, in later republic usu. an ex-consul; (under empire) governor of senatorial province; || (rhet.) governor of modern colony etc.; (*pro-consul*) deputy consul. Hence or cogn. ~AR¹ a., ~ATE¹(1), ~SHIP, nn. [ME, f. L, earlier *pro consule* (one acting) for consul]

procrăs'tin|āte, v.i. & t. Defer action, be dilatory; (rare) postpone (action). Hence or cogn. ~**ātinGLY²** adv., ~**A'TION,** ~**ātor,** nn., ~**ātive,** ~**ātory,** aa. [f. L PRO¹(*crastinare* f. *crastinus* of tomorrow f. *cras*), see -ATE³]

prŏc'rĕ|āte, v.t. Beget, generate, (offspring, or abs). Hence or cogn. ~ANT, ~**ātive,** aa., ~**A'TION** n. [f. L PRO¹(*creare* CREATE)]

Procrŭs'tĕan, a. Tending to produce uniformity by violent methods. [f. Gk *Prokroustēs*, lit. stretcher, name of fabulous robber who fitted victims to his bed by stretching or mutilation, see -AN]

|| prŏc'tor, n. (Camb. & Oxf. Univv.) each of two officers (*senior, junior,* ~) appointed annually & charged with various functions esp. discipline of persons *in statu pupillari*; (law) person managing causes in court (now chiefly eccl.) that administers civil or canon law; *King's, Queen's, P*~, official who has right to intervene in probate, divorce, & nullity cases when collusion or suppression of facts is alleged. Hence **prŏctŏr'IAL** a., ~SHIP n. [late ME syncopation of PROCURATOR]

|| prŏc'toriz|e, -is|e (-īz), v.t. Exercise proctor's authority on (undergraduate etc.). Hence~**A'TION** n. [-IZE]

procŭm'bent, a. Lying on the face, prostrate; (bot.) growing along the ground. [f. L PRO¹(*cumbere* lay oneself) fall forwards, -ENT]

prōcūrā'tion, n. Procuring, obtaining, bringing about, so **procūr'AL**(2), **procūr'ANCE,** nn.; function, authorized action, of attorney; || (eccl.) provision of entertainment for bishop or other visitor by incumbent etc., now commuted to money payment; (fee for) negotiation of loan; procurer's trade or offence. [ME, f. OF, or f. L *procuratio* (as PROCURE, see -ATION)]

prŏc'ūrātor, n. (Rom. hist.) treasury officer in imperial province; agent, proxy, esp. one who has power of attorney; magistrate in some Italian cities; || ~ *fiscal*, public prosecutor of district in Scotland. Hence or cogn. **prŏcūrātŏr'IAL** a., ~SHIP n. [ME, f. OF (-*tour*) or L *procurator* (as PROCURE, see -OR)]

prŏc'ūratory, n. Authorization to act for another, esp. *letters of* ~. [f. LL *procuratorium* neut. adj. (as PROCURE, see -ORY)]

prŏc'ūrātrix, n. Inmate of nunnery managing its temporal concerns. [L, as foll., -TRIX]

procūre', v.t. & i. Obtain by care or effort, acquire, as *must* ~ *a copy, cannot* ~ *employment*; (arch.) bring about, as ~*d his* *death by poison*; act as procurer or procuress. Hence **procur′**ABLE a., ~MENT (-ūrm-) n. [ME, f. OF *procurer* f. L PRO¹- (*curare* see to)]

procur̄′|**er**, n. In vbl senses, esp. man or woman who procures women for gratification of another's lust. So ~ESS¹ n. [ME & AF *procurour* f. L as PROCURATOR]

pr͞od, v.t. & i. (-dd-), & n. **1.** Poke with pointed instrument, end of stick, etc.; (fig.) stimulate to action; make ~ding motion *at*. **2.** n. Poke, thrust, pointed instrument. [16th c., perh. imit.]

pr͞od͞eli′sion (-zhn), n. Elision of initial vowel (as in *I'm* for *I am*). [f. L *prod-* = PRO-¹ + ELISION]

pr͞od′igal, a. & n. Recklessly wasteful (person); lavish *of*; ~ *son*, repentant sinner, returned wanderer, etc. (*Luke* xv. 11–32). Hence or cogn. ~ITY (-ăl̆-) n., ~LY² adv. [obs. F, or f. LL *prodigalis* f. L *prodigus* wasteful, see -AL]

pr͞od′igalize, **-ise** (**-īz**), v.t. Spend lavishly. [-IZE]

prodi′gious (-jus), a. Marvellous, amazing; enormous; abnormal. Hence ~LY² adv., ~NESS n., (-jus-). [f. L *prodigiosus* (as foll., see -OUS)]

pr͞od′igy̆, n. Marvellous thing, esp. one out of the course of nature; wonderful example *of* (some quality); person endowed with surprising qualities, esp. precocious child, as (attrib.) *a* ~ *violinist*. [f. L *prodigium* portent]

pr͞od′rom|**e**, n. Preliminary book or treatise (*to* another); (med.) premonitory symptom (*of*), whence ~AL, **prodr͞om′ic**, aa. [F, f. mod. L f. Gk PRO² (*dromos* running)]

pr͞od′ūce¹, n. Amount produced, yield, esp. in assay of ore; (also *raw* ~) agricultural & natural products collectively; result (*of* labour, efforts, etc.). [f. foll.]

prod͞uce′², v.t. Bring forward for inspection or consideration, as *will* ~ *evidence*, *witnesses*, *reasons*, ~ *your tickets*; bring (play, performer, book, etc.) before the public; (geom.) extend, continue, (line *to* a point); manufacture (goods) from raw materials etc.; bring about, cause, (a sensation etc.); (of land etc.) yield (produce) (of animal or plant) bear, yield, (offspring, fruit). So **prod͞ucibil′ity** n., **prod͞u′cible** a. [ME, f. L PRO¹(*ducere duct-* lead)]

prod͞u′cer, n. In vbl senses, esp.: (pol. econ.) one who produces article of consumption (cf. CONSUMER); (cinemat.) person generally responsible for production of a film (apart from direction of the acting); ~ *gas*, combustible gas, properly that formed by passing air through red-hot carbon, but often used for the 'semi-water gas' formed by passing steam and air through red-hot carbon. [f. prec. + -ER¹]

pr͞od′uct, n. Thing produced by natural process or manufacture; result, as *the* ~ *of his labours*; (math.) quantity obtained by multiplying quantities together;

(chem.) compound not previously existing in a body but formed during its decomposition. [ME, as PRODUCE²]

prod͞uc′tion, n. Producing; total yield; thing produced, esp. literary or artistic work. [ME, f. OF, f. L *productionem* (as prec., see -ION)]

prod͞uc′tive, a. Producing, tending to produce, as ~ *of figs*, ~ *of great annoyance*; (pol. econ.) producing commodities of exchangeable value, as ~ *labour(er)*; producing abundantly, as *a* ~ *soil*, *mine*, *writer*. Hence ~LY² adv., ~NESS n., **pr͞oductiv′ity** n., capacity to produce, quality or state of being ~, production per man-hour, (loosely) intensified production. [f. F (-*if*, -*ive*), or LL *productivus* (as PRODUCE², see -IVE)]

pr͞o′em, n. Preface, preamble, to book or speech, beginning, prelude. Hence **pr͞oēm′ial** a. [ME, f. OF *pro(h)eme* f. L f. Gk *prooimion*]

profāne′¹, v.t. Treat (sacred thing) with irreverence or disregard; violate, pollute, (what is entitled to respect). So **pr͞ofan′**A′TION n. [ME *prophane* f. OF *prophaner* f. L *profanare*, as foll.]

profāne′², a. Not belonging to what is sacred or biblical, as ~ *history*, *literature*, *writer*, *sacred and* ~ *love*; not initiated into religious rites or any esoteric knowledge; (of rites etc.) heathen; irreverent, blasphemous, so **profān′ity** n. Hence ~LY² adv., ~NESS n. [ME, f. OF *prophane* or med. L -*phanus* f. L PRO¹(*fanus* f. *fanum* temple) before i.e. outside the temple]

profess′, v.t. & i. Lay claim to (quality, feeling), pretend (*to* be or do), as *they* ~ *extreme regret*, *does not* ~ *to be a scholar*; openly declare, as *they* ~ *themselves quite content*, *I* ~ (*that*) *this is news to me*; affirm one's faith in or allegiance to (religion, God, Christ); make (law, medicine, flute-playing, the flute, etc.) one's profession or business; teach (subject) as professor; perform duties of a professor. [ME, f. L PRO¹(*fitēri fess-* = *fatēri* confess,)]

profess′ed′ (-st), a. Self-acknowledged, as *a* ~ *Christian*; alleged, ostensible, whence **profess′ed**LY² adv.; claiming to be duly qualified, as *a* ~ *anatomist*; ~ *monk*, *nun* (that has taken vows of religious order). [p.p. of prec.]

profe′ssion (-shn), n. Declaration, avowal, as *in practice if not in* ~, *accept my sincere* ~*s of regard*, *spare me these* ~*s*; declaration of belief in a religion; vow made on entering, fact of being in, a religious order; vocation, calling, esp. one that involves some branch of learning or science, as *the learned* ~*s* (divinity, law, medicine), *the military* ~, *a carpenter by* ~, whence ~LESS a.; *the* body of persons engaged in this, esp. (theatr. sl.) actors, as *lets apartments to the* ~. [ME, f. OF, f. L *professionem* (as PROFESS, see -ION)]

profe′ssional (-sho-), a. & n. **1.** Of,

belonging to, connected with, a profession, as ~ *men, etiquette, jealousy*; ~ *politician, agitator*, etc. (making a trade of politics etc.); ~ *cricketer, golfer*, etc. (playing for money, cf. AMATEUR). **2.** n. ~ man, esp. (abbr. *pro*)~ cricketer, golfer, etc. Hence ~LY² adv. [-AL]

profĕ'ssional|ism (-sho-), n. Qualities, stamp, of a profession; practice of employing professionals. So ~IZE(3) v.t. [-ISM]

profĕss'or, n. ‖ One who makes profession (*of* a religion); public teacher of high rank, esp. holder of a chair in university (prefixed as title, abbr. *Prof.*), whence ~ATE¹(1), ~ESS¹, **prŏfĕssŏr'**iATE¹(1), ~SHIP, nn., **prŏfĕssŏr'**IAL a., **professŏr'**ialLY² adv.; (as grandiose title)*P*~ *Smith's Boxing Dormice* etc., (sl.) professional. [ME, f. AF -*our* or L (as PROFESS, see -OR)]

prŏff'er, v.t., & n. **1.** Offer (gift, services, etc., arch. for do; esp. in p.p.). **2.** n. Offer. [ME; (n. f. AF *profre*) f. AF *proffrir* (PRO-¹ + *offrir* OFFER)]

profi'cient (-shnt), a. & n. Adept, expert, (*in, at*, an art etc., *in* doing). Hence **profi'ci**ENCY n., ~LY² adv., (-shn-). [f. L as PROFIT¹, see -ENT]

prŏf'il|e (-fēl, -fīl), n., & v.t. **1.** Drawing, silhouette, or other representation, of side view esp. of human face, whence ~IST n.; *drawn* etc. *in* ~*e* (as seen from one side); side outline esp. of the human face; (journalism) short biographical or character sketch; (fortif.) transverse vertical section of fort, comparative thickness of earthwork etc.; flat outline piece of scenery on stage. **2.** v.t. Represent in ~e, give a ~e to. [(n. f. It. *profilo* now *proff-*) f. It. (now *proff-*) PRO¹(*filare* spin f. L *filare* f. *filum* thread)]

prŏf'it¹, n. Advantage, benefit, as *have studied it to my* ~, *no* ~ *in such pursuits*; pecuniary gain, excess of returns over outlay; (book-keep.) ~ *& loss account*, account in which gains are credited & losses debited so as to show net ~ or loss at any time; ~*-sharing* (of ~s esp. between employer & employed). Hence ~LESS a., ~lĕssLY² adv., ~lĕssNESS n. [ME, f. OF, f. L *profectus -ūs* f. PRO¹(*ficere fect-* = *facere* do) advance]

prŏf'it², v.t. & i. (Of thing) be of advantage to (person etc. orig. indirect object), as *it will not* ~ *him, what will it* ~ *him?* ; be of advantage; (of person etc.) be benefited or assisted, as *hope to* ~ *by your advice*, ~*ed by the confusion to make my escape*. [ME, f. OF *profiter* as prec.]

prŏf'itable, a. Beneficial, useful, as ~ *conservation*; yielding profit, lucrative, as *a* ~ *speculation*. Hence ~NESS n., **prŏf'it**abLY² adv. [ME, f. OF (PROFIT¹ + -ABLE)]

prŏfiteer', v.i., & n. **1.** Make inordinate profits out of the State's or the consumer's straits (esp. of contractors & traders in

times of scarcity). **2.** n. ~ing person. [PROFIT, -EER]

prŏf'lig|ate, a. & n. **1.** Licentious, dissolute; recklessly extravagant. **2.** n. ~ate person. Hence ~ACY n., ~ateLY² adv. [f. L PRO¹(*fligare* = *fligere* strike down) overthrow, ruin, see -ATE³]

profound', a. & n. **1.** Having, showing, great knowledge or insight, as ~ *statesman, inquiry, treatise*; demanding deep study or thought, as ~ *doctrines*; (of state or quality) deep, intense, unqualified, as *fell into a* ~ *sleep, take a* ~ *interest, simulated a* ~ *indifference*; having, coming from, extending to, a great depth, as ~ *crevasses, a* ~ (deep-drawn) *sigh*, ~ (deep-seated) *gangrene*. **2.** n. (poet.). *The* vast depth (*of* ocean, futurity, the soul, etc.). Hence or cogn. ~LY² adv., ~NESS, **profūn'd**ITY, nn. [ME, f. OF *profund, -fond* f. L PRO¹(*fundus* bottom) deep]

profūse', a. Lavish, extravagant, (*in, of*, gifts, promises, expenditure, etc.); (of things) exuberantly plentiful. Hence or cogn. ~LY² (-sl-) adv., ~NESS (-sn-), **profū'**SION (-zhn), nn. [f. L PRO¹(*fundere fus-* pour)]

prŏg¹, n. (sl.). Food, esp. for journey or excursion. [17th c.; prob. f. obs. (exc. dial.) *prog* to forage etc.]

‖ **prŏg²**, ‖ **prŏgg'ins** (-ginz), nn. & vv.t. (sl.). Proctor at Oxford or Cambridge; (v.t.) proctorize. [abbr.]

progĕn'itive, a. Capable of, connected with, the production of offspring. [as foll., -IVE]

progĕn'it|or, n. Ancestor of person, animal, or plant; (fig.) political or intellectual predecessor, original of a copy. Hence ~ōr'IAL a., ~ORSHIP, ~RESS¹, nn. [ME, f. OF *progeniteur* or L *progenitor* f. PRO¹(*gignere genit-* beget), see -OR]

progĕn'iture, n. (Begetting of) offspring. [as prec., see -URE]

prŏ'gĕnȳ, n. Offspring of person, animal, or plant; descendants; (fig.) issue, outcome. [ME, f. OF *progenie* f. L *progenies* f. PRO¹(*gignere* beget)]

‖ **prŏggins.** See PROG².

proglŏtt'|is, n. (pl. ~*idēs*). Segment of tapeworm. [f. Gk PRO²(*glōssis* f. *glōssa*, *-tta*, tongue), from its shape]

prŏg'nath|ous (*or* -nă²), a. With projecting jaws; (of jaws) projecting. So **prŏgnăth'**IC a., ~ISM(2) n. [f. PRO-² + Gk *gnathos* jaw + -OUS]

prŏgnōs'is, n. (pl. -*osēs*). Prognostication, esp. (med.) forecast of course of disease. [LL, f. Gk PRO²(*gnōsis* f. *gnō-* know)]

prŏgnōs'tic, n. & a. **1.** Pre-indication, omen, (*of*); prediction, forecast. **2.** adj. Foretelling, predictive, (*of*). [(n. ME, f. OF *pronostique*) f. L f. Gk *prognōstikon* f. PRO²(*gignōskō* learn), -IC]

prŏgnōs'tic|āte, v.t. Foretell (event, *that*); (of things) betoken. Hence or cogn.

~ABLE, ~ātive, ~ātory, aa., ~A'tion, ~ātor, nn. [f. med. L *pro(g)nosticare* (as prec.), see -ate³]

prōg'ramme, -ăm, n., & v.t. 1. Descriptive notice of series of events, e.g. of course of study, concert, etc.; definite plan of intended proceedings; (colloq.) *what is the ~ for* (what are we going to do) *today?*; ~-*music* (intended to suggest series of scenes or events); ~ *picture* (cinemat.), film of some length forming part, but not the main feature, of the ~. 2. v.t. Make a ~ or definite plan of. [f. LL f. Gk *programma* f. pro²(*graphō* write) write publicly; -*me* now usu., but cf. *diagram, telegram*, etc.]

prōg'rèss¹, n. Forward or onward movement in space, as *made slow ~, continued his ~*; *an inquiry is now in ~* (going on); advance, development, as *made no ~ in his studies, the ~ of civilization, disease made rapid ~*; ‖ (arch.) state journey, official tour, esp. *royal ~*. [ME, app. f. OF *progresse*, f. L pro¹ (*gredi gress-* = *gradi* walk)]

progrèss'², v.i. Move forward or onward; be carried on, as *the controversy still ~es*; advance, develop, as *we ~ in knowledge, science~es*. [f. prec.; Amer. revival of obs. E, later re-adopted into E]

progrĕ'ssion (-shn), n. Progress, as *mode of ~*; (math.) arithmetical, geometrical, harmonic, ~; (mus.) passing from one note or chord to another. Hence ~al (-sho-) a. [ME, f. OF or L *progressio* (as progress¹, see -ion)]

progrĕ'ssionist (-sho-), n. Advocate of progress e.g. in political or social matters (also **prŏg'rĕssist** n.); one who holds that life on the earth has been marked by gradual progression to higher forms. [-ist]

progrĕss'ive, a. & n. 1. Moving forward, as ~ *motion*; proceeding step by step, successive; ~ *whist* etc. (played by several sets of players at different tables, certain players passing after each round to next table); advancing in social conditions, character, efficiency, etc., as *a ~ nation*; (of disease) continuously increasing; favouring progress or reform, as ~ *principles, party*, whence **progrĕss'ivism** n. 2. n. Advocate of ~ policy. Hence ~ly² adv., ~ness n. [f -*if, -ive*), as progress¹, see -ive]

prohib'it, v.t. Forbid, debar, (action, thing, person *from doing*). Hence or cogn. ~er¹, ~or, nn. [ME, f. L pro¹(*hibēre hibit-* = *habēre* hold)]

prohibi'tion (-ŏĭb-), n. Forbidding; edict, order, that forbids; forbidding by law of sale of intoxicants, whence ~ist (-ŏĭbisho-) n.; (law) writ from High Court of Justice forbidding inferior court to proceed in suit as being beyond its cognizance. [ME, f. OF, or L *prohibitio* (as prec., see -ion)]

prohib'itive, a. Prohibiting; serving to prevent the use or abuse or purchase of a thing, as ~ *tax, published at a ~ price.* Hence or cogn. ~ly² adv., ~ness n., **prohib'itory** a. [F (-*if, -ive*), as prohibit, see -ive]

project'¹, v.t. & i. Plan, contrive, (scheme, course of action, etc.); cast, throw, impel, (body *into* space etc.); ~ one*self*, go out of oneself *into* another's feelings, the future, etc., (spirit.) make a phantom of oneself visible to a distant person; (chem.) cast (substance *into, on*, etc.); cause (light, shadow) to fall on surface etc.; (fig.) cause (idea etc.) to take shape; (geom.) draw straight lines from a centre through every point of (given figure) to produce corresponding figure on a surface by intersecting it, draw (such lines), produce (such corresponding figure); make projection of (earth, sky, etc.); (intr.) protrude. [f. L pro¹(*jicĕre ject-* = *jacĕre* throw)]

prŏj'ĕct², n. Plan, scheme. [ME, as prec.]

projĕc'tile, a. & n. 1. Impelling, as ~ *force*; capable of being projected by force, esp. from gun. 2. n. = missile. [as prec. +-ile]

projĕc'tion, n. 1. Throwing, casting. 2. Transmutation of metals, as *powder of ~*, alchemists' powder of philosophers' stone. 3. Planning. 4. Protruding; protruding thing; thrusting forward. 5. (geom.). Projecting of a figure (see project¹); ~ *of a point*, point in derived figure corresponding to point in original figure. 6. Representation on plane surface of (any part of) surface of earth or of celestial sphere, as *Mercator's ~* (in which points of compass preserve same direction all over the map). 7. Mental image viewed as objective reality. 8. (cinemat.). Display of films by throwing image on screen, whence ~ist (-sho-) n. [f. L *projectio* (as prec., see -ion), or f. F]

projĕc'tive, a. (Geom.) of, derived by, projection, ~ *property* of a figure (unchanged after projection); mentally projecting or projected, as ~ *imagination.* Hence ~ly² adv. [[as prec., see -ive]

projĕc'tor, n. One who forms a project; promoter of speculative companies; apparatus for projecting rays of light or throwing image on cinematograph screen. [as prec., see -or]

prolăpse', v.i., & n. (path.). Slip forward or down out of place; (n.) = foll. [f. L pro¹(*labi laps-* slip); n. f. foll.]

prolăp'sus, n. (path.). Slipping forward or down of part of organ esp. of uterus or rectum. [LL, gen. -*ūs*, as prec.]

prōl'āte, a. (Geom., of spheroid) lengthened in direction of polar diameter (cf. oblate); growing, extending, in width; (fig.) widely spread; (gram.)=foll. Hence ~ly² adv. [f. L pro¹(*ferre lat-* carry) prolong]

prolăt'ive, a. (gram.). Serving to extend or complete predication, as in '*you can go*' *go is a ~ infinitive.* [f. LL *prolativus* (prec., -ive)]

prŏlĕgŏm'ĕn|on, n. (usu. in pl. ~a). Preliminary discourse or matter prefixed to book etc., introduction. Hence ~ARY[1], ~OUS, aa. [Gk *prolegomenon* neut. pass. part. of PRO[2](*legō* say)]

prolĕp'sis, n. (pl. *-psēs*). Anticipation; (gram.) anticipatory use of adjectives, as in *So those two brothers & their murdered man Rode past fair Florence.* Hence or cogn. **prolĕp'tic** a., **prolĕp'tically** adv. [L, f. Gk *prolēpsis* f. PRO[2](*lambanō* take)]

prŏletaire', n. = foll. n. Hence **prŏlètair'**ISM(2) n. [f. F *prolétaire*, as foll.]

prŏlětar'ian, a. & n. (Member) of the proletariate. Hence or cogn. ~ISM(2) n., **prŏl'ĕt**ARY[1] n. [f. L *proletarius* one who served the State not with property but with offspring (*proles*), see -ARY[1] & -AN]

prŏlètar'iat(e), n. (Rom. hist.; & mod., freq. derog.) lowest class of community; (pol. econ.) indigent wage-earners, labouring classes; *dictatorship of the* ~, Communist ideal of domination by the ~ after the suppression of capitalism & the *bourgeoisie*. [f. F *prolétariat* (as prec., see -ATE[1])]

prŏl'icide, n. Killing of offspring, esp. before or soon after birth. Hence **prŏlicid'**AL a. [f. L *proles* offspring + -CIDE]

prolif'er|āte, v.i. & t. Reproduce itself, grow, by multiplication of elementary parts; produce (cells etc.) thus; increase rapidly. So ~A'TION n., ~ātive a. [back form. f. *proliferation* f. F *prolifération* (as foll., see -ATION)]

prolif'erous, a. (Bot.) producing leaf or flower buds from leaf or flower, (also) producing new individuals from buds; (zool.) multiplying by budding; (path.) spreading by proliferation. [f. L *proles* offspring, see -FEROUS]

prolif'ic, a. Producing (much) offspring; abundantly productive *of*, abounding *in*. Hence ~ACY [irreg.], **prōlifi'city**, ~NESS, nn. [f. F *-ique* or med. L *prolificus* (as prec., see -FIC)]

proli'gerous, a. Bearing offspring, generative. [as prec. + L *-ger* -bearing + -OUS]

prŏl'ix (*or* prolĭks'), a. Lengthy, tediously wordy, as ~ *speech, writer.* Hence or cogn. **prolix'ity** n., ~LY[2] adv. [ME, f. OF *prolixe* or L *prolixus* (*liquere* be liquid)]

prŏl'ocutor (*or* prolŏ'-), n. Chairman ‖ esp. of lower house of convocation of either province of Church of England. Hence~SHIP n. [ME, L, f. PRO[1](*loqui locut*- speak), -OR]

prŏl'ogize (-j-), **-guize** (-gīz), **-ise** (-īz), vv.i. Write, speak, a prologue. [(-*gize*) f. Gk *prologizō* as foll., (-*gu*-) f. foll. + -IZE]

prŏl'ogue (-ŏg), n., & v.t. Preliminary discourse, poem, etc., esp. introducing play (cf. EPILOGUE); (fig.) act, event, serving as introduction (*to*); (v.t.) introduce, furnish, with a ~. [ME, f. OF, f. L f. Gk PRO[2](*logos* speech)]

prolōng', v.t. Extend (action, condition, etc.) in duration; extend in spatial length; lengthen pronunciation of (syllable etc.). So~ABLE (-nga-) a., **prōlonga**A'TION (-ngg-) n. [ME, f. LL PRO[1](*longare*, as LONG[1])]

prolu'sion (-ōozhn), n. Preliminary essay, article, or attempt. So **prolus'ory** (-ōo-) a. [f. L *prolusio* f. PRO[1](*ludere lus-* play) practise beforehand]

prŏm, n. (colloq.). = PROMENADE concert. [abbr.]

prŏmenade' (-ahd, -äd), n., & v.i. & t. 1. Walk, ride, drive, taken for exercise, amusement, or display, or as social ceremony; place, esp. paved public walk, for this; ~ *concert*, one at which (part of) audience is not seated and can move about; ~ *deck*, an upper deck on a liner, where passengers may ~. 2. v.i. Make a ~, whence **prŏmenad'**ER[1] (-ahd-, -äd-) n. 3. v.t. Make a ~ through (place); lead (person) about a place esp. for display. [F, f. *promener* take for walk f. L PRO[1](*minare* threaten) drive (beasts), -ADE]

Promēth'ean, a. Of, like, Prometheus in his skill or punishment. [f. Gk *Promētheus* (demigod who made man from clay, stole fire from Olympus & taught men the use of it & various arts, & was chained by Zeus to rock in Caucasus), see -AN]

prŏm'in|ent, a. Jutting out, projecting; conspicuous; distinguished. Hence or cogn. ~ENCE, ~ENCY, nn., ~ently[2] adv. [f. L PRO[1](*minēre*, see EMINENT)]

promis'cuous, a. Of mixed & disorderly composition, as *a* ~ *mass*; (w. pl. n.) of various kinds mixed together; indiscriminate, as ~ *massacre, hospitality*; ~ *bathing* (of both sexes together); ~ *sexual relations* (unrestricted by marriage or cohabitation); (colloq.) casual, as *took a* ~ *stroll.* Hence or cogn. **prŏmiscū'ity** n., ~LY[2] adv. [f. L PRO[1](*miscuus* f. *miscēre* mix) + -OUS]

prŏm'ise[1], n. Assurance given to a person that one will do or not do something or will give or procure him something; thing promised, as *I claim your* ~; BREACH[1] *of* ~; *land of* ~ (see foll.); (fig.) ground of expectation of future achievements or good results, as *book, writer, of great* ~. [ME, f. L *promissum* p.p. of PRO[1](*mittere* send) put forth, promise]

prŏm'ise[2], v.t. & i. Make (person) a promise to give or procure him (thing), as *I* ~ *you a fair hearing*; make (person) a promise (*to do, that* thing shall be done etc.); (abs.) *cannot positively* ~; ~ one- *self*, look forward to (a pleasant time etc.); (colloq.) *I* ~ (assure) *you, it will not be so easy*; (fig.) afford expectation of, as *these discussions* ~ *future storms*, seem likely (to do); (abs.) ~ well etc., hold out good etc. prospect; ~d land (also land of promise), Canaan (Gen. xii. 7 etc.), heaven, any place of expected felicity. Hence **prŏm'isER**[1] n. [ME, f. prec.]

prŏmisee', n. (law). Person to whom promise is made. So **prŏm'isOR** n. [-EE]

prŏm'ising, a. Likely to turn out well, hopeful, full of promise, as ~ boy, sky, beginning. Hence ~LY[2] adv. [-ING[2]]

prŏm'issorỹ, a. Conveying or implying a promise; (rare) full of promise (of); ~ note, signed document containing written promise to pay stated sum to specified person or to bearer at specified date or on demand. [f. med. L promissorius (as PROMISE[1], see -ORY)]

prŏm'ontor|ỹ, n. Point of high land jutting out into sea etc., headland; (anat.) kinds of protuberance in the body. Hence ~iED[2] (-rĭd) a. [f. med. L promontorium altered (on mons -ntis mount) f. L promunturium]

promōte', v.t. Advance, prefer, (person to position, higher office; was ~d major, to be major, to the rank of major, to majority, not to major); help forward, encourage, (process, result); support actively the passing of (law), take necessary steps for passing of (local or private act of parliament); *publicize & sell (product); (chess) raise (pawn) to rank of queen etc. Hence or cogn. **promō'TION** n., **promōt'IVE** a. [ME, f. L PRO[1](movēre mot- move)]

promōt'er, n. In vbl senses, esp. (also company-~) one who promotes formation of joint-stock company (freq. derog., whence ~ISM n.). [-ER[1]]

prŏmpt[1], a. & n. 1. Ready in action, acting with alacrity, as a ~ assistant, made, done, etc., readily or at once, as ~ reply, decision, payment, whence or cogn. ~'ITUDE, ~'NESS, nn., ~'LY[2] adv.; for ~ cash (on the spot); (commerce., of goods) for immediate delivery ,& payment, as ~ iron. 2. n. Time limit for payment of account, stated on ~-note, as what is the ~? [ME; (n. f. adj.) OF, or f. L promptus f. promere prompt- produce (PRO-[1] + emere take)]

prŏmpt[2], v.t., & n. 1. Incite, move, (person etc. to action, to do); supply (actor, reciter, or abs.) with the words that come next, assist (hesitating speaker) with suggestion; inspire, give rise to, (feeling, thought, action). 2. n. Thing said to help the memory esp. of actor; ~-book, copy of play for prompter's use; ~-(prompter's) box on stage; ~ side of stage (usu. to actor's left; abbr. p.s.). [ME, f. med. L *promptare, as prec.]

prŏmpt'er, n. One who prompts, esp. (theatr.) person stationed out of sight of audience to assist actor's memory. [-ER[1]]

prŏmp'ting, n. In vbl senses, esp. the ~s of conscience etc. [-ING[1]]

prŏm'ulg|āte, v.t. Make known to the public, disseminate (creed etc.), proclaim

(decree, news). Hence or cogn. ~A'TION, ~ātoR[2], nn. [f. L promulgare, see -ATE[3]]

promŭlge' (-j), v.t. (arch.). = prec. [as prec.]

pronā'ŏs, n. (Gk ant.). Space in front of body of temple, enclosed by portico & projecting side walls. [L, f. Gk PRO[2](naos temple)]

prŏn'|āte, v.t. (physiol.). Put (hand, fore limb) into prone position (cf. SUPINATE). So ~A'TION n. [f. LL pronare (as PRONE), see -ATE[3]]

prōnāt'or, n. (anat.). Muscle that effects or helps pronation. [med. L (as prec., see -OR)]

prōne, a. Having the front or ventral part downwards, lying face downwards, (loosely) lying flat, prostrate, as fell ~, whence ~'LY[2] (-nl-) adv.; (of ground) having downward aspect or direction, (loosely) steep, headlong; disposed, liable, (to quality, action, or condition, to do). Hence ~'NESS (-n-n-) n. [ME, f. L pronus]

prōneur' (-nér), n. Extoller, eulogist. [F]

prŏng, n., & v.t. Forked instrument, e.g. hay-fork; each pointed member of fork, whence (-)~ED[2] (-ngd) a.; (v.t.) pierce, stab, turn up (soil etc.), with ~; ~-buck, -horn, -horned antelope, N.-Amer. deer-like ruminant. [c. 1500, of unkn. orig.]

pronŏm'inal, a. Of (the nature of) a pronoun. Hence ~LY[2] adv. [f. LL pronominalis f. L PRO[1](nomen -minis noun), see -AL]

prōn'oun, n. Word used instead of (proper or other) noun to designate person or thing already mentioned or known from context or forming the subject of inquiry (used also to include pronominal & other adjectives, see below); personal ~s (I, we, thou, you, he, she, it, they); interrogative ~s (who, what, which); relative ~s (who, that, which); possessive ~s, adjectives representing possessive case (my, her, our, etc., with absolute forms mine, hers, ours); demonstrative ~s (this, that); distributive ~s (each, every, either, etc.); indefinite ~s (any, some, etc.). [PRO-[1] + NOUN, after F pronom, L pronomen (prec.)]

pronounce', v.t. & i. 1. Utter, deliver, (judgement, sentence, curse, etc.) formally or solemnly, state, declare, as one's opinion, as I ~ the pears unripe, cannot ~ him (or that he is) out of danger, whence ~MENT (-sm-) n. 2. Pass judgement, give one's opinion, (on, for, against, in favour of). 3. Utter, articulate, (words, or abs.), as ~ more distinctly, esp. with reference to different modes, as how do you ~ 'fulsome'?, cannot ~ French, whence ~ABLE (-sabl) a. [ME, f. OF pronuncier f. L PRO[1]-(nuntiare announce f. nuntius messenger)]

pronounced' (-st), a. In vbl senses, also, strongly marked, decided, as ~ tendency, magenta, flavour. Hence **pronoun'cedLY[2]** adv. [-ED[1]]

pronoun'cing, n. In vbl senses; (attrib.)

~ *dictionary* (in which pronunciation is indicated). [-ING[1]]

*°prŏn'tŏ, adv. (sl.). Promptly, quickly. [Sp.]

prŏn'tosii, n. One of the sulphonamide group of drugs. [P]

pronŭnciamĕn'tŏ, n. (pl. ~s). Proclamation, manifesto, esp. (in Spanish-speaking countries) one issued by insurrectionists. [f. Sp. *pronunciamiento*, also used in E, f. L as PRONOUNCE, see -MENT]

pronŭnciā'tion, n. Mode in which a word is pronounced; a person's way of pronouncing words, as *his ~ is often faulty*. [ME, f. OF, or f. L *pronuntiatio* (as PRONOUNCE, see -ATION)]

prŏŏf[1], n. 1. Evidence sufficing or helping to establish a fact, as *this requires no ~*, *as a ~ of his esteem*, *~ positive of his intention* or *that he intended*, whence *~'LESS a.*; spoken or written legal evidence. 2. Proving, demonstration, as *not capable of ~*, *in ~ of my assertion*. 3. ‖ (Sc. law). Trial before judge instead of by jury. 4. Test, trial, as *must be brought to the ~*, *will stand a severe ~*, *the ~ of the pudding is in the eating*. 5. (Place for) testing of fire-arms or explosives. 6. (arch.). Proved impenetrability, as *armour of ~*. 7. Standard of strength of distilled alcoholic liquors. 8. (*First*) ~, trial impression taken from type, in which corrections etc. may be made (cf. REVISE); *~-reader, -reading*, (person employed in) reading & correcting *~s*; *~-sheet*, sheet of *~*. 9. Each of a limited number of careful impressions made from engraved plate before printing of ordinary issue & usu. (also *~ before letters*) before inscription is added; *artist's, engraver's, ~* (taken for examination or alteration by him); *signed ~*, early *~* signed by artist. 10. Test-tube. 11. *~-plane*, conductor fixed on insulating handle & used in measuring electrification of a body. [ME & OF *proeve, preve*, later *prŏf*, f. LL *proba*, as PROVE]

prŏŏf[2], a., & v.t. 1. (Of armour) of tried strength; impenetrable, as *~ against the severest weather, the pricks of conscience*, esp. in comb., as *bomb, bullet, burglar, fire, FOOL[1], rain, sound, weather, -~, WATER[1]-~*. 2. v.t. Make (thing) *~*, esp. make (fabric etc.) waterproof. [adj. f. prec., app. by ellipsis of *of*; vb f. prec., or f. adj.]

prŏp[1], n., & v.t. & i. (-pp-). 1. Rigid support, esp. one not forming structural part of thing supported, e.g. pole; ‖ CLOTHES-~; (fig.) person etc. who upholds institution etc. 2. v.t. Support (as) by ~ (lit. & fig.), hold *up* thus. 3. v.i. (Of horse etc.) come to a dead stop with fore-legs rigid. [15th c., prob. f. MDu. *proppe*; vb f. n., or MDu. *proppen*]

prŏp[2]. See PROPOSITION.

prŏp[3], n. (colloq.). Aircraft propeller. [abbr.]

prŏp[4], n. (theatr.). Stage property. [abbr.]

prōpaedeut'ic, a. & n. (Subject, study) serving as introduction to higher study; (n. pl.) preliminary learning. Hence *~AL* a. [f. Gk PRO[2](*paideuō* teach f. *pais paidos* child), see -IC]

prōpagăn'da, n. 1. (*Congregation, College, of*) *the P~*, committee of cardinals in charge of foreign missions. 2. Association, organized scheme, for propagation of a doctrine or practice; doctrines, information, etc. thus propagated; efforts, schemes, principles, of propagation. [It., f. mod. L *congregatio de propaganda fide* congregation for propagation of the faith]

prōpagăn'd|ist, n. Member, agent, of a propaganda, whence *~ISM* n., *~is'tic* a., *~IZE*(2, 4) v.i. & t.; proselytizer; missionary, convert, of the Propaganda. [-IST]

prŏp'ag|āte, v.t. 1. Multiply specimens of (plant, animal, disease, etc.) by natural process from parent stock; (of plant etc.) reproduce (*itself*, or abs.). 2. Hand down (quality etc.) from one generation to another. 3. Disseminate, diffuse, (statement, belief, practice). 4. Extend operation of, transmit, (vibration, earthquake, etc.). Hence or cogn. *~A'TION, ~ātor,* nn., *~ātive* a. [f. L *propagare* multiply plants from LAYERS, f. PRO[1](*pago* f. root of *pangere* fix, set), see -ATE[3]]

prōparŏx'ytone, a. & n. (Gk gram.). (Word) with acute accent on antepenult. [f. Gk PRO[2](*paroxutonos* PAROXYTONE)]

propĕl', v.t. (-ll-). Drive forward, give onward motion to, (lit. & fig.); JET[2]-*~led*. [ME, f. L PRO[1](*pellere puls-* drive)]

propĕll'ant, -ent, a. & n. Propelling (agent); explosive that propels bullet or shell from fire-arm. [-ANT, -ENT]

propĕll'er, n. In vbl senses, esp., revolving shaft with blades usu. (*screw ~*) set at an angle & twisted like thread of screw, for propelling ship or aircraft; *~ turbine* or *prop'-jet engine*, aircraft engine having a turbine-driven *~*. [-ER[1]]

propĕn'sitỹ, n. Inclination, tendency, (*to* condition, quality, thing, *to do, for doing*). [f. now rare *propense* f. L *propensus* inclined, p.p. of PRO[1](*pendēre* hang) +-ITY]

prŏp'er, a. 1. (arch.). (Usu. w. possessive pron. & occas. w. *own*) own, as *with my own ~ eyes*. 2. (astron.). *~ motion*, that part of the apparent motion of fixed star etc. supposed to be due to its actual movement in space. 3. Belonging, relating, exclusively or distinctively (*to*, or abs. as *~ psalms, lessons, ~* to particular day). 4. (gram.). *~ noun* or *name*, name used to designate an individual person, animal, town, ship, etc. (e.g. Jane, Neddy, London, Victory). 5. Accurate, correct, as *in the ~ sense of the word*. 6. (Usu. foll. its noun) strictly so called, real, genuine, as *within the sphere of architecture ~* ; *~*

fraction (less than unity). **7.** (colloq.). Thorough, complete, as *will be a ~ row about this*. **8.** (arch.). Handsome, as *a ~ man*. **9.** Fit, suitable, right, as *choose the ~ time, do it the ~ way*. **10.** In conformity with demands of society, decent, respectable, as *she is so distressingly ~, would it be quite ~?* **11.** In the natural, not conventional, colours, as *a peacock ~*. [ME & OF *propre* f. L *proprius*]

pröpĕrĭspŏm'ĕnon, a. & n. (Gk gram.). (Word) with circumflex accent on penult. [Gk PRO²(PERISPOMENON)]

prŏp'erlў, adv. Fittingly, suitably, as *do it ~ or not at all*; rightly, duly, as *he very ~ refused*; with good manners, as *behave ~*; (colloq.) thoroughly, as *puzzled him ~*. [-LY²]

prŏp'ertў, n. **1.** Owning, being owned, as *~ has its duties*; thing owned, possession(s), as *the book is his ~, regards him as her exclusive ~, a man of* (great) *~, has a small ~* (estate) *in Norfolk*, PERSONAL, REAL², *~*; *~ qualification* (based on possession of *~*), *~ tax* (levied directly on *~*). **2.** (theatr.; abbr. *prŏp*). Article of costume, furniture, etc., used on stage; *~-man, -master*, man in charge of stage properties. **3.** Attribute, quality, as *the properties of soda, has the ~ of dissolving grease*; (log.) quality common to a whole class but not necessary to distinguish it from others, cf. DIFFERENTIA. [ME, f. OF *propriete* f. L *proprietatem* (as PROPER, see -TY)]

prŏph'ĕcў, n. Faculty of a prophet, as *the gift of ~*; prophetic utterance; foretelling of future events. [ME, f. OF *profecie* f. LL f. Gk *prophēteia* (as PROPHET)]

prŏph'esў, v.i. & t. Speak as a prophet; foretell future events; (arch.) expound the Scriptures; foretell (event, *that, who*, etc.). [ME, f. OF *profecier*, as prec.]

prŏph'ĕt, n. Inspired teacher, revealer or interpreter of God's will; *the ~s*, prophetical writers of O.T., *major ~s*, Isaiah, Jeremiah, Ezekiel, Daniel, *the 12 minor ~s*, Hosea to Malachi; *the P~*, Mohammed, (also) Joseph Smith, founder of Mormons; *Saul among the ~s*, person revealing unexpected gifts or sympathies (see 1 *Sam.* x. 11); spokesman, advocate, (of principle etc.); one who foretells events, as *am no weather-~*; (sl.) tipster. Hence *~*ESS¹, *~*HOOD, *~*SHIP, nn. [ME, f. OF *prophete* f. L (-*ta*) f. Gk PRO²(*phētēs* speaker f. *phēmi* speak) spokesman]

prŏphĕt'ic, a. Of a prophet; predicting, containing a prediction *of* (event etc.). Hence *~*AL a., *~*alLY² adv. [f. F (-*ique*) or LL f. Gk *prophētikos* (prec., -IC)]

prŏphўlăc'tic, a. & n. (Medicine, measure) tending to prevent disease. [f. Gk *prophulaktikos* f. PRO²(*phulassō* guard)]

prŏphўlăx'is, n. Preventive treatment of disease. [f. PRO-² + Gk *phulaxis* a guarding, after prec.]

propĭn'quĭtў, n. Nearness in place; close kinship; similarity. [f. ME & OF *propinquite* f. L *propinquitatem* (*propinquus* near f. *prope* near, see -TY)]

propĭ'tiāte (-shĭ-), v.t. Appease (offended person etc.); make propitious. [f. L *propitiare* (as PROPITIOUS, see -ATE²)]

propĭtiā'tion (-shĭ-), n. Appeasement; atonement; (arch.) gift etc. meant to propitiate, as *he is the ~ for our sins*. [ME, f. LL *propitiatio* (as prec., see -ATION)]

propĭ'tiātor|ў (-sha-), a. & n. Serving, meant, to propitiate, as *a ~y smile*; (n.) the mercy-seat (esp. fig. of Christ). Hence *~*ĭLY² adv. [ME, f. LL *propitiatorius* (as PROPITIATE, see -ORY)]

propĭ'tious (-shus), a. Well-disposed, favourable, as *the fates were ~*; (of omens etc.) favourable; (of weather, occasion, etc.) suitable *for*, favourable *to*, (purpose). Hence *~*LY² adv. [la'e ME, f. OF *propicieus* f. L *propitius*, -OUS]

prŏp'olis, n. Red resinous substance got by bees from buds to stop up crevices with. [L, f. Gk PRO²(*polis* city) suburb, bee-glue]

propŏn'ent, a. & n. (Person) that puts forward a motion, theory, or proposal. [f. L as PROPOUND, see -ENT]

propŏr'tion, n., & v.t. **1.** Comparative part, share, as *a large ~ of the earth's surface, of the profits*; comparative relation, ratio, as *the ~ of births to the population, price will be raised in ~* (*to the labour* etc., or *abs.*); due relation of one thing to another or between parts of a thing, as *windows are in admirable ~, his success bore no ~ to his abilities*, whence *~*LESS (-sho-) a.; *was out of* (*all*) *~ to*, too great for; (pl.) dimensions, as *athlete, building, of magnificent ~s*; (math.) equality of ratios between two pairs of quantities, as *3, 5, 9, & 15 are in ~*, set of such quantities, (arith.) RULE of three. **2.** v.t. Make (thing etc.) proportionate *to*, as *must ~ the punishment to the crime*, whence (-)*~*ED¹ (-shond) a., *~*MENT (-sho-) n. [ME; n. OF, or L PRO²(*portio* PORTION); vb f. OF *proporcioner* or med. L -*are*]

propŏr'tion|al (-sho-), a. & n. **1.** In due proportion, corresponding in degree or amount, as *a ~al increase in the expense, resentment ~al to his injuries, ~al* REPRESENTATION, so *~*ABLE, *~*ATE², aa., *~*abLY², *~*ateLY², advv. **2.** n. One of the terms of a proportion, as *5, 3, 10, 6, are ~als, 6 is a mean ~al between 3 & 12*. Hence or cogn. *~*ăl'ITY n., *~*alLY² adv., (-sho-). [f. L *proportionalis* (as prec., see -AL)]

propŏr'tionalist (-sho-), n. One who plans proportions; advocate of proportional representation. [-IST]

propōs'al (-z-), n. Act of proposing something; offer of marriage, as *have had a ~*; scheme of action etc. proposed, as *the ~ was never carried out*. [-AL]

propōse' (-z), v.t. & i. Put forward for consideration, propound; set up as an aim, as *the object I ~ to myself*; nominate (person) as member of society etc.; offer (person's health, person) as toast; make offer of marriage (*to*); put forward as a plan, as *we ~* (to make) *a change, that a change should be made*; intend, purpose, (*to do, doing*); (abs.) *man ~s, God disposes*. [ME, f. OF PRO¹(*poser*, see COMPOSE)]

prŏposi'tion (-z-), n. Statement, assertion, as *a ~ too plain to need argument*, esp. (log.) form of words consisting of predicate & subject; (math., abbr. *prŏp*) formal statement of theorem or problem, often including the demonstration, as *Euclid, Book I, ~ 5*; proposal, scheme proposed; (sl.) task, job, problem, objective, occupation, trade, opponent, prospect, etc. Hence ~AL (-zisho-) a. [ME, f. OF, or L *propositio* (as foll., see -ION)]

propound', v.t. Offer for consideration, propose, (question, problem, scheme, matter, etc., *to* person); produce (will) before proper authority in order to establish its legality. Hence ~ER¹ n. [replacing *propone* f. L PRO¹(*ponere posit-*place), cf. *compound* etc.]

propraet'or, n. (Rom. hist.). Ex-praetor with authority of praetor in province not under military control. [L, earlier *pro praetore* (one acting) for praetor]

propri'etarў, a. & n. 1. Of a proprietor, as *~ rights*; holding property, as *the ~ classes*; held in private ownership, as *~ medicines* (sale of which is restricted by patent etc.). 2. n. Proprietorship, as *an exclusive ~*; body of proprietors, as *the landed ~*. [f. LL *proprietarius* (as PROPERTY, see -ARY¹)]

propri'ĕt|or, n. Owner. Hence ~ŏr'iAL a., ~ŏr'iaLŬ² adv., ~ORSHIP, ~RESS¹, nn. [altered in 17th c. f. prec.]

propri'ĕt|ў, n. Fitness, rightness, as *doubt the ~y of the term, of refusing him*; correctness of behaviour or morals, as *a breach of ~y*; (pl.) details of correct conduct, as *must observe the ~ies*. [ME; (in earlier senses ' ownership, peculiarity ') f. OF *propriete* PROPERTY]

prŏp'rĭŏ mŏt'ŭ (or *mŏt'ū prŏp'rĭŏ*), n. Form of papal bull without seal & used in the administration of the papal court. [L, = of our own motion, wds included in the formula]

prŏptōs'|ĭs, n. (path.). Prolapse, protrusion, esp. of eye. Hence ~ED¹ (-st) a. [LL, f. Gk *proptōsis* f. PRO²(*piptō* fall)]

propŭl's|ion (-shn), n. Driving or pushing forward; JET²(-*ion* (; (fig.) impelling influence. So ~IVE a. [F (as PROPEL, see -ION)]

prŏpўlae'|um, n. (pl. ~a). Entrance to temple; *the P~a*, entrance to Acropolis at Athens. [L, f. Gk PRO²(*pulaion* f. *pulē* gate)]

prŏp'ўl|īte, n. Volcanic rock found in some silver-mining regions. Hence ~ĭt'IC

a. [f. foll. + -ITE¹, as opening a volcanic epoch]

prŏp'ўlŏn, n. (pl. *-ons, -a*). = PROPYLAEUM. [L, f. Gk PRO²(*pulon* f. *pulē* gate)]

prorŏgue' (-g), v.t. & i. Discontinue meetings of (British parliament etc.) without dissolving it; (of parliament etc.) be ~d. So **prŏroga'**TION n. [ME *proroge* f. OF *proroger, -guer* f. L PRO¹(*rogare* ask) prolong]

pros- in comb. = Gk *pros* to, towards, in addition.

prŏsā'ic (-z-; *also* pro-), a. Like prose, lacking poetic beauty; unromantic, commonplace, dull, as *a ~ life, person, view of ' things*. Hence **prŏsā'**ICALLY adv., ~NESS n. [f. F (-*ique*) or LL *prosaicus* (as PROSE, see -IC)]

prŏs'ā|ist (-z-), n. Prose writer; prosaic person. So ~ISM(4) n. [as PROSE, see -IST]

prŏscĕn'ium (*or* pro-), n. (pl. *-ia*). (In ancient theatre) the stage; (mod.) space between curtain or drop-scene & orchestra, esp. with the enclosing arch. [L, f. Gk PRO²(*skēnion* f. *skēnē*, as SCENE)]

proscrībe', v.t. Put (person) out of protection of law; banish, exile, (esp. fig.); reject, denounce, (practice etc.) as dangerous etc. So **proscrip'**TION n., **proscrip'**TIVE a. [f. L PRO¹(*scribere* script-write)]

prōse (-z), n., & v.i. & t. 1. Ordinary non-metrical form of written or spoken language (*Milton's ~ works*); (eccl.)= SEQUENCE; *~ poem*, ~ work of poetical style; plain matter-of-fact quality, as *the ~ of existence*; tedious discourse. 2. v.i. Talk prosily (*about* etc.), whence **prōs'**ER¹ (-z-) n. 3. v.t. Turn (poem etc.) into ~. [ME, f. OF, f. L *prosa* (*oratio*) straightforward (discourse), fem. of *prosus*, earlier *prorsus*]

prosĕc'tor, n. One who dissects dead bodies in preparation for anatomical lecture etc. [LL, = anatomist, f. PRO¹(*secare sect-* cut), prob. after F *prosecteur*]

prŏs'ĕcūte, v.t. Follow up, pursue, (inquiry, studies); carry on (trade, pursuit); institute legal proceedings against (person), as *trespassers will be ~d*, (abs.) *shall not ~*. [ME, f. L PRO¹(*sequi secut-* follow)]

prŏsĕcū'tion, n. Prosecuting (*of* pursuit etc.); (law) institution and carrying on of criminal charge before court; carrying on of legal proceedings against person; prosecuting party, as *the ~ denied this*; ‖ *director of public ~s*, public prosecutor. [ME, f. OF, or f. LL *prosecutio* (prec., -ION)]

prŏs'ĕcūtor, n. One who prosecutes esp. in criminal court; *public ~*, law officer conducting criminal proceedings in public interest. Hence **prŏsĕcū'**RIX n. (pl. *-ices* pr. -īsēz). [med. L (as PROSECUTE, see -OR)]

prŏs'ĕlўt|e, n., & v.t. 1. Convert from

one opinion, creed, or party, to another, as *made many* ~es; Gentile convert to Jewish faith, ~*e of the gate* (not submitting to circumcision etc.). **2.** v.t. (now rare). Make a ~e of (person, or abs.). Hence ~ISM(1, 2), ~ĪZER[1], nn., ~IZE(2) v.t. (often abs.). [ME, f. LL f. Gk PROS(*ēlutos* f. st. *eluth-* come) one who has come, convert]

prŏsĕn'chyma (-ngk-), n. (bot.). Tissue of elongated cells placed with their ends interpenetrating (cf. PARENCHYMA); esp. fibro-vascular tissue. Hence ~TOUS (-ĕngkǐm²) a. [f. Gk *pros* toward, as PARENCHYMA]

prŏs'ǐfy (-z-), v.t. & i. Turn into prose, make prosaic; write prose. [-FY]

prōs'ǐt, int. used in drinking person's health, wishing him success, etc., lit. = may it benefit you. [f. G f. L]

prŏs'od┃y̆, n. Science of versification, laws of METRE[1]. Hence ~ĭ'ACAL, prosŏd'ĬAL, prosŏd'ĬC, aa., ~IST n. [ME, f. L f. Gk PROS(*ŏidia* as ODE)]

prŏsōpopoe'ia (-pē'a, -pē'ya), n. (rhet.). Introduction of pretended speaker; personification of abstract thing. [L, f. Gk *prosōpopoiia* (*prosōpon* person + *poieō* make)]

prospect, n., & v.i. & t. **1.** (prŏs'pĕkt). Extensive view of landscape etc., as *a fine, striking,* ~; mental scene, as *opened a new ~ to his mind;* expectation, what one expects, as *offers a gloomy* ~, *his* ~*s were brilliant, no ~ of success, have nothing in* ~ *at present,* whence ~LESS a.; (mining) spot giving ~s of mineral deposit, sample of ore for testing, resulting yield; possible or probable customer, subscriber, etc. **2.** (prospĕkt'). v.i. Explore region (*for* gold etc.), so **prospĕc'TOR** (*or* prŏs'-) n.; (fig.) look out *for,* (of mine) promise (*well, ill*); (v.t.) explore (region) for gold etc., work (mine) experimentally, (of mine) promise (specified yield). [ME; (vb f. n.) as PROSPECTUS]

prospĕc'tive, a. Concerned with, applying to, the future (cf. RETROSPECTIVE), as *the law was held to be exclusively* ~, *implies a* ~ *obligation;* expected, future, some day to be, as ~ *peer, bridegroom, profit.* Hence ~LY² adv., ~NESS n. [f. obs. F (-*if*, -*ive*) or LL *prospectivus* (as foll., see -IVE)]

prospĕc'tus, n. (pl. ~es). Circular describing chief features of school, commercial enterprise, forthcoming book, etc. [L, gen. -*ūs*, = prospect, f. PRO¹(*specere* = *specere* look)]

prŏs'per, v.i. & t. Succeed, thrive, as *cheats never* ~, *nothing will ever* ~ *in his hands;* make successful, as *Heaven* ~ *our attempt.* [ME, f. OF *prosperer* or L *prosperare,* as foll.]

prŏs'perous, a. Flourishing, successful, thriving, as *a* ~ *merchant, enterprise,* whence or cogn. **prŏspĕ'rITY** n., ~LY² adv.; auspicious, as *a* ~ *gale, in a* ~ *hour.* [ME, f. OF *prosperus* f. L *prosper(us),* see -OUS]

prŏs'tāte, n. Large gland, each of several small glands, accessory to male generative organs in mammals. Hence **prostāt'IC** a. [F, or f. mod. L (-*la*) f. Gk PRO²(*statēs* f. *sta-* stand) one who stands before]

prŏs'thĕsis, n. (Gram.). addition of letter or syllable at beginning of word; (surg.) making up of deficiencies (e.g. by false teeth or wooden leg) as a branch of surgery. So **prŏsthĕt'IC** a. [LL, f. Gk *prosthesis* f. PROS(*tithēmi* put)]

prŏs'tītūte, n., & v.t. **1.** Woman who offers her body to indiscriminate sexual intercourse esp. for hire. **2.** v.t. Make a ~ of (one*self*); (fig.) sell for base gain (one's honour etc.), put (abilities etc.) to infamous use. So **prŏstītū'TION** n. [f. L PRO¹(*stituere* -*ut-* = *statuere* set up, place) offer for sale; n. = L *prostituta*]

prŏs'trāte¹ (*or* -āt), a. Lying with face to ground, esp. as token of submission or humility; lying in horizontal position; overcome, overthrown, as *had laid the Tory party* ~; physically exhausted; (bot.) lying flat on ground. [ME, f. L p.p. as foll.]

prostrāte'² (*or* prŏs'-), v.t. Lay (person etc.) flat on ground; cast one*self* down prostrate (*at* shrine, *before* person etc.); (fig.) overcome, make submissive; (of fatigue etc.) reduce to extreme physical weakness. So **prostrā'TION** n. [ME, f. L PRO¹(*sternere strat-* lay flat)]

prŏs'tyle, n. & a. Portico of not more than four columns in front of Greek temple; (adj.) having a ~. [f. L (-*os*) f. Gk PRO²(*stulos* STYLE²)]

prŏs'y̆ (-z-), a. Commonplace, tedious, dull, as ~*y talk(er)*. Hence ~ILY² adv., ~ĬNESS n. [f. PROSE + -Y¹]

prŏtăg'onist, n. Chief person in drama or plot of story, cf. DEUTERAGONIST; leading person in contest, principal performer; (erron.) advocate, champion, *of course,* method, etc. [f. Gk *prōtagōnistēs* (*prōtos* first + *agōnistēs* actor, as AGONIZE)]

prŏt'asis, n. (pl. -*asēs*). Introductory clause, esp. clause expressing condition (cf. APODOSIS). So **protăt'IC** a. [L, f. Gk PRO²(*tasis* f. *teinō* stretch) proposition]

prŏt'ēan (*or*-ē'an), a. Variable, versatile; of or like PROTEUS. [-AN]

protĕct', v.t. Keep safe, defend, guard, (person, thing, *from, against,* danger, injury, etc.); (pol. econ.) guard (home industry) against competition by imposts on foreign goods; (commerc.) provide funds to meet (bill, draft); provide (machinery etc.) with appliances to prevent injury from it, as ~*ed rifles*. [f. L PRO¹(*tegere tect-* cover)]

protĕc'tion, n. Protecting, defence, as *is safe under your* ~, *affords* ~ *against weather;* patronage, as *book was indebted to your kind* ~; protecting person or thing, as *man, dog, is a great* ~ *against burglars; live under X's* ~, (of a woman) be kept by X; safe-conduct; U.S.

certificate of American citizenship issued to seamen; (pol. econ.) system of protecting home industries, whence ~ISM(3), ~IST(2), nn., (-sho). [ME, f. OF, or LL *protectio* (as prec., see -ION)]

protĕc'tive, a. Serving or intended to protect; (of foods) protecting against deficiency diseases; ~ *custody*, (usu.) detention of persons in order to protect the State from their (real or suspected) subversive activities. Hence ~LY[2] adv., ~NESS n. [-IVE]

protĕc'tor, n. Person who protects; regent in charge of kingdom during minority, absence, etc., of sovereign, *Lord P~ of the Commonwealth*, title of Oliver Cromwell (1653–8) & Richard Cromwell (1658–9), whence ~AL a., ~SHIP n.; thing, device, that protects, as CHEST-~, point-~ (for pencil). Hence **protĕc'trESS**[1] n. [ME, f. OF *protectour* f. LL *protector* (as PROTECT, see -OR)]

protĕc'torate, n. Office of protector of kingdom or State; period of this, esp. of the ~ of O. & R. Cromwell; protectorship of weak state by stronger one, esp. of territory inhabited by backward tribes; such territory. [-ATE[1]]

protĕc'torў, n. (Rom. Cath.). Institution for care of destitute or vicious children. [as PROTECT, see -ORY]

protégé (prŏt'ĕzhă), n. (fem. ~e). Person to whom another is (usu. permanent) protector or patron. [F, p.p. of *protéger* PROTECT]

prŏt'ĕïd, n. = PROTEIN (1st sense). [-ID[4]]

prŏt'ĕïfŏrm, a. Very changeable in form. [f. PROTEUS + -FORM]

prŏt'ĕïn (*or* -tēn), n. (chem.). (Now preferred in scient. use to *proteid*) albuminoid, kinds of organic compound (containing carbon, hydrogen, oxygen, & nitrogen, freq. also sulphur, occas. phosphorus) forming an important part of all living organisms, and the essential nitrogenous constituent of the food of animals; (orig.) supposed basis of albuminoids. Hence ~A'CEOUS (-āshus), prŏtĕïn'IC, prŏtĕ'inOUS, aa. [f. F *protéine*, G *protein*, f. Gk *prōteios* primary, see -IN]

prŏter|(o)-, comb. form of Gk *proteros* former, anterior, as ~*an'drous*, ~*o'gўnous*, having stamens (pistil) mature before pistil (stamens).

prŏt'ĕst[1], n. Formal statement of dissent or disapproval, remonstrance, as *made a ~, paid it under ~*; ‖ written statement of dissent from motion carried in H. of Lords signed by any peer of minority (hist.); written declaration usu. by notary public that bill has been duly presented & payment or acceptance refused; solemn declaration. [ME, f. OF *protest* f. *protester* (foll.)]

protĕst'[2], v.t. & i. Affirm solemnly (one's innocence etc., *that*, or abs.); write a

protest in regard to (bill, see prec.); make (often written) protest *against* (action, proposal), whence ~ER[1], ~OR, nn., ~inglY[2] adv. [ME, f. OF *protester* f. L PRO[1](*testari* aver f. *testis* witness)]

prŏt'ĕstant, P-, n. & a. (Member, adherent) of any of the Christian bodies that separated from the Roman communion in the Reformation (16th c.) or their offshoots, whence P~ISM(3) n., P~IZE(3) v.t. & i.; (hist., pl.) those who dissented from decision of Diet of Spires (1529), adherents of reformed doctrines in Germany; (*also* protĕs[L]) making, maker of, a protest. [1539, G or F (as prec., -ANT)]

prŏtĕstā'tion, n. Solemn affirmation (*of, that*); protest (*against*). [ME, f. OF, f. LL *protestatio* (as prec., see -ATION)]

Prŏt'eus (-tūs), n. Changing or inconstant person or thing; (earlier name for) amoeba; kinds of bacteria; kinds of tailed amphibian with eel-like body & four short legs. [L, f. Gk *Prōteus* sea-god taking various shapes]

prŏthalăm'ĭum, -ĭŏn, n. (pl. *-ia*). Preliminary nuptial song. [(-*on*) made by Spenser on EPITHALAMIUM (PRO-[2])]

prŏth'ĕsis, n. (Placing of eucharistic elements on) credence-table, part of church where this stands; (gram.) = PROSTHESIS, so **prŏthĕt'IC** a. [Gk *prothesis* f. PRO[2](*tithĕmi* place)]

prŏtis'ta, n. pl. Kingdom of organized beings not distinguished as animals or plants. [Gk *prōtista*, neut. pl. superl. f. *prōtos* first]

prŏt'ĭum, n. (chem.). Ordinary hydrogen as dist. from heavy hydrogen (DEUTERIUM). [f. PROT(O)-, -IUM]

prŏto- (bef. a vowel *prot*-), comb. form of Gk *prōtos* first. **1.** = chief, original, primitive, as: ~*A'rabic*, ~*Cel'tic*, etc. of the original Arabs etc.; ~*genĕt'ic*, ~*gĕn'ic*, of first period of formation of growth; *prŏt'ogine*, kind of granite found in Alps, assumed to be the most ancient; ~*hipp'us*, extinct quadruped related to horse; *prŏ'tomartyr* (-ter), first martyr (esp., of Christians, St Stephen); *prŏtŏph'ўta* n. pl., the most simply organized plants, each consisting of a single cell, *prŏt'ophўte*, such plant; ~*thĕr'ia* n. pl., mammals of the lowest subclass, their hypothetical ancestors; ~*zō'a* n. pl., great division of animal kingdom comprising animals of simplest type consisting of single cell & usu. microscopic, ~*zō'on*, such animal; ~*zō'al* a., ~*zō'an* a. & n., (animal) of the ~zoa, (of disease) caused by parasitic ~zoon; ~*zō'ic*, (geol.) of strata) containing earliest traces of living beings, (also) ~*zoal*; ~*zōöl'ogy*, study of ~zoa. **2.** In chem. names of compounds in which the element or radical combines in smallest proportion with another element, as ~*chlor'ide*, ~

sulph'ide, **prŏt'oxide**, compound containing minimum of chlorine, sulphur, oxygen.

prŏt'ocŏl, n., & v.i. & t. (-ll-). **1.** Original draft of diplomatic document, esp. of terms of treaty agreed to in conference & signed by the parties; formal statement of transaction; (in France etc.) etiquette department of Ministry of Foreign Affairs; diplomatic etiquette; official formulas at beginning & end of charter, papal bull, etc. **2.** vb. Draw up ~s; record in ~. [16th c. *prothocol* f. OF -*cole* f. med. L f. Gk PROTO(*kollon* f. *kolla* glue) fly-leaf glued to (book-)case]

prŏt'ŏn, n. (phys.). Unit of positive electricity, forming part (or, in hydrogen, whole) of the nucleus of the atom (cf. ELECTRON). [neut. of Gk *prōtos* first]

prŏtonŏt'ar|y̆, **prŏtho-**, (or protŏn'o-), n. Chief clerk in some law courts, esp. (hist.) Chancery, Common Pleas, & King's Bench, (orig. in Byzantine court); P~*ies Apostolic(al)*, twelve prelates who register papal acts, direct canonization of saints, etc. [f. LL f. late Gk PROTO(*notarios* NOTARY)]

prŏt'oplăsm, n. Semifluid semitransparent colourless substance consisting of certain complex organic compounds, basis of life in plants & animals. Hence **prŏtoplăsmăt'ic**, **prŏtoplăs'mĭc**, aa., (-z-). [f. G PROTO(PLASMA)]

prŏt'oplăst, n. The first created man; original, model; unit or mass of protoplasm. Hence **prŏtoplăs'tĭc** a. [f. F -*plaste* or LL f. Gk PROTO(*plastos* moulded, as PLASMA)]

prŏt'o|type, n. The original thing or person in relation to any copy, imitation, representation, later specimen, improved form, etc. Hence ~**typal**, ~**typ'ic**(AL), aa. [F, f. Gk PROTO(*tupon* f. *tupos* TYPE)]

protrăct', v.t. Prolong, lengthen out, as ~*ed their stay for some weeks*, whence ~**ĕdly²** adv.; draw (plan of ground etc.) to scale. [f. L PRO¹(*trahere* tract- draw)]

protrăc'tile a. (zool.). (Of organ etc.) that can be extended. [-ILE]

protrăc'tion, n. Protracting; action of protractor muscle; drawing to scale. [F, or LL *protractio* (as PROTRACT, see -ION)]

protrăc'tor, n. Instrument for measuring angles, usu. in form of graduated semicircle; muscle serving to extend limb etc. [med. L (as prec., see -OR)]

protrude' (-ōōd), v.t. & i. Thrust forth, cause to project; (fig.) obtrude; stick out, project. Hence or cogn. **protru'DENT**, **protru'SIBLE**, **protru'SIVE**, aa., (-ōō-), **protru'SION** (-ōōzhn) n. [f. L PRO¹(*trudere trus-* thrust)]

protru'sile (-ōō-), a. (Of limb, etc.) that may be thrust forth. [as prec., see -ILE]

protŭb'er|ant, a. Bulging out, prominent (lit. & fig.). Hence ~**ANCE** n. [f. LL PRO¹-(*tuberare* f. *tuber* hump), see -ANT]

prŏt'yle, n. (chem.). Supposed original undifferentiated matter of which chemical elements may be composed. [f. PROTO-+-YL]

proud, a. & adv. **1.** Valuing oneself highly or too highly, esp. on the ground *of* (qualities, rank, possessions, etc.); (also ~-*hearted*) haughty, arrogant; feeling oneself greatly honoured, as *am ~ of his acquaintance*, *of knowing him*, *to know him*; having a proper PRIDE, as *too ~ to complain*; HOUSE¹-~; (of actions etc.) showing pride, of which one is or may be justly ~, as *a ~ day for us*, *a ~ sight*; (of things) imposing, splendid; (of waters) swollen, in flood; ~ *flesh*, overgrown flesh round healing wound. **2.** adv. (colloq.). *You do me ~* (honour me greatly). Hence ~'**LY²** adv. [late OE *prūt*, *prūd*, = ON *prúthr* f. OF *prud*, *prod* (mod. *preux*) valiant, f. LL *prode* f. L *prodesse* be of value; cf. PROW², PRUDE, PRIDE]

prov|e (prōōv), v.t. & i. (arch. p.p. ~*en*). (Arch.) test qualities of, try; subject (gun etc.) to testing process; (arith.) test accuracy of (calculation); *the* EXCEPTION ~*es the rule*; take proof impression of (stereotype plate etc.); make certain, demonstrate, (*fact, the truth of*, thing etc. *to be*, *that*), whence ~'**ABLE** a., ~'**ableNESS** n., ~'**ably²** adv., (-ōōv-); (Sc. law, as verdict in criminal trial) *not proven*; establish genuineness & validity of (will); (intr.) turn out (*to be*, *to do*), turn out to be, as *will ~e (to be) the heir*, *to know nothing about it*. [ME, f. OF *prover* f. L *probare* test]

provĕd'itor, **provĕdōre'**, nn. (-*tor*) officer of Venetian republic; caterer, purveyor. [f. obs. It. *proveditore*, Port. *provedor*, ult. f. L as PROVIDE, see -OR]

prŏv'ĕnance, n. (Place of) origin, as *vases of doubtful ~*. [F, f. *provenir* f. L PRO¹-(*venire* come), see -ANCE]

Provençal (see Ap.), a. & n. (Inhabitant, language) of Provence. [F, as PROVINCIAL]

prŏv'ĕnder, n. Fodder; (joc.) food for human beings. [ME, f. OF *provend(r)e*, ult. f. LL *praebenda*, see PREBEND]

provĕn'ience, n. = PROVENANCE. [f. L as PROVENANCE, see -ENCE]

prŏv'erb, n. Short pithy saying in general use, adage, saw; *ignorant* etc. *to a ~* (notoriously); *their fickleness is a ~* (notorious), *he is a ~* (byword) *for inaccuracy*; play (usu. French) based on ~; (pl.) kinds of round game; (*Book of*) P~*s* (in O.T.). [ME, f. OF *proverbe* or L PRO¹-(*verbium* f. *verbum* word)]

provĕrb'ial, a. Of, expressed in, proverbs, as ~ *wisdom*; that has become a proverb, notorious. Hence ~**ITY** (-ăl¹) n., ~**LY²** adv. [f. L *proverbialis* (as prec., see -AL)]

prŏv'iant, n. Food supply esp. of army. [17th c., f. G; ult. as PROVENDER]

provid|e, v.i. & t. **1.** Make due preparation (*for* person's safety, entertainment, etc., *against* attack etc., occas. *for* undesirable thing); (of person, law, etc.)

stipulate (*that*); supply, furnish, (person *with* thing, thing *for* or *to* person); equip with necessaries, as *you must ~e your-selves*; make provision, esp. secure maintenance, (*for* oneself, family, etc.). 2. (hist.). Appoint (incumbent *to* benefice); (of pope) appoint (successor *to* benefice not yet vacant). 3. *~ing* (*that*) conj., = foll. [ME, f. L PRO¹(*vidēre* vis- see)]

provid'ed, a. & conj. 1. In vbl senses, as ‖ *~ school*, public elementary school *~* by local authority. 2. conj. On the condition or understanding, as *~* (*that*) *all is safe, ~* (*that*) *he does no harm.* [-ED¹]

prov'idence, n. Foresight, timely care; thrift; beneficent care of God or nature, *special ~*, particular instance of this; (P*~*) God. [ME, f. OF, or L *providentia* (as foll., see -ENCE)]

prov'ident, a. Having or showing foresight; thrifty. Hence *~*LY² adv. [ME, f. L, as PROVIDE, see -ENT]

providen'tial (-shl), a. Of, by, divine foresight or interposition; opportune, lucky. Hence *~*LY² (-sha-) adv. [f. as PROVIDENCE + -IAL]

provid'er, n. In vbl senses; *lion's ~*, jackal (lit. & fig.); ‖ *universal ~*, tradesman dealing in all or many kinds of goods etc. [-ER¹]

prov'ince, n. (Rom. hist.) territory outside Italy under Roman governor; principal division of country etc.; (eccl.) district under archbishop or metropolitan, e.g. Canterbury, York; *the ~s*, whole of a country outside the capital; sphere of action, business, as (*is not within*) *my ~*; branch of learning etc., as *in the ~ of polite letters.* [ME, f. OF, f. L *provincia* charge, province]

provin'cial (-shl), a. & n. 1. Of a province; of the provinces; having the manners, speech, narrow views, etc., prevalent in these, whence *~*ITY (-shĭăl²) n. 2. n. Inhabitant of a province or the provinces (also *~*IST n.); countrified person; (eccl.) head of, chief of religious order in, a province. Hence *~*IZE v.t., *~*LY² adv., (-sha-). [ME, f. OF, or f. L *provincialis* (as prec., see -AL)]

provin'cialism (-sha-), n. Provincial manner, fashion, mode of thought, etc.; word, phrase, peculiar to county etc.; attachment to one's province rather than country. [-ISM]

provi'sion (-zhn), n., & v.t. 1. Providing (*for, against*), esp. *make ~*; provided amount of something. 2. pl. Supply of food, eatables & drinkables, whence *~*LESS (-zho-) a. 3. Legal or formal statement providing for something, clause of this. 4. (hist.). Appointment to benefice not yet vacant; P*~s of Oxford*, ordinances for checking king's misrule drawn up by barons under Simon de Montfort in 1258. 5. v.t. Supply with *~s*,

whence *~*MENT (-zho-) n. [ME, f. OF, f. L *provisionem* (as PROVIDE, see -ION)]

provi'sional (-zho-), a. For the time being, temporary. Hence **provisional'-**ITY, *~*NESS, nn., *~*LY² adv., (-zho-). [-AL]

provis'o (-zō), n. (pl. *~s*). Stipulation; clause of stipulation or limitation in document. [L, neut. abl. p.p., = PROVIDED *that*]

provis'or (-z-), n. 1. (hist.). Holder of a PROVISION; *Statute of P~s* (preventing pope from granting provisions). 2. (R.-C. Ch.) vicar general. [ME, f. AF *provisour* f. L *provisorem* (as PROVIDE, see -OR)]

provis'or|y̆ (-z-), a. Conditional; making provision, as *~y care.* Hence *~*iLY² adv. [f. F *provisoire* (as prec., see -ORY)]

provoca'tion, n. Incitement, instigation, irritation, as *did it under severe ~.* [ME, f. OF, or L *provocatio* (as PROVOKE, see -ATION)]

provoc'ative, a. & n. (Thing) tending to provocation (*of* curiosity etc.); intentionally irritating. [f. F (-*if, -ive*), or LL *provocativus* (foll., -IVE)]

provok|e, v.t. Rouse, incite, (person *to* anger, *to* do); irritate; instigate, tempt, allure; call forth (indignation, inquiry, a storm, etc.; cause, as *will ~e fermentation.* Hence *~'*ING² a., *~'*inGLY² adv. [ME, f. OF *provoker* f. L PRO¹(*vocare* call)]

prov'ost (*in* mil. *senses* provŏ'), n. 1. ‖ Head of some colleges at Oxford, Cambridge, etc.; (hist.) head of chapter or religious community. 2. ‖ Head of Scottish municipal corporation or burgh (in some cities, Lord P*~*). 3. Protestant clergyman in charge of principal church of town etc. in Germany etc. 4. *~ marshal*, head of military police in camp or on active service, master-at-arms of ship on which court martial is to be held, chief police official in some colonies, (hist.) French semi-military officer; *~ sergeant*, sergeant of military police. Hence *~*SHIP n. [OE *profost, pra-*, in ME reinforced by AF & OF *provost, pre-*, f. med. L *propositus* for *praepositus*, see PRAEPOSTOR]

prow¹, n. Fore-part immediately about stem of boat or ship; (zool., also *prora*) *~*-like projection in front. [f. F *proue* f. L *prora* f. Gk *prō̆(i)ra*]

‖ **prow²**, a. (arch.). Worthy, gallant. [ME, f. OF *prou, prod*, (F *preux*) f. LL as PROUD]

prow'ess, n. Valour, gallantry. [ME, f. OF *proece* (as prec., see -ESS³)]

prowl, v.i. & t., & n. 1. Go about in search of plunder or prey (also fig.); traverse (streets, place) thus. 2. n. *~ing*, esp. *on the ~*. Hence *~'*ER¹ n. [ME *prolle*, of unkn. orig.]

prox'imal, a. (anat.). Situated towards centre of body or of point of attachment (cf. DISTAL). Hence *~*LY² adv. [f. L *proximus* nearest + -AL]

For other words in *pro-* see PRO-¹.

prŏx′imate, a. Nearest, next before or after (in place, order, time, connexion of thought, etc.); approximate. Hence ~LY[2] adv. [f. L *proximare* draw near (as prec.), see -ATE[2]]

‖*prŏx′ĭmē accĕss′ĭt* (aks-), sent., & n. (pl. *-ĕssēr′unt*). (Placed in list after name of candidate for prize etc.) he came very near (the winner); (n.) *I was, he got a,* ~ (was very near). [L]

prŏxim′ity, n. Nearness in space, time, etc. (*to*); ~ *of blood*, kinship; ~ *fuse*, radio device causing projectile to explode when near target. [f. F *proximité* f. L *proximitatem* (as PROXIMAL, see -TY)]

prŏx′ĭmō, a. (abbr. *prox.*). Of next month, as *the 3rd prox.* [L, = in next (*mense* month)]

prŏx′y, n. Agency of substitute or deputy, as *married, voted, by* ~; person authorized to act for another, as *made me his* ~; writing authorizing person to vote on behalf of another, vote so given; (attrib.) done, given, made, by ~. [15th c. contr. f. obs. *procuracy* f. med. L *procuratia* (as PROCURATION, see -ACY)]

prud|e (prŏŏd), n. Woman of extreme (esp. affected) propriety in conduct or speech. Hence or cogn. ~ERY(4), ~ish-NESS, nn., ~′ISH[1] a., ~′ishLY[2] adv., (-ŏŏ-). [c. 1700, as adj. & n., f. F *prude*, in OF *prude, prode*, back formation f. *prude-femme*; see PROW[2], PROUD]

pru′d|ent (-ŏŏ-), a. (Of person or conduct) sagacious, discreet, worldly-wise. Hence or cogn. ~ENCE n., ~entLY[2] adv. [ME, f. OF or L *prudens* = *providens* PROVIDENT]

prudĕn′tial (-ŏŏ-, -shl), a. & n. Of, involving, marked by, prudence, as ~ *motives, policy*; (n. pl.) ~ considerations or matters. Hence ~ISM(2), ~IST(2), nn., ~LY[2] adv., (-ŏŏ-, -sha-). [f. L *prudentia* PRUDENCE + -AL or med. L *-alis*]

pru′inōse (-ŏŏ-), a. (nat. hist.). Covered with white powdery substance, frosted. [f. L *pruinosus* (*pruina* hoar-frost, see -OSE[1])]

prune[1] (prŏŏn), n. Dried plum; colour of its juice, dark reddish purple (esp. attrib.); ~*s & prism* (of mincing way of speaking etc., Dickens' *Little Dorrit* II. v). [ME, f. OF *prune* f. Rom. **pruna* f. L *prunum* PLUM]

prune[2] (prŏŏn), v.t. Trim (tree etc., often *down*) by cutting away superfluous branches etc.; hence **prun′ER**[1] (-ŏŏn-) n.; lop *off, away* (branches etc.); (fig.) remove (superfluities); *pruning-hook* (used for this purpose); clear (book etc. *of* what is superfluous). [ME *prouyne* f. OF *proŏing-(n)ier, proignier*]

prune[3] (prŏŏn), v.t. (now rare). = PREEN. [ME *prune, pruyne, proyne*, prob. of OF orig.; cf. PREEN]

prunĕll′a[1] (prŏŏ-), n. Strong silk or worsted stuff used formerly for barristers' gowns etc. & later for uppers of women's shoes; LEATHER *&* ~. [17th c., = mod. F *prunelle*, of obsc. orig.]

prunĕll′a[2] (prŏŏ-), n. Kinds of fever & of throat disorder; ~ *salt*, preparation of fused nitre used for ~; kinds of plants including the weed self-heal used to cure ~. [17th c., f. mod. L, earlier *br*-, dim. of med. L *brunus* BROWN]

prunĕll′ō (prŏŏ-), n. (pl. ~s). Finest kind of prune, made esp. from greengages. [f. obs. It. *prunella* dim. of *pruna* PRUNE[1]]

prŭnt, n. Piece of (esp. blackberry--shaped) ornamental glass laid on to vase etc., tool for applying this. [perh. dial. form of *print*]

prur′i|ent (-oor-), a. Given to indulgence of lewd ideas; (rare) having morbid desire or curiosity. Hence ~ENCE, ~ENCY, nn., ~entLY[2] adv. [f. L *prurire* itch, be wanton, see -ENT]

prurig′ō, -it′us, (-oor-), nn. (Diseased state of skin marked by) violent itching (*-tus*). So **pruri′ginous** (-oor-) a. [L (gen. *-ginis, -tūs*), = itching, as prec.]

Prū′ssian (-shn), a. & n. (Native, inhabitant) of Prussia; ~ *blue*, a deep blue pigment, ~ *brown, green* (derived from or allied to this); ~ (small kind of) *carp*. Hence ~IZE(3) (-sha-) v.t., (esp.) assimilate to the ~ system of sacrificing the individual to the State. [17th c., f. mod. L *Prussianus* f. *Prussia*, see -AN]

prŭss′ic, a. Of, got from, Prussian blue; ~ *acid* (HYDROCYANIC). [f. F *prussique* (*Prusse* Prussia, see -IC)]

prȳ[1], v.i. Look, peer, inquisitively (often *into, about* adv.); inquire impertinently *into* (person's affairs, conduct, etc.). Hence ~′ING[2] a., ~′ingLY[2] adv. [ME *prie*, of unkn. orig.]

prȳ[2], v.t. Var. of PRIZE[3].

prȳtanē′um, n. (Gk ant.). Public hall, esp. one in Athens for entertainment of ambassadors, presidents of senate, & specially honoured citizens. [L, f. Gk *prutaneion* f. *prutanis* president etc.]

psalm (sahm), n. Sacred song, hymn; *the (Book of) P~s*, (pop.) the *P~s of David*, book in O.T.; ~*book*, book containing the P~s, metrical version of these for public worship. [OE (*p*)*sealm* f. LL f. Gk *psalmos* song sung to harp (*psallō* twang, sing to harp)]

psalm′ist (sahm-), n. Author of a psalm (also as title of book of psalmody); *the P~*, David or author of any of the Psalms. [f. LL *psalmista* (as prec., see -IST)]

psal′mod|y (sahm-, sălm-), n. Practice, art, of singing psalms, hymns, anthems, etc., esp. in public worship, whence **psalmōd′IC** (săl-) a., ~IST n., ~IZE(2) v.i., (sahm-, sălm-); arrangement of psalms for singing, psalms so arranged. [ME, f. LL *psalmodia* f. Gk *psalmōidia* singing to harp (as PSALM + *ō*(*i*)*dē* song)]

psal′ter (sawl-), n. The Book of Psalms; version of this, as *Latin, English, Prayer--book, Scotch Metrical, P~*; copy of the Psalms esp. for liturgical use. [ME & AF *sauter*, OF *-ier*, f. L f. Gk *psalterium* stringed instrument (*psallō* twang), in eccl. L *Book of Psalms*; OE (*p*)*saltere* dir. f. LL]

psal′terỹ (sawl-), n. Ancient & medieval instrument like dulcimer but played by plucking strings with fingers or plectrum. [ME, f. OF *sauterie* etc. f. L as prec.]

psĕph′ism (*or* s-), n. (Gk ant.). Decree enacted by vote of (esp. Athenian) public assembly. [f. Gk *psēphisma* (*psēphizō* vote f. *psēphos* pebble)]

psĕph|ŏl′ogỹ (*or* s-), n. Study of elections and voting. Hence ~ŏl′OGIST n. [f. Gk *psēphos* pebble, vote, -LOGY]

pseud′ĕchis (s- *or* ps-, -k-), n. (zool.). Kinds of venomous snakes, as ~ *poisoning*. [f. PSEUDO- + Gk *ekhis* viper]

pseudĕpig′raph|a (s- *or* ps-), n. pl. Spurious writings, esp. Jewish writings ascribed to various O.T. prophets etc. Hence ~AL, **pseudĕpig′raph′**IC(AL), aa. [neut. pl. of Gk PSEUD(*epigraphos*, see EPIGRAPH)]

pseud|(o)- (s- *or* ps-), comb. form f. stem of meaning false(ly), seeming(ly) or professed(ly) but not real(ly), in compp. f. Gk, & as living pref. (occas. written separately without hyphen as adj., as *the*~*o penitent*), as : ~*o-archa′ic*, artificially archaic in style etc., so ~*o-arch′aism*, ~*o-arch′aist*; ~′*o-carp* (bot.), fruit formed from other parts besides the ovary; ~*o-cath′olic*; ~′*o--Christ*; ~*o-Chris′tian*; ~*o-class′ic*, pretending or wrongly held to be classic; ~*o-Goth′ic*, sham Gothic in style; ~*o--mart′yr*; ~*o-proph′et*.

pseud′ograph (s- *or* ps-, -ahf), n. A spurious literary work. [f. LL f. Gk PSEUDO- (*graphos* -GRAPH)]

pseudŏl′og|er (s- *or* ps-), n. (joc.). Systematic liar. So **pseudolŏ′gICAL** a., ~IST n. [f. Gk PSEUDO(*logos*, see -LOGER)]

pseud′o|mŏrph (s- *or* ps-), n. False form, esp. (mineral.) crystal etc. consisting of one mineral with form proper to another. Hence ~mŏrph′IC, ~mŏrph′OUS, aa., ~mŏrph′ISM(2), ~mŏrphos′IS, nn. [f. PSEUDO- + Gk *morphē* form]

pseud′onỹm (s- *or* ps-), n. Fictitious name, esp. one assumed by author. [f. F (-*me*), f. Gk neut. adj. as foll.]

pseud|ŏn′ỹmous (s- *or* ps-), a. Writing, written, under a false name. Hence ~onỹm′ITY n. [f. Gk PSEUD(*ōnumos* f. *onoma* name) + -OUS]

pseud′o|scōpe (s- *or* ps-), n. Optical instrument making convex object seem concave & vice versa. Hence ~scŏp′IC a. [SCOPE]

pshaw (psh-, sh-), int., n., & v.i. & t. Int. expr. contempt or impatience; (n.) this exclamation; (v.i.) say ~ (often *at*); (v.t.) show contempt for (thing etc.) thus. [natural]

psī, n. Greek letter (Ψ, ψ) = ps. [Gk]

psīlăn′throp|ism (*or* s-), n. Doctrine that Christ was a mere man. So **psīlan-thrŏp′**IC a., ~IST n. [f. eccl. Gk *psilan-*

thrōpos merely human (*psilos* bare, mere, + *anthrōpos* man) + -ISM]

psīlōs′is (*or* s-), n. (path.). Stripping bare, e.g. of hair or flesh ; = SPRUE². [Gk (prec., -OSIS)]

psitt′acine (*or* s-), a. Of parrots, parrot--like. [f. L *psittacinus* (*psittacus* parrot, see -INE¹)]

psittacōs′is (s- *or* ps-), n. Epidemic disease somewhat resembling typhoid fever and pneumonia said to be caught by human beings from parrots. [f. L *psittacus* parrot + -OSIS]

psō′ás (*or* s-), n. ~ *magnus*, *parvus*, two hip muscles. [Gk, acc. pl. of *psoa*, taken as sing.]

psōr′a (*or* s-), n. A contagious skin disease, itch. [L, f. Gk *psōra*]

psōri′asis (s- *or* ps-), n. Skin disease marked by red patches covered with scales. [Gk, see prec. & -ASIS]

psyche (sīk′ī, ps-), n. 1. Soul, spirit, mind, (in Gk myth. personified as beloved of Eros, & represented with butterfly wings). 2. Kinds of dayflying moths. [f. Gk *psu-khē* breath, life, soul]

psychi′atr|ist (sīk-, psīk-), n. One who treats mental disease. So **psychiăt′rI**-C(AL) aa., ~Y¹ n., (sīk-, psīk-). [f. Gk as prec. + *iatros* physician + -IST]

psych′ic (sīk-, psīk-), a. & n. 1. = foll. ~ *force*, non-physical force assumed to explain spiritualistic phenomena. 2. n. Person susceptible to ~ influence, medium; (pl.) psychology; psychical research. [f. Gk *psukhikos* (PSYCHE, -IC)]

psych′ical (sīk-, psīk-), a. Of the soul or mind, whence ~LY² adv.; of the animal life of man; of phenomena & conditions apparently outside domain of physical law, esp. ~ *research*, so **psych′icISM**, **psych′ic**IST, nn., (sīk-, psīk-). [AL-]

psych|o- (sīk-, psīk-), comb. form of Gk *psukhē* soul, mind, as : ~*ō-anăl′ỹsis*, the psychology of Freud, Jung, & Adler, dividing the mind into conscious & unconscious elements, & investigating the interactions of these (so ~*ō-ăn′alÿse* v.t., ~*ō-ăn′alÿst* n., ~*ō-ănalÿt′ic* a.); ~*ō-dÿnăm′ic*(s), (science) of the mental powers; ~*ōgen′esis*, ~*ŏg′ony*, genesis of soul or mind, so ~*ōgenĕt′ic*(al), ~*ōgŏn′ical*, aa.; ~′*ogram*, writing supposed to come from a spirit, ~′*ograph*, instrument for writing this; ~*ŏg′raphy*, descriptive branch of psychology, (also) spirit-writing; ~*ōmancy*, occult communication between souls or with spirits; ~*ōm′etry*, faculty of divining from physical contact or proximity the qualities of an object or of persons etc. that have been in contact with it, so ~*ōmĕt′ric*(al) aa., (also) measurement of mental states or processes, so ~*ōmĕt′rics* n. pl. ; ~*ōmŏt′or* a., inducing movement by psychic action; ~*ōneurōs′is*, mental disease consisting in loss of balance between instincts & controlling power; ~′*ōpath*, mentally deranged person, ~*ōpath′ic*,

~*op'athist*, ~*ōpathōl'ogy*, ~*ŏp'athy*, of, one who treats, science of, mental disease; ~*ōphys'ics*, science of general relations between mind & body, so ~*ōphys'ical* a., ~*ōphys'icist* n.; ~*ōphysiōl'ogy*, branch of physiology dealing with mental phenomena, so ~*ōphysiolo'gical* a., ~*ōphysiŏl'ogist* n.; ~*ōsomăt'ic* a., of mind & body, (of bodily disease) caused or made worse by worry; ~*ōtherapeut'ic*,~*ōthĕ'rapy*, (of) treatment of mental illness.

psycholŏ'gical (sĭk-, psĭk-), a. Of psychology; ~ *moment* [f. F mistransl. of G *moment* neut. potent element as *moment* masc. moment of time], the ~ly appropriate moment, (improp., esp. joc.) nick of time. Hence ~LY² adv. [-ICAL]

psychŏĭ'og|y̆ (sĭk-, psĭk-), n. Science of nature, functions & phenomena, of human soul or mind; treatise on, system of, this. So ~IST n., ~IZE(2, 3) v.t. & i. [f. mod. L *psychologia* (PSYCHO-, -LOGY)]

psychōs'is (sĭk-, psĭk-), n. (pl. ~*osēs*). Severe mental derangement involving the whole personality, mental disease. Hence **psychŏT'IC** (sĭk-, psĭk-) a. & n., of or relating to, (person) suffering from, a ~. [f. late Gk *psukhōsis* (*psukhoō* give life to, as PSYCHE, see -OSIS)]

psychrŏm'ĕter (sĭk-, psĭk-), n. Wet-&-dry-bulb thermometer. [f. Gk *psukhros* cold +-METER]

ptârm'igan (t-), n. Bird of grouse family, with black or grey plumage in summer & white in winter. [= Gaelic *tarmachan*, *p*- is pseudo-etym. after Gk wds in *pt*-]

ptĕrid|ŏl'ogy̆ (pt-, t-), n. Study of ferns. So ~olŏ'gICAL a., ~ŏl'ogIST n. [f. Gk *pteris -idos*, a feathery fern (*pteron* wing) +-O-+-LOGY]

ptĕr|o- (pt-, t-), comb. form of Gk *pteron* wing, as: ~*odac'tyl*, extinct winged reptile;~*ŏg'raphy*, description of feathers, so ~*opod*, mollusc with middle part of foot expanded into pair of wing-like lobes; ~*osaur*, extinct flying saurian reptile.

ptĕ'ropus (pt-, t-), n. (pl. ~*pi*). FLYING fox. [f. Gk PTERO(*pous* foot) wing-footed]

ptĕ'ry̆goid (pt-, t-), a. ~ *process*, each of two processes descending from junction of body & great wing of sphenoid bone; connected with these. So **ptĕ'ry̆go-** (pt-, t-) comb. form. [f. Gk *pterugoeidēs* wing-like (*pterux -ugos* wing, -OID)]

ptisan (tĭ'zn, tĭzăn'), n. Nourishing decoction, esp. barley-water. [ME & OF *tizanne* etc. f. L f. Gk *ptisanē* peeled barley]

Ptŏlĕmā'ic (t-), a. Of Ptolemy, Alexandrine astronomer of 2nd c., esp.~ *system* (of astronomy, in which earth was held to be the stationary centre round which sun and stars revolved, cf. COPERNICAN); of the Ptolemies, rulers of Egypt from death of Alexander the Great to Cleopatra. [f. L f. Gk *Ptolemaios* +-IC]

ptomaine (tōm'ān, tomān'), n. Kinds of

(often poisonous) alkaloid body in putrefying animal & vegetable matter, esp. ~ *poisoning*. [f. It. *ptomaina* irreg. f. Gk *ptōma* corpse (*piptō* fall), -INE⁵]

ptōs'is (pt-, t-), n. Drooping of upper eyelid from paralysis of a muscle. [Gk *ptōsis* f. *piptō* fall]

‖ **pŭb**, n. (colloq.). Public house. [abbr.]

pŭb'erty̆, n. Being functionally capable of procreation; *age of* ~ (at which ~ begins; in England, legally, 14 in boys, 12 in girls). [ME, f. L *pubertas* (*puber* of the age of ~), see -TY)]

pūbĕs'c|ence, n. Arrival at puberty; soft down on leaves & stems of plants, downiness; soft down on parts of animals esp. insects. So ~ENT a. [F, or f. L *pubescens*, see -ENCE]

pŭb'lic, a. & n. 1. Of, concerning, the people as a whole, as ~ *offence, holiday*, (Parl.) ~ *act, bill*; ~ *utility*, a supply or undertaking usu. available in large towns, e.g. water, gas, electricity, etc. 2. Done by or for, representing, the people, as ~ *prosecution, prosecutor, assembly*. 3. ‖ (Univv.) of, for, acting for, the university, as ~ *orator, lecture, examination*. 4. Open to, shared by, the people, as ~ *baths, library, road*. 5. ‖ ~ *house*, inn, tavern, providing food & lodging, esp. alcoholic liquors to be consumed on premises; ~ *education* (at school, also, at ~ school); ~ *school*, one under ~ management, ‖ esp. endowed grammar (usu. boarding-) school preparing pupils chiefly for universities or ~ services, often maintaining discipline with help of pupils. 6. Open to general observation, done or existing in ~, as *made a* ~ *protest*, *gave it* ~ *utterance*, whence ~LY² adv. 7. Of, engaged in, the affairs or service of the people, as ~ *life*, *a* ~ *man*, *notary* ~; ~ *relations*, relations of a department, organization, etc. with the general ~ (~ *relations officer*, abbr. *P.R.O.*, person who gives out information to the ~ in connexion with some department etc.); ~ *spirit*, patriotism, so ~-*spirited* a., -*spi'ritedly* adv., -*spi'ritedness* n. 8. Of the nations, international, as *proscribed Napoleon as a* ~ *enemy*. 9. n. The (members of the) community in general, as *the* ~ *is the best judge*, *are the best judges*, *the British, American*, ~; section of the community, as *the reading* ~, *the most gullible of* ~*s*; ‖ ~ *house* (colloq.); *in* ~, openly, ~ly. [ME, f. OF (-*ique*), or f. L *publicus*, see -IC]

pŭb'lican, n. (Rom. hist., & in N.T.) tax-farmer, tax-gatherer; ‖ keeper of public house. [ME & OF *publicain* f. L *publicanus* (as prec., see -AN)]

pŭblicā'tion, n. Making publicly known; issuing of book, engraving, music, etc., to the public; book etc. so issued. [ME, f. OF, or f. L *publicatio* (as PUBLISH, see -ATION)]

pŭb'lic|ist, n. Writer on, person skilled

in, international law; writer on current public topics, esp. journalist. So ~ISM n., ~IS′TIC a., ~IZE v.t. [f. F *publiciste* f. L (*jus*) *publicum* public law, see -IST]

pŭbli′citȳ, n. Openness to general observation, notoriety, (*avoid, court,* ~; *give* ~ *to*); the business of advertising (both goods and persons); ~ *agent,* person employed to keep the name of an actor etc. constantly before the public. [f. F *-ité* f. med. L *publicitatem* (PUBLIC, -ITY)]

pŭb′lish, v.t. Make generally known, noise abroad; announce formally, promulgate (edict etc.); ask, read, (banns of marriage); (of author, editor, or publisher) issue copies of (book, engraving, etc.) for sale to the public. Hence ~ABLE a. [ME *puplise, -ish, publisce,* etc. f. OF *puplier, publier* f. L *publicare* (as PUBLIC), see -ISH²]

pŭb′lisher, n. In vbl senses, esp. one who produces copies of book etc. & distributes them to booksellers or to the public. [-ER¹]

pŭccoōn′, n. N.-Amer. plant yielding red or yellow dye. [native]

pūce, a. Flea-colour, purple-brown. [F, = flea (-colour), f. L *pulicem* (nom. *-ex*)]

pŭck¹, n. (P~) the goblin *Robin Goodfellow* or *Hobgoblin*; any mischievous sprite or (fig.) child. Hence ~ISH¹, ~LIKE, aa. [OE *pūca* = ON *pūki* mischievous demon; ult. orig. unkn.]

pŭck², n. (Disease in cattle attributed to) nightjar, goatsucker. [orig. unkn.]

pŭck³, n. Rubber disc used for ice hockey. [orig. unkn.]

pŭck′a, pŭkk′a, a. (Anglo-Ind.). Of full weight; genuine; permanent, solidly built. [Hind. (*pakkā*), = cooked, ripe]

pŭck′er, v.i. & t., & n. 1. Contract, gather, (t. & i. of brow, seam, material, often *up*) into wrinkles, folds, or bulges, intentionally or as fault e.g. in sewing. 2. n. Such bulge etc. Hence ~Y² a. [vb c. 1600, prob. rel. to POKE¹, POCKET (cf. PURSE²), see -ER⁵]

pŭd, n. (nursery). Child's hand; fore-foot of some animals. [orig. unkn.; cf. PAD³ (4)]

pu′dding (poŏ-), n. Soft or stiffish mixture of animal or vegetable ingredients, esp. mixed or enclosed in flour or other farinaceous food, cooked by boiling, steaming, or baking (*batter, beefsteak, bread-&-butter, currant,* HASTY, *lemon,* MILK¹, PLUM, *suet,* YORKSHIRE, ~); intestine of pig etc. stuffed with oatmeal, blood, etc. (BLACK, *hog's, white,* ~); *more praise than* ~ (material reward); *the* PROOF¹ *of the* ~ etc.; thing of ~-like appearance etc.; (sl.) drugged liver etc. given by burglars etc. to dogs; (naut., also *pu′ddening*) pad, tow binding, to prevent chafing etc.; ~-*cloth,* cloth in which some ~s are tied up for boiling; ~ *face,* large fat face; ~-*head,* dolt; ~-*heart,* coward; ‖ ~ *pie,* forms of pastry; ~-*stone,* composite rock of rounded pebbles in silicious matrix.

Hence ~Y² a. [ME *poding,* of obsc. orig.; cf. syn. OF *bodin,* mod. F *boudin*]

pŭd′dle¹, n. Small dirty pool esp. of rain on road etc.; (colloq.) muddle, mess; clay (& sand) mixed with water as watertight covering for embankments etc. Hence **pŭdd′LY¹** a. [ME *podel, puddel,* dim. of OE *pudd* ditch; cf. LG *pudel,* G *pfudel*]

pŭd′dle², v.i. & t. Dabble, wallow, (often *about*) in mud or shallow water; busy oneself in untidy way; make (water, also fig.) muddy; knead (clay & sand) into, make, line (canal etc.) with, PUDDLE¹; stir about (molten iron) to produce wrought iron by expelling carbon. Hence **pŭdd′LER** (1, 2) n. [ME f. prec.; cf. Du. *poedelen,* LG *pud(d)eln* splash in water (see POODLE)]

pŭd′encȳ, n. Modesty. [f. LL *pudentia* (as foll., see -ENCY)]

pŭdĕn′dum, n. (usu. in pl. *-da*). Privy parts. Hence or cogn. **pŭdĕn′dAL, pŭd′ic, aa.** [L (*pudēre* be ashamed)]

pŭdge, n. (colloq.). Short thick or fat person, animal, or thing. Hence **pŭdg′Y²** a. [cf. PODGE]

pŭd′sȳ (-z-), a. Plump. [cf. prec. & PUD]

pue′blŏ (pwĕ-), n. (pl. ~s). Spanish (-Amer.) town or village, esp. settlement of Indians. [Sp.]

pū′erile, a. Boyish, childish; trivial, whence or cogn. ~LY² adv., **pūeril′ITY** n.; ~ *breathing* (with loud pulmonary murmur as in children, usu. sign of disease in adult). [F, or f. L *puerilis* (*puer* boy, -ILE)]

pūĕrp′eral, a. Of, due to, childbirth. [f. L *puerperus* (*puer* child + *-parus* bearing) + -AL]

pŭff¹, n. 1. Short quick blast of breath or wind; sound (as) of this; small quantity of vapour, smoke, etc., emitted at one ~. 2. Round soft protuberant mass of material in dress, of hair of head, etc. 3. (Also *powder-~*) small pad of down or the like for applying powder to skin. 4. Piece, cake, etc., of light pastry esp. of ~ *paste.* 5. Unduly or extravagantly laudatory review of book, advertisement of tradesman's goods etc., esp. in newspaper. 6. ~-*adder,* large venomous African viper inflating upper part of body when excited; ~-*ball,* fungus with ball-shaped spore-case; ~-*box* (containing powder & ~); ~ *paste,* light flaky paste; ‖ ~-~ (nursery), steam-engine, train. [ME *puf,* init., see foll.]

pŭff², v.i. & t. 1. Emit puff of air or breath; (of air etc.) come *out, up,* in puffs; breathe hard, pant, esp. ~ *& blow;* put out of breath, as *was rather* ~ed; ~ *out,* utter pantingly; (of steam-engine, person smoking, etc.) move with puffs, as ~ed *away at his cigar,* ~ed *out of the terminus.* 2. Blow (dust, smoke, light object, *out, up, away,* etc.) with puff; smoke (pipe) in puffs. 3. Blow *out, up,* inflate; become inflated, swell *up, out;* ~ *up,* elate, make proud, (esp. in p.p.

with pride etc.). **4.** Advertise (goods) with exaggerated or false praise; ‖ bid at auction to raise price. Hence ~'ER¹ n. [ME *puffe*, imit., see prec.]

puff'erỹ, n. Advertisement, puffing; puff frilling, puffs. [-ERY]

puff'in, n. N.-Atlantic sea-bird with large furrowed particoloured bill. [ME *poffin*, of unkn. orig.]

puff'|ỹ, a. Gusty; short-winded; puffed out; corpulent. Hence ~INESS n. [-Y²]

pŭg¹, n. **1.** (Also ~*dog*) dwarf squat--faced breed of dog like bulldog, whence ~g'ISH¹,~g'Y², aa.,(-g-);~-*nose(d)*, (with) short squat or snub nose. **2.** ‖ (Among servants) upper servant in large establishment. **3.** (Quasi-proper name for) fox. **4.** ‖ Small locomotive for shunting etc. [orig. unkn.]

pŭg², n., & v.t. (-gg-). Loam or clay mixed & prepared for brickmaking etc.; (v.t.) prepare (clay) thus, pack (space esp. under floor, to deaden sound) with ~, sawdust, etc.; ~-*mill* (for preparing ~). Hence ~g'ING¹(3) (-g-) n. [orig. unkn.]

pŭg³, n., & v.t. (Anglo-Ind.). Footprint of beast; (v.t.; -gg-) track by ~s. [f. Hind. *pag* footprint]

pŭg⁴, n. (sl.). Pugilist. [abbr.]

pŭgg'(a)ree (-rĭ), n. Indian's light turban; thin scarf of muslin etc. worn round hat & sometimes falling down behind to keep off sun. Hence **pŭgg'(a)reED²**(-rĭd) a. [f. Hind. *pagri* turban]

pū'gil|ist, n. Boxer, fighter; (fig.) vigorous controversialist. So ~ISM n., ~is'TIC a., ~is'TICALLY adv. [f. L *pugil* boxer (*pugnus* fist) +-IST]

pŭgnā'cious (-shus), a. Disposed to fight, quarrelsome. Hence or cogn. ~LY² adv., **pŭgnă'CITY** n. [f. L *pugnax* (*pugnare* fight, see -ACIOUS)]

puisne (pūn'ĭ), a. & n. ~ (*judge*), judge of superior court inferior in rank to chief justice; (law) later, subsequent (*to*), as ~ *mortgagee, mortgagees* ~ *to the plaintiff*. [OF *puis* after f. L *postea* +*né* born f. L *natus*); cf. PUNY]

pū'iss|ant (*or* pūĭs⁴ *or* pwĭs⁴), a. (arch.). Having great power or influence, mighty. Hence or cogn. ~ANCE n., ~antLY² adv. [ME, f. OF f. Rom. **possiantem* f. *posse*; see POTENT]

pu'ja (poō-), **poō'ja**, n. Hindu religious rites (generally); (Anglo-Ind. sl., usu. pl.) prayers. [Hind. f. Skr. *pūjā*]

pūke, v.i. & t., & n. Vomit. [16th c., orig. unkn.]

pukka(h), = PUCKA.

pŭl'chritude (-kr-), n. Beauty. [ME, f. L *pulchritudo* (*pulcher* beautiful, -TUDE)]

pūle, v.i. Cry querulously or weakly, whine. Hence **pūl'ingLY²** adv. [16th c., imit., perh. f. F *piauler*]

pull¹ (poŏl), v.t. & i. **1.** Exert upon (thing) force tending to draw it to oneself, as *don't* ~ *my hair*, ~ *his ears* or *him by the ear* (as chastisement), ~ *his nose* or *him by the nose* (as insult), ~ *his sleeve* or *him by the sleeve* (to gain attention), ~ *the* (bell-rope or handle to ring the) *bell*, ~ person's LEG, ~ (= *draw*) *the* LONG¹-*bow*, ~ *the* STRINGS, WIRES. **2.** Draw (thing etc.) towards oneself or in direction so regarded, as ~ *it nearer*, ~ *him into the room*, ~ *your cap over your ears*, ~ *off* one's *hat* (as salutation), ~ *on* one's *stockings*. **3.** Attract or secure (support, custom). **4.** ~ (thing) *to pieces*, separate its parts forcibly, (fig.) criticize (person, thing) unfavourably. **5.** Exert ~ing force, as *horse* ~*s well*, ~*ed* (*away*) *at the handle*; exert influence in favour of person. **6.** Proceed with effort (*up* hill etc.); (of horse) strain, esp. habitually, against bit; ~ *devil*, ~ BAKER. **7.** Draw, suck, *at* (pipe, tankard). **8.** Pluck (plant, often *up*) by root. **9.** ~*ed*, reduced in health or spirits; ~*ed bread*, pieces from inside of new loaf, rebaked till crisp. **10.** ~ *caps*, *wigs*, scuffle, quarrel. **11.** Tear, pluck, *at* (thing). **12.** Print upon (sheet), print (copy, proof), orig. in old hand-press by ~ing bar towards one. **13.** Move boat, move (boat), by ~ing oar; (of boat) be rowed, be rowed by (so many oars), as *she* ~*ed inshore*, ~*s 6 oars*; ~ (row with effect in proportion to) one's *weight*. **14.** (sl.). Arrest; make raid on (gambling-house etc.). **15.** Check (horse) esp. so as to make him lose .race; ~ one's *punches* (boxing), fail to give full force to one's blows, also fig. **16.** (Crick.) strike (ball, or abs.), strike ball bowled by (bowler), from off to leg; (golf) drive (ball, or abs.) widely to left (of right-handed player). **17.** ~ *a* FACE¹; ~ *a sanctimonious* etc. *face*, assume such expression. **18.** ~ *about*, ~ from side to side, treat roughly; ~ *down*, demolish (building etc.), lower in health, spirits, price, etc.; ~ *in*, (of train) enter station; ~ *off*, win (prize, contest); ~ *out*, row out, (of train) move out of station; ~ *out of the fire*, save (game etc.) when the case seems hopeless; ~-*out* n., page or plate in book that folds out from front edge of leaves to facilitate reference; ~-*over* n., sweater put on over head; ~ *through* adv. & prep., get (person), get oneself, safely through (danger, illness, etc., or abs.); ~-*through* n., cord with which cleaning-rag is drawn through rifle; ~ *oneself together*, rally, recover oneself; ~ *together*, work in harmony; ~ *up*, cause (person, horse, vehicle) to stop, reprimand, check oneself, advance one's relative position in race etc.; ~-*up* n., house of call for travellers. **19.** ~-*back*, retarding influence, check, contrivance for ~ing fullness of woman's skirt to back. [late OE *pullian*, of unkn. orig.]

pull² (poōl), n. **1.** Act of pulling, wrench, tug; force thus exerted; (fig.) means of exerting influence, interest with the powerful. **2.** (print.). Rough proof. **3.** Pulling at bridle to check horse esp. in racing. **4.** Spell of rowing. **5.** (Crick., golf) pulling stroke. **6.** ‖ (In public house) supply of beer etc. exceeding that asked for. **7.** *Have the* ~ (advantage) *of* (person). **8.** Deep draught of liquor. **9.** Handle etc. by which ~ is applied, as BEER¹, BELL¹, -~. [f. prec.]

pu'ller (pŏŏ-), n. In vbl senses, esp.: kinds of instrument or machine for pulling; horse that pulls esp. against bit. [-ER¹]

pu'llet (pŏŏ-), n. Young fowl, esp. hen from time she begins to lay till first moult. [ME, f. OF *poulet* dim. of *poule*]

pu'lley (pŏŏ-), n. (pl. ~s), & v.t. **1.** Grooved wheel(s) for cord etc. to pass over, mounted in block & used for changing direction of power, one of the simple mechanical powers; wheel, drum, fixed on shaft & turned by belt, used esp. to increase speed or power. **2.** v.t. Hoist, furnish, work, with ~. [ME & OF *polie* ult. f. Gk *polidion pivot dim. of *polos* POLE²]

Pu'llman (pŏŏ-), a. & n. ~ (*car*), railway saloon carriage usu. arranged for use as sleeping-car. [G. M. ~, designer (d. 1897)]

pull'ŭl|āte, v.i. (Of shoot, bud) sprout out, bud; (of seed) sprout; (fig., of doctrines etc.) develop, spring up. Hence ~ANT a., ~A'TION n. [f. L *pullulare* sprout (*pullulus* dim. of *pullus* young of animal), see -ATE³]

‖ **pu'lly-haul'y** (pŏŏ-), a. & n. (colloq.). (Of) pulling & hauling. So **pu'lly-haul** (pŏŏ-) v.t. & i. [-Y²]

pŭlm|o-, shortened f. *pulmoni-*, comb. form of L *pulmo -monis* lung, as: ~*obranch'iate*, with gills modified for air--breathing; ~*ŏm'eter*, instrument measuring capacity of lungs, so ~*ŏm'etry*.

pŭl'monary, a. Of, in, connected with, the lungs, as ~ *artery*, main artery conveying blood from heart to lungs, ~ *disease*; having lungs or lung-like organs, so **pŭl'monATE²** a.; affected with, subject to, lung-disease. So **pŭlmŏn'ic** a. [f. L *pulmonarius* (prec., -ARY¹)]

pŭlp, n., & v.t. & i. **1.** Fleshy part of fruit; any fleshy or soft part of animal body, e.g. nervous substance in interior cavity of tooth; soft formless mass, esp. that of rags, wood, etc., from which paper is made; ore pulverized & mixed with water. **2.** vb. Reduce to ~, remove ~ from (coffee-beans), whence ~'ER¹(2) n.; become ~y. Hence or cogn. ~'IFY v.t., ~'INESS n., ~'LESS, ~'OUS, ~'Y², aa. [f. L *pulpa*]

pu'lpit (pŏŏ-), n. Raised enclosed platform usu. with desk & seat from which preacher in church or chapel delivers sermon; *the* profession of preaching; preachers; (in title of book) collected sermons; (attrib.) ~ *eloquence, orator, style*. [ME, f. L *pulpitum* scaffold, platform]

pulpit|eer' (pŏŏ-), n., & v.i. Professional preacher (usu. derog.), so ~AR'IAN a. &

n.; (v.i.) preach, whence ~eer'ING¹ n. [-EER]

pulque (pŏŏl'kĕ), n. Mexican fermented drink from sap of agave etc.; ~ *brandy*, intoxicant made from ~. [Sp.-Amer.]

pŭlsāte' (*or* pŭl²-), v.t. & i. **1.** Expand & contract rhythmically, beat, throb (lit. & fig.); vibrate, quiver, thrill; agitate (diamonds) with machine (pŭlsāt' or n.) to separate them from earth in which they are found. Hence or cogn. **pŭlsA²TION** n., **pŭl'saTORY** a. [f. L *pulsare* frequent. of *pellere puls-* drive, beat, see -ATE³]

pŭl'satile, a. Of, having the property of, pulsation; (of musical instrument) played by percussion. [as prec. + -ILE]

pŭlsatill'a, n. The pasque-flower, its extract used in pharmacy. [med. L, dim. of *pulsata* fem. p.p. (as prec.), as quivering in wind]

pŭlse¹, n., & v.i. & t. **1.** Rhythmical throbbing of arteries as blood is propelled along them esp. as felt in wrists, temples, etc.; *feel* person's ~ (as indicating by its rate & character his state of health, fig., sound his intentions etc.); each successive beat of arteries or heart; (fig.) throb, thrill, of life or emotion; rhythmical recurrence of strokes e.g. of oars; (mus.) beat; single beat or vibration of sound, light, etc. **2.** v.i. Pulsate (lit. & fig.); (v.t.) send *oul, in*, etc., by rhythmic beats. Hence ~'LESS a., ~'lèssness n. [(n.) ME & OF *pous* f. L *pulsus -ūs* f. *pellere puls-*drive; vb f. L *pulsare* (as PULSATE)]

pŭlse², n. (Collective sing., sometimes with pl. vb) edible seeds of leguminous plants e.g. peas, beans, lentils; (with pl.) any kind of these. [ME, f. OF *po(u)ls* f. L *puls -ltis* pottage of meal etc.]

pŭlsim'ĕter, n. Instrument for measuring rate or force of pulse. [f. PULSE¹ + -I- + -METER]

pŭlsŏm'ĕter, n. Steam-condensing vacuum pump, so called from pulsatory action of the steam. [P; irreg. as prec., -o-]

pŭltā'ceous (-shus), a. Of (the nature of) pap or a poultice, soft, pulpy. [as PULSE², see -ACEOUS]

pŭl'veriz|e, -is|e (-ĭz), v.t. & i. Reduce to powder or dust, divide (liquid) into spray, whence ~ātor, ~ER¹(2), nn.; (fig.) demolish, crush, smash; (intr.) crumble to dust. Hence ~ABLE a., ~A'TION n. [f. LL *pulverizare* (*pulvis -eris* dust, see -IZE)]

pŭlvĕ'rulent (-rŏŏ-), a. Powdery, of dust; covered with powder; (of rock etc.) of slight cohesion, apt to crumble. [f. L *pulverulentus* (as prec., see -LENT)]

pŭl'vinate, -āted, aa. (Archit., *-ed*) swelling, esp. (of frieze) with convex face; (bot., entom.) cushion-like, having cushion-like swelling. [f. L *pulvinatus* (*pulvinus* cushion), see -ATE²(2)]

pŭm'a, n. = COUGAR. [Sp. f. Peruv.]

pŭm'ice(-stōne), n., & v.t. (Piece of) light spongy kind of lava used for removing stains from hands etc., polishing, etc.; (v.t.) rub, clean, with ~; ~ *hoof* of horse, made spongy by disease. So **pŭmi'cĕous** a. [ME & OF *pomis* f. Rom. **pōmicem*, L *pūmex*; cf. POUNCE²]

pŭmm'el, v.t. (-ll-). Strike repeatedly esp. with fist. [altered f. POMMEL]

pŭm(m)'elō. Var. of POMELO.

pŭmp¹, n. **1.** Machine, usu. cylinder in which piston etc. is moved up & down by rod, for raising water; kinds of machine for raising or moving liquids, compressing or rarefying gases, etc. (fig. of heart, insect's suckers, etc.); AIR¹, FORCE¹, STOMACH, -~; *bicycle*-~ (for inflating tires); pumping, stroke of ~; attempt, person skilful, at pumping others. **2.** ~-*brake*, handle of ship's ~ esp. with transverse bar for several persons to work at; ~-*handle* v.t. (colloq.), shake (person's hand) effusively; ~-*room*, building where ~ is worked esp. at spa where medicinal water is dispensed. [ME *pumpe, pompe,* = early mod. Du. *pompe*, LG *pump(e)*; prob. imit.]

pŭmp², v.i. & t. Work a pump; remove, raise, (water etc., usu. *out, up*) thus; make (ship, well, etc.) *dry* by ~ing; ~ *up*, inflate (pneumatic tire), inflate tires of (bicycle etc.); bring out, pour forth, (abuse etc. *upon*) as by ~ing; elicit information from (person), elicit (information, usu. *out of* person), by artful or persistent questions; (of exertion) put completely out of breath (esp. pass.); (of mercury in barometer) rise & fall instantaneously; ~'*ship* (not in polite use), (v.i.) make water, (n.) urination. Hence ~'ER¹ n. (esp., rail TROLLEY). [f. prec.]

pŭmp³, n. Kind of light shoe now usu. of patent leather & without fastening, worn with evening dress & for dancing. [orig. unkn.]

pu'mpernickel (pŏŏ-), n. German wholemeal rye bread. [G, f. earlier sense boor, 'stinker']

pŭmp'kin, n. (Cucurbitaceous plant bearing) large egg-shaped or globular fruit with edible layer next to rind, used in cookery & for cattle. [alt. f. 16th c. *pompon, pumpion,* f. obs. F *po(m)pon* f. L f. Gk *pepōn*]

pŭn¹, n. & v.i. (-nn-). **1.** Humorous use of word to suggest different meanings, or of words of same sound with different meanings, play on words. **2.** Make ~s (*upon* word, subject). Hence ~n'ing-LY² adv. [17th c., of obsc. orig.]

‖ **pŭn²**, v.t. (-nn-). Consolidate (earth, rubble) by pounding or ramming; work *up* to proper consistency with PUNNER. [dial. var. of POUND³]

pu'na (pŏŏ-), n. High bleak plateau in Peruvian Andes; difficulty in breathing caused by rarefied atmosphere. [Peruv., in first sense]

pŭnch¹, n. Instrument or machine for cutting holes in leather, metal, paper, etc.,

driving bolt etc. out of hole (*starting*-~), enlarging hole, forcing nail beneath surface (*driving*-~), etc.; tool or machine for impressing design or stamping die on material; *bell*-~, conductor's ticket-~ with bell to announce punching of ticket. [app. var. of POUNCE¹, or short f. PUNCHEON¹]

pŭnch², v.t., & n. **1.** Strike esp. with closed fist, as ~ *his head*; ~*ing-ball*, inflated ball held by elastic bands etc. & ~ed as form of exercise; prod with stick etc., esp. *drive (cattle) thus; pierce (metal, leather, bus-ticket, etc.) as or with punch; pierce (hole) thus; drive (nail etc. *in, out*) with punch. **2.** n. Blow with fist (*a* ~ *on the head*; PULL¹ one's ~*es*; ~-*drunk*, dazed through being severely ~ed, also transf.); (sl.) vigour, momentum, effective force. Hence ~'ER¹(1, 2) n. [vb var. of POUNCE¹ (16th c. in same senses), see prec.; n. f. vb]

pŭnch³, n. Drink usu. of wine or spirits mixed with hot water or milk, sugar, lemons, spice, etc., as *brandy, rum, milk,* ~; bowl of ~; party at which ~ is drunk; ~-*bowl,* bowl in which ~ is mixed, round deep hollow in hill(s). [f. 1632, orig. unkn.; perh. abbr. of PUNCHEON²]

pŭnch⁴, n. **1.** ‖ (*Suffolk*) ~, short-legged thickset draught horse; ‖ (dial.) short fat man or thing. **2.** (*P*~) grotesque humpbacked figure in puppet-show called P~ & *Judy*, esp. as title of a London weekly comic paper; *as pleased, as proud, as P*~ (much, very). [abbr. of PUNCHINELLO]

pŭn'cheon¹ (-shn), n. Short post esp. one supporting roof in coal-mine; (now rare) = PUNCH¹. [ME, f. OF *poinçon, poinchon,* f. Rom. **punctionem* or **punctiare* (L *pungere punct-* prick), see -ION]

pŭn'cheon² (-shn), n. (hist.) Large cask for liquids etc. holding from 72 to 120 gals. [ME, f. OF *poinçon, poinchon,* etc., of unkn. orig.]

Pŭnchĭnĕll'ō, n. (pl. ~s). Chief character in Italian puppet-show; short stout person. [17th c. *polichinello* f. Neapolitan dial. *Polecenella,* of uncert. orig.]

pŭnc't|āte, a. (nat. hist., path.). Marked or studded with points, dots, or spots. So ~A'TION n. [f. L as POINT¹, see -ATE²(2)]

pŭnctil'io (-lyō), n. (pl. ~s). Nice point of ceremony or honour; petty formality. [ĭ. It. *puntiglio* & Sp. *puntillo* dim. of *punto* POINT¹]

pŭnctil'ious (-lyus), a. Attentive to punctilios. Hence ~LY² adv., ~NESS n. [f. F *pointilleux* f. *pointille* (f. It. as prec., see -OUS]

pŭnc'tūal, a. Observant of appointed time; in good time, not late; (arch.) punctilious; (geom.) of a point. Hence ~ITY (-ăl²) n., ~LY² adv. [ME, f. med. L *punctualis* (*punctus -ūs* POINT¹ see -AL)]

pŭnc'tūat|e, v.t. Insert stops in (writing), mark or divide with stops; (fig.) interrupt (speech) *with* exclamations etc.; (improp.)

emphasize, accentuate, as *flung it on the ground to* ~*e his refusal.* Hence or cogn. ~IVE a., ~OR n. [f. med. L *punctuare* (as prec.), see -ATE[3]]

pŭnctŭā′tion, n. Insertion of vowel & other points in Hebrew etc.; practice, art, of punctuating. [f. med. L *punctuatio* (prec., -ATION)]

pŭnc′t|um, n. (pl. ~a). Speck, dot, spot of colour or elevation or depression on surface. So ~ULE n., whence ~ŭlATE[2](2) a., ~ŭla′TION n. [L, = POINT[1]]

pŭnc′ture, n., & v.t. & i. 1. Pricking, prick, esp. accidental pricking of pneumatic tire; hole thus made. 2. v.t. Prick, pierce; (v.i. of tire, bicycle etc., rider etc.), experience a ~. [ME, f. L *punctura* (*pungere punct-*, see POINT[1], -URE)]

pŭn′dĭt, n. Hindu learned in Sanskrit & in philosophy, religion, & jurisprudence, of India; (joc.) learned teacher. [f. Hind. *paṇḍit*]

pŭn′gent (-j-), a. (Nat. hist.) sharp-pointed; (of reproof, satire, etc.) biting, caustic; mentally stimulating, piquant; affecting organs of smell or taste, or skin etc., with pricking sensation, as ~ *gas, smoke, sauce.* Hence **pŭn′gency** n., ~LY[2] adv., (-j-). [f. L *pungere* prick, -ENT]

Pŭn′ic, a. & n. Carthaginian; ~ *Wars* (between Rome & Carthage); ~ FAITH; (n.) ~ language. [f. L *Punicus, Poen-* (*Poenus* f. Gk *Phoinix* Phoenician, see -IC)]

pŭn′ish, v.t. 1. Cause (offender) to suffer for offence; chastise; inflict penalty on (offender); inflict penalty for (offence). 2. (colloq.) Inflict severe blows on (opponent in boxing); (of race, competitor) tax severely the powers of (competitor); take full advantage of (weak bowling, bowler, stroke at tennis); make heavy inroad on (food etc.); whence ~ING[2] a. Hence ~abīL′ITY, ~ER[1], ~MENT, nn., ~ABLE a., ~abLY[2] adv. [ME, f. OF *punir* (-ISH[2]) f. L *punire* (*poena* PAIN)]

pŭn′itive, a. Inflicting punishment, retributive, as ~ *justice, expedition*; ~ *police* (India), detachment of police sent to a particular district and paid for by the inhabitants as punishment for lawlessness. So **pŭn′itory** a. [f. F (*-if, -ive*) or med. L *punitivus* (as prec., see -IVE)]

‖ **pŭnk[1],** n. (arch.). Prostitute. [c. 1600, of unkn. orig.]

*** pŭnk[2],** n. & a. 1. Rotten wood, fungus growing on wood, used as tinder; worthless stuff, rubbish, tosh. 2. adj. (sl.). Worthless, rotten. [16th c., of obsc. orig.; cf. SPUNK]

pŭnk′a(h) (-ka), n. (E.-Ind.). Portable fan usu. of leaf of palmyra; large swinging cloth fan on frame worked by cord. [f. Hind. *pankha*]

pŭnn′er, n. Tool for ramming earth about post etc. [f. PUN[2] + -ER[1]]

pŭnn′ĕt, n. Small chip basket for fruit or vegetables. [orig. unkn.]

pŭn′ster, n. Inveterate maker of puns. [-STER]

pŭnt[1], n., & v.t. & i. 1. Flat-bottomed shallow boat, broad & square at both ends, propelled by long pole thrust against bottom of river etc. 2. vb. Propel with or use ~-pole; convey in a ~. Hence **pŭn′ter[1]** [-ER[1]], **pŭn′tist,** nn. [ME, f. MLG *punte,* MDu. *ponte,* f. L *ponto,* kind of Gallic transport, whence OE *punt*]

pŭnt[2], v.t., & n. 1. Kick (football) after it has dropped from the hands & before it reaches ground. 2. n. Such kick; ~-*about,* kicking about of football for practice, ball so used. [prob. dial. orig.]

pŭnt[3], v.i., & n. 1. (At faro & other card-games) lay stake against bank; (colloq.) bet on horse etc. 2. n. Player who ~s; point in faro. Hence **pŭn′ter[2]** [-ER[1]] n. [c. 1700, f. F *ponte(r)*]

pŭn′tў, pŏ-, n. Iron rod used in glass-blowing. [app. f. F *pontil* f. It. *puntello* dim. of *punto* POINT[1]]

pŭn′|ў, a. Undersized; weak, feeble; petty. Hence ~ĬNESS n. [f. 16th c., phonetic sp. of PUISNE]

pŭp, n., & v.t. & i. (-pp-). 1. Young dog; *in* ~, pregnant; *conceited* etc. ~ (boy, young man); *sell* person a ~, swindle him esp. by selling thing on prospective value. 2. vb. Bring forth ~s; give birth to. [shortened f. PUPPY]

pūp′|a, n. (pl. ~ae). Chrysalis. Hence ~AL a. [L, = girl, doll]

pūp′|āte, v.i. Become a pupa. Hence ~A′TION n. [-ATE[3]]

pūp′il, n. 1. One who is taught by another, scholar; (law) person below age of puberty & under care of guardian; ~-*teacher,* boy, girl, teaching in elementary school under head teacher & concurrently receiving general education from him or elsewhere. 2. Circular opening in centre of iris of eye regulating passage of light to the retina. So ~(ĭ)AR[1], ~(ĭ)ARY[2], aa. [f. OF *pupille* f. L *pupillus, -la,* ward, minor, (*-la*) ~ of eye]

pūp′il(l)|age, n. Nonage, minority (fig. of country, language, etc.), so ~ā′rITY n. (law); being a pupil. So **pūp′il|ship** n. [-AGE]

pūp′il(l)īze, -ise (-īz), v.t. & i. Take pupils; coach (pupil). [-IZE]

pūpip′arous, a. (entom.). Bringing forth young already advanced to pupal state. [f. PUPA + L -*parus -bearing*]

pŭpp′ĕt, n. Figure, usu. small, representing human being, esp. one with jointed limbs moved by wires etc. in ~-*show*; person whose acts are controlled by another; ~-*play, -show* (with ~s as characters); ~-*clack, -valve,* disc valve opened by lifting bodily from its seat, not hinged; ~ *state,* country professing to be independent but actually under the control of some greater power, so ~ *king, ruler.* Hence ~RY(4, 5) n. [16th c., var. of POPPET]

pŭpp'ỹ, n. Young dog (also, childish, ~*-dog*); vain empty-headed young man, coxcomb, whence ~ISM n. Hence ~DOM, ~HOOD, nn., ~ISH¹ a. [ME, perh. f. OF *poupée* doll, plaything, toy]

pur-, pref. AF form of OF *por-*, *pur-*, f. L *por-*, PRO-¹ (*purchase*, *purport*, *pursue*).

purā'na (poorah-), n. Any of a class of Sanskrit sacred poems. Hence **purā'nic** (poorah-) a. [f. Skr. *puraṇá* of former times (*pura* formerly)]

Pŭrb'ĕck, a. ~ *stone*, hard limestone from ~ in Dorset; ~ *marble*, finer qualities of this.

pŭrb'lind, a., & v.t. Partly blind, dim-sighted; (fig.) obtuse, dull; (v.t.) make~. Hence ~NESS n. [ME *pur*(*e*) *blind*; *pur-* = PURE in sense 'quite', w. assim. to PUR-]

pŭrch'ase¹, n. **1.** Buying; ~*-money*, price (to be) paid; (hist.) practice of buying commissions in army; thing bought; annual return from land, as *sold at 20 years'* ~; (fig.) *life is not worth an hour's* ~, cannot be trusted to last an hour; (law) acquisition of property by one's personal action, not by inheritance. **2.** Mechanical advantage, leverage, (often fig.); appliance for gaining this, esp. (naut.) rope, windlass, pulley (*single, double, treble*, ~ *pulley*, with 1, 2, 3, sheaves). [ME, f. OF *porchas*, *pur-*, as foll.]

pŭrch'as|e², v.t. **1.** Buy; acquire (victory, freedom, etc., *with* one's blood, toil, etc.). **2.** (naut.). Haul up (anchor etc.) by means of pulley, lever, etc. So ~ABLE a., ~ER¹ n. [ME, f. AF PUR(*chacer* CHASE¹) procure, bring about]

pŭrd'ah(-da), n. (E.-Ind.). Curtain, esp. one serving to screen women from sight of strangers; (fig.) Indian system of secluding women of rank; striped material for curtains. [f. Hind. & Pers. *pardah*]

pūre, a. **1.** Unmixed, unadulterated, as ~ *white, air, alcohol, water*; (of sounds) not discordant, esp. (mus.) perfectly in tune. **2.** Of unmixed descent, ~*-blooded*; ~ *mathematics* (not including practical applications, opp. to *applied*, *mixed*); (gram., of vowel) preceded by another vowel, (of stem) ending in vowel, (of consonant) not accompanied by another. **3.** Mere, simple, nothing but, sheer, as *knowledge* ~ *& simple*, ~ *nonsense*, *prejudice*. **4.** Not corrupt, as *his taste was severe & ~*; morally undefiled, guiltless, sincere; sexually undefiled. Hence ~LY² (-ūrl-) adv. (rare exc. in senses exclusively, solely, entirely), ~'NESS (-ūrn-) n. [ME, f. OF *pur*, fem. *pure*, f. L *purus*]

purée (pūr'ā, & see Ap.), n. Soup of vegetables, meat, etc., boiled to pulp & passed through sieve. [F]

pūr'fle, n., & v.t. (arch.). **1.** Border, esp. embroidered edge of garment. **2.** v.t. Adorn (robe) with ~; ornament (edge of building *with* crockets etc.); beautify.

Hence **pūrf'ling¹** n., (esp.) inlaid bordering on back & belly of fiddles. [ME, f. OF *porfil*(*er*), as PROFILE]

pūrgā'tion, n. Purification; purging of bowels; spiritual cleansing, esp. (R.-C. Ch.) of soul in purgatory; (hist.) clearing of oneself from accusation or suspicion by oath or ordeal. [ME, f. OF *purgacion* or L *purgatio* (as PURGE, see -ATION)]

pūrg'ative, a. & n. Aperient (medicine); serving to purify. [ME, f. OF (*-if*, *-ive*), or LL *purgativus* (as PURGE, see -ATIVE)]

pūrg'atorỹ, n. & a. **1.** Condition, place, of spiritual purging, esp. (R.-C. Ch.) of souls departing this life in grace of God but requiring to be cleansed from venial sins etc.; place of temporary suffering or expiation. **2.** adj. Purifying. So **pūrgatōr'IAL** a. [ME, f. AF *-orie*, OF *-oire* f. med. L *purgatorium*, neut. of LL *-orius* adj. (as foll., see -ORY)]

pūrge, v.t., & n. **1.** Make physically or spiritually clean (*of*, *from*, impurities, sin, etc.); remove by cleansing process (lit. & fig., often *away*, *off*, *out*); (of medicine) relieve (bowels, or abs.) by evacuation; clear (person, one*self*, *of* charge, suspicion); (law) atone for, wipe out, (offence, sentence) by expiation & submission; rid (political party, army, etc.) of persons regarded as undesirable. **2.** n. Such clearance, purgation, (*Pride's* ~, hist., exclusion by Col. Pride of Presbyterian & Royalist members from Long Parliament); aperient. [ME; vb f. OF *purger* f. L *purgare*; n. f. vb, partly f. F *purge*]

pūrifica'tion, n. Purifying; ritual cleansing, esp. that of woman after childbirth enjoined by Jewish law, as *the P~* (*of the Virgin Mary*), Feb. 2nd (*Luke* ii. 22). So **pūr'ificātorỹ** a. [ME, f. OF, or f. L *purificatio* (as PURIFY, see -ATION)]

pūr'ificātor, n. (eccl.). Cloth used at communion for wiping chalice & paten & fingers & lips of celebrant. [as foll., see -OR]

pūr'if|ỹ, v.t. Make pure, cleanse, (*of*, *from*, impurities, sin, etc.); make ceremonially clean; clear of foreign elements, whence ~IER¹(2) n. [ME, f. OF *purifier* or L *purificare* (as PURE, see -FY)]

Pūr'im, n. Jewish festival commemorating defeat of Haman's plot (*Esth.* ix). [Heb., pl. of *pur*, perh. = lot]

pūr'|ist, n. Stickler for, affecter of, scrupulous purity esp. in language. So ~ISM n., ~is'tic(AL) aa. [f. F *puriste* (PURE, -IST)]

pūr'itan, n. & a. **1.** (Hist.; *P~*) member of the party of English Protestants who regarded reformation of Church under Elizabeth as incomplete & sought to abolish unscriptural & corrupt ceremonies etc.; member of any non-religious purist party; person of or affecting extreme strictness in religion or morals. **2.** adj. Of the P~s; scrupulous in religion or morals. Hence **pūritan'ic(AL)** aa., **pūritān'icalLY²** adv., ~ISM n., ~IZE(2, 3) v.i.

& t. [f. L *puritas* (foll.)+-AN; cf. F *puritain*]

pūr′ity, n. Pureness, cleanness, freedom from physical or moral pollution. [ME & OF *pur(e)te* f. LL *puritatem* (PURE, -TY)]

purl[1], n., & v.t. & i. 1. Cord of twisted gold or silver wire for bordering; chain of minute loops, each loop of this, ornamenting edges of lace, ribbon, etc.; (knitting, also *pearl*) inversion of stitches, producing ribbed appearance. 2. vb. Border (material or abs.) with ~; invert (stitches or abs.); invert stitches of (stocking etc.). [cord sense app. Sc. *pirl* twist; other senses perh. different wds]

purl[2], v.i., & n. 1. (Of brook etc.) flow with whirling motion & babbling sound. 2. n. Such motion or sound. [16th c., prob. imit.; cf. Norw. *purla* bubble up]

purl[3], n. (hist.). Ale or beer with wormwood infused; hot beer mixed with gin as morning draught, dog's-nose. [orig. unkn.]

purl[4], v.t. & i., & n. (colloq.). 1. Turn (t. & i.) upside down, upset. 2. n. Cropper, heavy fall. [prob. var. of *pirl* (see PURL[1])]

purl′er, n. (colloq.). Throw, blow, that hurls one head foremost (*come, take, a ~, fall headlong*). [prec.+-ER[1]]

purl′ieu (-lū), n. Tract on border of forest esp. one earlier included in it & still partly subject to forest laws; one's bounds, limits; (pl.) outskirts, outlying region (lit. & fig.); squalid street or quarter of town. [ME, prob. altered after LIEU f. *pur(a)ley* f. obs. & AF PUR(*alé* ALLEY) perambulation to settle boundaries]

purl′in, n. Horizontal beam running along length of roof, resting on principals & supporting common rafters or boards. [ME, orig. unkn.]

purloin′ (-per-), v.t. Steal, pilfer. Hence ~ER[1] n. [ME, f. AF PUR(*loigner* f. *loing* far f. L *longe*) put away, do away with]

pūr′ple, n., a., & v.t. & i. 1. (Of) a colour mixed of red & blue in various proportions with some black or white or both; (anciently, also *Tyrian ~*) (of) the colour got from the molluscs *purpura* & *murex*, crimson; *~-red* etc., red etc. inclining to ~. 2. ~ robe, esp. as dress of emperor, king, consul, etc., as *born in the ~*, or of cardinal, as *raised to the ~* (cardinalate). 3. pl. Swine fever; disease in wheat. 4. ~ *emperor*, a butterfly; ~ *patch*, ornate passage in literary composition. 5. vb. Make, become, ~. Hence pūr′p′lish[1], pūr′p′ly[2], aa. [OE *purple*, ME *purpul* etc., altered f. OE *purpure*, ME *purpur* etc. f. L PURPURA; cf. *marble* f. *marbre*]

purpoint. See POURPOINT.

pūrp′ort[1], n. Meaning, sense, tenor, of document or speech; (rare) object, purpose. [ME, f. AF, as foll.]

purpōrt′[2] (-per-), v.t. (Of document or speech) have as its meaning, convey,

state, (fact, *that*); profess, be intended to seem (*to do*), as *a letter ~ing to be written by you*, to contain your decision. Hence ~ɛ́dLY[2] adv., professedly. [ME, f. AF & OF PUR*porter* f. med. L *proportare* f. PRO-+L *portare* carry]

pūrp′ose[1], n. Object, thing intended, as *could not effect my ~, this will answer* (or *serve*) *our* (or *the*) ~, *what was the ~ of this law?*; fact, faculty, of resolving on something, as *honesty of ~, is wanting in ~; novel with a ~, ~-novel*, (written to defend some doctrine etc.); *on ~*, in order (*to do, that*), (abs., also *of set ~*) designedly, not by accident, whence ~LY[2] (-sl-) adv.; *to the ~*, relevant, useful for one's ~; *to little, some, no, ~*, with such result or effect. Hence ~FUL (-sf-), ~LESS (-sl-), aa., ~fulLY[2], ~lessLY[2], advv., ~fulNESS, ~lessNESS, nn. [ME, f. AF & OF *purpos*, f. *purposer*, as foll.]

pūrp′ose[2], v.t. Design, intend, as *I ~* (*arranging* or *to arrange*) *an interview, ~ that an interview shall be arranged*; (arch.) *am ~d*, intend (*to do, doing, that*). [ME, f. OF PUR*poser = proposer* PROPOSE]

pūrp′osive, a. Having, serving, done with, a purpose; (of person or conduct) having purpose & resolution. [-IVE]

pūrp′ura, n. Disease marked by purple or livid spots on skin; kinds of molluscs including some from which purple dye was derived. [L, f. Gk *porphura* (shellfish yielding) purple]

purpūr′ic (per-), a. Of purpura, as *~ fever*; ~ *acid*, an acid the salts of which are purple. [-IC]

pūrp′ūrin, n. Red colouring-matter orig. got from madder. [f. PURPURA+-IN]

pūrr, v.i. & t., & n. 1. (Of cat or other feline animal, fig. of person) make low continuous vibratory sound expressing pleasure; utter, express, (words, contentment) thus. 2. n. Such sound. [imit.]

pū′rree, n. Yellow colouring-matter from India & China. [f. Hind. *peori*]

pur sang (see Ap.), adv. (appended to classifying n. or adj.). Of the full blood, without admixture, through & through, genuine, (*is Welsh* or *a Welshman, militarist, a cynic, ~; the artist ~ is a rarity*). [F]

pūrse[1], n. 1. Small pouch of leather etc. for carrying money on the person, orig. closed by drawing strings together; (fig.) money, funds, as *a common ~* (fund), *heavy* or *long ~*, wealth, *light ~*, poverty, *the public ~*, national treasury; || PRIVY ~; sum collected, subscribed, or given, as present or as prize for contest, as *will any gentleman give* or *put up a ~?*; *bag-like natural or other receptacle*, pouch, cyst, etc. 2. *~-bearer*, one who has charge of another's or a company's money, || official carrying Great Seal before Lord Chancellor in ~; *~-net*, bag-shaped net for catching rabbits etc., mouth of which can be closed with cords; *~-proud*, puffed up by wealth; ~-*seine*, ~-*net* for fishing; ~-*strings*, strings for closing mouth of ~, (*hold the* ~-*strings*, have control of expenditure; *tighten, loosen, the* ~-*strings*, be sparing, generous, of money). Hence ~'FUL (-sf-) n., ~'LESS (-sl-) a. [OE *purs* app. f. LL *bursa* purse f. Gk *bursa* hide]

pŭrse[2], v.t. & i. Contract (lips, brow, often *up*) in wrinkles; become wrinkled; (rare) put (often *up*) into one's purse. [f. prec.]

pŭrs'er, n. Officer on ship who keeps accounts esp. in passenger vessel. Hence ~SHIP n. [f. PURSE[1] + -ER[1]]

pŭrs'lane (-in), n. Low succulent herb used in salads & pickled. [ME, f. OF *porcelaine* altered f. L *porcil(l)aca, portulaca*, on PORCELAIN]

pursū'ance (per-), n. Carrying out, pursuing, (of plan, object, idea, etc.), esp. *in* ~ *of*. [as foll., see -ANCE]

pursū'ant (per-), a. & adv. Pursuing; (adv.) conformably *to* (*the Act* etc.), whence ~LY[2] adv. [f. OF *porsuiant* part. as foll.]

pursūe' (per-), v.t. & i. Follow with intent to capture or kill; (fig., of consequences, penalty, disease, etc.) persistently attend, stick to; seek after, aim at, (pleasure etc., one's object); proceed in compliance with (plan etc.); proceed along, continue, (road, inquiry, conduct); follow (studies, profession); go in pursuit (*after*, or abs.). Hence **pursū'ABLE** (per-) a. [ME, f. AF PURSiwer, -*suer*, = OF *porsievre, -sivre* etc., f. pop. L pro-, *persequere* f. L *sequi* follow; see SUE]

pursū'er (per-), n. In vbl senses, also || (civil & Sc. law) prosecutor. [-ER[1]]

pursuit' (persūt), n. Pursuing, esp. *in* ~ *of* (animal, person, one's object); ~ *plane*, fighter aircraft; profession, employment, recreation, that one follows. [ME, f. AF *purs(e)uite*, OF *porsuite* f. *porsuivre* PURSUE after *suite* SUIT]

|| pŭrs'uivant (-sw-), n. Officer of College of Arms below herald; (poet.) follower, attendant. [ME, f. OF *porsivant* (as PURSUE, see -ANT)]

pŭrs'|y̆[1], a. Short-winded, puffy; corpulent. Hence~INESS n. [ME & AF *porsif* f. OF *polsif* f. *polser* breathe with labour (as PULSATE, see -IVE)]

pŭrs'y̆[2], a. Puckered. [f. PURSE[1] + -Y[2]]

pŭrt'enance, n. (arch.). Inwards, pluck, of animal. [earlier form of PERTINENCE]

pŭr'ul|ent (-rŏŏ-), a. Of, full of, discharging, pus. Hence or cogn. ~ENCE, ~ENCY, nn., ~entLY[2] adv. [f. L *purulentus* (PUS, see -LENT)]

purvey' (pervā), v.t. & i. Provide, supply, (articles of food) as one's business; make provision, act as purveyor, (*for* person, army, etc.). [ME, f. AF PURveier f. L *providere* PROVIDE]

purvey'ance (pervā'ans), n. Purveying; || right of crown to provisions etc. at fixed price & to use of horses etc. [ME, f. AF *porveance* f. L *providentia* PROVIDENCE]

purvey'or (pervā'er), n. One whose business it is to supply articles of food, esp. dinners etc. on large scale, as *P*~ *to the Royal Household*; (hist.) officer making purveyance for sovereign. [ME, f. AF *purveour* (as PURVEY, see -OR)]

pŭr'view (-vū), n. Enacting clauses of statute; scope, intention, range, (of act, document, scheme, book, occupation, etc.); range of physical or mental vision. [ME, f. AF *purveu* provided, p.p. as PURVEY]

pŭs, n. Yellowish viscid matter produced by suppuration. [L, gen. *puris*]

Pŭs'ey|ism (-zǐ-), n. (Hostile term for) TRACTARIANISM. So ~ITE[1] (-zīt) n. [E. B. *Pusey* d. 1882 + -ISM]

push[1] (pŏŏsh), v.t. & i. 1. Exert upon (body) force tending to move it away; move (body *up, down, away, back,* etc.) thus; exert such pressure, as *do not* ~ *against the fence*; (billiards) make push--stroke; (of person in boat)~ *off*, ~ *against* bank with oar to get boat out into stream etc. 2. (bibl.). Butt (t. & i.) with the horns. 3. (Cause to) project, thrust *out, forth,* etc., as *plants* ~ *out new roots, cape* ~*es out into sea.* 4. Make one's way forcibly or persistently, force (one's *way*) thus. 5. Exert oneself esp. to surpass others or succeed in one's business etc., whence ~'ING[2] a., ~'ingLY[2] adv., (pŏŏ-). 6. Urge, impel, (often *on, to do, to* effort etc.). 7. Follow up, prosecute, (claim etc., often *on*); engage actively in making (one's *fortune*); extend (one's *conquests* etc.); ~ (matter) *through,* bring it to a conclusion. 8. Press the adoption, use, sale, etc. of (goods etc.) esp. by advertisement. 9. Press (person) hard, as *do not wish to* ~ *him for payment,* esp. in pass., as *am* ~*ed for* (can scarcely find) *time, money.* 10. ~-*button war,* = PRESS[2]- *button war;* *~*over* n.,* an opponent easily defeated, a gullible person, an easy problem; ~-*pin,* a child's game, *drawing-pin.* Hence ~'ER[1] (1, 2) (pŏŏ-) n. (~*er aeroplane,* with air-screw behind, opp. *tractor*). [ME, f. OF *pousser,* earlier *polser* f. L *pulsare* as PULSATE]

push[2] (pŏŏsh), n. 1. Act of pushing, shove, thrust; (billiards) stroke in which ball is pushed, not struck; exertion of influence to promote person's advancement. 2. Thrust of weapon or of beast's horn. 3. Vigorous effort, as *must make a* ~ *to get it done, for home,* (mil.) attack in force. 4. Continuous pressure of arch etc.; pressure of affairs, crisis, pinch. 5. Enterprise, determination to get on, self--assertion, whence ~'FUL (pŏŏ-) a. 6. (sl.). Gang of thieves, convicts, etc. 7. (sl.). *Give, get, the* ~, dismiss, be dismissed. 8. ~-*ball,* game played with enormous ball, pushed, not kicked, towards opponents' goal; || ~-*bike* (sl.), bicycle worked by pedalling (opp. *motor-bike*). [f. prec.]

Pŭsh'tōō, -tu (-ōō), n. Afghan language. [f. Pers. *pashto*]

pŭsĭllăn'ĭmous (-z-), a. Faint-hearted, mean-spirited. Hence or cogn. **pŭsĭllanĭm'ITY** n., **~LY**[2] adv. [f. eccl. L *pusillanimis* (*pusillus* petty + *animus* soul) + -OUS]

puss (pŏŏs), n. Cat (esp. as call-name); (quasi-proper name for) hare, tiger; (colloq.) girl, as *sly ~*; *~ moth*, large European moth. [prob. f. MLG *pūs*, Du. *poes*, cf. Norw. *puse*, perh. orig. a call]

pu'ssў (pŏŏ-), n. (nursery). *~(-cat)*, cat; (nursery) soft furry thing, e.g. willow catkin; (sl.) *~foot*, *P~foot*, liquor-prohibition, advocate of this, (from nickname of a *U.S.* prohibitionist), **(v.i.)* move stealthily, act cautiously. [-Y[3]]

pŭs'tūl|āte, v.t. & i. Form into pustules. So **~ATE**[2] *(-at)* a., **~A'TION** n. [f. LL *pustulare*, as foll.]

pŭs'tūl|e, n. Pimple; *malignant ~e*, disease caused by anthrax bacillus; (bot., zool.) wart, wart-like excrescence. Hence or cogn. **~AR**[1], **~OUS**, aa. [ME, f. L *pustula*]

put[1] (pŏŏt), v.t. & i. (*put*). **1.** General senses. **1.** Propel, hurl, (*the weight, stone*) from hand placed close to shoulder as athletic exercise. **2.** Thrust (weapon), send (missile), as *~ a knife into*, stab, *put a bullet through*, shoot. **3.** (coal-mining). Propel (tram or barrow of coal). **4.** (naut.). Proceed, take one's course, *back, forth, in* (*to* harbour etc.), *off* (*from* shore etc.), *out*, in ship. **5.** Move (thing etc., lit. & fig.) so as to place it in some situation, as *~ it in your pocket, on the table, up the chimney, down the well*; *~* (mark, write) *a tick against his name, your signature to it*; *~ the horse to* (*the cart*), harness him; *~ bull to cow* or *cow to bull* (for breeding); *~* (convey) *him across the river, ~ the children to bed, ~ him in prison*; *has ~* (infused) *new life into him*; *will ~* (present) *the matter clearly before her*; *~ a* SPOKE *in his wheel, ~ the words into his* MOUTH[1], *~ one's* FOOT[1] *in it*, one's SHOULDER *to the wheel, hand to the* PLOUGH[1], *the* LID *on*. **6.** (With less or no idea of physical motion in space) bring into some relation or state, as *~ yourself, the matter, in(to) my hands*; *time he was ~* (began to go habitually) *to school*; *~ it to* (offer it for) *sale, on the market*; *~ 'Othello' on* (*the stage*), produce it; *~* (add) *milk to your tea*; *should ~* (price) *it at 2/6*; *~s* (estimates) *the circulation at 60,000*; *~* (translate) *it into Dutch*; *cannot ~ it into* (express it in) *words*; *what a way you have of ~ting things!*; *~s* (sets) *no value on my advice*; *I ~* (base) *my decision on the grounds stated*; *~* (apply) *it to a good use*; *~* (imagine) *yourself in his place*; *~* (substitute) *the will for the deed*; *~ a good* FACE[1] *on it*; *~ an end, period, stop, to it, stop it*; *~ a check* or *stopper on it, a veto on it*, check it, forbid it; *~ an end to* (destroyed) *himself* or *his life*; *~ the wind*

up one (sl.), frighten him; *~* (stake) *money on a horse*; *~ his money into* (invested it in) *land*; *~ & take* (name of a gambling game with teetotum); *~* (submit) *the case to him, to the vote*; *I ~ it* (appeal) *to you*; (esp. of examining counsel) *I ~ it to you* (invite you to acknowledge) *that you were after no good*; *dues were ~* (imposed) *on cattle*; *every insult was ~* (inflicted) *on him*; *don't be ~ upon* (victimized) *by him*; *~* (lay) *the blame on me*; *~ him* (caused him to be) *at his ease, in fear of his life, out of temper, on his guard, on his mettle*; *~ him* (make him speak) *on* (*his*) *oath*; *~ the servants on* (allow them) *board wages*; *~ the proposal into shape*; *~ his* NOSE[1] *out of joint*; *~* thing *out of court* (make it not worth discussing etc.); *~* thing *out of* one's *head* (forget, make him forget, it); *a few words will ~* (make) *the matter right*; *always manages to ~ me* (make me appear) *in the wrong*; *~ out of* COUNTENANCE[1]; *must have ~* (made) *the clock fast* (by advancing hands); **~ wise* (sl.), disabuse or enlighten; *~* (subject) *them to death, torture, ransom, expense, inconvenience, the test or trial, the rack, the sword, confusion, shame*; *land was ~ into* or *under* (sown with) *turnips*; *~* (set) *him to mind the furnace*; *~ my horse to* or *at* (invited him to jump) *the fence*; (of horse & fig. of person) *must be ~ through* (made to perform) *his paces*; *~ him* (make him read) *through a book of Livy*; *was ~* (forced, driven) *to flight, to his shifts, to the* BLUSH[2]; *was ~ to* (forced to play) *his trumps*; *surprising what he can do when he's ~ to it* (pressed); *was hard ~ to it to* (could scarcely) *keep them off*. **II.** Special senses with advv. **1.** *~ about*: lay (sailing vessel) on opposite tack, cause (horse, body of men) to turn round, (of vessel) go about; (chiefly Sc.) trouble, distress. **2.** *~ across*, execute or establish successfully (*~ it across*, succeed in doing). **3.** *~ away*: (arch.) divorce; lay by (money etc.) for future use; (sl.) consume (food, drink); (sl.) imprison; (sl.) pawn. **4.** *~ back*: check the advance of, retard; move back the hands of (clock); restore to former place. **5.** *~ by*: evade (question, argument); *~ off* (person) with evasion; lay aside esp. for future use. **6.** *~ down*: suppress by force or authority; take down, snub, put to silence; cease to maintain (expensive thing); account, reckon, as *I ~ him down for nine years old, at nine, as a fool, for a fool*; attribute, as *~ it down to his nervousness*; *~* one's FOOT[1] *down*. **7.** *~ forth*: exert (strength, effort, eloquence); *~ in* circulation; (of plant) send out (buds, leaves, or abs.). **8.** *~ forward*: thrust (oneself etc.) into prominence; advance, set forth, (theory etc.). **9.** *~ in*: install in office etc., as *~ in a caretaker, bailiff*, (hence) *distress, execution*; present formally (document, evidence, plea, claim, bail) as in law-court; *~ in* (make) *an appearance*; make a claim (*for* election etc.); interpose (blow, shot, remark, quoted words), ~ *in* one's OAR; throw in (additional thing); perform (piece of work) as part of a whole; (colloq.) pass, spend, (time). **10.** ~ *off*: postpone; postpone engagement with (person); evade (person, demand, often *with* excuse, compromise); hinder, dissuade, *from*; foist (thing *upon* person); remove, take off, (clothes); (of boat, crew, etc.) leave shore; ~-*off* n., evasion, postponement. **11.** ~ *on*: clothe oneself or another with; (colloq.) ~ *it on*, overcharge, simulate exaggerated emotion, suffering, etc.; assume, take on, (character, appearance); develop additional (flesh, weight); add (so much *to* price, runs etc. *to* score); stake (money *upon* horse etc.); advance the hands of (clock); bring into action, exert, (force, pressure, speed, STEAM[1], *the* SCREW[1]); appoint, arrange for, (person) to bowl etc., (train) to run etc. **12.** ~ *out*: dislocate (shoulder etc.); (crick.) cause (batsman) to be out; extinguish (candle, gas, fire, etc.); disconcert, confuse, annoy, irritate; ~ to inconvenience; exert (strength etc.); lend (money) at interest, invest; give (work) to be done off the premises. **13.** ~ *over*, secure appreciation for (film, play, etc.); ~ (oneself) *over*, impress one's personality on (an audience). **14.** ~ *through*: carry out (task); place (person) in telephonic connexion with (*to*) another through exchange(s). **15.** ~ *together*: form (whole) by combination of parts; ~ TWO *& two together*; ~ (*our* etc.) *heads together*, consult; (crick.) compile (score). **16.** ~ *up*: ~ person's *back up*, enrage him; ~ one's HAIR *up*; employ (person) as jockey; produce (play) on stage; cause (game) to rise from cover; raise (price); offer (prayer), present (petition); propose for election; publish (banns); offer for sale by auction or for competition; pack up in parcel, place in receptacle for safe keeping; sheathe (sword); lodge & entertain (man, horse); take up one's lodging (*at* inn etc.); ~ *up a* (*good* etc.) *fight*, make a good etc. fight of it; ~ *up with* (arch. ~ *up*), submit to, tolerate, (insult, annoying person or thing); ~ (person) *up to*, inform him of, instruct him in, (also) instigate him (*to* do, to *do*ing, or action); construct, build; concoct (underhand piece of work); ~-*up a.*, fraudulently concocted. Hence **pu'ttER**[1] (pŏŏ-) n. [late OE **putian* (? **pūtian*, also (*ā*)*pȳtan*, *potian*, of unkn. orig.]

put² (pŏŏt), n. **1.** Throw, cast, of the weight or stone. **2.** Option of delivering fixed amount of a stock at fixed price within fixed time. [f. prec.]

pŭt³, pŭtt, v.i. & t. (*pŭtted*), & n. **1.** Strike golf-ball, strike (golf-ball) gently with club to get it into hole on smooth piece of ground called *putting-green.* **2.** n. Such stroke. Hence **pŭtt'ER**¹(1, 2) n. [differentiated f. PUT¹·²]

pŭt⁴, n. (old sl.). Duffer, queer person, countryman, etc. [17th c., of unkn. orig.]

pūt'ative, a. Reputed, supposed, as *his* ~ *father.* Hence ~LY² adv. [ME, f. OF (-*if*, -*ive*), or LL *putativus* (*putare* think, see -ATIVE)]

pūte, a. (arch.). Pure (*&*) ~, mere. [f. L *putus* in phr. *purus ac putus*]

pŭt'éal, n. (Rom. ant.). Stone curb round mouth of well. [L (*puteus* well, see -AL)]

pŭt'lŏg, -lŏck, n. Short horizontal timber on which scaffold-boards rest. [orig. unkn.]

pŭt'rė|fy̆, v.i. & t. Become putrid, rot, go bad; fester, suppurate; become morally corrupt; (rare) cause to ~fy. So ~FAC'TION n., ~fāctive a. [ME, f. L *putrefacere* (*putrēre* be rotten, see -FY)]

pūtrĕs'c|ent, a. In process of rotting; of, accompanying, this process. Hence ~ENCE n., ~IBLE a. [f. L *putrescere* incept. of *putrēre* rot, see -ENT]

pŭt'rid, a. Decomposed, rotten; foul, noxious; (fig.) corrupt; (sl.) of poor quality, highly distasteful; ~ *fever*, typhus; ~ *sore throat*, gangrenous pharyngitis, diphtheria. Hence ~ITY (-ĭd⁴), ~NESS, nn., ~LY² adv. [f. L *putridus* (*putrēre* rot, -ID¹)]

putsch (-ŏŏ-), n. Revolutionary attempt, *coup de main.* [G (Swiss)]

putt. See PUT³.

pŭtt'ee (-ĭ), n. Long strip of cloth wound spirally round leg from ankle to knee for protection & support. [f. Hind. *paṭṭi* bandage]

pŭtt'ŏŏ, n. (Anglo-Ind.). Fabric, plain or patterned, produced in Cashmere from coarse goat-wool. [native name]

pŭtt'y̆, n., & v.t. **1.** (Also *jewellers'* ~) powder of calcined tin (& lead) for polishing glass or metal; (also *plasterers'* ~) fine mortar of lime & water without sand; (also *glaziers'* ~) cement of whiting, raw linseed oil, etc., for fixing panes of glass, filling up holes in woodwork, etc.; ~ *medal*, fit reward for small service (*you deserve a* ~ *medal*). **2.** v.t. Cover, fix, join, fill *up*, with ~. [f. F *potée* lit. POTful, see -Y⁴]

puy (pwē), n. Small volcanic cone esp. in Auvergne. [F]

pŭz'zle¹, n. Bewilderment, perplexity; perplexing question, enigma; problem, toy, contrived to exercise ingenuity & patience, as *Chinese* ~; ~-*head*(ed), -*pate*(d), (person) with confused ideas; ‖~-*peg*, piece of wood so fixed to dog's lower jaw as to prevent him from putting nose close to ground. [app. f. foll.]

pŭz'zle², v.t. & i. Perplex; be perplexed (*about, over,* problem etc.); make *out* (solution of problem etc.); MONKEY-~. Hence ~DOM (-ld-), ~MENT (-lm-), **pŭzz'-lER**¹(2), nn., **pŭzz'lingLY²** adv. [orig. unkn.]

puzzolana. See POZZOLANA.

py̆aem'|ia, n. Blood-poisoning marked

by formation of pus-foci. Hence ~ɪᴄ a. [f. Gk *puon* pus +*haima* blood + -ɪᴀ¹]

pўc′no-, comb. form of Gk *puknos* thick, dense, as ~*style* a. & n., (building) with close arrangement of columns, i.e. at interval of one diameter & a half.

pўe′dŏg, pĭ(e)-, n. Ownerless mongrel of the East. [f. Anglo-Ind. *pye, paĕ*, Hind. *pāhī* outsider]

pўg′m|ў, pĭ-, n. & a. 1. One of a diminutive race of men said to have inhabited parts of Ethiopia or India; *the P~ies*, a dwarf people in equatorial Africa; dwarf (fig. of intellectual inferiority etc.); elf, pixy. 2. adj. Of the ~ies, dwarf. So **pўgm(a)e′ᴀɴ** (-ē′*an*) a. [ME, f. L f. Gk *pugmaios* (*pugmē* length from elbow to knuckles, also the fist)]

‖ **pўja′mas, *paj-**, (-ahmaz), n. pl. Loose silk or cotton trousers tied round waist, worn by both sexes among Mohammedans & adopted esp. for night wear by Europeans; sleeping-suit of loose trousers & jacket; also attrib. in sing. form *pўja′ma* (-ah-), as *pyjama jacket, trousers*. [f. Pers. *pae jamah* (*pae, pay*, foot, leg, + *jamah* clothing)]

pўk′nic, a. & n. (anthrop.). (Person) characterized by a thick neck, large abdomen, and relatively short legs. [f. Gk *pyknos* compact + -ɪᴄ]

pўl′ŏn, n. Gateway esp. of Egyptian temple; tall compound structure erected as support (esp. for power-cables) or boundary or decoration. [f. Gk *pulōn* (*pulē* gate)]

pўlŏr′us, n. (anat.). Opening from stomach into duodenum; part of stomach where this is. Hence **pўlŏ′ʀɪᴄ** a. [LL, f. Gk *pulōros* gatekeeper (*pulē* gate + *ouros* warder)]

pўo-, comb. form of Gk *puon* pus, as ~*gen′esis*, formation of pus; ~*rrhoe′a* (-rēa), purulent discharge (esp. as a dental disease). So **pў′oɪᴅ** a.

pўr′acănth, n. Evergreen thorny shrub with white flowers & scarlet berries. [f. Gk *purakantha*]

pў′ramid, n. 1. Monumental (esp. ancient Egyptian) structure of stone etc. with polygonal or (usu.) square base, & sloping sides meeting at apex. 2. Solid of this shape with base of three or more sides. 3. ~-shaped thing or pile of things; fruit-tree trained in ~ shape. 4. Poem whose successive lines increase or decrease in length. 5. ‖ pl. (billiards). Game played with (usu. 15) coloured balls & one cue-ball. Hence or cogn. **pўrăm′idᴀ**L a., **pўrăm′idᴀ**Lʏ², ~wɪsᴇ, advv. [f. L f. Gk *puramis -idos*, perh. of Egypt. orig.]

pў′rāmidist, n. Student of structure & history of Egyptian pyramids. [-ɪsᴛ]

pўre, n. Heap of combustible material, esp. funeral pile for burning corpse. [f. L f. Gk *pura* (*pur* fire)]

pўrĕth′rum, n. Name of kinds of chrysanthemum. [L, f. Gk *purethron*]

pўrĕt′ic (*or* pī-), a. Of, for, or producing, fever. [f. Gk *puretos* fever + -ɪᴄ]

pўrĕx′|ia (*or* pī-), n. (path.). Fever. Hence ~ɪᴀʟ, ~ɪᴄ(ᴀʟ), aa. [f. Gk *purexis* (*puressō* be feverish, as prec.)]

pyrhĕliŏm′eter (*per*-), n. Instrument for measuring heat given off by sun. [f. Gk *pur* fire + *hēlios* sun + -ᴍᴇᴛᴇʀ]

pўr′idine (*or* pī-), n. (chem.). A volatile liquid alkaloid from dry distillation of bone-oil, used for asthma. [f. Gk *pur* fire + -ɪᴅ⁴ + -ɪɴᴇ⁵]

pўrit′ĕs (-z), n. (Also *iron*~) either of two sulphides of iron; *copper* ~, double sulphide of copper & iron. Hence **pyrit′ɪᴄ**, **pyritɪF′ᴇʀᴏᴜs**, aa., **pyr′ɪᴛᴢᴇ** v.t., (pīr-, *or* pī-). [L, f. Gk *puritēs* of fire (*pur*, see -ɪᴛᴇ¹)]

pyro. See ᴘʏʀᴏ*gallic*.

pўr|o-, comb. form of Gk *pur* fire, as: ~*o-elec′tric*, ~*o-electri′city*, (property of) becoming electrically polar when heated; ~*ogall′ic acid* (abbr. *pyro*), acid used as reducing agent in photography etc.; ~*ogenĕt′ic*, productive of heat, esp. in the body, or (also ~*ogĕn′ic*) of fever; ~*ŏ′genous*, (of rock) igneous, (of substance) produced by combustion of another; ~*ŏg′raphy*, = ᴘᴏᴋᴇʀ¹ -*work*; ~*ogravure′*, piece of poker-work; ~*ŏl′atry*, fire-worship; ~*olig′neous*, produced by action of fire or heat on wood, as ~*oligneous acid*; ~*omān′ia*, incendiary mania, so ~*omān′iac* n., ~*omani′acal* a.; ~*ŏm′eter*, instrument for measuring high temperatures, so ~*omet′ric(al)* aa., ~*omet′rically* adv., ~*ŏm′etry* n.; ~*ŏph′orus*, substance that takes fire spontaneously on exposure to air, so ~*ophŏ′ric*, ~*ŏph′orous*, aa.; ~*ophŏt′ograph*, one burnt in on glass or porcelain, so ~*ophotogrăph′ic* a., ~*ophotŏg′raphy* n. Also in scientific wds denoting (chem.) new substance formed from another by destructive distillation etc., (min.) minerals etc. showing some property or change under action of heat, or having fiery red or yellow colour.

pўr′ope, n. A deep-red garnet. [ME, f. OF *pirope* f. L f. Gk *purōpos* gold-bronze, lit. fiery-eyed (*pur* fire + *ōps* eye)]

pўrōs′is, n. (med.). Burning sensation in the stomach with eructation of watery fluid, water-brash. [mod. L f. Gk *purōsis* f. *pur* fire]

pўrotech′n|ic (-tĕk-), a. & n. 1. Of (the nature of) fireworks, as ~*ic display*; (fig., of wit etc.) brilliant, sensational. 2. n. pl. Art of making, display of, fireworks (lit. & fig.). Hence or cogn. ~ɪᴄᴀʟ a., ~ɪᴄᴀʟʏ² adv., ~ɪsᴛ, **pўr′otechny**¹, nn., (-tĕk-). [f. ᴘʏʀᴏ- + Gk *tekhnikos* (*tekhnē* art, see -ɪᴄ)]

pўr′ŏxĕne, n. (Kinds of) mineral composed mainly of the silicates of calcium and magnesium, a common component of igneous rocks. [f. ᴘʏʀᴏ- + Gk *xenos* stranger (because supposed alien to igneous rocks)]

pўrŏx′ўlin, n. Nitrates of cellulose, esp.

the explosive, gun-cotton, or the lower nitrate which when dissolved in ether & alcohol forms collodion & serves as the basis of varnishes, artificial leather, etc. [f. F (-*ine*) f. PYRO- + Gk *xulon* wood + -IN]

Pȳ′rrhic[1] (-rĭk), p-, n. & a. **1.** ~ (*dance*), war dance of ancient Greeks. **2.** The metrical foot ⌣ ⌣ ; (adj.) consisting of such feet. [(1) f. L or Gk *purrhikhḗ*, said to be named from one *Purrhikhos*, the inventor; (2) f. L f. Gk *purrhikhios* (*pous*) pyrrhic foot]

Pȳ′rrhic[2] (-rĭk), a. ~ *victory* (gained at too great cost, like that of Pyrrhus king of Epirus over the Romans at Asculum in 279 B.C.). [f. Gk *purrhikos* (*Purrhos* Pyrrhus, see -IC)]

Pȳ′rrhon|ism (-ro-), n. Sceptic philosophy of Pyrrho of Elis (c. 300 B.C.), doctrine that certainty of knowledge is unattainable; scepticism, philosophic doubt. Hence or cogn. **Pȳrrhon′IAN** (-rō-), **Pȳrrhon′IC** (-rō-), aa. & nn., ~IST (-ro-) n. [f. Gk *Purrhōn* Pyrrho + -ISM]

Pȳr′us, n. Genus of rosaceous trees & shrubs including pear & apple, esp. ~ *japonica*, scarlet or crimson ~. [med. & mod. L erron. sp. of L *pirus* pear-tree]

Pȳthăgore′an, a. & n. (Follower) of Pythagoras, philosopher of Samos (6th c. B.C.) said to have believed in transmigration of souls; ~ *proposition*, Euclid I. 47. [f. L f. Gk *Puthagoreios* + -AN]

Pȳth′ian (-dh-), a. & n. Of (Apollo's oracle & priestess at) Delphi; the ~, Apollo, his priestess at Delphi. [f. L f. Gk *Puthios* (*Puthō*, older name of Delphi) + -AN]

pȳth′on[1], n. (Gk myth.) huge serpent or monster slain near Delphi by Apollo; large snake that crushes its prey. So **pȳthŏn′ic**[1] [-IC] a. [f. L f. Gk *Puthōn*]

pȳth′on[2], n. Familiar spirit; person possessed by this. Hence or cogn. ~ESS[1] n., **pȳthŏn′ic**[2] [-IC] a. [f. LL *pytho* or late Gk *puthōn*]

pȳx, n., & v.t. **1.** (eccl.). Vessel in which consecrated bread is kept. **2.** ‖ Box at Royal Mint in which specimen gold & silver coins are deposited to be tested at the annual *trial of the* ~ by jury of Goldsmiths' Company; ‖ (v.t.) deposit (coin) in ~, test (coin) by weight & assay. [ME, f. L PYXIS]

pȳxid′ium, n. (bot.; pl. -*ia*). Capsule of which the top comes off like lid of box. [f. Gk *puxidion*, dim. as foll.]

pȳx′is, n. Small box, casket; = prec. [L, f. Gk *puxis* f. *puxos* box-tree]

Q

Q (kū), letter (pl. *Q*s, Q's). (Skating) change of edge followed by turn (*reverse Q*, turn followed by change of edge); *mind* one's *P*s & *Q*s, see P; *Q-boat, Q-ship,* = MYSTERY[1]-*ship*; *Q department*, that of Q.M.G.

quā, conj. As, in the capacity of, (*objects to the Church not* ~ *Church, but* ~ *Establishment*). [L, abl. fem. sing. of *qui* rel. pron.]

quăck[1], v.i., & n. (Utter) harsh sound made by ducks; talk loudly & foolishly; ~-~ (nursery), duck. [imit.; cf. Du. *kwakken*, G *quacken* croak, quack]

quăck[2], n., & v.i. & t. **1.** Ignorant pretender to skill esp. in medicine or surgery, one who offers wonderful remedies or devices, charlatan, (often attrib., as ~ *doctor, remedies*); hence ~′ERY(4) n., ~′ISH[1] a. **2.** vb. Play the ~; talk pretentiously; puff or advertise (cure etc.). [abbr. of foll.]

quăck′sălver, n. (Orig. form, now rare, of) QUACK[2] n. [Du. (QUACK[1], SALVE, -ER[1])]

quad (kwŏd), n. See QUADRANGLE, QUADRAT, QUADRUPLET.

qua′drable (-ŏd-), a. (math.). Capable of being represented by an equivalent square or expressed in finite number of algebraic terms. [as QUADRATE[2], -ABLE]

quadragênār′ian (-ŏd-), a. & n. (Person) forty years old. [f. L *quadragenarius* (*quadrageni* distrib. of *quadraginta* forty, -ARY[1])]

Quadragĕs′ima (-ŏd-), n. (Also ~ *Sunday*) first Sunday in Lent. [LL (Lent, first Sunday in Lent), fem. of L -*us* fortieth (*quadraginta* forty)]

quadragĕs′imal (-ŏd-), a. Lasting forty days (of fast, esp. Lent); Lenten. [f. med. L *quadragesimalis* (prec., -AL)]

quadrangle (kwŏd′rănggl), n. Four-sided figure, esp. square or rectangle; so **quadrăng′ūlAR**[1] a., **quadrăng′ūlar**LY[2] adv., (-ngg-); ‖ (also *quad*, pr. kwŏd) four-sided court (partly) enclosed by parts of large buildings, such court with buildings round it. [ME, f. OF f. LL *quadrangulum* square (QUADRI-, ANGLE)]

qua′drant (-ŏd-), n. Quarter of circle's circumference; plane figure enclosed by two radii of circle at right angles & arc cut off by them; quarter of sphere; thing, esp. graduated strip of metal, shaped like quarter-circle, instrument properly so shaped & graduated for taking angular measurements. Hence **quadrăn′tAL** a. [ME, f. L *quadrans* -*antis* (QUADRI-)]

qua′drat (-ŏd-), n. (Also *quad*, pr. kwŏd) small metal block used by printers in spacing (*em* ~, *en* ~, broader, narrower, size). [var. of foll.]

qua′drate[1] (-ŏd-), a. & n. **1.** Square, rectangular, (chiefly in anat. names, as ~ *bone* in birds' & reptiles' heads, ~ *muscle* in loins, thigh, forearm, etc.). **2.** n. Rectangular block or plate (rare); ~ bone or muscle. [ME, f. L *quadratus* (foll., -ATE[2])]

quadrāte′[2] (*or* kwŏ′-), v.t. & i. (rare). Make square (math.) square (circle etc.); correspond or conform (*with*, or abs. of pl. subj.); make conform *with* or *to* or abs. [f. L *quadrare* (QUADRI-, -ATE[3])]

quadrăt′ic, a. & n. **1.** Square (rare); (math.) involving second & no higher power of unknown quantity or variable (esp. ~ *equation*). 2. n. = equation; (pl.) branch of algebra dealing with these. [QUADRATE¹, -IC; perh. f. F *-ique*]

qua′drature (-ŏd-), n. (Math.) finding of square with area precisely equal to that of figure bounded by curve (esp. ~ *of the circle*); (astron.) one of two points in space or time at which moon is 90° from sun, position of heavenly body in relation to another 90° away. [f. F, or L *quadratura* (QUADRATE², -URE)]

quadrĕnn′ial, a. Occurring every, lasting, four years. [irreg. f. L *quadriennium* four-year period (foll., *annus* year), -AL]

qua′dri- (-ŏd-), (bef. a vowel *quadr*-; in a few wds *quadru*- bef. *p*), L comb. form = four-, in a few L words (*quadriduum* period of four days, *quadripartitus* ~-partite), & in many of later L & mod. formation, esp. in scientific use: ~**fĭd**, a., cleft into four divisions or lobes; ~**lăt′eral**, a. & n., four-sided (figure or area; *the Q~lateral*, four fortresses in N. Italy & district protected by them); ~**ling′ual** (-nggw-), a., using, in, four languages; **quadrill′ion** (kwadril′yon), n., ∥ fourth power of million (1 followed by 24 ciphers), *fifth power of a thousand (cf. BILLION); ~**nŏm′ial**, n., consisting of four algebraic terms; ~**pärt′ite**, a., consisting of four parts, shared by or involving four parties; ~**rēme**, n., ancient galley with four banks of oars; ~**sўllăb′ic**, a., four-syllabled; ~**sўll′able**, n., word of four syllables; **quadriv′alent** (kwa-), a. (chem.), capable of combining with four univalent atoms; **quadriv′ium** (kwa-), n. (hist.), medieval university course of arithmetic, geometry, astronomy, & music (cf. TRIVIUM).

qua′dric (-ŏd-), a. & n. (solid geom.). (Surface) of second degree. [as prec., -IC]

quadrig′a, n. (pl. *-ae*). Ancient chariot with four horses abreast. [L (QUADRI-, *jugum* yoke)]

quadrille′¹ (ka-, kwa-), n. Fashionable 18th-c. game for four persons with forty cards. [F, perh. f. Sp. *cuartillo* w. assim. to foll.]

quadrille′² (ka-, kwa-), n. Square dance for four couples & containing five figures (also *set of ~s*); piece of music for such dance. [F, f. Sp. *cuadrilla* (*cuadra* square) squadron, band]

quadroōn′, n. Offspring of white & mulatto, person of quarter-Negro blood; hybrid of similarly proportioned descent between other human, animal, or vegetable stocks. [f. Sp. *cuarteron* (*cuarto* fourth) w. assim. to QUADRI-]

quadru′manous (-rōō-), a. Four-handed, belonging to the order *Quadrumana* of mammals with opposable digit on all four limbs. [after foll. f. L *manus* hand]

qua′druped (-ŏdrōō-), n. & a. 1. Four-footed animal, esp. four-footed mammal; so **quadru′pĕdal** (-rōō-) a. 2. adj. Four-

-footed. [f. F *-pède*, or L *quadrupes -pedis* a. & n. (*quadru-* form of QUADRI- occas. used before p-, *pes* foot)]

qua′druple (-ŏdrōŏ-), a., n., & v.t. & i. 1. Fourfold, consisting of four parts or involving four parties, (~ *algebra*, using four independent units; ~ *rhythm* or *time*, with four beats to a measure; ~ *alliance* etc.); amounting to four times the amount or number *of*, equivalent to fourfold the amount of, superior by four times in amount or number *to*, (*has a light & heat* ~, or ~ *of* or *to*, *that of the earth*); hence **qua′drupLY²** (-ŏdrōŏ-) adv. 2. n. Number or amount four times greater than another (esp. *the* ~ *of*). 3. vb. Multiply (t. & i.) by four. [F, f. L *quadruplus* (prec., *-plus* as in *duplus* DOUBLE)]

qua′druplĕt (-ŏdrōŏ-), n. (Pl. four children at a birth (colloq. *quads*, pr. kwŏdz); four things working together; bicycle for four. [f. prec. after TRIPLET]

quadru′plicate¹ (-ōŏ-), a. & n. 1. Fourfold, four times repeated or copied. 2. n. *In* ~, in four exactly similar examples or copies; (pl.) four such copies. [f. L *quadruplicare* (*quadruplex* fourfold, cf. QUADRUPED, DUPLEX), -ATE²]

quadru′plic|āte² (-ōŏ-), v.t. Multiply by four; make four specimens of. Hence ~A′TION n. [as prec., -ATE³]

quadrupli′city (-ŏdrōŏ-), n. Fourfold nature, being fourfold. [as prec., -TY]

quaere (kwēr′ĭ), v.t. imperat., & n. (abbr. *qu.*). 1. Inquire (imperat.), it is a question, I should like to know, (*most interesting, no doubt; but* ~, *is it true?*). 2. n. A question, query. [L, imperat. of *quaerere* ask]

quaes′tor, n. Ancient-Roman official, state-treasurer, paymaster, etc.; treasurer. Hence or cogn. **quaestōr′ial** a., **quaes′torship** n. [L (*quaerere quaesit-* seek, -OR)]

quaff (-ah-), v.i. & t. Drink (t. & i.), drain (cup etc.), in copious or long draughts. [prob. imit.]

quăg, n. Marshy or boggy spot, quaking bog. Hence ~**g′y¹** (-g-) a. [rel. to dial. *quag* vb, prob. imit.; cf. *wag*, *swag*]

quăgg′a, n. S.-Afr. quadruped related to ass & zebra, less striped than latter; Burchell's zebra. [S.-Afr.]

quăg′mire, n. Quaking bog, fen, marsh, slough (lit. & fig.). [app. f. QUAG, MIRE]

*quahog′, -haug′ (kwahŏg), n. Edible round clam of Atlantic coast of N. America. [abbr. of Amer.-Ind. *poquauhock*]

∥ **quaich**, **quaigh** (kwāχ), n. (Sc.). Kind of drinking-cup, usu. of wood & having two handles. [f. Gael. *cuach* cup]

Quai d'Orsay′ (kādŏr-), n. (Used for) the French Foreign Office.

quail¹, n. Kinds of migratory bird allied to partridge esteemed as food; ~-*call*, ~-*pipe*, whistle with note like~'s for luring. Hence ~′ERY(3) n. [ME, f. OF *quaille* f. med. L *coacula* (imit.); cf. MDu., MLG *quackele*]

quail[2], v.i. & t. (Of person, or his heart, courage, spirit, or eyes) flinch, be cowed, give way *before* or *to*; (rare) cow, daunt. [ME *quayle*, of unkn. orig.]

quaint, a. Attractive or piquant in virtue of unfamiliar, esp. old-fashioned, appearance, ornamentation, manners, etc., daintily odd. Hence ~'LY[2] adv., ~'NESS n. [earlier senses *wise*, *cunning*; ME, f. OF *cointe* f. L *cognitus* p.p. of *cognoscere* learn]

quāk|e, v.i., & n. **1.** Shake, tremble, rock to & fro, (of earth with earthquake, person usu. *for* or *with* fear or cold, bog when trodden on, etc.); ~*ing-grass*, kinds with slender foot-stalks trembling in wind. **2.** n. Act of ~ing, (colloq.) earthquake. Hence ~'ing**LY**[3] adv., ~'Y[2] a. [OE *cwacian*]

quāk'er, n. **1.** (*Q*~). (Outsiders' name for) member of Society of Friends founded by George Fox 1648–50, & devoted to peace principles, plainness of dress (esp. the use of drab or grey), simplicity of speech (esp. the use of *thee* & avoidance of titles & words, such as the names of the days, suggestive of paganism), & peculiar priestless religious meetings. **2.** *Dummy gun in ship or fort. **3.** (Also ~*-bird*, *-moth*) kinds of plain-coloured bird & moth. **4.** ~, or ~*s*', *-meeting*, religious meeting of Friends, silent till some member is moved by the spirit, (transf.) silent meeting, company in which conversation flags. Hence ~DOM, ~ESS[1], ~ISM (3, 4), nn., ~ISH[1], ~LY[1], aa. [f. prec. + -ER[1]]

qualifica'tion (-ŏl-), n. **1.** Modification, recognition of contingency, restricting or limiting circumstance, detraction from completeness or absoluteness, (*statement with many* ~*s*; *hedged with* ~*s*; *requires* ~; *his delight had one* ~). **2.** Quality fitting person or thing (*for* post etc., or abs.); condition that must be fulfilled before right can be acquired or office held (*the* ~ *for citizenship may be a certain income*), document attesting such fulfilment. **3.** Attribution of quality (*the* ~ *of his policy as opportunist is unfair*). So **qua'lifica̅tory** (-ŏl-) a. [f. F, or med. L *qualificatio* (foll., -FICATION)]

qua'lify (-ŏl-), v.t. & i. **1.** Attribute some quality to, describe as, (~ *documents as heretical*, *person as a scoundrel*, *proposal as iniquitous*; *adjectives* ~ *nouns*). **2.** Invest or provide with the necessary qualities, make competent, fit, or legally entitled, (*for* be*ing* or do*ing*, *to* be or do, *for* post or sphere, or abs.; ~*ing examination*, to ascertain that candidates are not below a fixed standard, often followed by competitive; (intr.) fulfil some condition, esp. pass examination or take oath, to make oneself eligible (*for* office, or abs.). **3.** Modify (statement, opinion), make less absolute or sweeping, subject to reservations or limitation. **4.** Moderate, mitigate, make less complete or pleasing or un-

pleasing; diminish strength or flavour of (spirit etc. with water, also joc. water with spirit). [f. F *qualifier* or med. L *qualificare* (L *qualis* such as, -FY)]

qua'litative (-ŏl-; *or* -tā-), a. Concerned with, depending on, quality (opp. QUANTITATIVE; esp. ~ *analysis*). [f. LL *qualitativus* (foll., -ATIVE)]

qua'lit|y̆ (-ŏl-), n. **1.** Degree of excellence, relative nature or kind or character, (opp. QUANTITY; *of good*, *high*, *poor*, etc., ~*y*; *is made in three* ~*ies*; ~*y matters more than quantity*); general excellence (*has* ~*y*, is excellent). **2.** Faculty, skill, accomplishment, characteristic trait, mental or moral attribute, (*give a taste of* one's ~*y*, show what one can do; *has many good* ~*ies*, *the* DEFECTS *of his* ~*ies*, *the* ~*ies of a ruler*, *the* ~*y of inspiring confidence* or *of courage*, *the* ~*y of mercy*). **3.** (arch. or vulg.). High rank or social standing (*people of*, *the*, ~*y*, the upper classes). **4.** (log.). (Of proposition) being affirmative or negative. **5.** (Of sound, voice, etc.) distinctive character apart from pitch & loudness, timbre. [ME & OF *qualite* f. L *qualitatem* (*qualis* of what kind, -TY)]

qualm (-ahm, -awm), n. Momentary faint or sick feeling, queasiness; misgiving, sinking of heart; scruple of conscience, doubt of one's own rectitude in some matter. Hence ~'ISH[1] a. [16th c., of obsc. orig.; cf. G *qualm*, MLG *quallem*, Du., LG *kwalm* (G *qualm*) vapour, smoke]

quandar'y̆ (-ŏn-; *also* kwŏn'dari), n. A state of perplexity, difficult situation, practical dilemma, (*am in a* ~). [16th c., of unkn. orig.]

quand même (see Ap.), adv. Despite consequences, even so, all the same. [F]

‖ **quant** (kwŏnt), n., & v.t. & i. Punting-pole with prong to prevent its sinking in mud, used by E.-coast bargemen etc.; (vb) propel (boat), propel boat, with ~. [15th c., perh. f. L f. Gk *kontos* pole]

qua'ntic (-ŏn-), n. (math.). Rational integral homogeneous function of two or more variables. [f. L *quantus* how much, -IC]

qua'nti|fy̆ (-ŏn-), v.t. (Log.) define application of (term, proposition) by use of *all*, *some*, etc.; determine quantity of, measure, express as quantity. Hence ~**fIABLE** a., ~**fICA̅'TION** n. [f. med. L *quantificare* (prec., -FY)]

qua'ntitative (-ŏn-; *or* -tā-), a. Measured or measurable by, concerned with, quantity (opp. QUALITATIVE; esp. ~ *analysis*); of, based on, the quantity of syllables (~ *scansion*, *verse*, etc.). Hence ~**LY**[2] adv. [f. med. L *quantitativus* (QUANTITY, -ATIVE)]

qua'ntitive (-ŏn-), a. = prec. (rare). [foll., -IVE]

qua'ntit|y̆ (-ŏn-), n. **1.** The property of things that is estimable by some sort of measure, the having of size, extension, weight, amount, or number, (*mathematics is the science of pure* ~*y*; *stated in* *terms of ~y).* **2.** Amount, sum, *(the ~y of the current depends on the size of the plates).* **3.** Specified or considerable portion or number or amount of something, *the amount of something present, (a small ~y of blood; a ~y of baskets; buys in large ~ies; the ~y of heat in an animal body);* (pl.) large amounts or numbers, abundance, *(is found in ~ies on the shore).* **4.** Length or shortness of vowel sounds (see LONG¹; *~y-mark,* put over vowel to indicate ~y; FALSE *~y*). **5.** (log.). Extension given to subject of proposition. **6.** (math.). Thing having ~y, figure or symbol representing it, *(incommensurable ~ies have no aliquot parts; unknown ~y,* transf., person or thing whose action cannot be foreseen; *negligible ~y,* transf., person etc. that need not be reckoned with). **7.** ‖ BILL⁴ *of ~ies;* ‖*~y surveyor,* one whose business it is to prepare bills of ~ies, measure and price work done, etc. [ME & OF *quantite* f. L *quantitatem (quantus* how much, -TY)]

quantiv'alence (-ŏn-, -ăn-), n. (chem.). Extent to which one of element's atoms can hold other atoms in combination. [f. L *quantus* how much, after *equivalence* see EQUIVALENT]

qua'ntum (-ŏn-, *in* L *phrr.* -ăn-, -ŏn-), n. (pl. *-a,* rare). Amount; share, portion; required, desired, or allowed amount; ~ *lib'ĕt* or *plă'cĕt,* abbr. *q.l., q.p.,* as much as is desired (in prescriptions); ~ *sŭff'icit,* abbr. *quant. suff.,* or *q.s.,* as much as suffices (in prescriptions), (gen.) sufficient quantity, to sufficient extent; ~ *theory* (phys.), the hypothesis, accounting for the stability of the atom & other phenomena, that in radiation the energy of electrons is discharged not continuously but in discrete amounts or quanta. [L, neut. of *quantus* how much]

quăquavĕrs'al, a. (geol.). Pointing in every direction. [f. LL *quaquaversus (quaqua* wheresoever, *versus* towards)]

quarantine (kwŏ'răntēn), n., & v.t. **1.** (Period of) isolation imposed on voyagers, travellers, sick persons, or infected ship, that might spread contagious disease. **2.** v.t. Impose such isolation on, put in ~. [prob. f. It. *quarantina* forty days f. *quaranta* forty]

quār'ĕ im'pĕdĭt, n. Writ issued in cases of disputed presentation to benefice against objector. [L, = why does he hinder?]

‖ **qua'renden, -der,** (kwŏ-), n. Kind of Devonshire & Somerset apple. [15th c., of unkn. orig.]

qua'rrel¹ (kwŏ-), n. (hist.). Short heavy arrow or bolt used in crossbow or arbalest. [ME, f. OF *quarel,* f. Rom. **quadrellus* dim. of *quadrus* square (L *-um*)]

qua'rrel² (kwŏ-), n. **1.** Occasion of complaint against person or his actions *(have no ~ against* or *with him; find ~ in a straw,* be captious; *pick a ~,* invent or eagerly avail oneself of such occasion to commence hostilities; *espouse* one's ~, *fight* one's*~s for him,* assist him in getting redress; *in a good ~,* justly taken up). **2.** Violent contention or altercation between persons, rupture of friendly relations. Hence ~SOME a., ~SOMELY² adv., ~SOMENESS n. [ME, f. OF *querele* f. L *querela* complaint *(queri* complain)]

qua'rrel³ (kwŏ-), v.i. (-ll-). Take exception, find fault *with (I never ~ with Providence; ~ with* one's *bread & butter,* abandon employment by which one lives); contend violently *(with* person, *about* or *for* thing), fall out, have dispute, break off friendly relations. [ME, f. prec.]

qua'rry¹ (kwŏ-), n. Object of pursuit by bird of prey, hounds, hunters, etc.; intended victim or prey. [ME, f. OF *cuiree (cuir* skin f. L *corium,* -Y⁴), orig. sense, parts of deer placed on hide & given to hounds]

qua'rry² (kwŏ-), n., & v.t. & i. **1.** Excavation made by taking stone for building etc. from its bed; place whence stone, or fig. information etc., may be extracted; floor-tile; *~man,* worker in ~. **2.** vb. Extract (stone) from ~; extract (facts etc.) laboriously from books etc.; expend toil in searching documents etc. *(~ing in the Harleian MSS.).* [ME, f. med. L *quareia* etc. f. OF *quarriere* f. **carre* f. L *quadrum* square]

qua'rry³ (kwŏ-), n. Diamond-shaped pane of glass as used in lattice-windows. [later form of QUARREL¹]

quart¹ (kwŏrt), n. Measure of capacity, quarter of gallon or two pints *(put ~ into pint pot,* make less contain greater); pot or bottle containing this amount *(~ bottle* of wine or spirit, ⅓ gal.); (abs. for) ~ of beer *(still takes his~); ~-pot.* [ME, f. OF *quarte* f. fem. of L *quartus* fourth]

quart² (kûrt), n., & v.i. & t. **1.** A position in fencing, CARTE, *(~ & tierce,* fencing-practice); sequence of four cards in piquet etc. *(~ major,* ace, king, queen, knave). **2.** vb. Use the position ~; draw back (head etc.) in this. [f. F *quarte* f. fem. L as prec.]

quar'tan (kwôr-), a. & n. (Ague or fever) with paroxysm every third (by inclusive reckoning fourth) day. [ME & OF *quartaine* f. L *(febris) quartana (quartus* fourth, -AN)]

quartā'tion (kwôr-), n. Combining of three parts of silver with one of gold as preliminary in purifying gold. [L *quartus* fourth, -ATION]

quarte (kârt). Var. of QUART² (see etym.)

quar'ter¹ (kwôr-), n. **1.** Fourth part, one of four equal or corresponding parts, fourth part of, *(divide the apples into ~s; ~ of a century,* any period of 25 years; *second* etc. ~ *of the century,* 26th to 50th etc. years of it; *~ of an hour,* any consecutive 15 minutes; *bad ~ of an hour,* short unpleasant experience; *can get it at* the stores for a ~ the or of the, or for ~ the, price; is not a ~ as good as it should be; ~ mile, yard, etc., ~ of a mile etc.). **2.** (U.S., Can.). 25 cents or ~ dollar, as amount or coin. **3.** One of four parts, each including leg or arm, into which beast's or bird's carcass is divided (of beast, often fore, hind, ~); (pl.) similar parts of traitor quartered after execution; (usu. in pl., often hind-~s) haunch(es) of living animal or man. **4.** Either side of ship aft of main-chains (on the ~, between astern & on beam). **5.** (her.). One of four divisions of quartered shield (dexter & sinister chief, dexter & sinister base); charge occupying ~ placed in chief. **6.** ‖ Grain-measure of eight bushels, used in stating large quantities, prices, etc.; (abbr. qr) fourth of cwt, 28 lb. **7.** Fourth of fathom (& a ~ five, 5¼ fathoms; a ~ less five, 4¾). **8.** Fourth of year for which payments become due on ~-day; instalment of allowance etc. for the ~; school term. **9.** Fourth of lunar period; moon's position between first & second or third & fourth of these. **10.** Point of time 15′ before or after any hour o'clock (at a ~ to, past, six; it is not the ~ yet, strikes the hours, half-hours, & ~s; it has gone the ~, clock has sounded for it). **11.** ‖ (Channel I.). Unit of property or income, reckoned as £25, for assessment of taxes etc. **12.** (Region lying about) point of compass, direction, district, locality, source of supply or help in information, (wind blows from all four ~s at once; what ~ is the wind in? lit., & fig. how are things going? etc.; flocked in from all ~s; no help to be looked for in that ~; had the news from a good ~). **13.** Division of town, esp. one appropriated to or occupied by special class (the Jewish, manufacturing, residential, etc., ~). **14.** pl. Lodgings, abode, esp. place where troops are lodged or stationed (HEAD-~s; winter ~s, occupied, esp. by troops, for winter; take up one's ~s, lodge in, with, etc.; BEAT¹ up ~s of; beat to ~s, naut., summon crew to appointed stations as for action; at CLOSE¹ ~s). **15.** Exemption from death offered or granted to enemy in battle who will surrender (give, receive, ~; ask for or cry ~; no ~ to be given). **16.** ~-mile race or running-distance (won the ~; has done the ~ in 50″). **17.** ~-bell, sounding the ~-hours; ~ binding of book, with narrow leather at back & none at corners, so ~-bound a.; ~-butt in billiards, cue shorter than half-butt; ‖ ~-day, on which quarterly payments are due, tenancies begin & end, etc. (Lady Day 25 Mar., Midsummer Day 24 June, Michaelmas 29 Sep., & Christmas 25 Dec.; in Scotland, Candlemas 2 Feb., Whitsunday 15 May, Lammas 1 Aug., Martinmas 11 Nov.); ~-deck, part of upper deck between stern & after-mast, the officers (cf. LOW¹er deck) of ship or navy; ~-ill,

cattle & sheep disease causing putrefaction in one or more of the ~s; ~ left, right, (mil.), ~ of a right angle to left, right; ~-light, window in body of closed carriage apart from door-window; ~-line (naut.), disposition in which bow of each ship is abaft beam of one in front; ~-master, (naut.) petty officer or rating in charge of steering, binnacle, signals, hold-stowing, etc., (mil., abbr. Q.M.) regimental officer with duties of assigning ~s, laying out camp, & looking after rations, clothing, etc. (Q~master-General, abbr. Q.M.G., military member of the Army Council and head of department controlling quartering, equipment, etc.); ~-miler, runner whose distance is the ~; ~-plate, photographic plate 3¼ in. × 4¼, photograph produced from it; ‖ ~ sessions, court of limited criminal & civil jurisdiction & of appeal held quarterly by justices of peace in counties & by recorder in cities and boroughs; ~-staff, stout pole 6–8 ft long formerly used by peasantry as weapon; ~-tone (mus.), half a semitone; ~-wind, blowing on ship's ~ (most favourable sailing wind). [ME, f. AF quarter, OF -ier, f. L quartarius fourth part (of a measure) f. quartus fourth, see -ER³(2)]

quar'ter² (kwôr-), v.t. **1.** Divide into four equal parts, divide (traitor's body) into quarters. **2.** (her.). Place or bear (charges or coats of arms) quarterly on shield; add (another's coat) to one's hereditary arms; place in alternate quarters with; divide (shield) into quarters or into divisions formed by vertical & horizontal lines. **3.** Put (esp. soldiers) into quarters, station or lodge in specified place. **4.** (Of dogs) range or traverse (ground) in every direction. [ME, f. prec.]

quar'terage (-ŏr-), n. Quarterly payment, a quarter's wages, allowance, pension, etc. [-AGE]

quar'tering (-ŏr-), n. In vbl senses; esp. (her., pl.) coats marshalled on shield to denote alliances of family with heiresses of others; square lengths of timber made by sawing planks into four lengths. [-ING¹]

quar'terlÿ (-ŏr-), a., n., & adv. **1.** Occurring every quarter of a year. **2.** n. ~ review or magazine. **3.** adv. Once every quarter of a year; (her.) in the four, or in two diagonally opposite, quarters of shield (~-quartered, with one or more quarters divided in four). [-LY¹,²]

‖ **quar'tern** (-ŏrt-), n. (Also ~-loaf) four-pound loaf. [f. AF quartrun, OF quart(e)ron, f. quart(e) fourth]

quartĕt(te)' (-ŏr-), n. Musical composition for four voices or instruments, players or singers rendering this (piano ~, 3 stringed instruments with piano); set of four. [F (-te), f. It. quarietto (quarto fourth f. L quartus) -ET¹]

quar'tile (-ŏr-), a. & n. (astrol.). **1.** Connected with or relating to an aspect of two heavenly bodies which are 90° distant from each other. **2.** in. A ~ aspect. [f. med. L *quartilis* f. L *quartus* fourth]

quar′tŏ (-ôr-), n. (also written 4to, 4°; pl. ~s). Size given by folding sheet of paper twice; book consisting of sheets so folded; ~ *paper*, so folded. [L (*in*) *quarto* (in) fourth (of sheet); abl. of *quartus* fourth]

|| **quar′tus** (-ôr-). See PRIMUS[1].

quartz (-ôr-), n. Kinds of mineral, massive or crystallizing in hexagonal prisms, consisting in pure form of silica or silicon dioxide, & occas. containing gold. [f. G *quarz*, of unkn. orig.]

quash (kwŏsh), v.t. Annul, make void, reject as not valid, put an end to, (esp. by legal procedure or authority). [ME, f. OF *quasser* (now *casser*) f. L *quassare*]

Qua′shee (kwŏ-), n. Negro (as national nickname). [f. Ashantee or Fantee *Kwasi* common personal name]

quãs′ĭ, conj. & pref. **1.** (Introducing etymological explanation, abbr. *qu.*) that is to say, as if it were, (*Earls of Wilbraham*, ~ *Wild boar ham*). **2.** (Hyphened esp. to noun or adj.) seeming(ly), not real(ly), practical(ly), half-, almost, (*engaged in a ~-war*; *the ~-art of making enemies*; *has a ~-episcopal position*). [L, = as if]

quãss′ia (*or* -ãsh′a, -ŏsh′a), n. S.-Amer., esp. Surinam, tree; (wood, bark, or root of this & other trees, yielding) bitter medicinal decoction. [f. name of Negro (cf. QUASHEE) who discovered its virtues 1730]

quăt′ercĕntĕn′arӯ, n. Four-hundredth anniversary. [L *quater* four times]

quatėr′narӯ, a. & n. **1.** Having four parts, esp. compounded of four chemical elements or radicals; concerned with the number four; (geol.) (*Q*~) belonging to most recent period, subsequent to Tertiary. **2.** n. Set of four things; the number four; *the Pythagorean* ~, 1 + 2 + 3 + 4 = 10, with mystic significance in Pythagoreanism. [ME, f. L *quaternarius* (*quaterni* distrib. of *quatuor* four, -ARY[1])]

quatėr′nion, n. Set of four; quire of four sheets folded in two; Pythagorean quaternary, mystic number 4 or 10 (see prec.); (math.) quotient of two vectors or operator that changes one vector into another (named as depending on four geometrical elements), (pl.) form of calculus of vectors in which this operator is used. [ME, f. LL *quaternio* (prec.)]

quatėr′nitӯ, n. Being four; set of four persons (esp. of the Godhead in contrast to *Trinity*). [f. LL *quaternitas*]

quatorzain (kăt′erzān), n. Fourteen-line poem, irregular sonnet. [f. F *quatorzaine* (*quatorze* fourteen f. L *quatuordecim*)]

quatrain (kwŏt′rĭn), n. Stanza of four lines occas. with alternate rhymes. [F (*quatre* four f. L *quatuor*)]

quatre (kăt′er), n. = CATER[1].

quat′refoil (kătre-, kăter-), n. Four-cusped figure, esp. as opening in archi-tectural tracery, resembling symmetrical four-lobed leaf or flower. [ME, f. AF *quatrefoil* (*quatre* four, FOIL[1])]

quattrocĕn′tĭst (-ahtrŏch-), n. & a. (Artist etc.) of the quattrocento. [-IST]

quattrocĕn′tŏ (-ahtrŏch-), n. Fifteenth century as period in Italian art. [It., lit. 400, but used = 1400]

quāv′er¹, v.i. & t. Vibrate, shake, tremble, (esp. of voice or musical sound); use trills in singing; sing (note, song) with trills, say (usu. *out*) in trembling tones. Hence ~**ĭnglӯ²** adv. [15th c., f. ME (obs.) *quave* + -ER[5]; orig. imit., cf. QUIVER²]

quāv′er², n. Trill in singing; tremulous-ness in speech, whence ~**Y¹** a.; || (mus.) note equal in length to half crotchet. [f. prec.]

quay (kē), n. Solid stationary artificial landing-place usu. of stone or iron lying alongside or projecting into water for (un)loading ships. Hence ~**AGE**(1, 4) (kē′ĭj) n. [ME *key(e)*, *kay* f. OF *kay* f. Gaulish **kagio, *kajo*]

quean, n. (arch.). Impudent or ill-behaved girl, jade, hussy. [OE *cwene*, OS, OHG *quena*, ON *kvenna*, Goth. *qino* woman f. Gmc **kwenōn* cogn. w. QUEEN]

queas′ӯ (-z-), a. (Of food) unsettling the stomach, causing or tending to sickness, fulsome; (of person, his stomach, or his conscience) easily upset, weak of diges-tion, over scrupulous or tender or delicate, in fastidious condition. Hence ~**ĭNESS** n. [15th c. *coisy*, of obsc. orig.; cf. OF *coisier* hurt]

quebra′chŏ (kābrah-), n. (Kinds of) American tree yielding very hard timber and medicinal bark; bark of this tree. [Sp., = axe-breaker]

queen¹, n. **1.** King's wife (also ~ *consort* for distinction from next sense; ~ *dowager*, wife of late king; ~ *mother*, ~ *dowager* who is mother of sovereign, & see next sense; also prefixed as title, as *Q*~ *Elizabeth*). **2.** Female sovereign of king-dom (~*mother*, ~ having child or children; also prefixed as title, as *Q*~ *Victoria*; *Q*~ *Anne is dead*, retort to stale news; *Q*~ *Anne's* BOUNTY; *Q*~*-Anne*, in the archi-tectural or decorative style of *Q*~ *Anne's* time; *Q*~ *of Scots*, Mary Stuart). **3.** Wor-shipped female, e.g. the Virgin Mary (*Q*~ *of grace* etc.); ancient goddess (*Q*~ *of heaven*, Juno, *of love*, Venus, *of night*, Diana, etc.); person's sweetheart or wife or mistress; majestic woman; belle, mock sovereign, on some occasion (*Q*~ *of the* MAY[3] etc.). **4.** Personified best example of anything that can be regarded as fem. (*the* ~ *of watering-places, roses, nurses*). **5.** Person, country, etc., regarded as ruling over some sphere (~ *of hearts*, any beautiful woman; ~ *of the Adriatic*, Venice; ~ *of the seas*, Gt Britain; ~ *of the meadows*, meadowsweet). **6.** (Also ~ *bee, wasp, ant*) perfect female of bee etc. **7.** Piece in chess (~*'s bishop, knight*, pawn, etc., those placed nearest ~ at start; ~'s GAMBIT; 8. One of court-cards in each suit. 9. ~-*cake*, small soft currant cake often heart-shaped; ~-*posts*, two upright timbers between the-beam & principal rafters of roof-truss; ‖ Q~'s BENCH, BOUNTY; ‖ Q~'s COLOUR¹, COUNSEL¹, ENGLISH¹, EVIDENCE, HEAD¹; ~'s *pin-cushion*, flower of guelder rose; ‖~'s SHILLING; ~-*stitch*, fancy stitch in embroidery; ~'s-*ware*, cream-coloured Wedgwood; ‖~'s *weather*, sunshine. Hence ~'DOM, ~'HOOD, ~'SHIP, nn., ~'LESS, ~'LIKE, aa. [OE *cwēn*, OS *quān*, ON *kvæn*, *kván*, Goth. *qēns* wife f. Gmc *kwæniz* cogn. w. QUEAN]

queen², v.t. & i. Make (woman) queen; ~ *it*, play the queen; (chess) advance (pawn) to opponent's end of board & have it converted to queen or other piece, (intr., of pawn) be converted thus. [f. prec.]

‖ **queen'ing**, n. Kind of apple. [-ING³]

queen'l|y̆, a. Fit for, appropriate to, queen; majestic, queenlike. Hence ~ʹNESS n. [-LY¹]

Queens'berr|y̆ (-z-), n. ~ *Rules*, standard rules of boxing drawn up by 8th Marquis of ~ in 1867.

queer, a., n., & v.t. 1. Strange, odd, eccentric; of questionable character, shady, suspect; homosexual (also as n.); out of sorts, giddy, faint, (esp. *feel* ~); ‖ (sl.) drunk; in *Q~ Street* (sl.), in a difficulty, in debt or trouble or disrepute; hence ~'ISH¹ a., ~'LY² adv., ~'NESS n. 2. v.t. (sl.). Spoil, put out of order, (‖ esp. ~ *the pitch for* one, spoil his chance beforehand; *make feel* ~. [(1) orig. unkn.; (2) thieves' cant, orig. unkn.]

quĕll, v.t. (poet. & rhet.). Suppress, forcibly put an end to, crush, overcome, reduce to submission, (fear, opposition, rebellion, rebels, etc.). Hence (-)~'ER¹ n. [OE *cwellan* kill, OS *quellian*, OHG *quellen*, ON *kvelja* f. Gmc *kwaljan*]

quĕnch, v.t. Extinguish (fire, light, eyesight; chiefly poet. or rhet.); ~ *smoking flax*, cut short promising development (see *Is.* xlii. 3); cool, esp. with water (heat, heated thing; poet. or rhet.); stifle, suppress, (desire, speed, motion; poet. or rhet.); slake (thirst); (sl.) reduce to silence, shut up, (opponent); cool (hot metal) in water. Hence ~'ABLE, ~'LESS, aa. [ME, f. OE -*cwencan* causative f. -*cwincan* (= Fris. *kwinka*) be extinguished]

quĕn'cher, n. In vbl senses; esp. (sl.) something to drink (usu. *a modest* ~). [-ER¹]

quenĕlle' (ke-), n. Seasoned ball of fish or meat reduced to paste. [F, orig. unkn.]

quĕr'ist, n. Person who asks question. [f. L *quaerere* ask, -IST]

quĕrn, n. Hand-mill for grinding corn; small hand-mill for pepper etc.; ~-*stone*, millstone. [OE *cweorn*, OS *quern*, OHG *quirn*, ON *kvern*, Goth. -*qairnus*]

quĕr'ulous (-rōō-), a. Complaining, peevish. Hence ~'LY² adv., ~'NESS n. [f. LL *querulosus* (L *querulus*, f. *queri* complain, -OSE¹)]

quĕr'y̆, n., & v.t. & i. 1. (Used abs. to introduce question; abbr. *qu.*) pray, one would like to know, (Q~, or *qu.*, *was the money ever paid?*). 2. A question, esp. of the nature of objection (*was prepared to suppress all queries*); mark of interrogation or the word ~ or *qu.* written against statement, or the word ~ interjected in speech, to question accuracy. 3. vb. Ask, inquire, (*whether, if,* etc.); put a question; call (thing) in question in speech or writing, question accuracy of. [17th c., anglicized form of QUAERE]

quĕst¹, n. 1. ‖ Official inquiry or jury etc. making it (now only in vulg. *crowner's* ~, coroner's inquest). 2. Seeking or thing sought by inquiry or search, esp. object of medieval knight's pursuit (*in* ~ *of*, seeking). [ME, f. OF *queste* f. Rom. *quæsita* p.p. of L *quaerere* seek]

quĕst², v.i. & t. (Of dogs etc.) search for game (often *about*); go (*about*) in search of something; (poet.) search for, seek *out*. [ME, f. OF *quester* (prec.)]

ques'tion¹ (-chon), n. 1. Sentence adapted by order of words, use of interrogative pronoun or stop, or other means, to elicit answer, interrogative sentence, (*put a* ~ *to* one, ask him something; ~ *& answer*, alternation of ~s & answers, catechetic procedure; LEADING³, RHETORICAL, ~; *indirect, oblique*, ~, made into dependent clause; ~-*mark* or -*stop*, mark of interrogation). 2. (Raising of) doubt about or objection to thing's truth, credibility, advisability, etc. (*allowed it without* ~; *beyond all* or *beyond, out of, past, without,* ~, certainly, undoubtedly; *call in* ~, raise objections to; *make no* ~ *of* fact etc., but *that it is* so etc., admit it; *there is no* ~ *but that* . . .), whence ~'LESS (-cho-) adv. & a. 3. Problem requiring solution, matter or concern depending on conditions of, (*a difficult* ~; BEG the ~; *success is merely a* ~ *of time*, will certainly come, but may come sooner or later; *it is only a* ~ *of putting enough coffee in*). 4. Subject being discussed or for discussion, thing to be voted on, (*the person in*~, that we are referring to; *come into* ~, be discussed, become of practical importance; *that is not the* ~, is irrelevant; *the* ~ *is*, introducing or recalling exact matter of debate; Q~ ! in public assemblies, used to recall speaker from digression; *the* PREVIOUS ~; *out of the* ~, too impracticable to be worth discussing; *put the* ~, require supporters & opponents of proposal to record their votes, divide meeting etc.; OPEN ~). 5. (arch.). Torture to elicit confession (*was put to the* ~). [ME, f. OF f. L *quaestionem* (*quaerere* seek, -TION)]

ques'tion² (-chon), v.t. Ask questions of, interrogate, subject to examination, (person); seek information from study of (phenomena, facts); call in question, throw doubt upon, raise objections to, (~ *the honesty, accuracy, fitness,* etc., *of*; *it cannot be* ~ed *but that* or *but,* it is certain that), whence ~ABLE a. (esp., doubtfully true, not clearly consistent with honesty or honour or wisdom), ~abLY² adv. (-cho-). Hence~ingLY² (-cho-) adv. [ME, f. OF *questionner* (prec.)]

questionnaire' (kěstǐŏ-, kwěscho-), **quěs'-tionary** (rare; -cho-), n. Formulated series of questions, an interrogatory. [(-aire F) f. med. L *questionarium,* see QUESTION, -ARY¹]

quět'zal, n. Beautiful Central-Amer. bird. [Sp., f. Aztec *quetzalli* the bird's tail-feather]

queue (kū), n., & v.t. & i. **1.** Hanging plaited tail of hair or wig, pigtail; line of persons, vehicles, etc., awaiting their turn to be attended to or proceed. **2.** vb. Dress (hair) in ~; (of persons etc.) form *up* in, join *on* to, a~. [F, f. L *cauda* tail)]

quib'ble, n., & v.i. **1.** Play on words, pun; equivocation, evasion, unsubstantial or purely verbal argument etc. esp. one depending on ambiguity of word. **2.** v.i. Use ~s; hence **quibb'lER¹** n., **quibb'lING²** a. [perh. dim. of obs. *quib* f. L *quibus* abl. pl. of *qui* who (familiar f. use in legal documents)]

quick, a., n., & adv. **1.** Living, alive, (arch.; esp. *the* ~ *& the dead, go down* ~ *into hell;* ~ *with child,* orig. *with* ~ *child,* at stage of pregnancy when motion has been felt). **2.** Vigorous, lively, ready, sensitive, prompt to act, perceive, be affected, learn, think, or invent, (*a* ~ *child,* intelligent; ~ *temper,* easily irritated, whence ~temperED² a.; ~ *sight,* acute or alert, whence ~sightED² a.; *has a* ~ *eye, ear,* etc., whence ~-eyED², ~-earED², aa.; *is* ~ *to take offence; has* ~ *wits,* is ready at grasping situation, making repartees, etc., whence ~wittED² a.; N.B. these compounds have ~ stressed when attrib., unstressed when pred.). **3.** Moving rapidly, rapid, swift, done in short time or with little interval, (~ *succession; at a* ~ *trot; a* ~ *way of doing it; his* ~ *growth; a* ~ *one, a* ~ *drink; be* ~, make haste; *did a* ~ *mile; was followed by* ~ *vengeance*), whence ~LY² adv. **4.** ~-*change,* (of actor etc.) ~ly changing costume or appearance to play another part; ~'LIME¹; ~ *march* (mil.), march in ~ time (see below; esp. as word of command for starting at usual pace); ~*'sand,* (bed of) loose wet sand readily swallowing up ships, animals, etc.; ~*'set,* (adj., of hedge) formed of living plants esp. hawthorn, (n.) live slips of plants esp. hawthorn set in ground to grow, hedge formed of these; ~*'silver,* (n.) mercury, (fig.) mobility of temperament or mood, (v.t.) coat (mirror-glass) with amalgam of

tin; ~ *step,* step used in ~ *time* (mil.), rate of marching reckoned at 128 paces of 33 in. to the minute or four miles an hour, the usual British-army rate; ~*'step* (dancing), a fast foxtrot. **5.** n. Tender or sensitive flesh below skin or esp. nails, tender part of wound or sore where healthy tissue begins, seat of feeling or emotion, (*bites his nails to the* ~; *probed it to the* ~; *the insult stung him to the* ~; *is a Tory to the* ~, through & through); = ~*set* a. & n. **6.** adv. (~*er,* ~*est,* always after vb). At rapid rate, in comparatively short time, (*ran as* ~ *as I could; who will be there* ~*est?*); (ellipt. for imperat. of *go, come, be,* ~) make haste; ~-(prefixed to partt. esp. in -*ing*)-ly, soon, (~-*fading,* -*forgotten,* etc.; ~*-firing gun,* or ~-**fir'ER¹** n., gun with special mechanism for firing shots in ~ succession); ~*-freeze,* freeze (food) rapidly so as to preserve its natural qualities (also as n. & attrib.). [OE *cwicu,* OS *quik,* OHG *quec,* ON *kvikr,* f. Gmc **kwikwaz* f. **kwiw-,* cogn. w. Goth. *qius,* L *vivus*]

quick'en, v.t. & i. Give or restore natural or spiritual life or vigour to, animate, stimulate, rouse, inspire, kindle, whence ~ING² a.; receive, come to, life; (of woman or embryo) reach QUICK stage in pregnancy; accelerate, make or (of pace, motion, etc.) become quicker. [-EN⁶]

quick'ie, n. (colloq.). Cheap film made to satisfy the Films Quota Act. [QUICK, -Y³]

quick'ness, n. Readiness or acuteness of perception or apprehension; speed, rapidity, suddenness, (rare; esp. of single gesture or motion); hastiness *of temper.* [-NESS]

quicun'què vult, n. *The*~, the Athanasian creed. [initial L wds, = whosoever will]

|| **quid¹,** n. (sl.; pl. ~). A sovereign, £1, (*at two* ~ *a week*). [17th c., of unkn. orig.]

quid², n. Lump of tobacco held in mouth & chewed. [var. of CUD]

quidd'ity, n. Essence of a thing, what makes a thing what it is; quibble, captious subtlety. [f. med. L *quidditas* (L *quid* what, -ITY)]

quid'nunc, n. Newsmonger, person given to gossip. [f. L *quid* what, *nunc* now]

quid pro quo, n. Blunder made by using or putting one thing for another (now rare); compensation, return made, consideration, (*must get, must find him, a* ~). [f. L *quid* something *pro quo* something]

quies'cent, a. Motionless, inert, silent, dormant. Hence or cogn. ~ENCE, ~ENCY, nn., ~entLY² adv. [f. L *quiescere* (*quies* QUIET¹, -ESCENT)]

qui'et¹, n. Undisturbed political condition, public tranquillity; silence, stillness; being free from disturbance or agitation or urgent tasks, rest, repose, peace of mind; unruffled deportment, calm. [ME, f. AF *quiete* f. OF *quiet* (as foll.)]

qui'et², a. (~*er,* ~*est*). With no or slight or gentle sound or motion; of gentle or

quiet inactive disposition; (of colour, dress, etc.) unobtrusive, not showy; not overt, private, disguised, (~ *resentment*; *had a* ~ *dig at him*; esp. *on the* ~, or sl. abbr. *on the q.t.*, secretly); undisturbed, not interfered with or interrupted, free or far from strife or uproar; informal (*a* ~ *dinner--party*); enjoyed in quiet, tranquil, not anxious or remorseful. Hence ~LY³ adv., ~NESS, qui′ETUDE, nn. [ME, f. OF *quiet(e)* or L *quietus* p.p. f. *quiescere* (QUIESCENT)]

qui′et³, v.t. & i. Reduce to quietness, soothe, calm; become quiet (rare; usu. ~ *down*). [f. LL *quietare* (partly f. prec.)]

qui′eten, v.t. & i. = prec. [-EN⁶]

qui′et|ism, n. Passive attitude towards life with devotional contemplation & abandonment of the will as form of religious mysticism, non-resistance principles. So ~IST(2) n. & a., ~is′tic a. [f. It. *quietismo* (QUIET², -ISM)]

quiĕt′us, n. Acquittance, receipt, given on payment of account etc. (now rare); release from life, death, extinction, final riddance, (*got, gave him, his* ~). [f. med. L *quietus* (*est* he is) quit (QUIET²) used as receipt form]

‖ **quiff**, n. Curl plastered down on the forehead, tuft of hair over forehead. [orig. unkn.]

quill¹, n. Hollow stem of feather, (also ~-*feather*) whole large feather of wing or tail; pen (also ~ *pen*), plectrum, fishing--float, or toothpick, made of this; one of porcupine's spines; bobbin of hollow reed, any bobbin; musical pipe made of hollow stem; curled-up piece of cinnamon or cinchona bark; ~-*coverts*, feathers covering base of ~-feathers; ~-*driver*, clerk or journalist or author. [prob. f. (M)LG *quiele*; cf. MHG *kil*, G *kiel*]

quill², v.t. & i. Form into quill-like folds, goffer, whence ~′ING¹(2) n.; wind thread or yarn on bobbin. [f. prec.]

‖ **quill′ĕt**, n. (arch.). Quibble, nice distinction. [perh. abbr. of obs. *quillity* alt. of QUIDDITY]

quilt, n., & v.t. **1.** Bed-coverlet made of padding enclosed between two layers of linen etc. & kept in place by cross lines of stitching; any coverlet or counterpane (PATCH*work* ~). **2.** v.t. Cover with padded material; make or join together after the manner of a ~; sew up (coin, letters, etc.) between two layers of garment etc.; ‖ compile (literary work) out of extracts or borrowed ideas; (sl.) thrash. Hence ~′ING¹(1, 3) n. [ME, f. OF *cuilte* f. L *culcita* cushion]

quin′ary, a. Of the number five; consisting of five things. [f. L *quinarius* (*quini* distrib. of *quinque* five, -ARY¹)]

quin′ate, a. (bot.). (Of leaf) composed of five leaflets. [f. L *quini* (prec.), -ATE²]

quince, n. Hard acid yellowish pear--shaped fruit used as preserve or as flavouring, tree bearing it. [ME; orig. pl.

of obs. *coyn*, f. OF *cooin* f. L *cotoneum* var. of *cydonium* neut. of *Cydonius* of Cydonia in Crete]

quincĕntēn′ary, irreg. for quing-.

quinc′ŭnx, n. (Arrangement of) five objects set so that four are at corners of square or rectangle & the other at its centre (e.g. the five on dice or cards; *plantation is laid out in* ~*es*, in the diagonal cross lines given by combining ~es). So **quincŭn′cial** (-shl) a., **quincŭn′cialLY²** (-sha-), adv. [L, = 5/12 (*quinque* five, *uncia* OUNCE), also ~ pattern]

quingĕntēn′ary (-j-; *or* -jĕn′te-), a. & n. Of, in, 500th year; (n.) 500th anniversary. [f. L *quingenti* 500 after CENTENARY]

quin′ia (med.). = QUININE. [f. Sp. *quina* f. Peruv. *kina* bark]

quinine′ (-ēn, -īn), n. Alkaloid found esp. in cinchona bark & used as febrifuge and tonic; (pop.) sulphate of ~, the usu. form in which ~ is taken. So **quin′ize(4) v.t.**, **quin′ism(5)** n. [as prec., -INE⁵]

quinquagĕnār′ian, a. & n. (Person) fifty years old. [f. L *quinquagenarius* (*quinquageni* distrib. of *quinquaginta* fifty, -ARY¹), -AN]

quinquagĕn′ary (*or* -kwăj′e-), a. & n. = prec. a. & n.; fiftieth anniversary. [prec.]

Quinquagĕs′ima, n. (Also ~ *Sunday*) Sunday before Lent. [f. LL fem. of L *quinquagesimus* fiftieth]

quinqu(e)-, comb. form of L *quinque* five, in some wds taken f. L, & in many mod., esp. bot. & zool., formations. So ~**ăng′ular** (-ngg-) five-angled; ~**ĕcŏs′tāte** five-ribbed; ~**ĕnn′iad**, ~**ĕnn′ium** (pl. -a), five-year period; ~**ĕnn′ial** five-year--long, five-yearly, whence ~**ĕnn′ialLY²** adv.; ~**ĕlăt′eral** a. & n., five-sided (figure or object); ~**ĕlŏb′āte** five-lobed; ~**ĕpărt′īte** divided into, consisting of, five parts; **quin′quĕrēme** ancient galley with five banks of oars; ~**ĕvăl′vular** five-valved; **quin′quifĭd** cleft in five; ~**ĭv′alent** capable of combining with five univalent atoms.

quinqui′na (kĭnkē², kwĭnkwī²), n. (Kinds of) tree producing) Peruvian bark yielding quinine & other febrifuge alkaloids. [f. Peruv. *kinkina* redupl. form as QUINIA]

quins (-z), n. pl. (colloq.). Five children at a birth. [short for QUINTUPLETS]

quin′s|ў (-z-), n. Inflammation of throat, suppuration of tonsils. Hence ~iED² (-ïd) a. [ME, f. med. L *quinancia* f. Gk *kunagkhē* (*kun-* dog, *agkhō* throttle)]

quĭnt (*in sense 2 usu.* kĭnt), n. **1.** Musical interval of fifth; organ-stop of tone one--fifth above normal. **2.** (piquet). Sequence of five of same suit (~ *major*, of ace to ten; ~ *minor*, of knave to seven). [f. F *quinte* f. L fem. of *quintus* fifth]

quin′tain (-tĭn), n. (hist.). (Medieval military exercise of tilting at) post set up as mark & often provided with sandbag to swing round & strike unskilful tilter.

[ME, f. OF *quintaine* perh. ult. f. L *quin-tana* (*quintus* fifth) camp market]

quin'tal, kin-, n. 100 lb.; 112 lb. or hun-dredweight; 100 kilograms. [ME, f. OF, f. Arab. *qintar*]

quin'tan, a. & n. (Ague or fever) with paroxysm every fourth (by incl. reckon-ing fifth) day. [f. L (*febris*) *quintana* (*quintus* fifth, -AN) fifth-day (fever)]

quinte (kahnt), n. Fifth fencing thrust or parry. [as QUINT]

quintĕss'ence, n. **1.** (Ancient philos.) fifth substance, apart from four elements, composing the heavenly bodies entirely & latent in all things. **2.** Most essential part of any substance, refined extract; purest & most perfect form, manifesta-tion, or embodiment, *of* some quality or class. Hence **quintĕssĕn'tiAL** (-shl) a. [ME, f. OF or med. L *quinta essentia*]

quintĕt(te)', n. (Performers of) piece for five voices or instruments (*piano, clarinet,* etc. ~, four stringed instruments plus instrument named); set of five. [F (-*te*), f. It. *quintetto* (*quinto* fifth f. L *quintus*)]

quintill'ion (-lyon), n. ‖ Fifth power of million (1 with 30 ciphers); (U.S. & France) cube of million (1 with 18 ciphers). [L *quintus* fifth, BILLION]

quin'tŭp|le, a., n., & v.t. & i., ~lȳ, adv., ~lĕt, n., **quintŭp'licate** (-*at*), a., n. (-āt), v.t., **quintŭplicā'tion**, n. Fivefold etc. (for detailed senses see QUADRUPLE & wds in *quadrupl-*, substituting *five* for *four*). [-*uple* F, f. L *quintus* fifth, after QUADRUPLE]

‖ **quin'tus**. See PRIMUS[1].

quip, n., & v.i. (-pp-). Sarcastic remark, clever hit, smart saying, verbal conceit; equivocation, quibble; (v.i.) make ~s. [var. of obs. *quippy* perh. f. L *quippe* forsooth]

quipu (kē'pŏŏ, kwē-), n. Ancient-Peru-vian substitute for writing by variously knotting threads of various colours. [Peruv., = knot]

quīre[1], n. Four sheets of paper etc. folded to form eight leaves as in mediaeval MSS.; any collection of leaves one within another in MS. or book (*in ~s*, unbound, in sheets); 24 sheets of writing-paper. [ME, f. OF *quaer* (now *cahier*) f. Rom. *quaternum* f. L *quaterni* set of four, see QUATERNION]

quīre[2], n., & v.t. & i. See CHOIR.

Qui'rinal, n. (Used for) the Italian Government (esp. as opp. VATICAN). [name of palace]

quirk, n. Quibble, quip; trick of action or behaviour; twist or flourish in drawing or writing; (archit.) acute hollow between convex part of moulding & soffit or fillet. [16th c., of unkn. orig.]

*quirt, n., & v.t. Short-handled riding--whip with braided leather lash; (v.t.) lash with this. [perh. f. Sp. *cuerda* CORD]

quis'ling (-z-), n. Person co-operating with an enemy who has occupied his country, (pop.) traitor. Hence ~ITE[1] a. & n. [f. Q~, renegade Norwegian Army officer]

quit[1], pred. a. Free, clear, absolved, (arch.; *the others can go* ~; *was* ~ *for a ducking*, got off with that); rid *of* (*glad to be* ~ *of the trouble*); ~'*claim*, (n.) renuncia-tion of right, (v.t.) renounce claim to, give up (thing) *to*; ~'*rent*, (usu. small) rent paid by freeholder or copyholder in lieu of service. [ME, f. OF *quit(l)e* f. L *quietus* QUIET[2]]

quit[2], v.t. (~*ted*, rarely ~ exc. U.S.). **1.** Rid one*self of* (arch.). **2.** (refl.). (Usu. w. archaic refl. pron. without *self*) behave, acquit, conduct, oneself *well* etc. (esp. ~ *you like men*; arch.). **3.** Give up, let go, abandon, (~ *hold of*, loose; ~ *office* etc.); *cease, stop, as ~ *grumbling*. **4.** Depart from, leave, (place, person, etc.; ~*ted Paris at midnight*; ~*ted him in anger*); (abs., of tenant) leave occupied premises (esp. *give, have,* etc., *notice to* ~). **5.** (poet.). Requite, repay, clear off, (~ *love with hate*; *death* ~*s all scores*). Hence *~'t'ER[1] n., one who deserts his job or his post, shirker, poltroon. [ME, f. OF *quit(l)er* QUIET[2]]

qui tăm, n. (legal). (Action brought by) informer. [L, = who as well (for the King as for himself sues)]

quitch, n. (Also ~-*grass*) COUCH[3]-*grass*. [OE *cwice* = MLG *kwēke*, Du. *kweek*, cogn. w. QUICK]

quite, adv. Completely, wholly, entirely, altogether, to the utmost extent, nothing short of, in the fullest sense, positively, absolutely, (~ *covers it*; *was* ~ *by myself*; ~ *other*, very different; ~ *another*, a very different; *is* ~ *a hero, disappointment, good thing*; *I* ~ *like him*; *is* ~ *too delightful*, colloq., i.e. to be done justice to in words; *is* ~ *the thing*, fashionable; *not* ~ *proper*, rather improper); rather, to some extent, (*it took* ~ *a long time*; ~ *a few*, a fair number); ‖ (ellipt., colloq.) *he, she, isn't* ~, he, she, isn't ~ a gentleman, lady; ~ *so* (& improp.~), I grant the truth of that. [ME, f. obs. *quite* a. = QUIT[1]]

quits, pred. a. On even terms by retalia-tion or repayment (*will be* ~ *with him yet*, will have revenge; *now we are* ~; *cry* ~, acknowledge that things are now even, agree not to proceed further in quarrel etc.; DOUBLE[2] *or*~). [perh. abbr. of med. L *quittus*=*quietus* QUIT[1]; or=QUIT[1]+-ES]

quitt'ance, n. (arch., poet.). Release *from* something; acknowledgement of payment, receipt, (*omittance is no* ~, debt is not annulled by not being pressed); re-quital. [ME, f. OF *quitance* (*quiter* QUIT[2])]

quiv'er[1], n. Case for holding arrows (*have an arrow, shaft, left* in one's ~, not be re-sourceless; ~ *full of children*, large family, see Ps. cxxxvii. 5). Hence ~FUL(2) n. [ME, f. OF *quivre* f. WG *kokar* (OE *cocer*, OS *cocāre*, OHG *kochar*)]

quiv'er[2], v.i. & t., & n. **1.** Tremble or

vibrate with slight rapid motion (of person, leaf, wing, voice, light, etc.; *with* emotion, *in* the wind etc.); (of birds, esp. skylark) make (wings) ~; hence ~ing⁴ adv. **2.** n. ~ing motion or sound. [prob. imit.; cf. QUAVER]

qui vive (kēvēv'). *On the* ~, on the alert, watching for something to happen. [F, = lit. (*long*) *live who?*, i.e. *on whose side are you?*, as sentry's challenge]

Quix'ote, n. Enthusiastic visionary, pursuer of lofty but impracticable ideals, person utterly regardless of his material interests in comparison with honour or devotion. Hence **quixōt'IC** a. (*quixotics* n. pl., quixotic sentiments), **quixōt'I-CALLY** adv., **quix'otism(2)**, **quix'otRY(4)**, nn., **quix'otIZE(2, 3)** v.t. & i. [hero of Cervantes's *Don* ~]

quiz, n., & v.t. (-zz-). **1.** ‖ Odd or eccentric person, person of ridiculous appearance, (now rare); person given to ~zing; (orig. U.S.) interrogation, questionnaire, examination; test of general knowledge in radio or television programme; hoax, ridicule, thing done to expose or burlesque another's oddities, (now rare); hence ~z'icAL a., ~z'icalLY² adv. **2.** v.t. Make sport of (person or his ways), whence ~z'ABLE a.; regard with mocking air; look curiously at, observe the ways or oddities of, survey through an eye-glass or (now rare) ~*zing-glass*; *examine by questioning; hence ~z'inGLY² adv. [appears as a vogue-word (n. 1782, vb 1796, of unkn. orig.]

quō'ăd, prep. As regards; ~ *hŏc*, in this respect, so far as this goes. [L (*quo* whither, *ad* to)]

quŏd¹, n., & v.t. (sl.; -dd-). Prison (*in, out of,* ~); (v.t.) imprison. [c. 1700, orig. unkn.]

quŏd², neut. of L *qui* which (~ *ĕ'răt dēmōnstrăn'dum* abbr. *Q.E.D.*, ~ *ĕ'răt faciĕn'dum* (·shì·) abbr. *Q.E.F*, ~ *ĕ'răt invĕniĕn'dum* abbr. *Q.E.I.*, which was the thing to be proved, made or done, found; formulae in geometrical demonstrations, &, esp. *Q.E.D.*, in gen. use; ~ *vid'ē*, abbr. *q.v.*, which see, in cross & other references).

quoin (koin), n., & v.t. **1.** External angle of building; stone or brick forming angle, corner-stone, whence ~'ING¹(3) n.; internal corner of room; wedge for locking type in forme, raising level of gun, keeping barrel from rolling, etc. **2.** v.t. Secure or raise with ~s. [var. of COIN]

quoit (kolt, kwoit), n., & v.t. & i. Heavy flattish sharp-edged iron ring thrown to encircle iron peg or to stick in ground near it in game of ~s; (vb; rare) fling like ~, play ~s. [ME, of unkn. (prob. F) orig.]

quŏn'dăm, a. That once had but no longer has the specified character, sometime, former, (*a* ~ *friend of mine*). [L, = formerly]

quōr'um, n. Fixed number of members

that must be present to make proceedings of assembly or society or board valid. [L, = of whom (we will that you etc. be)]

quŏt'a, n. Share that individual person or company is bound to contribute to or entitled to receive from a total; quantity of goods which under government controls must be manufactured, exported, imported, etc.; number of yearly immigrants allowed to enter the United States from any one country; ~ QUICKIE. [f. med. L *quota* (*pars*) how great (a part); fem. of *quotus* (*quot* how many)]

quotā'tion, n. (Print.) quadrat used for filling up blanks; quoting, passage quoted; amount stated as current price of stocks or commodities; ~*marks*, inverted commas & apostrophes, single (' ') or double (" "), used to mark beginning & end of quoted passage. [f. med. L *quotatio* (QUOTE, ·ATION)]

quŏt'ative, a. Of quoting; given to quotation. [foll., ·ATIVE]

quōte, v.t., & n. **1.** Cite or appeal to (author, book) in confirmation of some view, repeat or copy out passage(s) from; repeat or copy out (borrowed passage) usu. with indication that it is borrowed, (abs.) make quotations, (*from* author, book, speech, etc.); enclose within quotation-marks; adduce or cite *as*; state price of (usu. *at* figure); hence quōt'ABLE, ~' WORTHY, aa. **2.** n. (colloq.). Passage quoted; (usu. pl.) quotation-mark(s). [earlier (ME) sense *mark with numbers*, f. med. L *quotare* (QUOTA)]

quŏth, v.t. 1st & 3rd pers. past indic. (arch.). Said *I, he, she,* & rarely *we* or *they* (placed amidst, after, or before the words quoted; *quŏth'a*, arch. for ~ *he*, used in quoting contemptuously = forsooth). [past of obs. *quethe*, OE *cwethan*]

quotid'ian, a. & n. **1.** Daily, of every day, (~ *fever, ague,* recurring every day); commonplace, trivial. **2.** n. ~ ague or fever. [ME, f. OF *cotidien*, ·*ian*, or L *cot-, quotidianus* (*quotidie* daily, ·AN)]

quō'tient (·shnt), n. Result given by dividing one quantity by another; INTELLIGENCE ~. [erron. f. L *quotiens* how many times, by confusion w. ·ENT]

quō warrăn'tō (wŏ-), n. (hist.). Writ formerly issued by the King's Bench Division calling on a person to show by what warrant he held or exercised an office or franchise. [med. L, = by what warrant]

R

R (är), letter (pl. *Rs, R's*). *The* r *months*, those with **r** in their names (Sep.–Ap.) as season for oysters; *the three* Rs, reading, (w)riting, & (a)rithmetic, as basis of elementary education.

răbb'ĕt, n., & v.t. **1.** Step-shaped reduction cut along edge or face or projecting angle of wood etc. usu. to receive edge or tongue of another piece. 2. Elastic beam arranged to give rebound to hammer striking it in ascent. 3. v.t. Join or fix with ~, make ~ in. [ME, f. OF *rabat* abatement, recess, (*rabattre* REBATE[1])]

rabb′i, n. Jewish doctor of the law (as form of address by itself or prefixed to name, or as ordinary noun), esp. one authorized by ordination to deal with law & ritual & perform certain functions; *Chief R~*, ‖ ecclesiastical head of British Jewish communities. [ME; LL f. Gk f. Heb. = my master (*rabh* master + pronom. suf.)]

rabb′in, n. Rabbi (usu. *the ~s*, chief Jewish authorities on law & doctrine, most of them between 2nd & 13th cc.). Hence ~ATE[1], ~ISM(3), ~IST(2, 3), nn., **rabbin′ICAL** a., **rabbin′icaLY**[2] adv. [f. F *rabbin* or med. L *rabbinus* (prec.; *-n* obso.)]

rabb′it[1], n., & v.i. 1. Burrowing mammal of hare family, brownish grey in natural state, also black or white or pied in domestication; ‖ (colloq.) a poor performer at any game (esp. cricket, golf, or lawn tennis); *~-hutch*, *-warren*; WELSH[2] *~*; hence *~-Y*[2] a. 2. v.i. Hunt *~s*. [ME, app. f. northern F; cf. dial. *rabotte*, Walloon *robett*, Flem. *robbe*]

rabb′it[2], v.t. (vulg.) *Odd~it* etc., form of imprecation. [perh. alt. of *-rat* in *od rat*, DRAT]

rab′ble[1], n. Disorderly crowd, mob; contemptible or inferior set of people; the lower part of the populace. [orig. unkn.; ME sense *pack* or *string of animals* etc.]

rab′ble[2], n. Iron bar with bent end for stirring molten metal. [f. F *râble* f. L *rutabulum* (*ruere rut-* rake up) fire-shovel]

rab′blement (-lm-), n. (now rare). (Tumult as of) a rabble. [-MENT]

Rabelais′ian, -aes′ian, (-zyan), a. & n. 1. Of, like, Rabelais or his writings, marked by exuberant imagination & language & coarse humour & satire. 2. n. Admirer or student of Rabelais. [*Rabelais*, French humorist (d. 1553), -IAN]

rab′id, a. Furious, violent, (*~ hate*); unreasoning, insensate, headstrong, (*~ democrat*); (esp. of dog) affected with rabies, mad; of rabies. Hence rabid′ITY, ~NESS, nn., ~LY[2] adv. [f. L *rabidus* (*rabere* rave)]

rab′ies (-bēz, -biēz), n. Canine madness, hydrophobia. [L (prec.)]

race[1], n. 1. Onward sweep or movement, esp. strong current in sea or river (*tide set with a strong ~*; *the R~ of Alderney* etc.). 2. Course of sun or moon, course of life, (*ere he had run half his~*). 3. Channel of stream (esp. in comb., as *mill-~*); channel along which shuttle moves. 4. Contest of speed between runners, ships, horses, etc., or persons doing anything; (pl.) series of these for horses at fixed time on regular course (SELLing *~*; *~ ball*, dance held in connexion with *~s*; *~-card*, programme of *~s*; *~-course*,

ground for horse-racing; *~-horse*, bred or kept for racing; *~-meeting*, horse-racing fixture. [ME, f. ON *rás* running, race, etc., = OE *rǣs*]

race[2], v.i. & t. Compete in speed *with*; indulge in horse-racing (*a racing man*; *the racing world*, the turf); go at full speed, (of propeller, paddle-wheel, etc.) work violently from diminished resistance when out of the water; have race with, try to surpass in speed; cause (horse etc.) to ~ (*~d his bicycle against a motor-car*); make (person, thing) move at full speed (*~d me along at five miles an hour*; *~d the Bill through the House*). [f. prec.]

race[3], n. 1. Group of persons or animals or plants connected by common descent, posterity *of* (person); house, family, tribe or nation regarded as of common stock; distinct ethnical stock (*the Caucasian, Mongolian*, etc., *~*); genus or species or breed or variety of animals or plants, any great division of living creatures (*the human, feathered, four-footed, finny*, etc., *~*). 2. Descent, kindred, (*of noble, Oriental*, etc., *~*; *separate in language & ~*). 3. Class of persons etc. with some common feature (*the ~ of poets, dandies*, etc.). [F, f. It. *razza* of unkn. orig.]

race[4], n. Root (of ginger). [f. OF *rais* f. L *radicem* nom. *-ix* root]

racéme′, n. (bot.). Flower-cluster with the separate flowers attached by short equal stalks at equal distances along central stem. Hence **rā′cémosE**[1] a. (bot., also anat. of compound glands). [f. L *racemus* grape-bunch]

rā′cer, n. In vbl senses; esp: racehorse, yacht, bicycle, etc., used for racing; circular horizontal rail along which traversing-platform of a heavy gun moves. [-ER[1]]

rā′chis, rhā-, (-k-), n. (pl. *-ides* pr. -ēz). Stem of grasses etc. bearing flower-stalks at short intervals; axis of pinnately compound leaf or frond; vertebral column or cord from which it develops, whence **rā′chi(o)-** (-k-) comb. form; feather-shaft, esp. the part that bears the barbs. [f. Gk *rhakhis* spine; the E pl. *-ides* is erron.]

rachit′is (-k-), n. (Learned form for) RICKETS. [f. Gk *rhakhitis* (prec., -ITIS)]

rā′cial (-shl), a. Of, in regard to, due to, race. Hence ~ISM (-sha-) n., tendency to ~ feeling, antagonism between different races of men, ~LY[2] adv. [RACE[3], -IAL]

rack[1], n., & v.i. 1. Driving clouds. 2. v.i. (Of clouds) drive before wind. [ME, prob. of Scand. orig.; cf. Norw. & Sw. dial. *rak* wreckage etc., f. *reka* drive]

rack[2], n., & v.t. & i. 1. Fixed or movable frame of wooden or metal bars for holding fodder; framework with rails, bars, pegs, or shelves, for keeping articles on or in (*plate, hat, tool, pipe*, etc., *~*); cogged or indented bar or rail gearing with wheel or pinion or worm, or serving with pegs etc. to adjust position of something; ~-*railway*, with cogged rail between bearing rails; ~-*wheel*, cog-wheel. 2. vb. Fill *up stable*-~ with hay or straw (also trans., ~ *up horse*, provide it thus); fasten (horse) *up* to ~; place in or on ~. [ME, f. Du. *rak*, also MDu. *rec*, MLG *rek(ke)* rail etc., f. *recken* (foll.)]

răck³, v.t., & n. **1.** Stretch joints of (person) by pulling esp. with instruments of torture made for the purpose; (of disease or bodily or mental agony) inflict torture on (a ~*ing headache*; ~*ed with pain*); shake violently, injure by straining, task severely, (*cough that seemed to* ~ *his whole body*; ~ *one's brains for something to say, a plan*, etc.). **2.** Exact utmost possible amount of (rent), oppress (tenants) with excessive rent, exhaust (land) with excessive use; ~-*rent*, (n.) full economic rent, (also) excessive rent, (v.t.) exact this from (tenant) or for (land) ; ~-*renter*, tenant paying or landlord exacting ~-rent. **3.** n. Instrument of torture, a frame with roller at each end to which victim's wrists & ankles were tied so that his joints were stretched when rollers were turned (*on the* ~, being ~ed, lit., or fig. of person in distress or under strain). [ME, f. MDu., MLG *recken* stretch (= OE *reccan*); n.f. prec.]

răck⁴, n. Arrack (esp. ~ *punch*). [for ARRACK]

răck⁵, n., & v.i. **1.** Horse's gait between trot & canter, both legs of one side being lifted almost at once, & all four feet being off ground together at moments. **2.** v.i. Progress thus. [orig. unkn.]

răck⁶, v.t. Draw off (wine etc.) from the lees (often *off*). [ME, f. Pr. *arracar* (*raca* stems & husks of grapes, dregs)]

răck⁷, n. Destruction (usu. *go to* ~ & *ruin*). [var. of WRACK, WRECK]

răck′ĕt¹, **răc′quet** (-kĭt), n. Cat-gutted bat used in tennis, rackets, etc. ; (pl.) ball-game for two or four persons played in plain four-walled court with ~s; snow-shoe resembling ~ ; ~-*ball*, small hard kid-covered ball of cork & string ; ~-*press*, for keeping ~s taut & in shape ; ~-*tail*, kinds of small bird with ~-shaped tail. [f. F *raquette* f. It. *racchetta* f. Arab. *rāha* palm of hand]

răck′ĕt², n., & v.i. **1.** Disturbance, uproar, din; social excitement, gaiety, dissipation. **2.** (sl.). Dodge, game, line of business, lay; (orig. U.S.) scheme for obtaining money, or effecting some other object, by illegal (and often violent) means, so ~*eer′ING¹* n., organized black-mail of traders etc. by intimidation & violence, ~EER′ n., one who practises this. **3.** Ordeal, trying experience, (*stand the* ~, come successfully through test, face consequences of action). Hence ~Y², a. **4.** v.i. Live gay life (often *about*), move about noisily. [prob. imit.]

raconteur (see Ap.), n. (fem. -*euse*). Teller of anecdotes (usu. *good, skilful*, etc., ~). [F]

rac(c)ōōn′, n. Greyish-brown furry bushy-tailed sharp-snouted American nocturnal carnivore. [Algonquin]

ră′clȳ, a. Having the qualities that characterize the kind in high degree (esp. ~*y flavour*); of distinctive quality or vigour, not smoothed into sameness or commonness, retaining traces of origin (esp. ~*y of the soil*, of homely directness. spirited, lively, piquant). Hence ~ILY² adv., ~INESS n. [RACE³, -Y²]

‖ **răd**. See RADICAL n.

răd′ăr, n. System for ascertaining direction & range of aircraft, ships, coasts, and other objects, by means of the electromagnetic waves which they reflect; apparatus used for this. [f. initial letters of *radio detection and ranging*]

răd′dle, n., & v.t. **1.** Red ochre. **2.** v.t. Paint with ~; plaster with rouge. [var. of RUDDLE]

răd′ial, a. & n. **1.** Of, in, rays; arranged like rays or radii, having position or direction of a radius (~ *axle*, maintaining such direction to curve of track as car etc. travels round it); having spokes or radiating lines, whence ~īzed (-zd) a., ~izā′tion n.; acting or moving along lines that diverge from a centre; relating to the radius of the forearm (~ *artery, vein, nerve*); hence ~LY² adv. **2.** n. ~ nerve or artery. [f. med. L *radialis*, or RADIUS + -AL]

răd′ian, n. Angle at centre of circle subtended by an arc whose length is equal to the radius. [RADIUS, -AN]

răd′iant, a. & n. **1.** Emitting rays of light, (of eyes or looks) beaming with joy or hope or love, (of light) issuing in rays, (of beauty) splendid or dazzling, whence or cogn. **răd′iANCE**, **răd′iANCY** (rare), nn., ~LY² adv.; operating radially (esp. ~ *heat*); (bot. etc.) extending radially, radiating; ~ *point*, from which rays or radii proceed, (astron.) apparent focal point of meteoric shower. **2.** n. Point or object from which light or heat radiates; (astron.) ~ point. [ME, f. L *radiare* (RADIUS), -ANT]

răd′iate¹, a. Having divergent rays or parts radially arranged. Hence ~LY² adv. [as foll., -ATE²]

răd′i|ăte², v.i. & v.t. Emit rays of light or heat, (of light or heat) issue in rays; emit electromagnetic waves; diverge or spread from central point; emit (light or heat) from centre; disseminate (life, love, joy, etc.). Hence or cogn. ~A′TION n., ~ATIVE a. [f. L *radiare* (RADIUS), -ATE³]

răd′iātor, n. In vbl senses; esp.: apparatus for heating room etc. consisting of metal case containing winding pipe through which hot water circulates; oil or electric stove, usu. portable; engine-cooling apparatus in motor-car. [-OR]

răd′ical, a. & n. **1.** Of the root(s). **2.**

Naturally inherent, essential, funda-mental, (~ *humour, heat,* etc., in mediaeval philos., moisture, heat, etc., essential to life; *a ~ error; the ~ rottenness of human nature*). 3. Forming the basis, primary, *(the ~ idea* or *principles of a system*). 4. Affecting the foundation, going to the root, root-&-branch, (~ *change, cure, reform*); (of politicians) desiring such reforms, ‖ belonging to extreme section of Liberal party (hist.), (of measures etc.) advanced by or according to principles of ~ politicians, whence ~ISM(2) n., ~IZE(3) v.t. & i., ~ĪZA'TION n. 5. (math.). Of the root of a number or quantity (~ *sign,* √, ³, ⁴, etc., indicating that square, cube, fourth, etc. root of number following is to be extracted). 6. (philol.). Of the roots of words (~ *word,* not analysable into root & other known element). 7. (mus.). Belonging to the root of a chord. 8. (bot.). Of, springing direct from, the root or the main stem close to it. Hence ~LY² adv. 9. n. (Philol.) root; fundamental prin-ciple; (math.) quantity forming or ex-pressed as root of another, also the ~ sign; (chem.) element or atom, or group of these, forming base of compound & remaining unaltered during compound's ordinary chemical changes; (pol.) person holding ~ views or belonging to ~ party. [ME, f. LL *radicalis* (*radix -icis* root, -AL)]

răd'icle, n. Part of plant embryo that de-velops into primary root; rootlet; (anat.) rootlike subdivision of nerve or vein; (chem.) = prec. n. Hence **radic'ŭlAR¹** a. [f. L *radicula* (prec., -ULE)]

răd'iō, n. (pl. ~s), & v.t. & i. (orig. U.S.). 1. Wireless telegraphy or telephony; message so sent; broadcasting; a wireless receiving-set. 2. (attrib.), Of or relating to, sent by, used in or using, ~ (~ *altimeter, beacon, compass,* navigational aids; ~ *cab, car,* vehicles equipped with ~; ~ *direc-tion-finder,* abbr. R.D.F., instrument for determining direction of ~ waves from a ~ transmitter, so *-finding*); of stars or extra-terrestrial sources from which ~ waves are received (~ *source*); ~ *telescope,* used in ~ *astronomy* (dealing with ~ waves transmitted to or received from celestial objects; so ~ *astronomer*). 3. vb. Send (message), send message to (person), communicate, broadcast, by ~. [short for *radio-telegraphy* etc.]

răd'i|o-, comb. form of RADIUS. 1. (anat.). Belonging to the radius in conjunction with some other part, as ~*o-carp'al,* of radius & wrist, ~*o-di'gital,* ~*o-ul'nar.* 2. (phys.). Connected with rays or radia-tion, as ~*o-balance,* instrument for measuring intensity of heat radiation; ~*o-caesium,* ~*o-cobalt,* radio-active iso-topes, prepared artificially; ~*o-carbon,* radio-active isotope of carbon, esp. = carbon 14, an isotope decaying in dead organic matter at a fixed rate, used by archaeologists to determine date of

ancient deposits; ~*o·* (radio-active) *element;* ~*o-fre'quency,* (of) the frequency of radio waves; ~*ogĕn'ic,* produced by radio-activity, suitable for being broad-cast by radio; ~*ogoniom'eter,* apparatus for finding the direction of ships & air-craft from their radio signals; ~*ogram,* picture obtained by X-rays, (also) = ~*o-telegram,* (also, in full ~*o-gram'ophone*) combined radio receiving-set & gramo-phone reproducing records through loud speaker; ~*ograph,* instrument recording intensity & duration of sunshine, (also) picture obtained by X-rays, (v.t.) secure such image of, & so ~*ŏg'rapher,* ~*ŏg'raphy,* ~*ogrăph'ic*(ally); ~*o-*(radio-active) *iso-tope;* ~*o-loca'tion,* = RADAR; ~*ŏl'ogy,* scientific study of X-rays, ~*o-activity,* ~*o-therapy,* etc., so ~*ŏl'ogist,* ~*olŏ'gical;* ~*ŏm'eter,* instrument illustrating con-version of radiant energy into mechanical force, (also) instrument for measuring intensity of radiation; ~*ŏph'ony,* pro-duction of sound by radiant light or heat; ~*ŏs'copy,* examination by X-rays; ~*osŏnde,* miniature radio transmitter, carried aloft in a balloon and descending by parachute, for broadcasting pressure, temperature, & humidity at various levels [G *sonde* sounding-line]; ~*o-tel'egram,* message by wireless telegraphy; ~*o-thĕ'rapy,* treatment of disease with X-rays or other forms of radiation, so ~*o-thĕrapeut'ic*(s).

răd'io(-)ăc'tive, a. Capable of emitting spontaneously rays consisting of material particles travelling at high velocities. So **răd'io(-)activ'itў** n. [f. prec. + ACTIVE]

răd'ish, n. (Cruciferous plant with) fleshy pungent root often eaten raw as relish in salads. [OE *rǣdic* f. L *radicem* (nom. *-ix*) root; in 15th c. readopted f. OF *radis*]

răd'ium, n. Radio-active metallic ele-ment obtained from pitchblende, widely used in radio-therapy; ~ *emanation,* RADON; ~*-therapy,* treatment of disease by the use of ~ or its products. [f. L *radius* ray, see -IUM]

răd'ius, n. (pl. *-ii*). 1. Thicker & shorter bone of forearm in man, corresponding bone in beast's foreleg or bird's wing. 2. (math.). Straight line from centre to circumference of circle or sphere; radial line from focus to any point of curve (~ *vector,* variable line drawn to curve from fixed point, esp. in astron. from sun or planet to path of satellite). 3. Any of a set of lines diverging from a point like radii of circle; object of this kind, e.g. spoke. 4. Circular area as measured by its ~ (*knows everyone within a ~ of 20 miles;* ‖ *the four-mile ~,* that of which Charing Cross is centre). 5. (bot.). Outer rim of composite flowerhead, e.g. daisy, also radiating branch of umbel. [L, = staff, spoke, ray]

răd'ix, n. (pl. *-ices* pr. *-ĭsēz*). Number or symbol used as basis of numeration scale *(ten is the ~ of decimal numeration, & of common logarithms)*; source or origin of. [L, = root]

rād'ome, n. Dome or covering on outer surface of aircraft protecting radar equipment. [f. RA(DAR), DOME]

rād'on, n. Gaseous radio-active element arising from the disintegration of radium (formerly known as *niton*). [f. RADIUM after *argon* etc.]

räff. = RIFF-RAFF.

Raffaelesque. = RAPHAELESQUE.

räff'ia, n. Kind of palm; fibre from its leaves used for tying up plants and making hats, baskets, mats, etc. [Malagasy]

räff'ish, a. Disreputable, dissipated, fast--looking. Hence ~LY² adv., ~NESS n. [-ISH¹]

räf'fle¹, n., & v.i. & t. 1. Sale of article by taking entrance-fee from any number of persons & assigning it by lot to one of them. 2. vb. Enter one's name in ~ for article; sell by ~. [ME, kind of dice-game, f. OF *rafle* of unkn. orig.]

räf'fle², n. Rubbish, refuse, lumber, debris. [ME; cf. OF *ne rifle, ne rafle* nothing at all]

raft (-ah-), n., & v.t. & i. 1. Collection of logs, casks, etc., fastened together in the water for transportation; flat floating structure of timber or other materials for conveying persons or things, esp. as substitute for boat in emergencies; floating accumulation of trees, ice, etc.; ~s'man, worker on ~. 2. vb. Transport as or on ~; form into a ~; cross (water) on ~(s); work ~. [ME, f. ON *raptr* RAFTER²]

ra'fter¹ (-ah-), n. Man who rafts timber. [-ER¹]

ra'fter² (-ah-), n., & v.t. 1. One of the sloping beams forming framework on which slates etc. of roof are upheld. 2. v.t. (Usu. in p.p.) provide with ~s; || plough (land) so that contents of furrow are turned over on same breadth of unploughed ground next it, half-plough. [OE *ræfter*, = MLG *rafter*, rel. to ON *raptr* RAFT]

räg¹, n. 1. Torn or frayed piece of woven material, one of the irregular scraps to which cloth etc. is reduced by wear & tear (*in* ~s, torn); (pl.) tattered clothes (*in* ~s, in old clothes); GLAD ~s; (usu. with neg.) smallest scrap of cloth or sail (*not a* ~ *to cover him*; *spread every* ~ *of sail*); (collect.) ~s used as material for paper, stuffing, etc. 2. Remnant, odd scrap, irregular piece, (*flying* ~s *of cloud*; *cooked to* ~s, till it falls to pieces; *not a* ~ *of evidence*). 3. (derog.). Flag, handkerchief, curtain, newspaper, etc. 4. Jagged projection (rare). 5. ~-baby, doll made of ~s; ~-bag, in which scraps of linen etc. are kept for use; ~-bolt, (n.) with barbs to keep it tight when driven in, (v.t.) join together with these; ~-paper, made of ~s; ~'tag, ~'tag & bob-tail, the riff-raff, ragged or low or disreputable people;

~'time, popular music of U.S. Negro origin with much syncopation, (attrib.) farcical (*a* ~time army); ~-wheel, with projections catching in links of chain that passes over it, sprocket-wheel; ~'wort, yellow-flowered ragged-leaved plant. [ME, perh. repr. OE *ragg* f. ON *rogg* tuft or strip of fur]

räg², n. Large coarse roofing-slate; || kinds of hard coarse stone breaking up in thick slabs (esp. CORAL-~, *Kentish*, *Rowley*, ~). [ME, of unkn. orig.]

|| räg³, v.t. & i. (-gg-), & n. (sl.). 1. Scold, reprove severely; tease, torment, play rough jokes upon, disarrange (person's room etc.) by way of practical joke; engage in bally-ragging, be noisy & riotous. 2. n. Noisy disorderly scene. [cf. BALLYRAG, BULLYRAG]

räg'amüffin, n. Ragged dirty fellow. Hence ~LY¹ a. [prob. f. RAG¹ w. fanciful termination]

räge¹, n. 1. (Fit of) violent anger; violent operation of some natural force or some sentiment (*the* ~ *of the wind, of faction*). 2. Vehement desire or passion *for* (*has a* ~ *for, or for collecting, first editions*); object of widespread temporary enthusiasm or fashion (*Miss Siddons, the open-air cure, was the or all the* ~). 3. Poetic or prophetic or martial ardour. [ME, f. OF f. Rom. *rabia* f. L RABIES]

räge², v.i. & refl. Rave, storm, speak madly or furiously, (*at, against, or abs.*), be full of anger; (of wind, sea, passion, feeling, battle, pain, disease, etc.) be violent, be at the height, operate unchecked, prevail, whence **rä'gingLY²** adv.; (refl., esp. of storm etc.) ~ *itself out*, cease raging. [ME, f. OF *rager* (prec.)]

rägg'ed (-g-), a. Rough, shaggy, hanging in tufts; of broken jagged outline or surface, full of rough or sharp projections; faulty, imperfect, wanting finish or smoothness or uniformity, (~ *rhymes*, *time* in rowing, etc.); rent, torn, frayed, (of persons) in ~ clothes; ~ *robin*, crimson-flowered campion with tattered petals; || ~ *school* (obs.), free school for poor children. Hence ~LY² adv., ~NESS n. [RAG¹, -ED²]

rag(g)ee (rah'gē), n. A coarse kind of millet, the staple food in parts of India. [Hind. *rāgī*]

Räg'lan, n. Overcoat without shoulder seams, the sleeve running up to the neck; also attrib. as ~ *sleeve*. [f. Lord ~ (d. 1855), commander in Crimean war]

ragout' (-ōō), n., & v.t. Meat in small pieces stewed with vegetables & highly seasoned; (vb) cook thus. [f. F *ragoût* (*ragoûter* revive taste of, see RE-, GUST²)]

raid, n., & v.i. & t. 1. Sudden attack made by military party (orig. of mounted men), ship(s), or aircraft; predatory incursion in which surprise & rapidity are usu. relied upon, foray, inroad; sudden descent of police etc. upon suspected premises or illicit goods. **2. vb.** Make ~ *into* etc.; make ~ on (person, place, cattle); hence ~'ER¹ n. [Sc. form of OE *rǣd* ROAD¹]

rail¹, n., & v.t. & i. **1.** Horizontal or inclined bar or continuous series of bars of wood or metal used to hang things on, as top of banisters, as part of fence, as protection against contact or falling over, or for similar purpose. **2.** Any horizontal piece (cf. STILE²) in frame of panelled door. **3.** Iron bar or continuous line of bars laid on ground as one side or half of ~way track (*off the* ~s, disorganized, out of order, not working right; *by* ~, by ~way). **4.** ~-*chair*, iron holder, attached to sleeper, in which railway ~ rests; ~'*head*, farthest point reached by a ~way under construction, (mil.) point on ~way at which road transport of supplies begins; ~-*motor*, self-propelled ~way coach (also attrib.); *~'road*, (n.) ~way, (v.t.) rush (person, thing) *to, into, through,* etc.; ~'*way,* ‖ road laid with ~s for heavy horse-carts, track or set of tracks of iron or steel ~s for passage of trains of cars or trucks drawn by locomotive engine & conveying passengers & goods, (also ~*way line*) the tracks of this kind worked by single company or the whole of the organization & persons required for their working, (attrib. in many phrr., as ~*way accident*; ~*way act*, regulating duties & rights of ~way companies; ~*way bill*, proposal in Parliament esp. for constructing new ~way; ~*way bridge, carriage, company, contractor, director, engine, journey, shares*; at ~*way speed*, very quickly; ~'(*way*)*man*, ~way employee; ~*way rug, station, stock, system, train, travelling, tunnel*), whence ~'wayLESS a., ~*way* v.i., travel by ~; hence ~'AGE(4) n., ~'LESS a. **5. vb.** Furnish or enclose (place) with ~ (often *in, off*), provide (bench etc.) with ~, whence ~'ing¹ [-ING¹(3, 4)] n.; lay (~way route) with ~s; convey (goods), travel, by ~. [ME, f. OF *reille* [L *regula* RULE)]

rail², n. Kinds of bird, esp. LAND¹~, *water*-~. [ME, f. OF *raale* (now *râle*), f. Rom. **rascula*, prob. imit.]

rail³, v.i. Use abusive language (usu. *at* or *against*, or arch. *upon*). Hence ~'ER¹ n., ~'ing² [-ING²(1)] n., ~'ing³ [-ING²] a., ~'ingLY² adv. [ME, f. OF *railler* (RALLY²), f. Rom. **ragulare*]

rail'ler̆y̆, n. (Piece of) good-humoured ridicule, rallying. [f. F *raillerie* (prec., -ERY)]

raim'ent, n. (poet. & rhet.). Clothing, dress, apparel. [ME; aphetic f. obs. *arrayment* (ARRAY¹, -MENT)]

rain¹, n. **1.** Condensed moisture of atmosphere falling visibly in separate drops, fall of such drops (~ *or shine*, whether it rains or not); (pl.) showers of ~, esp. *the* ~*s*, rainy season in tropical countries, (naut.) *the R*~*s*, rainy region of Atlantic 4–10° N. lat.; (~-like descent of) falling

liquid or solid particles or bodies (*a* ~ *of ashes, frogs, pearls, rice, fire*; also fig. *a* ~ *of melody, kisses, congratulations*). **2.** ~-*bird*, kinds of bird, esp. green woodpecker; ~-*box*, theatre contrivance imitating sound of ~; ~'*coat*, waterproof; ~-*doctor*, producer of ~ by magic; ~'*drop*, single drop of ~; ~'*fall*, shower, quantity of ~ falling within given area in given time (usu. in inches of depth per annum); ~-*gauge*, instrument measuring ~*fall*; ~-*water*, collected from ~, not got from wells etc.; ~-*worm*, common earthworm. Hence ~'LESS. ~'PROOF², ~'TIGHT, aa. [OE *regn*, OS, OHG *regan*, ON *regn*, Goth. *rign*]

rain², v.i. & t. *It* ~*s*, rain comes down (*it* ~*ed blood, frogs, invitations, tracts*, etc., there was a shower of them; *it* ~*s cats & dogs*, violently; *it never* ~*s but it pours*, events usu. happen several together; *it* ~*s in*, rain penetrates house etc.; *it has* ~*ed itself out*, rain has ceased); *God, the sky, the clouds,* ~, send down rain; fall or send down in showers or like rain (*flowers* ~*ed from their hands*; *tears* ~*ed down her cheeks*; *blows* ~ *upon him*; *his eyes* ~ *tears*; ~ *influence*; *he* ~*ed benefits upon us*). [OE *regnian* (prec.)]

rain'bow (-ō), n. Arch showing prismatic colours in their order formed in sky (or across cataract etc.) opposite sun by reflection, double refraction, & dispersion of sun's rays in falling drops of rain (*lunar* ~, similar effect from moon's rays, rarely seen; *sea* ~, formed on sea spray; *secondary* ~, additional arch with colours in reverse order formed inside or outside of ~ by double reflection & double refraction; *all the colours of the* ~, many colours); (attrib.) many-coloured; ~ *trout*, Californian kind. [OE *rēnboga* (RAIN¹, BOW¹)]

rain'|y̆, a. In or on which rain is falling or much rain usually falls (~*y weather, climate, day, month, county*, etc.; ~*y day*, fig., time of esp. pecuniary need, as *provide against a* ~*y day*); (of clouds, wind, etc.) laden with, bringing, rain. Hence ~*i*LY² adv., ~*i*NESS n. [-Y²]

raise (-z), v.t. (often followed by *up* in most senses), & n. **1.** Set upright, make stand up, restore to or towards vertical position, rouse, (~*d him from his knees*; ~ *the standard of revolt*; ~*d pastry, pie*, etc., standing without support of dish at sides; ~ *one from the dead*, restore him to life; ~ *the country, city*, etc., rouse inhabitants in some emergency, often *against* or *upon* enemy etc.; *the danger* ~*d his spirits*; ~ *the wind*, fig., procure money for some purpose; ~ *a dust*, lit., & fig. cause turmoil, also obscure the truth). **2.** Build up, construct, create, produce, breed, utter, make audible, start, give occasion for, elicit, set up, advance, (~ *palace, large family, blister*, one's *own vegetables, storm, shout, hymn, controversy, prejudice, claim, demand, objection, question*; *a deliverer* *was* ~*d up,* caused by Providence to appear; ~ *a laugh,* cause others to laugh; *no one* ~*d his voice,* spoke). **3.** Elevate, put or take into higher position, extract from earth, direct upwards, promote to higher rank, make higher or nobler, cause to ascend, make (voice) louder or shriller, (naut.) come in sight of (land, ship), increase amount of, heighten level of, (~ one's *hat, bow;* ~ one's *glass to,* drink health of; *thousands of tons of coal were* ~*d;* ~ one's *eyes,* look upwards; ~ one's *eyebrows,* look supercilious or shocked; ~*d him to the see of York; trying to* ~ *a degraded class; undertook to* ~ *the spirit of King Solomon,* cf. LAY[3]; ~ *Cain, hell, the devil, the mischief,* etc., make disturbance; *their voices were* ~*d as in anger;* ~ *income-tax from 8s. 6d. to 10s.;* ~ *cloth,* make nap on it; ~ *bread,* cause it to rise with yeast; ~ one's *reputation,* add to it; *the price of the 2lb. loaf is* ~*d a penny;* ~ *colour* in dyeing, brighten it). **4.** Levy, collect, bring together, procure, manage to get, (~ *tax, loan, subscription, money, army, fleet).* **5.** Relinquish, cause enemy to relinquish, (siege, blockade); remove (embargo). **6.** p.p. *(vulg.).* Brought up, educated. **7.** n. Increase in salary, stakes at poker (also as vb), bid at bridge, etc. [ME, f. ON *reisa* f. Gmc *raizjan* (whence OE *rǣran* REAR[2]), causative of *rīsan* RISE[1]]

rais'in (-zn), n. Partially dried grape. [ME, f. OF *raisin* f. L as RACEME]

raison d'être (see Ap.), n. Purpose etc. that accounts for or justifies or originally caused thing's existence. [F]

rait. See RET.

raj (rahj), n. (Anglo-Ind.; hist.). Sovereignty *(the British* ~ *in India).* [Hind.]

raja(h) (rah'ja), n. Indian king or prince (also as title of petty dignitary or noble in India, or Malay or Javanese chief). Hence **ra'jah**SHIP (rahj'ash-) n. [Hind. *rājā* f. Skr. *rājan* king *(rāj* to reign)]

Rajpoot, -put, (rahj'pōot), n. Member of Hindu soldier caste claiming descent from Kshatriyas. [Hind. *(-ut),* f. prec., *putra* son]

rāke[1], n. Implement consisting of pole with cross-bar toothed like comb at end for drawing together hay etc. or smoothing loose soil or gravel, wheeled implement for same purpose; kinds of implement resembling ~ used for other purposes, e.g. by croupier drawing in money at gaming-table. [OE *raca,* MLG, MDu. *rāke,* cogn. w. MLG *rēke,* OHG *recho,* ON *reka* spade]

rāke[2], v.t. & i. Collect, draw *together,* gather *up,* pull *out,* clear *off,* (as) with rake (~ *out the fire;* ~ *up* or *together all possible charges;* ~ *off the leaves);* clean or smooth with rake; search (as) with rake, ransack, *(has* ~*d all history for proofs);* make *level, clean,* etc., with rake; scratch, scrape; sweep with shot,

enfilade, send shot along (ship) from stem to stern, sweep with the eyes, (of window etc.) have commanding view of; use rake, search as with rake *(have been raking among* or *in* or *into old records);* ~*-off* (colloq.), commission, rebate, share of profits (usu. in bad sense). [ME, f. ON *raka* cogn. w. prec.]

rāke[3], n. Dissipated or immoral man of fashion. [for RAKEHELL]

rāke[4], v.i. & t., & n. **1.** (Of ship or its bow or stern) project at upper part of bow or stern beyond keel; (of masts or funnels) incline from perpendicular towards stern; give backward inclination to *(bicycle's front forks are* ~*d).* **2.** n. Amount to which thing ~s, raking position or build; slope of stage or auditorium in theatre. [17th c., of unkn. orig.]

‖ **rāke'hĕll** (-kh-), n. (arch.). = RAKE[3]. Hence ~Y[2] a. (arch.). [RAKE[2], HELL]

rāk'ish[1], a. (As) of, like, a RAKE[3]. Hence ~LY[2] adv., ~NESS n. [-ISH[1]]

rāk'ish[2], a. (Of ship) smart & fast-looking, seeming built for speed & therefore open to suspicion of piracy. [perh.=prec., assoc. w. RAKE[4]]

râle (rahl), n. (path.). Sound additional to that of respiration heard in auscultation of unhealthy lungs. [F, f. *râler* to rattle]

rǎllentǎn'dō, mus. direction. Gradually slower. [It.]

‖ **rǎll'icǎr(t),** n. Light two-wheeled driving-trap for four. *[Ralli,* first purchaser, 1885]

rǎll'y[1], v.t. & i., & n. **1.** Reassemble, get together again, (t. & i.; esp. of army or company) after rout or dispersion, (cause to) renew conflict; bring or come together as support or for concentrated action *(rallied his party, his party rallied, round* or *to him);* revive (faculty etc.) by effort of will, pull oneself together, assume or rouse to fresh energy; throw off prostration or illness or fear, regain health or consciousness, revive. **2.** n. Act of ~ing (intr.), reunion for fresh effort; recovery of energy after or in the middle of exhaustion or illness; (in tennis, rackets, etc.) series of strokes before point is decided. [n. f. vb, f. F *rallier* (RE-, ALLY[1])]

rǎll'y[2], v.t. Banter, chaff. Hence ~**ing**-LY[2] adv. [f. F *railler* RAIL[3]]

rǎm[1], n. **1.** Uncastrated male sheep, tup. **2.** *(Ram)* zodiacal sign Aries. **3.** = BATTER[1]-*ing*-~; (battleship with) projecting beak at bow for charging side of other ships; falling weight of pile-driving machine; rammer; hydraulic water-raising or lifting machine; piston of hydrostatic press; plunger of force-pump. **4.** ~*'s-horn,* lit., also scroll ornament imitated from ~'s head & horns. [OE *ram(m), rom(m),* = MDu., MLG, OHG *ram (ramm-),* perh. rel. to ON *rammr* strong]

rǎm[2], v.t. (-mm-). Beat down (soil etc.) into solidity with wooden block etc., (abs.) use ~mer; make (post, plant, etc.) firm by ~ming soil round it; drive (pile etc.) *down, in, into*, by heavy blows; force (charge) home, pack (gun) tight, with ~rod; squeeze or force into place by pressure (*~med his clothes into a bag, his hat down on his head; had the list ~med into me by repetition*; ~ *the argument home*, lay sufficient stress on it); cram *with* stuffing etc.; (of ship) strike (as) with ram; dash or violently impel (thing) *against, at, on,* or *into* (*~med his head against the wall, his horse at a fence*); ~*rod*, for ~ming home charge of muzzle-loader. Hence ~m'ER¹(2) n. [ME, f. prec.]

räm³, n. (naut.). Boat's length over all. [orig. unkn.]

Ramadän', n. Ninth month of Mohammedan year, during all daylight hours of which rigid fasting is observed. [Arab. (*ramada* be hot); perh. orig. one of hot months, now passing through all seasons owing to lunar reckoning]

räm'al, a. (bot.). Of, proceeding from, a branch. [f. L *ramus* branch, -AL]

räm'ble, v.i., & n. 1. Walk (v. & n.) for pleasure, with or without definite route. 2. Wander in discourse, talk or write disconnectedly. [17th c., of unkn. orig.]

räm'bler, n. In vbl senses; also, kinds of climbing rose, esp. the crimson ~. [-ER¹]

räm'bling, a. Peripatetic, wandering; disconnected, desultory, incoherent; (of plants) straggling, climbing; (of house, street, etc.) irregularly planned. Hence ~LY² adv. [-ING²]

rämbut'an (-ōot-), n. Red fruit of an E.-Indian tree, covered with soft spines and with pleasant sub-acid pulp. [Malay, f. *rambut* hair, in allusion to spines]

räm'ekin, -quin (-kǐn), n. Small quantity of cheese with bread-crumbs, eggs, etc., baked in small mould. [c. 1700, F *ramequin*, of Gmc orig.; cf. LG *ramkin* cheese-cake]

räm'ie (-mē), n. Fine strong fibre obtained from a Chinese and E.-Indian nettle-like plant, woven into a durable material. [Malay *rāmǐ*]

rämificā'tion, n. Ramifying, (arrangement of) tree's branches; subdivision of complex structure comparable to tree's branches (*the ~s of a river, society, trade, plot, inquiry,* etc.). [as foll., -ATION, perh. after F]

räm'ifȳ, v.i. & t. Form branches or subdivisions or offshoots, branch out; (usu. pass.) cause to branch out, arrange in branching manner (*railways were ~ied over the country*). [f. F *ramifier* f. med. L *ramificare* (L *ramus* branch, -I-, -FY)]

rämm'ish, a. Rank-smelling. [RAM¹, -ISH¹]

ramōse' (or räm'ōs), a. Branched, branching. [f. L *ramosus* (*ramus* branch, -OSE¹)]

rämp¹, n. Slope, inclined plane joining

two levels of ground esp. in fortification, or of wall-coping; difference in level between opposite abutments of rampant arch; upward bend in stair-rail. [18th c., f. F *rampe* f. *ramper* creep(?)]

rämp², v.i. & t. 1. (Chiefly of lion) stand on hind-legs with fore-paws in air, assume or be in threatening posture; (now usu. joc.) storm, rage, rush about. 2. (Archit., of wall) ascend or descend to different level; (archit., mil.) furnish or build with ramp. [ME, f. OF *ramper* creep]

‖ rämp³, n., & v.i. & t. (sl.). Attempt to extort payment of fictitious debt from bookmaker; (transf.) levying of exorbitant prices, as *the black-market ~ in whisky*; swindle, racket; (vb) engage in, subject (person etc.) to, ~. [orig. unkn.]

rämpāge', v.i., & n. 1. Behave violently, storm, rage, rush about. 2. n. Violent behaviour (esp. *be on the ~*). Hence ~OUS (-jus) a., ~OUSLY² adv., ~OUSNESS n. (-jus-). [vb perh. f. RAMP²]

rämp'ant, a. (Chiefly of lion, esp. in her.) ramping (in her., & in allusive imitations, placed after nouns, as *lion ~, the snob ~*); violent or extravagant in action or opinion, arrant, aggressive, unchecked, prevailing, (*is a ~ theorist; popery is ~ among us*); rank, luxuriant, (*a rich soil makes nasturtiums too ~*); (of arch etc.) having one abutment higher than the other, climbing. Hence rämp'-ANCY n., ~LY² adv. [ME & OF *rampant* (RAMP², -ANT)]

rämp'ärt, n., & v.t. Broad-topped & usu. stone-parapeted walk on top of defensive wall; (fig.) defence, protection; (vb) fortify or defend (as) with ~. [f. F *rempart* (*remparer* fortify, f. RE-, *emparer* take possession of, f. L *ante* before, *parare* prepare)]

rämp'ion, n. Kind of bell-flower with white tuberous roots used as salad. [cf. F *raiponce*, It. *ramponzolo*]

‖ rämp'ire, n., & v.t. (arch.). = RAMPART.

räm'shackle, a. Tumbledown, crazy, rickety, (usu. of house or vehicle). [earlier -ed, p.p. of obs. *ransackle* RANSACK]

räm'son (-sn), n. (Root, eaten as relish, of) broad-leaved garlic. [pl. in -en of OE *hramsa*, cogn. w. G *rams*]

rän¹, n. A certain length of twine. [orig. unkn.]

ran², See RUN¹.

ränce, n. Kind of red marble with blue & white veins & spots. [prob. of F orig.]

ränch, n., & v.i. 1. Cattle-breeding establishment in U.S. & Canada. 2. v.i. Conduct ~. [f. Sp. *rancho* mess, persons feeding together]

rän'cid, a. Smelling or tasting like rank stale fat. Hence räncid'ITY, ~NESS, nn. [f. L *rancidus* stinking]

ränc'our (-ker), n. Inveterate bitterness, malignant hate, spitefulness. Hence ränc'orous a., ränc'orously² adv. [ME, f. OF, f. LL *rancorem* (prec., -OR)]

rănd, n. 1. Strip of leather between heel & shoe or boot. 2. (S.-Afr.) highlands on either side of river valley (*the R~*, district round Johannesburg). [OE *rand* = OHG *rant*, ON *rönd* bank, rim]

rǎndǎn'¹, n. Style of rowing for three men, the middle using sculls & the others oars; boat for such use. [orig. unkn.]

rǎndǎn'², n. Spree (esp. *on the ~*). [var. of RANDOM]

rǎn'dem, adv. & n. With three horses harnessed tandem; (n.) carriage or team so driven. [prob. formed on *random & tandem*]

rǎn'dom, n. & a. 1. *At ~*, at haphazard, without aim or purpose or principle, heedlessly. 2. adj. Made, done, etc., at ~ (*~ sample, selection*); (of masonry) with stones of irregular size & shape; hence ~LY² adv. (rare). [ME & OF *random* etc. great speed (*randir* gallop); -*m* as in *ransom*]

rǎn'd|y̆, a. ‖ Loud-tongued, boisterous, lusty, (Sc.); (of cattle etc.; dial.) wild, restive; lustful, in lustful mood. Hence ~INESS n. [perh. f. obs. *rand* var. of RANT, -Y²]

ranee (rahn'ī), n. Hindu queen. [f. Hind. *rani* f. Skr. *rajnī* fem. of RAJAH]

rang. See RING².

rǎnge¹ (-j-), v.t. & i. 1. Place or arrange in a row or ranks or in specified situation or order or company (usu. pass. or refl.; *~d their troops*; *~d themselves on each side*; *was ~d against, among, on the side of, with*, etc.; *trees ~d in an ascending scale of height*; *~ oneself*, imit. F, take up definite position in society, settle down, e.g. by marrying). 2. Run in a line, reach, lie spread out, extend, be found or occur over specified district (often *from ... to*), vary between limits, (*~s north & south, along the line*; *nightingale ~s from the Channel to Warwickshire*). 3. Be level (*with*; *a 12mo does not ~ well with a folio*); rank or find right place *with* or *among* (*~s with the great writers*). 4. Rove, wander, (often *over, along, through*, etc., district or coast; *his thoughts ~ over past, present, & future*; *ranging fancy*, inconstant affections). 5. (Of gun) throw projectile over, (of projectile) traverse, (distance; *~s over a mile*). 6. Go all about (place), sail along or about (coast, sea). [ME, f. OF *ranger* (*rang* RANK¹)]

rǎnge² (-j), n. 1. Row, line, tier, or series, of things, esp. of buildings or mountains. 2. Lie, direction, (*the ~ of the strata is east & west*; *keep the two buoys in ~ with the lighthouse*). 3. Stretch of grazing or hunting ground. 4. Piece of ground with targets for shooting. 5. Area over which plant etc. is distributed, area included in or concerned with something, sphere, scope, compass, register, limits of variation, limited scale or series, distance attainable by gun or projectile, distance between gun etc. & objective, (*gives the*

~s of all species; *the thorniest question in the whole ~ of politics*; *the ~ of her voice is astonishing*; *his reading is of very wide ~*; *the ~ of the barometer readings is about 2 in.*; *Hebrew is out of my ~*; *there is a lower ~ of prices today*; *the enemy are out of ~, have found the ~ of our camp*). 6. Cooking fireplace usu. with oven(s), boiler(s), & iron top plate with openings for saucepans etc. 7. *~-finder*, instrument for estimating distance of object, esp. one to be shot at. [ME, f. OF, = row, rank, (prec.)]

rǎn'ger (-j-), n. In vbl senses; also: keeper of a royal park, whence ~SHIP n.; *(R~)* member of U.S. COMMANDO; (pl.) body of mounted troops or other armed men; senior girl guide. [-ER¹]

rǎnk¹, n. 1. Row, line, queue, (now chiefly of cabs standing; in chess, row of squares across board, opp. FILE³). 2. Number of soldiers drawn up in single line abreast (*the ~s were broken*, could not keep the formation; *the ~s* or *the ~ & file*, common soldiers, i.e. privates & corporals, & transf. lower classes or ordinary undistinguished people; *rise from the ~s*, said of common soldier or sergeant who is given commission, or of selfmade man). 3. Order, array, (*keep ~, break ~*, remain, fail to remain, in line). 4. Distinct social class, grade of dignity, station, high station, (*people of all ~s*; *persons of ~*, members of nobility; *~ & fashion*, high society; *the pride of ~*). 5. Place in a scale. [f. obs. F *ranc* (mod. *rang*), OF *renc*, f. WG **hring* RING¹]

rǎnk², v.t. & i. Arrange (esp. soldiers) in rank; classify, give certain grade to; *take precedence of* (person) in respect to rank; have rank or place (*~s among the Great Powers, next to the king*, etc.); have a rightful place on the list of claims on, or claimants against, a bankrupt estate; (mil.) march *past* or *off*. [f. prec.]

rǎnk³, a. Too luxuriant, gross, coarse, over-productive, choked with or apt to produce weeds, (*roses are growing ~*, running too much to leaf; *land too ~ to grow corn*); foul-smelling, offensive, rancid; loathsome, indecent, corrupt; strongly marked, unmistakable, flagrant, virulent, gross, (*~ treason, pedantry, poison, nonsense*). Hence ~LY² adv., ~NESS n. [OE *ranc*, = ON *rakkr* bold, slender; cf. MLG *rank* long & thin]

rǎnk'er, n. (Commissioned officer who has been) a soldier in the ranks. [-ER¹]

rankle (rǎng'kl), v.i. (Of wound, sore, etc.) fester, continue painful, (arch.); (of envy, disappointment, etc., or their cause) be bitter, give intermittent or constant pain. [ME, f. OF *rancler* (*rancle, drancle, draoncle*, festering sore f. med. L *dracunculus* dim. of *draco* serpent)]

rǎn'sǎck, v.t. Thoroughly search (place, receptacle, person's pockets, one's conscience, etc.); pillage, plunder, (house, country, etc.). [ME, f. ON *rannsaka* (*rann* house, *sǽkja* seek]

ran'som, n., & v.t. **1.** (Liberation of prisoner of war in consideration of) sum of money or value paid for release (*hold one to* ~, be willing to release him for such consideration; *worth a king's* ~, of immense value); blackmail, sum etc. exacted in return for privilege or immunity, (*graduated income-tax & death-duties are no more than a fair* ~ *paid by the rich*); ~*-bill, -bond*, undertaking, esp. on part of captured ship, to pay ~; hence ~LESS a. **2.** v.t. Redeem, buy freedom or restoration of; atone for, expiate; hold to ~, release for a ~; exact ~ from. [ME, f. OF *ranson(ner)* f. L *redemptionem* REDEMPTION]

rant, v.i. & t., & n. **1.** Use bombastic language; declaim, recite theatrically; preach noisily, whence (esp. of Primitive Methodists) ~'ER[1] n. **2.** n. Piece of ~ing, tirade; empty turgid talk. [f. obs. Du. *randten, ranten, randen* (cf. RANDY) rave]

ranun̄c'ul̄|us, n. (pl. ~*uses,* ~*ī*). Kinds of plants including the buttercups, crowfoot. Hence ~A'CEOUS (-āshus) a. [L, orig. dim. of *rana* frog]

ranz-des-vaches (see Ap.), **n.** Swiss herdsman's melody made of harmonic notes of Alpine horn. [Swiss dial.]

rap[1], n., & v.t. & i. (-pp-). **1.** Smart slight blow (*a* ~ *on the knuckles,* punishment inflicted on child, also fig. reproof); (sl.) blame, punishment, etc., esp. *take the* ~ (freq. in another's place); sound made by knocker on door etc., or by some agency on table or floor in spiritualistic seances. **2.** vb. Strike (esp. person's knuckles) smartly; make the sound called **a** ~ (~*ped at the door, on the table,* etc.); ~ *out* (oath, pun, etc.), utter abruptly or on the spur of the moment, (v.i.) use strong language; (of spirits) ~ *out* (message, word), express by ~s. [ME, prob. imit.]

rap[2], n. Skein of 120 yds of yarn. [orig. unkn.]

rap[3], n. An atom, the least bit, (*don't care a* ~). [earlier sense *18th-c.* Irish counterfeit halfpenny, short. f. Ir. *ropaire*]

rapā'cious (-shus), a. Grasping, extortionate, predatory. Hence or cogn. ~LY[2] adv., rapā'CITY n. [f. L *rapax* (*rapere* seize, -ACIOUS)]

rape[1], v.t., & n. **1.** Take by force (poet.); ravish, force, violate, (woman). **2.** n. Carrying off by force (poet.); ravishing or violation of a woman (also fig. of a country, as *the* ~ *of Austria*). [ME, f. AF f. L *rapere* seize]

‖ **rape[2],** n. Any of six divisions of Sussex. [first in Domesday Book; orig. unkn.]

rape[3], n. Plant grown as food for sheep; plant cultivated for its seed from which oil is made, coleseed; *wild* ~, charlock; ~*-cake,* ~*-seed* pressed into flat shape after extraction of oil & used as manure; ~*-oil,* made from ~*-seed* & used as lubri-

cant & in making soap & indiarubber. [ME, f. L *rapum, rapa* turnip]

rape[4], n. Refuse of grapes after wine-making used in making vinegar; vessel used in river-making. [f. F *răpe, =* Pr. *raspa,* It. *raspo,* med. L *raspa*]

Rǎphǎēlěsque' (-sk), Rǎff-, a. In style of Raphael. [*Raphael* (It. *Raffaello*), -ESQUE]

rǎph'ia, n. (Bot. name of) RAFFIA.

rǎp'id, a. & n. **1.** Speedy, quick, swift; acting or completed in short time; (of slope) descending steeply; hence or cogn. rapid'ITY n., ~LY[2] adv. **2.** n. (usu. pl.). Steep descent in river-bed, with swift current. [f. L *rapidus* (*rapere* seize)]

rǎp'ier, n. Light slender sword for thrusting only, small-sword, (~*-thrust,* often fig. of delicate or witty repartee). [prob. f. Du. *rapier,* f. F *rapière,* of unkn. orig.]

rǎp'ine, n. (rhet.). Plundering, robbery. [ME, f. OF, or L *rapina* (*rapere* seize, -INE[4])]

rǎpparee', n. (hist.). 17th-c. Irish irregular soldier or freebooter. [f. Ir. *rapaire* short pike]

rǎppee', n. Coarse kind of snuff. [f. F (*tabac*) *răpé* RASPed (tobacco)]

rapport' (*or* rapōr'), n. Communication, relationship, connexion, (*be in,* or F *en* pr. ahn, ~ *with*). [F (*rapporter* f. RE-, APporter f. L *portare* carry)]

rapprochement (see Ap.), **n.** Re-establishment or recommencement of harmonious relations, esp. between States. [F]

rǎpscǎll'ion (-lyon), n. (arch.). Rascal, scamp, rogue. [earlier *rascallion,* f. RASCAL]

rǎpt, p.p., & a. Snatched away bodily or carried away in spirit from earth, from life, from consciousness, or from ordinary thoughts & perceptions (often *away, up,* etc.); absorbed, enraptured, intent, (esp. *listen with* ~ *attention*). [ME, f. L *raptus* p.p. of *rapere* seize]

rǎptōr'ial, a. & n. (zool.). Bird (usu. large) which preys upon other birds, mammals, etc.; bird of prey as eagle, falcon, owl, etc.; predatory (animal or bird); adapted for seizing prey. [f. L *raptor* (prec., -OR) plunderer + -IAL]

rǎp'ture, n. Mental transport, ecstatic delight, (*be in, go into,* ~s, be enthusiastic, talk enthusiastically; ~*s,* vehement pleasure or the expression of it); (esp. theol.) act of transporting a person from one place to another (esp. heaven). Hence **rǎp'turous,** a., **rǎp'turousLY**[2] adv. (-tyer-). [f. med. L *raptura* (RAPT, -URE)]

rǎp'tured (-tyerd), a. Enraptured, in ecstasy. [f. obs. *rapture* vb (prec., -ED[1])]

rar'a av'is, n. Rarity, kind of person or thing rarely encountered. [L, = rare bird]

rāre[1], a. **1.** Of loosely packed substance, not dense, (*the* ~ *atmosphere of the mountain tops*). **2.** Few & far between, uncommon, unusual, exceptional, seldom found or occurring, (*it is* ~ *for* person etc. *to do,* or *it is* ~*ly that* he etc. *does*). **3.** Of uncommon excellence, remarkably good, very amusing, *(a miracle of ~ device; had ~ fun with him)*. 4. ~ **earths**, oxides of certain metals (e.g. cerium, lanthanum, yttrium) found in a few ~ minerals. Hence ~'LY² (-ărĭ-) adv., (esp.) seldom, not often, finely, in an unusual degree, ~'NESS (-ărn-) n. [ME, f. L *rarus*]

•rāre², a. (Of meat) underdone. [var. of obs. *rear* half-cooked (of eggs), f. OE *hrēr*]

rare'bĭt (rārb-), n. See WELSH¹ *rabbit*.

rār'ee-show (-ō), n. Show carried about in a box; any show or spectacle. [app.= *rare show* as pronounced by Savoyard showmen]

rār'e|fỹ, v.t. & i. Lessen density or solidity of (esp. air); purify, refine, (person's nature etc.); make (idea etc.) subtle; become less dense. So ~FAC'TION, ~FICA'TION nn., ~făctive a. [ME, f. OF *rarefier* or L *rarefacere* (*rarus* rare, *facere* make)]

rār'itỹ, n. Rareness (see RARE¹); uncommon thing, thing valued as being rare. [f. F *rareté*, or L *raritas* (RARE¹, -TY)]

ra'scal (rah-), n. & a. 1. Rogue, knave, scamp, (often playfully to child etc.; *you lucky ~ !*). 2. adj. Belonging to the rabble (arch.; *the ~ rout*, the common people). Hence ~DOM, ~ISM(2), răscăl'ITY nn., ~LY¹ a. [ME, f. OF *rascaille* rabble]

rase. See RAZE.

răsh¹, n. Eruption of the skin in spots or patches. [c. 1700, corresp. to OF *rache* scurf, eruptive sores, = It. *raschia* itch]

răsh², a. Hasty, impetuous, overbold, reckless, acting or done without due consideration. Hence ~'LY² adv., ~'NESS n. [ME, =MDu. *rasch*, OHG *rasc*, ON *rǫskr*]

răsh'er, n. Thin slice of bacon or ham. [orig. obsc.; perh. f. obs. *rash* to slash]

rasp (rah-), v.t. & i., & n. (Scrape with) coarse kind of file having separate teeth raised with pointed punch; scrape roughly; grate upon (person or his feelings), irritate; scrape *off* or *away*; make grating sound. Hence ra'spER¹ (rah-) n., (esp., hunting) high difficult fence. [ME, f. OF *raspe(r)*, now *râpe(r)*, f. WG *hraspōn* scrape together]

ra'spatorỹ (rah-), n. Rasp used in surgery. [f. med. L *raspatorium* (*raspare* RASP, -TORY)]

ra'spberry (rahzb-), n. 1. (Plant bearing) yellow or red berry of numerous drupels on conical receptacle. 2. (sl.). Sound, gesture, or sign expressing dislike, derision, or disapproval; dismissal. 3. ~*-canes*, the plants; ~ *vinegar*, kind of syrup. [f. 16th c. *rasp* (now Sc. & north.) & *raspis* (obs.; pl. *-es*) of unkn. orig.]

rasse (răs'ĭ, răs), n. Kind of civet-cat. [f. Javanese *rase*]

răt¹, n., & v.i. (-tt-). 1. Rodent of some larger species of the mouse kind (MUSK, WATER, ~; *black* or *old-English ~*, variety now largely ousted by common *grey, brown*, or *Norway ~; smell a ~*, have suspicions; *like a drowned ~*, said of

person wet through; *Rats!*, sl., nonsense!, incredible!, etc.). 2. (pol.) Person who deserts his party in difficulties as ~s are said to desert doomed house or ship, turncoat. 3. Workman who refuses to join strike, takes striker's place, or accepts less than trade-union wages. 4. ~*-catcher* (who rids houses of ~s), (sl.) unorthodox hunting dress; ~*s'bane*, ~-poison (now only in literary fig. use); ~ *race*, fiercely competitive struggle; ~*'s-tail*, thing shaped like ~'s tail, e.g. kind of file; ~*-tail*, (horse with) hairless horse's tail, whence ~*'tailED²* a. (~*-tail spoon*, with tail-like prolongation of handle along back of bowl); ~*-trap*, list, also (cycle pedal) made of two parallel iron plates with teeth; hence ~*t'Y²* a. (in n. senses, & sl., snappish, irritable, touchy). 5. v.i. Hunt or kill ~s (of person or dog); play the ~ in politics; ~ *on* (desert) person; hence ~t'ER¹ n. [OE *ræt*; in ME f. OF *rat* f. Rom. *ratтus*]

răt², v.t. 3rd sing. pres. subj. (vulg.). = DRAT.

ra'ta (rah-), n. Large handsome New Zealand tree with crimson flowers & hard red wood. [Maori]

răt'|able, a. Proportional (arch.); ‖ liable to payment of local rates, whence ~ABIL'ITY n. Hence ~ABLY² adv. [RATE², -ABLE]

rătafi'a (-ĕa), -fee', n. Liqueur flavoured with almonds or kernels of peach, apricot, or cherry; kind of biscuit similarly flavoured; kind of cherry. [F (-*ia*), prob. rel. to TAFIA (Creole)]

răt'al, n. Amount on which rates are assessed (also attrib., as *the ~ qualification for vestries*). [f. RATE¹, prob. after RENTAL]

rătaplăn', n., & v.t. & i. (-nn-). 1. Drumming sound. 2. vb. Play (as) on drum; make ~. [F, imit.]

rătch'ĕt, rătch, nn., & vv.t. 1. Set of teeth on edge of bar or wheel in which a pawl engages to ensure motion in one direction only; (also ~*-wheel*) wheel with rim so toothed. 2. v.t. Provide with ~, give ~ form to. [f. F *rochet* kind of lance-head, (later) ratchet etc.]

rāte¹, n. 1. Statement of numerical proportion prevailing or to prevail between two sets of things either or both of which may be unspecified, amount etc. mentioned in one case for application to all similar ones, standard or way of reckoning, (measure of) value, tariff charge, cost, relative speed, *(going at the ~ of six miles an hour; can have them at the ~ of 1/- a thousand; the death-~ was 19 per mille; the ~ of interest, wages*, etc., *is to be regulated; the high ~s charged by the railways; at that ~*, colloq., if this is a fair specimen, if this assumption is true, etc.; *at any ~*, in each or any possible case, even if a stronger statement is doubtfully true, etc.; *the low ~ at which you value it; sell at a high ~; win success at an easy ~*;

went off at a great ~, speed; *pauperism increases at a fearful ~). 2. || Assessment levied by local authorities for local purposes (~s & taxes; a 6d. ~ is raised for the public library service). 3. Class (in FIRST, SECOND, THIRD, etc., -~). 4. ||~payer, person liable to have municipal ~s exacted from him. [ME, f. OF, f. med. L *rata* (L *pro rata parte* according to the proportional share), f. *ratus* p.p. of *rērī* reckon]

rāte², v.t. & i. 1. Estimate worth or value of (*I do not ~ his merits high*; *each offence is ~d at a fixed sum by way of penalty*; esp. in *over~*, *under~*), assign fixed value to (coin, metals) in relation to monetary standard (*the copper coinage is ~d much above its real value*); consider, regard as, (*I ~ him among my benefactors*). 2. || (Usu. in pass.) subject to payment of a local rate, value for purpose of assessing rates on, (*we are highly ~d for education*, have to pay a high rate; *houses are ~d at a sum smaller than the rent*, the sum on which rates are charged is less). 3. ~ *up*, impose higher insurance rate on (persons etc., liable to exceptional risks). 4. (naut.). Class under a certain RATING¹, (intr.) rank or be ~d *as*. [ME, f. prec.]

rāte³, v.t. & i. Scold (trans.) angrily; (rare) storm *at*. [ME, of unkn. orig.]

rate⁴. See RET.

rateable. Var. of RATABLE.

rāt'el, n. African and Indian nocturnal carnivorous burrowing mammal, honey-badger. [Afrikaans, orig. unkn.]

•**rāt'er**, n. Racing yacht of specified tonnage (*10-~*, *2½-~*, etc.). [RATE¹, -ER¹]

|| **rath** (rahth), n. (Ir. ant.). Prehistoric hill-fort. [Ir.]

|| **rāthe** (-dh), a. (poet.). Coming, blooming, etc., early in the year or day; ~*ripe*, *rāth'rīpe*, ripening early, precocious, (n.) early kinds of pea, apple, etc. [OE *hrǣth* adj., quick, eager]

ra'ther (rahdh-), adv. 1. More truly, to a greater extent, as a more accurate description or preferable account of the matter, *or* to be more precise, (*is ~ good than bad*; *derived ~ from imagination than reason*; *orderliness is not the result of law*, ~ *it is the cause of it*; *late last night*, *or ~ early this morning*); *the ~ that*, so much the more because. 2. In a modified way, to some extent, slightly, somewhat, (*I ~ think you know him*; *the performance was ~ a failure*, *was ~ good*, *fell ~ flat*). 3. By preference, for choice, sooner, as an alternative chosen sooner *than* another of same grammatical form or *than* to (*would much ~ not go*; *he would ~ have died than refused*; *use soft water ~ than hard*; *the desire to seem clever ~ than honest*; *he resigned ~ than stifle his conscience*; also with *had*, as *I had ~ err with Plato than be right with —*). 4. || (colloq.). (In answers) most emphatically, yes without doubt, assuredly, (*Have you been here before?—*

R~!); freq. pr. **rahdhĕr'**. [ME, f. OE *hrathor*, comp. of *hrǣthe* adv. f. *hrǣth* adj.; see prec.]

•**ra'thskĕller** (rahts-), n. Beer-saloon or restaurant in basement. [G, = town-hall cellar]

rāt'i|fy̆, v.t. Confirm or make valid (compact made in one's name) by formal consent, signature, etc. So ~FICA'TION n. [ME, f. OF *ratifier* f. med. L *ratificare* (RATE¹, -FY)]

ratine' (-ēn), n. [F] Dress fabric resembling sponge cloth. [F]

rāt'ing¹, n. In vbl senses of RATE²; also or esp.: || amount fixed as municipal rate; (naut.) person's position or class on ship's books, || non-commissioned sailor, || (collect.) all persons of a particular ~; any of the classes into which racing yachts are distributed by tonnage. [RATE², -ING¹]

rāt'ing², n. Angry reprimand. [RATE³, -ING¹]

rā'tio (-shiō), n. (pl. ~s). Quantitative relation between two similar magnitudes determined by the number of times one contains the other integrally or fractionally (*are in the ~ of three to two or 3:2*; *the ~s 1:5 & 20:100 are the same*). [L (RATE¹, -ION)]

rātiō'cin|āte (or -shi-), v.i. Go through logical processes, reason formally, use syllogisms. So ~A'TION n., ~ATIVE a. [f. L *ratiocinari* (prec.), -ATE³]

rā'tion (*rā-), n., & v.t. 1. (Usu. pl.) fixed daily allowance of food served out esp. for members of Services (& formerly of forage for animals); fixed allowance of food etc. for civilians in time of shortage (~ *book*, *card*, entitling holder to ~); single portion of provisions, fuel, clothing, etc.; (pl.) provisions. 2. v.t. Limit (persons, food, clothing) to fixed ~. [f. F, or L RATIO]

rā'tional (-sho-), a. & n. 1. Endowed with reason, reasoning; sensible, sane, moderate, not foolish or absurd or extreme; of, based on, reasoning or reason, rejecting what is unreasonable or cannot be tested by reason in religion or custom, (~ *dress*, esp. formerly of knickerbockers worn by women instead of skirts; *has ~ leanings in religion*, has doubts about the truth of revelation, the possibility of miracles, etc.). 2. (math.). (Of quantity or ratio) expressible without radical signs (opp. SURD); hence or cogn. ~ITY (-ăl⁴) n., ~LY² adv. 3. n. pl. ~ dress. [ME, f. L *rationalis* (prec., -AL)]

rātionāl'e (-sho-), n. Reasoned exposition, statement of reasons, (now rare); fundamental reason, logical basis, *of*. [L, neut. as prec.]

rā'tional|ism (-sho-), n. Practice of explaining the supernatural in religion in a way consonant with reason, or of treating reason as the ultimate authority in religion as elsewhere; theory that reason is the foundation of certainty in knowledge (opp. *empiricism, sensationalism*). So ~IST(2) n. & a., ~IS'TIC a., ~IS'TICALLY adv. [-ISM]

rä'tionaliz|e (-sho-), -is|e (-īz), v.t. & i. Explain, extenuate *away*, by rationalism, bring into conformity with reason; be or act as a rationalist; (math.) clear from surds; (econ.) reform (an industry) by eliminating waste in labour, time, & materials, whence ~A'TION n. [-IZE]

rät'īte, a. (ornith.). Belonging to the *Ratitae*, a genus including ostrich, emu, cassowary, etc., with keelless breastbone (opp. CARINA*te*). [f. L *ratis* raft, -ITE[2]]

rät'lin(e), **-ling**, n. (usu. pl.). (One of) small lines fastened across ship's shrouds like ladder-rungs. [ME; orig. unkn.]

ratoōn', n., & v.i. New shoot springing from sugar-cane root after cropping; (vb) send up ~s. [f. Sp. *retoño* sprout]

rat(t)än', n. Kinds of E.-Indian climbing palm with long thin many-jointed pliable stems; piece of ~ stem used as cane or for other purposes; ~s used as a material in building etc. [f. Malay *rotan* (*raut* pare)]

rät-tät', **rätatät'**, **rät-tat-tät'**, n. Rapping sound, esp. of knocker. [imit.]

‖ **rätt'en**, v.t. Molest (workman or employer) by abstracting or injuring tools or machinery etc. in disputes. [orig. unkn.]

rät'tle[1], v.i. & t. Give out rapid succession of short sharp hard sounds, cause such sounds by shaking something (*he ~d at the door*); talk in lively thoughtless way (often *on, away, along*); move or fall with rattling noise, drive vehicle or ride or run briskly, (usu. *down, along, past*, etc.); (part.) brisk, vigorous, (*a rattling wind, pace*), (preceding *good* etc.) remarkably (*had a rattling good run, dinner*, etc.); make (chain, window, crockery, etc.) ~ (~ *the sabre*, threaten war); say or recite (verses, stories, lists, oaths) rapidly (usu. *off, out, over, away*, etc.); stir *up* from dullness; (sl.) excite, agitate, fluster, make nervous, frighten; make move quickly (~ *fox*, hunt it close; ~ *up the anchor*; ~ *bill through the House*). [ME, ·prob. f. MDu., LG *ratelen* (imit.)]

rät'tle[2], n. **1.** Instrument or plaything made to rattle esp. in order to give alarm or to amuse babies; set of horny rings in ~snake's tail; kinds of plant with seeds that rattle in their cases when ripe (esp. *yellow, red,* ~); rattling sound, uproar, bustle, noisy gaiety, racket, (*death-*~, such sound in throat immediately before death; *the* ~s, croup); noisy flow of words, empty chatter, trivial talk; lively incessant talker. **2.** ~*bag, -bladder, -box,* ~s constructed of bag etc. with objects inside to rattle; ~*-brain, -head, -pate,*(person with) empty brain etc., whence ~**brain**-ED[2], ~**head**ED[2], ~**pat**ED[2], aa.; ~*snake,* venomous American snake with rattling apparatus in tail; ~*trap* n. & a., rickety (vehicle etc.), (pl.) curiosities, odds & ends. [f. prec.]

rätt'ler, n. In vbl senses; esp.: remarkably good specimen of anything; *rattle-snake. [-ER[1]]

ratty. See RAT[1].

rauc'ous, a. Hoarse, harsh-sounding. Hence ~LY[2] adv. [f. L *raucus*, -OUS]

‖ **raughty.** See RORTY.

‖ **rauque** (rawk), a. (rare). Raucous. [F (RAUCOUS)]

räv'age, v.t. & i., & n. **1.** Devastate, plunder, (t. & i.), make havoc. **2.** n. Devastation, damage; (esp. pl.) destructive effects *of*. [f. F *ravager, ravage,* alt. f. *ravine* rush of water; see -AGE]

räve[1], n. Rail of cart; (pl.) permanent or removable framework added to sides of cart to increase capacity. [also *rathe* (dial.), of unkn. orig.]

räve[2], v.i. & t., & n. **1.** Talk wildly or furiously (as) in delirium (often *about, against, at, of, for; raving mad,* uncontrollably, so as to ~); (of sea, wind, etc.) howl, roar; speak with rapturous admiration *about,* go into raptures; utter with ravings (~ *one's grief* etc.); ~ *oneself* hoarse, *to* sleep, etc.; *storm* ~ *itself out,* to an end; hence (often pl.) **räv'**ING[1](1) n. **2.** n. Raving sound *of* wind etc.; (sl.) enthusiastic review (of film, play, etc.); (sl.) infatuation, ' crush '. [ME, perh. f. OF *raver,* rel. to (M)LG *reven* be senseless, rave]

räv'el, v.t. & i. (-ll-), & n. **1.** Entangle or become entangled, confuse, complicate, (thread etc., or fig. question, problem; esp. in p.p., as *the* ~*led skein of life*); fray (i. & t.) *out,* whence ~LING[1](2) n.; disentangle, unravel, distinguish the separate threads or subdivisions of, (often *out*). **2.** n. Entanglement, knot, complication; frayed or loose end. [app. f. Du. *ravelen, raf-,* tangle, fray out, unweave, LG *rebbeln* to ripple flax]

räv'elin (-vl-), n. (fortif.). Outwork of two faces forming salient angle outside main ditch before curtain. [F, f. It. *ravellino,* now *riv*-, of unkn. orig.]

räv'en[1], n. & a. **1.** Large glossy blue--black-plumaged hoarse-voiced bird of crow kind feeding chiefly on flesh, often kept tame, & popularly held of evil omen. **2.** adj. Of glossy black (esp. ~ *locks,* black hair). [OE *hræfn,* OHG *(h)raban,* ON *hrafn* f. Gmc *hrabhnaz]

räv'en[2], v.i. & t. Plunder (intr.), go plundering *about,* seek *after* prey or booty, prowl for prey; eat(t. & abs.) voraciously; have ravenous appetite (*for*). [f. OF *raviner* f. *ravine* RAVIN]

räv'enous, a. Rapacious (now rare); voracious (esp. ~ *hunger, eagerness,* etc.); famished, very hungry. Hence ~LY[2] adv., ~NESS n. (rare). [ME, f. OF *ravineus* (foll., -OUS)]

räv'in, n. (poet., rhet.). Robbery, rapine; seizing & devouring of prey (*beast of* ~, of prey); spoil. [ME & OF *ravine* (this sense obs. in mod. F) f. L *rapina* RAPINE]

ravin|e′ (-ēn), n. Deep narrow gorge, mountain cleft. Hence ~ED² (-ēnd′) a. [= mod. F *ravine*, = prec.]

rav′ish, v.t. **1.** Carry off (person, thing) by force (now rare); (of death, circumstances, etc.) take from life or from sight. **2.** Commit rape upon, violate, (woman), whence ~ER¹ n. **3.** Enrapture, charm, entrance, fill with delight, whence ~ING² a., ~ingLY² adv., so ~MENT n. [ME, f. OF *ravir* f. Rom. *rapire f. L *rapere*, see -ISH²]

raw, a., n., & v.t. **1.** Uncooked (~ *cream*, got without scalding of milk; ~ *brick*, not hardened by fire); unripe; in unwrought state, not or not completely manufactured, (~ *silk*, as reeled from cocoons; ~ *cloth*, unfulled; ~ *hide*, untanned leather, also rope or whip of this; ~ *spirit*, undiluted; ~ *grain*, unmalted; ~ *material*, that out of which any process of manufacture makes the articles it produces, as *the finished product of one industry is the ~ material of another*; *the ~ material of an army is men*); artistically crude; inexperienced, untrained, unskilled, fresh to anything, (*is a ~ lad*; ~ *recruits*); stripped of skin, having the flesh exposed, excoriated, sensitive to a touch from being so exposed; ~ *edge* of cloth, without hem or selvage; (of atmosphere, day, etc.) damp & chilly occas. with fog; ~-*boned*, with bones almost exposed, gaunt; ~ DEAL²; ~ *head & bloody bones*, nursery bugbear, death's-head & cross-bones, (attrib., of narrative style etc.) crudely horrible; hence ~′ISH¹ (2) a., ~′NESS n. **2.** n. ~ place on person's or esp. horse's skin; *touch* one *on the* ~, wound his feelings on the points on which he is sensitive. **3.** v.t. Rub (esp. horse's back) into ~ness. [OE *hrēaw*, OS, OHG (*h*)*rāo*, OHG *rāu*-, ON *hrár* f. Gmc *hrawaz, cogn. w. Gk *kreas* flesh]

ray¹, n. **1.** Single line or narrow beam of light; (in scientific use) straight line in which radiant energy capable of producing sensation of light is propagated to given point (*Röntgen*, pr. rŭn′tyen, or *X*, ~*s*, form of radiation penetrating many substances impervious to ordinary light; *Becquerel* ~*s*, ~*s* emitted by RADIO-ACTIVE bodies). **2.** Analogous propagation-line of heat or other non-luminous physical energy; (fig.) fragment or remnant or beginning of enlightening or cheering influence (*a* ~, *not a* ~, *of hope, truth, genius*, etc.). **3.** Radius of circle (rare); any of the lines forming a pencil or set of straight lines passing through one point, any of a set of radiating lines or parts or things. **4.** (Bot.) marginal part of composite flower, as daisy; radial division of starfish. Hence ~ED² (rād), ~′LESS, aa., ~′LET n. [ME, f. OF *rai*, acc. of *rais*, f. L RADIUS]

ray², v.i. & t. (Of light etc., or fig. of thought, hope, etc.) issue, come *forth*, or off or *out*, in rays; radiate (t. & i.; poet.). [f. prec., or F *rayer*, f. L *radiare* (RADIUS)]

ray³, n. Kinds of large sea-fish allied to shark, with broad flat body, used as food, esp. the skate. [ME, f. OF *raie* f. L *raia*]

ray⁴. See RE¹.

ray′ah (rī′a), n. Non-Moslem subject of the Ottoman Empire. [f. Arab. *ra′iyah* flock (*ra′a* feed)]

ray′on, n. Artificial silk made from cellulose. [P; arbitr. f. RAY¹]

rāze, rāse (-z), v.t. Wound slightly, graze, (rare); erase, scratch *out*, (rare exc. fig. as ~ *person's name from remembrance*); completely destroy, level with the ground, (town, house, walls, etc.; usu. *to the ground*). [ME *rase* (f. 16th c. *raze*) f. OF *raser* f. Rom. *rasare f. L *radere* *ras*-scrape]

razee′, n., & v.t. (hist.). Ship reduced in height by removal of upper deck(s); (vb) turn into a ~. [f. F *rasée* fem. p.p. as prec.]

rāz′or, n., & v.t. **1.** Instrument used in shaving hair from skin (*safety* ~, kinds with guard to obviate risk of gashing skin). **2.** ~-*back*, back sharp as ~'s edge (often attrib., as ~-*back whale* or RORQUAL, ~-*back hill*, etc.), whence ~-*back*ED² a.; ~-*bill*, kinds of bird with ~ *bill* (bill shaped like ~), whence ~-*bill*ED² a.; ~-*edge*, keen edge, sharp mountain ridge, critical situation, sharp line of division (*keep on the* ~-*edge of orthodoxy*; *be on a* ~-*edge* or ~'*s edge*, imit. Gk, be in great danger); ~-*fish*, ~-*shell*, kinds of bivalve with shell like handle of ordinary ~; ~-*grinder*, lit., ‖ also kinds of bird; ~-*strop*. **3.** v.t. (rare). Use ~ upon, shave, cut *down* close. [ME, f. OF *rasor* (prec., -OR)]

rāzz′ia, n. Raid, plundering or slave-collecting expedition, esp. as carried out by African Mohammedans. [F, f. Algerian Arab. *ghazīah* (*ghasw* make war)]

rāz′zle(-dăz′zle), n. (sl.). Excitement, bustle, stir, spree; undulating merry-go-round. [redupl. of DAZZLE]

R-boat, n. Fast German motor mine-sweeper. [R f. G *räumen* to clear]

re¹ (rā), ray, n. Second note of octave (rare) note D, the second in natural scale of C major. [See GAMUT]

rē², abl. of RES. (As prep.) in the matter of (chiefly in legal & business use as first word of headline stating matter to be dealt with; also vulg. as substitute for *about*, *concerning*, in ordinary use); *re infēc′tā*, without having accomplished one's object (esp. *return re infecta*).

re- (see †Pronunciation, **Hyphen, below), pref. f. L *re-*, *red-*, again, back, un-. *Re-* both forms part of large numbers of already compounded words borrowed f. L or Rom., & is treated as a living pref. In the latter capacity it may be prefixed for the occasion to any vb or vbl derivative; this is esp. common in such phrr. as *traverse & re-traverse* = traverse again & again, *reckoning & re-reckoning, translation & re-translation;* but many vbs etc. that originated as nonce-wds have become established, often with restriction to one or some only of the simple word's senses; the more common or important words of this class, & others whose simplicity of meaning allows them to be grouped with it, are given with any necessary information under senses 8, 9, below. Those senses are the simple ones, found also in many of the wds compounded before being adopted by E; but in others of the pre-E compds the sense of the pref. has been so developed as to be obscure or unrecognizable, & senses 1–7 are given as a rough classification.

†Pronunciation:—rē in all wds (esp. all given under senses 8, 9) that are historically, or are capable of being taken for, simple modifications of existing E wds by one of those senses (even when a similarly spelt compd exists in senses not capable of being so regarded; so *rĕcover*= cover again, cf. RECOVER[1], *rĕcount*=count again, cf. RECOUNT[1], *rĕcreation* second or new creation, cf. *recreation* in RECREATE[1]); rĕ before vowels, and before h (exc. in *rehearse*); rē also in *reflex, regress* n., *rescript, retail* n.; rē also in *recalesce, recrudesce, regelate,* & their derivv., & *recantation, retardation, retraction,* †*retractility:* elsewhere, rĭ when the next syllable bears the word-accent (*reflect'*, *repos'itory*), & otherwise rĕ (*recollect'*, *rev'ocable*).

**Hyphen:—The hyphen is often used when a writer wishes to mark the fact that he is using not a well-known compd vb, but *re-* as a living prefix (senses 8, 9) attached to a simple vb (*re-pair* = pair again, cf. *repair* mend); also usu. before e (*re-emerge*), & occas. before other vowels (*re-assure*, usu. *reassure*); also when the idea of repetition is to be emphasized, esp. in such phrr. as *make & re-make*.

1–7: Special senses chiefly in pre-E compds.

1. In return, mutual(ly): *react, reciprocal, recompense, recrimination, rejoinder, remunerate, repartee, repay, requite, result, revenge,* etc.

2. Opposition: *rebel, recalcitrant, recusant, reluctance, remonstrate, repugnant, resist, revolt,* etc.

3. Behind, after: *relic, relinquish, relish, remain, remorse,* REST[3, 4], etc.

4. Retirement, secrecy: *recluse, recondite, recourse, refuge, remote, repository, reticent,* etc.

5. Off, away, down: *rebate, relax, release, relegate, remiss, renounce, repress, repudiate, rescind, reside, resolve, retail,* etc.

6. Frequentative or intensive: *redolent,*

redouble, redoubtable, redound, reduplicate, refine, refulgent, regard, rejoice, remark, renown, repine, repute, research, respect, resplendent, revere, revile, revolve, etc.

7. Negative, un-: *reproach, reproof, reprobate, resign, reveal.*

8, 9: Ordinary senses as living prefix.

8. Once more, again, anew, afresh, repeated, (often with implication that previous doing etc. was deficient or erroneous or now requires alteration or improvement or renewal; many wds may be classed indifferently under 8 or 9): *readdress'* v.t., change address of (letter); *readjust'* v.t.; so *readjust'ment* n.; *reaffirm'* v.t.; so *reaffirma'tion* n.; *reappa'rel* v.t.; *reapprais'al* n., second or fresh appraisal, revaluation; *rearm'* v.i. & t., provide (troops) with arms of new pattern, restore (country) to military strength; so *rearm'ament* n.; *rearrange'* v.t.; so *rearrange'ment* n.; *reassert'* v.t.; so *reasser'tion* n.; *reassess'* v.t.; so *reassess'ment* n.; *reassign'* v.t.; so *rebaptize'* v.t., lit., & fig. give new name to; so *rebap'tism* n.; *rebirth'* n., esp. fresh incarnation; so *reborn'* p.p.; *rebite'* v.t., (defective parts of etched etc. plate with acid); *rebuild'* v.t.; *recapit'ulate* v.t., go over headings of, summarize, go quickly through again; so *recapitula'tion* n. (spec. in biol., reproduction in embryos of successive type-forms in line of development), *recapit'ulative, recapit'ulatory,* aa.; *recast'* v.t., & n., (put into) new shape, improve(d) arrangement etc. (of); *rechri'sten* v.t., = rebaptize above; *reclothe'* v.t.; *recoal'* v.t.; *recoat'* v.t., put new coat of paint on; *recoin'* v.t.; so *recoin'age* n.; *recol'onize* v.t.; so *recoloniza'tion* n.; *recol'our* v.t.; *recombine'* v.t.; so *recombina'tion* n.; *recommence'* v.t. & i.; so *recommence'ment* n.; *recommit'* v.t., esp. refer back (bill etc.) for further consideration to committee; so *recommit'ment, recommit'al,* nn.; *recompose'* v.t.; *recompound'* v.t.; *reconsid'er* v.t.; so *reconsidera'tion* n.; *reconstit'uent* a. & n., (remedy) that builds up strength or tissue anew; *recon'stitute* v.t., esp. piece together (past events) into an intelligible whole; so *reconstitu'tion* n.; *reconstruct'* v.t.; so *reconstruc'tion* n., *reconstruc'tive* a.; *re--count'* v.t., (esp. votes at election as security against error), & see RECOUNT[1]; so *re-count'* n.; *re-cov'er* v.t., (esp. umbrellas etc.), & see RECOVER[1]; *recreate'* v.t., create over again, & see RECREATE[1]; so *recrea'tion,* & see in RECREATE[1]; *redirect'* v.t., esp. = readdress above; so *redirec'tion* n.; *redistrib'ute* v.t.; so *redistribu'tion* n., esp. of seats in Parliament or voting-power in elections, *redistrib'utive* a.; *redivide'* v.t.; so *redivi'sion,* n.; *redo'* v.t.; *redye'* v.t.; *re--ed'it* v.t.; so *re-edi'tion* n.; *re-enforce'* v.t. (cf. REINFORCE); *re-en'gine* v.t., supply (ship etc.) with new engine(s); *re-exam'ine* v.t., esp. of opening side's second examination of witness after opponents' cross-examination; so *re-examina'tion* n.; *reface'* v.t., put new facing on (building); *refa'shion* v.t.; so *refa'shionment* n.; *refil'* v.t. & i., restore (ship) by, (of ship) undergo, renewal & repairs; so *refit'*, *refit'ment*, nn.; *refoot'* v.t., supply new foot to (stocking); *refurn'ish* v.t.; *regen'esis* n.; *regroup'* v.t.; *rehan'dle* v.t., esp. = *recast* above; *rehang'* v.t., (esp. pictures, curtains); *rehash'* v.t., & n., (put) stale materials esp. of literary kind in new shape; *rehear'* v.t., (case in lawcourt); *rehear'ing* n.; *rehouse'* v.t., provide with new house(s); *reincarn'ate* v.t.; so *reincarna'tion* n., entrance of the soul, after death, into another human (or animal) body, *reincarn'ate* (-at) a.; *reink'* v.t.; *reinsure'* v.i. & t. (esp. of underwriter re. devolving risk upon another); so *reinsur'ance* n.; *reinter'* v.t.; *reinvest'*[1] (see also sense 9) v.t., shift (money) to other investment; so *reinvest'ment* n.; *reiss'ue* v.t.; so *reiss'uable* a. (esp. of bills or notes), *reiss'ue* n., esp. part of already published edition to be sold with change of form or price; *reit'erate* v.t., say or do over again or several times, repeat; so *reitera'tion* n., *reit'erative* a.; *relab'el* v.t.; *relive'* v.i. & t.; *reload'* v.t.; *remake'* v.t.; *reman'*[1] (see also sense 9) v.t., equip with fresh men; *remar'gin* v.t., (esp. of secondhand bookseller repairing worn book); *rema'rry* v.i. & t.; so *rema'rriage* n.; *remast'* v.t.; *remint'* v.t.; *remod'el* v.t.; *remould'* v.t.; *remount'* (see also REMOUNT[2]) v.t., esp. provide with fresh horse etc.; *rem'ount* n., supply of fresh horses for regiment etc., fresh horse; *rename'* v.t.; *renum'ber* v.t., esp. change numbers of series etc.; *reorg'anize* v.t.; so *reorganiza'tion*, *reorg'anizer*, nn.; *repap'er* v.t., *reparti'tion* v.t.; *reperuse'* v.t.; so *reperus'al* n.; *replant'* v.t.; so *replanta'tion* n.; *repot'* v.t. (esp. plant into larger pot); *reprint'* v.t.; *rep'rint* n., book, article, etc., reprinted; *reproduce'* v.t. & i., esp. (trans.) produce copy or representation of, (intr.) multiply by generation; so *reproduc'tion* n., *reproduce'able*, *reprodu'cible*, *reproduc'tive*, aa., *reproduc'tively* adv., *reproduc'tiveness* n.; *reprovi'sion* v.t.; *repub'lish* v.t. (esp. book etc.); so *republication* n.; *reread'* v.t.; *reseat'* v.t., esp. provide church, theatre, etc., with fresh seats; *reseek'* v.t.; *reset'* v.t. (esp. gems); *reset'tle* v.t.; so *reset'tlement* n.; *reshape'* v.t.; *reshuf'fle* v.t. (esp. cards, also n.); *resole'* v.t.; *respell'* v.t., esp. spell phonetically; *restamp'* v.t.; *restart'* v.t. & i., & n.; *restate'* v.t., esp. put into more intelligible or convincing words; so *restate'ment* n.; *restock'* v.t. & i., provide with or take in fresh stock; *resumm'ons* n., renewed legal summons; *resurvey'* v.t.; so *resurv'ey* n.;

retaste' v.t.; *retell'* v.t.; *retouch'* v.t. (esp. composition, picture, etc.), & n.; *retrim'* v.t.; *retry'* v.t., = *rehear* above; so *retri'al* n.; *returf'* v.t.; *reurge'* v.t.; *revac'cinate* v.t.; so *revaccina'tion* n.; *reval'ue* v.t., assess value of anew; so *revalua'tion* n.; *revic'tual* v.t.; *revis'it* (often rī-) v.t.; *reword'* v.t., change wording of; *rewrite'* v.t.

9. Back, with return to previous state after lapse or cessation or occurrence of opposite state or action, (often corresponding to compounds in DIS- or UN-; many words may be assigned indifferently to 9 or 8); *reaffo'rest* v.t.; so *reafforesta'tion* n.; *rean'imate* v.t.; so *reanima'tion* n.; *reappear'* v.i.; so *reappear'ance* n.; *reappoint'* v.t.; so *reappoint'ment* n.; *rearise'* v.i.; *rearouse'* v.t.; *reascend'* v.i. & t.; *reassem'ble* v.i. & t.; *reassume'* v.t. (now rare, ousted by RESUME); so *reassump'tion* n.; *reassure'* v.t., restore to confidence, dispel apprehensions of; so *reassur'ing* a. (of words, manner, etc.), *reassur'ingly* adv.; *rebarb'arize* v.t.; *rebind'* v.t. (esp. book); *recap'ture* v.t., & n.; *re-cede'* v.t.; so *re-ce'ssion* n.; *recharge'* v.t.; *rē'charge* n., amount of substance, actual piece, used in recharging; *reciv'ilize* v.t.; so *reciviliza'tion* n.; *recom'fort* v.t.; *reconduct'* v.t.; *recon'quer* v.t.; so *recon'quest* n.; *reconvert'* v.t.; so *reconver'sion* n.; *recross'* v.t.; *redescend'* v.i. & t.; *redisco'ver* v.t.; so *redisco'very* n.; *re-elect'* v.t.; so *re-elec'tion* n.; *re-el'igible* a.; *re-embark'* v.i. & t.; so *re-embarka'tion* n.; *re-emerge'* v.i.; so *re-emer'gence* n., *re-emer'gent* a.; *re-ena'ble* v.t.; *re-enact'* v.t.; so *re-enact'ment* n.; *re-en'ter* v.i. & t. (part. occas. = RE-ENTRANT); *re-en'trance* n.; *re-estab'lish* v.t.; so *re-estab'lishment* n.; *re-exist'* v.i.; *re-export'* v.t.; *re-ex'port* n., commodity imported & then exported esp. without further manufacture; so *re-exporta'tion* n.; *refill'* v.t.; *rēf'ill* n., = *recharge* above; *refloat'* v.t. (stranded ship); *rēf'lux* n., backward flow; *refo'rest* v.t., turn into forest again; so *reforesta'tion* n.; *refurb'ish* v.t.; *regerm'inate* v.i.; so *regermina'tion* n.; *regild'* v.t.; *rehabil'itate* v.t., restore to privileges, reputation, or proper condition; so *rehabilita'tion* n.; *rehum'anize* v.t.; *reignite'* v.t. & i.; *reimport'* v.t., import (same goods) after exporting; so *reim'port* n.; *reimpose'* v.t.; so *reimposi'tion* n.; *reincorp'orate* v.t.; *reingra'tiate* v.t.; *reinsert'* v.t.; so *reinscr'tion* n.; *reinvest'*[2] (see also sense 8) v.t., replace *in* office, *with* privilege; so *reinves'titure* n.; *reinvig'orate* v.t.; so *reinvigora'tion* n.; *rekin'dle* v.t. & i.; *reline'* v.t., renew lining of (esp. garment); *reman'*[2] (see also sense 8) v.t., restore to manhood or courage; *remigrate'* v.i., esp. return after migrating; so *remigra'tion* n.; *reocc'upy* v.t.; so *reoccupa'tion* n.; *reop'en* v.t. & i.; *repag'anize* v.t.; *repaint'*

v.t., restore paint or colouring of; *repass'* **v.t.** & i., esp. pass again on way back; so *repass'age* n.; *repeo'ple* v.t.; *repercu'ssion* n., echo, recoil after impact, indirect effect or reaction of event or act; so *repercuss'ive* a.; *repiece'* v.t., put pieces of together again, reconstruct; *repoint'* v.t. (joints of masonry); *repol'ish* v.t.; *repop'ulate* v.t.; *repossess'* v.t.; so *re-posse'ssion* n.; *repurch'ase* v.t., & n.; *repur'ify* v.t.; *requick'en* v.t.; *resad'dle* v.t. & abs.; *resale'* n., esp. sale of thing bought; so *resal'able* n.; *reseize'* v.t.; so *reseiz'ure* n.; *resell'* v.t., esp. sell after buying; *reship'* v.t. & i., put, go, on board ship again; so *reship'ment* n.; *restuff'* v.t.; *retake'* v.t.; *rĕt'ake* n. (cinemat.), a second photograph(ing) of a scene; *retransfer'* v.t.; so *rctrans'fer* n.; *retransform'* v.t.; *retranslate'* v.t. (esp. back into the original language); so *retransla'tion* n.; *retread'* v.t.; *reunite'* v.t. & i.; *revit'alize* v.t.; *rewin'* v.t.

're, colloq. abbr. of *are* appended to *we, you, & they* (*we're, you're, they're*).

reach[1], v.t. & i. **1.** Stretch out, extend, (t. & i.; often *out* etc.; *~ed out his hand, its branches; a dominion ~ing from the Ebro to the Carpathians*). **2.** Stretch out the hand etc., make ~ing motion or effort lit. or fig., (*you must ~ out further; mind ~es forward to an ideal; ship ~es ahead in race*). **3.** Get as far as, attain to, arrive at, (specified point or object of destination; also abs.), succeed in affecting, either simply or with the hand or instrument or missile or influence, (~ BOTTOM[1]; *~ed land; could not ~ his enemy*, esp. in fencing, boxing; *how is her conscience to be ~ed?; libels that the ordinary law ~es; the steps by which you ~ the entrance; your letter ~ed me today; every syllable ~ed the audience; has ~ed middle age, its eighth edition; cannot ~ so high, far enough, down, up to it*, etc.; *as far as eye could ~; my income will not ~ to it*). **4.** Hand, pass or take with outstretched hand, (*~ed him the book; ~ed down his hat*). **5.** (naut.). Sail with the wind abeam. **6.** ‖*~-me-down* a. & n. (sl.), ready-made (garment). Hence *~'ABLE* a. [OE *rǣcan*, MDu., MLG *reiken*, OHG *reichen* f. WG **raik-jan*]

reach[2], n. **1.** Act of reaching out. **2.** Extent to which hand etc. can be reached out, influence be exerted, motion be carried out, or mental powers be used, range, scope, compass, (*within, above, out of, beyond*, one's ~, possible, impossible, of attainment or performance; *has a wide ~; within easy ~ of the railway; no help was within~*). **3.** Continuous extent, esp. part of river that can be looked along at once between two bends. **4.** (naut.). Length of tack. [f. prec.]

reǎct', v.i. **1.** Produce reciprocal or responsive effect, act upon the agent, (*they ~ upon each other; tyranny ~s upon the tyrant*, has effects upon him as well as upon his victims); (chem., of substance applied to' another) call out activity, cause manifestation, (*nitrous oxide ~s upon the metal*). **2.** Respond to stimulus, undergo change due to some influence. **3.** (mil.). Make counter-attack(s). **4.** Be actuated by repulsion *against*, tend in reverse or backward direction. Hence **reǎc'tive** a., **reǎctiv'ity** n., **reǎc'tor** n., atomic PILE[2] (also *nuclear ~or*). [RE- 1]

reǎc'tance, n. (electr.). That component of the impedance of an alternating--current circuit due to capacitance or inductance or both. [f. prec., -ANCE]

reǎc'tion, n. **1.** Responsive or reciprocal action (esp. *action & ~*); (chem.) action set up by one substance in another; CHAIN ~. **2.** Response of organ etc. to external stimulus; responsive feeling (*what was his ~ to this news?*); immediate or first impression. **3.** Return of previous condition after interval of opposite (e.g. glow felt after cold bath, depression after excitement). **4.** (mil.). Counter-stroke. **5.** Retrograde tendency esp. in politics, whence *~ARY*[1] (-sho-) a. & (= ~ary person) n., *~IST*(2) (-sho-) n. & a. **6.** (radio). Method by which weak signals are strengthened. [RE- 1]

reǎc'tiv|āte, v.t. Restore to a state of activity. Hence *~A'TION* n. [RE- 8]

read (rĕd), v.t. & i. (*read*, pr. rĕd), & n. **1.** Interpret mentally, declare interpretation or coming development of, divine, (~ *dream, riddle, omen, futurity, men's hearts or thoughts or faces; ~* person's *hand*, as palmist; *~ the sky*, as astrologist or meteorologist). **2.** (Be able to) convert into the intended words or meaning (written or printed or other symbols or things expressed by their means, or abs.; *~s* or *can ~ hieroglyphs, shorthand, the clock, the Morse system, music, several languages; does not ~ or write*). **3.** Reproduce mentally or (often *aloud, out, off,* etc., or with ind. obj.) vocally, while following their symbols with eyes or fingers, the words of (author, book, tale, letter, etc., or abs.; often *over, through,* advv.; *~s well*, with good intonation etc., expressively; *was ~ ing Plato; ~ it through six times; does he preach extempore or ~?; have no time to ~; the Bible is the most ~ of all books; ~ one a lesson*, admonish him; *the Bill was ~ for the first* etc. *time*, was allowed its first etc. READING; *invalid is ~ to for several hours daily; seldom ~s French*, anything written in it). **4.** Study (t. & i.) by *~*ing (often *up; is ~ing law; shall not ~ for honours;* ‖*~ing man*, who devotes most of his time to study; *has ~ much*); (p.p. in active sense as adj. with *well, deeply, slightly, little,* etc.) versed in subject by *~*ing, acquainted with literature. **5.** Find (thing) stated, find statement, in print etc. (*revenge, we ~, is wild justice; I have ~ somewhere that . . ., have*

~ of it). **6.** Interpret (statement, action) in certain sense (*may be ~ several ways; my silence is not to be ~ as consent*). **7.** Assume as intended in or deducible from writer's words, find implications, (*you ~ too much into the text; in their pleas for reform I ~ Protection*; ~ *between the lines*, search for or discover hidden meanings). **8.** (Of editor or text) give as the word(s) probably used by author (*Bentley ~s* peraeque; also joc. in correcting statements, as *for* white *~* black, *& the account may be accepted*). **9.** Bring into specified state by ~ing (*~ me to sleep, himself stupid, hoarse,* etc.; ‖ *~* oneself *in,* of incumbent, enter upon office by public reading of xxxix articles etc.). **10.** (Of recording instrument) present (figure etc.) to one ~ing it (*thermometer ~s* 33°). **11.** Sound or affect hearer or reader *well, ill,* etc., when ~ (*play ~s better than it acts; ~s like a threat, translation,* etc.). **12.** n. Time spent in ~ing (*have a short, long, good, quiet, ~*). [OE *rǣdan* consider, discern, = OS *rādan,* OHG *rātan,* ON *rātha,* Goth. *·rēdan* f. Gmc **rǣdhan*]

read'ab|le, a. Capable of being read with pleasure or interest; (rare) legible. Hence **readaBIL'ITY,** ~leNESS, nn., ~LY² adv. [-ABLE]

readdress. See RE- 8.

read'er, n. In vbl senses; also or esp.: person employed by publisher to read & report on offered MSS.; printer's proof- -corrector; person appointed to read aloud, esp. (often *lay ~*) parts of service in church; ‖ higher grade of lecturer in some universities etc. (*~ in Roman law* etc.); book of selections for use by students of a language etc. Hence~SHIP n. [-ER¹]

rea'dily (rĕd-), adv. Without showing reluctance, willingly; without difficulty (*the facts may ~ be ascertained*). [READY, -LY²]

rea'diness (rĕd-), n. Prompt compliance, willingness; facility, prompt resourcefulness, quickness in argument or action; ready or prepared state (*all is in ~*). [READY, -NESS]

read'ing, n. In vbl senses; also or esp.: literary knowledge (*a man of vast ~*); *first, second, third, ~,* successive occasions on which Bill must have been presented for acceptance to each House before it is ready for royal assent (*first ~,* permitting introduction; *second,* approving general principle; *third,* accepting details as amended in committee); entertainment at which something is read to audience (‖ *penny ~,* formerly for poor of parish etc.); word(s) read or given by an editor or found in text of a passage (*the right, true, best, MS.,* etc., ~; *various ~s*); (specified quality of) matter to be read (*is good, dull, ~; there is plenty of ~ in it*); figure etc. shown by graduated instrument (*40° difference between day & night ~s*);

interpretation, view taken, rendering, (*what is your ~ of the facts?; his ~ of Iago was generally condemned*); ~*desk,* for supporting book etc., lectern; ~*room,* in club, library, etc. for persons wishing to read. [-ING¹]

readjust etc. See RE- 8.

rea'dy (rĕd-), a., adv., n., & v.t. **1.** With preparations complete, in fit state, with resolution nerved, willing, apt, inclined, about *to,* prompt, quick, facile, provided beforehand, within reach, easily secured, unreluctant, easy, fit for immediate use, (*Are you ~? Go!,* formula for starting race; ~, *present, fire,* successive orders, the first = make rifle ~; *dinner is ~; are ~ to march; am ~ to risk my life; is too ~ to suspect; was ~ to swear with rage; a bud just ~ to burst; is ~ for death; the ~ ministers of vengeance; is very~ at excuses, has a ~ pen, wit,* whence ~-witTED² a., etc.; *gave a ~ consent; found ~ acceptance; its ~ solubility in water; found an instrument ~ to hand, a ~ source of revenue; the readiest way to do it; make ~,* prepare i. & t., as *they made ~ for the attempt* or *to fight,* or *made everything ~*; ~ *money,* actual coin, also payment on the spot); ~ *reckoner,* book of ~-reckoned (see adv.) computations of kind commonly wanted in business. **2.** adv. (chiefly with p.p., usu. hyphened, prop. a pred. use of adj.). Beforehand, so as not to require doing when the time comes, (*please pack everything ~; boxes are ~ packed* or *packed ~*; ~*-built houses*; ~*-made clothes,* made in standard shapes & sizes, not to customer's individual measure; ~*-made shop,* selling these); (rare exc. in comp. & superl.) quickly (*the child that answers readiest*). **3.** n. Position in which rifle is held before the present (*come to the ~* etc.); (sl.) ~ money (*planked down the ~*). **4.** v.t. Make ~, prepare. [ME *rǣdi(g), re(a)di,* f. OE *rǣde* + -Y², f. Gmc **raidh-* put in order, prepare; cf. OHG *bireiti* (G *bereit*) prepared]

reaffirm etc., see RE- 8; **reafforest** etc., RE- 9.

reä'gency, n. Reactive power or operation (see REACT).

reä'gent, n. (Chem.) substance used to detect presence of another by REACTION; reactive substance or force (see REACT).

re'al¹ (rē-, rä-), n. Former silver coin & money of account used in Spain and Spanish-speaking countries (the ~ *de plata* being worth 6½*d.,* and the ~ *de vellon,* of base metal, 2½*d.*). [Sp., n. use of adj. f. L *regalis* REGAL]

re'al², a. **1.** Actually existing as a thing or occurring in fact, objective, genuine, rightly so called, natural, sincere, not merely apparent or nominal or supposed or pretended or artificial or hypocritical or affected, (*~ money,* coin, cash; *the ~*

presence, of Christ's body & blood in the Eucharist as disputed by theologians; *a ~ object & its image*; *~ & paper roses*; *effected a ~ cure*; *should like a ~ fine day*; *~ life*, that lived by actual people, opp. fictitious & dramatic imitations; *there is no ~ doubt about it*; *who is the ~ manager?*; *is a ~ man*, unaffected, also worthy of the name; *the ~ thing*, not a makeshift or inferior article). 2. (law; cf. PERSONAL). Consisting of immovable property such as lands or houses (esp. ~ *estate*). 3. (philos.). Having an absolute & necessary & not merely contingent existence. 4. abs. *The ~*, what is ~, esp. opp. the ideal (also rarely as n. with pl. *= ~ thing*, as *I deal only with ~s*). [f. OF *real, reel,* or LL *realis* (*res* thing, -AL)]

rěăl'gar, n. Disulphide of arsenic, red arsenic, red orpiment, used as pigment & in fireworks. [ME, f. med. L, f. Arab. *rehj alghār* powder of the cave]

rē'al|ism, n. **1.** Scholastic doctrine that universals or general ideas have objective existence (cf. *nominalism, conceptualism*). **2.** Belief that matter as object of perception has real existence (cf. *idealism*). **3.** Practice of regarding things in their true nature & dealing with them as they are, freedom from prejudice & convention, practical views & policy, (cf. *idealism*). **4.** Fidelity of representation, truth to nature, insistence upon details. So~IST(2) n. & a.,~is'TIC a.,~is'TICALLY adv. [-ISM]

rěăl'ĭty, n. Property of being real; resemblance to original (*reproduced with startling ~*); real existence, what is real, what underlies appearances, (*in ~*, in fact, opp. *in words, in appearance*, etc.); existent thing; real nature *of*. [f. med. L *realitas,* or F *réalité* (REAL², -TY)]

rē'aliz|e, -is|e (-ĭz), v.t. **1.** Convert (hope, plan, etc.) into fact (usu. pass.). **2.** Give apparent reality to, make realistic, present as real, (*these details help to ~e the scene*); conceive as real, apprehend clearly or in detail (noun, *that, how,* etc.). **3.** Convert (securities, property) into money (often abs., = sell one's property); amass (fortune, specified profit); fetch as price. Hence ~ABLE a.,~A'TION n. [-IZE, after F *réaliser*]

really (rĭ'ali), adv. In fact, in reality, (often *~ & truly*); positively, indeed, I assure you, I mean what I say, I protest; *~?*, do you mean it?, is that so? [ME, after med. L *realiter*; see -LY²]

realm (rělm), n. Kingdom (chiefly rhet., & in some legal phrr., as *the laws of the ~, persons who are out of the ~*); sphere, province, domain, (*the ~s of fancy, poetry,* etc.). [ME, f. OF *realme, reaume,* f. L *regiminem* REGIMEN infl. by *reial* ROYAL]

real-politik (rāahl' pŏltěk'), n. Policy of placing the material greatness and success of one's own nation before all other considerations. [G]

•rē'ăltŏr, n. Real-estate agent (prop. one who is a member or affiliated member of the National Association of Real Estate Boards). [U.S., f. foll. +-OR]

rē'alty, n. Real estate (cf. *personalty*). [-TY]

ream¹, n. Twenty quires or 480 sheets of paper (often 500, to allow for waste; *printers' ~*, 516); (often pl.) large quantity of paper (*wrote ~s & ~s of verse*). [ME *rem* (= OF *rayme, reyme*), *rim* (= Du. *riem*), ult. f. Arab. *rizmah* bundle (cf. It. *risma*)]

ream², v.t. Widen (hole in metal) with borer or ~'ER¹(2) n.; turn over edge of (cartridge-case etc.); (naut.) open (seam) for caulking. [19th c., of obsc. orig.]

|| ream³, n. (dial., esp. SW. Eng.). Raw cream. [OE *rēam,* MHG *roum,* G *rahm*]

reanimate etc. See RE- 9.

reap, v.i. & t. Cut (grain or similar crop), cut grain etc., with sickle in harvest; gather in thus or with machine or fig. as harvest (*~ as one has sown, sow wind & ~ whirlwind, ~ the fruits of,* take consequences of one's actions; *~ where one has not sown,* profit by others' toil); harvest crop of (field etc.); *~ing-hook,* sickle; *~ing-machine,* for cutting grain & often binding sheaves without manual labour. Hence ~'ER¹(1, 2) n. [OE *ripan, reopan,* excl. E]

reapparel, see RE- 8; **reappear** etc., **reappoint** etc., RE- 9; **reappraisal,** RE- 8.

rear¹, n. Hindermost part of army or fleet (*hang on the ~, of,* follow with view to attacking); back of, space behind, position at back of, army or camp or person (*bring, close, up the ~,* come last; *take enemy in ~,* attack from behind; *saw them far in the ~,* behind; *was sent to the ~ for safety*); back part of anything (*at the ~ of,* behind); || (colloq.) water-closet or latrine; ~-, *~ attrib.,* hinder, back-; so ~'MOST a.; *~-admiral,* flag-officer below vice-admiral; *~'guard,* body of troops detached to protect ~ esp. in retreats (*~guard action,* engagement between ~-guard & enemy); *~'ward* n. [f. AF *rerewarde = ~guard*], ~ (esp. in prep. phrr., as *to ~ward of, in the ~ward*); *~'ward* a. & adv., *~'wards* adv., towards the ~ [-WARD(S)]. [aphestic f. ARREAR]

rear², v.t. & i. **1.** Raise, set upright, build, uplift, hold upwards, (rhet.; *~ a pillar, cathedral,* etc.; *~ed his mighty stature; ~ one's head,* one's *voice, a hand,* etc.). **2.** Raise, bring up, breed, foster, nourish, educate, cultivate, grow, (cattle, game, children, crops, etc.). **3.** (Of horse etc.; intr. & rarely refl.) rise, raise itself, on hind legs. Hence ~'ER¹ n. [OE *rēran, = ON reisa,* Goth. -*raisjan*; see RAISE]

rear-'ārch, rēre-', n. Inner arch of window or door opening distinct from the outer.

rearise, see RE- 9; **rearm** etc., RE- 8; **rearouse,** RE- 9; **rearrange** etc., RE- 8.

rear-vault, n. Vault between arched

window or door head and arch in inner face of wall.

reascend. See RE- 9.

reas'on[1] (-z-), n. **1.** (Fact adduced or serving as) argument, motive, cause, or justification (*give ~s for; prove with ~s; the woman's~*, repetition of fact as its own explanation, as in *I love him because I love him; for no other ~ than that I forgot, but this; there is no ~ to suppose; ~ of State*, political justification esp. for immoral proceeding; *the ~ of your isolation, of eclipses, is that —; failed by ~ of its bad organization; there was ~ to believe; I saw ~ to suspect him; he complains with~*, not unjustifiably). **2.** (log.). One of premisses of syllogism, esp. minor premiss when given after conclusion. **3.** The intellectual faculty characteristic esp. of human beings by which conclusions are drawn from premisses (*whether dogs have ~ is really a question of definition; there can be no opposition between ~ & common sense*). **4.** Intellect personified (*God & ~ are identical*); (as transl. of G *Vernunft* in Kant) faculty transcending the understanding (*Verstand*) & providing *a priori* principles, intuition. **5.** Sanity (*has lost his, is restored to, ~*). **6.** Sense, sensible conduct, what is right or practical or practicable, moderation, (*without* RHYME *or ~; bring to ~*, induce to cease from vain resistance; *will do anything in ~*, within the bounds of moderation; *it stands to ~*, cannot be denied without paradox, would be generally admitted; *hear* or *listen to~*, suffer oneself to be persuaded; *as ~ was*, as good sense bade; *have ~*, arch. or transl. of F, be right; *there is ~ in what you say*). Hence ~LESS a. [ME, f. OF *raisun* f. L *rationem* (*rēri rat-* consider, -ION)]

reas'on[2] (-z-), v.i. & t. **1.** Use argument *with* person by way of persuasion. **2.** Form or try to reach conclusions by connected thought silent or expressed (*from* premisses; *about, of, upon*, subject), whence ~ER[1] n.; discuss *what, whether, why*, etc.; conclude, assume as step in argument, say by way of argument, *that* (or parenth.). **3.** Express in logical or argumentative form (*a ~ed exposition, manifesto, article; ~ed amendment*, in which reasons are embodied with a view to directing course of debate). **4.** Persuade by argument *out of, into* (*tried to ~ him out of his fears; ~ed himself into perplexity*). **5.** Think *out* (consequences etc.). Hence ~ING[1](1) n. [ME, f. OF *raisoner* f. Rom. **rationare* (prec.)]

reas'onab|le (-z-), a. **1.** Endowed with reason, reasoning, (rare). **2.** Sound of judgement, sensible, moderate, not expecting too much, ready to listen to reason. **3.** Agreeable to reason, not absurd, within the limits of reason, not

greatly less or more than might be expected, inexpensive, not extortionate, tolerable, fair. Hence ~leNESS n., ~LY[2] adv. [ME, f. OF *raisonable* (REASON[1], -ABLE), after L *rationabilis*]

reassemble, see RE- 9; **reassert, reassess** etc., **reassign,** RE- 8; **reassume** etc., **reassure** etc., RE- 9.

Réaumur (see Ap.), n. Name of French physicist appended (abbr. R.) to readings of the thermometer introduced by him with freezing-point 0° & boiling-point 80° (*a temperature of more than 55° R. or ~*). [F]

‖ **reave, reive,** (rēv), v.i. & t. (arch., poet.; *réft*). Commit ravages (usu. *reive*), whence **reiv'**ER[1] (rēv-) n.; forcibly deprive *of* (esp. in p.p.); take by force, carry off, (*away, from*). [OE *rēafian*, OS *rōbōn*, OHG *roubōn*, Goth. *-raubōn* f. Gmc **raubhōjan*]

rebaptize etc., see RE- 8; **rebarbarize,** RE- 9.

rebarb'ative, a. Repellent, unattractive. [f. F *rébarbatif, -ive* f. *barbe* beard]

‖ **rebāte'**[1], v.t. (arch.). Diminish, reduce force or effect of; blunt, dull. [f. OF *rabattre* (RE- 5, ABATE)]

rēb'āte[2] (*also* rĭbāt'), n. Deduction from sum to be paid, discount, drawback. [f. F *rabat* (prec.)]

rebate[3] (răb'ĭt, rĭbāt'), n., & v.t. = RABBET.

rēb'ĕc(k), n. Medieval three-stringed instrument, early form of fiddle. [f. F *rebec* var. of OF *rebebe* f. Arab. *rebab*]

rĕb'el[1], n. Person who rises in arms against, resists, or refuses allegiance to, the established government; person or thing that resists authority or control; (attrib.) rebellious, of ~s, in rebellion. [orig. a & n.; the pred. a. use now obs.; f. ME, f. OF *rebelle* f. L *rebellis* (RE- 2, *bellum* war)]

rĕbĕl'[2], v.i. (-ll-). Act as rebel (*against*); feel or manifest repugnance to some custom etc. (*against*). [ME, f. OF *rebeller* f. L *re(bellare* make war), revolt, RE- 2]

rĕbĕll'ion (-lyon), n. Organized armed resistance to established government (*the Great R~*, period of English history 1642–-60); open resistance to any authority. [ME, f. OF f. L *rebellionem* (REBEL[1], -ION)]

rĕbĕll'ious (-lyus), a. In rebellion, disposed to rebel, insubordinate, defying lawful authority; (of diseases, things) difficult to treat, unmanageable, refractory. Hence ~LY[2] adv., ~NESS n. [as REBEL[1] or prec. +-OUS]

rĕbĕll'ow (-ō), v.i. & t. (poet.). Re-echo loudly. [RE- 6; after L *re(boare* bellow), 'RE- 6]

rebind, see RE- 9; **rebirth** etc., **rebite,** RE- 8.

rĕb'ōant, a. (poet.). Rebellowing, resounding, re-echoing. [f. L *reboare* RE-BELLOW, -ANT]

For pronunciation & hyphening of *re-* see RE- ; for words in *re-* not given see RE- 8, 9.

rĕbound'[1], v.i. Spring back after impact; have reactive effect, recoil upon agent, (*our evil example will ~ upon ourselves*). [ME, f. OF *rebonder* (RE- 1, BOUND³)]

rĕbound'[2], n. Act of rebounding, recoil; reaction after emotion (*take* one *on* or *at the ~*, utilize such reaction to persuade him to contrary action etc.). [f. prec.]

rĕbuff', n., & v.t. 1. Check given to one who makes advances, proffers help or sympathy, shows interest or curiosity, makes request, etc., repulse, snub. 2. v.t. Give ~ to. [f. obs. F *rebuffe(r)* f. It. *rabbuffo, rabbuffare,* (RE- 2, *buffo* puff)]

rebuild. See RE- 8.

rĕbūk|e', v.t., & n. 1. Reprove, reprimand, censure authoritatively; hence ~'ing_LY² adv. 2. n. ~ing or being ~ed; a reproof. [ME, f. ONF *re(buker* = OF *bucher* beat), RE- 5]

rĕb'us, n. Enigmatic representation of name, word, etc., by pictures etc. suggesting its syllables. [prob. = abl. pl. of L *res* thing; origin of sense (in F & E) doubtful]

rĕbŭt', v.t. (-tt-). Force or turn back, give check to; refute, disprove, (evidence, charge), whence ~t'AL(2), ~MENT, ~t'ER⁴ (see SURREBUT), nn. [f. OF *re(buter* BUTT⁴), RE- 9]

rĕcǎl'cĭtr|āte, v.i. Kick *against* or *at* rules etc., refuse compliance, be refractory. So ~ANT(1) a. & n., ~ANCE, ~A'TION, nn. [f. L *re(calcitrare* strike with heel f. *calx -cis* heel), RE- 2, -ATE³]

rĕcal|ĕsce', v.i. Grow hot again (esp. in techn. use of iron allowed to cool from white heat, which recovers heat at certain point for short time). Hence ~ĕs'CENCE n. [f. L *re(calescere* grow hot), RE- 9]

rĕcall'[1] (-awl), v.t. Summon back from a place or from different occupation, inattention, digression, etc.; cancel appointment of (official sent to distance, esp. overseas); bring back to memory, serve as reminder of, recollect, remember; revive, resuscitate; revoke, annul, (action, decision), take back (gift). Hence ~ABLE a. [RE- 9]

rĕcall'[2] (-awl), n. Summons to come back; cancelling of appointment abroad; signal to ship etc. to return; possibility of recalling esp. in sense of annulling (esp. *beyond, past, ~*). [RE- 9]

rĕcǎnt', v.t. & i. Withdraw & renounce (opinion, statement, etc.) as erroneous or heretical; disavow former opinion, esp. with public confession of error. Hence rĕcǎnta'TION n. [f. L *re(cantare* sing) revoke, RE- 7]

rē'căp, v.t. & n. (colloq.). Recapitulate; (n.) recapitulation. [abbr.]

recapitulate etc., see RE- 8; **recapture,** RE- 9; **recast,** RE- 8.

recce (rĕk'ĭ), n. (mil. sl.). Reconnaissance. [abbr.]

rĕcēde', v.i. Go or shrink back or farther off; be left by observer's motion at in-

creasing distance; slope backwards; withdraw (*from* engagement, opinion, etc.); decline in character or value. [f. L *re(cedere* go), RE- 5]

rĕceipt' (-sēt), n., & v.t. 1. = RECIPE. 2. Amount of money received. 3. Fact or action of receiving or being received into person's hands or possession (*on ~ of a postal order for 10|- the goods will be sent; beg to acknowledge ~ of your book; entrusted with the ~ of subscriptions*); written acknowledgement of such ~ esp. of payment of sum due. 4. (arch.). Place where money is officially received, esp. ~ *of custom,* custom-house. 5. v.t. Write or print ~ on (bill). [ME *receit* f. ONF *receite* f. L *recepta* fem. p.p. of *recipere* RECEIVE w. *-p-* inserted on L]

rĕceive' (-sēv), v.t. 1. Accept delivery of, take (proffered thing) into one's hands or possession, (*Lord, ~ my soul,* dying man's prayer; *~ stolen goods,* as thief's accomplice; ~ person's *confession, oath,* consent to hear; *~ a petition,* take it to consider; *~ the sacraments,* eat & drink the bread & wine, also abs., as *attend without receiving*). 2. Bear up against, stand force or weight of, encounter with opposition, (*~d his body in their hands; arch ~s weight of roof; ~d the sword-point with his shield; prepare to ~ cavalry,* order to infantry). 3. Admit, consent or prove able to hold, provide accommodation for, submit to, serve as receptacle of, (*had to ~ the visits, attentions, of; ~ an impression, stamp, mark,* etc., be marked lit. or fig. more or less permanently with it; *sensitive paper ~s the record of signals; the basin that ~d his blood; the house ~d a new guest; hole large enough to ~ two men; fitted to ~ the knowledge of God; has ~d our yoke; town ~s a French garrison; was ~d into the Church,* admitted to membership). 4. Entertain as guest, greet, welcome, give specified reception to, (*shall not be ~d at my house; he that ~th me ~th him that sent me; you stay here & ~ him; how did she ~ his offer?; was ~d with cries of Judas; news was ~d with horror; I ~ it as certain, as a prophecy,* regard it in that light); (abs.) ~ company, hold reception. 5. Give credit to, accept as true, (*an axiom universally ~d; they ~ not our report*), whence rĕceivED' (-sēvd') a. (*~d pronunciation,* abbr. *R.P.,* form of speech used, with local variations, by the majority of cultured people). 6. Acquire, get, come by, be given or provided with, have sent to or conferred or inflicted on one, (*have not yet ~d my dividend; ~ a letter, news; a window that has not ~d a frame; ~ the name of John; ~ Christ in baptism,* have Christian character conferred; *pleasant to ~ sympathy; deserves more attention than it ~s; ~ orders to march; ~d many insults, a thrust, a broken jaw, the contents of his pistol*); partake of. Hence rĕceiv'ABLE (-sēv-) a. [ME, f. ONF

receivre f. L *re(cipere = capere* take) recover, RE- 9]

receiv'er (-sĕv-), n. In vbl senses, esp.: person appointed by court's *receiving- -order* to administer property of bankrupt or property under litigation, whence ~-SHIP n.; person who receives stolen goods, fence; receptacle etc. for receiving something in machine or instrument, esp. earpiece of telephone; apparatus for transforming broadcast waves into sound or light, wireless receiving-set. [ME, f. AF *receivere, -our*; later, prec.+-ER¹]

recen'sion (-shn), n. Revision of, revised, text. [f. L *recensio* f. *re(censēre* review), RE- 8]

re'cent, a. Not long past, that happened or existed lately, late; not long established, lately begun, modern. Hence re'CENCY n., ~LY² adv., ~NESS n. [f. L *recens -entis* or F *récent*]

recep'tacle, n. Containing vessel, place, or space; (bot.) common base of floral organs, axis of cluster. [ME, f. OF, or L *receptaculum* (recept- p.p. st. of *recipere* RECEIVE)]

recep'tion, n. **1.** Receiving or being received (rare in gen. sense); receiving esp. of person, being received, into a place or company (*the rooms were prepared for his ~; was honoured by ~ into the Academy*; ‖~ *order*, authorizing ~ of lunatic in asylum). **2.** Formal or ceremonious welcome (*the ~ of the delegates is arranged for Monday next*); occasion of receiving guests, assembly held for this purpose, (*after the review there will be a ~*; ~-*room*, available for receiving company, esp. opp. *bedroom*). **3.** Receiving of ideas or impressions into the mind (*has a great faculty of ~, but little originative power*); (rare) mental acceptance, recognition of something as true or advisable, (*the general ~ of the Newtonian hypothesis*). **4.** Welcome or greeting of specified kind, demonstration of feeling towards person or project, (*warm ~*, vigorous resistance or enthusiastic welcome; *his ~ was frigid, all that he could desire*; *proposal, book, had a favourable ~*). **5.** Receiving of wireless signals, or the efficiency with which they are received. Hence ~IST (3) (-sho-) n., person employed by photographer, dentist, etc., to receive clients. [ME, f. OF, or f. L *receptio* (as prec., -ION)]

recep'tive, a. Able or quick to receive impressions or ideas (*a mind more ~ than retentive or creative*); (rare) concerned with receiving. Hence ~LY² adv., ~NESS, recĕptiv'ITY, nn. [f. med. L *receptivus* (as prec., -IVE)]

recess', n., & v.t. & i. **1.** Temporary cessation from work, vacation, esp. of Parliament; receding of water, land, glacier, etc., from previous limit, amount by which it recedes, recession, (rare);

retired or secret place (*in the inmost ~es of the Alps, of the heart*); receding part of mountain chain etc., niche or alcove of wall; (anat.) fold or indentation in organ. **2.** v. Place in a ~, set back; provide with ~(es); *(v.i.)* take a ~, adjourn. [f. L *recessus* (recess- p.p. st. of RECEDE*re*)]

reces'sion (-shn), n. Receding, withdrawal, from a place or point; receding part of object, recess; *slump in trade. So **reces'sIVE** a. & n., (also, Mendelism, of a) characteristic appearing in the second or later generation of hybrids, inherited from one of the original parents but suppressed in the first generation (cf. DOMINANT). [f. L *recessio* (as prec., -ION)]

reces'sional (-sho-), a. & n. ~ *hymn* or ~, hymn sung while clergy & choir withdraw after service; of the parliamentary recess. [-AL]

Rĕch'abĭte (-k-), n. Total abstainer. [*Rechab*, see *Jer.* xxxv. 6, -ITE¹(1)]

recharge. See RE- 9.

réchauffé (rĭshōf'ā, & see Ap.), n. Warmed-up dish; rehash (RE- 8). [F]

recherché (reshärsh'ā, & see Ap.), a. Devised or got with care or difficulty, choice, far-fetched, thought out, (esp. of meals or words). [F]

rechristen. See RE- 8.

recĭd'ivĭst, n. One who relapses into crime. So ~ISM n. [f. F *récidiviste* f. L *recidivus* f. *re(cidere = cadere* fall), RE- 9, -IVE, -IST]

re'cĭpe, n. Medical prescription or remedy prepared from it; statement of ingredients & procedure for preparing dish etc.; expedient, nostrum, device for effecting something. [2nd sing. imperat. as used (abbr. **R.**) in prescriptions of L *recipere* RECEIVE].

recĭp'ĭ|ent, a. & n. **1.** Receptive, whence ~ENCY n. **2.** n. Person who receives something. [f. L *recipere* RECEIVE, -ENT]

recĭp'rocal, a. & n. **1.** In return (*if I helped him, I had ~ help from him*); mutual (~ *love, protection, injuries*); inversely correspondent, complementary, (*I took the chamois for a man, & it made the ~ mistake*); (gram.) expressing mutual action or relation (*‘each other’ is a ~ pronoun*), (formerly also) reflexive; hence ~LY² adv. **2.** n. (math.). Function or expression so related to another that their product is unity (*1/5 is the ~ of 5*). [f. L *reciprocus* (prob. f. *re-* back & *pro* forward), -AL]

recĭp'roc|āte, v.t. & i. (Mech.) go with alternate backward & forward motion (~*ating engine* etc., with work done by part that moves thus, opp. *rotatory* see ROTATE²), give such motion to; give & receive mutually, interchange, (influence etc.); return, requite, (affection etc.), make a return (often *with* thing given in return). So ~A'TION n. [f. L *reciprocare* (prec.), -ATE³]

rĕcĭprŏ'cĭtў, n. Reciprocal condition, mutual action; principle or practice of give-&-take, esp. interchange of privileges between States as basis of commercial relations. [f. F *réciprocité* (RECIPROCAL, -ITY)]

rĕcĭt'al, n. 1. Detailed account *of a* number of connected things or facts, relation *of* the facts of an incident etc., a narrative. **2.** Part of document stating facts. **3.** Act of reciting; performance of programme by one musician (*vocal, pianoforte,* etc., ~). [RECITE, -AL]

rĕcĭtatĭve' (-ēv), n. Musical declamation of kind usual in narrative & dialogue parts of opera & oratorio; words, part, given in ~. [f. It. *recitativo* (foll., -IVE)]

rĕcĭte', v.t. & i. Repeat aloud or declaim (poem, passage) from memory esp. before audience, give recitation (*reciting-note,* that held on for indefinite number of syllables in chanting); (law) rehearse (facts) in document; mention in order, enumerate. So rĕcĭtA'TION n. [ME, f. OF *reciter* or L *re(citare* CITE), RE- 8]

rĕcĭt'er, n. Person who recites; book of passages for recitation. [-ER¹]

recivilize etc. See RE- 9.

rĕck, v.i. & t. (rhet., poet., **in** neg. & interrog. sentences only). ~ *of,* pay heed to, take account of, care about; care, be troubled, concern oneself, (*if, though, that, how, whether,* etc., or abs.; also impers. with same construction following, as *what ~s it him that . . .?*). [OE *reccan,* OS *rōkjan,* OHG *ruoh(h)en,* ON *rækja* f. Gmc **rōkjan*]

rĕck'lĕss, a. Devoid of caution, regardless of consequences, rash; heedless *of* danger etc. Hence ~LY² adv., ~NESS n. [OE *receleás* (prec., -LESS)]

rĕck'on, v.t. & i. 1. Ascertain (number, amount), ascertain number or amount of, by counting or usu. by calculation, compute; start *from,* go on *to,* in counting (t. & i.); count *up,* sum *up* character of; arrive at as total (*I ~ 53 of them*). **2.** Include in computation, count *in,* place in class *among* or *with* or *in,* take *for,* regard *as,* consider *to be* (or with obj. & compl. as ~ *him wise, beyond redemption*). **3.** Conclude after calculation, be of the confident opinion, (*that;* also, chiefly U.S., parenth., cf. *calculate, guess*). **4.** Make calculations, cast up account or sum, (~ *without* one's HOST²), settle accounts *with* person. **5.** Rely or count or base plans *upon.* [OE (*ge)recenian,* MDu., MLG *rekenen,* OHG *rechenōn* f. WG **rekenōjan*]

rĕck'oner (-kn-), n. In vbl senses; esp., READY ~. [-ER¹]

rĕck'oning (-kn-), n. In vbl senses; esp.: tavern bill; *day of* ~, time when something must be atoned for or avenged; DEAD ~; *out in* one's ~, mistaken in a calculation or expectation. [ME; -ING¹]

rĕclaim', v.t. & i., & n. 1. Win back or away from vice or error or savagery or waste condition, reform, tame, civilize, bring under cultivation esp. from flooding by sea or marsh, whence ~ABLE a.; make protest, say in protest, (rare); so **rĕclam·** A'TION n. **2.** n. ~ing, reclamation, (rare, chiefly in *past* or *beyond* ~). [ME, f. OF *reclamer* f. L *re(clamare* shout) cry out against, RE- 2]

rĕclame (rāk'lahm, & see Ap.), n. Art or practice by which notoriety is secured. [F]

rĕc'lĭnate, a. (bot.). Bending downwards. [f. L *reclinatus* (foll., -ATE²)]

rĕclĭne', v.t. & i. Lay (esp. one's head, body, limbs) in more or less horizontal or recumbent position (p.p., of person, lying thus); assume or be in recumbent position, lie or lean, sit with back or side supported at considerable inclination; (fig.) rely confidently *upon.* [ME, f. OF *recliner* or L *reclinare* (RE- 9), see DECLINE¹]

reclothe. See RE- 8.

rĕcluse' (-lōōs), a. & n. (Person) given to or living in seclusion or retirement or isolation, esp. as religious discipline, hermit, anchorite or anchoress. [ME, f. OF *reclus, -use* p.p. of *reclure* f. L *re(cludere=claudere* shut), RE- 4]

recoal, recoat. See RE- 8.

rĕcognĭ'tion, n. In vbl senses (RECOGNIZE). So **rĕcŏg'nĭtORY** a. (rare). [f. L *recognitio* (RECOGNIZE, -ION)]

rĕcŏg'nĭzance (or -kŏn²), n. Bond by which person· engages before court or magistrate to observe some condition, e.g. to keep the peace, pay a debt, or appear when summoned; sum pledged as surety for such observance. [ME, f. OF *reconoissance* (*reconoistre* RECOGNIZE, -ANCE)]

rĕcŏg'nĭzant (or -kŏn²), a. Showing recognition (*of* favour etc.), conscious or showing consciousness of something. [as foll., see -ANT]

rĕc'ognĭz|e, -is|e (-īz), v.t. **1.** Acknowledge validity or genuineness or character or claims·or existence of, accord notice or consideration to, discover or realize nature of, treat *as,* acknowledge *for,* realize or admit *that.* **2.** Know again, identify as known before. Hence~ABLE a., ~ABIL'ITY n., ~ABLY² adv. [ME, f. OF *reconiss-* part. st. of *reconoistre* f. L *re(cognoscere -gnitum* learn), RE- 8, w. assim. to -IZE]

rĕcoil', v.i., & n. 1. Retreat before enemy (now rare); start or spring back, shrink mentally, in fear or horror or disgust; rebound after impact, (of gun) be driven backwards by discharge, spring back. **2.** n. Act or fact or sensation of ~ing. [ME, f. OF *reculer* (RE- 9, *cul* posteriors f. L *culus*)]

recoin etc. See RE- 8.

rĕcollĕct', v.t. Succeed in remembering, recall to mind, remember. [f. p.p. st. of L *re(colligere* COLLECT²), RE- 8]

recollec′t|ion, n.. Act, power, of recollecting; thing recollected, reminiscence; person's memory, time over which it extends, (*it is in my ~ion that*, I remember that; *happened within my ~ion*). So **~ive a.** [F, or f. med. L *recollectio* (prec., -ION)]

recolonize etc., **recolour**, **recombine** etc., see RE- 8; **recomfort**, RE- 9; **recommence** etc., RE- 8.

recommend′, v.t. **1.** Give (one*self*, one's spirit, a child, etc.) in charge *to* God or a person or his care etc. **2.** Speak or write of or suggest as fit for employment or favour or trial (*to* person, or with ind. obj. as *can you ~ me a cook, a book?*; *as* servant etc.; *for* post, promotion, decoration). **3.** (Of qualities, conduct, etc.) make acceptable, serve as recommendation of. **4.** Advise (course of action or treatment, person to do, *that* thing should be done). Hence or cogn. **~A′TION** n., **~ABLE**, **~atory**, aa. [ME, f. med. L *re(commendare* COMMEND), RE- 5]

recommit etc. See RE- 8.

rec′ompēnse, v.t., & n. **1.** Requite, reward or punish, (person, action, person *for* action, action *to* person or with ind. obj.); make amends to (person) or for (another's loss, injury, etc., or rarely one's own misconduct). **2.** n. Reward, requital, atonement or satisfaction given for injury, retribution. [ME, f. OF *recompenser* f. LL *re(compensare* COMPENSATE), RE- 1]

recompose, **recompound**. See RE- 8.

rec′oncil|e, v.t. **1.** Make friendly after estrangement (persons to one another, person *to* or *with* another, person to oneself). **2.** Purify (consecrated place etc.) by special service after desecration. **3.** Make resigned or contentedly submissive (*to* disagreeables, *to doing*, or abs.; usu. in pass.). **4.** Heal, compose, (quarrel etc.). **5.** Harmonize, make compatible, show compatibility of by argument or in practice, (apparently conflicting facts, statements, qualities, actions, or one such *with* or *&* or rarely *to* another). Hence or cogn. **~ABLE** a., **~ABIL′ITY**, **~EMENT** (-lm-), **rēconciliA′TION**, nn. [ME, f. OF *reconcilier* or f. L *re(conciliare* CONCILIATE), RE- 9]

rec′ondīte (*or* rĭkŏn²), a. (Of subjects or knowledge) abstruse, out of the way, little known; (of author or style) dealing in ~ knowledge or allusion, obscure. Hence **~LY²** adv., **~NESS** n. [f. L *re(conditus* p.p. of *condere* hide), RE- 4]

recondi′tion, v.t. Overhaul & refit, rehabilitate, renovate. [RE- 8]

reconduct. See RE- 9.

rĕcŏnn′aissance (-nĭs-), n. Military, naval, etc. examination of tract by detachment to locate enemy or ascertain strategic features (*~ in force*, made by strong party); reconnoitring party; preliminary survey made by anyone for any purpose. [F (earlier -*oissance*), as foll. -ANCE]

rĕconnoi′tr|e (-ter), v.t. & i., & n. **1.** Make reconnaissance of (enemy, district), approach & try to learn position & condition etc. of; make reconnaissance. **2.** n. (rare). Reconnaissance. Hence **~ER¹** n. [f. F *reconnoître* (now -*aître*) f. L *recognoscere* RECOGNIZE]

reconquer etc., see RE- 9; **reconsider** etc., **reconstitute** etc., **reconstruct** etc., RE- 8; **reconvert** etc., RE- 9.

rĕcŏrd′¹, v.t. **1.** (Of birds) practise (tune, or abs.) by singing in an undertone. **2.** Register, set down for remembrance or reference, put in writing or other legible shape, represent in some permanent form, (*his thoughts have been ~ed for us by himself, his features by Watts, & his voice by the phonograph*; *~ing angel*, who registers men's good & bad actions; *minimum thermometer ~ed 10° below zero*); (radio) register & reproduce (item, programme) by RECORDING. Hence **~ABLE** a. [ME, f. OF *recorder* f. L *recordari* remember (RE-, *cor* heart)]

rĕc′ōrd², n. **1.** State of being recorded or preserved in writing esp. as authentic legal evidence (*is on ~*, legally or otherwise recorded; *matter of ~*, something established as fact by being recorded; *court of ~*, whose proceedings are recorded & valid as evidence of fact). **2.** Official report of proceedings & judgement in cause before court of ~, copy of pleadings etc. constituting case to be decided by court (*travel out of*, *keep to*, *the ~*, introduce, abstain from introducing, irrelevant matter). **3.** ‖ (*Public*) R~ *Office*, building in London in which State papers and other public documents are stored, calendared, etc. **4.** Piece of recorded evidence or information, account of fact preserved in permanent form, document or monument preserving it; **off the ~*, unofficial(ly); object serving as memorial of something, portrait etc.; series of marks etc. given by recording instrument or plate etc. containing these (*second-hand gramophone ~s for sale*); *~-player*, gramophone, esp. one with electrical pick-up. **5.** Facts known about person's past (*has an honourable ~ of service*; *his ~ is against him*). **6.** Best performances or most remarkable event of its kind on ~ (*break* or *cut* or *beat the ~*, outdo all predecessors); (attrib.) best hitherto recorded (*at ~ pace*; *the ~ height*). [ME, f. OF *record*, f. *recorder* (prec.)]

rĕcōrd′er, n. In vbl senses; also: city or borough magistrate with criminal & civil jurisdiction ‖ & holding court of Quarter sessions, whence **~SHIP** n.; recording-apparatus in instruments; vertical (English) flute. [orig. f. AF *recordour*; later, partly f. RECORD¹+-ER¹]

For pronunciation & hyphening of *re-* see RE-; for words in *re-* not given see RE- 8, 9.

recōrd'ing, n. 'In vbl senses, esp. (radio) process of registering sound for subsequent reproduction, material (disc, film, magnetic steel or plastic tape) on which sound has been registered, sound-programme registered & reproduced. [-ING[1]]

recount'[1], v.t. Narrate, tell in detail. [f. ONF & AF re(conter COUNT[2]), RE- 8]

re-count'[2]. See RE- 8.

recoup' (-ōōp), v.t. & i. (Law) deduct, keep back, (part of sum due), make such deduction; compensate (person loss, person *for* loss, loss; ~ one*self*, recover what one has expended or lost). Hence ~MENT n. [f. F re(couper cut, see COUP), RE- 5]

recourse' (-ōrs), n. Resorting or betaking of oneself *to* possible source of help (~ *to brandy is deprecated*; usu. in phr. *have* ~ *to*, adopt as adviser, helper, or expedient); thing resorted to (rare; *their usual* ~ *is perjury*); *without* ~ (commerce, law), formula used by indorser of a bill etc. to indicate that he disclaims responsibility for non-payment. [ME, f. OF *recours* f. L *re(cursus* COURSE[1]), RE- 9]

recō'ver[1] (-kŭ-), v.t. & i., & n. 1. Regain possession or use or control of, acquire or find (out) again, reclaim, (*has* ~*ed his kingdom, his friends' affection, the meaning of the hieroglyphs, the track, health, his appetite, his voice, much land from the sea*; ~ oneself, regain consciousness or calmness or control of limbs or senses; *horse* ~*s itself after stumble*; ~ one's *legs*, stand up after fall). 2. Secure restitution or compensation, secure (damages), by legal process (*plaintiff shall* ~ *according to verdict*; *his remedy is to* ~ *in a court of law*; *an action to* ~ *damages for false imprisonment*). 3. Bring or come back to life, consciousness, health, or normal state or position (*he* ~*ed slowly*; *the mention of a bucket of water* ~*ed her*; *I* ~*ed the heat of his body with fomentations*; *corpse cannot be* ~*ed to life*; ~*ed me from a lingering illness*; *am quite* ~*ed from my cold*; *sat down to* ~ *from his agitation*; ~ *sword*, bring it back after thrust etc., or, mil., hold it upright with hilt opposite mouth). 4. Retrieve, make up for, get over, cease to feel effects of, (*must try to* ~ *lost time*; *never* ~*ed the blow, his losses, this* faux pas). 5. Make one's way back to (rare; ~*ed the shore with difficulty*); hence ~ABLE a. 6. n. Position to which sword etc. is brought back in fencing or drill, act of coming to this. [ME, f. AF, OF *recov(e)rer* f. L *recuperare* RECUPERATE]

re-cover'[2]. See RE- 8.

recō'very (-kŭ-), n. Act or process of RECOVER[1]ing or being recovered. [ME, f. AF *recoverie* or OF *recovree* (RECOVER[1], -Y[4])]

rec're|ant, a. & n. (rhet., poet.). Craven, coward(ly), apostate. Hence ~ANCY n., ~antLY[2] adv. [ME, f. OF, part. of *recroire* f. med. L (*se*) *recredere*, RE- 6, yield in trial by combat]

rec're|āte[1], v.t. & i. (Of pastime, relaxation, holiday, employment, etc., or refl. of person indulging in them) refresh, entertain, agreeably occupy, (*it* ~*ates him to invent histories for his neighbours*; ~*ates himself with cricket, climbing, lying in a hammock, political argument*; amuse oneself, indulge in ~ation. So ~A'TION n., ~ATIVE a. [f. L re(creare CREATE), RE- 8, -ATE[3]]

re-create[2] etc. See RE- 8.

rec'rement, n. Waste product, refuse, (now rare); (physiol.) fluid separated from blood & again absorbed in it, e.g. saliva, bile. Hence ~I'TIOUS[1] (-ishus) a. [f. F *récrément* or L re(crementum f. cernere cret- sift, RE- 5, -MENT]

recrim'in|āte, v.i. Retort accusation, indulge in mutual or counter charges. So ~A'TION n., ~ATIVE, ~ātORY, aa. [f. med. L re(criminari f. crimen, CRIME), RE- 1]

recross. See RE- 9.

recrud|ĕsce' (-ōō-), v.i. (Of sore, disease, etc., or fig. of discontent etc.) break out again. So ~ES'CENT a., ~ĕs'CENCE n. [f. L re(crudescere f. crudus raw, see -ESCENT), RE- 8]

recruit'[1] (-rōōt), n. Newly enlisted & not yet trained soldier; person who joins a society etc.; tiro (often *raw* ~). [earlier sense *reinforcement*, f. obs. F *recrute*= *recrue* fem. p.p. of re(croître, OF *creistre*, f. L *crescere* increase), RE- 8]

recruit'[2] (-rōōt), v.t. & i. 1. Enlist recruits for (army, regiment, crew, society, party), enlist (person) as recruit, get or seek recruits (esp. ~*ing-sergeant*). 2. Replenish, fill up deficiencies or compensate wear & tear in, refresh, reinvigorate. 3. (Seek to) recover health etc. (*has gone to the country to* ~), whence ~AL(2) n. Hence ~MENT (-rōō-) n. [f. F *recruter* (obs. *recrute*, see prec.)]

rec'tal, a. Of or by the rectum. [-AL]

rec'tângle (-nggl), n. Plane rectilinear four-sided figure with four right angles, esp. one with adjacent sides unequal. [F, or f. LL *rectiangulum* (*rectus* straight, ANGLE[1]) right-angled]

rectăng'ūlar (-ngg-), a. Shaped, having base or sides or section shaped, like rectangle; placed, having parts or lines placed, at right angles. Hence ~ITY (-ă'r-) n., ~LY[2] adv. [as prec., -AR[1]]

rec'ti|fy, v.t. 1. Put right, correct, amend, reform, adjust, (method, calculation, statement, position, instrument). 2. Abolish, get rid of, exchange for what is right, (abuse, anomaly, error, omission, grievance). 3. (chem.). Purify or refine by renewed distillation or other process. 4. (geom.). Find straight line equal to (curve). Hence or cogn. ~fiABLE a., ~FICA'TION n., ~fiER[1] (1, 2) n., (also, radio) thermionic valve or other device transforming an alternating to a direct current. [ME, f. OF *rectifier* f. med. L *rectificare* (L *rectus* right, -FY)]

rĕctilin'|ĕar, -ĕal, aa. In or forming a straight line; bounded or characterized by straight lines. Hence ~ĕă'rɪᴛʏ n., ~ĕarʟʏ² adv. [f. LL *rectilineus* (L *rectus* straight, *linea* ʟɪɴᴇ²), -ᴀʀ¹, -ᴀʟ]

rĕc'titūde, n. Moral uprightness, righteousness; (rare) correctness, rightness. [ME, f. OF or LL *rectitudo* (L *rectus* right, -ᴛᴜᴅᴇ)]

rĕc'tō, n. (pl. ~s). Right-hand page of open book; front of leaf (opp. ᴠᴇʀsᴏ). [f. L *recto* (*folio*) on the right (leaf)]

rĕc'tor, n. 1. ‖ Incumbent of parish still in enjoyment of tithes (cf. ᴠɪᴄᴀʀ). **2.** Head of university, college, school, or religious institution (esp. abroad; in England only of heads of Exeter & Lincoln Colleges, Oxford; in Scotland of headmasters of some secondary schools etc., & see ʟᴏʀᴅ¹ ~), whence rĕc'ᴛʀᴇss¹ n. Hence ~ᴀᴛᴇ¹, ~sʜɪᴘ, nn., rĕctōr'ɪᴀʟ a. (‖ also as n. = ~ial election). [ME, f. L, = ruler (*regere rect-* rule, -ᴏʀ)]

rĕc'tory, n. ‖ Rector's benefice; rector's house. [f. OF *rectorie* or med. L *rectoria* (prec., -ʏ¹)]

rĕc'tum, n. Final section of large intestine, terminating at anus. [f. L *rectum* (*intestinum*) straight (intestine)]

rĕcŭm'b|ent, a. Lying back, reclining. Hence ~ᴇɴᴄʏ n., ~ᴇɴᴛʟʏ² adv. [f. L *re*(*cumbere* lie), ʀᴇ- 9, -ᴇɴᴛ]

rĕcŭp'er|āte, v.t. & i. Restore, be restored or recover, from exhaustion, illness, loss, etc. So ~ᴀ'ᴛɪᴏɴ n., ~ᴀᴛɪᴠᴇ a. [f. L *recuperare* ʀᴇᴄᴏᴠᴇʀ, see -ᴀᴛᴇ³]

rĕcŭr', v.i. (-rr-; *part. pr.* -ū'rĭng *or* -ĕr'ĭng). Go back in thought or speech *to*; (of idea etc.) come back to one's mind etc., return to mind; (of problem etc.) come up again; occur again, be repeated, (~*ring decimals*, figures in decimal fraction that ~ in same order again & again); ~*ring curve*, that returns upon itself, e.g. circle. So rĕcŭ'ʀʀᴇɴᴄᴇ n. [f. L *re*(*currere* run), ʀᴇ- 9]

rĕcŭ'rrent, a. & n. 1. (Of nerve, vein, branch, etc.) turning back so as to reverse direction; occurring again or often or periodically; hence ~ʟʏ² adv. **2.** n. = artery or nerve, esp. one of the two ~ laryngeal nerves. [as prec., -ᴇɴᴛ]

rĕcūrv|e', v.t. & i. Bend backwards. So ~ᴀᴛᴇ² a., ~'ᴀᴛᴜʀᴇ n. [f. L *re*(*curvare* bend), ʀᴇ- 9]

rĕc'ūs|ant (-z-), n. & a. (Hist.) (person) who refused to attend Church-of-England services; (person) refusing submission to authority or compliance with regulation (*against*). Hence ~ᴀɴᴄᴇ, ~ᴀɴᴄʏ, nn. [f. L *recusare* ʀᴇᴄᴜsᴇ]

rĕcūse' (-z), v.t. (now rare). Reject (person, his authority); object to (judge) as prejudiced. [ME, f. OF *recuser* f. *recusare* (ʀᴇ- 2, *causa* ᴄᴀᴜsᴇ) refuse]

rĕd, a. & n. 1. Of or approaching the colour seen at least refracted end of spectrum, of shades varying from crimson to bright brown & orange, esp. those seen in blood, sunset clouds, rubies, glowing coals, human lips, & fox's hair, (~ as a *rose* etc.; *blood, fiery, yellowish, deep,* etc., ~; ~ *with anger* etc., flushed in face; *with* ~ *hands*, bloodstained; ‖ *all-*~ *route*, *line, cable,* etc., traversing British territory or under British control, w. ref. to ~ in maps as British colour; ~ *gold,* arch. & poet., real gold, money; ***~ *cent,* smallest coin orig. of copper, esp. *don't care a* ~ *cent*; ~ *eyes,* bloodshot, or with lids sore from weeping, also of bird etc. with ~ iris; as distinctive epithet with many varieties of animal & plant & mineral, as ~ *deer, partridge, mullet, ant,* ᴄᴜʀʀᴀɴᴛ, *campion,* ᴀʀsᴇɴɪᴄ). **2.** Having to do with bloodshed, burning, violence, or revolution (~ *battle, ruin;* sᴇᴇ'~; *a* ~*republican, radical, anarchist*). **3.** Russian, Soviet, (*the Red Army, Air Force*). **4.** ~ ᴀᴅᴍɪʀᴀʟ; ~ *bark,* superior kind of cinchona; ~ *blind,* colour-blind to ~; ‖ ~ *book* (containing list of nobility & gentry); ~ *box,* used by Ministers for official documents; ~ *breast,* the robin; ~'*brick,* (of university) of modern foundation (*Red'brick,* opp. ᴏxʙʀɪᴅɢᴇ); ~'*cap,* ‖ military policeman; ~'*coat,* British soldier; ~ *cross,* St George's cross or national emblem of England, also Christian side in crusades, also (emblem of) ambulance etc. service organized according to Geneva Convention; ‖ ~ ᴇɴsɪɢɴ (also, sl., ~ *duster*), used by British merchant ships; ~'*eye,* the fish rudd; ~'*fish,* male salmon in spawning season, also (market name for) salmon (opp. *white fish* of all other kinds); ~ *flag,* symbol of revolution (*the Red Flag,* a modern revolutionary song), danger-signal on shooting-ranges, railways, etc.; ~ *gum,* teething-rash in children, also (kinds of eucalyptus yielding) ~dish resin; ~'*hand'ed,* in the act of crime (*take* ~'*handed*); ~ *hat,* cardinal's, ‖ (also nickname for) British staff-officer; ~ *heat,* being ~-hot lit. & fig., temperature of ~-hot thing; ~ *herring,* herring(s) .~-dened by being cured in smoke (*neither fish, flesh, nor good* ~ *herring,* of ambiguous indefinite nature; *draw a* ~ *herring across the track,* divert attention from subject in hand by starting irrelevant but exciting question, with ref. to use of ~ herring in exercising hounds); ~-*hot,* heated to ~ness, highly excited, enthusiastic, furious; ~-*hot poker,* garden plant with flame-coloured spikes of flower; ‖ ~ *lamp,* night-sign of doctor or chemist; ~ *lane,* (nursery name for) throat; ~ *lead,* pigment made from ~ oxide of lead (v.t., coat with this); ~-*legged,* with ~ legs (of birds etc., esp. the ~-*legged* or *French partridge*); ~-*legs,* kinds of bird, also the plant bistort; ~-*letter,* (of day) marked with ~ letter(s) in calendar as saint's day or festival, (fig.) memorable as date of joyful occurrence, (v.t.), record as memorable for joy); ~ *light*, danger-signal on railways etc. (*see the ~ light*, fig., realize approach of disaster), brothel; ~ *man*, N.--Amer. Indian; ~ *meat*, beef, mutton, etc. (opp. veal & pork & chicken); ~ *mass*, at which priest wears ~; ~'*pŏll*, kinds of ~-crested bird similar to linnet, also (pl.) ~-haired polled cattle; ~ *rag*, thing that excites person's rage as ~ object enrages bull (*is a ~ rag to him*), ‖ also kind of rust in grain; ~ *rattle*, louse-wort; ‖ ~ *ribbon*, ribbon, membership, of Order of Bath; ~ *sanders*, wood of E.--Ind. tree used in dyeing; ~'*shank*, large kind of sandpiper; ~-*short*, (of iron) brittle while ~-hot; ~'*skin*, = ~ *man* above; ~ *snow*, ~dened by kind of alga & common in Arctic & Alpine regions; ~ *soldier*, (pig affected with) kind of swine fever with ~ness of skin; ~ *spider*, insect infesting hothouse plants esp. vines; ~'*start*, ~-tailed European songbird [OE *stcort* tail]; ~-*streak*, kind of cider apple; ~ *tape*, excessive use of or adherence to formalities esp. in public business, whence ~-tăp'ERY, ~-tăp'ISM, ~-tăp'IST, nn.; ~ *triangle*, (emblem of) the Y.M.C.A.; ~-*water*, malarial cattle & sheep disease with ~ urine; ~ *weed*, corn poppy; ~-*wing*, kinds of thrush & other birds; ~'*wood*, kinds of tree etc. esp. Californian *sequoia* (*sempervirens*); ~ *worm*, kind used as fishing-bait; hence ~d'EN⁶ v.t. & i., ~d'ISH¹(2), ~d'Y², aa., ~'LY² adv. (rare), ~'NESS n. 5. n. = colour; *a* shade of ~; the ~ colour in roulette & rouge-et-noir; *the* ~ ball at billiards; *the debtor side of an account (*in the* ~, in debt); ~ cloth or clothes (*dressed in* ~); one of former three squadrons or divisions (*the ~, white, blue*) of British fleet; radical or republican or anarchist or communist. [OE *read*, OS *rōd*, OHG *rōt*, ON *rauthr*, Goth. *rauths* f. Gmc *rauthaz*, cogn. w. L *rufus*]

red-, pref. = RE-, only in wds of L origin.

rĕdăct', v.t. Put into literary form, arrange for publication, edit. So rĕdăc'tor n. [in mod. use a back formation f. foll.]

rĕdăc'tion, n. Preparing or being prepared for publication, revision, editing, rearrangement; new edition. [f. F *rédaction* f. L *red*(*igere* -*act-* = *agere* bring), RE-8, -ION]

rĕdăn', n. Field-work with two faces forming salient angle. [F *redan* for *redent* (RE-, *dent* tooth)]

‖ rĕdd, v.t. (Sc.). Clear up, arrange, tidy, put right, settle, compose. [= syn. MLG, Du. *redden*, but in ME perh. independent form rel. to READY]

rĕd'dle, n., & v.t. Red ochre, ruddle; (vb) colour with ~. [var. of RUDDLE]

‖ rēde¹, n. (arch.). Counsel, advice; resolve, design; narrative. [OE *ræd*, f. Gmc *rædhaz* f. *rædhan* READ]

‖ rēde², v.t. (arch.). Advise (person, with inf. with or without *to*, or with imperat.); read (riddle, dream). [same wd as READ, the common ME sp. being retained for the arch. senses of the wd]

rēdeem', v.t. 1. Buy back, recover by expenditure of effort or by stipulated payment, (~ one's *rights, position, honour, mortgaged land, pledged goods*); compound for, buy off, (charge or obligation) by payment. 2. Perform (promise). 3. Purchase the freedom of (another, *oneself*), save (one's life) by ransom. 4. Save, rescue, reclaim; (of God or Christ) deliver from sin & damnation. 5. Make amends for, compensate, counterbalance, (fault, defect; *has one ~ing feature*); save *from* a defect (*the eyes ~ the face from ugliness*). Hence ~ABLE a., (esp. of Christ, see above) ~ER¹ n. [ME, f. OF *redimer* or L *red*(*i-mere* -*empt-* = *emere* buy), RE-8]

rēdĕmp'tion, n. 1. REDEEMing or being redeemed, esp. the deliverance from sin & damnation wrought by Christ's atonement (*past, beyond, without,* ~, so that ~ is hopeless; *in the year of our* ~ *1963* etc., A.D. 1963 etc.). 2. Thing that redeems (*that blow was* or *proved his* ~). 3. ‖ Purchase (*became a member of a livery company by* ~). Hence rēdĕmp'tIVE a. [ME, f. OF, or L *redemptio* (prec., -ION)]

rēdeploy'ment, n. Improved physical arrangements in factories as means of increasing output. [RE-8]

redescend. See RE-9.

rĕd'ingōte (-ngg-), n. Woman's long double-breasted outer coat with skirts sometimes cut away in front. [F, f. E *riding-coat*]

rĕdin'tĕgr|āte, v.t. Restore to wholeness or unity; renew or re-establish in united or perfect state. So ~A'TION n. [ME, f. L *red*(*integrare* INTEGRATE²), RE-9, -ATE²]

redirect etc., see RE-8; rediscover etc., RE-9; redistribute etc., redivide etc., redo, RE-8.

rĕd'ol|ent, a. Fragrant (now rare); having a strong smell, (fig.) strongly suggestive or reminiscent, *of*. Hence ~ENCE n. [ME, f. OF, or L *red*(*olēre* smell), RE-6, -ENT]

rĕdou'bl|e (-dŭbl), v.t. & i., & n. 1. Intensify, increase, make or grow greater or more intense or numerous, (~*e* one's *efforts; the clamour ~ed*). 2. (bridge). Double again a bid already doubled by adversary; (n.) act or instance of ~ing. [f. F *re*(*doubler* DOUBLE³), RE-6]

rĕdoubt' (-owt), n. (fortif.). Outwork or fieldwork usu. square or polygonal & without flanking defences. [f. F *redoute* f. It. *ridotto* f. med. L *reductus* refuge f. p.p. of L REDUCEre; -*b-* after DOUBT (cf. foll.)]

rĕdoubt'able (-owt-), a. (Of opponent, warrior, controversialist, etc.) formidable. [ME, f. OF *redoutable* f. re(*douter* DOUBT²) fear, RE-6]

rĕdoubt'ĕd ·(-owt-), a. (arch.). Dreaded, redoubtable. [f. obs. *redoubt* f. F as prec.]

rĕdound', v.i. Contribute in the end, make great contribution, *to* one's advantage, credit, etc. (*this procedure will ~ to our advantage*; *the tale, fact, ~s to their credit*); come as final result *to*, come back or recoil *upon*, person (*the benefits that ~ to us from his self-sacrifice*). [ME also = *overflow*, f. OF *redonder* f. L *red*(*undare* f. *unda* wave), RE- 6]

rĕdrĕss', v.t., & n. 1. Readjust, set straight again, (usu. *~ the balance*, restore equality); set right, remedy, make up for, get rid of, rectify, (distress, wrong, damage, grievance, abuse). 2. n. Reparation for wrong, *~ing of* grievances etc. [ME, f. OF *redrecier* (RE- 8, DRESS)]

rĕdūce', v.t. & i. 1. Restore to original or proper position, remedy by such restoration, (now only surg.; *had the shoulder, dislocation, ~d*); bring back to (*~ person to discipline*). 2. Convert physically or mentally *to* other form, subject to such conversion, make suitable or conformable or adapted *to*, bring by classification or analysis *to*, (*~ rule to practice*, act on it; *observations taken at surface must be ~d to centre*; *~ anomalies to rule*, discover formula covering them; *the facts may all be ~d to three heads*; *~ it to English orthography & spell it* employee; *~ dissimilar quantities to one denomination, integer to form of fraction*; *can we ~ these ripples to their mechanical elements?*; *~ clods to powder, ore to metal, compound to components, surface by harrowing*, or simply *~ clods, compound*, etc.; *~ syllogism of one form to another*). 3. Compel *to* do (rare); bring by force or necessity *to* some state or action, subdue, bring back to obedience, (*~ the Crown to submission, the revolted towns, all the other Powers of the continent*; *~d him to assert* or usu. *asserting an absurdity*; *was ~d to despair, to weakness, to borrow* or usu. *borrowing clothes, to borrowing*). 4. Bring down, lower, weaken, impoverish, diminish, contract, (*~ Pope to place of chief bishop*; *N.C.O. was ~d to the ranks*, made a private; *is in a very ~d state*, feeble; *~ liquid to two-thirds of its bulk*; *this ~s the temperature*; *the 16 may be ~d to 5*, by omission of 11, or by reclassification etc.; *have ~d our outfit to almost nothing*; *he ~d himself into the least possible compass*; *to be sold at ~d prices*; *~d circumstances*, poverty after prosperity; *~ the establishment*, dismiss officials or cut down expenses; *~d officers* etc., dismissed in such reduction). 5. intr. Lessen one's weight. Hence rĕdū'CER[1] n., (esp. photog.) an agent for reducing the density of negatives, rĕdū'CIBLE a. [ME, f. L *re*(*ducere duct-* bring), RE- 9]

rĕdūc'tiō ăd absŭrd'um (-shĭ-), n. Reduction to absurdity (see foll.). [L]

rĕdūc'tion, n. Reducing or being RE-DUCED; also: reduced copy of picture, map, etc.; *~ to absurdity*, proof of the falsity of a principle etc. given by producing a logical consequence of it that is absurd, (loosely) pushing of a principle to unpractical lengths. [ME, f. OF, or f. L *reductio* (REDUCE, -ION)]

reduit (redwē'), n. (fortif.). Keep for garrison to retire to & hold when outworks are taken. [f. F *réduit* REDOUBT]

rĕdŭn'd|ant, a. Superfluous (freq. of workers in industry), excessive, pleonastic; copious, luxuriant, full. Hence or cogn. *~ANCE*, *~ANCY*, nn., *~ant*LY[2] adv. [f. L as REDOUND, -ANT]

rĕdŭp'lic|āte, v.t. Make double, repeat; (gram.) repeat (letter, syllable), form (tense) by reduplication. So *~ATIVE* a. [f. LL *re*(*duplicare* DUPLICATE[2]), RE- 8, -ATE[3]]

rĕdūplicā'tion, n. Doubling, repetition; counterpart; (gram.) repetition of syllable or letter in word-formation (esp. in perf. in Gk & L, as *tetigi* from *tango*), part so repeated. [f. LL *reduplicatio* (prec. -ATION)]

redye. See RE- 8.

ree. = REEVE[2].

reeb'ok, n. Small S.-African antelope with sharp horns. [Du., = roebuck]

rē-ĕch'ō (-k-), v.i. & t. Echo (t. & i.), echo (t. & i.) again & again, resound. [RE- 6]

reed, n., & v.t. 1. (Tall straight stalk of) kinds of firm-stemmed water or marsh plant (*broken ~*, unreliable person or thing; *lean on a ~*, put trust in weak thing or person), whence *~'ED*[2] a.; (collect.) *~s* growing in a mass or used as material esp. for thatching, ‖ wheat-straw prepared for thatching. 2. (poet.). Arrow; musical pipe of *~* or straw; pastoral poetry. 3. Vibrating part, of various shape & material, inserted in some musical wind-instruments (esp. oboe, bassoon, clarinet, bagpipe, & some organ-pipes) to produce the sound; (usu. pl., cf. *strings*, *brass*) *~* instrument(s). 4. Weaver's implement for separating warp-threads & beating up weft; (usu. pl.) set of semicylindrical adjacent mouldings like *~s* laid together. 5. *~-babbler* or *-warbler* or *-wren*, *~-bunting* or *-sparrow*, two kinds of bird; ‖*~-mace*, cat's-tail; *~-pheasant*, bearded tit; *~-pipe*, musical pipe of *~*, also *~ed* organ-pipe; *~-stop*, organ-stop consisting of *~-*pipes. 6. v.t. Thatch with *~*; make (straw) into *~*; decorate with *~-*moulding; fit (musical instrument or organ-pipe) with *~*. [OE *hrēod*, OS *hriod*, OHG *(h)riot* f. Gmc **hreudham*]

rē-ĕd'ify, v.t. Rebuild (house etc.); build up again (hopes, wasted tissue, etc.). [RE- 8]

rē-ĕd'it etc. See RE- 8.

For pronunciation & hyphening of *re-* see RE-; for words in *re-* not given see RE- 8, 9.

reed'ling, n. Bearded tit. [-LING¹]

reed'ly, a. Abounding with reeds; made of reed (chiefly poet., as ~y *pipe, couch*); like a reed in weakness, slenderness, or (of grass etc.) thickness; (of voice) like reed--instrument in tone, scratchy, not round & clear. Hence ~INESS n. [-Y²]

reef¹, n., & v.t. **1.** One of three or four strips across top of square & bottom of fore-&-aft sail that can be taken in or rolled up to reduce sail's surface (*take in a ~,* lit., & fig. proceed cautiously); ~-knot, consisting of two bights each enclosing the other's parallel laid shanks, ordinary double-knot made symmetrically for easy casting off (opp. GRANNY); ~-point, one of the short pieces of rope attached to a sail to secure it when ~ed. **2.** v.t. Take in ~ (s) of (sail; *single, double, treble,* -~ed, with 1, 2, 3, ~s taken in); shorten (topmast, bowsprit, also paddles of paddle-wheel by shifting them nearer centre). [ME *riff,* f. Du. *reef, rif,* f. ON *rif,* RIB, in same sense (cf. foll.)]

reef², n. Ridge of rock or shingle or sand at or just above or below surface of water (gold-mining) lode of auriferous quartz, also the bedrock. [16th c. *riff(e)* f. MDu., MLG *rif, ref,* f. ON *rif* (as prec.)]

reef'er¹, n. One who reefs; (sl.) midshipman; REEF¹-knot; (also *reefing-jacket*) close double-breasted stout jacket. [REEF¹, -ER¹]

reef'er², n. See MARIJUANA. [orig. unkn.]

reek¹, n. Smoke (Sc. & literary); vapour, visible exhalation, (chiefly Sc. & lit.); foul or stale odour (*the ~ of tobacco*), fetid atmosphere (*amid ~ & squalor*). Hence ~'Y² a. (chiefly Sc. & literary; *Auld Reek'ie,* Edinburgh). [OE *rēc,* OS *rōk,* OHG *rouh,* ON *reykr* f. Gmc **raukiz*]

reek², v.i. Emit smoke (chiefly of houses after conflagration or object that has been burning in open air); emit vapour, steam, (of hot drink or food, sweating person etc., or shed blood or thing smeared with it); smell unpleasantly (usu. *of;* ~s *of patchouli, tobacco, blood,* or fig. *of murder, affectation,* etc.). [OE *rēocan,* OHG *riohhan,* ON *rjúka,* f. Gmc **riukan* cogn. w. prec.]

reel¹, n., & v.t. & i. **1.** Kinds of rotatory apparatus on which thread, silk, yarn, paper, wire, etc., are wound at some stage of manufacture; contrivance for winding up & unwinding line as required, esp. in fishing (*off the ~,* fig., straight off, without hitch or pause, in rapid succession); ‖ small cylinder on which sewing-cotton etc. is wound for convenience; revolving part in various machines; (cinemat.) quantity of positive film rolled on one ~ (often as rough unit of length, about 1,000 ft, complete films being termed *two-, three-, four-,* etc., ~ers). **2.** vb. Wind (thread, fishing-line, etc.) on ~; take (cocoon silk etc.) off, draw (fish, logline, etc.) *in* or *up,* by use of ~; rattle

(story, list, verses) *off* without pause or apparent effort; (of grasshopper etc.) make clicking noise like ~ in motion. [OE *hrēol,* not in cogn. langg.]

reel², v.i., & n. **1.** (Of eyes, mind, head) be in a whirl, be dizzy, swim; sway, stagger, stand or walk or run unsteadily, be shaken physically or mentally, rock from side to side, swing violently, (*his mind, the front rank, the ship, the tower,* ~ed *under the shock;* ~ *to & fro like a drunken man; went* ~ing *down the street; the State was* ~ing *to its foundations*); seem to shake (*the mountains ~ before his eyes*); hence ~'ingLY² adv. **2.** n. ~ing motion lit. or fig. (*without a ~ or a stagger; the ~ of vice & folly around us*). [ME (chiefly north. & Sc.), f. prec.]

reel³, n., & v.i. **1.** Lively esp. Scottish dance, usu. of two couples in line & describing circular figures. **2.** v.i. Dance ~. [f. REEL² n.]

re-elect etc., **re-embark** etc., **re-emerge** etc. See RE- 9.

reen, n. = RHINE¹.

re-enable, re-enact etc., see RE- 9; **re--engine,** RE- 8; **re-enter** etc., RE- 9.

rē-ēn'trant, a. & n. (Angle) that points inward (opp. SALIENT; esp. in fortification). [RE- 9, ENTRANT]

rē-ēn'try, n. Act of entering again, esp. (of space vehicle, missile, etc.) of re--entering earth's atmosphere; (law) a retaking possession; *card of* ~ (whist & bridge), high card that can be relied on to give holder the lead by winning a trick. [RE- 9, ENTRY]

re-establish etc. See RE- 9.

reeve¹, n. (Hist.) chief magistrate of town or district; (Canada) president of village or town council. [OE *gerēfa,* orig. unkn.]

reeve², ree, n. Female of RUFF².

reeve³, v.t. (naut.; past & p.p. *rōve* or ~d). Thread (rope, rod, etc.) *through* ring or other aperture; pass rope through (a block etc.); fasten (rope, block, or other object) *in, on, round, to,* something by reeving; (of ship) thread (shoals, ice--pack). [f. Du. *reeven* to reef]

re-examine etc., see RE- 8; **re-exist, re--export** etc., RE- 9; **reface, refashion** etc., RE- 8.

rēf, n. (colloq.). Football referee. [abbr.]

refěc'tion, n. Refreshment by food or drink (*milk & eggs were offered for our ~*); slight meal, repast. [ME, f. OF f. L *refectionem* f. *reficere* (foll.), RE- 8]

refěc'tory (*or in monastic use* rěf'I-), n. Room used for meals in monasteries etc. [(in ME *fraitur* FRATER) f. LL *refectorium* f. L *re(ficere -fect- = facere* make) refresh, RE- 8, -ORY]

refėr', v.t. & i. (-rr-). **1.** Trace or ascribe *to* person or thing as cause or source, assign *to* certain date or place or class, (~ one's *victories to Providence, miraculous tales to ignorance, ill temper to indigestion, the lake-dwellings to the sixth century, the*

*origins of sculpture to Egypt, barnacles to
the molluscs*), whence rĕf'erABLE a. 2.
Commit, hand over, (one*self*, question for
decision) *to* person etc. (*I ~ myself to your
generosity*; *let us ~ the dispute to Socrates*;
~ to drawer, abbr. R.D.), banker's note
suspending payment etc. of cheque).
3. Send on or direct (person), make appeal
or have recourse, *to* some authority or
source of information, (abs.) cite authority or passage, (*for my proof I ~ to the
facts of human nature, to* 1 Kings *iii.* 7;
~red to his watch for the exact time). 4. (Of
statement etc.) have relation, be directed,
(of hearer etc.) interpret (statement etc.)
as directed, *to* (*these remarks ~ only to
deliberate, are not to be~red to involuntary,
offences*). 5. (Of person speaking etc.)
make allusion, direct attention, *to* (*he
several times ~red to the modern increase
in expenditure; found myself on the peak
~red to*). [ME, f. OF *referer* or L re(*ferre
latum* bring), RE- 9]

refe**ree**', n., & v.i. & t. 1. Arbitrator,
person to whom dispute is to be or is referred for decision; *Official R~*, attached
to Supreme Court, to whom questions
arising in an action may be referred for
inquiry and report or for trial where
parties consent; umpire esp. in football.
2. vb. Act as~ (for) esp. in football. [-EE]

rĕf'erence, n., & v.t. 1. Referring of
matter for decision or settlement or
consideration to some authority, scope
given to such authority, (*the peerage was
allowed without ~ to the House of Lords*;
the ~ is very wide, strictly limited; *the
Commission must confine itself to, that is
a question outside, the terms of~*). 2. Relation, respect, correspondence, *to* (*the parts
of a machine all have~ to each other*; *success
seems to have little ~ to merit*; *in, with, ~
to*, regarding, as regards, about; *without
~ to*, irrespective of). 3. Allusion *to* (*~, a
or no ~, several ~s, to a previous conversation was* or *were made*). 4. Direction
more or less precise to (page etc. of) book
etc. where information may be found
(*loads his pages with, does not give, ~s*;
cross ~, to another passage in same book;
~ bible, with marginal cross~s; ‖ *legislation by ~*, use in bill-drafting of ~s to
previous statutes instead of restatement);
mark used to refer reader of text to note
or to part of diagram (usual ~ marks:
asterisk *, obelisk †, double obelisk ‡,
section §, parallel ‖, paragraph ¶). 5. Act
of looking up passage etc., or of referring
another or applying to person, for information (*~ or a~ to the dictionary would
have enlightened him*; *please give me a ~,
I should like to make ~, to your last employer*; *book of ~*, to be used not for
continuous reading but to consult on
occasion; *~ library*, where books may be
consulted without being taken away, opp.

lending library): person named by one
applying for post or offering goods etc. as
willing to vouch for him or them (*who are
your ~s?*; (loosely) testimonial; hence
rĕferĕn'tIAL (-shl) a. 6. v.t. Provide
(book) with ~s to authorities. [-ENCE]

‖ rĕferĕn'darў, n. (rare). Referee;
assessor to commission; reporting or
revising official. [f. LL *referendarius*
(foll., -ARY[1])]

rĕferĕn'dum, n. Referring of certain
political questions or of such questions
under certain circumstances to the electorate for direct decision by a general
vote on the single question. [L (REFER*re*)]

refill. See RE- 9.

refin|e', v.t. & i. Free from dross or im-
purities or defects, purify, clarify; make
elegant or cultured, imbue with delicacy
of taste, polish manners or appearance of;
become pure or clear or improved in
polish or delicacy; employ subtlety of
thought or language, make fine distinctions, discourse subtly (*up*)*on*; improve
(*up*)*on* by refinements. Hence ~'ĕDLY[2]
adv. [RE- 6, FINE[2] v., partly after F
raffiner]

refine'ment (-nm-), n. Refining or being
refined; fineness of feeling or taste,
polished manners etc.; subtle or ingenious
manifestation *of*, piece of elaborate
arrangement, (*all the ~s of luxury*; *a
countermine was a ~ beyond their skill*);
piece of subtle reasoning, fine distinction.
[-MENT, after F *raffinement*]

refin'|er, n. In vbl senses: esp., person
whose business is to refine crude oil, metal,
sugar, etc., whence ~ERY(3) n. [-ER[1]]

refit etc. See RE- 8.

reflā'tion, n. Inflation of currency after
a deflation, undertaken to restore the
system to its previous condition. [f.
RE-[9], after INFLATION, DEFLATION]

reflĕct', v.t. & i. 1. Fold back (rare; *~ the
corner of the paper*). 2. (Of surface or
body) throw (heat, light, sound, rarely
ball etc.) back, cause to rebound, (*shine
with ~ed light*, not one's own, borrowed).
3. (Of mirror etc., or transf.) show image
of, reproduce to eye or mind, exactly
correspond in appearance or effect to,
(*laws ~ the average moral attitude of a half
century earlier*). 4. (Of action, result, etc.)
bring back or cause to redound (credit,
discredit, etc.), (abs.) bring discredit,
(*up*)*on* person or method responsible.
5. Go back in thought, meditate, or
consult with oneself (*on, upon*, or abs.),
remind oneself or consider (*that, how,
etc.*), whence ~ingLY[2] adv. 6. Make disparaging remarks *upon*. [ME, f. OF
reflecter or L re(*flectere flex-* bend), RE- 9]

reflĕc'tion, -ĕ'xion (-kshn), n. (-x- etym.
correct but now rare exc. in scientific
use). 1. REFLECTing or being reflected
(*angle of ~*, made by reflected ray with

perpendicular to surface); reflected light, heat, colour, or image. **2.** Reflex action. **3.** (Piece of) censure (usu. *on* or *upon*); thing bringing discredit (*up*) *on*. **4.** Reconsideration (*on ~, I doubt whether I was right*). **5.** Mental faculty dealing with products of sensation & perception. **6.** Idea arising in the mind, mental or verbal comment, apophthegm, (often *on* or *upon*). Hence ~**AL**, ~**LESS**, aa., (-sho-). [ME f. OF, or f. LL *reflexio* (prec., -**ION**) w. assim. to *reflect*]

reflec'tive, a. **1.** (Of surface etc.) giving back reflection or image; (of light etc.) reflected (rare). **2.** (gram.). Reflexive (now rare). **3.** (Of action) reflex, reciprocal, (now rare). **4.** (Of mental faculties) concerned in reflection or thought; (of person, mood, etc.) thoughtful, given to meditation. Hence ~**LY**² adv., ~**NESS** n. [REFLECT, -**IVE**]

reflec'tor, n. **1.** Body or surface reflecting rays, esp. piece of glass or metal usu. concave for reflecting in required direction; (telescope etc. provided with) apparatus for reflecting images. **2.** Person, book, etc., that gives or affords conscious or unconscious representation *of* prejudices, habits, etc. [-**OR**]

reflet' (-lě), n. Lustre, iridescence, esp. on pottery. [F]

ref'lex¹, n. **1.** Reflected light or colour or glory (*the fame of Greece was a ~ from the glory of Athens*); (paint.) part of picture represented as affected by the light or colour of another part. **2.** Image or reflection in mirror etc. **3.** Reproduction, secondary manifestation, correspondent result, (*legislation should be a ~ of public opinion; lamb & mint sauce is a popular ~ of the passover with bitter herbs*). **4.** A reflex action (*doctor tested patient's ~es*). CONDITIONED ~. [f. L *reflexus -ūs* (REFLECT)]

ref'lex², a. **1.** (rare). Recurved; (of light etc.) reflected. **2.** (Of thought etc.) introspective, directed back upon itself or its own operations; (of effect or influence) reactive, coming back upon its author or source. **3.** (physiol.). ~ *action*, independent of the will, excited as involuntary response to nerve-stimulation. **4.** (gram.). Reflexive (now rare). **5.** ~ (*camera*), a hand camera in which, by means of a pivoted surface-silvered mirror, the reflected image can be seen and focused up to the moment of exposure. Hence ~**LY**² adv. [f. L *reflexus* p.p. (REFLECT)]

reflexed' (-kst), a. (bot.). Recùrved. [f. obs. *reflex* vb = REFLECT]

reflex'|ible, a. Capable of being reflected. Hence ~**IBIL'ITY** n. [as prec., -**IBLE**]

reflexion. See REFLECTION.

reflex'ive, a. & n. (gram.). (Word, form) implying agent's action upon himself; (verb) indicating identity of subject & object; (pers. pronoun or poss. adjective) referring to subject. Hence ~**LY**² adv. [f. mod. L *reflexivus* (as REFLECT, -**IVE**)]

refloat. See RE- **9.**

ref'luent (-ŏŏ-), a. Flowing back (*~ tide, blood*). Hence **ref'luENCE** (-ŏŏ-) n. [f. L *re(fluere* flow), RE- **9,** see -**ENT**]

reflux, see RE- **9; refoot,** RE- **8; reforest** etc., RE- **9.**

reform'¹, v.t. & i. Make (person, institution, procedure, conduct, one*self*) or (of person or body of persons) become better by removal or abandonment of imperfections, faults, or errors (*~ed churches,* see REFORMATION²); abolish, cure, (abuse, malpractice). Hence ~**ABLE** a. [ME, f. OF *reformer* or L *re(formare* FORM²), RE- **8**]

reform'², n. Removal of abuse(s) esp. in politics (*R~ Bill, Act,* esp. those of 1831–2 amending parliamentary representation); improvement made or suggested. [f. prec. or F *réforme*]

reform'³, v.t. & i. Form again. So **reforma'tion**¹ n. [RE- **8**]

reforma'tion², n. Reforming or being reformed, esp. radical change for the better in political, religious, or social affairs; *the R~,* 16th-c. movement for reform of abuses in Roman Church ending in establishment of Reformed or Protestant Churches, whence ~**AL** (-sho-) a. [ME, f. OF or L *reformatio* (REFORM¹, -**ATION**)]

reform'ative a., **reform'atory** a. & n. **1.** Tending or intended to produce reform. **2.** n. Institution to which juvenile offenders are sent for ~ purposes, approved school. [REFORM¹, -**ATIVE**, -**ORY**]

reform'er, n. In vbl senses; esp.: leader in the 16th-c. REFORMATION²; advocate of the REFORM² bill. [-**ER**¹]

refract', v.t. (Of water, air, glass, etc.) deflect (light) at certain angle when it enters obliquely from another medium of different density (*~ing telescope,* with object--glass converging rays to focus). Hence or cogn. **refrac'tion** n., **refrac'tional** (-sho-), **refrac'tive**, aa. [f. L *re(fringere -fract- = frangere* break), RE- **5**]

refrac'tor, n. Refracting medium or lens or telescope. [-**OR**]

refrac'tor|y, a. & n. **1.** Stubborn, unmanageable, rebellious; (of wound, disease, etc.) not yielding to treatment; (of substances) hard to fuse or work. **2.** n. Substance specially resistant to heat, corrosion, etc. Hence ~**ILY**² adv., ~**INESS** n. [alt. of obs. *-ary* (after -**ORY**), f. L *refractarius* (REFRACT, -**ARY**¹)]

refrain'¹, n. Recurring phrase or line esp. at end of stanzas. [ME, f. OF, ult. f. Rom. **refrangere* = *refringere* REFRACT]

refrain'², v.t. & i. Put restraint upon, curb, withhold, (one*self,* one's tears, soul, etc.; arch.); abstain from doing something, abstain *from* act or do*ing.* [ME, f. OF *refrener* f. L *re(frenare* f. *frenum* bridle), RE- **9**]

refran'g|ible (-j-), a. That can be refracted. Hence ~**IBIL'ITY** n. [RE- **5,** L *frangere,* -**IBLE;** cf. FRANGIBLE]

refrĕsh′, v.t. & i. Make cool again (rare); reanimate, reinvigorate, (of food, drink, rest, amusement, etc., or person providing these esp. in ~ one*self*; ~*ing innocence* etc., interesting to blasé observer); freshen up (memory); restore (fire, electric battery, etc.) with fresh supply; take esp. liquid refreshment. Hence ~ing-LY² adv. [ME, f. OF *refreschier*, see FRESH, RE- 9]

refrĕsh′er, n. In vbl senses; esp.: extra fee to counsel in prolonged case; (colloq.) a drink; attrib., as ~ *course* (of instruction in modern methods etc.). [-ER¹]

refrĕsh′ment, n. Refreshing or being refreshed in mind or body; thing, esp. (usu. in pl.) drink or food, that refreshes (*the sight was a* ~ *to him*; *take some* ~ or ~*s*; ~ *room* at railway station or *car* on train); *R*~ *Sunday*, 4th in Lent with gospel f. *John* vi. [ME, f. OF *refreschement* (RE-FRESH, -MENT)]

refri′gerāte, v.t. & i. 1. Make, rarely become, cool or cold. 2. Expose (provisions) to extreme cold in order to freeze or preserve, whence ~āTOR n. Hence or cogn.~ANT(2) a. & n., ~A′TION n. [f. L re(*frigerare* f. *frigus -oris* cold), RE- 9, -ATE³]

refri′geratŏrў, n. & a. 1. Cold-water vessel attached to still for condensing vapour; refrigerator. 2. adj. Refrigerant. [f. L *refrigeratorius* (prec., -ORY)]

reft. See REAVE.

refūge, n., & v.t. & i. 1. (Place of) shelter from pursuit or danger or trouble (*seek* ~; *has found a* ~; *take* ~ *in a cave, in lying; city of* ~, see *Josh.* xx; *house of* ~, institution for the homeless etc.); person, thing, course, that gives shelter or is resorted to in difficulties (*he is the* ~ *of the distressed*; *books are the* ~ *of the destitute*); raised piece in middle of busy road for crossers to halt on. 2. vb (rare). Give ~ to; take ~. [ME, f. OF f. L re(*fugium* f. *fugere* flee), RE- 4]

refugee′, n. Person escaped to foreign country from religious or political persecution. [f. F *réfugié* p.p. of *réfugier* (prec.)]

refŭl′g|ent, a. Shining, gloriously bright. Hence or cogn. ~ENCE n., ~entLY² adv. [f. L re(*fulgēre* shine), RE- 6, -ENT]

refŭnd′, v.t. & i., & n. 1. Pay back (money received or taken, expenses incurred by another); reimburse; make repayment; hence ~MENT n. 2. n. (rē′fŭnd). ~ment. [ME sense *pour back*, f. OF *refunder* or L re(*fundere fus-* pour), RE- 9]

refurbish, see RE- 9; refurnish, RE- 8.

refūs′al (-z-), n. In vbl senses (*will take no* ~, is importunate); also, right or privilege of deciding to take or leave a thing before it is offered to others (*have, stipulate for, give* person, *the* ~ *of*). [foll., -AL(2)]

refūs|e′¹ (-z), v.t. & i. 1. Say or convey by action that one will not accept or submit to or give or grant or gratify or consent (~*e offer, gift, chance, office, candidate*, person as husband, etc.; *horse* ~*es fence* etc., or abs., will not jump, whence ~′ER¹ (-z-) n.; ~*e orders, control,* etc.; ~*e obedience, compliance*; ~*ed me satisfaction, tribute to suzerain, my request*; ~*e* one, not grant his request; *have never been* ~*ed*, had request rejected; ~*e to do*). 2. Make refusal; (cards) not follow suit. Hence ~ABLE (-z-) a. [ME, f. OF *refuser* f. Rom. *refusare f. L *refundere*, see REFUND]

rĕf′ūse², a. & n. (What is) rejected as worthless or left over after use. [ME, app. OF *refuse* p.p. as prec.]

rē-fūse′³ (-z), v.t. Fuse again. [RE- 9]

refūt|e′, v.t. Prove falsity or error of (statement, opinion, argument, person advancing it), rebut or repel by argument. Hence or cogn. **rĕf′ūtable** a., ~′AL(2), rĕfūtA′TION, nn. [f. L re(*futare* see CONFUTE), RE- 9]

regain′, v.t. Recover possession of (esp. ~ *consciousness*); reach (place) again; recover (one's *feet* or *footing* or *legs*). [f. F re(*gagner* GAIN²), RE- 9]

rēg′al, a. Of or by kings (~ *government, title, office*); fit for a king, magnificent, (*lives in* ~ *splendour*). Hence ~LY² adv. [ME, f. OF *regal* or L *regalis* (*rex regis* king, -AL)]

regāle′¹, n. Choice repast lit. or fig., feast *of* some dainty; a dainty (rare); choice flavour (rare; *viands of higher* ~). [f. obs. F *régale* (mod. -*al*) f. OF *gale* pleasure]

regāle′², v.t. & i. Entertain choicely (often iron.) with food or *with* talk etc.; (of beauty, flowers, etc.) give delight to; feed oneself choicely (usu. *on*). Hence ~MENT (-lm-) n. [f. F *régaler* (prec.)]

regāl′ia¹ (-lya), n. pl. Royal privileges (now rare); insignia of royalty used at coronations; insignia of an order, e.g. of Freemasons. [med. L, f. L, neut. pl. of REGALis]

regāl′ia² (-lya), n. Large cigar of good quality. [f. Sp. *regalia* royal privilege]

rēg′alism, n. Doctrine of sovereign's ecclesiastical supremacy. [-ISM]

regăl′itў, n. Attribute of kingly power, being king, (*things that touch his* ~); monarchical State, kingdom, (rare); royal privilege. [ME, f. AF, OF *regalite* or med. L *regalitas* (REGAL, -ITY)]

regărd′¹, v.t. & i. 1. Gaze upon (usu. with adv. phr. or adv.; *found him* ~*ing me with curiosity, intently*). 2. Give heed to, take into account, let one's course be affected by, (esp. in neg. context; *fears not God nor* ~*s man*; *does not* ~ *my advice*); give heed, pay attention, take notice. 3. Look upon or contemplate mentally *with* reverence, horror, etc., or with adv. specified sentiment (*I still* ~ *him kindly*). 4. Consider (usu. *as* with compl., also *in* *the light of, under an aspect,* etc., also vulg. with compl. & without *as*=consider; *is to be ~ed as a wild beast; ~ it as madness or indispensable, him as among my friends).* **5.** (Of things) concern, have relation to, (*does not ~ me* etc., has nothing to do with; esp. *as ~s,* or *~ing* as part. or prep., = about, touching; *as ~s wheat, prices are rising; considerations ~ing peace; am innocent ~ing the former).* [ME, f. F re(garder GUARD²), RE- 6, cf. REWARD]

règard'², n. **1.** Gaze, steady or significant look. **2.** Respect, point attended to, (in *this* etc. ~; esp. *in ~ to* or *of, with ~ to, regarding,* as touching, about; *in* one's ~, concerning or about or towards him). **3.** Attention, heed, care, (*to, for; ~ must be had* or *paid to general principles; the next object of ~ is his conduct; act without ~ to* or *for decency; pays no ~ to expostulations* or *adviser*), whence ~FUL a. (*of*), ~LESS a. & adv. (*of*; also sl. as ellipt. adv. **=** ~less of expense, as *got up ~less,* expensively dressed), ~fuLLY² (rare), ~lessLY², advv., ~fulNESS (of), ~lessNESS, nn. **4.** Esteem, kindly feeling or respectful opinion, (*for; have little, a great, ~ for him, no, a high, ~ for his judgement or advice*); (pl.) expression of friendliness in letter etc., compliments, (*kind ~s to you all; give him my ~s* or *best etc. ~s*). [ME & OF regard f. *regarder* (prec.)]

règard'ant, a. (Her.) looking backward; observant, with steady or intent gaze. [AF & OF (REGARD¹, -ANT)]

règatt'a, n. Meeting for boat or yacht races. [It. (Venetian)]

règel|āte', v.i. (Of fragments of ice, heaped snow, etc.) be fused by temporary thawing of surfaces into frozen mass. Hence ~A'TION n. [RE- 9, L *gelare* freeze, -ATE³]

rè'gency, n. Rule, control, (rare); office of regent; commission acting as regent; regent's or regency-commission's period of office (*the R~* in Eng. Hist., 1810–20). [ME, f. LL *regentia,* or REGENT + -ENCY]

règěn'er|āte, v.t. & i. Invest with new & higher spiritual nature; improve moral condition of, breathe new & more vigorous & higher life into, (person, institution, etc.); generate again, bring or come into renewed existence, (*must ~ate his self-respect; polypus ~ates after extraction*); reform oneself. Hence or cogn. ~ATE² (-at), ~ATIVE, aa., ~A'TION n. [f. L re(generare GENERATE), RE- 8]

règěn'erātor, n. In vbl senses; also, fuel-saving fire-brick device in furnaces. [-OR]

regenesis. See RE- 8.

rè'gent, n. & a. **1.** Ruler, ruling principle, (rare); person appointed to administer kingdom during minority, absence, or incapacity of monarch; ‖ (Oxford and Cambridge Univv.) Master of Arts who presided over disputations in the Schools (hist.); *member of the governing body of a State University. **2.** adj. (following n.). Acting as ~ (*Queen, Prince,* etc., *R~*).

[ME, f. OF *regent* or L *regere* rule, -ENT; n.f.adj.]

regerminate etc. See RE- 9.

rè'gicide, n. Killer or participator in killing of a king (*the ~s,* those concerned in trying & executing Charles I); king-killing. Hence **règicid'AL** a. [L *rex regis* king, -CIDE]

régie (rāzhě'), n. State monopoly or control of tobacco, salt, etc. [F]

regild. See RE- 9.

régime, regime, (rāzhěm'), n. Method of government, prevailing system of things, (*ancien régime,* see Ap., system of government in France before the revolution, also transf. any now abolished or past method); *under the ~ of purchase, privilege, protection, competition, Tory ascendancy,* etc. [F (*ré-*) f. L REGIMEN]

rè'gimen, n. Rule, system of government, régime, (now rare); (med.) prescribed course of exercise, way of life, & esp. diet; (gram.) relation of syntactic dependence between words, government. [L (*regere* rule, -MEN)]

rè'giment (or -jm-), n., & v.t. **1.** Rule, government, (now rare). **2.** Permanent recruiting & training unit of army usu. commanded by (Lieut.-)Colonel & divided into several companies or troops or batteries & often into two, or in war-time into many, battalions; operational unit of artillery, tanks, armoured cars, etc.; *Royal R~ (of Artillery),* Royal Artillery; (often pl.) large array or number, legion, (usu. *of*). **3.** v.t. Form (men) into ~ or ~s; organize (workers, labour) in groups or according to a system, whence **règiměntA'TION** n. [ME, f. OF f. LL *regimentum* (prec., -MENT)]

règiměn'tal, a. & n. **1.** Of a regiment; hence ~LY² adv. **2.** n. pl. Dress worn by regiment, military uniform. [-AL]

Règin'a, n. (abbr. *R.*). Reigning queen (in signatures to proclamations, as *V.R.,* Victoria ~, titles of crown law-suits, as ~ *v. Jones,* ~ versus Jones, etc.). [L (*rex regis* king, -INA¹)]

règin'al, a. (rare). Queenly, of or befitting a queen. [f. med. L *reginalis* (prec., -AL)]

rè'gion (-jn), n. Tract of country, space, place, of more or less definitely marked boundaries or characteristics (*a desert, fertile, ~; the ~ between the Elbe & the Rhine; earth is divided into ~s characterized by different fauna & flora*); separate part of world or universe (often pl.; *lower ~s,* hell, realm of the dead; *upper ~s,* sky, heaven; *the ~ beyond the grave*); sphere or realm of (*you are getting into the ~ of metaphysics*); *upper, middle, lower,* layer of atmosphere or sea; part of the body round or near some organ etc. (the *lumbar, abdominal,* etc., ~; *the ~ of the eyes*). Hence ~AL (-jo-) a. [ME, f. OF *region* f. L *regionem* nom. *-o* direction (*regere* direct, -ION)] rĕ′gister¹, n. **1.** Book in which entries are made of details to be recorded for reference; official or authoritative list kept e.g. of births, marriages, & burials or deaths, of shipping, of qualified voters in constituency (~ *office*, or in mod. use ~, a registry). **2.** Slider in organ controlling set of pipes; compass of voice or instrument, part of voice-compass (*head, chest, throat, upper, middle, lower,* ~). **3.** Adjustable plate for widening or narrowing an opening & regulating draught esp. in fire-grate; recording indicator of speed, force, etc. **4.** (Print.) exact correspondence of printed matter on two sides of leaf (*in* ~, so corresponding); (photog.) correspondence of focusing screen with plate or film. [ME & OF *registre, -istre*, or f. med. L *regestrum, -istrum* for *regestum* (LL *regesta* things recorded f. RE- 8, L *gerere* carry)]

rĕ′gister², v.t. & i. **1.** Set down (name, fact, etc.) formally, record in writing; (fig.) make mental note of. **2.** Enter or cause to be entered in particular register (~ *letter*, entrust to post-office with special precautions for safety; ‖ ~ *luggage*, on railway etc.; ~ one*self* or abs., put one's name on electoral register). **3.** (Of instrument) record automatically, indicate; (cinemat.) express facially or by gesture (emotion). **4.** (print. etc.). Correspond, make correspond, exactly. Hence or cogn. rĕ′gistrABLE a., rĕgistrA′TION n. [ME, f. OF *registrer*, or f. med. L *registrare* (prec.)]

rĕ′gistrar, n. Official recorder, person charged with keeping register. Hence ~SHIP n. [prec., -AR²]

rĕ′gistrary, n. Registrar of Cambridge University. [f. med. L *registrarius* (REGISTER¹, -ARY¹)]

rĕ′gistry, n. Registration; place, office, where registers are kept; *married at a* ~ or ~ *office* or *register office*, i.e. without religious ceremony; *servants'* ~ (*office*), shop etc. where lists of vacant situations & servants seeking them are kept; register (rare). [REGISTER¹, -RY]

‖ Rē′gius, a. ~ *professor of Greek* etc., holder of chair at Oxf. or Camb. instituted by Henry VIII, (or, in Scotland, by the Crown), or of later one placed on same footing. [L, = royal (*rex regis* king)]

rĕg′nal, a. Of a reign (~ *year*, beginning with king's accession or an anniversary of it; ~ *day*, anniversary of accession). [f. med. L *regnalis* (REIGN, -AL)]

rĕg′nant, a. Reigning (Queen *R*~, ruling in her own right & not as consort); (of things, qualities, opinions, etc.) predominant, prevalent. [f. L *regnare* REIGN², -ANT]

regŏrge′, v.t. & i. Bring or cast up again, vomit, disgorge; gush or flow back from pit, channel, etc.; swallow again. [f. F *regorger*, or RE- 9 + GORGE²]

regrāt|e′, v.t. (hist.). Buy up (goods, esp. victuals) with view to retailing at a profit (a practice formerly prohibited). Hence ~ER¹, ~′OR, nn. [ME, f. OF *regrater* (now *regratter*) of obsc. orig.]

rĕg′rĕss¹, n. Going back; declension, backward tendency. [ME, f. L *regressus* (foll.)]

rĕgrĕss′², v.i. Move backwards (chiefly astron.). [f. L *re*(*gredi=gradi gress-* step), RE- 9]

rĕgrĕ′ssion (-shn), n. Backward movement, retreat; return of curve; relapse, reversion. So rĕgrĕss′IVE a., rĕgrĕss′ivELY² adv., rĕgrĕss′iveNESS n. [f. L *-io* (prec., -ION)]

rĕgrĕt′, v.t. (-tt-), & n. **1.** Be sorry for loss of, wish one could have again; be distressed about or sorry for (event, fact), grieve at, repent (action etc.); be sorry *to* say etc. or *that* (esp. in polite refusal of invitation etc.); hence ~t′ABLE a., ~t′abLY² adv. **2.** n. Sorrow for loss of person or thing (often *for*); repentance or annoyance concerning thing (left un)done (*has no* ~*s*; *express* ~ *for*, esp. make apology or ask pardon for); vexation or disappointment caused by occurrence or situation (*hear with* ~ *of* or *that*; *refuse with much* ~ or *many* ~*s*); hence (of person or feeling) ~FUL a., ~fulLY² adv. [(1) ME, f. OF *regreter*, perh. f. ON *grāta* GREET²; (2) 16th c., f. F *regret*, f. (1)]

regroup. See RE- 8.

rĕg′ulable, a. Admitting of regulation. [f. med. L *regulabilis* (REGULATE, -ABLE)]

rĕg′ular, a. & n. **1.** (eccl.) Bound by religious rule, belonging to religious or monastic order, (cf. SECULAR; *the* ~ *clergy* in R.-C. countries, monks as opp. parish priests etc.). **2.** (Of shape, structure, arrangement, or objects in these respects) following or exhibiting a principle, harmonious, consistent, systematic, symmetrical, (~ *nomenclature, formation, features, curve, figure, flower; the five* ~ *solids*, tetrahedron or triangular pyramid bounded by 4 equal triangles, hexahedron or cube by 6 equal squares, octahedron by 8 equal triangles, dodecahedron by 12 equal pentagons, & icosahedron by 20 equal triangles). **3.** Acting, done, recurring, uniformly or calculably in time or manner, habitual, constant, not capricious or casual, orderly, (~ *working, steps, procedure, sequence, pulse, bowels, salary, orbit, bedtime, employ; keep* ~ *hours,* do same thing at same time daily; *a* ~ *life,* lived in orderly manner, esp. without excesses; ~ *people,* living ~ lives; also vulg. as adv., as *comes, happens,* ~). **4.** Conforming to a standard of etiquette etc., not transgressing conventions, in order, (*had no* ~ *introduction; the attitude of the Foreign Office has been quite* ~).

For pronunciation & hyphening of *re-* see RE- ; for words in *re-* not given see RE- 8, 9.

5. (gram.). (Of verbs, nouns, etc.) following a normal type of inflection. **6.** Properly constituted or qualified, not defective or amateur, devoted exclusively or primarily to its nominal function, (*cooks as well as a ~ cook; has no ~ profession*; ~ *soldiers*, opp. volunteers or militia or temporary levies; ~ *army*, of ~ soldiers); (colloq.) complete, thorough, indubitable, (*is a ~ rascal, brick, hero; a ~ royal queen; had a ~ smash, overhauling*, etc.; also vulg. as adv., as *is ~ angry*); hence **rĕgŭlā′rity** n., ~**IZE**(3) v.t., ~**IZA‑TION** n., ~**LY²** adv. **7.** n. One of the ~ clergy; ~ soldier; (colloq.) ~ customer, visitor, etc.; (colloq.) person permanently employed. [ME & OF *reguler* f. L *regularis* (*regula* rule); later dir. f. L; see -**AR¹**]

rĕg′ŭlāte, v.t. Control by rule, subject to restrictions, moderate, adapt to requirements; adjust (machine, clock) so that it may work accurately. Hence ~**ātoR** n., ~**ATIVE** a. [f. LL *regulare* (*regula* rule, f. *regere* direct), -**ATE³**]

rĕgŭlā′tion, n. Regulating or being regulated; prescribed rule, authoritative direction; (attrib.) fulfilling what is laid down by ~s, of correct pattern etc., ordinary, usual, formal, (*of the ~ size; exceed the ~ speed; a ~ sword, cap; the ~ mourning*). [prec., ~**ATION**]

rĕg′ŭlus, n. (pl.~ī). **1.** (*R‑~us*) bright star in Leo. **2.** (chem.). Purer or metallic part of mineral separated by sinking to bottom in crucible, impure metallic product of smelting various ores, whence ~**INE¹** a. **3.** Golden‑crested wren. [L, dim. of *rex regis* king; sense 2 orig. of metallic form of antimony, perh. as title of honour due to its readiness to combine with gold]

rĕgŭr′git|āte, v.i. & t. Gush back; (of stomach or crop or receptacle) pour or cast up again. Hence ~**A′TION** n. [f. med. L *re(gurgitare* f. L *gurges ‑itis* whirlpool), **RE‑** 9, -**ATE³**]

rehabilitate. [f. med. L *rehabilitare* (**RE‑** 9, **HABILITATE**)]; **rehandle, rehang, rehash, rehear**, etc., **RE‑** 8.

rėhears′al (‑hĕr‑), n. Rehearsing; preparatory performance of play or other entertainment (*dress* ~, such ~ in costume, i.e. when practice is far advanced). [‑**AL** (2)]

rėhearse′ (‑hĕrs), v.t. Recite, say over, repeat from beginning to end, give list of, recount, enumerate; have rehearsal of (play etc. or part in it), practise for later public performance. [ME, f. OF *rehercer*, app. f. **RE‑** 8, *herser* harrow f. *herse*; see **HEARSE**]

rehouse, see **RE‑** 8; **rehumanize**, **RE‑** 9.

Reich (rīk), n. The German commonwealth as a whole (*First* ~, Holy Roman Empire, 962–1806; *Second* ~, 1871–1918; *Third* ~, Nazi regime, 1933–45); ~*s′wehr* (‑vār), (formerly) German armed forces. [G, = empire]

Reichstag (rīks′tahk), n. (hist.). The German parliament; parliament of the late Transleithan Austria‑Hungary. [G]

rė′ifȳ, v.t. Convert (person, abstract concept) into thing, materialize. So **rēIFI‑CA′TION** n. [f. L *res* thing, -**I‑**, -**FY**]

reign¹ (rān), n. Sovereignty, rule, sway, (*under the ~ of Queen Victoria; his ~ was a gentle one; the ~ of law in nature; night resumes her ~; R~ of* **TERROR**); realm, sphere, (rare); period during which sovereign reigns (*in the ~ of John; during five successive ~s*). [ME, f. OF *regne* f. L *regnum* (*regere* rule)]

reign² (rān), v.i. Hold royal office, be king or queen lit. or fig., (~*ed over Great Britain for 60 years; a king who desired to rule as well as ~; better to ~ in hell than serve in heaven*; ~*ing beauty*, acknowledged as supreme for the time); hold sway, prevail, (*dissension & improvidence ~ed; silence ~s*, all is quiet). [ME, f. OF *regner* f. L *regnare* (prec.)]

reignite. See **RE‑** 9.

rėimbūrse′, v.t. Repay (person who has expended money, out‑of‑pocket expenses, person expenses). Hence ~**MENT** (‑sm‑) n. [**RE‑** 9, obs. *imburse* put in purse f. med. L *imbursare* (**IM‑¹**, **BOURSE**)]

reimport, reimpose etc. See **RE‑** 9.

rein (rān), n., & v.t. **1.** Long narrow strap with each end attached to bit used to guide or check horse etc. in riding or driving, (fig.) means of control, (often pl. in same senses; *draw ~*, stop one's horse, pull up, abandon effort, retrench expenditure, etc.; *give horse the ~s* or ~, let it go its own way; so *throw the ~s to; give ~ or the ~s to* one's *imagination* etc., let it have free scope; *assume, drop, the ~s of government*, enter upon, resign, office); hence ~′**LESS** a. **2.** v.t. Check or manage with ~s; (fig.) govern, restrain, control; *pull up* or *back* with ~s, hold *in* with ~s or fig. [ME, f. OF *rene*, earlier *resne*, f. Rom. **retina* f. L *retinere* **RETAIN**]

reincarnate etc., see **RE‑** 8; **reincorporate**, **RE‑** 9.

rein′deer (rān‑), n. (collect. sing. usu. for pl.). Subarctic deer used for drawing sledges & kept in herds for its milk, flesh, & hide. [ME, f. ON *hreindȳri* (*hreinn* reindeer, **DEER**)]

rēinfôrce′, v.t., & n. **1.** Strengthen or support by additional men or material or by increase of numbers, quantity, size, thickness, etc. (~ *fortress, army, provisions, party, the basses* etc. in band or chorus, person's *health* etc. with food etc., one's *argument* with fresh points); ~*d concrete* (with metal bars, gratings, or wire, embedded in it); (rare) enforce again, re‑enforce. **2.** n. Thicker part of gun next breech; strengthening part, band, etc., added to object. [**RE‑** 8, *inforce* = **ENFORCE**]

rēinfôrce′ment (‑sm‑), n. Reinforcing or being reinforced; (often pl.) additional men, ships, etc., for military or naval force; anything that reinforces. [-MENT]

reingratiate, see RE- 9; **reink**, RE- 8.

‖ **reins** (rānz), n. pl. (arch.). The kidneys; the loins. [ME, f. OF, f. L *renes* pl.]

reinsert etc. See RE- 9.

rëinstāte′, v.t. Restore to, replace *in*, lost position, privileges, etc.; restore to health or proper order. Hence ~MENT (-tm-) n. [RE- 9, obs. *instate* (IN-¹, STATE n.)]

reinsure etc., **reinter**, see RE- 8; **reinvest** etc., RE- 8, 9; **reinvigorate** etc., RE- 9.

reis (rās), n. pl. Former Portuguese and Brazilian money of account of very small value. [Port. (pl. of *real* REAL¹)]

reissue etc., **reiterate** etc. See RE- 8.

reiver. See REAVE.

reject, v.t., & n. 1. (rǐjĕkt′). Put aside as not to be accepted, practised, believed, chosen, used, complied with, etc. (~ *doctrine*, *custom*, *evidence*, *candidate*, *literary contribution*, *food*, *request*, *suitor*, *vote*; *sorting-machine* ~s *all defective specimens*); cast up again, vomit, evacuate. 2. n. (rē′jĕkt). Somebody or something that has been ~ed (e.g. person unfit for military service, article sold cheaply as not up to standard). Hence or cogn. **rejĕct′ABLE** a., **rejĕc′tER¹**, **rejĕc′tION**, **rejĕc′tor**, nn. [ME, f. L *re*(*jicĕre -ject-* == *jacĕre* throw), RE- 9]

rëjĕctamĕn′ta, n. pl. Refuse, waste matters; things cast up by the sea; excrements. [mod. L (prec., -MENT)]

rējoice′, v.t. & i. Cause joy to, make glad, (*the news* ~d *him*; *I am* ~d *to hear it*, *that it should be so*, *at it*, etc.); feel great joy, whence **rējoi′cingLY²** adv.; be glad *that* or *to do*, take delight *in* or *at*, (~ *in*, be blessed in the possession of, often joc. for *have*); make merry, celebrate some event, whence **rējoi′cings** (-z) [-ING¹] n. pl. [ME, f. OF *re*(*joir -iss-* JOY²), RE- 6]

rējoin′¹, v.i. & t. (Law) reply to charge or pleading, esp. to plaintiff's replication; say in answer, retort; join (one's companion, regiment, etc.) again. [ME, f. OF *rejoindre* JOIN), RE- 9]

rē-join′², v.t. & i. Join (t. & i.) together again, reunite. [RE- 9 + JOIN, or as prec.]

rējoin′der, n. What is REJOIN′ed or said in reply, retort. [as REJOIN¹, see -ER⁴]

rējuv′ĕn|āte, **rējuv′ĕn|īze**, -|ise (-ōō-; -īz), vv.t. & i. Make or become young again. Hence ~A′TION, ~ātor, nn., (-ōō-). [RE- 9, L *juvenis* young, -ATE³, -IZE]

rējuvĕn|ĕsce′ (-ōō-), v.i. & t. Become young again (biol., i. & t. of cells) get, fill with, fresh vitality. So ~ĕs′CENT a., ~ĕs′CENCE n., (-ōō-). [f. LL *re*(*juvenescere* f. L *juvenis*, -ESCENT), RE- 9]

rekindle. See RE- 9.

-rel, also *-erel*, suf. of dim. & depreciating tendency, occas. repr. OF *-erel*, mod. F *-ereau*, but usu. in native wds of obscure origin.

relabel. See RE- 8.

rēlăps|e′, v.i., & n. 1. Fall back, sink again, into wrong-doing, error, heresy, weakness or illness, quiescence or indolence, (often *into*). 2. n. Act or fact of ~ing, esp. deterioration in patient's condition after partial recovery. [f. L *re*(*labi laps-* slip), RE- 9]

rēlāt|e′, v.t. & i. 1. Narrate, recount, whence ~′ER¹ n. 2. Bring into relation, establish relation between, (*to*, *with*, or abs.; *cannot* ~*e the phenomena with* or *to anything we know* or *to each other*); (p.p.) connected, allied, akin by blood or marriage, (*the law extends to several* ~ed *groups*; *is* ~ed *to the royal family*), whence ~′ĕdNESS n. 3. Have reference *to*, stand in some relation *to*, (*notices nothing but what* ~es *to himself*; *how parts* ~*e to parts*). [f. L *relat-* (REFER)]

rēlā′tion, n. 1. Narration, a narrative; (law) laying of information before Attorney-General for him to take action upon (*proceeding at the* ~ *of the Board of Trade*). 2. What one person or thing has to do with another, way in which one stands or is related to another, kind of connexion or correspondence or contrast or feeling that prevails between persons or things, (*the* ~s *primarily expressed by prepositions are those of place & time*; *the outlay seems to bear no* ~, *is out of all* ~, *to the object aimed at*; *the* ~ *between them is that of guardian & ward*; ~s *are rather strained*, cordiality is impaired; *the report has* ~ *to a state of things now past*; *in* or rarely *with* ~ *to*, as regards), whence ~AL a., ~alLY² adv., (-sho-). 3. Kinship lit. or fig. (rare, now usu. ~SHIP n.). 4. Kinsman, kinswoman, relative (occas. with mixture of prec. sense, as *is he any* ~, *what* ~ *is he*, *to you?*; *he is no* ~). Hence ~LESS (-sho-) a. [ME, f. OF, or L *relatio* (prec., -ION)]

rĕl′ative, a. & n. 1. (gram.). Referring, & attaching a subordinate clause, to an expressed or implied antecedent (~ *pronoun*, as in *The man* whom *you saw*; ~ *adjective*, as in Which *things are an allegory*; ~ *adverb*, as in *The place* where *he died*); (of clause) attached to antecedent by ~ word. 2. Having mutual relations, corresponding in some way, related to each other, (*different yet* ~ *designs*). 3. Pertinent, relevant, related to the subject, (*without some more* ~ *proof*). 4. Comparative (*what are the* ~ *merits of the two?*; *made the next attempt with* ~ *coolness*); in relation to something else (*their* ~ *positions are the same though they are miles apart*); proportioned to something else (*supply is* ~ *to demand*); implying comparison (heat, speed, strength, *are* ~ *words*); correlative or essentially involving a different but corresponding idea (*the conceptions of husband & wife are*

~ *to each other*); not having absolute existence but conditioned (*she is beautiful to me, but beauty is* ~ *to the beholder's eye*). **5.** Having reference, relating, *to* (*detailed the facts* ~ *to the matter*; also loosely as adv., as *I wrote to him* ~ *to renewal of the lease*); hence ~LY[2] (·vl·)adv. **6.** n.(Gram.) ~ word, esp. pronoun (*the principal* ~*s are* who, which, that, what), whence **relativ′AL** a.; (philos.) ~ thing or term. **7.** Kinsman, kinswoman, relation by blood or marriage. [ME, f. OF (·*if*, ·*ive*), or LL *relativus* (RELATE, ·IVE)]

rĕl′ativ|ism, n. Doctrine that knowledge is of relations only. So ~IST(2) n. [prec., ·ISM]

rĕlativ′itў, n. Relativeness; (philos.) Einstein's theory of the universe, based on the principle that all motion is relative, regarding space-time as a four-·dimensional continuum, & invalidating previous conceptions of gravitation, geometry, & other matters. [·ITY]

rĕlāt′or, n. Relater (now rare); (law) maker of RELATION (legal sense). [L (RELATE, ·OR)]

rĕlăx′, v.t. & i. Cause or allow to become loose or slack or limp, enfeeble, enervate, mitigate, abate, (~ *the bowels, the muscles*, one's *grasp, discipline, a rule*, one's *attention*, one's *efforts*; ~*ed throat*, form of sore throat; *place has a* ~*ing climate*, opp. *bracing*); grow less tense or rigid or stern or ceremonious or energetic or zealous (*his hold, hands, severity, features, manner, endeavours,* ~*ed*; *must not* ~ *in* one's *efforts*). [ME, f. L re(laxare see LAX), RE- 9]

rĕlaxā′tion, n. Partial remission *of* penalty, duty, etc.; cessation from work, recreation, amusements; diminution of tension, severity, precision, etc. [f. L *relaxatio* (prec., ·ATION)]

rĕlay′[1], n., & v.t. & i. **1.** Set of fresh horses substituted for tired ones; gang of men, supply of material, etc., similarly used (~·*race*, between teams of which each person does part of the distance, the 2nd etc. members of teams starting when the 1st etc. end); (teleg.) instrument reinforcing long-distance current with local battery. **2.** vb. Arrange in, provide with, replace by, get, ~(s); (radio) broadcast (a message, programme, originating at, and received from, another station). [ME, f. OF *relai* n., *relaier* vb, ult. f. L *laxare*, cf. DELAY]

rē-lay′[2], v.t. Lay again. [RE- 8]

rĕleas|e′[1], v.t. **1.** (law). Remit, surrender, make over to another, (debt, right, property), whence ~EE′, ~′OR, nn. **2.** Set free, liberate, deliver, unfasten, (*from*); (cinemat.) issue (film etc.) for general exhibition. Hence ~′ABLE a. [ME, f. OF *relesser* f. L RELAXARE]

rĕlease′[2], n. **1.** Deliverance, liberation, from trouble, sorrow, life, duty, confinement, or fixed position. **2.** Written dis-

charge, receipt; legal conveyance of right or estate to another, document effecting this. **3.** Handle, catch, etc., that releases part of machine etc. [ME, f. OF *reles* (prec.)]

rĕl′ég|āte, v.t. Banish *to* some place of exile; consign or dismiss *to* some usu. inferior position, sphere, etc.; transfer (matter) for decision or execution, refer (person) for information etc., *to*. Hence ~ABLE a., ~A′TION n. [f. L re(*legare* send), RE- 5, ·ATE[3]]

rĕlĕnt′, v.i. Relax severity, become less stern, abandon harsh intention, yield to compassion. Hence ~ĭngLY[2] adv., ~LESS a., ~lĕssLY[2] adv., ~lĕssNESS n. [ME, ult. f. RE- 9, L *lentus* soft; cf. L *relentescere* slacken]

rĕl′év|ant, a. Bearing upon, pertinent *to*, the matter in hand. Hence ~ANCE, ~ANCY, nn., ~antLY[2] adv. [f. med. L *relevans*, part. of L *relevare* RELIEVE, ·ANT]

rĕli′|able, a. That may be relied upon, of sound & consistent character or quality. Hence ~ABIL′ITY n. (~*ability trials*, long-·distance trials of motor vehicles designed to test dependableness, endurance, etc. rather than speed), ~ableNESS n., ~abLY[2] adv. [RELY, ·ABLE; from 16th c.; an established wd avoided by some purists as of irreg. formation]

rĕli′ance, n. Trust, confidence, (usu. *upon, on, in*; *have, place, feel,* ~ *upon* etc.; *my* ~ *is upon God*); thing depended upon (*the well is our chief* ~). So **rĕli′ANT** a. [RELY, ·ANCE]

rĕl′ic, n. **1.** Part of holy person's body or belongings kept after his death as object of reverence; memento, souvenir. **2.** pl. Dead body, remains, of person; what has survived destruction or wasting, remnant, residue, scraps. **3.** Surviving trace or memorial *of* a custom, belief, period, people, etc.; object interesting for age of associations. [ME *relike* etc., f. OF *relique*, f. L RELIQUIAE]

rĕl′ict, n. Widow (usu. *his* etc. ~, or ~ *of*); geological or other object which has survived in a primitive form; animal or plant known to have existed in the same form in previous geological ages; (rare) = prec. [f. p.p. of L re(*linquere* -*lict*-leave), RE- 3]

rĕlief′[1], n. **1.** Alleviation of or deliverance from pain, distress, anxiety, etc. (*the medicine brought* ~; *it is a* ~ *to come across an optimist*). **2.** Feature etc. that diversifies monotony or relaxes tension (*a blank wall without* ~; *a comic scene follows by way of* ~). **3.** Assistance given to the poor esp. ~). ‖ formerly under the Poor Law (*recipients of public* ~ *shall not be eligible*) or to persons in special danger or difficulty (*a* ~ *fund for the earthquake victims*; ~*works*, building etc. operations started to give work to the unemployed). **4.** Reinforcement & esp. raising of siege of besieged town. **5.** (Replacing of person or persons on duty by) person(s) appointed to take turn of duty. **6.** Redress of hardship or grievance. [ME, f. AF *relef*, OF *relief* (*relever* RELIEVE)]

relief'², n. Method of moulding or carving or stamping in which design stands out from plane or curved surface with projections proportioned & more or less (*high*, *low*, ~) closely approximating to those of objects imitated (*the profile of Julius in* ~); piece of sculpture etc, in ~; appearance of being done in ~ given by arrangement of line or colour or shading, distinctness of outline lit. or fig., vividness, (*stands out in* ~; *bring out the facts in full* ~); ~ *map*, map-model showing the elevations and depressions of the area dealt with, usu. on an exaggerated relative scale, (also) ordinary map indicating hills and valleys by shading, colouring, or hachures, rather than by contour lines alone. [f. F *relief* & its source It. *rilievo* (*rilevare* raise f. L as RELIEVE)]

relieve', v.t. **1.** Bring, give, be a, RELIEF¹ to (*town was* ~*ed*; *am much* ~*ed to hear it*; *devotes himself to* ~*ing distress or the distressed*; ‖ ~*ing officer*, official charged with care of the poor; ~*ing arch*, built in substance of wall to ~e part below from weight; ~e one's *feelings*, by strong language or some ebullition; ~e *nature*, evacuate bladder or bowels; *a black bodice* ~*ed with white lace*; ~e *guard*, come & take one's turn on guard; *you shall be* ~*ed at 10.30*; ~e one of *load*, take it off him, also joc., as *a tramp* ~*ed him of his purse*). **2.** Bring into RELIEF², exhibit with appearance of solidity or detachment, (esp. in p.p., often *against* background). Hence ~'ABLE a. [ME, f. OF *relever* f. L *re(levare* f. *levis* light), RE- 9]

relievo, n. (pl. ~s). = RELIEF² esp. in lit. senses (ALTO, BASSO, MEZZO, ~-~). [f. It. *rilievo* RELIEF² w. anglicized spelling & pronunc.]

reli'gion (-jn), n. **1.** Monastic condition, being monk or nun, (*enter into*, *be in*, ~); (rare) a monastic order. **2.** (rare). Practice of sacred rites. **3.** One of the prevalent systems of faith & worship (*the Christian*, *Mohammedan*, ~; *established* ~, that of established CHURCH¹; NATURAL, REVEAL¹*ed*, ~; *all* ~s *are the same to him*). **4.** Human recognition of superhuman controlling power & esp. of a personal God entitled to obedience, effect of such recognition on conduct & mental attitude, (*get* ~, vulg. or joc., be converted to such belief). **5.** Action that one is bound to do (*make a* ~ *of doing*). Hence ~LESS (-jon-) a. [ME, f. AF *religiun*, OF *-ion*, or L *religio*)]

reli'gioner (-jon-), n. Member of monastic order; person zealous for religion. [-ER¹]

reli'gion|ism (-jon-), n. Excessive religious zeal. So ~IST(2) n. [-ISM]

reli'gionize (-jon-), -**ise** (-īz), v.t. & i. Convert to or imbue with religion; exhibit religious zeal. [-IZE]

reli'giose, a. Morbidly religious. [as RELIGIOUS, -OSE¹]

religios'ity, n. Being religious or religiose. [ME, f. L *religiositas* (foll., -ITY)]

reli'gious (-jus), a. & n. **1.** Imbued with religion, pious, god-fearing, devout; of, belonging to, a monastic order; of, concerned with, religion; scrupulous, conscientious, (*with* ~ *care*, *exactitude*, etc.); hence ~LY² adv., ~NESS n., (-jus-). **2.** n. (As sing. with *a* etc., & as pl. in same form with *the*, *some*, *several*, etc.) person bound by monastic vows. [ME, f. AF *religius*, OF *-ieus*, or L *religiosus* (RELIGION, -OUS)]

reline. See RE- 9.

relin'quish, v.t. Give up, abandon, cease from, resign, surrender, (habit, plan, hope, belief, right, possession); loose hold of (object held). Hence ~MENT n. [ME, f. OF *relinquir* f. L *re(linquere* leave), RE- 3, -ISH²]

rel'iquary, n. Receptacle for relic(s). [f. F *reliquaire* (RELIC, -ARY¹)]

rel'ique (-ik; *or* relēk'), n. (arch.). Relic. [F]

reli'quiae, n. pl. Remains; (geol.) fossil remains of animals or plants; (bot.) withered remains of leaves decaying on stem. [L (*reliquus* remaining, f. *relinquere* RELINQUISH, -IA¹)]

rel'ish¹, n. **1.** Flavour, distinctive taste *of*; slight dash or tinge *of* some quality. **2.** Appetizing flavour, attractive quality, (*meat has no* ~ *when one is ill*; *horseplay loses its* ~ *after childhood*); thing eaten with plainer food to add flavour. **3.** Enjoyment of food or other things, zest, liking *for*, (*eat*, *read*, *appreciate jest*, etc., *with great* ~; *has no* ~ *for poetry*). [16th c. alt. (w. assim. to -ISH²) of obs. *reles* f. OF *reles* remainder f. *relaisser* (RELEASE¹)]

rel'ish², v.t. & i. Serve as relish to, make piquant etc.; get pleasure out of, like, be pleased with, (*thought he could* ~ *a lobster*; *does not* ~ *the prospect*), whence ~ABLE a.; taste, savour, smack, suggest presence, *of*; affect the lit. or fig. taste *well*, *badly*, etc. [f. prec.]

relive, reload. See RE- 8.

relu'cent (-ōō-), a. (rare). Shining, bright. [f. L *re(lucēre* shine), RE- 6, -ENT]

reluct', v.i. (now rare). Feel or show reluctance, make opposition, (*at*, *against*). So ~ATE³ (in same sense) v.i., reluctaTION n. [f. L *re(luctari* struggle), RE- 2]

reluc'tant, a. Struggling, offering resistance, hard to work or get or manage, (esp. poet.); unwilling, disinclined, *to do* or abs. (*am very* ~ *to admit*; *gave me* ~ *assistance*). Hence reluc'tANCE n., ~LY² adv. [as prec., -ANT]

relume' (*or* -ōōm), v.t. (poet.). Rekindle (light or flame lit. or fig.); make (eyes etc.) bright again; light (sky etc.) up again. [RE- 9, & as ILLUME]

rely', v.i. Put one's trust, depend with confidence, (*up*)*on* person or thing (*is* ~*ing upon a broken reed*; *I* ~ *upon you to do it, its being done, today*; *you may* ~ *upon it that he will be here*). [ME; earlier senses *rally, be vassal of*; f. OF *relier* bind together, f. L *re(ligare* bind), RE- 9]

remain'¹, v.i. 1. Be left over after abstraction or use of or dealing with the rest (*the few pleasures that* ~ *to an old man*; *worse things* ~ *to be told*; *nothing* ~*s but to draw the moral*). 2. Abide, stay in same place or condition, continue to exist, be extant, be left behind, (~ *three weeks in Paris*; *let it* ~ *as it is*; *as things have been they* ~; *the Parthenon* ~*s to attest* or *as a proof of it*; *this visit will always* ~ *in my memory*; *the luggage unfortunately* ~*ed on the platform*; *victory* ~*ed with the Thebans*). 3. (With compl.) continue to be (*one thing* ~*s certain*; ~ *faithful* etc.; *I* ~ *yours truly* etc., formula concluding letter). [ME, f. AF *remeyn-* f. OF *remanoir* (also *remaindre*) f. L *re(manēre* stay), RE- 3]

remain'², n. 1. (Usu. pl.) what remains over, surviving members or parts or amount, (*the* ~*s of a nation, family, meal, stock, building*, of one's *conscience* or *strength*, etc.; also in pl. as sing., & in sing., as *here there is the* ~*s, a* ~, *of a temple*): (usu. pl.) relics or relic of obsolete custom or of antiquity (*Roman* ~*s*). 2. pl. Works, esp. those not before or yet published, left by author (rarely in sing. of single work). 3. pl. Dead body, corpse. [ME, f. OF (prec.)]

remain'der, n., & v.t. 1. (law). Residual interest in estate devised to another (cf. REVERSION) simultaneously with creation of estate (~ *man*, devisee of ~), right of succession to title or position on holder's decease, whence ~SHIP n. 2. Residue, remaining person or things; (arith.) number left after subtraction or division; (bookselling) copies left unsold when demand has ceased & often offered at reduced price, (vb) treat or dispose of (edition) as ~; (attrib.) left over. [ME & AF, = OF *remaindre*, see REMAIN¹, -ER⁴]

remake, see RE- 8; **reman**, RE- 8, 9.

remand' (-ah-), v.t., & n. 1. Send back *to*, reconsign, (now rare in gen. sense); send back (prisoner) into custody to allow of further inquiry. 2. n. Recommittal to custody; ~ *home*, temporary institution for juvenile offenders. [ME, f. OF *remander* or LL *re(mandare* commit), RE- 9]

rem'anent, a. Remaining, residual, (now rare exc. in ~ *magnetism*, that left in iron after electric excitation). [ME, f. L *part.* as foll., see -ENT]

rem'anet, n. Remaining part, residue; postponed lawsuit or parliamentary bill. [L, 3rd sing. of L *remanere* (REMAIN¹)]

remargin. See RE- 8.

remark'¹, v.t. & i. Take notice of, perceive, regard with attention, observe, (person, thing, fact, *that* etc.); say by way of comment; make comment (*up*)*on*. [f. F *re(marquer* MARK²), RE- 6]

remark'², n. Noticing, observing, (*worthy of* ~, remarkable), commenting (*is the theme of general* ~; *let it pass without* ~); a written or spoken comment, anything said, (*his* ~*s are often interesting*; *make a* ~, speak). [f. F *remarque* (prec.)]

remark'ab|le, a. Worth notice, exceptional, striking, conspicuous. Hence ~leNESS n., ~LY² adv. [f. F *remarquable* (REMARK¹, -ABLE)]

remarque (rĭmàrk'), n. Mark, usu. marginal sketch, indicating certain state of engraving plate. [F]

remarry etc., **remast.** See RE- 8.

remblai (rahṅblā'), n. (Fortif.) earth used to form ramparts, parapets, etc.; earth brought to form railway embankments etc. [F, f. *remblayer* embank]

Rembrändtèsque' (-sk), a. & n. (After) the style of Rembrandt (d. 1669), with marked effects of light & shade. [-ESQUE]

rem'edy, n., & v.t. 1. Cure for disease, healing medicine or treatment, means of removing or counteracting or relieving any evil (*for*), redress, legal or other reparation, whence or cogn. **remed'IAL** a., **remed'ially²** adv., (now poet. or rhet.) **rem'edILESS** (or rĭmĕd'-) a., **rem'edíléss-LY²** adv. 2. Margin within which coins as minted may differ from the standard fineness and weight. 3. v.t. Cure medically (now rare); rectify, make good; so **remed'iABLE** a. [ME; vb f. OF *remedier* or L *remediare*, n. f. AF *remedie*, f. L *re(medium* f. *medēri* heal), RE- 1]

remem'ber, v.t. 1. Retain in the memory, not forget, recall to mind, recollect, know by heart, (person, thing, fact, *that*, *to* do, *how* to do, *when*, *why*, etc., or abs.; ~ *oneself*, bethink oneself of one's manners or intentions after a lapse; also refl. with *me, him*, etc., arch., as *I* ~ *me that, they* ~*ed them of*), whence ~ABLE a. 2. Make present to, tip, (~*ed me in his will*; ~ *the waiter*). 3. Mention in one's prayers. 4. Convey greetings from (person) *to* another (~ *me kindly to them*; *begs to be* ~*ed to you*). [ME, f. OF *remembrer* f. LL *re(memorari* f. L *memor* mindful), RE- 9]

remem'brance, n. 1. Remembering or being remembered, memory, recollection, (*has escaped my* ~; *have in, call to,* ~; *put in* ~, remind; *have no* ~ *of it*; *more than once within my* ~; *a pillar in* ~ *of the exploit*); *R* ~ *Day*, day (11th November, ARMISTICE *Day*, or the Sunday immediately preceding it) commemorating those who fell in the wars of 1914–18 & 1939–45. 2. Keepsake, souvenir, memorial. 3. pl. Greetings conveyed through third person. [ME, f. OF (prec., -ANCE)]

rĕmĕm′brancer, n. **1.** ‖ *King's, Queen's, R~*, officer collecting debts due to sovereign; ‖ *City R~*, representing Corporation of City of London before parliamentary committees etc. **2.** Reminder, memento, memorial. [ME, f. AF (prec., -ER¹)]

remigrate etc. See RE- 9.

rĕmind′, v.t. Put (person) in mind *of, to do, that, how*, etc., or abs. [RE- 8, MIND vb]

rĕmin′der, n. Thing that reminds or is memento, *of*. [ME, f. AF (prec., -ER¹)]

rĕmind′ful, a. Acting as a reminder, reviving the memory, *of*. [-FUL]

rĕminis′cence, n. **1.** Remembering, recovery of knowledge by mental effort, (*Platonic doctrine of ~*, that all knowledge is such recovery of things known to the soul in previous existences). **2.** Remembered (& related) fact or incident; (pl.) collection in literary form of incidents that person remembers. **3.** Point in thing reminding or suggestive of other thing (*there is a ~ of the Greek type in her face*). Hence **rĕminiscĕn′tIAL** (-shl) a. [F, or f. LL *reminiscentia* f. *reminisci* remember, RE- 9, -ENCE]

rĕminis′cent, a. Recalling past things, given to or concerned with retrospection, mindful or having memories *of*; reminding or suggestive *of*. Hence **~LY²** adv. [as prec., -ENT]

remint. See RE- 8.

rĕmise′¹ (-ēz), n., & v.i. **1.** (arch.). Coach-house, carriage hired from livery-stable. **2.** (fenc.). Second thrust made for recovery from first; (v.i.) make **~**. [F, vbl n. f. *remettre* REMIT]

rĕmise′² (-īz), v.t. (legal). Surrender, make over, (right, property). [f. F *remis(e)* p.p. as prec.]

rĕmiss′, a. Careless of duty, lax, negligent; lacking force or energy. Hence **~LY²** adv., **~NESS** n. [f. L *remissus* p.p. of REMIT*tere*]

rĕmiss′ible, a. That may be remitted. [F, or f. LL *remissibilis* (REMIT, -IBLE)]

rĕmi′ssion (-shn), n. **1.** Forgiveness *of* sins etc., forgiveness of sins; remitting of debt, penalty, etc. **2.** Diminution of force, effect, degree, violence, etc. **3.** Act of remitting in other senses (rare). So **rĕmiss′IVE** a. [ME,. f. OF, f. L *remissionem* (foll., -ION)]

rĕmit′, v.t. & i. (-tt-), & n. **1.** (Usu. of God) pardon (sins etc.); refrain from exacting or inflicting or executing (debt, punishment, sentence). **2.** Abate (t. & i.), slacken, mitigate, partly or entirely cease from or cease, (*~ one's anger or efforts, the siege*; *pain, enthusiasm, begins to ~*). **3.** Refer (matter for decision etc.) *to* some authority, send back (case) to lower court. **4.** Send or put back (*into*) previous state; postpone, defer, *to* or *till*. **5.** Transmit (money etc.), get conveyed by post etc., whence **~t′er¹** [-ER¹], **~TEE′**, nn. Hence

~t′AL(2) n. **6.** n. (*Also* rēm′it) item **~ted** for consideration. [ME, f. L *re(mittere miss-* send), RE- 5]

rĕmitt′ance, n. Money sent to person; consignment of goods sent (rare); sending of money; **~-man**, emigrant subsisting on **~s** from home, person paid to stay abroad. [prec., -ANCE]

rĕmitt′ent, a. & n. (Fever) that abates at intervals (cf. INTERMIT*tent*). [REMIT, -ENT]

rĕmitt′er², n. (legal; for *remitter¹* see REMIT). Substitution, in favour of holder of two titles to estate, of the more valid for the other by which he entered on possession; remitting of case to other court; restoration to rights, rehabilitation, (rare). [-ER⁴]

rĕm′nant, n. *The* little or few that remain(s), small remaining quantity or piece or number of persons or things; surviving trace *of*; fragment, scrap, esp. piece of cloth etc. offered at reduced price when greater part has been used up. [ME, contr. f. obs. & OF *remenant*, *-manant*, (*remanoir* REMAIN¹, -ANT)]

remodel. See RE- 8.

rĕmŏn′ĕtĭz|e (*or* -mŭn²), **-is|e** (-īz), v.t. Restore (metal etc.) to former position as legal tender. Hence **~A′TION** n. [RE- 9]

rĕmŏn′strance, n. (Hist.) formal statement of public grievances (*the Grand R~*, from House of Commons to Crown 1641); remonstrating, expostulation, *a* protest. [OF (foll., -ANCE)]

rĕmŏn′str|āte (*or* rĕm′on-), v.i. & t. Make protest, expostulate, (*against* course, *with* person, *on* or *upon* matter, or abs.); urge in remonstrance (*that* or parenth.). Hence or cogn. **~ANT** a. & n., **~antLY²**, **~āting-LY²** advv., **~atIVE** a., **~ātOR** n. [f. med. L *re(monstrare* show), RE- 2, -ATE³]

rĕmŏn′tant, a. & n. (Rose) blooming more than once in year. [F (*remonter* REMOUNT², -ANT)]

rĕm′ora, n. The sucking-fish, formerly supposed to stay course of ship to which it adhered; obstruction, impediment, (now rare). [L (RE- 2, *mora* delay), = impediment, sucking-fish]

rĕmŏrse′, n. Bitter repentance for wrong committed, whence **~FUL** (-sf-) a., **~fulLY²** adv.; compunction, compassionate reluctance to inflict pain or be cruel, (chiefly in *without ~*), whence **~LESS** (-sl-) a., **~lĕssLY²** adv., **~lĕssNESS** n. [ME, f. OF *remors* f. LL *re(morsus -ūs* f. *mordēre mors-* bite), RE- 3]

rĕmōte′, a. (**~r**, **~st**). **1.** Far apart. **2.** Far away or off in place or time, not closely related, distant or widely different or by nature separate *from*, (*lies ~ from the road*; *came from the ~st parts of the earth*; *memorials of ~ ages*; *a ~ ancestor, descendant, kinsman*; *~ causes, effects*; *introduces considerations ~ from the subject*); *~ control*, control of apparatus etc.

from a point some distance away by means of electrically operated device, radio waves, etc. 3. Out-of-the-way, secluded, (a ~ *village*; *lives*~). 4. (Chiefly superl., of idea etc.) slight(est), faint(est), least, (*have not the*~*st, have only a very*~, *conception of what he means*). Hence ~LY² (-tl-) adv., ~NESS (-tn-) n. [ME, f. L *remotus* (REMOVE⁷)].

remould, remount¹. See RE- 8.

rĕmount'², v.t. & i. Go up, get on to, (hill, ladder, horse, etc.) again; go up again, get on horseback again, make fresh ascent; go back to specified date, period, source. [ME, f. OF *re*(*monter* MOUNT²), RE- 9; later dir. f. MOUNT²]

rĕmo'v|able (-mōō-), a. In vbl senses; esp., (of magistrate or official) subject to removal from office, holding office during pleasure of Crown or other authority. Hence ~ABIL'ITY n. [foll., -ABLE]

rĕmove'¹ (-ōōv), v.t. & i. 1. Take off or away from place occupied, convey to another place, change situation of, get rid of, dismiss, (~ one's *hat, the tea-things, all traces*; ~ *mountains*, do miracle; *cardinal was* ~*d by poison*; ~ *magistrate from office*; *boy is* ~*d from school*, taken away by parents etc.; *this will* ~ *all apprehension, the last doubts*; ~ *furniture*, for persons changing house, as special trade, whence **rĕmo'vER¹** (-mōō-) n.); ‖ (pass., of course at dinner etc.) be succeeded by (*boiled haddock* ~*d by hashed mutton*). 2. Change one's residence, go away from, (*am removing from London to Oxford*; *truth has* ~*d from earth*). 3. p.p. Distant or remote from (*is not many degrees* ~*d from the brute*); (of cousins) *once, twice*, etc., ~*d*, with difference of one, two, etc., generations (*my first cousin once, twice*, ~*d*, cousin's child or parent's cousin, cousin's grandchild or grandparent's cousin). Hence **rĕmo'vAL** (-mōō-) n. (not of cousinship). [ME, f. OF *removeir* f. L *re*(*movère* MOVE), RE- 4]

rĕmove'² (-ōōv), n. 1. ‖ Dish that succeeds another at table. 2. ‖ Promotion to higher form at school (*has not got his* ~); ‖ (in some schools) a certain form or division. 3. (rare). Change of residence, departure, removal; distance (*at a certain* ~ *its shape seems to change*). 4. Stage in gradation, degree, (*is but one* ~, *few* ~*s, from*), esp. in consanguinity (cf. prec.). [f. prec.]

rĕmūn'er|āte, v.t. Reward, pay for service rendered; serve as or provide recompense for (toil etc.) or to (person). Hence or cogn. ~A'TION n., ~ATIVE a., ~ATIVELY² adv., ~ATIVENESS n. [f. L *re*(*munerari* f. *munus -eris* gift), RE- 1, -ATE³]

rĕnaiss'ance (& see Ap.), n. Revival of art & letters under influence of classical models in 14th–16th cc., period of its progress, style of art & architecture developed by it, (often attrib., as ~ *painters*,

architecture, church); any similar revival. [F (*renaître* be born again) after *naissance* birth, cf. RENASCENCE]

rĕn'al, a. Of the kidneys. [f. F *rénal* or LL *renalis* (*renes* kidneys, -AL)]

rename. See RE- 8.

rĕnăs'cence, n. Rebirth, renewal; = RENAISSANCE. [foll., -ENCE]

rĕnăs'cent, a. Springing up anew, being reborn. [f. L *re*(*nasci* be born), RE- 8, -ENT]

rĕncoun'ter, rĕncŏn'tre (-ter, & see Ap.), n. (now rare). Encounter, battle, skirmish, duel; casual meeting. [f. F *rencontre* (*rencontrer*, see RE-, ENCOUNTER)]

rĕnd, v.t. & i. (*rĕnt*). 1. Tear or wrench (*off, away, out of, from, asunder, apart*, etc., or abs.; arch. or rhet.; *a province rent from the empire*; ~ *one's garments, hair*, in sign of grief etc.; *turn &* ~ one, fig., abuse him unexpectedly). 2. Split or divide (t. & i.) in two or in pieces or usu. into factions (~ *laths*, make them by splitting wood; *Europe was rent in two by the question*; *shouts* ~ *the air*, sound explosively; *heart is rent by contending emotions*; *the veil was rent*). [OE *rendan*, = OFris. *renda*, not otherwise represented]

rĕn'der, v.t., & n. 1. Give in return (~ *thanks, good for evil*). 2. Give back (arch.); hand over, deliver, give up, surrender, (chiefly arch.; ~ *to Caesar the things that are Caesar's*; *grave* ~*s up its dead*; *fortress was* ~*ed on terms*). 3. Pay (tribute etc.), show (obedience etc.), do (service etc.), (usu. *to* or with ind. obj.). 4. Produce for inspection, submit, present, send in, (account, reason, etc.; *will have to* ~ *an account of*; *account* ~*ed*, bill previously sent in & not yet paid, phr. used as substitute for repetition of items). 5. Reproduce, portray, give representation or performance or effect of, execute, translate, (*painter has hardly* ~*ed the expression*; *the quartet, Iago, the dramatist's conception, were well* ~*ed*; *how would you* ~ *solvitur ambulando?*; *poetry can never be adequately* ~*ed in another language*), whence ~ING¹ (1, 2) n. 6. (With obj. & compl.) make, cause to be, convert into, (*age had* ~*ed him peevish*; *the tone* ~*ed it an insult*). 7. Melt (fat) down, extract by melting, clarify, also ~ *down*. 8. Cover (stone, brick) with first coat of plaster; ~-*set* v.t., plaster (wall etc.) with two coats, n. & a., (plastering) of two coats. 9. n. (legal). Return in money or kind or service made by tenant to superior. [ME, f. OF *rendre* f. Rom. *rendere f. L *reddere reddit-* (RE- 1, *dare* give)]

rendezvous (rŏn'dĭvōō), n. (pl. same, pr. -ōōz), & v.i. (~*es*, ~*ed*, ~*ing*, pr. -ōōz, -ōōd, -ōōing). 1. Place appointed for assembling of troops or ships; place of common resort; meeting-place agreed on, meeting by agreement (*place of* ~). 2. v.i. Meet at ~. [F, f. *rendez vous* (*rendre*, see prec.) betake yourselves]

rĕndi′tion, n. 1. Surrender of place or person (now rare). 2. A translation; interpretation, rendering, of dramatic role, musical piece, etc. [F (obs.), f. *rendre* RENDER, -ION]

rĕn′egāde, n. & v.i., **rĕnĕgād′ō** (arch.), n. 1. Apostate, esp. from Christianity to Mohammedanism; deserter of party or principles, turncoat. 2. v.i. Turn ~; so **rĕnĕgA′TION** n. [Sp. (-o), f. med. L *re(negatus* f. *negare* deny), RE- 9]

rénég(u)e′ (-ĕg), v.i. & t. (Cards) revoke (arch.) deny, renounce, abandon. [f. med. L *renegare* f. RE- + *negare* deny]

renew′, v.t. & i. 1. Restore to original state, make (as good as) new, resuscitate, revivify, regenerate, (*nature dies & is ~ed*), ~ *person's life, sorrow, energy*; ~ *the golden age*; *rose from her knees ~ed by the Holy Spirit*; ~*ed by baptism*). 2. Patch, fill up, reinforce, replace, (*coat ~ed in places*); ~ *the water in the bowl*; ~ *garrison, tires*, etc.). 3. Get, begin, make, say, or give, anew, continue after intermission, (~ *one's youth, strength, etc., grow young* etc. *again*; ~ *attack, correspondence, speech, game, efforts*; ~ *one's vows, statements*, etc.; ~ *lease, bill, grant* or be granted continuation of it); (abs.) ~ *lease or bill*. 4. (rare). Become new again (*the clamour ~ed*; *feel my youth ~ing*). Hence ~ABLE a., ~AL(2) n. [RE-, NEW]

rĕn′ifŏrm, a. Kidney-shaped. [REINS, -FORM]

rĕnn′ĕt[1], n. Curdled milk found in stomach of unweaned calf, or preparation of stomach-membrane or of kinds of plant, used in curdling milk for cheese etc. [ME, f. *renne* obs. form of RUN[1]]

‖ **rĕnn′ĕt**[2], n. Kinds of dessert apple. [f. F *reinette*, f. *reine* queen f. L REGINA, -ETTE]

renounce′, v.t. & i., & n. 1. Consent formally to abandon, surrender, give up (claim, right, possession). 2. Repudiate, refuse to recognize longer, decline association with or disclaim relationship with, withdraw from, discontinue, forsake, (~ *treaty, principles*, person's *authority, all thought of, design, attempt, son* etc., *friend, friendship*; ~ *the world*, abandon society or temporal affairs). 3. (law). Refuse or resign right or position esp. as heir or trustee. 4. (cards). Follow with card of another suit for want of right one (cf. REVOKE); (n.) playing of such card, opportunity of doing so. Hence ~MENT (-sm-) n. [ME, f. OF *renoncer* f. L *re(nuntiare* ANNOUNCE), RE- 5]

rĕn′ovāte, v.t. Make new again, repair, restore to good condition or vigour. So ~A′TION, ~āTOR, nn. [f. L *re(novare* f. *novus* new), RE- 9, -ATE[3]]

renown′, n. Celebrity, fame, high distinction, (*man, town*, etc., *of* ~ or *great* etc. ~, famous). [ME, f. AF *renoun* = OF *renon* f. *renomer* make famous f. L *re-* RE- 8 + *nominare* NOMINATE]

renowned′ (-nd), a. Famous, celebrated. [ME, f. prec. + -ED[2], after OF *renomé* (p.p.)]

rĕnt[1]. See REND.

rĕnt[2], n. Large tear in garment etc., opening in clouds etc. resembling tear; cleft, fissure, gorge. [f. obs. *rent* vb, var. of REND]

rĕnt[3], n., & v.t. & i. 1. Tenant's periodical payment to owner or landlord for use of land or house or room; payment for hire of machinery etc.; ~-*charge*, periodical charge on land etc. reserved by deed to one who is not the owner; ~-*free* a. & adv., with exemption from ~; ~-*roll*, register of person's lands etc. with ~s due from them, sum of one's income from ~; ‖ ~-*service*, (tenure by) personal service in lieu of or addition to ~; hence (of land etc., with *low, high*, etc.) -*rĕn′tED*[2] a. 2. vb. Take, occupy, use, at a ~; let or hire for ~; be let *at* specified ~; impose ~ on (tenant; ~*s his tenants low*); make ~*-*ABLE a., *rĕn′tER*[1] n., (esp.) wholesaler in the film trade. [ME, f. OF *rente* f. Rom. **rendita* fem. p.p. as RENDER]

rĕn′tal, n. Income from rents; amount paid or received as rent. [AF (prec., -AL)]

rente (rahn̄t), n. Income, esp. that consisting of life-annuity or dividends. [F]

rentier (rahn̄′tiā), n. Person living on *rente*, person not needing to earn his living. [F]

renŭm′ber. See RE- 8.

renŭncia′tion, n. Renouncing, document expressing it; self-denial, giving up of things. So **renŭn′ciANT**(1) n. & a. (-shĭ-), **renŭn′ciATIVE** (-sha-), **renŭn′ciatory** (-shatrĭ), aa. [ME, f. L *renunciatio* (RENOUNCE, -ATION)]

reo-. See RHEO-.

reoccupy etc., **reopen**, see RE- 9; **reorganize** etc., RE- 8.

rĕp[1], **rĕpp**, **rĕps**, n. Textile fabric with ..corded surface used in upholstery. [f. F *reps* of unkn. orig.]

rĕp[2], n. (school sl.). Verse etc. learnt by heart. [abbr. of *repetition*]

rĕp[3], n. (sl.). Person of loose character. [perh. for REPROBATE[2]; cf. RIP[1]]

rĕp[4], n. (sl.). Repertory theatre or company. [abbr.]

repaganize etc., **repaint**. See RE- 9.

repair′[1], v.i., & n. 1. Resort, have recourse, go often or in numbers, *to*. 2. n. (arch.). Resort (*have* ~ *to*); haunt; being visited by numbers (*a place of great, little*, ~). [ME, f. OF *repairer(r* f. LL *re(patriare* f. L *patria* native land), RE- 9]

repair′[2], v.t. Restore (building, machine, garment, tissue, strength, etc.) to good condition, renovate, mend, by replacing or refixing parts or compensating loss or exhaustion, whence ~ABLE a.; remedy, set right again, make amends for, (loss, wrong, error). [ME, f. OF *reparer* or L *re(parare* make ready), RE- 9]

repair'³, n. Restoring to sound condition (*health, bicycle, house, boots, need ~*; *shop is closed during ~s; ~s done while you wait; running ~s,* minor replacements); good condition, relative condition, for working or using (*is in, out of, ~*; *must be kept in good, is in bad, ~*). [f. prec.]

repänd', a. (bot., zool.). With undulating margin, wavy. Hence ~o- comb. form. [f. L *re(pandus* bent), RE- 9]

repaper. See RE- 8.

rep'arable, a. (Of loss etc.) that can be made good. [F, f. L *reparabilis* (REPAIR², -ABLE)]

reparä'tion, n. **1.** Repairing or being repaired, repair, (pl.) repairs, (now usu. *repair, repairs*). **2.** Making of amends, compensation (esp., pl., for war damages). So **rěp'araTIVE** (or **rĭpä'r-**) a. [ME, f. OF *reparacion* f. LL *reparationem* (REPAIR², -ATION)]

r̄epartee', n., & v.i. Witty retort; (making of) witty retorts (*a great power, a storehouse, of ~*); (vb, now rare) make ~s. [f. F *repartie* fem. p.p. of *re(partir* PART²) start again, reply promptly, RE- 8]

repartition, see RE- 8; **repass** etc., RE- 9.

rěpast' (-ah-), n. (Food supplied for or eaten at) meal (usu. *rich, plentiful, slight, delicate, luxurious,* etc., ~). [ME, f. OF, f. *repaistre* f. LL *re(pascere past-* feed), RE- 8]

rěpat'ri|āte, v.t. & i. Restore or return to native land. Hence ~ATE¹ (-at) n., one who has been ~ated, ~A'TION n. [f. LL *re(patriare* f. L *patria* fatherland), RE- 9]

rěpay', v.t. & i. (-*paid*). Pay back (money); return, retaliate, (blow, visit, service, etc.); give in recompense *for*; make repayment to (person); make return for, requite, (action); make repayment. Hence ~ABLE a., ~MENT n. [f. OF *re(paier* PAY²), RE- 9]

rěpeal', v.t., & n. **1.** Revoke, rescind, annul, (law etc.); hence ~ABLE a. **2.** n. Abrogation, ~ing; (Irish pol.) cancelling of the Union of 1801 demanded by O'Connell etc., whence ~ER¹ n. (hist.). [ME, f. AF *repel(l)er* = OF *rapeler* (RE- 9, APPEAL¹)]

rěpeat', v.t. & i., & n. **1.** Say or do over again, recite, rehearse, report, reproduce, give imitation of, (~ *action, statement, poem, conversation, attempt, pattern, signal,* etc.; *action was ~ed several times,* whence ~edLY² adv.; *language will not bear ~ing,* is too foul etc. to ~); (of watch etc., alss.) strike last quarter etc. over again when required (so *~ing watch* etc. or ~ER¹ n.); (of fire-arms) fire several shots without reloading (*~ing rifle* etc.). **2.** Recur, appear again or ~edly; (*the last three figures ~*; *food ~s,* is tasted intermittently over time). **3.** (refl.). Recur in same form, say or do same thing over again, (*history*

~*s itself; does nothing but ~ himself*); hence ~ABLE a. **4.** n. ~ing, esp. of item in programme in response to encore; (radio) ~ed programme; (mus.) passage intended to be ~ed, mark indicating this; pattern ~ed in wallpaper etc.; (commerc.) fresh consignment similar to previous one, order given for this. [ME, f. OF *repeter* f. L *re(petere* seek), RE- 8]

rěp'ěchage (-eshahzh), n. (rowing). Extra race in which runners-up in the eliminating races compete for a place in the final. [F]

rěpěl', v.t. (-ll-). **1.** Drive back, repulse, ward off, refuse admission or acceptance or approach to, (~ *assailant, attack, temptation, weapon, blow, suggestion, plea, offer,* person's *advances; first attracts & then ~s the magnet*). **2.** Be repulsive or distasteful to, exert mental repulsion upon, whence ~l'ENT a. & n., ~l'entLY² adv. [ME, f. L *re(pellere* puls- drive), RE- 2]

rěp'ent¹, a. (chiefly bot.). Creeping, esp. growing along or just under surface of ground. [f. L *repere* creep, -ENT]

rěpěnt'², v.t. & i. **1.** (arch.). (Refl., with arch. refl. pron.) feel regret or penitence about something or of (*I now ~ me; he ~eth him of the evil*); (impers.) affect with penitence or regret (*it ~s me that I did it*). **2.** Think with contrition of, think with contrition of, be regretful about or of, be contrite, wish one had not done, (*you shall ~ this, of this,* or abs.; *have nothing to ~ of; ~ my kindness, setting off when I did*). So **rěpěn'tance** n., **rěpěn'tant** a., **rěpěn'tantLY²** adv. [ME, f. OF *repentir* f. *re-* RE- 3 + *pentir* f. Rom. **penitire* f. L *poenitēre*]

repeople. See RE- 9.

repercussion etc. See RE- 9.

rěp'ertoire (-twár), n. Stock of pieces etc. that company or performer knows or is prepared to give. [F (*ré-*), f. L as foll.]

rěp'ertorÿ, n. **1.** Place for finding something, store or collection, esp. of information, instances, facts, etc. **2.** = prec. (~ *theatre, company, system,* relying on ~ & not on long runs). [f. LL *repertorium* f. L *reperire -pert-* find]

reperuse etc. See RE- 8.

rěpětěnd', n. Recurring figures of decimal; recurring word or phrase, refrain. [f. L as REPEAT]

rěpěti't|ion, n. REPEATING or being repeated; piece set to be learnt by heart; copy, replica; ability of musical instrument, to repeat note quickly. Hence ~ionAL, ~ionARY¹, (-sho), ~ious (-shus), **rěpět'itIVE**, aa. (rare). [f. F, or L *repetitio* (RE- 8, PETITION)]

repiece. See RE- 9.

rěpin|e', v.i. Fret, be discontented, (*at, against,* or abs.). Hence ~'ingLY² adv. [RE- 6, PINE²]

rěpique' (-ēk), n., & v.t. & i. **1.** Winning

of 30 points on cards alone before beginning to play in piquet. **2.** vb. Score ~ against (opponent); make ~. [f. F *repio* (RE-, PIQUE²)]

replace′, v.t. Put back in place; take place of, succeed, be substituted for, (pass.) be succeeded or have one's or its place filled by, be superseded; fill up place of (*with*, *by*), find or provide substitute. for. Hence ~ABLE (-sa-) a., ~MENT (-sm-) n., (also) person or thing that ~s another. [RE- 9, PLACE²]

replant etc. See RE- 8.

replay′, v.t. Play (a match) over again; hence **rep′lay** n., a ~ed match. [RE- 8]

replen′ish, v.t. Fill up again (*with* or abs.); (p.p.) filled, fully stored, full, (*with* or abs.). Hence ~MENT n. [ME, f. OF *re(plenir* ult. f. L *plenus* full), RE- 9, -ISH²]

replēte′, a. Filled, stuffed, fully imbued, well stocked, *with*; gorged, sated, (*with*). So ~ē′TION n. (esp. *full to* ~*etion*). [ME, f. OF *replet* or L *re(plēre plet-* fill), RE- 6]

replev′in, n. Restoration or recovery of distrained goods on security given for submission to trial & judgement; writ granting ~; action arising out of ~. [ME, f. AF, f. OF as foll.]

replev′y, v.t. Recover by replevin. [f. OF *re(plevir* f. Frank. *pligi PLEDGE¹), RE- 9]

rep′lica, n. Duplicate made by original artist of his picture etc.; facsimile, exact copy. [It. (*replicare* REPLY)]

rep′licate¹, n. Tone one or more octaves above or below given tone. [as foll.]

rep′licate², a. (bot.). Folded back on itself. [as foll., -ATE²]

rep′licate³, v.t. (rare). Repeat; make replica of; fold back. [L *re(plicare* fold), RE- 9, -ATE³]

replica′tion, n. **1.** Folding back, fold, (rare). **2.** Replying, rejoinder, answer, esp. reply to answer; (law) plaintiff's reply to defendant's plea. **3.** Echo. **4.** Copy, copying. [ME, f. OF, f. L *replicationem* (prec., -ATION)]

reply′, v.i. & t., & n. **1.** Make answer, respond, in word or action (*to*; abs., *that* etc., or parenth.; *rose to* ~ *for the ladies*, represent them in returning thanks for toast; *the batteries replied to our fire*; *he replied that I must please myself*; '*Please yourself*' *he replied*). **2.** n. Act of ~ing (*what he says in* ~); what is replied, response; ~ *paid*, (of telegram) with cost of ~ prepaid by sender. [ME, f. OF *replier* f. L as REPLICATE³]

repoint, repolish. See RE- 9.

répondez s'il vous plaît (see Ap.), formula appended (usu. in abbr. *R.S.V.P.*) to invitation or other letter, = please answer. [F]

repopulate. See RE- 9.

rep̄ort′¹, v.t. & i. **1.** Bring back account of, state as ascertained fact, tell as news,

narrate or describe or repeat esp. as eye-witness etc. (*to*), relate as spoken by another, make official or formal statement about, inform against (offence, offender) *to* authorities or abs., announce one*self* or abs. as returned or arrived, (~*s open water at pole, pole to be accessible, that he reached pole*; *it is* ~*ed*, commonly said; ~*ed all details of the scene to me*; *my actual words & those* ~*ed to you were quite different*; ~*ed speech*, oblique oration; *chairman of committee* ~*s bill to House*, announces conclusion of committee's dealings with it between 2nd & 3rd reading; ‖ ~ *progress*, state what has been done so far, *move to* ~ *progress* in House of·Commons, propose that debate be discontinued, often for obstructive purposes; *all variations are to be* ~*ed daily*; *shall* ~ *you, your unpunctuality, to senior partner*). **2.** Take down word for word or epitomize or write description of for publication (~ *law case, proceedings, meeting*; also abs., as *reports for* The Times). **3.** Make, draw up, or send in report. **4.** Give report of conveying that one is *well* or *badly* impressed (~*s well of the prospects*; *is badly* ~*ed of*). Hence ~ABLE a., ~AGE n., (typical style of) ~ing events for the press, ~ER¹ n. [ME, f. OF *reporter* f. L *re(portare* bring), RE- 9]

rep̄ort′², n. **1.** Common talk, rumour, (*mere* ~ *is not enough to go upon*; *the* ~ *goes*, it is said); way person or thing is spoken of, repute, (*things of good* ~; *faithful through good & evil* ~). **2.** Account given or opinion formally expressed after investigation or consideration, description or epitome or reproduction of scene or speech or law case esp. for newspaper publication, ‖ (~ *stage* in House of· Commons, treatment of bill when committee has reported, see prec.); periodical statement on a pupil's work, conduct, etc. at school. **3.** Sound of explosion (*went off with a loud* ~). [ME, f. OF, f. L *reporter* (see prec.)]

repōse′¹ (-z), v.t. Place (trust etc.) *in*. Hence ~′AL (-zl) n. [f. RE- 4 + POSE¹, after L *re(ponere posit-* place)]

repōse′² (-z), v.t. & i., & n. **1.** Rest (one*self* or abs.); lay (one's *head* etc.) to rest (often *on* pillow etc.); give rest to, refresh with rest; lie, be lying or laid, esp. in sleep or death (*in, on*, or abs.), be supported or based *on* (*the whole system* ~*s on fear*); (of memory etc.) dwell *on*. **2.** n. Rest, cessation· of activity or excitement, respite from toil, sleep, peaceful or quiescent state, stillness, tranquillity; restful effect, harmonious combination in art, composure or ease of manner, esp. in *lacks* ~); hence ~FUL (-zf-) a., ~fulLY² adv. [ME, f. OF *repos(er)* f. LL *re(pausare* PAUSE; RE- 5); meaning infl. by prec.]

repōs′itory (-z-), n. **1.** Receptacle; place

where things are stored or may be found, museum, warehouse, store, shop, (*book, person*, etc., *is a ~ of curious information*); burial-place. 2. Recipient of confidences or secrets. [f. obs. F *repositoire* or L *repositorium* (REPOSE[1], -ORY)]

repossess etc. See RE- 9.

repost. See RIPOSTE.

repot. See RE- 8.

repoussé (repōōs'ā), a. & n. (Ornamental metal work) hammered into relief from reverse side. [F, p.p. of *re(pousser* PUSH[1]), RE- 3]

repp. See REP[1].

repped (-pt), a. Having surface like rep. [-ED[2]]

reprehend', v.t. Rebuke, blame, find fault with. So ~**en'sible** a., ~**en'sibly[2]** adv., ~**en'sion** (-shn) n. [ME, f. L *re(prehendere* seize), RE- 2]

represent' (-z-), v.t. 1. Call up by description or portrayal or imagination, figure, place likeness of before mind or senses, serve or be meant as likeness of, (*can you ~ infinity to yourself?*; *can only ~ it to you by metaphors*; *picture ~s murder of Abel*; *is ~ed in hunting costume*). 2. Try to bring (facts influencing conduct) home (*to*), state by way of expostulation or incentive, (*~ed the rashness of it, that it could not succeed*). 3. Make out to be etc., allege *that*, describe or depict *as*, (*am not what you ~ me to be* or *as*; *in the corner is the Pope ~ed as a beggar*; *~s that he has* or *himself to have seen service*). 4. Act (play etc.), play part of on stage. 5. Symbolize, act as embodiment of, stand for, correspond to, be specimen of, (*sovereign ~s majesty of State*; *inch of rain ~s 100 tons to acre*; *globe ~s totality*; *camels are ~ed in the New World by llamas*; *Welsh football is ~ed in the team by Morgan*). 6. Fill place of, be substitute or deputy for, be entitled to speak for, be sent as member to House of Commons by, (*King was ~ed by the Duke of Norfolk*; *members ~ing urban constituencies*). Hence or cogn. ~**ABLE** a., ~**A'TION** (-z-) n. (*proportional ~ation*, electoral system so arranged that minorities are ~ed in proportion to their strength), ~**ā'tionAL** (-shon-) a. [ME, f. OF *representer* or L *re(praesentare* PRESENT[4]), RE- 8]

represen'tative (-z-), a. & n. 1. Serving as portrayal or symbol of (*a group ~ of the theological virtues*); that presents or can present ideas to the mind (*imagination is a ~ faculty*); typical of a class or classes, containing typical specimens of all or many classes, (*the truth of an allegory is ~, not literal*; *call a meeting of ~ men*; *a very ~ selection, collection*); consisting of elected deputies or ~s (*~ chamber, house,* etc.), based on representation by such deputies (*~ government, institutions*); hence ~**LY[2]** adv., ~**NESS** n. 2. n. Sample, specimen, typical embodiment, analogue, of; person's agent, delegate, substitute,

successor, or heir; deputy in ~ chamber (*House of R~s*, lower house of U.S. Congress). [ME, f. OF (-*if, -ive*) or med. L *repraesentativus* (REPRESENT, -ATIVE)]

repress', v.t. Check, restrain, put down, keep under, quell, suppress, prevent from sounding or bursting out or rioting. So **reprē'ssion** (-shn) n. (esp., in psych., of natural promptings), ~**IVE** a. [ME, f. L *re(primere = premere* PRESS[2]), RE- 5]

repriev|e', v.t., & n. 1. Suspend or delay execution of (condemned person); (fig.) give respite to. 2. n. ~ing or being ~ed; (warrant for) remission or commutation of capital sentence; respite. [15th c. as p.p. *repryed*, app. f. AF *repris* p.p. of *re(prendre* f. L *prehendere* take), RE- 8; *-v-* unexpl.]

rep'rimand (-ah-), n., & v.t. Official(ly) rebuke (*for* fault). [f. F *réprimande* f. L *reprimenda* f. *reprimere* REPRESS]

reprint. See RE- 8.

repris'al (-zl), n. 1. (hist.). Forcible seizure of foreign subjects' persons or property in retaliation (*letters of ~*, official warrant authorizing this). 2. Act of retaliation (usu. *make ~s* or *~*). [ME, f. OF *reprisaille* as foll. +-AL(2)]

reprise' (-z), n. 1. (law). Rent-charge or other payment to be made yearly out of estate (*beyond, besides, above, ~s*, remaining after all ~s have been paid). 2. (rare). Resumption of action, one of the times devoted to something not done all at once. [F, fem. of *repris* see REPRIEVE]

reproach', v.t., & n. 1. Upbraid, censure, (person, often *with* offence); rebuke (offence); (of look etc.) convey protest or censure to (*his eyes ~ me*); hence ~**ingLY[2]** adv. (rare for ~*fully*). 2. n. Thing that brings disgrace or discredit (*to*; *the state of the roads is a ~ to civilization*), whence ~**LESS** a. (rare for *irreproachable*); opprobrium, disgraced or discredited state, (*live in ~ & ignominy*; *the things that had brought ~ upon him*; *has taken away my ~*); upbraiding, rebuke, censure, (*abstain from ~*; *heap ~es on*; *the mute ~ in his eyes*; *term of ~*, word implying censure), whence ~**FUL** a., ~**fulLY[2]** adv., ~**fulNESS** n.; (pl.) Good-Friday chiefly R.-C. set of antiphons & responses representing ~es of Christ to people. [ME, f. OF *reproche(r)* f. Rom. **repropiare* (*prope* near)]

rep'rob|āte[1], v.t. Express or feel disapproval of, censure; (of God) cast off, exclude from salvation. So ~**A'TION** n. [f. L *re(probare* approve), RE- 7, -ATE[3]]

rep'robate[2], a. & n. (Person) cast off by God, hardened in sin, of abandoned character, immoral. [as prec., -ATE[2]]

reproduce etc. See RE- 8.

reproof'[1], n. Blame (*a word, glance, of ~*; *spoke in ~ of idleness*); a rebuke or expression of blame. [ME, f. OF *reprove (re-prover* REPROVE)]

reproof'[2], v.t. Render (coat etc.) waterproof again. [RE- 9]

reprov|e' (-ōōv), v.t. Rebuke, chide, (person, rarely sin etc.). Hence ~'ingLY² (-ōōv-) adv. [ME, f. OF *reprover* f. L *reprobare* disapprove, as REPROBATE¹]

reprovision. See RE- 8.

reps. See REP¹.

rep'tant, a. (nat. hist.). Creeping. [f. L *reptare* frequent. of *repere* crawl, -ANT]

rep'tile, n. & a. **1.** Member of the *Reptilia* or class of animals including snakes, lizards, crocodiles, turtles, & tortoises, whence **reptil'IAN** (-lyan) a. & n., **reptilif'EROUS, reptil'IFORM,** aa.; mean grovelling person. **2.** adj. (Of animals) creeping; mean & grovelling (*the ~ press,* subservient semi-official newspapers). [ME, (n. f. *reptile* neut.) f. LL *reptilis* (*repere rept-* crawl, -IL)]

repub'lic, n. A State in which the government is carried on nominally & usu. in fact also by the people or through its elected representatives, commonwealth; (in France) *Third R~* 1871-1940, *Fourth R~* 1947-58, *Fifth R~* 1958-; (fig.) society of persons or animals with equality between members (*the ~ of letters,* literary men, literature). [f. F *république* or L *respublica* (abl. *republica*) f. *res* concern, PUBLICUS]

repub'lican, a. & n. **1.** Of, constituted as, characterizing, republic(s). **2.** (Person) advocating or supporting ~ government. **3.** (*R~*). *(Member) of U.S. political party favouring liberal interpretation of constitution, extension of central power, & protective tariff, opp. DEMOCRAT(IC). **4.** (Of birds) social, living in large communities. Hence ~ISM(3) n., ~IZE(3) v.t. [-AN]

republish etc. See RE- 8.

repud'i|ate, v.t. & i. **1.** Divorce (one's wife; esp. of the ancients or non-Christians). **2.** Disown, disavow, reject, refuse dealings with, deny. **3.** Refuse to recognize or obey (authority) or discharge (obligation, debt); (of State) ~ate public debt. So ~A'TION, ~ātor, nn. [f. L *repudiare* (*repudium* divorce, -ATE²)]

repugn' (-ūn), v.i. & t. (rare). Offer opposition; strive *against*; strive against; affect disagreeably, be repugnant to. [ME, f. OF *repugner* or L *re(pugnare* fight) oppose, RE- 2]

repug'nance, n. Inconsistency, incompatibility, of ideas, statements, tempers, etc. (*of, between, to, with*); antipathy, dislike, aversion, (*to, against*). [ME, f. OF or L *repugnantia* (prec., -ANCE)]

repug'nant, a. Contradictory (*to*), incompatible (*with*); (poet.) refractory, resisting; distasteful (*to*). [ME, f. OF or L as REPUGN + -ANT]

repull'ul|ate, v.i. (rare). Sprout afresh, shoot out again; (of diseases) start again, recur. Hence ~A'TION n. [f. L *re(pullulare* PULLULATE), RE- 9, -ATE³]

repuls|e', v.t., & n. **1.** Drive back, (attack, attacking enemy) by force of arms, (fig.) foil in controversy; rebuff (friendly advances or maker of them), refuse (request, offer, or maker of it). **2.** n. ~ing or being ~ed, rebuff, (*inflict, meet with, suffer,* etc., ~e or usu. *a ~e*). [(n. f. L *repulsus* or -sa); vb f. *repuls-* as REPEL]

repul'sion (-shn), n. **1.** Repulsing (rare). **2.** (phys.). Tendency of bodies to repel each other or increase their mutual distance (opp. ATTRACTION; also fig.); *capillary ~,* tendency in some liquids (e.g. quicksilver in glass) to shrink from wall of capillary tubes so that upper surface is convex. **3.** Dislike, aversion, repugnance. [f. LL *repulsio* (REPEL, -ION)]

repul'sive, a. **1.** Offering resistance (poet.). **2.** (phys.). Exercising repulsion. **3.** (Of behaviour etc.) repellent, cold, unsympathetic, (arch.). **4.** Exciting aversion or loathing, loathsome, disgusting, whence ~LY² adv., ~NESS n. [f. F (-*if, -ive*) or REPULSE v. + -IVE]

repurchase, repurify. See RE- 9.

rep'utab|le, a. Of good repute, respectable. Hence ~LY² adv. [REPUTE n., -ABLE]

repūtā'tion, n. What is generally said or believed about a person's or thing's character (*has not justified his ~*); state of being well reported of, credit, distinction, respectability, good fame, (*persons of ~; has a ~ for integrity*); the credit or discredit *of* doing or *of* being (*has the ~ of racking his tenants, of being or of the best shot in England*). [ME, f. L *reputatio* (REPUTE, -ATION)]

repute', v.t., & n. **1.** (Rare in active) consider or reckon, (pass.) be generally considered or reported of, (with compl., *to be,* or *as; is ~d the best doctor* or *to be* or rarely *as the best*); (pass.) be generally *well, ill,* etc., thought or spoken *of*; (p.p.) passing as but probably not being (*his ~d father, clemency,* etc.; ||*~d pint* etc., bottle of beer etc. sold as pint etc. but not guaranteed as imperial pint etc.); hence **repūt'edLY²** adv. **2.** n. Reputation. [ME, f. OF *reputer* or L *re(putare* think), RE- 6]

request', n., & v.t. **1.** Act of asking for something, petition made, thing asked for, (*came at his ~; shall make two ~s; you shall have your ~; make ~ for; by ~,* in response to·expressed wish); state of being sought after, demand, (*is now in great, came into, ~*). **2.** v.t. Seek permission to do; ask to be given or allowed or favoured with (*~ candid consideration,* person's *presence,* etc.); ask *that*; ask (person) *to* do. [ME, f. OF *requeste(r),* see RE- 6, QUEST]

requicken. See RE- 9.

re'quiëm, n. Special mass for repose of souls of the dead; musical setting for ~;

dirge. [ME; initial L wd (= rest) of the mass]

rĕquĭĕs′c|ăt, n. Wish for dead person's repose; ~*ăt*, ~*ănt, in pā′ce,* abbr. R.I.P., inscription = may he or she, they, rest in peace, used esp. on R.-C. tombs. [L, = may he rest]

require′, v.t. & i. **1.** Order (person), demand (*of* or *from* person), *to* do (*they ~ me* or *of me to appear*); demand or ask in words (person's action, act *of* person, thing *at* person's *hands, that,* etc.) esp. as of right (*they ~ my appearance, an oath of me, a gift at my hands, that I should appear*). **2.** Lay down as imperative (*had done all that was ~d by the Act*). **3.** Need, call for, depend for success etc. on, (*the emergency ~s it, that it should be done; irony ~s care in its use; land ~s 10 lb. of seed to the acre; place would ~ an army to take it; machine ~s no attention; it ~d all his authority to keep them in hand*). **4.** (rare). ‖ Be necessary (*do not tie it more tightly than ~s*). Hence ~MENT (-īrm-) n. [ME, f. OF *requerre* f. L re(*quirere -quisit-* = *quaerere* seek), RE- 6]

rĕ′quisite (-z-), a. & n. **1.** Required by circumstances, necessary to success etc., called for; hence ~NESS (-zĭtn-) n. **2.** n. Requirement, thing needed for accomplishment of some purpose (*for*). [ME, f. L p.p. as prec.]

rĕquisi′tion (-z-), n., & v.t. **1.** Requiring, demand made, esp. formal & usu. written demand that some duty should be performed; order given to town etc. to furnish certain military etc. supplies; being called or put into service (*is under* or *in ~*, being used or applied; *put in, call in to, ~*, have recourse to). **2.** v.t. Demand use or supply of esp. for war purposes; demand such supplies etc. from (town etc.); press into service, call in for some purpose. [F, or f. L *requisitio* (REQUIRE, -ION)]

requit|e′, v.t. Make return for, reward or avenge, (service, wrong, injury, treatment; often *with*); make return to, repay with good or evil, (person; often *for* treatment received, *with* treatment given); give in return (*~e like for like*). Hence ~′AL(2) n. [RE- 1, *quite* var. of QUIT²]

re-read. See RE- 8.

rere′dŏs (rērd-), n. Ornamental screen covering wall at back of altar. [ME, f. AF **reredos* (REAR¹, F *dos* back f. L *dorsum*)]

rēs (-z), n. Thing (*~ jŭdĭcāt′a* (jōō-), = CHOSE JUGÉE); property (*~ ăngŭs′ta* (-ngg-) *domī′*, poverty). [L]

resaddle, resale etc. See RE- 9.

rescind′, v.t. Abrogate, annul, revoke, cancel. So **resci′ssion** (-zhn) n. [f. L re(*scindere sciss-* cut), RE- 5]

rēs′cript, n. **1.** Roman emperor's written reply to appeal for guidance esp. from magistrate on legal point; Pope's decretal epistle in reply to question, any

papal decision. **2.** Ruler's or government's or official edict or announcement. **3.** Thing rewritten, rewriting; palimpsest. [f. L *rescriptum,* p.p. neut. of re(*scribere script-* write), RE- 1]

rĕs′cū|e, v.t., & n. **1.** Deliver from or *from* attack, custody, danger, or harm; (law) unlawfully liberate (person), forcibly recover (property); hence ~ER¹ n. **2.** n. ~ing or being ~ed, succour, deliverance, illegal liberation, forcible recovery; *~e* (*bid*), a bid at bridge made to get one's partner out of a difficult situation. [ME *rescowe* f. OF *rescoure* f. Rom. **reexcutere* (L RE-, EXcutere = *quatere* shake)]

research′ (-sĕr-), n., & v.i. **1.** Careful search or inquiry *after* or *for*; (usu. pl.) endeavour to discover new facts etc. by scientific study of a subject, course of critical investigation, (*his ~es have been fruitful; is engaged in ~*). **2.** v.i. Make ~es; hence ~ER¹ n. [f. obs. F *recerche*(r), now *recherche*(r), see RE- 6, SEARCH]

reseat. See RE- 8.

rĕsĕct′, v.t. (surg.). Pare down (bone, cartilage, etc.). So **rĕsĕc′tion** n. [f. L re(*secare sect-* cut), RE- 5]

rĕsēd′a, n. **1.** Kinds of plants including mignonette & dyer's weed. **2.** (usu. *réséda* F, pr. rāzădah′). Pale green colour as of mignonette. [L]

reseek, see RE- 8; **reseize** etc., **resell,** RE- 9.

rĕsĕm′bl|e (-z-), v.t. Be like, have similarity to or feature(s) in common with or same appearance as, & so ~ANCE (*to, between, of*) n., ~ANT (*to*) a. (rare); (arch.) liken *to*. [ME, f. OF re(*sembler* f. L *simi-lare, simulare,* f. *similis* SIMILAR), RE- 1]

rĕsĕnt′ (-z-), v.t. Show or feel indignation at or retain feelings about (insult or injury sustained). Hence ~FUL [perh. through obs. *resent* ~ment] a., ~fULLY² adv., ~MENT n. [f. F *ressentir* (RE- 1, L *sentire* feel)]

rĕserva′tion (-z-), n. In vbl senses; also or esp.: (eccl.) right reserved to Pope of nomination to vacant benefice, power of absolution reserved to superior, practice of retaining for some purpose a portion of the Eucharistic elements (esp. the bread) after celebration; (law) right or interest retained in estate being conveyed, clause reserving it; ***tract of land reserved esp. for exclusive occupation by native tribe; express or tacit limitation or exception made about something (*mental ~*, qualification tacitly added in making statement, oath, etc.); ***booking (of berth on steamer, room in hotel, seat in train, etc.). [ME, f. OF, or f. LL *reservatio* (foll., -ATION)]

rĕsĕrv|e′¹ (-z-), v.t. **1.** Postpone use or enjoyment or treatment of, hold over, keep back for later occasion, (*~e oneself for,* not put forth one's energies till). **2.** Secure or retain possession or control of esp. by legal or formal stipulation (*for* or *to* oneself or another; ~*ed seals* at entertainment etc., that may be booked; ||~*ed list*, of naval officers removed from active service but liable to be called out); (pass.) be left by fate *for*, fall first or only *to*. 3. Set apart, destine, *for* some use or fate. 4. (p.p. as adj.). Reticent, slow to reveal emotions or opinions, uncommunicative, whence ~'ėdLY² (-z-) adv. [ME, f. OF *reserver* f. L *re*(*servare* keep), RE- 3]

rèsėr̀ve'² (-z-), n. 1. Something reserved for future use, extra stock or amount, (*banker's* ~, amount kept on hand to meet probable demands; *has a great* ~ *of energy*; often attrib., as *his* ~ *strength*). 2. (Mil., sing. or pl.) troops withheld from action to reinforce or cover retreat, forces outside regular army & navy & air force liable to be called out in emergencies, member of such forces (also rèsèr̀v'IST (-z-) n.); (in games) extra player chosen in case substitute should be needed. 3. Being kept unused but available (*has it in* ~). 4. Place reserved for some special use (*game* ~). 5. (At exhibitions) distinction conveying that exhibit will have prize if another is disqualified. 6. Limitation, exception, restriction, or qualification, attached to something (*I accept your statement without* ~, fully ; *sale or auction without* ~, not subject to a fixed price's being reached ; ~ *price*, than which less will not be accepted ; *we publish this with all* ~, *all proper* ~*s*, without endorsing it). 7. Self-restraint, abstinence from exaggeration or ill-proportioned effects, in artistic or literary expression; reticence, avoidance of plain speaking, coolness of manner, lack of cordiality; intentional suppression of truth. [f. prec., partly thr. F]

rès'ervoir (-zervwàr), n., & v.t. 1. Receptacle constructed usu. of earthwork or masonry in which large quantity of water is stored. 2. Any natural or artificial receptacle esp. for or of fluid, place where fluid etc. collects ; part of machine or organ of body holding fluid (~ *pen*, containing its own supply of ink); reserve supply or collection *of* something e.g. knowledge or facts, etc. 3. v.t. Store in ~. [F, f. *réserver* see prec., -ORY(2)]

|| rèsèt'¹, v.t. & i. (-tt-). Receive (stolen goods); receive stolen goods. So ~t'ER¹ n. [ME, f. OF *receter* f. L *receptare* frequent, of *recipere* RECEIVE]

reset², resettle etc., reshape, see RE- 8; reship etc., RE- 9; reshuffle, RE- 8.

rèsíde' (-z-), v.i. (Of persons) have one's home, dwell permanently, *at, in, abroad*, etc.; (of officials) be 'in residence; (of power, rights, etc.) rest or be vested *in* person etc.; (of qualities) be present or inherent *in*. [ME, f. OF *resider* or L *re*(*sidēre* = *sedēre* sit), RE- 3]

rĕs'ídence (-z-), n. 1. Residing (*have, take up*, one's ~, begin to dwell; *honoured the place with her* ~ ; ~ *is required*,-- official etc. must live on the spot for certain periods or altogether; so *in* ~). 2. Place where one resides, abode *of*; house esp. of considerable pretension, mansion, (*desirable family* ~ *for sale*). [ME, f. OF f. med. L *residentia* (prec., -ENCE)]

rĕs'ídencÿ (-z-), n. (hist.). Official residence of Governor-general's representative at Indian native court. [as prec., -ENCY]

rĕs'ídent (-z-), a. & n. 1. Residing (*whether* ~ *at home or abroad*; *the* ~ *population*) ; (of birds etc.) non-migratory ; bound to residence, having quarters on the spot, (~ *surgeon, tutor, political agent*); inherent, located, *in* (*a right* ~ *in the nation*; *powers of sensation* ~ *in the nerves*). 2. n. Permanent inhabitant of town or neighbourhood (opp. *visitor*); Indian Governor-general's political agent residing at native court (hist.), British government agent in other semi-dependent State, whence ~SHIP n. [ME, f. OF or L (RESIDE, -ENT)]

rĕs'ídĕn'tial (-z-, -shl), a. Suitable for or occupied by private houses (~ *estate, street, quarter*); connected with residence (*the* ~ *qualification for voters*). [RESIDENCE, -AL]

rĕs'ídĕn'tiarÿ (-z-, -sha-), n. & a. 1. Ecclesiastic bound to residence. 2. adj. Bound to, requiring, of or for, official residence (usu. after n.; *Canon, Canonry*, ~; *at his* ~ *house*). [f. med. L *residentiarius* (RESIDENCE, -ARY¹)]

rèsíd'úal (-z-), a. & n. 1. (math.). Resulting from subtraction (n., ~ *quantity*). 2. Remaining, left over, left as residuum, (n., remainder, substance of the nature of a residuum). 3. (Of error in calculations) still unaccounted for or not eliminated. [f. RESIDUE + -AL]

rèsíd'úarÿ (-z-), a. Of the residue of an estate (~ *bequest, clause, legatee*, etc.); of, being, a residuum, residual, still remaining, (*mere* ~ *substances*; *the* ~ *aberration*; *some* ~ *odds & ends*). [RESIDUUM, -ARY¹]

rĕs'ídue (-z-), n. Remainder, rest, what is left or remains over; what remains of estate after payment of charges, debts, & bequests ; (chem. etc.) residuum. [ME, f. OF *residu* f. L RESIDUUM]

rèsíd'úum (-z-), n. (pl. -*dua*). What remains, esp. (chem. etc.) substance left after combustion or evaporation, (in calculations) amount not accounted for or residual error; lowest stratum or dregs of population. [L, neut. of *residuus* remaining (RESIDE)]

rèsígn'¹ (-zĭn), v.t. & i. 1. Relinquish, surrender, give up, hand over, (office, right, claim, property, charge, task, life, hope; often *to* person, *into* person's hands etc.; ~ one*self to* another's *guidance, to sleep, rest, meditation,* etc.). **2.** Reconcile one*self,* one's *mind,* etc. (*to* one's *fate* etc., *to doing,* or abs. =. accept the inevitable without repining), whence ~ED¹ (-zīnd') a., ~ēdLY² (-zīn-) adv. **3.** Give up office, retire. [ME, f. OF *resigner* f. L *re*(*signare* seal) unseal, cancel, RE- 7]

rē'-sign'² (-sīn), v.t. &i. Sign again. [RE- 8]

rĕsignā'tion (-z-), n. In vbl senses (RE-SIGN¹); esp.: resigning of an office, document conveying it (*give, send in,* one's ~); being resigned, uncomplaining endurance of sorrow or other evil. [ME, f. OF f. med. L *resignatio* (RESIGN¹, -ATION)]

rĕsīle' (-z-), v.i. (Of elastic bodies) recoil, rebound, resume shape & size after stretching or compression; have or show elasticity or buoyancy or recuperative power. Hence or cogn. rĕsil'iENCE, rĕsil'iENCY, nn., rĕsil'iENT a., (-zīlyen-). [f. obs. F *résiler, -ir,* or L *re*(*silire = salire* -jump), RE- 9]

rĕs'in (-z-), n., & v.t. **1.** Adhesive substance insoluble in water (cf. GUM²) secreted by most plants & exuding naturally or upon incision esp. from fir & pine; kinds of similar substance got by chemical process. **2.** v.t. Rub or treat with ~. Hence ~iF'EROUS ~iFORM, ~OUS, aa., ~OID a. & n., ~ATE¹(3) n., ~iFY v.t. & i., ~iFICA'TION n̄., ~O- comb. form. [ME *resyn, rosyn,* f. L *resina,* med. L *rosina*]

rĕsipis'c|ence, n. Recognition of error, return to good sense. So ~ENT a. [F, or f. LL *resipiscentia* f. *re*(*sipiscere* f. *sapere* see SAPIENT), RE- 9]

rĕsist' (-z-), v.t. & i., & n. **1.** Stop course of, successfully oppose, keep off or out, prevent from penetrating, repel, be proof against or unaffected or uninjured by, abstain from, (projectile, weapon, edge, frost, heat, moisture, attack, temptation, power, infection, influence, suggestion, etc.; *who can ~ God's will?; cannot ~ a joke,* must make it if it suggests itself, or must be amused by it), whence ~IBLE a., ~LESS a. (poet.), ~lĕssLY² adv. **2.** Strive against, oppose, try to impede, refuse to comply with, as ~ *arrest.* **3.** Offer resistance, make opposition, whence or cogn. ~ANT, ~ENT, ~IVE, aa., ~ER¹ n. (‖ *passive ~er,* person refusing on grounds of justice to pay education rate imposed by Act in 1902), ~OR n., device offering electrical resistance. **4.** n. Composition applied to surfaces for protection from some agent employed on them, esp. to parts of calico that are not to take dye. [ME, f. OF *resister* or L *re*(*sistere* redupl. of *stare* stand), RE- 2]

rĕsis'tance (-z-), n. **1.** (Power of) resisting (*passive ~,* refusal to comply; *something with greater ~ for its weight than steel*); ~ *movement* (esp. of unconquered people in a conquered country). **2.** Hindrance,

impeding or stopping effect, exercised by material thing upon another (*overcome the ~ of the air;* ~ *of fluids varies with their specific gravity; line of* ~, direction in which it acts; *take line of least* ~, fig., adopt easiest method or course). **3.** (Electr., magnet., heat) non-conductivity; (electr.) part of apparatus used to offer definite ~ to current. [ME, f. OF *resist-ance* f. LL *resistantia* (prec., -ANCE)]

rĕsistibil'ity (-z-), n. Being resistible; power of offering resistance. [RESIST*ible,* -BILITY]

resole. See RE- 8.

rĕs'oluble (-zolŏō-, -lŭ-), a. That can be resolved, (usu.) analysable *into,* resolvable. [f. LL *resolubilis* (RESOLVE, & see SOLUBLE)]

rĕs'olute (-zolŏŏt, -ūt), a. (Of person or his temper or action) determined, decided, bold, not vacillating, unshrinking, firm of purpose. Hence ~LY² adv. [f. L *resolutus* p.p., see RESOLVE]

rĕsolu'tion (-zolŏō-, -lŭ-), n. **1.** Separation into components, decomposition; analysis, conversion *into* other form; (med.) disappearance of inflammation without suppuration; (pros.) substitution of two short syllables for one long; (mus.) making of discord to pass into concord; (mech.) replacing of single force by two or more jointly equivalent. **2.** Solving of doubt, problem, question, etc. **3.** Formal expression of opinion by legislative body (cf. MOTION) or public meeting, form proposed for this. **4.** Resolve, thing resolved on, (*good* ~s, intentions that one formulates mentally for virtuous conduct). **5.** Determined temper or character, boldness & firmness of purpose. [ME, f. OF or L *resolutio* (RESOLVE, -ION)]

rĕs'olutive (-zolŏō-, -lŭ-), a. & n. **1.** Having dissolving power, disintegrating, (chiefly med.); (n.) ~ application or drug. **2.** (law). ~ *condition,* whose fulfilment terminates contract etc. [f. med. L *resolutivus* (as prec., -IVE)]

rĕsŏlve' (-z-), v.t. & i., & n. **1.** Dissolve (t. & i.; *into*),. disintegrate, analyse, break up into parts, dissipate, convert or be converted *into;* reduce by mental analysis *into,* (used *vinegar to ~ the rocks; blood first coagulates & then* ~s; ~ *thing, thing is* ~d or ~s *itself* or ~s, *into its elements; telescope* ~s *nebula into stars; inflammation, tumour, is* ~d or ~s, passes away without suppuration; *House* ~s *itself into a committee; might ~ Christianity into a system of morality*); (mus.) convert (discord) or be converted into concord. **2.** Solve, explain, clear up, settle, (*all doubts were* ~d; ~ *me this,* arch., answer this question; *the problem of its origin has not yet been* ~d). **3.** Decide upon, make up one's mind *upon* action or *doing* or *to* do, form mentally or (of legislative body or public meeting) pass by vote the resolution *that,* (of circumstances etc.) bring (person) to resolution *to* do or *upon* action or doing, (he ~d upon or rarely ~d amendment; ~d that nothing should induce him, that he would do, upon doing; the House began by resolving that . . . ; this discovery ~d us on going or to go; p.p. used in minutes of meeting, = the following resolution was passed, namely that; p.p. as adj., resolute, whence rĕsŏl'vĕd-LY² (-z-) adv.); hence rĕsŏl'VABLE (-z-) a. 4. n. Resolution come to in the mind (& she kept her ~); (poet.) resolution, steadfastness, (a mind, deeds, of high ~). [ME, f. L re(solvere solut- SOLVE), RE- 5]

rĕsŏl'vent (-z-), a. & n. (chiefly med. & chem.). (Drug, application, substance) effecting resolution of tumour etc. or division into component parts. [prec., -ENT]

rĕs'on|ant (-z-), a. (Of sound) echoing, resounding, continuing to sound, reinforced or prolonged by vibration or reflexion; (of bodies, rooms, etc.) tending to reinforce or prolong sounds esp. by vibration; (of places) resounding with. Hence or cogn. ~ANCE n., ~antLY² adv. [F, or f. L re(sonare sound), RE- 6, -ANT]

rĕs'onātor (-z-), n. Instrument responding to single note & used for detecting it in combinations; appliance for giving resonance to sounds. [as prec., -OR].

rĕsōrb', v.t. Absorb again. Hence ~ENCE n., ~ENT a. [f. L re(sorbēre sorpt- ABSORB), RE- 9]

rĕsŏr'cin (-z-), n. Compound got by action of potash on resin used chiefly as dye-stuff. [RESIN, ORCIN]

rĕsōrp'tion, n. Resorbing or being resorbed. [RESORB, -ION]

rĕsōrt'¹ (-z-), v.i. 1. Turn for aid to (~ to force, experiment, etc., or rarely concrete object or person). 2. Go in numbers or often to (visitors ~ed to him, to the shrine, by the hundred; watched the inn to which he was known to ~). [ME, f. OF re(sortir come or go out) rebound etc., RE- 8]

rĕsōrt'² (-z-), n. 1. Thing to which recourse is had, what is turned to for aid, expedient, (a carriage, repetition. of the experiment, was the only ~). 2. Recourse (cannot be done without ~ to compulsion; in the last ~, when all else has failed, as final attempt). 3. Frequenting or being frequented (encouraged the ~ of scholars; a place of great ~). 4. Place frequented usu. for specified purpose or quality (health, holiday, ~; mountain, seaside, ~). [ME, f. OF f. resortir (prec.)]

rē-sōrt'³, v.t. Sort again. [RE- 8]

rĕsound' (-z-), v.i. & t. 1. (Of place) ring or echo (with); (of voice, instrument, sound, etc.) produce echoes, go on sounding, fill place with sound. 2. (Of fame, event, etc.) be much talked of, produce sensation, (often through Europe etc.). 3. Repeat loudly (usu. the praises etc. of); (of place) give back (sound). Hence

~ingLY² adv. [ME; RE- 9, SOUND, after OF resoner or L resonare (RESONANT)]

rĕsource' (-sōrs), n. 1. (Usu. in pl.) means of supplying a want, stock that can be drawn on; (pl.) country's collective means for support & defence. 2. (after French; now rare). Possibility of aid (lost without ~). 3. Expedient, device, shift, (flight was his only ~; am at the end of my ~s). 4. Leisure occupation (reading is a great ~; a man of no ~s). 5. Skill in devising expedients, practical ingenuity, quick wit, (is full of ~). Hence ~FUL (-ōrsf-), ~LESS (-ōrsl-), aa., ~fulNESS, ~lessNESS, nn., ~fulLY² adv. [f. F ressource f. OF re(s)sourdre f. RE- 9, L surgere rise]

rĕspĕct'¹, n. 1. Reference, relation, (to; the terms have ~ to position alone; is true with ~ to the French; with ~ to possible routes, there are three; ablative, accusative, of ~ in Lat. gram., those translatable by with ~ or as to). 2. Heed or regard to or of, attention to, (have not had or paid ~ to anything but colour; did it quite without ~ to the results; ~ of persons, partiality or favour shown esp. to the powerful). 3. Particular, detail, point, aspect, (of; is admirable in ~ of style; in all, many, some, ~s; in one, this, ~). 4. (arch.). Consideration that (is out of the question, in ~ that it stultifies the whole plan). 5. Deferential esteem felt or shown towards person or quality (has won the ~ of all; have the greatest ~ for him; is held in ~; SELF-~). 6. pl. (With my, his, etc.) polite messages or attentions (give him my, sends his, ~s; went to pay his ~s to). [ME, f. OF or L respectus -ūs (respicere see foll.)]

rĕspĕct'², v.t. 1. Pay heed to (arch.; ~ persons, discriminate unfairly between them under influence of wealth etc., whence ~ER¹ n. of persons). 2. Relate to, be concerned with, (now rare exc. in part., as legislation ~ing property, also used as prep., as am at a loss ~ing his whereabouts). 3. Regard with deference; avoid degrading or insulting or injuring or interfering with or interrupting, treat with consideration, spare, (~ oneself, refrain from unworthy conduct or thoughts, have self-respect; ~ innocence or the innocent, refrain from offending or corrupting or tempting; ~ed my silence, let me remain silent; ~ privileges, property, neutral territory, etc.). [f. L re(spicere spect- = specere look at), RE- 6]

rĕspĕctabil'itў, n. Being, those who are, a person who is, socially respectable. [foll., -BILITY]

rĕspĕc'table, a. & n. 1. Deserving respect (did it from ~ motives). 2. Not inconsiderable in amount etc., of some merit or importance, fairly good or many or much, tolerable, passable, (a ~ hill, antiquity, painter, minority; ~ talents). 3. Of fair social standing, having the qualities necessary for such standing, not disreputable, honest & decent in conduct; (of pursuits, clothes, etc.) befitting ~ persons; hence **respec'tably**[2] adv. **4.** n. A ~ person (usu. in pl.). [-ABLE]

respect'ful, a. Showing deference (~ *behaviour; stood at a ~ distance*). Hence ~LY[2] adv., ~NESS n. [-FUL]

respec'tive, a. Each's own, proper to each, individual, several, comparative, (*go to your, put them in their, ~ places*; *were given places according to their ~ rank or ranks; A & B contributed the ~ sums of 4d. & 3d.; the election depends on the ~ popularity of the candidates*). Hence ~LY[2] (-vl-) adv. [f. med. L *respectivus* (RESPECT[2], -IVE)]

respell. See RE- 8.

res'pirable (*or* rispir[2]), a. (Of air, gas, etc.) that can, fit to, be breathed. [f. RESPIRE + -ABLE, *or* F *respirable*]

respira'tion, n. Breathing; single inspiration & expiration; plant's absorption of oxygen & emission of carbon dioxide. [ME, f. OF *or* L *respiratio* (RESPIRE, -ATION)]

res'pirator, n. Apparatus of gauze etc. worn over mouth (& nose) to warm or filter inhaled air; (mil.) kinds of chemical filtering-apparatus worn for defence against poison-gas. [as foll.; see -OR]

respire', v.i. & t. Breathe, inhale & exhale, air, whence **res'piratory** (*or* rispir'at-) a.; breathe (air etc.); (rare) exhale (perfume, amiability, etc.); breathe again, take breath, recover hope or spirit, get rest or respite. [ME, f. OF *respirer or* L *re(spirare* breathe), RE- 9]

res'pite, n., & v.t. **1.** Delay permitted in the discharge of an obligation or suffering of a penalty; interval of rest or relief. **2.** v.t. Grant ~ to, reprieve, (condemned person); postpone execution or exaction of (sentence, obligation); give temporary relief from (pain, care) or to (sufferer). [ME, f. OF *respit* f. L RESPECT[1]*us*]

resplen'd|ent, a. Brilliant, dazzlingly or gloriously bright. Hence *or* cogn. ~ENCE, ~ENCY, nn., ~entLY[2] adv. [ME, f. L *re(splendēre* glitter), RE- 6, -ENT]

respond'[1], v.i. **1.** Make answer (esp. of congregation making set answers to priest etc.); perform answering or corresponding action (~*ed with a drop-kick, left--hander,* etc.). **2.** Show sensitiveness *to* by behaviour or change (*does not ~ to kindness; nerve ~s to stimulus, string to note,* etc.). **3.** (rare). Correspond, be analogous, whence *or* cogn. ~ENCE, ~ENCY, nn. [f. L *re(spondēre* spons- pledge) answer, RE- 1]

respond'[2], n. **1.** (eccl.). = RESPONSORY, also response to versicle. **2.** (archit.). Half-pillar or half-pier attached to wall to support arch. [ME, f. OF (*respondre* answer, as prec.)]

respon'dent, a. & n. **1.** Making answer; responsive *to*; in position of defendant. **2.** n. One who makes answer, defends

thesis, etc.; defendant esp. in divorce case. [as RESPOND[1], -ENT]

response', n. Answer given in word or act, reply, retort, (*in ~ to; made no ~; the ~s of the oracles; his ~ was the proclamation of martial law*); feeling, movement, etc., elicited by stimulus or influence (*called forth no ~ in his breast*); (eccl.) = RESPONSORY, also any part of liturgy said or sung in answer to priest. [ME, f. OF *respons(e)*; later f. L *responsum* neut. p.p. (RESPOND[1])]

responsibil'it|y, n. Being responsible (*declines all ~y for it; will take the ~y of doing it; did it on his own ~y,* without authorization; *is not afraid of ~y,* of having to act without detailed guidance); charge for which one is responsible (*a family is a great ~y; asked to be relieved of his ~y or ~ies*). [foll., -BILITY]

respon'sib|le, a. Liable to be called to account, answerable (*to* person, *for* thing, or abs.; ~*le ruler, government,* not autocratic), morally accountable for actions, capable of rational conduct; of good credit or position or repute, respectable, apparently trustworthy; involving responsibility (*a ~le office*). Hence ~LY[2] adv. [obs. F (L RESPOND[1]*ēré*, -IBLE)]

|| **respon'sions** (-shnz), n. pl. First of three examinations for Oxford B.A. degree, abolished in 1960 (also *smalls* colloq.; cf. *moderations, greats, final schools*). [f. L *responsio* (RESPOND[1], -ION)]

respon'sive, a. Answering, by way of answer, (of liturgy etc.) using responses; responding readily to *or* to some influence, impressionable, sympathetic. Hence ~LY[2] adv., ~NESS n. [f. F *responsif, -ive or* LL *responsivus* (RESPOND[1], -IVE)]

respon'sory, n. Anthem said or sung by soloist & choir after lesson. [f. LL *responsorium* (RESPOND[1], -ORY)]

rest[1], v.i. & t. **1.** Be still, cease or abstain or be relieved from exertion or action or movement or employment, lie in sleep or death, be tranquil, be let alone, (*waves that never ~; ~ (up)on one's oars,* temporarily cease rowing or any exertion; *never let your enemy ~; let us ~ here,* cease walking etc.; ~ *from one's labours; actor is ~ing,* is out of work; ~*s in the churchyard,* lies buried; *let her ~ in peace; is too feverish to ~; could not ~ under an imputation, till he got his wish; land was allowed to ~,* left fallow; *the matter cannot ~ here,* must be further examined etc.); give relief or repose to (*stayed a day to ~ myself; ~ your men for an hour; says the goggles ~ his eyes; must ~ the ground; ~ or God ~ his soul,* may God give it repose); (p.p.) refreshed or reinvigorated by ~ing (*are you quite ~ed?*). **2.** Lie, be spread out, be supported or based, depend, rely, (of eyes etc.) alight or be steadily directed, (up)on (*shadow, light, ~s on his face; roof ~s on four arches; their left ~ed on the river; hand ~ing on the table; science ~s on* *phenomena*; *I ~ upon your promise*; *his gaze ~ed on a strange object*); be propped *against*; repose trust *in* (*be content to ~ in God*); place for support or foundation (*up*)*on* (~ one's *elbow*, *load*, *on the table*; ~ one's *case on equity*, *unimpeachable evidence*). **3.** *~ing-place*, provided or used for *~*ing (*last ~ing-place*, the grave). [OE *ræstan*, = OS *restian*, OHG *restan*]

rĕst², n. 1. Repose or sleep esp. in bed at night (*go*, *retire*, *to ~*; *take ~* or one's *~*). **2.** Abstinence or freedom from or absence of exertion or activity or movement or care or molestation, a period of such abstinence etc., (*day of ~*, Sunday; *a ~ from work* etc.; *give person*, *horse*, *machine*, etc., *a ~*; *take a short ~*; *at ~*, still, not agitated or troubled, often of the dead; *set question*, person's *mind*, *at ~*, settle, relieve; *lay to ~*, bury). **3.** Lodging-place or shelter provided for sailors, cabmen, or other class. **4.** Prop or support or steadying-piece, e.g. for gun in aiming, telephone-receiver, billiard-cue, cutting-tool in lathe, or foot on bicycle. **5.** (Mus.) appointed interval of silence or sign denoting it; pause in elocution, caesura in verse. **6.** *~-balk*, ridge left unploughed between furrows; *~-cure*, *~* usu. of some weeks in bed as medical treatment; *~-day*, day spent in *~*, (rare) Sunday; *~-house*, (in India) DAWK bungalow. [OE *ræst(e)*, = OS, OHG *resta* etc.]

rĕst³, v.i. Remain over (arch.: *whatever ~s of hope*); *~ with*, be left in the hands or charge of (*it ~s with you to propose terms*; *the management of affairs ~ed with Wolsey*); remain in specified state (*the affair ~s a mystery*; *~ assured*, *satisfied*, etc.; also arch. in epistolary forms, as *I ~ your devoted friend*). [ME, f. OF *rester* f. L re(*stare* stand), RE- 3]

rĕst⁴, n. 1. *The* remaining part(s) or individuals of, *the* remainder of some quantity or number, *the* others, (*& the* or *all the ~ of it*, all else that might be mentioned; *for the ~*, as regards anything beyond what has been specially mentioned). **2.** ‖ (Banking) reserve fund; (commerc.) stocktaking & balancing; (tennis etc.) spell of continuous returns. [ME, f. OF *reste* f. *rester* (prec.)]

rĕst⁵, n. (hist.). Check holding butt of mediaeval tilter's spear when couched for charging (*with*, *lay*, or *set* one's *lance in ~*). [ME, aphetic f. ARREST¹]

restamp, **restart**, **restate** etc. See RE- 8.

rĕs'taurant (-tor-, & see Ap.), n. Place where meals or refreshments may be had. [F (*restaurer* RESTORE, -ANT)]

restaurateur (rĕstoratér'), n. Restaurant-keeper. [F]

rĕst'ful, a. Favourable to repose, free from disturbing influences, soothing. Hence *~*LY² adv., *~*NESS n. [-FUL]

rĕst'-hărrow .(-ō), n. A tough-rooted

shrub, cammock. [obs. *rest* v. as REST⁵, HARROW¹]

‖ **restiff.** See RESTIVE.

rĕs'titūte, v.t. & i. (rare). Make restitution (of). [f. L re(*stituere -lut-* = *statuere* set up), RE- 8]

rĕstitū'tion, n. Restoring of or *of* thing to proper owner, reparation for injury, (esp. *make ~*; *~ of conjugal rights*, name of a matrimonial lawsuit); restoring of thing to its original state (esp. theol. *the ~ of all things*); resumption of original shape or position by elasticity. [ME, f. OF or L *restitutio* (prec., -ION)]

rĕs'tive, ‖ **rĕs'tiff** (arch.), a. (Of horse) refusing to advance, stubbornly standing still or moving backwards or sideways, jibbing, refractory; (of person) unmanageable, rejecting control; (erron.) restless. Hence **rĕs'tive**LY² (-vl-) adv., **rĕs'tiveness** (-vn-) n. [ME *restif* f. OF (REST³, -IVE)]

rĕst'less, a. Finding or affording no rest, uneasy, agitated, never still, ever in motion, unpausing, fidgeting. Hence *~*LY² adv., *~*NESS n. [REST², -LESS]

restock. See RE- 8.

rĕstorā'tion, n. In senses of RESTORE; also or esp.: (period of) re-establishment of monarchy in 1660 (*the R~*); model or drawing representing supposed original form of extinct animal, ruined building, etc. [17th c. alt. (after *restore*) f. ME *restauracion*, f. OF, or LL *restauratio* (RESTORE, -ION)]

rĕstorā'tion|ism (-shon-), n. Doctrine that all men will ultimately be restored to happiness in the future life. So *~*IST(2) n. [-ISM]

rĕstŏ'rative, a. & n. 1. Tending to restore health or strength. **2.** n. *~* food, medicine, or agency. Hence *~*LY² adv. [ME also *-au-* f. OF *restauratif*, *-ive* (foll., -ATIVE)]

rĕstōr|e', v.t. 1. Give back, make restitution of. **2.** (Attempt to) bring back to original state by rebuilding, repairing, repainting, emending, etc. (*church*, *picture*, *text*, has been *~ed*, *spoilt in ~ing*, *~ed out of all recognition*, etc.); make representation of supposed original state of (extinct animal, ruin, etc.). **3.** Reinstate, bring back *to* dignity or right; bring back *to* or *to* health etc., cure (person). **4.** Re-establish, renew, bring back into use. **5.** Reinsert by conjecture (missing words in text, parts of extinct animal, etc.). **6.** Replace, put back, bring *to* former place or condition. Hence *~*'ABLE a., *~*'ER¹ n. [ME, f. OF *restorer* f. L *restaurare*]

rĕstrain'¹, v.t. Check or hold in *from*, keep in check or under control or within bounds, repress, keep down; confine, imprison. Hence *~*ABLE a., *~*édLY² adv. (esp., with self-restraint). [ME, f. OF *restrai(g)n-* st. of *restraindre* f. L re(*stringere strict-* tie), RE- 2]

rē-strain'[2], v.t. Strain again. [RE- 8]

rėstraint', n. Restraining or being re-strained, stoppage, check, controlling agency or influence, confinement esp. in asylum, (*without* ~, freely, copiously; *is under* ~, esp. as lunatic); constraint or reserve of manner; self-control, avoid-ance of excess or exaggeration, austerity of literary expression. [ME, f. OF *restraint(e)* (RESTRAIN[1])]

rėstrict', v.t. Confine, bound, limit, (*to, within; has a very* ~*ed application; am* ~*ed to advising; is* ~*ed within narrow limits*). Hence or cogn. **rėstric'tion** n., **rėstric'tive** a. (~*ive practices,* ~*ing out-* put in industry),~ėDLY[2], **rėstric'tively**[2], advv. [f. L *restrict-*, see RESTRAIN[1]]

rėstuff'. See RE- 9.

rėsult' (-z-), v.i., & n. **1.** Arise as actual or follow as logical consequence (*from* con-ditions, causes, premisses, etc., or abs.); have issue or end in specified manner esp. *in* failure etc. (~*ed badly, in a large profit*). **2.** n. Consequence, issue, or outcome of something (*without* ~, in vain, fruitless), whence ~FUL, ~LESS, aa.; quantity, formula, etc., given by calculation. [ME, f. med. L f. L *re*(*saltare* = *saltare* frequent. of *salire* jump), RE- 9]

rėsul'tant (-z-), a. & n. **1.** Resulting, esp. as total outcome of more or less opposed forces. **2.** n. Composite effect of two or more forces acting in different directions at same point (esp. in mech., also transf.). [prec., -ANT]

rėsume' (-z-), v.t. & i. **1.** Get or take again or back, recover, reoccupy, (~ one's *spirits, sway, liberty, seat;* ~ *gift, grant, territory*). **2.** Begin again (upon), go on (with) after interruption, begin to speak or work again, recommence t. & i., (*the House* ~*d work or its labours, or* ~*d;* ~ *thread of* one's *discourse;* ~ *pipe,* go on smoking again; *'No, it is hopeless' he* ~*d*). **3.** Make résumé of, recapitulate, sum-marize. [ME, f. OF *resumer*, or L *re*(*sumere sumpt-* take), RE- 8]

résumé (rāz'ŏomā, & see Ap.), n. Sum-mary, epitome, abstract. [F, p.p. of *résumer* RESUME]

rėsummons. See RE- 8.

rėsump'tion (-z-), n. Resuming. So ~IVE a., ~IVELY[2] adv. [ME, f. OF, or LL *resumptio* (RESUME, -ION)[2]]

rėsup'inate, a. (bot.). (Of leaf etc.) In-verted, bottom up. Hence ~A'TION n. [f. L *re*(*supinare* make SUPINE[1]), RE- 9]

rėsurge', v.i. (rare exc. joc.). Experience resurrection, revive, rise or arise again. So (in ordinary use) rėsur'gent(1) n. & a., rėsur'gence n. [f. L *re*(*surgere surrect-* rise), RE- 9]

rėsurrect' (-z-), v.t. (colloq.). Raise from the dead (rare); revive practice or memory of; take from grave, exhume. [back form. f. foll.]

rėsurrec'tion (-z-), n. **1.** (*R*~). (Festival in memory of) rising of Christ from the grave; rising again of men at the last day. **2.** Exhumation lit. or fig., resurrecting (~ *man*, BODY-snatcher), whence ~IST(1) (-sho-) n. **3.** Revival from disuse or inactivity or decay, restoration to vogue or memory. Hence ~AL (-sho-) a. [ME, f. OF, or LL *resurrectio* (RESURGE, -ION)]

rėsur'vey. See RE- 8.

rėsus'citate, v.t. & i. Revive, return or usu. restore to life, consciousness, vogue, vigour, or vividness. Hence or cogn. ~A'TION, ~ātor, nn., ~ATIVE a. [f. L *re*(*suscitare* CITE), RE- 9, -ATE[3]]

rėt, rāte, rait, v.t. & i. Soften (flax, hemp) by soaking or exposing to moisture; (of hay etc., in pass. or intr.) be spoilt by wet, rot. [hist. obsc.; 15th c. *ret*(*t*)*en* corresp. to MDu. *re*(*e*)*ten*]

rėta'ble, n. Shelf, or frame enclosing de-corated panels, above back of altar. [f. F *rétable*, cf. med. L *retrotabulum* rear table]

rėt'ail[1], n. Sale of goods in small quanti-ties (esp. *by* ~, or attrib., as ~ *trading, dealer;* also adv., esp. in conjunction w. *wholesale*, as *do you buy wholesale or* ~?). [ME, f. OF *retail*(*le*) piece cut off f. *re*(*tailler* cut, see TAIL[2]), RE- 5]

rėtail'[2], v.t. & i. **1.** Sell (goods) by retail; (of goods) be ~ed (esp. *at* or *for* specified price). **2.** Recount, relate details of. Hence ~ER[1] n. [ME, prob. f. prec.]

rėtain', v.t. **1.** Keep in place, hold fixed, (~*ing wall*, supporting & confining mass of earth or water; ~*ing force*, mil., posted to keep part of enemy inactive etc.). **2.** Secure services of (esp. barrister) by engagement & preliminary payment (~*ing fee*, retainer). **3.** Keep possession of, not lose, continue to have; continue to practise or recognize, allow to remain or prevail, not abolish or discard or alter. **4.** Succeed in remembering, not forget. Hence ~ABLE a. [ME, f. OF *retenir* f. L *re*(*tinēre tent-* = *tenēre* hold), RE- 3]

rėtain'er, n. **1.** (Law) formal retention of something as one's own, authorization to retain thus; being retained to serve in some capacity; fee paid to barrister etc. for right to his services if required. **2.** In vbl senses; esp. (hist.), dependant or fol-lower of person of rank; *old* ~ (joc.), old and faithful servant. [RETAIN +(sense 1) -ER[4], (sense 2) -ER[1]]

rėtake. See RE- 9.

rėtal'iate, v.t. & i. **1.** Repay (injury, insult, etc., rarely kindness etc.) in kind; retort (accusation) *upon* person. **2.** Do as one is done by, esp. return evil, make reprisals, (pol. econ.) impose duties on imports from foreign State in return for its import duties. Hence or cogn. ~A'TION n., ~ATIVE, ~atory, (-lya-), aa. [f. L *re*(*taliare* f. *talis* such), RE- 1]

rėtard', v.t. & i., & n. **1.** Make slow or late, delay progress or development or arrival or accomplishment or happening of. **2.** (Esp. of physical phenomena, e.g.

motion of tides, waves, or celestial bodies) happen, arrive, behind normal or calculated time; hence or cogn. rētārdA'TION, ~MENT, nn., ~ATIVE, ~ATORY, aa. 3. n. ~ation (~ *of tide* or *high water*, interval between full moon & following high water). [f. F *retard(er)* or L *re(tardare* f. *tardus* slow), RE- 3]

retaste. See RE- 8.

rētch, v.i., & n. 1. Make motion of vomiting esp. ineffectually & involuntarily. 2. n. Such motion or sound of it. (16th c., var. of (now dial.) *reach,* f. OE *hrǣcan* spit f. *hrǣca* spittle]

retell. See RE- 8.

rētĕn'tion, n. RETAINING; esp. (med.) failure to evacuate urine or other secretion. [ME, f. OF, f. L *retentionem* (RETAIN, -ION)]

rētĕn'tive, a. (Of memory, or rarely of person in that respect) tenacious, not forgetful; (of substances) ~ *of* moisture etc., apt to retain it (also ~ abs., ~ of moisture); (surg., of ligature etc.) serving to keep something in place. Hence ~LY[2] adv., ~NESS n. [ME, f. OF (-*if, -ive*), see RETAIN, -IVE]

retenue' (-nōō), n. Reserve, self-control. [F.]

rē'tiary̆ (-sha-), n. Net-making or geometrical spider. [f. L *retiarius* (gladiator) with net (*rete* net, -ARY[1])]

rĕt'ic|ence, n. Reserve in speech, avoidance of saying all one knows or feels, abstinence from over-emphasis in art; holding back of some fact; disposition to silence, taciturnity. So ~ENT a. (*on, upon, about*), ~ENTLY[2] adv. [F, or f. L *reticentia* f. *re(ticēre = tacēre* be silent), RE- 4]

rĕt'icle, n. Network of fine threads or lines in object-glass of telescope to help accurate observation. [f. L RETICULUM]

retic'ulăte, v.t. & i. Divide or be divided in fact or appearance into a network, arrange or be arranged in small squares or with intersecting lines. So (see etym.) ~ATE[2] (-at) a., ~ateLY[2] adv., ~A'TION n., ~āto- comb. form. [vb by back form. f. *reticulated* f. *reticulate* a. f. L *reticulatus* (RETICULUM, -ATE[2])]

rĕt'icule, n. 1. = RETICLE. 2. Lady's netted or other bag carried or worn to serve purpose of pocket. 3. (astron.) A Southern constellation. [f. F *réticule* f. L (foll.)]

retic'ul|um, n. (pl. ~a). 1. Ruminant's second stomach or honeycomb. 2. Net-like structure, reticulated membrane etc., whence ~AR[1], ~OSE[1], aa., ~0- comb. form. [L (*rete* net, -CULE)]

rĕt'iform, a. Netlike, reticulated. [f. L *rete* net, -I-, -FORM]

rĕt'in|a, n. (pl. ~as, ~ae). Layer at back of eyeball sensitive to light. Hence ~AL a., ~IT'IS n. [ME, f. med. L, f. L *rete* net]

rĕt'inŭe, n. Suite or train of persons in attendance upon someone. [ME, f. OF *retenue* fem. p.p. of *retenir* RETAIN]

retīre', v.i. & t., & n. 1. Withdraw (intr.), go away, retreat, seek seclusion or shelter, recede, go (as) to bed, (~ *from the world,* become recluse; ~ *into* one*self,* be uncommunicative or unsociable, whence **retīr'ING[2]**a., **retīr'ingLY[2]**adv., **retīr'ingNESS** n.;. *the ladies* ~, leave dining-room after dessert; *always* ~s *before midnight,* often *to rest, to bed, for the night,* etc.; *general, army, was forced to* ~, ~d *in good order,* often *from* position, *to* place, *before* enemy, etc.; *background does not* ~ *as it should;* ' *retiring-room,* for retiring to, esp. lavatory); (p.p., f. obs. trans. use; pr. rĭtīrd') withdrawn from society or observation, secluded, (*lives* ~d; *a* ~d *life; in a* ~d *valley),* whence ~d'NESS (-īrdn-) n. 2. Cease *from* or give up office or profession or employment or candidature, (crick.) voluntarily terminate.one's innings, compel (officer, employee) to ~, (~ *from the army, from business, on a* pension; *batsman* ~d *hurt; was compulsorily* ~d *as incompetent; retiring age,* age at which person ~s; *retiring pension,* allowed to one who ~s at normal time); (p.p., see -ED[1](2) for sense) that has ~d (*a* ~d *general, grocer;* ~d *pay,* pension; ~d *list,* of ~d officers). 3. (Mil.) order (troops) to ~; (finance) withdraw (bill, note) from operation or currency. 4. n. (mil.). Signal to troops to ~ (usu. *sound the* ~). [f. F *retirer* f. *tirer* draw, RE- 9]

retīre'ment (-īrm-), n. In vbl senses; also: seclusion, privacy; secluded place. [F (prec., -MENT]

retort'[1], v.t. & i., & n. 1. Requite (humiliation, insult, attack) in kind; turn (mischief etc.), fling (charge, sarcasm, jest), back (*on* or *upon* author or aggressor), make (argument) tell against or *against* its user; make, say by way of, repartee or counter-charge or counter-argument; (p.p.)' recurved, twisted or bent backwards. 2. n. Incisive reply, repartee; turning of charge or argument against its author; piece of retaliation. [f. L *re(torquēre tort-* twist), RE- 9]

retort'[2], n., & v.t. 1. Vessel usu. of glass with long downward-bent neck used in distilling liquids; kinds of receptacle of various shapes & materials used in purifying mercury & making gas & steel. 2. v.t. Purify (mercury) by heating in ~. [f. F *retorte* f. med. L *retorta* fem. p.p. as prec.]

retor'tion, n. Bending back (lit. & fig.); (Internat. law) retaliation by State upon subjects of another. [f. med. L *retortio, -sio* (RETORT[1], -ION)]

retouch. [prob. f. F *retoucher* (RE- 8, TOUCH)]

retrāce', v.t. Trace back to source or

beginning; look over again; recall the course of memory; go back over (one's *steps* or *way*; often fig. of undoing actions). [f. F *retracer* (RE- 8, TRACE v.)]

rĕtrăct', v.t. & i. **1.** Draw (esp. part of one's body) back or in, (of such part etc.) shrink back or in or be capable of being ∼ed, (*snail* ∼*s its horns*; *cat's claws* ∼ *or can be* ∼*ed*; *surgeon* ∼*s skin with instrument, organ is* ∼*ed by muscle, called* **rĕtrăc'toR** n.; *if the piston is suddenly* ∼*ed*); hence or cogn. **rĕtrăc'table** [-ABLE] & (in same sense) **rĕtrăc'tILE** a., **rĕtrăctIl'ITY** n., **rĕtrăc'tIVE** a., **rĕtrăc'tion**[1] [-ION] n. **2.** Withdraw, revoke, cancel, refuse to abide by, acknowledge falsity or error of, expressly abandon, (statement, promise, opinion), (abs.) ∼ opinion or statement; hence or cogn. **rĕtrăc'table**[2] [-ABLE] a., **rĕtrăctA'TION**, **rĕtrăc'tion**[3] [-ION], nn. [sense 1 f. L *re(trahere tract-* draw), RE- 4; sense 2 partly as 1, but chiefly f. L *re(tractare* draw, frequent. of *trahere* draw), RE- 9, & L *re(tractare* pull about or handle), RE- 8, as in arch. *retractation* rehandling, now only in title of Augustine's *Retractations*]

rēt'ral, a. (nat. hist. etc.). Hinder, posterior, at the back. [RETRO-, -AL]

retransfer, retransform, retranslate etc., **retread**[1]. See RE- 9.

rē-tread'[2] (-ĕd), v.t., & n. Furnish (tire) with a new tread; (n.) tire so renewed. [RE- 9]

rĕtreat', v.i. & t., & n. **1.** Go back, retire, relinquish a position, (esp. of army etc.); (trans., chiefly in chess) move (piece) back from forward or threatened position; recede (*a* ∼*ing chin, forehead*). **2.** n. Act of, (mil.) signal for, ∼ing (*sound the or a* ∼, mil.; *beat a* ∼, ∼, abandon undertaking; *make good* one's ∼, get safely away; *intercept* ∼ *of*, cut off; *are in full* ∼); (mil.) bugle-call at sunset. **3.** Withdrawing into privacy or security, (place of) seclusion; (eccl.) temporary retirement for religious exercises;' asylum for inebriates or lunatics or pensioners; lurking-place, place of shelter. [vb (15th c.) f. OF *retraiter*; n. ME & OF *retret(e)* f. p.p. of *retraire* f. L *retrahere* (RETRACT)]

rĕtrĕnch', v.t. & i. **1.** Cut down, reduce amount of, (expenses, things causing outlay); cut off, deduct, (∼*ed a year from the established period*); make excisions in or of, shorten or remove, (literary work or passages in it); cut down expenses, introduce economies. **2.** (fortif.). Furnish with inner line of defence usu. consisting of trench & parapet. Hence ∼MENT n. [f. obs. F *retrencher*, mod. *retrancher* (RE-, TRENCH)]

retrial. See RE- 8.

rĕtribū'tion, n. Recompense for evil or rarely for good done, vengeance, requital. So **rĕtrib'ūtIVE** a., **rĕtrib'ūtIVELY** adv. [ME f. OF, or f. LL *re(tributio* f. *tribuere* -*ut*- assign, -ION), RE- 1]

rĕtriev|e', v.t. & i., & n. **1.** (Of dogs, esp. of special breed) find & bring in (killed or wounded bird etc., or abs.), whence ∼'ER[1] n. **2.** Recover by investigation or effort of memory, restore to knowledge or recall to mind. **3.** Regain possession of. **4.** Rescue *from* bad state etc.; restore to flourishing state, revive, (esp. one's fortunes etc.). **5.** Make good, repair, set right, (loss, disaster, error); hence ∼'ABLE a., ∼'AL(2) n. **6.** n. Possibility of recovery (*beyond, past,* ∼*e*). [ME, f. OF *retroeve*-stressed st. of *re(trover* find), RE- 9]

retrim. See RE- 8.

retro- (usu. rē- exc. in the commoner wds, esp. *rĕtrograde, rĕtrospect*), pref. f. L *retro* adv. & pref.: (1) chiefly in L derivatives (∼*act*, ∼*grade*) or wds formed on L anal. of L elements (∼*flex*, ∼*ject*) with senses *backwards, back again, in return*; (2) chiefly in anat. and path. terms with sense *behind* (∼*sternal* a., behind the breastbone), *situated behind*.

rĕtro|ăct', v.i. React; operate' in backward direction; have retrospective effect. Hence or cogn. ∼ăc'tIVE a., ∼ăc'tIVELY adv., ∼ăctIV'ITY, ∼ăc'tION, nn. [f. L RETRO(*agere act*- act)]

rĕt'ro|cēde'[1], v.i. Move back, recede; (of gout) strike inward. So ∼cēd'ENCE n., ∼cēd'ENT a. [f. L RETRO(*cedere cess*-go)]

rĕtrocēde'[2], v.t. Cede (territory) back again. [f. F *rétrocéder* (RETRO-, CEDE)]

rĕtrocĕ'ssion (-shn), n., **rĕtrocĕss'ive**, a. In vbl senses (RETROCEDE[1, 2]). [f. LL *retrocessio* (RETROCEDE[1], -ION)]

rĕt'rochoir (-kwīr), n. Part of cathedral or large church behind high altar. [f. med. L RETRO(*chorus* CHOIR)]

rĕtroflĕc'tĕd, rĕt'roflĕx, -flĕxed (-kst), aa. (anat., path., bot., etc.). Turned backwards. So **rĕtroflĕ'xION** (-kshn) n. [f. L RETRO(*flectere flex*- bend)]

rĕtrogradā'tion, n. (Astron.) apparent backward motion of planet in zodiac, motion of heavenly body from E. to W., backward movement of lunar nodes on ecliptic; = (the now usu.) RETROGRESSION. [f. LL RETRO(*gradatio* f. LL -*gradare* walk), -ATION]

rĕt'rogrāde, a., n., & v.i. **1.** (Astron.) in or showing RETROGRADATION; directed backwards (∼ *motion*), retreating; reverting esp. to inferior state, declining; inverse, reversed, (*in* ∼ *order*; ∼ *imitation* in music, with notes of passage repeated backwards); hence ∼LY[2] adv. **2.** n. (rare). Degenerate person; backward tendency. **3.** v.i. (Astron.) show RETROGRADATION; move backwards, recede, retire, decline, revert. [a. (& n.) f. L RETRO*gradus* (*gradus* step); vb f. L *retrógradi* or LL -*gradare* (prec.)]

rĕtrogrĕss', v.i. Go back, move backwards, deteriorate. Hence ∼IVE a., ∼IVELY[2] adv. [f. L RETRO(*gradi gress*-walk)]

rĕtrogrĕ′ssion (-shn), n. (Astron.) retrogradation; backward or reversed movement; return to less advanced state, reversal of development, decline, deterioration. [as prec., -ION]

rĕt′roject, v.t. Cast back (chiefly as opp. *project* in lit. senses). [RETRO-, & as PRO-JECT¹]

rĕtropŭl′sion (-shn), n. (path.). Shifting of external disease to internal part. [RETRO-, L *pellere puls-* drive, -ION]

rĕt′ro-rŏck′ĕt, n. Auxiliary rocket for slowing down space vehicle etc. when re-entering earth's atmosphere. [RETRO-, ROCKET²]

retrŏrse′, a. (nat. hist.). Turned back, reverted. Hence ~LY² (-sl-) adv. [f. L *retrorsus*=RETRO(*versus* p.p. of *vertere* turn)]

rĕt′rospĕct, n. Regard (to be) had *to* precedent or authority or previous conditions; (rare) retrospective force, retroaction; backward view (rare); survey of past time or events (*is pleasant in the* ~, when looked back on; *a short* ~ *is now necessary*). [f. L RETRO(*spicere spect-*=*specere* look) after PROSPECT n.]

rĕtrospĕc′tion, n. Action of looking back esp. into the past, indulgence or engagement in retrospect. [as prec., -ION]

rĕtrospĕc′tive, a. Of, in, proceeding by, retrospection; (of statutes etc.) not restricted to the future, licensing or punishing etc. past actions, having application to the past, retroactive; (of view) lying to the rear. Hence ~LY² adv. [as prec., -IVE]

retroussé (retrōōs′ā), a. Turned up (of nose). [F]

rĕt′rovĕrt, v.t. Turn backwards (esp. path. in p.p., of womb). So **rĕtrovĕr′sion** (-shn) n. [f. LL RETRO(*vertere vers-* turn)]

retry etc. See RE- 8.

rĕtt′erў, n. Flax-retting place. [RET, -ERY]

returf. See RE- 8.

rĕtūrn′¹, v.i. & t. **1.** Come or go back (*gone never to* ~; ~ *home, the way one came*; p.p. occas. as in -ED¹(2), as *a* ~*ed emigrant, they are* or usu. *have* ~*ed*). **2.** Revert (*shall* ~ *to the subject*; *unto dust shalt thou* ~; ~ *to* 'one's old habits'; *property* ~*s to original owner*). **3.** Bring, convey, give, yield, put, send, or pay, back or in return or requital (*fish must be* ~*ed to the water*; ~ *borrowed book* or *sum*; *investments* ~ *a profit*; ~ *sword to scabbard*, or ~ *swords* (mil.); ~ *ball*, strike etc. it back in tennis etc.; ~ *like for like, the compliment, a blow, an answer*; ~ *thanks*, express them esp. in grace at meals or in response to toast; ~ *person's love, greeting*, etc., reciprocate it; ~*ed empties*, packing-cases etc. sent back; ~ *clubs* etc. or *partner's lead* at cards, lead from same suit). **4.** Say in reply, retort. **5.** State, mention, or describe, officially esp. in answer to writ or formal demand (*liabilities were* ~*ed at £5000*; *were all* ~*ed guilty, unfit for work*; || ~*ing officer*, official conducting election & announcing name of person elected); (of constituency) elect as M.P. Hence ~ABLE a. [ME, f. OF re(*torner* TURN), RE- 9]

rĕtūrn′², n. **1.** Coming back (*his* ~ *was the signal for riots*; ~ *of* POST²; || ~ *ticket* or ~, ticket for there-&-back journey, as *took a first-class* ~ *to Leeds*; ~ *passenger, voyage, cargo*, etc.; *many happy* ~*s of the day* or ~*s*, birthday or festival greeting; *have had a, no,* ~ *of the symptoms*). **2.** (archit.). Part receding from line of front, e.g. side of house or of window-opening (~ *angle, side, wall*, etc.); termination of dripstone. **3.** (Coming in of) proceeds or profit of undertaking (often pl.; *the* ~*s were large*; *brings an adequate* ~; *small profits & quick* ~*s*, motto of cheap shop etc. relying on large trade). **4.** Giving, sending, putting, or paying, back, or thing so given etc., || esp. sheriff's report on writ, (returning officer's announcement of) candidate's election as M.P., or formal report with statistics etc. compiled by order (*sheriff made a* ~ *of* nulla bona; *secured his* ~ *for Colchester*; *table littered with* ~*s & pamphlets*; *must ask for the* ~ *of the book* or *loan*; *received a ticket in* ~ *for his fare, neglect in* ~ *for attention*; *fencer's* ~, i.e. riposte, *is slow*; *fielder has a good* ~ in cricket, sends ball in fast & straight; ~ *match* or *game*, or ~, between same sides as before). **5.** pl. || Kind of mild pipe-tobacco (orig. sense *refuse of* tobacco). Hence ~LESS a. [ME, f. AF (prec.)]

rĕtūse′, a. (bot., entom.). With broad end & central depression (of leaf or similar part). [f. L re(*tundere tus-* beat), RE- 9]

rĕūn′ion (-nyon), n. **1.** Reuniting or being reunited, reunited state. **2.** Social gathering, esp. of intimates or persons with common interest. [RE- 8, UNION; cf. F *réunion*]

rĕūn′ionist, -ism, (-nyon-), nn. Seeker, seeking, of reunion between R.-C. & Anglican Churches. [-IST, -ISM]

reunite etc. See RE- 9; **reurge, revaccinate** etc., RE- 8.

rĕv, n., & v.i. & t. (colloq.; -vv-). **1.** =REVOLUTION (of engine). **2.** vb. Revolve (with *up*, to increase in speed of revolution); (often with *up*) cause (engine) to run quickly (esp. when first starting). [abbr.]

rĕvalĕn′ta, n. Food prepared from lentil & barley flour. [orig. *eru*- (L *ervum lens* LENTIL)]

rĕvaloriza′tion, -is- (-ĭz-), n. Restoration of the value of a country's currency. [RE-9+VALORIZATION]

revalue etc. See RE- 8.

rĕvēal′¹, v.t. **1.** (Esp. of God) make known by inspiration or supernatural means (~*ed religion*, opp. *natural*). **2.** Disclose, divulge, betray; display, show, let appear (~ *itself*, come to sight or knowledge). Hence ~ABLE a. [ME, f. OF *reveler* or L *re*(*velare* f. *velum* VEIL), RE- 7]

réveal'², n. Internal side surface of opening or recess, esp. of doorway or window--aperture. [f. obs. vb *revale* lower f. OF *re*(*valer* f. *avaler* VAIL¹), RE- 4]

révei'lle (-vĕll, -väll), n. Military waking--signal sounded in morning on bugle or drums etc. [f. F *réveillez* imperat. pl. of *réveiller* (RE-, *veiller* f. L *vigilare* watch)]

rĕv'el, v.i. & t. (-ll-), & n. 1. Make merry, be riotously festive, feast, carouse, whence ~IER¹ n.; take keen delight *in*; throw *away* (money, time) in ~ry. 2. n. ~ling, (occasion of indulgence in) merry-making, (often pl., as *the* ~*s began*; ~ *rout*, party of ~lers, f. obs. f. OF *revel*(*er*) riot f. L REBEL²-*lare*]

rĕvĕlā'tion, n. Disclosing of knowledge, knowledge disclosed, to man by divine or supernatural agency (*the R*~, also pop. *R*~*s* or *the R*~*s*, abbr. *Rev.*, last book of N.T.', Apocalypse), whence ~AL (-shon-)a.; striking disclosure (*it was a* ~ *to me*; *what a* ~*!*); revealing of some fact. [ME, f. OF, or LL *revelatio* (REVEAL¹ -ATION)]

rĕvĕlāt'ionist (-shon-), n. *The R*~, author of Apocalypse; believer in divine revelation. [-IST]

revenant (rev'enahṅ), n. One returned from the dead or from exile etc. [F]

rĕvĕndicā'tion, n. (diplom.). Formal claiming back, or recovery by such claim, of lost territory etc. [F (RE-, VINDICATION)]

révĕnge'¹ (-j), v.t. & i. Satisfy one*self*, (pass.) be satisfied, with retaliation (*for* offence, *on*, *upon*, *of*, offender); retaliate, requite, exact retribution for, (offence to oneself or another; *on*, *upon*, offender); avenge (person); take vengeance. [ME, f. OF *re*(*venger* f. L *vindicare* VINDICATE), RE- 1]

révĕnge'² (-j), n. 1. Revenging, act done in revenging; desire to revenge, vindictive feeling, whence ~FUL (-jf-) a., ~ful-LY² adv., ~fulNESS n. 2. (In games) opportunity given for reversing former result by return game (*give* one his ~). [f. prec. or obs. F *revenge* (as prec.)]

rĕv'ĕnūe, n. 1. Income, esp. of large amount, from any source (pl. collective items of it, usu. w. possess. as *his* ~*s*). 2. State's annual income from which public expenses are met (INLAND ~; ~ *tax*, imposed to raise ~, not to affect trade, opp. *protective*; ~ *cutter*, *officer*, etc., employed to prevent smuggling); department of civil service collecting it. [ME, f. OF, p.p. of *revenir* f. L *re*(*venire* come) return, RE- 9]

révĕrb'er|āte, v.t. & i. 1. Return, beat back, echo, reflect, (t. & i. of sound, light, heat; ~*ating furnace* or *kiln*, constructed to ~ate heat on substance dealt with,

whence ~atORY a. & n.). 2. (rare). (Of emotion etc.) react *upon*; (of ball etc.) rebound. So ~A'TION n., ~ATIVE, ~ANT (poet.), aa. [f. L RE- 9(*verberare* lash), -ATE³]

révĕrb'erātor, n. Reflector, reflecting lamp. [-OR]

révēre', v.t. Regard as sacred or exalted, hold in deep & usu. affectionate or religious respect, venerate. [f. F *révérer* or L RE(*vereri* fear)]

rĕv'erence, n., & v.t. 1. Revering (see prec.; *hold in*, *regard with*, ~; *feel* ~ *for*, *pay* ~ *to*); capacity for it (*the rising generation lacks* ~); (arch.) gesture showing it, bow, curtsy, obeisance; so rĕverĕn'tIAL (-shl) a., rĕverĕn'tialLY² adv. 2. Being revered (*saving your* ~, arch., apology for use of coarse term; *your*, *his*, ~, arch. or vulg. or joc., titles used to, of, clergyman). 3. v.t. Regard with ~, venerate. [ME f. OF, or L *reverentia* (prec., -ENCE)]

rĕv'erend, a. & n. 1. Deserving reverence, revered, (esp. as title, abbr. *Rev.*, or otherwise, of clergyman; *Very R*~, of dean; *Right R*~, of bishop; *Most R*~, of archbishop; *the Right R*~ *John Smith* or *the Right R*~ *the bishop of* —; *Rev.* or *the Rev. John* or *J. Smith*, or *the Rev. Mr Smith*; *the* ~ *gentleman*, the.clergyman in question; as n., usu. pl., = clergyman etc., as ~*s & right* ~*s*, clergy & bishops). 2. Of the clergy (~ *utterances* etc.). 3. (arch.). = foll. [ME, f. OF or L *reverendus* (REVERE, -ND¹)]

rĕv'erent, a. Feeling or showing reverence. Hence ~LY² adv. [ME, f. L *reverens* (REVERE, -ENT)]

rĕv'erie, n. (Fit of) musing, day-dream(ing), (*was lost in* ~ or *a* ~); (arch.) fantastic notion or theory, delusion; (mus.) dreamy instrumental piece. [ME, f. OF, f. *rever* to revel (mod. *rêver* dream), of obsc. orig.; see -ERY & cf. RAVE²]

revers (revār'), n. (pl. the same). Turned--back edge of coat, bodice, etc., displaying lining. [F]

révĕrse'¹, a. Opposite or contrary (*to*, or abs.) in character or order, inverted, back or backward, upside down, (*in the* ~ *direction to the time before*; *the* ~ *side* etc. *of a coin*, *picture*, etc.; ~ *fire*, *battery*, etc., playing on enemy's rear or into works from rear; ~ *flank*, opposite to pivot end in wheeling). Hence ~LY² (-slī) adv. [ME, f..OF *revers* or L *reversus* p.p. of *re*(*vertere vers*- turn), RE- 9]

révĕrse'², v.t. & i. 1. Turn (trans.) the other way round or up or inside-out, invert, transpose, convert to opposite character or effect, (~*e arms*, hold rifles butt upwards; ~*e motion*, *policy*, *order*, etc.; ~*e engine*, make it work backwards; ~ *the charge*, make recipient of telephone call responsible for payment. 2. Revoke, annul, (decree, attainder, etc.). 3. (Danc., esp. in waltz) begin to revolve in opposite direction. Hence ~'AL(2) n., ~'IBLE a., ~ĪBIL'ITY n. [ME, f. OF *reverser* f. LL RE(*versare* frequent. of *vertere* turn)]

re̅ve̅rse'[3], n. 1. *The* contrary (*of*, or abs.; *with others the* ~ *of this* or *the* ~ *happens*; *in* ~ in motoring, with car moving backwards; often w. adj. as periphr. for its opposite, as *made remarks the* ~ *of complimentary*). 2. (Device on) subordinate side of coin etc. (opp. OBVERSE; = VERSO. 3. = REVERSE[1] *side* (*take in* ~, subject to REVERSE[1] *fire*). 4. Piece of misfortune, disaster, esp. defeat in battle (*the* ~*s of fortune*; *suffered a* ~). [ME, f. OF (*-rs, -rse*) as REVERSE[1]]

re̅ve̅r'si, n. Game on draught-board with counters coloured differently above & below. [F]

re̅ve̅r'sion (-shn), n. 1. (Return fo grantor or his heirs or passing to ultimate grantee or ~ER[1] (-sho-) n. of, also right of ultimate succession to) estate granted till specified date or event, esp. death of original grantee (*in* ~, on such conditions). 2. Sum payable on person's death esp. by way of life-insurance. 3. Thing to which one has a right or expects to succeed when relinquished by another. 4. Return to a previous state, habit, etc., esp. (biol.) to ancestral type. Hence ~AL, ~ARY[1], aa., ~alLY[2] adv., (-sho-). [ME, f. OF, or L *reversio* (as REVERSE[1], -ION)]

re̅ve̅rt', v.i. & t., & n. 1. Go back (rare). 2. (Of property, office, etc.) fall in by REVERSION, whence ~ER[4] n. (legal). 3. Return to former state etc. (cf. prec.; n. after *convert*, *pervert*, person who readopts his original faith); (abs.) fall back into wild state. 4. Recur to subject in talk or thought. 5. Turn (eyes, rarely steps) back. [ME, f. OF *revertir* or L as prec.]

re̅ve̅rt'ible, a. (Of property) subject to reversion. [ME, f. med. L *revertibilis* (prec., -IBLE)]

re̅ve̅t', v.t. (-tt-). Face (rampart, wall, etc.) with masonry etc. esp. in fortification. [f. F *revêtir* f. LL re(*vestire* clothe f. VESTis), RE- 8]

re̅ve̅t'ment, n. Retaining-wall or facing (as prec.). [f. F *revêtement* (prec., -MENT)]

revictual. See RE- 8.

re̅vie̅w'[1] (-vū), n. 1. Revision (esp. legal; *is not subject to* ~; *court of* ~, before which sentences etc. come for revision). 2. Display & formal inspection of troops, fleet, etc. (~ *order*, dress & arrangement usu. at ~s, & transf., full fig; *pass in* ~, fig. t. & i., examine or be examined). 3. Retrospect, survey of the past. 4. Critique of book etc.; periodical publication with articles on current events, new books, art, etc. 5. Second view. [16th c. f. F *reveue* (now *-vue*) f. *revoir* (RE- 9, VIEW)]

re̅vie̅w'[2] (-vū), v.t. & t. 1. View again.

2. Subject to esp. legal revision. 3. Survey, glance over, look back on. 4. Hold review of (troops etc.). 5. Write review of (book etc.), write reviews, whence ~ER[1] (-vūer) n. Hence ~ABLE a., ~AL(2) n., (-vūa-). [f. RE- 9 + VIEW, after F *revoir*]

re̅vi̅le'[e', v.t. & i. Call by ill names, abuse, rail at; talk abusively, rail. Hence ~'ER[1], ~'ING[1](1), nn., ~'ingLY[2] adv. [ME, f. OF *reviler* (RE- 6, VILE)]

re̅vi̅s[e'[e' (-z), v.t., & n. 1. Read or look over or re-examine or reconsider & amend faults in (literary matter, printers' proofs, law, constitution, etc.; *R* ~*ed Version*, abbr. R.V., revision made 1870–84 of Authorized or 1611 Version of Bible); hence or cogn. ~'ABLE, ~'ORY, (-z-), aa., ~'AL(2) (-z-), re̅vi̅'sion (-zhn), nn., re̅vi̅'sionAL (-zho-) a., ~'ER[1] (-z-) n. (esp. in pl. of authors of R.V.). 2. n. Revision, ~ing, (rare); ~ed form (rare); (print.) proof-sheet embodying corrections made in earlier proof. [f. F *reviser* look at, or f. L *revisere* (*vidēre vis-* see), RE- 8]

revisit, see RE- 8; revitalize, RE- 9.

re̅vi̅v'al, n. 1. Bringing or coming back into vogue (~ *of learning, letters*, etc., at Renaissance; ~ *of architecture*, 19th-c. reversion to Gothic; ~ *of book, play, word, custom*, etc.). 2. (Special effort with meetings etc. to promote) reawakening of religious fervour, whence ~ISM(3), ~IST(2), nn. 3. Restoration to bodily or mental vigour or to life or consciousness. [foll., -AL(2)]

re̅vi̅v[e'[e', v.i. & t. Come or bring back to consciousness, life, existence, vigour, notice, activity, validity, or vogue; (chem.) restore (metal, esp. mercury) to natural form. Hence ~'ABLE a. [ME, f. OF *revivre* or LL re(*vivere* live), RE- 8]

re̅vi̅v'er, n. In vbl senses; esp.: (sl.) stimulating drink; preparation for restoring faded colour etc. [-ER[1]]

re̅vi̅v'i[fy̅, v.t. Restore to animation, activity, vigour, or life; (chem.) = REVIVE. Hence ~FICA'TION n. [f. F *revivifier* or LL re(*vivificare* VIVIFY), RE- 8]

re̅vi̅vis'cence, n., re̅vi̅vis'cent, a. Returning to life or vigour. [f. LL *reviviscentia* f. re(*viviscere* incept. of *vivere* live), RE- 8, -ENCE, -ENT]

‖ re̅vi̅v'or, n. (law). Proceeding for revival of suit after death of party etc. [REVIVE, -OR]

re̅vo̅ke', v.t. & i., & n. 1. Repeal, annul, withdraw, rescind, cancel, (decree, consent, promise, permission; also rarely abs., withdraw promise etc.), so re̅v'oc-ABLE, re̅v'ocatory, aa., re̅voca'tion n.; (cards) make ~. 2. n. Card-player's failure to follow suit though he could; (rare) revocation (*beyond* ~). [ME, f. OF *revoquer* or L re(*vocare* call), RE- 9]

re̅vo̅lt', v.i. & t., & n. 1. Cast off allegiance, make rising or rebellion, fall away *from* or rise *against* ruler, go over *to* rival power, (n., act of ~ing or state of having ~ed, rising, insurrection; so *in* ~; p.p. as -ED[1](2), as *his* ~*ed subjects*). **2.** Feel revulsion or disgust *at*, rise in repugnance *against*, turn in loathing *from*, (*common sense*, one's *heart*, ~*s at* or *against* or *from it*; n., sense of loathing, rebellious or protesting mood). **3.** Affect with strong disgust, nauseate, whence ~ING[2] a., ~ingLY[2] adv. [f. F *révolte(r)* f. Rom. *revolvitare* intensive of *revolvere* REVOLVE; RE- 2]

rĕv'olute[1] (-ŏŏt, -ūt), a. (bot. etc.). With back-rolled edge. [f. L REVOLVE*re*]

rĕvolute'[2] (-ŏŏt), v.i. (sl.). Engage in political revolution. [back formation f. foll.]

rĕvolu'tion (-lŏŏ-, -lū-), n. **1.** Revolving, motion in orbit or circular course or round axis or centre, rotation, single completion of orbit or rotation, time it takes, cyclic recurrence. **2.** Complete change, turning upside down, great reversal of conditions (INDUSTRIAL ~), fundamental reconstruction, esp. forcible substitution by subjects of new ruler or polity for the old (*the R*~, expulsion of James II 1688; *French R*~, overthrow of monarchy 1789 etc.; *American R*~, overthrow of British rule 1775 etc.), whence ~IZE(1, 3) v.t., ~ISM(3), ~IST(2), nn., (-ŏŏsho-, -ŭ-). [ME f. OF, or LL *revolutio* as REVOLVE, -ION]

rĕvolu'tionarў (-ŏŏsho-, -ŭ-), a. & n. (Instigator) of revolution; involving great & usu. violent changes; (rare) of rotation or revolving. [-ARY[1]]

révŏlve', v.t. & i. Turn (t. & i.) round or round & round, rotate, go in circular orbit, roll (intr.) along, (~ *problem*, *fact*, *in the mind* etc. or abs., ponder over it; *mechanism for revolving the turntable*; *Earth* ~*s both round or about sun & on its axis*; *seasons*, *years*, ~). [ME, f. L *re(volvere volut-* roll), RE- 6]

révŏl'ver, n. Pistol with revolving chambers enabling user to fire several shots without reloading (*policy of the big* ~, of threatening foreign States with retaliatory tariff). [-ER[1]]

révūe', n. Loosely constructed play or series of scenes or spectacles presenting or satirizing current events. [F]

révūl'sion (-shn), n. **1.** Counter-irritation, treatment of one disordered organ etc. by acting upon another. **2.** (rare). Drawing or being drawn away (*the* ~ *of capital from other trades*). **3.** Sudden violent change of feeling, sudden reaction in taste, fortune, trade, etc. [F, or f. L *revulsio* (*vellere vuls-* pull), RE- 9]

révūl'sive, a. & n. (chiefly med.). **1.** Of, producing, revulsion. **2.** n. Counter-irritant application. [prec., -IVE]

rĕward' (-wôrd), n., & v.t. **1.** Return or recompense for service or merit, requital

for good or evil, retribution; sum offered for detection of criminal, restoration of lost property, etc.; hence ~LESS a. **2.** v.t. Repay, requite, recompense, (service or doer of it, offender, offence). Hence ~ING[2] a., (of task, book, etc.) well worth doing, reading, etc. [ME, f. ONF *re-ward(er)* = OF REGARD[1](*er*)]

rewin, see RE- 9; **reword**, **rewrite**, RE- 8. **Rĕx**, n. (abbr. *R.*). Reigning king (in use as REGINA). [L]

Rey'nard (rĕn-, rān-), n. (Proper name for) the fox; a fox. [ME, f. OF *Renart* name of fox in the *Roman de Renart*]

rhăb'domăncў, n. Use of divining-rod, esp. for discovering subterranean water or ore. [f. Gk *rhabdomanteia* (*rhabdos* rod, -MANCY)]

Rhădămăn'th|us, n. Stern & incorruptible judge. Hence ~INE[2] a. [name of judge in Gk Hades]

Rhae'tian (rēshn), a. & n. ~ *Alps*, part of Alps about the Engadine; = RHAETO-ROMANIC a. & n. [L *Rhaetia*, -IAN]

Rhaet'ic, a. & n. (Of) *the* set of strata intermediate between Lias & Trias prevailing in Rhaetian Alps. [f. L *Rhaeticus* (prec., -IC)]

Rhaeto-Romăn'ic, -ănce', aa. & nn. (Of, in) any of the Romance dialects of SE. Switzerland & Tyrol, esp. Romansh & Ladin. [L *Rhaetus* Rhaetian, -O-]

rhăp'sŏde, n. Ancient-Greek minstrel or reciter of epic poems. [f. Gk *rhapsō(i)dos* (*rhaptō* stitch, ODE)]

rhăp'sod|ize, -|ise (-ĭz), v.t. & i. Recite (t. & i.) as rhapsode; talk or write rhapsodies (usu. *about*, *on*, etc.). So ~IST(1) n. [foll., -IZE]

rhăp'sodў, n. **1.** (Gk ant.) epic poem, or part of it, of length for one recitation. **2.** Enthusiastic extravagant high-flown utterance or composition, emotional irregular piece of music, whence rhăp-sŏd'ICAL a., rhăpsŏd'icalLY[2] adv. Hence rhăpsŏd'IC a. [f. L *rhapsodia* f. Gk *rhapsōidia* (RHAPSODE, -IA[1])]

rhăt'anў, n. (Extract, used medicinally & in adulterating port, of root of) S.-Amer. shrub. [f. Port. *ratanhia* f. native *rataña*]

rhe'a (rēa), n. S.-Amer. three-toed ostrich. [name of Gk goddess]

Rhĕm'ish, a. Of Rheims (~ *Bible*, *Testament*, *version*, *translation*, N.T. translated by Roman Catholics of English College at Rheims 1582). [obs. E *Rhemes*, -ISH]

Rhĕn'ish, a. & n. (arch.). **1.** Of the Rhine & districts on its banks (now usu. *Rhine* attrib.). **2.** n. ~ wine (now usu. *Rhine wine* or *hock*). [14th c. *rynis*, -*isch*, etc., f. MDu. *rijnisch*, G *rheinisch*, w. assim. to L *Rhenus* Rhine]

rhen'ium, n. Rare metallic element of manganese group, discovered in 1925. [f. L *Rhenus* Rhine, -IUM]

In words beginning with *rh* h is mute.

rhĕo-, rēo-, comb. form in chiefly electr. terms of Gk *rheos* stream, = current-, as *rheŏl'OGY*, study of flow & deformation of matter; *rhe'ostat*, apparatus for controlling supply of current, esp. to electric motors when starting up, by introducing variable resistance.

rhĕs'us, n. Small catarrhine monkey common in N. India; *R~ factor* (abbr. *Rh-factor*), substance occurring in red blood cells of most persons and some animals (as in the ~ monkey, in which it was first observed). Subjects in which this substance is present, absent, are said to be *Rh-positive, Rh-negative*. [arbitr. use of Gk *Rhēsus*, mythical king of Thrace]

rhĕt'or, n. Ancient Greek or Roman teacher or professor of rhetoric; (mere) orator (rare). [ME, f. L f. Gk *rhētōr*]

rhĕt'oric, n. (Treatise on) the art of persuasive or impressive speaking or writing; language designed to persuade or impress (often w. implication of insincerity, exaggeration, etc.); persuasiveness of or *of* looks or acts. [ME, f. OF *rethorique* or L f. Gk *rhētorikē* (*tekhnē* art) of RHETOR, -IC]

rhĕtŏ'rical, a. Expressed with a view to persuasive or impressive effect, artificial or extravagant in language, of the nature of rhetoric, (~ *question*, asked not for information but to produce effect, as *who cares?* for *nobody cares*); of the art of rhetoric; given to rhetoric, oratorical. Hence ~LY[2] adv. [ME, f. L f. Gk *rhētorikos* (RHETOR, -IC) + -AL]

rhĕtori'cian (-shn), n. = RHETOR; rhetorical speaker or writer. [ME, f. OF *rethoricien* (RHETORIC, -ICIAN)]

∥ **rheum** (rōōm), n. (arch.). Watery secretion or discharge of mucous membrane etc. such as tears, saliva, or mucus; catarrh; (pl.) rheumatic pains. [ME, f. OF *reume* f. LL f. Gk *rheuma -atos* stream (*rheŏ* flow)]

rheumăt'|ĭc (-ōō-), a. & n. **1.** Of, suffering from, subject to, producing, or produced by, rheumatism (~*ic fever*, non-infectious fever with inflammation & pain in joints; ~*ic walk* etc., impeded by ~ic stiffness); hence ~ICALLY adv., ~ĭcky[2] a. (colloq.), **rheu'mato-** comb. form, **rheu'matoID** a., (-ōō-). **2.** ~ic patient; (pl., colloq.) rheumatism. [ME, f. OF *reumatique* or L f. Gk *rheumatikos* (prec., -IC)]

∥ **rheu'mў** (-ōō-), a. (arch.). Consisting of, flowing with, rheum; (of air) damp, raw. [-Y[2]]

rhin'al, a. (anat. etc.). Of nostril or nose. [f. Gk *rhis rhinos* + -AL]

∥ **rhine**[1] (rēn), n. (SW. dial.). Large open ditch. [app. repr. OE *ryne* stream]

Rhine[2], n. German river (~ *wine*, kinds esp. of white wine from ~ vineyards, cf. RHENISH; ~'*stone*, kind of rock-crystal, also paste gem imitating diamond).

rhin'ō[1], n. (sl.). Money (often *ready* ~).

rhin'ō[2], n. (sl.; pl. ~*s*). (Short for) rhinoceros.

rhin|o-, comb. form of Gk *rhis rhinos* nostril, nose, as ~*opharyn'geal*, of nose & pharynx; ~*oplas'tic, rhin'oplasty*, (of) plastic surgery of the nose; *rhin'*OSCOPE, ~*oscŏp'ic,* ~*ŏs'copY*[1].

rhinŏ'ceros, n. Large pachydermatous African & S.-Asian quadruped with horn or two horns on nose & thick folded & plated skin. So **rhĭnŏcerŏt'IC** a. [ME, f. L f. Gk RHINO(*kerŏs* f. *keras* horn)]

rhiz'o-, comb. form of Gk *rhiza* root chiefly in bot. terms as ~*carp*, plant with perennial root but perishing stems.

rhiz'ōme, n. Prostrate rootlike stem emitting roots, rootstock. [f. Gk *rhizōma* (*rhizoomai* take root, as prec.)].

rhō, n. Greek letter (P, ρ) = r. [Gk]

Rhōde Isl'and (īl-) **Rĕd,** n. American breed of reddish-black domestic fowl. [f. *Rhode Island*, State of U.S.]

Rhodes schŏl'ar (rōdz sk-), n. Holder of any of a number of scholarships awarded annually & tenable at Oxford by candidates from certain Commonwealth countries, South Africa, and the United States. [Cecil *Rhodes*, founder]

Rhŏd'ian, a. & n. (Native) of Rhodes. [L *Rhodius* f. L f. Gk *Rhodos* Rhodes + -AN]

rhŏd'ium[1], n. (Also ~-*wood*) scented wood of Canary convolvulus, (*oil of* ~, oil got from it). [mod. L, neut. adj. (sc. *lignum* wood) = roselike f. Gk *rhodon* rose]

rhŏd'|ium[2], n. Hard white metal of platinum group (~*ium pen*, steel pen tipped with it). Hence ~IC, ~OUS, aa. (chem.). [Gk *rhodon* rose, -IUM, from colour of solution of its salts]

rhŏdo-, comb. form of Gk *rhodon* rose, found chiefly in names of mineral and chem. substances, as ~*chrŏ'site* (-kr-), carbonate of manganese occurring in rose-red crystals.

rhŏdoden'dron, n. Kinds of large-flowered evergreen shrubs akin to azalea. [L f. Gk (prec., *dendron* tree)]

rhŏmb (-b usu. mute exc. before vowel), n. Oblique equilateral parallelogram, as ace of diamonds on playing-card, object or part with such outline; (cryst.) rhombohedron. Hence **rhŏm'bIC** a., **rhŏm'bo-** comb. form. [f. F *rhombe*, or L f. Gk *rhombos*]

rhŏmbohĕd'r|on, n. (chiefly cryst.; pl. ~*a*, ~*ons*). (Crystal in shape of) solid bounded by six equal rhombs. Hence ~AL a. [RHOMBO- (prec.), Gk *hedra* base]

rhŏm'boid, a. & n. **1.** Of or near the shape of a rhomb (~ *muscle*, connecting scapula with vertebrae). 2. n. Quadrilateral of which only opposite sides & angles are equal; ~ muscle. [f. F *rhomboïde* or LL f.˙Gk *rhomboeidēs* (RHOMB, -OID)]

rhŏmboid'al, a. Having shape of a rhomboid (prec.).); = prec. (adj.). Hence ~LY² adv. [prec., -AL]

rhŏm'bus, n. (pl. *-buses, -bī*). 1. = RHOMB. 2. Kinds of flat-fish including turbot & brill. [L (RHOMB)]

rhŏt'acism, n., **rhŏt'acize** (*or -ise, pr. -īz*), v.i. (Speak with) excessive or peculiar pronunciation of *r*; conversion of, convert, other sounds into *r*. [f. Gk *rhōtakizō* (RHO, -IZE, -ISM)]

rhu'barb (rōō-), n. 1. (Purgative made from) root of Chinese & Tibetan plant (usu. *Chinese, East Indian, Russia,* or *Turkey* ~, from channels of importation). 2. (Fleshy leaf-stalks of) kinds of garden plant, cooked in spring as substitute for fruit (occas. *English, French, common,* or *garden*~). 3. attrib. (Of colour) yellowish-brown like Chinese ~. Hence ~Y² a. [ME, f. OF *rubarbe* f. med. L *rhabarbarum* foreign 'rha' or rhubarb (*rha* Gk, perh. f. *Rha* the Volga, BARBAROUS), w. assim. to L f. Gk *rhēon* rhubarb]

rhŭmb (-m), n. (naut.). (Also ~*-line*) line cutting all meridians at same angle, line followed by ship sailing on one course; angular distance between two successive points of compass, 11° 15′. [f. F *rumb* or Sp. *rumbo* f. L RHOMBUS]

rhyme¹, rime, n. 1. Identity of sound between words or verse-lines extending from the end to the last fully accented vowel & not further (greet & deceit, shepherd & leopard, quality & frivolity, stationary & probationary, is it & visit, give ~s, but seat & deceit, station & crustacean, visible & invisible, do not; single or male or masculine, double or female or FEMININE, treble or triple, quadruple,~, according to number of syllables included; *imperfect* ~, as in love & move, phase & race; *without* ~ *or reason,* quite unaccountable, -bly). 2. Verse marked by ~s (pl. or sing.), a poem with ~s, the employment of ~, (*should be written in* ~; *prefer blank verse to* ~; *am sending you some* ~s; NURSERY ~; *was reading an old* ~; ~ *royal,* stanzas of seven ten-syllable lines with ~s as *ababbcc,* as· in Chaucer's *Clerkes Tale* etc.). 3. Word providing a ~ (*to another; can't find a* ~ *to* teacups; *English is badly off for double* ~s). Hence ~'LESS (-ml-) a., ~'lèssNESS n. [17th c. var. (w. assim. to RHYTHM) of ME f. OF *rime* f. L f. Gk *rhuthmos* RHYTHM]

rhyme², rime, v.i. & t. Write rhymes, versify (intr.), whence rhym'ER¹, rhyme'-STER (-ms-), nn.; put or make (story etc.) into rhyme (~*d verse,* opp. *blank verse*); while (time) *away* in rhyming; (of words or lines) exhibit rhyme, (of word) supply or act as rhyme *to* or *with,* (of person)

treat (word) as rhyming *with,* select rhymes, (~s *carelessly*; ~s law *with* four; *rhym*ING¹*-dictionary,* of words arranged by terminations for versifiers' use), whence rhym'IST(1) n. [17th c. var. of ME *rime* f. OF *rimer* (see prec.)]

rhy'thm (-dhm, -thm), n. 1. Metrical movement determined by various relations of long & short or accented & unaccented syllables, measured flow of words & phrases in verse or prose. 2. That feature of musical composition concerned with periodical accent & the duration of notes. 3. (art). Harmonious correlation of parts. 4. (Phys., physiol., & gen.) movement with regular succession of strong & weak elements. Hence or cogn. rhyth'mIC(AL) aa., rhyth'micaLLY² adv., rhythm'LESS a., rhyth'mIST(3) n., (-dh--th-). [f. L f. Gk *rhuthmos* cf. *rheō* flow]

ri'ant, a. Smiling, cheerful, (of face, eyes, etc., & esp. of landscape). [F (*rire* f. L *ridēre* laugh, -ANT)]

rib, n., & v.t. (-bb-). 1. One of curved bones reaching from spine round upper part of body (*true, sternal,* ~, joined also to breastbone, opp. *false, floating, short,* ~; *poke one in the* ~s, to draw his attention facetiously; *smite under fifth* ~, bibl., *stab mortally; ~ or ~s of beef* etc., as joint of meat; SPARE-~); (joc. w. ref. to *Gen.* ii. 21) wife, woman. 2. Ridge or long raised piece often of thicker material across thinner surface serving to support as part of framework or strengthen or adorn, e.g. vein of leaf, shaft of feather, spur of mountain, vein of ore, ridge between furrows, wave-mark on sand, raised line in knitting, one of ship's curved timbers to which planks are nailed or corresponding ironwork, arch supporting vault, groin, raised moulding on groin or across ceiling etc., wooden or iron beam helping to carry bridge, hinged rod of umbrella-frame. 3. ~*-grass,* ~*'wort,* PLANTAIN¹ with long narrow leaves. Hence (~)~bED²(-bd), ~'LESS, aa. 4. v.t. Provide with ~s, act as ~s of, whence ~b'ING¹(3, 6) n.; mark with ridges; plough with ~s between furrows, half-plough, rafter; (sl.) make fun of, tease. [OE *rib(b),* OHG *rippi,* ON *rif,* also OS *ribba,* OHG *rippa,* f. Gmc **rebja-*]

rib'ald, n. & a. 1. Irreverent jester, user of scurrilous, blasphemous, or indecent language; so ~RY(4, 5) n. 2. adj. (Of language or its user) scurrilous, obscene, irreverent. [ME, earlier sense *low-born retainer,* f. OF *ribaut, ribault,* f. *riber* pursue licentious pleasures]

rib'and n., **rib'andèd** a. = RIBBON(*ed*). [ME, f. OF *riban* (now *ru-*)]

ribb'and, n. Wale, strip, scantling, or light spar, of wood, used esp. in shipbuilding to hold ribs in position, launching, & making of gun-platform or pontoon-bridge. [f. RIB, BAND¹, or f. prec.]

ribb'on, n. **1.** (Piece or length of) silk or satin or other fine material woven into narrow band esp. for adorning costume; ~ of special colour etc. worn to indicate membership of knightly order, club, college, athletic team, etc. (BLUE¹~; R~ *Society* (hist.), Irish R.-C. secret society formed in early 19th c. & associated with agrarian crime, whence R~ISM n.). **2.** Long narrow strip of anything, (pl.) driving-reins, (*hang in, torn to,*~s, ragged strips; *handle, take, the* ~s, drive). **3.** ~ *building,* ~ *development,* the building of houses along a main road, extending outwards from a town; ~*-fish,* long slender flat kinds; ~*-grass,* slender-leaved kind; ~*-man,* member of R~ Society. Hence (-)~ED²(-nd) a. [ME, var. of RIBAND]

rīb'ēs (-z), n. (bot.). Currant or gooseberry plant; (pop.) flowering currant. [med. L, = sorrel, f. Arab. *ribas*]

Rib'ston pipp'in, n. Kind of dessert apple. [*Ribston* Park in Yorks.]

Ricard'ian, a. & n. (Adherent) of the political economist Ricardo (d. 1823), according to his views. [-IAN]

rīce, n. (Pearl-white seeds, used as staple food in many Eastern countries, & in Britain in puddings, cakes, etc., or as table-vegetable, of) chiefly oriental plant grown in marshes; ~*-bird,* Java sparrow, also bobolink; ~*-milk,* boiled & thickened with ~; ~*-paper,* kind made from pith of a Formosan plant & used by Chinese artists for painting on (named after ~ in error). [ME, f. OF *ris* f. It. *riso* f. Rom. *orizum* f. L f. Gk *oruza* of Oriental orig.]

rich, a. **1.** (Of persons, societies, States, etc.) wealthy, having riches, (also as n. in *the* ~, ~ *& poor*). **2.** (Of countries, periods, soil, etc.) abounding in or *in* natural resources or some valuable possession or production, fertile. **3.** Valuable (~ *offerings, a* ~ *harvest*). **4.** (Of dress, furniture, buildings, banquets, etc.) splendid, costly, elaborate, (*with* lace, sculpture, etc.). **5.** (Of food or diet) containing or involving large proportion of fat, oil, butter, eggs, spice, etc. **6.** (Of colours, sounds, smells) mellow, deep, full, not thin. **7.** Abundant, ample. **8.** (Of incidents) highly amusing, full of entertainment or material for humour. **9.** (Of mixture in internal--combustion engines) highly combustible. **10.** ~-, richly (~*-clad, -bound, -glittering,* etc.). Hence ~'EN⁶ v.i. & t. (rare), ~'NESS n. [OE *rīce,* OS *rīki,* OHG *rīchi,* ON *rīkr,* Goth. *reiks,* f. an early Gmc adoption of Celt. **rīx* = L *rex* king]

Rich'ard, pers. name. ~ *Rōe,* fictitious character in law (cf. JOHN *Doe*); ~*'s himself again* (f. interpolation in Cibber's version of Shaks. ~ *III*), said by or of person recovered from despondency, fear, illness, etc.

rich'es (-ĭz), n. (usu. as pl.). Abundant means, wealth, valuable possessions,

being rich. [ME *richesse* f. OF (*riche* RICH, -ESS²), apprehended as pl.]

rich'lȳ, adv. In adj. senses; also (chiefly with *deserve*) fully, thoroughly, (~ *deserves a thrashing, to succeed*). [-LY²]

rick¹, n., & v.t. **1.** Stack of hay, corn, peas, etc., esp. one regularly built & thatched; ||~*-barton,* = ~*-yard;* ~*-cloth,* canvas cover for unfinished ~; ~*-stand,* short wooden or stone pillars bearing joists to raise ~ from ground; ~*-yard,* enclosure for ~s. **2.** v.t. Form into ~(s). [OE *hrēac* = MDu. *rooc,* ON *hraukr,* of unkn. orig.]

rick². See WRICK.

rick'ets, n. (as sing. or pl.; *-et* in comb. etc., as *ricket-producing, rickety*). Children's disease with softening of bones, esp. of spine, & bow-legs etc., rachitis. [described as 'The Rickets' by D. Whistler (1645); assoc. w. Gk RACHITIS, adopted as its scientific name]

rick'etȳ, a. **1.** Suffering from, of (the nature of), rickets. **2.** Feeble, shaky, tottering, weak-jointed, fragile, insecure, (of persons or things, esp. furniture). Hence ~INESS n. [-Y²]

ricksha(w). See JINRICKSHA.

ric'ochet (-shā, -shĕt), n., & v.i. & t. (-t- or -tt-, *pr.* -shåd *or* -shĕtĭd, -shåing *or* -shĕtĭng etc.). **1.** Skipping on water or ground of projectile esp. shell or bullet, hit made after it, (often attrib., as ~ *fire, shot*). **2.** vb. (Of projectile) skip once or more; (of gun, gunner, etc.) hit or aim at with ~ shot(s). [F, of unkn. orig.]

ric'tus, n. Expanse or gape of person's or animal's mouth, bird's beak, or flower with two-lipped corolla. [L *rĭngi* open the mouth)]

rid, v.t. (past **ridded, rid**; p.p. **rid,** rarely **ridded**). Make (person, place) free, disencumber, *of* (usu. in p.p. with *be* or *get; glad to be, must get,* ~ *of him*); (arch.) abolish, clear away, get ~ of, (pest). Hence ~**d'**ANCE n. (esp. *a good* ~*dance,* as excl. of joy; person etc. *is a good* ~*dance,* better away). [ME, earlier sense *clear* (land etc.); f. ON *rythja*]

rid(d)'el, n. (eccl.). Altar-curtain. [ME, f. OF *ridel* (F *rideau*) curtain]

ridden. See RIDE.

rid'dle¹, n., & v.i. & t. Question, statement, or description, designed or serving to test ingenuity of hearers in divining its answer or meaning or reference, conundrum, enigma; puzzling or mysterious fact, thing, or person. **2.** vb. Speak in, propound, (part.) expressed in, ~s, whence **rĭdd'lĭng**LY² adv.; solve (~; often ~ *me* as challenge²). [OE *rǣdels*(e) (= OS *rādisli, -lo,* OHG *rādisle*) f. *rǣdan* READ +*-els* as in BURIAL]

rid'dle², n., & v.t. **1.** Coarse sieve for corn, gravel, cinders, etc.; plate with pins used in straightening wire. **2.** v.t. Pass (corn etc.) through ~, sift, (fig.) test (evidence, truth); fill (ship, person) with holes esp. of gunshot, (fig.) pelt with questions, refute (person, theory) with facts. [OE *hriddel*, earlier *hrid(d)er* f. *hrid*-shake, cogn. w. OHG (*h*)*ritera* sieve]

ride, v.i. & t. (*rōde*, arch. *rid*; *ridden* pr. ri'dn, arch. *rid*), & n. **1.** Sit on & be carried by horse etc., go on horseback etc. or on bicycle etc. or in train or other public conveyance (cf. DRIVE¹), sit or go or be *on* something as on horse esp. astride, sit on & manage horse, lie at anchor, float buoyantly, (of sun etc.) seem to float, (of things normally level or even) project or overlap, (~ *a-*COCK-HORSE, BODKIN, ROUGH-*shod*, *50 miles*, *full speed*, *a race*; ~ *to hounds*, hunt; ~ *for a fall*, ~ or fig. act recklessly, court defeat; ~ *12 st.* etc., weigh that in riding-trim; ~ *over*, in horse-racing as WALK *over*; ~ one *down*, overtake him by riding, also put one's horse at him; ~ one *off* at polo, edge him away; ~ *off on* a side issue, use it to evade the main point; ~ & *tie*, of two or more travellers sharing horse, one riding ahead & then leaving it tied to await the other; *riding on his father's shoulders*, *back*, *knee*, *foot*; ~*s well*, *cannot* ~, *learn to* ~, *riding*--*lessons* or -*school*; *bird*, *ship*, ~*s on the wind*, *waves*; *ship rode at anchor*; ~ *out the storm* lit. & fig., come safely through it; *moon was riding high*; *bone* ~*s* in fracture, one part overlaps other; *rope* ~*s*, has one turn crossing over another); traverse on horseback etc., ~ over or through, (~ *the country*, *desert*, etc.; ~ *a ford*, pass through it on horseback). **2.** ~ on, sit heavily on, oppress, haunt, dominate, tyrannize over, (~ *horse*; ~ one's *horse at* fence or enemy, urge it forward; ~ one's *horse*, & fig. hobby or method or jest, *to death*, kill or overdo it; *nightmare* ~*s* sleeper; ~ *the whirlwind*, direct it; *ship* ~*s the waves*; *ridden by fears*, *prejudices*, etc.; *priest* etc. -*ridden*). **3.** Give ~ to, cause to ~, (~ *child on* one's *back*; ~ one *on rail*, carry him astride on it as torture). **4.** (Of ground) be of specified character for riding on (~*s well*, *soft*, *hard*, etc.); hence rid'ABLE a. **5.** n. Journey in public conveyance, spell of riding on horse, bicycle, person's back, etc.; *take for a* ~ (sl.), drive (person) away in a motor-car prior to murdering him. **6.** Road esp. through wood for riding on. **7.** (mil.). Batch of mounted recruits. [OE (OS) *ridan*, OHG *ritan*, ON *ritha* f. Gmc *ridan*]

rid'el. See RIDDEL.

rid'er, n. In vbl senses; also or esp.: **1.** (naut.). (Pl.) additional set of timbers or iron plates strengthening ship's frame; (sing.) overlying rope or rope-turn. **2.** (curl.). Stone that ousts another. **3.** Additional clause amending or supplementing document, esp. parliamentary bill at third reading; corollary, naturally arising supplement; expression of opinion, recommendation etc., added to verdict.

4. (math.). Problem testing student's mastery of principles on which its solution depends. **5.** Piece in machine etc. that surmounts or bridges or works over others. Hence ~LESS a. [OE *ridere* (RIDE)]

ridge, n., & v.t. & i. **1.** Line of junction of two surfaces sloping upwards towards each other (*the* ~ *of a roof*, *the nose*, etc.); long narrow hill-top, mountain range, watershed; (agric.) one of a set of raised strips separated by furrows; (gard.) raised hotbed for melons etc.; any narrow elevation across surface; ~-*piece*, beam along ~ of roof; ~-*pole*, horizontal pole of long tent, also = ~-*piece*; ~-*tile*, used for roof~; ~-*tree*, = ~-*piece*; ~-*way*, road along ~; hence ridg'Y² a. **2.** vb. Break up (land) into ~s; mark with ~s; plant (cucumbers etc.) in ~s; gather (t. & i. esp. of sea) into ~s. [OE *hrycg*, MDu. *rugghe*, MLG *rugge*, OHG *hrucci*, ON *hryggr* f. Gmc **hrugjaz*]

rid'icule, n., & v.t. **1.** Ridiculous thing, ridiculousness, (arch.); holding or being held up as laughing-stock, derision, mockery. **2.** v.t. Make fun of, subject to ~, laugh at. [F, or f. L *ridiculum* neut. of *ridiculus* laughable (*ridēre* laugh)]

ridic'ulous, a. Deserving to be laughed at, absurd, unreasonable. Hence ~LY² adv., ~NESS n. [as prec.+-OUS, or f. L *ridiculosus*]

rid'ing¹, n. In vbl senses; also, road for riders, esp. green track through or beside wood; ~-*breeches*; ~-HABIT¹; ~-*lamp*, -*light* (borne by ship at anchor). [-ING¹]

‖ rid'ing², n. Administrative division (*East*, *W.*, or *N.*, *R*~) of Yorkshire; similar division of other U.-K. or colonial county. [for *thriding* (f. ON *thrithjungr* THIRD, -ING³) third part, with loss of *th*-owing to preceding -t(h) of *east* etc.]

Ries'ling (ree-), n. A dry white table--wine. [G]

rīfaci̇́měn'tō (-ahch-), n. (pl. -*ti* pr. -tē). Remodelled form of a literary work or the like. [It.]

rife, pred. a. Of common occurrence, met with in numbers or quantities, prevailing, current, numerous, (usu. *be*, also *grow*, *wax*, etc., ~); well provided *with* (*language is* ~ *with maxims*). Hence ~'NESS (-fn-) n. [OE *rȳfe* = MDu., MLG *rive*, ON *rífr*]

Riff, a. & n. (Of) a Berber of the *Rif* district of Morocco. So ~'IAN a. & n.

rif'fle, n. (In gold-washing) groove or slat set in the trough or sluice to catch the gold particles. [orig. unkn.]

riff'-raff, n. *The* rabble, disreputable persons. [ME *rif & raf* f. OF *rif et raf*]

ri'fle¹, v.t. & i. **1.** Search & rob, esp. of all that can be found in various pockets or storing-places; carry off as booty. **2.** Make spiral grooves in (gun or its barrel or bore) to produce rotatory motion in projectile (p.p. of projectile, with projections fitting such grooves). **3.** Shoot (t.

& i.) with rifle. Hence **rif′ling**[1] n. [(1)ME,
f. OF *rifler* graze, scratch, plunder; (2)
from 1635, f. obs. Flem. *riffelen* scrape,
LG *rifeln* to groove f. *rife* groove; (3) f.
foll.]

ri′fle[2], n. **1.** One of the grooves made in
rifling a gun (obs.). **2.** (Formerly ~-*gun*)
fire-arm with rifled barrel esp. one fired
from shoulder; (pl.) troops armed with
~s. **3.** ~-*bird*, dark-green Australian
bird; ‖ *R*~ *Brigade*, regiment of British
army; ~-*corps*, of volunteer ~men;
~(-)*green* n. & a., (of) dark green as in
~man's uniform; ~-*GRENADE*; ~*man*,
soldier armed with ~, esp. member (*R*~-
man when prefixed = Private) of some
~ regiments in British army, also = ~-
-*bird*; ~-*pit*, excavation as cover for ~
men firing at enemy; ~-*range*, distance
~ carries, place for ~-*practice*; ~-*shot*,
distance ~ carries, *good* etc. ~-*marksman*,
shot fired with ~. [f. prec.; cf. obs. Flem.
rijffel, LG *riffel* groove]

rift, n., & v.t. **1.** Cleft, fissure, chasm, in
earth or rock; rent, crack, split in an
object, opening in cloud etc. (*little* ~
within the lute, often fig. of incipient madness or dissension); ~-*valley*, steep-sided
formed by subsidence of earth's crust;
hence ~′LESS, ~′Y[2], aa. **2.** v.t. (Usu. in
p.p.) rend apart, cleave. [ME, of Scand.
orig.; cf. Da., Norw. *rift* cleft, OIcel. *ript*
breach; cogn. w. RIVE]

rig[1], v.t. & i. (-gg-), & n. **1.** Provide (ship),
(of ship) be provided, with necessary
spars, ropes, etc., or ~g′ING[1](3) (-g-) n.,
prepare (t. & i.) for sea in this respect;
assemble & adjust parts of (aircraft);
fit (*out*, *up*, or rarely abs.) with or *with*
clothes or other equipment; set *up*
(structure) hastily or as makeshift or by
utilizing odd materials; ~-*ging-loft*, gallery
in dockyard for fitting ~*ging*, (theatr.)
space over stage from which scenery is
manipulated. **2.** n. Way ship's masts,
sails, etc., are arranged, whence ~~gED[2]
(-gd) a.; (transf.) person's or thing's look
as determined by clothes etc. (~-*up*, *-out*,
such accessories); *in full* ~ (colloq.),
smartly dressed. [ME, of unkn. orig.; the
syn. Norw., Sw. *rigga*, Da. *rigge* are prob.
f. E]

rig[2], n., & v.t. (-gg-). **1.** Trick, dodge, way
of swindling; (commerc.) = CORNER. **2.**
v.t. Manage or conduct fraudulently (~
the market, cause artificial rise or fall in
prices). [orig. unkn.]

‖ **rig**[3], n. Imperfectly developed or
partially castrated male animal. [late
ME, f. ON *hyrggr* = OE *hrycg* back,
RIDGE]

Rig′a (*or* rē-), n. A port of the Baltic (~
deal, *hemp*, etc.; = *balsam*, essential oil
distilled from kind of pine & used
medicinally).

rigadoon′, n. Lively dance for two persons; music for this dance. [F *rigaudon*]

rig′es′c|**ent**, a. Growing rigid, rather stiff.

So ~ENCE n. [f. L *rigescere* (*rigēre* be stiff,
-ESCENT)]

rigg′er (-g-), n. In vbl senses (RIG[1,2]); also
or esp.: one who attends to the rigging
of aircraft; (mech.) band-wheel; = OUT-
RIGGER; = THIMBLE-~; ~, ship rigged in
specified way. [-ER[1]]

right (rīt), a., v.t. & i., n., & adv. **1.** (arch.).
Straight (now only in ~ *line*, ~-*lined*).
2. (Of angle) neither acute nor obtuse,
of 90°, made by lines meeting not
obliquely but perpendicularly, (*at* ~
angles, turning or placed with such angle),
whence ~-*ángl*ED[2] (-nggld) a.; involving
~ angle(s), not oblique, (~ *sailing*, due
N., S., E., or W.; ~ ASCENSION; ~ *cone*,
cylinder, *prism*, etc., with ends or base
perpendicular to axis). **3.** (Of conduct
etc.) just, morally good, required by
equity or duty, proper, (*acted a* ~ *part*;
it is only ~ *to tell you*, *that you should
know*), whence ~-*mind*ED[2] a., ~-
-*mind*′ed*ED*NESS ñ. **4.** Correct, true, (~ *use
of words*; *did not give a* ~ *account of the
matter*; *your opinions are* ~ *enough*);
the preferable or most suitable, the less
wrong or not wrong, (*which is the* ~ *way
to* —?; *the* ~ *man in the* ~ *place*; *does not
do it the* ~ *way*; *the* ~ *heir*; *took the* ~
way to offend us; *a fault on the* ~ *side*; *the
~ side of a fabric etc.*, that meant for
show or use; so ~ *side up*; *on the* ~ *side of
forty* etc., not yet 40 years old). **5.** In
good or normal condition, sound, sane,
satisfactory, well-advised, not mistaken,
(*in one's* ~ *mind*, not mad etc.; *is not* ~ *in
his head*; *are you* ~ *now?*, comfortable,
recovered, etc.; *all's* ~ *with the world*; *is
as* ~ *as a trivet*, *as rain*, etc., quite; *set* or
put ~, restore to order, health, etc., also
correct mistaken ideas of, also justify
oneself usu. *with* person; *get* ~, bring or
come into ~ state; ~, ~ *you are*, forms of
approval, or, & so also *all* ~, ‖ ~ *oh!* sl.,
of assent to order or proposal), whence
‖ ~′EN[6] (rīt-) v.t. (rare). **6.** (arch.). Rightful, real, veritable, properly so called, (~
WHALE; ~ *cognac* etc.). **7.** (Of position)
having the relation to front & back that
equinoctial sunrise has to north & south,
on or towards that side of human body of
which the hand is normally more used,
on or towards that part of an object
which is analogous to person's ~′*side* or
(with opposite sense) which is nearer to
spectator's ~ *hand*, (cf. LEFT[1]; ~ *side*, *eye*,
etc.; ~ *wing* or *flank* of army etc.; ~ *bank*,
on ~ *side* of one looking down stream; ~
CENTRE[1]). **8.** ~ *& left*: adv., to or on both
sides, on all hands, as *the crowd divided*,
he was abused, ~ *& left*; adj., with or of or
to both hands or sides, as *a* ~-*& -left shot*,
with both barrels, ~-*& -left screw*, with
contrary threads at two ends; n., ~-*&*-
-*left shot*, also pugilist's two blows in
quick succession with different hands.
9. ~ *arm*, (fig.) one's most reliable helper.
10. ~ *hand*: hand of ~ *side*; this as the

better hand, as *put* one's ~ *hand to the work*; this w. ref. to handshaking, and *give the* ~ *hand of fellowship*; region or direction on this side of person, as *at, on, to,* one's ~ *hand*; one's indispensable or chief assistant; ~-*hand,* placed on the ~ hand; ~-*hand man,* soldier on one's ~ hand in line, also assistant as above; ~--*hand screw,* with thread turning to ~; ~--*handed,* using ~ hand more than left; ~-*handed blow* etc., struck with ~ hand; ~-*handed tool* etc., made to suit ~ hand; ~-*handed rotation* etc.; ~-*hander,* ~--*handed* blow or person. 11. ~ *turn,* that brings one's front to face as one's ~ side did before; ~-*about turn* or *face,* ~ turn prolonged to rear (see ABOUT¹ for mil. use); ~-*about,* = ~-about turn, reversal of front, hurried retreat as in *send to the* ~-*about,* send packing; also as v.t. & i. = reverse or make reverse front; hence ~'NESS (rīt-) n. 12. vb. Restore to proper .or straight or vertical position (~ *helm,* put it amidships; *boat* ~s *herself; could not* ~ *the boat, car*); ~ *oneself,* recover balance, (of ship) recover vertical position. 13. Make reparation for or to, avenge, (wrong, wronged person); vindicate, justify, rehabilitate. 14. Correct (mistakes etc.), correct mistakes in, set in order, (often refl., as *that is a fault that will* ~ *itself*); hence ~'ABLE (rīt-) a. 15. n. What is just, fair treatment, (~ *& might,* ~ *& wrong; do one* ~, treat or think of him fairly; *by*~ or now usu. ~s, *if* ~ *were done; the*~, the juster cause, as *God defend the*~; *be in the*~, have justice or truth on one's side). 16. Justification, fair claim, being entitled to privilege or immunity, thing one is entitled to, (*has a, the, no,* ~ *to thing, to do, of doing, of search* etc.; ~ *divine* or DIVINE~; *claims in*~ *of his wife; reigns by*~ *of worth; belongs to him of or by* ~; ~s *& duties; woman's* ~s, of equality with men; ~ *of way,* ~ established by usage to pass over another's ground, also path subject to such ~, precedence in passing granted to one vehicle etc. over another; *Declaration* or *Bill of R*~s, ‖ constitutional settlement of 1689; *assert* or *stand on one's* ~s, refuse to relinquish them; *peeress in her own*~, not by marriage; *admiration is her*~), whence ~'LESS (rīt-) a. 17. pl. ~ condition, true state, (*set* or *put to* ~s, arrange properly; *have not heard, do not know, the* ~s *of the case*). 18. ~-hand part or region or direction (*is on your* or *the, to the,* ~; *to, from,* ~ *& left; work round the enemy's* ~); (pol., usu. R~) conservative members of (orig. continental) parliament etc., whence ~'WARD a. & adv., ~'WARDS adv., (rīt-). 19. adv. Straight (*wind was* ~ *behind us; go* ~ *on; went* ~ *at him;* ~ *off, away,* chiefly U.S., immediately, without pause). 20. All the way to, round, etc., completely off, out, etc., (*sank* ~ *to the bottom; veranda* ~ *round house; took gate* ~ *off hinges; turned* ~ *round*). 21. Exactly, quite, (~ *in the middle*). 22. Very, to the full, (*know* ~ *well; banqueted* ~ *royally; was* ~ *glad to hear;* ‖~ HONOURABLE, REVEREND; ~-*down,* thorough, -ly, *as is a* ~-*down scoundrel, was* ~-*down sorry*). 23. Justly, properly, correctly, aright, truly, satisfactorily, (*whether they act* ~ *or wrong; does not hold his pen, do the sum,* ~; *serves him* ~, is no worse than he deserves; *nothing goes* ~ *with me; if I remember* ~; *guessed* ~). 24. To ~ hand (*eyes* ~ !, order to soldiers dressing; *looks neither* ~ *nor left*). [OE *riht* adj., = OS, OHG *reht,* ON *rétlr;* Goth *raihts,* rel. to L *rectus*]

righteous (rīch'us), a. Just, upright, virtuous, law-abiding, (of person, life, action). Hence ~LY² adv., ~NESS n. [OE *rihtwis* (prec. n. + WISE a., or prec. a. + WISE n.) w. assim. to bounteous etc.]

right'ful (rīt'-), a. (Of actions etc.) equitable, fair; (of persons) legitimately entitled to position etc. (*the* ~ *king, heir, owner*), (of office, property, etc.) that one is entitled to. Hence ~LY² adv., ~NESS n. [-FUL]

right'ly (rīt-), adv. Justly, fairly, properly, correctly, accurately, justifiably. [-LY²]

ri'gid, a. Not flexible, stiff, unyielding, (*a* ~ *bar, stem, frame, airship*); inflexible, harsh, strict, precise, punctilious, (~ *justice, principles, Catholics, adherence to rules, economy*). Hence or cogn. **rigid'ITY** n., ~LY² adv. [f. L *rigidus* (as RIGOR)]

rig'marole, n. Rambling or meaningless talk or tale; (attrib.) incoherent. [alt. f. obs. *ragman roll* = catalogue, orig. unkn.]

rig'or, n. (path.). Sudden chill with shivering before fever etc.; ~ *mort'is,* stiffening of body after death. [L (*rigēre* be stiff, -OR)]

rig'our (-ger), n. Severity, strictness, harshness, (pl.) harsh measures; strict enforcement of rules etc. (*with the utmost* ~ *of the law*); extremity or excess of weather, hardship, famine, etc., great distress; austerity of life, Puritanic strictness of observance or doctrine, so **rig'orISM**(3), **rig'orIST**(2), nn.; logical accuracy, exactitude. So **rig'orous** a., **rig'orousLY²** adv. [ME, f. OF f. L *rigor* (prec.)]

rigs'dåg (-z-), n. Former name of Danish parliament (now *folketing*). [Da.]

Rig-ve'da (-vā-), n. The chief VEDA. [f. Skr. *rigveda* (ric praise)]

riks'dåg, n. Swedish parliament. [Sw.]

rile, v.t. (sl.). Raise anger in, irritate. [var. of obs. & U.S. *roil* make muddy]

rilie'vo (rēlyā-), n. = RELIEF², RELIEVO. [It.]

rill, n., & v.i. 1. Small stream, runnel, rivulet; hence ~'ET¹ n. 2. v.i. Issue or flow as ~. [ME, f. LG *ril, rille*]

rille, n. (astron.). Trench or narrow valley of moon's surface. [G, as prec.]

rillettes', -êttes' (-êts), n. pl. Preparation of minced ham, chicken, fat, etc. [F (-es)]

rim¹, n., & v.t. (-mm-). 1. Outer ring of

wheel's framework, not including tire; frame of sieve; (poet.) circular object (*golden* ~, crown); (naut.) surface of the water; raised edge or border, margin, verge, esp. of something more or less circular; ~-*brake*, acting on ~ of wheel; hence ~'LESS, (-)~MED[2] (-md), aa. 2. v.t. Furnish with ~, serve as ~ to, edge, border. [OE *rima*, = ON *rimi* ridge]

‖ rim[2], n. (arch.). ~ (*of the belly*), peritoneum. [OE *rēoma*, OS *reomo*, OHG *riumo*, strap]

rime[1], n., & v.t. & i. = RHYME[1,2]. [ME *rime*, now normally RHYME[1,2], but revived in literary use since *c.* 1870]

rime[2], n., & v.t. (chiefly poet.). 1. Hoar-frost; hence rim'y[2] a. 2. v.t. Cover with ~. [OE *hrim*, MDu. *rijm*, ON *hrīm*]

rim'er, n. = REAM[2]*er*. [dial. *rime* var. of REAM[2], -ER[1]]

Rimm'on, n. Ancient deity worshipped at Damascus (*bow down in the house of* ~, compromise one's convictions). [2 *Kings* v. 18]

rim'ose, rim'ous, aa. (bot. etc.). Full of chinks or fissures. [f. L *rimosus* (*rima* chink, -OSE[1]), -OUS]

rind, n., & v.t. Bark of tree or plant (vb, strip ~ from); peel of fruit or vegetable; harder enclosing surface of cheese or other substance; skin of bacon etc.; external aspect, surface. Hence ~'ED[2] a. [OE *rind*, OS, OHG *rinda*]

rin'derpest, n. Disease of ruminants esp. oxen, cattle-plague. [G (*rinder* pl. of *rind* ox)]

ring[1], n., & v.t. 1. Circlet usu. of precious metal & often set with gem(s) worn round finger as ornament or token (esp. of betrothal or marriage) or signet, or (usu. *nose*, *arm*, etc., ~) hung to or encircling other part of body. 2. Circular appliance of any material & any (but esp., cf. *hoop*, no great) size. 3. Raised or sunk or otherwise distinguishable line or band round, rim of, cylindrical or circular object. 4. Circular fold, coil, bend, structure, part, or mark (~s of tree, concentric bands of wood corresponding in number to tree's years; *has livid* ~s *round his eyes*; *puffing out* ~s *of smoke*; ~s in water, circular ripples expanding from centre of agitation). 5. Persons, trees, etc., disposed in a circle, such disposition; (commerce. etc.) combination of traders or politicians acting together for control of market or policy. 6. Circular enclosure or space for circus-riding, prize-fighting (PRIZE-~; ~'*side seat* or *view*, also fig.), betting at races (*the*~, bookmakers), showing of cattle, etc. 7. Circular or spiral course (*make* ~s *round*, go or do things incomparably quicker than). 8. ~-*bark* v.t., cut ~ in bark of (tree) to kill it or to check its growth & bring it into bearing; ~-*bolt*, bolt with ~ attached for fastening rope to etc.; ~-*bone*, (horse-disease with) deposit of bony matter on

pastern-bones; ~-*cartilage*, CRICOID; ~-*dove*, wood-pigeon; ~-*fence*, completely enclosing estate etc., also fig.; ~-*finger*, third esp. of left hand; ~-*goal*, game in which light hoop is thrown towards goal with sticks; ~-*hunt*, in which beasts are driven inwards by ~ of fire; ~'*leader*, (one of) chief instigator(s) in mutiny, riot, etc.; ~-*lock*, opened by right adjustment of several grooved ~s; ‖ ~-*man*, bookmaker; ~-*master*, manager of circus performance; ~-*neck*, ~-*necked* plover or duck; ~-*necked*, with band(s) of colour round neck; ~-*net*, kind of salmon net, also of lace; ~ *ouzel*, kind of bird allied to blackbird; ~-*snake*, common European grass-snake (from coiling); ~-*stand*, for keeping finger-~s on; ~'*tail*, female of hen-harrier, also golden eagle till its third year, also ~-*tailed* opossum or phalanger; ~-*tailed*, with tail ~ed in alternate colours, also (of phalanger) with tail curled at end; ~-*taw*, game with marbles in ~; ~-*wall*, as ~-*fence*; ~'*worm*, skin-disease esp. of children in circular patches; hence (-)~ED[2] (-ngd), ~'LESS, aa. 9. vb. (Of hawk etc.) rise in spirals; (of hunted fox) take circular course. 10. Encompass (usu. *round*, *about*, *in*; often in p.p.), hem in (game, cattle) by riding or beating in circle round them. 11. Put ~ upon, put ~ in nose of (pig, bull), (~-*the-bull*, game with ~ to be thrown or swung on to hook). 12. = ~-*bark* above. 13. Cut (onions, apples) into ~s. [OE, OS, OHG *hring*, ON *hringr* f. Gmc *hrengaz*]

ring[2], v.i. & t. (*rang*, now rarely *rung*; *rung*), & n. 1. Give forth clear resonant sound (as) of vibrating metal (*bell*, *trumpet*, *coin*, *sound*, ~s, often *out* etc.; *with a* ~*ing laugh*; *a shot rang out*; *a* ~*ing frost*, in which ground ~s under foot; ~ *true*, *false*, of coin tested by throwing on counter, & fig. of sentiments etc.); (of bell) ~ *to* or *for* prayers, dinner, etc., convey summons by ~ing. 2. (Of place) resound, re-echo, (*with* sound, *to* sound or its cause, *with* fame etc. or its theme, *with talk of*; often *again*). 3. (Of utterance or other sound) ~ *in* one's *ears*, *heart*, etc., linger in one's hearing, haunt the memory. 4. (Of ears) be filled with sensation as of bell-~ing (so *has a* ~*ing in the ears*) or *with* sound. 5. Make (bell) ~ (~ *the bell*, esp. as summons to servant; ~ *the bell* (colloq.), be successful [from use of bell in machines for testing strength or skill], (also) strike a sympathetic note; ~ *up bell*, raise church bell over beam & ~ it there; ~*ing engine*, pile-driver worked by ropes like peal of bells); throw (coin) on counter to test it. 6. ~ bell as summons (~ *at door*, to get admittance etc.; ~ *for* servant, coffee, etc.; *did you* ~, *sir*?). 7. Sound (peal, knell, BOB[1]· *major*, the CHANGE's) on bells (or with *bell* or *bells* as subj.; ~ *the knell of*, announce or herald abolition etc. of). 8. Announce (hour etc.)

by sound of bell(s). **9.** Summon *up* etc. by ~ing bell (~ *up* on telephone, get or seek communication with; ~ *off*, terminate telephone interview; ~ *curtain up* or *down* in theatre, direct it by bell to be raised or lowered. **10.** Usher *in*, *out*, with bell-~ing, esp. *new*, *old*, *year*. **11.** n. Set of (church) bells. **12.** ~ing sound, ~ing tone in voice etc., resonance of coin or vessel. **13.** Act of ~ing bell, sound so produced, (*three* ~*s for the hall porter*; *give bell a* ~; *heard a loud* ~ *at the door*); call on the telephone (*give me a* ~). [OE *hringan*, ON *hringja*, perh. imit.]

rin'gent (-j-), a. Gaping, grinning, (esp. bot. of wide labiate corolla). [as RICTUS, -ENT]

ring'er, n. **1.** Quoit that falls round pin; fox that runs in ring when hunted. **2.** Bell-~; device for ringing bell. [RING[1,2], -ER[1]]

ring'let, n. **1.** (rare). Small ring, fairy ring on grass, ring-shaped mark etc. **2.** Curly lock of hair, curl, whence ~ED[2], ~Y[2], aa. [-LET]

rink, n., & v.i. **1.** Stretch of ice used for game of curling; sheet of natural or artificial ice, floor, for (roller-)skating. **2.** v.i. Skate on ~ esp. with roller-skates, whence ~'ER[1] n. [orig. North ME, = *jousting-ground*; app. f. OF *renc* RANK[1]]

rinse, v.t., & n. **1.** Wash out or *out* (vessel, mouth) by filling with water etc., shaking, & emptying; pour liquid over, or wash lightly; put (clothes) through clean water to remove soap; clear (impurities) *out* or *away* by rinsing; wash (food) *down* with liquor. **2.** n. Rinsing (*give it a* ~); kind of hair tint. [ME, f. OF *rincer*, *reincier*]

ri'ot, n., & v.i. & t. **1.** Loose living, debauchery. **2.** Loud revelry, a revel; unrestrained indulgence in or display or enjoyment of something. (*a* ~ *of emotion*, *colour*, *sound*). **3.** (hunt.). Following of any scent indiscriminately (*run*~, orig. of hounds doing this, now usu. fig. of person or his tongue or fancy throwing off all restraint). **4.** Disorder, tumult, disturbance of the peace, outbreak of lawlessness, on part of a crowd ‖ (*R*~ *Act*, by which persons not dispersing after official reading of part of it incur guilt of felony; *read the R*~ *Act*, lit., & joc. of parent etc. announcing that noise etc. is to cease); hence or cogn. ~OUS a., ~OUSLY[2] adv., ~OUSNESS, (rare) ~RY(2), nn. **5.** vb. Live wantonly, revel. **6.** Throw *away* (time, money), wear *out* (life), in dissipation. **7.** Make or engage in a political ~ or offence against the R~ Act, whence ~ER[2](4) n. [ME, f. OF *riote*(r), orig. unkn.]

rip[1], n. Worthless horse, screw; dissolute person, rake. [perh. var. of REP[3]]

rip[2], v.t. & i. (-pp-), & n. **1.** Cut or tear (thing) quickly or forcibly away from something (~ *out the lining*; ~ *the boards off*); make long cut or tear in, cut or tear

vigorously apart (often *up*; *had his belly* ~*ped up*). **2.** Split (wood, rock), saw (wood) with the grain (~*saw*, used thus). **3.** Strip (roof) of tiles or slates & laths. **4.** Make (fissure, passage) by ~ping. **5.** Open *up* (wound, quarrel, sorrow, the past) again. **6.** Come violently asunder, split (intr.). **7.** Rush along (of ship, & transf.; so *let her* ~, do not check speed or interfere). **8.** ‖ (part.; sl.; cf. *rattling*). Fine, splendid, enjoyable, first-rate, (also as adv. with *good* etc., as *a* ~*ping good time*), whence ~p'ingLY[2] adv. **9.** ~-cord (aeron.), cord for releasing parachute from its pack. **10.** n. Act of ~ping; long tear or cut. [orig. obsc.; cf. Fris. *rippe*]

rip[3], n. Stretch of broken water in sea or river, overfall. [perh. rel. to RIPPLE[2]]

ripar'ian, a. & n. **1.** Of, on, river-bank (esp. ~ *proprietor*, *rights*). **2.** n. ~ proprietor. [L *riparius* (*ripa* bank, -ARY[1]) + -AN]

ripe, a., & v.t. & i. **1.** Ready to be reaped, gathered, eaten, drunk, used, or dealt with, fully developed, mellow, mature, prepared or able *to* undergo something, in fit state *for*, (~ *corn*, *fruit*, *cheese*, *wine*, *seed*; ~ *lips*, red & full like ~ fruit; ~ *beauty*, of grown woman; ~ *scholar*, *judgement*, *experience*, *understanding*; *die at a* ~ *age*, old; *persons of* ~*r years*, not immature; *opportunity* ~ *to be seized*; *is* ~ *to hear the truth*; *mood or person*, *plan*, *disease*, ~ *for mischief*, *execution*, *treatment*; *soon* ~ *soon rotten*, prov. depreciating precocity); hence rip'EN[6] v.t. & i., ~'LY[2] (-pl-) adv., ~'NESS (-pn-) n. **2.** vb. (chiefly poet.). = ~n. [OE *ripe*, OS *ripi*, OHG *rifi*; perh. rel. to REAP]

ripôste', n., & v.i. **1.** Quick return thrust in fencing; (transf.) counterstroke, retort. **2.** v.i. Deliver ~. [F, f. It. *risposta* RESPONSE]

ripp'er, n. In vbl senses; esp.: tool for ripping roof; ripp-saw; (sl.) ripping person or thing. [-ER[1]]

rip'ple[1], n., & v.t. **1.** Toothed implement used to clear away seeds from flax. **2.** v.t. Treat with ~. [corresp. to MDu., MLG *repel(en)*]

rip'ple[2], n., & v.i. & t. **1.** Ruffling of water's surface, small wave(s); wavy or crinkled appearance in hair, ribbons, etc.; gentle lively sound that rises & falls (esp. *a* ~ *of conversation*); ~-*cloth*, soft woollen washing fabric with ~d surface used for dressing-gowns etc.; ~-*mark*, ridge, ridged surface, left on sand or mud or rock by water or wind; hence rip'LET[1] n., rip'ly[2] a. **2.** vb. Form, flow in, show, agitate or mark with, sound like, ~s. [vb 17th c., orig. unkn.; n. f. vb]

Ripuar'ian, a. Of the ancient Franks living on Rhine between Meuse & Moselle (esp. ~ *law*, code observed by them). [f. med. L *Ripuarius* (*Ribu*-) + -AN; connex. w. L *ripa* very doubtful]

Rip van Winkle (wĭng'kl), n. Person of

utterly antiquated ideas or information. [hero of tale by W. Irving who slept 20 years]

rise¹ (-z), v.i. & t. (*rose* pr. rōz; ~*n* pr. rĭ'zn; p.p., see -ED¹(2), often with *is* etc.). 1. Get up from lying or sitting or kneeling position, get out of bed, (of meeting etc.) cease to sit for business, recover standing or upright position, become erect, leave ground, come to life again or usu. *again* or *from the dead*, (~ *from table*, leave meal; *all rose to receive him*; *house*, i.e. theatre audience, ~*s* at actress etc., in universal applause; *found he could not, was too weak to*, ~; ~, *Sir Thomas* etc., formula in knighting; ~ *betimes, at 5 a.m., with the lark*; ~ *up early*; *Parliament will* ~ *next week*; *fell never to* ~ *again*; *the hair rose on his head*; *horse* ~*s on its hind-legs*; *horse* ~*s to a fence*, takes off for leap; *birds* ~ *well today*). 2. Cease to be quiet, abandon submission, make revolt, (*if a wind should* ~; ~ *in arms, rebellion*, etc., *against oppression, oppressor*; *town rose on its garrison*; *gorge, stomach*, ~*s*, indignation or disgust is felt; *my whole soul* ~*s against it*, finds it intolerable). 3. Come or go up, grow upwards, ascend, mount, soar, project or swell upwards, become higher, reach higher position or level or amount, increase, incline upwards, come to surface, become or be visible above or *above* surroundings, develop greater energy or intensity, be progressive, (*sun, star, morning, dawn*, ~*s*; *the* ~*n sun*; *rising cupboard*, kitchen lift; *the rising generation*, the young; *smoke* ~*s straight up*; *tree* ~*s 20 ft*, attains that height; *building rose like a dream*; *blisters* ~, form; *bread will not* ~, swell with yeast; *balloon* ~*s*; *should* ~ *above petty jealousies*, be superior to; *picture, idea*, ~*s before the mind*; *river, tide, flood, level, rose 6 ft, is rising*; *the mercury, barometer* or *glass, is rising*; *spirits* ~, become more cheerful; *prices, demands*, ~; *a rising lawyer*; *a man likely to* ~; ~ *in the world*, attain higher social position; ~ *to greatness*; *rising ground*, sloping up; *in a rising series*; ~*s in a gentle curve*; *the interest* ~*s with each act*; *bubbles* ~; *fish* ~*s*, comes to surface to feed; *drowning man* ~*s three times*; *in the foreground* ~*s a castle*; *does not* ~ *above mediocrity*; *the wind is rising*; *her colour rose*, became bright or deeper; || *rising 5, 14*, getting on for that age). 4. Develop powers equal *to* (*does not* ~ *to an occasion*; *rose to the emergency, requirements*, etc.). 5. Have origin, begin to be, flow, *from, in, at*, etc. (*river* ~*s from a spring, in the Grampians*, etc.; *earth & heaven rose at His word*; *the difficulty* ~*s from misapprehension*). 6. (rare, usu. poet.). Arise (*a feud, rumour, rose*). 7. (Causative in spec. senses) make or see ~ (*did not* ~ *a fish, a bird, all day*; ~ *ship*, see it appear from top downwards in approaching it). [OE *rīsan*, OS, OHG *rīsan*,

ON *rīsa*, Goth. *~reisan* f. Gmc *°rīsan*; see RAISE, REAR²]

rise² (-z), n. 1. Coming up *of* sun etc. (rare; *at* ~ *of sun, day*; cf. SUN~ etc.). 2. Ascent, upward slope, knoll, hill, (*came to a* ~ *in the road*; *chapel stands on a* ~). 3. Social advancement, upward progress, increase in power, rank, value, price, amount, height, pitch, || *wages*, etc., (*has had a* ~ *in life*; *the* ~ *& fall of statesmen*; *the* ~ *of the tide is 30 ft*; || *asks for a* ~, increasing). 4. Movement of fish to surface (*not a sign of a* ~; fig., *get* or *take a* ~ *out of* one, draw him into display of temper or foible). 5. Vertical height of step, arch, incline, etc., (also **rĭs'ER**¹ (-z-) n. f. prec.) vertical piece connecting two treads of staircase. 6. Origin, start, (*has, takes, its* ~ *in, from*; *give* ~ *to*, occasion, suggest). [f. prec.]

ris'ible (-z-), a. Inclined to laugh, so **risi**BIL'ITY (-z-) n.; of laughter (~ *nerves, faculties*, etc.); (rare) laughable, ludicrous. [f. LL *risibilis* (*ridēre ris-* laugh, -IBLE)]

ris'ing (-z-), n. In vbl senses; esp.: ~ (-*again*), resurrection; insurrection, revolt; boil, pimple. [-ING¹]

risk, n., & v.t. 1. Hazard, chance of or *of* bad consequences, loss, etc., exposure to mischance, (*there is the* ~ *of his catching cold*; *run* ~*s, a* ~, *the* ~, often *of*, expose oneself or be exposed to loss etc.; *take* ~*s* etc., expose oneself so; *at the* ~ *of his life*; *at owner's* etc. ~, he to bear any contingent loss); ~*-money*, allowance to cashier to cover accidental deficits; hence ~'FUL, ~'LESS, aa. 2. v.t. Expose to chance of injury or loss; venture on, take the chances of, (~ *the jump, a battle, a sprained ankle*). [f. F *risque(r)* f. It. *risco, riscare*]

ris'ky, a. 1. Hazardous, full of risk. 2. (Also, & after, F *risqué* pr. rĭs'kā) involving suggestion of indecency, offending against propriety, (of story, dramatic situation, etc.). Hence ~ILY² adv., ~INESS n. [-Y²]

risött'ō (rĕ-), n. Stew made with rice, chicken, onions, etc. [It.]

risqué. See RISKY.

riss'ōle, n. Fried ball or cake of meat or fish mixed with bread-crumbs etc. [F, OF *ruissole*, f. LL *russeolus* reddish]

ritardan'dō (rē-), mus. direction. Slower. [It.]

rite, n. (Form of procedure, action required or usual, in) a religious or solemn ceremony or observance (*the* ~*s of hospitality*; *the* ~ *of confirmation*; *burial* or *funeral* ~*s*; *conjugal* or *nuptial* ~*s*, sexual intercourse between husband & wife; *the Latin, Anglican*, etc., ~, body of usages characteristic of a Church). Hence ~'LESS (-tl-) a. [ME, f. OF *rit(e)* or L *ritus* -*ūs*]

rit'ual, a. & n. 1. Of, with, consisting in, involving, religious rites; hence ~LY² adv. 2. n. Prescribed order of performing religious service; book containing this;

performance of ∼ acts, whence (w. implication of excess) ∼ISM(3), ∼IST(2), nn., ∼is'TIC a., ∼is'TICALLY adv., ∼IZE(2, 3) v.i. & t. [f. L *ritualis* (prec., -AL)]

‖ riv'age, n. (poet.). Coast, shore, bank. [ME, f. OF, f. *rive* f. L *ripa* bank, -AGE)]

ri'val, n., attrib. a., & v.t. & i. (-ll-). 1. Person's competitor for some prize (esp. a woman's or man's love) or in some pursuit or quality (also of things; *without a* ∼, unapproached for excellence etc.); hence ∼RY(2, 4), ∼SHIP, nn. 2. adj. That is a ∼ or are ∼s. 3. vb. Vie with, be comparable to, seem or claim to be as good etc. as; (rare) be in ∼ry. [f. L *rivalis* (*rivus* stream, -AL) orig. = on same stream]

rive, v.t. & i. (∼d; ∼n pr. ri'vn, rarely ∼d). Rend, cleave, wrench *away* or *off* or *from*, strike asunder, (arch., poet.); (of artisan) split (wood, stone), make (laths) by splitting, whence riv'er[1] [-ER[1](1)]] n.: be split, gape under blow etc., (of wood etc.) admit of splitting. [ME, f. ON *rifa*]

‖ riv'el, v.i. & t. (arch.; -ll-). Wrinkle, crumple, shrivel. [ME, back formation f. *rivelled*, OE *rifelede* app. f. **rifel* a wrinkle + -ED[2]]

riven. See RIVE.

riv'er[2], n. (for *river*[1] see RIVE). Copious stream of water flowing in channel to sea or lake or marsh or another ∼ (‖ *the∼* often prefixed to name, as *the* ∼ *Thames*); *the* boundary between life & death; copious flow or stream *of* (*a* ∼ *of lava*; ∼*s of blood*, much bloodshed); (attrib., prefixed to many names of animals, plants, & things) living in, situated or used on, ∼(s); ∼-BED[1](2); ∼-*god*, mythological being dwelling in & personifying a ∼; ∼-*horse*, hippopotamus; ∼-*side*, ground along ∼'s bank (often attrib., as *a* ∼*side villa*). Hence (-)∼ED[2] (-*erd*), ∼LESS aa. [f. AF *rivere*, OF -*iere* f. Rom. **riparia* (L *ripa* bank, -ARY[1])]

riv'erain, a. & n. 1. Of river or its neighbourhood; situated, dwelling, by river. 2. n. Person dwelling by river. [F (*rivière* as prec., -AN)]

riv'erine, a. Of, on, river or its banks, riparian. [-INE[1]]

riv'et, n., & v.t. 1. Nail or bolt for holding together metal plates etc., its headless end being beaten out or pressed down after passing through two holes. 2. v.t. Clinch (bolt); join or fasten with ∼s (*together, down, to, into, on* adv. or prep., etc.); fix, make immovable, (∼ *error* etc.); concentrate, direct intently, (eyes, attention, etc., *upon*); engross (attention), engross attention of; hence ∼ER[1](1, 2) n. [ME, f. OF, f. *river* clinch, of unkn. orig.]

riv'ière (-lār, or rēvyār'), n. Gem necklace, esp. of more than one string. [F, as RIVER[2]]

riv'ulet, n. 1. Small stream. 2. Kinds of

moth. [perh. f. It. *rivolello* (L *rivus* stream, -UL-, -ET[1])]

rix'-dollar, n. (hist.). Silver coin & money of account (4/6–2/3) of 16th–19th cc. in some continental States. [f. Du. *rijcks-daler*, see REICH, DOLLAR]

roach[1], n. Small freshwater fish allied to carp (*sound as a* ∼, in first-rate health etc.); ∼-*backed*, -*bellied* (convex in profile). [ME, f. OF *roche*, of unkn. orig.]

roach[2], n. (naut.). Upward curve in foot of square sail. [18th c., orig. unkn.]

roach[3], n. = COCKROACH. [abbr.]

road[1], n. 1. (Usu. pl.; also ∼'*stead*) piece of water near shore in which ships can ride at anchor. 2. Line of communication between places for use of foot-passengers, riders, & vehicles (*on the* ∼, travelling, esp. as a commercial traveller; *take the* ∼, set out; *the* ∼, the highway; ‖ *take to the* ∼, arch., become highwayman; *rule of the* ∼, custom regulating side to be taken by vehicles, riders, or ships, meeting or passing each other). 3. Way of getting *to* (*the* ∼ *to York, ruin, success*; *royal* ∼ *to*, way of attaining without trouble). 4. One's way or route (*in the, my,* etc., ∼, colloq., obstructing someone or something; so *get out of the, my,* etc., ∼). 5. ∼-*bed*, foundation structure of a railway, whole material laid down of an ordinary ∼; ∼-*book*, describing ∼s of country etc., itinerary; ∼ *fund* (for construction & maintenance of ∼s & bridges): ∼-*hog*, reckless or inconsiderate motorist or cyclist; ∼ *house*, inn on main ∼ in country district; ∼'*man* (repairing ∼s); ∼-*metal*, broken stone for ∼-making; ∼-*sense*, capacity for safe handling of vehicles on the ∼; ∼'*side*, border of ∼ (esp. attrib., as ∼*side plants, inn*); ∼'*stead*, see sense 1; ∼'*way*, ∼, central part of ∼ (opp. *side-path*), part of bridge or railway used for traffic; ∼'*worthy*, fit to be used on the ∼, (of person) fit to travel. Hence (-)∼ED[2], ∼'LESS, aa. [OE *rād* (*rīdan* RIDE); cf. RAID]

road[2], v.t. (Of dog) follow up (game-bird, or abs.) by foot-scent. [19th c.; orig. unkn.]

road'ster, n. Ship at anchor in roadstead; horse, bicycle, etc., for use on the road; experienced traveller. [-STER]

roam, v.i. & t., & n. Ramble (v., & rarely n. as *a half-hour's* ∼), wander; walk or travel unsystematically over or through or about (country, seas). [ME, orig. unkn.]

roan[1], a. & n. 1. (Of animal) with coat of which the prevailing colour is thickly interspersed with another, esp. bay or sorrel or chestnut mixed with white or grey (often with chief colour prefixed, as *black, blue, red,* ∼). 2. n. ∼ horse, cow. [OF *roan* (now *rouan*), f. Sp. *roano*]

roan[2], n. Soft sheepskin leather used in bookbinding as substitute for morocco. [ME, perh. *Roan*, old name of *Rouen*]

roar (rōr), v.i. & t., & n. **1.** (Utter, send forth) loud deep hoarse sound (as) of lion, person or company in pain or rage or loud laughter, the sea, thunder, cannon, furnace, etc. (*the ~ of the waves*; *~s of laughter*; *lions~ing after their prey*; *~ed with pain* or *laughter* or *for mercy*; *you need not ~*, talk so loud; *set table in a ~*, make company laugh loud). **2.** (Of horse) make loud noise in breathing due to disease, whence *~'ER*[1], *~'ING*[1], (rōr-), nn. **3.** (Of place) be full of din, re-echo, (often *again*). **4.** Say, sing, utter, (words, chorus, oath, etc., often *out*) in loud tone. **5.** Make *deaf, hoarse*, etc., put *down*, by *~ing*. **6.** (part.). Riotous, noisy, boisterous, brisk, (*a ~ing night*, stormy, also spent in revelry; *a ~ing blade*, arch., fast liver; *the ~ing game*, curling; *~ing forties*, see FORTY; *in ~ing health*; *drive a ~ing trade*). [OE *rārian*, = MDu. *reeren*, MLG *rāren, rēren*, OHG *rēren*, prob. imit.]

roast, v.t. & i. (p.p. in vb forms *~ed*, as adj. *~*), & n. **1.** Cook (esp. meat) by exposure to open fire or now ' usually in oven (*prefers ~ beef, his meat ~ed*); heat or calcine (ore) in furnace; heat (coffee-beans) as preparation for grinding; expose (victim for torture, one*self* or some part for warmth) to fire; ridicule, banter, chaff; undergo *~ing*; (part.) very hot; *~ing-jack*, appliance keeping meat in motion while *~ing*. **2.** n. *~* meat or a dish of it (*rule the ~*, be master); *joint of meat; operation of *~ing*. [ME; n. partly f. OF *rost*, partly f. vb, f. OF *rostir* f. WG (OFrank. *hraustjan*; cf. OHG *rōsten* f. *rōst(e)* gridiron)]'

roast'er, n. In vbl senses; esp.: kind of oven for roasting; ore-roasting furnace; coffee-roasting apparatus; pig, potato, etc., fit for roasting. [-ER[1]]

rob, v.t. (-bb-). Despoil (person etc.) of or *of* property by violence, feloniously plunder (person, place, often *of*), deprive *of* what is due; *~ PETER*; (abs.) commit *~bery*. So*~b'er* [-ER[1], -ER[2](4)], *~b'ERY*(2, 4), nn. [ME, f. OF *rob(b)er* f. Gmc *raubh* (cf. OS *rōbon*) REAVE]

robe, n., & v.t. & i. **1.** Any long loose outer garment (rare, poet., metaph.); (trade name of) kind of lady's dress in one piece; *dressing-gown; outer garment of baby in long-clothes; (often pl.) longer outer garment.worn as indication of wearer's rank, office, profession, etc., gown, vestment, '(*the long ~*, legal or clerical dress; *gentlemen of the ~*, lawyers); *~-de-chambre* (F, see Ap.), dressing-gown, wrapper. **2.** vb. Invest (person) in *~*, dress; assume one's *~s* or vestments. [ME, f. OF, conn. w. prec., orig. sense *booty*]

‖ **Rob'ert, n.** (colloq.). A policeman. [see BOBBY]

rob'in, R-, n. (Also *~ redbreast*) small red-breasted bird; (with or without distinctive epithet) kinds of Amer., Colonial, & Indian bird; *~-*, *~'s-*, in plant names, as ‖ *R~-run-the-hedge*, ground-ivy, ‖ *~'s--eye*, kind of geranium; *R~ Goodfellow*, a mischievous sportive sprite, alias *Puck*; *R~ Hood*, (type of) medieval forest outlaw; ROUND[1] *~*. [ME, f. OF, fam. for *Robert*]

rob'orant, a., & n. (med.). Strengthening (drug). [L *roborare* (*robur -oris* strength), -ANT]

rob'ot, n. 1. An apparently human automaton, an intelligent & obedient but impersonal machine; (transf.) machine-like person. **2.** Automatic traffic signal. **3.** Flying bomb. [term in Čapek's play *R.U.R.* (*Rossum's Universal Robots*), 1920; f. Czech *robota* forced labour]

rob'urite (-ber-), n. A strong flameless explosive. [L *robur* strength, -ITE[1](2)]

robust', a. (*~er, ~est*). Of strong health & physique, not slender or delicate or weakly, (of persons, animals, plants, body, health, etc.); (of exercise, discipline, etc.) tending to or requiring strength, invigorating, vigorous; (of intellect etc.) sensible, straightforward, not given to nor confused by subtleties. Hence *~LY*[2] adv., *~NESS* n. [f. F *robuste*, or L *robustus* (*robur* strength)]

robus'tious, a. Boisterous, self-assertive, noisy. [earlier in common use = prec.; now chiefly w. ref. to *Hamlet* III. ii. 10]

roc, n. Gigantic bird of Eastern tales. [f. Arab. *rokh*]

roc'ambole, n. Kind of leek used for seasoning. [F]

roch'et, n. Surplice-like vestment used chiefly by bishops & abbots. [ME, f. OF, dim. f. WG (cf. OE *rocc*, OS, OHG *rok*, ON *rokkr*); cf. FROCK]

rock[1], n. **1.** Solid part of earth's crust underlying soil (*dug down to the living ~*; often *bed-~*; *built, founded, on the ~*, lit., & fig., secure; *R~ of ages*, Christ); mass of this projecting & forming a hill, cliff, etc., or standing up into or out of sea etc. from bottom (*the R~*, Gibraltar; *run upon the ~s, see ~s ahead*, etc., of lit. or fig. shipwreck or danger of it; *on the ~s*, sl., hard up; *~ of water* etc., ref. to *Numb.* xx. 11). **2.** Stone as a substance (*a mass, needle, of ~*); large detached stone, boulder; (geol.) any particular igneous or stratified mineral constituent of earth's crust including sands, clays, etc. **3.** Kinds of hard sweetmeat (usu. *almond etc. ~*). **4.** (Also *blue ~*) *= ~-pigeon*. **5.** *~-bed*, base of *~*, rocky bottom; *~-bird*, esp. puffin; *~-bottom*, (colloq., of prices etc.) very lowest; *~-cake*, bun with hard rough surface; *~-cork*, variety of asbestos; *~-crystal*, transparent colourless silica or quartz usu. in hexagonal prisms; *~-dove, ~-pigeon; ~-drill, ~-boring tool or machine; *R~ English*, mixed language of Gibraltar; *R~ fever*, kind of enteric prevalent at Gibraltar; *~-fish*, kinds of goby, bass, wrasse, etc.; *~-garden*, artificial mound or bank of stones with ~-plants etc. planted in the interstices, garden in which ~eries are the chief feature; ~-goat, ibex; ~-hewn, cut out of the ~; ~-leather, as ~-cork; ~-ling [-LING¹], kinds of fish esp. sea-loach; ~-oil, native naphtha; ~-paper, as ~-cork; ~-pigeon, kind of dove haunting ~s & supposed source of domestic pigeon; ~-rabbit, hyrax; ~-ribbed, (of earth, coast, etc.) with ribs of ~; ~-rose, kinds of cistus with yellow, rose, or salmon flowers; ~-salmon, (trade name for) dogfish; ~-salt, found stratified in free state; R~ scorpion, (nickname for) person born at Gibraltar; ~-silk, as ~-cork; ~-sucker, sea lamprey; ~-tar, petroleum; ~-whistler, Alpine marmot; ~-wood, as ~-cork; ~-work or ~'ERY(3)n., pile of rough stones with soil in interstices for growing ferns etc. on, also natural group or display of ~s. Hence ~'LESS, ~'LIKE, aa., ~'LET n. [ME, f. OF roke, roque (also roche), f. Gallo-Rom. rocca]

rŏck², n. (hist.). Distaff. [ME, f. MDu. rocke, MLG rocken, OHG rocco, ON rokkr]

rŏck³, v.t. & i., & n. 1. Move (t. & i.) gently to & fro (as) in cradle, set or keep (cradle etc.) or (of cradle etc.) be in such motion, (~ him to sleep; ship ~ing on, ~ed by the waves; sat ~ing himself or ~ing in his chair; ~ed in security, hopes, etc.); (gold-min.) work (CRADLE), work cradle, shake in cradle; sway (t. & i.) from side to side, shake, oscillate, reel, (earthquake ~s house, house ~s, a ~ing gait). 2. ~'ing-chair, mounted on rockers, or with seat arranged to ~; ~'ing-horse, wooden horse on rockers for child; ~'ing-stone, poised boulder easily ~ed; ~'ing-turn in skating, from any edge to same in opposite direction with body revolving away from convex of first curve (counter-~ing-turn or -rocker or counter, same turn with body revolving away from concave); ~-shaft, that oscillates about axis without making complete revolutions; ~-staff, part of apparatus working smith's bellows. 3. n. ~ing motion, spell of ~ing; ~-'n' (= and) -roll, (dancing to) kind of swing music. [OE roccian, app. f. Gmc *rukk- to move; cf. MDu., MLG rocken, rucken]

rŏck'er, n. In vbl senses; esp.: one of the curved bars on which cradle etc. rocks (off one's ~, sl., crazy); gold-miner's cradle; skate with highly curved blade; (skat.)~, counter-~, = (counter-)ROCK³ing-turn. [ROCK³, -ER¹]

rŏck'ĕt¹, n. Kinds of plant of which some are used as salad & some grown for flowers (base ~, wild mignonette; blue ~, kinds of wolfsbane & larkspur, also bluebell; yellow ~, winter cress). [f. F roquette f. It. ruchetta (ruca f. L eruca, -ETTE)]

rŏck'ĕt², n., & v.t. & i. 1. Cylindrical paper or metal case that can be projected to height or distance by ignition of contents, used in firework displays, for signalling, to carry line to ship in distress,

etc.; projectile containing its own propellant & depending for its flight on the reaction set up by a continuous jet of rapidly expanding gases released in the propellant by ignition (e.g. of cordite) or by the mixture of two liquids (e.g. alcohol & liquid air), whence ~RY n., study or use of ~s; ~ engine, jet, motor, (operated on same principle); ~-propelled, ~ propulsion; ~ range (for testing ~ missiles). 2. (sl.). Reprimand. 3. vb. Bombard with ~s; (of horse or its rider) bound upwards or dart like ~; (of prices etc.) rise steeply; (of pheasant etc.) fly straight upwards, fly fast & high, whence ~ER¹ n. [f. F roquet(te) f. It. rocchetta (rocca ROCK², w. ref. to cylindrical shape), -ETTE]

rŏck'|y̆, a., & n. (pl.). 1. Of rock, full of or abounding in rocks, (the R~y Mountains, or as n. the R~ies, western N.-Amer. range); like rock in ruggedness, firmness, solidity, etc. 2.(sl.). Unsteady, tottering. Hence ~ĭLY² adv., ~ĬNESS n. [ROCK¹, ³, -Y²]

rŏcŏc'ō, a. & n. 1. Of a style of art prevalent in Europe c. 1730–80. 2. (Of furniture, architecture, etc., also of literary style) highly ornamented, florid. 3. (obs.). Antiquated, out of date. 4. n. The ~ style of art. [F, joc. alt. f. rocaille pebble-work]

rŏd, n. 1. Slender straight round stick growing as shoot on tree or cut from it or made from wood, switch, wand, (occas. as symbol of office etc., see esp. BLACK¹ ~; AARON'S- ROD; divining, dowsing, ~, see DOWSING). 2. Such stick, or bundle of twigs, for use in caning or flogging (the ~, use of this; spare the ~ & spoil the child; make etc. a ~ for one's own back, prepare trouble for oneself; kiss the ~, take punishment meekly or gladly; have a ~ in pickle for, be ready to punish when time comes). 3. = FISH²ing-~. 4. (Also ~'man & ~'STER n.) angler. 5. (As measure)=PERCH². 6. Slender metal bar, connecting bar, shaft, (curtain, piston, etc., ~~). 7. *(sl.). Pistol or revolver. 8.(physiol.). ~-shaped structure. Hence ~'LESS, ~'LIKE, aa., ~'LET n. [OE rodd, prob. rel. to ON rudda club]

rōde¹. See RIDE.

rōde², v.i. (Of wildfowl) fly landward in the evening, (of woodcock) fly in the evening during breeding season. [orig. unkn.]

rōd'ent, a. & n. 1. (Animal) of the order Rodentia with strong incisor & no canine teeth (e.g. rat, mouse, hamster, squirrel, beaver, porcupine), whence rodĕn'tIAN (-shl) a. 2. Gnawing (esp. in path. of ulcers). [f. L rodere ros- gnaw; see -ENT]

rōde'o (-dāō, or rōd'iō; pl. ~s), n. A round-up of cattle on a western American ranch for branding etc., enclosure for this; exhibition of cowboys' skill; (transf.) exhibition of motor-cycle feats etc. [Sp., f. rodear go round]

rŏdomontãd|e', n., a., & v.i. **1.** Boastful, bragging, (saying or talk). **2.** v.i. Brag, talk big; hence~'ER¹n. [F(*Rodomont* f.It. *Rodomonte* character in *Orlando Furioso*, -ADE)]

rŏe¹, n. (collect. sing. occas. for pl.). Small kind of European & Asian deer; ~'*buck*, male ~; ~-*deer*, ~. [OE *rāha*, OS, OHG *rĕho*, ON *rá*]

rŏe², n. Mass of eggs (also *hard* ~) in female fish's ovary (~-*corn*, one egg); *soft* ~, male fish's milt (~-*stone*, oolite. Hence (-)roED²(rŏd) a. [ME *roughe*, MLG *rogen*, OHG *rogo, rogan*, ON *hrogn*]

rogā'tion, n. **1.** (eccl.). (Usu. pl.) litany of the saints chanted on the three days before Ascension Day (*R~ days*, these; *R~ week, Sunday*, including, preceding, them; ~ *flower*, milkwort), whence ~AL (-shon-) a. **2.** (Rom. ant.). Law proposed before the people. by consul or tribune (*Licinian* etc. ~s, proposed by Licinius etc.). [f. L *rogatio* (*rogare* ask, -ATION)]

Rŏ'ger, n. Male name (*the jolly* ~, pirates' black flag; ~ or *Sir* ~ *de Coverley* (de kŭv'erli), a country-dance & tune).

rŏgue (-g), n., & v.t. **1.** Idle vagrant (arch.); knave, rascal, swindler, (often playfully of mischievous child or waggish or arch-mannered person). **2.** Inferior plant among seedlings (vb, weed out ~s from). **3.** (Also ~ *elephant, buffalo*, etc.) wild beast, esp. elephant, driven or living apart from the herd & of savage temper. **4.** Shirking racehorse or hunter. Hence rŏg'uERY(4) (-ge-) n., rŏg'uISH¹ (-gĭ-) a., rŏg'uishLY² adv., -ATION. n. [16th-c. cant wd, of unkn. orig.]

roi (rwah), n. (F for) king; ~ *fainéant* (see Ap.; lit. = King Do-nothing), ruler. chairman, etc., who is a mere figure-head like the Merovingian kings whose power was usurped by mayors of the palace; *le* ~. *le veult, le ~ s'avisera*, (see Ap.), forms of giving, refusing, the royal assent to parliamentary bill, ꞊ the king wills it, will consider.

roi'nĕk. See ROOINEK.

rois'ter, v.i. Revel noisily, be uproarious, (esp. in part. as adj.). Hence~ER¹, ~ING¹, nn. [f. obs. *roister* roisterer f. F *rustre* var. of *ruste* f. L RUSTICUS]

Rŏl'and, n. Name of nephew of Charlemagne celebrated in legend often with his comrade Oliver (*a* ~ *for an Oliver*, effective retort).

rŏle, rôle (rŏl), n. Actor's part; one's function, what one is appointed or expected or has undertaken to do. [F *rôle*, ꞊ foll.]

rŏll¹, n. **1.** Cylinder formed by turning flexible fabric such as paper or cloth over & over upon itself without folding (~*s of carpet, paper*, etc.; SWISS ~); (in Ionic capital) volute. **2.** Document, esp. official record, in this form (‖ *Master of the R~s*, one of the judges of the Court of Appeal, Keeper of the Records at the Public Record Office; ‖ *the R~s*, buildings in which these were formerly kept now superseded by Public Record Office); register or catalogue (*in the* ~ *of saints*; *a long* ~ *of heroes; on the* ~s *of fame*; RENT³-~; ~ *of honour*, esp. list of those who have died for their country in war); ‖ the official list of qualified solicitors (*strike off the* ~s, debar from practising for dishonesty etc.); a list of persons esp. soldiers or schoolboys used to detect absentees (~-*call*, calling over of this). **3.** More or less (semi)cylindrical straight or curved mass of anything however formed (*a* ~ *of butter, soap, straw, tobacco, hair; has* ~s *of fat on him*; ~ *of bread* or usu. ~, small loaf esp. for breakfast use); (archit., also ~-*moulding*) moulding of convex section. **4.** Turned-back edge of something, e.g. coat-collar. **5.** (book-bind.). Revolving patterned tool for marking cover. **6.** Cylinder or roller. [ME, f. OF *rolle, role* (now *rôle*) f. L *rotulus*]

rŏll², v.t. & i., & n. **1.** Move (t. & i.) or send or go in some direction by turning over & over on axis often with aid of gravitation (~ *barrel; barrel started* ~*ing; ball, coin*, ~*ed under the table, into a hole; river* ~s *down stones*; ~*ing stone* GATHERS *no moss; planets* ~ *on their courses; years* ~ *on* or *by*, go smoothly; ~ *one over*, send him ~*ing* or sprawling); make revolve between two surfaces (~*ing a marble between his palms*); wrap usu. *up in* by ~*ing* motion (~*ed himself up in the blankets*). **2.** Change direction (of) with rotatory motion (*his eyes* ~ *strangely*; ~*ed his eyes on us*). **3.** Wallow, turn about in fluid or loose medium, (of horse etc.) lie on back & kick about, (*porpoise, swimmer*, ~s *in the water*; ~*ing in money, luxury, ease; mule tried to* ~, as way of getting rid of rider or load). **4.** Sway or rock (t. & i.), walk with swaying gait as of sailor, reel, (~*ed himself from side to side; ship* ~s *& pitches; he* ~*ed up to her*). **5.** Undulate, show undulating surface or motion, go or propel or carry with such motion, (*sea, river*, ~s; *river* ~s *its waters to sea; waves* ~ *in; smoke* ~s *up; chimney* ~s *up smoke; the mist* ~*ed away; a* ~*ing expanse* or *plain*). **6.** Utter or be uttered, sound, with vibratory or undulating or trilling effect (~ *out verses, song*, etc.; *thunder, drum, organ, voice, echo*, ~s; ~ *one's rs*). **7.** (Of wheeled vehicle) advance or convey usu. *along, by*, etc., (of person) be so conveyed, (*carriage* ~*ed along*, ~*ed them by; he* ~*ed past in his carriage*; ~*ing-stock*, railway engines and vehicles). **8.** Flatten by passing roller over or by passing between rollers (~*s of lawn, metal, paste for pies*, etc.; ~*ed gold*; thin coating so applied; ~*ing-pin*, roller for paste; ~*ing-press*, copperplate-printer's press with revolving cylinder, also press with rollers for various purposes).

9. Turn (t. & i.) over & over upon itself into more or less cylindrical shape (usu. *up*; *the way to ~ a greatcoat*; *hedgehog ~s itself into a ball or ~s up*). **10.** Form (t. & i.) in(to) cylindrical or spherical shape, or accumulate into mass, by ~ing (~ *cigarettes, a huge snowball, snow into ball*; *the reckoning is ~ing up*, increasing, in amount; *saint & philosopher~ed into one*). **11.** *~-top desk*, with flexible cover sliding in curved grooves. **12.** *~ up*, (mil.) drive flank of (enemy line) back & round so that line is shortened or surrounded, (intr., colloq.) appear on the scene, turn up; hence ~ABLE a. **13.** n. ~ing motion (*the ~ of the sea, ship*); (aeron.) complete revolution about the longitudinal axis; spell of ~ing (*a ~ on the grass*); ~ing gait; ROCK[3] *-'n'- ~*. **14.** Quick continuous beating of drum; long peal of thunder or shout; rhythmic flow of words. [ME, f. OF *rol(l)er* f. Rom. *rotulare* f. *rotula* (*-us*) dim. of ROTA]

roll'er, n. In vbl senses; esp.: cylinder of wood, stone, metal, etc., & of various proportions used alone or as rotating part of machine for lessening friction, smoothing ground, pressing, stamping, crushing, spreading printer's ink, rolling up cloth on, etc.; (usu. ~ *bandage*) long surgical bandage rolled up for convenience of applying; kind of tumbler-pigeon; long swelling wave; brilliant-plumaged bird allied to crows, also German breed of canary, [G, f. *rollen* to roll]; ~ SKATE[2], *skating*; ~ *towel*, endless, working on ~. [-ER[1]]

roll'ey. See RULLEY.

roll'ick, v.i., & n. **1.** Be jovial, indulge in high spirits, enjoy life boisterously, revel, (esp. in part. as adj.). **2.** n. Exuberant gaiety; frolic, spree, escapade. [orig. unkn.]

rol'y-pol'y, n. & a. **1.** (Also ~ *pudding*) pudding made of sheet of paste covered with jam etc., formed into roll, & boiled. **2.** adj. (Usu. of child) podgy, plump. [prob. formed on ROLL[2]]

Rŏm, n. (pl. ~*a*). Male gipsy, (pl.) gipsies. [Romany wd]

Romā'ic, a. & n. (Of, in, etc.) the vernacular language of modern Greece. [f. Gk *Rōmaïkos* Roman (used esp. of Eastern empire)]

Romā'ika, n. National dance of modern Greece. [mod. Gk (*-kē*), orig. fem. adj. (prec.)]

Rŏm'an[1], n. **1.** Citizen, soldier, native, or inhabitant, of ancient Rome, member of ancient-~ State, (*King, Emperor, of the~s*, sovereign head of Holy Roman Empire); inhabitant of medieval or modern Rome. **2.** pl. Christians of ancient Rome (~*s*, or in full *Epistle to the ~s*, N.-T. book, abbr. *Rom.*). **3.** (print.) ROMAN[2] type (abbr. in press-correcting, *rom.*). **4.** = ROMAN CATHOLIC. [f. L *Romanus* (ROME, -AN); ME *romain(e)* f. OF *romain*]

Rŏm'an[2], a. **1.** Of ancient Rome or its territory, people, or (rarely; usu. *Latin*) language (~ *Empire*, that established by Augustus 27 B.C. & divided by Theodosius A.D. 395 into WESTERN or Latin & eastern or Greek empires, of which the eastern lasted till 1453, & the western, after lapsing in 476, was revived 800 by Charlemagne & continued to exist as the *Holy ~ Empire* till 1806; ~ *law*, code developed by ancient Romans & forming basis of many modern codes; ~ *pottery, bricks, road*, etc., surviving from period of ~ rule; ~ *cement*, trade name for a hydraulic cement named after ancient-~ kind; ~ *balance, beam, or steelyard*, ordinary steelyard; ~ *simplicity, honesty, virtue, patriotism*, etc., as of Romans of early Republic; ~ *nose*, with high bridge, aquiline, whence, of person or horse, ~-nŏSED[2] (*-zd*) a.; ~ *letters or type*, of the plain upright type used in ordinary print, opp. *Gothic* or *black letter & italic*; ~ *alphabet*, that used by Romans & still with slight modifications in W. Europe; ~ *numerals*, the letters I, V, etc. used in composing number-symbols, see below[†] for mod. use, & cf. ARABIC; ~ *architecture*, COMPOSITE, & see ORDER[1]; ~ *history, historian*, etc., of ancient Rome). **2.** Of papal Rome, esp. = ROMAN CATHOLIC, whence ~ISH[1](2) a., ~īZER[1] n. **3.** Of medieval or modern Rome (~ *school*, painting school of Raphael; ~ *fever*, malaria, formerly prevalent at Rome; ~ SNAIL; ~ *vitriol*, sulphate of copper; ~ CANDLE). Hence ~ISM(3, 4), ~IST(2, 3), ·nn., ~is'tic a., ~IZE(2, 3, 4) v.t. & i., ~īZA'TION n., Romān'o- comb. form. [†Mod. use of ~ numerals, differing in some respects from the ancient: The only symbols now used are I = 1, V = 5, X = 10, L = 50, C = 100, D = 500, M = 1000; the letters composing a number are ranged in order of value, & the number meant is found by addition, e.g. MDCLXVI = 1666; if a letter or set of letters is placed before a letter of higher value, it is to be subtracted from it before the addition is done, e.g. IX = 9, MCM = 1900; IIII is usu. preferred to IV on clock-faces. [ME *romain(e)*, later *roman* (as prec.)]

roman-à-clef (rōmahn' ah klā'), n. Novel in which real persons or events appear in disguise. [F, = novel with a key]

Rŏm'an Căth'olic, a. & n. (Member) of the Church of Rome. Hence Rōman--Cathŏl'icALLY, Rōman-Căth'olicLY[2], advv., Rōman-Cathŏl'icISM(3) n. [f. c. 1600, perh. orig. as non-controversial compromise between *Roman(ist), Romish,* etc., & *Catholic*]

rŏmance', n. & a., & v.i. **1.** (R~). Vernacular language of old France mainly developed but distinguished from Latin; corresponding language of Italy, Spain, Provence, etc.; (collect.) the languages descended from Latin. **2.** adj. (R~; of languages) thus descended. **3.** Medieval tale usu. in verse of some hero of chivalry (named as written in R~). **4.** Prose or rarely verse tale with scene & incidents remote from everyday life, class of literature consisting of such tales; set of facts, episode, love affair, etc., suggesting such tales by its strangeness or moving nature; atmosphere characterizing such tales, mental tendency to be influenced by it, sympathetic imaginativeness, whence ~LESS (-sl-) a. **5.** (An) exaggeration, (a) picturesque falsehood. **6.** (mus.). Short piece of simple character. **7.** v.i. Exaggerate or distort the truth, draw the long-bow. [ME, f. OF *romanz* f. Rom. **romanice* (opp. *Latine* in Latin) adv. f. ROMANICUS]

romăn′cer, n. Medieval or other writer of romances; fantastic liar. [f. *romance* vb (prec.) partly in obs. sense]

Rŏm′anĕs, n. Gipsy language. [Gipsy (adv.)]

Rŏmanĕsque′ (-k), a. & n. = ROMANCE 1 & 2. **2.** (archit.). (In) style of building prevalent in Romanized Europe between the classical & Gothic periods. [-ESQUE]

Rŏmān′ian, **Roum-** (rōō-), **Rum-** (rōō-), n. & a. (Native or language) of Romania. [-AN]

Rŏmăn′ic, a. & n. **1.** Descended from Latin, Romance (a. & n.). **2.** Descended from, inheriting civilization etc. of, the Romans, Romance-speaking. [f. L *Romanicus* (ROMAN 1, -IC)]

Rŏmăn′itў, n. (rare). Civilization & influence of Roman empire. [f. LL *Romanitas* (ROMAN 2, -ITY)]

Rŏmănsh′, **Rou-**, **Ru-**, (ro-, rōō-), n. & a. (In) the RHAETO-ROMANIC dialect spoken in the Grisons, E. Switzerland; = *Rhaeto-Romanic*. [as ROMANCE]

romăn′tic, a. & n. **1.** Characterized by or suggestive of or given to romance, imaginative, remote from experience, visionary, (*a ~ story, scene, adventure, girl*). **2.** (Of music) subordinating form to theme, imaginative, passionate. **3.** (Of projects etc.) fantastic, unpractical, quixotic, dreamy. **4.** (Of literary or artistic method etc.) preferring grandeur or picturesqueness or passion or irregular beauty to finish & proportion, subordinating whole to parts or form to matter, (opp. CLASSIC, CLASSICAL), whence ~IST(2) n.; hence **romăn′tically** adv., ~ISM(2, 3) n., ~IZE(2, 3) v.i. & t. **5.** n. A ~ist; (pl.) ~ ideas or talk. [f. ROMAUNT, f. OF *romant* (mod. *roman*) f. *romanz* ROMANCE, -IC]

Rŏm′anў, n. & a. **1.** Gipsy (n. & a.); (pl., also collect. sing.) *the* gipsies, (pl.) gipsies. **2.** The gipsy language. [f. Gipsy *Romani* fem. & pl. of *Romano* adj. (ROM)]

romaunt′, n. (arch.). A romance or tale of chivalry etc. [f. OF *romant* see ROMANTIC]

Rōme, n. **1.** City or ancient State of ~ (~ *was not built in a day*, encouragement to fainthearted; *do in ~ as ~ does, as the Romans do*, adapt oneself to surroundings); Roman empire. **2.** Church of ~, whence ~′WARD a. & adv., ~′WARDS adv., (-mw-), **Rŏm′ISH** 1 a. (chiefly derog.). [ME, f. OF, f. L *Roma*; OE f. L]

rŏmp, v.i. & n. **1.** (Of children etc.) play about together, chase each other, wrestle, etc.; (racing sl.) get *along, past,* etc., without effort, come *in* or *home* as easy winner. **2.** n. Child or woman fond of ~ing, tomboy; spell of ~ing, boisterous play, (often *game of* ~s); hence ~′Y 2 a. [perh. (n. f. vb) var. of RAMP 2]

rŏmp′er, n. (Sing. or pl.) child's overall. [prec., -ER 1(2)]

rŏn′deau (-dō), n. Ten-line or thirteen-line poem with only two rhymes throughout & opening words used twice as refrain. [F, earlier RONDEL]

rŏn′del, n. (Special form of) RONDEAU. [ME, f. OF, f. *rond* ROUND 1, -LE(2); cf. ROUNDEL]

rŏn′dō, n. (pl. ~s). Piece of music with leading theme which returns from time to time. [It., f. F RONDEAU]

rŏn′dure, n. (poet.). Round outline or object. [f. F *rondeur* (ROUND 1, -URE), after *roundure*]

‖ **rŏne**, n. (Sc.). Gutter to carry off rain from roof. [orig. unkn.]

‖ **Rŏn′eŏ**, n., & v.t. Machine for duplicating letters, circulars, etc., in numbers; (v.t.) reproduce with a ~. [P]

Rönt′genŏgrăm (rüntyen-), n. Photograph taken by Röntgen rays. [foll., -O-, GRAM]

Röntgen rays. See RAY 1..

rōōd, n. **1.** The cross of Christ (arch.; often in oaths, as *by the R*~); crucifix, esp. one raised on middle of ~-*screen*, wooden or stone carved screen separating nave & choir; ~-*arch*, between nave & choir; ~-*beam*, cross-beam, usu. as head of ~-*screen*, supporting ~; ~-*cloth*, veiling ~ in Lent; ~-*loft*, gallery on top of ~-*screen*. **2.** Quarter of an acre (esp. as loose term for small piece of land; *not a ~ remained to him*). [OE *rōd*, OS *rōda*, cross; also, in sense 'rod, pole ', OE *rōd*, OS *rōda*, OHG *ruota* (cf. OE *seglrōd* sail-yard)]

rōōf, n., & v.t. **1.** Upper covering of house or building usu. supported by its walls (*under* one's ~, in one's house, esp. w. ref. to hospitality; *a ~ over* one's *head*, somewhere to live; also fig., as *the ~ of heaven*; ~ *of the world*, high mountain range; ~ *of the mouth*, palate; *under a ~ of foliage*; top of covered vehicle esp. when used for outside passengers; ~-*garden*, on flat ~ of building; ~-*tree*, ridge-pole of ~; hence ~′AGE(1)n., (-)~ED 2 (-ft), ~′LESS, aa. **2.** v.t. Cover with ~, be ~ of, (often *in, over*); hence ~′ING 1(3) n. [OE *hrōf*, = OFris. *rhoof*, MDu. *roof*]

‖ **rōōf′er**, n. (colloq.). Letter of thanks

for entertainment sent by departed visitor. [prec., -ER[1]]

rōō'ĭnĕk, roi'nĕk, n. Newcomer, esp. British or European immigrant, in S. Africa; (in Boer war) British soldier. [Afrikaans (*rooi-*), = red-neck]

rook[1], n., & v.t. **1.** Black hoarse-voiced bird of crow tribe nesting in colonies; sharper, esp. at dice or cards, person who lives on inexperienced gamblers etc., (cf. PIGEON); ~ *pie*, of young ~s; ~*rifle*, of small bore for ~-shooting; hence ~'LET, ~'LING[1], nn., ~'Y[2] a. **2.** v.t. Win money from at cards etc. esp. by swindling; charge (customer) extortionately. [OE *hrōc*, MDu. *roec*, MLG *rōk*, OHG *hruoh*, ON *hrókr*, prob. imit.]

rook[2], n. (chess). = CASTLE[1]. [ME, f. OF *roc(k)* ult. f. Pers. *rukh*]

rook'erў, n. **1.** (Clump of trees with) colony of rooks. **2.** Colony of penguins etc. or seals. **3.** Crowded cluster of mean houses or tenements. [-ERY]

rook'ie, n. (army sl.). Recruit.

room, n., & v.i. **1.** Space that is or might be occupied by something, capaciousness or ability to accommodate contents, (*takes up too much* ~; *there is plenty of* ~; *no* ~ *to turn in, to swing a* CAT[1]; *would rather have his* ~ *than his company*, wish him away; *we have no* ~ *here for idlers*; *make* ~, vacate standing-ground etc. or post etc. for or *for* another, withdraw, retire, also clear a space *for* person or thing by removal of others; ~ *for*, arch., ellipt. command to make way for some one; *in one's* ~, *in the* ~ *of*, instead of, in succession to, as substitute for), whence ~'Y[2] a., ~'INESS n., ~'ĬLY[2] adv. **2.** Opportunity, scope, to do or for (~ *to deny ourselves*; *no* ~ *for dispute*; *leave* ~ *for evasion*; *there is* ~ *for improvement*, things are not as good as they should be). **3.** Part of house enclosed by walls or partitions, floor, & ceiling; (pl.) set of these occupied by person or family, apartments or lodgings; (transf.) the company in a ~ (*set the* ~ *in a roar*); whence ~'FUL(2) n., ~'ED[2] (-md) a. **4.** *v.i. Have ~(s), lodge, board, whence ~'ER[1] n.; ~*ing-house*, lodging-house. [OE *rūm*, OS, OHG, ON, Goth. *rūm*]

roost[1], n., & v.i. & t. **1.** Bird's perching or resting place, esp. hen-house or part of it in which fowls sleep, (transf.) sleeping-accommodation, bed(room), (*go to* ~, retire for the night; *at* ~, perched, in bed; *curses come home to* ~, recoil upon curser). **2.** vb. (Of birds or persons) settle for sleep, be perched or lodged for the night; provide with sleeping-place. [OE *hróst*, = MDu. *roest*; cf. OS *hróst* roof-spars]

∥ **roost**[2], n. Tidal race about Orkneys & Shetlands. [f. ON *rost*]

roos'ter, n. Domestic cock. [-ER[1]]

root[1], n. **1.** Part of plant normally below earth's surface & serving to attach it to earth & convey nourishment from soil to it, (pl.) such part divided into branches or fibres, corresponding organ of epiphyte, part attaching ivy to its support (also. ~'LET r.), permanent underground stock of plant, small plant with ~ for transplanting, (plant, such as turnip or carrot, with) edible ~, (*pull up by the* ~s, uproot lit. & fig.; *take, strike,* ~, begin to draw nourishment from soil, fig. get established; *lay axe to* ~ *of* tree or institution, set about destroying it; ~ *&* BRANCH[1]). **2.** (bibl.). Scion, offshoot, (*there shall be a* ~ *of Jesse*). **3.** Imbedded part of some bodily organ or structure, part of thing attaching it to greater or more fundamental whole, (~ *of tongue, tooth, nail,* etc.; ~ *of a gem*, esp. of emerald, cloudy part by which it adhered to stone; ~s *of mountain*, its base). **4.** Source or origin (*of; love of money is the* ~ *of all evil*; a ~ *of bitterness*; ~ *fallacy, idea,* etc., the one from which the rest originated). **5.** Basis, dependence, means of continuance or growth, (*has its* ~ *or* ~s *in selfishness*; *has no* ~ *in the nature of things*). **6.** Bottom, essential substance or nature, (*get at the* ~s *of things*; *has the* ~ *of the matter in him*, is essentially sound, w. ref. to *Job* xix. 28). **7.** (math.). ~ *of*, number or quantity that when multiplied by itself a usu. specified number of times gives (specified number etc.; *square or second* ~ *of 4*, or ellipt. ~ *of 4* or ~ *4*, symbol √4, is 2; √3 *is irrational*; *cube or third* ~ *of 27*, symbol √27, *is 3*). **8.** (philol.). Ultimate unanalysable element of language, basis (whether itself surviving as a word or not) on which words are made by addition of prefixes or suffixes or by other modification, (symbol √, as *sopor* is *from* √SWEP). **9.** (mus.). Fundamental note of chord. **10.** ~-*stock*, = RHIZOME, also primary form whence offshoots have arisen. Hence ~'AGE(1, 3) n., ~'LESS, ~'Ў[1] [-Y[2]], aa. [OE *rōt* f. ON *rót* f. *wrōt*- cogn. w. WORT & L *radix*]

root[2], v.t. & i. **1.** (Cause to) take root, fix firmly to the spot, establish, (*some kinds* ~ *freely*; *take care to* ~ *them firmly*; *fear* ~*ed him to the ground*; esp. in p.p., as *her affection was deeply* ~*ed*, ~*ed objections to, obedience* ~*ed in fear*, whence ~'ĕDLY[2] adv., ~'ĕDNESS n.). **2.** Drag or dig *up* by the roots; ~ *out*, exterminate; uproot, tear away, *from* (poet.). [ME, f. prec.]

root[3], *rout*, v.i. & t. **1.** (Of swine etc.) turn up ground with snout, beak, etc., in search of food; turn *up* (ground) thus. **2.** (transf.). Search *out*, hunt *up*, rummage (*among, in*). **3.** *(sl.). Be active *for* another by giving encouraging applause or support. [alt. (w. assim. to ROOT[1]) f. *wroot* f. OE *wrōtian* f. *wrōt* snout; cf. ROUT[2]]

root'erў, n. Pile of roots & stumps for growing garden plants on (cf. ROCK[1]*ery*). [-ERY]

∥ **rōō'tle,** v.i. & t. = ROOT[3]. [-LE(3)]

‖ **rōōt′ẏ²**, n. (for *rooly¹* see ROOT¹). (mil. sl.). Bread.· [Anglo-Ind., f. Hind. *rōṭī*]

rōpe, n., & v.t. & i. 1. (Piece of) stout cordage (prop. over 1 in. in circumf., cf. CABLE¹, CORD) made by twisting strands of hemp, flax, hide, or wire, into one (*the ~*, halter for hanging person, also = TIGHT-~; *on the* HIGH *~s*; *the ~s*, those enclosing prize-ring or other area; *know, learn, put* one *up to, the ~s*, the conditions in some sphere of action; *give* one *~, ~ enough to hang* him*self, plenty of ~*, etc., not·check him, trust to his bringing about his own discomfiture; *~ of sand,* delusive security; *~ of onions, ova, pearls*, these strung together; *on the ~*, of mountaineers,.~d together). 2. Viscid or gelatinous stringy formation in beer or other liquid. 3. *~-dancer, ·dancing*, performer, performing, on tight·~; *~-drill*, in which a ~ stretched by two men represents company etc.; *~-ladder*, two long·~s connected by short cross·~s as ladder; *~′manship*, skill in ~-walking or ~-·climbing; *~-moulding*, cut spirally in imitation of ~-strands; *~-quoit*, ring of ~ used in quoits played on board ship; *~′s-end*, short piece of ~ used to flog (esp. sailor) with; *~-walk*, long piece of ground used for twisting ~; *~-walker, ·walking, = ~-dancer, ·dancing*; *~-yard, ~-making* establishment; *~-yarn*, (piece of the) material (esp. when unpicked) of which *~-*strands consist, mere trifle; hence **rōp′ING¹**(6) n., **rōp′ẏ²** a., **rōp′INESS** n. 4. vb. Fasten or secure with ~; (mountaineering) connect (party) with~, attach (person) to ~, put on ~; use ~s in towing etc.; enclose, close *in*, (space) with ~; ~ *in*, secure adherence of, decoy. 5. ‖ (In racing) check (horse), check horse, (of athlete) not put forth full powers, in order to lose race. 6. Become ropy or viscid. [OE *rāp*, MDu., MLG *rēp*, OHG *reif*, ON *reip*, Goth. *raip* f. Gmc **raip-*]

Rŏ′quefort·(-kfŏr), n. Kind of French cheese of goats' & ewes' milk. [~ in France]

rŏ′quelaure (-kelōr), n. (hist.). Man's cloak reaching to knees (18th c.). [F (Duke of *R~*)]

rŏ′quet (-kǐ), v.t. & i. (*~ing, ~ed*, pr. ·ǐng, ·ǐd), & n. 1. Cause one's ball to strike, (of ball) strike, another ball at croquet; strike another ball thus. 2. n. Act or fact of *~ing*. [arbitrary f. CROQUET² & orig. in same sense]

rŏr′qual, n. Whale with dorsal fin, finback. [F, f. Norw. *röyrkval*, repr. OIcel. *reythr* the specific name + *hvalr* whale]

rōrt′ẏ, raught′ẏ (-awt·), a. (sl.). Enjoyable (*had a ~ time*); fond of amusement & excitement. [orig. unkn.]

rōs′āce (-z-), n. Rose-window; rose-·shaped ornament or design. [F (ROSE)]

rosā′ceous (-zāshʊs), a. Of the family *Rosaceae*, of which the rose is the type.

So **rosA′CEAN** (-zāshan) n. [f. L *rosaceus* (ROSE, ·ACEOUS)]

rōsăn′iline (-z-), n. (Kinds of red dye obtained from) an organic base derived from aniline. [ROSE, ANILINE]

rosār′ian, n. 1. Rose-fancier. 2. (R.-C. Ch.). Member of a Confraternity of the Rosary. [f. L *rosarium* ROSARY, ·AN]

rosār′ium, n. Rose-garden. [L (foll.)]

rōs′arẏ (-z-), n. 1. Rose-garden, rose-bed. 2. (R.-C. Ch.) form of prayer in which fifteen decades of Aves are repeated, each decade preceded by Paternoster & followed by Gloria; book containing this; string of 165 beads for keeping count in this (*lesser~*, of 55). [15th c., f. L *rosarium* (ROSE, ·ARIUM)]; R.-C. sense f. LL sense *chaplet*]

Rōs′cian (-shǐ-), a. Like or worthy of Roscius, famous Roman actor of 1st c. B.C. [·AN]

rōse¹ (-z), n., a., & v.t. 1. (Prickly bush or shrub bearing) a beautiful & usu. fragrant flower usu. of red or yellow or white colour (BLUSH², BRIER¹, CABBAGE, DAMASK, DOG¹, MONTHLY, MOSS¹, MUSK, TEA, etc., ·~; also in names of other flowering plants, as ROCK¹~, CHRISTMAS ~, ~ *of Jericho*, the Resurrection plant with dried fronds unfolding under moisture, ~ *of Sharon*, unidentified eastern flower, ~ *of May*, white narcissus; ATTAR, OTTO, *of ~s*; *red as a ~*; *gather ~s* or *life's ~s*, seek pleasure; *path strewn with ~s*, life of delights; *bed of ~s*, pleasant easy post or condition, esp. in *is no bed of ~s*; so *is not all ~s*; ~ *without a thorn*, impossible happiness, unalloyed delight; *the white ~ of virginity, innocence*, etc.; *the ~ of* with place-name, most beautiful girl or woman in; *Wars of the R~s*, 15th-c. civil wars between Yorkists with white & Lancastrians with red ~ as emblem; *under the ~*, = SUB² *rosa*), whence **rōs′ERY**(3) (-z-) n. 2. Representation of the flower in heraldry or decoration (esp. as national emblem of England, cf. THISTLE, SHAMROCK, LEEK or DAFFODIL; *Golden ~*, ornament blessed by Pope on 4th Sunday in Lent & sent as compliment to some R.-C. sovereign, city, etc.); *~*-shaped design. 3. Rosette worn on shoe or clerical hat. 4. Protuberance round base of animal's horn or some birds' eyes. 5. Sprinkling-·nozzle of watering-pot or hose, whence (·)**rōsED²** (·zd) a. 6. = ~ *diamond*; = *~-window*. 7. Light crimson colour, pink, (usu. pl.) rosy complexion (*has quite lost her, spoiled her natural, ~s*). 8. *The ~*, erysipelas. 9. *~-apple*, tropical tree cultivated for foliage & fruit, its fruit; *~-bay*, oleander, rhododendron, azalea, species of willow-herb; *~′bud*, bud of ~ (often attrib., as *~bud mouth*), pretty girl, *débutante*; *~-bush, ~ plant*; *~-·chafer*, green or copper-coloured beetle frequenting *~s*; *~-colour*, rosy red, pink, (fig.) pleasant state of things or outlook *(life is not all ~-colour)*; ~*-coloured*, rosy, (fig.) optimistic, sanguine, cheerful, (*takes ~-coloured views; see things through ~-coloured spectacles*); ~*-cut*, cut as a ~ *diamond*, hemispherical with curved part in triangular facets; ~*-drop*, skin-disease with red blotches; ~*-engine*, appendage to lathe for engraving curved patterns; ~*-gall*, excrescence on dog-~ etc. made by·insect; ~*-leaf*, leaf, usu. petal, of ~ (*crumpled ~-leaf*, slight vexation alloying general felicity); ~*-lipped*, with rosy lips; ~*-mallow*, hibiscus; ~ (or ~*-head*) *nail*, with head shaped like ~ diamond; ~ *noble*, 15th–16th c. gold coin of varying value stamped with ~; ~*-pink*, pigment of chalk or whiting coloured with Brazil-·wood decoction, also = ~*-colour(ed)* lit. & fig.; ~*-rash*, = ROSEOLA; ~*-red* a. & n., red as (of) a ~; ~*-root*, kinds of plant with root smelling like~ when dried or bruised; ~*-tree*; ~ *vinegar*, infusion of~s in vinegar for application in headache etc.; ~*-water*, perfume made from~s, (fig.) compliments, gentle handling, etc. (~*-water surgery*) *revolutions are not made with ~-water*); ~*-window*, circular, usu. with spokelike tracery; ~*'wood*, kinds of cabinet wood named from their fragrance; hence ~'LESS, ~'LIKE, (-z-), aa. **10.** adj. Coloured like a pale red~, of warm pink. **11.** v.t. Make (face, snow-slope, etc.) rosy (esp. in p.p.). [OE *rose*, *rōse*, f. L *rosa*; in ME reinforced f. OF *rose*]

rose². See RISE¹.

rōs'eate (-z-), a. = ROSE-*coloured* (lit. & fig.). Hence ~LY² adv. [f. L *roseus* (ROSE¹) *rosy*+-ATE²]

rōse'mary̆ (-zm-), n. Evergreen fragrant shrub with leaves used in perfumery etc. & taken as emblem of remembrance. [ME, earlier *rosmarine* f. L *rosmarinus* (*ros* ·dew, MARINE) w. assim. to ROSE & the name of the Virgin]

rōs'eo- (-z-), comb. form in names of salts & alkalis of L *roseus* rose-coloured, as ~*·cobalt*.

rōse'ol|a (-z-), n. Rosy rash in measles etc.; German measles. Hence ~AR¹, ~OUS, aa. [mod. L (prec., -*ola* dim. termination)]

rosĕtt|e' (-z-),.n. Rose-shaped ornament for dress or harness made of ribbons, leather strips, etc.; (archit.) carved or moulded conventional rose on wall etc., also rose-window; (biol.) roselike cluster or organs, markings resembling rose; = ROSE *diamond*; roselike object or arrangement of parts. Hence ~'ED² a. [F (ROSE¹, -ETTE)]

Rōsicru'cian (-zĭkrōōshn), n. & a. (Member) of an order devoted to occult lore said to have been founded 1484 by Christian Rosenkreuz. Hence ~ISM(3) n. [f. mod. L *rosa crucis* (or *crux*), as latinization of G *Rosenkreuz*, +-IAN]

rŏs'in (-z-), n., & v.t. **1.** = RESIN (esp. of solid residue after distillation of oil of

turpentine from crude turpentine); hence ~Y² a. **2.** v.t. Smear, seal up, rub (esp. bow or string of fiddle etc.), with~. [ME, alt. f. RESIN]

Rŏsinăn'tè (-z-), Rŏz-, n. Worn-out ·horse, jade. [f. Sp. *Rocinante* (*rocin* jade, cf. obs. E *rouncy* riding-horse), Don Quixote's horse]

rosŏl'iō (-z-), n. A S.-Europ. sweet cordial. [It., f. L *ros* dew, *solis* of the sun, cordial being orig. made from plant sun-dew] ·

rŏs'ter, n. List or plan showing turns of duty for individuals or companies esp. of a military force. [f. Du. *rooster* list, orig. gridiron (*roosten* ROAST), w. ref. to parallel lines]

rŏs'tral, a. (Of column etc.) adorned with beaks actual or sculptured etc. of ancient war-galleys; (zool. etc.) of, on, the rostrum. [f. LL *rostralis* (ROSTRUM, -AL)]

rŏsträt'ĕd, a. (Of column etc.) = prec.; (zool. etc.) having, ending in, a rostrum. [f. L *rostratus* (ROSTRUM, ·-ATE²)]

rŏs'tr|um, n. (pl. ~*a*, ~*ums*). **1.** (Sing., or pl. ~*a* of single specimen but usu. w. pl. constr.; pl. in pl. sense, ~*a* or ~*ums*) platform for public speaking (orig. that in Roman forum adorned with beaks of captured galleys; pulpit, office, etc. that enables one to gain the public ear, esp. *auctioneer's* ~. **2.** (Rom. ant.). Beak of war-galley (pl. usu.~*a*). **3.** (zool., entom., bot.). Beak, stiff snout, beaklike part, whence ~ATE², ~IF'EROUS, ~IFORM, aa., ~o- comb. form. [L, = beak (*rodere* gnaw)]

rŏs'ŭlate (-z-), a. (bot.). (Of leaves) packed over each other like rose-petals. [LL *rosula* (ROSE¹, -ULE), -ATE², see -UL-]

rōs'y̆ (-z-), a. Coloured like a red rose (esp. of complexion as indicating health, of blush, wine, sky, light, etc.), (fig.) = ROSE-·*coloured*; (now rare) smelling like a rose, made of or covered or strewn with roses; ~ *cross*, emblem of ROSICRUCIANS; ~*-fingered*, epithet of *dawn* etc. Hence rōs'ILY² adv., rōs'INESS n., (-z-). [ME; -Y²]

rŏt¹, n. & int. **1.** Decay, putrefaction, rottenness, (esp. in timber, cf. DRY¹-~). **2.** Virulent liver-disease of sheep (usu. *the* ~). **3.** (sl.). (Also *tommy* ~) nonsense, absurd statement or argument or proposal (often as int. of incredulity or ridicule), foolish course, undesirable state of things, (*don't talk* ~; *it is perfect* ~ *to trust him*; *what tommy* ~ *that it is not open on Sundays!*). **4.** (crick., war, etc.). Sudden series of (freq. unaccountable) failures on one side (*a* ~ *set in*). [ME, prob. f. Scand.; cf. Icel., Norw. *rot*]

rŏt², v.i. & t. (-tt-). **1.** Undergo natural decomposition, decay, putrefy, (~ *off*, drop from stem etc. through rottenness); (fig., of society, institutions, etc.) gradually perish from want of vigour or use, (of prisoner) pine away (*left to* ~ *in gaol*),

2. Cause to ~, make rotten; (sl.) spoil or disconcert (*has ~ted the whole plan*). 3. || (sl.). Chaff, banter, tease; (abs.) talk ironically (*he is only ~ting*). 4. ~*-gut* a. & n., (liquor) injurious to stomach. [OE *rotian*, = MDu., MLG *roten*, OS *rotōn*, OHG *rozzēn*; see RET, ROTTEN]

röt′a, n. 1. List of persons acting, or duties to be done, in rotation, roster. 2. (R.-C. Ch.; *R*~). Supreme ecclesiastical & secular court. [L, = wheel]

röt′ary, a. & n. 1. Acting by rotation. 2. n. ~ machine; *traffic roundabout. 3. (*The*) *R*~, *R*~ *Club*(*s*), a world-wide society with many branches for international service to humanity, orig. named from clubs entertaining in rotation, whence Rotār′IAN a. & n., (member) of R~. [f. LL *rotarius* (prec., -ARY¹)]

röt′ate¹, a. (bot.). Wheel-shaped. [ROTA, -ATE²]

rotāte′², v.i. & t. Move (t. & i.) round axis or centre, revolve; arrange (esp. crops) or take in rotation. So röt′ATIVE, röt′atORY, ~′ABLE, aa. [f. L ROTA*re*, -ATE³]

rotā′tion, n. Rotating; recurrence, recurrent series or period, regular succession in office etc., (often *in, by,* ~; ~ *of crops,* growing of different crops in regular order to avoid exhausting soil). Hence ~AL (-sho-) a. [f. L *rotatio* (prec., -ATION)]

rotāt′or, n. (Anat.) muscle that rotates a limb etc.; revolving apparatus or part. [L (ROTATE², -OR)]

rötch(e), n. The little auk. [later form of Du., Fris. *rotge* of unkn. orig.]

röte, n. Mere habituation, knowledge got by repetition, unintelligent memory, (only *by* ~, as *say, know, do, by* ~). [ME *rote*, of unkn. orig.]

röt′ifer, n. Wheel-animalcule, member of class *Rotifera* with rotatory organs used in swimming. [L ROTA, -FEROUS]

röt′ograph (-ahf), n. Print of MS. page etc. got by sensitized roll. [prec., -GRAPH]

röt′or, n. Rotary part of machine; horizontally-rotating vane of helicopter. [irreg. for ROTATOR]

rött′en, a. 1. Decomposed or decomposing, putrid, perishing of decay, falling to pieces or friable or easily breakable or tearable from age or use. 2. (Of sheep). affected with the rot. 3. Morally, socially, or politically corrupt, effete, (||~ BOROUGH; *something is* ~ *in the state of Denmark, Haml.* I. iv. 90, things are unsatisfactory). 4. Inefficient, worthless; (sl.; of state of things, plan, etc.) disagreeable, regrettable, beastly, ill-advised. 5. ~*-stone,* decomposed siliceous limestone used as polishing-powder. Hence ~LY² adv., ~NESS n. [ME, f. ON *rotinn* cogn. w. ROT², RET]

Rött′en Row (rō), n. (Now usu. *the Row*) track in Hyde Park, fashionable resort for riding. [app. f. prec.]

|| **rött′er,** n. (sl.). One who is objectionable on moral or other grounds, useless or inefficient or disliked person. [ROT²*, -ER¹]

rotünd′, a. Circular, round, (rare), whence **rotün′d**ATE² a., **rotün′d**I-, **rotün′d**O- comb. forms, (bot.); (of mouth) rounded in speaking etc., (of speech, literary style, etc.) as from ~ mouth, sonorous, sounding, grandiloquent; (of persons) plump, podgy. Hence or cogn. **rotün′d**ITY n., ~LY² adv. [f. L *rotundus* cogn. w. ROTA]

rotün′da, n. Building of circular ground--plan, esp. one with dome; circular hall or room. [earlier *rotonda,* It., fem. of *rotondo* = prec.]

roturier (see Ap.), n. Plebeian. [F (*roture* plebeian tenure, f. L *ruptura* breaking, -IER]

rou′ble (roo-), **ru-** (roo-), n. Russian monetary unit and silver coin, = 100 copecks. [F, f. Russ. *ruble*]

roucou (rōōkōō′), n. (W.-Ind. tree yielding) orange dye. [F, f. Braz. *urucú*]

roué (rōō′ā), n. Debauchee, rake. [F, **p.p.** of *rouer* break on wheel, = one deserving this]

rouge¹ (rōōzh), a., n., & v.t. & i. 1. Red (only in *R*~ *Croix* pr. krwah, *R*~ *Dragon,* two pursuivants of English College of Arms, & in ~*-royal marble,* reddish Belgian kind). 2. n. Fine red powder made from safflower & used for colouring cheeks & lips; plate-powder of oxide of iron; revolutionary politician; ~*-et-noir* (-ā-nwah′r), card-game played on table with red & black marks on which money staked is laid (~, the red in this). 3. vb. Colour, adorn oneself, with ~. [F, f. L *rubeus* cogn. w. RED]

|| **rouge²** (rōōj), n. Scrummage, also touch--down counting as point to opponents, in Eton football (field game). [orig. unkn.]

rough (rŭf), a., adv., n., & v.t. 1. Of uneven or irregular surface, not smooth or level or polished, diversified or broken by prominences, hairy, shaggy, coarse in texture, rugged, (~ *skin, hands, paper, bark, road, cloth, country; book with* ~ *edges,* in which edges of original sheets are left untrimmed; ~ *leaf,* || first true leaf of springing plant after the smooth leaves or cotyledons, *in the* ~ *leaf,* at this stage; ~ *rice,* unhusked rice, paddy). 2. Not mild or quiet or gentle, unrestrained, violent, stormy, boisterous, disorderly, riotous, inconsiderate, harsh, unfeeling, drastic, severe, grating, astringent, (~ *manners, soldier, play;* ~ *water, sea, weather, wind;* ~ *words;* ~ *element of the population, quarter of the town;* ~ *usage, handling;* ~ *remedies;* ~ *baritone voice;* ~ *claret;* ~ *tongue,* habit of rudeness; *gave him a lick with the* ~ *side of my tongue,* spoke severely to him; ~ *passage,* crossing over ~ sea; ~ *work,* violence, also task requiring it, & see below; *have a* ~ *time,* suffer ~ handling or hardship; *horse has* ~ *paces,* jolts rider; *fact etc. is* ~ *luck,* or ~, *on person,* worse luck than he deserves; ~ MUSIC. **3.** Deficient in finish or elaboration or delicacy, incomplete, rudimentary, entirely or partly unwrought, merely passable, inexact, approximate, preliminary, (~ *nursing, style, welcome, kindness, plenty, accommodation, sketch, drawing*; ~ *work*, & see above; ~ *state, attempt, makeshift, circle*; ~ *stone*, not dressed; ~ DIAMOND; ~ *justice*; ~ *translation, estimate*; ~ *copy* of picture etc., reproducing only essentials; ~ *draft*; ~ COPY¹; ~ *coat*, first coat of plaster laid on; ~ *coating*, ~cast; ~ *& ready*, not elaborate, just good enough, not over-particular, ~ly efficient or effective). **4.** ~-*&-tum'ble*, (adj.) irregular, scrambling, disorderly, regardless of procedure-rules, (n.) haphazard fight, scuffle; ~'*cast*, (adj., of wall etc.) coated with mixture of lime & gravel, (of plan etc.) imperfectly elaborated, (n.) plaster of lime & gravel for walls, (v.t.) coat (wall) with ~cast, prepare (plan, essay, etc.) in outline; ~-*dry*, dry (clothes) without ironing etc.; ~-*footed*, with feathered feet (in names of birds); ~-*grind*, give preliminary grinding to (edged tool etc.); ~-*hew*, shape out ~ly, give crude form to, (p.p., uncouth, unrefined); ~-*hound*, kind of dogfish; ~ *house* (sl.), disturbance, row, horseplay; ~-*house*, (v.t.) handle (person) ~ly, (v.i.) make a disturbance, act violently; ~-*legged*, with hairy or feathered legs (of breeds of horse & bird); *~- neck* (sl.), a rowdy; ~-*rider*, horsebreaker, man who can ride unbroken horses, (mil.) irregular cavalryman; ~'*shod*, (of horse) having shoes with the nail-heads projecting (*ride* ~*shod*, domineer *over*); ~- -SPOKEN; ~-*wrought*, with the earlier processes done; hence ~EN⁶ (rŭ'fn) v.t. & i., ~'ISH¹(2) a., ~'LY² adv. (~*ly* SPEAK*ing*), ~'NESS n., (rŭf²). **5.** adv. In ~ manner (*land should be ploughed* ~; *play*~; chiefly in compds, of which some are given above). **6.** n. ~ ground (esp. *'over* ~ *& smooth*), (golf) *the* ~ ground outside the fairway between tees &ˌgreens; one of the spikes inserted in ~ing horse; hard part of life, piece of hardship, (usu. *take the* ~ *with the smooth, the* ~*s & the smooths*); ‖ rowdy, hooligan, man or boy of lower classes ready for lawless violence; *the* unfinished or *the* natural state, *the* general way, (*shape it from the* ~; *have seen it only in the* ~; *is true in the* ~). **7.** v.t. Turn *up* (feathers, hair, etc.) by rubbing against the grain (~ *one up the wrong way*, irritate *him*); secure (horse or its shoes) against slipping by insertion of spikes or projecting nails in shoes; ~ *it*, do without ordinary conveniences of life; break *in* (horse); shape or plan *out* ~ly; sketch *in* ~ly; tune *up* (piano) ~ly; give first shaping to (gem, lens, etc.). [OE *rūh*, MLG *rūch*, OHG *rūh*, f. Gmc **rūh(w)a*-]

roughage (rŭf'ij), n. (In dietetics) bran of cereals and other forms of cellulose con-

sidered valuable as a mechanical stimulant to the bowels. [-AGE (1)]

roulade (rōōlahd'), n. Florid passage of runs etc. in solo vocal music, usu. sung to one syllable. [F (*rouler* ROLL², -ADE)]

rouleau (rōōlō'), n. (pl: ~*x* or ~*s*, pr. -z). Cylindrical packet of coins; coil or roll. [F (*rôle* ROLL¹)]

roulĕtte' (rōō-), n. **1.** Gambling game on table with revolving centre. **2.** (math.). Curve generated by point on rolling curve. **3.** Device for keeping hair in curl. **4.** Revolving toothed wheel used in engraving, similar wheel for perforating postage stamps. [F, dim. of *rouelle* dim. of *roue* f. L *rota* wheel]

Roumān'ian (rōō-), n. & a. See ROMANIAN.

Roumansh. See ROMANSH.

R(o)umēl'iŏte (rōō-), n. Native of R(o)u-melia. [-OT²]

roun'cival, n. (Also ~ *pea*) large variety of pea. [from 16th c.; perh. f. *Ronces-valles* place-name]

round¹, a. **1.** Spherical or circular or cylindrical or approaching these forms, presenting convex outline or surface, (*the* ~ *world*; ~ *shot* (hist.), spherical ball for smooth-bore cannon; ~ *buckler, hole, mat*, of circular outline; ~ *table*, with disc top; *the R*~ *Table*, at which Arthur & his knights sat that none might have precedence; ~-*table conference*, held at ~ table for same purpose, (also) any informal confidential conference; ~ *game*, proper for ~ table, players being of any number & without sides or partners; ~ *face*, as broad as long; ~ *jacket*, cut level below, without skirts; ~ *hand* or *text*, writing with bold curves; ~ *tower, post, limbs*; ~ *arch*, semicircular as in Romanesque, opp. *pointed*; ~ *cheeks*, plump, not hollow; ~ *shoulders*, so bent forward that back is convex, whence ~'*shoul'derED*² (-shŏl'derd) a.; ~ *vowel* in phonet., pronounced with rounded lips). **2.** Done with or involving circular motion (~ *dance*, waltz; ~ *trip, voyage*, with return to starting-point; ~ or ~-*arm* or ~-*hand bowling*, with arm swung horizontally, cf. *underhand, overhand*; ~ *towel*, endless on roller; ~ *robin*, written petition with signatures in circle to conceal order in which they were written). **3.** Entire, continuous, all together, not broken or defective or scanty, sound, smooth, plain, genuine, candid, outspoken, (~ *dozen, score*, that & no less, so many together; ~ *numbers*, tens, hundreds, etc., with neglect of minor denominations, whence=roughly correct; *a* ~ *sum*, considerable; *a* ~ *style*, flowing; *at a* ~ *trot*, vigorous; *a* ~ *voice*, not harsh; ~ *unvarnished tale*, the plain truth; *be* ~ *with* one, arch., speak home-truths to him; *a* ~ *oath*, unmistakable). **4.** ~'*head*, member of Parliament party in 17th-c. civil war (from custom of wearing hair close cut); ~-*house*, (hist.) lock-up or place of detention, (naut.) cabin or set of cabins on after part of quarterdeck chiefly in old sailing-ships; ~-*top*, platform about masthead, formerly circular; ~ *turn* (naut.), single turn of rope round post etc. (hence, transf., *bring up with a* ~ *turn*, check with a sudden jerk, check abruptly). Hence ~'ISH¹(2) a., ~'NESS n. [ME, f. OF *rund*, *round*, f. L ROTUNDUS]

round², n. **1.** Round object (*this earthly* ~, earth; ~*s of ladder*, rungs; ~ *of beef*, thick disc from haunch as joint; ~ *of toast*, disc etc. cut across loaf). **2.** (sculpt.), Solid form as opp. *relief*; *in the* ~ (fig.), with all the features etc. fully shown. **3.** Circumference, bounds, extent, *of* (*in all the* ~ *of Nature*). **4.** Revolving motion, circular or circuitous or recurring course, circuit, cycle, series, (*the earth in its daily or yearly* ~; *a milk* (milkman's) ~; *the daily* ~, ordinary occupations of the day; *go for a good* ~, long walk out & home; *a* ~ *of days, pleasures, visits*; *make, go, one's* ~*s*, take customary walk esp. of inspection; *make the* ~ *of*, go round; *news, story, goes the* ~, is passed on); (mil., pl.) watch that goes round inspecting sentries or circuit it makes (*visiting, grand,* ~*s*, orderly, field, officer's inspection of guard & sentries); (golf) playing of all holes in course once; (mus.) kind of perpetual canon at the unison for equal voices. **5.** Allowance of something distributed or measured out, one of set or series, one bout or spell, one stage in competition, (*serve out a* ~ *of spirit, 20* ~*s of ball cartridge*; *never fired a single* ~; ~ *after* ~ *of cheers*; *a fight of ten* ~*s*; *threw up the sponge after the third* ~; *the winners in the first* ~ *are paired for the second*). **6.** ‖ ~*s'man*, tradesman's employee going round for orders & with goods. [ME, f. OF *rond(e)* n. (as prec.), partly f. ROUND¹]

round³, adv. & prep. **1.** With more or less circular motion, with return to starting-point after such motion, with rotation, with change to opposite position lit. or fig., (*sun goes, summer comes,* ~; *brings us* ~ *to winter*; *sleep the clock* ~, for twelve or twenty-four hours; *all the year* ~; *6 in.* ~, in girth; *wheels go* ~; *he turned short* ~; *soon won him* ~). **2.** To or at or affecting all or many points of a circumference or area or members of a company etc., in every direction from a centre or within a radius, (*glasses* ~, for all present to drink; *tea was served* ~; *send* ~ *the HAT*; *Home Rule all* ~, for each nationality; *an all-man*, one of varied talents; *show one* ~, take him to all points of interest; *room hung* ~ *with portraits*; *spread destruction* ~; *all the neighbours for a mile* ~). **3.** By circuitous way. (*will you jump or go* ~?; *go a long way* ~; *ask* one ~, out of his house into one's own; *order the car* ~, from garage to door). **4.** *All* ~, *right* ~, ~ *&* ~, emphatic forms of ~; ~ *about*, in a ring (about), all ~ (adv. & prep.); on all

sides (of), with change to opposite position, circuitously, approximately (*it will cost* ~ *about £10*); ~'*about*, (n.) circuitous way, place where all traffic has to follow a circular course (also attrib.), piece of circumlocution, ‖ merry-go-~ (‖ *lose on the swings what you make on the* ~*abouts*, end where you began after ups & downs), (adj.) circuitous, circumlocutory, plump or stout. **5.** prep. So as to encircle or enclose (*tour* ~ *the world*; *has a wrapper* ~ *her*). **6.** With successive visits to, at or to points on the circumference of, (*hawks them* ~ *the cafés*; *station them* ~ *the field*; *seated* ~ *the table*). **7.** In various directions from or with regard to (*diffuses cheerfulness* ~ *her*; *shells bursting* ~ *me*). **8.** Having as axis of revolution or central point (*turns* ~ *its centre of gravity*; *argue* ~ *&* ~ *subject*, not come to close quarters with it; *write book* ~ *a subject*). **9.** So as to double or pass in curved course, having thus passed, in the position that would result from thus passing, (*go, be, find person,* ~ *the corner*; GET ~). **10.** *All* ~, *right* ~, ~ *&* ~, emphatic forms of ~. [ME, f. ROUND¹, ², perh. partly aphetic f. AROUND]

round⁴, v.t. & i. **1.** Invest with, assume, round shape (~*ed eyes, mouth*; *her form is* ~*ing*; ~ *vowel*, pronounce it with ~*ed lips*; ~ *off* or ~ *the angles*, make them less sharp; ~ *dog's ears*, crop them). **2.** Bring to complete or symmetrical or well-ordered state (often *off*; ~ *off* or ~ *a sentence, estate, career*). **3.** Gather *up* (cattle, & transf.) by riding round, gather *up* (stragglers, criminals, etc.), whence ~'-*ŭp* n. **4.** Pass round, double, (cape etc.). **5.** Turn (t. & i.) round (rare, chiefly naut.; ~*ed on his heel to look at me*; ~ *boat off* etc., turn her to meet wave etc.; *ship* ~*s to*, comes to wind & heaves to). **6.** ~ *on*, make unexpected retort to (friend etc.), (of informer) peach upon. [f. ROUND¹; in ME perh. after OF *rondir*]

‖ **round⁵**, v.i. & t. (arch.). Whisper (t. & i.; chiefly w. double obj., as ~*ed him in the ear that*, told him secretly that). [OE *rūnian* (= OS *rūnōn*, OHG *rūnēn*) f. *rūn* RUNE; -*d* as in SOUND²]

roun'del, n. Small disc, esp. decorative medallion etc.; rondeau or rondel. [ME, f. OF *rondel(le)*, see ROUND¹, -LE(2)]

roun'delay, n. Short simple song with refrain; bird's song. [f. F *rondelet* (RONDEL, -ET¹) w. assim. to LAY¹]

roun'der, n. In vbl senses of ROUND⁴: ‖ also, (pl.) game with bat & ball between two sides with ~ (or complete run of player through all the bases arranged in a round) as unit of scoring. [ROUND⁴, ², -ER¹]

round'lỹ, adv. In thorough-going manner (*go* ~ *to work*); bluntly, with plain speech, without qualification, severely, (*told him* ~ *that he would not*; ~ *asserts that it is true*; *was* ~ *abused*); in circular way (*swells out* ~). [-LY²]

‖ **roup**[1] (rowp), v.t., & n. (Sc. & north.).
1. Sell by auction. **2.** n. An auction. [ME
'to shout', of Scand. orig.; cf. Icel.
raupa boast, M Swed. *röpa* shout]

roup[2] (roop), n. Kinds of poultry-disease
(a) with swelling on rump, (b) with purulent catarrh. Hence **rou′py**[2] (roo-) a.
[(a) orig. unkn., (b) prob. imit.]

‖ **rouse**[1] (-z), n. (arch.). Draught of liquor,
bumper, toast, revel, drinking-bout, (*take
one's ~, carouse*; *give a ~*, propose or
drink toast). [prob. for CAROUSE, perh. f.
wrong division of *drink carouse*]

rouse[2] (-z), v.t. & i., & n. **1.** Startle (game)
from lair or cover. **2.** Wake or stir up or
startle (person) from sleep or inactivity
or confidence or carelessness (often *up,
from, out of, to* action, *to* energy, *to* do,
etc.; ~ *oneself*, overcome one's indolence;
wants rousing, is indolent; *a rousing cheer,
song, sermon, lie*). **3.** Provoke temper of,
inflame with passion, (*is terrible when
~d*). **4.** Evoke (feelings). **5.** Stir (liquid,
esp. beer while brewing). **6.** (naut.). Haul
vigorously in, *out, up*. **7.** Cease to sleep,
become active, (usu. *up*). **8.** n. (mil.).
‖ The reveille. [orig. as hunting term, so
prob. f. AF or OF; orig. unkn.]

rouse[3] (-z), **roose** (-z), v.t. Sprinkle
(herring etc.) with salt in curing. [apheticо
f. *arrouse* f. OF *arouser* f. pop. L *arrosare*
f. LL AD(*rorare* f. *ros roris* dew)]

rous′er (-z-), n. In vbl senses of ROUSE[2];
esp.: implement for rousing beer; outrageous or rousing lie. [-ER[1]]

Rousseau′|ism (rōōsō-), n. (Adherence
to) views on religion, politics, education,
etc., of Jean-Jacques Rousseau, French
author 1712–78. So ~IAN, ~ISH[1], ~AN, aa.,
~IST(2), ~ITE(1), nn. & aa. [-ISM]

roust′about, n. *Wharf labourer; deck
hand; (Austral., also *rouseabout*) handy
man. [f. dial. & U.S. *roust* rout out]

rout[1], n., & v.t. **1.** Assemblage or company esp. of revellers or rioters, (law)
assemblage of three or more persons
engaged in unlawful act; riot, tumult,
disturbance, clamour, fuss. **2.** (arch.).
‖ Large evening party or reception (~-
-*seat*, light bench hired out for ~s). **3.**
Disorderly retreat of defeated army or
troops (*put to ~*, utterly defeat). **4.** v.t.
Put to ~. [ME, f. OF *route*, see ROUTE]

rout[2], v.i. & t. = ROOT[3]; also, force or
fetch *out* (*of bed* or from bed or house
or hiding-place). [var. of ROOT[3]]

route (root, mil. freq. rowt), n., & v.t.
1. Way taken in getting from starting-
-point to destination; (mil.) marching
orders (*get, give, the ~*), *column of ~*,
formation of troops on the march, ~-
-*march*, training march of battalion etc.;
en ~ (F; pr. ahṅ), on the way (*is, did it,
en ~*). **2.** v.t. Send, forward, direct to
be sent, by a certain ~. [ME, f. OF *route*
road f. L *rupta* (*via*) fem. p.p. of *rumpere*
break; see ROUT[1]]

routin|e′ (rōōtēn), n. Regular course of

procedure, unvarying performance of
certain acts, (theatr.) dancer's or comedian's act; (attrib.) performed by rule
(~*e duties* etc.). Hence ~ISM(3), ~IST(2),
nn., (-ēn²). [F (prec., -INE[2])]

rove[1], v.i. & t., & n. **1.** Wander without
settled destination, roam, ramble (*roving
sailor*, kinds of creeper); (of eyes) look
in changing directions; wander over or
through; *roving commission*, authority
given to person(s) conducting an inquiry
to travel as may be necessary; (angling)
troll with live bait. **2.** n. Act of roving
(esp. *on the~*). [ME; orig. term in archery
= shoot at casual mark with range not
determined; of obsc. orig.]

rove[2], n., & v.t. **1.** Sliver of cotton, wool,
etc., drawn out & slightly twisted. **2.** v.t.
Form into ~s; hence **rōv′er**[1] [-ER[1]] n.
[orig. unkn.]

rove[3], n. Small metal plate or ring for
rivet to pass through & be clinched over.
[f. ON *ró*, w. excrescent *v*]

rove[4]. See REEVE[3].

rōv′er[2] (for *rover*[1] see ROVE[2]), n. **1.** (Archery) mark chosen at undetermined range,
also mark for long-distance shooting,
(usu. *shoot at ~s*); wanderer; (croquet)
ball that has passed all hoops but not
pegged out, its owner. **2.** Sea robber,
pirate; senior boy scout. [ME; (1) f. ROVE[1],
-ER[1]; (2) f. MDu., MLG *rover* (*roven* rob
cogn. w. REAVE, -ER[1])]

row[1] (rō), n. Number of persons or things
in a more or less straight line (*in a ~, ~s*,
so arranged); ~ of houses, street with
this on one or each side (‖ often in street
names); *~-house*, terrace-house; ‖ *the
Row*, ROTTEN ROW; line of seats in theatre
etc. (*in the front, third, etc., ~*); ~ of plants
in garden (*a hard~ to hoe*, difficult task).
[ME *raw, row*, f. OE *~raw*, poss. rel. to
MDu. *rie*, G *reihe*]

row[2] (rō), v.i. & t., & n. **1.** Propel boat,
propel (boat), convey (passenger) in boat,
with oars or sweeps (~ *over*, WALK over in
boat-race; also with cogn. obj., as ~ *a
race, a few strokes, a fast stroke, 30 to the
minute*); ~ race with; ~ *down*, overtake
in ~ing, esp. bumping, race; ~ *out*,
exhaust by ~ing (*the crew were completely
~ed out at the finish*); be oarsman of
specified number in boat (~*s 5 in the
Oxford crew*); (of boat) be fitted with (so
many oars); ~-*boat*, ~ing-boat. **2.** n.
Spell of ~ing, boat-excursion. Hence
~ER[1] (rō′er) n. [OE *rōwan*, =MDu., MLG
rojen, ON *róa*; cogn. w. RUDDER, L *remus*
oar]

row[3], n., & v.t. (colloq.). **1.** Disturbance,
commotion, noise, dispute, (*what's the ~?*,
what is the matter?; *make, kick up, a ~*,
raise noise, also make protest); shindy,
free fight, (*town-&-GOWN ~*); being
reprimanded (*shall get into a ~*). **2.** v.t.
Reprimand, rate; hence ~ING[1](1) n.
[sl., *c.* 1800, of unkn. orig.]

row′an (rō-, row-), n. (Sc. & north.).

(Scarlet berry of) mountain ash (also ~-*tree*). [f. Scand., corresp. to Norw. *raun*, Sw. *rön*]

row-de-dow', n. Din, uproar. [imit.]

rowd'|y̌, n. & a. Rough & disorderly & noisy (person); so ~*y-dowdy* a. Hence ~**ĭ**NESS, ~**y̌**ISM(2), nn., ~**y̌**ISH¹(2) a. [U.S., orig. unkn.; orig. sense *backwoodsman*]

row'èl, n., & v.t. (-ll-). 1. Spiked revolving disc at end of spur (vb, urge with ~). 2. Circular piece of leather etc. with hole in centre inserted between horse's skin & flesh to discharge humours (vb, insert ~ in). [ME, f. OF *ro(u)el* f. LL *rotella* f. L *rota* wheel, -LE(2)]

row'lock (rŭl-), n. Pair of thole-pins or other contrivance on boat's gunwale serving as fulcrum for oar. [alt. of earlier *oarlock*, OE *ārloc* (OAR, LOCK²), to ROW²]

Röx'burghe (-ŭru), n. Style of bookbinding with plain leather gilt-lettered backs, cloth or paper sides, & leaves with untrimmed edges & bottoms. [Duke of ~ 1740–1804]

roy'al, a. & n. 1. Of, from, suited to, worthy of, belonging to family of, in service or under patronage of, a king or queen (after its noun in some phrr., as *the blood* ~, ~ *family*, RHYME¹~, PRINCESS *R*~; cf. *R*~ *Princess* used of any of ~ family; ~ *charter*, *warrant*, etc.; *the* ~ *anger*, *hands*, etc., the sovereign's; *R*~ ACADEMY; *R*~ AIR¹ *Force*; *R*~ *Armoured Corps*, armoured fighting vehicles and tanks; *R*~ *Army* ORDNANCE *Corps*; *R*~ *Army Service Corps*, commissariat and transport branch of army; *R*~ *Artillery*; ~ *blue*, a deep pure vivid shade; ~ *burgh*, holding charter from Crown; ~ COMMISSION; *R*~ *Corps of Signals*, army organization dealing with communication in the field; *R*~ *Courts of Justice*, building in Strand, London, in which superior courts of law & appeal are held; *R*~ *Electrical & Mechanical Engineers*, instituted in 1942 to do some of the work previously done by the *R*~ *Army Ordnance Corps* & the *R*~ *Army Service Corps*; *R*~ *Engineers*, engineer branch of army; ~ *evil*, =KING'*s evil*; *R*~ *Exchange*, building in Cornhill, London, for dealings between merchants; *R*~ *Flying Corps*, now absorbed by *R*~ *Air Force*; *R*~ HIGHNESS; *R*~ HORSE¹ *Artillery*; *R*~ HUMANE *Society*; *R*~ *Institution*, founded 1799 for diffusion of scientific knowledge; *R*~ *Irish Constabulary*, Imperial semi--military police in Ireland, disbanded 1921; *R*~ *Marine Artillery*, *R*~ *Marine Light Infantry*, now united in *R*~ *Marines*, corps trained for service at sea and on land; *R*~ *Military Academy*, formerly at Woolwich for Engineer & Artillery cadets, *R*~ *Military College*, formerly at Sandhurst for infantry & cavalry cadets, now amalgamated into *R*~ *Military Academy* at Sandhurst; *R*~ *Naval Air Service*, former naval branch of *R*~ *Air Force*; *R*~ *Naval Division*, military force raised

in the 1914–18 war from surplus sailors & marines; *R*~ *Naval Reserve*, drawn from mercantile marine; *R*~ *Naval Volunteer Reserve*, drawn from landsmen used to the sea; *R*~ *Navy*; ~ *oak*, in which Charles II hid after Worcester; *R*~ *Observer Corps*, civilian organization for reporting & tracking aircraft movements & radio-active fall-out; ~ ROAD *to*; *R*~ SOCIETY; ~ *standard*, square banner with ~ arms). 2. Kingly, majestic, stately, splendid, first-rate, on great scale, of exceptional size etc., (~ *magnanimity*; *gave us* ~ *entertainment*; *in* ~ *spirits*; *had a* ~ *time*; BATTLE¹ ~; ~ *paper*, 24 × 19 in. for writing & 25 × 20 for printing; ~ *octavo* etc., folded from this; ~ *fern*, osmund; ~ *stag*, with head of 12 or more points; ~ *sail*, *mast*, above topgallant sail & mast; ~ *arch*, degree in freemasonry); hence ~LY² adv. 3. n. Member of ~ family (colloq.); ~ *stag*; ~ *sail* or *mast*; *the R*~*s*, the *R*~ Scots, (also) the *R*~ Marines. [ME, f. OF *roial* f. L *regalis* (*rex* king, -AL)]

roy'al|ist, n. 1. Monarchist, supporter of monarchy as an institution or of the royal side in civil war etc. (also attrib.). 2. *Die-hard (esp. in phr. *economic* ~*ist*). So ~ISM(3) n., ~*is'*TIC a. [-IST]

roy'alty̌, n. 1. Office or dignity or power of king or queen, sovereignty; royal persons; member of royal family (usu. in pl.); (usu. in pl.) prerogative(s) or privilege(s) of the sovereign. 2. Royal right (now esp. over minerals) granted by sovereign to individual or corporation; (hist.) lessee's payment to land-owner for privilege of working mine; sum paid to patentee for use of patent or to author etc. for each copy of his book etc. sold. [ME, f. OF *roialte* (ROYAL, -TY)]

‖ **Roy'ston crow** (-ō), n. Hooded or grey crow. [place-name]

rŭb¹, v.t. & i. (-bb-), & n. 1. Subject to friction, slide one's hand or an object along over or up & down the surface of (~ one's *hands*, each with the other usu. in sign of keen satisfaction; ~ *shoulders*, come into contact *with* other people; ~ *noses*, of some savages & animals, greet each other; ~ *the wrong way*, stroke against the grain, irritate or repel as by stroking cat upwards). 2. Polish, clean, abrade, chafe, make *dry*, *sore*, *bare*, etc., by ~*bing*. 3. Reproduce design of (sepulchral brass or stone) by ~*bing* paper laid on it with coloured chalk etc., whence ~**b'**ING¹(2) n. 4. Slide (hand, object) *against* or *on* or *over* something, (objects) *together* or *together*, with friction. 5. Bring (stain etc.) *out*, (nap etc., or fig. novelty, shyness, etc.) *off* or *away*, force (liniment etc., or fig. lesson, humiliating fact, etc.) *in* or *into*, reduce *to* powder etc., force *through* sieve, bring size or level of *down*, spread (ointment etc.) *over*, groom (horse, *oneself*) *down*, freshen or brush (tarnished object, or fig. one's memory,

Greek, etc.) *up*, mix (chocolate, pigment, etc.) *up* into paste, by ~ *bing* lit. or fig. **6.** Come into or be in sliding contact, exercise friction, *against* or *on*. **7.** (Of bowl) be retarded or diverted by un-evenness of ground, (fig., of person, process, etc.) go *on, along, through*, with more or less restraint or difficulty. **8.** (Of cloth, skin, etc.) get frayed or worn or sore or bare with friction. **9.** ~-*stone*, (piece of) stone used for sharpening, smoothing, etc. **10.** n. Spell of ~*bing* (*give it a* ~, ~-*up*, ~-*down*, etc.). **11.** (Bowls) inequality of ground impeding or diverting bowl, the being diverted etc. by this (prov., *those who play at bowls must look for* ~*s*); (transf.) impediment or difficulty *there's the* ~, that is the point at which doubt or difficulty arises; *the* ~*s & worries of life*); (golf) ~ *of* or *on the green*, accidental interference with course or position of ball. [ME *rubben* prob. f. LG *rubben*; orig. unkn.]

rub². See RUBBER².

rub'a-dŭb, n., & v.i. (Make) rolling sound of drum. [imit.]

ruba'tŏ (rōōbah-), a. & n. (mus.). (*Tempo*) ~, time varied for expression. [It., = robbed]

rŭbb'er¹, n., & v.t. In vbl senses; also or esp.; masseur or masseuse; Turkish-bath attendant; implement used for, part of machine operating by, rubbing; caout-chouc or india-~ (often attrib.; vb, coat with ~); superior soft brick that can be rubbed down to any desired shape; *(pl.) galoshes; *-neck* (sl.), gaping sightseer, inquisitive person. [-ER¹, india-~ sense from use in rubbing out pencil-marks]

rŭbb'er², n. Three successive games be-tween same sides or persons at whist, bridge, cribbage, backgammon, etc. (*have a* ~ *of whist* etc. or *a* ~); *the* ~ (also abbr. *the rub*), winning of two games in ~, third game when each side has won one. [orig. unkn.; as term in bowls from c. 1600; in early use often *a rubbers*]

rŭbb'ish, n. & int. Waste material, debris, refuse, litter; worthless material or ar-ticles, trash, (*good riddance to bad* ~, esp. at departure of person one dislikes), absurd ideas or suggestions, nonsense (often as excl. of contempt), whence ~Y² & colloq. in same sense ~**ing**, aa. [ME & AF *rubbous, robous(e)*, etc.; app. rel. to RUBBLE, w. unexpl. diff. ending; orig. unkn.]

rŭb'ble, n. Waste fragments of stone, brick, etc., from old houses; pieces of un-dressed stone used, esp. as filling-in, for walls; (geol.) loose angular stones etc. as covering of some rocks, also water-worn stones. Hence **rŭbb'lY²** a. [ME *robyl, rubel*, of unkn. orig.; see prec.]

***rube** (rōōb), n. (colloq.). Country bump-kin, hick. [abbr. of *Reuben*]

ru'bĕfȳ, -ify, (rōō-), v.t. Make red; (med., of counter-irritant) stimulate (skin etc.)

to redness, so **rubĕfA'CIENT** (-āshent) a. &, see -ENT(2), n., **rubĕfAC'TION** n., (rōō-). [ME, f. OF *rubifier* f. L *rubefacere* (*rubēre* be red, -FY)]

ru'bicĕlle (rōō-), n. Orange-red precious stone, kind of spinel ruby. [F, prob. dim. of *rubis* or *rubace* RUBY]

Ru'bicon (rōō-), n., & v.t. **1.** *The* boundary by passing which one becomes committed to an enterprise (usu. *pass* or *cross the* ~). **2.** (*r*~; in piquet) winning of game before opponent has scored 100; (v.t.) defeat (opponent) thus. [name of stream limiting Caesar's province & crossed by him before war with Pompey]

ru'bicund (rōō-), a. (Of face, complexion, or person in these respects) ruddy, high--coloured. Hence ~ITY (-ŭn²) n. [f. F *rubicond* or L *rubicundus* (*rubēre* be red)]

rubid'ium (rōō-), n. Soft silvery metallic element grouped with caesium, lithium, potassium, & sodium. [L *rubidus* red (w. ref. to spectrum lines), -IUM]

rubi'ginous (rōō-), a. Rust-coloured. [f. LL *rubiginosus*, f. L *rubigo -inis* rust, -OUS]

ru'bious (rōō-), a. (poet.). Ruby-coloured. [RUBY, -OUS]

ru'ble (rōō-), n. See ROUBLE.

ru'bric (rōō-), n. **1.** Heading of chapter, section, etc., also special passage or sen-tence, written or printed in red or in special lettering. **2.** Direction for conduct of divine service (prop. in red) inserted in liturgical book, whence ~AL a., ~alLY² adv., **rubri'CIAN** (-Ishn), ~ISM(3), ~IST(2), nn., (rōō-). **3.** (Red-letter entry in) calen-dar of saints (now rare). [ME, f. OF *ru-brique* or L *rubrica* (*ruber rubr-* red)]

ru'bric|ate (rōō-), v.t. Mark with, print or write in, red; furnish with rubrics. Hence ~A'TION, ~ātOR, nn. [L *rubricare*, -ATE³]

ru'bȳ (rōō-), n. & a., & v.t. **1.** Rare precious stone (also *true* or *Oriental* ~) of colour varying from deep crimson or purple to pale rose (*balas, spinel*, ~, stones of less value resembling ~; *above rubies*, of inestimable value). **2.** (Of) glowing purple-tinged red colour. **3.** Red pimple on nose or face. **4.** Red wine; (pugil.) blood. **5.** A size of TYPE. **6.** ~ *glass*, coloured with oxides of copper, iron, lead, tin, etc.; ~-*tail*, insect of deep metallic bluish-green with upper side of abdomen bright red (also *gold wasp*); ~ *wedding*, fortieth anniversary. **7.** v.t. Dye or tinge ~-colour. [ME, f. OF *rubi(s)*, obsc. rel. to L *rubeus* red]

ruche (rōōsh, & see Ap.), n. Frill or quilling of gauze, lace, etc. Hence **ruchED²** (rōōsht) a. [F]

rŭck¹, n. Main body of competitors left out of the running. [ME 'stack of fuel, heap, rick'; app. Scand., = Norw. *ruka* w. same meanings]

rŭck², ‖ **rŭc'kle¹**, nn., & vv.i. & t. Crease,

wrinkle, (as vb usu. ~ *up*). [*ruck* vb f. n., f. ON *hrukka*; *ruckle* f. *ruck*, -LE(3)]

rŭc′kle², v.i. & n. (Make) gurgling sound esp. in throat of dying person. [f. Scand. (Norw. dial. *rukla* vb)]

ru′cksäck (rŏŏ-), n. Bag slung by straps from both shoulders & resting on back for carrying walker's or climber's necessaries. [G]

rŭc′tion, n. (sl.). Disturbance, tumult, row, (*there will be* ~s, things will not be allowed to proceed quietly). [1825, of unkn. orig.]

rŭdbĕck′ia, n. (Kinds of) composite garden plant of the aster family native to N. America. [f. *Rudbeck*, surname of two Swedish botanists (c. 1700), -IA¹]

rŭdd, n. Freshwater fish resembling roach, red-eye.· [app. rel. to *rud* red colour]

rŭdd′er, n. Broad flat wooden or metal piece hinged to vessel's stern-post for steering with, (fig.) guiding principle etc.; (brewing) paddle for stirring malt in mash-tub; ~*fish*, kinds that follow ships. Hence ~LESS a. [OE *rōthor*, MDu., MLG *roder*, OHG *ruodar* f. Gmc *rōthra-* f. st. of ROW²]

rŭd′dle, n., & v.t. 1. Red ochre, esp. of kind used for marking sheep. 2. v.t. Mark or colour (as) with ~. [rel. to obs. *rud* (see RUDD)]

rŭdd′ock, n. Robin redbreast. [OE *rudduc*, as prec., -OCK]

rŭdd′|y̆, a., & v.t. & f. 1. (Of face or its owner) freshly or healthily red, rosy, (~*y health*, *youth*, etc., marked by ~iness); (of light, fire, sky, object lighted up, etc., also in animal names as ~*y plover*, *squirrel*) reddish; ‖ (sl.) bloody, damnable; hence ~ĬLY² adv., ~ĬNESS n. 2. vb. Make or grow ~y. [OE *rudig* (*rud* see RUDD, -Y²)]

rude (rŏŏd), a. 1. Primitive, simple, unsophisticated, in natural state, rugged, unimproved, uncivilized, uneducated, roughly made or contrived or executed, coarse, artless, wanting subtlety or accuracy, (~ *times*, *men*, *simplicity*, *ignorance*, *chaos*; ~ *produce*, *ore*; ~ *scenery*; ~ *plough*, *beginnings*, *methods*; ~ *path*, *verses*, *drawing*; ~ *fare*, *plenty*; ~ *writer*, *style*; ~ *observer*, *version*, *classification*). 2. Violent, not gentle, unrestrained, startling, sudden, abrupt, (~ *passions*, *blast*, *shock*, *awakening*, *reminder*). 3. Vigorous, hearty; (~ *health*). 4. Insolent, impertinent, offensive, (~ *remarks*; *say* ~ *things*; *be* ~ *to*, insult). Hence ~LY² adv., ~′NESS, (colloq.) ru′DERY(4), nn., ru′d-ISH¹(2) a., (rŏŏ-). [ME, f. OF *ru(i)de* or L *rudis*]

Ru′desheimer (rŏŏdĕs-hī-), n. A white Rhine wine. [G (*Rü*-)]

ru′diment (rŏŏ-), n. (Pl.) elements or first principles of or *of* knowledge or some subject; (pl.) imperfect beginning *of* something that will develop or might under other conditions have developed,

(sing.) part or organ imperfectly developed as having no function (e.g. the breast in males). Hence **rudimĕn′tAL** (rare), **rudimĕn′tARY¹**, aa., (rŏŏ-). [F, or f. L *rudimentum* (RUDE, -MENT)]

rue¹ (rŏŏ), v.t., & n. 1. Repent of, bitterly feel the consequences of, wish undone or non-existent, (*you shall* ~ *it*; ~ *the day*, *hour*, etc., *when* —). 2. n. (arch.). Repentance, dejection at some occurrence, whence (in ordinary & esp. joc. use) ~′FUL (rŏŏf-) a. (*Knight of the* ~*ful countenance*, Don Quixote), ~′fulLY² adv., ~′fulNESS n.; compassion, ruth. [OE *hrēow(an)*, OS *hrewan*, OHG *hriuw(an)*]

rue² (rŏŏ), n. Perennial evergreen shrub with bitter strong-scented leaves formerly used in medicine. [ME, f. OF *rue* f. L *ruta* f. Gk *rhutē*]

‖ **rue-răddy̆** (rŏŏ-), n. Belt or rope passed over shoulder to drag something with. [orig. unkn.]

rufĕs′cent (rŏŏ-), a. (zool. etc.). Reddish. [L *rufescere* (*rufus* red, -ESCENT)]

rŭff¹, n. 1. Deep projecting frill of several folds of linen or muslin starched & separately goffered worn round neck esp. in 16th c.; projecting or conspicuously coloured ring of feathers or hair round bird's or beast's neck; whence (~)-ED² (-ft) a. 2. Kind of domestic pigeon. [perh. f. ROUGH; cf. RUFFLE]

rŭff², n. (fem. *reeve*). Bird of sandpiper kind of which male has RUFF¹ & ear-tufts in breeding season. [perh. f. prec., but that leaves the similarity to the fem. REEVE² unexpl.]

rŭff³, n. Small freshwater fish of perch family with prickly scales. [perh. f. ROUGH]

rŭff⁴, n., & v.i. & t. Trump(ing) at cards; (also *cross* or *double* ~) state of game in which partners out of different suits give each other alternate chances of trumping. [perh. f. *ruff* obs. card-game f. OF *roffle*, *ronfle*, perh. corrupt. of *triomphe* TRIUMPH, cf. TRUMP²]

rŭff′ian, n. Brutal violent lawless turbulent person, desperado, bully, rough. Hence ~ISM(2) n., ~LY¹ a. [f. F *rufian*, *-en* = Pr. & Sp. *rufian*, f. It. *ruffiano*]

rŭf′fl|e, v.t. & i., & n. 1. Disturb smoothness or tranquillity of (feathers, hair, water, temper or person in regard to it, brow; *bird* ~*es up its feathers*, in anger or to keep off cold; *nothing ever* ~*ed him*); (of sea,. hair, temper, etc.; rare) suffer ~ing, lose smoothness or calmness; swagger about, behave arrogantly or quarrelsomely, whence ~ER¹ n. 2. n. Perturbation, bustle, (rare; *without* ~*e or excitement*); rippling effect on water; ornamental gathered or goffered frill of lace etc. worn at opening of garment esp. about wrist or breast or neck, RUFF¹ of bird etc., whence ~ED² (-feld) a.; (now rare) a contention, dispute; (mil.) vibrating drum-beat. [ME, of unkn. orig.]

ru′f|ous (rōō-), a. (chiefly nat.-hist.). Reddish-brown. So ~**i-**, ~**o-**, comb. forms. [L *rufus*, -OUS]

rŭg, n. 1. Large wrap or coverlet of thick woollen stuff. 2. Floor-mat of shaggy material or thick pile, esp. (often *hearth-* ~) laid down before fireplace. [perh. f. Scand. (Norw. dial. *rugga* coverlet, Sw. *rugg* ruffled hair)]

Rŭgbei′an (-bēan), n. & a. (Member) of Rugby School.

Rŭg′bў, r-, n. ~ *football* or ~, also **rŭgg′ER**[1] (-g-) n. (sl.), one of the two chief forms of football, distinguished from *Association* or *soccer* esp. by players' being permitted to carry the ball & to hold opponent doing this; ~ *Union*, as clubs using ~ football rules. [~ school]

rŭgg′ed (-g-), a. Of rough uneven surface (~ *bark*; ~ *ground*, *country*, full of abrupt ups & downs, craggy, wooded, etc.; ~ *features*, strongly marked, of irregular outline); unsoftened, unpolished, lacking gentleness or refinement, harsh in sound, austere, unbending, involving hardship, (~ *manners*, *grandeur*, *individualist*, *kindness*, *honesty*, *character*, *verse*, *times*, *life*); robust, sturdy. Hence ~LY[2] adv., ~NESS n. [ME, prob. f. Scand.; cf. RUG, & Sw. *rugga* roughen]

rugger. See RUGBY.

rugōse′ (rōō-), a. (chiefly nat.-hist.). Wrinkled, corrugated. Hence or cogn. ~LY[2] adv., **ru′gATE**[2], **ru′gous**, aa., **rugŏs′ITY** n., (rōō-). [f. L *rugosus* (*ruga* wrinkle, -OSE[1])]

ru′in (rōō-), n., & v.t. & i. 1. Downfall or fallen or wrecked or impaired state, lit. (of building or structure; *the crash of* ~; *tumble*, *lie*, *lay*, *in* ~) or fig. (*the* ~ *of my hopes*; *bring to* ~, complete loss of property or position; *dates her* ~ *from his arrival*; RACK[7] & ~); (often pl.) what remains of building, town, structure, etc., or fig. of person, that has suffered ~ (*the* ~**s** *of Rome*, remains of ancient Rome or of the Roman imperial system; *is but the* ~ *of what he was*; *lies in* ~**s**; *is a* ~; *lives in an old* ~); what causes ~, destroying agency, havoc, (*will be the* ~ *of us*; BLUE[1] ~; *rapine & red* ~), so [f. obs. *ruinate* vb] **ruinA′TION** (rōō-) n. 2. vb. Reduce (place) to ~**s** (esp. in p.p.); bring to ~ (*her extravagance* ~*ed him*; so ~ *oneself*; ~ *girl*, seduce her; ~ *one's new hat, prospects*); (poet.) fall headlong or with a crash. [ME; (1) f. OF *ruine* f. L *ruina* (*ruere* fall, -INE[4]); (2) f. F *ruiner* or med. L *ruinare*]

ru′inous (rōō-), a. In ruins, dilapidated; bringing ruin, disastrous, (~ *folly*, *expense*), whence ~LY[2] adv. Hence ~NESS n. [ME, f. OF *ruineux* or L *ruinosus* (prec., -OSE[1])]

rule (rōōl), n., & v.t. & i. 1. Principle to which action or procedure conforms or is bound or intended to conform, dominant custom, canon, test, standard, normal state of things, (*deduce* ~**s** *of action*; *the*

~**s** *of decorum, cricket*, etc.; ~ *of the* ROAD[1]; *there was a* ~ *that* —; *standing* ~, made by corporation to govern its procedure; ~ *of thumb*, based on experience or practice, not theory, often ~-*of-thumb* attrib.; ~ *of three*, method of finding number that bears same ratio to one given as exists between two others given, also attrib., as ~-*of-three sum*; GOLDEN ~; *by* ~, in regulation manner, mechanically; WORK[2] *to* ~; *hard & fast* ~, rigid formula; EXCEPTION *proves* ~; *large families are the exception & not the* ~; *as a* ~, usually, more often than not). 2. Sway, government, dominion, (*bear* ~, hold sway; *under British* ~; *the* ~ *of force*; *entrusted with the* ~ *of half the tribe*). 3. (eccl.). Code of discipline observed by religious order. 4. (law). Order made by judge or court w. ref. to particular case only (~ NISI; ~ *absolute*, making ~ *nisi* no longer contingent). 5. (hist.). *The* ~**s**, limited area outside Fleet & King's-Bench prisons in which prisoners were allowed to live on certain terms. 6. Graduated often jointed straight measure used by carpenters etc. (often *foot-*~, 2 *ft* ~, etc.); SLIDE[1]-~. 7. (print.). Thin slip of metal for separating headings, columns, etc., also short (*en* ~) or long (*em* ~) dash in punctuation etc. 8. ~-*joint*, of kind usual in jointed carpenter's ~; hence ~′LESS (rōōl-l-) a. 9. vb. Exercise sway or decisive influence over, keep under control, curb, (person, conduct, one's passions; *ruling passion*, motive that habitually directs one's actions); (pass.) consent to follow advice, be guided *by*. 10. Be the ruler(s) or have the sovereign control of or *over*, bear~, (~ *the* ROAST; ~**s** *over many millions*; *kings should* ~ *by love*). 11. (Of prices, or goods etc. in regard to their or to quality etc.) have a specified general level, be for the most part, (*corn*, *prices*, *the market*, ~*d high* etc.; *crops* ~ *good*; *ruling prices*, those current). 12. Give judicial or authoritative decision (usu. *that*; also ~ person or thing *out of order*; ~ *out*, exclude, pronounce, irrelevant or ineligible), whence **ru′lING**[1](2) (rōō-) n. 13. Make parallel lines across (paper), make (straight line), with ruler or mechanical help. [ME, f. OF *riule(r)* f. L *regula*, LL *regulare*, see REGULAR]

ru′ler (rōō-), n. 1. Person or thing bearing (esp. sovereign) rule (often *of*), whence ~SHIP n. 2. Straight strip or cylinder of wood or metal or plastic material used in ruling paper or lines. [ME; -ER[1]]

‖ **rŭll′ey**, **rŏl-**, n. (pl. ~**s**). Flat four-wheeled dray, lorry. [orig. unkn.]

rŭm[1], n. 1. Spirit distilled from sugarcane; ~-SHRUB[2]. 2. *Any intoxicating liquor (usu. with hostile sense); ·~-·runner (colloq.), smuggler of intoxicants, or ship engaged in the traffic; ·~ *row* (colloq.), position outside the prohibited area taken up by ~-*running vessels.*

[c. 1650, perh. abbr. of contemporary forms *rumbullion, rumbustion*; orig. unkn.]

rŭm², **rŭmm' y¹**, aa. (sl.). Odd, strange, queer; ~ *customer*, (esp.) person or animal that is dangerous to meddle with; ~ *start* (sl.), surprising occurrence. Hence **rŭm´ ly²**, **rŭmm'ily²**, advv., **rŭm'ness**, **rŭmm'iness**, nn. [16th-c. cant, orig. = *fine, spirited*, perh. var. of ROM; -y²]

Rumān'ian (rōō-), a. & n. See ROMANIAN.

Rumansh. See ROMANSH.

rŭm'ba (or rōō-), n. Cuban Negro dance; ballroom dance imitative of this. [Sp.]

rŭm'ble¹, v.i. & t., & n. **1.** Make sound (as) of thunder, earthquake, heavy cart, air in the bowels, etc.; go *along, by*, etc., making or in vehicles making such sound; utter, say *out*, give *forth*, with such sound. **2.** n. Rumbling sound; hind part of carriage arranged as extra seat or for luggage; ~ *tumble*, lumbering vehicle, rough motion. [ME *romble*, prob. f. MDu. *rommelen* (imit.).]

‖ **rŭm'ble²**, v.t. (sl.). Get to the bottom of, see through, detect. [orig. unkn.]

rŭmbŭs'tious, a. (colloq.). Boisterous, uproarious. [prob. var. of ROBUSTIOUS]

Rumeliote. See R(O)UMELIOTE.

ru'mĕn (rōō-), n. Ruminant's first STOM-ACH. [L, = throat]

ru'minant (rōō-), n. & a. **1.** Animal that chews cud. **2.** adj. Belonging to the ~s; contemplative, given to or engaged in meditation. [foll., -ANT]

ru'min|āte (rōō-), v.i. & t. Chew the cud; meditate, ponder, (i., rarely t.; often *over, about, of, on*), whence or cogn. ~ATIVE a., ~ātively² adv., ~ātor n. So ~A'TION (rōō-) n. [f. L *ruminari* (RUMEN), -ATE³]

rŭmm'ag|e, v.t. & i., & n. **1.** Ransack (ship, house, pockets, records, book), make search in or *in*, make search; fish *out* or *up* from among other things; disarrange, throw *about*, in searching. **2.** n. Things got by ~ing, miscellaneous accumulation; ~ing, search (esp. of ship by Customs officer); ~e *sale*, clearance sale of unclaimed articles at docks etc., sale of odds & ends contributed to raise money for charity bazaar. [n. in mod. senses f. vb; vb (16th c.) f. n. in obs. sense *arranging of casks etc. in hold*, f. F *arrumage* (now *arri-*) f. *arrumer* to stow]

rŭmm'er, n. Large drinking-glass. [f. WFlem. *rummer* or Du. *roemer* (= G *römer*) f. *roemen* extol, boast]

rummy¹. See RUM².

rŭmm'y², n. Simple card game resembling COON-CAN, played with two packs. [orig. unkn.]

rumour (rōōm'er), n., & v.t. **1.** General talk, report, or hearsay, of doubtful accuracy; *a* or *the* current but unverified statement or assertion (often *that, of*). **2.** v.t. (usu. in pass.). Report by way of ~ (*it is* ~*ed that*—; *he is* ~*ed to* be etc.; *the* ~*ed*

disaster). [ME, f. OF, f. L *rumorem* nom. *-or*]

rŭmp, n. **1.** Tail-end, posterior, buttocks, of beast or bird or rarely of person, whence (of tailless fowl) ~'LESS a. **2.** Small or contemptible remnant of a parliament or similar body, esp. *the R*~ (hist.), that of Long Parliament either after its restoration 1659 or from Pride's Purge 1648 to its first dissolution 1653. **3.**~ *steak*, cut from ox's ~. [ME, prob. f. Scand.; cf. MDa. *rumpe*, MSw. & Norw. *rumpa*]

rŭm'ple, v.t. Wrinkle, crease, tousle, disorder, (fabric, leaves, garment, hair, etc.). [f. obs. *rumple* n. (f. MDu.), or MDu. *rompelen*, MLG *rumpelen*]

rŭm'pus, n. (sl.). Disturbance, brawl, row, uproar. [prob. fanciful]

‖ **rŭm'py**, n. Manx tailless cat. [RUMP, -y²]

rŭm'-tŭm', n. Light sculling-boat on lower Thames. [fanciful]

rŭn¹, v.i. & t. (răn, rŭn; p.p. rarely as -ED¹(2), as *a fresh-*~ *salmon*). I. General senses. **1.** (Of men) progress by advancing each foot alternately never having both on ground at once (cf. WALK¹; ~*ning jump*, in which jumper ~s to the take-off); (of animals) go at quicker than walking pace, amble, trot, canter, gallop, etc. **2.** (Start to) cross cricket pitch to score run. **3.** Flee, abscond, (chiefly now in ~ *for it, cut & ~* sl.; ~*ning fight*, naut., kept up by retreating ship or fleet with pursuer). **4.** Go or travel hurriedly, precipitately, etc. (~ *to meet* one's *troubles*, anticipate them; ~ RIOT; ~ *to help* another; ~ *over* or *down* or *up*, to place for flying visit; *he who* ~*s may read*, said of easily intelligible exposition etc.). **5.** Be allowed to grow or stray *wild*. **6.** Compete in or *in* race (~ *second* etc., come in so); seek election etc. (*for* parliament, president, etc.). **7.** (Of fish, ship, etc.) go straight & fast (*a* ~*ning whale*; *salmon* ~, go up river from sea; *ship* ~*s before the wind, into port, ashore, on the rocks*, FOUL *of* or *aboard* another). **8.** Advance (as) by rolling or on wheels, spin round or along, revolve (as) on axle, go with sliding or smooth or continuous or easy motion, be in action, work freely, be current or operative, (*ball, carriage, wheel, spindle, sledge, time,* ~*s; rope* ~*s in pulley; his life* ~*s smoothly*; ~*ning knot*, that slips along rope & enlarges or diminishes ~*ning noose*; ~*ing hand*, writing in which pen etc. is not lifted after each letter; *how your tongue* ~*s!*, how incessantly you talk!; *verse* ~*s*, is smooth; *tune* ~*s in head*, seems to be heard over & over again; *lease, contract,* ~*s for seven* etc. *years*; *play ran 100 nights*, was kept on stage; *courage* ~*s in the family*, is found in all members of it; *the works have ceased* ~*ning; place where writs do not* ~, are not valid or respected). **9.** (Of public conveyance by land or water) ply (*from, to*, *between*); (of fire, news, enthusiasm, etc.) spread rapidly from point to point (*news ran like wildfire*; *a cheer ran down the line*; *~ning fire*, successive shots from different points). **10.** (Of colour in fabric) spread from the dyed to the undyed parts, (of ink) spread beyond proper place. **11.** (Of thought, eye, memory, etc.) pass in transitory or cursory way (*thoughts ~ through one's head*; *eyes ~ over object*; *~ning commentary*, touching on a point here & there, broadcast report by eye-witness of ceremonial, sporting event, etc.; *~ back over the past*, survey it summarily). **12.** (Of liquid, grain, sand, etc., also of vessel containing or object emitting etc., & fig.) flow, be wet, drip, flow with, (*till the blood ran*; *ran blood*; *fountains ~ wine*; *is ~ning with oil*; *tide ~s strong*; *river~s clear, thick*; *feeling ran high*; one's *blood ~s cold*, he is horrified; *the sands are ~ning out*, time of grace etc. is nearly up; *~ning sore*, suppurating; *nose, eyes, ~*, drop mucus or tears; *~ at the nose*; *~ with sweat*; *~ dry*, cease to flow, be exhausted; *~ low, short*, become scanty; *candle ~s*, gutters). **13.** Extend, be continuous, have a certain course or order, progress, proceed, have a tendency or ˙common characteristic or average price or level, (*fence ~s round the house*; *~ning headline, head*, or *title*, repeated or different heading of page; *whereof the memory of man ~neth not to the contrary*, phr. applied to immemorial tradition or custom; *~ning account*, = current ACCOUNT[2]; *road ~s at right angles to, along, the ridge*; *story, title, document, ~s in these words*; *must not ~ to extremes*; *~s to sentiment*; *our pears ~ big this year*, are so for the most part; *prices ~ high*; *oats ~ 44 lb. to the bushel*); (in part., placed after pl. n.) following each other without interval, in succession, (*happened three days, hit the bull's-eye seven times, ~ning*). **14.** (With cogn. obj.) pursue, follow, traverse, cover, make way swiftly through or over, wander about in, perform, essay or be exposed or submit to, (course, way, race, a mile, run at cricket; *things must ~ their course*, be left to themselves; *~ a scent*, follow it up; *~ the streets*, be street arab; *~ errands, messages*, be a messenger; *the Derby was ~ in a snow-storm*; *~ the* GAUNTLET[2]; *~* RISKS; *~s a chance of being*, may be; *~ rapids*, shoot them; *~ croquet-hoop*, send ball clear through it; *~* BLOCKADE[1]). **15.** Sew (fabric) slightly. **16.** Chase, hunt, have *~*ning race with, (*~ fox five miles*; *~ to earth*, chase to its lair, & often fig. ═ discover after long search; *will ~ you for £50 a side*; *~ one hard* or *close*, press him severely in race, competition, or comparative merit etc.). **17.** (In causative senses) make *~* or go (*~ cattle* etc., turn out to graze; *~ brandy* etc., smuggle it in by evading coastguard etc.; *~ ship aground, to New York*; *~ boat*

down to the water; *~ train through*; *~ one's head against*; *~ cart into wall*; *~ sword, pin, into*; *~ one's hand, eye, along, down, over*, something; *~ rope through eyelet*; *~ coach, steamer, business, person*, keep them going, manage them, conduct their operations; *~ the show*, sl., dominate in an undertaking etc.; *~ horse*, send him in for race, so *~ candidate*; *~ metal into mould*; *~ the water off*; *~ parallel, simile*, etc., *too far*; *ran his fingers, comb, through his hair*; *~ thing fine*, leave very little margin of time or amount concerning it). **18.** Allow (account, bill) to accumulate for some time before paying. **19.** *~'about*, (a.) roving, (n.) light motor-car; *~'away* n. &., fugitive, bolting (horse), *~away match* or *marriage*, after elopement, *~away ring* or *knock*, given at door by practical joker who immediately makes off. **II.** With prepp. **1.** *~ across*, fall in with. **2.** *~ after*, pursue with attentions, seek society of, give much time to (pursuit etc.). **3.** *~ against*, fall in with. **4.** *~ at*, assail by charging or rushing. **5.** *~ in* (incur) *debt*. **6.** *~ into*, fall into (practice, absurdity, etc.), be continuous or coalesce with, have collision with, reach or attain (*some length, five editions*, etc.). **7.** *~ on*, be concerned with (*talk, mind, ~s on* a subject). **8.** *~ over*, review, glance over, peruse, recapitulate; touch (notes of piano etc.) in quick succession; (of vehicle) pass over (prostrate person). **9.** *~ through*, examine cursorily, peruse, deal successively with; consume (estate etc.) by reckless or quick spending, pervade. **10.** *~ to*, reach (amount, number, etc.); have money or ability or (of money etc.) be enough for (some expense or undertaking); fall into (ruin); (of plants) tend to develop chiefly (seed); (of persons) indulge inclination towards (coarseness etc.). **11.** *~ upon*, (of thoughts etc.) be engrossed by, dwell on; (of person) encounter suddenly. **III.** With advv. **1.** *~ about*, bustle, hurry from one person etc. to another, (esp. of children) play or wander without restraint. **2.** *~ away*, flee, abscond, elope; (of horse) bolt, (of horse or person) get clear away *from* competitors in race. **3.** *~ away with*, carry off (person, stolen property, etc.); accept (notion) hastily; (of expense etc.) consume (money etc.); (of horse etc.) bolt with (rider, carriage or its occupants). **4.** *~ down*, (of clock etc.) stop for want of winding; (of person or his health etc.) become enfeebled from overwork, poor feeding, etc. (also in p.p. as *is, feels, much ~ down*); knock down or collide with (person, ship, etc.); overtake (game, person) in pursuit, discover after search; disparage. **5.** *~ in*, (of combatant) rush to close quarters; (rugby footb.) carry ball over opponents' goal-line & touch it down; pay short visit (*to* person or house); (colloq.) arrest & take to prison; (colloq.) secure election of (candidate); bring (new machinery) into good working order by ~ning it. **6.** ~ *off*, flee, flow away, digress suddenly; write or recite (poem, list, etc.) fluently; drain (liquid) off; decide (race) after tie or trial heats. **7.** ~ *on*, be joined together (of written characters); continue in operation; elapse; speak volubly, talk incessantly; (print.) begin (t. & l. of sentence etc.) in same line as what precedes. **8.** ~ *out*, come to an end (of period, also of stock of something or its owner; ~ *out of*, exhaust one's stock of); escape from containing vessel; advance from block to hit ball in cricket; pass or be paid out (of rope); jut out; come out of contest in specified position etc. or complete required score etc.; complete (race); advance (gun etc.) so as to project; put down wicket of (batsman while ~ning); exhaust one*self* by ~ning. **9.** ~ *over*, overflow (of vessel or contents); recapitulate, review, glance over. **10.** ~ *through*, pierce with sword etc.; draw line through (written words). **11.** ~ *up*, grow quickly, rise in price, amount *to*; be RUNNER-up; accumulate (number, sum, debt) quickly; force (rival bidder) to bid higher, force up (price or commodity in that respect); erect (wall, house) to great height or in unsubstantial or hurried way; add up (column of figures). [OE rare *rinnan* (usu. metath. *irnan*) intr., & *ærnan, earnan* (metath. f. **rennan*) trans., f. Gmc **rinnan* & **rannjan*; ME *rinne, renne* prob. f. ON]

run², n. **1.** Act or spell of RUN¹ning (*have a ~ for* one's *money*, get some enjoyment etc. out of expenditure or effort, orig. w. ref. to scratching of horse after bets; *had a good ~*, esp. in hunting or on ship, train, etc.; *on the ~*, fleeing, also bustling about; *at a ~*, running; *a ~ on the Continent, to Paris*, etc., short excursion or visit); distance travelled by ship in specific time (usu. 24 hours). **2.** (crick.). Traversing of pitch by both batsmen without either's being put out, point scored thus or otherwise. **3.** Rhythmical motion, way things tend to move, direction, (*cannot get the ~ of the metre*, or *of* some process or operation, see how it goes; *the ~ of the market was against us; the ~ of the hills is NW.*). **4.** Rapid fall (*come down with a ~*, of building etc., person, mercury in barometer etc., prices, etc.). **5.** (mus.). Rapid scale passage. **6.** Continuous stretch or spell or course, long series or succession, general demand, (*a 500 ft ~ of pipe; a long ~ of power, office; a ~ of luck; in the* LONG¹ ~; *a ~ on the bank*, sudden demand from many customers for immediate payment; ~ *on rubber, book*, etc., great demand for it; so *book* etc. *has a considerable ~; ~ on the red* in rouge-et-noir, its coming many times running; *play has a ~ of 50 nights, a long ~*, etc.). **7.** Common, general,

average, or ordinary type or class (*the common ~ of men*, average men; ~ *of the mill or mine*, ordinary or average product or specimen, not specially selected or distributed); class or line of goods; batch or drove of animals born or reared together, shoal of fish in motion. **8.** Regular track of some animals, enclosure for fowls etc., range of pasture (usu. *sheep* etc. ~). **9.** Trough for water to run in. **10.** Part of ship's bottom narrowing towards stern. **11.** Licence to make free use of (*allowed him the ~ of their books, house; the ~ of* one's *teeth*, free board). **12.** (Of aircraft) flight on a straight and even course at a constant speed before or while dropping bombs (also ~-*in* or ~-*up*). **13.** ~-*down*, reduction in numbers esp. of armed forces by demobilization; ~-*in*, act of running in (see prec.) at football, see also sense 12; ~-*off*, deciding race after dead heat; ~-*up*, race between greyhounds up to hare's first turn, see also sense 12. [f. prec.]

run′agate, n. (arch.). Vagabond. [assim. of RENEGADE to *run* & obs. *agate* away]

run′cible spoon, n. Kind of fork with three broad prongs, one with a cutting edge, and hollowed out like a spoon. [*runcible*, nonsense word of Edward Lear (d. 1888), SPOON¹]

run′cinate, a. (bot.). Saw-toothed, with lobes curved towards base. [L *runcina* plane (formerly taken to mean saw), -ATE²]

‖ **run′dale**, n. Joint occupation of (esp. Irish) land, each holder having several strips not contiguous. [RUN¹, obs. *dale* north. var. of DOLE¹]

rune (rōōn), n. **1.** Any letter of earliest Teutonic alphabet used esp. by Scandinavians & Anglo-Saxons, dating from as early as 2nd c. & formed by modifying Roman or Greek characters to suit carving; similar mark of mysterious or magic significance. **2.** (Division of) Finnish poem. **3.** ~-*staff*, magic wand inscribed with ~s, also runic calendar. [f. ON & Icel. *rún*, cogn. w. OE *rún*, OS, OHG, Goth. *runa*; see ROUND⁵]

rung¹, n. Short stick attached at each end as rail, spoke, or cross-bar in chair etc. or esp. in ladder (often fig., as *the lowest, topmost, ~ of Fortune's ladder*). Hence ~ED² (-gd), ~′LESS, aa. [OE *hrung*, = MLG *runge*, Goth. *hrugga*]

rung². See RING².

ru′nic (rōō-), a. & n. **1.** Of, in, marked with, runes; (of poetry etc.) of the ancient -Scandinavian type; (of ornament) interlacing as on ~ monuments & metal-work. **2.** n. ~ inscription; kinds of moth; (print.) ornamental type of thick face & condensed form. [-IC]

run′let¹, n. (arch.). Cask of varying size for wine etc. [f. OF *rondelet* dim. of *rondelle* dim. of *ronde* (ROUND¹)]

run′let², n. Small stream. [RUN², -LET]

rŭnn'el, n. Brook, rill; gutter. [later form (after *run*) of *rinel*, OE *rynel* (RUN[1], -LE(1))]

rŭnn'er, n. In vbl senses; also or esp.: **1.** Messenger, scout, collector, or agent for bank etc., tout; (hist., esp. BOW- -STREET ∼) police-officer. **2.** The bird water-rail. **3.** =BLOCKADE[1]-∼. **4.** Revolving millstone. **5.** (naut.). Rope in single block with one end round tackle-block & other having hook. **6.** Creeping stem that issues from main stem of strawberry etc. & takes root; (also ∼ *bean*) kinds of twining bean, esp. SCARLET ∼. **7.** Ring etc. that slides on rod, strap, etc.; one of the long pieces of wood etc. on which sledge etc. slides, (blade of) FEN[1]-∼; groove or rod for thing to slide along; roller for moving heavy article. **8.** ∼-*up*, dog beaten only in final heat at coursing, competitor similarly beaten at golf etc. [ME; -ER[1]]

rŭnn'ing, n. In vbl senses; esp.: (w. ref. to racing) *make, take up, the* ∼, take the lead, set the pace, (lit., & fig. of talk etc.), *in, out of, the* ∼, (of competitor) with good, no, chance of winning; ∼-*board*, footboard on either side of a locomotive, motor-car, etc.; ∼ *commentary*, oral description of event(s) in progress; ∼ *powers*, right granted by railway to another to run trains over its line. [-ING[1]]

∥ **rŭn'rig**, n. (Sc.). = RUNDALE. [RUN[1], Sc. & north. *rig* RIDGE]

rŭnt, n. Ox or cow of small esp. Scottish- -Highland or Welsh breed; large breed of domestic pigeon; small pig; weakling or undersized person. [orig. unkn.]

rŭn'way, n. **1.** Trail to animals' watering- -place. **2.** Incline down which logs are slid. **3.** Gangway (usu. of special kind). **4.** Specially prepared surface in airfield, for taking off and landing. [RUN[1]]

rupee' (rōō-), n. Monetary unit; in India = 100 *Naye Paise*; in Pakistan formerly = 16 annas; in Ceylon = 100 cents; pl. abbr. *Rs*; *Rx*, tens of ∼s, in statistics etc, [f. Hind. *rupiyah* f. Skr. *rupya* wrought silver]

rŭp'ture, n., & v.t. & I. **1.** Breach of harmonious relations, disagreement & parting; (path.) tumour formed by protrusion of part of an organ through breach in wall of containing cavity esp. in abdomen, hernia; breaking, breach. **2.** vb. Burst, break, (cell, vessel, membrane); sever (connexion, marriage, etc.); affect with hernia; suffer ∼. [ME, f. OF, or f. L *ruptura* (*rumpere rupt-* break, -URE)]

rur'al (roor-), a. In, of, suggesting, the country (opp. URBAN), pastoral or agricultural, (∼ DEAN[1]; *in* ∼ *seclusion*; ∼ *policeman, constituency, sports,* etc.). Hence **rurāl'ITY** n., ∼IZE(2, 3) v.i. & t., ∼īZA'TION n., ∼LY[2] adv. [ME f. OF, or f. LL *ruralis* (*rus ruris* country, -AL)]

ruridēcān'al (roor-; *also* -dĕk'a-), a. Of

rural DEAN[1] or deanery. [L *rus* (prec.), -I-]

Ruritān'∣ia (roor-), n..Imaginary Central- -European kingdom, the novelist's and dramatist's locale for court romances in a modern setting; hence ∼IAN a. & n. [scene of Anthony Hope's novel *The Prisoner of Zenda* (1894)]

ru'sa (rōō-), n. Large E.-Ind. deer. [Malay]

ruse (rōōz, & see Ap.),n. Stratagem, feint, trick. [ME, f. OF, f. *ruser*, see RUSH[2]]

rusé (see Ap.), a. (fem. *-ée*). Given to ruses, sly, cunning, (of person, procedure, look, etc.). [F]

rŭsh[1], n., & v.t. **1.** Marsh or waterside plant with naked slender tapering pith- -filled stems (prop. leaves) formerly used for strewing floors & still for making chair-bottoms & plaiting baskets etc., a stem of this, (collect.)∼es as a material; thing of no value (*don't care, not worth, a* ∼). **2.** ∥ ∼-*bearing*, annual northern festival on occasion of carrying ∼es & garlands to strew floor & decorate walls of church; ∼ *candle*, made by dipping pith of a ∼ in tallow; ∼-*light*, ∼ candle (usu. fig. of feeble glimmer of intelligence, scanty information, etc.); ∼ *ring*, made of ∼(es) formerly used in (esp. mock) weddings; hence ∼'L!KE, ∼'Y[2], a a. **3.** v.t. Supply (chair-bottom), strew (floor), with ∼es. [OE *risc* & rare *rysc*, corresp. to MDu., MLG *risch* etc. & *rusch*, MHG *rusch(e)*; ult. orig. unkn.]

rŭsh[2], v.t. & i., & n. **1.** Impel, drag, force, carry along, violently & rapidly (∼*ed them into danger, round the sights*; *ball is* ∼*ed down the field*; ∼ *bill through*, get it hurriedly passed; *refuse to be* ∼*ed*, insist on doing things at one's own pace). **2.** (mil.). Take by sudden vehement assault. **3.** Pass (obstacle, stream, fence, etc.) with a rapid dash. **4.** Swarm upon & take possession of (goldfield, platform at meeting, etc.). **5.** (sl.). Charge (customer) exorbitant price (*they* ∼ *you shockingly, ∼ed us £1 a head*). **6.** Run precipitately, violently, or with great speed, go or resort without proper consideration (*in*)*to*, (∼ *into, out of, the room;* ∼ *at*, charge; *dark horse* ∼*ed past the favourite;* ∼ *into extremes;* ∼ *into print,* write to newspaper, publish book, etc.). **7.** Flow, fall, spread (intr.), roll (intr.), impetuously or fast (*river* ∼*es past; a* ∼*ing mighty wind; avalanches* ∼ *down; blood* ∼*ed to his face; his past life* ∼*ed into his memory*). **8.** n. Act of ∼ing, violent or tumultuous advance, spurt, charge, onslaught, (*the* ∼ *of the tide; carry the citadel with a* ∼; *a* ∼ *of blood to the head; a great* ∼ *of business*); (cinemat.) first print or preliminary showing of film before cutting; (footb.) combined dash of several players with the ball; sudden migration of large numbers esp. to new goldfield; strong run *on or for* some commodity; ∼-*hours* (at which traffic is busiest). [ME, f. AF *russcher*, = OF *re*(h)*user*, *ruser*; ult. orig. unkn.]

rusk, n. Piece of bread pulled or cut from loaf & rebaked. [f. Sp. or Port. *rosca* twist, coil, roll of bread]

Rusk|in'ian, a. & n. After the manner or principles, follower, of John Ruskin writer on art & social subjects d. 1900. So ~**inese**′ (-ēz), ~**inesque**′ (-ĕsk), aa. & nn., ~′**inism**(3) n., ~′**inize**(2, 3, 4) v.i. & t. [-IAN]

Russ, n. & a. (arch.). 1. A Russian; the Russian language. 2. adj. Russian. Hence ~′**ify** v.t., ~**ifica′tion** n., ~′o- comb. form, ~′**ophil** n. & a., ~**oph′ilism**(3) n., ~′**ophobe** n. & a., ~**ophob′ia** n. [f. Russ. *Rusi* Russian people or country]

Russ′ell (cŏrd), n. Ribbed fabric of cot- ton & wool used for scholastic gowns etc. [orig. unkn.]

russ′et, n. & a. 1. (Hist.) coarse home- spun reddish-brown or grey cloth worn by peasants; reddish brown; kind of rough- -skinned ~-coloured apple. 2. adj. Red- dish-brown (also ~y² a.); (arch.) rustic, homely, simple. [ME, f. OF *rousset* (*rous* red f. L *russus*, -ET¹)]

Ru′ssia (lea′ther) (-shα; lĕdh-), n. Dur- able bookbinding leather from skins im- pregnated with birch-bark oil. [*Russia*]

Ru′ssian (-shn), n. & a. 1. Native, language, of Russia. 2. adj. Of or from Russia (~ *boots*, loosely enclosing calf); (of or in ~; hence ~**ize**(3) (-shα-) v.t. [f. med. L *Russianus* (prec., -AN)]

Russ′niăk, n. & a. (Member, language) of the Little Russian or Ruthenian people in Galicia. [f. native *Rusnyak*]

rust, n., & v.i. & t. 1. Yellowish-brown coating formed on iron or steel by oxida- tion esp. as effect of moisture & gradually corroding the metal, similar coating on other metals; (fig.) impaired state due to disuse or inactivity, inaction as deterio- rating influence. 2. (Plant-disease with ~-coloured spots caused by) kinds of fungus, blight, brand; hence ~′**less** a. (~*less steel*, esp. ferro-chromium alloys used for stainless cutlery etc.). 3. vb. Contract ~, undergo oxidation or blight; (of bracken etc.) become ~-coloured; lose quality or efficiency by disuse or inacti- vity (*better wear out than* ~ *out*, exhorta- tion to maintain activity in old age etc.); affect with ~, corrode. [OE *rūst*, = OS, OHG *rost* f. Gmc *rudhs-to-*, f. *rudh-*, cogn. w. RED]

rus′tic, a. & n. 1. (Now less usual for) rural. 2. Having the appearance or manners of country-people, character- istic of peasants, unsophisticated, un- polished, unrefined, uncouth, clownish. 3. Of rude or country workmanship (~ *seat, bridge, work*, of untrimmed branches or rough timber); (of lettering) irregularly formed; (archit.) with rough-hewn or roughened surface or with chamfered joints (~-*work*, such masonry); hence or

cogn. **rus′tically**, ~**ly³** (rare), advv., **rusti′city** n. 4. n. Countryman, peasant. [ME, f. L *rusticus* (*rus* the country)]

rus′tic|āte, v.i. & t. 1. Retire to, sojourn in, the country, lead a rural life; send down temporarily from university as punishment; countrify. 2. Mark (mason- ry) with sunk joints or roughened surface. Hence ~**a′tion** n. [f. L *rusticari* live in the country (prec.), -ATE³]

ru′stl|e (-sl), v.i. & t., & n. 1. (Give forth) sound (as) of dry leaves blown, rain pat- tering, or silk garments in motion; go with ~e (*along* etc.; ~*e in silks*, be clad in silk); cause to ~e by shaking etc.; hence ~**ingly²** (-sl-) adv. 2. *(colloq.). Hustle, move energetically; steal (cattle or horses); hence ~**er¹**(-sl-)n. [ME *rustel* etc., imit.; cf. Flem. *ruysselen*, Du. *ridselen*]

rus′t|y̆¹, a. Rusted, affected with rust; of antiquated appearance; (of voice) croak- ing, creaking; stiff with age or disuse, antiquated, behind the times, impaired by neglect, in need of furbishing, (*his Greek is a little* ~y); (of black clothes) dis- coloured by age; rust-coloured. .Hence ~**ily²** adv., ~**iness** n. [ME; -Y²]

rus′ty̆², a. Rancid (esp. of bacon). [dial., = obs. *resty* & dial. *reasty* f. OF *reste* left over, stale]

rut¹, n., & v.t. (-tt-). 1. Track sunk by passage of wheels; established mode of procedure, beaten track, groove; hence ~**t′y²** a. 2. v.t. Mark with ~s (usu. in p.p.). [16th c., perh. f. OF *rote* ROUTE]

rut², n., & v.i. (-tt-). 1. Periodic sexual excitement of male deer (also of goat, ram, etc.), heat. 2. v.i. Be affected with ~. Hence ~**t′ish¹**(1) a. [ME, f. OF, also *ruit*, f. L *rugitus -ūs* (*rugire* roar)]

ruth (rōŏth), n. (arch.). Pity, compassion. Hence (mod.) ~′**less** a., ~′**lessly²** adv., ~′**lessness** n., (rōō-). [ME, f. RUE¹ vb +-TH¹]

ruthēn′ium (rōō-), n. Rare metallic ele- ment of the platinum group. [f. med. L *Ruthenia* Russia (from its discovery in the Urals)]

‖ **rŭx** n. (school sl.). Temper, passion.

-ry, suf., shortened form of -ERY (which see for numbered meanings), as in *chantry* (ME *chaunterie*), *jewry*, *bottomry*, *foundry*, *poultry*, *jewel*(le)*ry*; occas. also in direct formations, as *rivalry*.

rȳe, n. (Grain of) a N.-Europ. cereal used for bread in northern Continental coun- tries & for fodder in U.K.; (also ~ *whisky*) whisky distilled from ~. [OE *ryge*, = ON *rugr* f. Gmc *rugiz*; cogn. w. OS *roggo*, OHG *rocko*]

rye′-grass (rīgrahs), n. Kinds of fodder grass. [f. obs. *ray-grass*; orig. unkn.]

‖ **rye-pĕck** (rīp-), n. Ironshod pole for se- curing punt etc. [orig. unkn.]

‖ **rȳm′er**, n. One of the posts in weir or lock holding paddles. [orig. unkn.]

rȳ′ot, n. Indian peasant. [f. Hind. *raiyat* f. Arab. as RAYAH]

S

S (ĕs), letter (pl. *Ss*, *S's*). (Also) S-shaped object (COLLAR[1] of *S*, *Ss*, *SS*, or *esses*) or curve (*river makes a great S*).

's, used for (1, arch.) *God's* in *'sblood* & other oaths; (2, colloq.) *is* in *he's*, *she's*, *it's*, *Smith's*, etc.; (3, colloq.) *has* as in (2), esp. before p.p. as *he's done it*; (4, colloq.) *us* in *let us*, as *let's go*; (5, colloq.) *does*, as *what's he say about it?*

Sab(a)e'an (-bē-), a. & n. (Native) of ancient Yemen; (erron.)=SABIAN. [f. L f. Gk *Sabaios* (*Saba* f. Arab. *Saba'* people of Yemen) +-AN]

Säb'aism, n. Star-worship. [f. Heb. *çābā* host, -ISM]

Säb'äŏth, n. pl. *Lord of* ~ in N.T. & *Te Deum*, Lord of Hosts. [LL, f. Gk f. Heb. pl. (prec.)]

săbbatär'ian, n. & a. **1.** Sabbath-keeping Jew; Christian who accepts (& inculcates) the obligation to observe Sunday strictly as sabbath; Christian individual or member of sect observing Saturday as sabbath, seventh-day baptist etc.; hence ~ISM(3) n. **2.** adj. Of ~ tenets. [f. L *sabbatarius* (foll., -ARY[1]) +-AN, see -ARIAN]

săbb'ath, n. **1.** (Also ~ *day*) seventh day of week as day of religious rest appointed for Israel (~-*day's journey*, distance Israelite might travel on ~, about ⅔ m. also transf. easy journey). **2.** (Also ~ *day*) Christian Sunday esp. as day of obligatory abstinence from work & play (chiefly in Presbyterian, nonconformist, & distinctively protestant use, or joc.; *keep, break, the* ~; ~-*breaker*), whence ~LESS a. **3.** Period of rest. **4.** (Usu. *witches'* ~) general meeting of the devil and witches. [f. L *sabbatum* & OF *sab(b)at*, f. Gk -*ton*, f. Heb. *shabbāth* (*shābath* to rest)]

sabbät'ĭc|(al), aa. Of, appropriate to, the sabbath (~*al river*, one in Jewish legend flowing except on sabbath; ~*al year*, seventh year in which Israelites were to cease tilling & release debtors & Israelite slaves, (also) year's leave granted to university professor etc. for study, travel, etc.). Hence ~alLY[2] adv. [f. F *sabbatique* or LL f. Gk *sabbatikos* (prec., -IC), -AL]

săbb'atize, **-ise** (-īz), v.i. & t. Keep the, have a, sabbath; make (day) into, keep as, a sabbath. [f. LL *sabbatizare* f. Gk *sabbatizō* (SABBATH, -IZE)]

Sabĕll'ian[1], a. & n. (Rom. hist.). (Member) of the group of tribes in ancient Italy including Sabines, Samnites, Campanians, etc. [f. L *Sabelli* SABINES +-IAN]

Sabĕll'ian[2], a. & n. (Holder) of the doctrine of Sabellius (3rd c.) that the three Divine persons are merely aspects of one. [f. LL *Sabellianus* (-AN)]

Säb'ian, a. & n. **1.** (Member) of a sect classed in Koran with Moslems, Jews, & Christians, as believers in the true God.

2. (erron.). (Adherent) of SABAISM. [f. Arab. *çabi'* +-AN]

säb'icu (-kōō), n. Cuban timber-tree; its valuable hard durable wood. [Cuban Sp.]

Säb'ine, a. & n. (One) of the ~s, ancient Italians of central Apennines. [f. L *Sabinus*]

sä'ble[1], n. Small brown-furred arctic & subarctic carnivorous quadruped allied to martens; its skin or fur; fine paint-brush made of ~ hair. [ME, f. OF, prob. f. Slav., cf. Pol. & Czech *sobol*]

sä'ble[2], n. & a. **1.** Black as a heraldic colour; (poet., rhet.) the colour black; (poet. & rhet.; pl.) mourning garments, whence sä'blED[2] (-beld) a. **2.** (Also ~ *antelope*) large stout-horned antelope of which male is black. **3.** adj. (poet. & rhet.). Black, dusky, gloomy, dread, (of Negro, sky, sea, night, Fate, etc.; *his* ~ *Majesty*, the devil); hence säb'LY[2] adv. [ME, f. OF (her.), perh. f. prec.]

säb'ot (-ō), n. **1.** Shoe hollowed out from one piece of wood worn by French lower classes; wooden-soled shoe. **2.** (mil.). Wooden disc riveted to spherical, metal cup strapped to conical, projectile; (mech.) shoe or armature of pile, boring-rod, etc. Hence ~ED[2] (-bŏd) a. [F, alt. f. *savate* shoe]

säb'otage (-ahzh, -īj), n., & v.t. & i. **1.** Malicious or wanton destruction, esp. doing of damage to plant etc. by workmen on bad terms with their employers (*the derailing of the train is attributed to* ~; *acts of* ~). **2.** vb. Commit ~ (on); (fig.) destroy, render useless, as ~ *a scheme*. [F, f. *saboter* (prec., -AGE)]

säb'oteur (-tẽr), n. One who commits sabotage. [F]

sä'bre (-er), n., & v.t. **1.** Cavalry sword with curved blade (*the* ~, military force or rule); (in pl., hist.) cavalry unit (cf. *rifle*), cavalry soldier & horse, (*had 3,000* ~*s*); copper tool for skimming molten glass; ~-*bill*, -*wing*, kinds of bird; ~-*cut*, blow with ~, wound made or scar left by it; ~-*toothed lion* or *tiger*, extinct mammal with long ~-shaped upper canines. **2.** v.t. Cut down or wound with ~. [F, earlier *sable* f. G *sabel* f. Pol. *szabla* or Magyar *száblya*]

sä'bretache (-ertäsh), n. Cavalry officer's satchel on long straps from left of waist-belt. [F, f. G *säbeltasche* (prec., *tasche* pocket)]

sabreur (sahbrẽr'), n. Cavalryman with sabre, esp. (often *beau* ~) cavalry officer of dashing appearance. [F]

säb'ulous, a. Sandy, of sand, (pedant.); (med., of secretions esp. in urinary organs) granular. [f. L *sabulosus* (*sabulum* sand, -OSE[1])]

sabü'rra, n. (med.). Foul granular matter deposited in stomach. [L, =sand, ballast, cf. prec.]

săc, n. Baglike membrane-enclosed cavity in animal or vegetable organism;

membranous envelope of hernia, cyst, tumour, etc.; (of dress) = SACK¹. [F, or f. L *saccus* SACK¹]

sacc′āte, a. (Bot.) dilated into bag; contained in sac. [f. mod. L *saccatus* (prec., -ATE²)]

sacc′har|(o)- (-ka-), comb. form of med. L f. Gk *sakkharon* SUGAR, of many words chiefly in scientific use; ~ATE¹(3), salt of *sacchā′rıc acid*, a dibasic acid formed by the action of nitric acid on dextrose; ~IDE, (now more commonly used in chem. for) ~ose; ~ĬF′EROUS, sugar-bearing; ~ĭFY, convert (starch) into sugar; ~iFICA′TION; ~ĬM′ETER, instrument for testing sugars by polarized light; ~ĬM′ETRY; ~IN(e) n., intensely sweet substance got from coal-tar & used to sweeten food for the gouty, diabetic, etc.; ~INE¹ a., sugary, of or containing or like sugar; ~O-, sugar-&-; ~OID a. (geol.), granular like sugar, (n.) sugarlike substance; ~ŏ-M′ETER, hydrometer used, esp. in brewing, to estimate amount of sugar in solution by specific gravity; ~OSE², ordinary sugar, cane-sugar.

sac′ciform (-ks-), a. Sac-shaped. [SAC, -FORM]

sacc′ūl|e, n. Small sac or cyst. Hence (see -UL-) ~AR¹, ~ATE², ~āted, aa., ~A⁴ TION n. [f. L *sacculus* (SAC, -ULE)]

sä′cerdŏçy, n. (rare). Sacerdotalism; priestly function. [f. L *sacerdotium* (*sacerdos -otis* priest lit. sacrifice-giver f. *sacer* holy, *dare* give)]

sä′cerdōtage, n. (joc.). Sacerdotalism; priest-ridden state. [as prec. w. ref. to *dotage*, cf. *anecdotage*]

sacerdōt′al, a. Of priest(s) or priesthood, priestly; (of doctrines etc.) ascribing sacrificial functions & supernatural powers to ordained priests, claiming excessive authority for the priesthood. Hence ~LY² adv., ~ISM(3), ~IST(2), nn., ~IZE(3) v.t. [ME, f. OF, or f. LL *sacerdotalis* as SACERDOCY, -AL)]

sǎch′em, n. Supreme chief of some Amer.-Ind. tribes; big-wig, eminent person. [Amer.-Ind.]

sä′chet (-shä), n. Small perfumed bag; (packet of) dry perfume for laying among clothes etc. [F, dim. of *sac* f. L SACCUS]

sǎck¹, n., & v.t. 1. Large usu. oblong bag for storing & conveying goods usu. open at one end & made of coarse flax or hemp (*give* one, *get, the* ~, dismiss him, be dismissed, from service, cf. '*On luy a donné son sac*, hee hath his pasport given him' in Cotgrave), whence ~′ING¹(3) n.; ~ with contents (usu. *of*; also ~′FUL n.); amount (of corn, coal, flour, wool, potatoes, etc.) usu. put in ~ as unit of measure or weight (*at 12/- the* ~). 2. (Of dress; also as pseudo-F *sacque, sac*) kind of lady's loose gown (arch.); pleated silk appendage attached to shoulders of dress & falling to ground & forming train; man's or woman's loose-hanging coat not shaped to

back. 3. ~′*cloth*, coarse fabric of flax or hemp, ~ing, (fig.) mourning or penitential garb (esp. *in ~cloth & ashes* bibl.); ~-*race*, between competitors tied in ~s up to the neck. 4. v.t. Put into ~(s); (colloq.) give the ~ to, dismiss from service; (colloq.) defeat in match or fight. [OE *sacc* f. L f. Gk *sakkos* f. Heb. *saq*]

sǎck², v.t., & n. 1. (Of victorious army or its commander) plunder, give over to plunder, (captured city etc.); (of burglars etc.) carry off contents of. 2. n. ~ing of captured place. [16th c., f. F' *sac* in phr. *mettre à sac* put to sack, f. It. *sacco*; vb f. n.]

sǎck³, n. (hist.). Kinds of white wine formerly imported from Spain & the Canaries (*sherry, Canary*, etc., ~; ~ *posset, whey*, etc., beverages containing it; *halfpennyworth of bread to intolerable deal of* ~, absurd excess of the unessential, w. ref. to *1 Henry IV*, II. iv. 592). [16th c. *wyne seck*, f. F *vin sec* dry wine]

sǎck′but, n. (Old name for) trombone. [f. F *saquebute* sackbut from 15th c., = ONF *saqueboute* hook for pulling man off horse (*saquer* pull, *boute* as BUTT⁴)]

∥ **sǎck′lèss,** a. (arch., Sc. & north.). Innocent (*of*), harmless, feeble-minded. [OE *saclēas* f. ON *saklauss* (SAKE, -LESS)]

sacque (sǎk). See SACK¹.

sǎc′ral, a. (Anat.) of the sacrum; (anthropol.) of or for sacred rites. [SACRUM, -AL]

sǎc′rament, n., & v.t. 1. Religious ceremony or act regarded as outward & visible sign of inward & spiritual grace (applied by the Eastern, pre-Reformation Western, & R.-C. Churches to the seven rites of baptism, confirmation, the eucharist, penance, extreme unction, orders, & matrimony; restricted by most Protestants to baptism & the eucharist; *the* ~, *the* ~ *of the altar, the Blessed* or *Holy S*~, the eucharist, also the consecrated elements esp. the bread or Host; *take, receive, the* ~ *to* do or *upon*, as confirmation of some promise or oath). 2. Thing of mysterious & sacred significance, sacred influence, symbol, etc. 3. Oath or solemn engagement taken. 4. v.t. (esp. in p.p.). Bind by oath. [ME, f. OF *sacrement* f. L *sacramentum* military oath, legal caution-money, f. *sacrare* (*sacer sacr-* SACRED), -MENT, used in Christian L as transl. of Gk *mustērion* MYSTERY¹]

sǎcramen′tal, a. & n. 1. Of (the nature of) a or the sacrament, whence ~ITY (-ăl⁴) n.; (of doctrine etc.) attaching great importance to the sacraments, whence ~ISM(3), ~IST(2), nn.; hence ~LY² adv. 2. n. Observance analogous to but not reckoned among the sacraments, e.g. use of holy water or sign of the cross. [ME, f. OF, or f. LL *sacramentalis* (prec., -AL)]

sǎcramentār′ian, a. & n. 1. (hist.). (Also *sacramentary*) denying, denier of, the Real Presence (as holding that 'body &

blood of Christ' was used only in a sacra-mental, i.e. symbolic, sense). 2. Holding or involving, holder of, high sacramental doctrine, whence ~ISM(3) n. [f. med. L SACRAMENT(*arius* -ARY¹), see -ARIAN]

sacrār′ium, n. (pl. *-ia*). (Rom. ant.) shrine, adytum, room of Penates in house; (also *sanctuary*) part of church within altar-rails; (R.-C.) piscina. [L (*sacer sacr-* holy, -ARIUM)]

sā′crĕd, a. (rarely ~*est*). **1.** Consecrated or held dear *to* a deity, dedicated or reserved or appropriated *to* some person or purpose; made holy by religious association, hallowed, (~ *book, writings,* embodying laws etc. of a religion; ~ *history,* related in Bible; ~ *number,* associated with religious symbolism, e.g. 7; ~ *poetry, music,* on religious themes; ~ *concert,* of ~ music; as specific epithet of beasts etc. now or once ~ to some god, as ~ *ibis, monkey, beetle*). **2.** Safeguarded or required by religion or reverence or tradi-tion, indefeasible, inviolable, sacrosanct, (*His most S~ Majesty the King; the ~ right of insurrection; regards it as a ~ duty; their property, persons, will be held* ~; *no place was ~ from him, from outrage*). Hence ~LY² adv., ~NESS n. [ME, p.p. of obs. *sacre* consecrate f. OF *sacrer* f. L *sacrare* (*sacer sacr-* holy)]

sā′crĭfĭce, n., & v.t. & i. **1.** Slaughter of animal or person, surrender of a posses-sion, as offering to a deity, (fig.) act of prayer or thanksgiving or penitence as propitiation; what is thus slaughtered or surrendered or done, victim, offering; (theol.) the Crucifixion, the Eucharist as either a propitiatory offering of the body & blood of Christ or an act of thanks-giving. **2.** Giving up of thing for the sake of another that is higher or more urgent, thing thus given up, loss thus entailed, (*will gain nothing by the* ~ *of your prin-ciples; at some* ~ *of regularity; surplus stock for sale at a large* ~; *his health was the* ~ *demanded of him; the great or last* ~, esp., death for one's country in war; SELF-~); so **sā′crĭfĭ′cĭAL** (-shl) a., **sā′crĭfĭ′cĭALLY²** (-sha-) adv. **3.** vb. Offer (as) ~ (*to*); give up, treat as secondary or of inferior importance, devote, *to* (*has* ~*d herself, her whole life, her pleasures, to his interest;* ~ *accuracy to vividness*); resign oneself to parting with. [ME, f. OF f. L *sacrificium* (*sacrificus* as prec., -FIC); vb f. n.]

sā′crĭlĕge, n. Robbery or profanation of sacred building, outrage on consecrated person or thing, violation of what is sacred. Hence **săcrĭlē′gĭOUS** (-jus; *or* -lj′us) a., **săcrĭlē′gĭOUSLY²** (-jus-) adv., **săcrĭlē′gĭST**(1) n. (rare). [ME, f. OF f. L *sacrilegium* f. *sacrilegus* (SACRED, *legere* collect)]

sā′crĭng, n. (arch.). Consecration of elements in the mass; ordination & con-secration of bishop, sovereign, etc.; ~-

-bell, rung at elevation of Host. [ME, f. obs. *sacre* (SACRED), -ING¹]

sā′crĭst, n. Official keeping sacred vessels etc. of religious house or church. [OF (*-e*), or f. med.L *sacrista* (SACRED, -IST)]

sā′crĭstan, n. Sexton of parish church (arch.); = prec. [ME, f. med. L SACRIST*anus* SEXTON]

sā′crĭstў, n. Repository for vestments, vessels, etc., of a church. [F (*-ie*), or f. med. L *sacristia* (SACRIST, -IA¹)]

sā′crōsănct, a. (Of person, place, law, etc.) secured by religious sanction against outrage, inviolable. Hence **sā̆crōsănc′tĭTY** n. [f. L *sacrosanctus* (*sacro* abl. of *sacrum* SACRED rite, SAINT a.)]

sā′cr|um, n. Composite triangular bone of anchylosed vertebrae forming back of pelvis. Hence ~AL a., ~o- comb. form. [f. L *os sacrum* sacred bone (from sacri-ficial use)]

săd, a. (-dd-). Sorrowful, mournful, show-ing or causing sorrow, (*a ~der & a wiser man,* of one who has had distressing experience; *in ~ earnest,* seriously); (derog., usu. joc.) shocking, deplorably bad, incorrigible, (*is a ~ slut, coward,* etc.; ~ *dog,* rake, scapegrace; *writes ~ stuff*); (of pastry, bread, etc.) heavy, doughy; (of colour) dull, neutral-tinted; ~*-iron,* solid flat-iron. Hence ~**d′EN**⁴ v.t. & i., ~′LY² adv., ~′NESS n., ~**d′ISH**⁴(2) a. [OE *sǣd,* OS *sad,* OHG *sat,* ON *sathr,* Goth. *saths* f. Gmc **sadhaz* full, cogn. w. L *satis*]

săd′dle, n., & v.t. **1.** Rider's seat placed on back of horse etc. (usu. concave-shaped of leather with side-flaps & girths & stir-rups) or forming part of bicycle etc. or of some agricultural machines (PACK¹, SIDE, ~; *in the* ~, mounted, fig. in office or control; *put* ~ *on right, wrong, horse,* blame right, wrong, person). **2.** Part of shaft-horse's harness that bears shafts. **3.** ~-shaped thing, e.g. ridge between two summits, support for cable or wire on top of suspension-bridge pier or telegraph--pole, joint of mutton or venison consist-ing of the two loins. **4.** ~*-back,* (archit.) tower roof with two opposite gables, ~-backed hill, kinds of bird (esp. the grey crow) & fish, (adj.) ~*-backed;* ~*-backed,* with upper outline concave, (archit.) having ~-*back,* one of pair of bags laid across horse behind ~, kind of carpeting (in imitation of Eastern ~-bags of camels) used in upholstering chairs etc.; ~*-boiler,* of concave form used in heating-apparatus; ~*-bow* (-bō), arched front of ~ [BOW¹]; ~*-cloth,* laid on horse's back under ~; ~*-fast,* firmly seated in ~; ~*-horse,* for riding; ~*-pin,* by which bicycle etc. ~ fits into socket; ~*-tree,* frame of ~, also N.-Amer. tulip-tree (with ~-shaped leaves); hence ~LESS a. **5.** v.t. Put ~ on (horse etc.); burden (person) *with* task, responsibility, etc.; put (bur-den) *on* or *upon* (person). [OE *sadol,* OHG

satal, ON *sǫthull* f. Gmc* *sadhulaz*; vb f.
OE *sadolian*]

sådd′l|er, n. Maker of or dealer in saddles
& other equipment for horses; (mil.) man
in charge of mounted regiment's ~ery.
Hence ~ERY(1, 2, 3) n. [-ER¹]

Sådd′ucee, n. Member of a Jewish sect or
party (cf. PHARISEE, ESSENE) of time of
Christ that denied resurrection of the
dead, existence of spirits, & obligation of
the traditional law. Hence or cogn.
Sådduce′an a., ~ISM(2) n. [f. LL f. Gk
Saddoukaios f. Heb. *Çadduqi* prob. =
descendant of *Zadok* (2 *Sam.* viii, 17)]

sadhu (sah′dōō), n. (India) holy man.
[Skr., = pious]

sa′d|ism (sah-), n. Form of sexual perver-
sion marked by love of cruelty; pleasure
derived from inflicting or watching
cruelty. So ~IST(2) n., ~is′tic a. [f. F
sadisme (Count de *Sade* 1740–1814, -ISM)]

safa′ri (-ahr-), n. Hunting expedition in
Africa (esp. in phr. *on* ~); sportsman's or
traveller's caravan. [Swahili, f. Arab.
safar journey]

safe¹, n. (Also *meat-*~) ventilated cupboard for provisions; fireproof & burglar-
-proof receptacle for valuables. [orig.
save, f. SAVE¹]

safe², a. 1. (Pred., after *come, arrive, bring,
keep*, etc.) uninjured (*parcel came* ~; *saw
them* ~ *home*; often ~ *& sound*); secure,
out of or not exposed to danger (*from*),
(*now we are, can feel*, ~; *is* ~ *from his
enemies*). 2. Affording security or not involving danger (*put it in a* ~ *place*; *is it* ~
to leave him?; ~ *custody, convoy*, etc.; *err,
error, on the* ~ *side*, with margin of security against risks; *dog is not* ~ *to touch*;
it is ~ *to say*, may be said without risk
of exaggeration or falsehood); debarred
from escaping or doing harm (*have got
him* ~). 3. Cautious & unenterprising,
consistently moderate, that can be
reckoned on, unfailing, certain *to* do or
be, sure to become, (*a* ~ *critic, statesman*;
~*methods*; *a* ~ CATCH², *winner*; *is a* ~ *first*,
sure to take a first class; *is* ~ *to win*, be
there); hence ~′NESS (-fn-) n. 4. ~ *conduct*,
(document conveying) privilege granted
by sovereign, commander, etc., of being
protected from arrest or harm on particular occasion or in district; ~ *deposit*,
building containing strong-rooms and
safes let separately; ~′*guard*, = ~ *conduct*,
(also & usu.) proviso or stipulation or
quality or circumstance that tends to
prevent some evil or protect, (v.t.) guard,
protect, (esp. rights etc.) by precaution
or stipulation (∥ ~*guarding duties*, on
imports, against competition held to be
unfair); ~ *keeping, custody*. Hence
~′LY² (-fl-) adv. [ME & OF *sauf* f. L
salvus]

safe′ty (-ft-), n. 1. Being safe, freedom
from danger or risks, (*there is* ~ *in numbers* prov.; *is in* ~; *cannot do it with* ~;
play for ~, avoid risks in game or fig.;

~ *first!*, motto inculcating caution).
2. Safeness, being sure or likely to bring
no danger, (*is the* ~ *of the experiment
certain?*; *factor* or *coefficient of* ~ in
engineering, ratio of material's strength
to strain to be allowed for). 3. (Also ~-
-*catch*) contrivance for locking gun-trigger,
gun with this. 4. (Also ~-*bicycle*) bicycle
of usual low-saddled modern form (opp.
ordinary). 5. ~-*belt*, strap securing occupant to seat, in aeroplane, motor-car, etc.;
~ *curtain*, fireproof curtain cutting off the
auditorium in a theatre from the stage;
~ *film*, cinematographic film on slow-
-burning or non-inflammable base (esp. in
sub-standard sizes); ~ *fuse*, FUSE² containing a slow-burning composition for
firing detonators from a distance, (electr.)
protective FUSE¹; ~-*glass*, TRIPLEX glass;
~ *lamp*, miner's so protected as not to
ignite fire-damp; ~ *match*, only igniting
on prepared surface; ~-*pin*, with point
that returns to head & is caught in a guard
so that wearer may not be pricked nor
pin come out; ~ *razor*, kinds with guard
to prevent cutting skin; ~-*valve* in steam-
-boiler, opening automatically to relieve
excessive pressure, (fig.) means of giving
harmless vent to excitement etc. (*sit on
the* ~-*valve*, follow policy of repression).
[ME, f. OF *sauvete* f. med. L *salvitatem*
(prec., -TY)]

säff′ian, n. Leather of goatskin or sheepskin tanned with sumach & dyed in
bright colours. [f. Russ. *safiyanu*]

säf′flower (-owr), n. A thistle-like plant
yielding red dye used esp. in rouge; its
dried petals; the dye made from them.
[f. Du. *saffloer* f. OF *safleur* f. early It.
saffiore, orig. unkn.]

säff′ron, n., a., & v.t. 1. Orange-coloured
stigmas of the autumnal crocus used for
colouring & flavouring confectionery &
liquors (*bastard* ~, the plant safflower);
MEADOW ~. 2. adj. & n. ~-colour(ed),
whence ~Y² a.; ~ *cake*, cake flavoured with
~, also tablet of pressed ~. 3. v.t. Colour
with or like ~. [ME, f. OF *safran* ult. f.
Arab. *za′faran*]

säf′ranin, n. Colouring-matter of saffron;
yellowish-red coal-tar colour. [prec., -IN]

säg, v.i. & t. (-gg-), & n. 1. Sink or subside
under weight or pressure; hang sideways,
be lopsided, (*gate, bridge*, ~s); have downward bulge or curve in middle (*ceiling,
beam, stretched rope, ladder*, ~s), (trans.)
cause to curve thus; (commerc.) decline
in price; (of ship) drift from course (esp.
~ *to leeward*); hence ~g′Y² (-g-) a. 2. n.
Amount that rope etc. ~s, distance from
middle of its curve to straight line between supports; sinking, subsidence;
decline in price; (naut.) tendency to leeward. [15th c., app. rel. to MLG *sacken*,
Du. *zakken* subside]

sa′ga (sah-), n. A mediæval Icelandic or
Norwegian prose narrative, esp. one embodying history of Icelandic family or

Norwegian king, (transf.) story of heroic achievement or adventure; series of connected books giving the history of a family etc. [ON, = narrative, cogn. w. SAW²]

saga'cious (-shus), a. Mentally penetrating, gifted with discernment, practically wise, acute-minded, shrewd; (of sayings, plans, etc.) showing sagacity; (of animals) exceptionally intelligent, seeming to reason or deliberate. Hence or cogn. ~LY² adv., sagā'CITY n. [f. L sagax (sagire discern acutely), -ACIOUS]

sag'amore, n. = SACHEM (1st sense). [f. Amer.-Ind. sagamo]

sage¹, n. Aromatic herb with dull greyish-green leaves; its leaves used in cookery (~ & onions, stuffing used for goose, duck, pork, etc.); ~-brush, growth of alkaline plants characterizing some sterile districts of U.S. (~-cock, -grouse, -hare, etc., found in this); ~ cheese, flavoured & mottled by addition of ~-infusion to the curd; ~-green, colour of ~-leaves; ~ tea, medicinal infusion of ~-leaves. Hence sā'gy² a. [ME & OF sauge f. L salvia]

sage², a. & n. 1. Wise, discreet, judicious, having the wisdom of experience, of indicating profound wisdom, (often iron.) wise-looking, solemn-faced; hence ~'LY² (-jl-) adv., ~'NESS (-jn-) n. 2. n. Profoundly wise man (often iron.), esp. any of the ancients traditionally reputed wisest of their time (the seven ~s, 7 Greeks each credited with a notable saying); hence ~'SHIP (-jsh-) n. [ME & OF, f. Gallo-Rom. *sapius (L sapere be SAPIENT)]

sagg'ar, n. Case of baked fireproof clay enclosing pottery while it is baked. [prob. contr. of safeguard]

Sagitt'a, n. A northern constellation, the Arrow. [L, = arrow]

Sāgittār'ius, n. Constellation & ninth sign of zodiac, the Archer. [L (prec., -ARY¹)]

sā'gittāte, -ātĕd, aa. (bot., zool.). Shaped like arrow-head. [SAGITTA, -ATE²]

sāg'ō, n. (pl. ~s). (Kinds of palm & cycad with pith yielding) kind of starch used as food in puddings etc. [f. Malay sagu]

ǁ sahaa' (sa-hah'), int. Goodbye. [Maltese]

Sahār'ǀa (sa-h-), n. Great Libyan desert; arid tract (lit. & fig.). Hence ~AN, ~IAN, ~IC, aa. [f. Arab. çahra]

Sah'ib, n. (fem. mĕm'sahib). 1. (India). European as spoken of or to by Indians; an honorific affix (Colonel ~, Jones ~, Raja ~, Khan ~). 2. (colloq.; s~). Gentleman (pukka s~). [Hind., f. Arab. çahib friend]

said¹. See SAY².

Said² (säd). Var. of SEID.

saig'a (or sī-), n. Antelope of steppes. [Russ.]

sail¹, n. 1. Piece of canvas or other textile material extended on rigging to catch wind & propel vessel, (collect.) some or all of ship's ~s (CARRY, CROWD², hoist,

lower, MAKE¹, SET¹, SHORTEN, STRIKE, ~; take in ~, fig., moderate one's ambitions; take WIND¹ out of ~s; full ~ adv., with all ~ spread lit. & fig.; under ~, with ~s set). 2. (collect.). Ships (in giving number of ships in squadron or company; a fleet of twenty ~). 3. Ship (esp. in ~ ho!, cry announcing that ship is in sight). 4. pl. (naut. sl.; hist.). ǁ Chief petty officer in charge of rigging; one who makes or repairs ~s. 5. Wind-catching apparatus, now usu. set of boards, attached to arm of windmill. 6. ~-fish's dorsal fin, tentacle of nautilus. 7. (Also wind-~) funnel-shaped bag on ship's deck or above mine giving ventilation. 8. ~-arm, arm of windmill; ~-axle, on which ~-arms revolve; ~-cloth, canvas for ~s, also dress-material; ~-fish, kinds with large dorsal fin, esp. basking shark. Hence (-)~ED² (-ld), ~'LESS, aa. [OE, OS segel, OHG segal, ON segl, f. Gmc *saglam]

sail², v.i. & t., & n. 1. (Of vessel or person on board) travel on water by use of sails (~ing-ship, -vessel, opp. steamer; ~ close to or near the wind, nearly against it, also fig. come near transgressing a law or moral principle); (of vessel or person on board) travel on water by use of sails or engine-power, start on voyage, (we ~ next week; list of ~ING¹s from London; ~ing orders, instructions to captain for departure, destination, etc.). 2. (Of bird, cloud, moon, etc.) glide in air; (esp. of women) walk in stately manner. 3. Travel over or along, navigate, glide through, (the sea, Spanish main, sky, etc.). 4. Control navigation of (ship; plain ~ING¹, used pred. to describe task etc. that is not perplexing; ~ing-master, officer navigating yacht); set (toy-boat) afloat. 5. ~ into (sl.), inveigh against, scold, rate, attack. 6. n. Voyage or excursion in ~ing-vessel (go for a ~); voyage of specified duration (is ten days' ~ from Plymouth); ~'plane, glider. [OE siglan, segl(i)an, (prec.)]

sail'er, n. Ship of specified sailing-power (fast, good, bad, ~). [-ER¹]

sail'or, n. Seaman, mariner, esp. one below rank of officer (good, bad, ~, person not, very, liable to sea-sickness); ~ hat, of straw with straight narrow brim & flat top worn by women, also with turned-up brim in imitation of ~'s worn by children; ~-man, (vulg. & joc. for) ~; ~s' home, institution for lodging ~s cheaply ashore; ~'s knot, way of tying necktie. Hence ~ING¹(1) n., ~LESS, ~LY¹, aa. [var. of prec., see -ER¹, -OR]

ǁ sain, v.t. (arch.). Make sign of the cross on, bless, protect by divine power or enchantment. [OE segnian, = OS segnōn, OHG seganōn, ON signa, f. L signare mark (SIGN¹um)]

sain'foin, n. Plant of pea family grown for forage. [F (sain SANE, foin hay f. L faenum)]

saint, a. (*unstressed* sent, snt; *abbr.* St, S., *in pl.* Sts, SS.), n., & v.t. **1.** Holy, canonized or officially recognized by the Church as having won by exceptional holiness a high place in heaven & veneration on earth, (usu. as prefix to name of person or archangel as *St Paul, St Michael*, whence ellipt. names of churches as *St Peter's*, & of towns called after their churches often with loss of possessive sign as *St Andrews* & *St Albans*, & many Christian & family names taken either from patron ~ or from local names as above; also in some names of churches not called after ~s, as *St Saviour's, Sepulchre's, Faith, Cross*); *St* —*'s day*, Church festival in memory of particular ~. **2.** *St Andrew*, patron ~ of Scotland (*St A.'s day*, 30th Nov.); *St Anthony's, Elmo's*, FIRE[1]; *St Bartholomew*; *St B.'s*, (used for) St B.'s Hospital in London, abbr. *Bart's*; *massacre of St B.*, of Huguenots in France on St B.'s day, 24 Aug., 1572. *St Bernard* (*the Great, Little, St B.*, Alpine passes); *St Bernard dog* or *St Bernard*, breed kept by monks of Hospice on Great St Bernard pass for rescue of travellers. *St Cecilia*, patron ~ of music; *St Charles*, King Charles I as canonized martyr; *St David*, patron ~ of Wales (*St D.'s day*, 1st Mar.); *St Denis*, patron ~ of France. *St George*, patron ~ of England (*St G.'s day*, 23rd Ap.); *St G.'s*, (used for) St G.'s Hospital in London; *St G.'s, Hanover Square*, London church at which many West-end weddings take place; *St G.'s cross*, the *Greek* CROSS[1]. *St Germain* (or *Faubourg St G.*), aristocratic quarter of Paris; *St Gotthard* (*the St G*, the Alpine pass of St G. or the tunnelled railway used instead of it). *St Helen'a*, (used for) place of exile (w. ref. to Napoleon, 1815–21). *St James's* (or *the Court of St James's* or *St James*), the British court (esp. in distinction from foreign courts; w. ref. to St James's Palace in London); (also) fashionable district in London about St James's Palace. *St-John's--wort*, kinds of yellow-flowered wild & garden plant. *St Leger*, horse-race at Doncaster for three-year-olds, f. founder's name; *St Lubbock's day*, any of the BANK[3]-holidays instituted 1871 by Sir J. Lubbock's Act; *St Luke's* SUMMER. *St Mark's*, (used for) St M.'s church in Venice; *St Martin's-le-Grand*, (used for) the General Post Office; *St* MARTIN'*s summer*; *St Michael & St George*, order of knighthood; *St Michael*, kind of orange, f. one of the Azores so called; *St* MONDAY. *St Patrick*, patron ~ of Ireland (*St P.'s Day*, 17th Mar.; *order of St P.*, Irish order of knighthood); *St Paul's*, cathedral of see of London; *St Peter's*, (used for) the church of St Peter in the Vatican in Rome; *St Peter's chair*, (used for) the office of Pope. *St Sophia* (used for) the mosque of St S. in Constantinople; *St*

Stephen's, (used for) Parliament (w. ref. to former use of St S.'s chapel, Westminster, for meetings of House of Commons); *St Swithin's*, the day (15th July) whose rain or absence of rain is said to presage the same for 40 days. *St Thomas's*, (used for) St Thomas's Hospital in London. *St* VALENTINE'*s day*; *St Vitus's* DANCE[2]. **3.** n. One of the blessed dead or other member of the company of heaven (*departed* ~, phr. used by or attributed to mourners, = deceased person); canonized person (see adj. sense; *patron* ~, selected as heavenly protector of person or place, esp. church, often named after him); (bibl., arch., & with some mod. sects) one of God's chosen people, member of the Christian Church or speaker's branch of it; person of great real or affected holiness (*would provoke, try the patience of, a* ~; *young* ~*s old devils* or *sinners*, early piety is no good sign; LATTER-*day* ~s); ~*'s-day*, Church festival in memory of a ~, often observed as holiday at schools etc.; hence ~'DOM, ~'HOOD (-t-h-), ~'SHIP, ~'LING[1], nn., ~'LIKE, ~'LY[1], aa., ~'liNESS n. **4.** v.t. Canonize, admit to the calendar of ~s; call or regard as a ~; (p.p.) worthy to be so regarded, of ~ly life, (of place etc.) sacred. [ME, f. OF, f. L *sanctus* p.p. of *sancire* consecrate]

Saint-Simōn'ian, a. & n. (Advocate) of the socialism of the Comte de Saint--Simon (1760–1825) with State control of property & distribution of produce. So **Saint-Sim'on**IST(2), **Saint-Sim'on**ITE[1] (1), **Saint-Sim'on**ISM(3), ~ISM(3), nn. [-IAN]

saith. See SAY[2].

saithe (sāth), n. (Sc.). Coal-fish. [f. ON *seithr*]

Säit'ic, a. Of Sais, ancient capital of Lower Egypt (~ *dynasties*, 26th–30th of Egyptian kings). [f. L f. Gk *Saïtikos* (*Saïlēs* f. *Sais*, -ITE[1])]

sāke, n. *For the* ~ *of* —, *for* —*'s* or *my* etc. ~, out of consideration for, in the interest of, because of, owing to, in order to please or honour or get or keep, (common n. with sibilant ending does not take the extra syllable of the possessive before ~, but has usu. the apostrophe, as *for peace', conscience', goodness'*, ~, cf. *for God's, the children's, Phyllis's*, ~; *for my own* ~ *as well as yours*; *for both, all, our* ~*s* or rarely ~; *for his name's* ~, because he bears the name he does or in the interest of his reputation; *persecuted for opinion's* ~; *for any* ~ in entreaties, for one reason if not for another; *for old* ~*'s* ~, in memory of old days). [OE *sacu* contention, charge, fault, sake, = OS *saka*, OHG *sahha*, ON *sǫk*, also OE *sæc*(c), Goth. *sakjō*]

sä'ké (-ā), n. Japanese fermented liquor made from rice. [f. Jap. *sake*]

sāk'er, n. **1.** Large lanner falcon used in hawking, esp. the female larger than the male or ~ET[1] n. **2.** (hist.), Old form of cannon. [ME, f. OF *sacre* (in both senses) f. Sp., Port., *sacro*, f. Arab. *çaqr*]

sa'ki (sah-), n. S.-American monkey with long non-prehensile tail, and neck-ruff. [native name, through F]

sa'kia (sah-), n. Eastern water-wheel for irrigation. [Arab. *sāqiya* (*saqā* irrigate)]

sal (sahl), **saul**, n. Valuable Indian timber (tree). [Hind.]

salaam' (-lahm), n., & v.i. & t. **1.** Oriental salutation ' Peace '; Indian obeisance with or without this, low bow of head & body with right palm on forehead. **2.** vb. Make ~ (to). [f. Arab. *salam*]

sāl'able, -lea-, a. Fit for sale, finding purchasers; ~ *price*, that article will fetch. Hence **sālabIL'ITY** (*or* **-lea-**) n. [-ABLE]

salā'cious (-shus), a. Lustful, lecherous. Hence *or comp.* ~LY[2] adv., ~NESS, sālā'CITY, nn. [f. L *salax* (*salīre* leap), -ACIOUS]

sãl'ad, n. Cold dish of various mixtures of raw or cooked vegetables or herbs usu. seasoned with oil, vinegar, etc., & eaten with or including cold fish, meat, hard--boiled eggs, etc.; vegetable or herb suitable for eating raw; ~*days*, inexperienced youth; ~*-dressing*, mixture of oil, vinegar, cream, etc., taken with ~; ~*-oil*, kinds of oil for ~-dressing. [ME, f. OF *salade* ult. f. L *sal* salt, -ADE(1)]

sãl'amänder, n. **1.** Lizard-like animal supposed to live in fire; person who can endure great heat, fire-eating soldier etc.; spirit living in fire (cf. *sylph*, *gnome*, *nymph*); (zool.) kinds of tailed amphibian, whence **sãlamän'droID** a. & n. **2.** Red--hot iron for firing gunpowder, hot iron plate for browning omelettes etc. Hence **sãlamän'drIAN**, **sãlamän'drINE**[1], aa. [ME, f. OF (*-dre*), f. L f. Gk *salamandra*]

sala'mè (-lah-), n. Italian sausage highly salted and flavoured often with garlic. [It.]

sãl-ammōn'iäc, n. Ammonium chloride. [L *sal* salt, AMMONIAC]

sãl'angāne (-ngg-), n. Swallow making edible nest. [F, f. *salamga* name in Luzon]

salār'iät, n. The salaried class. [F]

sãl'ar|y̆, n., & v.t. **1.** Fixed periodical payment made to person doing other than manual or mechanical work (cf. *wages*). **2.** v.t. Pay ~y to (chiefly in p.p. ~*ied* pr. -rid). [ME, f. AF (*-ie*), = OF *salaire* f. L *salarium* orig. soldier's salt-money (*sal* salt, -ARY[1])]

sãle, n. Exchange of a commodity for money or other valuable consideration, selling (*on*, *for*, ~, offered for purchase; ~ *&*, *or or*, *return*, arrangement by which retailer takes quantity of goods with right of returning all that he fails to sell); amount sold (*the* ~*s were enormous*); public auction (*put up for* ~, offer at auction); rapid disposal at reduced prices of shop's stock at end of season; BILL[3] *of* ~; ~*-ring*, ring of buyers at auction; ~*s'man*, ~*s'woman*, person engaged in selling goods in shop or as middleman between producer & retailer, whence ~*s'manSHIP* (-lz-) n., skill in this art; ~*s resistance*, the opposition or apathy of the prospective customer etc., to be overcome by ~smanship; ~*s tax*, tax on (receipts from)~s. [OE *sala* prob. f. ON *sala* f. root *sal-* SELL]

saleable. Var. of SALABLE.

‖ **Sãl'em**, n. Nonconformist chapel. [*Heb.* vii. 2]

sãl'ep, n. Nutritive meal from dried tubers of some orchidaceous plants. [F f. Turk., f. Arab. *tha'leb*]

'sälerāt'us, n. Impure bicarbonate of potash or sodium bicarbonate as ingredient in baking-powders. [f. mod. L *sal aeratus* AERATED salt]

Sāl'ian[1], a. Of the Salii or priests of Mars. [L *Salii* pl. (*salīre* leap), -AN]

Sãl'ian[2], a. & n. (Member) of Frankish tribe near Zuyder Zee from which the Merovingians were descended. [LL *Salii* the tribe, -AN]

Sãl'ic, Salique' (-ŏk), aa. (Form *-ic* = prec.), adj. (~ *law*, Frankish law-book extant in Merovingian & Carolingian times); (*-ic*, *-ique*) ~ *law*, law excluding females from dynastic succession, esp. as alleged fundamental law of French monarchy (based on a quotation, not referring to such succession, from the law--book above). [f. F *Salique* or med. L *Salicus* f. *Salii* (prec.), -IC]

sãl'icin, n. Bitter crystalline principle got from willow-bark & used medicinally. So **sãl'icYL** n., **sãlicyl'ic** a. (*salicylic acid*, used as antiseptic & for rheumatism), **sali'cy̆lATE**[1](3) n., **sali'cY̆lIZE**(5) & in same sense **sali'cY̆lATE**[3] vv.t., **sali'cy̆l-ISM**(5) n., **sali'cy̆lOUS** (chem.) a. [F (*-ine*), f. L *salix -icis* willow, -IN]

sali'cional (-shon-), **sãl'icĕt**, nn. Organ stop of soft reedy tone as of willow pipe. [G, f. L *salix* (prec.) w. suff.]

sãl'ient, a. & n. **1.** Leaping or dancing (pedant., joc.), (of water etc., poet.) jetting forth, (~ *point*, arch., initial stage or origin or first beginning, from old med. use = heart as it first shows in an embryo); (of angle, esp. in fortif., opp. RE-ENTRANT) pointing outwards; jutting out, prominent, conspicuous, most noticeable, (~ *points*, *features*, *characteristics*). **2.** n. A ~ angle or part in fortification (*the S~*, that at Ypres in the 1914–18 war). Hence **sāl'iENCE**, **sāl'iENCY**, nn., ~LY[2] adv. [f. L *salīre* leap, -ENT]

salif'erous, a. (geol.). (Of strata) containing much salt. [L *sal* salt, -I-, -FEROUS]

sãl'ine (*or* salīn'), a. & n. **1.** (Of natural waters, springs, etc.) impregnated with salt or salts, whence **sãlinŎM'ETER** n.; (of taste) salt; (of chemical salts, of the nature of a salt; (of medicines) containing salt(s) of alkaline metals or magnesium; hence **salin'ITY** n., **salin'o-** comb. form. **2.** n.

Salt lake, spring, marsh, etc.; salt-pan, salt-works; ~ substance; ~ purge; solution of salt & water. [ME; prec., -INE¹]

Salique. See SALIC.

saliv′a (-ī), n. Colourless liquid given by mixed secretions of salivary & mucous glands discharged into mouth & assisting mastication, spittle. So **săl′IVARY¹ a.** [L]

săl′iv|āte, v.t. & i. Produce unusual secretion of saliva in (person) usu. with mercury; secrete or discharge saliva esp. in excess. So **~A′TION n.** [f. L SALIVAre, -ATE³]

salle (sahl), n. Hall, room, (of foreign countries); ~-à-manger (see Ap.), dining-room, coffee-room; ~-d'attente (see Ap.), waiting-room at station. [F]

săll′enders, n. pl. Dry eruption inside hock of horse's hind-leg (cf. MALANDERS). [orig. obsc.; in F *solandre*]

săll′ow¹ (-ō), n. Willow-tree, esp. of low-growing or shrubby kinds, whence ~Y² (-ōī) a.; a shoot, the wood, of this. [OE *sealh*, f. Gmc **salhaz*, cogn. w. OHG *salaha*, ON *selja*, L *salix*]

săll′ow² (-ō), a. (~*er*, ~*est*), n., & v.t. & i. 1. (Of human skin or complexion or person in these respects, rarely of foliage) of sickly yellow or pale brown; hence ~ISH¹(2) (-ōī-) a., ~NESS (-ōn-) n. 2. n. ~ hue. 3. vb. Make or grow~. [OE *salo*, = MDu. *salu*, OHG *salo*, ON *sǫlr* f. Gmc **salwa-*]

săll′y¹, n., & v.i. 1. Rush of besieged upon besiegers, sortie; a going forth, excursion; sudden start into activity, outburst; escapade (rare); witticism, piece of banter, lively remark esp. by way of attack upon person or thing or of diversion in argument; ~-*port*, opening in fortification for making ~ from. 2. v.i. Make military ~ (often *out*); go *forth* or *out* on a journey, for a walk, etc.; issue, come out, suddenly (rare). [vb f. n., f. F *saillie* (*saillir* issue, f. L *salire* leap)]

săll′y², n. First movement of bell when set for ringing (also *hand-stroke*, opp. *back-stroke*), bell's position when set; part of bell-rope prepared with inwoven wool for holding; ~-*hole*, through which bell-rope passes. [perh. f. prec. in sense *leaping motion*]

Săll′y³, fam. for *Sarah* (AUNT~; || ~ *Lunn*, sweet light tea-cake served hot, perh. f. name of girl hawking them at Bath *c.* 1800).

sălmagŭn′dĭ, n. Dish of chopped meat, anchovies, eggs, onions, etc., & seasoning; general mixture, miscellaneous collection, of articles, subjects, qualities, etc. [f. F *salmigondis* of unkn. orig.]

săl′mi (-ē), n. Ragout esp. of game-birds. [F, short for prec.]

salmon (săm′on), n. (collect. sing. usual for pl.), & a. 1. Large silver-scaled pink-fleshed anadromous fish much prized for food & sport; ~-*colour*(*ed*), (of) the orange-pink colour of ~-flesh; ~-*ladder*, -*leap*, -*pass*, -*stair*, series of steps or other arrangement for allowing ~ to pass dam & ascend stream; ~ *peel* (or *peal*), (in Ireland) grilse, (in England) sea-trout; ~ *steak*, fried slice of ~; ~ *trout*, N.-Europ. fish resembling ~; hence **săl′monOID a.** & n. 2. adj. ~-coloured, orange-pink. [ME, f. AF *samoun* f. L *salmonem* (-*mo*)]

Sălomōn′ic, Sălomōn′ian, aa. Of, as of, Solomon. [LL *Salomon* Solomon, -IC, -IAN]

salon (see Ap.), n. Reception-room in continental, esp. French, house; (re-union of notabilities in) reception-room of (esp. Parisian) lady of fashion (hist.); *the S~*, annual exhibition of living artists' pictures in Paris; ~ *music*, light music for drawing-room. [F]

saloōn′, n. 1. Hall or large room, esp. in hotel or place of public resort, fit for assemblies, exhibitions, etc. 2. Large cabin for first-class or for all passengers on ship; cabin for passengers in large aircraft. 3. || (Also ~*car, carriage*) luxurious railway carriage without compartments furnished as drawing-room etc. (also *sleeping, dining,* -~). 4. || Public room(s) or gallery for specified purpose (*billiard, dancing, shaving, shooting,* etc., -~). 5. *Drinking-bar. 6. || ~ *bar*, first-class bar in English public-house; || ~ *car*, (also) motor-car with closed body and no partition behind driver; ~ *deck*, reserved for ~ passengers; *~-keeper*, of bar; || ~ *pistol, rifle,* adapted for short-range practice in shooting-~. [f. prec., f. It. *salone* (*sala* hall f. Gmc, -OON)]

saloōp′, n. = SALEP; hot drink of salep or sassafras formerly sold as substitute for coffee at London street-stalls. [var. of SALEP]

Salōp′ian, a. & n. (Native) of Shropshire; (member) of Shrewsbury school. [*Salop* Shropshire f. AF *Sloppesberie* corrupt. of OE *Scrobbesbyrig* Shrewsbury, -IAN]

sălpiglŏss′ĭs, n. Herbaceous showy-flowered garden-plant allied to petunia. [irreg. f. Gk *salpigx* trumpet, *glōssa* tongue]

săl′sify, n. British & Continental plant with long cylindrical fleshy roots eaten as vegetable, purple goat's-beard. [f. F *salsifis*, app. f. It. *sassefrica* of unkn. orig.]

salt (sawlt, sŏlt), n., a., & v.t. 1. (Also *common* ~) substance that gives sea-water its characteristic taste got in crystalline forms from strata consisting of it or by evaporation of brine pumped from these or of sea-water & used for seasoning or preserving food & other purposes, sodium chloride, (BAY-SALT, SEA-~, ROCK¹-~; *while* ~, refined for household use from the brownish rock-~; *table* ~, powdered or easy to powder for the ~-*cellar*; *in* ~, sprinkled with ~ or immersed in brine as preservative; *eat* ~ *with*, be guest of; *eat* one's ~, be his guest or dependant; *is not, any one, worth his* ~, efficient, worth keeping; *drop pinch of* ~ *on tail of*, capture, w. ref. to directions given children for catching bird; *take with a grain of* ~, regard as exaggerated, be incredulous about, believe only part of; *am not made of* ~, can go out in rain without fear of dissolving; *the* ~ *of the earth*, people or classes for whose exis-tence the world is better, moral élite, see *Matt.* v. 13). 2. Sting, piquancy, pun-gency, wit, (*no* ~ *in such tears*; *talk full of* ~; ATTIC[1] ~). 3. (Old chem.) solid soluble non-inflammable sapid substance (obs. exc. in some compd names, as ~ *of* LEMON[1], GLAUBER'S SALT, SMELL*ing* ~s, EPSOM ~); (chem.) compound of basic & acid radicals, acid with whole or part of its hydrogen replaced by a metal. 4. =~-*-cellar* (chiefly now in trade use; & hist. in *above, below*, etc., *the* ~, seated at table among the family & their equals, among the servants & dependants). 5. (Also ~-*-marsh*, ~*ING*[1] n.) marsh overflowed by sea, often used as pasture or for collecting water for ~-making. 6. pl. Exceptional rush of sea-water up river. 7. Experienced sailor (esp. *old* ~). 8. ~*cat* [*cat* unexpl.], mass of ~ mixed with gravel, urine, etc., to attract pigeons & keep them at home; ~*cellar* [assim. of obs. *saler* (f. OF *salier* ~-box f. L as SALARY) to *cellar*], vessel holding ~ for table use, (also, colloq.) specially deep hollow above collar-bone in woman's neck (regarded as disfigure-ment; usu. pl.); ~-*glaze*, glaze on stone-ware made by throwing ~ into furnace; ~-*lick*, place where animals collect to lick earth impregnated with ~; ~-*mine*, yielding rock-~; ~-*pan*, depression near sea, vessel, used for getting ~ by evapora-tion; ~-*pit*, pit yielding ~; ~-*pond*, natural or artificial for evaporating sea-*-water*; ~-*spoon*, usu. with short handle & roundish deep bowl for helping ~; ~-*-well*, bored well yielding brine; ~-*works*, ~ manufactory; ~*wort*, kinds of maritime & ~-marsh plants; hence ~*LESS*, ~*Y*[2], aa., ~*INESS* n. 9. adj. Impregnated with, containing, tasting of, cured or preserved or seasoned with, ~ (cf. FRESH); (of plants) growing in sea or ~-marshes; (of tears, grief, etc.) bitter, afflicting; (of wit etc. pungent; (of stories, jests, etc.) indecent, spicy; (of bill, charge, etc.; sl.) exorbitant; ~ *horse* (naut. sl.), ~ *beef*; ~ JUNK[1]; ~ *water*, sea-water, (sl.) tears; ~-*water*, of, living in, the sea; hence ~*ISH*[1](2) a.,' ~*LY*[2] adv., ~*NESS* n. 10. v.t. Cure or preserve money with ~ or brine (~ *down money* or *stock*, sl., put it by); sprinkle (esp. snow to melt it in street) with ~; make ~, season, (lit. & fig.); (p.p.; of horses or persons) proof against diseases incident to climate or special conditions by habitu-ation, hardened; treat (esp. paper in photog.) with solution of ~ or mixture of ~s; (commerc., sl.) ~ *an account* etc., put

down extreme price for articles, ~ *the books*, represent receipts as larger than they have been; (mining, sl.) ~ *a mine*, introduce extraneous ore etc. to make it seem rich. [OE *seall*, OS, ON, Goth. *salt*, OHG *salz* f. Gmc **saltam*; cogn. w. L *sal*, Gk *hals*; vb f. OE *sealtan*]

săltărĕll'ō, n. Italian & Spanish dance with sudden skips for one couple. [It. & (-*elo*) Sp.]

săltā'tion, n. Leaping, dancing, a jump; sudden transition or movement. So **săl'tatory**, **sāltatŏr'IAL**, aa. [f. L *salta-tio* (*saltare* frequent. of *salire* salt- leap, -ATION)]

salt'er (sawl-, sŏl-), n. Manufacturer of, dealer in, salt; = DRY[1]-~; workman at salt-works; person who salts fish etc. [OE *sealtere* (SALT n. & v., -ER[1])]

salt'ern (sawl-, sŏl-), n. A salt-works; set of pools for natural evaporation of sea-*-water. [OE *sealtærn* (SALT, *ærn* hut)]

săl'tigrāde, a. & n. (Spider) with legs adapted for jumping. [L *saltus* -*ūs* leap (*salire* salt-), -*gradus* -walking]

săltimban'cō, n. Mountebank, quack. [It.]

săl'tire, n. (her.). Ordinary formed by bend & bend sinister crossing like a St Andrew's cross (*in* ~, *per* ~, so arranged). Hence ~*WISE* (-īrwiz) adv. [ME, f. OF *sautoir* stile, saltire, f. med. L *saltatorium* (SALTATION, -ORY)]

saltpetre (sawltpēt'er, sŏl-), n. Potassium nitrate, nitre, white crystalline salty substance used as constituent of gun-powder, in preserving meat, & medicinally (*Chili* or *cubic* ~, sodium nitrate); ~-*-paper*, TOUCH-paper; ~ *rot*, white efflores-cence on new or damp walls. [ME & OF *salpetre* f. med. L *salpetra* prob. for *sal petrae* salt of stone (i.e. found as incrustation) w. assim. to *salt*; *petrae* f. LL f. Gk *petra* rock]

săl'tus, n. (pl. -*ūs*). Sudden transition, breach of continuity. [L, = leap]

salu'brious (-lōō-, -lū-), a. Healthy (chiefly of climate, air, etc.; rarely of food, exercise, etc.). Hence or cogn. ~*LY*[2] adv., **salu'brity** n., (-lōō-, -lū-). [L *salubris* (as SALUTARY), -OUS]

Salu'ki (-lōō-), n. Breed of dog, Arabian gazelle-hound. [Arab.]

săl'utary, a. Salubrious (now rare); pro-ducing good effects, beneficial. [f. F *salutaire* or L *salutaris* (*salus* -*utis* health, -AR[1]), -ARY[2]]

sălūtā'tion, n. (Use of) words spoken or written to convey interest in another's health etc., pleasure at sight of or com-munication with him, or courteous recog-nition of his arrival or departure, (rarely, now usu. *salute*) gesture of similar import, (*the Angelic S*~, the Ave Maria). Hence or cogn. ~*AL* (-sho-), **salu'tatory** (-lōō-, -lū-), aa. [ME, f. OF (-*cion*), or L *saluta-tio* (foll., -ATION)]

salute' (-ōōt, -ūt), v.t. & i., & n. 1. Make

salutation to, greet; (rare) hail as (king etc.); perform ~ to or to, perform ~; (arch.) kiss (person, cheek, hand) esp. at meeting or parting; accost or receive *with* a smile, oath, volley, etc.; become perceptible to (eye, ear, person arriving). **2.** n. Gesture expressing respect, homage, or courteous recognition, to person esp. when arriving or departing; (mil., naut.) prescribed movement or position of body or weapons, or use of flag(s) or discharge of gun(s) in sign of respect, (*a ~ of 7 guns was fired*; *the ~*, attitude taken by individual soldier, sailor, policeman, etc., in saluting; *take the ~*, esp. of highest officer present, acknowledge it as meant for him by gesture); (fenc.) formal performance of certain guards etc. by fencers before engaging; kiss given, prop. as greeting (arch. or joc.; often *a chaste ~*). [ME; vb f. L *salutare* (*salus -utis* health); n. f. OF *salut*, partly f. E vb]

salutif′erous (-lŏo-, -lū-), a. (now rare). Promoting health. [f. L *salutifer* (prec., -FEROUS)]

sal′vage, n., & v.t. **1.** (Payment made or due for) saving of a ship or its cargo from loss by wreck or capture (also attrib., as *~ money*); rescue of property from fire etc.; property *~d*; saving & utilization of waste paper, scrap-metal, etc.; materials *~d*. **2.** v.t. Make ~ of, save from wreck, fire, etc. [f. med. L *salvagium* or OF *salvage* (LL *salvare* SAVE¹, -AGE)]

sal′varsän, n. Drug used esp. in syphilis. [P]

sälvā′tion, n. **1.** Saving of the soul; deliverance from sin & its consequences & admission to heaven brought about by Christ (*find ~*, be converted, also joc. discover formula that will enable one to abandon one's principles etc.). **2.** Preservation from loss, calamity, etc., thing that preserves from these (esp. *be the ~ of*). **3.** *S~ Army*, organization on military model for revival of religion among the masses, welfare work, etc., whence (& w. ref. to religious revivals in general) *~ISM*(3), *~IST*(2), nn., (*-sho-*. [ME & OF *sau-*, *salvation* f. LL *salvationem* (SAVE¹, -ATION)]

salve¹ (sahv, sälv), n., & v.t. **1.** Healing ointment for sores or wounds (now chiefly poet. & in *lip-~*). **2.** Mixture of tar & grease for smearing sheep. **3.** Something that soothes wounded feelings or uneasy conscience or (arch.) glozes over discrepancy or palliates fault (usu. *for*). **4.** v.t. Anoint (wound etc.; arch. exc. in fig. use=*soothe* as below). **5.** Smear (sheep). **6.** Smooth over or make good (defect, disgrace, etc.; arch.); soothe (pride, self-love, conscience, etc.). **7.** Account for, dispose of, harmonize, vindicate, (difficulty, doubt, discrepancy, person's honour). **8.** Save (ship, cargo) from loss at sea or (property) from fire, whence

säl′vable a. [OE *sealf*, OS *salba*, OHG *salba* f. Gmc *salbō*; vb f. OE *sealfian*, in senses 6 & 7 partly f. L *salvare* SAVE¹ & in last sense back formation f. SALVAGE]

säl′vē¹, n. (Also *S~ regina*) R.-C. antiphon beginning with ~ recited after Divine Office from Trinity Sunday to Advent, music for it. [L (vb imperat.= hail)]

säl′ver, n. Tray usu. of gold, silver, brass, or electroplate, on which servants hand refreshments, letters, cards, etc. [f. F *salve* tray for presenting certain things to king f. Sp. *salva* assaying of food (*salvo* SAFE²) +-ER¹]

säl′via, n. (Kinds of) plant of the sage family (including several garden flowering plants). [L, = SAGE¹]

säl′vō¹, n. (pl. *~s*). Saving clause, reservation, (often *of*; *with an express ~ of their rights*); tacit reservation, quibbling evasion, bad excuse; expedient for saving reputation or soothing pride or conscience. [f. L abl. of *salvus* SAFE² as used in *salvo jure* etc. without prejudice to the right etc.]

säl′vō², n. (pl. *~es*, *~s*). Simultaneous discharge of pieces of artillery or other fire-arms esp. as salute, or in seafight; number (*of bombs*) released from aircraft at the same moment, cf. STICK; round or volley of applause. [earlier & It. *salva* salutation, as SAVE²]

säl volät′ilĕ, n. (Aromatic solution, taken for faintness etc., of) ammonium carbonate. [mod. L, = volatile salt]

säl′vor, n. Person, ship, making or assisting in salvage. [SALVE¹ vb, -OR]

Säm, n. (sl.). *Stand ~*, bear the expense esp. of drink; ‖ *upon my ~*, asseveration. [orig. unkn.]

Samā′ritan, n. & a. **1.** Native, language, of Samaria (*good ~*, genuinely charitable person, w. ref. to *Luke* x. 33 etc.); adherent of the ~ religious system. **2.** adj. Of Samaria or the *~s* (*the ~ pentateuch*, recension used by *~s* of which MSS. are in ~ or archaic-Hebrew characters). Hence *~ISM*(2, 3, 4) n. [f. LL *Samaritanus* f. Gk *Samareitēs* (*Samareia* Samaria)+-AN]

säm′ba, n. Brazilian native dance; ball-room dance imitative of this. [Braz.]

säm′bō, n. (pl. *~s*, *~es*). Half-breed esp. of Negro & Indian or European blood; (*S~*; nickname for) Negro. [1st sense f. Sp. *zambo* perh. = *zambo* bandy-legged; 2nd sense prob. a diff. wd]

Säm Browne, n. Army officer's belt & straps. [f. Gen. Sir *S. J. Browne* (d. 1901)]

säm′būr, n. Kinds of large S.-E.-Asian deer. [f. Hind. *sa(m)bar*]

säme, a. **1.** Monotonous, uniform, unvarying, (*the life is perhaps a little ~*; *the ~ old story*), whence *~′NESS* (-mn-) n.; (with *this*, *these*, *that*, *those*; often w. depreciatory intention) aforesaid, previously alluded to or thought of, (*what is the use of this ~ patience?*); (vulg. or commerc.) = *the ~*

(pron. & adv., as specified below). 2. *The* ~, a., pron., & adv.: (adj.) identical, not different, indifferent, unchanged, (also *the very* ~, *just the* ~, & in sing. *one & the* ~; *the* ~ *causes produce the* ~ *effects*; *the difference between a body in motion & the* ~ *body at rest*; *the* ~ *observations are true of the others also*; *all planets travel in the* ~ *direction*; *belong to one & the* ~ *class*; *say the* ~ *thing twice over*; *several of the very* ~ *birds*; *bigotry is the* ~ *in every age*; *she was always the* ~ *to me*; *it is all, just, the* ~ *to me*, makes no difference; *much the* ~, not appreciably different; *at the* ~ *time*, often introducing fact etc. in apparent conflict with what precedes but also true or to be remembered; *by the* ~ TOKEN); identical *with* (*words of the* ~ *nature with those he had first heard*; *expectation of pleasure is the* ~ *thing with desire*); (emphatic substitute—before full or elliptical relative clause with *that*, *where*, etc., or esp. *as* which often replaces *that* under its influence—for) the, that, those, (*at the* ~ *time that I am endeavouring*; *to the* ~ *place where I had found it*; *on the* ~ *grounds that he would defend suicide*; *I have the* ~ *Bible my mother gave me*; *Rhenish wine at the* ~ *price as French is sold at*; *sailors received the* ~ *pay as soldiers*; *gave the* ~ *answer as before*); (pron.) the ~ person (now rare exc. in *To*, *From*, *the* ~ as heading of letter or poem addressed to or coming from ~ person as the preceding one), the ~ thing (*we must all say, do, the* ~; *would do the* ~ *again*), the aforesaid thing or person (arch., legal, commerc., & vulg.; occas. in commerc. & vulg. use with omission of *the*; *grace & power faithfully to fulfil the* ~; *he that shall endure unto the end, the* ~ *shall be saved*; *& never met, found, the* ~ *again*; *to repairing sleeve of* ~ 1/3); (adv.) in the ~ manner (*think the* ~ *of, feel the* ~ *to*, remain in the ~ mind regarding; *we take what pleasure we can get, the* ~, or vulg. ~, *as you do*; *all the* ~, nevertheless, notwithstanding, even under different circumstances; *just the* ~, in spite of changed conditions). [ME, f. ON *same*, = OHG, Goth. *sama*, cogn. w. Gk *homos*]

săm'el, a. (Of brick, tile) imperfectly baked, soft, from being outmost in the baking. [perh. f. OE *sam-* half, cogn. w. SEMI-, *ǣlan* burn]

Sām'ian, a. & n. (Native) of Samos (~ *ware*, fine pottery found on Roman sites). [L f. Gk *Samios* (*Samos*), -AN]

săm'isĕn, n. Long three-stringed Japanese guitar, played with plectrum. [Jap., f. Chin. *san-hsien* (*san* three, *hsien* string)]

săm'ite, n. (arch.). Rich medieval dress--fabric of silk occas. interwoven with gold. [ME, f. OF *samit* f. med. L f. med. Gk *hexamiton* f. *hex* six + *mitos* thread; cf. DIMITY]

săm'lĕt, n. Young salmon. [SALMON, -LET]

Săm'nite, n. & a. 1. Member of an ancient-Italian people at war with republican Rome. 2. adj. Of the ~s. [ME, f. L *Samnites* pl.]

Samō'an, a. & n. (Native, language) of Samoa. [-AN]

sămovár', n. Apparatus with interior heat-tube for keeping water at boiling--point for making tea. [f. Russ. *samovar* = self-boiler]

Săm'oyĕd (-mo-), n. Member of a people of Siberian Mongols (also attrib.); their language; white Arctic breed of dog. [f. Russ. *Samoyedu*]

Sămoyĕd'ic (-mo-), a. & n. Of the Samoyeds; (n.) their language. [-IC]

săm'păn, n. Any small boat of Chinese pattern. [f. Chin. *san-pan* (*san* three, *pan* board)]

săm'phīre, n. Cliff plant with aromatic saline fleshy leaves used in pickles. [16th c. *sampere* f. F (*herbe de*) *St Pierre* St Peter('s herb)]

sa'mple (sah-), n., & v.t. 1. Small separated part of something illustrating the qualities of the mass etc. it is taken from, specimen, pattern, (esp. as offered by dealer in commodities sold by weight or measure; also of immaterial things, as *if that is a fair* ~ *of his proceedings*); ~-*card*, card with ~(s) of goods attached. 2. v.t. Take or give ~s, try the qualities, get a representative experience, of; hence **sa'mpler¹** [-ER¹] n. [ME; aphetic f. OF *essample* EXAMPLE]

sa'mpler² (sah-), n. 1. Piece of embroidery worked by girl as specimen of proficiency & often preserved & displayed on wall etc. 2. Young tree left standing when others are cut down. [aphetic f. OF *essamplaire* f. LL *exemplarium* (EXAMPLE, -ER²)]

Săm'son, **-pson**, n. Person of great strength or resembling ~ (*Judg.* xiii-xvi) in some respect; (naut.) ~'*s-post*, strong pillar passing through hold or between decks, post in whale-boat to which harpoon rope is attached. [LL, f. Gk (-*psōn*) f. Heb. *Shimshon*]

săm'urai (-ōōri), n. (Jap.; pl. same). Military retainer of daimios, member of military caste, (hist.); army officer. [Jap.]

săn'ative, **-tory̌**, aa. Healing, of or tending to physical or moral health, curative. [(1) ME, f. OF (-*if*, -*ive*) or LL *sanativus* (*sanare* cure, -IVE); (2) mod. .form. as (1), -ORY, cf. LL *sanatorius*]

sănatōr'ium, n. (pl. -ia). Establishment for treatment of invalids esp. convalescents & consumptives; place with good climate etc. frequented by invalids. [mod. L, as prec., -ORY(2)]

sănbēni'tō (-nē-), n. (pl. ~s). Penitential scapular-shaped yellow garment with red St Andrew's cross before & behind worn. by confessed & penitent heretic under Spanish Inquisition; similar black garment painted with flames & devils worn by impenitent heretic at auto-da-fé. [Sp.

(samb-), f. *San Benito* St Benedict (shaped like scapular introduced by him)]

sănc′ti|fў, v.t. Consecrate, set apart or observe as holy; purify or free from sin (p.p. often iron. = *sanctimonious; such ~fied airs*); impart sanctity to, make legitimate or binding by religious sanction, give colour of innocence to, justify, sanction (*the end ~fies the means*); make productive of or conducive to holiness. So ~FICA′TION n. [ME, f. OF *saintifier* f. eccl. L *sanctificare* (L *sanctus* holy, -FY)]

sănctimōn′ious, a. Making a show of sanctity or piety. Hence ~LY² adv., ~NESS n. [foll., -OUS]

sănc′timonў, n. Sanctimoniousness. [f. OF (-*ie*), or L *sanctimonia* sanctity (*sanctus* SAINT, -MONY)]

sănc′tion, n., & v.t. **1.** Law, decree, (hist.; PRAGMATIC ~). **2.** Penalty (also *vindicatory* or *punitive* ~) or reward (also *remuneratory* ~) for (dis)obedience attached to a law, clause containing this; (eth.) consideration operating to enforce obedience to any rule of conduct. **3.** Confirmation or ratification of law etc. by supreme authority, express authoritative permission, countenance or encouragement given to action etc. by custom etc.; hence ~LESS a. **4.** v.t. Ratify, invest with authority, make binding; authorize; countenance (action etc.); attach penalty or reward. to (law). [F, or f. L *sanctio* (*sancire sanct-* make sacred, -ION)]

sănc′titūde, n. (now rare). Saintliness. [ME, f. L *sanctitudo* (SAINT, -TUDE)]

sănc′tit|ў, n. Holiness of life, saintliness, (ODOUR of~*y*); sacredness, being hallowed, right to reverence, inviolability; (pl.) sacred obligations, feelings, etc. (*the ~ies of the home*). [ME, f. OF *sain(c)tete* or L *sanctitas* (SAINT, -TY)]

sănc′tūarў, n. **1.** Place recognized as holy, church, temple, tabernacle, HOLY place, HOLY of holies. SACRARIUM, penetralia, inmost recess, (lit. & fig.); part of chancel between altar rails and east window or screen, containing high altar. **2.** Sacred place by retiring to which fugitive from law or debtor was secured by medieval Church law against arrest or violence, place in which similar immunity was established by custom or law, asylum or place of refuge (*London, the ~ of political refugees*); (right of affording) such immunity (*violate* or *break ~*), arrest or use violence to person in a ~; *take, seek,* etc., ~, resort to a ~; *rights* etc. of ~). **3.** Place for preservation and protection of birds & wild animals. [ME, f. OF *sain(c)tuarie, -aire* f. L *sanctuarium* (eccl. L=shrine), irreg. f. *sanctus* (SAINT, -ARY¹)]

sănc′tum| (sănctŏr′um), n. **1.** Holy place (~), HOLY of holies (~ *sanctorum*), in Jewish temple (usu. transf. of inner retreat, esoteric doctrine, etc.). **2.** Person's private room, study, den. [eccl. L, transl. of Heb.]

sănc′tus, n. The hymn 'Holy, holy, holy' closing the Eucharistic preface, music for this; ~ *bell,* bell in turret at junction of nave & chancel, or handbell, rung at the ~. [L, = holy]

sănd, n., & v.t. **1.** Minute fragment resulting from wearing down of esp. silicious rocks & found covering parts of the seashore, riverbeds, deserts, etc., (also pl.) shoal or submarine bank of ~, (usu. in pl.) grain of ~, (pl.) expanse or tracts of ~, (*numberless as the ~* or *~s*; ROPE *of ~; built* etc. *on ~*, unstable; PLOUGH *the ~* or *~s; the ~s are running out* etc., time of grace etc. is nearly at end, w. ref. to hour-glass etc.; *children playing on the ~s; scour saucepan, adulterate sugar, dry ink* or *writing, with ~*). **2.** *(colloq.).* Firmness of purpose, grit. **3.** ~-*bag* n., filled with ~ for use (a) in fortification for making temporary defences, (b) as ballast esp. for boat or balloon, (c) as ruffian's weapon inflicting heavy blow without leaving mark, (d) as support for engraving-place, (e) to stop draught from window or door; ~'*bag* v.t., barricade or defend, provide (window, chink), with ~-bag(s), fell with blow from ~-bag; ~'*bank,* shoal in sea or river; ~-*bar,* ~ bank at mouth of harbour or river; ~-*bath,* vessel of heated ~ as equable heater in chem. processes; ~-*bed,* stratum of ~; ~-*blast,* jet of ~ impelled by compressed air or steam for giving rough surface to glass etc.; ~-*box,* castor for sprinkling ~ over wet ink (hist.), mould of ~ used in founding, box of ~ on locomotive for sprinkling slippery rails; ~'*boy,* (prob.) boy hawking~ for sale (now only in *jolly as a ~boy*); ~-*cloud,* driving ~ in simoom; ~-*crack,* disease of horses' hoofs, crack in human foot from walking on hot ~, crack in brick due to imperfect mixing; ~-*eel,* an eel-like fish; ~-*fly,* kind of midge, kind of fishing-fly; ~-*glass,* wasp-waisted reversible glass with two bulbs containing enough ~ to take a definite time (*hour, minute,* etc., -*glass*) in passing from upper to lower bulb; ~-*hill,* dune; ~-*hopper,* small marine crustacean, common on seashore; ~'*man,* (also *dustman*) power causing children's eyes to smart towards bedtime; ~-*martin,* kind nesting in side of ~-pit or sandy bank; ~'*paper,* with ~ stuck to it for polishing, (v.t.) polish with ~paper; ~'*piper,* kinds of bird haunting open wet sandy places; ~-*pump,* for clearing drill-hole, caisson, etc., of wet ~; ~-*shoes,* usu. of canvas with rubber or hemp soles for use on ~s; ~-*spout,* pillar of ~ raised by desert whirlwind; ~'*stone,* rock of compressed ~ (*old, new, red, ~stone,* series of British rocks below, above, carboniferous); ~-*storm,* desert storm of wind with clouds of ~. **4.** v.t. Sprinkle with ~; overlay with, bury under, ~; adulterate (sugar, wool, etc.) with ~; polish with ~. [OE,

OS *sand*, OHG *sant*, ON *sandr* f. Gmc *sand-*]

săn'dal[1], n., & v.t. (-ll-). **1.** Sole without uppers attached to foot by thongs passing over instep & round ankle (worn chiefly by ancient Greeks & Romans, by some Orientals, & as modern revival esp. by children & women); strap for fastening low shoe passing over instep or round ankle. **2.** v.t. Put ~s on (feet, person; esp. in p.p.); fasten or provide (shoe) with ~. [ME, f. L f. Gk *sandalion*]

săn'dal[2](wŏŏd), n. Kinds of scented wood (*white, yellow, red*, ~); *sandal-tree*, the white ~ tree of S.W. India. [ME, f. med. L *sandalum*, ult. f. Skr. *čandana*]

săn'dărăc, n. Orpiment (arch.); resin of N.-African conifer, used in making varnish. [f. L f. Gk *sandarakē*]

sănd'-blind, a. (arch.). Dim-sighted, purblind. [ME, prob. f. OE **samblind* (cf. SAMEL) after SAND]

săn'derling, n. A small wading bird. [perh. f. OE **SAND- (*yrthling* ploughman, also name of some bird)]

săn'ders, saun-, n. ||=SANDALWOOD; RED ~. [ME, f. OF *sandre* var. of *sandle* SANDAL[2]]

Sănd'hŭrst (-d-h-), n. (Used for) Royal Military College or Academy, ~, for army cadets. [~ in Berkshire]

săn'diver, n. Glass-gall, liquid saline matter given off in glass-making. [ME, corresp. to F *suin de verre* exhalation (*suer* sweat) of glass]

sănd'wich, n., & v.t. **1.** Two slices of bread with meat or other relish between (*ham, egg, caviare, cucumber*, etc., ~; also fig., as *a ~ of good & bad*); (usu. ~-*man*, -*boy*, etc.) man etc. walking street with two advertisement-boards hung one before & one behind; ~-*board*, one of such boards; ||~-*boat* in bumping race, boat rowing last in higher & first in lower division on same day; ~ *course,*of training (with alternate periods of practical & theoretical instruction). **2.** v.t. Insert (thing, statement, etc.) between two of another character. [f. Earl of *S*~ (said to have eaten slices of bread & meat while gaming for 24 hrs)]

sănd'|ў[1], a. In n. senses; also, (of hair) yellowish-red, (of person) with such hair. Hence ~ĬNESS n., ~ўISH[1](2) a. [-Y[2]]

Săn'dў[2], n. (Nickname for) Scotsman. [usual Sc. shortening of *Alexander*]

săne, a. Of sound mind, not mad; (of views etc.) moderate, sensible. Hence ~'LY[2] (-nl-) adv. [f. L *sanus* healthy]

sang. See SING.

săng'a(r) (-ng-), n. Stone breastwork used by Indian hill-tribes. [f. Hind. *sunga*]

săngaree' (-ng-), n. Cold drink of wine diluted & spiced. [f. Sp. *sangria* (lit. bleeding) drink of lemon-water & red wine]

sang-de-bœuf (sahǹdebŭf'), n. & a. (Of a deep red colour found on old Chinese porcelain. [F, = bullock's blood]

sang-froid (see Ap.), n. Composure, coolness, in danger or under agitating circumstances. [F, = cold blood]

sangrail, -real. See GRAIL[2].

sănguifică'tion (-nggwĭ-), n. Formation of, conversion of food into, blood. [F, or f. mod. L (L *sanguis* blood, -FICATION)]

săng'uinar|ў (-nggwĭ-), a. Attended by, delighting in, bloodshed or slaughter, bloody, bloodthirsty, (of laws) inflicting death lightly; || (euphem., substituted in reporting strong language, or used orig. as milder form, for) bloody. Hence ~ĬLY[2] adv., ~ĬNESS n. [f. L *sanguinarius* (*sanguis -inis* blood, -ARY[1])]

săng'uine (-nggwĭn), a., n., & v.t. **1.** Blood-red (literary, & in nat. hist. = L *sanguineus*, as ~ *ant, sponge, turtle*); of blood (rare; ~ *rain*), sanguinary (rare; ~ *slaughter*); (hist.) of the temperament in which the blood predominates over the other HUMOUR[1]s, with ruddy complexion & courageous hopeful amorous disposition; (of complexion) bright, ruddy, florid; habitually hopeful, confident, expecting things to go well, whence (& rarely in other senses) ~LY[2] adv., ~NESS n. **2.** n. Crayon coloured red with iron oxide; a drawing in red chalk. **3.** v.t. (poet.). Stain with blood, stain red. [ME, f. OF *sanguin* f. L *sanguineus* (prec.)]

sănguin'ěous (-nggwĭ-), a. Of blood (med.); blood-coloured (esp. bot.); full--blooded, plethoric. [f. L as prec., -OUS]

săn'hédrim (-nĭ-), -**in**, n. Highest court of justice & supreme council in ancient Jerusalem, of 71 members. [f. late Heb. *sanhedrin* f. Gk *sunedrion* (SYN-, *hedra* seat)]

săn'icle, n. An umbelliferous plant of parsley family formerly believed to have healing properties. [ME, OF, f. med. L *sanicula* prob. f. L *sanus* SANE]

săn'ifў, v.t. Make healthy, improve sanitary state of, (place). [f. L *sanus* healthy, -I-, -FY]

săn'itar|ў, a. Of the conditions that affect health esp. with regard to dirt & infection; free from or designed to obviate influences deleterious to health; ~*y towel* (of kind used in menstruation). Hence sănitAR'IAN (-ār-) n. & a., ~ĬLY[2] adv., ~ĬNESS, ~ĬST(2), nn. [f. F *sanitaire* (L as SANITY, -ARY[1])]

sănită'tion, n. (Improving of) sanitary conditions. Hence ~ĬST(2) (-sho-) n., (by back formation) săn'itāte v.t. & i. [irreg. f. SANITARY, -ATION]

săn'itў, n. Being sane, mental health; tendency to avoid extreme views. [ME, f. OF *sanite* or f. L *sanitas* (SANE, -TY)]

săn'jăk, n. (hist.). One of the administrative districts of a Turkish vilayet. [Turk.]

sank. See SINK[1].

san(n)yasi (sŭnyah'sĭ), n. (Also *sunnyasee*) Indian religious mendicant. [Hind., f. Skr. *saṃnyāsin* laying aside]

sans, prep. Without (as E wd, pr. sănz, now chiefly w. ref. to Shaks. *A. Y. L.* II. vii: 166, ~ *teeth*, ~ *eyes*, ~ *taste*, ~ *everything*. As F wd, pr. as F, in phrr. & compounds, for pronunc. of which see Ap.: ~ *cérémonie* adv., with rude or hurried or kindly neglect ·of usual formalities; ~*culôtte'*, pr. as F or E, lit. = breechless, republican of Parisian lower classes in French Revolution, any extreme republican or revolutionary, whence~*culôtt'erie* [-ERY(4, 5)] n., ~*culôtt'*IC a., ~*culôtt'*ISM n.; ~ *façon* adv., outspokenly, unceremoniously; ~*gêne* n., absence of constraint, familiarity, making oneself at home; ~ *peur et* ~ *reproche* a., of chivalrous character, cf. BAYARD; ~ *phrase* adv., in a word, without qualification; ~*souci* n., gay carelessness, unconcern). [ME *sa(u)n*, *sa(u)ns*, f. OF, f. L *absentia* AB-SENCE, perh. infl. by *sine* without]

sănse'rif, n. & a. (Form of type) without serifs. [app. f. prec.+SERIF]

Săn'skrit, **-scrit**, n. & a. (Of, in) the ancient & sacred language of India, oldest known member of INDO-European family. Hence **Sănskrit'**IC a., **Săn'**skrĭtIST(3) n. [f. Skr. *saṃskṛta* composed (*saṃ* together, cogn. w. SAME, *kṛ* make)]

Săn'ta Claus' (-z), n. Personage who fills children's stockings with Christmas presents by night. [U.S., f. Du. dial. *Sante* (Du. *Sint*) *Klaas* St Nicholas]

sǎn'tŏn, n. Mohammedan monk or hermit. [f. F or Sp. *santon* (Sp. *santo* SAINT)]

săntŏn'ica, n. Kind of wormwood. [L (*Santones* Aquitanian tribe, -IC)]

săn'tonin, n. Extract of santonica used as anthelmintic. [-IN]

Saorstat Eireann (sayor'stath ār'an), n. Republic of Ireland. [Ir.]

săp¹, n., & v.t. (-pp-). 1. Vital juice circulating in plants (also fig., as *the* ~ *of youth*, *there is no* ~ *in a written constitution*; (also ~-*wood*) soft outer layers of wood, alburnum; ~-*green* n. & a., pigment made from buckthorn berries, (of) colour of this; ~-*lath*, made of ~-wood; hence ~'FUL, ~'LESS, ~p'Y², aa., ~p'INESS n. 2. v.t. Drain or dry (wood) of ~; (fig.) exhaust vigour of (*his energy*, *constitution*, *belief*, *had been* ~*ped by*; cf. foll.); remove ~- -wood from (log). [OE *sæp*, MDu., MLG *sap*, OHG *saf*, perh. cogn. w. L *sapere* taste]

săp², n., & v.i. & t. (-pp-). 1. Making of trenches to cover assailants' approach to besieged place, (fig.) insidious or slow undermining of belief, resolution, etc.; covered siege-trench; ~-*head*, front end of ~; ~-*roller*, large gabion covering ~-head. 2. vb. Dig ~, approach (i. & t.) by ~; undermine, make insecure by removing foundations, (fig.) destroy insidiously (cf. prec.), (*walls*, *cliffs*, ~*ped by the stream*, *tide*; *health* ~*ped by the damp climate*; *science was* ~*ping old beliefs*). [(vb f. F *saper*) f. F *sappe* & It. *zappa* spade, sap]

săp³, v.i. (-pp-), & n. (school sl.). 1. ‖ Be studious, work hard at books or lessons. 2. n. ‖ Studious or hardworking person; ‖ tiresome task, trouble, grind, (*it is such a*, *too much*, ~); *(sl.) simpleton. [prob. fig. use of prec.]

săp'ajou (-jōō), n. Small S.-Amer. monkey often kept as pet. [F, earlier *-iou*, said to be Cayenne wd]

săp'an-wŏŏd, -pp-, n. A red dye-wood obtained from an E.-Ind. tree. [f. Du. *sapan*, f. Malay *sapang*, cf. Tamil *shappangam*]

săp'id, a. Having (esp. agreeable) flavour, savoury, palatable, not insipid; (of talk, writing, etc.) not vapid or uninteresting. So **sapid'**ITY n. [f. L *sapidus* (*sapere* taste, -ID¹)]

săp'ient, a. Wise (now rare); would-be wise, of fancied sagacity, aping wisdom. Hence or cogn. **săp'**IENCE n., ~LY² adv. [ME, f. OF, or L part. st. of *sapere* be wise] ·

săpiĕn'tial (-shl), a. Of wisdom (esp. *the* ~ *books*, Prov., Eccl., Ecclus., Cant., Wisd., etc.). [ME, f. OF, or eccl. L *sapientialis* (L *sapientia* wisdom as prec., -AL)]

săp'ling, n. Young tree; (fig.) a youth, greyhound in first year (~ *stakes* in coursing). [SAP¹, -LING¹]

săpodill'a, n. Large evergreen tropical- -Amer. tree with durable wood & edible fruit (~ *plum* or NASEBERRY). [f. Sp, *zapotilla* dim. of *zapote* f. Mex. *zapotl*]

săponā'ceous (-shus), a. Of, like, containing, soap, soapy (lit. &, in joc. use, fig.). [f. L *sapo -onis* soap, -ACEOUS]

sapŏn'i|**fy**, v.t. & i. Turn (t. & i. of fat or oil) into soap by decomposition with alkali. Hence or cogn. ~fiABLE a., ~FICA'TION n. [f. F *saponifier* (prec., -FY)]

săp'ŏr, n. Quality perceptible by taste, e.g. sweetness; distinctive taste of substance; sensation of taste. [ME, f. L *sapere* taste, -OR)]

săpp'er, n. In vbl senses of SAP¹ ² ³; also, ‖ officer or man of Royal Engineers, as official term, private (*Royal S*~*s & Miners*, former title of R.E.). [-ER¹]

Sapphic (săf'ik), a. & n. 1. Of Sappho (Lesbian lyric poetess 600 B.C.; ~ *vice*, also **Sapph**ISM (săf'izm) n., unnatural sexual relations between women; ~ *verse*, *stanza*, in Gk metres invented by Sappho & imitated in L by Horace, esp. the four- -line stanza with short fourth line incorrectly copied in E light verse as *Needy knife-grinder*, *whither do you wander?*). 2. n. pl. Verse in ~ stanzas. [f. F *saphique* f. L f. Gk *Sapphikos* (*Sapphō*, -IC)]

sapphire (săf'ir), n. & a. 1. A transparent usu. blue precious stone, (mineral.) any precious native crystalline alumina including~ & ruby; bright blue of~, azure; kinds of humming-bird; so **sapphir**INE² (săf'ir-) a. 2. adj. Of~ blue. [ME, f. OF *safir* f. L f. Gk *sappheiros* lapis lazuli]

sappy. See SAP¹.

săp′r|(o)-, comb. form of Gk *sapros* rotten in scient. terms: ~*aem′ia*, septic poisoning, so ~*aem′ic* a., [Gk *haima* blood]; ~*ogen′ic*, causing or produced by putrefaction; ~*ophile* a. & n., (bacterium) inhabiting putrid matter; ~*ophyte*, vegetable organism living on decayed organic matter.

‖ **săr,** n.. A fish, the sea bream. [F, f. L *sargus*]

să′rabănd, n. Stately old Spanish dance; music for this or in its rhythm, in triple time freq. with long note on second beat of bar. [F (-*de*), f. Sp. *zarabanda*]

Să′racen, n. & a. **1.** (General name among later Greeks & Romans for) nomad of Syro-Arabian desert; Arab or Moslem of time of crusades; ~ *corn*, buckwheat; ~*'s head*, as heraldic charge or inn-sign; hence (esp. of Moslem archit.) **Săracēn′ic** a. **2.** adj. = ~*ic*. [ME, f. OF *Sar(r)acin* f. LL f. late Gk *Sarakēnos*; OE f. LL]

Săratŏg′a (trŭnk), n. Lady's large travelling-trunk. [prob. f. *Saratoga* Springs, New York watering-place]

sărc′ăsm, n. Bitter or wounding remark, taunt, esp. one ironically worded; language consisting of, faculty of uttering, use of, such remarks; so **sărcăs′tic** a., **sărcăs′tically** adv. [f. LL f. late Gk *sarkasmos* (*sarkazō* gnash the teeth, tear flesh, see SARCO-, -*asm* corresp. to -ISM)]

sărcĕlle′, n. Kinds of small duck or teal. [ME, f. OF *cercelle* f. L *querquedula*]

sarcenet. See SARSENET.

sărc′|o-, comb. form of Gk *sarx sarkos* flesh; ~*ŏl′ogy*, anatomy of fleshy parts of body; ~*oplasm*, interfibrillar substance of muscle.

sărc′ōde, n. Animal protoplasm. [prec., -ODE]

sărcōm′a, n. (pl. ~*ta*). Tumour of embryonic connective tissue. [f. Gk *sarkōma* (*sarkoō* see SARCO- become fleshy); see -OMA]

sărcŏph′agus, n. (pl. -*gī*, pr. -*gī*, -*jī*). Stone coffin usu. adorned with sculpture in inscription. [L, f. Gk *sarkophagos* orig. = flesh-consuming (stone) as SARCO- + -*phagos* -eating]

sărc′ous, a. Consisting of flesh or muscle. [SARCO-, -OUS]

sărd, n. Yellow or orange cornelian. [f. F *sarde* f. L *sarda* = LL *sardius* f. Gk *sardios* (*Sardis* in Lydia)]

Sărdanapāl′ian, a. As of, like, Sardanapalus king of Nineveh notorious for effeminate luxury. [-IAN]

sărdĕlle′, n. Fish like & treated like sardine. [f. It. *sardella* dim. of L *sarda* SARDINE²]

sărd′ine¹, n. Precious stone in *Rev.* iv. 3. [ME, f. L (Vulg.) *sardinus* transl. Gk *sardios* (whence R.V. *sardius*)]

sardine′² (-ēn), n. Small fish of herring kind found off Sardinia & Brittany, or young pilchard of Cornish coast, cured & tinned in oil (*packed like* ~*s*, of crowded company). [ME, f. OF, f. It. f. L *sardina* (*sarda* f. Gk *sardē* perh. f. *Sardō* Sardinia)]

Sărdin′ian, a. & n. (Inhabitant) of the island or of the kingdom (1720–1861, including also Piedmont etc.) of Sardinia. [-AN]

sărdŏn′|ic, a. Bitter, scornful, mocking, sneering, cynical, (of laugh, laughter, affected merriment, etc.). Hence ~I-CALLY adv. [f. F (-*ique*) f. L f. Gk *sardonios* (= Sardinian) alt. of *sardanios*, Homeric epithet of bitter or scornful laughter]

sărd′onyx, n. Onyx with white layers alternating with sard. [ME, f. L f. Gk *sardonux* (SARDios, ONYX)]

sărgăss′ō, n. (pl. ~*s*, ~*es*). (Also *gulf-weed*) kinds of seaweed with berry-like air-vessels found floating in island-like masses in the Gulf-stream & esp. in N.-Atlantic region called S~ *Sea*. [f. Port. *sargaço*]

sa′ri (sah-), n. Length of cotton or silk wrapped round body, worn as main garment by Hindu women. [Hind. *sāri*]

sariss′a, n. (Gk ant.; pl. -*ae*). Long lance of ancient Macedonians. [Gk]

‖ **sărk,** n. (Sc.). Shirt or chemise. Hence ~*'ING¹* n., boarding between rafters & roof. [ME *serk* f. ON *serkr* f. Gmo *sarkiz*]

Sărmā′tian (-shn), a. & n. (Inhabitant) of ancient Sarmatia (Russia & Poland); (poet.) Pole, Polish. [-AN]

sărm′entōse, -ĕn′tous, aa. (bot.). With long thin trailing shoots. [f. L *sarmentosus* (*sarmenta* pl. twigs, brushwood, f. *sarpere* prune, -MENT, -OSE¹, -OUS)]

sarŏng′, n. Malay national garment, a long strip of (often striped) cotton or silk worn by both sexes tucked round waist. [Malay *sārung*]

sărsaparill′a, n. Kinds of tropical-American smilax esp. the Jamaica ~ (so called as chief source of the medicinal ~ for which Jamaica was emporium); dried roots, or extract of these used as tonic etc., of (esp. Jamaica) ~. [f. Sp. *zarzaparilla* (*zarza* bramble, perh. + dim. of *parra* vine)]

sărs′en, n. Sandstone etc. boulder, relict carried by ice in glacial period. [prob. f. SARACEN]

sărs′enĕt, săr′c-, (-sn-), n. Fine soft silk material now used chiefly for linings. [ME, f. AF *sarzinett* (prob. f. *sarzin* SARACEN + -ET¹ after OF *drap sarrasinois* Saracen cloth)]

sărtōr′ial, a. Of tailor, tailoring, or men's clothes. [f. L *sartor* tailor + -IAL]

Sār′um, eccl. name of Salisbury (~ *use*, order of divine service used in diocese of Salisbury from 11th c. to Reformation). [med. L, prob. f. misread abbr. of L *Sarisburia* Salisbury, cf. *viz* for *videlicet*]

sash[1], n. Ornamental scarf worn by man usu. as part of uniform or insignia over one shoulder or round waist or by woman or child round waist. Hence ~ed[1] [-ED[2]] (-sht) a. [16th c. *shash* f. Arab. *shāsh* muslin, turban]

sash[2], n. Frame usu. of wood holding pane(s) of glass & usu. made to slide up & down in grooves of window aperture, glazed sliding light of glasshouse or garden-frame, (opp. CASEMENT); (rare)= casement; ~-*cord*, -*line*, strong cord attaching ~-weights to ~; ~-*pocket*, space on each side of window-frame in which ~-weights run; ~-*pulley*, for ~-cord to work over; ~-*tool*, kinds of glazier's & painter's brush; ~-*weight*, attached to each end of ~ to balance it at any height; ~-*window*, with ~ or usu. two ~es, of which one or each can be slid over the other to make opening. Hence ~ed[2] [-ED[2]] (-sht), ~'LESS, aa. [corrupt. of CHASSIS app. mistaken for pl.]

sas'in, n. Indian antelope. [Nepalese]

sassäb'y̆, n. Large S.-Afr. antelope. [native]

sass'afras, n. (Small N.-Amer. tree yielding) a bark used medicinally; infusion of this. [Sp. *sasafras*, of unkn. orig.]

Sässän'ian, Säss'anĭd, nn. & aa. (Member, esp. a king) of family of Sa(s)san, rulers of Persian empire A.D. 211–651. [-IAN, -ID[3]]

Säss'enach (see Ap.), n. & a. (Sc. & Ir. for) English(man). [thr. Gael. & Ir. f. *Saxon*]

sastru'gi (sahstrōō'gĭ), n. pl. Wavelike irregularities on the surface of hard snow caused by winds. [Russ.]

sat. See SIT.

Sāt'an, (arch.) **Sät'anăs**, n. The Devil, Lucifer. [LL f. Gk. f. Heb. *ṣaṭan* enemy]

Satän'ic, a. Of, like, or befitting Satan, diabolical, hellish, (*his* ~ *majesty*, Satan; ~ *school*, orig. Byron, Shelley, etc., also any set of writers accused of defiant impiety etc.). Hence ~aLLY[2] adv. [-IC, -ICAL]

Sät'anĭsm, n. Deliberate wickedness, pursuit of evil for its own sake, diabolical disposition, so ~IZE(3) v.t.; characteristics of SATANIC school; (esp. French 19th-c.) professed worship of Satan. So ~IST(2) n. [-ISM]

Sätanŏl'oğy̆, n. (History or collection of) beliefs concerning the Devil. [-O-, -LOGY]

satär'a, n. Heavy broadcloth with horizontal rib. [*S*~ in India]

sätch'el, n. Small bag usu. of leather & hung from shoulder with strap for carrying books etc. esp. to & from school. Hence ~IED[2] (-ld) a. [ME, f. OF *sachel* f. L *saccellus* (SACK[1], -EL)]

sāte[1], v.t. Gratify (desire, person feeling it) to the full; cloy, surfeit, weary with over-abundance (~*d with*). Hence ~'LESS (-tl-) a. (poet.). [f. (now dial.) *sade*, OE *sadian* (SAD), assim. to L *sat(is)* enough]

sate[2] (sǎt, sāt). Arch. past & p.p. of SIT.

sateen', n. Cotton or woollen fabric with glossy surface. [f. SATIN after VELVETEEN]

sät'ellĭte, n. Person's follower or henchman or hanger-on, member of great man's retinue, underling; heavenly body revolving round another (often fig.), whence~it'IC a.; artificial body launched from and encircling the earth; (attrib.) minor, secondary; ~ *state*, country subservient to or controlled by a greater power; ~ *town*, smaller town dependent on a larger town a short distance away. [F, or f. L *satellit-* nom. -*les* guard]

sati. See SUTTEE.

sā'tiate[1] (-shyat), a. Satiated. [L *satiare* (SATIS), -ATE[2]]

sā'tiate[2] (-shĭ-), v.t. = SATE[1]. So **sā'tiABLE** (-sha-) a. (rare), **satia'TION** (sǎsĭ-, sǎshĭ-) n. [as prec., -ATE[3]]

sati'ety̆, n. Glutted or satiated state, feeling of having had too much of something, cloyed dislike *of*, (*to* ~, to extent beyond what is desired); (rare) over-abundance. [f. F *satiété* f. L *satietatem* (*satis* enough, -TY)]

sät'in, n. & a., & v.t. 1. Silk fabric with glossy surface on one side got by catching warp-threads only at intervals (*Denmark* ~, smooth worsted material used for ladies' slippers); *white*~, the plant honesty, also kind of moth; ~ or *white* ~, sl., gin. 2. adj. Smooth as ~. 3. ~ *beauty, carpet*, kinds of moth; ~ *cloth*, a woollen cloth woven like ~; ~ *finish*, polish given to silver with metallic brush; ~-*flower*, honesty, also greater stitchwort; ~ *gypsum*, fibrous kind with pearly lustre; ~ *paper*, fine glossy writing-paper; ~ *pug, pygmy*, kinds of moth; ~-*sheeting*, fabric of waste silk & cotton; ~-*spar*, fibrous carbonate of lime; ~-*stitch*, giving appearance of ~ in embroidery & woolwork; ~-*stone*, ~ gypsum; ~-*straw*, soft & flexible for hats; ~ *white*, artificial sulphate of lime; ~-*wood*, choice timber of a tropical tree; hence ~Y[2] a., ~ETTE'(2) & in same sense ~ET[1] nn. 4. v.t. Give glossy surface to (paper). [ME, f. OF, f. Arab. *zaituni*]

sät'ire, n. (Rom. ant.) poetic medley, esp. poem aimed at prevalent vices or follies; a composition in verse or prose holding up vice or folly to ridicule or lampooning individual(s), this branch of literature, (often *upon*); thing that brings ridicule upon something (*our lives are a* ~ *upon our religion*); use of ridicule, irony, sarcasm, etc., in speech or writing for the ostensible purpose of exposing & discouraging vice or folly. [F, or f. L *satira* later form of *satura* medley]

sati'ric, a. Of satires or satire, containing satire, writing satires, (~ *verse, poem; poet, writer, intent, stroke*). [F (-*ique*), or f. LL *satiricus* (prec., -IC)]

sati'rical, a. = prec.; given to the use of satire in speech or writing or to cynical observation of others, sarcastic, humorously critical. Hence ~LY² adv. [as prec., see -ICAL]

săt′irist, n. Writer of satires; satirical person. [-IST]

săt′irize, -ise (-īz), v.t. Assail with satire, write satire(s) upon, describe satirically. .[f. F *satiriser* (SATIRE, -IZE)]

săt′ĭs, Latin adv. & n. = enough, used in phrr. *jăm* ~, already enough, ~ *superque* (pr. sŭpêrk′wĭ), enough & too much.

sătisfăc′tion, n. **1.** Payment of debt, fulfilment of obligation, atonement (*for*), thing accepted by way of ~, (eccl.) performance of penance, (theol.) atonement made by Christ for sins of men, (*make* ~; *in* ~ *of*; *enter* ~, legal, place on record of court that payment ordered has been made; *Christ is the* ~ *for our sins*). **2.** Opportunity of fighting duel with person one complains of (*give, demand,* ~). **3.** Satisfying or being satisfied in regard to desire or want or doubt, thing that satisfies desire or gratifies feeling, (*find* ~ *in*; *give* ~; *to the* ~ *of*; *heard it with great* ~; *their* ~ *at* or *with the results*; *if you can prove it to my* ~; *the* ~ *of not having to do it*; *it is a great* ~ *that it need not be done*; *would be a* ~ *to me*; *thinks only of present* ~). [ME, f. OF, f. L *satisfactionem* (SATISFY)]

sătisfăc′tor|y̆, a. **1.** (theol.). Serving as atonement for sin. **2.** Satisfying expectations or needs, leaving no room for complaint, causing satisfaction, adequate, (~*y proof, method, result, pupil, pair of boots, expedition, marriage, compromise*). Hence ~ĬLY² adv., ~ĬNESS n. [f. F *satisfactoire* or LL *satisfactorius* (SATISFY, -ORY)]

săt′isf|y̆, v.t. & i. **1.** Pay (debt, creditor), fulfil (obligation), comply with (demand); (of Christ) make atonement for sins of men. **2.** Meet the expectations or desires of, come up to (notion, preconception, etc.), be accepted by (person, his taste, etc.) as adequate, content, (~*y the examiners* at univ., receive pass without honours). **3.** pass. Be content or pleased (*with*), demand no more than or consider it enough *to do*, (*rest* ~*ied*, make or take no further demands or steps). **4.** intr. Give satisfaction, leave nothing to be desired. **5.** Dispose of (an appetite or want), rid (person) of an appetite or want, by sufficient supply. **6.** Furnish with adequate proof, convince, (*of fact, that it is so*; ~*y* one*self*, attain to practical certainty). **7.** Adequately meet (objection, doubt, request, conditions). Hence ~Ĭ-ABLE~, ~Y̆ING,² aa., ~Y̆ĬNGLY² adv. [ME, f. OF *satisfier* f. L SATISfacere *fact*- (-FY)]

≠atrangi (sŭt′ranjĭ, satrŭn′jĭ), n. Cheap Indian cotton carpet. [Hindi]

≠ăt′răp, n. Holder of provincial governorship or ~Y¹ n. in ancient-Persian empire, viceroy; modern subordinate ruler, colonial governor, etc. (rhet. with implication of luxury or tyranny). [ME, f.

OF, or L f. Gk *satrapēs* f. OPers. *khsatrapava* province-guardian]

Săt′suma, n. (Also ~ *ware*) cream-coloured Japanese pottery. [name of province]

săt′ŭr|āte (or -cher-), v.t. Impregnate, soak thoroughly, imbue *with*; overwhelm (defences, target area) by concentrated bombing; (chem. etc.) charge (substance, air, vapour, metal) with or cause to combine with or absorb or hold the greatest amount possible of another substance, moisture, magnetism, electricity, etc.; (p.p., of colour) free from admixture of white, full, rich. Hence or cogn. ~ATE³ (-at) a. (poet. exc. of colour), ~ABLE a., ~A′TION n. [f. L *saturare* (*satur* full cogn. w. SATIS), -ATE³]

Săt′urday (-erdĭ), n. Seventh day of week (HOLY, HOSPITAL, ~; ~*-to-Monday,* the now usu. WEEK-*end*). [OE *Sætern(es)dæg* transl. of L *Saturni dies* day of SATURN]

Săt′ŭrn, n. **1.** (Rom. ant.). Italic god of agriculture later identified with Greek Cronos father of Zeus, ruler of the world in a golden age of innocence and plenty. **2.** A planet, the farthest off of the 7 anciently known, with 10 moons & broad flat ring, credited in astrology with producing cold sluggish gloomy temperament in those born under its influence. [f. L *Saturnus* (*serere sat-* sow)]

săturnāl′ia (-ter-), n. pl. & (see below) sing. Ancient-Roman festival of Saturn in December observed as time of unrestrained merrymaking extending even to slaves, predecessor of modern Christmastide (*S*~); scene or time of wild revelry or tumult (also *S*~; often as sing. as *a* ~ *of crime*). Hence **săturnāl′ian** (-ter-) a. [L, neut. pl. of *Saturnalis* (prec., -AL)]

Săturn′ian, a. & n. **1.** Of the god or the planet Saturn; ~ *age*, GOLDEN age; ~*metre, verse,* metre used in early Latin poetry before introduction of Greek metres. **2.** n. Inhabitant of Saturn; (pl.) ~ verse. [f. L SATURN*ius*, -AN]

saturn′ic, a. (path.). Affected with lead-poisoning. So **Săt′urn**ISM(5) (-ter-) n. [SATURN in alch. sense *lead*, -IC]

săt′urnīne (-ter-), a. Of sluggish gloomy temperament, (of looks etc.) suggestive of or produced by such temperament, whence ~LY² adv.; of lead (*a* ~ *poultice* etc.); of, affected by, lead-poisoning (~ *patients, symptoms*). [ME, f. OF -*ine* f. med. L -*inus* (as prec., -INE¹)]

satyagraha (sahtyah′grahah), n. (Indian pol.). Passive resistance. [Skr., f. *satya* truth + *āgraha* firm grasping]

săt′yr (-er), n. One of a class of Greek woodland deities in human form with horse's ears & tail (or, as represented by Romans, with goat's ears, tail, legs, & budding horns); lustful or beastly-minded man; (rare) orang-utan. [ME, f. OF *satyre* or L f. Gk *saturos*]

sătyrī′asis (-ter-), n. Excessive sexual

desire in males. [f. LL f. Gk *saturiasis* (prec., -ASIS)]

saty′ric, a. Of satyrs (esp. ~ *drama*, kind of Greek comic play with chorus of satyrs, see TETRA*logy*). [f. L f. Gk *saturikos* (SATYR, -IC)]

sauce, n., & v.t. 1. Liquid preparation taken as relish with some article of food (*bread, egg, mint, parsley, tomato*, etc., ~, with these as prominent ingredient; *white* ~, .of melted butter, flour, etc.; *hunger is the best* ~; ~ *for the* GANDER; *serve with the same* ~, subject to same usage).; (fig.) something that adds piquancy (*is tame without the* ~ *of danger*). 2. Solution of salt & other ingredients used in some manufacturing processes. 3. Sauciness, impertinent speech, cheek, (*none of your* ~ *l*). 4. ~-*alone*, hedge-weed formerly used to flavour salads &~s; ~-*boat*, vessel in which ~ is served; ~*box*, impudent person; ~*pan* (*-an*), metal vessel usu. cylindrical with long handle projecting from side for boiling things in cookery; hence ~*LESS* a. 5. v.t. Season with ~s or condiments (rare); (fig.) make piquant, add relish to; (vulg.) be impudent to, cheek, (person). [ME, f. OF f. Rom. *salsa* fem. of *salsus* (*salere sals-* to salt f. *sal* salt)]

sau′cer, n. Shallow vessel for standing cup on to intercept spillings of tea etc. (~ *eye*, large & round as a ~, whence ~-*eyeD²* a.); vessel placed under flowerpot to prevent water from running away at once; any small shallow round vessel resembling tea~. Hence ~*FUL*(2) n., ~*LESS* a. [ME = *condiment-dish*, f. OF *saussier* f. LL *salsarium* (SAUCE, -ARY²)]

sau′cy, a. Impudent to superiors, cheeky; (sl.) sprightly, smart, stylish. Hence ~*ILY²* adv., ~*INESS* n. [earlier sense *savoury*; SAUCE, -Y²]

sauerkraut (sowr′krowt), n. German dish of pickled cabbage. [G]

saul. See SAL.

saumur (sōm′ūr), n. White wine produced near S~ in France.

saunders. See SANDERS.

saun′ter, v.i., & n. 1. Walk in leisurely way or without destination, stroll, (also fig., as ~ *through life*); hence ~*ER¹* n., ~*ingLY²* adv. 2. n. Leisurely ramble or gait. [orig. unkn.]

saur′|ian, a. & n. (One) of the *Sauria* or order of lizards including crocodiles, alligators, & extinct kinds such as ichthyosaurus & plesiosaurus. So ~*o*- comb. form, ~*oID* a. & n. [Gk *sauros* lizard, -IAN]

saur′y, n. A long-billed sea-fish. [prob. f. mod. L f. Gk *sauros* lizard]

sau′sage (sŏs-), n. Pork or other meat minced, seasoned, & stuffed into long cylindrical cases prepared from entrails & divided when full into lengths of a few inches by twisting or tying, a length of this, (*Bologna* ~, large kind made of

bacon, veal, pork-suet, etc., & sold ready for eating cold); ~*filler, -grinder, -machine*, ~-*making appliances*; ~*meat*, meat & bread etc. minced & seasoned for use in ~s or as a stuffing etc.; ~ *roll*, ~-meat enclosed in pastry & cooked. [ME, f. ONF *saussiche* f. LL *salsicia* (L *salsus* see SAUCE)]

sauté (sŏt′ā), a. (in fem. -*ée*; pl. -*és*, fem. -*ées*; pronunc. the same in all forms). Quickly fried in hot pan with little grease. [F]

Sauterne(s) (sōtärn′), n. Kinds of sweet white French wine. [f. *Sauternes*, name of district]

sauve-qui-peut (sōvkēpėr′), n. Precipitate flight in various directions. [F *sauve qui peut* save (himself) who can]

sav′age, a., n., & v.t. 1. Uncultivated, wild, (arch.; *a* ~ *scene*); uncivilized, in primitive state, (~ *tribes, life*); fierce, cruel, furious, (~ *persecution, persecutor, revenge, criticism, blow*); (colloq.) angry, out of temper; (her.; of human figure) naked; hence or cogn. ~*LY²* (-IjlI) adv., ~*NESS* (-Ijn-), sav′a*gERY*(2, 4) (-IjrI), nn. 2. n. Member of ~ tribe esp. of one living by hunting & fishing, whence ~*DOM* (-Ijd-) n.; brutally cruel or barbarous person. 3. v.t. (Of horse) attack & bite or trample (person; *was* ~*d by his horse*). [ME & OF *sal-*, *sauvage* f. LL *salvaticum* (L *sil-*) f. *silva* a wood, -ATIC]

savann′a(h) (-na), n. Grassy plain with scattered trees in tropical & subtropical regions. [f. Sp. *zavana* perh. of Carib orig.]

savant (see Ap.), n. Man of learning, esp. distinguished scientist. [part. of F *savoir* know, as SAPIENT]

savate′ (-aht), n. French boxing, in which feet & head are used as well as fists. [F]

save¹, v.t. & i., & n. 1. Rescue, preserve, deliver, from or *from* danger or misfortune or harm or discredit (~*d my life, me from drowning, the State*; ~ *me* or *God* ~ *me from my friends* etc., comment upon well-meant inopportune officiousness; ~ *us!*, excl. of surprise; ~ *one's*. BACON, FACE¹; ~ *the situation*, find or provide way out of difficulty, avert disaster; ~ *appearances*, put a good face on something; (footb. etc.) prevent opponents from scoring. 2. Bring about spiritual salvation of, preserve from damnation, (*who then can be* ~*d?*; *the saving of souls*); (part.) redeeming (*by the saving grace of God*; *has the saving grace of humour*). 3. Keep for future use, husband, reserve, abstain from expending, lay by money, live economically, (~ *one's breath*, be silent; *a saving housekeeper*; *is saving his strength*; *has never* ~*d*, put by money; ~ *up*, try to .accumulate money by economy; *you may* ~ *your pains or trouble*, need not take, will take in vain), whence sav′*ER*¹(1) n., sav′*ING*¹(2) n. (usu. in pl.), sav′*ingLY¹* adv. 4. Relieve (person) from need of expending (money, trouble, etc.) or from exposure to (annoyance etc.), obviate need of, reduce requisite amount of, (that will ~ me £50; his secretary ~d him much time or labour, many interviews; ~ the follow-on in cricket, get enough runs to prevent it; stitch in time ~s nine; soap ~s rubbing), whence (-)sāvER¹(2) n. (time-~r), (-)sāvING² a. (labour-saving). **5.** Avoid losing, be in time for, succeed in catching, (write hurriedly to ~ the post; shall we ~ the tide?, get in or out while it serves). **6.** Make reservation concerning, make reservation, (esp. saving clause, containing stipulation of exemption etc.; saving your reverence, apology for unseemly expression etc., cf. ~ the MARK¹); (part. as prep.) except, with the exception of, SAVE². **7.** n. (Footb. etc.) act of preventing opponents from scoring; (bridge) action taken to prevent heavy losses. **8.** ~-all (hist.), pan with spike for burning up candle-ends; savings-bank, receiving small deposits & conducted solely in depositors' interests (Post-office savings-bank, with branches at local post offices). Hence sāv′ABLE a. [ME, f. OF salver, sauver f. LL salvare (salvus safe)]

sāve², prep. & conj. **1.** Except, but, (with n. in obj. case, or with that clause; arch., poet., or with formal or pretentious effect in ordinary writing, also pleonast, in ~ & except; forty stripes ~ one; all ~ him, & see conj.; I am well ~ that I have a cold). **2.** conj. (arch.). Unless, but, (thou seest no beauty ~ thou make it; all the conspirators ~ only he; happy ~ for one want). [ME, f. OF sauf, sauve f. L salvō (see SALVO¹), salvā SAFE²]

sav′eloy, n. Highly seasoned dried sausage. [corrupt. of F cervelas, -at, f. It. cervellata (cervello brain)]

sav′in, n. (Kind of juniper with) tips of shoots yielding a volatile oil used medicinally. [ME, f. OF savine f. L sabina (herba) SABINE (herb)]

sav′iour (-vyer), n. Deliverer, redeemer (the, our, S~, Christ), person who saves a State etc. from destruction etc. [ME & OF sauveour f. LL salvatorem (salvare SAVE¹), see -IOUR]

savoir faire (săv′wăr făr′), n. Quickness to see & do the right thing, address, tact. [F]

savoir vivre (săv′wăr vē′vr), n. Good breeding, being at home in society. [F]

sav′ory, n. Herb of mint family used in cookery. [ME saverey, ult. f. L satureia]

sav′our (-ver), n., & v.i. & t. **1.** Characteristic taste, flavour, relish, or (now rare) smell, power to affect the taste (lit. or fig.); quality suggestive, perceptible admixture, suspicion, smack, of (a not unpleasing ~ of preciosity); hence ~LESS (-ver-) a. **2.** vb. Appreciate or perceive the lit. or fig. taste of (arch.); give flavour to

(rare); smack, offer suggestion, suggest presence, of (the offer ~s of impertinence). [ME; (1) OF, f. L saporem (sapere taste, -OR); (2) f. OF savourer f. LL saporare]

sav′our|ў (-verĭ), a. & n. **1.** With appetizing taste or smell; (of places etc.; only w. neg.) free from bad smells; (of dishes etc.) of salt or piquant & not sweet flavour (sweet or ~y omelette); hence ~ĭLY² adv., ~ĭNESS n. **2.** n. ‖ ~y dish, esp. one served at beginning or end of dinner as stimulant or digestive. [ME, f. OF savoure p.p. (prec.); see -Y⁴]

savoy′, n. Kind of cabbage with wrinkled leaves. [S~ in France]

Savoy′ard (-oi-), n. & a. **1.** (Native) of Savoy. **2.** Member of the Savoy Theatre company who acted in the original productions of the Gilbert and Sullivan operas. [F (Savoie Savoy, -ARD)]

săv′ў, corrupt. of Sp. sabe knows, in sl. use = do you understand? (no ~, I do, he etc. does, not know or understand), also as n. = understanding, wits, savoir faire.

saw¹, n., & v.t. & i. (p.p. ~n, rarely ~ed). **1.** Implement usu. of steel worked by hand or mechanically & with variously shaped blade or edge having teeth of various forms cut in or attached to it for dividing wood, metal, stone, etc., by reciprocating or rotatory motion (annular, crown, cylinder, ~, cylinder with toothed edge for making circular hole; BAND¹, BOW¹, FRAME², FRET¹, -~; CIRCULAR ~; cross-cut, rip-, ~, for cutting wood across, along, the grain; hand-~, held with one hand; HACK²-~; jig′~, frame-~ worked mechanically in connexion with table holding the wood etc. (jig~ puzzle, of pieces sawn with jig~ to be put together); musical or singing ~, ordinary ~ played on by performer by means of violin bow; pit-~, worked by two men one above & one in pit; reciprocating ~, worked mechanically with backward & forward strokes; stone-~, toothless frame-~ cutting stone by friction with sand & water). **2.** (zool. etc.). Serrated organ or part. **3.** ~-doctor, machine for making teeth of ~; ~′dust, wood fragments produced in ~ing used in packing, pugging, stuffing, drying moisture, etc. (let the ~dust out of, fig., expose pretentiousness or unsubstantial character of, w. ref. to doll's stuffing); ~′fish, large kind with toothed snout used as weapon; ~-fly, kinds injurious to plants with serrated ovipositor; ~-frame, in which ~-blade is held taut; ~-gate, ~-frame; ~-gin, cotton-GIN¹ with ~-teeth; ~-horse, rack supporting wood for ~ing; ~′mill, driven by water or steam for mechanical ~ing; ~-pit, in which lower of two men working pit-~ stands; ~-set, tool for wrenching ~-teeth in alternate directions to give kerf wider than blade & let ~ work freely; ~-wort, plant yielding yellow dye named from

serrated leaves; ~-*wrack*, a serrated seaweed; ~-*wrest*, ~-set. **4.** vb. Cut (wood
etc.) with, make (boards etc.) with, use
~; move (t. & i.) backward & forward,
divide (the air etc.), with motion as of ~
or person ~ing; (quasi-pass.) admit of
being ~n *easily, badly,* etc.; (bookbind.)
make incisions to receive binding-bands
in (gathered sheets); ~'*bones* (sl.), surgeon.
[OE *sagu, saga,* OHG *saga,* ON *sǫg* f.
Gmc *sagō*; cogn. w. L *secare* cut]

saw², n. Proverbial saying, old maxim,
(usu. *old* or *wise*~). [OE *sagu,* OHG, ON
saga, f. Gmc *sag-* SAY²; cf. SAGA]

saw³. See SEE¹.

sawd'er, n. *Soft* ~, compliments, flattering speeches, blarney. [= SOLDER]

Sawn'ey, n. (Nickname for) Scotsman;
simpleton. [prob. as SANDY²]

saw'yer, n. Man employed in sawing
timber (TOP-~); * uprooted tree floating
or stranded in river (named as sawing
up & down); kinds of wood-boring larva.
[-YER]

săx, zăx, n. Slater's chopper, with point
for making nail-holes. [OE *seax,* OS *saks,*
OHG *sahs,* ON *sax* f. Gmc *sah-, *sag-
cogn. w. SAW¹]

săx'atile, a. (nat. hist.). Living, growing,
on or among rocks. [F, or f. L *saxatilis*
(*saxum* rock, -ATILE)]

săxe, n. ‖ Kind of photographic paper;
a colour, = SAXON *blue.* [F, = Saxony
(place of origin)]

săx'hŏrn, n. Brass instrument made in
seven sizes, the lowest three being considered tubas. [A. *Sax,* inventor (d. 1894)]

săxic'oline, -lous, aa. (nat. hist.). =
SAXATILE. [f. mod. L *saxicolus* (*saxum*
rock, *colere* inhabit) +-INE, -OUS]

săx'ifrage (or -āj), n. Kinds of Alpine or
rock plant with tufted foliage & panicles
of white or yellow or red flowers. [ME,
f. OF, or LL *saxifraga (herba)* f. *saxum*
rock +*frangere* break]

Săx'on, n. & a. **1.** Member, language
(often *Old* ~), of the Germanic people by
which Britain was conquered in 5th & 6th
cc.; = ANGLO-SAXON, whence ~DOM n.;
native of modern Saxony; Germanic
(opp. Latin or Romance) elements of
English. **2.** adj. Of the ~s (~ *architecture,*
rude Romanesque preceding Norman in
England); in ~ (~ *words* in English, of
Germanic origin), whence ~ISM(2, 4),
~IST(2), nn.; ~ *blue,* solution of indigo in
sulphuric acid as dye; hence ~IZE(2, 3)
v.i. & t. [ME, f. OF f. LL *Saxonem* f. WG
Saxon- (OE *Seaxan, Seaxe* pl.)]

săx'onў, n. Fine kind of wool, cloth made
from it. [f. *S*~ in Germany]

săx'ophŏne, n. Keyed brass instrument
in several sizes, having a reed like that of
a clarinet. [as SAXHORN, Gk *phōnē* sound]

săx'tuba, n. Large SAXHORN. [TUBA]

say¹, n. (now rare). Fine serge-like cloth.
[ME, f. OF *saie* f. L *saga* pl. of *sagum*
military cloak]

say², v.t. & i. (*said* pr. sĕd; 3rd sing. pres.
says pr. sĕz, arch. *saith* pr. sĕth; arch.
2nd sing. pres. ~*st* or ~*est,* past *saidst*
rarely *saidest*), & n. **1.** Utter, make (specified remark), recite, rehearse, in ordinary
speaking voice (~ *the word,* give the order
etc.; ~ WHEN; ~ *no more,* cease speaking;
~ *a good word for,* commend or excuse;
to be said or sung; ~ *no, yes,* refuse, grant,
request, also deny, confirm or accept,
statement; ~ *out,* express fully or candidly; ~ one *nay,* refuse him something; *has
said his* ~, finished what he had to ~;
~ *lesson,* repeat it to teacher; ~ *grace,
prayer*; ~ *something,* make a short speech;
that is to ~, in other words, as *the whole
family, that is to* ~ *four persons,* also = or
at least, as *he never went, that is to* ~ *it is
not recorded that he did,* also ellipt. ~ in
giving sum in words after figures, as
£*500* ~ *five hundred pounds*; *he said 'You
lie '*; ~*s* or *said he* etc., *said I,* ~*s I* colloq.,
forms inserted in repeating conversation;
~*ing & doing,* speech & action; ‖ *I* ~,
excl. used to draw attention, open a conversation, or express surprise, as *I* ~,
who was that?, I ~, *what a beauty!,* or in
same sense *I* ~ *!* alone). **2.** State, promise,
prophesy, (*he* ~*s all men or that all men are
liars*; *you said you would*; DARE ~; *they* ~,
it is said, forms introducing rumour; *it*
~*s in the Bible,* the Bible ~*s*; *goes without
*~*ing,* is too obvious to need mention;
hear ~, hear it reported; *so he* ~*s, he* ~*s
so*; *you may well* ~ *so,* your statement is
fully justified). **3.** Speak, talk, (rare; ~
away, ~ what you have to ~; *he said, &
turned his back,* in narrative poetry etc.).
4. Put into words, express (*that was well
said*). **5.** Adduce or allege in argument or
excuse (*there is much to be said on both
sides*; *have you anything to* ~ *for yourself?*).
6. Form & give opinion or decision as to
or abs. (*there is no* ~*ing, it is hard to* ~,
who it was; *I cannot* ~, do not know
whether etc. or abs.; *do* ~ *which you will
have*; *what* ~ *you to a theatre?,* are you
inclined for it ?; *& so* ~ *all of us,* & that is
our opinion too). **7.** Select as example,
assume, take (specified number etc.) as
near enough, (*let us* ~, or usu. ellipt. ~;
any country, let us ~ *Sweden, might do the
same*; *well,* ~ *it were true, what then?*; *a
few of them,* ~ *a dozen or so*). **8.** n. (Opportunity of ~ing) what one has to ~, share
in decision, (~ *your* ~; *let him have his* ~;
had no ~ *in the matter*). [OE *secgan,* OS
seggian, OHG *sagēn,* ON *segja,* f. Gmc
*sagjan, *sagǣjan*]

say'ing, n. In vbl senses; esp., sententious
remark, maxim, adage, (*as the* ~ *is or
goes,* form used in quoting proverb or
phrase). [-ING¹]

Say(y)id (sā'yĭd), **Said** (săd), nn. Varr. of
SEID. [f. Arab., see SIDI, SEID]

sbĭr'rō (zb-), n. (pl. *-ri* pr. -ē). Italian
policeman. [It.]

scăb, n., & v.i. (-bb-). **1.** Dry rough

incrustation formed over sore in healing, cicatrice; mange, itch, or similar skin--disease; kinds of fungous plant-disease; mean dirty fellow (arch.); (trade unionism) workman who refuses to join strike or union or takes striker's place, black-leg; ~'wort, elecampane; hence ~bED² (-bd), ~b'Y², aa., ~b'ĬLY² adv., ~b'ĬNESS n. 2. v.i. (Of sore) form ~, heal over. [ME, f. ON skabbr = OE sceabb, see SHABBY]

scǎbb'ard, n. Sheath of sword, bayonet, etc. (*fling, throw, away the* ~, commit oneself to fighting a matter out to the end); ~*-fish,* silvery-white sea-fish shaped like sword-~. [ME scauberc etc., f. AF, OF escauberc, escauberge of WG orig.]

scǎb'ies (-z), n. The itch. [L (scabere scratch)]

scǎb'ious, a. & n. 1. Scabby, affected with mange, itch, etc. 2. n. Kinds of wild & cultivated annual or perennial herb with blue, pink, or white, pincushion-shaped flowers, as *devil's-bit.* [(n. f. med. L scabiosa herba, named as specific against itch) f. F scabieux or L scabiosus (prec., -OUS)]

scǎb'rous, a. (Zool., bot., etc.) with rough surface, scurfy; (literature; of subject, situation, etc.) requiring tactful treatment, hard to handle with decency. Hence ~NESS n. [f. F scabreux or LL scabrosus (L scaber rough, -OUS)]

scǎd, n. Kind of fish called also horse--mackerel. [orig. unkn.]

scǎff'old, n., & v.t., **scǎff'old|ǐng,** n. 1. Elevated platform of timber usu. for execution of criminals (~; *the* ~, death by executioner's hands) or rarely (~, ~*ing*) for display of something or accommodation of spectators; (usu. ~*ing*) temporary structure of poles & planks providing workmen with platform(s) to stand on while building or repairing house etc., (~*ing*) materials for this; (anat., embryol.; ~, ~*ing*) framework outlining parts to be formed on it later (*the* ~ *of the skull*); ~*ing-pole,* mastlike pole helping to support building-platform. 2. v.t. Attach ~ing to (house). [ME, f. NF forms corresp. to OF eschaffaut, earlier escadafaut f. EX- + Rom. *catafalcum CATAFALQUE]

scǎg'lia (or skǎl'ya), n. Reddish Italian limestone. [It.]

scagliola (skǎlyōl'a), n. Imitation stone of plaster mixed with glue & variously coloured or diversified. [It. (-iuola)]

scǎl'able, a. In vbl senses of SCALE¹˒²˒³. [-ABLE]

scalā'rǐfŏrm, a. (bot., zool.). Ladder--shaped (of veins in insect's wings, or of alternating thick & thin strips in structure). [f. mod. L scalariformis f. scalaris SCALE³, -AR¹, -FORM]

scǎl'awǎg, scǎll'a-, scǎll'y̆-, n. Under-sized or ill-fed animal; good-for-nothing person, scamp, scapegrace. [U.S. sl., of unkn. orig.]

scald¹ (-aw-), v.t., & n. 1. Injure or pain (skin, or person or animal or part in regard to it) with hot liquid or vapour (*was* ~*ed to death by the steam*; ~*ing tears,* of bitter grief); raise (milk) to near boiling--point (~*ed cream,* from milk ~ed & allowed to stand), whence ~'ER¹(2) n.; cleanse (vessel; often *out*) by rinsing with boiling water. 2. n. Injury to skin by ~ing (*for* ~s *& burns*). [ME, f. ONF escalder f. LL EX(caldare f. L calidus hot)]

scald² (-aw-), **sk-,** n. Ancient-Scandinavian composer & reciter of poems in honour of great men. Hence **sca'ldiᴏ** (-awl-) a. [ON skáld, of unkn. orig.]

scald'-head (-awld-hĕd), n. Scalp-disease of children. [SCALD, -ED²]

scāle¹, n., & v.t. & i. 1. One of the thin horny overlapping plates protecting the skin of many fishes & reptiles. 2. Plate or thin outer piece with some resemblance to fish-~ in organic or other object, e.g. pod, husk, rudimentary leaf or feather, bract, metamorphosed hair of lepidoptera, bulb-layer, flake of skin, scab, lamina on surface of rusty iron. 3. (Without *a*) incrustation inside boiler etc., tartar on teeth. 4. ~*-armour,* of metal ~s attached to leather etc.; ~*-board,* very thin for back of mirror, picture, etc.; ~*-borer,* machine for removing ~ from boiler-tubes; ~*-fern,* ceterach; ~*-insect,* kinds that cling fast to plants & secrete a shieldlike ~ as covering; ~*-moss,* kinds of plant with ~like leaves resembling moss; ~*-winged,* lepidopterous; ~*-work,* overlapping arrangement, imbrication; hence (-)scālED(-ld),~'LESS(-l-l-), scāl'y², aa., scāl'iNESS n. 5. vb. Take away ~(s) from (~ *fish, almonds, teeth, iron*); (of skin, metal, etc.) form, come off in, drop, ~s; (of ~s) come *off.* [ME, f. OF escale f. WG *skala, see foll.]

scāle², n., & v.t. 1. Dish of simple balance (*throw sword into* ~, back claim with arms; *turn the* ~, of motive or circumstance, be decisive); (astron.) *the S~s,* = LIBRA; (pl.) a simple balance (also *pair of* ~s) or weighing-instrument (*hold the* ~s *even,* be impartial judge). 2. v.t. Weigh in ~s (rare); (of thing weighed) show (specified weight) in the ~s (~s *10 st.,* *100 lb.*). [ME, f. ON skál bowl = OHG skâla f. Gmc *skælô var. of *skalô whence OE scealu SHALE; see also SHELL¹]

scāle³, n., & v.t. & i. 1. Series of degrees, ladderlike arrangement or classification, graded system, (*is high in the* ~ *of creation* or *social, intellectual,* etc., ~; *sink in 'the* ~, fall to lower rank or level; *at the top, bottom, of the* ~; *sliding* ~, see SLIDE¹). 2. (mus.). Steplike ordered arrangement of all notes used in any system of music (DIATONIC, CHROMATIC, MAJOR², MINOR, ~; *play, sing, run over* one's, ~s, as exercise for fingers or voice). 3. (Often ~ *of notation*) basis of numerical system as shown in ratio between units in different places of number (the *ordinary* or *denary* or *decimal* ~, with successive places denoting units, tens, hundreds, etc.; *binary* ~, denoting units, twos, fours, etc.; *ternary* ~, denoting units, threes, nines, etc.; thus fourteen is written in binary ~ 1110 i.e. nought+two+four+ eight, in ternary ~ 112 i.e. two+three+ nine, in septenary ~ 20 i.e. nought+two sevens, & in denary ~ 14 i.e. four+ten). **4.** Relative dimensions, ratio of reduction & enlargement in map etc., (*philanthropy, armies, on a vast ~; a building of small ~ but fine proportions; large, small, -~ map; to ~*, with uniform reduction or enlargement; *the ~ to be one to fifty thousand, an inch to the mile, 1/1000*, etc.). **5.** Set of marks at measured distances on a line for use in measuring or making proportional reductions & enlargements, rule determining intervals between these, piece of metal etc. or apparatus on which they are marked (GUNTER'S ~). **6.** vb. Climb (wall, steep place, or abs.) with ladder (*scaling-ladder*) or by clambering. **7.** Represent in dimensions proportional to the actual ones, reduce to common ~, (*~up, down*, make larger, smaller, in due proportion; *increase, reduce*, in size). **8.** (Of quantities etc.) have common ~, be commensurable. [ME (= ladder), f. L *scala* (*scandere* climb)]

scalene′, a. & n. **1.** Unequal-sided (*~ triangle*, with no two sides equal; *~ cone, cylinder*, with axis inclined to base; *~ muscle*, any of several connecting spine & ribs). **2.** n. ~ triangle or muscle. [f. LL f. Gk *skalēnos*]

scall (-awl), n. (arch.). Scaly eruption on skin (*dry ~*, the itch; *moist ~*, eczema). [ME, prob. f. ON *skalli* bald head, f. Gmo **skal-* (SHALE, SHELL¹)]

scaliawag. See SCALAWAG.

scăll′ion (-yon), n. Kind of onion or shallot. [ME, f. AF *scal(o)un* = OF *eschalo(i)gne*, see SHALLOT]

scăll′op, scŏ-, n., & v.t. **1.** Bivalve mollusc with shell divided into grooves & ridges radiating from middle of hinge & edged all round with small semicircular lobes; (also ~*-shell*) one valve of this (hist.) as pilgrim's badge, (mod.) as utensil in which oysters, shredded fish, mince, etc., are cooked & served, small shallow pan similarly used; (pl.) ornamental edging cut in material in imitation of ~*-edge*. **2.** v.t. Cook in ~; ornament (edge, material) with ~s or ~ING¹(6) n. [ME, f. OF *escalope* f. Gmo f. MDu. *schelpe, schulpe* shell]

scallywag. See SCALAWAG.

scălp, n., & v.t. **1.** Top of head; skin with hair etc. of head excluding face; this or part of it cut as trophy from enemy's head by Red Indians (*take ~; out for ~s*, on the warpath, often fig. = in aggressive or pugnacious or savagely critical mood); bare rounded hill-top; whale's

head without lower jaw; ~*-lock*, single lock on Red Indian's shaven head left as challenge to enemies; hence ~*'LESS* a. **2.** v.t. Take ~ of; criticize savagely. [north. ME, app. f. Scand.; cf. ON *skálpr* sheath, Da. dial. *skalp* shell, husk]

scăl′pel, n. Surgeon's small light knife shaped for holding like pen. [F, or f. L *scalpellum* (*scalprum* chisel, f. *scalpere* scrape, -EL)]

scăl′per, scaup′er, n. Gouge used by engravers. [f. L *scalprum* (prec.)]

scăl′priform, a. Chisel-shaped (of incisor teeth). [as prec., -I-, -FORM]

scămm′onў, n. (Kind of Asian convolvulus yielding) a gum resin used as drastic purgative. [ME, f. OF *scamonee*, *escamonie* f. L f. Gk *skammōnia*]

scămp¹, n. Rascal, knave, (also in playful use as term of endearment). Hence ~*'ISH¹* a. [prob. of same orig. as SCAMPER]

scămp², v.t. Do (work etc.) in perfunctory or inadequate way. [prob. dial.; cf. SKIMP]

scăm′per, v.i., & n. **1.** Run impulsively like (or of) frightened animal or playing child; take ~ *through*. **2.** n. Hasty run; gallop on horseback for pleasure; rapid tour or course of reading (*through Normandy, Dickens*, etc.). [f. 16th c. (obs.) *scamp*, f. MDu. *schampen* decamp +-ER⁵]

scăn, v.t. & i. (-nn-). **1.** Test metre of (line etc.) by examining number & quantity of feet & syllables, read over with emphasis on rhythm; be metrically correct (*line does not ~*), admit of rhythmic reading (*line will not ~, ~s smoothly, badly*). **2.** Look intently at all parts successively of (face, horizon, etc.). **3.** (television). Resolve (a picture) into its elements of light and shade for purposes of transmission. **4.** (radar). Cause (a particular region) to be traversed by a controlled beam. [ME, f. L *scandere* climb, in LL scan verses]

scăn′dal, n. (Thing that occasions) general feeling of outrage or indignation esp. as expressed in common talk, opprobrium, (*it is a ~ that such things should be possible; a grave ~ occurred; gave rise to ~*); malicious gossip, backbiting, whence ~MONGER n.; (law) public affront, irrelevant abusive statement in court, (cf. LIBEL, SLANDER). So ~OUS a., ~OUSLY² adv., ~OUSNESS n. [ME *-dle*, f. ONF *escandle* f. eccl. L f. Gk *skandalon* snare, stumbling-block]

scăn′dalize¹, -ise (-īz), v.t. Offend moral feelings, sense of propriety, or ideas of etiquette, of, shock. [f. F *scandaliser* f. eccl. L f. Gk (-izō) as prec., see -IZE]

scăn′dalize², -ise (-īz), v.t. (naut.). Reduce area of (a sail). [alt. f. obs. *scantelize* = obs. *scantle* (SCANT vb +-LE(3))]

scăn′dalum măgnāt′um, n. (hist.). Defamation of magnates. [med. L]

Scăndināv′ian, a. & n. (Native, family of

languages) of Scandinavia (Denmark, Norway, Sweden, & Iceland). [-AN]

scăn'sion (-shn), n. Metrical scanning, way verse scans. [f. L *scansio* (LL of metre) f. *scandere scans*- climb, -ION]

scănsōr'ial, a. Habitually climbing, adapted for climbing, (of birds, their feet, etc.). [L *scansorius* (prec., -ORY), -AL]

scănt, a., & v.t. 1. Barely sufficient, deficient, with scanty supply *of*, (arch., poet., & in isolated phrr., as *with ~ courtesy*, *~ of breath*); hence ~'LY² adv. 2. v.t. (arch.). Skimp, stint, provide grudgingly, (supply, material, person). [ME, f. ON *skamt* short]

scăn'ties (-tĕz), n. pl. (colloq.). Abbreviated panties. [f. prec., after PANTIES]

scănt'ling, n. Specimen, sample, (arch.); modicum, small amount, one's necessary supply *of*; small beam under 5 in. in breadth & depth; size to which stone or timber is to be cut; set of standard dimensions for parts of structure esp. in shipbuilding; trestle for cask. [alt. f. obs. *scantillon* (after -LING¹) f. OF *escantillon*]

scăn't|y̌, a. Of small extent or amount, barely sufficient, (opp. *ample*). Hence ~iLY² adv., ~iNESS n. [-Y²]

scăpe¹, n., & v.t. (arch.). Escape (still in *hairbreadth ~s*). [aphetic f. ESCAPE]

scăpe², n. (Bot.) radical stem bearing fructification & no leaves as in primrose; (entom.) base of antenna; shaft of feather; spring, usu. with curve, of column from base. [f. L f. Gk *skapos* cogn. w. SCEPTRE]

scăpe'goat (-pg-), n. (O.T.) goat allowed to escape when Jewish chief priest had laid sins of people upon it (*Lev.* xvi); person bearing blame due to others. [SCAPE¹]

scăpe'grāce (-pg-), n. Harebrained person, esp. child, who constantly gets into trouble. [= one who escapes the grace of God (SCAPE¹)]

scapement = ESCAPEMENT.

scăph'oid, a. & n. (anat.). 1. Boat-shaped (*~ bone*, one in tarsus & oné in carpus). 2. n. ~ bone. [f. Gk *skaphoeidēs* (*skaphē*, *skaphos*, bowl, boat, -OID)]

scăp'ūla, n. (pl. *-ulae*). SHOULDER-blade. [LL, sing. of L *scapulae*]

scăp'ūlar, a. & n. 1. Of shoulder or shoulder-blade (*~ arch*, = shoulder--GIRDLE¹; *~ feathers*, growing near insertion of wing). 2. n. Monastic short cloak covering shoulders; badge of admission to an ecclesiastical order, consisting of two strips of cloth hanging down breast & .back & joined across shoulders (also *~y*); bandage for shoulder-blade; ~ feather. [n. f. LL *scapulare* (prec., -AR¹); adj. f. mod. L *scapularis*]

scăp'ūlo-, comb. form of SCAPULA, as *~-hŭm'eral*, *~-răd'ial*, *~-ŭl'nar*, of scapula & humerus, & radius, & ulna. [-O-]

scăr¹, n., & v.t. & i. (-rr-). 1. Mark left after healing of wound or burn or sore, cica-

trice, (also fig. of abiding effects of grief etc.); mark on plant left by fall of a leaf etc., hilum; hence ~'LESS a. 2. vb. Mark with ~ or ~s (esp. in p.p.); heal (i. & t.) over, form ~. [ME, f. OF *escare* f. LL *eschara* (also *scara*) scar]

scăr², scaur (-ōr), n. Precipitous craggy part of mountain side; sea-cliff. [ME, f. ON *sker* low reef in sea, cogn. w. SHEAR¹]

scă'rab, n. Sacred beetle of ancient Egypt; =foll.; ancient-Egyptian gem cut in form of beetle & engraved with symbols on flat side. [f. L f. Gk *scarabaeus*]

scărabae'id, n. Member of *Scarabaeidae*, family of beetles including prec., cock-chafer, etc. [prec., -ID³] .

scărabae'oid, a. & n. Like a· scarab or a scarabaeid; (n.) counterfeit scarab. [-OID]

scă'ramouch, n. (arch.). Boastful poltroon, braggart. [17th c., f. It. *Scaramuccia* stock character in Italian farce (= SKIRMISH); pres. sp. f. F *-mouche*]

scarce, a. & adv. 1. Insufficient for the demand or need, not plentiful, scanty, (usu. pred., & of food, money, or other necessaries of life), whence scar'CITY n. (*of*, or abs.=dearth of food); seldom met with, rare, hard to find, (*a ~ book, moth*); *make oneself ~*, colloq., retire, make off, keep out of the way, whence ~'NESS (-sn-) n. 2. adv. (arch., poet., rhet.). Scarcely. [ME & ONF *skars* f. Rom. **excarpsus* f. L *excerptus* EXCERPT]

scarce'ly (-slĭ), adv. Hardly, barely, only just, (*is ~ seventeen years old*; *had ~ arrived when he was told that —*; *I ~ know him*); surely not; not unless the unlikely happens or is true, (*you will ~ maintain that*; *he can ~ have said so*); (mild or apologetic substitute for) not (*I ~ think so, know what to say*). [-LY²]

scarce'ment (-sm-), n. Set-back in a wall, ledge resulting from this. [SCARCE + -MENT]

scare, v.t., & n. 1. Strike (esp. child, foolish person, or animal) with sudden terror, frighten (as) with a bugbear, (*~d face, expression*, etc., betraying terror; *~ away*, drive off by fright); keep (birds) away from sown land etc.; *~'crow*, figure of man hung with old clothes & set up in field to keep birds away, bugbear, badly dressed or grotesque-looking or skinny person. 2. n. Unreasoning terror, esp. baseless general apprehension of war, invasion, etc., whence ~'MONGER n.; commercial panic; *~-head(ing)*, extravagantly sensational newspaper headline. [ME *skerre*, f. ON *skirra* (*skjarr* timid)]

scärf¹, n. (pl. *-fs, -ves*). Long narrow strip of material worn for ornament or warmth round neck, over shoulders, or baldric--wise; man's necktie (|| ~-*pin*, *-ring*, usu. of gold or jewelled for holding ends of this together); *~-loom*, for weaving narrow fabrics; *~-skin*, outermost layer of skin constantly scaling off (esp. of that adhering to base of nails); *~-wise*, baldric-wise. Hence ~ED² (-ft) a. [f. ONF *escarpe* = OF *escharpe* sash etc., prob. same wd as *escharpe* SCRIP¹]

scarf², v.t., & n. 1. Join ends of (pieces of timber, metal, or leather) by bevelling or notching so that they overlap without increase of thickness & then bolting, brazing, or sewing them together; flench (whale). 2. n. Joint made by ~ing timber or leather (also ~-*joint*) or metal (also ~-*-weld*); notch, groove. [n. ME, perh. f. Scand., cf. Sw. *skarf*, Norw. *skarv* joint or seam; vb f. n.]

scä'rificātor, n. In vbl senses; esp., surgical instrument for scarifying, in which several lancet-points protrude at once from plane surface on touching of trigger. [mod. L, see SCARIFY, -OR]

scä'rifier, n. In vbl senses; esp.: = prec.; agricultural machine with prongs for stirring without turning soil; spiked road-breaking machine. [foll., -ER¹]

scä'ri|fy, v.t. (Surg.) make superficial incisions in, cut off skin from, (fig.) pain by severe criticism etc.; stir (soil) with scarifier. So ~FICA'TION n. [f. F *scarifier* f. LL *scarificare* f. L *scarifare*]

scar'ious, a. (bot.). Thin, dry, & membranaceous (of bracts etc.). [f. F *scarieux*]

scärlati'na (-tē-), n. Scarlet fever. [It. (-*tt*-), f. *scarlatto* SCARLET]

scär'l'et, n. & a. (Of) brilliant red colour inclining to orange; ~ cloth or clothes (*dressed in* ~); ~ *fever*, infectious fever with ~ rash, (joc.) tendency to fall in love with soldiers; ~-*grain*, scale-insect from which red dye is made in Russia & Turkey; ~ *hat*, cardinal's, (allus.) cardinalate; ~ *rash*, roseola; ~ *runner*, ~-*flowered* climbing bean-plant; ~ *woman*, *whore*, pagan Rome, papal Rome, or the worldly spirit (acc. to interpretation put on *Rev.* xvii). [ME, f. OF *escarlate*, med. L *scarlatum*; ult. orig. unkn.]

scä'roid (*or* skär-), a. & n. (Fish) of scarus genus, resembling scarus. [-OID]

scärp, n., & v.t. 1. Inner wall or slope (cf. COUNTERSCARP) of ditch in fortification; any steep slope. 2. v.t. Make (slope) perpendicular or steep, provide (ditch) with steep ~ & counter~; (p.p., of hillside etc.) steep, precipitous. [f. It. *scarpa* ESCARP]

scär'us, n. Kinds of bright-hued fish with parrotlike beak (also *parrotfish*) of wrasse family. [L, f. Gk *skaros*]

scät, int., & v.i. & t. (-tt-; colloq.). Begone! (vb) say ~, drive away thus. [perh. abbr. of *scatter*]

scäth|e (-dh), v.t., & n. 1. Injure esp. by blasting or withering up (now rare exc. in part. used by exag. of severe speech, as ~*ing* sarcasm, ridicule, remarks, whence ~'ingLY² (-dh-) adv.); (in neg. context) do the least harm to (*shall not be* ~*ed*; esp. *unscathed*). 2. n. (rare, & usu. in neg. context). Harm, injury, (*without, guard from*, ~*e*), whence ~'e'LESS (-dhl-) a. (usu. pred.). [ME, f. ON *skathi* n., *skatha* vb,

= OE *sc(e)atha*, *-lan*, OHG *skado*, *-ōn* f. Gmc **skath-*]

scatöl'ogy, n. Study of coprolites or of obscene literature. [Gk *skōr skatos* dung, -LOGY]

scatöph'agous, a. Feeding on dung. [prec., Gk *-phagos* -eating]

scätt'er, v.t. & i., & n. 1. Throw here & there (~ *seed*), strew (~ *gravel on road*, *road with gravel*), sprinkle; disperse (t. & i.), turn (t. & i.) in dispersed flight, rout, be routed; dissipate (cloud, hopes); diffuse (light); (of gun) send charge, send (charge), in spreading manner; (p.p.) not situated together, wide apart, sporadic, (~*ed hamlets, garrisons, instances*); ~-*brain*, heedless person; ~-*brained*, heedless, desultory. 2. n. Act of ~ing, extent of distribution esp. of shot. Hence ~ingLY² adv. [ME, metath. par. of SHATTER]

scätt'ÿ, a. (sl.). Feeble-minded, hare-brained. [orig. unkn.]

scaup(-dŭck), n. Kinds of duck named from frequenting mussel-scaups or beds of mussels exposed at low tide. [perh. f. *scaup*, Sc. var. of SCALP]

scaup'er. Var. of SCALPER.

scaur. See SCAR².

scäv'ëng|er (-j-), n., & v.i. 1. Person employed to keep streets clean by carrying away refuse; animal feeding on carrion (esp. ~*er-beetle, -crab*), writer etc. delighting in filthy subjects or dealing in scandal; hence ~e (-j; by back formation) v.t. & i., (also) expel exhaust gases etc. from cylinder of internal-combustion engine, ~ERY (2, 5) (-j-) n. 2. v.i. Be, act as, ~er. [ME *scavager* (cf. *messenger*) inspector of imports f. AF *scawager* f. *scawage* f. ONF *escauwer* inspect f. Flem. *scauwen* cogn. w. SHOW¹]

scäz'on, n. Greek & Latin iambic, ending with ∪ − − ⊻ instead of ⊻ − ∪ ⊻, used in short poems, choliamb; other metres of limping character. [L f. Gk *skazōn* (*skazō* limp)]

scena (shā'nah), n. (mus.). Scene or portion of opera; elaborate dramatic solo usu. including recitative. [It.]

scenār'ĭŏ (shā-), n. (pl. ~s). (Table of) scene-distribution, appearances of characters, etc., in dramatic work, skeleton libretto; (*usu. pr.* sēnär'ĭŏ) written version of play, details of scenes, etc., in film production. [It.]

scend. See SEND².

scëne, n. 1. Stage of theatre (arch.; still in fig. use *quit the* ~, esp. = die); place on which something is exhibited as on the stage (*this world is a* ~ *of strife*). 2. Place in which events set forth in drama or tale are supposed to occur, locality of event, (*the* ~ *is laid in India*; *the* ~ *of the disaster was the North Sea*). 3. Portion of a play during which action is continuous or (esp. of French plays) in which no intermediate entries or exits occur, subdivision (or rarely the whole) of an act, (*in the* third ~ of Act II; Act II, ~ iii, l. 220; the famous duel ~ ; CARPENTER-~); (transf.) description with more or less abrupt beginning & end of an incident or part of person's life (~s of clerical life, from a goldfield, etc.), actual incident that might occasion such description (distressing ~s occurred), agitated colloquy esp. with display of temper (now don't make a ~). 4. Any of the pieces of painted canvas, woodwork, etc., used to help in representing ~ of action on stage, or whole of these together (behind the ~s, among the stage machinery or the actors off the stage, usu. fig. = having information not accessible to the public; CARPENTER-~; ~s painted by —; set ~, made up of many parts fitted together; DROP-SCENE); (transf.) landscape or view spread before spectator like ~ in theatre (a silvan, desolate, ~; a ~ of destruction; change of ~, variety of surroundings esp. secured by travel). 5. ~-dock, space near stage where ~s are stored; ~-painter, -painting, of theatre ~s; ~-shifter, person helping to change ~s in theatre. [f. F scène f. L f. Gk skēnē tent, stage]

scён'erў, n. Accessories used in theatre to make stage resemble supposed scene of action; spectacles presented by natural features of a district (the ~ is imposing, tame). [17th c. scenary f. It. scenario f. LL scenarius (prec., -ARY¹) of the stage, assim. to -ERY]

scён'ic, a. Of, on, the stage (~ performances); of the nature of a show, picturesque in grouping; (of picture etc.) telling a tale, crystallizing an incident; (of emotion etc.) dramatic, affected, put on; ~ railway, miniature railway running through artificial picturesque scenery, as attraction at large fairs etc. Hence scён'ICALLY adv. [f. F scénique, or f. L f. Gk skēnikos (SCENE, -IC)]

scён|ŏg'raphў, n. Drawing or painting in perspective (esp. of representing building not in ground-plan or elevation, but as spectator sees it). So ~'OGRAPH(1), ~ŏG'RAPHER nn., ~OGRAPH'IC a., ~ogräph'ICALLY adv. [f. F (-ie) or L f. Gk skēnographia (SCENE, -GRAPHY)]

scёnt, v.t. & i., & n. 1. Discern by smell (~ game etc.), (fig.) begin to suspect presence or existence of (~ treachery, a job); ~ out, discover by smelling about or search; make fragrant or rank (rose, carrion, ~s the air), apply perfume to (handkerchief etc.; ~ed soap, tobacco); exercise sense of smell, apply this to, (goes ~ing about; lifts its head & ~s the air). 2. n. Odour, esp. of agreeable kind, proceeding from or belonging to something (the ~ of hay), whence ~'LESS a.; (hunt.) trail perceptible to hounds' sense of smell left by animal (often fig.; follow up, lose, recover, etc., the ~, lit., & of investigation; on the ~, having clue; put off the ~, deceive by false indications;

COLD¹, HOT¹, ~), paper strewn by paper-chase hares (false ~, laid to deceive about course, also fig.); power of detecting or distinguishing smells or of discovering presence of something, flair, (some dogs have practically no ~; keen-~ed; has a wonderful ~ for snobbery, young talent, etc.); liquid perfume distilled from flowers etc. 3. ~-bag, pouch containing special odoriferous substance in some animals, also bag of aniseed etc. as substitute for fox in hunting; ~-bottle, for perfume; ~-gland, secreting musk, civet, etc.; ~-organ, ~-bag or ~-gland; hence (-)~'ED² a. (~ed caper, kind of tea; ~ed fern, kind smelling like citron). [ME sent f. OF sentir perceive, smell, f. L sentire]

scёp'sis (sk-), *sk-, n. Philosophic doubt, sceptical philosophy. [f. Gk skepsis inquiry (skeptomai examine)]

scёp'tic (sk-), *sk-, n. Ancient or modern holder of PYRRHONISM; person who doubts truth of the Christian or of all religious doctrines, agnostic, (pop.) atheist; person of sceptical habit of mind, or unconvinced of truth of particular fact or theory, or who takes cynical views. So ~ISM(3) (sk-) n. [f. F sceptique or L f. Gk skeptikos (prec., -IC)]

scёp'tical (sk-), *sk-, a. Inclined to suspense of judgement, given to questioning truth of facts & soundness of inferences, critical, incredulous; accepting PYRRHONISM, denying possibility of knowledge; holding, designed to support, inspired by, the ideas of SCEPTICS. Hence ~LY² adv. [-AL]

scёp'tr|e (-ter), n. Staff borne as symbol of personal sovereignty; royal or imperial authority. Hence ~ED² (-terd), ~ELESS (-terl-), aa. [ME, f. OF, f. L f. Gk skēptron]

schadenfreude (shah'denfroide), n. Malicious enjoyment of others' misfortunes. [G, f. schade damage+freude joy]

schappe (shǎp, shah'pe), n. Fabric or yarn made from waste silk. [G, = silk waste]

schёd'üle (‖ sh-, *sk-), n., & v.t. 1. Tabulated statement of details, inventory, list, etc., esp. as appendix or annexe to principal document; *time-table; ~ time, that stated in time-table (on ~, to ~ time). 2. v.t. Make ~ of, include in ~. [ME & OF cedule f. LL scedula (L sceda papyrus-strip, -ULE); sch- f. med. L]

scheel'ite (sh-), n. (min.). Calcium tungstate, found in varicoloured brilliant crystals. [K. W. Scheele (d. 1786), -ITE¹(2)]

scheik. = SHEIKH.

schём'|a (sk-), n. (pl. ~ata). Synopsis, outline, diagram; (log.) syllogistic figure; (gram., rhet.) figure of speech; (Kantian philos.) general type, essential form, conception of what is common to all members of a class. So ~ăt'IC a., ~ăt'ICALLY adv., (sk-). [L, f. Gk skhēma -atos]

scheme 1126 **school**

schēm|e (sk-), n., & v.i. & t. **1.** Systematic arrangement proposed or in operation (~*e of colour*, principle on which colours have been chosen & grouped in picture etc.), table of classification or of appointed times, outline, syllabus; plan for doing something; artful or underhand design. **2.** vb. Make plans, plan esp. in secret or underhand way (*to do, for,* or abs.), intrigue, whence ~'ER[1] n., ~'ING[2] a., (sk-); plan to bring about. [f. L SCHEMA]

scherzăn'dō (skărts-), mus. direction. In playful manner. [It.]

scherzo (skărt'sō), n. (pl. ~*s*). Vigorous (prop. light & playful) composition, independent or as movement in works of sonata type. [It., f. Gmc (G *scherz* jest)]

Schiedăm' (skĭd-), n. Holland gin. [place]

schĭll'ing (sh-), n. Austrian monetary unit and coin, = 100 groschen. [G]

schipp'erkĕ (sk-, sh-), n. Kind of lapdog. [Du.]

schism (sĭ'zm), n. Division of a community into factions (rare in gen. sense), esp. separation of a Church into two Churches or secession of part of a Church owing to difference of opinion on doctrine or discipline; offence of causing or promoting such separation. [ME & OF *scisme* f. LL f. Gk *skhisma -atos* (*skhizō* split)]

schismăt'ĭc (sĭz-), a & n., -ĭc|al, a. **1.** Tending or inclined to, guilty of, schism; hence ~alLY[2] adv. **2.** n. Holder of ~ opinions, member of ~ faction or seceded branch of a Church. [ME, f. OF *scismatique* f. LL f. Gk *skhismatikos* (prec., -IC), -AL]

schist (sh-), n. Kinds of foliated rock presenting layers of different minerals & splitting in thin irregular plates. Hence **schĭs'tose**[1] (sh-) a. [f. F *schiste* f. L f. Gk *skhistos* split (SCHISM)]

schĭzăn'thus (sk-), n. Kinds of plant with handsome white, violet, or crimson flowers & much-divided leaves. [Gk *skhizō* split, *anthos* flower]

schiz'oid (sk-), a. & n. Of or resembling schizophrenia or a schizophrenic; (n.) ~ person. [as prec., -OID]

schizomycēte' (sk-), n. Any of the *Schizomycetae*, a class of minute often single-cell vegetable organisms between algae & fungi multiplying by fission, including bacilli, bacteria. microbes, etc. [Gk *skhizō* split, *mukēs -ētos* mushroom]

schizophr|ēn'ĭa (sk-), n. Mental disease marked by disconnexion between thoughts, feelings, & actions. Hence ~ĕn'ĭc a. & n. [as prec., Gk *phrēn* mind]

•schmaltz (shmawlts), n. (sl.). Sugary sentimentalism in art. [thr. Yiddish f. G *schmalz* dripping, lard]

schnăp(p)s (shn-), n. A spirit resembling Holland gin. [G]

schnauzer (shnow'tser), n. German breed of house-dog with close wiry coat. [G]

Schneid'er Trŏph'ў (shnī-), n. International trophy open to seaplanes of all nations presented in 1913 by Jacques Schneider, in 1931 won outright by Great Britain.

Schnŏrk'el (shn-), n. (German name for) SNORT[2]. [G *schnorchel*]

schnŏ'rrer (shn-), n. Jewish beggar. [Yiddish, f. G dial. *schnurrer* beggar]

schŏl'ar (sk-), n. **1.** Schoolboy, schoolgirl, (arch. or vulg.). **2.** Person's disciple (rhet.). **3.** Person who learns (*proved an apt, dull,* ~; *at 90 he was still a* ~). **4.** Learned person, person versed in literature esp. that of ancient Greece & Rome, (*a* ~ *& a gentleman*, person of good education & breeding), whence ~LY[1] a., ~SHIP (3) n. **5.** (Univv., pub. schh.) undergraduate or child admitted to foundation usu. after competitive examination & receiving education gratis or for reduced fees (RHODES, ~), whence ~SHIP(1) n. [ME, f. AF *escoler* (OF -*ier*) f. LL *scholaris* (SCHOOL, -AR[1]); OE dir. f. L]

scholăs'tic (sk-), a. & n. **1.** Of universities, schools, schooling, dons, or schoolmasters, educational, academic, pedantic, formal, (*a* ~ *education, post*; ~ *attire, manners, precision, life*; ~ *agent*, finding posts for teachers). **2.** (As) of the SCHOOL[1]men, dealing in logical subtleties, (~ *theology*, much concerned with precise definition of & deduction from dogma); hence or cogn. **scholăs'tically** adv., ~ISM (2, 3) n. **3.** n. SCHOOL[1]man; modern theologian of ~ tendencies; Jesuit between novitiate & priesthood. [f. L f. Gk *skholastikos* (*skholē*, see SCHOOL[1], -IC)]

schŏl'ĭ|ăst (sk-), n. Commentator, esp. ancient grammarian who wrote scholia on the classics. Hence ~ăs'tĭc a. [f. med. L f. Gk *skholiastēs* (*skholiazō* write scholia) (foll.)]

schŏl'ĭum (sk-), n. (pl. -*ĭa*). Marginal note, explanatory comment, esp. one by ancient grammarian on passage in classical author. [f. med. L f. Gk *skholion* (*skholē* see foll.)]

schōol[1] (sk-), n., & v.t. **1.** Institution for educating children or giving instruction usu. of more elementary or more technical kind than that given at universities (APPROVED, BOARD[1], BOARDING, COMPREHENSIVE, DAY, GRAMMAR, MIXED, NIGHT, NORMAL, PRIMARY, PRIVATE, PUBLIC, SECONDARY, SUNDAY, ~; ‖ *national* ~, one founded by the National Society started 1811 to promote education of the poor; *continuation* ~, at which those who have left esp. primary ~ for an occupation can have further teaching in leisure time; *evening*-~, = *night-*~; *free* ~, open without fees; *high* ~, secondary ~, or chief ~ of a town etc.; *technical* ~, giving TECHNICAL education; *keep a* ~, manage private ~); buildings of such institution, any of its rooms used for teaching in (*the fifth-form, chemistry,* ~), its pupils (*the whole* ~

knows); time during which teaching is done (*there will be no* ~ *today*; *go to* ~, attend lesson). **2.** Being educated in a ~ (*go to, leave,* ~, begin, cease, this; *go to* ~ *to,* transf., imitate or learn from); (fig.) circumstances or occupation serving to discipline or instruct (*in the* ~ *of adversity*; *learnt his generalship in a severe* ~; *the duel is a good* ~ *of manners*). **3.** Medieval lecture-room (*the*~s, medieval universities & their professors & teaching & disputations; *the theology of the* ~*s*; ~ *doctors,* ~men); ‖ any of the branches of study with separate examinations at university (*the history, mathematical, Greats,* ~); hall in which university examinations are held; (pl.) such examination (*in the* ~*s,* undergoing or conducting this at Oxford; ‖ *in for his* ~*s,* of candidate). **4.** Disciples or imitators or followers of philosopher, artist, etc., band or succession of persons devoted to some cause or principle or agreeing in typical characteristics, (*left no* ~ *behind him*: ~ *of Epicurus, Raphael,* etc.; *Bolognese, Venetian, Roman, British,* etc., ~, of painters; *lake, romantic,* etc., ~, of literature; *peripatetic, Hegelian,* etc., ~, of philosophy; *laissez-faire, blue-water,* etc., ~, of politics, strategy; *Tübingen* ~, of rationalistic theological criticism; *a gentleman of the old* ~, according to the older acceptation of the word). **5.** (mus.). Manual of (—*'s violin* ~, ~ *of counterpoint*). **6.** ‖ *Old* ~ *tie,* necktie worn by former members of a ~, (fig.) sentimental or excessive local or class loyalty; ~*-board,* local education authority ‖ responsible (1870–1902) for providing BOARD[1]~*s*; ~*-book,* for use in ~*s*; ~*'boy,* boy at ~ (often attrib., as ~*boy slang, mischief, spirits*); ‖ ~*-dame,* keeper of old-fashioned DAME-~ ; ~*-days,* time of being at ~ esp. as looked back upon; ~ *divine,* scholastic theologian, so ~ *divinity*; ~ *fee(s),* amount periodically paid by pupil's parent etc.; ~*'fellow,* member past or present of same ~; ~*'girl* (as ~*boy*); ~*'house,* building of esp. village ~; ‖ ~ *house,* headmaster's or central boarding-house at public ~; ~*-inspector,* reporting on efficiency of ~s; **~-ma'am, -marm* colloq., ~*mistress*; ~*'man,* teacher in medieval European university, theologian dealing with religious doctrines by rules of Aristotelian logic; ~*'master,* head or assistant male teacher in ~, pedagogue; ~*'mate,* contemporary at same ~; ~ *miss,* inexperienced or bashful girl; ~*'mistress* (as ~*master*); ‖ ~ *pence,* money formerly brought weekly by elementary-~ child as fee; ~*'room,* used for lessons in ~ or private house; ~*-ship,* training-ship; ~*-teacher,* master or mistress esp. in primary ~; ~*-teaching*; ~*-time,* lesson-time at ~ or home, also = ~*-days.* **7.** v.t. Send to ~, provide for education of, (rare), whence (in common use)~*'ING*[1] n.;

discipline, bring under control, deliberately train or accustom *to,* induce to follow advice, (*must* ~ *his temper*; ~ oneself *to patience, to take an interest in*; *will not be* ~*ed*). [OE *scōl* f. L *schola* school f. Gk *skholē* leisure, philosophy, lecture-place]

school[2] (sk-), n., & v.i. **1.** Shoal of or of fish; ~*-fish,* kinds that ~, esp. the menhaden. **2.** v.i. Form ~s. [ME, f. MDu. *schole,* = OS *scola,* OE *scolu* troop]

school'able (sk-), a. Liable by age etc. to compulsory education. [-ABLE]

schoon'er (sk-), n. **1.** Fore-&-aft-rigged vessel with two or more masts; PRAIRIE-~. **2.** *Tall beer-glass; ‖ measure for beer. [orig. *scooner,* supposed to have been given by the first designer (c. 1713) f. an alleged New-England vb *scun, scoon* skim or skip]

schorl (sh-), n. Black tourmaline. [f. G *schörl*]

schöttische (shŏtēsh'), n. (Music for) kind of slower polka. [G *-sch*), = *Scottish*]

sciäg'raphy (sī-), ski-, n. Art of shading in drawing etc.; photography by X-rays (usu. *sk-*); (archit.; also & usu. *-graph*) vertical section showing interior of house etc.; (astron.) finding of time by shadows as in sundial. So **sci'agram** n., X-ray picture, **sciagrammät'ic** a., **-icallý** adv., **sci'agRAPH(1, 2, 3) n. & v.t., sciä-GRAPHER** n., **sciagRAPH'ic** a., **sciagräph-ICALLY** adv., (sī-). [f. F (-*ie*) f. L f. Gk *skiagraphia* (*skia* shade, *-GRAPHY*)]

sciäm'achy (sī-, -kǐ), sciŏ-, n. Fighting with shadows, imaginary or futile combat. [f. Gk *skiamakhia* (prec., *-makhos* -fighting f. *makhomai* fight, *-IA*[1])]

sciät'ic (sī-), a. Of the hip (~ *nerve, artery,* etc.); of, affecting, the ~ nerve; suffering from or liable to sciatica. Hence **sciät'IC-ALLY** adv. [f. F *sciatique* f. LL *sciaticus* f. L f. Gk *iskhiadikos* subject to sciatica (*iskhias -ados* loin-pain f. *iskhion* socket of thigh-bone)]

sciät'ica (sī-), n. Neuralgia of hip & thigh, pain in sciatic nerve. [ME, f. med. L *sciatica* (*passio*), fem. of LL as prec.]

sci'ence (sī-), n. **1.** Knowledge (arch.), whence (in mod. use) **scien'tIAL** (-shl) a., **scien'tIALLY**[2] adv. **2.** Systematic & formulated knowledge (*moral, political, natural,* etc., ~, such knowledge in reference to these subjects); pursuit of this or principles regulating such pursuit (*man of* ~). **3.** (Also *natural* ~) the physical or natural ~s collectively (~ *now shares the curriculum with literature, history, & mathematics*). **4.** (With *a* & pl.) branch of knowledge, organized body of the knowledge that has been accumulated on a subject, (*the* ~ *of optics, ethics, philology*; *exact* ~, admitting of quantitative treatment; *pure* ~, one depending on deductions from self-evident truths, as mathematics, logic; *natural, physical,* ~, one dealing with material phenomena &

based mainly on observation, experiment, & induction, as chemistry, biology, whence esp. **sci'ent**IST, **sci'ent**ISM, nn.; *the dismal ~*, political economy). 5. Expert's skill as opp. strength or natural ability, esp. in pugilism or other fighting. 6. *~ fiction*, fanciful fiction dealing with space travel, life on other planets, etc. [ME, f. OF f. L *scientia* (*scire* know, -ENCE)]

scien'ter (sī-), adv. (legal). Wittingly. [L (prec., -ENT, *-er* adv. term.)]

scientif'|ic (sī-), a. (Of investigations etc.) according to rules laid down in science for testing soundness of conclusions, systematic, accurate; of, used or engaged in, esp. natural science (*~ic instruments*, *books*, *terminology*, *men*); (of act or agent) assisted by expert knowledge (*a ~ic boxer*, *game*; *~ic cruelty*). Hence **~**ICALLY adv. [f. LL *scientificus*, see SCIENCE, -FIC]

scil'icet (sī-), adv. (abbr. *sc.*, *scil.*). To wit, that is to say, namely, (introducing word to be supplied or explanation of ambiguous one). [L, = *scire licet* it is permitted to know]

Scillōn'ian (sī-), a. & n. (Native, inhabitant) of the Scilly Isles. [f. *Scill*(*y*)+ *-onian* (perh. after *Devonian*)]

scim'itar (sī-), n. Oriental curved sword usu. broadening towards point. (16th c. f. Pers. *šešmīr* sabre, F *cimeterre*, It. *scimilarra* etc.; ult. orig. unkn.]

scintill'a (sī-), n. Spark, atom, (esp. *not a ~ of evidence* etc.). [L]

scin'till|āte (sī-), v.i. Sparkle, twinkle, emit sparks; also fig. of witty talk etc. So **~**ANT a., **~**A'TION n. [f. L *scintillare* (prec.), -ATE[3]]

sci'ol|ist (sī-), n. Superficial pretender to knowledge, smatterer. Hence or cogn. **~**ISM(2) n., **~is'tic** a. [f. LL *sciolus* smatterer (*scire* know), -IST]

sciol'tŏ (shŏ-), mus. direction. In free manner, according to taste; staccato. [It.]

sciomachy. See SCIAMACHY.

sci'on (sī-), n. Shoot of plant, esp. one cut for grafting or planting; descendant, young member of (esp. noble) family. [ME, f. OF *cion*, *sion*, (mod. *scion*), ult. f. Frank. *kitho* KID[1]]

Sci'ŏt(e) (sī-), a. & n. (Inhabitant) of Scio, the ancient Chios. [-OT[2]]

scir'e fā'ciās (sīrī, -shī-), n. Writ to enforce or annul judgement, patent, etc. [L, = let (party) know]

scirocco. See SIROCCO.

scirrh|us (sī'rus, skī-), n. Hard tumour as early stage of cancer. Hence or cogn. **~**'OID, **~**'OUS, aa., **~**ŏs'ITY, n. [L, f. Gk *skir*(*r*)*os* (*skiros* hard)]

sciss'el (sī-), n. Waste clippings of metal or remainder of metal plate from which discs have been punched in coining. [f. F *cisaille* f. *ciseau* CHISEL, -AL(2)]

sciss'ile (sī-), a. Able to be cut. [f. L *scissilis* (*scindere sciss-* cut, -IL)]

scission (sī'shn), n. Cutting, being cut, division, split. [F, f. LL *scissionem* (prec., -ION)]

sciss'or (sīz'or), v.t. Cut (*off*, *up*, *into*, etc.) with scissors; clip out or *out* (cutting from book etc.), whence **~**ING[1](2) n. [f. foll.]

sciss'ors (sīz'orz), n. pl. Instrument for cutting fabrics, paring nails, etc., made of two blades with handles for thumb & one finger or the fingers & so pivoted that their cutting edges work by leverage against each other (often *pair of ~*; *I want a pair of*, *some*, *~*; *where are my ~?*; *buttonhole ~*, with gaps in blades near pivot so that cutting begins inside edge of cloth; *lamp*, *nail*, *~*, of special shapes for trimming wicks, nails; *~ & paste*, compiling of books out of cuttings from others); *scissor-bill*, the bird SKIMMER; *scissor-bird* or *-tail*, kinds of bird with long forked tail esp. fork-tailed fly-catcher; *scissor-tooth*, tooth in carnivora acting like *~* against one in other jaw. Hence **sciss'or**WISE (sīz'or-) adv. [ME *sisoures* f. OF *cisoires* f. LL *cisoria* pl. of *cisorium* (as CHISEL, -ORY)]

sci'ūr|ine (sī-), a. Of the squirrel tribe; squirrel-like. So **~**OID a. [f. L f. Gk *skiouros* squirrel + -INE[1]]

Sclav, Sclavonic, etc. See **Slav** etc.

scler'|a, n. = SCLEROTIC n. (anat.). Hence **~**IT'IS, **~**ŏT'OMY, nn. [f. fem. of Gk *sklēros* hard]

sclerī'asis, n. (path.). Hardening of tissue. [mod. L (foll., -ASIS) after *elephantiasis*]

sclēr'(o)-, comb. form of Gk *sklēros* hard: *~ench'yma* (-ngk-), hard tissue of coral, tissue forming hard parts of plants such as nut-shell or seed-coat; *~oderm'*(*at*)*ous*, with hard outer skin (of reptiles, fish, etc.); *~'ogen*, hard matter deposited on inner surface of plant-cells, e.g. that lining walnut shell; *~omēn'inx*, DURA MATER; *~oskel'eton*, hard parts resulting from ossification of tendons as in turkey's leg etc.; *~os'teous*, of the nature of *~*o-skeleton.

sclēr'oid, a. (bot., zool.). Of hard texture. [f. Gk *sklēros* hard + -OID]

sclērōm'a, sclērōs'is, nn. (pl. *~mata*, *-sēs*). Morbid hardening of tissue; (bot.; *-sis*) hardening of cell-wall by SCLEROgen. Hence **sclēr'**ŌSED[2] (-st) a. [Gk (*sk*-), see SCLERO-, -OMA, -OSIS]

sclērŏt'ic, a. & n. 1. Of, with, sclerosis; of the *~*. 2. n. Membrane coating eye round iris, white of eye; hence **sclērŏt**IT'IS n. [SCLERO-, -OTIC]

sclēr'ous, a. (path., anat., bot.). Indurated, bony. [Gk *sklēros* hard, -OUS]

scŏbs, n. Sawdust, shavings, filings, dross. So **scŏb'**IFORM a. (bot., of seeds). [L]

scŏff[1], n., & v.i. 1. Mocking words, taunt, gibe; object of ridicule, laughing-stock. 2. v.i. Speak derisively esp. of religion or object of respect; aim ~s or mockery *at*; hence ~'ER[1] n., ~'ingLY[2] adv. [vb f. n., ME *scof*, perh. f. Scand.; cf. early mod. Da. *skuf*, *skof* jest, mockery]

scŏff[2], n., & v.t. & i. (sl.). 1. Food, meal, grub. 2. vb. Eat greedily. [(1) Afrikaans (now *skof*), repr. Du. *schoft* quarter of a day (hence, meal); (2) vb orig. a var. of dial. *scaff* (16th c.) & assoc. w. (1)]

scŏld, v.i. & t., & n. 1. Find fault noisily, rail; rate, rebuke, (chiefly of parent, employer, speaking to child, servant), whence scŏl'dING[1](1) n. 2. n. Railing or nagging woman. [vb f. n., ME, app. f. ON *skáld* SCALD[2]]

scŏl'ex, n. (pl. *-ĕ'cēs*). Head of larval or adult tapeworm. [f. Gk *skōlēx* worm]

scŏli|ōs'is, n. Lateral curvature of spine. Hence ~ŏT'IC a. [mod. L, f. Gk f. *skolios* crooked, -OSIS]

scollop. See SCALLOP.

scŏlopā'ceous (-shus), scŏl'opacĭne, aa. Of, like, the snipes. [f. LL f. Gk *skolopax* snipe, see -ACEOUS, -INE[1]]

scŏlopĕn'drine, a. Of, like, related to, centipede(s). [f. L f. Gk *skolopendra* millepede, -INE[1]]

scŏlopĕn'drium, n. Kinds of fern, hart's--tongue etc. [L, f. Gk *skolopendrion* (prec.)]

scŏm'b|er, n. Mackerel or kinds of fish allied to it. Hence ~rID[3](1) n., ~roID a. & n. [L, f. Gk *skombros*]

scŏn. Var. of SCONE.

scŏnce[1], n. Flat candlestick with handle; bracket candlestick to hang on wall. [ME, f. OF *esconse* lantern or med. L *sconsa* f. L *absconsa* fem. p.p. of ABSCOND- *ere* hide]

scŏnce[2], n. (Old joc. term for) head, crown of head (*a crack on the* ~). [perh. a use of prec. or foll.]

scŏnce[3], n. Small fort or earthwork, usu. covering a ford, pass, etc.; (arch.) shelter, screen. [16th c., f. Du. *schans*]

‖ scŏnce[4], v.t., & n. 1. (At Oxford) inflict forfeit of beer etc. for offence against table etiquette upon (member of company or his offence; *Jones was, Latin quotations are*, ~*d*); (hist., of university officials etc.) fine for breach of discipline (*Vice-Chancellor* ~*d all that were without their hoods*). 2. n. The forfeit. [orig. unkn.]

‖ scŏne, n. Soft cake of barley-meal or wheat-flour of size for single portion cooked on griddle. [perh. f. MDu. *schoon(brot)*, MLG *schon-* fine (bread)]

scŏŏp, n., & v.t. 1. Short-handled deep shovel for taking up & transferring such things as grain, sugar, coal, specie; large long-handled ladle-shaped dipping-vessel for liquids; gouge-like instrument e.g. for surgical use or for helping cheese; coal-scuttle; motion as of, act of, ~ing (*with a, at one*, ~); large profit made quickly or by anticipating competitors; exclusive piece of news for newspaper;

~*net*, formed for sweeping river-bottom, also hand-net for catching bait; ~*wheel*, with buckets on circumference raising water for irrigation etc. 2. v.t. Lift (usu. *up*), hollow (usu. *out*), (as) with ~ ; secure (large profit etc.) by sudden action or stroke of luck; forestall (rival newspaper, reporter, etc.) with ~. [ME, f. MDu., MLG *schōpe* bucket etc., & MDu. *schoppe*, MLG *schuppe* shovel]

scoop'er, n. In vbl senses; esp.: engraver's tool; kind of avocet. [-ER[1]]

scoot, v.i. (sl.). Run, dart, make off. Hence ~'ER[1](2) n., child's toy propelled by foot and consisting of a footboard with two wheels set tandemwise and a long steering-handle, (also, in full *motor* ~*er*) simple motor cycle. [18th c. (naut.) *scout*; later *scoot* from U.S.]

scŏp'a, scŏp'ŭla, nn. (entom.; pl. *-ae*). Small brushlike tuft of hairs esp. on bees' legs. Hence scŏp'ATE[2], scŏp'ŭLATE[2], scŏp'iFORM, scŏp'ŭliFORM, scŏpiF'EROUS, aa. [*scopa* sing. of L *scopae*, = twigs, broom; *-la* LL dim.]

scōpe, n. 1. End aimed at, purpose, intention, (now rare). 2. Outlook, purview, sweep or reach or sphere of observation or action, tether, extent to which it is permissible or possible to range, opportunity, outlet, vent, (*mind, undertaking, of wide* ~ ; *is beyond my* ~ ; *gives no, ample*, ~ *for expatiating, to ability*; *seeks* ~ *for his energies*). 3. (naut.). Length of cable out when ship rides at anchor. [f. It. *scopo* f. Gk *skopos* target (*skeptomai* look at)]

-scope, suf. repr. L f. Gk -*skopion* f. *skopein* observe. *Horoscope* is f. Gk *hōroskopos*, (watcher of) a nativity. *Telescope* is f. Gk *tēleskopos*, far-seeing. In wds of mod. formation the suf. usu. has the sense *instrument for observing or showing*, as *stetho*~, *gyro*~, *laryngo*~, and the hybrid *muto*~. Hence -*scŏp'ic*, adj. suf., pertaining to the -scope, occas. w. extended meaning also, as in TELESCOPIC, MICROSCOPIC; -*scopy*, n. suf., use of or examination by the -scope, as *laryngoscopy*.

scŏrbūt'|ic, a. & n. Of, like, (person) affected with, scurvy. Hence ~ICALLY adv. [f. obs. *scorbut(e)* f. F *scorbut* scurvy prob. f. MLG *schorbūk* (*schoren* break, *būk* belly) +-IC]

scŏrch, v.t. & i., & n. 1. Burn surface of with flame or heat-rays so as to discolour or injure or pain, affect with sensation of burning (*a wit that* ~*es*), whence ~'ING[3] a., ~'ingLY[2] adv.; ~*ed earth policy*, burning crops etc. and removing or destroying anything that might be of use to an enemy occupying the country; become discoloured etc. with heat. 2. (sl.). (Of motorist or cyclist) go at utmost speed; (n.) spell of such driving or riding. [ME, of obsc. orig.; cf. ME *skorken*, *skorkle* in same sense]

scŏrch'er, n. In vbl senses; (also, (sl.) fine specimen of its kind. [-ER¹]

scōre, n., & v.t. & i. **1.** Notch cut or line cut or scratched or drawn (*rock covered with ~s or striations; the ~s of the whip showed on his back; made a ~ in the tally; lightning had made ~s in the mountain side*); mark showing starting-point in race or standing-place in shooting-match (now rare; hence perh. *go off at ~*, start off vigorously esp. to discourse on pet subject); (naut.) groove in block or dead--eye to hold strap. **2.** Running account kept by ~s against customer's name esp. for drink in old inns, reckoning esp. for entertainment, (*pay · one's ~*, settle reckoning; *death pays all~s ; pay off old~s*, fig., pay person out for past offence; so *quit~s with*). **3.** Number of points made by player or side in some games, register of items of this, (*make a good ~ ; what is the~ now? ; ~-book, -card, -sheet*, prepared for entering esp. cricket-~ in; *keep ~*, register it as it is made). **4.** (mus.). Copy of a composition on set of staves braced & barred together (named from bar drawn through all staves; *full ~*, with separate staff for each part; *compressed, close, short, ~* in vocal music, with treble & alto on one staff, tenor & bass on another; *in ~*, with parts arranged below each other & corresponding. **5.** Twenty, set of twenty, (for use of ~, ~s, see DOZEN; *three ~ & ten*, phr. for normal length of human life; *~s of people*, great numbers); weight of twenty (or twenty-one) pounds, esp. in weighing pigs or oxen. **6.** Category, head, (*rejected on the ~ of absurdity*, as being absurd; *you may be easy on that ~*, so far as that matter is concerned). **7.** ‖ (sl.). Remark or act by which person ~s off another (*given to making cheap ~s*); piece of good fortune (*what a ~!*). **8.** vb. Mark with notches or incisions or lines, slash, furrow, make (line etc.) with something that marks, (*~ out words*, draw line through them; *~ under*, underline); *criticize severely. **9.** Mark *up* in inn-~, enter (item of debt *against* or *to* customer; often *up*); (fig.) mentally record (offence *against* or *to* offender); record (point in cricket etc. ~; abs., keep the~, whence **scōr'ER¹** n.). **10.** Win & be credited with (*has ~d a success, a century at cricket*), make points in game (*failed to ~*), secure an advantage or have good luck (*that is where he ~s ; we shall ~ by it*); ‖ *~ off* (sl.), worst in argument or repartee, inflict some humiliation on. **11.** (mus.). Orchestrate, whence **scōr'ING¹** (6) n., arrange *for* another instrument, write out in ~. [OE *scoru* f. ON *skor* notch, tally, twenty, f. Gmc **skur-*, **sker-*, see SHEAR]

scŏr'|ia, n. (pl. *~iae*). Cellular lava or fragments of it. Hence ~**ıA'CEOUS** (-*āshus*) a. [L, f. Gk *skŏria* refuse (*skŏr* dung)]

scŏr'i|fŷ, v.t. Reduce to dross, assay (precious metal) by ~fying a portion of its ore fused with lead & borax. Hence~**FICA²-TION, ~fiER¹** (2), nn. [prec., -FY]

scŏrn, n., & v.t. **1.** Disdain, contempt, derision, (*think ~ of*, despise; LAUGH to ~), whence ~**'FUL** a., ~**'fulLY²** adv., ~**'fulNESS** n.; object of contempt, (usu. *a ~ to, the ~ of*, persons etc.). **2.** v.t. Hold in contempt, consider beneath notice, abstain from or refuse to do as unworthy (*~s lying, a lie, to lie*); hence ~**'ER¹** n. (arch. exc. w. *of*). [ME *skarn, scorne*, etc. f. OF *esc(h)arn(ir)* f. WG, cf. OS, OHG *skern* mockery]

Scŏrp'iō, n. Zodiacal constellation & eighth sign of zodiac, the Scorpion. [L, also *scorpius* f. Gk *skorpios* scorpion]

scŏrp'ioid, n. & a. (bot.). (Inflorescence) curled up at end like scorpion's tail & uncurling as flowers develop. [f. Gk *skorpioeidēs* (prec., -OID)]

scŏrp'ion, n. **1.** Arachnid with lobster-like claws & jointed tail that can be bent over to inflict poisoned sting on prey held in claws, falsely reputed to sting itself to death if encircled with fire & to contain a substance serving as antidote for its poison. **2.** (bibl.). Whip armed with metal points (1 *Kings* xii. 11). **3.** (*S~*)=SCORPIO. **4.** Kind of ballista. **5.** *~-broom*, kind of genista; *~-fish*, kind with spines on head & fins; *~-plant*, Javan orchid with creamy white flower, also *~-broom*; *~--shell*, kind of shellfish with long spines fringing outer lip of aperture; *~-thorn, ~-broom*. [ME, f. OF, f. L *scorpionem* SCORPIO]

scŏrzonē̆r'a, n. Black salsify or viper's--grass, a plant with parsnip-like root used as vegetable. [It., f. *scorzone* venomous snake]

Scŏt¹, n. (hist.). Payment corresponding to modern tax, rate, or other assessed contribution (*pay ~ & lot*, share pecuniary burdens of borough etc.); *~-free* (in mod. use), not having to pay (rare), (usu.) unharmed, unpunished, safe, (esp. *go ~--free*). [ME, f. ON *skot* (also, partly, f. OF *escot* f. same Gmc orig.), corresp. to OE *sc(e)ot*, see SHOT³]

Scŏt², n. (Pl.) Gaelic tribe that migrated from Ireland to Scotland about 6th c. (often PICTS *& ~s*); native of Scotland. [OE *Scottas* pl., f. LL *Scottus*]

Scŏtch¹, a. & n. **1.** Of Scotland or its inhabitants, in the dialect(s) of English spoken in Lowlands of Scotland, (the ~ themselves usu. prefer the form *Scottish* also used by the English esp. in dignified style or context, or *Scots* rare in Engl. use exc. in compliment to ~ hearers; *the ~, ~ people or nation*; ~ FIR, KALE, MIST; POUND¹ *Scots*; ~ *broth*, soup or liquid stew with pearl barley and vegetables; ~ *cap*, of shapes worn with Highland costume, Glengarry, Tam-o'-Shanter, etc.; ~ *catch* or *snap* in music, short note on the beat followed by long one occupying remainder of beat; ~ *collops*, steak & onions; ~ *pebble*, kinds of agate & jasper, cairngorm, etc.; ~ *terrier*, small rough-haired short-legged kind; ~ *whisky*, kind distilled in Scotland esp. from malted barley; ~ *woodcock*, eggs on anchovy toast; ‖ ~-*&-English*, prisoners' base); ~'*man*, *Scots'man*, ~'*woman*, *Scots*-*woman*, natives of Scotland (*Flying Scots-man*, a London–Edinburgh express). 2. n. The ~ dialect of English (Sc. *Scots*; also *Lowland* ~; BROAD ~); ~ whisky (~ *& soda*, glass of this with soda-water). [contr. of SCOTTISH]

scotch[2], v.t., & n. (arch.). **1.** Make incisions in, score, wound without killing, slightly disable, (esp. ' We have ~'d the snake, not killed it ', see *Macbeth* III. ii. 13). **2.** n. Slash, mark on ground for HOP[2]-~. [ME; orig. unkn.]

scotch[3], n., & v.t. **1.** Wedge or block placed before wheel etc. to prevent motion downhill. **2.** v.t. Hold up (wheel, barrel) with ~. [orig. unkn.]

scot'er, n. Large sea-duck. [orig. unkn.]

sco'tia (-sha), n. Concave moulding esp. in base of column. [L, f. Gk *skotia* darkness (SCOTO-) w. ref. to shadow produced]

Scot'|ism, n. (hist.). Metaphysical doctrines of Duns Scotus (d. 1308). So ~IST(2) n. [L *Scotus* the Scot, -ISM]

Scot'land Yard. (Used for) the Criminal Investigation Department of the Metropolitan Police, the headquarters of the detection of crime. [*Great, New*, ~, successive headquarters of Metropolitan Police]

scot'o-, comb. form of Gk *skotos* darkness; ~*din'ia*, giddiness [Gk *dinē* whirl]; ~*graph*, machine for writing in darkness. **scotom'a**, n. (path.; pl. ~*ta*). Obscuration of part of the field of vision. [LL, f. Gk *skotōma* f. *skotoō* darken (prec., -OMA)]

Scots. See SCOTCH[1]; (in regimental titles) *Reyal* ~, *Royal* ~ *Fusiliers*, ~ *Greys*, ~ *Guards*. [orig. *Scottis*, north. var. of SCOTTISH]

Scot(t)ice (skŏt'ĭsē), adv. In Scotch. [mod. L (LL *Scot(t)icus* Scotch)]

Scott'icism, -ŏti-, n. Scotch phrase, word, or idiom. [as prec., -ISM(4)]

Scott'icize, -ise (-īz), -ŏti-, v.i. & t. Imitate the Scotch in idiom or habits; imbue with, model on, Scotch ways. [prec., -IZE]

Scott'ish, a. See SCOTCH[1]; (in regimental titles) *King's Own* ~ *Borderers*, ~ *Rifles*, *London* ~. [SCOT[2], -ISH[1]]

scoun'drel, n. Unscrupulous person, villain, rogue, rascal. Hence ~-DOM, ~ISM(3), nn., ~LY[1] a. [16th c., of unkn. orig.]

scour[1] (-owr), v.t., & n. **1.** Cleanse or brighten by friction (~ *metal*, with sand etc.; ~ *clothes* etc., with soap or chemicals); (of water, or person with water) clear out (channel, harbour, pipe, etc.) by

flushing or flowing through or over; (of drug, physician, etc.) purge (bowels) drastically (~ *worms*, purge them by placing in damp moss etc. to fit them for bait); clear (rust, stain, etc.) *away, off*, by rubbing etc. (also fig.); ~*ing-rush*, kind of HORSE[1]-tail with silicious coating used for polishing wood etc.; hence (-)~'ER[1](1, 2) n. **2.** n. Clearing action of swift current on channel etc. (*the* ~ *of the tide*); diarrhoea in cattle; substance used for ~ing fabrics. [ME; prob. f. MDu., MLG *schüren* f. OF *escurer* f. LL *excurare* clean (off) (EX-, L *curare* CURE)]

scour[2] (-owr), v.i. & t. Rove, range, go along hastily, esp. in search or pursuit; hasten over or along, search rapidly, (~ *the plain, coast, woods*). [ME, of obsc. orig.; cf. Norw. *skura* rush violently]

scourge (skêrj), n., & v.t. **1.** Whip for chastising persons (arch.); person or thing regarded as instrument or manifestation of divine or other vengeance or punishment (e.g. barbarian conqueror, pestilence, war; *the white* ~, consumption as an endemic disease). **2.** v.t. Use whip on (arch.); chastise, afflict, oppress, harass. [ME; n. f. AF *escorge*, rel. to OF *escorgiee*; vb f. OF *escorgier*; both ult. f. L *corrigia* thong, whip]

scout[1], n., & v.i. **1.** (Mil. etc.) man sent out to get information about enemy or surroundings (*boy* ~, member of organization intended to develop character, resourcefulness, & public spirit); ‖ A.A. or R.A.C. patrol-man; ship designed for reconnoitring; small fast aircraft; ‖ (Oxf.) college servant (cf. GYP[1], SKIP[2]); ‖ (crick.; arch.) fielder; act of seeking (esp. mil.) information (*on the* ~); kinds of bird, auk, guillemot, puffin; ~'*master*, officer directing ~s or boy ~s. **2.** v.i. Act as ~ (esp. *out* ~*ing*). [ME, f. OF *escouter* listen, f. L as AUSCULTATION; n. f. vb]

scout[2], v.t. Reject (proposal, notion) with scorn or ridicule. [f. Scand.; cf. ON *skúta, skúti* taunt]

scow, n. Kind of flat-bottomed boat. [f. Du. *schouw* ferry-boat]

scowl, v.i. & t., & n. **1.** Wear sullen look, look sour, frown ill-temperedly; ~ *down*, master or overbear (person, opposition, etc.) with ~; hence ~'ingLY[2] adv. **2.** n. ~ing aspect, angry frown. [ME, prob. f. Scand.; cf. Da. *skule*]

scrab'ble, v.i. Scrawl, scribble, (bibl.); scratch or grope about to find or collect something (usu. *about*). [f. Du. *schrabbe-len* frequent. of *schrabben* SCRAPE]

scrag, n., & v.t. (-gg-). **1.** Lean skinny person, animal, plant, etc.; bony part of animal's carcass as food, ‖ esp. neck of mutton or inferior part of it; (sl.) person's neck; hence ~g'Y[2] (-gĭ) a., ~g'ĭLY[2] adv., ~g'ĭNESS n., (-gĭ-). **2.** v.t. Put to death by hanging, garotte, wring neck of, (sl.); (footb.) tackle by the neck; (school sl.) squeeze neck of with arm by way of torture. [prob. alt. f. (now dial.) *crag* neck, rel. to MDu. *krāghe*, MHG *krage*]

*scräm, int. (sl.). Be off! [f. foll.]

scrăm'ble, v.i. & t., & n. 1. Make way as best one can over steep or rough ground by clambering, crawling, etc.; take part in physical or other struggle to secure as much as possible of something from competitors (usu. *for*; ~ *for pennies*, of children etc. among whom coin is thrown; ~ *for place, wealth, a living*); (of aircraft) take off; throw (coins etc.) to be ~d for; cook (eggs) by breaking into pan with butter, milk, etc., stirring slightly, & heating; alter frequency of transmitted speech of (telephone conversation) so as to make it unintelligible to an eavesdropper; hence **scrăm'bling**LY² adv. 2. n. Climb or walk over rough ground etc.; kind of motor-cycle race or trial over fields etc., eager struggle or competition for or *for* something. [f. 16th c., symbolic, cf. dial. *scamble, cramble*]

scrăn, n. (sl.). Food, eatables, broken victuals; *bad ~ to —!* (Anglo-Ir.), bad luck to —. [18th c., of unkn. orig.]

‖ **scrănn'el**, a. (arch.). (Of sound) weak, reedy, feeble, (chiefly w. allus. to Milton, *Lycidas* 124). [cf. Norw. *skran* thin, lean]

scrănn'ў, ***scrawn'ў**, a. (chiefly dial.). Lean, scraggy. [cf. prec.]

scrăp¹, n., & v.t. (-pp-). 1. Small detached piece of something, fragment, remnant, (pl.) odds & ends, useless remains, whence ~p'ʏ² a., ~p'ɪLʏ² adv., ~p'ɪNESS n.; picture, paragraph, etc., cut from book or newspaper for keeping in a collection (~-*book*, for pasting these into); ~ *of paper*, negligible promise etc. (w. ref. to violation of Belgian neutrality 1914); (collect.) rubbish, waste material, metal collected for reworking (also ~-*iron*, -*metal*), (~-*heap*, collection of waste stuff, also fig.; ~-*heap policy*, practice of discarding promptly what is past its prime); (sing. or pl.) residuum of melted fat or of fish with the oil expressed (~-*cake*, compressed fish ~). 2. v.t. Consign to ~-heap, condemn (ships, supplies, etc.) as past use, discard. [ME, f. ON *scrap* f. *scrapa* SCRAPE]

scrăp², n., & v.i. (sl.; -pp-). 1. Fight, scrimmage, esp. of unpremeditated kind (*had a bit of a ~ with*). 2. v.i. Have a ~.

scrāpe, v.t. & i., & n. 1. Level surface of, clear of projections, abrade, smooth, polish, shave, or graze, by drawing sharp or angular edge breadthwise over or by causing to pass over such edge (~ *ship's bottom*, clear of barnacles etc.; ~ one's *chin*, shave; ~ one's *boots*, remove dirt from soles by drawing over scraper; ~ one's *plate*, leave no food on; *ship ~d her side, paint, against the pier*; ~ *away*, reduce by scraping; ~ *down*, ~ *away*, also ~ *all over*, & see below). 2. Take (projection, stain, etc.) *off, out*, or *away*, by scraping (~ *off the paint*). 3. Excavate

(hollow) by scraping (often *out*). 4. Draw along with scraping sound, produce such sound from, emit such sound, (~ one's *feet*, in restlessness or to drown speaker's voice, also ~ abs., esp. = draw back foot in making clumsy formal bow; ~ *down*, silence by scraping feet; ~ *bow across fiddle-strings*, ~ *fiddle*, also ~ abs. = play fiddle etc.; *branches scraping against the window*). 5. Pass along something so as to graze or be grazed by it or just avoid doing so (~*d against, along, the wall*; ~ *through* adv. or prep., get through with a squeeze or narrow shave, often fig. of passing examination etc.). 6. Amass by scraping or with difficulty or by parsimony, contrive to gain, (usu. *up, together*; *must ~ up enough for*; ~-*penny*, miser; ~ *acquaintance with*, thrust one's acquaintance on); (abs.) practise economy (*work & ~ as one may*); hence **scrāp'ing**¹ (esp. 2), **scrāp'er**¹(1, 2), nn. 7. n. Act or sound of scraping (*a ~ of the pen*, writing of a, esp. important, word or two e.g. signature); scraping of foot in bowing; awkward predicament esp. resulting from escapade. [ME, repr. OE *scrapian* or f. ON *skrapa* f. Gmc **skrap-, *skrep-*]

scrătch¹, v.t. & i., n., & a. 1. Score surface of, make long narrow superficial wounds in, with nail, claw, or something more or less pointed (*threatened to ~ my face*; ~ *the surface of*, not penetrate far into, also fig.; ~ *a Russian, & you find a Tartar*; *stones ~ed with rude letters or pictures*; *much ~ed with thorns*), get (some part of one) ~ed (*have ~ed my hands badly*); form (letters, representation), excavate (hole), by ~ing, scribble (*a few lines etc.*); scrape without marking esp. with nails to relieve itching (~ one's *head*, esp. as sign of perplexity; ~ *my back & I will ~ yours*, = CLAW² *me*), (abs.) ~ oneself, ~ ground etc. in search (~ *about for stray seeds, evidence*, etc.); scrape *together* or *up*; score (written words etc.) *out* or *through*, strike *off* with pencil etc., ‖ erase (horse's name in list of entries for race, competitor's name), withdraw (horse, candidate, or intr. for refl.) from competition; ~ *along*, sl., manage to live etc. 2. n. Mark or sound made by ~ing (*a ~ of the pen*, signature or written order easily given); spell of ~ing oneself; slight wound (*got off with a ~ or two*); line from which competitors in race start (*toe, come to* or *up to*, the ~, put in appearance at right time, not shirk, often transf.; ~ *race*, with all on equal terms, opp. handicap; ~ *man* or ~, competitor in handicap receiving no start); (pl.) horse-disease with dry chaps above heel; (also ~-*wig*) wig covering part only of head; ~-*cat*, spiteful child or woman; ~-*work*, graffito decoration. 3. adj. Collected by haphazard, ~ed together, heterogeneous, (*a ~ crew, lot, team*). [15th c., app. confus. syn. ME (now dial.) *scrat*, & ME (now obs.)

cratch, both of obsc. orig.; cf. MLG *kratsen*, OHG *krazzōn*]

Scrätch[2], n. *Old* ~, the devil. [f. obs. *scrat* hermaphrodite = ON *skrat(t)i* goblin]

scrätch'|ỹ, a. (Of drawing etc.) done in scratches, careless or unskilful; (of pen) making sound of scratching or given to catching in paper; (of crew etc.) of scratch character, not well matched or working well together. Hence ~ĭLY[2] adv., ~ĭNESS n. [-Y[2]]

scrawl, v.i. & t., & n. **1.** Write (t. & i.) in hurried more or less illegible way; mark (paper etc.) *over, all over,* with bad writing or lines like writing. **2.** n. Piece of bad writing, hurried note or letter. [perh. alt. f. CRAWL[2]]

‖ **scray**, n. Common tern, sea swallow. [cf. W *yscraen*]

scream, v.i. & t., & n. **1.** Utter piercing cry expressing terror, pain, or pretence of these, (of steam-engine etc.) whistle or hoot shrilly; laugh uncontrollably (usu. ~ *with laughter*; ~'ING[1] *farce, fun,* etc., causing spectators to ~, intensely funny); utter, say, in ~ing tone (usu. *out*; ~*ed that she did not dare jump*; ~ *out a curse, order,* etc.); hence ~'ĭngLY[2] adv. **2.** n. ~ing cry or sound (~*s of pain, laughter*); (sl.) irresistibly comical affair. [ME *scræme*, perh. f. OE *scræman*; cf. WFris. *skrieme* weep]

scream'er, n. In vbl senses; also or esp.: kinds of bird, e.g. the swift; (sl.) tale etc. that raises screams of laughter, extraordinarily fine specimen of anything. [-ER[1]]

‖ **scree**, n. (Mountain slope covered with) small stones that slide down when trodden on (often pl. in same sense). [f. ON *skritha* (*skritha* glide)]

screech, v.i. & t., & n. Scream (vb & n.) with, of, fright or pain or anger, or in harsh or uncanny tones (usu. derog. or joc., & esp. w. ref. to disagreeable nature of sound); ~*-owl*, kinds that ~ instead of hooting, ‖ esp. the BARN-owl. [16th c. var. of ME *scritch* (imit.)]

screed, n. Long tiresome harangue (esp. list of grievances) or letter; ‖ one of the fillets of mortar or strips of wood by which a surface to be plastered is divided into compartments. [ME, var. of SHRED]

screen, n., & v.t. **1.** Partition of wood or stone separating without completely cutting off one part of church or room from another, esp. that between nave & chancel '(ROOD-~), decorated wall enclosing court etc. **2.** Movable piece of furniture designed to shelter from excess of heat, light, draught, etc., or from observation (*fire, window, folding,* etc., -~). **3.** Any object utilized as shelter esp. from observation, expression of face or measure adopted for concealment, protection afforded by these, (*prepared the attack behind a* ~ *of trees*; *put on a* ~ *of indifference*; *a cavalry* ~, cavalry thrown out to keep enemy's scouts from getting in touch with main body; *under* ~ *of night*). **4.** Board, often with wire-netting or glass cover, on which notices are posted. **5.** White surface on which moving or televised· pictures or lantern slides are projected; *the* ~, moving pictures collectively. **6.** Body proof against electric or magnetic induction or having property of interrupting other such physical processes. **7.** Large sieve or riddle esp. for sorting coal etc. into sizes. **8.** (photog.). Transparent finely-ruled plate used in process of half-tone reproduction. **9.** (crick.). One of two large movable white wood or canvas erections placed near boundary in line with wicket to assist batsman's sight of the ball. **10.** v.t. Afford shelter to, hide partly or completely, (*from*; often fig. of protecting another from deserved censure etc. by taking blame upon oneself or diverting it). **11.** Show (object, scene) on lantern or cinema ~. **12.** Riddle (coal etc.; ~*ed coal,* from which dust etc. has been removed; ~*ings,* refuse separated by sifting); (fig.) sift & investigate (persons). **13.** Prevent from causing electrical interference. [of obsc. orig.; perh. f. AF var. of OF *escran* in same sense]

screeve, v.i., **screev'er**, n. (sl.). (Be) pavement artist. [ult. f. L *scribere* write]

screw[1] (-ōō), n., & v.t. & i. **1.** Cylinder with spiral ridge called the thread running round it outside (MALE or *exterior* ~) or inside (FEMALE or *interior* ~), metal male ~ with slotted head & sharp point for fastening pieces of wood together with more security than nail (also *wood-, common,* ~) or with blunt end to receive nut & bolt things together (also ~*-bolt*), wooden or metal male or female ~ as part of appliance or machine acting as one of the MECHANICAL powers to exert pressure in various ways, (ARCHIMEDEAN ~; *endless* or *perpetual* ~, threaded revolving shaft engaging with & working cogwheel; *differential* or *Hunter's* ~, arrangement of ~s with threads of different pitch working inside each other giving great lifting-power; *left-handed* ~, advanced by turning leftwards contrary to usu. arrangement; *right-&-left* ~, cylinder with threads in opposite directions at the two ends; *interrupted* ~, with parts of thread cut away; *have, there is, a* ~ *loose,* phrr. suggesting that something, esp. person's brain, is out of working order; *put the* ~ *on,* exert pressure esp. in way of extortion or intimidation). **2.** (Also ~*-propeller*) revolving shaft with spiral blades projecting from ship or airship at stern & propelling it by acting on ~ principle upon water or air. **3.** (Also ~ *steamer,* abbr. *s.s.*) steamer propelled by ~ or ~s. **4.** One turn of a ~ (*give it another* ~). **5.** ‖ Oblique curling motion or tendency as of billiard-ball struck sideways. **6.** ‖ Small twisted-up paper *of* tobacco etc. **7.** Miser, stingy or extortionate person. **8.** ‖ (sl.). Amount of salary or wages. **9.*** ~'*ball* (sl.) a. & n., mad, crazy (person); ~ *coupling*, right-&-left female ~ for joining ends of pipes or rods; ~-*cutter*, hand-tool for cutting ~s; ~'*driver*, tool like blunt chisel for turning ~s by the slot; ~-*eye*, ~ with loop for passing cord etc. through instead of slotted head; ~ *gear*, endless ~ with cogwheel or pinion; ~-*hook*, hook to hang things on with ~ at end of shank to fasten it in with; ~-*jack*, dentist's implement for regulating distance between crowded teeth, (also) carriage JACK[1] worked by ~; ~-*pile*, with ~ at lower end, & sunk by rotation; ~-*pine*, plant with leaves arranged spirally & resembling those of pineapple; ~-*plate*, metal plate for holding ~-cutting dies, also steel plate with threaded holes for making male ~s; ~-*pod*, kind of mesquit with spirally twisted pods; ~ *press*, press worked by simple ~ used esp. by printers & binders; ~-*tap*, tool for making female ~s; ~ *valve*, stopcock opened & shut by ~, valve moved by ~; ~-*wheel*, worked by endless ~; ~-*wrench*, for turning ~s with angular head or nuts, also wrench with jaws worked by ~. **10.** vb. Fasten, tighten, etc., by use of ~ or ~s (~ *up door*, make fast, esp. as practical joke at university; ~ *up person*, ~ up his door; *boards are* ~*ed down*; *his head is* ~*ed on the right way*, he has sense). **11.** Turn (~), twist round like ~, (w. ref. to twisting pegs of fiddle; usu. *up*) make tenser or more efficient (~ one's *courage to the sticking-place*, ~ *up* one's *courage*, gather resolution; *he, the management, wants* ~*ing up*). **12.** Put the ~ upon, press hard on, oppress. **13.** Be miserly. **14.** Squeeze, extort, (consent, money, etc.) *out of*. **15.** Contort, distort, contract, (~ one's *face into wrinkles*; ~ *up* one's *eyes*). **16.** (Of ~) revolve (~ *stiffly, to the right*, etc.). **17.** (Of rolling ball, also of person etc.) take curling course, swerve; hence ~'ABLE (-ōōa-) a. [app. f. OF *escroue*, (mod. *écrou*), female screw, nut, f. L *scrofa* SOW]

screw² '(-ōō), n. Vicious, unsound, or worn-out horse. Hence ~'Y² (-ōōi) a. (also, sl., slightly crazy, having a screw loose). [perh. f. prec.]

screwed (-ōōd), a. (sl.). Drunk, drunken. [prob. f. SCREW¹, -ED¹]

scribā'cious (-shus), a. (rare). Given to writing. [f. L *scribere* write, -ACIOUS]

scrib'ble¹, v.t. & i., & n. **1.** Write (t. & i.) hurriedly or carelessly in regard either to handwriting or composition; be a journalist or author (w. implication, often mock-modest, of inferiority), write poetry etc., whence **scribb'ler¹** [-ER¹] n.; ‖ *scribbling-paper*, *-diary*, for casual jottings; hence ~MENT n. (rare). **2.** n. Careless handwriting or thing written in it, scrawl,

hasty note, etc. [ME, f. med. L *scribillare* dim. of L *scribere* write]

scrib'ble², v.t. Card (wool, cotton) coarsely, pass through scribbling-machine or **scribb'ler²** [-ER¹] n. [prob. f. LG, cf. syn. G *schrubbeln*, see SCRUB²]

scribe, n., & v.t. **1.** Person who writes or can write (rare; *am no great* ~, do not write well); ancient or medieval copyist of manuscripts. **2.** (bibl.). Ancient-Jewish maker & keeper of records etc., also Jewish theologian & jurist of type prevalent in time of Christ; hence **scrib'AL** a. **3.** (Also ~-*awl*) pointed instrument for marking lines on wood, bricks, etc., to guide saw etc., or writing words on barrel etc. **4.** v.t. Mark with ~; *scribing-compass*, for scratching circles etc.; *scribing-iron*, **scrib'ER¹** n., = ~ (sense 3). [ME, f. L *scriba* (*scribere* write)]

scrim, n. Lining-cloth in upholstery etc. [orig. unkn.]

scrimm'age, **scru-**, n., & v.i. & t. **1.** Tussle, confused struggle, row, brawl, skirmish, (usu. *scri-*). **2.** (Rugby footb.; usu. *scru-*; also abbr. *scrum*) tight mass of all the forwards with ball on ground in middle; *scrum half*, the half-back who puts the ball into the scrum. **3.** vb. Engage in a ~; put (ball) in a ~. [varr. of SKIRMISH]

scrimp, v.t. & i. Skimp. Hence **scrimp'y²** a. [18th c., of obsc. orig.; cf. MHG *schrimpfen* contract, wrinkle, & see SHRIMP]

‖ **scrim'shank**, v.i. (mil. sl.). Shirk duty. Hence ~ER¹ n. [orig. unkn.]

scrim'shaw, v.t. & i., & n. **1.** Adorn (shells, ivory, etc.), adorn shells etc., with carved or coloured designs (as sailors' amusement at sea). **2.** n. Piece of such work. [perh. f. person's name]

scrin'ium, n. (Rom. ant.; pl. *-ia*). Cylindrical or other box for rolled MSS. [L, see SHRINE]

‖ **scrip¹**, n. (arch.). Beggar's or traveller's or pilgrim's wallet, satchel. [ME, f. OF *escrep(p)e* wallet, var. of *escherpe*, mod. *écharpe* SCARF¹, f. WG *skerpa*]

scrip², n. Provisional certificate of money subscribed to bank or company entitling holder to formal certificate in due time & to dividends etc.; (collect.) such certificates. [abbr., = (sub)scrip(tion) receipt)]

script, n. **1.** (In law) original document (opp. *copy*). **2.** Handwriting, written characters (opp. *print*); printed cursive characters, imitation of handwriting in type; kind of non-cursive handwriting imitating print. **3.** Text of broadcaster's announcement or talk; typescript of film-play. **4.** ‖ Examinee's written answer. [ME, f. L *scriptum* thing written (*scribere script-* write)]

scriptōr'ium, n. (pl. *-s*, *-ia*). Room set apart for writing esp. in monastery. [med. L (prec., -ORY)]

scrip'tural (-chōō-), a. Founded on,

reconcilable with, laying stress on, appealing to, doctrines contained in the Bible; whence ~ISM(3), ~IST(2), nn.; of, taken from, the Bible (rare; usu. now *scripture* attrib.). Hence ~LY² adv., ~NESS n. [foll., -AL]

scrip'ture, n. **1.** The Bible with or without the Apocrypha (usu. without article; also *Holy S~* or the *S~s*; *a doctrine not found in S~* or the *S~s*; *a* or the quotation from the Bible; (attrib.) taken from or relating to the Bible (*a ~ text, lesson*; cf. SCRIPTURAL). **2.** Sacred book of non--Christian community. **3.** (arch.). ‖ Inscription. **4.** ~*-reader*, person employed to read the Bible to the poor in their homes. [ME, f. L *scriptura* (SCRIPT, -URE)]

scriv'ener, n. (hist.). Copyist, drafter of documents, notary, broker, money--lender; (in mod. use) ~*'s palsy*, WRITER'S cramp. [ME, f. obs. *scrivein* f. OF *escrivain* (SCRIBE, -AN) + -ER¹]

scrobic'ulate, -āted, aa. (bot., zool.). Pitted, furrowed. [L *scrobiculus* (*scrobis* ditch, -CULE), -ATE²]

scrŏf'ul|a, n. Morbid constitutional condition with glandular swellings & tendency to consumption. Hence ~OUS a., ~OUSLY² adv., ~OUSNESS n. [ME, f. med. L sing. f. LL *scrofulae* scrofulous swelling, dim. of *scrofa* a sow]

scrŏll, n., & v.t. & i. **1.** Roll of parchment or paper, book or volume of the ancient roll form; (arch.) schedule or list. **2.** Ornamental design esp. in architecture carved or drawn or otherwise made to imitate ~ of parchment more or less exactly, volute of Ionic capital or of chair etc., head of fiddle, flourish in writing, ribbon bearing heraldic motto, etc. **3.** Any tracery of spiral or flowing lines. **4.** ~*-bone*, turbinated; ~ *gear*, with ~-wheel; ~*-head*, volute at ship's bow; ~*-lathe*, for spiral work; ~*-saw*, fretsaw; ~*-wheel*, cogwheel in shape of disc with cogs in spiral lines on one side causing variation of pace according as outer or inner parts are in action; ~*-work*, ornament of spiral lines esp. as cut by ~-saw. **5.** vb. Curl up (p. & i.; rare) like paper; adorn with ~s (chiefly in p.p.). [15th c. *scrowle* alt. f. ME *scrowe* aphetic f. AF *escrowe* (ESCROW), OF *escro(u)e* strip of parchment etc., f. Gmc, cogn. w. SHRED]

scrōōp, n., & v.i. (Make) grating noise. [imit.]

scrŏt'|um, n. (pl. ~*a*). Bag containing testicles. Hence ~AL a., ~IT'IS, ~OCELE, nn. [L]

scrounge (-j), v.t. & t. (sl.). Appropriate things, cadge; acquire thus. Hence **scroun'gᴇʀ¹** (-j-) n. [cf. dial. *scrunge* steal]

scrŭb¹, n. (Ground covered with) brushwood or stunted forest growth; worn or short-bristled brush or moustache; stunted or insignificant person, animal, or plant; ~*-oak*, American dwarf kinds.

Hence ~b'ʏ² a., ~b'ɪNESS n. [var. of SHRUB¹]

scrŭb², v.t. & i. (-bb-), & n. **1.** Rub hard to clean or brighten esp. with soap & water applied with ~bing-brush; use such brush (*would rather ~ for my living*); (sl.) cancel, scrap; eliminate, or extract for use, certain components from (coal--gas); hence ~b'ᴇʀ¹ (esp., apparatus for ~bing gas), ~b'ɪNG¹, nn. **2.** n. ~bing or being ~bed (*give it, he wants, a good ~*). **3.** *(colloq.).* Player not belonging to regular team; second or weaker team; game of baseball with less than full complement of players; also attrib., as ~*-team*. [ME, prob. f. MLG, MDu. *schrobben, schrubben*, perh. rel. to SCRAPE]

scrŭbb'er, n. In vbl senses: also, apparatus for purifying coal-gas from ammonia & tar by spraying with water. [-ER¹(1, 2)]

scrŭff, n. Back *of the neck* as used to grasp & lift or drag animal or person by (*take by the ~ of the neck*). [corrupt. of SCUFF²]

scrum(mage). See SCRIMMAGE.

scrŭmp'tious (-shus), a. (sl.). Delightful, delicious, firstrate. [arbitrary; cf. GOLUPTIOUS]

scrŭnch. = CRUNCH. [s- as in SCRAG etc.]

scru'ple (-ōō-), n., & v.i. & t. **1.** Weight--unit (in apothecaries' wt) of 20 grains; very small quantity (arch.); feeling of doubt or hesitation on grounds of morality or propriety about acting or approving of action, conscientious objection, (*make no ~ to do*, do without such hesitation or with easy conscience; *have ~s about doing*; *man of no ~s*, unscrupulous; *did it without ~*). **2.** vb. Feel or be influenced by ~s (rare); be deterred from or hindered in (*doing* or n. of action; arch.; *would ~ lying or a lie*) by ~s; hesitate owing to ~s *to do* (esp. w. neg.; *does not ~ to say*). [f. L *scrupulus* (*scrupus* pebble, -ULE); fig. sense thr. F *scrupule*]

scru'pulous (-ōōp-), a. Careful to offend in nothing, conscientious even in small matters, not neglectful of details, punctilious, marked by extreme thoroughness, unfailing, (~ *persons*; ~ *honesty, cleanliness, care, methods, respect, attention*, etc.); over-attentive to details, esp. to small points of conscience, whence **scrupulos**-ITY (-ōōp-) n. Hence ~LY² adv., ~NESS n. [f. F *scrupuleux* or L *scrupulosus* (prec., -OSE¹)]

scrutāt'or (-ōō-), n. Person given to scrutiny (chiefly as signature to newspaper letters etc.). [L (SCRUTINY, -OR)]

scrutin (skrōōtǎn'), n. ~ *d'arrondissement, de liste*, (dǎrawndesmahn', de lēst'), contrasted methods by which voter votes for one or more representatives of small district only, or for large number representing wide area. [F]

‖ **scrutineer'** (-ōō-), n. Person examining ballot papers for irregularities. [SCRUTINY, -EER]

scru'tiniz|e (-ōō-), **-is|e** (-īz), v.t. Look closely at, examine in detail. Hence ~**ingly**[2] adv. [foll., -IZE]

scru'tiny (-ōō-), n. Critical gaze, close investigation, examination into details; official examination of votes cast in election to test their validity when closeness of contest or suspicion of irregularity makes it desirable (*demand a* ~). [ME, f. L *scrutinium* (*scrutari* search)]

scry̆, v.i. Use the crystal in CRYSTAL-*gazing*. Hence ~'ER[1] n. [= (DE)SCRY]

scŭd, v.i. (-dd-), & n. **1.** Run or fly straight & fast esp. with smooth or easy motion, skim along; (naut.) run before the wind. **2.** n. Spell of ~ding; vapoury driving clouds. [16th c., of obsc. orig.]

scu'dō (*or* -ōō-), n. (pl. -*di* pr. -dē). Old Italian silver coin of about 4/-. [It., f. L *scutum* shield]

scuff[1], v.i. Walk with dragging feet, shuffle with the feet. [18th c., of obsc. orig.]

scuff[2], n. Nape (now usu. *scruff*). [18th c., of obsc. orig.]

scu'ffle, v.i., & n. (Engage in) confused struggle in which disputants chiefly push each other about, disorderly fight. [perh. f. Scand.; cf. Sw. *skuffa* to push, cogn. w. SHOVE]

‖ **scŭg**, n. (school sl.). Person lacking spirit, sociability, manners, sportsmanship, etc. [orig. unkn.]

sculduggery. See SKUL(L)DUGGERY.

scŭll, n., & v.t. & i. **1.** One of pair of small oars used by single rower each with one hand; oar resting in nick on boat's stern & worked with twisting strokes to propel like ship's screw. **2.** vb. Propel (boat), propel boat, with ~(s). [ME, of unkn. orig.]

scŭll'er, n. User of scull(s); boat intended for sculling. [-ER[1]]

scŭll'ery̆, n. Back kitchen, room for washing up dishes etc. [ME, f. AF *squillerie*, OF *escuelerie* f. *escuelé* dish f. L *scutella*, see -ERY]

‖ **scŭll'ion** (-yon), n. (arch., poet., rhet.). Cook's boy, washer of dishes & pots. [ME; perh. assim. to prec. of F *souillon* scullion, orig. dirty fellow (as SOIL[2])]

scŭlp, v.t. (Colloq. for) SCULPTURE. [f. L *sculpere*; now regarded as abbr.]

scŭl'pin, n. Kinds of small American sea-fish with large spiny head. [perh. f. obs. *scorpene* f. L f. Gk *skorpaina* a fish]

scŭlp'sit, **scŭlpser'unt**, (abbr. *sc.* or *sculps.*), v. sing. & pl. 3rd pers. (So-&-so) carved or sculptured or engraved (this work; used with artist's signature). [L]

scŭlp't|or, n. One who sculptures. Hence ~FESS[1] n. [L (foll., -OR)]

scŭlp'tur|e, n., & v.t. & i. **1.** Art of forming representations of objects in the round or in relief by chiselling stone, carving wood, modelling clay, casting metal, or similar processes; a work of ~e; (zool., bot.) raised or sunk markings on

shell etc.; hence ~**AL**, ~**ESQUE** (-ěsk'), aa., ~**alLY**[2] adv., (-cher-). **2.** vb. Represent in ~e; adorn with ~e; be a sculptor, do ~e; (p.p., zool. & bot.) having ~e. [ME, f. L *sculptura* (*sculpere sculpt-*, -URE)]

scŭm, n., & v.t. & i. (-mm-). **1.** Impurities that rise to surface of liquid esp. in boiling or fermentation, floating film; (fig.) worst part, refuse, offscouring, (*of*); hence ~**m'y**[2] a. **2.** vb. Take ~ from, skim; be or form a ~ on; (of liquid) develop ~. [ME, f. MLG, MDu. *schŭm* (= OHG *scŭm*), f. Gmc **skūma*; vb f. n.]

scŭm'ble, v.t., & n. **1.** Modify (oil-painting) by painting a thin tint or colour over a darker one. **2.** n. Thin layer of paint over a darker one, modifying the underlying paint. [perh. frequent. of *scum* vb (-LE(3))]

scŭn'cheon (-chn), n. Stones or arches across angles of square tower supporting alternate sides of octagonal spire. [ME, f. OF *escoinson* (EX-, COIN[1])]

‖ **scŭnn'er**, n., & v.t. & i. (Sc.). **1.** Strong dislike (esp. *take a* ~ *at*, *against*), object of loathing. **2.** vb. Sicken, disgust; feel sick, be nauseated. [n. f. vb, ME, of obsc. orig.]

scŭpp'er[1], n. Hole in ship's side to carry off water from deck. [ME, perh. f. OF *escopir* spit; cf. G *speigat*]

‖ **scŭpp'er**[2], v.t. (sl.). Surprise & massacre, sink (ship, crew), do for. [orig. unkn.]

scŭrf, n. Flakes on surface of skin cast off as fresh skin develops below, esp. those of head (also *dandruff*); any scaly matter on a surface. Hence ~'Y[2] a., ~'iNESS n. [late OE *scurf* f. Scand. (cf. OSw. *skorver*), earlier *sceorf* (= OHG *scorf*) f. root of *sceorfan* gnaw]

scŭr'ril|ous, (arch.) **scŭ'rril|e** (e), aa. Grossly or obscenely abusive (of person or language), given to or expressed with low buffoonery. Hence or cogn. ~**ousLY**[2] adv., ~**ITY** (-il'-) n. [f. obs. *scurrile* (. F, or L *scurrilis* (*scurra* buffoon), -OUS]

scŭ'rry̆, v.i., & n. **1.** Run hurriedly esp. with short quick steps, scamper, (*the* ~*ing mice*). **2.** n. Act or sound of ~ing; short fast horse-race (*polo-*~, race for polo-ponies). [perh. shortened f. *hurry-scurry* redupl. of *hurry*]

scŭr'v|y̆, a. & n. **1.** Paltry, low, mean, dishonourable, contemptible, (*a* ~*y trick*, *fellow*); hence ~**ILY**[2] adv. **2.** n. Deficiency disease with swollen gums, livid spots, & prostration, attacking sailors & any who feed on salt meat & lack vegetables; ~*y-grass* [corrupt. of *-cress*], plant of mustard family used against ~y; hence ~**iED** (-vīd) a. [-adj. f. SCURF + -Y[2]; n. subst. use of adj., perh. assoc. w. obs. *scorbut*(e) (SCORBUTIC)]

scŭt, n. Short tail esp. of hare, rabbit, or deer. [orig. unkn.]

scŭt'age, n. (hist.). Money paid by feudal landowner in lieu of personal service. [ME. f. med. L *scutagium*, after OF *escuage* f. *escu* (L *scutum*, shield) +·AGE]

scŭtch, v.t., & n. **1.** Dress (fibrous material, esp. retted flax) by beating; ~·*blade*, ~·*ing-sword*, ~·*ER*¹(2) n., implements for ~ing flax. **2.** n. ~er; coarse tow separated in ~ing flax. [vb f. OF *escoucher, escousser*, f. pop. L *excussare* f. L EX(*cutere cuss-* = *quatere quass*-shake); n. f. OF *escouche*]

scŭtch′eon (-chon), n. = ESCUTCHEON; ornamented brass etc. round keyhole; plate for name or inscription. [ME. aphetic f. ESCUTCHEON]

scute. See SCUTUM.

scŭtĕll′|um, n. (nat. hist.; pl. ~*a*). Small shield, plate, or scale, in plants, insects, birds, etc., esp. one of the horny scales on birds' feet. Hence **scŭt′ĕll**ATE², ~AR¹, aa., ~A′TION n. [mod. L, dim. of SCUTUM]

‖ **scŭtt′er**, v.i., & n. Scurry. [perh. alt. of SCUTTLE³ (·ER⁵)]

scŭt′tle¹, n. (Usu. *coal-*~) metal or other vessel in which small supply of coal esp. for single fireplace is brought & kept. [OE *scutel* = ON *skutill*, OHG *scuzzila* f. L *scutella* dish]

scŭt′tle², n., & v.t. **1.** Hole with lid in wall or roof of house or ship's deck, side, or hatchway-covering; section of motor-·car connecting bonnet and body; ~·*butt*, ·*cask*, water-butt usu. on deck with hole in top for dipping from. **2.** v.t. Make hole(s) in (ship), open sea-cocks of (ship), esp. for purpose of sinking. [ME; identical w. F *escoutille* = Sp. *escotilla* hatchway]

scŭt′tle³, v.i., & n. **1.** Hurry along, scurry, run away, make off, fly from danger or difficulty. **2.** n. Hurried gait, precipitate flight or departure. [cf. dial. *scuddle* f. SCUD +·LE(3)]

scŭt′|um, n. (pl. ~*a*). (Rom. ant.) legionary's shield of oblong, oval, or semi-cylindrical shape; (anat.) knee-pan; (zool. etc.; also *scute*) shieldlike plate or scale, piece of bony armour in crocodile, sturgeon, turtle, armadillo, etc., whence ~AL, ~ATE², aa. Hence ~iFORM a. [L]

Scy̆ll′a, n. ~ & *Charybdis*, six-headed monster living on a rock, & whirlpool, so placed on opposite sides of Straits of Messina that it was hard to steer clear of one without being caught by the other (see Homer, *Od.* xii); *between* ~ & *Charybdis*, between two dangers, between the devil & the deep sea.

scy̆ph′|us, n. (pl. ~*ī*). (Gk ant.) footless drinking-cup with two handles not higher than rim; (bot.) cup-shaped part as in narcissus flower or in lichens; whence ~OSE¹ a. Hence ~iFORM a. [L, f. Gk *skuphos*]

scythe (sīdh), n., & v.t. **1.** Mowing & reaping implement of long slightly curved blade swung over ground by usu. crooked pole about 5 ft long with two short

handles projecting at right angles from it; blade continuing axle of ancient war-·chariot at each end, whence **scy̆thED**³ (-dhd)′a. **2.** v.t. Cut with ~. [OE *sīthe*, ON *sigthr* f. Gmc **segithjaz* f. **seg-* cut, cogn. w. L *secare*]

Scyth′ian (sĭdh-, -th-), a. & n. (Inhabitant) of ancient Scythia, the region north of the Black Sea; = TURANIAN. [L f. Gk *Skuthia* (*Skuthēs* a~), -AN]

‖ **′sdeath** (zdĕth), int. (arch.) expressing anger, surprise, etc. [short for *God's death*]

se-, L pref. = apart, without.

sea, n. **1.** Expanse of salt water that covers most of earth's surface & encloses its continents & islands, the ocean, any part of this as opposed to dry land or fresh water, (*by* ~ & *land*; *at the bottom of the* ~; *jumped into the* ~; *on the* ~, in ship etc., also situated on ~shore; *go to* ~, become sailor; *follow the* ~, be sailor; *put to* ~, leave port or land; *arm of the* ~, deep gulf; *at* ~, away from & esp. out of sight of land, also fig. = perplexed, not knowing conditions etc. or what to do; *between* DEVIL¹ & *deep* ~; *as good* FISH¹ *in the* ~; *when the* ~ *gives up its dead*, at the resurrection; also pl. in same sense, as *beyond, over,* ~ *or* ~*s*, to or in countries separated by ~; *the high* ~*s*, the open ~ outside the three-mile limit to which nearest country's jurisdiction extends; *mistress of the* ~ *or* ~*s*, chief naval power at any time). **2.** Particular tract of ~ partly or sometimes wholly enclosed by land & usu. distinguished by special name (*the North, Mediterranean, Caspian, Dead, Sea*; *inland* ~, entirely landlocked as the Caspian, also rarely of great freshwater lakes; *closed* ~, = MARE¹ *clausum*; *the seven* ~*s*, Arctic, Antarctic, N. Pacific, S. Pacific, N. Atlantic, S. Atlantic, & Indian, Oceans; ‖ *the four* ~*s*, those enclosing Great Britain). **3.** Local motion or state of the ~, swell, great billow, (*a heavy* ~, with great waves; ~*s mountains high*; (of boat etc.) *ship a* ~, be flooded by a wave; *long* ~, with long regular waves; *short* ~, choppy & irregularly agitated; ~ *like looking-glass* or *sheet of glass*, quite smooth; *half* ~*s over*, having drunk too much). **4.** Vast quantity or expanse of (*a* ~ *of troubles, care, flame, upturned faces*; also pl., as ~*s of blood*, ruthless bloodshed). **5.** (bibl.). *Brazen* or *molten* ~, = LAVER². **6.** (attrib. & in comb.). Living or used in or on, of, near, like, the ~ (often prefixed to name of animal, fruit, etc., to form name of marine thing with merely superficial resemblance to what it is named after, as ~ *canary, cucumber, ·fox, raven,* below); ~ *acorn*, barnacle; ~ *air*, air at ~side esp. as recommended for invalids etc.; ~·*anchor*, DRAG²-anchor; ~ ANEMONE; ~·*angel*, ANGEL-fish; ~·*arrow*, flying squid; ~ *asparagus*, kind of soft-shelled crab;

~-*barrow*, skate's egg-case; ~ *bathing*, in ~; ~ *bear*, polar bear, also kind of fur--seal; ~-*bells*, ~shore bindweed; ~-*belt*, sweet fucus, a ~weed with beltlike fronds; ~'*board*, ~shore, coast region, line of coast; ~-*boat*, ship etc. of specified ~going qualities (*is a good, bad*, etc., ~-*boat*), boat which can be lowered quickly in an emergency at ~; ~-*born*, born of the ~ (poet., esp. of Aphrodite); ~-*borne*, conveyed by ~ (~-*borne commerce, goods*); ~-*bow*, rainbow effect in ~-spray; ~'-*breeze*, blowing landward from ~ esp. during day in alternation with land-breeze at night; ~ *breeze*, any breeze at ~; ~-*calf*, common seal; ~ *canary*, white whale (from its whistling); ~ *captain*, (poet., rhet.) great sailor or commander at ~, (in ord. use, chiefly where army-captain is to be excluded) past or present captain of ship in navy or merchant service; ~ *change*, transformation (w. ref. to *Tempest* I. ii. 400); ~ *chestnut*, ~-urchin; ~-*cloth*, used in theatre to represent shore; || ~ *coal*, arch., coal (orig. of coal brought from Newcastle by ~, opp. charcoal etc.); ~ *coast*; ~-*cock*, kinds of bird & fish, also valve by which ~-water can be let into ship's interior; ~ *colander*, brown ~weed with fronds perforated like colander; ~ *cook*, naut. term of abuse; ~-*cow*, sirenian, also walrus; ~ *crow*, kind of gull; ~ *cucumber*, any holothurian, esp. *bêche-de--mer*; ~-*devil*, kinds of fish; ~-*dog*, kinds of seal, also dogfish, also old sailor (esp. of the Elizabethan ~-captains), & see ~-DOG[1]; ~ *eagle*, kinds of fishing eagle; ~-*ear*, ormer; ~ *elephant*, large kind of seal with proboscis; ~-*fan*, kind of coral; ~'*faring* a. & n., traversing the ~ esp. habitually (~-*faring man*, sailor), so ~'faRER[1] n. (rare); ~ *fennel*, samphire; ~-*fight*, between warships; ~-*flower*, ~ anemone; ~ *fog*, caused by difference of land & ~ temperature & extending only short way inland; ~-*food*, edible salt-water (shell)fish; ~-*fowl*; ~-*fox*, long-tailed shark; ~ *front*, part of town facing ~; ~ *furbelow*, kinds of brown ~weed; ~-*gauge*, ship's draught, also kind of sounding--instrument; ~ *gherkin*, ~ cucumber; ~ *gilliflower*, ~ pink; ~-*girt*, surrounded by ~ (poet., rhet., of island etc.); ~-*god(dess)*; ~'*going*, (of ship) for crossing ~, not coasting, (of person) ~faring; ~ *grape*, glasswort, also gulf-weed, also (pl.) cuttle--fish eggs; ~-*green* a. & n., (of) bluish green as of ~; ~-*gull*; ~ *hedgehog*, ~--urchin; ~-*hog*, porpoise; ~-*horse*, creature harnessed to ~-god's chariot having horse's head & fish's tail, also walrus, also hippocampus; ~-*island cotton*, fine quality of long-stapled cotton originally grown on islands off Georgia and S. Carolina; ~ *kale*, kind of perennial with young shoots used as table vegetable; ~ *kidney*, kidney-shaped polypidom; ~-*king*, medi-

eval Scandinavian pirate chief; ~ *lace*, kind of ~weed with long cordlike fronds; ~ *lawyer*, (naut. term of contempt for) captious person; ~-*legs*, ability to walk on deck of rolling ship (*has not yet got his* ~-*legs*); ~ *lemon*, a yellow oval mollusc; ~ *leopard*, kinds of spotted seal; ~--*letter*, official protective letter carried by neutral ship in wartime, describing her cargo, crew, etc.; ~ *level*, level continuous with that of ~ halfway between high & low water (also *mean* ~ *level*) as used in reckoning height of hills etc. & for barometric standard (*corrected to* ~ *level*); ~ *lily*, crinoid; ~-*line*, horizon at ~; ~ *lion*, kinds of large eared seal, esp. one with mane; || *Sea Lord*, naval member of the Board of Admiralty; ~'*man* (pl. -*men*), sailor, (nav.) rating of executive or upper-deck branch (ABLE-*bodied* ~*man*; *ordinary* ~*man*, below rating of A.B.), person expert in the practice of nautical matters, whence ~'*man*LIKE, ~'*man*LY[1], aa., ~'*man*SHIP(3) n.; ~-*mark*, beacon, lighthouse, etc., or elevated conspicuous object, used to direct course at ~; ~-*mat*, polyzoan forming flat matted coralline; ~ *melon*, kind of holothurian; ~-*mew*, gull; ~ *mile*, geographical MILE; ~ *monster*, any huge, terrible, or strange ~--*animal*; ~ *moss*, mosslike polyzoan or ~weed; ~-*mouse*, an iridescent ~-worm; ~ *mud*, saline deposit of salt marshes etc. used as manure; ~ *necklace*, string of whelk egg-cases; ~ *needle*, garfish; ~ *nettle*, jellyfish; ~-*nymph*; ~ *oak*, kind of ~weed; ~ *ooze*, ~ mud; ~ *orange*, globose orange-coloured holothurian; ~-*orb*, globe-fish; ~ *otter*, kind with very valuable fur; ~-*owl*, = LUMP[2]; ~-*ox*, walrus; ~-*pad*, starfish; ~ *parrot*, puffin; ~ *pass*, neutral ship's passport in time of war; ~-*pay*, for active service at ~; ~ *peach*, *pear*, kinds of ascidium; ~-*pen*, feather--shaped polyp; ~ *pie*, sailors' pie of salt meat etc., || also a shore-bird, the oyster--catcher; ~-*piece*, picture of scene at ~; ~*pi'et*, ~ pie (bird); ~-*pig*, porpoise, also dugong; ~-*pike*, garfish, hake, & other fish; ~ *pilot*, ~ pie (bird); ~ *pincushion*, skate's egg-case; ~ *pink*, ~shore or alpine plant with bright pink flowers, thrift; ~'*plane*, aeroplane constructed for rising from & alighting on water; ~ *poacher*, a small fish; ~'*port*, town with harbour; ~ *power*, ability to control and make successful use of the ~; ~ *pumpkin*, ~ melon; ~-*purse*, skate's egg-case; ~ *raven*, sculpin; ~ *robin*, red gurnard; ~-*room*, clear space at ~ allowing ship to turn etc.; ~ *rover*, pirate or piratical ship; ~-*salt*, got by evaporating ~-water; ~-*scape*, ~-piece; ~ *scouts*, maritime auxiliary to *boy* SCOUT[1]s; ~ *serpent*, kinds of snake living in ~, also (*the* ~ *serpent*) enormous serpentine ~ monster occasionally reported as seen but disbelieved in by naturalists; ~ *shell*, shell of any salt-

-water mollusc; ~-*shore'*, land close to ~, (law) space between high & low water marks; ~'*sick*, vomiting or inclined to vomit from motion of ship etc., whence ~'SICKNESS n.; || ~-*side'*, places or some unspecified place close to ~ as permanent or esp. as holiday residence (*do you like the* ~-*side? ; must go to the* ~-*side*); ~-*sleeve*, cuttlefish; ~ *slug*, ~ cucumber; ~ *snail*, small slimy fish, the unctuous sucker, also periwinkle or similar shellfish; ~ *snipe*, the dunlin, also the snipefish; ~ *squirt*, any ascidium; ~ *strawberry*, kind of polyp; ~ *sunflower*, ~ anemone; ~ *swallow*, tern; ~-*tang(le)*, kinds of ~weed; ~-*toad*, the angler; ~-*trout*, kinds of salt--water trout; ~-*urchin*, echinus; ~-*wall*, wall or embankment made to check encroachment of ~; ~-*ware*, ~weed collected for manure or other uses; ~--*water*; ~-*way*, ship's progress, also place where ship lies in open water (*in a* ~-*way*), also inland waterway; ~'*weed*, any alga or other plant growing in ~; ~-*whip*, whip-shaped coral; ~ *whipcord*, kind of ~-weed; ~-*wife*, fish allied to wrasse; ~-*wind*, = ~-*breeze*; ~-*wing*, a bivalve mollusc; ~'*withwind*, ~-bells; ~-*wolf*, ~ elephant, also kinds of fish, also viking or pirate; ~'*worthy*, (of ship) in fit state to put to ~, strong & well rigged etc., whence ~'**worthi**NESS n. Hence ~'WARD a., adv., & n., ~'WARDS (-z) adv. [OE *sǣ*, OS, OHG *sēo*, ON *sǣr*, Goth. *saiws* f. Gmc *saiwiz*]

seal[1], n., & v.i. **1.** Kind of carnivorous amphibious marine mammal with short limbs modified to serve chiefly for swimming but having fur or hair & beastlike face (*eared* ~ or *otary*, distinguished from *common* ~ by having visible external ears, & including the larger kinds, as sea bear, sea lion, sea elephant, & the fur-~s); = ~ *skin*; ~-*fishery* or ~'ERY n.; ~-*rookery*, ~s' breeding-place; ~'*skin*, skin of ~, or usu. prepared fur of ~s as material for women's jackets etc., jacket of this. **2.** v.i. Hunt ~s. [OE *seolh*, MLG *sēl*, OHG *selah*, ON *selr* f. Gmc *selhaz*]

seal[2], n., & v.t. **1.** Piece of wax, lead, or other such material, impressed with device & attached in some way to document usu. in addition to signature as guarantee of authenticity (*given under my hand &* ~, signed & ~ed by me; *set* one's ~ *to*, authorize or confirm) or to envelope or to any receptacle such as box or room or house to prevent its being opened without knowledge of owner etc. (*leaden* ~, stamped piece of lead holding ends of a wire used as fastening; *under* ~ *of confession, confidence, secrecy, silence*, etc., fig. of communications for which secrecy is stipulated or obligatory); impression stamped on or paper disc stuck to document as symbol equivalent to wax ~. **2.** (fig.). Significant or prophetic mark (*has the* ~ *of death in his face*). **3.** Gem,

piece of metal, etc., serving as stamp to produce ~ on wax etc. or paper (~-*ring*, finger-ring with ~; || *the* ~s, those held during tenure of office by Lord Chancellor or Secretary of State; || *Great S*~, ~ in charge of Lord Chancellor or Lord Keeper used in ~ing Parliament-writs, treaties, & important State papers; || PRIVY *S*~; *Fisher's S*~, papal~ with St Peter fishing as device). **4.** Act done, thing given, event regarded, as confirmation or guarantee *of* (~ *of love*, kiss, birth of child, etc.; *baptism & the Lord's Supper are* ~s *of God's covenant with us*). **5.** Substance used to close aperture etc., esp. water standing in drain-trap to prevent ascent of foul air (~-*pipe*, DIP[2]-pipe). **6.** ~-*wort*, SOLOMON'S ~. **7.** v.t. Affix~ to, stamp or fasten with~, certify as correct with ~ or stamp (*S*~ed *Book*, one of the presumed perfect copies of Book of Common Prayer certified by Great S~ in 1662 under Charles II); show genuineness of (devotion etc.) *with* one's life etc. **8.** Close securely or hermetically, stop up or up, (*my lips are* ~ed, I must not speak; *sleep* ~ed *his eyes*; *is u* ~ed *book to me*, is something of which I have & can get no knowledge; *windows must be* ~ed *up*, e.g. by pasting paper along all crevices; ~ *up tin*, solder it so that air has no access; ~ *pipe* etc., provide it with water~ by means of trap etc.). **9.** Set significant mark on, set apart, destine, decide irrevocably, (*death has* ~ed *her for his own*; *is* ~ed *to* or *for salvation, damnation*, etc.; *his fate is* ~ed); (of Admiralty etc.) officially adopt (design); ß ~ed *pattern*, standard pattern of equipment, clothing, etc., approved for issue by the Admiralty etc. (also fig.). **10.** Confine securely (often *up*); fix (staple etc.) into wall etc. with cement etc. **11.** ~*ing-wax*, mixture of shellac & rosin with turpentine & pigment used for~s. [ME, f. AF *seal*, OF *seel* f. L *sigillum*]

seal'er, n. In vbl senses of SEAL[1], [2]; esp., ship or man engaged in seal-hunting. [-ER[1]]

Seal'yham (-llam), n. ~ (*terrier*), a breed of terrier. [place]

seam, n., & v.t. **1.** Line of junction between two edges esp. those of two pieces of cloth etc. turned back & sewn together or of boards fitted edge to edge, fissure left by gaping of parallel edges (*ship's* ~s *want caulking*); scar, cicatrice; line of separation between two strata; stratum of coal etc.; (anat.) suture; ~ *bowler* in cricket, one who makes the ball move off the ~ when it bounces (also ~'ER[1]); ~-*lace*, ~ing-lace; ~-*presser*, agricultural implement for flattening down furrow-ridges after the plough, also tailors' goose; hence ~'LESS a. **2.** v.t. Unite with ~ (rare); mark or score with ~, fissure, or scar (chiefly in p.p.; ~ed *with wounds, cracks*, etc.); (knitting) make ridges in (stocking etc.); ~ing-lace, galloon or other trimming sewn over ~s in upholstery etc. [OE *sēam*, MDu. *sōm*, OHG *soum*, ON *saumr* f. Gmc **saumaz* f. **sau-*, **su-* SEW]

seam′stress, semp′, (sĕms-), n. Sewing--woman. [OE *sēamestre* (prec., -STER) + -ESS[1]]

seam′y, a. Showing seams (~ *side*, inside of garment etc. where turning-back of seams is visible; chiefly fig. of the less presentable or attractive aspect of life etc.). [-Y[2]]

Seanad Eireann (shăn′adh āī′an), n. Upper Chamber of the legislature of Eire. [Ir., = senate of Ireland]

sē′ance (sā-), *séance* (see AP.), n. Sitting of a society or deliberative body; meeting for exhibition or investigation of spiritualistic phenomena. [F, f. L *sedēre* sit]

sear[1], a. & v.t., sēre, a. 1. (Of leaves, flowers, etc., & fig. of age etc.) withered, dried up (*the ~, the yellow leaf*, old age). 2. v.t. Wither up, blast, (rare); scorch surface of esp. with hot iron, cauterize, brand; make callous (*a seared conscience*); *searing-iron*, for cauterizing. [OE *sēar*, MLG *sōr* f. Gmc **sauza-*; hence OE *sēarian* = OHG (*ar-)sōrēn* vb]

sear[2]. See SERE[1].

search (sĕr-), v.t. & i., & n. 1. Look or feel or go over (person or his face or pockets, receptacle, place, book) for what may be found or to find something of which presence is suspected, probe (lit. & fig.; ~ *a wound, men's hearts*); *~ me !*, int. implying that the speaker does not know (the answer to some inquiry, what to do, etc.); (of shrapnel, gunners) penetrate all recesses of (trench etc.); (arch.) look for, seek out or (still current) *out*; make ~ or investigation (*for* or abs.); (part., of examination etc.) thorough, leaving no loopholes, whence ~′ingLY[2] adv.; hence ~′ER[1](1, 2) n., ~′LESS a. (poet.). 2. n. Act of ~ing, investigation, quest, (*am in ~ of*, trying to find; *the ~ for* or *of*; *right of ~* in internat. law, belligerent's right to stop neutral vessel & ~ it for contraband); *~′light*, electric arc-light with concentrated beam that can be turned in any direction for use esp. for discovering hostile aircraft, enemy movements, etc.; *~-party*, persons going out to look for lost or concealed person or thing; *~-warrant*, granted by justice of peace to enter premises of person suspected of concealing stolen property etc. [ME, f. OF *cerchier* (F *chercher*) f. LL *circare* go round (CIRCUS)]

search′ing (sĕr-), n. In vbl senses; esp., *~s of heart*, misgivings caused by guilt or otherwise. [-ING[1]]

seas′on (-zn), n., & v.t. & i. 1. Proper time, favourable opportunity, time at which something is plentiful or in vogue or active, (*a word in ~*, advice given when it is likely to be taken or is needed;

in ~ & out of ~, at all times without selection; *oysters, venison, strawberries, are in ~*, to be had in good condition & without special difficulty; *the holiday ~*, any of the times when most people keep holiday, ‖ esp. Christmas, Easter, Whitsuntide, or August; *the London, Parisian, ~*, when society is busy or visitors many there; *London in the ~, the theatrical, publishing, cricket, ~*; *close, open, ~*, when hunting etc. of some animal is prohibited, permitted). 2. Period of indefinite or various length (*may endure for a ~*; *a ~ of inaction*; ‖ *~-ticket*, issued at reduced rates for any number of journeys taken, performances attended, etc., within a year, six months, or other period). 3. One of the divisions of the year with distinguishable characteristics of temperature, rainfall, vegetation, etc. (*the four ~s*, spring, summer, autumn, winter, beginning astronomically each at an equinox or solstice but popularly having different dates in different countries; *the dry, rainy, ~*, two ~s recognized in the tropics instead of the four of temperate countries); hence ~AL, ~LESS, aa., ~alLY[2] adv., (-z-). 4. vb. Bring into efficient or sound condition by habituation, acclimatization, exposure, special preparation, use, or lapse of time, inure, mature, (*~ed soldiers, timber*). 5. Make palatable or piquant by introduction of salt, condiments, wit, jests, etc., give zest to, flavour, (*highly ~ed dishes; conversation ~ed with humour*), whence ~ER[1](2), ~ING[1](4), nn., (-z-); temper, moderate, (*let mercy ~ justice*). 6. Become fit for use by being ~ed. [ME, f. OF *seson*, f. L *sationem* (*serere sat-* sow, -ION) in Rom. sense *season*]

seas′onab|le (-z-), a. Suitable to, of the kind usual at, the season (esp.*~le weather*, frost etc. in winter); opportune, meeting the needs of the occasion, (*~le aid, caution*, etc.; *the ~le arrival of*). Hence ~leNESS n., ~LY[2] adv. [ME; prec., n., -ABLE]

seat, n., & v.t. 1. Thing used, esp. one made, for sitting on, chair, throne, stool, bench, or other sitting-accommodation, (*the ~s are uncomfortable*), occupation of a ~ (*took his ~ on the throne, a rock*; *pray take a ~*, sit down), whence ~′ING[1](6) n., *~-ER*[1] n. (motor-car, aeroplane, etc. with ~s for specified number). 2. Part of chair etc. on which sitter's weight directly rests, part of machine that supports another part (*~ of valve*, surface etc. on which it slides or works). 3. The buttocks, part of trousers etc. covering them. 4. Site or location, temporary or permanent scene, abiding-place, of (*the liver is the ~ of disease; the disease has its ~ in the liver; the ~ of war is mountainous; an ancient ~ of learning*). 5. Country mansion esp. with park or large grounds (*has a ~ in Norfolk; the country ~s. of England*). 6. Right to sitting-accommodation or to sit as member of board or esp. House of Commons (*have taken two ~s for* Macbeth; *has a ~ on the Board; lost his* or *the ~,* failed to secure re-election to Parliament). **7.** Manner of sitting horse, bicycle, etc. (*has a good, firm, graceful, ~*); hence ~'LESS a. **8.** v.t. Make sit, place one*self* in sitting posture, (p.p.) sitting, (*took up the child & ~ed him on the bookcase; ~ candidate,* elect him to Parliament; *~ed himself in state; found him ~ed on a reversed bucket; pray be ~ed,* sit down). **9.** Fit or provide (church, room, etc.) with ~s (*is ~ed for 5000*); (of room etc.) have ~s for (number). **10.** Mend ~ of (chair, trousers). **11.** Establish in position, fix in particular place (*~ machinery,* put it on its supports; *a deep-~ed disease*). [ME, f. ON *sæti* = MDu. *gesæte,* OHG *gasāzi* f. Gmc. *(ga)sætjam* cogn. w. SIT]

sèbā′ceous (-shŭs), a. Of tallow or fat, fatty, (*~ gland, follicle, duct,* secreting or conveying oily matter or *~ humour* to lubricate hair & skin). [L *sebaceus* (*sebum* tallow), -OUS]

sèbĕs′tan, -en, n. Plumlike fruit of the tree *Cordia Myxa,* used medicinally in the East & formerly in Europe. [Arab. *sabastān*]

sĕc, a. (Of wine) dry. [F]

sĕc′ant, a. & n. (math.). **1.** Cutting. **2.** n. ~ line, esp. radius of circle produced through end of arc to meet tangent to other end, ratio of this to radius, *~ of angle,* ratio of greater to less of its containing lines as bounded by a perpendicular to either (abbr. *sec; sec 60° = 2*). [L *secare* cut, -ANT]

secateurs (sĕk′atĕrz), n. Pair of pruning clippers. [F, irreg. f. L *secare* cut]

sĕcc′ō, n. Tempera-painting. [It.]

sĕcc′otine (-ēn), n., & v.t. A liquid substitute for glue; (v.t.) stick with ~ (*on, together,* etc.). [P]

sĕcēd|e′, v.i. Withdraw formally from membership of some body, esp. a Church or federal or other State. Hence ~'ER[1] n. [f. L SE(*cedere cess-* go)]

sĕcĕrn′ent, a. & n. (physiol.). **1.** That secretes or can secrete. **2.** n. Secreting organ; drug that promotes secretion. [as SECRETE, -ENT]

sĕcĕ′ssion (-shn), n. Act of seceding (*War of S~,* American civil war of 1861–5 caused by ~ of eleven Southern States). Hence ~ISM(3), ~IST(2), nn., (-shon-). [f. L *secessio* (SECEDE, -ION)]

sĕclud|e′ (-ōōd), v.t. Keep (person, place, esp. one*self*) retired or away from company or resort (*~e* one*self from society; a ~ed spot, life,* etc.). Hence ~'ĕdLY[2] (-ōō-) adv. [ME, f. L SE(*cludere -clus-=claudere* shut)]

sĕclu′sion (-ōōzhn), n. Secluding or being secluded, retirement, privacy, avoidance of intercourse, whence ~IST(2) n.; secluded place. [f. med. L *seclusio* (prec., -ION)]

sĕc′ond, a., n., & v.t. **1.** Next after first (*the, a,~,* often as n. with ellipse of n., esp. = ~ day of month; often further defined, as *the ~ man you meet, was the ~ to come; in the ~ place,* secondly; *~ to none,* surpassed by no other; ~ CLASS; *~ cabin,* ~-class accommodation in passenger-ship; *come in, finish, ~,* be ~ in race; *~ floor,* that two floors above ground-floor; ||*~ distance,* space in landscape between foreground & background). **2.** Other besides one or the first, additional, supplementary, (*~ advent,* return of Christ, esp. as preliminary to His expected personal reign on earth, whence ~-ăd′ventIST n.; *~ ballot,* electoral method by which, if the winner on the first ballot has not polled more than half the votes cast, a ~ is taken in which only he & the next candidate are eligible; *~ chamber,* upper House in bicameral parliament; *~ coming,* ~ advent; *~* DIVISION; *~ nature,* acquired tendency that has become instinctive, as *habit is ~ nature, self-sacrifice is now ~ nature with him;* ~ SELF; *~ teeth,* those of adults, cf. MILK[1]-*teeth;* ~ *thoughts,* opinion or resolution formed on reconsideration; ~ WIND[1]). **3.** Of secondary kind, subordinate, derived, unoriginal, imitative, metaphorical, (*~ cause,* that is itself caused; ~ CHILDHOOD, COUSIN; *~ Daniel, Solomon,* etc., person comparable to these; *~ fiddle, violin,* etc., lower of two employed in score, esp. fig. in *play ~ fiddle,* be of only secondary importance, often *to* other person; *at ~ hand,* by hearsay, not actual observation etc.; ~ INTENTION, SIGHT[1]). **4.** ~-*best,* of ~ quality (*come off ~-best,* get the worst of it); ~-*class,* of ~ or of inferior position or quality (||*~-class passenger, ticket,* using, entitling to use of, ~-class railway-carriage etc.); ||*~-hand,* (of clothes, books, furniture, etc.) bought after use by a previous owner, (of information etc.) taken on another's authority & not got by original observation or research; ~ *lieutenant,* army OFFICER; ||*~-pair back, front,* room on ~ floor in back, front, of house (see PAIR[1]); ~ PERSON (gram.); ~-*rate,* not of superior quality, (of ship, also as n.) rated in ~ class. **5.** n. ~ person etc. in race etc. (*a good ~,* close up); ||~ class in examination for honours, person who takes this. **6.** Another person or thing besides the previously mentioned or principal, whether regarded as next, inferior, or equal. **7.** (mus.). Interval of which the span involves only two alphabetical names of notes, harmonic combination of the two notes thus separated. **8.** pl. Goods of ~ quality, esp. coarse flour or bread made from it. **9.** Supporter chosen by principal in duel or pugilism to see fair play etc. **10.** Sixtieth part of a MINUTE of time or angular measurement (see etym.), (loosely) short time (*wait a ~*). **11.** ~ *in command,* officer next in rank to commanding officer; ~ *of* EX-CHANGE[1]; ~*-hand*, extra hand in some watches & clocks recording ~s; ~*-mark*, mark (″) used with ~-figures in statements of angular measurement or time (*1° 6′ 40″* ; *1 h. 35′ 15″*), or denoting linear inches. **12.** v.t. Supplement, support, back up, (~ *words with deeds*; *will you* ~ *me if I ask him?*). **13.** (Of member of debating body) give the necessary formal support to (motion etc. or its proposer) by rising with or without speech to show that mover is not isolated, whence ~ER[1] n. **14.** (*pr.* sikŏnd′). ‖ (Mil.) put (officer) into temporary retirement with a view to staff or other extra-regimental appointment; ‖ transfer (official) temporarily to another department. [(adj.) ME f. OF *second* f. L *secundus* (*sequi* follow); (time etc.) ME f. OF *seconde* f. med. L *secunda minuta* secondary minute, i.e. minute of a minute; (vb) f. F *seconder* f. L *secundare*]

sĕc′ondar|y, a. & n. **1.** Next below, coming in place or time after, depending on or derived from, of less importance or originality than, what is primary, of the second rank etc., supplementary, of inferior rank or importance *to*, (~*y* COLOUR[1]; ~*y education, school*, for those who have received elementary or primary instruction but not yet proceeded to university or occupation, esp. boys & girls from 11 to 15 years old; ~*y grammar school* (giving an academic education); ~*y modern school* (giving a general and practical education); ~*y technical school* (for those whose abilities are of a more practical character); (geol.) = MESOZOIC; ~*y planet*, planet's satellite); (geol.) = MESOZOIC; hence ~iLY[2] adv. **2.** n. Deputy or delegate; ‖ minor cathedral dignitary; ~*y planet*; feather growing on second joint of wing; insect's hind wing; ~*y strata*. [ME, f. L *secundarius* prec., -ARY[1]]

seconde′ (-awnd), n. Fencing-position. [F (SECOND)]

sĕc′ondly, adv. In the second place (in enumerations. [-LY[2]]

sĕcŏn′dŏ, n. Second performer or lower part in duet (cf. PRIMO[1]). [It. (as SECOND)]

sĕc′recy, n. Keeping of, ability to keep or habit of keeping, secrets (*he promised* ~; *can rely on his* ~; *the gift of* ~; *done with great* ~); tendency to concealment, secretiveness; unrevealed state, being kept secret, (*there can be no* ~ *about it*; *in* ~, in secret). [alt. f. 15/16th c. *secretee*, *-tie* app. f. obs. *secre* or *secret* adjj. + -TY or -Y]

sĕc′rĕt, a. & n. **1.** (To be) kept private, not (to be) made known or exposed to view, privy, (~ *treaty, understanding, errand, door, passage, sin, process, influence*; *the* ~ *parts*, parts of body of which exposure is avoided, esp. the genitals; ‖ ~*-service money*, applied by Government to securing information etc. without obligation to state details of expendi-

ture), whence ~LY[2] adv.; given to or having faculty of secrecy (~ or ~*-service agent*, superior kind of spy), secretive, close, rĕticent, not leaky; (of place etc.) secluded, retired. **2.** n. Thing (to be) kept ~ (*keep a* or *the* ~, abstain from revealing it); thing known only to a limited number (*in the* ~, among the number of those allowed to know it; *open* ~, thing ~ only to those who do not trouble to learn it); mystery, thing of which explanation is sought in vain, (*the ~s of nature*); true but not generally recognized method for attainment *of* (*the* ~ *of health, success, happiness, salvation, is temperance, to try again*, etc.); secrecy (only in *in* ~, ~ly); (R.-C. Ch.) celebrant's private prayer in Mass; (pl.) ~ parts of body. [ME, f. OF f. L *secretus* f. SE(*cernere cret-* sift) put apart]

sĕcrétaire′, n. Escritoire. [F, as foll.]

sĕcrétār′iat(e), n. Office of secretary; members of a government administrative office collectively; administrative office collectively; administrative office building. [F, as foll., -ATE[1]]

sĕc′retary, n. **1.** Person employed by another to assist him in correspondence, literary work, getting information, & other confidential matters (often *private* ~; *unpaid* ~, esp. of person acting as ~ to prominent politician for sake of experience). **2.** Official appointed by society or company or corporation to conduct its correspondence, keep its records, & deal in the first instance with its business (‖ *honorary* ~, abbr. *hon. sec.*, unpaid ~ usu. of society not conducted for profit). **3.** Minister in charge of a Government Office (‖ *the* S~ *of State for Air, the Colonies, Commonwealth Relations, Foreign Affairs, Home Affairs, Scotland, War*, or *the Colonial, Foreign, Home*, etc., S~; *under-* ~, ‖ one of two attached to each S~ of State, one as permanent manager of the connected office, the other usu. as representative in other House of the S~ of State; ‖ *permanent* ~, *under-* ~ as above; ~ *of legation* or *embassy*, ambassador's chief subordinate & deputy); S~ *of State*, (in U.S. & Vatican) chief ~ & foreign minister. **4.** Secretaire, escritoire. **5.** (print.). Script type imitating engrossing-hand. **6.** ~*-bird*, African bird preying on snakes, with crest likened to pen stuck over writer's ear. Hence sĕcrétār′IAL a., ~SHIP(1) n. [ME, f. LL *secretarius* (SECRET, -ARY[1])]

sĕcrĕt|e′, v.t. Put (object, person, one*self*) into place of concealment; (physiol.; of gland or organ or the person etc. of which it is part) produce by secretion, whence ~′OR n., ~′ORY a. [f. L *secret-* (as SECRET); partly f. foll.]

sĕcrē′tion, n. Act of concealing (*the* ~ *of stolen goods*); (physiol.) process by which special substances are separated from blood or sap for service in the organism or for rejection as excretions, any substance produced by such process, as saliva, urine, resin. [F (*sécré-*), or f. L *secretio* (SECRET, ·ION)]

sĕc′rĕtive (*or* sĭkrē⁴·), a. Given to making secrets, intentionally uncommunicative, needlessly reserved. Hence ~LY² adv., ~NESS n., (*or* sĭkrē⁴·). [f. SECRET + -IVE]

sĕct, n. Body of persons agreed upon religious doctrines usu. different from those of an established or orthodox Church from which they have separated & usu. having distinctive common worship, nonconformist or other Church as described by opponents, party or faction in a religious body, religious denomination, so ~AR′IAN a. & n., ~ār′ianISM(2, 3) n., ~ār′ianIZE(3) v.t.; followers of a particular philosopher or philosophy or school of thought. [ME, f. OF *secte*, or f. L *secta* f. stem of *sequi secut-* follow]

sĕc′tarў, n. (arch.). Member of a sect, esp. of the Independents, Presbyterians, etc., at time of the Civil War. [f. F *sectaire* or med. L *sectarius* (prec., -ARY¹)]

sĕc′tile, a. Able to be cut (esp. of soft minerals such as talc). [F, f. L *sectilis* (*secare sect-* cut, -IL)]

sĕc′tion, n., & v.t. **1**. Separation by cutting. **2**. Part cut off from something, one of the parts into which something is divided arbitrarily or may naturally be considered as divided (e.g. length of cane- -stem between two rings), one part of a structure such as boat or wooden house that is made in parts for transportation, one of the minor subdivisions of a book usu. indicated by the ~-*mark* (§; § 20), (mil.) subdivision of the platoon, part of community having separate interests or characteristics (whence ~alISM n., ~alIZE v.t.), (*microscopic* ~, thin slice cut from something for examination with microscope; *subject falls into five* ~s; *last* ~ *of the journey*; *conveyed to Tanganyika in* ~s; ~s *have been preferred to chapters*; ~- *commanders will be responsible*; *popular with all* ~s & *classes*). **3**. Cutting of solid by plane (*conic* ~s, study of curves of intersection produced by allowing plane to cut cone at various angles), representation of internal structure of something supposed to be cut thus (*vertical, horizontal, longitudinal, oblique*, etc., ~, according to position chosen for plane). **4**. (nat. hist.). Group, esp. sub-genus. **5**. The ~ mark (see above) used as mark of marginal reference or with or without number to indicate beginning of ~; hence ~AL (-shon·) a., ~alLY² adv. **6**. v.t. Arrange in, divide into, ~s. [F, or f. L *sectio* (prec., -ION)]

sĕc′tor, n. **1**. Plane figure enclosed between two radii of circle, ellipse, etc., & the arc cut off by them (~ *of sphere* etc., solid generated by revolution of plane ~ round one radius). **2**. (mil.). Any of the parts into which the space occupied by opposing armies is distributed according as each lies within the tactical purview of a headquarters at the focus or centre in rear (also transf., as *the private* ~ *of industry*). **3**. Mathematical rule of two flat pieces working on rule-joint with lines representing sines, tangents, etc., radiating from centre of joint for use in making diagrams etc. Hence ~AL a. [LL, = sector f. L = cutter (prec., -OR)]

sĕctōr′ial, a. & n. (Carnivore's tooth) acting with tooth in opposite jaw like scissors (of specialized molar or premolar). [prec., -IAL]

sĕc′ūlar, a. & n. **1**. Occurring once in or lasting for an age or a century (~ *games*, ancient-Roman festival held at long intervals; ~ *hymn*, composed for this; *the* ~ *bird*, phoenix). **2**. Lasting or going on for ages or an indefinitely long time (opp. *periodical, cyclic*; ~ *change*, going on slowly but persistently; ~ *cooling* or *refrigeration*, that of the earth from fluid state; ~ *acceleration*, slow increase in motion of heavenly body; ~ *fame*, enduring; *the* ~ *rivalry between France & England, Church & State*, etc.). **3**. Concerned with the affairs of this world, worldly, not sacred, not monastic, not ecclesiastical, temporal, profane, lay, (~ *affairs, education, music*; *the* ~ *clergy*, parish priests etc., opp. *regular*; *the* ~ *arm*, hist., civil jurisdiction to which criminal was transferred by ecclesiastical courts for severer punishment); sceptical of religious truth or opposed to religious education etc., whence ~ISM(3)n., ~IST(2)n. & a., ~IZE(3) v.t., ~IZA′TION n.; hence **sĕcŭlă′rITY** n., ~LY² adv. **4**. n. ~ priest. [ME; (in senses lay, worldly, f. OF *seculer*) f. L *saecularis* (*saeculum* generation, age)]

sĕcŭnd′, a. (bot., zool.). Arranged on one side only (as flowers in lily-of-the-valley). Hence ~LY² adv. [f. L as SECOND]

sēcŭn′dō. See PRIMO².

sĕcŭn′dum, L prep. = according to: ~ *art′ĕm*, artificially, also skilfully or scientifically; ~ *natūr′ām*, naturally, not artificially; ~ *quid*, in some respect only, not absolutely or generally, with limitations. **sĕcŭn′dus**. See PRIMUS¹.

sĕcūre′, a., & v.t. **1**. Untroubled by danger or apprehension (*a quiet* ~ *existence*; *dwell* ~); (arch.) confident or unsuspecting (*a* ~ *fool*, dupe etc.; *the* ~ *hope of salvation*); safe against attack, impregnable; reliable, certain not to fail or give way, (*a* ~ *foundation, fastening, foothold, grasp*); (usu. pred.) in safe keeping, firmly fastened, (*have got him* ~; *are you sure it is* ~?); having sure prospect of, safe against or from, (~ *of victory*; ~ *against assault*; ~ *from interruption*); hence ~LY³ (-rlī) adv. **2**. v.t. Fortify (town, harbour, etc., usu. *with* wall etc.); confine, enclose, fasten, or close, (~ *prisoner, valuables, buckle, window*; ~ *vein* etc. in surgery, compress to prevent bleeding; ~ *arms*, mil., hold rifles with lock in armpit to guard from rain); guarantee, make safe against loss, (*loan ~d on landed property* etc.; *how can I ~ myself against the consequences?*; *to ~ the labourer the or in the fruits of his labour*); succeed in getting, obtain, (esp. something coveted or competed for, as *have ~d front places, a first-class cook, the prize, my ends*); hence **secur'ABLE** a. [vb **f. a., f. L** SE(*curus* f. *cura* care)]

secur'iform, a. (esp. nat. hist.). Axe-shaped. [L *securis* axe (*secare* cut), -I-, -FORM]

secur'ity, n. In adj. senses; also or esp.: over-confidence; thing that guards or guarantees (*pride should at least be a ~ against meanness*; *in ~ for*, as guarantee for); organization for preventing leakage of information to enemy (*~-minded*; *~ police* etc.; *~ risk*, person of doubtful loyalty whom it is considered risky to employ on state service); *S~* Council, a body of the United Nations set up to maintain peace and *~*, consisting of five permanent members (China, France, U.K., U.S.A., U.S.S.R.) and six non-permanent members elected for a two-year term; thing deposited or hypothecated as pledge for fulfilment of undertaking or payment of loan to be forfeited in case of failure, document as evidence of loan, certificate of stock, bond, exchequer bill, etc. [ME, f. L *securitas* (SECURE, -TY)]

sedan', n. (Also *~-chair*) 17th & 18th c. vehicle seated for one & carried by two chairmen with poles; enclosed motor-car for four or more persons including driver. [17th c., of obsc. orig.]

sedate', a. (Of person or his manner, look, speech, or writing) tranquil, equable, composed, settled, not impulsive or lively. Hence *~*LY² adv., *~*NESS n. [L *sedare* settle (*sedēre* sit), -ATE²]

sed'ative, a. & n. (Drug, influence, etc.) tending to soothe. [ME, f. OF *sedatif* or med. L *sedativus* (as prec., -IVE)]

sē dēfendēn'dō, adv. In self-defence (as plea in cases of homicide). [L]

sed'entar|y, a. & n. 1. Sitting (*~y posture, statue*); (of person) inclined by nature or driven by occupation to, (of occupation) involving, (of life etc.) characterized by, much sitting, whence *~*iLY² adv., *~*iNESS n.; (zool. etc.) not migratory, free-swimming, etc., (of spider) lying in wait till prey is in web. 2. n. *~*y person; *~*y spider. [f. F *sédentaire* or f. L *sedentarius* (*sedēre* sit, -ENT, -ARY¹)]

sed'er (sā-), n. Ritual for the first night of the Passover. [Aram.]

sēdēr'ūnt, n. Sitting of ecclesiastical assembly or other body, or of a company over the wine or in talk (*had a long ~*). [L, = (the following persons) sat]

sedge, n. Kinds of grasslike plant with jointless stems growing in marshes or by waterside, bed of such plants; *~-warbler, ~-wren,* kind of warbler frequenting *~*.

Hence **sedg'y²** a. [OE *secg* (cf. LG *segge*) f. Gmc **sagjaz* f. **sag-,* cf. SAW¹]

sedil'ia, n. pl. (sing. *sēdil'e,* rare). Set of usu. three stone seats for priests in S. wall of chancel often canopied & otherwise decorated. [f. L *sedile* seat (*sedēre* sit)]

sed'iment, n. Matter that settles to bottom of liquid, lees, dregs. Hence *~*ARY¹ (-ĕn²) a. [F (*sé-*), or f. L *sedimentum* (prec., -MENT)]

sedi't|ion, n. Agitation directed against the authority of a State's executive, conduct or speech tending to rebellion or breach of public order. So *~*ioUS (-shus) a., *~*iousLY² adv., *~*iousNESS n. [ME, f. OF, or f. L *seditio* (*sed-* = SE-, *ire* *it-* go, -ION)]

sedūce', v.t. Lead astray, tempt into sin or crime, corrupt; persuade into surrender of chastity, debauch. Hence *~*'IBLE a., *~*'iNGLY² adv., *~e*'MENT (-sm-; rare), *~*'ER¹, nn. [f. L SE(*ducere* *duct-* lead)]

sedūc't|ion, n. Seducing or being seduced; thing that tends to seduce, tempting or attractive quality of (often with merely playful or no imputation of blame), (*the ~ions of a great capital, beauty, the country,* etc.), so *~*IVE a., *~*iVELY² adv., *~*iveNESS n. [F (*sé-*), or f. L *seductio* (prec., -ION)]

sed'ūlous, a. Diligent, persevering, assiduous, (of action etc.) deliberately & consciously continued, painstaking, (*with ~ care; ~ flattery, attentions; play the ~ ape,* acquire literary style by imitation). Hence or cogn. *~*LY² adv., **sedūl'ITY,** *~*NESS, nn. [L *sedulus,* -OUS]

see¹, v.i. & t. (*saw, seen*). 1. Have or exercise the power of discerning objects with the eyes (*~s best at night*; *cannot ~ till the ninth day*; *~ into millstone, through brick wall,* fig. of preternatural acuteness of intelligence; *~ing is believing,* one's own observation is the best evidence; *~ DOUBLE¹ adv.; ~ red, ~* things as blood-coloured, be filled with fury; *~ing ye shall ~ & shall not perceive; ~ through,* fig., not be deceived by, penetrate, detect nature of). 2. Descry, discern by sight, observe, look at or over, (*come where we cannot be ~n; children should be ~n & not heard; please ~ whether it is there, where it is; ~ the light,* be born or alive, also of conversion etc.; *things ~n,* not imaginary etc.; *~ visions,* be a seer etc.; *~ things,* have hallucinations etc.; *~ stars,* have dancing lights before eyes from blow on head; *was ~n to fall or falling; saw him fall or falling; ~ the back,* be quit of visitor, invader, etc.; *cannot ~ my way; ~* one's *way* to do or to doing, manage, contrive; *~ the sights, town,* etc., as SIGHT¹-seer; *~ over* house etc., go round examining; *worth ~ing,* notable; *~ p. 15* etc., look at, *vide; ~* thing done, supervise doing of it). 3. Learn from newspaper etc. (*I ~ that another speed record was broken yesterday*). 4. Discern mentally, attain to comprehension of, apprehend, excogitate, ascertain by search or inquiry or reflection, consider, (*cannot ~ a* or *the joke, point*; *do you ~ what I mean?*, also ~? ellipt. in same sense' colloq.; *you ~*, parenth., as you no doubt understand, also = I must explain; *I ~*, now that you have explained I understand; *as far as I can ~*, to the best of my understanding or belief; *must ~ what can be done*; *do not ~ the, good, fun, advantage*, etc., *of doing*; *do not ~ how to do it*; *you ~ what it is to have faith*); (part. as prep. or conj.) considering or inasmuch as (*~ing that you do not know it yourself*; *~ing no other course is open to us*). 5. Experience, go through more or less observantly, have presented to one's attention, contemplate & abstain from interference with, (*shall never ~ death*; *have ~n five reigns*; *will never ~ 50* etc. *again*, is over that age; *~ life*, gain experience of men & manners esp. by dissipation etc.; so perh. *well ~n*, arch., accomplished *in*, as intr. p.p.; *have ~n the day when*, in drawing attention to past state of affairs; *never saw such doings*; *has ~n service*, is expert or worn; *has ~n better*, or *its* etc. *best, days*, has declined; *you will not ~ me shot like a dog?*; ~ person or thing *blowed* or *damned first*, before one will do what he asks or trouble about it; *~ thing through* or *out*, not abandon undertaking before it is completed). 6. Grant interview or be at home to, pay visit to, secure interview with, (*refused to ~ me*; *can I ~ you on business?*; *when will you come & ~ us?*; *must ~ the lawyer, doctor*, etc.; *can ~ you for five minutes*). 7. Call up picture of, imagine, (*cannot ~ myself submitting to it*). 8. Recognize as tolerable, consent willingly to, (*do not ~ being made use of*). 9. Escort, conduct, stand by & countenance, (*may I ~ you home?*; *mind you ~ him off the premises*; *saw him off by the Mauretania*; *will you ~ me through*, or *through the difficulty?*). 10. Take view of, have opinion, (*I ~ life, things, it, differently now*; *~ good*, consider it right or expedient *to do*; ~ EYE¹ *to eye*). 11. Make provision, take care, give attention, make sure, (*~ that it is done*; *~ you don't catch your foot*; *~ to* one's *business*; *will ~ about it*, & see below; *~ after*, take care of; *~ to it that*, take care that). 12. Make examination, hold inquiry, (*must ~ into it*). 13. Reflect, take time to consider, (esp. *let me ~*, appeal for time to think before making answer or giving particulars, or confession that coming statement may need reconsideration; *will ~ about it*, form for declining to act at once, & see above). 14. (In gambling etc.) accept or take on (challenge to bet or competition, person offering it). 15. *~-bright*, the plant clary (w. ref. to use as eye-salve founded on pop. etym. of *clary* as = clear-eye). Hence sē′ER¹ n. [OE

sēon, OS, OHG *sehan*, ON *sjá* (f. *séa*), Goth. *saihwan* f. Gmc **sehw-*]

see², n. What is committed to (arch)-bishop, (archi-)episcopal city, (usu. *the ~ of Norwich, Canterbury, Rome*, etc.; *Holy See, See of Rome*, the Papacy or Papal court; cf. BISHOPRIC, DIOCESE; *several new ~s were created*). [ME. f. AF *se(d)* = OF *sie(d)* f. Rom. **sēdes* f. L *sēdes* (*sedēre* sit)]

seed, n., & v.i. & t. 1. Flowering plant's unit of reproduction or germ capable of developing into another such plant, (collect.) *~s* in any quantity esp. as collected for sowing, (*its ~s are, ~ is, black*; *is full of ~*; *drops its ~s* or *~ everywhere*; *to be kept for* or *as ~*; *go, run, to ~*, cease flowering as *~ comes*, fig. grow shabby etc.). 2. Male fecundating fluid, semen, milt. 3. (bibl.). Offspring, progeny, (*raise up ~*, beget children; *the ~ of Abraham*, Hebrews). 4. Germ, prime cause, beginning, *of* (*~s of strife, vice*; *sow the ~s of*, initiate). 5. (colloq.). *~ed* competitor. 6. *~-cake*, containing whole *~s* esp. caraway as flavouring; *~-coral*, in small *~like* pieces; *~-corn*, reserved for *~*; *~-drill*, DRILL²; *~-eater*, kind of bird; *~-fish*, ready to spawn; *~-leaf*, primary leaf or developed cotyledon; *~-lobe*, cotyledon; *~-oysters*, young ones for planting; *~-pearl*, small; *~-plot*, piece of nursery-ground, (fig.) hotbed *of* sedition etc.; *~s′man*, dealer in *~s*; *~-time*, sowing season; *~-vessel*, pericarp; *~-wool*, raw cotton before *~s* have been removed from fibre; hence *~′LESS* a. 7. *vb*. Go to *~*, produce or let fall *~*; sprinkle (as) with *~*. 8. Remove *~s* from (fruit etc.). 9. Separate *~* from straw of (flax); (sport) sort stronger from weaker (competitors) to secure good later matches in tournament. 10. *~ing-machine*, mechanical *~-sower*; *~ing-plough*, with hopper depositing *~* in furrow as made. [OE *sǣd*, OS *sād*, OHG *sāt*, ON *sáth*, Goth. *-sēths* f. Gmc **sǣdh-* f. **sǣ-* SOW]

seed′er, n. Seed-drill; apparatus for seeding raisins etc.; ‖ spawning fish. [-ER¹]

seed′ling, n. Plant raised from seed & not from cutting etc.; young tender plant. [-LING¹]

seed′ly̆, a. Full of seed, going to seed; (of brandy) having flavour attributed to weeds among the vines; (colloq.) shabby-looking, in worn clothes, ‖ out of sorts, feeling ill, whence *~ILY²* adv.; *~y-toe*, disease of horse's foot. Hence *~INESS* n. [-Y²]

seek, v.t. & i. (*sought* pr. sawt). 1. Make search or inquiry for, try or be anxious to find or get, ask (thing *of* person), aim at, pursue as object, endeavour *to do*, make for or resort to (place, person, for advice, health, etc.), (*what are you ~ing?*; *~s a situation as cook, wealth, scope for his energies*, etc.; *sought of him a sign*; *~s my aid*; *~s my life* or *to kill me*; *came ~ing advice*; *sought his bed, a fortune-*

-*teller, the shore*; ~ *dead?*, order to retriever to find killed game; ~ *out*, single out for pursuit etc., esp. make special efforts to secure society of). 2. Search (place, receptacle) *through*. 3. Make search or inquiry *after* or *for* (*sought-after*, much in demand, generally desired or courted). 4. (arch.). Resort in numbers *to* (person, place). 5. *Is* etc. *to* ~ or *much to* ~, is deficient, wanting, or not yet found (*politeness is much to* ~ *among them*; *is to* ~ *in intelligence, grammar*; *an efficient leader is yet to* ~). Hence (·)~'ER[1] n. [OE *sēcan*, OS *sōkian*, OHG *suohhan*, ON *sǿkja*, Goth. *sōkjan* f. Gmc **sōk-*; cf. BESEECH]

seel, v.t. (arch.). Close (eye), close eyes of (hawk), by sewing up lids; (fig.) hoodwink. [later form of obs. *sile* f. OF *siller* f. *cil* eyelash f. L as CILIA]

seem, v.i. 1. Have the air or appearance or sensation of being, appear or be apparently perceived or ascertained *to* do or have done, (*be what you* ~ *to be* or ~; *the man who* ~*ed the ringleader*; ~*s to be tired, a hopeless absurdity*; ~*s to be a good fellow, saint,* etc.; *I* ~ *to be* or ~ *deaf today,* ~ *to see him still*; *do' not* ~ *to*, colloq., somehow do not, as *I do not* ~ *to like him, fancy it*; ~ *good to*, be adopted as best course by; *what* ~*eth him good, arch.*, what he chooses; ~*s to have died at* 35). 2. Appear to be true or the fact (with anticipatory *it* & following *that*-clause, or parenth. with *it* only, often with implication of anger or remonstrance; *it* ~*s to me that it will rain, such talk is absurd, we had better make up our minds to it*; *so we are to get nothing, it* ~*s*; *it* ~*s you were lying*; also *it should* or *would* ~ in same senses; *me*~*s*, ~*eth*, ~*ed*, arch., it ~*s*, ~*ed*, to me). 3. (part.). Ostensible, apparent only, apparent but perhaps not real, apparent & perhaps real, (*the* ~*ing & the real*; *a* ~*ing friend*; *with* ~*ing sincerity*; ~*ing-virtuous* etc., usu. with suggestion of falsity), whence ~'ingLY[2] adv. [ME *seme* f. ON *sœma* f. *sœmr* seemly; cogn. w. SAME]

seem'l|ỹ, a. & adv. 1. Decent, decorous, becoming; hence ~iNESS n. 2. adv. (rare). Decorously. [ME, f. ON *sœmiligr* (prec., -LY[2])]

seen. See SEE[1].

seep, v.i. Ooze out, percolate slowly; also fig. Hence ~'AGE(3) n. [with *sipe*, of dial. orig.; cf. OE *sipian* to soak]

seer[1], n. Prophet, person who sees visions, person of preternatural insight esp. as regards the future. [ME; f. SEE[1] + -ER[1]]

seer[2], n. Indian (varying) measure of weight (in most parts = 2 lb.); Indian liquid measure (about one litre). [Hind. *ser*]

seer'·fish, seir- (sēr-), n. Common Indian scombroid fish. [corruption of Port. *serra* saw]

seer'sucker, n. Crimped striped material

of linen or cotton. [f. Pers. *shīr o shakkar* lit. milk & sugar]

see'saw, a., adv., n., & v.i. 1. With backward & forward motion as of a saw (~ *motion*; *go* ~, vacillate or alternate). 2. n. Game in which two persons sit one at each end of long board balanced on central support & move each other up & down alternately, board thus balanced. 3. v.i. Play at ~; move up & down as in ~; vacillate in policy etc. [redupl. of SAW[1]]

seeth|e (·dh), v.t. & i. (~*ed*) arch. past *sod*; arch. p.p. SODDEN). Cook (t. & i.) by boiling (arch.; prov. *thou shalt not* ~*e a kid in his mother's milk*); (fig.) boil, bubble over, be agitated, (*the* ~*ing waters*; *India was* ~*ing with discontent*; *madness, enthusiasm,* ~*ing in his breast*). [OE *sēothan*, OHG *siodan*, ON *sjótha* f. Gmc **seuth-*]

segar. (Incorrect for) CIGAR.

seg'ment, n., & v.i. & t. 1. Part cut off or separable or marked off as though separable from the other parts of something (e.g. one ring of a worm, one division of a limb or the skull, one wedge of orange-·pulp); (geom.) part cut off by line or plane from any figure (~ *of circle*, part enclosed between arc & chord; ~ *of sphere*, part cut off by any plane not passing through centre), ~ *of line*, part included between two points; ~*-gear*, ·*rack*, ·*wheel*, with cogs occupying arc of circle only; ~*-saw*, with teeth extending over ~ of circle, also circular saw made up of ~al saw-plates, also saw for cutting into ~al shapes; ~*-valve*, closed by slide turning radially across seat; hence ~AL (·ĕn[2]), ~ARY[1], aa., ~aLLY[2] (·ĕn[2]) adv. 2. vb. Divide (i. & t.) into ~s, (of embryo) undergo cleavage or divide into parts; (physiol.) reproduce by gemmation; hence ~A'TION n., (esp.) formation of many cells from a single cell. [f. L *segmentum* (*secare* cut, ·MENT)]

seg'reg|āte[1], v.t. & i. Put apart from the rest, isolate; (intr.; crystallog.) separate from a mass & collect about centres or lines of fracture. Hence or cogn. ~A'TION n., ~ATIVE a. [f. L SE(*gregare* f. *grex gregis* flock), ·ATE[3]]

seg'regate[2], a. Set apart, separate, (arch.); (zool.) simple or solitary, not compound; (bot.) ~ *polygamy*, inflorescence in which each floret within common calyx has its own perianth also. [prec., -ATE[2]]

seiche (sāsh), n. Oscillation of lake waters due to changes in barometric pressure. [Swiss F, perh. = G *seiche* sinking (of water)]

Se'id (sā-, or sēd), n. Descendant of Mohammed through Fatima & Ali. [f. Arab. *sayyid* prince, see SAYYID, SIDI]

Seid'litz powd'er (sĕd-), n. Aperient medicine of two powders mixed separately with water & then poured together.

[named as substitute for mineral water of *Seidlitz* in Bohemia]

seigneur (sānyêr'), **seignior** (sān'yor), n. Feudal lord, lord of manor, whence **seignior'ial** (sānyôr²-) a.; *grand seigneur* (see Ap.), person of high rank or whose demeanour etc. correspond to popular ideal of great nobleman; *the Grand Seignior,* = GRAND *Signior.* [ME, f. L *seniorem* SENIOR]

seign(i)orage (sān'yorĭj), n. (hist.). Something claimed by sovereign or feudal superior as prerogative, esp. Crown's right to percentage on bullion brought to mint for coining. [ME, f. OF (*-norage*), see prec., -AGE]

seigniory (sān'yorĭ), n. Lordship, sovereign authority; seignior's domain; municipal council of medieval Italian republic. [ME, f. OF *seignorie* (SEIGNEUR, -Y¹)]

seine (sān, sēn), n., & v.t. & i. 1. Fishing--net for encircling, with floats at top & weights at bottom edge, & usu. hauled ashore; ~*gang,* set of men working ~; ~*-needle,* for netting ~ s ; ~*-roller,* cylinder over which ~ is hauled. 2. vb. Fish, catch, with ~, whence sein'ER¹ n. [OE *segne,* OS, OHG *segina* f. L f. Gk *sagēnē*]

seise, seisin. See *seiz-.*

seis'mic, seis'mal (rare), (sīz-), aa. Of earthquake(s). [Gk *seismos* earthquake (*seiō* shake), -IC]

seis'm|o- (sīz-), comb. form of Gk *seismos* (prec.); ~*ogram,* record given by ~OGRAPH (2) or ~ŏM'ETER or ~OSCOPE, instruments showing force, place, etc., of earthquake; so ~*ŏg'raphy,* ~*ŏg'rapher,* ~*ogrăph'ic(al),* ~*ŏm'etry,* ~*omĕt'ric(al),* ~*oscŏp'ic* ; ~*ŏl'ogy,* ~*ŏl'ogist,* ~*olŏ'gical(ly).*

seize (sēz), v.t. & i. 1. (law). (Also *seise*) put in possession *of* (chiefly in p.p. ~*d* or *seised* of, having in legal possession, &, fig., aware or informed of; often *stand* ~*d of*). 2. Take possession of (contraband goods, documents, etc.) by warrant or legal right, confiscate, impound, attach, whence *seiz'OR* n. (legal), *seiz'ABLE* a., (sēz-). 3. Lay hold of forcibly or suddenly, snatch, grasp with hand or mind, comprehend quickly or clearly, (~ *fortress, sceptre,* person *by the neck* etc., person's *hand, opportunity* or *occasion,* an *idea, a distinction,* the *point,* the *essence of* the *matter; was* ~*d by* apoplexy, *with remorse* or *panic*). 4. Lay hold eagerly *upon* (~ *upon a chance* or *pretext*). 5. (naut.). Lash, fasten with several turns of cord, (~ one *up,* lash him to rigging for flogging; ~ *ropes together*), whence *seiz'ING¹*(4) (sēz-) n. (usu. pl.). 6. (Of machinery) become stuck, jam, from undue heat or friction. [ME, f. OF *saisir* give seizin f. Frankish L *sacire* f. *°sakjan* quarrel, claim at law, cf. OS *sakan* (*saka* lawsuit) SAKE]

seiz'in, seis'in, (sēz-), n. (legal). Possession of land by freehold; act of taking such possession; what is so held. [ME, f. OF *saisine* (prec.)]

seizure (sēzh'er), n. In vbl senses; esp., sudden attack of apoplexy etc., stroke. [ME, f. SEIZE + -URE]

sej'ant, a. (her.). (Of animal) sitting upright on haunches. [prop. *seiant* f. OF var. of *seant* f. *seoir* f. L *sedēre* sit, -ANT]

sēk'ŏs, n. (archaeol.). Sacred enclosure esp. of ancient temple, adytum. [Gk]

sēlăch'ian (-k-), n. & a. 1. Any fish of shark or dogfish kind. 2. adj. Of or like such fishes. [Gk *selakhos* shark, -IAN]

sela'dăng (-ahd-), n. Large wild ox of Malay countries; Malayan tapir. [native name]

sēl'ah, Hebrew word of unknown meaning retained in Bible version of Psalms & supposed to be a musical direction.

sēla'mlĭk (-ah-), n. Men's part of Mohammedan house. [Turk.]

sēl'dom, adv. (rarely ~*er,* ~*est*). Rarely, not often, (~ *or never; very* ~; *not* ~). [OE *seldan* (OHG *seltan,* ON *sjaldan*), alt. to *-um* after adv. dat. ending as in WHILOM]

sēlĕct', a., & v.t. 1. Chosen for excellence, choice, picked, got by rejection or exclusion of what is inferior; (of society etc.) exclusive, cautious in admitting members; hence ~NESS n.; ‖ ~ *committee,* small parliamentary committee appointed to conduct some special investigation; *°*~*man,* one of the annually elected councillors in a New England town(ship). 2. v.t. Pick out as best or most suitable; hence **sēlĕc'tIVE** a. (*°*~*ive service,* conscription), **sēlĕc'tIVEly** adv., **sēlĕc'tOR** n. [f. L SE(*ligere lect-* = *legere* pick)]

sēlĕc'tion, n. Selecting, choice; what is selected (*a fine* ~ *of summer goods; what is your* ~ *for the Derby?; the new headmaster is a good* ~); (biol.) sorting out in various ways (*natural, sexual, physical, artificial, methodical, unconscious,* ~) of the types of animal or plant better fitted to survive or multiply regarded as a factor in evolution. [f. L *selectio* (prec., -ION)]

sēlĕctiv'itў, n. (Of wireless receiving--sets etc.) power to respond to any particular wave-length without interference from others. [SELECTIVE + -ITY]

selenite. n. 1. (sĕl'In-). Sulphate of lime or gypsum occurring as transparent crystals or thin plates; (chem.) salt of selenium. 2. (S~; sĭlē-). Inhabitant of moon. Hence **sēlēnīt'ıc** a. [(1) f. L f. Gk *selēnītēs* (*lithos*) moon(-stone) f. *Selēnē, -ITE¹*; (2) f. Gk *selēnītēs*]

sēlēn'ium, n. Non-metallic element of sulphur-tellurium group, characterized by the fact that its electrical resistance varies with the intensity of the illumination falling on it. Hence **sēlēn'ıc** a., **sēl'ēnATE¹**(3) n., **sēlēn'ıous** (chem.) a. [Gk *Selēnē* moon, -IUM; named w. ref. to TELLURIUM]

sēlēn'|(o)-, comb. form of Gk *sclēnē* moon;

~*ocen'tric*, as seen etc. from centre of moon; ~*odont*, (mammal) with crescent-ridges on crowns of teeth; *sélēnŏg'*RAPHY, study or mapping of the moon, so ~*o*-GRAPH(1), *sélēnŏg'rapher*, ~*ograph'ic*; *sélēnŏl'*OGY, *sélēnŏl'ogist*; ~*otrŏp'ic*, curving towards the moon (of plant-organs influenced in growth thus), so *sélēnŏt'ropism*, *sélēnŏt'rop*Y[1].

Sèleu'cïd, n. (pl. ~*s*, ~*ae*). One of the dynasty founded by Seleucus that governed Syria c. 312–64 B.C. [-ID[3]]

sĕlf, n. (pl. *-ves*) & a. 1. Person's or thing's own individuality or essence, person or thing as object of introspection or reflexive action, (*the study of the* ~; *the consciousness of* ~; one's *former, better*, etc., ~, oneself as one formerly was, one's nobler impulses etc.; one's *second* ~, intimate friend, right-hand man; chiefly *his, its*, etc., *own* or *very* ~ as form of *himself* etc. when divided; *Caesar's, pity's*, etc., ~, rhet. for *Caesar himself, pity itself*); one's own interests or pleasure, concentration on these, (*cares for nothing but, refers everything to*, ~; ~ *is a bad guide to happiness*); flower of uniform, or of the natural wild, colour; (commerc., vulg., joc.) = *myself, yourself, himself*, etc. (*cheque drawn to* ~; *a ticket admitting* ~ *& friend*); *our noble selves* (joc., as toast). 2. adj. (Of colour) uniform, the same throughout, (of flower) ~-coloured. 3. HERSELF, HIMSELF, ITSELF, MYSELF, ONE~, OURSELF, THEMSELVES, YOURSELF. [OE, OS *self*, OHG *selb*, ON *sjalfr*. Goth. *silba*; orig. appended, as adj. or in apposition, to pronoun & declined with it, *he self, his selfes*, dat. *him selfum*, acc. *hine selfne*; in ME also adj. = same, very]

sĕlf-, pref. (prec.) expr. direct or indirect reflexive action, automatic or independent action, or sameness; freely used as living pref.; the more established wds are given alphabetically with references to the numbered classes following:

1. Expressing direct reflexive action with part. of any vb that can have *self* for object, & hence with the p.p. in sense *by oneself* or *itself*, & with vbl nn. & adjj. & advv. in sense of *-self*; so from 'I accuse myself' come ~*accusing*, *-accused*, aa., *-accuser, -accusation*, nn., *-accusatory* a., *-accusingly, -accusatorily*, advv.

2. By extension it is prefixed also to any word, whether participle or other vbl deriv. or not, to which *self* might be attached by a preposition; in a large class (2a) the sense is *without external agency or assistance*; so from 'acts by or of itself' come ~*acting*, ~*action*, ~*activity*; from 'evident of itself' comes ~*evident*; in other wds (2b) the relation expressed is various; so from 'conceited about one self' ~*conceited* & ~*conceit*, from 'be absorbed, confide, in oneself' ~*absorbed, -absorption, -confidence*, from 'inflict on oneself' ~*-inflicted*, from 'be conscious,

despair, of oneself' ~*consciousness, -despair*, from 'depend on oneself' ~*-dependence*, from 'righteous as seen by oneself' ~*-righteous*, from 'seek things for oneself' ~*-seeker, -seeking* a. & n., from 'suffice, use violence, to oneself' ~*-sufficing, -sufficient*, ~*-violence*.

3. To a few nn. & their derivv. in *-ED*[2] *self-* is prefixed with sense *uniform*, or *natural & not artificially produced.*

~*-aban'donment*, ~*-abase'ment*, ~*-abho'rrence*, ~*-abnega'tion*, 1; ~*-absorbed'*, ~*-absorp'tion*, 2b; ~*-abuse'* 1, solitary sexual indulgence; ~*-accusa'tion*, ~*-accus'atory*, etc., 1; ~*-ac'ting*, ~*-ac'tion*, ~*-activ'ity*, 2a, automatic. (action); ~*-adjust'ing*, ~*-adjust'ment*, 1, of machinery etc.; ~*-admira'tion* 1; ~*-affirma'tion* 1 (psych.), recognition and assertion of the existence of the conscious self; ~*-aggran'dizement, -appoin'ted, -apprecia'tion, -approv'al, -approba'tion*, 1; ~*-*ASSERT'*ing, -assert'ive, -asser'tion*, etc., 1; ~*-assumed'* 2b, of title etc. not conferred but taken esp. without right; ~*-begott'en* 1, by exag. for *not begotten by another*; ~*-betray'al* 1; ~*-bin'der* 2a, reaping-machine with automatic arrangement for binding sheaves; ~*-blind'ed* 1; ~*-born* 1, as ~*-begotten*; ~*-cen'tred*(ness) 2b, preoccupied with one's own personality or affairs; ~*-clos'ing* 1; ~*-cock'ing* 1, of gun in which hammer is raised by trigger, not by hand; ~*-collect'ed* 2b, having or showing presence of mind or composure; ~*-col'our*(ed) 3, of flower or material in which colour is uniform throughout, or flower whose colour has not been changed by cultivation etc.; ~*-command'* 1, power of controlling one's emotions; ~*-commun'ion* 2b, meditation esp. upon one's own character or conduct; ~*-compla'cent, -compla'cency*, 2b, of person too easily pleased with himself; ~*-conceit'*(ed) 2b; ~*-condemned', -condemna'tion*, 1; ~*-con'fidence, -con'fident*(ly), 2b; ~*-congratula'tion, -con'quest*, 1; ~*-con'scious*(ness) 2b, esp. of person embarrassed or made theatrical by inability to forget himself in society, also philos. etc. of man as having faculty of ~*-contemplation*; ~*-consis'tent, -consis'tency*, 2b; ~*-con'stituted* 1, esp. of person who assumes function without right to it; ~*-consum'ing* 1; ~*-contained'* 1, not communicative, also compact or complete in itself; ~*-contempt', -contemp'tuous*(ly), 1; ~*-content'* n., *-conten'ted*, 2b; ~*-contradic'tion, -contradic'tory, -control', -convict'ed*, 1; ~*-creat'ed, -crea'tion*, 1, as ~*-begotten*; ~*-crit'ical, -crit'icism, -cul'ture, -deceiv'ing, -deceiv'er, -deceit', -decep'tion*, 1; ~*-defence'* 1 (*in* ~*-defence*, not by way of aggression; *art of* ~*-defence*, boxing); ~*-delu'sion* 1; ~*-*DENY'*ing* (~*-denying ordinance*, resolution of Long Parliament 1645 depriving members of Parliament of civil & military office; also often used allusively),

·deni'al, 1; ~-depen'dent, -ence, 2b; ~-depre'cia'tion, -depre'ciative,1;~-despair' 2b; ~-destroy'ing, -destruc'tion, etc., 1; ~-determ'ining, -determina'tion, etc., 1, esp. w. ref. to free will as opp. fatalism etc., &, in pol., of a nation's right to determine its own polity; ~-devel'opment 1;~-devo'tion 1, devoting of oneself to person or cause; ~-dis'cipline, -dispa'ragement, -display', -dispraise', -distrust'(ful), -ed'ucated, -educa'tion, -efface'ment, 1; ~-elec'tive 1, esp. = proceeding etc. by co-optation;~-esteem' 1;~-ev'ident(ly) 2a, without need of demonstration; ~-examina'tion 1; ~-ex'ecuting 1, not needing legislation etc. to enforce it; ~-exis'tent 2a; ~-explain'ing, -explan'atory, 1; ~-faced 3, (of stone) unhewn, undressed; ~-feed'ing, -feed'er, 1, (furnace, machine, etc.) that renews its own fuel or material automatically; ~-fert'ilizing, -fert'ilized, 1, -fert'ile, -fertil'ity, 2a, of plants fertilized by their own pollen, not from others; ~-flatt'ering, -flatt'ery, 1; ~-forget'ful(ness) 1, unselfish-(ness); ~-gen'erating 1; ~-glazed 3, (of porcelain) covered with glaze of one tint; ~-glorifica'tion 1; ~-go'verning (esp. the ~-governing colonies opp. CROWN¹-colony), -go'vernment, 1; ~-gratula'tion 1;~-heal 1, kinds of plant named as enabling patient to do without doctor; ~-help' 1, working for oneself without waiting for external aid; ~-humilia'tion, -immola'tion, 1; ~-import'ant, -import'ance, 2b, in one's own eyes, & hence pompous etc.; ~-imposed' 2b, of task etc.; ~-im'potent 2a, opp. ~-fertile; ~-improve'ment 1; ~-induc'tive, -induc'tion, 2a, (electr.) (capable of) production of extra current in circuit by variation of current in that circuit; ~-indul'gent, -indul'gence, etc., 1, yielding to temptations of ease or pleasure; ~-inflict'ed 2b;~-in'terest(ed) 2b, (actuated by or absorbed in) what one conceives to be for one's own interests; ~-invit'ed 1, having had to ask for, having come without, an invitation; ~-involved' 2b, wound up in oneself; ~-justifica'tion, -kind'led, -know'ledge, -lauda'tion, 1; ~-love' 1, selfishness, impulse towards ~-indulgence, vulnerable conceit, also rarely desire of ~-development etc.; ~-lum'inous 2a; ~-made 1, of person who has risen by his own exertions, often with implication of vulgarity etc.; ~-mas'tery, -mortifica'tion, 1; ~-mov'ing, -mo'tion, -murd'er(er), 1; ~-opin'ion, -opin'ioned, -opin'ionated, 2b, of stubborn adherence to one's own opinions; ~-par'tial, ~-partial'ity, 2b; ~-pit'y, -pleas'ing a. & n., 1; ~-poised' 2a; ~-pollu'tion 1, ~-abuse; ~-port'rait 2a, portrait (literary or pictorial) made by a person of himself;~-possessed', -posse's-sion, 1, cool(ness), composed, composure, in agitating circumstances etc.; ~-praise' 1 (~-praise is no recommendation); ~-preserva'tion 1, esp. the primary instinct impelling conscious beings to go on living & avoid injury; ~-prof'it 2b; ~-prop'agating 1;~-propelled' 1;~-rak'er 2a, reaping-machine with set of rakes automatically preparing corn for binding; ~-realiza'tion 1, development of one's faculties esp. as ethical first principle; ~-record'ing 2a, of scientific instrument etc.; ~-regard'ing, -regard', 1, opp. altruism etc. without the censure implied in selfish etc.; ~-re'gistering 2a, as ~-recording;~-reg'ulating 1, of machinery; ~-reli'ant, -ance, 2b; ~-renuncia'tion 1, unselfishness; ~-repre'ssion, -reproach'(ful), 1; ~-repug'nant 2b, inconsistent; ~-respect'ing, -respect', -respect'ful, 1, of person who has & acts up to a standard of worthy conduct; ~-restrained', -restraint', -reveal'ing a., -revela'tion, 1; ~-rev'erent, -rev'erence, 1, rhet., poet., theol., etc., for ~-respect etc.; ~-right'-eous(ness) 2b;~-right'ing a. 1, of boat; ~-sac'rificing a., -sac'rifice, 1, postponing private interest & desires to those of others;~'same 3, emphatic form of same; ~-sat'isfied, -satisfac'tion, 2b, conceit(ed); ~-scorn' 1; ~-seek'ing a. & n., -seek'er, 2b; ~-service 1, (attrib., of restaurant, shop, etc.) in which customers help themselves to food or goods & afterwards pay a cashier, thereby reducing the need for sales assistants, (n.) this kind of service; ~-slaught'er 1; ~-sown' 1, sprung from seed that has dropped without human agency; ~-start'er 2a, electric appliance for starting motor-car without use of crank-handle; ~-ste'rile, -steril'ity, 2a, as ~-impotent; ~-styled' 1, having taken the name without right etc., pretended, would-be; ~-suffi'cing 2b, requiring nothing from outside, independent; ~-suffi'cient, -ency, 2b, = ~-sufficing, also & usu. sufficient in one's own opinion, presumptuous; ~-sugges'tion 2b, reflexive suggestion of the mesmeric or hypnotic kind; ~-support'(ing), -surren'der, -sustain'ing, -sustained', -laught', -torment'ing etc., -tor'ture etc., 1; ~-vi'olence 2b, esp. suicide; ~-will(ea¸ 2b, as ~-opinion etc.; ~-wind'ing 1, of clock with automatic winding apparatus; ~-wor'ship 1.

self'hood, n. (rare). Personality, separate & conscious existence. [-HOOD]

self'fish, a. Deficient in consideration for others, alive chiefly to personal profit or pleasure, actuated by self-interest, (of motives etc.) appealing to self-interest (~ theory of morals, that pursuit of pleasure of one kind or another is the ultimate spring of every action). Hence ~-LY² adv., ~-NESS n. [-ISH¹]

self'less, a. Oblivious of self, incapable of selfishness. Hence ~-NESS n. [-LESS]

self'ness, n. (rare). = SELFHOOD. [-NESS]

Sèljuk' (-ook), n. Member of 11th–13th-c. Mohammedan dynasties in central & Western Asia descended from the chieftain Seljuk. Hence ~-IAN a. & n.

sèll, v.t. & i. (sôld), & n. 1. Make over or

dispose in exchange for money (cf. BUY, BARTER; ~ one's *life dearly*, fig., kill or wound assailants before being killed; ~*ing-race, -handicap*, etc., in which winning horse must be sold to highest bidder; ~ one *a pup*, sl., swindle him). 2. Keep stock of for sale or be a dealer in (*do you* ~ *candles?*; *bookselling* etc.). 3. Betray for money or other reward (~ one's *country* etc.), also ~ *down the river*. 4. Prostitute for money or other consideration, make a matter of corrupt bargaining, (~ *justice*, oneself, one's *honour* or *chastity*). 5. (sl.). Disappoint by not keeping engagement etc., by failing in some way, or by trickery (*sold again!*, excl. used by or to disappointed person). 6. Advertise or publish merits of; give (person) information *on* value of something, inspire with desire to possess something; *be sold on*, be enthusiastic about. 7. (Of goods) find purchasers (*will never* ~; ~*ing like wildfire, hot cakes*). 8. ~ *off*, ~ remainder of (goods), clear out stock, at reduced prices; ~ *out*, leave army by ~ing commission (hist.), ~ (all or some of one's shares in company, whole stock-in-trade, etc., or abs.); ~*out* n., betrayal, ~ing of all tickets etc. for a show etc., commercial success; ~ *up*, ~ goods (of debtor) by distress or legal process. 9. n. (colloq.). Disappointment (*what a* ~ *!*). Hence (-)~*ER*[1] n. (~*ers' market*, one in which goods are scarce and high prices favour ~ers). [OE *sellan*, OS *sellian*, OHG *sellen*, ON *selja*, Goth. *saljan*, cf. SALE]

sellanders. See SALLENDERS.

selt'zer, n. (Also ~ *water*) medicinal mineral water from *Selters* in Germany; artificial substitutes for this, soda-water.

selt'zogĕne, n. = GAZOGENE. [f. F *selzo-gène* (prec., -GEN)]

sel'vage, -edge, n. Edge of cloth so woven that it cannot unravel, border of different material or finish along edge of cloth intended to be torn off or hidden, list; edge-plate of lock with opening for the bolt. Hence **sel'vageD**[2] (-ĭjd) a. [15th c., f. SELF + EDGE, after MDu. *selfegge*]

selvagee' (-j-), n. Hank of rope-yarn bound together, used as a sling etc. [f. prec.]

selves. See SELF.

sĕmăn'tic, a. & n. 1. Relating to meaning in language. 2. n. pl. Branch of philology concerned with meanings. [f. F (-*ique*) f. Gk *sēmantikos* significant (*sēmainō* mean)]

sĕm'aphŏre, n., & v.t. & t. 1. Signalling apparatus of post with oscillating arms, arrangement of lanterns, etc., for use (esp. now on railways) by day or night; military signalling by operator's two arms or two flags. 2. vb. Signal, send, by ~. Hence **sĕmaphŏ'rıo** a., **sĕmaphŏ'rı-CALLY** adv. [F, f. Gk *sēma* sign + -PHORE]

sĕmási̱|ŏl'ogy̆, n. Semantics. So ~o-

lŏ'gical a. [G, f. Gk *sēmasia* meaning + -LOGY]

sĕmăt'ic, a. (nat. hist.). (Of colour or markings in animals) significant, serving to warn off enemies or attract attention. [f. Gk *sēma-atos* sign + -IC]

|| **sĕm'blable**, a. (arch.). Having semblance of something, seeming. [ME, f. OF (foll., -ABLE)]

sĕm'blance, n. What looks like, the outward appearance of, something (*put on a* ~ *of anger*; *bears the* ~ *of an angel & the heart of a devil*). [ME, f. OF f. *sembler* f. L *simulare* SIMULATE]

semée, semé, (sĕm'ĭ), a. (her.). Covered with small bearings of indefinite number (e.g. stars, fleurs-de-lis) arranged over field. [F, p.p. of *semer* sow (SEMEN)]

semeiology, semeiotics. See semio-.

sĕm'ĕn, n. Generative fluid of male animals. [L, genit. *-inis*, = seed (*serere* sow, -MEN)]

sĕmĕs'ter, n. Half-year course or term in German & other universities. [G, f. L *semestris* six-monthly (*sex* six, *mensis* month)]

sĕm'i-, pref. = L *semi-* half, cogn. w. Gk *hēmi-* HEMI-, attached to any E wd as living pref. (cf. BI-, DI-[2], DEMI-, HEMI-); the more established or illustrative wds are given alphabetically w. reff. to the following numbered senses: 1. the half of (~*circle*); 2. on one of two sides (~*-detached*), in one of two directions (~*-infinite*), in some particular (~*vowel*); 3. little more or better than (~*barbarism*); 4. rather less than (~*-official*), in low degree (~*civilized*), not quite deserving the description (~*-smile*); 5. imperfect(ly)(~*-bull*, ~*-double*); 6. occurring, published, etc., each half — or twice in a — (~*-annual*; cf. BI- 1e): ~*-ann'ual*(ly) 6); ~*-barbār'ian, -barb'arism*, 3; || ~*'brĕve* 1, longest note in common use, equalling two minims (see BREVE); ~*-bull* 5, issued by Pope after election & before coronation with one side of seal left blank; ~*-centenn'ial* 6, occurring etc. every fifty years; ~*-chor'us* 1, half or part of choir, passage given by it; ~*circle*, ~*circ'ular* a., 1, (amounting to, arranged as or in, shaped like) half of a circle or of its circumference, set of objects ranged in or object forming a ~*-circle*, instrument for measuring angles; ~*-cōl'on* 4, punctuation-mark (;) now used as the chief stop (the colon being mostly reserved for special uses) of intermediate value between comma & full stop; ~*-cyl'inder*, ~*cylin'drical*, 1, (of, forming, etc.) half of a cylinder cut longitudinally; || ~*-demi-semiquaver* 1; ~*-detached'* (-cht) 2, (of house) joined to another by party-wall on one side only; ~*-documen'tary* a. & n. 1, (cinema film) having an actual background and a fictitious story; ~*-dome* 1, 4, half-dome formed by vertical section, part of structure more or less resembling dome; ~*-dou'ble* 5 (bot.), having outer stamens only converted to petals; ~*fin'al* 4, match or round preceding the final (~*fin'alist*, competitor in this); ~*flu'id* a. & n. 4, viscous (fluid); ~*-fused* 5; ~*-in'fidel* 3; ~*-in'finite* 2, limited in one direction & stretching to infinity in the other; ~*-lun'ar* 1, 4, half-moon-shaped, crescent-shaped, (esp. in anat. names, as ~*-lunar bone, cartilage, fold, fossa, lobe, valve*); ~*-month'ly* 6; ~*-mute* a. & n. 3, (person) practically dumb owing to (esp. congenital) deafness; ~*-offi'cial(ly)* 4, esp. of communications made to newspapers by official with stipulation that they shall not be formally attributed to him; ~*'plume* 2, feather with firm stem but downy web; ~*pre'cious* 4, of stones; || ~*'quaver* 1 (mus.), note half length of quaver; ~*-ri'gid* 4, (of airship) having a stiffened keel attached to a flexible gas container; ~*-smile* 4; ~*'tone* 1 (mus.), smallest interval in normal European music, half length of tone (*diatonic* ~*tone*, occurring in major or minor scale; *chromatic* ~*tone*, not so occurring); ~*transpār'ent* 4; ~*trop'ical* 4, (as) of regions bordering on the tropics; ~*-tūb'ular* 1, shaped like half a tube cut longitudinally; ~*-un'cial* 5, between uncial & minuscule; ~*'vowel*, ~*vōc'al* a., 2, sound, or letter representing it, intermediate between vowel & consonant (e.g. *y*, *w*), consonant that is not mute (e.g. *l*, *m*, *z*); ~*-week'ly* 6.

sĕm'inal, a. Of seed or semen or reproduction, germinal, reproductive, propagative, (~ *fluid*, semen; *in the* ~ *state*, rudimentary, still undeveloped; ~ *principles*, pregnant with consequences). Hence ~LY² adv. [ME, f. OF, or f. L *seminalis* (SEMEN, -AL)]

sĕm'inār, n. Small class at university for discussion and research; *conference of specialists; short intensive course of study. [G, as foll.]

sĕm'inar|ў, n. Place of education (formerly in pretentious use for *school*, cf. ACADEMY; now rare exc. either fig. as *a* ~*ў of vice* etc., or of R.-C. & esp. Jesuit schools, whence ~IST n.). [ME, f. L *seminarium* seed-plot (SEMEN, -ARY¹)]

sēminā'tion, n. (bot.). Process, plant's manner, of seeding. [f. L *seminatio* (*seminare* f. SEMEN, -ATION)]

sēminif'erous, a. Bearing seed; conveying semen. [SEMEN, -I-, -FEROUS]

sēmiŏl'ogў, **sēmiŏt'ics**, -meio- (-miŏ-), nn. Branch of pathology concerned with symptoms. [Gk *sēmeion* sign (*sēma* mark), *sēmeiōlikos* of signs, -LOGY, -ICS]

Sĕm'|ite, n. & a. (Member) of any of the races supposed to be descended from Shem (*Gen.* x. 21 foll.) including esp. the Hebrews, Arameans, Phoenicians, Arabs, & Assyrians. So **Sĕmit'ic** a. (also n. = ~itic languages), ~**itism**(2, 4), ~**itist**(3), nn., ~**itize**(3) v.t. [f. mod. L *semita*, f. LL f. Gk *Sēm* Shem, -ITE¹]

|| **sĕmm'it**, n. (Sc.). Undershirt.

sĕmoli'na (-lē-), **sĕm'ola**, n. Hard grains left after bolting of flour, used in puddings etc. [-*ina* f. It. *semolino* dim. of *semola* bran]

sĕmpitērn'al, a. (Rhet. for) eternal; everlasting, never to end, (rare). [ME, f. OF (-*el*) or LL *sempiternalis*, f. L *sempiternus* (*semper* always + *aeternus* eternal), -AL]

sĕm'plīce (-chā), mus. direction. Simple in style of performance. [It., = SIMPLE]

sĕm'pre (-ā), mus. direction. Throughout (with other direction, as ~ *forte*). [It.]

sempstress. See SEAMSTRESS.

sĕn, n. Japanese copper coin, 1/100 of yen.

sēnār'ius, n. (pl. -*ii*). Latin verse of six feet, usu. iambics. [f. L (*versus*) *senarius* (*seni* six each, -ARY¹)]

sĕn'arў, a. On basis of six, by sixes, (~ SCALE³, cf. BINARY). [f. L as prec.]

sĕn'ate, n. 1. State-council of the ancient -Roman republic & empire dividing legislation with the popular assemblies, administration with the magistrates, & judicial power with the equites. 2. Upper & less numerous branch of the legislative assembly in various countries; (rhet.) any legislature or its proceedings or members (*the* ~, *the pulpit*, & *the press*). 3. Governing body of Cambridge Univ. & other institutions; *S*~*-house* (esp. at Cambridge). [ME, f. OF *senat*, *senaz* f. L *senatus* (*sen-* old, -ATE¹)]

sĕn'ator, n. Member of senate. Hence or cogn. **sĕnatōr'IAL** a., **sĕnatōr'iALLУ** adv., ~SHIP n. [ME, f. OF (-*eur*), f. L *senatorem* nom. -*or* (prec., -OR)]

sĕnāt'us, n. 1. The ancient-Roman senate (~ *pŏp'ulusque Roman'us*, the senate & people of Rome, abbr. S.P.Q.R., official name of ancient Rome as a State; ~*-consult'(um)*, decree of the ~). 2. || (In full ~ *acadēm'icus*) governing body in some universities. [L, = SENATE]

sĕnd¹, v.t. & i. (*sent*). 1. Bid go, secure conveyance of, to some destination (destination given by *to* or other prep. or by ind. obj. of person, or merely implied; ~ *message* or *messenger to*; *sent me a book*; *will* ~ *an army*; ~ *goods all over* or *round the world*; ~ COALS *to Newcastle*; ~ *word*, have message taken *that*, *to do*, etc.; ~ *up* or *in* one's name, an exhibit, etc., enter oneself or it for competition). 2. (Of God, providence, etc.) grant, bestow, inflict, bring about, cause to be so-&-so, (~ *rain*, *a judgement*, *pestilence*; *God* ~ *it may not be so!*; ~ *her victorious!*). 3. Propel, cause to move, (~ *bullet*; *sent his temperature up*, *down*; ~ *out* or *forth leaves*, *steam*, *odour*). 4. Dismiss, with or without force (with *off*, *away*, or compl. or adv. phr.; *sent him away*, *packing*, *flying*, *about his business*, *to the right-about*; ~ *to* COVENTRY; || ~ *down*, rusticate or expel from university; ~ *off letter*, *parcel*, etc., get it off one's own hands & started on its way; ~ *off* person, witness his departure as sign of respect etc., so ~-*off* n., also laudatory review of book etc.). **5.** Drive *mad* or *crazy*; (jazz sl.) put into ecstasy. **6.** ~ message or letter (*sent to warn me, depose him, to me to take care*; ~-*for him*, telling him to come; ~ *for the book*, ordering it as purchase). Hence ~'ER¹ n. [OE *sendan*, OS -*ian*, OHG -*en*, ON -*a*, Goth. *sandjan* f. Gmc *°sandh*-]

send², sc-, n., & v.i. (naut.; ~*ed*). **1.** Impulse given by the down slope of a wave (usu. ~ *of the sea*). **2.** v.i. (Of vessel) plunge or pitch owing to this. **3.** n. Such plunge. [f. prec.]

sen'dal, n. Medieval silken fabric used for rich dresses, pennons, etc. [ME, f. OF *cendal*, *sen*-, prob. f. Gk *sindōn* fine linen]

sen'ega, -ka, n. (Drug, used in cough- -mixtures, made from root of) American plant called also S~-*snake-root*. [f. name of *Seneca* Indians]

senĕs'c|ent, a. Growing old. Hence ~ENCE n. [f. L *senescere* (SENIOR, -ESCENT)]

sen'eschal (-shl), n. Steward or major- -domo of mediaeval great house. [ME, f. OF, f. med. L *seniscalcus* f. WG *°siniskalk* (*°sini*- old, *°skalk* servant); cf. MARSHAL]

sen'green (-n-g-), n. = HOUSE¹-*leek*. [OE *singrēne* evergreen]

senhor, senhora, senhorita, (sānyōr', -ōr'a, -orēt'a), used of or to Portuguese as SIGNOR etc.

sen'ile, a. Showing the feebleness etc. of, incident to, old age (~ *atrophy, apathy, garrulity, dementia*, etc.). Hence **senil'**ITY n. [f. L *senilis* (foll., -IL)]

sen'ior, a. & n. **1.** More advanced in age or older in standing, superior in age or standing *to*, of higher or highest degree, (opp. JUNIOR; ‖ *the ~ service*, Navy as opp. Army; *the ~ members of the family, university*, etc.; *the ~ partner*, head of firm; ‖~ *optime*, see WRANGLER; ‖~ *classic*, competitor placed highest in classical tripos when names were arranged according to merit; ‖~ WRANGLER; ‖~ *man* at university, opp. FRESHman; *is two years ~ to me*), so **seniŏ'**rity n. **2.** (Appended to name for distinction; abbr. *sen., sr*; opp. JUNIOR) ~ to another of same name (esp. with father's Christian name & surname when son has same, as *John Smith sen.*, or at school with surname when two or more boys have same, as *Smith sen.*). **3.** n. Person of advanced age or comparatively long service etc.; one's elder or superior in length of service, membership, etc. (*is my ~*); ‖ ~ wrangler, ‖ classic or man. [L, = older, old(ish) man, compar. f. st. of *senex senis* old(man)]

seniŏr'es priŏr'es (-z, -z), L sentence (= elders first) used in reminding the young of precedence due to seniority.

senn'a, n. (Dried leaflets, used as laxative, of) kinds of cassia. [f. Arab. *sanā*]

senn'ĕt, n. (hist.). Signal call on trumpet (in stage-directions of Shakspearean & other plays). [app. var. of SIGNET 'sign']

senn'ight (-it), n. (arch.). Week (esp. *Tuesday* etc. ~). [OE *scofon nihta* seven nights]

senn'it, sinn'ĕt, n. (naut.). Braided cordage made in flat or round or square form from 3-9 cords (*common* i.e. flat, *round, square,* ~). [c. 1600 *sinnet*, of unkn. orig.]

señor, señora, señorita, (sĕnyōr', -ōr'a, -orēt'a), used of or to Spaniards as SIGNOR etc.

Sĕnous(s)'ī (-ōō-), n. Religious & political Mohammedan fraternity in N. Africa named after founder (usu. *the* ~ as sing. or pl.).

sensā'tion, n. **1.** Consciousness of perceiving or seeming to perceive some state or affection of one's body or its parts or senses or of one's mind or its emotions, contents of such consciousness, (*had a* ~ *of giddiness, heat, pain, comfort, thirst, falling, sourness, deafness, pride, stupidity; pressing the eyeball in the dark will produce the ~ of light or of seeing light; in search of a new* ~). **2.** Stirring of the emotions common to many people or of eager interest among them, display of intense common emotion or interest, literary or other use of material calculated to excite it, (*made a great* ~, was eagerly discussed or viewed; ~ *among the audience*, shown by deep silence, applause, or other general manifestation; *a three- -days'* ~; *what is the latest* ~?; *the essence of melodrama is* ~; *deals largely in* ~). Hence ~AL (-shon-) a., ~ally² adv. [f. LL *sensatio* (in med. L sense) f. L *sensus* SENSE, -ATION]

sensā'tional|ism (-shon-), n. (Philos.) theory that ideas are derived solely from sensation; pursuit of the sensational in literature, political agitation, etc. So ~IST(2) n. [-ISM]

sĕnse, n., & v.t. **1.** Any of the special bodily faculties by which sensation is roused (*the five* ~s, sight, hearing, smell, taste, & touch; *sixth* or *muscular* ~, producing sensation of muscular effort; *has quick, keen,* ~s, *a dull* ~ *of smell*); (pl.) person's sanity or ordinary state of mind regarded as secured by possession of these (*have you taken leave of, are you out of, your* ~s?, are you mad?; *he will soon come, we must bring him, to his* ~s, out of mad folly; *frightened out of his* ~s, into loss of faculties; *in* one's ~s, sane). **2.** Ability to perceive or feel or to be conscious of the presence or properties of things, sensitiveness of all or any of the ~s, (~-*perception; errors of* ~, mistakes in perception; *the pleasures of* ~, those depending on sensation; *has a plant* ~?). **3.** Consciousness of (*a* or *the* ~ *of pleasure, pain, gratification, having done well*, one's *own importance, shame, responsibility; labouring under a* ~ *of wrong*, feeling wronged). **4.** Quick or accurate appreciation *of*, instinct regarding or insight into specified matter or habit of squaring conduct to such instinct, (~ *of locality, distance, the ridiculous, humour, duty, beauty, gratitude; a keen ~ of honour; the religious, moral, aesthetic,*~). 5. Practical wisdom, judgement, common ~, conformity to these, (*sound, good,* COMMON[1], ~; *a man of* ~, sagacious; *had not the* ~ *to do; has plenty of* ~; *what is the* ~ *of talking like that?; has more* ~ *than to do; now you are talking* ~). 6. Meaning, way in which word etc. is to be understood, intelligibility or coherence or possession of a meaning, (*in what exact* ~ *we shall rise again is doubtful; the* ~ *of the word is clear; does not make* ~, is unintelligible; *in the strict, limited, literal, figurative, moral, metaphorical, legal,* PICKWICKIAN, *proper, full,* ~; *in a vague, in every,* ~; *in a* ~, provided the statement is taken in a particular way, under limitations, as *what you say is true in a* ~; *make* ~ *out of nonsense*). 7. Prevailing sentiment among a number of people (*take the* ~ *of the meeting*, ascertain this by putting question etc.). 8. ~-*body,* -*capsule,* -*cavity,* -*cell,* -*centre,* -*organ,* parts of animals concerned in producing sensation; hence ~'LESS (-sl-) a. (esp.=foolish; *knock* ~*less,* stun), ~'**lèssLY** adv., ~-**lèssNESS** n. 9. v.t. Perceive by ~, (esp.) be vaguely aware of. [ME, f. OF *sens* or L *sensus* -*ūs* (*sentire sens*- feel)]

sĕnsibil'itў, n. Capacity to feel (*skin lost its* ~); exceptional openness to emotional impressions (*sense & ~*), delicacy of feeling, susceptibility (~ *to kindness* etc.), over-sensitiveness; (pl.) susceptibility in various directions. [ME, f.LL *sensibilitas* (foll., -TY)]

sĕn'sible, a. Perceptible by the senses (~ *phenomena, things*); great enough to be perceived, appreciable, (*a* ~ *difference, increase*); (arch.) sensitive (*to*); aware, not unmindful, *of,* (*was* ~ *of his peril, your kindness*); of good sense, reasonable, judicious, moderate, practical, (*a* ~ *man, course, compromise; that is very* ~ *of him*). Hence **sĕn'sibLY**[2] adv., ~NESS n. [ME f. OF, f. L *sensibilis* (SENSE, -IBLE)]

sĕn'sit|ive, a. & n. 1. Of the senses, sensory, (rare); having sensibility *to,* very open *to* or acutely affected by external impressions esp. those made by the moods or opinions of others in relation to oneself; (of instrument etc.) readily responding *to* or recording slight changes of condition (~*ive market,* liable to quick changes of price); (chem.) readily affected by or responsive *to* appropriate agent, (photog.) ~*ive paper,* prepared to receive impressions from light, whence ~IZE(3) v.t., ~ĪZA'TION, ~ĪZER[1](2), ~ŏM'ETER, nn.; ~*ive plant,* kind of mimosa whose leaves curve downwards & leaflets fold together at nightfall or when touched; hence ~**ivELY**[2] adv., ~**ivENESS,** ~**iv'ITY** (chem.,

photog., physiol., psychol.), nn. 2. n. (hypnotism etc.). Person ~ive to hypnotic etc. influences. [ME f. OF, or f. med. L *sensitivus,* irreg. f. L *sentire sens*-feel, -IVE]

sĕnsŏr'ium, n. (pl. -*ia,* -*s*). The seat of sensation, the brain, brain & spinal cord, or grey matter of these; (biol.) whole sensory apparatus including nerve-system etc. [LL *sensorium* (SENSE, -ORY)]

sĕn'sorў, sĕnsŏr'ial, aa. Of the sensorium or sensation or the senses. [after prec.; see -ORY]

sĕn'sŭal (*or* -shŏŏ-), a. Of sense or sensation, sensory, (rare); of or depending on the senses only & not the intellect or spirit, carnal, fleshly, (~ *pleasures*); given to the pursuit of ~ pleasures or gratification of the appetites, self-indulgent in regard to food & sexual enjoyment, voluptuous, licentious; (philos.) holding the doctrine of, according to, of, sensationalism. Hence or cogn. ~IZE(3) v.t., ~ĪZA'TION, ~ISM(2, 3), ~IST(1, 2), ~ITY (-ăl[2]), nn., ~LY[2] adv. [ME, f. L *sensualis* (SENSE, -AL)]

sĕn'sŭous, a. Of, derived from, affecting, the senses (chiefly as substitute, free of implied censure, for prec.; cf. *non-moral* & *immoral*). Hence ~LY[2] adv., ~NESS n. [f. L *sensus* SENSE + -OUS]

sent. See SEND[1].

sĕn'tence, n., & v.t. 1. (arch.). One's opinion for or against some course or conclusion (*my* ~ *is for war*); pithy saying, briefly expressed thought, maxim, proverb. 2. Verdict (rare); (declaration of) punishment allotted to person condemned in criminal trial (also transf.). 3. (gram.). Set of words complete in itself, containing subject & predicate (either, or part of either or both, occas. omitted by ellipsis), & conveying a statement, question, or command (e.g. *I go, will you go?, go*=go thou or you, *what?* = what did you say ?, *hearts trumps*=hearts are trumps; *simple* ~, with single subject & predicate; *compound* ~, with more than one of either or both; *complex* ~, with subordinate clause or clauses), so **sĕntĕn'tiAL** (-shl) a. (rare); (loosely in gram.; usu. *subordinate* ~) subordinate clause. 4. Amount of speech, usu. that between two full stops often including several grammatical ~s (e.g. *I went & he came*). 5. v.t. State ~ of (condemned criminal, or transf.), declare condemned *to.* [ME, f. OF, f. L *sententia* f. *sentire* be of opinion, -ENCE]

sĕntĕn'tious (-shŭs), a. Aphoristic, pithy, given to the use of maxims, affecting a concise impressive style; (of style) affectedly formal; (of persons) fond of pompous moralizing. Hence ~LY[2] adv., ~NESS n. [f. L *sententiosus* (as prec., -OUS)]

sĕn'tient (-shi-), a. Having the power of sense-perception. Hence **sĕn'tiENCE** (-shi-) n., ~LY[2] adv. [L *sentire* feel, -ENT]

sĕn'timent, n. 1. A mental feeling, the sum of what one feels on some subject, a tendency or view based on or coloured with emotion, such feelings collectively as an influence, (*the* ~ *of pity, patriotism*; *animated by noble* ~*s*; *my* ~ *towards him is one of respect*; ~ *unchecked by reason is a bad guide*; *these are*, often joc. *them's, my* ~*s*, that is what I think about it). **2.** (In art) moving quality resulting from artist's sympathetic insight into what is described or depicted. **3.** Tendency to be swayed by feeling rather than by reason, emotional weakness, mawkish tenderness or the display of it, nursing of the emotions, whence **sĕntĭmĕn'tAL** a., **sĕntĭmĕn'talLY**[2] adv., **sĕntĭmĕntāl'ITY, sĕntĭmĕn'talIsM, sĕntĭmĕn'talIsT**, nn., **sĕntĭmĕn'talIzE**(2, 3) v.i. & t. **4.** (Sense intended to be conveyed by) the expression of some desire or view esp. as formulated for a toast etc. (*the* ~ *is good though the words are injudicious* etc.; *conclude one's speech with a* ~; *I call upon Mr Jones for a song or a* ~). [ME, f. OF (*-lement*), f. med. L *sentimentum* (L *sentire* feel, -MENT)]

sĕn'tĭnel, n., & v.t. (-ll-). **1.** Soldier posted to keep guard (cf. foll.); (also ~ *crab*) Indian-Ocean crab with long eye-stalks. **2.** v.t. Keep guard over or in (poet.); station ~s at or in (rare). [16th c., f. F *sentinelle* f. It. *-ella*; orig. unkn.]

sĕn'trÿ, n. (Term in ordinary mil. use for sentinel; ~-*board*, platform for ~ outside ship's gangway; ~-*box*, wooden cabin large enough to hold ~ standing; ~-*go*, duty of pacing up & down as ~. [perh. f. *centrinel* 16th-c. var. of prec.]

Sĕnuss'ĭ (-ōō-), n. (Now usu. form of) SENOUS(S)I.

sĕn'za (-tsa), It. prep. = without, in mus. directions as ~ *tĕm'pŏ*, not in strict time.

sĕp'al, n. One of the divisions of the calyx, calyx-leaf, (cf. PETAL). [f. F *sépale*, mod. L *sepalum*, formed by H. J. de Necker 1790 after *petalum* PETAL f. Gk *skepē* covering]

sĕp'arate[1], a. & n. **1.** Physically disconnected, forming a unit that is or may be regarded as apart or by itself, distinct, individual, of individuals, (*from*, or abs.; *the* ~ *members of the body*; *the* ~ *volumes may be had singly*; *live in* ~ *rooms*; *live* ~; *the two questions are essentially* ~; *one is quite* ~ *from the other*; ~ & *corporate* or *common ownership*; ~ *estate*, married woman's property when not subject to husband's control; ~ *maintenance*, husband's allowance to wife from whom he lives ~ by consent, cf. *alimony*; hence ~LY[2] adv., ~NESS n., & (esp. w. ref. to political or ecclesiastical independence, opp. *unionism*, *-ist*) **sĕp'aratISM**(3) n., **sĕp'aratIST**(2) n. & a. **2.** n. Copy of single article etc. reprinted from proceedings of society, magazine, etc., for ~ distribution; either of the articles of women's dress (blouse or jumper, or skirt or slacks) that

may be worn ~ly or with the other. [f. L SE(*parare* arrange), -ATE[2]]

sĕp'ar|āte[2], v.t. & i. Make separate, sever, disunite, keep (trans.) from union or contact, part (t. & i.), secede *from*, go different ways, disperse (intr.); sort or divide (milk, grain, ore, fruit, light, etc.) into constituent parts or sizes, get (cream etc.) by such process for use or rejection, whence ~ātOR n. Hence ~ABLE, ~ATIVE, ~atORY (rare), aa., ~abLY[2] adv., ~abIL'ITY, ~ableNESS, nn. [as prec., -ATE[3]]

sēparā'tion, n. In vbl senses; esp. partial divorce, divorce from bed & board without dissolution of marriage tie (*judicial* ~, ordered by court); ~ *allowance*, that made by soldier etc., with larger Government augmentation, to his wife etc. [ME, f. OF, f. L *separationem* (prec., -ION)]

Sĕphărd'ĭ, n. (pl. *-im*). Spanish or Portuguese Jew. [f. Heb. *Sephārād* (see *Obad.* XX) Spain]

sĕp'ĭa, n. Black fluid of CUTTLE-fish; brown pigment prepared from this used in monochrome drawing & in water-colours (*warm* ~, mixture of this with some red), dark reddish-brown colour; (also ~-*drawing*) a drawing done in ~. [L f. Gk (*sē-*), = cuttle or its ink]

sĕp'oy, n. Indian soldier disciplined by European methods, esp. one of those serving in British-Indian army (~ *mutiny*, = *Indian* MUTINY). [f. Hind. f. Pers. *sipahi* soldier (*sipah* army)]

sĕps, n. Kinds of skink, serpent lizard. [L, f. Gk *sēps* (*sēpō* make rotten)]

sĕp'sĭs, n. (med.). Putrefaction, contamination from festering wound etc., blood-poisoning. [Gk *sēpsis* (as prec.)]

sĕpt, n. Clan, esp. in Ireland; in Scotland, tribe within a clan. [prob. 16th c. var. of SECT; cf. obs. F *septe*]

sĕpt-, sĕpt|ĕm-, sĕpt|ĭ-, comb. forms of L *septem* seven: *sĕp'tan*, (of fever) recurring every 6th (inclus. 7th) day; *sĕp'tangle*, ~*ang'ular*, heptagon(al); ~*ĕmpart'ite*, divided into 7 parts; ~*ĕnn'ial*(ly), of, for, (recurring) every, 7 years; ~*ĕnn'ium* (pl. *-ia*), period of 7 years; ~*ĭlat'eral*, seven-sided; ~*isyll'able*, word of 7 syllables.

sĕpta. See SEPTUM.

sĕp'tal, a. Of sept(s), septum, or septa. [-AL]

sĕp't|āte, a. (bot., zool., anat.). Having septum or septa, partitioned. Hence ~A'TION n. [SEPTUM, -ATE[2]]

Sĕptĕm'ber, n. Ninth month of year. [ME, f. L *september* (*septem* seven) the seventh month of the old Roman year]

Sĕptĕm'brĭst, n. Participator in the massacres in Paris Sept. 2, 3, 1792. [F (*-e*), see -IST]

sĕptĕnār'ius, n. (pl. *-rĭ̄*). Verse (esp. Latin) of 7 feet esp. trochaic tetrameter catalectic. [L, f. *septeni* seven each]

sĕptĕn'arÿ (or *sĕp'tin-*), a. & n. Of or

involving the number 7, on basis of 7, by sevens; (n.) a 7, group or set of 7 (esp. years), a septenarius. [f. L *septenarius* (prec.), -ARY]

sěp'těnate, a. (bot.). Growing in sevens, having 7 divisions. [f. L *septeni* seven each, -ATE²]

sěptěnn'ate, n. (Arrangement made for) period of 7 years. [f. F (-*at*) f. L *septennis* (*septem* seven, *annus* year), -ATE¹]

sěptět(te)', n. (Composition for) group of 7 singers or players, (transf.) any set of 7. [G (-*ett*), f. L *septem*, see -ET¹, -ETTE]

sept'foil (sĕt⁴), n. The plant tormentil (now rare); seven-lobed figure esp. as R.-C. symbol of the 7 sacraments. [f. LL *septifolium* as if thr. OF; see SEPTI-, FOIL¹]

sěp'tic, a. & n. (med.). 1. Of or involving sepsis, putrefying; ~ *tank* (in which sewage is disintegrated through bacterial activity); hence **sěp'TICALLY** adv., **sěp-ti'CITY** n. 2. n. ~ substance. [f. L f. Gk *sēptikos* (*sēptos* f. *sēpō* rot, -IC)]

sěpticaem'|ia (-sēm-), n. (path.). Blood--poisoning. Hence ~IC a. [mod. L, f. Gk *sēptikos* see prec., *haima* blood, & -IA¹]

sěptill'ion (-yon), n. ‖ Seventh power of a million, 1 with 42 ciphers; *eighth power of a thousand, 1 with 24 ciphers. [f. F f. L *septem* seven, after *million*]

sěp'timal, a. Of the number 7. [f. L *septimus* seventh (*septem* seven) +-AL]

sěp'time (-ēm), n. Fencing-position. [f. L *septimus* (prec.)]

sěp'timus. See PRIMUS¹.

sěptūăgenār'ian, a. & n. (Person) between 69 & 80. [foll., -AN]

sěptūăgēn'arў, a. Of seventy. [f. L *septuagenarius* (*septuageni* seventy each f. *septuaginta* seventy, -ARY¹)]

Sěptūăgēs'ima, n. (Also ~ *Sunday*) Sunday before Sexagesima. [ME, f. L, = seventieth (day), prob. named loosely as before SEXAGESIMA]

sěp'tūagint, n. Greek version of O.T. including the Apocrypha said to have been made about 270 B.C. by seventy-two 'translators. [f. L *septuaginta* seventy]

sěp'tum, n. (anat., bot., zool.; pl. -*ta*). Partition such as that between the nostrils or the chambers of a poppy-fruit, dissepiment. [L (also *sae-*), = fence (*saepire saept-* f. *saepes* hedge)]

sěp'tūple, a. & n., & v.i. & t. Sevenfold (amount); (vb) multiply by 7, increase sevenfold. [f. LL *septuplus* f. L *septem* seven]

sěpǔlch'ral (-kral), a. Of sepulchre(s) or sepulture (~ *mound, pillar,* etc.; ~ *customs*); suggestive of the tomb, funereal, gloomy, dismal, (*a* ~ *look, voice*). Hence ~LY² adv. [f. L *sepulcralis* (foll., -AL)]

sěp'ulchre (-ker), n., & v.t. 1. Tomb esp. cut in rock or built of stone or brick, burial vault or cave, (*the Holy S*~, in which Christ was laid; *whited* ~, hypocrite, w. ref. to *Matt.* xxiii. 27). 2. v.t.

Lay in ~, serve as ~ for. [ME, f. OF (-*cre*), f. L *sepulc(h)rum (sepelire sepult-* bury)]

sěp'ulture, n. Burying, putting in the grave. [ME, f. OF, f. L *sepultura* (prec., -URE)]

sèquā'cious (-shus), a. (pedant.). Inclined to follow, lacking independence or originality, servile; (of reasoning or reasoner) not inconsequent, coherent. Hence ~LY² adv., **sèquā'CITY** n. [L *sequax (sequi* follow), -ACIOUS]

sē'quel, n. What follows after, continuation or resumption of a story or process or the like after a pause or provisional ending, (*in the* ~, as things developed afterwards); after effects, upshot; (rare) result of a chain of argument, logical inference, conclusion. [ME, f. OF (-*lle*), or f. L, as foll.]

sèquēl'a, n. (path.; usu. in pl. -*ae*). Morbid condition or symptom following upon some disease. [L (*sequi* follow)]

sē'quence, n. 1. Succession, coming after or next, set of things that belong next each other on some principle of order, series without gaps, (*shall follow the* ~ *of events, give the facts in historical* ~; *calamities fall in rapid* ~; *a* ~ *in clubs* etc. in cards, three or more next each other in value; *the* ~ *spring, summer, autumn, winter*). 2. Mere succession without implication of causality (~ *is related to* consequence *as* post hoc *to* propter hoc; *is causality, is a law of nature, anything beyond invariable* ~?), so (& rarely in other senses) **sē'quENT, sèquěn'tIAL** (-shl), aa., **sèquěn'tIALLY²** adv., **sèquěn-tiāl'ITY** (-shi-) n. 3. (cinemat.). ·Incident in a film story recorded consecutively (corresponding to a scene in a play). 4. (mus.). Succession of similar melodic phrases at different pitches. 5. (gram.). ~ *of tenses* or *moods*, accommodation of subordinate vb in tense or mood according to certain rules to tense or mood of principal vb (e.g. *I think you* are, *thought you* were, *wrong*). 6. (eccl.). Hymn said or sung after the Alleluia that precedes the Gospel (also *prose*). [f. LL *sequentia* f. part. of *sequi* follow, see -ENCE]

sēquěn'tēs, sèquěn'tia (-shia), (abbr. *seq.* or *seqq.*), L wds = (&) the following lines, (&) what follows, appended (with or without *et* and) to line or page numbers in references. [pl. part. of L *sequi* follow]

sèques'ter, v.t. & i. 1. Seclude, isolate, set apart, (~ *oneself from the world*; esp. in p.p.; *as a* ~*ed life, retreat, cottage*). 2. (law). (Also **sèquěs'trATE³**, *or* sĕk²wĭs-, v.t.) seize temporary possession of (debtor's estate etc.), remove (debatable property) from control of party to lawsuit, (intr.; of widow) renounce concern in husband's estate. 3. (Also *sequestrate*) confiscate, appropriate; hence or cogn. **sèquěstrA'TION, sē'quèstrātor,** nn., **sèquěs'trABLE** (*or* sĕk'wĭs-) a. [f. LL *sequestrare* commit for safe keeping (L *sequester* trustee, agent, cf. *secus* apart)]

sĕquĕs'tr|um, n. (pl. ~a). Piece of dead bone detached from living bone but remaining in place. Hence ~AL a., sĕquĕs-trŏt'omy n. [neut. of L *sequester* adj. standing apart]

sĕ'quin, n. (Hist.) Venetian gold coin of about 9/4; coinlike ornament of silver, jet, etc., sewn on to dresses etc. [F, f. It. *zecchino* (*zecca* mint f. Arab. *sikka* die)]

sĕquoi'a, n. Kinds of Californian coniferous tree of great height, redwood. [f. *Sequoiah*, a Cherokee pers. name]

sérac (sĕrăk'), n. One of the castellated masses into which a glacier is divided at steep points by the crossing of crevasses (usu. in pl.). [Swiss F, orig. name of a cheese]

sera'glio (-ahlyŏ), n. (pl. ~s). Walled palace, esp. (hist.) that of Sultan with government offices etc. at Constantinople; harem. [f. It. *serraglio*, f. Turk.-Pers. *serāī* palace; cf. foll.]

serai' (-rī, -rah'ī), n. = CARAVANSERAI.

serăng', n. (Anglo-Ind.). Native head of a Lascar crew. [f. Pers. *sarhang* commander]

sĕra'pe (-ahpā), n. Shawl or blanket worn by Spanish-Americans. [Sp.]

sĕ'raph, n. (pl. ~im, ~s). Celestial being; one of the highest ORDER[1] of ninefold celestial hierarchy gifted esp. with love & associated with light, ardour, & purity; (*Order of the S~im*, Swedish order of knighthood). Hence seraph'ic a. (*the S~ic Doctor*, St Bonaventura), seraph'ically adv. [back formation f. *seraphim* (cf. CHERUB) f. LL f. Gk f. Heb. *seraphim* pl. of *saraph*]

sĕ'raphine (-ēn), n. Early form of harmonium. [prec., -INE[1]]

sĕraskier', n. Turkish general commanding, commander-in-chief, or minister of war; ~at, war office. [Turk. f. Pers. *ser'asker* head of army]

Sĕrb, a. & n., Sĕrb'ian, a. & n. (Native, language) of Serbia. Hence Sĕrbo-comb. form. [f. Serb. *Srb, Serb*]

Serbon'ian bŏg, n. Treacherous bog formerly existing between delta of Nile & isthmus of Suez, (fig.) situation from which escape is difficult. [Gk *Serbōnis*, -IAN]

sĕre[1], sear[2], n. Catch of gun-lock holding hammer at half or full cock. [of uncert. orig.; usu. referred to OF *serre* lock, bolt, grasp, f. *serrer* (LL *serare*, bolt, bar)]

sere[2]. See SEAR[1].

serein (serăn'), n. Fine rain falling in tropical climates from cloudless sky. [F]

sĕrĕnăd|e', n., & v.t. 1. Evening song or instrumental piece sung or played by lover at his lady's window; = foll. 2. v.t. Sing or play ~e to; hence ~ER[1] n. [F, f. It. *serenata* (*sereno* open air f. L as SERENE); see -ADE]

sĕrĕna'ta (-nah-), n. (mus.). Cantata with pastoral subject; simple form of orchestral or wind-band suite. [It. (prec.)]

sĕrĕndip'ity, n. The faculty of making happy and unexpected discoveries by accident. [coined by Horace Walpole after *The Three Princes of Serendip* (Ceylon), a fairy-tale]

serēne', a. & n., & v.t. 1. (Of sky, air, etc.) clear & calm, (of sea etc.) unruffled; placid, tranquil, unperturbed, (*a ~ temper, look, life*); || (sl.) *all ~*, all right; *His, Her, Their, Your, S~ Highness(es)*, abbr. H.S.H., T.S.H., titles used of or to certain continental princes; hence or cogn. ~LY[2] adv., serĕn'ity n. (*your etc. Serenity, S~ Highness*). 2. n. ~ expanse of sky, sea, etc. 3. v.t. (poet.). Make (sky, brow, etc.)~. [f. L *serenus*]

sĕrf, n. Villein, person whose service is attached to the soil & transferred with it (cf. SLAVE); oppressed person, drudge. Hence ~AGE, ~DOM, ~HOOD, nn. [OF, f. L *servus* slave]

sêrge, n. Kind of durable twilled worsted fabric used esp. for rough wear (*silk ~*, used for tailor's linings). [ME, f. OF *sarge, serge* f. pop. L **sarica* f. L *serica* (*lana*), see SILK]

sergeant, -j-, (sâr'jant), n. 1. (hist.). *Serjeant-at-law*, barrister of superior rank. 2. (mil.; -*g*-; abbr. *Sgt*). Non-commissioned officer above corporal, employed to teach drill, command small detachments, etc. (~*-major* or *regimental ~-major*, R.S.M., warrant officer assisting adjutant of regiment or battalion; *company ~-major*, C.S.M., highest non-comd officer of company; *lance-~*, corporal acting as ~). 3. Police officer ranking between inspector & constable (-*g*-). 4. *Serjeant-at-arms*, title of certain court, parliamentary, & city officials with mainly ceremonial duties; *Common Serjeant*, judicial officer of City of London; ~-*fish* (-*g*-), sea-fish with lateral stripes suggesting chevron. Hence ~SHIP n. [ME, f. OF *sergent* f. L *servientem* nom. -*ens* servant (L *servire* SERVE, -ENT)]

sĕrgette' (-j-), n. Thin serge. [F (SERGE, -ETTE)]

sĕr'ial, a. & n. 1. Of, in, forming, a series, whence ~ITY (-ǎl[2]) n.; (of story etc.) issued in instalments (~ *rights*, copyright in regard to story etc. so issued), whence ~IST (1) n.; (of publication) periodical; hence ~LY[2] adv. 2. n. ~ story; a ~ publication, periodical, (rare). Hence ~IZE v.t. [SERIES, -AL]

sĕr'iate, -ātĕd, aa., sĕr'iāte, v.t (Arrange) in the form of a series, in orderly sequence. So sĕriA'TION n. [L SERIES, -ATE[2,3]]

sĕriāt'im (or sēr-), adv. Point by point, taking one subject etc. after another in regular order, (*consider, examine, discuss, take*, etc., ~). [med. L f. L *series* after *gradatim*, LITERATIM]

Sĕr'ic, a. (rhet. etc.). Chinese. [f. L *sericus*, see SERGE, SILK]

sĕri'ceous (-shus), a. (bot., zool.). Of

silky or satiny surface, soft & shiny, covered with glossy down [as prec., see -EOUS; cf. LL *sericeus*]

sě′ri(cǐ)|cùlture, n. Silkworm-breeding, production of raw silk. Hence~cŭl′tùraL a., ~cŭl′tùrIST(3) n., (-cher-). [F (-*ci*-), see prec., -I-, CULTURE]

sěriēm′a, n. Sonorous-voiced Brazilian bird of heron size preying on serpents. [native]

ser′ies (sēr′ēz), n. (pl. same). 1. Number of things of which each is similar to the preceding or related to it as it to its predecessor, sequence, succession, order, row, set, (*a ~ of kings, misfortunes; in ~*, in ordered succession; *~ of stamps, coins*, etc., of different denominations but issued at one time, in one reign, etc.; *the whole ~ of reform acts*). 2. (bibliog.). Set of successive issues of a periodical, of articles on one subject or by one writer, etc., esp. (*first, second*, etc., *~*) when numbered differently from a preceding or following set, also set of independent books in common *format* or under common title or supervised by common general editor, (*Guesses at Truth, 2nd S~*; *the Men-of--Letters ~*). 3. (geol.). Set of strata with common characteristic. 4. (chem.). Set of elements with common properties or compounds with common radical. 5. (math.). Set of terms constituting a progression or having the several values determined by a common relation (*arithmetical, geometrical, ~*, one in ARITHMETICAL, GEOMETRICAL, progression). 6. (electr.). Set of batteries etc. having positive electrode of each connected with negative of next. 7. (zool.). Number of connected genera, families, etc. (used vaguely like GROUP). [L *series* row, chain, f. *serere* join, connect]

sě′rif, (now rare) cě′riph, n. Cross-line finishing off a stroke of a letter (esp. in SANSERIF; This has ~s: This is sanserif). [orig. unkn.]

serig′raph|y̆, n. Art or process of printing designs by means of a silk screen, silk screen printing. So sě′rigraph (-ahf) [-GRAPH], ~ER[1], nn. [irreg. f. L *sericum* silk, -GRAPHY]

sě′rin, n. Central-Europ. finch related to canary. [F, of unkn. orig.]

sěrinětte′, n. Instrument for teaching cage-birds to sing; kind of small barrel-organ, musical box, etc. [F (*seriner* teach to sing f. prec., -ETTE)]

sering′a (-ngg-), n. = SYRINGA; kinds of Brazilian rubber-tree. [F, = Pg. *seringa* f. mod. L; see SYRINGA]

sērio-cŏm′|ic, a. Combining the serious & the comic, jocular in intention but counterfeiting seriousness or vice versa. Hence ~ICALLY adv. [-O-]

sěriōs′ō, mus. direction. With solemnity. [It.]

sēr′ious, a. 1. Thoughtful, earnest, sober, sedate, responsible, not frivolous or reckless or given to trifling, (*has a ~ look, air*; *a ~ young person*; *~ politician*, who gives his best energies to politics; *~ thought*, real deliberation). 2. Important, demanding consideration, not to be trifled with, not slight, (*this is a ~ matter, question, step*; *made a ~ alteration*; *have a ~ rival in her affections*; *~ illness, danger, wound, damage, accident, defeat*). 3. Sincere, not ironical or jesting in earnest, (*are you ~?*, do you mean what you say ?; *made a ~ attempt*, not merely perfunctory; *& now to be ~*). 4. Concerned with religion or ethics, not worldly or secular, (*~ subjects* etc.); (now chiefly joc.) religious-minded, with thoughts concentrated on salvation. Hence ~LY[2] adv. (esp. as preface to sentence implying that irony etc. is now to cease), ~NESS n. [ME, f. OF *serious* or LL *seriosus* (L *serus*, see -OUS)]

sě′riph, n. = SERIF.

serjeant. See SERGEANT.

sěrm′on, n., & v.t. 1. Extempore or written discourse delivered from the pulpit by way of religious instruction or exhortation, similar discourse (often *lay ~*) on religious or moral subject delivered elsewhere or published, (*S~ on the Mount*, discourse of Christ reported *Matt.* v–vii); moral reflection suggested by natural objects etc. (esp. *~s in stones*); piece of admonition or reproof, lecture. 2. v.t. Administer such ~ to. Hence ~ETTE′, ~ET[1], nn., ~IZE(1, 2) v.t. & i., ~ĪZER[1] n. [ME, f. AF *sermun*, OF *-on*, f. L *sermonem* nom. *-o* speech]

sēro-, comb. form of SERUM: ~*pū′ulent*, of serum & pus; ~*sanguin′olent*, & blood; ~THERAPY.

sě′rotine, n. Chestnut-coloured European bat. [F (*sé*-), f. L *serotinus* late(*serus* late)]

sěrōt′inous, a. (bot.). Appearing late in season. [f. L *serotinus* (prec.) + -OUS]

sēr′ous, a. Of or like serum, watery, whey-like. Hence sēros′ITY n. [f. F *séreux* f. L SERUM + *-eux* -OUS]

sěrp′ent, n. Scaly limbless reptile, snake esp. of the larger kinds, (preferred to SNAKE chiefly in rhet. use; *the, the old, S~*, the devil, w. ref. to *Gen.* iii, *Rev.* xx), (fig.) treacherous person esp. one who worms himself into favour for base ends; *the S~*, a northern constellation; obsolete wind--instrument, a wooden tube with several bends giving powerful note; *Pharaoh's ~*, chemical toy of small cone that when ignited issues in long coiling ~like ash; ~*-charmer*, person who charms ~s esp. by music; ~*-eater*, SECRETARY-bird; ~*-grass*, Alpine bistort; ~ *lizard*, seps; ~*'s-tongue*, ADDER's-*tongue*. Hence serpěn′tIFORM, ~LIKE, aa. [ME, f. OF, f. L *serpentem* nom. *-ens*, part. of *serpere* creep; see -ENT]

sěrp′entine, a. & n., & v.i. 1. Of or like a serpent lit. or fig.; writhing, coiling, tortuous, sinuous, meandering, cunning, subtle, treacherous, (*~ windings*, of stream, road, etc., or of insinuation; ~ *motion*; ~ *wisdom*, profound, w. ref. to *Matt.* x. 16; ~ *dance*, with sinuous movements enhanced by special drapery; ~ *verse*, line beginning & ending with same word; ‖ *the S~*, ornamental water in Hyde Park). **2. n.** Kinds of hydrous silicate of magnesium, soft rocks of dark green & other colours sometimes mottled or spotted like serpent's skin, taking high polish & used as decorative material; (skating) wavy line produced by changes of edge. **3.** v.i. Move sinuously, meander. [(1) ME, f. OF *serpentin* f. LL *serpentinus* (prec., -INE¹); (2) OF *serpentin(e)* f. med. L *serpentina, -um* abs. use of adj.]

serpi′ginous, a. (path.). Affected with herpes; (of skin-disease etc.) creeping from one part to another. [f. med. L *serpigo -ginis* ringworm (L *serpere* creep), -OUS]

serp′ula, n. (pl. *-ae*). Kinds of marine worm inhabiting beautifully coloured tortuous calcareous tubes often massed together. [LL, = small serpent (L *serpere* creep)]

se′rra, n. (anat., bot., zool.; pl. *-ae*). Serrated organ, structure, or edge. [L, = saw]

se̍rradill′a, n. Kind of clover grown as fodder. [Port., dim. of *serrado* SERRATE a.]

se′rrate, a., **se̍rrate′,** v.t. (chiefly anat., bot., zool.). **1.** Notched like saw. **2.** v.t. (Usu. in p.p. as adj.) provide with saw-like edge. Hence **se̍rra′tion** n. [f. L SERRA*tus* (-ATE²), -ATE³]

se′rrefile, n. (mil.; usu. in pl.). Person in, (pl.) the line of supernumerary & non-commissioned officers in, rear of squadron or troop of cavalry. [F, f. *serrer* (see SERRIED) + *file* (see FILE³)]

se′rri-, comb. form (-I-) of SERRA: ~*corn*, (beetle) with serrate antennae; ~*F′EROUS*; ~FORM; ~*ros′trate*, (of bird) with serrated bill.

se′rried (-rĭd), a. (Of ranks of soldiers, rows of trees, etc.) shoulder to shoulder, without gaps, close. [f. 16th c. *serry* (app. f. F *serré* p.p. of *serrer* close f. LL *serare*) + -ED¹]

se̍rrul∣ate (-rōō-), **-ated,** aa. Finely serrate, with series of small notches. Hence ~A′TION n. [L *serrula* (SERRA, -ULE), -ATE²]

se̍r′um, n. Whey; amber-coloured liquid which separates from clot when blood coagulates; blood ~ as anti-toxin or therapeutic agent; watery animal fluid; ~ *sickness*, skin eruption, fever, etc., sometimes following injections of ~. [L, = whey]

se̍rv′al, n. Tawny black-spotted African tiger-cat. [F, f. Port.]

se̍rv′ant, n. **1.** Person who has undertaken usu. in return for stipulated pay to carry out the orders of an individual or corporate employer, esp. one who lives in house of master or mistress receiving board & lodging & wages & performing domestic duties (*public~s*, State officials; *civil ~*, member of the civil service; *outdoor ~*, groom, gardener, etc.; *indoor ~*, cook, butler, footman, housemaid, etc.; *domestic*, GENERAL, LIVERY¹, ~; ~*-girl, -maid; the ~ question*, problem of getting & controlling ~s; *keeps three ~s*; ~*s′ hall*, room in which ~s of large household have meals etc.; ~ *of ~s*, lowest of dependants, esp. as title assumed by Popes, transl. of *servus servorum Dei*; *a good ~ but a bad master*, of things that should be treated as means & not ends). **2.** Devoted follower, person willing to serve another, (*a ~ of Jesus Christ*; ‖ *your humble~*, arch., form of ironical courtesy; ‖ *your obedient~*, epistolary form preceding signature now used only in letters of official type). [ME, f. OF (SERVE, -ANT)]

se̍rve, v.t. & i., & n. **1.** Be servant (to), do service (to), be useful (to), (~ *two masters*, be divided between two conflicting principles etc.; ~ *the Lord* or *God*, be religious or virtuous; ~ *the devil*, be wicked; ~ *tables*, postpone spiritual to bodily needs, see *Acts* vi. 2; ~ *at table*, act as waiter; *has ~d his generation; would do much to ~ you; indiscretion sometimes ~s us well*; ~ *in army*, *navy*, etc., be employed in it; *has ~d in India*, been employed esp. as soldier). **2.** Meet needs (of), avail (t. & i.), suffice (t. & i.), satisfy, perform function, be suitable, do what is required for, (~ *a purpose*; ~ *the purpose of*, take place of, be used as; *to ~ some private ends*; ~*s the* or one's *turn* or *need*, does well enough; *it will ~*, do what is absolutely necessary; *that excuse will not ~ you*; *it ~s to show the folly of*; 1 lb. ~*s him for a week*; *nothing would ~ him* or ~ *but absolute submission*; *a sofa serving him*, or *serving, as* or *for (a) bed*; *as memory ~s*, whenever one remembers; *as occasion ~s*, when it is favourable; *the tide ~s*, is suitable for getting out of harbour etc.; *curate ~s two parishes*, does the work; ~ *an office*, go through a tenure of it; ~ one's *apprenticeship*, go through training; ~ *a sentence*, undergo it for the full time; ~ one's *time*, hold office for normal period, also ~ a sentence; ~ *time*, undergo imprisonment etc.; ~ *gun*, *battery*, keep it firing; ~ *mare* etc., cover, esp. of stallion etc. hired for purpose; ~ *rope* etc., naut., bind with small cord to save fraying). **3.** Dish *up*, set (food) on table, set out ready, distribute (trans. & abs.), supply (person *with*), make legal delivery of (writ etc.), set ball or set (ball) in play, (*fish ~d up nearly cold*; *asparagus ~d with butter*; ~ *up dinner*; *dinner is ~d*, servant's announcement that it is ready; ~ *ammunition*, *rations*, etc., *out* or *round*; *was serving a customer with stockings*, *serving in the shop*; *have them ~d with soup*; ~ *with the same sauce*, fig., retaliate upon; ~ *person*, *the town*, etc., *with gas*, *water*; ~ *with*

writ etc., = ~ writ etc. on; ~ *warrant,
writ, notice, process, attachment,* etc., usu.
on person, deliver document to person
concerned in legally formal manner;
tennis, racquet, etc., *player* ~s *a ball,
~s well, badly,* etc., sends ball to opponent
in first stroke of round). 4. Treat, treat
to, pay (person) *out,* (*has* ~d *me shamefully; you may* ~ *me as you will;* ~d *them
a trick,* played it on them; ~ *or* ~s *him
right!,* excl. of satisfaction at sight of
offender getting his deserts; *shall manage
to* ~ *him out,* retaliate). 5. ‖ *Serving-man,*
male servant. Hence (-)sĕrv′ER¹(1, 2) n.,
(also, eccl.) celebrant's assistant, sĕrv′ERY
(3) n., room from which meals etc. are ~d
& in which utensils are kept. 6. n. (In
tennis etc.) first stroke of round, turn
for delivering this (*whose* ~ *is it?*). [ME,
f. OF *servir* f. L *servire* (*servus* slave)]

Sĕrv′ian¹. Var. of, & till 1914 more usual
than, SERBIAN.

Sĕrv′ian², a. (Rom. ant.). Of **Servius**
Tullius sixth king of Rome (~ *wall,* built
by him & still existing in parts). [-AN]

sĕrv′ice¹, n., & v.t. 1. Being servant,
servant's status, master's or mistress's
employ, (*girl* etc. *goes out to, goes into,
tries, is in,* ~; *take* ~ *with,* become servant
to; *take into* one's ~, employ). 2. Department of royal or public employ or of
work done to meet some general need,
persons engaged in it, employment in it,
(*the fighting,* or *the,* ~s, navy, army, & air
force; *the public* ~s; *the* CIVIL, COVENANTED,
consular, SECRET, *bus, railway,* etc., ~; *the
preventive* ~, coastguards, custom-house,
etc.; *is on* ~, *in active* ~, actually engaged
in such employ; *see* ~, have experience
esp. as soldier or sailor; (attrib.) of the
kind issued to the ~ (*the* ~ *rifle).* 3. Person's disposal or behalf (*at your* etc. ~,
ready to obey orders or be used; ‖ *on his,
her, Majesty's* ~, abbr. O.H.M.S., frank
stamped on official letters etc.). 4. What
employee or subordinate is bound to,
work done or doing of work on behalf of
employer, benefit conferred on or exertion made on behalf of someone, expression of willingness to confer or make
these, (*personal* ~, feudal obligation of
homage etc.; *feudal, menial, willing,* YEO-
MAN('s), ~; *has a right to my* ~; *asks for my*
~s; *will you do me a* ~?; *exaggerates his
own* ~s; *has seen* ~, been much used,
shows signs of wear; *my* ~ *to him,* form of
respectful message). 5. Use, assistance,
(*can I, will it, be of* ~ *to you?*). 6. Liturgical form or office appointed for use on
some occasion, (whole proceedings, usu.
including one such ~ or more, of) single
meeting of congregation for worship,
musical setting of all or several of the
invariable parts of a liturgy adapted for
such treatment, (*the communion, burial,*
etc., ~; *special* ~s; *divine* ~ usu. without
a, meeting for worship; *holds four* ~s
every Sunday; are you going to ~ *or the*

~?; —'s ~, setting by particular composer; *full* ~, performed by choir without solos, also ~ with music wherever
possible; *plain* ~, read or monotoned; ~-
-*book,* book of offices of a Church, e.g. the
Book of Common Prayer; CHURCH¹-~).
7. Legal serving of or of writ etc. (*personal*
~, delivery with announcement of contents to person affected; ~ *by publication,
substitution,* publishing of writ etc. by
posting up or insertion in newspaper or
by handing to neighbour etc. recognized
as sufficient under some conditions;
ACCEPT ~). 8. Set of dishes, plates, etc.,
required for serving meal (*dinner, dessert,
tea,* etc., ~). 9. Set of trains, steamers,
buses, etc., plying at stated times.
10. (Single act of) serving in tennis
etc., serve, manner of serving, person's
turn to serve, game in which one serves,
(*his* ~ *is weak, terrific; whose* ~ *is it?; he
lost his* ~; ~-*line,* marking line short
of which serve must fall). 11. Expert
assistance or advice given to customers
after sale by manufacturers or vendors
of an article, e.g. a motor-car or wireless
set (so .~ *department, depot, station).*
12. ~ *area,* area round broadcasting
station within which satisfactory reception may be expected; ~ *dress,* ordinary
uniform (opp. *full dress*); ~ *flat* (in which
domestic ~ and meals are provided by
the management); ‖ ~ *hatch* (through
which dishes are passed to dining-room);
~ *pipe* (conveying water or gas from the
main to a building). 13. v.t. Maintain or
repair (car etc.) after sale. [ME, f. OF,
f. L *servitium* (*servus* slave)]

sĕrv′ice², n. (Usu. ~-*tree*) European tree
rare in England with leaves like those of
mountain-ash, cream-coloured flowers, &
small pear-shaped fruit (~-*berry* or ~)
eaten when over-ripe. [orig. *serves,* pl. of
obs. *serve,* OE *syrfe,* f. L *sorbus* SORB]

sĕrv′iceab‖le (-sabl), a. Of use, useful,
willing & able to render or capable of
rendering service, (*a* ~*le person, reminder,
instrument*); durable, suited for rough use
or ordinary wear rather than for ornament. Hence ~LY² adv., ~leNESS n. [ME,
f. OF *servisable* (SERVICE¹, -ABLE)]

sĕrviètte′, n. Table-napkin. [F]

sĕrv′ile (*or* -ĭl), a. Of, being, a slave or
slaves, slave-, (~ *war,* between revolted
slaves & their owners; ~ *class, labour;* ~
letter, fig., having no other function than
to indicate pronunciation of another, as
e in manageable, saleable); as of a slave,
slavish, cringing, mean-spirited, menial,
completely dependent, (~ *spirit, creature,
submission, flattery, fear, imitation),* so
sĕrvil′ITY n.; ~ *works* (eccl.), menial or
mechanical work forbidden on Sundays
and major Church festivals. Hence ~LY²
adv. [ME, f. L *servilis* (*servus* slave, -IL)]

Sĕrv′ite, n. One of the order of 'Servants
of Blessed Mary'. [f. med. L *Servitae*
f. L *servus* servant, see -ITE¹(1)]

sĕrv'ĭtor, n. Attendant, henchman, servant, (arch., poet.); || (Oxf. Univ.; hist.) undergraduate assisted from college funds & performing menial duties in return, whence ~SHIP n. [ME, f. OF f. LL (SERVE, -OR)]

sĕrv'ĭtūde, n. Slavery lit. or fig., subjection esp. involuntary to a master, bondage (PENAL ~); (law) subjection of tenement to an easement. [ME, f. OF f. L *servitudinem* (*servus* slave, -TUDE)]

sĕrv'o-mōt'or, n. Auxiliary motor, esp. one for operating the reversing gear of a large marine engine. [f. F *servo-moteur* (L *servus* slave)]

sĕs'amē, n. Annual herbaceous tropical & subtropical plant with seeds used in various ways as food & yielding an oil used in salads & as laxative; its seeds; *open* ~, (w. ref. to Arabian-Nights tale) magical or mysterious means of commanding access to what is usu. inaccessible. [f. L f. Gk *sēsamē*]

sĕs'amoid, a. & n. **1.** Shaped like a sesame-seed, nodular, (esp. of small independent bones developed in tendons passing over angular structure, as the knee-pan & the navicular bone). **2.** n. Such bone. [f. L f. Gk *sēsamoeidēs* (prec., -OID)]

sĕs'eli, n. Kinds of white-flowered umbelliferous perennial plants. [f. L f. Gk *seselis, seseli,* cf. CICELY]

sĕs'qui-, L pref. (perh. f. *semis-que* & a half), = one & a half (~*pedalis* a foot & a half long), proportioned as 1½:1 or 3:2 (~*alter*), proportioned as n+1: n (~*tertius,* ~*quartus,* etc., in ratios 4:3, 5:4, etc.). Hence in E: **1.** Chem. wds for compounds in which there are three equivalents of the named element to two others, as ~*ox'ide,* ~*sulph'ide;* ~*bas'ic,* (of salt) with three of base to two of acid. **2.** Math. wds expressing ratios as above, ~*al'teral* 3:2, ~*ter'tial* 4:3, ~*quar'tal,* ~*quin'tal,* ~*sex'tal,* ~*sep'timal,* ~*octav'al,* ~*non'al* 10:9. **3.** Mus. wds in -a corresponding to the above & expressing intervals (~*al'tera* interval having ratio 2:3, ~*ter'tia* 3:4, etc.). **4.** Miscellaneous wds, as ~*centenn'ial,* (of) a one-hundred- -&-fiftieth anniversary; ~*ocell'us* (entom.), large spot with smaller one within it (also ~*alter*); ~*pedāl'ian,* (of word) 1½ ft long, cumbrous & pedantic; ~*tone,* musical interval of 1½ tone.

sess. See CESS.

sĕss'ĭle, a. (bot., zool.). (Of flower, leaf, eye, etc.) attached directly by the base without stalk or peduncle. [f. L *sessilis* (*sedēre sess-* sit, -IL)]

sĕ'ssion (-shn), n. **1.** Being seated, sitting posture, (rare). **2.** Being assembled esp. for transaction of deliberative or judicial business, single uninterrupted meeting for such purpose, period during which such meetings are held daily or at short or regular intervals, period (usu. one in a year) between meeting & prorogation of Parliament, (*in* ~, sitting or assembled for business, not keeping vacation; *had a long* ~, sat assembled a long time; *autumn* ~, resumption of ~ of Parliament occas. required by pressure of business after long adjournment in summer without prorogation); (esp. Sc. & U.S.) university term. **3.** || QUARTER-~s; || BREW-STER-SESSIONS: || *petty* ~s, meeting of two or more justices of the peace for summary trying of certain offences; || *Court of S*~, supreme civil court of Scotland; KIRK-~. Hence ~AL (-shon-) a. (~*al order,* Parl., valid only for, renewable each, ~). [ME, f. OF, or f. L *sessio* (prec., -ION)]

sĕs'tĕrce, sĕstĕr'tius (-shus; pl. *-tĭ*), nn. Ancient-Roman silver (& later bronze) coin & money of account = ¼ denarius or 2½ (later 4) asses. [f. L (*-ius*) orig. adj. with *nummus* coin = 2½ (*semisertius* half-third)]

sĕstĕr'tium (-shm), n. (pl. *-ia*). Ancient- -Roman money of account = 1000 sesterces. [orig. gen. pl. of prec. after *millia* thousands]

sĕstĕt', n. = SEXTET; last six lines of sonnet. [f. It. *sestetto* (*sesto* f. L *sextus* sixth, -ET[1])]

sĕsti'na (-tē-), n. Form of rhymed or unrhymed poem with six stanzas of six lines & final triplet, each stanza having same words as the others ending its lines but in different order. [It. (prec., -INE[1])]

sĕt[1], v.t. & i. (*set*). **I.** General senses. **1.** Put, lay, stand (trans.), (usu. with adv. or advl phr.; ~ *load* or *passenger down, statue up, meat before* person, *flowers in water, one brick on another;* ~ *foot,* tread *on;* ~ thing *against* another, balance, reckon as counterpoise or compensation; ~ *apart,* reserve, separate; ~ *aside,* reserve, reject, disregard, annul; ~ *by,* reserve, save for future use; ~ *stone out,* lay it with edge projecting beyond one below; ~ person *over* others or thing, put in authority). **2.** Apply (thing) *to* (~ *pen to paper, bugle* to one's *lips, spurs* to *horse;* ~ one's *hand, seal,* to document, sign, seal; ~ one's *hand to* task, begin; ~ *fire to,* kindle; ~ *the axe to,* begin to cut down or destroy; ~ one's *wits to* question, try to solve; ~ one's *wits to* another's, argue with him; ~ SHOULDER *to wheel*). **3.** Station, place ready, place or turn in right or specified position or direction, dispose suitably for use or action or display, (~ *a* or naut. *the watch,* put sentinels etc. in place; ~ *chairs,* · for visitors etc.; ~ *clock* or *watch,* put hands to right time; ~ *alarum,* provide for its sounding at desired time; ~ *hen,* cause to sit on eggs; ~ *eggs,* place for hen to sit on; ~ *seed, plant,* put in ground; QUICK~; ~ *butterfly* etc., arrange as specimen; ~ *sail,* hoist, also = start on voyage; ~ *trap;* ~ *razor,* give even edge to after grinding;

~ *saw,* give teeth alternate outward inclination; ~ *table,* lay for meal; ~ or ~ *up type,* arrange it in words etc.; ~ *up book* etc., put it in type; ~ *close, wide,* etc., print with small, large, spaces between words or letters; ~ *out,* ~ *wide;* ~ one's CAP[1] *at).* 4. Join, attach, fasten, fix, determine, decide, appoint, settle, establish, (~ *leg, bone, joint,* put parts into right relative position after fracture or dislocation, also by extension ~ *fracture* or *dislocation;* ~ *eyes on,* catch sight of; ~ *diamond* etc., insert in gold etc. as frame or foil; ~ *stake in ground; close-~,* with little interval; ~ one's *heart, mind, hopes,* etc., on, long for, expect, be resolved to get; ~ one's *life on a chance* etc. metaph. from gambling, risk it; ~ *price on,* announce salable value of; ~ *person against* another or a thing, fill with settled dislike for; ~ *price on* one's *life* or *head,* offer specified reward for his killing; ~ *store* or *much by,* & ellipt. ~ *by,* estimate or value highly; ~ one's *face* or one*self against,* steadfastly oppose or discountenance; ~ one's *teeth,* clench them, esp. fig.=make up one's mind inflexibly; often in p.p., = unmoving, fixed, as ~ *smile, eyes, look, purpose;* of ~ *purpose,* intentionally, deliberately; ~ *time,* prearranged; ~ *scene,* built up of more or less solid material; ~ *piece* in fireworks, built up on scaffolding; ~ *forms of prayers* etc., not extempore; ~ *speech,* composed beforehand; ~ *fair,* of weather, fine without sign of breaking; ~ *on* or *upon,* de-·termined to get, absorbed in; *batsman is* ~, has got his eye in). 5. Fix (hair) when damp so that it dries in waves. 6. Bring by placing, arranging, impelling, or other means, into specified state (~ *things right, to rights, in order, in motion;* ~ one's *house in order,* often fig., introduce reforms; ~ *question,* person's *heart, at rest;* ~ *machine going, cask abroach;* ~ person *on his feet* lit. & fig., *box on its end;* ~ one *in the way,* direct him; ~ one *on his way,* arch., go part way with him; ~ one *right,* disabuse him of error, correct, often with implication of officiousness etc.; ~ one *at ease,* relieve his anxieties or bashfulness; ~ *at liberty,* ~ *free,* release; ~ persons *by the ears, at variance* or *loggerheads,* produce quarrel; ~ *on fire,* kindle; ~ *Thames on* FIRE[1]; ~ *movement* etc. *on foot,* start it; ~ *table, company,* etc., *laughing* or *on* or *in a roar,* stir laughter; ~ *teeth on* EDGE[1]); ~ *at defiance,* defy; ~ *at naught,* mock, disregard. 7. Make sit down *to* task, order to apply energies *to doing,* cause *to work,* apply oneself *to work,* (~ *him to dictation, wood-chopping, work at his Greek; shall* ~ *to work now,* begin; ~ one*self to* do, make up one's mind, resolve or undertake). 8. Exhibit or arrange as pattern or as material to be dealt with (often w. ind. obj.; ~, ~ person, *an example, task, prob-*

lem, etc., to be followed, done, solved, by him; ~ *the fashion, the pace,* determine it by leading; ~ *paper,* draw up questions to be answered by examinees; ~ *the* TEMPERAMENT in piano-tuning, arrange intervals of one octave as standard for the rest). 9. ~ (*to music*), provide (song, words) with music usu. composed for the purpose. 10. Make insertions in (surface) *with* (*gold, field, sky,* ~ *with gems, daisies, stars; shall* ~ *top of wall with broken glass, this bed with geraniums*). 11. Turn (i., rarely t.) to solid or hard or rigid from liquid or soft or mobile state, curdle, solidify, harden, take shape, develop (usu. intr.) into definiteness or maturity, (*egg* ~*s,* by cooking or incubation; HARD-~; *blossom* ~*s,* forms into fruit; *fruit* ~*s,* develops out of blossom; *tree*~*s,* develops fruit; *plaster of Paris* ~*s quickly; the jelly, junket, has* or *is* ~; *when his body, character, has* ~; THICK~; *over-exercise* ~*s a boy's muscles prematurely; face* ~*s,* takes hard expression; *eyes* ~, become motionless in death, swoon, etc.). 12. Sink below horizon (*sun, moon,* ~*s; the star of Rome, his star, has* or *is* ~, greatness is departed). 13. (Of tide, current, etc., & transf. of feelings, customs, etc.) have motion, gather force, sweep along, show or feel tendency, (*tide* ~*s in, out; current* ~*s strongly, eastwards; opinion is* ~*ting against it; his soul* ~ *to grief*). 14. (Of sporting dog) take rigid attitude indicating presence of game; (of dancers) take position facing partners (often ~ *to partners*). 15. (Of garment) adapt itself to figure, sit, *well, badly,* etc. 16. (In some games) fix the number of points to decide the game. 17. SHARP[1]~. II. Special senses with advv. & prepp. 1. ~ *about,* begin, take steps towards, (task, do*ing*). 2. ~ *back,* impede or reverse progress of, *(sl.) cost (person) so much. 3. ~ *down,* put in writing, attribute *to,* explain or describe to oneself as. 4. ~ *forth,* make known, declare, expound, adorn, begin journey or expedition. 5. ~ *forward,* assist progress of, begin going forward (arch.). 6. ~ *in,* arise, get vogue, become established, (*reaction, rain,* ~ *in; it* ~ *in to rain*). 7. ~ *off,* act as adornment or foil to, enhance, make more striking, start (person) laughing or talking on pet subject, begin journey. 8. ~ *on* adv., instigate, advance to the assault; ~ *on* prep., urge (dog etc.) to attack (person etc.), attack. 9. ~ *out,* embellish, demonstrate, exhibit, declare, begin journey. 10. ~ *to* adv., begin doing something vigorously, esp. (usu. w. pl. subj.) fighting or arguing. 11. ~ *up,* develop figure of by physical training (esp. in p.p., as *a well* ~-*up man*), start (institution, business, one's carriage, etc.), occasion (soreness etc.), establish (person) or provide with means of establishment or establish oneself in some capacity (*his* *father*, £500, ~ *him up as a tobacconist* or *in the tobacco trade*; *shall* ~ *up as a dentist*), provide adequately *in* or *with* some article (*am* ~ *up with novels for the winter*), place (standard, notice, etc.) in view, begin uttering (protest, shriek, etc.) loudly, propound (theory), restore from ill-health or depression; ~ *up for* (colloq.), make pretensions to the character of (~*s up for a scholar, moralist*, etc.). **12.** ~ *upon*, = ~ *on* prep. [OE *settan*, OS -*ian*, OHG *sezzan*, ON *setja*, Goth. *satjan* causal of Gmc **setjan* (**siljan*) SIT]

set², n. **1.** Number of things or persons that belong together as essentially similar or as complementary to each other, group, clique, collection, (~ *of studs, chairs, golf-clubs, fire-irons, lectures*; ~ *of teeth*, natural or artificial; *a fine* ~ *of men, players, officers*, etc.; *dinner* ~, dinner SERVICE¹; *toilet* ~, vessels of wash-hand-stand; *the fast, best, racing, smart, literary, political*, etc., ~, sections of society consorting together; ~ *of quadrilles* or ~, figures that make up a quadrille; ~ *of dancers* or ~, number needed to make up square dance; *a, the first*, etc., ~ in tennis etc., group of games counting as unit to side that wins more than half the games in it; ~ *point*, state of a ~ in lawn tennis when one side needs only one more point to win it; ~ *of exchange*, first etc. of EXCHANGE¹ col-lectively). **2.** Slip or shoot for planting; young fruit just set. **3.** Setting *of* sun or day (poet.). **4.** Way current or wind or opinion etc. sets, drift or tendency *of*, (*the* ~ *of the current, public feeling*, etc.; *the* ~ *of his mind is towards intolerance*). **5.** Configuration, conformation, habitual posture, way head etc. is set on or carried, way dress etc. sits or flows, (usu. *of*; *the* ~ *of the hills, his head, the drapery*); warp or bend or displacement caused by con-tinued pressure or position (*has got a* ~ *to the right*). **6.** (Amount of) alternate defec-tion of saw-teeth. **7.** Last coat of plaster on wall. **8.** Timber frame supporting gallery etc. in coal-mine. **9.** Amount of margin in type causing letters to be close or wide set. **10.** Number of eggs in nest, or number laid before bird sits, clutch. **11.** Setter's pointing in presence of game (often *dead* ~; *make a dead* ~ *at*, transf., attack esp. by argument or ridicule). **12.** ‖ Badger's burrow. **13.** Granite paving-block. **14.** Kinds of wrench & punch. **15.** (Theatr.) set scene; (cinemat.) built-up scene. **16.** Radio receiving apparatus. **17.** ~-*back*, reversal or arrest of progress, relapse; ~-*down*, rebuff, snub; ~-*off*, thing set off against another, thing of which the amount or effect may be deducted from that of another of opposite tendency, counterpoise, counter-claim, thing that embellishes, adornment *to* something, (archit.) sloping or horizontal member connecting lower and thicker

part of wall etc. with upper receding part; ~-*out*, commencement or start (esp. *at the first* ~-*out*), things set out, equip-ment, display of food or utensils or goods; ~-*to*, combat esp. with fists; ~-*up*, erect-ness or carriage of body, (colloq., orig. U.S.) structure, or arrangement of an organization etc. [sense 1 f. OF *sette* f. L *secta* SECT; remainder f. prec.]

sētā′ceous (-shus), a. Bristly, having bristles, shaped like a bristle. Hence ~LY² adv. [f. L *seta* bristle, -ACEOUS]

sētif′erous, sēti′gerous, sētōse′, aa. Having bristles. [L *seta* bristle, *setiger, setosus*, bristly, -FEROUS, -GEROUS, -OSE¹]

sēt′on, h. (surg.). Skein of cotton or the like passed below skin and left with ends protruding to maintain an artificial issue as counter-irritant etc. esp. in veterinary practice; ~-*needle*, for inserting ~. [f. med. L *seto* silk, app. f. L *seta* bristle, med. L also silk]

sēt square, n. Draughtsman's appliance consisting of a triangular plate of wood or metal or plastic with angles of 90°, 60°, 30°, or of 90°, 45°, 45°, for drawing lines at such angles. [p.p. of SET¹]

sētt. Arbitrary var. of SET² in some of its more technical senses.

sēttee′¹, n. Long seat variously con-structed to seat more than one person, esp. kind of double armchair or short sofa with ends alike for tête-à-tête. [perh. fanciful var. of SETTLE¹; see -EE]

sēttee′², n. Mediterranean sharp-prowed lateen-sailed vessel with two or three masts. [f. It. *saettia* (*saetta* f. L SAGITTA)]

sētt′er, n. In vbl senses; esp., breeds (English, Irish, Gordon, ~) of long-haired dog trained to stand rigid on scenting game; dog named from native habit of crouching on same occasion; ~-*on*, instigator. [SET¹, -ER¹]

sētt′erwort (-ĕrt), n. A plant, bear's-foot or fetid hellebore. [f. MLG *siterwort* etc.; first element of unkn. orig.]

sētt′ing, n. In vbl senses; esp.; the music of a song etc.; the metal or other frame in which a gem is set, (transf.) surround-ings of any object regarded as its frame-work or as accessories setting it off, en-vironment, (theatr.) way a play is put on the stage, scenery, properties, costumes, etc.; ~-*board*, on which entomological specimens are set; ~-*box*, in which ~-boards are kept like shelves or drawers; ~-*lotion*, used to damp the hair before it is set; ~-*needle*, needle in wooden handle used in setting specimens; ~-*rule*, brass rule or steel plate with which type is kept temporarily in place as it is set up; ~-*stick*, used in setting type. [-ING¹]

sēt′tle¹, n. Bench with high back & arms & often with chest from seat to floor. [OE *setl*, OHG *sezzal*, Goth. *sitls* f. Gmc **set-* SIT]

sēt′tle², v.t. & i. **1.** Establish or become established in more or less permanent abode or place or way of life (often *down*), (cause to) sit down or *down* to stay for some time, cease from wandering or motion or change or disturbance or turbidity (often *down*), bring to or attain fixity or composure or certainty or clarity or decision, determine, agree upon, decide, appoint, (*he ~d detachments of Jews in Assyria*; *shall ~ in London, Australia*; *~ feet in stirrups, plant's root well down in ground, invalid among pillows, oneself in chair*; *~ down to dinner, whist, reading, married life*; *~d down to defensive play, a series of skirmishes*; *marry & ~ down*; *cannot ~ to work, to anything*, of restless or excited or desultory person; *bird ~s on tree*, alights; *stand beer to ~*, get clear; *let the excitement ~ down*; *things will soon ~ into shape*; *must get it ~d up*, finally arranged; *~ coffee, soup, with white of egg*, clarify; *man, expression, of ~d convictions, melancholy*; *~d order, state, habitation, government, weather*; *a liqueur to ~ one's dinner*, facilitate digestion; *~ the day*, fix date; *~ quarrel, question, doubts, the pattern of, waverers*; *what have you ~d on or ~d?*; *~ the succession*, determine who shall succeed; *that ~s the matter or question*, there is no more to be said; *~ one's affairs*, esp. before death by making will etc.). 2. Colonize, establish colonists in, *~ as colonists in*, people, (country); **thickly ~d* (built-up) area. 3. Subside, (*the solid matter soon ~s*; *soil, house, foundation, ~s*, comes gradually to lower level; *ship ~s*, shows loss of buoyancy, begins to sink). 4. Deal effectually with, dispose or get rid of, do for, pay (bill), pay bill, (*~ person*, get rid of his importunity or obstruction by argument or conflict or killing; *let us ~ up our accounts or ~ up*, draw up & liquidate balance; *~ person's* HASH[2] *or business*; *~d*, written on paid bill in acknowledging payment; *will you ~ for me?*, pay the bill; *~ with creditors*, pay their bills or such proportion as they will agree to accept; || *settling-day*, esp. fortnightly account day at Stock Exchange). 5. Bestow legally for life on (*~d an annuity on him*; *~d all his property on his wife*; *~d estate*, held by tenant for life under specified conditions). [OE *setlan* f. *setl* (prec.)]

set′tlement (-tlm-), n. In vbl senses; esp.: (law) conveyance of, or creation of estate(s) in, property to make provision for one or more beneficiaries differing from what would result from simple conveyance or statutory inheritance (*marriage ~*, usu. made in favour of wife, her children, etc.); company of persons aiming at social reform who establish themselves in a poor district to live in intimate relations with the working class; newly settled tract of country, colony; subsidence of wall, house, etc.; *Act of S~*, statute of 1701 vesting crown in Sophia of Hanover & her heirs. [-MENT]

sett′ler, n. In vbl senses: esp.: one who settles in new colony, early colonist; (sl.) decisive blow, argument, or event. [-ER[1]]

sett′lor, n. (law). One who makes a settlement esp. of property. [-OR]

set′wall (-awl), n. Kind of valerian formerly in medicinal use. [ME & AF *zedewal* = OF *citoual* f. med. L **zedoale*, var. of *zedoarium* ZEDOARY]

sev′en, a. & n. 1. One more than six, 7, vii, VII, (often agreeing with understood n., as ~ *of the men, ~ of them, ~ o'clock or ~*; *one & ~, 1/7*; *~ & six, 7/6*; *twenty-~ or ~-&-twenty*, & so on to *~ - & - ninety*; *was ~ last birthday*, years old; *one-&-~penny* etc., costing 1/7 etc.; *the ~* SAGE[2]*s or wise men*; *the ~ sleepers*, Christians who fell asleep in a cave while hiding from Decian persecution & woke 200 years later when Roman Empire was Christian; *the ~* VIRTUES, *deadly* SINS, WONDER[1]*s of the world*; *~-league boots*, giving wearer power of going 7 leagues at each stride; *seventy times ~*, large indefinite number, w. ref. to *Matt.* xviii. 22); *~-gills*, kind of shark; hence *~FOLD* a. & adv., *~TEEN[1]* a. & n. (*sweet ~teen*, age of girlish beauty), *~teenTH[2]* a. & n. 2. n. The number 7, the symbol 7, set of 7 persons or things esp. 7-pipped card, (*twice ~ is 14*; *make a large ~*; *by ~s*, in sets of 7; *at* SIXES *& ~s*). [OE *seofon*, OS, OHG *sibun*, ON *sjau*, Goth. *sibun* f. Gmc **sebhun* cogn. w. L *septem*]

sev′enth, a. & n. 1. Next after sixth (*the, a, ~*, often as n. with ellipse of n., esp. *the ~* = 7th day of month; *~ day*, Saturday in Quaker speech & with sects keeping Saturday instead of Sunday as sabbath (*~-day*, sabbatarian; *S~-day Adventists*, a millenarian sect); *in the ~* HEAVEN, in the greatest happiness or satisfaction; *~ part*, one of 7 equal parts into which thing may be divided). 2. n. = ~ part; (mus.) interval of which the span involves 7 alphabetical names of notes, harmonic combination of notes thus separated. [OE *seofunda*, ME *sevende*; ME *seventhe* f. prec. + -TH[2]]

sev′enthly, adv. In the 7th place (in enumerations). [-LY[2]]

sev′enty, a. & n. 1. Seven times ten, 70, lxx, LXX, (*~y-one* etc., or *one-&-~y* etc.; *~y-first* etc.; *the ~y*, the disciples of *Luke* x, also the sanhedrim, also the Septuagint translators); *~y-four* (hist.), warship with 74 guns; *~y-five*, French 75 mm. gun, = *soixante-quinze*; hence *~*IETH a. & n. 2. n. The number or symbol 70; *the ~ies*, years between 69 & 80 in life or century. [OE *-seofontig* (SEVEN, -TY[2])]

sev′er, v.t. & i. Separate, divide, part, disjoin, disunite, (t. & rarely i.; *~ husband & wife, friends or friendship, rope, neck, connexion*; *sea ~s England & or from France*; *the rope ~ed under the strain*); cut or break off, take away, (part) from or *from* whole (*~ed his head, his head from his body*; *~* oneself *from the Church*); (law; of person in joint action) conduct case independently of the rest. Hence ~ABLE a., ~ANCE n. [ME, f. AF, OF *severer* f. pop. L **seperare* f. L *separare* SEPARATE]

sev'eral, a. & pron. **1.** Separate, diverse, distinct, individual, respective, (*all of us in our ~ stations*; *each has his ~ ideal*; *went their ~ ways*; *indictment of three ~ counts*; *the ~ members of the Board*; *each ~ ship sank her opponent*; *collective & ~ responsibility*, of persons as a body & as individuals; *joint & ~ bond* etc., signed by more than one person, of whom each is liable for whole sum; *~ estate*, not shared with others), whence ~LY² adv.; a few, more than two but not many, (*have called ~ times*; *myself & ~ others*). **2.** pron. A moderate number, more than two but not many, of the previously mentioned or implied persons or things (*~ of you have seen him*; *went mushroom--hunting & found~*). [ME, f. AF, f. med. L *separalis* (L *separ* SEPARATE, -AL)]

sev'eralty, n. Individual or unshared tenure of estate etc. (usu. *in ~*). [ME, f. AF *severalle* (as prec., -TY¹)]

sevēre', a. (-er, -est). **1.** Austere, strict, harsh, rigorous, unsparing, (*~ look, discipline, critic, master, sentence, inspection, self-control*; *~ upon*, hard on). **2.** Violent, vehement, extreme, (*~ weather*, very cold or stormy; *a ~ winter*; *~ attack of gout*). **3.** Trying, making great demands on endurance, energy, skill, or other quality, (*~ test, pain, competition, requirements*). **4.** Unadorned, stripped of all that is unessential, without redundance, restrained, terse, (*~ architecture, beauty, simplicity, style*). **5.** Sarcastic or satirical (*~ remarks*; *you are pleased to be ~*). Hence or cogn. ~LY² (-rlī) adv. (*leave* or *let ~ly alone*, abstain from dealing with as mark of disapproval, also joc. avoid meddling with as too formidable or difficult), sevē'rĭTY n. (w. pl. = ~ treatment). [F, or f. L *severus*]

sev'ery, n. (archit.). Compartment of vaulted celing. [f. AF **civorie*, OF *civoire* CIBORIUM]

Sev'ille o'range (-Inj), n. The bitter orange, used for marmalade. [*Seville, in* Spain]

Sèvres (see Ap.), n. Porcelain made at ~.

sew (sō), v.t. & i. (p.p. *sewn, sewed*, pr. sōn, sōd). Fasten (material, pieces) by passing thread again & again through holes made with threaded needle or with awl etc. (*~ cloth, calico, leather, pieces together, sheets of book*), whence ~'ING¹ (5) (sōi-) n.; make by ~ing (*~ seam, pleat, shirt, book, boot, buttonhole*); fasten *on* or *in*, attach, by ~ing (*~ on a button*; *can you~ buttons?*; *~ in a patch, band, gusset, rib*, etc.); close *up* (hole, rent, wound, bag) by ~ing; enclose, fasten *up*, by

~ing receptacle (*~ up money in a bag*; *~ money into* one's *belt*); *~* one *up*, sl., utterly exhaust, (esp. in p.p.) intoxicate; use needle & thread or ~ing-machine; *~ing-machine*, apparatus in which needle is worked mechanically by crank or treadle; *~ing-press*, apparatus for ~ing books. Hence ~'er¹ [-ER¹] (sō'er) n. [OE *si(o)wan*, OHG *siuwen*, ON *sýja*, Goth. *siujan* f. Gmc **siwjan* cogn. w. L *suere*]

sew'age, n., & v.t. **1.** Matter conveyed in sewers; *~-farm*, on which ~ is used as manure, esp. one that utilizes & disposes of a town's *~*; *~-grass*, grown on ~d land. **2.** v.t. Manure with ~. [formed f. SEWER³ by change of (supposed) -ER¹ for -AGE]

sewĕll'el, n. Small burrowing rodent of the W. coast of U.S. [Amer.-Ind.]

sewer¹. See SEW.

sew'er², n. (hist.). Person who set out table, placed guests, carried & tasted dishes, etc. [ME, f. AF *asseour* f. OF *asseoir* to seat, f. L AS(*sidēre=sedēre* sit) *sit beside*]

sew'er³, n., & v.t. **1.** Conduit or channel usu. covered over for carrying off the drainage & excrementitious matter of a town, public drain; *~-gas*, foul air of ~s; *~ rat*, common brown or Norway rat; hence ~AGE(1) n. **2.** v.t. Drain, provide, with ~s. [ME, f. AF, ONF *se(u)wiere* channel to carry off overflow from a fishpond f. L **EXAQUARIA* (*aqua* water, -ARY¹); cf. EWER]

sew'in, -ĕn, n. Kind of bulltrout. [orig. obsc.]

sewn. See SEW.

sĕx, n. Being male or female or hermaphrodite (*what is its~?*; *~ does not matter*; *without distinction of age or ~*), whence ~'LESS a., ~'lĕssNESS n., ~'Y² a., immoderately concerned with ~; males or females collectively (*all ranks & both ~es*; *the fair, gentle, softer, weaker, ~*, & joc. the *~*, women; *the sterner ~*, men; *is the fairest of her ~*); (attrib.) arising from difference, or consciousness, of ~ (*~ antagonism, ~ instinct, ~ urge*); *~ appeal*, attractiveness arising from difference of *~*. [f. L *sexus -ūs*; partly thr. F]

sĕx-, also occas. **sĕx|i-**, comb. forms of L *sex* six, in derivatives of L compds & in mod. formations: ~'*angle*, hexagon; ~*ang'ular*(*ly*), hexagonal(ly); ~*centĕn'ary* (or -sē'-) a. & n., of 600, 600--year, 600th anniversary; ~*di'gitate*, six--fingered; ~*enni'al*(*ly*), lasting, (occurring) once in, six years; ~'*ifid* (bot.), cleft in 6; ~'*foil*, 6-lobed figure in architectural or other decoration, also 6-leaved plant; ~*isyllab'ic*, ~*isyll'able*, (word) of 6 syllables; *~ (i)vāl'ent* (chem.), combining with 6 atoms of hydrogen, having 6 combining equivalents; ~*part'ite*, divided in 6.

sĕxagēnār'ian, a. & n. (Person) between 59 & 70. [L *sexagenarius* (foll.), -AN]

sĕxagēn′ary, a. Of 60, going by sixties. [f. L *sexagenarius* (*sexageni* 60 each f. *sexaginta* 60, -ARY[1])]

Sĕxagēs′ima, n. (Also ~ *Sunday*) Sunday before Quinquagesima. [ME (-*ime*), f. L, fem. adj. = 60th (day), prob. named loosely as preceding QUINQUAGESIMA]

sĕxagĕs′imal, a. & n. Sixtieth, of 60, proceeding by sixties, (~ *fractions*, or ~s n., with denominators proceeding in ratio of 60 as in the divisions of the circle & hour). Hence ~LY[2] adv. [f. med. L *sexagesimalis* f. L *sexagesimus* 60th (*sexaginta* 60), -AL]

sĕxill′ion (-lyon), n. ‖6th power of a million, 1 with 36 ciphers; *7th power of a thousand, 1 with 21 ciphers. [f. SEX-, after *million*]

sĕxt, sĕxte, n. (eccl.). The office of the 6th hour, recited at noon. [ME, f. fem. *sexta* (*hora* hour) of L *sextus* sixth]

sĕx′tain, n. = SESTINA. [perh. alt. f. obs. F *sestine*, after *quatrain*, *sixain*]

sĕx′tan, a. (Of fever etc.) recurring every fifth (by inclusive reckoning sixth) day. [f. mod. L *sextana* (*febris* fever) f. *sextus* sixth, -AN]

sĕx′tant, n. Sixth part of circle (obs.); instrument used in navigation and surveying for measuring the angular distance of objects by means of reflection. [f. L *sextans* -*ntis* sixth part (*sextus* sixth, -ANT)]

sĕxtĕt(te)′, n. (Musical work for) 6 voices, singers, instruments, or players, in combination; (transf.) any set of 6. [alt. of SESTET after L *sex* six]

sĕxtill′ion (-lyon), n. = SEXILLION. [F, f. L *sex* six, after *septillion*]

sĕx′tō, n. (pl. ~s). Book formed by folding sheets in six. [f. L *sextus* sixth, as QUARTO]

sĕxtodĕ′cimō, n. (abbr. 16mo, usu. read *sixteenmo*). Sheet of paper folded in 16 leaves; this way of folding (*in* ~); book made by folding thus. [orig. *in* ~ L (IN[5], *sextus decimus* 16th)]

sĕx′ton, n. Officer charged with care of church & churchyard, & often with duties of parish clerk & grave-digger; ~ *beetle*, kinds that bury carrion to serve as nidus for eggs. [ME *segerstane* f. AF *segerslaine*, OF *segreslein* f. med. L *sacristanus* SACRISTAN]

sĕx′tuple, a. & n., & v.t. & f. Sixfold (amount); (vb) multiply by 6. [f. med. L *sextuplus*, irreg. f. L *sex* six, after LL *quintuplus* QUINTUPLE]

‖ **sĕx′tus**. See PRIMUS[1].

sĕx′ūal (or -kshŏŏ-), a. Of sex, a sex, or the sexes (~ *organs*, genitals; ~ *intercourse* or *commerce*, copulation; ~ *affinity*, mutual attraction of two individuals of opposite sexes; ~ SELECTION; ~ *appetite*, *indulgence*, for, in, ~ intercourse); (bot.; of classification) based on the distinction of sexes in plants, whence ~IST(2) n. Hence ~ITY (-ăl[1]) n., ~LY[2] adv. [f. LL *sexualis* (SEX, -AL)]

sĕx′ūalīz|e (or -kshŏŏ-), -is|e (-īz), v.t. Attribute sex to. Hence ~A′TION n. [-IZE]

sfŏr̄zăn′dō (-ts-), mus. direction. With sudden emphasis. [It.]

sfuma′tō (-ŏŏmah-), a. (paint.). With indistinct outlines. [It., lit. smoked]

shăbb′|ў̆, a. Scurvy, contemptible, paltry, dishonourable, (*played me a* ~*y trick*); close-fisted, mean; worn, threadbare, dilapidated, seedy, in bad repair or condition; ~*y-genteel*, retaining traces of better days, attempting to keep up appearances. Hence ~ĬLY[1] adv., ~ĬNESS n., ~ỸISH[1](2) a. [f. (now dial.) *shab* f. OE *sceabb* (Gmc **skabh-* SHAVE)+-Y[2]; cf. SCAB]

shăb′răck, n. Cavalry saddlecloth. [f. G *schabracke* of E.-Europ. orig.]

shăck, n. Rough hut. [orig. unkn.]

shăc′kle, n., & v.t. 1. Metal loop or staple, bow of padlock, link closed by bolt for connecting chains etc., coupling link; long link joining pair of wrist or ankle rings, (pl.) fetters, impediments, or restraints (*the* ~*s of convention*); kind of insulator for telegraph wires; ~*-bolt*, for closing ~, also bolt with ~ at its end; ~*-joint*, in some fishes, formed by bony ring passing through hole in other bone. 2. v.t. Fetter, impede, trammel. [OE *sceacul*, fetter, corresp. to LG *schake*, *schäkel* link, coupling]

shăd, n. Kinds of anadromous deep-bodied fish, of which the American or white ~ is much esteemed as food. [OE *sceadd*, of unkn. orig.]

shădd′ock, n. (Fruit, sometimes weighing 15 lb., of) orig. Malayan & Polynesian tree of orange kind. [*S*~, introducer to W. Indies]

shāde[1], n. 1. Comparative darkness (& usu. coolness) caused by interception of light (& usu. heat) rays; (fig.) comparative obscurity (*throw into the* ~, outshine). 2. (Often pl.) place sheltered from sun, cool or sequestered retreat; (pl.) wine vaults; (pl.) darkness *of* night or evening. 3. Darker part of picture (*without light &* ~, of paintings, also fig. of descriptions or characters, monotonous, uniformly glaring or sombre). 4. A colour esp. with regard to its depth or as distinguished from one nearly like it, gradation of colour, material so coloured, (*in all* ~*s of purple*; *I want the same colour in a lighter* ~; *all the newest* ~*s in stock*; also fig., as *people of all* ~*s of opinion*, *delicate* ~*s of meaning*). 5. Slight difference, small amount, (*am a* ~ *better today*). 6. Unsubstantial or unreal thing (*is the shadow of a* ~, delusive). 7. Soul after death (*spoke with the* ~ *of Homer*; *went down to the* ~*s*, died, visited Hades; *S*~ *of Priscian* etc.!, exclamation at grammatical blunder etc., that would have outraged person invoked). 8. Screen excluding or moderating light, heat, etc. (usu. in comb., as SUN, *candle*, *lamp*, ~), eye-shield, glass

cover for object; *window-blind. Hence
~'LESS (-dl-) a. [ME *schade* f. OE *sceadu*,
OS *scado*, OHG *scato*, Goth. *skadus* f.
Gmc *skadhw-* cogn. w. Gk *skotos*; see
SHADOW]

shăde², v.t. & i. **1.** Screen from excessive
light (~*d his eyes with his hand*; *trees* ~
the street). **2.** Cover, keep off, or moderate
power of (luminous object, light) with
or as intervening object. **3.** Make dark
or gloomy (*a sullen look* ~*d his face*). **4.**
(In drawing) darken (parts of object represented) esp. with parallel pencil lines to
give effects of light & shade or gradations
of colour, whence shăd'ING¹(6) n. **5.** (Of
colour or light, &c; fig. of opinion, practice,
etc.) pass *off* by degrees into (or *into*)
other colour or variety, make (colour etc.)
pass thus *into* another. **6.** Modify pitch
of (organ-pipe). [ME, f. prec.]

shadoof', n. Pole with bucket & counterpoise used esp. in Egypt for raising water.
[f. Arab. *shādūf*]

shăd'ow¹ (-dō), n. **1.** Shade (*sitting in the*
~; *the* ~ *of death is on his face*; VALLEY *of
the* ~ *of death*; *the* ~*s of night*; *under the*
~ *of misfortune*); dark part of picture,
room, etc. **2.** Patch of shade, dark figure
projected by body that intercepts light
rays, this regarded as person's or thing's
appendage (*may your* ~ *never grow less!*);
(fig.) one's inseparable attendant or companion. **3.** Reflected image. **4.** Type,
faint representation, adumbration, pre-
monition (*coming events cast their* ~*s
before*). **5.** Slightest trace (*without a* ~ *of
doubt*). **6.** Unsubstantial or unreal thing
or counterfeit (*what* ~*s we are!*; *catch at
*~*s; having only the* ~ *of freedom*); phantom, ghost, (*is but the* ~ *of his former self*;
worn to a~; *a terrible*~*with uplifted hand*).
7. Privacy, obscurity, (*content to live in
the* ~). **8.** Shelter, protection, (*under the
~ of the Almighty*). **9.** ~-*boxing* (against
imaginary opponent as form of training);
|| ~- CABINET ; ~ *factory*, one planned or
built for possible reserve production
against the emergency of war; ~-*stitch*,
kind of ladder-work in lace-making.
Hence ~LESS (-ŏl-), ~Y² (-ōl), aa., ~ĪNESS
(-ŏl-) n. [repr. OE *scead(u)we*, obl. case of
sceadu SHADE¹]

shăd'ow² (-dō), v.t. Overspread with
shadow (chiefly poet.); set *forth* dimly, in
outline, allegorically, or prophetically;
dog, secretly watch all movements of.
[ME, f. prec.]

shăd'ŷ, a. Giving, situated in, shade; (of
actions, conduct, etc.) shunning the light,
disreputable, of dubious honesty; *on the
~y side of forty* etc., more than. Hence
~ĪLY² adv., ~ĪNESS n. [-Y²]

shaft (-ah-), n. **1.** (Slender pole of) lance
or spear. **2.** Long-bow arrow (often
CLOTH-*yard* ~; also fig., as ~*s of satire,
ridicule, envy*). **3.** Ray of light, bolt or
stroke *of* lightning. **4.** Stem, stalk,
column between base & capital, one of

group of clustered columns, spire, part of
chimney above roof, rib of feather, part
more or less long & narrow & straight
supporting or connecting part(s) of greater
thickness etc. **5.** (mech.). Large axle,
revolving bar transferring force by belts
or cogs, whence ~ING¹(3, 6) n. **6.** Handle
of tool etc. **7.** One of pair of bars between
which horse of vehicle is harnessed (~-
-*horse*, so placed, opp. LEADER in tandem).
8. Vertical or inclined excavation giving
access to mine; tunnel of blast-furnace;
(also • *ventilating* ~) upward vent for
smoke or bad air from tunnel, drain, etc.
[OE *sceaft*, OS *skaft*, OHG *scaft*, ON *skapt*
f. Gmc *skaft-*; cf. L *scapus*]

shăg¹, n. **1.** Rough growth or mass of
hair etc., whence ~g'ED² (-gĭd) a. (rare).
(arch.) long-napped rough cloth. **2.**
Coarse kind of cut tobacco. [OE *sceacga*,
cogn. w. ON *skegg* beard, OE *sceaga*
coppice, SHAW; f. Gmc *skag-*]

shăg², n. Crested cormorant. [prob. f.
prec.]

*shăg'bark, n. The white hickory.
[SHAG¹]

shăgg'|ŷ (-g-), a. Hairy, rough-haired;
(of hair) coarse, wildly abundant, unkempt; (of land etc.) overgrown with
forest or rough vegetation; (of trees etc.)
with rough branches or twigs; (bot.,
biol.) villous; ~ *dog* (long rambling would-
-be funny) *story*. Hence~ĪLY² adv.,~ĪNESS
n., (-g-). [-Y²]

shagreen', n. Kind of untanned leather
with artificially granulated surface made
from skin of horse, ass, camel, etc., & usu.
dyed green; shark-skin rough with natural papillae used for rasping & polishing.
[var. of CHAGRIN]

shah, n. King of Persia, padishah. [Pers.,
= ruler; cf. CHECK¹]

shāke¹, v.t. & i. (*shŏŏk, shāken*). **1.** Move
(thing, person) violently or quickly up &
down or to & fro with the hand(s) etc.
(*like a terrier shaking a rat*; *deserves a
good* shăk'ING¹(1) n.; ~ *hands*, ~ one *by
the* hand, clasp right hands with or without shaking at meeting or parting, in
reconciliation or congratulation, or over
concluded bargain; ~ *a mat*). **2.** (Make)
tremble or rock or quiver or vibrate or
wave, jolt, jar, brandish, (~ *the house*;
the earth shook; *hand* ~*s*, is unsteady;
~ *one's fist, stick*, etc., *in* person's *face* or
at, threaten with fist etc.; ~ *a* LEG; ~
one's *head*, move it from side to side in
refusal, denial, disapproval, or concern
over or *at* or abs.; ~ *with fear, cold*, etc.,
tremble violently; ~ *in* one's *shoes*,
tremble with apprehension). **3.** Agitate,
shock, disturb, (*was much*~*n by, with, at,
the news*; ~ *him out of his lethargy*; *shook
my composure*); (colloq.) upset composure
of (person). **4.** Weaken, impair, make
less convincing or firm or stable or
courageous, (*the firm's credit was* ~*n;
shook the witness's evidence*; *his faith in*

Providence was greatly ~n; *the ranks were ~n but not broken*). **5.** (Of voice, musical note, singer, etc.) make tremulous sounds, change pitch or power with rapid alternations, trill, (*his voice shook with emotion*; *must learn to ~*). **6.** (imperat.; colloq., chiefly U.S.).~ hands. **7.**~ *down*, fetch or send down by shaking (fruit from tree; straw or blankets etc. on floor for bed, whence ~'**down** n.; grain etc. in vessel into least compass), (intr.) become compact, get comfortably settled or into harmony with associates or circumstances (~*down cruise* of new ship, made to run in the engines and accustom the crew to the ship); ~ *off*, get rid of (dust etc., & fig. undesirable companion or worry) by shaking (~ *off the* DUST[1] *from one's feet*); ~ *out*, empty (vessel, garment, etc.) of contents or dust, (contents) from vessel etc., spread or open (sail, flag, reef); ~ *up*, mix (ingredients), restore (pillow etc.) to shape, by shaking, rouse from stagnant or lethargic or convention·ridden state. Hence shāk'ABLE a. [OE *scacan*, = OS *skakan*, ON *skaka* f. Gmc *skakan*]

shāke[2], n. **1.** Shaking or being shaken (see prec.; *with a ~ of the head*; *give it, had, a ~*; *all of a ~*, trembling; *the ~s*, ague); jolt, jerk, shock. **2.** *A glass of milk, or milk and egg, flavoured and shaken up (short for *milk·~*). **3.** Trill, quick alternation of two notes with voice or on instrument. **4.** Moment (*in two* etc. *~s of a lamb's tail* etc. or *~s*, very quickly, in no time; *in a brace of ~s*). **5.** Crack in growing timber. **6.** (sl.). *Is no great ~s*, not very good or efficient. **7.** *~·out* (St. Exch.), crisis in which weaker speculators are driven out of market; *~·up*, shaking or being shaken up. [f. prec.]

shāk'er, n. In vbl senses; also (*S~*) member of religious sect founded in Manchester, & still existing in U.S., holding that Christ's second coming has taken place (named from religious dances), whence **Shāk'er**ESS[1], **Shāk'er**ISM(3), nn. [-ER[1]]

Shāk(e)spe(a)r'i|an (-kspēr-), a. & n. (In the style) of Shakespeare; (n.) student of Shakespeare. So ~AN'A n. pl. [-IAN]

shāk'ō, n. (pl. ~s). Form of military hat, more or less cylindrical with peak & upright plume or tuft. [f. Magyar *csákó*]

shāk'|ў, a. Unsteady, apt to shake, trembling, unsound, infirm, unreliable, tottering, wavering, (*a ~y hand, table, old man, house*; *~y credit, voters, courage*; *feel, look, ~y*). Hence ~ILY[2] adv., ~INESS n. [-Y[2]]

shāle, n. Kinds of clayey stone splitting readily into thin plates & resembling slate but softer & less solid; *~·oil*, kind of naphtha got from bituminous ~. Hence shāl'Y[2] a. [perh. = dial. *shale* scale f. OE *scealu* cogn. w. ON *skal* SCALE[2]]

shāll (*unstressed* shal, shl), v. aux. (pres.

I, he, we, you, they, ~, thou shalt; past & condit. *I, he, we, you, they, should* pr. shŏŏd, *thou shouldst* pr. shŏŏdst, or *shouldest* pr. shŏŏd'lst; neg. forms *shall not* or *shan't* pr. -ah-, *should not* or *shouldn't*; no other parts used). ~ & *should* are used: **1** in first person (the others having *will, would*) to form a plain future or conditional statement or question (*we~ hear about it tomorrow*; *I should have been killed if I had let go*; ~ *I hear from you soon?*); **2** in 2nd & 3rd persons (1st having *will, would*) to form a future or conditional statement expressing speaker's will or intention (*you ~ not catch me again*; *he should not have gone if I could have prevented it*); **3** alternatively with *will, would*, in sentences of type 1 changed in reporting from 1st to other person (*he says* or *said, you say* or *said, that he, you, ~* or *should never manage it*; now more usu. *will, would*) or from other person to 1st (*he says I ~* or *will never manage it*, reporting *you will never*; *will* now rare); **4** in reporting sentences of type 2 that contained ~ or *should* (*you promised I, he, should not catch you at it again*); **5** in 2nd-person questions corresponding to type 1, by attraction to expected answer (~ *you be going to church?*); **6** in any person to form statements or questions involving the notions of command & future or conditional duty, obligation, etc. (*thou shalt not steal*; *I, you, he, should really have been more careful*; *~I, he, open the door?* *why should I, you, he, obey?*); **7** in all persons to form conditional protasis or indefinite clause (*if, when, we ~ be defeated* or *defeat~ overtake us*; *any one who should say*; *if you should happen to be there*; & with inversion *should I, you, he, be there, it would·be talked about*); **8** alternatively with *may, might*, in all persons in final clauses (*to the end that I, you, he ~* or *should not be able*); **9** in some miscellaneous idioms (*it should seem*, it seems; *you ~ find*, arch., be sure you will find; *it is surprising* etc. *that I, you, he, should be* or *have been so foolish*). [OE *sceal*, OHG *scal, sal*, OS, ON, Goth. *skal*, a preterite-present vb f. Gmc **skal-*, **skul-* owe]

shalloon', n. Light cloth for coat-linings & women's dresses. [f. *Châlons* in France]

shall'op, n. Light open boat. [f. F *chaloupe* SLOOP]

shal(l)ŏt', n. Plant of onion kind with cloves like, but of milder flavour than, those of garlic. [aphetic f. 18th c. *eschalot* f. F *eschalotte* alt. of *eschaloigne* (SCALLION) f. L *ascalonia* f. *Ascalon* in Palestine]

shăll'ow (-ō), a. (~*er*, ~*est*), n., & v.i. & t. **1.** Of little depth (lit. & fig.; ~ *water, a ~ stream, dish*; *a ~ mind, argument, love, man*, superficial, trivial; so ~·*brained, -hearted, -pated*); hence ~LY[2] adv., ~NESS n. **2.** n. ~ place, shoal. **3.** vb. Become

~er, make ~. [15th c. *schalowe*, prob. rel. to *schald*, OE *sceald* SHOAL[1]]

shalt. See SHALL.

sham, v.t. & i. (-mm-), n., & a. **1.** Feign, simulate, (~ *illness, sleep, a faint, fear*; *is only ~ming*); pretend to be (~*med ill, dead, asleep*); hence ~m'ER[1] n. **2.** n. Imposture, pretence, humbug, (*this age of ~s*); person or thing pretending or pretended to be something that he or it is not; (also *sheet, pillow, ~*) embroidered linen laid on bed in day for show. **3.** adj. Pretended, counterfeit, (~ *fight,* imitation battle for training troops; ~ *plea* etc. in law, advanced only to gain time). [17th-c. sl. of obsc. orig.]

Sham'anism, n. Religion of Siberian tribes involving belief in secondary gods & in power of shamans or priests to influence these. [f. G *schamane* of Mongol origin, -ISM]

sham'bl|e, v.i., & n. **1.** Walk or run in shuffling or awkward or decrepit way (~*ing gait,* of person who ~es). **2.** n. ~ing gait. [prob. f. *shamble* adj. straddling, wry, perh. f. *shamble* bench (see foll.) w. ref. to straddling trestles]

sham'bles (-lz), n. pl. (often w. sing. constr.). Butchers' slaughter-house; scene of carnage (*the place became a ~*); (loosely, esp. in journalistic use) mess, muddle (with no implication of blood or death). [pl. of *shamble* stool, stall, OE *sc(e)amel,* OS *skamel,* OHG *scamel* f. WG f. L *scamellum* dim. of *scamnum* bench]

shame[1], n. **1.** Feeling of humiliation excited by consciousness of guilt or shortcoming, of having made oneself or been made ridiculous, or of having offended against propriety, modesty, or decency, (*flushed with ~*; *begin with ~ to take the lowest room*). **2.** Restraint imposed by desire to avoid such humiliation (*for ~!*, appeal to person not to disregard or reproof for disregarding this; *cannot do it for very ~*; *is quite without* or *lost to ~*), whence ~'LESS (-ml-) a., ~'less-LY[2] adv., ~'lessNESS n. **3.** State of disgrace or ignominy or discredit (~ *on you!*; *put* one *to ~*, disgrace him esp. by exhibiting superior qualities etc.), person or thing that brings disgrace (*is a ~ to his parents*; *would think ~ to do it*; *is a sin & a ~*), whence ~'FUL (-mf-) a., ~'fulLY[2] adv., ~'fulNESS n [OE *sc(e)amu,* OS *skama,* OHG *scama,* ON *skǫmm* f. Gmc *skamō*]

shame[2], v.i. & t. Be ashamed, refuse from shame, *to* (arch.; usu. with negative, as he ~*d not to say*); bring shame on, be a shame to, make ashamed; put (superior) to the blush by outdoing (*a dog's fidelity ~s us*); frighten by shame *into* or *out of* doing, conduct, etc. [OE *sc(e)amian,* Goth. *skaman* (prec.)]

shame'faced (-āmfāst), a. Bashful, shy; (poet., of virtue, flowers, etc.) modest, retiring, inconspicuous. Hence ~LY[2]

adv., ~NESS n., (-āmfāsĭd-, -āst-). [16th c. etym. misinterpretation of *shamefast* f. OE *sceamu* SHAME[1] + *fæst* FAST[3]]

shamm'ў, shăm'oy, n. = CHAMOIS(2).

shampoo', v.t., & n. **1.** Subject (body etc.) to kneading or massage after hot bath (orig. sense, now rare); lather, wash, & rub (head, hair). **2.** n. A ~ing of the head; *dry ~,* alcoholic saponaceous preparation for cleaning the hair, powder for similar purpose, ~ing with these. [prob. f. Hind. *shāmpo,* imper. of *shāmpnā* to press]

shăm'rŏck, n. Kinds of trefoil or clover serving as national emblem of Ireland (cf. ROSE, THISTLE, LEEK). [f. Ir. *seamróg* trefoil, dim. of *seamar* clover]

shăn'drỹdăn, n. Light two-wheeled cart; old rickety vehicle. [orig. unkn.]

shăn'dỹ(găff), n. Mixed drink of beer & ginger-beer or lemonade. [orig. unkn.]

shănghai' (-hī), v.t. (naut. sl.). Drug & ship as sailor while unconscious. [*S~* in China]

shănk, n., & v.i. & t. **1.** Leg (*S~s's mare,* one's own legs as opp. riding etc.); leg from knee to ankle; shin-bone; upright part of bird's foot; footstalk of flower; ǁ leg of stocking; shaft of pillar etc., shaft of tool between head etc. & handle, stem of key, spoon, anchor, etc., straight part of fish-hook, narrow middle of boot-sole; hence (-)~ED[2] (-kt) a. **2.** vb. ~ *off,* (of flowers) fall off by decay of ~; (golf) strike (ball) with heel of club. [OE *sc(e)anca* (WG *skank-*) cogn. w. MHG *schenkel,* OHG *scinko* thigh (G *schinken* ham)]

shănn'ỹ, n. Oblong olive-green European sea-fish, the smooth blenny. [also (18th c.) *shan*; orig. unkn.]

shan't. See SHALL.

shăn'tŭng', n. A soft undressed Chinese silk (usu. undyed). [*S~,* Chin. province]

shăn'tỹ[1], n. Hut, cabin, mean dwelling. [f. Canad.-F *chantier* log hut f. F = workshop]

shăn'tỹ[2], n. Sailor's song (with alternating solo by ~*man,* & chorus) in heaving. [perh. a corrupt. of F *chantez,* imperat. pl. of *chanter* CHANT]

shape[1], v.t. & i. (p.p. ~*d,* arch. ~*n*). Create, form, construct; model, mould, fashion, bring into desired or definite figure or form (p.p., having such figure, as ~*d like a pear*); adapt, make conform, *to*; plan, devise; direct, aim, (one's course etc.); frame mentally, imagine, call up image of; assume form, develop into shape, give signs of future shape (~*s well,* is promising). Hence **shăp'ABLE** a. [OE *sciepan,* OS *sceppian,* Goth. *gaskapjan* create, f. Gmc **skapjan*; *shape* is a new ME form after the p.p.]

shape[2], n. **1.** Configuration, form, total effect produced by thing's outlines, (*spherical in ~*; *has the ~ of a boat*). **2.** Appearance, guise, (*monster in human*

~). **3.** Concrete presentment, embodiment, (*intention took ~ in action*; *showed me politeness in the ~ of an invitation*). **4.** Kind, description, sort, (*made no overtures in any ~ or form*). **5.** Symmetrical or definite form, orderly arrangement, proper condition, (*get* one's *ideas into ~*; LICK *into ~*; *give ~ to*), whence ~'LESS (-pl-) a., ~'lessLY² adv., ~'lessNESS n. **6.** Person considered as impressing the sight, & esp. as indistinctly seen or imagined, apparition, ghost, (*a ~ loomed through the mist*; *a grim mysterious ~ stalked towards me*). **7.** Pattern for workman etc., mould for shaping hats etc.; jelly, blancmange, etc. shaped in mould; padding worn by actor. Hence (-)shāp-ED² (-pt) a. [OE *gesceap* (Y-, prec.)]

shāpe'l|y (-pli), a. Well formed or proportioned, of the right or a pleasing shape. Hence ~iNESS n. [ME; -LY¹]

shāp'er, n. In vbl senses; esp., kinds of machine for turning, planing, stamping, moulding, etc. [-ER¹]

shārd, shĕrd, n. (arch.). Potsherd (still used by gardeners of fragment put over hole of flowerpot); beetle's wing-cover. [OE *sceard*, ON *skarthr* f. Gmc *skardaz* notched f. *skar- SHEAR¹; cf. SHARE]

shāre¹, n. **1.** Portion detached for individual from common amount (*must get a ~ of the plunder*). **2.** Part one is entitled to have or bound to contribute, equitable portion, (*that is your fair ~*; *took, bore, my or more or less than my ~ of the burden*; *go ~s*, make equitable division with others; *~ & ~ alike*, with equal division; LION'S *~*). **3.** Part one gets or contributes (*had a large ~ in bringing it about, but no ~ of the credit*). **4.** Part-proprietorship of property held by joint owners (*has a ~ in the bank, estate, etc.*), esp. one of the equal parts into which company's capital is divided entitling holder to proportion of profits (*hold 50 ~s in*; *an issue of 10,000 ~s*); *deferred ~s*, on which lower dividend or none is to be paid till fixed date or contingent event; *preference* or *preferred ~s*, on which fixed dividend is guaranteed before payment begins on *ordinary ~s*; ~'*holder*, owner of ~s; ‖ ~-*list*, of current prices of ~s in various companies; ~-*pusher*, colloq., pedlar of (usu. worthless) ~s. **5.** *~'cropper*, tenant farmer who pays his rent with a part of his crop. [ME *share* f. OE *scearu* division f. WG *skarō* f. *skar- SHEAR¹]

shāre², v.t. & i. Apportion (food, property, task, etc.) among others, give each a share of; give away part of (*would ~ his last crust*); get or have share of, possess or use or endure jointly with others; have share(s), be sharer(s), (*will ~ with you in the undertaking*; *we must ~ alike*); ~ *out*, distribute, whence ~-*out* n., provident club's distribution. Hence shār'ER¹ n. [16th c., f. prec.]

shāre³, n. Ploughshare; blade of seeding--machine or cultivator; ~-*beam*, part of plough in which ~ is fixed. [OE *scear*, *scær*, OHG *scar*, f. Gmc *skar-*, *sker- SHEAR¹]

shārk, n., & v.i. & t. **1.** Kinds of long--shaped lateral-gilled inferior-mouthed sea-fish many species of which are large & voracious (*basking, man-eating, white, blue, dusky, bonnet-headed,* etc., ~); rapacious person, swindler, (LAND-~); *(college sl.) brilliant student; ~-*moth*, kinds of moth named from shape; ~-*oil*, got from ~'s liver & used like cod-liver oil; ~'s-*mouth*, opening in awning for mast etc. **2.** vb. Play the swindler, adventurer, etc. (*~s for a living*), whence ~'ING² a.; gather *up* by dishonest or dishonourable means; swallow voraciously. [f. 16th c., of unkn. orig.]

shārp¹, a., n., & adv. **1.** With fine edge or point, not blunt; keen-edged, pointed, edged, (*~ gable, summit, ridge*). **2.** Well-defined, clean-cut, (*~ outline, distinction, impression, features; so ~-cut*). **3.** Abrupt, angular, (*~ turn, incline*). **4.** Keen, pungent, acid, tart, shrill, piercing, biting, harsh, acrimonious, severe, intense, painful, (*~ flavour, wine, voice, cry, frost, air, words, tongue, temper, reproof, contest, attack of gout*). **5.** Acute, sensitive, quick to see or hear or notice, keen-witted, vigilant, clever, (*~ eyes, ears, intelligence, attention*; ~-*sighted, -witted*, etc.; *keep a ~ look-out*; *a ~ remark, child*; *as ~ as a needle*, very intelligent). **6.** Quick to take advantage, bent on winning, artful, unscrupulous, dishonest, (*was too ~ for me*, overreached me; ~ *practice*, barely honest dealings). **7.** Vigorous, speedy, not loitering, impetuous, (*take a ~ walk*; ~'s *the word*, exhortation to be quick; ~ *work*, said of matter quickly dispatched or fight etc. that takes all one's energy). **8.** (phonet.). (Of mutes) unvoiced, hard. **9.** (mus., opp. FLAT²). Above true pitch (*piano is ~*; *B, D,* etc., ~, a semitone higher than B, D, etc.), (of key) having ~(s) in signature. **10.** ~-*shooter*, skilled shot posted where marksmanship is required; hence ~'EN⁶ v.t. & i., (-)~'en-ER¹(1, 2) n., ~'LY² adv., ~'NESS n. **11.** n. Sewing-needle of slender make; (mus.) note raised a semitone above pitch, symbol indicating this raising, ~s & FLAT²s; ~ *consonant*; (colloq.) swindler, cheat (*billiard-~*); *(joc.) expert (*mining-~*); ‖ (pl.) middlings (between flour & bran). **12.** adv. Punctually (*at six o'clock ~*); (mus.) above true pitch (*is singing ~*); LOOK¹ *~*; ~-*set*, hungry; ~-*shod*, calked. [OE *scearp*, OS *skarp*, OHG *scarpf*, ON *skarpr* f. Gmc *skarpaz*]

shārp², v.t. & i. Sharpen, whet, (arch. or vulg.); raise pitch of (note) or mark as sharp; play unfairly, swindle, at cards etc., whence ~'ER¹ n. [OE *scierpan*, f. prec.]

Sha'stra (-ah-), n. One of the sacred Hindu writings. [Skr. *çāstra*]

shătt′er, v.t. & i. Break (t. & i.) suddenly & violently in pieces; utterly derange, destroy, dissipate, (~ed nerves, constitution, hopes). [14th c., obsc. rel. to earlier SCATTER]

shave¹, v.t. & i. (p.p. ~d &, chiefly as adj., ~n). 1. Remove (hair), free (chin etc.) of hair, relieve (person) of hair on chin etc., with razor (has ~d off or ~d his beard, now wears none; a ~n chin); (intr.) ~ oneself (he does not ~ every day). 2. Pare surface of (wood etc.) with SPOKE-shave, plane, etc., whence **shăv′ing¹**(2) n. 3. Pass close to without touching, skirt, miss narrowly, nearly graze. 4. ~-hook, tool for scraping surface of metal before soldering; shaving-brush, for lathering chin etc. before shaving; shaving-horse, bench with clamp for holding wood to be ~d. [OE sceafan, OS scavan, OHG scaban, ON skafa, Goth. skaban f. Gmc *skabh-]

shāve², n. 1. Having one's beard etc. shaved (must have a ~; shilling ~). 2. Close approach without contact, narrow miss or escape or failure, (had a close ~ of it). 3. Knife-blade with handle at each end for shaving wood etc. 4. ‖ Trick, deception, hoax. [(the tool f. OE sceafa) f. prec.]

shāve′ling (-vl-), n. (arch.). Shaven person, monk, friar, priest. [-LING¹]

shăv′er, n. In vbl senses; also (colloq.), lad, youngster, (usu. young ~). [-ER¹]

Shāv′ian, a. (In the manner) of G. B. Shaw, dramatist (d. 1950). [-IAN]

‖ **shaw¹,** n. (arch. & poet.). Thicket, wood. [OE sc(e)aga = ON skagi; see SHAG¹]

‖ **shaw²,** n. (Sc.). Stalks and leaves of some plants, esp. potatoes and turnips. [of obsc. orig.]

shawl, n. & v.t. 1. Rectangular garment, often square to be folded into triangle, chiefly worn by women as outer covering for shoulders; ~-dance, in which dancer waves a ~; ~-pattern, variegated design like that of Oriental ~. 2. v.t. Put ~ on (person). [f. Pers. shdl]

shawm, n. Obsolete musical instrument with reed. [ME, f. OF chalemie f. L f. Gk kalamos reed]

shay, n. (Arch. joc., or vulg., for) CHAISE. [back form. f. chaise taken for pl.]

shē, pron. (obj. HER¹, possess. HER², HER²s, pl. THEY etc.), n., & a. 1. The female (or thing personified as female, e.g. ship or train) previously mentioned or implied or easily identified. 2. n. Female, woman, (the not impossible ~, woman one might love; is the child a he or a ~?; had a litter of two ~s & a he, two bitches & a dog). 3. adj. (usu. hyphened). Female (~-goat, -ass, -bear, etc.; ~-devil, -cat, malignant or spiteful woman; ~-oak, kinds of Australian shrub, esp. BEEFwood; ~-pine, Australian conifer). [prob. an alt. form of OE fem. demonstr. pron. sio, sēo, sie]

shea (shē), n. W.-Afr. tree yielding a vegetable butter (~-butter). [native si, se, sye]

shead′ing, n. Any of the six administrative divisions of the I. of Man. [SHED¹, -ING¹]

sheaf, n. (pl. -ves), & v.t. 1. Bundle of things laid lengthwise together & usu. tied (~ of papers, arrows, etc.), esp. armful of corn-stalks tied after reaping (~-binder, tool for tying these). 2. v.t. Make into sheaves, sheave. [OE scēaf, OS skōf, OHG scoub, ON skauf f. Gmc *skaubh-, see SHOVE]

sheal′ing. Var. of SHIELING.

shear¹, v.t. & i. (past ~ed & arch. shore; p.p. shorn, rarely ~ed). 1. Cut with sword etc. (poet.; t. & i.; shore off his plume; shore through the bone); (fig.) cut with scissors or shears, (trans.; ~ sheep, clip its wool; also abs., shall be ~ing, i.e. my sheep, tomorrow); ~ cloth, remove or reduce nap by clipping; (fig.) fleece, strip bare, (come home shorn; shorn of wool, glory, etc.). 2. (Of structure, material, etc.) be distorted or broken by the strain called a shear, (of pressure) distort or break thus. 3. ~′water, kinds of low-flying sea-bird. Hence ~ER¹ n. [OE, OS, OHG sceran, ON skera f. Gmc *sker-, *skar-, *skær-, *skur-, cogn. w. SHARD, SHARE, SCAR², etc.]

shear², n. 1. (Pl.) clipping-instrument with two meeting blades pivoted as in scissors or connected by spring & passing close over each other edge to edge (want a pair of ~s; ~ in comb. or attrib., as ~′bill, the bird scissorbill or skimmer; ~-grass, kind with sharp-edged leaves; ~-legs, SHEER³s; ~ steel, of special quality fit for ~s & other cutting tools; ~′tail, humming-bird with tail like ~s). 2. (mech.). Kind of strain produced by pressure in structure of a substance, its successive layers being shifted laterally over each other. [OE scēar, OHG scâra, also OE scērero pl., f., Gmc *skær-(prec.)]

shear′ling, n. Sheep once shorn. [-LING¹]

sheat′-fish, n. Largest European freshwater fish. [c. 1600, f. G scheidfisch or unkn. orig.; 16th c. sheath-fish prob. f. SHEATH]

sheath, n. (pl. pr. -dhz). Close-fitting cover, esp. for blade of weapon or tool; (bot., zool., anat.) investing membrane, tissue, skin, horny case, etc.; structure of loose stones for confining river within banks. Hence ~′LESS a. ·[OE scǣth, scēath, OS skēdia, OHG sceida, ON skeithir pl. f. Gmc *skaithjō; cf. SHED¹]

sheathe (-dh), v.t. Put into sheath (~ the sword, cease from war, & fig.); encase, protect with casing or **sheath′ing**(3) n. [ME, f. prec.]

sheave¹, n. Grooved wheel in pulley etc. for rope to run on. [ME, cogn. w. OS sciva, OHG sciba]

sheave², v.t. Gather (corn etc.) into sheaves, sheaf. [f. SHEAF]

sheaves. See SHEAF.

*shĕbăng', n. (sl.). House (esp. gambling--house), store, saloon; any matter of present concern; business (*the whole* ~). [orig. unkn.]

‖ shĕbeen', n. Pot-house, **unlicensed** house selling drink. [Ir.]

shĕd¹, v.t. (*shed*). Part with, let fall off, (*tree, stag, snake, crab, Prime Minister,* ~s *leaves, horns, skin, shell, colleagues*); drop (~ *tears*, weep; ~ one's *blood for* one's *country*, be wounded or killed); cause (others' blood) to flow; disperse, diffuse, spread abroad, (~ *light on*, illuminate, esp. fig.; ~ *love, radiance, perfume,* etc., *around* one); (electr.) reduce (the LOAD¹). Hence ~**d'ER¹** n. [OE *sc(e)ădan*, OS *skĕdan*, OHG *sceidan*, Goth. *skaidan* f. Gmc **skaith-* etc., prob. cogn. w. Gk *skhizō*, L *scindere*]

shĕd², n. One-storeyed shelter for storing goods or vehicles or keeping cattle etc. or for use as workshop etc. & consisting of roof with some or all o̅r no sides open. Hence ~**d'ING¹**(3) n. [app. var. of SHADE]

sheen, n. Splendour, radiance, brightness. Hence ~**'y̆¹** [-Y²] a. (poet.). [f. obs. adj. *sheen* beautiful, OE *sciene*, OS, OHG *skōni*, Goth. *skauns* f. Gmc *skau-SHOW¹; sense assim. to unrelated *shine*]

sheen'y̆², n.(sl.). Jew(derog.). [orig. unkn.]

sheep, n. (pl. the same). **1.** Kinds of wild or domesticated timid gregarious woolly occas. horned ruminant of which male is named *ram*, female *ewe*, & young *lamb* (~ *& goats*, the good & the bad, see *Matt.* xxv. 33; BLACK¹ ~; *cast* ~'s *eyes*, glance amorously *at*; *follow like* ~, said of persons with no initiative or independence; *as well be hanged for a* ~ *as a* LAMB¹; ~ *that have no shepherd*, helpless crowd etc.; WOLF *in* ~'s *clothing*). **2.** Bashful embarrassed person (so ~'ISH¹ a., ~'ishLY² adv., ~'ishNESS n.). **3.** (Usu. pl., now chiefly joc.) member(s) of minister's flock, parishioners etc. **4.** = ~-skin leather. **5.** ~-*bot*, fly & larva injurious to ~; ~-*cote* (arch.), -*fold*, -*pen* (rare), enclosure for penning ~; ~-*dip*, preparation for cleansing ~ of vermin or preserving their wool; ~-*dog*, collie, also breed of rough-coated short-tailed dog used by shepherds; ‖ ~-*farmer*, -*master*, breeder of ~; ~-*hook*, shepherd's crook; ~-*louse*, -*tick*, kinds of parasite on ~; ~-*pox*, ~-*disease* resembling smallpox; ~-*run*, extensive ~-*walk*, esp. in Australia; ~'s-*bit*, plant resembling scabious; ~'s *fescue*, a pasture grass; ~'*shank*, bight & hitches used to shorten rope's length temporarily; ~'s-*head* lit., also kind of sea-fish used for food; ~-*shearing*, (festival at) shearing of ~; ~'*skin*, garment or rug of ~'s skin with wool on, also leather of ~'s skin used in bookbinding etc., also parchment of it or deed or diploma

engrossed on this; ~-*walk*, tract of land on which ~ are pastured; ~-*wash*, lotion for killing vermin or preserving wool on ~. [OE *scēap*, OS *scāp*, OHG *scāf*, WG f. Gmc *skæpam]

sheer¹, a. & adv. **1.** Mere, simple, unassisted, undiluted, uncompounded, neither more nor less than, absolute, (*did it by* ~ *force; is* ~ *waste, nonsense, folly;* *a* ~ *impossibility*); (of rock, fall, ascent, etc.) perpendicular, unrelieved by slope; (of textiles) diaphanous. **2.** adv. Plumb, perpendicularly, outright, (*fell 3000 ft* ~; *torn* ~ *out by the roots; rises* ~ *from the water*). [ME *schēre* prob. f. ON *skærr* f. Gmc *skairjaz f. **skī-* SHINE (cf. OE *scīr* bright)]

sheer², v.i. (Naut.) deviate from course; (also in gen. use) ~ *off*, part company, depart, esp. from person or topic one dislikes or fears or is offended by. [perh. a use of SHEAR¹, but sense development is obsc.; cf. (M)LG *scheren*]

sheer³, n. Upward slope of ship's lines towards bow & stern; deviation of ship from course. [perh. f. SHEAR²·¹]

sheer⁴, n. (Pl.; also ~-*legs* or *shear-legs*) hoisting-apparatus of two (or more) poles attached at or near top and separated at bottom for masting ships or putting in engines etc., used in dockyards.or on ~-*hulk*, dismasted ship used for the purpose. [var. of SHEAR²; named from resemblance to pair of shears]

sheet¹, n. **1.** Rectangular piece of linen used in pairs as inner bed-clothes (*between the* ~s, in bed), whence ~'ING¹(3) n.; WHITE¹~. **2.** Broad more or less flat piece of some thin material (*a* ~ *of iron, glass,* etc.). **3.** Wide expanse *of* water, snow, ice, flame, colour, etc. **4.** Complete piece of paper of the size in which it was made (*book is in* ~s, printed but not bound; ~ *of notepaper*, freq. folded once for writing on; ~ *of quarto* etc., the four etc. leaves given by folding a ~ twice etc.); newspaper (*a penny, scurrilous,* etc., ~). **5.** Rope or chain at lower corner of sail for regulating its tension etc. (*flowing* ~, not close-hauled, eased for free wind; *a* ~, *three* ~s, *in the wind*, sl., rather, very, drunk). **6.** ~-*anchor*, second anchor orig. carried outside waist of ship for use in emergencies, (fig.) main dependence or security, something that may hold when all else has failed; ~ *copper, iron, metal,* etc., spread by rolling, hammering, etc., into thin ~s; ~ *glass*, kind made first as hollow cylinder, which is cut open & flattened in furnace; ~ LIGHTNING; ~ *music* (published in ~s, not in book form). [(1–4) OE *scīete* f. Gmc *skautjōn f. **skaut-* SHOOT¹; (5) OE *skēata* f. same source; (6) ~-*anchor* of obsc. orig.]

sheet², v.t. Furnish with sheets; cover with sheet (*the* ~*ẹd dead*); form into sheets (~*ẹd rain*); secure (sail) with sheet (esp. ~ *home*). [f. prec.]

sheik(h) (-ēk, -ăk), n. Chief, head of Arabian or Mohammedan tribe, family, or village; (transf.) masterful husband or lover, (sl.) dashing or attractive man; *S~ ul Islam* (hist.), grand mufti at Constantinople, chief authority on sacred law in Turkey. [Arab. *shaikh*, = elder, chief]

shekarry. See SHIKAREE.

shĕk'el, n. Ancient Jewish weight & silver coin; (pl., colloq.) money, riches, pelf. [f. Heb. *sheqel* (*shāqal* weigh)]

Shĕkin'ah, -ch-, n. Visible glory of Jehovah resting over mercy-seat. [Heb. (-k-), f. *shākan* dwell]

shĕl'drāke n. (fem. & pl. *shelduck*). Kinds of (usu. bright-plumaged) wild duck. [ME, prob. f. dial. *sheld* (f. or cogn. w. MDu. *schillede* variegated) +DRAKE]

shĕlf, n. (pl. *-ves*). Projecting slab of stone or board let into or hung on wall to support things, one of the boards in cabinet, bookcase, etc., on which books etc. stand, (on the ~, put aside, done with, esp. of person past work and of woman now unlikely to be married); ledge, horizontal steplike projection in cliff face etc.; reef or sandbank under water. Hence **shĕlved²** (-vd) a., **~'FUL**(2) n. [ME, f. (M)LG *schelf*, cogn. w. OE *scylfe* (? ledge, floor), *scylf* crag]

shĕll¹, n. 1. Hard outer case enclosing nuts, kinds of seed or fruit, eggs, some animals or parts of them, etc., husk, crust, pod, carapace, scale, conch, wing-case, pupa-case, (*come out of* one's ~, throw off reserve, become communicative). 2. Walls of unfinished or gutted house, ship, etc. 3. Outline of plan etc. 4. Inner coffin. 5. Light racing-boat. 6. Hollow metal or paper case to contain explosives for fireworks, cartridges, etc.; explosive projectile or bomb for use in big gun or mortar, whence **~'PROOF²** a.; *cartridge. 7. Handguard of sword. 8. Lyre (poet.). 9. ‖ (At schools) intermediate form. 10. Outward show, mere semblance. 11. (Short for) ~-jacket. 12. *~'back* (naut. sl.), old sailor; *~-bark*, kinds of hickory; *~-bit*, gouge-shaped boring-bit; ~ *button*, made of two metal discs enclosed in cloth etc.; *~'fish*, aquatic ~ed mollusc (oyster etc.) or crustacean (crab, shrimp, etc.); *~-heap* or *-mound*, kitchen MIDDEN; *~-jacket*, army officer's undress jacket reaching only to waist behind; *~-lime*, fine quality produced by burning sea-~s; *~-marble*, kinds containing fossil ~s; *~-shock*, disorganization of mental faculties, power of speech, etc., resulting from exposure to bombardment & other war strains; *~-work*, ornamentation of ~s cemented on wood etc. Hence (-)~ED³ (-ld), **~'LESS**, **~'Y²**, aa. [OE *sci(e)ll*, MDu., MLG *schelle*, ON *skel*, Goth. *skalja* f. Gmc *skaljō* f. *skal-* SCALE¹,², SHALE]

shĕll², v.t. & i. 1. Take out of shell,

remove shell or pod from, (~ *peas*). 2. Provide, cover, or pave, with shell(s). 3. Bombard (town etc.), fire at (troops), with shells, whence **~'ING¹**(1) n. 4. (Of metal etc.) come off in scales. 5. *~ out* (sl.), pay up (t. & i.), hand over required sum; **~-out** n., the game of pyramids played by three or more persons. [f. prec.]

shellăc', n., & v.t. (*~king*, *~ked*). 1. LAC¹ melted into thin plates, used for making varnish. 2. v.t. Varnish with ~. [transl. F *laque en écailles* LAC in thin plates]

shĕl'ta, n. Ancient hybrid cant language of Irish gipsies and pipers, Irish and Welsh travelling tinkers, etc. (largely BACK¹-slang). [orig. unkn.]

shĕl'ter¹, n. Thing serving as shield or barrier against attack, danger, heat, wind, etc. (ANDERSON, MORRISON, ~); screen or cabin built to keep off wind & rain (*cabman's* ~); place of safety or immunity; shielded condition (*find, take*, ~). Hence **~LESS** a. [16th c., of obsc. orig.; perh. f. *sheld* SHIELD + -TURE, after *jointure* etc.]

shĕl'ter², v.t. & i. Act or serve as shelter to, protect, conceal, harbour, defend *from* blame, screen, shield; ~ one*self under*, *beneath, behind*, etc., use the protection afforded by; take shelter *under, in, from*; ‖ ~*ed trades*, those not exposed to foreign competition, e.g. building & inland transport. [f. prec.]

‖ **shĕl'tỹ, -tie,** n. (Sc.). Shetland pony. [prob. repr. ON *Hjalti* Shetlander]

shĕlve¹, v.t. Put on shelf (books etc.), (fig.) abandon or defer consideration of (plan etc.), cease to employ (person); fit (cupboard etc.) with shelves, whence **shĕl'VING¹**(3) n. [f. *shelves* pl. of SHELF]

shĕlve², v.i. Slope gently. [16th c., of obsc. orig.; cf. WFris. *skelf* oblique]

shelves. See SHELF.

Shema' (-ah), n. The *Hear, O Israel*, Jews' confession of faith. [the initial wd, Heb. = hear]

shĕmŏz'zle, n. (sl.). Rumpus, brawl, muddle. [Yiddish]

shĕnăn'ĭgan, n. (colloq.). Nonsense, trickery.

Shē'ŏl, n. Hebrew Hades, place of the dead, the grave. [Heb.]

shĕp'herd (-perd), n., & v.t. 1. Man who tends sheep at pasture, pastor (lit., & fig. esp. of minister in relation to his flock; *the good S~*, Christ); ~'s *crook*, staff with hook at one end used by ~s; ~'s *needle*, white-flowered common weed; ~'s *pie*, minced meat baked under mashed potatoes; ~'s *plaid*, small black & white check pattern in cloth; ~'s *purse*, white-flowered cornfield weed; hence **~ESS¹** (-per-) n. 2. v.t. Tend (sheep, also fig.) as ~, marshal or conduct or drive (crowd etc.) like sheep. [OE *scēaphirde* (SHEEP, HERD²)]

Shĕ'raton, n. Severe 18th-c. style of

furniture (often attrib., as ~ *chairs*). [T. ~ maker & designer (d. 1806)]

sherb′et, n. Eastern cooling drink of diluted fruit-juices (in pop. Engl. use, made effervescent). [Turk. & Pers., f. Arab. *shariba* to drink]

sherd. See SHARD.

sherif′ (-ēf), **-eef,** n. Descendant of Mohammed through Fatima, entitled to wear green turban or veil; chief magistrate of Mecca. [f. Arab. *sharif* noble]

she′riff, n. ‖ Chief officer of crown in county or shire, charged with the keeping of the peace, administering justice under direction of the courts, executing writs by deputy, presiding over elections, etc.; (in Scotland) chief judge of county or district; *elective officer responsible for keeping the peace in his county. [OE *scīr-gerēfa* (SHIRE, REEVE[1])]

she′riffalty, she′riffdom, she′riffhood, she′riffship, nn. Shrievalty, office of sheriff. [*-alty* after shrievalty; -DOM, -HOOD, -SHIP]

Sher′pa, n. One of a Himalayan people living on the borders of Nepal and Tibet. [native]

she′rry, n. White wine from Jeres in Southern Spain (*brown* ~, dark varieties); ~*-glass*, wineglass containing about four table-spoons; ~ COBBLER. [16th c. *sherris* f. Sp. (*vino de*) *Xeres* (now *Jerez de la Frontera*); cf. CHERRY]

Shet′land, n. Group of islands NNE of Scotland (~ *lace*, openwork woollen trimming; ~ *pony*, small hardy breed; ~ *wool*, fine kind).

shew. See SHOW[1]; ~*′bread*, see SHOW[1].

Shi′ah, Shi′ite, (shē-), nn. Member of the Mohammedan sect (cf. *Sunni*, see SUNNAH) that regards Ali as first imam or successor of Mohammed & rejects first three Sunni Caliphs. [Arab., = sect]

shibb′olĕth, n. Test word or principle or behaviour or opinion, the use of or inability to use which betrays one's party, nationality, etc. (see *Judg.* xii. 6); old-fashioned & generally abandoned doctrine once held essential. [Heb.]

shield, n., & v.t. 1. Variously shaped & sized detached piece of armour made of leather, wood, or metal, for wearing on left arm to receive thrust or stroke, esp. (cf. *buckler, target*) one of elongated form large enough to cover most of body (*the other side of the* ~, the aspect of a question etc. that is less obvious, or that is not the one lately presented); protective plate or screen in machinery etc.; person or thing that protects one; ~*-like* part in animal or plant; (her.) drawing etc. of ~ used for displaying person's coat of arms; ~*-fern*, common handsome fern with ~*-*-shaped covers to fruit-dots; ~*-hand* (arch.), left hand; hence ~*′LESS* a. 2. v.t. Protect, screen, esp. from censure or punishment (often with implication of illegitimate concealment of facts). [OE

sceld, OS, OHG *scild,* ON *skjǫldr,* Goth. *skildus* f. Gmc *skelduz*]

‖ **shiel′ing,** ·n. (Sc.). Grazing-ground for cattle; cottage with earth floor; roughly constructed hut for shepherds or sportsmen; sheep-shelter. [f. Sc. *shiel* hut, of obsc. orig., +-ING[1]]

shi′er, -est. See SHY[1].

shift[1], v.t. & i. 1. Change or move (t. & i.) from one position to another, substitute one specimen of for another, undergo such substitution, change form or character, (~ one's *ground*, take up new position in argument etc.; ~ one's *lodging*; ~ *load into other hand*; ~ *the scene, the scene* ~*s*, in theatre, novel, etc.; ‖ ~ one's *shirt* etc., arch., change it; *cargo* ~*ed*, got shaken out of place; often ~ *about*; ~ *off* responsibility etc., get rid of, transfer to another; *wind* ~*s round to the E*). 2. Use expedients, take whatever course is available, contrive to do something, manage or get along or make a livelihood, (*must* ~ *as I can, for himself*). 3. Equivocate, practise evasion, (rare; ~*s & prevaricates*). [OE *sciftan* arrange, divide, etc., = MLG *schiften,* ON *skipta* f. Gmc *skiftjan*]

shift[2], n. 1. Change of place or character, substitution of one thing for another, vicissitude, rotation, (rare; *the* ~*s & changes of life*; ~ *of crops*, rotation). 2. Relay of workmen, time for which it works. 3. New device, expedient, resource, whence ~*′LESS* a., ~*′lĕssLY* adv., ~*′lĕssNESS* n. 4. Dodge, trick, artifice, piece of evasion or equivocation, whence ~*′Y*[2] a. (~*y eyes*, deceitful), ~*′iLY*[2] adv., ~*′iNESS* n. 5. *Make* ~ or *a* ~, manage or contrive (*to* do, or abs.), get along somehow (*must make* ~ *without it*). 6. (arch.). Chemise. 7. Arrangement by which joints of successive tiers in brickwork etc. do not coincide. [ME *schift,* f. prec.; cf. ON *skipti*]

Shiite. See SHIAH.

shikār′, n. (Anglo-Ind.). Hunting. [Hind.]

shikār′ee (-rī), **-rī, shekā′rry,** n. (Anglo-Ind.). Hunter. [Hind. (-ī), f. prec.]

shille′lagh (-āla), **-ālah,** n. Irish cudgel of blackthorn or oak. [*Shillelagh* in Ireland]

‖ **shill′ing,** n. (abbr. *s.*, as 3*s.*). British silver coin & money of account=1/20 of pound or twelve pence (1/6, a ~ & sixpence; £1 1s. 1d.; *take King's* or *Queen's* ~, enlist as soldier, w. ref. to now obs. method of recruiting; *cut off* one's *heir* etc. *with a* ~, leave one's property to others; ~*s′-*WORTH[1]). [OE, OS, OHG *scilling,* ON *skillingr,* Goth. *skilliggs* f. Gmc *skillingaz*]

shill′y-shăllў, n., a., & v.i. 1. Inability to make up one's mind, indecision, vacillation. 2. adj. Vacillating. 3. v.i. Vacillate, be undecided, hesitate to act or choose one's course. [orig. *shill I, shall I*; cf. *dilly-dally*]

shily. See SHY[1].

shim, n., & v.t. (-mm-). Thin slip or wedge used in machinery etc. to make parts fit; (vb) fit or fill up thus. [orig. unkn.]

shimm'er, v.i., & n. (Shine with) tremulous or faint diffused light. [OE *scymrian*, MDu. *schēmeren*, G *schimmern*; rel. to obs. *shim*, OE *scimian* shine]

shimm'y[1], n. (Colloq., nursery, etc., for) CHEMISE.

•shimm'y[2], n., & v.i. 1. Kind of fox-trot accompanied by tremulous motions of body; vibration of (front) wheels of car. 2. v.i. Dance a~; vibrate. [orig. unkn.]

shin, n., & v.i. & t. (-nn-). 1. Front of leg below knee (~-*bone*, tibia; ~ *of beef*, ox's shank); ~-*guard*, worn at football. 2. vb. Climb *up* (tree, wall, ladder, etc.; or with *up* adv.); kick ~s of, hack. [OE *scinu*, MDu. *schēne*, OHG *scina*]

shin'dy, n. Brawl, disturbance, row, noise, (often KICK[2] *up a* ~). [perh. **alt. f.** SHINTY]

shine[1], v.i. & t. (*shōne*). Emit or reflect light, be bright, glow, (lit. & fig.; *face shone with soap* or *with gratitude* etc.); be brilliant, be a luminary, excel, in some respect or sphere (*does not* ~ *in conversation, society*; *is a shining example*); (colloq.) make bright, polish, (boots, fireplace, brass, etc.). [OE (OS, OHG) *scinan*, ON *skina*, Goth. *skeinan* f. Gmc *•skīnan* f. *•skī-*]

shine[2], n. Light, brightness, (chiefly colloq.; *rain or* ~, whatever the weather; *put a good* ~ *on* boots etc.; *take the* ~ *out of*, impair brilliance or newness of, also throw into the shade by surpassing); (sl.) disturbance, shindy, sensation; *•take a* ~ *to* (sl.), take a fancy for. [f. prec.]

shin'er, n. (sl.). A coin, esp. sovereign, (pl.) money. [SHINE[1], -ER[1]]

shingle[1] (shǐng'gl), n., & v.t. 1. Rectangular slip of wood used like roof-tile on roofs, spires, etc.; *•small signboard; ~d* hair, this style of hairdressing. 2. v.t. Roof with ~s; cut (hair of head) so that all ends are exposed like roof~s, cut hair of (head, person) thus. [ME, app. f. L *scindula*, earlier *scandula*]

shingle[2] (shǐng'gl), n. Small rounded pebbles lying on sea-shore. Hence **shing'ly**[2] (-ngg-) a. [16th c. *chingle* (cf. SHIVER[1]), of obsc. orig.; perh. imit.]

shingles (shǐng'glz), n. pl. Acute skin-inflammation occurring along nerve-•tracks. [ME, f. med. L *cingulus* f. L *cingulum* girdle (*cingere* gird)]

•shinn'y[1], v.i. (colloq.). Shin tree etc., usu. *up*. [SHIN]

Shin'tō, n. Japanese religion partly ousted by Buddhism. Hence ~ISM, ~IST, nn. [f. Chin. *shin tao* way of the gods]

shin'ty, **shinn'y**[2], n. Variation of hockey played in Scotland and N. England; stick or ball used in it. [17th c. *shinny*, app. f. the cry used in the game *shin ye*, *shin you*, of unkn. orig.]

shin'|** y**, a. Glistening, polished, rubbed bright, (~*y hat, boots*, etc.; ~*y coat, seams*, with nap worn off). Hence ~INESS n. [-Y[2]]

ship[1], n. (regarded as fem., w. pron. *she, her*). 1. Vessel with bowsprit & three, four, or five square-rigged masts (cf. BARQUE, BRIG, SCHOONER, SLOOP); any sea-going vessel of considerable size (BATTLE[1]-~, ~ *of the* LINE[2], MERCHANT-~, SAIL[2]*ing-*~, WAR[1]~; *sister* ~, built on same plan as another; ~ *of the desert*, camel; ABOUT[2]~; PUMP[2]-~;*take* ~, embark; *on* BOARD[1] ~; *when my* etc. ~ *comes home*, when I etc. make my etc. fortune; (sl.) boat, esp. racing-boat; *•aircraft*; *on* ~*board*, on board ~. 2. ~ *('s)* biscuit, hard coarse kind made for keeping used on board ~; ~-*breaker*, contractor who breaks up old ~s; ~-*broker*, agent in buying and selling and insuring ~s; ~'*builder*, ~'*building*; ~-*canal*, for conveying ~s inland; ~--CHANDLER(y); ~-*fever*, typhus; ~'*load*, quantity of something forming whole cargo; ~'*mate*, person belonging to or sailing on same ~ as another, esp. fellow sailor; ~-*money* (hist.), impost for providing ~s for navy, revival of which by Charles I was a cause of Great Rebellion; ~'*owner*, person owning (shares in) ~(s); ~-*railway*, for transportation of ~s over land from water to water; ~-*rigged*, as ~ in first sense; ~'s *articles*, terms on which seamen take service on her; ~'s COMPANY[1]; ‖~'s CORPORAL[3]; ~'*shape* adv. or pred. a., in good order (& see BRISTOL); ~'s *husband*, agent appointed by the owners to see that a ~ in port is well found in all respects; ~'s *papers*, documents establishing ownership, nationality, nature of cargo, etc., of ~; ~-*way*, inclined structure on which ~ is built & down which it slides to be launched; ~-*worm*, mollusc boring into ~ timbers; ~'*wreck* n., destruction of ~ by storm, foundering, stranding, striking rock, etc., (fig.) ruin (*make* ~*wreck*, be ruined; *make or suffer* ~*wreck of* one's *hopes* etc.); ~'*wreck* v.t. & i., inflict ~wreck lit. or fig. on (person, hopes, etc., rarely ~), suffer ~wreck; ~'*wright*, ~-*builder*; ~-*yard*, ~-building establishment. Hence ~'LESS a. [OE *scip*, OHG *scif*, OS, ON, Goth. *skip*; ult. orig. unkn.]

ship[2], v.t. & i. (-pp-). Put, take, or send away (goods, passengers, sailors) on board ship; (commerc.) deliver (goods) to forwarding agent for conveyance by land or water; step (mast), fix (rudder etc.), in its place on ship (~ *oars*, take from rowlocks & lay inside boat); (of ship or boat) ~ *a sea*, be flooded by wave; take ship, embark, (of sailor) take service on ship. [OE *scipian* f. prec.]

-ship, suf. f. OE *-scipe* (cogn. w. (M)Du. *-schap*, OHG *-scaf*, (G *-schaft*), ON *-skapr*) f. Gmc *•skap-* SHAPE[1], forming abstract nn. on adjj. as *hard*~, *wor-* ~ (*worth* adj.),

& on nn. as *lord~, friend~, scholar~, apprentice~*; in the latter use it is a living suf.; meaning, (1) being so-&-so, status, office, honour, (2) tenure of office, (3) skill in certain capacity. *Landscape* also contains the suf.

ship′ment, n. Putting of goods etc. on ship; amount shipped, consignment. [SHIP², -MENT]

‖ **shipp′en, -on**, n. (chiefly dial.). Cowhouse, cattleshed. [OE *scypen* f. Gmc *skup-* (see SHOP)+-EN²; cf. MLG (G) *schuppen*]

shipp′er, n. Merchant etc. who sends or gets goods by ship. [-ER¹]

shipp′ing, n. In vbl senses; also: ships, esp. the ships of a country, port, etc.; *~-agent*, person acting for ship or line of ships at a port etc.; *~-articles*, agreement between captain & seamen as to wages etc.; *~-bill*, manifest of goods shipped; ‖*~-master*, official in whose presence *~-articles* are signed, paying off is done, etc.; *~-office, ~-agent's* or *~-master's.* [-ING¹]

‖ **shire** (*as suf. pr.* -sher), n. County (chiefly now as suf. in names of certain counties & districts, as *Hamp~, Hallam~,* with some of which it is omissible, as *Devon~* or *Devon &,* & in pl. the *~s,* band of counties stretching NE from *Hamp~* & *Devon~* ending in *~,* also loose term for midland counties, & for the hunting district including Leics. & Rutland & Northants.); *~-bred horse, ~-horse,* largest breed of draught horse raised esp. in Lincoln~ & Cambridge~; KNIGHT *of the ~.* [OE *scir,* OHG *scira* care, official charge; orig. unkn.]

shirk, v.t., & n. 1. Avoid meanly, get out of, shrink selfishly from, (duty, responsibility, fighting, etc.; also abs.); hence *~'ER¹* n. 2. n. *~er.* [f. obs. *shirk* n. sponger, sharper, perh. f. G *schurke*]

*****shir(r)**, n., & v.t. 1. Elastic webbing; elastic thread woven into fabric; gathered trimming, gathering in costumery. 2. v.t. Gather (material) with parallel threads run through; hence **shir′ring¹** n. [orig. unkn.]

shirt, n. Man's sleeved under-garment worn under cloth clothes, extending from neck to thighs, usu. visible at collar & wristbands, & made of linen, cotton, flannel, or silk (NIGHT-~; *in* one's *~-sleeves,* without coat; *near is my ~, but nearer is my skin,* self is the first consideration; *keep* one's *~ on,* sl., keep one's temper; *get* one's *~ off,* sl., make him angry; *put* one's *~ on, upon,* sl., bet all one has upon; *give* one *a wet ~,* work him till he sweats); woman's blouse with stiff collar & cuffs; *~-front,* breast of *~,* usu. stiffened & starched (*~-front wicket,* absolutely true & smooth cricket pitch), also dicky. Hence *~-ED²,* *~-LESS,* aa., *~'ING¹*(3) n., *~'Y²* a. (sl.), in a rage, annoyed. [OE *scyrte,* corresp. to ON

skyrta (whence SKIRT) f. Gmc *skurtjōn* prob. f. *skurt-* SHORT]

shit, v.i., & n. (vulg.). 1. Evacuate bowels. 2. n. Ordure (& as term of abuse). [OE *scītan,* MLG *schīten,* OHG *scīzan,* ON *skīta* f. Gmc *skit-*]

shiv′er¹, v.i., & n. 1. Experience or show quick slight vibrating movement (such as is) caused by sensation of cold, tremble with cold; *~ing-fit,* as in ague; hence *~ingLY²* adv. 2. n. Momentary *~ing* movement (often pl., as *gives me the ~s*), whence *~Y²* a. [ME *chivere,* orig. obsc.]

shiv′er², n. (usu. pl.), & v.t. & i. 1. (One of) the many small pieces into which thing is shattered by blow or fall. 2. vb. Break (t. & i.) into *~s* (*~ my timbers,* reputed naut. imprecation). [ME *scifre,* cogn. w. OHG *scivero* splinter (G *schiefer(stein)* slate) f. Gmc *skif* to split; cf. dial. *shive* slice]

shoal¹, a., n., & v.i. 1. Shallow, not deep, (only lit., of water). 2. n. Shallow place, submerged sandbank esp. one that shows at low water, (fig., usu. pl.) hidden danger(s) or impediment(s), whence *~'Y²* a., *~'INESS* n. 3. v.i. Get shallower. [OE *sceald* f. *skaldaz,* rel. to SHALLOW]

shoal², n., & v.i. 1. Multitude, crowd, great number, esp. of fish swimming in company (also SCHOOL²), (*~s of people; gets letters in ~s*). 2. v.i. (Of fish) form *~s.* [16th c., perh. re-adoption of MDu. *schole* SCHOOL²]

shock¹, n. 1. Violent collision, concussion, or impact (*three ~s of earthquake were felt; clashed with a mighty ~; ~ tactics,* (orig.) use of cavalry to charge in masses, (fig.) sudden and violent action; *~-troops,* troops specially trained for the offensive). 2. Sudden & disturbing physical or mental impression (*news came upon me with a ~, was a great ~; electric ~,* stimulation of nerves by passage of current through body); (path.) state of prostration following overstimulation of nerves by sudden pain as of wound etc. or violent emotion (*died of ~; the ~ is more dangerous than the loss of blood*); *~ therapy, treatment,* method of treating certain mental disorders by means of an electrical shock or powerful drug. 3. Injury inflicted on credit, stability, etc., great disturbance of organization or system. 4. *~-brigade, -workers,* (in U.S.S.R.) body of workers selected or volunteering for some specially arduous task; *~ stall,* excessive strain produced by air resistance on aircraft when speed approximates to that of sound. [app. f. F *choc* f. *choquer* (foll.)]

shock², v.t. & i. Affect with indignation, sorrow, disgust, or horror, appear improper or outrageous or scandalous to (*was ~ed at, by, to hear,* etc.), whence *~'ING²* a. & adv. (*~ing bad* etc. colloq.), *~'ingLY²* adv., *~'ingNESS* n.; collide violently (poet.). [f. F *choquer,* of obsc. orig.]

shŏck³, n., & v.t. **1.** Group of usu. twelve corn-sheaves stood up close together in field. **2.** v.t. Arrange (corn) in ~s. [ME, = OS *scok*, MDu., MLG *schok* shock of corn, sixty; cf. MHG *schoc* heap, sixty]

shŏck⁴, n. Unkempt or shaggy mass of hair; ~ *head*, rough head of hair, whence ~-head ᴇᴅ² a. [cf. obs. 17th c. *shock*(-*dog*), (16th c. *shough*) shaggy-haired poodle]

‖ **shŏck′er**, n. (colloq.). Very bad specimen of anything; sensational cheap novel. [-ᴇʀ¹]

shod. See SHOE².

shŏdd′y, n. & a. **1.** Fibre made from old cloth etc. shredded; inferior cloth made partly of such fibre; anything of worse quality than it claims or seems to have. **2.** adj. Counterfeit, pretentious, trashy. [19th c., of unkn. orig.]

shoe¹ (-ōō), n. **1.** Outer foot-covering not reaching above ankle (*that's another pair of* ~*s*, another matter; *dead men's* ~*s*, property or position as looked forward to by expectant successor; *be in* person's ~*s*, in his plight; *die in* one's ~*s*, by violence, esp. hanging; *where the* ~ *pinches*, hardships of one's own lot; *put the* ~ *on the right foot*, apportion blame etc. truly). **2.** Metal rim nailed to hoof of horse etc. **3.** Thing like ~ in shape or use, e.g. wheel-drag, socket, ferrule, mast-step. **4.** ~*s & stockings*, bird's-foot trefoil; ‖ ~'*black*, boy or man who blacks ~s of passers-by; ~-*buckle*, for fastening ~ over instep (now usu. worn only as ornament); ~'*horn*, instrument of horn, metal, etc., for helping ~ on to foot; ~-*lace*, -*string*, for lacing up ~; ~-*latchet* (bibl.), fastening of ~; ~-*leather*, leather for ~s, ~s (*as good a man as ever trod* ~-*leather*, lived); ~-*lift*, = ~*horn*; ~'*maker*, maker of boots & ~s; ~-*string*, *(also, colloq.) a small or inadequate amount of money, (attrib.) precarious, just adequate, as a ~-*string majority*. Hence ~'LESS (-ōō-) a. [OE (OS) *scōh*, OHG *scuoh*, ON *skór*, Goth. *skohs* f. Gmc *skōh(w)az*]

shoe² (-ōō), v.t. (*shŏd*; part. ~*ing*). Fit with shoe(s) (esp. with *horse* etc. as obj., or in p.p. as *neatly shod* (feet), *pole shod with iron*). [OE *scōgan*, f. prec.]

shōg′un (-ōōn), n. (hist.). Japanese hereditary commander-in-chief & virtual ruler for some centuries until the office was abolished 1868. Hence ~ATE¹ n. [Jap., = general]

shone. See SHINE¹.

shōō, int., & v.i. & t. (Utter) sound used to frighten birds away; drive *away* thus. [imit.]

shook¹. See SHAKE¹.

shook², n., & v.t. **1.** Set of staves & headings for cask ready for putting together. **2.** v.t. Pack in ~s. [prob. p.p. of *shake*; *shaken cask* is used in same sense]

shoot¹, v.i. & t. & n. (*shŏt*). **1.** Come vigorously or swiftly *out*, *forth*, *along*, *up*, etc., or

abs., sprout, dart. (*boat shot out from the creek*; ~*ing* STAR¹; *flash* ~s *across sky*; ~ *ahead*, come quickly to front of competitors etc.; *buds are* ~*ing*; *tree* ~s, puts forth buds; *fountain*, *flame*, ~s *up*; *prices shot up*, rose suddenly; *cricket-ball* ~s, darts along ground when it touches, instead of bouncing; *child is* ~*ing up*, growing tall; *pain* ~s *through nerves* etc.; *corn*, *tooth*, ~s, inflicts intermittent pain). **2.** Project abruptly *out* (*mountain-spur*, *cape*, ~s *out*). **3.** Send out, discharge, propel, emit, violently or swiftly (~ *rubbish* etc., let it slide from cart or receptacle; *bow*, *gun*, ~s *arrow*, *shell*; *passengers were shot out of coach*; *sun* ~s *its rays*; ~ *out* one's *lips*, bibl., protrude in scorn; ~ one's *linen*, display wristbands by shaking them down; ~ *the cat*, sl., vomit; ~ *fishing-net*, extend it across river etc.; ~ *bolt* of door, send it home; *tree* ~s *out branches*; *~ !* (sl.), say what you have to say. **4.** Discharge (bullet etc.) from gun etc., cause (bow, gun, etc.) to discharge missile, discharge gun etc., make use well etc. of gun etc., kill or wound (person, animal) with missile from gun etc., hunt game etc. habitually or on one occasion with gun, ~ *the game over* estate etc., ~ *game on* (estate etc.), (of gun etc.) go off; *send missile straight* etc., (*fool's* BOLT¹ *is soon shot*; *I'll be shot if* —, form of negative asseveration; *can army or sportsman does gun*, ~ *straight?*; *was shot for a spy*; ~ *a match*, engage in ~*ing-match*; *will* ~ *the coverts tomorrow*; *neither rides nor* ~s; *was out* ~*ing*; *have shot away all our ammunition*). **5.** (cinemat.). Photograph. **6.** (assoc. footb., hockey, etc.). Take a shot at goal. **7.** ~ *up*, terrorize (village, district) with punitive rifle-shooting, firing of houses, etc.; ~ *a line* (sl.), tell a tall story; ~ *the sun*, take its altitude with the sextant at noon; ‖ ~ *the moon* (sl.), remove one's goods by night to avoid paying rent. **8.** Be, have one's boat, swept swiftly under or down (bridge, rapid fall; ~ *Niagara*, attempt desperate enterprise). **9.** (joinery). Plane (edge of board) accurately (hence *shot edges*). **10.** p.p. (Of coloured material) so woven etc. as to show different colours at different angles (*shot silk*; *crimson shot with maize-colour*). **11.** ‖ ~*ing-box*, sportsman's lodge for use in ~*ing-season*; ~*ing-brake*, ESTATE car; ~*ing-coat*, -*jacket*, -*boots*, of patterns useful in ~*ing game*; ~*ing-iron* (sl.), fire-arm; ~*ing-range*, ground with butts for rifle practice; ~*ing-stick*, walking-stick which may be adapted to form a seat; ~*ing war*, one in which there is ~*ing* (opp. *cold war* or WAR¹ *of nerves*). Hence ~'ABLE a. [OE *scēotan*, OS *skietan*, OHG *sciozzan*, ON *skjóta* f. Gmc *skeut-*, *skaut-*, *skut-*, cf. SHEET¹, SHOT¹, SHUT]

shŏōt², n. Young branch or sucker; rapid in stream; inclined plane down which water etc. may flow or things slide, chute;

shooting party or expedition or practice or (= SHOOTING) land. [f. prec.]

shoot′er, n. In vbl senses; esp.: ball that shoots at cricket; (in comb.) shooting-implement (PEA-~; *six* etc. ~, revolver firing six etc. shots). [ME; -ER[1]]

shoot′ing, n. In vbl senses (for compounds see SHOOT[1]); esp.: right of ~ over particular land; estate etc. rented to shoot over. [-ING[1]]

shŏp, n., & *v.i.* & *t.* (-pp-). **1.** Building, room, etc., for retail sale of some commodity (*chemist's, butcher's, fruit-, ~; come to the wrong ~,* transf., apply to wrong person etc.), or in which manufacture or repairing is done (*engineering-~; fitting, pattern,* etc., ~, departments of manufactory). **2.** ‖ (sl.). Institution, establishment, etc., (e.g. one's school, university, etc.; esp. formerly of R.M.A., Woolwich; *the other* ~, rival institution). **3.** One's profession, trade, or business, things connected with it, or talk about it, (CLOSE[3]*d* ~; *shut up* ~, cease doing something; *talk* ~; *sink the* ~, refrain from talking ~, also conceal one's occupation; SMELL *of the* ~), whence ~p′Y[2] a. **4.** *All over the* ~ (sl.), in disorder, in every direction, wildly, (*have looked for it all over the* ~; *my books are all over the* ~; *hitting, steering,* etc., *all over the* ~). **5.** ~-*bell,* on door to give notice of customer's entrance; ~-*boy, -girl,* assistants in ~; ~′*keeper,* owner of ~ (*nation of* ~-*keepers,* the English); ~-*lifter,* pretended customer who steals goods in ~; ~′*man* ~keeper or his assistant; ~-*soiled,* = ~-*worn;* ‖ ~-*steward,* person .elected by his fellow workmen in a factory or branch of it as their spokesman on conditions of work etc.; ‖ ~′*walker,* attendant in large ~ who directs customers; ~ *window,* window of ~ used for display of wares (*has everything in the* ~ *window,* transf., is superficial); ~-*worn,* soiled or faded by being shown in ~. **6.** vb. Go to ~(s) to make purchases (*or inspect goods), whence ~p′ING[1] n.; (sl.) imprison, (of informer) cause (accomplice) to be imprisoned. [ME, f. OE *sceoppa* (cf. OHG *scopf*) f. Gmc *skuppan-,* cf. SHIPPEN]

shōre[1], n. Land that skirts sea or large body of water (*in* ~, on the water near or nearer to ~); (law) land between ordinary high & low water marks. Hence ~′LESS (-ōr̃l-) a., ~′WARD (-ōr̃w-) a. & adv. [ME *schore* f. MDu., MLG *schore,* prob. f. root of SHEAR[1]]

shōre[2], n., & *v.t.* **1.** Prop, beam set obliquely against ship, wall, tree, etc., as support. **2.** *v.t.* Support, hold *up,* with ~(s). Hence shŏr̃′ING[1](3) n. [ME *schore,* f. MDu., MLG *schōre,* prop, of unkn. orig.; cf. syn. ON *skortha*]

shōre[3], shorn. See SHEAR[1].

shŏrt, a., adv., *n.,* & *v.t.* **1.** Measuring little from end to end in space or time, soon traversed or finished, (*a* ~ *way off;*

a ~ *time ago;* ~ *story,* of the character of a novel but less length; ~ CUT[1]; ~ *circuit,* electric circuit made through a small resistance, esp. one acting as a shunt to one of greater resistance, form of this due to a fault that allows current's escape to earth; ~-*circuit* v.t., establish ~ circuit in, cut off current from thus; ~ DIVISION; ~ *drink,* cocktail etc. esp. before a meal; ~*er* CATECHISM; ~ *rib,* = *false* RIB; ~ SHRIFT; ~ WHIST[2]; *a* ~ *sea,* ~ broken waves; *make* ~ *work of,* dispose of or destroy or consume quickly; *he, his joy* etc., *had but a* ~ *life,* whence ~-liveD[2] a.; ~ *temper,* self-control that is soon or easily lost, whence ~-temperED[2] a.; ~ *waist* in dress, made high up, whence ~-waistED[2] a.; ~ *wind,* easily exhausted breathing-power, inability to run long or fig. to talk or write at any length, whence ~-windED[2] a., ~-wind′edNESS n.; ~ *clothes* or *coats,* dress of child too old for long-clothes, whence ~-′coat v.t.). **2.** Of small stature, not tall, (usu. of human beings, or of upright things, as chimney, tower, tree). **3.** Not far-reaching, acting near at hand, deficient, scanty, in want *of,* below the degree *of,* abruptly finished, (~ *sight,* not seeing clearly at distance or fig. into .the future, whence ~-sightED[2] a., ~-sight′edLY[2] adv., ~-sight′edNESS n.; *at* ~ *range; take* ~ *views,* consider the present only; ~ *date,* early date for maturing of bill etc., whence ~-datED[2] a.; ~ *bill, paper,* etc., dated for early payment; ~ LEG, SLIP, in cricket; *has a* ~ *memory; are* ~ *of hands,* have not enough workmen, whence ~-handED[2] a.; ~ *of breath,* panting, ~-winded; ~ COMMONS; *in* ~ *supply,* scarce; ~ *weight,* less than it is represented to be; *a* ~ *ten miles, mile, hour,* etc., less or seeming less than that; *cut* ~, bring to end before natural time; *come* ~, disappoint expectations etc., fail *of* one's duty or proper development, whence ~-′comING[1] n.; *fall* ~, be insufficient or inadequate; *run* ~, have or be too little, as *our tea ran* ~, *we ran* ~ *of tea; an escape nothing* ~ *of marvellous*). **4.** Concise, brief, curt, sullenly or snappishly reticent, (*the* LONG[1] & *the* ~ *of it; in* ~, to use few words, without circumlocution, to give the conclusion briefly; *is called Bob for* ~, by way of ~ name; *was very* ~ *with me,* uncivil). **5.** (phonet., pros.). (Of vowel or syllable) (prop.) having the less of the two recognized durations, (pop.) unstressed, (also, of vowel) having the or an other sound, than that called LONG[1] (e.g. those in *met, pill, but*). **6.** (Of pastry, clay, etc.) friable, crumbling, not tenacious, (cf. COLD-SHORT). **7.** (St. Exch. etc.) of stocks, stockbroker, crops, etc., sold, selling, etc., when the amount is not in hand in reliance on getting the deficit in time for delivery. **8.** *Something* ~, a drink of spirits etc.; ~′*bread,* ~′*cake,* brittle dry cake made with flour & much butter & sugar; ~'*fall*, deficit; ~'*hand*, methods of compendious writing used for taking verbatim reports of speeches etc., stenography; ~ *head* (racing), distance of less than length of horse's head (also ~-*head* v.t., beat by this distance); ~'*horn*, name of ~-horned breed of cattle; ~ *metre*, hymn stanza of 4 lines (6, 6, 8, 6 syllables); ~ *suit* (of less than four cards); ~ *time*, condition of working less than the regular number of hours per day or days per week; ~ TON¹; ~ *wave* (radio), having a wave--length of from 10 to 100 metres; hence ~'ISH¹(2) a., ~'NESS n. 9. adv. Abruptly, before the natural or expected time, in ~ manner, (*look him up* ~, interrupted him; *stop* ~, suddenly cease, not go on to the end; *bring*, or *pull*, *up* ~, check or pause abruptly; *be taken* ~, have sudden motion of bowels; ~-*spoken*, given to brevity of speech; *sell* ~, when one has not the articles in hand, see the adj.); ~ *of*, except, putting out of the question, (*all aid* ~ *of war*; ~ *of committing suicide he does his best to keep out of the way*). 10. n. ~ syllable (LONG¹s & ~s) or vowel; mark indicating that vowel is ~, as ǎ; ~ film; (colloq.) a ~ circuit; (colloq.) a ~ drink esp. of spirits; (pl.) garment like trousers cut ~ worn by athletes, boys, etc. 11. v.t. (colloq.). To ~-circuit. [OE *sc(e)ort*, OHG *scurz*, f. Gmc *skurtaz, perh. alt. f. L *curtus* (whence OS, OHG *kurt*, OHG(G) *kurz*); cf. SHIRT, SKIRT]

short'age, n. (Amount of) deficiency (*there is no* ~, *a* ~ *of 100 tons*). [-AGE]

short'en, v.i. & t. Become or make actually or apparently shorter or short, curtail; reduce the amount of *sail* spread; put (child) into short clothes. Hence ~ING¹(3) n., fat used for making pastry crisp. [-EN²]

short'ly, adv. Before long, a short time *before* or *after*; in few words, briefly; curtly. [ME; -LY²]

shot¹, n. (pl. ~s, also ~ see below), & v.t. (-tt-). 1. Single missile for fire-arm or big gun, non-explosive projectile, (usu. with qualification or in comb., as *round*, *solid*, CHAIN, GRAPE-, CASE²-, BUCK¹-, ~; *chilled* ~, case-hardened for armour-piercing; *a* ~ *in the* LOCKER); (pl. usu. ~) small lead pellets of which a quantity is used for single charge or cartridge esp. in sporting guns, such pellets collectively, (~ *does* or *do well for cleaning decanters*; *put three* ~ or ~*s of different sizes on the gut*; ~ *is made in various ways*; *about a dozen nº 10* ~ *were extracted from his leg*). 2. Discharge of fire-arm or big gun (*several* ~*s were fired*, *heard*, etc.); attempt to hit with projectile or missile or fig. to make stroke in game or guess or do something (*at each* ~ *he was nearer the bull's-eye*; *a beautiful* ~ *from cover-point took off the bails*; *a lucky* ~ *at goal*; *like a* ~, willingly; *made a bad* ~, guessed wrong; *am going to have a good* ~ *at winning*; *snap* ~, discharging of rifle etc. with momentary aim, cf. SNAP*shot*; *flying* ~, at bird on wing or moving object; PARTHIAN, *random*, ~; (·)~, range, reach, distance to or at which thing will carry or act, as *bow*, *rifle*, *ear* ~~). 3. Possessor of specified skill with rifle, gun, pistol, etc. (*is a good*, *bad*, *crack* or *first-class*, or *no*,~). 4. Dose of cocaine, injection of morphine, etc.; (colloq.) dram of spirits. 5. Photograph taken with cinematograph camera. 6. ~-*firer*, one who fires the ~ in blasting; ~-*gun*, smooth-bore gun, for firing small ~ at short range; ~-*tower*, in which ~ was made from molten lead poured through sieves at top & falling into water at bottom; hence ~'PROOF² a. 7. v.t. Load, weight, etc.; with ~. [OE *sc(e)ot*, *gesc(e)ot*, OHG *scoz*, ON *skot* f. Gmc *skut- SHOOT¹]

shot², p.p. of SHOOT¹.

shot³, n. Reckoning, (one's share of) bill at inn etc., (usu. *pay* one's ~). [ME, = SHOT¹ (cf. OE *scēotan* SHOOT, pay, contribute); cf. SCOT¹]

should. See SHALL.

shoul'der (shōl-), n., & v.t. & i. 1. Part of body at which arm or foreleg or wing is attached, either lateral projection below or behind neck, (also ~-*joint*) combination of end of upper arm with those of collarbone & blade-bone, (pl.) upper part of back, (pl.) body regarded as bearing burdens, (of slaughtered animal) foreleg with parts usu. kept with it in dismembering, (HEAD¹ & ~s; *dislocate* one's ~; ~ *to* ~, with closed ranks or united effort; *has broad* ~s, is strong, can bear much weight or responsibility; *old head on young* ~s, youthful wisdom, wise young person; *put*, *set*, ~ *to wheel*, make effort; *straight from the* ~, said of well-delivered blow or telling invective; ~-*of-mutton sail*, triangular fore-&-aft sail hoisted abaft mast; COLD¹ ~; COLD¹~ v.t.; *lay the blame*, *burden*, etc., *on the right* ~s). 2. Part of mountain, bottle, tool, etc., projecting like human ~. 3. (mil.) Position of soldier who has ~ed arms (see vb). 4. ~-*belt*, baldric, bandolier, or other band passing over one~ & under opposite arm; ~-*blade*, either large flat bone of upper back, scapula; ~-*brace*, contrivance for flattening round back of child etc.; ~-*knot*, of ribbon or metal lace worn on ~ by livery servant; ~-*pegged*, (of horse) stiff in ~s; ~-*strap*, band from ~--tip in soldier's uniform, keeping ~-belts in place & bearing name or number of regiment etc., (also) one of two strips of cloth suspending a garment from the wearer's ~s; hence (·)~ED²(-erd) a. 5. vb. Push (t. & i.) with ~, jostle, make way thus; take (burden lit. or fig.) on one's ~s; (mil.) ~ *arms*, hold rifle vertical supported by right hand at lock (cf. SLOPE v.). [OE *sculdor*, OFris. *skuldere*, OHG *sculter(r)a*; orig. unkn.]

shout, v.i. & t., & n. **1.** Make loud articulate or inarticulate cry or vocal sound, speak loudly,·(~*ed with laughter*; ~ *for joy*; ~ *at*, speak loudly to etc.; *all is over but the ~ing*, contest is virtually decided); say loudly, call out, express in loud tones, (~ *approbation*; ~*ed that the coast was clear*; ~*ed to* or *for me to come*; '*Go back* ' *he ~ed*). **2.** n. Loud utterance or vocal sound from individual or company expressing joy, (dis)approval, defiance, etc., or calling attention (*my etc.* ~, sl., turn to order drink etc. for the company). [ME, formally corresp. to ON *skúta* SCOUT²; prob. f. root of SHOOT¹]

shove (·ŭv), v.t. & i., & n. **1.** Push (t. & i.) vigorously, move (t.) along by hard or rough pushing; make one's way *along, past, through*, etc., by pushing, jostle (person); ~*-halfpenny*, modern gambling form of shovelboard; (colloq.) put somewhere (~ *it in the drawer*); ~ *off*, start from shore in boat. **2.** n. Push (*give one a ~ off*, help him to start); woody centre of flax-stem. [OE *scúfan*, MDu. *scūven*, OHG *scioban*, ON *skúfa*, Goth. *·skiuban* f. Gmc *skeubh-*, *skaubh-*, *skŭb-*]

sho'vel (·ŭv-), n., & v.t. (-ll-). **1.** Scooping implement for shifting coal, earth, etc., often in form of spade with sides of blade turned up; ~ *hat*, broad-brimmed as worn by Anglican dignitaries; ~*-head*, kinds of sturgeon & shark, also ~*-nose*; hence ~FUL(2) (shŭv'elfŏŏl) n. (pl. ~*fuls*). **2.** v.t. Shift (coal etc.) with or as with ~ (~ *food into* one's *mouth*, eat greedily). [OE *scofl*, MLG *schuffel*, cogn. w. OS, OHG *skūfla* (G *schaufel*), f. Gmc *skŭbh-* (prec.)]

shovelboard (shŭv'elbōrd), n. Game played (now esp. on ship's deck) by impelling discs (formerly coins) with hand or mace over marked surface. [earlier *shoveboard, -groat* (SHOVE)]

sho'veller (·ŭv-), n. In vbl senses; also, kind of duck with broad shovel-like beak. [-ER¹]

show¹ (·ō), v.t. & i. (p.p. ~*n*, rarely ~*ed*; also spelt, now rarely, *shew, shewn, shewed,* w. pron. shō etc.). **1.** Let be seen, disclose, manifest, offer (thing, person thing, thing *to* person) for inspection, exhibit, produce, give (treatment, person treatment, treatment *to* person), reveal, (*clothes ~ signs of wear*; *an aperture ~s the inside*; ~*ed neither joy nor anger, that he was annoyed, how much he felt it*, etc.; ~ *oneself*, be seen in public; ~ *me, I was ~n*, a specimen; *has nothing to ~ for it*, no token of achievement etc.; ~ *your tickets, please*; *got prizes for all the dogs he ~ed*; ~ CAUSE¹; ~ *favour, mercy, to*; ~*ed me kindness* or *unkindness*; ~ *fight*, not yield tamely; ~ one's COLOUR¹s; ~ one's *hand* orig. in cards, let out one's designs; ~ *the hoof* or *cloven hoof*, see CLEAVE¹; ~ *the white* FEATHER¹; ~ *a* CLEAN¹ *pair of heels*; ~ *a leg*, get out of bed; ~ *thing the fire*, slightly heat it). **2.** Be visible or noticeable, come into sight, appear in public, have some appearance, (*the blood ~s through her skin*; *stain will never ~*; *buds are just ~ing*; *her husband never ~s (up) at her at-homes*, colloq.; ~*s white, like a disc, from here*). **3.** Demonstrate, prove, expound, point out, cause (person) to understand (thing), (*has ~n the falsity of the tale, that it is false, how false it is, it to be false*; ~ one *the way*, by words, pointing, or going with or before him, also encourage by doing thing first; ~ *person how to write, what to do*, etc.; ~ *person the* DOOR; *it only ~s how little you know*; *on your own ~ing*, even according to your own admission or contention). **4.** Conduct (~*ed us round the house*; ~ one *out* or *in*, esp. open door for his exit or entrance). **5.** ~*-down*, (poker) laying down of cards with faces up, (fig.) final test, disclosure of achievements or possibilities; ~ *forth* (arch.), exhibit, expound; ~ *off*, (trans.) display to advantage, (intr.) try to make impression by exhibiting one's wealth or skill; ~ *up*, make or be conspicuous or clearly visible, expose (fraud, impostor), (colloq.) appear, be present; *shew'bread*, twelve loaves displayed in Jewish temple & renewed each sabbath; ~*-case*, glazed case for exhibiting goods, curiosities, etc.; ~*-room, -window*, in which wares are kept, hung up, for inspection; ~*-place*, that tourists etc. go to see. [OE *scēawian*, OS *skawon*, OHG *scouwōn* f. WG *skauwōjan* f. Gmc *skau-*, see SHEEN]

show² (·ō), n. **1.** Showing (*voted by ~ of hands*; DUMB¹ ~). **2.** Spectacle, exhibition, pageant, display, collection of things shown esp. for money to entertain, (*flower, horse*, etc., *-~*; || Lord *Mayor's ~*, procession of symbolic cars etc. in London; *a fine ~ of blossom*); (colloq.) any kind of public entertainment. **3.** Outward appearance, semblance, impression produced, parade, ostentation, pomp, display, (*pierce beneath the ~s of things*; *there is a ~ of reason in it*; *good enough in outward ~*; *did it for ~*; *is fond of ~*), whence ~'Y² (·ōī) a., ~'ILY² adv., ~'INESS n. **4.** (sl.). Concern, undertaking, organization, (RUN¹ or BOSS³ *the ~*; *give away the ~*, betray its inadequacy or pretentiousness; *good ~ !*, well done!). **5.** (sl.). Opportunity of acting, defending oneself, etc. (*had no ~ at all*; *give him a fair ~*). **6.** (obstetr.) Discharge indicating approach of labour. **7.** ~'*boat* (orig. U.S.), (river) steamboat in which theatrical performances are given; ~'*girl*, actress whose role is decorative rather than histrionic; ~'*man*, proprietor or manager of menagerie or other such ~; ~'*manship*, the art of the ~man, (fig.) capacity for exhibiting one's wares or oneself to the best advantage. [ME, f. prec.]

show'er, n., & v.t. & i. **1.** Brief fall of rain, hail, sleet, or snow, or *of* arrows, bullets, dust, stones, etc. (also fig., as a ~ *of gifts, honours; letters come in* ~s); ~-*bath* (colloq. ~), in which water descends from above through perforated plate; hence ~Y² a., ~iNESS n. **2.** vb. Discharge (water, missiles, etc.) in a ~, bestow (gifts etc. usu. *upon*); descend or come in a ~. [OE (= OS, OHG, ON) *scūr*, Goth. *skūra* f. Gmc *skūr-*, of unkn. orig.]

‖ **shråm**, v.t. (dial.; -mm-; usu. in p.p.), Benumb with or *with* cold. [cf. 15th c. (now dial.) *scram*, dial. *shrim* (OE *scrim̄man*) shrivel]

shrank. See SHRINK.

shrăp′nel, n. Bullets or pieces of metal contained in shell timed to burst slightly short of objective & let them fly on in shower; part of fragmentation bomb etc. so scored as to break & scatter. [f. inventor H. *S*~ (d. 1842)]

shrĕd, n., & v.t. (~*ded*, arch. ~). **1.** Scrap, fragment, rag, strip, torn or broken piece, small remains, least amount, (*tore it to* ~s; *without a* ~ *of clothing on him; not a* ~ *of evidence, reputation,* etc.; *tear* an argument etc. *to* ~s, completely refute it). **2.** v.t. Tear or cut into ~. [OE *scrēade* (= OHG *scrōt*) piece cut off, *scrēadian* (= OHG *scrōtan*) f. Gmc *skraudh-*, (*skreudh-, *skrūdh-): see SHROUD, SCREED]

shrew (-ōō), n. **1.** Scolding woman, whence ~′ISH¹ (-ōō-) a., ~′ISHLY² adv., ~′ISHNESS n. **2.** (Also ~-*mouse*) small long-snouted mammal, like mouse, feeding chiefly on insects. [OE *scrēawa* ~-mouse, not found elsewhere in Gmc]

shrewd (-ōōd), a. (Of pain, cold, etc.) sharp, biting, (literary, esp. ~ *blow, knock, thrust, turn*); sagacious, sensible, discriminating, astute, judicious, (*can make a* ~ *guess; a* ~ *observer; a* ~ *face* etc., sagacious-looking). Hence ~′LY² adv., ~′NESS n. [ME *shrewed* (prec., -ED², cf. *dogged, crabbed*)]

shriek, v.i. & t., & n. (Utter) shrill & usu. inarticulate cry of terror, pain, etc., screech, scream; laugh uncontrollably (usu. ~ *with laughter*); ~ *out*, say in shrill agonized tones. [16th c. parallel to *screak* (f. ON *skrækja*, imit.); cf. ME (now dial.) *shrike, scrike, scritch,* SCREECH]

shriev′altý, n. Sheriff's office or jurisdiction, tenure of this. [f. *shrieve*, obs. var. of SHERIFF, + -*alty* as in *admiralty* etc.]

shrift, n. (Arch.) confession to priest, confession & absolution, (now only in *short* ~, little time between condemnation & execution or punishment). [OE *scrift*, vbl n. f. SHRIVE; so OHG *scrift*, ON *skript*]

shrike, n. Kinds of bird called also *butcher-bird* with strong hooked & toothed bill & habit of impaling its prey of small birds & insects on thorns. [app. repr. OE *scrīc, scrēc* (imit., cf. SHRIEK) thrush or perh. any shrill-voiced bird]

shrill, a., & v.i. & t. **1.** Piercing & high-pitched in sound; (fig.) importunate; hence shril′LY² (-l-lli) adv., ~′NESS n. **2.** vb. (poet. or rhet.). (Of cry etc.) sound ~y; (of person etc.) utter, send *out*, (song, complaint, etc.) ~y. [ME, rel. to LG *schrell* of sharp tone or taste]

shrimp, n., & v.i. **1.** Small aquatic (esp. marine) edible crustacean, grey-green when alive, pink when boiled; diminutive person. **2.** v.i. Go catching ~s; hence ~′ER¹ n. [ME, prob. cogn. w. MHG (MG) *schrimpen* shrink up; cf. SHRAM]

shrine, n., & v.t. **1.** Casket, esp. one holding sacred relics; tomb usu. sculptured or highly ornamented of saint etc.; altar or chapel of special associations; place hallowed by some memory. **2.** v.t. (poet.). Enshrine. [OE *scrīn,* OHG *scrini,* ON *skrin,* f. L *scrinium* case for books etc.]

shrink, v.i. & t. (*shrănk; shrŭnk* & rarely in vbl, commonly in adj., use *shrŭnken*), & n. **1.** Become of less dimensions, grow smaller, whence ~′AGE(3) n.; recoil, retire from observation, (~ *into one*self, become reserved), flinch *from*, whence ~′ingLY² adv.; be averse *from doing*; make smaller (esp. in pass.; *his face has a shrunken look*), make ~ (flannel etc., in order that it may not do so later; ~ *wheel-tire* etc. *on*, slip it on while expanded with heat & let it tighten as it cools), whence ~′ABLE a. **2.** n. (rare). ~ing (*how much must we allow for the* ~?). [OE *scrincan,* cf. Sw. *skrynka* to wrinkle]

shrive, v.t. (arch.; *shrōve, shrĭven*). Hear confession of, assign penance to, & absolve; (of penitent) submit one*self* to priest for this purpose. [OE *scrīfan,* OS *skrīban,* OHG *scrīban,* ON *skrifa* f. L *scribere* write]

shriv′el, v.i. & t., & t. (-ll-). Contract or wither (i. & t.) into wrinkled, folded, rolled-up, contorted, or dried-up state. [16th c., perh. of Scand. orig.; cf. Sw. dial. *skryfla* to wrinkle]

shrŏff, n., & v.t. **1.** Banker or money-changer in the East; (Far East) native expert employed to detect base coin. **2.** v.t. Examine (coin). [Anglo-Ind. corrupt. of Pers. *saraf*]

shroud, n., & v.t. **1.** Winding-sheet, garment for the dead, whence ~′LESS a.; concealing agency (*wrapped in a* ~ *of mystery*); (pl.) set of ropes forming part of standing rigging & supporting mast or topmast. **2.** v.t. Clothe (corpse) for burial; cover & conceal or disguise. [OE *scrūd,* ON *skrūth* f. Gmc *skrūdh-* see SHRED]

Shrŏve Tues′day (tūz′dĭ), n. Day before Ash Wednesday, on which & the preceding days or *Shrovetide* it was customary to be shriven. [rel. to SHRIVE]

shrŭb¹, n. Woody plant of less size than tree & usu. divided into separate stems from near the ground. Hence ~b′Y² a., ~b′ERY(3) n. [ME, app. repr. OE *scrubb,*

scrybb; cf. NFris. skrobb, WFlem.
schrobbe, Norw. skrubba; cf. SCRUB[1])

shrŭb[2], n. Cordial made of fruit-juice &
spirit (usu. rum-~). [f. Arab. sharāb;
cogn. w. SHERBET, SYRUP]

shrŭg, v.t. & i. (-gg-), & n. 1. Slightly
& momentarily raise (shoulders), raise
shoulders, to express indifference, helplessness, contempt, vexation, etc. 2. n.
This motion (of the shoulders, or abs.). [c.
1400, of unkn. orig.]

shrunk(en). See SHRINK.

shŭck, n., & v.t. 1. Husk, pod; *~s!, int.
of disgust or regret. 2. v.t. Remove ~s
of, shell. [17th c., of unkn. orig.]

shŭdd'er, v.i., & n. (Experience) sudden
shivering due to fear, horror, repugnance,
or cold; feel strong repugnance etc. (I ~
to think what might happen). Hence ~ing-
LY[2] adv. [ME shod(d)re, rel. to MDu.
schŭderen, MLG schŏderen f. skŭdh- shake,
+ -ER[5]]

shŭf'fle, v.i. & t., & n. 1. Move (t. & i.)
with scraping or sliding or dragging or
difficult motion (~s along rheumatically;
~s his or with his feet; ~ cards, slide
them over one another so as to change
their relative positions; so ~ things of
any sort, intermingle, confuse; ~ the
cards, fig., change the parts, try new
policy, etc.); slip (clothes, burden) off or
on (~ off responsibility upon others;
~d on his clothes); keep shifting one's
position lit. or fig., fidget, vacillate, prevaricate, whence shŭff'lER[1] n.; ~-board,
= SHOVELBOARD; hence shŭff'lingLY[2] adv.
2. n. Shuffling movement; shuffling of
cards, general change of relative positions; piece of equivocation or sharp
practice; quick scraping movement of
feet in dancing (double ~, executed twice
with one & then the other foot). [f. or
cogn. w. LG schŭffeln, f. Gmc root *skuf-
(*skubh-) SHOVE]

shŭn, v.t. (-nn-). Avoid, keep clear of,
eschew. Hence ~'LESS a. (poet.). [OE
scunian, not found in other Gmc langg.]

'shŭn!, abbr. of attention! as word of
command.

shŭnt, v.t. & i., & n. 1. Divert (train,
electric current, etc.), || (of train etc.) di-
verge, on to a side track, esp. to clear
line for more important traffic, whence
~'ER[1] n.; postpone or stifle discussion
of (subject), lay aside (project), leave
(person) inactive. 2. n. Turning or being
turned on to side track; (electr.) conductor joining two points of circuit, over
which more or less of current may be
diverted. [ME, perh. f. SHUN]

shŭt, v.t. & i. (shut). 1. Move (door, sash,
lid, lips, etc.) into position to stop an
aperture (~ the door upon, refuse to consider, make impossible). 2. ~ door etc. of
(room, window, box, eye, mouth, etc.; ~
your eyes; ~ one's eyes or by extension
ears to, pretend not or refuse to see or
hear). 3. Become or admit of being closed,

swing or fall or contract into closed
position, (the door ~ with a bang; lid ~s
automatically; pimpernels ~ in rainy
weather). 4. Keep (person, sound, etc.)
out or in by ~ting door etc., send (person)
into or out of room etc. & fasten door etc.
against him, bar (person) out from hope
etc. 5. Be ~ of person (sl.), be rid of.
6. Catch or pinch (finger, dress, etc.) by
~ting something on it (~ his finger into
the door-hinge). 7. Bring parts of together
(~ his teeth, a knife, etc.). 8. ~ down,
push or pull (window-sash etc.) down into
closed position, (of factory etc.) cease
working; ~ in, (of hills, houses, sea, etc.)
encircle, prevent free prospect or egress
from or access to; ~ off, stop flow of
(water, gas, etc.) by ~ting valve, separate
from society etc.; ~ out, exclude (landscape etc.) from view, prevent (possibility
etc.); ~-out bid (bridge), pre-emptive
bid; ~ to adv., close (door etc., or intr. of
door etc.) tight; ~ up, close all doors &
windows of or bolt & bar (house; ~ up
shop, cease business for the day or permanently), close (box etc.) securely or deci-
sively or permanently, imprison (person),
put (thing) away in box etc., desist
(colloq.; esp. ~ up imperat.), reduce to
silence by rebuke or refutation. [OE
scyttan f. *skuttjan f. Gmc *skut- SHOOT[1];
cf. MDu., MLG schutten]

shŭtt'er, n., & v.t. In vbl senses of prec.;
esp.: one of a set of wooden panels or
iron plates, hinged, sliding, folding, or
detachable, placed inside or outside glass
of window to keep out light or burglars
(put up the ~s, cease business for the day
or permanently); structure of jointed
laths or metal slats on rollers serving
same purposes; blind of swell-box in
organ for regulating loudness; piece that
opens & closes lens of photographic
camera; hence ~LESS a.; (v.t.) provide
with ~s, put up ~s of. [-ER[1]]

shŭt'tle, n. Weaving-implement shaped
like cigar with two pointed ends by which
weft-thread is carried or shot across between threads of warp; carrier of lower
thread in lock-stitch sewing-machine;
~ armature (electr.), armature with a
single coil wound on an elongated iron
bobbin; ~cock, cork stuck with feathers
& struck to & fro in BATTLEDORE & ~
[-cock prob. f. flying motion]; ~ train
(running a short distance to and fro, usu.
on branch-line), so ~ service. [OE scytel
f. Gmc *skut- SHOOT[1] + -LE(1)]

shȳ[1], a. (~er, ~est, rarely shi-). (Of
beasts, birds, fish, etc.) easily startled,
timid, avoiding observation; bashful,
coy, uneasy in company; avoiding company of person, chary of doing, (FIGHT[1]~
of); elusive, hard to find, catch, interpret,
etc.; (sl.) short (of), in the position of
having lost (I'm ~ three quid); -shy, (in
combb.) indicating fear of or distaste for
(first element of comb.), as in GUN-~,

WORK¹·~. Hence ~'LY² adv., ~'NESS n.
[OE *scēoh*, = MHG *schiech*, f. Gmc
**skeuhw-* fear, terrify]

shy², v.i., & n. Start suddenly aside (*at*
object or noise, or fig. *at* proposal etc.) in
alarm (usu. of horse, or fig. of person).
Hence ~'ER¹ n. [f. prec.]

shy³, v.t. & i., & n. (colloq.). 1. Fling,
throw, (stone etc., or abs.). 2. n. Act of
~ing (*have a ~ at*, try to hit with missile,
jeer at, make an attempt to get). [18th
c., of unkn. orig.]

Shỹl'ŏck, n. Hard-hearted money-lender.
[character in *Merchant of Venice*]

*shỹs'ter, n. (sl.). Person without pro-
fessional honour, esp. tricky lawyer.
[orig. unkn.]

si (sē), n. (mus.). Seventh note of octave.
[added perh. *c.* 1600 to names of hexachord; see GAMUT; perh. f. initials of
Sancte Johannes in sapphics given under
gamut]

sī'amăng (*or* sē-), n. Kind of gibbon from
Sumatra & Malay peninsula. [Malay]

Siamēse' (-z), a. & n. (pl. same). (Native,
language) of Siam (Thailand); ~ *twins*,
two ~ (d. 1874) joined by cartilaginous
band from one's right to other's left side,
any similar monstrosity, (fig.) inseparable
friends etc.; ~ *cat*, cream-coloured short-
-haired breed with brown or blue points.
[-ESE]

sib, a. (chiefly Sc.), & n. (genetics; usu. pl.).
1. Related, akin, (*to*). 2. n. A brother or
sister (disregarding sex). Hence ~'LING
n., one of two or more children having one
or both parents in common (usu. pl.),
~'SHIP n., the group of children (disregarding sex) from the same two parents.
[OE *sib*(*b*), MDu. *sib*(*be*), OHG *sippi*,
Goth. *-sibjis*]

Sibēr'ian, a. & n. (Inhabitant) of Siberia
(~ *dog*, of breed much used for sledging).
[-AN]

sib'il|ant, a. & n. 1. Hissing, sounded
with a hiss (esp. of letter or set of letters,
as s, sh); hence ~ANCE, ~ANCY, nn. 2. n.
~ant letter(s). [f. L *sibilare* hiss, -ANT]

sib'il|āte, v.t. & i. Pronounce with hissing
sound. Hence ~A'TION n. [as prec., -ATE³]

sib'ỹl, n. One of the women who in
ancient times acted at various places
(*Cumaean, Erythraean*, etc., ~) as mouthpiece of some god, & to whom many
collections of oracles & prophecies were
attributed, pagan prophetess; old fortune-teller, sorceress, or hag. [ME, f. OF
Sibile or med. L *Sibilla* f. L f. Gk *Sibulla*]

sib'ỹllīne, a. Issuing from an ancient
sibyl, oracular, mysteriously prophetic;
the ~ *books*, collection of oracles belonging
to ancient-Roman State & often consulted by magistrates for guidance, (fig.,
with ref. to story of their acquisition)
thing that one refuses & is afterwards
glad to get on worse terms. [f. L *Sibyl-
linus* (prec., -INE¹)]

sīc, Latin adv. = so, appended in brackets

after a word or expression in a quoted
passage as guarantee that it is quoted
exactly, though its incorrectness or absurdity would suggest that it was not.
Also in the phrr. ~ *vŏl'ŏ ~ jub'eŏ* (jŏō-;
such is my will & command) used as n. =
arbitrary order; ~ *vōs nŏn vōb'īs* (so ye
not for yourselves) used w. ref. to work of
which the credit etc. falls to another than
the doer.

sicc'ative, a. & n. (Substance etc.) of drying properties, esp. one mixed with oil-
-paint to dry it. [f. LL *siccativus* f.
siccare dry, see -ATIVE]

sice¹, n. The six on dice. [ME, f. OF *sis*
SIX]

sice², sỹce, n. (Anglo-Ind.). Groom. [f.
Hind. f. Arab. *sā'īs*]

Sicil'ian, a. & n. 1. Of Sicily or its
inhabitants (~ *Vespers*, massacre of
French residents by natives in 1282, with
vesper bell as signal). 2. n. Native of
Sicily. [f. L *Sicilia* Sicily +-AN]

sick¹, a. 1. Ill, incapacitated by illness,
feeling effects of some disease, (*a ~ man*;
the S~ Man (*of Europe*), Turkish Empire
(hist.); ~ *of a fever*; *the* ~, those who are
ill; || *be, feel, make*, ~ in mod. use, vomit,
be disposed or cause to vomit; *turn* ~,
feel as if about to vomit). 2. Disordered, perturbed, suffering effects *of*,
disgusted, pining *for*, (*am ~ at heart*; ~ *of
love*, love~; *makes me ~ to think of it*; *is
awfully ~ at being beaten*; ~ *for a sight
of home*). 3. Surfeited & tired of (~ *of
flattery, rain, waiting*). 4. (Of ship) needing repair (esp. of specified kind, as *nail-
-~, paint-~*). 5. ~-BAY³; ~-*bed*, invalid's
bed, invalid state; ~-*benefit*, allowance
made to person absent from work through
illness; ~-*call*, military summons on
bugle etc. for ~ men to attend; ~-*flag*,
yellow, indicating presence of disease at
quarantine station or on ship; ~ *headache*,
due to biliousness; ~-*leave*, leave of
absence granted for reason of health;
~-*list*, of the ~ esp. in regiment, ship, etc.
(*on the ~-list*, laid up); ~-*making* (colloq.);
~-*room*, occupied by ~ person, or kept
ready for the ~. Hence ~'ISH¹(2) a. [OE
sēoc, OS *siok*, OHG *sioh*, ON *sjúkr*, Goth.
siuks]

sick², v.t. Set upon (usu. in imperat. ~
him! etc. urging dog to worry rat etc.).
[19th c., dial. var. of SEEK]

sick'en, v.i. & t. Begin to be ill, show
symptoms of illness (*child is ~ing for
something*); feel nausea or disgust *at, to
see*, etc.; affect with inclination to vomit,
loathing, or disgust (*a ~ing sight*) or
with weariness or despair *of* (*was ~ed of
trying to make peace*), whence ~ER¹(2) n.,
~ingLY² adv. [ME, f. SICK¹ +-EN⁶]

sic'kle, n. Reaping-hook, short-handled
semicircular-bladed implement now
chiefly used for lopping & trimming,
formerly for cutting corn; *the* constellation Leo; ~*bill*, kinds of bird with ~

-shaped bill; ~*-feather*, one of long middle feathers of cock's tail; ~*-wort*, the plant heal-all. [OE *sicol*, *-el*, MDu., MLG *sekele*, OHG *sihhila*, f. L *secula* f. *secare* cut]

sick′l|ỹ, a., & v.t. **1.** Apt to be ill, chronically ailing, of weak health; suggesting sickness, as of sick person, languid, faint, pale, (~*y look*, *smile*, *complexion*); causing ill health, inducing or connected with nausea, (~*y climate*, *smell*, *taste*); mawkish, weakly sentimental. **2.** v.t. Cover *over* or *o'er* with a ~*y* hue (w. ref. to *Haml.* III. i. 85). Hence ~iNESS n. [ME ; -LY¹]

sick′ness, n. **1.** Being ill, disease. **2.** A disease (FALL¹*ing* ~; *sleeping-*~, fatal African disease, *morbus dormitivus*, marked by somnolence & nerve-paralysis, caused by certain trypanosomes introduced by kinds of tsetse; *sleepy* ~, epidemic encephalitis or *encephalitis lethargica*, acute inflammation of the brain, not yet traced to a parasitic cause, but distinct from sleeping-~, though lethargy is a mark of both). **3.** Vomiting or inclination to vomit. [ME ; -NESS]

Sic′ulo-, comb. form of L *Siculi* Sicilians, as ~*-Arabian*, Arabian as modified in Sicily. [-O-]

side¹, n. **1.** One of the flat(tish) surfaces bounding an object (*cube has six* ~*s*), esp. a more or less vertical outer or inner surface (~ *of house*, *cave*, *mountain*, etc.; so perh. COUNTRY~); such surface as distinguished from top & bottom, or front & back, or ends (*four*, or *two*, ~*s of box*; *two* ~*s of house*). **2.** Either surface of thing regarded as having only two (*two* ~*s of sheet of paper*, *board*, etc.; *sent him six* ~*s of argument*, pages of notepaper so filled; *the* INSIDE *&* OUTSIDE *of a bowl*; *right*, *wrong*, ~ *of cloth* etc., surface, meant, not meant, to be visible; BACK¹*side*, SHADY, SEAMY, SILVER¹, ~). **3.** (math.). Bounding line of plane rectilinear figure (*opposite* ~*s of a parallelogram*). **4.** Part of person or animal that is on his or its right or left, esp. that of it which extends from armpit to hip or from foreleg to hindleg (~ *of mutton*, *bacon*, etc., this part of carcass; BLIND¹~; ~ *by* ~, standing close together, esp. for mutual support; *shake one's* ~*s*, laugh heartily; ~*-splitting*, causing violent laughter, amusing). **5.** Part of object turned in same direction as observer's right or left & not directly towards or away from him, or turned in specified direction (*right*, *left*, ~; *debit*, *credit*, ~, in account book; *epistle*, *gospel*, ~, south, north, end of altar; DECANI, CANTORIS, ~; *the north*, *landward*, ~). **6.** Part or region near margin and remote from centre or axis of thing, subordinate or less essential or more or less detached part, (~ *of room*, *road*, *table*, etc.); (attrib.) subordinate (~ *issue*, point that distracts attention; ~ *line*, work etc. carried on apart from one's main work, see also

sense 14); *on the* ~, as a ~ line, in addition to one's regular work. **7.** Region external but contiguous to, specified direction with relation to, person or thing (*on one* ~, aside; *look on all* ~*s*; *came from all* ~*s* or *every* ~; *standing at my* ~; *on the north* ~ *of*). **8.** Partial aspect of thing, aspect differing from or opposed to other aspects (*study all* ~*s of the question*; *has many* ~*s to his character*; *the* ~ *of the moon visible to us*; *on the* (so-and-so) ~, rather (so-and-so), as *prices were on the high* ~. **9.** (Cause represented by, position in company with) one of two sets of opponents in war, politics, games, etc. (*the Lord is on my* ~; *there is much to be said, there are faults, on both* ~*s*; *take* ~*s*, decide to espouse one or other cause; *join the winning* ~; ON¹, OFF, ~; *Cambridge has a strong* ~, team for cricket, football, etc.). **10.** Position nearer or farther than, right or left of, dividing line (*on this* ~ *of*, or *on this* ~, *the Alps*; *on this* ~ *the grave*, in life; *on the right*, *wrong*, ~ *of forty*, below, above, 40 years of age; *on the wrong* ~ *of the door*, shut out; *on the wrong* ~ *of the* BLANKET¹). **11.** Line of descent through father or mother (*well descended on the mother's* or *maternal* ~; DISTAFF or *spindle*, SPEAR, ~). **12.** ‖(bill.). Spinning motion given to ball by striking it on ~. **13.** ‖(sl.). Assumption of superiority, swagger, (*puts on*, *has too much*, ~), whence **sīd′y²** a. **14.** ~*-arms*, swords or bayonets; ~*-bet*, bet between opponents, freq. in card-games, over & above the ordinary stakes; ~*′board*, table or flat--topped chest at ~ of dining-room for supporting and containing dishes, decanters, etc., (pl., sl.) ~*-whiskers*; ~*‛bone*, (in carving fowls) either small forked bone under wing; *~*′burns*, short ~*-whiskers*; ~*-car*, = JAUNT*ing-car*, (also) car for passenger(s) attachable to ~ of (motor-) cycle; ~*-chapel*, in aisle or at~ of church; ~*-dish*, extra dish often of elaborate kind at dinner etc.; ~*-drum*, small double--headed drum in military band hung at drummer's ~; ~*′light*, light from ~, (fig.) incidental illustration etc., (naut.) red port or green starboard light on ship under way; ~*-lines*, (space immediately outside) lines bounding football-pitch, tennis--court, etc., at the ~s, see also sense 6; ~*-note*, marginal note; ~*-saddle*, for rider, usu. woman, with both feet on same ~ of horse; ~*-seat* in vehicle etc., in which occupant has back against ~ of vehicle; ~*-show*, minor show attached to principal one; ~*-slip*, skid v. & n., (aeron.) move (vb) or motion broadside on instead of forward, also shoot of tree & (fig.) illegitimate child, also (theatr.) division at ~ of stage for working scenery; ~*s′man*, deputy churchwarden; ~*-step*, (n.) step taken sideways, step for getting in & out of carriage etc., (v.t.) avoid by stepping sideways (esp. in football), (fig.) evade;

~-*stroke*, stroke towards or from a ~, incidental action, kinds of swimming action opp. breast-stroke; ~-*track*, siding, (v.t.) turn into siding, shunt, postpone treatment or consideration of; ~-*view*, view obtained sideways, profile; ~'*walk*, path at ~ of road for foot-passengers (chiefly U.S.); *~-*wheeler*, steamer with paddle-wheels; ~ *wind*, wind from a ~, indirect agency or influence. Hence (-)sĭd'ED²a.,(-)sĭd'ĕdLY²adv.,(-)sĭd'ĕd-NESS n., ~'LESS (-dl-) a. [OE (OS) *sīde*, OHG *sīta*, ON *sítha*; perh. f. the adj., OE *sīd*, ON *sīthr* extensive etc.]

side², v.i. Take part, be on same side, *with* disputant etc. [f. prec.]

side'lŏng (-dl-), adv. & a. Inclining to one side, oblique(ly), (*move*~; *a*~ *glance*). [-LONG]

sidēr'ĕal, a. Of the constellations or the fixed stars (~ *day*, time between successive meridional transits of star, esp. of first point in Aries, about 4' shorter than solar day; ~ *year*, time in which earth makes one complete · revolution round sun, longer than tropical year by difference due to precession; ~ *time*, measured by apparent diurnal motion of stars). [f. L *sidereus* (*sidus -eris* star), -AL]

siderŏg'raphў, n. A process of engraving on steel. [f. Gk *sidēros* iron, -GRAPHY]

side'ward(s) (-dw-), adv. & a. Lateral(ly), to or from a side, (*moved* ~; ~ *motion*). [-WARD(S)]

side'ways (-dwāz), adv. & a. = prec. [-WAYS]

sīd'ing, n. Short track by side of railway line & opening into it at one end or both for shunting purposes. [-ING¹]

sī'dle, v.i. Walk obliquely, esp. in timid or cringing manner (often *along*, *up*). [back formation f. obs. *sideling* (now SIDELONG)]

siege, n., & v.t. 1. Operations of encamped attacking force to take or compel surrender of fortified place, period during which these last, besieging or being besieged, (often fig.: *raise the* ~ *of*, abandon attempt to take; *lay* ~ *to*, begin besieging; ~ *lasted 100 days*; *stood a long* ~, before or without surrendering); persistent attempt to force or persuade reluctant person to do something; ~-*basket*, gabion; ~-*gun* (hist.), used in ~s, too heavy for field use; ~-*train* (hist.), artillery & other appliances for besieging; ~-*works*, trenches, shelters, etc., of besiegers. 2. v.t. (arch.). Besiege. [ME & OF *sege* seat f. pop. L *sedicum f. L *sedem*]

Sieg'fried line, n. German fortified line along Franco-German border, constructed prior to 1939–45 war. [person]

Sien(n)ēse' (-z), a. & n. (pl. same). (Inhabitant) of Sienna (~ *school*, of 13th–14th-c. painters). [-ESE]

siĕnn'a, n. Ochrous earth used raw or burnt as pigment of brownish-yellow (*raw* ~) or reddish-brown (*burnt* ~) colour.

[f. It. (*terra di*) *Sienna* (earth of) Sienna]

siĕ'rra, n. Long jagged mountain-chain; Spanish mackerel. [Sp., f. L *serra* saw]

siĕs'ta, n. Midday nap or rest in hot countries. [Sp., f. L *sexta* (*hora*) sixth hour]

sieve (sĭv), n., & v.t. 1. Sorting utensil with network or perforated bottom through which liquids or fine particles can pass while solid or coarser matter is retained; coarsely plaited basket often used as measure; person who cannot keep secrets. 2. v.t. Put through, sift with, ~. [OE *sife*, MDu., MLG *seve*, OHG *sib*; cf. SIFT]

siffleur (sēflẽr'), n. (fem. *-euse*, pr. *-ẽrz*). Whistling artiste. [F]

sift, v.t. & i. Separate into finer & coarser parts with sieve, separate (finer parts) *from* material or its coarser parts or *out*, sprinkle (sugar etc.) from perforated spoon etc.; closely examine details of (evidence, facts, etc.) with regard to credibility or authenticity or relevance, analyse character of; (of snow, light, etc.) fall as from sieve. Hence (-)~'ER¹ (1, 2) n. [OE *siftan*, MDu., MLG *siften*, cf. SIEVE]

sigh (sī), v.i. & t., & n. 1. Draw deep audible breath expressive of sadness, weariness, aspiration, relief from tension, cessation of effort, etc.; yearn *for* (person or thing desired or lost); utter or express with ~s (usu. *out*); (of wind etc.) make sound like ~ing; hence ~'ingLY² (sī'ī-) adv. 2. n. Act of, sound made in, ~ing (*a*~ *of relief*). [ME *sihen*, prob. back form. on *sihte* past of obs. *siche* f. OE *sīcan*]

sight¹ (sīt), n. 1. Faculty of vision (*long*, *short* or *near*, ~, requiring objects to be unusually far, near, for clear definition; *short* ~, fig., lack of discernment or foresight; *has good*, *bad*, ~; *know by* ~, be familiar with appearance only of; *loss of* ~, becoming blind; *second* ~, power of internal vision by which future or distant occurrences are presented), whence (-)~'ED² (sĭt-), a., (-)~'ĕdLY² adv., (-)~'ĕdNESS n. 2. Seeing or being seen, way of looking at or considering thing, (*catch*, *lose*, ~ *of*, begin, cease, to see; *have lost* ~ *of Jones*, no longer know his movements etc.; *get a* ~ *of*, manage to see; *take a* ~ (*of*, *at*), sl., cock a snook; *at*, *on*, ~, as soon as person or thing has been seen; *plays music at* ~, without preliminary study or practice of piece; ~-*singing*, reading vocal music at ~; *payable at* ~, of draft etc.; *at first* ~, prima facie; *the* ~ *of her distress unmanned him*; *she found favour in his* ~; *do what is right in* one's *own* ~). 3. Range or unobstructed space within which person etc. can see or object be seen (*is in*, *out of*, ~, visible, not visible; HEAVE¹ *in* ~; *the millennium is in* ~, clearly near at hand; *put out of* ~, hide, ignore; *came in* ~ *of the fort*, so as to see it or be seen from it; *out of ~ out of mind*, we forget the absent; *out of my ~ !*, rhetorical order to depart). **4.** Thing seen, visible, or worth seeing, display, show, spectacle, (*a sad ~ awaited us*; *a ~ for sore eyes*, person or thing one is glad to see, esp. welcome visitor; *went to see the ~s*, noteworthy features of town etc., whence *~'*sēer[1], *~'*seeing[1], nn.; *the daffodils were a ~ to see or a ~*; *his face is a perfect ~*, disfigured with wounds etc.; *make a ~ of oneself*, dress in bizarre fashion etc.). **5.** (colloq.). Great quantity (*will cost a ~ of money*; *is a long ~ better*). **6.** (Kinds of device for assisting precise aim with gun or observation with optical instrument (*forgot to put up the leaf of his back ~*, in rifle-shooting; *took a careful ~ before firing*; *the ~s of*, *a ~ with, quadrant or compass*). **7.** *~'worthy*, worth seeing. [OE (*ge*)*sihth*, MDu., OHG *siht*, f. *sih*-stem of see[1]+-th[1]]

sight² (sīt), v.t. Get sight of, esp. by coming near (*~ land, game*); take observation of (star etc.) with instrument; provide (gun, quadrant, etc.) with sights; adjust sights of (*~ing shot*, experimental one to guide rifleman etc. in this); aim (gun etc.) with sights. [f. prec.]

sight'less (sīt-), a. Blind; (poet.) invisible. [ME; -less]

sight'lⁱly̌ (sīt-), a. Not unsightly. Hence *~*iness n. [-ly[1]]

si'gillate, a. (Of pottery) with impressed patterns; (bot.) having seal-like marks. [f. L *sigillatus* (*sigillum* seal dim. of sig*num*, -ate²)]

sig'ma, n. Greek letter (Σ or C, σ or, when final, s) corresponding to s. [Gk]

sig'mate¹, a. Sigma-shaped; S-shaped. [-ate²]

sig'm|āte², v.t. Add sigma or s to. Hence *~*a'tion n. [-ate³]

sigmăt'ic, a. Formed with sigma (esp. *~ aorist*). [sigma *-atos*, -ic]

sig'moid, a. & n. **1.** (Chiefly anat.) curved like the uncial sigma (C), or (now usu.) like S. **2.** n. Reversed or inverted curve. [-oid]

sign¹ (sīn), n. **1.** Mark traced on surface etc. (esp. *the ~ of the cross*, made by Christian priests in blessing or laymen in reverence with finger on forehead or breast; *~ manual*, signature written in person's own hand). **2.** Written mark conventionally used for word or phrase, symbol, thing used as representation of something, (*positive* or *plus ~*, +; *negative* or *minus ~*, −; *words are the ~s of ideas*; *a sacrament is an outward & visible ~ of an inward & spiritual grace*). **3.** (Thing serving as) presumptive evidence or indication or suggestion or symptom *of* or *that*, distinctive mark, token, guarantee, password, miracle evidencing supernatural power, portent, (*violence is a ~ of weakness* or *that one is weak*; *shows all the ~s of decay*; *gave earth & water in ~*

of submission; *by this ~ ye shall know them*; *did ~s & wonders*; *~ & counter~*, secret words etc. by which confederates recognize each other; *~s of the times*, things showing the tendency of affairs); (path.) objective evidence or indication of disease (often with defining word, as *Babinski's, Oppenheim's, ~*). **4.** (Often *~'board*) fanciful device usu. painted on a board displayed formerly by traders of any sort & still by many inns & some barbers etc. as advertisement of their business (*at the ~ of the White Hart* etc., arch., formerly used as address). **5.** Natural or conventional motion or gesture used instead of words to convey information & esp. order or request (*gave him a ~ to withdraw*; *deaf-&-dumb ~s*, those used in finger-talk; *make no ~*, seem unconscious, not protest, etc.). **6.** Any of twelve divisions of zodiac named from constellations formerly situated in them. **7.** *~-painter, -writer*, of *~*boards, shop-front inscriptions, etc.; *~'post*, at cross-roads etc. with names of places on each road. [ME & OF *signe* f. L *signum*]

sign² (sīn), v.t. & i. **1.** Mark with sign (esp. *~ infant* etc. *with the sign of the cross* in baptism). **2.** Acknowledge or guarantee (letter, deed, picture, book, article, petition, etc., or abs.) as one's own production or as having one's authority or consent by affixing or having affixed one's name or initials or recognized mark (*the will had never been ~ed*; *a ~ed masterpiece of Turner's*; *~ed as usual with a dicky-bird*; *does not ~ his contributions to the press*; *nothing shall induce me to ~*), whence *~'*able (sīn-) a. **3.** Write (one's name) as signature; convey (right, property, etc.) *away* by *~*ing deed etc.; take, acknowledge being taken, *on* for some employment to which employee binds himself by signature. **4.** Communicate by gesture (*~ assent*), give order or make request by gesture *to* person *to do* (*~ed to me to come*). **5.** *~ off*, (bridge) indicate by a conventional bid that one is ending the bidding, (radio) cease transmitting; so *~-off* n. [ME, f. OF *signer* or L *signare* (*signum*, see prec.)]

sig'nal¹, a. Remarkably good or bad, conspicuous, noteworthy, exemplary, condign, (*~ victory, defeat, reward, punishment, virtue, example*). Hence *~*ly² adv. [f. F *signalé* f. It. p.p. *segnalato* distinguished (foll., *-ato* -ate²)]

sig'nal², n., & v.t. & i. (-ll-). **1.** Preconcerted or intelligible sign conveying information or direction esp. to person(s) at a distance, message made up of such signs, (*the ~ was to be the dropping of a handkerchief*; *~s are made by day with flags & by night with lights*; *gave the ~ for advance*; fog²*-~*; *~ of distress*, appeal for help, esp. from ship made by firing guns; *storm-~*, cone etc. hoisted at meteorological station; *code of ~s, ~-book*, body of ~s arranged for sending complicated messages esp. in naval & mil. use); immediate occasion *for* some general movement (*the earthquake was the ~ for an outbreak of the primitive instincts*); ‖ ROYAL *Corps of S~s*; *~box*, hut on railway with ~ling-apparatus; *~man*, ~ler; *~ strength*, strength of reception of radio ~s (varying with the time of day etc.). **2. vb.** Make ~(s), make ~(s) to, transmit (order, information) by ~, announce (event, *that*) by ~, direct (person *to* do) by ~; hence ~¹ER¹ n. [ME, f. OF, f. med. L *signale* (LL *signalis*) f. L *signum* SIGN¹, -AL]

sig′nalize, -ise (-īz), v.t. Make noteworthy or remarkable, lend distinction or lustre to, (*his accession was ~d by an amnesty*). [SIGNAL¹, -IZE]

sig′nator|y̆, a. & n. (Party, esp. State) that has signed an agreement esp. a treaty (*the ~ies or ~y powers to the treaty of Berlin*). [f. L *signatorius* of sealing (*signare* mark, -TORY)]

sig′nature, n. 1.(arch.). Significant appearance or mark (*has the ~ of passion, of early death, in his face*; *herb's yellow flowers are a ~ indicating that it will cure jaundice*). **2.** Person's name or initials or mark used in SIGN²ing. **3.** Letter or figure placed by printer at foot of (now, usu. only first) page of each sheet of book as guide in making up for binding, such sheet after folding. **4.** (mus.). *Key ~*, clef with sharps or flats at beginning of each staff; *time ~*, fraction placed at beginning of composition, numerator giving number of beats in each bar and denominator duration of each. **5.** *~ tune*, special tune used in broadcasting to announce a particular turn etc. [f. med. L *signatura* (LL = marking of sheep), or F *signature*; (as prec., -URE)]

sig′nĕt, n. Private seal for use instead of or with signature as authentication (*the ~*, royal seal formerly used for special purposes; ‖ WRITER *to the ~*); *~-ring*, finger-ring with seal set in it. [ME, f. AF, OF *signet*, or med. L *signetum* (SIGN¹, -ET¹)]

signif′icance, n. Being significant, expressiveness, (*there is no ~ in his eyes*; *with a look of deep ~*); covert or real import, what is meant to be or may be inferred, (*those were the words, but what is their ~?*); importance, noteworthiness, (*what he thinks about it is of no ~*). [OF, or f. L *significantia* (SIGNIFY, -ANCE)]

signif′icant, a. Having a meaning (-*kin is a ~ termination*); expressive, suggestive, with pregnant or secret sense, inviting attention; noteworthy, of considerable amount or effect or importance, not insignificant or negligible, (usu. in negative contexts, as *the only ~ event was —*). Hence ~LY² adv. [as SIGNIFY, -ANT]

significā′tion, n. Act of signifying (rare); exact meaning or sense (usu. *of* something, esp. of a word or phrase). [ME, f. OF, or f. L *significatio* (SIGNIFY, -ATION)]

signif′icātive, a. Offering signs or presumptive evidence *of*. [ME, f. OF (-*if*, -*ive*), or f. LL *significativus* (as foll., -ATIVE)]

sig′nif|y̆, v.t. & i. Be a sign or indication or presage of (*a long upper lip ~ies obstinacy*; *a halo ~ies rain*); mean, have as meaning, (*D.D. ~ies doctor of divinity*); communicate, make known, (*he ~ied his reluctance, that he could not consent*); be of importance, matter, (esp. in negative contexts, as *it does not ~y*). [ME, f. OF *signifier* f. L *significare* (SIGN¹, -FY)]

Signor, Signora, Signorina, (sēn′yŏr, sēnyōr′a, sēnyŏrēn′a), nn. (pl. -*ri* pr. -*rē*, -*re* pr. -*rā*, -*ne* pr. -*nā*). Titles used of or to Italians corresponding to Sir & Mr, Madam & Mrs, young lady & Miss. [It.]

Sikh (sēk, sĭk), n. Member of Hindu community founded as monotheistic sect *c.* 1500 in Punjab & after achieving independence annexed 1849 to British India. Hence ~′ISM n., the (religious) tenets of the ~s. [Hind., = disciple]

sil′age, n., & v.t. **1.** = ENSILAGE. **2.** v.t. Put into silo. [alt. f. ENSILAGE after SILO]

sil′ence, n., & v.t. **1.** Abstinence from speech or noise, being silent, taciturnity, non-betrayal of secret etc., fact of not mentioning a thing, (*the ~ of Scripture on the subject*; *~ gives consent*; *~ is golden*; *keep, break, ~*, abstain from speaking; *speak*; *put to ~*, esp. refute in argument); absence of sound, stillness, (*in ~*, without speech or other sound); oblivion, state of not being mentioned, (*have passed into ~*); *S~!* (order to cease from speech or noise). **2.** v.t. Make silent by force, superior argument, etc. (*~d the enemy's batteries, the best debaters in the House, the voice of conscience*). Hence **sil′encer¹** n., kinds of device for rendering (comparatively) noiseless the escape of gas from gun, oil-engine, etc. [ME, f. OF, f. L *silentium* (*silēre* be silent)]

sil′ent, a. Not speaking, not uttering or making or accompanied by any sound, (*~ letter*, one written but not pronounced, e.g. *b* in *doubt*; *~ film*, without sound accompaniment; *~ partner*, with no voice in management of business; *the ~ system* in prisons, by which prisoners are never allowed to speak); taciturn, speaking little; saying nothing on some subject (*history is ~ upon it*). Hence ~LY² adv. [f. L *silēre* be silent, -ENT]

Silē′nus, n. Rollicking drunken bloated old man. [L, f. Gk *Seilēnos* name of one of Bacchus's attendants]

silē′sia (-sha), n. Kinds of thin cloth used for blinds & dress-linings. [orig. made in Silesia]

silhouette′ (-lŏo-), n., & v.t. **1.** Portrait of person in profile showing outline only, all inside the outline being usu. black on white ground or cut out in paper; appearance of person or object as seen against light so that outline only is

distinguishable (*in* ~, so seen or placed).
2. v.t. Represent or (usu. pass.) exhibit
in ~. [f. Etienne de *Silhouette* (1709–67),
French author & politician]

sil'ic|a, n. Silicon dioxide, occurring as
quartz & as principal constituent of sandstone & other rocks (~ōs'ɪs n., disease
caused by inhalation of quartz dust, so
~ōt'ɪc a. & n.). Hence **sili'ɢɪc,**~ɪf'ɛʀous,
sili'cious or **sili'cɛous** (-shus), aa.,
~ate[1](3) n., ~ɪ-, ~o-, comb. forms. [f. L
silex -icis flint]

sil'icātèd, a. Coated, mixed, combined,
or impregnated, with silica. [prec., -ate[3],
-ed[1]]

sili'ci|fy, v.t. & i. Impregnate with silica,
turn (t. & i.) into silica, petrify. Hence
~fica'tion n. [SILICA, -FY]

sil'icon, n. Non-metallic element of very
common occurrence in the compound
SILICA. [f. L *silex -icis* flint, (after *carbon*,
boron), replacing *silicium*]

sil'iqua (pl. -*ae*), **silique'** (-ēk), n. Pod of
plants of mustard family. Hence **sil'iqu-
ose[1], sil'iquous,** (-kw-), aa. [L]

silk, n. 1. Fine soft thread produced in
making cocoon by ~'*worm* or larva of
kinds of moth feeding esp. on mulberry
leaves (*spun* ~, see SPIN ; *thrown* ~, ORGAN-
ZINE); similar thread spun by some
spiders etc. or (*artificial* ~, now usu.
rayon) thread or yarn made from cellulose.
2. Cloth woven of ~ (|| *take* ~, become
K.C. or Q.C. & exchange stuff for ~
gown); (pl.) kinds, or garments made, of
such cloth. **3.** || (colloq.). K.C. or Q.C.
4. Peculiar lustre seen in some sapphires
& rubies. **5.** (attrib., now usu. preferred
to *silken*). Made of ~ (~ *stockings* etc.;
make a ~ purse out of a sow's ear, get
better results from a person than his
qualities admit of). **6.** || ~-*fowl*, breed
with silky plumage; ~-*gland*, secreting
the substance produced as ~; ~-*reel*,
-*winder*, for unwinding ~ from cocoon &
winding it as thread; ~-*screen printing*, a
stencil printing process. [OE *sioloc* (cf.
ON *silki*) prob. ult. f. L, or Gk *sērikos* f.
Sēres, prob. the Chinese, -ɪc]

sil'ken, a. Made of silk (arch., poet.);
clad in silk; soft, lustrous, as silk; (of
manner etc.) suave, insinuating. [ME; -en[5]]

sil'k|y, a. Like silk in smoothness, soft-
ness, fineness, or lustre (~*y manner* etc.,
suave). Hence ~ɪness n. [-y[2]]

sill, n. Shelf or slab of stone or wood at
foot of door or esp. window; horizontal
timber at bottom of dock or lock entrance, against which the gates close.
[OE *syll(e)*, = MDu., MLG *sulle*, cogn. w.
ON *syll*, OHG *swelli*, Goth. *gasuljan* to
found]

sill'abub, n. Dish made of cream or milk
mixed with wine etc. into soft curd &
sometimes whipped or solidified with
gelatine. [16th c. also *sillibucke*, *sillub*,
etc., of unkn. orig.]

|| **sill'er,** n. (Sc.). Silver; money. [=SILVER]

Sill'ery, n. Kinds of sparkling & still
champagne. [place-name]

sill'|y, a. & n. 1. || Innocent, simple, help-
less, (arch.); foolish, weak-minded, im-
prudent, unwise, imbecile; || *the* ~*y
season*, August & September as the
season when newspapers start trivial
discussions for lack of news; ~*y point*,
short leg (placed close up to batsman).
2. n. (colloq.). A ~*y* person. Hence ~ɪLY[2]
adv., ~ɪness n. [later form of ME *sely*
(dial. *seely*) f. OE *sǣlig, OS, OHG *sālig*,
f. WG *sǣli luck, happiness]

sil'o, n. (pl. ~s), & v.t. 1. Pit or airtight
structure in which green crops are pressed
& kept for fodder, undergoing fermentation. **2.** v.t. Make ensilage of. [Sp., f. L
f. Gk *siros*]

silt, n., & v.t. & i. 1. Sediment deposited
by water in channel, harbour, etc. **2.** vb.
Choke or be choked with ~ (usu. *up*; *the
passage has* or *is* ~*ed up*). [ME, of obsc.
orig.; cf. Da., Norw. *sylt*, OLG *sulla*,
OHG *sulza* salt marsh, cogn. w. SALT]

Silūr'ian, a. & n. 1. Of the Silures, a
people of ancient Britain. **2.** (Of) a series
of rocks forming a subdivision of the
Palaeozoic immediately underlying the
Devonian, named as first investigated in
district of the Silures. [f. L *Silures*, -ɪan]

sil'van, sȳ-, a. Of the, having, woods;
rural. [16th c., f. L *silva* wood +-an, thr.
F *sylvain*; cf. L *Silvanus* woodland deity]

sil'ver[1], n. **1.** A white lustrous precious
metal used chiefly with alloy of harder
metals for coin, plate, & ornaments, &
in chem. combinations for photography
etc. (*German* ~, *nickel* ~, etc., white alloys
used as substitutes for ~ in table articles
etc., or for coating with ~; *fulminating* ~,
an explosive powder; OXIDIZE*d* ~). **2.** ~
coins (*have you any* ~ *on you?*). **3.** ~ vessels or implements or articles of furniture
(*melted down all his* ~ *in the king's service*).
4. Any of the salts of ~ used in sensitizing
photographic paper. **5.** attrib. or adj.
(usu. now preferred to ~n a. arch. see
-en[5]). Made of ~, second-best, (*the* ~ *age*,
see BRAZEN[1], also spec. the period of Latin
literature that followed the Augustan;
so ~ *Latin*; *a* ~ *cup*; *speech is* ~ *or* ~*n*,
but silence is golden, better be silent than
speak); (as substitute for ~y[2] a., whence
~ɪness n.) resembling ~ in whiteness,
lustre, ringing sound, etc. (~ *hair*, white
& lustrous; *has a* ~ *or* ~*y tone*; *has a* ~
tongue, is eloquent, whence ~-tongᴜᴇᴅ[2]
a.; *every cloud has a* ~ *lining*, misfortune
has its consolations). **6.** ~-*bath*, (tray for
holding) solution of ~ nitrate used for
sensitizing; ~ *fir*, kind with two ~ lines
on under side of leaves; ~-*fish*, kinds of
fish, esp. a colourless variety of goldfish,
(also) ~y insect found in books & mouldy
places; ~ FOIL[1]; ~ *fox*, variety of common
fox with black grey-tipped fur; ~ *gilt*, ~
gilded over, also imitation gilding of
yellow lacquer over ~ leaf; ~-*grey*,

lustrous grey; ~ LEAF; ~ *paper*, fine
white tissue-paper, (loosely) tin foil; ~
plate, vessels, spoons, etc., of ~; ~ *point*,
(process of sketching on prepared paper
with) ~-pointed style (*a head in ~ point*);
~ *print*, photographic positive on paper
sensitized by a salt of ~; ~ *sand*, fine
kind used in gardening; ~ *screen*, superior
type of cinematographic screen, (also)
film-pictures collectively; ~*side*, best
side of round of beef; ~*smith*, worker in
~, manufacturer of ~ articles; ~ *solder*,
solder for joining ~; ~ *standard*, use of ~
money alone as full legal tender; ||~-*stick*,
field-officer of Life Guards on palace duty;
|| ~ *streak, the* English Channel; ~ *thaw*,
glassy coating on the ground, exposed
woodwork, etc., caused when rain freezes
as it falls, or when a sudden thaw (after
hard frost) is succeeded by a light frost;
~-*top*, a disease in grasses; ~ *wedding*,
twenty-fifth anniversary; ~-*weed*, yellow-
-flowered roadside plant with ~y lower
leaf-surfaces. [OE *seolfor*, OS *sil(u)bar*,
OHG *sil(a)bar*, Goth. *silubr*, of obsc. orig.]

sil'ver², v.t. & i. Coat or plate with silver;
provide (mirror-glass) with backing of
tin foil, mercury, etc.; (of moon or white
light) give silvery appearance to; (with
hair as obj. or subj.) turn (t. & i.) grey or
white. [f. prec.]

sil'viculture, sŷ-, n. The growing and
tending of trees as a branch of forestry.
[f. L *silva* a wood + CULTURE]

sim'ian, a. & n. **1.** (zool.). (Of) one of the
Simiidae or anthropoid apes. **2.** Ape-
(like), monkey(-like). So ~OID a. [f. L
simia ape, -AN]

sim'ilar, a. & n. **1.** Like, alike, having
mutual resemblance or resemblance *to*,
of the same kind; (geom.) shaped alike;
hence or cogn. ~ITY (-ă'r-) n., ~LY² adv.
2. n. Thing resembling another; (pl.) ~
things. [f. F *similaire* or med. L *similaris*
(L *similis* like, -AR)]

sim'ile, n. The introduction, esp. in
poetry or poetical style, ostensibly for
explanatory or illustrative purposes but
often in fact for ornament only, of an
object or scene or action with which the
one in hand is professedly compared &
usu. connected by a comparative conjunction such as *as* (*a style rich in ~ &
metaphor*); a comparison of this kind (*the
~ of the dome of many-coloured glass*); cf.
METAPHOR, ALLEGORY, PARABLE). [f. L
neut. of *similis* like]

simil'itude, n. Likeness, guise, outward
appearance, (*in, assume, the ~ of*); simile,
comparison, (*talks in ~s*); counterpart,
facsimile, (rare; *is the very ~ of*). [ME, f.
OF, or f. L *similitudo* (prec., -TUDE)]

sim'ilize, -ise (-iz), v.i. & t. Use simile;
illustrate by simile(s). [SIMILE, -IZE]

simm'er, v.i. & t., & n. **1.** Be, keep
(trans.), on the point of boiling, boil (t. &
i.) very gently; (fig.) be in a state of suppressed anger, indignation, or laughter.

2. n. ~ing state (esp. *at a* or *on the ~*).
[alt. f. 16th c. (now dial.) *simper*, prob.
imit.]

|| sim'nel-cake, n. Rich ornamental
boiled cake made esp. at Easter, Christmas, and Mid Lent. [ME, f. OF *simenel*,
rel. in some way to L *simila* finest flour]

simŏn'iăc, n. Person guilty of simony.
[ME, f. OF, or f. med. L *simoniacus*
(SIMONY, -AC)]

simoni'acal, a. Guilty, of the nature, of
simony. Hence ~LY² adv. [-AL]

Sim'on Pūre, n. The real or genuine person or article (usu. *the real ~*). [character
in Centlivre's *Bold Stroke for a Wife*]

sim'onў, n. Buying or selling of ecclesiastical preferment. [ME, f. OF *simonie* f.
LL *simonia* f. *Simon* (*Magus*), see *Acts* viii.
18, -Y¹]

simŏŏm', n. Hot dry suffocating dust-
-laden wind moving in straight narrow
track and passing in a few minutes,
chiefly in Arabian desert. [f. Arab. *semūm*
samm to poison)]

***simp**, n. (colloq.). Simpleton. [abbr.]

sim'per, v.i. & t., & n. **1.** Smile affectedly,
smirk; express by or with ~ing (~*ed
consent*); hence ~**ingLY²** adv., ~**ER¹** n.
2. n. Affected smile. [16th c., orig. obsc.;
cf. Da., Norw., Sw. dial. *semper, simper*,
MDu. *simperlijk* nice, affected]

sim'ple, a. & n. **1.** Not compound, consisting of one element, all of one kind,
involving only one operation or power,
not divided into parts, not analysable,
(~ SENTENCE; ~ INTEREST¹; *a ~ quantity*,
expressible by single number; *induction
by ~ enumeration*, based merely on random examples without selection or tests;
~ *addition*, of numbers of one denomination; ~ *equation*, not involving the second
or any higher power of unknown quantity, cf. QUADRATIC; ~ *machine*, any of the
MECHANICAL powers; ~ *leaf*, of one blade;
~ *pistil*, of one carpel; ~ *eye* of insect,
OCELLUS; ~ *fracture*, breaking of bone
only, cf. COMPOUND²; ~ *idea*, that cannot
be analysed into elements). **2.** Not complicated or elaborate or adorned or involved or highly developed (*the style is
~ and devoid of ornament*; ~ *diet*; *the ~
life*, practice of doing without servants
& luxuries, attempt to return to more
primitive conditions; *the greatest works of
art are the ~st*; *in ~ beauty*, unadorned; *a
~ form of pump*; ~ *forms of life*, creatures
low in scale of evolution). **3.** Absolute,
unqualified, mere, neither more nor less
than, just, (*to give an infant alcohol is ~
murder or madness*; *his ~ word is as good
as an oath*; *pretends to be no more than a
~ gentleman*; FEE ~). **4.** Plain in appearance or manner, unaffected, unsophisticated, ingenuous, natural, artless, (*a ~
person*; ~ *attire*; *a ~ heart or mind*, whence
~-**heartED²**, ~-**mindED²**, aa., ~-**mind**-
edNESS n.). **5.** Foolish, ignorant, inexperienced, (*am not so ~ as to suppose*).

6. Easily understood or done, presenting no difficulty, (*gave a ~ explanation; the problem is very ~; can: be cured by a ~ device*). **7.** Of low rank, humble, insignificant, trifling, (GENTLE *& ~; her ~ efforts to please*); hence or cogn. ~NESS (rare), simpli′city, nn., sim′pLY² adv. **8. n.** A herb used medicinally, the medicine made from it; *be cut for the ~s*, undergo operation for cure of folly. [ME, f. OF, f. L *simplus* or *simplex*]

sim′pleton (-plt-), n. Foolish, gullible, or half-witted person. [fancy noun f. prec.]

slmpll′clter, adv. Absolutely, universally, without limitation, not relatively or in certain respects only (cf. SECUNDUM *quid*). [L]

sim′pli|fў, v.t. Make simple, make easy to do or understand. So ~FICA′TION n. [f. F *simplifier* f. med. L *simplificare* (SIMPLE, -FY)]

sim′plism, n. Affected simplicity. [-ISM]

simūlāc′rum, n. (pl. *-ra*). Image of something; shadowy likeness, deceptive substitute, mere pretence. [L (SIMULATE)]

sim′ūlant, a. Having the appearance of (esp. biol., as *stamens ~ of petals*). [foll., -ANT]

sim′ūlāte, v.t. Feign, pretend to have or feel, put on, (*~ virtue, indignation,* etc.); pretend to be, act like,. resemble, wear the guise of, mimic, (of word) take or have an altered form suggested by (word wrongly taken for its source), (*actor ~s king* etc.; *chameleon ~s its surroundings*; *amuck, for amok, ~s the English muck*). So simŭlā′TION n. [f. L *simulare* (*similis* like), -ATE³]

simultān′eous, a. Occurring or operating at the same time (*with*); *~ equation* (involving two or more variables). Hence simŭltānē′ITY, ~NESS, nn., ~LY² adv. [f. L *simul* together, -ANEOUS after *in-stantaneous* or (obs.) *momentaneous*]

simŭrg′, n. Monstrous bird of Persian myth. [f. Pers. *sīmurgh*]

sin, n., & v.i. & t. (-nn-). **1.** Transgression, *a* transgression, against divine law or principles of morality (ORIGINAL ~; *living in open ~; deadly* or *mortal ~*, such as kills the soul or is fatal to salvation; *the seven deadly ~s*, pride, covetousness, lust, anger, gluttony, envy, sloth; *one's besetting ~*, to which one is especially tempted; *for my ~s*, joc., as a judgement for something or other; *the unpardonable ~*, that described *Matt.* xii. 31–32; *man of ~*, arch. or joc., reprobate, also Antichrist; *like ~*, sl., vehemently); offence against good taste, propriety, etc.; *~-eater*, one hired to take on himself a dead person's ~s by eating bread and drinking ale placed on the bier; *~-offering*, sacrifice etc. in expiation of ~; hence ~′FUL, ~ᴸ LESS, aa., ~′fuLLY², ~′lèssLY² advv., ~′fulNESS, ~′lèssNESS, nn. **2. vb.** Commit ~; offend *against* (*more ~ned against than ~ning*, see *King Lear* III. ii. 60, often

of victim of seduction); *~ one's mercies,* be ungrateful for good luck; hence ~n′ER¹ n. (often joc., as *you young ~ner; as I am a ~ner*, form of asseveration). [OE *syn*(n), rel. to OS *sundea*, OHG *sunt*(e)*a*, ON *synth*; cf. L *sons sontis* guilty]

Sināit′ic, a. Of Mount Sinai or the peninsula of Sinai. [f. mod. L *Sinaiticus*]

Sināanthrōp′us, n. Apelike man of the type represented by remains found near Peking. [mod. L, f. SINO- + Gk *anthrōpos* man]

sin′apism, n. Mustard plaster. [f. F *-isme* or LL f. Gk *sinapismus* f. *sinapi* mustard]

since, adv., prep., & conj. **1.** After specified or implied past time, throughout (usu. *ever ~*) or at some or any point in the period between such time & that which is present or being dealt with, (*has* or *had been healthy ever ~; then more flourishing than ever before or ~; has ~ been cut down; have* or *had not seen him ~*); ago (*happened many years ~; how long ~ is it?; saw him not long ~*). **2. prep.** After (specified past time or event), through or in period between time present or being dealt with & (such time), (*has* or *had been going on, has happened, ~ 1900* or *Christmas; have eaten nothing ~ yesterday; ~ seeing you I have* or *had heard ~*). **3. conj.** From the past time when, through or in the period between time present or being dealt with & that when (*what have you done ~ we met?; nothing has happened, there had been a disturbance, ~ we parted*); seeing that, inasmuch as, (*~ that is so, there is no more to be said*); (ellipt.) as being (*a more dangerous, ~ unknown, foe*). [reduced form of obs. *sithence* (or f. dial. *sin* (f. *sithen*) adv. + -ES), f. OE *siththon* (prop. *sith thon* after that) + -ES; cf. OHG *sīd* since etc., Goth. *seithus* late]

sincēre′, a. Free from pretence or deceit, the same in reality as in seeming or profession, not assumed or put on, genuine, honest, frank. Hence or cogn. sincē′rITY n., ~LY² (-rlī) adv. (esp. in *yours ~ly* before signature of letter). [f. L *sincerus*]

sin′ciпŭt, n. Head from forehead to top (cf. OCCIPUT). [L (*semi-* half, *caput* head)]

sīne¹, n. (trigon.). (*~ of arc*) line drawn from one extremity of arc perpendicularly to radius which meets other extremity; (*~ of angle*) ratio of above line to radius (abbr. *sin*, as *sin A*, ratio of the perpendicular subtending the angle A to the hypotenuse; *versed ~*, abbr. *vers*, unity minus the cosine). [f. L *sinus* curve]

sin′e², L prep. Without (*~ di′ē*, without date, of business indefinitely adjourned; *~ quā nōn*, indispensable condition or qualification).

sin′ēcūr|e, n. Office of profit or honour without duties attached, esp. benefice without cure of souls. Hence ~ISM (3), ~IST(2), nn. [f. L *sine cura* without care]

sin'ew, n., & v.t. **1.** (Piece of) tough fibrous tissue uniting muscle to bone, tendon; (pl., loosely) muscles, bodily strength, wiriness, (fig.) what forms the strength of or sustains or holds together, framework, resources, (esp. *the ~s of war*, money, armaments, etc.); hence ~LESS, ~Y², aa., ~ÌNESS n. **2.** v.t. (poet.) Serve as ~s of, sustain, hold together. [OE *seon(o)we* obl. form of *si(o)nu* f. Gmc **senawō*; = OS *senewa*, OHG *-awa*, ON *sin*]

sinfoni'a (-ē'a), n. (In early Italian operas) overture. [It., = symphony]

sing, v.i. & t. (*săng* or, now rare, *sŭng*; *sung*). **1.** Utter words, utter (words), in tuneful succession, esp. in accordance with a set tune (~ *one's praises*, be always praising him), whence ~'ABLE a. **2.** Produce vocal melody, utter (song, tune), (*birds were ~ing*; ~ *another song* or *tune*, ~ *small*, become more humble, be crestfallen). **3.** Make inarticulate melodious or humming or buzzing or whistling sounds (*wind, kettle, bee, ~s*); (of ears) be affected as with buzzing sound (also *have a ~ing in* one's *ears*). **4.** Compose poetry, celebrate (hero, beauty, great event, etc.) in verse. **5.** Usher (esp. old or new year) *out* or *in* with ~ing; put *to sleep, into good humour*, etc., with ~ing; ~ *out* t. & i., call out loudly, shout. **6.** ∥*~ing-man* [-ING²], paid~*er*; *~ing-master* [-ING¹], teacher of ~ing; *~ing-voice* [-ING¹], voice as modulated in ~ing. Hence ~'ER¹ n. [OE (= OS, OHG) *singan*, ON *syngva*, Goth. *siggwan* f. Gmc **singwan*]

singe (-j), v.t. & i. (*~ing*), & n. **1.** Burn (t. & i.) superficially (~ *person's hair*, burn off tips as hairdressing operation; ~ *pig, fowl*, burn off bristles, down, after killing or plucking; *your dress is ~ing*; *his reputation is a little ~d*; ~ *one's feathers* or *wings*, take some harm esp. in venturesome attempt). **2.** n. Superficial burn (rare). [OE *sencgan*, = OFris. *senga*, MLG, MHG *sengen*, perh. causative f. SING (Gmc **sangjan*), w. ref. to hissing sound produced in burning]

Singhalese (-nggalēz'), a. & n. Var. of SINHALESE.

single¹ (sïng'gl), a. & n. **1.** One only, not double or multiple, united, undivided, designed for or used or done by one person etc. or one set or pair, (~ COMBAT, ENTRY, FILE³; ~ *flower*, that grows one on a stem, also that has not DOUBLE¹ corolla; ~ *game*, with one player on each side; ~ *wicket*, rudimentary form of cricket; ~ *court* in lawn tennis, fives, etc., of size etc. for ~ game; ~ *bed, room*, for one person; ~ *eye-glass*, for one eye, monocle; *a multitude inspired with a ~ purpose*; (of ticket) valid for outward journey only. **2.** Solitary, lonely, unaided, (a ~ *tree stands on the ridge*; *paid either by instalments or in a ~ sum*; ~ *life, state, man, woman*, unmarried; ~ *blessedness*, joc., unmarried

state). **3.** (In negative contexts) not to speak of more (*did not see a ~ one, a ~ person*; *can a ~ argument be advanced for it?*). **4.** Free from duplicity, sincere, consistent, guileless, ingenuous, (*a ~ eye*, devotion to one purpose, whence ~-eyED² a.; ~ *heart* or *mind*, simplicity of character, whence ~-heartED², ~-mindED², aa., ~-mind'edNESS n.). **5.** ~-acting, (of engine etc.) with steam admitted only to one side of piston; ~-breasted, (of coat etc.) with only one set of buttons & buttonholes, not overlapping; ~-cut, (of file) with grooves cut in one direction only, not crossing; ~-fire, (of cartridge) not meant to be recharged after use; ~-handed a. & adv., (done etc.) without help from other persons (*by his ~-handed efforts*; *cannot be done ~-handed*), also with or for one hand (*the men played ~-handed against the women with both hands*; *two-handed* & ~-handed *swords*); ~-loader, breechloading rifle without magazine; ~-stick, (fencing with) basket-hilted stick of about sword's length; hence ~NESS n., **sing'LY²** adv. (-ngg-). **6.** n. ~ game; ~ ticket; hit for one in cricket; (short whist) game won by 5–4; (pl.) twisted ~ threads of silk. [ME, f. OF, f. L *singulus*]

single² (sïng'gl), v.t. Choose *out* as an example or as distinguishable or to serve some purpose. [f. prec.]

∥ **sing'let** (-ngg-), n. Garment worn below shirt, vest. [SINGLE¹, -ET¹; prob. orig. = unindented garment on anal. of DOUBLET]

sing'leton (-ngglt-), n. The only card of a suit at bridge etc.; single thing, only child, etc. [f. SINGLE on anal. of *simpleton*]

sing'song, a. & n., & v.i. & t. **1.** In, recited with, monotonous rhythm. **2.** n. Monotonous rhythm; monotonous cadence in speaking; ∥ impromptu vocal concert, meeting for amateur singing. **3.** vb. Recite (verse etc.), speak, in ~ manner. [SING, SONG]

sing'ular (-ngg-), a. & n. **1.** (Gram.) of the form used in speaking of a single person or thing, not dual or plural; single, individual, (esp. *all* & ~, all whether taken together or separately); unexampled, unique, (now rare); unusual, remarkable from rarity, much beyond the average in degree, extraordinary, surprising; eccentric, unconventional, strangely behaved. **2.** n. (gram.) The ~ NUMBER²; a word in the ~ number. Hence ~LY² adv. [ME, f. OF *singuler*, *-ier*, *-aire*, or f. L *singularis* (*-arius*), as SINGLE, -AR¹]

singŭlă'ritў (-ngg-), n. In adj. senses: esp., uncommonness, being remarkable, odd trait or peculiarity. [ME, f. OF *singularite* or LL *singularitas* (prec., -TY)]

sing'ularize (-ngg-), -ise (-ïz), v.t. Strip (word) of termination mistaken for that of plural (*pease* & *Chinese are ~d into* pea, Chinee). Hence ~A'TION n. [-IZE]

Sinhalese' (-nalēz'), a. & n. (Member, language) of an Aryan people deriving from N. India and now living in Ceylon. [f. Skr. *Sinhala* Ceylon +-ESE]

sin'ister, a. (Her.) on left side of shield etc. (i.e. on right as seen by observer; BATON, BEND[1], ~; cf. DEXTER); (joc.) left; of evil omen; (usu. of person in regard to his appearance, or of his face or look) ill-looking, of malignant or villainous aspect; wicked, flagitious, (a ~ *design*). Hence ~LY[2] adv. [ME, f. OF *sinistre* or L *sinister* left]

sin'istral, a. Of, on, the left (rare); (of spiral shells) with whorls going to left & not as usu. to right. Hence ~LY[2] adv. [f. med. L *sinistralis* (prec., -AL)]

sin'istro-, comb. form of L *sinister* left, as ~*ce'rebral*, of the left hemisphere of the brain; ~*rse*, with leftward motion or aspect (esp. in bot. of climbing plants etc.).

sink[1], v.i. & t. (*sānk* or now rarely *sŭnk*; *sŭnk* or in adj. use usu. *sŭnken*). 1. Fall slowly downwards, decline, disappear below surface of liquid or below horizon, come gradually to lower level or pitch, droop, despond, subside, settle down, gradually expire or perish or cease, (*sun is ~ing*, *sank*; *my heart*, *spirits*, *sank*; *ship ~s*, goes to the bottom; *her eyes sank*, were turned downwards; *his head*, *chin*, *sank on his shoulder*, *chest*; *voice ~s*, becomes lower-pitched, or quieter; *sick man*, *life*, *is ~ing*, becoming weaker, dying; *prices ~*, become lower; *storm*, *river*, *~s*, subsides; *ground ~s*, slopes down, also comes to lower level by subsidence; *darkness sank upon the scene*, descended; *~ into feebleness*, *degradation*, *the grave*, *a quicksand*, *a chair*; *~ in* one's *estimation*, lose credit with him; *his eyes*, *cheeks*, *have sunk in* or *sunk*, fallen inwards, become hollow; so *sunken cheeks*, *eyes*; *here goes*, *~ or swim*, said in running risks & taking chances). 2. Penetrate (intr.), make way, *in* or *into* (*bayonet sank in to the hill*; *impression*, *lesson*, *~s into the mind* or *memory*, becomes fixed; *dye ~s in*, is absorbed). 3. Cause or allow to ~, send below surface of liquid or ground, lower level of, keep (trans.) in obscurity or background, conceal, put out of sight, make no reference to, excavate, make by excavating, engrave, (*would sooner ~ the ship than surrender*; *~ shaft*, *well*, dig or bore it; *~* one's *head on* one's *chest*, let it droop; *drought had sunk the streams*; *~* one's *title*, *name*, *office*, etc., keep it temporarily secret, not obtrude it; *~ the* SHOP; *~ a fact*, keep it quiet; *~* one*self* or one's *own interests*, be altruistic; SINKING-*fund*; *~ a die*, engrave it; *~ money*, invest it in undertaking from which it cannot be readily withdrawn, also lose it by such investment; *sunk* FENCE[1]). Hence ~'ABLE a. [OE *sincan*, OS, OHG *sinkan*, ON *søkkva*, Goth. *sigqan* f. Gmc *sinkwan*]

sink[2], n. Place in which foul liquid collects (now usu. fig.; *the Chinese quarter is a ~ of iniquity*); basin or box of porcelain etc. with outflow pipe into which slops are thrown in kitchens etc.; pool or marsh in which river's water disappears by evaporation or percolation; opening in stage through which scenery is raised & lowered. [f. prec.]

sink'er, n. In vbl senses; esp.: weight used to sink fishing or sounding line (HOOK[1], *line*, & ~); DIE[1].~. [-ER[1]]

sink'ing, n. In vbl senses; also: internal bodily sensation caused by hunger or apprehension; ~*-fund*, moneys set aside for the purpose of sinking or wiping out a State's or corporation's debt by degrees (*the ~-fund*, surplus of revenue over expenditure, devoted to reduction of national debt; *raid the ~-fund*, use such surplus in any year for other purposes). [-ING[1]]

sinn'er. See SIN.

sinn'et. See SENNIT.

Sinn Fein (shǐn fān), n. A 20th-c. patriotic movement & party in Ireland aiming at national revival in language etc. as well as political independence. [Ir., = we ourselves]

Sin'o-, comb. form of Gk *Sinai*, the Chinese; ~PHOBE n. & a., hater of, hating, the Chinese; ~PHOB'IA; also with another adj. of nationality, with the meaning 'Chinese and' (~*Japanese*).

Sin'ologue (-ŏg, -ōg), n. Person versed in Sinology. [F (foll., -LOGUE)]

Sinŏl'ogy, n. Knowledge of the Chinese language, history, customs, etc. Hence Sinŏl'OGIST n. [SINO-, -LOGY]

sin'ter, n. Siliceous or calcareous rock formed by deposit of springs. [G, = Eng. *sinter*; see CINDER]

sin'uate, a. (esp. bot.). Wavy-edged, with distinct inward & outward bends along edge. Hence ~LY[2] adv., sinūA'TION n. [f. L *sinuare* (SINUS) bend, -ATE[2]]

sinuŏs'ity, n. Being sinuous; a bend, esp. in a stream or road. [f. med. L *sinuositas* or F *-ité* (foll., -ITY)]

sin'uous, a. With many curves, serpentine, tortuous, undulating. Hence ~LY[2] adv. [f. L *sinuosus* (SINUS, -OUS)]

sīn'us, n. (pl. *-uses*, *-ūs*). (Anat., zool.) cavity of bone or tissue, pouch-shaped hollow; (path.) fistula; (bot.) curve between lobes of leaf. [L, = bosom, recess]

-sion (-shn, -zhn), suf. of nn. of action or condition thr. F *-sion* (or direct) f. L *-sionem* (nom. *-sio*) a compd suf. of p.p. stems in -s- + -ION (e.g. *mansion*, *mission*).

Sioux (sōō, sū), n. (pl. the same, pr. sōō, sū, sōōz, sūz), & a. 1. Member of a N.-Amer.-Indian tribe. 2. adj. Of the ~. [F, f. native name]

sip, v.t. & i. (-pp-), & n. 1. Drink (t. & i.) in repeated tiny mouthfuls or by spoonfuls. 2. n. Small mouthful of liquid imbibed (a ~ *of brandy*). [ME, perh. a modification of SUP]

siph'on, n., & v.i. & t. 1. Pipe or tube shaped like inverted V with unequal legs for conveying liquid over edge of vessel & delivering it at lower level by utilizing atmospheric pressure; (also ~-*bottle*) aerated-water bottle from which liquid is forced out by pressure of gas through ~-tube; (zool.; also *siphuncle*) canal or conduit esp. in molluscs or shells, sucking-tube of some insects etc.; ~ *baro-meter*, with tube bent at bottom like inverted ~; ~-*cup*, lubricating apparatus with oil led over edge of reservoir by capillary action through wick; ~ *gauge*, glass ~ attached to reservoir & containing mercury for indicating pressure etc. inside reservoir; hence ~AL, **siphŏn'**IC, aa. 2. vb. Conduct or flow (as) through ~ (*water is* ~*ing from the vase on to the tablecloth*); hence ~AGE(3) n. [f. F, or L f. Gk *siphōn* tube]

siph'onĕt, n. One of two tubes through which aphides exude honeydew. [prec., -ET¹]

siph'uncle (-ŭngkl), n. See SIPHON. [f. L *siphunculus* (SIPHON, -UNCLE)]

sipp'ĕt, n. Small piece of bread etc. soaked in liquid; one of the pieces of toast or fried bread served round mince etc. [app. dim. of SOP, see -ET¹]

si quis, n. Notice posted in ordination-candidate's parish church serving similar purpose to banns. [L, = if anyone (know an impediment)]

sīr, n., & v.t. (-rr-). 1. Used as vocative in addressing the king, a royal prince, archduke, a master or superior, the Speaker of the House of Commons either in his own person on points of order or as embodiment of the House in ordinary debate, any male whose name is or is to be understood to be unknown to speaker, or boy etc. who is to be rebuked (pl. ~s, for which *gentlemen* is usu. substituted). 2. Used as titular prefix to name of knight or baronet, always followed by Christian name, or its initial & surname, or the whole name (*Sir John Moore, Sir J. Moore*, or, in familiar use esp. as vocative, *Sir John*). 3. v.t. Address as ~ (*don't ~ me*). [ME; reduced form of SIRE]

sīrc'ar, n. (Anglo-Ind.). Government; head of government or household; house-steward; native accountant. [f. Hind. f. Pers. *sarkār* (*sar* head, *kār* work)]

sīrd'ar, n. (In India etc.) person in command, leader; (in Egypt) commander-in-chief (formerly a British officer) of army. [f. Hind. f. Pers. *sardār* (prec., -*dār* possessor)]

sīre, n., & v.t. 1. Father or male ancestor (poet.): male parent of beast, esp. stallion kept for breeding. 2. v.t. Beget (esp. of stallions). [ME, f. OF, f. pop. L *seior* f. L SENIOR]

sīr'ĕn, n. 1. (Gk myth.; pl.) women, or half women & half birds, living on a rocky isle to which they lured unwary seafarers with enchanting music. 2. Sweet singer. 3. Dangerously fascinating woman, temptress, tempting pursuit etc.; (attrib.) irresistibly tempting, as of a ~. 4. = SIRENIAN. 5. Instrument used in acoustic experiments & for making loud sound as warning etc. by revolution of perforated disc over jet of compressed air or steam; instrument for giving warning of air raids. [ME, f. OF *sereine* & LL *Sirena* f. L f. Gk *Seirēn*]

sīrēn'ian, a. & n. (Member) of the *Sirenia*, an order of fishlike mammals resembling cetaceans, including manatee & dugong. [mod. L *Sirenia* (prec.), -AN]

sīrg'ăng, n. Bright-green Asian bird, the green jackdaw. [E.-Ind.]

siri'asis, n. Sunstroke; sun-bath as medical treatment. [L, f. Gk *sciriasis* (*seiriaō* be hot, -ASIS)]

Si'rius. See DOG¹. [L, f. Gk *Seirios*]

sīrk'ar. = SIRCAR.

sīrl'oin, n. ‖ Upper part of loin of beef, with meat both above & (*undercut* or *fillet*) below the bone. [16th c. *surloin* f. OF **surloigne* var. of *surlonge* (SUR-², LOIN)]

sīrocc'ō, sci-, n. (pl. ~s). (Italian name for) Sahara wind or simoom when it reaches Italy, (also for) warm sultry rainy wind prevailing in winter. [It., f. Arab. *sharq* the East]

si'rrah (arch.), ***sir(r)ee'** (U.S. & dial.), nn. voc. replacing *sir* in imperious or contemptuous use. [f. SIR; -*ah* of uncert. orig.; w. -*ee* cf. dial. *sirry, surry*, etc.]

sirup. See SYRUP.

sirvente (sẽrvahnt'), n. Medieval usu. satirical lay of special metrical form. [f. F *sirvente* f. Prov. *sirventes, ser-*; E & F sp. due to taking -*es* as pl.]

sis'al, n. Fibre prepared from leaves of agave, used for cordage, ropes, etc.; the plant. [S~, port of Yucatan]

sis'kin, n. Olive-green songbird, kind of finch, often kept in cage. [16th c., f. MDu. *siseken*, dim. of *sijs*]

siss'ōō, n. Valuable Indian timber (-tree). [Hind. *sīsū*]

siss'ȳ. See CISSY.

sis'ter, n. 1. Daughter of same parents (also ~ *german*), or (strictly *half-*~) parent, as another person (the latter usu. specified by *my* etc. or possessive case; *the Fatal S~s* or *S~s three* or *three S~s*, the Fates; *S~ Anne*, person watching on behalf of another for an arrival, w. ref. to *Bluebeard*); (prop. ~-*in-law*) one's husband's or wife's ~ or brother's wife. 2. Close female friend, female fellow member of class or sect or human race. 3. Member of religious community of women (~ *of* CHARITY; ~ *of mercy*, member of nursing sisterhood, esp. of R.-C. one founded in Dublin 1827; *little S~s of the poor*, French R.-C. charitable sisterhood; LAY² ~). 4. Hospital nurse in authority over others. **5.** Personified quality or thing regarded as female that closely resembles another (*prose, younger ~ of verse; ~ ships,* built on same design). **6.** ~*-hook,* double hook that opens to admit rope etc. & closes into a figure 8. Hence ~LESS, ~LY[1], aa., ~liNESS n. [OE *sweoster,* OS *swestar,* OHG *-ter,* Goth. *swistar* f. Gmc **swestr-,* cogn. w. L *soror;* the current form *sister* is ME f. ON *systir*]

sis'terhŏŏd, n. Being a sister or sisters, relation between sisters; society of women bound by monastic vows or devoting themselves to religious or charitable work. [-HOOD]

Sis'tine, a. Of one of the popes called *Sixtus* (~ *chapel,* in Vatican, with frescoes by Michelangelo; ~ *Madonna,* picture by Raphael removed from church of San Sisto in Piacenza). [f. It. *Sistino* (*Sisto* Sixtus, -INE[1])]

sis'trum, n. (pl. *-tra*). Jingling instrument or rattle used by ancient Egyptians esp. in rites of Isis. [L, f. Gk *seistron* (*seiō* shake)]

sisȳphē'an, a. As of Sisyphus, Greek condemned in Tartarus to push a stone up hill & begin again when it rolled down, everlastingly laborious. [f. L f. Gk *Sisupheios* (*Sisuphos*), -AN]

sit, v.i. & t. (*săt,* arch. *sāte*). **1.** Take or be in position in which body is supported more or less upright by buttocks resting on ground or raised seat (~*s well,* has good seat in riding; ~ *tight,* colloq., remain firmly in one's place, not be shaken off or move away or yield to distractions); be engaged in some occupation in which this position is usual (~ *in judgement,* assume right of judging others, be censorious; ~ *for* one's *portrait,* give painter interviews or sittings; ǁ ~ *for fellowship* etc., undergo examination for it; ~ *for borough* etc., represent it in Parliament; *Parliament, Courts, are ~ting,* in session; ~ *at home,* be inactive). **2.** (Of birds & some animals) rest with legs bent & body close to ground or perch (*shoot bird, hare, ~ting,* when not on wing or running); remain on nest to hatch eggs (~*ting hen,* engaged in hatching; *wants to ~,* is broody). **3.** (Chiefly of inanimate things) be in more or less permanent position (~*s the wind there?,* is it in that quarter?, is that the state of affairs?; *food ~s heavy on the stomach,* is not soon digested; *her dress, imperiousness,* etc., ~*s well on her,* suits, fits; ~*ting tenant,* one in present occupation; *his principles ~ loosely on him,* do not bind him much). **4.** Keep one's seat on (horse etc.; *he could not ~ his mule*). **5.** Undergo, be a candidate at, (examination etc.). **6.** ~ *down,* take seat after standing (also refl. arch., as *sat him, pray ~ you, down*), (mil.) encamp *before* place to besiege it; ~*-down strike,* one in which strikers refuse to leave the place where

they are working; ~ *down under,* submit tamely to (insult etc.). **7.** ~ *in* (colloq.), act as ~*ter-in* (= BABY-~*ter*). **8.** ~ *on* or *upon,* (of jury etc.) hold session concerning; ~ *on his head* (as way of keeping fallen horse quiet); (sl.) repress or rebuke or snub (*he wants ~ting upon*). **9.** ~ *out,* take no part in something, esp. in particular dance (also trans., as *sat out the next dance*), also ~ *outdoors,* (trans.) outstay (other visitors) or stay till end of (performance). **10.** ~ *over* (player), (bridge) be on his left hand (and so in advantageous position). **11.** ~ *under,* be one of congregation preached to by (minister). **12.** ~ *up,* rise from lying to ~ting posture, remain (*late, nursing,* etc.) out of bed, ~ erect without lolling (*make one ~ up,* colloq., subject him to hard work, pain, surprise, etc.); ~ *up & take notice* (colloq.), have one's interest (suddenly) aroused. **13.** ~*fast* n., horny sore on horse's back. [OE *sittan,* OS *-ian,* OHG *sizzan,* ON *sitja* (Goth. *sitan*), f. Gmc **sitjan* f. **set-* cogn. w. L *sedēre*]

site, n., & v.t. **1.** Ground on which town or building stood, stands, or is to stand. **2.** v.t. Locate, place. [ME, f. AF, or f. L *situs*]

ǁ **sith,** conj. (arch., bibl.). Since. [see SINCE]

siti|o-, sit|o-, comb. form of Gk *sitos, sition,* food, as ~*ŏl'ogy* dietetics, ~*ophŏb'ia* morbid aversion to food.

sitt'er, n. In vbl senses; esp.: person sitting for portrait; *good, bad,* ~, hen that sits well etc.; (sl., from *to shoot bird sitting*) easy shot, thing easily done. [-ER[1]]

sitt'ing, n. In vbl senses; esp.: time during which one sits continuously (*wrote the whole poem at a ~; all-night ~ of House of Commons; can you give me six ~s?,* for portrait); clutch of eggs; seat in church appropriated to a person; ~*-room,* space enough to accommodate seated persons, also a room used for sitting in (opp. *bedroom*). [-ING[1]]

sit'ūātĕd, sit'ūate (arch.), aa. In specified situation (*situated on the top of the hill; awkwardly situated,* in a difficulty). [f. LL *situatus* (L *situs* SITE, -ATE[2, 3])]

situā'tion, n. Place, with its surroundings, occupied by something (*house stands in a fine ~; unrivalled for ~*); set of circumstances, position in which one finds oneself, (*came out of a difficult ~ with credit*); critical point or complication in drama (*curtain falls on a strong ~*); employee's, esp. domestic's, place or paid office (*cannot find a ~*). [F, or f. med. L *situatio* (as prec., -ATION)]

sitz-bath. See BATH[1].

Si'va (sē-), n. Hindu god held supreme by his special votaries, & by others associated as principle of destruction with Brahma & Vishnu in a triad. Hence ~**is'tic** [-IST, -IC] a., ~**ITE**[1](1) n. & a. [Hind., f. Skr. *çiva* propitious]

six, a. & n. **1.** One more than five, 6, vi, (often agreeing with understood noun, as ~ *of the men*, ~ *of them*, ~ *o'clock* or ~; ~ *to one*, long odds; *two &* ~, half-a--crown; ‖~ *& eight(pence)*, common item in solicitors' bills; ‖~ *&* ~, 6/6; *it is* ~ *of one & half-a-dozen of the other*, difference is merely nominal; *twenty-*~ or ~-*&--twenty*, & so on to ~-*&-ninety*; *am not* ~ *yet*, years old); ~*-footer*, person 6 ft in height, thing 6 ft long; ‖~*'pence*, (silver coin worth) 6*d*. (*have not got a* ~*pence*); ‖~*'penny* a., costing or worth 6*d*. (~*-penny bit*, or ~*penny* as n., the coin ~*-*pence; ‖ *seven-&-*~*'penny* etc., costing 7/6 etc.); ~*-shooter*, ~*-chambered* re-volver; hence ~*'FOLD* a. & adv. **2.** n. The number ~ (*twice* ~ *is twelve*; *at* ~*es & sevens*, in confusion); card or die-face of ~ pips (*the* ~ *of spades*; (*double*) ~*es*, die--throw of two ~es); ‖ (pl.) candles made ~ to the lb. [OE, ON *sex*, OS, OHG *sehs*, Goth. *saihs*, cogn. w. L *sex*]

six'ain, n. Six-line stanza. [F, see -AN]

six'er, n. Hit for six in cricket. [-ER¹]

sixte, n. One of the positions in fencing. [F, f. L *sextus* sixth]

sixteen, a. & n. **1.** One more than fifteen, 16, xvi; ~*mo* or *16mo*, = SEXTODECIMO; hence ~TH² a. & n. **2.** n. The number ~ (*twice* ~ *is thirty-two*). [-TEEN]

sixth, a. & n. **1.** Next after fifth (*the*, *a*, ~, often as n. with ellipse of noun, esp. *the* ~ = 6th day of month; ‖~ FORM¹); ~ *part*, one of six equal parts into which thing may be divided. **2.** n. = ~ part; ‖ *the* ~ *form*; (mus.) interval of which the span involves six alphabetical names of notes, harmonic combination of notes thus separated. [OE *sixta*, see -TH²]

sixth'lỹ, adv. In the sixth place (in enu-merations). [-LY²]

six'tỹ, a. & n. **1.** Six times ten, 60, lx, (~*-one*, *-eight*, etc.; ~*-first*, *-fourth*, etc.); ~*-four-mo*, (size of) book or page given by folding sheet six times into 64 leaves (for L *in quarto et sexagesimo*); hence **six'ti-**ETH a. & n. **2.** n. The number ~; *the sixties*, years between 59 & 70 in life or century. [OE *siextig* (-TY²)]

siz'able, a. Of large size; (angling) above prescribed size limit. [SIZE¹, -ABLE]

‖ **siz'ar**, n. Student at Cambridge or Trinity College, Dublin, paying reduced fees & formerly charged with certain menial offices, cf. SERVITOR. Hence ~SHIP n. [foll. = ration, -ER¹ (cf. *scholar*)]

size¹, n., & v.t. & i. **1.** (hist.). Standard of weight or measure for some article esp. of food or drink; ‖ (Camb. Univ.; also siz'ING¹ n.) ration of food or drink from buttery. **2.** Dimensions, magnitude, (*is of vast, diminutive*, ~, very large or small; ~ *matters less than quality*; *are both of a*, i.e. the same, ~; *is the* ~ *of*, i.e. as big as, *an egg*; *what* ~, i.e. how big, *is it?*; *that's about the* ~ *of it*, colloq., a true account of the matter); **one of the usu. numbered**

classes into which things, esp. garments, otherwise similar are divided in respect of ~ (*is made in several* ~*s*; *takes* ~ 7 *in gloves*; *is quite a* ~, *three* ~*s, too big*; OUT ~). **3.** Implement for sizing pearls. **4.** ~*-stick*, shoemaker's measure for taking length of foot; hence (-)SIZED² (-zd) a. **5.** v.t. Group or sort in ~s or according to ~, whence siz'ER¹(2) n.; ~ *up*, estimate ~ of, (colloq.) form judgement of (person etc.); **6.** v.i. ‖ (Camb. Univ.) order ~. [ME, f. OF *sise* aphetic f. *assise* ASSIZE]

size², n., & v.t. **1.** Gelatinous solution used in glazing paper & stiffening textiles & in many manufacturing processes; hence siz'Y² a. **2.** v.t. Glaze or stiffen or treat with ~. [ME, perh. = prec.]

siz'zle, v.i., & n. (colloq.). **1.** Make sputtering sound as in frying. **2.** n. Such noise. [imit.]

sjäm'bŏk (sh-), n., & v.t. **1.** Rhinoceros--hide whip. **2.** v.t. Flog with ~. [Afri-kaans (now *sambok*) f. Malay *chambog* f. Urdu *chābuk*]

skald. See SCALD².

skat (-aht), n. A three-handed card-game popular in Germany. [G, f. It. *scarto* a discard]

skāte¹, n. Kinds of ray-fish, esp. rhom-boidal long-tailed kind. [ME, f. ON *skata*]

skāt|e², n., & v.i. & t. **1.** One of pair of implements, each with steel blade or set of rollers, attached beneath boots & enab-ling wearer to glide in curves over ice or (*roller-*~*e*) hard floor. **2.** vb. Move, per-form (specified figure), on ~*es* (~*e over thin ice*, talk on subject needing tactful treatment); ~*ing-rink*, piece of ice arti-ficially made, or floor reserved, for ~ing; hence ~*'ER¹* n. [17th c. *schates* pl. f. Du. *schaats* (pl. *schaatsen*) f. ONF *escache* stilt]

skean, skēne, skain, n. Gaelic dagger used in Ireland & Scotland; ~*-dhu* (-dōō), dagger stuck in stocking as part of High-land costume. [f. Gael. *sgian* knife, *dubh* black]

skėdăd'dle, v.i., & n. (colloq.). **1.** Run away, disperse in flight. **2.** n. Hurried flight or dispersal. [U.S., of unkn. orig.]

skee. See SKI.

skein (-ān), n. Bundle of yarn or thread or silk made by coiling it many times, drawing it out to the coil's length, & folding it; flock of wild geese etc. in flight; (fig.) tangle, confusion. [ME, f. OF *escaigne*, of unkn. orig.]

skěl'ěton, n. **1.** Hard internal or external framework of bones, cartilage, shell, woody fibre, etc., supporting or contain-ing an animal or vegetable body, whence skěl'ětAL a., skěl'ěto- comb. form, skělětŏG'RAPHY n., etc. **2.** Dried bones of human being or other animal fastened together in same relative positions as in life (~ *at the feast*, something that alloys pleasure, intrusive care; ~ *in the cup-*

board, family ~, discreditable or humiliating fact concealed from strangers); part of anything that remains after its life or usefulness is gone. **3.** Framework or essential part of anything (~ *crew, regiment,* etc., permanent nucleus ready for filling up, cadre; ~ *drill,* with companies etc. represented by two men separated by long rope; ~ *key,* fitting many locks by having interior of bit hollowed; ~ or ~*-face type,* with thin strokes). **4.** Outline sketch, epitome, abstract. **5.** (By exag.) thin person. [f. Gk neut. of *skeletos* dried-up, whence L *sceletus*]

skĕl'ĕtonize, -ise (-ĭz), **v.t.** Reduce to skeleton or abstract by destroying flesh, the tissue between veins of leaves, etc., or by omitting details. [-IZE]

‖ **skĕlp, v.t. & i., & n.** (chiefly Sc.). **1.** Slap, smack; (v.i.) hurry along. **2. n.** (Noise made by) a slap or smack. [ME, prob. imit.]

skene. See SKEAN.

skĕp, skip, n. Kinds, varying locally, of wooden or wicker basket; straw or wicker beehive. [ME, f. ON *skeppa,* rel. to OHG *sceffil* (G *scheffel* bushel)]

skepsis, skeptic, etc. See **sce-.**

skĕ'rry, n. Reef, rocky isle. [f. ON *sker*]

skĕtch, n., & v.t. & i. 1. Preliminary, rough, slight, merely outlined, or unfinished drawing or painting often as experiment for, or memorandum for use in, regular picture; brief account without many details conveying general idea of something, rough draft, general outline; slight play often of musical kind or short descriptive article; musical composition of single movement; ~*-block, -book,* arrangements of drawing-paper leaves for doing series of ~es on; ~*-map,* with outlines but little detail; hence ~'y² a., ~'ĭLY² adv., ~'ĭNESS n. **2. vb.** Make or give ~ of; make ~es esp. of landscape (*went out* ~*ing*); hence ~'ER¹ n. [f. Du. *schets* or G *skizze* f. It. *schizzo,* perh. f. L f. Gk *skhedios* extempore]

skew, a. & n. 1. Oblique, slanting, sideways, distorted, (now chiefly in archit., mech., & math.; ~ *bridge,* with line of arch not at right angles to abutment; ~ *chisel,* with oblique edge; ~ *wheel,* bevel wheel with oblique teeth; ~ *curve,* in three dimensions); (math.) having symmetry distorted by reversal of some element on opposite sides; ~*'back,* sloping face of an abutment on which the extremity of an arch rests; ~*'bald,* (esp. of horse) with irregular patches of white & some colour (prop. not black, cf. *piebald*); ~*-eyed,* squinting; ‖~*-whiff* (colloq. & dial.), askew. **2. n.** Sloping top of buttress; coping of gable; stone built into bottom of gable to support coping. [17th c., rel. to ME *skew* vb ' turn aside ' etc., f. ONF *eskiu(w)er* = OF *eschiver,* see ESCHEW; cf. ASKEW]

skew'er, n., & v.t. 1. Pin of wood or iron

for' holding meat compactly together while cooking; (joc.) sword etc. **2. v.t.** Fasten together, pierce, (as) with ~. [17th c., var. of dial. *skiver,* of unkn. orig.]

ski (skē, shē), **n.** (pl. ~, ~s), **& v.i.** (~*'d* pr. skēd, shēd; ~*ing* pr. skē'ĭng, shē'). **1.** One of pair of wooden runners about 8 ft long & 4 in. broad fastened under feet for travelling over snow esp. in Scandinavia; ~*-joring* (-yēr'ĭng), winter sport in which the skier is towed by a horse. **2. v.i.** Go on ~. [Norw., f. ON *skith* billet, snowshoe]

skiagraphy etc. See **scia-.**

skid, n., & v.t. & i. (-dd-). **1.** Piece of frame or timber serving as buffer, support, inclined plane, etc.; wooden or metal shoe preventing wheel from revolving used as drag (also ~*-pan*), other kinds of wheel-locking contrivance; slip or slide of wheel on muddy ground. **2. vb.** Support or move or protect or check with ~; (of wheel or vehicle) slide forwards or backwards or sideways on slippery ground. [17th c., of obsc. orig.]

skier (skē'er, shē'er), **n.** Person using SKI (cf. SKYER). [-ER¹]

skiff, n. Light rowing or sculling boat. [16th c., f. F *esquif,* Sp., Port. *esquife,* or It. *schifo,* of Gmc orig.]

skif'fle, n. Kind of music played by a ~ *group* (a band accompanying a single singing guitarist or banjoist on a variety of instruments). [perh. imit.]

skil'ful, a. Having or showing skill (*at, in*), practised, expert, adroit, ingenious. Hence ~LY² adv. [foll., -FUL]

skill, n. Expertness, practised ability, facility in doing something, dexterity, tact. [ME, f. ON *skil* distinction, cf. SKILLS]

skilled (-ld), **a.** Having or showing skill, skilful, (rare exc. in phrr. ~ *labour, workman,* etc., = highly-trained, or followed by *in*). [-ED²]

skill'ĕt, n. Small metal pot with long handle & usu. legs used in cooking. [ME, of unkn. orig.]

skill'lĕss, a. (rare). Without skill, knowing nothing *of.* [-LESS]

skills, v.i. 3rd sing. impers. (arch.). *It* ~ *not,* makes no difference, is of no use, (usu. *to do*). [ME, f. ON *skilja* distinguish, or *skila* decide, see SKILL]

‖ **skill'y̆, n.** Thin broth or soup or gruel (usu. of oatmeal & water flavoured with meat). [abbr. f. *skilligalee,* prob. fanciful]

skim, v.t. & i. (-mm-), **& a. 1.** Take scum or cream or floating layer from surface of (liquid), take (cream etc.) from surface of liquid, (~ *the cream off,* often fig., take best part of; ~*ming-dish,* sl., flat-bottomed racing yacht, fast light motor-boat); keep touching lightly or nearly touching (surface) in passing over; (intr.) go, thus *over* or *along* surface, glide along in air; read (t. & i.) superficially, look over cursorily, gather salient facts contained in. **2.** adj. ~ *milk*, from which cream has been ~med. [ME, back form. f. SKIMMER, or f. OF *escumer* f. *escume* f. WG *skūm SCUM]

skimm'er, n. In vbl senses: esp.: ladle etc. for skimming liquids; fast light motor-boat; kinds of water-bird, esp. *black* ~, with flat mandibles. [ME, f. OF *escumoir*, *-eur* (prec.); later f. prec. + -ER¹]

skimp, v.t. & i. Supply (person with or *in* food, money, etc.; material, expenses, etc.) meagrely, stint; be parsimonious. Hence ~'Y² a., ~'ingLY² adv. [19th c.; also 18th c. *skimp* adj. scanty; orig. unkn., cf. SCRIMP]

skin¹, n. **1.** Flexible continuous covering of human or other animal body (*with a whole* ~, unwounded; *save* one's ~, get off safe; *change* one's ~, undergo impossible change of character etc.; *get under* one's ~, colloq., take strong hold on one, interest or annoy one intensely; *would not be in his* ~, should not like to be he; *is only* ~ *& bone*, very thin, & so ~n'Y² a., ~n'INESS n.; *escape with the* ~ *of* one's *teeth*, narrowly; *thick, thin,* ~, imperviousness, sensitiveness, to affront or criticism; *fair, dark,* etc., ~, complexion; *near is my* SHIRT, *nearer my* ~); (anat.) one layer of this (*true* or *inner* ~, derma; *outer* ~, epidermis). **2.** Hide of flayed animal with or without the hair etc.; material prepared from ~s esp. of smaller animals (cf. *hide*). **3.** Vessel for wine or water made of animal's whole ~. **4.** Outer coating of plant, fruit, etc., rind. **5.** Planking or plating of ship or boat inside or outside ribs. **6.** GOLD-*beaters'* ~; ~-*bound*, with ~ tightly stretched over flesh; ~-*deep*, (of wound, also of emotion, impression, beauty, etc.) superficial, not deep or lasting; ~-*diver*, one who dives without a diving-suit, usu. in deep water with AQUALUNG; ~ *effect* (electr.), tendency of high-frequency alternating current to flow through the outer layer only of a conductor; ~-*friction*, lateral resistance to way of ship etc. passing through water; ~'*ful* (of wine etc., or abs.), as much liquor as one can hold; * ~-*game* (sl.), swindle; ~-*grafting*, surgical substitution of ~ cut from another part or person for damaged part. Hence (-)skinnED² (-nd), ~'LESS, aa. [ME, f. ON *skinn*; cf. OHG *scindan* flay]

skin², v.t. & i. (-nn-). Cover (sore etc., usu. *over*) as with skin, (of wound etc.) form or become covered with new skin, cicatrize, (usu. *over*); strip of skin, withdraw skin from, flay, (*keep your eyes* ~*ned*, sl., be watchful or cautious); (colloq.) strip oneself, strip (another), of tight garment such as jersey; (sl.) fleece, swindle; ~'*flint*, niggard, miser. [f. prec.]

skink, n. Kinds of small-limbed lizard. [f. older F *scinc*, or L f. Gk *skingkos*]

skinn'er, n. In vbl senses; esp., (now chiefly in name of a CITY company) dealer in skins, furrier. [-ER¹]

skip¹, v.i. & t. (-pp-), & n. **1.** (Of lambs, kids, children, etc.) jump about, gambol, caper, frisk, move lightly from one foot on to the other; (of children, esp. girls) use ~ping-rope; shift quickly from one subject or occupation to another, be desultory, (usu. *off, from,* etc.); (sl.) make off, disappear; omit, make omissions, in dealing with a series or in reading (*do them all without* ~*ping any* or ~*ping; always* ~ *the descriptions;* ~*s as he reads;* ~ *every tenth row*); ~'*jack*, jumping toy made of bird's merrythought, also kinds of fish & butterfly & beetle named from their movements; ‖ ~*ping-rope*, length of rope with two wooden handles used in girls' game of ~ping; hence ~p'ingLY² adv. **2.** n. ~ping movement, esp. quick shift from one foot to other (HOP³, &c. *jump*). [ME, app. f. Scand., cf. MSw. *skuppa, skoppa* in same sense]

‖ **skip**², n. College servant, scout, esp. at Trinity College, Dublin. [prob. f. obs. *skip-kennel* lackey (prec.)]

skip³, n. Captain or director of side at bowls & curling. [abbr. of SKIPPER²]

skip⁴, n. Cage, bucket, etc., in which men or materials are lowered & raised in mines & quarries. [var. of SKEP]

skip⁵. See SKEP.

skipp'er¹, n. In vbl senses of SKIP¹; esp. (zool.) kind of usu. small brown butterfly. [-ER¹]

skipp'er², n. Sea captain, esp. master of small trading vessel; ~'*s daughters*, (with pun on prec.) tall white-crested waves; captain of an aircraft; (transf.) captain of side in games. [ME, f. MDu. or MLG *schipper* (*schip* SHIP¹, -ER¹)]

skipp'et, n. (hist.). Small cylindrical wooden box used to enclose and protect large seal attached by ribbon to deed. [ME, with var. *skibbet* (now dial.), of unkn. orig.]

‖ **skirl**, v.i., & n. (Make) sound characteristic of bagpipes. [prob. Scand., cf. Norw. dial. *skrylla*]

skir'mish, n., & v.i. **1.** Piece of irregular or unpremeditated fighting esp. between small or outlying parties, slight engagement; encounter of wit, argument, etc. **2.** v.i. Fight in small parties, loose order, or unpremeditated way; hence ~ER¹ n. [ME, f. OF *eskirmir*, also *escremir* f. WG *skirmjan (cf. OHG *scirmen* f. *scirm* shield), see -ISH]

skir'ret, n. Kind of water parsnip formerly much used as table vegetable. [ME *skirwhit*(e), app. alt. f. OF *eschervis*, var. of *carvi* CARAWAY]

skirt, n., & v.t. & i. **1.** Part of coat or shirt that hangs below waist; woman's outer garment shaped like petticoat from waist downwards (*divided* ~, loose trousers resembling ~), whence ~'ING¹(3) n.; (vulg. sl.) woman (esp. in *bit of* ~); edge, border, extreme part, (often pl.; *on the* ~*s of London*, just inside or outside of it); ~ *of beef* etc., the diaphragm & other membranes as cheap food-material; ~-*dance(r)*, -*dancing*, with full ~ waved about giving graceful effects; hence ~ED², ~LESS, aa. 2. vb. Go along or round or past the edge of, be situated along; *as along* coast, wall, etc.; ~*ing* or ~*ing-board*, along bottom of room-wall. [ME, f. ON *skyrta*, corresp. to OE *scyrte* SHIRT]

skit¹, n. Light piece of satire, burlesque, literary squib, (often *upon*). [18th c., rel. to 17th c. *skit*, vb, move lightly & rapidly, perh. f. ON *skyt-* cogn. w. *skjóta* SHOOT]

skit², n. (colloq.). A number, crowd (esp. in pl., heaps, lots). [orig. unkn.]

skitt'er, v.i. (Of wild-fowl) go splashing along water in rising or settling; fish by drawing bait along surface. [app. frequent. of dial. *skite*, perh. f. ON *skýt-* modified stem of *skjóta* shoot; cf. SKIT¹]

skitt'ish, a. (Of horses etc.) nervous, inclined to shy, excitable, playful, fidgety; (chiefly of women) capricious, coquettish, flirting, lively, given to amusement, gadding about, affecting youthfulness. Hence ~LY² adv., ~NESS n. [ME, of obsc. orig., perh. f. ON *skyt-* SKIT¹ + -ISH]

skit'tle, n., & v.t. 1. ‖~*s*, game played with nine pins (~*s* or ~-*pins*) set up at end of ~-*alley* or ~-*ground* to be bowled down with ~-*ball* (*beer* & ~*s*, amusement, as *life is not all beer* & ~*s*); (in full *table* ~*s*) game played with nine pins set up on board to be knocked down by swinging suspended ball; (sl., as int.)~*s!*, rubbish, nonsense. 2. v.t. ~ *out*, (crick.) get (batsmen) out rapidly in succession. [17th c. (also *kittle-pins*), of unkn. orig.]

skive, v.t. Split or pare (hide, leather); grind away surface of (gem). [f. ON *skifa*, rel. to ME *schive* (now dial. *shive*), slice]

skiv'er, n. Knife for skiving leather; thin leather got by skiving. [-ER¹]

‖ skivv'y, n. (colloq.). Female domestic servant (usu. derog.). [alt. f. *slavvy*, SLAVEY]

sku'a, n. Kinds of gull-like predatory sea-bird which pursue other birds and make them disgorge the fish they have caught. [f. ON *skúfr*]

*skŭldŭgg'erў (-g-), sc-, n. (joc.). Trickery; corrupt behaviour. [orig. unkn.]

skŭlk, v.i. Lurk, keep oneself concealed esp. in cowardice or with evil intent, stay or sneak away in time of danger, shirk duty, avoid observation. Hence ~'ER¹ &(in same sense) skŭlk, nn., ~'inGLY² adv. [ME, app. f. Scand., cf. Norw. *skulka* lurk, Da. *skolke*, Sw. *skolka* shirk, play truant]

skŭll, n. Bony case of the brain, frame of the head, cranium, (~ & *cross-bones*, representation of bare ~ with two thigh-bones crossed below it as emblem of death); ~-*cap*, close-fitting cap usu. of velvet worn indoors chiefly by old men, also kinds of plant with helmet-shaped flower. Hence (-)~ED² (-ld) a. [ME *scolle*, of unkn. orig.]

skŭnk, n. Black white-striped bushy-tailed American carnivorous animal about size of cat able to emit powerful stench from liquid secreted by anal glands as defence; its fur; stinking or contemptible fellow. [f. Amer.-Ind. *segankw*, *segongw*]

Skup'shtina (-ōŏp-), n. Jugoslav parliament. [Serb., = assembly]

skў, n., & v.t. 1. (The vault of) heaven (*blue, clear, cloudy, overcast*, etc., ~; *if the* ~ *fall we shall catch larks*, unlikely cataclysms are not worth providing against; *under the open* ~, out of doors; often pl., as *laud to the skies*, highly; *was raised to the skies*, taken up to heaven). 2. Climate, atmosphere, (*try what a warmer* ~, *warmer skies, will do for you*). 3. ~-*blue* a. & n. colour(ed) like clear ~; ~-*born*, poet., of divine birth; ~-*clad*, joc., naked; ~-*high* adv. & a., so as to reach, reaching, the ~; ~'*lark* n., lark that flies spirally upwards singing, v.i. (with pun on LARK¹,², & perh. of naut. orig., w. ref. to clambering about rigging), frolic, play tricks or practical jokes, ballyrag, etc.; ~'*light*, window set in plane of roof or ceiling; ~'*line*, outline of hill etc. defined against ~ (*is on the* ~*line*, seen outlined on ~); ~ *marker*, parachute flare dropped to mark target area; ~ *pilot*, sl., parson; ~-*rocket*, discharged upwards, (v.i., fig., of prices etc.) rise steeply; ~'*sail*, light sail above royal in square-rigged ship; ~-*scape*, picture chiefly representing ~; ~ *scraper*, = ~*sail*, also very tall building, tall chimney, etc.; ~'*way*, airways; ~-*writing*, legible smoke-trails made as advertising method by aeroplane; hence ~'EY², ~'LESS, aa., ~'WARD(S) adv. & a. 4. v.t. Hit (cricket-ball) high up; hang (picture) high on wall, treat picture of (artist) so. [ME *ski(es)* cloud(s) f. ON *sky* (f. *skiuja*), rel. to OE *skio*, OE *sceo*]

Skўe (tĕ'rrier), n. Small long-bodied short-legged long-haired slate or fawn coloured variety of Scotch terrier, named from Skye.

skў'er, n. High hit at cricket (cf. SKIER). [*sky* + -ER¹]

slăb¹, n., & v.t. (-bb-). 1. Thin flat usu. square or rectangular piece of stone or other rigid material; (of timber) outer cut sawn from log; ~-*sided*, long & lank; ~-*stone*, kinds of stone that split readily into ~*s*. 2. v.t. Remove ~*s* from (log, tree) to prepare it for sawing into planks; ~-*bing-gang*, set of saws for doing this. [ME, of unkn. orig.]

‖ slăb², a. (arch.). Viscous, (of liquid) thick & sticky, (chiefly w. ref. to *Macbeth* IV. i. 32). [rel. to *slab* ooze, sludge, app. f. Scand., cf. older Da. *slab* mud, Norw., Sw. *slabb* wet filth]

slabber. = SLOBBER. [16th c., prob. of Du. or LG orig., cf. Du., LG *slabber(e)n*]

slack, a., adv., n., & v.t. & i. **1.** Sluggish, remiss, relaxed, languid, loose, inactive, negligent, (~ *water*, about turn of tide, esp. low tide; ~ *in stays*, naut., slow in going about; *a* ~ *rope*, not taut; *keep a* ~ *hand* or *rein*, ride, or fig. govern, carelessly; ~ *trade*, *business*, *market*, with little doing; ~ *weather*, inclining to indolence); ~ *lime*, slaked lime; hence ~'EN⁶ v.t. & i., ~'LY² adv., ~'NESS n. **2.** adv. (In comb. **w.** *dry*, *bake*, etc.) slowly, insufficiently, (~-*dried hops*; to ~-*bake bread*). **3.** n. part of rope (*haul in the* ~); ~ *time* in trade etc.; (colloq.) spell of inactivity or laziness (*I'm going to have a good* ~ *this afternoon*); (dial.) cheek, impertinence; (pl.) trousers; coal-dust used chiefly for making briquettes etc. **4.** vb. ~en; make loose (rope; often *off*, *away*); (colloq.) take **a** rest, be indolent, whence ~'ER¹ n.; ~ SLAKE (lime); ~ *off*, abate vigour; ~ *up*, reduce speed of train etc. before stopping. [OE *sleac*, *slæc*, adj., = MDu., MLG *slak*, OHG *slach*, ON *slakr*, cogn. w. L *laxus*; the sense 'coal-dust' is of obsc. orig.]

slag, n., & v.i. (-gg-). **1.** Dross separated in fused state in reduction of ores, vitreous smelting-refuse, clinkers; BASIC ~; volcanic scoria; ~-*wool*, = mineral WOOL; hence ~g'Y² (-g-) a. **2.** v.i. Form~, cohere into ~like mass. [16th c., f. MLG *slagge* of obsc. orig.]

slain. See SLAY.

slake, v.t. Assuage, satisfy, (thirst, & rhet. revenge etc.), whence ~'LESS (-kl-) a. (poet.); (also *slack*) combine (lime) chemically with water. [OE *sleac-*, *slacian* f. *slæc* SLACK adj.]

sla'lom (-ah-), n. Ski-race down course defined by artificial obstacles; obstacle race in canoes. [Norw.]

slam, v.t. & i. (-mm-), & n. **1.** Shut (t. & i., of door etc; often *to* adv.) with loud bang; put *down* (object) with similar sound; (sl.) hit, beat, gain easy victory over. **2.** n. Sound (as) of ~med door; gaining of every trick in whist, bridge, etc. (*grand*, *little*, ~, winning of 13, 12, tricks in bridge). [perh. f. Scand., cf. Sw., Norw., Icel. *slamra*]

sla'nder (-ah-), n., & v.t. **1.** False report maliciously uttered to person's injury; uttering of such reports, calumny; (law) false oral defamation (cf. LIBEL, SCANDAL); hence or cogn. ~ous a., ~ously² adv., ~ousness n. **2.** v.t. Utter ~ about, defame falsely; hence ~ER¹ n. [ME *sclaundre* f. AF (OF) *escla(u)ndre*, alt. f. OF *escandle* f. LL SCANDALum]

slang, n., & v.t. **1.** Words & phrases in common colloquial use, but generally considered in some or all of their senses to be outside of standard English; words & phrases either entirely peculiar to or used in special senses by some class or profession, cant, (*racing*, *thieves'*, *artistic*,

schoolboy, etc., ~). **2.** v.t. Use abusive language to. [18th c. cant, of unkn. orig.]

slang'ǀy̆, a. Of the character of, given to the use of, slang. Hence ~iLY² adv., ~iNESS n. [-Y²]

slant (-ah-), v.i. & t., a., & n. **1.** Slope (i. & t.), diverge from a line, lie or go obliquely to a vertical or horizontal line; hence ~'ing² adv. (at right angles); *present* (news) from a particular angle; *(on perpendicular)* ~in(g)dic'ular or ~endic'ular a. **2.** adj. (chiefly poet.). Sloping, inclined, oblique. **3.** n. Slope, oblique position, (*on the* or *a* ~, aslant), whence ~'WISE (-ahntwīz) adv.; ∥ (arch.) indirect censure, disparaging remark; (naut.) *a* ~ *of wind*, favourable breeze; *way of regarding a thing, point of view*. [1 vb: later var. of ME (now dial.) *slent*, f. ON *slenta* (Norw. *slenta*) to slant, slope, prob. infl. by ASLANT; 2 adj.: 17th c. aphetic f. ME *aslonte*, *o-slante* ASLANT adv.; 3 n.: 17th c., goes w. (1) & (2) (cf. Norw. *slent*); relation of forms is obsc.]

slap, v.t. (-pp-), n., & adv. **1.** Strike with palm of hand, smack; (colloq., also ~ *down*) reprimand; (part. as adj. & adv.) very fast, big, good, etc. (*a* ~*ping pace*, *great girl*, *dinner*). **2.** n. Such stroke (~ *in the face* lit., also fig. rebuff, insult). **3.** adv. With the suddenness or effectiveness or true aim of a blow, suddenly, just quite, full, (*ran* ~ *into him*; *hit me* ~ *in the eye*). **4.** ~-*bang*', violently, noisily, headlong; ~*dash*' adv., vehemently, recklessly; ~*dash*, (adj.) impetuous, random, happy-go-lucky, (n.) such action or work, also = ROUGHcast, (v.t.) = ROUGHcast; ~-*happy* (sl.), recklessly happy; ~-*up* a. (sl.), quite up to date, in the latest fashion, with all modern appliances. [17th c.: n. & adv. f. LG *slapp* (imit.); vb f. the E n. or adv.]

slap'jack, n. Kind of pancake cooked on a griddle; = FLAPJACK. [SLAP v. + JACK]

slap'stick, n. Flexible divided lath used by harlequin; (fig.) boisterous low comedy of the roughest kind (also attrib.). [SLAP v. + STICK]

slash, v.i. & t., & n. **1.** Make sweeping or random cut(s) with sword, knife, whip, etc. (~*ing criticism*, with outspoken condemnation); make long narrow gashes in (~*ed sleeve* etc., with slits cut to show lining or puffing of other material); reduce or cut drastically (prices etc.); lash (person etc.) with whip, crack (whip); (mil.) fell (trees) to form abatis. **2.** n. (Wound or slit made by) ~ing cut; debris resulting from the felling or destruction of trees. [ME, perh. f. OF *esclachier* break in pieces]

slat¹, n. Thin narrow piece of wood, esp. used in sets in Venetian blinds, lath. [ME *s(c)lat* f. OF *esclat* splinter etc., rel. to *esclater* burst; cf. SLATE¹]

slat², v.i. & t. (-tt-). (Of sails, cordage,

etc.) flap against mast etc. with reports; strike noisily with or on a surface. [orig. unkn.]

slate¹, n., a., & v.t. **1.** Kinds of grey, green, or bluish-purple rock easily split into flat smooth plates; piece of such plate used as roofing-material; piece of it usu. framed in wood used for writing on with ~-*pencil* or small rod of soft ~ (*clean the* ~, rid oneself of or renounce obligations); ~-*black, -blue, -grey*, modifications of these tints such as occur in ~; || ~-*club*, mutual benefit society with small weekly contributions; ~-*colour*(ed), (of) dark bluish or greenish grey; hence slāt'Y² a. **2.** adj. (Made) of ~. **3.** v.t. Cover with ~s esp. as roofing; hence slāt'ER¹ n. [ME *s(c)late* f. OF *esclate*, fem. of *esclat* SLAT¹]

slate², v.t. (colloq.). Criticize severely (esp. author in reviews), scold, rate; *nominate, propose for office etc. Hence slāt'ING¹(1) n. [app. f. prec.]

slätt'ern, n. Sluttish woman. Hence ~LY¹ a., ~liNESS n. [17th c., rel. to *slattering* (woman etc.) slovenly, f. dial. *slatter* to spill, slop, waste]

slaught'er (-awt-), n., & v.t. **1.** Slaying, esp. of many persons or animals at once, carnage, massacre, (~ *or massacre of the* INNOCENTS); ~-*house*, shambles, place for killing cattle or sheep, place of carnage; hence ~OUS a. (rhet.), ~OUSLY² adv. **2.** v.t. Kill (people) in ruthless manner or on great scale; butcher, kill for food; hence ~ER¹ n. [ME *slahter* f. ON **slahtr* (ON *slátr* butcher-meat), f. *slah*- see SLAY]

Slav (-ahv), n. & a. **1.** One of a people spread over most of Eastern Europe and including Russians, Bulgarians, Illyrians, Poles, Silesians, Pomeranians, Bohemians, etc.; hence ~'OPHIL, ~'OPHOBE, nn. & aa., ~ISM(2, 3) n., (-ahv-). **2.** adj. Of the ~s, Slavonic, Slavonian. [ME *Sclave* f. med. L *Sclavus*, late Gk *Sklabos*, f. Slavonic]

slave, n., & v.i. **1.** Person who is the legal property of another or others and is bound to absolute obedience, human chattel (WHITE¹ ~); helpless victim *to* or *of* some dominating influence (*is a* ~ *to drink, the* ~ *of his wife's caprices*, etc.; *the* ~*s of fashion*); drudge, person of no leisure; mean contemptible person. **2.** ~-*bangle* (of gold, glass, etc., worn by ladies above elbow); ~-*born* (in slavery, *of* ~ parents); ~-*driver*, overseer of ~s at work, (transf.) hard taskmaster; ~-*grown*, (of commodities) produced by ~-*labour*; ~-*holder*, owner of ~s; ~-*hunter*, person who hunts esp. Negroes to sell them as ~s; ~-*ship*, employed in ~-trade; ~ *States* (hist.), southern States of N. America in which slavery prevailed before civil war; ~-*trade*, procuring, transporting, & selling as ~s, of human beings, esp. African Negroes; so ~-*trader*. **3.** v.i. Work like ~, drudge. [ME, f. OF *esclave* = med. L *sclavus, sclava* Slav (captive), see prec.]

slāv'er¹, n. Ship or person engaged in slave-trade. [-ER¹]

slāv'er², v.i. & t., & n. **1.** Let spittle flow from mouth; let one's spittle fall upon (garment etc., or another's cheek in kissing). **2.** n. Spittle running from mouth, (fig.) fulsome or servile flattery; hence ~ȳ¹ [-Y²] a. [ME, app. Scand., cf. Icel. *slafra*, rel. to LG *slabbern* SLABBER, SLOBBER]

slāv'erȳ², n. Condition of a slave; slave-holding; exhausting labour, drudgery. [-ERY]

|| **slāv'ey**, n. (sl.; pl. ~s). Maid-servant, esp. in lodgings or boarding-house. [-Y³]

Sla'vĭc (-ah-), a. & n. (Language) of the Slavs, Slavonic. [-IC]

slāv'ish, a. As of, having the characteristics of, slaves, abject, servile, base, (~ *imitation*, without any attempt at development or originality). Hence ~LY² adv., ~NESS n. [-ISH¹]

Slavōn'ian, a. & n. (Language, member) of the Slav people; (inhabitant) of the former Austrian district Slavonia. [f. med. L *S(c)lavonia* country of Slavs, -AN]

Slavōn'ic, a. & n. (Language) of the Slavs. Hence ~IZE(3) v.t. [as prec., -IC]

*slaw, n. Salad of sliced cabbage. [Du. *sla*, shortened f. *salade* SALAD]

slay, v.t. (*slew* pr. -ōō, *slain*). Kill (chiefly poet., rhet., or joc.; often abs., as *went forth~ing & spoiling*). Hence (-)~'ER¹ n. [OE *slēan*, OS, OHG *slahan*, ON *slá*, Goth. *slahan*]

sleaz'ȳ, a. (Of textiles, & rarely transf.) flimsy; (colloq.) slatternly. [17th c., of unkn. orig.]

slĕd, slĕdge¹, **sleigh** (slā), nn., & vv.i. & t. **1.** Vehicle on runners instead of wheels for conveying loads or passengers esp. over snow, drawn by horses or dogs or reindeer or pushed or pulled by hand, toboggan, (*sled* now little used in England except of structure on runners for dragging loads in agriculture; *sleigh* chiefly of runner-carriage for driving over snow; *sledge* in all senses); *sleigh-bell*, one of the tinkling bells often attached to harness of ~-horse etc. **2.** vv.i. & t. Travel, go, convey, in ~. [14th c. *sled* f. MFlem. or MLG *sledde*; 17th c. *sledge* f. MDu. *sleedse*, rel. to *slede*, whence E dial. *slead*; *sleigh*, orig. U.S., f. Du. *slee*, contr. f. *slede*]

slĕdge², n. (Also ~-*hammer*) blacksmith's large heavy hammer (~-*hammer* often attrib. & fig., as ~-*hammer blows, arguments, style*). [OE *slecg*, = MDu. *slegge*, cogn. w. ON *sleggja*, f. stem of SLAY]

sleek, a., & v.t. **1.** Smooth & soft & glossy (of hair, fur, skin, or animal or person with such hair etc.); hence ~LY² adv., ~NESS n. **2.** v.t. Make ~ esp. by stroking or pressing down. [later var. of SLICK]

sleep¹, n. Bodily condition, normally recurring every night & lasting several hours, in which nervous system is inactive, eyes are closed, muscles relaxed, & consciousness nearly suspended, prolonged similar condition of hibernating animals, (BEAUTY ~; in one's ~, while asleep; *the ~ of the just*, sound; ~ *that knows not breaking*, death; *broken~*, with disturbed intervals; *go to ~*, fall asleep; *fall on ~*, arch., go to ~, fig. die); a period of or single indulgence in ~ (*shall try to get a~*); (fig.) rest, quiet, negligence, death, etc.; ~*-walker*, *-walking*, somnambulist, *-ism*. Hence ~'LESS a., ~'lĕssLY² adv., ~'lĕssNESS n. [OE *slēp*, *slǣp*, OS *slāp*, OHG *slāf*, Goth. *slēps*]

sleep², v.i. & t. (*slĕpt*). 1. Be immersed in sleep, fall or be asleep, (*let ~ing dogs lie*, avoid stirring up trouble; ~ *like a log or top*, soundly; ~ *in*, live in, (Sc.) ~ *late*, *over~* oneself; ~ *on*, *upon*, *over*, a question, leave it till tomorrow). 2. Spend in or affect by ~ing (~ *the hours away*; *slept off his vexation, headache, debauch*). 3. Be inactive or dormant (*sword ~s in the scabbard*; *top ~s*, spins so steadily as to seem motionless; ~*ing partner*, not sharing management). 4. Lie in the grave. 5. Sojourn for the night *at*, *in*, etc.; have sexual intercourse *with*; ~ *around*, be sexually promiscuous. 6. Provide ~ing accommodation for (*lodging-house ~s 300 men*). 7. ~*ing-bag*, for ~ing out of doors in; ~*ing-car(riage)*, railway coach provided with beds; ~*ing-draught*, opiate; ~*ing-*SICKNESS; ~*ing-suit*, pyjamas. [OE *slēpan*, *slæpan*, OS *slāpan*, OHG *slāfan*, Goth. *slēpan*]

sleep'er, n. In vbl senses; also, ‖ wooden beam or piece of other material used as support for rails etc.; = (berth in) SLEEP²-*ing-car*. [ME; -ER¹]

sleep'|ў, a. Drowsy, ready for sleep; habitually indolent, unobservant, etc.; without stir or bustle (*a ~y little town*); (of fruit, esp. pears) insipid & dry with incipient decay; ~*yhead*, ~*y* or inattentive person (esp. in voc.); ~*y* SICKNESS. Hence ~iLY² adv., ~iNESS n. [ME; -Y²]

sleet, n., & v.i. impers. 1. Snow and rain together, or snow melting while falling. 2. vb. *It ~s* etc., ~ *falls*. Hence ~'Y² a., ~'iNESS n. [prob. repr. OE *slet* (f. *slēati-*), rel. to MLG *slōte*, MHG *slōz(e)* (G *schlosse*)]

sleeve, n. 1. Part of garment that covers arm (LAWN¹ ~s; LEG-*of-mutton* ~; *mandarin*~, loose & open below elbow; *laugh in one's* ~, slyly, secretly; *have card, plan*, etc., *up one's* ~, in reserve, concealed but ready for use; *turn, roll, up one's* ~s, prepare to fight or work; *wear one's* HEART *upon* one's ~). 2. Tube enclosing rod or smaller tube. 3. = WIND¹-*sock*. 4. ~*-coupling*, tube for connecting shafts or pipes; ~*-fish*, kind of cuttlefish, squid; ~*-link*, two buttons linked for fastening wristband; ~*-nut*, long nut with right-hand & left-hand screw-threads for drawing together pipes or shafts conversely

threaded; ~*-valve* (in the form of a cylinder with sliding movement). Hence (-)**sleeved²** (-vd), ~'LESS (-vl-), aa. [OE *slieve*, *slȳf*, = NFris. *slēv*, *sliv*]

sleigh. See SLED.

sleight (slīt), n. Dexterity, cunning, deceptive trick or device or movement, (arch.); ~*-of-hand*, juggling, legerdemain, prestidigitation, quickness of hand in fencing etc. [ME *slĕgth* f. ON *slægth* (*slǣgr* SLY, -TH¹)]

slĕn'der, a. Of small girth or breadth, slim, not stout, (~ *stem, waist, pillar, girl, hand*); scanty, slight, meagre, inadequate, relatively small, (~ *hopes, means, store, income, acquaintance with subject, foundations for belief*). Hence ~LY² adv., ~NESS n. [ME *s(c)lendre*, of unkn. orig.]

slept. See SLEEP².

sleuth'hound (-lōō-, -lū-), n. Bloodhound (lit. & fig.); (also *sleuth*, esp. U.S.) detective. [ME *sleuth* f. ON *slóth* track, trail; see SLOT²]

slew¹, **slue**, (slōō), v.t. & i., & n. 1. Turn or swing forcibly or with effort out of the forward or ordinary position (often *round, to the left*, etc.). 2. n. Such change of position. [18th c. naut., of unkn. orig.]

slew². See SLAY.

slice, n., & v.t. & i. 1. Thin broad piece or wedge cut off or out esp. from meat, bread, or cake; share, part taken or allotted, (*a ~ of territory, of the profits*, etc.); kinds of implement with thin broad blade e.g. (also *fish~*) for helping fish, (also ~*-bar*) for clearing furnace-bars of clinker, or for lifting things out of frying-pan etc. 2. vb. Cut (often *up*) into ~s, cut (piece) *off* adv. or prep., go through (air etc.) with cutting motion; make incorrect slicing motion with oar (also trans. ~ *the water*) or golf-club (also trans. ~ *the ball*, hit it a glancing blow so that it curves off to the right of a right-handed player). [ME, f. OF *esclice* splinter, f. *esclicer* f. WG *slitjan*, see SLIT]

slick, a. & adv. (colloq.), & v.t. 1. Dextrous, not marred by bungling, carried smoothly through; superficially or pretentiously smooth and dextrous. 2. adv. Directly, exactly, completely, (*came ~ into the middle of them*; *hit him~ in the eye*; *bowled his middle stump ~ out of the ground*). 3. v.t. Make sleek. Hence *~ER n.*, plausible cheat, (also) waterproof coat. [ME *slike(n)*, f. OE *slice*, *slician*; cf. SLEEK]

slid|e¹, v.i. & t. (*slid*). 1. Progress along smooth surface with continuous friction on same part of object progressing (cf. ROLL; *slid sitting down a grass slope*; *piston ~es noiselessly up & down*), make move thus (~*e the drawer into its place*). 2. Glide over ice on both feet without skates with momentum got by running (~*e over delicate subject*, barely touch upon it); glide, go smoothly along. 3. Take its own course (*let it ~e*). 4. Go unconsciously or by imperceptible degrees (~*es into sin*; ~*e from one note to another* in music). **5.**~*ing door*, drawn across aperture on slide instead of turning on hinges; || ~*ing keel*, CENTRE-board; ~*ing*, ~*e*-, *rule*, graduated, with ~ing part for doing certain mathematical processes automatically; ~*ing scale*, schedule for automatically varying one thing (esp. tax, wages, prices) in direct or inverse proportion to fluctuations of another; ~*ing seat*, mounted on runners esp. in racing boats to lengthen rower's or sculler's stroke. Hence ~'ER¹ (1, 2) n., ~'ABLE a. [OE *slīdan*, older LG *slīden*, MHG *slīten*]

slide², n. **1.** Track on ice made by persons sliding; slope prepared with snow or ice for tobogganing. **2.** Act of sliding. **3.** Inclined plane down which goods etc. slide to lower level, chute. **4.** (Also ~-*way*) part(s) of machine on or between which sliding part works. **5.** Part of machine or instrument that slides, (also ~-*valve*) sliding piece that opens and closes aperture by sliding across it. **6.** Thing slid into place, esp. glass holding object for microscope or magic-lantern picture. [f. prec.]

slight¹ (-it), a. Slender, slim, frail-looking, (*saw a* ~ *figure approaching*; *supported by a* ~ *framework*); *a or some* inconsiderable (*has a* ~ *cold*; *took a* ~ *repast*; *have made a* ~ *inquiry*, *some* ~ *inquiries, into it*); not much or great or thorough, inadequate, scanty, *not* even *the* smallest, (*after* ~ *inquiry*; *did it with* ~ *inconvenience to himself*; *there is not the* ~*est excuse for it*; *a conclusion based on very* ~ *observation*; *a structure raised on* ~ *foundations*; *paid him* ~ *attention*). Hence ~'ISH¹(2) a.,~'LY² adv.. ~'NESS n., (-it-). [ME *slight, sleght*, f. ON **slehtr, sléttr* = OS *sliht*, OHG *sleht*, Goth. *slaihts*]

slight² (-it), v.t., & n. **1.** Treat or speak of (person, branch of study, etc.) as not worth attention, fail in courtesy or respect towards, markedly neglect; hence ~'ingLY² (-it-) adv. **2.** n. Marked piece of neglect, omission of due respect etc., (*put a* ~ *upon*, slight). [f. prec.]

sli'lỹ. Var. of SLYly.

slim, a., & v.i. (-mm-). **1.** Of small girth or thickness, slenderly built, of slight shape; clever in stratagem, crafty, unscrupulous. **2.** v.i. Reduce one's figure by dieting and exercises. Hence ~'LY² adv., ~m'ISH¹(2) a., ~'NESS n. [17th c., f. Du. or LG *slim*, = MHG *slim* (G *schlimm*) crooked, bad, etc.]

slime, n., & v.t. & i. **1.** Fine oozy mud or other substance of similar consistence, e.g. liquid bitumen or mucous exudation of fish etc.; ~-*gland* in molluscs etc., secreting ~; ~-*pit*, of liquid bitumen. **2.** vb. Cover with ~ (esp. of snake preparing prey for gorging); || (sl.) get *through, away, past, out of it*, etc., by physical or moral slipperiness. [OE *slīm*,

MDu.; MLG, MHG *slīm*, ON *slīm*, prob. cogn. w. L *limus* mud]

slim'lỹ, a. Of the consistence of slime; covered or smeared with or full of slime; slippery, hard to hold; cringingly dishonest; repulsively meek or flattering. Hence ~iLY² adv., ~iNESS n. [ME : -Y²]

sling¹, v.t. & i. (*slŭng*), & n. **1.** Throw (rare; ~ *ink*, sl., be an author or journalist, write); hurl (stone etc.) from ~, use ~, whence ~'ER¹ n.; suspend with ~, allow to swing suspended, arrange so as to be supported from above, hoist or transfer with ~; ~ one's HOOK¹; ~-*cart*, in which load is slung from axletree; *slung shot*, metal ball attached by thong etc. to wrist & used esp. by criminals as weapon. **2.** n. Strap or string used with the hand to give impetus to small missile; kinds of apparatus used to support hanging weight, e.g. injured arm, rifle, ship's boat, goods being transferred; ~-*dog*, one of pair of hooks used to grapple goods for hoisting. [vb f. ON *slyngva*; n. app. f. LG or Scand.]

sling², n. (chiefly U.S.). Kind of toddy (esp. *gin*-~). [orig. unkn.]

slink¹, v.i. (*slŭnk* or rarely *slank, slunk*). Go in secretive manner or with guilty or ashamed or sneaking air (usu. *off, away, by*, etc.). Hence ~'Y² a., gracefully slender and flowing, sinuous. [OE *slincan* = LG *slinken*]

slink², v.t. & i., & n. **1.** (Of animal) miscarry, produce (young, or abs.) prematurely. **2.** n. Animal, esp. calf, so born; its flesh; ~-*butcher*, who deals in ~. [app. = prec.; cf. *cast, sling*]

slip¹, v.i. & t. (-pp-). **1.** Slide unintentionally for short distance, lose footing or balance or place by unintended sliding, (~*ped in the mud* or *over the edge and fell*; *blanket* ~*ped off bed*; *foot* ~*s out of stirrup, ring off finger*). **2.** Go with sliding motion (*as the door closes the catch* ~*s into place*; ~ *along*, sl., go at great speed; ~ *into*, sl., pummel, belabour, eat heartily of). **3.** Escape restraint or capture by being slippery or hard to hold or by not being grasped (*eel, opportunity*, ~*ped through his fingers*; *let reins* ~ *out of his hands*; *let* ~ *the dogs of war*, poet., begin war). **4.** Make way unobserved or quietly or quickly (*how time* ~*s away!*; ~ *by, past*; ~ *out of the room*; ~ *off* or *away*, depart without leave-taking etc.; *just* ~ *across to the baker's*; *errors will* ~ *in*). **5.** Make careless mistake (~*s now & then in his grammar*); deteriorate, lapse; ~ *up* (colloq.), fail, make a mistake. **6.** Let go from restraint of some kind (~ *greyhounds*, from leash; ~ *anchor*, detach ship from it; *cow* ~*s its calf*, produces it prematurely). **7.** Pull (garment etc.) hastily *on, off*. **8.** Insert stealthily or casually or with gliding motion (~*ped half a crown into the porter's hand, a white powder into her glass, the papers into his pocket, a marker between*

U

the pages). **9.** Escape from, give the slip to, (*dog* ~*s his collar, prisoner his guard*; *the point had* ~*ped my attention*). **10.** ~*ped disc*, layer of cartilage between vertebrae that has ~ped from its place. [ME, prob. f. MLG *slippen*, ≈ OHG *slipfan*; cf. SLIPPERY]

slip², n. **1.** Act of slipping, blunder, accidental piece of misconduct, (*a* ~ *on a piece of orange-peel may be fatal*; *there's many a* ~ *'twixt the cup & the lip*, nothing is certain till it has happened; *give one the* ~, escape from him; ~ *of the tongue, pen*, thing said or written accidentally for something else; *a few* ~*s in youth are inevitable*). **2.** Kinds of loose covering or garment, e.g. pillow-case, under-bodice, petticoat, pinafore. **3.** Leash for slipping dogs, device for suddenly loosing clip or attachment. **4.** Artificial slope of stone as landing-stage; inclined plane on which ships are built or repaired. **5.** Long narrow strip of thin wood, paper, etc.; printer's proof on such paper (see GALLEY). **6.** Cutting taken from plant for grafting or planting, scion (*a* ~ *of a boy*, slim boy). **7.** One of the fielders (*short, long*, ~) stationed for balls glancing off bat to off side behind batsman; (sing. or pl.) this part of ground (*was caught in the* ~*s or at* ~). **8.** (Without pl. or article) semifluid clay for coating or making pattern on earthenware. **9.** (theatr.; pl.) Part from which scenes are slipped on, part where actors stand before entering. **10.** pl. Bathing-drawers. **11.** Small sole (flat-fish). **12.** Loss of distance travelled by aircraft arising from nature of medium in which its propeller revolves. [chiefly f. prec.; sense 8 f. OE *sly(p)pe* (cf. COWSLIP); senses 5, 6, 11 app. f. MDu. or MLG *slippe* cut, strip, etc.]

slip-, the stem of SLIP¹ in comb.: ‖ ~-*carriage, -coach*, railway carriage on express for casting loose at station where rest of train does not stop; ~-*cover*, of calico etc. for furniture out of use; ~-*galley*, long narrow tray for holding composed type; ~-*hook*, with contrivance for loosing it readily at need; ~-*knot*, that can be undone by a pull, also knot that slips up & down string & tightens or loosens loop; ~-*road*, minor & local by-pass; ~-*rope*, with both ends on board so that casting loose either end frees ship from moorings; ~'*shod*, having shoes down at heel, slovenly, (fig., of speech, writing, speaker, writer, method of work, etc.) negligent, careless, unsystematic, casual, loose in arrangement; ~'*slop*, ≈ ~*shod* (fig.), (as n.) ~shod writing etc., also (as redupl. of *slop*) washy stuff lit. or fig., weak drink, slops, sentimental talk or writing; ~-*stream*, stream of air driven astern by aircraft's propeller(s); ~-*up* n. (colloq.), blunder; ~'*way*, shipbuilding or landing slip.

slipp'er, n., & v.t. **1.** Loose comfortable indoor shoe (HUNT¹-*the-*~; *bed-*~, ~-shaped BED¹-pan), whence ~ED²(-*erd*) a.; skid or shoe placed under wagon-wheel as drag; person who slips greyhounds in coursing-match; ~-*bath*, shaped like ~, with covered end; ~*wort*, calceolaria. **2.** v.t. Chastise (child etc.) with ~; hence ~ING¹(1) n. [ME; -ER¹]

slipp'er|y̆, a. (Of ground) hard to stand on, causing slips by its smoothness or muddiness, (fig., of subject) requiring tactful handling; (of object or person) hard to hold firmly owing to polish or sliminess or elusive motion, (fig.) unreliable, incalculable, shifty, unscrupulous. Hence ~iLY² adv., ~iNESS n. [alt. (perh. after LG *slipperig*) f. (now dial.) *slipper* (OE *slipor*)+-Y²]

slipp'y̆, a. Slippery (colloq.); *look or be* ~ (sl.), look sharp, make haste. [-Y²]

slit, v.t. & i. (*slit*), & n. **1.** Cut or (t. & i.) tear lengthwise, make long incision or rent in, cut into strips, (*threatened to* ~ *his nose, tongue*, etc.; ~ *one's weasand*, cut his throat; ~ *hide into thongs, sheet of metal into strips or rods*; *if you strain it too hard it will* ~; *has* ~ *my coat-sleeve from shoulder to wrist*); ~*ting-rollers*, ribbed pair fitting into each other & ~*ting* metal sheet by pressure. **2.** n. Long incision; long narrow opening comparable to cut (*a* ~ *is provided for the coin to drop through*; *the windows are mere* ~*s*; *the* ~*s on the neck are gill-openings*); ~*trench*, narrow trench for soldier or weapon. [ME *slitte*, rel. to OE *slitan* (dial. *slite*), OHG *sliz(z)an* (G *schleissen*), ON *slita*; cf. SLICE]

slith'er (-dh-), v.i. (colloq.). Slide unsteadily, go with irregular slipping motion. [ME var. of (now dial.) *slidder* (cf. *hither*) f. OE *slid(e)rian* frequent. f. *slid-*, weak grade of *slid-* SLIDE]

sliv'er, n., & v.t. & i. **1.** Piece of wood torn from tree or tree, splinter (esp. of exploded shell), (vb, break t. & i. off as ~, break t. & i. up into ~s). **2.** (In fishing) side of small fish cut off as bait (vb, cut ~s from). [ME, f. (now dial.) *slive* cleave (OE **slifan*)+-ER¹]

slobb'er, v.i. & t., & n. **1.** Run at the mouth in infantile helplessness or maudlin emotion; wet (clothes, other person in kissing) with saliva; do (task) badly, botch, bungle. **2.** n. Running saliva; maudlin talk, emotion, or kisses; hence ~Y² a., ~iNESS n. [rel. to SLABBER, SLUBBER; cf. Du. *slobberen*]

slob'ice, n. (Newfoundland). Floating ice mixed with snow. [*slob* var. of *slab* mud, cf. SLAB²]

sloe, n. (Small bluish-black wild plum, fruit of) BLACK¹*thorn* (~-*gin*, liqueur of ~s steeped in gin). [OE *slā(h)*, MDu., MLG *slee*, OHG *slēha*]

‖ **sloe-worm**. Var. of SLOW-WORM.

slŏg, v.i. & t. (-gg-), & n. **1.** Hit (i. & t.) hard & wildly esp. in boxing & at cricket;

slogan walk or work doggedly (usu. *on*, *away*); hence ~g'ER¹ (-g-) n. 2. n. Hard random hit. [orig. unkn.; cf. SLUG²]

slog'an, n. Highland war-cry; party cry, watchword, motto; short catchy phrase used in advertising. [f. Gael. *sluagh-ghairm* (*sluagh* host, *gairm* outcry)]

sloid, sloyd, n. A system (orig. Swedish) of manual training, esp. by means of wood-carving, used in schools. [f. Sw. *slöjd*, corresp. to ON *slœgth* SLEIGHT]

sloop, n. Small one-masted fore-&-aft-·rigged vessel with mainsail & jib, & usu. gaff topsail & forestaysail; ‖ small war-ship used for general purposes & esp. for police work on foreign stations; ‖ ~ *of war* (hist.), cutter-rigged ship mounting guns; ~-*rigged*, rigged like ~. [17th c., f. Du. *sloep*, older *sloepe*, LG *slûp*(*e*), whence F *chaloupe*; see SHALLOP]

sloot. Var. of SLUIT.

slop¹, n. (in pl. only), & v.i. & t. (-pp-). 1. (Pl.) dirty water or liquid, waste contents of kitchen or bedroom vessels; (pl.) liquid food, as broth, gruel, etc., non-alcoholic drinks; ~-*basin*, for receiving dregs of cups at table; ~-*pail*, for removing bed-room ~s. 2. vb. Spill (i. & t.), (allow to) flow over edge of vessel, (often *over*, *out*); make mess with ~s (or with ~s as subj.) upon (clothes, floor); ~ *over* (fig.), gush, be maudlin. [earlier ' slush ', prob. repr. OE *sloppe*, rel. to *slyppe*; see SLIP²(8)]

slop², n. (in pl. only). (Arch.) wide knickerbockers; ready-made clothing, clothes & bedding supplied to sailors in navy; ~-*room*, from which ~s are issued aboard ship; ~-*seller*, -*shop*, of ready-·made clothes. [ME; cf. OE *overslop* surplice, MDu. (*over*)*slop*, OIcel. *sloppr* gown]

‖ **slop³**, n. (sl.). Policeman. [f. *ecilop*, back sl. for *police*]

slope, n., & v.i. & t. 1. Inclined position or direction, the having of one end or side at higher level than the other, difference in level between two ends or sides of thing, the lying in a line neither parallel nor perpendicular to level ground or a line serving as standard, (*there is always a certain* ~ *in a ship's deck*; *cut this side straight & the other with a* ~ *to the right*; *the whole* ~ *may amount to 2 ft*); piece of rising or falling ground, incline; position of soldier with rifle ~d (*come to the* ~); hence ~'WISE (-pwiz) adv. 2. vb. Have or show ~, lie or tend obliquely esp. to ground level, slant esp. up or down, whence **slop'ing**LY² adv.; place or arrange or make in or at a ~ (~ *arms*, place rifle at a ~ over shoulder; *must* ~ *the sides of the pit*); (sl.) make *off*, go away, also saunter, walk about. [n. (17th c.) aphetic f. ASLOPE; vb (16th c.) f. (now poet.) *slope* adj. (16th c.) f. as n.]

slopp'|ȳ, a. (Of road) wet with rain, full of puddles; (of floor, table, etc.) wet with slops, having water etc. spilt on it; (of work) unsystematic, not thorough; (of sentiment or talk) weakly emotional, maudlin. Hence ~ILY³ adv., ~iNESS n, [SLOP¹, -Y²]

slosh, n., & v.t. 1. = SLUSH. 2. v.t. (sl.)· Beat, thrash. [see SLUSH]

slot¹, n., & v.t. (-tt-). 1. Groove, channel, slit, or long aperture, made in machine etc. to admit some other part, esp. slit for penny or other coin that sets working a ~-*machine* or automatic retailer of small wares; stage trapdoor. 2. v.t. Provide with ~(s). [f. OF *esclot* hollow of the breast, of unkn. orig.]

slot², n. Track of deer etc. esp. as shown by footprints. [f. AF & OF *esclot* 'hoof-·print prob. f. ON *slóth*, trail, cf. SLEUTH-·HOUND]

sloth, n. 1. Laziness, indolence, whence ~'FUL a., ~'fuLLY² adv., ~'fuLNESS n. 2. Kinds of S.-Amer. mammal with curved long-clawed feet living entirely in trees & capable only of very slow motion on ground. 3. ~-*bear*, large-·lipped black shaggy honey-eating bear of India & Ceylon; ~-*monkey*, kind of loris. [ME *slowthe* (SLOW, -TH¹)]

slouch, v.i. & t., & n. 1. Droop, hang down negligently; go or stand or sit with loose ungainly attitude; bend one side of brim of (hat) downwards (opp. *cock*); hence ~'inGLY² adv. 2. n. ~ing attitude or walk, stoop, downward bend of hat-brim (opp. *cock*); (sl.) incompetent or slovenly worker or operator or per-formance (esp. *is no* ~ *at, this show etc. is no* ~); ~ *hat*, with ~ed brim. [16th c., of unkn. orig.; cf. dial. *slouk*, Norw. *slôk*, Icel. *slókr*; vb app. f. n.]

slough¹ (slow), n. Quagmire, swamp, miry place, (*the S*~ *of Despond*, state of hopeless floundering in sin). Hence ~'y¹ [-Y²] (-owi) a. [OE *slôh*, of unkn. orig.]

slough² (slŭf), n., & v.i. & t. 1. Snake's cast skin, any part that an animal casts or moults; dead tissue that drops off from living flesh etc.; (fig.) habit etc. aban-doned; hence ~'y² [-Y²] (slŭf) a. 2. vb. Drop off (t. & i.; often *off*, *away*, esp. in intr. sense) as ~; cast off ~. [ME *slo*(*u*)*h*, perh. rel. to LG *sluwe*, *slu* husk]

Slov'ăk, n. & a. (Member) of a formerly Hungarian Slavic people. [Slovak & Czech]

slo'ven (-ŭv-), n. Personally untidy or dirty, careless & lazy, or unmethodical person. Hence ~LY¹ a., ~liNESS n., ~LY² adv. (arch.), ~RY n., (-ŭv-). [ME, perh. an AF formation on Flem. *sloef* dirty, or Du. *slof* careless]

Slovēne' (*or* slōv-), n., Sloven'ian, a. & n. (Member) of a southern Slavic people in Jugoslavia; (-*ian*) language of the Slo-venes. [G, f. OSlav. (*slovo* word), whence also SLAV]

slow (-ō), a., adv., & v.i. & t. 1. Not quick, deficient in speed, taking a long time to

traverse a distance or do a thing, (~ &
steady wins the race; ~ & sure, haste is
risky; ~ march, of troops in funeral procession etc.; ~ music), gradual (~ growth,
progress), whence ~LY² (-ŏlī) adv.; tardy,
reluctant, lingering, (was not ~ to defend
himself), not hasty or easily moved (is ~
to anger); (of clock etc., usu. pred.) behind
correct time (is 20'~); dull-witted, stupid,
(is ~ of speech, of wit); deficient in interest
or liveliness, dull, tedious, (entertainment
was voted ~); (of a photographic lens)
of small aperture (and so necessitating
long exposure); (of surfaces) tending to
cause ~ness (a ~ pitch, tennis-court,
billiard-table); ~coach, person~ in action,
dull of wit, or behind the times in opinions
etc.; ~match, ~-burning for igniting
explosives; ~motion, (attrib., of a film)
with the number of exposures per second
greatly increased (~ing down the motion
when projected at the normal rate);
~worm, see foll.; hence ~'NESS (-ŏn-) n.
2. adv. (~er, ~est). At ~ pace, ~ly,
(being ousted by ~ly, but still common
when the adv. & not the vb gives the
essential point, as how ~ he climbs!,
please read or go~ or ~er, watch goes~,
cf. I saw a man climb ~ly up; placed
always after vb exc. in excl. with how or
in comb. with part. as ~-going, -moving).
3. vb. Reduce one's speed, reduce speed
of (train, ship, etc.), (usu. down, up, off).
[OE slāw, OS slêu, OHG slêo, ON slǽr,
sljár f. Gmc *slaiwaz]

slow-worm (slŏ´wĕrm), n. Small harmless reptile between snakes & lizards,
blindworm. [OE slā-wyrm; first element
obsc., cf. MSw. slā, Norw. slo, etc., slow
-worm]

sloyd. See SLOID.

slub, n., & v.t. (-bb-). 1. Wool slightly
twisted as preparation for spinning.
2. v.t. Twist thus. [orig. unkn.]

slubb'er, v.t. & i. Do carelessly or bung-
lingly; slaver, slobber. [16th c., prob. f.
Du. or LG, cf. LG slubbern; cf. SLOBBER]

sludge, n. Thick greasy mud; sewage.
Hence slŭdg'Y² a. [see SLUSH]

slue. See SLEW¹.

slug¹, n., & v.i. (-gg-). 1. Kinds of shell-
less snail destructive to small plants;
(vb) collect & destroy ~s in garden etc.
2. Bullet of irregular shape; roundish
lump of metal; line of type in linotype
printing. [ME slugg(e) sluggard, perh.
f. Scand.; cf. Norw. dial. sluggje heavy
slow person, Sw. dial. slogga be slow]

*slug², v.t. & i. (-gg-), & n. = SLOG. [orig.
unkn., cf. SLOG]

slug'-abèd, n. (arch.). Person who lies
late in bed. [f. slug vb (foll.) +ABED]

slug'gard, n. Lazy sluggish person.
[ME, f. slug vb be slothful (perh. f. Scand.,
see SLUG¹)+-ARD]

slug'gish (-gĭ-), a. Inert, inactive, torpid,
indolent, slow-moving, (a ~ stream, circulation, temper, person). Hence ~LY² adv.,

~NESS n. [ME, f. SLUG¹ or slug vb (see
prec.)+-ISH¹]

sluice (-ōōs), n., & v.t. & i. 1. (Also ~-
-gate, -valve) sliding gate or other contrivance for changing level of a body of
water by controlling flow into or out of it,
floodgate; water above or below or issuing
through floodgate; (also ~-way) artificial
water-channel; a rinsing. 2. vb. Provide
with ~(s); flood with water from ~;
rinse; pour or throw water freely upon;
(of water) rush out etc. (as) from ~. [ME,
f. OF escluse f. LL exclusa, sclusa floodgate (orig. fem. p.p. see EXCLUDE)]

sluit (-ōōt), slōōt, n. (S. Africa). Narrow
water-channel. [Du. sloot ditch]

slum¹, n., & v.i. (-mm-). 1. Overcrowded
and squalid back street or court or alley
or district in city. 2. v.i. Go about the
~s to visit or examine condition of
inhabitants; hence ~m'ER¹ n. [c. 1800,
cant wd of unkn. orig.]

slum², n. Non-lubricating part of crude
oil; gummy residue formed in lubricating
oil during use. [orig. unkn.]

slum'ber, v.i. & t., & n. Sleep (distinguished in sense only by an implication
of comfort or ease, which is not invariable,
e.g. fell into a troubled ~; & in use by a
rhet. or poet. tinge; the n. is often in pl.,
as his ~s were interrupted by a knock); ~
away, waste (time) in ~; ~-wear (shop),
pyjamas. Hence slŭm'b(e)rous a.,
slŭm'b(e)rously² adv., ~ER¹ n. [ME
slūmeren, slombre, etc., f. slūmen vb or slūme
n. (OE slūma)+-ER⁵; -b- as in NUMBER; cf.
MDu. slummeren, MHG slum(m)ern]

slumm'ock, v.t. & i. (colloq.). Swallow
greedily, wolf down; move or speak in
awkward disorderly way. [var. of dial.
slommack, slammack]

slump, n., & v.i. 1. Sudden or rapid
or great fall in prices or values, or
diminution of demand for commodity or
interest taken in subject or undertaking.
2. v.i. Undergo ~, fall in price, fall
through, fail utterly; subside limply (he
~ed into a chair). [in 17th c. 'fall into a
bog', prob. imit., cf. PLUMP²]

slung. See SLING¹.

slunk. See SLINK¹.

slur, v.t. & i. (-rr-), & n. 1. Write (t. & i.)
or pronounce (t. & i.) indistinctly with
letters or sounds running into one another; (mus.) perform legato, mark
(notes) as to be so performed; pass (fault,
fact, etc.) lightly over, conceal or minimize; (arch.) put~ upon (person, character), make insinuations against. 2. n.
Imputation, blame, stigma, (he put a ~
upon me; it is no ~ upon his reputation
that he should have or to say that); piece
of ~ring in handwriting, pronunciation,
or singing; curved mark used in music-
-writing to show that two or more notes
are to be sung to one syllable or played
or sung legato. [17th c., f. 15th c. (now
dial.) slur thin mud, of unkn. orig.]

slŭ′rrў, n. Liquid mixture of materials for Portland cement manufacture; sticky muddy residue separated from coal at the pithead washing plants; semi-fluid mixture of ganister and fire-clay used in repairing converter-linings etc. [rel. to prec.]

slŭsh, n. Watery mud or thawing snow (cf. SLUDGE); (fig.) silly sentiment. Hence ~′ɣ² a. [f. 17th c., w. varr. *sludge* & *slutch*, also 19th c. *slosh*; orig. unkn.]

slŭt, n. Slovenly woman, slattern; (joc.) girl. Hence ~t′ERY(4) n., ~t′ISH¹ a., ~t′ishLɣ² adv., ~t′ishNESS n. [ME; orig. unkn.]

slȳ, a. (~*er*, ~*est*). Cunning, wily, hypocritical; practising concealment (~ *dog*, person who keeps his peccadilloes or pleasures quiet), done etc. in secret (*on the* ~, privately, without publicity); knowing, arch, bantering, insinuating, ironical; ~′*boots*, ~ person (in playful use, esp. to or of child or animal). Hence ~′Lɣ² adv., ~′NESS n. [ME *slēgh* f. ON *slǣgr* cunning, orig. ' able to strike ' f. *slōg*- pret. stem of *slā* SLAY; cf. SLEIGHT]

slȳpe, n. Covered way or passage from cathedral transept to chapter-house. [cf. WFlem. *slipe*, *slijpe* secret path]

smăck¹, n. & v.i. 1. Flavour, taste that suggests presence of something; barely discernible amount of some food-material etc. or of a quality etc. present in dish or person's character, tinge, tincture, spice, dash, of, (has a ~ *of ginger, of the cask, in it, of recklessness, of the old Adam, in him*). 2. v.i. Have a slight curious or unexpected or secondary taste (rare); taste slightly *of*, suggest by taste or otherwise the presence or effects *of*, (*wine* ~*ing of the cork; his manner* ~*ed of superciliousness*). [OE *smæc*, = MDu., OHG *smac*; vb f. n.]

smăck², n., v.t. & i., & adv. 1. Slight explosive report of surface struck with palm, of lips parted suddenly, or of whip cracked; blow with palm, slap; hard hit at cricket; loud kiss (*gave her a hearty* ~); *have a* ~ *at* (colloq.), make trial of (something), have a go at. 2. vb. Slap (person's face etc.) with palm; part (t. & i. of lips) noisily in eager anticipation or enjoyment of food or other delight; crack (t. & i. of whip). 3. adv. (colloq.). With a ~, in sudden direct violent way, outright, exactly, (*went* ~ *through windows, into ditch; hit him* ~ *on the nose*). [16th c., prob. imit.; cf. MDu. *smak*, MDu., MLG *smacken*]

smăck³, n. Sloop esp. for fishing; ~s² *man*, sailor on ~. [f. Du. *smak*, earlier *smacke*, LG *smak(ke)*]

smăck′er, n. (sl.). Loud kiss; sounding blow; ‖ large or remarkable specimen of anything; *dollar. [SMACK², -ER¹]

small (-awl), a., n., & adv. 1. Not large, of deficient or comparatively little size or strength or power or number, consisting

of minute units (~ *rain*), (of agent) not doing thing on large scale, (usu. without emotional implications of LITTLE, e.g. not *a dear* ~ *pony* or *a dirty* ~ *scoundrel*; ~ *farmer, shopkeeper*, on ~ scale; *has a* ~ *voice*; ~ FRY¹; ~ HOURS; ~ *& early*, party with few guests & not kept up late; *the still* ~ *voice*, conscience; *coat is* ~ or *too* ~ *for me*; ~ *craft*, boats; *came in* ~ *numbers; this beer is very* ~, weak, watery). 2. (As distinctive epithet) of the ~er kind (~*-sword*, rapier or sword for thrusting only; ~ *beer*, arch., of light kind; *think no* ~ *beer of oneself*, be conceited; *chronicle* ~ *beer*, talk of trifles as important; *look, feel*, ~, be humiliated; ~ *change*, copper & silver coins, (transf.) trivial remarks; ~ *gross*, ten dozen; ~*-ARM²s*, portable fire-arms; ~ *letters*, not capitals; ~ *capitals*, of less height than the fount's regular capitals; ~ *pica*, size of TYPE; ~ *hand*, ordinary writing, opp. *text-hand*; ‖~ *debt*, not above largest amount recoverable in county court; ~*-clothes*, arch., knee-breeches; ‖~ *holding*, piece of land between one and fifty acres in extent let or sold by a county council to a ~ *holder* for cultivation. 3. Not much of (*& ~* blame to him, *& ~* wonder, comments on conduct etc. just described; *there was no* ~ *excitement about it; has* ~ *Latin*, knows little of it). 4. Unimportant, trifling, (~ *talk*, ordinary society conversation; *the* ~ *worries of life; is great in* ~*matters*). 5. Socially undistinguished, poor, obscure, humble, (*great & ~*, all classes; *lives in a* ~ *way*, unpretentiously; *have experimented with radium in a* ~ *way*; ~ *people love to talk of great*). 6. Morally mean, ungenerous, petty, paltry, (*his* ~ *spiteful nature; only a* ~ *man would think of that at such a time; I call it* ~ *of him to remind me of it*), whence ~′mīnd′ED² a. 7. ~′*pox*, highly contagious & fatal disease with fever & pustules; hence ~′ISH¹(2) a., ~′NESS n., (-awl-). 8. n. *The* slenderest part of something, esp. ~ *of the back*, hinder part of waist; ‖ (pl., at Oxford) former responsions; ‖ (pl., colloq.) ~ articles of laundry. 9. adv. SING ~. [OE *smæl*, OS, OHG *smal*, ON *smalr*, Goth *smals*]

small′age (-awl-), n. Wild celery. [ME, f. SMALL +obs. *ache* f. OF *ache* f. L f. Gk *apion* parsley]

smalt (-awlt), n. Glass coloured blue with cobalt; pigment made by pulverizing this. [F, f. It. *smalto* f. Gmc, cogn. w. SMELT¹]

‖ **smärm′ў, a.** (colloq.). Unctuously ingratiating, fulsome. [f. *smarm* var. of dial. *smalm* smooth down (as with grease), -ɣ²]

smärt¹, v.i., & n. 1. (Of person or part of him, or of wound lit. or fig. or the missile or insult etc. that has inflicted it) feel or give acute pain, rankle, (*my finger* ~s; *rushed off* ~*ing with nettle-stings, under disappointment*, etc.; *with the gibe yet*

~*ing in his brain*; ~ *for*, be paid out for, suffer consequences of, esp. as threat *you shall* ~ *for this*). **2.** *n.* Bodily or mental sharp pain, stinging sensation. **3.** ~-*money*, paid or exacted as penalty or compensation; ~'*weed*, the water-pepper. [vb f. OE *smeortan* = MDu., LG *smerten*, OHG *smerzan*; *n.* ME, app. f. OE *smiertu* f. smeart adj. (foll.)]

smart[2], *a.* **1.** Severe, sharp, vigorous, lively, brisk, (*gave him a* ~ *rap over the knuckles*; *had a* ~ *skirmish, walk, bout of toothache*; *went off at a* ~ *pace*). **2.** Clever, ingenious, showing quick wit or ingenuity, keen in bargaining, quick to take advantage, (*a* ~ *talker, retort, saying, device, invention*; *a* ~ *officer, servant, lad*, ready & intelligent; ~ *dealing*, selfishly clever to verge of dishonesty); unscrupulously clever; •~ *alec(k)*, a would-be clever person. **3.** Bright & fresh in appearance, spruce, in perfect order or repair, in gay or fashionable clothes, well groomed, showing bright colours or new paint, (~ *clothes, a* ~ *garden; person, house, ship, looks quite* ~). **4.** Conspicuous in society, leading the fashion, stylish, (~ *people; the* ~ *set*). Hence ~'EN[5] *v.t.* & *i.*, ~'LY[2] *adv.*, ~'NESS *n.* [OE *smeart*, rel. to *smeortan* (prec.)]

smash, *v.t.* & *i.*, *n.*, & *adv.* **1.** Break (*t.* & *i.*) utterly to pieces (often *up*), shatter, bash *in* with crushing blow, (*a* ~*ing blow*, of irresistible force); utterly rout & disorganize (enemy); hit (lawn-tennis ball) downwards over net with great force; (of business firm) break, go bankrupt, come to grief; (of vehicle etc.) crash *into* another or an obstacle; (sl.) utter false coin; ~-*and-grab raid* (in which thief ~es shop-window· and grabs valuables behind it). Hence~'ING[2]*a.* (sl.), unusually good, superlative. **2.** *n.* Breaking to pieces; violent fall or collision or disaster (*go to* ~, be spoilt or disorganized or ruined); ~ing stroke in lawn tennis (see vb); violent blow with fist etc.; bankruptcy, series of commercial failures; drink of spirit & water·iced & flavoured (usu. *brandy*~); ~-*hit* (sl.), success; ~-*up*, complete ~. **3.** *adv.* (With vbs of motion) with a ~ (*went* ~ *into a goods train*). [prob. imit.]

smash'er, *n.* In vbl senses; esp. (sl.), someone or something excellent, convincing argument or smashing blow or heavy fall. [-ER[1]]

‖ **smatch**, *n.* (now rare). **=** SMACK[1] *n.* [ME var. of SMACK[1] *n.*]

smatt'er|ing, *n.* Slight superficial knowledge of a language or subject. So ~ER[1] *n.* [f. ME *smatter* talk ignorantly, prate, of unkn. orig.]

smaze, *n.* Mixture of smoke and haze, cf. SMOG. [portmanteau wd]

smear, *v.t.* & *i.*, & *n.* **1.** Daub with greasy or sticky substance or with something that stains, (of grease etc.) make

marks on, make a ~; blot, obscure outline of, (writing, drawing); defame, sully. **2.** *n.* Blotch made by ~ing; defamation; hence ~'Y[2] *a.*, ~'INESS *n.* [OE *smerian* f. *smeoru* fat = OS, OHG *smero*, ON *smjor*]

smec'tite, *n.* Kind of whitish clay used for taking out grease from cloth etc. [f. Gk *smēktis* fuller's earth, -ITE[1](2)]

‖ **smeech**, **smitch**, *n.* (dial.). Smell of burning or smouldering. [OE *smēc, smíc*, cogn. w. *smoke*]

smeg'|ma, *n.* Sebaceous soaplike secretion in folds of the skin, esp. of the prepuce. Hence ~**mat'IC** *a.* [f. Gk *smēgma -atos* soap (*smēkhō* = cleanse)]

smell, *n.*, & *v.t.* & *i.* (*smelt* or rarely ~*ed*). **1.** Nasal sense by which odours are perceived (~ *is less acute in man than in most animals; has a fine sense of* ~; *is perceptible to* ~ *as well as sight*); quality in substances that affects this sense, odour, (*has no, a sweet, pungent, disgusting, peculiar, close,* ~; *the* ~ *of thyme, carrion*); bad odour, whence ~'Y[2] *a.* (colloq.); act of inhaling in order to ascertain (*take a* ~ *at it*); hence ~'LESS *a.* **2.** *vb.* Perceive ~ of, detect presence of by ~, (*am sure I* ~ *gas*; *horses smelt the water a mile off*; *a rat*, fig., suspect foul dealing etc.), whence ~'ABLE *a.*; inhale ~ of, set one's sense of ~ to work at (*smelt it or at it to see if it was high*; *came up & smelt at my calves*); (of dog) hunt *out* by ~, (fig. of person) find *out* (secret, plotter, etc.) by investigation, (of dog or fig. of person) sniff or search *about*; perceive ~s, have sense of ~ (*can, do, fishes* ~?); emit ~ usu. of kind specified by adj. or adv., suggest or recall the ~ *of*, (*flowers that do not* ~; ~*s sweet, nice, disgustingly, of garlic, of brandy*; ~ *of the lamp*, seem to have been composed laboriously at night; ~ *of the shop*, be over-technical; ~ *of jobbery, nepotism*, etc., suggest these); stink, be rank; seem from the ~ to be (*dish, milk,* ~*s good, sour*); ~*ing-bottle*, pocket phial of ~*ing-salts*, ammonium carbonate mixed with scent to be sniffed as cure for faintness etc. [ME *smel(len)*, excl. E]

smell'er, *n.* In vbl senses; (also) the nose (sl.). [-ER[1]]

smelt[1], *v.t.* Extract metal from (ore) by melting; extract (metal) from ore by melting. [f. MDu. or MLG *smellen*; cogn. w. MELT[2]]

smelt[2], *n.* Small fish allied to salmon & prized as food. [OE, = obs. G *schmelt, schmelz*, Da. *smelt*]

smelt[3]. See SMELL.

smew, *n.* Kind of fishing duck. [also *smee, smeath*, orig. unkn.]

smil'ax, *n.* Kinds of climbing shrubs some of which yield sarsaparilla; climbing kind of asparagus much used in decoration. [L f. Gk]

smil|e, *v.i.* & *t.*, & *n.* **1.** Relax features often by parting lips into pleased or kind or gently amused or indulgently contemptuous or sceptical expression or forced imitation of these, look (up)on or at with such expression, (~e sweetly, indulgently, cynically, bitterly; ~e at the claims of, ridicule or show indifference to them), whence ~'ingLY² adv.; express by ~ing (~e welcome, consent, appreciation, etc.); give a ~e of specified kind (~ed an ironical, a curious, ~e); drive (person's vexation etc.) away, bring (person) into or out of a mood, by ~ing; come up ~ing, face fresh difficulty (w., ref. to boxer beginning new round); be or appear propitious, have bright aspect, seem to look propitiously (up)on, (fortune, occasion, ~es on us; all nature looks ~ing & gay). 2. n. Act of ~ing, ~ing expression or aspect; hence ~e'LESS (-l-l-) a. [ME, perh. f. MLG *smilen = OHG smîlan]

smirch, v.t., & n. Stain, soil, smear, spot, (lit., & fig. as a ~ed reputation). [15th c., of unkn. orig.]

smirk, v.i., & n. (Put on or wear) affected or silly smile, simper. [OE sme(a)rcian; f. *smar-, *smer- as in OE smerian laugh at; for -k cf. TALK]

smite, v.t. & i. (smôte & arch. smit, smitten & arch. smit), & n. 1. Strike, hit, (chiefly arch. or joc.; whosoever shall ~ thee on thy right cheek; smote his hands together; smote the harpstrings; ~ off his head; smote the first ball for four; an idea smote him, suddenly came); inflict severe defeat on (~ them hip & thigh, utterly defeat them; we hope to ~ them); chastise (God shall ~ thee; his conscience smote him); (chiefly in p.p.) strike or seize or infect or possess with disease or desire or fascination (city, person, smitten with plague, palsy; am smitten with her charms or her or abs.; smitten with a desire to); come forcibly or abruptly (up)on (wave smote upon the cliff; sun's rays smiting upon him; sound ~s upon the ear); hence smit'ER¹ n. 2. n. (colloq.). Blow, stroke, attempt. [OE smîtan, MDu., MLG smîten, OHG smîzan, Goth. -smeitan]

smith, n. Worker in metal esp. one who forges iron, blacksmith, (the gen. sense chiefly in comb., as gold, silver, tin, white, -~). [OE smith, MDu., MLG smit, OHG smid, smit, ON smithr, Goth. smitha]

smithereens' (-dherênz), smith'ers (-dh-), nn. pl. Small fragments (smash etc. to or into ~). [f. syn. smithers +-een (Ir. dim. ending); orig. unkn.]

smith'ery, n. Smith's work; (esp. in Admiralty dockyards) smithy. [-ERY]

Smith'field, n. (Used for) the London meat market. [~ in London]

smi'thy (-dhǐ), n. Blacksmith's workshop, forge. [ME, f. ON smithja, = OE smiththe, (Gmc *smithjön) whence obs. smithe]

smitten. See SMITE.

smock, n., & v.t. 1. Chemise (arch.); child's overall; blouse worn by artists etc.; ~(-frock), field-labourer's former outer linen garment of shirtlike shape & with upper part closely gathered; ~-mill (hist.), windmill of which the cap only & not the body revolves. 2. v.t. Adorn with SMOCKING. [OE smoc, OHG smoccho, ON smokkr, prob. rel. to OE smûgan creep, ON smjúga put on a garment]

smock'ing, n. Honeycomb ornamentation on garment of which the basis is close gathers as on smock-frock. [-ING¹]

smog, n. Mixture of smoke and fog, cf. SMAZE. [portmanteau wd]

smoke¹, n. 1. Volatile products of combustion, esp. visible vapour with carbon etc. in suspension emitted by burning substance (a column, cloud, of ~; end, go up, in ~, come to nothing; no ~ without FIRE¹; from ~ into smother, from one evil to another or a worse; like ~, sl., without check or difficulty, rapidly, easily; the big ~, sl., London or any large town). 2. Spell of tobacco-smoking (must have a ~). 3. (sl.). Cigar(ette). 4. ~-ball, projectile filled with material emitting dense ~ used to conceal military operations etc., also ball used in trap-shooting & giving puff of ~ when struck, also medical appliance for inhaling vapour from in asthma etc.; ~-bell, suspended over lamp etc. to protect ceiling; ~-consumer, apparatus for utilizing instead of releasing ~ of furnace or fireplace, & so ~-consuming a.; ~-dried, cured in ~; ~-jack, machine for turning roasting-spit by use of current of hot air in chimney; ~-plant, -tree, ornamental shrub with feathery ~like fruit-stalks; ~-rocket, contrivance for injecting ~ into drain to discover leak; ~-screen (mil., nav.), ~ diffused to hide operations; ~-stack, funnel & steam-escape pipes of steamer; ~-stone, cairngorm. Hence smŏk'ō n. (Australia & New Zealand), break for a ~ during working hours, ~'LESS (-kl-) a., ~'lêssLY² adv. ~'lêssNESS n. [OE smoca, f. weak grade of stem of smēocan, smēcan; see SMEECH]

smŏke|², v.i. & t. 1. Emit smoke or visible vapour, reek, steam, (his ~ing blade, steeds; meat ~ing on the board; lamp is ~ing, not burning clear), (of chimney or fire) discharge smoke into room. 2. Colour or darken or obscure, spoil taste of in cooking, preserve or cure, suffocate, rid of insects etc., with smoke (lamp ~es ceiling; ~ed wood, fumed; ~ed glass, darkened with smoke for looking at sun etc.; the porridge is ~ed; ~ed ham, haddock, etc.; ~e insects, plants, kill, cleanse, them by fumigation; *~e out, discover by thorough investigation; ~e out wasps, wasps'-nest, etc., destroy by injecting smoke). 3. Breathe in and out smoke of (tobacco-pipe, cigar, cigarette, tobacco, opium, stramonium, cane, brown paper; put that in your pipe & ~e it, reflect upon what has been said, esp. some admonition or rebuke), whence ~'ABLE a.; ~e tobacco (~es too much or like a chimney; will you

~*e?*), bring one*self* into specified state by ~ing (*has* ~*ed himself ill, sick, stupid, into tranquillity*). **4.** Get inkling, become suspicious or aware, of; ‖ (arch.) quiz, make fun of, (person etc.). **5.** ‖~*e-room*, ~*ing-room*; ~*ing-cap*, *-jacket*, of ornamental kind formerly worn while one ~ed; ~*ing-car(riage)* or *compartment*, reserved for smokers on railway-train; ‖~*ing-concert*, concert at which ~ing is allowed; ~*ing-mixture*, blend of tobaccos for ~ing in pipe; ~*ing-room*, in hotel or house kept for ~ing in (~*ing-room talk* etc., esp. such as is suited for men only). [OE *smocian* f. *smoca* (prec.)]

smok′er, n. In vbl senses; also or esp.: person who habitually smokes tobacco (~*'s heart, throat*, ailments due to excessive smoking; CHAIN-~); smoking-compartment on train; ‖ smoking-concert. [-ER¹]

smok′|y̆, a. Emitting, veiled or filled with, obscure (as) with, stained with or coloured like, smoke (*a* ~*y fire, city, room, hue, ceiling*). Hence ~ĬLY² adv., ~ĬNESS n. [-Y²]

smŏlt, n. Migratory stage of young salmon or sea-trout whilst leaving fresh water for first visit to sea. [ME; orig. unkn.]

smooth¹ (-dh), a. **1.** Of relatively even & polished surface, free from perceptible projections or lumps or indentations or roughness or (of liquid) undulations, not wrinkled or pitted or scored or hairy, that can be traversed without check, (~ *skin, surface, morocco, brow, chin; am now in* ~ *water*, have passed obstacles or difficulties; *bring the paste to a* ~ *consistence; had a* ~ *passage*, across sea; *course of true love never did run* ~; ~ *hair*, esp. flattened down on head). **2.** Free from harshness of sound or taste (~ *verse*, with easy & correct rhythm; ~ *claret, spirit*, etc.; ~ BREATHING). **3.** Equable, unruffled, polite, conciliatory, complimentary, flattering, (~ *temper, manners*; ~ *face*, esp. hypocritically friendly, whence ~FACED² a.; ~ *things*, esp. flattery or insincere encouragement, whence ~SPOKEN, ~-tongUED², aa.). **4.** ~-*bore*, gun with unrifled barrel. Hence ~′LY² adv., ~′NESS n., (-dh-). [OE *smōth* (once, usu. *smēthe* whence dial. *smeeth*); not in cogn. langg.]

smooth² (-dh), v.t. & i., & n. **1.** Make smooth (often *out, over, down, away*; ~ *over* or *away* differences, perplexities, difficulties, etc., reduce or get rid of in fact or appearance); free from impediments or discomfort (~ *the way; will* ~ *his declining years*); cloak *over* faults etc.; become smooth (usu. *down; sea presently* ~*ed down*). **2.** n. ~ing touch or stroke (*gave his hair a* ~); ~*ing-iron*, implement usu. heated to ~ linen etc.; ~*ing-plane*, small plane for finishing the planing of wood. [ME, f. prec.]

smörgăsbord (smĕr′gŏsboord), smör-

găsbŏrd, n. Scandinavian hors-d'œuvres. [Sw., f. *smör* butter, *găs* goose, *bord* table]

smote. See SMITE.

smo′ther (-ŭdh-), n., & v.t. & i. **1.** Smouldering ashes etc. (arch.; *from the* SMOKE into *the* ~); cloud of dust, spray, smoke etc., or obscurity caused by it (rare). **2.** vb. Suffocate, stifle, kill by stopping breath of or excluding air from, (~*ed mate* in chess, when king having no vacant space to move to is checked by knight); overwhelm *with* kisses, gifts, kindness, etc.; put out or keep down (fire) by heaping with ashes etc.; suppress, conceal or secure concealment of, keep from notice or publicity, burke, (often *up*; ~ *a yawn, with* ~*ed curses; the facts, the recommendations of the committee, were* ~*ed up*); cover entirely in (*strawberries* ~*ed in cream*); (rare) perish of suffocation, have difficulty in breathing. [ME *smorther* f. st. of *smorian* suffocate (dial. *smore*, = MDu. MLG *smoren*, G *schmoren*); vb f. n.]

smo′thery (-ŭdh-), a. Stifling. [-Y²]

smoul′der (smōl-), v.i., & n. **1.** Burn without flame, burn inwardly or in suppressed way or unseen, (of feelings etc.) exist, operate, be nursed, undetected or without conspicuous effects (~*ing discontent, hatred, rebellion*). **2.** n. ~ing combustion (*the* ~ *will soon be a flame*). [ME *smolder* n., of obsc. orig.; vb f. n.]

smŭdge¹, **smŭtch** (arch.), v.t. & i., & n. **1.** Smear or blot or blur lines of (writing, drawing); make dirt-mark or confused blot or smear on (face, paper, surface); (usu. *-tch*) defile, sully, stain with disgrace, impair purity of, (person's record, fame, etc.); (of ink, drawing, etc.) become blurred (*smudges easily*). **2.** n. Dirt-mark lit. or (esp. *-tch*) fig., blotted line, blurred mark; hence **smŭdg′y̆²** a., **smŭdg′ĭLY²** adv., **smŭdg′ĭNESS** n. [*-ge* older as vb (1430), *-tch* as n. (1530); orig. unkn.]

smŭdge², n. Outdoor fire with dense smoke made to keep off insects etc. [rel. to prec.]

smŭg, a. & n. **1.** Of commonplace respectable narrow-minded self-satisfied comfortable unambitious unimaginative character or appearance; hence ~′NESS n. **2.** n. (chiefly univ. sl.) ‖ Person ill fitted for society or without athletic pursuits or interests. [16th c., of unkn. orig.]

smŭg′gl|e, v.t. Import or export (goods, or abs.) illegally, esp. without payment of customs duties (often *in, out, over*), whence ~ER¹, ~ING¹, nn.; convey secretly *in, out*, etc., or put *away* etc. into concealment. [17th c. *smuckle, smuggle*, f. LG *smukkeln* (Du. *smokkelen*), *smuggeln* (G *schmuggeln*)]

smŭt, n., & v.t. & i. (-tt-). **1.** (Spot or smudge made by) small flake of soot; *ditto, brother* ~ (nursery etc.), tu quoque retort to criticism; lascivious talk or words or stories; disease of corn by which parts of the ear change to black powder; ~-*ball*, kinds of fungus; ~-*mill*, machine for cleansing grain from ~; hence ~t′y² a., ~t′ĭLY² adv., ~t′ĭNESS n. **2. vb.** Mark with ~(s); infect (corn) with, (of corn) contract, ~. [rel. to LG *smutt*, G *schmutz* the corn-disease, MHG *schmuz*, G *schmutz* dirt]

smutch. See SMUDGE.

Smyrn′iot(e) (-ĕr-), a. & n. **(Native or in-habitant)** of Smyrna. [-OT²]

snăck, n. Slight or casual or hurried meal (~ *bar* or *counter*, place where ~s are served); *go* ~*s*, go shares (~*s!*, claim to share). [orig. (15th c.) a snap or bite, f. *snack* vb.; f. MDu. *snac(k)*, *snacken* snap (of a dog)]

snăf′fl|e¹, n. Bridle consisting of ~*e-bit*, or plain slender jointed bit without curb, & single rein; *ride* one *on the* ~*e* (fig.), manage him gently. Hence ~ED² (-ld) a. [16th c., perh. conn. w. (M)Du., (M)LG *snavel* beak, mouth]

‖ **snăf′fle², v.t.** (sl.). Appropriate, purloin, pinch. [*c.* 1700, cant of unkn. orig.]

*•**snăfu′** (-fŏŏ), a. & n. (Service sl.). **1.** Chaotic. **2. n.** Utter confusion. [f. initial letters of 'situation normal, all fouled up']

snăg, n., & v.t. (-gg-). **1.** Jagged projecting point, e.g. irregular or broken tooth, stump of branch remaining on tree, pointed root or stump poking out of ground, piece of rough timber or rock embedded in river or sea bottom & impeding navigation; (fig.) unexpected obstacle or drawback; hence ~gED² (-gd), ~g′y² (-gĭ), aa. **2. v.t.** Run (ship) on ~; clear (land, waterway, tree-trunk) of ~s. [prob. f. Scand. (Norw. *snag* spike)]

snail, n., & v.t. & i. 1. Kinds of slimy slow-creeping gasteropod mollusc, most of them with spiral shell & horns or retractile eye-stalks, some used as food esp. in France, whence ~′ERY(3) n., & many destructive in gardens (*Roman* ~, the chief edible kind; ~′*s gallop, pace*, very slow locomotion); (also ~-*wheel*) notched wheel in clock resembling ~ in outline determining number of strokes in striking the hours; (also ~-*clover, -trefoil*) kinds of leguminous plant including lucerne with spiral pods; ~-*fish*, with ventral sucker for clinging; ~-*slow*, slow as a ~; hence ~′LIKE a. **2. vb.** Rid (garden) of, hunt for, ~s. [OE *snægel* etc., MLG *sneil*, OHG *snegil* (G dial. *schnegel*), ON *snigill*]

snake, n., & v.i. 1. Serpent (commoner in ordinary speech, more loosely applied so as to include ~like lizards etc., & specially used of the common British harmless kind; ~ *in the grass*, hidden danger or secret enemy; *warm, cherish*, etc., *a* ~ *in* one's *bosom*, meet with ingratitude or receive evil for good; SCOTCH² *the* ~; *see* ~*s*, have delirium tremens; *raise* or *wake* ~*s*, make disturbance, start violent quarrel; *S*~*s!*,

int. of anger). **2.** Treacherous cold-hearted person. **3.** ~-*bird*, fish-eating bird with long slender neck; ~-*charmer*, *-charming*, see SERPENT; ~-*fence* (of horizontal tree-trunks only, laid zigzag with overlapping ends to support each other); ~ *lizard*, kinds of lizard with rudimentary or no legs; ~-*locked*, with ~s instead of hair; ~-(-)*root*, one of several American plants having roots reputed to be ~-poison antidotes; ~*s'head*, the fritillary plant (from resemblance of bud to head of ~); ~-*stone*, ammonite; ~-*weed*, bistort; ~-*wood*, (wood of) a S.-American timber-tree (from its ~like markings). **4. v.i.** Move, twist, etc. like a ~. [OE *snaca*, = MLG *snake*, ON *snākr*, *snōkr*]

snāk′|ỹ, a. Infested with snakes; snake-like in appearance or in such attributes as venom, guile, coldness, ingratitude; ~*y hair* (of the Furies with snakes for hair). Hence ~ĭNESS n. [-Y²]

snăp, v.t. & i. (-pp-), & n. **1.** Make sudden audible bite (*dog* ~*ped viciously*; ~ *at*, try to bite, also speak irritably to; ~ *at* bait, offer, chance, etc., accept eagerly), (fig.) say ill-tempered or spiteful things (~ *out*, say irritably), whence ~p′ĭsh¹ a., ~p′ĭshLY² adv., ~p′ĭshNESS n.; bite *off* (~ *off* one's *nose*, esp. fig. interrupt him angrily or rudely). **2.** Pick *up* (scraps, or fig. bargain etc.) hastily, whence ~p′ER¹-up n.; take *up* (interlocutor) without letting him finish. **3.** (crick.). Catch (batsman) smartly at the wicket. **4.** Break (t. & i.) with sharp crack (~ *the string, a stick; oar, wire*, ~s). **5.** Produce report from, emit report or crack, (~ *pistol, whip*; ~ one's *fingers*, make audible fillip esp. *at* person etc. in contempt; ~ one's *fingers at*, fig., defy; *pistol* ~s, either in going off or in missing fire); close (t. & i.) etc. with ~ping sound (~ *the clasp*, one's *teeth together*; *the door* ~*ped to*). **6.** Take instantaneous photograph of (esp. unconscious or unwilling subject). **7.** *•*~ *into it* (sl.), start moving quickly; *•*~ *out of it* (sl.), get rid of a mood, habit, etc. **8.** ~*ping turtle*, ferocious American freshwater kind. **9. n.** Act or sound of ~ping (also quasi-adv., as ~ *went an oar*). **10.** Spring-catch fastening bracelet etc. **11.** ‖ Kinds of small crisp cake; BRANDY-~. **12.** A card-game. **13.** (Usu. *cold* ~) sudden spell of frost. **14.** Crispness of style, fresh vigour or liveliness in action, go, dash, spring, whence ~p′y² a. (*make it* ~*py*, colloq.; be quick about it). **15.** = ~*shot* n. (see below). **16.** *•*(sl.). Easy task (esp. *soft* ~). **17.** (theatr.). Short engagement as actor. **18.** attrib. (Esp. of parliamentary or other deliberative proceedings) taken by surprise, brought on without notice, etc. (*a* ~ *division, debate, crisis, vote*, etc.). **19.** ~-*bolt, -lock*, going home automatically with spring on closing of door etc.; ~′*dragon*, kinds of plant with bag-shaped

flower like a dragon's mouth, antir-
rhinum, also Christmas game of plucking
raisins from dish of burning brandy;
~-hook, **-link**, with spring allowing
entrance but barring escape of cord, link,
etc.; ~ *shot* n., shot taken with little or
no delay in aiming; **~'shot**, (n.) instantaneous photograph taken with hand
camera, (v.t., also -*shoot*) take such photograph of. [f. MDu. or MLG *snappen*;
partly echoic]

snare, n., & v.t. 1. Trap for catching
birds or animals, esp. one made with
wire; (surg.) wire loop for catching &
extracting polypi etc.; device for tempting enemy or dupe to expose himself to
capture, defeat, failure, disgrace, loss,
etc.; thing that acts as a temptation
(*popularity is often a* ~); (pl.) twisted
strings of gut or hide stretched across
lower head of side-drum to produce
rattling sound. 2. v.t. Catch (bird etc.)
in ~, whence (-)**snārER¹** n.; get (person)
into ~ (less common, & with more of the
lit. sense, than *ensnare*). [ME, f. ON
snara, rel. to OS *snari*, OHG *snar(ahha)*;
sense 'drum-snare' prob. f. Du.. or
LG]

snark, n. Chimerical animal of ill-defined
characteristics and potentialities. [from
The Hunting of the S~ by 'Lewis Carroll'
(1876)]

snarl¹, v.i. & t., & n. 1. (Of dog) make
high-pitched quarrelsome growl; (of
person) speak cynically, make ill-
-tempered complaints or criticisms; ~ *out*,
utter in ~ing tone; express (discontent
etc.) by ~ing; hence **~'ER¹** n., **~'ingLY²**
adv. 2. n. Act or sound of ~ing; hence
~'Y² a. [frequent. of 16th c. *snar*, f.
MDu., (M)LG *snarren*; see -LE(3)]

snarl², v.t. & i., & n. 1. Twist, entangle,
become entangled, (*a* ~*ed skein*, intricate
business); adorn exterior of (narrow
metal vase) with raised work made by
indirect internal hammering with ~-*ing*-
-*iron*. 2. n. Knot, tangle. [ME; n..f.
SNARE n. or vb (see -LE(3)); vb f. n.]

snatch, v.t. & i., & n. 1. Seize quickly,
eagerly, or unexpectedly, esp. with
suddenly outstretched hand(s), rescue
narrowly *from*, secure with difficulty,
carry suddenly *away* or *from*, (~*ed his
gun up, down*; *wind* ~*ed my cap off*; *child
~es its food*; ~ *kiss, opportunity*, etc.; *was
~ed from the jaws of death*; ~ *a half-hour's
repose*; ~ *victory out of defeat*; ~*ed away,
from us, by premature death*); shoot out
hand(s) *at* to seize (also fig., as ~ *at offer,*
take it eagerly); **~-*block*** (naut.), block
with hinged flap admitting rope to
sheave. 2. n. Act of ~ing (*made a* ~ *at it*);
(usu. pl.) fragment(s) or short burst(s) of
song or recitation or talk, short spell(s) of
action (*only works by* ~*es*, fits & starts),
whence **~'Y²** a., **~'ILY²** adv. [ME
snecchen, sna(c)che, of unkn. orig.; perh.
rel. to SNACK]

sneak, v.i. & t., & n. 1. Slink, go furtively,
(often *in, out, past, round, about, off,
away*, etc.), whence **~'ers** n. pl. (sl.),
silent shoes; (part.) furtive, not avowed,
(*have a* ~*ing kindness for him*, an affection
that one cannot justify by reason);
‖ (school sl.) peach, tell tales; (sl.) make
off with, steal; hence **~'ingLY²** adv.
2. n. Mean cowardly underhand person;
‖ (school sl.) informer, telltale; (crick.)
ball bowled along the ground; **~-*thief***
(stealing from open doors or windows).
[16th c., obsc. rel. to ME *snike*, OE *snīcan*
creep]

‖ **sneck**, n., & v.t. (chiefly Sc.). Latch.
[ME; cf. ME *snatch* in same sense]

sneer, v.i. & t., & n. 1. Smile derisively
(often *at*); utter derisive words esp. of a
covert or ironical kind (usu. *at*); put
(person) *down, out of countenance*, etc.,
take *away* (person's reputation etc.), by
~ing; hence **~'ER¹** n., **~'ingLY²** adv.
2. n. ~ing look or remark. [16th c., prob.
imit.]

sneeze, v.i., & n. 1. Make explosive sound
in involuntarily expelling anything that
irritates interior of nostrils (*not to be* ~*d
at*, passable, not contemptible); ~ *into a
basket* (euphem.), be guillotined. 2. n.
Act or sound of sneezing. [c. 1500 *snese*,
app. alt. f. obs. *fnese* (OE **fnēosan*) due to
misreading or misprinting *f* as *ʃ* after the
initial combination *fn-* had become unfamiliar, & *fnese* had been replaced (early
15th c.) by (now dial.) *neese*]

snib, n., & v.t. (-bb-; chiefly Sc.). 1. Bolt,
fastening, catch, of door, window, etc.
2. v.t. Bolt, fasten. [Sc.; orig. obsc.]

snick, v.t., & n. 1. Cut small notch or
make small incision in; (crick.) slightly
deflect course of (ball) with bat. 2. n.
Slight notch or cut; (crick.) ~ing touch
with bat. [18th c., prob. suggested by
SNICKERSNEE etc.]

snick'er, v.i., & n. Whinny, neigh; =
SNIGGER. [imit.]

snickersnee', n. (joc.). Knife, esp. one
usable as weapon. [alt. f. earlier *snick-or-
-snee* a fight with knives, earlier *stick or
snee*, f. Du. *steken* thrust, *snijen* cut]

snide, a. & n. (sl.). 1. Counterfeit, bogus;
insinuating, slyly derogatory. 2. n. ~
jewellery or coin(s); **~*s'man***, utterer of
false coin. [19th c. cant, of unkn. orig.]

sniff, v.i. & t., & n. 1. Draw up air
audibly through nose to stop it from
running or as expression of contempt (~
at, try the smell of, also show contempt
for or discontent with, also, of dog, show
disposition to bite person's *calves*); draw
up or *up* (air, liquid, scent), draw up scent
of (flower, brandy, meat, etc.), into nose.
2. n. Act or sound of ~ing, amount of air
etc. ~*ed up*. [ME, imit.; cf. SNUFF¹]

sniff'y, a. (colloq.). Disdainful, contemptuous; (of thing that should be odourless)
slightly malodorous. [-Y²]

snift'ing-valve, n. Air-escape valve in

steam-engine cylinder. [f. (now dial.) *snift* = SNIFF]

snig′ger (-g-), v.i. & n. (Give) half-suppressed secretive laugh. [imit., cf. SNICKER]

snig′gle, v.i. Fish *for* eels by pushing bait into hole. [f. *snig* small eel; orig. unkn.]

snip, v.t. & i. (-pp-), & n. **1.** Cut with scissors or shears esp. in small quick strokes (~ *cloth, a hole*; ~ *off the ends*; ~ *at*, make ~ping strokes at), whence ~p′ING¹(2) n. **2.** n. Act of ~ping; piece ~ped off; (sl.) tailor; (racing sl.) certainty (also *dead* ~). [16th c., f. Du. or LG *snippen*]

snipe, n. (collect. sing. usu. for pl.), & v.i. & t. **1.** Kinds of gamebird with long straight bill & angular flight frequenting marshes (*common* or *whole, great* or *double* or *solitary, small* or *half* or *jack*, ~, British kinds); GUTTER-~; ~-*eel, -fish*, etc., kinds with long slender snout; hence **snip′Y²** a. **2.** vb. Go ~-shooting; (mil.) fire shots from hiding usu. at long range into enemy's camp or at individuals, kill or hit thus, whence **snip′ER¹** n. [ME *snipe*, corresp. to Scand. *snipa* in Icel. *mȳrisnipa*; cf. MDu., MLG *snippe*, OHG *snepfa*]

snipp′et, n. Small piece cut off, snipping; (pl.) detached fragments of knowledge or information, short extracts from books, odds & ends, whence ~Y² a., ~INESS n. [-ET¹]

snip-snăp-snŏr′um, n. A round card-game. [18th c., f. LG *snipp-snapp-snorum*]

sniv′el, v.i. (-ll-), & n. **1.** Run at the nose; be lachrymose, show maudlin emotion; hence ~lER¹ n., ~lING² a. **2.** n. Running mucus; whining & weeping; hypocritical talk, cant. [ME, f. OE *snyflan* f. *snofl* mucus; n. f. vb]

snŏb, n. ‖ Man of low birth or breeding or social position (arch.); ‖ (at universities & public schools; arch.) townsman; person with exaggerated respect for social position or wealth & a disposition to be ashamed of socially inferior connexions, behave with servility to social superiors, & judge of merit by externals, whence ~b′ISH¹ a., ~b′ishLY² adv., ~b′ishNESS, ~b′ERY(4, 5), ~′lING¹(2), ~ŏc′RACY, nn. [18th c. (still colloq.) *cobbler*; orig. unkn.]

snoek (-ōŏk), n. (S. Afr.). Large edible sea-fish (cf. SNOOK¹). [Du.]

snŏŏd, n. **1.** (Sc. & literary) fillet worn by maidens in Scotland to confine hair, whence ~′ED² a. **2.** Any of the short lines attaching hooks to a main line in sea fishing. [OE *snōd*, of unkn. orig.]

snŏŏk¹, n. Kinds of fish esp. the sea pike (cf. SNOEK). [f. Du. *snoek*]

snŏŏk², n. (sl.). Contemptuous gesture with thumb to nose & fingers spread out (*cock, cut, make, a* ~ or ~*s*; *S~s*!, int. of contempt). [orig. unkn.]

snŏŏk′er, n. Game on billiard-table combining pool & pyramids (~*ed*, having one's object-ball covered by another; (fig.) beaten, defeated). [orig. unkn.]

snŏŏp, v.i. & t. (orig. U.S., colloq.). Pry into matters one is not concerned with; sneak *around* looking for infractions of the law; steal. Hence ~′ER¹ n. [f. Du. *snoepen* enjoy stealthily]

snooty. See SNOUT.

snŏŏze, v.i. & t., & n. (Take) short sleep esp. in day-time; pass time in lazy indifference; ~ *time* etc. *away*, spend it indolently. [18th c. cant, of unkn. orig.]

snŏr|e, v.i. & t., & n. (Make) hoarse rattling or grunting noise in breathing esp. during sleep; pass time *away* in ~ing; bring one*self awake, into a nightmare*, etc., by ~ing. Hence ~′ER¹ n. [ME, prob. imit.; cf. foll.]

snŏrt¹, v.i. & t., & n. (Make) explosive noise due to sudden forcing of breath through nose & usu. expressing anger or indignation or incredulity, or (of steam-engine etc.) noise resembling this; express (defiance etc.) by ~ing (often *out*), throw *out* (words) with ~ing. [ME, prob. imit.; cf. prec.]

Snŏrt², n. Device for enabling submarines to take in air for engines & crew when submerged to periscope depth. [orig. unkn.]

snŏrt′er, n. In vbl senses; also (sl.): boisterous gale; performance etc. conspicuous for vigour or violence. [-ER¹]

snŏt, n. (vulg.). Mucus of the nose (also of person as low term of abuse); ~-*rag*, handkerchief. [ME *snot(te)* (cf. OE *gesnot*), prob. f. MDu., MLG *snotte*]

snŏtt′|y, a. & n. **1.** Running or foul with snot (vulg.; also as low abusive epithet); (colloq.) annoyed, short-tempered; hence ~iLY² adv., ~iNESS n. **2.** n. (nav. sl.). Midshipman. [-Y²]

snout, n. Nose (& mouth) of animal or (derog.) human being; pointed front of something, nozzle, (~ *of glacier, of battleship's ram*, etc.); ~-*beetle*, kinds with beaked head; ~-*ring*, inserted in pig's ~ to prevent rooting. Hence (-)~ED² a., ~′Y², like a ~, having a (prominent) ~, (colloq., also **snŏŏt′y**) supercilious, conceited. [ME, f. MDu., MLG *snûte*]

snow¹ (-ō), n., & v.i. & t. **1.** Atmospheric vapour frozen into ice crystals & falling to earth in white flakes or spread on it as a white layer (*red* ~, ~-*plant*, see below); (pl.) falls or accumulations of ~ (*where are the* ~*s of yester-year?*). **2.** Substance etc. resembling ~ esp. in whiteness (*her breast of* ~; *the* ~*s of seventy years*, white hair; *apple, chestnut*, etc., ~, kinds of pudding); (sl.) cocaine. **3.** ~′*ball*, (n.) mass of ~ pressed into hard ball esp. for use as missile, ‖ fund each subscriber to which finds *n* others, ‖ kinds of pudding e.g. apple enclosed in rice, (v.t. & i.) pelt or have pelting-match with ~balls;

~*ball-tree*, guelder-rose; ~*-berry*, garden shrub with white berries; ~*-bird*, kinds of white or partly white finch, esp. the ~ *bunting*; ~*-blind(ness)*, unable, inability, to see owing to exhaustion of retina by reflection of light endured in traversing ~-fields etc.; ~*-blink*, reflection in sky of ~ or ice fields; ~*-boots*, over-boots of rubber & cloth; ~*-bound*, kept from going out or travelling by ~; ~*-cap*, white-crowned humming-bird; ~*-capped*, (of móuntain) covered at top with ~; ~*-drift*, bank of ~ heaped by wind; ~*'drop*, early spring white-flowered plant; ~*-fall*, esp. amount of ~ that falls on one occasion or in a year at any place as measured by ~*-gauge*; ~*-field*, esp. permanent wide expanse of ~ in mountainous or polar regions; ~*-flake*, one of the small collections of crystals in which ~ falls; ~*-goggles*, darkened spectacles worn by mountaineers etc. to prevent ~-blindness; ~*-goose*, arctic white goose with black-tipped wings, the wavy; ~*-grouse*, ptarmigan; ~*-ice*, opaque white ice formed from ~-slush; ~*-leopard*, ounce; ~*-line*, level above which ~ lies permanently at any place; ~ *man*, figure made of ~ by children etc. & set up (Abominable Snowman, (sub)-human animal alleged to have been seen, or supposed to leave tracks in the ~, on the higher Himalaya mountains, YETI); ~*-on-the-mountain*, kinds of white-flowered garden plant; ~*-*, or usu. ~*y*, *owl*, the great white owl; ~*-plant* or red~, microscopic alga growing in ~ & colouring it red; ~*-plough*, contrivance for clearing road or track by pushing ~ aside; ~ *plume*, fringe of blown ~ wind-driven from mountain-top or ridge; ~*-shoes*, racket-heads or (also SKI) long narrow boards attached to feet & enabling wearer to traverse ~ without sinking in; ~*-shovel*, large wooden shovel for~; ~*-slip*, avalanche; ~*-storm*, heavy fall of ~ esp. with wind; ~*-white*, white as ~; hence ~'LESS (-ŏl-), ~'Y² (-ōī), aa., ~'ILY² adv., ~'INESS n., (-ōī-). 4. vb. (Impers.) *it* ~*s*, *will*~, etc., ~ *falls* etc.; sprinkle or scatter, come, blow ~; *'*~ *under*, cover (as) with ~, overwhelm with numbers etc. (esp. in pass. of election cǎndidate defeated by huge majority); ~*ed up*, *in*, ~*-bound*, blocked up with ~. [OE *snǎw*, OS *snēu*, OHG *snēo*, ON *snǽr*, Goth *snaiws* f. Gmc *snaiwaz*, cogn. w. L *nix nivis*]

snow² (-ŏ), n. Small brig-like sailing vessel with supplementary trysail mast. [f. Du. *sna(a)uw* or LG *snau*]

snub¹, v.t. (-bb-), & n. 1. Rebuff, reprove, put down, humiliate, with sharp words or marked want of cordiality, whence ~b'ING(1) n., ~b'ingLY² adv.; check way of (ship) esp. by rope wound round ~(*bing*)-*post* or bollard. 2. n. ~*bing*, rebuff. [ME, f. ON *snubba chide*]

snub², a. & n. 1. (Of nose) short & stumpy

or turned up, whence ~-NOSED² a. 2. n. (rare). ~ nose. [f. prec. vb in old sense *check growth of*]

snuff¹, v.i. & t., & n. 1. ~ (the now more usu.) SNIFF vb; also, take ~, whence ~'ER¹ n. 2. n. = (the now more usu.) SNIFF n.; also: powdered tobacco taken by sniffing as stimulant or sedative (*give person* ~, *deal sharply with him*; *take thing in* ~, arch., take offence at it; *up to* ~, sl., not childishly ignorant or innocent, whence ~'Y² a., ~'INESS n.; medicinal powder taken by sniffing; ‖~*-&-butter*, brownish-yellow; ~*-box*; ~*-colour(ed)*, (of) dark yellowish-brown; ~*-mill*, for grinding ~, ‖ also ~*-box*; ~*-taker*, *-taking*. [vb prob. f. MDu. *snoffen*, *snuffen*; n. 'tobacco' f. Du. *snuf*, *snuif*, app. abbr. f. *snuiftabak* snuffing-tobacco]

snuff², v.t. & i., & n. 1. Trim ~ from (candle or its wick) with fingers or scissors or esp. ~'ers n. pl., kind of scissors with box to catch ~ (~ *out* v.t., extinguish by trimming, also fig. as *I was nearly*, *his hopes were*, ~*ed out*; ~ *out* v.i., sl., die; *can* ~ *a candle with a pistol*, shoot off top of wick without putting flame out); ~*er-tray*, holding ~ers. 2. n. Charred part of candle-wick, esp., in bad wick; ~*-dish*, ~*er-tray*. [ME *snoffe*, *snuffe*, of unkn. orig.; cf. LG *snuppe*; vb f. n., cf. LG *snuppen*]

snuf'fl|e, v.i. & t., & n. 1. Sniff (intr.), make sniffing sounds; speak nasally, whiningly, or like one with a cold, esp. as form of religious affectation ascribed to puritans & dissenters, whence ~ER¹ n.; ~*e out*, utter with ~ing; hence ~ingLY² adv. 2. n. Sniff; ~ing sound, tone, or talk. [prob. f. Du., Flem. *snuffelen*; see SNUFF¹, -LE(3)]

snug, a. Sheltered from weather & cold, well enclosed or packed in or fixed in place, comfortably situated, cosy, (*as* ~ *as a bug in a rug*); (of income, dinner, etc.) good enough for modest requirements. Hence ~'LY² adv., ~'NESS n. [16th c., orig. naut.; orig. unkn.]

snugg'erỹ (-g-), n. Snug place, esp. person's private room or den; bar-parlour of inn. [-ERY]

snug'gle, v.i. & t. Shift one's position or lie close *up to* for warmth; draw (child etc.) close *to* one, cuddle. [f. 16th c. vb *snug* (of unkn. orig., later assoc. w. SNUG) +-LE(3)]

so, adv., conj., int., & pron. 1. To the extent or in the manner set forth by preceding or following *as*-clause or implied in context, thus, equally, similarly, analogously, (now used to express degree before *as*-clause only with negative, as *I am not so eager*, *but I am as eager*, *as you*; *as the tree falls*, *so must it lie*; *as bees love sweetness*, *so flies love rottenness*; rarely used twice correlatively, as *so many men so many minds*; *when he saw her so frightened*; *why are you panting* so?; so & so only can it be done; stand just so; did not expect to live so long; did not get it by force & ought not to be so deprived of it; often in sentence appended as explanation, as I paid him double, I was so pleased; ever or never so bad etc. in condit. clause, as bad etc. as possible; so far, up to this time or point or extent, as so far it has not happened, so far you are right; so or in so far as or arch. so far forth as, to whatever extent; & so forth, & so on, et cetera, & the like; so long as, with the proviso, on the condition, that; so be it, form of acceptance, resignation, etc.; so long, good-bye till we next meet; so much for, that is all that need be done or said about; is only so much rubbish, all rubbish; at so much a week, a head; etc., a definite but unspecified sum etc.; similarly so much of one ingredient & so much of another; not so much as, less than, not even; is not so much discontented as unsatisfied. 2. To the degree or in the manner or with the intent or result set forth by following that-clause or but-clause or as to (so high that you cannot reach it; so run that ye may obtain; warned him so that he might avoid the danger; all precautions have been taken, so that we expect to succeed; not so deaf but he can hear a gun; was so fortunate as to escape; put it so as not to offend him; it so happens that he was not there). 3. To a degree that demands exclamatory emphasis (so many worlds, so much to do!; I am so glad, tired!; she is so beautiful!; so kind of you!; also colloq. or vulg. with ever, as that is ever so much better, he is ever so angry!). 4. On condition that or that, on condition set forth in as-clause or implied, (so that or so it is done, it matters not how; so may you find forgiveness as now you forgive me!; so help me God!, form of asseveration). 5. Accordingly, consequently, therefore, as appears or results from preceding or implied statements or fact, (he says he was not there, so he doubtless was not; so or and so I cannot come; so you are back again; so that's that, colloq. winding up of statement or discussion; so WHAT?; so look to yourself). 6. (Accompanying emphasis on some later word) moreover, also, as well, in actual fact, (well, so I did; you said it was good, & so it is; yes, I denied it, but or & so did you; ' your birthday? yes, so it is '). 7. (As substitute, often preceding vb, for obj. of say, call, speak, tell, think, hope, suppose, do, etc.) it, this, that, the same, this is what, (so he said; so spake Achilles, i.e. what precedes, & Patroclus so, i.e. what follows; also ellipt., as So Satan, whom the archangel thus rebukes; do you think so?; & so say all of us; I suppose so, form of agreement; I told you so, warned you in vain; she is ill & he thinks himself so; so-called, epithet questioning accuracy

of description; so to say or speak, apology for exaggeration, metaphor, neologism, etc.; you don't say so?, formula of surprise). 8. In that state or condition, actually the case, (he, it, is better so; God said Let there be light, & it was so; must it be so?; but perhaps it is not, even if it were, so; though it was, or things were, ever or never so, vulg., however bad the state of things; also with omission of it is etc., as how so?, why so?, if so, not so; also ellipt. for is that so? chiefly in imit. of German, as 'He went off yesterday'. 'So?'; quite so, just so, forms of agreement). 9. (arch.). And so, after which I, they, etc., proceeded (& so to dinner, to bed, etc.); so please you, by your favour, if you please. 10. (Ellipt. after conditional clause; arch.) let it be so, very well, (if you are content, so). 11. (As int., also soh) that will do, stay as you are, stand still, be quiet. 12. (In comb. with relative words) -ever (also with -ever appended, as whoso, whosoever). 13. So-&-so (pl. so-&-so's), particular person or thing not needing to be specified (never mind what so-&-so says; tells me to do so-&-so); so so, pred. adj. or adv., not more than passable, -bly; or so, or thereabouts (after expressions of quantity or numbers; send me ten or so; 1 lb. or so will do). [OE swā etc., OS, OHG sō, ON svá, Goth. swa, swē]

soak, v.t. & i., & n. 1. (Of absorbent substance) take up or suck in (liquid); place or leave or lie in or in liquid for saturation, steep tr. & i., make or be wet through, (of rain etc.) drench, whence ~'ING¹(1) n.; (of moisture) make way in(to) or through, make its way, by saturation, whence ~'AGE(3) n.; (sl.) extract money from by extortionate charge, taxation, etc. (~ the rich); drink persistently, booze. 2. n. ~ing; drinking-bout; hard drinker. [OE socian cogn. w. sūcan SUCK]

soak'er, n. In vbl senses; esp.: hard drinker; drenching shower. [-ER¹]

soap, n., & v.t. & i. 1. Compound of fatty acid with soda or potash or (insoluble ~s) with an earth or metallic oxide, of which the soluble kinds yield when rubbed in water a lather used in washing (soft ~, made with potash & remaining liquid, also fig. flattery); ~-berry, -nut, -plant, -pod, -root, -wort, kinds of plant yielding substances serving purpose of ~; ~-boiler, -boiling, manufacture(r) of ~; ~-box, box for holding ~, makeshift stand for street orator; ~-bubble, iridescent globe of air enclosed in film of soapy water made by blowing through pipe dipped in ~-suds; ~-earth, ~-stone, steatite; '~ opera (sl.), radio serial; ~-SUDS; ~-works, ~ manufactory; hence ~LESS a. 2. vb. Apply ~ to, scrub or rub with ~; use ~ upon oneself. [OE sāpe, MDu. seepe, OHG seifa f. Gmc *saipōn whence. L sapo]

soap'| y̆, a. Like, smeared or impregnated with, suggestive of, soap; (of person or his manners or talk) unctuous, flattering. Hence ~ĭLY² adv., ~ĭNESS n. [-Y²]

soar (sōr), v.i. Fly high (lit. & fig.), mount to or be at a great height above earth, hover or sail in the air without flapping of wings, (~ing eagle, spire, thoughts, ambition, ideals). Hence ~'ingLY² adv. [ME, f. OF essorer f. pop. L *EX (aurare f. aura breeze)]

sŏa'vĕ, sŏavĕmĕn'tĕ, (-ah-), mus. direction. With tenderness. [It.]

sŏb, v.i. & t. (-bb-), & **n. 1.** Draw breath in convulsive gasps usu. with weeping under mental distress or physical exhaustion; ~ out, utter with ~s; hence ~b'ingLY² adv. **2. n.** Convulsive drawing of breath esp. in weeping; *•~stuff,* pathos, sentimental writing. [ME sobbe(n), prob. imit.]

sŏb'er, a., & v.t. & i. 1. Not drunk (as ~ as a judge; appeal from Philip drunk to Philip ~, suggest that opinion etc. represents passing mood only); temperate in regard to drink (is a ~ man); moderate, well-balanced, sane, tranquil, self-controlled, sedate, not vehement or passionate or excited or wayward or fanciful or exaggerated, (of colour) quiet & inconspicuous, (in ~ fact, in fact as opp. fancy; a ~ estimate; ~-minded; ~-sides, sedate person; ~-suited, poet., clad in ~ colours; whence ~LY² adv. **2. vb.** Make or become ~ or less wild, reckless, enthusiastic, visionary, etc. (often down). [ME, f. OF sobre f. L sobrius]

Sŏbra'nje (-ahnyĕ), **n.** Bulgarian national assembly. [Bulg.]

sobri'ĕty, n. Being SOBER. [ME, f. OF sobriete or L sobrietas (SOBER, -TY)]

sŏb'riquet (-kă), **sou-** (sŏ̄o-), **n.** Nickname, assumed name. [F]

sŏc(c)'age, n. Feudal tenure of land involving payment of rent or other service to superior. [AF, f. soc f. OE sōcn SOKE + -AGE]

sŏcc'er (-k-), **n.** (colloq.). ASSOCIATION football. [ASSOCIATION, -ER¹]

sŏ'ciab|le (-sha-), **a. & n. 1.** Fitted for companionship, ready & willing to converse, not averse to society, communicative, liking company; (of meeting etc.) marked by friendliness, not stiff or formal; hence sŏciabIL'ITY n., ~LY² adv., (-sha-). **2. n.** Open carriage with facing side seats; tricycle for two riders side by side; S-shaped couch allowing two occupants to face each other. [F, or f. L sociabilis (sociare to unite, -ABLE)]

sŏ'cial (-shl), **a. & n. 1.** Living in companies, gregarious, not fitted for or not practising solitary life, interdependent, co-operative, practising division of labour, existing only as member of compound organism, (man is a ~ animal; ~ bees, wasps, kinds having common nests etc.; ~ birds, building near each other in com-

munities; ~ plants, kinds that grow thickly together & monopolize ground they grow on; ~ polyp etc.). **2.** Concerned with the mutual relations of men or classes of men (~ problems, science, morality, students, philosophers; the ~ contract or rarely compact, agreement among men to exchange the individual freedom of the state of nature for legal restriction, assumed by 18th-c. thinkers as basis of political society; ~ democrat, politician aiming at improving condition of lower classes by gradual advance towards socialism; ~ security, freedom from unemployment & want; ~ services, education, health, housing, insurance, pensions; the ~ evil, prostitution). **3.** Of or in or towards society (~ intercourse, life, code, etiquette, pleasures, duties; one's ~ superiors & inferiors; ~ rank, position, distinctions; has ~ tastes; a ~ evening, gathering). **4.** Of or with allies (the S~ war in Rom. hist.). **5. n.** ~ gathering, esp. one organized by club, congregation, etc. Hence or cogn. ~ITE¹(-sha-) n., prominent society person, sŏciäl'ITY (-shĭ-) n., ~LY² adv. [F, or f. L socialis (socius friend, -AL)]

sŏ'cial|ism (-sha-), **n.** A political and economic theory of social organization which advocates State ownership and control of the means of production, distribution, and exchange; a policy or practice based on this theory; Christian ~ism, attempt to apply Christian precepts in ordinary life resulting in some approximation to the aims of ~ism. Hence ~IST(2) n. & a., ~ĭs'TIC a., ~ĭs'TICALLY adv., (-sha-). [f. F -isme, or f. prec. +-ISM]

sŏ'cializ|e (-sha-), **-is|e** (-īz), **v.t.** Make social; arrange socialistically. Hence ~A'TION n. [-IZE]

soci'ĕty, n. 1. Social mode of life, the customs & organization of a civilized nation, (the progress of ~ is an evolution; pests of ~, persons who prey on the community). **2.** Any social community (no ~ can retain members who flout its principles). **3.** The upper classes of a community whose movements & entertainments & other doings are more or less conspicuous, the socially distinguished, fashionable & well-to-do & well-connected people, (was welcomed by ~; the customs of polite ~; ~ does not approve; leaders of ~; often attrib., as ~ lady, people, gossip, news, journal; ~ verse, of light topical witty kind). **4.** Participation in hospitality, other people's houses or company, (goes a great deal into, avoids, is at his best or embarrassed in, ~). **5.** Companionship, company, (~ & solitude; always enjoy his ~; seek, avoid, the ~ of). **6.** Association of persons united by a common aim or interest or principle (S~ of Friends, Quakers; S~ of Jesus, abbr. S.J., see JESUIT; BUILDING, CO-OPERATIVE, FRIENDLY ~; Royal S~, founded

1662 for improving natural knowledge; DORCAS ~). [f. F *société* f. L *societatem* (*socius* friend, -TY)]

Socin'ian, a. & n. (Follower, following or according to doctrine) of the 16th-c. Italian theologians Laelius & Faustus Socinus, whose opinions resemble those of modern unitarians. Hence ~ISM(3) n. [-IAN]

sōciŏl'ŏgȳ, n. Science of the development & nature & laws of human society. Hence **sōcioLO'GICAL** a., **sōciolŏ'gicalLY²** adv., (-sho-), **sōciŏl'OGIST** n. [F (-*gie*), f. L *socius* see SOCIABLE, -LOGY]

sŏck¹, n. (shop pl. *sox*). Short stocking not reaching knee (|| *pull up your ~s!*, brace yourself for an effort); removable inner sole put into shoe for warmth etc.; ancient comic actor's light shoe (also used allusively for comedy etc., cf. BUSKIN). [OE *socc* f. L *soccus* comic actor's shoe]

sŏck², v.t., n., & adv. (sl.). 1. Fling (ball, stone) *at*; hit (person) with hand-flung missile. 2. n. Blow inflicted by missile or fist (esp. *give him~s!*). 3. adv. With such blow, plump, right, (*hit him~ in the eye*). [c. 1700, cant, of unkn. orig.]

|| **sŏck³**, n., & v.t. & i. (school sl.). 1. Sweets, pastry, etc., eaten at odd times, tuck, grub. 2. vb. Treat to ~, indulge in ~; give (person thing). [orig. Eton sl., of unkn. orig.]

*****sŏckdŏl'oger**, **-lag-**, n. (sl.). Decisive blow or argument. [prob. fanciful]

sŏck'ét, n., & v.t. 1. Natural or artificial hollow for something to fit into or stand firm or revolve in (*eye-~*; ~ *of the hip*; *candle too large for* ~; BALL¹ *&* ~); ~-*joint*, = BALL¹-*&-~ joint*; ~-*pipe*, with enlarged end to receive another. 2. v.t. Place in, fit with, ~; (golf) hit (ball) with heel of club. Hence ~ED² a'. [15th c., AF, dim. of *soc* ploughshare, prob. of Celt. orig.]

sŏck'eye (-kī), n. The blue-back salmon. [Amer.-Ind. *sukai*]

sŏ'cle, n. (archit.). Plain low rectangular block serving as support for pedestal, vase, statue, etc. [F, f. It. *zoccolo* f. L *socculus* (*soccus* SOCK¹, -ULE)]

Socrăt'|ĭc, a. & n. 1. Of, like, following, etc., Socrates (*~ic method*, dialectic, procedure by question & answer; *~ic irony*, pose of ignorance assumed in order to entice others into display of supposed knowledge). 2. n. Follower of Socrates. Hence~ICALLY adv. [f. L f. Gk *Sōkratikos* (*Sōkratēs*, -IC)]

sŏd¹, n., & v.t. (-dd-). 1. Turf, upper layer of grass land including blades & roots & earth, (*under the* ~, in the grave); piece of turf pared off; hence ~d'Y² a. 2. v.t. Cover (ground) with ~s (*~ding mallet, spade*, implements used); pelt with ~s. [15th c., f. MDu. or MLG *sode*, = OFris. *sātha, sāda*, of unkn. orig.]

sŏd². See SEETHE.

sŏd³, n. (vulg.). Sodomite (esp. as vague term of abuse). [abbr.]

sŏd'a, n. 1. One of the compounds of sodium in common use, esp. sodium carbonate or bicarbonate. 2. (Also ~-*water*) water made effervescent by impregnation with carbonic acid under pressure & used alone or with spirit or wine or milk as a drink (orig. made with sodium bicarbonate; *some ~-water*; *some* or *a brandy & ~*; *~-fountain*, vessel in which ~-water is stored under pressure to be drawn out, shop, *store, or counter equipped with this apparatus). [med. L, f. *sodanum* glasswort, f. Arab. *suda'*]

sŏdăl'itȳ, n. A confraternity or association esp. of religious character (chiefly in titles of R.-C. societies). [f. F -*ité* or L *sodalitas* (*sodalis* comrade, -ITY)]

sŏdd'en, a., & v.t. & i. 1. Saturated with liquid, soaked through; (of bread) doughy, heavy & moist; stupid or dull in fact or appearance with habitual drunkenness; hence ~NESS n. 2. vb. Become or make ~. [orig. p.p. of SEETHE]

sŏd'ium, n. A soft silver-white metallic element found in soda, salt, & other compounds, which in its pure form decomposes water; ~ *bicarbonate*, baking powder; ~ *carbonate*, washing soda; ~ *chloride*, common salt; ~ *silicate*, water-*glass*; ~ *sulphate*, Glauber's salt. Hence **sŏd'ic** a. [SODA, -IUM]

Sŏd'om, n. (Type of) wicked town. [*Gen.* xviii, xix]

sŏd'omite, n. Person practising sodomy. [ME, f. OF, or f. LL f. Gk *Sodomitēs* inhabitant of Sodom, see -ITE¹(1)]

sŏd'omȳ, n. Copulation between male persons; unnatural connexion between human beings and animals. [ME, f. OF *sodomie* (LL *Sodoma*, -IA¹)]

sŏëv'er, suf. occas. separable usu. appended to relative pronouns, adverbs, or adjectives, but sometimes following them at an interval, to give indefinite meaning (*whosoever*, *howsoever*, etc.; *how great ~ it may be*; *with what end ~ he did it*). [SO, EVER]

sŏf'a, n. Couch with raised ends & back on which several persons can sit or one lie; ~ *bed*(*stead*), piece of furniture serving as ~ by day & bed by night. [F, f. Arab. *suffah*]

sŏff'it, n. Lower surface of architrave, arch, balcony, etc. [f. It. *soffitta*, -*itto*, & F *soffite*, ult. f. L SUB² (*figere* fix)]

sofi(sm). See SUFI(sm).

sŏft (*or* saw-), a., n., adv., & int. 1. Comparatively wanting in hardness, yielding to pressure, malleable, plastic, easily cut, (~ *as butter*; ~ *stone, iron*; ~ *coal*, bituminous, opp. *anthracite*; ~ *corn*, moist thickening of skin between toes confused with CORN³; ~ (opp. HARD) *currency*; ~ *tissues* of body, not bony or cartilaginous; ~ *palate*, hinder part of palate; ~ *wicket* at cricket, moist or sodden turf; ‖~ *goods*, textiles; ~ *solder*, kinds used for easily fusible metal, cf. ~ SAWDER; ~ SOAP; ~ *tack*, naut., bread, opp. *hard tack* or biscuit; ~ *roe*, of male fish; ~ *wood*, (wood of) coniferous tree). **2.** Of smooth surface or fine texture, not rough or coarse, (~ *skin, hair, raiment*). **3.** Mellow, mild, balmy, not noticeably cold or hot, (~ *air; a~ winter*). **4.** ‖ Rainy or moist or thawing (~ *weather; a~ day*). **5.** (Of water) free from mineral salts & so good for washing or cooking. **6.** Not astringent or sour or bitter (~ *claret* etc.). **7.** Not crude or brilliant or dazzling (~ *colours, light, eyes*); not sharply defined (~ *outline*); not strident or loud, low-toned, (*a~ voice*; ~ *music*; PEDAL[1]; ~-*pedal* v.i. & t., play with ~ pedal down, tone down, refrain from emphasizing; ~ *whispers, murmurs*); (phonet.) sibilant (*g is ~ in* gin), voiced (*b, g, d, are~ mutes*), unaspirated (~. or *smooth* BREATHING[1]). **8.** Gentle, quiet, conciliatory, complimentary or amorous, (~ *rain*; ~ *drink*, colloq., non-alcoholic; ~ *manners*; *a ~ answer*, esp. a good-tempered one to abuse or accusation; ~-*spoken*, see SPEAK; ~ *nothings*, amorous talk). **9.** Sympathetic, compassionate, (*has a ~ heart*, whence ~-*heart'ED*[2] a., ~-*heart'edNESS* n.). **10.** Tranquil (~ *slumbers*). **11.** (sl.). Easy (*has a ~ job*; *a ~ option*; a thing, light well-paid office etc.). **12.** Flabby, weak, feeble, unstrung, effeminate, silly, (*the national character has gone ~*; *a ~ luxurious people*; ~ *muscles*; ~-*headed*, ~-*willed*, half idiotic); hence ~'*ISH*[1] a., ~'*LY*[2] adv., ~'*NESS* n. **13.** n. Silly weak person, also ~'*Y*[3] n. **14.** adv. (commoner in compar. than in posit.). ~*ly* (*play ~, ~er*; ~-*whispering* etc.). **15.** int. (arch.). Wait a moment; hush! [OE *sŏft(e)*, older *sēft(e)*, = OHG *semfti*; cf. also MDu., MLG *sacht*, MHG *sanft*]

sŏf'ta, n. Moslem student of sacred law & theology. [Turk.]

soften (sŏ'fn, saw[2]), v.i. & t. Become or make SOFT or softer; (also ~ *up*) reduce strength of (defences) by bombing etc.; ~*ing* (morbid degeneration) *of the brain.* Hence ~ER[1](1, 2) n. [ME; -EN[5]]

sŏgg'∣y̆ (-g-), a. Sodden, saturated, dank. Hence ~*iNESS* n. [f. dial. *sog* a swamp]

soh. See SOL[2].

sohŏ'[1], int. used in quieting horse etc. [AF hunting-cry]

Sohŏ'[2], n. District in London associated with foreign restaurants etc.

soi-disant (see Ap.), a. Self-styled, pretended. [F]

soigné (swahn'yā), (fem. ~*e*), a. (Chiefly of a woman's toilet) exquisite in detail, carefully finished or arranged. [p.p. of F *soigner* take care of (*soin* care)]

soil[1], n. The ground, upper layer of earth in which plants grow consisting of disintegrated rock usu. with admixture of organic remains, mould, (*good, poor, clayey, alluvial, light, rich*, etc., ~ ~~; one's *native~*, ground of one's native land or place). Hence (·)~ED[2] (-ld) a. [ME, f. AF, app. f. L *solium* taken in sense of L *solum* ground]

soil[2], v.t. & i., & n. **1.** Make dirty, smear or stain with dirt, tarnish, defile, (~*ed linen*; *would not ~ my hands with it* fig.), so ~'URE n. (arch.); admit of being ~ed (~*s easily*). **2.** n. Dirty mark, stain, smear, defilement. **3.** ~-*pipe*, discharge-pipe of water-closet; hence ~'LESS (-l-l-) a. [ME, f. OF *suill(i)er, soill(i)er*, f. Rom. *·suculare* f. *sucula* dim. of *sus* pig; cf. SULLY]

soil[3], v.t. Feed (cattle) on fresh-cut green fodder (orig. for purging). [perh. f. SOIL[3] in sense *dung* (cf. NIGHT-*soil*)]

soirée (swär'ā), n. Social evening, evening gathering esp. for music, conversation, the advancement of some society's objects, or the like. [F]

soixante-quinze (see Ap.), n. French 75 mm. gun. [F]

sojourn (sŏj'ern, sŏ-, sŭ-), v.i. & n. (Make) temporary stay in or *in* place or *with* or *among* person(s). Hence ~ER[1] n. [ME, f. OF *sojorner* etc., f. Rom. *·subdiurnare* (SUB-, *diurnum* daily, day); n. f. OF *sojorn* etc.]

‖ **sŏke**, n. A right of local jurisdiction (hist.); district under a particular jurisdiction and administration, as the *S~ of Peterborough*. [f. OE *sōcn*]

Sŏl[1], n. (joc.). The sun. [L]

sŏl[2], **soh** (sō), n. (mus.). Fifth note of octave. [1st syl. of L *solve*, see GAMUT]

sŏl'a, n. Pithy-stemmed tropical swamp plant (~ *tŏp'ĭ*, Indian sun-helmet of the pith). [f. Hind. *sholā*]

sŏl'ace, n., & v.t. Comfort (v. & n.) in distress or disappointment or tedium (~ *oneself with*, find compensation or relief in; *tobacco, once the poor man's ~*; *found~ in religion*). [ME, f. OF *solas* f. L *solacium* (*solari* CONSOLE[1])]

sŏl'an(-gōōse), n. The gannet. [f. ON *súla* gannet, perh. +*ǫnd, and-* duck]

Sŏlān'um, n. Large genus of plants including potato, nightshade, & many kinds (often spoken of as ~) cultivated as ornamental creepers or for flowers or foliage. [L, = nightshade]

sŏl'ar, a. Of, concerned with, determined by, the sun (~ DAY, *eclipse, spectrum, time*, YEAR; ~ *flowers*, that remain open only for some hours in the day; ~ *month*, an exact twelfth of the year; ~ *myth*, tale explained as symbolizing ~ phenomena; ~ *plexus*, the complex of nerves at pit of stomach; ~ *system*, our sun & the heavenly bodies whose motion is directly or indirectly determined by it). [ME, f. L *solaris* (*sol* sun, -AR[1])]

sŏl'ar∣ism, n. Belief in solar myths as chief source of mythology. So ~IST(2) n. [-ISM]

solā̆r'ium, n. (pl. *-ia*). Place often enclosed in glass for enjoyment or esp. medical use of sun's rays. [L, =sun-dial, sunning-place (SOLAR, -ARY[1])]

sōl'ariz|e, -is|e (-īz), v.i. & t. (photog.). Spoil (i. & t.) by. long exposure. Hence ∼A'TION n. [-IZE]

solā'tium (-shǐ-), n. (pl. *-tia*). Thing given as compensation or consolation. [L, = SOLACE]

sold. See SELL.

sŏldanĕll'a, n. Kinds of Alpine plant some of which are grown in gardens. [mod. L, f. It.]

sŏl'der (*or* sŏd'er), n., & v.t. 1. Kinds of fusible alloy used to join edges of less fusible metals (*hard*, SOFT, ∼, fusible at higher, lower, temperature & so serving for different metals), (fig.) cementing agency. 2. v.t. Join with ∼; ∼*ing-iron*, tool used hot for applying ∼. [ME, f. OF *soudure* (*souder* f. L *solidare* f. SOLIDUS, -URE)]

sōl'dier (-jer), n., & v.i. 1. Member of army (lit. & fig.; ∼*s & sailors*; *play at* ∼*s*, of children, also of volunteers etc.; *tin*, *toy*, ∼*s*; ∼ *of Christ*, active or proselytizing Christian; *the unknown S*∼, see WARRIOR; *old* ∼, lit., also person of experience, also empty bottle, also cigar-end; *come the old* ∼ *over*, claim to dictate to in virtue of greater experience, seek to impose on; ∼ *of fortune*, ready to take service under any State or person that will hire him; *red* ∼, pig-disease; ∼*'s wind*, naut., fair wind for going & returning); private or N.C.O. in army (*both officers & ∼s*; often *common* ∼); military commander of specified ability (*a great, fine, poor,* ∼; *no*∼), whence ∼SHIP(3) n.; hence ∼LIKE a., ∼LY[1,2] a. & adv., (-jer-). 2. (sl.). (Naut.) man, esp. sailor, who shirks work; red herring. 3. (Also ∼ *ant*) one of fighting section of ant or termite colony; (also ∼ *beetle*) kinds of reddish-coloured insect with carnivorous larvae; (also ∼ *crab*) kind of hermit crab; ∼ *orchis*, kind with helmet-shaped sepals. 4. v.i. Serve as ∼ (chiefly in gerund, as *go, tired of,* ∼*ing*); (naut., sl.) shirk work; ∼ *on*, persevere doggedly. [ME *souder* etc., f. OF *soud(i)er*, *soldier* (*soude* pay f. SOLIDUS, -ARY[1]); cf. med. L *solidarius*]

sōl'diery (-jerǐ), n. *The* soldiers (of a State, in a district, etc.); *a* set of troops of specified character (*a wild, licentious,* etc., ∼). [-ERY]

sŏl'do, n. (pl. *-di*, pr. -dē). Italian coin, one-twentieth of lira. [It., f. SOLIDUS]

sōle[1], n., & v.t. 1. Lower surface of human or other plantigrade foot; part of shoe, sock, etc. below foot; bottom or foundation of various things, e.g. plough, carpenter's plane, wagon, golf-club head; ∼*-channel*, groove in ∼ of boot etc. in which sewing is sunk; ∼*-leather*, compressed for use in ∼s; ∼*-plate*, bed-plate of engine etc.; hence -SŌLED[2] (-ld) a.

2. v.t. Provide (shoe etc.) with ∼. [ME, f. OF, f. Rom.-*sola* f. L *solea* sandal]

sōle[2], n. Kind of flat-fish much esteemed as food (LEMON[2] ∼). [ME, f. OF, same wd as prec., in sense = L *solea* flat-fish]

sōle[3], a. On̄* & only, exclusive, (*his* ∼ *reason is this*; *on my own* ∼ *responsibility*); (law) unmarried (only in FEME SOLE); ‖ (arch.) alone, unaccompanied, (*went forth* ∼; CORPORATION ∼). Hence ∼'LY[2] (-l-l-) adv. [ME, f. OF *so(u)l* f. L *solus*]

sŏl'éc|ism, n. Offence against grammar or idiom, blunder in the manner of speaking or writing; piece of ill breeding or incorrect behaviour. So ∼IST(1) n., ∼is'tic a. [f. L f. Gk *soloikismos* f. *soloikos* speaking incorrectly]

sŏl'emn (-m), a. Accompanied with ceremony, done etc. in due form, formally regular, (∼ *feast-day, sacrifice, oath*; *the S*∼ *League & COVENANT*; *probate in* ∼ *form*); mysteriously impressive (∼ *silence*; *a* ∼ *cathedral*); sacred, full of importance, weighty, (*a* ∼ *occasion, truth, warning*); grave, sober, deliberate, slow in movement or action, (∼ *music, a* ∼ *promise,* ∼ *looks*; *a* ∼ *pace*); pompous, affecting gravity or importance, dull, (*put on a* ∼ *face*; *a* ∼ *fool*). Hence ∼LY[2] (-mlǐ) adv., ∼NESS n. (rare). [ME & OF *solem(p)ne*, or f. L *so(l)lemnis* customary etc.]

solĕm'nitў, n. Rite, celebration, festival, piece of ceremony; being solemn, solemn character or feeling or behaviour. [ME, f. OF *solem(p)nite* f. L *sollemnitatem* (prec., -TY)]

sŏl'emniz|e, -is|e (-īz), v.t. Celebrate (festival etc.); duly perform (marriage ceremony); make solemn. Hence ∼A'TION n. [ME, f. OF *solem(p)niser* or med. L *solemnizare* (SOLEMN, -IZE)]

sōl'en, n. A bivalve, the razor-shell. [L, f. Gk *sōlēn* tube, shellfish]

sōl'enoid, n. Cylindrical coil of wire which, when an electric current is passed through it, behaves as a bar magnet, & can magnetize a piece of iron or steel placed inside it. [f. F *solénoïde* (prec., -OID)]

sŏl'-fa' (-ah), v.i. & t., & n. = SOLMIZATE, SOLMIZATION; TONIC ∼. [SOL[2], FA]

sŏlfĕ'ggio (-jō), n. (pl. *-gi*, pr. -jē). Solmization, sol-fa; sol-fa exercise for voice. [It., (prec.+suf. *-eggio*)]

sŏlferi'nō (-rē-), n. A purplish-red colour made from rosaniline. [discovered in year of battle of *S*∼ (1859), cf. MAGENTA]

soli'cĭt, v.t. & i. Invite, make appeals or requests to, importune, (*marvels* ∼ *his attention* or *senses*; *we* ∼ *you for your custom*; *was known to have* ∼*ed the judges*), (of prostitute) entice (man, or abs.) in public place; ask importunately or earnestly for (∼ *favours, office, custom*). So ∼A'TION n. [ME, f. OF *sol(l)iciter* or L *sollicitare* (*sollicitus* anxious)]

soli'cĭtor, n. One who solicits (rare); ‖ member of the legal profession competent to advise clients & instruct &

prepare causes for barristers but not to appear as advocate except in certain lower courts (cf. BARRISTER, LAWYER, ATTORNEY); *canvasser; ‖ S~-*General*, Crown law officer below Attorney-General (in Scotland below Lord Advocate), & like him appointed by the Government of the day & advising & representing it in legal matters. [ME, f. OF *sol(l)iciteur* (prec., -OR)]

soli′citous, a. Eager *to* do; desirous *of*; anxious, troubled, (*about, concerning, for*, etc., or abs.). Hence ~LY² adv. [f. L *sol(l)icitus* see SOLICIT, -OUS]

soli′citude, n. Being solicitous, anxiety, concern. [ME, f. OF, or f. L *sol(l)icitudo* (prec., -TUDE)]

sŏl′id, a. & n. **1.** Of stable shape, not liquid or fluid, having some rigidity, (~ *food*; *water becomes* ~ *at* 32° F.). **2.** Of ~ substance throughout, not hollow, without internal cavities or interstices, uninterrupted, whole (~ *sphere* or *ball*; ~ *tire*, without central tube; ~ *square*, mil., formation of equal depth & length; ~-*hoofed, -horned*, etc.; ~-*drawn*, of tubes etc., pressed or drawn out from a ~ bar of metal; ~ *printing*, without leads between lines; *a* ~ *hour, day*, etc.). **3.** Strongly constructed, not flimsy, (~ *house, pier, furniture; man of* ~ *build*). **4.** Homogeneous, alike all through, (*of* ~ *silver* etc.; ~ *colour*, covering the whole of an object, without pattern etc.; *a* ~ *vote* etc., unanimous, undivided; *go or be* ~ *for*, be united in favour of; *the* ~ *South*, southern States of U.S. consistently voting for Democratic party). **5.** Well grounded, sound, reliable, real, genuine, not fancied or pretended or showy, (~ *arguments, sense, comfort; a* ~ *man*, sensible but not brilliant, also of sound financial position; *have* ~ *grounds for supposing*; ~ *consideration*, thing that can fairly be regarded as an inducement in contracts etc.). **6.** Of three dimensions (~ *foot* etc., cubic; ~ *angle*, formed by three or more plane angles in different planes meeting at point; ~ *number*, integer with three prime factors). **7.** Concerned with ~s (~ *geometry*; ~ *measure*; ~ *problem*, math., involving curves that are sections of ~s & requiring cubic equation); hence or cogn. SOLID′IFY v.t. & i., solidIFICA′TION n., solid′ifiABLE a., solid′ITY n., ~LY² adv. **8.** n. Body consisting of particles that maintain their relative positions against some degree of pressure; (geom.) body or magnitude having three dimensions (cf. *point, line, surface*; REGULAR ~). [ME; adj. f. OF *solide* or L *solidus*; n. f. adj. or f. F *solide* f. L *solidum*]

sŏlidă′ritў, n. Holding together, mutual dependence, community of interests, feelings, & action. So **sŏl′idarў** a. [f. F *solidarité* (*solidaire* f. *solide* = prec., -ARY¹, -TY)]

sŏlidŭng′ūlar (-ngg-), **-ate**, aa. Solid-hoofed, of horse family, equine. [f. L SOLID*us*, *ungula* hoof, -AR¹, -ATE²]

sŏl′idus, n. (pl. *-dī*). (Hist.) gold coin introduced by Roman Emperor Constantine; (only in abbr. *s.*) shilling(s), as 7*s.* 6*d.*, £1. 1*s.*; the shilling line (for ʃ or long s) as in 7/6, used also in writing fractions as in 3/4. [L, a noun use of SOLID*us*]

sŏlifid′ian, a. & n. (Holder) of doctrine that faith by itself suffices for salvation. [L *solus* alone, *fides* faith, +-IAN]

solil′oqu|ў, n. Talking without or regardless of the presence of hearers (*a* ~*y*, piece of this esp. on part of character in play). Hence ~IZE(2) v.i., ~IST(1) n. [f. LL *soliloquium* (*solus* alone, -I-, *loqui* speak)]

sŏl′ipĕd, a. & n. Solidungulate (animal). [L *solus* alone, *pes pedis* foot, or alt. f. L *solidipes* (SOLID); cf. F *solipède*]

sŏl′ips|ism, n. (metaphys.). View that the self is the only knowable, or the only existent, thing. So ~IST n. [f. L *solus* alone, *ipse* self, -ISM]

sŏlitaire′, n. Ear-ring, shirt-stud, etc., having a single gem; shirt-cuff fastening in one piece; game played by one person with marbles on special board; (now usu. *patience*) kinds of card-game for one player; kinds of W.-Ind. & Amer. thrush; (now rare) a recluse. [F, f. L *solitarius* (foll.)]

sŏl′itar|ў, a. & n. **1.** Living alone, not gregarious, without companions, unfrequented, secluded, single, lonely, sole, (~*y* ants, bees, etc., kinds not living in communities; *a* ~*y life, walk, valley, instance*; ~*y confinement*, isolation in separate cell); hence ~ILY² adv., ~INESS n. **2.** n. Recluse, anchorite. [ME, f. L *solitarius* (*solus* alone)]

sŏl′itŭde, n. Being solitary; lonely place. [ME, f. OF, or f. L *solitūdo* (SOLE³, -TUDE)]

sŏl′mizăte, v.i., **sŏlmizā′tion**, n. (Use) system of associating each note of scale with particular syllable (see GAMUT), in *fixed-do* system C always being do & other syllables accordingly, in *movable-do* system key-note always being do & other syllables accordingly. [f. F *solmiser*, *-ation* (SOL², MI, -IZE)]

sŏl′ō, n. (pl. *-os*, in sense 1 also *-i* pr. -ē), a., & adv. **1.** Vocal or instrumental piece or passage performed by one person with or without subordinate accompaniment (also attrib., as ~ *passage*; ~ *stops* on organ, stops specially suitable for playing ~ passages accompanied by other stops; ~ *organ*, fourth manual on large organ, with stops of this kind); whence ~IST(1) n. **2.** (cards). Kind of whist in which one player opposes three or undertakes other tasks; similar varieties of other games; declaration or playing to win five tricks at ~ whist. **3.** (aviation). An unaccompanied flight; (adj. & adv.) unaccompanied, alone, (a ~ *flight*; *flying* ~). [It., f. L *solus* SOLE[3]]

Sŏl'omon, n. King of Israel reputed wisest of men (*is no* ~; SONG *of* ~), whence **Sŏlomŏn'IC** a.; ~'s *seal*, kinds of flowering plant of family of lily of the valley

Sŏl'on, n Sage, wise legislator. [name of Athenian lawgiver (d. 558 B.C.)]

sŏl'stice, n. Either time (*summer*, *winter*, ~, about 21st June, 22nd Dec.) at which sun is farthest from equator & appears to pause before returning; (also *solstitial point*) point in ecliptic reached by sun at ~. So **sŏlsti'tIAL** (-ĭshl) a. [ME, f. OF, f. L *solstitium* (SOL[1]. *sistere* -*stit*- make stand f. *stare* stand)]

sŏl'ūble, a. That can be dissolved in some fluid; that can be solved; ~ *glass*, (also WATER-*glass*) preparation of silicate of soda used for hardening artificial stone, preserving eggs, etc. Hence **sŏlūbIL'ITY n.** [ME, f. OF, f. LL *solubilis* (SOLVE, -BLE)]

sŏl'us, pred. a. (fem. *sola*). Alone, unaccompanied, (esp. in stage directions, as *enter king* ~; also joc., as *found myself* ~). [L]

solu'tion (-lōō-, -lŭ-), n., & v.t. **1.** Separation, dissolution, abolition of union, (chiefly in ~ *of continuity*, surg., separation of tissues by fracture etc., & transf.). **2.** Dissolving or being dissolved, esp. conversion of solid or gas into liquid form by mixture with liquid called the solvent or menstruum (*chemical* ~, involving change in chem. properties of components; *mechanical* ~, without such change; state resulting from this (*held in* ~ etc.; *his ideas are in* ~, in a state of flux, unsettled); liquid & solid or gas so mixed (a ~ *of alum*; *strong*, *weak*, ~, with small, large, proportion of solvent). **3.** Resolution, solving, answer, method for the solving, of a problem, puzzle, question, doubt, difficulty, etc. (*of*, *for*, *to*). **4.** (In full *rubber* ~) dissolved caoutchouc. **5.** v.t. Coat with rubber ~. [ME, f. OF, or f. L *solutio* (as SOLVE, -ION)]

solu'tionist (-lōōshon-, -lŭ-), n. Professional solver of newspaper puzzles. [prec. +-IST (3)]

Solūt'rian, a. (archaeol.). Of the palaeolithic period represented by remains found at the Solutré cave, Saône-et--Loire, France.

sŏlve, v.t. Untie, loosen, unravel, dissolve, (knot, tangle, cohesion, etc.; arch.); find answer to (problem) or way out of (difficulty). Hence **sŏl'vABLE a.**, **sŏlvABIL'ITY n.** [ME, f. L *solvere solut*-]

sŏl'vent, a. & n. **1.** Having the power of dissolving or forming SOLUTION with something or fig. of weakening the hold of traditions or beliefs; having money enough to meet all pecuniary liabilities, whence **sŏl'vENCY n. 2.** n. ~ liquid or substance, menstruum, (see SOLUTION; *water is the commonest* ~; *alcohol is the*

~ *of resinous substances*); dissolving or weakening agent (*science as a* ~ *of religious belief*). [f. L SOLVEre, -ENT]

-som. See -SOME.

sŏmăt'ic, a. Of the body, corporeal, physical, (opp. *mental*, *spiritual*, *psychic*; ~ *death*, of the body as a whole). [f. Gk *sōmatikos* (*sōma* -*atos* body, -IC)]

sŏm'at|o-, comb. form of Gk *sōma* (prec., -o-) used in a number of scientific terms, = of body or the human body, as ~*ogĕn'ic*, originating in the body, ~ŏL'OGY, science of living bodies physically considered.

sŏm'bre (-ber), a. Dark, gloomy, dismal, as a ~ *sky*, ~ *prospect*, *man of* ~ *character*. Hence ~LY[2] adv., ~NESS n., **sŏm'brous** (poet.) a. [F, app. f. **sombrer* to shade f. LL *subumbrare* (SUB-, *umbra* shade)]

sŏmbrer'o (-ārŏ), n. (pl. ~s). Broad--brimmed felt hat common in America. [Sp., f. *sombra* shade, see prec.]

some (sŭm, sum), a., pron., & adv. **1.** Particular but unknown or unspecified (person or thing), as ~ *fool has locked the door*, *saw it in* ~ *book* (*or other*), *ask* ~ *experienced person*, ~ (*people*) *say yes* & ~ (or *others or other people*) *say no.* **2.** A certain quantity or number of (~thing), as *drink* ~ *water*, *eat* ~ *bread*, *bring* ~ *pens*, *I have* ~ *already*, *have* ~ *more*, ~ *of it is spoilt*, ~ *of them were late*, *can we or can't we have* ~ *milk?* (but *we cannot have any milk*), *if I find* ~ (or *any*) *I will send them*; **& then* ~ (sl.), & plenty more than that. **3.** An appreciable or considerable quantity of, as *went* ~ *miles out of our way*, *had* ~ *trouble in arranging it*, ~ *years ago*, *that is* ~ *help.* **4.** Such to a certain extent, as *that is* ~ *guide*, *test*, *proof*; (emphat. in meiosis, U.S. & sl.) such in the fullest sense, ~thing like (a), as *this is* ~ *war!*, *I call that* ~ *poem.* **5.** (Usu. stressed) not quite no, as *do have* ~ *mercy on our nerves*, *has after all* ~ *sense of decency.* **6.** Approximately so many or much of (~thing), as *waited* ~ *20 minutes*, *scales* ~ *15 stone*, *we were* ~ *60 in all*; ALL *&* ~. **7.** adv. (sl.). In ~ degree, as *he seemed annoyed* ~. **8.** ~'*body*, ~ person, (w. pl. -*dies*) person of consequence. **9.** ~'*how*, in ~ unspecified or unexplained manner, for ~ reason or other, as *he* ~*how dropped behind*, ~*how or other I never liked him*, (stressed) no matter how, as *must get it finished* ~*how.* **10.** ~'*one*, = ~*body* (not in pl.); ~ *one*, any particular (one), as *choose* ~ *one place as a centre*, *take* ~ *one as a type.* **11.** ~'*thing*, ~ thing (esp. *or* ~*thing* as vague substitute for noun, adj., vb, or adv.), as *have* ~*thing to tell you*; *we hope to see* ~*thing of* (occasionally meet) *them*, *has lost* ~*thing or other*, *take a drop of* ~*thing* (liquor), *he is* or *has* ~*thing* (~ official, ~ employment) *in the record office*, *can spare* ~*thing out of so much*, *there is* ~*thing* (truth, point) *in what you say*, thinks himself ~thing (of ~ consequence), felt there was a little ~thing wanting, ~thing of preciosity in his style, an ~thing of (am in ~ sense or degree) a carpenter, it is ~thing (~ comfort) to be safe home again, his temper is, his fads are, ~thing awful, was made a bishop or ~thing, has sprained his ankle or ~thing (~ other part), is neurotic or ~thing, lost his train or (did) ~thing, turned the tap too soon or too hard or (too) ~thing; (adv., arch. exc. ~thing like) in ~ degree, as was ~thing impatient, ~thing troubled, shaped ~thing like a cigar; (colloq., w. stress on like) this is ~thing like a (is a large or good) pudding, that's ~thing like (is capital)/ 12. ~ time adv., for ~ time, as have been waiting ~ time, at ~ time, as must see him about it ~ time; ~'time adv. & a. (arch.), former(ly), as was ~time mayor of Barnstaple, (the) ~time sheriff; ~'times adv., at ~ times, as have ~times thought, is ~times hot & ~times cold. 13. ~'way, in ~ way. 14. ~'what, (adv.) in ~ degree, as it is ~what difficult, was ~what puzzled, answered ~what hastily, (pron., arch. exc. when indisting. f. adv.) found ~what to detain him, loses ~what (perh. adv.) in the telling, loses ~what of its force. 15. ~ʻ when (rare, affected), at ~ time or other. 16. ~'where, in, at, to, ~ place, as lives ~where near us, sent him ~where, Burton says ~where in the Anatomy, will see him ~where (in hell etc.) first. 17. ~'whither (arch.), to ~ place. [OE, OS, OHG sum, ON sumr, Goth. sums]

-some, -som, suf. forming adjj., OE -sum, cogn. w. OS, OHG -sam; joined to nn. w. sense 'adapted to, productive of', as quarrelsome, gladsome (f. obs. glad n.), to adjj., as lithesome (also lissom), blithesome, fulsome, & to trans. vbs w. sense ' apt to ', as tiresome, winsome, wearisome, gruesome (f. grue in impers. trans. use it grues me). Written -om in lissom, buxom, etc.; in two, three, four, -some the suf. was orig. the pronoun OE sum some; -som in RANSOM is of diff. orig.

so'mersault, -sět[1], (sŭ'-), n., & v.i. 1. Spring, bound, in which person turns heels over head (double, treble, ~, twice, thrice) in the air; turn a ~, make such spring. 2. v.i. Turn ~. [f. OF sombresau(l)t alt. f. sobresault f. L supra above + saltus -ūs leap (salire)]

‖ so'mersět[2] (sŭ-), n. Padded saddle esp. for one-legged rider. [f. Lord F. S~ (d. 1855), who used one]

So'mersět House (sŭ-), n. Building in London containing chief place of deposit of proved wills, & inland revenue offices, & often mentioned allusively in these connexions.

sŏm'ite, n. Each body-division of a segmented animal, metamere. Hence sŏmit'ic[10] a. [f. Gk sōma body + -ITE'(2)]

sŏmnăm'būl|ism, n. Walking or performing other action during sleep; con-

dition of brain inducing this; artificial ~ism, hypnotism. Hence or cogn. ~ANT (rare), ~is'tic, aa., ~ATE[3] v.i. (rare), ~IST n. [f. L somnus sleep + ambulare walk]

sŏmnī-, comb. form of L somnus sleep, as: ~f'erous, inducing sleep, narcotic; ~l'oquence, ~l'oquism, ~l'oquy, habit of talking in sleep; ~l'oquous, ~l'oquist, (person) given to this; ~p'athist, hypnotic subject; ~p'athy, hypnotic sleep.

sŏm'nol|ent, a. Sleepy, drowsy; inducing drowsiness; (path.) in state between sleeping & waking. Hence or cogn. ~ENCE, ~ENCY, nn., ~entlY[2] adv. [ME, f. OF, or f. L somnolentus (somnus sleep, -LENT)]

sŏm'nolism, n. Hypnotic sleep. [f. prec. + -ISM]

son (sŭn), n. 1. Male child of a parent (~ & heir, esp. eldest ~); ~-in-law, one's daughter's husband; he is his father's ~ (like, worthy of, his father). 2. The Son of Man, (N.T.) Christ, the Messiah, (O.T.) descendant of Adam, esp. as form of address in Ezekiel; the ~s of men, mankind; the Son (of God), = GOD[1] the Son. 3. ~ of a GUN; every MOTHER[1]'s ~. 4. Descendant, as ~s of Abraham. 5. (As form of address esp. of old man to young man, confessor to penitent, etc.) my ~. 6. ~ of the soil, recognizable native of a district, worker on the land, dweller in the country. 7. Native of a country, as Britain's ~s. 8. Person viewed as inheriting an occupation, quality, etc., as ~ of toil, ~ of Mars (soldier), ~ (= man) of BELIAL, ~s of light, darkness, etc.; Sons of Liberty, of the (American) Revolution, etc., American patriotic etc. organizations. Hence ~'LESS a., ~'SHIP n. [OE, OS, OHG sunu, ON sunr, Goth. sunus f. Gmc *sunuz]

sŏn'|ant, a. & n. (Sound, letter) accompanied by vocal vibration, voiced, not surd, (e.g. b, d, g, j, v, z). Hence ~ANCY n. [f. L sonare sound (sonus, -ANT)]

*sŏn'ar, n. = ASDIC. [sound navigation ranging]

sona'ta (-nah-), n. Composition for one instrument (e.g. piano) or two (e.g. piano & violin), normally with three or four movements (one or more being usu. in ~ form) contrasted in rhythm & speed but related in key; ~ form, type of composition in which two themes ('subjects') are successively set forth, developed, & restated. [It. (as SONANT, see -ADE)]

sŏnati'na (-tē-), n. Simple or short form of sonata. [It., dim. of prec.]

sŏng, n. 1. Singing, vocal music, as burst forth into ~; musical cry of some birds (~-birds). 2. Short poem set to music or meant to be sung; short poem in rhymed stanzas; poetry, verse, as renowned in ~. 3. (mus.) ~ form, mode of composition usu. in three sections, the first & third being nearly the same & the second contrasted with the first. **4.** *Bought, sold, it for a* ~ *or an old* ~ (mere trifle); *nothing to make a* ~ *about* (colloq.), of very trifling importance; *S*~ *of* DEGREES or *ascents* (in O.T., Psalms 120-134); *S*~ *of S*~*s, S*~ *of Solomon*, O.T. book once attributed to Solomon; ~- -PLUG²*ing*; ~-THRUSH¹; ~-*sparrow*, hedge- -sparrow & other birds. Hence ~'LESS a. [OE, OS *sang*, OHG *sang*-, ON *sǫngr*, Goth. *saggws* f. Gmc *sangwaz* f. pret. stem of *singwan* SING]

sŏng'st|er, n. Singer; song-bird; poet. Hence ~rESS¹ n. [ME; -STER]

sŏn'ic, a. Of or relating to sound or sound-waves (~ *boom*, loud noise made when aircraft crashes the sound barrier; ~ *barrier*, excessive resistance offered by air to objects moving at speed near that of sound). [f. L *sonus* sound, -IC]

sonif'erous, a. Conveying or producing sound. [f. L *sonus* sound + -FEROUS]

sŏnn'ĕt, n. Poem of 14 lines (usu. rhyming thus; *pig bat cat wig jig hat rat fig*; lie *red sob die bed rob* or *lie red die bed pie wed*; or otherwise e.g. as in Shakespeare's ~s); ~ *sequence*, a set of ~s connected in theme; (now rare) any short lyric. So ~EER' (usu. derog.), (n.) composer of ~s, (v.i. & t.) compose ~s, celebrate in ~s, address ~s to. [F, or f. It. *sonetto* (*suono* SOUND² n., -ET¹)]

so'nny (sŭ-), n. Familiar form of address to a boy. [f. SON + -Y³]

sŏn'obuoy (-boi), n. Buoy for detecting submarines, dropped by parachute from aircraft and equipped with hydrophone and radio for transmitting sounds to aircraft and surface vessels. [f. L *sonus* sound + BUOY¹]

sonŏm'ĕter, n. Kinds of instrument for testing deaf person's hearing, measuring sounds, etc. [f. L *sonus* sound + -METER]

sŏnorĕs'c|ent, a. (Of hard rubber etc.) emitting sounds corresponding to pulsations of radiant heat or light. So ~ENCE n. [as SONOROUS + -ESCENT]

sonŏrif'ic, a. Producing (esp. other than vocal) sound. [as foll. + -FIC]

sonŏr'ous (*or* sŏn'o-), a. Resonant; loud- -sounding; (of speech, style, etc.) high- -sounding, imposing; ~ *figures* (formed in layer of sand etc. by sound-vibration); ~ *râle* (heard in some diseases). Hence *or* cogn. **sonŏr'ITY**, ~NESS, nn., ~LY² adv. [f. L *sonorus* (*sonor* sound) + -OUS]

‖ **sŏn'sў**, a. (Sc.). Plump, buxom; of cheerful disposition (esp. in phr. ~ *lass*). [ult. f. Gael. *sonas* good fortune]

sōon, adv. **1.** Not long after the present time or time in question or *after* specified time, in a short time, as *shall* ~ *know the result, was* ~ *convinced of his error, arrived* ~ *after four,* ~ *after the gate was closed, least said* ~*est mended.* **2.** *As* (or *so*, esp after negative, or when causality or other close connexion is suggested)

~ *as*, the moment that, not later than, as early as, as *came as* (or *so*) ~ *as I heard of it, will get there as* ~ *as they* (do), *did not arrive so* (or *as*) ~ *as I expected, drops his fine theories so* (or *as*) ~ *as they clash with his interests, so* ~ *as* (ever) *there is any talk of paying he cools down.* **3.** (With expressed or implied comparison) willingly, as *I would just as* ~ *stay at home* (as *go*), *would* ~*er die than let him* (or *than that he should*) *find it out, which would you* ~*est do?* **4.** Early, as *what makes you come so* ~?; *you spoke too* ~; *we had no* ~*er sat down than* (the moment we sat down) *she burst into tears; no* ~*er said than done*, it was done the moment it was proposed etc.; *the* ~*er the better; you will repent it* ~*er or later* (some day). [OE *sōna*, OS, OHG *sān(o)*]

sōot, n., & v.t. **1.** Black substance rising in fine flakes in the smoke of wood, coal, oil, etc., during combustion & sticking to sides of chimney etc., used as fertilizer; ~-*cancer,* -*wart*, disease of scrotum in sweeps. Hence ~'ILY² adv., ~'iNESS n., ~'LESS, ~'Y², aa. **2.** v.t. Cover with ~. [OE, MLG *sōt*, MDu. *soet*, ON *sōt*]

‖ **sōot'erkin**, n. (arch.). Dutch woman's false birth produced by sitting over stove; (fig.) abortive scheme. [perh. f. prec.; there is app. no similar term in Dutch]

‖ **sōoth**, n. (arch.). Truth, fact, esp. *in* (*good*), really, truly. [OE, f. *sōth* adj. (= OS *sōth*, ON *sannr, sathr*), f. *santh*-, cogn. w. Goth. *sunjis* true]

sōoth|e (-dh), v.t. Calm (person, nerves, passions); soften, mitigate, (pain); flatter, humour, (person, his vanity). Hence ~'ER² (-dh-) n. (in vbl senses, & esp. rubber teat for child to suck), ~'iNGLY (-dh-) adv. [OE *sōthian* verify, f. *sōth* adj. (prec.)]

‖ **sōoth'fast** (-ah-), a. (arch.). Truthful; true; loyal, steadfast. [OE *sōthfæst* (SOOTH, FAST³), cf. STEADFAST]

sōoth'sayer, n. One who foretells the future, diviner. Hence **sōoth'say** v.i. [ME; SOOTH + SAY + -ER¹]

sŏp, n., & v.t. & i. (-pp-). **1.** Piece of bread etc. dipped in broth etc. (~ *in the pan*, fried bread); MILK¹~; something given (*to* formidable or troublesome animal, person, etc., esp. *to Cerberus*) to pacify, bribe. **2.** v.t. Soak (bread etc. in broth etc.), take *up* (water etc.) by absorption in towel etc., wet thoroughly. **3.** v.i. Be drenched, as *am* ~*ping with rain, clothes are* ~*ping* (vbl n. as adv.) *wet*, whence ~p'Y² a., ‖ also (colloq.) full of mawkish sentiment. [OE *sopp*, corresp. to MLG *soppe*, OHG *sopfa*, f. weak grade of *sūpan* SUP]

sŏph'ism, n. False argument intended to deceive (cf. PARALOGISM). [ME, f. OF *sophi(s)me* f. L f. Gk *sophisma* (foll.)]

sŏph'ist, n. Ancient-Greek paid teacher of philosophy & rhetoric; captious or

fallacious reasoner, quibbler. Hence or
cogn. **sophis'tic**(AL) aa., **sophis'tical**LY
adv., **~RY**(4, 5) n. [f. L f. Gk *sophistēs*
(*sophizō* instruct f. *sophos* wise, -IST)]

sŏph'ister, n. (hist.). Student of varying
seniority at some English & American universities. [ME, f. OF *sophistre* as prec.]

sophis'tic|**āte**, v.t. & i. Involve (subject)
in sophistry; mislead (person) thus;
deprive (person, thing) of simplicity,
make artificial; (p.p., of person) worldly-
-wise; tamper with (text etc.) for purposes
of argument etc.; use sophistry; adulterate (wine etc.). So **~A'TION** n. [f. OF
(*-quer*), or med. L *sophisticare* (*sophisticus*
sophistic), see -ATE[3]]

*****sŏph'omŏre**, n. Second-year university
student. [app. f. *sophom* obs. var. of
SOPHISM + -OR]

Sŏph'y̆, n. (hist.). Ruler of Persia in
16th & 17th cc. [f. Pers. *Çafī* surname
of dynasty]

sŏpor|if'ic, a. & n. (Drug) tending to
produce sleep. So **~if'EROUS** a. [f. L
sopor sleep + -I- + -FIC; cf. L *soporifer*]

sopra'n|ō (-rah-), n. (pl. *-nos*, *-ni* pr. -nē).
(Music for) highest female or boy's voice,
treble (often attrib.); (also **~IST** n.) singer
with this. [It. (*sopra* above f. L *supra*)]

sŏr'a, n. Bird frequenting marshes of
Carolina etc. in autumn & used as food.
[native]

sŏrb, n. Service-tree; (also **~-apple**) its
fruit. Hence **~age'**AL[3] n., **~'ic** a., (chem.).
[f. F *sorbe*, or L *sorbus* service-tree]

sŏrbèfā'cient (-shnt), a. & n. (med.).
(Drug etc.) causing absorption. [f. L
sorbēre suck in + -FACIENT]

sŏrb'ĕt, n. Flavoured water-ice; = SHER-
BET. [F, as SHERBET]

Sŏrbŏnne', n. Theological faculty in
University of Paris having great influence
in 16th & 17th cc. (hist.); the seat of the
Académie of Paris & of the faculties of
science & literature. [F, f. R. de *Sorbon*,
founder about 1250]

sŏr'cer|er, n. User of magic arts, wizard,
enchanter (often fig.). So **~ESS**[1], **sŏr'cery**
(4, 5), nn. [f. obs. *sorcer* f. OF *sorcier* f.
Rom. **sortiarius* caster of lots (*sors -rtis*
lot, see -ARY[1]) + -ER[1]]

*****sŏrdamĕn'tĕ**, adv. (mus.). In a muffled
manner. [It.]

sŏrd'id, a. Mean, niggardly; ignoble,
base; (bot., zool., of colours) impure,
muddy, as **~** *blue*; dirty, squalid. Hence
~LY[2] adv., **~NESS** n. [f. F *sordide* or L
sordidus (*sordēre* be dirty, *sordes* filth, see
-ID[1])]

sŏrd'ine (-ēn), n. (mus.). Mute for bowed
or wind instruments; damper of piano
string. [f. It. *sordina* f. L as SURD]

sŏre, a., n., & adv. 1. (Of parts of body,
person) morbidly tender, as *has a* **~**
arm, is FOOT[1]**~**, (*clergyman's*) **~** THROAT,
touched him on a **~** *place* (often fig.), *a
sight for* **~** *eyes* (welcome, pleasant), *like
a bear with a* **~** *head* (grumpy); irritated,

aggrieved, touchy, as *is very* **~** *about his
defeat*; arousing painful feelings, irritating, esp. a **~** *subject*; (arch., poet.)
distressing, grievous, severe, as *in* **~**
distress, a **~** *struggle, affliction* **~** *long time
he bore*, whence **~LY**[2] (-rl-) adv. 2. n. **~**
place on body e.g. where skin or flesh
is bruised or inflamed; (fig.) **~** subject,
painful memory, esp. *re-open old* **~s**;
BED[1]**~**; EYE[1]**~**. 3. adv. Grievously,
severely, as **~** *oppressed, bested, afflicted*.
Hence **~'NESS** (-rn-) n. [(n. & adv. f. adj.)
OE *sār* painful, OS, OHG *sēr*, ON *sárr*
(Goth. *sair* n.), f. Gmc **sairaz*]

sorel. See SORREL[2].

sŏr'ghum (-gum), n. Kinds of tropical
cereal grasses including millet. [mod. L,
f. It. *sorgo*]

sŏr'icine, a. Of, related to, the shrew-
-mouse. [f. L *soricinus* (*sorex -icis* shrew-
-mouse, -INE[1])]

sorīt'ēs (-z), n. Chain-syllogism (e.g. a cat
is a quadruped, quadruped is an animal,
animal is a substance; therefore a cat
is a substance); form of sophism leading
by gradual steps from truth to absurdity
& based on the absence of precise, esp.
numerical, limits to terms (e.g. a man
with only 1 hair is bald, therefore a man
with 2, 3, 4, . . . 10,000, hairs is bald). So
sorit'ICAL a. [L f. Gk *sōritēs* lit. heaper
(*sōros* heap, see -ITE[1])]

‖ **sŏrn**, v.i. (Sc.). Obtrude oneself *on* (person) for bed & board. Hence **~'ER**[1] **n.**
[f. obs. Ir. *sorthan* free quarters]

sorŏp'timist, n. Member of an international association of women's clubs.
[app. f. L *soror* sister + OPTIMIST]

sorŏr'ity̆, n. Devotional sisterhood;
*women's society in college or university.
[f. med. L *sororitas* (L *soror* sister), after
fraternity]

sorōs'is, n. (bot.). Fleshy compound
fruit, e.g. pineapple, mulberry. [mod. L
f. Gk *sōros* SORUS + -OSIS]

‖ **sŏ'rra**, adv. (Ir., sl.). Not, never, (**~** *a
one, a bit*, etc., = the devil a). [= *sorrow*]

sŏ'rrel[1], n. Kinds of acid-leaved herb
allied with dock. [ME, f. OF *surele, sorele*
f. *sur* f. WG **sūr* SOUR]

sŏ'rrel[2], a. & n. (Of) reddish-brown
colour; **~** animal esp. horse; (also *sorel*)
buck of third year. [ME, f. OF *sorel* f.
sore (mod. *saur*) f. WG **saur* dry,
yellowish; see -LE(2)]

sŏ'rrow (-ō), n., & v.i. 1. Grief, sadness,
caused by loss of good or occurrence of
evil, whence **~FUL** (-rof-) a., **~ful**LY[2] adv.,
~fulNESS n.; occasion of this, misfortune,
trouble, as *has had many* **~s**, *much* **~**; *the
Man of S*~**s**, Christ; **~-stricken** (with **~**);
lamentation, as *his* **~** *was loud & long*.
2. v.i. Grieve, feel **~**, (*at, over, for*, misfortune etc., *for*, i.e. on behalf of, person
etc.), mourn (*after, for*, lost person or
thing), whence **~ER**[1] (-ōer) n., **~ING**[3]
(-rōl-) a. [OE *sorh, sorg*, OS, OHG *sorga*,
ON *sorg*, Goth. *saurga*]

so'rrў, a. Feeling regret, regretful, as *will be ~ for this some day, felt ~ for him* (on his account), *~ for one*self (colloq. = depressed), *am ~ for* (regret) *that, am so ~ (that) you must go, am ~ to hear it,* (as informal apology for trifling offence) *~!*; (literary) wretched, paltry, shabby, of poor quality, as *a ~ fellow, in a ~ plight, in ~ clothes, a ~ excuse,* whence **so'rrIlў**[2] adv., **so'rrINESS** n. [OE *sárig* (SORE, -Y[2])]

so̅rt[1], n. 1. Group of things etc. with common attributes, class, kind, species, as *biscuits of several ~s, a new ~ of bicycle, people of every ~ & kind*; of *~s,* (in inventories etc.) unassorted, mixed. **2.** (In foll. uses = KIND[1]) *nothing of the ~, coffee of a ~, what ~ of tree?,* (colloq.) *these ~ of men, a ~ of stockbroker* etc., *I ~ of expected it; a ~ of war* etc., *a war* etc. *of a ~* or colloq. *of ~s,* not fully deserving the name; (colloq.) *an awfully good ~* (of person), *that's your ~* (the way to do it). **3.** (arch.). Manner, way, as *in seemly, courteous,* etc., *~*; *after* or *in a ~* (= FASHION); *in some ~* (literary), to a certain extent. **4.** (print.). Any letter or piece in fount of type, as *copy is hard* (or *runs*) *on ~s* (requires many of some *~s*). **5.** *Out of ~s,* out of health, spirits, or temper, (print.) short of *~s.* [ME, f. OF *sorte* f. Rom. *sorta alt. f. L *sors sort-* lot]

so̅rt[2], v.t. & i. 1. Separate into sorts (often *over, out*); select (things of one sort) from miscellaneous group, as *~ed out those of the largest size.* **2.** (arch.). Correspond or agree *with* (*his actions ~ ill, well, with his professions*). Hence *~'ABLE a., ~'ER[1]* n. [ME, f. OF *sortir,* L *sortire,* & prec.]

so̅rt'e̅s (-z), n. pl. *~ Virgilian'ae, Bib'licae* or *Sāc'rae, Home'ricae,* divination by chance selection of passages from Virgil, the Bible, or Homer. [L, pl. as SORT[1]]

so̅rt'ie (-tē), n. **1.** Sally esp. of beleaguered garrison. **2.** Operational flight by one aircraft. [F, f. *sortir* go out]

so̅rt'ile̅ge, n. Divination by lots. [ME, f. OF *sortilege* or med. L *sortilegium* f. L *sortilegus* a. (as SORT[1] + *legere* choose)]

so̅rti'tion, n. Casting of lots. [f. L *sortitio* (*sortiri* cast lots)]

so̅r'us, n. (bot.; pl. *sor'i*). Heap, cluster, esp. of spore-cases on back of fern-frond. [f. Gk *sōros* heap]

-sory, suf., a spec. form of -ORY in aa. or nn. f. L vbs that form p.p. in -s-, as *accessory* (*cedere cess-*), *promissory* (*mittere miss-*).

S O S (ĕs'o̅ĕs'), n. Radio code-signal of extreme distress; broadcast appeal to (otherwise untraceable) person (to visit dying relative etc.); (transf.) any despairing cry or action. [Morse ⌣⌣⌣---⌣⌣⌣]

so̅'so̅, pred. a. & adv. Not very good. [SO]

so̅stenu'to̅ (-no̅o̅-), adv. (mus.). In sustained or prolonged manner. [It.]

so̅t, n., & v.i. (-tt-). **1.** Confirmed drunkard, person stupefied by habitual drunkenness. **2. v.i.** Tipple. Hence *~t'ISH[1] a., ~t'ishLў[2] adv., ~t'ishNESS n.* [f. OF *sot, sote* fool(ish), of unkn. orig.]

Soth'ebў's (sŭdhe-), n. A sale-room in London for books, MSS., etc.

So̅th'ic, a. Of the dog-star, esp. *~ year* (Egyptian, fixed by heliacal rising of dog-star), *~ cycle* (of 1460 ~ or 1461 solar years). [f. Gk *Sōthis* f. Egypt. name of dog-star]

so̅tt'o vo̅'ce (-chĕ), adv. In an undertone, aside. [It. *sotto* under + *voce* voice]

sou (so̅o̅), n. (pl. **-s** pr. -z). (Hist.) French coin of various values; (loosely) five--centime piece; (colloq.) *hasn't a ~* (a farthing, any money). [F, f. L as SOLIDUS]

soubrette (so̅o̅brĕt'), n. Maid-servant or similar character (esp. w. implication of pertness, coquetry, intrigue, etc.) in comedy. [F]

sou'câr (sow-), **sow'kâr, n.** Hindu banker or money-lender. [Hind. *sāhūkār* great merchant]

sou'cho̅ng (so̅osh-), n. Kind of black tea made from youngest leaves. [F, f. Chin. *siao* small + *chung* sort]

Soudanese' (so̅o̅-; -ēz). = SUDANESE.

souffle (so̅o̅'fl), n. (med.). Low murmur heard in auscultation of various organs etc. [F, f. *souffler* blow f. L SUF(*flare* blow)]

soufflé (so̅o̅f'lā), a. & n. **1.** Made light & frothy, as *omelet ~.* **2.** n. Such dish, usu. made with beaten whites of eggs. [F, p.p. as prec.]

sough (sŭf, sow, Sc. so̅o̅χ), n., & v.i. (Make) moaning, whistling, or rushing sound as of wind in trees etc. [OE *swōgan,* OS *swōgan,* move with a rushing sound]

sought. See SEEK.

soul (sōl), n. **1.** The immaterial part of man, as *immortality of the ~, commend one's ~ to God* (of person at point of death), *'pon my ~* (asseveration). **2.** Moral & emotional part of man, as *his whole ~ revolted from it,* CURE[1] *of, has a ~ above sherry & bitters.* **3.** Intellectual part of man, vital principle & mental powers of animals including man, as *keep* BODY[1] *& ~ together, cannot call his ~ his own* (is dominated by another). **4.** Animating or essential part, person viewed as this, as *he was the* (*life &*) *~ of the enterprise, of the party.* **5.** Person viewed as embodying moral or intellectual qualities, as *the greatest ~s of antiquity, left that to meaner ~s.* **6.** (Often without *a*) emotional or intellectual energy e.g. as revealed in work of art, as *the fellow has no ~, his pictures lack ~.* **7.** (Of persons) personification or pattern of (*is the ~ of honour,* is incapable of dishonourable conduct). **8.** Departed spirit, as ALL *S~s' Day*; disembodied spirit. **9.** Person, as *not a ~ to speak to for miles round, ship went down with 200 ~s*; (expr. familiarity, patronage, pity, contempt, etc.) *my good ~, there's a good ~, the poor little ~ had lost her way,* *a simple* ~. **10.** (In comb.) ~-*destroying, -stirring, -subduing,* etc. Hence (-)~ED² (sŏld), ~′LESS (sōl-l-), aa., ~′lèssLY² adv., ~′lèssNESS n. [OE *sāwol* = Goth. *saiwala;* cf. OS *sēola,* OHG *sē(u)la,* ON *sála*]

soul′ful (sōl-), a. Having, expressing, appealing to, the (esp. higher) emotional or intellectual qualities (occas. derog.). Hence~LY² adv.,~NESS n. [-FUL]

sound¹, a. & adv. **1.** Healthy, not diseased nor injured nor rotten, as *a ~ body, ~ mind, ~ in wind & limb, ~ fruit, timbers, ship;* correct, logical, well-founded, judicious, as ~ *doctrine, theologian, argument, views, policy, is he ~ on free trade?* (commerc., of company etc.) solvent; thorough, unqualified, as *a ~ sleep(er), flogging.* **2.** adv. ~ly, as ~ (fast) *asleep, will sleep the~er for it.* Hence ~′LY² adv., ~′NESS n. [ME *sund,* repr. OE (= G) *gesund;* cf. MDu. *ghesont,* MLG *(ge)sunt*]

sound², n., & v.i. & t. **1.** The sensation produced through the ear, what is or may be heard; vibrations causing this sensation; *musical ~* (produced by continuous & regular vibrations, opp. to *noise*); any of a series of articulate utterances, as *vowel, consonant,* ~s; mere words (~ & *fury*); (fig.) mental impression produced by oral or other statement etc., as *will have a queer ~, don't like the~ of it.* **2.** ~-*board,* = ~*ing-board;* ~-*bow,* thick edge of bell against which tongue strikes; ~-*film,* cinema film with audible dialogue, songs, etc. recorded on ~-*track;* ~-*hole, -post,* hole in belly, small prop between belly & back, of some stringed instruments; ~-PROOF²; ~-*track,* on side of cinema film recording ~; ~-*wave* (of condensation & rarefaction, by which ~ is propagated in elastic medium e.g. air). **3.** vb. Give forth ~, as *the trumpets* ~; (w. ref. to impression created, often fig.) ~*s to me like something cracking,* ~*s as if a tap were running,* ~*s as if he wanted to back out of it, will ~ very strange to say you hadn't time, that* (excuse etc.) ~*s very hollow, that* (report, explanation) ~*s all right* (promising, plausible, etc.); (part.) having more ~ than sense or truth, as ~*ing rhetoric, promises,* imposing, as ~*ing titles;* make (trumpet etc.) ~; utter, as ~ *a note of alarm;* pronounce (*the h in hour is not* ~ed); give notice of (*an alarm, the retreat,* etc.) with bell etc.; cause to resound, make known, as ~ *his praises far & wide;* test (railway-carriage wheel etc., lungs etc.) by noting ~ produced by hammer, by auscultation. **4.** ~*ing-board,* canopy over pulpit etc. serving to direct ~ towards audience, thin plate of wood in musical instrument increasing ~. Hence ~′LESS a. [ME; (n.) AF *soun* f. OF *son* f. L *sonus,* for -*d* cf. LEND, ROUND⁵, HIND²; (vb) f. OF *soner* f. L *sonare*]

sound³, v.t. & i., & n. **1.** Test the depth of (sea, channel, pond, etc., or abs.) & the quality of its bottom with ~*ing-line* or -*apparatus* or -*machine* (often furnished with cup etc. for bringing up sample); find depth of water in (ship's hold) with ~*ing-rod;* get records of temperature, humidity, pressure, etc. from (upper atmosphere) with ~*ing-balloon;* (med.) examine (bladder etc.) with probe; (of fish, esp. whale) dive to the bottom; inquire esp. in cautious or reserved manner into the sentiments or inclination of (person *about, on, as to*). **2.** n. Surgeon's probe. [ME, f. OF *sonder* f. Rom. **subundare,* f. *sub-* SUB-+*unda* wave]

sound⁴, n. **1.** Narrow passage of water connecting two seas or sea with lake etc., strait. **2.** Fish's air-bladder; cuttle-fish. [partly OE *sund,* partly f. ON *sund* swimming, sea, strait, f. stem of SWIM]

sound′er¹, n. ‖(Arch.) herd of wild swine; (pseudo-arch.) young wild boar. [ME, f. OF *sundre* f. Gmc, cf. OE *sunor,* OHG *swaner,* ON *sonar*]

sound′er², n. In vbl senses of SOUND³, esp. telegraphic receiving instrument for reading message by sound. [-ER¹]

sound′er³, n. In vbl senses of SOUND³; *echo-*~, apparatus for sounding by measuring time-interval between transmission of a note & receipt of its echo from the sea-bed; *flying* ~, sounding-apparatus that can be used without reducing ship's speed. [-ER¹]

sound′ing, n. In vbl senses of SOUND³, also (pl.) place near enough to shore to admit of ~, as *be in, come into,* ~s. [-ING¹]

soup (sōōp), n. Liquid food made of stock & other ingredients (*in the* ~, sl., in difficulties); ‖ (legal sl.) prosecution brief given to junior barrister at Quarter Sessions etc.; ~-*kitchen,* public establishment for supplying ~ gratis to the poor; ~-*ticket* (entitling holder to ~ at ~-kitchen); ~ *maigre* (-ger), thin ~ chiefly of vegetables; ~-*plate,* deep kind for ~; PEA ~. Hence ~′Y² a. [f. F *soupe* sop, broth, f. LL *suppa;* rel. to OE *sopp* (SOP) not clear]

soupçon (see Ap.), n. Very small quantity, dash, (*of* flavouring, quality, etc.). [F]

sour (sowr), a., & v.i. & t. **1.** Of acid taste, esp. as result of unripeness, as ~ *apples,* ~ GRAPES, or of fermentation, as ~ *milk, bread;* (of smell) suggestive of fermentation; (of soil) dank; (of person or temper) harsh, peevish, morose; ~ *dock,* common sorrel; ~′*puss* (sl.), ~-tempered person. **2.** vb. Make, become, ~ (esp. fig.), as *soured by misfortune.* Hence ~′ISH¹ a., ~′LY² adv., ~′NESS n. [OE *sūr,* OS, OHG *sūr,* ON *surr*]

source (sōrs), n. Spring, fountain-head, from which stream issues, as *the* ~s *of the Nile;* origin, place from which thing comes or is got, as *the* ~ *of all our woes, reliable* ~ *of information, drawn from all*

~s; ~-book [transl. of G *quellenbuch*], book or collection of original documents serving as material for the historical study of a subject. [ME, f. OF *sors, sourse*, p.p. as n. of *sourdre* rise f. L *surgere*]

sourdine (soordēn'), n. Harmonium stop producing soft effect; = SORDINE. [F, cf. SORDINE]

*****sourdough** (sowr'dō), n. One who has spent one or more winters in Alaska; old-timer. [dial., = leaven; SOUR + .DOUGH]

sour-sop (sowr-), n. A W.-Ind. fruit & tree. [SOUR+SOP]

souse[1], n., & v.t. & i. 1. Pickle made with salt; food in pickle, esp. head, feet, & ears, of swine; dip, plunge, drenching, in water. 2. vb. Put in pickle, as ~d mackerel; plunge (t. & i., *into* liquid), soak (thing *in* liquid), throw (liquid *over* thing); (p.p.) drunk (sl.). [ME; vb f. n., OF *souz* pickle f. WG *****sultja* (= OS *sultia*, OHG *sulza*), cogn. w. SALT]

souse[2], adv. With swift descent, head-long, as *came* ~ *into our midst*. [f. obs. *souse* swoop, alt. f. obs. SOURCE (in hawking)]

soutache (soo'tahsh), n. Ornamental braid for sewing on fabric in designs. [F, f. Magyar *sujtás*]

soutane (sootahn'), n. (R.-C. Ch.). Priest's cassock. [F]

souteneur (sootenēr'), n. Man cohabiting with & living on the earnings of a prostitute. [F, = protector]

|| **sout'er** (soo-), n. (Sc. & north.). Shoe-maker, cobbler. [OE *sūtere* f. L *sutor* (*suere, sut-* sew)]

south, adv., n., a., (abbr. *S*.), & v.i. 1. (Towards, at, near) point of horizon directly opposite to north; point of compass opposite north; DUE[1] ~; ~ BY[1] *east* or *west*; ~ *of*, farther ~ than; ~*-east*, ~-*-west*, etc., advv., aa., & nn., POINT[1]s of the compass, corresponding regions, (with uses & derivatives corresp. to those of ~, e.g. ~-~*-easterly*); || southern part of England, Scotland, Wales, Ireland, or Europe; the Southern STATE[1]s; ~ (*wind*), wind from the ~. 2. adj. Situated or dwelling in, looking towards, the ~; *S*~ *Downs* (of Hampshire & Sussex); ~'*down* a. & n., (sheep) of a breed originating on the ~ Downs esteemed for their flesh; *S*~ *Kensington*, (used for) the museums of S~ Kensington or the atmosphere of culture & art & instruction associated w. them; ~'*paw* a. & n. (sl.), left-handed (person), esp. in sport; *S*~ *Sea* (hist.), the Pacific; *S*~ *Sea Bubble*, scheme for trading in Spanish America, which collapsed in 1720. 3. v.i. Move towards ~, (of moon etc.) cross the meridian of a place. Hence ~'WARD a. & n., ~'WARD(S) adv. [OE *sūth*, OS *sūth*, OHG *sund-*, ON *sŭthr*]

southeas'ter, south'er, nn. Wind from SE, from S. [-ER[1]]

sou'therly (sŭdh-), a. & adv. Towards the south; (of wind) blowing from the south. [f. SOUTH, as EASTERLY]

sou'thern (sŭdh-), a. & n. 1. Of, in, the south; *S*~ HEMISPHERE, CROSS[1], CONFEDER-ACY, STATES; looking south, as *a* ~ *aspect*; (of wind, rare)=prec. 2. n. Inhabitant of the south, esp. of the S~ States, whence ~ER[1] n.; ~*wood*, kind of wormwood with scented leaves. Hence~MOST a. [OE; -ERN]

south'ing, n. In vbl senses, also (naut.) difference of latitude made in sailing south. [-ING[1]]

sou'thron (sŭdh-), a. & n. (arch. Sc.). English, Englishman, (usu. derog.). [var. of SOUTHERN]

southwes'ter, n. (Also *sou'wĕs'ter*) wind from SW.; (usu. *sou'wĕs'ter*) waterproof hat with broad brim behind to protect neck. [-ER[1]]

souvenir (soov'enēr), n. Thing given, kept, etc., to recall the past, memento (*of* occasion, place, etc.). [F, f. vb = remember, f. L SUB(*venire* come) occur to the mind]

sov'ereign (-vrĭn), a. & n. 1. Supreme, as ~ *power, the* ~ *good* (= SUMMUM BONUM); lofty, as *with* ~ *contempt*; possessing ~ power, as ~ *States*, royal, as *our* ~ LORD, whence ~TY (-vrĭn-) n.; very good, esp. *a* ~ *remedy*; hence ~LY[2] adv. (arch.). 2. n. Supreme ruler, esp. monarch; || (colloq. abbr. *sov*) British gold coin (now hardly in use) worth nominally £1. [(n. f. adj.) f. OF *soverain* f. Rom. *****SUPER-(*anus* -AN); *-g-* by assoc. w. *reign*]

sov'iĕt, S-, n. Any of the councils elected by the workers & soldiers of a district in revolutionary Russia, or of a smaller number elected by these, or the all--Russian congress of delegates from these latter; *Union of S*~ *Socialist Republics* (abbr. U.S.S.R.), the revolutionary government of Russia; *the S*~, Russia; (attrib., usu *S*~) Russian. [Russ.]

sow[1] (sō), v.t. (~*ed*, ~*n* or ~*ed*). Scatter (seed, or abs.) on or in the earth for purpose of growth; (fig.) ~ (*the seeds of*) *dissension* etc., *must reap what you have* ~*n*, ~ *the wind* (see WHIRL); plant (field etc. *with* seed) by ~ing; (fig.) cover thickly *with*. Hence ~'ER[1](1, 2), ~'ING[1], nn. [OE *sāwan*, OS *sāian*, OHG *sājan*, ON *sá*, Goth. *saian* f. Gmc *****sǣ-, cf. SEED]

sow[2], n. 1. Adult female hog; *get the wrong* ~ *by the ear*, fix on wrong person or thing, reach wrong conclusion; *as drunk as a* ~ (completely). 2. (Also ~-*bug*) wood--louse. 3. Main trough through which molten iron runs into side-channels to form pigs, large block of iron that solidifies in this. 4. ~'*back*, low ridge of sand etc.; ~'*bread*, kind of cyclamen; ~'*thistle*, plant with small yellow flowers & milky juice. [OE *sugu*, MDu., MLG *soge*, rel. to OHG *sū*, ON *sўr*, L *sus*]

soy, n. Kind of sauce made in Japan & China from the SOYA BEAN. [f. Jap. *shoyu*]

soy'a, (now rarely) **soy, bean**, n. (Seed of) a leguminous plant of south-eastern Asia, yielding an edible oil (~ *oil*) & *soya meal* or *flour* used for cattle & human food. [prec.]

sŏz'zled (-ld), a. (sl.). Very drunk. [p.p. of *sozzle* dial., to mix sloppily (prob. imit.)]

spa (-ah, -aw), n. (Place where there is a) mineral spring. [*Spa*, place in Belgium]

spāce[1], n. 1. Continuous extension viewed with or without reference to the existence of objects within it. 2. Interval between points or objects viewed as having one, two, or three dimensions, as *separated by a* ~ *of 10 ft, clear a* ~ (area), *box occupies too much* ~, *would take up too much* ~ (on paper) *to go into detail*; large region (*the wide open* ~s). 3. (print.). Blank between words etc., type securing this. 4. Interval of time, as *in the* ~ *of an hour, after a short* ~, *let us rest a* ~. 5. ~-*bar*, bar in typewriter for making ~ between words; ~ *craft* (for travelling through interplanetary ~ beyond the earth's atmosphere); ~ *fiction*, fanciful fiction about travel through ~; ~ *flight, flying*; ~ *helmet, suit*, worn by ~'*man* (traveller in outer ~); = ~ *craft*; ~-*time* (philos.), a fusion of the concepts of ~ & time, regarded as a continuum in which the existent exists; ~ *travel(ler), travelling*; ~ *vehicle*, = ~ *craft*; ~-*writer, -writing* (in newspaper, paid according to area occupied). Hence ~'LESS (-sl-) a. [ME, f. OF *espace* f. L *spatium*]

spāce[2], v.t. & i. Set at intervals, put spaces between, (esp. words, letters, lines, in printing); make a space between words on typewriter etc., as *don't forget to* ~, whence **spā'CER**[1](2) n.; ~ *out* (print.), put more or wider spaces between. Hence **spā'CING**[1](1) n. [f. prec.]

spā'cious (-shus), a. Enclosing a large space, roomy. Hence ~LY[2] adv., ~NESS n. [ME, f. L *spatiosus* (as SPACE[1], see -OUS)]

spāde[1], n., & v.t. 1. Tool for digging & cutting ground, turf, etc., with sharp-edged iron blade & wooden handle used with both hands; *call a* ~ *a* ~, call things by their names, speak plainly or bluntly; tool of similar shape for various purposes, e.g. for removing blubber from whale; ~ *bayonet* (with broad blade, used as both ~ & weapon); ~ *husbandry* (with deep ~-digging instead of subsoil-ploughing). 2. ~-*work*, (fig.) hard preparatory work. 3. v.t. Dig over (ground), cut blubber from (whale), with ~. Hence ~'FUL (-dfool) n. [OE *spadu, spada*, = OFris. *spada*, OS *spado*, rel. to Gk *spathē* blade, whence L *spatha*]

spāde[2], n. (Playing-card with) black figure(s) shaped like heart with small handle; (pl.) suit of these cards; ~

guinea (of George III with shield shaped like ~ on cards). [f. It. *spade* pl. of *spada* sword f. L *spatha*, as prec.]

‖ **spädg'er**, n. (sl.). Fanciful alt. of SPARROW.

spadille', n. Ace of spades in ombre & quadrille. [F, f. Sp. *espadilla* dim. of *espada* sword, see SPADE[2]]

spād'|ix, n. (bot.); pl. ~*ices* pr. -Is'ēz). Spike of flowers closely arranged round fleshy axis & usu. enclosed in a spathe. Hence or cogn. ~**i'CEOUS** (-Ishus), ~**iCOSE**[1], aa. [L f. Gk, = palm-branch]

spād'ō, n. (law). Person incapable of procreation. [L, f. Gk *spadōn* eunuch]

‖ **spae** (spā), v.i. & t. (Sc.). Foretell, prophesy; ~'*wife*, female fortune-teller. [f. ON *spá*]

spaghett'i (-gĕ-), n. Kind of macaroni. [It.]

spahi, -ee (spah'hē), n. (hist.). Member of 14th-c. Turkish irregular cavalry; member of native Algerian cavalry in French service. [f. Turk. f. Hind. *sipahi* SEPOY]

spake. See SPEAK.

spall (-awl), v.t. & i., & n. Splinter, chip; (mining) prepare (ore) for sorting by breaking it up. Hence **spal'd**ER[1] (-awl-) n. [also *spale* (both 15th c.), of unkn. orig.; cf. LG *spallern*, G *spellen* to split]

‖ **spälpeen'**, n. (Ir.). Mean fellow, rascal.

spăm, n. Tinned foodstuff imported from U.S. [P; f. *spiced ham*]

spăn[1], v.t. & i. (-nn-). (Of bridge, arch, etc., fig. of memory etc.) stretch from side to side of, extend across, (river etc., fig. period etc.), (of builder etc.) bridge (river etc.); measure, cover, the extent of (thing) with one's grasp etc.; (naut.) confine (booms etc.) with ropes; move in distinct stretches like span-worm. [ME, f. MDu. or MLG *spannen*, = OE, OHG *spannan*; see foll.]

spăn[2], n. 1. Full extent from end to end, as ~ *of a bridge, of an arch, our brief* ~ (of *life*), *the whole* ~ *of Roman history*. 2. Each part of a bridge etc. between piers or supports. 3. Greenhouse or similar structure with ~ *roof*. 4. Maximum distance between tips of thumb & little finger, esp. as a measure = 9 in. 5. Short distance, as *our life is but a* ~. 6. (naut.). Rope fastened by both ends to take a purchase in the loop, double rope connected with thimbles. 7. Pair of horses or mules, yoke of oxen. 8. ~-*dogs*, pair of iron bars with claws for grappling timber; ~ *roof* (with two inclined sides, opp. to pent-roof or lean-to); ~*worm*, larva of geometer. [OE *span(n)*, MDu. *spanne*, OHG *spanna*, ON *spann*- rel. to OE *spannan* (prec.); in ME prob. reinforced by OF *espan*; senses 6 & 7 f. (M)Du., (M)LG *span*]

spăn'drel, n. Space between shoulder of arch & surrounding rectangular moulding or framework, or between shoulders of adjoining arches & moulding above; ~ *wall* (built on curve of arch, filling in ~).

[app. a dim. of AF *spaundre, -dere*, perh. identical w. (*e*)*spaundre* expand]

spangl|e (spăng'gl), n., & v.t. **1.** Small piece of glittering material esp. one of many as ornament of dress etc.; any small sparkling object; (also *oak-~e*) spongy excrescence on oak-leaves, oak--apple. **2.** v.t. Cover with ~es (esp. in p.p.; STAR¹*~ed*). Hence ~Y² a. [ME, f. *spang*, f. MDu. *spange*, +-LE]

Spän'iard (-yard), n. Native of Spain. [f. OF *Espaignart* (*Espaigne* Spain, -ARD)]

spän'iel (-yel), n. Kinds of dog with long silky coat, drooping ears, & docile & affectionate disposition, some used by sportsmen & some kept as pets (*King Charles's* ~, small black-&-tan kind); (fig.) fawning or cringing person. [ME, f. OF *espaignol, -eul* Spanish (dog) f. Rom. *hispaniolus* f. *hispania* Spain]

Spän'ish, a. & n. **1.** Of Spain or the Spaniards or their language; ~ (= *Invincible*) ARMADA; ~ *black, brown, red, white*, pigments; ~ CHESTNUT; ~ *fly*, bright green insect dried & used for raising blisters, as aphrodisiac, etc.; ~ *fowl*, breed of domestic fowl with glossy greenish-black plumage; ~ *grass*, esparto; ~ *main* (hist.), NE coast of S. America between Orinoco river & Panama, & adjoining part of Caribbean sea; ~ *windlass*, use of stick as lever for tightening cord or bandage. **2.** n. ~ language. [ME *Spainisc* (*Spain*, see -ISH¹)]

spänk, v.t. & i., & n. **1.** Slap on buttocks with open hand or slipper etc., whence ~'ing¹ [-ING¹] n.; urge forward esp. by slapping or whipping; (of horse etc.) move briskly esp. at a step between trot & gallop. **2.** n. Slap, blow with open hand etc., on buttocks. [imit.]

spänk'er, n. In vbl senses; also or esp.: fast-going horse; (colloq.) person or thing of notable size or quality, stunner, whopper; (naut.) fore-&-aft sail set on after side of mizzenmast. [-ER¹]

spanking¹. See SPANK.

spänk'ing², a. & adv. In vbl senses; also: (colloq.) striking, notable, excellent, as *had a ~ time, a ~* (strong) *breeze*, (adv.) *a ~ fine woman*. [-ING², cf. *whacking, thumping, whopping*]

spän'less, a. (poet.). Beyond measure. [-LESS]

spänn'er, n. Instrument for turning nut on screw etc. (*throw a ~ into the works*, fig., introduce an upsetting element or influence); cross-brace of bridge etc.; connecting-rod in parallel motion of engine; = SPAN²-*worm*. [f. G *spanner* f. *spannen* draw tight (see SPAN²)]

spär¹, n., & v.t. (-rr-). **1.** Stout pole esp. such as is used for mast, yard, etc., of ship; ~-*buoy* (made of a ~ with one end moored so that other stands up); ~-*deck*, upper deck extending from bow to stern, including quarterdeck and forecastle. **2.** v.t. Furnish with ~, help (ship) over

shallow bar with ~s. [ME *sparre, sperre*, f. MDu., MLG *sparre, sperre*, = OS, OHG *sparro*, ON *sparri, sperra*; poss. also f. OF *esparre*, f. Gmc]

spär², n. Kinds of crystalline mineral, easily cleavable & non-lustrous, as *calcareous* ~, calcite, *Derbyshire* (= FLUOR) ~, *Iceland* ~, transparent calcite much used for optical purposes. [f. MLG *spar*, cogn. w. OE *spæren* gypsum]

spär³, v.i. (-rr-), & n. **1.** Make motions of attack & defence with closed fists, use the hands (as) in boxing, (often at opponent; ~*ring partner*, boxer employed to practise with another in training for a fight); (fig.) bandy words, as *they are always ~ring (at each other)*; (of cocks) fight esp. with protected spurs. **2.** n. ~ring motion, boxing-match, cock-fight. [ME, f. OE *sperran*, of unkn. orig.]

spä'rable, n. Headless nail for soles & heels of boots. [reduced f. *sparrow-bill*]

späre¹, a. & n. **1.** Scanty, frugal, as ~ *diet*, lean, thin, as *man of ~ frame*, whence ~'LY² (-rl-) adv., ~'NESS (-rn-) n.; ~'*rib*, upper part of row of ribs of pork with small amount of meat adhering; that can be spared, not required for ordinary use, as *how to use your ~ time, have no ~ cash*; reserved for emergency or extraordinary use, as *always take a ~ cap, ~ room* (bedroom for visitor). **2.** n. ~ part for substitution in machine. [ME, corresp. to OE *spær*, OHG *spar*, MDu. *spaer* sparing, f. *spar* (foll.); n. f. adj. & vb]

späre², v.t. & i. Be frugal or grudging of, as ~ *the rod & spoil the child, must not ~ expense*, whence **spär'ingLY²** adv., **spär'ing**NESS n.; dispense with, do without, as *cannot ~ him just now, ~ me a pound, could have ~d the explanation*; ‖ (arch.) forbear (*to* do); abstain from inflicting (with double object), as ~ *me these protestations*; abstain from killing, hurting, wounding, etc., as ~ (do not kill) *me, ~ my life, ~ his feelings*, (loosely) ~ (do not provoke) *his blushes*; be frugal. [OE *sparian*, OS, OHG *sparōn*, ON *spara* f. Gmc *spar-* (prec.)]

spär'ger, n. Sprinkling-apparatus, esp. in brewing. [f. *sparge* to sprinkle (L *spargere*) +-ER¹]

spärk¹, n. **1.** Fiery particle thrown off from burning substance, or still visibly alight in ashes, or struck out by impact from flint etc. (*as the ~s fly upward*, with the certainty of a law of nature). **2.** Small bright object or point e.g. in gem. **3.** (fig.). Brilliant emanation of wit etc., esp. *strike ~s out of* person, provoke him to lively or original conversation. **4.** (Usu. neg. or quasi-neg.) particle of fire or. (fig.) of a quality etc., as *not a ~ of life remained, if you had a ~ of generosity in you*. **5.** (electr.). Luminous effect of sudden disruptive discharge, electric ~ serving to fire explosive mixture in oil-engine of motor etc., as *advance, retard, the ~* (in

the cycle of operation in the engine).
6. (nickname for) radio operator; *fairy ~s*, phosphorescent light from decayed vegetable matter etc.; *~-arrester*, device for preventing (injury from) SPARK[2]ing in electrical apparatus, netting etc. to catch *~s* on steam-engine. Hence *~'LESS* a., *~'LET* n., small *~*, carbonic-acid charge for use in some gazogenes. [OE *spærca, spearca*, = MDu., MLG *sparke*, of unkn. orig.]

spárk[2], v.i. & t. Emit sparks of fire or electricity; || *~(ing)-plug*, device for firing explosive mixture in motor-engine; (electr.) produce sparks at point where continuity of circuit is interrupted; (v.t.; also *~ off*) stir into activity. [ME, rel. to prec.; cf. MDu., MLG *sparken*]

spárk[3], n., & v.i. & t. **1.** Gay fellow; gallant. **2.** v.i. Play the gallant. Hence *~'ISH[1]* a. [(vb f. n.) prob. fig. use of SPARK[1]]

spár'kl|e, v.i., & n. **1.** Emit sparks, (of gems etc. & fig. of wit etc.) glitter, glisten, scintillate, whence *~ER[1]* n., *~inGLY[2]* adv.; *~ing* wines (giving out carbonic-acid gas in small bubbles, cf. STILL). **2.** n. *~ing*, gleam, spark. [ME, f. SPARK[1,2] +-LE (1,3); cf. MDu. *sparkelen* vb]

spá'rrow (-ō), n. Kinds of small plain-coloured bird, esp. *house ~*, European kind noted for attachment to human dwellings, prolificness, and pugnacity; *~-bill*, = SPARABLE; *~-grass* (vulg.), asparagus; *~-hawk*, kinds of small hawk preying on *~s* etc. [OE *spearwa*, MHG *sparwe*, Goth. *sparwa*; also OHG *sparo*, ON *spǫrr*]

spár'rý, a. Of, like, rich in, SPAR[2]. [-Y[2]]

spárse, a. (Of population etc.) thinly scattered, not dense; (bot., zool.) placed, occurring, at distant or irregular intervals. Hence *~'LY[2]* (-sl-) adv., *~'NESS* (-sn-) n. [f. L *sparsus* (*spargere sparsscatter*)]

Spárt'acist, a. & n. (Member) of the Spartacus group of extremists in the German revolution in 1918. [*Spartacus*, leader in anc.-Roman servile war, -IST]

Spárt'an, a. & n. (Native) of Sparta (esp. w. allusion to supposed characteristics of *~s*, as *~ endurance, simplicity*). [ME, f. L *Spartanus*, f. Gk *Spartā*, *-lē*, see -AN]

spá'sm, n. Excessive muscular contraction (CLONIC, TONIC, *~*); sudden convulsive movement, wrench, or strain, as *a ~ of coughing*, (fig.) *~s of grief* etc.; *functional ~*, nervous disorders caused by occupation, e.g. writer's cramp. Hence *~ŏL'OGY* (-āz-) n. [ME, f. OF *spasme* or L f. Gk *spasmos* (*spaō* draw)]

spasmŏd'|ic (-āz-), a. Of, caused by, subject to, spasm(s), as *a ~ic jerk, ~ic asthma*; occurring, done, by fits & starts, as *~ic efforts*. Hence *~ICALLY* adv. [f. Gk *spasmōdēs* (as SPASM, see -ODE) +-IC]

spás'tic, a. & n. (med.). **1.** = prec. **2.** n. Person suffering from cerebral palsy. [f.

L f. Gk *spastikos* drawing (*spaō* draw, see -IC)]

spãt[1], n., & v.i. & t. (-tt-). **1.** Spawn of shellfish esp. oyster. **2.** vb. (Of oyster etc.) spawn; shed (spawn). [AN *spat* (14th c.), of unkn. orig.]

spãt[2], n. (usu. pl.). Short gaiter covering instep & reaching little above ankle. [abbr. of (17th c.) SPATTER*dash*]

spat[3]. See SPIT[2].

spãtch'cŏck, n., & v.t. **1.** Fowl killed & cooked in a hurry. **2.** v.t. (colloq.). Insert (words) hastily in telegram etc. [orig. in Ir. use, expl. by Grose (1785) as f. *dispatch-cock*; cf. SPITCHCOCK]

spãte, n. || River-flood, esp. *river is in ~*; (fig.) excessive amount, as *a ~ of words*. [ME, Sc. & north., of unkn. orig.]

spãthe (-dh), n. (bot.). Large bract or pair of bracts enveloping spadix or flower-cluster. Hence *spāth'OSE[1]*, *spāth'OUS*, aa. [f. L f. Gk *spathē* broad blade etc.]

spãth'ic, a. Of SPAR[2], like spar esp. in cleavage. So *spãth'iFORM* a. [f. obs. *spath*, f. G *spath* spar +-IC]

spã'tial (-shl), a. Of space, as *~ relations, extent*. Hence *spātiăl'ITY* (-shi-) n., *~LY[2]* adv. [f. L *spatium* SPACE +-AL]

spãttee', n. Woollen legging worn by women and children over shoes and stockings. [f. SPAT[2] after *pullee*]

spãtt'er, v.t. & i., & n. **1.** Scatter (liquid, mud, etc.) here & there in small drops; splash (person *with* mud, slander, etc.) thus; (of liquid) fall here & there in drops. **2.** n. *~ing*, splash (*of* mud etc.), quick succession of light sounds, pattering. **3.** *~dashes* (or now usu. *spãts*), cloth or other leggings to protect stockings etc. from mud etc. [app. frequent. of stem found in Du., LG *spatten* etc.; cf. WFlem. *spetteren* spatter]

spãt'ula, n. Broad-bladed instrument for working pigments etc.; surgeon's instrument for pressing tongue down or to one side. [L, dim. of *spatha* SPATHE]

spãt'ūl|e, n. (zool.). Broad racket-shaped formation or part, esp. end of bird's tail-feather. Hence *~AR[1]*, *~ATE[2]*, *~iFORM*, aa. [ME, f. OF, f. L as prec.]

spãv'in, n. Disease of horse's hock-joint; *blood, bog, ~*, distension of the joint by effusion of lymph within it; *bone ~*, deposit of bony substance uniting the bones. Hence *~ED[2]* (-nd) a. [ME, f. OF *espavain*, var. of *esparvain*, perh. of Gmc orig.]

spawn, v.t. & i., & n. **1.** (Of fish, frog, mollusc, crustacean, derog. of human being or other animal) produce (eggs, or abs.), generate; (of eggs or young of fish etc.) be produced, issue. **2.** n. Eggs of fish etc.; (derog.) human or other offspring (*~ of the devil, of Cobden*, scoundrels, free-traders); white fibrous matter from which fungi are produced, mycelium, as *mushroom ~*. [ME, f. AF *espaundre*, OF *espandre* EXPAND; n. f. vb]

spay, v.t. Castrate, remove ovaries of, (female animal). [ME, f. AF *espeier*, OF *espeer* cut with a sword (*espee* sword)]

speak, v.i. & t. (*spŏke*, arch. *spăke*; *spōken*). **1.** Use articulate utterance in ordinary (not singing-) voice, as *child is learning to ~, wish you would ~ distinctly*; (p.p., as stage direction) to be said, not sung (also as n., such part). **2.** Hold conversation (*with, to*, person, *of, about*, thing), as *have heard him ~ of it, will ~ to him about it*; *portrait ~s* (is lifelike), so *~ing likeness*. **3.** Make oral address, deliver speech, before assembly, magistrate, tribunal, etc. **4.** Utter (words); make known (one's opinion, *the truth*, etc.) thus, esp. ~ *one's mind* (bluntly etc.). **5.** Use (specified language) in ~ing, as *cannot ~ French*, whence **French'** etc. -~ER[1] n., -~ING[2] a. **6.** *Strictly, roughly, generally, ~ing* (quasi-adv.), in the strict, rough, etc., sense of the word(s), as *am not strictly ~ing a member of the staff*; *legally* etc. *~ing*, from the legal etc. point of view. **7.** (As an apology for loose or strong or figurative expression) *so to ~*, if I may use such an expression. **8.** Hail & hold communication with (ship). **9.** (arch.). (Of conduct, circumstance, etc.) show (person) to be (so-&-so), as *his conduct ~s him generous*; be evidence of, as *this ~s a little mind*. **10.** (Of fact etc.) ~ *volumes*, be very significant; *~ volumes* etc. *for*, ~ *well for*, be abundant evidence of, place in favourable light, as *~s volumes for his forbearance*. **11.** (Of dog) bark esp. when ordered. **12.** fig. (Of mus. instrument etc.) sound. **13.** Make mention in writing of. **14.** ~ *by the* or *like a* BOOK[1]; ~ (person) *fair*, use polite language to; ~ *for*, act as spokesman of, state the sentiments of; ~ *of*, mention; *nothing to ~ of*, nothing worth mentioning, practically nothing; ~ *out* (also *up*), ~ *freely*, ~ *one's whole opinion*; ~ *to*, address (person etc.), ~ *in* confirmation of or in reference to, as *I can ~ to his having been there, will ~ to that point later*; ~ *up* (also *out*), ~ *loud*(er); ~ *without book*, give facts etc. from memory; *fair, smooth, ill, well*, etc., *-spoken* [as if *-speech*ED[2]], (given to) using such language; *~-easy* (sl.), illicit liquor shop. [OE *sprecan*, later *specan*, OS *sprekan*, OHG *sprehhan*]

speak'er, n. One who speaks esp. in public; (*S~*) presiding officer in House of Commons charged with preservation of order etc. & having casting vote in case of equal division, similar officer in U.S. House of Representatives etc., whence *S~*-SHIP n.; LOUD ~. [ME; -ER[1]]

speak'ing, n. In vbl senses: ~ *acquaintance*, person one knows well enough to exchange conversation with him, this degree of familiarity; *not on ~ terms*, not, esp. no longer, having ~ acquaintance *with* (usu. implying estrangement); ~ *-trumpet*, instrument for conveying voice to a distance; *~-tube*, tube for conveying voice from one room or building to another. [ME; -ING[1]]

spear, n., & v.t. & i. **1.** Hunter's or foot-soldier's thrusting or hurling weapon consisting of stout staff with point usu. of steel (cf. LANCE, PIKE); (poet.) = *~man*; sharp-pointed & barbed instrument for stabbing fish etc.; ~ (long stiff) *grass*; *~head*, (esp. fig.) individual or group chosen to lead a thrust or attack, (v.t.) act as *~head* of (attack etc.); *~'man*, person esp. soldier who uses ~; *~'mint*, common garden mint; ~ *side*, male branch of family (cf. DISTAFF). **2.** v.t. Pierce, strike, with ~. **3.** v.i. Shoot into a long stem. [OE *spere*, OS, OHG *sper*, ON *spjǫr*]

spĕc, n.(colloq.). Speculation, speculative enterprise, as *it turned out a good ~, did it on ~*. [abbr. of SPECULATION]

spē'cial (-shl), a. & n. **1.** Of a particular kind, peculiar, not general, (cf. ESPECIAL), as *lacks the ~ qualities required, word used in a ~ sense, what is your ~ work?, its ~ charm did not appeal to him, ~ anatomy* (of particular organs of human body), ~ JURY, ~ *hospital* (for particular class of diseases). **2.** For a particular purpose, as *appointed ~ agents, received ~ instructions*. **3.** (Also *especial*) exceptional in amount, degree, intensity, etc., as *took ~ trouble, found no ~ excellence in his work*. **4.** ~ *case*, written statement of facts submitted by litigants to court, (also) exceptional or peculiar case; ~ *constable* (sworn in to assist in maintaining public peace in time of emergency); ~ *correspondent* (appointed by newspaper to report on ~ facts); ~ *edition* (including later news than ordinary edition of newspaper); ‖~ *licence* (enabling priests to marry parties without publication of banns or at time or place other than those usually necessary); ~ *logic*, rules for thinking concerning ~ class of objects; ~ *pleader*, member of Inns of Court whose business it is to give verbal or written opinions on matters submitted to him & to deal with various proceedings out of usual course; ~ *pleading*, (law) allegation of ~ or new matter as opp. to denial of allegations of other side, (pop.) specious but unfair argument, statement of case designed to favour speaker's point of view rather than to discover the truth; ~ *train*, extra train for ~ purpose; ~ VERDICT. **5.** n. ~ constable, train, examination, edition of newspaper (esp. EXTRA-~), etc. Hence ~LY[2] (-sha-) adv. [ME, f. OF *especial* (ESPECIAL) or L *specialis* (SPECIES, -AL)]

spē'cial|ist (-sha-), n. One who devotes himself to particular branch of a profession, science, etc. Hence or cogn. ~ISM n., ~is'TIC a. [-IST]

spĕciál'itý (-shǐ-), n. Special feature or characteristic; (also *specialty*) special pursuit, product, operation, etc., thing to which a person gives special attention, as *jam-making*) *is our* ~. [ME, f. OF *(e)specialite* or LL *specialitas* (as SPECIAL, see -TY)]

spē'cializ|e (-sha-), -is|e (-ĭz), v.t. & i. Make specific or individual; modify, limit, (idea, statement); (biol.) adapt, set apart, (organ etc.) for particular purpose, differentiate; be differentiated, become individual in character; be(come) a specialist. Hence ~A'TION n. [f. F *spécialiser* (SPECIAL, -IZE)]

spē'cialtȳ (-shl-), n. (Law) instrument under seal, sealed contract; = SPECIALITY (2nd sense). [ME, f. OF *(e)specialte* (SPECIALITY)]

spēciā'tion (*or* -shī-), n. (zool.). Formation of SPECIES by evolutionary process. [-ATION]

spē'cie (-shĭē, -shē), n. (no pl.). Coin as opp. to paper money, as ~ *payments, paid in* ~, *shortness of* ~. [f. L abl. of foll. in phr. *in specie*]

spē'cies (-shĭēz, -shēz), n. (pl. same). 1. (Nat. hist.) group subordinate in classification to *genus* (cf. CLASS) & having members that differ only in minor details; *the* or *our* ~, mankind. 2. (log.). Group subordinate to GENUS & containing individuals agreeing in some common attribute(s) & called by a common name. 3. Kind, sort, as *has a* ~ *of cunning, a* ~ *of dogcart*. 4. (law). Form, shape, given to materials. 5. (eccl.). The sensible form of each of the elements of consecrated bread and wine used in the Eucharist. [L, = appearance, kind, beauty, f. *specere* look]

spēcif'ic, a. & n. 1. Definite, distinctly formulated, as *a* ~ *statement, has no* ~ *aim*; of a species, as *the* ~ *name* of plant etc.; ~ *difference* (what differentiates a species); possessing, concerned with, the properties that characterize a species, as *the* ~ *forms of animals, draws a* ~ *distinction between them*; relating to particular subject; peculiar, as *has a* ~ *style, a style* ~ *to that school of painters*; (of a duty or tax) assessed by quantity or amount, not *ad valorem*; ~ *cause* (producing a particular form of disease); ~ *centre*, place or period at which differentiation from a common stock takes place; ~ GRAVITY, HEAT[1]; ~ *medicine*, having distinct effect in curing a certain disease. 2. n. ~ medicine or remedy. Hence **spēcif'IC- ALLY** adv., **spēcifi'CITY**, ~NESS, nn. [f. LL *specificus* (as SPECIES, see -FIC)]

spēcificā'tion, n. Specifying; specified detail, esp. (pl.) detailed description of construction, workmanship, materials, etc., of work undertaken by architect, engineer, etc.; description by applicant for patent of the construction & use of his invention; (law) working up of materials into a new product not held to be the property of the owner of the materials. [f. med. L *specificatio* (foll., -FICATION)]

spē'cif|ȳ, v.t. Name expressly, mention definitely, (items, details, ingredients, etc.; often abs.); include in (e.g. architect's) specifications, as *a slate-course was not* ~*ied*. Hence ~IABLE a. [ME, f. OF *specifier* f. LL *specificare* (as SPECIFIC, see -FY)]

spē'cimĕn, n. Individual or part taken as example of a class or whole, esp. individual animal or plant or piece of a mineral etc. used for scientific examination, as ~*s of copper ore, zoological* ~*s, fine* ~ *of the swallow-tail, of mosaic work, a* ~ *of his skill, generosity,* ~ *page* (of book, printed in prospectus etc.); (colloq. derog.) *what a* ~ (person)*!* [L, *(specere* look, -MEN)]

spēci|ŏl'ogȳ (-shī-), n. Science of (origin etc. of) species. Hence ~olŏ'gICAL a. [-LOGY]

spē'cious (-shŭs), a. Of good appearance, plausible, fair or right on the surface, as ~ *argument, tale, pretence, person, appearance*. Hence or cogn. **spēcios'ITY** (-shĭ-), ~NESS, nn., ~LY[2] adv. [f. L *speciosus* beautiful (SPECIES, see -OUS)]

spĕck[1], n., & v.t. 1. Small spot, dot, stain; particle (*of* dirt etc.); spot of rottenness in fruit. 2. v.t. Mark with ~s (esp. in p.p.). Hence ~'LESS a. [OE *specca*, not in cogn. langg.; cf. SPECKLE]

spĕck[2], n. (U.S. & S. Afr.). Fat meat, bacon, pork; fat of seals, whales, etc., blubber. [f. Du. *spek* or G *speck*, rel. to OE *spic* bacon]

spĕc'kle, n., & v.t. 1. Small spot or stain. 2. v.t. Mark with ~s or patches (esp. in p.p.). [ME, corresp. to MDu. *speckel*, see SPECK[1], -LE]

spĕcktioneer', -si-, (-shon-), n. (whaling). Chief harpooner. [f. Du. *speksnijer*, for -*snijder*, (SPECK[2], *snijden* cut, -ER[1])]

spĕcs, n. pl. (colloq.). Pair of spectacles. [abbr.]

spĕc'tacle, n. 1. Public show, whence **spĕctăc'ūlAR[1]** a., **spĕctăc'ūlarLY[2]** adv. 2. Object of sight, esp. of public attention, as *a charming* ~ *drunken woman is a deplorable* ~, *sure to make a* ~ (= EXHIBI- TION) *of himself*. 3. (*Pair of*) ~s or colloq. *specs*, pair of lenses to correct or assist defective sight, set in frame without spring (cf. EYE[1]-*glass*) constructed to rest on nose & ears; (fig.) *sees everything through rose-coloured etc.* ~*s*, takes cheerful etc. views; (crick.) *pair of* ~*s*, two DUCK[1]s. [ME, f. OF, or f. L *spectaculum* (*spectare* look)]

spĕc'tacled (-ld), a. Wearing spectacles; (of animals) marked in a way that suggests spectacles, esp. ~ *bear*, the S.-Amer. bear. [-ED[2]]

spĕctāt'or, n. One who looks on esp. at a show, game, etc., as *the* ~*s were moved to tears, was a mere* ~, *an unconcerned* ~, (as title of paper) *The S*~. Hence **spĕc- tāt'RESS[1]** n. [L (*spectare*, see SPECTACLE & -OR)]

spĕc'tral, a. Ghostlike, of ghosts; of spectra or the spectrum, as ~ *colours*, *analysis*. Hence ~LY² adv. [f. L *spectrum* SPECTRE + -AL]

spĕc'tre (-ter), n. Ghost; haunting presentiment (*of* ruin, war, madness, etc.); ~ *of the Brocken*, huge shadowy image of the observer projected on mists about mountain-top, first observed on the Brocken; (in names of animals compared to ~ from thinness of body etc.) ~-*bat*, -*crab*, -*insect*, -*lemur*, -*shrimp*. [F, or f. L SPECTRUM]

spĕc'tr|o- in comb. = SPECTRUM, as: ~*o-graph*, apparatus for photographing or otherwise reproducing the spectrum, ~*ogram*, representation obtained by this, so ~*ograph'ic* a., ~*ŏg'raphy* n.; ~*ohĕl'iograph*, instrument for taking photographs of the sun from light of one wave-length only; ~*ohĕl'ioscope*, spectroscope provided with a pair of oscillating slits which exclude from the observer's eye all light except that of the red hydrogen line; ~*ŏm'eter*, instrument for measuring refraction of light-rays in passing through prism.

spĕc'tr|oscōpe, n. Instrument for forming & analysing the spectra of rays, consisting usu. of collimating tube, prism or diffraction grating, small telescope, and measuring apparatus. Hence ~*oscŏp'ic*(AL) aa., ~*oscŏp'icalLY*² adv., ~*ŏs'cop-*IST (*or* spĕ²), ~*ŏs'copy*¹ (*or* spĕ²), nn. [F (SPECTRO- + -SCOPE)]

spĕc'trum, n. (pl. -*ra*). (Also *ocular* ~) image of something seen continuing when the eyes are closed or turned away; image formed by rays of light or other radiation in which the parts are arranged in a progressive series according to their refrangibility, i.e. according to wave-length; *diffraction*, *prismatic*, ~ (produced by means of diffraction grating, by means of prism); *solar* ~ (formed from rays of sun); ~ (or *spectral*) *analysis*, chemical analysis by means of spectroscope. [L; = appearance, image, f. *specere* look]

spĕc'ular, a. Of (the nature of) a speculum, esp. reflecting, as ~ *surface*. [f. L *specularis* (SPECULUM, see -AR¹)]

spĕc'ŭlāt|e, v.i. 1. Pursue an inquiry, meditate, form theory or conjectural opinion, (*on*, *upon*, *about*, subject, the nature, cause, etc., of a thing, or abs.). 2. Make investment, engage in commercial operation, that involves risk of loss, as *has been* ~*ing in stocks, in rubber*, (esp. w. implication of rashness) *is believed to* ~*e a good deal*. Hence or cogn. ~IVE a., ~IVELY² adv., ~IVENESS, ~OR, nn. [f. L *speculari* spy out, observe, (*specula* watch-tower as SPECULUM), see -ATE³]

spĕcŭlā'tion, n. 1. Meditation on, inquiry into, theory about, a subject, as *much given to* ~, *sorry to disturb your* ~*s*. 2. Speculative investment or enterprise,

practice of speculating, in business, as *ruined by (a single unlucky)* ~, *bought it as a* ~ (or *on* SPEC, rarely *on* ~). 3. Game in which cards are bought & sold. [ME, f. LL *speculatio* (as prec., see -ATION)]

spĕc'ŭlum, n. (pl. -*la*). (Surg.) instrument for dilating cavities of human body for inspection; mirror, usu. of polished metal e.g. ~-*metal* (alloy of copper & tin), esp. in reflecting telescope; (ornith.) specially coloured area on wing of some birds, also = OCELLUS. [L, = mirror (*specere* look)]

sped. See SPEED.

speech, n. 1. **Faculty of speaking.** 2. Thing said, remark, as *after this unlucky* ~ *he remained silent*. 3. Public address, as *after-dinner*, MAIDEN, ~, ~ *for the defence, a set* ~ (studied, prepared), *make* (deliver) *a* ~; ‖ *Queen's* or *King's* (*gracious*) ~, ~ *from the throne*, brief statement of foreign & domestic affairs & of the chief measures to be considered by Parliament, prepared by Government & read by sovereign in person or by commission at opening of Parliament. 4. Language of a nation. 5. Act of sounding in organ-pipe etc. 6. FIGURE¹ *of* ~; PART⁷ *) of* ~; ~-*reading*, deaf person's interpretation of ~ by watching speaker's lips; ‖ ~-*day*, annual day for delivering prizes in schools usu. marked by ~es etc. [OE *sprǣc*, *sprēc*, later *spǣc*, *spēc*, OS *sprāka*, OHG *sprāhha* f. st. of *sprecan* SPEAK]

speech'i|fy̆, v.i. (derog.). Make speeches, hold forth in public. Hence ~*FICA'TION*, ~*fiER*¹, nn. [-FY]

speech'less, a. Dumb; temporarily deprived of speech by emotion etc., as ~ *with rage*; (sl.) dead drunk. Hence ~LY² adv., ~NESS n. [OE *spǣclēas*, see -LESS]

speed, n., & v.t. & i. (*spĕd*, exc. as below). 1. Rapidity of movement, as *with all* ~, *more haste less* ~, *at full* ~; rate of progress or motion, as *attains a high* ~, *depends on the* ~ *required*, *three-* ~ *engine*, *bicycle*, etc. (with adaptable gear for going at different ~s); AIR¹, GROUND¹, ~. 2. (arch.). Success, prosperity, as *send me good* ~ (cf. GOD¹-~). 3. ~-*boat*, motor-boat designed for high ~; ~-*cone*, contrivance for adjusting ratio of ~ between parallel shafts by means of belt; ~-*cop* (orig. U.S., sl.), police motor-cyclist detailed to check motorists' ~; ~-*way*, arena for motor-cycle racing, •road or track reserved for fast motor traffic; ~-*well*, kinds of herb with creeping or ascending stems & bright-blue flowers. 4. vb. Go fast, as *sped down the street* (now chiefly literary); (arch.) send fast, send on the way, as ~ *an arrow from the bow*, ~ *the parting guest*. 5. (arch.). Be or make prosperous, succeed, give success to, as *how have you sped?*, *God* ~ *you!* 6. (past & p.p. ~*ed*). Regulate ~ of (engine etc.), cause to go at fixed ~; ~ *up*, cause to work at greater ~ (*the train service wants ~ing up*); (of motorists) travel at illegal or dangerous ~. [(n.) OE *spēd*, earlier *spœ̄d*, (OS *spōd*, OHG *spuot*) f. OE *spōwan* (OHG *spuon*) prosper; (vb) OE *spēdan* (OS *spōdian*, OHG *spuoten*) f. st. *spōd*- (as n.)]

speed'er, n. Kinds of device for regulating or increasing speed of machinery. [-ER¹]

speedŏm'ēter, n. Appliance indicating the speed of a vehicle etc. [SPEED, -O-, -METER]

speed'|ȳ̆, a. Rapid; expeditious, prompt, coming without delay, as *~y answer, vengeance*. Hence ~**iLY²** adv., ~**iNESS** n. [ME; -Y²]

speiss (-īs), n. Compound of arsenic, iron, etc., found in smelting some lead ores. [f. G *speise* food, amalgam, f. pop. L *spesa* EXPENSE]

spēlae'|an, a. Of, dwelling in, caves. So ~**ŏl'OGIST**, ~**ŏl'OGY**, nn. [f. L f. Gk *spēlaion* cave +-AN]

spelicans. See SPILLIKIN.

spĕll¹, n. Words used as charm, incantation or its effect (*under a ~*, mastered by or as by a ~); attraction, fascination, exercised by person, pursuit, quality, etc.; *~'binder*, political speaker who can hold audiences *~bound*; *~'bound*, bound (as) by a ~. [OE *spel(l)*, OS, OHG *spel*, *spell-*, ON *spjall*, Goth. *spill*]

spĕll², v.t. (*spelt* or *~ed* pr. -lt). Write or name the letters that form (a word), as *how do you* ~ ' *analyse* '?, *must not be spelt with a z, can't* ~ *his own name*, (abs.) *wish you would learn to* ~ (*correctly*); ~ *out* or *over*, make out (words, writing) laboriously letter by letter; ~ *backward*, repeat or write the letters of (word) in reverse order, (fig.) misinterpret, pervert meaning of; (of letters) make up, form, (word), as *what does* c a t *~?*; (fig., of circumstances, schemes, etc.) have as necessary result, involve, as *these changes* ~ *ruin to the farmer*. [ME, f. OF *espeler* f. WG **spellōn* discourse f. *spell*- (prec.)]

spĕll³, n., & v.t. 1. Turn of work, as *did a* ~ *of carpentering*; short period, as *wait (for) a* ~. 2. v.t. (rare). Relieve, take the place of, (person) in work etc. [later form of dial. *spele* f. OE *spelian*, of unkn. orig.; n. f. vb]

spĕll'er, n. In vbl senses of SPELL²; also = SPELLING-*book*. [-ER¹]

spĕll'ing, n. In vbl senses, as *his* ~ *is weak, not sure of the* ~ *of* ' *aneurysm* ', *another* ~ *of the same word*; *~-bee*, competition in ~; *~-book* (for teaching ~); *~-pronunciation*, artificial pronunciation based on ~ (as *forehead* pron. fŏr'hĕd instead of fŏ'rĕd). [15th c.; -ING¹]

spĕlt¹, n. Kind of wheat giving very fine flour, German wheat. [OE *spelt*, OS *spelta*, OHG *spelza* f. LL *spelta*]

spelt². See SPELL².

spĕl'ter, n. (now commerc.). Zinc.

[corresp. to OF *espeautre*, MDu. *speauter*, LG *spialter*; rel. to PEWTER]

|| **spĕnce, -se**, n. (arch.). Buttery, larder. [ME; aphetic f. OF *despense* (see DISPENSE)]

spĕn'cer¹, n. Short woollen jacket. [perh. f. Mr Knight S~ (fl. 1803)]

spĕn'cer², n. (naut.). = TRYsail. [orig. unkn.]

Spĕn'cerism, n. Doctrine of Herbert Spencer (d. 1903) referring the ordered universe to the necessary laws of mechanics, synthetic philosophy. So **Spĕncēr'IAN** a., **Spĕncēr'ianISM** n. [-ISM]

spĕnd, v.t. & i. (*spent*). 1. Pay out (money) for a purchase etc. (also abs., as ~ *profusely*); ~ *a penny* (colloq.), evacuate bladder or bowels; **~ing money*, pocket--money. 2. Use, use up, consume, as *our ammunition was all spent, shall* ~ *no more breath, trouble*, etc., *on him, how do you* ~ *your time?, spent a pleasant day*; exhaust, wear out, as *his anger will soon* ~ *itself, storm is spent, spent cannon-ball* (with little impulse left). 3. (naut.). Lose (mast). 4. Be consumed, as *candles* ~ *fast in draught*. 5. Emit spawn; *spent herring* etc. (that has deposited its spawn). 6. *~'thrift*, extravagant person, prodigal, (often attrib.). Hence *~'ABLE a.*, *~'ER¹* n. [OE *spendan*, (OS), OHG *spendōn* f. L EX(*pendere* weigh); ME *spende* perh. also aphetic f. OF *despendre* (obs. *dispend*, cf. DISPENSE)]

Spĕn'low and Jŏrk'ins (-lō, -z), n. Plan of attributing one's (S.'s) hard dealings to a supposed hard partner (J.) kept in background. [persons in Dickens's *David Copperfield*]

|| **spense**. See SPENCE.

Spĕnsēr'ian, a. & n. 1. Of the poet Edmund Spenser (d. 1599), esp. ~ *stanza*, that used in the *Faerie Queen*. 2. n. pl. ~ *stanzas*. [-IAN]

spent. See SPEND.

spērm¹, n. Male generative fluid. [ME, f. OF *esperme* or LL f. Gk *sperma -matos* seed]

spērm², n. (Also *~-whale*) cachalot, whale yielding spermaceti; = foll.; *~-oil*, lubricant from *~-whale*. [abbr.]

spērmacēt'i, n. White brittle fatty substance contained in solution in heads of sperm-whale etc., used for candles & ointments. [med. L, f. *sperma* SPERM¹ + *ceti* of whale f. Gk *kētos* (~ being regarded as whale-spawn)]

spērm'arȳ̆, n. Male germ-gland, testicle or equivalent organ. [SPERM¹+-ARY¹]

spērmăt'ic, a. Of SPERM¹ or the spermary. [f. OF *spermatique* or LL f. Gk *spermatikos* (as SPERM¹, see -IC)]

spērm'at|o-, comb. form of Gk *sperma* SPERM¹, as: *~o- blast*, germ of a *~ozoon*; *~ogen'esis*, development of *~ozoa*, so *~o'genous a.*, *~o'geny n.*; *~ŏl'ogist*, *~ŏl'ogy*, student, study, of sperm, so *~olŏ'gical a.*; *~ophore*, capsule containing

~ozoa; ~orrhoe'a (-rēa), involuntary seminal discharge; ~ozō'ŏn (pl. -zōa), male fertilizing element contained in semen of animals, similar element in lower plants, so ~ozo'al, ~ozo'an, aa.

spĕrm'|o-, irreg. comb. form (for prec.) of Gk sperma seed, semen, as: ~oblast = SPERMATOblast; ~ŏl'ogy, = SPERMATOLOGY, (bot.) study of seeds, so ~olō'gical a., ~ŏl'ogist n.

spew, spūe, v.t. & i. Vomit (t. & i.); (of gun) droop at muzzle from too quick firing. [OE spiwan, spēowan, OS, OHG spiwan, ON spýja, Goth. speiwan, cogn. w. L spuere]

sphă'cĕl|āte, v.t. & i. Affect, be affected, with gangrene or necrosis. Hence~A'TION n. [f. Gk sphakelos gangrene +-ATE³]

sphaer(o)-, comb. form of Gk sphaira SPHERE, in many scientific esp. nat. hist. terms.

sphăg'num, n. (bot.; pl. -na). Kinds of moss growing in bogs and peat, and used as packing etc. [mod. L, f. Gk sphagnos a moss]

sphĕn'|(o)-, comb. form of Gk sphĕn wedge, chiefly in sense 'of the sphenoid bone'; also: ~ogram, cuneiform character, so ~ograph'ic a.

sphĕn'oid, a. & n. (anat.). Wedge-shaped, esp. ~ (bone), compound bone at base of skull. Hence sphēnoid'AL a., sphē-noid'ŏ- comb. form. [f. Gk sphenoeidēs (sphēn wedge, -OID)]

sphēre, n., & v.t. 1. Solid figure generated by revolution of semicircle about its diameter, every point on whose surface is equidistant from a point within called the centre. 2. Ball, globe; (poet.) the heavens, the sky; any heavenly body; globe representing the earth or the apparent heavens. 3. Each of the revolving globe-shaped shells in which the heavenly bodies were formerly supposed to be set, esp. music, harmony, of the ~s (produced by movements of the ~s). 4. One's field of action, influence, or existence, one's natural surroundings, one's place in society, as has done much within his peculiar ~, earnest young lady in search of a ~, great mistake to take him out of his ~, moves in quite another ~, State's ~ (claimed or recognized area) of influence in Africa. 5. Celestial ~, surface on which heavenly bodies appear to lie; doctrine of the ~, spherical geometry & trigonometry; great, small, circle of ~, section made by plane passing, not passing, through its centre; oblique, right, parallel, ~, ~ of apparent heavens at a place where there is oblique angle, right angle, no angle, between equator & horizon. 6. v.t. Enclose (as) in ~, make ~-shaped; (poet.) exalt to the (celestial) ~. Hence sphēr'Y² a. (poet.). [ME sper(e) f. OF espere or LL sphera, L f. Gk sphaira ball]

sphĕ'ric, a. & n. 1. (Poet.) of the heavens,

celestial, exalted; (rare) = foll. 2. n. pl. Geometry & trigonometry of the sphere. [f. LL f. Gk sphairikos (as prec., see -IC)]

sphĕ'rical, a. Shaped like a sphere, globular, whence or cogn. ~LY² adv., sphĕri'CITY n.; of spheres, as ~ geometry; ~ lune, triangle, polygon (bounded by arcs of great circles of sphere). [-AL]

sphēr'ograph (-ahf), n. Stereographic projection of the earth on disc, with meridians & parallels of latitude marked in single degrees. [SPHERE+-O-+-GRAPH]

sphĕr'oid, n. Sphere-like but not perfectly spherical body; solid generated by revolution of ellipse about its major (prolate or oblong ~) or minor (oblate ~) axis, as the earth is an oblate ~. Hence sphē-roid'alLY² adv., sphēroid'(IC)AL aa., ~i'CITY n. [f. L f. Gk sphairoeidēs (as SPHERE, see -OID)]

sphĕrŏm'ēter, n. Instrument for finding radius of sphere & for exact measurement of thickness of small bodies. [f. F sphéromètre, see SPHERE, -METER]

sphĕ'rul|e (-ool), n. Small sphere. Hence ~AR¹, ~ATE²(2) (entom.), aa. [f. LL sphaerula (as SPHERE, see -ULE)]

sphĕ'rul|īte (-roo-), n. Vitreous globule as constituent of some rocks. Hence ~it'IC a., ~ītIZE(3) v.t. [f. prec.+-ITE¹]

sphinc'ter, n. Muscle surrounding & serving to close an opening or tube. Hence ~AL, sphinctēr'IAL, sphinctē'rIC, aa. [LL, f. Gk sphigktĕr (sphiggō bind tight)]

sphinx, n. 1. (Gk myth., S~) winged monster of Thebes with woman's head & lion's body who proposed a riddle to the Thebans, killed all who could not guess it, & on Oedipus' solving it threw herself from the rock on which she sat & died. 2. (Egypt. ant.) figure with lion's body & man's or animal's head (the S~, colossal ~ near the pyramids at Gizeh). 3. Enigmatic person (the ~ is silent). 4. Hawk-moth; kind of baboon. [L, f. Gk sphigx, app. f. sphiggō draw tight]

sphragis'tics, n. pl. (often treated as sing.). Study of engraved seals. [f. F -ique or Gk sphragistikos (sphragis seal, -IC(2))]

sphyg'm|o-, comb. form of Gk sphugmos SPHYGMUS, as: ~ograph, instrument for showing character of pulse in series of curves, ~ogram, record so produced, so ~ograph'ic a., ~ŏg'raphy n.; ~ŏl'ogy, study of the pulse; ~omanŏm'eter, instrument for measuring blood-pressure; ~ophone, ~oscope, instrument for making audible, visible, the action of the pulse.

sphyg'mus, n. (physiol.). Pulse, pulsation. [f. Gk sphugmos f. sphuzō throb]

spīc'|a, n. (Bot.) spike, whence ~ATE², ~āt̄ed, aa.; (surg.) spiral bandage with reversed turns. [L, = spike, ear of grain]

spice, n., & v.t. 1. Aromatic or pungent vegetable substance used to flavour food, e.g. cloves, pepper, mace; ~s collectively, as dealer in ~, sugar & ~ & all that's nice, so spi'cery(1) n.; (fig.) smack, dash, flavour, (of malice etc. in person's character, writings, etc.); ~'bush, aromatic American shrub of laurel family. 2. v.t. Flavour with ~. [ME, f. OF espice spice f. L SPECIES]

spick, a. ~ & span, smart & new, brand-new. [16th c. spick & span new, emphatic extension of ME span new f. ON spán-nýr = chip-new]

spic'ul|e, n. Small sharp-pointed body; (zool.) small hard body esp. in framework of sponge; (bot.) small or secondary spike. Hence ~AR¹, ~ATE²(2), aa. [F, or f. mod. L spicula, L spiculum, see -ULE]

spi'c|y, a. Of, flavoured or fragrant with, spice; (fig.) piquant, pungent, improper (~y story), showy, smart. Hence ~ILY² adv., ~INESS n. [-Y²]

spid'er, n. 1. Eight-legged animal of the order Araneida, many species of which spin webs esp. for capture of insects as food (~ & fly, fig., ensnarer & ensnared); kinds of arachnid like ~. 2. Thing compared to ~ esp. as having prominent legs, e.g. kind of three-legged gridiron. 3. Sulky with very large light wheels. 4. ~-catcher, kinds of bird; ~-crab, crab with long thin legs; ~-line, thread of ~'s web substituted for wire in scales etc. for minute work; ~-monkey, kind with long limbs & long prehensile tail; ~-wasp, wasp that stores its nest with ~s for its young. Hence ~LIKE a., ~Y² a. (esp. of writing, legs, spokes, etc.) very thin. [OE spithra (SPIN¹ +-ther agent suf.)]

spieg'eleisen (-līzn), n. Kind of cast iron containing manganese, much used in Bessemer process. [G (spiegel mirror f. L speculum +eisen iron)]

*spiel, n., & v.i. & t. (sl.). 1. Speech, story. 2. vb. Hold forth, orate; reel off (patter, yarn, tale of misfortune). [G, = play, game]

spif(f)'lic|āte, v.t. (sl.). Trounce, do for. Hence ~A'TION n. [fanciful]

spig'ot, n. Small peg or plug esp. one for insertion into gimlet-hole in cask; plain end of pipe fitting into socket of next one. [ME, perh. f. OPr. *espigot f. espiga SPICA]

spike¹, n., & v.t. 1. Sharp point; pointed piece of metal e.g. one of a set forming top of iron fence etc. or worn in bottom of shoe to prevent slipping; large stout nail esp. as used for railways; ‖ (colloq.) a 'spiky' Anglican [back formation f. spiky]; ~ plank, bridge before mizzen-mast of vessel meant for arctic service. 2. v.t. Fasten with ~s, furnish with ~s; fix on or pierce with ~; plug up vent of (gun) with ~, (fig.) make useless, *put an end to (idea etc.). Hence ~'WISE (-kw-) adv., spik'Y¹ [-Y²] a. (also, colloq.) of hard unyielding 'high-church' views. [ME, ult. f. L spica, perh. thr. MSw. spik, Sw. & Norw. spik nail]

spike², n. (bot.). Flower-cluster of many sessile flowers arranged closely on long common axis; separate sprig of any plant in which flowers form ~like cluster; [f. F spic) kind of lavender; ~ oil (got from lavender). Hence ~'LET (-kl-) n., spik'Y² [-Y²] a. [f. L spica ear of corn, plant-~]

spike'nard (-kn-), n. (Ancient costly aromatic ointment made chiefly from) perennial herb allied to valerian; ploughman's ~, composite fragrant plant with purplish-yellow flower-heads; kinds of fragrant oil. [ME, f. med. L SPICA nardi (NARD)]

spile, n., & v.t. 1. Wooden peg, spigot, large timber for driving into ground, pile. 2. v.t. Make ~-hole in (cask). [f. MDu. or MLG spile wooden peg etc.; in sense pile app. alt. f. PILE¹]

spil'ing, n. Set of piles; (naut.) edge-curve of plank in vessel's hull. [f. prec. +-ING¹; naut. sense, earlier spoiling, orig. unkn.]

spill¹, v.t. & i. (spilt or ~ed), & n. 1. Allow (liquid, substance in small particles) to fall or run out from vessel, as spill the salt, no use crying over spilt milk, (of liquid etc.) fall or run out; ~ blood, be guilty of bloodshed; ~ the blood of, kill; ~ money (sl.), lose it in betting etc.; (naut.) empty (belly of sail) of wind; *~ the beans (sl.), give the show away, divulge information indiscreetly; throw from saddle or vehicle, as horse spill him, was spilt from a cycle; ~ over (of surplus population of towns), cf. overspill n. 2. n. Such throwing, as had a nasty ~; fall (e.g. from cycle); ~way, passage for surplus water from dam. [OE spillan, = MDu., MLG spillen, rel. to syn. OE spildan, = OS spildian, OHG spilden]

spill², n. Thin strip of wood, spiral tube etc. of paper for lighting candles etc. [ME, of unkn. orig.; app. rel. to SPILE]

spill'er, n. Seine put into a larger one to take out fish when the larger cannot be hauled ashore. [orig. unkn.]

spill'ikin, n. Splinter of wood, bone, etc., used in some games; (pl., also spel'icans) game played with ~s. [f. SPILL², see -KIN]

spilt. See SPILL¹.

spilth, n. (arch.). What is spilt; excess, surplus. [-TH¹]

spin¹, v.t. & i. (spun or span, spun). 1. Draw out & twist (wool, cotton, or abs.) into threads; make (yarn) thus. 2. (Of spider, silkworm, etc.) make (web, gossamer, cocoon, or abs.) by extrusion of fine viscous thread. 3. Form (cup etc.) in lathe or similar machine. 4. (fig.) Produce, compose, (narrative, literary article, etc.; often out i.e. at great length), esp. ~ a yarn (orig. naut.), tell a story. 5. ~ out, spend, consume, (time, one's life, etc., by discussion etc., in occupation etc.), prolong (discussion etc.), (crick.) dismiss (batsman, side) by spin bowling. **6.** Cause (top etc.) to whirl round, (of top) whirl round, turn (person, thing) quickly round; (of person etc.) turn thus, e.g. as result of blow, as *sent him~ning*. **7.** Fish in (stream, pool) with swivel or spoon-bait. **8.** ‖ (sl.). Reject (candidate) after examination. **9.** p.p. (sl.). Tired out, done. **10.** *Spun glass* (spun when heated into filaments that remain pliant when cold); *spun gold, silver*, gold, silver, thread prepared for weaving; *spun silk*, cheap material of short-fibred & waste silk often mixed with cotton; *spun yarn* (naut.), line formed of rope-yarns twisted together. [OE, OHG, Goth. *spinnan*, ON *spinna*]

spin², n. Spinning motion, whirl; (aviation) diving descent combined with rotation; secondary revolving motion esp. as developed in rifle bullet, or in billiard or tennis ball struck aslant; (crick.) twisting motion given to ball when bowled (~ *bowler*, expert at this); brisk or short run or spell of driving, rowing, cycling, etc., as *went for a* ~; ~ *drier*, machine which dries clothes etc. by rapid spinning in a rotating aerated drum. [f. prec.]

spin′ach, -age, (-nij), n. Garden vegetable with thick succulent leaves used when boiled as food; other plants similarly used; ~ *beet*, kind of beet used like ~. Hence **spinā′ceous** (-āshŭs) a. [prob. f. MDu. *spinaetse*, *spinag(i)e*, f. OF *espinage; (e)spinache*]

spin′al, a. Of the spine, as ~ *curvature, complaint*; ~ *column*, spine; ~ *cord*, cylindrical structure within ~ canal, a part of the central nervous system. [f. LL *spinalis* (SPINE, -AL)]

spin′dle, n., & v.i. **1.** Pin in spinning--wheel used for twisting & winding the thread; small bar serving same purposes in hand-spinning; pin bearing bobbin of spinning-machine; pin, axis, that revolves or on which a thing revolves; *live* (revolving) ~, *dead* (non-revolving) ~; slender thing or person; varying measure of length for yarn. **2.** ~*-shanked*, with long thin legs, ~*-shanks*, person with such legs; ~*-shaped*, of circular cross-section & tapering towards each end; ~*-tree*, shrub or small tree with greenish-white flowers and hard wood used for ~s; hence **spind′ly²** a., slender, attenuated. **3.** v.i. Have, grow into, long slender form. [OE *spinel,* = OHG *spin(n)ila*, f. SPIN¹ + -LE(1); cf. MHG, G *spindel*]

spin′drift, n. Spray blown along surface of sea; ~ *clouds*, light feathery clouds. [Sc. var. of *spoon-, (spoom-) drift,* f. (16th c., now obs.) *spoon* run before wind or sea, +DRIFT]

spin|e, n. The series of the vertebrae, backbone; (bot.) stiff sharp woody process due to degeneracy or modification of some organ; sharp ridge or projection; the part of a book's cover or jacket visible when it is in place on a shelf; ~*e′back*, kinds of fish with ~es in or in front of dorsal fins. Hence ~ED² (-nd), ~′OSE¹, ~′OUS, aa., ~OS′ITY n. [ME, f. OF *espine* or L *spina* thorn, backbone]

spin′el, n. Kinds of mineral of various colours occurring in regular crystals; ~ *ruby*, valuable red variety. [f. F *spinelle,* f. It. *spinella*]

spine′less (-nl-), a. Having no spine, invertebrate; (fig.) limp, weak, having no backbone; (of fish) having no fin-spines. [-LESS]

spin′ét (*or* -ĕt′), n. (hist.). Small wing--shaped harpsichord with one string to each note. [f. obs. F *espinette* f. It. *spinetta*, prob. f. G *Spinetti*, inventor]

spin′|i-, comb. form of L *spina* thorn, backbone, as: ~*ice′rebrate*, having brain & spinal cord; ~*if′erous*, having or producing spines; ~*iFORM*.

spinn′aker, n. Large ‖jib-shaped sail carried on mainmast of racing-yacht running before wind. [fanciful f. *Sphinx*, name of yacht first using it]

spinn′er, n. In vbl senses, esp.: thread--spinning machine; person who shapes vessels etc. in lathe; (also ~ET¹ n.) spinning-organ in spider, silkworm, etc. [ME; -ER¹]

‖ spinn′ey, n. (pl. ~s). Small wood, thicket. [f. OF *espinnei (espine*, see SPINE)]

spinn′ing, n. In vbl senses; ~*-house* (hist.), house of correction for prostitutes; ~*-jenny*, mechanism for spinning more than one strand at a time; ~*-machine*, (esp.) machine that spins fibres continuously; ~*-wheel* (hist.), household implement for spinning yarn or thread, with fly-wheel driven by crank or treadle. [ME; -ING¹]

Spinoz′|ism, n. Doctrine of B. de Spinoza, a Spanish Jew (d. 1677), that there is one sole & infinite substance of which extension & mind are attributes & individual beings are changing forms. So ~IST n., ~′is′tic a. [-ISM]

spin′ster, n. Unmarried (esp. elderly in pop. use) woman. Hence ~HOOD n. [ME, orig.=woman who spins (SPIN¹, see -STER)]

spinthä′riscŏpe, n. Screen of zinc blende showing incidence of alpha particles (of ALPHA rays) by fluorescent flash. [irreg. f. Gk *spintharis* spark +-SCOPE]

spin′ŭl|e, n. (bot., zool.). Small spine. Hence ~iF′EROUS, ~OSE¹, ~OUS, aa. [f. L *spinula* (as SPINE, see -ULE)]

spin′|y, a. Full of spines, prickly, esp. in names of animals, as ~*y crab, lobster, rat*; (fig.) perplexing, troublesome, thorny. Hence ~iNESS n. [-Y²]

spir′acle, n. (zool.). External orifice of trachea in insects; blow-hole of whales etc. Hence **spirăc′ūlAR**, **spirăc′ū-lATE²(2)**, aa. [f. L *spiraculum* (also used in E) f. *spirare* breathe]

spīrae′a, n. Kinds of rosaceous plant

with white or pink flowers. [L, f. Gk *speiraia* meadowsweet (*speira* coil)]

spir'al, a., n., & v.t. & i. (-ll-). **1.** Coiled; winding continually about & constantly receding from a centre, whether remaining in same plane like watch-spring or rising in a cone; winding continually & advancing as if along cylinder, like thread of screw; ~ *balance* (measuring weight by torsion of ~ spring); ~ *wheel* (with teeth cut at angle to axis). **2.** n. Plane or other ~ curve, ~ spring, ~ formation in shell etc.; (fig.) gradual but progressive rise or fall (*the vicious ~ of rising prices and wages*). **3.** vb. Make ~; move in a ~ course. Hence ~ITY (-ăl²) n., ~LY² adv. [f. med. L *spiralis* (as SPIRE², see -AL)]

spir'ant, a. & n. (phonet.). (Consonant) uttered with perceptible expulsion of breath & in producing which the organs are near together but not wholly closed, continuable (consonant) (cf. EXPLOSIVE), e.g. *f, v, th, dh*, & occas. *w, y*, & others. [f. L *spirare* breathe, see -ANT]

spire¹, n., & v.i. & t. **1.** Tapering structure in form of tall cone or pyramid rising above tower; continuation of tree trunk above point where branching begins; any tapering body, e.g. stalk of grass. **2.** v.i. Shoot up. **3.** v.t. Furnish with~. Hence **spir'y²** a. [OE *spīr*, MDu. *spier*, MLG, MHG *spīr*]

spire², n. Spiral, coil; single twist of this. Hence **spir'y²** a. [F, or f. L f. Gk *speira* coil]

spirill'um, n. (pl. *-la*). Group of bacteria characterized by a spiral structure; any member of this. [mod. L, dim. of L *spira* SPIRE²]

spi'rit¹, n. **1.** Intelligent or immaterial part of man, soul; *in* (*the*) ~, inwardly, *as groaned in* ~, *was vexed in* ~, *shall be with you in* (*the*) ~. **2.** Person viewed as possessing this, esp. w. reference to particular mental or moral qualities, as *one of the most ardent* ~s *of his time, a meeting of choice* ~s; *a master-*~, person of commanding intellect etc. **3.** Rational or intelligent being not connected with material body, disembodied soul, incorporeal being, elf, fairy, as *God is a* ~, *the Holy S~* (third person of the Trinity), *has seen a* ~, ~s *must have been at work*, ASTRAL~s, FAMILIAR~, *peace to his departed* ~. **4.** Person's mental or moral nature or qualities, as *a man of an unbending* ~; *the poor in* ~; the meek. **5.** Courage, self-assertion, vivacity, energy, dash, as *if you had the* ~ *of a mouse, do show a little* ~, *went at it with* ~, *infused* ~ *into his men, people of* ~. **6.** Person viewed as supplying this (= *soul*, but usu. w. adj.), as *was the animating* ~ *of the rebellion*. **7.** Mental or moral condition or attitude, mood, as *took it in a wrong* ~, *depends on the* ~ *in which it is done, did it in a* ~ *of mischief, objections made in a captious* ~. **8.** Real meaning opp. to verbal expres-

sion, as *must consider the* ~ *of the law, not the letter, have followed out the* ~ *of his instructions*. **9.** Animating principle or influence, mental or moral tendency, as *cannot resist the* ~ *of the age or times*. **10.** (Formerly) immaterial principle governing vital phenomena, whence (mod.) ANIMAL ~s; *high* or *great* ~s, cheerfulness & buoyancy; *poor* or *low* ~s, depression. **11.** (Usu. pl.) strong distilled liquor esp. alcohol, e.g. brandy, whisky, gin, rum, as *glass of* ~s *& water*, ARDENT~s, *touches no* ~ *but gin*. **12.** Solution (*of* volatile principle) in alcohol, tincture; ~s *of salt*, hydrochloric acid; ~ *or* ~s *of wine*, alcohol; METHYLATED ~. **13.** ~ *blue*, aniline blue soluble in alcohol; ~ *duck*, kinds of duck diving rapidly at flash of gun etc.; ‖~-*lamp* (burning methylated ~ instead of oil); ~-*level*, glass tube partly filled with ~ for testing horizontality; ~-*rapper*, person professing to hold intercourse with departed ~s by means of their raps on table etc., so ~-*rapping*; ~-*room* (naut.), paymaster's store-room, formerly used for ~s. [ME, f. AF *spirit*(*e*), OF *esperit*, or L *spiritus* breath, spirit, f. *spirare* breathe]

spi'rit², v.t. Convey (usu. *away, off*, etc.) rapidly and secretly (as) by agency of spirits; cheer (person, usu. *up*). [f. prec.]

spi'rited, a. Full of spirit, animated, lively, brisk, courageous, as *a* ~ *translation, attack, reply*; having specified spirit, as *high, mean, proud, jealous,* -~; having specified spirits, as *low-*~. Hence (-)~LY² adv., ~NESS n. [-ED²]

spi'ritless, a. Wanting in courage, vigour, or vivacity. Hence ~LY² adv. [-LESS]

spīrĭtŏs'ō, adv. (mus.). With spirit. [It.]

spi'ritual, a. & n. **1.** Of spirit as opp. to matter; of the soul esp. as acted on by God, as ~ *life*; of, proceeding from, God, holy, divine, inspired, as ~ *songs, the* ~ *law*; *the* ~ *man*, inner nature of man, (also esp. in N.T.) regenerate man (opp. to *natural, carnal*); concerned with sacred or religious things, as *our* ~ *interests*, ~ (*ecclesiastical*) *courts*, ~ *corporations*; *lords* ~, bishops & archbishops in House of Lords, cf. TEMPORAL; having the higher qualities of the mind. **2.** n. Religious song peculiar to American Negroes (also (*Negro* ~). Hence ~LY² adv., ~NESS n. [ME, f. OF *spirituel* or L *spiritualis* (as SPIRIT, see -AL)]

spi'ritual|ism, n. Belief that departed spirits communicate with & show themselves to men, esp. (also *modern* ~*ism*) at seances by means of spirit-rapping, -handwriting, etc., so **spi'ritism**, **spi'ritIST**, nn.; (philos.) doctrine that spirit exists as distinct from matter or that spirit is the only reality (cf. MATERIALISM). Hence or cogn. ~IST n., ~**is'**tIc a. [-ISM]

spiritual'ity, n. Spiritual quality; (usu. pl.) what belongs or is due to the Church or to an ecclesiastic as such, as *the ~ies of his office, ~y of benefices,* tithes of land etc. [ME, f. OF (*e*)*spiritualite* or LL *spiritualitas* (as SPIRITUAL, see -TY)]

spi′ritūaliz|e, -is|e (-īz), v.t. Make spiritual, elevate, (character, person, thoughts); (rare) infuse life into, animate; attach spiritual as opp. to literal meaning to. Hence ~A′TION n. [f. SPIRITUAL +-IZE, or f. F *spiritualiser*]

spiritūĕl(le)′, a. (Chiefly of women) marked by refinement, grace, or delicacy of mind. [F, as SPIRITUAL]

spi′ritūous, a. Containing much alcohol, distilled not fermented, as ~ *liquors* (also used loosely of beer etc.). Hence ~NESS n. [f. L *spiritus* SPIRIT +-OUS, or f. F *spiritueux*]

spī′rĭtus, n. (Gk gram.). ~ ăs′per, lēn′ĭs, = *rough, smooth,* BREATHING¹. [L]

spīr′ĭvălve, a. Having spiral shell; (of shell) spiral. [F, f. L *spira* SPIRE² + *valva* VALVE]

spĭrk′ĕtĭng, n. (naut.). Inside planking between top of waterways & lower sills of ports. [f. obs. *spurkelt* (17th c.), *spirkelt* (18th c.), of unkn. orig.]

spīro-¹, comb. form of Gk *speira* coil, as ~*chaete* (-kēt′ē), spiral-shaped bacterium.

spīr′|o-² in comb. (irreg.)=L *spiro* breathe in sense 'breath', as: ~*ograph*, instrument for marking breathing movement; ~*ŏm′eter*, ~*oscope*, instrument for measuring lung capacity, so ~*omet′ric* a., ~*ŏm′etry* n.; ~*ophore*, instrument for inducing respiration in cases of suspended animation.

spĭrt, spŭrt, v.i. & t., & n. 1. Gush out in a jet or stream; cause (liquid etc.) to do this. 2. n. Sudden gushing out, jet. [vb 16th c., of unkn. orig.]

spit¹, n., & v.t. (-tt-). 1. Slender bar on which meat that is to be roasted is made to rotate before fire; skewer; small point of land running into sea; long narrow underwater bank. 2. v.t. Thrust a ~ through (meat etc.); (fig.) pierce, transfix, with sword etc. [OE *spitu*, MDu., MLG *spit*, OHG *spiz* (G *spiess*)]

spit², v.i. & t. (*spat* or arch. *spit*), & n. 1. Eject saliva (‖~ *& polish,* furbishing work of soldier etc.); eject (saliva, blood, food, etc. *out*) from mouth; (fig.) utter (oaths, threats, etc.) vehemently (~ *it out*, sl., exhortation to speak or sing louder); (of cat etc., fig. of person) make noise as of ~ting as sign of anger or hostility; (of rain) fall lightly, (of fire, candle, pen) send out sparks, stray ink, etc.; ~ *at* or *upon*, (fig.) treat with ignominy; ~*fire*, person of fiery temper, (also ~*devil*) toy cone of wet gunpowder ~ting when ignited. Hence ~t′ER¹ n. 2. n. ~ting (esp. of cat), spawn of some insects; spittle; *the* (*very*) ~ *of* (exact counterpart of, likeness of, as *he is the very* ~ *of his father*). [OE *spittan* = G dial. *spitzen*, of imit. orig.; cf. OE *spǣtan* (whence

past & p.p. *spat*); ON *spýta* = MHG *spiutzen*]

spit³, n. Spade-depth (*dig it two* ~*s or* ~ *deep*). [f. MDu., MLG *spit*, also *spitten* dig, = OE *spittan*, dial. *spit* vb]

spitch′cŏck, n., & v.t. 1. Eel split & broiled. 2. v.t. Prepare thus (eel, fish, bird). [16th c., of unkn. orig.; cf. SPATCHCOCK]

spite, n., & v.t. 1. Ill will, malice, as *did it from pure* ~ or *in* or *out of* ~; grudge, as *has a* ~ *against me*; (*in*) ~ *of*, notwithstanding. 2. v.t. Thwart, mortify, annoy, as *does it to* ~ *me, cut off one's nose to* ~ *one's face,* injure oneself by vindictive or resentful conduct. Hence ~′FUL (-tf-) a., ~′fulLY adv., ~′fulNESS n. [ME; aphetic f. *despite* n. & vb]

spit′tle, n. Saliva esp. as ejected from mouth. [alt. f. ME (now dial.) *spatile* (OE *spǣtl*), *spettle*, after SPIT²]

spittōōn′, n. Vessel to spit into, usu. round metal or earthenware vessel with funnel-shaped top. [irreg. f. SPIT² +-OON]

spitz, n. (Also ~-*dog*) small kind of dog with pointed muzzle, Pomeranian. [G *spitz*(*hund*) f. *spitz* pointed, *hund* dog]

‖**spiv**, n. (sl.). Shady character who avoids honest work & lives by his wits esp. in black-market traffic. [orig. unkn.]

splănch′n|ic (-ngk-), a. Of the entrails, intestinal. So ~o- comb. form, ~ŏL′OGY, ~ŏT′OMY, nn. [f. Gk *splagkhnikos* (*splagkhna* entrails, see -IC)]

splash, v.t. & i., & n. 1. Bespatter (person etc. *with* water, mud, etc.); dash, spatter, (liquid *about, on* or *over* person etc.); (of liquid) fly about in drops or scattered portions; (of person) cause liquid to do this, make one's *way,* move *across, along,* etc., thus; step, fall, plunge, etc., *into* (water etc.) so as to ~ it; decorate with scattered ornamentation. 2. n. ~ing; quantity of liquid ~ed; resulting noise, as *we heard a* ~; WATER¹-~; ‖(colloq.) small quantity of soda-water etc. (diluting whisky etc.); spot of dirt etc. ~ed on to things; patch of colour esp. on animal's skin; *make a* ~, (fig.) attract much attention, create sensation; complexion powder usu. of rice-flour; ~*-board,* guard over or beside wheel of vehicle to keep mud off occupants; ~ *headline* (conspicuous, designed to attract attention). Hence ~′Y² a.[alt. f. PLASH²]

splash′er, n. In vbl senses; also: kinds of guard placed over wheels of locomotive etc. to keep off mud etc.; screen behind wash-stand to protect wall. [-ER¹]

splătt′er, v.i. & t. Make continuous splashing sound; speak (a language, or abs.) unintelligibly; ‖~-*dash,* noise, clamour; ‖~-*dashes,* = SPATTERdashes. [imit.]

splay, v.t. & i., n., & a. 1. Construct (aperture) with divergent sides (~*ed loop-hole, window, doorway,* with opening wider at one side of wall), (of aperture or its sides) be so shaped or set; dislocate (esp. horse's shoulder). 2. n. Surface making oblique angle with another, e.g. ~ed side of window, embrasure. 3. adj. Wide & flat, turned outward; ~-*foot* n. & a., (having) broad flat foot turned outward; ~ *mouth*, wide mouth, mouth stretched wide in grimace. [aphetic f. DISPLAY vb]

spleen, n. 1. Organ producing certain modifications in the blood of most vertebrates, situated in mammals at left of stomach. 2. Lowness of spirits, ill temper, spite, as *a fit of* ~, *vented his* ~, whence ~'FUL, ~'ISH¹, ~'Y², aa., ~'fulLY², ~'ishLY², advv. 3. ~'*wort*, kinds of fern formerly used for ~ disorders. Hence ~'LESS a, [ME, f. OF *esplen,* or L f. Gk *splēn*]

splēn|(o)-, comb. form of Gk *splēn* spleen, as : ~*ăl'gia,* pain in (region of) spleen, so ~*ăl'gic* a.; ~*ĕc'tomy,* excision of spleen; ~*ĭt'is,* inflammation of spleen, so ~*ĭt'ic* a.; ~*ŏl'ogy,* study of spleen, so ~*olŏ'gical* a.; ~*ŏt'omy* incision into, dissection of, spleen.

splēn'dent, a. (mineral., entom.). Having bright metallic lustre. [ME, f. L *splendēre* shine, see -ENT]

splēn'did, a. Magnificent, gorgeous, sumptuous, glorious, brilliant, as *a* ~ *palace, gift, achievement, victory*; (of person) affecting splendour (*in* surroundings etc.); (colloq.) excellent, capital, as *here is a* ~ *chance of escape.* Hence ~LY² adv, [f. F (-*ide*) or L *splendidus* (prec., -ID¹)]

splēndif'erous, a. (colloq.). Splendid. [irreg. f. foll. +-FEROUS]

splēn'dour (-der), n. Great or dazzling brightness; magnificence, grandeur; (her.) *sun in* ~ (with rays & human face). [ME, f. AF (e)*splend*(o)*ur* or L *splendor* (as SPLENDENT, see -OR)]

splēnĕt'|ic, a. & n. 1. Ill-tempered, peevish, whence ~ICALLY adv.; of the spleen. 2. n. Medicine for sufferer from, disease of the spleen. [f. LL *spleneticus* (as SPLEEN, see -ETIC)]

splēn'ial, a. (anat.). Acting like a splint; of the splenius muscle. [f. L f. Gk *splēnion* +-AL]

splēn'ic, a. Of, in, the spleen, as ~ *fever,* anthrax. So **splēn'OID** a. [f. L f. Gk *splēnikos* (as SPLEEN, see -IC)]

splēn'ius, n. (pl. *-ii*). (Either section of) muscle on back & sides of neck serving to draw back the head. [f. Gk *splēnion* bandage]

splēnīzā'tion, -īs-, n. Conversion of lung into substance resembling spleen. [f. F *splénisation* or mod. L *splenisatio* (SPLEEN, -IZE, -ATION)]

splice, v.t., & n. 1. Join ends of (ropes) by interweaving strands; join (pieces of timber etc.) in overlapping position; (colloq.) join in marriage, as *when did he or they get* ~*d?*; ~ *the* MAIN³ *brace.* 2. n. Junction of two ropes or pieces of wood etc. by splicing; EYE¹~; *sit on the* ~ (crick.

sl.), play a cautious defensive game, stonewall. [f. MDu. *splissen* of uncert. orig.; perh. rel. to SPLIT]

spline, n., & v.t. 1. Rectangular key fitting into grooves in hub & shaft of wheel & allowing longitudinal play; slat; flexible wood or rubber strip used in drawing large curves esp. in railway work. 2. v.t. Fit with ~. [orig. E. Angl. dial., perh. for *splind,* & rel. to *splinder,* SPLINTER]

splint, n., & v.t. 1. Strip of rigid or flexible material for holding broken bone when set or for basketwork etc.; (anat. also ~-*bone*) either of two small bones in horse's foreleg lying behind & in close contact with cannon-bone, (in man) fibula; tumour on, callus due to disease of, ~-bone of horse; ~-*coal,* cannel coal of slaty structure. 2. v.t. Confine (broken limb etc.) with ~s. [ME *splent*(e), f. MDu. *splinte* or MLG *splinte, splente* metal plate or pin; cf. prec.]

splin'ter, v.t. & i., & n. 1. Split (t. & i.) into long thin pieces, shiver. 2. n. Sharp-edged or thin piece broken off from wood, stone, etc.; ||~-*bar,* cross-bar in vehicle supporting springs or to which traces are attached; ~-*bone,* fibula; ~ *party* (pol.), a party that has broken away from a larger one, esp. when very small in numbers; ~-*proof* (against ~s of bursting shells or bombs). [ME, f. MDu. (= LG) *splinter, splenter*; rel. to prec. & dial. *splinder*]

splin'terỹ, a. Of splinters; splinter-like; apt to splinter. [-Y²]

split¹, v.t. & i. (*split*). 1. Break forcibly, be broken, into parts esp. with the grain or plane of cleavage. 2. Divide into parts, thicknesses, etc., as ~ *it into three layers, the job, sum,* etc., *was* ~ (usu. *up*) *among 6 of us,* ~ *one's vote,* vote for opposed candidates, ~ *the difference,* take mean quantity etc. between two proposed; ~ *hairs,* draw over-subtle distinctions, so HAIR-~*ting.* 3. Divide (t. & i.) into disagreeing or hostile parties (*on* question etc.). 4. ~ (*one's sides* or intr.), be convulsed with laughter, so *side-*~*ting* a. & n., *side-*~*ter* (person or joke); *head is* ~*ting* (feels acute pain), *a* ~*ting* (acute) *headache.* 5. ~ *on* (sl.), betray the secrets of (accomplice etc.). 6. ~ *cloth* (surg.), bandage with several tails esp. for head & face; ~ *gear, wheel* (made in halves for removal from shaft); ~ *infinitive* (with adverb etc. inserted between *to* and verb, e.g. *seems to partly correspond*); ~ *moss,* kinds of which capsules ~ at maturity; ~*peas*(e) (dried & ~ in half for cooking); ~ *personality,* alteration or dissociation of personality such as may occur in some mental illnesses esp. schizophrenia and hysteria; ~ PIN¹; ~ *ring* (usu. of steel on the pattern of those used for bunches of keys); ~ *second,* a very short period of time; ~ *shot, stroke,* stroke at croquet driving two touching balls in different directions. Hence (-)~ter¹(1, 2) n. [16th c., orig. naut., f. MDu. *splitten*, obsc. rel. to *spletten*, *spliten* (G *spleissen*), & E dial. *splet*, *spleet*]

split², n. 1. Splitting; fissure, rent, crack. 2. Separation into parties, schism, rupture. 3. Split osier etc. for parts of basket-work; each of the strips of steel, cane, etc., of reed in loom; single thickness of split hide. 4. (In faro) turning up of two cards of equal value so that stakes are divided. 5. Half bottle of aerated water, half glass of liquor. 6. pl. Trick of sitting on ground with legs spread out, as *do the* ~s. [f. prec.]

splosh, n. (colloq.). A quantity of water suddenly dropped or thrown down; ‖ (sl.) money. [imit.]

splotch, **splodge**, nn. Daub, smear. Hence **splotch'y**² a. [-*lch* f. 17th, -*dge* 19th, c.; perh. imit.]

*****splurge**, n., & v.i. (Make) noisy display or effort. [U.S. wd, prob. imit.]

splutt'er, v.i. & t., & n. = sputter. Hence ~er¹ n. [imit.; for -*l*- cf. sp(l)atter]

Spöde, n. A fine pottery. [J. ~, maker, d. 1827]

spöff'ish, a. (sl.). Bustling, fussy. [orig. unkn.]

spoil¹, n. 1. (Usu. pl. or collect. sing.) plunder taken from enemy in war, (fig.) profit, advantage accruing from success in contest etc., (joc.) emoluments of public office etc. 2. *~s system*, practice of giving public offices to adherents of successful party, whence *~s'man*, advocate of, one who seeks to profit by, this. 3. A draw in the game of *~-five*, in which each player has five cards. 4. Earth etc. thrown or brought up in excavating, dredging, etc. [ME, f. OF *espoille*, or f. foll.]

spoil², v.t. & i. (~*t* or ~*ed*). 1. (arch., literary; never ~*t*). Plunder, deprive (person of thing), by force or stealth, as ~ *the Egyptians* (persons regarded as one's natural enemies etc.; *Exod.* xii. 36). 2. Impair the qualities of, or person's enjoyment of, as *was quite* ~*t by the rain*, *will* ~ *all the fun*, *always* ~ *a joke in the telling*, *the news* ~*t his dinner*, ~ *one's beauty for him* (with black eye etc.). 3. Injure character of (person etc.) by indulgence, as *spare the rod* & ~ *the child*, *are determined to* ~ *me*, *is the* ~*t child of fortune*. 4. (sl.). Maim or kill or do for (person). 5. (Of fruit, fish, etc., fig. of joke etc.) decay, go bad, as *will not* ~ *with keeping*, (only in part.) *dog is* ~*ing* (ripe, eager) *for a fight*. 6. ~*-sport*, one who ~s sport. Hence ~*er¹* n. [ME, f. OF *espoil-lier* f. L *spoliare* f. *spolium* spoil, plunder]

spoil'age, n. Paper spoilt in printing. [-age]

spöke¹, n., & v.t. 1. Each of the bars running from hub to rim of wheel, whence ~'wise (-kw-) adv.; rung of ladder; each

radial handle of steering-wheel of vessel; bar used to prevent wheel from turning esp. in going down hill, as (fig.) *put a* ~ *in* person's *wheel*, thwart his purposes; ~*-bone*, radius of forearm; ~'*shave*, plane-bit between two handles, used for ~s & other esp. curved work where ordinary plane is not available. 2. v.t. Furnish with ~s, check (wheel) with ~; *spoking--machine* (for giving uniform inclination to ~s of wheel. [OE *spāca*, OS *spéca*, OHG *speicha*]

spoke², **spoken**, **-spoken**. See speak.

spökes'man (-ks-), n. (pl. *-men*). One who speaks for others, representative. [irreg. f. spoke² + -es + man]

spöl'ïa opïm'a, n. (Rom. ant.) arms stripped from hostile general by Roman commander in single combat; (fig.) supreme achievement or distinction. [L, = rich spoils]

spölïä'tion, n. Plunder, pillage, esp. of neutral vessels by belligerent, (fig.) extortion; (eccl.) taking of fruits of benefice under pretended title, *writ of* ~ (for recovery of these); (law) destruction, mutilation, alteration, of document to prevent its being used as evidence. Hence or cogn. **spöl'ïätor** n., **spöl'ïatory** a. [ME, f. L *spoliatio* (as spoil², see -ation), or f. OF]

spöndä'ic, a. Of spondees; (of hexameter) having spondee as fifth foot. [f. F *spondaïque* or *spondaicus* = LL f. Gk *spondeiakos* (as foll., see -ac)]

spön'dee (-dï), n. Metrical foot – –. [ME, f. L f. Gk *spondeios* (*pous* foot) f. *spondē* solemn drink-offering; or f. OF *spondee*]

*****spöndül'icks**, n. pl. (sl.). Money.

spön'dyl|(e), n. Joint of backbone, vertebra. Hence ~(o)- comb. form. [OF (-*le*), or f. L f. Gk *sp-*, *sphondulos*]

sponge¹ (-ŭnj), n. 1. Aquatic animal of low order with pores in the body-wall, whence **spöngöl'ogist**, **spöngöl'ogy**, (-ngg-), nn. 2. Skeleton of a ~ or colony of ~s (whence **spo'ngiform** (-ŭnj-) a.), esp. elastic kind chiefly from the Levant used as absorbent in bathing, cleansing surfaces, etc.; *throw up the* ~, (of boxer or his attendant) throw into the air as token of defeat the ~ used between rounds, (fig.) abandon contest, own oneself beaten; *pass the* ~ *over*, agree to forget (offence etc.). 3. Thing of ~like absorbency or consistence, e.g. piece of leavened dough, ~*-cake*, absorbent pad used in surgery, kind of mop for cleaning bore of big gun, iron or other metal in finely divided condition. 4. (fig.). Parasite, person who contrives to live at another's expense. 5. ~*-bath*; ~*-cake*, light cake of ~like consistence; ~ *cloth*, soft loosely woven fabric with wrinkled surface; ~ *cucumber*, *-gourd*, *vegetable* ~, kind of gourd used in Turkish baths as rubber or towel, loofah; ~ *tent*, compressed ~ for keeping wound etc. open; ~*-tree*, spiny tropical leguminous shrub with globose heads of fragrant yellow flowers. [OE *sponge*, *spunge*, f. L f. Gk *spoggia* later var. of *spoggos*]

sponge[2] (-ŭnj), v.t. & i., & n. **1.** Wipe, cleanse, with sponge; sluice water over (parts of body etc., or abs., often *down*, *over*) with sponge; wipe out, efface, (writing, fig. memory of thing etc., usu. *out*) with sponge; absorb, take *up*, (water etc.) with sponge; gather sponges; procure by sycophantic arts; ~ *on*, live as the parasite of, be meanly dependent on (person *for* thing). **2.** n. Sponging, bath with sponge, as *had a* ~ *down*. Hence **spo'ngER**[1](1, 2) (-ŭnj-) n. [ME, f. prec., or OF *esponger* f. LL *spongiare* (as prec.)]

spo'nging (-ŭnj-), n. In vbl senses; ~-*house* (hist., in arch. sense *squeezing*), bailiff's house for temporary lodging of arrested debtor. [-ING[1]]

spongiopi'line (spŭnj-), n. Substitute for poultice made of sponge & fibre backed with rubber. [as SPONGE[1] + Gk *pilos* felt + -INE[4]]

spo'ngy (-ŭnj), a. Like sponge; porous, compressible, elastic, absorbent, as sponge; (of metal) finely divided & loosely coherent. Hence ~**iNESS** n. [-Y[2]]

spon'sion (-shn), n. Being surety for another; (internat. law) engagement made on behalf of State by agent not specially authorized. [f. L *sponsio* (*spondēre spons-* promise, see -ION)]

spon'son, n. Projection from side of warship to enable gun to be trained forward & aft; triangular platform before & abaft paddle-box. [orig. unkn.]

spon'sor, n., & v.t. **1.** Godfather or godmother; person who makes himself responsible for another; advertiser who pays for a broadcast or televised programme into which advertisements of his wares are introduced. **2.** v.t. Be ~ for. Hence **sponsŏr'IAL** a., ~**SHIP** n. [L (*spondēre spons-* promise, see -OR)]

spontän'eous, a. **1.** Acting, done, occurring, without external cause; voluntary, without external incitement, as *made a* ~ *offer of his services*; (of sudden movements etc.) involuntary, not due to conscious volition; growing naturally without cultivation; (biol., of structural changes in plants, muscular activity in esp. young animals) instinctive, automatic, prompted by no motive; (of bodily movements, literary style, etc.) gracefully natural & unconstrained. **2.** ~ *combustion*, ignition of mineral or vegetable substance (e.g. heap of rags soaked with oil, mass of wet coal) from heat engendered by rapid oxidation; ~ *generation*, production of living from non-living matter as inferred from appearance of life (due in fact to bacteria etc.) in some infusions; ~ *suggestion* (from association of ideas without conscious volition). Hence or cogn. **spŏntanē'ITY**, ~**NESS**, nn., ~**LY**[2]

adv. [f. LL *spontaneus* (*sponte* of one's own accord, see -ANEOUS)]

spŏntoon', n. (hist.). Kind of halberd used by some British infantry officers. [f. F *sponton* f. It. *spontone* f. *puntone*, *punto*, point]

spoof, v.t.t., & n. (sl.). Swindle, humbug, hoax; (attrib.) faked or fabricated. Hence ~'ER[1] n. [invented by Arthur Roberts (d. 1933), comedian]

spook, n. (joc.). Ghost. Hence ~'ISH[1], ~'Y[2], aa. [f. Du. *spook*, G *spuk*]

spool, n., & v.t. Reel for winding yarn, photographic film, etc., on; revolving shaft of angler's reel. **2.** v.t. Wind on ~. [ME, f. ONF *espole* or its source, MDu. *spole*, *spoele*, (M)LG *spōle*]

spoon[1], n., & v.t. & i. **1.** Utensil consisting of round or usu. oval bowl & a handle for conveying esp. liquid food to mouth, usu. of silver or plated metal for table use (*tea*, *dessert*, *table*, ~, of small, medium, large, size, esp. as recognized measure for medicine; APOSTLE ~, EGG[1], *salt*, *mustard*, ~; *marrow*~, for getting marrow from bones) & of wood or iron for cooking etc.; BORN *with silver* ~ *in mouth*; *long* ~ *& the devil* (see SUP); *wooden* ~, (wooden ~ given to) last man in Cambridge mathematical tripos (hist.), (fig.) booby prize; EGG[1]-*&-*~ *race*; ~-shaped thing, esp. (oar with) broad curved blade, wooden golf-club with more loft than driver & brassie. **2.** ~ (-*bait*), bright revolving ~-shaped piece of metal used as lure in fishing; ~*beak*, -*bill*, kinds of bird; ~-*drift*, see SPINDRIFT; ~-*fed*, (fig., of industries etc.) artificially encouraged by bounties or import duties, (of pupil) crammed with information; ~-*meat*, liquid food, food for infants (also fig.); ~-*net*, angler's landing-net. **3.** vb. Take (liquid etc., usu. *up*, *out*) with ~; fish with ~-bait; (croquet) make pushing stroke; (crick.) strike (ball) feebly, send *up* (ball, a catch) thus, with bat. Hence (-)~'FUL n. [OE *spōn* chip of wood, = (M)LG *spān*, ON *spónn*; cf. OHG *spān*, ON *spánn*]

spoon[2], n., & v.i. & t. (sl.). **1.** Simpleton; silly or demonstratively fond lover; *be* ~*s on*, be sillily in love with. **2.** vb. Behave amorously, behave thus towards (girl etc.). [f. prec.]

spoon'er(ism), n. Accidental transposition of initial letters etc. of two or more words (e.g. *has just received a blushing crow*, for *real enjoyment give me a well-boiled icycle*). [f. Rev. W. A. *Spooner* (d. 1930), esteemed for ~s, + -ISM]

spoon'|y, a. & n. (sl.). **1.** Soft, silly; sentimental, amorous, sweet (*up*)*on*. **2.** n. Mild simpleton. Hence ~**iLY**[2] adv., ~**iNESS** n. [prob. f. SPOON[2], -Y[2]]

spoor, n., & v.t. & i. **1.** Track, scent, of animal. **2.** vb. Follow by ~. Hence ~'ER[1] n. [Du. (S.A.) *spoor*, = G *spur*]

sporăd'ic, a. Occurring only here & there,

separate, scattered. Hence ~AL a. (rare), ~ALLY² adv., ~alNESS n. [f. med. L f. Gk *sporadikos* (*sporas* -*ados* scattered, cf. *speirō* sow, see -IC)]

sporän'gium, n. (bot.). Case in which spores are produced. [f. Gk *spora* SPORE + *aggeion* vessel]

spore, n. (Bot., in cryptogamous plants) single cell that becomes free & capable of individual development; (biol.) minute organic body that develops into new individual; (fig.) seed, germ, of anything. [f. Gk *spora* sowing, seed, f. *speirō* sow]

spor|o-, comb. form of Gk *spora* SPORE, as: ~*ogen'esis*, spore-formation; ~*ŏ́genous*, producing spores.

spŏ'rran, n. Pouch, usu. covered with fur etc., worn by Highlander in front of kilt. [f. Gael. *sporan*]

spŏrt, n., & v.i. & t. **1.** Amusement, diversion, fun; *in* ~, jestingly; *make* ~ *of*, turn into ridicule, make fun of; *be the* ~ (plaything, butt) *of Fortune* etc.; pastime, game; outdoor pastime, e.g. hunting, fishing, racing; *have good* ~, esp. make good bag or basket when shooting etc.; *athletic* ~s, running, jumping, putting weight, etc., meeting of athletes to compete in these, as *school*~s, *inter-university* ~s (~s *coat, jacket*, giving freedom of movement; ~s *field*; ~s *car*, for racing); animal, plant, deviating suddenly or strikingly from normal type; (sl.) good fellow, ~sman; ~s'*man*, ~s'*woman*, person fond of ~s esp. hunting, shooting, or fishing, (fig.) person who regards life as a game in which opponents must be allowed fair play, person ready to play a bold game, whence ~s'*manship* n.; ~s'*manlike*, befitting, worthy of, a ~sman. **2. vb.** Divert oneself, take part in pastime; (part.) interested in ~, as a ~*ing man*, ~smanlike, as ~*ing conduct*, ~*ing offer*, whence ~'*ingly²* adv.; (bot., zool.) become or produce a ~; wear, exhibit, produce, esp. ostentatiously, as ~*ed a gold tie-pin*; || ~ *one's* OAK. [ME; aphetic f. DISPORT]

spŏrt'ive, a. Playful. Hence ~LY² adv., ~NESS n. [-IVE]

spŏ'rŭl|e, n. Spore; small spore. Hence ~AR¹ a. [F, or f. mod. L *sporula* (SPORE, -ULE)]

spŏt¹, n. **1.** Particular place, definite locality, as *dropped it on this precise* ~, *the* ~ *where William III landed*; *a tender* ~, (fig.) subject on which one is touchy. **2.** Small part of the surface of a thing distinguished by colour, texture, etc., usu. round or less elongated than a streak or stripe, small mark or stain, pimple, as *a blue tie with pink* ~s, SUN~, *can the* LEOPARD *change his* ~s?; (fig.) moral blemish, stain, as *without a* ~ *on his reputation.* **3.** Kinds of fish & domestic pigeon. **4.** (sl.). Act of spotting winner etc.; horse etc. so spotted. **5.** (colloq.).

Small quantity of anything (*a* ~ *of leave, lunch*); a drink. **6.** (billiards). Small round black patch near each end of table equidistant from sides; || ~-*stroke*, pocketing red ball when placed on ~ remote from balk; || ~-*barred game* (in which successive ~-strokes are not allowed); ~ (-*ball*), white ball distinguished from the other by black ~. **7.** *On the* ~, without delay or change of place, then & there, (of person) wide awake, equal to the situation, in good form at game etc.; **put on the* ~ (sl.), decide on the assassination of, murder. **8.** (commerc.). ~ *cash, cotton, wheat, prices* to be paid or delivered immediately on sale); ~s, commodities sold for ~ cash. **9.** ~'*light* (theatr.), beam of light thrown on a particular actor, or the projector used for this purpose (also fig., as LIMELIGHT). Hence ~'LESS, ~t'Y², aa., ~'lèsslY³ adv., ~'lèssNESS, ~t'iNESS, nn. [ME = MDu. *spotte, spot*, ON *spotti*]

spŏt², v.t. & i. (-tt-). **1.** Mark, stain, soil, with spots (lit., & fig. of character etc.); (of material etc.) be (liable to be) marked with spots. **2.** (colloq.). Single out beforehand (winner of race etc., horse etc. as winner *for* event); detect, recognize nationality etc. of, as ~*ted him at once as an American, can always* ~ *a dun.* **3.** (mil.). Locate (enemy's position), esp. from the air; whence ~t'ER¹ n., airman detailed for such work, also person trained in aircraft recognition. **4.** (p.p.). Marked with spots, esp. in names of animals; ||~*ted dog* (sl.), =PLUM *duff*; ~*ted fever*, cerebro-spinal meningitis. Hence ~t'ĕdNESS n. [ME, f. prec.]

spouse (-z), n. Husband or wife. [ME & OF *sp(o)us*, *sp(o)use*, varr. of OF *espus* masc., -*se* fem., f. L p.p. of *spondēre*, see ESPOUSE]

spout, v.t. & i., & n. **1.** Discharge, issue, forcibly in a jet, as *blood* ~s *from wound, wounds* ~ *blood, whale* ~s *water*; utter (verses etc., or abs.) in declamatory manner, speechify; (sl.) pawn. **2.** n. Projecting tube through which liquid etc. is poured from teapot, kettle, gutter of roof, etc.; sloping trough down which thing may be shot into receptacle, esp. shoot in pawnbroker's shop, as *his watch is up the* ~ (in pawn); jet, column, of liquid or grain etc.; WATER¹-~; (also ~-*hole*) spiracle of whale. Hence ~'ER¹ n., ~'LESS a. [ME, of doubtful orig.; cf. Du. *spuit*, MDu. *spouten*; stem *spūt*- also in ON *spyta* SPIT²]

sprăg, n. Billet of wood or similar device for checking wheel of car etc. [orig. unkn.]

sprain, v.t., & n. **1.** Wrench (ankle, wrist, etc.) violently so as to cause pain & swelling but not dislocation. **2.** n. Such wrench, resulting inflahmation & swelling. [17th c., of unkn. orig.]

|| spraints, n. pl. Otter's dung. [ME, f.

OF *espraintes* f. *espraindre* squeeze out f. L EX(*primere* = *premere* press)]

sprang. See SPRING[1].

sprat, n., & v.i. (-tt-). **1.** Small European herring-like fish much used as food; other kinds of fish, e.g. sand-eel, young herring; *throw a ~ to catch a herring* or *mackerel* or *whale*, risk a little to gain much; (joc.) thin child; ‖ *~day*, Nov. 9, on which ~ season begins in England. **2.** v.i. Fish for ~s, whence ~t'ER[1], ~t'ING[1], nn. [later form of OE *sprot*, = MDu., MLG *sprot*)

sprawl, v.i. & t., & n. **1.** Spread oneself, spread (one's limbs), out in careless or ungainly way; (of writing, plant, etc.) be of irregular or straggling form; open out (troops) irregularly. **2.** n. ~ing movement or attitude. [OE *spreawlian*, = NFris. *spraweli*]

spray[1], n. Branch of tree with branchlets or flowers, esp. slender or graceful one, sprig of flowers or leaves; ornaments in similar form, as *a ~ of diamonds* etc.; *~-drain*, drain in field etc. made by filling trench with branches. Hence ~'ey[1] a. [cf. CLAYEY]. [ME, of unkn. orig.]

spray[2], n., & v.t. **1.** Water or other liquid flying in small drops from force of wind, dashing of waves, or action of atomizer etc.; medical or other liquid preparation to be applied in this form with atomizer etc. **2.** v.t. Throw (liquid, or abs.) in form of ~, sprinkle (object) thus, esp. fruit-trees etc. with insecticides. **3.** *~'board* (on boat's gunwale to keep off ~). Hence ~ER[1](1, 2) n., ~'ey[2] a. [n. (17th c.) app. rel. to MDu. *sprayen*, = MHG *spræjen*, to sprinkle]

spread[1] (-ĕd), v.t. & i. (*spread*). **1.** Extend the surface of, cause to cover larger surface, by unrolling, unfolding, smearing, flattening out, etc., (fig.) display thus to eye or mind, as *peacock ~s its tail, ~ oneself* (sl., = talk bumptiously), *~ a banner, ~ out a rug on the grass, ~ butter on bread, map lay ~ out on the table, the view ~ out before us,* whence ~ER[1](2) n. **2.** Show extended or extensive surface, as *river here ~s out to a width of half a mile, on every side ~ a vast desert, ~ing yews*. **3.** Diffuse, be diffused, as *his name ~ fear in every quarter, rumour ~ from mouth to mouth, has ~ a malicious report.* **4.** Cover surface of, as *slices of bread ~ with jam, a table ~ with every luxury, meadow ~ with daisies*: **5.** ~ *eagle,* figure of eagle with legs & wings extended as seen on coins etc., skating movement on both inside edges at once one forward & the other back, (colloq.) fowl split open down the back & broiled, (naut.) person lashed in rigging with arms and legs ~ out as punishment, (v.t., *~-eagle*) lash (man) thus, ~ out, outrun, (adj., *~-eagle*) bombastic, esp. noisily patriotic, whence *~-ea'gleism* n. **6.** *~-over*(*system*), elasticity in accommodating restricted work-hours

to special needs. [OE *sprædan*, MDu., MLG *sprēden*. OHG *spreitan*; ult. orig. unkn.]

spread[2] (-ĕd), n. Spreading; capability of expanding, as *inferior to the eagle in ~ of wings*; increased bodily girth, as *middle-age(d) ~*; breadth, compass, as *arches of equal ~*; diffusion (of education etc.); (colloq.) feast, meal, as *had no end of a ~*; *(commerc.) difference between cost of manufacture & selling price. [f. prec.]

spree, n., & v.i. Lively frolic, bout of drinking etc., as *is on the* (having a) ~; *buying ~*, bout of lavish spending; (v.i.) have a ~. [19th-c. sl., orig. unkn.]

‖ **sprent,** a. (arch.). Sprinkled, over-spread, (*with* drops, particles, etc.). [p.p. of obs. *sprenge* f. OE *sprengan* make SPRING[1]]

sprig, n., & v.t. (-gg-). **1.** Small branch, shoot; ornament of ~ form; small tapering headless tack; (usu. derog.) youth, young man, as *who is this ~?, a ~ of (the) nobility*. **2.** v.t. Ornament with ~s, as *~ged muslin*. **3.** *~'tail*, kinds of duck & grouse with pointed tail. Hence ~g'y[2] (-g-) a. [sense *nail* f. 14th, *shoot* f. 15th, c.; two unrelated wds of unkn. orig.]

spright'l‖ȳ (-it-), a. Vivacious, lively, gay. Hence ~iNESS n. [f. *spright*, var. of SPRITE + -LY[1]]

spring[1], v.i. & t. (*sprang, sprung*). **1.** Leap, jump, move rapidly or suddenly, (often *up, down, out, over, through, away, back,* etc.), as *sprang (up) from his seat, sprang through the gap, at his throat, to their assistance, blood sprang to her cheeks*. **2.** Move rapidly as from constrained position or by action of a spring, as *branch sprang back, door sprang to.* **3.** Come into being (usu. ~ *up*), arise (often *from* source), appear, as *a breeze sprang up, the piers from which the arches ~, is sprung from* or *of a royal stock, the buds are ~ing, the belief has sprung up, his actions ~ from a false conviction*; (to person arriving suddenly or unexpectedly or whose presence is only now realized) *where do* or *did you ~ from?* **4.** (Of wood) warp; (t. & i. of wood) split, crack, as *bat is* or *has sprung, have sprung my racket*. **5.** p.p. (colloq.). Tipsy. **6.** Rouse (game) from earth or covert. **7.** Cause to act suddenly by means of a spring, produce or develop suddenly or unexpectedly, as *~ a trap, has sprung a new theory, loves to ~ surprises on us.* **8.** Provide (motor vehicle etc.) with springs (usu. as p.p.). **9.** Cause (mine) to burst. **10.** (naut.). (Of ship) *~ a butt*, loosen end of plank by labouring in heavy sea, *~ a leak,* develop leak from starting of timbers, ‖ *~ the* or *her luff,* yield to helm & sail nearer to wind. [OE, OS, OHG *springan*, ON *springa*]

spring[2], n. **1.** Leap, as *took a ~, rose with a ~*. **2.** Season in which vegetation begins, the first season of the year.

(astron., from vernal equinox to summer solstice). **3.** Place where water or oil wells up from earth, basin so formed, as *hot*, *mineral*, ~*s*. **4.** Backward movement from constrained position, recoil, e.g. of bow. **5.** Elasticity, as *his muscles have no* ~ *in them*. **6.** Elastic contrivance usu. of bent or coiled metal used esp. as motive power in clockwork etc. or for preventing jar as in vehicle, as *bow* ~ (bow-shaped), CEE ~, *air* or *pneumatic* ~ (working by compression of air), HAIR-~, MAIN²-~, **7.** (fig.). Motive actuating person etc., source, origin, as *the* ~*s of human action*, *the custom had its* ~ *in another country*. **8.** Upward curve of beam etc. from horizontal line. **9.** Starting of plank. **10.** Springing of leak. **11.** Mooring-rope. **12.** pl. Period of ~ tide. **13.** ~ *balance* (measuring weight by tension of ~); ~*-beam*, beam stretching across wide space without intermediate support, elastic bar used as ~ in tilt-hammer etc.; ~ *bed*, *mattress*, mattress formed of spiral ~s in wooden frame; ~*-board*, elastic board giving impetus in leaping, diving, etc.; ~*-carriage*, *-cart* (mounted on ~s); ~*-clean* v.t., clean (house, room) thoroughly, esp. in ~; ~*-cleaning* n.; ~ *gun* (contrived to go off when trespasser or animal stumbles on it); ~*-halt*, convulsive movement of horse's hind leg in walking; ~ *tide*, high tide occurring shortly after new & full moon in each month; ~*'tide* (poet.), ~*'time*, season of ~; ~ *water* (from ~, opp. to river or rain water). Hence ~*'LESS*, ~*'LIKE*, aa., ~*'LET* n. [OE, f. prec.]

‖ **spring'al(d)**, n. (arch.). Youngster. [15th c., perh. f. SPRING¹]

spring'bok, n. S.-Afr. gazelle with habit of springing in play or when alarmed; *S*~*s*, (nickname for) S. Africans, S.-African football team etc. [Afrikaans]

springe (-j), n. Noose, snare, for small game. [ME, app. repr. OE *sprencg*, rel. to obs. *sprenge* factitive f. SPRING¹]

spring'er, n. In vbl senses; also or esp.: (archit.) part of arch where curve begins, lowest stone of this part, bottom stone of coping of gable, rib of groined roof or vault; kind of field spaniel used for spring game; grampus; springbok. [-ER¹]

spring'|ly̆, a. (Of movement or substance) elastic. Hence ~*INESS* n. [-Y²]

sprinkle (spring'kl), v.t. & i., & n. **1.** Scatter (liquid, ashes, crumbs, etc.) in small drops or particles, whence **sprink'**-lER¹(2) n.; subject (ground, object) to sprinkling (*with* liquid etc.); (of liquid etc.) fall thus on. **2.** Light shower (*of* rain etc.), so **sprink'**lING¹(2) n. (esp., fig., *a* few here & there *of*). [ME also *sprenkle*, rel. to Du. *sprenkelen*, LG *sprinkeln*, MDu. *sprenkel*, *sprinkel*]

sprint, v.i. & t., & n. **1.** Run short distance, run (specified distance), at full speed. **2.** n. Such run. Hence ~*'ER¹* n. [f. early Scand. *sprinta*, cf. ON *spretta*]

sprit, n. Small spar reaching diagonally from mast to upper outer corner of sail: ~*'sail* (-sāl, -sl), sail extended by ~, (formerly) sail extended by yard set under bowsprit. [OE *sprēot* pole, MDu., MLG *spriet*, *spret*, cogn. w. SPROUT]

sprite, n. Elf, fairy, goblin. [ME, f. OF *esprit*, or similarly reduced f. OF *esperit(e)*, AF *spirit(e)* SPIRIT]

spröck'ĕt, n. Each of several teeth on wheel engaging with links of chain; ~*-wheel*, such wheel, e.g. for engaging bicycle chain. [16th c., of unkn. orig.]

sprout, v.i. & t., & n. **1.** Begin to grow, shoot forth, put forth shoots; spring up, grow to a height; produce by ~ing; as *has* ~*ed horns*, *a moustache*. **2.** n. Shoot of plant; BRUSSELS ~*s*. [OE **sprūtan*, MDu., MLG *spruten*, MHG *spriezen*; rel. to OE *spryttan*]

spruce¹ (-ōōs), a., & v.t. **1.** Neat in dress & appearance, trim, smart. **2.** v.t. Smarten (one*self* etc., usu. *up*). Hence ~*'LY²* adv., ~*'NESS* n. [perh. f. foll., in the collocation *spruce* (leather) *jerkin*]

spruce² (-ōōs), n. Coniferous tree related to pine; (also ~ *fir*) kinds of fir; ~*-beer* (made from leaves and small branches of ~, useful as antiscorbutic). [alt. f. AF (ME, now obs.) *Pruce* Prussia; cf. med. L *Sprucia*]

sprue¹ (-ōō), n. Passage through which metal is poured into mould; metal filling ~. [19th c., of unkn. orig.]

sprue² (-ōō), n. Tropical disease (also *psilosis*) with ulcerated mucous membrane of mouth & chronic enteritis. [f. Du. *spruw* THRUSH² (*Indische spruw* = psilosis)]

spruit (-rāt), n. (S. Africa). A small watercourse, usu. almost dry except in the wet season. [Du. *spruit* cogn. w. SPROUT]

sprung. See SPRING¹.

sprȳ, a. (~*er*, ~*est*). Active, lively. [18th c., dial. & U.S., of unkn. orig.]

spŭd, n., & v.t. (-dd-). **1.** Kinds of small spade for cutting roots of weeds etc.; short thick thing, whence ~*d'Y²* a.; (sl.) potato. **2.** v.t. Remove (weeds, often *up*, *out*) with ~. [ME; orig. unkn.]

‖ **spŭd'dle**, v.i. (dial.). Dig lightly, dig about, (of amateur gardeners etc.). [orig. alt. of *puddle*; now assoc. w. prec.]

spue. See SPEW.

spūm|e, n., & v.i. Froth, foam. Hence ~*ěs'CENCE*, ~*'iNESS*, nn., ~*ES'CENT*, ~*'OUS*, ~*'Y²*, aa. [ME, f. OF (*e*)*spume* or L *spuma*]

spun. See SPIN¹.

spunge. (Arch. for) SPONGE.

spŭnk, n. (colloq.). Courage, mettle, spirit; anger. Hence ~*'Y²* a. [16th c. 'spark, tinder', prob. rel. to obs. *funk* & PUNK²]

spŭr, n., & v.t. & i. (-rr-). **1.** Pricking instrument with point or (also *rowel*-~) rowel worn on horseman's heel (*put or* *set* ~*s to*, = ~ vb; *need the*~, be sluggish, also of persons); *win* one's ~*s*, (hist.) gain knighthood, (fig.) gain distinction, make a name; (fig.) stimulus, incentive; *on the* ~ *of the moment*, impromptu, on a momentary impulse; ~-shaped thing, e.g. hard projection on cock's leg, steel point fastened to this in cockfight, projection from mountain (range), climbing--iron, wall crossing part of rampart and joining it to interior work, slender hollow projection from some part of flower. 2. ‖ ~ *royal*, coin of James I bearing ~like sun with rays; ~-*wheel*, cog-wheel with radial teeth; ~'*wort*, plant with whorls of leaves like rowel of ~. 3. vb. Prick (horse) with ~s (~ *a willing horse*, fig., be needlessly importunate), incite (person *on to* effort, *to* do, etc.), furnish (person, boots, gamecock, esp. in p.p.) with ~s; (intr.) ride hard (*on, forward*, etc.). Hence ~'LESS a. [OE *spora, spura*, OS *spora*, OHG *sporo*, ON *spori*; cf. SPURN]

spurge, n. Kinds of plant with acrid milky juice. [ME, f. OF *espurge* (*espurgier* purge, as EXPURGATE)]

spur'ious, a. Not genuine, not being what it pretends to be, not proceeding from the pretended source, as ~ *coin*, (*reading in*) *MS.*, *affection*; (zool.) resembling an organ etc. but not having its function, having the function of organ etc. but morphologically different, as ~ *eyes, legs*. Hence ~LY[2] adv., ~NESS n. [f. L *spurius* + -OUS]

‖ **spurl'ing-line**, n. (naut.). Line from steering-wheel to telltale in cabin for showing position of helm. [orig. unkn.]

spurn, v.t. & i., & n. 1. Repel, thrust back, with foot; (also arch. ~ *at*) reject with disdain, treat with contempt, (offer, advances, person, etc.). 2. n. ~ing, contemptuous rejection. [OE *spurnan, spornan*, prob. f. stem of SPUR]

spur'rier (*or* spū[4]), n. Spur-maker. [-IER]

spu'rry, -rey, n. Kinds of herb of pink family, esp. *corn*-~, a weed in cornfield etc. [f. Du. *spurrie*, prob. rel. to med. L *spergula*]

spurt[1], v.i., & n. (Make) short sudden violent effort esp. in racing. [var. of SPIRT in same sense]

spurt[2]. See SPIRT.

sput'nik (-ŏŏt-), n. Russian earth SATELLITE. [Russ., = travelling companion]

sputt'er, v.t. & i., & n. 1. Emit with spitting sound; speak, utter, (words, threats, a language, etc.) rapidly or incoherently; speak in hurried or vehement fashion (often *at* person etc.). 2. n. Such speech. Hence ~ER[1] n., ~ingLY[2] adv. [16th c., = Du. *sputteren*, imit.]

sput'um, n. (pl. -*ta*). Saliva, spittle; expectorated matter esp. as diagnostic of disease. [L, neut. p.p. of *spuere* spit]

spy, n., & v.t. & i. 1. Person who goes, esp. in disguise, into enemy's camp or territory to inspect works, watch movements, etc., & report the result; person who keeps (esp. secret) watch on movements of others, as *refuse to be a* ~ *on his conduct*. 2. v.t. Discern, make out, esp. by careful observation, as *spied a horseman approaching, is quick at* ~*ing his neighbours' faults, I* ~ STRANGERS; ~ *out*, explore secretly, discover by this means; (v.i.) play the ~, keep close & secret watch (*upon* person, movements, etc., *into* secret etc.); ~'*glass*, small telescope; ~'*hole*, peep-hole. [ME *spie* n., *spien* vb, f. OF *espie* n., *espier* vb ESPY]

squab (-ŏb), a., adv., & n. 1. Short & fat, squat, whence ~b'Y[2] (-ŏ-) a. 2. adv. With heavy fall, as *come down* ~ *on the floor*. 3. n. Short fat person; young esp. unfledged pigeon; stuffed cushion; ottoman; ~-*chick*, unfledged bird; ~ *pie*, pigeon-pie, pie of mutton, onions, & apples. [17th c., of unkn. orig.; cf. obs. *quab* shapeless thing, Sw. dial. *squabba*, Norw. dial. *skvabb* in similar senses]

squa'bbl|e (-ŏ-), v.i. & t., & n. 1. Engage in petty or noisy quarrel (*with* person *about* thing); (print.) disarrange (composed type). 2. n. Petty or noisy quarrel. Hence ~ER[1] n. [prob. imit., cf. Sw. dial. *skvabbel* n. dispute]

squacc'o, n. (pl. ~*s*). Small crested heron of S. Europe, Africa, & Asia. [f. It. *sguacco*]

squad (-ŏd), n. (Mil.) small number of men assembled for drill etc. (~ *drill*, elementary); *awkward* ~ (of recruits not yet competent to take place in regimental line, also fig.); small party of persons; FLYING ~. [f. F *escouade* var. of *esquadre* f. It. *squadra* SQUARE]

squa'dron (-ŏd-), n., & v.t. 1. Principal division of cavalry regiment or mechanized formation, consisting of two troops. 2. Any orderly body of persons. 3. Detachment of warships employed on particular service, as *flying* ~ (equipped for rapid cruising). 4. Unit of Royal Air Force (10 to 18 machines); ~-*leader* (see AIR[1] *Force*). 5. v.t. Form (men) into ~s. [f. It. *squadrone* (prec.), -OON)]

‖ **squail**, n. (Pl.) game with small wooden discs (~*s*) on round table or board (~--*board*). [orig. unkn.]

‖ **squail'er**, n. Stick with leaded knob for striking or throwing at squirrels etc. [f. dial. *squail* strike with ~ + -ER[1]]

squa'lid (-ŏl-), a. Dirty, mean, poor, in appearance. Hence or cogn. ~ITY (-ĭd[4]), ~NESS, squa'lor[1], nn., ~LY[2] adv., (-ŏl-). [f. L *squalidus* (*squalēre* be stiff or dirty, -ID[1])]

squall (-awl), v.i. & t., & n. 1. Cry out, scream, violently as in fear or pain; utter in screaming or discordant voice. Hence ~'ER[1] n. 2. n. Sudden & violent gust or successive gusts of wind, esp. with rain or snow or sleet (*arched* ~, ~ occurring near equator with sudden collection of black clouds in form of arch & usu. violent thunderstorm; *black ~*, with dark cloud; *white ~*, arising in fair weather without formation of clouds), whence ~'Y² (-aw-) a.; *look out for ~s*, (fig.) be on one's guard against danger or trouble; [f. the vb] discordant cry, scream. [imit.]

squal'oid, a. Like a shark. [f. L *squalus*, kind of sea-fish, (mod. L) genus of sharks. +-OID]

squam'|a, n. (bot., zool.; pl. *~ae*). Scale, scalelike feather or part of bone. Hence or cogn. ~I·, ~O·, comb. forms, ~OSE¹, ~OUS, aa., ~ULE n. [L]

squa'nder (-ŏn-), v.t. Spend (money, time, etc.) wastefully; dissipate (fortune etc.) thus. Hence ~ER¹ n., ~ingLY² adv., ~MAN'IA n. (craze for extravagant expenditure). [16th c., of unkn. orig.]

square, n., a., adv., & v.t. & i. **1.** Equilateral rectangle; object (approximately) of this shape; (usu. quadrilateral) area planted with trees etc. or ornamentally laid out & surrounded with buildings esp. dwelling-houses, as *Trafalgar S~, Russell S~, lives in the next ~*; block of buildings bounded by four streets; L-shaped or (*T·~*) T-shaped instrument for obtaining or testing right angles; *out of ~*, not at right angles; standard, pattern, (usu. fig., & arch. exc. *on the ~*, fairly, honestly, as *can be trusted to act on the ~, by the ~*, exactly); product of a number multiplied by itself, as *the ~ of 9 is 81, of x² is x⁴, 9 is a perfect ~* (has rational root); body of infantry drawn up in rectangular form, *hollow ~* (hist.), so drawn up with space in middle; (also *word-~*) set of words (to be guessed from description &) arranged in a ~ so as to read alike across & downwards (e.g. *cab ace bed*); (sl.) old-fashioned person; MAGIC ~; 100 ~ ft as measure of flooring etc. **2.** adj. Of ~ shape; ~ *foot, inch*, etc., (area equal to that of) ~ whose side is a foot, inch, etc.; ~ *measure* (expressed in ~ feet etc.); *a table 4 ft ~ has an area of 16 ~ ft*; rectangular, as *table with ~ corners*; at right angles *to*; ~ *number*, of an integer, e.g. 1, 4, 9, 16, etc.; ~ *root* of a given number, number of which it is the ~, as *the ~ root of 9 is 3, of x⁶ is x³, of 2 is irrational*; ~ *dance, game* (in which four couples, players, face inwards from four sides); having the breadth more nearly equal to the length or height than is usual, as *a man of ~ frame*; angular, not round, as ~ *peg in round* HOLE¹, *has a ~ jaw*; properly arranged, in good order, as *must tidy up & get things ~*; thorough, uncompromising, as *was met with a ~ refusal, made a ~ meal*; fair, honest, as *his play is not always quite ~*, *a ~ deal*, fair bargain, fair treatment; (sl.) old-fashioned; *be on the ~*, be a freemason; on a proper footing, even, quits, as *am now ~ with all the world, get ~ with* (pay, compound with) *our creditors*; (golf) *they were ~ or all ~* (had won the same

number of holes) *at the turn*. **3.** ~ *built*, of comparatively broad shape; ||~'*face* (sl.), gin; *~'head*, Scandinavian in U.S. or Canada; ~ *leg* (crick.), fielder at some distance on batsman's leg-side & nearly opposite wicket, his place, as *was put at ~ leg*; ~ *rigged*, with principal sails at right angles to length of ship & extended by horizontal yards slung to mast by the middle, opp. to *fore-&-aft rigged*; ~ *sail*, four-cornered sail extended on yard slung to mast by middle; ~ *shouldered*, with broad & not sloping shoulders, esp. opp. to *round-shouldered*; ~ *toed*, (having boots) with ~ toes, (fig.) formal, prim; ~ *toes*, ~ *toed* person. Hence ~'LY² (-rl-) adv., ~'NESS (-rn-) n., squar'ISH¹ a. **4.** adv. ~ly, as *sat ~ on his seat, hit him ~ on the jaw, do you think he plays ~* (fair)?, FAIR² & ~. **5.** vb. Make ~; make rectangular, give rectangular edges to (timber); multiply (number) by itself, as *3 ~d is 9, x ~d is written x²*; adjust, make or be suitable *to* or consistent *with*, reconcile, as *decline to ~ my conduct to* or *with his interests, his practice does not ~* or *he does not ~ his practice with his principles*; settle, pay, (bill etc.), esp. ~ *accounts with* (fig. have revenge on), (abs. in some senses) ~ *up*; (colloq.) pay, esp. bribe, as *can you ~ the porter?, has been ~d to hold his tongue*; secure acquiescence etc. of (person) thus; assume attitude of boxer, move *up to* (person) thus; ~ *up to difficulties* or *problems*, face and tackle them resolutely; ~ *the circle*, construct ~ equal in area to given circle, express area of circle exactly in ~ measure, (fig.) perform demonstrable impossibility; (golf) make the score of (a match) equal, make the scores equal; (naut.) lay (yards) at right angles with keel making them at same time horizontal, get (dead-eyes) horizontal, get (ratlines) horizontal & parallel to one another; *~ away*, tidy up (orig. naut.). [ME, f. OF *esquarre* etc., n., *esquarrer* vb; *esquarre* p.p. adj.; f. pop. L *EX(quadra* n., *-are* vb, square; cf. QUADRI·)]

squa'rrose, -ous, (-ŏr-), aa. (bot., zool.). Rough with scalelike processes. [f. L *squarrosus* scurfy, scabby]

||**squars'on**, n. (joc.). Squire & parson in one. [portmanteau wd]

squash¹ (-ŏ-), v.t. & i., & n. **1.** Crush, squeeze flat or into pulp; pack tight, crowd; (fig.) silence (person) with crushing retort; squeeze one's way (*into* etc.). **2.** n. ~ed thing or mass, whence ~'INESS n., ~'Y² a.; crowd, crowded assembly; (sound of) fall of soft body; (also ~ *rackets*) game played with rackets & soft ball in fives-court; LEMON¹ ~; ~ *hat* (of soft felt etc.). [f. OF *esquasser* f. pop. L *EX(quassare* see QUASH)]

squash² (-ŏ-), n. Kinds of gourd. [f. Amer.-Ind. *askutasquash*]

squat (-ŏt), v.i. & t. (-tt-), a., & n. **1.** Sit

on ground etc. with knees drawn up & heels close to or touching hams, crouch with hams resting on backs of heels; put (one*self*, person) into this position; (of animals) crouch close to ground; (colloq.) sit (*down*, *on*, etc.). 2. adj. In ~ting posture; (of person etc.) short & thick, dumpy. 3. n. ~ting posture; *hot ~ (sl.), electric chair; ~ person. [ME; (adj. & n. f. vb) f. OF *esquatir* flatten (es- EX- +*quatir* f. L coactus, see COGENT)]

squa´tter (-ŏt-), n. In vbl senses; also: (Austral.) person who gets right of pasturage from government on easy terms, also, any stock-owner; person who settles on new esp. public land without title; person who takes unauthorized possession of unoccupied premises. [f. prec. +-ER¹]

squaw, n. Amer.-Indian woman or wife; ~-*man*, white married to ~. [Amer.-Ind. *squaws, squa,* etc.]

squawk, v.i. & n. **1.** (Chiefly of birds) utter harsh cry of pain or fear. **2.** n. Such cry. [imit.]

squeak, v.i. & t., & n. **1.** Utter short shrill cry as of mouse or unoiled hinge; utter (words) shrilly; (sl.) turn informer, peach. **2.** n. Short shrill sound, whence ~´ILY² adv., ~´Y² a.; (*narrow*) ~, narrow escape, success barely attained; BUBBLE¹- -*and*-~. [ME; imit., cf. Sw. *sqväka* croak]

squeak´er, n. In vbl senses; also, young bird esp. pigeon. [-ER¹]

squeal, v.i. & t., & n. **1.** Utter shrill cry as of child from pain, fear, anger, joy, etc.; utter (words) thus; (sl.) protest excitedly e.g. against taxation; (sl.) turn informer; *make* one ~ (sl.), blackmail him. **2.** n. Shrill cry of child, pig, etc. [ME; imit.]

squeal´er, n. In vbl senses; also, young bird esp. pigeon. [-ER¹]

squeam´ish, a. Easily nauseated; fastidious, overnice, overscrupulous in questions of propriety, honesty, etc. Hence ~LY² adv., ~NESS n. [ME var. of (now dial.) *squeamous,* f. AF *escoymo(u)s,* of unkn. orig.]

squee´gee (or -ē´), **squil´gee,** nn., & vv.t. **1.** Rubber-edged implement for sweeping wet deck or road; small similar instrument or roller used in photography. **2.** v.t. Treat with ~. [*squeegee* perh. f. *squeeze,* strengthened form of SQUEEZE; *squil* unexpl. var.]

squeeze, v.t. & i., & n. **1.** Exert pressure upon (sponge, lemon, etc.) esp. in order to e x tract moisture, compress with hand or between two bodies, as ~ person's *hand* (as sign of sympathy, affection, etc.), ~*d orange* (fig.), person, thing, from whom or which no more is to be had, *was ~d to death in the crowd*; thrust (one*self*, person, thing, *into* vehicle, room, etc., *out of,* etc.) forcibly; make one's way by squeezing (*into* etc.); harass by exactions, extort money etc. from; constrain, bring pressure to bear on, as *could* ~ *the government to any extent*; get (money etc. *out of*

person etc.) by extortion, entreaty, etc.; produce with effort (*a tear* etc.); take impression of (coin etc.) esp. with sheets of damp paper or prepared wax. **2.** n. Application of pressure, as *gave him a* ~ (of the hand); crowd, crush, as *we all got in, but it was a* (*tight*) ~; a restriction; impression of coin etc., esp. as above; forced exaction by Asian official, illicit commission, percentage on goods purchased extorted by native servant. **3.** ~ *play,* (bridge) leading winning cards until opponent is forced to discard important card, (baseball) hitting ball short to infield to enable runner on third base to get home as soon as ball is pitched. Hence **squeez-** ABIL´ITY n., **squeez´**ABLE a. [c. 1600, perh. strengthened form of (15th c., now obs.) *quease,* of unkn. orig.; cf. obs. *squiss, squize*]

squeez´er, n. In vbl senses; also or esp.: machine for expressing air-bubbles etc. from puddled iron; (pl.) playing-cards with value shown at top right-hand corner so that they need not be opened out. [-ER¹]

squelch, v.t. & i., & n. (colloq.). **1.** Stamp on, crush flat, put an end to; disconcert, silence; make sucking sound as of hoof drawn out of thick mud. **2.** n. Act or sound of ~ing. [imit.]

squib, n., & v.t. & i. (-bb-). **1.** Firework thrown by hand & exploding like rocket or burning with hissing sound; tube of gunpowder used to fire a charge; short satirical composition, lampoon. **2.** vb. Write, attack with, lampoons. [16th c., of unkn. orig.; perh. imit.]

squid¹, n., & v.i. (-dd-). **1.** Kind of cuttle- -fish used as bait; kinds of artificial bait. **2.** v.i. Fish with ~. [17th c., of unkn. orig.]

squid², n. Anti-submarine mortar with several barrels firing depth-charges ahead of ship. [orig. unkn.]

|| **squiff´er,** n. (sl.). Concertina. [orig. unkn.]

squiff´y, a. (sl.). Slightly drunk. [fanciful]

squilgee. See SQUEEGEE.

squill, n. Plant of lily family; its bulb, used as diuretic, purgative, etc.; (also ~-*fish*) a crustacean. [f. L *squilla* f. Gk *skilla*]

squinch, n. Straight or arched structure across interior angle of square tower as support for side of octagon. [var. of obs. *scunch* abbr. of SCUNCHEON]

squint, v.i. & t., & n. & a. **1.** Have the eyes turned in different directions, have strabismus; look obliquely (*at* etc.); close (eyes) quickly, hold (eyes) half-shut. Hence ~ER¹ n. **2.** n. Affection of eyes in which their axes are differently directed, as *has a fearful* ~; stealthy or sidelong glance; (colloq.) glance, look, as *let's have a* ~ *at it*; leaning, inclination, (*to, towards,* policy etc.); oblique opening through wall of church affording view of altar. **3.** adj. ~ing, looking different ways; ~-*eyed*, (fig.) malignant. [vb aphetic f. *asquint*; n. f. adj. or vb; adj. f. obs. *squint* adv. (f. ASQUINT) or inferred f. ~-*eyed*]

squīre, n., & v.t. **1.** Country gentleman, esp. *the* chief landed proprietor in a district; woman's escort or gallant; ~ *of dames*, man who is attentive to or frequents company of women; attendant on knight (hist.). **2.** v.t. (Of man) attend upon, escort, (woman). Hence ~'HOOD, ~'LET, ~'LING¹, ~'SHIP, nn., ~'LY¹a, f. OF *esquier* ESQUIRE]

squīr(e)'|árchy (-kǐ), n. Government by, influence of, landed proprietors esp. before Reform Bill of 1832; the class of landed proprietors, so ~**árch** (-k) n. Hence ~**árchAL**, ~**árch'ICAL**, aa., (-k-). [f. prec. + Gk -*arkhia* rule f. *arkhō*]

‖ **squīreen'**, n. Small landed proprietor esp. in Ireland. [f. SQUIRE + -*een* dim. suf.]

squīrm, v.i., & n. **1.** Wriggle, writhe; (fig.) show, feel, embarrassment or discomfiture. **2.** n. Wriggling movement; (naut.) twist in rope. [imit.]

squi'rrel, n. Kinds of rodent of arboreal habits with bushy tail carried over back & pointed ears; *barking* ~, prairie-dog; ~-*fish*, kinds of fish covered with sharp spines; ~-*hawk*, large hawk preying on ~s; ~-*monkey*, marmoset & other small monkeys; ~-*tail*, kinds of grass allied to barley. [ME, f. AF *esquirel*, OF -*euil*, f. Rom. **scuriolus*, dim. of L f. Gk *skiouros*]

squīrt, v.t. & i., & n. **1.** Eject (liquid, powder) in a jet as from syringe; (of liquid etc.) be discharged thus. **2.** n. Syringe; jet *of* water etc.; (also ~-*gun*) kind of toy syringe; (colloq.) insignificant self-assertive fellow. [ME, prob. imit.; cf. LG *swirtjen*, EFris. *kwirtjen*]

squish, n. (colloq.). Marmalade. [imit.]

squit, n. (sl.). Small insignificant person. [cf. dial. *squit* vb 'to squirt', & *squirt* in same sense]

St. For St Andrew etc. see SAINT.

stăb, v.t. & i. (-bb-), & n. **1.** Pierce, wound, with (usu. short) pointed weapon e.g. knife or dagger; aim blow with such weapon (*at*); (fig.) inflict sharp pain on (person, his feelings, conscience, etc.), aim blow *at* (reputation, person, etc.); ~ (vb & n.) *in the back*, slander; roughen (brick wall) with pick before plastering. **2.** n. Blow, thrust, with knife etc., wound thus made, blow or pain inflicted on person's feelings; (sl.) an attempt, try. Hence ~'b'ER¹ n. [n. 15th c., vb 16th c., rel. to syn. (now dial.) *stob* vb, prob. f. *stob*, cogn. w. STUB]

Stăb'ăt Măt'er (or stah-, mah-), n. (Musical setting for) Latin hymn on agony of the Virgin Mary at the crucifixion. [f. the opening wds, L *stabat*

mater dolorosa 'Stood the Mother, full of grief']

stā'ble¹, a. Firmly fixed or established, not easily to be moved or changed or destroyed, as *doubt whether the structure is* ~; firm, resolute, not wavering nor fickle, as *the only* ~ *politician of his day*; ~ EQUILIBRIUM. Hence or cogn. staBIL'ITY, **stăbiliza'TION** (also, esp.) maintenance of the purchasing power of a country's currency by fixing its value in terms of gold, ~NESS, nn., **stăb'ilize(3)** v.t., **stăb'ilizER¹** n. (esp., one of a pair of retractable fins on sides of ship's hull below water-line to prevent rolling, aircraft's horizontal tailplane), **stā'bLY²** adv. [ME, f. AF *stable*, OF *estable* f. L *stabilis* (*stare* stand, see -BLE)]

stā'ble², n., & v.t. & i. **1.** Building set apart & adapted for lodging & feeding horses or (less usu.) cattle; racehorses of particular ~; (pl., mil.) duty or work in the ~s, (also) = ~-*call*; AUGEAN~s; ~-*boy*, -*man* (-mn), (employed in ~); ~-*call*, cavalry signal for grooming & watering horses; ~-*companion*, horse of same ~, (colloq.) member of same school, club, etc. **2.** v.t. Put, keep, (horse) in ~, as *where can we* ~ *our horses?*; (v.i., of horse etc., fig. of person) be ~d, as *must* ~ *where they can*. [ME, f. OF *estable* f. L *stabulum* (*stare* stand)]

stā'bling, n. In vbl senses of prec., esp. accommodation for horses etc. [-ING¹]

‖ **stă'blish**, v.t. (arch.). Fix firmly, establish, set up. [var. of ESTABLISH]

stacca'tō (-aht-), a. & adv. (To be played) in abrupt sharply detached manner, cf. LEGATO; ~ *mark*, dot above or below ~ note. [It.]

stăck, n., & v.t. **1.** Circular or rectangular pile of grain in sheaf or of hay, straw, etc., usu. with sloping thatched top; ~-*funnel*, pyramidal frame ventilating centre of ~; ~-*stand* (on which ~ is built for dryness & exclusion of vermin); (as measure of wood) pile of 108 cub. ft; pile, heap, of anything; (colloq.) large quantity, as *have* ~s, *a whole* ~, *of work to get through first*; pyramidal group of rifles, pile; number of chimneys standing together; isolated tall factory chimney; (also *smoke*~) chimney, funnel, of locomotive or steamer; ‖ high detached rock esp. off coast of Scotland & Orkneys. **2.** v.t. Pile in ~; arrange (cards) secretly for cheating; instruct to fly round at different levels (aircraft waiting to land at aerodrome); ~ (= PILE³) arms. [ME, f. ON *stakkr* haystack]

stăc'tē, n. A sweet spice used by ancient Jews in making incense. [ME, f. L f. Gk *staktē* (*stazō* drip)]

stăctŏm'eter, n. Tube for measuring a liquid in drops. [f. Gk *staktos* vbl adj. f. *stazō* drip + -METER]

stā'dium, n. (pl. -*ia*). **1.** (Gk ant.) measure of length, about 202 yds; course for foot-race and chariot-race. **2.** Modern athletic or sports ground. **3.** (med.), Stage, period, of disease. **4.** Interval between moults of an insect. [L, f. Gk *stadion* (*sta*- stand)]

stad(t)'hölder (stahd-, staht-, stá-), n. (hist.), Viceroy or governor of province or town in Netherlands; chief magistrate of United Provinces. Hence ~SHIP n. [f. Du. *stadhouder* deputy (*stad* STEAD + *houder* HOLDER)]

staff[1] (-ahf), n. (pl. now ~s exc. mus. *stáves*), & v.t. **1.** Stick, pole, for use in walking or climbing or as weapon (now chiefly fig.), as *bread is the ~* (support) *of life, you are the ~ of his old age*, QUARTER[1]-~. **2.** This as sign of office or authority, as *pastoral ~* (borne by or before bishop etc.). **3.** Shaft, pole, as support or handle, as FLAG[4]~. **4.** Stick used in surveying etc., esp. JACOB'S ~. **5.** Kinds of instrument for taking altitude at sea, as *back, cross, fore, -~.* **6.** Surgeon's steel instrument for guiding knife into bladder. **7.** Token delivered to engine-driver on single-line railways as authority to proceed over a given section of line (~ *system*, this method of working). **8.** (mil.), Body of officers assisting officer in high command & concerned with army or regiment as a whole, as *regimental ~; general ~* (at main headquarters of army, acting as personal ~ of commander-in--chief); ~ *captain, officer,* (serving on ~); ~ *college* (in which officers are prepared for ~ as opp. to regimental duties). **9.** Body of persons carrying on work under manager etc., as *editorial ~ of newspaper, diplomatic ~;* those in authority, opp. students, pupils, etc.; whence (-)~ED[2] (-ahft) a. **10.** (mus.), Set of five parallel lines on any one or between any two of which a note is placed to indicate its pitch; ~ *notation* (by means of ~, esp. opp. to TONIC *sol-fa*). **11.** v.t. Provide (institution etc.) with ~. [OE *stæf*, OS *staf*, OHG *slab*, ON *stafr* f. Gmc *stabhaz*]

staff[2] (-ahf), n. Mixture of plaster of Paris, cement, etc., as building-material. [orig. unkn.]

stăg, n. **1.** Male of red deer or of other large kinds of deer; bull castrated when (nearly) full-grown. **2.** || (St. Exch.) person who applies for allotments in new concerns with a view to selling at once at a profit; || (sl.) irregular dealer in stocks. **3.** ~-*beetle* (with branched mandibles like ~'s antlers); ~-*evil*, lockjaw in horses; ~-*horn*, kinds of club-moss & coral; ~-*hound*, large kinds of hound hunting deer by sight or scent; ~-*party* (of men only). [prob. repr. OE **stacga, *stagga*, cf. *docga* dog, *frocga* frog, **picga* pig]

stăge[1], n. **1.** Raised floor or platform, e.g. scaffold for workmen's use in building, *hanging ~* (suspended on ropes for painters' use), *landing-~* (at quay etc.

for landing from vessel); surface on which object is placed for inspection through microscope. **2.** Platform on which plays etc. are exhibited. **3.** (fig.). The drama, dramatic art or literature, actor's profession, as *went on the ~, became actor, the French ~.* **4.** (fig.). Scene of action, as *quitted the ~ of politics, the ~ of his operations, a larger ~ opened to him.* **5.** Point or period in development etc., as *reached a crucial ~, at this ~ an interruption occurred, passed through a long ~ of inactivity, is in the hoyden ~, larval ~.* **6.** Regular stopping-place in route, distance between two of these, as *travelled by easy ~s, got down at the next ~.* **7.** ~-*coach*, coach running regularly by ~s between two places, ~-*coachman*, driver of this; ~-*craft*, skill or experience in writing or staging plays; ~ *direction*, written or printed instruction in play as to movement, position, tone, etc. of actor; ~ *door*, actors' & workmen's entrance at back of ~; ~ *effect*, effect produced in acting or on the ~, artificial or theatrical effect produced in real life; ~ *fever*, inordinate desire to go on the ~; ~ *fright*, nervousness on facing audience esp. for first time; ~ *manager*, person responsible for lighting and other mechanical arrangements, costumes, etc. of play; ~ *rights*, exclusive rights to perform particular play; ~-*struck*, struck with ~ fever; ~ *whisper*, aside, whisper meant to be heard by others than the person addressed. [ME, f. OF *estage* f. Rom. **staticum* (*stare* stand)]

stăge[2], v.t. & i. Put (play) on stage; arrange to take place dramatically (~ a COME[1]-*back, recovery*); (of play) lend itself to representation, as *does not ~ well.* [f. prec.]

stä'ger, n. *Old ~*, experienced person, old hand. [STAGE[1] + -ER[1]]

stăgg'ard, -t, n. Stag four years old. [ME; -ARD]

stăgg'er (-g-), v.i. & t., & n. **1.** Walk or stand unsteadily, totter; hesitate, waver in purpose; cause to totter, as *received a ~ing blow;* cause to hesitate or waver, as *the question ~ed him, his resolution;* arrange in zigzag order, esp. set (spokes of wheel) leaning alternately to right & left; arrange (holidays, hours of work, etc.) so that they differ from those of others. Hence ~ING̣LY[2] adv. **2.** n. Tottering movement; (mech.) overhanging or slantwise or zigzag arrangement of like parts in a structure etc.; (pl., also *blind ~s*) kinds of disease of brain & spinal cord esp. in horses & cattle; (pl.) giddiness. [alt. of ME (now dial.) *stacker* f. ON *stakra* frequent. of *staka* push, stagger]

stăgg'erer (-g-), n. In vbl senses, esp. disconcerting argument, objection, event, etc. [-ER[1]]

stä'ging, n. Putting play on stage; driving or running stage-coaches;

scaffolding; ~ *post*, regular stopping place on air route. [-ING²]

Stā′girite, n. *The* ~, Aristotle. [f. L f. Gk *Stageirītēs* native of *Stageira* (-ITE¹)]

stăg′n|āte, v.i. (Of liquid) be(come) motionless, have no current, cease to flow; (of life, action, mind, business, person) be(come) dull or sluggish. Hence or cogn. ~ANCY, ~A′TION, nn., ~ANT a., ~antly² adv. [f. L *stagnare* (*stagnum* pool), -ATE³]

stăgnic′olous, a. Living in swamps or stagnant water. [f. L *stagnum* pool + *colere* inhabit + -OUS]

stā′g|ỹ, a. Theatrical in manner, style, appearance, etc. Hence ~INESS n. [f. STAGE¹ + -Y²]

staid, a. Of steady & sober character; sedate. Hence ~LY² adv., ~′NESS n. [= *stayed* p.p. of STAY]

stain, v.t. & i., & n. 1. Discolour, make foul, soil, as *cigarettes ~ the fingers*, *wine will ~ the cloth*, *warranted not to ~ clothes*; (fig.) sully, blemish, (reputation, name, person; p.p. often in comb., as *guilt*, *sin*, *~ed*); colour (wood, glass, etc.) by process other than painting or covering the surface; impregnate (substance) for microscopic examination with colouring matter that acts more powerfully on some parts than on others; print colours on (wallpaper). Hence ~′ABLE a., ~′ER¹ n. 2. n. Discoloration, spot or mark caused esp. by contact with foreign matter, as *cloth is covered with tea-~s*; ~ing-material; (fig.) blot, blemish, as *without a ~ on his character*. Hence ~′LESS a. (usu. of reputation, also of kind of chromium-steel alloy immune to rusting & corrosion); ~′lèssLY² adv. [ME; aphetic f. OF *desteign-*, *desteindre* (obs. E *distain*), f. DIS- + *teindre* (L *tingere* dye)]

stair, n. Each of a set of (now usu. indoor) steps, as *the top ~ but one*; (now usu. pl.) set of these, as *passed him on the ~s*, *down a winding ~*; *flight*, *pair*, *of ~s*, set of ~s in continuous straight line or from one landing to another; *below ~s*, in the basement of house esp. as part belonging to servants, as *was coolly discussed below ~s* (by the servants); *down*, *up*, ~s, on, to, the lower, upper, floor(s) of house; BACK¹-~; ~′case, (part of building containing) flight of ~s, *corkscrew ~case* (winding round NEWEL); ~′rod (for securing ~carpet in angle between two steps); ~′way, way up a flight of ~s, ~case. [OE *stæger* f. Gmc *staig-*, *stīg-* to climb; cf. (M)Du., LG *steiger* landing- -stage, WFlem. *steeger* ~case]

‖ **staith, staithe** (-dh), n. Waterside coal depot equipped for loading vessels. [ME, f. ON *stǫth* (f. *stathwō*) landing-stage]

stāke, n., & v.t. 1. Stick sharpened at one end & driven into ground as support, boundary mark, etc.; post to which person is bound to be burnt alive, (fig.) death by burning, as *was condemned to*, *suffered at*, *the* ~. 2. Tinsmith's small anvil fixed on bench by pointed prop. 3. Money etc. wagered on an event, esp. deposited with third party (~′holder) by each of those who make a wager, (pl.) money to be contended for esp. in horse- -race, (pl.) such race, as *maiden*, *trial*, ~s; *have a ~ in the country*, be materially concerned in its welfare, e.g. as landowner; (fig.) principle etc. contended for, as *consider the immensity of the* ~; *at* ~, at issue, in question, risked, as *life itself is at* ~. 4. ~-*boat* (anchored to mark course for boat-race etc.); ~-*net*, fishing-net hung on ~s. 5. v.t. Fasten, secure, support, with ~ or ~s; mark *off*, *out* (area) with ~s, as ~ *out a claim*. 6. Wager, risk, (money etc. *on* event etc.). [OE *staca*, = MDu., (M)LG *stake*, f. WG *stak-*, *stek-* pierce, cogn. w. STICK]

stăkhan′ovīte (-kahn-), n. A (Russian) worker who increases his output to an exceptional extent; also attrib. [f. *Stakhanov*, a Russian miner, + -ITE¹(1)]

stăl′actīte (*or* stală²), n. Deposit of carbonate of lime, usu. in form like large icicle, hanging from roof of cave etc. & formed by trickling of water. Hence **stalăc′tIC**, **stalăc′tiFORM**, **stălactīt′IC**, aa. [f. mod. L *stalactītēs* (Gk *stalaktos* vbl adj. f. *stalassō* drip, see -ITE³)]

Stăl′ăg, n. German prison camp, esp. for non-commissioned officers and men. [G]

stăl′agmīte (*or* stală²), n. Deposit as STALACTITE on floor of cave etc. often uniting with stalactite. Hence **stălagmit′IC** a., **stălagmit′ICALLY** adv. [f. mod. L *stalagmītēs* (Gk *stalagmos* dripping, as STALACTITE)]

stāle¹, a., & v.t. & i. 1. Musty, insipid, or otherwise the worse for age, not fresh; ~ *bread* (musty; also, not of the day's baking, as ~ *bread is best for toast*); (fig.) lacking novelty, trite, as ~ *joke*, *news*, *devices*; (of athlete) overtrained, also transf., e.g. of a crammed pupil. Hence ~′LY² (-l-ll-) adv., ~′NESS (-ln-) n. 2. vb. Make or become ~ or common. [prob. ult. f. the Gmc root *sta-* STAND]

‖ **stāle²**, n. (arch.). Decoy bird; dupe, laughing-stock. [prob. f. AF *estale* of Gmc orig. cf. OE *stæl(hrān* reindeer) decoy reindeer f. *stellan* to place]

stāle³, v.i. (arch. & dial.), & n. 1. (Esp. of horses and cattle) urinate. 2. n. Urine of horses and cattle. [late ME, perh. f. OF *estaler* = It. *stallare*]

stāle′māte (-lm-), n., & v.t. 1. (In chess) a draw resulting from a player's having no move available, his king not being in check; (fig.) deadlock. 2. v.t. Reduce (player) to ~; (fig.) bring to a standstill. [f. obs. *stale* (f. AF *estale* perh. f. *estaler*; cf. STALL²), + MATE¹]

Stal′in|ism (-ah-), n. Political theories and practices of the Russian Communist dictator Josef V. *Stalin* (d. 1953). So ~IST n. & a., ~ITE¹ n. & a. [-ISM]

stalk¹ (-awk), v.i. & t., & n. **1.** Stride, walk in stately or imposing manner (often *along* etc.); steal up to game under cover; pursue (game) stealthily; ~*ing-horse*, horse behind which hunter conceals himself, (fig.) pretext. **2.** n. ~ing of game, imposing gait. Hence (-)~ER¹ n. [ME *stalke* f. OE **stealcian* frequent. of **stal-*, **stel-* STEAL]

stalk² (-awk), n. (Bot.) stem, main axis, of plant, (loosely) any support of an organ; ~like support of organ etc. in animals; stem of wineglass etc.; (archit.) ornament like ~ of plant; tall chimney of factory etc.; ~*-eyed*, (of crab etc.) having the eyes mounted on ~s. Hence (-)~ED² (-awkt), ~'LESS, aa., ~'LET n. [ME *stalke*, app. dim. f. *stal-* in OE *stalu* side or rung of ladder, now dial. *stale* long handle]

stall¹ (-awl), n., & v.t. & i. **1.** (Single compartment for one animal in) stable, cowhouse; FINGER-~; booth in bazaar, market, etc., compartment in a building, for sale of goods, table in this on which goods are exposed, as *picked it up in* or *on a book-*~; fixed seat in choir or chancel of church more or less enclosed at back & sides & often canopied, esp. one appropriated to clergyman, as *canon's, dean's,* ~, (fig.) office, dignity, of canon etc., as *how long has he had his* ~?; ‖ each of a set of seats in theatre usu. between pit & stage; working-compartment in coal-mine; ~*-feed*, fatten (cattle) in ~, so ~*-fed* a. **2.** vb. Place, keep, (cattle etc.) in ~ esp. for fattening, as *a* ~*ed ox*; furnish (stable etc.) with ~s; (of horse or cart) stick fast as in mud or snow, (of motor-engine) stop working, (of aeroplane or airman) become unstable by loss of air-speed. [OE *steall*, MDu., MLG, OHG *stal*, ON *stallr* f. Gmc **stalla-* f. **sta-* STAND]

stall² (-awl), n., & v.i. & t. **1.** Pickpocket's confederate who diverts attention during theft & assists thief's escape etc. **2.** vb. **Fence conversationally; *block, delay, obstruct, (~ off, get rid of by evasive tactics or trick). [var. of STALE²]

‖ **sta'llage** (-awl-), n. Space for, rent for, right to erect, stall(s) in market etc. [ME, f. AF *estalage* (*estal* STALL¹, *-AGE*)]

stä'llion (-yon), n. Uncastrated male horse, esp. one kept for breeding. [ME, f. OF *estalon* = It. *stallone* f. Rom. **stallonem* f. Gmc **stalla-* STALL¹]

sta'lwart (-awl-), a. & n. **1.** Strongly built, sturdy; courageous, resolute, determined, as ~ *supporters*. **2.** n. (pol.) Strong party man. Hence ~LY² adv., ~NESS n. [16th c. Sc. var. of obs. *stalworth*, OE *stælwierthe* (*stæl* place, WORTH¹)]

stä'm'en, n. Male organ of flowering plants, organ containing pollen. Hence (-)~ED² (-nd), stamin'ĕAL, stamin'ĕous, stäminIF'EROUS, aa. [L, gen. *-minis*, = warp in upright loom, thread]

stä'm'ĭna, n. Staying-power, power of endurance. [L pl. of prec. now usu. as sing.]

stä'm'ĭnal, a. Of stamens or stamina. [-AL]

stä'm'ĭnate, a. Having stamens but no pistils; having stamens. [-ATE²(2)]

stämm'er, v.i. & t., & n. **1.** Speak (habitually, or on occasion from embarrassment etc.) with halting articulation esp. with pauses or rapid repetitions of same syllable, whence ~ER¹ n., ~ingLY² adv.; utter (words) thus, as ~*ed out an excuse.* **2.** n. ~ing speech, tendency to ~. [OE *stamerian* f. Gmc **stam-*, see STEM²]

stämp, v.t. & i., & n. **1.** Impress pattern, name, mark, upon (metal, butter, paper, etc.) with die or similar instrument of metal, wood, rubber, etc.; affix postage or other ~ to (envelope, document); crush, pulverize, (ores etc.); bring down one's foot, bring down (foot), heavily on ground; ~ *out*, put an end to, crush, destroy, (rebellion etc.); assign a character to, characterize, as *this alone* ~*s the story* (*as*) *a slander;* impress on the memory. Hence (-)~ER¹(1, 2) n. **2.** n. Instrument for ~ing pattern or mark; mark made by this; impression of official mark required to be made for revenue purposes on deeds, bills of exchange, etc., as evidence of payment of tax; piece of paper impressed with official mark as evidence of payment of tax or fee & meant to be affixed to letter, postcard, receipted account, etc.; POSTAGE ~; mark impressed on, label etc. affixed to, commodity as evidence of quality etc., (fig.) characteristic mark, impress, as *bears the* ~ *of genius*; character, kind, as *avoid men of that* or *his* ~; block that crushes ore in ~-mill; heavy downward blow with foot. **3.** *S*~ *Act*, act concerned with ~-duty, esp. that imposing duty on American colonies in 1765 & repealed in 1766; ~*-collector* (of postage-~s as curiosities); ~*-duty* (imposed on certain kinds of legal instrument); ~*-machine* (for issuing postage-stamps); ~*-mill* (for crushing ore etc.); ~*-office* (for issue of government ~s & receipt of ~-duty etc.). [(vb) ME *stampen* f. Gmc **stampaz* pestle f. **stamp-*, prob. cogn. w. **slap-* STEP; (n.) partly f. vb, partly f. OF *estampe* f. same Gmc source]

stämpēde', n., & v.i. & t. **1.** Sudden fright & scattering of a number of horses or cattle; sudden flight or hurried movement of people due to panic; **(pol.)* unconcerted movement of many persons by common impulse. **2.** vb. (Cause to) take part in ~. [f. Sp. *estampida* crash]

stänce, n. (golf, crick.). Position taken for stroke. [F, f. It. STANZA]

stanch¹, **staunch**, (-ah-, -aw-), v.t. Check the flow of (esp. blood); check the flow from (esp. wound). [ME, f. OF *estanchier* (mod. F *étancher*) dam up, make watertight), of disputed orig.]

stanch² etc. See STAUNCH¹ etc.

sta′nchion (-ahnshn), n., & v.t. **1.** Post, pillar, upright support, vertical strut; upright bar, pair of bars, for confining cattle in stall. **2.** v.t. Supply with ~, fasten (cattle) to ~. [15th c., f. OF *estanchon*, *-son*, f. *estance* prop, f. Rom. *stantia*; see STANZA]

stănd[1], v.i. & t. (stŏŏd). **1.** Have or take or maintain upright position, be set upright, as *tell him to ~ up*, ~ *at* EASE[1], ‖~ EASY, ~ *in* person's LIGHT[1], *in the* BREACH[1], *stood there till I was tired*, *was too weak to ~, chair will not ~ on two legs, hair ~s on end* (with terror). **2.** Be of specified height, as ~*s six foot three.* **3.** Be situated, be, as *on each side ~ two pillars, a stranger stood in the doorway, the cups ~ on the top shelf, here once stood a huge oak.* **4.** Assume stationary position, as ~ *still, was commanded to ~; ~ (& deliver)!*, highwayman's order. **5.** Maintain position, avoid falling or moving or being moved, as *don't ~ there arguing, house will ~ another century, whether we ~ or fall, has stood through worse storms, ~ on* one's *own* BOTTOM[1], *~ fast, ~ firm; all ~ing* (naut. & transf.), without time to lower sails or prepare, taken by surprise. **6.** *It ~s to reason*, it is logically demonstrable (*that*), (pop.) I shall lose my temper if you deny (*that*). **7.** Hold good, remain valid or unaltered, as *the former conditions may ~, the passage must ~, the same remark ~s good.* **8.** Be, find oneself, in specified situation, rank, etc., as ~*s convicted of treachery, in need of help, in an awkward position, under heavy obligations; I ~ corrected* (accept correction); *thermometer stood at 90° ; corn ~s higher* (is dearer) *than ever; the matter ~s thus; he ~s first on the list, alone among his contemporaries, in the same relation to both parties, ~s well* (is on good terms or in good odour) *with the authorities; how do we ~ in the matter of* (have we enough or suitable) *horses?; I ~ prepared to dispute it, ~ in awe of, have often stood his friend, ~ at* BAY[4]. **9.** Move to & remain in specified position, as ~ *back, clear, aside, aloof, away*; (naut.) hold specified course, as ~ *in for the shore*; (of dog) point, set. **10.** Place, set, in upright or specified position, as ~ *the jug on the table, ~ it against the wall, shall ~ you in the corner* (as punishment). **11.** Endure without succumbing or complaining, as *nerves could not ~ the strain, how does he ~ pain?, could never ~ the fellow, shall ~ no nonsense, can't ~ these French matches; ~ fire* (receive fire of enemy without giving way); *failed to ~ the test; ~* one's *ground*, maintain one's position (lit., & fig. of argument etc.). **12.** Undergo (trial), be faced with (CHANCE[1]). **13.** Provide at one's expense, as *stood him a drink, stood a bottle to the company, who is going to ~ treat?* **14.** ~ *by* (prep.), uphold, support, side with, (person), adhere to, abide by,

(terms, promise), (naut.) take or ~ ready to take hold of (anchor etc.); ~ *by* (adv.), ~ near, be a bystander, ~ & look on, as *will not ~ by & see him ill-treated*, (orig. naut.) ~ ready, be on the alert; ~*-by*, thing, person, that one can depend upon, machine etc. kept for emergency. **15.** ~ *down*, retire from witness-box or similar position, (mil.) go off duty after ~ing to. **16.** ~ *for*, represent, signify, imply, as *P.O. ~s for postal order, tariff reform ~s for a great deal more than that*, ‖ be candidate for (office), be candidate for representation of (constituency) in Parliament, espouse the cause of (free trade etc.), (colloq.) endure, tolerate, acquiesce in. **17.** ~ (person) *in* (sum), cost, as *coat stood me in £20, wife ~s him in £50 yearly for motor tires*; ~ (person) *in good* STEAD; ~ *in*, deputize *for* (~*-in* n., deputy, substitute); ~ *in with*, be in league with. **18.** ~ *off*, move away, keep one's distance, (v.t.) dispense with the services of (employee) temporarily; ~*-off* (*half*), (rugby football) half-back who forms a link between the scrum-half and the three--quarters; ~ *off & on* (naut.), sail alternately away from & towards shore so as to keep a point in sight. **19.** ~ *on* (prep.), insist on, observe scrupulously, esp. ~ *on ceremony*; ~ *on* (adv., naut.), continue on same course. **20.** ~ *out*, hold out, persist in opposition (*against*) or endurance, be prominent or conspicuous or outstanding. **21.** ~ *over*, be postponed. **22.** ~ *to* (prep.), abide by (promise etc.), stick to, not desert, (one's *post, guns*, esp. fig., *duty*, etc.), ~ *to it*, maintain stoutly (*that*), ~ *to sea* (naut.), sail out to sea ; ~ *to* (adv.), (arch.) fall to, set to work, (mil.) take post in preparation for an attack (esp. before dawn & after dark); ~ *to win, lose*, have one's bets or other dispositions so made that one is sure to win or lose something or a specified amount (*whoever loses, I ~ to win; how much do you ~ to lose?*). **23.** ~ *up*, rise to one's feet from sitting or other position, maintain erect position; ~ *up for*, side with, maintain, support, (person, cause); ~ *upon*, = ~ *on*; ~ *up to*, meet, face, (opponent) courageously, (of things) remain unimpaired despite the effects of (hard wear etc.). **24.** ~*-off′ish* a., distant, reserved, not affable, whence ~*-offishly* adv., ~*-offishness* n.; ~*-up* a., (of collar) upright, high, opp. to *turn-down*, (of fight) thorough, fair & square. [OE, OS, Goth. *standan*, OHG *stantan*, ON *standa* f. Gmc *sta-*, *stŏ-*, cogn. w. L *stare*]

stănd[2], n. **1.** Cessation from motion or progress, stoppage, as *came, was brought, to a ~; be at a ~* (arch.), be unable to proceed, be in perplexity. **2.** Stationary condition assumed for purpose of resistance, esp. *make a ~* (*against* enemy, *for, against*, principle etc.). **3.** Position taken up, as *took his ~ near the door, I take my ~* (base argument etc., rely) *on the precise* *wording of the act.* **4.** Table, set of shelves, rack, etc., on or in which things may be placed, as *music, hat, umbrella,* ~; INK~; (WASH-*hand*-)~. **5.** Stall in market etc., as *fruit-*~. **6.** Standing-place for vehicles etc., as CAB¹-~. **7.** Raised structure for persons to sit or stand on, as BAND¹~, GRAND ~; *witness-box, as *take the* ~. **8.** Standing growth (*of* clover etc.). **9.** (theatr.). Each halt made on a tour to give performances (*a one-night* ~). **10.** (Austral.). A forest, or its timber, regarded commercially. **11.** ~ *of arms*, complete set for one man; ~ *of colours*, regiment's flags. **12.** ~ *camera* (for use on a tripod); ~-*pipe*, vertical pipe for various purposes; ~*point*, point of view; ~-*rest*, high stool with sloping top for supporting person standing at easel etc.; ~*'still*, stoppage, inability to proceed, as *am brought to a* ~*still.* [ME, f. prec.]

stăn'dard, n. **1.** Distinctive flag, esp. flag of cavalry regiment (opp. to *colours* of infantry); *the Royal* ~, flag with Sovereign's personal coat of arms; rallying principle (*raise the* ~ *of revolt, free trade*). **2.** Weight or measure to which others conform or by which the accuracy of others is judged (often attrib., as ~*pound, yard,* etc.); thing serving as basis of comparison. **3.** Degree of excellence etc. required for particular purpose (*does not come up to the* ~; *must set a low* ~; ~ *of living,* minimum of material comfort with which a person or class or community may reasonably be content); thing recognized as model for imitation etc., esp. attrib., as *the* ~ *work on the subject,* ~ *novels* (those of admitted merit); grade of classification in primary schools. **4.** Average quality, as *work was of a low* ~. **5.** *Monetary* ~, proportion of weight of fine metal & alloy in gold or silver coin (*gold, silver,* ~) or in both (*double* ~); *multiple, tabular,* ~, ~ of value obtained by averaging prices of a number of products. **6.** Measure (165 cub. ft) of timber. **7.** Upright support (often attrib., as ~ *lamp,* set on tall freq. telescopic pillar); upright water or gas pipe; tree, shrub, that stands alone without support; shrub grafted on upright stem & trained in tree form. **8.** ~-*bearer,* soldier who bears~, (fig.) prominent leader in a cause; ‖~ *bread* (wheaten, of mixed flours). [ME, f. OF *estandard* prob. f. Rom. *estendere* (f. L as EXTEND + -ARD); partly assoc. w. STAND¹]

stăn'dardĭz|e, -is|e (-iz), v.t. Make to conform to standard; (chem.) obtain by analysis specific value of (solution etc.) for purposes of comparison. Hence ~A'TION n. [-IZE]

stăn'ding¹, n. In ·vbl senses; esp.: estimation in which one is held, repute, position, as *men of high* ~, *is of no* ~; duration, as *a dispute of long* ~; ~-*rocm,* space to stand in. [ME; -ING¹]

stăn'ding², a. In vbl senses, esp.: established, as *a* ~ *rule, has become a*~ (stock) *jest;* permanent, not made, raised, etc., for the occasion, as ~ *army,* ~ *orders* (esp. those respecting manner in which business shall be conducted in Parliament); ~ *rigging* (fixed stays); ~ *corn* (not cut); ~ *jump* (performed without preliminary run); ~ (stagnant) *water.* [ME; -ING²]

stăn'dish, n. (arch.). Inkstand. [ME, commonly thought to be f. STAND² + DISH]

*stănd'pătter, n. Politician who is for strict adherence to party platform, esp. on tariffs. [f. *stand* PAT³]

stăn'hope (-nop), n. Light open carriage of 2 or 4 wheels; (also S~ *press*) iron printing press invented by Lord S~; S~ *lens* (with convex surfaces of different curves). [name of inventors]

stăn'iel (-yel), n. Kestrel. [OE *stăngella* (*stăn* stone + *gellan* YELL)]

stank. See STINK v.

‖**stănn'arў**, n. & a. Tin-mine; tin-mining district; ~ *court* (hist.; for regulation of tin-mines in Cornwall & Devon). [f. med. L *stannaria* n. (LL *stannum,* tin, see -ARY¹)]

stănn'ĭc, a. (chem.). Of tin esp. in its higher valence, as ~*ic acid.* So ~ATE¹(3) n., ~ĬF'EROUS, ~OUS, aa. [f. LL *stannum* tin + -IC]

stăn'za, n. Group of (usu. four or more) rhymed lines, as SPENSERIAN ~; group of four lines in some Greek & Latin metres, esp. *Alcaic, Sapphic,* ~. Hence (-)~'d, ~ED² (-ad), stănză'ĭc, aa. [It., = chamber, stanza, f. Rom. *stantia* abode (*stare* stand, see -ANCE)]

stăphўlŏcŏcc'us, n. (bacteriol.; pl. -*cocci,* pron. -kŏk'sī). Form of pus-producing bacteria characterized by grapelike clusters. [mod. L, f. Gk *staphulē* bunch of grapes + *kokkos* berry]

stā'ple¹, n., & v.t. **1.** U-shaped piece of metal bar or wire with ends pointed for driving into wood etc. to take hasp of padlock or hook, or to secure netting, electric wire, etc.; metal tube holding the reeds of oboe & similar instruments; bent wire used in wire-stitching. **2.** v.t. Furnish, fasten, with ~; *stapling-machine*, bookbinder's wire-stitching machine. [OE *stapol,* OS *stapal,* OHG *staffal,* f. Gmc **stapulaz* f. **stap-* STEP]

stā'ple², n., a., & v.t. **1.** Important or principal article of commerce, as *the* ~*s of that country, of British industry;* raw material; (fig.) chief element or material, as *formed the* ~ *of conversation;* fibre of cotton, wool, etc., viewed as determining its quality, as *cotton of fine, short,* ~. **2.** adj. Principal, as ~ *commodities.* **3.** v.t. Sort, classify, (wool etc.) according to fibre, whence **stăp'lER¹** n. [ME, f. OF *estaple* market f. MLG, MDu. *stapel* market]

stăr¹, n. **1.** Celestial body appearing as luminous point; (also *fixed* ~) such body so far from earth as to appear motionless except for diurnal revolution of the heavens; *double, multiple*, ~, group of two, of three to six, fixed ~s appearing to naked eye as one; *binary* ~, two ~s revolving round one another; EVENING, MORNING, ~; *day'*~ (poet.), morning ~, sun; LODE~; *north, polar*, (= POLE²-) ~; *shooting* ~, small meteor appearing like ~ moving rapidly and disappearing. 2. Thing suggesting ~ by its shape, esp. figure or object with radiating points e.g. as decoration of an order; *S*~*s & Stripes*, U.S. national flag; asterisk; white spot on forehead of horse etc. 3. ‖ (pool). Additional life bought by player whose lives are lost. 4. Principal actor or actress in a company (*film* ~; *the* ~ *system*, of relying on a ~ or two to make up for weak company); ~ *turn*, principal item in an entertainment or performance; brilliant or prominent person, as *literary* ~, *bright particular* ~ (object of one's devotion). 5. Heavenly body considered as influencing person's fortunes etc., as *born under an unlucky* ~, *his* ~ *was in the ascendant, you may thank your* ~*s you were not there, the* ~*s were against it* (cf. ILL-~*red*). 6. ~*apple*, edible applelike fruit of W.-Indian tree, with a stellate section; *S*~ *Chamber* [perh. diff. wd], court of civil & criminal jurisdiction primarily concerned with offences affecting crown interests, noted for summary & arbitrary procedure, & abolished 1640; ~*drift*, common proper motion of a number of fixed ~s in same region; ~*finch*, redstart; ~*fish*, echinoderm with five or more radiating arms; ~*gazer* (joc.), astronomer; ~*light*, light of ~s, as *walked home by* ~*light*, (adj., also ~*lit*) lighted by the ~s, as *a* ~*light night*; ~ *of Bethlehem*, plant of lily family with ~-like white flowers striped with green on outside; *S*~ *of India* (hist.), order instituted 1861 to commemorate assumption of direct government of India; ~ *shell*, kind designed to burst in air & light up enemy's position; ~*spangled*, spangled with ~s (esp. of U.S. flag); ~*stone*, kind of sapphire; ~*stream*, either of two systematic drifts of ~s (one of which comprises the nearer ~s and moves towards Orion). Hence ~'LET n., little ~, young film actress who shows promise of becoming a ~, ~'LESS, ~'LIKE, ~r'Y² aa. (~*ry--eyed*, colloq., visionary, impractical). [OE *steorra*, OS, OHG *sterro* f. Gmc *sterron* f. *ster-*, cogn. w. Gk *astēr*]

star², v.t. & i. (-rr-). 1. Set, adorn, (as) with stars (esp. in p.p.); affix asterisk to (name in list etc.). 2. Appear as star actor; present as a theatrical, film, etc., star. 3. ‖ (pool). Buy additional life. [f. prec.]

starb'oard (-berd), n., & v.t. 1. Right side of vessel looking forward (cf. PORT⁵, LARBOARD; often attrib.). 2. v.t. Turn, put, (helm) to ~. [OE *stēorbord* (*stēor* rudder,

see STEER¹, +*bord* BOARD), early Teut. ships being steered with a paddle over the right side]

starch, a., n., & v.t. 1. (now rare). Precise, prim, whence ~'LY² adv., ~'NESS n. 2. n. White odourless tasteless powder procured chiefly from corn & potatoes but found in all plants except fungi & valuable in digestion; preparation of this with usu. boiling water for stiffening linen etc. before ironing; (fig.) stiffness of manner, formality. Hence ~'iNESS n., ~'Y² a., (lit. & fig.). 3. v.t. Stiffen with ~ (often fig. esp. in p.p.), whence ~'ĕDLY² adv., ~'ĕDNESS n.); CLEAR¹-~. Hence (-)~ER¹ n. [adj. f. n. f. vb ME *sterche* f. OE *stearcian* stiffen f. *stearc* STARK]

star|e, v.i. & t., & n. 1. Look fixedly with eyes wide open (*at, upon*, etc., or abs.) from surprise, admiration, bewilderment, stupidity, horror, impertinent curiosity, etc.; (chiefly in part.) be unpleasantly prominent or striking, as *a* ~*ing waistcoat, tie was of a* ~*ing red*, (adv.) *stark* ~*ing mad*; reduce (person) to specified condition by ~ing, as ~*ed him out of countenance, into silence, dumb*; ~*e down*, outstare; ~*e*(person) *in the face*, be evident or imminent, as *the facts* ~*e us in the face, ruin* ~*ed him in the face*. Hence ~'ingLY² adv. 2. n. ~ing gaze. [OE *starian*, OHG *starēn*, ON *stara* f. Gmc *star-* be rigid]

stark, a. & adv. 1. Stiff, rigid, as ~ *& stiff, lies* ~ *in death*; (poet.) strong; (poet.) stubborn, resolute; downright, sheer, as ~ *madness*; = foll. 2. adv. Quite, wholly, as ~ *crazy*. [OE *stearc*, OS, OHG *stark*, ON *sterkr* f. Gmc *starkuz*]

stark nāk'ĕd, a. Utterly naked, absolutely without clothing. [16th c. alt. f. ME (now dial.) *start naked* (*start* = tail, as in RED*start*)]

starl'ing¹, n. Small gregarious partly migratory bird with blackish-brown speckled plumage inhabiting chiefly cultivated areas, a good mimic. [OE *stærlinc* f. *stær* (now dial. *stare*) = OHG *star*, f. Gmc *staraz*, **starōn* cogn. w. L *sturnus*; see -LING¹]

starl'ing², n. Protective piling round pier of bridge. [perh. corrupt. of (now dial.) *staddling* in same sense]

starry. See STAR¹.

start¹, v.i. & t. 1. Make sudden movement from pain, surprise, etc., as ~*ed in his seat*, ~*ed at the sound of my voice*; change position abruptly as from shock or sudden impulse, as ~ *aside, from* one's *chair*. 2. (Of timbers etc.) spring from proper position, give way. 3. Set out, begin journey, as *we* ~ *at six*; make a beginning (on journey, enterprise, book, cigar, etc.); begin, commence, (*work* etc., *doing, to do*). 4. ~ *in* (colloq.), begin (*to do*); ~ *out* (colloq.), take steps as intending (*to do*); ~ *up*, rise suddenly e.g. from seat, arise, come into existence or action, occur to the mind, as *many difficulties, rivals, have*

~*ed up*, (trans.) cause (engine) to begin running. **5.** Rouse (game) from lair etc. **6.** Originate, set going, (enterprise, newspaper, business, clock after winding, objections, quarrel, etc.); cause to begin doing (*this* ~*ed me coughing*); cause or enable (person) to commence business etc.; give signal to (persons) to ~ in race. **7.** Cause or experience the starting of (timbers, tooth, etc.). **8.** (naut.). Pour out (liquor) from cask. **9.** *To* ~ *with*, in the first place, as *you have no right to be here, to* ~ *with*; at the beginning, as *had 6 members to* ~ *with*. [OE *styrtan* = OHG *sturzen*; ME *sterte* = MHG *sterzen*; f. Gmc **sturt-*, **stert-*]

start[2], n. **1.** Sudden movement of surprise, pain, etc.; (pl.) intermittent or spasmodic efforts or movements, esp. (*works*) *by fits & ~s*. **2.** Beginning of journey or action or race, as *shall make an early* ~ *for town, is difficult work at the* ~, *the* ~ *is fixed for 3 p.m.*; starting-place of race. **3.** Advantage conceded in race, as *will give you 60 yards* ~, *15 seconds* ~; advantageous position gained in business etc., as *got a good* ~ *in life, got the* ~ *of* (gained advantage over) *his rivals*. **4.** *A rum* ~ (colloq.), surprising occurrence. [ME *stert(e)*, f. prec.]

start'er, n. In vbl senses, esp.: one who gives signal to start in race; horse, competitor, starting in race, as *list of probable* ~*s*; SELF-~. [-ER[1]]

start'ing, n. In vbl senses; ~*-gate*, removable barrier for securing fair start in horse-races; ~*-post* (from which competitors start in race); ~ *prices* in horse-races, final odds at start. [-ING[1]]

star'tle, v.t. Cause (person etc.) to start with surprise or sudden alarm, give shock to, take by surprise, whence (of person, news, etc.) **start'ler**[1] n.; (part.) surprising, alarming, as *startling news, discovery, development*, whence **start'lingly**[2] adv. [ME *stertle* f. START[1] + -LE(3)]

starve, v.i. & t. **1.** Die of hunger; suffer from lack of food; suffer extreme poverty; (colloq.) feel hungry, as *am simply starving*; ‖ (now rare) perish with, suffer from, cold; (fig.) suffer mental or spiritual want, feel strong craving *for* (sympathy, amusement, knowledge, etc.). **2.** Cause to perish with hunger; deprive of, keep scantily supplied with, food (lit. & fig.); compel (garrison etc. *into* surrender etc.) thus; ‖ cause to perish, affect severely, with cold. Hence **starva'tion** n. [OE *steorfan* die, OS *sterban*, OHG *sterban* f. Gmc **sterbh-*]

starve'ling (-vl-), n. & a. **1.** Starving or ill-fed person or animal. **2.** adj. Starving. [-LING[1]]

stas'is, n. (path.). Stoppage of circulation of any of the fluids of the body. [Gk, = standing]

-stat, terminal element in names of cer-tain instruments, f. Gk *statos* stationary; as AERO~, PHOTO~, THERMO~.

state[1], n. & a. **1.** Condition in which a thing is, mode of existence as determined by circumstances, as ~ *of life* (one's rank & occupation), *a precarious* ~ *of health, found him in the same* ~, *in a* ~ *of deep depression, things were in an untidy* ~, *in a bad* ~ *of repair, what a* (dirty, untidy) ~ *you are in!*, (colloq.) *he was in quite a* ~ (quite excited or anxious) *about it*. **2.** (Often *S*~) organized political community with government recognized by the people, commonwealth, nation; such community forming part of federal republic, esp. *the United S~s* (*of America*). **3.** pl. Legislative body in Jersey, Guernsey, and Alderney. **4.** Civil government, as *Church & S*~. **5.** Rank, dignity, as *in a style befitting his* ~. **6.** Pomp, as *arrived in great* ~; *keep* ~, maintain one's dignity, be difficult of access; *in* ~ (with all due ceremony). **7.** (arch.). Throne (also *chair of* ~), dais, canopy over throne. **8.** (Of dead person) *lie in* ~, be placed on view in public place. **9.** (bibliog.). One of two or more differing portions of a single edition of a book. **10.** (Impression taken from) an etched or engraved plate at a particular stage of its progress. **11.** **Free, slave, S*~, *S*~ in which slavery did not, did, exist; *Southern S~s* (in southern part of U.S.); *S~s of the Church, Papal S~s*, former temporal dominions of Pope chiefly in central Italy; *S~s General*, legislative bodies of (1) the Netherlands (2) France before 1789; ~*'craft*, art of conducting affairs of *S*~. Hence ~*'HOOD* (-ăt'h-) n. **12.** adj. Of, for, concerned with, the S~, as ~ *criminal*, political offender; ~ *documents, service*; ~ *prisoner*, person under arrest for felony, also political prisoner; ~ *trial*, prosecution by *S*~ esp. for political offence; **S*~ *Department* (of foreign affairs); **S*~ *rights*, rights & powers not assumed by United *S*~s but reserved to individual S~s; *S*~ *socialism, socialist*, policy, advocate, of S~ control of manufactures, railways, etc. for the benefit of the masses. **13.** Reserved for, done on, occasions of ceremony, as ~ *apartments, carriage*; ~ *call* (colloq.), formal visit; ~ *room*, room so reserved, also, private sleeping-apartment on steamer. [ME; partly var. of ESTATE, partly dir. f. L STATUS]

state[2], v.t. Express, esp. fully or clearly, in speech or writing, as *have* ~*d my opinion, must* ~ *full particulars, this condition was expressly* ~*d, no precise time was* ~*d, did not* ~ *why*, ~*s that arrangements are complete*; fix, specify, (date etc.), as *at* ~*d intervals*, whence **stat'edly**[2] adv.; (alg.) express the conditions of (problem, relation, etc.) in symbols. Hence **stat'able** a. [f. prec.]

state'ly (-tl-), a. (Of manner, language,

person, literary style, rhythm, building, proportions, etc.) dignified, imposing, grand. Hence~INESS n. [ME, f. STATE¹ + -LY¹]

state′ment (-tm-), n. Stating, expression in words, as *requires clearer* ~; thing stated, as *the* ~ *is unfounded*; formal account of facts, e.g. of liabilities & assets, as *the Bank issues monthly* ~*s*. [-MENT]

stat′er, n. Ancient Greek coin of various values, esp. gold coin worth 20 drachmae. [LL, f. Gk *statēr*]

states′man (-ts-), n. Person taking prominent part, person skilled, in management of State affairs; sagacious far-sighted practical politician; ‖ (north.) small working landowner; *the Elder Statesmen*, the Japanese statesmen who mainly directed the evolution of Japan between the re-establishment of the Mikado (1868) & the end of the 19th c., also transf. Hence ~LIKE, ~LY¹, aa., ~SHIP(3) n. [= *state's man*]

stat′ic(al), a. Concerned with bodies at rest or forces in equilibrium, whence **stat′ics** n. pl. (or as sing.), also = atmospherics; acting as weight but not moving, as ~ *pressure*; ~ *electricity* (at rest); *static ataxia*, inability to stand without falling or swaying; *static water*, local supply not under pressure. Hence **stat′ically²** adv. [f. Gk *statikos* (sta- stand, see -IC & -AL)]

sta′tion, n., & v.t. 1. Standing, being still, (opp. *motion*; now rare; *a* ~ *like the herald Mercury*). 2. Place, building, etc., in which person or thing stands or is placed esp. habitually or for definite purpose, as *was assigned a* ~ *in the valley, returned to their several* ~*s*, *took up a convenient* ~, *coastguard* ~ (occupied by coastguardsmen), POLICE ~, ‖ *lifeboat* ~ (where lifeboat is kept); *naval* ~, place affording shelter or harbour for ships with dockyard etc.; (pl., nav.) posts assigned to members of ship's complement in readiness for battle. 3. Subordinate depot or office serving local needs. 4. Stopping--place on railway with buildings for accommodation of passengers & goods or ‖ (*goods*-~) of goods only. 5. Position in life, (high) rank, status, employment, as *occupied a humble* ~, *men of* (*exalted*) ~, *the duties of his* ~. 6. (surv.). Point from which measurements are made, standard distance usu. 100 or 66 ft. 7. Military post esp. in India, officers or society residing there. 8. (Austral.). Sheep-run or its building. 9. (eccl.). Fast on Wed. & Frid. (hist.); (also ~ *of the cross*) each of series of 14 images or pictures representing Christ's passion before which devotions are performed in some churches; church esp. in Rome to which pilgrims etc. go for devotions. 10. (bot., zool.). Nature of the habitat of plant or animal in respect of climate, soil, etc. 11. ~-*bill* (naut.), list of appointed posts of ship's

company; ‖ ~-*calendar*, board showing successively the starting-time of trains at each platform; ~-*house*, police-station; ‖ ~-*master*, official in charge of railway-~; ~-*pointer*, three-armed ′protractor for locating place on chart from certain data; ~-*wagon*, = ESTATE *car*. 12. v.t. Assign ~ to, place (person, *oneself*) in ~. [ME, f. OF f. L *stationem* (*stare* stand, -ATION)]

sta′tionary (-sho-), a. & n. 1. Remaining in one place, not moving, as *balloon was now* ~; not meant to be moved, not portable, as ~ *engine, troops*; (of planet) having no apparent motion in longitude; not changing in magnitude, number, quality, efficiency, etc., as ~ *temperature, population, intelligence*; ~ *air* (remaining in lungs during ordinary respiration); ~ *diseases*, local diseases due to atmospheric conditions & disappearing after a period. 2. n. ~ person, esp. (pl.) ~ troops. Hence **sta′tionariness** (-sho-) n. [ME, f. L *stationarius* (as prec., see -ARY¹)]

sta′tioner (-sho-), n. One who sells writing-materials etc.; ‖ *S*~*s' Hall* (of S~s' Company in London, at which book was formerly *entered*, i.e. registered, for purposes of copyright). ·Hence **sta′tionery** (1) (-sho-) n. [ME = bookseller (as prec. in med. L sense *shopkeeper* (esp. *bookseller*) as opp. pedlar)]

stat′ist, n. Dealer in statistics. [16th c.= politician, f. L *status* STATE¹ + -IST]

statis′tics, n. pl. Numerical facts systematically collected, as ~*ics of population, crime*; (treated as sing.) science of collecting, classifying, & using ~ics. So ~IC(AL) aa., ~**ically²** adv., **statisti′cian** (-Ishn), **statistol′ogy**, nn. [f. G *statistik* n., -*isch* adj., f. mod. L *statisticus* f. **statista* STATIST]

stat′or, n. (electr.). Stationary portion of a generator or motor; ~ *armature* (non--rotating). [mod. L, f. *stare* stand + -OR]

stat′oscope, n. Aneroid barometer for showing minute variations of pressure. [f. Gk *statos* fixed (sta- stand) + -SCOPE]

stat′uary, a. & n. 1. Of or for statues, as ~ *art*, ~ *marble* (fine-grained white). 2. n. Sculptor; (art of making) statues. [f. L *statuarius* (as foll., see -ARY¹)]

stat′ue, n. Sculptured or cast or moulded figure of person or animal (esp. one not much below life size, opp. to ~ETTE′ n.); EQUESTRIAN ~*e*. Hence ~ED² (-ūd) a. [ME, f. OF, f. L *statua* (*stare* stand)]

statuesque′ (-k), a. Like, having the dignity or beauty of, a statue. Hence ~LY² (-kl-) adv., ~NESS (-kn-) n. [-ESQUE]

stat′ure (-yer), n. Height of (esp. human) body, as *increased in* ~*e*, *of mean* ~*e*; (fig.) stage of advancement. Hence (-)~ED² (-yerd) a. [ME, f. OF, f. L *statura* (*stare* stat- stand, see -URE)]

stat′us, n. (pl. prob. not used). Social position, rank, relation to others, relative importance, (*his* ~ *is a matter of* doubt, *their* ~ *is wholly different, his* ~ *among* *novelists*; ~ *symbol*, possession etc. denoting person's ~); (law) person's relation to others as fixed by law; position of affairs, esp. ~ (*in*) *quo*; unchanged position (cf. IN[5] *statu quo*) or (also ~ *quo ante*) the previous position. [L, gen. *-ūs*, = standing (*stare* stand)]

stat'ūtab|le, a. = STATUTORY. Hence~LY[2] adv. [-ABLE]

stat'ūte, n. A written law of a legislative body, e.g. Act of Parliament; *S~ of Westminster* (in 1931, conferring equality of status on the self-governing British Dominions); ~ *law*, a ~, (collect.) the ~s (opp. to CASE[1] *law* and COMMON[1] *law*); ordinance of corporation, founder, etc., intended to be permanent, as *University ~s*; (bibl.) divine law, as *kept thy ~s*; *declaratory* ~ (fixing interpretation of existing law); *private* ~ (affecting individuals, opp. to *general, public*, ~); ~*-book*, book(s) containing the ~ *law*; ~*-roll*, engrossed ~, ~*-book*; ~*s at large* (in full as originally enacted). [ME, f. OF *statut* f. LL *statutum* neut. p.p. as n. of L *statuere* set up (*stare* stand)]

stat'ūtory, a. Enacted, required, imposed, by statute, as ~ *provisions, minimum*. [-ORY]

staunch[1], stanch, (-aw-, -ah-), a. Trustworthy, loyal, as ~ *friend, supporter*; (of ship, joint, etc.) watertight, airtight. Hence ~LY[2] adv., ~'NESS n. [ME, f. OF *estanche* fem. of *estanc* f. *estanchier* STANCH[1]]

staunch[2]. See STANCH[1].

staur'oscōpe, n. Instrument for examining effects of polarized light on crystals. [f. Gk *stauros* cross + -SCOPE]

stāve[1], n. Each of the curved pieces of wood forming sides of cask etc.; each of the boards forming curb of well or hollow cylinder; rung of ladder; stanza, verse; (mus.) = ʹSTAFF; ~*-rhyme*, alliteration esp. in old Teut. poetry. [var. of STAFF, due to pl. *staves*]

stāve[2], v.t. (*stōve* or ~*d*). Break a hole in (cask, boat; often *in* adv.); (usu. ~ *in*) crush or bash (hat, box) out of shape; furnish, fit, (cask etc.) with staves; ~ *off*, avert, ward off, defer, (ruin, exposure, etc.); make (metal etc.) firm by compression. [f. prec.]

stāves'acre (-vzăker), n. Kind of larkspur whose seeds are used as poison for vermin. [back form. f. *staves* pl. of STAFF[1]]

stay[1], v.t. & i., & n. 1. (Now chiefly literary) check, stop, (progress, inroads of disease etc.). 2. ~ one's *stomach*, appease hunger esp. temporarily. 3. Postpone (judgement, decision). 4. Support, prop (often *up*) as or with buttress etc. 5. Remain, as ~ *here till I return, will not ~ where it is put* (also, *will not ~ put*), *has come to ~* (colloq.), must be regarded as permanent; (w. adv.) ~ *away, on, out*, etc.; ~*-in strike*, (of miners) ~*-down strike*, = SIT-*down strike*; (colloq.) wait long en-

ough to partake of (*can you ~ to supper?*); dwell temporarily (*at* hotel etc., *in* town etc., *with* person). 6. Pause in movement, action, speech (esp. in imperat.), etc., as *get him to ~ a minute, ~!—you forget one thing*. 7. Show endurance esp. in race, as *does not seem able to ~*, whence ~'ER[1] n. . 8. ~*-at-home* a. & n., (person) remaining habitually at home. 9. n. Remaining, esp. dwelling, in a place, duration of this, as *made a long ~ in London, your ~ has been very short*. 10. Suspension of judicial proceedings (esp. ~ *of execution*, i.e. of carrying out judgement given). 11. (Chiefly literary) check, restraint, (*will endure no ~, a ~ upon his activity*). 12. Endurance, ~ing-power. 13. Prop, support, (*you have been the ~ of my old age*). 14. pl. Corset, whence ~[L] LESS a. 15. ~*-bar, -rod*, support in building or machinery; ~*-lace, -maker* (of corsets). [senses *remain, endure*: n. prob. f. vb f. OF *ester* f. L *stare* stand; sense *support* (4, 13–15) ult. f. OF *estaye(r)* prop, prob. = naut. vb *estayer* f. Gmc (foll.)]

stay[2], n., & v.t. (naut.). 1. Rope supporting mast or spar; *ship is* (*hove*) *in ~s* (going about from one tack to another); *miss ~s*, fail in endeavour to tack; ~*'sail* (-sāl, *naut.* -sl), any sail extended on ~. 2. v.t. Support (mast etc.) by ~s; put (ship) on other tack. [vb f. n., OE *stæg*, LG (G), ON *stag*, f. Gmc *stag-, *stah-* be firm, cf. STEEL]

stead (stĕd), n. (now chiefly literary). *Stand* (person) *in good ~*, be advantageous or serviceable to; *in* person's ~, instead of him, as his substitute. [OE *stede*, OS *stedi*, OHG *stat*, ON *stathr*, Goth. *staths* f. Gmc *stadhiz* f. *sta-* STAND]

stead'fast (stĕd-), a. Constant, firm, unwavering. Hence ~LY[2] adv., ~NESS n. [OE *stedefæst* (prec., FAST[3])]

|| **stea'ding** (stĕd-), n. Farmstead. [-ING[1]]

stea'dy (stĕd-), a., n., & v.t. & i. 1. Firmly fixed or supported or standing or balanced, not tottering, as *not ~ on his legs, must level table's legs to make it ~*, ~ *as a rock, has not acquired a ~ seat on bicycle*; done, moving, acting, happening, in uniform & regular manner, as *went off at a ~ pace, had a ~ wind behind us, requires a ~ light, observe a ~ increase in the numbers*; (as command or warning) ~*!*, be ~, abstain from erratic or boisterous behaviour, premature action, hasty inference, etc., (naut., also *keep her ~*) keep direction of ship's head unchanged; ~ *on!*, stop!; constant in mind or conduct, not changeable, as ~ *in his principles, allegiance*; of industrious & temperate habits. 2. n. Kinds of support for hand or tool; *(colloq.) regular sweetheart. Hence stea'dILY[2] adv., stea'diNESS n., (stĕd-). 3. vb. Make, become, ~, as ~ *the boat, boat steadied, adversity will ~ him, he will soon ~* (down). [STEAD + -Y[2]]

steak (stāk), n. Slice of beef, pork, venison, or fish, cut for broiling etc., as *beef*~, RUMP-, PORTER²-*house*, ~, *fillet* ~ (from undercut of sirloin); *Hamburg* ~, cake of chopped & seasoned beef cooked in covered frying-pan. [ME, f. ON *steik*, cogn. w. *sleikja* roast on spit]

steal, v.t. & i. (*stōle, stōlen*). **1.** Take away (thing, or abs.) secretly for one's own use without right or leave, take feloniously, as *who* ~*s my purse* ~*s trash, stolen fruit*; obtain surreptitiously or by surprise, as *stole a kiss, a stolen interview*; ~ *one's* THUNDER; (also ~ *away*) win, get possession of, (esp. person's *heart*) by insidious arts, attractions, etc.; ~ *a march on*, get the start of, anticipate. **2.** intr. Move (*in, out, away, up, by*, etc.) secretly or silently, as *stole out of the room, mist stole over the valley*. Hence (·)~ER¹ n. [OE *stëam* = WFris. *steam*, Du. *stoom* f. Gmc *staumaz*]

stealth (stĕl-), n. Secrecy, secret procedure, esp. *by*~, surreptitiously. Hence ~'ILY² adv., ~'INESS n., ~'Y² a. [ME; -TH¹]

steam¹, n. **1.** Vapour of water, esp. the gas into which water is changed by boiling, largely used as motive power owing to its elasticity; *saturated* ~ (in contact with, & at same temperature as, boiling water); *superheated* ~ (having higher temperature at given pressure, & greater volume for a given weight, than saturated ~); *wet, dry*, ~ (containing, not containing, mechanically suspended particles of water); visible particles of water resulting from condensation of ~; any vaporous exhalation. **2.** (colloq.). Energy, as *get up* ~, summon energy for special effort, so *put on, let off, work off*, ~. **3.** ~'*boat*, vessel propelled by ~; ~·*boiler*, vessel in which water is boiled to generate ~ esp. for working engine; ~·*box, -chest* (through which ~ passes from boiler to cylinder); ~ *brake, crane, gun, hammer, plough, whistle, winch*, etc. (worked by ~); ~·*coal* (used in heating ~·boilers); ~·*colour* (fixed on printed cloth by action of ~); ~·*cylinder* (in which piston of ~·engine moves); ~·*engine*, locomotive or stationary engine in which the motive power depends on elasticity & expansion or rapid condensation of ~; ~·*gas*, superheated ~; ~·*gauge* (attached to boiler to show pressure of ~); ~·*heat*, heat required to produce ~ from water at freezing-point, also, heat given out by ~ from radiators etc.; ~·*jacket*, casing round cylinder etc. with space between to be filled by ~ for heating the cylinder etc.; ‖ ~ *navvy*, excavating machine; ~·*port*, each of two oblong passages from ~·chest into cylinder, any passage for ~; ~·*power*, force of ~ applied to machinery etc.; ~ *radio* (sl.), sound radio; ~·*roller*, heavy slow-moving locomotive with wide wheels used in road-·making, (fig.) a crushing power or force

(v.t., crush as with a ~·roller); ~·*ship* (propelled by ~); ~·*tight*, capable of resisting passage of ~; ~ *tug*, steamer for towing ships etc.; ~ *turbine* (in which a high-velocity jet of ~ rotates a bladed disc or drum). Hence ~'INESS n., ~'Y² a. [OE *stëam* = WFris. *steam*, Du. *stoom* f. Gmc *staumaz*]

steam², v.t. & i. Cook (food) by steam; treat with steam, soften (timber) for bending by steam; give out steam or vapour, as *a sirloin* ~*ed on the table, water* ~*ing hot*; rise in vapour; move by agency of steam, as *we, the vessel,* ~*ed down the river*; (colloq.) work vigorously, make great progress, esp. ~ *ahead, away*. [OE *stěman, stýman* rel. to prec.]

steam'er, n. In vbl senses; also or esp.: vessel propelled by steam; vessel in which things are steamed, esp. cooked by steam; *boiler is a bad* ~ (generator of steam). [-ER¹]

stē'arin, n. Chief ingredient of suet & tallow; (pop.) stearic acid separated from ~ by steam & used for candles. Hence **stē'araTE¹**(3) n., **stēâ'ric** a. [f. F *stéarine* f. Gk *stear* stiff fat +-IN]

stē'atite, n. Kind of talc, soapstone. Hence **stēatit'ic** a. [f. L *steatites* (f. Gk as foll., -ITE¹)]

stēat(ō)-, comb. form of Gk *stear* -*atos* fat, as: ~*ōpy'gia* n., excessive development of fat on the buttocks, esp. of women [Gk *pȳgē* buttock], ~*ōpy'gous* (or ·ōp'ĭgus) a.; ~*ōs'ĭs*, fatty degeneration.

steed, n. (poet., rhet., or joc.). Horse, esp. war-horse. Hence ~'LESS a. [OE *stēda* stallion cogn. w. *stōd* STUD²]

steel, n., & v.t. **1.** Kinds of malleable alloy of iron & carbon largely used as material for tools, weapons, etc., & capable of being tempered to many different degrees of hardness (often attrib., as ~ *pen*), whence ~'IFY v.t.; BESSEMER ~; *cold* ~, sword etc. as opp. to fire-arm; *a grip, muscles, a heart, of* ~ (very tight, strong, hard); *rod of* ~, usu. tapering & roughened, for sharpening knives; *strip of* ~ for stiffening corset or expanding skirt; (poet., rhet., not in pl.) sword (*a foe worthy of one's* ~). **2.**~ *cap*, simple form of helmet; ~·*clad*, clad in armour; ~ *engraving*, engraving on, impression taken from, ~ plate; ~ *wool*, fine shavings of ~ massed together, used esp. for cleaning pots and pans; ~'*work*, ~ articles, ~ for these. **3.** v.t. Harden (one*self*, one's *heart*, etc., *to do, to* action, *against* compassion etc.). [OE *stýle*, OS *stehli*, also OHG *stahal*, ON *stál*, ult. f. Gmc *stahla*- f. *stah*-, *stag*- be rigid, see STAY²]

steel'|y, a. Of, hard as, steel; inflexibly severe, as ~*y glance, composure*. Hence ~INESS n. [·Y²]

steel'yard, n. Kind of balance with short arm to take the thing weighed & long graduated arm along which a weight is moved till it balances this. [f. STEEL + YARD[1], prob. suggested by the *steelyard beam* or public scales at the Hanseatic ' steelyard ' (mistranslation of MLG *stâlhof* = sample-house) in London]

steen′bŏk (stän-, stēn-), n. Kinds of small African antelope. [Du., lit. stone buck]

steen′ing, n. Stone lining of well. [f. (now dial.) *steen* (OE *stǣnan* to STONE) + -ING[1]]

steen′kĭrk, n. (hist.). Cravat, other articles of dress etc., named in allusion to Battle of *Steenkerke* in Belgium 1692.

steep[1], a. & n. 1. Having decided slope, sheer, as ~ *hills*; (colloq., of demand, price, etc.) exorbitant, unreasonable, as *seems a bit* ~ *that we should have both the trouble & the expense*, (of story etc.) exaggerated, incredible. 2. n. ~ slope, precipice. Hence ~′EN[2] v.i. & t., ~′LY[2] adv., ~′NESS n., ~′Y[2] (poet.) a. [OE *stēap* adj. f. Gmc *staupaz*- cogn. w. STOOP[1]]

steep[2], v.t., & n. 1. Soak in liquid; bathe with liquid; ~ *in* (fig.), impregnate with, pervade with, as ~*ed in Greek & Latin, misery, slumber*. 2. n. Process of ~ing (esp. *in* ~), liquid in which thing is ~ed. [ME *stepe, stipa*, repr. OE **stiepan, stēpan* f. *stēap* STOUP[1]]

steep′er, n. Vessel in which things are steeped. [-ER[1]]

stee′ple, n. Lofty structure, esp. tower surmounted with spire, rising above roof of church; ~*chase*, horse-race (perh. orig. with ~ as goal) across tract of country with ditches, hedges, etc., to jump, (also) cross-country foot-race; ~*chaser*, rider in ~chase, horse trained for ~chase; ~*chasing*, the sport of riding in ~chases; ~*-crowned hat* (with tall pointed crown); ~*jack*, man who climbs ~s etc. to do repairs etc.; ~*-top*, polar whale with spout-holes ending in cone. Hence **stee′plĕD[2]** (-ld) a., ~WISE adv. [OE *stēpel & stȳpel* (as STEEP), see -LE(1)]

steer[1], v.t. & i. Guide (vessel) by rudder or helm, guide vessel in specified direction, (~*ing-wheel*, vertical wheel with handles along rim for controlling rudder, wheel for controlling front wheels of motor-car); guide (motor, aircraft, etc.) by wheel etc.; (chiefly colloq. or poet.) direct (one's course), direct one's course, in specified direction, as ~*ed his flight heavenwards, we* ~*ed (our course) for the railway station*, ~ *clear of* (avoid) *the local meteorologist*; ~*s′man*, one who ~s vessel, ~*s′manship*, skill in ~ing. Hence ~′ABLE a., ~′ER[1] (1, 2) n., ~′ING[1] n. (~*ing committee*, one that decides in what order items of business are to be dealt with). [OE *stieran*, OHG *stiuren*, ON *stýra* f. Gmc **steurjan* f. **steurō* (OE *stēor*) rudder]

steer[2], n. Young male of ox kind, esp. castrated bullock raised for beef. [OE *stēor*, OHG *stior*, Goth. *stiur*, f. Gmc **steuraz*]

steer′age, n. (Now rare) steering; (naut.)

effect of helm on ship, as *ship went with easy* ~; part of ship allotted to ~ *passengers* (travelling at cheapest rate), variously placed; (hist.; in warship) part of berth-deck just forward of wardroom, quarters of junior officers, clerks, etc.; ~*-way*, amount of headway required by vessel to enable her to be controlled by helm. [ME ;-AGE]

steeve[1], v.i. & t., & n. (naut.). 1. (Of bowsprit) make angle with horizon; cause (bowsprit) to do this. 2. n. Such angle. [orig. unkn.]

steeve[2], n., & v.t. (naut.). 1. Long spar used in stowing cargo. 2. v.t. Stow with this. [ME, f. OF *estiver* or Sp. *estivar* f. L *stipare* pack tight; cf. STEVEDORE]

stein (stīn), n. Beer mug. [G, = stone]

Stein′berger (stīn-, -ger), n. White wine grown on Rhine near Wiesbaden.

stein′bŏck (stīn-), n. A wild goat, the Alpine ibex. [G, = stone buck]

stĕl′ē, n. (Gk archaeol.; pl. -*ae*). Upright slab or pillar usu. with inscription & sculpture, esp. as gravestone. [Gk]

stĕll′|ar, a. Of stars. So ~IF′EROUS, ~I-FORM, aa. [f. LL *stellaris* (*stella* star, see -AR[1])]

stĕll′ate, -ātĕd, aa. Arranged like a star, radiating, esp. (bot.) ~ *leaves* (surrounding stem in a whorl). Hence **stĕll′ateLY** adv. [f. L *stellatus* (*stella* star, -ATE[2])]

|| **stĕll′enbŏsch** (-sh), v.t. (hist.; mil. sl.). Supersede without formal disgrace by appointing to unimportant command. [f. *S*~ in S. Africa, military base so utilized]

stĕll′ūl|ar, a. Shaped like, set with, small stars. So ~ATE[2] a. [f. LL *stellula* dim. of *stella* star + -AR[1]]

stĕm[1], n., & v.t. & i. (-mm-). 1. Main body or stalk (usu. rising into light & air but occas. subterranean) of tree, shrub, or plant; slender stalk supporting fruit, flower, or leaf, & attaching it to main stalk or branch or twig. 2. ~*-shaped* part, e.g. slender part of wineglass between body & foot, vertical line rising or falling from head of note in music, various winding-parts of watch (~*-winder*, watch wound by turning head on end of ~, not by key), tubular part of tobacco-pipe. 3. Part of noun, verb, etc. (derived from & occas. identified with a root) to which case-endings etc. are added, part that appears or would originally appear unchanged throughout the case of a noun, persons of a tense, etc. 4. Line of ancestry, branch of family, as *descended from an ancient, a collateral*, ~. 5. Curved timber or metal piece to which ship's sides are joined at fore end, piece joined to & forming upright continuation of keel at fore end, as *from* ~ *to stern*, from end to end; *false* ~, sharp-edged piece in front of ~ serving as cutwater. 6. vb. Remove ~ of (esp. tobacco, whence ~m′ER[1](1) n,); *spring from*, originate *in*. Hence

~'LESS, (-)~MED² (-md), aa., ~'LET n. [OE *stemn*, *stefn* f. Gmc *stamniz*, cogn.w. OHG *stam*, ON *stamn*, *stafn*; f. root STA-STAND]

stĕm², v.t. (-mm-). Check, dam up, (stream etc., lit. & fig.); make headway against (tide, current, etc., lit. & fig.). [(1) *check*: f. ON *stemma* (= OHG, G *stemmen*) f. Gmc *stamjan* f. *stam*-, cf. STAMMER; (2) *make headway* f. STEM¹(5)]

stĕmm'a, n. (pl. ~ta). Family tree, pedigree; lineal descent; (zool.) simple eye, facet of compound eye. [L, f. Gk *stemma* wreath (*stephō* wreathe)]

stĕm'ple, n. Each of several cross-bars in shaft of mine serving as supports or steps. [orig. obsc.; cf. MHG *stempfel*, (G) *stempel* in similar sense]

Stĕn (gŭn), n. A light-weight machine--gun. [f. *S* and *T* (initials of inventors' surnames, Shepherd and Turpin) + *-en* after BREN)]

stĕnch, n. Offensive smell; ~-*trap* (in sewer etc., to prevent upward passage of gas). [OE *stenc* (any) smell, = OS *stanc*, OHG *stanch*, f. Gmc *stankw-* var. of *stinkw-* STINK]

stĕn'cil, n., & v.t. (-ll-). 1. (Also ~-*plate*) thin plate of metal etc. in which pattern (interrupted when necessary by a thin bar of the material left to prevent piece from falling out) is cut out; decoration, lettering, etc., produced by ~. 2. v.t. Produce (pattern) on surface, ornament (surface) with pattern, by brushing paint etc. over a ~-plate laid on the surface. Hence ~lER¹ n. [f. OF *estanceler* sparkle, cover with stars, f. *estencele* f. Rom. *stincilla*, see TINSEL]

stĕno-, comb. form of Gk *stenos* narrow, chiefly in scientific wds.

stĕnŏch'romy (-k-), n. Art of printing in several colours at one impression. [f. STENO- + Gk *khrōma* colour +-Y¹]

stĕn'ograph (-ahf), n. Character used, piece of writing, in shorthand; kinds of machine for writing in shorthand. So stĕnŏg'raphER¹, stĕnŏg'raph-IST, stĕnŏg'raphY¹, nn., ,stĕnŏgrăph'IC a., stĕnŏgrăph'ICALLY adv. [STENO- + -GRAPH]

Stĕn'tŏr, n. Person with powerful voice. Hence stĕntŏr'IAN a. [L f. Gk *Stentōr*, herald in Trojan war]

stĕp¹, v.i. & t. (-pp-). 1. Shift & set down foot or alternate feet (~ *out*, *short*, take long, short, steps; ~ *through a dance*, perform its steps; ~ *high*, lift feet high esp. of trotting horse, so HIGH-*stepp'er*); go short distance or progress in some direction by ~ping (~ *back*, *forward*, *across the road*, *into the boat*; ~ *this way*, polite formula for *come here*; ~ *in*, *out*, enter, leave, room or house; ~ *in*, fig., intervene to help or hinder; ~ *up*, *down*; ~ *aside*, lit., & fig. = make digression; ~ *on the* GAS; hence ~ *on it* (sl.), hurry. 2. Perform (dance; also ~ *it*, dance),

measure (distance), by ~ping. 3. (naut., prob. f. n.). Set up (mast) in step. 4. ~'*in* n. & a., (garment, esp. woman's undergarment) put on by being ~ped into; ~*ping-stone*, raised usu. as one of set in stream or muddy place to enable passengers to cross dryshod, (fig.) means to an end; ~ *up* (trans.), increase the rate, volume, etc. of, (electr.) increase voltage of (current) by transformer. [OE *stæppan*, *steppan* = OHG *stepfen* f. Gmc *stapjan* f. *stap-* (foll.)]

stĕp², n. 1. Complete movement of one leg in walking or running or dancing, distance gained by it, mark left by foot on ground, sound made by setting foot down, manner of stepping as seen or heard, simultaneous stepping with corresponding legs by two or more persons or animals, (fig.) measure taken esp. as one of a series in some course of action, (*took* a ~ *back* or *forward*; ~ *by* ~, gradually, cautiously, by degrees; *that is a long* ~ *towards success*; *it is but a* ~ *to my house*, *from life to death*, exagg. for short distance or quick transition; *do not move a* ~; *turn* one's ~s, go in a specified direction; *found his* ~s *or* usu. *foot*~s *in the soil*; *in his* etc.. ~s, following his etc. example; *do you hear a*, *know her*, ~?; *walks with a rapid*~; *one*~, *two*~, dance names; *in*, *out of*, ~, stepping, not stepping, in time with others or with drum-beat etc.; *keep*, *break*, ~, keep in, get out of, ~; *keep* ~ *with* person, *to* band etc.; FALSE ~; *must take* ~s *in the matter*, *to prevent it*, etc.; *a rash*, *ill-advised*, *prudent*, etc., ~; *mind*, *watch*, *your* ~, be careful). 2. Surface provided or utilized for placing foot on in ascending or descending, e.g. tread or riser & tread of staircase, block of stone or other platform before door or altar etc., rung of ladder, notch cut for foot in ice climbing, attached piece of vehicle for stepping up or down by, (pl., also ~-*ladder* or *pair* or *set of* ~s) kind of short ladder with flat ~s & prop used without being leant against wall etc., (fig.) one of the degrees in some scale of precedence or advancement, advance from one of these to another, (*staircase of 50* ~s; *stone*, *oak*, ~s; *door*, *altar*, ~; *on the top* ~ *of the ladder*; *run down the* ~s; *cutting* ~s *with his ice-axe*; *when did you get your* ~?, promotion esp. in army; *give him a* ~ *in the peerage*). 3. (Naut.) socket or platform supporting mast; (carpentry) piece of timber with another fixed upright in it; (mech.) lower socket or bearing for shaft. 4. ~-*dance*, in which the ~s are peculiar or difficult or of more importance than the figure, usu. danced as display by one performer. Hence ~pED² (-pt) a., ~'WISE adv. [OE *stæpe*, *stepe* f. *stapiz* f. Gmc *stap-*]

stĕp-, pref., = holding nominal relationship analogous to that specified owing to death of one and remarriage of the other of a married pair; ~'*child*, ~'*son*, ~'*daughter*, one's wife's or husband's child by previous marriage; ~'*father*, ~ *mother*, ~'*parent*, one's parent's later husband or wife; ~'*mother* or arch. ~ *dame*, harsh or neglectful mother lit. or fig., whence ~'*mother*LY[1] a.; ~'*brother*, ~'*sister*, child of previous marriage of one's ~parent. [OE *steop-*, = OHG *stiof-*, ON *stjúp-* f. Gmc *steupo-*]

stĕphanŏt′is, n. Climbing hothouse plant with fragrant waxy flowers. [Gk fem. adj. = fit for a wreath (*stephanos*)]

stĕp′ney, n. (hist.; pl. ~*s*). Spare spokeless wheel formerly carried by motorists. [said to be from *S*~ Street, Llanelly, where made]

stĕppe, n. Level plain devoid of forest esp. in Russia & Siberia. [f. Russ. *stepi*]

-ster, suf. forming agent nn.; OE *-estre*, cf. Du. & Fris. *-ster*. In OE the suf. was orig. confined to the fem., but this restriction appears in mod. E only in *spinster*. Exx.: *brew~*, *huck~* (which however seems to have existed before the obs. vb *huck*), *game~*, *malt~*, *pun~*, & perh. *hol~*, *bol~*. In *seamstress* -ESS[1] is added to *-ster*; *-ster* in *lobster* is of different orig., but perh. assimilated.

stẽrcorā′ceous (-shŭs), **stẽrc′oral**, aa. Of ordure or faeces. [L *stercus -oris* dung, -ACEOUS, -AL]

stēre, n. A cubic metre (about 35·3 cu. ft). [F (*-ère*), f. Gk *stereos* solid]

stĕ′rĕō, n. & a. (colloq.; pl. ~*s*). Stereotype (often attrib., as ~ *plate*); stereoscope; (adj.) stereoscopic. [shortening]

stĕ′rĕo- (or stĕr⁴-), comb. form of Gk *stereos* solid, stiff: ~*bate*, solid platform on which a building is erected; ~*chem′istry*, branch dealing with composition of matter as affected by relations of atoms in space; ~*gram*, ~*graph*, (one of) a pair of photographs for use in a ~scope; ~*phŏn′ic* a., (of sound reproduced) giving the effect of coming from more than one direction; ~*scope*, instrument for viewing pair of photographs of scene, object, etc. taken at slightly different angles, each with one eye, thus producing by the combination of these images an impression of depth & solidity, so ~*scŏp′ic*(ALLY), ~*scopy*[1] (-ŏs²).

stĕ′rĕotȳp|e (or stĕr⁴-), n., & v.t. **1.** Printing-plate cast from a papier-mâché or other mould of a piece of printing composed in movable type; making, use, of such plates; (fig.) fixed mental impression; ~*e-block*, on which ~e is mounted for use; hence ~IST(1), ~Y[1], ~ŏG′RAPHY, nn. **2.** v.t. Make ~es of; print by use of ~es; (fig.) make unchangeable, impart monotonous regularity to, fix in all details, formalize; hence ~ER[1] n. [f. F *stéréotype* a. (prec., TYPE)]

stĕ′ril|e, a. Unfruitful, unproductive, barren, not producing crop or fruit or young or complete seed or result (~*e land, cow, plant, year, effort, discussion*);

free from living germs esp. bacilli or bacteria· or microbes (usu. ~*ized*); (of style) jejune, bald. Hence or cogn. ~IZE(3) (-II-) v.t., (esp.) render free from micro-organisms, render incapable of producing offspring, ~IZA′TION, ~IZER[1](2), steril′ITY, nn. [f. F *stérile* or L *sterilis*]

stĕr′lĕt, n. Kind of small sturgeon. [f. Russ. *sterlyadi*]

stĕr′ling, a. & n. **1.** (Of coins & precious metals) genuine, of standard value· or purity, (abbr. *stg*); with coins, chiefly appended to sum expressed in pounds without odd money, as *£20 stg*; *is of* ~ *gold, silver*); (transf.) of solid worth, not showy, that is what it seems to be, (*is a* ~ *fellow*; ~ *sense, qualities, character*; *the* ~ *nature of*). **2.** n. Genuine British money; British money as dist. from foreign money; ~ *area*, group of countries keeping their reserves in ~ and not in gold or dollars, and transferring money freely between each other. [of uncert. orig., but prob. a late OE formation in -LING[1], perh. **steorling* coin with a star (OE *steorra*), some of the early Norman pennies having on them a small star]

stĕrn[1], a. Severe, grim, rigid, strict, enforcing discipline or submission, not compassionate or indulgent or yielding, (~ *countenance, ruler, treatment, rebuke, virtue, father, tutor; made of* ~*er stuff;* ~*er* SEX). Hence ~′LY[2] adv., ~′NESS n. [OE *styrne*, f. Gmc *sternjaz*, repr. only in E]

stĕrn[2], n. **1.** Hind part of ship or boat (opp. *bow*, *stem*; *from stem to* ~, throughout ship; ~ *chase*, pursuit of ship by another straight behind it; ~ *foremost*, moving backwards; ~ *on*, with ~ presented; BY[1] *the* ~). **2.** Buttocks, rump; tail esp. of foxhound. **3.** ~*fast*, rope or chain securing ~ to quay etc.; ~*post*, central upright timber or iron of ~ usu. bearing rudder; ~ *sheets*, space in boat aft of rowers' thwarts often with seats for passengers [perh. f. SHEET in naut. sense *rope*]; ~*way*, backward motion or impetus of ship; ~*wheel′er*, steamer propelled by one large paddle-wheel at ~. Hence (-)~ED[2] (-nd), ~′MOST, aa., ~′WARD a. & adv., ~′WARDS (-z) adv. [prob. f. ON *stjórn* steering f. Gmc *steurjan* STEER[1]]

stĕrn|(o)-, comb. form of foll. esp. in names of muscles etc. connecting sternum with other part; ~*al′gia*, chest-pain, esp. angina pectoris; ~*oclavic′ular*, of sternum & clavicle; ~*ofa′cial*; ~*othyr′oid*.

stĕr′|um, n. (pl. ~*a*). Bone running from neck to stomach & having ribs articulated with it, the breastbone. Hence ~AL a. [mod. L, f. Gk *sternon* chest]

stĕrnūtā′tion, n. Sneezing, sneeze. [f. L *sternutatio* (*sternutare* frequent. of *sternuere* sneeze cf. Gk *ptarnumai*, -ATION)]

stĕrnūt′ative, a., **sternūt′atorȳ**, a. & n. (Substance, e.g. snuff) causing to sneeze. [L *sternutare* (prec.), -IVE, -ORY]

stĕrt′orous, a. (Of breathing or breather,

esp. in apoplexy etc.) making snorelike sounds. Hence ~LY² adv., ~NESS n. [L *stertere* snore, -OR, -OUS] .

stĕt, proof-correcting direction, & v.t. **1.** Let it (i.e. the original form) stand (in margin to cancel a correction). **2.** v.t. Write ~ against, cancel correction of. [L, 3 sing. subj. of *stare* stand]

stĕth'|oscŏpe, n., & v.t. **1.** Instrument used in auscultation esp. of the heart. **2.** v.t. Examine with ~oscope. Hence ~-**ŏs'copIST**, ~**ŏs'copY¹**, nn., ~**oscŏp'IO** a., ~**oscŏp'ICALLY** adv. [F (*sté-*), f. Gk *stēthos* breast, -SCOPE]

stĕt'son, n. Broad-brimmed slouch hat. [*S*~, maker's name]

stĕv'ĕdôre, n. Man employed in loading & unloading ships. [f. Sp. *estivador* f. *estivar* stow a cargo (L *stipare* see STEEVE²)]

stew¹, n. (arch.). Brothel (usu. *the* ~s). [ME; orig. bath-room or house (cf. BAGNIO), f. OF *estuve*, rel. to foll.]

stew², v.t. & i., & n. **1.** Cook (t. & i.) by long simmering in closed vessel with little liquid (*let* person, thing, ~ *in his* etc. *own juice* or *grease*, abstain from helping etc.; ~ING¹ *pears* etc., fit for eating ~ed, not raw; *the tea is* ~*ed*, is bitter or strong with too long soaking); (fig.) be oppressed by close or moist warm atmosphere, (sl.) = SWOT; ~*-pan*, *-pot*, shallow saucepan, covered crock, used for ~ing. **2.** n. Dish made by ~ing (*Irish* ~, of mutton, potato, & onion); (fig., colloq.) *in a* ~, agitated with perplexity, anxiety, or anger. [ME, f. OF *estuver*, rel. to prec.]

stew³, n. ‖ Fishpond, tank for keeping fish alive in; artificial oyster-bed. [ME, f. OF *estui* (*estuier* shut up)]

stew'ard, n. **1.** Person entrusted with management of another's property, esp. paid manager of great house or estate. **2.** Purveyor of provisions etc. for a college, club, guild, ship, etc. **3.** Passengers' attendant & waiter on ship or aircraft. **4.** Any of the officials managing a race-meeting, ball, show, etc. **5.** ‖ *Lord High S*~ *of England*, high officer of state; ‖ *Lord S*~ *of the Household*, high court officer. Hence ~ESS¹, ~SHIP, nn. [OE *stiweard* f. *stig* (prob.) house, hall, +*weard* WARD¹; cf. STY¹]

sthĕn'ic, a. (path.). (Of disease etc.) with morbid increase of vital action esp. of heart & arteries. [Gk *sthenos* strength +-IC, after *asthenic*]

stich'omȳth, **stichomȳth'ia**, (-k-), n. Dialogue in alternate lines of verse as employed in Greek plays. [f. Gk *stikho-muthia* (*stikhos* line, MYTH)]

stick, v.t. & i. (*stuck*), & n. **1.** Thrust point of *in(to)* or *through* (~ *the spurs in*; ~ *bayonet*, *pin*, *into* or *through*). **2.** Insert pointed thing(s) into, stab, (~ *pigs*, of butcher, also of mounted sportsman spearing wild pig; *will pull out a knife & ~ you*; *tipsy-cake stuck over* or *stuck with almonds*; *cushion stuck full of pins*). **3.** Fix

(*up*)*on* pointed thing, be fixed (as) by point *in(to)* or *on* (*to*), (colloq.) put in specified position, (*heads were stuck on spikes of gateway*; *arrows* ~ *in target*; *work with needle* ~*ing in it*; ~ *feather*, *rose*, *in cap*, *buttonhole*; ~ *pen behind* one's *ear*; ~ *up a target*, erect it; ~ *your cap on*; ~ *them in your pocket*; ~ *a few commas in*; *just* ~ *it on the table*, *down anywhere*). **4.** (With *out*, *up*) protrude, (cause to) project, be or make erect, (~ one's *head out of window*; *his hair* ~*s straight up*; ~*-up collar*, not turned down; ~ *out* one's *chest*; ~ one's *chin* (or *neck*) *out* (colloq.), ask for trouble, expose oneself to danger; *how his stomach* ~*s out!*; *this* ~*s out a mile*, sl., is very obvious; *stuck--up*, conceited, insolently exclusive, prob. f. carriage of head; ~ *up to*, not humble oneself before, offer resistance to; ~ *up for*, maintain cause or character of esp. absent person). **5.** Fix or become or remain fixed (as) by adhesion of surfaces, (cause to) adhere or cleave, (~ *postage--stamp on*; *this envelope will not* ~; *if you throw* MUD *enough*, *some of it will* ~, innocence is not proof against scandal; *limpet* ~*s to rock*; ~ *to the point*, not digress; ~ *to business*, avoid distractions; *the name stuck to him* or *stuck*, was not forgotten; *friend that* ~*eth closer than a brother*; *can you* ~ *on a horse?*, escape being thrown; *some of the money stuck in* or *to his fingers*, was appropriated or embezzled by him; *friends should* ~ *together*; ~ *to friend*, *resolve*, *promise*, *word*, etc., abide by, remain faithful to; ‖ ~ *bills*, post placards on wall etc., esp. ~ *no bills*, notice forbidding placarding of wall; ~ *to it*, persist, not cease trying; ~ *in photograph*̣, ̣paste them in book etc.; ~*s like a bur*, is not to be got rid of; *are you going to* ~ *in* or *indoors all day?*, remain at home; so perh. ~ *out for higher price*, *better terms*, etc., refuse to take lower). **6.** ~ *it out* or ~ *it* (sl.), endure the conditions (*could not* ~ *it any longer*). **7.** ~ *it on* (sl.), make high charges, exaggerate in narration. **8.** Lose or deprive of power of motion through friction, jamming, suction, difficulty, or other impediment (~ *in the mud* lit., & fig. be unprogressive; ~*-in-the-mud*, (adj.) slow, unprogressive, (n.) person of such kind; also sl. *Mrs* etc. *S*~*-in-the-mud*, Mrs. etc. So-&-so; ~*s in my throat*, I cannot swallow it lit. or fig.; ~*s in* one's *gizzard*, cannot be digested fig.; ~ *fast*, be hopelessly bogged etc.; *is stuck on a sandbank*; *got up to the fourth form*, *through some ten lines*, *& there stuck*; ~ *at nothing*, allow nothing, esp. no scruples, to deter one; ‖ *stuck up*, sl., completely at a loss; *that will* ~ *him up*, puzzle him; ~ *up bank*, *mail-van*, etc., sl., terrorize officials etc., in order to rob). **9.** Provide (plant) with ~ as support or to climb up. **10.** Set (type) in COMPOSING-~, whence ~'FUL(2) n.

11. ~*ing-place, -point,* at which screw becomes jammed (usu. fig. w. ref. to *Macbeth* I. vii. 60); ~*ing-plaster,* adhesive plaster for wounds etc.; ‖ ~*jaw* (sl.), toffy etc. hard to masticate. **12.** n. Shoot of tree cut to convenient length for use as walking-cane or bludgeon, staff, wand, rod, piece of wood whether as part of something or separate more or less resembling these in shape & size, (*cut a* ~ *from the hedge; cannot walk without a* ~; *gathering* ~*s to make a fire,* twigs; *any* ~ *to beat a dog,* hatred makes unscrupulous; BROOM, DRUM[1], FIDDLE, GOLD, *rocket,* SHOOTING, SINGLE[1], SWORD, *umbrella,* ~~; *riding on broom*~, witch's way of transporting herself through air; *house was pulled down & not a* ~ *left standing; a few* ~*s of furniture,* chairs etc. of simple kind; *wants the* ~, should be caned; *as* CROSS[3] *as,* DEVIL[1] *on, two* ~*s; in a cleft* ~, see CLEAVE[1]; CUT[2] *one's* ~); (naut., joc.) mast or spar; (mus.) conductor's baton; (fig.) person of no vigour or intelligence or sexual qualities, incompetent actor or actress. **13.** Slender more or less cylindrical piece of sugar-candy, sealing-wax, shaving-soap, etc. **14.** (Short, with aid of context, for) fiddle-~, drum-~, composing-~, etc. **15.** Number (*of bombs*) released in rapid succession from aircraft, cf. SALVO[2]. **16.** ~*-insect,* = WALKing-~ *insect.* [(vb) OE *stician* (= OHG *stehhōn*) f. Gmc **stik-* cogn. w. Gk STIGMA; (n.) OE *sticca,* OHG *stecko* f. **stikkon* f. Gmc **stik-*]

stick′er, n. In vbl senses; also or esp.[*] *pig-*~, long-bladed sharp-pointed knife; BILL[4]-~; batsman who scores slowly & is hard to get out; person who stays too long on visit; **adhesive label;* (organ- -build.) wooden rod transmitting motion between ends of two reciprocating levers. [-ER[1]]

‖ **stick′it,** a. (Sc.). ~ *minister,* licentiate who has failed to get a pastoral charge. [Sc. form of p.p. of STICK]

stic′klebăck (-klb-), n. Small fish with sharp spines on back. [ME, f. OE *sticel* a prickle, sting, see STICK, -LE(1), BACK[1]]

stick′ler, n. ~ *for,* person who insists on or pertinaciously supports or advocates (*is a great, am no,* ~ *for authority, precision,* etc.). [f. obs. *stickle* be umpire, ME *stightle* frequent. of *slight* f. OE *stihtan* (= OHG *stiften*) set in order]

stick′|ў, a. Tending to stick to what is touched, glutinous, viscous; unbending, critical, making or likely to make objections (*he was very* ~*y about giving me leave*); (sl.) highly unpleasant & painful (*he'll come to a* ~*y end*); ~*y-back,* small photograph with gummed back. Hence ~iLY[2] adv., ~iNESS n. [-Y[2]]

stiff, a. & n. **1.** Rigid, not flexible, unbending, unyielding, uncompromising, obstinate, (~ *shirt-front; lies* ~ *in death; has a* ~ *leg,* incapable of bending at knee; ~- -*necked,* stubborn; *keep a* ~ *upper lip,*

show firmness of character; ~ *ship,* heeling little under sail, not crank; ~ *market,* with prices remaining firm; *met the charge with a* ~ *denial*). **2.** Lacking ease or grace or graciousness or spontaneity, constrained, reserved, haughty, formal, (~ *manners; a* ~ *reception, bow,* etc.; ~ *movement, attitude,* etc.; *writes in a* ~ *style*). **3.** Not working freely, sticking, offering resistance, (*a* ~ *hinge, piston,* etc.; ~ *un,* veteran athlete etc., (sl.) *corpse;* ~ *neck,* rheumatic affection in which patient cannot turn head without pain); (of muscle, limb, etc., or person in regard to them) aching when used as result of previous exertion. **4.** Hard to cope with, calling for strength or capacity of some kind, trying, (~ *examination, climb, slope, breeze; a* ~ *price,* high; *a* ~ *glass of rum,* strong; *a* ~ *subject,* requiring application to master it). **5.** (Of moist clay, batter, etc.) thick & viscous, not fluid, in or approaching plastic state. **6.** (colloq.). (In pred. use) to the point of exhaustion, almost to death, as *bore, scare,* ~. **7.** ~- -*bit,* horse's bit made of unjointed bar with rings at ends; hence ~LY[2] adv., ~′NESS n., ~ISH[1](2) a., ~′EN[6] v.t. & i., ~′enER[1] (2), ~′enING[1](1, 4), nn. **8.** n. (sl.). Negotiable paper; *corpse;* hopeless or incorrigible person. [OE *stif,* = MLG *slif* f. Gmc **stifaz,* cogn. w. L *stipare* to crowd]

sti′fle[1], v.t. & i. = SMOTHER vb. Hence (preferred to corresp. wds f. *smother*) **stif′liNG[1]** a., **stif′liNGLY[2]** adv. [orig. obsc.; w. 14th c. form *stuf(f)le* cf. OF *estouffer* smother]

sti′fle[2], n. (Also ~*-joint*) joint of horse's hind leg between hip & hock; disease of ~*-joint* or ~*-bone,* whence **stif′lED[2]** (-ld) a.; ~*-bone,* bone of ~*-joint,* horse's knee- -pan; ~*-shoe,* kind with which ~d horse is shod on sound leg to make it use & so strengthen the weak one. [orig. unkn.]

stig′ma, n. (pl. ~*s,* & ~*ta* as specified below). **1.** (arch.). Mark branded on slave, criminal, etc. **2.** Imputation attaching to person's reputation; stain on one's good name. **3.** (Path.) definite characteristic of some disease; (anat., zool.) spot, pore, small natural mark on skin etc., small red spot on person's skin (pl. ~*ta*) that bleeds periodically or under mental stimulus; (bot.) part of style or ovary-surface that receives pollen in impregnation, so **stig′mătIC,** ~tOSE[1], aa. **4.** (eccl.; pl. ~*ta;* usu. in pl.). Mark(s) corresponding to those left by the nails & spear at the Crucifixion said to have been impressed on the bodies of St Francis of Assisi & others (whence ~tIST n.) & attributed to divine favour. [L f. Gk *stigma -atos* mark made by pointed instrument, brand]

stig′matiz|e, -is|e (-īz), v.t. Use opprobrious terms of, describe opprobriously as, (*shall not* ~*e him as he deserves;* ~*e him, it, as a coward, cowardice*); produce stigmata on (person) by hypnotic suggestion etc. Hence ~A'TION n. [f. F -*iser* or med. L f. Gk *stigmatizō* (prec., -IZE)]

stile[1], n. Steps or some provision other than gate enabling passengers to get over or through fence or wall but excluding cattle etc. (*help lame* DOG[1] *over* ~). [OE *stigel* f. *stīgan* climb, -LE(1); cf. STIRRUP]

stile[2], n. Vertical piece (cf. RAIL[1]) in frame of panelled door, wainscot, etc. [perh. f. Du. *stijl* pillar, door-post]

stilett'ō, n. (pl. ~s), & v.t. **1.** Small dagger (vb, stab with ~). **2.** Pointed implement for making eyelets etc.; ~ *heel* of shoe (long and pointed). [It., dim. of *stilo* f. L *stilus* STYLE[1], -ET[1]]

still[1], a., n., v.t. & i., & adv. **1.** Without or almost without motion or sound or both (*stand, sit, lie, keep*, ~, motionless; *a* ~ *lake*, unruffled; ~ WATER[1]*s run deep*; ~ *as the grave*; *a* ~ *evening*; *how* ~ *everything is!*; *in* ~ *meditation*; ~ *small voice*, that of conscience, w. ref. to 1 *Kings* xix. 12; *all sounds are* ~, hushed; ~ *life* in painting, representation of inanimate things such as fruit & furniture; ~ *hock* etc., not sparkling; ~ *birth*, delivery of dead child, so ~-*born*); ~-*bugle*, naval call requiring crew to remain motionless till next call; hence ~'y̆ (-l-lĭ) [-LY[2]] adv. (rare), ~'NESS n. **2.** n. Deep silence (*in the* ~ *of night*); an ordinary photograph, as distinct from a motion picture. **3.** vb. Quiet, calm, appease, assuage, silence; (rare) grow calm (*when the tempest* ~s). **4.** adv. Constantly, habitually, (arch.); then or now or for the future as before, even to this or that past or present or future time; nevertheless, for all that, on the other hand, all the same; (with compar.) even, yet. [OE *stille* adj., OS, OHG *stilli* f. Gmc **stell-*, *stilljaz f. **stel-* be fixed; vb f. OE *stillan*]

still[2], n., & v.t. Distilling-apparatus, esp. for making spirituous liquors, consisting essentially of a boiler & a condensing chamber, the vapour from the former passing into a spiral tube or worm surrounded by cold water or other refrigerating matter that fills the latter & issuing in drops as it condenses; ‖~-*room*, room for distilling, housekeeper's store-room in large house. **2.** v.t. Distil (poet.); make (spirit) in ~. [aphetic f. DISTIL; n. f. vb]

still'age, n. Bench, frame, etc., for keeping articles off floor while draining, waiting to be packed, etc. [app. f. Du. *stellagie*, -*age* (*stellen* to place, -AGE)]

still'ing, still'ion (-yon), n. Support for cask. [perh. f. Du. *stelling* scaffold (as prec., -ING[1])]

stilly[1]. See STILL[1].

still'y̆[2], a.(poet.). Still, quiet. [STILL[1],-LY[1]]

stilt, n. Pole with rest for foot used generally in pairs with upper part of pole bound to leg or held with hand & raising

user from ground (*on* ~*s* lit., & fig. = bombastic, stilted); (also ~-*bird* or -*plover* or -*walker*) long-legged bird resembling plover in having three-toed feet; ~-*petrel*, -*sandpiper*, long-legged kinds. [ME *stilte*, cogn. w. MDu., (M)LG *stelte*, OHG *stelza*]

stil'tĕd, a. (As) on stilts; (of literary style etc.) pompous, bombastic, whence ~LY[2] adv., ~NESS n.; (of arch) with pieces of upright masonry between imposts & feet of the true arch. [-ED[2]]

Stil'ton, n. Superior kind of veined cheese named from ~ in Huntingdonshire.

stilus. See STYLUS.

stim'ŭlant, a. & n. **1.** Stimulating (rare in gen. sense); (med.) producing rapid transient increase of vital energy in organism or some part of it. **2.** n. ~ agent or substance, as warmth, electricity, joy, etc., or exciting drug or article of food esp. alcoholic drink; *never takes* ~*s*, usu. = drinks no alcohol. [f. L as foll., -ANT]

stim'ŭl|āte, v.t. Apply stimulus to, act as stimulus upon, animate, spur on, excite to (more vigorous) action. Hence or cogn. ~āting[2], ~ATIVE, aa., ~A'TION, ~ātoR, nn.: [L *stimulare* (foll.), -ATE[3]]

stim'ŭl|us, n. (pl. ~ī). **1.** Thing that rouses to activity or energy (*so lethargic that no* ~*us affects him*); rousing effect (*under the* ~*us of hunger*). **2.** (Physiol.) thing that evokes functional reaction in tissues; (bot.) sting, whence ~OSE[1] a. **3.** (eccl.). Point at end of crosier, pastoral staff, etc. [L, = goad]

stim'y̆, n., & v.t. (Var. of) STYMIE.

sting, v.t. & i. (*stung*), & n. **1.** Wound with ~ (*a bee, nettle, stung him, his finger*); affect with tingling physical or sharp mental pain (*pepper* ~*s one's tongue; the cane, his bat-handle, the blow, his conscience, the imputation, stung him; stung by reproaches, with envy or desire*; *a* ~*ing insult*), whence ~'ing**LY** adv.; (of part of one's body) feel acute pain or communicate it to sensorium (*my hand, tooth*, ~*s*); be able to ~, have a ~ (*some bees do not* ~; ~*ing-nettle*, opp. DEAD-*nettle*); (sl.) involve in expense, (usu. pass.) be caught, swindled, involved in expense (*he was stung for a fiver*). **2.** n. Sharp-pointed weapon often tubular & connected with poison-gland in some insects & other animals (in tail as with bee; also of snake's poison-fang) & plants (projecting as hair from surface as in nettle); infliction of wound with ~, wound so made; pain caused by it, wounding quality or effect, rankling or acute pain of body or mind, keenness or vigour, (*was hurt by a* ~; *face covered with* ~*s; the* ~ *of hunger*, ~*s of remorse; the* ~ *is in the postscript*; *this air, bowling, has no* ~ *in it*, is relaxing, feeble). **3.** ~-*bull* or -*fish*, kind of weever; ~-*nettle*, ~ing-nettle; ~-*ray*, kinds of fish with flexible tail having sharp serrated projecting spine used as weapon;

~-**winkle**, beaked shellfish that bores holes in other shellfish; hence ~'LESS a. [OE *stingan*, ON *stinga*, f. Gmc **stengpierce*]

sting'aree (-ngg-), n. = STING-*ray*. [corrupt.]

sting'er, n. In vbl senses; esp., smart painful blow. [-ER¹]

sting'o (-nggō), n. (arch.). Strong beer. [STING, w. ref. to pungency, with fancy ending]

stin'gi|y (-jĭ), a. Meanly parsimonious, niggardly. Hence ~ILY², ~INESS n. [17th c. also = stinging, perh. f. dial. *stinge* sting]

stink, v.i. & t. (*stank* or *stunk*, *stunk*), & n. 1. (Have or emit) strong offensive smell (~ *in* NOSTRILS *of*; ~ *one out*, drive him from room etc. by ~), whence ~'**ingly²** adv.; (sl.) ~ *of money*, be notoriously rich; (sl.) perceive ~ of (*can ~ it a mile off*); ǁ (n. pl., sl.) chemistry, natural science, as subject of study; (part., sl.) objectionable in any way, that one dislikes; (part., as distinctive epithet of animals or plants) having recognizable & usu. disagreeable smell (~*ing camomile*, ~*ing cedar* or *yew*, savin & allied trees; ~*ing crane's-bill*, *hellebore*, *horehound*, *nightshade*, etc.; ~*ing-weed* or *-wood*, kind of cassia; ~*ing badger*, teledu). 2. ~-*alive*, the fish bib (from rapid putrefaction after death); ~-*ball*, vessel containing explosives etc. generating noxious vapours used formerly in naval warfare; ~-*bomb* (emitting nauseating smell on exploding); ~-*horn*, kinds of ill-smelling fungus; ~-*pot*, any receptacle containing something that ~s, also = ~-*ball*, also as abusive term for person or thing; ~-*stone*, kind of limestone giving off fetid smell when quarried; ~-*trap*, appliance to prevent escape of effluvia from drains when opened. [OE *stincan*, (M)Du., (M)LG, G *stinken*, OHG *stinkan* f. Gmc **stinkw-*; cf. STENCH]

stink'ard, n. Stinking person or animal, esp. the teledu. [-ARD]

stink'er, n. Stinkard, stinkpot; kinds of large petrel; (sl.) anything peculiarly offensive, irritating, or rousing (esp. of a letter, as *I wrote him a* ~). [-ER¹]

stint, v.t., & n. 1. Cease do*ing* or *to do* (arch.); keep on short allowance (~ *oneself* or person or animal *in* food etc.); supply or give in niggardly amount or grudgingly (~ *food*, *money*, *service*, etc.); hence ~'**ingly²** adv. 2. n. Limitation of supply or effort (usu. *without*, *no*, ~; *laboured without* ~, without sparing effort), whence ~'LESS a. 3. Fixed or allotted amount of or of work (*do one's daily* ~); area of coal-face to be worked in a shift. 4. Kinds of small sandpiper, (pop.) dunlin. [OE *styntan* to blunt, dull, f. Gmc **stuntjan* f. **stuntaz* adj. STUNT²]

stip'āte, a. (bot.). Crowded, close-set. [L *stipare* pack, -ATE²]

stīpe, stīp'ēs (-z), n. (bot., zool.). Stalk or stem (in bot. esp. support of carpel, stalk of frond, stem of fungus). Hence **stip'iFORM**, **stip'iTATE²**, **stip'itiFORM**, aa. [F *stipe*, L *stipes* tree-trunk etc.]

stip'el, n. (bot.). Secondary stipule at base of leaflets of compound leaf. Hence ~IATE² a. [f. F *stipelle* (prec., -EL)]

stip'ēnd, n. Fixed periodical money allowance for work done, salary, esp. clergyman's official income. [ME, f. OF *stipende* f. L *stipendium*]

stipĕn'diary, a. & n. (Person) receiving stipend, paid, not serving gratuitously; ǁ ~ (*magistrate*), paid magistrate in large provincial towns, cf. METROPOLITAN. [f. L *stipendiarius* (prec., -ARY¹)]

stipes. See STIPE.

stip'pl|e, v.t. & i., & n. 1. Engrave (plate, thing portrayed), paint or draw, in dots, not lines; use this method; hence ~ER¹(1, 2), ~ING¹, nn. 2. n. Dotted work; ~*e- -graver*, engraver's ~ing-tool. [f. Du. *stippelen* (*stippen* to prick, f. *stip* point)]

stip'ul|āte¹, v.i. & t. ~*ate for*, mention or insist upon as essential part of agreement; demand as part of bargain or agreement *that*; (p.p.) laid down as part of the terms of an agreement (*is not of the ~ated quality*). So ~ā'tion¹ [-ATION], ~ātOR, nn. [f. L *stipulari*, -ATE³]

stip'ul|e, n. Small leaflike appendage to leaf usu. at base of leaf-stem. Hence ~A'CEOUS (-āshus), ~AR¹, ~ARY¹, ~ate² [-ATE²], ~iFORM, aa., ~ā'tion² [-ATION] n. [F, f. L *stipula*, see STUBBLE]

stīr¹, v.t. & i. (-rr-), & n. 1. Set, keep, or (begin to) be, in motion (*not a breath ~s the lake*, *leaves*; *sit without ~ring a foot* etc. or ~*ring*; *if you~*, *I shoot*; *never ~red abroad* or *out of the house*, went out; *is not ~ring yet*, is still in bed; ~ *the fire*, use poker; ~ *your stumps*, colloq., make haste, walk etc. faster; ~ *tea*, *porridge*, *soup*, etc., move spoon etc. round; ~ round in to mix ingredients, keep from burning in pot, etc.; *there is no news~ring*, going about; *lead ~ring life*, be busy; ~ *up*, mix well by ~*ring*; ~ *up the mud*, *sediment*, etc., make it rise from bottom of liquid by ~*ring*); rouse (*up*), excite, animate, inspirit, (~ *up strife*, *mutiny*, *discontent*, *curiosity*; *person wants ~ring up*, is indolent or torpid; ~ *one's blood*, excite him to enthusiasm, desire, etc.; ~ *one's wrath*, *bile*, etc., enrage, disgust, etc.; ~*ring events*, *times*, *music*, etc., exciting, stimulating; *a ~ring speech*, *picture*, *tale*), whence ~'**ringLY²** adv.; ~*- -about*, (n.) porridge, (adj.) bustling; hence ~'rER¹(1, 2) n. 2. n. Commotion, bustle, disturbance, excitement, sensation, (*full of* ~ *- & movement*; *person*, *event*, *makes a great* ~, is much discussed etc.); slightest movement (*not a* ~), whence ~'LESS a.; act of ~ring (*give the fire a* ~). [OE *styrian*, MSw. *styra* f. Gmc **sturjan*; cogn. w. OHG *stören*]

stif², n. (sl.). Prison. [orig. unkn.]

stirk, n. (Sc. & dial.). Yearling bullock or heifer. [OE *stirc*, app. dim. of *stēor* STEER²]

stirp'iculture, n. Breeding of special stocks or strains. [foll., -I-, CULTURE]

stirps, n. (Law) progenitor of family; (zool.) classificatory group. [L, = stock]

sti'rrup, n. Rider's foot-rest usu. consisting of iron loop with flattened base hung by a strap or ~-*leather* from ~-*bar*, iron attachment let into saddle; ~ & ~-*leather* as a whole; (naut.) rope with eye giving hold in reefing; ~-*bone*, small bone, ~-shaped in man, in mammal's ear; ~-*cup*, of wine etc. presented to person mounted for departure; ~-*iron*, ~ without ~-leather; ~-*piece* in carpentry etc., hanging support; ~-*pump* (with foot-rest & nozzle for producing either jet or spray of water, used for extinguishing small fires). [OE *stirāp* (*stīgan* climb, cf. STILE, ROPE)]

stitch, n., & v.t. & i. **1.** Acute internal pain in the side such as often results from running etc. soon after eating. **2.** Single pass of needle in sewing (*a ~ in time* SAVE¹*s nine*); result of it or of single complete movement in knitting, crochet, embroidery, etc. (*if one ~ gives the rest will*; *what long ~es!*; *has not a dry ~ on him*, is wet through; *drop a ~* in knitting, let loop fall off needle-end spoiling the continuity; *put a ~* or ~*es in* in surgery, sew up wound with gut, silk, wire; etc.); method followed in making ~es or kind of work produced (*am learning a new ~*; LOCK³, *buttonhole*, HERRING-*bone*, etc., ~, CROSS-STITCH). **3.** ~-*wheel*, harness-maker's notched wheel for pricking leather in places where ~es are to go; ~'*wort*, kinds of chickweed, esp. one with erect stem & white star flowers (named as cure for ~ in side). **4.** vb. Sew (t. & i.; ~ *up*, usu. mend by sewing; ~*ing-horse*, harness--maker's clamp for holding work). [OE *stice*, OS *stiki*, OHG *stih*, Goth. *stiks* f. Gmc **stikiz* f. **stik-* STICK; vb f. n.]

stith'y (-dhĭ), n. (arch. & poet.). Smith's shop, forge. [ME, f. ON *stethi* f. **stathjon* (*sta-* STAND)]

stiv'er, n. Even the smallest coin (usu. *don't care, has not, a ~*). [f. Du. *stuiver* small obsolete coin]

stō'a, n. (pl. -ae). Portico in ancient--Greek architecture (*the ~*, the PORCH, see STOIC). [Gk]

stoat¹, n. Kinds of ermine, esp. in its summer coat. [ME, of unkn. orig.]

stoat², v.t. Sew up (tear, cloth edges) with invisible stitches. [orig. unkn.]

stock, n., & v.t. & i. **1.** Stump, butt, main trunk, plant into which graft is inserted, body-piece serving as base or holder or handle for working parts of implement or machine, (source of) family or breed, raw material of manufacture, store ready for drawing on, equipment for trade or pur-suit, (*they nest in the ~s of trees*, arch. use; ~*s & stones*, inanimate things, lethargic persons; *laughing, gazing*, etc., ~, butt for ridicule etc.; *must be grafted on a sound ~*; ~ *of rifle, plane, plough*, main part, usu. of wood, into which barrel, blade, share, etc., are fastened; ~ *of bit*, brace; ~ *of anvil*, base it rests on; ~ *of anchor*, cross-bar; *lock, ~, & barrel*, fig., completely, root & branch; *cousins of a good, Puritan, treacherous*, etc., ~, family of distinct character; *polyp* etc. ~ in zool., aggregate organism; *paper*, etc. ~, rags etc. from which paper etc. is made; *soup-~* or usu. ~, liquor made by stewing bones etc. as basis for any sort of soup; *has a great ~ of information, hardware*; ROLL²*ing ~*; *take over a farm with the ~*, its animals, also *live~*, & implements, also *dead ~*; *fat ~*, ~ fit for slaughter as food; ~-*in-trade*, all requisites for a trade, also fig., as *the politician's ~-in-trade of a dozen catchwords*; *renew one's ~*; *lay in a ~ of*; *have in ~*, have ready without need of procuring specially; *take ~*, review one's ~ for accurate knowledge of what one has in ~; so ~-*taking* n.; *take ~ of*, fig., observe with a view to estimating character etc. of; ~ *argument, comparison, response, joke*, etc., one that requires no fresh thought but is always at hand & perpetually repeated whether by individual or by people in general). **2.** Kinds (*common* or *ten-weeks*, *Virginia*, etc., ~) of fragrant-flowered usu. hoary-leaved garden plant (orig. ~-*gilliflower*, named as having stronger stem than clove-gilliflower or pink). **3.** pl. (hist.). Timber frame with holes for feet & occas. hands in which petty offenders were confined in sitting position. **4.** pl. Timbers on which ship rests while building (*on the ~s*, in construction or preparation, often transf.). **5.** Stiff wide band of leather or other material formerly worn round neck, now displaced in general use by collar & tie, but surviving in some military uniforms & clerical dress & occas. revived in modified forms by fashion. **6.** ‖ (Finance) money lent to a government & involving payment of fixed interest to lenders or whomsoever their rights have passed to by purchase etc. (*buy, hold, ~*, the right to receive such interest on some amount of ~; ‖ *the ~s*, State's funded debts as a whole; *has money, £50,000, in the ~s*; *take ~ in*, fig., concern oneself with); capital of corporation or company contributed by individuals for prosecution of some undertaking & divided into shares entitling holders to proportion of profits (also JOINT²-~; *bank, railway*, etc., ~; PREFERENCE or *preferred ~*; ~ *certificate*; WATER² ~). **7.** Best quality clamp-burnt brick (also of certain kiln-burnt bricks, as *malm ~*). **8.** ‖ ~-*account*, *-book*, showing amount of goods laid in & amount disposed of;

|| ~*-breeder*, raiser of live~; ~*-broker*, ~*-broking*, (person engaged in) buying & selling for clients on commission of ~s held by ~jobbers; ~*-car*, cattle-truck; ~*-car racing*, motor-racing in which ordinary cars, not racing-cars, are used; ~ *company*, one semi-permanently engaged at a particular theatre; ~*-dove*, European wild pigeon smaller & darker than wood-pigeon [perh. from breeding in ~s of trees]; ~ *exchange*, place where ~s & shares are publicly bought & sold, || esp. *the S~ Exchange*, (building in London occupied by) association of dealers in ~s conducting business according to fixed rules (*is on the S~ Exchange*, a member of this association); ~*-farm(er)*, that breeds live~; ~*-fish*, cod & similar fish split & dried in sun without salt; ~*-gang*, gang of saws in frame cutting log into boards at one passage; ~*-jobber*, ~*-jobbing*, ~*-jobbery*, || (person engaged in) speculating in ~s with view of profiting by fluctuations in price, cf. ~*broker*; ~*-list*, daily or periodical ~-exchange publication giving current prices of ~s etc.; ~ *lock* (enclosed in wooden case, usu. on outer door); ~*-man* (Austral.), man in charge of live~; ~*-market*, ~ exchange or transactions on it; || ~*-owl*, the great eagle owl; ~*-piling*, accumulating ~s of commodities, raw materials, etc. to be held in reserve, so ~*-pile* n. & v.t.; ~*-pot*, for making or keeping soup~; ~*-rider* (Austral.), herdsman on unfenced station; ~*-still*, motionless; ~*-whip*, with short handle & long lash for herding cattle; ~*-yard*, enclosure with pens etc. for sorting or temporary keeping of cattle; hence ~'LESS a. (esp. of gun, anchor, etc.). **9.** vb. Fit (gun etc.) with ~. **10.** (hist.). Confine in the ~s. **11.** Provide (shop, farm, etc.) with goods or live~ or requisites (*a well-~ed 'larder, library,* etc.); keep (goods) in ~ (*we do not ~ the out sizes*). **12.** Fill or cover (land) with permanent growth esp. of pasture-grass; (of plant) = TILLER[3]. [OE *stoc(c)*, OS *stok*, OHG *stoc*, ON *stokkr* f. Gmc **stukkaz*]

stockāde, n., & v.t. (Fortify with) breastwork or enclosure of upright stakes. [f. obs. F *estocade*, alt. of *estacade* f. Sp. *estacada* (rel. to STAKE)]

Stock'holm tār (-hōm), n. Kind of tar prepared from resinous pinewood, used esp. in shipbuilding. [*Stockholm* in Sweden]

stŏck'inĕt, n. Elastic knitted material used esp. for underclothing. [prob. perversion of *stocking-net*]

stŏck'ing, n. Tight covering usu. knitted or woven of wool or cotton or silk or nylon for foot & leg (usu. in pl., esp. *pair of* ~s; *is or stands six feet in his* ~s *or* ~*-feet,* when measured without his shoes; *elastic* ~, surgical appliance of elastic webbing like ~ or part of it worn for

varicose veins, strained muscles, etc.; *while* etc. ~ in horse etc., lower part of leg differently coloured from rest); ~*-frame,* -*loom, -machine,* knitting-machine. Hence ~LESS a. [f. STOCK, in 16th c. (now dial.) sense 'stocking', +-ING[3]]

stŏck'ist, n. One who stocks (certain) goods for sale. [-IST (3)]

stŏck'|ȳ, a. Thickset, short & strongly built, (of person; also in bot. & zool.). Hence ~ILY[2] adv., ~INESS n. [f. STOCK +-Y[2]]

stŏdge, n., & v.i. & t. (school sl.). **1.** Food esp. of heavy kind; full meal, feast; greedy eater. **2.** vb. Eat greedily. [n. f. vb, of unkn. orig.; perh. imit.]

stŏdg'|ȳ; a. (Of food) heavy, filling, indigestible; (of receptacle) packed, bulging; (of book, style, etc.) over-full of facts or details, wanting in lightness or interest. Hence ~INESS n. [-Y[2]]

stoep (-ōōp), n. (S. Afr.). Terraced veranda in front of house. [Du., cogn. w. STEP]

*stŏg'y, -**gie,** (-gĭ), n. Kind of heavy boot or shoe; long roughly-made cigar. [orig. *stoga,* short for *Conestoga* (Pa.)]

stō'ic, n. Philosopher of the school founded at Athens c. 308 B.C. by Zeno making virtue the highest good, concentrating attention on ethics, & inculcating control of the passions & indifference to pleasure & pain (*S~;* often attrib., as *S~ philosopher, doctrines, indifference*); person of great self-control or fortitude or austerity, whence ~AL a., ~ALLY[2] adv. Hence S~ISM(2, 3), ~ISM, n. [f. L f. Gk *stōikos* (*stoa* porch, w. ref. to Zeno's teaching in *Stoa Poekile* Painted Porch at Athens, -IC)]

stōke, v.t. & i. Feed & tend (furnace), feed furnace of (engine etc.), act as stoker; (fig.; colloq.) take food esp. in hurried way; ~*-hole,* ~*-hold,* compartment in which steamer's fires are worked. [back form. f. foll.]

stōk'er, n. Man who tends furnace esp. that of steamer or steam-engine (*mechanical* ~, automatic feeder for furnace). [17th c., Du., f. *stoken* stoke]

stōle[1], n. (Rom. ant.; also L *stola* pl. *-ae*) outer dress of ancient-Roman matron; ecclesiastical vestment, a strip of silk or other material hanging from back of neck over shoulders & down to knees (worn by deacon over left shoulder only); woman's wrap similarly worn; || *groom of the* ~ [orig. *stoole,* i.e. king's close-stool], first LORD of the Bed-chamber. Hence (-)stōlED[2] (-ld) a. [ME, f. L f. Gk *stolē* robe (*stellō* array)]

stole[2], = STOLON.

stole[3], stolen. See STEAL.

stŏl'id, a. Phlegmatic, unemotional, lacking animation, not easily agitated, hard to stir, obstinate, apparently stupid. Hence or cogn. stolid'ITY n., ~LY[2] adv. [f. F *stolide* or L *stolidus*]

stōl'ŏn, stōle, n. Reclined or prostrate

branch that strikes root & develops new plant; underground shoot of mosses developing leaves; (zool.) rootlike creeping growth. Hence **stŏl'onATE²**, **stŏlonIF⸍EROUS**, aa. [f. L *stolo -onis*]

sto'mach (-ŭmak), n., & v.t. **1.** Internal organ in which chief part of digestion is carried on, being in man a pear-shaped enlargement of the alimentary canal extending from end of gullet to beginning of gut (*coat of the* ~, its mucous inmost lining; *coats of the* ~, the peritoneum or serous coat, the muscular, submucous, & mucous layers); (in some animals, esp. ruminants), one of several digestive organs either of similar character or differing in action or function (*ruminant's* ~*s*, first ~ or paunch or rumen, second ~ or honeycomb or reticulum, third ~ or psalterium or omasum, fourth or true ~ or reed or abomasum; *muscular* ~, acting by grinding or squeezing, as the gizzard; *glandular* ~, acting esp. by gastric juices); (loosely) belly, abdomen, lower front of body, (*pit of the* ~, depression below bottom of breastbone; *what a* ~ *he has got!*, corporation). **2.** Appetite for or for food (STAY¹ one's ~). **3.** Taste or readiness or sufficient spirit *for* (or arch. *to*) controversy, conflict, danger, or an undertaking (*had no* ~ *for the fight*), *proud* or *high* ~, haughtiness. **4.** ~*-ache*, pain in belly, esp. in bowels; ~*-cough*, caused by irritation of ~ or small intestine; ~*-pump*, kind of syringe for emptying ~ or forcing liquid into it; ~*-staggers*, apoplexy in horses due to paralysis of ~; ~*-tooth*, lower canine milk-tooth in infants, cutting of which often disorders ~; ~*-tube*, for introducing through gullet into ~ to wash it out or empty it by siphon action; hence ~AL, ~LESS, aa., ~FUL (2) n. **5.** v.t. Eat with relish or toleration, find sufficiently palatable to swallow or keep down, (fig.) pocket or put up with (affront etc.), (usu. w. neg., as *cannot* ~ *it*). [ME *stomak* f. OF *estomac* f. L f. Gk *stomakhos* gullet f. *stoma* mouth]

sto'macher (-ŭmach-), n. (hist.). Front--piece of 15th-17th-c. woman's dress covering breast & pit of stomach, ending downwards in point often lapping over skirt, & often set with gems or richly embroidered. [ME, app. f. prec. +-ER¹; but pronunc. supports deriv. f. an AF *esto-machier*]

stomăch'ic (-k-), a. & n. **1.** Of the stomach; aiding ~ action, promoting digestion or appetite. **2.** n. ~ draught or drug, bitters etc. [f. L f. Gk *stomakhikos* (STOMACH, -IC)]

stŏmatit'is, n. Inflammation of the mucous membrane of the mouth. [as foll. +-ITIS]

stŏmato-, comb. form of Gk *stoma -atos* mouth, as ~*gas'tric*, of mouth & stomach; ~*logy* (-ŏl⁴) n. (med.), science of (diseases of) the mouth.

stŏne, n., a., & v.t. **1.** Piece of rock of any shape usu. detached from earth's crust & of no great size, esp. a pebble, a cobble, or a single piece used or usable in building or roadmaking or as missile (STOCKS & ~*s*; *built of great* ~*s*; *as hard as a* ~; ROLL²*ing* ~; ROCK²*ing* ~; SERMONS *in* ~*s*; ~*s will cry out*, wrong is great enough to move inanimate things; *give a* ~ *for bread*, offer a mockery of help; *mark with a white* ~, record as a joyful day, w. ref. to ancient-Roman use of chalk; *meteoric* ~, meteorite; *leave no* ~ *unturned*, try every possible means, often *to* do; *break* ~*s*, get.living by preparing road metal, as phr. for being reduced to extremities; *cast*, *throw*, ~*s* or *a* ~ *at*, or *the first* ~, lit., & = make aspersions on character etc. of; *those who live in glass houses should not throw* ~*s*, aspersion provokes retort; *shower of* ~*s*, thrown, or rolling down hill etc.; *kill two* BIRDS *with one* ~; ~*'s cast or throw*, distance ~ can be thrown). **2.** (Usu. *precious* ~) a gem (*no* ~ *in it worth less than £100*; *Bristol* ~, Bristol DIAMOND; CAIRNGORM ~). **3.** ~*s* or rock as a substance or material (often with defining pref., as SAND, LIME¹, ~; *Bath, Caen, Portland*, ~, kinds of building-~; *built of* ~; ~ *buildings* etc.; ~ *jar* etc., of ~ware; ~ JUG¹; HOLYSTONE; *artificial* ~, kinds of concrete; *Cornish* ~, kaolin; *has a heart of* ~, is hard--hearted; *harden into* ~, petrify lit. or fig.; *the* ~ *age*, stage of civilization at which implements & weapons were of ~, not metal; PHILOSOPHERS' ~). **4.** Piece of ~ of definite & designed shape (often with purpose specified by word in comb., or easily supplied from context; GRIND, GRAVE¹, HEARTH, MILL¹, WHET, ~; *Moabite, Rosetta*, ~, stelae with historically important inscriptions). **5.** Thing resembling ~ in hardness or pebble in shape, e.g. calculus (as single concretion or as the malady), hard case of kernel in drupe or ~*-fruit*, seed of grape, testicle, pellet of hail, (GALL¹~; *underwent an operation for* ~ or *the* ~, remove the ~*s from plums*, *grapes*, etc.; *hail-storm with* ~*s as big as marbles*). **6.** || Weight of 14 lb. or of other amounts varying with the commodity (*rides 12* ~, weighs that in the saddle; *give a* ~ *& a beating to*, orig. racing sl., surpass easily; ~ *of meat or fish* 8 lb., ~ *of cheese* 16 lb., etc.). **7.** ~*-axe*, with two obtuse edges for hewing ~; ~*-blind* (quite); ~*-blue*, compound of indigo with starch or whiting; ~*-boiling*, primitive method of boiling by putting heated ~s into water; ~*-borer*, kinds of mollusc; ~*-break*, saxifrage; ~*-buck*, steenbok; ~*-butter*, kind of alum; ~*-cast*, = ~*'s cast* above; ~*-CHAT²*; ~*-coal*, anthracite; ~*-cold* (quite); ~*-crop*, kinds of low creeping plant growing esp. on walls & rocks; ~*-curlew*, thick-knee or thick-kneed plover; ~*-dead, -deaf*, (quite); ~*-eater*, = ~*-borer*; ~*-fence* (sl.), whisky & cider, or similar mixed drink; ~*fern*, ceterach; ~*fly*, insect with aquatic larvae found under ~s, used as bait for trout; || ~ *frigate*, naval establishment ashore bearing name of ship; ~*fruit*, with seeds enclosed in hard shell surrounded by pulp, drupe, e.g. plum, peach, cherry; ~*gall*, round mass of clay in variegated sand~; ~*horse* (arch.), stallion; ~ *man*, cairn; ~ *marten*, = BEECH *marten*; ~'*mason*, dresser of or builder in ~; ~*parsley*, umbelliferous hedge plant of carrot family; ~*pine*, S.-Ital. kind with branches at top spreading like umbrella; ~*pit*, quarry; ~ *pitch*, inspissated pitch; ~*plover*, large kind called also *thick-knee* & ~*curlew*; ~*race* (of runners who must pick up ~s laid at intervals); || ~*rag*, kind of lichen; ~*rue*, kind of fern; ~*saw*, untoothed iron blade stretched in saw-frame for cutting ~ with aid of sand; ~*weed*, gromwell; ~*snipe*, large N.-Amer. kind; ~*wall'* v.i. & t., obstruct by ~walling; ~*wall'ing*, (crick.) excessively cautious batting, (pol., esp. Austral.) parliamentary obstruction; ~'*ware*, pottery made from very silicious clay or from composition of clay & flint; ~'*work*, masonry; ~'*wort*, kinds of plant, esp. ~*parsley*; hence (-)stŏnĕD² (-nd), ~*LESS* (-nl-), aa. 8. adj. Made of ~. 9. v.t. Pelt with ~s (~ *to death*). 10. Free (fruit) from ~s. 11. Face, pave, etc., with ~. [OE *stān*, OS *stēn*, OHG *stein*, ON *steinn*, Goth. *stains* f. Gmc **stainaz*]

stŏn'|y̆, a. & adv. 1. Full of, covered with, having many, stones; hard, rigid, fixed, as stone (a ~*y stare*, refusing response or recognition; ~*y heart*, obdurate or unfeeling heart, also hard core or interior, whence ~y̆-hearted² a.); hence ~ILY² adv., ~INESS n. 2. adv. Utterly (only in ~y̆-BROKE²). [ME; -Y²]

stood. See STAND.

stŏŏge, n., & v.i. (sl.). 1. *Butt, foil, esp. for a comedian; a deputy; subordinate, puppet; person learning to fly. 2. v.i. Move, esp. fly, *about*, *around*, etc. [orig. unkn.]

stŏŏk, n., & v.t. (chiefly Sc. & north.). = SHOCK³. [ME *stouk*, f. or cogn. w. MLG *stūke*, WFlem. *stuik*]

stŏŏl, n., & v.i. 1. Backless seat for one, often consisting of wooden slab on three legs (*office* ~, high ~ used by clerks etc.; MUSIC, CAMP¹, ~; *three-legged* ~; *folding* ~, made to fold up; ~ *of repentance*, orig. that on which fornicators etc. were set to receive rebuke in churches in Scotland, & now transf.; *fall between two* ~s, fail from vacillation between two courses etc.); *low bench for kneeling on*; = FOOT-~. 2. (archit.). Window-sill. 3. (Place for) evacuation of bowels, faeces evacuated, (*go to* ~; CLOSE¹, NIGHT¹, ~). 4. Root or stump of plant from which shoots spring. 5. Piece of wood to which decoy-bird is attached. 6. ~*ball*, old game resembling cricket still played in Sussex esp. by girls;

~*pigeon*, pigeon used, person acting, as decoy. 7. v.i. Throw up shoots from root; (arch.) go to ~, evacuate bowels. [OE *stōl*, OS *stōl*, OHG *stuol*, ON *stóll*, Goth. *stōls* f. Gmc **stōlaz* (**stō-*, **sta-* STAND)]

stŏŏp¹, v.i. & t., & n. 1. Bring one's head nearer the ground by bending down from standing position, (fig.) deign or condescend *to* do, descend or lower oneself *to* some conduct (~ *to conquer*, gain power or one's end by preliminary self-abasement); carry one's head & shoulders bowed forward, whence ~'ingLY² adv.; (of hawk etc., & transf.) swoop, pounce; incline (head, neck, shoulders, back) forward & down; tilt (cask) forward. 2. n. ~ing carriage of body; (arch.) swoop of hawk etc. [OE *stūpian*, MDu. *stūpen*, ON *stúpa* rel. to Gmc **staupo-* STEEP¹]

stŏŏp², n. = STOUP.

stŏŏp³, n. (U.S., Can.). Unroofed platform in front of house. [f. Du. STOEP]

stŏp¹, v.t. & i. (-pp-). 1. Stuff up or *up*, prevent or forbid passage through, make impervious or impassable, close, bar, stifle, stanch, (~ *a leak*, *hole*, etc.; ~*ped pipe* in organ, with upper end plugged, giving note an octave lower; ~ one's *ears*, put fingers in to avoid hearing, also fig. refuse to listen; || ~ *a tooth*, fill cavity in it with ~p'ING¹ n. of gold, amalgam, cement, etc.; ~ *a wound*, stanch its bleeding; ~ one's *mouth*, fig., induce him by bribery or other means to keep silence about something; ~ *a gap*, serve to meet a temporary need; ~ *the way*, be or act as obstruction, prevent progress). 2. Put an end to (motion etc.), completely check progress or motion or operation of, effectively hinder or prevent, (~ *progress* etc.; ~ *horse* etc., esp. when running away; ~ *ball*, esp. of batsman or field in cricket; ~ *thief!*, cry of pursuer; ~ *blow*, parry it in boxing; ~ *blow with* one's *head* etc., joc., receive it, esp. ~ *a bullet*, (sl.) ~ *one*, be shot; *thick walls* ~ *sound*, render it inaudible; ~ one's *breath*, kill him by smothering or otherwise; ~ *clock*, *factory*, etc., make it cease working; ~ *person's doing*, person *from doing*; *shall* ~ *that nonsense*, not allow it to go on). 3. Cut off, suspend, decline customary giving of or permission for, (*shall* ~ *your wages*, *holidays*, *meetings*; *the cost must be* ~*ped out of his salary*; ~ *payment of a cheque*, direct one's banker not to cash; ~ *payment*, declare oneself unable to meet obligations, break financially; *why has our gas*, *water*, *been* ~*ped?*). 4. Obtain desired note from (string of violin etc.) by pressing finger, so shortening vibrating length. 5. Cease, come to an end, cease from *doing*, discontinue (one's action), cease from motion or speaking or action, make a halt or pause, (*noise*, *annuity*, ~s; *do not* ~, go on, continue; ~ *dead or short*, cease abruptly; *shall* ~ *playing*, *subscribing*, *my visits*, *my endeavours*; *do* ~

grumbling, your complaints, that noise; he ~ped in the middle of a sentence; my watch has ~ped; train does not ~ at, before, Exeter; he never ~s to think). 6. (colloq.). Remain, stay, sojourn, *(shall ~ in bed, at home; ~ up,* not go to bed; *shall you ~ for the sermon?; have been ~ping in Cornwall with friends).* 7. Provide with stops, punctuate, *(a badly spell & ~ped letter).* 8. (Naut.) make fast, stopper, (cable etc.); (etching) ~ *out,* cover (parts that are to be protected from action of acid) with defensive coating *(~ping-brush,* for doing this); (photog.) ~ *down,* obscure part of (lens) with diaphragm; (founding) ~ *off,* fill in (part of mould not to be used) with sand. *9. ~ off, ~ over,* break one's journey; *~'off, ~'over,* nn., a break in one's journey. Hence ~p'AGE(3) n. (also, path., obstruction in bodily organ). [ME, f. OE *-stoppian* = OLFrank. *-stuppôn,* MDu., MLG. *stoppen* f. WG **stoppôn* f. Rom. **stuppare* (L *stuppa* tow; see STUFF]

stŏp², n. 1. Stopping or being stopped, pause, check, *(put a ~ to; make, come to, bring to, a ~; is at a ~,* not proceeding or unable to proceed; *train runs from London to Crewe without a ~).* 2. Punctu-ation-mark, esp. comma, semicolon, colon, or period *(full ~,* period; *come to a full ~,* transf., cease completely). 3. (Mus.) change of pitch effected by stopping (see prec.), (in organ) row of pipes of one character brought into action by a ~ *-knob* or small *~key;* (fig.) manner of speech adopted to produce particular effect *(can put on* or *pull out the pathetic, blustering, virtuous,* etc., ~ *at will).* 4. Batten, peg, or the like, meant to stop motion of something at fixed point. 5. (Opt., photog.) diaphragm; (phonet.) mute consonant sound made by closure of organs concerned (as k, t, p); (naut.) small line used as lashing, also projection of lower mast-head supporting trestle--trees. Hence ~'LESS a. [f. prec.]

stŏp-, comb. form of STOP^{1,2}: *~'cock,* externally-operated valve inserted in pipe to regulate passage of contents; *~-collar,* ring checking motion of shaft; *~-cylinder,* kind of printing-press; *~-drill,* with shoulder limiting depth of penetration; *~'gap,* · temporary substitute; *~-key, -knob,* see prec. (sense 3); *~-order,* order to stockbroker to buy or sell on stock's reaching specified price; *~-plate,* limiting play of axle on bearings; || *~-press,* (news) inserted in paper after printing has begun; *~-valve,* closing pipe against passage of liquid; *~-volley* (lawn tennis), checked volley close to net, dropping ball dead on other side; *~-watch,* with mechanism for starting & stopping it at will, used in timing races etc.

stŏpp'er, n., & v.t. In vbl senses: esp.: plug for closing bottle etc. usu. of same material as the vessel *(put a ~ on* some-thing, bring about cessation of it); *tobacco-*

~. implement for pressing down tobacco in pipe-bowl; (naut.) rope, clamp, double claw, etc., for checking & holding rope cable or chain cable; ~ *bolt,* ring-bolt in deck to which ~s are secured; *~-knot,* finishing of end of ~-rope made by inter-lacing its strands; (vb) close or secure with ~. [-ER¹]

stŏp'ple, n., & v.t. 1. Stopper of bottle or other vessel. 2. v.t. Close with ~. [ME; partly f. STOP¹+-LE(1), partly aphetic f. ESTOPPEL]

stŏr'age, n. Storing of goods, method of doing this *(cold ~,* in refrigerators etc., also transf.); space available for it; cost of warehousing; ~ *cell, battery* (electr.), apparatus for storing electrical energy in a chemical form, accumulator. [STORE +-AGE]

stŏr'ax, n. (Tree yielding) a resinous vanilla-scented balsam formerly much used in medicine & perfumery; *liquid ~,* a balsam got from the Oriental sweet--gum-tree. [ME; LL var. of STYRAX]

store, n., & v.t. 1. Abundance, provision, stock of something ready to be drawn upon, (sing. with or, arch. exc. of intangible things, without *a,* & pl.; *has ~, good ~, a ~,* or *~s,* of *wine, wit, anecdote, wisdom; in ~,* laid up in readi-ness, about to come, destined, as *I have, tomorrow has, a surprise in ~ for you).* 2. Place where things are kept for sale, **ordinary shop* (~ *clothes* etc., esp. = ready-made; *book* etc. *~),* || large com-mercial establishment selling goods of many different kinds (the ~s, these opp. ordinary shops, as *I get most things at the ~s;* CHAIN, DEPARTMENT, ~; CO-OPERATIVE ~ or ~s; *Army & Navy,* etc., ~s, orig. selling only to members, who must have specified qualification). 3. pl. Articles of particular kind or for special purpose accumulated for use, supply of things needed, *(military, naval,* etc., ~s; *marine ~s,* old ship materials). 4. attrib. Kept for future use (~ *cattle* etc., not yet being fattened). 5. *Set ~ by,* reckon precious or important, esp. *set no great ~ by.* 6. *~ house,* place where things are ~d up, granary etc., esp. fig. *(person, book, is a ~house of information* etc., cf. MINE¹); *~'keeper,* *shopkeeper; *~-room,* in which household supplies are kept; *~-ship,* carrying ~s for fleet, garrison, etc. 7. v.t. Stock or furnish with or *with* something (usu. with knowledge or the like, *store your mind with facts; a well-~d memory).* 8. Lay up or *up* for future use *(harvest has been ~d,* got in; ~ *up a saying* in one's *heart);* deposit (furniture etc.) in a warehouse for temporary keeping. 9. (Of receptacle) hold, keep, contain, have storage-accom-modation for *(a single cell can ~ 2,000,000 foot-pounds of energy);* hence **stŏr'ABLE** a. [ME; aphetic f. obs. *astore* sb f. OF *estore,* f. *estorer* (whence E vb), f. L *instaurare,* cf. RESTORE]

stŏr′|ey (pl. ~*eys*), **stŏr′|ÿ** (pl. ~*ies*), n. Any of the parts into which a house is divided horizontally, the whole of the rooms etc. having a continuous floor, (*fell from a third~ey window; a house of five* ~*eys; upper* ~*ey* or ~*eys,* fig., the brain, as *is a little wrong in the upper* ~*ey*); ~*ey-post,* upright supporting a beam on which rests a floor or wall. Hence (-)~ eYED², ~ied, (-rĭd), a. [aphetic f. Anglo-L *historia* (perh. orig. meaning a tier of STORIED windows or sculpture), hence prob. same wd as STORY¹]

stŏr′iāted, a. (Of title-pages etc.) with elaborate decorative designs. [for HISTORIATED]

stŏr′ied (-rĭd), a. Celebrated in legend, associated with legends or stories or history; adorned with legendary or historical representations. [f. STORY¹ & *story* vb +-ED²]

stŏrk, n. Tall stately wading bird allied to heron, the best-known species pure white except for black wing-tips & reddish bill & feet, occas. half domesticated & nesting on buildings, & credited with peculiar affection both to its young & its parents (*King S~,* oppressively active ruler, cf. *King* LOG¹); ~*'s-bill,* kinds of geranium. [OE *storc,* OS *stork,* OHG *storah,* ON *storkr* f. Gmc *sturkaz*]

stŏrm, n., & v.i. & t. **1.** Violent disturbance of the atmosphere with thunder, strong wind, or heavy rain or snow or hail, a tempest, (*cyclonic* ~; *thunder, rain, snow, wind,* ~; ~ *in a teacup,* great excitement over small matter); (meteorol.) atmospheric disturbance intermediate between whole gale & hurricane. **2.** Violent disturbance of the established order in human affairs, tumult, agitation, war, invasion, dispute, etc. (~ *& stress,* period of fermenting ideas & unrest in person's or nation's life, f. G *Sturm und Drang,* name of a play characteristic of the literary movement in Germany 1770–82). **3.** Vehement shower *of* missiles or outbreak of hisses, applause, indignation, etc. **4.** Direct assault by troops on fortified place, capture *of* place by such assault, (*take by* ~, of such capture, & transf. of captivating audience or person rapidly). **5.** ~*-beaten,* battered by lit. or fig. ~s; ~*-bell,* tract in which ~s are frequent; ~*-bird,* stormy petrel; ~*'bound,* prevented from leaving port or continuing voyage by ~s; ~*-card,* chart assisting navigator of ship in ~ to conjecture position of ~-centre & so to direct course; ~*-centre,* point to which wind blows spirally inward in cyclonic ~, (fig.) subject etc. upon which agitation or disturbance is concentrated; ~*-cloud,* heavy rain-cloud, state of affairs that threatens disturbances; ‖~*-cock,* kinds of bird, esp. missel-thrush, fieldfare, or green woodpecker; ‖~*-cone,* tarred-canvas cone hoisted as warning of high wind, upright for north & inverted for south; ~*-door,* additional outer door for protection in bad weather or winter; ~*-drum,* cylinder added to ~-cone for expected ~ of great violence; ‖~*-finch,* stormy petrel; ~*-glass,* sealed tube containing a solution of which the clarity is affected by temperature, formerly regarded as efficient weather-glass; ~*-petrel,* stormy petrel; ~*-sail,* of smaller size & stouter canvas than the corresponding one used in ordinary weather; ~*-signal,* ~-cone, ~-drum, or other device for warning of an approaching ~; ~*-tossed,* lit. & fig.; ~*-troops,* shock-troops, (also) a Nazi semi-military organization (~*-trooper,* member of this); ~*-wind;* ~*-window,* as ~-*door;* ~*-zone,* ~-belt; hence ~*LESS,* ~*'PROOF²,* aa. **6.** vb. (Of wind, rain, etc.) rage, be violent. **7.** Talk violently, rage, bluster, fume, scold (intr.), (often *at* object of displeasure). **8.** Take by ~ (~*ing-party,* detachment told off to begin assault; so ~*'ER¹* n.). [OE, ¨OS *storm,* OHG *sturm,* ON *stormr* f. Gmc *sturmaz* f. *stur-* STIR¹]

stŏrm′|ÿ, a. Of marked violence, raging, vehement, boisterous, (~*y wind, sea, waves, passions, temper, abuse*); infested or troubled with lit. or fig. storms (*a* ~*y coast, sea, night, debate, life*); associated with or threatening storms (~*y petrel; a* ~*y sunset*). Hence ~*ILY²* adv., ~*INESS* n. [ME; -Y²]

stŏr′t(h)ing (-tǐ-), n. Norwegian Parliament. [Norw. (-*ti*-), f. *stor* great, *t(h)ing* assembly]

stŏr′ÿ¹, n. **1.** History (arch.; *versed in classic* ~). **2.** Past course of person's or institution's life (*his* ~ *is an eventful one; in our rough island*~). **3.** Account given of an incident (*they all tell the same* ~; *according to his own* ~, suggestion of doubt as to his veracity; *to make a long* ~ *short,* formula excusing omission of details; *it is quite another* ~ *now,* we now hear a different account, esp. = things have changed; *the* ~ *goes,* it is said); any narrative or descriptive article in a newspaper. **4.** Piece of narrative, tale of any length told or printed in prose or verse of actual or fictitious events, legend, myth, anecdote, novel, romance, (*tell me a* ~; *but is the* ~ *true?; short* ~, relating usu. a single incident & published as article in magazine or as one of a collection; *good, funny,* ~, amusing anecdote often embodying witticism or ludicrous situation; *but that is another* ~, formula for breaking off & tantalizing reader with allusion). **5.** Main facts or plot of novel or epic or play (*reads only for the* ~; *the* ~ *is the least part of the book*). **6.** Facts or experiences that deserve narration (*that face must have a* ~ *belonging to it*). **7.** (nursery.) Lie, fib, liar (*oh you* ~*!*). **8.** ~*-book,* containing ~ or stories; ~*-teller,* Eastern making a living by telling stories to audience, writer of stories, retailer of anecdotes in society, (nursery) liar. [ME *storie* f. AF *estorie* (OF *estoire*) f. L as HISTORY]

story². See STOREY.

|| **stôt**, n. (north. dial.). Young ox, steer. [OE *stot(t)*; cf. ON *stutr* bull]

stoup (-ōop), n. (arch.). Flagon, beaker, drinking-vessel; holy-water basin. [f. ON *staup* = OE *stéap*, OHG *stouf* f. Gmc *staupaz, -am*]

stout, a. & n. 1. Brave, doughty, resolute, vigorous, sturdy, stubborn, staunch, strongly built, (~ *fellow*, arch., also colloq., good at fighting etc.; *a ~ heart*, courage, whence ~**heart'**ED² (-hār-) a., ~**heart'**edLY² adv., ~**heart'**edNESS n.; *made a ~ resistance*; *a ~ opponent*; *a ~ stick, ship*, etc.); corpulent, bulky, tending to fatness; hence ~'ISH¹(2) a., ~'LY² adv., ~'NESS n. 2. n. Kind of strong dark-brown beer brewed (esp. in Dublin) with roasted malt. [ME *st(o)ute*, f. OF*estout* adj. f. WG *stulla-* (= MHG, G *stolz* proud)]

stove¹, n., & v.t. 1. Kinds of closed apparatus in which heat is produced by consumption of wood, coal, charcoal, oil, gas, or other fuel, for use in warming rooms, cooking, etc.; (gardening) hot-house with artificial heat; ~*-pipe*, conducting smoke & gases from~ to chimney (*~-pipe hat*, tall silk hat). 2. v.t. Force, raise, (plants) in ~. [ME = sweating-room; f. MDu., MLG *stove*, corresp. to OE *stofa*, OHG *stuba*]

stove². See STAVE².

stow (-ō), v.t. Pack (goods etc.) in right or convenient places without waste of room (~ *thing away*, place it where it will not cause obstruction); fill (receptacle) with articles compactly arranged; (sl., usu. in imperat.) abstain from, cease to indulge in, (~ *larks, that nonsense*, etc.); ~'*away*, person getting free passage by hiding aboard ship (~ *away* as v.i., do this); ~'*wood*, billets used for chocking casks in ship's hold. Hence ~'AGE(1, 3, 4) (-ōĭj) n. [ME *stow, stouwe*, etc., f. OE *stōw* a place; in (16th c.) naut. sense perh. infl. by Du. *stouwen*]

strabis'm|us (-z-), n. Squinting, squint, (*cross-eyed* ~*us*, with eye or eyes turning inward; *wall-eyed* ~*us*, outward). Hence ~IC, ~AL, aa. [mod. L, f. Gk *strabismos* (*strabos* squinting, -ISM)]

strabot'omy̆, n. Operation of cutting eyeball muscle to cure squint. [prec., -TOMY]

strǎd'dl|e, v.i. & t., & n. 1. Take or be in attitude with legs wide apart; stand or sit across (thing) thus (*cannot~e his horse*; *stood* ~*ing the ditch*); part (one's legs) widely; (nav.) drop shots short of & beyond (target, enemy) esp. to find range; drop bombs from side to side across (target); (fig.) vacillate between two policies etc., sit on the fence. 2. n. Act of ~ing lit. or fig.; (St. Exch.) contract giving holder the right of either calling for or

delivering stock at fixed price. [frequent. of *strad-*, var. of *strid-* STRIDE, see -LE(3)]

Strădivăr'ius (*or* -ār-), (colloq.) **Străd**, n. Violin or other stringed instrument made by ~ of Cremona (d. 1737).

strafe (-ahf; *-āf), v.t., & n. (sl.). 1. Bombard, worry with shells, bombs, sniping, etc.; reprimand or abuse or thrash. 2. n. Piece of strafing (*the morning* ~, gunfire at dawn). [joc. adaptation of G 1914 catchword *Gott* ~ (God chastise) *England*]

strǎg'gl|e, v.i. Stray from the main body, fail to remain compact, get dispersed, proceed in scattered irregular order, be sporadic, occur here & there, (*crowd* ~*ed along*; *plant* ~*es*, grows long & weedy; ~*ing village, houses*, etc.). Hence ~ER¹ n., ~ingLY² adv., ~Y² a. [perh. alt. f. *strackle* frequent. of dial. *strake* rel. to STRETCH]

straight (-āt), a., n., & adv. 1. Without curve or bend, extending uniformly in same direction, (~ *line* in geom., lying evenly between any two of its points; ~ *arch*, shaped like inverted V, without curves; *a ~ back*, not bowed; *a ~ knee*, not bent; ~ *.legs*, not bandy or knock-kneed; ~ *hair*, not curly; (of aim, look, blow, course) going direct to the mark; upright, honest, candid, (~ *dealings, speaking*; *is perfectly ~ in all his dealings*; ~ *thinking*, logical, not swayed by emotion); in proper order or place, level, symmetrical, (*are the pictures* ~? *put things* ~, get rid of disorder; *accounts are* ~, made up in due form; *a ~ race* etc., in which competitors do their best to win); direct from source (~ *tip*, hint esp. as to likely winner of race or prospects of investment got from good authority); *neat (a whisky* ~), undiluted, unmixed; *the ~ ticket*, the party programme without modification; ~ *jet*, jet aircraft with no propeller; ~*for'ward*, honest, open, frank, (of task etc.) presenting no complications; so ~*for'wardly* adv., ~*for'wardness* n.; ~'*way* (arch.), at once, immediately; hence ~EN⁶ v.t. & i., ~'NESS n., (-āt-). 2. n. ~ condition (*is out of the* ~, crooked); ~ part of something, esp. concluding stretch of racecourse (*they were even as they reached the* ~); sequence of five cards in poker. 3. adv. In a ~ line, direct, without deviation or circumlocution, (*go* ~; *hit* ~ *from the shoulder*, in boxing, also fig.; *ride* ~, taking fences etc. instead of going round; *comes* ~ *from Paris*; *is making* ~ *for a precipice*; *told it him* ~ *out*)* in right direction, with good aim, (*shoot* ~); correctly (*does not see* ~); (arch.) at once (also in ~ *away*, sl., immediately; ~ *off*, without hesitation, deliberation, etc., as *cannot tell you* ~ *off*). 4. ~*-cut*, (tobacco) cut lengthwise into long silky fibres; ~*-edge*, bar with one edge accurately ~, used for testing; ~*-eight*, motor vehicle with eight cylinders in line; ~ *eye*, ability to detect deviation from the ~; ~ *face* (intention-ally inexpressive); ~ *fight* (pol.), direct contest between two candidates. [ME *stregt*, p.p. of *strecche* STRETCH]

strain[1], v.t. & i. 1. Stretch tightly, make taut, exercise to greatest possible or beyond legitimate extent, press to ex-tremes, wrest or distort from true in-tention or meaning, (~ *parchment across the aperture*; ~ *rope to breaking-point*; ~ *every nerve*, do one's utmost; ~ *one's ears, eyes, voice*, etc., listen etc. to best of one's power, & see below; ~ *one's authority, powers, rights*, etc., or *the law* etc., apply them beyond their province or in violation of their true intention; ~ *a point*, go further than one is entitled or can be expected to, esp. in the way of concession, to effect a purpose; *a ~ed interpretation* or *sense*, got by pressing some rule of grammar etc. too far; *~ing-beam, -piece,* horizontal beam used as strut between tops of queen-posts). 2. Hug (person) *to* oneself or one's breast etc. 3. p.p. Pro-duced under compulsion or by effort, artificial, forced, constrained, not spon-taneous, (*the quality of mercy is not ~ed,* mercy should be spontaneous; *~ed man-ner, laugh, cordiality,* etc.). 4. Overtask, injure or try or imperil by over-use or making of excessive demands, (*take care not to ~ your eyes, voice,* etc.; *for fear of ~ing his followers' loyalty*; *has ~ed a muscle, his leg, his heart,* etc.; *ship is ~ed,* has had parts wrenched out of rigid state; *~ed relations,* over-sensitiveness between parties who have tried each other's for-bearance too far). 5. Make intense effort, strive intensely *after,* tug *at*, hold out with difficulty under or *under* pressure, (*the ~ing horses, masts*; *plants ~ing upwards to the light*; *dogs, horses, rowers,* ~ *at the leash, collar, oar*; *porter ~ing under his load*; *~s too much after epigram, effect,* etc.). 6. Clear (liquid) of solid matter by passing through sieve or other *~'*ER[1](2) n.; filter (solids) *out* from liquid; (of liquid) perco-late. 7. ~ *at a gnat,* be over-scrupulous (ref. to *Matt.* xxiii. 24, prop. ~ *out,* see R.V., in prec. sense). Hence *~'*ABLE a. [ME *streine* f. OF *estreindre estreign-* f. L *stringere strict-*]

strain[2], n. 1. Pull, stretching force, ten-sion, demand upon or force that tries cohesion or strength or stability or re-sources, exertion required to meet such demand or to do something difficult, in-jury or change of structure resulting from such exertion or force, (*the ~ on the rope was tremendous*; *was a great ~ on my resources, attention, credulity*; *the ~ of modern life*; *is suffering from~* or *over-~*; *all his senses were on the ~*, exerted to the utmost; *is epigrammatic without ~*, ap-pearance of undue effort; *has a ~ in his leg*). 2. (phys., mech.). Condition of a body subjected to stress, molecular dis-placement. 3. (poet. & rhet., usu. in pl.).

Burst or snatch or spell of music or poetry (*martial, inspiriting, pathetic,* etc., *~s,* music or poetry of such character; *the ~s of the harp, of the Elizabethan poets,* etc.). 4. Tone or style adopted in talking or writing, tendency of discourse, (*he went on in another ~; & much more in the same ~*). 5. Moral tendency forming part of a character (*there is a ~ of weakness, ferocity, mysticism, in him*). 6. Breed of animals, human stock or family, (*comes of a good ~*). [ME; senses 1–5 f. prec.; sense 6 f. OE *strēon* gain, progeny]

strait, a. & n. 1. Narrow, limited, confined or confining, (arch. exc. in ~ *gate* w. ref. to *Matt.* vii. 14,~ *jacket* or usu. *waistcoat,* strong garment put on maniacs to confine arms, which are either in sleeves so long that the ends can be tied or are strapped within body of jacket, & in *~-laced* now fig. only, severely virtuous, morally scrupulous, puritanic). 2. Strict (arch. exc. in *~est sect of* w. ref. to *Acts* xxvi. 5); hence *~'*LY[2] adv. (arch.), *~'*NESS n. (arch.), *~'*EN[2] v.t. (*~ened circumstances,* poverty; *is ~ened for,* ill supplied with). 2. n. Narrow passage of water connecting two seas or large bodies of water (usu. in pl. when used of particular ~ with name, as *the S~s of Messina, Dover*; *S~s Settle-ments,* former Crown colony on S~s of Malacca & Singapore; *the S~s,* formerly of Gibraltar, now usu. of Malacca); (usu. pl.) difficult position, need, distress, (esp. *in ~s*). [ME *streit,* f. OF *estreit* f. L *strictus* STRICT]

strāke, n. Continuous line of planking or plates from stem to stern of ship (GAR-BOARD ~). [ME, app. f. *strak-* whence Gmc *strakkjan* STRETCH]

stramin'eous, a. (arch.). Of, light or worthless as, coloured like, straw. [f. L *stramineus* (*stramen* -*inis* straw)+-OUS]

stramōn'ium, n. (Drug, much used in asthma, from seeds or leaves of) kind of datura. [mod. L, of uncert. orig.]

strānd[1], n., & v.t. & i. 1. Margin of sea, lake, or river (rhet., poet.). 2. vb. Run (t. & i. of ship) aground; (p.p.) in diffi-culties, unable to get along esp. for want of funds or other resources, left behind while others advance. [OE *strand,* MLG *strand-,* ON *strond*]

strānd[2], n., & v.t. 1. One of the strings or wires by twisting which a rope is made; (fig.) element or strain in any composite whole. 2. v.t. Break a ~ in (rope). [15th– –18th c. also *strond*; orig. unkn.]

strānge (-j), a. 1. Foreign, alien, not one's own, not familiar or well known (*to*), novel, queer, peculiar, eccentric, singular, surprising, unaccountable, unexpected, (*in a ~ land*; *worship ~ gods*; *cannot play on a ~ ground, with a ~ racket*; *the place, work, handwriting, is ~ to me*; *it is a ~ thing, story*; *how ~ that you should not have heard!*; *wears the ~st clothes*; *is very ~ in his manner*, seems mad etc.; *truth is*

~*r than fiction*; *repeating the question with* ~ *persistency*; *feel* ~, not in one's usual condition, esp. dizzy etc.; *it feels* ~, is a novel sensation), whence ~'LY² (-jll) adv. **2.** Fresh or unaccustomed *to*, unacquainted, bewildered, (*am* ~ *to the work*; *am quite* ~ *here*, do not know my way about or the people etc.; *feel* ~, not at home, out of one's element etc.). Hence ~'NESS (-jn-) n.; [ME *strang, straung*(*e*), f. OF *estrange* f. L EXTRAneus]

strān′ger (-j-), n. Foreigner, person in a country or town or company that he does not belong to, person unknown to or *to* one (in U.S. as rustic voc. = *sir* etc.), person entirely unaccustomed *to* some feeling or practice or experience, (*am a* ~ *here*, do not know my way about etc.; ‖ *spy* or *see* ~*s* in House of Commons, demand withdrawal of all but members or officials; *make a, no,* ~ *of,* treat distantly, cordially; *you are quite a* ~, seldom show yourself here; *is no, a,* ~ *to me,* I know, do not know him; *is a, no,* ~ *to fear, court-intrigues*, has had no, much, experience of; *the little* ~, newborn child). [ME *straunger*(*e*), f. OF *estrangier*, as prec., -ER²(2)]

strangle (străng′gl), v.t. Throttle, kill by squeezing windpipe; (of collar etc.) squeeze (neck); (fig.) suppress (movement, impulse, etc.); ~*hold*, deadly grip (usu. fig. in pol. or commerce). [ME *strangel, -ul*, f. OF *estrangler* f. L *strangulare* f. Gk *straggalaō*]

strangles (străng′glz), n. pl. (usu. treated as sing). Infectious catarrh in horse, ass, etc. [f. prec.]

străng′ūl|āte (-ngg-), v.t. Strangle (rare); (path., surg.) prevent circulation through (vein, intestine, etc.) by compression. Hence ~A′TION n. [f. L as STRANGLE, -ATE³]

străng′ūrȳ (-ngg-), n. Disease in which urine is passed painfully & in drops; disease produced in plants by bandaging. So **străngūr′ious** (-ngg-) a. [f. L f. Gk *straggouria* (*stragx -ggos* drop squeezed out, *ouron* urine)]

străp, n., & v.t. (-pp-). **1.** Strip of leather; strip of leather or other flexible material with buckle or other fastening for holding things together or other purpose (SHOULDER-~; *rug, umbrella,* etc., ~*,* pair of ~s with holder joining them for making bundle); strip of metal used to secure or connect, leaf of hinge, etc.; (bot.) tongue-shaped part in ligulate floret; *the* ~, chastisement with a ~. **2.** ~*hanger,* bus or train passenger who has to stand & hold on by ~ for want of sitting space; ~*laid,* (of rope) made by laying ropes side by side & joining them into a flat band; ~*oil,* beating given with ~; ~*work,* ornamentation imitating plaited ~s; ~*wort,* kind of white-flowered knotgrass. Hence ~′LESS a., (of dress) without shoulder-~s. **3.** v.t. Secure with ~ (often *up, down,* etc.; ~*ped*

trousers, held down by ~ passing below instep for riding etc.); strop, whet, (razor, knife); (surg.) close (wound), bind (part), up or *up* with adhesive plaster or ~p′ING¹(4) n.; flog with ~; (part. as adj., cf. *thumping, whacking, whopping* big, lusty, tall, (*a* ~*ping girl, fellow*), whence ~p′ER¹ n. [dial. form of STROP]

strappād′ō, n. (pl. ~s), & v.t. **1.** Torture inflicted by securing person's hands or other part in ropes, raising him, & letting him fall till brought up by taut rope. **2.** v.t. Subject to ~. [f. F *strapade* f. It. *strappata* (*strappare* pull); for *-o* see -ADO(2)]

strāss, n. Paste used in making artificial gems. [G, f. name of inventor, Josef *Strasser*]

strata. See STRATUM.

străt′agĕm, n. (An) artifice, trick(ery), device(s) for deceiving enemy, (*devised a* ~; *must be effected by* ~). [15th c., f. F *stratagème* f. L f. Gk *stratēgēma* (*stratēgeō* be STRATEGUS)]

strate′gic, a. Of, dictated by, serving the ends of, strategy (~ *skill, considerations, movement, position*); (of bombing) designed to disorganize the enemy's internal economy & to destroy morale. Hence ~AL a. (now rare), ~alLY² adv., **strate′gics** n. [f. F *-ique* f. Gk *stratēgikos* (foll., -IC)]

stratēg′us, n. (Gk ant.; pl. *-gi* pr. *-gī* or *-jī*). Military commander, esp. one of annually appointed board of ten at Athens. [L, f. Gk *stratēgos* (*stratos* army, *agō* lead)]

străt′ēgȳ, n. Generalship, the art of war, (lit. & fig.); management of an army or armies in a campaign, art of so moving or disposing troops or ships or aircraft as to impose upon the enemy the place & time & conditions for fighting preferred by oneself, (cf. TACTICS). Hence ~IST(3) n. [f. F *stratégie* f. Gk *stratēgia* (prec., -IA¹)]

străth, n. (Sc.). Broad mountain valley; ~*spey′* (-ā), (music for) a lively Scottish dance (named f. *Strathspey* valley of the Spey). [f. Gael. *srath*]

stratic′ulate, a. (geol.). Arranged in thin layers. [STRATUM, -I-, -CULE, -ATE²]

străt′i|fȳ, v.t. Arrange in strata (esp. p.p.). So ~FICA′TION n. [f. F *stratifier* f. med. L *stratificare* (STRATUM, -FY)]

strāto-, comb. form of STRATUS, as ~*cī′rrus*, ~*cūm′ulus*.

stratŏc′racȳ, n. Military government, domination of soldiers. [Gk *stratos* army, -CRACY]

străt′osphēre, n. The layer of atmospheric air lying above the TROPOSPHERE, in which the temperature ceases to fall with height, remaining constant. [STRATO- +SPHERE]

străt′|um, n. (pl. ~*a*). (Geol.) layer, or set of successive layers, of any deposited substance; (transf.) social grade (*the various* ~*a of society*). Hence ~AL, **străt′iFORM, aa., stratiĠ′RAPHY(2) n.,**

strătĭGRAPH'IC a., strătĭgrăph'ICALLY
adv. [L, = something spread or laid
down, neut. p.p. of *sternere* strew]

strāt'us, n. (pl. *-ti*). Continuous horizontal sheet of cloud. [assim. of prec. to
termination of *cumulus* & other CLOUDS]

straw, n., & v.t. **1.** Dry cut stalks of kinds
of grain as material for bedding, thatching, packing, hats, etc. (*made of, thatched
etc. with*, ~ ; *a load of* ~ ; ~ *mattress, hat,
rope*, etc.; *in the* ~, arch., in childbed;
man of ~, stuffed effigy, imaginary person
set up as opponent etc., person without
substantial means); ~ *hat*; single stalk or
piece of ~, insignificant trifle, (*with a* ~ *in
his mouth*; *lemonade sucked through* ~*s*;
draw ~*s*, draw lots with ~*s* of different
lengths; *make bricks without* ~, of persons
set to work without adequate means, see
Exod. v. 7; *catch at a* ~, resort to utterly
inadequate expedient like drowning man;
the last ~, slight addition that makes
something no longer tolerable as with
camel's load; *a* ~ *shows which way the
wind blows*, slight hint may suggest much;
is not worth, don't care, a ~). **2.** ~*-board*,
coarse cardboard made of ~ ; ~*-colour(ed)*,
(of) pale yellow; ~*-stem*, wineglass with
stem not made separately & attached but
drawn out of bowl; *~ vote* (pol.), unofficial balloting as test of strength;
~*-worm*, caddis; hence ~'Y² a. **3.** v.t.
(arch.). Strew. [OE *strēaw*, OS, MDu.,
MLG, OHG *strō*, ON *strá* f. Gmc *strāwam*
f. *strau-, *strew- STREW]

straw'berry, n. (Kind of perennial plant
throwing out runners & producing) pulpy
red fruit having surface studded with
yellow seeds (*crushed* ~, kind of dull
crimson; || *the* ~ *leaves*, ducal rank, w. ref.
to ornamentation of duke's coronet);
~*-mark*, soft reddish birthmark; ~ *pear*,
(fruit of) W.-Ind. cactaceous plant; ~
roan, red ROAN¹; ~*-tree*, evergreen arbutus
bearing ~*-like* fruit. [OE *strēaw-,
strēowberige* (STRAW, BERRY)]

stray, v.i. (p.p. as -ED¹, 2), n., & a. **1.** Wander, go aimlessly, deviate from the right
way or from virtue, lose one's way, get
separated from flock or companions or
proper place. **2.** n. ~ed domestic animal;
WAIFS & ~*s*; || property of deceased
person escheating to crown in default of
heirs; (radio, usu. in pl.) = ATMOSPHERICS.
3. adj. (no comp. & sup.). ~ed; scattered,
sporadic, occurring or met with now &
then or casually or unexpectedly, (*a few
~ instances; a* ~ *customer or two came in;
hit by a* ~ *bullet*). [(vb) ME, aphetic f.
astray, estray vbs f. OF *estraier* f. Rom.
estravagare f. L *extra vagari* EXTRAVAGATE;
(n.) ME, f. AF *stray, estrai,* f. *estraier,*
partly f. the vb; (adj.) 17th c., partly f.
ASTRAY, partly f. n.]

streak, n., & v.t. & i. **1.** Long narrow
irregular line or band or layer-edge, esp.
one distinguished by colour, visible on a
surface (*black with red* ~*s; a* ~ *of light

above the horizon; bacon with ~*s of fat &
lean;* ~ *of lightning,* flash; *like a* ~ *of
lightning,* or *a* ~, swiftly; || *the silver* ~,
English Channel; *has a* ~ *of humour,
superstition,* etc., *in him,* strain or element); hence ~'Y² a., ~'ILY² adv., ~'INESS
n. **2.** vb. (Usu. in p.p.) mark with ~(s);
(intr.) move very rapidly (*like a* ~ *of
lightning*). [OE *strica*, = OHG *strich,*
Goth. *striks,* f. Gmc *strik- STRIKE]

stream, n., & v.i. & t. **1.** Body of water
running in bed, river, or brook, (*on the
banks of a* ~; *up, down,* ~, moving or
situated upwards, downwards, on river),
whence ~'LESS a., ~'LET n.; flow of any
liquid, onward moving fluid mass or
crowd, (sing. or pl.) large quantity of or
of something that flows or moves along,
(*saw a* ~ *of lava; came out, went by, in a
~ or* ~*s; a* ~, ~*s, of blood, tears, people*);
current, direction of flow, (GULF-~; *with,
against, the* ~; *go with the* ~, do as others
do; *the* ~ *of tendency, thought, is the other
way*). **2.** ~*-anchor,* intermediate between
bower & kedge esp. for use in warping;
~*-line,* (n.) natural course of water or air
currents (~*line shape* in aircraft, motor-
-car, etc., that calculated to cause least
resistance), (v.t.) give a ~*line* form to;
hence ~'Y² a. (rare). **3.** vb. Flow or move
as a ~; run with liquid (~*ing eyes, windows, umbrella*); (of banner, loose hair,
etc.) float or wave in the wind; emit ~ of
(blood etc.). [OE *strēam,* OS *strōm,* OHG
stroum, ON *straumr* f. Gmc *straumaz*]

stream'er, n. Pennon, ribbon attached
at one end & floating or waving at the
other; column of light shooting up in
aurora. [ME; -ER¹]

street, n. Town or village road that has
(mainly) contiguous houses on one side
or both, this with the houses, (*go down,
across, the* ~; *main, side, broad,* etc., ~;
live in the ~, be constantly outside one's
house; *lives in a fashionable* ~; MAN¹ *in
the* ~; *not in the same* ~ *with,* colloq.,
utterly inferior to in ability etc.; *window
looks on the* ~; *in the* ~, said of St.-Exch.
business done after closing hours; *on the
~s,* living by prostitution; KEY¹ *of the* ~;
GRUB-STREET; HIGH, LOMBARD, QUEER, ~;
~ ARAB; || ~ *cries,* of hawkers; || ~ *orderly,*
scavenger); (arch.) paved road, highway
(as *Watling S~*); WALL STREET; *the* ~,
= *Fleet S~, Wall S~*; ~*-car,* tram-car;
~*-door,* opening on ~; ~*-sweeper,* esp.
machine with revolving brush for cleaning ~*s*; ~*-walker,* common prostitute.
Hence (-)~ED² a., ~'WARD adv. & a. [OE
strǣt, OS *strāta,* OHG *straza* f. LL *strata*
(ellipt. f. *via strata* paved road), f. *sternere
strat-* lay]

strength, n. **1.** Being STRONG, degree in
which person or thing is strong, (*the* ~ *of
a man, rope, beam, fortress, current, argument, fleet; the* ~ *of wine, acid, tea, evidence;* ~ *of body, mind, will, memory,
judgement; his* ~ *is in endurance; has the

~ *of a horse*, is as strong; *has not the* ~ *to lift a cup, walk upstairs; that is beyond human, too much for my,* ~; MEASURE[3] one's ~ *with; on the* ~ *of,* encouraged by or relying on or arguing from, as *I did it on the* ~ *of your promise*). 2. What makes strong (*God is our* ~; *his* ~ *is patience*). 3. Proportion of whole number present (*were there in great, full,* ~); full complement (*up to, below,* ~). 4. ‖ (mil. etc.). *On the* ~, on the muster-roll (*was taken, is, on the* ~). [OE *strengthu* (*strang* STRONG, -TH[1])]

streng'then, v.t. & i. Make or become stronger; ~ *one's hands* (fig.), encourage him to vigorous action. [-EN[6]]

stren'uous, a. Energetic, unrelaxing, ardently persistent; requiring exertion. Hence ~LY[2] adv., ~NESS n. [f. L *strenuus* + -OUS]

Streph'on, n. Fond lover (~ *& Chloe*, pair of lovers). [character in Sidney's *Arcadia*]

strepitos'o, mus. direction. Noisily. [It.]

streptocŏcc'us, n. (pl. -*ci*). Any of a group of bacteria which, as they remain attached after fission, are usu. found in chains. [Gk *streptos* twisted (*strephō* turn), *kokkos* a grain]

streptomy'cin, n. An antibiotic produced by the *Streptomyces* group of bacteria, effective against some groups of disease- -producing bacteria which are immune to penicillin. [f. Gk *streptos* (prec.), *mukēs* fungus, -IN]

Strep'yan, a. Of the stage of palaeolithic culture represented by remains found at Strépy in Belgium. [-AN]

stress, n., & v.t. 1. Constraining or im- pelling force *of* (*under, driven by,* ~ *of weather, poverty,* etc.). 2. Effort, demand upon energy, (STORM *& ~; subjected to great ~; times of slackness & times of* ~). 3. Emphasis (*lay* ~ *on*, convey that one attaches importance to); accentuation, emphasis laid on syllable or word, *a* or the accent, (~ *& quantity are different metrical principles; the* ~ *is on the first syllable, on the word 'permissive'*). 4. (mech.). Force exerted between contiguous bodies or parts of a body. Hence ~'LESS a. 5. v.t. Lay the ~ on, accent, emphasize; subject to mechanical ~. [ME; vb in present sense f. n., which is prob. aphetic f. DISTRESS[1]]

stretch, v.t. & i., & n. 1. Make taut, tighten, straighten, place somewhere in tight-drawn or outspread state, (*the rope must be ~ed tight; ~ a wire across the road; with a canopy ~ed over them;* ~ *trousers,* remove creases etc. by pulling out in frame; ~ *oneself* or ~ abs., tighten muscles after sleeping etc. by extending limbs etc. in various directions; ~ *one's legs,* straighten them by walking as relief from sitting etc.; ~ *one on the ground,* knock him sprawling; (p.p.) lying *at full length, on the lawn,* etc.; ~ *out hand, foot,*

etc., extend it by straightening arm or leg; ~ *out,* abs., reach out hand, also begin to lengthen stride). 2. Strain, exert to utmost or beyond legitimate extent, make the most of, do violence to, exagger- ate, (~ *a point, a principle,* one's *powers,* one's *credit,* = *strain;* ~ *the truth* or ~ abs., exaggerate, lie). 3. Have specified length or extension, be continuous between points or to or from a point, (~*es from end to end, across the sky, to infinity; road ~es away, memory ~es down, from* or *to* place or period). 4. Draw, be drawn or admit of being drawn, out into greater length or extension or size (*gloves, boots, want ~ing; it ~es like elastic*); (sl.) hang (person). 5. n. ~*ing* or being ~ed (*with a* ~ *& a yawn,* whence ~Y[2] a., ~'INESS n.; *by a* ~ *of authority, language,* etc.; *with every faculty on the* ~). 6. Continuous expanse or tract or spell (~ *of road, open country,* etc.; *works ten hours at a* ~); (naut.) distance covered on one tack; (sl.) imprisonment for a year, any term of imprisonment. [OE *streccan,* OHG *strecken,* f. WG *strakkjan* f. *strak-* straight]

stretch'er, n. In vbl senses: esp.: brick or stone laid with side in face of wall (cf. HEADER); board in boat against which rower presses feet; appliance, often of canvas stretched on oblong frame, for carrying disabled person on; wooden frame over which canvas of picture is stretched; (sl.) exaggeration, lie; ~-*bond,* method of building in which all bricks are ~s but joints of contiguous courses do not coincide. [-ER[1]]

strew, v.t. (-*ōō*) (p.p. ~*n,* ~*ed*). Scatter (sand, flowers, small objects) over a sur- face; (partly) cover (surface, object) with small objects scattered. [OE *strewian* etc., OS *stroian,* OHG *strouwen,* ON *strá,* Goth. *straujan* f. Gmc **strau-,* perh. rel. to L *sternere strat-*; cf. STRAW]

stri'a, n. (anat., zool., bot., geol.; pl. ~*ae*). Linear mark on surface, slight ridge or furrow or score. Hence ~ATE[2] a., ~ATE[3] v.t., ~ately[3] adv., ~A'TION[3] ~ature, nn. [L]

stricken. See STRIKE.

stric'kle, n. Rod used in STRIKE-*measure;* whetstone. [OE *stricel* (STRIKE)]

strict, a. Precisely limited or defined, accurate, tense, without irregularity or exception or deviation, requiring implicit obedience or exact performance, not lax, (*in the* ~ *sense; keep* ~ *watch; lives in* ~ *seclusion; was told me in* ~ *confidence; gave* ~ *orders; a* ~ *code of laws or customs; ~ morals,* admitting no laxity; ~ *parents, schoolmaster, discipline*). Hence ~'LY[6] adv. (~*ly speaking,* if one is to use words in their ~ sense), ~'NESS n. [f. L *strictus* STRAIT (*stringere strict-* tighten]

stric'tur|e, n. (Usu. in pl.) piece of cen- sure, critical remark, (usu. *on* or *upon*); (path.) morbid contraction of some canal or duct in the body, whence ~ED[6]

(-kcherd) a. [ME, f. L *strictura* (prec., -URE)]

stride, v.i. & t. (past *strode*, rare p.p. *stridden* or *strid*), & n. 1. Walk with long steps; pass over (ditch etc.) with one step; bestride, straddle (trans.). 2. n. Single step esp. in respect of length, gait as determined by length of ∼, (*walks with vigorous* ∼s *or a vigorous* ∼; *take* obstacle *in* one's ∼, clear it without changing step to jump, (fig.) find no serious impediment in it; *get into* one's∼, (fig.) settle down steadily to the job in hand); distance between feet parted either laterally or as in walking. [OE *stridan* = (M)LG *striden* in same sense; formally rel. to & prob. identical w. OS *stridian,* OHG *stritan,* ON *stritha* strive, quarrel]

strid'ent, a. Loud & harsh in sound. Hence ∼LY[2] adv. [L *stridere* creak, -ENT]

strid'ŭl|āte, v.i. (entom.). Make shrill jarring sound (of cicadas, grasshoppers, etc.). So ∼ANT a., ∼A'TION, ∼ātor, nn. [L *stridulus* creaking (prec.), -ATE[3]]

strife, n. Contention, state of conflict, struggle between opposed persons or things. [ME, aphetic f. OF *estrif,* cf. *estriver* STRIVE]

stri'gil, n. Skin-scraper used by ancients at bath. [f. L *strigilis* (*stringere* graze)]

strig'ōse, strig'ous, aa. (bot.). With short stiff hairs or scales. [L *striga* swath, -OSE[1], -OUS]

strike, v.t. & i. (*struck, struck* & as specified below *stricken*), & n. 1. Hit, hit upon or (*up*)*on,* deliver blow(s) or stroke(s), (*struck me in the mouth, with his fist;* ∼ *ball out of court* etc., send it with blow; ∼ *weapon up* or *down* or *aside,* divert it by blow; ∼ one's *foot against a stone,* one's *hand on the table;* ∼ while IRON[1] *is hot; striking--force,* esp. military body ready to deliver blow at short notice; *within striking--distance,* near enough to ∼; ∼ *a blow,* or ∼, *for freedom; hammer* ∼s on or ∼s *bell; ship* ∼s *rock* or on *rock* or ∼s, runs on it; ∼ *hands,* arch., touch or clasp them in sign of agreement made; *was struck by a stone, lightning; a stricken heart,* afflicted by strokes of grief; *stricken with fever, pesti-lence, paralysis,* etc.; *a stricken field,* pitched battle or scene of it; *stricken in years,* enfeebled by age; ∼ *out,* hit from the shoulder, also use arms & legs in swimming or feet in skating; ∼ *upon an idea, plan,* etc., have it luckily occur to one; ∼ OIL[1]; *light* ∼s *upon* object, illu-minates it; ∼ *at,* aim blow at; ∼ *at the root of,* threaten destruction to; ∼ *back,* return blow; ∼ *home,* get blow well in; ∼ *all of a heap,* colloq., dumbfound; ∼ *fish* or ∼ abs., jerk tackle in order to secure hook in mouth; ∼ *the track,* come upon it). 2. Produce or record or bring into speci-fied state by stroke(s) or striking (∼ *coin,* make it by stamping; ∼ *bargain,* make it as by striking hands; ∼ *sparks, fire,*

light, out of flint; ∼ *a match,* ignite by striking against something; ∼ *a light,* produce by striking match; *match will not* ∼, give light when struck; *clock* ∼s *the hour, five,* etc.; *the hour has struck,* clock has struck it, & fig. the critical moment has come or gone; ∼ one *blind, deaf,* etc., blind, deafen, etc., him at one stroke; ∼ *me dead!,* vulg., form of as-severation; ∼ *down,* fell with blow lit. or fig.; ∼ *his head off,* behead; ∼ *out plan* etc., forge or devise; ∼ *out a line for* one-*self,* be original; ∼ *item* or *name out* or *off,* ∼ *word through,* expunge with pen-stroke; ∼ *up an acquaintance,* start it rapidly or casually; band or person ∼s *up a tune* or ∼s *up,* starts playing or singing as by stroke of drum). 3. Arrest attention of, occur to mind of, produce mental im-pression on, impress *as,* (*what struck me was the generosity of the offer; it* ∼s me he *or that he may have misunderstood; an idea suddenly struck me; how does it* ∼ *you?,* what do you think about it?; *it* ∼s me as *ridiculous, absolutely perfect*); (part.) sure to be noticed, arresting, impressive, whence **strik'ingLY**[2] adv., **strik'ingNESS** n. 4. Lower or take down (flag, sail, tent), signify surrender by striking flag, sur-render, (∼ one's *flag,* surrender ship or fortress to enemy, also resign a naval command; ∼ *tents,* break up camp; *town, ship,* ∼s, surrenders). 5. Cease (work), cease work, (of workmen) refuse to go on working unless employer accedes to some demand (cf. LOCK[3] *out;* ∼ *for higher pay, against long hours,* etc.). 6. (Cause to) penetrate (*struck a knife, terror, into his heart; cold* ∼s *through his clothes, into his marrow, the wind* ∼s *cold; plant* ∼s *its roots into the soil;* ∼s *root,* or ∼s abs.; *oysters* ∼, attach themselves to bed; *rays* ∼ *through fog; struck with terror, panic, dizziness,* etc., suddenly filled with). 7. Direct one's course somewhere, take specified direction, diverge *to,* start *into,* (*then* ∼ *to the right;* ∼ *into* or *out of a track, subject,* etc.; ∼ *in,* intervene in talk, often *with suggestion* etc.; *gout* ∼s *in,* attacks interior instead of extremities; ∼ *into a gallop,* begin galloping). 8. Level (grain etc. or the measure) in ∼ *measure* (see n.); ascertain (balance) by deducting credit or debit from the other; arrive at (average) by equalizing all items; compose (jury) by allowing both sides to reject same number. 9. Suddenly & dramatically assume (attitude). 10. ∼*-a-light,* appara-tus for getting light from flint. Hence **strik'ER**[1] (1, 2) n. 11. n. Concerted refusal to work by employees till some grievance is remedied (*on* ∼, acting on such refusal; ∼*'bound,* immobilized by ∼; ∼*-breakers,* workmen brought in to replace strikers; ∼ *pay,* allowance for subsistence made by trade union to workmen who have struck; *general* ∼, by workmen of all or most trades with a view' to securing some common object by paralysing business; SIT-*down*, STAY[1]-*in*, ~; *sympathetic* ~, by unaggrieved trade to give moral support to one on ~). **12.** = STRICKLE (~ *measure*, when grain etc. is measured by passing a rod across top of heaped vessel to secure that it shall be full & no more). **13.** *Sudden success at finding petroleum, gold, etc., or in financial operations. **14.** (In baseball) batsman's actual or constructive attempt to hit pitched ball. **15.** Attack, esp. from the air. [OE *strican* go, OHG *strîhhan*, f. WG *strîk-* cogn. w. L *stringere strict-* touch lightly]

string, n., & v.t. & i. (*strung*). **1.** Twine or fine cord, piece of this or of leather, ribbon, webbing, or other material, used for tying up, lacing, drawing or holding together, actuating puppet, etc., (*want some ~ & brown paper*; APRON, *bonnet*, BOW[1], *kite*, etc., ~; *two ~s to* one's BOW[1]; *first*, *second*, ~, person or thing that one's chief, alternative, reliance is set on, w. ref. to prec. phr.; *pull the ~s*, be the real actuator of what another does; *have person on a ~*, have under one's thumb; HEART-~*s*). **2.** Tough piece connecting two halves of pod in beans etc. **3.** Stretched piece of catgut, cord, or wire, yielding musical tone(s) in piano, harp, violin, & other instruments (*harp-*, *fiddle-*, ~; *touch the ~s*, play; *harp on one ~*, dwell on single subject; *touch a ~*, fig., excite particular feeling in person's heart; *the ~s*, the ~ed instruments in a band or part contributed by them to the effect, cf. *the* WIND[1]), whence (-)~ED[2] (-ngd) a. **4.** Set of or usu. *of* objects strung together or persons or things of one kind coming one after another (*a ~ of beads, onions, pearls; filed past in a long ~; a ~ of porters, horses, oaths, lies*). **5.** (billiards). Scoring-board with buttons sliding on wires. **6.** The racehorses, collectively, under training at a particular stable. **7.** pl. *Conditions attached to a gift, offer, etc. **8.** ~ *alphabet*, code for the blind in which special knots on ~ represent letters; ~ *band*, (prop.) of ~ed instruments only; ~-*bark*, STRINGY-*bark*; ~-*board*, supporting timber in which ends of staircase steps are set; ~-*course*, (also ~) raised horizontal band or course on a building; ~-*halt*, = SPRING[2]-*halt*; ~-*piece*, long timber supporting & connecting the parts of a framework; ~ *tie*, very narrow tie. Hence ~'LESS a. **9.** vb. Supply with ~(s), tie with ~. **10.** Secure (bow) in state ready for use by bending it & slipping loop of ~ into notch; (fig., chiefly in p.p.) tighten *up* or make ready or sensitive or excited (senses, nerves, resolution, or person in regard to them; *was strung up to do the deed; high-strung* or *highly strung nerves* or *person*, neurotic, susceptible, over-sensitive). **11.** Thread (beads etc.) on a ~; strip ~s from (beans). **12.** *(colloq.). Hoax. **13.** (colloq.). ~ (*per-*

son) *along*, deceive; ~ *along with*, accompany; ~ *up*, kill by hanging. **14.** (Of glue etc.) become stringy. **15.** (billiards). Make the preliminary strokes that decide which player shall begin. [OE *streng*, MLG *strenge*, ON *strengr* f. Gmc *strangiz*; cf. OHG *stranc* rope; see STRONG]

strin'gĕn'dō (-j-), mus. direction. With increasing speed. [It.]

strin'g|ent (-j-), a. (Of rules, stipulations, etc.) strict, precise, requiring exact performance, leaving no loophole or discretion; (of money-market etc.) tight, hampered by scarcity, unaccommodating, hard to operate in. Hence ~ENCY n., ~entLY[2] adv. [L *stringere* draw tight, -ENT]

string'er (-ng-), n. In vbl senses; also, STRING-board. [-ER[1]]

string'|y (-ngĭ), a. Fibrous, like string, (~*y-bark*, kinds of gum-tree); (of liquid) viscous, ropy. Hence ~iNESS n. [-Y[2]]

strip[1], v.t. & i. (-pp-). **1.** Denude, lay bare, deprive *of* covering or appurtenance or property, (~ one *to the skin*, leave him no clothes; ~*ped*, naked; ~*ped of fine names, it is a swindle*; ~ *house, ship, tree*, remove furniture, rigging, bark & branches; ~ *cow*, milk to last drop; ~ *tobacco*, remove stems from; ~ *screw*, tear thread from it); pull or tear (covering lid, or fig., appurtenance, property) off or *off* from or *from* something; put off one's clothes, undress (~*-tease*, an entertainment in which a woman gradually ~s before an audience, also as vb). **2.** (Of screw) lose thread; (of projectile) issue from rifled gun without spin. **3.** ~*-leaf*, tobacco with stems removed. Hence ~p'ER[1](1, 2) n. [ME, f. OE -*strÿpan* despoil, = MDu., MLG *ströpen*, OHG *stroufen* f. WG *straupjan*]

strip[2], n. Long narrow piece (*a ~ of card, paper, cloth, garden, territory, board*); narrow space in newspaper for small pictures telling a comic or serial story (~ *cartoon*); AIR[1] ~. [ME, f. or cogn. w. MLG *strippe* strap, thong, prob. rel. to STRIPE]

stripe, n. **1.** Long narrow band usu. of uniform breadth on a surface from which it differs in colour or texture (*black with a red ~*; STAR[1]*s & ~s*; ~*s on soldier's trousers*; *sergeant's, corporal's, ~s*, chevrons on sleeves denoting rank; *get, lose, a ~*, be promoted, degraded; *zebra's ~s*), whence (-)stripED[2] (-pt), strip'Y[2], aa.. strip'iNESS n. **2.** (arch.). Blow with scourge (usu. in pl.); (pl.) flogging. **3.** pl. (colloq.). Tiger. [17th c., perh. back form. f. an earlier *striped*, f. MDu., MLG *strîpe* = MHG *strife*, ON *strîp* f. Gmc *strîp-* (cf. prec.); sense 2 ME, perh. f. Du. or LG; cf. MLG *strippe* whip-lash]

strip'ling, n. Lad, young man whose figure has not yet filled out. [ME, prob. f. STRIP[2], -LING[1]]

strive, v.i. (*strŏve*, *strĭven*). Struggle,

endeavour, try hard, make efforts, contend, vie (*to do, for* or *after* desired end,
with or *against* opponent or temptation
or difficulty; ~ *together*, or *with each other*,
quarrel, dispute pre-eminence etc.). [ME,
aphetic f. OF *estriver*, of disputed orig.]

strōb'lle, n. Cone of pine etc. [f. LL f. Gk
strobilos (*strephō* twist)]

strode. See STRIDE.

strōke[1], n., & v.t. **1.** Blow, shock given
by blow, (*to receive* 20 ~*s of the birch*;
with one ~ of his sword; *killed by a ~
of lightning* or *lightning-~*; *finishing ~*,
coup de grâce, final & fatal blow; ~ *of
paralysis* or *apoplexy*, or ~, sudden dis-
abling attack; SUN~). **2.** Single effort
put forth, one complete performance of
a recurrent action or movement, time
or way in which such movements are
done, (*has not done a ~ of work*; ~ *of
wing, oar,* etc., whole of motion till
starting-position is regained; ~ *of piston,*
whole motion in either direction; *golfer
does hole in five* ~*s,* successive single
dealings with ball; *row a fast, slow, long,*
etc., ~; *vary the* ~; *second boat is gaining
at every* ~ or ~ *by* ~). **3.** Method of striking in games etc., specially successful or
skilful effort, (*invented a new* ~ *in cricket*;
~ *of genius,* original idea; ~ *of wit,*
diplomacy, etc.; ~ *of business,* profitable
transaction; *a clever* ~; MASTER[1]-~); ~ *of
luck,* unforeseen opportune occurrence.
4. Mark made by movement in one
direction of pen or pencil or paint-brush,
detail contributing to general effect in
description, (*up, down,* ~, part of letter
so written; HAIR-~; *thick, thin, horizontal,*
etc., ~; *dash off picture with a few* ~*s*;
could do it with a ~ of the pen by exag.,
by writing signature; *finishing* ~*s,* finishing touches; *description is full of* ~*s from
the life*). **5.** Sound made by striking clock
(*it is on the ~ of nine,* nine is about to
strike; *was there on the ~,* punctually).
6. (Also, now rarely, ~ *oar*) oarsman rowing nearest stern & setting time of ~ (*row,
pull,* ~, act as ~). **7.** v.t. Act as ~ to
(boat, crew). [ME, f. OE *strāc =
(M)LG *strēk,* MHG *streich* f. Gmc *straik-
var. of *strik- STRIKE]

strōk|e[2], v.t., & n. **1.** Pass the hand
gently, & usu. repeatedly in same direction, along surface of (~*e* one or one's *hair
the wrong way,* irritate him; ~*e* one *down,*
mollify his anger etc.); hence ~**'ingLY**[2]
adv. **2.** n. Act or spell of ~ing. [OE
strācian, = MDu., MLG *strēken,* OHG
streihhōn f. Gmc *straik- (prec.)]

strōll, v.i. & t., & n. **1.** Saunter, go for
short leisurely walk; go from place to
place giving performances etc., traverse
the country thus, (~*ing players*; *a* ~*ing
company*). **2.** n. Short leisurely walk (*go
for, take, a* ~). Hence ~'**ER**[1] n. [c. 1600,
perh. a soldier's wd f. obs. G (17th c.)
strollen, strolchen (*strolch* vagabond)]

strōm'a, n. (biol.; pl. ~*ta*). Framework

of an organ or cell, usu. of connective
tissue. Hence **stromăt'ic** a. [LL, f. Gk
strōma coverlet]

strŏng, a. (comp. *& sup. pr.* -ngg-).
1. Having power of resistance, not easily
broken or torn or worn or injured or
captured, tough, healthy, firm, solid, (~
china, stick, cloth; *a* ~ *constitution,* not
liable to, able to overcome, disease; ~
nerves, proof against fright, irritation,
etc.; ~ *fortress, town,* etc.; ~*-box,* -*room,*
proof against burglars etc. for keeping
valuables in; ~ *conviction, faith, character; the* ~, those who have good health;
are you quite ~ *again?,* restored to health;
a ~ *foundation*; *a* ~ *market,* steadily high
or rising prices; ~ *meat,* doctrine or
measures acceptable only to vigorous or
instructed minds; ~ *suit,* suit at cards
that is able to take tricks, (fig.) thing at
which one excels). **2.** Capable of exerting
great force or doing much, muscular,
powerful by size or numbers or resources
or quality or ability, convincing, striking,
powerfully affecting the senses, (~ *to do,
suffer, labour, save,* etc.; *is* ~ *enough to*; ~
in judgement, Greek, numbers, health, well
equipped in these respects; ~ *eyes,
memory,* etc.; *a* ~ *man,* muscular; *by the*
~ *arm* or *hand,* by force; *is as* ~ *as a
horse,* can do or stand much work; *the*
~, those who have might on their side; ~
army, fleet, etc., numerous & well
equipped; *a* ~ *detachment,* numerous; *a
company* 200 ~, numbering 200; *how
many* ~ *are you?,* what are your numbers?; *a* ~ *combination,* set capable of
doing much when united; *a* ~ *candidate,*
formidable, likely to win; ~ *drink,
waters,* alcoholic liquors; ~ *tea, toddy,*
made with large proportion of the
flavouring element; ~ *situation,* conjuncture in play or story calculated to
move audience deeply; ~ *voice,* loud or
penetrating; ~ *mind,* capable of sound
reasoning; ~-*minded,* having such mind;
~ *evidence, argument, case*; ~ *light,*
shadow, colour, flavour; ~ *cheese, onion,*
pungent; ~ *butter, bacon,* rancid; ~
breath, ill-smelling). **3.** Energetic, effective, vigorous, decided, (*a* ~ *tide, attraction*; *have a* ~ *hold upon* or *over,* be able to
influence; *a* ~ *literary style,* vivid & terse;
has a ~ *inclination to*; ~ *language,* forcible
expressions esp. of abusive or blasphemous kind; ~ *wind,* very fresh; *give* ~
support to, support with all one's power;
a ~ *partisan, Tory, advocate*; ~ *man,*
administrator who acts without hesitation, masterful person; ~ *measures,*
drastic action; *is* ~ *against compromise,*
will have nothing to do with it; *going
~,* sl., continuing race or other occupation
vigorously, also in good health or trim;
come or *go it* ~, sl., go to great lengths in
something). **4.** (gram.). (Of vbs) forming
inflexions by vowel-change within stem
rather than by addition of suffix (e.g.

swim swam, give gave, break broke, cf.
float floated). **5.** ~'*hold*, fort, fastness,
citadel, place where some cause or sentiment prevails (*Liverpool was a ~hold of
protestantism*). Hence ~'ISH[1](2) a., ~'LY[2]
adv. [OE *strang, strong* = OS *strang*, ON
strangr f. Gmc **strangaz*; cf. STRING]

strŏn'tia (-sha), n., **strŏn'tian** (-shn), n. &
a. An oxide of strontium of which the
nitrate is used in fireworks to colour
flame red; (adj.) of strontia or strontium.
[*-an* (orig. adj.) f. *Strontian* in Argyll;
hence *-ia* (-IA)]

strŏn'tium (-shm), n. A soft silver-white
metallic element; ~ *90*, product of atomic
fission, concentrating selectively on the
bones. [f. STRONTIA, see *-*IUM]

strŏp, n., & v.t. (-pp-). **1.** Strip of leather
on which razor is sharpened, implement
or machine serving same purpose; collar
of leather or spliced rope or iron used in
slinging pulley etc. **2.** v.t. Sharpen on or
with ~. [ME, f. (M)Du., (M)LG *strop*,
OHG *strupf*, WG f. L *stroppus, struppus*
STRAP]

strophăn'thin, n. Poisonous drug ex-
tracted from varieties of the tropical plant
Strophanthus, used as a heart-tonic. [f.
Gk *strophos* twisted cord +*anthos* flower
+ -IN]

strŏph'e, n. (Lines sung during) turn
made in dancing by ancient-Greek chorus
(~, *antistrophe, epode*, three sections of
a choral ode or of one division of it, ~
& antistrophe exactly corresponding in
metre). So **strŏph'ıc** a. [Gk (-*ē*), orig.=
turning (*strephō* turn)]

strove. See STRIVE.

strow (-ō), v.t. (p.p. ~*n* or ~*ed*). (Arch.
for) STREW.

struck. See STRIKE.

strŭc'tur|e, n. Manner in which a build-
ing or organism or other complete whole
is constructed, supporting framework or
whole of the essential parts of something,
make, construction, (*the ~e of a house,
machine, animal, poem, sentence, society; a
sentence of loose, a rock of columnar, ~e;
its ~e is ingenious; ornament should emphasize & not disguise the lines of ~e*),
whence ~AL (-*cher-*), ~eLESS, (-)~ED[2]
(*-cherd*), aa., ~aLY[2] adv.; thing constructed, complex whole, a building, (*a
fine marble ~e; a lumbering ~e drawn by
six horses*). [f. L *structura (struere struct-*
build, -URE)]

strŭg'gl|e, v.i., & n. **1.** Throw one's limbs
about in violent effort to get free or
escape grasp (*child ~ed & kicked*); make
violent or determined efforts under
difficulties, strive hard *to* do, contend *with*
or *against* opponent or obstacle or difficulty, (*~ed to express himself, control his
feelings; ~ing with his infirmity, against
superior numbers* or *the forces of nature*);
make one's way with difficulty *through,
up, along, in,* etc. (*light ~ed in through
dirty panes*); (part.) experiencing difficulty

in making a living or getting recognition
(*a ~ing artist* etc.); hence ~**ingLY**[2] adv.,
~ER[1] n. **2.** n. Spell of ~ing, confused
wrestle or jostling, mêlée, hard contest,
effort under difficulties; *the ~e for existence*, the competition between organisms
esp. as an element in natural selection.
[ME *strugle, strogel*, etc., frequent.
formation of obsc. orig.]

strŭld'brŭg, n. One of those cursed
with immortality in Swift's *Gulliver's
Travels.* [arbitrary]

strŭm, v.i. & t. (-mm-), & n. **1.** Touch
notes or twang strings of piano or other
stringed instrument (esp. unskilfully); ~
on (piano, guitar, etc.). **2.** n. Sound made
by ~ming (*the ~ of a guitar*). [imit., cf.
THRUM]

strum'|a (-ōō-), n. (pl. ~*ae*). Scrofula;
goitre; (bot.) cushion-like dilatation of an
organ. So ~OSE[1], ~OUS, aa. [L, = scrofu-
lous tumour]

strŭm'pĕt, n. Prostitute. [ME, of unkn.
orig.]

strung. See STRING.

strŭt[1], v.i. (-tt-), & n. (Walk with) pompous or affected gait. Hence ~t'**ingLY**[2]
adv. [ME 'bulge, swell, strive', OE
strūtian prob. f. **strūt* = OHG *strūz*
strife]

strŭt[2], n., & v.t. (-tt-). **1.** Piece of wood
or iron inserted in a framework & in-
tended to bear weight or pressure in the
direction of its length, brace, esp. one set
obliquely from rafter to king-post or
queen-post. **2.** v.t. Brace with ~(s).
[16th c., ult. rel. to OE **strūt* (prec.);
cf. LG *strutt* rigid]

strŭth'ious (-ōō-), a. Of or like an ostrich,
of the ostrich tribe. [L *struthio* f. Gk
strouthiōn ostrich (*strouthos* sparrow),
-OUS]

strych'n|ine, (arch.) **strych'n|ia**, (-k-),
nn. Vegetable alkaloid got from plants of
genus *Strychnos*, very bitter to the taste
& highly poisonous & used in minute
doses as nerve-stimulant. Hence ~ıc a.,
~(in)ISM(5) nn. [L *strychnos* f. Gk (s)*trukh-
nos* kind of nightshade, -INE[5]]

Stū'art, n. The ~s, sovereigns James I,
Charles I & II, James II, Mary & Anne,
& members of their families.

stŭb, n., & v.t. (-bb-). **1.** Stump of tree,
tooth, etc., left projecting; remnant of
pencil, cigar, dog's tail, or similar object;
counterfoil; ~-iron, used for gun-barrels
& made of old horseshoe or other nails;
~-mortise, -tenon, going only part of the
way through; hence ~b'**y**[2] a. **2.** v.t.
Grub up (~) by the roots; clear (land) of
~s; ~ one's *toe*, hurt it by striking against
something; (also ~ *out*) extinguish (cigar,
cigarette) by pressing lighted end of ~
against some object. [OE *stub(b)*=MDu.,
(M)LG *stubbe*, ON *stubbr, stubbi*]

stŭb'ble, n. Short stalks of cereal plants
left sticking up after harvest, cropped hair
or beard, hair on unshaved chin or cheek,

Hence **stubb′ly²** a. [ME, f. OF (e)stuble f. L stup(u)la var. of stipula straw]

stubb′orn, a. Obstinate, unyielding, obdurate, inflexible, refractory, intractable, (facts are ~ things, will not adapt themselves to theory). Hence~LY² adv., ~NESS n. [ME stiborn, stoburn, etc., of unexpl. orig.]

stucc′o, n. (pl. ~es), & v.t. 1. Kinds of plaster or cement used for coating wall surfaces or moulding into architectural decorations. 2. v.t. Coat with ~. [It., perh. f. Gmc (cf. OHG stukki crust)]

stuck(-up). See STICK.

stud¹, n., & v.t.(-dd-). 1. Large-headed nail, boss, or knob, projecting from a surface esp. for ornament, rivet, cross-piece in each link of chain-cable; two-headed button for use with two button-holes ∥ esp. in shirt-front (collar-~, long kind going through two or four holes); post to which laths are nailed, whence ~d′ing¹ n., woodwork of lath-&-plaster wall. 2. v.t. Set with ~s by way of strengthening or usu. of decorating, (p.p.) thickly set or strewed with (door, lawn, sea, sky, ~ded with nails, daisies, islands, stars); be scattered over or about (surface). [OE studu, stuthu, MHG stud, ON stoth f. Gmc *studh-, *stuth- prop]

stud², n. Number of horses kept for some purpose as breeding, racing, hunting, coaching; ~-book, containing pedigrees of horses; ~ farm, place where horses are bred; ~-horse, stallion. [OE stōd, OHG stuot (G stute mare), ON stóth f. Gmc *stōdh- f. *stō- *sta- STAND]

studding-sail (stŭn′sl), n. Sail set on small extra yard & boom beyond leech of square sail in light winds. [16th c., of unkn. orig.]

stud′ent, n. 1. Person studying in order to qualify himself for some occupation or devoting himself to some branch of learning or under instruction at university or other place of higher education or technical training (medical, theological, historical, ~; ~ interpreter, civil servant qualified or qualifying for consular service in China, Persia, etc., by study of the language required; a ~ of archaeology, law, botany, manners; numbers its ~s by the thousand). 2. Person of studious habits. 3. ∥(At some colleges) recipient of stipend from foundation, fellow or scholar, whence ~SHIP n. [f. L studēre (studium STUDY¹), -ENT; ME studiant, aphetic f. OF estudiant]

stud′io, n. (pl. ~s). Working-room of painter, sculptor, photographer, etc., often with skylights or windows specially designed to secure suitable light; room in which cinema-play is staged; (pl.) cinema-~s of a film company with auxiliary buildings; one of the rooms in a broadcasting station used for transmissions. [It., f. L as STUDY¹]

stud′ious, a. Given to study, occupied with reading; taking care to do (more ~ to divide than to unite—Pope), anxiously desirous of doing; studied, deliberate, intended, zealous, anxious, painstaking, (with ~ care, attention, politeness). Hence ~LY² adv., ~NESS n. [ME, f. L studiosus (foll., -OUS)]

stud′y¹, n. 1. Thing to be secured by pains or attention (it shall be my ~ to please, to write correctly; your comfort was my ~; make a ~ of, try to secure). 2. (Now usu. brown ~) fit of musing, reverie, (there he stood for an hour in a ~; is in a brown ~, too intent on his thoughts to observe what is passing). 3. Devotion of time & thought to acquiring information esp. from books (often pl.), pursuit of some branch of knowledge, (gives his hours to ~; make a ~ of, investigate carefully; my studies have convinced me that; the ~ of mathematics, morals; continue your studies, go on with your lessons). 4. Thing that is or deserves to be investigated (the proper ~ of mankind is man; his face was a ~). 5. (Paint. etc.) sketch made for practice in technique or as preliminary experiment for picture or part of it (his studies are exquisite, but his finished work disappointing; a ~ of a head); (mus.) composition designed to develop skill in some particular branch of execution; (theatr.) good, slow, etc., learner of parts (UNDERSTUDY). 6. Room used for literary occupation, transaction of business, etc. (you will find him in his, the, ~). [ME studie, f. AF & OF estudie f. L studium zeal, study]

stud′y², v.t. & i. 1. Make a study of, take pains to investigate or acquire knowledge of (subject) or to assure (result sought), scrutinize or earnestly contemplate (visible object), (~ law, French, philosophy; ~ book, read it attentively; ~ one's part, try to learn it by heart; ~ up, get up for examination etc.; ~ out, succeed in finding out by hard thinking; studies others' convenience, his own interests; ~ person's face or character, a map, the stars). 2. Apply oneself to study esp. reading (~ for the bar, read law). 3. (arch.) Meditate, muse. 4. Be on the watch, try constantly to manage, to do (studies to avoid disagreeable topics). 5. p.p. Deliberate, intentional, affected, (a studied insult; with studied politeness, rudeness, unconcern, abandon), whence **stud′iedly²** (-did-) adv. [ME studie, f. OF estudier f. med. L studiare f. L as prec.]

stuff, n., & v.t. & i. 1. Material that thing is made of or that is or may be used for some purpose (the ~ that dreams, heroes, are made of; has good ~ in him, sterling qualities; some ~ they call beer; this punch, book, is good, sorry, ~; household ~, arch., furniture etc.; bread, food, ~s, things made of bread, used as food; green, garden, ~, vegetables; doctors' ~, physic; inch ~, boards 1 in. thick; thick ~, planking over 4 in. thick; the ~, colloq., available supply of something, e.g. timber, money, shells). **2.** Any woollen fabric (opp. silk, cotton, linen; ‖ ~ *gown*, worn by barrister who has not taken SILK). **3.** Valueless matter, refuse, trash, nonsense (n. & int.), (*take that* ~ *away*; *Smith a liar?* ~ *& nonsense!*; *what* ~ *he writes!*). **4.** (sl.). *Do your* ~, perform your tricks, get on with your job; *know* one's ~, be a master of one's subject, trade, etc.; *the* ~ *to give 'em or the troops*, the way to proceed etc. **5.** vb. Pack, cram, stop *up*, fill, distend, (~ one's *ears with wool*, *cushion with down*; ~*ed birds, beasts*, skin with interior removed & replaced by enough material to restore original shape; ~*ed fowl, turkey, haddock, veal*, with minced seasoning inserted before cooking; *•~ed shirt*, colloq., a pompous nonentity; ~ *child, goose*, etc., make it eat largely; *a head* ~*ed with romance, facts, folly*), whence ~'ING¹(4) n. (~*ing-box*, chamber in machinery through which rod can work without allowing passage of air etc., all vacant space being filled with ~ing). **6.** Ram or press into receptacle (~*ed his necessaries into a small bag, his fingers into his ears, the food into his mouth*). **7.** Gull with lies, hoax. **8.** Gorge oneself, eat greedily; hence (-)~ER¹ n. [ME *stoffe* f. OF *estoffe* f. *estoffer* equip, furnish f. Rom. *•stuppare* STOP¹ up]

stŭff′| y̆, a. (Of valley, room, etc., or atmosphere in it) lacking fresh air or ventilation, close, hard to breathe in, fusty; angry, sulky; narrow-minded. Hence ~ĭNESS n. [-Y²]

stŭl′tĭ|fȳ, v.t. (Of act, statement, agent, speaker) reduce (previous act etc.) to absurdity, exhibit (act etc. or one*self*) in ridiculous light, make (act etc.) of no effect, neutralize (one*self*) as agent, by later inconsistent act etc. Hence ~FICA′TION n. [f. LL *stultificare* (L *stultus* foolish, -I-, -FY)]

stŭm, n., & v.t. (-mm-). **1.** Unfermented grape-juice, must. **2.** v.t. Prevent from fermenting, secure (wine) against further fermentation in cask, by introduction of antiseptic. [17th c., f. Du. *stom* n., *stommen* vb. f. *stom* adj. dumb]

stŭm′bl|e, v.i. & t., & n. **1.** Lurch forward, have partial fall, from catching or striking foot or making false step (~*e along*, go with frequent ~es); make blunder(s) in doing something (~*es in his speech*; ~*e through a recitation*); be offended, feel scruples, *at*; come accidentally (*up*)*on* or *across*; (arch.) give pause to, excite scruples in; ~*ing-block*, obstacle, circumstance that causes difficulty or hesitation or scruples; hence ~ĭNGLY² adv. **2.** n. Act of ~ing. [ME *stomble*, *stumble* (-*b*- is euphonic) corresp. to Norw. *stumla*, cogn. w. *stam*- STAMMER]

‖ **stŭm′er**, n. (sl.). Worthless cheque, counterfeit coin or note. [orig. unkn.]

stŭmp, n., & v.i. & t. **1.** Projecting rem-

nant of cut or fallen tree, corresponding remnant of broken branch or tooth or amputated limb, useless end of cigar or pencil, worn-down brush or other implement, stub; (pl., joc.) legs (usu. STIR one's ~s). **2.** ~ of tree used by orator to address meeting from (*on the* ~, colloq., engaged in political speech-making or agitation; ~ *oratory*, of kind suitable for such speeches). **3.** (crick.). One of the three uprights of a wicket (OFF, *middle*, LEG, ~). **4.** Cylinder of rolled paper or other material with conical ends for softening pencil-marks & other uses in drawing. **5.** vb. Walk stiffly & noisily as on wooden legs. **6.** (Of question etc.; colloq.) pose, be too hard for, (*am* ~*ed*, at a loss, at my wits' end), whence ~'ER¹(2) n. **7.** (crick.). Put (batsman who is not in his ground) out by disturbing wicket while holding ball, whence ~'ER¹(1) n. (sl., = wicket-keeper). **8.** Make ~ speeches, traverse (district) doing this. **9.** Use~ on (drawing, line, etc.). **10.** ‖~ *up* (sl.), pay over the money required, produce (sum). [ME *stompe*, f. (M)Du. *stomp*, MLG *stump(e)*, corresp. to OHG (G) *stumpf* stump]

stŭmp′|y̆, a. Thickset, stocky, of small height or length in proportion to girth, (*a* ~*y man, book, tail, pencil*). Hence ~ĭLY² adv., ~ĭNESS n. [-Y²]

stŭn, v.t. (-nn-). (Of sound) deafen temporarily, bewilder; (of blow lit. or fig.) knock senseless, reduce to insensibility or stupor, benumb, overwhelm; (part. as adj., sl.) ravishingly good in some respect, splendid, delightful, ripping, whence ~n′ĭNGLY² adv., & so ~n′ER¹ n. [ME; aphetic f. OF *estoner* ASTONISH]

Stun′dism, Stun′dist, (-ōō-), nn. Doctrines, adherent, of a religious body in Russia, orig. of peasants, rejecting ceremonies of Orthodox Church & basing itself on the Bible as translated 1861 into modern Russian. [G *stunde* hour, lesson (the movement originating with German colonists), -ISM, -IST]

stung. See STING.

stunk. See STINK.

stŭn′sail, stŭns′l, n. ⸗ STUDDING-SAIL.

stŭnt¹, v.t. Check growth or development of, dwarf, cramp, (esp. in p.p.). [f. OE *stunt* adj. foolish, corresp. to MHG *stunz*, ON *stuttr* short]

stŭnt², n., & v.i. (colloq.). **1.** Special effort, feat, show performance, display of concentrated energy; advertising device. **2.** v.i. Perform ~s esp. aerobatics. [orig. unkn.; first in U.S. college athletics]

stūpe¹, n., & v.t. **1.** Flannel etc. wrung out of hot water & applied as fomentation; pledget of soft material used as surgical dressing. **2.** v.t. Apply ~ to, foment. [ME, f. L *stup(p)a* tow]

stūpe², n. (sl.). Fool. [for STUPID]

stŭp′é|fȳ, v.t. Make stupid or torpid, deprive of sensibility, (~*fied with drink, narcotics, grief*, etc.). Hence or cogn.

~FA'CIENT (-ăshnt) a. & n. (med.), ~FAC⁴ TION, ~fIER¹(1, 2), nn., ~făctIVE a. [f. F *stupéfier* f. L *stupefacere* (*stupēre* be amazed, -FY)]

stüpĕn'dous, a. Amazing, prodigious, astounding, esp. by size or degree (*a ~ structure, error, achievement*; ~ *folly*). Hence ~LY² adv., ~NESS n. [L *stupendus* (*stupēre* be amazed at), -OUS]

stüp'id, a. & n. 1. In a state of stupor or lethargy; dull by nature, slow-witted, lacking in sensibility, obtuse, crass, characteristic of persons of this nature, (*a ~ person, joke, idea, book*; *what a ~ place to put it in!*), so stüpid'ITY n.; uninteresting, dull, (*a ~ place, visit, time*). 2. n. (colloq.). ~ person. Hence ~LY² adv. [f. F *stupide* or L *stupidus* (as STUPENDOUS, -ID¹)]

stüp'or, n. Dazed state, torpidity, whence ~OUS a. (med.); helpless amazement. [L (as STUPENDOUS, -OR)]

stŭrd'ў¹, a. Robust, hardy, vigorous, lusty, strongly built, (~*y child, opponent, legs, frame, resistance, courage*; ~*y beggar*, arch., able-bodied but not working). Hence ~iLY² adv., ~iNESS n. [ME ' reckless, violent ', aphetic f. OF *estourdi* p.p. of *estourdir* stun, daze]

stŭrd'ў², n. Vertigo in sheep caused by tapeworm in brain. Hence ~iED² (-ĭd) a. [f. OF *estourdie* giddiness (prec.)]

stŭr'geon (-jn), n. Kinds of large anadromous fish resembling shark in general shape, having mailed body & head, yielding caviare & isinglass, & esteemed as food. [ME, f. AF (e)*sturgeon* f. Rom. *sturionem* nom. -o f. WG *sturjo whence OHG *sturjo*, OE *styrga*]

Sturm und Drang (shtoorm ŏŏnt drahng'). See STORM & stress.

stŭtt'er, v.i. & t., & n. 1. Keep repeating parts, esp. initial consonants, of words in effort to articulate; utter in this way (often *out*); hence ~ER¹ n., ~ingLY² adv. 2. n. Act or habit of ~ing. [f. ME (now dial.) *stutt*, cogn. w. OHG *stōzen* knock, +-ER⁵; cf. MDu., MLG *stoteren*]

stў¹, n. (pl. -*ies*), & v.t. & t. 1. (*Pig*')~, enclosure for keeping pig(s) in, (fig.) mean or dirty hovel or room, place of debauchery. 2. vb. Lodge (t. & i.) in ~. [OE *stī*, prob. = *stīg* (see STEWARD), ON (*svin*) *stī*]

stў² (pl. -*ies*), stўe, n. Inflamed swelling on edge of eyelid (usu. *a ~ in* one's *eye*). [prob. f. obs. *styany* (= *styan eye* f. OE *stigend* sty, lit. riser, f. *stīgan* rise + *eye*) shortened as though = sty on eye]

Stў'gian, a. (As) of the Styx or of Hades, murky, gloomy. [L f. Gk *Stugios* (STYX), -AN]

stўle¹, n., & v.t. 1. Ancient writing-implement, a small rod with pointed end for scratching letters on wax-covered tablets & blunt end for obliterating (whence stўl'IFORM a.); (poet.) pen or pencil; (transf.) thing of ~-like shape as etching-needle or styloid process in anat. 2. Manner of writing, speaking, or doing, esp. as opposed to the matter to be expressed or thing done (*the ~ is better than the matter*; *written in a florid, cumbrous, lucid, delightful, ~*; *different ~s of rowing*; *slashed about him in fine ~*; *good, bad, ~, = good, bad, FORM¹*). 3. Collective characteristics of the writing or diction or artistic expression or way of presenting things or decorative methods proper to a person or school or period or subject, manner exhibiting these characteristics, (*in the ~ of Shakespeare, Raphael, Wagner*; *the epic, lyric, dramatic, ~*; *lapidary* or *monumental ~*, fit or resembling that fit for inscriptions on stone; *pre-Raphaelite, impressionist, ~*, in painting; *baroque, Louis XIV, rococo, renaissance, ~*, in architecture or furniture or dress; GOTHIC, *classical*, ROMANESQUE, ~, in architecture; *Norman, early English, decorated, perpendicular, ~s*, kinds of esp. ecclesiastical architecture prevailing successively in England 1066–1189, 1189–1272, 1272–1377, 1350–1600, & marked respectively by round arches & heavy pillars, pointed arches & lancet windows & simple tracery, flowing tracery & elaborate ornament, slender pillars & vast windows divided by vertical & horizontal lines; *Tudor, Jacobean, Queen Anne, ~s*, kinds of esp. domestic architecture). 4. Descriptive formula, designation of person or thing, full title, (*is entitled to the ~ of* Right honourable, King, Esquire; *did not recognize him under his new ~*; *my ~ is plain* John Smith; *regret that I am not acquainted with your proper ~*; *old, new, ~*, abbr. O.S., N.S., appended to dates, = so called when reckoned by the Julian, GREGORIAN, CALENDAR¹). 5. Noticeably superior quality or manner esp. in regard to breeding or fashion, distinction, (*there is no ~ about her*, she looks commonplace; *let us do the thing in ~ if we do it at all*), whence stўl'ISH¹ a., stўl'ishLY² adv., stўl'ishNESS n. 6. Kind, sort, esp. with regard to appearance (*what ~ of house, servant, do you require?*; *a gentleman of the old ~*). 7. Make, shape, pattern, (*this ~ 2/6*; *in all sizes & ~s*). 8. v.t. (usu. pass.). Use specified designation of (*is ~d king, folly*). [ME & OF *stile, style* f. L *stilus*; sp. *style* w. assim. to foll.]

stўle², n. Gnomon of sun-dial; (bot.) narrowed extension of ovary supporting stigma. [app. f. Gk *stulos* pillar]

stўle³, n. (Incorrect spelling for) STILE.

stўl'ĕt, n. Slender pointed instrument, stiletto; (surg.) stiffening wire of catheter, probe. [F, f. It. STILETTO]

stўl'ist, n. Person with or aiming at good literary style. [-IST]

stўlis'tlic, a. Of literary style. Hence ~ICALLY adv. [-IC]

stўl'ite, n. Medieval ascetic living on top

of a pillar. [f. late Gk *stulítēs* (STYLE², -ITE¹)]

stỹl'ize, -ise (-īz), v.t. (Usu. in p.p.) conform (artistic representation) to the rules of a conventional style. [-IZE (G *stilisieren*)]

stỹl'ō, n. (colloq; *pl.* ~*s*). Stylograph. [abbr.]

stỹlo-, comb. form of *styloid* in names of muscles = of the styloid process & —, as ~*hy'oid*, ~*maxill'ary*. [f. L as STYLE¹, -0-]

stỹl'obāte, n. Continuous basement supporting a row or rows of columns. [f. L f. Gk *stulobatēs* (STYLE², *bainō* walk)]

stỹl'o|graph (-ahf), n. Kind of pen containing reservoir of ink & marking with point instead of split nib. Hence ~**gräph'IC** a., ~**gräph'ICALLY** adv. [STYLE¹, -0-, -GRAPH]

stỹl'oid, a. & n. ~ (*process*), spine projecting from base of temporal bone. [STYLE¹, -OID]

stỹl'us, stil'us, n. **1.** = STYLE¹ (writing-implement). **2.** = STYLE². [see STYLE¹]

stỹm'ie, n., & v.t. (golf; ~ abolished in 1952). **1.** Condition on putting-green when a player's ball lay between opponent's ball & the hole, if the balls were at least six inches apart, as *I laid him a* ~. **2.** v.t. Put (opponent, opponent's ball, one*self*) into the position of having to negotiate a ~; also fig. [orig. unkn.]

stỹp'tic, a. & n. (Substance) that checks bleeding. [f. L f. Gk *stuptikos* (*stuphō* contract)]

stỹr'äx, n. Kinds of tree & shrub, some of which yield valuable gums. [L, f. Gk *sturax*; cf. STORAX]

Stỹ'rian, a. & n. (Native) of Styria. [-AN]

Stỹx, n. (Gk myth.). River encompassing Hades (*cross the* ~, die; *black etc. as* ~). [L, f. Gk *Stux -ugos*]

Suabian. See SWABIAN.

sū'able, a. That can be sued. Hence **sūabIL'ITY** n. [-ABLE]

suasion (swā'zhn), n. Persuasion as opposed to force (esp. *moral* ~). So **suas- IVE** (swā-) a. [ME, f. OF or L *suasio* (*suadēre suas-* urge)]

suave (swāv), a. Bland, soothing, mollifying, polite, (~ *person, speech, manners, wine, medicine*). Hence or cogn. ~'LY³ adv., **suäv'ITY** (sw-) n. [F, or f. L *suavis* cogn. w. SWEET]

suav'Iter (swā-). ~ *in mŏd'ō, fŏrt'Iter in rē*, gently but firmly, with iron hand in velvet glove. [L]

sŭb¹, n., & v.i. (-bb-; colloq.). **1.** Subaltern; submarine; subscription; substitute. **2.** v.i. Act as substitute *for* someone. [abbr.]

sŭb², L prep., = under, in some L phrs.: ~ *fin'em* (abbr. *s.f.*), towards the end (of the chapter etc. referred to); ~ *ju'dicĕ* (jōō-), under judicial consideration (*newspaper comment on cases* ~ *judice is pro-*

hibited), not yet decided, still debatable (*the matter is still* ~ *judice*; cf. RES *judicata*); ~ *rōs'a* (-z-), (of communications, consultations, etc.) in confidence, under express or implied pledge of secrecy [lit. under the rose, as emblem of secrecy]; ~ *stlĕn'tio* (-tĭō, -shĭō), in hushed-up manner, privately; ~ *vō'cĕ*, abbr. *s.v.*, (in references to dictionaries etc.) under the word in question, under the word —.

sub- (sŭb, sub), pref. f. L *sub* prep. & *sub-* pref. = under.

1. Many words are from L compounds, in which ~ (or often by assim. etc. *suc-, suf-, sug-, sum-, sup-, sur-, sus-*) expresses clearly or obscurely the ideas of lower position (~*jacent,* ~*ordinate,* ~*scribe,* ~*sist,* ~*stance*), motion to this (~*ject,* ~*jugate,* ~*junctive,* ~*merge,* ~*mit,* ~*side, succumb, suppose, suppress*) or from this (~*tract, succinct, suspect, suspend, suspire*), covertness or secrecy or tacitness (~*audition,* ~*orn, summon, surreptitious*), inclusion (~*sume*), closeness (~*join,* ~*junctive,* ~*lime,* ~*sequent,* ~*urb, succeed*), inferiority (~*altern,* ~*serve, succentor*), support (~*sidy,* ~*vention, succour, suffer, suffice, sustain*), addition (*suffix, supplement*), or substitution (~*stitute, supplant, surrogate*).

2. ~, without the above changes into *suc-* etc., is also used as a living pref. after L models or prefixes to wds of E or other orig.:

a. Adjj. are formed from *sub*, the abl. of any L noun, & an adj. ending, esp. as anat. terms with sense *situated under the* — (~*sternal* below the breastbone); in others ~ has the secondary sense *below in degree* (~*normal* below normal), & in some having this sense, as in b below, ~ is prefixed directly to a derived E adj. (~*human* less than human).

b. Adjj. & rarely nn. are formed by prefixing ~ to E adjj. & nn., the pref. having an effect equivalent to rather (~*acid*), more or less (~*aquatic*), roughly (~*cylindrical*), incipient (~*delirium*), not quite (~*conscious*), approaching the specified character (~*erect*), on the borders of (~*alpine*).

c. ~ is prefixed to nn. & vv. with sense *under-, subordinate(ly), secondary -ily, further,* (~*prefect,* ~*heading,* ~*species,* ~*divide,* ~*let*).

d. ~ is rarely prefixed to E nn. with sense *underlying* (~*soil,* ~*way*).

The following list contains, with letters of reference & further explanation when necessary, the words in ~ whether compounded in L or in E that fall under 2; the L wd needed to give the meaning of wds marked a will be found by reference to the simple adj. that is left when ~ is removed, or to wd added in brackets:— ~*abdom'inal*, a; ~*a'cid,* ~*acid'ity*, b, (lit., & fig. of words etc.); ~a'gent, ~a'gency, c; ~al'pine, b; ~ān'al, a; ~ande'an, b (of Andes mountains); ~ap'ennine, b; ~apostol'ic, b, of period after that of apostles; ~aquat'ic, b, of more or less aquatic habits or kind, also a, underwater; ~āq'ueous, a; ~arc'tic, b; ~as'tral, a, terrestrial; ~aur'al, a; ~ax'illary, a; ~¹branch, ~²breed, nn., c; ~caud²al, a; ~cen'tral, a, b; ~ce'rebral, a (esp. of reflex action in which the spinal cord is concerned, but not the brain); ~'class, c; ~clāv'ate, b; ~clāv'ian, ~clavic'ular, a (CLAVICLE); ~commi'ssion(er), ~committ'ee, c; ~conc'ave, ~con'ical, ~con'scious(ly, -ness), b; ~con'tinent n., b, region whose size & importance would justify the name continent if it were not part of one, e.g. India, S. Africa; ~con'tract n., ~con-tract' v.i., ~contrac'tor n., c; ~con'trary a. & n. pl., ~contrari'ety n., b, contrary in some degree only (esp. in logic, as ' some men are mortal ' & ' some men are not mortal ' are ~contraries, whereas ' all men are mortal ' & ' no man is mortal ' are contraries); ~con'vex, b; ~cord'ate, b; ~corn'eous, b, rather horny, also a, placed under horn, nail, etc.; ~cort'ical, ~cos'tal, ~crān'ial, a; ~crys'talline, b; ~cūtān'e-ous(ly), ~cutic'ular, a; ~cylin'drical, b; ~deac'on, ~deac'onship, ~dean', ~dean'ery, ~decān'al, c; ~deli'rium, b, incipient or mild or intermittent; ~derm'al, a (DERM); ~dīac'onate, c; ~divide' v.t. & i. [f. L subdividere], ·divi'sion, c; ~dom'i-nant n. (mus.), a, note below dominant, fourth of diatonic scale; ~dors'al, a; ||~ed'it, ~ed'itor, c; ~epiderm'al, a (EPIDERMIS); ~e'qual, b (esp. of quanti-ties in a group such that no one is as large as the sum of the rest); ~equi-lat'eral, b; ~erect', b; ~fam'ily, c (in zool. classif.); ~feb'rile, b; ~'flavour, d; ~'form, c; ~'fusc, b, dusky, dull-coloured [f. L suffuscus see FUSCOUS]; ~gelat'inous, b; ~gēnus, ~gene'ric, c; ~gla'cial, a; ~glob'ular, ~grallator'ial, b; ~'group, ~'head (in classif.), ~head'ing, c; ~hep-at'ic, a, b; ~himalay'an, b; ~hūm'an, a; ~hūm'eral, a (HUMERUS); ~infeuda'tion, ~inspec'tor, c; ~intes'tinal, a (INTESTINE¹); ~'joint, c, one of ~divisions of regular joint in leg etc. of insect etc.; ~'kingdom, c, main division of animal or vegetable kingdom; ~lan'ceolate, b; ~'lease n., ~-lease' v.t., ~lessee', ~less'or, ~let' v.t., ~librar'ian, ||~lieuten'ant, c; ~ling'ual, a; ~litt'oral, b; ~lun'ar (poet.), ~lun'ary, a, of this world, earthly; ~-machine-gun, a, large automatic pistol; ~mamm'ary, a (MAMMA²); ||~'master, c, second master in some schools; ~maxill'ary, a (MAXILLA); ~mēd'iant n. (mus.), a, sixth note of diatonic scale; ~men'tal, a (MENTAL²); ~metall'ic, b; ~mon-tane, a; ~muc'ous, b; ~narcot'ic, b;

~nās'al, ~na'tural (opp. *supernatural*), ~norm'al, ~occip'ital (OCCIPUT), ~ocean'ic, a; ~ocell'ate, b (OCELLUS), ~oc'ular, ~oesopha'geal(OESOPHAGUS),~orb'ital(ORBIT), a; ~'order, ~ord'inal, c (in bot. & zool. classif.); ~ov'al, b; ~pari'etal, ~pharyn'geal (PHARYNX), ~phren'ic, a; ~pil'ose, b; ~pleur'al, a; ~pol'ar, b, of nearly polar character or situation, also a, directly below pole of heavens (astron.); ~prēf'ect(ure), ~pri'or, c; ~pyram'idal, ~quadran-g'ular, ~quad'rate, b; ~ram'ose, b; ||~'reader, c (in Inns of Court); ~rec-tang'ular, b; ~'rector, c, rector's deputy; ~'region, c, division of faunal region; ~'rent v.t., c; ~ret'inal, a (RETINA); ~rhombo'id'al, b; ~sac'ral, a (SACRUM); ~sal'urated, ~satura'tion, b; ~scap'ular, a; ~'section, c; ~sen'sible, a, below the reach of the senses; ~ser'ous, ~sess'ile, b; ~'soil, d; ~'species, ~specif'ic a., c; ~sphe'rical, ~spin'ous (SPINE), b; ~'station, c; ~stern'al, a (STERNUM); ~strāt'um (pl. -la rare), d, what underlies something, lower layer, foundation, basis, (often fig., as it has a ~stratum of truth); ~struc'tion or~struc'ture, ~struc'tural, d; ~tem'perate, b (of climate etc.); ~'tenant, ~'tenancy, c; ~term'inal, b, nearly at the end; ~terrā-n'ean, a, underground (lit. & fig.), so ~terran'eously; ~thora'cic, a (THORAX); ~ˡtitle, c, (also) film-caption; ~ton'ic n. (mus.), a, note next below tonic; ~trans-par'ent, ~triang'ular, b; ~'tribe, a (zool. & bot. classif.); ~trop'ical, b (of climate, fauna, flora, etc.); ~ung'ulate, b, hoofed, but with several digits; ~urs'ine, b; ~'variety c, (in classif.); ~vert'ebral, a; ~vert'ical, ~vit'reous, b; ~'way, d, || covered usu. underground way, •under-ground railway.

subahdar' (sooba-), n. (Anglo-Ind.). Chief Indian officer of company of sepoys. [Hind. (*subah* province, *dār* master)]

sub'altern, a. & n. 1. Of inferior rank, (log., of propositions) particular, not universal. 2. n. (mil.). Officer below rank of captain. [f. LL SUB(*alternus* ALTERNATE)]

subaud'i, v. imperat. Supply (specified word or words) by way of subaudition. [L]

subaudi'tion, n. Mental supplying of omitted word(s), understanding of what is not expressed, reading between the lines. [f. LL *subauditio* f. SUB(*audire* hear) understand]

|| **subdūce'**, **subdūct'**, vv.t. (rare). With-draw, deduct, subtract. So **subdūc'tion** n. [f. L SUB(*ducere* -duct- draw)]

subdūe', v.t. Conquer, subjugate, over-come, vanquish, master, tame, bring into subjection, discipline, (~ *enemies, nature, rough land, one's passions*; ~*d by kind-ness*); soften, make gentle, tone down, mitigate, (esp. in p.p., as ~*d colour, light,*

tone, effect, mood, manners, satisfaction,
whence ~d'NESS (-dŭd-) n.]. Hence **sub-**
dū'ABLE a., **subdū'AL**(2) n. [ME *sodewe*
repr. AF **soduer, *su(b)duer* = OF
soduire repr. in form L SUBDUCE*re*, but in
sense L SEDUCE*re*, while the E vb has the
sense of L SUB²(*dere* put) conquer]

sŭbēr'ēous, sŭbē'ric, sŭb'erŏse, aa.
Corky, of or like cork. [(-*ose* f. L
subereus +-OUS) f. L *suber* cork, -IC, -OSE¹]

subjā'cent, a. Underlying, situated below. [f. L SUB(*jacēre* lie), -ENT]

sŭb'jĕct¹, a. & adv. 1. (arch., poet.). Sub-
jacent (*survey the ~ plains*). **2.** Under
government, not independent, owing
obedience *to,* (*a ~ province, tribe; is held
~,* in subjection; *has long been ~ to
France; States ~ to foreign rule; we are all
~ to the laws of nature, the law of the land*).
3. Liable or exposed or prone to (thing;
*persons ~ to gout; is very ~ to damage,
envy,* etc.). **4. ~** (a. & adv.) *to,* condi-
tional(ly) upon, on the assumption of,
without precluding, (*treaty is ~ to ratification,* not valid unless ratified; *the
arrangement is made, or is, ~ to your
approval; ~ to your consent, I propose to
try again; ~ to correction, these are the
facts*). [ME & OF *suget* etc., f. L p.p. of
SUB(*jicĕre -ject- = jacĕre* throw)]

sŭb'jĕct², n. 1. Person subject to political
rule, any member of a State except the
Sovereign, any member of a subject State,
(*rulers & ~s; the ~s of the Sultan; the
liberty of the ~,* such immunities as are
secured to ~s under constitutional rule;
fig., *as the ~s of King Shakespeare*). **2.** (log.,
gram.). That member of a proposition
about which something is predicated, the
noun or noun-equivalent with which the
verb of a sentence is made to agree in
number etc., (*~ & predicate are the
essential parts of a sentence; every verb has
a ~ expressed or understood, not every verb
has an object*). **3.** (philos.). Thinking &
feeling entity, the mind, the ego, the
conscious self, as opp. all that is external
to the mind (*~ & object,* the ego & the
non-ego, self & not-self, the consciousness
& what it is or may be conscious of); the
substance or substratum of anything as
opp. its attributes. **4.** Theme or of
discussion or description or representation, matter (to be) treated of or dealt
with, (*never talks on serious ~s; proposed
a ~ for the debate; on the ~ of,* concerning,
about; *a tabooed, ticklish, interesting,
dull, ~; what is the ~ of the poem, story,
picture?; constantly wanders from the ~;
pastoral, genre, marine, historical,* etc., *~*
in painting; *~ of piece of music,* theme of
fugue or sonata, leading phrase, motif;
~ for dissection, or ~, dead body; *was
made the ~ of an experiment; could write
if I could think of a ~; change the ~,* talk
of something else, esp. as way out of embarrassment). **5.** Circumstance that gives
occasion *for* specified feeling or action

*(is a ~ for ridicule, pity, rejoicing, con-
gratulation).* **6.** Person of specified usu.
undesirable bodily or mental tendencies
(*a sensitive, bilious, plethoric, hysterical,
ill-conditioned,* etc., *~*). **7. ~**-*heading,* in
index collecting references to a *~; ~-
-matter,* matter treated of in book etc.;
~-object, object of sense or thought as it is
conceived of (opp. *object-object,* as it is in
fact. Hence ~LESS a. [ME & OF *suget*
etc. f. L masc. & neut. p.p. (prec.)]

subjĕct'³, v.t. Subdue (nation etc. usu. *to*
one's sway etc.); expose, make liable,
treat, *to* (*rudeness ~s one to retorts in print;
must be ~ed to great heat; shall ~ it to
criticism*). So **subjĕc'tion n.** [ME, f. OF
subjecter or L *subjectare* as SUBJECT¹]

subjĕc'tive, a. & n. 1. (Philos.) belonging
to, of, due to, the consciousness or thinking or perceiving subject or ego as opp.
real or external things; (pop.) imaginary.
2. (Of art & artists, literature, & history)
giving prominence to or depending on
personal idiosyncrasy or individual point
of view, not producing the effect of
literal & impartial transcription of external realities, whence ~NESS, **sŭb-**
jĕctiv'ITY, nn. 3. (gram.). Of the subject (*~ case, or ~* as n., the nominative;
~ genitive, as in ' by the act *of God* ', cf.
OBJECTIVE). Hence ~LY² adv. [ME, f. L
subjectivus (SUBJECT², -IVE)]

subjĕc'tiv|ism, n. Doctrine that know-
ledge is merely subjective & that there is
no external or objective test of truth. So
~IST(2) n. & a. [prec., -ISM, -IST]

subjoin', v.t. Add at the end, append,
(illustration, anecdote, etc.). [f. obs. F
subjoindre f. L SUB(*jungere junct-* join)]

sŭb'jug|āte (-jōŏ-), **v.t.** Subdue, van-
quish, bring under bondage or into subjection. Hence or cogn.~ABLE a.,~A'TION,
~ātOR, nn. [ME, f. LL *subjugare* bring
under the yoke (SUB², *jugum* yoke),
-ATE³]

subjŭnc'tive, a. & n. ~ mood or ~, a
verbal MOOD², obsolescent in English,
named as being used in the classical
languages chiefly in subordinate or sub-
joined clauses (cf. CONJUNCTIVE; the two
names denote the same forms & are occas.
used indifferently; occas. ~ is restricted
to the subordinate uses while *conjunctive*
either includes all uses or is restricted to
principal-clause verbs, as in apodosis of
conditional sentence). Hence ~LY² adv.
[f. LL *subjunctivus* (SUBJOIN, -IVE)]

sŭblāpsār'ian, a. & n. = INFRALAPSARIAN.
[SUB- 2a]

sŭb'lim|āte¹, v.t. Convert from solid
state to vapour by heat & allow to solidify again; (fig.) refine, purify, idealize.
Hence ~A'TION n. [as foll., -ATE³]

sŭb'limate², a. & n. Sublimated (substance); *corrosive ~,* mercuric chloride.
[f. L *sublimare* SUBLIME², -ATE²]

sublīme'¹, a. Of the most exalted kind,
so distinguished by elevation or size or

nobility or grandeur or other impressive quality as to inspire awe or wonder, aloof from & raised far above the ordinary, (~ *mountain, scenery, tempest, ambition, virtue, heroism, self-sacrifice, love, thought, beauty, genius, poet,* etc.; ~ *indifference, impudence,* etc., as of one too exalted to fear consequences; *the S~* PORTE; *the ~,* all that is ~, sublimity), whence or cogn. ~LY[2] adv., sublim'ITY n.; (anat.) lying near the surface, not deep-sunk. [f. L *sublimis*]

sublim|e'[2], v.t. & i. Sublimate (lit.), whence~'ER[1](2) n.; undergo sublimation; purify or elevate, become pure, as by sublimation; make sublime. [ME, f. OF *sublimer* f. L *sublimare* in med. L sense *sublimate* (prec.)]

sublim'inal, a. (psych.). Below the threshold of consciousness, (of sensations) so faint that subject is not conscious of them; ~ *advertising,* technique of flashing an advertisement on a screen for a fraction of a second, so that the image penetrates to the viewer's subconsciousness though it makes no impression on his conscious mind; ~ *self,* the subconscious mind as a distinct part of the individual's personality. [f. SUB- 2a, L *limen -inis* threshold, -AL]

sub'man, n. Man of markedly inferior development or capacity (opp. SUPERMAN). [SUB- 2c]

sub'marin|e (-ēn; *adj. also* -ēn'), a. & n. 1. Existing, acting, used, constructed, etc., under the surface of the sea, as ~*e plant, volcano, cable.* 2. n. A ~*e* vessel, esp. a warship capable of operating either on or under the surface, equipped with torpedo-tubes, guns, & periscope, & propelled by diesel engines or electric motors or atomic power. Hence ~ER[1] (-mȧ'rēn·) n. [SUB- 2a]

submerge', v.t. & i. Place below water, flood with water, inundate, (also fig.; *the ~d tenth,* the part of the population that is sunk in poverty or permanently in distress); (of submarine or its crew or commander) dive, go below surface. Hence or cogn. submer'gENCE, submer'sION (-shn), nn. [f. L SUB(*mergere mers-* dip)]

submers|e', v.t., & a. (rare). 1. Submerge (rare exc. in p.p. used in bot. of parts of plants growing under water). 2. adj. (rare; bot.). ~ed. Hence (in common use) ~'IBLE a. [f. L p.p. (prec.)]

submi'ssion (-shn), n. Submitting or being submitted (*shall be satisfied with nothing short of complete ~ ; demands the ~ of the signature to an expert*); (in legal use) theory etc. submitted by counsel to judge or jury (*my ~ is that,* I submit that); humility, meekness, resignation, acceptance of authority, obedient conduct or spirit, so **submiss'IVE** a., **submiss'ive-**

-LY[2] adv., **submiss'iveNESS** n. [ME, f. OF, or L *submissio* (foll., -ION)]

submit', v.t. & i. (-tt-). Surrender oneself for control etc. *to* (*wives ~ yourselves unto your own husbands*); present for consideration or decision (*should like to ~ it to your inspection; ~ a case to the court*); urge or represent deferentially that (*I ~ that a material fact has been passed over*; also parenth., as *that, I ~, is a false inference*); give way, make submission, yield, cease or abstain from resistance, (*will never ~, ~ to indignity, ~ to being parted from you; had to ~ to defeat, God's will*). [ME, f. L SUB(*mittere miss-* send)]

subord'inate[1], a. & n. 1. Of inferior importance or rank, secondary, subservient, (*to; ~ clause,* sentence made by addition of a conjunction or by position to serve as a noun or adj. or adv. in another sentence); hence ~LY[2] adv. 2. n. Person working under another (*leaves everything to, never trusts, ~s* or *his ~s*). [f. med. L SUB(*ordinatus* f. L *ordinare* ORDAIN), -ATE[2]]

subord'in|āte[2], v.t. Make subordinate, treat or regard as of minor importance, bring or put into subservient relation, (*to*). Hence or cogn. ~A'TION n., ~ATIVE a. [f. med. L *subordinare* (as prec., -ATE[3])]

subordina'tionism (-sho-), n. (theol.). Doctrine that second & third persons of Trinity are inferior to the Father as regards (orthodox view) order only or (Arian view) essence. [-ISM]

suborn', v.t. Induce by bribery or otherwise to commit perjury or other unlawful act. Hence or cogn. suborna'TION, ~ER[1], nn. [f. L SUB(*ornare* equip or incite secretly)]

subpoen'a (-pēn-), n., & v.t. (~*ed* pr. -*ad*, ~'d). 1. Writ commanding person's attendance in court of justice. 2. v.t. Serve ~ on. [ME; *orig.* two words, L, = under penalty, the first in the writ]

subrep'tion, n. Obtaining of something by surprise or misrepresentation. [f. L *subreptio* purloining f. SUB(*ripere rept-* = *rapere* snatch)]

subrogā'tion, n. (law). Substitution of one party for another as creditor. [f. LL *subrogatio -onis,* see SURROGATE]

subscrib|e', v.t. & i. 1. Write (one's name or rarely other inscription) at foot of document etc. (*the ~ed names carry weight; someone has ~ed a motto;* also refl.); write one's name at foot of, sign, (document, picture, etc.). 2. Express one's adhesion *to* an opinion or resolution (*cannot~e to that*). 3. Enter one's name in a list of contributors, make or promise a contribution, contribute (specified sum), to or *to* a common fund *or for* a common object, raise or guarantee raising of by ~*ing* thus, (~*e to a charity, for a testimonial,* £10; ~*e for a book,* engage before it is published to take copy or copies; ~e to a newspaper, engage to take it for specified time; *the sum needed was ~ed several times over*). Hence or cogn. ~ER¹ (*the ~er*, the undersigned), subscrip⁴ TION, nn. [ME, f. L SUB(*scribere script-* write)]

sub′script, a. (Gk gram.). Written below (only in *iota ~*, small iota written below ᾱ, ē, & ō). [f. L p.p. (prec.)]

subsell′ium, n. (pl. *-ia*). = MISERICORD (last sense). [L (SUB², *sella* seat)]

sub′sequ|ent, a. That follow(s) or followed the event etc. indicated in the context, of later time or date than something, posterior in time *to*. Hence ~ENCE n., ~ently² adv. [ME, f. OF, or f. L SUB²(*sequi* follow), -ENT]

subserve′, v.t. Serve as means in promoting (purpose, end, etc.). [f. L SUB²(*servire* SERVE)]

subserv′i|ent, a. Useful as means, having merely instrumental relation, (*to*); cringing, obsequious. Hence ~ENCE, ~ENCY, nn., ~ently² adv. [f. L as prec., -ENT]

subside′, v.i. (Of water, esp. flood) sink in level, run off, disappear; (of ground) cave in, sink; (of building, ship, etc.) settle down lower in ground or water; (of suspended matter) fall to bottom, be precipitated; (of person, usu. joc.) sink into sitting or kneeling or lying posture (*~d into an armchair*); cease from activity or agitation, become tranquil, abate, (*storm, tumult, apprehension, excitement, ~s*). Hence **sub′sID**ENCE (or *subsi̅*) n. [f. L SUB²(*sidere* settle cogn. w. *sedēre* sit)]

subsid′iar|y̆, a. & n. **1.** Serving to assist or supplement, auxiliary, supplementary, whence ~ILY² adv.; (of company) controlled by another holding more than 50 per cent. of its issued share capital; (of troops) subsidized, hired by another nation. **2.** n. (Usu. pl.) ~y thing or person, accessory; ~y company. [f. L *subsidiarius* (SUBSIDY, -ARY¹)]

sub′sidize, -ise (-ı̄z), v.t. Pay subsidy to. [foll., -IZE]

sub′sidy̆, n. (Hist.) parliamentary grant of money to the sovereign for State needs, tax levied on particular occasion; money grant from one State to another in return for military or naval aid or other equivalent; money contributed by State to keep down price of commodities etc. (*food, housing, ~*) or to expenses of commercial undertaking, charitable institution, etc., held to be of public utility. [ME, f. AF *subsidie* = OF *subside* f. L *subsidium*]

subsist′, v.i. & t. Exist, continue to exist, remain in being; keep oneself alive, support life, be kept in life, find sustenance, (*on vegetables, charity*, etc., *by begging* etc.); provide sustenance for (*undertook to clothe, arm, & ~ 1000 men*). [f. L SUB²-(*sistere* set, stand, causal f. *stare* stand)]

subsis′tence, n. Subsisting; means of

supporting life, livelihood, what one lives on or by; ~ *money*, allowance or advance of pay granted for maintenance; ~ *wage*, merely enough to provide the bare necessities of life. [f. LL *subsistentia* substance (prec., -ENCE)]

sub′stance, n. **1.** (Metaphys.) the substratum that the cognizable properties or qualities or attributes or accidents of things are conceived as inhering in or affecting, the essential nature underlying phenomena, (*~ & accidents in metaphysics correspond to subject & predicate in logic*; *a ~ is a being subsisting in itself & subject to accidents*; *being of one ~ with the Father*); essence or most important part of anything, pith, purport, real meaning, (*I agree with you in ~*, generally, apart from details; *can give you the ~ of his remarks*; *the ~ of religion*). **2.** Material as opposed to form (*the ~ is good, but the style repellent*). **3.** Reality, solidity, solid worth, actual possessions, (*sacrifice the ~ for the shadow*; *there is no ~ in him*; *an argument of little ~*; *a man of ~*, with property, cf. *man of* STRAW; *waste one's ~*, be spendthrift). **4.** Particular kind of matter (*a heavy, porous, yellow, transparent, ~*; *the small number of ~s that make up the world*). [ME, f. OF, f. L *substantia* (SUB², *stare* stand, -ANCE)]

substan′tial (-shl), a. Having substance, actually existing, not illusory, (*the ghost proved ~ after all*); of real importance or value, of considerable amount, (opp. *nominal, verbal*; *a ~ argument, point*; *made a ~ contribution, ~ progress, ~ concessions*); of solid material or structure, not flimsy, stout, (*a ~ house*; *a man of ~ build*); possessed of property, well-to-do, commercially sound, (*a ~ yeoman*; *deal only with ~ firms*); deserving the name in essentials, virtual, practical, (*~ truth, agreement, success, performance of contract*). Hence or cogn. ~ITY (-shiăl′) n., ~LY³ adv. [ME, f. OF *substanciel* or LL *substantialis* (prec., -AL)]

substan′tial|ism (-sha-), n. (philos.). Doctrine that behind phenomena there are substantial realities. So ~IST(2) n. [-ISM]

substan′tialize (-sha-), -ise (-ı̄z), v.t. & i. Invest with or acquire substance or actual existence. [-IZE]

substan′ti|āte (-shǐ-), v.t. Prove the truth of, give good grounds for, (charge, statement, claim). Hence ~A′TION (-sǐ-, -shǐ-) n. [17th c., see SUBSTANCE, -ATE³]

sub′stantive, a. & n. **1.** Expressing existence (*the ~ verb*, the vb *be*); having a separate & independent existence, not merely inferential or implicit or subservient or parasitic, (*~ enactment, motion*, etc., made in due form as such; *noun ~*, old name for the noun in the now usual sense distinguishing it from the *noun adjective* now called *adjective* simply); ~ *rank* (mil.), permanent rank in the holder's branch of the army (as opp. brevet, honorary, acting, or temporary rank); hence ~LY² adv. (esp. in gram., = *substantivally*). 2. n. Noun ~, noun in the now usual sense excluding adjectives; so **sŭbstantiv'AL** a., **sŭbstantiv'alLY²** adv. [ME, f. OF (-*if*, -*ive*), or LL *substantivus* (SUBSTANCE, -IVE)]

sŭb'stit|ūte, n., & v.t. 1. Person or thing performing some function instead of another. 2. v.t. Make (person or thing) fill a place or discharge a function for or *for* another; (vulg.) replace (person or thing) *by* or *with* another; put in exchange (*for*); so ~ū'TION n., ~ū'tionAL (-sho-), ~ū'tionARY¹ (-sho-), ~ūtive, aa., ~ū'tionalLY² adv. [ME, f. L SUB(*stituere* -*ut*- = *statuere* .see STATUTE)]

subsūme', v.t. Include (instance etc.) under a rule or class. Hence **subsŭmp'TION** n. [SUB-, L *sumere sumpt*- take]

subtĕnd', v.t. (geom.). (Of chord, side of triangle) be opposite to (arc, angle). [f. L SUB(*tendere tens*- stretch); cf. TEND]

subtĕnse', n. Line subtending arc or angle. [f. L p.p. (prec.)]

sŭbter-, pref. = under, less than, esp. in wds formed as opposites to compounds of SUPER-, as ~*position*, ~*human*, ~*natural*. [L (SUB², -*ter* as in INTER²)]

sŭb'terfūge, n. Attempt to escape censure or defeat in argument by evading the issue, statement etc. resorted to for such purpose, use of such statements etc. [f. LL -*fugium* f. L SUBTER(*fugere* flee)]

sŭbtil(e) (sū'tl, sŭb'til), a. (Arch. for) SUBTLE. Hence or cogn. **subt'ilIZE**(2, 3) v.t. & i., **subtilizA'TION** n., (sŭt-), **subtilTY** (sŭt'ltī) n. (arch.). [ME & OF *subtil* f. L *subtilis* f. SUB² + *tela* web]

subtle (sū'tl), a. Tenuous or rarefied (arch.), pervasive owing to tenuity, (*the ~ air, a ~ vapour*; *of ~ texture, a ~ perfume*); evasive, mysterious, hard to grasp or trace, (~ *magic, charm, power, art*; *a ~ distinction*); making fine distinctions, having delicate perception, acute, (~ *senses, perception, insight*; *a ~ observer, philosopher, intellect, mind*); ingenious, elaborate, clever, (*a ~ device, fancy, workman, explanation, policy*; ~ *fingers*); crafty, cunning, (*now the serpent was more ~ than any beast*; *a ~ enemy*). Hence **subt'LY²** (sŭt-) adv. [ME & OF *sotil* f. L as prec.]

subtlety (sŭt'ltī), n. In adj. senses; also, a fine distinction, a piece of hair-splitting. [ME, f. OF *s(o)utilite* f. L *subtilitatem* (SUBTIL, -TY)]

sŭbtŏp'i|a, n. (derog.). Term applied to urban and rural areas disfigured by ill-planned and ugly building development; unsightly suburbs regarded as encroaching upon the natural scene; also fig. Hence ~AN a. [f. SUB- 2a + (U)TOPIA]

subtrăct', v.t. Deduct (part, quantity,

number) from or *from* whole or greater quantity or number, esp. in arithmetic or algebra. Hence or cogn. **subtrăc'tION** n., **subtrăc'tIVE** a. [f. L SUB(*trahere tract*- draw)]

sŭb'trahĕnd, n. What is to be subtracted in a subtraction sum. [L as prec.]

sŭb'ūlate, **sŭb'ūlifōrm**, aa. (bot., zool.). Awl-shaped. [L *subula* awl (*suere* sew), -ATE², -I-, -FORM]

sŭb'ûrb, n. Outlying district of city (*the ~s*, all or one of such districts, as *a house in the ~s*, also the environs). So **suburb'AN** a. [ME, f. OF *suburbe* or L SUB(*urbium* f. *urbs urbis* city)]

Suburb'ia, n. (usu. derog.). (Quasi-proper name for) the suburbs (esp. of London) & their inhabitants. [-IA¹]

subvĕn'tion, n. Grant of money in aid, subsidy. [ME, f. OF, f. LL *subventionem* f. SUB(*venire vent*- come) assist, -ION]

subvĕrt', v.t. Overturn, upset, effect destruction or overthrow of, (religion, monarchy, the constitution, principles, morality). Hence or cogn. **subvĕr'sION** (-shn) n., **subvĕr's'IVE** a. [ME, f. OF *subvertir* or L SUB(*vertere vers*- turn)]

suc-, = SUB- in L compounds of *sub* with words in c- & their derivatives.

succāde', n. Candied fruit in syrup. [ME, f. AF *sukade* = OF *succade*, *chuc(c)ade*]

sŭccĕdān'e|um (-ks-), n. (pl. ~a). Substitute, thing or rarely person that one falls back on in default of another. So ~OUS a. [neut. of L *succedaneus* (foll., -ANEOUS)]

succeed' (-ks-), v.t. & i. 1. Take the place previously filled by, follow (t. & i.) in order, come next (to), ensue, be subsequent (to), come by inheritance or in due order to or to office or title or property, (*day ~s day* or *to day*; *agitation ~ed calm*; *~ing ages will reverence his memory*; *Elizabeth ~ed Mary*, *~ed to the throne, ~ed*). 2. Have success (*in doing* etc.), be successful, prosper, accomplish one's purpose; (of plan etc.) be brought to successful issue. [ME, f. OF *succeder* or L SUC(*cedere cess*- go)]

succĕn'tor (-ks-), n. Precentor's deputy in some cathedrals. [LL, f. L SUC(*cinere -cent*- = *canere* sing), -OR]

succès d'estime (see Ap.), n. Passably cordial reception given to performance or work from respect rather than appreciation. [F]

succès fou (see Ap.), n. Success marked by wild enthusiasm. [F]

success' (-ks-), n. Issue of undertaking (rare; *with good* or *bad ~*); favourable issue, accomplishment of end aimed at, attainment of wealth or fame or position, (*have inquired for it without ~*; *military ~es*; *spoilt by ~*; *nothing succeeds like ~*; *one ~ leads to others*), whence ~FUL a., ~fulLY² adv.; thing or person that turns out well (*the experiment is a ~*; *was a great*

~ *as a bishop*): pupil who passes his examination. [f. L *successus -ūs* (SUCCEED)]

succe'ssion (-ksĕshn), n. **1.** A following in order (esp. *in* ~; *three great victories in* ~, running, without intervening defeat). **2.** Series of things in ~ (*a* ~ *of disasters*, several running). **3.** (Right of) succeeding to the throne or any office or inheritance, set or order of persons having such right, (*laws regulating the* ~; *claimed*, *was excluded from, the* ~; *in* ~ *to*, as successor of; *the* ~ *must not be broken*; *is second in the* ~; *was left to him & his* ~, heirs; *apostolic* ~, uninterrupted transmission of spiritual authority through bishops from the apostles downwards; *law of* ~, regulating inheritance esp. in cases of intestate decease; *the S*~ *States*, those resulting from the partition of Austria--Hungary. **4.** (biol.). Order of descent in development of species. Hence ~AL (-ksĕsho-) a. [ME, f. OF, or L *successio* (SUCCEED, -ION)]

succe'ssive (-ks-), a. Following one after another, in uninterrupted succession, running, consecutive. Hence ~LY² adv. [ME, f. med. L *successivus* (SUCCEED, -IVE)]

succe'ssor (-ks-), n. Person or thing that succeeds to another (*to, of*; cf. PREDECESSOR). [ME, f. OF f. L (SUCCEED, -OR)]

succinct' (-ks-), a. Terse, concise, briefly expressed. Hence ~LY² adv., ~NESS n. [ME, f. L *succinctus* f. SUC(*cingere cinct*-gird) tuck up]

succ'ory, n. = CHICORY. [alt. f. *cicoree* etc., old forms of CHICORY]

•**succ'otash**, n. Dish of green maize & beans (& salt pork) boiled together. [f. Amer.-Ind. *msiquatash*]

succ'our (-ker), v.t., & n. **1.** Come to the assistance of, give aid to, (person in danger or difficulty). **2.** n. Aid given at time of need; (pl., arch.) reinforcements, troops coming to the rescue; hence ~LESS a. [vb ME, f. OF *sucurre* f. L SUC(*currere curs-* run); n. ME & OF *sucurs* etc. f. med. L *succursus -ūs* (succurrere)]

succ'uba, -bus, n. (pl. *-bae*, *-bī*). Female demon having sexual intercourse with sleeping men. [LL (*-ba*) & med. L (*-bus*) f. SUC(*cumbere* lie)]

succ'ulent, a. Juicy (of lit. or fig. food); (bot.) thick & fleshy, having such leaves or stems. Hence ~ENCE n., ~entLY² adv. [f. L *succulentus* (*succus* juice, -LENT)]

succumb' (-m), v.i. Be overcome, have to cease from resistance or competition or other effort, be forced to give way to, die owing *to*, die, (~ *to* one's *enemies, superior numbers, grief, temptation*). [ME, f. OF *succomber* or f. L SUC(*cumbere* lie)]

succu'rsal, a. (Of chapel of ease) subsidiary. [f. F (*église*) *succursale* subsidiary (church) f. med. L as SUCCOUR, -AL]

such, a. (no comp. or sup.; placed not between *a* & its n. but before or after them), & pron. **1.** Of the same kind or degree *as* (~ *people, people* ~, *as these*; ~ *beauty as yours*; *experiences* ~ *as this are rare*; ~ *grapes as you never saw*; ~ *as also* = of the or a kind that, as ~ *a scarlet as makes the eyes ache*). **2.** So great, so natured in some respect, *as to* do or *that* (*is* ~ *as to make one despair*; *had* ~ *a fright that she hardly survived it*). **3.** Of the kind or degree already described or implied or intelligible from the context or circumstances (*never had* ~ *sport*; *there are no* ~ *doings now*; ~ *things make one despair*; ~ *are the privileges of fatherhood*; *don't be in* ~ *a hurry*; *how could you leave him at* ~ *a time?*; *saw just* ~ *another yesterday*; *long may he continue* ~ *!*; often colloq. preceding adj. & n. with the effect of *so* modifying the adj., as ~ *horrid language*, language so horrid, *was it* ~ *a long time ago?*, *don't want* ~ *a big one* or ~ *big ones*; also rarely used twice as relative & correl., as ~ *master* ~ *servant*, the servant is ~ as the master is). **4.** (In legal or formal style) the aforesaid, of the aforesaid kind (*whoever shall make* ~ *return falsely*). **5.** So great!, of a kind that demands exclamatory description, (*we have had* ~ *sport!*, ~ *an enjoyable evening!*). **6.** Of a kind or degree sufficient to account for the preceding or following statement (*he cannot come too often, he gives* ~ *pleasure*; *there was* ~ *draught, it is no wonder he caught cold*). **7.** (Also ~*-&-*~) particular, of particular kind, but not needing to be specified (~ *an one*, ~ *a one*, arch., ~*-&-*~ *a person*, someone, so-&-so; ~*-&-*~ *results will follow from* ~*-&-*~ *causes*). **8.** ~*'like*, of ~ kind (now chiefly vulg.; & see below). **9.** pron. ~ *as*, those who (chiefly arch. or poet. or rhet.; ~ *as sit in darkness*). **10.** That, the action etc. referred to, (*I may have offended, but* ~ *was not my intention*). **11.** *As* ~, as being what has been named (*in country places a stranger is welcome as* ~); *all* ~, persons of ~ character (*so perish all* ~ *!*). **12.** (Also ~*like*; chiefly vulg.) things of ~ kind (*do not hold with theatres & balls & ~ or ~like*). **13.** (vulg. or commerc.). The aforesaid thing(s), it, they or them, (*those who leave parcels in the train cannot expect to recover* ~). [OE *swylc*, OS *sulik*, OHG *sulih*, ON *slíkr*, Goth. *swaleiks* f. Gmc. *•swalik-* (SO, LIKE)]

suck, v.t. & i., & n. **1.** Draw (milk, liquid) into mouth by making vacuum with muscles of lips etc., (fig.) imbibe or gain (knowledge, advantage, etc.; also ~ *in knowledge*, ~ *advantage out of*); draw milk or liquid or sustenance or advantage from (~ *dry*, exhaust of contents thus; ~ *the breast of*; *the mother whom he* ~*ed*; ~*ed orange*, thing in which there is no goodness left; ~ one's *brains*, extract his ideas for one's own use); roll the tongue about, squeeze in the mouth, (~ *sweets*, one's *teeth*, etc.); (of absorbent substance) ~ *in* or *up*, absorb; (of whirlpool etc.) ~

in, engulf; ~ the breast or udder (part., not yet weaned, as ~*ing child*, ~*ing-pig*; also fig., unpractised, budding, as ~*ing barrister, saint*); ~ something, use ~*ing* action, make ~ing sound, (*sat* ~*ing at his pipe*; *pump* etc. ~*s*, makes gurgling or drawing sound; ~*ing-disc*, sucker); ~ *in* (sl.), deceive, ~*in*, n., disappointment; ‖ ~ *up* (schoolboy sl.), play toady (*to*; ~*-up* n., a toady). 2. n. Opportunity of ~ing the breast (*give* ~, of mother or nurse or animal suckling child etc.); drawing action of whirlpool etc.; spell of ~ing with lips or in mouth (*take a* ~ *at it*); small draught of or of liquor; ‖ (schoolboy sl., pl.) sweets; (sl.; also ~*in*) disappointment, fiasco, (*what a* ~!, ~*s!*, intt. expr. amusement at another's failure after confidence). [OE *sūcan*, cogn. w. L *sugere*; cf. SOAK]

suck′er, n., & v.t. & i. 1. Person or thing that sucks, esp. sucking-pig or new-born whale; (sl.) person of immature mind, greenhorn; kinds of fish that suck in food or have mouth suggesting suction or adhere by sucking-disc. 2. Piston of suction-pump; pipe through which liquid is drawn by suction. 3. (Also *sucking-disc*) flat or concave surface (as organ in some animals, also *acetabulum*, or artificial of rubber etc. in machinery or appliances) that adheres by suction & atmospheric pressure to what it is placed against. 4. (bot.). Shoot springing from subterranean part of stem, from part of root remote from main stem, from axil, or abnormally from bole or branch. 5. vb. (bot.). Remove ~s from; produce ~s. [-ER¹]

suc′kle, v.t. Give suck to. [ME, perh. back form. f. foll.]

suck′ling, n. Unweaned child or animal (*babes & ~s*, the utterly inexperienced). [ME, f. SUCK vb; -LING¹]

suc′rose, n. Cane-sugar or any of the sugars of the same composition & properties. [F *sucre* SUGAR, -OSE²]

suc′tion, n. Sucking; production of partial vacuum by removal of air etc. for purpose of enabling external atmospheric pressure to force in liquid or produce adhesion of surfaces; ~*-chamber*, *-pipe*, in ~*-pump*; ~*-fan*, for withdrawing chaff etc. from grain by ~; ~*-plate*, holding set of artificial upper teeth & adhering to palate by ~; ~*-pump*, drawing water through pipe into chamber exhausted by piston. [f. LL *suctio* (L *sugere suct-* SUCK, -ION)]

suctōr′ial, a. (zool.). Adapted for or capable of sucking, having sucker for feeding or adhering. [mod. L *suctorius* (prec., -ORY), -AL]

Sudanese (soōdaněz′), a. & n. (pl. same). (Inhabitant, language) of the Sudan, region of Africa south of Egypt. [-ESE]

sudār′ium, n. (pl. *-ia*). Kerchief of St Veronica miraculously stamped with face

of Christ; any miraculous portrait of Christ; napkin about Christ's head (*John* xx. 7). [L, = napkin (*sudor* sweat, -ARY¹)]

sūdatōr′ium, n. (pl. *-ia*). Hot-air bath. [L neut. as foll.]

sūd′atorў, a. & n. 1. Promoting perspiration. 2. n. ~ drug; = prec. [f. L *sudatorius* (*sudare* SWEAT, -ORY)]

sŭdd, n. Floating plants, trees, etc., impeding navigation of White Nile. [Arab., = barrier]

sŭdd′en, a. & n. 1. Occurring or come upon or made or done unexpectedly or without warning, abrupt, abnormally rapid, hurried, (~ *death, need, fear*; *a* ~ *resolve, departure, change, turn of the wrist, bend in the road*; *is very* ~ *in his movements*); ~ *death*, (also, colloq.) decision by a single toss of a coin (as against the best of three), decision of a level set at lawn tennis by the issue of the next game; hence ~LY² adv., ~NESS n. 2. n. *Of* or *on a*, rarely *on the*, ~, ~ly. [ME, f. AF *sodein, sudein* = OF *soudain* f. L *subitaneus* (*subitus* sudden, -ANEOUS)]

sūdorif′erous, a. Sweat-producing (of glands). [f. LL *sudorifer* (*sudor* sweat, -FEROUS)]

sūdorif′ic, a. & n. (Drug) causing sweat. [L *sudor* sweat, -I-, -FIC]

Sud′ra (soō-), n. Lowest of four great Hindu castes; cf. BRAHMIN, KSHATRIYA, VAISYA. [Skr.]

sŭds (-z), n. pl. Froth of soap & water (usu. *soap-*~). [16th c. also = fen waters etc., of uncert. orig.; cf. MDu., MLG *sudde*, MDu. *sudse* marsh, bog]

sūe, v.t. & i. Prosecute (person) in law-court; entreat (person), make entreaty or application *to* person or law-court, (*for* redress or a favour, esp. woman's hand in marriage); ~ *out*, make petition in law-court for & obtain (writ, pardon, etc.). [ME, f. AF *suer*, *siuer* = OF *sivre* etc. f. Rom. *°sequere* f. L *sequi* follow]

suède (swād), n. Kid-skin dressed with flesh side rubbed to a nap (usu. attrib.). [F. f. (*gants de*) *Suède* (gloves of) Sweden]

sū′et, n. Hard fat of kidneys & loins of oxen, sheep, etc. Hence ~Y² a. [ME, app. f. AF *°suet*, *°sewet* f. OF *seu, sieu* (mod. *suif*) f. L *sebum* tallow, -ET¹]

suf-, = SUB- in L compds with wds in f- & their derivations.

sŭff′er, v.t. & i. 1. Undergo, experience, be subjected to, (pain, loss, grief, defeat, change, punishment, wrong, etc.); undergo pain or grief or damage or disablement (~*s acutely*; ~*ing mortals*; *was* ~*ing from neuralgia*; *your reputation will* ~; *the engine* ~*ed severely*; *trade is* ~*ing from the war*), whence ~ER¹, ~ING¹(1), nn. (often pl.). 2. (Of condemned man) be executed (*was to* ~ *the next morning*). 3. Permit to do, allow to go on, put up with, tolerate, (~ *them to come*; *should not* ~ *it for a moment*; *how can you* ~ *him or his insolence?*), whence, chiefly w. neg., ~ABLE a.). [ME. f. AF *suffrir* = OF *sof(f)rir* f. L SUF(*ferre* bear)]

süff'erance, n. ‖ (Arch.) submissiveness; tacit consent, permission or toleration implied by abstinence from objection, (esp. *on* ~, in virtue of such toleration). [ME. f. AF, OF *suf(f)rance* f. LL *sufferentia* (SUFFER, -ENCE)]

süff'ète, n. One of two chief magistrates of ancient Carthage. [f. L *sufes -etis* f. Punic]

suffice', v.i. & t. Be enough (*to do*, *for* person or purpose, or abs.), be adequate, (*your word will* ~; *that* ~s *to prove it*; ~ *it to say that*, I will content myself with saying that); satisfy, meet the needs of, (*half a dozen* ~d *him*). Hence **suffi'c-ingly²** adv. [ME., f. OF *suffire* (*suffis-*) f. L SUF(*ficere* = *facere* make)]

suffi'ciency (-shn-), n. ‖ (Arch.) being sufficient, ability, efficiency; adequate resources, a competence, a sufficient amount of or of something. [f. OF *sufficience* or LL *sufficientia* (foll., -ENCY)]

suffi'cient (-shnt), a. & n. 1. Sufficing, adequate esp. in amount or number to the need, enough, (*is* ~ *to feed a hundred men*; *had not* ~ *courage for it*; *has impudence* ~ *for anything*; *have you* ~ *provisions?*), whence ~LY² adv.; ‖ (arch.) competent, of adequate ability or resources; SELF-~. 2. n. Enough, a ~ quantity, (chiefly vulg. for *enough*; *have you had* ~?). [ME, f. OF, or f. L *sufficiens* (SUFFICE, -ENT)]

suffix'¹, v.t. Append (letter, syllable) in word-formation. [f. foll.]

süff'ix², n. Suffixed letter or syllable (cf. *prefix, affix*). [f. mod. L *suffixum* f. neut. p.p. of L SUF(*figere fix-* fasten)]

süff'oc|āte, v.t. & i. Choke or kill by stopping respiration (of person, superincumbent mass, fumes, etc.); produce choking sensation in, impede breath or utterance of, (~*ated by* or *with grief, excitement,* etc.); feel ~ated, gasp for breath. Hence or cogn. ~**ātingly²** adv., ~**A'TION** n. [f. L *suffocare* (SUB², *fauces* throat)]

süff'ragan, a. & n. ~ *bishop* or *bishop* ~ or ~, bishop appointed to help diocesan bishop in administration of diocese, also any bishop in relation to his archbishop or metropolitan (~ *see* etc., *of* ~ *bishop*). Hence ~**SHIP** n. [ME. f. AF, OF *suffragan*, repr. med. L *suffraganeus* assistant (bishop) f. stem of *suffragium* (foll.)]

süff'rage, n. Vote, approval or consent expressed by voting, (*the electors gave their* ~*s for free trade*; also transf., as *the horse has my* ~, I think it preferable); the right of voting in political elections (*the* ~, or *manhood, woman, universal,* etc., ~; *manhood* ~, extended to all adult males without property tests etc.; *woman* ~, extended to women as well as men; *universal* ~, extended to all adults); (eccl.) short petition of congregation, esp. one said in response to priest, (arch.) an inter-

cessory prayer. [ME. f. L *suffragium*, partly thr. F *suffrage*]

süffragètte', n. Woman who agitated for woman suffrage. [irreg. f. SUFFRAGE + -ETTE]

süff'ragist, n. One who attaches importance to (esp. some extension of) the suffrage (*woman-* etc.). [-IST]

suffūse' (-z), v.t. (Of colour or moisture) well up from within & colour or moisten (a *blush, tears,* ~*d her cheeks, eyes*; often in p.p., as *skies* ~*d with amethyst*). So **suffū'sion** (-zhn) n. [f. L SUF(*fundere fus-* pour)]

suf'|i (sōō-), **sōf'|ī,** n. Mohammedan pantheistic mystic. Hence ~IC a., ~ISM (3) n. [f. Arab. *çūfī* man of wool (*çūf* wool)]

sug-, = SUB- in L compds w. wds in g- & their derivatives.

su'gar (shŏō-), n., & v.t. & i. 1. Kinds of sweet crystalline substance prepared from various plants esp. the ~-cane & beet for use in cookery, confectionery, brewing, etc. (*cane, beet, maple,* etc., ~, named from plant of origin; *brown, white, granulated, powdered,* LUMP¹, CASTOR², LOAF¹, ~). 2. Sweet words, flattery, anything serving purpose of ~ put round pill in reconciling person to what is unpalatable. 3. (chem.). Kinds of soluble sweet-tasting fermentable carbohydrate divided according to their composition into glucoses & saccharoses. 4. ‖ ~-*basin,* holding ~ for table use; ~-*bean,* kinds of pulse & kidney-bean; ~-*beet,* kinds from which ~ is extracted; ~-*bird,* kinds that suck flowers; ~-CANDY; ~-*cane,* a grass with jointed stems 18–20 ft high from which ~ is made; *~-daddy* (sl.), elderly protector and source of revenue of a (female) GOLD-*digger;* ~-*gum,* Australian gum-tree with sweet foliage; ~-*house,* establishment in which raw ~ is made; ~-LOAF¹; ~-*maple,* tree from sap of which ~ is made; ~-*mill,* for crushing ~-cane & expressing ~; ~-*mite,* kind infesting unrefined ~; ~-*orchard,* of ~-maples; ~*plum,* sweetmeat, esp. small ball of boiled ~; ~-*refiner(y),* (establishment of) manufacturer who refines raw ~; ~*-tongs,* small tongs for taking up lump-~ at table; hence ~Y², ~LESS, aa., ~INESS n. 5. vb. Sweeten with ~ lit. or fig. 6. (sl.). Used in pass. as euphem. imprecation. 7. ‖ (sl.). Work lazily, not do one's full share of work, not put forth all one's strength, whence ~ER¹ n. [ME, f. OF *çucre, zuchre,* etc., f. med. L *zuc-, succarum,* f. Arab. *sukkar*]

suggèst' (suj-), v.t. Cause (idea) to present itself, call up the idea of by mention or association, (*thing* ~s *itself,* comes into the mind); propose (theory, plan, often expressed in *that*-clause) for acceptance or rejection, set up the hypothesis *that,* (~*ed a retreat, that they should retreat;* *I* ~ *that,* formula of examining counsel in imputing motives etc. = *I put it to you,* as

I ~ that you had a secret understanding with them). [f. L SUG(*gerere gest-* bring)]

sugges't|ible (suj-), a. That may be suggested; open to hypnotic suggestion.
Hence ~IBIL'ITY n. [-IBLE]

sugges'tĭŏ făl'sī (suj-), n. Positive misrepresentation not involving direct lie but going beyond concealment of the truth (cf. SUPPRESSIO VERI). [L]

suggestion (sujĕs'chon), n. Suggesting (*full of ~*, suggesting many ideas, stimulating reflection); theory or plan suggested; suggesting of prurient ideas; insinuation of a belief or impulse into the mind of a hypnotic subject, such belief or impulse. So **sugges'tive** a. (*of*), **sugges'tively** adv., **sugges'tiveness** n. (suj-). [ME, f. OF, f. L SUGGESTIonem (-ION)]

sū'ī, genit. of L *suus* his, her, its, or their, own: *~ gĕn'eris* pred. a., not classifiable with others, unique; *~ jur'is* (-oor-) pred. a., of full age & capacity, independent.

sū'icide, n. 1. Person who intentionally kills himself; (law) ~ of years of discretion & sane mind. 2. Intentional self-slaughter (in law, as in 1; esp. *commit ~*, kill oneself); action destructive to one's own interests or continuance in some capacity (*commit political ~*, ruin one's prospects as a politician; *race-~*, failure of a people to maintain its numbers); hence **sūicid'AL** a., **sūicid'ally** adv. [f. mod. L *suicida*, *suicidium*, f. *sui* of oneself +-CIDE]

sū'illine, a. Of the hog family. [f. LL *suillinus* f. L *suillus* (*sus* pig), -INE¹]

suit (sūt), n., & v.t. & i. 1. Suing, petition, seeking of woman's hand in marriage, (*make ~*, urge a humble request; *with lowly ~*; *has a ~ to the king*; *press, push,* etc., one's *~*; *prosper in* one's *~*). 2. Legal prosecution of a claim, action in law-court, (also *law~*, ~ *at law*; *criminal, civil,* etc., *~*). 3. Any of the four sets (spades, hearts, diamonds, clubs) into which pack of cards is divided (*follow ~*, play from ~ that was led, fig. conform to another's movements); player's holding in it (*long, short, ~* in whist, of more than three, less than four, cards). 4. Set of man's clothes esp. when of same cloth, consisting usu. of coat, waistcoat, & trousers or knickerbockers or breeches (often *~ of clothes*; *dress ~*, for evening dress; *~ of* DITTOS; *~'case*, kind of small portmanteau), whence *~'ING¹*(3) n.; (usu. 2, 3, 4, *-piece~*) woman's costume. 5. Set *of* sails, set of armour, for simultaneous use. 6. vb. Accommodate, adapt, make fitting or appropriate, *to* (*~ the action to the word*, carry out promise or threat at once; *~* one's *style* to one's *audience*); (p.p.) appropriate *to*, well adapted or having the right qualities *for*, *is not ~ed to be* or *for an engineer*). 7. Satisfy, meet the demands or requirements or interests *of*, (*does not ~ all tastes*; *it ~s me* or, prob.

w. ref. to betting, *my book to put up with him*; *~ yourself*, do as you choose, also find something that satisfies you, esp. as servant's formula in giving warning); (of food, climate, etc.) improve or be consistent with the health of, agree with, (*cold, asparagus, does not ~ me*). 8. Comport with or *with*, go well with appearance or character of, become, (*red does not ~ with* or *~s her complexion*; *the part ~s him admirably*; *mercy ~s a king*). 9. Be convenient (*that date will ~*). [f. AF *siute* etc., = OF *sieute* f. Gallo-Rom. **sequita* f. Rom. **sequere* SUE]

suit'|able (sūt-), a. Suited *to* or *for*, well fitted for the purpose, appropriate to the occasion. Hence ~ABIL'ITY, ~ableness, nn., ~ably² adv. [prec., -ABLE]

suite (swēt), n. Retinue, set of persons in attendance; set of things belonging together, esp. *~ of rooms* or *furniture*; (mus.) instrumental composition, orig. succession of movements in dance style. [F, f. SUIT]

suit'or (sūt-), n. Party to lawsuit; petitioner; wooer, man who asks for woman's hand in marriage. [ME, f. AF *seutor, suitour*, etc., f. L *secutorem* (*sequi, secut-* follow, -OR)]

suivez (swēv'ā), mus. direction instructing accompanist to suit his time etc. to soloist's performance. [F]

sul'cāte, a. (bot., anat.). Grooved, fluted, channelled. [f. L *sulcare* (*sulcus* furrow), -ATE²]

sulk, n., & v.i. 1. Sulky fit (usu. pl., esp. *in the ~s*). 2. v.i. Be sulky. [18th c., of unkn. orig.; cf. NFris. *sulke*]

sul'k|y̆, a. & n. 1. Sullen, morose, silent or inactive or unsociable from resentment or ill temper; hence ~ILY² adv., ~INESS n. 2. n. Light two-wheeled one-horse vehicle for single person. [-Y²; cf. NFris. *sulkig*]

sull'age, n. Filth, refuse, sewage. [16th c., of unkn. orig.]

Sull'an, a. (Rom. hist.). Of, enacted by, L. Cornelius Sulla. [-AN]

sull'en, a. & n. 1. Passively resentful, unforgiving, gloomy-tempered, unsociable, not responding to friendliness or encouragement or urging, stubbornly ill-humoured, morose, of dismal aspect; hence ~LY² adv., ~NESS n. 2. n. pl. *The ~s*, ~ frame of mind, ill temper, depression. [16th c. alt. f. ME *solein* f. AF **solein* ult. f. L *solus* SOLE³, -AN]

sull'y̆, v.t. Soil, tarnish, (chiefly poet.); diminish the purity or splendour of (reputation, character, victory, etc.), disgrace. [c. 1600, app. f. F *souiller*, see SOIL²]

sul'ph|(o)-, comb. forms of SULPHUR: *~ăm'ic*, derived from an amic acid of sulphuric acid, so *~amATE*¹(3); *~āte*, salt of sulphuric acid (*~ate of copper*, blue vitriol; *~ate of iron*, green vitriol; *~ate of magnesium*, Epsom salts; *~ate of sodium*, Glauber's salts; *~ate of zinc*, white vitriol); *~ĭde*, compound of sulphur with element or radical; ~*ile*, salt of sulphurous acid; ~*ocyăn'ic*, containing sulphur & cyanogen; ~*onal*, a hypnotic & anaesthetic drug; ~*ŏn'amîdes*, group of synthetic chemical compounds acting as anti-bacterial agents when circulating in the blood-stream or applied locally; ~*ŏn'ic acid*, any of a group of acids produced by the action of sulphuric acid (~*ona'tion*) on various aromatic compounds; ~*ovĭn'ic*, of sulphuric acid & alcohol.

sŭl'phur (-er), n., a., & v.t. 1. Pale-yellow non-metallic element occurring in crystalline & amorphous modifications, burning with blue flame & stifling smell, & used in making gunpowder, matches, vulcanite, & sulphuric acid, & in medical treatment of skin-diseases (*flowers, milk, of* ~, yellow, white, powders got by treating ~ in certain ways; *roll, stick,* ~, ~ refined & cast in moulds, brimstone). 2. Kinds of yellow butterfly. 3. Material of which hell-fire & lightning were held to consist. 4. ~*-bottom* (*whale*), Pacific rorqual with yellow belly; ~ *ore*, iron pyrites; ~*-spring*, of water impregnated with ~ or its compounds; ~*-wort*, yellow-flowered herb formerly used in medicine; hence ~Y[2] a. 5. adj. Of pale slightly greenish yellow. 6. v.t. Apply ~ to, fumigate with ~. [ME, f. AF *sulf(e)re* = OF *soufre* f. L *sulfur(em), sulphur(em)*]

sŭl'phur|āte, v.t. Impregnate or fumigate or treat with sulphur, esp. in bleaching. Hence ~A'TION, ~ātor, nn. [f. prec. +-ATE[3]]

sŭlphūr'éous, a. Of, like, suggesting, sulphur; (bot.) sulphur-coloured. [L *sulphureus* (SULPHUR), -OUS]

sŭlphūrětt'ĕd, a. Having sulphur in combination (chiefly in ~ *hydrogen*, H₂S, a transparent colourless fetid gas). [f. *sulphuret* (SULPHUR, -URET) +-ED[2]]

sŭlphūr'ic, a. (chem.). Containing sulphur in its higher combining proportion (cf. SULPHUROUS; ~ *acid*, H₂SO₄, oil of vitriol, a dense oily colourless highly acid & corrosive fluid much used in many processes in chemical industry; ~ *ether*, = ETHER in chem. sense). [f. F *sulfurique* see SULPHUR, -IC (chem.)]

sŭl'phuriz|e, -is|e (-īz), v.t. = SULPHURATE. Hence ~A'TION n. [f. F *sulfuriser* (as prec., -IZE)]

sŭl'phurous, a. = SULPHUREOUS; (chem.; *pr.* -ŭr'us) containing sulphur in its lower combining proportion (cf. SULPHURIC; ~ *acid*). [f. L SULPHUR(*osus* -OUS), or f. SULPHUR +-OUS]

sŭl'tan, n. 1. Moslem sovereign (*the S*~, hist., ~ of Turkey), whence ~ATE[1] n. 2. Kinds of gorgeously coloured bird of rail family; variety of white domestic fowl from Turkey; *sweet, yellow,* ~, kinds of garden flower. [F, or f. med. L *sultanus*, f. Arab.]

sŭlta'na (-tah-), n. 1. Sultan's mother,

wife, or daughter. 2. Mistress of king etc. 3. Sultan-bird. 4. Kind of seedless raisin used in puddings & cakes. [It., f. *sultano* (prec.)]

sŭl'tanĕss, n.=prec. (first sense). [-ESS[1]]

sŭl'tr|ў̆, a. (Of atmosphere or weather) hot & close or oppressive; (of temper etc.) passionate. Hence ~ILY[2] adv., ~INESS n. [f. obs. *sulter* vb (perh. f. *swulter* cogn. w. SWELTER) +-Y[2]]

sŭm, n., & v.t. & i. (-mm-). 1. Total amount resulting from addition of items, brief expression that includes but does not specify details, substance, summary, (also ~ *total*; *the* ~ *of all my wishes is happiness; the* ~ *of two & three is five;* ~, *remainder, product, quotient,* results of addition, subtraction, multiplication, division; *the* ~ or ~ *& substance of his objections is this; in* ~, briefly & comprehensively put); particular amount of money (*what* ~ *would you give for it? for the* ~ *of* 15/-; *a good, round, considerable,* ~; LUMP[1] ~); (working out of) an arithmetical problem (*good at* ~*s; did a rapid* ~ *in his head*). 2. vb. Collect into or express or include as one total or whole (often *up*), gather *up* (evidence, points of argument etc., already treated in detail) into brief review; ~ *up* (intr.), make recapitulation of evidence or argument (esp. of judge after both sides have been heard; so ~*ming-up* n.), (trans.) form or express idea of character of (person). [ME, f. AF, OF *summe, somme* f. L *summa* fem. of *summus* highest; vb f. OF *sommer* or LL *summare*]

sŭm'ăc(h) (-k; *also* shŏŏm'ăk), n. (Dried & ground leaves, used in tanning & dyeing, of) kinds of shrub. [ME, f. OF *sumac* f. Arab. *summāq*]

Sŭmēr'ian, a. & n. (archaeol.). 1. Of the non-Semitic element in the civilization of Babylonia. 2. n. The ~ language, a ~ person. [f. F (-*ien*), f. *Sumer* in Babylonia]

sŭmm'ar|ize, -ise (-īz), v.t. Make or be a summary of, sum up. So ~IST(1) n. [foll., -IZE]

sŭmm'ar|ў̆, a. & n. 1. Compendious, brief, dispensing with needless details or formalities, done with dispatch, (*a* ~*y account;* ~*y methods, jurisdiction,* etc.); hence ~ILY[2] adv. 2. n. Brief account, abridgement, epitome. [n. f. L *summarium*, adj. f. med. L *summarius*, (L *summa*, -ARY[1])]

summā'tion, n. Addition, finding of total or sum. [f. SUM vb +-ATION]

sŭmm'er[1], n., & v.i. & t. 1. Second season of the year, June–August (astron., from ~ solstice to autumnal equinox; INDIAN, ‖ *St* MARTIN'S, ~; ‖ *St Luke's* ~, period of fine weather expected about 18th October. 2. (poet.). (Usu. in pl. with number etc.) year of life or age (*a child of ten* ~*s*). 3. attrib. Characteristic of or fit for ~ (~*-house,* light building in garden etc. for sitting in; ~ *lightning,*

distant sheet lightning; ~ *school*, long-
-vacation meeting for lectures etc., esp. at
university; ~*-time* or ~*time*, the weather
or season of ~ ; || ~ *time*, that indicated by
clocks advanced in ~ to prolong use of
daylight; || (*British*) *double* ~ *time*, two
hours in advance of Greenwich mean
time); hence ~LY¹, ~Y², ~LESS, aa. 4. vb.
Pass the ~ usu. *at* or *in* place; pasture
(cattle) *at* or *in*. [OE *sumor*, OS, OHG,
ON *sumar*]

summ'er², n. (Also ~*-tree*) horizontal
bearing beam, esp. one supporting joists
or rafters. [ME, f. AN *sumer*, *somer* pack-
-horse, beam, = OF *somier* f. Rom.
*saumarius, LL *sag-*, f. LL f. Gk *sagma*
pack-saddle; see BREASTSUMMER]

summersault, -set. = SOMERSAULT.

summ'it, n. Highest point, top, apex,
highest degree, (*the icy* ~*s of the Alps*; *at
the* ~ *of power*; *the* ~ *of my ambition is*);
a ~ *meeting*; (attrib., of meetings, talks,
etc.) taking place between heads of
governments. Hence ~LESS a. [ME, f.
OF *somet*, *sommette*, (*som* top f. L *summum* neut. of SUMMUS, -ET¹)]

summ'on, v.t. Demand the presence of,
call upon to appear, esp. as defendant or
witness in lawcourt, cite, convoke, invite; call upon (town etc.) to surrender;
~ *up*, gather *courage*, *spirit*, etc., usu. *to
do* or *for* undertaking. [ME, f. OF
somondre f. L SUB(*monēre*, warn), in med.
L = call]

summ'ons (-z), n. (pl. ~*es*), & v.t. **1.**
Authoritative call or urgent invitation to
attend on some occasion or to something.
2. Citation to appear before judge or magistrate. **3.** v.t. Serve with ~. [ME, f. OF
somo(u)nse fem. p.p. of *somondre* as prec.]

summ'um bŏn'um, n. The chief good,
esp. as the end or ultimate determining
principle in an ethical system. [L]

sump, n. Pit or well for the reception of
(esp. superfluous) water, oil, or other
liquid in mines, machines, etc.; cesspool.
[ME = *marsh*, f. MDu., MLG *sump*, or
(mining) G *sumpf*, rel. to SWAMP]

sump'ter, n. (Arch.) pack-horse or its
driver; ~*-horse*, *-mule*, *-pony*, pack-
-animals. [ME, f. OF *som(m)etier* f. Rom.
*sagmatarius f. LL f. Gk *sagma* *-atos*
pack-saddle; see SUMMER²]

sump'tion, n. Major premiss of syllogism.
[f. L *sumptio* f. *sumere* *sumpt-* take, -ION]

sump'tūary, a. Regulating expenditure
(~ *law*, *edict*, etc., limiting private expenditure in the interest of the State).
[f. L *sumptuarius* (*sumptus* *-ūs* cost as
prec.)]

sump'tūous, a. Rich & costly, suggesting
lavish expenditure. Hence ~LY² adv.,
~NESS n. [ME, f. OF *somptueux* or L
sumptuosus (prec., -OUS)]

sŭn, n., & v.t. & i. (-nn-). **1.** The heavenly
body that the earth travels round &
receives warmth & light from, such
light or warmth or both, (~ *rises*, *sets*,

is brought by earth's revolution above,
below, the horizon; *his*, *its*, etc., ~ *is set*,
time of prosperity or existence is over;
rise with the ~, get up early; *Order of the
Rising Sun*, Japanese order; *hail* or *adore
the rising* ~, curry favour with new or
coming power; *empire* etc. *on which the* ~
never sets, world-wide; *let not the* ~ *go
down upon your wrath*, limit it to one day;
the midnight ~, seen in arctic & antarctic
regions; *nothing new under the* ~, in the
world; *mock* ~, parhelion; *Sun of righteousness*, Christ; *see the* ~, be alive; *make
HAY while the* ~ *shines*; *hold a candle to the*
~, prov. of superfluous action; *take*, or sl.
shoot, *the* ~ (naut.), ascertain its altitude
in order to fix latitude; *with*, *against*, *the*
~, CLOCK¹WISE, counterclockwise, whence
~'WISE (-z) adv.; ~'s *eyelashes*, ~'s *back-
stays* (naut.), ~ *drawing water*, phenomenon given by rays piercing aperture in
cloud & illuminating suspended particles
in parallel lines; ~ *& planet*, system of
gearing in which cogged wheel on reciprocating rod both rotates on its axis &
travels round the wheel that it engages &
communicates motion to; *exclude*, *let in*,
the ~; *in the* ~, exposed to ~'s rays; *a
place in the* ~, fig., favourable situation or
conditions; *take the* ~, expose oneself to
~light). **2.** Any fixed star with satel-
lite(s). **3.** (poet.). Day or year. **4.** (Also
~ *burner*) set of gas-jets, electric lights,
etc., massed as one great light in ceiling.
5. ~*-bath*, exposure of body to ~; ~'*beam*,
ray of ~; ~*-bird*, kinds of small bright-
-plumaged Old-World birds with resem-
blance to humming-birds; || ~*-blind*,
window-shade; ~*-bonnet*, of linen etc.
with projection & pendent back to shade
face & neck; ~*-bow*, prismatic bow given
by ~light on spray etc.; ~'*burn*, tanning
of skin by exposure to ~, so ~'*burnt* or
-*burned* a.; ~'*burst*, firework or piece of
jewellery imitating ~ and rays; ~*-dance*,
of N.-Amer. Indians in honour of ~;
~'*dew*, kinds of small bog-plant with
hairs secreting drops of moisture; ~-
DIAL; ~-DOG¹; ~'*down*, ~set; ~'*downer*,
Australian tramp who times his arrival
at a station for the evening, (colloq.) a
drink at ~set; ~*-dried*, dried by ~ & not
by artificial heat; ~'*fish*, large fish of almost spherical shape; ~'*flower*, kinds of
tall garden-plant with showy golden-
-rayed flowers, plant grown for its seeds
which yield an edible oil; ~*-glasses*, for
protecting the eyes from direct ~light
or glare; ~'*glow*, whitish or faintly
coloured corona of light occas. seen
round ~; ~*-god*, the ~ worshipped as a
deity; ~*-hat*, *-helmet*, adapted by material
or shape to keep ~ off; ~'*light*; ~'*lit*;
~*-myth*, SOLAR myth; ~*-rays*, ultra-violet
rays used therapeutically as substitute
for ~light; ~'*rise*, (moment of) ~'s rising;
~'*set*, (moment of) ~'s setting, western
sky with colours characterizing ~set

(attrib., resembling these), (fig.) declining period of life; ~'*shade*, parasol, also awning of shop-window; ~'*shine*, light of ~ (~*shine recorder*, instrument recording duration of ~shine; ~*shine roof*, sliding roof of saloon motor-car), surface illuminated by it, fair weather, (fig.) cheerfulness or bright influence, so ~'*shiny* a.; ~-*snake*, ornament found in early N.-Europ. art shaped like S with small circle at centre; ~-*spot*, one of the dark patches, changing in shape & size & lasting for varying periods, occas. observed on ~'s surface; ~-*star*, red starfish with many rays; ~-*stone*, kinds of quartz (esp. cat's-eye) & feldspar; ~'*stroke*, acute prostration from excessive heat of weather; ~-*up* (dial.), ~*rise*; ~-*worship(per)*; hence ~'*LESS* a., ~'*lèssNESS* n., ~'*LIKE*, ~'*PROOF*², aa., ~'*WARD* a. & adv., ~'*WARDS* (-z) adv. **6. vb.** Expose to the ~ (~ *oneself*, bask in ~light, also fig.); ~ oneself. [OE *sunne*, also OE; ON -*a*, OS, OHG -*o*, -*a*, Goth. -ð f. Gmc *sunnon, -ōn*]

***sūn'dae** (-di), n. Portion of ice-cream mixed with crushed fruit, nuts, etc. [arbitrary]

Sŭn'day (-di), n. First day of week, Lord's day, observed as day of rest & worship (HOSPITAL, LOW¹, PALM¹, ROGATION, SHOW², ~; *month of* ~s, long period; ~ *letter*, DOMINICAL letter; ~ *best*, ~ *go-to-meeting clothes*, usu. joc., best clothes kept for ~ use; ~-*school*, for religious instruction on ~s). [OE *sunnan dæg*, transl. LL *dies solis* day of the sun]

sŭn'der, v.t. & i. (arch., rhet., poet.). Separate (t. & rarely i.), sever, keep (trans.) apart. Hence ~ANCE n. (rare). [OE *sundrian*, f. *āsundrian*, f. *sundor*, esp. in *on sundran* ASUNDER]

sŭn'drỹ, a. & n. **1.** Divers, several, (chiefly arch. & joc.; *all & ~*, each & all, everyone collectively & individually). **2. n.** (Austral.) an extra in cricket; (pl.) oddments, accessories or items not needing special mention. [OE *syndrig* (*sundor* see prec., -Y²)]

sung. See SING.

sunk(en). See SINK¹.

sŭnn, n. (Also ~ *hemp*) E.-Ind. hemplike fibre. [f. Hind. *san* f. Skr. *sana*]

Sŭnn'ǀla(h) (-na), n. Traditionary portion of Mohammedan law based on Mohammed's words or acts, but not written by him, accepted as authoritative by the orthodox (~ITE¹ or ~i pr. -ē, nn.) & rejected by the Shiites. [Arab. *sunnah* (*sunnal*) tradition]

sunnud. Var. of SANAD.

sŭnn'ǀlỹ, a. Bright with or as sunlight; of the sun (rare); exposed to, warm with, the sun (*the* ~*y side*, side of house etc. that gets sun, also fig. the more cheerful aspect of circumstances etc.); cheery, bright in disposition, diffusing cheerful-

ness. Hence ~ĪLY² adv., ~ĪNESS n. [ME; -Y²]

sunnyasee. Var. of SAN(N)YASI.

sŭp, v.t. & i. (-pp-), & n. **1.** Take (soup, tea, etc.) by sips or spoonfuls (*he must have a long spoon that ~s with the devil*, parleying with doubtful characters is risky); take supper (*on, off*, specified food); (of food or host) provide supper for. **2. n.** Mouthful of liquid (esp. *neither bit or bite nor ~*). [(sense ' sip ') OE *sūpan* (MLG *sūpen*, OHG *sūfan*), *suppan* (OHG -*supphen*, G *supfen*), *sūpian* f. sŭp- cf. SOP; (sense ' take supper ') ME f. OF *soper, super* see SUPPER]

sup-, = SUB- in L compds w. wds in p- & their derivatives.

sŭp'er, n. & a. (colloq., shop). **1.** Supernumerary actor, (fig.) extra or unwanted or unimportant person etc.; superintendent; expensively produced film designed for exhibition as the principal item in cinema programmes (in full ~-*film*); (commerc.) superfine cloth or manufacture. **2. adj.** Superfine; (of measure) superficial, in square (not linear or solid) measure (*120 ~ ft*, or *120 ft ~*); (sl.) splendid. [abbr. *supernumerary,. superfine, superficial*]

sŭp'er-, pref. f. L *super* prep., *super-* pref., over, beyond. **1.** In adjj. & their derivv. varieties of meaning are:

a. situated directly over, as ~*columnar* above columns, ~*humeral* over the shoulder;

b. not in or under but above, as ~*aqueous*, ~*terrene*, ~*celestial*, above water, earth, sky;

c. exceeding, going beyond, more than, transcending, too exalted for contact or connexion with, as ~*normal* beyond the norm, ~*natural* beyond what nature will account for, ~*sensible* out of reach of sense, ~*ethical* above the sphere of ethics. **2.** In vbs & adjj. & their derivv. varieties of meaning are:

a. on the top of something, as ~*impose*, ~*scribe*, ~*stratum*;

b. observation from above, as ~*intend*, ~*stition*, ~*vise*;

c. besides, in addition, as ~*add*, ~*erogation*, ~*fetation*;

d. to a degree beyond the usual or the right, as ~*eminent*, ~*saturate*, ~*subtle*. **3.** In nn. & their derivv. varieties of meaning are:

a. upper or outer, as ~*canopy*, ~*cilious*, ~*hive*;

b. of higher kind, higher in degree, expressing addition, in higher than the ordinary sense, esp. in names of classificatory divisions, as ~*class* group including more than one class;

~*abound'* v.i., ~*abūn'dance* n., ~ *abūn'dant* a., ~*abūn'dantlỹ* adv., 2d; ~*ădd'* v.t., ~*addi'tion* n., 2c; ~*altar*

For words in *super-* not given see SUPER-.

(-awl-) n., 3a, slab of stone consecrated & placed on unconsecrated altar; ~ăn′al a., 1a(ANUS);~ăngĕl′ĭc a., 1c;~ănn′ūāte v.t., 1c (L *annus* year), declare too old for work or use or continuance, dismiss or discard as too old, require the removal from school of (a pupil who has failed to reach a certain educational standard), send into retirement with pension, (p.p.) past work or use, so ~ănnŭā′tion n.; ~ā′quĕous a., 1b; ~căl′endered a., 2d;~căn′opў n.,3a;~cārgō n. (pl. *-oes*), 1, person in merchant ship managing sales etc. of cargo [f. Sp. *sobrecargo*];~cĕlĕs′tial a., 1b, also 1c = ~*angelic*;~chārger n., 2d, pump used in motor-cars & aeroplanes to force an extra quantity of explosive mixture into cylinders of engine & so increase the power output; ~cil′iarў a., 3a (L *supercilium* eyebrow f. *cilium* eyelid), of the brows, over the eye; ~cil′ious a., ~cil′iouslў adv., ~cil′iousnĕss n., 3a [f. L *superciliosus* w. ref. to raised eyebrows, see prec.], contemptuous, showing haughty indifference, assuming superiority; ~civ′ilized (-zd) a., 2d; ~class (-ah-) n., 3b;~colŭm′nar a., 1a;~colŭmniā′tion n., 1a, placing of one architectural order over another;~cōōl v.t., 2d, cool (a liquid) below its freezing-point, without solidification; ~dread′nought (-drĕd′nawt) n., 1c, battleship more powerful than the Dreadnought type (hist.); ~ĕlĕvā′tion n., 3b, amount by which outer rail at a curve is higher than inner; ~ĕm′inent a., 2d;~ĕrogā′tion n., 2c [f. LL *supererogare* pay out beyond what is expected], doing of more than duty requires (esp. *works of*~*erogation* in theol., such as form a reserve fund of merit that can be drawn on in favour of sinners), so ~ĕrŏg′atorў a.; ~ĕth′ical a., 1c; ~ĕx′cellent a., ~ĕx′cellence, ~ĕxcitā′tion, nn., 2d; ~fămilў n. (biol.), 3b; ~fătt′ĕd a., 2d (of soap); ~fēcundā′tion, ~fētā′tion, nn., 2c, second conception occurring during gestation; ~fi′cial (-Ishl) a., ~ficiăl′itў (-shĭ-) n., ~fi′ciallў adv., 3a (foll.), of or on the surface only, not going deep, without depth, (~*ficial colour*, *resemblance*, *knowledge*, *wound*, *accomplishments*; *a* ~*ficial person*, with no reserve of knowledge or feeling behind what he shows), (of measure) square (see SUPER a.); ~fi′cies (-shĭĕz) n. (pl. the same), 3a (L, f. *facies* face), a surface; ~fine a., 2d, (commerc.) of extra quality, (gen.) affecting great refinement; ~flu′itў (-lōō-) n., 2d (foll.),~fluous amount (*give of one's*~*fluity*), thing not needed;~fluous (sŏōpĕr′flŏō-) a. ~fluouslў adv., ~fluousnĕss n., 2d (L *superfluus* f. *fluere* flow), more than enough, redundant, needless; ~heat′ v.t., 2d, (esp.) heat (steam) to temperature higher than that

of boiling water, so ~heat′ER¹(2) n.; ~hive n., 3a, removable upper compartment of hive; ~hŭm′an a., ~hŭm′anlў adv., 1c; ~hŭm′eral n., 1a (L HUMERUS), Jewish ephod, also AMICE¹, also archiepiscopal pallium; ~impōse′ (-z) v.t., 2a, lay on or *on* something else;~imprĕgnā′tion n., 2c, ~fecundation;~incŭm′bent a., 2a, lying on something; ~indūce′ v.t., 2c, develop or bring in as an addition; ~institū′tion n., 2c, institution of person into benefice already occupied; ~intĕnd′ v.t. & i., 2b (L INTEND*ere* attend to), have the management (of), arrange & inspect working (of), so ~intĕn′dence n., ~intĕn′dent n., person who ~intends, || police officer above rank of inspector; ~jā′cent a., 2a (L *jacēre* lie), ~incumbent; ~lative (sŏōpĕr^c) a. & n., 2d [f. LL *super(lativus* f. *ferre lat-* carry)], of the highest degree (~*lative wisdom*, *beauty*, etc.; ~*lative degree* in gram., the forms of the adjective & adverb by which the highest or a very high degree of a quality is expressed, as *bravest*, *most absurdly*), so ~lativelў adv., ~lativenĕss n., (n.) the ~lative degree or form (*not used in the* ~*lative*; *what is the* ~*lative of shy?*), a word in the~lative (*his talk is all*~*latives*, he exaggerates);~lun′ar(ў) (-lōō-) a., 1b, (esp.) not of this world; ~man n., 3b, OVERMAN; ~mārkĕt, n., 3b, large, usu. self-service, store selling food & domestic goods; ~mĕd′ial a., 1a; ~mŏl′ĕcule n., 3b, compound molecule, combination of molecules acting as physical unit; ~mŭn′dāne a., 1c, superior to earthly things; ~năc′ulum adv. & n., 1 [16th c. L rendering of G *auf den Nagel* (*trinken*)], || *drink* ~*naculum* to the bottom (w. ref. to pouring of the last drop on thumbnail), (n.) choice wine worthy of being so drunk; ~năt′ant a., 2a (NATATION), floating on surface; ~nă′tural (-cher-) a.,~nă′turallў adv.,~nă′turalnĕss n., 1c, due to or manifesting some agency above the forces of nature, outside the ordinary operation of cause & effect, so ~nă′turalism, ~nă′turalist, belief, believer, in the ~natural, ~nă′turalize, -ise (-īz), elevate into the ~natural region; ~nŏrm′al a., 1c; ~nŭm′erarў a. & n., 1c, (person or thing) in excess of the normal number, esp. extra person engaged for odd jobs; ~nūtri′tion n., 2d; ~ŏctave (-īv) n., 3b, organ-stop two octaves above open diapason; ~ōrder n., ~ōrd′inal a., 3b (in classif.); ~ōrd′inarў a., 1c; ~ōrgăn′ic a., 1c (of psychical things considered apart from the organisms in which they are manifested), also, 3b, social, organic in a higher metaphorical sense; ~ŏxўgĕnā′tion n., 2d;~pă′rasite n., parasite of a parasite, ~părasit′ic a., 3b; ~phŏs′phāte n., 2d, phosphate with greatest possible proportion of phosphoric acid; ~**phys′ical** (-z-) a., 1c; ~**pōse′** (-z) v.t., ~**posi′tion** (-z-) n., 2a, lay (thing) on or (up)on another; ~**săc′ral** a., 1a (SACRUM); ~**săt′ūrāte** v.t., ~**sătūrā′tion** n., 2d; ~**scribe** v.t., 2a [f. L super(scribere script-write)], write (inscription) at top of or outside something, write inscription over or on (thing), so~**script** a., written above the line, superior, ~**scrip′tion** n., ~scribed word(s); ~**sēde′** v.t. [f. OF *superseder* desist f. L super(sedēre sess-sit) desist from], set aside, cease to employ, adopt or appoint another person or thing in place of, (of person or thing appointed or adopted) take the place of, oust, supplant; ~**sĕn′sible** a., 1c; ~**sĕn′sĭtive** a., 2d; ~**sĕn′sŭal**, ~**sĕn′-sŭous**, aa., 1c, sensible; ~**sĕ′ssion** (-shn) n., ~seding or being ~seded; ~**sōl′ar** a., 1b; ~**sōlid** n., 3b, a solid of more than three dimensions; ~**sŏn′ic** a. & n., 1c (L *sonus* sound), relating to sound-waves of such a high frequency as to be inaudible, (of speed) greater than that of sound, (of aircraft etc.) travelling at ~sonic speed, (n. pl.) high-frequency sound-waves, study of these; ~**sound** n., 1c, vibrations of same type as sound but too rapid to be audible; ~**spi′ritŭal** a., ~**spiritŭăl′it̆y** n., 2d; ~**strāt′um**, ~**strŭc′tion** or ~**strŭc′ture** nn., ~**strŭc′tural** (-cher-) a., 2a; ~**sub-stăn′tial** (-shl) a., 1c; ~**subtle** (-sŭ′tl) a., ~**subtlety** (-sŭt′ltĭ) n., 2d; ‖~**tăx** n., 3b, (1909–29) graduated tax on incomes above £5,000 p.a. levied in addition to ordinary income tax; ~**tellūr′ic** a., 1b (L *tellus -uris* the earth); ~**tĕm′poral** a., 1a, above the temples of the head, also 1c, transcending time; ~**tĕrrēne′**, ~**terrĕs′-trial**, aa., 1b; ~**tŏnĭc** n., 1c, tone in musical scale next above tonic; ~**tŭberā′-tion** n., 3b, formation of tubers on tubers; ~**vacān′eous** a., 2d [f. L super(vacaneus f. *vacare* be empty)], ~fluous, unnecessary; ~**vēne′** v.i., 2a [f. L super(venire *vent-* come)], occur as an interruption to or change from some condition or process, so ~**vĕn′tion** n.; ~**vise′** (-z) v.t., 2b (L *vidēre vis-* see), direct or watch with authority the work or proceedings or progress of, oversee, so ~**vi′sion** (-zhn) n., ~**visor** (-z-) n., ~**vis′ory** (-z-) a. [repr. L *super-* = adv. & prep. *super* above, rel. to OVER, Gk *huper*, Skr. *upari*]

sŭp′erable, a. Not insuperable. [f. L *superabilis* f. *superare* overcome (*super* over, see prec.), -ABLE]

superb′ (sōō-, sŭ-), a. Of the most impressive or splendid or exalted kind, grand, (~ *beauty, courage, impudence; a ~ view, display, collection, specimen, voice, binding*). Hence ~LY² adv. [f. F *superbe* or L *superbus* proud]

sŭperhĕt′erody̆ne, n. & a. (Using) a system of wireless reception in which a local variable oscillator is tuned to beat at a constant ultrasonic rate with carrier-wave frequencies, thus making it unnecessary to tune the amplifier & securing great selectivity; abbr. *sŭperhĕt′*. [f. SUPER(SONIC)+HETERODYNE]

supēr′ior (sōō-, sŭ-), a. & n. 1. Upper, in higher position, of higher rank, (~ *officer, rank, court;* ~ LIMIT¹; ~ *genus,* higher in the classificatory series & so more comprehensive; ~ *wings,* folding over others; ~ *figures* or *letters,* written or printed above the line; ~ *limb* of sun etc., upper edge; (bot., of calyx or ovary) placed above the ovary or calyx). 2. Better or greater in some respect, related as the better or greater *to,* (*by* ~ *wisdom, cunning,* etc.; *is* ~ *in speed to any other machine;* ~ *numbers,* esp. more men or their presence, as *was overcome by* ~ *numbers*). 3. Of quality or qualities above the average, having or showing consciousness of such qualities, (*made of* ~ *leather; my cook is a very* ~ *woman;* ~ *persons,* the better educated etc., also & usu. iron., prigs; *he remarked with a* ~ *air*). 4. Above giving attention or yielding or making concessions *to* (~ *to bribery, temptation, revenge, fortune; rise* ~ *to,* be unaffected by); hence or cogn. **supēr̆iŏ′rĭty** (*or* -pĕ-) n., ~LY² adv. (chiefly in describing position in bot., anat., etc.). 5. n. One's better, person ~ to one, in rank or *in* some respect (*is deferential to his* ~*s; you are my* ~ *in ability & I yours in application; has no* ~ *in courage*). 6. Head of monastery etc. (often *Father, Mother, Lady, S~*), whence ~ESS¹ n. (rare). [ME, f. OF, f. L *superiorem* nom. *-or,* comp. of *superus* high (*super* above, see SUPER-)]

supērn′al, a. (poet., rhet.). Heavenly, divine, of the sky, lofty. [ME, f. OF, or med. L *supernalis* f. L SUPERNus, -AL]

sŭpersĕd′eăs, n. Writ staying proceedings. [L 2 sing. pres. subj. as SUPERsede]

sŭpersti′t|ion, n. Credulity regarding the supernatural, irrational fear of the unknown or mysterious, misdirected reverence; a religion or practice or particular opinion based on such tendencies. So ~**IOUS** (-shus) a., ~**iousLY²** adv., ~**iousNESS** n., (-shus). [ME, f. OF, or f. L *superstitio* f. *stare stat-* stand]

sŭp′in|āte, v.t. Turn (hand) palm upward (cf. PRONATE). Hence or cogn. ~**A′TION** n., ~**ātoR** n. (as name of two muscles). [L *supinare* (foll.), -ATE³]

sŭp′ine¹ (*or* -īn′), a. Lying face upward (cf. PRONE); disinclined for exertion, indolent, lethargic. Hence **sŭpine′LY²** adv., **sŭpine′NESS** n. [f. L *supinus* (st. of SUPER-, -INE¹)]

sŭp′ine², n. (L gram.). Verbal noun with accusative in *-um* & ablative in *-u* formed from p.p. st. of L vbs & used in special constructions. [f. LL (*verbum*) *supinum,* transl. Gk *hyptios* passive]

sŭpp'er, n. A meal taken at the end of a day, the last meal of the day when dinner is not the last. Hence ~LESS a. [ME, f. OF *soper*, *super*, subst. use of inf. (-ER¹), f. Rom. *suppare f. Gallo-Rom. *suppa* SOP, SOUP; cf. SUP]

supplant' (-ah-), v.t. Oust & take the place of esp. by underhand means. Hence ~ER¹ n. [ME, f. OF *supplanter* or L SUP(*plantare* f. *planta* sole) trip up]

sŭp'ple, a., & v.t. & i. **1.** Easily bent, pliant, flexible; given to compliance, avoiding overt resistance, wanting in sturdiness of character, artfully submissive, fawning; ~*jack*, (walking-cane of) kinds of strong twining shrub; hence ~NESS n., sŭp'plY² adv. **2.** vb. Make or grow ~ *horse*, train him to obey slightest touch of rein). [ME *souple*, f. OF, f. Rom. *supples f. L SUP(*plex* -*plicis* f. *plicare* fold) submissive]

sŭp'plement¹, n. Thing added to supply deficiencies, esp. fuller treatment of special subject issued with or in addition to newspaper etc.; (math.) the angle that added to another will make the sum two right angles. Hence ~AL, ~ARY¹, aa., (-měn⁴). [ME, f. L SUP(*plementum* f. *plēre* fill, -MENT)]

sŭp'plement'², v.t. Make addition(s) to. Hence ~A'TION n. [f. prec.]

sŭp'pliant, a. & n. **1.** Supplicating, expressive of supplication; hence ~LY² adv. **2.** n. Humble petitioner. [ME, f. OF (*supplier* f. L as foll., -ANT)]

sŭp'plicāte, v.t. & i. Make humble petition to or *to* person or for or *for* thing. Hence or cogn. ~ātinGLY² adv., ~A'TION n., ~atorY a. [ME, f. L *supplicare* (*supplex* SUPPLE, -ATE³]

supplỹ', v.t., & n. **1.** Furnish, provide, (thing needed, or person, receptacle, etc., with or *with* thing needed), whence **suppli'ER¹** n.; make up for, meet, serve to obviate, (deficiency, need, loss); fill (place vacancy, pulpit) as substitute. **2.** n. Providing of what is needed (*Committee of S~*, House of Commons discussing details of estimates for public service); stock, store, amount of something provided or at hand or get-at-able, (~ *& demand*, in pol. econ., chief factors regulating price of commodities; *an inexhaustible* ~ *of fish, coal*, etc.; *goods are in short* ~, scarce; *water etc.* ~), (pl.) collected necessaries for army etc.; (pl.) grant of money by Parliament for cost of government, money allowance to person (*his father cut off the supplies*). [ME, f. OF *so(u)pleer, souplier*, f. L SUP(*plēre* fill)]

support', v.t., & n. **1.** Carry (part of) weight of, hold up, keep from falling or sinking, (*foundation, buttress, ~s house, wall*; ~*ed by a lifebelt*; *had to be ~ed home*). **2.** Enable to last out, keep from failing, give strength to, encourage, (*what ~ed him* or *his strength was a glass of* brandy, *a good conscience, hope, your approval*; *too little food to* ~ *life*). **3.** Endure, tolerate, (~*s fatigue well*; *I can* ~ *life, such insolence, no longer*), whence ~ABLE a., ~abLY² adv. **4.** Supply with necessaries, provide for, (~ *a family*). **5.** Lend assistance or countenance to, back up, second, further, (~ *a cause, policy, team, leader, candidate*; ~ *actor* or other performer, take secondary part to him; ~*ing film, picture*, less important one in programme; ~ *resolution* etc., speak in favour of it; ~ *lecturer* etc., appear on his platform; ~ *institution*, subscribe to its funds). **6.** Bear out, tend to substantiate, bring facts to confirm, (statement, charge, theory, etc.). **7.** Keep up or represent (part, character) adequately. **8.** n. ~ing or being ~ed (*give* ~ *to*; *requires* ~; *gets no* ~; *troops stationed in* ~, as reserve; ~ *trench*, the second of three lines, between fire-trench & reserve trench; *speak in* ~ *of*, advocate); person or thing that ~s (*shelf must have another* ~; *he is the chief* ~ *of the cause*); hence ~LESS a. [ME, f. OF *supporter* f. L SUP(*portare* carry)]

support'er, n. In vbl senses; esp., (her.) representation of living creature holding up or standing (usu. as one of pair) beside an escutcheon. [15th c.; -ER¹]

suppose' (-z), v.t. **1.** Assume as a hypothesis (*let us* ~ *a second flood*; *well,* ~ *it was so*; in part. or imperat. with conjunctional force = *if*, as *supposing white were black you would be right*; ~ *your father saw you what would he say?*; also in imperat. as formula of proposal, as ~ *we went for a walk,* ~ *we try another*). **2.** (Of theory, result, etc.) require as a condition (*that ~s mechanism without flaws*; *design in creation ~s a creator*). **3.** Take for granted, presume, assume in default of knowledge, be inclined to think, accept as probable, (*I* ~ *we shall be back in an hour*; *you cannot* ~, *it is not to be ~d, that*; *I* ~ *he won't* or *I don't* ~ *he will come*; *what do you* ~ *he meant?*; *I* ~ *so*, form of hesitating assent; also abs. in parenth., as *you will not be there, I* ~). **4.** *Be* ~*d*, have as a duty (*he is not* ~*d to clean the boots*). **5.** p.p. Believed to exist, believed to have specified character, (*the* ~*d music of the spheres*; *his* ~*d brother, generosity*), whence **suppos'edLY²** (-z-) adv. Hence or cogn. **suppos'ABLE** (-z-) a., **supposi'TION** (-zĭ-) n. [see below], **supposi'tionAL** (-zǐsho-) a., **supposi'tionalLY²** adv.; **supposi'tious(2)** (-zǐshus) a., hypothetical, assumed. [ME, f. OF SUP(*poser* POSE¹); *supposition* etc. f. L SUP(*positio* (in LL 'hypothesis') f. L *ponere* *posit*-place, -ION)]

suppositi'tious (-zĭtĭshŭs), a. Substituted for the real, spurious, (~ *child, writings*). Hence ~LY² adv., ~NESS n. [f. L *suppositicius* f. SUP(*ponere* *posit*- place) substitute, -ITIOUS¹]

suppōs'itorў (-z-), n. (med.). Cone or cylinder of medicinal substance introduced into rectum or vagina or uterus & left to dissolve. [ME, f. med. L *suppositorium*, subst. use of LL *-orius* (as prec., -ORY)]

suppréss', v.t. Put down, quell, put an end to activity or existence of, (rebellion, sedition, agitators, etc.); conscience, piracy, monasteries, etc.); restrain, keep in, not give vent to, withhold or withdraw from publication, keep secret, not reveal, (groan, yawn, feelings, name, book, evidence, facts); (p.p., of a disease) checked in its normal course (*~ed measles* etc.). So ~IBLE a., **suppré'ssion** (-shn) n., ~OR n., (esp.) device for counteracting electrical interference. [ME, f. L SUP- (*primere press- = premere* Suppression)]

supprés'siŏ vēr'i, n. Suppression of truth, misrepresentation by concealment of facts that ought to be made known (cf. SUGGESTIO FALSI). [L]

sŭpp'ūr|āte, v.i. Form pus, fester. So ~A'TION n., ~ATIVE a. [L SUP(*purare* f. PUS), -ATE[3]]

sŭp'ra, adv. Above; previously, before (in a book or writing). [L, = above]

sŭpra-, pref. f. L *supra* adv. & prep. above, freely used in forming anat. terms indifferently with SUPER- 1a, as *~clavic'ular* above the clavicle, *~-orb'ital* above the eye-sockets, *~rēn'al* above the kidney, or with SUPER- 3a as *~maxill'ary* a. & n., (of) the upper jaw; also in other wds w. sense *over, beyond, before, after*, often in contrast with compds of INFRA-, SUB-, as *~mun'dane* above or superior to the world, *~lapsar'ian(ism)* a. & nn., (holding, holder of) doctrine that God's decrees of election & reprobation were not due to the Fall but preceded it & his prescience of it (cf. INFRALAPSARIAN); *~prot'est*, acceptance or payment of bill by third person after protest for non--acceptance or non-payment.

suprēm'acў (sŏō-, sū-), n. Being supreme, highest authority, (*Act, oath, of ~*, securing ecclesiastical *~* to the Crown & excluding the authority of the Pope). [foll., -ACY(2)]

suprēme' (sŏō-, sū-), a. & n. Highest in authority or rank (*the S~ Being* or *the S~* as n., God; *S~ Council of the Allies*, small body, also *the Big Four, Five*, settling by conference the Allied common policy 1919–21, each Great Power having a representative; *S~ Court of* JUDICATURE; *~ end* or *good*, SUMMUM BONUM; *~ Pontiff*, the Pope); greatest possible, uttermost, extreme, last & greatest or most important, (*~ wisdom, courage*, etc.; *the ~ test of fidelity; a* or *the ~ hour, moment*, etc.). Hence *~*LY[2] adv. [f. L *supremus* superl. of *superus* f. *super* above]

sur-, = SUPER- in many wds taken into E f. OF, as *surcharge, surface, surloin, surprise, surrender*, also sometimes for

super-, supra-, in anat. wds as *surrenal* SUPRArenal.

sura(h[1]) (soor'a), n. Chapter of Koran. [Arab.]

sūr'ah[2] (-a), n. Kind of soft twilled usu. one-coloured silk. [f. F pron. of *Surat* in India]

sūr'al, a. Of the calf of the leg (*~ artery* etc.). [L *sura* calf, -AL]

surăt' (sŏō-), n. Kind of cotton grown, kind of cotton cloth made, in the Bombay Presidency. [place-name]

surcease' (*ser-*), n., & v.i. (arch.). **1.** Cessation. **2.** v.i. Cease. [AF *sursise* delay, [ME, f. OF *sursis*, fem. *-ise* (cf. AF *sursise* omission), p.p. of OF *surseoir* f. L as SUPERSEDE, w. assim. to *cease*]

surcharge, n., & v.t. **1.** (sẽr'chärj). Excessive or additional load or burden or amount of money charged; supply of force, electricity, etc., in excess of what is required; additional charge made by assessors as penalty for false returns of taxable property; mark printed on postage-stamp changing its value; amount in official account not passed by auditor & having to be refunded by person responsible; showing of omission in account for which credit should have been given. **2.** v.t. (serchärj'). Overload, fill or saturate to excess; (of assessor, auditor) exact *~* from, exact (sum) as *~*, fine (person sum) as *~*; show omission of credit in (account). [ME, f. OF *surcharge(r)*, see SUR-]

sūr'cingle, n., & v.t. Band round horse's body rarely as saddlegirth, usu. to keep blanket etc. in place; girdle of cassock; (vb) gird (horse), fasten (blanket etc.), with *~*. [ME, f. OF SUR(*cengle* girth f. L *cingula* f. *cingere* gird)]

sūrc'oat, n. (hist.). Loose robe worn over armour; 15th–16th-c. woman's jacket. [ME, f. OF SUR(*cot, -cote* COAT)]

sūrc'ūlōse, **-lous**, aa. (bot.). Producing suckers. [f. L *surculosus* (*surculus* sucker, -OSE[1]), -OUS]

sŭrd, a. & n. **1.** (math.). Irrational (a. & n.). **2.** (phonet.). (Consonant, consonantal sound) uttered with the breath & not the voice (as p, f, s, cf. *voiced* or *vocal* of b, v, z). [f. L *surdus* deaf, noiseless; math. sense by mistransl. into L of Gk *alogos* irrational, speechless thr. Arab. *jaðr açamm* deaf root]

sure (shoor), a. & adv. **1.** Having or seeming to have adequate reason for belief, convinced *of* or *(that)*, having certain prospect or confident anticipation or satisfactory knowledge *of*, free from doubts *of*, (*are you ~?; you may be ~ of his honesty, he is* or *that he is honest; he feels* or *is ~ of success; I did not feel ~ of my company, could not feel ~ about it; if one could be ~ of living to 70; I'm ~ I didn't mean to hurt you*, form of asseveration; *well, I'm ~!*, excl. of surprise). **2.** Safe, reliable, trusty, unfailing, (*sent it by a ~*

hand; put it in a ~ place; a ~ shot, marksman who never misses; *a ~ draw,* covert certain to yield fox, remark etc. certain to draw person; ~ *card,* scheme etc. certain to succeed; SLOW *& ~; there is only one ~ way;* ~-*footed,* never stumbling or making false step lit. or fig.). **3.** To be relied on, certain, *to do (is ~ to turn out well; would be ~ to dislike him).* **4.** Undoubtedly true or truthful (*one thing is ~; to be ~,* formula of concession = to avoid over-statement, *as to be ~ she is not perfect, is pretty,* also as excl. of surprise, *as so it is, to be ~!, well, to be ~!; make ~,* ascertain absolutely that something is as supposed, take measures to secure that something is as desired; *make ~ of,* establish the truth or ensure the happening of; also *make ~ of or that,* have confident but often false anticipation of or that); hence ~'NESS n. **5.** adv. (Arch.) I admit, you will admit, (*'tis pleasant, ~, to see one's name in print*); *(colloq.) certainly (it ~ was cold); as certainly as (as ~ as eggs is eggs, as ~ as a gun,* colloq. forms of asseveration); ~ *enough,* in fact as well as in prospect (*I said it would be, & ~ enough it is*), with practical certainty (*he will come~ enough*); *~ *thing* (colloq.), a certainty, (as int.) certainly! [ME, f. OF *sur, sëur* f. L *securus* SECURE]

sure'ly (shoor'li), adv. With certainty or safety (*he knows full ~ that; will diminish slowly but ~; mule plants its feet ~*); (of strong belief or experience or probability or right is to count for anything (*it ~ cannot have been he; ~ I have met you before; there is no truth in it, ~; ~ you will not desert me*); (in answers, arch.) certainly, undoubtedly, (*'Should you be willing to try?' 'S~ '*). [-LY²]

sure'ty (shoor'ti), n. (Arch.) certainty (esp. *of a ~,* certainly); thing pledged as security for payment or performance (now rare); person who makes himself responsible for another's appearance in court or payment of sum or performance of engagement (*stand ~,* become so responsible, go bail, *for another; find ~ or sureties,* said of person primarily liable), whence ~SHIP n. [ME, f. OF *surte, sëurte* f. L *securitatem* (SURE, -TY)]

surf, n., & v.i. **1.** Foam & commotion of sea breaking on shore or reefs; ~-*bird,* coast-bird related to sandpiper; ~-*boat,* of buoyant build for use in ~; ~-*man,* skilled in managing ~-boats; ~-*riding* (on boards, as a sport). **2.** v.i. Go ~-riding. Hence ~'Y² a. [earlier *suff* (c. 1600), poss. of Indian orig.]

surf'ace (-is), n., & v.t. & i. **1.** The outside of a body, (any of) the limits that terminate a solid, outward aspect of material or immaterial thing, what is apprehended of something upon a casual view or consideration, (*has a smooth, uneven, ~; presents a large ~ to view; its upper ~ is*

as cold as ice; looks only at the ~ of men & things; his politeness is only of or on the ~; one never gets below the ~ with him), (attrib.) of the ~ only (~ *plausibility, impressions,* etc.); the ~ of the sea (~ *mail,* opp. air mail; ~ *craft, raider, ship,* opp. submarine). **2.** (geom.). That which has length & breadth but no thickness (*plane ~,* that contains the whole of the straight line connecting any two points in it; *curved ~,* that may be so cut by a plane through any point in it that the line of section shall be a curve; *developable ~,* that may be unfolded into a plane without doubling or separation of parts, e.g. ~ of cone or cylinder). **3.** ~-*colour,* used in ~-*printing,* printing from raised ~ as with ordinary type or woodcuts ~ not from incised lines; ~-*man,* keeping permanent way of railway in order; ~-*tension,* tension of a liquid causing it to act as an elastic enveloping membrane seen in drop or bubble; ~-*water,* that collects on & runs off from ~ of ground etc.; hence (-)*surfaceD²* a. **4.** vb. Put special ~ on (paper etc.); bring (submarine) to the ~; (of submarine) rise to the ~. [F (SUR-, FACE)]

surf'eit (-fit), n., & v.t. & i. **1.** Excess esp. in eating or drinking, oppression or satiety resulting. **2.** vb. Overfeed (t. & i.), (cause to) take too much of something, cloy, satiate *with.* [ME, f. OF *sor-, surfeit,* f. SUR- + *fail* p.p. of *faire* (L *facere fact-* do); cf. LL *superficies* excessive]

surge, v.i., & n. **1.** Move up & down or to & fro (as) in waves (of sea, crowd, standing corn, emotion, etc.); (naut., of rope or chain on windlass) slip back with a jerk; (of wheel) revolve without advancing on rail or road. **2.** n. Waves, a wave, surging motion. [n.: orig. obsc., in sense 2 f. vb; vb partly f. OF *sourdre (sorge-)* or obs. F *sorgir* f. L *surgere* rise, partly f. n.]

sur'geon (-jn), n. Medical man treating injuries & deformities & diseases by manual operation (*house-~,* on staff of hospital), person skilled in surgery; medical practitioner having a diploma qualifying him to practise surgery (~ *dentist,* dentist thus qualified); (formerly, opp. *physician*) general practitioner dispensing drugs & attending out-patients & not confining himself to consultation; medical officer in navy or army or military hospital; ~-*fish,* kind named from lancet-shaped spines on each side of tail. [ME, f. AF *surgien,* f. OF *ser-, cirurgien* f. *cirurgie* f. L f. Gk *kheirourgia* handiwork, surgery (*kheir* hand, -o-, *ergō* work)]

sur'gery, n. **1.** Manual treatment of injuries or disorders of the body, operative therapeutics, surgical work, (*antiseptic, clinical, plastic,* etc., ~; *conservative ~,* avoiding amputations etc.). **2.** Doctor's consulting-room & dispensary.

[ME, f. OF *surgerie*, contr. f. *ser-, cirurgerie* (*cirurgie* see prec., -ERY)]

sur'gical, a. Of surgeons or surgery (~ *skill, operations, instruments*; ~ *fever*, caused by ~ operation through sepsis). Hence ~LY² adv. [as SURGEON, -ICAL]

sur'icāte, n. S.-Afr. animal resembling polecat & ferret. [f. F *surikate*, f. native African]

surloin, obs. form of SIRLOIN.

surl'|y̆, a. Uncivil, given to making rude answers, showing unfriendly temper, churlish. Hence ~ILY² adv., ~INESS n. [alt. sp. of obs. *sirly* (SIR, -LY¹)]

‖ **surm'aster** (-ah-), n. Second master or vice-master in St Paul's School. [alt. f. orig. *submaster* (*hypodidascalus* in Erasmus lett.) f. med. L *submagister* (SUB- 2b)]

surmise (sermĭz'), n., & v.t. & i. 1. Conjecture, suspicion of the existence or guess at the nature of something. 2. vb. Infer doubtfully, suspect the existence of; make a guess, try to divine something. [ME, f. OF p.p. of SUR(*mettre* put f. L *mittere* miss- send) accuse]

surmount' (-ser-), v.t. Cap, be on the top of, (usu. in pass.; *peaks ~ed with snow*); overcome, get over, (difficulty, obstacle), whence ~ABLE a. [ME, f. OF *so(u)rmonter* f. med. L *supermontare* (SUR-, MOUNT²)]

surmull'et (ser-), n. The red mullet. [f. F *surmulet*]

surn'āme, n., & v.t. 1. Additional name of descriptive or allusive kind attached to a person & occas. becoming hereditary; the name common to all members of a family (cf. CHRISTIAN *name*). 2. v.t. Give ~ to; give (person ~); (p.p.) called by way of additional name, having as family name. [ME; SUR-, NAME, after AF, OF *surnum, sornom*]

surpass' (serpahs'), v.t. Outdo, excel. Hence ~ING² a., ~INGLY² adv. [f. F SUR(*passer* PASS¹)]

surp'lic|e, n. Loose full-sleeved white-linen vestment descending to hips or knees or ankles & worn usu. over cassock by clergy & choristers at divine service; ~e *choir*, wearing ~es; ‖ ~e-*fee*, paid to clergy for marriages, funerals, etc. Hence ~ED² (-st) a. [ME, f. AF *surpliz*, OF *sourpeliz*, f. med. L *superpellicium* (SUPER-, *pellicia* PELISSE)]

surp'lus, n. What remains over, what is not required for the purpose in hand, esp. excess of public revenue over expenditure for the financial year, (opp. *deficit*; often attrib., as ~ *population*). So ~AGE(1) n. [ME, f. OF, f. med. L SUPER(PLUS)]

surprise (serprĭz'), n., & v.t. 1. Catching of person(s) unprepared (*the fort was taken, the truth must be elicited, by* ~; *determined to attempt a* ~; *a* ~ *visit*, without notice); emotion excited by the unexpected, astonishment, (*full of* ~; *his* ~ *was visible*; *to my great* ~, much against my expectations); ‖ ~ *packet*, with unexpected contents, e.g. packet of sweets with coin, also often fig.); event etc. that excites ~ (*was a great* ~ *to me*; *I have a* ~ *for you*, piece of unexpected news, unexpected gift, etc.; *what a* ~ *!*). 2. v.t. Capture (place, person) by ~, attack at unawares, come upon (person) off his guard (~*d him in the act*); affect with ~, astonish, turn out contrary to expectations of, be a ~ to, (*should you be* ~*d to learn* —?; *I am* ~*d at you*, shocked, scandalized; *more* ~*d than frightened*), whence surprīs'ING² a., surprīs'ingLY², surpris'edLY², advv., (serprĭz-); hurry (person) by ~ *into* conduct or act or doing (~*d me into rudeness, consent, dropping the reins*); hence surpris'AL(2) (serprĭz-) n. [OF, fem. p.p. of SUR(*prendre* f. L *prehendere* take)]

surra (sū'ra, soor'a), n. Form of pernicious anaemia affecting horses & cattle in the tropics. [Marathi *sūra*]

surré'al|ism, n. Twentieth-century movement in art & literature purporting to express the subconscious mind by images etc. in sequences or associations such as may occur in dreams. So ~IST a. & n. [SUR-², REAL², -ISM]

surrebut' (-tt-), v.i. (Of plaintiff) reply, make surrebutt'ER⁴, surrejoin'DER⁴, nn., to defendant's rebutter, rejoinder (order of pleadings at common law: Plaintiff's *declaration*, Defendant's *plea*, P.'s *replication*, D.'s *rejoinder*, P.'s *surrejoinder*, D.'s *rebutter*, P.'s *surrebutter*). [SUR-]

surren'der, v.t. & i., & n. 1. Hand over, give into another's power or control, relinquish possession of, esp. upon compulsion or demand (~ *fortress, army, ship, freedom, hopes, chastity, privilege, office*, etc.; ~ *insurance policy*, abandon claim in return for repayment of part of premiums); give *oneself* over to habit, emotion, influence, etc.; (of fortress, ship, or force, or its commander) accept enemy's demand for submission; give oneself up, cease from resistance, submit, (~ *to* one's *bail*, appear in court after being admitted to bail). 2. n. ~ing or being ~ed (~ *value*, amount payable to one who ~s insurance policy). [ME, f. OF *sur*(rendre RENDER)]

surrep'ti'tious (-Ishus), a. Underhand, kept secret, done by stealth, clandestine. Hence ~LY² adv. [ME; L *surrepticius* f. *sur*(ripere -rept-=rapere snatch), -ITIOUS¹]

*****sur'rey**, n. (pl. ~s). Light two-seater four-wheeled carriage. [Engl. county]

sur'rogate, n. ‖ Deputy, esp. of bishop or his chancellor for granting licences for marriages without banns. Hence ~SHIP n. [L *sur*(rogare ask) elect as substitute, -ATE²]

surround', v.t., & n. 1. Come or be all round, invest, enclose, encompass, encircle, environ, (*the* ~ing *country*, the neighbouring district; ~*ed with* or *by*). 2. n. Floor-covering between walls &

carpet. [ME = *overflow*, f. OF *suronder* f. LL SUPER(*undare* flow f. *unda* wave); cf. ABOUND]

surroun'dings (-z), n. pl. Sum total or general effect of all that is in the neighbourhood of a person or thing (*picturesque, healthy, degraded, cultured, ~*). [-ING[1]]

sūr̃'sum cōrd'a, L phr. Priest's exhortation to the people before the Preface in the Latin Mass. [in Book of Common Prayer 'Lift up your hearts']

sūrt'ax, n., & v.t. (Impose) additional tax (on); ‖ graduated tax on incomes above a certain figure in addition to ordinary income tax, imposed since 1929--30 in place of supertax. [f. F SUR(*taxe, -taxer*, TAX)]

sūrt'out (-tōō), n. (now rare). Overcoat, esp. of frock-coat shape. [F, f. *sur tout* over all]

surveill'ance (servăl'ans, -l'yans), n. Supervision, close observation, invigilation, (esp. *under~*, not trusted to work or go about unwatched). [F, f. SUR(*veiller* f. L as VIGILANT)]

survey'[1] (servă'), v.t. Let the eyes pass over, take general view of, form general idea of the arrangement & chief features of; examine condition of (building etc.); collect by measurement etc. all facts needed for determining the boundaries, size, position, shape, contour, ownership, value, etc., of (country, coast, district, estate, etc.), whence ~ING[1](1) n. [ME, f. AF *surveier* = OF *-vëeir*, f. med. L SUPER-(*vidēre* see)]

sūr̃'ey[2] (-vă), n. General view, casting of eyes or mind over something; inspection of the condition, amount, etc., of something, account given of result of this; department carrying on, operations constituting, piece of, surveying of land etc. (see prec.), map or plan setting forth results of such ~ (ORDNANCE ~). [f. prec.]

survey'or (servă'er), n. Official inspector of (*~ of weights & measures* etc.), whence ~SHIP n.; person professionally engaged in SURVEY[1]ing. [ME, f. AF *surve(i)our* (SURVEY[1], -OR)]

surviv'al (ser-), n. Surviving (*~ of the fittest*, process or result of *natural* SELECTION); person or thing that has remained as a relic of an earlier time. [foll., -AL(2)]

survive' (ser-), v.t. & i. Outlive, be still alive or in existence after the passing away of, come alive through or continue to exist in spite of, (*~ one's children, contemporaries*, etc.; *~ one's usefulness; ~ all perils*); continue to live or exist, be still alive or existent. Hence surviv'OR (ser-) n., surviv'ORSHIP n. (esp. right of joint tenant to whole estate on other's death). [ME, f. AF *survivre* f. L SUPER-(*vivere* live)]

sus-, = SUB- in L compds w. wds in c- (also SUC-, cf. *succeed, susceptible*), in p- (also SUP-, cf. *suppose, suspend*), & in t-,

& their derivatives. [for *subs* var. of *sub*; cf. ABS-]

suscĕp'tib|le, a. (Pred.) admitting of (*passage is ~le of another interpretation; facts not ~le of proof*), open or liable or accessible or sensitive *to* (*very ~le to pain, injury, kindness, female charms*); impressionable, sensitive, readily touched with emotion, touchy. Hence or cogn. **suscĕptibIL'I̱TY** n. (often in pl. = sensitive points of person's nature), ~LY[2] adv. [f. LL *susceptibilis* f. L SUS(*cipere -cept- = capere* take), -IBLE]

suscĕp'tive, a. Concerned with the receiving of emotional impressions (cf. prec. & *receptive*; *the ~ faculties, nature*). [f. LL *susceptivus* as prec., -IVE]

sus'i (sōō-), n. E.-Ind. cotton fabric with stripes of different-coloured silk. [Hind.]

suspĕct'[1], v.t. 1. Have an impression of the existence or presence of (*danger, a plot, foul play, collusion, a causal relation*); half believe *to be* (*I ~ him to be my brother, a liar, dying*); be inclined to think that or *that* (*I ~ you once thought otherwise*; also parenth., as *you, I ~, don't care*). 2. Incline to mentally accuse *of* or inculpate, doubt the innocence of, distrust, (*I ~ him of lying, of deep designs; a ~ed criminal*, person ~ed of being one; *~ed persons; the ignorant ~ everybody*). 3. Hold to be uncertain, mistrust, doubt the genuineness or truth of, (*~ the authenticity of the evidence*). Hence ~ABLE a. (rare). [ME, f. L *suspect-* (foll.)]

sŭs'pĕct[2], pred. a. & n. 1. Of suspected character, subject to suspicion, not unimpeachable, (*the statement of an interested party is naturally ~*). 2. n. Suspected person (*political ~s are kept under surveillance*). [ME, f. L *suspectus* p.p. of *suspicere* f. *specere* look; partly after OF *sospet*, F *suspect*]

suspĕnd', v.t. 1. Hang up, (p.p., of solid particles or body in fluid medium) sustained somewhere between top & bottom (*a balloon ~ed in mid-air; ~ed particles of dust*), so suspĕn'sIBLE a., suspĕnsIBIL'ITY n. 2. Keep in undecided or inoperative state for a time, defer, temporarily annul, adjourn, debar temporarily from office or function or privilege or membership, (*~ judgement*, one's indignation, the rules, the Habeas-Corpus Act, proceedings, a clergyman; *~ payment*, fail to meet financial engagements, admit insolvency; *~ed animation*, state of insensibility without death). [ME, f. OF *suspendre* or L SUS(*pendĕre pens-* hang)]

suspĕn'der, n. In vbl senses; esp., (pl.) *pair of braces, ‖* pair of (sets of) attachments to which tops of socks or stockings are hung. [-ER[1]]

suspĕnse', n. State of usu. anxious uncertainty or expectation or waiting for information (*keep one in ~*, delay acquainting him with what he is eager to know); (law) suspension, temporary

cessation of right etc.: ~ *account* in book-
-keeping (in which items are temporarily
entered till proper place is determined).
[ME, f. OF *suspens*, p.p. of L SUSPEND*ere*]

suspen'|sion (-shn), n. In vbl senses
(SUSPEND); esp. ~*sion bridge*, in which
roadway is hung across stream etc., usu.
on wire or chain cables passing over
towers & anchored, without support from
below. So ~SIVE a. (~*sive veto*, operating
only for a time, not definitive), ~SORY
a., ~SIVELY² adv. [f. L *suspensio* (SUS-
PEND, -ION)]

sus. per coll., n. The entry recording that
a person is to be hanged (often joc. =
hanged, hanging). [abbr. of L *suspendatur
per collum* let him be hanged by the neck]

suspi'cion (-shn), n., & v.t. **1.** Feeling of
one who suspects, suspecting or being
suspected (*above* ~, too obviously good
etc. to be suspected), partial or unconfirmed belief esp. that something is wrong
or someone guilty; soupçon *of*; hence
~LESS a. **2.** v.t. (dial.). Have ~ that or
that. [ME, f. AF *suspecioun* (OF *sous-
peçon*) f. med. L *suspectionem* f. L *suspicere*
SUSPECT, -ION]

suspi'cious (-shus), a. Prone to, feeling,
indicating, suggesting or justifying,
suspicion (*the ignorant are* ~; *he became*
~; *with a* ~ *glance*; *under* ~ *circumstances*).
Hence ~LY² adv., ~NESS n. [ME, f. OF
f. L *suspiciosus* (prec., -OUS)]

suspire', v.i. (poet.). Sigh. So **suspira'-**
TION n. [f. L *suspirare* (SUB-, *spirare*
breathe)]

sustain', v.t. **1.** Bear weight of, hold up,
keep from falling or sinking (cf. *support*).
2. Enable to last out, keep from failing,
give strength to, encourage, (exx. as in
SUPPORT; ~*ing food*, that keeps up the
strength). **3.** Endure without giving
way, stand, bear up against, (~*ed the
shock of the enemy's tanks*; *will not* ~
comparison with). **4.** Undergo, experience, suffer, (~ *a defeat, severe contusion,
loss*, etc.). **5.** (Of court or other authority)
allow validity of, give decision in favour
of, uphold, (~ *the objection, the applicant
in his claim*, etc.). **6.** Bear out, tend to
substantiate or corroborate, confirm,
(statement, charge, theory, etc.). **7.** Keep
up or represent (part, character) adequately. **8.** Keep (sound, effort, etc.)
going continuously (*a* ~*ed note, effort*).
Hence ~ABLE a., ~MENT n. (rare). [ME, f.
AF, OF *sus-*, *sostenir* f. L SUS(*tinēre* tent-
= *tenēre* hold)]

sus'tenance, n. Nourishing (now rare;
given for the ~ *of our bodies*); nourishing
quality, subsistence, food lit. or fig.,
(*there is no* ~ *in it*; *how shall we get* ~?;
lived a week without ~ *of any kind*). [ME,
f. AF *sustenaunce* f. *sustenir* (prec.,
-ANCE)]

sustenta'tion, n. Support of life (rare;
~ *fund*, collected to support indigent
clergy). [ME, f. OF, or f. L *sustentatio*

(*sustentare* frequent. of *sustinēre* SUSTAIN,
-ION)]

susurra'tion, n., **susu'rrous**, a., (rare).
Whispering, rustling. [f. LL *susurratio*
(L *susurrare*), L *susurrus* a. or n., -ATION,
-OUS]

sut'ler, n. Camp-follower selling provisions etc. [f. early mod. Du. *soeteler* f.
soetelen befoul, perform mean duties]

Sut'ra (soo-), n. Set of aphorisms in
Sanskrit literature. [Skr. *sutra* thread,
(hence) rule, f. *siv* SEW]

suttee', sati' (-ē), n. Hindu widow who
immolates herself on her husband's
funeral pyre; custom requiring such im-
molation, also **suttee'**ISM(2) n. [f. Skr.
sati virtuous wife]

su'tur|e, n., & v.t. **1.** Seamlike articula-
tion of two bones at their edges, esp.
one of those in the skull, similar junction
of parts in bot., entom., etc.; (surg.)
uniting of edges of wound by stitching,
thread or wire used for this. **2.** v.t. Stitch
(wound). Hence ~AL (-che-) a., ~ally³
adv., ~A'TION n., ~ED² (-cherd) a. [F,
or f. L *sutura* (*suere sut-* SEW, -URE)]

suz'erain, n. Feudal lord, lord paramount, sovereign or State having nominal
sovereignty or right of general control
over semi-independent or internally
autonomous State. So ~TY n. [F, app. f.
sus above f. L *su(r)sum* upward, after
souverain SOVEREIGN]

svelte, a. Lightly built, lissom, supple,
(chiefly of human, esp. female, figure).
[F]

swab (-ŏb), v.t. (-bb-), & n. **1.** Mop or
other arrangement of absorbent material
on handle for cleaning; absorbent pad
used in surgery; specimen of morbid
secretion etc. taken with a ~ for bacterio-
logical examination. **2.** (naut. sl.).
Officer's. epaulet; clumsy fellow, also
~b'ER¹ n. **3.** v.t. Clean with ~, as ~
(*down*) *the deck*; take up (moisture) with
~. [n. f. vb, back form. f. *swabber* f. early
mod. Du. *zwabber* f. *zwabben* (MLG
swabben) splash in water or mire]

Swab'ian, Sua-, a. & n. (Inhabitant) of
Swabia (~ *emperors*, Hohenstaufens,
1138-1254). [*Suabia* (mod. L f. G
Schwaben), -AN]

swa'ddl|e (-ŏ-), v.t. Swathe in bandages
or many or thick wraps or garments
(~*ing-bands, -clothes*, in which infants are
wrapped, also fig. influences that restrain
freedom of action or thought). [ME;
SWATHE, -LE]

Swade'shi (-ahdā-), n. Movement in
India, originating in Bengal, advocating
the production of home-made, and the
boycott of foreign, goods. [Hindi, = own
country]

swag, n. (sl.). Booty carried off by
burglars etc., (transf.) gains made by
political or other jobbery; (Austral.)
tramp's, miner's, or bush-traveller's
bundle. [f. now dial. *swag* vb hang

swaying (of bundle, fat belly, etc.), prob. Scand., cf. Norw. dial. *svag(g)a*]

swâge, n., & v.t. 1. Kinds of die or form for shaping wrought iron etc. by hammering or pressure; ~-*block*, with variety of perforations, grooves, etc., for this purpose. 2. v.t. Shape with ~. [f. F *suage*, *souage*]

swägg'er (-g-), v.i. & t., & n. & a. 1. Walk like a superior among inferiors, show self-confidence or self-satisfaction by gait, go *about*, *in*, *out*, etc., with such walk; behave in domineering or defiant way; talk boastfully (*about* prep.) or in hectoring manner; bluff (person) *into*, *out of*, etc.; hence ~ER[1] n., ~inGLY[2] adv. 2. n. ~ing gait or manner or talk; dashing or confident air or way of doing something, freedom from tameness or hesitancy, smartness; || ~-*cane*, carried by soldiers when walking out. 3. adj. (colloq.). Smart, fashionable, (~ *clothes*, *society*, etc.). [app. f. SWAG vb + -ER[5]]

Swahili (swahhēl'I), n. A Bantu people (or one of them) inhabiting Zanzibar and the adjacent coasts; (also *Kiswahili*) their language. [f. Arab. *sawāḥil* pl. of *sāḥil* coast]

swain, n. Young rustic; bucolic lover; (joc.) lover, suitor. [ME *swein* f. ON *sveinn* lad = OE *swān* swineherd]

|| **swāle**, sweal, v.t. & i. (dial.). Burn, set fire to (esp. gorse, brushwood, etc.); be scorched; (of candle) melt away. [OE *swǣlan* = (M)LG *swelen* to burn (trans.)]

|| **swa'llèt** (-öl-), n. (dial.). Underground stream; hole into which a stream flows, SWALLOW[1]-hole. [obsc. f. foll.]

swa'llow[1] (-ŏlō), v.t. & i., & n. 1. Cause or allow (food etc.) to pass down one's throat (~ *a* CAMEL, make no difficulty about something incredible or impossible or outrageous); engulf, absorb, exhaust, draw in, make away with, (usu. *up*; *the earth* ~*ed them up*; *the expenses more than* ~ *up the earnings*; *death is* ~*ed up in victory*); accept (statement) with ready credulity (*will* ~ *anything you tell him*); put up with, pocket, stomach, (affront); recant (one's words); perform muscular operation of ~ing·something. Hence ~-ABLE a. 2. n. Gullet; act of ~ing; amount ~ed at once; || (also ~-*hole*) funnel-shaped cavity in limestone. [OE, OS *swelgan*, ON *svelga*, f. Gmc *swelg-*, *swalg-*]

swa'llow[2] (-ŏlō), n. 1. Kinds of usu. migratory, long-winged, swift-flying, wide-gaped, weak-legged, fork-tailed, insectivorous bird associated with summer (*one* ~ *does not make a summer*, warning against hasty inference). 2. || ~ *dive* (with arms outspread till close to water); ~-*fish*, kind of gurnard; ~-*hawk*, -*plover*, -*shrike*, etc., fork-tailed kinds of hawk etc.; ~-*tail*, deeply forked tail, kinds of butterfly & humming-bird having this, points of burgee, (sing. or pl.) ~-tailed coat; ~-*tailed*, with deeply forked tail (of butter-

flies, birds, etc.; ~-*tailed coat*, kind with tapering tails formerly worn in ordinary costume & still in evening dress); ~-*wort*, milkweed, also celandine. [OE *swealwe*, OS *suala*, OHG *swalwa*, ON *svala* f. Gmc *swalwōn*]

swam. See SWIM.

swa'mi (-ah-), n. Hindu idol; Hindu religious teacher (esp. as form of address to Brahmin); ~ *work*, silver articles ornamented with figures of Hindu deities. [Hind., = master, prince, f. Skr. *svāmin*]

swamp (-ŏ-), n., & v.t. & i. 1. Piece of wet spongy ground, bog, marsh,· (attrib., in many names of plants & animals found in ~s); hence ~Y[2] a. 2. vb. Entangle in ~ (usu. in p.p.); (of water) overwhelm, flood, soak, (boat or its crew or contents, house, provisions, etc.); make helpless with excessive supply of something (*am* ~*ed with letters*, *applications*, *work*); (of greater quantity or numbers) swallow up, make invisible etc., prevent from being noticed or taking effect; (v.i.) become ~ed. [17th c., usu. referred to root *swamp-*, *swamb-*, *swamm-* sponge or fungus (as in G *schwamm*); cf. SUMP]

swan (-ŏn), n. 1. Kinds of large water-bird with long flexible neck, webbed feet, and in most species snow-white plumage, formerly supposed to sing melodiously at point of death (*white*, *black-necked*, *black*, *mute* or *tame* or *common*, *trumpeter*, *whooper*, etc., ~; *black* ~, name given before discovery of black species to extreme rarity; *all his geese are* ~*s*, see GOOSE). (fig., w. ref. to sweetness of dying song) poet (esp. *S*~ *of Avon*, Shakespeare). 2. The constellation Cygnus. 3. *~ dive*, = SWALLOW[2] *dive*; ~-*flower*, kind of orchid; ~-*goose*, long-necked China goose; ~-*herd*, royal officer having charge of ~-*marks*; ~-*mark*, cut in skin of beak to show ownership; ~-*neck*, curved end of discharge-pipe; ~'*s-down*, down of ~ used in trimmings & esp. in powder-puffs, also kind of thick cotton cloth with soft nap on one side; ~-*shot*, of large size; ~-*skin*, kind of fine twilled flannel; ~ *song*, of dying ~, also person's last production etc.; || ~-*upping*, annual taking up & marking of Thames ~s. Hence ~'LIKE a., ~n'ERY(3) n. [OE, OS *swan*, OHG *swan(a)*, ON *svanr* f. Gmc *swan-*]

swänk, n., & v.i. (sl.). Show(ing) off, swagger, bounce, bluff. Hence ~'Y[2] a., marked by ~, ostentatiously smart. [*c.* 1800, orig. midl. & s.w. dial.]

swap. See SWOP.

Swaraj' (-ahj), n. Self-government, independence, for India. Hence **swaraj'**IST (-ahj-) n. & a. [Skr. = self-ruling (RAJ)]

sward (-ôrd), n. Expanse covered with short grass, lawnlike ground; turf, whence ~'ED[2] a. [OE *sweard*, MDu., MLG *swarde*, MHG *swarte*, ON *svǫrthr* f. Gmc *sward-*, *swardh-*, *swarth-*]

sware. See SWEAR.

swarf (-ôrf), n. Chips or filings of wood, metal, etc. [f. ON *swarf* file-dust]

swarm[1] (-ôrm), n., & v.i. 1. Large number of insects, birds, small animals, sharp-shooters, horsemen, etc., moving about in a cluster or irregular body esp. round prey or enemy (~s, great numbers of children, stars, people, bills, etc.); cluster of honey-bees emigrating from hive with queen bee to establish new home; ~-*cell*, -*spore*, zoospore. 2. v.i. Move in a ~ (~ *round*, *about*, *over*, etc., prepp.), (of bees) cluster for emigration; congregate in numbers, be very numerous; (of places) be overrun, be crowded, abound, *with* (*road*, *hills*, *house*, ~*ing with beggars*, *rebels*, *fleas*). [OE *swearm*, OS, OHG *swarm*, ON *svarmr* f. Gmc *swarmaz*]

swarm[2] (-ôrm), v.i. & t. Climb rope or tree or pole (always *up*), climb (rope etc., or *up* rope etc.), by clipping with knees & hands. [16th c., of unkn. orig.]

swart (-ôrt), a. (arch.). Dark-hued, swarthy. [OE *sweart*, OS *swart*, OHG *swarz*, ON *svartr*, Goth. *swarts* f. Gmc *swartaz*]

swar'th|y (-ôrdhĭ), a. Dark-complexioned. Hence ~ILY[2] adv., ~iNESS n. [obsc. var. of obs. *swarty* (prec., -Y[2])]

swash (-ŏ-), v.t. & i., & n. 1. (Arch.) strike violently (~'*buckler*, bully, bravo; ~*ing blow*, hard); (of water etc.) wash about, make sound of washing or rising & falling; ~-*plate*, inclined disc revolving on axle & communicating up-&-down motion to bar whose end rests on it. 2. n. Motion or sound of ~ing water. [imit.]

swäs'tika (or swŏs[c]-), n. Fylfot. [Skr., f. *svastī* well-being (*sū* good, *asti* being)]

swat (-ŏt), v.t. (-tt-). Slap, crush (fly etc.). [c. 1600 = sit down, north. dial. & U.S. var. of SQUAT]

swatch (-ŏ-), n. (chiefly Sc. & north.). Sample of cloth or fabric. [orig. unkn.]

swath (-aw-; *pl. pron.* -dhz), n. Ridge of grass, corn, etc., lying after being cut, or space left clear after one passage of mower etc. [OE *swæth*, *swathu*, = MDu., MLG *swāde*, G *schwade* f. Gmc *swath-*]

swäthe (-dh), v.t., & n. 1. Bind with bandages, enclose in wraps or cloths or warm or many garments. 2. n. (rare). A bandage or fold. [OE *swathian* f. *swæth* n.; cf. SWADDLE]

sway, v.i. & t., & n. 1. Lean unsteadily to one side or in different directions by turns, have unsteady swinging motion, oscillate irregularly, waver, vacillate; give ~ing motion to, govern the motion of, wield, control direction of, have influence over, govern, rule over, (*wind* ~*s trees*; ~ *sceptre*, *cricket-bat*, *sword*; *his speech* ~*ed votes*; *is too much* ~*ed by the needs of the moment*; ~*s a fifth of mankind*); (p.p., of horse, also ~-*backed*) with back abnormally hollowed. 2. n. ~ing motion or position; rule, government. [c. 1500,

app. f. LG *swājen* be blown to and fro, Du. *zwaaien* swing, wave]

swear (swār), v.t. & i. (*swŏre* or arch. *swūre*; *sworn*), & n. 1. State something on oath, take oath (*to*, *that* or *that*), promise (conduct, *to* do) on oath, take (oath), (colloq.) say emphatically that, (*will you* ~, ~ *it*, *to it*, ~ *you* or *that you were not there*; *on the Testament?*; ~ *eternal fidelity*; *had sworn*, or *sworn a solemn oath*, *to return*; *I* ~ *it is too bad of him*; ~ *to* or *by*, appeal to as witness & guarantee of oath; ~ *by*, colloq., profess or have great belief in, regularly resort to or recommend; ~ *off drink* etc., take oath to abstain). 2. Use profane oaths to express anger or as expletives (often *at*). 3. Cause to take oath, administer oath to, (~ *witness* etc.; ~ person *to secrecy*; sworn brothers or *friends*, close intimates; *sworn enemies*, open & irreconcilable; *sworn broker*, admitted to profession with oath against fraud etc.; ~ *in*, induct into office by administering oath); (p.p., of evidence etc.) given on oath. 4. Make sworn affirmation of (offence) *against* (~ *treason against*; ~ *the peace against*, make oath that one is in danger of bodily harm from); hence ~'ER[1] n. 5. n. Spell of profane ~ing (*relieved his feelings by a hearty* ~); (colloq., also ~-*word*) a profane oath. [OE, OS, OHG *swerian*, ON *sverja*, f. Gmc *swarjan* f. *swar-* (Goth. *swaran*)]

sweat (-ĕt), n., & v.i. & t. 1. Moisture exuded from the skin, perspiration, (*running*, *dripping*, *wet*, *with* ~; *in* or *by the* ~ *of* one's *brow* or *face*, by dint of toil; *bloody* ~, exudation of blood mixed with ~); ~ing state, spell of ~ing, piece of exercise that induces ~, (*in a*, colloq. *all of a*, ~; *nightly* ~*s*; *a cold* ~, as in death, swoon, terror, etc.; *a* ~ *will do him good*); (colloq.) state of anxiety (*in a* ~); (chiefly colloq.) drudgery, toil, effort, a laborious task or undertaking, (*cannot stand the* ~ *of it*; *says it is a horrid* ~; *will not take the* ~); *old* ~ (sl.), old soldier; drops exuding from or condensing on any surface. 2. ~-*band*, leather or flannel lining of hat or cap; ~-*cloth*, esp. thin blanket under horse's saddle or collar; ~-*duct*, by which ~ exudes from ~-*gland*, secreting ~ below skin; ~ *shirt*, short-sleeved sweater; ~-*shop*, in which ~ed workers are employed; hence ~'LESS, ~'Y[2], aa., ~'ILY[2] adv., ~'iNESS n. 3. vb. Exude ~, perspire; (fig.) be in state of terror or suffering or repentance (*he shall* ~ *for it*, repent it); emit (blood, gum, etc.) like ~; (of wall etc.) exhibit surface moisture; toil, drudge; make (horse, athlete, etc.) ~ by exercise; employ (labour, workers) at starvation wages for long hours, exploit to the utmost by utilizing competition, (~*ed clothes* etc., made by ~ed workers), (of workers) work on such terms; subject (hides, tobacco) to fermentation in manufacturing; deprive (coins) of part of metal by shaking in bag; remove ~ from (horse) by scraping; fasten (metal part) on or in by partial fusion. 4. ~ing-bath, for producing ~; ~ing-iron, for scraping ~ from horse; ~ing-room, in Turkish bath; ~ing-sickness, epidemic fever prevalent in 15th & 16th cc. [ME swel(e), alt. (after swete vb f. OE swætan f. swāt) f. swole f. OE swāt (OS swēt, OHG sweiz, ON sveiti) f. Gmc *swait-]

swea'ter (-ĕt-), n. In vbl senses; esp.: sweating employer; thick woollen jersey worn during or after exercise to reduce weight or prevent chills; ~ girl (colloq.), girl or woman with well-developed bust. [-ER¹]

swēde, n. Native of Sweden (S~); Swedish turnip. [MLG, MDu.]

Swēdenbŏr'ġian, a. & n. (Adherent) of the Swedish philosophical & religious mystic Emanuel Swedenborg (1688--1772) or his doctrines or New Church. Hence ~ISM(3) n. [-IAN]

Swēd'ish, a. & n. (Language) of Sweden or its inhabitants. [SWEDE, -ISH¹]

*sweenّ'y̆, n. Atrophy of muscle, esp. of shoulder, in horse. [prob. f. dial. G schweine atrophy]

sweep, v.i. & t. (swĕpt), & n. 1. Glide swiftly, speed along with impetuous unchecked motion, go majestically, extend (intr.) in continuous curve or line or slope, (eagle ~s past; wind ~s along; cavalry ~s down on the enemy; she swept out of the room; his glance ~s from right to left; with a ~ing stroke; coast ~s northward; plain sweeps away to the sea). 2. (part.). Of wide range, regardless of limitations or exceptions, (~ing remark, generalization, etc.), whence ~'ingLY² adv., ~'ingNESS n. 3. Impart ~ing motion to, carry along or down or away or off in impetuous course, clear off or away or out of existence etc. or from, (swept his hand across; river ~s away bridge, ~s logs down with it; was swept away by an avalanche; the plague swept off thousands; ~ away slavery, feudalism, abolish swiftly; he swept his audience along with him, won enthusiastic support; ~ all obstacles from one's path). 4. Traverse or range swiftly, pass lightly across or along, pass eyes or hand quickly along or over, scan, scour, graze, (~ the seas, traverse in all directions, & see below; wind ~s the hillside; ~ the strings, lute, etc., of hand or its owner; ~ the horizon, of eyes or their owner; ~ river-bottom etc., drag it to find something; dress ~s the ground). 5. (Of artillery etc.) include in line of fire, cover, enfilade, rake, (battery ~s the approaches, glacis, street). 6. Clear everything from, clear of dust or soot or litter with broom (often up), gather up or collect (as) with broom, push away etc. (as) with broom, (~ the seas, drive all enemies from them, & see above; ~ floor, carpet,

chimney; ~ up the room; ~ away the snow; swept & garnished, generally renovated. w. ref. to Luke xi. 25; ~ the board, win all the money on gaming-table, & transf. win all possible prizes etc.; ~ a constituency etc., receive nearly all votes, have large majority; ~s everything into his net, seizes all that comes; ~ up litter etc., whence ~'ING¹(2) n. usu. in pl.). 7. Propel (barge etc.) with ~s. 8. ~-net, long fishing-net, also entomologist's net; ~-seine, large seine; ~'stake(s), form of gambling on horse-races etc. in which the sum composed of participators' stakes goes to the drawer(s) of winning or placed horse(s) etc.; hence ~'ER¹(1, 2) n., (also, India) domestic servant employed on sanitary & scavenging duties. 9. n. ~ing motion or extension, curve in road etc., piece of curving road etc., (with a ~ of his arm, eyes, scythe; a ~ of mountain country; river makes a great ~ to the left; house is approached by a fine ~ or carriage ~). 10. Range or compass of something that has ~ing motion (within, beyond, the ~ of the scythe, net, telescope, eye, human intelligence). 11. Act of ~ing (as) with broom (give it a thorough ~ or ~-up or ~-out; make a clean ~, have complete riddance of old furniture, officials, etc.); sortie by aircraft. 12. Long oar worked by standing rower(s) on barge, becalmed sailing-ship, etc. (had to get out the ~s). 13. Long pole mounted as lever for raising bucket from well. 14. Man who ~s chimneys (often chimney-~). 15. (colloq.). = ~stake. 16. ~'back, angle at which aircraft's wing is set back relatively to the axis; swept-back wing or swept-wing a., (of aircraft) having the outer portion of the wing aft of the inner portion. [ME swepe, replacing obs. swope SWOOP f. OE swāpan; see SWIFT]

sweet, a. & n. 1. Tasting like sugar or honey (~ apples etc.; ~ stuff, ~meats; likes her tea ~, with much sugar; a ~ tooth, a liking for ~ things; ~ wine, opp. DRY¹; tastes ~, has ~ taste). 2. Smelling like roses or perfumes, fragrant, (smells ~; so ~-scentED² a.; air is ~ with thyme; ~ violet, of scented kind, opp. dog-violet; ~ breath). 3. Melodious or harmonious in sound (has a ~ voice; sounds ~; ~ song, singer, etc.). 4. Fresh & sound, not salt or salted or sour or bitter or rancid or high or stinking, (~ water, fit for drinking, neither salt nor bitter nor putrid; is the meat, milk, butter, still ~?; keep the room clean & ~). 5. Highly agreeable or attractive or gratifying, inspiring affection, dear, beloved, amiable, gentle, easy, (colloq.) pretty or charming or delightful, ('tis ~ to hear one's own praises; ~ toil, that one loves; ~ love, dalliance, idleness, sleep; what a ~ blouse, moustache, collie!; ~ temper, amiability, whence ~-temperED² a.; a ~ nature, face, etc.; a ~ girl, lovable, affectionate; ~ one, voc., darling;

a ~ *one*, sl., painful blow with fist etc.; ~ *going*, travelling over well-laid road or in smooth-going carriage). **6.** *At* one's *own* ~ *will*, just as or when one pleases, arbitrarily, at random; ~ (*up*)*on* (colloq.), (inclined to be) in love with, very fond of. **7.** ~'*bread*, pancreas (*belly* ~*bread*) or thymus-gland (*throat* or *neck* ~*bread*) esp. of calf as food; ~BRIER¹; ~ GALE¹; ~'*heart*, either of pair of lovers, (vb) be engaged in love-making (esp. *go* ~*heart-ing*); ~-*john*, kinds of pink or of narrow-leaved ~-william; ~'*meat*, shaped morsel of confectionery usu. consisting chiefly of sugar or chocolate, a fruit preserved in sugar, bonbon, sugarplum, goody; ~ *oil*, (esp.) olive oil; ~ *pea*, garden annual with showy variously-coloured ~-scented flow-ers; ~ POTATO; ~-*root*, liquorice; ~ *rush*, kind of sedge with thick creeping aromatic rootstock used in medicine & confection-ery; ~-*sop*, (~-pulped fruit of) an ever-green shrub of tropical America; ~ SULTAN; ~-*water*, kind of white hothouse grape; ~-*will'iam*, a garden-plant, kind of pink with close-clustered flowers often particoloured in zones; ~ *willow*, ~ *gale*; hence ~'EN⁶ v.t. & i., ~'enING¹(4) n., ~'ISH¹(2) a., ~'LY² adv., ~'NESS n. **8.** n. ~ *part* (*the* ~ *& the bitter* or ~*s & bitters of life*); ǁ a ~*meat*, bonbon, (also ~'Y³ h.); ~ *dish* such as pudding, tart, cream, jelly, forming a course at table; (usu. pl.) fragrance (*flowers diffusing their* ~*s on the air*); (pl.) delights, gratifications, pleasures, (*the* ~*s of office*, *domestication*, *flattery*, *success*); (chiefly in voc.) darling. [OE *swēte*, OS *swōti*, OHG *s(w)uozi*, ON *sǣtr* f. Gmc *swōtja-*, *swōti-*, cogn. w. L *suavis*, Goth *suts*]

sweet'ing, n. Kind of sweet apple; (arch.) darling. [-ING³]

swell, v.i. & t. (p.p. *swollen*, arch. *swoln*, rarely ~*ed*), & n. & a. **1.** (Cause to) grow bigger or louder, dilate, expand, rise or raise *up* from surrounding surface, bulge *out*, increase in volume or force or intensity, (*river swollen with melted snow*; *the injured wrist began to* ~ *up* or ~, whence ~'ING¹(2) n.; *the* ~*ing sails*; *toad* ~*ing himself to size of ox*; ~*ing oratory*, of inflated kind; *sound* ~*s on the breeze*; *murmur* ~*ed into a roar*; *ground* ~*s into an eminence*; *heart* ~*s*, feels like bursting with emotion; ~ *with pride*, *indignation*, etc., be or seem hardly able to contain it; ~ *like a turkey-cock*, put on blustering air; *wind* ~*s the sails*; *the* ~*ing tide*; *expendi-ture swollen by extravagance*; *swollen estimates*, inordinately high; *a thousand voices* ~ *the sound*; *items* ~ *the total*; ~ *note* in music, sing or play it with alternate crescendo & diminuendo; *emotion* ~*s & subsides*; ~*ed* or *swollen head*, sl., conceit). **2.** n. Act or condition of ~*ing* (*the* ~ *of the hymn floated past*; *the* ~ *of the ground*). **3.** Heaving of sea with waves that do not break after storm. **4.** Part of any more

or less cylindrical object that ~*s* out (*the* ~ *of the fore-arm*). **5.** (mus.). Mechanism in organ (operated by ~-*pedal*) for ob-taining crescendo or diminuendo by opening or closing slats in front of ~-*box* containing pipes of the ~-*manual*. **6.** (colloq.). Person of distinction or ability, first-class person, member of good society, person of dashing or fashionable appear-ance, (*is a* ~ *in politics*, *at cricket*, etc.; *what a* ~ *you are!*, how finely dressed; *has been asked to dinner by some* ~*s*), whence ~'DOM n. **7.** ~-*fish*, kinds that can inflate themselves into nearly globu-lar form; ~ *mob*(*smen*), (class of) pick-pockets dressed like gentlemen; ~-*organ*, set of pipes enclosed in ~-box; ~-*rule* in printing, dash ~ing into. diamond in middle & tapering towards ends. **8.** adj. (colloq.). Of distinction (*a* ~ *pianist*; ~ *parties*, *society*, etc.); fine, splendid; smart, finely dressed, (~ *clothes*; *looks very* ~); hence ~'ISH¹(2) a. [OE, OS, OHG *swellan*, ON *svella* f. Gmc *swellan*]

swel'ter, v.i., & n. **1.** Be faint or moist or languid or oppressive with heat (of atmosphere etc., or of things or persons suffering from it; *under a* ~*ing sky*; *city* ~*ed in the plain*; *the* ~*ing horses*). **2.** n. ~*ing* atmosphere or conditions (*in the* ~ *of the Indian night*). [f. root of (now dial.) *swelt*, f. OE (= OS) *sweltan* perish, OHG *swelzan*, ON *svelta*, Goth. *swiltan*, see -ER¹]

swept. See SWEEP.

swerve, v.i. & t., & n. **1.** Diverge from regular line of motion, go off in changed direction, dodge, (*never* ~*s an inch from his duty*; *bird*, *ball*, ~*s in the air*; *horse*, *three-quarters* at football, ~*d suddenly*); cause (ball) to ~ in the air. **2.** n. Diver-gence from course, swerving motion; hence ~'LESS (-vl-) a. [ME *swerve*, repr. OE *sweorfan*, OS, OHG *swerban* wipe etc., ON *sverfa*, Goth. *-swairban*]

swift, a., adv. (~*er*, ~*est*), & n. **1.** Fleet, rapid, quick, soon coming or passing, not long delayed, (now chiefly poet. & rhet.; ~ *runner*, *movement*, *feet*, *retribution*, *anger*, *laughter*, *response*, *riddance*; so ~-footED², ~-wingED², aa.); prompt, quick to do, (*has a* ~ *wit*; ~ *to anger*; *be* ~ *to hear*, *slow to speak*; so ~-handED² a.); hence ~'LY² adv., ~'NESS n. **2.** adv. ~*ly* (*he answered* ~; *they that run* ~*est*; esp. in comb., as ~-*coming*, -*passing*). **3.** n. Kinds of very long-winged & ~-flying insectivorous bird with resemblances to swallows, whence ~'LET n. (small kind); kinds of small lizard; the common newt; ǁ breed of pigeons; kinds of moth; revolving frame for winding yarn etc. from. [OE *swift*, prehist. *swipt-* f. Gmc *swaip-*, *swip-*; see SWOOP, SWEEP]

swig, v.t. & i. (-gg-), & n. (sl.). **1.** Take draughts (of). **2.** n. (Act of taking) a draught of liquor. [vb f. n. (16th c.) in obs. sense *liquor*, of unkn. orig.]

swill, v.t. & i., & n. **1.** Rinse, pour water over or through, flush, (often *out*); drink (t. & i.) greedily. **2.** n. Rinsing (*give it a ~ or ~ out*); bout of drinking (rare); inferior liquor; hog-wash, slops. [OE *swillan, swilian,* of unkn. orig.]

swim, v.i. & t. (*swăm, swŭm*), & n. **1.** Float on or at surface of liquid (SINK[1] *or ~; vegetables ~ming in butter; with bubbles ~ming on it*). **2.** Progress at or below surface of water by working legs, arms, tail, webbed feet, fins, flippers, wings, body, etc., traverse or accomplish (stream, distance, etc.) thus, compete in (race) thus, compete with thus, cause (horse, dog, etc.) to progress thus, (fig.) go with gliding motion, (*~ on one's chest, back, side,* methods of human *~ming; ~ across, out, back, the channel, a mile, a race,* person *a hundred yards,* one's *horse across; cannot ~ a stroke; ~ with the tide* or *stream,* act with the majority; *~ to the bottom* or *like a stone* or *tailor's goose,* joc., sink; *she swam into the room; moon ~s in sky*), whence *~'m'ER[1]* n. **3.** Appear to undulate or reel or whirl, have dizzy effect or sensation, (*everything swam before his eyes; my head ~s; has a ~ming in the head*). **4.** Be flooded or overflow with or *with* or *in* moisture (*eyes, deck, ~ming with tears, water; ~ming eyes; floor ~ming in blood*). **5.** *~ming-bath,* large enough to ~ in; *~ming-bell,* bell-shaped ~ming organ of jellyfish etc.; *~ming-belt,* to keep learner afloat; *~ming-bladder,* fish's sound; *~ming-stone,* kind of spongy quartz. **6.** n. Spell of ~ming; *~ming-bladder* (rare); deep pool frequented by fish in river; (fig.) main current of affairs (esp. *in the ~,* engaged in or acquainted with what is going on); *~-suit,* bathing-dress. [OE, OS, OHG *swimman,* ON *svimma*]

swimm'erĕt, n. Swimming-foot in crustaceans. [*swimmer,* -ET[1]]

swimm'ingly, adv. With easy & unobstructed progress (esp. *go on ~*). [-LY[2]]

swin'dl|e, v.t. & i., & n. **1.** Cheat (person, *money out of* person, person *out of* money etc., or abs.); so *~ER[1]* n., *~ingLY[2]* adv. **2.** n. Fraudulent scheme, imposition, piece of *~ing,* person or thing represented as what it is not. [back form. f. *swindler* f. G *schwindler* visionary projector, swindler, (*schwindeln* be dizzy)]

swine, n. (pl. the same). Kinds of ungulate non-ruminant omnivorous mammal, pig (which name has displaced it exc. in poet., rhet., zool., agricult., & U.-S. use), whence **swin'ERY[3]** n.; person of greedy or bestial habits; *~-bread,* the truffle, also = sow[2]*-bread; ~-fever, ~-plague; ~-herd,* tender of ~; *~-plague,* infectious lung-disease of ~; *~-pox,* form of chicken-pox; *~'s-snout,* dandelion. Hence **swine'ISH[1]** a., **swin'ishLY[2]** adv., **swin'ishNESS** n., (chiefly of persons & their habits). [OE *swin,* OS, OHG *swin,* ON *svin,*

Goth. *swein* f. Gmc **swinam,* neut. of adj. form, cf. L *suinus* f. *su-* SOW[2]]

swing, v.i. & t. (*swŭng* or rarely *swăng, swung*), & n. **1.** Move (t. & i.) with to-&-fro or curving motion of object having fixed point(s) or side but otherwise free, sway (t. & i.) or so hang (t. & i.) as to be free to sway like a pendulum or door or branch or tree or hammock or anchored ship, oscillate, revolve, rock, wheel, (*he shall ~ for it,* be hanged; *door swung to,* closed; *boat, boom, ~s round, across; ship ~s at anchor; ~ child* etc., work the ~ in which he sits; *sat on table ~ing his legs; ~ one's arms, a bell, Indian clubs, bat, basket; ~ a hammock,* suspend it by ends; *no room to ~ a* CAT[1]). **2.** part. (Of gait, melody, etc.) vigorously rhythmical (*at a long ~ing trot; a ~ing chorus*). **3.** Go with *~ing* gait (*he swung out of the room; ~ along, past, by,* etc.), whence *~'ingLY[2]* adv. ‖ *~ the lead* (Service sl.), malinger or scrimshank. **5.** n. Act of *~ing,* oscillation, *~ing* movement, (*work is in full ~,* active; *the ~ of the pendulum,* fig., tendency to alternation, esp. tendency of electorate to put parties in power alternately). **6.** *~ing* gait or rhythm (*goes with a ~*); (also ~ *music*) kind of jazz in which time of melody is freely varied, with simple harmonic accompaniment in rigid rhythm. **7.** Normal duration of activity (*let it have its ~,* have free course till it rests of itself like pendulum). **8.** Seat slung by ropes or chains for *~ing* in (*~s & ROUND[3]-abouts*), spell of *~ing* in this. **9.** Compass to which thing ~ (*has a ~ of 3 ft*). **10.** *~-boat,* boat-shaped carriage hung from frame for *~ing* in; ~ *bridge,* that can be swung aside as a whole or in sections to let ships etc. pass; ~ *plough,* without wheels. [OE, OHG *swingan,* f. Gmc **swingw-, *swangw-*]

swinge (-j), v.t. (*~ing*). Strike hard, beat, (arch. exc. in *a ~ing blow* etc.); (part.) huge (*~ing majority, lie, damages;* cf. *thumping, whopping,* etc.), [alt. f. ME *swenge* f. OE *swengan,* causal(**swangwjan*) of prec.]

swingle (swing'gl), n., & v.t. **1.** Wooden instrument for beating flax & removing woody parts from it; swinging part of flail; ‖ *~tree,* crossbar pivoted in middle to ends of which traces are fastened in cart, plough, etc. **2.** v.t. Clean (flax) with ~; *swingling-tow,* coarse part of flax. [ME, f. MDu. *swinghel,* as SWING, -LE(1)]

swink, v.i., & n. (arch.). Toil. [OE *swincan* (whence n.), parallel form. to *swingan* SWING]

swipe, v.i. & t., & n. **1.** Hit at or hit cricket-ball etc., hit (cricket-ball etc.), hard & recklessly, slog; (sl.) steal by snatching; hence **swip'ER[1]** n. **2.** n. Reckless hard hit or attempt to hit at cricket etc., slog. [var. of SWEEP]

‖ **swipes** (-ps), n. pl. Washy or turbid or

otherwise inferior beer. [f. prec. in obs. sense *drink off*]

swirl, v.i. & t., & n. **1.** Eddy, carry (object) or be carried with eddying motion. **2.** n. Eddying motion of water, air, etc.; commotion made by fish etc. rushing through water. [orig. Sc., of uncert. orig.; cf. Norw. dial. *svirla*, Du. *zwirrelen* to whirl, G dial. *schwirrlen* totter]

swish¹, v.t. & i., & n. ‖ Flog with birch; audibly cut the air with (cane etc.), cut (flower etc.) *off* thus; make such audible cut *with* cane etc.; (make, move with) sound as of cane or lash or swift bird cutting the air or of scythe cutting grass; ‖ a stroke of a birch or cane or lash. [imit.] ‖ **swish**², a. (colloq.). Smart, swagger.

Swiss, a., & n. (pl. the same). (Native) of Switzerland (~ *French, German*, dialects of French & German spoken in Switzerland; *German* ~, a patois; ~ *guards*, ~ mercenaries formerly employed in France etc. & still at the Vatican; ~ *roll*, kind of jam sandwich baked & rolled up). [f. F *Suisse* f. MHG *Swiz*]

switch, n., & v.t. & i. **1.** Flexible shoot cut from tree, tapering rod resembling this. **2.** Tress of dead hair tied at one end used in hairdressing. **3.** Kinds of mechanism for making & breaking connexion between corresponding parts of a system by which railway trains are diverted from one line to another, electric circuits completed or interrupted, etc. **4.** ‖ ~'*back*, zigzag railway for ascending or descending steep slopes, also railway (chiefly used for amusement at fairs etc.) in which train's ascents are effected solely by momentum acquired in previous descents; ~-*bar*, part of railway or electric ~; ~'*board*, arrangement for varying the connexion between a number of electric circuits; ~-*lever*, handle & lever operating a ~; ~-*man*, in charge of railway ~es; ~-*signal*, flag or lantern or semaphore board indicating position of railway ~. **5.** vb. Whip with ~. **6.** Swing (thing) round quickly, snatch suddenly, whisk, (cow ~es her tail; *I ~ed my head round*; *he ~ed it out of my hand*). **7.** Transfer (train, current) with ~, (fig.) direct (thoughts, talk) to another subject; race (horse) under another's name; (bridge) change to another suit in bidding. **8.** Turn (electric light, current) *off* or *on*; put (user of telephone) *on* to or cut (him) *off* from another (~ *off* intr., cut off connexion). [early forms *swits, switz*, prob. f. Flem. or LG, cf. Hanoverian *swutsche*, LG *zwukse* long thin stick, switch]

‖ **swith'er** (-dh-), v.i., & n. (Sc.). **1.** Hesitate, be uncertain. **2.** n. Flurry, doubt, uncertainty. [16th c. Sc., of unkn. orig.]

Switz'er, n. (arch.). A Swiss. [f. MHG *Switzer*, or MDu. *Switser* f. *Switz*(*en*) Switzerland, -ER¹]

swiv'el, n., & v.i. & t. (-ll-). **1.** Ring & pivot serving as connexion between two

parts of something & enabling one of them to revolve without the other (~ *chain, bookrest, gun, -hook, -joint, rowlock*, etc., provided with ~); ~-*eye*(*d*), (with) squinting eye. **2.** vb. Turn (t. & i.) on ~. [ME, f. weak grade *swif*- of OE *swifan* copulate +·LE(1)]

swiz'zle, n. Compounded intoxicating drink (~-*stick*, with brushlike end used for frothing or flattening drinks). [orig. unkn.]

swob(**ber**), var. of. SWAB(*ber*).

swollen, swoln (arch.), p.p. of SWELL.

swoon, v.i., & n. **1.** (Have) fainting-fit (~*ed for joy, with pain*, etc.); (of music etc.) die languidly away, whence ~'**ing**-LY² adv. [ME *swoune* perh. back form. f. *swogning* n. f. OE p.p. *geswōgen* in a swoon]

swoop, v.i. & t., & n. **1.** Come down or *down* with the rush of a bird of prey, make sudden attack from a distance, (often *upon* prey, place, etc.); (colloq.) snatch *up*, snatch, the whole of, at one ~. **2.** n. Sudden attack or downward plunge as of bird of prey; snatching action carrying off many things at once; *at one fell* ~ (in describing completeness & extent & suddenness of catastrophe etc., see *Macb.* IV. iii. 219). [app. dial. var. of obs. *swope* f. OE *swāpan*, see SWEEP, SWIFT]

swop, swap (-ŏp), v.t. & i. (-pp-), & n. (sl.). Exchange (v.t. & i., & n.) by way of barter (*never ~ horses while crossing the stream*, leave changes till crisis is past; ~*ped my knife for bread; will you ~ places etc.?*, or abs.; *shall we try a ~?*). [f. 14th c. in obs. sense *hit*, prob. imit., hence (16th c.) 'strike' a bargain]

sword (sōrd), n. **1.** Offensive weapon consisting of long variously shaped blade for cutting or thrusting or both & hilt with hand-guard (BROAD~; *cavalry* ~, sabre; *court, dress*, ~, worn with court dress; *double-edged, two-handed*, etc.,~; *duelling, small-*, ~, kind with straight edgeless blade of triangular section used for thrusting only; SCUTCH*ing*-~; ‖ ~ *of State*, borne before sovereign on State occasions; *the* ~ *of the spirit*, the word of God; *cross or measure ~s*, have fight or controversy or open rivalry, often *with*; *draw, sheathe, the* ~, begin, cease from, war; *throw one's ~ into the scale*, back claim etc. with arms; *put to the* ~, kill, esp. of victors or captors; *fire & ~*, rapine, destruction spread by invading army; *the ~ of justice*, judicial authority; *the* ~, war, the arbitrament of war, military power, sovereign power); (army sl.) bayonet. **2.** ~-*arm*, right; ~-*bayonet*, kind with short ~-blade & hilt; ‖ ~-*bearer*, person carrying sovereign's or other great person's ~ on some occasions; ~-*belt*, to which scabbard is attached; ~-*bill*, long-billed humming-bird; ~-*cane*, hollow walking-stick enclosing ~-**blade**;

~-*cut*, wound given with ~-edge, scar left by it; ~-*dance*, in which~s are brandished, or women pass under men's crossed ~s, or performer treads about ~s laid on ground; ~-*fish*, fish with upper jaw prolonged into sharp ~like weapon; ~-*flag*, esp. yellow iris; ~-*flighted*, (of birds) having flight-feathers of separate colour & looking when closed like ~ worn at side; ~-*grass*, gladiolus, kinds of sedge with ~like leaves; ~-*guard*, part of ~-hilt that protects hand; ~-*hand*, right; ~-*knot*, ribbon or tassel attached to ~-hilt orig. for securing it to wrist; ~-*law*, military domination; ~-*lily*, gladiolus; ~-*play*, fencing, (fig.) repartee, cut-&- -thrust argument; ~*s'man*, person of (usu. specified) skill with ~, whence ~**s'man**-SHIP(3) (sŏrdz-) n.; ~-*stick*, ~-cane. Hence (-)~'ED², ~'LESS, ~'LIKE, ~'PROOF³, aa. [OE *sweord*, OS *swerd*, OHG *swert*, ON *sverth* f. Gmc **swerdam*]

swore, sworn. See SWEAR.

‖ **swŏt**, v.i. & t. (-tt-); & n. (school sl.). **1.** Work hard esp. at books, sap; ~ (subject) *up*, study it hurriedly. **2.** n. Hard study; (thing that demands) effort, a sweat, (*it is too much* ~; *what a* ~!); person who works hard esp. at learning, a sap. [dial. var. of SWEAT]

swum, swung. See SWIM, SWING.

sўb'ar|īte, n. & a. **1.** (*S~ite*). Inhabitant of ancient-Greek colony of Sybaris in Italy noted for luxury. **2.** Luxurious & effeminate (person). Hence ~**it'ic** a., ~**ītism**(2) n., ~**it'ically** adv. [f. L (-*ta*) f. Gk *Subaritēs* (*Subaris*, -ITE¹)]

sўb'il, n. (Erron. for) SIBYL.

sўc'amine, n. (bibl.). The black mulberry-tree. [f. L f. Gk *sukaminos* mulberry-tree f. Heb. *shiqmah* sycamore]

sўc'amŏre, n. (Also ~ *fig* or *Egyptian* or *oriental* ~) kind of fig-tree growing in Syria & Egypt; (also ~ *maple*) large timber-tree allied to maple; **plane-tree. [ME, f. OF *sicamore* f. L f. Gk *sukomoros* (*sukon* fig, *moron* mulberry)]

sўce, sīce, n. (Anglo-Ind.). Groom. [f. Hind. f. Arab. *sā'is*]

sўcee', n. (Also ~ *silver*) ingots of pure silver bearing banker's or assayer's seal & used in China for payments by weight. [f. Chin. *si sz'* fine silk (as capable of being drawn out fine)]

sўchnocărp'ous (-k-), a. (bot.). Bearing fruit several times before dying, perennial. [Gk *sukhnos* numerous, *karpos* fruit, -OUS]

sўcōn'ium, n. (bot.; pl. -*ia*). Fleshy hollow receptacle developing into multiple fruit as in fig. [mod. L (Gk *sukon* fig)]

sўc'oph|ant, n. Flatterer, toady, parasitic person. So ~ANCY n., ~**ăn'tic** a. [f. L f. Gk *sukophantēs* informer, f. *sukon* fig, *phainō* show; reason for name unkn.]

sўcōs'is, n. Skin-disease of bearded part of face or scalp also called *barber's itch*. [f. Gk *sukōsis* (*sukon* fig, -OSIS)]

sў'en|īte, n. Grey crystalline rock of

feldspar & hornblende with or without quartz. Hence ~**it'ic** a. [F (*syé-*), f. L *Syenites* (*lapis* stone) of Syene in Egypt, see -ITE¹]

sўll'abary, n. List of characters representing syllables & serving the purpose, in some languages or stages, of an alphabet. [f. mod. L *syllabarium* f. med. L -*ius* adj. (as SYLLABLE, -ARY¹)]

sўllăb'|ic, a. Of syllable(s) (often in comb., as *mono, di, tri, quadri*, -~*ic*, having 1, 2, 3, 4, syllables); (of symbols) representing a whole syllable; articulated in syllables. Hence ~**ICALLY** adv. [f. LL f. Gk *sullabikos* (SYLLABLE, -IC)]

sўllăb'icāte, sўllăb'ifў, sўll'abīze, -ise (-īz), vv.t. Divide into or articulate by syllables. Hence **sўllăbICA'TION, sўllăbi-FICA'TION,** nn. [Gk *sullabē* see foll., -IC, -ATE³, -FY, -IZE]

sўll'abl|e, n., & v.t. **1.** Unit of pronunciation forming a word or part of a word & containing one vowel sound & often consonant(s) preceding or following or preceding & following this; (transf.) so much as a word, the least amount of speech, (*not* a ~*el*, do not speak); hence (-)~ED² (-ld) a. **2.** v.t. Pronounce by ~es, articulate distinctly; (poet.) utter (name, word). [ME, f. AF *sillable* f. OF *sillabe* (cf. *participle, principle*) f. L f. Gk *sullabē* (*syl-, lambanō* take)]

syllabub. See SILLABUB.

sўll'abus, n. (pl. -*bī*, -*buses*). **1.** Abstract giving heads or main subjects of a lecture, course of teaching, etc., conspectus or programme of hours of work etc. **2.** (R.-C. Ch.) summary of points decided by an ecclesiastical decree, esp. catalogue of eighty heretical doctrines or practices or institutions condemned by Pius IX in 1864. [mod. L *syllabus*, orig. misreading of L f. Gk *sittuba* title-slip or label]

sўllĕp'|sis, n. (gram.; pl. -*sēs*). Application of a word to two others in different senses (e.g. *in a flood of tears & a sedan- -chair*) or to two of which it grammatically suits one only (e.g. *neither you nor he knows*; cf. ZEUGMA. So ~**tic** a., ~**tically** adv. [LL, f. Gk *sullēpsis* (*sullambanō* see SYLLABLE)]

sўll'og|ism, n. Form of reasoning in which from two given or assumed propositions called the premis(s)es & having a common or middle term a third is deduced called the conclusion from which the middle term is absent (FIGURE¹, MOOD² of ~*ism*; *false* ~*ism*, one whose conclusion does not necessarily follow from its premisses because it fails to fulfil the rules of logic regarding the nature & mutual relations of the major & minor & middle terms necessary if the inference is to be sound); (transf.) deductive reasoning as opp. induction. So ~**is'tic** a., ~**is'tically** adv. [ME, f. OF *silogi(s)me* or L f. Gk *sullogismos* f. *sullogizomai* (*syl-, logizomai* to reason f. *logos* reason), -ISM]

syll'ogize, -ise (-īz), v.i. & t. Use syllogisms; throw (facts, argument) into syllogistic form. [ME, f. OF *sil(l)ogiser* or LL *syllogizare* f. Gk *sullogizomai* (prec.)]

sylph, n. Elemental spirit of the air (cf. *nymph, gnome, salamander,* of water, earth, fire) in Paracelsus's system, whence ~'LIKE a.; (transf.) slender girl; kinds of long-tailed humming-bird. [f. mod. L *sylphes,* G *sylphen* (pl.), prob. invented by Paracelsus]

sylvan. See SILVAN.

sylviculture. See SILVICULTURE.

sym-, = SYN- in Gk compds with words in b-, m-, p-, as: ~'*bion(t),* organism living in ~biosis [Gk *biōn -ountos* part. of *bioō* f. *bios* life]; ~*biōs'is,* permanent union between organisms each of which depends for its existence on the other as the fungus & alga composing lichen [f. Gk as *symbion,* -OSIS], whence ~*biŏt'*IO a.,~*biŏt'*ICALLY adv.; ~*pal'mograph,* apparatus exhibiting sound-curves usu. by double pendulum with style attached [Gk *palmos* vibration f. *pallō* brandish]; ~*pel'mous,* (of bird) having tendons of toe-flexors united at a point [Gk *pelma* sole]; ~*pet'alous,* having petals united; ~*phyll'ous,* with leaves united [Gk *phullon* leaf]; ~*phỹsis,* growing togéther, (place or line of) union between two corresponding bones or other parts, coalescence, [Gk *phuō* grow], whence ~*phys'*eAL a.; ~*plĕsōm'eter,* instrument for measuring force of current of water, also barometer in which atmospheric pressure is balanced partly by column of liquid & partly by elastic pressure of confined gas [Gk *piesis* pressure f. *piezō* press]; ~*pŏd'ium,* stem whose successive sections are strictly branches each springing from the preceding, as in the vine [Gk *pous podos* foot], so ~*pŏd'*iAL a., ~*pŏd'*iaLY² adv.

sym'bol, n., & v.t. (-ll-). 1. = CREDO. 2. Thing regarded by general consent as naturally typifying or representing or recalling something by possession of analogous qualities or by association in fact or thought (*white, the lion, the thunderbolt, the cross, are ~s of purity, courage, Zeus, Christianity; values the handle to his name only as a ~*). 3. Mark or character taken as the conventional sign of some object or idea or process, e.g. the astronomical signs for the planets, the letters standing for chemical elements, letters of the alphabet, the mathematical signs for addition & infinity, the asterisk; hence or cogn. symbŏl'IC(AL) aa., symbŏl'icALLY² adv., symbŏl'ICS n., ~ISM(3), ~IST(3), nn. (esp. denoting certain schools of painters & of French poets), ~IZE v.t. (see Vb), ~IZA'TION, symb(ol)ŏl'OGY, symb(ol)ŏl'ATRY, nn. 4. vb (rare, also & usu.~*ize*). Be the ~ of; represent by means of ~, speak of under a ~; (~*ize* only) treat (story etc.) as ~ic & not literal, import ~ism

into. [15th c., f. L f. Gk *sumbolon* mark, token, f. SYM(*ballō* throw); in eccl. L ' creed']

symm'ĕtr|ỹ, n. 1. (Beauty resulting from) right proportion between the parts of the body or any whole, balance, congruity, harmony, keeping. 2. Such structure as allows of an object's being divided by a point or line or plane or radiating lines or planes into two or more parts exactly similar in size & shape & in position relatively to the dividing point etc., repetition of exactly similar parts facing each other or a centre, whence (in art) ~OPHOB'IA n. 3. Approximation to such structure, possession by a whole of corresponding parts correspondingly placed; (bot.) possession by flower of sepals & petals & stamens & pistils in (multiples of) the same number. Hence or cogn. symmĕt'ric(AL) aa., symmĕt'ricaLY² adv., ~IZE(3) v.t., ~īzA'TION n. [f. obs. F -*ie* or L f. Gk *summetria* (SYM-, *metron* measure)]

sympathet'ic, a. & n. 1. Of, full of, exhibiting, expressing, due to, effecting, sympathy (~ *heart, person, conduct, words;* ~ *landscape* etc., that touches the feelings by association etc.; ~ *pain* etc., caused by pain or injury to someone else or in another part of the body; ~ *sound, resonance, string,* sounding by vibration communicated through the air or other medium from vibrating object; ~ STRIKE; ~ *nerve,* any, esp. either of two extending the length of the vertebral column, of a system of nerves uniting viscera & blood-vessels in common nervous action; ~ *ink,* writing done with which is invisible till brought out by warmth or other agency); capable of evoking sympathy, appealing *to* reader etc.; hence sympathĕt'ICALLY adv. 2. n. ~ nerve or system; person peculiarly sensitive to hypnotic or similar influence. [f. mod. L f. Gk *sumpathētikos* (SYMPATHY, PATHETIC)]

sym'pathiz|e, -is|e (-īz), v.i. Feel or express sympathy, share feeling or opinion *with* person etc., agree *with* sentiment. Hence ~ER¹ n. [f. F *sympathiser* (foll., -IZE)]

sym'pathỹ, n. Being simultaneously affected with the same feeling, tendency to share or state of sharing another person's or thing's emotion or sensation or condition (*with*), mental participation in another's trouble (*with*), compassion (*for*), agreement in opinion or desire. [f. L f. Gk *sumpatheia* f. SYM(*pathēs* f. *pathos* feeling) sympathetic]

sym'phonỹ, n. (Arch.) harmony, consonance of sounds, whence symphŏn'ious a. (rare); (mus.) SONATA for full orchestra, (also) opening or closing instrumental passage in song. Hence symphŏn'ic a. [ME, f. OF *simphonie* f. L f. Gk *sumphōnia* f. SYM(*phōnos* f. *phōnē* sound) harmonious]

sȳmpŏs′iȧrch (-k), n. President of symposium, toast-master, feast-master. [f. Gk *sumposiarkhos* (foll., -*arkhos* -ruler f. *arkhō* rule)]

sȳmpŏs′i|um (-z-), n. (pl.~a). **1.** Ancient--Greek after-dinner drinking-party with music, dancers, or conversation; any drinking-party. **2.** Philosophical or other friendly discussion; set of contributions on one subject from various authors & points of view in magazine etc. Hence ~AL a. [f. L f. Gk *sumposion* f. SYM(*pinō* drink, cf. *posis* drinking) drink together]

sȳmp′tom, n. Perceptible change in the body or its functions indicating disease (*subjective*, *objective*, ~s, directly perceptible only to patient, to others); sign or token of the existence of something. Hence or cogn. ~ăt′IC a., ~ȧtŏl′OGY n. [14th c. f. med. L *sinthoma*; later f. F -*tome* or LL f. Gk *sumptōma* -*atos* chance, symptom, f. SYM(*piptō* fall, -M)]

sȳn-, pref. (assim. to *syl-* before l, to *sym-* before b, m, p; to *syr-* before r, to *sys-* before simple s, to *sy-* followed by s plus consonant, and before z. The Gk change of *sun-* to *sug-* before gutturals is disregarded in mod. derivatives) repr. Gk *sun* prep. & pref., with, together or alike, in wds derived directly f. Gk wds (*syncope*) or made f. Gk (*syngnathous*):—~(*a)er′esis* (-nĕr-), contraction of two vowels or syllables into one [Gk *haireō* take]; ~*allagmăt′ic*, (of treaty or contract) imposing reciprocal obligations [Gk *allassō* exchange]; ~*al(o)eph′a* (-lē-), elision or obscuration of final before initial vowel [Gk *aleiphō* smear]; ~*an′therous*, with stamens coalescent by the anthers; ~*an′thous*, with flowers & leaves appearing simultaneously [Gk *anthos* flower]; ~*aphe(i)′a* (-ēa), continuity between lines in verse, allowing the ordinary rules of elision & quantity to operate with the final syllable [Gk *haptō* join]; ~*arthrōs′is* (pl. -*osēs*), immovable articulation, as in sutures of skull & socketing of teeth; ~*carp*, aggregate or multiple fruit, e.g. blackberry, fig, so ~*carp′ous* a. [Gk *karpos* fruit]; ~*chondrōs′is* (-k-), (nearly) immovable articulation of bones by layer of cartilage, as in spinal vertebrae; ~*clas′tic*, concave, or convex, all over (opp. *anticlastic*, partly concave & partly convex) [Gk *klaō* break]; ~*clin′al*, (of strata) dipping towards a common line or point (opp. *anticlinal*, dipping away); ~*cotylēd′onous*, with cotyledons united; ~*′cretism*, attempt to sink differences & effect union between sects or philosophic schools, so ~*crĕt′ic*, ~*′cretist*, ~*cretis′tic*, ~*′cretize* v.t. & i. [Gk *sugkrētizō* combine against common enemy]; ~*cȳt′ium* (pl. -*ia*), mass of protoplasm with several nuclei but forming one cell [-CYTE]; ~*dac′tyl(ous)* aa., with digits united as in webbed feet etc., so ~*dac′tylism*; ~*desmŏs′is*, articulation by ligaments, so

~*desmŏt′ic*, ~*desmol′ogy*, ~*desmog′raphy* [Gk *desmos* bond f. *deō* bind]; ~*dĕt′ic* of, using, conjunctions [ASYNDETON]; ~*′drōme* (or -mǐ), concurrence of, set of concurrent, symptoms in disease; ~*ec′doche* (-kǐ), extended acceptation by which when a part is named the whole it belongs to is understood, as in *50 sail* (for *ships*) [Gk *ek* out *dekhomai* accept]; ~*′esis*, violation of grammatical rule due to influence exerted by the sense (as *neither of them* are *right*) [Gk *sunesis* understanding]; ~*gen′esis*, formation of embryo partly from the male & partly from the female element; ~*′gnathous*, (of fish) with jaws united into tubular snout; ~*izēs′is* (pl. -*esēs*), pronunciation of two vowels not making a diphthong as one syllable [Gk *hizō* to seat]; ~*oe′cious* (-nēshus), having male & female organs in one inflorescence or receptacle, as in composite flowers & mosses [Gk *oikos* house]; ~*osteol′ogy*, science of the joints of the body; ~*ost(e)ōs′is*, anchylosis, so ~*ostŏt′ic* a.; ~*ōv′ia*, albuminous fluid secreted by membranes in interior of joints & in other places needing lubrication, so ~*ōv′ial* a. [invented by Paracelsus from unknown elements].

sȳn′agogue (-ŏg), n. Jewish congregation with organized religious observances & instruction, its place of meeting. Hence **sȳnagŏ′g**ICAL (-gǐ-, -jǐ-) a. [ME, f. OF *sinagoge* or LL f. Gk *sunagōgē* f. SYN(*agō* bring)]

sȳnch′romĕsh, a. & n. (System of gear--changing, esp. in motor-cars) in which the sliding gear-wheels are provided with small friction clutches which make contact with the non-sliding wheels before engagement, thus facilitating gear--changing by making both wheels revolve at the same speed. [for *synchronized mesh*]

sȳnchrŏn′ic (-ngk-), a. See DIACHRONIC.

sȳnch′ron|ize (-ngk-), |-ise (-īz), v.i. & t. Occur at the same time, be simultaneous or ~OUS a. (whence ~OUSLY[2] adv.), (*with*); ascertain or set forth the correspondence in date of (events); cause (clocks) to show, (of clocks) show, a standard or uniform time. Hence or cogn. ~ISM(1) n., (also) co-ordination of the audible and visible components in cinematography, television, etc., ~IZA′TION n. [f. *synchronism* f. mod. L f. Gk -*ismos* (SYN-, *khronos* time), -IZE]

sȳn′cop|āte, v.t. Shorten (word) by dropping interior letter(s) or syllable(s), as in *symbology* for *symbology*, *Gloster* for *Gloucester*; (mus.) displace beats or accents in (passage) so that what was 'strong' becomes 'weak', & vice versa. So ~A′TION n. [LL *syncopare* swoon (foll.). -ATE[3]]

sȳnc′opĕ, n. (Gram.) syncopated spelling or pronunciation; (med.) fainting, loss of consciousness from fall of blood-pressure, whence **sўncŏp′(t)ıc** a.; (mus.) syncopation, also such combination of voice-parts that two or more notes in one coincide with one in another. [f. LL f. Gk *sugkopē* (SYN-, *koptō* strike)]

sўn′dic, n. Official of kinds differing in different countries & times; ‖ (Camb. Univ.) member of special committee of senate. [F, f. LL f. Gk *sun(dikos* f. *dikē* justice) advocate]

sўn′dicalism, n. A movement among industrial workers having as its object the transfer of the means of production & distribution from their present owners to unions of workers. [f. F -*isme* (prec., -AL, -ISM)]

sўn′dicate, n. (-*at*), & v.t. (-āt). 1. Body of syndics (esp. at Camb.); combination of commercial firms etc. associated to forward some common interest; combination of persons for the acquisition of literary articles etc., and their simultaneous publication in a number of periodicals; group of people who combine to rent a shooting, fishing, etc. 2. v.t. Form (parties) into ~; deal with (news etc.) by ~. Hence **sўndicA′TION** n. [f. F -*at* f. med. L -*atus* (SYNDIC, -ATE¹)]

sўne, Sc. for *since* (*auld lang* ~, the days of long ago, esp. as title & refrain of song sung at parting etc.).

sўn′od, n. 1. Ecclesiastical council (*oecumenical* or *general*, *national*, *provincial*, *diocesan*, ~, attended by bishop(s) & delegated clergy of all nations, a nation, a province, a diocese); (Presb.) ecclesiastical court above presbyteries & subject to General Assembly; any meeting for debate. 2. (astron.). Conjunction of planets or stars. So ~AL, **sўnŏd′ıc(AL)**, aa., **sўnŏd′ıcALLY** adv. [ME, f. LL f. Gk *sunodos* (SYN-, *hodos* way) meeting]

sўn′onym, n. Word identical & coextensive in sense & usage with another of the same language (as *caecitis*, cf. *typhlitis*); word denoting the same thing(s) as another but suitable to different context (as *leap*, *slay*, cf. *jump*, *kill*) or containing different suggestion (as *blind-worm*, cf. *slow-worm*); word equivalent to another in some only of either's senses (as *ship*, cf. *vessel*). Hence or cogn. **sўnŏnym′ITY** n., **sўnŏn′ўmous** a. (*with*), **sўnŏn′ўmousLY²** adv. [f. L f. Gk *sunōnumon* (SYN-, *onoma* -*atos* name)]

sўnonym′ıc, a. Of or using synonyms. [prec., -IC]

sўnŏn′ўmў, n. Synonymity; collocation of synonyms for emphasis (as *in any shape or form*); system or collection of, treatise on, synonyms. [f. LL f. Gk *sunōnumia* (SYNONYM, -Y¹)]

sўnŏp′sis, n. (pl. -*psēs*). Summary, conspectus. [f. LL f. Gk SYN(*opsis* seeing)]

sўnŏp′tic, a. & n. 1. Affording a conspectus or general survey (~ *gospels*, those of Matthew, Mark, & Luke); of the ~ gospels; ~ *chart* (meteor.), weather map;

hence ~AL a., ~alLY² adv. 2. n. (Also **sўnŏp′tıst**) writer of a ~ gospel. [f. Gk *sunoptikos* (prec., -IC)]

sўnovit′ıs, n. Inflammation of the membrane that secretes the lubricating fluid in a joint. [f. SYNOVIA + -ITIS]

sўntăc′t|ıc, a. Of, according to, syntax. Hence ~ICALLY adv. [f. Gk *suntaktikos* (foll.)]

sўn′tăx, n. Sentence-construction, the grammatical arrangement of words in speech or writing, set of rules governing this, cf. ACCIDENCE. [F (-*xe*), or f. LL f. Gk *suntaxis* (SYN-, *tassō* order) marshalling, syntax]

sўn′the|sis, n. (pl. ~*sēs*). Combination, composition, putting together, (opp. *analysis*); building up of separate elements esp. of conceptions or propositions or facts, into a connected whole, esp. a theory or system; (chem.) artificial production of compounds (called 'synthetic rubber, indigo, cream', etc.) from their constituents as opp. extraction from plants etc.; (gram.) making of compound & derivative words, preference of composition & inflexion to use of prepositions etc.; (surg.) joining of divided parts. Hence or cogn. **sўnthĕt′ıc(AL)** aa., **sўnthĕt′ıcALLY** adv., ~SIZE(1), ~tīze, vv.t., ~tıST(1), ~sist, nn. [L, f. Gk *sunthesis* (SYN-, *tithēmi* put); the irreg. ~*size* more used than the correct ~*tize*]

sўph′er, v.t. Join (planks) with overlapping edges into flush surface; ~-*joint*, thus made. [var. of CIPHER in obs. sense]

sўph′il|is, n. Pox, a contagious venereal disease affecting first some local part (*primary* ~*is*), secondly the skin & mucous membrane (*secondary* ~*is*), & thirdly the bones & muscles & brain (*tertiary* ~*is*). Hence ~it′ıc, ~ous, ~OID, aa., ~IZE(5) v.t., ~ŏL′OGY n. [mod. L, f. title (*Syphilis*, *sive Morbus Gallicus*) of Latin poem (1530), f. *Syphilus*, a character in it, first sufferer from the disease]

syphon, syren, erron. for si-.

Sў′rıăc, n. & a. (In) the language of ancient Syria, western Aramaic. Hence ~ISM(4) n. [f. L f. Gk *Suriakos* (*Suria* Syria f. *Suros* a Syrian, -AC)]

Sў′rian, a. & n. (Native) of Syria. [*Syria*, -AN]

sўring′a (-ngga), n. The mock orange, a shrub with strong-scented white usu. clustered flowers; (bot.) lilac. [mod. L, as SYRINX (w. ref. to use of stems cleared of pith as pipe-stems), -A; cf. SERINGA]

sў′rınge (-j), n., & v.t. 1. Cylindrical tube with nozzle & piston into which liquid is first drawn by suction & then ejected in fine stream used in surgery, gardening, etc., squirt, (*hypodermic* ~, needle-pointed for hypodermic injections). 2. v.t. Sluice or spray (ears, plants, etc.) with ~. [f. med. L *siringa* f. Gk as foll.]

sў′rınx, n. (pl. -*es*, -*ngēs*). Pan-pipe;

(archaeol.) narrow rock-cut . gallery in Egyptian tombs; (anat.) Eustachian tube from throat to drum of ear supplying latter with air, whence **sўrĭng**ɪᴛ'ɪꜱ (-j-) n.; lower larynx or song-organ of birds, whence **sўrĭn'gē**ᴀʟ (-j-) a.; (surg.) fistula, whence **sўrĭng**ŏᴛ'ᴏᴍʏ n. [L, f. Gk *surigx surigg*- pipe]

Sўro-, comb. form f. Gk *Suros* Syrian, as ∼*arab'ian*, ∼*phoeni'cian*. [-ᴏ-]

sýr'tĭs (sêr-), n. (pl. *-tēs*). Quicksand. [L, f. Gk *surtis* (*surō* draw)]

sў'rup, *si-, n. Water (nearly) saturated with sugar, this combined with flavouring as beverage or with drug(s) as medicine; condensed sugarcane-juice, part of this remaining uncrystallized at various stages of refining, molasses, treacle, (|| *golden* ∼, trade name for pale kind). Hence ∼ʏ**²** a. - [ME, f. OF *sirop* or med. L *siropus* f. Arab. *sharāb* beverage, cf. ꜱʜᴇʀʙᴇᴛ, ꜱʜʀᴜʙ²]

sўssarcōs'ĭs, n. Connexion between bones by intervening muscle. [f. Gk *sussarkōsis* (ꜱʏɴ-, *sarkoō* f. *sarx sarkos* flesh, -ᴏꜱɪꜱ)]

sўssit'ĭa, n. pl. (Gk ant.). Public messes of Spartans & some other Dorians at which citizens were required to feed with a view to the promotion of patriotism, military efficiency, discipline, & simplicity. [Gk (*su-*) pl. of *sussition* (ꜱʏɴ-, *sitos* food)]

sўstăl'tic, a. Contracting & dilating by turns, having systole & diastole, pulsatory. [f. LL f. Gk *sustaltikos* (*sy-*=ꜱʏɴ-, *stellō* place, -ɪᴄ)]

sўs'tĕm, n. 1. Complex whole, set of connected things or parts, organized body of material or immaterial things, (∼ of *pulleys*, several arranged to work together; ∼ of *philosophy*, set of co-ordinated doctrines; *mountain* ∼, range or connected ranges; *river*, *railway*, ∼, river, railway, with its tributaries or branches, also rivers, railways, of a country, continent, etc.; *solar* ∼, sun & planets; *nervous*, *muscular*, etc., ∼, the nerves, muscles, of a person's or animal's body; *digestive* etc. ∼, all bodily parts subserving digestion etc.; the ∼, the body as a functional whole, as *the poison has passed into the* or *his* ∼; *Ptolemaic* etc. ∼, set of hypotheses or principles composing Ptolemy's etc. theory; *Devonian* etc. ∼, set of strata etc. so named). 2. Method, organization, considered principles of procedure, (principle of) classification, (∼ of *government*; *what* ∼ *do you go on?*; *lacks*, *works with*, ∼; *Linnaean*, *natural*, etc., ∼, classifications with different criteria), whence ∼ʟᴇꜱꜱ a. 3. (mus.). Braced staffs of score. [f. F *systême* or LL f. Gk *sustēma -atos* (*sy-* = ꜱʏɴ-, *histēmi* set, -ᴍ)]

sўstĕmăt'|ĭc, a. Methodical, according to a plan, not casual or sporadic or unintentional, classificatory, (∼*ic worker*, *liar*, *insolence*, *nomenclature*). Hence or cogn.

∼ɪᴄᴀʟʟʏ adv., **sўs'tĕmatɪz**ᴇ(3) v.t., **sўs'tĕmatɪꜱᴍ**(1), **sўs'tĕmatɪꜱᴛ**(1), **sўs'tĕmatɪz**ᴇʀ¹, **sўstĕmatɪzᴀ'ᴛɪᴏɴ**, nn. [f. LL f. late Gk *sustēmatikos* (prec., -ɪᴄ)]

sўstĕm'|ĭc, a. (physiol.). Of the bodily system as a whole, not confined to a particular part; (of insecticides, fungicides, etc.) entering the plant via roots or shoots and passing through the tissue. Hence ∼ɪᴄᴀʟʟʏ adv. [irreg. f. ꜱʏꜱᴛᴇᴍ+-ɪᴄ]

sўs'tolė, n. (physiol.). Contraction of heart etc. alternate with ᴅɪᴀꜱᴛᴏʟᴇ. Hence **sўstŏl'ĭc** a. [f. Gk *sustolē* (*sustellō*, see ꜱʏꜱᴛᴀʟᴛɪᴄ)]

sўs'tўle, a. With columns set comparatively close together. [f. L f. Gk ꜱʏ(*stulos* ꜱᴛʏʟᴇ²)]

sўs'tўlous, a. (bot.). With styles united. [as prec., -ᴏᴜꜱ]

sўz'ўgў, n. (astron.). Conjunction or opposition. [f. LL f. Gk *suzugia* f. *suzeugnumi* (*sy-*=ꜱʏɴ-, *zeugnumi* f. *zugon* yoke)]

T

T, t, (tē), letter (pl. *T*s, T's). T-shaped thing, esp. attrib., as *T-bandage*, *-bar*, *-bolt*, *-joint*, *-pipe*, -ꜱQᴜᴀʀᴇ; *suits me*, *hit it off*, etc., *to a T*, exactly, to a nicety; *cross the T's*, (fig.) be minutely accurate, also, emphasize a point.

|| **ta** (tah), int. (nursery, vulg.). Thank you, as *ta muchly*, *must say ta*.

taal (tahl), n. *The* ∼ (hist.), term used for the earlier form of ᴀꜰʀɪᴋᴀᴀɴꜱ. [Du.; = language, cogn. w. ᴛᴀʟᴇ]

tăb, n., & v.t. (colloq.; -bb-). 1. Small flap, strip, tag, or tongue, as part of or appendage to garment etc., e.g. metallic binding at end of bootlace, (also *ear-*∼) flap at side of cap to protect ear; (mil.) mark on collar distinguishing ' staff-officer; (colloq.) account, tally, check (esp. in phr. *keep* ∼ (or ∼*s*) *on*, keep account of, have under observation or in check; **baggage-*∼, luggage-label. 2. v.t. Tabulate, record. [*c.* 1600, of unkn. orig.]

tăb'ard, n. (Hist.) coarse outer garment worn by the poor, knight's garment worn over armour; herald's coat blazoned with arms of sovereign. [ME, f. OF *tabart*, of unkn. orig.]

tăb'arĕt, n. Upholstery fabric of alternate satin & watered-silk stripes. [mod. trade wd, perh. f. ᴛᴀʙʙʏ]

tăbasheer', **-shir** (-ēr), n. Kind of opal found in joints of bamboo & used in E.-Ind. medicine. [f. Pg. or F f. Hind. & Arab. (-*ir*)]

tăbb'ў, n., & v.t. 1. Watered fabric esp. silk (often attrib.). 2. (Also∼*cat*) brindled or mottled or streaked cat, esp. of grey or brownish colour with dark stripes; cat, esp. female. 3. Gossiping woman esp. old maid. 4. (Also ∼ *moth*) kinds of moth. 5. Kind of concrete. 6. v.t. Give wavy appearance to (fabric). [sense 1 f. F *tabis*

f. Arab. *'attābīy* a quarter of Baghdad; remaining senses of obsc. orig.]

tăběfăc'tion, n. Emaciation due to disease. [f. LL *tabefacere* (*tabēre* f. TABES, see -FACTION)]

‖ **tăb'erdār,** n. Scholar of Queen's College, Oxford. [= *tabarder* (TABARD + -ER[1]), from former dress]

tăb'ernăcl|e, n., & v.t. & i. **1.** (Bibl.) fixed or movable habitation usu. of slight construction, (fig.) human body; *Feast of T~es,* Jewish autumn festival commemorating the dwelling of the Jews in wilderness ; (Jewish hist.) tent used as sanctuary before final settlement of Jews in Palestine. **2.** (freq. derog.). Place of public worship. **3.** Receptacle for pyx or eucharistic elements. **4.** (archit.). Canopied stall, niche, or pinnacle, *~e-work,* series, tracery characteristic, of such *~es,* whence *~*ED[2] (-ld) a. **5.** Socket or double post for hinged mast that requires lowering to pass under bridges. **6.** vb. (fig.). Provide with shelter; dwell temporarily. So **tăbernăc'ūl**AR[2] a. [ME, f. OF, or L *tabernaculum* tent (*taberna* hut, see -CULE)]

tăb'ēs (-z), n. (med.). Emaciation; *dorsal ~,* wasting disease of spinal cord, locomotor ataxia. [L]

tabĕt'ic, a. & n. **1.** Of, affected with, (esp. dorsal) tabes. **2.** n. *~* patient. So **tabēs'**CENCE, **tăb'**ITUDE, nn., **tabēs'**CENT, **tăb'**IC, **tăb'ID**[1], aa., **tăb'id**LY[2] adv. [irreg. f. prec. + -i- + -IC]

tăb'inĕt, n. Watered fabric of silk & wool. [as TABARET]

tăb'lature, n. (arch.). Mental picture; graphic description. [f. F (foll., -URE)]

tā'ble, n., & v.t. **1.** Article of furniture consisting of flat top of wood or marble etc. & one or more usu. vertical supports esp. one on which meals are laid out, articles of use or ornament kept, work done, or games played; *breakfast, luncheon, tea, supper, -~,-* *~* used for such meals or on which such meal is laid out (*at ~,* while taking meal at *~,* as *refused to talk politics at ~; under the ~,* esp. drunk after dinner); each half of folding backgammon*-~; billiard-~* (for billiards, with slate top covered with green cloth); LORD'S, ROUND[1], KNEE[1]*-hole,* DRESSING-, TOILET-, *~.* **2.** Part of machine--tool on which work is put to be operated on. **3.** Slab of wood, stone, etc. **4.** Matter written on this, esp. *the two ~s* or *the ~s of the law* or *covenant* or *testimony,* ten commandments, *the twelve ~s,* laws promulgated in Rome 451–450 B.C., principal source of Roman jurisprudence. **5.** Level area, plateau. **6.** (archit.). Flat usu. rectangular surface, horizontal moulding esp. cornice. **7.** Flat surface of gem, cut gem with two flat faces. **8.** Palm of hand, esp. part indicating character or fortune. **9.** Each of two bony layers of skull. **10.** Company seated at (dinner- etc.) *~,* as *kept the ~ amused.* **11.** (Quantity &

quality of) food provided at *~,* as *keeps a good~, expenses of his~.* **12.** List of facts, numbers, etc., systematically arranged esp. in columns, matter contained in this, as *mathematical~s* (of logarithms, trigonometrical ratios, etc.), *~s of weights & measures, knows his multiplication ~ up to 12 times 12, ~ of* (i.e. *prohibited*) DEGREES, *~ of* CONTENT[1]s. **13.** *Lay, lie, on the ~,* postpone (measure, report, etc., in Parliament etc.), be postponed, indefinitely; *turn the ~s* (on person, or abs.), reverse relations (between), esp. pass from inferior to superior position [f. backgammon sense of *~s*]. **14.** *~-beer,* ordinary beer used at *~; ~-book,* ornamental usu. illustrated book kept on esp. drawing--room *~; ~-clamp* (for fastening thing to *~*); *~-cloth* (of white linen etc. for use at meals, of coloured material for use at other times); *~-cut,* (of gem) cut with flat top; *~-flap,* hinged end of *~-*top, lowered when not in use; *~-knife,* steel knife for use at*~ ;~-land,* extensive elevated region with level surface, plateau; *~-leaf,* piece that may be inserted in top of *~* to increase its length, also, *~-flap ; ~-lifting, -moving, -rapping, -tipping, -turning,* lifting etc. of *~* apparently without physical force, as spiritualistic phenomenon; *~-linen, ~-*cloths, napkins, etc. ; *~-money,* allowance to higher officers in army etc. for official hospitality, charge to members of club for use of dining--room; *~-*SPOON; *~-talk,* miscellaneous talk at *~* (often as title of book); *~ tennis,* PING-PONG; *~-tomb,* flat-topped, chest-like tomb in Roman catacombs; *~-ware* (for use at*~*); *~-water,* mineral water bottled for use at *~.* Hence *~*FUL n. **15.** v.t. Lay (measure etc., as above) on the *~.* **16.** Set (timbers) together with alternate grooves & projections in each to prevent shifting. **17.** Strengthen (sail) with wide hems. Hence **tăb'ling**[1](1, 2) n. [ME & OF *table* f. L *tabula*; OE *tabule* dir. f. L]

tăb'leau (-lō), n. (pl. *-eaux* pr. *-ōz*). Picturesque presentation, esp. (also *~ vivant,* see Ap.; pl. *~x vivants*; lit. living picture) silent & motionless group of persons etc. arranged to represent a scene; dramatic or effective situation suddenly brought about; (as int., after description of incident) picture the scene!; *~ curtains* (theatr.), pair of curtains to draw across & meet in the middle of the stage in place of the usual drop-curtain. [F, = picture, dim. of prec.]

table d'hôte (tahbl-dōt'), n. Common table for guests at hotel; *~ dinner* etc. (served in hotel etc. at fixed hour & price), cf. À LA CARTE. [F, ⇒ host's table]

tăb'lĕt, n. **1.** Thin sheet of ivory, wood, etc., for writing on, esp. each of a set fastened together; (usu. pl.) such set. **2.** Small slab esp. with or for inscription, as *votive~.* **3.** Small flat piece of prepared substance, esp. fixed weight or measure of a drug brought by pressure or addition of gum into convenient shape. 4. (Also *tablette'*) projecting horizontal coping of wall. [ME, f. OF *tablete* (TABLE, -ETTE)]

tablier' (-lyā), n. Woman's small apron or apron-like part of dress. [F]

tab'loid, n. 1. = TABLET (sense 3; P). 2. Newspaper, usu. popular in style, printed on sheets of half normal size; also attrib., as ~ *journalism*. [-OID]

taboo', n., a., & v.t. 1. (Among Polynesians etc.) system, act, of setting apart person or thing as accursed or sacred; ban, prohibition. 2. adj. Under a ban, prohibited, consecrated. 3. v.t. Put (thing, practice, etc.) under ~, exclude or prohibit by authority or social influence, as *the subject was* ~*ed*. [f. Tongan *ta-bu*]

tab'or, n. (hist.). Small drum, esp. one used to accompany pipe. [ME, f. OF *tabour* f. Arab. *ṭabl*, pl. *ṭubûl*, cf. TAMBOUR]

tab'ouret (-borit), n. Small seat usu. without arms or back, stool; embroidery--frame. [F, = stool, dim. as prec.]

tabu. Var. of TABOO.

tab'ula, n. (pl. -ae). (Anat.) hard flat surface of bone etc.; ~ *rās'a*, erased tablet, (fig.) human mind at birth viewed as having no innate ideas. [L, = TABLE]

tab'ular, a. Of, arranged in, computed etc. by means of, tables, as a ~ *statement*, ~ *values, results, computations, arranged in* ~ *form*, ~ *difference* (between successive logarithms etc. in mathematical tables); broad & flat like a table, as ~ *surface*; (formed) in thin plates, as ~ *structure*. Hence ~LY² adv. [f. L *tabularis* (prec., see -AR¹)]

tab'ul|āte, v.t., & a. 1. Arrange (figures, facts) in tabular form, whence ~A'TION, ~ātoR, nn.; give flat surface to. 2. adj. (-at). Having flat surface, composed of thin plate. [f. LL *tabulare* f. TABULA + -ATE², ³]

tac'amahac (-*ama*-), n. Gum resin from some S.-Amer. & other trees; the balsam poplar. [Sp. (-*ca*), f. Aztec *tecomahiyac*]

tac'-au-tac' (-ō-), n. (fencing). Parry combined with riposte; rapid succession of attacks & parries. [F, imit.]

ta'cē, v.i. imperat. Be silent (~ *is Latin for a candle*, veiled injunction = MUM¹). [L]

ta'cět, mus. direction indicating silence of voice or instrument. [L, = is silent]

tach(e), n. (bibl.). A clasp, link. [ME, f. OF *tache* fibula; rel. to *attach, detach*; doublet of TACK]

tachŏm'eter (-k-), n. Instrument for measuring velocity. So **tachŏm'etry** n. [f. Gk *takhos* speed +-METER]

tăchycard'ia (-kI-), n. (path.). Abnormally rapid heart-action as a disease. [f. Gk as foll., & see CARDIAC]

tachÿg'raph|ÿ (-k-), n. Stenography, esp. that of ancient Greeks & Romans. Hence ~ER¹ n., **tăchÿgrăph'ic**(AL) aa. [f. Gk *takhus* swift +-GRAPHY]

tăch'ÿ|lÿte (-k-), n. A vitreous form of basalt. Hence ~lÿt'IC a. [as prec.+ -*lutos* f. *luō* loose, from ready fusion under blowpipe]

tachÿm'eter (-k-), n. Surveyor's instrument for rapid location of points. [as prec. +-METER]

ta'cit, a. Understood, implied, existing, without being stated, as ~ *consent, agreement, understanding*; abstaining from speech or action (~ *spectator*). Hence ~LY² adv. [f. L *tacitus* silent (*tacēre* be silent)]

ta'citurn, a. Reserved in speech, not given to much speaking. So **tăcitūrn'**ITY n. [f. F (-*ne*) or L *taciturnus* as prec.]

tăck, n., & v.t. & i. 1. Small sharp flat--headed nail of iron, copper, etc., for securing carpet etc. (tin-~, iron ~ coated with tin; BRASS ~s). 2. pl. Long stitches as temporary fastening in needlework. 3.(naut.). Rope for securing corner of some sails, corner to which this is fastened; direction in which vessel moves as determined by position of sails (*port, starboard*, ~, with wind on port, starboard, side); temporary change of direction in sailing to take advantage of side wind etc., esp. each of several alternate movements to port & starboard (~ *& ~*, by successive ~s). 4. (fig.). Course of action or policy, as *must change our* ~, *am on the right* or *wrong* ~, *try another* ~. 5. = foll. (Parl. sense). 6. Sticky condition of varnish etc., whence ~'INESS n., ~'Y² a. 7. [prob. diff. wd]. Food, fare, esp. HARD ~; *soft* ~, bread, good fare. 8. ~-*driver*, machine that automatically places & drives ~s; ~-*hammer*, light hammer for driving ~s, usu. with claw for extracting ~s. 9. vb. Fasten (carpet etc., often *down*) with~s, stitch (pieces or parts of cloth etc.) lightly together; (fig.) annex, append, (thing *to* or *on to* another, esp. as in foll.). 10. Change ship's course (often *about* by shifting ~s & sails (cf. WEAR³); (fig.) change one's conduct, policy, etc. Hence ~'ER¹(1, 2) n. [ME *tak* etc., of obsc. orig.; doublet of TACH(E), though no forms in *k* or *q* are recorded in OF]

tăck'ing, n. In vbl senses, esp.: (law) priority of a third or subsequent mortgage etc. to a second of which notice was not given; ‖ (Parl.) appending of an extraneous clause to a money bill to secure its passing House of Lords, which cannot amend money bills. [-ING¹]

tăc'kle, n., & v.t. & i. 1. (Also *block & ~*) mechanism esp. of ropes, pulley-blocks, hooks, etc., for lifting weights, managing sails or spars, etc. (*naut. pr.* tā'kl); windlass with its ropes & hooks; requisites for a task or sport, as *fishing-*~; grasping or holding or obstructing esp. of opponent in football; ~-*block*, pulley over which rope runs; ~-*fall*, rope connecting blocks of a ~. 2. vb. Grapple with, grasp with endeavour to hold or manage or overcome, (opponent, awkward thing or business problem); (footb.) obstruct or seize & stop (player running with ball); secure by means of ~; ~ *to* (colloq.), fall to work vigorously, set to. Hence **tăck′**ING[1](1, 3, 6) n. [ME, f. MLG, MDu. *takel*, f. *taken* lay hold of, see -LE(1)]

tăct, n. Intuitive perception of what is fitting esp. of the right thing to do or say, adroitness in dealing with persons or circumstances, whence ~′FUL, ~′LESS, aa., ~′FULLY[2] adv., ~′LESSNESS n. [F, f. L *tactus -ūs* (sense of) touch (*tangere tact-* touch)]

tăc′tical, a. Of tactics; (of bombing) carried out in immediate support of military or naval operations; adroitly planning or planned. Hence ~LY[2] adv. [f. Gk *taktikos* (foll.) +-AL]

tăc′tics, n. (As sing. or pl.) art of disposing military or naval or air forces esp. (cf. STRATEGY, LOGISTICS) in actual contact with enemy; (pl.) procedure calculated to gain some end, skilful device(s), as *cannot approve these* ~; so occas. in sing. form **tăc′tic** n. Hence **tăcti′**CIAN (-ĭshn) n. [f. Gk *taktika* neut. pl. (*tassō* arrange, see -IC)]

tăc′tile, a. Of, perceived by, connected with, the sense of touch, as ~ *impression, organ*, so **tăc′tu**AL a., **tăc′tu**ALLY[2] adv.; tangible; (paint.) producing or having to do with the effect of solidity (~ *values* etc.). Hence **tăctil′**ITY n. [f. L *tactilis* (*tangere tact-* touch, see -ILE)]

tăd′pōle, n. Larva of batrachian e.g. frog from time it leaves egg till loss of gills & tail; ~*-fish*, European fish with large flat head. [ME *taddepolle* (TOAD+POLL[1], f. size of head)]

taed′ium vit′ae, n. (path.). Weariness of life with tendency to suicide. [L]

tael (tāl), n. Chinese ounce (= 1⅓ oz avoirdupois) esp. of silver as former monetary unit. [Port., f. Malay *tahil* weight]

taen′i|a, n. (pl. ~ae). (Archit.) fillet on top of Doric epistyle; (anat.) ribbonlike part esp. of brain; roller bandage; tapeworm; (Gk & Rom. ant.) fillet, headband. Hence ~OID a. [L, f. Gk *tainia*]

tăff′ėta, n. Kinds of silk or linen fabric esp. thin glossy silk of plain texture. [ME, f. OF *taffetas* f. Pers. *taftah* (*tāftan* shine)]

tăff′rail, **tăff′erel** (-fril), n. Rail round stern of vessel; (-*erel*) upper part of stern. [f. Du. *tafereel* panel dim. of *tafel* f. L as TABLE, assim. to RAIL[1]]

Tăff′ÿ[1], n. (colloq.). Welshman. [W pronunc. of *Davy* = *David*]

taffy[2]. See TOFFEE.

tăf′ia, n. (W. Ind.). Kind of rum distilled from molasses etc. [native]

tăg, n., & v.t. & i. (-gg-). 1. Metal point at end of lace. 2. Loop at back of boot used in pulling it on. 3. Address label, esp. one for tying on. 4. Loose or ragged end of anything; ragged lock of wool on sheep. 5. Appendage; (theatr.) closing

speech addressed to audience; trite quotation, stock phrase, refrain of song. 6. (Tip of) animal's tail. 7. [perh. diff. wd]. Children's game in which one chases the rest (*cross-, long*, etc., ~, forms of this). 8. *~ day*, = FLAG[1]-*day*; ~*rag*, = RAG[1]~; ~*sore*, pustular disease of sheep; ~*′tail*, kind of worm, sycophant. 9. vb. Furnish (lace etc., literary composition) with a ~. 10. Join (thing, esp. piece of writing, *to* or *on to* another, things *together*), find rhymes for (verses), string (rhymes) together. 11. Shear away ~s from (sheep). 12. (colloq.). Follow closely or persistently. 13. Touch (person pursued) in game of ~. [ME, of unkn. orig.]

tağėt′ės (-jĕtēz), n. Kinds of plant of aster family with showy yellow or orange flowers. [f. L *Tages*, Etruscan divinity]

tăgg′er (-g-), n. In vbl senses; also or esp.: pursuer (also called *it*) in game of tag; (pl.) thin sheet iron, whether coated with tin or (*black* ~s) not. [-ER[1]]

tahsil′ (-ēl), n. Territorial subdivision in India for revenue purposes. Hence ~dăr n., native collector of revenue in ~. [Hind. & Arab., = collection; Pers. *dar* holder]

taiga (ti′gah), n. Coniferous forest between tundra & steppe. [Russ.]

tail[1], n., & v.t. & i. 1. Hindmost part of animal esp. when prolonged beyond rest of body, as *dog* WAG[1]*s his* ~, *tail* WAG[1]*s dog*, dog has *his* ~ *between his legs* (as sign of alarm or dejection; often fig. of person); ~*s up*, (of persons, fig.) in good spirits; *turn* ~, turn one's back, run away; *twist the* LION'*s* ~, *drop pinch of* SALT *on* ~ *of*, PASHA *of three* etc. ~*s*. 2. Thing like or suggesting ~ in shape or position, hind or lower or subordinate or inferior part, slender part or prolongation, as ~ (luminous train) *of comet*, ~ (outer corner) *of the eye*, ~ (end) *of procession* etc., ~ (weaker members) *of the cricket* XI (or other sports team), ~ *margin* (at foot of page), *followed by a* ~ (long train) *of attendants, at the* ~ (back) *of a cart*, ~ (string & paper appendage at lower end) *of a kite, cow's*~, frayed end of rope etc., ~ (= STEM[1]) *of musical note*, ~ (part below line) *of a g* etc., ~ (exposed end) *of slate* or *tile* in roof, ~ (unexposed end) *of brick* or *stone* in wall, ~ (slender backward prolongation) *of butterfly's wing*, ~ (comparative calm at end) *of a gale*, ~ (calm stretch following rough water) *of a stream*, ~ *of the trenches* (fortif.), part first made by advancing party, *make* HEAD[1] *or* ~ *of*, PIGTAIL. 3. pl. = ~*coat*, as *boys go into* ~*s at sixteen*. 4. (In tossing) ~ or usu. ~*s*, reverse of coin turned upwards (see HEAD). 5. ~*-bay*, part of canal lock between ~*-gate* & lower pond; ~*-board*, hinged or removable back of cart; ~*-braid* (for protecting hem of skirt); ~*-coat*, man's morning or evening coat with long skirt divided at back into ~s & cut away in front; ~-*gate*, lower gate of canal lock; ~-*light* (carried at back of train, car, cycle, etc.); ~-*piece*, decoration in blank space at end of chapter etc., triangular piece of wood to which lower ends of strings are fastened in some musical instruments; ~-*pipe*, suction--pipe of pump, (v.t.) fasten something to ~ of (dog, fig. person); ~-*race*, part of mill-race below water-wheel; ~-*spin* (aviation), kind of spinning dive. Hence (-)~ED² (-ld), ~LESS, aa. 6. vb. Furnish with ~. 7. Remove the stalks of (fruit); dock ~ of (lamb etc.). 8. (colloq.). Shadow, follow closely. 9. Join (thing on to another). 10. ~ *after*, follow closely; ~ *away* or *off*, (of persons, dogs, etc.) fall behind or away in scattered line; ~ *in*, fasten (timber) by one end into wall etc.; ~ *to the tide*, ~ *up and down stream*, (of anchored vessel) swing up & down with tide. [OE *tægel, tægl*, OHG *zagal*, ON *tagl* f. Gmc *taglaz*]

tail², n. & a. (law). 1. Limited ownership (*in* ~, on those terms); estate limited to a person & heirs of his body. 2. adj. So limited, esp. *estate* ~, FEE-~. [ME, f. OF *taille* notch, cut, tax, f. *taillier* cut f. LL *taliare* (L *talea* slip of wood); see TALLY]

tail′ing, n. In vbl senses of TAIL¹; also or esp.: unexposed end of brick or stone or beam in wall; (pl.) refuse or inferior part of grain, ore, etc.; blur or other fault in calico-printing. [-ING¹]

tail′or, n., & v.i. & t. 1. Maker of (esp. men's) garments esp. to order (*the* ~ *makes the man*; *nine* ~*s go to a man*; *ride like a* ~, badly); ~-*bird*, kinds of small bird sewing leaves together to form nest; ~-*made*, (esp. of woman's dress) made by ~ usu. w. little ornament & w. special attention to exact fit; ~'s *chair* (without legs), for sitting cross-legged as ~ at work; ~'s *cramp* (in fingers & thumbs); ~'s *twist*, kind of strong silk thread. Hence ~ESS¹ n. 2. vb. Be, work as, a ~, whence ~ING¹ n.; make clothes for (chiefly in p.p., as *well*-~*ed*). [ME & AF *taillour*, = OF *tailleor* f. Rom. *taliatorem* f. LL *taliare* TAIL², -OR]

tain, n. Thin tin plate; tin foil for backing mirror. [F, = *étain* tin]

taint, n., & v.t. & i. 1. Spot, trace, of decay or corruption or disease (lit. & fig.), corrupt condition, infection, as *there was a* ~ *of insanity in the family*, *the moral* ~ *had spread among all classes*, *without* ~ *of commercialism*. 2. vb. Introduce corruption or disease into, infect, be infected, as ~*ed meat*, ~*s all it touches*, *meat will* ~ *readily in hot weather*, *his mind was* ~*ed*; ~*ed goods* (in trade-unionism), goods that members of a union must not handle because non-union labour has been employed on them or for similar reasons. Hence ~'LESS a., ~'lèssLY² adv. [ME, f.

OF *teint* n. & p.p. of *teindre* TINGE; partly also aphetic f. ATTAINT]

Tai′-ping′, **Tae-**, (tī-), n. One of those who took part in a rebellion in China (1850–64). [f. Chin. *t'ai p'ing* great peace]

taj (tahj), n. Tall cap of Mohammedan dervish. [Pers. f. Arab.]

take¹, v.t. & i. (tŏŏk, ~n). I. General senses. 1. Lay hold of with the hand(s) or other part of the body or with any instrument (lit. & fig.), grasp, seize, capture, catch by pursuit or surprise, captivate, win, gain, as ~ *it between your finger & thumb*, *took him by the throat*, ~ *it up with the tongs*, ~ *the* BULL¹ *by the horns*, *deuce* ~ *it!*, ~ BIT¹ *between teeth*, ~ *a fortress*, ~ *by* STORM, *took 113 prisoners*, *was* ~*n prisoner* or *captive*, *took his bishop* (at chess), ~ *the odd trick* (at cards), ~*s* (gains, receives in payment) *£40 a week*, *took* (gained) *little by this move*, *took first prize*, ~ *the* CAKE or *biscuit* (sl.), *rabbit* ~ *n in trap*, *took* (surprised, caught) *him in the act* or *at a disadvantage*, *was* ~*n ill* or colloq. *bad*, ~*n aback*, *what* ~*s* (captivates) *my fancy*, *was much* ~*n* (charmed) *with* or *by her manners*, *novel did not* ~ (become popular), *vaccine did not* ~ (operate). 2. (See also 9 below). Assume possession of, procure e.g. by purchase, acquire, avail oneself of, use, use up, consume, require as instrument, material, agent, etc., as ~*s whatever he can lay his hand on*, *wish you would not* ~ *my bicycle*, ~ (assume or enjoy as one's right) *precedence*, *took his degree*, ~ ORDER¹s, ∥ ~ SILK, *shall* ~ *a holiday*, (cooking direction) ~ *1 oz of curry-powder*, *do you* ~ (buy regularly, subscribe to) *Punch?*, *am not taking any* (sl.), decline offer, *took* (engaged) *seats in advance*, *must* ~ *lessons*, *lodgings*, *a taxi*, *will* ~ (buy) *2 lb.*, ~ *legal*, *medical*, etc., *advice*, *consult lawyer* etc. (& see below), ~ (as instance) *the French Revolution*, *has* ~*n a partner*, *a wife*, (arch.) *took to* (as) *wife Jane Smith*, ~ *a* BACK¹ *seat*, *took his seat on the* WOOLSACK, *must* ~ *the liberty of differing from you*, *must* ~ *leave to differ*, *took a mean advantage*, *do not* ~ *advantage* (avail yourself unfairly) *of his youth*, ~ *the opportunity*, *will* ~ (drink) *a cup of tea*, ~*s too much alcohol*, *these things* ~ *time*, ~ *your time*, *do not hurry*, *it* ~*s a lot of doing* (is hard to do), ~*s a poet to translate Virgil*, *transitive verbs* ~ *an object*. 3. Cause to come with one, carry with one, conduct, convey, remove, dispossess person etc. of, as ~ *the letters to the post*, *the dog for a walk*, *the children to the pantomime*, *the corkscrew from the shelf*, ~ *for a* RIDE, ~*s his readers with him* (engrosses their attention), ~ *him through* (make him read) *a book of Livy*, *took him into partnership*, ~*s all the fun out of it*, ~ *to* TASK, ~ *in hand*, undertake, start doing or dealing with, undertake the control or reform of (*the boy wants taking in hand*), (see also special uses w. advv. & prepp.),

4. Catch, be infected with, (cold, fever, etc.). **5.** Conceive, experience, indulge, give play to, exert, as ~ *offence, umbrage,* ~ *a fancy to,* ~*s a pride in his work, a pleasure in contradicting,* ~ *pity on him,* ~ *no notice,* ~ *heed, pains, trouble.* **6.** Ascertain (person's measure, height, temperature, address, etc.) by inquiry, measurement, etc. **7.** Apprehend, grasp mentally, infer, conclude, understand, interpret, as *I* ~ *your meaning* or (arch.) *you, I* ~ *this to be ironical, I* ~ *it that we are to wait here,* ~ *person at his* WORD[1], *how would you* ~ (translate, interpret) *this passage?,* ~ *it for granted,* assume it, *do you* ~ *me for* (think me) *a fool?* **8.** Treat or regard in specified manner, adopt specified attitude towards, as ~ *things coolly,* ~ *it easy, should* ~ *it kindly of you* (be obliged) *if you would answer my letter, must not* ~ *it ill of him* (resent his conduct), ~ *to* HEART, ~ *as read,* dispense with the actual reading of (minutes etc.). **9.** (See also 2 above.) Accept, put up with, submit to, adopt, choose, receive, derive, as ~ *the offer,* ~ *what you can get, the bet was* ~*n,* ~*n & offered* (abbr. *t. & o.*), phr. used in recording betting odds), *I took him* (his bet), *must* ~ *us as you find us, will* ~ *no nonsense, will not* ~ *this treatment, took it like a lamb, will not* ~ *a hint,* ~ *advice,* act on it (& see above), *you may* ~ *it from me* or ~ *my word for it, I, a well-informed person, assure you,* ~ *sides,* join one of two parties, ~ (hold, adopt) *a different view,* ~*s its name from the inventor.* **10.** Perform, execute, make, undertake, negotiate, deal with, as *took work for a friend,* ~ *notes,* ~ *a photograph, took a sudden leap, horse will not* ~ *the fence,* ~ *a walk,* || ~ (be examined in) *the mathematical tripos,* ~ (conduct) *the evening service,* ~ *a glance round you, took a deep breath,* ~ *an oath.* **11.** Photograph, come out *well* etc. when photographed, as ~ *him in cap & gown, does not* ~ *well.* **12.** ~ *account of,* include in one's reckoning, not overlook; ~ *aim,* direct weapon or missile (*at* object); ~ *care,* be careful, be on one's guard, not neglect or fail, be cautious in arranging or deciding, as ~ *care!,* ~ *care to leave plenty of room,* ~ *care not to wake the baby,* ~ *care how you speak* or *what you say to him;* ~ *care of,* be careful of, be in charge of, *be adequate provision for, *be able to deal with; ~ *one's chance,* accept risk (*of*); ~ *earth,* (of fox etc., fig. of person) escape into hole; ~ EFFECT[1], EXCEPTION, HEART (*of grace*), HOLD[2]; ~ *it* (colloq.), endure punishment etc.; ~ LEAVE[1] (*of*); ~ *one's life in one's hand,* risk it; ~ *person's* esp. *God's name in vain,* use it lightly or profanely; ~ PART[1]; ~ *place,* happen; ~ STOCK (*of, in*); ~ *the* WALL, ~ WIND[1]. **II.** Spec. uses w. prepp., advv., & adv. phrr. **1.** ~ *after,* resemble (person, esp. parent) in character, feature, etc. **2.** ~ *back* (colloq.), retract

(words). **3.** ~ *down:* write down, as ~ *down his name & address, took down the sermon in shorthand;* humble, esp. ~ *person down a* PEG[1] *or two;* swallow (food etc.) esp. with difficulty or reluctance; remove (building, structure) by taking it to pieces. **4.** ~ *from,* diminish, lessen, weaken, as *such faults do not* ~ *from his credit as a historian.* **5.** ~ *in:* admit, receive, (lodgers, guest, etc.); ~ (lady) *in* (often *to dinner*), conduct from drawing-room to dining-room & sit beside; receive (washing, sewing, typewriting, etc.) to be done at home; include, comprise; reduce (garment etc.) to smaller compass, furl (sail); understand, digest mentally; believe (false statement); deceive; cheat; || ~ (newspaper etc.) by subscription; ~*'in* n., a fraud, deception, piece of humbug. **6.** ~ *into:* ~ *into* one's *confidence,* confide in; ~ *into* one's *head,* conceive, get hold of, (idea), imagine, adopt the belief, (*that, it . . . that*), resolve (*to* do). **7.** ~ *off:* remove (clothes, hat, etc.) from the body (~ *off one's hai to,* fig., applaud as admirable); remove, conduct away, as *took him off to the station, took himself off,* went off; deduct (part of price); drink off; ridicule by imitation, mimic; jump, spring, (*from, at,* place); (aviation) start from rest & become airborne; ~*-off* n., caricature, spot from which one jumps, (aviation) becoming airborne, (croquet) stroke causing one's own ball to go forward while touching but scarcely moving another. **8.** ~ *on:* undertake (work, responsibility); ~ *person on at golf* etc., play with him; (colloq.) show violent emotion, make a fuss. **9.** ~ *out:* cause to come out, bring or convey out, as ~ *him out for a walk, books must not be* ~*n out of the library;* remove (stain etc.); (bridge) remove (one's partner) from the suit he has called by bidding a fresh suit or no trumps; ~ *the nonsense* etc. *out of* person, cure him of it; accept payment of (debt etc.) or compensation for (injury etc.) *in,* as *took it out in cigars & drinks;* ~ *it out of,* have revenge on, get satisfaction from, exhaust the strength of; procure, get issued, (patent, summons, etc.). **10.** ~ *over,* succeed to management or ownership of (business etc.); ~*-over bid,* an offer to purchase shares which will secure for the bidder control of a company. **11.** ~ *to:* begin, fall into the habit of, begin to busy oneself with, as *took to humming a tune,* ~ *to bad habits, literature;* conceive a liking for (person etc.). **12.** ~ *up:* lift up; absorb, occupy, engage, as *sponges* ~ *up water,* ~*s up all my time, my attention; train stops to* ~ *up* (admit) *passengers;* ~ *into* custody; adopt as protégé; interrupt or correct (speaker); enter upon (profession, subject); pursue (matter, inquiry) further; secure, fasten, (dropped stitch, artery, etc.); furnish the amount of (loan etc.); ~ *up with*, consort with; ~ *up the* CUDGELS, GAUNTLET[1], GLOVE; ~*ᴸup* n. (mech.), kinds of device for tightening band etc. in machine, drawing up slack of thread, removing material that has been operated on, etc. **13.** ~ *(it) upon* or *on one to*, venture, presume, to. [late OE *tacan* f. ON *taka*, in ME superseding *niman*]

tāke², n. Amount *(of* fish, game, etc.) taken or caught; (print.) amount of copy set up at one time; takings, esp. money received at theatre for seats; (cinemat.) a scene that has been or is to be photographed; GIVE² *& ~*. [f. prec.]

tāk'er, n. In vbl senses, esp. one who takes a bet, as *no ~s, a few ~s at 5 to 4*. [-ER¹]

ta'kin (tah-), n. Tibetan horned ruminant. [native]

tāk'ing¹, n. In vbl senses, esp.: (pl.) money taken in business, receipts; (arch.) state of agitation, as *was in a great ~*. [-ING¹]

tāk'ing², a. Attractive, captivating; catching, infectious. Hence ~LY² adv., ~NESS n. [-ING²]

tăl'apoin, n. 1. Buddhist monk in Ceylon, Siam, etc. 2. Kind of monkey. [f. Port. *talapão*, of E.-Ind. orig.]

talar̄'ĭa, n. pl. Winged boots or sandals as attribute of Mercury, Iris, & others. [L]

tal'botȳpe (tawl-), n. Photographic process invented by W. H. Fox Talbot in 1840, the basis of that now used. [TYPE]

tălc, n., & v.t. 1. A magnesium silicate usu. found in flat smooth often transparent plates & used as lubricator etc.; (pop., commerc.) mica esp. as glazing-material. Hence tāl(c)k'Y², ~'OID, ~'OSE¹, ~'OUS, aa. 2. v.t. Treat with~. [F, or f. med. L *talcum* f. Arab. *talq*]

tăl'cite, n. A massive variety of talc. [-ITE¹]

tăl'cum, n. = TALC; ~ *powder*, powdered talc for toilet use, usu. perfumed. [med. L]

tāle, n. 1. True or usu. fictitious narrative esp. one imaginatively treated, story, as *tell him a ~, a true ~ of the* Crusades, *old wives' ~s, marvellous legendary ~s; ~ of a tub*, idle fiction; TELL *the ~; prefer to tell my own ~* (give my own account of the matter); *thing tells its own ~* (is significant, requires no comment, explains itself). 2. Malicious report whether true or false, as *all sorts of ~s will get about, if all ~s be true* (esp. as preface to scandal); *tell ~s (out of school)*, report esp. with malicious intention what is meant to be secret; ~ᴸ *bearer*, person who does this, so ~*'bearing* a. & n.; ~*'teller*, one who tells ~s (in either sense). 3. ‖ (arch., rhet., poet.). Number, total, as *the ~ is complete, shepherd tells his ~* (of sheep). [OE *talu*, OS, ON *tala*, OHG *zala*, f. Gmc **talō* f. **lal-* see TELL]

tăl'ent, n. 1. Special aptitude, faculty,

gift, *(for* music etc.), *for doing*; see *Matt.* xxv. 14–30), high mental ability, whence ~ED², ~LESS, aa. 2. Persons of ~, as *all the ~ of the country, looking out for local ~, ministry of all the ~s*; (sport. sl.) *the ~*, those who take odds etc. relying on their own judgement & knowledge, opp. to bookmakers. 3. Ancient weight & money of account among Greeks, Romans, Assyrians, etc., of varying value. 4. ~*-money*, bonus to professional cricketer etc. for especially good performance. [ME, f. OF f. L *talentum* f. Gk *talanton* balance, weight, sum of money]

tāl'ēs (-z), n. (law). Writ for summoning jurors, list of persons who may be so summoned, to supply deficiency; *pray a ~*, plead for completion of jury thus; ~*'man (or* -lz-), person so summoned. [ME; L ~ *(de circumstantibus)* such (of the bystanders), first wds of writ]

Tăliacō'tian (-shn), a. ~ *operation*, formation of new nose by means of flap taken from upper arm but severed only after union has taken place. [f. *Tagliacozzi*, Italian surgeon d. 1599 + -AN]

tăl'ion, n. (Also L *lex tăliōn'ĭs*) the law of retaliation inflicting punishment of same kind & degree as injury (see *Lev.* xxiv. 20). Hence tăliōn'IC a. [ME, f. OF, f. L *talio -onis (talis* such)]

tăl'ipĕd, a. & n. 1. Club-footed; (zool., of sloth etc.) having feet twisted into unusual position. 2. n. = person or animal. [as foll.]

tăl'ipēs (-z), n. Club-foot(edness); taliped formation. [mod. L (TALUS, *pes pedis* foot)]

tăl'ipŏt, -ŭt, n. A fan-leafed palm. [f. Hind. *tālpāt* f. Skr. *tālapattra (tāla* palm + *pattra* leaf)]

tăl'isman (-z-), n. Charm, amulet, thing capable of working wonders; (astrol.) magical figure cut or engraved & capable of benefiting its possessor. Hence **tălismăn'**IC (-z-) a. [F, = Sp., Port. *talisman*, It. *-mano*, ult. f. Arab. *ṭilsam* f. Gk *telesma*]

talk (tawk), v.i. & t., & n. 1. Converse, communicate ideas, by spoken words, as *was ~ing with* or to *a friend, what are you ~ing about?*, ~ BIG, TALL, *people will ~* (scandal), *now you're ~ing* (sl. = I welcome that offer etc.), *you can't ~* (colloq. = you are just as bad yourself); communicate by radio signals. 2. Have the power of speech, as *child is learning to ~, parrots can ~*; use this to excess, as *is always ~ing*. 3. Express, utter, discuss, in words, as *you are ~ing nonsense, ~ treason, philosophy*, SHOP; *~ (cold) turkey* (colloq.), tell the plain truth. 4. Use (language), as *they were ~ing French*. 5. Bring into specified condition etc. by ~ing, as *~ed himself hoarse, ~ person round*, persuade him, *~ed him out of his resolution, into his grave, would ~ the hind leg off a donkey*, is talkative. 6. ~ *about*, discuss, as *do not want to be ~ed about* (made subject of gossip); ~ *at*, address to one of a company remarks covertly hostile to & meant to be heard by (another); ~ *away*, consume (time) in ~ing; ~ *back*, reply defiantly; ~ *down*, silence (person) by superior loudness or persistency, bring (aircraft) to a landing by radioing instructions from the ground; ~ *of*, discuss, mention, as ~*ing* (while we are on the subject) *of muffins, what time do you have tea?*, express some intention of (do*ing*); || ~ *out* (bill, motion, in Parl.), get rid of it by prolonging discussion till time of adjournment; ~ *over*, discuss at some length, win over by ~ing; ~ *round*, discuss (subject) at length without reaching conclusion, also ~ over (person); ~ *through* one's *hat* (sl.), exaggerate or bluff or make wild statements; ~ *to*, speak to, (colloq.) reprove, give a piece of one's mind to, so *gave him a* ~*ing-to*; ~ *up*, discuss (subject) in order to rouse interest in it. Hence ~ER² (tawk-) n. **7**. n. Conversation, as *let us have a* ~, SMALL, TABLE-, TALL, ~, *it will end in* ~ (nothing will be done); short address or lecture in conversational style (esp. when broadcast by radio); theme of gossip, as *they, their quarrels, are the* ~ *of the town.* [ME *talkien, talken*, deriv. vb f. TALE or TELL, w. frequent. -*k* as in *stalk, walk, lurk*]

ta′lkative (tawk-), a. Fond of talking. Hence ~NESS n. [ME; -ATIVE]

ta′lkee-ta′lkee (tawkĭ), n. Incessant chatter; broken English of Negroes etc. [TALK]

ta′lkie (tawkĭ), n. (sl.). = SOUND²-*film*. [f. TALK, after MOVIES]

ta′lking (tawk-), a. In vbl senses, esp.: having the power of speech, as ~ *parrot*; expressive, as ~ *eyes*. [-ING²]

tall (tawl), a. & adv. **1**. (Of person) of more than average height; (of tree, steeple, mast, etc.) higher than the average or than surrounding objects; of specified height, as *he is six feet* ~ (now usu. *high*), *how* ~ *is it?*; ~*′boy*, || bedroom chest of drawers 5 ft or more high sometimes in lower & upper sections or mounted on legs or on dressing-table, kind of chimney-pot; (sl.) extravagant, boastful, excessive, as *a* ~ *story*, ~ *talk*, *a* ~ *order* (exorbitant or unreasonable demand). **2**. adv. (sl.). In a ~ way, as *talk* ~, boast. Hence ~′NESS n. [prob. repr. OE *getæl* swift, prompt]

tall′(i)age, n. (hist.). Form of taxation abolished in 14th c. [ME & OF *taillage* (*tailler* cut, see TAIL² & -AGE)]

tăll′ith, n. Scarf worn by Jews esp. at prayer. [Heb.]

tăll′ow (-ō), n., & v.t. **1**. Substance got by melting the harder & less fusible kinds of (esp. animal) fat, used for making candles & soap, greasing machinery, etc.; *vegetable* ~, kinds of vegetable fat similarly used; ~*-chandler*, maker, vendor, of ~ candles so ~ER¹ (-ŏer) n.; ~*-drop*, style of cutting precious stones with dome on one or both

sides; ~*-face*, pale person; ~*-tree*, kinds of tree yielding vegetable ~. Hence ~ISH¹, ~Y² (-ŏi), aa. **2**. v.t. Grease with ~; fatten (sheep). [ME *talg*(h), MLG (G) *talg*, MIcel. *tōlg, tōlk*; ult. orig. unkn.]

tăll′y, n., & v.t. & i. **1**. Piece of wood scored across with notches for the items of an account & then split into halves of which each party kept one; account so kept, score, reckoning; mark made to register a fixed number of objects delivered or received, such number used as unit, as *buy goods by the* ~ (dozen, hundred, etc.); (in counting goods aloud as delivered) *16, 18,* ~ (20), *96, 98,* ~ (100); ticket, label of wood or metal or paper with name etc. attached to thing for identification, as *horticultural tallies*, plant labels; corresponding thing, counterpart, duplicate, (*of*). **2**. || ~*man*, one who keeps a ~ or ~-shop, one who sells goods by sample; ~*-sheet*, paper on which ~ is kept; || ~*-shop*, conducted on ~ system; || ~ *system, trade* (of sales on short credit with account kept by ~). **3**. vb. Record, reckon, by ~; (naut.) haul (sheet) taut; agree, correspond, (*with*), as *goods do not* ~ *with invoice.* Hence **tăll′iER¹** n. [ME, f. AF *tallie* (= OF *taille*, whence doublet obs. *tail* = TALLY), f. L *talea*, see TAIL²]

tăll′y-hō′, int., n., & v.t. & i. **1**. Huntsman's cry to hounds on viewing fox. **2**. vb. Utter, urge (hounds) with, this. [cf. F *talaut*]

tăl′ma, n. Woman's or man's long cape or cloak in first half of 19th c. [F. J. *T*~, French tragedian, d. 1826)]

tăl′mi-gŏld, n. Brass thinly coated with gold. [f. G *talmi*(*gold*)]

Tăl′mud, n. Body of Jewish law & legend comprising the Mishnah (precepts of the elders codified *c.* 200 A.D.) & the Gemara (commentary on the Mishnah in recensions at Jerusalem *c.* 400 & at Babylon *c.* 500), (also, in limited sense) the Babylonian Gemara. Hence **Tălmŭd′IC(AL)** aa. [late Heb., ~ instruction]

Tăl′mud|ist, n. Compiler, adherent, of (now usu.) student, of the Talmud. Hence ~** is′tic** a. [-IST]

tăl′on, n. **1**. Claw esp. of bird of prey. **2**. Cards left after deal. **3**. Shoulder of bolt against which key presses in shooting it; ogee moulding; heel of sword-blade. Hence (-)~ED² (-nd) a. [ME, f. OF, = heel, f. Rom. *talo -onis* f. L *talus*]

taluk′ (-ōōk), -ōōk, n. District in India subject to revenue collection by native officer; tract of proprietary land in India; ~*dar*, such officer, proprietor of ~. [Hind. *ta′alluq*]

tāl′us, n. (pl. -*lī*). **1**. (Anat.) ankle(-bone); form of club-foot. **2**. Slope of wall that tapers to the top or rests against bank; (geol.) sloping mass of fragments at foot of cliff. [L, = ankle, heel; sense 2 f. F *talus* of unkn. orig.]

tamán'dūa, tăm'anoir (-wâr), nn. Kinds of ant-eater. [(-*ua*) Braz., (-*oir*) F corrupt.]

tăm'arăck, n. Kinds of Amer. tree, esp. = HACKMATACK. [Amer.-Ind.]

tăm'arin, n. Kinds of S.-Amer. marmoset. [F, f. native name]

tăm'arínd, n. (Tropical tree with) fruit whose pulp is used in making cooling drinks etc.; ~-*fish*, preparation of fish with ~ pulp. [ult. f. Arab. *tamr-hindi* date of India]

tăm'arisk, n. Kind of plant, esp. *common* or *French* ~, evergreen shrub with feathery branches & white or pink flowers suitable for planting near sea. [ME, f. LL *tamariscus*, L *tamarix*]

tama'sha (-mah-), n. (Anglo-Ind.). A show or entertainment or function. [Arab.]

tăm'bour (-oor), n., & v.t. **1.** Drum; circular frame on which silk etc. is stretched to be embroidered, stuff so embroidered; (archit.) cylindrical stone in shaft of column, circular part of various structures, ceiled lobby with folding doors in church porch etc. to obviate draught; kinds of fish making drumming noise or like drum in shape; (fortif.) palisaded defence for road, gate, etc. **2.** v.t. Decorate, embroider, (stuff or abs.) on ~. [F, later f. *tabour* TABOR]

tăm'bourin (-bor-), n. .Long narrow drum used in Provence; (music for) dance accompanied by this. [F, dim. of prec.]

tămbourine' (-borēn), n. **1.** Small drum made of wooden or metal hoop with parchment stretched over one end & loose jingling metal discs. **2.** Kind of African pigeon. [cf. prec.]

tāme, v.t., & a. **1.** Make gentle & tractable, domesticate, break in, (wild beast, bird, etc.); subdue, curb, reduce to submission, humble, (person, spirit, courage, ardour, etc.). Hence **tăm(e)a-** **BIL'ITY, tăm(e)'ableness,** (-)**tāmer**[1], nn., **tăm(e)'able,** ~'**less** (-ml-; poet.), aa. **2.** adj. Made tractable, domesticated, not wild, (~ *cat*, fig., person tolerated as useful hanger-on); (colloq., of land or plant) cultivated, produced by cultivation; submissive, spiritless, inert, feeble, flat, insipid, as *the~st of slaves*, ~ *acquiescence*, *scenery*, *description*. Hence ~'**LY** (-ml-) adv., ~'**NESS** (-mn-) n. [OE *tam*, OHG *zam*, ON *tamr* f. Gmc **tamaz* cogn. w. L *domare*; (vb) ME *tame* f. adj.]

Tăm'il, n. Language, member, of a people inhabiting S. India & Ceylon. Hence **Tamil'IAN** a. [native]

Tămm'anў, n. Organization of democratic party in ~ *Hall*, New York (often implying political corruption). Hence ~'**ISM** n.

tăm-o'-shăn'ter, tămm'ў, n. Round woollen or cloth cap fitting closely round brows but large & full above. [f. Burns's *Tam o' Shanter*]

tămp, v.t. Pack (blast-hole) full of clay etc. to get full force of explosion, whence ~'**ING**[1](3) n.; ram down (road material etc.). Hence ~'**ER**[1] (1, 2) n., (also) bricklayer's tool. [perh. back form. f. *lampin* (var. of TAMPION) taken as = *tamping*]

tăm'păn, n. Venomous S.-Afr. tick. [native]

tăm'per, v.i. ~ *with*: meddle with; make unauthorized changes in (will, MS., etc.); exert secret or corrupt influence upon, bribe. Hence ~**ER**[1] n. [var. of TEMPER]

tăm'pion, n. Wooden stopper for muzzle of gun; plug e.g. for top of organ-pipe. [15th c. -*on*, -*ion*, f. F *tampon*, nasalized var. of *tapon*; see TAP[1], -OON]

tăm'pon, n., & v.t. **1.** Plug used to stop haemorrhage; pad for the hair. **2.** v.t. Plug (wound etc.) with ~. [F, see prec.]

tămponade', n. Use of tampon for wound etc. So **tăm'ponAGE, tăm'ponMENT,** nn. [-ADE]

tamtam. See TOMTOM.

tăn[1], v.t. & i. (-nn-), n., & a. **1.** Convert (raw hide) into leather by soaking in liquid containing tannic acid or by use of mineral salts etc., whence ~n'**ABLE** a., ~n'**AGE**(3), ~n'**er**[1] [-ER[1](1)], ~n'**ERY**(2, 3), nn.; make, become, brown by exposure to sun; treat (imitation marble, fish-nets, etc.) with hardening process; (sl.) beat, thrash. Hence ~n'**ING**[1](1) n. **2.** n. Bark of oak or other tree bruised & used for ~ning hides; colour of this, yellowish--brown; the bronze of sunburnt skin; *the* ~ (sl.), the circus, floor of riding-school; (also *spent* ~) ~ from which tannic acid has been extracted, used for covering roads etc.; ~-*balls* (of spent ~, used for fuel); ~-*liquor*, -*ooze*, -*pickle*, liquid used in ~ning; ~-*yard*, ~nery. **3.** adj. Of ~ colour; BLACK[1] *& ~*. [(vb) late OE *tannian*, f. med. L *tan(n)are* f. *tan(n)um*; (n.) *c.* 1600, prob. f. F *tan*, = med. L *tan(n)um*, prob. f. Celt. orig., cf. Bret. *tann* oak]

tan[2]. See TANGENT.

ta'na (tah-), **tănn'a,** n. Military post, police-station, in India; *tan(n)adar*, chief officer of this. [f. Hind. *thāna*]

tăn'ag|er, n. Kinds of Amer. birds of finch family & mostly of brilliant plumage. Hence ~**rINE**[1], ~**ROID,** aa. [f. Braz. *tangara*]

Tăn'agra (or tanăg[2]), n. City of Boeotia in ancient Greece; (in full, ~ *statuette*, *figurine*) terracotta statuette found, or of the type found, in tombs near ~.

tăn'děm, adv., n., & a. **1.** (Of horses in harness) one behind another; *drive* ~ (with horses so harnessed). **2.** n. (Carriage with) horses ~; bicycle or tricycle with seats for two or more one behind another. **3.** adj. (Of bicycle) so arranged. [L, = at length (of time), used punningly]

tăng[1], n., & v.t. **1.** Point, projection, esp. part of chisel etc., that goes into handle. **2.** Strong taste or flavour, characteristic property, whence ~'Y² (-ngĭ) a. **3.** v.t. Furnish or affect with a ~. [ME, f. ON *tangi* point]

täng², n. Kinds of seaweed. [16th c., f. Scand., = Norw., Da., Færoese *tang*, Icel. *thang*]

täng³, v.t. & i., & n. **1.** Ring, twang, sound loudly, (t. & i.); induce (bees) to settle by striking pieces of metal together. **2.** n. Twang. [imit.]

tän'gent (-j-), a. & n. **1.** Meeting a line or surface at a point but not (when produced if necessary) intersecting it. **2.** n. Straight line ~ to a curve at any point; *fly, go, off at a ~*, diverge impetuously from matter in hand or from normal line of thought or conduct; (trig., abbr. *tan*) ~ *of an angle*, ratio of the perpendicular subtending it in any right-angled triangle to the base. **3.** ~-*balance* (showing weight by position of beam as shown on graduated arc). Hence **tän'gency** n., **tängën'tIAL** (-jĕnshl) a., **tängën'tIALLY²** adv. [f. L *tangere* touch, see -ENT]

Tängerine' (-jerĕn), a. & n. (Native) of Tangier; ~ (*orange*), small flattened kind. [f. *Tanger, Tangier* +-INE¹]

tän'ghin (-nggĭn), n. Madagascar tree the fruit of which has poisonous kernel formerly used in ordeals. [F, f. native *tangena*]

tän'g|ible (-j-), a. Perceptible by touch; definite, clearly intelligible, not elusive or visionary, as ~*ible advantages, scheme, distinction*; (law) corporeal. Hence or cogn. ~IBIL'ITY, ~IBLENESS, nn., ~IBLY² adv. [F, or f. LL *tangibilis* (*tangere* touch, see -BLE)]

tangle¹ (täng'gl), v.t. & i., & n. **1.** Intertwine (threads, hair, etc.), become involved, in confused mass; entrap, entangle; 'complicate, as *a* ~*d affair*; **~foot* (sl.), whisky or intoxicants. **2.** n. Confused mass of intertwined threads etc.; confused state, as *skein, business, is in a* ~; device used in dredging for delicate forms of marine life. Hence ~SOME, **täng'lY²** (-ngg-), aa. [ME var. of obs. *tagle*, prob. of Scand. orig.; cf. Sw. dial. *taggla* disarrange; 17th c. n. f. vb]

tangle² (täng'gl), n. = TANG².

täng'ō (-ngg-), n. (pl. ~s), & v.i. A S.-Amer. dance; (v.i.) dance the ~. [Sp.]

tän'gram (-ngg-), n. Chinese puzzle square cut into seven pieces to be combined into various figures. [orig. unkn.]

tän'ist, n. (hist.). Successor apparent to Celtic chief, usu. most vigorous adult of his kin. [f. Ir. *tánaiste* heir]

tän'istrў, n. Celtic mode of tenure according to which a lord's successor was chosen from his family by election (abolished in Ireland under James I). [-RY]

tänk, n. **1.** Large metal or wooden vessel for liquid, gas, etc.; part of locomotive tender containing water for boiler; (E.-Ind.) storage-pond, reservoir for water. **2.** (mil.). Armoured motor vehicle mov-

ing on caterpillar tracks & mounted with guns (~*-buster*, sl., aircraft with anti-~ cannon). **3.** ~ *drama* (theatr. sl.), sensational drama in which water is used for representing rescue from drowning etc.; ~ *engine*, railway engine carrying fuel & water receptacles on its own frame, not in tender. [cf. Gujerati *tänkh*; partly f. Port. *tanque* f. L *stagnum* pool]

tänk'age, n. (Charge for) storage in tanks; cubic content of tank(s); kind of fertilizer got from refuse fats etc. [-AGE]

tänk'ard, n. Large drinking-vessel usu. of silver or pewter & often with cover; contents of, amount held by, this, as *a* ~ *of ale*; COOL¹ ~; ~ *turnip*, kinds with oblong root usu. rising high above ground. [ME, = (M)Du. *tankaert*; orig. unkn.]

tänk'er, n. Ship with tank(s) for carrying liquids, esp. mineral oils, in bulk; road vehicle with large tank for conveying milk etc. in bulk; aircraft for refuelling other aircraft in air. [-ER¹]

tanner¹. See TAN¹.

‖ **tänn'er²**, n. (sl.). A sixpence. [orig. unkn.]

tänn'|ic, a. Of tan; ~*ic acid* (also ~IN n.), astringent substance got chiefly from bark etc. of oak & other trees & used in preparing leather & writing-ink & in medicine. So ~ATE¹(3) n. (chem.), ~IF'EROUS a. [f. *tannin* (F, *tan* +-IN) +-IC]

tanrec. See TENREC.

tän'sy (-zI), n. Herb with yellow flowers & finely-toothed bitter aromatic leaves used in medicine & cookery. [ME, f. OF *tanesie* f. med. L f. Gk *athanasia* immortality (*a*- not +*thanatos* death)]

tän'taliz|e, -is|e (-Iz), v.t. Torment, tease, (person etc.) with hopes that seem continually on point of fulfilment or with object almost within his grasp or with imperfect information etc. Hence ~A²-TION n., ~ingLY² adv. [f. TANTALUS +-IZE]

tän'talum, n. A rare white metallic element highly resistant to heat & to action of acids. [f. foll. w. ref. to its non-absorbent quality +-UM]

Tän'talus, n. **1.** (Gk myth.). Son of Zeus condemned in Tartarus to stand up to chin in water that receded whenever he stooped to drink. **2.** (*t*~). Kinds of ibis; spirit-stand in which decanters are locked up but visible. **3.** ~*-cup*, toy cup containing figure of man illustrating principle of siphon. [L, f. Gk *Tantalos*]

tän'tamount, a. Equivalent, as *his message was* ~ *to a flat refusal*. [orig. as vb, f. AF *tant amunter* AMOUNT to so much ·(*tant* f. L *tantus* so great)]

täntär'a, n. Succession of notes on trumpet or horn. [imit.]

täntiv'ў, n., a., adv., & v.i. (arch.). **1.** Hunting cry; swift movement, gallop, rush. **2.** adj. Swift. **3.** adv. Swiftly. **4.** v.i. Hurry, rush. [perh. imit. of hoof-strokes]

tăn'tra, n. Each of a class of Sanskrit religious works dealing chiefly with magic. Hence **tăn'trɪsм(3), tăn'trɪsт(2),** nn. [Skr., =loom, groundwork, doctrine]

tăn'trum, n. Display of temper or petulance, as *is in, went into, her~s.* [18th c., of unkn. orig.]

Taoiseach (tē'shăkh), n. Official title of Prime Minister of Eire. [Ir., = chief, leader]

Taoism (tah'ō-, tow²), n. Religious doctrine of Lao-tsze, Chinese philosopher (c. 500 B.C.). [f. Chin. *tao* way + -ɪsм]

tăp¹, n., a., & v.t. (-pp-). **1.** ‖ Cock through which liquid is drawn from cask or flows from pipe; plug used to close opening in cask; liquor of a particular brewing etc. w. ref. to quality, as *an excellent ~, you know the ~; =~room, as found him in the ~;* instrument for cutting threads of internal screws; *on ~,* (of cask) furnished with ~, (of liquor) in such cask, ready to be drawn, also fig., ‖ (of Treasury bills etc.) obtainable when & as required at a fixed rate; *~-borer,* auger for boring tapering hole in cask; ‖ *~'room* (in which liquor is sold & drunk); *~-root,* chief descending root of plant. **2.** v.t. Furnish (cask) with cock; pierce (cask etc.) to let out liquid, let out thus; (surg.) give vent to (fluid accumulated in body), operate thus on (person); draw sap from (tree) by cutting into it; penetrate to, get into communication with, establish trade etc. in, (district etc.); apply to, solicit, (person *for*); broach (subject); divert part of current from (telegraph wires etc.) to intercept message; make internal screw-thread in. [OE *tæppa*, OHG *zapfo*, ON *tappi* f. Gmc **tappon*; vb f. OE *tæppian*]

tăp², v.t. & i. (-pp-), & n. **1.** Strike lightly, as *~ the door with your knuckles, pavement with your stick, ~ped his forehead knowingly;* cause (thing) to strike lightly against etc., as *~ped his stick against the window;* strike gentle blow, rap, (*at door* etc.); apply leather to (heel of shoe). **2.** n. Light blow, rap; sound of this, as *heard a ~ at the door;* (pl.) men's dinner-call in barracks, *signal on drum or trumpet for lights to be put out in soldiers' quarters; *~-dancing,* stage-dancing characterized by rhythmical *~ping* of the feet. [ME *tappe,* imit., perh. thr. F *taper*]

ta'pa (tah-), n. Bark of a tree used in Pacific islands for clothes, mats, etc. [native]

tāpe, n., & v.t. 1. Narrow cotton or linen strip used for tying up parcels & in dressmaking etc. (RED); *such strip stretched across racing-track between winning-posts, as *breast the ~,* win race; narrow band of strong fabric rotating on pulleys etc. in machinery; continuous strip of paper in receiving instrument of recording telegraph; (also *magnetic ~*), metal strip or ribbon for the electromagnetic recording & reproduction of signals;

= *~-measure,* ~worm. **2.** *~-line, -measure,* strip of ~ or thin flexible metal marked for use as measure, & often coiled up in cylindrical case; *~ recorder,* apparatus for recording sounds etc. on magnetic ~ and afterwards reproducing them (*~ recording,* such reproduction); *~'worm,* kinds of ~-like many-jointed worm infesting alimentary canal of man & most vertebrates. Hence *~'LESS a.* **3.** v.t. Furnish, tie up, with ~; join sections of (book) with bands of ~; *have person ~d* (sl.), have summed him up. [OE *tæppa, -e,* ME *tappe, tāpe,* of unkn. orig.]

tāp'er, n., a., & v.i. & t. 1. Slender candle, wick coated with wax etc. **2.** adj. (now chiefly poet. or rhet.). Growing gradually smaller towards one end like cone or pyramid, as *~ fingers,* whence *~NESS* n., *~WISE* adv. **3.** vb. (Often *~ off*) make or become ~, (cause to) grow gradually less, as *the upper part ~s* or *is ~ed off to a point,* whence *~ingLY² adv.* [OE *tapur, -or, -er* wax candle; not in cogn. langg.; perh. f. Rom. **papyrus* wick]

tăp'ĕstr‖ў, n. Textile fabric in which woof is supplied with spindle instead of shuttle, with design formed by stitches across warp, used for covering walls, furniture, etc.; *Bayeux ~y,* ancient roll of linen representing scenes in life of William I preserved at Bayeux; *Russian ~y,* stout linen or hemp stuff used for blinds etc. Hence (-)*~ɪED²* (-rĭd) a. [15th c. alt. f. *tapissery* f. OF *tapisserie* (TAPIS, -ERY)]

tăpiŏc'a, n. Starchy substance in hard white grains got by heating cassava & used for puddings etc. [Port., Sp., F. f. Braz. *tipioca (tipi* dregs, *og, ók* squeeze out)]

tāp'ir (*-er*), n. Hoofed swinelike mammal with short proboscis, allied to rhinoceros. Hence *~OID* (-er-) a. & n. [f. Braz. *tapira*]

tāp'is (-ē, -ĭs), n. (Of subject) *be, come, on the ~* (under consideration or discussion). [15th c., f. OF *tapiz* f. LL f. Gk *tapēlion* dim. of *tapēs -ētos*]

tapôte'ment (-tm-), n. (med.). Percussion as part of massage treatment. [F (*lapoter* to tap, -MENT)]

tăpp'ĕt, n. Arm, collar, cam, etc., used in machinery to impart intermittent motion; *~ loom,* (in which hammers are worked by *~s*). [app. f. TAP² + -ET¹]

‖ **tăpp'ĭt, a.** (Sc.). *~ hen:* crested hen; large drinking vessel with knob on lid. [= *topped* p.p. of TOP²]

‖ **tăp rāte, n.** (financ.). Current rate for Treasury bills etc. [f. phr. *on* TAP²]

tăp'ster, n. Person employed at a bar to draw & serve liquor. [OE *tæppestre,* orig. fem. (TAP¹, -STER)]

tapu. See TABOO.

tār¹, n., & v.t. (-rr-). **1.** Dark viscid liquid got by dry distillation of wood, coal, etc., & used as preservative of timber & iron, antiseptic, etc.; *a touch of the ~ -brush,* admixture of Negro blood as shown by colour of skin; ~-*board*, stout millboard of ~-red rope etc.; ~ *macad'am*, road-materials of stone or slag with ~; ~-*sealed* (New Zealand), surfaced with ~ macadam, so ~-*seal* n.; ~-*water*, cold infusion of ~ used as medicine, also, tarry ammoniacal water obtained in gas-manufacture. **2.** v.t. Cover with ~; ~ *& feather*, smear with ~ & then cover with feathers as punishment; ~*red with the same brush* or *stick*, having the same faults. [OE *teru*, MLG *ter(e)*, ON *tjara*, f. Gmc *terwa-* f. *trew-* TREE]

tar², n. (Also *Jack* ~) sailor. [abbr. of TARPAULIN]

tă'radiddle, tarra-, n. (colloq.). Fib, lie. [cf. DIDDLE]

tăr'a(-fèrn), n. Edible fern of New Zealand etc. [Tasmanian]

taraki'hi (tahrakē'hē), **ter-,** n. A New Zealand sea-fish. [Maori]

tărantăss', n. Springless four-wheeled Russian vehicle. [f. Russ. *tarantasu*]

tărantĕll'a, -ĕlle', n. (Music for) rapid whirling Ital. dance once held a cure for tarantism. [f. It. (-*la*) dim. as foll.]

tă'rantism, n. Dancing mania, esp. that originating in S. Italy among those who (thought they) had been bitten by the tarantula. [f. It. *Taranto* f. L *Tarentum*, S.-Ital. town, -ISM]

tarăn'tŭl|a, n. Large spider of S. Europe whose bite was formerly held to cause tarantism; other kinds of spider. Hence ~AR¹ a. [f. med. L -*ula*, It. -*ola*, as prec.]

tăratăn'tara (or -ăntăr'a), n. Sound of trumpet or bugle. [imit., cf. TANTARA]

tarăx'acum, n. Kinds of plant of aster family including dandelion; drug prepared from this. [med. L f. Arab. f. Pers.]

tărbōosh', n. Cap like fez. [f. Arab. *tarbūsh*]

tărdamĕn'tĕ, adv. (mus.). Slowly. [It.]

Tărdenois'ean (-z-), a. (archaeol.). Of the mesolithic period represented by remains in Tardenois, Aisne, France. [-EAN]

tărd'igrăde, a. & n. (zool.). Slow-moving (animal). [F, or f. L *tardigradus* (*tardus* slow + *gradi* walk)]

tărd'ō, a. & adv. (mus.). Slow(ly). [It.]

tărd'|y, a. Slow-moving, slow, sluggish; late, coming or done late, as ~*y retribution, amends, reform*; (of person etc.) reluctant, hanging back. Hence ~ĭLY² adv., ~ĭNESS n. [f. F *tardif*, -*ive* f. Rom. *tardivus* f. L *tardus* slow, see -IVE]

tăre¹, n. Kinds of vetch, esp. common vetch (in *Matt.* xiii. 25, 36, perh. = darnel). [ME, of unkn. orig.]

tăre², n., & v.t. **1.** Allowance made for weight of box etc. in which goods are packed, as *real, customary, average*, ~; weight of motor vehicle without fuel etc.; ~ *& tret*, arithmetical rule for computing ~ etc.; (chem.) weight of vessel in which substance is weighed. **2.** v.t. Ascertain weight of (box etc.). [15th c., f. OF, f.

med. L *tara* f. Arab. *tarḥah* what is rejected (*taraḥa* reject)]

tăr'ge. See foll.

tărg'ét (-g-), n. **1.** Circular stuffed pad with concentric circles painted on surface as mark in archery; similar usu. rectangular mark for fire-arms; anything that is fired at (also attrib., as ~ *area*); (fig.) objective, result aimed at, as *export, fuel, savings*, ~ (also attrib.); (fig.) person, thing, serving as mark *for* (scorn etc.). **2.** Circular railway signal e.g. at a switch. **3.** Neck & breast of lamb as joint. **4.** (Also *large* arch.) shield, buckler, esp. small round one, whence ~ED² a. **5.** ~-*card* (coloured like ~, for keeping archer's score); ~ *ship*, old ship used as ~. [ME, dim. of ME & OF *targe* f. OFrank. *targa* shield, cogn. w. OE *targe, -a*, OHG *zarga*, ON *targa*]

Tărg'|um, n. Each of various ancient Aramaic or Chaldee paraphrases of the Hebrew scriptures. Hence ~ŭm'ĭc, ~ŭmis'tĭc, aa., ~ŭmIST(3) n. [Chald., = interpretation, *targēm* interpret)]

tă'riff, n., & v.t. **1.** List of duties or customs to be paid on imports or exports; such duties collectively; law imposing these; duty on particular class of goods; *preferential* ~, reduced duties on imports from favoured country; *retaliatory* ~, import duties levied by a nation to balance foreign duties imposed on its exports; ~ *reform* (hist.), removal of inequalities etc. in ~ (|| esp. as name given by opponents of free trade in U.K. to their policy); ~ *wall*, ~-created national trade barrier; list of charges, as *railway, telegraph*, || *refreshment-room*, ~. **2.** v.t. Make ~ of duties on (goods); put a valuation on. [f. F *tarif* f. It. *tariffa* arithmetic, rate-book, f. Arab. *tar'if* notification (*'arafa* notify)]

tărl'atan, n. Thin kind of muslin. [f. F *tarlatane* earlier *larn-*, prob. of Ind. orig.]

tărm'ăc, n. = TAR¹ *macadam*; part of airfield surface made of ~. [abbr.; P]

tărn¹, n. Small mountain lake. [ME *terne* f. ON **tarnu, tjǫrn*]

tărn². [dial. form of TERN¹]

*tărn'al, *tărnä'tion, aa. & advv. (sl.). Confounded(ly). [dial. pron. of *eternal*; -*ation* on *damnation*]

tărn'ish, v.t. & i., & n. **1.** Lessen or destroy the lustre of, lose lustre, as *has been* ~*ed by damp, will* ~ *if exposed, does not easily* ~, (fig.) a ~*ed reputation*. **2.** n. Loss of lustre, blemish, stain; (mineral.) film of colour formed on exposed surface of mineral. Hence ~ABLE a. [f. F *ternir* (*terne* dark), see -ISH²]

ta'rō (tah-), n. (pl. ~*s*). Kinds of tropical plant of arum family with root used as food esp. in Pacific islands. [native]

tă'rŏc, -ot (-ō), n. Game played with, each card of, a pack of 78 cards. [f. It. *tarocchi*, F *tarot*, of unkn. orig.]

tărp'ăn, n. Wild horse of Tartary. [native]

tarpaul′in, n. Waterproof cloth esp. of tarred canvas; sheet of this as covering; sailor's tarred or oiled hat; (arch.) sailor. [prob. f. TAR + PALL¹ + -ING¹, as in *netting* etc.]

Tarpei′an (-pēan), a. ~ *rock*, cliff from which ancient-Roman criminals were hurled. [f. L *Tarpeius* of Tarpeia (who was buried at foot of ~ rock) + -AN]

tarp′on, n. Large game-fish common on south coast of U.S. [so Du. *tarpoen*; orig. unkn.]

tă′rradiddle. See tara-.

tă′rragon, n. Plant allied to wormwood & used in salads & in making ~ *vinegar*. [= med. L f. Byzantine Gk f. Arab. *ṭarchōn*, perh. f. Gk *drakōn* DRAGON]

Tărragŏn′a, n. Spanish wine like port. [~ in Spain]

tă′rras, n. See TRASS.

tă′rrock, n. Young kittiwake; common tern; guillemot. [orig. unkn.]

tăr′rў¹, a. Of, like, smeared with, tar. [-Y²]

tă′rrў², v.i. & t. (now literary). Remain, stay, lodge, (*at, in*, etc.); wait (often *for*); delay to come or appear, be late; wait for. [ME, orig. unascert.]

tărs′ia, n. Kind of mosaic woodwork. [It.]

tărs′ier, n. Small large-eyed nocturnal lemur. [F (foll., from structure of foot)]

tărs′|us, n. (pl. ~ī). 1. Collection of bones between lower leg & metatarsus, ankle; shank of bird's leg; (entom.) terminal segment of limb. 2. Plate of connective tissue in eyelid. Hence ~AL a., ~I-, ~O-, comb. forms. [mod. L, f. Gk *tarsos* flat of the foot]

tărt¹, a. Sharp-tasting, acid; cutting, biting, as *a* ~ *rejoinder*. Hence ~LY² adv., ~NESS n. [OE *teart*, of unkn. orig.]

tărt², n., & v.t. & i. 1. ‖ Pie containing fruit, as *apple, cherry*, ~; *jam* ~, piece of pastry with jam on top. 2. (sl.). Girl, woman, esp. of immoral character. So ~′LET n. 3. vb. ~ *up*, dress up like a ~, deck gaudily; (fig.) smarten up. [ME & OF *tarte* = med. L *tarta*, of unkn. orig.]

tărt′an¹, n. & a. Woollen fabric with stripes of various colours crossing at right angles esp. as worn by Scottish Highlanders; (other fabric) so striped, as *silk* ~, ~ *velvet*; Scottish plaid with distinctive pattern of a clan. [*c.* 1500, perh. f. OF *tertaine, tiretaine*]

tărt′an², n. Kind of single-masted vessel used in Mediterranean. [f. F *tartane* f. It. *tartana*]

tărt′ar¹, n. Pink or red deposit from completely fermented wine, forming hard crust on side of cask, whence tărtă′rIC, ~OUS, aa. (chem.), ~ĪZA′TION n., ~IZE(5) v.t.; CREAM¹.*of* ~; incrustation of saliva, calcium phosphate, etc., forming on the teeth; ~ *emetic*, double tartrate of potassium & antimony used as emetic, purgative, etc. [ME, f. OF *tartre* f. med. L f. med. Gk *tartaron*]

Tărt′ar², **Ta′tar** (tah-), a. & n. 1. (Native) of Tartary, (member) of a group of peoples including Turks, Cossacks, etc., so **Tărtăr′ian** a. 2. (*Tar*-) intractable or savage person (*catch a* ~, meet with person who is more than a match for one). [ME *tartre* f. OF *tartare* or med. L *Tartarus*; in Pers. *Tātār*, perh. the native form, whence *Tar*-, the usu. spelling, by assoc. w. TARTARUS]

tăr′tar(e) sauce, n. A savoury sauce containing mayonnaise, chopped gherkins, etc. [F *sauce tartare*]

Tărt′arus, n. (Gk myth.). Abyss below Hades where Titans were confined; place of punishment in Hades. So **Tărtăr′ēAN** a. [L, f. Gk *Tartaros*]

tărt′rate, n. Salt of tartaric acid. [f. TARTAR¹ + -ATE¹]

Tărtuf(f)|e′ (-ōof), n. Religious hypocrite. Hence ~ISM n. [character in Molière's ~*e*]

Tăr′zan, n. Man of great agility and powerful physique. [name of a white man reared by African apes, in stories by E. R. Burroughs (d. 1950)]

task (tah-), n., & v.t. 1. Piece of work imposed; lesson to be learnt at school, as *has done his* ~; a work voluntarily undertaken, as *an arduous* ~, *undertook the* ~ *of classification*; *take* person *to* ~, accuse him of fault, rebuke him *for* (*doing*); *~ force*, specially organized unit for a special ~; *~′master, -mistress*, one who imposes ~. 2. v.t. Assign ~ to; exact labour from, put strain upon, tax, (*powers, intellect*, etc.). [ME, f. ONF *tasque* = OF *tasche* f. med. L *tasca*, perh. metath. f. *taxa* TAX]

Tăsmān′ian (-z-), a. & n. (Inhabitant) of Tasmania; ~ *devil*, DASYURE peculiar to the island; ~ *wolf*, nocturnal carnivorous wolflike marsupial. [after Abel *Tasman*, discoverer in 1642]

‖ tăss¹, n. (Sc.). Small draught (*of* brandy etc.). [15th c., f. OF *tasse* cup f. Arab. *ṭass* basin]

Tăss², n. Telegraph agency of the Soviet Union. [f. initials of Russian title]

tăss′el, n., & v.t. (-ll-). 1. Tuft of loosely hanging threads or cords as ornament for cushion, cap, etc.; ~-like head of some plants, esp. staminate inflorescence at top of stalk of Indian corn; ribbon sewn into book to be used as bookmark; = TORSEL. 2. v.t. Furnish with ~; remove ~s of (Indian corn) to strengthen plant. [ME, f. OF *tasel, tassel*, of unkn. orig.]

tăste¹, v.t. & i. 1. Learn flavour of (food etc., or abs.) by taking it into the mouth, as ~ *this cheese, he* ~s *teas* (professionally) *for Smith & Co.* 2. Eat small portion of ~ of (esp. after negative), as *must just* ~ *a snack, has not* ~d *food for 3 days.* 3. Perceive the flavour of, as *can* ~ *nothing when you have a cold, fancy I* ~ *garlic*. 4. (arch.). Relish, enjoy, as *cannot* ~ *a joke against himself*. 5. Experience, have experience *of*, as *shall not* ~ (*of*) *death,* *has never ~d (of) success.* 6. (Of food etc., or fig.) have a flavour *of*, smack *of*, as *~s of mint, his writings ~ of the schools.* Hence **tāst'**ABLE a. [ME, = touch, taste, f. OF *taster* touch, taste, f. Rom. **tastare*, f. **taxitare* f. L *taxare* touch, TAX]

tāste², n. 1. Sensation excited in certain organs of mouth by contact of some soluble things, flavour, as *cannot endure the ~ of onions, white of egg has no ~.* 2. Sense by which ·this is perceived. 3. (rare). Act of tasting. 4. Small portion (*of* food etc.) taken as sample (*give him a ~ of the whip*, enough to show how it feels). 5. Liking, predilection, *for*, as *has no ~ for sweet things, a ~ for drawing, scenery, argument, is not to my ~* (liking), *~s differ, there is no accounting for ~s,* add *pepper* etc. *to ~* (to the amount desired). 6. Faculty of discerning & enjoying beauty or other excellence esp. in art & literature, as *is a man of ~, true, false, ~.* 7. Disposition or execution of work of art, choice of language, conduct, etc., dictated by or seen in the light of this faculty, as *composed in admirable ~, the remark was in bad ~.* [ME, f. OF *tast*, f. *taster*, as prec.]

tāste'ful (-tf-), a. (Of person, work of art, etc.) having, showing, done in, good taste. Hence ~LY² adv., ~NESS n. [-FUL]

tāste'less (-tl-), a. Having no flavour; insipid; lacking the physical sense of taste; lacking artistic taste; (of language, conduct, etc.) not in good taste. Hence ~LY² adv., ~NESS n. [-LESS]

tās'ter, n. In vbl senses, esp.: person employed to judge of teas, wines, etc., by taste; (fig.) publisher's reader; (hist.) person employed to taste food before it was touched by his employer; small cup used by wine-~; instrument for extracting small cylindrical sample from a cheese. [-ER¹]

tās't|ȳ, a. (colloq.). Savoury, of pleasant flavour; (now vulg.; of dress, decoration, etc.) in good taste. Hence ~ILY² adv. [-Y²]

tăt¹, v.i. & t. (-tt-). Do tatting; make by tatting. [orig. unkn.]

tăt², **tătt'ōō¹**, nn. (Anglo-Ind.). Pony. [f. Hind. *taṭṭu*]

ta-ta (tătah'), int. Good-bye.

Tatar. See TARTAR².

Tāte Găll'erȳ, n. London public gallery with permanent exhibition of pictures & sculpture by British & modern foreign artists. [Sir H. *Tate*, donor (d. 1899)]

tatou (tah'tōō), n. An armadillo. [Braz.]

tătt'er, n. Rag, torn piece, of cloth, paper, etc. (usu. in pl.); *~demāl'ion*, ragged person. Hence ~ED² (-*erd*)~Y², aa. [ME, of Scand. orig.; cf. ON *tǫturr* (f. **laturr*), pl. *tǫtrar* rags]

Tătt'ersall's (-z), n. (Used for) head-quarters of horse-dealing & betting rendezvous (*knows his ~ better than his Greek Testament*). [R. *Tattersall*, founder of firm (d. 1795)]

tătt'ing, n. Kind of knotted work used for trimmings etc. [orig. unkn.]

tăt'tle, v.i. & t., & n. 1. Prattle, chatter, gossip, whence **tătt'lingLY²** adv.; utter (words) idly. 2. n. Trivial talk. [imit.; cf. MFlem. *tatelen*, LG *tatein*, *täteln* gabble, cackle]

tătt'ler, n. 1. Prattler, gossip, (arch. *Tatler*, periodical of Steele & Addison). 2. Sandpiper. [f. prec.+-ER¹]

tattōō¹ (tatōō'), n., & v.i. 1. Beat of drum, or bugle-call, at 10 p.m. recalling soldiers to quarters, elaboration of this with music & marching as entertainment; *beat the devil's ~,* drum idly with fingers etc. 2. v.i. Rap quickly & repeatedly, beat the devil's ~. [17th c. *tap-too* f. Du. *taptoe*, lit. ' close the tap ' (of the cask)]

tattōō² (tatōō'), v.t., & n. 1. Mark (skin etc.) with indelible patterns by inserting pigments in punctures. 2. n. Such mark. [(n. f. vb) f. Tahitian *tatau* n.]

tătt'ȳ¹, n. (Anglo-Ind.). Matting of cuscus-grass hung & kept wet to cool & perfume the air. [f. Hind. *taṭṭi* wicker frame]

tătt'|ȳ², a. (orig. dial.). Ragged, shabby; fussily ornate. So ~ILY² adv., ~INESS n. [app. rel. to OE *tættec* rag, TATTER]

tau (taw, tow), n. Greek letter (*T, τ*) = **t**; kinds of fish etc. marked with or suggesting this; (attrib.). T-shaped, as *~ cross.* [Gk]

taught. See TEACH.

taunt¹, v.t., & n. 1. Reproach, upbraid, (person etc. *with* conduct etc.) contemptuously, whence *~'ingLY²* adv. 2. n. Contemptuous reproach, object of this, as *endured the ~s of*, became a *~ to, his neighbours.* [16th c., in phr. *taunt pour* (for) *taunt* f. F *tant pour tant* tit for tat, hence, smart rejoinder; hence vb]

‖ **taunt²**, a. (naut.). (Of mast) tall. [16th c., of unkn. orig.; cf. obs. *ataunt* adv. with all sails set]

taur'|īne, a. Bull-like, bovine, so ~IFORM a.; of the zodiacal sign Taurus. [f. L *taurinus* (*taurus* bull, see -INE¹)]

taurŏm'achy (-kǐ), n. Bull-fight(ing). [f. Gk *tauromakhia* (*tauros* bull + *makhē* fight)]

Taur'us, n. Zodiacal constellation, the Bull; second sign of zodiac. [L, = bull]

taut, a. (naut.). (Of rope) tight, not slack; (of vessel etc.) in good order or condition. Hence ~'EN⁵ v.t. & i., ~'LY² adv., ~'NESS n. [ME *togt*, perh. alt. f. *tigt* (TIGHT) after *togen* drawn, p.p. of obs. *tee* (OE *tēon* draw]

taut|o-, comb. form of Gk *tauto* = *to auto*, the same, as: *~'ochrōne* (-k-) [f. Gk *khronos* time], curve on which body starting from state of rest under gravity will reach lowest point in same time from whatever point it starts, so *~ŏch'ronism* (-k-) n., *~ŏch'ronous* (-k-) a.; *~ŏph'onȳ*, repetition of same sound.

tautŏl'og|ȳ, n. Saying of the same thing

twice over in different words (e.g. *arrived one after the other in succession*). Hence **tautolo′gic**(al) aa., **tautolo′gical**ly[2] adv., ~ist(1) n., ~ize(2) v.i. [f. LL f. Gk TAUTO(*logia* -LOGY)]

tăv′ern, n. Public house for supply of food & drink. [ME, f. OF *taverne* f. L *taberna* hut, tavern]

taw[1], v.t. Make (hide) into leather without use of tannin, esp. by soaking in solution of alum & salt. Hence ~′ER[1], ~′ERY(3), nn. [OE *tawian*, MDu., MLG *touwen*, OHG *zouwen* f. Gmc **taw-*, **tōw-*, (cf. Goth. *taujan* do, make)]

taw[2], n. Game at marbles; limit line in playing marbles; a marble. [*c.* 1700; of unkn. orig.]

tawd′r|y, a. & n. **1.** Showy but worthless, gaudy, having too much or ill-judged ornament, whence ~ily[2] adv., ~iness n. **2.** n. Cheap or excessive or tasteless finery. [as n., short for *tawdry lace*, orig. *St Audrey's lace*, f. *Audrey* = *Etheldrida*, patron saint of Ely]

tawn′|y, a. Brownish-yellow, tan-coloured. Hence ~iness n. [ME, f. AF *taune*, OF *tane* f. *tan* TAN[1]]

‖ **taws(e)** (-z-), n. sing. or pl. (Sc.). Slit thong for chastising children. [app. pl. of obs. *taw* tawed leather, see TAW[1]]

tăx[1], v.t. Impose tax on (subjects, citizens, etc., commodity, land, etc.), so ~a′tion n.; (N.T.) register (person) for purpose of imposing tribute; make demands upon, demand exertion from, (person's resources, powers, ingenuity, etc.); *cannot ~ my memory*, cannot undertake to recollect the facts wanted; (law) examine & (dis)allow items of (costs etc.); ‖ ~*ed* (also ~-) *cart*, two-wheeled cart usu. for agricultural or trade purposes on which only reduced duty (& later none) was charged; charge (person *with* fault, *with* doing); ‖ ~*ing-master*, law-court official who ~es costs. Hence ~abil′ity, ~′able**ness**, nn., ~′able a., ~′ably[2] adv. [ME, f. OF *taxer* f. L *taxare* censure, charge, compute, cf. TASK, TASTE[1]]

tăx[2], n. Contribution levied on persons, property, or business, for support of government, as DIRECT[2], INDIRECT, *capitation*, INCOME, *poll-*, PURCHASE[1], ~; strain, heavy demand, (*up*)*on* (person, his energies etc.); ‖ ~*-cart*, see prec.; ~*-collector*, official who collects ~es; ~*-farmer*, one who buys from government the right to collect certain ~es; ~*-free*, exempt from ~es; ~*-gatherer*, = ~*-collector*; ~′*payer*. Hence ~′LESS a. [ME, f. prec.]

tăx′i, n., & v.i. & t. **1.** Motor-cab plying for hire & fitted with taximeter (also ~-*cab*), other motor-car of similar pattern; ~-*man*, driver of ~. **2.** vb. Go or convey in ~; (aeron., of aircraft or pilot) go along ground or water under machine's own power before or after flying. [abbr. TAXI-METER]

tăx′iderm|y, n. Art of preparing & mounting skins of animals in lifelike manner. Hence **tăxiderm′al**, **tăxiderm′ic**, aa., ~ist(3) n. [f. TAXIS+DERM]

tăxim′eter, n. Automatic device fitted to cab & indicating fare due at any moment. [f. F *taximètre* (*taxe* tariff, TAX[2], -METER)]

tăx′in, n. Resinous substance from yew leaves. [f. L *taxus* yew+-IN]

tăx′is, n. (Surg.) manual pressure applied to restore parts to their place; (Gk ant.) various divisions of troops; (zool.) classification; (gram., rhet.) arrangement. [Gk, f. *tassō* arrange]

tăx|**on′omy**, n. (nat. hist.). (Principles of) classification. Hence or cogn. ~ol′ogy, ~on′om**ist**(3), nn., ~onom′ic(al) aa., ~onom′ical**ly**[2] adv. [f. F *taxonomie* (TAXIS+Gk -*nomia* distribution)]

tazza (taht′sa), n. Saucer-shaped cup esp. one mounted on a foot. [It.]

tchick, n., & v.i. (Make) sound produced by pressing tongue against roof of mouth & quickly withdrawing it, esp. as used in urging horse. [imit.]

tĕ. See SI.

tea, n., & v.i. & t. **1.** (Also ~-*plant*) shrub or small tree of camellia family grown in China, India, etc.; leaves of this dried & prepared for use (*black, green,* ~, prepared by different processes; *bohea, congou, souchong, pekoe*, etc., ~, kinds of black; *hyson, gunpowder*, etc., ~, kinds of green; *tile* ~, in BRICK form). **2.** Infusion or decoction of ~-leaves as beverage; infusion etc. of leaves of other plants or of other substance, as BEEF, CAMOMILE, ~. **3.** Light afternoon meal with ~; (also *high* ~, *meat* ~) solid evening meal with ~. **4.** ~-CADDY; ‖ ~-*cake*, kinds of cake or bun eaten toasted or otherwise at ~; ~-*chest*, light lead-lined wooden box in which ~ is exported; ~-*cloth* (for ~-table or -tray, also drying-cloth for cups etc.); ~′*cup*, cup in which ~ is drunk (*storm in a* ~*cup*, commotion in circumscribed circle or about trivial matter), (as measure, also ~′*cupful*) gill; ~-*fight* (colloq.), ~-*party*; ~-*garden* (in which ~ is served to the public); ~-*gown*, woman's loose gown worn at ~ etc.; ~-*house* (in which ~ etc. is served in China & Japan); ~-*kettle* (used in making ~); ~-*leaf*, leaf of ~ esp. (pl.) after infusion or soaking, used in sweeping floors; ~-*party* (at which ~ is served); ~′*pot*, vessel in which ~ is made; ~-*rose*, kinds with scent compared to that of ~; ~-*service, -set*, ~pot, cups, etc., used in serving ~; ~-SPOON; ~-*table* (often attrib., as ~-*table conversation*); ~-*things*, = ~-*set*; ~-*tray* (on which ~-set is used or carried); ~-*urn*, for boiling or holding water for ~. **5.** vb. Take ~, as *we ~ at* 4; give ~ to (person). [17th c. *tay, tee*, prob. f. Du. *thee* f. Chin. (Amoy dial.) *t'e*, = Mandarin dial. *ch'a*]

teach, v.t. & i. (*taught* pr. tawt). **1.** Enable or cause (person etc. *to* do) by instruction

& training, as ~ *him to swim, dog was taught to beg, misfortune has taught him to be thankful for small mercies, this* (punishment) *will ~ you to speak the truth,* (colloq.) *I will ~ him* (not) *to meddle in my affairs.* 2. Give lessons at school or elsewhere in or on (subject, game, instrument, etc., *to* person, or w. double object), as *taught him Greek, ~es Greek for a living, ~es the violin, ~ me bridge, was never taught music, music was never taught to a more unwilling pupil, it is time the boy was taught something;* *~ *school,* be a ~er in a school. 3. Give instruction to, educate; (intr.) be a ~er. 4. Explain, show, state by way of instruction, (fact etc., *how, that,* etc., *to* person or w. double obj.), as *taught that we must forgive our enemies, I was taught that two sides of a triangle were greater than the third, was taught otherwise, was never taught this, who taught you that?* Hence ~'ER¹, ~'erSHIP, nn. [OE *tǣc(e)an* f. Gmc *taikjan, f. **taik-* TOKEN]

teach'|able, a. Apt to learn, docile; (of subject etc.) that can be taught. Hence ~ABIL'ITY, ~ableNESS, nn. [-ABLE]

teach'ing, n. In vbl senses, esp. what is taught, doctrines, as *the ~s of the Church.* [ME; -ING¹]

teak, n. (E.-Ind. tree with) heavy durable timber that does not warp or shrink or corrode iron, much used in shipbuilding. [f. Port. *teca* f. Malayalam *tēkka*]

teal, n. (pl. same). Kinds of small freshwater duck. [ME *tele* (WG *taili), cf. MDu. *tēling*]

team, n., & v.t. 1. Two or more beasts of burden harnessed together, whence ~'WISE adv.; set of players on one side in some games e.g. football; set of persons working together; ~*-work,* combined effort, organized co-operation. 2. v.t. Harness (horses etc.) in ~; give out (work) to contractor who employs ~ of workmen, whence ~'ING¹ n. [OE. *tēam* family, offspring, corresp. to OS *tôm,* OHG *zoum,* ON *taumr,* f. Gmc *taumaz prob. f. **taug-* cogn. w. L *ducere,* cf. TOW¹]

team'ster, n. Driver of a team. [-STER]

teap'oy, n. Small three- or four-legged table esp. for tea. [f. Hind. *tin* three + Pers. *pāē* foot; sense & spelling influenced by TEA]

tear¹ (tār), v.t. & i. (*tore, torn*), & n. 1. Pull apart, rend, lacerate, as *tore up the letter, has torn his coat, ~ it in half, in two, in pieces, torn to pieces by a tiger,* (fig.) *country was torn by factions, heart torn by conflicting emotions;* make (hole, rent) thus; ~ *it* (sl.), spoil one's chances, foil one's plans, put the lid on (*that's torn it*); pull violently (lit. & fig.), as *tore down the notice, ~ out a page, ~ off the cover, tree torn up by the roots, was torn* (forcibly parted) *from her parents, babe torn from the breast, could not ~ myself* (make up my mind to go) *away;* pull violently *at,* as *tore at the cover of the parcel; ~ one's hair,*

pull it in anger or perplexity or despair; lend itself to ~ing, as ~s *easily, will not ~.* 2. Run or walk hurriedly or impetuously, as *tore down the hill, was simply ~ing.* 3. ~'*away,* (adj.) impetuous, (n.) street ruffian. 4. n. Rent in cloth etc. [OE *teran,* OHG *zeran,* Goth. *gatairan* f. Gmc **teran,* cogn. w. Gk *derō* flay]

tear² (tēr), n. (Also ~*-drop*) drop of saline liquid ordinarily serving to moisten & wash the eye but falling from it as result of grief or other emotion or of coughing or laughter, as *the ~s fell down her cheeks, wept bitter ~s of remorse, laughed till the ~s came, ~s were her only argument, a ~- -stained face, found her in ~s* (weeping); ~like thing, e.g. drop of fluid, solid drop of resin etc.; ~*s of strong wine,* drops forming on inside of partly-filled glass of port etc.; CROCODILE ~*s;* ~*-gas,* lachrymatory poison gas used in warfare; ~*-jerker* n. (colloq.), song, story, film, etc. calculated to evoke sadness or sympathy; ~*-jerking* a.; ~· (= LACHRYMA-TORY) *shell.* [OE *tēar,* OHG *zahar,* ON *tár,* Goth. *tagr,* cogn. w. L *lacrima* (OL *dac-*), Gk *dakru*]

tear'ful (tēr-), a. Shedding tears, so *tear-*LESS a.; (of event, news, etc.) mournful, sad. Hence ~LY² adv., ~NESS n. [-FUL]

tear'ing (tār-), a. In vbl senses (TEAR¹), also, violent, overwhelming (~ *pace, rage*). [-ING²]

teas|e (-z), v.t., & n. 1. Assail playfully or maliciously, vex, with jests, questions, or petty annoyances, whence ~'inGLY² (-z-) adv.; importune (person *for* thing, *to* do); pick into separate fibres, comb, card, (wool, flax, etc.); dress (cloth etc.) with teasels. 2. n. Person given to ~ing. [OE *tǣsan* = MDu. *tēsen,* MLG *tēsen,* OHG *zeisan* f. WG *taisjan]

teas'el (-z-), **-zel, -zle,** n., & v.t. 1. Kinds of plant with large prickly heads used in dressing cloth; such head; machine substituted for ~s. 2. v.t. Dress (cloth) with ~s, whence ~ER¹ (-zel-), teaz'ler, nn. [OE *tǣs(e)l* (as prec. +-LE)]

teas'er (-z-), n. In vbl senses, esp.: teasing person; (colloq.) difficult question or problem or task, thing hard to deal with. [-ER¹]

teat, n. Mammary nipple through which milk passes, pap of woman, dug of beast. Hence (-)~ED², ~'LIKE, aa. [ME *tete, tette* f. OF *tete,* replacing OE *tit(t),* mod. dial. *tit*]

tĕc, n. (sl.). Detective (novel). [abbr.]

techne'tium (tĕknē'shm), n. (chem.). Artificially produced radio-active metallic element. [f. Gk *teknētos* artificial f. *tekhnē* art, +-IUM²]

tĕch'nic (-k-), a. & n. 1. adj. (rare). = foll. 2. n. = TECHNIQUE; (usu. pl.) doctrine of arts in general; (pl.) technical terms, details, methods, etc. Hence techni'cian (tĕkni'shn) n., person skilled in the technique of a particular craft, or in ~s

Y

generally, ~IST n. [f. L f. Gk *tekhnikos* (*tekhnē* art, see -IC)]

tĕch'nical (-k-), a. Of or in a particular art, science, handicraft, etc., as ~ *terms*, *skill*, *difficulty*; of, for, in, the mechanical arts, as ~ *education*, *school*; legally such, in the eyes of the law, as ~ *assault*. Hence ~LY² adv., ~NESS n. [-AL]

tĕchnical'it|y̆ (-k-), n. Technicalness, technical expression, distinction, etc., as *legal* ~*ies*. [-ITY]

Technicolor (tĕk'nǐkŭler), n. (cinemat.). Process of colour photography in which the colours are separately but simultaneously recorded & then transferred to a single positive print; (fig.) vivid colour, artificial brilliance. Hence ~ED² (-erd) a. [P; f. TECHNI(CAL)+COLOUR]

technique (tĕknēk'), n. Mode of artistic execution in music, painting, etc.; mechanical skill in art. [F, as TECHNIC]

tĕchnŏc'racy (-k-), n. Organization and management of a country's industrial resources by technical experts for the good of the whole community. Hence **tĕch'noCRAT** (-k-) n., advocate of this. [f. Gk *tekhnē* art +-CRACY]

tĕchnŏl'og|y̆ (-k-), n. Science of the industrial arts; ethnological study of development of arts. Hence **tĕchnolŏ'gICAL** a., ~IST n. [f. Gk *tekhnologia* (*tekhnē* art, -LOGY)]

techy. See TETCHY.

tĕctŏl'ŏgy̆, n. Structural morphology, i.e. that which treats an organism as composed of organic individuals. Hence **tĕctolŏ'gICAL** a. [f. G *tektologie*, f. Gk *tektōn* carpenter +-LOGY]

tĕctŏn'ic, a. & n. 1. Of building or construction; (geol.) due to a change in structural conditions caused by deformation. 2. n. pl. Whole art of producing useful & beautiful buildings, furniture, vessels, etc. [f. LL f. Gk *tektonikos* (*tektōn* *-onos* carpenter, see -IC)]

tĕctŏr'ial, a. Forming a covering, esp. ~ *membrane* (of ear). [f. L *tectorius* (as foll., see -ORY)+-AL]

tĕctrī'cēs (-z), n. pl. (ornith.). Covering feathers of wings & tail. [f. L *tegere tectcover*, -TRIX]

tĕd, v.t. (-dd-). Turn over & spread out (grass, hay) to dry. Hence ~d'ER¹(1, 2) n. [ME, f. ON *tethja* spread manure, rel. to OHG *zetten*; cf. TOD¹]

Tĕdd'y̆, n. Pet-form of Christian name *Edward*; (colloq., also ~ or *t*~ *boy*) youth affecting a style of dress held to be characteristic of reign of Edward VII (1901–10); ~ *girl*, female counterpart in behaviour but not dress.

Tĕdd'y̆ bear (bār), n. Child's toy bear (named after *Theodore* Roosevelt, d. 1919).

Tĕ Dē'um, n. (Music for) hymn beginning ~ *laudamus*, 'Thee, God, we praise', sung at morning service, or on special occasions as thanksgiving; *sing* ~, (fig.) exult, triumph. [L]

tēd'ious, a. Wearisome, irksome, tiresome. Hence ~LY² adv., ~NESS n. [ME, f. LL *taediosus* (as foll., see -OUS)]

tēd'ium, n. Tediousness. [f. L *taedium* f. *taedēre* to weary]

tee¹, n. Letter T; T-shaped thing esp. pipe.

tee², n., & v.t. & i. 1. Mark aimed at in quoits, bowls, curling. 2. (golf). Cleared space from which the ball is struck at beginning of play for each hole (also ~*ing-ground*); small pile of sand or small appliance of wood, rubber, etc. on which ball is placed before being struck. 3. v.t. Place (ball) on ~; (v.i.) ~ *off*, start from ~, (fig.) start, begin. [f. (17th c.) *teaz*, of unkn. orig.]

tee³, n. Umbrella-shaped usu. gilded ornament crowning tope or pagoda. [f. Burm. *h'ti* umbrella]

teem¹, v.t. & i. ‖ (Arch.) bear (offspring); be prolific, be stocked to overflowing *with*, as *forests* ~ *with snakes*, *book* ~*s with blunders*; be abundant, as *fish* ~ *in these waters*. [OE *tīeman* etc., f. *taumjan* f. Gmc *taumaz* TEAM]

teem², v.t. (dial., tech.). Empty, discharge, pour out, (vessel, cart, coal, molten metal, etc.). Hence ~'ER¹ n. [ME *teme* f. ON *tœma* (*tómr* adj. empty)]

‖ **teen** n. (arch.). Grief; trouble; harm. [OE *tēona*, OS *tiono*, ON *tjón*]

-teen, an inflected form of TEN (OE **-*tiene*, -*tȳne*, -*tēne*) added to the numerals 3 to 9 to form the names of those from 13 to 19.

teens (-z), n. pl. (Also *teen age*, *years*) years of one's age from 13 to 19, esp. *in* one's ~; *teen-age* a., in the ~; *teen-ager*, person of this age.

teeny. See TINY.

teet'er, v.i., & n. (U.S. & dial.). 1. Seesaw; move unsteadily. 2. n. A seesaw. [var. of dial. *titter* totter]

teeth. See TOOTH.

teethe (-dh), v.i. Grow or cut teeth. Hence **teeth'ING¹** (-dh-) n. [f. prec.]

teetŏt'al, a. Of, advocating, total abstinence from intoxicants, as ~ *meeting*, *pledge*, whence ~ISM n.; (colloq.) total, entire, whence ~LY² adv. [redupl. of *total*; from about 1833]

teetŏt'aller, n. Total abstainer. [-ER¹]

teetŏt'um, n. Children's four-sided top with sides lettered to determine gain or loss of the spinner; any top spun with the fingers (*like a* ~, spinning). [f. T (the letter on one side)+L *totum* the whole (stakes), for which it stood]

tĕg, n. Sheep in its second year. [16th c., perh. Scand.; cf. OSw. *takka* ewe]

tĕg'ŭl|ar, a. Of or like tiles. Hence or cogn. ~arLY² adv., ~āted [-ATE²] a. [f. L *tegula* tile (*tegere* cover)+-AR¹]

tĕg'ūment, n. Natural covering of (part of) animal body. Hence ~AL, ~ARY¹, aa., (-ĕn⁴). [f. L *tegumentum* (*tegere* cover, see -MENT)]

tehee′, n., & v.i. **1.** Restrained or contemptuous laugh. **2.** v.i. Laugh thus, titter. [imit.]

Te′ian, Te′an, a. Of (the poet Anacreon born at) Teos. [f. L *Teius* (L f. Gk *Teŏs*) +-AN]

‖ **teind** (tēnd), n. (Sc.). Tithe. [ME *tende*, = TEN*th*]

tĕknŏn′ȳm|ȳ, n. (anthrop.). Practice of naming parent from child. So ~OUS **a.** [f. Gk *teknon* child + *-ōnumos* -named +-Y¹]

tĕlaesth|ēs′ia, n. (psych.). Direct perception of distant occurrences or objects not effected by the recognized senses. Hence ~ĕt′IC **a.** [mod. L, f. TELE-, Gk *aisthēsis* perception, & -IA¹]

tĕl′amon, n. (archit.; pl. ~*es* pr. -ōn′ēz). Male figure as bearing pillar (cf. CARYATID). [L, f. Gk *Telamōn* mythol. person]

tĕlaut′o|graph (-ahf), n. Telegraph that reproduces writing etc. So ~GRAM (5) **n.** [f. TELE- + AUTOGRAPH, after *telegraph*]

tĕle-, comb. form of Gk *tēle-* far, esp. in names of instruments producing or recording results etc. at a distance, as ~*barŏm′eter*, ~*thermŏm′eter*; (also) abbr. for TELEVISION, as *tĕl′ecast* n., television broadcast programme or item, also as v.t.; *tĕl′ecaster*, television broadcaster; *tĕl′efilm*, cinema film transmitted by television; ~*gĕn′ic*, suitable for being televised; ~*promp′ter*, electronic device that slowly unrolls (television) speaker's text, in large print, outside the sight of the audience:~*record′* v.t., record (item or programme to be televised);~*record′ing* n.

tĕlecommūnicā′tion, n. Communication at a distance, as by cable, telegraph, telephone, or radio; (also, freq. in pl.) means or channel of so communicating (also attrib.). [TELE-]

tĕl′edu (-ōō), n. Stinking badger of Java and Sumatra. [native]

tĕlĕg′onȳ, n. (biol.). Supposed influence of previous sire seen in subsequent sire's progeny by same mother. Hence tĕlegŏn′IC **a.** [f. TELE- + Gk *-gonia* begetting]

tĕl′ĕgräm, n. Telegraphic message. [-GRAM]

tĕl′ĕgraph¹ (-ahf), n. **1.** Apparatus for transmitting messages or signals to a distance esp. by electrical impulses. **2.** Semaphore. **3.** (In titles of newspapers) *Daily T*~ etc. **4.** ~ (-*board*), board on which numbers of horses running in race, cricket scores, etc., are put up so as to be visible at distance;~-*key*, device for making and breaking electric circuit of ~; ~-*line*, -*pole* or -*post*, -*wire* (used in forming telegraphic connexion); ~-*plant*, E.-Ind. plant whose leaves have spontaneous jerking motion. [f. F *télégraphe* (TELE-, -GRAPH)]

tĕl′ĕgraph² (-ahf), v.t. & i. Send (message *to* person, or abs.) by telegraph, as ~ *the news to your father*, ~ *me the result*, ~ *to him to come, that we cannot come*; make

signals (*to* person *to* do, *that*, etc.). [f. prec.]

tĕlĕg′raph|er (*or* tĕl′I-), n. Person skilled or employed in telegraphy. So ~IST **n.** [-ER¹]

tĕlĕgraphēse′ (-z), n. & **a.** (In) the elliptical style usual in telegrams. [-ESE]

tĕlĕgräph′|ic, a. Of telegraphs or telegrams; of ~*ic* brevity, economically worded, with unessential words omitted; ~*ic address*, abbreviated or other registered address for use in telegrams. Hence ~ICALLY adv. [-IC]

tĕlĕg′raphȳ, n. Art of constructing, practice of communicating by, telegraph; *wireless* ~, transmission of signals through space by means of electromagnetic waves. [-Y¹]

tĕlĕkinēs′is, n. (psych.). Movement at a distance from the motive cause or agent without material connexion. [mod. L, f. TELE- + Gk *kinēsis* motion (*kineŏ* move)]

tĕl′ĕmärk, n. Expert swing turn in skiing used to change direction or to stop short. [f. *T*~, district in Norway]

tĕlĕmĕchăn′ics (-k-), n. pl. Art of transmitting power by radio, & so controlling machinery from a distance. [TELE-]

tĕl′ĕmēter, v.i. & t. Record readings of an instrument at a distance usu. by means of radio devices; (freq. ~ *back*) transmit (readings etc.) to a distant receiving set or station. Hence ~ED¹ **a.**, ~ING¹ n., tĕlĕm′ETRY n. [TELE-]

tĕlĕŏl′og|ȳ, n. Doctrine of final causes, view that developments are due to the purpose or design that is served by them. So tĕlĕolŏ′gic(AL) aa., tĕlĕolŏ′gicalLY² adv.,~ISM, ~IST, nn. [f. mod. L *teleologia* f. Gk *telos -eos* end +-LOGY]

Tĕleosaur′us (-sōr-), n. Genus of fossil crocodiles. [f. Gk *teleos* complete + *sauros* lizard]

tĕlĕp′athȳ|ȳ, n. Action of one mind on another at a distance through emotional influence without communication through senses. Hence tĕlĕpäth′IC **a.**, tĕlĕpäth′icalLY adv., ~IST(2) n., ~IZE(1, 2) v.t. & i. [TELE- +-PATHY]

tĕl′ĕphōne, n., & v.t. & i. 1. Apparatus for transmitting sound esp. speech to a distance by wire or cord, esp. by means of electricity; *the* ~, system of communication by a network of ~s (*on the* ~, having an instrument connected with this, also, by use of or while using the ~). **2.** vb. Send (message etc.), speak (*to* person) by ~. Hence tĕlĕphŏn′IC **a.**, tĕlĕphŏn′ICALLY adv., tĕlĕph′onIST(3), tĕlĕph′onY¹ n. [f. TELE- + Gk *phōnē* sound]

tĕlĕ|photŏg′raphȳ, n. Photographing of distant objects by means of a combination of telescope & ordinary photographic lens. So ~photŏgräph′IC **a.** [TELE-]

tĕl′ĕprinter, n. Telegraph instrument for transmitting messages by typing over the telephone exchange system. [TELE-]

tĕl′ergў, n. (psych.). Force conceived as operating on the brain in telepathy. [TELE-+(en)ergy]

tĕl′escōpe, n., & v.t. & i. **1.** Instrument for making distant objects appear nearer & larger, whence **tĕlĕs′copIST**(3), **tĕlĕs′copy**[1], nn. **2.** vb. Press, drive, (sections of tube, colliding trains, etc.) together so that one slides into another like sections of small ~; close, be driven, be capable of closing, thus. [17th c., f. It. *telescopio* or mod. L *-ium* (TELE-, -SCOPE)]

tĕlĕscŏp′ic, a. Of, made with, a telescope, as ~*ic observations*; visible only through telescope, as ~*ic stars*; consisting of sections that telescope, as ~*ic funnel* (of steamer), so ~**iFORM** a. Hence ~**iCALLY** adv. [-IC]

tĕl′evision (-zhn), n. A system employing photo-electrical & wireless processes by means of which an actual or recorded scene may be reproduced at a distance on a screen; vision of distant objects obtained thus. Hence **tĕl′eviewer** (-vūer) n., one who uses a ~ receiver, **tĕl′evīse** (-z) v.t. & i., transmit by ~, be suitable for ~ (*the play televised well*). [TELE-]

tĕl′ex, T~, n. System of telegraphy in which printed signals or messages are exchanged by teleprinters connected to public telecommunication network. [f. *teleprinter*+*exchange*]

tĕll, v.t. & i. (*tŏld*). **1.** Relate in spoken or written words, as ~ *me a tale*, *a story*. **2.** Make known, divulge, state, express in words, as ~ *me what you want*, ~ *me all about it*, *will* ~ *you a secret*, ~ *it not in Gath* (let this news not reach & gladden the enemy, usu. joc. w. ref. to 2 *Sam.* i. 20), ~ *that to the* (HORSE[1]-)*marines*, told *him my candid opinion*, ~ *me your name*, ~ TALES (*out of school*), *cannot* ~ *you how glad I was*, ~ FORTUNES. **3.** Utter, as *you told me a lie*, *a* STORY[1], *are you* ~*ing the truth?* **4.** Give information or description, as *told me of* or *about his difficulties*, he *told of foreign lands*, *that* ~*s a tale* (is significant, reveals something); (childish) *don′t* ~ *on* (inform against) *me*. **5.** Decide, determine, as *how do you* ~ *which button to press?*, *you never can* ~ (appearances & probabilities are deceptive). **6.** Distinguish, as *cannot* ~ *them apart*, *him from his brother*. **7.** Assure, as *I can* ~ *you*, *it is not so easy*. **8.** Produce marked effect, as *every blow* ~*s*, *strain begins to* ~ *on him*, whence ~**ING**[2] a., ~**inGLY**[2] adv. **9.** Count (votes esp. in House of Commons, one′s BEAD[1]s; *we were 18 men all told*; ~ *a hundred*; ~*s over his money every night*). **10.** Direct (person) *to* do something (~ *him to wait for me*). **11.** *~ person *good-bye*, say good-bye to; ~ *off*, count off, detach, for duty, as *6 of us were*, *I was*, *told off to get fuel*, *(sl.) ~ (person) home truths, ´recite misdoings of; ~ *the tale* (sl.), pitch a pitiful yarn to evoke sympathy; *~ *the world*,

announce openly, assert emphatically; *you′re* ~*ing me!* (sl.), I am fully aware of that. Hence ~′**ABLE** a. [OE *tellan*, OS *tellian*, OHG *zellen*, ON *telja* f. Gmc **taljan* f. **talō* TALE]

tĕll′er, n. In vbl senses, esp.: any of four persons appointed (two for each side) to count votes in House of Commons; person appointed to receive or pay out money in bank etc. Hence ~**SHIP** n. [ME; -ER[1]]

tĕll′tāle, n. One who tells about another′s private affairs, tattler; (fig.) thing, circumstance, that reveals person′s thoughts, conduct, etc., esp. attrib., as ~ *blushes*, *face*, *the* ~ *clay in his shoes*; kinds of mechanical device for recording person′s attendance at specified time etc., giving warning that cistern is full, etc.; (naut.) index near wheel to show position of tiller, (also ~ *compass*) compass hung usu. in captain′s cabin for checking ship′s course.

tĕllūr′ian, a. (Inhabitant) of the earth. So ~**AL** a. [as foll.+-IAN]

tĕllūr′ion, n. Instrument for illustrating succession of day & night & changes of seasons. [f. L *tellus -uris* earth]

tĕllūr′ium, n. (chem.). A rare brittle silver-white metallic element. Hence ~′**ūrATE**[1](3), ~′**URET**, ~′**ūrIDE**, nn., ~′**ūrĕtĕD**[1], ~**ūr′ic**, ~′**ūrous**, aa. [as prec. + -IUM]

tĕll′ў, n. (sl.). Television. [abbr.]

tĕ′lotýpe, n. Printing electric telegraph; telegram so printed. [TELE-, -O-, TYPE]

tĕl′pher, n. Serving to transport (esp. goods) by electric locomotion, as ~ *line*. Hence ~**AGE**(1, 2) n. [for TELE-(PHORE)]

tĕl′son, n. Last joint in abdomen of Crustacea. [Gk, = limit]

tĕm′enŏs, n. (Gk ant.; pl. *-nē*). Sacred enclosure, temple precinct. [Gk (*lemnō* cut)]

tĕmerār′ious, a. (literary). Reckless, rash. [f. L *temerarius* (*temere* rashly) + -OUS]

tĕmĕ′rity, n. Rashness. [f. L *temeritas* (*temere* at random, rashly, see -TY)]

tĕmp., abbr. (now usu. as playful pedantry) of L *tempore* in the time of, as ~ *Henry I.*

Tĕmpē′an, a. Of or like Tempe, beautiful vale in Thessaly celebrated by Gk & L poets. [-AN]

tĕm′per[1], v.t. & i. **1.** Prepare (clay etc.) by moistening, mixing, & kneading. **2.** Bring (metal, esp. steel), (of metal) come, to proper hardness & elasticity by successive heating & cooling. **3.** Modify, mitigate, (justice etc.) by blending *with* (mercy etc.); moderate, restrain, tone down. **4.**(mus.). Tune, modulate, (piano, organ) in particular TEMPERAMENT. Hence ~**ABLE**, ~**atIVE**, aa., ~**ER**[1] n. [OE *temprian* f. L *temperare*, in ME reinforced by OF *temprer*; cf. TAMPER]

tĕm′per[2], n. **1.** Mixture, esp. suitable combination of ingredients (*of* mortar etc.); resulting condition or consistence. **2.** Condition of metal as to hardness & elasticity. **3.** Habitual or temporary disposition of mind, as *was of a saturnine, frigid, fiery, placid,* ~, *persons of congenial* ~, *found him ·in a good* ~ (not irritable or angry), *in a bad* ~ (peevish, angry); irritation, anger, as *fit of* ~, *what a* ~ *he is in !, naughty* ~ *!; show* ~, be petulant; *lose* one's ~, become angry; *keep, control,* one's ~, not lose it; *out of* ~, angry. Hence (·)~ED² (·*érd*) a., (·)~edLY² adv. [ME *tempre,* f. prec.]

těm′pera, n. = DISTEMPER³. [It.]

těm′perament, n. **1.** Individual character of one's physical organization permanently affecting the manner of acting, feeling, & thinking, as a *nervous* ~, *the artistic* ~; *sanguine, lymphatic* or *phlegmatic, choleric* or *bilious, melancholic* or *atrabilious,* ~ (formerly attributed to predominance of blood, lymph, yellow bile, black bile). **2.** (mus.). Adjustment of tuning of piano etc. so as to fit the scale for all keys, esp. *equal* ~, in which the 12 semitones are at equal intervals. Hence ~AL (·*ēn²*) a. (in n. senses, & esp., of persons, liable to peculiar moods). [ME, f. L *temperamentum* (as TEMPER¹, see -MENT)]

těm′perance, n. Moderation, self--restraint, in speech, conduct, etc., esp. in eating & drinking; moderation in use of, total abstinence from, alcoholic liquors as beverages; ~ *hotel* (not supplying alcoholic drinks); ~ *movement, society, league* (for restriction or abolition of use of alcoholic drinks). [ME, f. AF (·*aunce*), f. L *temperantia* (as TEMPER¹, see -ANCE)]

těm′perate, a. Moderate; self-restrained; abstemious; of mild temperature, as *north, south,* ~ *zone* (between tropic of Cancer & arctic circle, Capricorn & antarctic). Hence ~LY² adv., ~NESS n. [ME, f. L TEMPER¹*atus,* -ATE²]

těm′perature, n. Degree or intensity of sensible heat of a body or of the atmosphere esp. as shown by thermometer, as *high, low,* ~; (med.) internal heat of the body (*normal* ~ in man, 98.4° F.; *take* one's ~, ascertain his variation from this in illness etc.); (colloq.) body ~ above normal; *absolute* ZERO *of* ~; ~ *curve* (showing variations of ~). [F, or f. L *temperatura* (as TEMPER¹, see -URE)]

těm′pest, n. Violent storm of wind often with rain, snow, etc.; (fig.) violent tumult or agitation. [ME, f. OF *tempeste* f. Rom. *tempesta* = class. L *tempestas* (*tempus* time)]

těmpěs′tŭous, a. (Of weather, time, etc., and fig. of person or mood) stormy, violent. Hence ~LY² adv., ~NESS n. [f. LL *tempestuosus* (prec., -OUS)]

těm′plar, n. **1.** (*T*~) member of religious military order (*Knights T*~s) for protection of pilgrims to Holy Land, suppressed in 1312. **2.** Lawyer, law student, with

chambers in the Temple. **3.** *Good T*~s, temperance society. [ME, f. AF *templer,* OF -*ier,* = med. L -*arius* (TEMPLE¹, -ARY¹)]

template. See TEMPLET.

těm′ple¹, n. **1.** Edifice dedicated to service of (esp. ancient Greek, Roman, Egyptian) god. **2.** Any of three successive religious edifices of the Jews in Jerusalem. **3.** Place of Christian public worship, esp. Protestant church in France; (fig.) place in which God resides (1 *Cor.* vi. 19). **4.** *Inner, Middle, T*~, two INNS *of Court* on site of the *T*~ (establishment of Knights Templars) in London; *T*~ *Bar,* gateway (removed 1879) that marked the westward limit of the City Corporation's jurisdiction, at junction of Fleet Street & Strand in London. [OE *temp*(*e*)*l,* reinforced in ME by OF *temple,* f. L *templum*]

těm′ple², n. Flat part of either side of head between forehead & ear. [ME, f. OF, f. Rom. *temp*(*u*)*là,* f. L *tempora* pl., in same sense]

těm′ple³, n. Device in loom for keeping cloth stretched. [15th c., OF, perh. orig. same wd as prec.]

těm′plět, -āte, n. Pattern, gauge, usu. thin board or metal plate, used as guide in cutting or drilling metal, stone, wood, etc.; timber or plate used to distribute weight in wall or under beam etc.; wedge for building-block under ship's keel; = prec. [prob. f. prec. +-ET]

těm′pō, n. (mus. pl. -*pi* pr. -pē). Time, rapidity of movement; (fig.) rate of motion or activity (*the* ~ *of the war is quickening*); characteristic style of movement, as ~ *di menuetto.* [It.]

těm′poral, a. & n. **1.** Of this life, secular, esp. opp. to *spiritual,* as ~ *affairs, interests,* whence ~LY² adv., ~NESS n.; ‖ ~ *lords,* peers of realm, cf. SPIRITUAL; ~ *power,* of ecclesiastic esp. Pope in ~ matters. **2.** Of or in or denoting time (~ *& spatial,* of time & space; ~ *conjunctions,* when etc.). **3.** Of the temple(s) of the head, as ~ *artery, bone.* **4.** n. ~ bone. [ME, f. OF, f. L *temporalis* (*tempus -oris,* see TEMPER¹, TEMPLE² +-AL)]

těmporăl′itў, n. A secular possession, esp. properties & revenues of religious corporation or ecclesiastic (usu. pl.); (law) temporariness. [ME, f. LL *temporalitas* (as prec., see -TY)]

těm′poraltў, n. The laity; = prec. (1st sense). [ME, app. f. AF *temporelte* = OF *temporalite* as prec.]

těm′porar|ў, a. & n. Lasting, meant, only for a time, as ~*y buildings, relief, possession, office;* (n.) person employed ~ily. Hence ~iLY² adv., ~iNESS n. [f. L *temporarius* (*tempus -oris* time, see -ARY¹)]

těm′poriz|e, -is|e (-ĭz), v.i. Pursue indecisive or time-serving policy; avoid committing oneself, act so as to gain time; comply temporarily with requirements of occasion. Hence ~A′TION, ~ER¹, nn.,

~ingly² adv. [f. F *temporiser* f. med. L *temporizare* (*tempus -oris* time, -IZE)]

těm'poro-, comb. form of L *tempora* temples of head, as *~fa'cial*, of temporal & facial regions.

těmpt, v.t. (Arch., bibl.) test, try the resolution of, as *God did ~ Abraham*; entice, incite esp. to sin, (*to do, to* action esp. evil one); *I am ~ed* (strongly disposed) *to question this*; allure, attract, whence **~'ingly²** adv.; (arch., bibl.) provoke, defy, as *shall not ~ the Lord*. Hence or cogn. **~abil'ity** n., **~'able** a. [ME, f. OF *tenter, tempter*, f. L *temptare, tentare* handle, test, try]

těmptā'tion, n. Tempting or being tempted (*the T~*, see *Matt.* iv); incitement esp. to sin; thing that attracts, attractive course. [ME, f. OF *temptacioun* f. L *temptationem* (prec., -ATION)]

těmp't|er, n. One who tempts; *the T~er*, the devil. So **~ress¹** n. [ME, f. OF *tempteor, -eur*, f. L *temptatorem* (as prec., see -OR)]

těn, a. & n. One more than nine, 10, X; (as round number) *~ times as easy*, *~* to *one he forgets it*; HART *of ~*; UPPER *~*; *~penny nail*; *~'pins*, ninepins; *~poun'der* (hist.), person having vote in parliamentary election by occupation of property of rental value of £10. Hence *~fold* a. & adv., *~th²* a. & n., *~th'ly²* adv. [OE *tien*, OS *tehan*, OHG *zehan*, ON *tiu*, Goth. *taihun* f. Gmc *taihan, -un* cogn. w. L *decem*]

těn'able, a. That can be maintained or defended against attack, as *a ~ position, fortress, theory*; (of office etc.) that can be held *for* specified time, *by* person, etc. Hence **těnabil'ity**, **~ness**, nn. [F (*tenir* hold f. L *tenēre*, see -ABLE]

těn'ace (-ĭs), n. (cards). (Holding of) two cards, one next above, the other next below, the opponents' highest of the suit (*major, minor, ~*, variations of this variously defined). [F, f. Sp. *tenaza* lit. pincers]

těnā'cious (-shŭs), a. Holding fast; keeping firm hold (*of* property, rights, principles, etc.); (of memory) retentive; adhesive, sticky; strongly cohesive. Hence or cogn. **~ly²** adv., **~ness**, **těnā'city**, nn. [f. L *tenax* (*tenēre* hold, see -ACIOUS)]

těnāc'ulum, n. (pl. *-la*). Surgeon's sharp hook for picking up arteries etc. [L, = holding instrument (*tenēre* hold)]

těn'ant, n., & v.t. **1.** One who occupies land or tenement under a landlord; (law) person holding real property by private ownership, also defendant in real action; occupant (*of* any place); *~ farmer* (cultivating farm he does not own); ||*~ right*, right of *~* to continue tenancy, as long as he pays rent & acts properly, without injurious increase of rent, & to receive compensation from landlord if turned off. **2.** v.t. Occupy as *~* (esp. in p.p.). Hence or cogn. **těn'ancy** n., **~less** a. [ME, f. OF, f. L *tenēre* hold, see -ANT]

těn'antable, a. Fit to be occupied by a tenant. [-ABLE]

těn'antry, n. Tenants. [-RY]

těnch, n. A European freshwater fish of carp family. [ME, f. OF *tenche* f. LL *tinca*]

těnd¹, v.i. Be moving, be directed, hold a course, lit. & fig., as *~s in our direction, downwards, this way, towards the coast, to the same conclusion*; be apt or inclined, serve, conduce, (*to* action, quality, etc., *to* do). [ME, f. OF *tendre* stretch f. L *tendere* tens- or *tent-*]

těnd², v.t. & i. Take care of, look after, (flocks, invalid, machine); wait *upon*; (naut.) watch (ship at anchor) so as to keep turns out of her cable. So **těnd'ance** n. (arch.). [ME, aphetic f. ATTEND]

těn'dency, n. Bent, leaning, inclination, (*towards, to*, thing, *to* do). [f. med. L *tendentia* (as TEND¹, see -ANCE)]

těnděn'tious (-shŭs), a. (derog.). (Of writing etc.) having an underlying purpose, calculated to advance a cause. [f. G *tendenziös* (TENDENCY, -OUS)]

těn'der¹, n. In vbl senses of TEND²; also: vessel attending larger one to supply her with stores, convey orders, etc.; carriage attached to locomotive & carrying fuel, water, etc.; small water reservoir fixed to mop etc. [-ER¹]

těn'der², v.t. & i., & n. **1.** Offer, present, give in, (one's *services, resignation*, etc.); offer (money etc.) as payment; make a *~* (*for* supply of thing or execution of work). **2.** n. Offer, esp. offer in writing to execute work or supply goods at fixed price, as *are open to receive~s for*; *plea of ~* (that defendant has always been ready to satisfy plaintiff's claim & now brings the sum into court); *legal ~*, currency that cannot legally be refused in payment of debt, as *silver is not legal ~ above 40s*. [f. OF *tendre* (TEND¹); for *-er* cf. RENDER & -ER¹]

těn'der³, a. (*~est*). **1.** Soft, not tough or hard, as *~ steak*; easily touched or wounded, susceptible to pain or grief, as *a ~ heart, conscience, place* (in body); delicate, fragile, (lit., & fig. of reputation etc.; *of ~ age*, immature, young); loving, affectionate, fond, as *~ parents, wrote ~ verses*; solicitous, considerate, (*of* one's honour, good name, etc.); afraid *of* (*doing* wrong thing); requiring careful handling, ticklish, as *a ~ subject*. **2.** *~-eyed*, having gentle eyes, weak-eyed; *~foot* (chiefly U.S. sl.), new-comer in bush etc., novice; *~-hearted*, having *~* heart, so *~-heart'edly* adv., *~-heart'edness* n.; *~loin*, undercut of sirloin, (*T~loin*) amusements district of New York & other cities. Hence *~ly²* adv., *~ness* n. [ME, f. OF *tendre* f. L *tener*]

těn'don, n. Strong band or cord of tissue forming termination or connexion of fleshy part of muscle; *~ of Achilles* (akil'ēz; L *tendo Achillis*), *~* connecting heel (where alone Achilles was vulnerable) with calf. So tĕn′dinous a. [F, or f. med. L *tendo -inis* f. LL f. Gk *tenōn* w. assim. to *tendere* stretch]

tĕn′dril, n. Slender leafless plant-organ attaching itself to another body for support. Hence ~led² (-ld) a. [16th c., prob. f. obs. F *tendrillon*, f. obs. *tendron* young shoot]

tĕn′ĕbrae, n. pl. (R.-C. Ch.). Matins & lauds for last three days of Holy Week, at which candles are successively extinguished. [L, = darkness]

tĕnĕbrif′ĭc, a. Making darkness, as ~ *stars* (believed to cause night). [f. prec., see -FIC]

tĕn′ĕbrous, a. (arch.). Dark, gloomy. [ME, f. OF *tenebrus* f. L *tenebrosus* (TENEBRAE, -OUS)]

tĕn′ĕment, n. Piece of land held by an owner; (law) any kind of permanent property, e.g. lands, rents, peerage, held of a superior, so ~ARY¹ (-měn² a. ; dwelling-house; set of apartments used by one family (~*-house*, containing ~s). Hence ~AL (-měn²) a. [ME, f. AF, OF, f. med. L *tenementum* (*tenēre* hold, see -MENT)]

tĕnĕs′mus (-z-), n. (path.). Continual inclination to void the bowels or bladder accompanied by painful straining. [L, f. Gk *tēnesmos* straining (*teinō* stretch)]

tĕn′ĕt, n. Principle, dogma, doctrine, of a person or school. [L, = he holds; formerly also *tenent*, = they hold]

tĕnn′er, n. (colloq.). ‖ Ten-pound, *ten-dollar, note. [-ER¹]

tĕnn′is, n. Game for 2, 3, or 4 persons played by striking ball with rackets over net stretched across walled court; = LAWN ~; ~ *arm, elbow*, affection of arm caused by ~; ~*-ball, -court* (for ~). [c. 1400 *tenetz, tenes*, app. f. OF *tenez* ‘take, receive’, called by server to his opponent]

tĕn′on, n., & v.t. 1. End of piece of wood fitted for insertion into corresponding cavity (esp. MORTISE) in another piece; ~*-saw* (small, with strong brass or steel back, for fine work). 2. v.t. Cut into a ~, join by means of ~, whence ~ER¹ (1, 2) n. [ME, f. OF, f. *tĕnir* hold f. L *tenēre*]

tĕn′or, n. 1. Settled or prevailing course or direction, esp. fig. of one's *life, way*, etc.; general purport, drift, (*of* speech, writing, etc.); (law) true intent, (also) exact copy. 2. (mus.). (Music for, singer with) highest ordinary adult male voice, between baritone & alto (often attrib., as ~ *voice*); instrument, esp. viola, of which range is roughly that of ~ voice; ~ *bell* (largest of peal or set). So ~IST(3) n. (mus.). [ME, f. OF *tenor, -our* f. L *tenorem* (nom. -or) f. *tenēre* hold, see -OR]

tenŏt′omý, n. Tendon-cutting, esp. as remedy for club-foot. [f. F *-mie*, irreg. f. Gk *tenōn -ontos* TENDON, see -TOMY]

tĕn′rĕc, tăn′-, n. Hedgehog-like tailless insectivorous mammal of Madagascar. [F (*tan-*), f. Malagasy *t(r)àndraka*]

tĕnse¹, n. (gram.). Form taken by verb to indicate the time (also continuance or completeness) of the action etc., as *present, future, past*, (im)*perfect, pluperfect, aorist*, ~, *primary, historic*, ~*s*; set of such forms for the various persons and numbers; SEQUENCE *of* ~*s*. Hence ~′LESS a. [ME, f. OF *tens* f. L *tempus* time]

tĕnse², a., & v.t. & i. 1. (Of cord, membrane, nerve, fig. of mind, emotion) stretched tight, strained to stiffness. 2. vb. Make or become ~. Hence ~′LY² adv., ~′NESS, tĕn′sITY, nn. [f. L *tensus*, p.p. of *tendere* stretch (TEND¹)]

tĕn′sĭle, a. Of tension, as ~ *force*; capable of being drawn out or stretched, whence or cogn. tĕnsĭBIL′ITY, tĕnsil′ITY, nn., tĕn′sIBLE a. [as prec., see -IL]

tĕn′sion (-shn), n., & v.t. 1. Stretching, being stretched; tenseness; mental strain or excitement; strained (political, social, etc.) state; (mech.) stress by which bar, cord, etc. is pulled when it is part of a system in equilibrium or motion; expansive force of gas or vapour; electromotive force. 2. v.t. Subject to ~. Hence ~AL a. [f. F *tension* or L *tensio* (TEND¹, -ION)]

tĕn′son, -zon, n. Contest in verse between troubadours; subdivision of poem composed for this. [F *tension*, = Prov. *tenso*, as prec.]

tĕn′sor, n. (anat.). Muscle that tightens or stretches a part. [mod. L, as TEND¹, see -OR]

tĕnt¹, n., & v.i. & t. 1. Portable shelter of canvas, cloth, etc., supported by pole(s) & stretched by cords secured to ~*-pegs* driven into ground; *bell* ~, circular ~ with one pole in middle; (photog., also *dark* ~) portable dark room for outdoor use. 2. ~*-bed* (with a ~like canopy); ~*-fly*, piece of canvas stretched over ridge pole of ~ leaving open space but keeping off sun & rain; ~*-pegging*, cavalry exercise in which rider tries at full gallop to carry off on point of lance ~*-peg* fixed in ground; ~*-stitch*, series of parallel diagonal stitches suggesting ~. 3. vb. Cover (as) with ~; encamp in ~. [ME & OF *tente* f. Rom. **tenta* neut. pl. p.p. as TEND¹]

tĕnt², n., & v.t. 1. Piece, bunch, roll, of linen etc. inserted into wound or natural opening to keep it open. 2. v.t. Keep open thus. [ME, f. OF *tente* f. *tenter* probe, as TEMPT]

tĕnt³, n. Deep red wine chiefly from Spain, used esp. as sacramental wine. [f. Sp. *tinto* deep-coloured f. L as TINGE]

tĕn′tacle, n. Feeler, long slender flexible process or appendage of animal, used for exploration, prehension, or locomotion; (bot.) sensitive hair or filament. Hence ~ED² (-ld), tĕntăc′ŭlAR¹, tĕntăc′ŭlATE², -ātĕd, tĕntăc′ŭlIFORM, tĕntăcŭlí′GEROUS, aa. [f. mod. L *tentaculum*, f. *tentare* = *temptare* (TEMPT) + *-culum* -CULE]

tĕn′tative, a. & n. **1.** Done by way of trial, experimental. **2.** n. Experimental proposal or theory. Hence ~LY[2] adv. [f. med. L *tentativus* (as TEMPT, see -IVE)]

tĕn′ter[1], n. Person in charge of something, ǁ esp. of machinery in factory. [f. obs. & Sc. *tent* var. of TEND[2]+-ER[1]]

tĕn′ter[2], n. Machine for stretching cloth to set or dry; ~(*hook*), each of the hooks that hold the cloth; *be on* ~*hooks* or (arch.) *on the* ~s (in state of suspense or mental torment). [ME, f. AF **tentur*, f. med. L *tentorium* f. *tent*- TEND[1], see -ER[2], -OR]

tĕn′ūis, n. (pl. *-es* pr. *-ēz*). Hard or surd mute (k, p, t), cf. MEDIA. [L, = thin]

tĕnū′ity, n. Slenderness; (of air, fluid) rarity, thinness; (of style) simplicity, absence of grandeur. [f. L *tenuitas* (as prec., see -TY)]

tĕn′ūous, a. (rare). Thin, slender, small; (of distinctions etc.) subtle, over-refined. [f. L TENUIS+-OUS]

tĕn′ure (*-yer*), n. Kind of right or title by which (esp. real) property is held, as ALLODIAL, FEUDAL, ~, *military* ~ (involving military service); (period of) holding, possession, enjoyment, as *during his* ~ *of office, holds life on a precarious* ~; (hist.) ~*-horn, -sword* (produced on certain occasions as evidence of ~ of estates). [ME, f. OF (*tenir* hold f. L *tenēre*, see -URE)]

tĕnu′tŏ (*-ōō-*), a. (mus.). Sustained, given its full time value (cf. STACCATO). [It., = held]

tēocāll′ĭ, n. Temple of Mex. & other Amer. aborigines, usu. on truncated pyramid. [Mex. (*teotl* god + *calli* house); also *teopan*]

tĕp′ee, teep′ee, n. Conical tent or lodge of the American Indians, formerly made of skins, now of cloth or canvas. [native name]

tĕp′e̯fȳ, v.t. & i. Make, become, tepid. Hence ~FAC′TION n. [f. L *tepefacere* (as TEPID, see -FY)]

tĕph′igrăm, n. (meteorol.). Diagram showing state of atmosphere at different levels in terms of temperature & entropy. [f. symbol *t* for temperature +symbol *phi* for entropy +-GRAM]

tĕph′rite, n. Kinds of modern volcanic rock. [f. Gk *tephra* ashes, -ITE[1]]

tĕp′id, a. Slightly warm, lukewarm (lit. & fig.). Hence or cogn. tĕpid′ITY, ~NESS, nn., ~LY[2] adv. [f. L *tepidus* (*tepēre* be lukewarm, see -ID[1])]

tĕpĭdā′rĭum, n. (Rom. ant.; pl. *-aria*). Intermediate room of moderate temperature in Roman baths; boiler for heating hot bath. [L (as prec., see -ARIUM)]

tĕr, adv. Three times (esp. mus. & med.). [L]

-ter. See -THER.

terai′ (*-rī*), n. Wide-brimmed felt hat, often with double crown, worn by white men in sub-tropical regions. [f. *T*~, belt

of marshy jungle between Himalayan foot-hills and plains]

tĕ′raph, n. (bibl.; only in pl. *~īm*, used as sing. or collective sing.). Small image(s) as domestic oracle of ancient Hebrews. [Heb.]

tĕrat|o-, comb. form of Gk *teras -atos* monster, as: ~*ogĕn′ic* a., ~*ŏ′geny* n., (of) production of monstrosities; ~*ŏl′ogy,* dealing in the marvellous, (biol.) study of animal or vegetable monstrosities, so ~*olŏ′gical* a., ~*ŏl′ogist* n.

terce. See TIERCE.

tĕr′cel, tier′cel, n. Male falcon. [ME, f. OF *tercel* etc., f. Rom. **tertiolus* dim. of L *tertius* third]

tĕrcĕn′tenary (*or -entēn*[2]), **-tĕnn′ial,** aa. & nn. Of 300 years; (n.) 300th anniversary. [TER]

tĕr′cĕt, n. (Mus.; pros., also *tiercet*) = TRIPLET. [f. It. *terzetto* (*terzo* third f. L *tertius*)]

tĕ′rĕbene, n. A hydrocarbon prepared by treating oil of turpentine with sulphuric acid, used as disinfectant etc. [f. foll.+-ENE]

tĕ′rĕbinth, n. Turpentine-tree, yielding Chian turpentine; *oil of* ~, oil of turpentine. [ME, f. OF *therebinthe* or L f. Gk *terebinthos*]

tĕrĕbin′thine, a. Of the terebinth; of turpentine, so **terĕb′ic** a. [f. L f. Gk *terebinthinos* (as prec., see -INE[2])]

tĕ′rĕbr|a, n. (pl. ~*ae*). Boring ovipositor of some insects. Hence ~ATE[2](2) a. [L, = borer]

teredō, n. (pl. ~s). Ship-worm, mollusc that bores ships etc. [L, f. Gk *terēdōn* (*teirō* rub)]

tĕrg′al, a. Of the back, dorsal. [f. L *tergum* back +-AL]

tĕrgĕm′inate, a. (bot.). (Of leaf) having at base a pair of leaflets & forking with a pair on each branch. [f. L TER(*geminus* born together) +-ATE[2]]

tĕr′givers|āte, v.i. Turn one's back on oneself, turn one's coat, apostatize, change one's party or principles; make conflicting statements. So ~A′TION, ~-ātor, nn. [f. L *tergiversari* turn one's back (*tergum* back + *vers*- f. *vertere* turn), see -ATE[3]]

tĕrm, n. **1.** (arch.). Boundary, limit, esp. of time, as *set a* ~ *to his encroachments, awaited the* ~ *of his existence,* whence ~′LESS a. (poet., rhet.). **2.** Limited period, as *for a* ~ *of 5 years, his* ~ *of office expired.* **3.** (Univv., school, law) period during which instruction is given ǁ or court holds sessions, as *Michaelmas, Hilary, Easter, Trinity,* ~ (w. ref. to administration of justice, now *sittings*), *will end it next* ~, *during* ~ (*-time*), ǁ EAT one's ~s. **4.** Appointed day, ǁ esp. QUARTER[1]-day. **5.** (law). (Also ~ *of* or *for years*) estate or interest in land to be enjoyed for fixed period. **6.** (math.). Antecedent or consequent of ratio, part of expression joined to the rest by + or − (e.g. $3ax^2 − b + cz$ *has three* ~s). **7.** (log.). Word(s) that may be subject or predicate of a proposition, as MAJOR[2], MINOR, MIDDLE[1], ~. **8.** Word used to express a definite conception esp. in particular branch of study etc., as *technical, scientific, law,* ~, *in* ~*s of* (in the language peculiar to), CONTRADICTION *in* ~*s, set* (definite) ~*s.* **9.** pl. Language employed, mode of expression, as *in the most flattering* ~*s.* **10.** pl. Conditions, as *cannot accept his* ~*s, do it on your own* ~*s* ; esp. charge, price, as *his* ~*s are 2 guineas a lesson,* INCLUSIVE ~*s* ; *come to* ~*s,* yield, give way, (also *make*~*s*) conclude agreement (*with*) ; *bring person to* ~*s,* cause him to accept conditions ; ~*s of reference,* points referred to an individual or body of persons for decision or report, scope of an inquiry ; ~*s of trade,* ratio between prices paid for imports and received for exports. **11.** pl. Relation, footing, as *am on good, bad, familiar,* ~*s with him, are not on speaking* ~*s.* [f. ME & OF *terme* f. L TERMINUS]

term[2], v.t. Denominate, call, as *the music* ~*ed plain-song, I forget how or what he* ~*s it, this he* ~*ed sheer robbery.* [f. prec.]

term'agant, n. & a. **1.** (hist. ; *T*~). Imaginary deity of violent and turbulent character, often appearing in morality plays. **2.** Brawling woman, shrew, scold. **3.** adj. Boisterous, turbulent, shrewish, whence **term'ag**ANCY n., ~LY[2] adv. [ME *Tervagant* f. OF *Tervagan,* proper name in *Chanson de Roland*]

term'inable, a. That may be terminated ; coming to an end after certain time, as ~ *annuity.* Hence ~NESS n. [f. obs. *termine* TERMINATE, see -ABLE ; cf. LL *-abilis*]

term'inal, a. & n. **1.** Of, forming, a limit or terminus, as ~ *station* ; (math.) ~ *value,* most concise form of an expression ; (bot.) borne at end of stem .etc. ; (zool. etc.) ending a series, as ~ *joints* ; of, done etc., each term, as ~ *accounts, subscription* ; ~ (TERMINUS) *figure.* **2.** n. Terminating thing, extremity, esp. point of connexion in electric circuit ; railway or airway terminus. Hence ~LY[2] adv. [f. L *terminalis* (TERMINUS, see -AL)]

term'in|āte[1], v.t. & i. Bound, limit ; bring, come, to an end ; (of word) end *in* (such letters or syllable). Hence or cogn. ~ative LY[2] adv. [f. L *terminare* (TERMINUS), see -ATE[3]]

term'inate[2], a. Coming to an end, bounded, as *a* ~ *decimal.* [as prec., see -ATE[2]]

termina'tion, n. (In vbl senses, see TERMINATE[1], & esp.) word's final syllable or letter or group of letters esp. as an element in inflexion or derivation ; *put a* ~ *to, bring to a* ~, make an end of. Hence ~AL a. (gram.). [ME, f. OF, or L *terminatio* (TERMINATE[1], -ATION)]

term'inātor, n. Person, thing, that terminates ; dividing line between light &

dark part of heavenly body. [f. TERMIN-ATE[1] + -OR ; cf. LL *terminator*]

term'iner. See OYER.

term'in|ism, n. Doctrine that everyone has limited term for repentance ; = NOMINALISM. So ~IST n. [f. TERMINUS + -ISM]

termin|ŏl'ogy̆, n. Science of proper use of terms ; terms used in an art etc. Hence ~olŏ'gical a. (~*ological inexactitude,* joc., lie), ~olŏ'gically[2] adv. [f. TERMINUS + -LOGY]

term'inus, n. (pl. *-uses, -ī*). **1.** (Now rare) final point, goal. **2.** ‖ Station at end of railway or bus route. **3.** (Rom. ant., *T*~) god of boundaries. **4.** Figure of human bust ending in square pillar. **5.** ~ *ăd quĕm, ā quō,* terminating, starting--point (of argument, policy, period, etc.). [L *terminus* end, limit, boundary]

termitār'ium, term'itary̆, nn. Nest of, cage for, termites. [f. foll. + -ARIUM, -ARY[1]]

term'ite, n. Social insect, chiefly tropical & very destructive to timber, pop. but erron. called *white ant.* [f. LL *termes -itis* alt. f. *tarmes* after *terere* rub, bore]

term'ly̆, a. & adv. (rare). (Occurring, paid, etc.) by the term, terminal(ly). [-LY[1]]

term'or, n. (law). One who holds lands etc. for a term of years, or for life. [ME, f. AF *termer* (TERM, see -ER[2], -OR)]

tern[1], **tärn,** n. Kinds of sea-bird like gull but usu. smaller & with long forked tail. [of Scand. orig., cf. Da. *terne,* Sw. *tärna* f. ON *therna*]

tern[2], n. & a. **1.** Set of three, esp. three lottery numbers that when drawn together win large prize ; such prize. **2.** adj. = TERNATE. [f. F *terne,* L *terni*]

tern'|ary̆, a. Composed of three, so ~AL a. ; (math.) having three variables. [f. L *ternarius* (L *terni* three each, see -ARY[1])]

tern'āte (*or -at*), a. Arranged in threes, esp. (bot., of leaves) having three leaflets, whorled in threes. Hence ~LY[2] adv. [mod. L *ternatus* (as prec., -ATE[2])]

terne, n. (Usu. ~*-plate*) inferior tin plate alloyed with much lead. [prob. f. F *terne* dull, see TARNISH]

Terpsich'ore (-ko-), n. The MUSE[1] of dancing. Hence **Terpsichore'**AN (-ko-) a. [Gk (*-khorē*)]

te'rra, n. Earth (in various L & It. phrr.) ; ~ *căriŏs'a,* tripoli, rotten-stone ; *terrae fĭl'ĭus,* son of the soil, humbly-born person ; ~ *fĭrm'a,* dry land ; ~ *incŏg'nĭta* (ĭn-k-), unknown region ; ~ *Japŏn'ĭca,* gambier [orig. thought to be earth from Japan] ; ~ *nera* (nār'a), pigment used by ancient artists [It., = black earth] ; ~ *verde* (vār'dā), green earth used as pigment [It.]. [L]

te'rrace, n., & v.t. **1.** Raised level space, natural or artificial ; (geol.) raised beach. **2.** ‖ Row of housing along top or face of slope, row of contiguous houses ; ~*-house,* one of row of houses joined by party-

-walls. 3. v.t. Form into, furnish with, ~;
~d roof, flat roof of an Indian or Eastern
house. [F, f. Rom. *terracea (prec.,
-ACEOUS)]

terracòtt'a, n. Hard pottery used as
ornamental building-material & in statuary (often attrib.); statue, figurine, of
this; (a. & n.) its brownish-red colour.
[It., = baked earth]

terrain', n. A tract of land as regarded
by the physical geographer or the tactician. [F, f. Rom. *terranum, f. L terrenum
TERRENE]

terramare' (-ahr, -ār), n. Kinds of earthy
deposit containing bones, phosphates,
etc., & useful as fertilizer; S.-Europ. prehistoric deposit like kitchen MIDDEN. [F,
f. dial. It. TERRA (mara = marna marl)]

terrän'eous, a. (bot.). Growing on land.
[f. L -terraneus (TERRA, -ANEOUS)]

te'rrapin, n. Kinds of freshwater tortoise,
esp. salt-marsh ~ (also diamond-back),
kind valued as food. [Algonquin dim. of
torope, turupe]

terrä'queous, a. (Of the earth) comprising
both land & water. [TERRA, AQUA, -EOUS]

terrène', a. Of earth, earthy; terrestrial.
[ME, f. AF, f. L terrenus (TERRA)]

terreplein (tar'plan), n. (fortif.). Surface
of rampart behind parapet, where guns
are mounted. [F (terre earth +plein f. L
plenus full); orig. sense talus]

terrès'trial, a. & n. 1. Of the earth, esp.
opp. to celestial, as the ~ seasons, the ~
globe, the earth, a ~ globe (representing
earth), ~ MAGNETISM; of this world, worldly, as ~ aims, interests; of land opp. to
water; (zool.) living on the ground, opp.
to aquatic, arboreal, aerial. 2. n. Inhabitant of earth. Hence ~LY² adv. [ME, f.
L terrestris (TERRA) +-AL]

te'rrèt, -ĭt, n. Each of loops or rings on
harness-pad for driving-reins to pass
through. [15th c. var. of (now dial.)
torret, turret, f. OF toret dim. of TOUR]

te'rrible, a. Exciting or fit to excite
terror, awful, dreadful, formidable;
(colloq.) excessive, as a ~ bore; (colloq.)
incompetent; ENFANT TERRIBLE. Hence
~NESS n., te'rribLY² adv. (esp., sl., very).
[ME, f. F, f. L terribilis (terrēre frighten,
see -BLE)]

terric'olous, a. Living on or in the earth,
esp. of the Terricolae, group of annelids
including earthworm. [f. L terricola
(TERRA +colere inhabit) +-OUS]

te'rrier¹, n. 1. Kinds of active & hardy
dog with digging propensity; black-&-tan,
BULL¹, FOX¹, ~, short-haired kinds;
Cairn, Irish, Scotch, Skye, Yorkshire, ~,
rough-haired kinds; Maltese, toy, ~, small
toy kinds. 2. (colloq.). || Member of
Territorial Army. [ME, f. OF (chien)
terrier (= burrow) f. med. L terrarius;
-ium (TERRA + -E² (2))]

te'rrier², n. Book recording site, boundaries, etc., of land of private persons
or corporations; (hist.) collection of

acknowledgements of vassals or tenants
of a lordship. [ME, f. OF (as prec.) =
rent-roll. = med. L terrarius (liber book)]

terrif'|ic, a. Causing terror, terrible.
Hence ~ICALLY adv. [f. L terrificus (terrēre
frighten, see -FIC)]

te'rrify, v.t. Fill with terror, frighten.
[f. L terrificare (as prec., see -FY)]

terri'gènous, a. Produced by the earth,
as ~ deposits; ~ metals, metallic bases of
earths, e.g. aluminium. [f. L terrigenus
earth-born, +-OUS]

terrine' (-ēn), n. Earthenware vessel
containing and sold with some table
delicacy. [orig. form of TUREEN]

territ. See TERRET.

territōr'ial, a. & n. 1. Of territory, as ~
possessions, acquisitions; limited to a
district, as the right was strictly ~; (T~)
of (any of) the U.S. Territories; (eccl.)
~ system (in which civil rule claims supremacy as a natural right, whence ~ISM n.);
|| T~ Army, volunteer force organized on
a ~ basis to provide a reserve of trained
and disciplined manpower for use in any
emergency; ~ waters, marginal waters
under the jurisdiction of a State, esp.
that part of the sea within three miles
of the shore measured from low-water
mark. 2. n. || Member of T~ Army.
Hence ~LY² adv. [f. LL territorialis (as
TERRITORY, see -AL)]

territōr'ialize, -ise (-īz), v.t. Extend by
addition of, reduce to state of, territory.
[-IZE]

te'rritory, n. Extent of land under jurisdiction of sovereign, State, city, etc.;
(commerc.) area over which a commercial traveller operates; large tract of
land; *(T~) organized division of the
country not yet admitted to full rights of
a State. [ME, f. L territorium (TERRA,
-ORY(1))]

te'rror, n. Extreme fear; ~-stricken,
-struck (with ~); person, thing, that
causes this, as a ~ to evildoers; (colloq.)
here comes this (holy) ~ (troublesome child)
again; king of ~s, death (Job xviii. 14);
Reign of T~, the T~, period of French
Revolution, 1793–4 (& of similar periods
marked by sanguinary excesses of revolu-
tionaries, also Red T~, or reactionaries,
also White T~). [ME & AF terrour, OF
-or f. L terrorem (terrēre frighten, -OR)]

te'rror|ist, n. One who favours or uses
terror-inspiring methods of governing or
of coercing government or community.
Hence or cogn. ~ISM(2, 3), ~IZA'TION, nn.,
~is'TIC a., ~IZE(1) v.t. [F (-e), prec., -IST]

te'rry, n. A pile fabric with the loops
uncut (also attrib.). [18th c., of unkn.
orig.]

tèrse, a. (Of speech, style, writer) free
from cumbrousness and superfluity,
smooth and concise. Hence ~'LY² (-sl-)
adv., ~'NESS (-sn-) n. [f. L tersus p.p. of
tergere wipe, polish]

tèr'tian (-shn), a. & n. (Fever, disease)

whose paroxysms occur every other day, as ~ ague. [ME (fevẹr) tertiane f. L (febris) tertiana (tertius third, -AN)]

tér′tiary (-sha-), a. & n. **1.** Of the third order, rank, formation, etc. **2.** n. (Ornith.) flight-feather of third row, so **tér′tiAL** (-shi) a. & n.; (T~) member of third order of monastic body; the T~, third geological period. [f. L tertiarius (prec., -ARY¹)]

tér′tio (-shiō). See PRIMO².

tér′tium quid (-shĭ-), n. A third something, esp. between mind and matter or between opposite things; (joc.) third party in the ETERNAL triangle. [L]

tér′tius (-shus), a. || (In schools) Jones etc. ~ (third of the name); ~ gaud′ĕns (L, = glad third), third party expecting to profit by two others' quarrel. [L]

terza rima (tārt′sa rēm′a), n. (pl. -ze -me, pr. -ā). Arrangement of (hen)decasyllabic triplets rhyming thus (bat pig cat fig box wig ox etc.) as in Dante's Commedia; such triplets. [It.]

terzett′ō (tārts-), n. (mus.). Vocal trio. [It.]

Tes′la, n. ~ coil, form of induction coil for high-frequency alternating currents such as are used in diathermy. [Nikola ~, Amer. scientist (d. 1943)]

tess′ell|āted, a. Formed of tesserae, as ~ated pavement; (bot., zool.) regularly checkered. So ~AR¹ a., ~A′TION n. [f. LL tessellare (tessella dim. of foll., see -ATE²), or It. tessellato, w. Engl. suf.]

tess′er|a, n. (pl. ~ae). Small square usu. cubic block used in mosaic, whence ~AL a.; (Rom. ant.) small square of bone etc. used as token, ticket, etc. [L]

tessitur′a (-oora), n. (mus.). Range within which most tones of a voice-part fall. [It., = TEXTURE]

test¹, n. **1.** Critical examination or trial of person's or thing's qualities, as has stood (undergone) the successive ~s of poverty and riches, must put it to the ~; a ~ case (serving to show the principle involved). **2.** Means of so examining, standard for comparison or trial, circumstances suitable for this, as success is not a fair ~. **3.** Ground of admission or rejection, as is excluded by our ~. **4.** (chem.). Reagent, substance employed to reveal presence of an ingredient in a compound, as galls are a ~ of or for iron. **5.** Movable hearth in reverberatory furnace used in separating silver from lead. **6.** (colloq.). ~-match. **7.** T~ Act (of 1672, requiring all persons before holding office to take the ~, i.e. the oaths of supremacy and allegiance or equivalent ~; repealed in 1828); ~-match, one of the matches in a cricket tour etc. that are to count towards the total result; ~-glass, -mixer, -paper, -tube, (for ~s or other chem. purposes; ~-tube baby, colloq., one conceived by artificial insemination). [ME, f. OF, f. L testu(m) earthen pot, collateral form of testa TEST³; in mod. use mainly f. foll.]

test², v.t. Put to the test, make trial of, (person, thing, quality); try severely, tax, (one's powers of endurance etc.); refine (metal); (chem.) examine by means of reagent. Hence ~′ABLE a., tĕs′ter¹ [-ER¹(1, 2)] n. [f. prec.]

test³, n. Shell, hard covering, of some animals. [f. L testa tile, jug, shell, etc., cf. TEST¹]

testā′ceous (-shus), a. Of shells or shellfish, so testA′CEAN (-āshn) a. & n., testăcĕŏl′OGY n.; with a hard continuous shell; (bot., zool.) of red brick colour. [f. L testaceus (TEST³, -ACEOUS)]

tes′tacȳ, n. Being testate. [f. TESTATE, after INTESTACY]

tes′tament, n. **1.** = WILL² (last sense), as MILITARY ~, so ~arĭLY² (-ĕn²) adv., ~ARY¹ (-ĕn²-) a. **2.** (Bibl.) covenant, dispensation; Old, New, T~, the portion of the Bible dealing with the Mosaic, Christian, dispensation; (T~) copy of the N.T. [ME, f. L testamentum will (TESTATE, -MENT); in early Christian L rendering Gk diathēkē covenant]

|| **testām′ur,** n. (univv.). Certificate that one has passed examination. [L, = we testify]

tes′tāte (or -at), a. & n. (Person) who has made a will (and died leaving it in force). So **testāt′OR, testār′RIX,** nn. [f. L testari testify, make will, (testis witness), see -ATE²]

tester¹ See TEST³.

tes′ter², n. Canopy, esp. over FOUR-poster. [ME; med. L testerium, testrum, testura (Rom. *testa head; cf. OF testre, testiere]

|| **tes′ter³,** n. Shilling of Henry VIII; (arch., joc.) sixpence. [var. of earlier and OF teston (as TEST³, see -OON)]

tes′ticle, n. Each of two glands in male that secrete spermatozoa etc. Hence **testic′ŭlAR¹** a. [15th c., f. L testiculus dim. of testis a ~]

testic′ŭlate, a. Having, shaped like, testicles; (bot.) having a pair of organs so shaped. [f. LL testiculatus (prec., -ATE²)]

tes′tifȳ, v.i. & t. (Of person or thing) bear witness (to fact, state, assertion, against person etc., arch. of or concerning matter); (law) give evidence; affirm, declare, (one's regret etc., that, how, etc.); (of things) be evidence of, evince. [ME, f. L testificari (testis witness, see -FY)]

testimōn′ial, n. Certificate of character, conduct, or qualifications; gift, money, presented to person, esp. in public, as mark of esteem, in acknowledgement of services, etc. [ME, f. OF (adj.), f. LL testimonialis (TESTIMONY, -AL)]

testimōn′ialize, -ise (-īz), v.t. Present (person) with testimonial. [-IZE]

tes′timonȳ n. Evidence, demonstration, as called him in ~, produce ~ (to, of), we have his ~ for that; (law) oral or written statement under oath, or affirmation; declarations, statements, as must rely *on the* ~ *of history, of historians;* (arch.) solemn protest, as *for a* ~ *against them;* (bibl.) the decalogue, esp. *the tables of the* ~, (sing. or pl.) the Scriptures. [ME, f. L *testimonium* (*testis* witness, see -MONY)]

tĕstūdinār′ious, a. Mottled with red, yellow, and black, like tortoise-shell. [f. TESTUDO +-ARIOUS]

tĕstūd′inate, a. Arched like carapace of tortoise. [f. L *testudinatus* (TESTUDO, see -ATE²)]

tĕstūdin′eous, a. Like carapace of tortoise. [f. L *testudineus* (foll., -EOUS)]

tĕstūd′|ō, n. (pl. ~*os*, ~*ines*). **1.** (Rom. ant.) screen formed by body of troops in close array with overlapping shields; similar screen used by miners when ground is likely to cave in. **2.** Kinds of tortoises, ′whence ~**inAL a.** [L, gen. -*dinis*, = tortoise-shell (TEST³)]

tĕs′t|ў, a. Irritable, touchy. Hence~**ĭLY²** adv., ~**ĭNESS n.** [ME & AF *testif,* f. *teste* head (TEST³), see -IVE]

tĕtăn′ic, a. n. 1. Of, such as occurs in, tetanus, as ~ *spasm.* **2. n.** Remedy acting on the muscles through the nerves, e.g. strychnine. [f. L f. Gk *tetanikos* (as foll., see -IC)]

tĕt′an|us, n. Disease marked by spasm of many or all muscles of voluntary motion, e.g. lockjaw; *artificial* ~*us* (induced by strychnine etc.). Hence or cogn. ~**ĭZA′TION n.,** ~**ĭZE(3) v.t.,** ~**OĬD a.** [L, f. Gk *tetanos* f. *teinō* stretch]

tĕ(t)ch′|ў, a. Peevish, irritable. Hence ~**ĭLY²** adv., ~**ĭNESS n.** [prob. f. *teche, tache* fault or vice, f. OF *teche* +-Y²]

tête-à-tête (tāt′ahtāt′), adv., a., & n. **1.** Together in private. **2.** adj. Private, confidential. **3. n.** Private interview or conversation usu. between two; sofa for two. [F, lit. head-to-head]

tĕth′er (-dh-), n. & v.t. **1.** Rope, chain, halter, by which grazing animal is confined; (fig.) scope, extent of one's knowledge, authority, etc. (*was beyond, at the end of, his* ~). **2. v.t.** Tie (esp. grazing animal) with ~. [ME, f. ON *tjóthr*]

tĕt′ra-, comb. form of Gk *tettares* four, as: ~*chord* (-k-), scale series of half-octave (esp. in ancient mus.), so ~*chord′al a.*; ~*cyc′lic* (bot.), of four circles or whorls; ~*dac′tyl* a. & n., ~*dac′tylous* a., four--toed (animal); ~*gon,* plane rectilineal figure of four angles & four sides, so *tĕtrăg′onal a.*; ~*grăm,* word of four letters, quadrilateral figure; ~*grămm′aton, Jehovah* or other sacred word written in four letters; *tĕtrā′gynous* (-j-), of four pistils; ~*hĕd′ron* (-*a*-h-), four-sided solid, esp. triangular pyramid, so ~*hĕd′ral* (-*a*-h-) a.; *tĕtrăl′ogy,* group of four literary or ′operatic works, esp. (Gk ant.) three tragedies & satyric drama; *tĕtrăm′eral, tĕtrăm′erous,* having four parts; *tĕtrăm′eter,* verse of four measures (cf. DIMETER); ~*morph* (Christian art), union of attri-

butes of four evangelists in one winged figure; ~*pet′alous,* ~*phyll′ous,* of four petals, leaves; ~*pŏd a. & n., tĕtrăp′odous* a., (butterfly) with only four perfect legs; *tĕtrăp′ody,* group, verse, of four feet; ~*stich* (-k), group of four lines of verse; ~*style a. & n.,* (building) with four pillars esp. forming portico in front or supporting ceiling; ~*syll′able,* word of four syllables, so ~*syllăb′ic a.*

tĕt′răd, n. The number four; set of four; atom, element, with combining-power of four atoms of hydrogen. [f. Gk *tetras -ados* (as prec., see -AD)]

tĕtrăn′drous, a. (bot.). Having four stamens. [f. TETRA- +Gk *anēr andros* male +-OUS]

tĕt′rārch (-k), n. (In Rom. empire) governor of fourth part of a country or province, subordinate ruler, whence or cogn. ~ATE(1), ~Y¹, nn., **tĕtrārch′ICAL a.,** (-k-); commander of subdivision of ancient Greek phalanx. [f. LL *tetrarcha,* class. L f. Gk *tetrarkhēs* (TETRA-, *arkhō* rule)]

tĕtt′er, n. Kinds of skin-disease; ~*wort,* larger celandine (supposed to cure these). [OE *teter,* cf. OHG *zitaroh,* G dial. *zitteroch*]

Teuc′rian, a. & n. Ancient Trojan. [f. L *Teucri* +-AN]

Teut′o-, comb. form (irreg.) of foll., as ~MAN′IA(C)), ~PHIL(E), ~PHOBE, ~PHOB′IA.

Teut′on, n. Member of any of the Teutonic nations or (hist.) of the tribe of ~*s* first mentioned in 4th c. B.C. & dwelling perh. near mouth of Elbe. [f. L *Teutones, Teutoni,* ethnic name]

Teutŏn′ic, a. & n. 1. Of the Teutons; of the Germanic peoples (including, in widest sense, Scandinavians & Anglo--Saxons as well as German races); ~ *languages,* High & Low GERMAN² & Scandinavian. **2. n.** Languages of the Teutons collectively. Hence ~ISM(4), **Teut′on**ISM(2, 4), **Teutonĭ**ZA′TION, nn., **Teut′on**IZE(3) v.t. [f. L*Teutonicus* (prec., -IC)]

tĕxt, n. Original words of author esp. opp. to paraphrase of or commentary on them, as *there is nothing about this in the* ~, *the* ~ *is hopelessly corrupt* (altered by copyists); passage of Scripture used as authority or esp. chosen as subject of sermon etc.; subject, theme; *stick to* one's ~, not digress; main body of book opp. to notes, pictures, etc.; *~book;* (pl.) books prescribed for study; (also ~*hand*) large kind of handwriting; CHURCH¹, GERMAN², ~; ~*book,* manual of instruction, standard book in a branch of study. [f. ME & OF *texte* f. L *textus -ūs* (in med. L = Gospel) f. L *texere text-* ′weave']

tĕx′tile, a. & n. 1. Of weaving, as *the* ~ *art;* woven, suitable for weaving, as ~ *fabrics, materials.* **2. n.** ~ material. [F, or f. L *textilis* (as prec., see -ILE)]

tĕx'tŭal, a. Of, in, the text, as ~ *criticism, errors*. Hence ~LY² adv. [ME & AF *textuel* (as TEXT, see -AL)]

tĕx'tŭal|ist, n. One who adheres strictly to the letter of the text, so ~ISM n.; ready quoter of scriptural texts. [-IST]

tĕx'tŭr|e, n. Arrangement of threads etc. in textile fabric, as *loose* ~*e*; arrangement of constituent parts, structure, (*of* skin, rock, literary work, etc.); representation of surface of objects in works of art; (biol.) tissue, structure of this. Hence ~AL (-cher-, -tūr-) a. [ME, f. L *textura* (as TEXT, see -URE)]

tĕx'tureless (-cherl-, -tūrl-), a. Without discernible texture, amorphous. [-LESS]

●**-th¹**, suf. forming nn. (a) f. vbs; in some, as *bath, birth, death*, Gmc, repr. var. Aryan suff. (*-tos* etc.), in others, going back to OE or ON, as *tilth*, or of later form. as *growth, spilth, stealth*; the suf. appears regularly as *-t* in *flight, gift, thirst* (f. Gmc), & in *sight* (in E). (b) f. adjj. (rarely nn.), OE *-thu, -tho, -th* (= Goth. *-itha*, Gmc*-ithō*), forming nn. of state, as *filth* (*foul*), *length* (*long*), etc., & by analogy *breadth, sloth*, etc. In some, *-th* is repr. by *-t*, as *height, slight, theft*.

●**-th²**, **-eth** after *-ty*, suf. forming ordinal numbers with all simple numbers from *fourth* onward in mod. E; repr. OE *-tha, -the*, or *-othā, -othe*, f. Aryan *-tos* (cf. Gk *pemptos*, L *quintus*).

thăl'amus, n. (pl. *-mī*). (Gk ant.) inner room, women's apartment; (anat.) place where nerve emerges from brain, esp. *optic* ~; (bot.) receptacle of flower. [L, f. Gk *thalamos*]

tha'ler (tah-), n. (hist.). German silver coin. [G, see DOLLAR]

Thali'|a, n. MUSE¹ of comedy & pastoral poetry; one of the Graces. Hence ~AN a. [L, f. Gk *Thaleia* (*thallō* bloom).]

thăll'|ium, n. Rare soft white metallic element used in making a highly refractive optical glass. Hence ~IC, ~OUS, aa.. [f. foll. (from green line given in spectrum) +-IUM]

thăll'|us, n. Plant-body not differentiated into root, stem, and leaves. Hence ~OID a. [L, f. Gk *thallos* green shoot (*thallō* bloom)]

than (dhan, -ăn), conj. (& quasi-prep.) introducing second member of comparison, as *you are taller* ~ *he* (*is*), (colloq.) *taller* ~ *him, I know you better* ~ *he* (*does*), *better* ~ (I know) *him, it is better to use hot water* ~ *cold, do anything rather* ~ *let him get off; would do anything rather* ~ *that he should get off, a man* ~ *whom no one is better able to judge.* [OE *thanne* etc., orig. same wd as THEN; *A is better* ~ *B* orig. = *A is better, then B*; so OS *than*, OHG *danne*]

thān'age, n. Rank of, land granted to, thane. [ME, f. AF *thanage*, f. THANE + -AGE]

thănat|(o)-, comb. form of Gk *thanatos* death, as ~*ophĭd'ĭa* n. pl., poisonous snakes.

thăn'atoid, a. Deathlike, apparently dead; deadly. [as prec. + -OID]

thāne, n. (In early Eng. hist.) member of a rank between ordinary freemen and hereditary nobles. Hence ~'DOM, ~'HOOD, ~'SHIP, nn. [OE *theg(e)n, thēn* servant, soldier, = OS *thegan*, OHG *degan*, ON *thegn* f. Gmc *thegnaz* cogn. w. Gk *teknon* child]

thănk¹, v.t. Express gratitude to (person *for* thing); ~ *you*, I ~ *you* (polite formula acknowledging gift, service, offer accepted or refused); (as contempt. refusal) ~ *you for nothing*; (anticipatory) ~ *you* (*for that ball*)!, please throw it here; (as polite formula, now usu. iron. implying reproach) *I will* ~ *you to shut the door, wipe your boots, leave my affairs alone; he may* ~ *himself, has only himself to* ~, *for that*, it is his own fault. [OE *thancian*, (OS *thankōn*, OHG *dankōn*), f. foll.]

thănk², n. (now only in pl.). (Expression of) gratitude, as *give* ~s *to Heaven, expressed his heartfelt* ~s, *she bowed her* ~s, *small* (iron. *much*)~s *I got for it*; ~*-offering* (bibl.), Jewish offering made as act of thanksgiving; (as formula) ~s, thank you; ~s *to* (as the result of) *my foresight, your obstinacy*. Hence ~'WORTHY a. (arch.). [OE *thanc, thonc*, OS *thank*, OHG *dank*, (ON *thǫkk*), Goth. *thagks* f. Gmc *thankaz* cogn. w. THINK]

thănk'ful, a. Grateful; (of words or act) expressive of thanks. Hence ~LY² adv., ~NESS n. [-FUL]

thănk'less, a. Not feeling or expressing gratitude; *a* ~ *task* (not likely to win thanks, unprofitable). Hence ~LY² adv., ~NESS n. [-LESS]

thănks'giving, n. Expression of gratitude esp. to God; form of words for this, as *General T*~ (in Book of Common Prayer); *T*~ *day* (set apart in U.S. for ~ to God, usu. last Thursday of November); (bibl.) offering made as ~.

thar (tär), n. Goat antelope of Nepal. [native]

that, a., pron., & adv. **1.** demonstr. adj. & pron. (pr. dhăt; pl. *those* pr. dhōz). The (person, thing), the person or thing, pointed to or drawn attention to by or observed by the speaker at the time, or already named or understood or in question or familiar, as *observe* ~ *dog in the next field, who is* ~ (*woman*) *in the garden?, what was* ~ *noise?, what noise is* ~?, *don't roll your eyes like* ~ (as you are doing) or *in* ~ *imbecile fashion, I knew all* ~ *before, talked about responsibilities & all* ~ (similar commonplaces), ~ (your action, the action you tell me of) *is not fair*, ~'*s right!* (formula of approval, also vulg. = yes), (colloq.; also *there's*) ~'*s* (you, in view of present or future compliance etc., are) *a dear!, I use* ~ (or *the*) *term in a special sense, much to the disgust of* ~ (or *the*) *monarch, was cured from* ~ *hour, things were easier in those* *days, so ~'s ~* (formula closing narrative or discussion), *come out of ~* (sl. form ordering person etc. to clear out), *wouldn't give ~* (a finger-snap) *for it, AT ~* ; (with feeling) *I will not see ~ boy put upon, why will you bring ~ woman here?, when you have done thumping ~ piano, shall not easily forget~ day* ; (coupled or contrasted with *this*, & applied esp. to the farther, less immediate or obvious, etc., of two) *this poker is much heavier than ~* (one), *went to this doctor & ~* or *to this & ~ doctor* (various doctors), *this, ~, & the other* (various things), *put this & ~* (various facts etc.) *together* ; (as pron. replacing *the* w. noun, w. sense completed by rel. pron. expressed or, in obj. case & arch. in subj., omitted) *those who drink water think water, those may try it who choose, had ~ in his eye which forbade further trifling, all those* (~) *I saw, all those* (usu. *the*) *specimens ~ I saw, those* (usu. *the*) *few* (*books*) *~ I had, a different pattern to ~* (*which*) *I was used to* ; (or by adj. or equivalent) *those unfit for use, those below the standard, a tunic like ~ described above, those* (usu. *the*) *persons most injured by the tax, like most of those issuing from German workshops, cost of oil is less than ~ of gas* ; (foll. by *that* conj.) such, such a, as has ~ *confidence in his theory that he would put it into practice tomorrow, was wounded to ~ degree that he resigned.* **2.** adv. (pr. dhăt). To such a degree, so, as (colloq.) *will go ~ far, have done ~ much,* (vulg.) *I was ~ angry I could have struck him.* **3.** rel. pron. (pl. same ; pr. dhat ; used, exc. arch., rhet., poet., only to introduce defining-clause essential or rhet. viewed as essential to identification ; now largely replaced by WHO & to some extent by WHICH, esp. after antecedent ; in obj. case, & in arch. use in subj., ~ is often omitted ; prep. governing ~ is always placed after it & usu. at end of clause). Exx. : *the book* (~ or *which*) *I sent you, the box* (~ or *which*) *you put them in, the man* (~ or usu. *whom*) *you stopped, the people* (~) *you got it from* or *from whom you got it, the meanest flower ~* (rarely *which*) *blows, the best ~* (not *which*) *you can do, no one* (~ ; not *whom*) *I ever heard of could see any difference* ; (coupled) *Mrs Smith, Mary Jones ~* (not *who*) *was* (=whose maiden name was Mary Jones). [OE *thæt*, nom. & acc. sing. neut. of the demonstr. pron. & adj. *se, sēo, thæt* ; see THE]

that² (dhat, occas. -ăt), conj. introducing subordinate clauses : (of statement or hypothesis) *they say* (~) *he is better, there is no doubt* (~) *he meant it, it is suggested ~ the mistake was intentional, it is hoped ~ all will go well, it is monstrous ~ he should expect further help, to think* (~) *he should use me so!* ; (of purpose) *he lives ~ he may eat, he withdrew* (in order) ~ *the dispute might cease* : (of result) *am so sleepy* (~) *I cannot keep my eyes open, his language was such ~ we declined further dealings with him, what have I done ~ he should cut me?, where is he, ~ you come without him?* ; (of reason or cause) *it is rather~ he has not the time, not~* (I do not say this because) *I have any objection* ; (of wish) (O) ~ *that were all!,* (O) ~ *I knew the truth!* ; (arch. or literary) *in ~,* since, in so far as : *now ~,* since now, as *you ought to write now ~ you know the address.* [uses of THAT¹ demonstr. or rel. pron., in which it becomes a mere relative or conjunctive particle ; cf. THE]

thătch, n., & v.t. **1.** Roof-covering of straw, reeds, or (in tropical countries) coconut & other leaves ; (colloq.) hair of the head. **2.** v.t. Cover (roof, house, or abs.) with ~. [(n.) late collateral form of (now dial.) *thack* (after the vb *thatch*, OE *thecc(e)an*), OE *thæc*, OHG *dach*, ON *thak* f. Gmc **thakam* cogn. w. L *tegere* cover]

thaum'atrŏpe, n. Disc etc. on which are depicted images that appear to go through various movements when disc revolves. [irreg. f. Gk *thauma* wonder + *-tropos* -turning]

thaum'atŭrg|e, n. Worker of miracles, wonder-worker. Hence or cogn. **thaumatŭr'gic(AL)** aa., ~IST, ~Y¹, nn. [f. med. L f. Gk *thaumatourgos* a. (*thauma -matos* wonder + -o- + *-ergos* -working)]

thaw, v.i. & t., & n. **1.** (Of ice, snow, frozen thing) pass to liquid state, melt, dissolve ; (of weather, *it*) become so warm as to melt ice etc., rise above 32° Fahr. ; (fig.) be freed from coldness or stiffness, unbend, become genial ; cause to ~ (lit. & fig.). **2.** n. ~ing, warmth of weather that ~s, as *a ~ has set in.* Hence ~'LESS, ~'Y², aa. [OE *thawian,* OHG *douwen,* ON *theyja*]

the (*before vowel* dhĭ, *before consonant* dhe, *emphat.* dhē), a. & adv. **1.** adj. Applied esp. to person(s) or thing(s) already mentioned or under discussion, or from the nature of the case actually or potentially existent, or unique (as class or individual), or familiar, or otherwise sufficiently identified, as *tried to soothe ~ child, gave ~ fellow a shilling, shall let ~ matter drop, how is ~ game* or *score?, what is ~ time?, depends on ~ weather, ~ Devil, sun, moon, stars, Thames, inflammation of ~ lungs, pulled ~ trigger, what was ~ result?, you will be ~ loser, revised by ~ author, find their way to ~ sea, went to ~ baths, theatre, rink, ~ King, ~ Home Secretary, ~ M*ᶜ*Gregor etc.* (chief of clan), *story does not lose in ~ telling* ; to sing. n. as repr. species, class, etc., as ~ *lion, domestic cat, philosopher, cucumber, gavotte, general reader, man in the street, new woman,* (rhet., esp. bibl.) ~ *oppressor, locust* ; to some nn. used in restricted sense, esp. fig. repr. a pursuit etc., as ~ *gloves, ribbons, table, stage, theatre, platform, hustings, bottle, pulpit, fancy* ;

to names of diseases etc. (now partly arch.), as ~ *smallpox, measles, toothache, gout, fidgets, blues* (depression), *hump,* (vulg.) ~ (habit of) *drink*; to nn. expr. a unit, as *10d.*~ (or a or per) *pound, yard,* etc., *£15* ~ *coat & skirt, allow 8 minutes* (to) ~ *mile, 16 oz to* ~ *pound*; with sense completed by rel. clause or adj. or equivalent, as ~ *book* (*that) you borrowed,* ~ *best* (*that) I can do for you, has not* ~ *nerve for motoring, wonder you have*~ *impudence* (*to ask it* expr. or understood), (exclam.)~ *impudence of*~ *fellow!,* ~ *cup on* ~ *top shelf,* ~ *one with a broken handle,* ~ *bottom of a well,* ~ *best way,* ~ *only way,* ~ *way out,* ~ *upper classes,* ~ *better man of the two*; w. adjj. used abs., as *none but* ~ *brave* (brave men) *deserve* ~ *fair,* ~ *beautiful* (beauty), ~ *sublime*; w. adjj. rhet. viewed as part of definition, as ~ *virtuous & talented Duchess of X., details of*~ *shocking disaster,* ~ *enraged animal*; (dhē; italics) applied to the person or thing best known or best entitled to the name, as *no relation to the Browning, the tobacco is* (advertiser's). 2. adv. (a) rel., only in comb. w. (b). In whatever degree. (b) In that degree, by that amount, on that account. Exx.: ~ *more he gets,* ~ *more he wants*; *I play* ~ *worse,* ~ *more I practise*; *am not* (or none)~ *more inclined to help him because he is poor, on that account, for what you tell me*; *none* ~. *better for seeing you*; *that makes it all* ~ *worse* (in the full degree to be expected from what you say etc.); (tautologically) *so much*~ *worse for him,* ~ worse, so much worse, for him. [late OE *the,* the reduced & flexionless stem of the OE demonstr. *se, sēo, thæt* (= THAT[1]), = ON *sá, sú, that,* Goth. *sa, sō, thata,* cogn. w. Gk *ho, hē, to,* Skr. *sa, sā, tat*; **2.** OE *thȳ, thē,* instrumental case]

theān'dric, a. Of the union, by joint agency, of divine & human nature in Christ. [f. eccl. Gk *theandrikos* (*theos* god, *anēr andros* man, -IC)]

theānthrōp'ic(al), aa. Both divine & human; tending to embody deity in human form. [f. eccl. Gk *theanthrōpos* god-man f. *theos* god + *anthrōpos* man + -IC]

thē'archy (-kI), n. Government by god(s); class, order, of gods, as *the Olympian* ~. [f. eccl. Gk *thearkhia* rule of god (Gk *theos* god + -*arkhia* f. *arkhō* rule)]

thē'atre (-ter), n. Building for dramatic spectacles, playhouse; ‖ *patent* ~ (established by letters patent, not licensed by Lord Chamberlain); room, hall, for lectures etc. with seats in tiers (*operating*-~, for surgical demonstrations); dramatic literature or art; scene, field, of operation, as *the* ~ *of war*; *good* ~ (pred.), effective on the stage; ~-*goer, -going,* frequenter, frequenting, of~s. [ME, f. OF, or L f. Gk *theatron* f. *theaomai* behold]

theāt'rical, a. & n. **1.** (Of manner, speech,

gesture, person) calculated for effect, showy, affected; of or suited to the theatre, of acting or actors, so **theāt'rical.** (rare). **2.** n. pl. ~ performances, esp. *private* (amateur) ~*s.* Hence ~ISM(2, 4), ~ITY (-ǎl⁴), nn., ~IZE(3) v.t., ~LY² adv. [f. LL f. Gk *theatrikos* (prec., -ICAL)]

Thēbā'id (or thē⁴), n. Territory around Thebes (in Egypt); poem on (siege of) Thebes (in Greece), esp. that of Statius. [f. L f. Gk *Thēbaïs -idos* (*Thēbai* Thebes)]

Thēb'an, a. & n. (Inhabitant) of Thebes. [-AN]

thé dansant (tā dahṅsahṅ), n. Afternoon tea with dancing. [F]

thee. See THOU.

theft, n. Stealing; larceny. [OE *thiefth, thēofth,* later *thēoft* (THIEF, -TH¹)]

thegn (-ān), n. (hist.). Older form of THANE.

thē'ine, n. = CAFFEINE. [f. mod. L *thea* tea + -INE¹]

their (dhār), possessive case of, & adj. corresponding to, THEY, with absolute form *theirs* (for uses cf. HER²). [f. ON *their(r)a* gen. pl. of *sā* = OE *se* THE]

thē'|ism, n. Belief in existence of a god supernaturally revealed to man (cf. DEISM) & sustaining a personal relation to his creatures. So ~IST n., ~is'TIC(AL) aa. [f. Gk *theos* god + -ISM]

them. See THEY.

thēmāt'ic, a. (Mus.) of themes, as ~ *treatment,* ~ *catalogue* (giving opening themes as well as names etc.); (gram.) of, belonging to, a theme, as ~ *vowel, form.* Hence **thēmāt'ICALLY** adv. [f. Gk *thematikos* (as foll., -IC)]

thēme, n. Subject on which one speaks, writes, or thinks; school composition, essay, on given subject; (gram.) stem of noun or verb, part to which inflexions are added; (mus.) melodic subject usu. developed with variations; (hist.) any of 29 provinces in Byzantine empire; ~ *song,* recurrent melody in musical play or film. [ME, f. L f. Gk *thema -matos* (*tithēmi* set, place, see -M); partly thr. OF]

Thēm'is, n. (Gk myth.) goddess of law & justice; these personified. [L f. Gk *Themis* law]

themselves (dhemsělz'), pron. Emphat. & reflex. form corresp. to THEY (for use, cf. HIMSELF). [see SELF]

then (dhěn), adv., conj., a., & n. **1.** adv. At that time, then (*was* ~ *too much occupied,* ~ *comes the trouble, the* ~ *existing ordinances*); next, afterwards, after that, as *it must* ~ *soak for two hours, & ~ the operation is complete*; *now & ~,* at one time & another, from time to time. **2.** conj. In that case, therefore, it follows that, (often *well,* ~), as ~ *you should have said so,* ~ *it is no use your going,* (*but) ~* (if what you say is true) *why did you take it?*; (of grudging or impatient concession) *if you must have it so,* as *take it* ~, *between you & I* . . . *'me'*, ~; (resumptively, not as first word) accordingly, as *the new Governor*, ~, *came prepared*; NOW ~. **3.** adj. Existing etc. at that time, as *the ~ Duke, secretary*. **4.** n. That time, as *before, till, by, from*, ~; *every now & ~*, from time to time. [OE *thanne, thenne*, etc., = OS *than(na)*, OHG *danne, denne*, (cf. Goth. *than*), adv. formation f. demonstr. root *tha-*; cf. THAT, THE]

then'ar, n. (anat.). Palm of hand, sole of foot; (also attrib.~ *prominence, eminence*) ball of thumb. [Gk *thenar*]

thence (dh-), adv. (Arch.) from that place, from there; (somewhat arch.) from that source, for that reason, as *a discrepancy ~ results*, *it ~ appears*; *~forth'*, *~for'ward*, advv. & nn., from (or *from*) that time forward. [ME *thannes, thennes*, f. *thenne* adv. (OE *thanon*(e) etc., f. *tha-* as THEN), +-ES]

the'o-, comb. form of Gk *theos* god, as: *~oc'racy*, government or State governed by God directly or through a sacerdotal class etc., *the Theoc'racy*, Jewish commonwealth from Moses to the monarchy; *the'ocrat*, ruler in, subject under, *~ocracy*, so *theocrat'ic* a.; *~oc'ratist*, believer in direct intervention & authority of God through revelation in government of society; *~oc'rasy* (or *the'ōkrāsi*) [f. Gk *krasis* mixture], union of soul with God through contemplation (among Neo-platonists, Buddhists, etc.); *~od'icy* [f. Gk *dikē* right], vindication of divine providence in view of existence of evil; *~og'ony*, (poem dealing with) genealogy of the gods, so *theogōn'ic* a., *~ōg'onist* n.; *~ōm'achy* (-kĭ), strife against or among the gods; *theomān'ia*, insane belief that one is God, also, religious insanity, so *theomān'iac* n.; *~ōph'any*, appearance of God to man, so *theophan'ic* a.; *theophilan'thropist*, one who professes to unite love to God with love to man, so *theophilanthrop'ic* a., *theophilan'thropist*, *theophilan'thropy*, nn.; *theopneus'ty*, divine inspiration, so *theopneus'tic* a.; *the'otechny* (-k-), supernatural machinery, so *theotech'nic* (-k-) a.

theod'ol|ite, n. Surveying-instrument for measuring horizontal and vertical angles by means of telescope. Hence ~**it'ic** a. [16th c. -*delitus*, of unkn. orig. (Engl.) orig.]

Theodōs'ian, a. Of the emperor Theodosius (I, II, or III), esp. ~ *code* (published under Theodosius II, d. 450). [-AN]

theolō'gian, n. Person skilled in, professor of, theology. [F (-*ien*), as foll. +-AN]

theol'ogy, n. Science of (esp. Christian) religion; *natural* ~ (dealing with knowledge of God as gained from his works by light of nature & reason); *positive*, ~ (based on revelation); *dogmatic* ~ (dealing with authoritative teaching of the Scriptures & the Church); *speculative* ~ (giving scope to human speculation, not confined to revelation);

systematic ~, methodical arrangement of the truths of religion in their natural connexion. Hence or cogn. **theolō'gical** a., **theolō'gically** [2] adv., **theol'ogize**(1, 2) v.t. & i. [ME & OF *theologie* f. L f. Gk THEO(*logia* -LOGY)]

theorb'o, n. (pl. ~s). Two-necked musical instrument of lute class much used in 17th c. [f. It. *tiorba*, of unkn. orig.; whence F *téorbe, théorbe*]

the'or|em, n. (Math.) proposition to be proved by chain of reasoning, a truth to be established by means of accepted truths, (cf. PROBLEM); algebraical or other rule, esp. one expressed by symbols or formulae, as BINOMIAL *~em*; a speculative truth. Hence *~ēmāt'ic*(AL) aa., *~ēm'atist*(3) n. [f. F, or LL f. Gk *theōrēma* (*theōreō*, see THEORY & -M)]

theor|ēt'ic, a. & n. **1.** = foll. **2.** n. pl. Speculative parts of a science etc., so *~ēti'cian* (-ĭshn) n. [f. LL f. Gk *theōrētikos* (as THEORY, see -ETIC)]

theorēt'ical, a. Concerned with knowledge but not with its practical application, speculative; based on mere theory, not dealing with facts as presented by experience. Hence *~*LY [2] adv. [-AL]

the'or|y, n. Supposition explaining something, esp. one based on principles independent of the phenomena etc. to be explained, opp. to HYPOTHESIS, as *atomic ~y*, *~y of gravitation, evolution*; speculative view, as *one of my pet ~ies* (often implying fancifulness); the sphere of speculative thought, as *this is all very well in ~y, but how will it work in practice?*; exposition of the principles of a science etc., as *the ~y of music*; (math.) collection of results designed to illustrate principles of a subject, as *~y of chances, equations*. Hence *~*IST(3), *~*IZA'TION, nn., *~*IZE(2) v.i. [f. LL f. Gk *theōria* f. *theōros* spectator f. *theōreō* behold]

theōs'oph|y, n. Any of various ancient & modern philosophies professing to attain to a knowledge of God by spiritual ecstasy, direct intuition, or special individual relations. Hence or cogn. **the'osoph**, *~*ER [1], *~*IST(2), nn., **theosoph'ic**(AL), **theosophis'tical**, aa., *~*IZE(2) v.i. [f. med. L f. late Gk *theosophia* f. THEO(*sophos* wise)]

-ther, -ter, suf. repr. (a) Aryan compar. suf. *-tero-*, Gk *-teros*, L *-ter* (*alter, neuter*), as in *after, further*; *either, other, whether*; (b) indicating direction (cf. Goth. *-thrō, -drē*, L *citro, ultro*), as in *hither, thither, whither*.

therapeut'|ic, a. & n. **1.** Curative; of the healing art. **2.** n. pl. Branch of medicine concerned with treatment of disease & action of remedial agents in disease or health. Hence *~*ICAL a., *~*ICALLY [2] adv., *~*IST(3) n. [f. LL f. Gk *therapeutikos* (*therapeuō* wait on, cure, f. *theraps* servant, see -IC)]

-the'rapy, suf. f. Gk *therapeia* service,

medical treatment, denoting medical treatment as indicated by first element of wd; also as n. (*occupational therapy*).

there (dhār, dher *as below*), adv., n., & int. **1.** In or at that place, as *put it down ~, what is that dog doing ~?, lived ~ some years, have been ~ before* (sl.), know all about it, *all ~* (sl.), in one's senses, sane, *~ it is—on the sofa*, (calling attention) *you ~!*; at that point in argument, progress of affairs, situation, etc., as *~ I agree with you, ~ is* (or *comes in*) *the rub, you had* (the advantage of) *him ~,~ it* (the trouble) *is, you see*; HERE *&~*, *neither* HERE *nor ~*; to that place, as *go ~ every day, got ~ in two minutes, get ~* (sl.), succeed; *~ or ~abouts*, (transf.) about that amount, time, etc. (*'was it two years ago?'* *'T~ or ~abouts'; will come to £100, ~ or ~abouts*); (merely expletive or introductory, usu. dher; preceding, or in interrog. or neg. or quasi-neg. sentence following, verb that normally precedes its subject, esp. *be*; in poet. or exclam. use subject may stand first) *~ was a cart close by, ~ was nothing ~, ~ was plenty to eat, what is ~ for supper?, not a sound was ~ to indicate their presence, seldom·has ~ been more fuss, ~. fell a deep silence, a knight ~ was, a nice mess ~ is or seems to be!; ~'s* (=THAT¹'s) *a dear* etc. **2.** n. That place, as *was brought from ~, lives somewhere near ~, tide comes up to ~, passed by ~.* **3.** int. Expr. confirmation, triumph, dismay, etc., as *~! what did I tell you?*, or used to soothe child etc., as *~, ~, never mind.* **4.** *~about(s)'*, near that place, as *ought to be somewhere ~abouts*, near that number, quantity, etc., as *two gallons or ~abouts; ~af'ter* (arch.), after that, according to that rule etc.; *~anent'* (Sc.), about that matter; *~at'* (arch.), at that place, on that account, after that; *~by'* (or dhār'bī), by that means, as result of that (*& ~by hangs a tale*, in which connexion there is something to be told, see *As You Like It*, II. vii. 28); *~for'* (arch.), for that object or purpose; *~'fore*, for that reason, accordingly, consequently; *~from'* (arch.), from that or it; *~in'* (arch.), in that place, in that respect; *~inaf'ter ~before'*, later, earlier, in same document etc.; *~in'to* (arch.), into that place; *~of'* (arch.), of that or it; *~on'* (arch.), on that or it (of motion & position); *~out'* (arch.), out of that, from that source; *~through'* (arch.), through that; *~to'* (arch.), to that or it, in addition, to boot; *~un'to* (arch.), to that or it; *~upon'*, in consequence of that, soon or immediately after that, (arch.) upon that (of motion or position); *~with'* (arch.), with that, *~upon*; *~withal'*, in addition, besides. [OE *thǣr, thēr*, OS *thār*, OHG *dār*, ON, Goth. *thar* f. demonstr. root *tha-* (THAT, THE)]

theri'ăc, n. (Also *theri'aca Andrŏm'achi* pr. -akī, *Venice treacle*) antidote to bites

of poisonous animals compounded of many drugs. [f. L f. Gk *thēriakē* antidote, fem. adj. as n. (*thērion* dim. of *thēr* wild beast, see -AC)]

theri|ănthrŏp'ic, a. Of, worshipping, beings represented under form of man & beast. So *~ăn'throp*ISM(3) n. [f. Gk *thērion* beast *+anthrōpos* man *+*-IC]

therm, n. Statutory unit of calorific value in gas-supply (100,000 B.Th. units; see THERMAL). [f. Gk *therm* as prec.]

therm'ae, n. pl. (Gk & Rom. ant.). Hot springs or (esp. public) baths. [L, f. Gk *thermai* pl. as prec.]

therm'al, a. & n. **1:** Of heat, as *~ unit* (for measuring heat); *British ~ unit* (abbr. *B.Th.U.*), amount of heat required to raise 1 lb. of water at maximum density through 1° Fahr.; *~ equator*, line along which greatest heat occurs on earth's surface; *~ springs*, hot springs; of thermac. **2.** n. Rising current of heated air (used by gliders). Hence *~LY²* adv. [f. F, as THERM *+*-AL]

thermăn'tidōte, n. Apparatus for cooling the air, used in India. [as THERM *+* ANTIDOTE]

therm'ic, a. Of heat, as *~rays, conditions*. [as THERM *+*-IC]

Thermidōr'ian, n. Any of those who effected or favoured Robespierre's overthrow on Thermidor 9th, 1794. [f. F *thermidorien* (*thermidor*, republican month July–August, as THERM *+* Gk *dōron* gift), see -IAN]

therm'ion, n. An ION emitted by an incandescent substance. Hence **thermiŏn'ic** a. (*~ic valve* or *vacuum tube*, appliance giving copious flow of electrons used esp. in wireless transmission & reception). [THERMO- *+*ION]

therm'ite, -mit, n. Mixture of finely powdered aluminium and oxide of iron that produces a very high temperature on combustion (used in welding and as a composition for incendiary bombs). [G (*-mit*), f. foll. *+*-ITE¹]

therm'o-, comb. form of Gk *thermos* warm, *thermē* heat, as: *~chem'istry* (-kĕm-), branch of chemistry dealing with the quantities of heat evolved or absorbed during chemical reactions; *~(electric) couple, = ~pile; ~dynam'ics*, science of the relations between heat & mechanical work; *~electri'city*, electricity produced by difference of temperature, so *~-elec'tric* a.; *~gen'esis*, production of heat esp. in human body, so *~genĕt'ic, ~gĕn'ic*, aa.; *~gram*, record made by *~graph* (self-registering thermometer); *~nuclear* (hydrogen) *bomb; ~pile, ~*-electric battery esp. arranged for measuring small quantities of radiant heat; *~scope*, instrument for detecting differences of temperature without measuring, so *~scop'ic(al)* aa.; *~setting*, (of plastics) setting when heated; *~stat*, automatic instrument for regulating temperature, so *~stăt'ic* a.;

~stăt'ics, theory of the equilibrium of heat; ~tăx'is, regulation of heat or temperature esp. in warm-blooded animals, so ~tăc'tic, ~tăx'ic, aa.; ther-mŏt'ropism, involuntary movement of animal or plant towards or away from source of heat.

thermŏm'eter, n. Instrument for measuring temperature, usu. glass tube with small bore containing mercury or alcohol, & variously graduated (Fahrenheit, Réaumur, Celsius or Centigrade, ~, with freezing-point at 32°, 0°, 0°, boiling-point of water at 212°, 80°, 100°); clinical ~ (small, with range of 25° or less, for taking temperature of the body); MAXIMUM, MINIMUM, ~. Hence thermomĕt'ric(AL) aa., thermomĕt'ricaLY² adv., ther-mŏm'etry n. [THERMO-+-METER]

therm'ŏs, n. T~ flask or ~, brand of VACUUM flask. [P]

ther'oid, a. (Esp. of idiot) having beast-like propensities. [f. Gk thēr wild beast +-OID]

therŏl'ogǀ|ў, n. Science of mammals, mammalogy. So ~IST n. [as prec.+ -LOGY]

thesaur'us, n. (pl. -rī). Elaborate lexicon, cyclopaedia. [L, f. Gk thēsauros treasure]

these. See THIS.

thēs'is (or thĕ- as below), n. (pl. thēses pr. -ēz). 1. Proposition to be maintained; dissertation, esp. one bʸ candidate for degree; school or college exercise. 2. (Also thĕ-) unaccented syllable in English scansion (cf. ARSIS). [L f. Gk thesis putting, placing; a proposition etc., f. the- root of tithēmi place]

Thēs'pian, a. & n. 1. Of Thespis, semi-legendary Greek dramatic poet of 6th c. B.C.; the ~ art, the drama. 2. n. Actor or actress. [f. Gk Thespis+-AN]

thĕt'a, n. Greek letter (Θ, θ) = th. [Gk]

thē'ūrgǀ|ў, n. Supernatural agency esp. in human affairs; art of securing this; magical science of Neoplatonists; production of effects by supernatural agency opp. natural magic. Hence or cogn. thēūr'gIC(AL) aa., ~IST(3) n. [f. LL f. Gk theourgia f. theos god+-ergos working]

thews (-z), n. pl. Sinews, muscles; (fig.) mental or moral vigour. Hence thewED² (-ūd), thew'LESS, thew'y², aa. [OE thēaw, =OS thau, OHG dau usage, custom]

they (dhā), pron. (obj. them pr. dhem, -ĕm, poss. THEIR). Pl. of HE, SHE, IT; ~ (the persons) who; ~ (people in general) say; ~ (those in authority) have raised the rates; (joc.) them's (those are) my sentiments. [OE their nom. pl. masc. of sd, sú, that THE]

thick, a., n., & adv. 1. Of great or specified depth between opposite surfaces, as bread is (cut) too ~, spread the butter ~, a board two inches ~, how ~ was it? (of line etc.) broad, not fine, (of script, type, etc.) consisting of ~ lines. 2. Arranged closely, crowded together, as ~ hair, forest, crowd grew ~er; numerous, as fell ~ as peas; abounding, packed, with, as trees ~ with leaves, air ~ with snow; of firm consistence, as ~ paste, soup; turbid, muddy, cloudy, not clear, as ~ puddles, weather is still ~. 3. Stupid, dull; (of voice) muffled, indistinct. 4. (colloq.). Intimate, esp. ~ as thieves. 5. Lay it on ~, (sl.) be profuse esp. in compliments; ǀǀ a bit ~, rather ~, a little too ~, etc. (sl.), going beyond what is reasonable, too much of a good thing; ǀǀ~ ear (sl.), external ear swollen as result of blow (esp. in give person a ~ ear). 6. ~'head, blockhead; ~-headed, stupid; ~'sĕt', set or growing close together, heavily or solidly built, (n., ~'set) kind of stout fustian, (also ~set hedge) close-grown hedge; ~-skinned, (fig.) not sensitive to reproach, insult, etc., stolid; ~-skulled, -witted, stupid; ǀǀ~'un (obs. sl.), sovereign (coin). 7. n. The ~ part of anything, esp. fig. in the ~ of it (of fight etc.); (colloq.) stupid person; through ~ & thin, under all conditions, resolutely, so ~-&-thin a., as ~-&-thin supporters. 8. adv. ~ly, as snow was falling ~, blows came fast & ~, heart beats ~. Hence ~'ISH¹ a., ~'LY² adv. [OE thicce, OS thikki, OHG dicki, ON thykkr f. Gmc *thik(k)uz]

thick'en, v.t. & i. Make or become thick; make (gravy etc.) of stiffer consistence, whence ~ING¹(3) n.; plot ~s (becomes more intricate). [-EN⁶]

thick'ĕt, n. Number of shrubs, trees, etc., growing close together. [OE thiccet f. THICK+-et denominative suf.]

thick'ness, n. Being thick; dimension other than length & breadth; piece of material of known ~, as three ~es of cardboard will suffice. [-NESS]

thief, n. (pl. -ves). 1. One who steals esp. secretly & without violence, whence thiev'ERY(4), thiev'ishNESS, nn., thiev-ISH¹ a., thiev'ishLY² adv.; thieves' LATIN. 2. Projection in wick of candle causing it to gutter. [OE thēof, OS thiof, OHG diob, ON thjófr, Goth thiufs f. Gmc *theubhaz]

thieve, v.i. & t. Be a thief, practise stealing; steal (thing). [OE thēofian (as prec.)]

thigh (thī), n. Part of human leg between hip & knee, corresponding part in other animals; smile HIP¹ and ~; ~-bone, single bone of ~, femur. Hence (-)~ED² (-id) a. [OE thēoh, OHG dioh, ON thjó f. Gmc *theuham]

thill, n. Shaft of cart or carriage; (also ~'ER¹ n.) ~-horse (put between ~s). [14th c., of uncert. orig.; cf. DEAL³]

thim'ble, n. 1. Metal cap (occas. open at end) worn to protect finger & push needle in sewing; (mech.) short metal tube, as ~ joint, coupling; metal ring concave on outside & fitting in rope to prevent chafing. 2. ~ful (-bl-fŏŏl), small quantity (of brandy etc.) to drink; ~-pie, rapping on head with ~, as punishment;

~rig n. & v.i., (play) sleight-of-hand trick with three ~-shaped cups & pea, by-standers betting which cup covers pea, **~rigger**, one who plays this, sharper. [OE *thȳmel*, as THUMB +-LE(1)]

thin¹, a. Having opposite surfaces close together, of small diameter, slender, as ~ *wire, string, board, sheet*; not dense, as ~ *air*; not full or closely packed, as ~ *house* (theatre); of slight consistency, as ~ *gruel*; lacking in important ingredient, as ~ *beer, blood, voice, humour, eloquence*; (fig.) shallow, transparent, flimsy, as ~ *disguise, excuse,* (colloq.) *that's too ~*; lean, not plump; (of lines) narrow, fine, (of script, type, etc.) consisting of ~ lines; (sl.) uncomfortable, distasteful, (esp. *have a ~ time*); *through* THICK *and* ~; ~-*skinned,* (fig.) sensitive. Hence ~'LY² adv., ~'NESS n., ~n'ISH¹ a. [OE *thynne*, OS *thunni*, OHG *dunni*, ON *thunnr* f. Gmc **thunnuz* cogn. w. L *tenuis*]

thin², v.t. & i. (-nn-). Make or become thin, reduce in bulk or numbers, as *his hair is* ~*ning, nation had* ~*ned under* (or *been* ~*ned by*) *proscription*; remove some young fruit from (vine, tree) to improve growth of rest (also ~ *out seedlings* etc.). [OE *thynnian*, as prec.]

thine. See THY.

thing, n. 1. Whatever is or may be an object of thought (including or opp. to *person*), as: (of animate objects, esp. persons, expr. contempt, pity, affection, etc.) *poor ~, spiteful ~, a dear old ~, dumb* ~*s,* (sl.) OLD ~*, &* ~*s* (colloq.=*& the like, etc.*); (of inanimate material object) *take those* ~*s off the table, platinum is a costly ~, got my* ~*s* (clothes) *wet, pack up your* ~*s* (personal belongings); (of act, fact, idea, course, task, affair, circumstance) *a foolish ~ to do,* SOFT ~, PUT¹-*up* ~, *strange* ~ *that you cannot hold your tongue, that is not the same ~, the only ~ now is to take a cab, the* ~ (to aim at) *is to improve the pace,* ~*s begin to look brighter, has made a mess of* ~*s, takes* ~*s too seriously*; (of specimen or type of work etc.) *the latest* ~ *in hats, a little* ~ *of mine I should like to read to you; not the* (conventionally proper) ~; *am not feeling at all the* ~ (well); (law) ~*s personal, real,* personal, real, property; (pl., with adj. following, often joc.) all that is so describable (~*s Japanese, political, feminine, scholastic,* etc.). 2. *Do the handsome* ~ *by,* treat handsomely; *have a* ~ *about* (colloq.), be obsessed by; *know a* ~ *or two,* be experienced or shrewd; *make a good* ~ *of,* make good profit by. [OE (= OS, ON) *thing,* OHG *ding* public assembly etc.]

thing'amy, thing'umajig, thing'um-bŏb, thing'ummy, nn. (colloq.). Person, thing, whose name one forgets or treats as known, what's-his-name, what-d'you--call-it. [prec.]

think, v.t. & i. (*thought* pr. thawt). 1. Consider, be of opinion, as *we* ~ (*that*)

he will come, we do not ~ *it probable, I* ~ *it a shame, it is not thought fair, is thought to be a fraud, I don't* ~ (sl. addition to ironical statement, as *you are a pattern of tact, I don't* ~). 2. Intend, expect, as ~*s to deceive us.* 3. Form conception of, as *cannot* ~ *the infinite,* (colloq.) *I can't* ~ *how you do it.* 4. Recognize presence or existence of, as *the child thought no harm.* 5. Reduce to specified condition etc. by ~ing, as *cannot* ~ *away a toothache, will* ~ *himself silly.* 6. Exercise the mind otherwise than by passive reception of another's ideas, as *let me* ~ (appeal for time before answering etc.), ~ *twice before doing* (avoid hasty action), ~ *in German* etc. 7. Have half-formed intention, as *I* ~ *I'll try.* 8. ~ *about,* consider, esp. consider the practicability of (scheme, doing); ~ *aloud,* utter one's thoughts in the order of their occurrence; ~ *fit* or *good,* choose (*to* do esp. arbitrary or foolish thing); ~ *of,* consider, imagine, propose to oneself, entertain the idea of, hit upon, as *have many things to* ~ *of, to* ~ *of* (one can hardly imagine) *his not guessing it!, must be* ~*ing of going, couldn't* ~ *of such a thing,* ~ *of a word beginning with B, would have telephoned if I had thought of it;* ~ *better of,* decide on second thoughts to abandon (intention), (also) have higher opinion of (person, esp. *than to believe* etc.); ~ *little* or *nothing of,* consider insignificant or contemptible, as ~ *nothing of 30 miles a day, I* ~ *nothing of your friend Jones;* ~ *much, well, highly, meanly, of,* esteem thus, ~ *no small* BEER *of;* ~ *out,* consider carefully, devise (plan etc.); ~ *over* (adv. or prep.), reflect upon, as ~ *over what I have said, will* ~ *it over;* ~ *up* (colloq.), devise. Hence ~'ABLE, ~'ING² (*all* ~*ing men,* all who accept my view), aa., ~'ER¹ n. [OE *thenc(e)an,* OS *thenkian,* OHG *denken,* ON *thekkja,* Goth. *thagkjan* f. Gmc **think-, *thank-* (whence also THANK), **thunk-*]

thi(o)-, comb. form of Gk *theion* sulphur, as ~*o-acid,* acid in which oxygen is replaced by sulphur.

third, a. & n. 1. Next after second, whence ~'LY² adv. 2. ***~ DEGREE, ‖~ ESTATE, *of* EXCHANGE¹; ~-*class,* -*rate,* (loosely) inferior, poor; (crick.) ~ *man,* (place of) fielder between slip(s) and point; ~ *party* or *person* (see PERSON for gram. sense), another besides the two principals, bystander etc., (~-*party risks* in insurance, damage to another than the insured, which the underwriter contracts to meet); ~ REPUBLIC. 3. n. One of three equal divisions of a whole. 4. Sixtieth of a second of time or angular measurement. 5. (mus.). Interval of which the span involves three alphabetical notes, harmonic combination of the notes thus separated. 6. ~ part of husband's personal property, formerly going to widow in certain cases. [OE *thridda*, OS *-io*, OHG *dritto*, ON *thrilhi*, Goth. *thridja* f. Gmc **thridhjaz* cogn. w. Gk *tritos*, L *tertius*]

thirst, n., & v.i. **1.** Suffering caused by want of drink, desire for drink (*have a* ~, colloq., want a drink); (fig.) ardent desire, craving, (*of, for, after*, glory, person's blood, etc.). **2.** v.i. Feel ~ (now chiefly fig. *for, after*). Hence ~'LESS a. [OE (OS) *thurst*, OHG *durst*, ON *thorsti*, Goth. *thaurstei* f. Gmc **thurs-* cogn. w. L *torrēre* parch; vb f. n., OE *thyrstan*]

thirs't|ў, a. Feeling thirst (*be~ў*, current E for *thirst* vb); fond of drink; (of country or season) dry, parched; (colloq.) causing thirst, as *this is ~у work*. Hence ~ILY² adv. [OE *thurstig* (prec., -Y¹)]

thir'teen', a. & n. One more than twelve, 13, xiii; *the ~ superstition* (that ~ as the number of persons at table, or of one's room etc., brings ill luck). Hence ~TH² a. & n. [OE *thrēotiene, -tēne* (as THREE, see -TEEN)]

thir't'ў, a. & n. Three times ten, 30, xxx; ~*-one* etc., ~*-first* etc.; *T~-nine Articles* (subscribed to by person taking orders in Ch. of Eng.); ~*-two-mo, 32mo*, book with 32 leaves to the sheet. Hence **thir't'ieth**, ~fold (see -FOLD), aa. /& nn. [OE *thritig* (thrī THREE, see -TY²)] /

this (dh-), a. & pron. (pl. *these* pr. dhēz). The (person, thing, the person or thing, close at hand or touched or pointed to or drawn attention to or observed by the speaker at the time, or already named or understood or in question or familiar (seldom idiomatically interchangeable with THAT¹, but often only equally applicable to the facts, the implication of greater nearness, familiarity, etc., being purely idiomatic), as *observe ~ dog on the hearth-rug, who are these people in the next room?, what is all ~ noise?, fold it like ~, I knew all ~ before, ~* (your action, the action I am speaking of) *is not fair, ~ term is liable to much abuse, things are easier in these days; ~ and* THAT¹; ~ *much*, ~ amount (esp. = what I am about to state, as *I know ~ much, that the thing is absurd*); ~, THAT¹, *& the other*; (of time) ~*-day*, today, *shall be or have been busy all ~ week, ought to be ready by ~* (time), *before ~* (time), *have been asking for it these* (or ~) *three weeks* (just past). [OE masc. *thes*, fem. *thēos*, neut. *this*, ult. f. root *tha-* (THAT¹); OE pl *thās* gave THOSE; the less common pl. *thæs*, ME *thēs*, later *these*, was ult. different. f. *those*]

this'ness (dh-), n. Quality of being this, = HAECCEITY. [-NESS]

thi'stle (-sl), n. Kinds of prickly composite plant with globular or cylindrical heads with purple, yellow, or white flowers, Scottish national emblem (cf. ROSE); *Order of the T~*, a Scottish order of knighthood. Hence **thi'stly²** (-sli) a. [OE *thistil, -el*, OHG *distil*, ON *thistell, -ill*]

thith'er (dhidh-), adv. (arch.). To that place, there (of motion). Hence ~WARD(s) adv. [OE *thider*, alt. (after HITHER) f. *thæder* f. root *tha-* (THAT¹, THE) +suf. -THER denoting motion towards, cf. HITHER, WHITHER]

tho'. See THOUGH.

‖ **thōle¹**, v.t. (arch., exc. Sc.). Undergo, endure, suffer, (pain, grief, etc., or abs.); permit, admit of. [OE *tholian*, OS *-ōn, -ian*, OHG *dolōn*, ON *thola*, Goth. *thulan* f. Gmc **thul-* cogn. w. L *tolerare*]

thōle², n. (Also ~*-pin*) pin in gunwale of boat as fulcrum for oar; each of two such pins between which oar plays. [OE *thol(l)*, MDu., MLG *dolle*, ON *thollr*]

Thom'|ism (tō-), n. Doctrine of Thomas Aquinas (died 1274), a scholastic philosopher and theologian, or of his followers. So ~IST n., ~is'tic(AL) aa. [-ISM]

thŏng, n., & v.t. **1.** Narrow strip of leather used as halter, reins, lash of whip, etc. **2.** v.t. Provide with ~, strike with ~. [OE *thwang, thwong* (cf. ON *thvengr*), f. Gmc **thwing-, *thwang-, *thwung-,* restrain (cf. G *zwingen*)]

Thōr, n. Scandinavian god of thunder, war, & agriculture; ~*'s hammer*, flint axe (-hammer). [f. ON *Thórr*]

thor'ăx, n. (Anat., zool.) part of trunk between neck & abdomen or tail, whence **thorǎ'cic** a., **thorǎ'ci-**, **thorǎ'cico-**, **thorǎc'o-**, comb. forms; (Gk ant.) breastplate, cuirass. [L, f. Gk *thōrax-akos*]

thor'ite, n. A black compact mineral found in Norway. [THOR +-ITE¹]

thor'ium, n. Radio-active metallic element, the oxide of which is used in gas-mantles. [THOR +-IUM]

thorn, n. **1.** Prickle, spiny process on plant, esp. abortive branch; kinds of ~y shrub or tree, as *haw~, while~, black~*; *a ~* in one's *flesh or side*, constant source of annoyance; *be, sit, on* ~s, be continuously uneasy esp. in expectation of being detected etc. at any moment. **2.** Name of the obs. E letter þ (th). **3.** ~*'back*, ray with spines on back and tail, British spider crab; ~*'bill,* ~*'tail*, kinds of humming-bird; ~*'tree* (S. Afr.), kinds of acacia. Hence ~*'LESS,* ~*Y²* (often fig. of affair, = hard to handle), aa. [OE, OS, ON *thorn*, OHG *dorn*, Goth. *thaurnus* f. Gmc **thurnuz*]

thorough (thǔ'rō), a., n., prep., & adv. **1.** Complete, unqualified, not superficial, out-&-out, as *his work is seldom ~, has caught a ~ chill, wants a ~ change, a ~ scoundrel*. **2.** n. (hist.). Uncompromising policy of Strafford & Laud under Charles I. **3.** prep. & adv. (arch.). Through (~ *bush, ~ brier*). **4.** ~*-bass*, bass part accompanied by signs esp. numerals to indicate the general harmony, such system of signs, (loosely) harmonic composition; ~*-brace*, strap between C-springs of vehicle; ~*-bred* a. & n., (animal, esp. horse) of pure breed, high-spirited, mettlesome, (also fig. of persons); ~fare, road, street, esp. one through which much traffic passes; no ~fare, (as notice at end of obstructed or private road) no passage; ~going, uncompromising, out--&-out; ~paced, (lit., of horse) trained to all paces, (fig.) complete, unqualified, as a ~paced rascal; ~pin, swelling in hollow of horse's hock. Hence~LY²(-ŭ'roll) adv., ~NESS (-ŭ'rōnĕs) n. [later OE thuruh, var. of thurh THROUGH]

thōrp(e), n. Village, hamlet. [OE, OS, ON thorp, OHG dorf, Goth. thaurp ƒ. Gmc *thorpam]

those. [pl. of THAT¹; see THIS]

thou (dhow), pron. (object. thee, pl. YE, YOU), & v.t. & i. Sing. pron. of 2nd pers., now arch. or poet. exc. in addressing God & (usu. thee as subject. with 3rd pers. vb) as used by Quakers; (v.t.) address (person) as ~; (v.i.) use ~ instead of you. [OE, OS thū, OHG dū, ON thū, Goth. thu ƒ. Gmc *thū cogn. w. L tu]

though (dhō), thō', conj. (Also although) notwithstanding the fact that, as he finished' first ~ he began last, ~ it was late we decided to go; (also although) on the supposition that, as it is better to ask him (even) ~ he (should) refuse or refuses; what ~ (what does it matter if) the way is (arch. be) long?; as ~, as if, as it is as ~ a man should ask alms of a beggar, he acts as ~ he were mad, it looks as ~ he meant (vulg. means) business; (introducing what is virtually an independent sentence) & yet, as I have no doubt he will understand ~ ~ you never know; (abs. or as adv.) however, as I wish you had told me, ~. [ME thoh etc. ƒ. ON thó (ƒ. *thauh), corresp. to OE thēah, thēh, OS thōh, OHG doh ƒ. Gmc *thauh]

thought¹ (thawt), n. 1. Process, power, of thinking; faculty of reason; sober reflection (in ~, meditating); consideration, as take ~ (consider matters), after serious ~, acts without ~; idea, conception, chain of reasoning, etc., produced by thinking, as an essay full of striking ~s, a happy ~, well-timed or apposite idea or suggestion; half-formed intention, as had (some) ~s of resigning, had no ~ of offending him; (usu. pl.) what one thinks, one's opinion, as will tell you my ~s of the matter; subject of one's ~, as his one ~ is how to get away, a PENNY for your ~s; you are much in my ~s, I often think of you. 2. A ~, a little, somewhat, as cut it a ~ shorter, seems to me a ~ arrogant; FREE¹~; quick as ~, very quick; second ~s, further consideration, as second ~s are best, on second ~s I will take a bus; ~-reader, -reading, reader, reading, of person's ~s by telepathy; ~-transference, telepathy; ~-wave, undulation of the supposed medium of ~-transference. Hence (-)~ED² (-awt-) a. [OE thoht ƒ. *thōht ƒ. *thanht ƒ. st. of thencan THINK +-t suff.]

thought². See THINK.

thought'ful (-awt-), a. Engaged in or given to meditation; (of book, writer, remark, etc.) giving signs of original thought; (of persons or conduct) considerate, not haphazard or unfeeling. Hence ~LY² adv., ~NESS n. [ME; -FUL]

thought'less (-awt-), a. Careless of consequences or of others' feelings; due to want of thought. Hence ~LY² adv., ~NESS n. [-LESS]

thous'and (-z-), a. & n. Ten hundred, 1000, M (for uses cf. HUNDRED); (loosely) many, as a ~ times easier, one in a ~ (esp. rare or excellent one); (a) ~ & one, myriad, numberless (the ~ & one small worries of life; made a ~ & one excuses); a ~ thanks, pardons, apologies, etc. (forms of polite exaggeration); UPPER ten ~. Hence ~FOLD a. & adv., (-)~TH² a. & n. [OE thūsend, OS -ind, OHG dūsunt, ON thūsund, Goth. thūsundi]

thrall (-awl), n., a., & v.t. 1. Slave (of, to, person or thing, lit. & fig.); bondage, esp. in ~. 2. adj. (arch.). Enslaved (to). 3. v.t. Enslave. Hence thra'lDOM (-awl-) n. [OE thrǣl ƒ. ON thrǣll]

thrāsh, thrēsh, v.t. & i. 1. (usu. -esh). Beat out or separate grain from (corn etc.) on threshing-floor or in threshing-machine; (fig.) ~ out, arrive at, obtain, (the truth, rhyme, etc.) by repeated trial. 2. (Of paddle-wheel, branch, etc.) act like flail, deliver repeated blows, (of ship) keep striking the waves, make against wind or tide (usu. -ash, as ~ to windward). 3. (-ash). Beat esp. with stick or whip, conquer, surpass, whence thrāsh'ING¹ n. [OE therscan, later threscan, OHG dreskan, ON threskja, Goth. thriskan]

thrāsh'er, thrē-, n. Kind of shark; (usu. thre-) person, machine, that threshes; (thra-) one who thrashes. [-ER¹]

thrasōn'ical, a. Bragging. Hence ~LY² adv. [ƒ. L Thraso -onis, character in Terence, ƒ. Gk thrasus bold, +-ICAL]

thread¹ (-rĕd), n. 1. Spun-out filament of cotton, flax, silk, wool, etc., yarn, (has not a dry ~ on him, is wet through); thin cord of twisted yarns; gold ~ (of silk etc. with gold wire wound round it); LISLE THREAD; ~ & THRUM¹; ~-shaped thing, long slender body, e.g. spiral part of screw; thin seam or vein of ore; (fig.) the ~ (course) of life; hang by a ~, (of person's life etc.) be in a precarious state, (of momentous issue etc.) be determinable either way by something still in doubt; lost the ~ (chain, connexion) of his argument; resume or take up the ~ of, proceed with after interruption; gather up the ~s, bring the divisions of subject etc. into relation after separate treatment. 2. ~'bare, (of cloth) worn so that nap is lost and ~ visible, wearing such clothes, (fig.) well-worn, hackneyed, whence ~'bareness n.; ~ lace (made of ~); ~-mark, mark made in bank-note paper with highly coloured silk fibres to prevent counterfeiting; ~-*needle*, children's game (OLD *Lady of T~needle St*); ~-*paper*, (strip of) soft thin paper used for rolling up ~; ~'*worm*, kinds of ~like worm, esp. one infesting rectum of children. Hence ~'ɪNESS n., ~'Y² a., (-rĕd-). [OE *thrǣd*, OHG *drāt*, ON *thrǣdhr*, f. Gmc **thrǣdhuz* f. *thrǣ*- THROW]

thread² (-rĕd), v.t. Pass thread through eye of (needle); string (beads etc.) on thread, make (chain etc.) thus; pick one's way through (maze, streets, crowded place, etc.), make one's *way* thus; streak (hair etc.) as with threads. [ME, f. prec.]

threat (-rĕt), n. Declaration of intention to punish or hurt; (law) such menace of bodily hurt or injury to reputation or property as may restrain person's freedom of action; indication of coming evil (*there is a ~ of rain*). [OE *threat* affliction etc., f. Gmc **thraulaz* f. **threut-*, **thraut-*, **thrut-* whence OHG *-driozan* (G *verdriessen*), Goth. *-thriutan*]

threa'ten (-rĕtn), v.t. & i. Use threats towards (person etc., or abs.; *with* the evil ~ed), as *~ed me with death, am ~ed with a visit*; give warning of the infliction of (injury etc., or abs.), announce one's intention (*to do*), as punishment or in revenge etc., as *~s every kind of torment, ~ to resign*, (fig.) *clouds ~ (an interruption* or *to interrupt us), the practice ~s to become general.* Hence ~ɪNGLY² adv. [OE *threatnian* f. prec. + -EN⁶]

three, a. & n. **1.** One more than two, 3, iii; (skat.) any of four turns in which direction & edge are both changed; (rugby footb.) ~-*quarter*; ~ *times* ~, ~ *cheers* thrice repeated; *the ~ R's*, reading, writing, arithmetic; RULE of ~. **2.** ~-*bottle man*, old-fashioned hard drinker; ~-*card trick* (in which bets are made on which is the queen among ~ cards lying face downwards; also *find the lady*); ~-*colour process* (of reproducing natural colours by combining photographs in red, blue, & yellow); ~-*cornered*, triangular, (of contest etc.) between ~ parties each for himself; ~-*deck'er*, war-vessel with ~ gun-decks, novel in ~ volumes, ~-*storeyed pulpit*; ~-*handed*, with ~ hands, played by ~ persons, as ~-*handed euchre*; ~ *halfpence*, 1½*d.*; *T~ in One*, the Trinity; ~-*lane*, wide enough for ~ lines of traffic; ~-*legged race*, of couples each having a right & left leg tied together; ~-*mast'er*, vessel esp. schooner with ~ masts; ‖~-*pair*, (of room) up ~ pair of stairs (usu., ~-*pair back* or *front*); ‖~-*pence* (thrĕp-, -ĭp-), sum of ~ pence; ‖~-*penny* (*bit*) (same pron.), coin worth ~ pence; (*the*) ~-*per-cents*, (government) bonds bearing that interest; ~-PHASE; ~-*ply*, of ~ strands, webs, or thicknesses, (as n.) ~-*ply* wood made by gluing together 3 layers with grain in different directions; ~-*point landing* (aeron.), landing of an aircraft on the two wheels & the tail skid

simultaneously; ~-*quart'er(s)*, (adj.) of ~ fourths of normal size or numbers, (of portrait) going down to hips, showing ~ fourths of face, (n.) any of 3 or 4 players behind HALF-backs; ~*score'*, (age of) sixty (~*score & ten*, age of 70 as normal limit of life). Hence ~'FOLD a. & adv. [OE *thrī*, fem. & neut. *thrīo*, *thrēo* f. Gmc **thriz* (f. **thrijiz*), **thrijō*, Aryan *treies*, *treja*, Skr. *trayas*, Gk *treis, tria*, L *tres, tria*]

three'some, n. & a. **1.** Set of three persons; game etc. for three. **2.** adj. Of three. [-SOME]

thrĕmmatŏl'ogȳ, n. Science of breeding animals & plants. [f. Gk *thremma -matos* nursling (*trephō* nourish, -M), -O-, -LOGY]

thren'|ōde, -odȳ, nn. (Song of) lamentation esp. on person's death. Hence or cogn. ~ET'IC, ~ĕt'ICAL, ~ōd'IAL, ~ōd'IC, aa., ~odIST(3) n. [f. Gk *thrēnōidia* (*thrēnos* wailing + *ōidē* ODE)]

thresh etc. See THRASH etc.

thresh'ōld, n. Plank or stone at bottom of door in dwelling-house, church, etc.; (loosely, esp. fig.) entrance, as *at the ~ of a discussion, on the ~ of a revolution, of a new century*; (psych.) limit of consciousness, limit below which a stimulus ceases to be perceptible. [OE *therscold*, *-wold*, etc., gen. referred to THRESH]

threw. See THROW.

thrice, adv. (arch. or literary). Three times (now chiefly in comb. = highly, as ~-*blessed, -favoured*). [ME *thriĕs* f. *thriĕ* adv. (OE *thriwa, thriga*) + -ES]

thrid, v.t.(arch.; -dd-). = THREAD².

thrid'ace, n. Inspissated juice of lettuce, used as sedative. [f. Gk *thridax -akos* lettuce]

thrift, n. **1.** Frugality, economical management, whence ~'LESS a., ~'lĕssLY² adv., ~'lĕssNESS n. **2.** n. Kinds of plant, esp. sea-pink. [ME, f. THRIVE + -t; cf. *drift, gift* (-TH ¹ (a))]

thrif'tȳ, a. Frugal, economical; thriving, prosperous. Hence ~ɪLY² adv. [ME; -Y²]

thrill, v.t. & i., & n. **1.** Penetrate (person etc.) with wave of emotion or sensation, as *his voice ~ed the listeners*; be thus penetrated or agitated (*with* horror etc.); (of emotion etc.) pass *through, over, along*, as *fear ~ed through my veins*; quiver, throb, (as) with emotion. **2.** n. Wave of emotion or sensation, as *a ~ of joy*; throb, pulsation; (med.) kinds of tremor or resonance observed in auscultation; (sl.) sensational story. Hence ~ER¹(2) n. (esp. sensational play or tale), ~'ɪNGLY² adv., ~'ɪNGNESS n. [metatheric f. (now dial.) *thirl* vb f. OE *thyrlian* pierce f. *thȳr(e)l* hole f. *thurh* THROUGH + -EL]

thrips, n. Kinds of insect, esp. (improp.) some injurious to vines etc. [L f. Gk, = woodworm]

thriv|e, v.i. (*thrōve* rarely ~*ed*, *thrĭven* rarely ~*ed*). Prosper, flourish; grow rich; (of animal or plant) grow vigorously.

Hence~**ingly**² adv., ~**ingness** n. [ME,
f. ON *thrifask* refl. thrive]

thro', thro. See THROUGH.

throat, n., & v.t. **1.** Front of neck between
chin & collar-bone, jugular region, (*cut
one's ~*, esp. with intent to kill him; *take
by the ~*, try to throttle); gullet; windpipe, as *words stuck in my ~*; ~-shaped
thing, e.g. narrow part of river between
rocks, (also in many naut. wds); *sore ~*,
inflammation of lining membrane of
gullet etc., *clergyman's (sore) ~*, form of
this affecting those who speak much in
public, often of nervous origin; *cut one's
own ~*, *one another's ~s*, adopt suicidal,
mutually destructive, policy; *lie in one's
~*, lie grossly; *give person the lie in his ~*,
accuse him of lying grossly; *thrust thing
down one's ~*, force it on his attention.
2. v.t. Channel, groove. Hence (-)~ED² a.
[OE *throte*, -*u*, app. f. Gmc. *thrut-, thrūt
(OE *thrūtian* to swell); cogn. w. OHG
drozza (G *drossel*)]

throat'|y̆, a. Guttural, uttered in the
throat; having prominent or capacious
throat. Hence ~iNESS n. [-Y²]

thrŏb, v.i. (-bb-), & n. **1.** (Of heart,
bosom, temples, etc.) palpitate, pulsate
esp. with more than usual force or
rapidity; (fig.) quiver, vibrate, (as) with
emotion. **2.** n. Palpitation, pulsation, as
heart~s, ~s of pleasure. Hence ~**b'ingly²** adv. [ME, app. imit.]

thrŏe, n., & v.i. **1.** (Usu. pl.) violent
pang(s), esp. of childbirth lit. & fig.,
anguish; (pop.) *in the ~s of* (struggling
with) *spring-cleaning*. **2.** v.i. (rare). Be
in agony. [17th c. alt. f. obs. *throwe*(*e*),
poss. rel. to THROW¹]

‖ **Thrŏgmŏrt'on** Street. (Used for) the
London Stock Exchange or its members
or operations.

thrŏmb|ōs'is, n. Coagulation of blood in
blood-vessel or organ. Hence ~**ŏt'ic** a.
[Gk *thrombōsis* curdling (*thrombos* lump,
see -OSIS)]

thrōne, n., & v:t. **1.** Chair of state for
sovereign, bishop, etc., usu. decorated &
raised on dais; sovereign power, as *came
to the ~, lost his ~*; (pl.) third ORDER¹ of
angels. **2.** v.t. (poet. exc. in p.p.). En-
throne (lit. & fig.). Hence ~'LESS (-nl-) a.
[ME, f. OF *trone* f. L f. Gk *thronos* seat,
chair]

thrŏng, n., & v.i. & t. **1.** Crowd of people;
multitude esp. in small space (*of people
or things*). **2.** vb. Come, go, press, (*round
etc.*) in multitudes; fill (street etc.) with
a crowd or as crowd does; (arch.) press
hard upon (person). [ME *thrang*(*e*),
throng(*e*), f. st. of OE *thringan* -*thrang
-thrungen* press]

thrŏ'stle (-sl), n. **1.** Song-thrush. **2.** (Also
~-*frame*) machine for spinning wool,
cotton, etc. [OE *throstle* f. root of Gmc
thrastuz (ON *throstr*), commonly referred
to Aryan *trozdus*, whence L *turdus*]

thrŏt'tle, n., & v.t. **1.** Throat, gullet,

windpipe; (also ~-*valve*) valve controlling
flow of steam etc. in engine. **2.** v.t. Choke,
strangle; control (steam etc., engine)
with ~-*valve*; ~ *down*, reduce speed of
(engine, car) thus. [vb (f. 1400) perh. f.
THROAT + -LE(3); n. (f. 1550) of obsc. hist.;
perh. f. vb]

through, thro', thro, (-rōō), prep., adv.,
& a. **1.** From end to end or side to side of,
between the sides or walls or parts of,
as *marched ~ the town, arrow went ~ his
arm, see ~ a telescope, look ~ the window,
pass ~ the doorway, swam ~ the waves,
pushes his fingers ~ his hair*; (fig.) *went ~
many trials, got ~ his examinations, saw ~
his hypocrisy, wait ~ ten long years,
flashed ~ his mind*; by reason of, by
agency, means, or fault of, as *it all came
about ~ his not knowing the way, concealed
it ~ shame, it was all ~ you that we were
late*; *up to and including (*from Friday
~ Tuesday*). **2.** adv. From side to side,
from end to end, from beginning to end,
as *let us stroll ~, would not let us ~* (gate
etc.), *ice gave & I went ~, read it carefully
~, read it ~ & ~* (~ again & again), *looked
him ~ & ~* (observed searchingly), *lasted
all ~* (all the time); (colloq.) *are you ~
(with that job)?*, have you finished (it)?;
CARRY, *drop or* FALL¹, PULL¹, ~; GO¹ ~
with. **3.** adj. Going, concerned with going,
~, as *a ~ bolt*, ~-*stone*, = BOND¹-*stone*;
esp. (of railway or steamboat travelling)
going all the way without change of line
etc., going over different companies' lines
with same ticket, as ~ *carriage, train,
passenger, ticket* (for ~ passenger), *fares.*
4. ~-*put* n., amount of material put ~ in
a manufacturing etc. process. [OE, OS
thurh, OHG *duruh*; cogn. w. Goth. *thairh*
(cf. *thairkō* hole), THRILL]

through'ly (-rōōll), adv. (arch.). Thoroughly. [15th c., f. THROUGH + -LY²]

throughout' (-rōō-owt), adv. & prep.
1. Right through, in every part, in all
respects, as *timber was rotten~, followed a
sound policy ~*. **2.** prep. Right through,
from end to end of, as ~ *the length &
breadth of the land*, ~ *the 18th century.*
[ME; OUT]

throve. See THRIVE.

throw¹ (-ō), v.t. & i. (*threw* pr. -ōō, ~*n*
pr. -ōn). **1.** Release (ball, object) after
imparting motion, propel through space,
send forth or dismiss esp. with some
violence, fling or hurl or cast (lit. & fig.),
as *must not ~ stones* (lit., & fig. = cast
imputations), *threw the ball over his head,
learnt to ~ a fly* (in fishing), *mortars ~
shells, hose ~s water, house ~n down by
earthquake, ship was ~n upon the coast,
~n from his horse, was ~n into a dilemma
or upon his own resources*, ~ COLD¹ *water
on*, ~ *a* SOP *to*; ~ *light on the matter*, help
to explain it; ~ *down the* GLOVE, ~ DUST¹
in person's eyes; ~ *oneself*, one's *daughter,
at the head of* (openly seek as husband);
~ (as FLING) *in one's teeth*; ~ *good money*

after bad (lose more in trying to recoup a loss); (w. ind. obj.) ~ *me a rope,* ~ one *a kiss* (wave hand to him after kissing it); (crick., of bowler) deliver ball with sudden straightening of elbow (*was no-balled for* ~*ing*). 2. (Of wrestler, horse) bring (antagonist, rider) to the ground. 3. Put (clothes etc.) carelessly or hastily *on, off, over* one's *shoulders* etc.; (of snake) cast (skin). 4. (Of animals, e.g. rabbits, pigeons) bring forth (young). 5. Make (specified cast) with dice, as *threw deuce--ace.* 6. Twist (silk etc.) into threads. 7. Shape (round pottery) on potter's wheel. 8. Turn, direct, move esp. quickly (esp. part of body), as *threw his eyes to the ground, a glance backwards, his arms up, his head back;* ~ *a chest* (sl.), stand erect with chest expanded. 9. *Lose (contest, race, etc.) intentionally. 10. Have (a fit); (sl.) give (a party). 11. ~ *away,* (fig.) part with needlessly or recklessly, lose by neglect, as *threw away all his advantages, an excellent offer*; (theatr.) speak (lines) with conscious under-emphasis; (p.p.) wasted, as *the advice was* ~*n away upon him.* 12. ~ *back,* revert to ancestral character; ~*ᴸback* n., reversion to ancestral character, example of this. 13. ~ one*self down,* lie down. 14. ~ *in,* (also ~ *into the bargain*) add (thing) to a bargain without extra charge; interpose (word, remark) by way of parenthesis or casually; ~ *in* one's *hand,* lit. in card games esp. poker, (fig.) give up, withdraw from a contest; ~ *in* one's *lot with,* decide to share the fortunes of. 15. ~ one*self into,* engage vigorously in. 16. ~ *off,* discard (acquaintance etc.); contrive to get rid of (illness, troublesome companion); aban- don (disguise); produce, deliver, (poem, epigram) in offhand manner; (of hounds or hunt, & transf.) begin hunting, make a start, begin speaking, playing, etc.; (& see above). 17. ~ one*self on, upon,* place one's reliance on (*the mercy of the court* etc.). 18. ~ *open,* open suddenly or wide; make accessible (*to* all comers etc.); ~ *open the door to,* make possible. 19. ~ *out,* cast out; build (wing of house, pier, pro- jecting or prominent thing); suggest, put forward tentatively; reject (bill in Parliament); distract (person speaking, thinking, or acting) from the matter in hand so that he blunders or stops; (crick., of fielder) put out (batsman) by ~*ing* at & hitting wicket. 20. ~ *over,* desert, abandon. 21. ~ *overboard,* see OVER-(2). 22. ~ *up,* lift up (window-sash); resign (office); vomit (t. & i.); ~ one's *eyes up* (as sign of horror or outraged propriety); ~ *up the* SPONGE. Hence (·)~'ER¹ (·ōer) n. [OE *thrāwan* twist, turn, OS *thrāian,* OHG *drāen* f. Gmc **thræ-* cogn. w. Gk *terō* bore, L *terere* rub; cf. THREAD]

throw² (·ō), n. 1. Throwing, cast; cast of dice; cast of fishing-line; distance a missile is or may be thrown, as *record* ~

with the hammer; a stone's ~, (loosely) slight distance; fall in wrestling; (crick.) bowler's illegitimately delivered ball. 2. (geol., mining). Fault, leap, in strata. 3. Machine, device, giving rapid rotary motion. 4. ~*-off,* start in hunt or race; ~*ᴸstick,* club, stick, meant to be whirled from the hand, e.g. boomerang. [f. prec.]

throw'ster (-rō-), n. One who throws silk. [-STER]

thrŭm¹, n., & v.t. (-mm-). 1. Fringe of threads remaining on loom when web has been cut off; single thread of this; any loose thread or tuft; *thread &* ~, all alike, good & bad. 2. v.t. Make of, cover with, ~s. Hence ~m'Y² a. [OE, = OHG *drum,* ON *thrǫmr* f. Gmc **thrum-, *thram-* cogn. w. L *terminus*]

thrŭm², v.i. & t. (-mm-), & n. 1. Play monotonously or unskilfully on or *on* (stringed instrument); drum, tap, idly on or *on* (table etc.). 2. n. Such playing, resulting sound. [imit.]

thrŭsh¹, n. Family or genus of birds, esp. European *song-*~, throstle. [OE *thrýsce* f. Gmc **thrūskjōn*]

thrŭsh², n. Disease, esp. of children, marked by pearl-coloured fungous vesi- cles in mouth & throat; disease affecting frog of horse's foot. [17th c., of unkn. orig.]

thrŭst, v.t. & i. (*thrust*), & n. 1. Push with sudden impulse or with force (lit. & fig.), as ~ *his fist into my face,* ~ *the letter into his pocket,* ~ *a pin into the cushion, I* ~ *out my hand,* ~ *him forth* (out of room etc.), *was* ~ *from his rights;* ~ one*self* or one's *nose in,* obtrude, interfere; pierce (person etc.) *through;* make sudden push *at* (person etc. *with* dagger etc.); force one- self *through, past,* etc.; make one's *way* thus; hence ~'ER¹ n. (‖ esp., foxhunter who endangers others or the hounds in securing a forward place). 2. n. Sudden or forcible push, strong attempt to penetrate enemy's line or territory; attack with point of weapon; remark aimed at a person (*a shrewd,* HOME¹, ~; *he parried the* ~); stress between two bodies esp. parts of structure, e.g. arch, rafters; crushing of coal-mine pillars by weight of roof; ~*-block,* (esp.) casting or frame carrying or containing the bearings on which the collars of a propeller-shaft press; ~*-hoe* (worked by ~, not pull). [ME *thruste, thryste,* f. ON *thrýsta*]

thŭd, v.i. (-dd-), & n. (Make, fall with) low dull sound as of blow on soft thing. [c. 1500, app. imit.]

thŭg, n. Member of a religious organiza- tion of assassins in India suppressed about 1825; cut-throat, ruffian. [f. Hind. *thag*]

thŭgg'|ee (-gē), n. (hist.). The practice of the thug. So ~ERY, ~ISM, nn., (-g-). [f. Hind. *thagi* as prec.]

Thŭl'ē, n. Name given by Pytheas of Massilia to some (is)land north of Gt

Britain; *ul'tima* (= farthest) ~, any far-
away unknown region.

thŭmb (-m), n., & v.t. **1.** Short thick
finger set apart from & opposite to the
others on human hand; digit of other
animals corresponding to this in position;
~s *up!* (sl. excl. of satisfaction); RULE
of ~; *his* FINGERs *are all* ~s; *under* person's~ (influence, domination). **2.** ~-*blue*,
washing indigo in small lumps; ~-*index*,
set of lettered grooves cut in front edges
of a book's leaves to facilitate reference;
~-*latch* (raised by pressing end of lever
with ~); ~-*mark* (made by ~ esp. on leaf
of book); ~-*nail sketch*, portrait of ~-*nail*
size, hasty word-picture; ~-*nut* (shaped
for ~ to turn); ~-*print*, impression of ~
esp. as used for identification; ~'*screw*,
instrument of torture for squeezing ~s;
~-*stall*, sheath, pad, etc., to protect ~;
•~'tack, drawing-pin. **3.** v.t. Wear, soil,
(pages etc.) with ~; handle (piano keys
etc.) or play (music) awkwardly; signal
(to) with the ~; ~ *a lift*, (try to) get a lift
from a passing motorist by such signal;
•~ one's *nose* (*at*), cock a SNOOK[2] (at).
Hence ~'LESS (-ml-) a. [OE *thūma*, OHG
dūmo f. Gmc *•thūmon* cogn. w. L *tumēre*
swell]

thŭmm'ĭm. See URIM.

thŭmp, v.t. & i., & n. **1.** Beat heavily esp.
with fist; deliver heavy blows *at*, *on*, etc.;
~ *the* or *a cushion* (of vehement preacher
emphasizing his words with blows on
pulpit cushion). **2.** n. Heavy blow, bang.
[16th c., imit.]

thŭm'p|er, n. In vbl senses, also : (colloq.)
large, striking, or impressive person **or**
thing, esp. lie, so ~ING[2] a. [-ER[1]]

thŭn'der, n., & v.i. & t. **1.** Loud noise
following flash of . lightning & due to
discharge of electricity through the
air; ~*bolt*, as *Jove's* ~s; (fig.) loud
noise, as ~s *of applause*, *blood-&-*~, (of
novel etc.) sensational, melodramatic;
(pl.) authoritative censure or threats (*the*
~s *of* The Times, *the Church*). **2.** v.i. Give
forth ~, usu. *it* ~s; make loud noise, as
voice~ed in my ears; utter violent threats
etc. *against* etc. **3.**v.t. Emit (threats etc.)
in loud or impressive manner. **4.** *Steal*
person's ~, (fig.) forestall him (by telling
the story he meant to tell, making profitable use of his invention before he can, &
the like; from remark of John Dennis
when the stage ~ he had intended for his
own play was used for another); ~*bolt*,
flash of lightning with crash of~, imaginary bolt or shaft viewed as substance of
lightning, kinds of stone or fossil supposed
to be such bolt, formidable threat etc.;
~*clap*, crash of ~ (esp. fig. or in simile of
sudden terrible event or news; *the* ~*clap*
of Napoleon's escape; *the news came on me
like a* ~*clap*); ~*cloud* (producing ~);
~*storm* (with ~ & lightning & usu. heavy
rain or hail); ~*struck*, struck by lightning,
amazed. Hence ~LESS, ~OUS, ~Y[2], aa.,

~OUSLY[2] adv. [OE *thunor*, OS -*er*, OHG
donar, ON *thórr* f. Gmc *•thonaraz* cogn.
w. L *tonare*]

thŭn'derer, n. In vbl senses, esp. *the T*~,
Jupiter (Tonans), || (joc.) *The Times* news-
paper. [-ER[1]]

thŭn'dering, a. & adv. In vbl senses,
also or esp.: (colloq.) unusual(ly), remarkable, remarkably, decided(ly), as *a*
~ *nuisance*, *was* ~ *glad to get back*, *a* ~
great fish; *the T*~ *Legion*, Roman legion
containing Christian soldiers whose
prayers were held to have procured a
thunderstorm that terrified the enemy.
Hence ~LY[2] adv. [-ING[2,1]]

thūr'|ĭ-, comb. form of L *thus thuris* frank-
incense, as : ~'*ifer*, acolyte who carries
censer; ~*if'erous*, producing frankincense; ~*ifica'tion*, burning of incense.

thūr'ible, n. Censer. [ME, f. OF, or L
l(*h*)*uribulum* (prec.) f. Gk *thuō* sacrifice]

Thŭrs'day (-zdĭ), n. Fifth day of week;
HOLY, MAUNDY, ~. [OE *thunres-*, *thur*(*e*)*s-
dæg*, day of Thor, rendering LL *dies Jovis*
day of Jupiter]

thŭs (dh-), adv. In this way, in the way
(to be) indicated, whence ~'NESS n. (joc.);
accordingly, as a result or inference; to
this extent, so, as ~ *far*, ~ *much*. [OE,
OS *thus* app. f. *tha-* (THAT[1])]

thwăck, v.t., & n. = WHACK. [imit.]

|| **thwaite**, n. Piece of wild land made
arable. [f. ON *thveit* paddock, f. *•thvĭta*
= OE *thwitan* cut (cf. WHITTLE)]

thwart (-ôrt), adv., prep., & a., (arch.),
v.t., & n. **1.** Across, athwart; (naut.) ~-
hawse, across the hawse,~-*ship* a., -*ships*
adv., (lying) across ship; (adj.) lying
across, transverse. **2.** v.t. Frustrate,
cross, (wish, purpose), whence ~'ING LY[2]
adv. **3.** n. Oarsman's bench placed across
boat. [ME *thwert* f. ON *thvert* adv., neut.
of *thverr* adj., f. *•thverh* = OE *thwerh*,
OHG *twerh* (G *zwerch-*), Goth. *thwairhs* f.
Gmc *•thwerhw-* cogn. w. L *torquēre* twist]

thȳ, thine, (dh-), pron. & a. Possessive
case of, & adj. corresp. to, THOU (now
arch. etc. as THOU; before vowel usu.
thine), also (*thine*) in abs. use, as *it was
thy fault*, *lift thine eyes*, *the fault is thine*,
do what thou wilt with thine own. [ME,
reduced f. *thin* (mod. *thine*), OE, OS, ON
thin, OHG *dīn*, Goth. *theins* f. Gmc
•thīnaz]

thȳl'acine, n. Zebra wolf, a Tasmanian
carnivorous marsupial. [F, f. Gk *thulakos*
pouch, -INE[1]]

thyme (tīm), n. Kinds of plant, esp.
common garden ~, shrub with pungent
aromatic leaves used in cookery, *shepherd's* or *wild* ~, kind with mildly
aromatic leaves. Hence thȳm'OL n. (a
powerful antiseptic), thym'Y[2] (tī-) a.
[ME, f. OF *thym* f. L f. Gk *thumon* (*thuō*
sacrifice)]

thȳm'us, n. (anat.; pl. -*mī*). (Usu. ~
gland) a ductless gland situated near the
base of the neck (in man disappearing

on the approach of puberty). [f. Gk *thumos*]

thyr′oid, a. & n. (anat., zool.). Shield-shaped, as ~ *cartilage*, large cartilage of larynx projection of which in man forms Adam's apple; connected with the ~ cartilage, as ~ *artery*; ~ *gland*, large ductless gland lying near larynx and trachea secreting hormone which regulates rate of metabolism (~ *gland* or ~, extract prepared from the ~ gland of animals and used in treating goitre, cretinism, etc.); having shield-shaped markings, as ~ *woodpecker*. Hence **thȳro-** comb. form (anat.). [f. obs. F -*ide*, irreg. f. Gk *thureoeidēs* (Galen) f. *thureos* shield, see -OID]

thȳrox′in(e), n. White active principle of thyroid gland. [f. THYR(OID)+OX-+-IN]

thyrs′us (-êr-), n. (Gk ant.; pl. -*si*). Staff tipped with ornament like pine-cone, an attribute of Bacchus. [L, f. Gk *thursos*]

thȳsĕlf′ (dh-), pron. Reflexive & emphat. form corresp. to *thou, thee*. [THY+SELF]

ti¹ (tē), n. Kinds of tree with edible roots. [Polynesian name]

ti² (tē). See SI.

tiar′a, n. Ancient Persian turban worn erect by king, depressed by others; Pope's diadem pointed at top & surrounded by three crowns, (fig.) the papal office; ornamental coronet. Hence ~'d [-ED²] a. [L f. Gk of unkn. orig.]

tib′i|a, n. (anat.; pl. ~*ae* pr. -ē). The shin-bone; fourth joint of leg in insects; drumstick of fowl. So ~AL a., ~o- comb. form. [L (*tī-*), = shin-bone, flute]

tic, n. Habitual spasmodic contraction of muscles esp. of face; (in full ~ *douloureux* pr. dōŏlˈrŏŏ′, & see Ap., lit. painful ~) severe form of facial neuralgia with convulsive twitchings. [F]

tical (*in Siam* tikahl′; *in Burma* tī′kl), n. Former Siamese silver coin (roughly = 1 rupee) or its weight; similar Burmese and Chinese weight. [Port. *tical* = Ind. *ṭankā, ṭakā*]

ticc′a, a. (Anglo-Ind.). Engaged on contract, hired (esp. in ~-*gharry*, hackney-carriage). [Hind. *ṭhīkā*, hire, fare]

tice, n. = YORKER. [f. obs. *tice* ENTICE]

tick¹, v.i. & t., & n. **1.** (Make) slight recurring click, esp. that of watch or clock (*to* or *on the* ~, with exact punctuality); (colloq.) moment, instant; ~-*lack*, pulsating sound esp. of the heart (see also TRICK-TRACK), kind of manual semaphore signalling practised by racecourse touts; ~~, (nursery for) watch. **2.** Small mark set against items in list etc. in checking; (v.t.) mark (item, usu. *off*) with ~. **3.** (Of clock etc.) ~ *away* (the time etc.); ~ *off* (sl.), reprimand; (of tape-machine) ~ *out* (news etc.); ~ *over*, (of int.-comb. engine) run slowly with gears etc. disconnected, also fig. [n. 15th c. (*tek*), cf. Du. *tik*, LG *tikk* touch, tick; vb 16th c., cf. Du., LG *tikken*, Norw. *tikke* touch lightly]

tick², n. Arachnid or insect parasitic on various animals, as *dog, sheep, cattle,* -~. [OE **tica*, ME *teke, tyke*, of obsc. orig.] cf. MDu., MLG *teke*, OHG *zecho*, G *zecke*]

tick³, n. Cover, case, of bedding; (also ~′ING¹ n.) stout usu. striped linen or cotton material used for this. [15th c. *tikke, teke* (= MDu., MLG *tēke*, OHG *ziëcha*), f. WG **lēka, *tika*, f. L f. Gk *thēkē* case]

tick⁴, n., & v.i. & t. (colloq.). **1.** Credit, as *buy goods on* ~. **2.** vb. Give ~; buy or sell (thing) on ~; give (person) ~. [app. abbr. of TICKET in phr. *on the ticket*]

tick′er, n. In vbl senses of TICK¹, esp.: (colloq.) watch, telegraphic tape; (joc.) the heart. [-ER¹]

tick′ĕt, n., & v.t. **1.** Written or printed piece of card or paper entitling holder to admission to place of entertainment etc., conveyance by train etc., or other right, as *concert, theatre, bath, lottery, railway, excursion,* SEASON, THROUGH, RETURN, ~; || (mil. sl.) discharge (*get* one's ~); label attached to thing & giving price or other particulars; notice, usu. of card, set up in window etc. of house to let etc.; *the* ~ (colloq.), the proper thing, as *not quite the* ~; *(pol.) list of candidates put forward by a party, (fig.) principles of a party, as *the democratic* ~. **2.** || ~ *of leave* (allowing liberty with certain restrictions to prisoner or convict who has served part of his time), || ~-*of-leave man*, holder of such ~; || ~-*day* (St. Exch.), day before settling-day, when names of actual purchasers are handed to stockbrokers; ~-*night*, performance at theatre proceeds of which are divided among several persons in proportion to number of ~s disposed of by each; || ~-*porter*, licensed porter identified by badge; ~-*punch* (for punching ~s). **3.** v.t. Put ~ on (article for sale etc.). [16th c., f. obs. F *etiquet* or (mod.) *étiquette* f. OF *estiquer* f. MDu. *steken* to STICK]

tick′ey, -kȳ, tikk′ie, -kȳ, n. (S.-Afr. colloq.). Threepenny-bit. [orig. unkn.]

tic′kle, v.t. & i., & n. **1.** Apply light touches to (person, part of his body, or abs.) so as to excite the nerves & usu. produce laughter. & in extreme case convulsion, as ~ *him with a feather*, ~ *the soles of her feet, don't* ~; feel this sensation, as *my foot* ~s; excite agreeably, amuse, divert, (person, his sense of humour, vanity, etc.), as *I was highly* ~*d at the idea, this will* ~ *his palate*; catch (trout etc.) with the hand. **2.** n. Act, sensation, of tickling. [ME *tikelle*, perh. by metath. f. ON *kitla*, cf. KITTLE]

tick′ler, n. In vbl senses, also: puzzling or delicate question or matter; feather used by revellers to tickle faces. [-ER¹]

tick′lish, a. Easily tickled, sensitive to tickling; (of question or thing to be dealt with) difficult, critical, delicate, requiring careful handling. Hence ~**LY**² adv., ~**NESS** n. [-ISH¹]

ticpolŏng′a (-ngg-), n. Venomous serpent of India & Ceylon. [f. Sinhalese *titpolongā* spot-viper]

tid′al, a. Of tide(s); ~ *air* (passing in & out of lungs at each respiration); ~ *basin, dock, harbour* (subject to rise & fall of tide); ~ *friction* (of ~ wave, retarding diurnal rotation of earth); ~ *river* (affected by tide to some distance from mouth); ~ *wave*, wave following sun & moon from east to west & causing tides, (improp.) any extraordinary ocean wave e.g. one attributed to earthquake, (fig.) widespread manifestation of feeling etc. Hence ~**LY**² adv. [-AL]

tidbit. See TITBIT.

‖ **tidd′ler**, n. (Nursery name for) stickleback. [orig. unkn.]

tidd′lў-winks, n. Game in which counters are flicked into tray etc. on centre of table. [orig. unkn.]

tide¹, n. **1.** Time, season, (now chiefly in *Whitsun*~, *Christmas*~, *yule*~, etc., otherwise arch.); period of time, as *work double* ~s (night & day). **2.** Periodical rise (*flood*-~) & fall (*ebb*-~) of sea due to attraction of moon & sun, whence **tidŏ-** **L′OGY** n.; *high, low,* ~, completion of flood, ebb, -~; *spring, neap,* -~, maximum, minimum, ~ when solar & lunar ~s act together, act 90° apart; LAG¹*ging,* PRIMING², *of the* ~s; *meteorological* ~ (due to regular alternations of wind etc.); (fig.) trend of opinion or fortune or events (*go with the* ~, *the* ~ *turns*). **3.** ~-*gate* (opened to admit water or let vessels pass during rising ~, closed to keep water in during ebb); ~-*gauge* (showing extremes or present level of ~); ~-*lock* (between tidal harbour & basin behind it); ~-*rip(s),* rough water caused by opposing ~s; ~-*waiter,* customs officer who boards ship on arrival to enforce customs regulations; ~*way,* channel where ~ runs, ebb or flow in such channel. Hence ~**LESS** (-dl-) a. [OE, OS *tīd* time, OHG *zīt,*’ ON *tīth* f. Gmc *tīdiz,* f. root *tī-,* cf. TIME]

tide², v.i. & t. Drift with tide, esp. work in or out of harbour with help of tide; get *over* (difficulty etc.), as ~ *over this business,* ~ *it over.* [(in obs. sense happen, betide) OE *tīdan;* mod. senses direct f. prec.]

tid′ings (-z), n. pl. (now chiefly literary; treated as sing. or pl.). (Piece of) news, as *the* ~ *come(s) too late.* [OE *tīdung* (as prec.), ME *tidinde* f. ON *tīthindi* f. corresp. ON vb]

tid′ў, a., n., & v.t. **1.** (Of dress, room, person, habits) neatly arranged, neat, orderly; (colloq.) pretty large, considerable, as *left a* ~ *sum behind him, a* ~ *day's work;* (dial.) fairly well in health, as *am feeling pretty* ~. **2.** n. Detachable usu. ornamental cover for chair-back etc., receptacle for odds & ends (*street* ~, bin

for paper etc.). **3.** v.t. Make (room, table, etc., one*self,* or abs.; often *up*) neat, put in good order. Hence **tid′iLY**² adv., **tid′iNESS** n. [ME, = timely etc., f. TIDE¹+-Y²]

tie¹, v.t. & i. (*lying*). **1.** Attach, fasten, with cord or the like, as ~ *the dog to the railings,* RIDE & ~, ~ *his legs together,* ~ *up a parcel;* secure (shoe, bonnet) by tightening & knotting its strings; arrange (string, ribbon, tie, etc.) to form knot, bow, etc., as ~ *your tie,* ~ *it in a bow;* form (knot, bow) thus; ~ (dress fish-hook to look like) *a fly;* bind (rafters etc.) by crosspiece etc.; restrict, bind, (person etc. *to, down to,* conditions, occupation, etc.). **2.** ~*d to* woman's APRON-*strings;* ~ person's *tongue,* secure, compel, his silence; ~ *up,* restrict, esp. annex conditions to (bequest etc.) to prevent its being sold or diverted from its purpose; ‖ ~*d garage, house,* garage, public house, bound to deal exclusively with one firm. **3.** (mus.). Unite (notes) by tie. **4.** Make equal score or run dead heat or draw game (*with* competitor, *for* place or prize). [OE *tīgan* f. *tēaggjan* f. *tēag* rope (foll.)]

tie², n. **1.** Cord, chain, etc., used for fastening; = NECK¹-~; *old* SCHOOL¹ ~; (fig.) thing that unites persons, bond, obligation, as ~s *of blood, friendship;* rod, beam, holding parts of a structure together, *rail sleeper;* ~-*beam,* horizontal beam connecting rafters; small fur necklet. **2.** (mus.). Curved line above two notes of same pitch that are to be joined as one. **3.** Equality of score or draw or dead heat among competitors in game or contest; *play, shoot,* etc., *off a* ~, play further game etc. to decide between such competitors; match between any pair of several competing players or teams, as *cup*-~s (in competition for cup). **4.** ~-*up,* obstructed situation, standstill, esp. *strike of railwaymen etc.; ~-*wig* (tied behind with ribbon). [OE *tēah, tēag,* ON *taug* rope f. Gmc *teuh-, tauh-, tuh-* to pull]

tier; n., & v.t. **1.** Row, rank, esp. one of several placed one above another as in theatre; ~s *of cable,* circles it forms when coiled. **2.** v.t. Pile (often *up*) in ~s. [16th c. *tire* f. F, f. *tirer* draw, elongate]

tierce, n. .One third of a pipe as old wine-measure, cask containing certain quantity (varying with the goods) esp. of provisions; (mus.) = THIRD; sequence of three cards; (fencing) third position for guard, parry, or thrust (~ & *quart,* fencing); (eccl., also *terce*) office of third hour. [ME, f. OF *terce, tierce,* fem. of *terz, tierz* third f. L TERT*ius*]

tiercel. See TERCEL.

tiercet. See TERCET.

tiers état (tyār̄z′ätah′), n. = *third* ESTATE. [F]

tiff¹, n., & v.t. Draught of liquor; (v.t.) sip, drink. [17th c., orig. unkn.]

tiff², ·n. & v.i. Fit of peevishness, slight

quarrel; (v.i.) be in a pet. [18th c., orig. unkn.]

tiff³, v.i. (Anglo-Ind.). = TIFFIN. [abbr.]

tiff'any̆, n. Kind of gauze muslin. [orig. dress for Twelfth Night, f. OF *tiphanie* f. LL THEO*phania* manifestation of God, EPIPHANY]

tiff'in, n., & v.i. (Anglo-Ind.). (Take) light meal esp. of curried dishes & fruit, lunch. [TIFF¹+-ING¹; orig. in sense 'drinking']

tige (tēzh), n. (Archit.) shaft of column; (bot.) stem, stalk. [F, f. L TIBIA]

tig'er (-g-), n. **1.** Large Asian striped feline quadruped, esp. *Bengal~*; *American ~*, jaguar; *red ~*, cougar; *work* etc. *like a ~* (with fierce energy); (colloq.) formidable opponent in a game, opp. RABBIT; dissolute swaggerer or bully, whence ~ISM(2) n.; groom accompanying master in light vehicle; •(sl.) yell supplementary to three cheers, final burst. **2.** *~-beetle*, predacious kinds with spotted or striped wing-covers; *~-cat*, any moderate-sized feline beast resembling the ~, e.g. ocelot, serval, margay; *~('s)-eye*, a gem of brilliant lustre; *~-lily*, garden kind with flowers of dull orange spotted with black or purple; *~-moth*, kinds with richly streaked hairy wings suggesting ~'s skin; *~-wood* (imported from Brit. Guiana for cabinet-making). So **tig'ress¹** n. [ME & OF *tigre* f. L f. Gk *tigris* of oriental orig.]

tig'erish (-g-), a. Like, cruel as, a tiger. [-ISH¹]

tight (tīt), a., n., & adv. **1.** Closely & firmly put together, as *~ ship*; impermeable, impervious, esp. (in comb.) to specified thing, as *air, gas, water, wind, ~*; closely held, drawn, fastened, fitting, etc., as *~ knots, cork is too ~, corn caused by a* (too) *~ shoe*; neat, trim, compact, as *a ~ lass* (arch.), *~ little island*; tense, stretched so as to leave no slack, as *~ rope* (*~'rope*, one on which rope-dancers etc. perform); (colloq.) drunk; *money is ~* (not easily obtainable), *a ~ money-market* (in which money is ~); produced by, requiring, great exertion or pressure, as *a ~ squeeze, am in a ~ place* (usu. fig., difficult situation); *~-fisted*, stingy; *•~wad* (sl.), close-fisted or stingy person. **2.** n. pl. Close-fitting garments as used by acrobat, dancer, etc. **3.** adv. ~ly, as *squeeze it, hold it,* ~. Hence ~'EN⁶ (tīt-) v.t. & i. (*~en* one's *belt*, go without food, also fig.), ~'enER¹(1, 2), ~'NESS, nn., ~'LY² adv. [app. alt. f. ME (now dial.) *thight* f. ON *•thehtr, thēttr*, cf. MLG (G) *dicht*]

tig'on, n. Offspring of tiger and lioness. [portmanteau wd]

tike. See TYKE.

tiki (tēk'ē), n. (New Zealand). Large wooden or small greenstone image of creator of man or of an ancestor. [Maori]

tikkie, -ky. See TICKEY.

til (tēl), n. The TILDE in Port. use (over vowel, repr. lost nasal n).

til'bury̆, n. (hist.). Kind of gig. [maker]

til'de (-ă), n. Swung dash, mark (~) put over Spanish *n* when it is pronounced ny (so *señor*). [Sp., var. of *tilulo* TITLE¹]

tile, n., & v.t. **1.** Thin slab of baked clay for roof, pavement, drain, etc.; similar slab glazed & often decorated for hearth, fireplace, wall, etc.; *have a ~ loose* (sl.), be rather mad; *on the ~s* (sl.), on a debauch; *Dutch ~* (painted usu. in blue & with scriptural subjects); PANTILE; *plain~*, flat roofing-~ usu. about 10½ × 6¼ in.; (colloq.) silk hat; *~ TEA*; *~'stone*, kinds of flagstone serving when split for *~s*. **2.** v.t. Cover (roof etc., or abs.) with *~s*; (freemasonry) guard (lodge, meeting) against intrusion by placing tiler at door, whence (gen.) bind (person) to secrecy; *~ in*, enclose in *~s*. Hence **til'ING¹**(1, 2, 6) n. [OE *tigule, -ele, OS tiegla, OHG ziagal, ON tigl,* f. L *tegula* f. *tegere* cover]

til'er, n. One who makes or lays tiles, whence **til'ERY**(3) n.; (freemasonry, also arch. *tyler*) doorkeeper of lodge. [-ER¹]

till¹, v.t. Prepare and use (soil) for crops. Hence ~'ABLE a., ~'AGE(3) n. [OE (OS) *tilian* strive, obtain, OHG *zilōn*, Goth. *gatilōn*, see TILL²]

till², prep. & conj. **1.** Up to, as late as, (specified day, hour, season), as *wait ~ evening, four o'clock, then, Monday, next week*; up to the time of (event expected to happen sooner or later), as *was true ~ death, waited ~ the end, ~ his return, arrival, departure*. **2.** conj. Up to the time when, as *ring ~ you get an answer, walk on ~ you come to the gate*. [f. ON *til* to, prob. orig. a noun *•til* (prec.) = OE *till* fixed point, OHG *zil* goal, Goth *til*]

till³, n. Money-drawer in shop counter. [15th c., cf unkn. orig.]

till⁴, n. Stiff clay with boulders, sand, etc., boulder-clay. Hence ~'Y² a. [orig. unkn.]

till'er¹, n. One who tills. [ME; -ER¹]

till'er², n. Lever fitted to head of rudder for steering; *~-chain, -rope* (connecting ~ with wheel). [ME, f. OF *telier* crossbow-stock, orig. weaver's beam, f. L *tela* web, -ARY¹]

till'er³, n., & v.i. **1.** Shoot of plant springing from bottom of original stalk; sapling; sucker. **2.** v.i. Put forth ~s. [app. repr. OE *telgor* extended f. *telga* bough, = ON *tjalga*, MHG *zelg(e)*]

tilt¹, v.i. & t., & n. **1.** (Cause to) assume sloping position, heel over, as *table is apt to ~ over, don't ~ the table, cask wants ~ing* (to facilitate emptying); (geol., t. & i. of strata) turn *up* at steep angle. **2.** Make a charge with lance (often *at* opponent, esp. fig.); *~ at the ring* (suspended for horseman to carry off on point of lance). **3.** Hammer (steel etc.) with ~. **4.** n. ~ing, sloping position. **5.** Charging with spear against antagonist or mark (*~-yard*, place used for this). **6.** Device of crossed sticks etc. for showing when fish has taken hook. **7.** *Full ~*, at full

speed, with full force, esp. *come, run, full
~ against.* 8. ~ (*-hammer*), heavy pivoted
hammer used in forging. Hence ~'ER[1]
(1, 2) n. [ME *tille* f. OE *tealt* unsteady,
shaky, cf. Norw. *tylten* shaky, Sw. *tulta*
waddle]

tilt[2], n., & v.t. 1. Covering of canvas etc.
esp. for cart. 2. v.t. Furnish with ~.
[collateral form of ME *tild*, OE *teld*,
OHG *zelt*, ON *tjald*, perh. infl. by *tent*]

tilth, n. Tillage, cultivation; depth of soil
affected by this. [OE (TILL[1]+-TH[1])]

tim'bal, -ul, tỹ-, n. Kettledrum. [f. F
timbale, earlier *attabale* f. Sp. f. Arab.
attabal the drum]

timbale (tăṅbahl'), n. Drum-shaped
raised pie in crust of paste or macaroni.
[F]

tim'ber, n. 1. Wood prepared for building, carpentry, etc.; trees suitable for
this; woods, forest; piece of wood, beam,
esp. (naut.) any of the curved pieces
forming ribs of vessel, whence (invoking
destruction) *shiver my ~s;* ‖ (hunting)
fences & gates. 2. ‖ ~*-cart* (high-wheeled
with tackle for lifting~); ~*-head*, top end
of ~ rising above deck & used for belaying
ropes etc.; ~*-hitch*, knot used in attaching
a rope to a spar; ~*-toe*(s), colloq., person
with wooden leg; ~*-wolf*, large American
grey wolf; ‖ ~*-yard* (lit., &, in cricket sl.,
batsman's wicket). Hence (·)~ED[2] (*-erd*)
a., ~ING[1](2, 3) n. [OE *timber* building,
OS *-ar*, OHG *zimbar*, ON *timbr*, Goth.
timr f. Gmc *timram* f. *tem-*, cogn. w.
Gk *demō* build, L *domus* house]

timbre (tăm'ber, & see Ap.), n. Characteristic quality of sounds produced by each
particular voice or instrument, depending
on the number & character of the over-
tones. [F, ult. f. L f. Gk as TYMPANUM]

tim'brel, n. Tambourine. [dim. of ME
timbre f. OF, as prec., see -LE(2)]

time[1], n. 1. Duration, continued existence; progress of this viewed as affecting
persons or things, as ~ *will show who is
right, has stood the test of* ~, (personified) *assaults of* (old, *Father*) *T~.* 2. More
or less definite portion of this associated
with particular events or circumstances,
historical or other period, as *the ~s of the
Stuarts, the ~ of the Black Death, for the
~* BEING, *prehistoric ~s, those godless ~s,
the good old ~s, things have changed since
those ~s, the scientists of the ~.* 3. Allotted
or available portion of ~, the ~ at one's
disposal, as *it will last our ~* (lives), *have
no ~ for such frivolities, had no ~ to discuss
it, spend, lose, waste,* ~; *will take you all
your ~* (colloq. = tax your powers); *give
me ~ & I will pay;* (colloq.) *got there ~*
(soon) *enough to see him; gain~*, procure it
esp. by temporizing measures. 4. Moment
or definite portion of ~ destined or suitable for a purpose etc., as *there is a ~ for
everything, will fix a ~ for seeing him, now
is the ~ to press your point, now is your ~*
(opportunity), *I must bide my ~, it is*

(HIGH) ~ *to go,* ~ *for lunch, lunch-~, it is ~
I was going* (for me to go), *in the* NICK[1] *of
~,* ~ (for boxing-round etc.) *is up,*
(umpire's call) ~*!, is serving his* ~ (as
apprentice etc.), *is doing ~* (in prison), *is
far on in her ~* (of gestation), *is near her
~* (of childbirth), *my ~* (death) *is drawing
near.* 5. (Often pl.) conditions of life,
prevailing circumstances, of a period, as
hard, bad, good, ~*s* (esp. hard etc. to get
a living in); *had a good~*, enjoyed myself;
those were (fine) ~*s!; what a ~* (trouble)
you will have getting him home! 6. Occasion, as *the first ~ I saw him, wait till next
~, did it seven ~s running, have told you
a dozen ~s, ~s out of number, ~ & again,
many a ~, ~ after ~, for the last ~ of
asking; three, four,* etc. ~*s* (but *twice,* not
two ~s) 9 is 27 etc., *is three ~s the size of
mine, ten ~s easier or as easy.* 7. *Past,
present, future,* ~, the portions into which
all ~ may at any moment be accurately
or loosely divided (esp., gram., with
reference to tenses). 8. (Amount of) ~
as reckoned by conventional standards,
as *the ~ allowed was four years, months,
minutes, did a mile in record ~, astronomical* (mean solar) ~, *apparent* (SOLAR) ~,
SIDEREAL ~, esp. stated in hours & minutes
of the day, as *the ~ fixed was 4.30, what is
the ~?, is that the correct* (GREENWICH) ~*?,
at this ~ of day* (fig., at this late stage
in history, in the negotiations, etc.). 9.
(mus.). Duration of a note as indicated by
semibreve, minim, etc.; style of movement
depending on number & accentuation
of beats in a bar, as *binary, ternary, ~*
(with two, three, beats in bar), COMMON[1]
~; rate of execution, =*tempo.* 10. *Against
~,* with utmost speed, as *working, riding,
against ~; ahead of,* (born) *before,* one's *~
or ~s,* having notions too enlightened to
be appreciated or put into practice; *all
the ~,* during the whole of the ~ referred
to (*they were laughing all the ~*), *at all
~s* (*is a business man all the ~*); *at the
same~,* simultaneously, notwithstanding,
all the same; *at ~s,* now & then; *at one ~,*
during a known but unspecified past
period (*at one ~ we met frequently*); *beat
~,* indicate, follow, ~ of music with stick,
hand, etc.; *civil ~* (expressed by CIVIL
year etc.); CLOSE[1] ~; *from ~ to ~,* occasionally; *in ~,* not late, early enough (*to
do, for* thing), eventually, sooner or later,
in accordance with, following, the ~ of
music etc.; *in no ~,* rapidly, in the twink-
ling of an eye; *keep ~,* walk, dance, sing,
etc., in ~, (of clock etc.) *keep good, bad,
~,* record ~ (in)accurately; *mean ~*
(regulated by average); *one, two,* etc., *at a
~,* each, each two etc., separately; *out of
~,* unseasonable, unseasonably, too late,
(of singing etc.) not in ~; ~ *immemorial*
or *out of mind,* (for, from) a longer ~ than
anyone can remember or trace; *the ~ of
day,* hour by clock, (colloq.) *pass the ~ of
day,* exchange greeting etc. (*with* person),

(sl.) *so that's the ~ of day* (the state of affairs, your little game, etc.)/; *the ~ of one's life*, a period of exceptional enjoyment or pleasant or unpleasant excitement (*have the ~ of one's, give one the ~ of his, life*); *what ~* (poet.), while, when; *The T~s*, the newspaper so named. **11.** ~-*ball* (dropped from top of staff at observatory to indicate fixed moment of mean ~); ~-*bargain*, contract for sale of stock etc. at future ~ (often a form of gambling); ~ *bomb* (designed to explode some ~ after being dropped or put in position); ~-*book*, -*card*, -*sheet* (for recording workmen's hours of work); ~-*fuse* (calculated to burn for or explode at given ~); ~-*honoured*, venerable by antiquity; ~'*keeper*, one who records ~ esp. of workmen, *watch* etc. *is good, bad*, ~*keeper* (keeps good, bad, ~); ~ *lag*, interval of ~ between cause etc. & result or consequence; ~-*limit* (within which something must be done); ~'*piece*, ~-measuring instrument esp. portable but stationary clock; ~-*server*, one who, esp. for selfish ends, adapts himself to opinions of the ~s or of persons in power, so ~-*serving* a. & n.; ~-*table*, scheme of school work etc., table showing ~s of trains; ~-*work* (paid for by ~, not PIECE--*work*). [OE *tima*, ON *timi*, f. Gmc root *tī-*, cf. TIDE]

time², v.t. & i. Choose the time for, do at chosen time, as *must ~ your blows, remark was ill, well*, ~*d*; arrange time of arrival of, regulate rate of travelling of, (train etc.); ascertain the time taken by (race, runner, etc.), whence **tim'ER¹**(1, 2), **tim'ING¹**, nn.; keep time, harmonize, *with*. [ME; f. prec.]

time'less (-ml-), a. (rare). Unending; untimely. [-LESS]

time'l|ў (-ml-), a. Seasonable, opportune. Hence ~iNESS n. [ME; -LY¹]

tĭm'ĕŏ Dăn'aŏs ĕt dŏn'a ferĕn'tēs, phr. inculcating or expressing distrust of a conciliatory enemy. [L, = I fear the Greeks, even when they bring gifts]

|| **time'ous** (-mus), **tim'ous**, a. (chiefly Sc.). Timely. Hence ~LY² adv. [f. TIME¹+-OUS]

tim'id, a. Easily alarmed; shy. Hence or cogn. **timid'ITY**, ~NESS, nn., ~LY² adv. [f. F -*ide* or L *timidus* (*timēre* fear, -ID¹)]

timŏc'racў, n. Form of government in which there is a property qualification for office. So **tĭmŏcrăt'IC** a. [f. OF *tymocracie* f. med. L f. Gk *timokratia* (*timē* honour, worth, value, see -CRACY)]

tim'orous, a. Timid, easily alarmed. Hence ~LY² adv., ~NESS n. [ME, f. OF *timoreus*, f. med. L *timorosus*, f. L *timor*, see -OUS]

tim'othў, n. (Also ~ *grass*) a fodder--grass. [T~ Hanson, who introduced it in N. America *c*. 1720]

|| **timous**. See TIMEOUS.

tim'pan|ō, n. (pl. ~*i* pr. -ē). A kettle--drum. So ~IST n., one who plays the percussion instruments in an orchestra. [It., see TYMPANUM]

tin, n., & v.t. (-nn-). **1.** White malleable metal, taking high polish & resisting corrosion, used mainly in alloys with lead, copper, or antimony to form solder, white-metal, pewter, bronze, etc., or in plating thin steel sheets to form ~ *plate* to make containers, kitchen utensils, toys, etc.; || vessel etc. of ~, esp. for preserving meat, fruit, etc., as *sardine-~*; (attrib.) made of ~ or of iron covered with ~; (sl.) money; *cry of ~*, crackling sound it makes if bent; *salt of ~*, ~--*liquor*, solutions of ~ used as mordants by dyers etc. **2.**~ *fish* (naut. sl.), torpedo; ~ *foil*, foil of ~ or alloy; ~ *god*, object of mistaken veneration; ~ *hat* (army sl.), modern soldier's steel helmet; ||~-*opener*, tool for opening ~s; ~-*pan alley*, (fig.) the world of the composers and publishers of popular music; ~-*plate* v.t., coat with ~; ~'*man*, ~-*smith*, worker in ~ and ~ plate, so ~'n'ER¹ n.; ~'*pot* a. (derog.), cheap, inferior; ~'*stone*, one of the ores of ~; ~'*ware*, vessels etc. of ~ or ~ plate; ~ *whistle*, = *penny* WHISTLE. Hence ~n'Y² a. **3.** v.t. Cover, coat, with ~; || pack (meat, fruit, etc.) in ~s for preservation. [OE, ON *tin*, OHG *zin*, f. Gmc *tinam*, not known outside Gmc]

tin'amou (-ŏō), n. S.-Amer. quail-like game-bird. [F, of S.-Amer. orig.]

tinc'al, -**kal**, (-ngkl), n. Unrefined borax. [f. Malay *tingkal* f. Skr. *ṭankaṇa*]

tinctōr'ial, a. Of colour or dyeing, producing colour. [f. L *tinctorius* (*tinctor* dyer), see TINGE, -ORY, -AL]

tinc'ture, n., & v.t. **1.** Alcoholic solution of some (usu. vegetable) principle used in medicine, as ~ *of quinine*; slight flavour, spice, smack, (*of* thing, fig. *of* moral quality etc.); tinge (*of* colour); (her.) inclusive term for the metals, colours, & furs in a coat of arms. **2.** v.t. Colour slightly, tinge, flavour; (fig.) affect slightly (*with* quality). [(vb f. n.) ME, f. L *tinctura* dyeing (as TINGE, see -URE)]

tin'dal, n. (India). Native petty officer of Lascars. [Malayalam *taṇḍal*]

tin'der, n. Dry substance readily taking fire from spark, esp. charred linen etc. used in ~-*box* (containing ~, flint, & steel, for kindling fire); *German* ~, = AMADOU. Hence ~Y² a. [OE *tynder*, -*re* f. Gmc *tund-*, *tind-* kindle; cf. ON *tundr*, OHG *zuntara*]

tine, n. Point, prong, e.g. of antler, harrow, or fork. Hence (-)tinED² (-nd) a. [OE *tind*, ON *tindr* f. Gmc *tindiz*]

ting, n., & v.i. (Make) tinkling sound as of bell. [imit.]

tinge (-j), v.t., & n. **1.** Colour slightly (*with* red etc.); (fig.) modify by mixture (*with* envy etc.). **2.** n. Tint, slight colouring, flavour (lit. & fig.). [ME, f. L *tingere tinct-* dye, stain]

tingle (tǐng'gl), v.i. & t., & n. (Feel)
prickling or stinging sensation; cause
this, as *the reply ~d in his ears;* (rare)
make (ear etc.) ~. [ME; var. of
TINKLE]

tink'er, n., & v.t. & i. 1. ‖ Mender (esp.
itinerant) of kettles, pans, etc. *(don't care
a ~'s damn* or *cuss,* at all); rough-&-ready
worker, botcher; patching, botching, as
had an hour's ~ at it. 2. Kinds of fish,
bird, & seal. 3. vb. Repair (metal-work),
patch (anything, lit. & fig., often *up*)
roughly; work in amateurish or clumsy
fashion *at* (thing) in the way of repair or
alteration. Hence ~LY[1] a. [ME, of unkn.
orig.]

tinkle (tǐng'kl), v.i. & t., & n. (Make)
succession of clinking sounds; make (bell
etc.) ~ ; (obs.) tingle. [ME, f. obs. *tink* to
chink + -LE(3)]

tink'ler, n. In vbl senses, esp.: (sl.) small
bell. [-ER[1]]

tinnit'us, n. (med.). Ringing in the ears.
[L, f. *tinnire -it-* ring, tinkle]

tinny. See TIN.

tin'sel, n., a., & v.t. (-ll-). 1. Kinds of
glittering metallic substance made in thin
sheets & used in strips, threads, etc., to
give sparkling effect; dress-fabric etc.
adorned with ~; (fig.) superficial brilliancy or splendour. 2. adj. Showy, gaudy,
cheaply splendid. 3. v.t. Adorn with ~
(lit. & fig.). [f. OF *estincelle* f. pop. L
stincilla f. L *scintilla* spark; cf. STENCIL]

tint, n., & v.t. 1. A variety of a colour, esp.
one made by diluting with white; (rare)
tendency towards, admixture of, a different colour, as *red of* or *with a blue ~;*
autumn ~s (of dying leaves); (engrav.)
set of parallel lines cut with ~-*tool* to give
uniform shading; ~-*block,* block bearing
design to be printed in faint colour as
background, *ruled, crossed,* ~, surface of
this with parallel, crossing, lines. 2. v.t.
Apply ~ to, colour. Hence ~'LESS a.
[app. alt. 'f. earlier *tinct* f. L (as TINGE),
perh. infl. by It. *tinta*]

tint'er, n. Person who tints; instrument
for tinting; magic-lantern slide of plain
coloured glass. [-ER[1]]

tintinnăbŭlā'tion, n. Tinkling of bells.
[f. foll. + -ATION]

tintinnăb'ŭl|um, n. (pl. ~a). Bell, esp.
small tinkling one, whence ~AR(Y)[1], ~OUS,
aa.; rattle made of small bells or metal
plates. [L, = bell, f. *tintinnare* redupl.
form as TINNITUS]

tintŏm'eter, n. Instrument for determining tints. [-METER]

tint'y, a. Discordantly tinted. [-Y[2]]

tin'y, teen'y (nursery), a. Very small, as
a ~ little boy, little ~ boy. [app. f. 15th c.
tine, tyne adj. & n., small, a little (of
unkn. orig.) + -Y[2]]

-tion, suf. of n. of action or condition,
thr. F *-tion* (or dir.) f. L *-tionem* (nom.
-tio), a compd suf. f. p.p. stems in *-t-* +
-ION. See -ATION, -ITION, -SION.

tip[1], n., & v.t. (-pp-). 1. Extremity, end,
esp. of small or tapering thing, as *the ~s
of the fingers, walk on the ~s of your toes,
~ of a cigar, bird measures 15 in. from
~* (of one wing) *to ~* (of other), *had it on
the ~ of my tongue,* was just going to say
it or was on the point of remembering it;
kinds of brush used in gilding; small
piece or part attached to end of thing,
e.g. ferrule. 2. ~'*staff* (hist.; pl. ~*staves*),
(metal-tipped staff as badge of) sheriff's
officer; ~*-tilted,* (of nose) turned up at
~ ; ~'*toe,* (adv., also *on ~toe*) on the ~s of
the toes, (v.i.) walk ~*toe;* ~*top',* (n.)
highest point of excellence, (a. & adv.)
first-rate. 3. v.t. Furnish with ~. [ME
(first in p.p.), f. ON *typpi* n., *typpa* vb,
typptr tipped; prob. reinforced by MDu.,
MLG *tip* = MHG *zipf*]

tip[2], v.t. & i. (-pp-), & n. 1. (Cause to) lean
or slant, tilt, topple, (*over, up,* etc.) esp.
with slight effort. 2. Strike or touch
lightly (~ *& run,* form of cricket in which
batsman must run if bat touches ball;
~*-&-run raid,* one in which the raider
appears suddenly and makes off immediately after attacking). 3. Overturn,
cause to overbalance, (person *into* pond
etc.); discharge (contents of jug etc. *out,
into,* etc.) thus. 4. (sl.). Throw lightly,
hand, give, communicate, in informal
manner, as ~ (throw) *us a copper,* ~ *us
your fin,* shake hands, ~ *us a song, a yarn,
might have ~ped me the wink* (given me
warning wink); ~ *off,* give (person) warning, hint, inside information, so ~*-off* n.,
a hint; (sport.) give secret information
about horse etc. to. 5. Make usu. small
present of money to, as *must ~ the porter,
~ped me* (now rarely *with*) *half-a-crown.*
6. n. Small money present. 7. Secret
information about horse-racing, money-
-market, etc., as *will give you the straight*
(correct) ~; good dodge or recipe for
doing something; *miss one's ~,* fail in
one's object. 8. Slight push; light stroke
esp. in baseball. 9. Place where refuse
is ~ped. 10. ~-*car, -cart* (pivoted for
~ping); ~'*cat,* (game with) short piece of
wood tapering at ends & struck with
stick; ~-*up seat,* of the kind used in
theatres etc. to allow of free passing.
Hence ~p'ER[1] (1, 2) n. [of various orig.]

Tipperăr'y, n. Refrain specially associated with the B.E.F. of 1914. [*It's a long
way to ~,* first wds of chorus]

tipp'ĕt, n. Cape, muffler, of fur etc. covering shoulders & coming down to some
distance in front, worn by women & as
part of official costume by judges, clergy,
etc. [ME, of unkn. orig.]

tip'ple, v.i. & t., & n. 1. Drink strong
drink habitually; drink (liquor) slowly &
repeatedly. 2. n. Strong drink. **tipp'lER**[1]
n. [ME *tippler,* of unkn. orig.; vb later,
prob. by back form.; cf. Norw. dial.
tippla to drink in small quantities]

tipp'y, a. (Of tea) containing a large

proportion of 'golden tips' (leaf-buds). [TIP¹ + -Y²]

tip′ster, n. One who gives tips about races etc. [-STER]

tip′s|ỹ, a. Slightly intoxicated; proceeding from, showing, intoxication, as *a ~y lurch*; *~y-cake*, sponge-cake soaked in wine & served with custard. Hence ~iFY v.t., ~iLY² adv., ~iNESS n. [prob. f. TIP², = inclined to lean, unsteady; for *-sy* cf. *tricksy, flimsy*]

tirāde′ (*or* tīr-), n. Long vehement speech esp. of censure; long passage of declâmation etc. [F, = long speech, f. It. *tirata*, f. It. *tirare* draw, see -ADE]

tirailleur′ (-ralĕr, & see Ap.), n. Sharpshooter, skirmisher. [F]

tire¹, v.t. & i. Make or grow weary; *am ~d*, have had enough *of*, am sick *of*, (thing, doing), am exhausted *with*. Hence ~d′NESS (tīrd-) n., also (rhet., poet.) ~′lèss¹ (tīrl-) [-LESS] a., ~′lèssLY² adv. [OE *tiorian*, *tē-*; excl. E]

tire², ‖ **tyre**, n., & v.t. **1.** Band of metal, rubber, etc., placed round rim of wheel to strengthen it or prevent jar; PNEUMATIC ~. **2.** v.t. Place ~ on (wheel). Hence (-)tirED² (tīrd), ~′lèss² (tīrl-) [-LESS], aa. [15th c., prob. = foll.]

‖ **tire³**, n., & v.t. (arch.). **1.** Head-dress; attire. **2.** v.t. Adorn, attire, as *she ~d her head*; *~′woman* (arch.), woman employed to dress another. [ME, aphetic f. ATTIRE]

tire′some (tīrs-), a. Tending to tire, fatiguing; tedious; annoying, as *how ~! —I have left my watch behind.* Hence~LY² adv., ~NESS n. [TIRE¹ + -SOME]

tīr′ō, tỹr′ō, n. (pl. ~s). Beginner, novice. [L (*ti-*), = newly levied soldier]

tīrocin′ium, n. (pedant.). Apprenticeship, first rudiments of an art. [L, = first service of soldier (prec.)]

'tis (-z), arch. or poet. contraction of *it is.*

tisane′ (-zăn), n. = PTISAN. [F]

tiss′ue (-sū, -shū, -shōō), n. Any fine woven fabric; (biol.) substance of an organ, fabric formed of cells & cell-products, as *adipose, connective, muscular, nervous, ~*; (fig.) interwoven series, set, collection, (*of* lies, absurdities, etc.); *~ (-paper)*, thin soft unsized paper for wrapping or protecting delicate articles, engraving in book, etc. Hence (-)tiss′uED² (-sūd, -shūd) a. [ME, f. OF *tissu* rich stuff, f. p.p. of *tistre* f. L *texere* weave]

tit¹, n. **1.** Kinds of small bird, including *~′lark* & *~′mouse* (both also called *~′ling*); *bearded, blue, coal* or *cole, crested, great, long-tailed, marsh, ~.* **2.** (arch.). Small or poor horse; child, girl. [prob. imit. of littleness; cf. Icel. *tittr* pin, titmouse]

tit², n. ~ *for tat*, blow for blow, retaliation. [perh., = earlier *tip for tap*]

tit³, n. (colloq.). = TEAT.

Tit′an, n. (Gk myth.) each of a gigantic race, the children of Uranus & Ge, (also) the sun-god, brother of Helios; person of superhuman size, strength, intellect, etc.,

whence ~ESS¹ n. So ~ESQUE′ (-ĕsk), tităn′IC, aa. [L f. Gk]

titān′ium, n. A dark-grey metallic element. Hence **tīt′an**ATE¹ (3) n. [prec. + -IUM]

tit′bit, n. Delicate bit, choice morsel. [17th c. *tid-bit*, f. dial. *tid* adj.]

tīthe (-dh), n., & v.t. **1.** Tax of one-tenth, esp. one payable in kind; ‖ (oîten pl.) tenth part of annual proceeds of land (*predial ~s*) & personal industry (*personal ~s*) taken for support of clergy & church; ‖ *mixed ~s* (from pigs, sheep, etc., fed on the land); ‖ *~ redemption commissioners* (arranging commutation of *~s* etc.); ‖ *~-pig*, tenth pig set apart for *~;* (rhet.) tenth part, esp. *not a ~ of.* **2.** v.t. Subject to *~s.* Hence **tīth′**ABLE (-dh-) a. [ME *tig(e)the, tithe* = OE *teogotha, tēotha* TENTH; vb f. *teogothian*]

tīth′ing (-dh-), n. Taking tithe; (hist.) ten householders living near together & bound over as sureties for each other's peaceable behaviour. [as prec., -ING¹]

Ti′tian (-shn), n. Venetian painter (d. 1576); one of his pictures; (attrib., esp. of hair) bright golden auburn. Hence ~ESQUE′ (-shanĕsk) a., in the style of ~.

tit′ill|āte, v.t. Tickle; excite pleasantly. So ~A′TION n. [f. L *titillare*, see -ATE³]

tit′ivāte, titt′i-, v.t. & i. (colloq.). Adorn, smarten, (oneself etc.); adorn oneself. [earlier *tid-*, perh. f. *tidy* after *cultivate*]

tit′lărk. See TIT¹.

ti′tle, n. **1.** Distinguishing appellation placed at head of chapter, poem, etc.; contents of *~-page* of book, short essential part of these used in reference (e.g. *Adam Smith's Wealth of Nations*); book or publication. **2.** Formula at head of legal document, statute, etc.; division of statute etc. **3.** Personal appellation, hereditary or not, denoting or implying office (e.g. *king, queen, judge, mayor, rector, captain*) or nobility (e.g. *duke, marquis, earl, viscount, baron,* any of which exc. *duke* may be COURTESY ~ of son etc. of duke etc.) or distinction or merit (e.g. *baronet, knight*) or (usu. *degree*) qualification (e.g. *D.D., M.A.*), or used in addressing or referring to person (e.g. *Lord, Lady, Sir, Mrs, Miss, Doctor, Professor,* prefixed to name; *your* or *her* or *his Majesty, Grace*, etc.). **4.** (Law) right to ownership of property with or without possession, the facts constituting this, (also *~-deed*) legal instrument as evidence of right; just or recognized claim (*to*), service, merit, etc., that constitutes this. **5.** Fineness of gold as expressed in carats. **6.** Fixed sphere of work & source of income as condition to ordination. **7.** (District attached to) parish church in Rome. **8.** *~-page*, page at beginning of book giving particulars of subject, authorship, publication, etc.; *~-role*, part in a play that gives it its name (e.g. *Othello*). Hence ~LESS a. [ME & OF *title* f. L *titulus*]

ti′tled (-ld), a. Having title of nobility. [-ED²]

tit′ling¹, n. See TIT¹. [f. TIT¹+-LING; cf. Norw. dial., Icel. *titlingr*]

tit′ling², n. Impressing of title in gold-leaf etc. on back of book. [-ING¹]

tit′mouse, n. (pl. *-mice*). = TIT¹. [ME *titmōse* (TIT¹+OE *māse* ~, = OHG *meisa*, G *meise*)]

Tit′ōǐism (tē-), n. President Tito's kind of Communism in Jugoslavia as dist. from that of Russia and her satellite countries. So ~IST(2) n. & a. [*Tito*, assumed name of Josip Broz (b. 1892), -ISM(3)]

tit′r|āte, v.t. Determine quantity of given constituent in (compound) by observing quantity of a standard solution necessary to convert this constituent into another form. So ~A′TION n. [f. F *titrer* (*litre* TITLE), see -ATE³]

tit′ter, v.i., & n. 1. Laugh, giggle, in restrained manner. 2. n. Such laugh. Hence ~ER¹ n. [imit.]

tit′tle, n. Particle, whit, esp. *not one jot or* ~. [ME, = stroke over word or letter, f. L as TITLE, cf. TILDE]

∥ **tit′tlebāt** (-lb-), n. Stickleback. [var. of childish orig.]

tit′tle-tāttle, n., & v.i. Gossip. [redupl. f. *tattle*]

tit′tup, v.i., & n. 1. Go *along* etc., move, conduct oneself, in lively or frisky fashion; ∥ (naut. etc. sl.) toss for drinks. 2. n. Spring, prance. Hence ~(p)Y² a. [perh. imit. of hoof-beat]

titūbā′tion, n. (med.). Fidgetiness esp. as caused by nervous irritation. [f. L *titubatio* (*titubare* totter, see -ATION)]

tit′ūlar, a. & n. 1. Held by virtue of a title, as ~ *possessions*; existing, that is such, only in name, as ~ *sovereign(ty)*; ~ *bishop*, (R.-C. Ch.) bishop bearing name of a former Christian see esp. in Mohammedan countries; ~ (*saint*), patron saint of church. 2. n. Holder of office etc. esp. benefice without corresponding functions or obligations. Hence ~LY² adv. [c. 1600, f. F *titulaire* (TITLE, -AR¹)]

†mēs′is, n. (gram.). Separation of the parts of a compound word by intervening word(s) (e.g. *to* us *ward*, *what* things *soever*). [LL f. Gk *tmēsis* cutting f. *temnō* cut]

to¹ (*before consonant* te, *before vowel* tōo, *emphat. or at end of clause* tōo), prep. 1. In the direction of (place, person, thing, condition, quality, etc.; with or without the implication of intention or of arrival), as *was walking over to Bath*, *on his way to the station*, *fled to Rome*, *throw it to me*, *got to the house by four*, *to bed with you!*, *fluttered to the pavement*, *was committed to the flames*, *house looks to the south*, *held it to the light*, *to arms!*, *hand to hand*, *told him to his face*, *was carried to destruction*, *letter has come to hand*, *fell to work*, *fell to musing*, *tends or has a tendency to indolence*, *slow to anger*, *appointed to a post*, *born to a great fortune*, *all to no purpose*, *to his shame be it said*. 2. As far as, not short of, as *true to the end*, *cut him to the heart*, *a Home-ruler to the core*, *fought to the last gasp*, *hit it to the boundary*, *correct to a hair's-breadth*, *suits him to a T*, *acted his part to perfection*, *might run to £5*, *drank himself to death*, *might argue to all eternity*, *& so on to the end of the chapter*. 3. (Of comparison, ratio, adaptation, reference, etc.) *this is nothing to what it might be*, *3 is to 4 as 6 is to 8*, *ten to one he will find it out*, *two to one is not fair play*, *not up to the mark*, *equal to the occasion*, *made to order*, *drawn to scale*, *not to the point*, *true to life*, *will speak to that question later*, *sang to his guitar*, *cannot do it to his liking*; *corresponding*, *compared*, *inferior*, etc., *to*. 4. (arch.). For, by way of, as *took her to wife*, *has a duke to his father-in-law*. 5. (Introducing indirect object of vb, recipient, possessor, etc., or person or thing affected by the action, quality, etc.; alternative constr. as shown) *lend it* or *them*, or *this* etc., *or your knife* etc., *to John* or *to him* (*also lend John* or *him this* etc. or *your knife* or rarely *it* or *them*, *lend it* or rarely *them him* or rarely *John*, but not *lend this* etc., *or your knife him*, or *John*, nor *lend to him* or *John it* or *them*, nor *in ordinary prose lend to him* or *John this* etc. or *your knife*); *write to me*, *explain it to me*, *apply to the secretary*, *seems to me absurd*, *to my mind* or *thinking*, *revolting to sane minds*, *pleasant to the taste*, *impervious to weather*, *obedient to command*, *unkind to him*, *has been a good father to them*, *what's that to you?*, *drink to me the only with thine eyes*, *here's to you* (your health), *broken in to the saddle*, *accustomed to it*, *next door to us*, *ready to his hand*, *has not a shilling to his name*, *takes no wine to his dinner* (arch.), *there is a moral to it*, *there is no end to it*; *would to God* (I wish it were or had been God's will) *that*. 6. (As sign of infinitive, expressing purpose, consequence, etc., limiting the meaning of adj., or merely forming verbal n.; omitted after *can*, *do*, *may*, *must*, *shall*, *will*, & as shown, cf. also DARE, NEED, GO) *he proposes to stay*, *declines to go*, *wants to know*, *began to sing* (or *began singing*), *fail to understand*, *does it to annoy*, *the matter is difficult to explain*, *it is useless to rebel* (rebellion is useless), *allow me to remind* (but *let me remind*) *you*, *was seen to fall* (but *I saw him fall*), *was heard to complain* (but *I heard him complain*), *floor was felt to tremble* (but *felt the floor tremble*), *was never known or found to fail*, *have sometimes known or found it* (*to*) *fail*, *make him repeat it*, *he was made* (usu. *to*) *repeat it*, *help me* (*to*) *lift this*, *please* (*to* usu. omitted) *shut the door*, *was pleased* (thought fit) *to be angry*, *I prefer to go* (but *had rather go*, *had as lief go*), *had my work to do*, *had to do my work* (but *will not have you talk such nonsense*), *was about to protest*, (arch.) *he is much to seek* (deficient) *in that respect*, (arch.) *what went ye out for to see?*, *to* WIT [1]. 7. (As substitute for infinitive) *meant to call but forgot to*, *had no time to*, *you promised to*. 8. Included, contained, or involved in (*that's all there is to it*, it's that and no more). [OE, (OS) *tō*, OHG *zuo* f. WG *[tō]*]

to [2] (tŏŏ), adv. To the normal or required position or condition, esp. to a standstill, as BRING, COME, FALL, GO, HEAVE, LIE [3], *to*; *the door is to* (just not shut); *to & FRO.* [f. prec.]

toad, n. 1. Amphibian like frog but with clumsy & usu. warty body & not aquatic except when breeding; detestable or disgusting person. 2. ~ *in a* (or *the*) *hole*, beef or sausages baked in batter. 3. ~- *-eater*, sycophant, obsequious parasite, so ~-*eating* a. & n.; ~'*flax*, perennial plant with spurred yellow flowers marked with orange spot (*ivy-leaved ~flax*, with lilac flowers & ivy-shaped leaves); ~'*spit*, = CUCKOO-*spit*; ~'*stone*, stone, occas. precious, supposed to resemble or to have been formed in body of ~, formerly used as amulet etc., [f. G *todtes gestein* dead rock] kind of volcanic rock; ~'*stool*, kinds of umbrella-shaped fungus. Hence ~'*ISH* [1] a. [OE *tādige*, *tadde*, of unkn. orig.]

toad'ȳ, n., & v.t. 1. = TOAD-*eater*. 2. v.t. Fawn servilely upon (person, or abs.). Hence ~*ISH* [1] a., ~*ISM* n. [19th c., f. TOAD- *-eater*+-Y [3]]

toast, n., & v.t. & i. 1. (Slice of) bread browned on each side esp. at the fire (*anchovies* etc. *on* ~, so served at table; MELBA ~; *have one on* ~, sl., have him at one's mercy; *as warm as a* ~, glowing with warmth); (arch.) *a* ~, piece of ~ in cup of wine. 2. Person esp. woman whose health is drunk, thing, sentiment, similarly named in drinking, as *was a great* ~ *in her day*. 3. ~-*list*, ~-*master*, (person who announces) ~s at public dinner; ‖~-*rack* (for holding slices of ~ at table); ~-*water* (in which ~ has stood, used as cooling drink; also ~ *& water*). 4. vb. Brown, cook, (bread, muffin, cheese, bacon, or intr. of persons) before fire; warm (one's feet etc.) thus. 5. Drink to the health or in honour of. Hence ~'*ER* [1] (1, 2) n. [ME, f. OF *toster* f. LL *tostare* grill, roast (L *torrēre tost-* parch); n. f. vb]

toast'ing, n. In vbl senses; ~-*fork*, long fork for making toast, (joc., also ~-*iron*) sword. [-ING [1]]

tobacc'ō, n. (pl. ~s). 1. (Also ~-*plant*) plant of Amer. origin with narcotic leaves used for smoking, chewing, or snuff; its leaves esp. as prepared for smoking etc. (abbr. *baccy*). 2. ~-*cutter*, instrument for shredding ~; ~ *heart*, disorder of heart caused by excessive use of ~; ~-PIPE [1]; ~-*pouch* (for carrying about small quantity of ~); ~-*stopper*, instrument for pressing down ~ in pipe. [f. Sp. *tabaco*, of native orig.]

tobacc'onist, n. Dealer in tobacco. [f. prec.+-IST w. inserted -*n*-]

tobŏgg'an, n., & v.i. 1. Long narrow sledge used for going downhill esp. over snow or ice; ~-*shoot*, -*slide*, slide for ~s, usu. divided into different courses to prevent collision. 2. v.i. Go in ~. Hence ~ER [1], ~ING [1], nn. [of Canadian Ind. orig.]

tŏb'ȳ, n. · Jug or mug usu. in form of old man with three-cornered hat (also *T~ Fillpot*); ‖~ *collar*, broad turned-down goffered collar like the frill of Punch's dog *T~*. [pers. name]

tocca'ta (-kah-), n. (mus.). Kind of rapid brilliant composition for piano, organ, etc. [It., f. *toccare* TOUCH, see -ADE]

Tŏc H, n. Society with many branches embodying Christian fellowship and service. [signallers' former letter T, + H, for *Talbot House* started by Rev. T. B. Clayton in Ypres Salient in 1915 in memory of Gilbert Talbot]

Tochār'ian (-k-), a. & n. (Of, in) an extinct Indo-European language. [f. F -*ien*, f. *Tochari* a Scythian tribe· (in Strabo)]

‖**tŏch'er** (-χ-), n. (Sc.). Marriage portion, dowry. [f. Gael. *tochar*]

‖**tŏc'ō**, -**kō**, n. (sl.). A thrashing; chastisement. [Hind. *thōcō*, imper. of *thocnā* censure]

tŏc'sin, n. (Bell rung as) alarm-signal (now chiefly fig.). [F, in OF *toquassen* f. Pr. *tocasenh* (*tocar* TOUCH+*senh* signal-bell f. L as SIGN)]

‖**tŏd** [1], n. (arch.). Bush; mass of foliage; weight for wool, usu. 28 lb. [ME, app. same wd as EFris., f. LG *todde* bundle, pack, ON *toddi* bit, piece; see TED]

‖**tŏd** [2], n. (dial.). Fox. [orig. unkn.]

today', **to-day'**, adv. & n. (On) this present day, as *saw* or *shall see him* ~, ~ *is his birthday*. [OE *tō dæg* on (this) day (*tō* TO [1]+DAY); so *tonight*, *tomorrow*]

tŏd'dl|e, v.i. & t., & n. 1. Walk with short tottering steps, as child learning to walk; make (one's *way*), perform (distance), thus; take casual or leisurely walk (*round*, *to*, etc.). 2. n. ~ing walk; (colloq.) ~ing child. Hence **tŏdd'ler** [1] n. [of obsc. orig.]

tŏdd'ȳ, n. Sap of some kinds of palm, from which when fermented arrack is obtained; sweetened drink of spirits & hot water. [f. Hind. *tāṛī* (*tār* palm f. Skr. *tāla* palmyra)]

to-do' (-dōō), n. Bustle, fuss. [f. *to do*, dat. inf. ' to be done ', as in *What's to do?*; cf. ADO]

tŏd'ȳ, n. W.-Ind. bird related to kingfisher. [f. F *todier* f. L *todus*, a small bird]

tōe, n., & v.t. & i. (part. ~*ing*). 1. Digit of foot; part of stocking, shoe, boot, that covers the ~s. 2. Fore part of hoof; piece of iron under front of horseshoe to prevent slipping. 3. Projection from foot of buttress etc. to give stability; outer end of head of golf-club; (mech.) lower end of vertical shaft resting in a step, arm on valve-lifting rod of steam-engine. 4. *Ball* (callous fleshy pad on under side) *of* ~; *great, little,* ~, largest, smallest, ~ of human foot; *tread on* person's ~*s*, offend his feelings or prejudices; *the light fantastic* ~, (joc.) dancing; *on* one's ~*s*, alert, eager; (sl.) *turn up* one's ~*s*, die; *from top to* ~, from head to foot, completely; *heel-&-*~ WALK [1]*ing*; ~-*cap*, outer covering of ~ in boot or shoe; ~-*drop*, inability to raise ~*s*, from paralysed muscles; ~-*nail*, nail of human ~, metal nail driven obliquely through end of board etc. 5. *vb.* Furnish with ~, mend ~ of, (stocking, shoe); touch *(the line, mark, scratch)* with ~ before starting in race (~ *the line*, fig., conform esp. under pressure to the requirements of one's party); (golf) strike (ball) with part of club toe near ~; ~ *in, out,* turn ~*s* in, out, in walking. Hence (-)toED (tōd), ~'LESS, aa. [OE *tā*, ON *tá*, OHG *zēha* f. Gmc **taih(w)ōn*]

to'fall (tōō'fawl), n. (arch., poet.). Close, decline, *(of* day etc.). [TO[2]+FALL]

‖ **tôff**, n. (sl.). Distinguished person, swell. [perh. perversion of TUFT]

‖ **tôff'ee** (-fi), -fў, n. Kinds of sweet made of sugar, butter, etc., as *almond* ~; *can't shoot* etc. *for* ~ (sl.), is no shot etc. (cf. NUT). [earlier, & still Sc. & U.S., *taffy*, of unkn. orig.]

‖ **tôft**, n. (law). Homestead; land once occupied by this; ~'*man* (hist.), occupier of ~. [OE, f. ON *topt*]

tŏg, n., & v.t. (sl.; -gg-). 1. (Usu. pl.) garment(s); (naut.) *long* ~*s*, shore-clothes. 2. v.t. Dress (person, one*self*, often *out*). Hence ~g'ERY(5) (-g-) n. [app. abbr. of *togeman(s), togman*, a 16th c. cant wd]

tŏg'a, n. Ancient Roman's loose flowing outer garment, esp. w. allusion to Roman citizenship, to civil career, or (also ~ *viril'is*, manly ~) to its assumption as sign of manhood (at age of 14). Hence ~'d, ~ED[2] (-ad), a. [L, cogn. w. *tegere* cover]

tŏgĕth'er (-dh-), adv. In company or conjunction, as *walking* ~, *lived* ~; simultaneously, as *both* ~ *exclaimed*; *compared* ~ (one with another); into conjunction, so as to unite, as *sew them* ~, *tied* ~, GET, HANG[1], ~, *put* TWO *& two* ~; uninterruptedly, on end *(he would keep sober for weeks* ~); ~ *with*, as well as, & also, as *sent a host of foot-soldiers* ~ *with some cavalry.* [OE *tōgædere tō* TO[1]+*gædre* together, cf. GATHER[1]]

‖ **tŏgg'er** (-g-), n. (Oxf. sl. for) TORPID n.

tŏg'gle, n. (Naut.) pin put through eye of rope etc. to keep it in place etc.; pair of rods or plates hinged together by ~-*joint* (knee-joint) so as to transmit pressure at right angles; ~-*iron*, harpoon with movable blade instead of fixed barbs; ~-*press* (acting by means of ~-*joints*); ~-*rope* (with wooden handle at

one end & loop at the other). [of unkn. orig.]

toil[1], v.i., & n. 1. Work long or laboriously *(at, on, through,* task); move painfully or laboriously *(up* hill etc., *along).* 2. n. Labour, drudgery; ~-*worn* (by ~). Hence ~'ER[1], ~'SOMENESS, nn., ~'FUL, ~'LESS (-l-l-), ~'SOME, aa., ~'fulLY[2], ~'somely[2], advv. [ME, f. AF *toiler* = OF *tooillier*, f. L *tudiculare* stir about, f. *tudicula* machine for bruising olives]

toil[2], n. (now only in pl.). Net, snare, (lit. & fig.), as *taken in the* ~*s*. [f. OF *toile* cloth, (pl.) toils, f. L *tela* web]

toile (twahl), n. ~ *cirée* (sērā'), fine kinds of oilcloth; ~ *côl'bert* (-bār), canvas for embroidery; ~ *d'Alsace'* (-ahs), *de Vichy* (vēshē'), linen materials for woman's summer dress. [F, see prec.]

toil'ĕt, n. 1. Process of dressing, arranging the hair, etc., as *make* one's ~; (style of) dress, costume, as *an elaborate* ~, *a* ~ *of white satin;* (also ~-*table*) dressing-table usu. with looking-glass; lavatory or water-closet; ~-*cover*, cover for ~-*table*; ~-*paper* (for water-closet); ~ *powder*, dusting powder used in making one's ~; ~-*roll* (of ~-*paper*); ~-*set* (of utensils for ~); ~ *soap* (for use in ~); ~ *vinegar* (aromatic kind for mixing with washing-water). 2. (med.). Cleansing of a part after operation. [F (-*ette*), orig. = cloth, wrapper, dim. of prec.]

toison d'or (twahzawn' dŏr'), n. = Golden FLEECE. [F]

Tokay', n. Rich aromatic wine made at Tokaj in Hungary; kind of grape.

‖ **tōke**, n. (sl.). Food (esp. dry bread).

tŏk'en, n. 1. Sign, symbol, evidence, *(of* affection etc.; often *in* ~ *of*); memorial of friendship, keepsake; ring, coin, etc., serving as proof of authenticity; BOOK[1] ~. 2. (bibl.). Preconcerted signal *(Mark* xiv. 44). 3. (hist.). Piece of metal like & used instead of coin, but worth much less than nominal value & issued by tradesmen, bank, etc., without sanction of government. 4. (arch. or joc.). *By (this, the same)* ~, *more by* ~, in corroboration of what I say. 5. ~ *money*, coins of higher nominal than intrinsic value but exchangeable for full-standard money at the higher rate; ~ *payment,* (pol.) payment of small proportion of sum due (esp. from one country to another) as indication that debt is not repudiated, (loosely) nominal payment; ~ *vote,* Parliamentary vote of money in which the amount stated *pro formâ* is not meant to be binding. Hence ~LESS a. [OE *tāc(e)n*, OS *tēcan*, OHG *zeihhan,* ON *teikn,* Goth. *taikns* f. Gmc **taik*- TEACH]

‖ **tōk'o**. See TOCO.

tōl'a, n. Unit of weight in India, = 180 grains troy. [Hind., f. Skr. *tulā*]

told. See TELL.

Tolĕd'o, n. (pl. ~s). Fine sword(-blade) made at ~ in Spain.

tol′erab|le, a. Endurable; fairly good, not bad, as *am in ~le health, had a ~le passage*. Hence **~leNESS** n., **~LY²** adv. [ME, f. OF, f. L *tolerabilis* (as foll., see -BLE)]

tol′er|āte, v.t. Endure, permit, (practice, action, person's *doing*); forbear to judge harshly or rigorously (person, religious sect, opinion); endure society of or intercourse with; sustain, endure, (suffering etc.), esp. (med.) sustain use of (drug etc.) without harm. Hence or cogn. **~ANCE** n., (also) permissible variation in dimension, weight, etc., **~ātOR** n., **~ANT** a., **~antLY²** adv. [f. L *tolerare*. -ATE³]

tolerā′tion, n. Tolerating; forbearance; recognition of right of private judgement in religious matters, liberty to uphold one's religious opinions & forms of worship or to enjoy all social privileges etc. without regard to religious differences, whence **~IST(2)** n.; *Act of T~* (conditionally freeing Dissenters from some restrictions on the exercise of their forms of worship, 1689). [F (-*lé-*), f. L *tolerationem* (as prec., see -ATION)]

toll¹, n., & v.i. **1.** Tax, duty, paid for use of market, public road, etc., or for service rendered; *road ~* (fig.), road casualties; (law) ‖*~ thorough* (taken by town for use of highway, bridge, etc.), ‖*~ traverse* (for passing over private land); ‖ grain retained by miller as compensation for grinding (still, fig., in *take ~=* abstract a portion *of*). **2.** *~-bar, -gate*, bar or usu. gate across road to prevent passage of person, vehicle, etc., without paying ~; ‖ *tol(l)′booth* [arch., Sc.], town gaol [orig. temporary structure for collection of market ~s & detention of those who did not pay & others]; *~′house* (occupied by collector at ~-gate). **3.** v.i. Take, pay, ~. [OE *toll, toln*, OS *tol, tolna*, OHG *zoll*, ON *iollr* f. pop. L *toloneum* f. LL f. Gk *telōnion* *~house* (*telos* tax)]

toll², v.t. & i., & n. **1.** Cause (bell, or abs.) to ring with slow uniform strokes; (of bell or clock) give out (stroke, knell, hour of day), give out measured sounds, ring on account of (person, his death, etc.). **2.** n. *~ing*, stroke, of bell. [15th c., spec. use of ME (now dial.) *toll* entice, pull]

toll′able, a. (Of person or goods) subject to toll. [TOLL¹+-ABLE]

‖ **tol(l)′booth**. See TOLL¹.

tŏl-lŏl′, a. (sl.) In fair state, so-so, middling. [f. *tol*(*erable*) w. redupl.]

‖ **tŏll′ỹ**, n. (school sl.). Candle. [perh. f. TALLOW]

Tŏl′tĕc, n. One of a people traditionally held to have ruled in Mexico before the Aztecs. Hence **~AN** a. [Mex.]

tolū′ (or *tō*²), n. Balsam got from a S.-Amer. tree & used in perfumery & medicine. Hence **~IC** a., **tŏl′ūENE** & **tŏl′ūOL** nn., colourless inflammable liquid hydrocarbon of the benzene series, used in the preparation of dyes & T.N.T. [name of place]

tŏm, n. **1.** (*Tom*) abbr. of *Thomas*; *Tom, Dick, & Harry*, persons taken at random, ordinary commonplace people. **2.** Male animal, esp. ~(-*cat*). **3.** *Long ~* (naut.), long gun esp. one carried amidships on swivel-carriage; *Old Tom*, strong kind of gin; PEEP²*ing Tom*; *°Tom & Jerry*, rum & water beaten up with eggs etc.; ~*′boy*, romping girl, hoyden; ~*′fool′*, fool, trifler, (v.i.) play the fool, act in trifling manner (~*fool′ery*, foolish trifling, foolish knick-knacks etc.); *Tom Fool* (type of witlessness), esp. in proverb *there 's more knows Tom Fool than Tom Fool knows* = notoriety is not honour); ~*nodd′y*, blockhead, fool; *Tom Thumb*, a legendary dwarf, any diminutive person, dwarf variety of various plants; *Tom Tiddler's ground*, children's game, place where money can be had for the picking up; ‖ ~*′tit′*, kinds of small bird, esp. titmouse.

tŏm′ahawk (-*a-h*-), n., & v.t. **1.** War-axe of N.-Amer. Indian, with head of horn, stone, or steel; *bury the ~* or HATCHET. **2.** v.t. Strike, kill, with ~; criticize savagely in review. [of native orig.]

tomäll′ey, -lỹ, n. Soft greenish substance (called the liver) in lobster, used as sauce. [Carib]

toman′ (-ahn), n. Persian gold coin. [Pers. *tuman*]

toma′tō (‖ -ah-, °-ā-), n. (pl. ~es). (Plant with) red or yellow pulpy edible fruit; *currant ~* (with small fruit about size of currant); *tree-~*, kind that grows erect & sustains fruit without support. [17th c. *tomate*, = F (2 syll.) or Sp. & Port. (3 syll.), f. Mex. *tomatl*]

tomb (tōōm), n., & v.t. **1.** Hole (made) in earth or rock to receive dead (esp. human) body, grave; subterranean or other vault for the dead; sepulchral monument; (fig.) *the ~*, death; ~*′stone*, monumental stone placed over grave. **2.** v.t. Enclose as or in or as in ~. Hence ~*′LESS* a. [ME *t(o)umbe* f. AF *tumbe* = OF *tombe* f. LL *tumba* f. Gk *tumbos*]

tŏm′băc, -k, n. Kinds of copper-&-zinc alloy, used under various names as material for cheap jewellery. [F (-*c*), f. Malay *tambâga* copper]

tŏm′bola, n. Kind of lottery. [F or It., f. *tombolare* TUMBLE]

tōme, n. Volume, esp. large heavy one. [F, f. L f. Gk *tomos* section f. *lemnō* cut]

-tome, suf. f. (1) Gk *tomē* a cutting, or (2) *-tomos* cutting, (1) denoting section, segment, & (2) used in designations of surgical instruments (for corresponding operations in -TOMY).

tomĕn′t|um, n. (Bot.) kind of pubescence composed of matted woolly hairs; (anat.) flocculent inner surface of pia mater. Hence **tōm′entOSE¹**, **~OUS**, aa. [L, *~* = padding of wool etc.]

tŏmm′ỹ, n. **1.** (*T~*) familiar form of TOM; ‖ *T~ Atkins*, the British soldier, whence *T~* or *~* (sl.), private in army.

2. (mech.). Kinds of wrench or turn-screw, (also ~-*bar*) short bar for working box-spanners. 3. Bread, provisions, esp. as given to workman in lieu of wages; this system of payment, truck system (now illegal); ~-*shop*, (formerly) in which ~ was enforced, (now) shop in works where provisions may be bought, any baker's shop; ‖ food carried by workmen. 4. *~-*gun*, sub-machine gun [f. inventor J. T. *Thompson*]; ~ ROT[1]; *soft* ~ (naut.), soft or fresh bread (cf. HARD *tack*). [-Y[3]]

tomŏr'row, to-mŏ'rrow, (-ō), adv. n. (On) the day after today, as *will write* ~, (prov.) ~ *never comes*; (attrib.) ~ *morning*, *afternoon*, etc. (used as nn. & advb.; ~ *week*, eight days hence). [TO[1]+MORROW, cf. TODAY]

tŏm'pion. Var. of TAMPION.

tŏm'tŏm, n., & v.i. (-mm-). 1. Indian drum; gong. 2. v.i. Beat ~. [f. Hind. *tamtam*, imit.]

-tomy, suf. = Gk -*tomia* -cutting (*temnō* cut), chiefly in names of surgical operations (*ana*~, *phlebo*~, *tracheo*~).

ton[1] (tŭn), n. 1. Measure of weight, 2240 or *(also *short* ~) 2000 lb. avoirdupois; *metric* ~, 1000 kilograms (2204·6 lb.). 2. Measure of capacity (often varying) for timber (40 ft), stone (16 cub. ft), salt (42 bushels), lime (40 bushels), coke (28 bushels), wheat (20 bushels), wine (see TUN), etc. 3. Unit of internal capacity (100 cub. ft) or carrying capacity (40 cub. ft) of ship. 4. (colloq.). Large number or amount, as *bag weighs (half) a* ~ (several pounds, ounces, etc.), ~*s of people, have asked him* ~*s of times*. 5. (sl.). Speed of 100 m.p.h. (~-*up boys*, motor cyclists who travel at this speed). [diff. f. TUN in 17th c.]

ton[2] (tawn), n. Prevailing mode, fashion, as *in the* ~, BON TON. [F]

tŏn'al, a. Of tone or tones; of tonality. Hence ~LY[2] adv. [f. med. L *tonalis* (TONE, -AL)]

tŏnăl'itў, n. (Mus.) character of tone, key; colour scheme of picture. [-ITY]

‖ **to'nāme** (tōō-), n. (chiefly Sc.). Name added esp. to person's Christian name & surname for distinction. [OE *tō-nama* (TO[1], NAME)]

tŏn'dō, n. (pl. -*di* pr. -dē). Easel painting, or relief, of circular form. [It., = round (plate), f. L *rotundus* round]

tōne[1], n. 1. Sound, esp. w. ref. to pitch, quality, & strength; *heart* ~*s*, sounds of heart heard in auscultation. 2. Modulation of voice to express emotion, sentiment, etc., as *impatient, lively, imploring, despondent, bantering, suspicious*, ~. 3. (phon.). Accent on one syllable of word. 4. (mus.). Musical sound, esp. with ref. to pitch, quality, & strength (FUNDAMENTAL ~); interval of major second, e.g. C–D, E–F sharp; *whole*~ *scale*, consisting entirely of ~s, with no semitones; *Gregorian* ~*s*, traditional

plain-song chants for psalms. 5. (med.). Proper condition of the bodily organs, state of health in which animal functions are duly performed, as *has lost, recovered,* ~. 6. Prevailing character of morals, sentiments, etc., as *the* ~ *of the nation must be raised, gave a flippant* ~ *to the debate*. 7. General effect of colour or of light & shade in picture; tint, shade of colour; degree of luminosity of colour; (photog.) colour of finished positive picture. 8. ~-*arm*, tubular arm connecting sound-box of gramophone to the horn; ~-*poem*, musical composition for orchestra illustrating or translating a poetic idea, painting in which the ~s are harmonized poetically. Hence ~'LESS (-nl-) a., ~'LESSNESS n. [ME, partly f. OF *ton* f. L f. Gk *tonos* f. *teinō* stretch, partly f. L]

tōne[2], v.t. & i. 1. Give tone or quality (of sound or colour) to (~*d paper*, esp. of pale amber tint). 2. (mus.). Adjust (part of instrument, e.g. padded surface of hammers of piano) so as to produce desired quality of sound. 3. (photog.). Give (picture), (of picture) receive, altered colour in finishing by means of chemical solution. 4. Harmonize (usu. intr.), as *does not* ~ *with the wallpaper*. 5. ~ *down*, soften colouring of (picture), render (statement, expression, etc.) less pronounced or confident, (intr.) become softer, less pronounced, etc.; ~ *up*, give, receive, higher tone or character or greater vigour. [ME, f. prec.]

tŏng, n. A Chinese guild, association, or secret society. [Chin. *t'ang* meeting-place]

tŏng'a (-ngg-), n. Light two-wheeled vehicle used in India. [f. Hind. *tāngā*]

tŏngs (-z), n. pl. (Also *pair of* ~) kinds of instrument for grasping & holding usu. with two limbs pivoted together near either end or connected by spring piece, as *fire*~ (for grasping coal etc.), *asparagus, sugar, blacksmith's, wire*, LAZY, ~~; HAMMER[1] *& ~; would not touch* (repulsive person or thing) *with a pair of* ~ (still less without). [OE *tang(e)*, OS *tanga*, OHG *zanga*, ON *tong* f. Gmc *tang-]

tongue[1] (tŭng), n. 1. Fleshy muscular organ in the mouth, serving purposes of taste, mastication, swallowing, & (in man) of speech (*put out* one's ~, as grimace, or for doctor's inspection; *on the* ~*s of men*, much talked of; *furred* or *dirty* ~, symptom of illness). 2. This as article of food, as *ox-, sheep's, reindeer's,* ~; *smoked, rolled,* ~. 3. Faculty of, tendency in, speech, *has a ready* or *fluent* ~, *sharp, caustic, dangerous, long* (talkative), ~; *have, speak with,* one's ~ *in* one's *cheek*, speak ironically, humour one's hearer; *keep a civil* ~ *in* one's *head*, avoid rudeness. 4. Language of a nation etc., as *the German* ~, one's *mother* ~; *gift of* ~*s*, power of speaking in unknown ~*s* esp. as miraculously conferred on early

Christians; *confusion of* ~s (*Gen.* xi. 1–9).
5. Thing like ~ in shape (esp. tapering) or
function, e.g. long low promontory, strip
of leather closing gap in front of shoe,
clapper of bell, pin of buckle, projecting
edge of MATCH¹-board, slip connecting two
grooved boards etc., index of scale or
balance, vibrating slip in reed of some
musical instruments, jet of flame, pointed
rail in railway-switch. **6.** *Have lost, find,*
one's ~, be too bashful, recover power of
speech; *give* or *throw* ~, (of hounds) bark
esp. on finding scent; *hold* one's ~, be
silent; *on the* TIP¹ *of* one's ~ ; *wag* one's ~,
talk indiscreetly or volubly; ~-*bit* (with
plate preventing horse from getting ~
over mouthpiece); ~-*bone*, = HYOID; ~-
-*tie*, impediment in speech due to shortness of fraenum of ~, ~-*tied*, having this,
(fig.) debarred from speaking out. Hence
(-)tongueED² (tŭngd), ~'LESS, aa., ~'LET n.
[OE *tunge*, OS, ON *tunga*, OHG *zunga*,
Goth. *tuggô* f. Gmc *tungôn*, held to be
cogn. w. L *lingua* (f. *dingua*)]

tongue² (tŭng), v.t. & i. Produce staccato etc. effects with (flute etc.) by use
of tongue, use tongue thus; ~ & *groove*,
furnish (MATCH¹-board etc.) with tongue
& groove. [f. prec.]

tŏn'ic, a. & n. **1.** (Of medicine, medical
treatment, etc., fig. of success, misfortune, punishment) serving to in-
vigorate, bracing; (mus.) of tones, esp.
of the keynote; ~ *accent*, accent on
syllable; ~ *sŏl-fa'* (-ah), system of sight-
-singing & notation in which keynote of
all major keys is *doh* (& other notes correspondingly, as *ray, me, fah, sol, lah, te*) &
keynote of all minor keys *lah* (& other
notes correspondingly, as *te, doh*, etc.),
with time-values shown by vertical lines,
colons, etc.; ~ *spasm*, continuous muscular contraction (cf. CLONIC). **2.** n. ~
medicine etc. (lit. & fig.); (mus.) keynote.
Hence tŏn'ICALLY adv. [f. Gk *tonikos* (as
TONE¹, see -IC)]

toni'citў, n. Tone; being tonic; healthy
elasticity of muscles etc. [-ITY]

tonight', **to-night'**, (-nīt), adv. & n. (On)
the present night, (on) the night of today.
[TO¹+NIGHT, cf. TODAY]

tŏn'ish, **tonn-**, a. (now rare). In the TON²,
modish, stylish. Hence ~NESS n. [-ISH¹]

tŏn'ite, n. A powerful gun-cotton explosive. [f. L *tonare* thunder+-ITE¹]

‖ **tŏnk**, v.t. (sl.). Hit (bowling, person)
hard, defeat easily in contest. [orig.
unkn.]

Tŏnk'a bean, t-, n. Fragrant seed of a
tree found in Guiana etc., used in perfumery etc. [native *tonka*, the bean]

to'nnage (tŭ-), n. Internal cubic capacity,
or freight-carrying capacity, of ship in
TON¹s; total freightage esp. of a country's
merchant marine; duty on vessels
formerly reckoned on ~, now on registered size; charge per ton on cargo or
freight; ~ & *poundage* (hist.), customs

duties on the tun of wine & the pound's-
-worth of merchandise imported or exported, granted as subsidies (orig. for the
defence of the realm) at intervals in the
14th–18th cc. & levied unconstitutionally
by Charles I without consent of Parliament; ~-*deck* (upper of two, second of
three or more). [in hist. sense ME f. OF;
in mod. use f. TON¹+-AGE]

tŏnn'eau (-nō), n. Part of some motor-
-cars that contains the back seats. [F,
lit. cask, tun]

tonŏm'ēter, n. Tuning-fork or other instrument for measuring pitch of tones.
[as TONE¹+-METER]

tŏn'sil, n. Either of two oral organs on
each side of the fauces. Hence tŏn'sillAR
a., tŏnsilLIT'IS n. [f. L *tonsillae* pl.]

tŏnsôr'ial, a. (joc.). Of a barber or his
work. [f. L *tonsorius* (*tondère tons-* shave,
see -OR)+-AL]

tŏn'sure (-sher), n., & v.t. **1.** Rite of
shaving the crown (R.-C. Ch.) or whole
head (Gk Ch.) of person entering priesthood or monastic order; bare part of
monk's or priest's head; (fig.) admission
to holy orders. **2.** v.t. Shave head of,
give ~ to. [ME, f. OF, or f. L *tonsura*
(prec., -URE)]

tŏntine' (-ēn), n. Annuity shared by subscribers to loan, the shares increasing as
subscribers die till last survivor gets all;
~*policy of insurance* (in which associated
policy-holders agree to receive no dividend, return-premium, etc., till end of
fixed period called ~ *period*). [F, f. name
of Lorenzo *Tonti*, originator of ~s in
France c. 1653]

tŏō, adv. & a. **1.** In a higher degree than is
admissible for a specified or understood
purpose, standard, etc. (not used to
qualify vb, cf. VERY), as ~ *ripe for cooking,*
~ *good to be true, allows* ~ *long an interval,*
~ *long intervals,* ~ *large for me, my taste,*
my purpose, is ~ *fond of comfort,* ~ MANY
for; ~ *much* (*of a good thing*), intolerable
(*this is really* ~ *much* or ~ *much of a good
thing*); (colloq.) very (*you are* ~ *kind; he is
not* ~ *well today*). **2.** (In affected or gushing use) *is quite* ~, *is* ~ ~, (*delightful* etc.,
often omitted). **3.** Also, as well, as *take
the others* ~, *mean to do it* ~ (as well as
threaten). **4.** Moreover, as *achieved,* ~, *at
small cost.* **5.** adj. ~ ~, gushing. [stressed
form of TO¹, f. 16th c. sp. *too*]

took. See TAKE.

tōol¹, n. **1.** Mechanical implement, as
*carpenter's, joiner's, gardener's, engraver's,
mason's,* ~*s* ; (pl.) implements & munitions
of war; machine used in making machinery, e.g. lathe. **2.** (fig.). Thing used in
an occupation or pursuit, as *literary* ~*s,
the* ~*s of* one's *trade*; person used as mere
instrument by another, cat's-paw. **3.**
Separate figure in tooling of book. **4.**
Broad ~, = TOOLER; EDGE¹-, *edged,* ~;
~-*holder*, device for holding ~ in lathe,
handle for use with different ~s; ~-*post,*

-*rest*, holder or support for cutting-~ in lathe. [OE *tōl* = ON *tól* pl., f. Gmc *tō(w)lam* f. *tōw-*, see TAW[1]]

tool[2], v.t. & i. Dress (stone) with chisel; ornament (sides & back of book-cover) with tooling; equip with tools; work with ~; (sl.) drive (coach etc.), (intr.) drive, ride, (often *along* etc.) esp. in casual or leisurely manner. [f. prec.]

tool'er, n. In vbl senses, esp.: stone--mason's broad chisel for tooling. [-ER[1]]

tool'ing, n. Stone-dressing in parallel lines; ornamentation of book-cover with designs impressed by heated tools (*blind* ~, without gilding). [-ING[1]]

toon, n. E.-Ind. tree with close-grained red wood much used for furniture etc. [f. Hind. *tun*]

toot, v.t. & i., & n. 1. Sound, esp. produce short rapid sound with, (horn, cornet, whistle, etc.); sound horn etc. thus; (of horn etc.) give out such sound; (of grouse) call. 2. n. Sound of horn, trumpet, etc. [c. 1500, imit., or f. (M)LG *tüten*]

tooth, n. (pl. *teeth*), & v.t. & i. 1. Each of several hard dense structures growing in jaws of vertebrates & used for mastication; CANINE, EYE[1], INCISOR, MILK[1], MOLAR[1], WISDOM, ~ *false, artificial*, ~ (made by dentist). 2. ~-shaped projection or thing, e.g. cog, point, etc., of gear-wheel, saw, comb, rake. 3. SWEET~; *cast* thing in person's *teeth*, reproach him with it; *in the teeth of*, in spite of (opposition etc.), in opposition to (directions etc.), in the face of (the wind etc.); *armed to the teeth* (completely, elaborately); *cut* one's *eye-teeth*, gain worldly wisdom; *escape by the skin of* one's *teeth* (narrowly); *fight, struggle, ~ & nail* (with utmost effort); *from the teeth outwards* (arch.), insincerely, not from the heart; LIE[2] *in* one's *teeth*; *long in the ~*, old (orig. of horses; from recession of gums with age); *put teeth into* (law, regulation, etc.), make it effective; *set* one's *teeth* on EDGE[1]; *show* one's *teeth*, take threatening tone; *take the* BIT[1] *between* one's *teeth*. 4. ~'*ache*, ache in ~; ~*-billed*, (of bird) having ~like process(es) on cutting edges of bill; ‖~*-brush* (for cleaning teeth); ‖~*-comb* (with fine close--set teeth; prop. *fine-~ comb*); ~ *ornament*, = DOG[1]-~; ~*-paste, -powder*, (for cleaning or preserving teeth); ~'*pick*, small sharp instrument of quill, wood, gold, etc., for removing matter lodged between teeth. 5. vb. Furnish with teeth; (of cog-wheels) interlock. Hence (-)~ED[2] (-thd), ~LESS, aa., ~LET n. [OE *tōth*, OS *tand*, OHG *zan*(d), ON *tǫnn*, Goth. *tunthus* f. Gmc *tanth-*, *tunth-* cogn. w. L *dens dentis*, Gk *odous -ontos*]

tooth'ful (-ŏŏl), n. Small draught of spirit etc., thimbleful. [-FUL]

tooth'ing, n. In vbl senses, esp.: projecting bricks or stones left at end of wall to provide for continuation; ~*-plane* (with serrated edge for roughing surface). [-ING[1]]

tooth'some, a. Pleasant to eat. Hence ~LY[2] adv., ~NESS n. [-SOME]

too'tle, v.i. Toot gently or repeatedly esp. on flute. [-LE(3)]

toot'sy(-wŏŏtsy), n. (nursery). Foot.

top[1], n. & a. 1. Summit, highest part, as ~ *of a hill, hill-~, at the ~ of the tree* (fig., of highest rank in profession etc.); *come to the ~*, win distinction; *on ~*, above; *on the ~ of*, in addition to. 2. Leaves etc. of plants grown for the root, as *turnip-~s*. 3. Surface (of ground), upper surface (of table etc.). 4. Upper part of shoe; cover of carriage; lid of saucepan etc.; head (of page in book); upper edges of book, as *gilt* ~. 5. (Person occupying) highest rank, foremost place, as *came out* (*at the*) ~ *of the school, the* ~ (upper end, head) *of the table*. 6. Utmost degree, height, as *realized the* ~ *of my ambition, called at the* ~ *of his voice, ran at the* ~ *of his speed*; crown of the head, as *from* ~ *to toe*; *the* ~ *of the morning* (*to you*), Irish morning greeting. 7. (naut.). Platform round head of lower mast serving to extend ~mast shrouds, as *main*~, *fore*~, *mizzen*~. 8. pl. Two highest cards of a suit in bridge etc. 9. (In motoring) highest gear (usu. *on* or *in* ~). 10. pl. Metal buttons plated etc. only on face. 11. Bunch of hair, fibres, etc., esp. as measure = 1½ lb. 12. adj. Highest in position or degree, as *the* ~ *rail, at* ~ *speed*, ~ *dog* (sl., = victor, master, opp. *under dog*), whence ~'MOST a. 13. ~*-boot* (also ~), boot with high ~ usu. of different material or colour & made to look as if turned down; ~'*coat*, overcoat; ~*-dress*, apply manure on the ~ of (earth) instead of ploughing it in; ~*-dressing*, this process, manure so applied; ~*gall'ant* (tŏpg-, tog-), mast, sail, yard, rigging, immediately above ~mast & ~sail; ~ *hamper*, light upper sails & rigging; ~ *hat*, tall silk hat; ~*-heavy*, overweighted at ~ so as to be in danger of falling (often fig. of scheme etc.); ‖~*-hole* (sl.), first-rate; ~'*knot*, knot, bow of ribbon etc., tuft, crest, worn or growing on head; ~*-lantern, -light*, light displayed from mizzen~ of flagship; ~'*man*, ~*-sawyer* (lit.), (naut., also ~s'*man*) man doing duty in a ~; ~'*mast* (-ăst) (next above lower mast); ~'*sail* (-sl), square sail next above lowest; ~*-saw'yer*, sawyer in upper position in saw-pit, (fig.) person in superior or high position; ~'*sides*, sides of ship above water-line. [OE *top*, OHG *zopf*, ON *loppr* f. Gmc *tuppaz*]

top[2], v.t. (-pp-). 1. Provide with top or cap; (naut.) raise one end of (yard etc.) above the other. 2. Remove top of (plant) to improve growth etc. 3. Reach the top of (hill etc.). 4. Be higher than; be superior to, surpass, as ~*s all I ever saw*, whence ‖~p'ING[2] a., ~p'ingLY[2] adv.; ~ one's *part*, act or discharge it to perfection. 5. (golf). Hit (ball) at top instead of true. 6. ~ *off* or *up*, put an end or a finishing touch to (thing, or abs.); **~** *up*, (also) fill up (partly empty container). 7. Be of (specified height), as *he ~s 6 ft.* 8. *~ping-lift*, each of a pair of lifts by which a yard may be topped. [ME, f. prec.]

tŏp³, n. Kinds of wooden or metal toy, usu. conical, spherical, or pear-shaped, rotating on sharp point at bottom when set in motion by hand, spring, or string; HUMMING, PEG, WHIP¹*ping* or *whip*, **~**; SLEEP² *like a* **~** (sound); *old* **~** (sl.), old chap, old fellow; **~**-*shell*, kinds of shellfish with **~**-shaped shell. [late OE *top*; cf. MDu. *dop(pe)*, Du. *top*, OHG *topfo*, G dial. *topf*]

tŏp′ăz, n. 1. A transparent or translucent mineral, a silicate of aluminium, yellow, white, green, blue, or colourless; *false* **~**, kind of yellow quartz. 2. Kind of humming-bird. [ME, f. OF *topaze* f. L f. Gk *topazos, -zion*]

topăz′olite, n. Yellow or green kind of garnet. [prec. + -O- + -LITE]

tōpe¹, v.i. Drink alcoholic liquors to excess esp. habitually. Hence **tōp′ER¹** n. [orig. unkn.; cf. earlier (obs.) *top*]

tōpe², n. (Anglo-Ind.). Mango or other grove. [f. Tamil *tōppu*]

tōpe³, n. Buddhist monument, usu. dome or tower. [f. Hind. *tōp* f. Skr. *stūpa* mound]

tōpe⁴, n. Small species of shark, dogfish. [perh. f. Cornish]

tŏph, tŏph′us (pl. *-phī*), nn. Gouty deposit of calcareous matter round teeth & at surface of joints. Hence **tophA′CEOUS** (-āshŭs) a. [L (*-us*), = sandstone, TUFA]

Tŏph′ĕt, n. Place in Valley of Hinnom near Jerusalem used for idolatrous worship & later for depositing refuse, for consumption of which fires were kept burning; hell. [f. Heb. *topheth*]

tŏp′ī, tŏp′ee (·ī), n. (Anglo-Ind.). Hat (see SOLA). [Hind. *ṭopī*]

tŏp′īa, n. Ancient-Roman style of mural decoration with heterogeneous landscape scenes. [L, f. Gk *topos* place]

tŏp′iar|y̆, a. The **~***y art* (of clipping shrubs etc. into ornamental shapes). Hence **tōpiar′ian** a., **~IST** n. [f. L *topiarius* landscape gardener (as prec., see -ARY¹)]

tŏp′ic, n. Theme for discussion, subject of conversation or discourse; (log., rhet.) class of considerations from which arguments can be drawn. [f. L f. Gk (*ta*) *topika* topics, as title of a treatise of Aristotle (*topos* place, see -IC)]

tŏp′ical, a. Of topics; dealing with esp. current or local topics, as **~** *allusion, song*; local, esp. (med.) affecting a part of the body. Hence **~LY²** adv. [-AL]

topŏg′raph|y̆, n. Detailed description, representation on map etc., of natural & artificial features of a town, district, etc.; such features; (anat.) mapping of surface of body with reference to the parts beneath. Hence **~ER¹** n., **tŏpo-**

grăph′IC(AL) aa., **tŏpogrăph′ically²** adv. [f. LL f. Gk *topographia* (*topos* place, see -GRAPHY)]

topŏn′y̆my̆, n. Study of the place-names of a region. [f. Gk *topos* place, *onuma* name, -Y¹]

tŏpp′er, n. In vbl senses, also: (colloq.) = TOP¹ *hat*; (colloq.) a good fellow, good sort; (commerc.) fine fruit etc. put at top of stock for show. [f. TOP² + -ER¹]

tŏp′ple, v.i. & t. (Cause to) totter & fall (often *over, down*). [f. TOP² + -LE(3)]

tŏpsy̆tŭrv′|y̆, adv., a., n., & v.t. 1. Upside down; (in) utter confusion. 2. v.t. Turn **~**y: Hence (joc.) **~y̆DOM**, **~IFICA′TION**, nn., **~IFY** v.t. [16th c., of obsc. hist., but app. f. TOP² + obs. *terve* overturn]

tōque (-k), n. 1. Small kinds of man's & woman's cap or bonnet (hist.); woman's small hat with little or no or turned-up brim. 2. Kinds of monkey with caplike arrangement of hair. [F, app. = It. *tocca*, Sp. *toca*]

tŏr, n. Hill, rocky peak, esp. on Dartmoor. [OE, perh. cogn. w. Gael. *tòrr* hill]

tŏr′ah, n. Revealed will of God, esp., Mosaic law; Pentateuch. [Heb. *torāh* instruction]

tŏrc, n. See TORQUE.

tŏrch, n. Piece of resinous wood or twisted flax etc. soaked in tallow etc. for carrying lighted (**~** *of Hymen*, passion of love); other appliance for this purpose, e.g. oil-lamp on pole; *electric* **~**, portable electric lamp; **~**-*fishing*, (also **~**ING¹ n.) mode of catching fish by **~**light; **~**-*race*, ancient-Greek festival performance of runners handing lighted **~**es to others in relays; **~**-*singer*, woman who sings **~**-*songs* (sentimental ditties of unrequited love); *hand on the* **~**, keep knowledge etc. alive (w. ref. to **~**-*race*). [ME, f. OF *torche* app. f. Rom. ***torca** f. L *torquēre* twist]

torchon (see Ap.), n. attrib. **~** *paper*, paper with rough surface used esp. for water-colours; **~** *board* (covered with **~** paper); **~** *mat*, MAT³ of **~** paper; **~** *lace*, peasants' bobbin lace with geometrical designs. [F, = dish-cloth (*torcher* wipe)]

tore¹. See TEAR¹.

tore². = TORUS (first sense).

tŏ′readŏr′, n. (hist.). Spanish (usu. mounted) bullfighter. [Sp., f. *toro* f. L *taurus* bull]

toreut′ic (-rōō-), a. & n. 1. Of chasing, carving, & embossing, esp. metal. 2. n. pl. This art. [f. Gk *toreutikos* (*toreuō* bore, chase, see -IC)]

tŏrg′ŏch (-x), n. Red-bellied char. [W (*tor* belly + *coch* red)]

torii (tŏ′rĭē, tŏr′ĭē), n. Gateway of Shinto temple. [Jap.]

tŏrm′ent¹, n. Severe bodily or mental suffering, as *was in* **~**, *suffered* **~**s; source of this, as (colloq.) *the child is a positive* **~**. [ME, f. OF, f. L *tormentum* (*torquēre* twist, see -MENT)]

tŏrmĕnt'[3], v.t. Subject to torment, as *~ed with neuralgia, suspense, inquiries.* Hence **~ĭngLY**[2] adv. [ME. f. OF *tormenter* f. LL *tormentare* f. L *tormentum* (prec.)]

tŏrm'entil, n. Low herb with bright yellow flowers & highly astringent root-stock used in medicine. [ME, = OF *tormentille* f. med. L *-illa* dim. of L *tormentum* TOR-MENT[1]; sense-connexion unkn.]

tŏrmĕn'tļor, n. Person, thing, that torments, whence **~rĕss**[1] n.; long fork used on ship for taking meat from coppers; kind of harrow on wheels. [ME & AF *tormentour*, OF *-teur* (TORMENT[2], *-OR*)]

tŏrm'ina, n. Griping pains in bowels, colic. [L, f. *torquēre* twist]

torn. See TEAR[1].

tŏrnăd'ō, n. (pl. *~es*). Violent storm of small extent, esp. in W. Africa at beginning & end of rainy season & in U.S. from April to July, having usually a rotary motion, & often accompanied by funnel-shaped cloud; (fig.) outburst or volley of cheers, hisses, missiles, etc. Hence **tŏrnăd'ĭc** a. [app. assim. of Sp.. *tronada* thunderstorm (*tronar* to thunder) to Sp. *tornar* to turn]

tŏr'ous, torōse', aa. (Bot.) cylindrical with bulges at intervals; (zool.) knobby. [f. L *torosus* (TORUS, see *-OSE*[1], *-OUS*)]

tŏrpēd'ō, n. (pl. *~es*), & v.t. 1. Electric ray, a fish with electric apparatus for numbing or killing its prey etc. 2. Kinds of explosive mine or petard; cigar-shaped. self-propelling submarine missile that can be aimed at a ship etc. & explodes on touching it (*aerial ~*, discharged from aircraft); *~-boat*, small fast warship for carrying or discharging *~es*; *~ gunboat*, large vessel intended to catch *~-boat* (*~-boat*) DESTROYER; *~-net* (hung round ship to intercept *~es* or *~-boat*); *~-tube* (from which *~es* are discharged). 3. v.t. Destroy, attack, with *~*; (fig.) paralyse, make (policy, institution, etc.) ineffective. [L *torpedo* electric ray (*torpēre* be numb)]

tŏrp'ļĭd, a. & n. 1. (Of hibernating animal) dormant; numb; sluggish, dull, apathetic. 2. n. pl. ‖ Hilary term boat-races at Oxford .between (orig. second crews of) colleges; (sing.) boat rowing in these. Hence or cogn. **~ĭd'ĭTY**, **~ĭdNESS**, **~OR**, nn., **~ĭdLY**[2] adv., **~ĭFY** v.t., **~orĭF'ĭC** a. [f. L *torpidus* (prec., *-ID*[1])]

Tŏrps, n. (nav. sl.). Ship's torpedo officer. [abbr.]

tŏr'quāte, -ātĕd, aa. (zool.). With ring of peculiar colour or texture of hair or plumage about the neck. [f. L *torquatus* (foll., *-ATE*[2])]

tŏrque (-k), **tŏrc**, n. Necklace of twisted metal, esp. of Gauls; (mech., *-que*) twisting-MOMENT. [f. L *torques* (*torquēre* twist)]

tŏ'rrelfỹ, v.t. Parch with heat, roast, dry, (metallic ores, drugs). So **~FAC'TION** n. [f. F *torréfier* f. L *torrefacere* (*torrēre* parch, see *-FY*)]

tŏ'rrent, n. Rushing stream of water etc.; (pl.) great downpour *of rain* (also *rain falls in ~s*); (fig.) violent flow (*of abuse, grief, questions*). Hence **tŏrrĕn'tĭAL** (-shl) a., **tŏrrĕn'tĭaLLY**[2] adv. [F, f. It. *-ente* f. L *torrentem* (*torrēre* parch, *-ENT*)]

Tŏrrĭcĕll'ian, a. *~ experiment* (with mercury in tube, leading to principle on which barometer is made); *~ tube* (used for this). [E. *Torricelli* d. 1647 +-AN]

tŏ'rrid, a. (Of land etc.) parched by sun, very hot; *~ zone*, part of earth's surface between tropics. Hence**~ĭTY** (-ĭd²), **~NESS**, nn. [f. F *-ide* or L *torridus* (*torrēre* parch, see *-ID*[1])]

tŏrs'el, n. Twisted ornament e.g. scroll; block of wood in brick wall for joist etc. to rest on. [var. of TASSEL]

tŏr'sion (-shn), n. Twisting; (bot.) state of being spirally twisted, so **tŏrs'ĭVE** a.; (med.) twisting of cut end of artery after operation etc. to check haemorrhage; *~ balance* (for measuring minute forces by means of fine twisted wire). Hence **~AL**, **~LESS**, aa., **~aĭLY**[2] adv., (-sho-). [ME, f. OF, f. LL *tortionem*, *-si-* (as TORT, see *-ION*)]

tŏrsk, n. Fish of cod family. [f. Norw. *torsk, tosk* f. ON *tho(r)skr*]

tŏrs'ō, n. (pl. *~s*). Trunk of statue apart from head & limbs; human trunk; (fig.) unfinished or mutilated work. [It., = stalk, stump, torso, f. THYRSUS]

tŏrt, n. (law). Private or civil wrong. [ME, f. OF, f. med. L *tortum* wrong f. L *torquēre* *tort-* twist]

tŏrtĭcŏll'is, n. (path.). Rheumatic affection of muscles of neck, stiff neck. [mod. L, f. *tortus* crooked (prec.) + *collum* neck]

tŏrt'ile, a. Twisted, curved; (bot.) coiled. Hence **tŏrtĭl'ĭTY** n. [f. L *tortilis* (TORT, *-ILE*)]

tŏrti'lla (-ĕlya), n. Flat maize cake, Mexican equivalent of bread. [Sp.]

tŏr'tious (-shus), a. (law). Constituting a tort, wrongful. Hence **~LY**[2] adv. [AF *torcious* (TORSION, *-OUS*), assoc. in sense w. *tort*]

tŏrt'oise (-tus), n. 1. Land (& freshwater) varieties of turtle, reptile encased in two scaly or leathery shields forming a box; ALLIGATOR *~*; (Rom. ant.) = TESTUDO. 2. *Hare & ~*, ability beaten by persistence; *~-shell*, mottled & clouded outer shell or scale of some sea-turtles used for combs etc., *~-shell cat, butterfly* (with black & yellow markings suggesting *~-shell*). [ME *tortuce* etc., *tortu* (thr. OF *tortue*) f. med. L *tortuca, tortua* app. f. L *tortus* (TORT) w. ref. to *~'s* crooked feet]

tŏrt'ŭous, a. Full of twists or turns, so **tŏrt'ŭosE**[1] a. (bot.); (fig., of policy etc.) devious, circuitous, crooked, not straightforward. Hence or cogn. **tŏrtŭŏs'ĭTY**, **~NESS**, nn., **~LY**[2] adv. [ME, f. AF, f. L *tortuosus* (*tortus -ūs* twist, foll., *-OUS*)]

tŏr'turļe, n., & v.t. 1. Infliction of severe

bodily pain e.g. as punishment or means of persuasion, as *was put to the ~e*, *instruments of ~e* (rack, thumbscrew, etc.); severe physical or mental pain. **2.** v.t. Subject to ~e, as *~ed with neuralgia, tight boots, anxiety*; (fig.) force out of natural position or state, pervert meaning of (words, passage). Hence ~ABLE, ~OUS, aa., ~ER¹ n., ~INGLY² adv. [F, f. LL *tortura* twisting (*torquēre tort-* twist, see -URE)]

tŏ′rūl|a, n. (pl. ~ae). Kinds of yeastlike fungus; chain of spherical bacteria, whence ~IFORM a.; (bot.) small torus. [mod. L dim. of TORUS]

tŏr′us, n. (pl. *-rī*). Large moulding of semicircular profile esp. as lowest member of base of column; (bot.) receptacle of flower, modified end of stem; (anat.) smooth ridge as of muscle. [L, = swelling, bulge, cushion, etc.]

Tŏr′ȳ, n. & a. (now chiefly in colloq. or hostile use). (Member) of the party that opposed the exclusion of the Duke of York (James II), inclined to the Stuarts after 1689, accepted George III and the established order in Church & State, opposed Reform Bill of 1832, & has been succeeded by Conservative party (cf. WHIG). Hence ~ISM n. [orig. = Irish robber, f. Ir. *tóraidhe, -aighe* pursuer (*tóir* pursue)]

-tory, suf., most freq. form of -ORY, in wds f. L vbs w. p.p. stem in *-t-* (*amatory, factory*).

tŏsh, n. (sl.). Rubbish, twaddle; (crick., lawn tennis, etc.) easy bowling or service. ‖ tŏsh′er, n. (sl.). Unattached student (see UNATTACHED). [corrupt.]

tŏss, v.t. & i. (*~ed* or poet. *tost*), & n. **1.** Throw up (ball etc.) with the hand esp. with palm upward, (of ball etc.) throw (person etc.) up with the horns. **2.** Throw (thing *to* person, *away, aside*, etc.) lightly or carelessly. **3.** Throw (coin) into air to decide choice etc. by way it falls, settle question or dispute with (person *for* thing) thus, as *will ~ you for* (or *who has*) *the armchair*. **4.** Toss (person) *in* blanket, jerk him upwards out of it by pulling suddenly on all corners; ~ one's *head*, throw it back esp. in contempt or impatience; ~ *a pancake*, jerk it up so that it returns upside down to pan. **5.** Throw (thing, one*self*) about from side to side, throw oneself about thus in bed etc., roll about restlessly; (of sea, ship, branch, etc.) roll or swing with fitful to-&-fro motion. **6.** Separate heavy from light parts of (tin ore) by agitation in vessel. **7.** ~ *oars* (of boat's crew bringing oars to upright position blades upward as salute); ~ *off*, drink off at a draught, dispatch (work) rapidly or without apparent effort; ~ *up*, ~ coin as above, prepare (food) hastily; ~*pot* (arch.), toper. **8.** n. ~ing of coin, head, etc., as *win the~*, have its decision in one's favour; *a contemptu-*

ous ~ of the head; *full ~*, a full pitch at cricket; *~-up*, ~ing up of coin, doubtful question, as *is quite a ~-up whether he comes or not*; PITCH²-&-~. **9.** ‖ Throw from horseback etc. (*take a ~*, be thrown). [c. 1500, of unkn. orig.]

tŏt¹, n. Small child, esp. *a tiny ~*; (colloq.) dram of liquor. [18th c., of unkn. orig.]

tŏt², n., & v.t. & i. (colloq.; -tt-). **1.** ‖ Set of figures to be added. **2.** vb. Add usu. *up*; (of items) mount *up* (~ *up to*, amount to). [abbr. of foll. or of L *totum* the whole]

tōt′al, a., n., & v.t. & i. (-ll-). **1.** Complete, comprising the whole, as *the ~ number of persons, ~ population, sum~, ~ tonnage*; absolute, unqualified, as *was in ~ ignorance of it; resulted in ~ loss of his fortune, ~* ABSTINENCE, *abstainer*; ~ *eclipse* (in which whole surface is obscured); ~ *war* (in which all available weapons & resources are employed). **2.** n. ~ number or amount. **3.** vb. Find the ~ of (things, set of figures), amount in number to, as *the visitors ~led 131*; amount *to*, mount *up to*. Hence totăl′ITY n. (esp., time for which an eclipse is ~), ~LY² adv. [ME, f. OF, f. med. L *totalis* (*tōtus* entire, see -AL)]

tōtălitār′ian, a. Relating to a polity that permits no rival loyalties or parties; ~ *State* (with only one, the governing, party). [-ARIAN]

tōt′alizātor, n. Device showing number & amount of bets staked on race with a view to dividing the total among betters on winner. [foll., -ATE³, -OR]

tōt′aliz|e, -is|e (-īz), v.t. & i. Collect into a total, find the total of; use totalizator in betting. Hence ~A′TION n. [-IZE]

tōte¹, n. (sl.). = TOTALIZATOR. [abbr.]

*tōte², v.t. Carry (a gun, supplies, timber, etc.). [U.S., f. 1676, of unkn. orig.]

tōt′em, n. Natural object esp. animal assumed among N.-Amer. Indians as emblem of clan or individual on ground of relationship; image of this; ~*-pole, -post* (on which ~s are carved or hung); ~ *stage*, stage of mental development in which ~s are taken as clan-names & objects of worship. Hence totēm′ic, ~is′tic, aa., ~ISM(3), ~IST(2), nn. [Algonquian]

t′o′ther, to′ther, (tŭdh-), a. & pron. The other; *tell ~ from which* (joc. variant of *tell one from the other*). [ME the tother, for earlier *thet other* ' the other'; now understood as = *the other* & usu. used without *the*]

tōt′ĭdĕm *vĕrb′ĭs*, adv. In so many words, in these very words, as *he said, ~, that he would write in either case*. [L]

tŏt′ĭēs quŏt′ĭēs (or tŏsh′iēs kwŏsh′iēs), adv. On each occasion, every time, as *offer was refused~*. [L, = as often as]

tōt′ō cael′ō (sē-), adv. *Differ ~* (by an immense distance). [L, = by the whole heaven]

tŏtt′er, v.i. Stand or walk unsteadily (esp. of child learning to walk); (part., of steps) unsteady; (of tower etc., fig. of

State, system, etc.) be shaken, be on the point of falling. Hence ~ER¹ n., ~ingLY² adv., ~Y² a. [ME, perh. f. Norse; cf. Norw. dial. *tutra*, *totra* quiver, shake]

toucan (tōōkahn′, tōō′kn), n. Kinds of tropical American bird with immense beak. [f. Braz. *tucana*]

touch¹ (tŭch), v.t. & i. **1.** Be separated at one or more points by no intervening space or object from (thing etc.), be in or come into contact with, bring part of body esp. hand into contact with, establish this relation towards (thing *with* one's *hand*, *stick*, etc.), cause (two things) to come into contact, (of two things) be in contact, as *two rocks ~ (each other) at the bases, you are ~ing wet paint, ~ pitch*, have to do with shady transaction or person, *he ~ed me on the shoulder, ~ the table with your stick, wouldn't ~ him* (unpleasant person) *with a barge-pole, just ~ed them together & they cracked, I never ~ed him* (hostilely), *can just ~ bottom* (of water with toes), *~ BOTTOM¹, ~ed his hat* (as salutation), *was ~ed by the king* (to cure KING¹'s evil), *~ wood* (to propitiate Nemesis after boasting etc.), *~ the spot* (find out, or do, exactly what is requisite). **2.** (geom.). Be a tangent to (circle etc.). **3.** Apply slight force to, as *he ~ed* (rang) *the bell*; strike (keys, strings, of musical instrument), strike keys or strings of. **4.** Delineate, mark lightly, put *in*, (features etc.) with brush, pencil, etc. **5.** Reach, as *can just ~ the ceiling*; (fig.) approach in excellence etc., as *no one can ~ him in light comedy, for purity of style*. **6.** Affect with tender feeling, soften, as *it ~ed me to the heart, was visibly ~ed by her appeal*; rouse painful or angry feeling in, as *~ed him home, ~ed him to the quick*, = *~ed him on a raw* or *tender place* (also lit.). **7.** Treat of (subject) lightly or in passing. **8.** Concern, as *the question ~es you nearly*. **9.** (Chiefly neg.) have to do with, as *refuses to ~* (risk capital in) *breweries, dare not ~* (drink) *beer*. **10.** Injure slightly, as *flowers are a little ~ed with the east wind*. **11.** p.p. Slightly crazy. **12.** Affect slightly, modify, as *morality ~ed with emotion*; (neg.) produce slightest effect on, cope with, as *brass polish won't ~ these candle-sticks, couldn't ~ the algebra paper*. **13.** (sl.). ~ one *for*, get (sum) out of him (*~ed me for £5*; cf. TAP¹). **14.** ~ *at* (naut.), call at (port etc.); ~ *down*, (rugby footb.) ~ ball on ground either behind one's own or the opponents' goal, (of aircraft) alight; ~ *off*, make (sketch) hastily, make hasty sketch of, (obs.) discharge (cannon); ~ *on* or *upon*, treat (subject) briefly; refer to or mention casually; ~ *up*, correct, give finishing touches to (picture, writing, etc.), strike (horse) with whip, jog (memory). **15.** ~*wood* (see also foll.), children's game in which ~ing wood gives immunity from pursuit. Hence

~'ABLE a. [ME, f. OF *tochier, tuchier*, f. Rom. **toccare*, prob. imit., f. **toc* imitating a knock]

touch² (tŭch), n. **1.** Act or fact of touching, contact, as *gave him a ~, felt a ~ on my arm, royal ~* (for KING¹'s evil), *at a ~* (if touched, however lightly). **2.** Sense by which contact is perceived, whence ~'LESS a. **3.** Light stroke with pencil, brush, etc., in drawing etc., as *added a few ~es, finishing ~es*, (often fig. of writing, management of business, etc.). **4.** Small amount, slight tinge or trace, as *wants a ~ of salt, an occasional ~ of irony, felt a ~ of rheumatism*. **5.** Performer's manner of touching keys or strings of musical instrument, manner or degree in which keys etc. respond to this, manner or style of workmanship in carving etc. or in writing, as *has a light* or *firm ~ on piano, piano is wanting in ~, writer has light ~* (produces required effect simply, without laboured emphasis, etc.); *the Nelson ~,* Nelson's masterly handling of a situation. **6.** Mental correspondence, sympathy, communication, esp. *keep in ~,* remain in sympathy or not cease from correspondence or personal intercourse (*with*), so *get in(to) ~ with*. **7.** Magnetization of steel bar by repeated contact with magnet. **8.** (arch.). ~stone, test, as *put it to the ~*. **9.** *Near ~,* close shave, narrow escape. **10.** (med.). Exploration of organs etc. by sense of ~. **11.** (footb.). Part of field outside the side limits (~*-lines*) & between goal-lines produced; ~*-in-goal*, each of the four outside corners enclosed by ~*-lines* & goal-lines; ~*-down*, touching down (as in prec.). **12.** ~*-&-go*, (adj.) of uncertain event, risky, placed in risky circumstances, as *it was ~-&-go whether we got past, a ~-&-go business, we were ~-&-go all the time*, (n.) such situation; ~*-body*, *-corpuscle* (concerned in sense of ~); ~*'hole*, small hole in cannon by which it was fired; ~*'last*, children's game; ~*-needle*, needle of gold alloy of known composition used as standard in testing other alloys on ~stone; ~ *of nature*, natural trait, (pop.) exhibition of feeling with which others sympathize (f. misinterpretation of Shakesp. *T. & C.* III. iii. 175); ~*'paper* (steeped in nitre, for firing gunpowder etc.); ~*'stone*, fine-grained dark schist or jasper used for testing alloys of gold etc., (fig.) standard, criterion; ~*'wood²* (see also prec.), soft substance into which wood is changed by some fungi, used as tinder. [ME, f. OF *touche* f. *tochier* (prec.); partly f. vb]

tou'cher (tŭ-), n. In vbl senses, also : ∥ (sl.) *near ~,* close shave, as *near as a ~,* very nearly, almost exactly. [ME; -ER¹]

tou'ching (tŭ-), a. & prep. **1.** Affecting, pathetic, as *a ~ incident, shows the most ~ confidence in us,* whence ~LY² adv., ~NESS n. **2.** prep. (arch. or literary). (Also *as~*) concerning, about. [ME; -ING²]

tou'ch|y (tŭ-), a. Apt to take offence, over-sensitive. Hence ~**iLY**[2] adv., ~**iNESS** n. [perh. alt. f. TETCHY]

tough (tŭf), a. & n. **1.** Flexible but not brittle, hard to break or cut, as *a beef-steak as ~ as leather, requires the ~est steel*; (of clay etc.) stiff, tenacious; able to endure hardship, hardy; unyielding, stubborn; difficult, as *found it a ~ job*; (colloq., of luck etc.) hard, severe, unpleasant; *ruffianly, turbulent & criminal. **2.** n. *Street ruffian. Hence ~**EN**[4] v.t. & i., ~**ISH**[1] a., ~**LY**[2] adv., ~**NESS** n., (tŭf-). [OE *tōh*, OHG *zāh* f. Gmc *tanhuz*; cf. OHG *zāhi* (G *zäh(e)*)]

toupee' (tōō-), n. Wig or artificial patch of hair worn to cover bald spot. [f. F *toupet* dim. of OF *loup* tuft (as TOP[1])]

toupet (tōōp'ā), n. Front of false hair. [F, see prec.]

tour (toor), n., & v.i. & t. **1.** Journey through a country from place to place; *the grand ~* (hist.), journey through France, Italy, etc., as finishing touch to education; rambling excursion, journey, walk, as *a ~ of observation through the town*; (mil.) spell of duty on service, time to be spent at a station; ~ *de force* (de), feat of strength or skill. **2.** vb. Make ~ (*through, about*, etc.); make a ~ of, travel through, (country etc.). Hence ~**ER**[1] n., ~**ing-car**. [ME, f. OF *tor, tour*, back form. f. pl. *tors* (cf. TURN), f. L f. Gk *tornos*]

tour'aco (toor-), n. (Kinds of) large African bird with crimson & green plumage & prominent crest. [F, f. native name]

tourbillion (toorbil'yon), n. Kind of firework spinning in air so as to look like scroll or spiral column of fire. [f. F *tourbillon* whirlwind]

tour'ist (toor-), n. Person who makes a tour, as *place is overrun with ~s*; ~ *ticket*, railway etc. ticket issued to ~ on special terms, esp. return ticket available for extended period. So **tour'ism** (toor-) n., organized touring. [f. TOUR+-IST]

tour'malin(e) (toor-), n. Mineral of various colours possessing powerful electric properties & used as gem; ~ *granite* (containing ~). [F, f. Sinhalese *tòramalli*]

tour'nament (toor-, tĕr-), n. **1.** (hist.). Pageant in which two parties of mounted & armed men contended with usu. blunted weapons. **2.** Any contest of skill between a number of competitors, as *chess, lawn-tennis*, ~. [ME, f. OF *torneiement* (*torneier* TOURNEY, see -MENT]

tour'nay (toor-), n. Printed worsted upholstering-material. [f. *Tournay*, in Belgium]

tournedos (toornedō'), n. Small fillet of beef within strip of suet etc. [F]

tour'ney (tĕr-, toor-), n. (pl. ~s), & v.i. (Take part in) tournament (esp. sense 1). [ME, f. OF *tornei* n., (f.) *torneier* vb, ult. f. L *tornus, tornare* see TURN]

tourniquet (toorn'ĭkĕt), n. Instrument for stopping flow of blood through artery by compression effected with screw. [F, f. *tourner* TURN]

tournure (toornūr'), n. Curve, contour; pad etc. worn by women to give rounded outline to hips, back drapery of dress. [F (as TURN, see -URE)]

tou'sle (-zl), v.t. Pull about, handle roughly, make (esp. hair) untidy. [f. *touse* (now dial.)+-LE(3); ME *t(o)use* f. OE *tūsian* cogn. w. OHG *-zūsōn* (G *zausen*)]

tous-les-mois (tōōlămwah'), n. Food starch got from tubers of species of canna. [F, lit. = every month, prob. corrupt. of S.-Amer. *toloman*]

tous'y (-z-), a. Rough, shaggy, dishevelled. [f. *touse* (TOUSLE)+-Y[2]]

tout (towt), v.i., & n. **1.** Solicit custom, pester possible customers with applications (*for* orders); spy out movements & condition of horses in training. **2.** n. Instance of, (also ~**ER**[1] n. rare) person employed in, ~ing. [ME *tūte* look out (OE *tūtian*) = ME (now dial.) *toot* (OE *tōtian*) f. Gmc *tūt-*, *tōt-* project]

tout court (tōō koor), adv. (Of name etc.) without addition or explanation. [F, lit. = quite short]

tout ensemble (see Ap.), n. See EN-SEMBLE. [F]

tow[1] (tō), v.t., & n. **1.** (Of vessel, horse on bank, etc.) pull (boat, barge, etc.) along in water by rope or chain; pull (person, thing) along behind one; drag (net) over surface of water, drag net over (water), to collect specimens. **2.** n. ~ing, being ~ed, esp. *take, have, in* or *on* ~, (fig.) assume direction of, take possession of, (person); ~(*ing*)-*line*, -*rope* (used in ~ing); ~(*ing*)-*net* (for dragging water); ~(*ing*)-*path* (along river or canal for use in ~ing). Hence ~**AGE**(3, 4) (tō'ĭj) n. [OE *togian*, OHG *zogōn*, ON *toga* f. Gmc *tog-* cogn. w. L *ducere*; cf. TUG]

tow[2] (tō), n. Coarse & broken part of flax or hemp. Hence ~**Y**[2] (tō'ĭ) a. [ME, f. MLG *touw*, f. OS *tou*, rel. to ON *tō* uncleansed wool or flax]

toward[1] (tō'erd), a. (arch.). Docile, apt. Hence ~**LY**[1] a., ~**NESS** n., (arch.). [as foll.]

towards, toward[2], (tōrdz, tō'erdz, twôrdz, towôrdz'), prep. (-s now more usu. in prose & colloq.). In the direction of, as *looks ~ the sea, set out ~ town, I look ~ you* (in drinking health); as regards, in relation to, as *felt some animosity ~ him, his altitude ~ Home Rule*; (arch. esp. bibl.) *to usward*, ~ us; for, for the purpose of, as *saved something ~ his education*; near, as ~ *noon*, ~ *the end of our journey*; (arch., as adv.) *feast is toward* (coming). [OE *tōweard* a. future, OS *tōward*, OHG *zuowart* (TO, -WARD, -ES)]

tow'el, n., & v.t. & i. (-ll-). **1.** Cloth for drying oneself after washing; *throw in the* ~ (boxing, & fig.), admit defeat (cf. SPONGE¹); *roller* ~, endless ~ on revolving bar; ~*horse*, frame for hanging ~s on; (old sl.) *lead* ~, bullet, *oaken* ~, cudgel. 2. vb. Wipe (one*self* etc.) with ~; ‖ (sl.) thrash; wipe oneself with ~. Hence ~LING¹ (1, 3) n. [ME, f. OF *toaille* f. WG *thwahlja* f. *thwahan* (= OS, Goth.) to wash]

tow′er, n., & v.i. **1.** Tall usu. equilateral (esp. square) or circular structure, often forming part of church or other large building; (fig.) place of defence, protector (~ *of strength,* champion, comforter, etc.); *ivory* ~, shelter from the harsh realities of life; MARTELLO ~; *water-*~, pipe used to secure high head of water at fires, (also)~ supporting tank for distribution of water at high pressure; ‖ *the T*~ *(of London),* assemblage of buildings now used as repository of objects of public interest, orig. a fortress & palace & later used as State prison. **2.** v.i. Reach high (*above* surroundings, often fig. of eminent person, as ~*s above his contemporaries*), (of eagle etc.) soar or be poised aloft, (of wounded bird) shoot straight up; (part.) high, lofty, (fig.) *a* ~*ing* (violent) *rage, passion.* Hence ~ED² (*-erd*), ~Y², aa. [ME & OF *tor, tur* f. L *turris;* OE *torr* dir. f. L]

town, n. **1.** (hist.). Collection of houses enclosed by wall or hedge. **2.** Considerable collection of dwellings etc. (larger than *village;* often opp. to *country*), esp. one not created a CITY. **3.** The people of a ~, as *the whole* ~ *knows of it, is the talk of the* ~ (talked about by everyone in the ~). **4.** (Without *the*) London or the chief city or ~ in speaker's neighbourhood, as *went up to* ~ (London) *from York, is not in* ~, *is out of* ~. **5.** *Man about* ~, fashionable idler esp. in London; PAINT² *the* ~. *red*; COUNTY ~; ~ *& gown*. **6.** ~ *clerk,* official who makes & keeps ~ records; ~ *council(lor),* (member of) governing body in municipality; ~ *crier*; ~ *hall,* building for transaction of official business of ~, often also used for public entertainment etc.; ~ *house,* one's ~ (as opp. to *country*) residence; ~ *major* (hist.), chief executive officer in a garrison-~ or fortress; ~*s*-*folk,* inhabitants of a particular ~ or of ~s; ~*s*′*man,* inhabitant of a town, fellow citizen; ~*s*′*people,* the people of a ~; ~ *talk,* the talk of the ~. Hence ~′LESS, ~′WARD, aa., ~′LET n., ~′WARD(S) adv. [OE, OS *tūn,* ON *tún,* OHG *zūn* (G *zaun* hedge) f. Gmc *tūn-,* cogn. w. Celt. *dūn* camp]

‖ **townee′,** n. (univ. sl.). Inhabitant of university town who is not a member of the university. [-EE]

town′ship, n. (Hist.) community inhabiting a manor, parish, etc., manor or parish as a territorial division, small town or village forming part of a large parish, or being one of the parishes into which a larger one had been divided; (U.S.

& Can.) division of county with some corporate powers, district six miles square; (Austral., New Zealand) small town, town-site. [OE *tūnscipe,* see TOWN, -SHIP]

towy. See TOW².

toxaem′ia, n. Blood-poisoning. [as TOXIC + Gk *haima* blood + -IA¹]

tox′ic, a. Of poison, as ~ *symptoms;* poisonous; ~ *anaemia, epilepsy,* etc. (caused by poison). Hence tox′ICALLY, ~olō′gICALLY², advv., ~ANT a. & n., ~olō′gICAL a., tŏxī′CITY, ~ŏl′ogIST, ~ŏl′ogY, ~OMAN′IA, ~OS′IS, tŏxīPHOB′IA, nn. [f. med. L *toxicus* f. L f. Gk *toxikon* poison for arrows (*toxa* pl. arrows, -IC)]

tox′in, n. A poison, esp. one secreted by a microbe & causing some particular disease. [f. TOXIC + -IN]

tŏxŏph′il|ite, n. & a. (Student, lover) of archery. Hence ~īt′ic a., ~ў n. [f. Gk *toxon* bow + -PHIL + -ITE¹]

toy, n., & v.i. **1.** Plaything esp. for child; knick-knack, thing meant rather for amusement than for serious use, as *the spinthariscope is a pretty* ~; occupation followed in trifling or unpractical manner, hobby, as *she makes a* ~ (amuses herself with needless elaboration) *of housekeeping.* **2.** ~*-box* (for keeping one's ~s in); ~ *dog, spaniel, terrier,* small kinds kept as pets or curiosities; ~′*shop*; ~ *soldier* (of lead etc., or of an army that has no fighting to do). **3.·** v.i. Trifle, amuse oneself; ~ *with,* deal with, handle, in trifling or fondling or careless manner, as ~*ed with a plate of strawberries,* whence ~′ingLY² adv. [16th c.; earlier = dallying, fun, jest, whim, trifle; orig. unkn.]

Toyn′bee Hall (hawl), n. Institution in Whitechapel founded in 1884 by members of Oxf. & Camb. Univv. as a SETTLEMENT in memory of A. Toynbee, social reformer (d. 1883).

trăbeā′tion, n. Use of beams (not arches or vaulting) in construction. So **trăb′éate** [-ATE²(2)], **-ātĕd,** aa. [f. L *trabs* beam + -ATION]

trabĕc′ul|a, n. (pl. ~*ae*). (Anat.) supporting band or bar of connective tissue etc.; (bot.) beamlike projection or process. Hence ~AR¹, ~ate [-ATE²(2)], ~ātĕd, aa. [L, dim. of *trabs* beam]

tracasseries (trahkahsrē′), n. pl. Petty worries & entanglements & quarrels. [F]

trāce¹, v.t., & n. **1.** Delineate, mark out, sketch, write esp. laboriously, as ~*d* (*out*) *a plan of the district,* ~*d the words with a shaking hand,* (fig.) *the policy* ~*d* (*out*) *by him, was never followed.* **2.** (Also ~ *over*) copy (drawing etc.) by following & marking its lines on superimposed sheet (esp. of *tracing-paper* made transparent with oil of turpentine etc.) through which they are visible or on sheet placed below with carbon paper between. **3.** Follow the track or path of (person, animal, footsteps, etc., *along, through, to,* etc.). **4.** Ascertain position & dimensions etc. of (ancient road, wall, etc.) by its remains. **5.** Observe or find vestiges or signs of, as *his resentment can be clearly ~d in many passages, cannot ~* (often = do not think·I received) *any letter of that date.* **6.** *~ back,* go back over the course of, as *have ~d his genealogy back to* (the time of) *William I, the report has been ~d back to you.* **7.** Pursue one's way along (path etc.). Hence ~ABIL'ITY (-sa-), ~'ABLENESS, nn., ~'ABLE a., ~'ablʏ adv., trā'cɪNG[1] n., reproduction made on tracing-paper or *tracing-cloth* (transparent linen sized on one side). **8.** n. Track left by person or animal walking or running, footprints or other visible signs of course pursued (usu. pl.). **9.** Visible or other sign of what has existed or happened, as *of these buildings no ~ remains, sorrow has left its ~s on her face, ~s of Italian influence abound in his earlier works;* (loosely) small quantity, as *contains ~s of soda; ~ elements* (occurring, or required to be present, esp. in soil, in ~s). Hence ~'LESS (-sl-) a., ~'lèssLʏ[2] adv. [ME; n. f. OF *trace,* vb f. OF *tracier* f. Rom. **tractiare* ult. f. L *trahere tract-* draw]

trace[2], n. Each of the two side-straps **or** chains by which horse draws vehicle; *in the ~s,* in harness (lit. & fig.); *kick over the ~s,* (fig., of person) become insubordinate; *~-horse* (that draws in ~s **or** by single ~, esp. one hitched on to help up hill etc.). [ME *trays* f. OF *trais,* pl. of *trait;* see TRAIT]

trā'cer, n. (Mil.) projectile whose course is made visible by flame etc. emitted, so *~ bullet, shell;* artificially produced radio-active isotope introduced into human body in food or otherwise and capable of being followed in its course by the radiations it produces. [f. TRACE[1], -ER[1]]

trā'cer∤ʏ, n. Stone·ornamental open-work esp. in head of Gothic window; decorative pattern or natural outline (e.g. in insect's wing) suggesting this. Hence ~ɪED[2] (-rid) a. [f. TRACE[1] + -ERY]

trache'a (-kēa; or trăk'ɪa), n. (pl. *-ae*). Principal air·passage of body from larynx to bronchial tubes; each of the passages by which air is conveyed from the exterior in insects, arachnids, etc.; (bot.) duct, vessel. Hence **trăch'eAL, trăch'eAN, trăch'eATE**[2](2), aa., **trăch'eo-** comb. form, **trăch'eOCELE, trăchĕŏT'OMY, trăchĕĭT'IS,** nn., (-k-). [med. L, = *trachia* f. Gk *trakheia* (*artēria*) 'rough artery', f. *trakhus* rough]

trachel'o- (-k-), comb. form of Gk *trakhēlos* neck.

trach∤ōm'a (-k-), n. Disease of eye marked by granular excrescences on inner surface of lids. Hence ~ōm'atous a. [17th c., f. LL f. Gk *trakhōma* (*trakhus* rough, see -OMA)]

trăchy- (-k-), comb. form of Gk *trakhus* rough, as *~phōn'ia* hoarseness.

trăch'yte (-kīt), n. Light-coloured volcanic rock rough to the touch. Hence **trachyt'ɪc** (-k-) a. [F. f.. Gk *trakhutēs* (prec.) + -ITE; cf. BARYTES]

trăck[1], n., & v.t. & i. **1.** Continuous line, series of marks, left by·person, animal, or thing, in passing along, (pl.) such marks, esp. footprints, as *watched the broad ~ of departing ship, followed his ~ through the snow, am on his ~* (in pursuit of him, fig. in possession of clue to his conduct, designs, etc., *presently came on some more of his ~s, keep ~ of* (follow the course or development of). **2.** Course taken, as *followed in his ~, indicated the ~ in which we were to go, ~ of a comet.* **3.** Path, esp. one beaten by use, (fig.) course of life or routine, as *a rough ~ runs round the hillside, covered with sheep-~s, afraid to leave the beaten~* (of ordinary life; also lit.). **4.** Prepared racing-path, esp. *cinder-~* (for runners). **5.** Continuous line of railway, as *single, double, ~,* one pair, two pairs, of rails. **6.** Wheelband of tank, tractor, etc., whence (of vehicle) ~ED[2] (-kt) a. **7.** Transverse distance between a vehicle's wheels. **8.** *In* one's *~s* (sl.), where one stands, there & then; *make ~s* (sl.), go or run away, make off; *make ~s for* (sl.), go in pursuit of, go after; *off the ~,* off the scent, (fig.) away from the subject; *~-clearer,* kinds of device attached to locomotive, mowing-machine, etc., for clearing *~* in front or behind. Hence ~'LESS a., ~'lèssLʏ[2] adv., ~'lèssNESS n. **9.** vb. Follow the *~* of (animal, person, *to lair* etc.); *~ down,* reach, capture, by *~ing;* trace, make *out,* (course, development, etc.) by vestiges. **10.** (Of wheels) so run that the hinder is exactly in the first's *~.* [vb f. n., ME, f. OF *trac,* of uncert. orig.; cf. MLG & Du. *tre(c)k* draught etc., Du. *trekken* to draw etc.]

trăck[2], v.t. & i. Tow (boat) by rope etc. from bank; (v.i.) travel by towing. [18th c., app. f. Du. *trecken* to draw etc.]

trăck'age, n. Towing; railway-tracks collectively, amount of these. [f. TRACK[1,2] + -AGE]

trăck'er, n. In vbl senses of TRACK[1,2]; wooden connecting-rod in organ mechanism. [-ER[1]]

trăct[1], n. Region, passage, of indefinite (usu. large) extent, as *a ~ of sand, pathless ~s;* (anat.) area of organ or system, as *olfactory, optic, respiratory, ~;* ‖ (arch.) period (of time, obs.). [f. L *tractus -ūs,* vbl n. f. *trahere tract-* draw]

trăct[2], n. Short treatise or discourse or pamphlet esp. on religious subject; (R.·C. Ch. etc.) a form of anthem; *T~s for the Times, Oxford T~s,* see TRACTARIANISM. [app. abbr. of L *tractatus* TRACTATE; sense 'anthem' f. med. L *tractus* (prec.)]

trăc't∤able, a. (Of persons, rarely of materials etc.) easily handled, manageable, pliant, docile. Hence ~**abil**'ity, ~**able**ness, nn., ~**ably**[2] adv. [f. L *tractabilis* (*tractare* handle, frequent. of *trahere tract-* draw, -**ble**)]

Tractā'rian, a. & n. (Adherent, promoter) of Tractarianism. [**tract**[2] + -**arian**]

Tractā'rianism, n. (Also *Oxford movement*) High-Church reaction towards primitive Catholicism & against rationalism & formalism, voiced by Newman, Pusey, Keble, Froude, etc., in 90 tracts (*Tracts for the Times*) published at Oxford 1833–41. [-**ism**]

trāc'tāte, n. Treatise. [f. L *tractatus -ūs* (*tractare*, see **tractable**)]

trāc'tion, n. Drawing of a body along a surface, as *electric*, *steam*, ~; *line of* ~, that in which the force of ~ acts, *angle of* ~ (between line of ~ & plane in which body is drawn); contraction e.g. of muscle, as ~ *aneurysm* (produced by ~); ~-*engine*, movable steam-engine for dragging heavy load on ordinary road, or gang of ploughs etc.; ~-*wheel*, driving-wheel of locomotive etc. Hence or cogn. ~**al** (-sho-), **trāc**'tive, aa. [F, or f. med. L *tractio* f. L *trahere tract-*, -**ion**]

trāc'tor, n. 1. Traction-engine; stationary or locomotive motor engine for hauling; self-propelled vehicle for hauling other vehicles, farm machines, etc. 2. Aeroplane with engine in front (opp. *pusher*). [mod. L, as prec., -**or**]

trāde, n., & v.i. & t. 1. Business, esp. mechanical or mercantile employment opp. to *profession*, carried on as means of livelihood or profit; *be in* ~, be a retailer, keep a shop; **jack**[1] *of all* ~*s*; *two of a* ~ *never 'gree*; *trick of the* ~, device for attracting custom, gaining advantage of rival, etc.; ∥ *the* ~, (colloq.) the licensed victuallers, (naut. sl.) submarine branch of Navy. 2. Exchange of commodities for money or other commodities, commerce, as *foreign* ~, exportation & importation of goods from & to home country or exchange of commodities of different countries, *domestic* or *home* ~ (carried on within a country); *is good, bad, for* ~, induces, discourages, buying; *carrying-*~, transportation of goods from one country to another by water or air. 3. The persons engaged in a ~, as *the* ~ *will never submit to it*, *is unpopular with the book* ~. 4. *Board of T*~, ∥ government department supervising commerce & industry; **bal**'**ance**[1] *of* ~; **free**[1] ~; **fair**[2] ~. 5. = ~ *wind* (chiefly pl.). 6. *T*~ *Board*, statutory body for the settlement of disputes, wage claims, etc., in certain industries; ~ *cycle*, recurring succession of ~ conditions alternating between prosperity & depression; ~ *hall* (for meetings of traders etc.); ~ *mark*, device or word or words legally registered (or, formerly, established by use) as distinguishing a manufacturer's or trader's goods; ~ *name*, that by which a thing is called in the ~,

(also) name given by manufacturer to proprietary article; ~ *price* (charged by manufacturer etc. to dealer for goods that are to be sold again); ~ *show*, private exhibition of new film to renters & critics; ~*s'man*, person engaged in ~, esp. shopkeeper; ~*s'people*, ~smen & their families; ~ *union*, organized association of workmen of a ~ formed for protection & promotion of common interests, ~-*un'ionism*, this system of association, ~-*un'ionist*, advocate of this, member of ~ union; ~ *wind*, wind blowing continually towards thermal equator within parallels 30° N. & 30° S. in Atlantic & Pacific & deflected westwardly by rotation of earth, (pl.) the ~ wind & the (30°–60°) **anti-trade**. 7. vb. Buy & sell, engage in ~ (*in* commodity, *with* person); have a transaction (*with* person *for* thing); carry, merchandise (*to* place); exchange in commerce, barter, (goods); make a ~ of one's political influence, make corrupt bargains in politics, (esp. in part.). 8. ~ *on*, take (esp. unscrupulous) advantage of (person's good-nature, one's knowledge of a secret, etc.). [ME, f. MLG *trade* track, f. OS *trada* f. *tredan* **tread**]

trād'er, n. Person engaged in, vessel regularly employed, in trade. [-**er**[1]]

tradi'tion, n. 1. Opinion or belief or custom handed down, handing down of these, from ancestors to posterity. 2. (theol.). Doctrine etc. supposed to have divine authority but not committed to writing, esp. (1) laws held by Pharisees to have been delivered by God to Moses, (2) oral teaching of Christ not recorded in writing by immediate disciples, (3) words & deeds of Mohammed not in Koran. 3. Artistic or literary principle(s) based on accumulated experience or continuous usage, as *stage* ~, *the* ~*s of the Dutch School*. 4. (law). Formal delivery. Hence or cogn. ~**al**, ~**ary**[1], aa., ~**ally**[2] adv. (-sho-). [ME, f. OF *tradicion* or L *traditio* f. *tra*(*dere dil-* = *dare*, give), -**ion**]

tradi'tion∣alism (-sho-), n. (Excessive) respect for tradition esp. in religion; philosophical system referring all religious knowledge to divine revelation & tradition. So ~(al)**ist** nn., ~**alis**'**tic** a. [-**ism**]

trād'itor, n. (pl. ~*s*, ~*es* pr. -ōr'ēz). Early Christian who to save his life surrendered copies of Scripture or Church property to persecutors. [L *tradere*, see **tradition**, -**or**)]

tradūce', v.t. Calumniate, misrepresent. Hence **tradū**'**cer**[1], ~**ment** (-sm-), nn., **tradū**'**cible** a. [f. L *tra*(*ducere duct-* lead) disgrace]

tradū'cian∣(ist), nn. One who believes that soul as well as body is propagated (cf. **creationism**, 1st sense). So ~**ism** n. [f. LL *traducianus* f. L *tradux -ucis* vine-shoot trained for propagation (as prec.), see -**an**]

trăff'ic, v.i. & t. (-ck-), & n. 1. Trade (*in*

commodity lit. & fig.), carry on commerce: barter (esp. fig.). Hence ~KER[1] n. **2.** n. Trade (*in* commodity lit. & fig.), as *the ~ in raw hides, unscrupulous ~ in lucrative appointments*; transportation of goods, coming & going of persons or goods by road, rail, steamship route, etc., number or amount of persons or goods conveyed, as *there is little ~ on these roads, the ~-returns* (periodical statements of ~) *on all railways show marked decrease, apply to the superintendent of ~* (on railway); *•~ circle*, roundabout; *~ lights*, series of coloured lights working automatically and regulating ~ usu. at cross-roads. Hence ~ātor n., movable direction-indicator on motor vehicle, ~LESS a. [16th c.; n. f. F traf(f)ic f. It. traffico; vb f. F -iquer f. It. -icare; ult. orig. obsc.]

trăg′acănth, n. White or reddish gum from certain herbs, used in pharmacy, calico-printing, etc. [f. F tragacante or L f. Gk tragakantha, name of shrub (tragos goat + akantha thorn)]

tragēd′i|an, n. Writer of tragedies; (w. fem. ~ĕnne′) actor in tragedy. [ME (TRAGEDY, -AN)]

tră′gĕdў, n. **1.** Drama in prose or verse of elevated theme & diction & with unhappy ending (~ queen, tragic actress); (T~) ~ personified. **2.** Sad event, calamity, serious accident or crime. [ME, f. OF tragedie f. L f. Gk tragōidia app. goat-song (tragos goat, ōidē song)]

tră′gic|(al), aa. **1.** (-ic). Of, in the style of, tragedy, as ~ drama, the ~ stage, in a ~ voice, ~ actor; ~ irony, used in Gk tragedy of words having an inner esp. prophetic meaning for audience unsuspected by speaker. **2.** Sad, calamitous, distressing, as a ~(al) tale, event, scene. Hence ~ally[2] adv., ~alness n. [f. F -ique f. L f. Gk tragikos (tragos see prec., -IC, -AL)]

trăgĭcŏm′|ĕdў, n. Drama of mixed tragic & comic elements. So~IC a., ~ICALLY adv. [f. F (-édie) f. LL tragicomoedia (L tragico-comoedia) as prec., see COMEDY]

trăg′opăn, n. Horned pheasant. [L f. Gk, reputed bird in Ethiopia (tragos goat, Pan, Gk god)]

trail, n., & v.t. & i. **1.** Part drawn behind or in the wake of a thing, long (real or apparent) appendage, as *engine left a ~ of smoke behind it*, *the ~ of a meteor*; lower end of gun-carriage; track left by thing that has moved or been drawn over surface, as *slimy ~ of a slug*; track, scent followed in hunting, as *got on, off, the ~*; beaten path esp. through wild region; *at the ~* (mil.), with arms ~ed (see vb); ~-net, drag-net. **2.** vb. Draw along behind one esp. on the ground, as *was ~ing a toy cart*, ~ed her dress through the mud, ~ing clouds of glory*; follow the ~ of, pursue; (mil.) ~ arms, let rifles hang balanced in one hand (right, left, ~) parallel to ground; tread down (grass

etc.) so as to make path; be drawn along behind, as *skirt ~s on the ground*; drag (one's limbs) along, walk wearily, lag, straggle; hang loosely; (of plant) grow to some length over ground, wall, etc.; ~ing edge, rear edge of aircraft's wing; ~ing wheel, either hind wheel of carriage. [ME trail(l)e, f. OF trailler to tow, or MLG, MDu. treilen haul, f. Rom. *tragulare f. L tragula drag-net, sledge]

trail′er, n. In vbl senses; also or esp.: trailing plant; set of short extracts from a film exhibited to advertise it in advance; wheeled vehicle drawn by another. [-ER[1]]

train, v.t. & i., & n. **1.** Bring (person, child, animal) to desired state or standard of efficiency etc. by instruction & practice, as ~ up a child in the way he should go, was ~ed for the ministry, a ~ed nurse, soldier, ~ed faculties, did not escape his ~ed eye. **2.** Teach & accustom (person, animal, to do, to action), as *dog is ~ed to jump through hoop, ~ed to all outdoor exercises, to obey or obedience*. **3.** Bring (horse, athlete, oneself), come, to physical efficiency by exercise & diet, as *is ~ing for the boat-race, ~s horses, is only half-~ed, is over, under, ~ed, ~ down* (to lower weight), *~ fine* (into exact condition required; t. & i.), *always ~s on vegetarian diet*; cause (plant) to grow in required shape (often up, over, wall etc.). **4.** Point, aim, (gun etc. upon object etc.). **5.** (arch.). || Entice, lure, (away, from, post etc.). **6.** (now rare). || Draw along (esp. heavy thing). **7.** (colloq.). Go by ~, perform (journey) thus, as *shall ~ from York to Leeds, ~ the rest of the way, we ~ed it all the way*. **8.**~ off, (of shot) go off obliquely. Hence ~′ABLE a., ~EE′ n. **9.** n. Thing drawn along behind or forming hinder part, esp. elongated part of woman's skirt trailing on ground or of official robe, long or conspicuous tail of bird. **10.** Body of followers, retinue, as *formed part of his ~, a ~ of admirers*. **11.** Succession or series of persons or things, as *long ~ of sightseers, of camels, by an unlucky ~ of events, suggested a whole ~ of ideas, painful ~ of thought, in the ~ of* (as a sequel of; *war with pestilence in its ~*). **12.** Series of railway carriages drawn by same engine(s), as *missed my ~, put on a special ~*, EXPRESS[1], *fast, slow*, UP, DOWN[3], THROUGH, CORRIDOR, PARLIAMENTARY, ~; *train de* LUXE (see Ap.). **13.** Line of combustible material to lead fire to mine etc. **14.** (arch.). Ordered arrangement, condition, as *matters were in a fine ~*. **15.** Series of connected wheels or parts in machinery. **16.** ~′band (hist.), each division of London citizen soldiery esp. in Stuart period; ~-bearer, person employed to hold up ~ of robe; ~-ferry, vessel that conveys a ~ across a piece of water; ~-mile, mile run by a ~, as unit of work in railway accounts. Hence

~'LESS a. [ME, f. OF *traîner*, *trahiner*, f. Rom. *°traginare*, ult. f. L *trahere* draw; n. repr. OF *traine*, *train*, f. *trainer*]

train'er, n. In vbl senses, esp. one who trains horses, athletes, etc., for races etc· [-ER¹]

train'ing, n. In vbl senses; *be in* (process of)~, *go into* ~, (for race etc.); ~*-bit*, gag-bit for vicious horse; ~*-college*, *-school*, (for training teachers); ~*-ship* (on which boys are taught seamanship etc.). [-ING¹]

train-oil, n. Oil got from blubber of whale (esp. of the right whale). [c. 1500 (now obs.) *trane*, f. syn. (M)LG *trān*, MDu. *traen*, app. = the wd meaning ' tear ', ' drop ', = OS *trahni* (pl.), OHG *trahan* (G *träne*)]

traipse. Var. of TRAPES.

trait (|| -ā, •-āt), n. Distinguishing feature in character, physiognomy, habit, or portrayal; stroke, touch (*of* humour etc.). [F, f. L *tractus* (as TRACT¹)]

trait'or, n. One who violates his allegiance or acts disloyally (*to* country, king, cause, religion, principles, him*self*, etc.). Hence or cogn. ~OUS a., ~OUSLY² adv., ~OUSNESS, **trait'RESS**¹, nn. [ME, f. OF, f. L *traditorem* (*tradere*, see TRADITION & -OR)]

trajec'tory (*or* trăj'e·), n. Path described by projectile moving under given forces; (geom.) curve or surface cutting system of curves or surfaces at constant angle. [f. med. L *trajectorius* f. L *tra(jicère ject-jacère* throw), see -ORY]

trăm¹, n., & v.i. & t. (-mm-). 1. || (Also ~*-car*) passenger car running on rails laid in public road; such rail; || (also ~'*way*, ~*-line*) line consisting of such rails; four-wheeled car used in coal-mines; || ~*-lines* (colloq.), either pair of long parallel lines bounding a lawn-tennis court, the inner of each pair being the single-court boundary; ~*-road* (hist.), road with wooden, stone, or metal wheel-tracks. 2. vb. Convey in ~, perform (journey) in ~: go in ~. [app. same wd as LG *traam* balk, beam, barrowshaft, MDu., MLG, EFris. *trame*]

trăm², n. Kind of double silk thread used for some velvets & silks. [f. F *trame* f. L *trama* weft]

trămm'el, n., & v.t. (-ll-). 1. Kinds of net for fish, esp. (also ~*-net*) triple drag-net; shackle, esp. one used in teaching horse to amble; hook in fireplace for kettles etc.; instrument for drawing ellipses etc.; beam-compass; (usu. pl.) impediment(s) to free movement or action (chiefly fig.), as ~*s of etiquette, official routine*. 2. v.t. Confine, hamper, with ~s (usu. fig.); (p.p., of horse) with white marks on fore & hind feet of same or (*cross*—*led*) different sides. [in sense ' net ' ME, f. OF *tramail* f. L *°tremaculum* usu. expl. as f. *tri-*triple ⊥*macula* MAIL¹; other senses obsc.]

tramonta'na (-ah-, -ah-), n. (In Mediterranean) north wind; cold blighting wind in the Archipelago. [It., see foll.]

tramŏn'tăne, a. & n. 1. (Situated, living) on other side of the Alps; (fig., from It. point of view) foreign, barbarous. 2. n. ~ person, also = prec. [f. It. *tramontano* f. L TRANS(*montanus* f. *mons -ntis* mountain) beyond the mountains]

trămp, v.i. & t., & n. 1. Walk heavily, as *heard him ~ing about overhead*; walk, go on foot, perform (journey), traverse (country), on foot (usu. w. implication of reluctance, weariness, etc.), as *have ~ed up & down all day looking for you*, *decline to ~ ten miles in this heat*, *have ~ed the whole country in my time*, *missed the train & had to ~ it*. 2. Be a~. 3. n. Sound of person(s) walking or marching or of horse's steps. 4. Journey on foot, walk. 5. Iron plate protecting sole of boot from wear & tear of spade in digging. 6. Person who ~s the roads in search of work or as vagrant, this mode of life (esp. *on the ~*). 7. Freight-vessel running on no regular line. 8. ~*-pick*, lever for turning up hard soil. [ME *trampe* f. Gmc *°tremp-*, *°tramp-*, whence MLG *trampen*, Goth. *ana-trimpan*]

trăm'pl|e, v.t. & i., & n. 1. Tread under foot, crush thus, as ~*ed to death by elephants*; ~*e on*, tread heavily on, (fig.) treat roughly or with contempt, show no consideration for, (person, feelings, etc.). 2. n. Sound, act, of ~ing. Hence ~ER¹ n. [ME, f. prec. +-LE(3); cf. LG, MHG *trampeln*]

trăm'pŏline, n. Elastic contrivance resembling spring-mattress used by acrobats etc. [It. *trampolino* spring-board]

trance (-ah-), n., & v.t. 1. State suggesting that the soul has passed out of the body; ecstasy, rapture, extreme exaltation; (path.) state of insensibility to external surroundings with partial suspension of vital functions, catalepsy, also, hypnotic state. 2. v.t. (poet.) = ENTRANCE². [ME; (vb f. n.) f. OF *transe* f. *transir* fall into trance f. L TRANS(*ire* go) over]

trăn'quil, a. Calm, serene, unruffled, not agitated, as *preserved a ~ mind*, ~*scene*, ~ *surface of pond*. Hence or cogn. ~l'ITY, ~lizA'TION n., ~lizE(3) v.t., ~lizER¹ n., (also) sedative drug, ~lizinGLY², ~LY², advv. [f. F *-ille*, or L *tranquillus*]

trans-, pref., the L prep. & pref. *trans* (in L wds usu. reduced to *tran-* before s, occas. to *tra-* before other consonants), across, beyond, on or to the other side, through, into a different state or place. Occurs in wds f. L, or in those formed on L elements, or on E or other wds of non-L origin; ~*fer*, ~*late* (*lation*), ~*marine*, ~*ocular*, *transcribe*, *transcript(ion)*, ~*uterine*; ~*border*, ~*fashion*, ~*ship*; in many geog. adjj., as ~*-African*, ~*atlantic*, ~*-Siberian*; esp. in sense beyond, surpassing, transcending, as ~*human*, ~*-material*.

trăns|ăct' (-z-), v.t. & i. Perform, carry

through, (business); carry on business (*with* person). So ~**ăc'tor** (-z-) n. [f. L TRANS(*igere act-·*= *agere* ACT)]

trănsăc'tion (-z-), n. Management of business, as *left the* ~ *of the matter to him*; piece of esp. commercial business done, *as the* ~*s of a firm, the* ~ *will not bear looking into, mixed up in shady* ~*s*; (pl.) reports of discussions, papers read etc., at meetings of some learned societies, as *Philosophical T*~*s* (esp. of Royal Society); (law) adjustment of dispute by mutual concessions, any act affecting legal rights. [ME, f. LL *transactio* (as prec., see -ION)]

trănsăl'pine (-z-), a. & n. (Person living) beyond the Alps (usu. from Ital. point of view). [f. L TRANS(*alpinus* ALPINE)]

trănsatlăn'tic (-z-), a. Beyond the Atlantic, American; crossing the Atlantic, as ~ *flight, line, steamer*. [TRANS-]

*•**trănsceiv'er** (-nsĕv-), n. Combined radio transmitter & receiver. [f. *trans-*(*mitter*) + (*re*)*ceiver*]

trănscĕnd', v.t. & i. Be beyond the range or domain or grasp of (human experience, reason, description, belief, etc.); (t. & i.) excel, surpass. [ME, f. OF *transcendre* or L *tran*(*scendere* = *scandere* climb)]

trănscĕn'd|ent, a. & n. 1. Excelling, surpassing, as ~*ent merit, genius*. 2. (scholastic philos.). Higher than, not included under any of, the ten categories. 3. (Kantian philos.). Not realizable in experience. 4. (Esp. of God) existing apart from, not subject to limitations of, the material universe, cf. IMMANENT. 5. n. (philos.). ~ent thing. Hence or cogn. ~ENCE, ~ENCY, nn., ~entLY² adv. [aş prec., see -ANT, -ENT]

trănscendĕn'tal, a. & n. 1. = prec. (second sense). 2. (Kantian philos.). Of *a priori* character, presupposed in & necessary to experience, as ~ *cognition, a priori* knowledge, ~ *object*, real (unknown & unknowable) object, ~ *unity* (brought about by cognition). 3. Explaining matter & objective things as products of the subjective mind (esp. in Schelling's philosophy). 4. (pop.). Abstruse, vague, obscure, visionary. 5. (math.). (Of functions) not capable of being produced by the algebraical operations of addition, multiplication, & involution, or the inverse operations; ~ *curve* (represented by ~ function). 6. n. ~ term, conception, etc. Hence ~LY² adv. [f. med. L *transcendentalis* (prec., -AL)]

trănscendĕn'tal|ism, n. Transcendental philosophy, esp. that of Schelling & his followers e.g. Emerson. So~IST n., ~IZE(3) v.t. [-ISM]

trănscŏntinĕn'tal (-z-), a. Extending across a continent, as ~ *railway*. [TRANS-]

trănscr|ibe', v.t. Copy out in writing; (radio) record for subsequent reproduction, broadcast by *transcription* (recorded programme). Hence or cogn. ~**īb'er¹**,

~**ĭp'tion**, nn., ~**ĭp'tion**AL, ~**ĭp'tive**, aa. [f. L *tran*(*scribere script-* write)]

trăn'script, n. Written or recorded copy. [as prec.]

trănscŭ'rrent, a. (nat. hist.). Set or running crosswise. [f. L TRANS(*currere* run), -ENT]

trănsĕc'tion, n. Cross-section. [TRANS-]

trăn'sĕpt, n. Transverse part of cruciform church, either arm (*north, south*, ~) of this. Hence **trănsĕp'tal** a. [16th c., f. med. or mod. (Anglo-) L *transseptum* f. TRANS- +SEPTUM]

trănsfĕr'¹, v.t. (-rr-). Convey, remove, hand over, (thing etc. *from* person or place *to* another); make over possession of (property, ticket etc. conferring rights, *to* person); convey (drawing etc.) from one surface to another esp. to lithographic stone by ineans of transfer--paper; remove (picture) from one surface to another esp. from wood or wall to canvas. Hence **trănsfera**BIL'ITY, **trăns-**ferEE', **trăns'fer**ENCE, **trăns'fer**or, ~**r'ER¹**, nn., **trăns'fer**ABLE a. (*the* ~*able vote*, electoral method for securing that elected candidate shall represent a majority, each voter signifying on his ballot-paper to which candidate his vote shall be ~red if no candidate has an absolute majority of first preferences), **trănsferĕn'**TIAL (-shal) a. [ME, f. OF *transferer* or L TRANS(*ferre lat-* bear)]

trăns'fer², n. 1. Transferring; conveyance of property or right, document effecting this; design etc. (to be) conveyed from one surface to another; small toy coloured picture or design transferable from paper on which it is sold to other surface; ‖ soldier exchanged from one regiment etc. to another. 2. ~-*book*, register of ~s of property, shares, etc.; ‖ ~-*days* at Bank of England, days for ~ of consols etc. free of charge (all but Sat. & Sun.); ~-*ink* (for making designs on lithographic stone or ~-paper); ~-*paper* (specially coated to receive impression of ~-ink & transfer it to stone). [f. prec.]

trănsfĭgŭră'tion, n. Change of form or appearance, esp. that of Christ (*Matt.* xvii. 1-9); (*T*~) festival of Christ's ~, Aug. 6. [ME, f. OF, or L *transfiguratio* (as foll., see -ATION)]

trănsfĭg'ure (-ger), v.t. Change in form or aspect esp. so as to elevate or idealize. [ME, f. L TRANS(*figurare* FIGURE) or OF *transfigurer*]

trănsfīx', v.t. Pierce with lance etc.; (of horror etc.) root (person) to the spot, paralyse faculties of. [f. L TRANS(*figere fix-* fix)]

trănsfī'xion (-kshon), n. Piercing through; (surg.) amputation by piercing transversely & cutting outwards. [-ION]

trănsfŏrm', v.t. Make (esp. considerable) change in the form, outward appearance, character, disposition, etc., of, as *caterpillar is* ~*ed into butterfly, 10 years in*

India have ~*ed him* (in character or physique), *a beard may* ~ *a man beyond recognition.* Hence ~ABLE, ~ATIVE, aa. [ME, f. OF, or L TRANS(*formare* FORM²)]

transforma'tion, n. Transforming, being transformed, as *has undergone a great* ~; metamorphosis esp. of insects; change from solid to liquid or from liquid to gaseous state or vice versa; (math.) change from one figure or expression to another equal in quantity; change in blood during passage through capillaries of vascular system; morbid change of tissue into form proper to some different part; (shop) woman's artificial head of hair; ~*-scene*, elaborate spectacular scene in which chief pantomime characters are supposed to change into chief actors of the harlequinade that follows. [ME, f. OF, or LL *transformatio* (as prec., see -ATION)]

transfòrm'er, n. In vbl senses, esp. apparatus for reducing or increasing the voltage of an alternating current. [-ER¹]

transfòrm'|ism, n. Fact, doctrine, of the development of one species from another; theory of development of complex animals from free organisms united into a colony & changed into organs of a complex whole. So ~IST n. [F (-*isme*), as TRANSFORM, -ISM]

trans|fūse' (-z), v.t. Cause (fluid, fig. quality etc.) to pass from one vessel etc. to another; (med.) transfer (blood) from veins of person or animal to those of another person, inject (liquid) into blood-vessel to replace lost fluid. Hence or cogn. ~fū'SION (-zhn) n., ~fūs'IVE a. [ME, f. L TRANS(*fundere fus-* pour)]

transgrèss' (-z-, -s-), v.t. Violate, infringe, (commandment, law; often abs.). So **trànsgrè'ssION** (-shn), ~OR, nn. [app. f. F *transgresser* f. L TRANS(*gredi gress-* = *gradi* walk)]

tranship. See TRANS-SHIP.

trànshūm'ance, n. Seasonal moving of live-stock to another region. [F, (TRANS-, L *humus* ground, -ANCE)]

trans'ient (-z-), a. Not permanent, as *the* ~ *affairs of this life*; of short duration, momentary, hasty, as *a* ~ *gleam of hope, snatched a* ~ *glance*; (mus.) ~ *chord, note* (unessential, serving only to connect). Hence **trans'iENCE, -ENCY**, nn., ~LY² adv., (-z-). [f. L TRANS(*ire* go), see -ENT]

trànsil'ient, a. Extending across from one point of support to another. [f. L TRAN(*silire* = *salire* leap), see -ENT]

trànsillūmina'tion (-z-), n. (med.). Throwing of strong light through organ etc. for purpose of diagnosis. [TRANS-]

‖ *trànsīr'è* (-z-), n. Custom-house permit for removal of goods. [L TRANS(*ire* go) go across]

trànsis'tor (-z-), n. Non-vacuum electronic device performing functions usu. performed by the thermionic valve; ~ *radio.* [*tran*(*sfer, re*)*sistor*]

trans'it (-z-), n., & v.t. **1.** Going, conveying, being conveyed, across or over or through, as *allowed 2 days for the* ~ *of the lake, improved methods of* ~ *by rail, goods delayed in* ~, *loses quality in* (the) ~; passage, route, as *the overland*~; = ~*-circle, -compass, -instrument*; apparent passage of heavenly body across meridian of place; passage of heavenly body across meridian (esp. of Venus as determining solar parallax, or of Mercury) across sun's disc etc. **2.** ~*-circle, -instrument*, instruments for observing ~ of heavenly body across meridian; ~*-compass*, surveyor's instrument for measuring horizontal angle; ~*-duty* (paid on goods passing through a country). **3.** v.t. Cross the disc of (sun etc.). [ME, f. L *transitus* f. TRANS(*ire it-* go)]

trànsi'tion (-z-), n. Passage, change, from one place or state or act or set of circumstances to another, as *came by an abrupt* ~ *into hilly country, made a hurried* ~ *to indifferent topics, is subject to frequent* ~*s from high spirits to depression*; (mus.) modulation of momentary character; (art) change from one style to another, esp. (archit.) from Norman to Early-English, as (attrib.) ~ *stage, period*; ~ *tumour* (tending, on recurrence after removal, to become malignant). Hence ~AL, ~ARY¹, aa., ~alLY² adv., (-zisho-). [f. F, or L TRANSITIO (-ION)]

trans'itive, a. & n. (gram.). (Verb) taking a direct object expressed or understood (e.g. *pick* in: *pick peas, pick till you are tired*; opp. to *intransitive* as in *picked at the hole to make it bigger*). Hence ~LY² adv., ~NESS n. [f. LL *transitivus* (as TRANSIT, see -IVE)]

trans'itor|ў, a. Not permanent, lasting only a short time; ~*y action* (law), one that can be brought in any country irrespective of where the transaction etc. occurred. Hence ~iLY² adv., ~iNESS n. [ME, f. AF *transitorie*, OF *transitoire* f. L *transitorius* (TRANSIT, -ORY)]

trànslāt|e' (-s-, -z-), v.t. **1.** Express the sense of (word, sentence, book) in or into another language, as *has* ~*ed Homer* (*into English, from the Greek*), *his own novels into French*; (fig.) kindly ~*e* (say what you mean in plain words); (quasi-pass., of language, style, etc.) *lend itself well* etc. to translation. **2.** Convey, introduce, (idea, principle) *from* one art etc. *into* another. **3.** Infer or declare the significance of, interpret, (signs, movements, conduct, hint, etc.), as *this I* ~*ed as a protest,* ~*ed his gestures to the bystanders.* **4.** Remove (bishop) to another see; (bibl.) convey to heaven without death; (arch.) transform; (teleg.) retransmit (message); (mech.) cause (body) to move so that all its parts follow same direction, impart motion without rotation to. Hence or cogn. ~'ABLE, **trànslā'tionAL** (mech.), aa., **trànslā'tION**, ~'OR, nn. [ME, f. L *translatus*, p.p. of TRANSFER¹, see -ATE²,³]

trănslit′er|āte (-z-), v.t. Represent (word, or abs.) in the more or less corresponding characters of a different language. Hence ∼A′TION, ∼ātor, nn. [f. TRANS- + L *littera* letter + -ATE³]

trănslu′c|ent (-zlōō-), a. Transmitting light but not transparent; (loosely) transparent. Hence ∼ENCE, ∼ENCY, nn., ∼ID¹ (rare) a. [f. L TRANS(*lucēre* shine), -ENT]

trănsmarine′ (-z-, -ēn), a. Situated beyond the sea. [f. L TRANS(*marinus* MARINE)]

trăns′migr|āte (or -ig̃²), v.i. (Of soul) pass into, become incarnate in, a different body; migrate. So ∼ANT a. & n. (esp., alien passing through one country on way to another), ∼ātor n., trănsmig̃′ratory a. [f. L TRANS(*migrare* MIGRATE)]

trănsmigrā′tion, n. = METEMPSYCHOSIS, whence ∼ISM(3) n.; migration. [ME, f. LL *transmigratio* (as prec., see -ATION)]

trăns|mit′ (-z-), v.t. (-tt-). Pass on, hand on, transfer, communicate, as *will* ∼*mit the parcel, shall* ∼*mit daily dispatches, will* ∼*mit the title, the disease, the faculty, to his descendants, his writings have* ∼*mitted the principle to posterity*; suffer to pass through, be a medium for, serve to communicate, (heat, light, sound, electricity, emotion, news). Hence or cogn. ∼missi-BIL′ITY, ∼mi′ssion (-zmĭshn), ∼mitt′AL, ∼mitt′ER¹(1, 2), nn., ∼miss′IBLE, ∼miss′IVE, ∼mitt′ABLE, aa. [ME, f. L TRANS *(mittere miss-* send)]

trănsmŏg̃′ri|fy (-z-), v.t. (joc.). Transform esp. in magical or surprising manner. Hence ∼FICA′TION n. [17th c., of unkn. orig.]

trănsmūtā′tion (-z-), n. Transmuting; change into another form, nature, or substance; (alch.) change of baser metals into gold etc.; (geom.) change of figure or body into another of same area or content; (biol.) change of one species into another, whence ∼IST(2) n.; ∼ *glaze*, iridescent porcelain glaze. [ME, f. OF, or f. L *transmutatio* (as foll., see -ATION)]

trănsmūt|e′ (-z-), v.t. Change the form, nature, or substance, of. Hence or cogn. ∼ABIL′ITY, ∼′ER¹, nn., ∼′ABLE, ∼′ative, aa., ∼′abLY² adv. [ME, f. L TRANS(*mutare* change)]

trănsnŏrm′al (-z-), a. Beyond, exceeding, what is normal. [TRANS-]

trănsoceăn′ic (-zōsh-), a. Situated beyond the ocean; crossing, concerned with crossing, the ocean, as ∼ *flight* of birds. [TRANS-]

trăn′som, n. ‖ Horizontal (cf. MULLION) bar of wood or stone across window or top of door; ∼ *window* (divided by ∼ or placed above ∼ of door); each of several beams fixed across stern-post of ship; beam across saw-pit; strengthening cross-bar. Hence ∼ED² (-md) a. [ME (13th–15th c.) *traversayn, 'transyn, -ing,* app. f. OF *traversin* in same sense, f. *traverse* TRAVERSE]

trăns′padăne, a. Situated beyond (usu. = north of) the Po. [f. L TRANS(*padanus* f. *Padus* Po, see -AN)]

trănspar′encў (or -ā′r-), n. Being transparent, so **trănspar′ENCE** (or -ā′r-) n.; picture, inscription, etc., painted on canvas or muslin & shown up by light behind, wooden framework supporting such picture; (photog.) positive picture on glass hung in window as ornament or used as lantern slide; porcelain relief whose parts vary in thickness & ∼; *his* etc. *T*∼ (burlesque title = G *Durchlaucht,* cf. SERENITY). [f. med. L *transparentia* (as foll., see -ENCY)]

trănspar′ent (or -ā′r-), a. Transmitting rays of light without diffusion so that bodies behind can be distinctly seen (cf. TRANSLUCENT); (fig., of disguise, pretext, etc.) easily seen through, (of motive, quality, etc.) easily seen through attempted disguise; bright, clear, (fig.) free from affectation or disguise, frank; ∼ *colours,* (in painting) such as when laid lightly on do not hide underlying colours & forms, (in stained glass) appearing only by transmission of light. Hence ∼LY² adv., ∼NESS n. [ME, f. OF, f. med. L *transparens* (TRANS-, *parēre* appear, -ENT)]

trănspierce′, v.t. Pierce through. [f. F TRANS(*percer* PIERCE)]

trănspīr|e′, v.t. & i. 1. Emit through excretory organs of skin or lungs, send off in vapour; be emitted thus, pass off as in insensible perspiration. 2. (Of gas or liquid) move through capillary tube under pressure; (bot., of plant or leaf) exhale watery vapour. 3. (fig.). (Of secret etc.) ooze out, come to be known; (vulg.) happen. Hence or cogn. ∼′ABLE, ∼′atory, aa., trănspira′TION n. [f. med. L *tran-(spirare* breathe), or F *transpirer*]

trănsplant′ (-lah-), v.t. Plant in another place; remove & establish, esp. cause to live, in another place; (surg.) transfer (living tissue) & implant in another part of body or in another person's body. Hence or cogn. ∼ABLE (-lah-) a., trănsplant-A′TION n. [ME, f. LL TRANS(*plantare* PLANT)]

trănspla′nter (-lah-), n. In vbl senses, esp.: hand-tool for lifting plants, machine for removing trees, with ball of earth about roots. [-ER¹]

‖ **trănspŏn′tine**, a. Of the part of London on Surrey side of Thames; cheaply melodramatic, like the plays formerly popular in ∼ theatres. [f. TRANS- + L *pons -ntis* bridge + -INE¹]

trănspŏrt′¹, v.t. 1. Convey (person, goods, troops, baggage, etc.) from one place to another, whence ∼ER¹ n. 2. (hist.) Convey (criminal) to penal colony. 3. Carry away by strong emotion (chiefly in pass., as ∼*ed with joy, anger, fear,* whence ∼ingLY² adv. [ME, f. OF *transporter,* or L TRANS(*portare* carry)]

trăns′port², n. 1. Conveyance, transportation, from place to place, carriage; means of ~, as *motor* ~. 2. Vessel employed to carry soldiers, stores, etc., to destination. 3. (hist.). Transported convict. 4. Vehement emotion, as *in a* ~ *of rage, was in* ~*s* (usu. of joy). [f. prec.]

transpōrt'|able, a. That may be transported, whence ~ABIL'ITY n.; (of offender or offence) punishable by transportation (hist.). [-ABLE]

transportā'tion, n. Conveying, being conveyed, from place to place; removal to penal colony (hist.). [-ATION]

transpōs|e' (-z), v.t. Cause (two or more things) to change places; (alg.) transfer (term) with changed sign to other side of equation; change the natural or the existing order or position of (words, a word) in sentence; (mus.) write, play, in different key, as ~*ed from G to B*; ~*ing instrument* (producing notes different in pitch from the written notes), ~*ing piano* (on which transposition may be effected mechanically). Hence ~'AL, ~'ER¹, nn., (-z-). [ME, f. OF TRANS(*poser*, see COM-POSE)]

transposi'tion (-zī-), n. Transposing, being transposed. Hence or cogn. ~AL, **transpŏs'itive**, aa., (-zī-). [F, or f. LL *transpositio* f. TRANS(*ponere posit*- place), see -ION; assoc. w. prec.]

trans-ship' (-nsh-), v.t. (-pp-). Transfer from one ship or conveyance to another. Hence ~MENT n. [TRANS-]

transubstăn'tiāte (-shĬ-), v.t. Change from one substance into another (esp. as foll.). [f. med. L TRAN(*substantiare*, as SUBSTANCE), see -ATE³]

transubstantiā'tion (-shĬ-, -sĬ-), n. Change from one substance into another, esp. (theol.) conversion of whole substance of eucharistic bread & wine into body & blood respectively of Christ (cf. CONSUBSTANTIATION). [ME, f. med. L *transubstantiatio* (as prec., see -ATION)]

transūd|e', v.i. (Of fluid) pass through pores or interstices of membrane etc. Hence ~A'TION n., ~'atORY a. [F *transuder* or mod. L, f. *tran-* = TRANS-+ *sudare* sweat]

transūrăn'ic, a. (chem.). (Of elements) having a higher atomic number than uranium. [TRANS-]

transvĕrs'al (-nz-), a. & n. 1. (Of line) cutting a system of lines. 2. n. ~ line. Hence ~ITY (-ăl-) n., ~LY² adv. [ME, f. med. L *transversalis* (foll., -AL)]

transvĕrse' (-z-; *also* trã-), a. & n. 1. Situated, arranged, acting, in crosswise direction, as ~ *artery, ligament, magnet* (whose poles are at sides not ends), *section, strain*. 2. n. ~ muscle. Hence ~LY³ adv., **transvĕrs'o-** (-z-) comb. form. [f. L TRANS(*vertere vers*- turn)]

transvĕst', v.t. (psychol.). Clothe in other garments, esp. those of opposite sex. Hence ~ISM n. [TRANS-, L *vestire* clothe]

‖ **trăn'ter**, n. (dial.). Carrier; hawker. [c. 1500, f. AF *traventer* f. med. (Anglo-) L *travetarius*, perh. f. **tra(ns)vectarius* transporter]

trăp¹, n., & v.t. & i. (-pp-). 1. Pitfall or enclosure or mechanical structure for catching animals, affording entrance but not exit & often baited & having door or lid actuated by spring; FLY¹, RAT¹, ~; (fig.) trick for betraying person into speech or act, as *is always setting* ~*s for me, walked straight into the* ~, *is this* (question etc.) *a* ~? 2. Contrivance for suddenly releasing bird, or throwing ball etc. into air, to be shot at; shoe-shaped wooden device with pivoted bar that sends ball from its heel into air on being struck at other end with bat, ~-*ball*, game played with this. 3. U-shaped or other section of pipe so arranged as to prevent return flow of gas by means of liquid replaced whenever ~ is used. 4. ‖ Kinds of wheeled vehicle, e.g. dog-cart. 5. = ~*door*. 6. ‖~-*cellar*, space under stage of theatre; ~*door*, door in floor or roof (~*door spider*, kind that makes hinged ~door at top of nest), (fig.) L-shaped tear in cloth etc. 7. vb. Catch (animal, fig. person) in ~; furnish (stage) with ~s for a play; set ~s in (wood, hedge, etc.); arrest (gas) in ~; supply (drain etc.) with ~; (of steam) be impeded in pipe etc. [OE *treppe, træppe*, ME *trapp(e)*; cf. syn. MDu. *trappe*, WFlem. *traap, trape*, also med. L (Rom.) *trappa*; ult. orig. obsc.]

trăp², n. (min.). Dark-coloured eruptive rock of columnar structure. [f. Sw. *trapp* f. *trappa* stair (the rock freq. presenting a stair-like appearance)]

trăp³, v.t. (-pp-). Furnish with trappings. [f. obs. *trap*, n., ME f. OF *drap*, see DRAPE]

‖ **trăp⁴**, n. (Sc.). Ladder leading to a loft. [app. = Du., MFlem. *trap* flight of steps]

trapan. See TREPAN².

trāpes (-ps), traipse, n., & v.i. (colloq. & dial.). 1. Slattern; a tiresome walk. 2. v.i. (Esp. of women) tramp or trudge wearily or in draggletailed way, go about on errands. [vb earlier (1593), of unkn. orig.]

trapēz|e', n. Cross-bar(s) suspended by cords used as swing for gymnastic exercises; = foll., whence ~'IFORM a. [f. F *trapeze* f. foll.]

trapēz'ium, n. 1. Quadrilateral with two sides parallel. 2. (U.S.) A trapezoid. [mod. L, f. Gk *trapezion* (*trapeza* table)]

trăp'ezoid, n. & a. 1. Quadrilateral with no two sides parallel. 2. (U.S.) A trapezium. 3. adj. Of, in the form of, a ~. Hence ~AL (-oid⁴) a. [f. late Gk *trapezoeidēs* (prec., -OID)]

trăpp'|ean, a. Of the nature of the rock TRAP². So ~OID, ~OSE¹, aa. [-EAN]

trăpp'er, n. One whose business is to trap animals esp. for furs; one who tends air-doors in mines. [f. TRAP¹+-ER¹]

trăpp′ings (-z), n. pl. Harness of horse esp. when ornamental; (fig.) ornamental accessories (*of* office etc.). [ME, f. TRAP³ +-ING¹]

Trăpp′ist, n. Member of a Cistercian order founded 1140 at Soligny-la-Trappe & noted for silence & other austerities. [-IST]

trăpp′istine, n. **1.** Liqueur made at Trappist abbey of Grâce-Dieu in France. **2.** (*T~*). Nun of an order affiliated with Trappists. [-INE¹]

trăpp′|ỹ, a. (colloq.). Tricky, treacherous, (chiefly of things). Hence ~INESS n. [f. TRAP¹+-Y²]

trăps, n. pl.(colloq.). Personal belongings, baggage. [app. shortened f. TRAPPINGS]

trăsh, n., & v.t. **1.** Worthless or waste stuff, rubbish, refuse; loppings of trees etc., (W. Ind.) stripped leaves of sugar-cane used as fuel; thing, e.g. literary production, of bad workmanship or material; nonsensical talk; *cane-~,* refuse of crushed sugar-canes & dried leaves & tops, used as fuel; *~-house* (on sugar--plantation, for storing bagasse & cane--~); *~-ice,* broken ice mixed with water; *white~,* the poor white population in the Southern States. **2.** v.t. Strip (sugar--canes) of outer leaves. Hence ~′ERY(1), ~′INESS, nn., ~′ILY² adv., ~′Y² a. [16th c., of unkn. orig.; cf. Norw. dial. *trask* trash etc., Icel. *tros* rubbish, fallen leaves & twigs]

trăss, tä′rras, n. A volcanic earth formerly imported as cement-material. [f. Du. *tras,* earlier *terras, tiras* f. Rom., cf. TERRACE]

trăttori′a (-*ēa*), n. Italian eating-house. [It.]

traum′a, n. (pl. *~ta, ~s*). Morbid condition of body produced by wound or external violence; (psych.) emotional shock. So ~TISM n. [f. Gk *trauma -matos* wound]

traumăt′ic, a. & n. Of, (medicine) for, wounds. [f. LL f. Gk *traumatikos* (as prec., see -IC)]

trăv′ail, n., & v.i. (Suffer) pangs of child-birth; (make) painful or laborious effort. [ME; vb f. OF *travaillier* app. f. Rom. *trepaliare* f. LL *trepalium* instrument of torture (L *tres* three, *palus* stake); n. f. OF n. f. vb]

trăv′el, v.i. & t. (-ll-), & n. **1.** Make a journey esp. one of some length to distant countries, as *ordered to ~ for his health, spent his life in ~ling;* act as COMMERCIAL traveller (*for* firm, *in* commodity); (of machine or part) move (*along* bar etc., *in* groove etc.); pass esp. in deliberate or systematic manner from point to point, as *his eye ~led over the scene, mind ~s over the events of the day;* (of deer etc.) move onwards in feeding; move, proceed, in specified manner or at specified rate, perform (distance), as *horse ~s slowly, light ~s faster than sound,*

~s thousands of miles per second, train ~led 1,000 miles a day; journey through, as *~led France from end to end;* cause (herds etc.) to ~; (p.p.) experienced in ~ling, as *is a ~led man; ~ out of the record,* wander from subject; *~ling-cap, -dress,* etc. (of form convenient for ~ling). **2.** n. ~ling esp. in foreign countries, as *is much improved by ~, has returned from his ~s, is going to publish* (account of) *his ~s, cannot read books of ~* or *~s;* range, rate, mode, of motion of a part in machinery, as *has extended, improved, the ~ of the valves;* (of person, clothes, etc.) *~-soiled, -stained, -worn,* etc. (as result of ~). [ME; differentiated f. prec.]

trăv′eller, n. In vbl senses, esp., kinds of moving mechanism (esp. overhead crane on rails); = COMMERCIAL; FELLOW-~; *tip person the ~,* impose on him, tell him-lies; *~'s tale,* presumable lie; *~'s joy,* a climbing shrub with greenish-white flowers, wild clematis. [ME; -ER¹]

trăv′elogue (-ŏg), n. Illustrated lecture--narrative of expedition etc. [f. TRAVEL, after *monologue* etc.]

trăv′erse, a., n., & v.t. & i. **1.** (Arch. in gen. use) = TRANSVERSE; (her.) crossing shield from side to side; *~ sailing* on zigzag track). **2.** n. Thing, esp. part of structure, that crosses another; (fortif.) earthwork in form of parapet protecting covered way etc., double or quadruple right-angle in trench (⌐, ⌐⌐) to prevent enfilading; gallery from side to side of church etc.; (geom.) transversal line; single line of survey (usu. plotted from prismatic-compass bearings & chained or paced distances between angular points); (naut.) zigzag line taken by ship owing to contrary winds or currents (*work, solve, a ~,* compute direct distance so covered); sideways movement of part in machine; sideways motion across face of precipice from one practicable line of ascent or descent to another, place where this is necessary; (law) denial esp. of allegation of matter of fact; ‖ (arch.) thwarting circumstance; turning of gun to required direction; *~-table,* nautical table used in solving ~s, platform for shifting engine etc. from one line of rails to another. **3.** vb. Travel or lie across, as *must ~ a vast extent of country, district ~d by canals, wall ~d by beam;* make a ~ in climbing; (fig.) consider, discuss, the whole extent of (subject); turn (gun); plane (wood) across grain; deny esp. (law) in pleading; thwart, frustrate, oppose, (plan, opinion); (of needle of compass etc.) turn (as) on pivot; (of horse) walk crosswise; *traversing pulley* (running over rope etc. that supports it). [n. f. OF *travers* f. pop. L *traversum* f. L *trans-* (TRANSVERSE), partly f. OF *traverse* f. *traverser* (see vb); vb f. OF *traverser* f. *travers* n. or adj.; adj. f. OF *travers* f. pop. L *traversus* (see n.)]

trăv′erṣer, n. In vbl senses, esp. railway traverse-table. [-ER¹]

trăv′ertin(e), n. Porous light-yellow rock, a calcareous deposit from springs, hardening on exposure. [f. It. *travertino* f. L *tiburlinus* (*lapis* stone) of Tibur (Tivoli), see -INE¹]

trăv′ĕstÿ, v.t., & n. **1.** Make (subject etc.) ridiculous (intentionally or not) by treatment of it; (of person or thing, e.g. literary work) be a ridiculous imitation of (another). **2.** n. Such treatment, such imitation, (*of*). [f. F *travesti* p.p. of *travestir* disguise, change the clothes of, f. It. *tra(vestire* clothe f. L *vestire*)]

trawl, v.t. & i., & n. **1.** Drag (~-net), catch fish in ~-net. Hence ~′ING¹ n. **2.** n. (Also ~-*net*) large bag-net with wide mouth held open by beam (*beam-*~) or otherwise, meant to be dragged along the bottom by boat; *(also ~-*line*) long sea-fishing line buoyed & supporting short lines with baited hooks; ~-*anchor* (for anchoring ~-line); ~-*boat* (for setting ~-line or drawing ~-net). [orig. & age obsc.; cf. MDu. *traghelen* to drag, f. *traghel* drag-net]

trawl′er, n. Person who trawls; trawl-boat. [-ER¹]

tray, n. Flat shallow vessel usu. of wood or metal for placing or carrying esp. small articles on, as *tea-*~, *pen-*~, *developing-*~ (in photography); metal or other container or desk for correspondence, as *in, out, ~*; shallow lidless box forming a compartment in trunk. Hence ~′FUL n. [OE *trig* f. Gmc **traujam*, cogn. w. TREE]

trea′cherous (-ĕch-), a. Violating allegiance, betraying trust, perfidious; not to be relied on, deceptive, as ~ *memory*, ~ *ice* (apt to give). Hence or cogn. ~LY² adv., ~NESS, **trea′chery¹** (-ĕch-), n. [ME, f. OF *trecherous* (*trechour* a cheat f. *trechier, trichier* (see TRICK)), -OUS]

‖ **trea′cle,** n. Syrup got in refining sugar; (loosely) = MOLASSES; kinds of saccharine fluid, e.g. sap of birch. Hence **treac′ly²** a. [ME *triacle*, in sense 'theriac', f. OF f. L *theriaca* THERIAC]

tread (-ĕd), v.i. & t. (*trŏd*, arch. *trode*; *trodden*), & n. **1.** Set down one's foot, walk, step, (of foot) be set down, as *do not ~ on the grass, trod on a snake*; ~ *lightly,* (fig.) deal cautiously with delicate subject; *where no foot may ~, where angels fear to ~*; ~ *in* person's (*foot*)*steps,* (fig.) follow his example; ~ *on* person's *corns* or *toes,* (fig.) offend him; ~ *on the heels of,* (lit., & fig. of event etc.) come closely or immediately after; ~ *or seem to ~ on air* (of person transported with joy); ~ *on* or *as on eggs* (of person in situation requiring much tact); ~ (set one's foot lit. or fig. as sign of supremacy) *on the neck of* person, ~ AWRY. **2.** Walk upon, press or crush with the feet, as ~*s a perilous path, trod the room from end to end,* ~ *grapes* (in making wine), *wine.* **3.** Perform, execute,

in walking etc., as *trod a dozen hurried paces,* ~ *a measure* (in dancing). **4.** (Of cock) copulate with (hen, or abs.). **5.** ~ *down,* press down with feet, trample on, destroy, as ~ *down the earth round the roots,* ~ *down Satan under our feet;* ~ *in,* press in or into earth etc. with feet; ~ *out,* stamp out (fire, fig. insurrection etc.), press out (wine, grain) with feet; ~ *the stage* or *boards,* be an actor, appear on stage; ~ *under foot,* (fig.) destroy, treat contemptuously; ~ *water,* maintain upright position in deep water. **6.** n. Manner, sound, of walking, as *recognized his heavy* ~, *approached with cautious* ~. **7.** (Of male bird) copulation. **8.** (Also ~-*board*) top surface of step or stair, each step of ~*mill.* **9.** Piece of metal or rubber placed on step to lessen wear or sound. **10.** Part of wheel that touches ground or rails, part of rail that wheels touch. **11.** Part of stilt on which foot rests. **12.** Part of boot-sole that rests on ground. **13.** Distance between pedals of bicycle. **14.** Cicatricule of egg (formerly supposed to appear only in fecundated eggs). **15.** ~*mill,* appliance for producing motion by the stepping of man or horse etc. on movable steps on revolving cylinder, esp. kind formerly used in prisons as punishment, (fig.) monotonous routine; ~-*wheel,* ~mill or similar appliance. [OE, OS *tredan,* OHG *tretan,* cogn. w. ON *trotha,* Goth. *trudan,* f. Gmc **tredh-, *tradh-, *trudh-*]

trea′dle (-ĕdl), n., & v.i. **1.** Lever moved by foot & imparting motion to machine, e.g. lathe, sewing-machine, bicycle, reed-organ; ~*machine,* ~*press,* printing-press worked by ~. **2.** v.i. Work ~. Hence **tread′lER¹** (-rĕd-)n. [ME, f. prec. +-LE(1)]

treas′on (-z-), n. **1.** (Also *high*~) violation by subject of allegiance to sovereign or to chief authority of State (e.g. compassing or intending sovereign's death, levying war against his enemies, killing his wife or heir, violating his wife or eldest unmarried daughter or heir's wife, killing chancellor or treasurer or justice, abetting marriage of sovereign under 18 years of age without written consent of regent & parliament). **2.** Breach of faith, disloyalty, (*to* cause, friend, etc.). **3.** *Constructive* ~ (held in law as equivalent to ~ though not intended or realized as such); MISPRISION¹ *of* ~; ‖~-*felony,* attempt to depose sovereign or levy war in order to compel change of measures, intimidate parliament, or stir up foreign invasion. Hence ~OUS a. [ME, f. AF *treisoun* etc., OF *traïson,* f. L as TRADITION]

treas′onab‖le (-z-), a. Involving the crime, guilty, of treason. Hence ~leNESS n., ~LY² adv. [ME; -ABLE]

trea′sure (-ĕzher), n., & v.t. **1.** Precious metals or gems, hoard of these, accumulated wealth, as *buried* ~, *had amassed* *great* ~ or ~*s, a voyage in quest of* ~, (not now in colloq. use); thing valued for rarity, workmanship, associations, etc., as *art* ~*s, absorbed in his latest* ~ (book, picture, etc.); (colloq.) beloved person esp. child, as (voc.) *my* ~; (colloq.) highly efficient or satisfactory person e.g. servant, as *the girl is a perfect* ~. 2. v.t. Store (usu. *up*) as valuable; receive, regard, as valuable, store (usu. *up*) in memory, (person's words, looks, etc.). 3. ~-*city* (bibl.), city for stores & magazines; ~-*house*, place where ~s (esp. fig.) are kept; ~ *trove* [see TROVER], gold etc. found hidden of unknown ownership. [ME, f. OF *tresor* f. Rom. **tresaurus* for L f. Gk *thēsauros*]

trea'surer (-ĕzhe-), n. Person in charge of funds of society, company, club, etc.; officer authorized to receive & disburse public revenues; *Lord High T*~ (hist.), crown officer with duties now discharged by Lords of the Treasury; ‖*T*~ *of the Household*, official ranking next to Lord Steward. Hence ~-SHIP n. [ME, f. ONF, AF *tresorer*, OF *-ier* f. *tresor* (prec., see -ARY[1], -ER[2]), after LL *thesaurarius*]

trea'sury (-ĕzhe-), n. 1. Place, building, where treasure is stored; (fig.) book, person, etc., viewed as repository of information etc. 2. Place where public revenues are kept; department managing public revenue of a country, officers of this; ‖ *T*~ *Board, Lords* (*Commissioners*) *of the T*~, board in charge of British public revenue, viz. Prime Minister (who is also *First Lord of the T*~), Chancellor of the Exchequer, & 5 junior lords; *T*~ *bench*, front bench on right hand of Speaker in House of Commons, occupied by Prime Minister, Chancellor of Exchequer, & other members of Government. 3. ‖*~ bill*, bill of exchange issued by the T~ to raise money for temporary needs & sold to highest bidder; ~ *note*, = CURRENCY *note*, *note issued by T~ & receivable for government dues; *T*~ *warrant* (issued by T~ for sums disbursed by Exchequer). [ME, f. OF *tresorie* (as TREASURE, see -Y[1])]

treat, v.t. & i., & n. 1. Act towards, behave to, as *how did they* ~ *you?*, ~*ed me abominably, kindly*, as *if I were a child, better* ~ *it as a joke*. 2. Deal with (person, thing) with view to result, apply process to, subject to chemical agent etc., as ~*ed him for smallpox, how would you* ~ *a sprained ankle?, must next be* ~*ed with sulphuric acid*. 3. Manipulate, present, express, (subject) in literature or art. 4. Give (person) food and drink or entertainment at one's expense, as *I will* ~ *you all, think you might* ~ *me to an ice, a theatre*, (of candidate for election) give food etc. or cause these to be given to (electors) in order to influence election, whence ~'ING[1] n. 5. Negotiate terms (*with* person); ~ *of*, handle, discuss,

(subject). 6. n. Thing that gives great pleasure, as *pantomime is a great* ~ *to him, what a* ~ *it is not to have to get up early*; entertainment designed to do this, as *school-*~, picnic etc. for (esp. Sunday-) school children; *stand* ~, bear expense of entertainment. Hence ~'ABLE a., ~'ER[1] n. [ME, f. OF *traitier* f. L *tractare* handle frequent. of *trahere tract-* draw]

treat'ise (-z, -s), n. Literary composition dealing more or less systematically with definite subject. [ME, f. AF *tretis* (*traitier* as prec.)]

treat'ment, n. (Mode of) dealing with or behaving towards a person or thing, as *received strange* ~ *from him, must vary the* ~, *is now ready for* ~ *with an acid*. [as TREAT, see -MENT]

treat'y, n. Formally concluded & ratified agreement between nations; agreement between persons (*to do* etc.); *be in* ~ (negotiating) *with* (person *for* purchase etc.); ~ *port*, one that a country is bound by ~ to keep open to foreign trade. [ME, f. AF *trete*, p.p. of *traiter* TREAT, & f. L *tractatum* TRACTATE]

tre'ble, a. & n., & v.t. & i. 1. Threefold, triple, whence **trĕb'LY**[2] adv.; multiplied by three, three times (amount etc., as *the enemy had* ~ *our numbers*); (esp. of boy's voice or boy) = SOPRANO; ~ *chance*, method of competing in football pool in which the aim is to pick all draws from a given selection of matches, a draw counting more than a home or away win. 2. n. (In short whist) game won by 5 to 0 counting three points; = SOPRANO. 3. vb. Multiply, be multiplied, by three, as *has* ~*d its value, its value has* ~*d*. [ME, f. OF, f. L *triplus* TRIPLE]

trĕb'uchĕt (-sh-), **trĕb'uckĕt**, n. (Hist.) military engine for throwing stones etc.; tilting balance for weighing light articles; kind of trap for small birds etc. [ME, f. OF, f. *trebucher* overthrow etc.]

trecĕn'to (-āch-), n. The 14th century in Italian art & literature. So ~IST(2, 3) n. [It., = three (for thirteen) hundred]

tree, n., & v.t. 1. Perennial plant with single woody self-supporting stem or trunk usu. unbranched (cf. SHRUB[1]) for some distance above ground; piece or framework of wood for various purposes, e.g. AXLE, BOOT[1], ROOF, SADDLE, SWINGLE, ~, CROSS-TREES; (arch.) gibbet, cross used for (esp. Christ's) crucifixion; CHRISTMAS ~; (math.) diagram of branching lines; *family* or GENEALOGICAL ~; *up a* ~, (fig.) cornered, nonplussed; *at the top of the* ~, at the top of one's profession. 2. ~ *agate* (with ~-like markings); ~ *calf*, calf binding for book stained with ~-like design; ~ -*creeper*, kinds of small bird; ~-*fern*, kinds of fern attaining size of ~; ~-*frog*, (pop. name for) ~-*toad*; ~-*goose*, = BARNACLE[2] (1); ~-*milk*, juice of a shrub used in Ceylon instead of milk; ~'*nail*, pin of hard wood for securing planks etc.; ~ *of*

heaven, ornamental Asian ~ with ill-
-scented flowers; ~ *of knowledge of good
& evil* (Gen. iii); ~ *of liberty* (dedicated to
liberty & set up in public place); ~ *of life*
(Gen. ii. 9); ~-*toad*, arboreal amphibian
with adhesive discs on digits enabling it
to climb. Hence ~'LESS a., ~'lèssNESS n.
3. v.t. Force (animal, fig. person) to take
refuge in ~; stretch (boot) on boot-~.
[OE *tréow*, OS *treo*, ON *tré*, Goth. *triu*,
f. Gmc **trewam*, cogn. w. Gk *drus* oak,
doru spear]

trḗf'oil, n. & a. Kinds of leguminous
plant with leaves of three leaflets &
flowers of various colours, clover; kinds
of plant with similar leaves; three-lobed
ornamentation in tracery etc.; (thing)
arranged in three lobes, whence ~ED² (-ld)
a. [ME, f. AF *trifoil* & L TRI(*folium* leaf)]

trḗha'la (-ah-), n. Manna of starch, sugar,
& gum, excreted in cocoon form by an
insect in Turkey & Persia. [f. native
tiqālah]

trĕk, v.i. (-kk-), & n. (S.-Afr.). 1. (Of ox)
draw vehicle, pull load; travel by ox-
-wagon; migrate; proceed slowly. 2. n.
Such journey, each stage of journey;
organized migration. Hence ~k'ER¹ n.
[f. Du. *trekken* vb, *trek* n.]

trĕll'is, n., & v.t. 1. (Also ~-*work*) lattice,
grating, of light wooden cross-bars nailed
together where they cross, similar structure of wire or metal; summer-house,
screen, etc., made of ~-work. 2. v.t.
Furnish, support (vine etc.), with ~. [ME,
f. OF *treliz*, *-is*, f. Rom. **trilicius* f. L
TRI(*lix* f.-*licium* warp-thread) three-ply]

trĕm'bl|e, v.i., & n. 1. Shake involun-
tarily from fear, agitation, physical
weakness, etc., as *he ~ed with anger, voice
~ed with excitement, hands ~e from over-
smoking* etc.; (fig.) be in state of extreme
agitation, fear, suspense, etc., as *I ~e to
think what has become of him, ~e at the
thought, no cause to ~e before his judge,
hear & ~e* (be duly impressed)*!, I ~e* (am
alarmed) *for his safety, in ~ing uncertainty*; move in quivering manner, as
leaves ~e in the breeze, ~ing POPLAR; (fig.)
his fate, life, etc., *~es in the balance* (has
reached a critical point, is in extreme
danger). Hence or cogn. ~eMENT n. (poet.,
rare), ~inGLY² adv., ~Y² a. 2. n. ~ing,
quiver, as *there was a ~e in her voice*,
(colloq.) *was all of a ~e* (~ing all over);
(pl.) kinds of (esp. cattle-) disease, with
~ing. [ME, f. OF *trembler* f. med. L
tremulare f. *tremulus* TREMULOUS]

trĕm'bler, n. In vbl senses; also or esp.:
automatic vibrator for making & breaking electric circuit; electric bell. [-ER¹]

trĕm'ellōse, a. (bot.). Jellylike, shaking
like jelly. [f. mod. L *Tremella*, genus of
jellylike fungi, +-OSE¹]

trĕmĕn'dous, a. Awful, fearful, overpowering, (colloq.) considerable, as *a ~
explosion, revolution, makes a ~ difference*,
a ~ (huge) *bluebottle*. Hence ~LY² adv.,

~NESS n. [f. L *tremendus* (*tremere* tremble)
+-OUS]

trĕmŏlän'dō, adv. (mus.). Tremulously.
[It.]

trĕm'olant, -ūlant, n. Device in organ
for producing tremolo effect. [(-*ol*- f. It.
tremolante) f. med. L as TREMBLE, see -ANT]

trĕm'olō, n. (mus.). Tremulous effect in
singing or in playing bowed instruments
etc.; = prec. [It, as TREMULOUS]

trĕm'or, n. (Of leaf, part of body, voice,
person) shaking, quivering; thrill (of fear,
exultation, etc.); *earth ~*, slight earthquake; *intention ~* (in part of body when
it moves to do something); *metallic ~*,
trembling palsy of metal-workers. Hence
~LESS a. [ME & OF, f. L *tremorem* (*tremere*
tremble, see -OR]

trĕm'ūlous, a. Trembling, quivering, as
~ leaves, voice, hand; *~ line* (drawn by ~
hand); timid, vacillating. Hence ~LY²
adv., ~NESS n. [f. L *tremulus*, LL *-osus*, f.
tremere tremble, see -OUS]

trenail. Var. of TREENail.

trĕnch, v.t. & i., & n. 1. Dig ditch in
(ground); turn over the earth of (field
etc.) by digging succession of contiguous
ditches; ‖ cut groove in (wood etc.); proceed, make one's way, (*down, along*, etc.)
by ~ing; encroach (*up*)*on* (person's rights,
privacy, etc.); verge or border closely
(*up*)*on* (heresy, vulgarity, etc.). Hence
~'er [-ER¹] n. 2. n. Deep furrow or
ditch; (mil.) ditch often 7 ft deep with
earth thrown up to form parapet, as *open*
(begin digging) *the ~es, mount* (guard in)
the ~es. 3.*~-cart*, hand-cart on low wheels
for use in ~es; *~ coal*, soldier's lined or
padded mackintosh; *~ fever*, form of fever
affecting soldiers in ~es, spread by lice;
~ foot, affection of feet or legs with
sloughing etc. caused by much standing in
water; *~ mortar*, light simple kind throwing heavy charge of high explosive short
distance for use in ~es. [ME, f. OF
trenchier (& *trenche* n.) cut f. Rom.
*trincare f. L *truncare* TRUNCATE]

trĕnch'ant, a. Sharp, keen, as *~ sword,
blade*, (now rare in lit. sense); (fig., of
style, language, policy, etc.) penetrating, incisive, decisive, vigorous. Hence
trĕnch'ANCY n., ~LY² adv. [ME, f. OF,
part. as prec.]

trencher¹. See TRENCH.

trĕnch'er², n. Wooden platter now
chiefly used for cutting bread on at table;
(arch.) the pleasures of the table, eating,
(chiefly attrib. or in comb., as *~ com-
panions, ~-valiant; good, poor*, etc., *~-man*,
great, small, etc., eater); *~ cap*, square
college cap; *~-fed*, (of hounds) kept by
separate members of the hunt, not all
together in hunt kennels. [ME, f. AF
trenchour, OF *-eoir*, f. *trenchier* (prec.) +
-oir = L *-atorium*]

trĕnd, v.i., & n. 1. Have specified general
direction, bend or turn away in specified
direction, as *coast ~s* (towards the) *south*;

(fig.) be chiefly directed, have general tendency, (*towards* etc.). 2. n. General direction & tendency (esp. fig. of events, opinion, etc.). [ME ' revolve ' etc., OE *trendan* f. Gmc **trend-*, **trand-*, **trund-*; cf. MLG *trint*, *trent*, *trunt* aa. round, & TRUNDLE]

trĕn′tal, n. Set of 30 successive daily masses for the dead. [ME, f. OF *trentel* & med. L *trentale* f. L *triginta* thirty + -AL]

trente-et-quarante (see Ap.), n. = ROUGE¹-*et-noir*. [F, = 30 & 40]

trĕpăn′¹, n., & v.t. (-nn-). 1. Surgeon's cylindrical saw for removing part of bone of skull to relieve brain; borer for sinking shafts. 2. v.t. Perforate (skull) with ~. So **trĕpanA′TION**, ~n′ING¹, nn. [ME, f. OF *trepan(er)* n. & vb f. med. L *trepanum* f. Gk *trupanon* (*trupaō* bore f. *trupa* hole)]

trĕpăn′², v.t. (-nn-). Trap, ensnare, beguile, (*into*, *from*, place etc., *into doing*). [17th c., f. earlier *trapan* a decoy, prob. thieves' sl. f. TRAP¹]

trĕpăng′, n. Edible sea-slug used in China for soup. [f. Malay *trīpang*]

trĕphine′ (-ēn, -ĭn), n., & v.t. 1. Improved form of trepan with guiding centre-pin. 2. v.t. Operate on (skull, eyeball, person) with this. So **trĕphinA′TION** n. [orig. *trafine*, f. L *tres fines* three ends, after TREPAN¹]

trĕpidā′tion, n. Alarm, flurry; trembling of limbs e.g. in paralysis; (hist.) oscillation of ecliptic formerly assumed to account for precession of equinoxes etc. [f. L *trepidatio* (*trepidare* be agitated, tremble, f. *trepidus* flurried, see -ATION]

trĕs′pass, v.i., & n. 1. Make unlawful or unwarrantable intrusion (*on*, *upon*, land, rights, etc., or abs.; ~ *on* one's *preserves*, fig., meddle in a matter that he has made his own); make unwarrantable claim *on* (chiefly in polite formulas, as *shall ~ on your hospitality*); offend (*against* person, law, principle, rights; now literary), as *forgive them that ~ against us*. Hence ~ER¹ n. 2. n. Transgression of law or right; (law) any transgression that is not (misprision of) treason or felony; ~ing (see vb, 1st sense) on another's land with damage; (also *action of ~*) common-law action for recovery of damages for ~; ~*offering*, sacrifice atoning for ~ against Mosaic law. [ME; n. f. OF *trespas* f. *trespasser* pass over, trespass, f. med. L TRANS(*passare* PASS); vb f. n., or OF *trespasser*]

trĕss, n., & v.t. 1. Portion, lock, plait, of hair of human esp. woman's or girl's head; (pl.) hair of esp. woman's or girl's head. Hence (-)~ED² (-st), ~′Y², aa. 2. v.t. Arrange (hair) in ~es (chiefly in p.p.). [ME, f. OF *tresce*, *tresse*; vb. f. OF *trecier*, *tresser* (f. n.)]

trĕ′stle (sl), n. Supporting structure for table or flat form or carpenter's work etc., consisting of bar supported by two divergent pairs of legs or of two frames fixed at an angle or hinged; (also ~-*work*) open braced framework of wood or metal for supporting bridge etc.; (naut., also ~-*tree*) each of a pair of horizontal pieces on lower mast supporting topmast etc. [ME, f. OF *trestel* f. Gallo-Rom. *transtellum beam, dim. of L *transtrum*]

‖ **trĕt**, n. (hist.). Allowance of extra weight formerly made to purchasers of some goods for waste in transportation. [ME, prob. f. AF, OF *tret*, var. of *trait* draught; see TRAIT]

trevet. See TRIVET.

‖ **trews** (-ōōz), n. pl. Tartan trousers, esp. as worn by some Scottish regiments. [f. Ir. *trius*, Gael. *triubhas* (sing.); see TROUSERS]

trey (trā), n. Card, die, with three spots. [ME, f. AF, OF *treis*, *trei* three f. L *tres*]

tri-, pref. = L & Gk *tri-* three-, comb. form of L *tres*, Gk *treis* three, Gk *tris* thrice, having or composed of three, triple, as: ~*adelph′ous*, with 3 stamens in 3 sets; ~*an′drous*, with 3 stamens; ~*ap′sidal*, with 3 apses; ~*bās′ic*, with 3 hydrogen atoms replaceable by base or basic radical; ~*brăch′ial* (-k-), three--armed implement etc., esp. a flint implement; ~*cap′sular* (bot., zool.), with 3 capsules (to each flower); ~*carp′ous*, bearing 3 fruits or carpels; ~*centēn′ary*, = TERCENTENARY; ~*chlōr′ide* (-kl-), compound of element or radical with 3 atoms of chlorine; ~*′chord* (-k-) a. & n., three--stringed (instrument esp. lute), (of piano) with 3 strings to each note; ~*chromat′ic* (-kr-), three-coloured (~-*chromatic photography*, THREE-*colour process*), (of the eye) having the normal three colour sensations, i.e. red, green, & purple, so ~*chrōm′atism* (-kr-) n.; ~*′corn*, having 3 horns, (n., also ~′*corne*) three-cornered cocked hat; ~*corp′oral*, ~*corp′orate*, (her.) having 3 bodies & one head; ~*cotylēd′onous*, with 3 cotyledons; ~*crŏt′ic*, (of pulse) with 3 beats; ~*cŭs′pid*, with 3 cusps or points, as ~*cuspid valve* of heart, ~*cuspid murmur* (heard when this is deranged); ~*dac′tyl(ous)*, with 3 fingers or toes; ~*den′tate*, with 3 teeth or prongs; ~*di′gitate*, = ~*dactyl*; ~*dimen′sional*, of 3 dimensions; ~*fā′cial* a. & n., (of) the trigeminus; ~*flor′al*, ~*flor′ous*, bearing 3 flowers; ~*fōl′iate*, ~*fōl′iolate*, (of compound leaf) with 3 leaflets, (of plants) having such leaves; ~*fōl′iated*, (bot.) = prec., (archit.) trefoiled; ~*′form(ed)*, formed of 3 parts, having 3 forms or bodies; ~*furc′ate* (-at) a., divided into three forks, (v.t. & i., -at) divide thus; ~*gĕm′inal* a. & n., triple, (of) the ~geminus; ~*gĕm′inus*, cranial nerve with the 3 functions of motion, common sensation, & taste; ~*′glot*, written in 3 languages; ~*goneut′ic* (entom.), having 3

For other words in *tri-* see TRI-.

broods in a year; ~'gram, ~'graph, group
of 3 letters representing one sound;
~gynous (trīj⁴), having 3 pistils; ~hĕd'ral,
with 3 surfaces; ~jug'ate,~jug'ous,(-jŏŏ-),
(bot.), having, arranged in, 3 pairs;
~lăb'iate, three-lipped; ~lăm'inar, of
3 layers; ~lăt'eral a. & n. (adv. -lly), of 3
sides, (of dealings) to which there are 3
parties, (n.) triangle; ~lemm'a, choice
between 3 things; ~lĭn'ear, of 3 lines;
~ling'ual (-nggw-), of, expressed in, 3
languages; ~lĭt'eral, of 3 letters, (of Semitic languages) having (most of) their
roots in 3 consonants, so ~lĭt'eralism,
~literal'ity, nn.; ~'lith, monument of 3
stones, esp. two upright & one across
their tops, so ~lĭth'ic a.; ~lŏb'ate, three-
-lobed; ~lŏc'ular, with 3 cells or compartments; ~men'sual, ~mes'tr(i)al, occurring
every 3 months; trim'erous, of 3 members
or joints (also 3-merous); ~morph'ism,
~morph'ous, (biol., bot.), crystallog.),
existence, existing, in 3 distinct forms;
~nerv'ate, three-nerved; ~nŏd'al (anat.,
bot.), having 3 joints; ~nŏm'ial a. & n.,
(technical name, algebraical expression)
consisting of 3 terms; ~nŏm'ialism, use
of 3 terms in naming objects in natural
history; ~oe'cious (-ēsh-), having male,
female, & hermaphrodite flowers each on
different plants; ~ox'ide, oxide containing
3 oxygen atoms; ~penn'ate, = ~pinnate;
~pĕt'alous, having 3 petals; trĭph'thong,
3 vowels forming one sound; trĭphthong'al
(-nggl), so formed; ~phyll'ous, three-
-leaved; ~pinn'ate, having 3 series of
leaflets; ~răd'ial, ~răd'iate(d), radiating
in 3 directions; ~sēr'ial, ~sĕr'iate, (anat.,
bot.) disposed in 3 rows; ~sperm'ous,
containing 3 seeds; ~spor'ous, ~spor'ic,
having 3 spores; trĭs'tichous (-k-), arranged in 3 vertical rows; ~stigmat'ic,
~styl'ous, (bot.), having 3 stigmas, styles;
~sulc'ate, (bot.) three-grooved, (zool.)
divided into 3 digits or hoofs; ~tern'ate,
(bot.) thrice ternate, having 27 leaflets;
~'tone, (mus.) interval of 3 tones;
triv'alent (chem.), having combining
power of 3.

tri'able, a. That may be tried. [ME,
f. AF, as TRY + -ABLE]

triacŏntahĕd'ral, a. Having 30 sides or
surfaces. [f. Gk triakonta 30 + hedra base,
side, -AL]

tri'ad, n. Group of three; (chem.) element, radical, with combining power of
three; (mus.) chord of three notes, common chord; Welsh form of literary composition depending on arrangement in
groups of three. Hence triăd'IC a. [f.
F triade or LL f. Gk trias -ados (treis three,
see -AD)]

‖ **tri'age,** n. Refuse of coffee-beans. [F,
= sifting (as TRY, see -AGE)]

tri'al, n. 1. Process or mode of testing the
qualities of a thing, experimental treatment, test, as made ~ of his strength, was
found on ~ to be incompetent, shall subject

or put it to further ~, will make the ~ (try
the experiment), has been making ~s or
(attrib.) ~ ascents with an aeroplane; ~ of
the PYX; bicycle is hired, clerk employed,
on ~ (to be retained only if efficient), will
give you a ~ (employ you on ~); = ~
HEAT¹; = ~ match. 2. Trying thing or
experience or person, esp. hardship,
trouble, as old age has many ~s, fear you
will find the boy, the piano next door, a
great ~. 3. Judicial examination &
determination of issues between parties
by judge with or without jury or by
referee etc., as was on his ~ or stood
or underwent ~ for murder, granted a
new ~ (on ground of error or injustice
in former ~, or because of jury's failure
to agree). 4. ~ balance (of ledger in
double-entry book-keeping), comparison
of Dr & Cr totals, inequality of which
reveals certain errors in posting; ~ eights,
two experimental crews tried against
each other with a view to selection of
crew for boat-race; ~ match, game of
cricket, football, etc., in which players
who may be selected for an important
team take part; ~ trip, new vessel's trip
to test sailing qualities etc., (fig.) experiment. [AF trial, triel (TRY, -AL)]

tri'ăngle (-nggl), n. 1. Figure (esp. plane)
bounded by three (esp. straight) lines, as
equilateral, isosceles, scalene, right-angled.
~, spherical ~ (formed on surface of
sphere by intersection of three great
circles); any three points not in one
straight line together with the imaginary
lines joining them. 2. Implement etc. of
this shape, e.g. right-angled ~ as drawing-
-implement, (naut.) device of three spars
for raising weights, (mus.) rod of polished
steel in form of ~ open at one angle
sounded by striking with steel rod, (hist.)
frame of three halberds joined at top to
which soldier was bound for flogging; the
ETERNAL ~; ~s of the neck (regions into
which it is divided for surgical purposes);
(T~) a northern constellation. 3. Solution
of a ~, finding of the remaining angles &
sides when some are given; ~ of forces, ~
whose sides represent in magnitude &
direction three forces in equilibrium, fact
that such forces can always be represented by a ~. [ME, f. OF, or f. L
triangulum f. TRI(angulus ANGLE) a.]

triăng'ular (-ngg-), a. Of the shape of a
triangle, three-cornered, so triăng'ulOID
(-ngg-) a.; ~ treaty, duel, etc., (between
three parties); ~ compasses (with three
legs); ~ numbers, sums of the series 1, 2,
3, etc., taken to any number of terms,
e.g. 1, 6, 28, 55 (w. ref. to mode of disposing
such number of points in form of equilateral triangle); ~ pyramid (with ~ base).
Hence ~ITY (-nggŭlă'r-) n., ~LY² adv. [f.
LL triangularis (as prec., see -AR¹)]

triăng'ul|āte¹ (-ngg-), v.t. Make tri-
angular; divide (area etc.) into triangles
for surveying purposes; determine

(height, distance, etc.) thus. Hence ~ᴬᴸ TION n. [f. L, as TRIANGLE + -ATE³]

triăng′ūlate² (-ngg-), a. (zool.). Marked with triangles. Hence ~LY² adv. [f. med. L *triangulatus* (prec., -ATE²)]

Tri′ăs, n. (geol.). Division of rocks underlying the Jurassic. Hence **Triăss′ic** a. [as TRIAD, f. threefold subdivision in Germany]

triăt′ic stay, n. (naut.). Stay connecting masts in fore-&-aft-rigged ships. [orig. unkn.]

trib′adism, n. Unnatural vice between women. [f. L f. Gk *tribas -ados* lewd woman (*tribō* rub) + -ISM]

trib′al|ism, n. Tribal organization. So ~IZE v.t. [-ISM]

tribe, n. **1.** Group of primitive clans under recognized chiefs; (Rom. hist.) each of the political divisions (orig. three, probably representing clans, ultimately 35) of the Romans; any similar division whether of natural or political origin, e.g. *the twelve ~s* of the Israelites (*the ten ~s*, these without Judah & Benjamin; *the lost ~s*, the ten ~s after deportation by Shalmaneser). **2.** (zool., bot.). Group of plants or animals usu. ranking between genus & order. **3.** (usu. derog.). Set, number, of persons esp. of one profession etc., as *the whole ~ of parasites, actors, the scribbling ~*. **4.** ~*s′man*, member of a ~ or of one's own ~. Hence **trib′AL** a., **trib′alLY²** adv. [ME *tribu*, *tribe*, f. OF *tribu* or L *tribus*]

trib′lĕt, **trib′olĕt**, n. Mandrel used in making tubes, rings, etc. [f. F *triboulet*]

trībŏm′ĕter, n. Sledlike apparatus for measuring friction. [f. F *tribomètre* f. Gk *tribos* rubbing + -METER]

trib′răch (-k), n. Metrical foot ᴗ ᴗ ᴗ. Hence **tribrăch′ic** (-k-) a. [f. L f. Gk TRI(*brakhus* short)]

tribūlā′tion, n. Severe suffering or trial. [ME, f. OF (-*cion*), f. LL *tribulationem* (*tribulare* press, oppress, f. *tribulum* sledge for threshing, f. *terere trit-* rub, see -ATION)]

tribūn′al, n. Judgement-seat, seat or bench for judge(s) or magistrate(s); court of justice (rhet., & often fig., as *before the ~ of public opinion*); ‖ (in the 1914–18 war) local board hearing claims for exemption from military service. [f. F, or L (as TRIBUNE) f. *tribunal* (as -AL)]

trib′ūn|e¹, n. **1.** (Rom. hist.). (Also ~*e of the people*) each of (orig. two, ultimately ten) officers chosen by the people to protect their liberties against senate & consuls; kinds of military, fiscal, & other officers. **2.** (transf.). Popular leader or demagogue (*the T~e*, often as newspaper title). Hence or cogn. ~ATE¹(1), ~ESHIP, nn., ~ARY¹, ~i′ciAL, ~i′tial, (-shl), ~i′ciAN (-ïshn), aa. [ME, f. L *tribunus* (as TRIBE)]

trib′ūne², n. Raised floor for magistrate's chair in apse of Roman basilica; bishop's

throne, apse containing this, in basilica; platform, pulpit, esp. that used by speakers in French Chamber of Deputies. [F, f. It., f. med. L *tribuna* (prec.)]

trib′ūtar|ў, a. & n. **1.** Paying, subject to, tribute, as ~*y States*; contributory, auxiliary; (of river) serving to swell a larger river. **2.** n. ~y State, person, stream. Hence ~iLY² adv., ~iNESS n. [ME, f. L *tributarius* (as foll., see -ARY¹)]

trib′ūte, n. Money or equivalent paid periodically by one prince or State to another in acknowledgement of submission or as price of peace or protection, or by virtue of treaty; state of being subject to ~, as *was laid under ~*; (fig.) contribution, esp. thing done, said, given, etc., as mark of respect etc., as *the ~ of a tear, will not withhold my ~ of praise, the ~s* (gifts, compliments, attentions) *of her admirers, floral ~s* (flowers to actress, at funeral, etc.); ‖ (mining) proportion of ore, its equivalent, paid to miner for his work, ~*-work* (so paid). [ME, f. L *tributum* (*tribuere -ut-* give)]

tric′ăr, n. Three-wheeled motor-car. [TRI-]

trice¹, v.t. (naut.). Haul up (usu. *up*); haul up & secure in place (usu. *up*); tie up (usu. *up*). [ME, f. MDu. *trīsen*, MLG *trissen*]

trice², n. *In a ~*, in a moment. [ME, f. prec.]

tri′cĕps, a. & n. **1.** (Of muscle) three-headed. **2.** n. ~ muscle, esp. large muscle of back of arm. [L, f. TRI- + -*ceps* (*caput* head)]

trich′i. See TRICHINOPOLI.

trichi′asis (-k-), n. Urinary disease in which hairlike filaments appear in urine; disease of breasts in child-bearing women; inversion of eyelashes; disease marked by matted state of hair. [LL, f. Gk *trikhiasis* (as foll., see -ASIS)]

trich′in|a (-k-), n. (pl. ~*ae*). Hairlike worm parasitic in body of man, swine, rat, etc., usu. introduced into human body by use of imperfectly cooked pork, & causing often fatal disease. Hence ~i′ASIS, ~iZA′TION, ~OS′IS, nn., ~IZE(3) v.t., ~ŌSED²(-sd), ~OT′IC, ~OUS, aa. [mod. L, f. Gk *trikhinos* of hair (TRICHO-, -INE²)]

trichinŏp′oli, **trich′i**, n. Kind of Indian cheroot. [*Trichinopoli* in India]

trich|(o)- (-k-), comb. form of Gk *thrix trikhos* hair, as: ~′*ogen* n., ~*ŏ′genous* a., (preparation) promoting growth of hair; ~*ŏl′ogy*, study of the hair; ~*opath′ic* a., ~*ŏp′athy* n., (treatment) of diseases of hair.

trich′ōme (-k-), n. Hair, scale, or other outgrowth from epidermis of plant. [f. Gk *trikhōma* (*trikhoō* furnish with hair, see prec.)]

trichōs′is (-k-), n. Any disease of hair. [f. Gk *trichosis*, as TRICHO- + -OSIS]

trĭchŏt′om|ў (-k-), n. Division into three, esp. of human nature into body, soul, & spirit. Hence ~ous a. [f. Gk *trikha* three-fold (*treis* three) + ·TOMY]

trick, n., & v.t. & i. 1. Fraudulent device or stratagem, as *I suspect some* ~, ~ *of the* TRADE, *shall not serve me that* ~ *twice*. 2. Feat of skill or dexterity, knack, precise mode of doing or dealing with a thing, as *conjurer's* ~*s*, *do the* ~ (sl., = accomplish one's purpose), *my dog knows no* ~*s*, *I know a* ~ *worth two of that* (better expedient), *shall soon get or learn the* ~ *of it* (best way of doing or handling it), (attrib.) ~ *cyclist* etc. 3. Peculiar or characteristic practice, habit, mannerism, as *has a* ~ *of repeating himself*, *these are private-school* ~*s*, *style is disfigured by* ~*s*, *must cure himself of the* ~ *of archaism*. 4. Mischievous or foolish or discreditable act, practical joke, prank, as *is always playing mad* ~*s*, *a dirty or shabby or dog's* ~ *to play on anyone*. 5. (cards). The cards played in a round, as *take up the* ~; such round, point gained as result of this, as *won*, *lost*, *saved*, *the* ~; *the* ODD ~. 6. (naut.). Man's turn at helm, usu. two hours. 7. ~ *cyclist* (sl.), psychiatrist; ~-*line*, cord used in making changes in pantomime; ~ *scene* (made without dropping curtain); ~ *wig* (of which hair can be made to stand on end). 8. vb. Deceive by ~, cheat, (person, often *out of* thing, *into doing*, etc.); (of thing) foil, baffle, disappoint the calculations of, take by surprise; play ~s; (usu. *out or up*) dress, decorate, deck. Hence ~′ER¹, ~′ERY (4, 5), ~′STER, nn., ~′ISH (now rare, = TRICKY) a. [ME, f. OF dial. *trique*, f. *trikier* = OF *trichier* (cf. TREACHEROUS); vb f. n.]

trĭc′kl|e, v.i. & t., & n. 1. (Of liquid) flow in drops or in small stream, as *tears* ~*ed down her cheeks*, *water* ~*es through crevice*, (fig.) *the information* ~*ed* (came gradually) *out*; cause (liquid) to do this, pour out in drops; ~*e charger*, accumulator charger that works at a low rate. 2. n. ~ing stream. Hence ~ET¹ n., ~Y² a. [ME *trekel*, *trikle*, prob. imit.]

trĭck′sў, a. Playful, frolicsome; quaint. [f. TRICK; for ·sў cf. TIPSY]

trĭck′-trăck, **tĭck′-tăck**, n. Complicated form of backgammon. [f. F *trictrac*, prob. imit. of sound]

trĭck′|ў, a. Crafty, prone to deceit; skilful at evasion, resourceful, adroit; (of task etc.) requiring adroitness, full of pitfalls, ticklish. Hence ~ILY² adv., ~INESS n. [TRICK + ·Y²]

trĭclin′ium, n. (Rom. ant.; pl. -*ia*). Dining-table with couches along three sides, room containing this. [L, f. Gk TRI(*klinion* f. *klinē* couch)]

trĭc′oline, n. Fine cotton poplin resembling silk. [P]

trī′colour, **-or**, (-ŭler), a. & n. 1. (Also ~ED² a.) of three colours. 2. n. Flag of three colours in about equal proportions,

esp. French national standard of blue, white, & red, adopted during Revolution. [f. F TRI(*colore* f. LL as COLOUR)]

trī′cot (trēk′ŏ), n. Hand-knitted woollen fabric, imitation of this; kind of ribbed cloth; ~-*stitch*, kind of crochet stitch. [F, = knitting]

trī′cўcl|e, n., & v.i. (Ride on) three--wheeled pedal-driven vehicle. Hence ~IST(1) n. [F]

trī′dent, n. Three-pronged implement e.g. fish-spear; such spear or sceptre as attribute of Poseidon or Neptune. [f. L TRI(*dens* -*ntis* tooth)]

Trīden′tine, a. & n. 1. Of the Council of Trent (1545–63) esp. as basis of Roman Catholic doctrine & practice, as ~ *theology*. 2. n. Roman Catholic. [f. med. L *Tridentum* Trent + ·INE¹]

trĭdu′o (trēd′ŏŏ), **trid′ūum**, n. (R.-C. Ch.). Three days' service of prayer in preparation for saint's day or for obtaining saint's intercession. [(-*o* It.) f. L TRI(*duum* f. *dies* day) three days]

trĭenn′ial, a. & n. 1. Lasting, happening or done every, three years, as ~ *plants*, *parliaments*; *T*~ *Act* (requiring ~ parliaments, repealed 1716). 2. n. ~ plant; mass performed daily for three years for soul of dead person; every third anniversary of event. Hence ~LY² adv. [f. L TRI(*ennis* f. *annus* year) + ·AL]

trī′er, n. In senses of TRY, esp. (also *trior*) person appointed to decide whether challenge to juror is well founded. [·ER¹]

trī′erarch (-k), n. (Gk ant.). Commander of trireme; wealthy person compelled to build & equip trireme at his own expense. Hence ~AL (-k-) a. [f. L Gk TRI(*er-arkhos* f. *triērēs* trireme + *arkhō* rule]

trī′erarchў (-k-), n. Office, duty, of trierarch; (Athenian formation of fleet at expense of) the trierarchs. [f. Gk *trierarkhia* (prec., -Y¹)]

trĭf′id, a. (bot., zool.). Partly or wholly divided into three, three-cleft. [f. L TRI(*fidus* f. root of *findere* cleave)]

trī′fle, n., & v.i. & t. 1. Thing, fact, circumstance, of slight value or importance, as *wastes time on* ~*s*, *the merest* ~ *puts him out*, (iron.) *shall probably break our necks*, *but that is a* ~; small amount esp. of money, as *spare a* ~ *for the porter*, (adv.) *seems a* ~ (rather) *angry*; confection of whipped cream or white of eggs, with pastry etc. soaked in wine, fruit, almonds, etc.; common pewter; ~-*ring*, kinds of puzzle-ring. 2. vb. Talk or act frivolously; ~ *with*, treat (person, thing, matter) with flippancy or derision, refuse to take seriously, (also) occupy oneself carelessly with, toy with, (novel, cigarette, etc.); throw or fool *away* (time, energies, money, etc., *on* object); (part.) *a trifling error*, *correction*, *circumstance*, etc. (unimportant). Hence trĭf′lER¹ n., trĭf′linglў¹ adv. [ME & OF *trufle* parallel form of *truf(f)e* deceit, of unkn. orig.]

trifōr'ium, n. (pl. *-ia*). Gallery, usu. in form of arcade, above arches of nave & choir (& transepts) of church. [c. 1185 in Anglo-L, of unkn. orig.]

trig¹, a., & v.t. (-gg-). 1. Trim, spruce, smart. 2. v.t. Smarten, deck, (often *up, out*). [ME adj., f. ON *tryggr* faithful etc., = Goth. *triggws* TRUE]

trig², v.t. (-gg-), & n. 1. Check, stop, (wheel) with skid, stone, etc.; prop *up*. 2. n. Obstacle etc. used. [perh. f. ON *tryggja* to secure, f. *tryggr* firm, see prec.]

trig³, school abbr. of *trigonometry*.

trig'am|ous, a. Thrice married or having three wives or husbands at once; so ~IST, ~Y¹, nn.; (bot.) having male, female, & hermaphrodite flowers in same head (cf. TRIO*ecious*). [f. Gk TRI(*gamos* wedding) + -OUS]

trigg'er (-g-), n., & v.t. 1. Device for releasing spring or catch & so setting mechanism in action, esp. projecting tongue in firearm that liberates hammer of lock; agent that sets off a chain reaction; HAIR ~; ~-*happy*, apt to shoot on slight provocation. 2. v.t. (Also ~ *off*) set in action, initiate or precipitate. Hence (-)~ED² (-gerd) a. [17th c. *tricker* f. Du. *trekker* (*trekken* pull, cf. TREK)]

trig'lyph, n. Each of the grooved tablets alternating with metopes in Doric frieze. Hence ~AL, **triglyph'ic**(AL), aa. [f. L f. Gk TRI(*gluphos* f. *gluphō* carve)]

trig'ŏn, n. (Astrol.) each of four groups (*watery, earthly, airy, fiery, ~*) of three signs of zodiac; triangular instrument used in dialling; = TRINE; (Gk ant., also *trigōn'on*) triangular lyre or harp; (math.) triangle, whence **trigŏn'ic** a. [f. L f. Gk TRI(*gōnon* f. *gōnia* angle) triangle]

trig'on|al, a. (Math.) triangular; (bot., zool.) triangular in cross-section, as ~*al stem, antennae.* Hence or cogn. ~alLY³ adv., ~ous a. [f. prec. + -AL]

trigonŏm'ĕter, n. Instrument for solution of plane right-angled triangles by inspection; one versed in trigonometry. [TRIGON + -O- + -METER]

trigon|ŏm'ĕtrȳ, n. Branch of mathematics dealing primarily with relations of sides & angles of a triangle, much used in astronomy, surveying, & navigation. Hence ~omĕt'ric(AL) aa., ~omĕt'ricalLY² adv. [f. mod. L *trigonometria* (TRIGON + -O- + -METRY)]

trike, n. & v.i. (colloq.). = TRICYCLE. [abbr.]

tril'bȳ, n. ‖ ~ (*hat*), soft felt kind (colloq.). [f. G. du Maurier's novel *T~* (1894)]

trill, v.i. & t., & n. 1. (Of person or thing) give forth sound with tremulous vibration, as ~*ing laughter*; sing (t. & i.) in quavering manner, esp. (mus.) with shake. 2. n. Quavering sound, esp. (mus.) quick alternation of two notes a (semi)tone apart, shake; consonant pronounced with ~ing sound, e.g. *r*. [f. It. *trillare* (imit.)]

trill'ing, n. Compound crystal of three individuals; each of three children born at a birth. [f. TRI- + -LING, app. after Da., Sw. *trilling*, Du. *drieling*, G *drilling*]

trill'ion (-lyon), n. & a. ‖ A million million million; *(after F) a million million. Hence ~TH² a. & n. [F, f. TRI- on *million*, after *billion*]

tril'obite, n. Member of a large group of extinct arthropods characterized by a three-lobed body. [f. mod. L *Trilobites* (TRI-, Gk *lobos* lobe, -ITE¹)]

tril'ogȳ, n. (Gk ant.) set of three tragedies to be performed in immediate succession; set of three literary compositions, speeches, etc., each complete in itself but with common theme. [f. Gk TRI(*logia* -LOGY)]

trim, a., v.t. & i. (-mm-), & n. 1. In good order, well arranged or equipped, neat, spruce, whence ~'LY² adv., ~'NESS n. 2. vb. Set in good order, make neat or tidy, remove irregular or superfluous or unsightly parts from, (lamp or strictly its wick, hedge, beard, etc.); remove (such parts, often *off, away*) by clipping, pruning, planing, etc.; make (person, one*self*, often *up*) neat in dress &. appearance; ornament (dress etc. *with* ribbon, lace, etc.); (of school of fish) ~ (move along close to) *the shore*; (naut.) adjust balance of (ship, boat) by distribution of cargo or passengers etc., arrange (yards, sails) to suit wind, as ~ BY¹ *the head, stern*; hold middle course in politics or opinion, attach oneself to neither of contesting parties, be a time-server; (colloq.) rebuke sharply, thrash, cheat out of money, worst in bargain etc.; (colloq.) ~ person's *jacket*, flog him. 3. n. State, degree, of adjustment or readiness or fitness, as *found everything in perfect ~, am in no ~* (state of dress, health, etc.) *for rough work, in fighting ~*, (of ship, & fig.) ready for battle; good order (esp. naut.), as *in, out of, ~*; (naut.) ~ (relative position) of the masts. [formally repr. OE *trymman, trymian* make firm, arrange, f. *trum* strong; but the **vb** is undocumented from OE to 1500]

trim'ĕter, n. & a. (Verse) consisting of three measures (see DIMETER), esp. *iambic ~*, six-foot iambic line usual in ancient Greek dramatic dialogue. Hence **trimĕt'ric**(AL) aa. [f. L f. Gk TRI(*metros* f. *metron* measure)]

trimm'er, n. In vbl senses, esp.: one who trims articles of dress, as *coat, hat, ~*; person who stands neutral, time-server, (orig. of party following Marquis of Halifax 1680–90); kinds of instrument for clipping etc.; piece of timber framed across opening (e.g. for hearth) to carry ends of the truncated joists. [-ER¹]

For other words in *tri-* see TRI-.

trimm′ing, n. In vbl senses, esp.: orna-mentation of lace etc. on dress etc.; (pl., colloq.) leg of mutton etc. & ~s (acces-sories). [-ING[1]]

trine, a. & n. **1.** Threefold, triple, made up of three parts, whence **trin′AL, trin′ARY**[1], aa.; ~ aspersion or immersion, thrice sprinkling in baptism; (astrol.) of a ~, in ~. **2.** n. (astrol.). Aspect of two planets 120° apart; in ~, so related (to). [ME, f. OF trin(e) f. L trinus threefold (tres three)]

tringle (trĭng′gl), n. Curtain-rod: support-ing rod for canopy of bedstead; (archit.) small square moulding or ornament; (gunnery) bar on traversing-platform to check recoil. [F, of unkn. orig.]

trinitrotŏl′ūēne, -ŭŏl, n. A high ex-plosive (abbr. T.N.T. or TNT). [f. TRI-, NITRO-, TOLU-, -ENE, -OL]

trin′ity, n. **1.** Being three; group of three; the T~, union of three persons (Father, Son, Holy Spirit) in one Godhead, doc-trine of this, whence **Trinitār′IAN(ISM)** nn.; symbolical representation of the T~ in art. **2.** ~ ring, kinds of ancient bronze ring with three bosses etc. found in Ireland; T~ Sunday, next after Whit-sunday; ‖ T~ Brethren, members of T~ House, association concerned with licens-ing of pilots, erection and maintenance of lighthouses, etc.; ‖ T~ TERM. [ME, f. OF trinite f. LL trinitatem f. trinus TRINE, see -TY]

trink′ĕt, n. Trifling ornament, jewel, etc., worn on the person; small fancy article. Hence ~RY(1, 5) n. [16th c., of unkn. orig.]

tri′o (-ēŏ, -ĭō), n. (pl. ~s). **1.** (mus.). Com-position for three vocal or instrumental parts; set of three performers; second division of minuet, march, etc., orig. performed by ~ of instruments; piano ~, for violin, violoncello, & piano. **2.** Set of three persons etc.; three aces, kings, queens, or knaves, in piquet. [F f. It., f. tre three, after duo]

tri′ōde, a. (Of radio valves) having three electrodes. [f. TRI-+(ELECTR)ODE]

tri′ōle (trē-), n. (mus.). = TRIPLET. [dim. of TRIO]

tri′olĕt (or trē[2]), n. Poem of 8 (usu. 8--syllabled) lines with rhymes as shown, first line recurring as fourth & seventh & second as eighth (cat dog bat cat fat hog cat dog). [F (-LET)]

Triŏn′ĕs (-z), n. pl. = CHARLES'S WAIN, [L, = plough-oxen]

trior. See TRIER.

trip, v.i. & t. (-pp-), & n. **1.** Walk or dance with quick light tread, (fig., of rhythm etc.) run lightly, whence ~p′ingLY[2] adv. **2.** (arch.). Take journey or excursion, whence (in mod. use) ‖ ~p′ER[1] n., person who goes on a ~ esp. for a day to sea-side or other resort. **3.** Make false step, stumble, (often over obstacle); make mistake, commit inconsistency or inac-curacy or moral delinquency, as caught

him ~ping in his dates, all apt to ~; (of person or obstacle) cause (person) to stumble by entangling or suddenly arresting his feet (often up); detect (per-son) in blunder (often up). **4.** (Naut.) loose (anchor) from bottom by means of cable, turn (yard etc.) from horizontal to vertical position; release (part of ma-chine) suddenly by withdrawing catch etc. **5.** n. Journey, voyage, excursion esp. for pleasure, as round ~ (to a place & back), cheap ~s to the Riviera. **6.** Nimble step. **7.** Stumble (lit. & fig.); ~ping or being ~ped up. **8.** The fish caught during a voyage. **9.** ~-hammer, kind of TILT[1]--hammer. [ME, f. OF treper, trip(p)er, f. MDu. trippen skip, hop]

tripart′ite (or trĭp[2]), a. Divided into 3 parts; (bot., of leaf) divided into 3 seg-ments almost to the base; ~ indenture (with 3 corresponding parts or copies); made, existing, between 3 parties, as ~ treaty. Hence ~LY[2] adv., **tripart′ition** n. [f. L TRI(partitus p.p. of partiri divide]

tripe, n. Principal part of stomach of ox etc. as food, as will stand anything but ~ (arch. a ~); (now vulg., usu. pl.) entrails, belly; ‖ (sl.) inferior stuff, nonsense, easy bowling etc.; ~-de-roche (trĕp′dĕrōsh′) [F, lit. rock-~], bitter nutritive vegetable substance obtained from some lichens & used at a pinch by hunters etc. as food; ~′man, man who prepares & hawks ~. Hence **trip′ERY**(3) n. [ME, f. OF trip(p)e, of unkn. orig.]

tri′plāne, n. Aeroplane with three planes. [TRI-, PLANE[3]]

tri′ple, a., & v.t. & i. **1.** Threefold, of three parts (often in comb., as ~-headed, -nerved); T~ Alliance, (1) between Eng-land, Sweden, & Netherlands, in 1668 against Louis XIV, (2) between France, Great Britain, & Netherlands, in 1717 chiefly against Spain, (3) between Ger-many, Austria, & Italy, in 1882–3 against Russia & France; ~ crown, pope's tiara; T~ ENTENTE; (mus.) ~ time (of 3 or 9 beats in bar). **2.** vb. Increase (t. & i.) threefold; be three times as great or many as; alter (engine) to ~ expansion. [adj. (16th c.) F, or f. L triplus f. Gk triplous; vb (14th c.) f. LL triplare]

trip′lĕt, n. Set of three things; 3 verses rhyming together; (mus.) 3 notes per-formed in the time of two; each of 3 children born at a birth; (naut.) 3 links of chain between cable & anchor-ring. [f. prec.+-ET[1], after DOUBLET]

trip′lex, a. & n. **1.** Triple, threefold; ~ glass (P; also ~) unsplinterable glass used in motor-cars etc., consisting of a transparent sheet of plastic material between two sheets of glass. **2.** n. (mus.). Triple time; composition in three parts. [L TRI(plex -plicis f. plicare fold)]

trip′licate[1], a. & n. **1.** Threefold, esp. of which three copies are made, as ~ certificate; ~ ratio of two numbers, ratio of their cubes. 2. n. Each of a set of 3 copies or corresponding parts, state of being ~, as *document drawn up in* ~. [ME, f. L *triplicare* (TRIBLE), -ATE²]

trip′lic|āte², v.t. Treble, make triplicate. So ~A′TION, ~āTURE, nn. [-ATE³]

tri̅p′lĭce (-chä), n. = TRIPLE *alliance* (3). [It., = triple]

tripli̅ci̅tȳ, n. State of being triple. [ME, f. OF -*ite* or LL *triplicitas* (TRIPLEX, -ITY)]

trip′ŏd, n. Stool, table, utensil, resting on three feet or legs, whence ~AL a.; three--legged stand for supporting camera etc.; (Gk ant.) bronze altar at Delphi on which priestess sat to utter oracles, imitation of this esp. as prize in Pythian games etc. [f. L *tripus* f. Gk TRI(*pous podos* foot)]

trip′oli, n. = ROTTEN-*stone*. [f. *T*~ in Africa]

∥ trip′ŏs, n. (Camb. Univ.). Honours examination for degree of Bachelor of Arts. [as TRIPOD, w. ref. to stool on which B.A. sat to deliver satirical speech at commencement]

tripper. See TRIP.

trip′tych (-ĭk), n. Picture or carving on three panels side by side, set of three associated pictures so placed; set of three writing-tablets hinged or tied together; triangular plate on motor-car serving as a customs international pass. [f. TRI- after DIPTYCH]

∥ tripŭd′iāte, v.i. (pedant.). Dance for joy; dance in triumph or contempt *upon*. [f. L *tripudiare* (*tripudium* a dance, perh. f. TRI-, *pes pedis* foot), -ATE³]

triquĕt′ra, n. (pl. *-ae*). Symmetrical ornament of three interlaced arcs. [L, fem. of *triquetrus*) three-cornered]

triquĕt′rous, a. Three-cornered, esp. (bot., of stem) having 3 acute angles. Hence ~LY² adv. [f. L as prec. + -OUS]

trir′ēme, n. Ancient esp. Greek warship with three banks of oars. [f. L TRI(*remis* f. *remus* oar)]

Trĭsăg′ion (-g-), n. Hymn esp. in Oriental Churches with triple invocation of God as holy. [f. Gk *trisagios* (*tris* thrice + *hagios* holy)]

trisĕct′, v.t. Divide into three (usu. equal) parts. Hence trisĕc′tion n. [f. TRI- + L *secare sect*- cut]

tris′mus (-z-), n. (path.). Lockjaw [mod. L, f. Gk *trismos* = *trigmos* a scream, grinding]

trist′ful, a. (arch.). Sad. [obs. *trist* adj. f. OF *triste* f. L *tristis* sad + -FUL]

trisyll′able, n. Word of three syllables. trisyllăb′ic a., trisyllăb′ically adv. [f. TRI- + SYLLABLE]

trităg′onist, n. Third actor in Greek play (cf. DEUTERAGONIST). [f. Gk *tritagōnistēs* (*tritos* third + *agōnistēs* actor)]

trite, a. (Of expression, sentiment, quotation, etc.) commonplace, hackneyed,

worn out. Hence ~LY² adv., ~′NESS n. [f. L *terere trit*- rub]

tri′the|ism, n. Doctrine that there are (esp. that Father, Son, & Holy Spirit are) 3 Gods. So ~IST II., ~is′tic(AL) aa. [TRI-]

trit′ium, n. (chem.). Heavy isotope of hydrogen with mass about three times that of ordinary hydrogen, cf. DEUTERIUM. [f. Gk *tritos* third + -IUM]

Trit′on, n. (Gk myth.) son of Poseidon & Amphitrite, each of a race of minor sea--gods usu. represented as men with fishes' tails & occas. with forefeet of horse & carrying shell-trumpet; ~ *among the* MINNOWS; (*t*~) kinds of gastropod & salamander. [L, f. Gk *Tritōn*]

trit′ūr|āte, v.t. Grind to fine powder; grind with molar teeth, masticate thoroughly. Hence or cogn. ~ABLE a., ~A′TION, ~ātoR, nn. [f. LL *triturare* f. L *tritura* rubbing, as TRITE, see -URE & -ATE³]

tri′umph, n., & v.i. 1. (Rom. ant.) procession & ceremony in honour of victory & victorious general; state of being victorious or successful, signal success, great achievement, thing that constitutes this, as *returned home in* ~, *has achieved great* ~s, *the* ~s *of science, hat is a* ~ *of ugliness*; joy at success, manifestation of this, exultation, as *great was his* ~ *on hearing* etc., *could detect no* ~ *in his eye*. 2. v.i. (Rom. ant.) enjoy a ~; gain victory, be successful, prevail, (*over* enemy, opposition, etc.); exult (*over* fallen enemy etc., or abs.), whence ~ĭNGLY² adv. [ME, n. f. OF *triumphe* f. L *triumphus*; vb f. OF *triumpher* f. L *triumphare*]

triūm′phal, a. Of, used in, celebrating, a triumph, as ~ *car, progress, hymn*; ~ *crown* (Roman general's laurel wreath); ~ *arch* (built to commemorate victory etc.). [ME, f. OF, or L *triumphalis* (as prec., -AL)]

triūm′phant, a. Victorious, successful; (of person, speech, voice, etc.) exulting. Hence ~LY² adv. [ME, f. OF, or L *triumphare* (as prec., -ANT²)]

triŭm′vir, n. (pl. ~s, ~ī). (Rom. ant.) each of three men united in office; (Rom. hist.) each member of first or second triumvirate. Hence ~AL a. [L (*trium*, gen. of *tres* three, +*vir* man)]

triŭm′virate, n. Office of a triumvir; set of triumviri; (Rom. hist.) *first* ~, (coalition 60 B.C. between) Pompey, Julius Caesar, & Crassus, *second* ~, (that in 43 B.C. between) Mark Antony, Octavian, & Lepidus; party, set, of three. [f. L *triumviratus* (prec., see -ATE¹)]

tri′ūne, a. Three in one, as ~ *Godhead*. Hence triūn′ITY n. [f. TRI- + L *unus* one]

triv′ĕt, n. Iron tripod for holding cooking--vessels by the fire; iron bracket designed to hook on to bars of grate for similar purposes; *right* (orig. = steady) *as a* ~, (colloq.) all right (adj. & adv.), in good health or position or circumstances; ~ *table* (with three feet). [ME *trevet*, app. f. L TRI(*pes pedis* foot) three-footed]

triv'ia, n. pl. Trifles, trivialities [mod. L, see foll.]

triv'ial, a. Of small value or importance, trifling, as ~ *matters*, *a* ~ *loss* (of something ~), *raised* ~ *objections*; (of person) trifling, shallow, lacking ability or moral qualities; commonplace, humdrum, as *the* ~ *round* (of daily life etc.); (bot., zool., of name) popular, not scientific, also, specific opp. to *generic*. Hence or cogn. ~ISM(2, 4), trivi̇āl'ITY, ~NESS, nn., ~IZE(3) v.t., ~LY² adv. [f. L *trivialis* commonplace f. TRI(*vium* f. *via* road) place where three ways meet, see -AL]

triv'ium, n. (hist.). (In medieval schools) the first three liberal arts, grammar, rhetoric, & logic. [see prec.]

-trix, suf. forming fem. agent nn. corresp. to masc. nn. in -*tor*, f. L -*trix* -*tricis*, chiefly in legal terms (*executrix*, *adminis-tratrix*).

troat, v.i., & n. (Make) cry of rutting buck. [cf. OF *trout*, *trut*, int. for urging on hunting dogs etc.]

trōc'ăr, n. (med.). Instrument used in dropsy etc. for withdrawing fluid from body. [f. F *troquart*, *trois-quarts*, *trocart* (*trois* three + *carre* side, face of instrument)]

trochā'ĭc (-k-), a. & n. **1.** (Composed) of trochees, as ~ DIMETER, TETRA*meter*. **2.** n. pl. ~ verse. [f. F (-*ique*) or L f. Gk *trokhaïkos* (as TROCHEE, see -IC)]

trŏch'al (-k-), a. (zool.). Wheel-shaped. [f. Gk *trokhos* wheel (*trekhō* run) + -AL]

trochăn'ter (-k-), n. (anat., zool.). Each of several bony processes on upper part of thighbone; second joint of insect's leg. [F, f. Gk *trokhantēr* (*trekhō* run)]

trŏche (-k, -sh, -ch, trŏk'ē), n. Small medicinal circular cake or lozenge. [back form. f. *troches*, pl. of obs. *trochisk* f. OF *trochisque* f. LL f. Gk *trokhiskos* dim. of *trokhos* wheel]

trŏch'ee (-kĭ), n. Metrical foot — ◡. [f. L f. Gk *trokhaios* (*pous*) running foot (*trekhō* run)]

trŏch'ĭl(us) (-k-), n. Kinds of small bird esp. (1) humming-bird, (2) bird mentioned by ancient writers as picking crocodile's teeth. [f. L f. Gk *trokhilos* (*trekhō* run)]

trŏch'lē|a (-k-), n. (anat.; pl.~*ae*). Pulley-like part or arrangement. Hence ~AR¹ (anat., bot.), ~ATE² (bot.), aa. [f. L *trochlea* pulley, f. Gk *trokhileia*]

trŏch'oid (-k-), a. & n. **1.** (Anat.) rotating on its own axis; (of curve) generated by a point in the plane of one curve that rolls on another; (conch.) top-shaped. **2.** n. ~ joint, ~ curve, kinds of gasteropod. Hence trochoid'AL (-k-) a. [f. Gk *trok-hoeidēs* wheel-like (TROCHAL, -OID)]

trochŏm'eter (-k-), n. = HODOMETER. [as TROCHAL + -METER]

trod(den). See TREAD.

trŏg'lody̆t|e, n. Cave-dweller, esp. of prehistoric W. Europe (often attrib.); (fig.) hermit; kinds of wren & anthropoid ape. Hence or cogn. trŏglodȳt'IC(AL) aa., ~ISM(2) n. [f. L (-*ta*) f. Gk *trōglodutēs* (*trōglē* cave + *duō* enter)]

troik'a, n. (Vehicle with) team of three horses abreast. [Russ.]

trois-temps (see Ap.), a. & n. ~ (*waltz*), waltz in ordinary time (cf. DEUX-TEMPS). [F, = three-time]

Trōj'an, a. & n. (Inhabitant) of Troy; ~ *War* (between Greeks under Agamemnon & ~s under Priam); (fig.) person who works or fights or endures courageously, esp. *like a* ~. [orig. *Troyan*, *Troian*, f. L *Troianus* f. *Troia* Troy]

trŏll¹, v.t. & i., & n. **1.** Sing out in care-free spirit; fish for, fish in (water), fish, with rod & line & dead bait or with spoon-bait (~*ing-spoon*) drawn along behind boat; (arch.) cause (bottle) to circulate at table etc. **2.** n. Reel of fishing-rod; ~ing-spoon. [ME ' stroll, roll '; cf. OF *troller* to quest, (M)HG *trollen* roll]

trŏll², n. Supernatural being, giant or (later) friendly but mischievous dwarf, in Scandinavian mythology. [f. ON & Sw. *troll*, Da. *trold*]

trŏll'ey (pl. ~s), **trŏll'y̆,** n. Kind of truck that can be tilted; ‖ costermonger's cart pushed by hand or drawn by donkey; ‖ low truck worked by hand-lever along the rails for conveying railwaymen to work; (also ~-*table*) small table usu. on castors for use in serving food; apparatus consisting of wheel, pole, etc. used for collecting current in electric street-railway (‖ ~ *bus*, trackless electric bus running on a highway and collecting current from overhead ~-wires; *~-car*, electric street-car); (also ~-*lace*) lace of which the pattern is outlined with thick thread. [of dial. orig., perh. f. TROLL¹]

trŏll'op, n. Slatternly woman; prostitute. Hence ~ISH¹, ~Y², aa. [perh. rel. to TROLL¹, or TRULL]

trŏm'ba, n. (mus.). Trumpet. [It.]

trŏm'bōn|e, n. Large musical instrument of trumpet family with sliding tube or with valves. Hence ~IST(3) n. [It. (as prec., see -OON)]

trŏmm'el, n. (mining). Revolving cylindrical sieve for cleaning ore. [G, = drum]

tromŏm'ĕter, n. Instrument for measuring very slight earthquake shocks. [f. Gk *tromos* trembling + -METER]

trŏmpe, n. Apparatus for producing blast in furnace. [F, = TRUMP¹]

troop, n., & v.i. & t. **1.** Assembled company, assemblage of persons or animals, as *a* ~ *of school-children*, *of antelopes*, *surrounded by* ~s *of friends*; (pl.) soldiers, as *lost a third of his* ~s, HOUSEHOLD ~s; cavalry unit consisting of usu. 60 troopers with two lieutenants & captain (cf. COMPANY), command of this (*get one's* ~, *be*

Z

promoted captain); unit of artillery & armoured formation; particular call of drum as signal for marching; company of performers, troupe; ~-carrier, large aircraft for transporting ~s; ~-horse, cavalry horse; ~-ship, transport. 2. vb. Assemble, flock together, (often up, together, etc.); move along in a ~ (along, in, out, etc.); (w. pl. subject) walk hurriedly off, away; form (regiment) into ~s; ‖ ~ing the colour, ceremony at public mounting of garrison guards. [f. F troupe f. med. L troppus flock, of Gmc orig.]

troop′er, n. Horse-soldier, private soldier in cavalry and armoured unit; swear like a ~ (much); cavalry horse; troopship. [-ER¹]

tropae′olum, n. Indian cress, kinds of trailing plant with spurred yellow or scarlet flowers including NASTURTIUM (2nd sense). [mod. L f. Gk tropaion TROPHY, w. ref. to likeness of flower & leaf to helmet & shield]

trōpe, n. Figurative (e.g. metaphorical, ironical) use of a word; (eccl.) phrase or verse introduced as embellishment into some part of the mass. [f. L f. Gk tropos turn, way, trope, (trepō turn)]

trŏph′ic, a. Concerned with nutrition, as ~ nerves. [f. Gk trophikos (trophē nourishment f. trephō nourish + -IC)]

trŏpho-, comb. form of Gk trophē food, as ~neurōs′is, defective nutrition due to nervous derangement.

trŏph′|ў, n. (Gk ant.) arms etc. of vanquished enemy set up on field of battle or elsewhere to commemorate victory; Roman memorial of victory in imitation of this but usu. permanent; anything, e.g. captured standard, kept as memorial of victory (lit. & fig.); prize; memento; ornamental group of symbolic or typical objects arranged on wall etc. Hence (-)~iED² (-ĭd) a. [f. F trophée f. L f. Gk tropaion (tropē rout f. trepō turn)]

trŏp′ic, n. & a. 1. Parallel of latitude 23° 27′ north (~ of Cancer) or south (~ of Capricorn) of the equator; the ~s, region between these; each of the two corresponding circles on celestial sphere where sun appears to turn after reaching greatest declination; ~-bird, kinds of bird like tern seen usu. in the ~s. 2. adj. = foll. exc. last sense. [ME, f. L f. Gk tropikos (kuklos) tropic (circle) f. tropē turning, solstice, (trepō turn), see -IC]

trŏp′ical, a. Of, peculiar to, suggestive of, the tropics, as ~ plants, diseases, heat, abscess (of liver, induced by residence in hot climate); ~ year (between two successive passages of sun through same equinox); (fig.) fervid, passionate; [f. TROPE] figurative. Hence ~LY² adv. [-AL]

trŏpĭcopŏl′ĭtan, n. & a. (Animal, plant) confined & common to the tropics. [f. TROPIC on cosmopolitan]

tropŏl′ogў, n. Figurative use of words; figurative interpretation esp. of the Scrip-

tures, so trŏp′ɪsT(2)n. Hence **trŏpolŏ′gɪ-CAL** a., **trŏpolŏ′gĭcally²** adv. [f. LL f. Gk tropologia (TROPE, -LOGY)]

trŏp′opause (-z), n. Narrow layer between troposphere & stratosphere. [f. Gk tropos turn + PAUSE]

trŏp′osphēre, n. Layer of atmospheric air extending about seven miles upwards from the earth's surface, in which temperature falls with height (cf. STRATO-SPHERE). [f. Gk tropos turn + SPHERE]

trŏpp′ō, adv. (mus.). Too, as andante etc. ma non ~ (but not too much so). [It.]

trŏt, v.i. & t. (-tt-), & n. 1. (Of horses etc.) proceed at steady pace faster than walk lifting each diagonal pair of legs alternately with brief intervals during which body is unsupported; cause (horse etc.) to do this; (of person) run at moderate pace esp. with short strides (often along etc.); perform (distance) by ~ting; bring (person, horse, etc.) to specified condition by ~ting, as ~led him off his legs, to death; ~ out, cause (horse) to ~ to show his paces, (fig.) produce, introduce, (person, thing, superior information, subject) to excite admiration. 2. n. Action, exercise, of ~ting, as proceeded at a ~, went for a ~; (fig.) brisk steady movement or occupation, as kept him on the ~ (busy); ‖ toddling child. [ME, f. OF troter f. n. f. OF trot]

trŏth, n. (arch.). Truth, esp. (in) ~, truly, upon my word; plight one's ~, pledge one's word esp. in betrothal. [ME trowthe, for OE trēowth TRUTH]

trŏtt′er, n. In vbl senses; also or esp.: horse of special breed noted for trotting; (pl.) animal's feet used as food, as pigs', sheep's, ~s; (joc.) human foot. [TROT, -ER¹]

trŏttoir′ (-twahr), n. Side pavement. [F]

trŏt′ўl, n. (chem.). Trinitrotoluene. [(trini)trol(oluene) + -YL]

trou′badour (-ōō-, -oor), n. Lyric poet of a class originating in Provence (cf. TROU-VÈRE) in 11th c. [F, f. Pr. trobador f. trobar (F trouver) find, invent, compose in verse]

trou′ble (trŭb-), v.t. & i., & n. 1. Agitate, disturb, be disturbed or worried, as ~d waters, don't let it ~ you, don't ~ about it, has been ~d about or with money matters, a ~d countenance; afflict, as am ~d with neuralgia, how long has it been troubling you?; subject, be subjected, to inconvenience or exertion (chiefly in polite formulas), as may I ~ you to shut the door?, to mind your own business?, will ~ you for (to pass) the mustard, sorry to ~ you, don't ~ (to explain etc., or abs.), why should I ~ (myself) to explain? 2. n. Vexation, affliction, as has been through much ~, till this great ~ came upon them, life is full of small ~s; disease, as liver, digestive, ~s; inconvenience, unpleasant exertion, source of this, as did it to spare you ~, shall not put you to any ~ in the matter, fear the child is a great ~ to you, will never take *the* ~ *to write, is incapable of taking* ~, *an omelette is no* ~ (*to make*), *French beans are a great* ~ *to prepare,* (as polite formula) *no* ~ (*at all*); *ask* or *look for* ~ (colloq.), meddle, be rash, etc.; *be in, get into,* ~, incur censure, punishment, etc.; (mining) small fault; **~-shooter* (colloq.), man employed to detect and correct (esp. mechanical) faults. [ME, f. OF *trubler* etc., f. Rom. **turbulare* = cl. L *turbidus*; n. f. OF *truble* (f. vb)]

trou'blesome (trŭbls-), *a.* (Of person or thing) causing trouble, vexatious. Hence ~LY² *adv.*, ~NESS *n.* [-SOME]

trou'blous (trŭb-), *a.* (arch.). Full of troubles, agitated, disturbed, as ~ *times.* [ME, f. OF *troubleus* (TROUBLE, -OUS)]

trough (-ŏf, -awf, -ŭf), *n.* Long narrow open wooden or other receptacle for holding water or food for sheep etc., kneading dough, washing ore, etc.; wooden or other channel for conveying liquid; ~ *of the sea,* hollow between two waves; ~ *of barometric depression,* line of greatest depression in area of moving barometric pressure. [OE, OS, ON *trog,* OHG *troc,* f. Gmc **trugaz,* cogn. w. TREE]

trounce, *v.t.* Beat severely, castigate, (lit. & fig.). Hence **troun'CING**¹ *n.* [16th c. ' afflict ', of unkn. orig.]

troup|e (-ōō-), *n.* Company of actors, acrobats, etc. Hence ~'ER¹ *n.*, member of a theatrical ~e. [F, see TROOP]

trous'er (-z-), *n.* (Pl., also *pair of* ~s) two-legged outer garment reaching from waist to ankles; (vulg.) pair of ~s, as *here, again, is a smart & dressy* ~; ~*-button* (of certain sizes & materials); ~ or ~s *pocket* (esp. as holding one's money, or hands when idle); ~*-stretcher,* apparatus for stretching ~s to preserve shape; early 19th-c. woman's long frilled drawers reaching to ankles. Hence ~ED²(-zerd) *a.*, ~ING¹(3) *n.* [extended pl. form, after *drawers,* of arch. *trouse* sing., f. Ir. (& Sc. Gael.) *triubhas* TREWS]

trousseau (trōōsō', trŏŏ'sō), *n.* (pl. ~*s,* or ~*x* pr. -z). Bride's outfit of clothes etc. [F, lit. bundle, dim. of *trousse* TRUSS]

trout, *n.* (pl. usu. same), & *v.i.* **1.** Kinds of freshwater fish esteemed as food & game; ~*-coloured,* (of white horse) speckled with black, bay, or sorrel. **2.** *v.i.* Fish for ~. Hence ~'LET, ~'LING¹, *nn.,* ~'Y² *a.* [OE *truht* f. LL *tructa*]

trouvaille (see Ap.), *n.* Lucky find, windfall. [F]

trouvère (trōōvār'), *n.* Epic poet of a class originating in N. France (cf. TROUBADOUR) in 11th c. [OF nom. form (acc. *trovèor*) used as equivalent of Pr. (acc.) *trobador,* see TROUBADOUR]

trove. See TREASURE.

trov'er, *n.* (law). Acquisition of personal property; common-law action to recover value of personal property wrongfully taken or detained. [OF = find (-ER⁴)]

‖ **trow** (-ō, -ow), *v.t.* (arch.). Think, believe; (added to question) *what ails him, (I)* ~ (I wonder)? [OE *trūwian* (*trūwa* faith), *trēowian* (*trēowe* faith)]

trow'el, *n.,* & *v.t.* (-ll-). **1.** Mason's or bricklayer's flat-bladed tool for spreading mortar etc.; *lay it on with a* ~, (fig.) flatter grossly; gardener's scoop for lifting plants etc. **2.** *v.t.* Apply (plaster etc.) dress (wall etc.), with ~. [ME, f. OF *truele* f. med. L *truella* f. L *trulla* dim. of *trua* ladle etc.]

troy, *n.* (Also ~ *weight*) system of weights used for gold & silver (cf. AVOIRDUPOIS); as *weighs 3 lb. 5 oz* ~, ~ *pound contains 12 oz, 5760 grains.* [ME, prob. f. *Troyes,* town in France]

tru'ant (-ōō-), *n., a.,* & *v.i.* **1.** One who absents himself from place of work, esp. child who stays away from school without leave; *play* ~, stay away thus; ~*-school* (hist.), industrial school for ~ children. **2.** *adj.* (Of person, conduct, character, thoughts, etc.) shirking, idle, loitering, wandering. **3.** *v.i.* Play ~. Hence **tru'ANCY** *n.,* ~LY² *adv.,* (-ōō-). [ME & OF, prob. f. Celt. (W *truan,* Gael. *truaghan,* wretched)]

truce (-ōō-), *n.* (Agreement for) temporary cessation of hostilities (FLAG⁴ *of* ~); respite from pain etc., rest from work etc. (*a* ~ *to* —, arch., demand that — shall cease); ~ *of God* (hist.), suspension of private feuds esp. during certain church festivals etc. Hence ~'LESS *a.,* **tru'CIAL** (-ōōshl) *a.,* of or bound by a ~ (only in ref. to ~ of 1835 between Britain & certain Sheikhs of Oman Peninsula, as in *trucial chiefs*). [ME *trewes,* pl. of *trewe,* f. OE *trēow* (Goth. *triggwa*) compact, faith, see TRUE]

truck¹, *v.i.* & *t.,* & *n.* **1.** Make an exchange, trade, bargain, (*with* person *for* thing); exchange (thing *for* another); hawk (wares) about. **2.** *n.* Exchange, barter, traffic, (*have no* ~ *with,* avoid dealing with); small wares; **market-garden produce*; (colloq.) rubbish, (fig.) nonsense, as *shall stand no* ~; (hist.; also ~ *system, tommy*) practice of paying workmen in goods instead of money or in money on the understanding that they will buy provisions etc. of their employers, *T*~ *Acts* (of 1831 & 1870, providing for suppression of or inquiry into ~ system), ~ *shop* (conducted on ~ system). [ME, f. OF *troquer,* = med. L *trocare*; n. f. AF *truk,* OF *troque* (f. *troquer*)]

truck², *n.,* & *v.t.* **1.** Strong usu. four or six wheeled vehicle for heavy goods; ‖ open railway wagon; motor vehicle for transporting goods, troops, etc.; porter's two, three, or four, wheeled barrow for luggage at railway station etc.; set of wheels in framework for supporting whole or part of railway-carriage etc.; (naut.) wooden disc at top of mast with holes for halyards; (now rare) small tireless wheel; ~*-bolster,* crossbeam on car~

supporting one end. 2. v.t. Convey on ~.
Hence ~'AGE(3, 4) n. [f. L f. Gk *trokhos*
wheel; or short for TRUCKLE in sense
' wheel, pulley ']

trŭc'kle, v.i. & n. 1. Submit obsequiously, cringe, (*to*), whence **trŭck'lER**[1] n.
2. n. (Usu. ~-*bed*) low bed on wheels that
may be wheeled under another, esp. as
formerly used by servants etc. [ME =
AF *trocle* f. L TROCHLEA; vb f. (to sleep in
a) *truckle-bed*]

trŭc'ŭl|ent (*or* trōō-), a. Of or showing
bellicose aggressive merciless temper.
Hence *or* cogn. ~ENCE, ~ENCY, nn.,
~entLY[2] adv. [f. L *truculentus* (*trux trucis*
fierce, see -LENT]

trŭdge, v.i. & t., & n. 1. Walk esp. laboriously, perform (distance) thus. 2. n. Such
walk. [16th c., of unkn. orig.]

trŭdg'en, n. ~ (*stroke*), swimming with
alternate right & left over-arm strokes &
ordinary leg action. [J. *T~,* person]

true (-ōō), a., adv., & v.t. 1. In accordance
with fact or reality, not false or erroneous,
as *his story is* ~, *that is only too* ~, *is it* ~
that he refused?; *a dream came* ~ (was
realized in fact); (as formula of concession), ~, *it would cost more.* 2. In accordance with reason or correct principles
or received standard, rightly so called,
genuine, not spurious or hybrid or
counterfeit or merely apparent, having
all the attributes implied in the name, as
could not form a ~ *judgement, frog is not a*
~ *reptile, is a* ~ *benefactor, the* ~ *heir,* ~
ribs (complete, articulating with breast-
bone, not floating), ~ HORIZON. 3. Accurately conforming *to* (type etc.). 4. (Of
voice) in perfect tune. 5. Loyal, constant,
adhering faithfully, (*to* one's word, friend,
one*self,* etc.; often ~ *as steel*). 6. (Of
wheel, post, beam,'etc.) in correct position,
balanced or upright or level. 7. (arch.).
Not given to lying, veracious; honest, as
~ *men.* 8. ~ *bill,* bill of indictment endorsed by grand jury as being sustained
by evidence; ~-*blue* a. & n., (person) of
uncompromising principles or loyalty;
~*-born,* of genuine birth, truly such by
birth, as *a* ~-*born Englishman;* ~*-bred,* of
genuine or good breed; ~-*hearted*(*ness*);
~*-love,* person truly loved or loving,
sweetheart, plant with four leaves
arranged like ~-*love*(*r's*) *knot* (kind of
double knot with interlacing bows on
each side); ~'*penny* (arch.), honest fellow.
9. adv. Truly (rare exc. w. certain vbs, as
tell me, aim, breed, ~). 10. v.t. Bring
(tool, wheel, frame, etc.) into exact position or form required. Hence ~'NESS n.
(rare). [OE *trēowe,* OS, OHG *triuwi,*
ON *tryggr,* Goth. *triggws,* f. n. repr. by
OE *trēow.* f. Gmc **triww-,* see TRUCE]

trŭf'fl|e (*or* trōō-), n. Subterranean fun-
gus used for seasoning dishes. Hence
~ED[2] (-ld) a. [prob.' f. MDu. *truffel,* f. obs.
F *truffel* (mod. *truffe*))

‖ **trŭg,** n. Wooden milk-pan; shallow gar-

den basket made **or** wood strips. [perh.
dial. var. of TROUGH]

tru'ism (-ōō-), n. A self-evident or indisputable truth; proposition that states
nothing not already implied in one of its
terms (e.g. *I don't like my tea too hot* = *I
don't like it hotter than I like it*); hackneyed
truth, platitude. [f. TRUE + -ISM]

trŭll, n. (arch.). Prostitute. [16th c.,
= G *trulle,* TROLLOP]

tru'lў (-ōō-), adv. Sincerely, genuinely, as
am ~ *grateful, a* ~ *alarming state of affairs,
a* ~ *courageous act*; (as purely neutral
formula for closing letter) *yours* (*very*) ~
W. Jones, (hence, joc.) *won't do for yours*
~ (me); (usu. parenthet., & now chiefly
literary or arch.) really, indeed, as ~, *I
should be puzzled to say*; faithfully, loyally,
as *has served him* ~; accurately, truth-
fully, as *it has been* ~ *stated, is not* ~
represented. [OE *trēowlīce* (TRUE, -LY[2])]

truneau (trōōmō'), n. (archit.; pl. ~*x*).
Piece of wall, pillar, between two open-
ings, e.g. pillar dividing large doorway.
[F]

trŭmp[1], n. (arch., poet.). Trumpet, its
sound, as *last* ~, ~ *of doom.* [ME & OF
trompe, of Gmc. orig.]

trŭmp[2], n., & v.t. & i. 1. Each card of a
suit temporarily ranking above others, as
a call for ~s (conventional signal to partner to lead ~s); ~ *card,* card turned up to
determine which suit shall be ~s, any
card of this suit, (fig.) valuable resource;
(colloq.) person of admirable courage, resource, generosity, etc., excellent fellow;
put person to his ~s, (fig.) reduce him to
his last resources; *turn up* ~s (colloq.),
turn out better than was expected, (also)
have a stroke of luck. 2. vb. Defeat (card)
with a ~, play a ~ (also fig.); ~ *up,* fabricate, forge, (story, excuses, etc.). [cor-
rupt. f. TRIUMPH in same (now obs.) sense]

trŭmp'erў, n. & a. 1. Worthless finery;
rubbish; nonsense. 2. adj. Showy but
worthless, delusive, shallow, as ~ *furniture, arguments.* [ME, f. OF *tromperie*
(*tromper* deceive, -ERY)]

trŭmp'ét, n., & v.t. & i. 1. Wind instrument of brass, the developed orchestral
form having valves (occas. slides) increasing the sounding length of the tube
& thus giving extra harmonic series, so
making all notes instantaneously available; reed-stop in organ imitating this;
trumpeter, esp. (hist.) one sent as envoy;
EAR, SPEAKING, ~; ~-shaped thing e.g.
kind of funnel; sound (as) of ~; *feast of*
~s, Jewish festival celebrating beginning
of year; FLOURISH[2] *of* ~s; BLOW[1] one's *own*
~. 2. ~-*call,* call by sound of ~, (fig.)
urgent summons to action; ~-*conch,*
-*shell,* sea-~, kinds of gasteropod with
turreted shell; ~-*flower,* -*leaf,* kinds of
plant with ~-shaped flowers, leaves;
~ *major,* head trumpeter of ca'alry
regiment. 3. vb. Proclaim (as) by sound
of ~ (usu. fig., = celebrate), blow ~, (of

elephant etc.) make loud sound as of ~. [ME, f. OF *trompete* dim. as TRUMP[1]]

trŭmp′éter, n. **1.** One who sounds a trumpet, esp. cavalry soldier giving signals with trumpet (*be one's own* ~, = BLOW[1] *one's own trumpet*). **2.** Kind of domestic pigeon with peculiar coo, other birds making trumpetlike sound, esp. (also ~ *swan*) a large N.-Amer. swan. [f. prec. +-ER[1], or F *trompeteur*]

trŭnc′al, a. Of the trunk of a body or tree. [f. L *truncus* TRUNK +-AL]

trŭnc′|āte, v.t., & a. **1.** Cut the top or end from (tree, body, cone, pyramid, fig. quoted passage etc.); (cryst.) replace (edge) by plane. **2.** adj. ~ated, (bot., zool., of leaf, feather, etc.) ending abruptly as if cut off at tip, whence ~ātely[2] adv. So ~A′TION, ~atURE (zool.), nn. [f. L *truncare* (TRUNK), -ATE[2, 3]]

trŭn′cheon (-shn), n. ∥ Short club or cudgel e.g. that carried by policeman; baton, staff of authority, esp. (her.) that of Earl Marshal. [ME, f. OF *tronchon* stump f. Rom. **truncionem* f. L *truncus* TRUNK]

trŭn′dle, n., & v.t. & i. **1.** Small broad wheel, e.g. castor; small wheel with cylindrical teeth; low-wheeled truck; (also ~-*bed*)=TRUCKLE-*bed*; head of lower drum of double capstan. **2.** vb. Roll (t. & i., of hoop, truck, etc., often *along*, *down*, etc.); (sl.) bowl at cricket; hence **trŭnd′lER[1]** n. (esp., sl., bowler). [var. of obs. or dial. *trendle*, *trindle*, OE *trendel* circle, see TREND]

trŭnk, n., & v.t. **1.** Main body of tree opp. to branches & roots; human or animal's body without head & limbs & tail; main part of any structure. **2.** (Also ~-*line*) main line of railway or canal, telephone main line (esp. of lines from town to town). **3.** Large box with hinged lid, often covered with leather, for carrying clothes etc. on journey. **4.** Kinds of shaft, conduit, or trough, usu. rectangular & of wood, for ventilation, separation of ores, etc. **5.** Open cylinder used instead of piston-rod in some marine & other engines (~-*engines*). **6.** Proboscis esp. of elephant. **7.** pl. (Also ~ *hose*) 16th-17th-c. breeches from waist to middle of thigh. **8.** ∥~-*call*, telephone call on ~-line with charges according to distance; ~ *drawers*, drawers reaching only to knees; ~-*nail*, nail with large ornamental head for ~, coffin, etc.; ~-*road*, main road. Hence ~′FUL n., ~′LESS a. **9.** v.t. Separate (ore) by use of ~. [ME, f. OF *tronc* f. L *truncus*]

trŭnn′ion (-yon), n. Supporting cylindrical projection on each side of cannon or mortar; hollow gudgeon supporting cylinder in steam-engine & giving passage to steam. Hence ~ED[2] (-yond) a. [f. F *trognon* core, stump]

trŭss, v.t., & n. **1.** Support (roof, bridge, etc.) with ~ (see below). **2.** Fasten (wings of fowl etc.), fasten wings etc. of (fowl etc.), before cooking, tie arms of (person) to his sides; (arch.) fasten, tighten, (garment, usu. *up*), hang (criminal, usu. *up*), (of hawk etc.) seize (bird). **3.** n. Supporting structure or framework of roof, bridge, etc., e.g. pair of rafters with tie-beam, king-post, & struts (~-*bridge* etc., so strengthened). **4.** Bundle of old (56 lb.) or new (60 lb.) hay or (36 lb.) straw. **5.** Compact terminal flower-cluster. **6.** Large corbel supporting monument etc. **7.** (naut.). Heavy iron fitting securing lower yards to mast. **8.** (surg.). Padded belt or encircling spring used in rupture. [ME; vb f. OF *trusser* (mod. *trousser*); n. f. OF *trusse* (mod. *trousse*)]

trŭst, n., & v.t. & i. **1.** Firm belief in the honesty, veracity, justice, strength, etc., of a person or thing, as *our* ~ *is in God*, *I repose considerable* ~ *in him, put no* ~ *in him*; confident expectation (*that*). **2.** Person, thing, confided in, as *he is our sole* ~. **3.** Reliance on truth of statement etc. without examination, as *takes everything on* ~. **4.** Commercial credit, as *supplied with goods on* ~. **5.** Responsibility arising from confidence reposed in one, as *am in a position of* ~. **6.** (law). Confidence reposed in person by making him nominal owner of property to be used for another's benefit; right of the latter to benefit by such property; property so held, legal relation between holder & property so held, as *have accepted a* ~, *the property is merely a* ~, *is held in* ~, (attrib.) ~-*money*. **7.** Thing, person committed to one's care, resulting obligation, as *would not desert his* ~, *have fulfilled my* ~. **8.** (commerc.). Organized association of several companies for purpose of defeating competition etc., the shareholders in each transferring all or most of the stock to central committee & losing their voting power while remaining entitled to profits. **9.** BRAINS *T*~; ~-*deed*, deed by debtor conveying property to trustee for payment of his debts, deed conveying property to creditor to sell & pay himself & restore the residue, any instrument of conveyance that creates a ~. **10.** vb. Place ~ in, believe in, rely on the character or behaviour of, as *have never* ~*ed him, if we may* ~ *this account, do not* ~ *him with* (let him use) *your typewriter, cat cannot be* ~*ed with* (will steal) *milk, would* ~ *him with untold gold*, whence ~′ingLY[2] adv. **11.** Consign (thing *to* person etc.), place or leave (thing *with* person etc., *in* place etc.), without misgiving. **12.** Allow credit to (customer *for* goods). **13.** Entertain an earnest or (rarely) confident hope, as *I* ~ *he is not hurt*(?), *I* ~ *to hear better news.* **14.** Place reliance *in*; ~ *to*, place (esp. undue) reliance on, as *we must* ~ *to meeting someone who knows, does not do to* ~ *to memory for these things.* [ME *troste*, *truste*; n. f. ON *traust* (*traustr* strong): vb f. ON *treysta*, w. assim. to n.]

trŭstee′, n. Person who holds property in trust for another (|| *the Public T~*, State official charged, since 1908, with executing wills & trusts when invited); each of a body of men, often elective, managing affairs of college etc. Hence ~SHIP n. [-EE]

trŭst′ful, a. Full of trust, confiding. Hence ~LY² adv., ~NESS n. [-FUL]

trŭst′worth|y (-ẽrdhĭ), a. Worthy of trust, reliable. Hence ~INESS n.

trŭs′t|y, a. & n. 1. (Chiefly arch.) trustworthy, as ~*y steed, sword, servant*, whence ~ILY² adv., ~INESS n.; *trustful. 2. n. Well-behaved & privileged convict. [ME; -Y²]

truth (-ōō-), n. (*pl. pr.* -dhz). Quality, state, of being true or accurate or honest or sincere or loyal or accurately shaped or adjusted, as *the ~ of the rumour is doubted, there is ~ in what he says, may depend on his ~, wheel is out of ~*; what is true, as *have told you the (whole) ~, the ~ is that I forgot, am a lover of ~* (or *T~* personified), *fundamental ~s, home ~s* (unpalatable facts about oneself), GOD'¹*s ~*, GOSPEL *~*, HALF-*~*; *in ~* (literary), *of a ~* (arch.), truly, really; *to tell the ~*, *~ to tell*, formulas introducing confession. [OE *trēowth* (as TRUE, see -TH¹)]

truth′ful (-ōōth-), a. Habitually speaking truth, veracious; (of tale etc.) true. Hence ~LY² adv., ~NESS n. [-FUL]

truth′lĕss (-ōōth-), a. (Of statement) false; (of person) faithless, not adhering to promise etc. Hence ~NESS n. [-LESS]

trŷ, v.t. & i., & n. 1. Test (quality), test the qualities of (person, thing) by experiment, subject (person etc.) to suffering or hard treatment (as if) for this purpose (whence ~′ING² a., ~′ĭnGLY² adv.), as ~ *(the effect of) soap & water*, ~ *(buy) our ginger ale, did you ever ~ quinine* (as cure) *for it?*, *(strength of) rope must be tried before it is used, each machine is tried before it leaves the shops*, ~ *your hand (skill) at, this will ~ his courage, patience has been sorely tried, should not ~ your eyes with that small print*. 2. Make experiment in order to find out, as ~ *how far you can throw, let us ~ which takes longest, whether it will break*; ~ CONCLUSIONS; a FALL². 3. Investigate (case, issue) judicially, subject (person) to trial (*for* murder etc., also *for his life*). 4. Settle (question, disputed point) by examination or experiment. 5. Attempt to achieve or perform, as *tried a jump & fell, better ~ something easier*; attempt, endeavour, (*to* do or abs.; colloq. often *&* do, seldom after neg. or quasi-neg. & never after past tense), as *do ~ to* (or *&*) *attend, must ~ to* (or *&*) *get it finished tonight, if at first you don't succeed ~*; ~, ~ *again, no use ~ing to persuade him, don't ~ to* (rarely *&*) *palliate it, have often tried to mend it*. 6. (Also ~ *up*) dress (roughly-planed board) with ~*ing-plane* to give fine sur-

face. 7. (Also ~ *out*) purify (metal, fat, oil) by melting or boiling. 8. ~ *back*, = HARK (intr.) *back*, lit. & fig.; ~ *for*, apply or compete for (appointment etc.); ~ *on*, put (clothes etc.) on to test fit, begin (*it*, one's *games, tricks*, etc., often *with* person) experimentally to see how much will be tolerated, as *no use~ing it on with me*; ~*⊥on* n. (colloq.), an attempt to deceive; ~ *out*, put to the test, test thoroughly; ~*⊥out* n., experimental trial, test of popularity etc. (*he gave the play a ~-out at Brighton*). 9. ~′*sail* (-sl), small fore-&-aft sail set with gaff in heavy weather on mainmast or foremast or supplementary mast instead of mainsail or foresail [f. obs. naut. sense of vb, = lie to]; ~′*(ing)-square*, carpenter's square usu. with one wooden & one metal limb; ~*-works*, apparatus for ~ing blubber. 10. n. Attempt (colloq.), as *have* (make) *a ~ at it, for it, to catch it*; (rugby footb.) touching-down of ball by player behind adversaries' goal-line. [ME 'separate, distinguish, etc.' f. OF *trier* of unkn. orig.]

trŷp′anosōme, n. Kinds of blood-parasite some of which cause sleeping-sickness & other diseases. [f. Gk *trupanon* auger, *sōma* body]

trŷp′sin, n. Chief digestive ferment of the pancreatic juice. [f. Gk *tripsis* friction (because first obtained by rubbing down the pancreas with glycerin) + -IN]

trŷst, n., & v.t. & i. (arch.). 1. Appointed meeting, appointment, as *keep, break*, ~. 2. vb. Engage to meet (person), appoint (time, place) for meeting; make a ~. [ME, = obs. *triste* f. OF *triste* appointed station in hunting, of obsc. hist.]

tsăr, czăr (z-), n. Emperor of Russia.

tsari′na, czarina (-ēna), n. Empress of Russia. [f. G. (c)*zarin* f. TSAR]

tsĕt′sè, n. African fly whose bite is often fatal to horses, cattle, dogs, etc. [native]

tsuna′mi (tsoōnah′mĭ), n. Sea wave caused by disturbance of ocean floor or seismic movement. [Jap.]

tuan (tōōahn′), n. Sir, master (used by Malayans as a respectful term of address). [Malay *tuan, tuwan*]

tuata′ra (tōōahtah′ra), n. Large iguana-like reptile, peculiar to New Zealand, having a dorsal row of yellow spines. [Maori, = spine on the back]

tŭb, n., & v.t. & i. (-bb-). 1. Open wooden usu. round vessel of staves held together by hoops used for washing (*wash-~*) or holding butter, liquids, etc. (*let every ~ stand on its own bottom*, everyone look to himself); varying measure of capacity for butter, corn, tea, etc. 2. Sponge-bath, (colloq.) bath of any kind, bath taken in this, as *jumped into his ~, seldom has a ~, a cold ~ would do him good*. 3. (mining). Kinds of bucket or box for conveying ore, coal, etc. 4. Clumsy slow boat (derog.); boat used for practice rowing, as ~*-pair*, *-eight*, etc. (for so many oarsmen). **5.** ~-*thumper*, ranting preacher or orator, so ~-*thumping* a. & n.; ~-*wheel*, bowl-shaped water-wheel, rotating drum for washing skins etc. in. Hence~'FUL n. **6.** vb. Bathe (t. & i.) in ~; plant in ~; row in ~, coach (oarsman, -men) in ~ -*pair*; (mining) line (shaft) with wood or iron casing. Hence~b'ING¹(1, 2) n. [ME *tubbe* = MDu., MLG *tubbe, tobbe*]

tūb'a, n. Bass brass instrument of various sizes & pitches; an organ reed-stop. [L, = trumpet]

tŭbb'|y̆, a. Tub-shaped, fat & round, corpulent, so ~-ISH¹ a.; (of musical instrument) sounding dull, lacking resonance. [-Y¹]

tūbe, n., & v.t. **1.** Long hollow cylinder esp. for conveying or holding liquids etc.; cylinder of thin flexible metal with screw cap for holding paint etc. (~ *colours*, kept in ~s). **2.** Main body of wind instrument. **3.** (anat.). Hollow ~-shaped organ, esp. one conveying air, as *bronchial* ~, whence **tūb'AL, tūb'AR¹,** aa. **4.** *Thermionic valve. **5.** ‖ Each of several tubular electric railways in London. **6.** *Crookes's* ~, vacuum ~ for showing certain phenomena connected with gases; *pneumatic* ~ (for pneumatic dispatch); TEST¹~; ~-*flower*, ornamental E.-Ind. shrub of vervain family; ~-*shell*, kinds of bivalve forming shelly ~; ~-*well*, iron pipe with sharp point & perforations at bottom for getting water from underground. **7.** v.t. Furnish with, enclose in, ~ or ~s; ~d *horse* (that has had a metallic ~ inserted in the air-passage). Hence **tūb'ING¹(2) n.** [F, or f. L *tubus*]

tūb'er, n. Short thick part of an underground stem covered with modified buds, e.g. potato, artichoke, whence ~IF'EROUS, ~IFORM, aa.; kinds of underground fungus, truffle; (anat.) swelling part, prominence. [L, = bump, tumour]

tūb'ercl|e, n. Small rounded projection esp. of bone; small granular tumour or nodule formed within the substance of an organ tending to degeneration & (in lungs etc.) to production of pulmonary consumption etc.; (bot.) wartlike excrescence, small tuber. Hence ~ED² (-ld), **tūbẽrc'ulAR¹, tūbẽrc'ulATE², aa., tūbẽrc'ulIN n.,** liquid prepared from cultures of ~e bacillus, used esp. as a test for tuberculosis, **tūbẽrc'ulOID, tūbẽrc'u-lOSE¹, tūbẽrc'ulOUS, aa.** [f. L TUBER-*culum* (-CULE¹)]

tūbẽrcŭlā'tion, n. Formation, set, system, of tubercles. [-ATION]

tūbẽrc'ul(ar)īz|e, -is|e (-iz), vv.t. Infect with tuberculosis. Hence ~A'TION n. [-IZE]

tūbẽrcŭlōs'īs, n. Disease affecting most tissues of the body marked by tubercles & the presence of a characteristic bacillus; *pulmonary* ~, consumption. Hence **tūbẽrc'ulOSED² (-st) a.** [-OSIS]

tūb'er|ōse, a. & (*pop. pron.* tūb'rōz) n.

1. Covered with tubers, knobby; of the nature of a tuber; bearing tubers. Hence or cogn. ~ŌS'ITY, ~OUSNESS, nn., ~OUS a. **2.** n. Garden & greenhouse bulb with creamy-white fragrant flowers. [(n. f. L fem. adj.) f. L *tuberosus* (TUBER, see -OSE¹)]

tūb'ĭ-, comb. form of L *tubus* tube, as: ~*corn* a. & n., (ruminant) with hollow horns; ~FORM; ~*ling'ual*, with tubular tongue.

tūb'ŭl|ar, a. Tube-shaped; having, consisting of, contained in, tube(s), as ~*ar boiler* (in which heat or water to be heated passes through many tubes), ~*ar bridge*, rectangular tube through which railway etc. passes; (of sound in breathing) like sound of air passing through tube. So ~OSE¹, ~OUS, aa. [f. as foll. + -AR¹]

tūb'ŭle, n. Small tube. Hence **tūb'ŭl-** comb. form. [f. L *tubulus* dim. as TUBE]

tŭck¹, v.t. & i., & n. **1.** Gather (material) into flat folds for stitching; draw or thrust or roll the parts of (cloth etc. *up, in*) close together, as ~ *in the loose ends*, ~*ed up his shirt-sleeves* (so as to leave arms bare); draw together into small compass, as ~*ed his legs under him like a tailor, bird* ~s *his head under his wing*; cover (person, oneself) snugly & compactly *up or in*, as ~*ed himself up in bed*; stow away (thing *in* corner etc., *away*, etc.); (of spare material etc.) be disposed of by ~ing away; empty (seine) by means of small one; (sl.) hang (criminal) *up*; ~ *in* (sl.), eat heartily (*at* food, or abs.). **2.** n. Flat fold, often one of several parallel folds, in fabric fixed in place by stitches as ornament or to dispose of spare stuff, as *make a* ~ *in sleeves* (when too long); (naut.) part of vessel's hull where after planks meet; ‖ (sl.) eatables esp. pastry & sweets, ~-*in*, -*out*, full meal, ‖~-*shop* (where~is sold); ~-*net*, -*seine*, small net for taking fish from larger one; ~-*pointing*, method of pointing brickwork with coloured mortar, a central groove in which is filled with fine white lime putty, projecting slightly. [ME *tukke, tokke*, f. MDu., MLG *tucken, tokken*, = OHG *zucken*, pull, pluck]

tŭck², n. (arch.). Blast, flourish, of trumpet; (Sc.) ~ (beat) *of drum*. [f. ME (now dial.) *tuck* vb f. ONF *to(u)ker* (OF *tochier*) TOUCH¹]

tŭck'er¹, n. In vbl senses; also or esp.: piece of lace, linen, etc., covering neck & shoulders of woman in 17th & 18th c. (*best* BIB² & ~); part of sewing-machine used in making tucks; ‖ (sl.) food. [TUCK¹ + -ER¹]

***tŭck'er²,** v.t. (colloq.). Tire, weary (usu. ~ *out*). [f. TUCK¹ (vb)]

tŭck'ĕt, n. (arch.). Flourish on trumpet. [conn. w. TUCK²]

tuc'um (tōō-), n. Brazilian palm with fibre used for cordage etc. [Braz.]

-tude, suf. repr. L *-tūdo̓, -tūdinem* (F *-tude*), forming abstract nn. f. adjj., pp., or vb stems; in E direct f. L (*alti-*), thr. F (*soli-*), or on L anal. (*exacti-*).

Tūd'or, a. Of the (period of the) ~**s**, English sovereigns from Henry VII to Elizabeth I, as ~ (late perpendicular) *style* in architecture, ~ *rose*, five-lobed flower, ~ *flower*, trefoil ornament, used in ~ style. [Owen ~ of Wales, grandfather of Henry VII]

Tuesday (tūz'dĭ), n. Third day of week; SHROVE ~. [OE *Tiwesdæg* (rendering L *dies Martis*) f. *Tīwes* genit. of *Tiw* ancient Teutonic deity identified w. the Roman *Mars*; so OHG *zīestac*, ON *týsdagr*]

tŭf'a, n. Rock of rough or cellular texture of volcanic or other origin. Hence **tūf**A̓CEOUS (-āshu̇s) a. [It., as foll.]

tŭff, n. Kinds of volcanic fragmentary rock; ~*cone* (of ashes etc. round volcanic opening). [f. F *tuf(fe)* f. It. *tufo* f. L *tofus* soft sandy stone]

tŭft, n., & v.t. & i. 1. Bunch, collection, of threads, grass, feathers, etc., held or growing together at the base, whence **tŭf'tY**[2] a.; (anat.) bunch of small blood-vessels; imperial (beard); ‖ tufted undergraduate [from ~ formerly worn on cap]; ~*-hunter*, *-hunting*, one who seeks, practice of seeking, society of titled persons. 2. vb. Furnish with ~ or ~s; make depressions at regular intervals in (mattress etc.) by passing thread through; grow in ~s. [ME, of obsc. orig.; perh. repr. F *touffe*]

tŭg, v.t. & i. (-gg-), & n. 1. Pull with great effort or violently; make vigorous pull *at*; tow (vessel) by means of steam ~, (of steam ~) tow (vessel); (fig.) drag (subject etc. *in* etc.) forcibly. 2. n. ~ging, violent pull, as *gave a* ~ *at the bell*; violent or painful effort, esp. fig., as *felt a great* ~ *at parting, parting was a* ~, *had a great* ~ *to persuade him.* 3. ‖ (Eton sl.) Colleger. 4. (Also ~*'boat*) small powerful steam-vessel for towing others. 5. Loop from saddle supporting shaft or (in double harness) trace; ~*-spring*, spring-frame to which this is fastened to lessen jerk in starting etc. 6. (mining). Iron hoop to which a tackle is fixed. 7. ~ *of war*, contest in which each of two groups of persons holding same rope tries to pull the other across line marked between them, supreme contest. [ME *togge, tugge*, intensive f. Gmc *teuh-*, *tauh-*, *tug-*, see TOW[1]]

tū'ism, n. Doctrine that all thought is addressed to a second person, esp. to one's future self as this. [f. L *tu* thou +-ISM]

tūi'tion, n. Teaching, esp. as a thing to be paid for; fee for this. Hence ~AL, ~ARY[1], aa., (-sho-). [ME, f. AF, OF, f. L *tuitionem* (*tuēri tuit-* watch, guard, see -ION)]

tul'a (tōō-), n. (Also ~*-work*) = NIELLO. [*Tula*, in Russia]

‖ **tŭl'chan, -in**, (-χ-), n. (Sc.). Calf-skin

stuffed with straw or spread on mound beside cow to make her give milk; ~ *bishops* (hist.), titular bishops in whose names revenues of Scottish sees were drawn by lay barons after Reformation. [Gael., = mound]

tūl'ip, n. Kinds of plant with brilliant bell-shaped flowers of various colours; bell-shaped outward swell of muzzle of gun; ~*root*, disease of oats causing base of stem to swell; ~*-tree*, N.-Amer. tree with flowers like large greenish-yellow ˏˏ⁸ₑ marked with orange inside. [16th c. *tulipa*, also *-pan, -pant* = F (obs.) *tulipan, tulipe*, f. Turk. *tulbant* f. Pers. *dulband* TURBAN]

tūlipo|**mān'ia**, n. Craze for tulips, esp. that in Holland about 1634. Hence ~MAN'IAC n. [prec. + o- + -MANIA]

tulle (tōōl, & see Ap.), n. Fine silk net used for veils & dresses. [T~, city in France]

tūl'wār, n. Sabre used by some N.-Indian tribes. [Hind. *talwār*]

tŭm, tŭm'tŭm, n. Sound of banjo or similar instrument. [imit.]

tŭm'ble, v.i. & t., & n. 1. Fall (*down, over, off, from*, etc.) suddenly or violently; (of waves, sick person, etc.) roll, toss, up & down or from side to side; move, walk, run, in headlong or blundering fashion (*came tumbling along,* ~*d up the stairs,* ~*d into* or *out of bed*); perform acrobatic feats; pull about, disorder, rumple, (clothes, hair, etc.); overturn, fling headlong, throw or push (*down, out, in*, etc.) roughly or carelessly; bring down (bird, hare, etc.) by shooting; polish (castings etc.) in tumbling-box. 2. ~ *in*, fit (piece of timber) into another, (naut., also ~ *home*, of ship's sides) incline inwards above extreme breadth, (sl.) go to bed; ~ *to* (sl.), understand, grasp, (idea etc.). 3. n. Fall, as *had a slight, nasty*, etc., ~ ; somersault or other acrobatic feat; untidy or confused state, as *things were all in a* ~. 4. ~*-bug*, kinds of dung-beetle; ~*down*, dilapidated. [ME *tumbel*, frequent. f. OE *tumbian* (-LE(3)); cf. MLG *tummeln*, OHG *tumalōn*]

tŭm'ler, n. In vbl senses; also or esp.: one who turns somersaults etc., acrobat; kind of pigeon that turns somersaults during flight; toy figure of sitting mandarin etc. contrived to rock when touched; flat-bottomed stemless drinking-glass (formerly with rounded bottom so as not to stand upright), whence ~FUL n.; part of the mechanism of a lock or gunlock. [ME; ~ER[1]]

tŭm'bling, n. In vbl senses; ~*-barrel, -box, -wheel*, revolving box or barrel containing emery-powder etc. in which castings etc. are cleaned by friction against each other or the walls of the box; ~*-bob*, weighted lever reacting when lifted to a certain point. [15th c.; -ING[1]]

‖ **tŭm'brel, -il**, n. (hist.). Two-wheeled covered cart for carrying tools, ammunition, etc.; dung-cart; open cart used in French Revolution to convey victims to the guillotine; instrument of punishment perh. the same as CUCKING-STOOL. [ME, f. OF *tumb-, tomberel*, f. *tomber* fall]

tūm′ė|fȳ, v.t. & i. (Cause to) swell, inflate; be inflated, (lit. & fig.). So ~FA′CIENT (-āshnt) a. (path.), ~FAC′TION n. (path.). [f. F *tuméfier* f. L *tumēre* swell, see -FY]

tūm′id, a. (Of parts of body etc.) swollen, inflated, so **tūmēs′CENCE** n., **tūmes′CENT** a.; (fig., of style etc.) inflated, bombastic. Hence or cogn. **tūmid′ITY**, ~NESS, nn., ~LY² adv. [f. L *tumidus* (*tumēre* swell, -ID¹)]

tŭmm′ȳ, n. (nursery). = STOMACH. [-Y³]

tūm′our (-mer), n. Local swelling esp. from morbid growth; *malignant* ~ (tending to recur after removal & cause death, opp. to *benign* ~). [f. L *tumor* (*tumēre* swell, -OR)]

tŭm′tŭm¹, n. W.-Ind. dish of boiled plantains beaten soft in a mortar; (Anglo-Ind.) light vehicle, dog-cart. [orig. unkn.]

tumtum². See TUM.

tŭm′ŭlt, n. Commotion of a multitude esp. with confused cries etc.; noisy uprising of mob etc.; uproar; confused & excited state of mind, as *the* ~ *within him had subsided*. Hence or cogn. **tūmŭl′tūARY**¹ (esp. undisciplined, riotous), **tūmŭl′tūous** (esp. vehement, uproarious), aa., **tūmŭl′tūousLY²** adv., **tūmŭl′tūousNESS** n. [ME, f. L *tumultus* f. *tumēre* swell]

tŭm′ŭl|us, n. (pl. ~ī). Sepulchral mound often enclosing masonry. Hence or cogn. ~AR(Y)¹ aa. [L (*tumēre* swell)]

tūn, n., & v.t. (-nn-). 1. Large cask for wine, beer, etc., esp. formerly as measure of capacity (252 wine gallons); brewer's fermenting-vat; ‖ ~′*dish*, kind of funnel esp. in brewing. 2. v.t. Store (liquor) in ~. [OE *tunne*, = OHG, ON *tvnna*, f. Gaulish *tunna*]

tūn′a, n. The Californian TUNNY. [f. Sp.-Amer. *atin* TUNNY]

tun′dra (tōō-), n. Barren arctic regions where subsoil is frozen. [Lappish]

tūne, n., & v.t. & i. 1. Melody with or without harmony, air, as *psalm, hymn,* ~; correct intonation in singing or playing, due adjustment of instrument for this, as *piano is out of* ~, *sings out of* ~, *must learn to sing in* ~. 2. Agreement, concord, harmonious relation, as *in, out of,* ~ *with* one's *surroundings* or *company*; suitable mood (*for* purpose etc.). 3. *Change* one's ~, *sing another* ~, assume a different style of language or manner, e.g. change from insolent to respectful tone; *to the* ~ (serious or exorbitant amount) *of £5* etc. 4. vb. Put (violin, piano, etc.) in ~, whence **tūn′ER**¹(1, 2) n.; (fig.) adjust, adapt, (thing *to* standard, purpose, circumstances, etc.); be in harmony (*with*, lit. & fig.); (poet.) produce

(music), as *lark* ~*s his song*; express, celebrate, in music. 5. ~ *in*, set wireless instrument to right wave-length; ~ *up*, (of orchestra) bring instruments to common pitch, begin to play or sing, (joc., of child) begin to cry. Hence **tūn′ABLE** a., **tūn′ableNESS** n., **tūn′abLY²** adv. [ME unexpl. phon. var. of TONE¹]

tūne′ful (-nf-), a. Melodious, musical. Hence ~LY² adv., ~NESS n. [-FUL]

tūne′less (-nl-), a. Not in tune; unmelodious; (of mus. instrument) not played, silent. [-LESS]

tŭng⁻oil, n. An oil used chiefly for varnishing woodwork, obtained from the Chinese *tung-tree*. [Chin. *yu t'ung*]

tŭng′st|en, n. Wolfram, a steel-grey heavy metallic element with very high melting-point, used for the filaments of electric lamps and for alloying steel etc. Hence ~ATE¹(3) n., ~IC, ~OUS, aa. (chem.). [Sw. (*tung* heavy + *sten* stone)]

tūn′ic, n. 1. Ancient Greek or Roman short-sleeved body-garment reaching about to knees; woman's loose blouse or coat gathered or belted at waist; close-fitting short coat of uniform of soldier, policeman, etc. 2. (Zool.) leathery envelope of ascidia etc.; (anat.) membrane enclosing an organ; (bot.) any of the layers of a bulb, integument of a part; whence ~ATE² a. (zool., anat., bot.), & n. (zool.); (eccl.) = foll. [f. F *tunique* or L *tunica*]

tūn′icle, n. Fine or delicate tunic (esp. bot., zool.); (eccl., esp. R.-C. Ch.) short vestment of subdeacon at eucharist etc., (pl.) this & dalmatic worn by bishop. [ME, f. L *tunicula* dim. as prec.]

tūn′ing, n. In vbl senses; ~*fork*, two-pronged steel fork designed to give particular note (esp. middle C) when struck; ~*hammer*, hammer-shaped wrench for altering tension of strings in piano etc. by turning the pegs (~*pegs*, ~*pins*) to which they are attached. [-ING¹]

tunnage. See TONNAGE.

tŭnn′el, n., & v.t. & i. (-ll-). 1. Artificial subterranean passage through hill etc. or under river etc.; subterranean passage dug by burrowing animal; (mining) adit or level open at one end; main flue of chimney; ~*borer*, kinds of machine for making ~s; ~*net*, fishing-net wide at mouth & narrow at other end. 2. vb. Make a ~ through (hill etc.); furnish with ~; make one's way (*through, into,* etc.), make one's *way*, by ~ling. [ME, f. OF *tonel* & *tonnelle*, dim. of *tonne* TUN]

tŭnn′ȳ, n. Large oceanic scombroid fish used as food. [f. F *thon* f. Prov. *ton*, f. L f. Gk *thunnos*]

tūn′|ȳ, a. (Of music) having marked or catchy tunes. Hence ~iNESS n. [TUNE, -Y²]

tŭp, n., & v.t. (-pp-). 1. Male sheep, ram; striking-face of steam hammer etc. 2. v.t. Copulate with (ewe). [ME *tope, tupe*, of unkn. orig.]

tūque (-k), n. Kind of Canadian cap. [Canad. F form of TOQUE]

tū quŏ'que, n. The retort *So are* (or *did* etc.) *you*. [L, = you too]

turacou, turako. Varr. of TOURACO.

Tūrān'ian, a. Of the Asian languages that are neither Semitic nor Indo-European, esp. of the Ural-Altaic group of languages. [f. Pers. *Turān* region beyond Oxus, + -IAN]

tŭrb'an, n. Oriental man's head-dress of scarf wound round cap; modification of this, esp. early-19th-c. European woman's head-dress; (later) woman's or child's hat with narrow or no brim; spire of univalve shell; ~-*shell*, kinds of gasteropod or shell; ~-*stone*, Mohammedan pillar tombstone with ~ carved on top; ~-*top*, kind of mushroom. Hence ~ED² (-nd) a. [16th c. also *tulbant* etc., f. Turk. *tulbant* f. Pers. *dulband*; see TULIP]

‖ **tŭrb'arў**, n. Right of digging turf on another's ground; place where turf or peat is dug. [ME, f. AF *turberie* f. OF *turb-, torberie* f. *tourbe* TURF]

tŭrb'id, a. (Of liquid or colour) muddy, thick, not clear; (fig.) confused, disordered. Hence ~ITY (-id²), ~NESS, nn., ~LY² adv. [f. L *turbidus* f. *turba* crowd, disturbance, see -ID¹]

tŭrb'in|ate, a. Shaped like a top or inverted cone, so ~IFORM, ~OID, aa.; (anat., esp. of some nasal bones) of scroll-like formation; whirling like a top. So ~AL a., ~A'TION n. [f. L *turbinatus* (as foll., see -ATE²)]

tŭrb'ine, n. Kinds of water-wheel driven by impact or reaction or both of a flowing stream of water; *air* ~, wheel of similar form driven by wind or by air from tube, *gas* ~ (driven by gas), *steam* ~ (driven by steam jets); ~ *boat* etc. (driven by ~s). [F, f. L *turbo -inis* top, whirlwind]

tŭrb'it, n. Kind of domestic pigeon with flat head & short beak. [app. f. L *turbo* top, from its figure; cf. TURBOT]

tŭrb'o-, comb. form of TURBINE; ~-*jet engine* (having a turbine-driven compressor for supplying compressed air to the combustion chamber); ~-*prop(eller)-engine* (having a turbine-driven propeller).

tŭrb'ot, n. Large kind of flat-fish esteemed as food. [ME, f. OF *turbot*, f. OSw. *lörnbut* f. *törn* thorn + *but* BUTT²; cf. E *thornback, -but*]

tŭrb'ŭl|ent, a. Disturbed, in commotion; tumultuous; insubordinate, riotous. Hence or cogn. ~ENCE n., ~entLY² adv. [f. L *turbulentus* (*turba* tumult, see -LENT)]

Tŭrc'ō, n. (hist.; pl. ~s). Algerian tirailleur in French service. [F]

Tŭrco-, Tŭrko-, in comb. Of the Turks. So **Tŭrc'OPHIL, Tŭrcŏph'iLISM, Tŭrc'OPHOBE**, nn. [f. med. L as TURK, -O-]

tŭrd, n. (not in polite lang.). Ball or lump of excrement. [OE *tord*, ON *tord(ў)fill*)]

tŭrd'|ïne, a. Thrushlike. So ~IFORM, ~OID, aa. [f. L *turdus* thrush + -INE¹]

tūreen', n. Deep covered dish for holding soup etc. at table. [c. 1700 *terrine*, *-ene* f. F *TERRINE* (L *terra*, -INE¹)]

turf, n., & v.t. 1. Surface earth filled with matted roots of grass etc.; piece of this cut from the ground, sod; (in Ireland) peat; *the* ~, the race-course, occupation or profession of horse-racing, esp. *on the* ~, so occupied; ~-*bound*, covered with close ~; ~ *drain* (covered with ~); ~*man*, person interested in horse-racing, so ~'ITE¹ n. 2. v.t. Plant (ground) with ~; (sl.) throw (person or thing) *out*. Hence ~'iNESS n., ~'Y² a. [OE, OS *turf*, ON *torf(a)*, OHG *zurf, zurba*, MDu., MLG (G) *torf*, f. Gmc *turbh-*]

tŭr'g|id, a. Morbidly swollen or inflated or enlarged, whence ~ĕs'CIBLE a.; (fig., of language) pompous, bombastic, inflated. Hence or cogn. ~ĕs'CENCE, ~ĭd'ITY, nn., ~Es'CENT a., ~ĭdLY² adv. [f. L *turgidus* (*turgēre* swell, see -ID¹)]

tūr'ion, n. (bot.). Young scaly shoot rising from ground as in asparagus, hops, etc. Hence ~IF'EROUS a. [f. L *turio -onis* shoot]

Tŭrk, n. 1. Ottoman, Osmanli; member of the people from whom the Ottomans are derived; (trans.) ferocious, wild, or unmanageable person (now chiefly joc. of children); (arch.) Mohammedan; Turkish horse. 2. ~'*s cap*, kinds of lily & other plants with turban-like flowers; ~'*s head*, head on post for sword displays, turban-like ornamental knot, kinds of round brush or broom, kind of baking-pan for cakes. Hence ~'ISM n. [ME, = F *Turc*, med. L *Turcus*, Pers. & Arab. *Turk*]

tŭrk'ey, n. (pl. ~s). 1. Large (esp. domestic) gallinaceous bird native of America related to pheasant, esteemed as food & associated with Christmas festivities. 2. (*T*~). Country of the Turks. 3. ~ *buzzard, vulture*, an American vulture; *T*~ *carpet* (made entirely of wool, & of velvety appearance); ~-*cock*, male of ~ (*red as a* ~-*cock*, of person flushed with anger etc.), (fig.) pompous or self-important person; *T*~ *corn*, maize; ‖ *T*~ *leather*, kind treated with oil before the hair side is removed; ~-*poult*, young of ~; *T*~ *red*, a pigment or colour, cotton cloth dyed with this; *T*~ *stone*, kind of oilstone for sharpening knives etc.; ~ *trot*, kind of dance. [16th c., short for *turkey-cock, -hen*, orig. applied to the guinea-fowl, as imported through Turkey, and then erron. to the American bird]

Tŭrk'ish, a. & n. 1. (Language) of Turkey or the Turks. 2. ~ *bath*, hot-air bath followed by soaping, washing, rubbing, kneading, etc., (also pl.) building used for this; ~ (= TURKEY) *carpet*; ~ *delight*, a sweetmeat in gelatinous slabs coated with powdered sugar; ~ *music* (produced with instruments of percussion); ~

pound (usu. written *£T*, as *£T50*), coin formerly worth about 18/2; ~ *towel* (rough with long nap usu. of uncut loops). [-ISH¹]

Tŭrk'oman, Tŭrk'man, Tŭrc'o-, n. (pl. ~s). Member of any of various Turkish tribes in Turkestan, Afghanistan, Persia, & Russia; ~ *carpet*, rich-coloured kind with soft long nap. [f. Pers. *Turkumān* (TURK, *mān-dan* resemble)]

tŭrm'alin(e). See TOURMALIN.

tŭrm'eric, n. E.-Ind. plant of ginger family: powdered root of this as dye-stuff, stimulant, & condiment esp. in curry-powder; ~-*paper* (saturated with ~ & used as test for alkalis). [16th c. forms *tarmaret* etc., perh. f. F *terre mérite* & med. L *terra merita*]

tŭrm'oil, n., & v.t. 1. Agitation, trouble. 2. v.t, (arch., chiefly in p.p.). Agitate, trouble. [16th c., of unkn. orig.]

‖ **tŭrm'ut**, var. of *turnip* used by writers as characteristic of rustic speech.

tŭrn¹, v.t. & i. I. General senses. **1.** Move (t. & i.) on or as on axis, give rotary motion to, receive such motion, as *crank* ~*s wheel*, *wheel* ~*s*, ~ *the key in the lock*, ~ *the tap*, *tap will not* ~, *he* ~*ed on his heel*(*s*), ~ person *round one's* FINGER, *everything* ~*s* (depends) *on his answer*. **2.** Execute (somersault etc.) with rotary motion. **3.** Change from one side to another, invert, reverse, (fig.) revolve mentally, as ~*s everything upside down or inside out* (into state of confusion), *whole world has* ~*ed topsy-turvy*, *umbrella* ~*s inside out*, ~*ed the body with its face upwards*, ~*ed* (inverted) *comma*, ~*ed period* (·), ~ TURTLE, ~ *the* TABLES *on*, ~ *over pages of book* (to read on other side), ~ *over new* LEAF, *not* ~ *a* HAIR, *dress must be* ~*ed* (the soiled outside becoming the inside), ~ one's COAT, ~ *an honest* PENNY, *have* ~*ed the matter over & over in my mind*. **4.** Give new direction to, take new direction, adapt, be adapted, as ~ *your face this way*, *river* ~*s to the right*, ~*ed his flight northwards*, *scarcely know where or which way to* ~ (fig. what course to follow, where to seek help), ~*ed to God in her trouble*, ~ one's BACK¹ *on*, ~ *a* DEAF *ear to*; ~ *the edge of* (knife etc., fig. remark etc.), blunt; ~ *your attention to this*; *have often* ~*ed my thoughts*, *thoughts have often* ~*ed*, *to the subject*; *can* ~ *his hand to* (learn to do) *anything*; ~*s even his errors to account* (profits by them); *all* ~*s* (tends) *to his profit*; *tide* ~*s* (at ebb or flow). **5.** Move to other side of, go round, flank, as ~ *the* CORNER; ~ *the scale*, cause it to sink, (fig.) decide question in suspense; ~ (*the flank or position of*) *an army*, pass round so as to attack it from flank or rear; ~ person's *flank*, outwit him, defeat him in argument etc. **6.** *Be* ~*ed* (have passed the age) (*of*) *40* etc. **7.** Cause to go, send, put, as *was* ~*ed adrift in the world*, ~ *it out into a basin*, *never* ~*ed* (*away*) *a beggar from his door*, *will* ~ (resist or divert) *a bullet*. **8.** Change (t. & i.) in nature, form, condition, etc., change for the worse, (cause to) become, as ~*ed water into wine*, *has been* ~*ed into a joint stock company*, *fear he will* ~ *crusty*, *has* ~*ed traitor*, *Mohammedan*, *botanist*, *joy is* or *has* ~*ed to bitterness*; ~ (translate) *it into French*, *how would you* ~ *this passage?*, *milk will* ~ (sour), *thunder will* ~ *milk* (sour), ~*ed pale at the thought*, *very thought* ~*s me pale*, *sight of rawmeat* ~*s* (nauseates) *my stomach*, *stomach* ~*s at the sight*, *success has* ~*ed his head* (intoxicated him), *head has* ~*ed with success*, *head* ~*s* (with giddiness), *overwork has* ~*ed his brain*. **9.** Shape (object) in lathe, (of material) lend itself (*easily*, *well*, etc.) to treatment in lathe. **10.** Give (esp. elegant) form to, as *can* ~ *a compliment*, *could* ~ *a Latin verse in my day*, *well-* ~*ed phrase*, *exquisitely* ~*ed wrist*. II. Spec. uses with advv. & prepp. **1.** ~ *about*, or, as mil. command, *about* ~ *!*, ~ so as to face in new direction. **2.** ~ *against*, become hostile to. **3.** ~ *down*, fold down; place (playing-card) face downwards; reduce flame of (gas, lamp, etc.) by ~*ing* tap etc.; reject (proposal, its maker, etc.). **4.** ~ *in*, fold inwards; hand in, give up; incline inwards, as *his toes* ~ *in*; (colloq.) go to bed. **5.** ~ *off*, check passage of (water, gas, etc.) by means of tap etc.; achieve, produce, (epigram, piece of work); dismiss (servant etc.) from employment; (sl.) hang (criminal), marry (couple). **6.** ~ *on* (adv.), give free passage to (water etc.) by ~*ing* tap; (colloq.) give free scope to, as ~ *on the waterworks*, begin to cry. **7.** ~ *on* (prep.), depend upon; face hostilely, become hostile to. **8.** ~ *out*, expel; cause to point or incline outwards, as ~ *out your toes*; produce (manufactured goods etc.); ~ inside out, bring to view, as *made him* ~ *out his pockets*; assemble for duty etc., as *15 men* ~*ed out*; get out of bed; (mil.) ~ *out the guard*, call them from guard-room; be found, prove to be the case, as *this* ~*s out to be true*, *he* ~*ed out a humbug*, *it* ~*s out that he was never there*, *we shall see how things* ~ *out*. **9.** ~ *over*, cause to fall over, upset; transfer the conduct of (thing *to* person); do business to the amount of, as ~*s over £500 a week*. **10.** ~ *round*, face about; adopt new opinions or policy. **11.** ~ *to* (prep.), apply oneself to, set about, (work, doing). **12.** ~ *to* (adv.) begin work. **13.** ~ *up*, disinter, as *plough* ~*s up skulls*; make one's appearance, as ~*ed up an hour late*, *unexpectedly*; (of event, opportunity, etc.) happen, present itself; (colloq.) cause to vomit, as *the sight* ~*ed me up*. **14.** ~ *upon*, = ~ *on*. III. Comb. ~-*bench*, watchmaker's portable lathe; ~-*buckle*, device for connecting parts of metal rod; ~-*cap*, revolving chimney-top; ~'*coat*, one who ~*s his* COAT; ~'*cock*, person employed to ~ on water for mains etc.; ~-*down*, (of collar) doubled down; ~'*key*, person in charge of prison keys; ~-*out*, ~ing-out esp. for duty, strike of employees, assembly of persons to see spectacle etc., equipage, quantity of goods manufactured etc. in given time; ~'*over*, upsetting of carriage etc., semicircular pie or tart, amount of money ~ed over in business, changing of labour in factories etc.; ‖ newspaper article running on to next page; ~'*pike*, defensive frame of pikes (hist.), gate set across road to stop carts etc. till toll is paid, such road; ~-*round*, (of ship) process of entering port, discharging cargo, reloading, & leaving port; ~-*screw*, screwdriver; ~'*side*, giddiness in dogs; ~'*sole*, kinds of plant supposed to ~ with the sun; ~'*spit*, long-bodied short-legged dog formerly used to ~ spit; ~'*stile*, post at entrance of building esp. where admission fee is charged with four horizontal arms that move round as person passes through; ~'*stone*, bird allied to plover; ~-*table*, circular revolving platform for reversing locomotives etc.; ~-*up*, thing ~ed up, (colloq.) commotion. [OE *tyrnan*, *turnian*, in ME reinforced f. OF *turner*, *torner*, f. L *tornare* turn in lathe (*tornus* f. Gk *tornos*)]

turn², n. 1. Rotary motion, changed or change of direction or position or tendency, deflection, deflected part, bend, as *a single ~ of the handle*, *a ~ of Fortune's wheel* (change of luck), *with a neat ~ of the wrist*, *took a sudden ~ to the left*, *complaint took a favourable ~*, *milk is on the ~* (just turning sour), *tide is on the ~* (turning), *gave a new ~ to the argument*, *path is full of ~s & twists*, *walked along a ~ of the river*; (mil. as wds of command) *right*, *left*, *about*, ~ *!*; any of the THREES (~ *A*, *B*, *C*, *D*) in figure-skating. 2. Character, tendency, disposition, formation, as *was of a humorous ~*, *do not like the ~ of the sentence*, *the ~ of an ankle*; *have a fine*, *pretty*, etc., ~ *of speed* etc., be able to go very fast etc. on occasion. 3. Short walk, stroll, drive, ride, or performance, as *take a ~ in the garden*, *on a bicycle*, *took a ~ of work*; *short ~s* (songs, recitations, etc., in music-hall etc.). 4. Opportunity, occasion, privilege, obligation, coming successively to each of several persons etc., as *it is your ~ to watch*, *it was now my ~ to be angry*, *must not speak out of* (before or after) *your ~*, *will hear you all in ~* (succession); *we dug by ~s* (in rotation of individuals or groups); *take ~s*, work etc. alternately; *work ~ & ~ about* (alternately), *went hot & cold by ~s*; *did not serve my ~* (purpose); *did me a good*, *an ill*, ~ (service, disservice); *one good ~ deserves another*). 5. (mus.). Kind of grace consisting of principal note with those above & below it. 6. pl. Menses. 7. Each round in coil of rope etc. 8. (print.). Inverted type as temporary substitute for missing letter, letter turned wrong side up. 9. (colloq.). Nervous shock, as *gave me quite a ~*. 10. *To a ~*, exactly, perfectly, as *meat is done to a ~* (enough & not too much). [ME, partly f. AF **torn*, **turn*, = OF *torn* (later *tor*, see TOUR), f. L *tornus* (prec.); partly f. prec.]

turn'|er, n. In vbl senses; also or esp.: one who works with lathe, so ~ERY (1, 2, 3) n.; ‖ kind of tumbler-pigeon. [-ER¹]

turn'ing, n. In vbl senses, esp.: use of lathe; place where road meets another, such road, as *stop at the next ~*, *take the second ~ to the left*; ~-*point*, point in place, time, development, etc., at which decisive change occurs, as *has reached the ~-point*, *this may be the ~-point of his life*. [ME]

turn'ip, n. Biennial plant of mustard family; its fleshy globular root used as vegetable & for feeding cattle etc.; ~-*top*, growing top of ~ used as vegetable. Hence ~Y² a. (esp. tasting of ~s). [16th c. *turnep(e)*, f. Sc. & dial. *neep* (OE *nǣp* f. L *napus*); first element uncert., perh. f. F *tour* or E *turn*]

turp'entine, n., & v.t. 1. Oleo-resin secreted by several coniferous trees & (*Chian ~*) by terebinth, used in mixing paints & varnishes & in medicine; (also pop. *turps*) oil or spirit of ~; ~-*tree*, terebinth. 2. v.t. Apply ~ to. [ME, f. OF *ter(e)bentine* f. L *terebinthina* (sc. *resina* resin) (as TEREBINTH, see -INE²)]

turp'eth, n. Cathartic root of an E.-Ind. plant. [ME, f. OF *turbith* or med. L *turbith(um)* f. Arab. & Pers. *turbid*]

turp'itūde, n. Baseness, depravity. [F, or f. L *turpitudo* (*turpis* base, see -TUDE)]

turps. See TURPENTINE.

tur'quoise (-koiz, -kwoiz), n. Opaque sky-blue or greenish-blue precious stone; ~-*green*, pale colour between green & blue. [ME *turkeis* etc., f. OF *turqueise*, later -*oise* Turkish (*Turc* TURK, see -ESE)]

tu'rret, n. Small tower connected with main building whether rising from ground or projecting from wall or corbels; (mil.) low flat usu. revolving tower for gun & gunners in ship or fort; (hist.) square many-storeyed building on wheels used in attacking fortified place; ~ *gun* (for use in revolving ~); ~-*ship* (with guns in ~s). Hence ~ED² a. [ME, f. OF *torete* dim. of *tor* TOWER, see -ET¹]

tur'ricūlate, -ātéd, aa. (conch.). (Of shell) having a long spire. [f. L *turricula* (*turris* tower, see -CULE, -ATE²)]

tur'tle¹, n. (Now usu. ~-*dove*) kinds of dove, esp. a common wild kind noted for soft cooing & affection for mate & young. [OE *turtla*, -*le* = OHG *turtulo*, -*la*, dim. or assim. form of L *turtur*]

tur'tle², n., & v.i. 1. Marine reptile encased as tortoise & with flippers used in swimming, esp. (also *green ~*) kind much used for soup; MOCK² ~; *turn ~* (naut. sl.), capsize; ~-*shell*, tortoise-shell, esp. dark

kind used for inlaying, (also ~-*cowry* ~), tūtŏr'ĭaĹĹŸ² adv. 2. vb. Act as ~ to,
large handsome kind of cowry. 2. v.i. instruct; exercise restraint over (one*self*,
Hunt for~s, whence tŭrt'lEr¹, tŭrt'lING¹, one's passions, another); make one's
nn. [app. correl. of earlier *tortue* (see living as ~. [ME, f. AF, OF *tutour* or L
TORTOISE), assim. to prec.] *tutor* (*tuēri tut-* watch, see -OR)]

Tŭs'can, a. & n. (Language, inhabitant) tŭt'san, n. St-John's-wort, plant once
of Tuscany; ~ ORDER¹; ~ *straw*, fine held to heal wounds etc. [ME, of AF or
yellow wheat-straw used for hats etc. OF (unkn.) orig.]
[f. L *Tuscanus* (L *Tuscus*, see -AN)] tutti (tŏŏt'ē), mus. direction, & n. All

tŭsh¹, int., n., & v.i. (arch.). Pshaw. (voices, instruments) together; (n.) pass-
[ME, imit.] age for these. [It.]

tŭsh², n. Long pointed tooth, esp. canine tutti-frutti (tŏŏt'ē frŏŏtē), n. Confection,
tooth of horse. [ME repr. of rare OE ice-cream, of mixed fruits. [It., = all
tusc TUSK] fruits]

tŭsh'erŷ, n. (literary). Use of *Wardour* tŭtt'ŷ, n. Impure zinc oxide used as
Street archaisms such as TUSH¹. [-ERY; polishing-powder. [ME, f. OF *tutie* f.
word made by R. L. Stevenson] med. L *tutia* f. Arab. *tūtiyā*]

tŭsk, n., & v.t. 1. Long pointed tooth, tu'tu (tŏŏ'tŏŏ), n. Ballet dancer's short
esp. protruding from closed mouth as projecting skirt. [F]
in elephant, walrus, etc.; ~like tooth or tŭ'um.' see MEUM.
part in harrow, lock, etc. Hence (~)~ED² tu-whit' (tŏŏ-) n., tu-whoo' (tŏŏ-) n., &
(-kt), ~'Ÿ², aa. 2. v.t. Gore, thrust, tear v.i. (Make) cry of owl. [imit.]
up, with ~ or ~s. [ME alt. of OE *tux* *tŭxĕd'ō, n. (pl. ~s, ~es). Dinner-jacket.
(*tusc*; see TUSH²)] [T'~, place-name]

tŭsk'er, n. Elephant with developed tuyère (twēyār', tŏŏyār', twēr), twŷ'er,
tusks. [-ER¹] n. Pipe through which air is forced into

tŭss'er, -ur, -ōre, n. Oak-feeding silk- furnace etc. [earlier *tewire*, *twire*, *tweer*
worm yielding strong but coarse silk; (also f. OF *toiere*, mod. F *tuyère*]
~-*silk*) silk of this & some other silkworms. twa'ddl|e (-ŏ-), v.i., & n. (Indulge in)
[f. Hind. *tasar* f. Skr. *tasara* shuttle] senseless, feeble, or prosy talk. Hence

tŭss'ive, a. (med.). Of a cough. [f. L ~ER¹ n., ~Ÿ² a. [alt. f. earlier *twattle*]
tussis cough, see -IVE] twain, a. & n. (arch.). Two; two persons

tŭs'sle, n., & v.i. Struggle, scuffle, (*with* or things; *cut* etc. *in* ~ (in two). [OE
person, *for* thing). [orig. Sc. & north., *twēgen*, masc. nom. & acc. of *twā* TWO]
dim. of *touse*, see TOUSLE] twăng, v.i. & t., & n. 1. (Cause to) make

tŭss'ock, n. Clump, hillock, of grass etc.; ringing metallic sound as of string of
tuft, lock, of hair etc.; (also ~-*moth*) kinds musical instrument or bow when plucked,
of moth with tufted larvae; ~-*grass*, tall (derog.) play on or *on* (fiddle etc.) thus,
elegant grass on boggy ground in Pata- as *the fiddles* ~*ed*, ~*ed* (*on*) *his fiddle*,
gonia etc. Hence~Ÿ² a. [16th c., perh. ~*ed his bow*, whence ~LE(3) (-ăng'gl) v.i.
alt. f. dial. *tusk* tuft] & t.; speak, utter, with nasal sound.

tŭss'ōre. See TUSSER. 2. n. Sound of tense string when plucked,
nasal tone. [imit.]

tŭt¹, tŭt-tŭt', int., n., & v.i. (-tt-). 1. Int. twănk'ay, n. Kind of green tea. [f.
expr. impatience, contempt, or rebuke. Chin. *Tun-ki*, name of a stream]
2. n. This exclamation. 3. v.i. Exclaim 'twas (-oz), arch. or poet. contr. of *it was*.
~. [a natural utterance] tway'blāde, n. Kinds of orchid with green

‖ tŭt², n. (mining). Job; ~-*work*, piece- or purple flowers & single pair of leaves.
-work (cf. TRIBUTE). [c. 1700, of unkn. (*tway* var. of TWAIN +BLADE]
orig.] tweak, v.t., & n. 1. Pinch & twist sharply,

tŭt'ėlage, n. Guardianship; (period of) pull with sharp jerk, twitch. 2. n. Twitch,
being under this. [f. L *tutela* (*tuēri tuit-* sharp pull, pinch. Hence ‖ ~ER¹ n. (sl.),
or *tut-* watch) +-AGE] boy's catapult. [prob. alt. f. dial. *twick*,

tŭt'ėlar(ŷ), aa. Serving as a guardian, TWITCH]
protective; of a guardian, as~*authority*. tweed, n. Twilled woollen or wool-&-
[f. LL *tutelaris*, L -*arius*, f. *tutela* (prec., -cotton fabric with unfinished surface &
-AR¹, -ARY¹)] usu. two colours combined in the yarn,

tŭt'ėnăg, n. Zinc imported from China used esp. for men's clothes & largely
& E. Indies; white alloy like German made in S. Scotland; (pl.) suit of ~. [a
silver. [f. Marathi *tuttināg* perh. f. Skr. trade name originating in a misreading of
tuttha blue vitriol +*nāga* tin] *tweel*, Sc. form of TWILL, helped by assoc.

tŭt'or, n., & v.t. & i. 1. Private teacher, w. the river *Tweed*]
esp. one having general charge of person's twee'dle, n. Sound as of fiddle; ~*dum' &
education; ‖ (Eng. Univv.) college official, ~*dee'* (-ld-), things differing only or
usu. a fellow, directing studies of under- chiefly in name. [imit.]
graduates assigned him; (law) guardian 'tween, adv. & prep. Between, esp.
of a minor. Hence or cogn. ~AGE(2), ~-*decks*, (space) between decks. [ME,
~ESS¹, ~SHIP, nn., tūtŏr'IAL a. (also n., abbr.]
period of instruction given by a college

‖ **tween′ÿ,¦** n. (colloq.). Servant assisting two others e.g. cook & housemaid. [prec. +-Y³]

tweet, n., & v.i. Chirp (of bird). [imit.]

tweez′er, n., & v.t. **1.** (Pl., also *pair of* ~s) minute pair of tongs for taking up small objects, plucking out hairs, etc. **2.** v.t. Extract (hair, thorn, etc.) with ~s. [extended form of *tweezes* (cf. TROUSERS), pl. of obs. *tweeze*, case for small instruments, aphetic f. *etweese* = *etuis*, pl. of ETUI]

twelfth, a. & n. **1.** Next in order after eleventh (*the* ~, of August, as beginning of grouse-shooting); *T*~-*day* (after Christmas, festival of Epiphany); *T*~-*night*, night of this, celebrated with various festivities etc.; *T*~-*cake*, prepared for T~- -*night*. **2.** n. Each of 12 equal parts. Hence ~′LY³ adv. [OE *twelfta* (foll. -TH²)]

twelve, a. & n. One more than eleven, 12, xii; *the T*~ (apostles); *T*~ TABLES; *in* ~s (duodecimo); *long, square,* ~s, duodecimo pages of sheet variously folded; ~′FOLD a. & adv.; ~′*mo, 12mo,* = DUODECIMO; ‖~ *month,* year, as *has been there a* ~*month,* (adv.) *this day* ~*month,* a year hence or ago; ‖~′*pence* (arch. exc. shop), a shilling; ‖~′*penny,* shilling (adj.). [OE *twelf,* OS *twelif,* OHG *zwelif,* ON *tólf,* Goth. *twalif* f. Gmc **twalibhi-* f. **twa* TWO + **libh-* prob. rel. to LEAVE² (as if = two over)]

twen′tÿ, a. & n. Twice ten, 20, xx; *have told him* ~ (several) *times;* ~-*one, -two,* etc., *or one, two,* etc., *& ~; ~-five,* (rugby footb., hockey), line drawn across ground 25 yds from each goal, ground between this & goal-line; ~*mo,* ~*four′mo,* (*20mo, 24mo*), leaf of sheet folded into 20, 24, equal parts, book made up of such leaves. Hence **twen′tiETH** a. & n., ~′FOLD a. & adv. [OE *twentig* f. *twen-* two + -*tig* -TY²]

′twere (-er), arch. or poet. contr. of *it were.*

‖ **twerp,** n. (sl.). Bounder, cad.

twi-, twy-, = two, double, f. OE *twi-,* comb. form expr. two, occas. twice, in TWILIGHT & in some arch. or pseudo-arch. forms, as: ~′*bill,* double-bladed battle- -axe, kind of mattock; ~′*blade,* = TWAY-BLADE; ~′*fold* a. & adv., twofold; ~′*folded;* ~′*forked;* ~′*formed.* [= OHG *zwi-,* ON *tvi,* cogn. w. L *bi-* BI-, Gk *di-* DI-]

twice, adv. Two times (esp. of multiplication), on two occasions, as ~ *3 is 6, told him* ~; doubly, in double degree or quantity, as ~ *as strong, has* ~ *the strength, is* ~ *the man he was* (~ as strong etc.); (colloq.) *did it in* ~ (two attempts or instalments). [OE *twiges* f. *twige* adv. twice +-ES]

‖ **twi′cer,** n. Compositor who is also pressman; (sl.) one who usu. goes to church twice on Sunday. [f. prec. +-ER¹]

twid′dle, v.t. & i., & n. **1.** Twirl idly, esp. ~ one's thumbs (for lack of occupation); trifle *with* (object); *twiddling-line,* string attached to compass-gimbal & pulled to make compass-card play freely. **2.** n. Slight twirl. [app. imit., after *twirl, twist,* & *fiddle, piddle*]

twig¹, n. Small shoot or branch of tree or plant; (anat.) small branch of artery etc.; (electr.) small distributing conductor; divining-rod, esp. *work the* ~; *hop the* ~ (colloq.), die. Hence (-)~gED² (-gd), ~′LESS, ~g′Y² (-g-), aa. [north. OE *twigge,* obsc. rel. to OE *twig, twi;* cf. OHG *zwig, zwi;* all f. stem TWI-]

twig², v.t. (colloq.; -gg-). Understand, catch the meaning of, (person, words, plan, *that* etc., or abs.); perceive, observe. [18th c., of unkn. orig.]

twi′light (-it), n., & v.t. (~ed). **1.** Light from sky when sun is below horizon in morning or (usu.) evening; faint light; (fig.) state of imperfect knowledge, understanding, etc.; ~ *arc(h)* or *curve* (bounding the brightest region of ~ where atmosphere receives solar rays direct); ~ *of the gods* (Norse myth.), conflict in which gods & giants destroyed each other; ~ *sleep,* name of a method of making child-birth painless. **2.** v.t. (rare). Illuminate faintly. [ME (TWI-+LIGHT¹)]

twill, n., & v.t. **1.** Textile fabric in which weft-threads pass alternately over one warp-thread & under (not one as in plain weaving but) two or more thus producing diagonal lines. **2.** v.t. Weave (material) thus (esp. in p.p.). [Sc. & north. var. of obs. *twilly,* OE *twili* = OHG *zwilih,* f. TWI- after L BI(*lix* f. *licium* thread)]

′twill, arch. or poet. contr. of *it will.*

twin, a., n., & v.t. & i. (-nn-). **1.** Forming, being one of, a closely related or associated pair esp. of children born at a birth, as ~ *children, brother(s), sister(s), the T*~ *Brothers* or *Brethren,* Castor & Pollux, ~ *bed(s);* (bot.) growing in pairs; consisting of two closely connected & similar parts; ~ *boat, steamer* (with two hulls supporting one deck & having paddle-wheel between them); ~-*screw,* steamer with two propellers on separate shafts having opposite twists; ~ *set,* woman's matching cardigan and jumper. **2.** n. Each of a closely related pair esp. of children born at a birth; exact counterpart of person or thing; compound crystal one part of which is in a reversed position with reference to the other; *The T*~s, Gemini; SIAMESE ~s. Hence ~′LING¹, ~′SHIP, nn. **3.** vb. Join intimately together, couple, pair, (*with;* t. & i.); ~*ning-machine, -saw* (for cutting out teeth of combs, these being cut in pairs). Hence ~n′ING¹ n., formation of ~ crystals. [OE *twinn* adj. double, f. TWI-; cf. ON *tvinnr*]

twin|e, n., & v.t. & i. **1.** String of two or more strands of hemp, manilla, etc., twisted together; coil, twist, as *snaky* ~*es;* interlacing, tangle. **2.** vb. Form (thread) by twisting strands together, whence ~′ER¹(2) n.; form (garland etc.) of interwoven material, garland (brow etc.)

with; interweave; coil, wind, (thing *about*, *round*, another); (of plant, snake) coil itself or its*elf* (*round*). Hence ~'in**g**l**y**² adv. [OE *twin*, Du. *twijn*, ult. f. stem of TWI-; vb ME *twine*, Du. *twijnen*, goes w. n.]

twinge (-j), v.t. (rare), & n. (Affect with) sharp darting pain, as *conscience* ~*d him*, *a* ~ *of toothache*, *rheumatism*, *conscience*, *remorse*. [OE *twengan*, = MLG *twengen*, OHG *zwengen*; n. (16th c.) f. vb]

twinkl|e (twing'kl), v.i. & t., & n. **1.** (Of light, star, etc.) shine with quick gleams, sparkle; (of eyelids, feet in dancing, etc.) move rapidly up & down or to & fro; blink, wink, (one's eyes, or intr. of person or eye); (of eyes) sparkle (*at* jest etc.); emit (light) in quick gleams. Hence ~er¹ n. **2.** n. Twitching of eyelid, blink, wink; sparkle, gleam, of the eyes, as *a humorous*, *mischievous*, ~*e*; short rapid movement e.g. of feet in dancing; quick tremulous light, glimmer. [OE *twinclian*, frequent. of **twincan*, repr. by ME *twinke*, MHG *zwinken*]

twink'ling, n. In vbl senses, esp. *in a* ~, *in the* ~ *of an eye*, *in the* ~ *of a* BED¹*post*, in a moment, very quickly. [-ING¹]

twirl, v.t. & i., & n. **1.** Revolve (t. & i.) rapidly, spin, whirl, (often *round*); turn (one's *thumbs* etc.) round & round in purposeless way, twiddle. **2.** n. Rapid or idle circular motion, flourish or curl made with pen etc. [16th c., prob. alt., after *whirl*, f. obs. *tirl* THRILL]

twirp. Var. of TWERP.

twist, n., & v.t. & i. **1.** Thread, rope, etc., made by winding two or more strands etc. about one another; kinds of strong silk thread & of cotton yarn; roll of bread, tobacco, etc. in form of ~; paper packet with screwed-up ends. **2.** Act of ~ing, condition of being ~ed, as *give it a* ~, *has a curious* ~, *full of turns & ~s*; jazzlike dance with vigorous bodily contortions. **3.** Manner or degree in which thing is ~ed, e.g. inclination of rifle-grooves, whirling motion given to ball in cricket etc. to make it take special curve. **4.** Peculiar tendency of mind, character, etc. (freq. derog.). **5.** ~ing strain, (angle showing) amount of torsion of rod etc., forward motion combined with rotation about an axis. **6.** ‖ Kinds of mixed drink, as *gin* ~. **7.** ‖ (colloq.). Appetite, as *had a tremendous* ~. **8.** *Damascus* ~, process of ~ing. Damascus iron to form gun-barrel; ~ *of the wrist*, (fig.) dexterity, knack. **9.** vb. Wind (strands etc.) one about another; form (rope etc.) thus; interweave (thing *with* or *in with* another). **10.** Give spiral form to (rod, column, etc.) as by rotating the ends in opposite directions; receive, grow in, spiral form. **11.** Cause (ball, esp. in billiards) to rotate while following curved path. **12.** Twine (flowers etc. *into* garland etc.), make (garland etc.) thus. **13.** Make one's way,

make one's *way*, (*through* crowd, etc., *along*, etc.) in winding manner; dance the ~. **14.** Wrench out of natural shape, distort slightly, as *limbs* ~*ed on the rack*, *features* ~*ed with pain*, (fig.) *wants to* ~ *my words into an admission of error*; ~ one's *arm*, force his hand or wrist round as torture. **15.** ~ *off*, break off (piece) by ~ing; ~ *up*, ~ (paper etc.) into spiral form. Hence ~'ABLE a. [ME, f. TWI-]

twis'ter, n. In vbl senses; also or esp.: untrustworthy person, swindler; twisting ball in cricket or billiards; girder; inner part of thigh as proper place to rest upon on horseback. [-ER¹]

twit, v.t. (-tt-). Reproach, upbraid, taunt, (person *with* fault etc.); tease. Hence ~t'in**g**l**y**² adv. [16th c. *twite*, aphetic f. *atwite* f. OE *ætwïtan* (*æt* at + *wïtan* blame)]

twitch¹, v.t. & i., & n. **1.** Pull (thing *off* etc.) with light jerk; pull at, jerk at, (person's sleeve etc.) esp. to call attention; (of features, muscles, limbs) move or contract spasmodically. **2.** n. Sudden involuntary contraction or movement, sudden pull or jerk; veterinary appliance for stilling horse during operation. [ME *twicche*, = LG *twikken*, MHG *zwicken*, OE *twiccian*, dial. *twick*]

twitch², n. = QUITCH. [dial. var.]

twite, n. Bird like linnet. [perh. imit. of cry]

twitt'er, v.i. & t., & n. **1.** (Of bird) utter succession of light tremulous sounds, chirp; utter, express, thus. **2.** n. Such series of sounds; (colloq., also ~A'TION n.) excited state. [ME, imit.; cf. OHG *zwizzirōn*]

'twixt, prep. = BETWIXT. [abbr.]

two (tōō), a. & n. **1.** One more than one, 2, ii ; *one or* ~, a few (also lit.); *cut*, *divide*, etc., *in* ~ (into ~ parts); ~ *can play at that game*, threat of retaliation; *put* ~ & ~ *together*, make inference from data; *in* ~ ~*s*, in a very short time. **2.** ~-*cleft* (bot.), divided nearly to the middle in ~ parts; ~-*edged*, (of sword etc.) having an edge on each side, (fig., of argument, compliment, etc.) cutting both ways, ambiguous; ~-*faced*, (fig.) insincere; ~*fold* a. & adv., double, doubly; ~-*handed*, having ~ hands, (of sword) requiring to be used with both hands, (of saw, game, etc.) to be worked, played, etc., by ~ persons; ~-*handled*, -*legged*, -*tipped*, -*masted*, -*petalled*, -*toothed*, etc., (having ~ handles etc.); ~-*line* a. (print.), having a depth double that of the size specified, as ~-*line pica* ; ‖ ~*pence* (tŭp'ns), sum of, silver coin (now only as maundy money) worth, ~ pence (~*pence coloured*, cheap &, as opp. *penny plain*, gaudy); ‖ ~*penny* (tŭp'eni), (adj.) worth or costing ~*pence*, cheap, worthless, (n.) kind of beer orig. sold at ~*pence* a quart (hist.), (sl.) *tuck in your* ~*penny* (head, at leap-frog); ‖ ~*penny-halfpenny* (tŭp'eni hāp'ni), contemptible, insignificant, trumpery; ~-*ply*, of ~ strands, layers, or thicknesses, as ~-*ply rope, carpet*; ~-*sided*, having ~ sides, aspects, etc.; ~-*speed*, adapted for ~ rates of speed, as ~-*speed gear, bicycle*; ~-*step*, kind of round dance in march or polka time; ~-*tongued*, double-tongued, deceitful; ~-*way*, (electr.) of switch) permitting current to be switched on or off from either of ~ points, (plumbing, of cock) permitting fluid to flow in either of ~ channels, (math.) having double mode of variation. Hence ~'NESS n. [fem. of the OE numeral *twegen* masc. (TWAIN), *twā* fem. & neut., *tū* neut.; cf. OS *twēne*; *twā, twō*: *twē*, OHG *zwēne*: *zwā, zwō*: *zwei*; cogn. w. Skr. *dwau, dwē*, Gk & L DUO]

two'some (tōō-), a. & n. (Game, dance, etc.) for two persons. [-SOME]

'twould, contr. of *it would*.

twy- pref., var. of TWI-.

twyer. See TUYÈRE.

-ty¹, suf. denoting quality or condition, repr. ME -*tie*, -*tè*, -*te* f. OF -*te* (mod. F -*té*) in pop. derivv. f. L -*itatem* (nom. -*itas*). Such L types as *bonitatem* became OF *bonte* (w. loss of atonic L -*i*-), whence ME *bonte* bounty; thus ME *plente* plenty, *poverte* poverty. Many of these older adoptives were refash. after the L, as ME *purte* purity (similarly in F, cf. OF *verte*, *amablete*, now *vérité, amabilité*. See -ITY.

-ty², suf. = tens, as *twenty, thirty, ninety*, (two, three, etc. tens); OE (OS) -*tig*, = OHG -*zug* etc. (G -*zig*), & the independent wds ON *tigr*, Goth. *tigus* TEN.

Tyb'urn, n. (hist.) Place of execution in London on site of Marble Arch; ~ *ticket* (hist.), exemption from parish offices etc. granted to one who prosecuted a felon to conviction; || ~ *tippet*, halter; || ~ *tree*, gallows. Hence **Tyburn'ia** n., fashionable London district north of Hyde Park.

Tychon'ic (-k-), a. Of the Danish astronomer Tycho Brahe (d. 1601) or his system. [-IC]

tycoon', n. Title applied by foreigners to shogun of Japan 1854-68; *(colloq.) business magnate. [f. Jap. *taikun* great prince]

tying. See TIE¹.

tyke, ti-, n. Cur; || low fellow; *Yorkshire* ~, Yorkshireman. [ME, f. ON *tik* bitch]

tyler. See TILER.

tyl'opŏd, a. & n. (Animal) with padded not hoofed digits, e.g. camel. Hence **tylŏp'odous** a. [f. Gk *tulos* knob or *tulē* callus, cushion + *pous podos* foot]

tylos'is, n. (Path.) inflammation of eyelids with hardening of the margins; (bot.) kind of growth formed in the cavity of a duct. So **tylŏt'ic** a. [mod. L, f. Gk f. *tulos* or *tulē* (prec., -OSIS)]

tyl'ote, n. (zool.). Cylindrical sponge-spicule knobbed at ends. [as prec.]

tymp, n. Crown of opening in front of hearth in blast-furnace; short horizontal roof-timber in mine. [abbr. of foll.]

tym'pan, n. Stretched sheet of membrane or thin material; frame for equalizing pressure in some printing-presses; (anat. archit.) = TYMPANUM. [f. F *tympan* or L TYMPANUM]

tympan'ic, a. Like, acting like, a tympan-head; (anat.) of the tympanum; ~ *membrane*, drum-membrane of ear; ~ (*bone*), bone of ear supporting this. [-IC]

tympanist. Var. of TIMPANIST.

tympan|it'ēs (-z), n. Swelling of abdomen caused by air in intestine etc. Hence ~*it'ic* a. [LL f. Gk *tumpanitēs* of drum (TYMPANUM, -ITE¹)]

tympanit'is, n. Inflammation of lining membrane of tympanum. [-ITIS]

tym'panum, n. (pl. -*na*). (Anat.) middle ear, (also *tympanic membrane*) ear-drum; modified end of trachea in ducks etc.; (archit.) triangular space forming field of pediment, similar space over door between lintel & arch, door-panel; drum-wheel for raising water from stream; kind of treadmill. [L, f. Gk *tumpanon* drum]

Tyn'wald (-ôld), n. Isle of Man legislature. [f. ON *thing-vǫllr* place of assembly (*thing* assembly + *vǫllr* field)]

type¹, n. n. 1. Person, thing, event, serving as illustration, symbol, prophetic similitude, or characteristic specimen, of another thing or of a class, as *water may serve as a ~ of instability, paschal lamb is a ~ of Christ, these things are a ~* (have a prophetic significance), *the treatment he received is but a ~ of what patriots must expect, he is an admirable ~ of modern athleticism or of the modern athlete*. 2. Class of things etc. having common characteristics, as *her beauty was of or belonged to another ~, dislike men of that ~*. 3. (biol. etc.). Plan of structure, as *deviates from the ~*; main division of animal or vegetable kingdom characterized by this, as *the vertebrate ~*; organism having the essential characteristics of its group (so ~ *genus*, genus giving its name to & having the characteristics of a higher group, e.g. a family); whence **typ'AL** a. 4. (chem.). Compound whose structure illustrates that of many others, esp. hydrochloric acid, water, ammonia, & marsh-gas. 5. Object, conception, work of art, serving as model for subsequent artists. 6. Device on either side of medal or coin. 7. (print.). Piece of metal or wood having on its upper surface a letter or character for use in printing, (collect. sing.) set or supply or (with pl.) kind of these, as *wooden ~s are or ~ is now used only for posters, ran short of ~, short of certain ~s, was printed in various ~s* (kinds or sizes of ~), *printed in large ~, a large-~ Bible*; brilliant, diamond, pearl, ruby, nonpareil, emerald, minion, brevier, bourgeois, long primer, small pica, pica, English, great primer, canon, ~ (principal sizes in ascending order); BLACK¹-letter, CHURCH¹-text, CLARENDON, GERMAN²-text,

GOTHIC, ITALIC, ROMAN², RUNIC, SCRIPT, ~; FOUNT² *of* ~. 8. ~*-bar*, line of ~s in solid bar as cast in some ~-setting machines; ~*-high*, (of woodcut etc.) of proper height to print with ~; ~*-metal*, alloy used for printing-~s; ~*'script*, ~written matter; ~*ᶥsetter*, compositor, (also) composing machine; ~*ᶥsetting*, setting of ~s in proper order for printing, ~*-setting machine* (for simplifying this process, occas. including the making of ~s as they are needed); ~*-wheel*, wheel bearing letters in relief as used in some ~writers & telegraphs; ~*ᶜ write*, print (copy etc., or abs.) with ~*-writer*; ~*'writer*, machine for producing printed characters on paper as substitute for handwriting, (now rare) typist. [F, or f. L f. Gk *tupos* impression, figure, type, f. *tuptō* strike]

typeᵌ, v.t. Be a type of; typewrite. [prec.]

typhlᶥit'ĭs, n. Inflammation of caecum & vermiform appendix. Hence ~*it'ĬC* a. [mod. L, f. Gk *tuphlon* caecum or blind gut (*tuphlos* blind) +-ITIS]

typh'oid, a. & n. Like typhus; ~ (*fever*), infectious fever with eruption of red points on chest & abdomen & severe intestinal irritation, enteric; ~ *bacillus*, germ causing ~; ~ *condition* (of depressed vitality, occurring in many acute diseases); ~ *pneumonia* (combined with ~). Hence typhoid'AL a. [f. TYPHUS + -OID]

typhomān'ĭa, n. Muttering delirium characteristic of typhus. [Gk (*tuphŏ-*) f. *tuphos* TYPHUS, -MANIA]

typhōon', n. Violent hurricane in the China seas occurring esp. from July to October. Hence typhŏn'ĬC a. [partly f. Arab. *tūfān* perh. f. Gk *tuphōn* whirlwind, partly f. Chin. *tai fung* big wind]

typh'us, n. Fever marked by eruption of purple spots, great prostration, & usu. delirium; *malignant, simple*, ~, severe, mild, form of ~. Hence typh'ous a. [mod. L f. Gk *tuphos* smoke, stupor]

typ'ĭc, a. = foll. (first sense). [f. F *typique* f. LL f. Gk *tupikos* (as TYPE¹, see -IC)]

typ'ical, a. Serving as a type or characteristic example, representative, symbolical, emblematic, (*of*), as *a* ~ *genus, plant, Scotsman, is* ~ *of the genus, was* ~ *of* (foreshadowed) *Christ's second coming*; characteristic of, serving to distinguish, a type, as ~ *markings, structure, phraseology*. Hence ~LY² adv., ~NESS n. [f. LL *typicalis* (prec., -AL)]

typ'ĭᶥfŷ, v.t. Represent by a type, foreshadow; be a type of, embody the characteristics of. Hence ~FICA'TION, ~fīER¹, nn. [f. L *typhus* TYPE¹+-FY]

typ'ist, n. User of typewriter. [f. TYPE¹ +-IST]

typ'ō, n. (sl.; pl. ~s). = TYPOGRAPHER. [abbr.]

typ'|o-, comb. form of Gk *tupos* TYPE¹, as: ~*ograph*, machine for making & setting type; ~*olite*, stone impressed with figure

of animal etc., fossil; ~*ŏl'ogy*, doctrine, interpretation, of (esp. biblical) types, so ~*olo'gical* a.; ~*onym* (biol.), name based on a type, so ~*ŏn'ĭmal*, ~*onĭm'ĭc*, aa.

typŏg'raph|ŷ, n. Art of printing, whence ~ER¹ n.; character, appearance, of printed matter, as *faults of* ~*y, the* ~*y was admirable*. Hence typŏgrăph'ĬC(AL) aa., typŏgrăph'ĬCALLY² adv. [F (-*ie*), = TYPE +-0- +-GRAPHY]

tyrănn'ᶥic(al), a. (~*ic* rare). Acting like, characteristic of, a tyrant; arbitrary, imperious, despotic. Hence or cogn. ~icALY², tyrannousLY², adv., ~ical-NESS n., ty'rannous a. [~*ic* f. L f. Gk *turannikos* (TYRANT, -IC) +-AL]

tyrănn'ᶥ|cĭde, n. Killer, killing, of a tyrant. Hence ~cĭd'AL a. [F, f. L *tyrannicida*, -*cidium* (as TYRANT, see -CIDE)]

ty'rannize, -ise (-iz), v.i. & t. Play the tyrant, rule despotically or cruelly (*over* person etc.); (now rare) rule (person etc.) despotically. [f. F *tyranniser* (TYRANT, see -IZE)]

ty'rannŷ, n. Despotic or cruel exercise of power; instance of this, tyrannical act or behaviour; rule of (Greek) tyrant, period of this. [ME, f. OF *tyrannie* f. med. L (-*ia*) f. Gk *turannia*, as foll., -Y¹]

tyr'ant, n. Oppressive or cruel ruler; (Gk hist.) absolute ruler usu. owing his office to usurpation, *Thirty T*~*s*, oligarchs ruling Athens 404–403 B.C.; ~*-bird*, ~ *fly-catcher*, kinds of Amer. passerine bird. [ME *tyran, -ant*, f. OF *tiran*, tyrant f. L f. Gk *turannos*]

tyre¹, n. (Anglo-Ind.). Curdled milk & cream. [Tamil *tayir*]

tyre². See TIRE².

tyr'ō. See TIRO.

Tyrolēse' (-z), a. & n. (pl. same). (Native) of the Tyrol. [-ESE]

Tyrŏliěnne', n. Dance of Tyrolese peasants, song suitable for this. [F]

tyrotŏx'ĭcŏn, n. A ptomaine produced in milk or cheese. [f. Gk *turos* cheese+ *toxikon* poison]

Ty'rrhēne, Tyrrhēn'ĭan, (-rē-), aa. & nn. Etruscan. [f. L f. Gk *Turrhēnos* +-IAN]

tzetze. See TSETSE.

Tzigane (tsĭgahn'), a. & n. **1.** Of the Hungarian gipsies or their music. **2.** n. Hungarian gipsy. [F, f. Magyar *czigány*]

U

U, u, (ū), letter (pl. U's, 'U's). *U-boat*, German submarine [G *untersee*, underwater]; *U-bolt, -tube*, etc. (shaped like U); U.P. (sl. pronunc. of *up* adv., esp. *it's all U.P.*).

ūbi'etŷ, n. Being in definite place, local relation, whereness. [f. L *ubi* where, see -TY]

ūb'ĭ ĭn'fra, adv. In the place (in book etc.) mentioned below. [L. lit. where below]

ūbiquītār′ian, a. & n. (theol.). Of, believer in, the omnipresence of Christ's body. Hence ~ISM n. [foll., -ARIAN]

ŭbi′quit|ў, n. Omnipresence; being everywhere or in an indefinite number of places at same time; ||~*y of the king* (law), his official presence in courts in the person of his judges. Hence ~OUS a., ~OUSLY² adv., ~OUSNESS n. [f. mod. L *ubiquitas* f. L *ubique* everywhere f. *ubi* where, -ITY]

ŭb′ĭ sŭp′ra, adv. In the place (in book etc.) above mentioned. [L, lit. where above]

ūd′al, n. Kind of freehold right based on uninterrupted possession prevailing in N. Europe before feudal system & still in Orkney & Shetland (often attrib., as ~ *tenure*); ~*man*, holder of property by ~, so -IER¹ n. [f. ON *ōthal*, = OE *ǣthel*, *ēthel*, OHG *uodil*]

ŭdd′er, n. Mammary glands of cattle etc. esp. when large & having more than one teat. Hence (-)~ED² (-erd), ~LESS, aa. [OE *ūder*, OS *ūdar*, OHG *ūtar*, f. Gmc *ūdhr-* cogn. w. L *uber*, Gk *outhar*]

ūdŏm′ĕter, n. Rain-gauge. Hence ūdo-mĕt′ric a. [f. F *udomètre* f. L *udus* damp +-o-+-METER]

ugh (ŏŏh), int. expr. disgust or horror.

ŭg′lў, a. & n. **1**. Unpleasing or repulsive to sight, as *an ~ beast of a bulldog, must not make ~ faces, the ugliest house I have seen, has an ~ scar on the forehead*; morally repulsive, vile, discreditable, unpleasant, unpleasantly suggestive, threatening, unpromising, as ~ *vices, his conduct has an ~ look, ~ rumours are about, an ~* (awkward) *job, an ~ customer*, formidable person, *cloud has an ~ look, have had ~ weather, an ~ gash*; ~ *duckling*, person who turns out the genius etc. of the family after being thought the dullard etc. (w. ref. to cygnet in brood of ducks in an Andersen tale). Hence ŭg′lĭFY v.t., ŭg′lĭLY² adv., ŭg′lĭNESS n. **2**. n. || Shade worn as appendage to bonnet about middle of 19th c. [ME, f. ON *ugglígr* to be dreaded, f. *ugga* to dread, see -LY¹]

Ŭg′rian, **Ŭg′rĭc** (ōō-), aa. Finnic. [f. name of a tribe +-IAN, -IC]

ŭh′lan (ōō-, ū-), n. (hist.). Cavalryman armed with lance in some European armies. [F, G, f. Pol. (*h*)*ulan* f. Turk. *oghlān* son, youth, servant]

Uitlander (āt′lŏnder), n. (S. Africa). Foreigner, alien. [Du., f. *uit* out + *land* land; cf. OUTLANDISH]

ūkāse′, n. Edict of Tsarist Russian government; any arbitrary order. [f. Russ. *ukaz′* ordinance, edict]

ukulele (ūkŭlā′lē), n. Four-stringed Hawaiian guitar. [native]

-ular, suf. repr. L -*ularis* (see -ULE, -AR²), in adjj. f. nn. in -*ulus*, -*ula*, -*ulum*. E adjj. in ~ are usu. f. L, med. or mod. L forms, some (*corpusc~, funic~*) dir. on L nn.

ŭl′cer, n. Open sore on external or internal surface of body with secretion of pus etc.; (fig.) moral blemish, corrupting influence, etc. Hence or cogn. ~ED² (-erd), ~OUS, aa., ~OUSLY² adv., ~OUSNESS n. [ME, f. OF *ulcere*, or f. L *ulcus -eris*, rel. to Gk *helkos*]

ŭl′cer|āte, v.i. & t. Form, convert or be converted into, affect with, an ulcer (lit. & fig.). Hence or cogn. ~ABLE, ~ATIVE, aa., ~A′TION n. [f. L *ulcerare* (prec.), -ATE²]

-ule, suf. of dimm. f. L wds in -*ulus*, -*ula*, -*ulum*, as *globule* (L *globulus* f. *globus*), *granule, pustule*, & in mod. wds on L anal. *anguillule*.

u′lēma (ōō-), n. Moslem doctors of sacred law & theology esp. in former Turk. empire. [f. Arab '*ulema* pl. of '*alim* learned *i.* '*alama* know]

-ulent, suf. of adjj. f. L, repr. L -*ulentus*, the normal form of -*lentus* -LENT, as in *fraud~, turb~, truc~*; meaning, 'abounding in, full of'. Hence n. suf. -*ulence*.

ūli′ginōse, a. (bot.). Growing in muddy places. [f. L *uliginosus* (*uligo -ginis* moisture, see -OSE¹)]

ŭll′age (commerce.). What a cask etc. wants of being full, loss by evaporation or leakage; (sl.) dregs. [ME, f. AF *ulliage*, OF *ouillage* (*ouiller* fill up, -AGE)]

ŭl′m|in, n. (chem.). Black gummy substance found on elm & other trees & in vegetable mould etc. Hence ~IC, ~OUS, aa. (chem.). [f. L *ulmus* elm +-IN]

ŭl′n|a, n. (pl. *-ae*). Inner of two bones of forearm (cf. RADIUS). Hence ~AR¹ a., ~o-comb. form. [L, cogn. w. Gk *ōlenē*, & ELL]

-ulose, suf. repr. L -*ulosus* (see -ULE, -OSE¹), forming adjj. on nn. in -*ulus*, -*ula*, -*ulum*. In E dir. f. L (*calc~*) or on L anal. (*glob~*). Where forms in ~ are paralleled by forms in -*ulous*, the former are either older forms now displaced by -*ulous*, or later forms different. for special senses.

ūlŏt′rich|an, a. & n., ~ous a., (-k-). Woolly-haired; (member) of the woolly-haired division of mankind. [f. Gk *oulos* woolly + *thrix trikhos* hair +-AN, -OUS]

-ulous, suf. repr. L -*ulosus* (see -ULOSE), as in *fab~, pop~*, & L -*ulus*, as in *garr~, trem~*.

ŭl′ster, n. Long loose overcoat often with belt orig. of U~ frieze, whence ~ED² (-erd) a.; U~ *custom*, form of tenant-right in Ireland. [U~ in Ireland]

ŭltēr′ior, a. Situated beyond; more remote, not immediate, in the future, in the background, beyond what is seen or avowed, (~ *views, motive, plans*). Hence ~LY² adv. [L, compar. adj., corresp. to the advv. *ultra, ultro*]

ŭl′tĭma, a. Last, most remote, (in phrr.: ~ *rā′tiō* (-shi-), final argument esp. force; ~ *ratio rēg′um*, last argument of kings, resort to arms; ~ THULE). [L, fem. of *ultimus*, superl. as prec.]

ŭl′timate, a. Last, final, beyond which

no other exists or is possible, as ~ *result*, *analysis*; fundamental, primary, as ~ *basis*, ~ *principles*, *truths*, ~ *cause* (beyond which no other can be found), *the ~ facts of nature* (beyond reach of analysis). Hence ~LY² adv., ~NESS n. [f. LL *ultimare* come to an end (*ultimus*, as prec.), see -ATE²]

ŭltĭmāt'um, n. (pl. *-tums*, *-ta*). Final proposal or statement of terms, rejection of which by opposite party may lead to rupture, declaration of war, etc.; ultimate conclusion; fundamental principle. [neut. p.p. as prec.]

ŭl'tĭmō, adj. (usu. abbr. *ult.*). In the month preceding that now current (cf. PROXIMO, INSTANT¹), *as your letters of the 28th ult. & 3rd inst.* [L, = in last (*mense* month), see ULTIMA]

ŭltĭmogĕn'ĭture, n. System in which youngest son (cf. PRIMOGENITURE) takes inheritance, = BOROUGH-ENGLISH. [f. L *ultimus* (see ULTIMA) on PRIMOGENITURE]

ŭl'tra, a. & n. Favouring, advocate of, extreme views or measures. [orig. as abbr. of F *ultra-royaliste*]

ŭltra-, pref. = L *ultra* beyond, on the other side of, as ~*montane*, ~*terrestrial*, ~*violet*; ~*microscope*, instrument devised to reveal objects too minute to be detected by the ordinary microscope; ~*microscopic*, beyond the power of conventional microscopes; ~*short wave* (radio), having a wave-length below 10 metres; ~*son'ic* a., relating to sound waves of such pitch as to be beyond the threshold of human audibility; ~*son'ics* n. pl.; esp. in sense 'excessively or extravagantly, beyond what is usual or natural or reasonable', as ~*classical*, ~*conservatism*, ~*conservative*, ~*cosmopolitan*, ~*critical*, ~*fashionable*, ~*partisan*, ~*Protestant*(ism), ~*religious*.

ŭl'tra|ist, n. Holder of extreme opinions in politics, religion, etc. So ~ISM n. [-IST]

ŭltramarine' ('-ēn), a. & n. 1. Situated beyond the sea. 2. n. Blue pigment got from lapis lazuli; *artificial* ~ (made by mixing clay, carbonate of soda, sulphur, & resin); ~ *ashes*, residuum of lapis lazuli after extraction of ~, used by old masters for neutral flesh-tints etc. [f. med. L ULTRA(*marinus* MARINE); n. sense from fact that lapis lazuli was brought from beyond sea]

ŭltramŏn't|āne, a. & n. 1. Situated south of the Alps; Italian; favourable to the absolute authority of the Pope in matters of faith & discipline, whence ~anISM, ~anIST, nn. 2. n. One who resides south of the Alps, person holding ~ane views. [f. med. L ULTRA(*montanus* f. L *mons* *-ntis* mountain+-ANE); earlier in senses, 'north of Alps', 'unfavourable to Pope', etc., cf. TRAMONTANE, CIS*montane*]

ŭltramŭn'dāne, a. Beyond the world or the solar system; of another life. [f. L ULTRA(*mundanus* MUNDANE)]

ŭltra-vī'olĕt, a. (Of invisible rays of the spectrum) beyond the violet rays. [ULTRA-]

ŭl'tra vīr'ēs (-z), adv. or pred. a. Beyond one's power or authority. [L]

ŭl'ŭl|āte, v.i. Howl; hoot. So ~ANT a., ~A'TION n. [f. L *ululare*, see -ATE³]

-um. See -IUM.

ŭm'bel, n. (bot.). Flower-cluster in which stalks nearly equal in length spring from common centre & form a flat or convex or concave surface as in parsley. Hence ~IAL, ~IAR¹, ~IATE²(2), ~LIF'EROUS, ŭm-bĕll'IFORM, aa., ~IET¹, ŭmbĕll'ULE, nn. [f. L *umbella* sunshade dim. of UMBRA]

ŭm'ber, n., a., & v.t. 1. Natural pigment like ochre but darker & browner (*raw* ~, this in natural state, of dark yellow colour, *burnt* ~, redder & deeper in colour), whence ~Y² a.; grayling; ~*bird* (also *umbrette*), Afr. bird allied to stork & heron. 2. adj. Of ~ colour, dark, dusky. 3. v.t. Colour with ~. [f. F (*terre d'*) *ombre* or It. (*terra di*) *ombra*, either = shadow (L *umbra*) or f. fem. of L *Umber* Umbrian]

ŭmbil'ical (or -ik'al), a. Of, situated near, the umbilicus, as ~ *cord*, ropelike structure passing from foetus to placenta; central; connected through the female line, as *an ~ ancestor*. [f. med. L *umbilicalis* (UMBILICUS, -AL)]

ŭmbil'ic|ate, a. Shaped like a navel, whence ~A'TION n.; having an umbilicus. [f. L *umbilicatus* (UMBILICUS, -ATE²)]

ŭmbilic'us (or -bil'I-), n. Navel, whence ŭmbiliF'EROUS, ŭm'biliFORM, aa.; (bot., zool., conch.) navel-like formation; (geom.) point in a surface through which all lines of curvature pass; (Rom. ant.) boss at each end of stick on which MS. was rolled. [L, cogn. w. Gk *omphalos*, & NAVEL]

ŭm'bles (-blz), n. pl. (obs.). Edible offal of deer; attrib. in *umble-pie* (cf. HUMBLE *pie*). [15th c.; var. of NUMBLES]

ŭm'bō, n. (pl. ~s, ~*nes* pr. -ōn'ēz). Boss of shield, esp. in centre; (bot., zool., etc.) boss, knob, protuberance. Hence ŭm-bonAL, ŭm'bonATE², ŭmbŏn'IC, aa. [L, gen. *-onis*]

ŭm'br|a, n. (pl. ~*ae*). (Astron.) total shadow (cf. PENUMBRA) cast by the earth or moon in an eclipse; dark central part of sun-spot (cf. PENUMBRA). (Rom. ant.) uninvited guest brought by a guest. Hence ~AL a. [L, = shade]

ŭm'brage, n. Sense of slight or injury, offence, as *give*, *take*, ~; (chiefly poet.) shade, what gives shade, so ŭmbrāge-OUS (-jus) a., F OF *ombrage* f. Rom. **umbraticum* (L *-us* adj.), see UMBRA, -AGE]

ŭmbrĕll'a, n. 1. Light circular canopy of silk or other material attached to radiating folding frame sliding on stick carried in the hand as protection against rain or (now usu. *sunshade, parasol*) sun; (fig.)

a screen of fighter aircraft or (in full ~ *barrage*) a curtain of fire put up as protection against enemy aircraft; gelatinous disc of jellyfish etc. by contraction & expansion of which it swims; (also ~-*shell*) gasteropod with ~like shell. 2. ~-*bird*, kinds of S.-Amer. bird with radiating crest; ~-*stand* (for holding closed ~s, usu. with pan at bottom to catch drippings); ~-*tree*, small kind of magnolia with leaves in ~like whorl at end of branch, (colloq.) tree so grafted or trained that its branches droop in ~ form. Hence ~'d [-ED²] a. [f. It. *ombrella*, dim. of *ombra* shade f. UMBRA]

umbrette. See UMBER.

Um'brian (ŭ-), a. & n. **1.** Of (ancient or modern) Umbria; ~ *school*, school of painting to which Raphael & Perugino belonged. **2.** n. Language, inhabitant, of ancient Umbria. [-AN]

ûmbrif'erous, a. Affording shade. [f. L *umbrifer* (UMBRA, see -FEROUS)]

ûmiak (ōōm'yăk), n. Eskimo boat worked by women. [Esk.]

umlaut (ōōm'lowt), n., & v.t. **1.** (In Germanic languages) vowel change due to *i* or *u* (now usu. lost or altered) in following syllable (e.g. German *mann* *männer*, *fuss* *füsse*, English *man* *men*). **2.** v.t. Modify (form, sound) by the ~. [G (*um-* about + *laut* sound)]

ûm'pīre, n., & v.i. & v.t. **1.** (Law) third person called in to decide between arbitrators who disagree; person chosen to decide question; person chosen to enforce rules & settle disputes in cricket or other game. Hence **ûm'pīrAGE**(3), ~SHIP, nn. **2.** vb. Act as ~ (*for* persons, *in* game etc.), act as ~ in (game). [ME; later form of *noumpere* f. OF *non-, nomper* not equal, in sense *odd man* (*non* not + *per* PEER¹); for loss of *n-* cf. ADDER]

ûmp'teen, a. (sl.). Several, many, a lot of. [joc. form. on -TEEN]

'un, pron. (colloq.). One, as *that's a good 'un, he's a tough 'un*.

ûn-¹, repr. OE *un-, on-,* (orig. *and-*, see ANSWER), OS *ant-,* OHG *ant-, int-* (G *-ent*), Goth. *and-,* cogn. with Gk *anti*; pref. of vbs w. neg. sense & usu. denoting action contrary to or annulling that of the simple vb. The pref. being unlimited in use, only a selection of the existing vbs & derivative wds is here given. Adjj. in *-able, -ed,* & *-ing,* are identical in form with wds in UN-², with or without material difference in meaning; *undoable, unstrappable,* may mean 'that can be undone, unstrapped', or 'that cannot be done, strapped'; *unbracing* may mean 'that unbraces' or 'that does not brace'; an *unbending* person is one fond of or averse to relaxation; an *un²coiled* rope must be coiled before it can be *un¹coiled*; an *un-bridlED¹* horse may (*un-¹*) or may not (UN-²) have been previously bridled, in either case he is now *un²bridlED²*. As a

rule, the UN-² forms of such adjj. are current, the others not. The stress in the foll. wds is not marked, being the same as in the simple vb or n. or, where that is monosyllabic, falling on the second syllable (*undeceive', unsay'*); but p.pp. or adjj. in *-ed,* whether in *un-¹* or UN-², tend in attrib. use to have stress on *un-* (cf. -ED²), as *an un'masked villain, an un-muzzled hound, villain was unma'sked, dog was unmuz'zled.*

1. Wds formed upon a simple verb & with contrary sense (rarely w. intensified negative sense, as *unloose*). The distinction between some of these & the vbs in sections 2, 3, & 4, which appear to be formed rather on a noun, is necessarily arbitrary, the assumed simple vb (identical in form with the noun, from which it is usu. derived) being often rare or non-existent in the required senses of 'furnish with', 'place in', etc.

Exx.: *unanchor* v.t. & i.; *unallire* v.t. & i.; *unbalance* v.t.; *unbank* v.t., cause (fire) to burn briskly by removing ashes from top; *unbar* v.t., remove bar from (gate etc.), unlock, open, (often fig.); *unbear* v.t., take off or relax bearing-rein of (horse); *unbend* v.t. & i., change from bent position, straighten, relax (mind etc.) from strain or exertion, rid oneself of constraint, be affable, whence *unbending¹* a., (naut.) unfasten (sails) from yards & stays, cast (cable) loose, untie (rope); *unbeseem* v.t., be unbecoming to; *unbias* v.t., free from bias; *unbind* v.t., release from bonds or binding; *unblindfold* v.t.; *unblock* v.i. & t. (cards), play high card to avoid interrupting partner's long suit, give free scope to (partner's suit) by such play; *unbolt* v.t., release (door etc.) by drawing back bolt; *unbonnet* v.i. & t., take off cap etc. e.g. in salutation, remove the bonnet of: *unbosom* v.i. & t., disclose one's secret feelings, disclose (thoughts etc.); *unbrace* v.t., remove the braces of, free from tension, relax (nerves etc.); *unbraid* v.t., separate the strands of; *unbreech* v.t., free the breech of (cannon) from fastenings etc.; *unbridle* v.t., remove bridle from (horse, fig. person, tongue, etc.); *unbuckle* v.t., release the buckle of (strap, shoe, etc.); *unburden* v.t., relieve of burden, relieve (*oneself*, conscience, etc.) by confession etc. *to* person; *unbutton* v.t., open (coat etc.) by withdrawing buttons from buttonholes; *unchain* v.t.; *unchristianize* v.t.; *unclasp* v.t., loosen the clasp of; *unclench, -inch,* v.t. & i.; *unclog* v.t.; *unclose* v.t. & i., open; *unclothe* v.t.; *uncock* v.t., let down hammer of (gun) softly so as not to explode charge; *uncoil* v.t. & i.; *uncord* v.t.; *uncork* v.t., draw cork from (bottle), (colloq.) give vent or expression to (feelings etc.); *uncouple* v.t., release (dogs, railway-cars, etc.) from couples or couplings; *uncover* v.t. & i., remove covering from, lay bare, disclose, **take off** one's hat or cap; *uncreate*[1] v.t., annihilate; *uncross* v.t., remove (legs, arms, knives, etc.) from crossed position; *uncurb* v.t.; *uncurl* v.t.; *undeceive* v.t., free from deception, whence *undeceived*[1] a.; *undeify* v.t.; *undo* v.t., annul (*cannot∼ the past, our past actions*), untie or unfasten or unloose (coat, button, parcel), unfasten the buttons or garments or stays of (person), ruin the prospects or reputation or morals of, whence *undoer, undoing*, nn., *undone*[1] a.; *undomesticate* v.t.; *undrape* v.t.; *undress*[1] v.t. & i., take off the clothes of, take off one's clothes, whence *undressed*[1] a.; *unegoize* v.t.; *unentangle* v.t.; *unequalize* v.t.; *unfasten* v.t., whence *unfastened*[1] a.; *unfetter* v.t., whence *unfettered*[1] a.; *unfeudalize* v.t.; *unfile* v.t., remove (paper) from file; *unfit* v.t., make unsuitable (*for*); *unfix* v.t., whence *unfixed*[1] a.; *unfold*[1] v.t. & i., open the folds of, spread out, (fig.) reveal (thoughts, designs), become opened out, develop; *unform* v.t.; *unfurl* v.t. & i., spread out (sail), become spread out; *ungear* v.t., strip of gear, throw out of gear; *ungild* v.t.; *ungird* v.t.; *unglaze* v.t.; *unhallow* v.t., profane, desecrate; *unhand* v.t., take one's hands off, release from one's grasp; *unhang* v.t., remove from hanging position, strip (wall etc.) of hangings; *unharness* v.t.; *unhasp* v.t., loose from hasp; *unhinge* v.t., take (door) off its hinges, disorder (mind etc.), whence *unhinged* a.; *unhitch* v.t.; *unhook* v.t., remove from hook, open (dress etc.) by detaching its hooks; *unhoop* v.t.; *unhouse* (-z) v.t., deprive of shelter, drive from house; *unhumanize* v.t.; *unjoin* v.t.; *unjoint* v.t., separate joints of (fishing-rod etc.); *unkink* v.t. & i.; *unknit* v.t.; *unknot* v.t.; *unlace* v.t., loose or open by undoing lace(s) of (boot, stays, etc.); *unlade* v.t.; *unlash* v.t. (naut.); *unlatch* v.t., release latch of (door); *unlay* v.t. (naut.), untwist; *unlearn* v.t., expel from one's memory, forget the knowledge of, rid oneself of (esp. false or misleading information, habit, etc.); *unline* v.t., remove lining of; *unlink* v.t.; *unload* v.t., remove load from (ship, cart, etc., or abs.), remove (load) from ship etc., (Stock Exch.) get rid of (stocks or shares), sell out, withdraw charge from (gun etc.); *unlock* v.t., release lock of (door, box, etc., fig. mind etc.), (fig.) disclose (secret etc.); *unlodge* v.t., dislodge; *unloose* v.t., loose; *unmake* v.t., destroy, annul; *unmask* v.t. & i., remove the mask from, expose (villain, villainy), take off one's mask, reveal one's true character etc.; *unmew* v.t. (poet., rhet.), release; *unmoor* v.t., loose the moorings of (vessel etc. or fig., also abs.), weigh one of two or more anchors of (vessel); *unmortise* v.t.; *unmould* v.t., change the form of; *unmuffle* v.t. & i., remove muffler from (face, bell,

etc.), remove muffler etc. from one's face; *unmuzzle* v.t., (esp., fig.) relieve of obligation to remain silent; *unnaturalize* v.t., make unnatural; *unnerve* v.t., deprive of nerve or strength or resolution, whence *unnerved* a.; *unpack* v.t., open & remove contents of (package, box, etc., or abs.), take out (contents) from package etc.; *unpeg* v.t., remove the peg(s) from or of, open thus; *unpeople* v.t., depopulate; *unpick* v.t., undo (stitches, garment, etc.) by picking, open with pick; *unpin* v.t., unfasten by removing pins; *unplait* v.t.; *unplug* v.t.; *unpreach* v.t. & i., recant in preaching; *unravel* v.t., separate (threads etc.), separate the threads of (material), disentangle (lit. & fig.); *unreel* v.t. & i., unwind, become unwound, from reel; *unreeve* v.t. (naut.); *unrein* v.t., give the rein to (often fig.); *unriddle* v.t., solve or explain (riddle, mystery); *unrig* v.t. (naut.); *unrip* v.t., rip open or apart; *unrivet* v.t.; *unroll* v.t. & i., open (roll of cloth etc.), (of roll) be opened, display, be displayed; *unromanize* v.t.; *unroot* v.t., pull up by root; *unsaddle* v.t. (often abs.); *unsay* v.t., retract (statement), whence *unsaid*[1] a.; *unscrew* v.t., unfasten by removing screws, loosen (screw); *unseal* v.t., break the seal of, open, (letter etc.); *unseam* v.t., rip open (garment etc.) at seam; *unseat* v.t., remove from seat, throw from seat on horseback, depose (M.P. etc.) from seat, whence *unseated*[1] a.; *unset* v.t., remove (gem) from its setting; *unsettle* v.t., disturb orderly arrangement of, discompose, disincline to routine etc. (*holidays ∼ me*), derange (intellect), whence *unsettled*[1] a.; *unshackle* v.t.; *unsheathe* v.t.; *unship* v.t., unload (cargo), disembark (passenger), (naut.) remove (oar, tiller, etc.) from place where it is fixed or fitted, whence *unshipped*[1] a.; *unsling* v.t. (esp. naut.); *unspeak* v.t., retract; *unsteel* v.t., soften, relax, (resolution, person); *unstick* v.t., separate (thing stuck to another; *come unstuck*, sl., come to grief, fail); *unstitch* v.t., undo stitches of; *unstock* v.t., deprive of stock, remove (gun-barrel) from stock; *unstop* v.t., free from obstruction, remove stopper from; *unstrap* v.t., remove or undo the strap(s) of; *unstring* v.t., remove the strings of, loosen strings of (harp etc.), take (beads etc.) off string, weaken (nerves), weaken nerves of (person etc.), whence *unstrung* a.; *unswaddle* v.t.; *unswathe* v.t.; *unswear* v.t., recant by oath; *untack* v.t., disjoin, separate, (thing tacked to another); *untangle* v.t.; *unteach* v.t.; *untemper* v.t., take away the temper of (metal etc.); *untether* v.t.; *unthink* v.t., retract in thought; *unthread* v.t., take thread out of (needle), find one's way out of (maze); *untie* v.t., undo (knot etc.), undo the cords etc. of (bundle, package, etc.), liberate from bonds, whence *untied*[1] a.;

untruss v.t.; *unluck* v.t.; *untune* v.t., put out of tune (lit. & fig.); *untwine* v.t. & i.; *untwist* v.t. & i.; *unveil* v.t. & i., remove veil from, remove one's veil, remove concealing drapery from (statue etc.) with ceremonies; *unvote* v.t., retract by vote (what has been voted); *unwarp* v.t., restore from warped state; *unweave* v.t., take to pieces (textile fabric), separate (woven threads); *unwill* v.t., will the reverse of (what one has willed); *unwind* v.t. & i., draw out at length (what is wound), become thus drawn out, whence *unwound*[1] a.; *unwork* v.t., undo, destroy, (fabric etc.); *unwrap* v.t.; *unwrinkle* v.t.; *unyoke* v.t. & i., release (as) from yoke, (fig.) cease work.

2. Vbs formed on n. or vb—see (1)—& having sense 'deprive of', 'separate from'. A simple vb sometimes exists in same sense, e.g. (*un*)*bone*, (*un*)*husk*, (*un*)*shell*.

Exx.: *unapparel* v.t.; *unarm* v.t., deprive of arms or armour, whence *unarmed*[1] a.; *unballast* v.t.; *unbelt* v.t.; *unbone* v.t.; *unboot* v.t. & i.; *unbowel* v.t.; *uncap* v.t.; *uncloak* v.t.; *uncowl* v.t., uncover (face) by removing cowl, unmonk; *uncrown* v.t., deprive (esp. fig. king etc.) of crown; *unedge* v.t., destroy edge of, blunt; *unface* v.t., expose; *unfeather* v.t.; *unfence* v.t.; *unflesh* v.t.; *unflower* v.t.; *unframe* v.t.; *unfrock* v.t., deprive of frock or (fig.) of ecclesiastical rank; *ungirdle* v.t.; *unglove* v.t. & i., deprive of, take off one's, gloves; *ungown* v.t.; *ungum* v.t.; *unhair* v.t.; *unhat* v.t.; *unhelm* v.t.; *unhusk* v.t.; *unlead* (-lĕd) v.t. (print.), remove leads from (types); *unlimber* v.t. & abs.; *unman* v.t., deprive (esp. ship) of men, see also (4); *unmantle* v.t.; *unnail* v.t., take nails out of, unfasten (box etc.) thus; *unplume* v.t., *unprop* v.t.; *unring* v.t.; *unrobe* v.t. & i., undress; *unroof* v.t.; *unrumple* v.t.; *unscale* v.t., remove scales of; *unself* v.t., rid of self, unegoize; *unsex* v.t., deprive (usu. woman) of the qualities of the sex; *unshell* v.t.; *unshoe* v.t., take shoe(s) off (horse etc.); *unshot* v.t., remove shot from (gun); *unshutter* v.t.; *unsinew* v.t.; *unsister* v.t.; *unsolder* v.t.; *unspar* v.t.; *unstarch* v.t., free from starch or (fig.) stiffness or reserve; *unstopper* v.t.; *untile* v.t.; *untin* v.t.; *untooth* v.t.; *unturf* v.t.

3. Vbs similarly formed with sense 're-lease from', 'take out of', 'displace from'.

Exx.: *unbag* v.t.; *unbed* v.t.; *unbitt* v.t. (naut.); *unbox* v.t.; *uncage* v.t.; *uncart* v.t.; *uncase* v.t.; *unchurch* v.t., excommunicate; *uncloister* v.t.; *uncoop* v.t.; *undock* v.t.; *unearth* v.t., drive (fox etc.) from an earth, dig up, (fig.) bring to light; *unfold*[2] v.t., release (sheep) from fold; *unhive* v.t.; *unhorse* v.t., throw from horse, (of horse) throw (rider), cause

to dismount; *unleash* v.t.; *unnesl* v.t.; *unpen* v.t.; *unperch* v.t.; *unroost* v.t.; *unsnare* v.t.; *unspell* v.t., release from spell; *unsphere* v.t.; *unstep* v.t. (naut.); *untent* v.t.; *unthrone* v.t.; *untomb* v.t.

4. Occasional vbs formed f. nouns with sense 'cause to be no longer', 'degrade from the position of '.

Exx.: *unbishop* v.t.; *unduke* v.t.; *unking* v.t.; *unlord* v.t.; *unman* v.t., deprive of manly qualities, break the courage of, dishearten, emasculate, see also (2); *unmonk* v.t.; *unpope* v.t.; *unprelate* v.t.; *unpriest* v.t.; *unprince* v.t.; *unqueen* v.t.; *unsquire* v.t.; *unvicar* v.t.

ŭn-[2], repr. OE *un-*, OS, OHG, Goth. *un-*, ON *ú-*, *ó-*, corresp. to L IN-[2], Gk *an-*, *a-*, Skr. *an-*; pref. giving neg. sense to adjj. with their derivative nn. & advv., & to a miscellaneous group of nn. not formed on adjj.; see (2).

1. Of the many adjj. formed with *un-*, esp. of those in *-able*, *-ed*, *-ing*, for which cf. UN-[1], only a selection is here given. The sense of *un-* is either simply 'not' (as in most adjj. in *-able*, *-ed*, *-ing*, & in some others, as *unofficial*) or more commonly 'the reverse of', with implication of praise, blame, etc. Between *un-* & IN-[2] a differentiation has been suggested according to which *inartistic* means 'contrary to rules of art', 'such as an artist would condemn', & *unartistic* means 'not concerned with rules of art'; & pairs of words may be found that bear out the distinction, esp. where one of the pair has long been restricted to the proposed sense & the other has been created or revived to supply its deficiencies (*immoral*, *unmoral*). But the purely neutral sense thus ascribed to *un-* is not that found in many of the most familiar adjj. (*unbeautiful*, *unfair*, *ungraceful*, *ungracious*, *unkind*, *unjust*, *ungenerous*, *untrue*, *unscrupulous*, *unmanly*, *unscholarly*, *unladylike*, *unchristian*), including some of the exact type of *unartistic* (*unscientific*, *unphilosophical*): when we say that a thing is *untrue*, we do not mean that it does not matter for our purpose whether it is true or not, but that it is culpably inconsistent with truth. Apart from the adjj. in *-able*, *-ed*, *-ing*, both *un-* & *in-* more commonly have this implication of blame etc., the purely neutral sense being often given by NON-(5). IN-[2] is preferred to *un-* with certain terminations of L orig., e.g. *-ate*, *-ite*, *-ant*, *-ent*, *-ble* (exc. *-able*, now a living E suf.). It is for the most part adorn. with *-ed*[1,2] (*indigested* etc., but cf. *inexperienced*), and is not used with *-ing*, *-ful*, *-like*, *-ly*, etc. Derivatives in *-ly*, *-ness*, *-ity*, etc., are briefly recorded; stress follows that of the simple adj.; but for adjj. in *-ed* see UN-[1].

Exx.: **unabashed**; *unabated*; *unabbreviated*; *unabetted*; *unabiding*; *unable*, not able (*to do*); *unabridged*; *unabsorbable*;

unabsorbed; *unabsorbent*; *unaccented*; *unaccentuated*; *unacceptable*; *unaccommodating*; *unaccompanied*, not accompanied, (mus.) without accompaniment; *unaccomplished*, not accomplished or achieved, lacking accomplishments; *unaccordant*; *unaccountable* (-*bility*, -*bleness*, -*bly*), that cannot be explained, strange, irresponsible; *unaccoutred*; *unaccredited*; *unaccused*; *unaccustomed*, not accustomed (*to*), not usual (*his ~ silence*); *unachievable*; *unachieved*; *unacknowledged*; *unacquainted*; *unacquirable*; *unacquired*; *unacted*; *unadaptable*; *unadapted*; *unaddicted*; *unaddressed*; *unadjudged*; *unadjusted*; *unadministered*; *unadmired*; *unadmonished*; *unadopted*, ‖ (esp., of new roads) not taken over for maintenance by the local authority; *unadorned*; *unadulterated*; *unadventurous*; *unadvisable* (-*bility*); *unadvised* (-*edly*), indiscreet, rash, without advice; *unaffable*; *unaffected* (-*ly*, -*ness*), free from affectation, genuine, sincere, not affected (*by*); *unaffiliated*; *unafflicted*; *unaggressive*; *unaided*; *unalarmed*; *unalleviated*; *unallotted*; *unallowable*; *unalloyed*; *unalterable* (-*bility*, -*bleness*, -*bly*); *unaltered*; *unamazed*; *unambiguous* (-*ly*, -*ness*); *unambitious* (-*ly*, -*ness*); *unamenable*; *unamendable*; *un-American*, not American, foreign to American customs or ideas; *unamiable* (-*bility*, -*bleness*, -*bly*); *unamusing*; *unanalysable*; *unanalysed*; *unanimated*; *unannounced*; *unanswerable* (-*bility*, -*bleness*, -*bly*), that cannot be answered or refuted; *unanswered*; *unanticipated*; *unapocryphal*; *unapostolic*, contrary to apostolic usage, not having apostolic authority; *unappalled*; *unapparelled*; *unapparent*; *unappeasable*; *unappeased*; *unappetizing* (-*ly*); *unapplied*; *unappreciated*; *unappreciative*; *unapprehended*; *unapprehensive*; *unapprised*; *unapproachable* (-*bility*, -*bleness*, -*bly*); *unappropriated* (~ *blessing*, joc., old maid); *unapproved*; *unapproving* (-*ly*); *unapt* (-*ly*, -*ness*); *unarmed*[2]; *unarmoured*; *unarranged*; *unarrayed*; *unarrested*; *unartificial* (-*ly*), not artificial, natural; *unartistic*; *unascertainable*; *unascertained*; *unashamed*; *unasked*; *unaspirated*; *unaspiring* (-*ly*); *unassailable*, not assailable, (of statement etc.) against which nothing can be said; *unassayed*; *unassignable*; *unassimilated*; *unassisted*; *unassuming*, making little of one's merits or status; *unattached*, not attached, (law) not seized for debt, (mil.) not assigned to regiment or company, (univ., of student) belonging to no college; *unattainable* (-*ness*); *unattempted*; *unattended*; *unattested*; *unattractive* (-*ly*, -*ness*); *unaugmented*; *unauthentic* (-*ity*); *unauthenticated*; *unauthorized*; *unavailable*; *unavailing* (-*ly*), ineffectual; *unavenged*; *unavoidable* (-*bly*); *unavowed*; *unaware*, not aware (*of*, *that*, etc.); *unawares* (ŭnáwārz′) [-ES] adv. & n., unexpectedly, by surprise, unintentionally, as *was taken ~ by his question*, *must have dropped it ~*, (n.) *at ~*, unexpectedly; **unbacked**, not supported, having no backers (esp. in betting), (of horse) unbroken, not taught to bear rider; *unbalanced*, (esp., of the mind) disordered, violently impulsive; *unbaptized*; *unbearable* (-*bly*); *unbeaten*, not beaten, not surpassed (~ *record* etc.); *unbeautiful*, ugly; *unbecoming* (-*ly*, -*ness*), indecorous (*an ~ speech*), not befitting (person, *to* or *for* person), not suited to the wearer (*an ~ hat*); *unbefitting*; *unbefriended*; *unbegotten*; *unbeknown*, -*knownst*, (colloq.), not known, esp. ~ *to* quasi-adv., without the knowledge of, as *did it ~ to him*; *unbelievable*; *unbelieving* (-*ly*), not believing esp. in divine revelation; *unbeloved* (-*vd*); *unbending*[2] (-*ly*, -*ness*), not bending, inflexible, firm, austere; *unbeneficed*; *unbeseeming* (-*ly*); *unbesought*; *unbespoken*; *unbias(s)ed*; *unbiblical*, not in or authorized by the Bible; *unbidden*, not commanded, not invited; *unbigoted*; *unbirthday* (joc., of a present) given on a day other than a birthday); *unbleached*; *unblemished*; *unblest*; *unblooded*, (of horse etc.) not thoroughbred; *unblushing* (-*ly*, -*ness*); *unbookish*; *unborn*; *unbounded* (-*ly*, -*ness*), not bounded (*by*, or abs.), infinite; *unbred*; *unbribable*; *unbridled*, not bridled, esp. fig., as ~ *insolence*, *tongue*; *unbroken* (-*ly*, -*ness*), not broken, not subdued, not interrupted (~ *slumber*, *peace*), not surpassed (~ *record*), not broken in (~ *horse*); *unbrotherly*; *unburdened*; *unburied*; *unbusinesslike*;

uncalled, not called, esp. ~ *for*, impertinently obtruded, as *the remark was ~ for*, *his ~-for remark*; *uncandid* (-*ly*); *uncanny* (-*iness*), weird, mysterious, not canny; *uncanonical* (-*ly*, -*ness*); *uncanonized*; *uncared-for*, disregarded, neglected; *uncarpeted*; *uncastrated*; *uncatalogued*; *uncaused*, not caused, not created, self-existent; *uncauterized*; *unceasing* (-*ly*); *unceremonious* (-*ly*, -*ness*), informal, familiar, abrupt in manner, wanting in courtesy; *uncertain* (-*ly*, -*ly*), not certainly knowing or known (*am ~ which he means*, ~ *of his meaning*, *is of ~ age*, *the result is ~*), not to be depended on (*is ~ in his aim*), changeable (~ *temper*, *weather*); *uncertificated*; *unchallenged*; *unchancy* (chiefly Sc.), unlucky, unseasonable; *unchangeable* (-*bly*, *ness*); *uncharitable* (-*bly*, -*ness*), censorious, severe in judgement; *unchartered*; *unchary*; *unchaste* (-*ly*, -*lity*); *unchastened*; *unchivalrous*; *unchristian* (-*ly*, -*ness*), not Christian, contrary to the Christian character; *uncircumcised*, (fig.) heathen, unregenerate; *uncircumstantial*, not going into details; *uncivil* (-*ly*), ill-mannered, rude; *uncivilized*; *unclad*; *unclaimed*; *unclean* (-*ness*), not clean, foul, unchaste, ceremonially impure (in Jewish law); *unclerical*; *unclothed*; *unclouded* (esp. of happiness etc., cf. *cloudless*); *uncoined*; *uncoloured*, not coloured, (fig.) not exaggerated or heightened in description (~ *account* etc.); *uncombed*; *uncome- -at-able* (-kŭmăt-), colloq., not accessible or attainable; *uncomely* (-*iness*); *uncomfortable* (-*bly*); *uncommercial*, not commercial, contrary to commercial principles; *uncommitted*; *uncommon* (-*ly*, -*ness*) a. & colloq. adv., not common, unusual, remarkable, (adv.) remarkably (*an ~ fine girl*); *uncommunicative* (-*ly*, -*ness*), reserved, taciturn; *uncompanionable*; *uncomplaining* (-*ly*, -*ness*); *uncomplaisant* (-*ly*); *uncomplicated*; *uncomplimentary*; *uncompounded*; *uncompromising* (-*ly*), not admitting of compromise, decided, inflexible, unyielding; *unconcerned* (-*édly*), not concerned (*in, with*), easy in mind, free from anxiety or agitation; *uncondemned*; *uncondensed*; *unconditional* (-*ity*, -*ness*, -*ly*), not subject to conditions, absolute, (~ *surrender, refusal*); *unconditioned*, not subject to conditions (*the U~*, philos., that which is not subject to the conditions of finite existence; ~ *reflex*, psych., instinctive or inborn response to a stimulus); *unconfirmed* (esp. of rumour etc.); *unconformable* (-*bly*, -*ness*); *uncongenial* (-*ly*); *unconnected*; *unconquerable* (-*bly*); *unconquered*; *unconscientious* (-*ly*, -*ness*); *unconscionable* (-*bly*, -*ness*), wholly unreasonable, not guided or restrained by conscience, (law) ~ *bargain*, contract too grossly unfair to be enforced, [prob. f. *conscion*, formed as sing. of *conscience* taken as pl.]; *unconscious* (-*ly*, -*ness*), not conscious, as *was ~ of any change, lay ~ for some hours*; ~ CEREBRATION, *the ~* (as n.; see PSYCHO-*analysis*); *unconsecrated*; *unconsidered*, disregarded; *unconstitutional* (-*ity*, -*ly*), (of measures, acts, etc.) opposed to a country's constitution; *unconstrained* (-*édly*); *unconsumed*; *uncontainable*; *uncontaminated*; *uncontemplated*, not expected; *uncontracted*; *uncontradicted*; *uncontrollable* (-*bly*, -*ness*); *uncontrolled* (-*édly*); *uncontroversial* (-*ly*); *uncontroverted*; *unconventional* (-*ity*, -*ly*), not bound by convention or custom, free in character or action or treatment; *unconversable*; *unconversant*; *unconverted*; *unconvinced*; *uncooked*; *uncorroborated*; *uncorroded*; *uncorrupted*; *uncountenanced*; *uncoupled*; *uncourtly*; *uncovenanted*, not promised by or based on a covenant (~ *mercies* of God), not enjoying a covenant; *uncovered*; *uncoveted*; *uncreated*, not yet created, (also arch. *uncreate*[2]) existing without being created; *uncritical* (-*ly*), disinclined or incompetent to criticize, not according to principles of criticism; *uncrossed*, not crossed (‖ ~ *cheque* etc.), not thwarted; *uncrowned* (~ *king*, not yet crowned, also, having power but not name of king); *unculled*; *uncultivable*; *uncultivated*; *uncultured*; *uncurbed*; *uncurtailed*; *uncushioned*; *uncustomed*, not liable to

duty, having paid no duty; *uncut*, not cut, esp. (of book) with full untrimmed margins, (loosely) unopened;

undamaged; *undated*, not dated; *undaunted* (-*ly*, -*ness*), not daunted, fearless; *undebated*; *undebauched*; *undeceived*[2]; *undecided* (-*ly*), not settled (*point is still ~*), irresolute (*he stood ~*); *undecipherable*; *undefended*, (esp., of suit) in which no defence is put in; *undefiled*; *undefined*; *undelivered*; *undemonstrated*; *undemonstrative*, not given to showing strong feelings, reserved; *undeniable* (-*bly*), that cannot be denied or disputed, decidedly good; *undenominational* (~ *education*); *undenounced*; *undependable*; *undeplored*; *undeposed*; *undepraved*; *undepreciated*; *undepressed*; *undescried*; *undeserved* (-*édly*); *undeserving*; *undesignated*; *undesigned* (-*édly*), not designed, esp. not intended; *undesirable* (-*bility*, -*bleness*, -*bly*) a. & n., not desirable, unpleasant, inconvenient, (n.) ~ *person*; *undesired*, not desired or solicited; *undesirous*; *undetachable*; *undetected*; *undetermined*, not settled, irresolute; *undeterred*; *undeveloped*; *undeviating* (-*ly*); *undevout*(-*ly*); *undifferentiated*; *undiffused*; *undigested* (esp. fig., of ill-arranged facts etc.); *undignified*, lacking or inconsistent with dignity; *undiluted*; *undiminished*; *undimmed*; *undiplomatic*; *undirected*; *undiscerned*; *undiscerning* (-*ly*); *undischarged*; *undisciplined*; *undisclosed*; *undiscomfited*; *undisconcerted*; *undiscoverable* (-*bly*); *undiscovered*; *undiscriminating*(-*ly*); *undiscussed*; *undisguised* (-*édly*), not veiled, open, (~ *reluctance* etc.); *undismayed*; *undispelled*; *undispersed*; *undisplayed*; *undisputed*; *undissected*; *undissembled*; *undissolved*; *undistinguishable* (-*bly*, -*ness*); *undistinguished*; *undistracted*; *undistressed*; *undistributed* (~ *middle*, fallacy resulting from failure to* DISTRIBUTE *middle term); *undisturbed* (-*édly*); *undiversified*; *undiverted*; *undivided*; *undivorced*; *undivulged*; *undomesticated*; *undone*[2], not done; *undoubted*; *undoubtedly* adv., without doubt (implying certainty on speaker's part, cf. DOUBTLESS); *undoubting* (-*ly*); *undraped*; *undreamed-of*, -*mt-of*; *undressed*[2]; *undrilled*; *undrinkable*; *undue* (-*duly*), excessive, disproportionate, (*spoke with ~ warmth*), improper (~ *influence*, by which person, e.g. testator, is induced to do what he would not of his own free will), (of bill etc.) not yet due; *undurable* (-*bly*); *undutiful* (-*ly*, -*ness*); *undying* (-*ly*,) immortal (~ *fame* etc.);

unearned, not earned (~ *increment*, increased value of land due to external causes e.g. increased population, not to owner's labour or outlay); *unearthly* (-*iness*), not earthly, supernatural, ghostly, weird, (~ *cry, pallor*), (colloq.) absurdly early (*why call me at this ~ hour?*); *uneasy* (-*ily*, -*iness*), disturbed or uncomfortable in body or mind (*you seem ~, passed an ~*

night), disturbing (*had an ~ suspicion*); *uneatable*; *uneaten*; *unecclesiastical*; *uneclipsed*; *uneconomic*, (esp., of rent) too low to repay owner & builder; *uneconomical*; *unedified*; *unedifying*, (esp.) tending. to suggest evil or offend moral delicacy; *unedited*; *uneducated*; *uneffaced*; *uneffected*; *unelated*; *unelected*; *unelucidated*; *unemancipated*; *unembarrassed*; *unemotional* (*-ly*); *unemphatic* (*-ally*); *unemployable* a. & n., (person) unfitted by character, by age, or otherwise, for paid employment; *unemployed*, not used, lacking employment, out of work & wages (*~ capital, energies, the ~*); *unempowered*; *unenclosed*; *unencumbered* (*~ estate*, having no liabilities on it); *unendangered*; *unending* (*-ly, -ness*), having no end; *unendorsed*; *unendowed*; *unendurable* (*-bly*); *unenforced*; *unenfranchised*; *unengaged*; *un-English*, not (characteristic of the) English; *unenjoyable*; *unenlightened*; *unenrolled*; *unenslaved*; *unenterprising* (*-ly, -ness*); *unentertaining* (*-ly, -ness*); *unenthusiastic*; *unenumerated*; *unenviable* (*-bly*); *unenvied*; *unequable* (*-ly*); *unequal* (*-ly*), not equal (*to*), of varying quality; *unequalled*; *unequipped*; *unequivocal* (*-ly, -ness*), not ambiguous, plain, unmistakable; *unerased*; *unerring* (*-ly, -ness*), not erring or failing or missing the mark (*~ judgement, wisdom, aim*); *unescapable*; *unespied*; *unessayed*; *unessential* a. & n., not essential, not of the first importance, (n.) *~* part or thing; *unestablished*; *unestimated*; *unestranged*; *unethical*; *unevangelical*; *unevaporated*; *uneven* (*-ly, -ness*), not level or smooth, not uniform or equable (*makes ~ progress, has an ~ temper*), (of number, rare) odd; *uneventful* (*-ly*); *unexamined*; *unexampled*, without precedent; *unexcelled*; *unexceptionable* (*-bly, -ness*), with which no fault can be found; *unexcised*, not subject to excise; *unexclusive* (*-ly*); *unexecuted*; *unexemplified*; *unexercised*; *unexhausted*; *unexpected* (*-ly, -ness*); *unexpensive*; *unexpiated*; *unexpired*, (of lease etc.) still running; *unexplained*; *unexplored*; *unexposed*; *unexpounded*; *unexpressed*; *unexpurgated*; *unextended*, not extended, occupying no space, dimensionless;

unfadable, that cannot fade; *unfading* (*-ly, -ness*); *unfailing* (*-ly, -ness*), not failing, not running short (*~ supply*), not disappointing one's expectations etc. (*~ resource, supporter*, etc.); *unfair* (*-ly, -ness*), not equitable or honest or impartial (*an ~ advantage, got by ~ means, ~ play*); *unfaithful* (*-ly, -ness*), (esp.) not faithful in wedlock; *unfaltering* (*-ly*); *unfamiliar* (*-ity, -ly*); *unfashionable* (*-bly, -ness*); *unfashioned*, not brought into shape; *unfastened*[2]; *unfathered*, (poet.) fatherless, (fig.) not acknowledged by its author (*~ theory* etc.); *unfatherly*; *unfathomable* (*-bly*); *unfathomed*; *unfavourable* (*-bly, -ness*); *unfeasible*; *unfed*; *unfeed*,

not FEED[3]; *unfeeling* (*-ly, -ness*), lacking sensibility, harsh, cruel; *unfeigned* (*-ēdly*); *unfelt*, not FELT[2]; *unfeminine*; *unfermented*; *unfertilized*; *unfettered*[2]; *unfigured*, not marked with figures (*~ muslin, vase*); *unfilial* (*-ly*); *unfilled*; *unfiltered*; *unfinished*; *unfit* (*-ly, -ness*), not fit (*to do*, *for* purpose, *for a doctor* etc., to be one); *unfitted*, not fit, not fitted, not furnished with fittings; *unfitting* (*-ly*); *unfixed*[2]; *unflagging*; *unflattering* (*-ly*); *unflavoured*; *unfledged*, not yet fledged or (fig., of person etc.) developed; *unfleshed*; *unflinching* (*-ly*); *unfordable*; *unforeseen*; *unforgettable*; *unforgivable*; *unforgiven*; *unforgiving* (*-ly, -ness*); *unforgotten*; *unformed*, not formed, shapeless; *unformulated*; *unfortified*; *unfortunate* (*-ly*) a. & n., the reverse of fortunate, unlucky, unhappy, (n.) *~* person; *unfounded*, without foundation (*~ rumour, hopes*), not yet founded; *unfrequented*; *unfriended*, lacking friends; *unfriendly* (*-iness*); *unfruitful* (*-ly, -ness*); *unfulfilled*; *unfunded*, (of debt) floating, not funded; *unfurnished*, not supplied (*with*), without furniture; *unfused* (FUSE[1,2]);

ungallant (*-ly*), not gallant to women; *ungalvanized*; *ungarbled*; *ungarnered*; *ungarnished*, not decorated; *ungauged*; *ungenerous* (*-ly*); *ungenial*; *ungenteel* (*-ly*); *ungentle* (*-ness, -tly*), harsh, rude, ill-bred; *ungentlemanly* (*-iness*), unworthy of a gentleman, rude, ill-bred; *unget-at-able*, inaccessible; *unglazed*; *unglutted*; *ungodly* (*-ily, -iness*); *ungovernable* (*-bly*), unruly, licentious, wild, violent, (*~ passions*); *ungraceful* (*-ly, -ness*); *ungracious* (*-ly, -ness*), not kindly or courteous (*~ reply, reception*); *ungraduated*; *ungrammatical* (*-ly*), contrary to rules of grammar; *ungrateful* (*-ly*); *ungrounded*, (of statement etc.) unfounded; *ungrudging* (*-ly*); *unguarded* (*-ly*), not guarded, incautious, thoughtless (*an ~ expression, admission*);

unhackneyed; *unhallowed*; *unhampered*; *unhandsome* (*-ly, -ness*), (of appearance, conduct, etc.) not handsome; *unhandy* (*-ily, -iness*), awkward to handle, inconvenient, (of person) clumsy; *unhanged*, (esp.) who has escaped hanging (*the greatest scoundrel ~*); *unhappy* (*-ily, -iness*), not happy, unlucky, wretched; *unharmed*; *unhatched* (HATCH[2,3]); *unhealthful* (*-ly, -ness*); *unhealthy* (*-ily, -iness*), (esp., mil. sl., of places) dangerous, exposed to fire; *unheard*, not heard (*~ of*, unprecedented); *unheeded*; *unheedful* (*-ly*); *unheeding*; *unhelpful* (*-ly*); *unhemmed*; *unheralded*; *unheroic*; *unhesitating* (*-ly*); *unhewn* (lit., & fig., rough, incondite; *unhidden*; *unhistoric(al)*, (esp.) merely legendary; *unholy* (*-ily, -iness*), not holy, impious, wicked, (colloq., as intensive epithet) frightful, hideous (*what an ~ row to kick up!*); *unhonoured*; *unhuman*, not human; *unhung*; *unhurt*;

unidea'd, having no ideas; *unideal,* not ideal, prosaic, ordinary, dull, inferior; *unidentified; unilluminated; unillustrated; unimaginable; unimaginative (-ly, -ness); unimpaired; unimpassioned; unimpeachable (-bility, -bleness, -bly),* giving no opening to censure, beyond reproach or question; *unimpeded; unimportant (-ance); unimposing; unimpressionable; unimpressive (-ly, -ness); unimproved,* (esp. of land) not improved; *unimpugned; unindexed; unindicated; uninflammable; uninflated; uninflicted; uninfluenced; uninfluential; uninformed,* (esp.) ignorant; *uninhabitable; uninhabited; uninitiated; uninjured; uninspired,* (esp., of oratory etc.) commonplace; *uninstigated; uninstructed; uninstructive; uninsulated; uninsured; unintelligent (-ly); unintelligible (-bility, -bly); unintentional (-ly); uninteresting (-ly, -ness); unintermittent (-ly); unintermitting (-ly); uninterpretable; uninterred; uninterrupted (-ly); uninventive (-ly); uninvestigated; uninvited; uninviting (-ly),* unattractive, repellent; *uninvoked; uninvolved; unirrigated; unisolated; unissued; unjaundiced; unjust (-ly),* contrary to justice, not just; *unjustifiable (-bly, -ness);*

unkind (*-ly, -ness*), not kind, harsh, cruel; *unkingly; unkneaded; unknightly (-iness); unknowable (-bility, -bleness, -bly) (the* U~, the First Cause or ultimate reality, which is beyond finite apprehension); *unknowing (-ly),* not knowing, unconscious, (*of,* or abs.); *unknown* a., n., & adv., not known (*he, his purpose, what he wanted, that district, was~ to me, a youth to fame~, of ~ ingredients,* x & y *denote~ quantities* in equation etc., *the* U~ WARRIOR), (n. or abs. adj.) *we all dread the ~, equation of two ~s,* (adv.) ~ *to,* without the knowledge of (*did it ~ to me*);

unlabelled; *unlaboured,* (of style etc.) easy, spontaneous; *unladylike; unlamented; unlawful (-ly, -ness); unlearnéd,* not LEARNED; *unlearnt, -ned (pr. -nd),* not learnt; *unleavened* (lit. & fig.); *unlettered,* illiterate; *unlicensed; unlicked,* not licked into shape, unmannerly; *unlike (-ness)* a. & prep., not like (*is ~ both his parents, the two are~, portrait is utterly ~, ~ signs,* + & —, *plays quite ~ anyone I have heard before*); *unlikely (-ihood, -iness),* improbable, unpromising, (~ *tale, errand*); *unlimited (-ly, -ness),* boundless, unrestricted, very great or numerous (*has ~ scope, possibilities, his powers are ~, ~ expanse of sea, drinks ~ coffee*); *unlined,* (esp.) with no lining, (of face etc.) not wrinkled; *unliquidated; unlit; unlocated; unlooked-for,* not expected; *unlopped; unlovable; unloved; unlovely (-iness),* not amiable or attractive; *unloverlike; unloving; unlucky (-ily),* not lucky or fortunate or successful, hapless, wretched, unsuccessful, bringing bad luck, ill-timed, ill-contrived, (~ *toss of coin, always ~ at*

cards, ~ *fellow, asked in an ~ hour, single magpie is ~, his ~ efforts to please, an ~ expedient*);

unmade; *unmaidenly; unmailable,* that must not or cannot be sent by post; *unmaimed; unmaintainable; unmalleable (-bility); unmanageable (-bly, -ness),* not (easily) to be managed or manipulated or controlled (~ *child, material, situation*); *unmanful (-ly); unmanlike,* not like a man, esp. womanish or childish; *unmanly (-iness); unmannerly (-iness),* .rude, ill-bred; *unmarked,* not marked, not noticed; *unmarketable; unmarriageable (-ness); unmarried; unmartial,* unwarlike; *unmasculine,* not masculine or manly; *unmasticable; unmatchable; unmatched; unmated; unmaterial,* not consisting of matter; *unmatured; unmeaning (-ly, -ness),* without meaning, senseless; *unmeant,* not intended; *unmeasured,* not measured, (poet.) immeasurable; *unmechanical; unmeet (-ly, -ness),* arch., not fit (*to do, for* purpose); *unmelodious (-ly, -ness); unmelled; unmendable; unmentionable (-ness)* a. & that it is improper to mention, (n. pl., joc.) trousers; *unmerchantable; unmerciful (-ly, -ness); unmerited; unmethodical; unmetrical (-ly),* not metrical, violating requirements of metre; *unmilitary; unmindful (-ly, -ness); unminted; unmirthful (-ly); unmistakable (-bly),* that cannot be mistaken or doubted, clear; *unmitigated,* unqualified, absolute, (~ *blackguard, lie*); *unmixed; unmodern; unmodified; unmodulated; unmolested; unmoral (-ity),* non-moral; *unmortgaged; unmotherly; unmounted,* not mounted (~ *police, picture, jewel*); *unmourned; unmoved,* not moved, not changed in purpose, not affected by emotion; *unmown; unmurmuring (-ly),* not complaining; *unmusical (-ity, -ly),* not pleasing to the ear, unskilled in or indifferent to music; *unmutilated;*

unnamable, (esp., of vices) too horrible to be named; *unnamed; unnational; unnatural (-ly, -ness),* contrary or doing violence to nature, monstrous, (~ *crimes, vices*), lacking natural feelings (~ *parent, child*), artificial, forced, affected; *unnaturalized,* not naturalized; *unnavigable; unnecessary (-ily)* a. & n., not necessary, more than is necessary (*with ~ care*), (n., usu. pl.) ~ thing(s); *unneedful (-ly); unnegotiable; unneighbourly (-iness); unnoticed; unnourished; unnumbered,* not marked with number, not counted, countless;

unobjectionable (*-bly*) *unobliging; unobliterated; unobscured; unobservant; unobserved; unobstructed; unobtainable; unobtrusive (-ly, -ness); unoccupied; unoffending,* harmless, innocent; *unoffered; unofficial,* (esp., of news) not officially confirmed; *unofficinal; unopened; unopposed; unordained; unorganized; unoriginal,* not possessing originality, derived;

unornamental, not ornamental, unsightly; *unornamented*; *unorthodox*; *unostentatious* (*-ly*, *-ness*); *unowned*;

unpacified; *unpaged*, with pages not numbered; *unpaid*, (of sum, bill, debt, or person) not paid (‖ *the great* ~, ~ *magistrates or justices*); *unpaired*; *unpalatable* (*-bly*); *unparalleled*, having no parallel or equal; *unpardonable* (*-bly*, *-ness*); *unpared*; *unparental*, unworthy of a parent; *unparliamentary* (*-ily*, *-iness*), contrary to parliamentary usage (~ *language*, oaths, abuse); *unpatented*; *unpatriotic* (*-ally*); *un-patronized*; *unpaved*; *unpawned*; *unpeaceful*; *unpedantic*; *unpedigreed*; *unpeeled*; *unpensioned*; *unperceived*; *unperforated*; *unperformed*; *unperjured*; *unpersuadable*; *unpersuaded*; *unpersuasive*; *unperturbed*; *unperused*; *unperverted*; *unphilosophical* (*-ly*, *-ness*), not according to philosophical principles, wanting in philosophy; *unpicked*, not selected, (of flowers) not plucked; *unpicturesque*; *unpiloted*; *unpitied*; *unpitying* (*-ly*); *unplaced*, not placed esp. in race or list; *unplagued*; *unplaned*; *unplanned*; *unplanted*; *unplastered*; *unplastic*; *unplated*; *unplausible* (*-bly*); *unplayable* (esp. of ball or serve in games); *unpleasant* (*-ly*), not pleasant, disagreeable; *unpleasantness* n., in adj. senses, also, misunderstanding, quarrel, *the late* ~ (joc.), the American civil war (1861–5); *unpleasing* (*-ly*); *unpliable* (*-bly*); *unpliant* (*-ly*); *unploughed*; *unplucked*; *unplumbed*; *unpoetical* (*-ly*, *-ness*); *unpointed*, having no point, not punctuated, without vowel points (in Hebrew etc.), (of masonry) not pointed; *unpolished*; *unpolitical*, not concerned with politics; *unpolled*, not polled (~ *elector*, *vote*); *unpolluted*; *unpopular* (*-ity*, *-ly*), not popular, esp. not liked by the public; *unportioned*, portionless; *unpossessed*, not possessed, not possessed *of*; *unposted*, uninformed, ‖ (of letter) not posted; *unpractical* (*-ity*, *-ly*), (of person, plan, method, etc.) not practical; *unpractised*, not experienced or skilled, not put into practice; *unpraised*; *unprecedented*, for which there is no precedent, unparalleled; *unprefaced*; *unprejudiced*, (esp.) impartial; *unprelatical*; *unpremeditated* (*-ly*), not previously thought over, not deliberately planned, unintentional; *unpreoccupied*; *unprepared* (*-ness*), not prepared (*found everything* ~, *was* ~ *for this objection*, *delivered an* ~ *speech*); *unprepossessing*; *unprescribed*; *unpresentable*, not presentable, not fit to be presented to company, not fit to be seen; *unpresuming*; *unpresumptuous*; *unpretending* (*-ly*), *unpretentious* (*-ly*, *-ness*), aa., not given to display, making little show; *unpreventable*; *unpriced*, with the price(s) not fixed or marked or stated (~ *goods*, *catalogue*); *unpriestly*; *unprimed*; *unprincely*; *unprincipled*, lacking or not dictated by good moral principles (~

person, *conduct*); *unprintable*, (esp.) too blasphemous, indecent, etc., to appear in print; *unprinted*; *unprivileged*; *unprized*, not valued; *unprobed*; *unproclaimed*; *unprocurable*; *unproductive* (*-ly*, *-ness*); *unprofaned*; *unprofessional* (*-ly*), not pertaining to one's profession, not belonging to a profession, contrary to professional etiquette etc., (*knows nothing of* ~ *matters*, *ask any* ~ *man*, ~ *conduct*); *unprofitable* (*-bly*, *-ness*; ~ *servants*, persons content to do no more than their duty); *unprogressive* (*-ness*), not progressive, conservative; *unprohibited*; *unprolific*; *unpromising*; *unprompted*, spontaneous; *unpromulgated*; *unpronounceable*; *unpropagated*; *unprophetic*; *unpropitious* (*-ly*, *-ness*); *unproportional*, not proportional; *unproposed*; *unprosperous* (*-ly*, *-ness*); *unprotected*; *unprotested*; *unprovable*; *unproved*, *-en*; *unprovided*, not supplied (*with money* etc.), not. prepared; *unprovoked*, (of person or act) without provocation; *unpruned*; *unpublished*, not made public, (of MS. etc.) not published; *unpunctual* (*-ity*, *-ly*); *unpunctuated*; *unpunishable*; *unpunished*; *unpurified*;

unquailing (*-ly*); *unqualified* (*-ly*), not competent, not legally or officially qualified, not modified, (*am* ~ *to serve*, *an* ~ *practitioner*, *gave his* ~ *assent*); *unquarried*; *unquelled*; *unquenchable* (*-bly*); *unquenched*; *unquestionable* (*-bly*, *-ness*), that cannot be questioned or doubted; *unquestioned*, not disputed or doubted, not interrogated; *unquestioning* (*-ly*), asking no questions (~ *obedience* etc., yielded without questions asked); *unquiet*, restless, agitated, (~ *spirit*, *times*); *unquilted*; *unquotable* (as *unprintable*); *unquoted*;

unransomed; *unrazored*, unshaven; *unreachable*; *unread*, (of book etc.) not read, (of person) not well-read; *unreadable* (*-ness*); *unready*, not ready, not prompt in action; *unreal* (*-ity*, *-ly*), illusive, sham, visionary; *unrealizable*; *unrealized*; *unreaped*; *unreasonable* (*-bly*, *-ness*), not reasonable, exceeding the bounds of reason (~ *demands*, *conduct*, etc.), not guided by or listening to reason; *unreasoned*, not rationally thought out; *unreasoning* (*-ly*), not using or guided by reason; *unrebuked*; *unrecallable*; *unrecalled*; *unreceipted*; *unreceived*; *unreciprocated*; *unreckoned*; *unreclaimed*; *unrecognizable* (*-bly*); *unrecognized*; *unrecompensed*; *unreconciled*; *unrecorded*; *unrectified*; *unredeemed*, not redeemed, (of promise) not fulfilled, (of bills etc.) not recalled by payment, not taken out of pawn, (of faults etc.) not mitigated or relieved (*by* merits etc., or abs.); *unredressed*; *unrefined*, not refined (~ *sugar*, *manners*); *unreflecting* (*-ly*); *unreformable*; *unreformed*; *unrefuted*; *unregal*; *unregarded*; *unregenerate*; *unregistered*; *unregretted*; *unregulated*; *unrehearsed* (esp. of results that surprise their authors); *unrelated*; *unrelaxed*; *unrelenting* (*-ly*, *-ness*); *unreliable* (*-bility*, *-bleness*, *-bly*); *unrelieved*, (esp.) lacking the relief given by contrast or variation; *unreligious*, not concerned with religion; *unremembered*; *unremitting* (*-ly*), not abating, incessant, (~ *care*, *exertions*); *unremunerative*, not profitable; *unrenewed*; *unrenounced*; *unrepealed*; *unrepentant* (*-ance*); *unrepining* (*-ly*); *unreplenished*; *unreported*; *unrepresentative*; *unrepresented*; *unreproachful*; *unreproved*; *unrequited*, not requited or returned (~ *affection*); *unrescinded*; *unresented*; *unresenting* (*-ly*); *unreserved* (*-édly*, *-ness*), without reservation (~ *compliance* etc.), open, frank, (*an* ~ *nature*), not reserved (~ *seats*); *unresisted*; *unresisting* (*-ly*); *unresolved*, not having formed a decision, not solved or cleared up (~ *doubts*, *problem*), not separated into constituent parts; *unrespected*; *unresponsive* (*-ness*); *unrestful* (*-ly*, *-ness*); *unresting* (*-ly*); *unrestored*; *unrestrainable* (*-bly*); *unrestrained* (*-édly*, *-ness*); *unrestricted* (*-ly*); *unretarded*; *unretentive*; *unrevenged*; *unreversed*; *unrevised*; *unrevoked*; *unrewarded*; *unrhetorical*; *unrhymed*; *unrhythmical*, without (satisfactory) rhythm; *unridable*; *unridden*; *unrighted*; *unrighteous* (*-ly*, *-ness*), not upright or honest or just, evil, wicked; *unripe* (*-ness*), not ripe (lit. & fig.); *unrisen*; *unrivalled*, having no equal, peerless; *unromantic* (*-ally*); *unroofed*; *unroyal* (*-ly*), unlike or unworthy of a king; *unruffled*; *unruled*, not governed, not ruled with lines; *unru'ly* (*-iness*), lawless, refractory, [f. rare *ruly* (RULE, -Y²)];

unsafe (*-ly*, *-ness*), dangerous; *unsaid*²; *unsaintly*; *unsal(e)able* (*-bility*, *-bleness*); *unsalaried*; *unsalted*; *unsanctified*; *unsanctioned*; *unsanitary*, unhealthy; *unsated*; *unsatisfactory* (*-ily*, *-iness*); *unsatisfied*; *unsatisfying* (*-ly*); *unsaved*, not saved (esp. in religious sense); *unsavoury* (*-ily*, *-iness*), uninviting, disgusting, (*an* ~ *dish*, *smell*, *theme*); *unsayable*; *unscalable*, that cannot be climbed; *unscannable*, that cannot be scanned (~ *verses*); *unscared*; *unscarred*; *unscathed*, without injury suffered; *unscented*; *unscheduled*; *unscholarly*; *unschooled*; *unscientific* (*-ally*), (esp.) transgressing scientific principles; *unscoured*; *unscourged*; *unscreened* (esp. of coal); *unscriptural* (*-ly*), not in accordance with Scripture; *unscrupulous* (*-ly*, *-ness*), having no scruples, shameless, unprincipled; *unsculptured*, not covered with sculpture, (zool.) smooth; *unsealed*; *unsearchable*, beyond the reach of search; *unsearched*; *unseasonable* (*-bly*, *-ness*); *unseasoned*; *unseated*², not provided or furnished with seat(s); *unseaworthy* (*-iness*); *unseconded*; *unsectarian* (*-ism*), free from sectarian limitations; *unsecured*; *unseduced*; *unseductive*; *unseeing*, blind, unobservant;

unseemly (*-iness*) a. & (arch.) adv.; *unseen* a. & n., not seen (*the* ~, the world of spirits), ~ (*translation*), translation of unprepared passages as school exercise; *unseizable*; *unselect*, promiscuous, mixed; *unselected*; *unselfish* (*-ly*, *-ness*), regardful of others' interests rather than of one's own; *unsensational* (*-ly*); *unsent*; *unsentenced*; *unsentimental*; *unseparated*; *unserviceable* (*-bly*, *-ness*); *unset*, not set (*sun*, *gem*, *trap*, *broken leg*, *is* ~); *unsettled*², not settled, liable to change, open to further discussion, not paid, having no fixed abode, (of lands) not occupied by permanent inhabitants, (*his mind is still* ~, *weather*; *the point*, *the bill*, *is* ~); *unsevered*; *unshackled*; *unshaded*; *unshadowed*; *unshaken*, not shaken esp. in resolution; *unshapely*; *unshared*; *unshaven*; *unshed*; *unsheltered*; *unshipped*²; *unshocked*; *unshod*; *unshorn*, not shorn or shaven; *unshown*; *unshrinkable*, that will not shrink (~ *flannel*); *unshrinking* (*-ly*), unhesitating, fearless, firm; *unshrunk*; *unshut*; *unshuttered*; *unsifted*; *unsighted*, not sighted (*ship is still* ~), not furnished with sights (~ *gun*), precluded from seeing (*the umpire was* ~ *when Jones was caught*); *unsightly* (*-iness*), repulsive to the sight, ugly; **unsight*, *unseen*, without examination or inspection; *unsigned*; *unsinged*; *unsisterly* (*-iness*); *unsized*, not stiffened with size; *unskilful* (*-ly*, *-ness*); *unskilled*, not possessing or requiring skill or special training (~ *labour*, simple forms of manual labour); *unslaked*; *unsleeping*, *unslumbering*, (fig.) watchful; *unsmoked*; *unsociable* (*-bility*, *-bleness*, *-bly*); *unsocial*; *unsoiled*; *unsolaced*; *unsold*; *unsoldierly*; *unsolicited* (esp. ~ *testimonial*); *unsolicitous*; *unsolid* (*-ity*); *unsolvable*; *unsolved*; *unsoothed*; *unsophistical*; *unsophisticated* (*-ness*), artless, innocent, simple, not adulterated, not artificial; *unsorted*; *unsought*; *unsound* (*-ness*), not sound, diseased, morbid, rotten, ill-founded, erroneous, fallacious, unreliable, (~ *lungs*, *fruit*, *doctrine*, *policy*, *argument*; *of* ~ *mind*, insane); *unsounded*, unfathomed; *unsoured*; *unsown*; *unsparing* (*-ly*, *-ness*), profuse, lavish, (~ *praise*, ~ *of* or *in praise*, ~ *in his efforts*), merciless; *unspeakable* (*-bly*, *-ness*), that words cannot express, good, bad, etc., beyond description (~ *joys*, *an* ~ *bore*); *unspecified*; *unspeculative*; *unspent*; *unspilt*; *unspiritual* (*-ity*, *-ly*); *unspliced*, *-lt*; *unspoken*; *unspontaneous*, forced, artificial; *unsportsmanlike* (colloq. also *unsporting*); *unspotted*, not spotted or (fig.) contaminated; *unsprung*, (of vehicles, furniture, etc.) not provided with springs; *unsquared*; *unstable*; *unstaid*; *unstained*, not stained (esp. fig.); *unstamped*, without stamp (~ *deed*, *letter*); *unstarched*; *unstartled*; *unstated*; *unstatesmanlike*; *unstatutable* (*-bly*), not warranted by statute; *unsteadfast* (*-ly*, *-ness*); *unsteady* (*-ily*,

-iness), not steady or firm, shaking, reeling, changeable, fluctuating, of irregular habits, (*an ~ hand, walked with ~ steps, ladder is ~, was ~ in his adherence, ~ winds, is notoriously ~,* dissipated); *unstigmatized*; *unstimulated*; *unstinted*; *unstirred*; *unstocked,* not stocked (*with,* or abs.); *unstopped*; *unstored*; *unstrained,* not forced, not subjected to strain, not put through a strainer; *unstratified*; *unstressed,* not pronounced with stress; *unstudied,* easy, natural, spontaneous, (*~ ease, eloquence*); *unstuffed*; *unstung*; *unsubdued*; *unsubjugated*; *unsubmissive* (*-ly, -ness*); *unsubscribed*; *unsubstantial* (*-ity, -ly*), having little or no solidity or reality (*~ air, visions, forms, an ~ building*); *unsubstantiated,* not confirmed or established (*~ rumours*); *unsuccessful* (*-ly*); *unsugared*; *unsuggestive*; *unsuitable* (*-bility, -bly*); *unsuited,* unfit (*for* purpose), not adapted (*to*); *unsullied*; *unsummed*; *unsummoned*; *unsung,* not sung or (poet.) sung of; *unsunned,* not lighted by sun; *unsupple*; *unsupplied*; *unsupportable* (*-bly, -ness*); *unsupported*; *unsuppressed*; *unsure*; *unsurgical*; *unsurmised*; *unsurmounted*; *unsurpassable* (*-bly*); *unsurpassed*; *unsurrendered*; *unsurveyed*; *unsusceptible*; *unsuspected* (*-ly*); *unsuspicious* (*-ly, -ness*); *unsustainable*; *unsustained*; *unswallowed*; *unswayed,* not controlled or influenced; *unsweetened*; *unswept*; *unswerving* (*-ly*); *unsworn,* not sworn (*~ oath, witness*); *unsymbolical*; *unsymmetrical* (*-ly*), failing in or not characterized by symmetry; *unsympathetic* (*-ally*); *unsympathizing* (*-ly*); *unsystematic* (*-ally*);

untainted; *untalented*; *untamable* (*-ness*); *untamed*; *untanned*; *untarnishable*; *untarnished*; *untasked*; *untasted*; *untaught,* (of person etc. or subject etc.) not taught, ignorant; *untaxed*; *unteachable* (*-ness*); *untearable*; *untechnical*; *untempered,* not tempered (*~ mortar, steel, severity*); *untempted*; *untenable* (*-bility, -bleness*); *untenantable,* not fit to be occupied; *untenanted*; *untended,* not offered; *unterrified*; *untested*; *untethered*; *unthanked*; *unthankful* (*-ly, -ness*); *unthatched*; *unthinkable,* that cannot be conceived in thought, (colloq.) unlikely; *unthinking* (*-ly*), thoughtless; *unthought,* not thought, esp. *~-of*; *unthoughtful* (*-ness*); *unthrashed*; *unthreadable*; *unthreaded*; *unthreshed*; *unthrifty*; *unthwarted*; *untidy* (*-ily, -iness*); *untied*[2]; *untiled*; *untillable*; *untilled*; *untimbered*; *untimely* (*-iness*) a. & adv.; || *untim(e)ous* (Sc.), untimely; *untinctured*; *untinged*; *untired*; *untiring* (*-ly*); *untithed,* not subject to tithes; *untitled*; *untold,* not told, not counted, beyond count (*~ gold*); *untormented*; *untorn*; *untortured*; *untouchable,* that may not be touched, (n.) a non-caste Hindu (whom a caste man may not touch); *untouched*; *untoward,* perverse, refractory, awkward, unlucky, (*an ~ generation, accident*);

untraceable; *untraced*; *untracked,* not followed by means of or marked with tracks; *untragic,* not tragic or suited to tragedy; *untrained,* not trained or practised or instructed, not prepared by exercise, diet, etc., for race etc.; *untrammelled*; *untransferable,* that cannot or must not be transferred; *untranslatable* (*-bility, -bleness, -bly*); *untransmutable*; *untransportable*; *untravelled,* that has not travelled; *untraversable*; *untried,* (esp.) inexperienced; *untrimmed*; *untrodden*; *untroubled,* not troubled, calm; *untrue* (*-uly*), not true, contrary to the fact, false, not faithful or loyal (*to* person, principle, etc.), deviating from correct standard; *untrussed* (*~ fowl* etc.); *untrustworthy* (*-iness*); *untruthful* (*-ly, -ness*); *untuned*; *untuneful* (*-ly*); *unturned,* not turned (*leave no* STONE *~*); *untutored,* not taught or schooled;

unused, *unusual* (*-ity* rare, *-ness, -ly*), not usual, remarkable; *unutilized*; *unutterable* (*-bly*), above or beyond description (*~ torment, joy, etc., an ~ fool*); *unuttered*; *unvaccinated*; *unvalued,* not esteemed or prized, not estimated or priced; *unvanquished*; *unvaried*; *unvarnished,* not varnished or embellished (*~ surface, the ~ truth*); *unvarying* (*-ly*); *unvenerable*; *unvenerated*; *unvenomous*; *unventilated*; *unveracious*; *unverifiable*; *unverified*; *unversed,* not versed or skilled (*in*); *unvexed*; *unvictualled*; *unvindicated*; *unviolated*; *unvisited*; *unvitiated*; *unvoiced,* not spoken or uttered, (phonet.) not voiced; *unvouched,* not vouched (usu. *-for*);

unwak(en)ed; *unwanted*; *unwarlike*; *unwarmed*; *unwarned*; *unwarped*; *unwarrantable* (*-bly, -ness*), indefensible, unjustifiable, improper; *unwarranted,* unauthorized, not guaranteed; *unwary* (*-ily, -iness*); *unwashed,* not washed (*the great ~,* the rabble); *unwatched*; *unwatchful* (*-ness*); *unwatered,* not watered or diluted or supplied with water (*~ milk, horse, capital*); *unwavering* (*-ly*); *unweaned*; *unwearable*; *unwearied*; *unweary*; *unwearying* (*-ly*), not growing weary, persistent, (*~ efforts* etc.); *unwedded*; *unweeded*; *unweighed*; *unwelcome*; *unwelcomed*; *unwell,* not in good health, indisposed, menstruating; *unwept* (rhet., poet.), not wept for; *unwetted*; *unwhipped*; *unwhitened*; *unwhitewashed*; *unwholesome* (*-ly, -ness*); *unwifely*; *unwilling* (*-ly, -ness*), not willing or inclined (*to do, for* thing, *for* thing *to* be done, *that,* or abs.); *unwinged*; *unwinking,* not winking, vigilant; *unwise* (*-ly*), foolish, imprudent; *unwished,* not wished (usu. *-for*); *unwithdrawn*; *unwithered*; *unwithering*; *unwitnessed*; *unwitting* (*-ly*), not consciously or intentionally [see WIT[1]]; *unwomanly*; *unwon*; *unwonted*; *unwooded*; *unwooed*; *unworkable*; *unworkmanlike*; *unworldly* (*-iness*), not worldly, spiritual, (*~-minded* etc.); *unworn,* that has not been worn or impaired by wear; *unworshipped*; *unworthy* (-*ily*, -*iness*), not worthy or befitting the character (*of*), discreditable, unseemly; *unwound*²; *unwounded*; *unwoven*; *unwreaked*; *unwrinkled*; *unwritable*; *unwritten*, not written (~ *law*, resting originally on custom or judicial decision, not on written statutes etc., also, assumption that homicide in defence of personal honour etc. is justifiable); *unwrought*; *unwrung*, not wrung (WITHERS ~); *unyielding* (-*ly*, -*ness*), firm, obstinate; *unyoked*; *unyouthful*; *unzealous*.

2. Nouns are occas. formed either directly on a simple noun (*unbelief*, *unfriend*, *unrepair*) or by back formation or otherwise on corresp. adj. In these the formation may not be ascertainable, e.g. *unchastity* may be from *un-*+*chastity* or from *unchaste*+-*ity*.

Exx.: *unbelief'*, incredulity, disbelief esp. in divine revelation or in a particular religion, so *unbeliev'er*; *unchas'tity*; *uncircumci'sion*, not being circumcised, (N.T.) *the* ~, the Gentiles; *unconcern'*, freedom from anxiety, indifference, apathy; *unconstraint'*, freedom from constraint; *undress'*², ordinary dress opp. to full dress or uniform, loose negligent dress, (often fig. & attrib.); *unease'* (arch.), uneasiness, distress, discomfort; *unemploy'ment*, lack of employment, state of things in which many workers cannot find work or wages (~ *benefit*, payment made to unemployed worker under an insurance act, or by a trade union); *unfaith'* (rare), want of faith; *unfriend'* (arch.), enemy; *unprej'udice*, freedom from prejudice; *unreas'on*, lack of reason, nonsense, folly (ABBOT *of U*~); *unrepair'*, dilapidation, want of repair; *unreserve'*, absence of reserve, frankness; *unrest'*, lack of rest, disturbed or agitated condition of person or nation; *unrestraint'*; *unright'* (arch.), wrong injustice; *unsuccess'*, want of success, failure; *unsuspi'cion* (rare); *unsymm'etry*, absence or violation of symmetry; *un'thrift* (arch.), prodigal(ity); *untruth'*, being untrue, falsehood, lie, (*the manifest* ~ *of this statement, told me an* ~); *unwis'dom*, lack of wisdom, folly, imprudence.

unadopted, see UN-²(1); **unanchor**, UN-¹(1).

ūnăn'imous, a. All of one mind, agreeing in opinion, as *we were, the meeting was*, ~ (*for reform, as to the policy to be pursued, in protesting*, etc.); (of opinion, vote, etc.) formed, held, given, with one accord. Hence or cogn. **ūnanim'ity**, ~NESS, nn., ~LY² adv. [f. L *unanimus*, LL -*mis*, (*unus* one+*animus* mind)+-OUS]

unapparel, unarm, unarmed¹, see UN-¹ (2); **unattire**, UN-¹(1).

ŭn'au (-aw), n. Brazilian two-toed sloth. [Braz.]

unbag, see UN-¹(3); **unbalance**, UN-¹(1); **unballast**, UN-¹(2); **unbank**, **unbar**, **unbear**, UN-¹(1); **unbed**, UN-¹(3); **unbeknown(st)**, UN-²(1); **unbelief**, **unbeliever**, UN-²(2); **unbelt**, UN-¹(2); **unbend**, **unbending**¹, UN-¹(1).

unberu'fen (ŏŏnberŏŏ-), a. Unsummoned (in E use as deprecating Nemesis after boastful remark etc.). [G]

unbeseem, unbias, unbind, see UN-¹; **unbirthday**, UN-²(1); **unbishop**, UN-¹(4); **unbitt**, UN-¹(3); **unblindfold**, **unblock, unbolt** UN-¹(1); **unbone**, UN-¹(2); **unbonnet**, UN-¹(1); **unboot**, UN-¹(2); **unbosom**, UN-¹(1); **unbowel**, UN-¹(2); **unbox**, UN-¹(3); **unbrace, unbraid**, **unbreech, unbridle, unbuckle, unburden**, **unbutton**, UN-¹ (1); **uncage**, UN-¹(3); **uncanny**, UN-²(1); **uncap**, UN-¹(2); **uncart, uncase**, UN-¹(3).

uncate. See UNCINATE.

unchain, see UN-¹(1); **unchastity**, UN-¹ (2); **unchristianize**, UN-¹(1); **unchurch**, UN-¹(3).

ŭn'cia (-shĭa), n. (Rom. ant.; pl. -*ae*). Twelfth part, esp. (as coin or amount) of the as; ounce; inch. [L]

ŭn'cial (-shl), a. & n. 1. Of, written in, a kind of majuscule writing found in MSS. of 4th to 8th c. with characters from which modern capitals are largely derived. 2. n. ~ letter or MS. [f. L *uncialis* (prec., see -AL), in LL sense *inch-high, large*]

ŭn'cin|ate, a. (Also **ŭnc'ate**) hooked, crooked. So **ŭncĭf'EROUS**, **ŭn'cĭFORM**, ~AL, aa. [f. L *uncinatus* (*uncinus* hook f. L *uncus* hook, see -ATE²)]

uncircumcision, see UN-²(2); **unclasp**, UN-¹(1).

uncle (ŭng'kl), n. Father's or mother's brother; aunt's husband; *(as familiar mode of address) U*~ *Tom's Cabin* etc., *U*~ *Sam* (colloq.), federal government or typical citizen of U.S.; (sl.) pawnbroker; (colloq., often w. name added, as voc. or not) elderly friendly person, e.g. B.B.C. announcer; *talk to* (person) *like a Dutch* ~ (with kindly severity). Hence ~SHIP n. [ME, f. AF, f. L *avunculus* maternal uncle (*avus* grandfather, see foll.)]

-uncle, suf. repr. OF -*uncle* (-*oncle*) & L -*unculus*; -*la*, a special form of -*ulus* -ULE. In E thr. (O)F (*carb*~) or dir. f. L (*fur*~); the L form is retained in *ranunculus*.

unclench, -inch, see UN-¹(1); **uncloak**, UN-¹(2); **unclog**, UN-¹(1); **uncloister**, UN-¹(3); **unclose, unclothe**, UN-¹(1).

‖ **ŭnc'ŏ**, a., n. (pl. ~*s*), & adv. (Sc.). 1. Strange, unusual; notable. 2. n. Stranger; (pl.) news. 3. adv. Remarkably, very; *the* ~ *guid*, rigidly religious people (usu. derog.). [dial. var. of UNCOUTH]

uncock, uncoil, see UN-¹(1); **unconcern**, UN-²(2); **unconditioned**, **unconscionable**, UN-²(1); **unconstraint**, UN-²(2);

For adjj. in un- not given see UN-²(1).

uncoop, UN-¹(3); **uncord, uncork, uncouple**, UN-¹(1).

uncouth' (-ōo-), a. (Obs. or arch.) not known of, unfamiliar, unusual; (of places; now literary) unfrequented, desolate, wild, (of life) uncivilized, comfortless; (of persons, looks, conduct, etc.) strange, awkward, clumsy, uncultured, (of language) harsh, rugged, pedantic. Hence ~LY² adv., ~NESS n. [OE *uncūth* unknown (UN-² + *cūth* p.p. of *cunnan* know, CAN²)]

uncover, see UN-¹(1); **uncowl**, UN-¹(2); **uncreate, uncross**, UN-¹(1); **uncrown**, UN-¹(2).

ŭnc'tion, n. Anointing with oil or unguent for medical purposes or as religious rite or ceremonial (EXTREME ~); thing used in anointing, unguent, (fig.) soothing or flattering words or thought or circumstance (see FLATTER); fervent or sympathetic quality in words or tone caused by or causing deep religious or other emotion; simulation of this, affected enthusiasm, gush; excessive suavity; keen or lingering enjoyment in narration, gusto, (*told the story with much* ~). [ME, f. L *unctio* (*ungere unct-* anoint, see -ION)]

ŭnc'tŭous, a. Full of (esp. simulated) unction; greasy, esp. (of minerals) having a soapy feel when touched. Hence ~LY² adv., ~NESS n. [ME, f. med. L *unctuosus* f. L *unctus -ūs* anointing (as prec.), see -OUS]

uncurb, uncurl, see UN-¹(1).

ŭn'dé (-ā), **ŭn'dee**, a, (her.). Wavy. [f. F *ondé* (L *unda* wave, -ATE²)]

undeceive, undeceived¹, **undeify**, see UN-¹(1).

ŭn'der, prep., adv., & a. **1.** In or to a position lower than, below, as *it lay, fell,* ~ *the table, assembled* ~ (at the foot of) *the castle wall, struck him* ~ *the left eye, nothing new* ~ *the sun* (anywhere), ~ FOOT¹, ~ HATCH¹*es*, ~ one's NOSE, ~ (in & covered by) *water,* ~ one's WING. **2.** Within, on the inside of, (surface etc.), as *inserted a knife-blade* ~ *the bark, was seen to blush* ~ *his dusky skin, with a good meal* ~ *his belt* (in his stomach), ~ *the* LEE *of.* **3.** Inferior to, less than, as *no one* ~ *a bishop, incomes* ~ *£400, cannot be done* ~ (at less cost than) *£5, total falls* ~ *what was expected, speak* ~ one's *breath* (in a whisper). **4.** In the position or act of supporting or sustaining, subjected to, undergoing, liable to, on condition of, subject to, governed or controlled or bound by, in accordance with, in the form of, in the time of, as *sank* ~ *the load* (lit. & fig.), ~ *a* CLOUD, *groaning* ~ *tyranny, is now* ~ *repair,* ~ *examination, a few acres* ~ (planted with) *corn,* ~ FIRE¹, ~ (propelled by) *sail,* ~ WAY, ~ ARM¹*s, forbidden* ~ *pain of death, a criminal* ~ *sentence of* (condemned to) *death, have sat* ~ (attended sermons of) *famous preachers, country prospered* ~ *him* or *his rule, might*

succeed ~ *other conditions, is* ~ *a delusion, was* ~ *the impression,* ~ *the circumstances,* ~ *the rose,* =SUB² *rosa,* ~ FAVOUR¹, ~ (attested by) one's *hand & seal, was* ~ *a vow, known* ~ *an assumed name, appears* ~ *various forms,* ~ *pretence of ignorance, lived* ~ *the Stuarts.* **5.** adv. In or to a lower place or subordinate condition, as BRING, KEEP¹, KNOCK¹, KNUCKLE, GO¹, ~, *a cloth should be spread* ~ (usu. ~*neath, beneath*). **6.** adj. Lower (now largely merged in foll.), as *the* ~ *jaw,* ~ *layers,* ~ *servants;* ~ *dog* (sl.), dog, person, who has the worst of an encounter, oppressed or (socially) inferior person. Hence ~MOST a. [OE *under*, OS *-ar*, OHG *untar*, ON *undir*, Goth. *undar*]

ŭnder-, pref.=prec. prep. or adv. or adj. **1.** As prep. governing the noun to which it is prefixed, w. sense 'below', *under-* forms a few advv. & adjj., as: *un'derarm* a., (crick.) = UNDERHAND, (lawn tennis, of service or stroke) made by swinging racket below shoulder-level; ~*co'ver* a., surreptitious (~*cover agent*, one trying to secure evidence of illegal activities by associating with the suspected wrongdoers); ~*foot'* adv., under one's feet; UNDERGROUND; UNDERHAND; *un'derproof* a., with less alcohol than proof spirit. **2.** *Under-* is prefixed to vbs & their derivatives w. adv. or prep. force in sense 'beneath', 'lower than', 'below', as: ~*bid'* v.t., make lower bid than (person). (bridge) bid less on (a hand) than its strength warrants; ~*cut'*¹ v.t., cut away material of (design etc. in carving) so as to make it stand out in relief, (golf) hit (ball) so that it rises high & does not roll far on alighting, (commerce.) offer lower terms than (competitor); ~*drain'*¹ v.t., drain (ground) by forming channels beneath it; ~*lay'* v.t. & i., lay something under (thing), esp. (print.) lay paper under (types) to raise them, (mining, intr.) incline from the vertical; *un'derlay* n., paper laid under types; waterproof paper, sheet, etc., for laying under carpet or mattress, (mining) = inclined lode or shaft; ~*let'* v.t., let below true value, sublet; ~*line'*¹ v.t., draw line under (word) to secure emphasis or to indicate italics, stress, emphasize; ~*men'tioned* a.; ~*pin'* v.t., place support of masonry etc. under (wall, overhanging bank, etc.); ~*play'* v.i. (cards), play low card while retaining high one of same suit; *un'derplay* n., ~*playing;* ~*prop'* v.t., put prop under; ~*quote'* v.t., quote lower prices than (person), quote lower prices than others for (goods etc.); ~*run'* v.t. & i., run or pass under, (naut.) overhaul or examine (a cable etc.) by lifting it on board and passing it along by hand; ~*score'* v.t., =~*line*¹; ~*sell'* v.t., sell cheaper than (person); *un'derseller* n.; ~*set'*¹ v.t., support (masonry etc.) by prop; *un'dershot* a., (of wheel) worked by water passing under it, = UNDERHUNG; ~signed' a., I, we, the ~signed, (whose signatures appear below).

3. *Under-* in sense ' insufficiently ', ' incompletely ', is prefixed to vbs (used in p.p.) & to some adjj., w. their derivatives. Adjj. & p.pp. tend in attrib. use (cf. UN-¹, -ED²) to take stress on first syllable (*beef was* ~*done*', *hate un'derdone beef*; *an un'der-exposed* or *un'der-exposed' negative*).

Exx. ~*act*' v.t., act (a part, or abs.) inadequately; ~*bred*' a., ill-bred, vulgar; ~*charge*' v.t., charge too little for (thing) or to (person), put insufficient charge into (gun etc.); *un'dercharge* n., insufficient charge; ~*devel'op* v.t. (photog.); ~*do*' v.t., cook insufficiently, esp. in p.p. ~*done*; ~*dose*' v.t.; ~*draw*' v.t., depict inadequately; ~*dress*' v.t. & i., dress too plainly or too lightly; ~*employ'ment* n., shortage of work; ~*es'timate* v.t., form too low an estimate of; ~*es'timate* (-*at*), -*ation*, nn.; ~*expose*' v.t., ~*exposure* n. (photog.); ~*feed*' v.t. & i.; ~*fired*' a., (of pottery) not baked enough; ~*grown*' a.; ~*man*' v.t., furnish (ship etc.) with too few men; ~*mas'ted* a.; ~*pay*' v.t., pay (workmen etc.) inadequately; ~*priv'ileged* (-ĭjd) a., less privileged than others, belonging to the lower classes of society; ~*-produc'tion* n., production less than is usual or required; ~*rate*' v.t., ~estimate; ~*reck'on* v.t.; ~*ripe*' a.; ~*sized*' a., of less than the usual size, dwarfish; ~*stale*' v.t.; ~*statement* n.; ~*stock*' v.t., supply (farm, shop, etc.) with insufficient stock; ~*valua'tion* n.; ~*val'ue* v.t.

4. *Under-* in adj. relation with noun replaces or is interchangeable with *under* a., in senses ' situated beneath ', ' subordinate '. In the less-established compounds the hyphen is usu. retained & the stress variously placed on either component or both.

Exx.: ~*-agent* n.; *un'derbrush* n., = ~*growth*; *un'dercarriage*, aircraft's landing gear; *un'derclay* n., clay bed under coal; ~*-clerk(ship)* nn.; *un'dercliff* n., terrace or lower cliff formed by a landslip; *un'derclothes*, *un'derclothing*, nn., clothes worn under others esp. next to skin; ~*drain*³ n., drain placed underground; *un'derflow* n., current flowing beneath surface; *un'dergarment* n., garment worn under others; *un'dergrowth* n., shrubs or small trees growing under larger ones; ~*-king* n., inferior or subordinate king; ~*-lease* n., lease granted by lessee for shorter term than his own; *un'derline²* n., advance announcement of production of subsequent play at foot of play-bill, descriptive line(s) under an illustration; *un'derlinen* n., linen or (loosely) other ~*garments*; *•un'derpass*, subway; *un'derplot* n., subordinate plot in play or novel; *un'der-*

For adjj. in *un-* not given see UN-²(1).

-*sec'retary(ship)* nn.; || (*Parliamentary Under-Secretary*, member of Government; *Permanent Under-Secretary*, member of Civil Service & head of a department); ~*-servant* n.; *un'derset²* n. (naut.), undercurrent in contrary direction to that of wind or surface water; ~*-sheriff* n., sheriff's deputy; ~*shirt* n.; *un'der-shrub* n., plant like shrub but smaller; *un'derskirt* n.; *un'dersleeve* n., sleeve, esp. detached one, worn under another; *un'dersoil* n.; *un'derstrapper* n., inferior agent, underling; ~*-stratum* n.; ~*-tenant* n., tenant's tenant; ~*-tenancy* n.; *un'dertint* n., subdued tint; *un'dertone* n., subdued tone esp. in speaking, thin or subdued colour, ~*lying* quality or element, ~current; *un'dertow* n., backward flow of wave breaking on beach, = ~*set*; *un'derwear* n., (clothes meant for) wearing underneath; *un'derwing* n., kinds of moth with conspicuous markings etc. on under wings; *un'derwood* n., = ~*growth*; *un'der-world* n., antipodes, infernal regions, lowest social stratum, world of crime.

underact, see UNDER- 3; under-agent, UNDER- 4; underarm, UNDER- 1; under-bid, UNDER- 2; underbred, UNDER- 3; underbrush, undercarriage, UNDER- 4; undercharge, UNDER- 3; underclay, undercliff, underclothes, underclothing, UNDER- 4; undercover, UNDER- 1.

ŭn'dercroft (-aw-), n. Crypt. [UNDER, ME croft f. L crupta CRYPT]

ŭn'dercurrent, n. Current below the surface; (fig.) unperceived influence or feeling of different or contrary tendency; (mining) large shallow box beside main hydraulic sluice serving to aid in saving gold. [UNDER- 4]

undercut¹. See UNDER- 2.

ŭn'dercut², n. || Under side of sirloin; upward blow in boxing. [UNDER- 4]

under-develop, underdo, underdose, see UNDER- 3; underdrain¹ v.t., UNDER- 2; underdrain² n., UNDER- 4; underdraw, underdress, underemployment, underestimate, underestimation, under-expose, under-exposure, underfeed, underfired, UNDER- 3; underflow, UNDER- 4; underfoot, UNDER- 1; undergarment, UNDER- 4.

ŭndergō', v.t. Be subjected to, suffer, endure esp. with firmness, as *has undergone many trials*, *underwent a rapid change*, *an operation*. [OE UNDER(gän GO)]

ŭndergrăd'ū|ate, n. Member of university who has not taken his first degree (often attrib.). Hence ~ateSHIP n., ~ETTE² n. (joc.), female ~ate. [UNDER- 4]

ŭnderground', adv., a., & n. 1. Beneath surface of earth. 2. adj. (*in attrib. use* ŭn²). Situated ~, as ~ *railway*; (fig.) hidden, secret, as ~ (secret resistance) *movement*. 3. n. (ŭn²). || ~ *railway*; ~ *movement*. [UNDER- 1]

For other words in *under-* see UNDER-.

undergrown, see UNDER- 3; **undergrowth**, UNDER- 4.

ŭnderhănd', adv. & a. (*in attrib. use* ŭn⁴). Clandestine(ly), secret(ly), not above--board; (crick., of bowling) (performed) with hand underneath both elbow & ball, as *bowls* ~, ~ *bowling*. [UNDER- 1, 4]

ŭnderhŭng' (*in attrib. use* ŭn⁴), a. (Of lower jaw) projecting beyond upper jaw; having ~ jaw. [UNDER- 2]

under-king, see UNDER- 4; **underlay** v.t. & i., & n., UNDER- 2; **under-lease**, UNDER- 4; **underlet**, UNDER- 2.

ŭnderlie', v.t. Lie, be situated, under (stratum etc., or abs.); (fig., of principle etc.) be the basis of (doctrine, law, conduct, etc., or abs. esp. in part.). [UNDER- 2]

underline¹ v.t., see UNDER- 2; **underline²**, **underlinen**, UNDER- 4.

ŭn'derling, n. Subordinate (usu. derog.). [ME (-LING¹)]

underman, undermasted, see UNDER- 3; **undermentioned**, UNDER- 2.

ŭndermin|e', v.t. Make mine or excavation under, wear away base or foundation of, as *rivers* ~*e their banks*, ~*e the walls*; injure (person, reputation, influence, etc.) by secret means; injure, wear out, (health etc.) insidiously or imperceptibly. Hence ~'ER¹ n. [UNDER- 2]

ŭnderneath', adv., prep., a., & n. 1. At or to a lower place (than), below (not in fig. senses). 2. adj. & n. Lower (surface, part). [OE *underneothan* (UNDER, cf. BENEATH)]

•**underpass**, see UNDER- 4; **underpay**, UNDER- 3; **underpin, underplay** v.i., & n., UNDER- 2; **underplot**, UNDER- 4; **underprivileged, under-production**, UNDER- 3; **underproof**, UNDER- 1; **underprop, underquote**, UNDER- 2; **underrate, under-reckon, under-ripe**, UNDER- 3; **underrun, underscore**, UNDER- 2; **under-secretary(ship)**, UNDER- 4; **undersell(er)**, UNDER- 2; **under-servant**, UNDER- 4; **underset¹** v.t., UNDER- 2; **underset²** n., **under-sheriff, undershirt**, UNDER- 4; **undershot**, UNDER- 2; **undershrub**, UNDER- 4; **undersigned**, UNDER- 2; **undersized**, UNDER- 3; **underskirt, undersleeve, undersoil**, UNDER- 4.

ŭnderstănd', v.t. & i. (-*stood*; arch. p.p. -*standed*). 1. Comprehend, perceive the meaning of, (words, person, or language etc.), as *does not* ~ *what you say*, *do you* ~ *me?, French? ; tongue not* ~*ed of the people*, foreign language. 2. Grasp mentally, perceive the significance or explanation or cause or nature of, know how to deal with, as *do not* ~ *why he came, what the noise is about, the point of his remark; quite* ~ *your difficulty; cannot* ~ *him, his conduct, his wanting to go; thoroughly* ~*s children, could never* ~ *mathematics;* (abs.) *you don't* ~ (the situation etc.). 3. Infer esp. from information received, take as implied, take

for granted, as *I* ~ *that doors open at 7.30, that they are almost destitute, him to be* or *that he is a distant relation, I quite understood that expenses were to be paid, no one could* ~ *that from my words, what did you* ~ *him to say* (~ from his words)? ; (expr. uncertainty or surprise or indignation) *do I* ~ (*you to say*) *that* or *am I to* ~ *that you refuse? ;* (introducing warning or threat) *now* ~ *me, he gave me* or *I was given to* ~ (I thought he said or meant) *that it was done.* 4. Supply (word) mentally, as *the verb may be either expressed or understood.* [OE UNDER(*standan* STAND)]

ŭnderstănd'ing¹, a. Having insight. [ME; -ING¹]

ŭnderstănd'ing², n. In vbl senses, esp.: intelligence, as *has an excellent* ~, *men without* ~ ; power of apprehension, power of abstract thought, (often opp. to *reason*); agreement, harmony, union of sentiments, convention, thing agreed upon, as *must come to an* ~ *with him, disturbed the (good)* ~ *between them, had a secret* ~ *with other firms, consented only on this* ~, *on the distinct* ~ *that;* (pl., sl.) feet, legs, shoes, etc. [ME; -ING¹]

understate(ment), understock, see UNDER- 3; **understrapper, under--stratum**, UNDER- 4.

ŭn'derstŭdy̆, n., & v.t. 1. One who studies theatrical part in order to play it at short notice in absence of the usual actor. 2. v.t. Study (part) thus, act as ~ to (actor). [UNDER- 4]

ŭndertāke', v.t. & i. Bind oneself to perform, make or-self responsible for, engage in, enter upon, (work, enterprise, responsibility); accept an obligation, promise, (*to* do); (arch.) engage with (person) in combat, argument, etc.; guarantee, affirm, as *I will* ~ *that he has not heard a word, that you shall* or *will be no loser by it;* (arch.) be guarantee *for* (person, fact); (colloq.) manage funerals. [ME, repl. OE *underniman*]

ŭn'dertāker, n. In vbl senses, esp.: one who manages funerals; (hist.) influential person who undertook to procure particular legislation esp. to obtain supplies from Commons if king would grant some concession. [-ER¹]

ŭndertāk'ing, n. In vbl senses, esp.: work etc. undertaken, enterprise, as *a serious* ~; management of funerals (ŭn⁴). [-ING¹]

under-tenant, under-tenancy, see UNDER- 4; **undertint, undertone, undertow**, UNDER- 4; **undervaluation, undervalue**, UNDER- 3; **underwear, underwing, underwood, underworld**, UNDER- 4.

ŭnderwrīte' (-erīt), v.t. & i. Execute & deliver (policy of insurance esp. on marine property), practise marine insurance, engage to buy all stock in (company etc.) not bought by the public, whence **ŭn'derwrīter** n.; undertake to finance;

write below, as *the underwritten names*.
[UNDER- 2]

ŭn'dies (-dĭz), n. pl. (colloq.). (Esp. women's) underclothing. [abbr., -Y³]

ŭndine' (-ēn), n. Female water-sprite who by marrying a mortal & bearing a child might receive a soul. [f. mod. L *Undina* f. L *unda* wave + -INE¹]

undo, see UN-¹(1); **undock**, UN-¹(3); **undoer, undoing, undomesticate, undone**¹, UN-¹(1).

undrape, undress¹ v.t. & i., see UN-¹ (1); **undress**² n., see -UN-²(2); **undressed**¹, UN-¹(1); **unduke**, UN-¹(4).

ŭn'dŭl|āte¹, v.i. Have wavy motion or look. Hence ~ANT a. (esp. ~*ant fever*, Malta fever), ~**ātĭngLY**² adv. [as foll., -ATE³]

ŭn'dūlate², a. Wavy, going alternately up & down or in & out, as *leaves with ~ margins*. Hence~LY² adv. [f. L *undulatus* (*unda* wave, see -UL-, -ATE²)]

ŭndūlā'tion, n. Wavy motion or form, gentle rise & fall, each wave of this; set of wavy lines; (path.) sensation of undulating movement in the heart. [as prec. + -ATION]

ŭn'dūlātorў, a. Undulating, wavy; of, due to, undulation; ~ *theory of light* (that light is propagated through the ether by wave-motion imparted to the ether by molecular vibrations of the radiant body), so **ŭndūlā'tion**IST(2) (-sho-) n. [-ORY]

unearth, see UN-¹(3); **unease**, UN-²(2); **unedge**, UN-¹(2); **unegoize**, UN-¹(1); **unemployment**, UN-²(2); **unentangle, unequalize**, UN-¹(1); **unethical**, UN-²(1); **unface**, UN-¹(2); **unfaith**, UN-²(2); **unfasten, unfastened**¹, UN-¹(1): **unfeather, unfence**, UN-¹(2); **unfetter, unfettered**¹, UN-¹(1); **unfeudalize, unfile, unfit, unfix, unfixed**¹, UN-¹(1); **unflesh, unflower**, UN-¹(2); **unfold**¹, UN-¹ (1); **unfold**², UN-¹(3); **unform**, UN-¹(1); **unframe**, UN-¹(2); **unfriend**, UN-²(2); **unfrock**, UN-¹(2); **unfurl**, UN-¹(1).

ŭngain'l|ў (-n-g-), a. & adv. (Of persons or animals or their movements) ill-made, awkward-looking, clumsy; (adv.) in ~y manner. Hence ~iNESS n. [UN-² + obs. *gain* a. f. ON *gegn* straight + -LY¹; rel. to AGAIN]

ungear, see UN-¹(1); **unget-at-able**, UN-²(1); **ungild, ungird**, see UN-¹(1); **ungirdle**, UN-¹(2); **unglaze**, UN-¹(1); **unglove, ungown**, UN-¹(2).

ŭng'ual (-nggw-), a. Of, like, bearing, a nail or hoof or claw. So **ŭnguic'ŭlAR**¹, **ŭnguic'ŭlATE**², [-CULE, usu. without dim. force], **ŭnguïf'EROUS, ŭng'uïFORM**, aa. [f. L *unguis* claw, nail, + -AL]

ŭng'uent (-nggw-), n. Any soft substance used as ointment or for lubrication. So ~ARY¹ a. [f. L *unguentum* (*unguere* anoint)]

ŭng'ūl|a (-ngg-), n. (pl. ~*ae*). Hoof, claw,

talon, whence ~ATE²(2) a. & n. (zool.); hooked instrument for extracting dead foetus; cone, cylinder, with top cut off by plane oblique to base. Hence ~AR¹ a. [L, dim. as UNGUAL]

ungum, unhair, see UN-¹(2); **unhallow, unhand, unhang, unharness, unhasp**, UN-¹(1); **unhat, unhelm**, UN-¹(2); **unhinge(d), unhitch**, UN-¹(1); **unhive**, UN-¹(3); **unhook, unhoop**, UN-¹(1); **unhorse**, UN-¹(3); **unhouse, unhumanize**, UN-¹(1); **unhusk**, UN-¹(2).

ūni-, comb. form of L *unus* one, as: ~*artic'ulate*, single-jointed; ~*ax'(i)al*, having a single axis, whence ~*ax'ially* adv.; ~*căm'eral*, of only one chamber (of Parliament etc.); ~*cap'sular*, of one capsule; ~*cell'ular*, one-celled; ~*col'our(ed)*, of one colour; ~*corn'ous*, one-horned; ~*cos'tate*, single-ribbed; ~*cus'pid* a. & n., (tooth) of one cusp; **ŭn'icycle**, single-wheeled vehicle; ~*flor'ous*, bearing one flower; ~*fol'iate*, having one leaf; ~*lăt'eral*, one-sided (~*lateral leaves*, leaning to one side of stem,~*lateral contract*, binding one party only), (of car-parking) restricted to one side of the street; ~*lat'erally* adv.; ~*lĭt'eral*, consisting of one letter; ~*loc'ular*, ~*loc'ulate*, (bot., zool.), single--chambered; *ūnĭp'arous*, producing one at a birth, (bot.) having one axis or branch; ~*part'ite*, not divided; **ŭn'iped**, single--footed; ~*pers'onal*, (of Deity) existing only in one person, (of verb) used only in one person; ~*plān'ar*, lying in one plane; ~*pol'ar*, (biol., of cell etc.) having only one pole, (electr.) showing only one kind of polarity, whence ~*pola'rily* n.; ~*răd'iate(d)*, having only one arm or process; ~*ser'ial*, set in one row; ~*sex'ual*, of one sex, not hermaphrodite, having stamens or pistil but not both, whence ~*sexual'ity* n., ~*sex'ually* adv.; ~*sul'cate* (bot., zool.), single-grooved; *ūnĭv'alent* (chem.), having a combining power of one, whence *ūnĭv'alence, ūnĭv'alency*, nn.; **ŭn'ivalve** a. & n., (mollusc) of one valve; *ūnĭv'ocal* a. & n., (word) of only one proper meaning, whence *ūnĭv'ocally* adv.

Un'iat, -āte, n. (ū-). Member of any community of Oriental Christians that acknowledges Pope's supremacy but retains own liturgy etc. [f. Russ. *uniyat* f. *uniya* union f. L *unus* one]

ŭn'icŏrn, n. **1.** Fabulous animal with horse's body & single straight horn (in *Deut.* xxxiii. 17 mistransl. of Heb. *re'em*, a two-horned animal); heraldic representation of this, with goat's beard & lion's tail. **2.** (Also ~-*fish*, -*whale*, *sea-~*) narwhal. **3.** Kind of single-horned beetle; caterpillar with hornlike prominence on back (~ *moth*, of this). **4.** Pair of horses with third horse in front, turn-out with these. **5.** (Also ~-*shell*) kinds of gasteropod with spine on lip of shell. [ME, f. OF *unicorne* or LL *unicornis*, *-us* n., f. L adj. UNI(*cornis* f. *cornu* horn)]

ūn′ifŏrm, a., n., & v.t. **1.** Not changing in form or character, the same, unvarying, as *present a ~ appearance*, *of ~ size & shape, keeps a ~ temperature, behaved with ~ moderation, ~ acceleration* (not varying with time); (of tax, law, etc.) not varying with time or place; conforming to same standard or rule. **2.** n. ~ dress worn by members of same body, e.g. by soldiers, sailors, policemen. **3.** v.t. Make ~, clothe in ~. Hence ~LY² adv. [f. F *uniforme* adj. or L UNI(*formis* -FORM)]

ūnifŏrm′ity, n. Being uniform, sameness, consistency; *Act of U~* (for securing ~ in public worship, esp. that of 1662); *doctrine of ~* (that ~ has prevailed in physical causes & effects in all ages, opp. to CATA-STROPHISM), whence **ūnifŏrmĭtăr′ian**(ISM) nn. [ME, f. OF *uniformite* or LL *uniformitas* (as prec., see -TY)]

ūn′ĭfy, v.t. Reduce (things, or abs.) to unity or uniformity. Hence or cogn. ~FICĀ′TION, ~fīER¹, nn. [f. F *unifier* or LL UNI(*ficare* -FY)]

Unĭgĕn′ĭtus (ū-), n. (hist.). Bull of Clement XI against Jansenism in 1713. [LL=only-begotten, rendering Gk *monogenēs*]

unintelligible. See UN-²(1).

ūn′ion (-yon), n. **1.** Uniting, being united, coalition, junction, as *effected a~*, *the ~ of the parts was imperfect, ~ by first or second* INTENTION; *the U~* (of England & Scotland in 1706, also, of Great Britain & Ireland in 1801). **2.** Matrimony, marriage. **3.** Concord, agreement, as *lived together in perfect ~*. **4.** A whole resulting from combination of parts or members, esp. (1) *the* U.S., (2) *the* United Kingdom, (3) South Africa; TRADE~; POSTAL~. **5.** ‖ (Formerly) two or more parishes consolidated for administration of poor-laws, (in full ~ *workhouse*) workhouse erected by such ~. **6.** ‖ Association of independent (esp. Congregational or Baptist) churches for purposes of co-operation. **7.** (*U~*) general club & debating society at some universities, buildings of such society. **8.** Part of flag with device emblematic of ~ normally occupying upper corner next staff (*ensign hoisted ~ down*, with ~ below as signal of distress); *U~ Jack* or *flag*, national ensign of United Kingdom formed by ~ of crosses of St George, St Andrew, & St Patrick. **9.** Kinds of joint or coupling for pipes etc.; shallow vat in which beer is left to clear; fabric of mixed materials, e.g. cotton with linen or silk or jute. **10.** *°~ suit*, combinations (garment). [ME, f. OF, f. LL *unio* unity (*unus* one, see -ION)]

ūn′ion|ist (-nyo-), n. **1.** Member of a trade union, advocate of trade unions. **2.** Person opposed to rupture of legislative union between Great Britain & Ireland, opponent of home rule in Ireland, as

LIBERAL *~ist*, (attrib.) *~ist party, principles*; °(hist.) one who during the civil war opposed secession. So ~ISM n., ~is′tic a. [-IST]

ūnique′ (-ēk), a. & n. **1.** Unmatched, unequalled, having no like or equal or parallel, as *his position was~*, *this vase is so far as is known ~*, (vulg.) *the most ~* (remarkable) *man I ever met*, *rather ~* (unusual). **2.** n. ~ thing. Hence ~LY² (-ēk′li) adv., ~NESS (-ēk′n-) n. [F, f. L *unicus* (*unus* one)]

ūn′ison, a. & n. **1.** (mus.). Coinciding in pitch, whence or cogn. **ūnis′onᴀʟ**, **ūnis′onᴀɴᴛ**, **ūnis′onous**, aa., **ūnis′on**ᴀɴᴄᴇ n.; *~ string* (tuned in ~ with another string & meant to be sounded with it). **2.** n. Unity of pitch in sounds or notes, (mus.) this regarded as an interval; state of sounding at same pitch, esp. *in~*; *= ~ string*; concord, agreement, as *acted in perfect ~*. [f. OF *unison* or LL UNI(*sonus* sound)]

ūn′it, n. Individual thing or person or group regarded for purposes of calculation etc. as single & complete, each of the individuals or groups into which a complex whole may be analysed, as *take the family as the ~ of society*; quantity chosen as a standard in terms of which other quantities may be expressed, as *abstract ~*, the number one (1), *C.G.S. system of ~s* (in which centimetre, gramme, second, are the ~s of length, mass, & time), *electrical, magnetic, thermal, ~*. [1570 (J. Dee), f. L *unus* repl. *unity*, perh. after *digit*]

ūnĭtăr′ian, n. & a. **1.** (*U~*) one who, member of a religious body that, maintains against the doctrine of the Trinity that God is one person, whence U~ISM n., U~IZE v.t.; advocate of unity or centralization e.g. in politics. **2.** adj. Of the U~s, as *U~ Church*; = foll. [partly f. mod. L *unitarius* (*unitas* UNITY)+-AN, partly f. UNITY+-ARIAN]

ūn′itary, a. Of a unit or units, as ~ *method*, a rule in arithmetic used for same purpose as rule of three; marked by unity or uniformity. [f. UNIT or UNITY + -ARY¹]

ūnite′, v.t. & i. **1.** Join (t. & i.) together, make or become one, combine, consolidate, amalgamate, as ~ *the parts with cement, give the parts time to ~, the two nations gradually (became) ~d, oil will not ~ with water*; *U~d Brethren*, the MORAVIAN sect; *U~d Irishmen*, Irish society formed in 1791 for purposes of parliamentary reform etc.; *U~d* KINGDOM; *U~d Nations*, (orig., in 1942) those ~d against the AXIS powers in the 1939–45 war, (later) an organization of almost all ‘ peace-loving States ’; *U~d Provinces*, Holland, Zealand, & 5 other provinces ~d in 1579 & forming basis of republic of Netherlands, (also, hist.) one of the major Indian administrative divisions,

comprising Agra and Oudh; *U~d* STATE¹*s*.
2. Agree, combine, co-operate, (*in* sentiment, conduct, doing). Hence **ūnit′ĕDLY²** adv., **ūn′ĭtīve** a. [f. L *unire -it-* (*unus* one)]

ūn′ĭtў̆, n. Oneness, being one or single or individual, being formed of parts that constitute a whole, due interconnexion & coherence of parts, as *disturbs the ~ of the idea, pictures lack ~, national ~*; thing showing such ~, thing that forms a complex whole, as a *person regarded as a ~*; (math.) the number one, factor that leaves unchanged the quantity on which it operates; *the dramatic unities, unities of time, place, & action,* limitation of supposed time of drama to that occupied in acting it or to a single day, use of same scene throughout, & abstention from all that is irrelevant to development of single plot; harmony, concord, between persons etc., as *dwell together in ~, at ~ with*; (law) joint tenancy of different tenants, joint possession by one person of different rights. [ME, f. OF *unite*, or L *unitas* (*unus* one, see -TY)]

ūnivĕrs′al, a. & n. **1.** Of or belonging to or done etc. by all persons or things in the world or in the class concerned, applicable to all cases, as *the terror was ~, met with ~ applause, has the ~ sanction of philosophers, the rule does not pretend to be ~, ~ agent* (empowered to do all that can be delegated), ~ PROVIDER, ~ *compass* (with legs that may be extended for large circles), ~ *coupling* or *joint* (transmitting power by a shaft at any selected angle), ~ *legatee* (to whom the whole of a property is bequeathed), ~ *proposition* (in which predicate is affirmed or denied of the entire subject). Hence or cogn. **ūnivĕrsăl′ITY**, ~īZA′TION, nn., ~IZE(3) v.t., ~LY² adv. **2.** n. (Log.) ~ proposition; (philos.) general notion or idea, thing that by its nature may be predicated of many. [ME, f. OF *universal, -el*, or L *universalis* (as UNIVERSE, see -AL)]

ūnivĕrs′al|ist, U-, n. One who holds, esp. member of an organized body of Christians who hold, that all mankind will eventually be saved. Hence or cogn. ~ISM n., ~is′tic a. [-IST]

ūn′ivĕrse, n. All existing things; the whole creation (& the Creator); all mankind; (log.) all the objects under consideration (usu. ~ *of discourse*). [f. F *univers* f. L *universum* neut. of UNI(*versus* p.p. of *vertere* turn) combined into one, whole]

ūnivĕrs′itў̆, n. Educational institution designed for instruction or examination or both of students in all or many of the more important branches of learning, conferring degrees in various faculties, & often embodying colleges & similar institutions; members of this collec-

tively; team, crew, etc., representing a ~, as *the ~ had four wickets to fall*; U~ EXTENSION; *U~ Test Act* (abolishing subscription to Thirty-nine Articles etc. as requisite to taking of degree, 1871). [ME, f. OF *universite* f. L *universitatem* the whole (world); in LL college, guild (as prec., -TY)]

ūnivers|öl′ogў̆, n. Science of all created things; science of all that is of human interest. Hence ~olö′ǴIGAL a., ~öl′oǴIST n. [f. UNIVERSE + -O- + -LOGY]

unjoin, unjoint, see UN-¹(1).

unkĕmpt′ (ŭn-k-), a. Uncombed, dishevelled; untidy, of neglected appearance; (of language) careless, rough, incondite. [UN-² + ME *kempt* p.p. of *kemben* COMB²]

unking, see UN-¹(4); **unkink, unknit, unknot, unlace, unlade, unlash, unlatch, unlay,** UN-¹(1); **unlead,** UN-¹(2); **unlearn,** UN-¹(1); **unleash,** UN-¹(3).

unlĕss′, conj. If not, except when, as *shall (not) go ~ I hear from him, ~ absolutely compelled, always walked ~ I had a bicycle*; ~ *& until* (verbose for *until* in condit. use, cf. *if & when*). [f. LESS preceded by *of, in, upon,* & *on*; unstressed on assim. to UN-²]

unlimber, see UN-¹(2); **unline, unlink, unload, unlock, unlodge, unloose,** UN-¹(1); **unlord,** UN-¹(4); **unmake,** UN-¹(1); **unman,** UN-¹(2, 4); **unmantle,** UN-¹(2); **unmask, unmew,** UN-¹(1); **unmonk,** UN-¹(4); **unmoor, unmortise, unmould, unmuffle, unmuzzle,** UN-¹(1); **unnail,** UN-¹(2); **unnaturalize, unnerve(d),** UN-¹(1); **unnest,** UN-¹(3); **unpack, unpeg, unpen,** UN-¹(1); **unpen,** UN-¹(3); **unpeople,** UN-¹(1); **unperch,** UN-¹(3); **unpick, unpin, unplait, unplug,** UN-¹(1); **unplume,** UN-¹(2); **unpope,** UN-¹(4); **unpreach,** UN-¹(1); **unprejudice,** UN-³(2); **unprelate, unpriest, unprince,** UN-¹(4); **unprop,** UN-¹(2); **unqueen,** UN-¹(4); **unravel,** UN-¹(1); **unreason,** UN-²(2); **unreel, unreeve, unrein,** UN-¹(1); **unrepair, unreserve, unrest, unrestraint,** UN-²(2); **unriddle, unrig,** UN-¹(1); **unright,** UN-²(2); **unring,** UN-¹(2); **unrip, unrivet,** UN-¹(1); **unrobe,** UN-¹(2); **unroll, unromanize,** UN-¹(1); **unroof,** UN-¹(2); **unroost,** UN-¹(3); **unroot,** UN-¹(1); **unrumple,** UN-¹(2); **unsaddle, unsaid¹, unsay,** UN-¹(1); **unscale,** UN-¹(2); **unscrew, unseal, unseam, unseat, unseated¹,** UN-¹(1); **unself,** UN-¹(2); **unset, unsettle, unsettled¹,** UN-¹(1); **unsex,** UN-¹(2); **unshackle, unsheathe,** UN-¹(1); **unshell,** UN-¹(2); **unship, unshipped¹,** UN-¹(1); **unshoe, unshot, unshutter,** UN-¹(2); **unsight, unseen,** UN-²(1); **unsinew, unsister,** UN-¹(2); **unsling,** UN-¹(1); **unsnare,** UN-¹(3); **unsolder, unspar,** UN-¹(2); **unspeak,** UN-¹(1); **unspell, unsphere,** UN-¹(3); **unsprung,** UN-²(2);

For adjj. in *un-* not given see UN-²(1). For other words in *uni-* see UNI-.

unsquire, UN-¹(4); **unstarch**, UN-¹(2); **unsteel**, UN-¹(1); **unstep**, UN-¹(3); **unstick**, **unstitch**, **unstock**, **unstop**, UN-¹(1); **unstopper**, UN-¹(2); **unstrap**, **unstring**, **unstrung**, UN-¹(1); **unsuccess**, **unsuspicion**, UN-²(2); **unswaddle**, **unswathe**, **unswear**, UN-¹(1); **unsymmetry**, UN-²(2); **untack**, **untangle**, **unteach**, **untemper**, UN-¹(1); **untent**, UN-¹(3); **untether**, **unthink**, **unthread**, UN-¹(1); **unthrift**, ŬN-²(2); **unthrone**, UN-¹(3); **untie**, **untied**¹, UN-¹(1).

until', prep. & conj. = TILL² (preferred when its clause or phrase stands first, as ~ *you told me I had no idea of it*, & occas. in leisurely or dignified style, as *unless* & ~). [orig. north. ME *untill* f. ON (= OS, Goth.) *und* as far as +TILL²]

untile, **untin**, see UN-¹(2).

ŭn'to (-ŏŏ), prep. (arch.). = TO¹ (in all uses except as sign of infinitive). [ME; formed on UNTIL, w. TO¹ repl. north. TILL²]

untomb, see UN-¹(3); **untooth**, UN-¹(2); **untouchable**, UN-²(1); **untruss**, UN-¹(1); **untruth**, UN-²(2); **untuck**, **untune**, UN-¹(1); **unturf**, UN-¹(2); **untwine**, **untwist**, **unveil**, UN-¹(1); **unvicar**, UN-¹(4); **unvote**, **unwarp**, **unweave**, UN-¹(1).

ŭnwiel'd|ў, a. Slow or clumsy of movement, difficult to use or manage, owing to size or weight or shape. Hence ~**ĬLY²** adv., ~**ĬNESS** n. [UN-² +(now dial.) *wieldy* active f. WIELD +-Y²]

unwill, **unwind**, see UN-¹(1); **unwisdom**, UN-²(2); **unwitting(ly)**, UN-²(1); **unwork**, **unwound**¹, **unwrap**, **unwrinkle**, **unyoke**, UN-¹(1).

ŭp, adv., prep., a., n., & v.i. **1**. To or in a high(er) place, position, degree, amount, value, etc., to or in a capital or university or place farther north or otherwise conventionally regarded as high(er), *as bird flew up to the eaves, high up in the air, what is he doing up there?, horse might have won with a better jockey up* (in saddle), *lives four floors up, a few feet farther up, flames mount up, total mounts up, tide is coming up, water came up to his chin, a hundred up* (on scoring-board, scored in game), *it is up to* (incumbent on) *us to foot the bill, sums up to £5, lives up to* (spends all) *his income, up to the* MARK¹, *up against* (confronted with) *a hard job, am not up to* (fit for) *travelling, custom is traced up* (back) *to the Stuarts, up to* DATE², *lift up your head, as far up* (north) *as Aberdeen,* || *Oxford men just going up,* || *stayed up* (at Oxford etc.) *for the vacation, ran up to town* (London) *for the day, was had up* (before magistrate) *on a charge of drunkenness, sailed up* (towards source) *as far as the river was navigable, corn is up* (at high price), *is high up in the school, went up three places in class, ran up a bill, have looked for it up & down* (in every direction). **2**. To the place in question or in which the speaker etc. is, *as child came up & asked me the time, went straight up to the door, sure to* TURN¹ *up late.* **3**. To or in erect or vertical position (lit. & fig.), as favourable to activity, out of bed or lying or sitting or kneeling posture, in(to) condition of efficiency or activity, as *sprang up from his seat, stand up,* (with *get, stand,* etc. understood) *up!, up with you,* get up, *get up with it,* put it up, *up* (opp. *down with*) *the Bolsheviks!, was* (already) *up early this morning, was* (still) *up late last night, must be up & doing, Home Secretary is up* (has risen to speak, is speaking), || *Parliament is up* (no longer sitting, prorogued), *stir up sedition,* GET *up, screw up your courage, wind up watch, put the helm up* (so place it as to force ship away from wind), *beer is not up* (is flat), *nation is up in arms* (armed & ready to fight lit. & fig., often *against*), *whole of the west was up* (in rebellion etc.), *his blood is up* (anger or spirit roused), *is well up* (instructed) *in mathematics, what is up* (going on)?, *what tricks have you been up to* (playing)?, *up to* SNUFF¹, *do not feel up* (equal) *to work, this cigar is not up to much* (is poor); || (at Eton Coll.) *he is up to* (in the form of) *Mr A.* **4**. (Expr. complete or effectual result etc.) *eat, drink, burn, dry, tear, up; speak up* (loudly); *hunt up,* find by hunting; *follow up; praise up; save up,* accumulate by saving; *pack,* PUT¹, *bind, store, up; lock, chain, tie, fasten, fix, nail, seal, up* (securely); *time is up* (exhausted); GIVE¹ *up, hurry up,* MAKE¹ *up, cheer up, clear up; it is all up* (& sl. *U.P.*) *with him,* his case is hopeless; HARD-*up.* **5**. prep. To a higher point of, on or along in ascending direction, as *climbed up the ladder, up the hill, smoke goes up chimney, sailed up* (towards source of) *the river, walked up* (towards higher or more central part of, or simply along) *the street, up hill & down dale,* up & down in every direction, taking the country as it comes; at or in a higher part of, as *lives farther up the road, somewhere up the river, saw him sitting half-a-mile up the hill, up a* TREE, *up the* POLE¹, *up the* SPOUT. **6**. adj. Moving, sloping, going, towards a higher point or to the capital, as *up stroke, line* (of railway) *train;* *up-and-coming, enterprising, alert. **7**. n. *On the up-&-up* (colloq.), improving, on the level, honest; *ups & downs,* rises & falls, undulating ground, alternately good & bad fortune. **8**. v.i. (colloq. & dial.; ·pp-). Start up, begin abruptly to say or do something (*he ups & says*); (with *with*) raise, pick up, as *he upped* (or *up*) *with his fist, with his stick.* [OE *upp, up* adv., OS *up*, ON *upp*, rel. to OHG *ûf* (G *auf*), Goth. *iup*]

ŭp-, pref. = prec. = PREC. **1**. Adv. pref. to vbs (esp. in p.p.) & vbl nn., chiefly arch., poet., or rhet., exc. a few given separately (UPBRAID etc.), as: *upbear'* v.t. hold up, sustain, aloft, esp. in p.p. *upborne*; *upbind'* v.t.; *upblaze'* v.i.; *up'bringing* n.

bringing up, education; *upcast'* (-ah-) v.t.; *up'cast* n., casting up, upward throw, (mining) shaft through which air passes out of mine; *up'growth* (-ōth) n., growing up, development, what grows up; *upheap'* (-p-h-) v.t.; *upheav'al* (-p-h-) n., heaving up, esp. (geol.) of part of earth's crust, (fig.) vast social or other change; *upheave'* (-p-h-) v.t. & i.; *up'keep* n. (mod.), (cost, means, of) maintenance; *uplift'* v.t.; *up'lift* n., elevating influence, edifying effect, moral inspiration; *upraise'* v.t.; *uprear'* v.t.; *uprise'* v.i.; *upris'ing* n., rising esp. from bed, rebellion, riot; *uproot'* v.t. (mod.), tear up by roots (lit. & fig.); *upstan'ding*, well set up, erect, (of wages) fixed, not variable; *up'take* n., lifting, (orig. Sc.) understanding, apprehension, as *quick in the uptake*; *up'throw* (-ō) n., throwing upward, esp. (geol., mining) upward displacement of rock on one side of fault; *up'thrust* n. (geol.), = *upheaval*; *upturn'* v.t., turn up (ground in ploughing etc.). 2. Pref. with prep. force forming advv. & adjj. f. nn., as : *up'country* (-kŭ-) a., toward the interior, inland, as *up-country districts* (cf. *up country* adv.); *uphill'* (-p-h-) adv., with upward slope along hill or slope in upward direction, as *road runs uphill, riding uphill*; *up'hill* (-p-h-) a., sloping upwards, (fig.) arduous, difficult, laborious, as *uphill work*; *up'stage* a. (colloq.), stand-offish; *upstairs'* (-z) adv., *up'stair(s)* a., on, to, an upper storey; *up-stream'* adv., *up'stream* a., (moving, done) against the current; *up'town* adv., to, in or the upper (*or residential) part of a town, also as adj. 3. With adj. force, as : *up'land* a. & n. (sing. or pl.), (of) the higher or inland parts of a country; *up'stroke*, upward line made in writing.

upa'nishad (ōōpah-, ōōpá-), n. Each of a series of Sanskrit philosophical treatises forming an exposition of the Vedas. [Skr.]

up'as, n. (Also ~-*tree, antiar*) Javanese tree yielding milky sap used as arrow-poison & held fatal to whatever came beneath its branches, (fig.) pernicious influence, practice, etc.; poisonous sap of this & other trees. [Malay, = poison]

upbraid', v.t. Chide, reproach (person etc. *with, for,* fault etc., or abs.). Hence ~ING[1] n., ~INGLY[2] adv. [OE UP(*bregdan* BRAID[2] in obs. sense)]

up-ĕnd', v.t. & i. (dial.). Set on end; sit, stand, or rise up. [UP adv.]

uphŏld' (-p-h-), v.t. Hold up, keep erect, support; give support or countenance to (person, practice, etc.); maintain, confirm, (decision, verdict). Hence ~ER[1] n. [ME; -UP-]

uphŏl'ster (-p-h-), v.t. Furnish (room etc.) with hangings, carpets, furniture, etc.; provide (chair etc.) with textile covering, padding, springs, etc., cover

(chair etc. *with, in,* tapestry etc.). [back formation f. foll.]

uphŏl'sterer (-p-h-), n. One whose trade it is to upholster; ~-*bee,* kind that furnishes its cell with cut leaves etc. So *uphŏl'stery*(1, 2) n. [f. obs. *upholster* n. (also obs. *upholder*) f. *uphold* (in obs. sense 'keep in repair') +-STER, +-ER[1]]

uph'rōe, n. (naut.). Long wooden block with holes through which cords are rove for adjusting an awning. [f. Du. *juffrouw* young lady, (naut.) ornamental pulley, etc. (*jong* young +*vrouw* woman)]

upŏn', prep. = ON (*on* & ~ are perhaps always idiomatically interchangeable; *on* is perhaps the commoner word esp. in colloq. use; ~ is perhaps preferred when the prep. follows its object, as *had no evidence to go* ~, *nothing to depend* ~, *not enough to live* ~, but cf. *which table did you leave it on?*; other idiomatic preferences are perhaps rightly shown in ~ *my word, on the whole, tier* ~ *tier of seats, fell* ~ *him unawares, had him on toast, came at once on receiving your message, take it on trust, will go on the chance, went on the spree, thrown* ~ *his own resources, stretched* ~ *the rack*). [formerly also as adv.; ME (UP +ON)]

upp'er, a. & n. 1. Higher in place, situated above, as ~ *lip,* ~ *storey* (of house, also fig.=brain, as *something wrong in his* ~ *storey*), ~ (right-hand side of) *keyboard,* ~ CASE[2], *have* or *get the* ~ *hand* (mastery); ~ *works* (naut.), parts of ship above water when she is balanced for voyage; ~-*cut* (boxing), short-arm blow delivered upwards inside opponent's guard, (v.t.) hit with ~-cut; ~ PARTIALS. 2. Higher in rank, dignity, etc., as *the* ~ *servants, the U~ House,* House of Lords, *the* ~ *ten* (thousand), the aristocracy, *the U~ Bench* (hist.), Court of King's Bench during exile of Charles II; ~ *crust* (colloq.), the aristocracy. 3. n. ~ part of boot or shoe, as *be on* one's ~s (poor, in difficulties); (pl.) cloth gaiters. [ME (UP +-ER[3])]

upp'ermost, a. & adv. 1. Highest in place or rank, so *up'MOST* a. 2. adv. On or to the top, as *said whatever came* ~ (first suggested itself). [prec.+-MOST]

upp'ish, a. Self-assertive, pert. Hence ~-LY[2] adv., ~NESS n. [f. UP +-ISH[1]]

up'right (-rīt; *in pred. use also* uprīt'), a., adv., & n. 1. Erect, vertical, as *an* ~ *post, posture,* PIANO[2], (pred. a. or adv.) *stood* ~, *set it* ~; righteous, strictly honourable or honest, whence ~-LY[2] adv., ~NESS n., (-rīt-). 2. n. Post or rod fixed ~ esp. as support to some structure. [OE UP(*riht* RIGHT)]

up'roar (-ōr), n. Tumult, violent disturbance, clamour. Hence *uproar'ious* a. (often of laughter, high spirits, etc.), *uproar'iously* adv., *uproar'iousness*

n., (-ōr-). [f. Du. *oproer* (*op* up + *roer* confusion, cf. G *aufruhr*); assoc. w. ROAR]

ŭp′rŭsh, n. An upward rush; (esp., psych.) a sudden emergence into consciousness from the subliminal. [UP- 1]

ŭpsĕt′[1], v.t. & i., & n. **1.** Overturn, be overturned, as *carriage (was)* ~; disturb the composure or temper or digestion of, as *the news quite* ~ *him, ate something that* ~ *him*; shorten & thicken (metal, esp. tire) by hammering or pressure. **2.** n. (ŭp′). ~ting, being ~. [UP-]

ŭp′sĕt[2], a. ~ *price*, lowest selling price of property in auction etc., reserve price. [ME; UP-]

ŭp′shŏt, n. Final issue, conclusion; general effect, the long & short, (*of a* matter). [UP-]

ŭp′sĭde-down′, adv. & a. With the upper part under, inverted, in total disorder, as *everything was (turned)* ~, *an* ~ *arrangement*. [altered f. ME *up so down*, lit. up as if down]

|| **ŭpsīdes′** (-dz), adv. (colloq.). *Get* ~ *with*, turn the tables on, avenge oneself upon. [UP, SIDE, -ES]

ŭpsĭl′on, n. Greek letter (Υ, v) = u. [Gk *u psilon* slender u, w. ref. to its later sound (ü)]

ŭp′stărt, n. Person who has risen suddenly from humble position (often attrib.); person who assumes arrogant tone. [UP-]

ŭp′ward, a., ŭp′ward|(s) (-z), adv. **1.** Directed, moving, towards a higher place (lit. & fig.), as *an* ~ *glance, prices show an* ~ *tendency*, whence ~LY[2] adv. **2.** adv. In ~ direction, as *look, move,* ~(s), followed *the stream* ~(s) (towards source); *children of 6 years old & ~(s)* (more); *found* ~(s) *of* (more than) *40 specimens*. [OE; -WARD(S)]

ur- (oor), pref. repr. G (MLG, MHG) *ur-*, denoting ' primitive, original, earliest '.

ūraem′|ĭa, n. (path.). Morbid condition of blood due to retention of urinary matter normally eliminated by kidneys. Hence ~IC a. [f. Gk *ouron* urine + *haima* blood]

ūrae′us, n. Serpent as head-dress of Egyptian divinities & kings. [mod. L f. Gk *ouraios* repr. the anc.-Egypt. wd for cobra]

Ur′al-Altā′ic (ūral-ăl-), a. Of (the people of) the Ural & Altaic mountain ranges; (philol.) of a family of Finnic, Mongolian, & other agglutinative languages of N. Europe & Asia.

Urān′ia (ūr-), n. The MUSE[1] of astronomy. [L, f. Gk *ouranos* heaven]

uranian. See VENUS.

ūrān′ium, n. Radio-active white metallic element, the heaviest of the elements occurring in nature, used as a source of atomic energy & (in the isotope U 235) in atomic bombs. Hence ūrān′ic, ūr′anous, aa. [f. URANUS + -IUM]

ūran|o-, comb. form of Gk *ouranos* heaven, as : ~*ŏg′raphy*, descriptive astronomy, so ~*ograph′ic(al)* aa., ~*ŏg′raphist* n.; ~*ŏl′ogy*, astronomy; ~*ŏm′etry*, measurement of

stellar distances, map showing positions and magnitudes of stars.

Ur′anus (ūr-; *or* ūrān[2]), n. (Gk myth.) son of Ge (Earth) & father of Cronus (Saturn), the Titans, etc.; planet discovered by Herschel in 1781, outermost of solar system except Neptune & Pluto. [L, f. Gk *ouranos* heaven, Uranus]

ŭrb′an, a. Of, living or situated in, a city or town, as ~ *districts, population*. Hence ~IZE (3) v.t., render ~, remove the rural character of (a district), ~ĭzā′TION n. [f. L *urbanus* (*urbs urbis* city, see -AN)]

ŭrbāne′, a. Courteous, suave, elegant or refined in manner. Hence~LY[2] adv. [f. F *urbain* or L *urbanus* (as prec.)]

ŭrbăn′itў, n. Courtesy, polished manners; || (arch.) polished wit or humour. [f. F *-ité* or L *urbanitas* (as prec., see -TY)]

ŭr′cĕolate, a. (bot.). Pitcher-shaped, with large body & small mouth. [f. L *urceolus* dim. of *urceus* pitcher + -ATE[2]]

ŭrch′in, n. **1.** Roguish or mischievous boy; boy, youngster. **2.** (Usu. *sea-*~) = ECHINUS; || (arch.) hedgehog, goblin. [ME var. of (now dial.) *hurcheon* n. ONF *herichon*, ult. f. L *ericius* hedgehog]

Urdu (oor′dōō), n. An Indic language, allied to Hindi but with large admixture of Persian, etc., widely used in Pakistan & India. [Hindi, lit. = 'camp language']

-ure, suf. repr. (O)F *-ure*, L *-ura* in many E wds of F or L orig. Many are f. OF (*figure*), a few f. L (*aperture*), some f. E stems of L orig. (*composure*). Senses in E : (1) action or process, its result (*enclosure, scripture*), (2) function, state, rank, dignity, office (*judicature, prefecture*), (3) collective body of agents (*legislature*), (4) that by which the action is effected (*closure, ligature*). To this form various (O)F suff. have been assimilated in E, as in *failure, leisure, pleasure, seizure, treasure, velure*.

ūr′ĕa, n. (chem.). Soluble colourless crystalline compound contained esp. in urine of mammals. [latinized f. F *urée* f. Gk *ouron* urine]

-uret, suf. (chem.) of nn. & their derivatives indicating combination, now for the most part replaced by -IDE. [mod. L *-uretum* first applied to F wds in *-ure*]

ūrĕt′er, n. Duct by which urine passes from kidney to bladder etc. [f. Gk *ourētēr* (*oureō* make water)]

ūrĕth′r|a, n. Duct by which urine is discharged from bladder. Hence ~AL a., ~IT′IS, ~OCELE, ~ŌT′OMY, nn. [LL, f. Gk *ourēthra* (as prec.)]

ūrĕt′ic, a. & n. = DIURETIC.

ŭrge, v.t., & n. **1.** Drive forcibly, impel, hasten, cause to proceed with effort, as ~*d his horse forward*, ~*d him on, we* ~*d our flight northwards*; entreat or exhort earnestly or persistently, as ~ *him to action, to take steps*; advocate (measure etc.) pressingly; ply (person etc.) hard with argument or entreaty; dwell persistently or emphatically upon, as *in vain you ~ his youth*, *~d the difficulty of getting supplies*, *argument was ~d in vain*. 2. n. Impulsion, yearning. [f. L *urgēre* press, drive]

ūr'gent, a. Pressing, calling for immediate action or attention, as *am in ~ need*, *the matter is ~*, *an ~ demand*; importunate, earnest & persistent in demand, as *was ~ with me for* (or *to disclose*) *further particulars*. Hence **ūr'gency** n., **~ly²** adv. [F (as URGE, see -ENT)]

ūr'ic, a. Of urine; *~ acid* (found in small quantities in healthy urine of man & quadrupeds, chief constituent in that of birds & reptiles). [f. F *urique* (URINE, -IC)]

-urient, suf. f. L *-urient-*, part. stem of desiderative verbs, forming aa. with meaning ' desiring (to do something) ', as ESURIENT.

ūr'im, n. *~ & thŭmm'im*, objects of unknown nature connected with breastplate of high priest (*Exod*. xxviii. 30). [Heb. *urim* pl. of *ōr* light, *tummim* pl. of *tōm* perfection]

ūr'inal, n. Fixed vessel or receptacle for use of persons requiring to pass urine; public or private place containing such receptacles; vessel used by invalid for passing water in bed; glass vessel for containing urine for inspection. [ME, f. OF f. LL *urinal* (URINE, -AL)]

ūr'inarў, a. & n. 1. Of urine, as *~ organs*, *diseases*. 2. n. Reservoir for urine as manure; (mil.) barrack building containing several urinals. [f. med. L *urinarius* (URINE, -ARY¹)]

ūr'in|āte, v.i. Pass urine. Hence **~A'TION** n. [f. med. L *urinare* (as foll.), see -ATE³]

ūr'in|e, n. Pale-yellow fluid secreted from the blood by the kidneys, stored in bladder, & discharged through urethra. So **~ous** a. [ME, f. OF, f. L *urina*, cogn. w. Gk *ouron*, see -INE²]

ūrin|o-, comb. form of prec., as: *~ōl'ogy*, study of the urine; *~ōm'eter*, instrument showing specific gravity of urine, so *~omĕt'ric* a., *~ōm'etry* n.; *~ŏs'copy*, inspection of urine, so *~oscŏp'ic* a.

ūrn, n., & v.t. 1. Vase with foot & usu. with rounded body, esp. as anciently used for storing the ashes of the dead or as vessel or measure; (fig.) anything in which dead body or its remains are preserved, e.g. grave; vase-shaped vessel with tap in which tea, coffee, etc., is kept hot, e.g. by means of spirit-lamp; *~-flower*, kinds of bulbous plant with *~-shaped flower. Hence ~'FUL n. 2. v.t. Enclose in~. [ME, f. L *urna*]

ūro-¹, comb. form of URINO-, as *ūrōl'ogy* etc.

ūro-², comb. form of Gk *oura* tail, in anat. terms.

Urs'a (ẽr-), n. *~ Major, Minor, Great,*

Little, BEAR¹; *~ Major*, (also) Dr Johnson. [L, = she-bear]

ūrs'ine, a. Of, like, a bear. [f. L *ursinus* (*ursus* bear, see -INE¹)]

Urs'uline (ẽr-), a. & n. (Nun) of an order founded in 1537 for nursing the sick & teaching girls. [f. St *Ursula*+-INE¹]

ūrticār'ia, n. (path.). Nettle-rash. [f. L *urtica* nettle]

ūrt'ic|āte, v.t. Sting like a nettle; whip (paralytic limb etc.) with nettles to restore feeling. So **~A'TION** n. [f. med. L *urticare* (L *urtica* nettle) see -ATE³]

urubu (ŏŏ'rŏŏbŏŏ), n. American black vulture. [Brazilian]

ūr'us, n. Kind of wild bull described by Caesar, = AUROCHS. [L, = Gk *ouros*, Gmc *ūrus*, see AUROCHS]

us (ŭs, us), pl. obj. of I² (abbr. *'s*, as *let's go*; occas. poet. & arch., = ourselves, as *let's get us from the walls*). [OE, OS *ūs*, ON *oss*, = OHG, Goth. *uns*, cogn. w. L *nos*, Skr. *nas*]

ūs'age (-z-), n. Manner of using or treating, treatment, as *met with harsh ~*, *damaged by rough~*; habitual or customary practice esp. as creating a right or obligation or standard, as *sanctified by~*, *an ancient ~*, *contrary to the ~ of the best writers*, *modern English ~*; (law) habitual but not necessarily immemorial practice. [ME, f. OF *usage* f. L *usus* (as USE², see -AGE)]

ūs'ance (-z-), n. (commerc.). Time allowed for payment of foreign bills of exchange, as *the ~ on Indian bills is 4 months*, *bill drawn at half or double ~*. [ME, f. OF (as USE², see -ANCE)]

use¹ (ūs), n. 1. Using, employment, application to a purpose, as *should recommend the ~ of a file*, *taught him the ~ of the globes*, *put it to a good ~*, *is meant for ~ not ornament*, *is in daily~*, *becomes easier with ~*, *worn & polished with ~*, *made ~ of* (employed) *a quibble*, *pray make ~ of my telephone*. 2. Right or power of using, as *stipulated for the ~ of the piano*, *lost the ~ of his left arm*. 3. Availability, utility, purpose for which thing can be used, as *a blunt knife is of ~ for this work*, *a foot-rule will be found of (great) ~*, *it is* (of) *no ~ talking or to talk*, *what is the ~ of talking?*, *talking is no ~*, *find a ~ for banana-skins*, *I have no ~ for it*. 4. Custom, wont, familiarity, as *long ~ has reconciled me to it*, *in such matters ~ is everything*, *according to his ~ in emergencies*, *~ & wont*. 5. Ritual & liturgy of a church, diocese, etc., as *Sarum, Anglican, Roman, ~*. 6. (law). Benefit or profit of lands & tenements in the possession of another who holds them solely for the beneficiary. [ME, f. OF *us* f. L *usus* (as foll.)]

use² (ūz), v.t. & i. 1. Employ for a purpose, handle as instrument, consume as material, exercise, put into operation, avail oneself of, as *seldom ~ a knife*, *should ~ oil for frying, we seem to ~ a great deal of butter, never ~ a dictionary, learn to ~ your hands, ~ your wits, must ~ the services of an agent, shall ~ every means, must ~ your opportunities, ~ your discretion, should at least ~ some moderation, may I ~ your name* (quote you as authority, reference, etc.)?, *do not fail to ~* (in argument, pleading, etc.) *this damaging fact, has ~d my absence to poison everyone against me.* **2.** Treat in specified manner, as *has ~d me like a dog, how did he ~ you?, ~d me ill, ill-~d me.* **3.** (Now only in past, usu. pron. ûst, esp. when followed immediately by *to*) be accustomed, have as one's constant or frequent practice, as *I ~d to take the bus, does not come as often as he ~d* (to), *bell ~d always to ring at one, what ~d he* (colloq. *did he ~*) *to say?, ~d not* (colloq. *didn't ~*) *to answer.* **4.** (Now only in p.p., pron. as last sense) accustomed, as *am not ~d to this sort of thing, to being called a liar, have become ~d to a vegetarian diet.* **5.** ~ *up,* consume the whole of (material etc.), find a use for (remaining material etc.), exhaust, wear out e.g. with overwork. Hence **ūs′ABLE** a., **ūs′er**[1] [-ER[1]] n., (-z-). [ME, f. OF *user* f. Rom. **ûsare* frequent. of L *uti us-* use]

ûse′ful (-sf-), a. Of use, serviceable, producing or able to produce good result, as ~ *arts, ratchet-brace will be found ~, gave me some ~ hints, must make himself generally ~* (perform miscellaneous services); (sl.) highly creditable or efficient, as *pretty ~ performance, is pretty ~ at Greek iambics.* Hence **~LY**[2] adv., **~NESS** n. [-FUL]

ûse′lèss (-sl-), a. Serving no useful purpose, unavailing, as *a mass of ~ erudition, contents were rendered ~ by damp, protest is ~*; (sl.) out of health or spirits, unfit for anything, as *am feeling ~.* Hence **~LY**[2] adv., **~NESS** n. [-LESS]

user[1]. See USE[2].

ūs′er[2] (-z-), n. (law). Continued use or enjoyment of a right etc.; *right of ~,* (1) right to use, (2) presumptive right arising from ~. [F *user* USE[2], or inferred f. NON- -USER]

ûsh′er, n., & v.t. **1.** Officer or servant acting as doorkeeper of a court etc., showing persons to seats in public hall etc., || or walking before person of rank, as (*gentleman ~ of the*) BLACK[1] *rod*; || (now usu. derog.) under-teacher, assistant schoolmaster. Hence **~ETTE′, ~SHIP,** nn. **2.** v.t. Act as ~ to, precede (person) as ~, announce, show *in* etc., as *was at length ~ed (in)to his presence, star~s in the dawn.* [ME, f. AF *usser,* OF *u(i)ssier,* var. of *huisier* f. *huis* door f. pop. L *ûstium* f. cl. L *ostium,* see -ARY[1], -ER[2]]

ûs′quèbaugh (-aw), n. Whisky; Irish cordial made of brandy etc. [f. Ir. & Sc. Gael. *uisge beatha* water of life, see WHISKY[1]]

ûstūlā′tion, n. Drying of moist substance to prepare it for pulverizing; burning of wine. [f. LL *ustulatio* f. L *ustulare* scorch f. *urere ust-* burn, -ATION]

û′sual (-zhoo-), a. Such as commonly occurs, customary, habitual, as *asked the ~ questions, with his ~ disregard of convention, the courtesy ~ with him, it is ~ to tip the waiter, came earlier than* (was) ~, *have forgotten something as* (is) ~ *or* (vulg. joc.) *as per ~*; also abs., as *may I have my ~* (drink etc.). Hence **~LY**[2] adv., **~NESS** n. [ME, f. OF *usual, -el* or LL *usualis* (as USE[1], see -AL)]

ûsūcăp′tion (-z-), **-cāp′ion,** n. (civil law). Acquisition of the title or right to property by uninterrupted & undisputed possession for prescribed term. [f. OF *usucaption* or med. L *usucaptio* f. L *usucapio -onis* f. *usucapere* acquire by prescription (*usu* by USE[1]+*capere capt-* take)]

ûs′ūfrŭct (-z-), n., & v.t. Right of enjoying the use & advantages of another's property short of destruction or waste of its substance; (vb) hold in ~. [f. med. L *usufructus* (cf. foll.) f. L *usus fructus* (*usus* USE[1]+*fructus* FRUIT)]

ûsūfrŭc′tūarў (-z-), a & n. Of, one who has, usufruct. [f. LL *usufructuarius* (prec., -ARY[1])]

û′surer (-zhu-), n. One who lends money at exorbitant interest. [ME, f. AF *usurer,* OF *-eor,* f. LL *usurarius* n. (as USURY see -ER[2])]

ûsŭrp′ (-z-), v.t. & i. Seize, assume, (throne, office, power, property, etc.) wrongfully; (rare) encroach (*up*)*on.* Hence or cogn. **ûsurpA′TION** (-zer-), **~ER**[1], nn., **~ĭnɡ**LY[2] adv. [ME, f. OF *usurper* f. L *usurpare*]

û′surў (-zhu-), n. Practice of lending money at exorbitant interest esp. at higher interest than is allowed by law, whence **ûsūr′ious** (-z-, -zh-) a., **ûsūr′iously**[2] adv., **ûsūr′iousness** n.; such interest; (now usu. fig.) interest, as *the service was repaid with ~.* [ME, f. AF **usurie* or med. L. *usuria* (-Y[1]), f. L *usura* (USE[1], -URE)]

ut[1] (ŏot), n. Key-note of a scale (now usu. DO[3]). [see GAMUT]

ŭt[2], adv. *Ut sŭp′ra, ĭn′fra,* as shown or stated above, below. [L]

ūtĕn′sil, n. Instrument, implement, esp. one in domestic use, as *kitchen, cooking-, ~s.* [f. OF *utensile* f. L *utensilis* usable]

ūt′erine, a. Of the uterus; born of same mother but not same father (*his ~ brother*). [15th c., f. OF *uterin(e)* or LL *uterinus* (foll., -INE[1])]

ūt′er|us, n. (pl. *~ī*). The womb. Hence **~ĭT′ĭs** n. [L]

ūtilitār′ian, a. & n. Of, consisting in, utility; (holder) of utilitarianism. [-ARIAN]

ūtilitār′ianism, n. Doctrine that actions are right because they are useful; doctrine that greatest happiness of greatest number should be sole end of public action. [-ISM]

util'ity̆, n. Usefulness, profitableness; useful thing; = *public* ~; = prec.; (theatr., also ~-*man*) actor of the smallest parts in plays; (attrib.) made or serving for ~, severely practical, (~ *clothes, furniture*). [ME, f. OF *utilite* f. L *utilitatem* (*utilis* useful f. *uti* use, see -TY)]

ŭt'iliz|e, -is|e (-īz), v.t. Make use of, turn to account, use. Hence ~ABLE a., ~A'TION n. [f. F *utiliser* f. It. *utilizzare*, see prec.]

ŭt'ĭ pŏssĭdēt'ĭs, n. Principle that leaves belligerents in possession of what they have acquired. [L, = as you possess]

ŭt'most, a. & n. **1.** Furthest, extreme, as *the* ~ *limits*; that is such in the highest degree, as *showed the* ~ *reluctance*. **2.** n. One's ~, all one can do. [OE *ūtemest*, double superl. of *ŭt* OUT, cf. AFTERMOST]

Utŏp'ia (ū-), n. (Book published by Sir T. More in 1516 describing) imaginary island with perfect social & political system; ideally perfect place or state of things. [= nowhere, f. Gk *ou* not +*topos* place]

Utŏp'ian (ū-), ŭ-, a. & n. (Inhabitant) of Utopia; (characteristic of an) ardent but unpractical reformer etc., whence **ūtŏp'ianISM** n. [-AN]

ŭt'ricle, n. Cell of animal or plant; small bag or cavity in the body, esp. one in the inner ear. Hence **ŭtric'ŭlAR¹** a. [f. F *utricule* or L *utriculus* dim. of *uter* leather bag]

ŭtt'er¹, a. Complete, total, unqualified, as ~ *misery, saw the* ~ *absurdity of it, an* ~ *denial*; ‖ ~ *barrister* (junior, addressing court from outside bar within which Q.C. pleads). Hence ~LY² adv., ~MOST a., ~NESS n. [OE *ūtera, ūttera*, compar. adj. f. *ŭt* OUT; cf. OUTER]

ŭtt'er², v.t. Emit audibly·(cry, groan, sigh, etc.); express in spoken or written wds (one's sentiments, a lie, the truth, etc.); put (notes, base coin, etc.) into circulation. [ME *utter* f. OE *ūtor* compar. of *ŭt* OUT; cf. OFris. *ūtria*, MLG *ūteren*, MHG *ūzeren* make known]

ŭtt'erance¹, n. Uttering, expressing in words, as *gave* ~ *to his rage*; power of speech, as *defective* ~; spoken words, as *his pulpit*~s. [ME, f. prec. +-ANCE]

ŭtt'erance², n. (literary). Fight etc. to *the* ~ (bitter end). [ME, f. OF *outrance* (*outrer* surpass, as ULTRA-)]

ŭv'ŭl|a, n. (pl. ~*ae*). Pendent fleshy part of soft palate; similar processes in bladder & cerebellum. Hence ~AR¹ a. [LL, dim. of L *uva* grape]

ŭxŏr'ious, a. Excessively fond of one's wife. Hence ~LY² adv., ~NESS n. [f. L *uxorius* (*uxor* wife) +-OUS]

Uz'bĕk, Uz'bĕg (ŭ-), n. Member of a Turkish people in central Asia. [native]

V

V, v, (vē), letter (pl. *V*s, V's, Vees). V-shaped thing, e.g. joint; (Roman numeral) 5, as IV 4, VI 6, viii 8, viiii (now usu. ix) 9, xv 15, lv 55; *V sign*, made by hand with fingers clenched except the first and second outspread to form the letter *V* (for *Victory*).

vāc'ancy̆, n. Being vacant or empty or unoccupied; emptiness of mind, idleness, listlessness; unoccupied post, as *has a* ~ *on his staff, in his warehouse, must fill the*~. [f. foll. +-ANCY, or med. L *vacantia*]

vāc'ant, a. Empty, not filled or occupied, as *house is empty*, ~, *a* ~ *smoking-compartment, have no* ~ *space, will amuse your* ~ *hours, applied for a* ~ *post in the Treasury*; not mentally active, not rationally occupied, empty-headed, thoughtless, listless, stupid, as *his mind seems completely* ~, *received the news with a* ~ *stare, given up to* ~ *frivolities*, whence ~LY² adv. [ME, f. OF, or f. L *vacare* (as foll., see -ANT)]

vacāte' (or vă-), v.t. Go away from so as to leave empty or unoccupied, give up occupation or possession of, (military position, place, house, throne, office); annul (law, contract, etc.). [f. L *vacare* be empty (cf. VACUOUS), see -ATE³]

vacā'tion (or vă-), n. Vacating (*of* house, post, etc.); holiday, fixed period of cessation from work, esp. in law-courts & universities, as *Christmas, Easter, Whitsun, long* or *summer*, ~. [ME, f. OF, or f. L *vacatio* (as prec., see -ATION)]

văc'cin|āte (-ks-), v.t. Inoculate with vaccine to procure immunity from smallpox or with modified virus of any disease in order to produce it in mild form & so prevent serious attack. Hence ~A'TION (-ks-), ~ā'tionIST(2) (-ks-, -sho-), ~ātoR (-ks-), nn. [f. foll. +-ATE³]

văc'cine (-ks-), a. & n. **1.** Of cows or cowpox or vaccination. **2.** n. Virus of cowpox as used in vaccination (*bovine, humanized*, ~), got direct from cow, got from human subject), modified virus of any disease similarly used, whence **văc'cinAL, văccin'ic** (-ks-), aa. [f. L *vaccinus* a.; n. f. F *vaccine* (*vacca* cow, see -INE¹)]

văccin'ia (-ks-), n. (med.). Cowpox, esp. inoculated. [mod. L, f. prec., -IA¹]

vă'cill|āte, v.i. Move from side to side, oscillate, waver; fluctuate in opinion or resolution. Hence or cogn. ~ātingLY² adv., ~A'TION n. [f. L *vacillare*, see -ATE³]

văc'ū|ŏle, n. (biol.). Minute cavity in organ etc. containing air, fluid, etc. Hence ~olAR¹, ~olATE²(2), aa. [F, f. L *vacuus* empty]

văc'ūous, a. Empty, void; unintelligent, expressionless, vacant, as *a* ~ *stare, remark*. Hence or cogn. **văcū'ITY, ~NESS**, nn. [f. L *vacuus* +-OUS]

văc′ūum, n. (pl. *-ums*, *-ua*). 1. Space entirely devoid of matter, as *nature abhors a ~*; space, vessel, from which air has been almost exhausted by air-pump etc. (*Guerickian, Torricellian, ~*, produced by air-pump, by mercury-pump as in mercurial barometer); (loosely) partial diminution of pressure below normal atmospheric pressure; (colloq.) ~ *cleaner.* 2. *~ brake*, continuous train-brake in which pressure is caused by exhaustion of air from bellows pulling brake-rod; ~ *cleaner*, apparatus for removing dust etc. by suction; ~ *flask*, vessel with double wall enclosing ~ so that liquid in inner receptacle retains its temperature; ~ -*gauge* (for testing pressure consequent on production of ~); ~*-tube*, sealed glass tube with almost perfect ~ for observing passage of electric charge (see also THER-MION). [L, neut. of *vacuus* empty]

văd′ė-mēc′um, n. Handbook or other thing carried constantly about the person (often in title of book). [L, = go with me]

vae vĭc′tĭs, int. Woe to the vanquished (expressing victor's intention of exacting full fruits of victory). [L]

văg′abŏnd, a., n., & v.i. 1. Having no fixed habitation, wandering; driven, drifting, to & fro; (of spider) not sedentary. 2. n. Wanderer, vagrant, esp. idle & worthless one; (colloq.) scamp, rascal. 3. v.i. (now colloq.). Wander about, play the ~. Hence ~AGE(2, 3), ~ISM(2), nn., ~ISH[1] a., ~IZE(2) v.i. [ME, f. OF, or f. L *vagabundus* (*vagari* wander)]

vagar′y̆, n. Whimsical or extravagant notion; caprice; freak. [f. L *vagari* wander]

vagīn′a, n. Sheath, sheathlike covering, esp. (anat.) sexual passage in female from uterus to external orifice, whence **văgīnIT′IS, văgĭnōT′OMY,** nn.; (bot.) sheath formed round stem by base of leaf. Hence **vă′gĭnAL, vă′gĭnATE[2], vă′gĭnātĕd,** aa. [L]

văg′rant, a. & n. 1. Wandering, roving, strolling, itinerant, as *a ~ musician, indulging in ~ speculations.* 2. n. Wanderer, idle rover, vagabond; (law) idle & disorderly person of any of three grades liable to various terms of imprisonment. Hence **văg′rANCY** n., ~LY[2] adv. [ME *vag(a)raunt*, perh. alt. f. AF *wakerant*, by assoc. w. L *vagari* wander]

văgue (-g), a. Indistinct, not clearly expressed or identified, of uncertain or ill--defined meaning or character, as *returned only a ~ answer, has some ~ idea of going to Canada, have not the ~st notion of his reasons, yield to ~ terrors, heard a ~ rumour to that effect.* Hence ~LY[2] (-gl-) adv., ~′NESS (-gn-) n. [F, or f. L *vagus* wandering]

vail[1], v.t. & i. (arch., poet.). ‖ Lower or doff (one's plumes, pride, crown, etc.) esp. in token of submission; yield, give place, uncover as sign of respect etc. [f. OF *valer*, or aphetic f. obs. *avale* f. OF *avaler* (*a val* down, f. *val* VALE[1]) lower]

‖ **vail[2]**, n. (arch.; usu. pl.). Gratuity, tip; present given for corrupt purpose. [ME, aphetic f. AVAIL[2]]

vain, a. 1. Unsubstantial, empty, trivial, as *~ boasts, ~ triumphs, distinctions*; useless, unavailing, followed by no good result, as *in the ~ hope of dissuading him, all resistance was ~, to resist is ~, it is ~ to resist*; conceited, having too high an opinion of one's beauty, ability, etc. 2. *In ~*, to no purpose, as *we protested in ~, it was in ~ that we protested*; TAKE[1] person's *name in ~.* 3. ~*glor′y*, boastfulness, excessive vanity, whence ~*glor′ious* a., ~*glor′iously* adv., ~*glor′iousness* n. Hence ~′LY[2] adv., ~′NESS n. (rare). [ME, f. OF, f. L *vanus* empty, vain]

vair, n. (her.). A fur represented by small shield-shaped figures alternately azure & argent. [ME, f. OF, f. L as VARIOUS]

Vaisya (vī′sya), n. (Member of) the third of the four great Hindu castes, comprising the merchants and agriculturists, cf. BRAHMIN, KSHATRIYA, SUDRA. [Skr. *vaisya* peasant]

văl′ance, văl′ence[1], n. Kind of damask used for furniture; short curtain round frame or canopy of bedstead. Hence **văl′anceD[2]** (-st) a. [ME, f. AF **valance* f. *valer* = OF *avaler* descend, see VAIL[1]]

vāle[1], n. Valley (now chiefly poet. or in names as *V~ of the White Horse*). [ME, f. OF *val* f. L *vallis*]

vāl′e[2], int. & n. Farewell. [L, imperat. of *valēre* be well, be strong]

vălēdic′t|ion, n. (Words used in) bidding farewell. So ~ORY a., (also, as n., **farewell oration delivered by senior scholar on graduation etc.). [f. L VALE(*dicere dict-* say) bid farewell, see -ION]

valence[1]. See VALANCE.

vāl′ence[2], n. (chem.). Combining or replacing power of an atom as compared with standard hydrogen atom, as *hydrogen, carbon, has a ~ of one,* four. [f. LL *valentia* strength (as VALE[2], see -ENCE)]

Valĕn′cia (-sha), n. Province of Spain; (usu. pl.) mixed fabric with wool weft and silk, cotton, or linen warp, usu. striped; (pl.) ~ almonds or raisins.

Vălenciennes′ (-sĕnz, & see Ap.), n. Rich. kind of lace. [~, in France]

văl′enc|y̆, n. (chem.). Unit of combining capacity, as *carbon has 4 ~ies*; = VALENCE[2]. [-ENCY]

văl′entine, n. *St V~'s day*, day on which St V~ was beheaded & on which birds were supposed to pair, Feb. 14; sweetheart chosen on this; amatory or satirical letter or picture sent to person of opposite sex on St V~'s day. [ME, f. OF *-in*, or L *Valentinus*, proper name]

valēr′ian, n. Kinds of plant, esp. *common ~*, herb with pink or white flowers & rather unpleasant smell; root of this used as mild stimulant etc., whence

văl′erATE¹(3) n., **valē′rıc** a., (chem.). [ME, f. OF *valeriane* f. med. L *-ana*]

văl′ĕt (or -lā), n., & v.t. 1. (Also ~ *de chambre*, pr. văl′ā de shahň′br) man-servant who attends on man's person; ~ *de place* (văl′ā de plahs), courier esp. in France. 2. v.t. Act as ~ to. [F, = OF *valet, vaslet,* rel. to VASSAL; cf. VARLET]

vălĕtūdinār′ian, a. & n. 1. Of infirm health; seeking to recover health; unduly solicitous about health. 2. n. ~ person. Hence or cogn. ~ISM n., **vălĕtūd′inARY¹** a. & n. [f. L *valetudinarius* (*valetudo -dinis* health f. *valēre* be well, see -TUDE & -ARIAN, -ARY¹)]

văl′gus, n. Deformity involving outward bending of distal part of limb; knock--kneed person. [L]

Vălhăll′a, n. (Norse myth.) palace in which souls of slain heroes feasted; building used as final resting-place of the illustrious, or containing their statues etc. [f. ON *valhǫll,* hall of the slain (*valr* slain + *hǫll* HALL)]

văl′iant (-ya-), a. (Of person or conduct) brave, courageous. Hence ~LY² adv. [ME, f. OF *vaillant* part. of *valoir* be worth f. L *valēre* be strong]

văl′id, a. (Of reason, objection, argument, etc.) sound, defensible, well-grounded; (law) sound & sufficient, executed with proper formalities, as ~ *contract, the marriage was held to be*~. Hence or cogn. **valid′ITY** n., ~LY² adv. [f. F *valide* or L *validus* strong (as prec., see -ID¹)]

văl′id|āte, v.t. Make valid, ratify, con-firm. So ~A′TION n. [f. LL *validare* (as prec.), see -ATE³; partly f. F *valider*]

valise′ (-ēs), n. Kind of small portman-teau; kitbag. [F, f. It. *valigia* corresp. to med. L *valisia,* of unkn. orig.]

văl′kyr (-ēr), **vălkÿ′ria,** -ie, n. (Norse myth.; pl. *-kyrs, -kyries*). Each of Odin's handmaidens who selected those destined to be slain in battle. Hence **vălkÿ′rIAN** a. [f. ON *valkyrja* lit. chooser of slain (*valr* slain + *-kyrja* chooser cogn. w. *kjósa* CHOOSE)]

văllĕc′ūl|a, n. (anat., bot.; pl. ~*ae*). Groove, furrow. Hence ~AR¹, ~ATE², aa. [LL, dim. of L *vallis* vale]

văll′ey, n. (pl. ~s). Low area more or less enclosed by hills & usu. with stream flowing through it; any depression com-pared to this; ~ *of the shadow of death,* (period of) extreme affliction (*Ps.* xxiii. 4); (archit.) internal angle formed by intersecting planes of roof. [ME, f. OF *valee* (as VALE¹, see -Y⁴)]

val(l)ōn′ia, n. Acorn-cups of the ~ *oak,* used in tanning, dyeing, & making ink. [f. It. *vallonia* ult. f. Gk *balanos* acorn]

văll′um, n. (Rom. ant.). Rampart. [L]

văl′orīz|e, -ise (-īz), v.t. Raise or stabilize the value of (a commodity etc.) by government action. Hence ~A′TION n. [f. L *valor* worth + -IZE (3)]

văl′our (-ler), n. (now chiefly poet., rhet.,

or joc.). Personal courage esp. as shown in fighting, prowess. So **văl′orous** a., **văl′orousLY²** adv. [ME, f. OF, f. LL *valorem* (*valēre* be strong, see -OR)]

valse (vahls), n. Waltz; ~ *à* DEUX-TEMPS, waltz with two beats (instead of three) in a bar, each divided into three smaller beats. [F, f. G as WALTZ]

văl′uable, a. & n. 1. Of great value or price or worth, as ~ *property, land, furni-ture, information, assistance*; capable of valuation, as *a service not* ~ *in money.* 2. n. (usu. in pl.). ~ thing(s), esp. small article(s) of personal property, as *sent all her*~s *to the bank.* [f. VALUE + -ABLE]

vălūā′tion, n. Estimation (esp. by pro-fessional valuer) of a thing's worth, worth so estimated, price set on a thing, as ~ *of land, disposed of at a low* ~, *sets too high a* ~ *on his abilities.* [16th c., f. foll. vb + -ATION]

văl′ūe, n., & v.t. 1. Worth, desirability, utility, qualities on which these depend, as *now learnt the* ~ *of fresh water, a friend, quinine, accuracy, regular exercise*; worth as estimated, valuation, as *sets a high* ~ *on his time*; *commercial, economic, ex-change(able)* ~, ~ *in exchange,* purchasing power, power of a commodity to pur-chase others, amount of (pop.) money or (pol. econ.) other commodities for which thing can be exchanged in open market; FACE¹, SURRENDER, ~; *surplus* ~, surplus production of labour after subsistence of labourer & family; the equivalent of a thing, what represents or is represented by or may be substituted for a thing, as ~ *received* (see BILL⁴ of *exchange*), *got good* ~ *for* (something well worth) *his money, paid him the* ~ *of his lost property, the precise* ~ (meaning) *of a word,* acute accent *has not always the same* ~, *give the note* (in music) *its full time*~ (the full time indicated by it); (paint.) relation of one part of picture to others in respect of light & shade, as *out of* ~, too light or dark; amount, quantity, denoted by algebraical term or expression; (biol.) rank in classification. 2. v.t. Estimate the ~ of, appraise (professionally, whence **văl′ūER¹** n., or otherwise), as *should* ~ *the whole at £2000*; have high or specified opinion of, attach importance to, prize, esteem, appreciate, pride oneself v̆n, as ~ *sincerity* (*beyond all things*), *a*~*d friend,* ~s *himself on his conversational powers, do not* ~ *that a brass farthing.* [ME, f. OF, fem. p.p. of *valoir* be worth f. L *valēre* be strong; vb f. n.]

văl′ūeléss (-ūl-), a. Worthless. Hence ~-NESS n. [-LESS]

vălve, n. Kinds of automatic or other device for controlling passage of liquid or gas or the like through pipe etc., as *clack, rotary², screw, sliding, throttle,* ~, *key* ~ (of organ, flute, etc.), SAFETY~, THERMIONIC~; (anat., zool.) membranous part of organ etc. allowing flow of blood etc. in one direction & not in another, as ~s *of the heart, veins, pulmonary* ~s, whence **vălvŭlīˈīs** [-UL-] n.; (conch.) each of two or more separable pieces of which shell consists, whole shell in one piece; (bot.) each of the segments into which a capsule dehisces, each half of an anther after its opening; (now rare) leaf of folding door. Hence or cogn. **văl′**VAL(bot.), **văl′**VAR¹, **văl′**VATE²(anat., bot.), (-)**vălVED²** (-vd), ~′LESS (-vl-), **vălvIF′**EROUS, **văl′**vIFORM, **văl′vŭlAR¹** [-UL-], aa.,~′LET(-vl-), **vălvŏT′**OMY(med.), **văl′**vULE(anat., bot.), nn. [f. L *valva* leaf of folding door]

vămˈbrăce, n. (hist.). Armour for fore--arm. [ME, f. AF *vaunt-bras* (*avaunt* before, see ADVANCE¹, + *bras* arm f. L *brachium*)]

***vamōse′**, -ōōs(e)′, v.i. & t. (sl.). Begone, decamp; decamp from (place). [f. Sp. *vamos* let us go]

vămp¹, n., & v.i. & t. 1. Upper front part of boot or shoe; patch designed to make old thing look new; improvised accompaniment. 2. vb. Put new ~ to (boot, shoe); repair, furbish usu. *up*; make *up* (literary article etc.) out of odds & ends; improvise accompaniment to, improvise accompaniments. Hence ~′ER¹ n. [ME, f. AF *vampe, *vanpe, = OF *avanpie* f. *avan(t)* before + *pie* foot]

vămp², n., & v.t. & i. (colloq.). 1. Adventuress, woman who exploits men; unscrupulous flirt. 2. vb. Allure, exploit; act as ~. [abbr. of foll.]

văm′pīre, n. Ghost or reanimated body (usu. of wizard, heretic, criminal, etc.) that leaves grave at night & sucks blood of sleeping persons; person who preys on others; = prec. n.; (in full ~ *bat*) kinds of bat, some of which suck blood of horses, cattle, & sleeping persons; (theatr.) small spring trap of two flaps used for sudden (dis)appearances of one person. Hence **vămpi′rIC** a. [F, f. Magyar *vampir* perh. of Turk. orig.]

văm′pīrīsm, n. Belief in existence of vampires; blood-sucking (lit. & fig.). [-ISM]

văm′plāte, n. (hist.). Iron plate protecting hand when lance was couched. [ME, f. AF *vaunt-* (as VAMBRACE) +PLATE]

‖ **văn¹**, n., & v.t. (-nn-). 1.(Arch.) winnowing-machine; (arch., poet.) wing. 2. v.t. Test quality of (ore) by washing on shovel or by machine, whence ~n′ER¹(1, 2) n.; (n.) such test. [ME, southern var. of FAN¹, perh. partly f. OF *van* or L *vannus*]

văn², n. Foremost division of army on the march or of fleet when sailing; front of army in line of battle; (fig.) leaders of a movement etc., as *in the* ~ *of civilization*. [abbr. of VANGUARD]

văn³, n., & v.t. (-nn-). Large usu. covered vehicle for conveying furniture or other goods; ‖ railway carriage for luggage (*luggage* ~) or for use of guard (*guard's*

~); (vb) convey in ~. [abbr. of CARAVAN, cf. *bus, wig*]

vanăd′ium, n. Hard grey metallic element used in small quantities for strengthening some steels. Hence **văn′ad**ATE¹(3) n., **vanăd′**IC, **văn′ad**OUS, aa., (chem.). [f. ON *Vanadis* name of the Scand. goddess *Freyja*, + -IUM]

Văn′dal, a. & n. (Member) of a Germanic people that ravaged Gaul, Spain, N. Africa, & Rome, destroying many books & works of art; (fig., also *v*~) wilful or ignorant destroyer of works of art etc., whence ~ISM(2), v-, n. Hence **Vandăl′**IC, v-, a. [f. LL *Vandalus* of Gmc orig.]

văndȳke′, n., a., & v.t. 1. (*V*~; prop. *Van Dyck*) Flemish painter d. 1641, picture by him; each of a series of large points forming a border to lace, cloth, etc., (also *V*~ *cape, collar*) cape, collar, with ~s. 2. adj. (usu. *V*~). In the style of dress, esp. with pointed borders, common in *V*~'s portraits; *V*~ (pointed) *beard*; *V*~ *brown*, deep rich brown. 3. v.t. Cut (cloth etc.) in ~s.

vāne, n. Weathercock; similar device exposed to current of water etc. as in water-meter; (also *dog*-~) cone or other device used on shipboard as weathercock; blade of windmill, screw propeller, etc.; sight of surveying instruments, sight of quadrant etc. Hence **vān**ED² (-nd), ~′LESS, aa. [ME, southern var. of obs. *fane* f. OE *fana*, banner; cf. GONFALON]

văng, n. (naut.). Each of two guy-ropes running from end of gaff to deck. [f. Du. *vang* in *vanglijn* painter; earlier *fang*]

văn′guard (-gärd), n. Foremost part of army etc.; (fig.) leaders of an intellectual etc. movement. [f. OF *avan(t)garde* (*avant* before), see ADVANCE¹, GUARD, WARD]

vanill′|a, n. Kinds of tall orchid with fragrant flowers; (also ~*a-bean*) fruit of this; extract obtained from ~*a-bean* & used for flavouring ices, chocolate, etc. Hence ~ATE¹(3) n., ~IC a., (chem.). [f. Sp. *vainilla* pod dim. of *vaina* sheath, pod, f. L. VAGINA]

vanill′ism, n. Eruptive itching skin-disease common among workers in vanilla. [-ISM(5)]

văn′ish, v.i., & n. 1. Disappear suddenly; disappear gradually, fade away; pass away; cease to exist; (math.) become zero (~*ing fraction*, one that becomes zero for a particular value of the variable it contains); (perspect.) ~*ing-point*, point in which all parallel lines in same plane tend to meet, ~*ing-line*, that which represents the line at infinity in which given plane cuts all parallel planes; ~*ing cream*, emollient that leaves no trace when rubbed into the skin. 2. n. (phonet.). Slight sound with which a principal sound ends (e.g. ŏŏ, ĭ, at end of ō, ă). [ME; aphetic f. OF *evanir* EVANISH]

văn′itȳ, n. Futility, unsubstantiality,

unreality, emptiness, unsubstantial or unreal thing, as *the* ~ *of worldly wealth, of political distinction, of human achievements, these things are* ~ *or vanities, all is* ~, *pomps & ~ of this wicked world, V~ Fair*, the world (allegorized in *Pilgrim's Progress*) as a scene of ~; empty pride, conceit, based on personal attainments or attractions or qualities (~ *bag, case*, carried on the person & containing small mirror, powder-puff, etc.); ostentatious display; (O.T.) heathen deity, as *the vanities of the Gentiles*. [ME, f. OF *vanite*, f. L *vanitatem* (as VAIN, see -TY)]

van′quish, v.t. Conquer, overcome, (lit. & fig.; now chiefly rhet.). Hence ~ABLE a., ~ER[1] n. [ME *venkus, -quis*, etc., f. OF *vencus* p.p., & *-quis* past tense of *veintre* f. L *vincere*; see -ISH[2]]

va′ntage (vah-), n. = ADVANTAGE (now chiefly in tennis use & in ~*-ground*, COIGN *of* ~). [ME, f. AF aphetic f. OF *avantage* ADVANTAGE]

vap′id, a. Insipid, flat, as ~ *beer, conversation, moralizings*. Hence vapid′ITY, ~NESS, nn., ~LY[2] adv. [f. L *vapidus*]

vap′or|ize, -ise (-īz), v.t. & i. Convert, be converted, into vapour. Hence or cogn. ~ABIL′ITY, ~īZA′TION, ~īZER[1](2), nn., ~(īz)ABLE aa. [-IZE]

vap′our (-per), n., & v.i. **1.** Moisture in the air e.g. mist, (loosely) light cloudy substance e.g. smoke, (phys.) gaseous form of a normally liquid or solid substance (cf. GAS), whence vāporIF′EROUS, vāporIF′IC, vāp′orIFORM, aa., vāpori-M′ETER n.; (med.) kinds of remedial agent to be inhaled, as ~ *of iodine*; unsubstantial thing, vain imagination; (arch.) empty boasting; ‖ (pl., arch.) depression, spleen, hypochondria, whence ~ISH[1] (-per-) a., ~ishNESS n.; ~ *bath* (also vāporAR′IUM n.), bath in ~ or steam, apparatus or apartment for this; ~*-burner*, apparatus for vaporizing a hydrocarbon for lighting or heating purposes; ~*-engine* (driven by steam or other elastic fluid). Hence or cogn. vāp′orOSE[1], vāp′orOUS, ~Y[2] (-per-), aa., vāporōS′ITY, vāp′orousNESS, nn., vāp′orousLY[2] adv. **2.** v.i. Emit ~; utter idle boasts or empty talk, whence ~ER[1] (-per-) n. [ME, f. OF, or f. L *vapor*; vb f. n. or L *vaporare*]

vāpūlā′tion, n. (rare). Flogging. So **vāp′ūlātory** a. [f. L *vapulare* be flogged +-ATION]

vaquer′ō (-kār-), n. (pl. ~s). Mex. or U.-S. herdsman. [Sp. (*vacca* cow, -ARY[1])]

Varän′gian (-j-), n. Norse rover, esp. of those who ravaged Baltic coasts about 9th c.; ~ *guard*, bodyguard of Byzantine emperors formed partly of ~s. [f. med. L *Varangus* f. ON *Vǣringi* lit. confederate (*várar* oaths)]

vă′rĕc, n. Seaweed; kelp. [f. F *varec, varech*, of Scand. orig., cf. WRECK]

vār′iable, a. & n. **1.** That can be varied or adapted, as *rod of* ~ *length, the pressure*

is ~, *a word of* ~ *construction*, ~ *gear* (designed to give varying speeds, e.g. slow advance & quick return); apt to vary, not constant, fickle, unsteady, as ~ *wind, mood, temper, fortune*; (astron., of stars) periodically varying in brightness or magnitude; (math., of quantity) indeterminate, able to assume different numerical values; (bot., zool., of species) including individuals or groups that depart from the type; (biol., of organism) tending to change in structure or function. Hence vāriaBIL′ITY, ~NESS, nn., vār′iabLY[2] adv. **2.** n. ~ thing esp. quantity; (naut.) shifting wind, (pl.) region between NE & SE trade-winds. [ME, f. OF, f. L *variabilis* (VARY, -BLE)]

vă′ria lĕc′tĭō, n. Variant reading. [L]

vār′iance, n. Disagreement, difference of opinion, dispute, lack of harmony, as *on that point we are at* ~ (*among ourselves*), *at* ~ *with the authorities, have had a slight* ~ *with him, this theory is at* ~ *with all that is known on the subject*; (law) discrepancy between pleadings & proof or between writ & declaration. [ME, f. OF, f. L *variantia* difference (as foll., see -ANCE)]

vār′iant, a. & n. **1.** Differing in form or in details from the one named or considered, differing thus among themselves, as *a* ~ *reading in some MSS., 40* ~ *types of pigeon*; variable, changing. **2.** n. ~ form, spelling, type, reading, etc., as *valet is a* ~ *of varlet, difficult to choose between these* ~*s*. [ME, f. OF (as VARY, see -ANT]

vāria′tion, n. Varying, departure from a former or normal condition or action or amount or from a standard or type, extent of this, as *is not liable to* ~, *repeated* ~*s of temperature, is subject to a* ~ *of several degrees, estimates the* ~ *in value at 20 per cent*; (astron.) deviation of heavenly body from mean orbit or motion (*periodic, secular,* ~, compensated in short, in very long, period); (of magnetic needle) = DECLINATION (~*-chart*, with lines drawn through places that have same~); (biol.) structural or functional deviation from type; (alg.) (theory of) relation between quantities that VARY as each other; thing that varies from a type, as *the scazon is a* ~ *of or on the ordinary iambic trimeter*, esp. (mus.) tune or theme repeated in a changed or elaborated form. Hence ~AL (-sho-) a. [ME, f. OF, or L *variatio* (VARY, -ATION)]

vă′ricātĕd, a. (conch.). Having varices. So **vărica′TION** n. [f. VARIX, see -ATE[2](2)]

văricĕll′|a, n. = CHICKEN-*pox*. Hence ~AR[1], ~OID, áa. [mod. L, irreg. dim. of VARIOLA]

vă′ricocēle, n. Tumour composed of varicose veins of spermatic cord. [as VARIX +-CELE]

vār′icoloured (-kŭlerd), a. Variegated in colour; of various or different colours. [f. L *varius* various + COLOURED]

vă′ricōs|e, a. Of, affected with, designed

for cure of, varix, as ~*e ulcer, vein, bandage*, whence ~ED[1] (-st) a., **văricŏs'ITY** n.; = VARICATED. [f. L *varicosus* (VARIX, see -OSE[1])]

văr'iĕg|āte, v.t. Diversify in colour, mark with irregular patches of different colours (chiefly in p.p., esp. bot. of leaves partly pale from suppression of chlorophyll or of plants with such leaves, as ~*ated geranium*). Hence ~A'TION n. [f. L *variegare* f. *varius* VARIOUS, see -ATE[3]]

vari'ĕtў, n. **1.** Being various, diversity, absence of monotony or uniformity, many-sidedness, as *was struck by the ~ of his attainments, of his conversation, of the scene, London has for me the charm of ~, cannot live without ~*. **2.** Collection of different things, as *turned over a ~ of silks, for a ~ of reasons; ~ entertainment* or *show* or simply ~ (consisting of dances, songs, acrobatic feats, etc.), ~ *theatre* (for ~ shows etc.). **3.** (Specimen, member, of a) class of things differing in some common qualities from the rest of a larger class to which they belong. **4.** (biol.). Individual or group usually fertile with any other member of the species to which it belongs but differing from the type in some qualities capable of perpetuation, subspecies, as *climatic* ~ (produced by climatic influences), *geographical* ~ (confined to given area), whence **vari'ĕtAL** a., **vari'ĕtALY**[2] adv. [f. F *variété* or L *varietas* (as VARIOUS, see -TY)]

văr'ifŏrm, a. Having various forms. [-FORM]

vari'ol|a, n. Smallpox. Hence ~AR[1], **văriŏl'IC**, ~OUS, aa. [med. L, as VARIOUS]

văriolā'tion, n. Inoculation with smallpox virus. [f. prec. + -ATION]

văr'i|ōle, n. (zool., bot.). Shallow pit like smallpox mark. Hence ~OLATE[2], ~OLĀTĔD, aa. [f. med. L VARIOLA]

văr'iol|ĭte, n. Rock with concretionary structure causing on surface an appearance like smallpox pustules. Hence ~it'IC a. [as prec. + -ITE[1]]

văr'ioloid, a. & n. **1.** Like smallpox. **2.** n. Mild form of smallpox esp. as modified by previous inoculation. [as prec. + -OID]

văriŏm'ēter, n. (electr.). Device for varying the inductance in an electric circuit. [as VARIOUS + -METER]

văriŏr'um, a. & n. **1.** With notes of various commentators, as *a ~ (edition of) Horace*. **2.** n. A ~ edition. [L, gen. pl. as VARIOUS; short for *cum notis* ~]

văr'ious, a. Different, diverse, as *the modes of procedure were* ~, *types so* ~ *as to defy classification*; separate, several, more than one, as *came across* ~ *people, for* ~ *reasons*. Hence ~LY[2] adv., ~NESS n. (rare). [f. L *varius* + -OUS]

văr'ix, n. (pl. *vă'rĭcēs*). (Path.) permanent abnormal dilatation of vein or other vessel, vein etc. thus dilated; (conch.) each of the ridges across the whorls of a univalve shell. [L]

vărl'ĕt, n. (Hist.) medieval page preparing to be a squire; (arch., esp. joc.) menial, low fellow, rascal. [ME, f. OF var. of *vaslet*, see VALET]

vărm'int, n. (vulg., joc.). Mischievous or discreditable person or animal; (hunt. sl.) *the* fox. [var. of *varmin*, VERMIN]

vărn'ish, n., & v.t. **1.** Kinds of resinous solution applied to wood, metal, etc., to give hard shiny transparent surface; glaze on pottery etc.; artificial or natural glossiness; superficial polish of manner; favourable appearance given to misconduct etc., palliation, whitewash; ~*-tree*, kinds from which ~ is obtained. **2.** v.t. Apply ~ to (wood, picture, etc., fig. character, person, action, account, or abs.); ~*ing-day*, day before exhibition of pictures on which exhibitors may retouch or ~ their pictures already hung. [ME, f. OF *vernis*, of unkn. orig.; vb f. OF *verniss(i)er* f. *vernis*; see -ISH[2]]

|| **vărs'al**, a. (colloq., now rare). = UNIVERSAL. [illit. abbr.]

vărs'itў, n. (colloq.). University (often attrib., as *the ~ boat*). [colloq. abbr.]

vărsovienne' (-vyĕn), n. (Music for) dance resembling mazurka. [F, = (dance) of Warsaw (*Varsovie*)]

văr'us[1], n. Deformity involving inward bending of distal part of limb; bandy-legged person. [L, = bent]

văr'us[2], n. = ACNE. [L, = pimple]

văr'|ў, v.t. & i. Change, make different, modify, diversify, as *can~y the* (direction, amount, etc., of) *pressure at will, seldom* ~*ies the routine,* ~*ies the treatment according to circumstances, never* ~*ies his style, style is not sufficiently* ~*ied, a* ~*ied scene*; (mus.) make VARIATIONS of (theme); suffer change, be(come) different in degree or quality, be of different kinds, as *he, his mood,* ~*ies from day to day, climate* ~*ies, tried with* ~*ying success,* ~*ies from the type, opinions* ~*y on this point;* ~*y* (directly) as, ~*y inversely as,* increase, decrease, in proportion or correspondingly to the increase of, as *attraction of bodies* ~*ies* (directly) *as their masses & inversely as the square of their distances, A* ~*ies as* (symbol ∞) *B, A* ~*ies as B & C jointly* (as their product). [ME, f. OF *varier* or L *variare* (as VARIOUS)]

văs, n. (anat.; pl. *văs'a*). Vessel, duct, as ~ *def'erens*, excretory duct of testicle. Hence **văs'AL** a., ~EC'TOMY n. [L, = vessel]

văs'cŭlar, a. Of, made up of, containing, vessels or ducts for conveying blood, sap, etc., as ~ *functions, tissue,* ~ (circulatory) *system,* ~ *plants.* Hence ~ITY (-ă'r-), ~IZA'TION, nn., ~IZE(3) v.t., ~LY[2] adv. [f. mod. L *vascularis* f. VASCULUM + -AR[1]]

văs'cŭlōse, n. & a. Chief substance of vessels of plants; (adj.) = prec. [foll., -OSE[2,1]]

văs'cŭlum, n. (pl. *-la*). Botanist's (usu.

tin) collecting-case; (anat.) small vessel, penis. [L, dim. of VAS]

vase (vahz; *arch.* vawz, *arch. & U.S.* vās, -z), n. Vessel of baked clay or other material used for various purposes but primarily ornamental, as *flower-~*; large usu. sculptured vessel of marble etc. used to decorate gate-post etc.; *~-painting*, decoration of *~*s with pigments esp. among ancient Greeks, instance of this. Hence *~'FUL* n. [F, f. L VAS]

väs'eline, n. Unctuous substance got from petroleum & used in ointments etc. [P; irreg. f. G *wasser* water + Gk *elaion* oil + -INE³]

väsi-, väso-, comb. forms of VAS, as: *vas'i-form*, tubular; *vasoconstric'tor, -dilat'or, -mot'or*, aa. & nn., (nerve, drug) causing constriction, dilatation, either, of blood-vessels; *vasosen'sory*, supplying sensation to vessels.

väss'al, n. (Hist.) holder of land by feudal tenure (*great, rear, ~*), holding directly from king, holding from great *~*); (rhet.) slave, humble dependant. [ME, f. OF, f. med. L *vassallus*, of Celt. orig., the simplex *vassus* corresp. to OBreton *uuas*, W *gwas*, Ir. *foss*; cf. VAVASOUR]

väss'al|age, n. (Hist.) condition, obligations, service, of a vassal; servitude, dependence; fief; (rare; also *~RY* n.) vassals collectively. [ME, f. OF *vassal-(l)age* (prec., see -AGE)]

vast (vah-), a. & n. 1. Immense, huge, very great, as *a ~ expanse of water, ~ plains, shook his ~ frame, a ~ multitude, scheme*; (colloq.) *gave him ~ satisfaction, makes a ~ difference.* Hence *~'LY²* adv. (esp. colloq.), *~'NESS* n. 2. n. (poet., rhet.). *~ space, as the ~ of ocean, of heaven.* [f. L *vastus* void, immense, or F *vaste*]

vät, n., & v.t. (-tt-). 1. Large tub, cistern, or other vessel, esp. for holding liquids or holding something in liquid in process of manufacture, as *fermenting, tan, ~*, whence *~'FUL* n. 2. v.t. Place, treat, in *~*. [ME; southern var. of *fat*, OE *fæt*, OS, ON *fat*, OHG *faz*, f. Gmc *fatam* container]

Vät'ican, n. Palace & official residence of Pope on *~* hill in Rome; (fig.) papal government; *~ Council*, oecumenical council held 1869–70 & proclaiming infallibility of Pope when speaking *ex cathedra*, whence *~ISM*(3), *~IST*(2), nn. [f. L *Vaticanus ~* hill]

vati'cin|āte, v.t. Prophesy (often abs.). So *~A'TION, ~ātoR*, nn. [f. L *vaticinari* (*vates* prophet + *canere* sing), -ATE³]

vaude'vill|e (vōdv-), n. ‖ Slight dramatic music-hall sketch interspersed with songs & dances; variety entertainment; French popular e.g. topical song with refrain; (hist.) convivial song esp. any of those composed by O. Basselin, poet born at Vau de Vire in Normandy, d. 1418. Hence *~IST*(3) n. [F, f. *Vau de Vire* Valley of the Vire]

Vaudois¹ (vōdwah'), a. & n. (pl. same). (Inhabitants, dialect) of Vaud in Switzerland. [F (*Vaud + -ois* -ESE)]

Vaudois² (vōdwah'), a. & n. (pl. same). (Member) of the Waldenses. [F, repr. med. L *Valdensis*, see WALDENSES]

vaudoo. See VOODOO.

vault¹, n., & v.t. 1. (Archit.) arched roof, continuous arch, set or series of arches whose joints radiate from central point or line; *~like* covering, as *the ~ of heaven*; arched apartment; arched or other cellar or subterranean chamber as place of storage (*wine-~* etc.), of interment beneath church or in cemetery (*family ~*), etc.; (anat.) arched roof of a cavity. 2. v.t. Make in form of, furnish with, *~* or *~*s (esp. in p.p.). Hence *~'ING¹*(6) n. [ME, f. OF *voute, vaulte*, f. Rom. **volvita* fem. p.p. of L *volvere* roll]

vault², v.i. & t., & n. 1. Leap, spring, esp. while resting on the hand(s) or with help of pole, as *~ over the gate, from the saddle, upon a horse*; spring over (gate etc.) thus; *~ing-horse*, wooden horse for practice in *~*ing. Hence *~'ER¹* n. 2. n. Leap so performed. [app. f. OF *volter* leap, w. assim. to prec.]

vaunt, v.i. & t., & n. 1. Boast, brag; boast of. 2. n. Boast. Hence or cogn. *~'ER¹* n., *~'ingLY²* adv. [ME; vb f. OF *vanter* f. LL *vanitare* f. L *vanus* VAIN; partly aphetic f. obs. *avaunt* f. OF *a + vanter*]

vaunt'-courier (-kŏŏ-), n. = AVANT-COURIER.

väv'asorý, n. (hist.). Tenure, lands, of a vavasour. [f. OF *vavasorie* or med. L *-oria* (foll., -Y¹]

väv'asour (-ŏr, -er, -oor), n. (hist.). Vassal holding of a great lord & having other vassals under him. [ME, f. OF *vavas-(s)our* or med. L *vavassor*, app. f. *vassus vassorum* VASSAL of vassals]

've, colloq. abbr. of *have* appended to *I, we, you, they, & who* (*I've* etc.).

veal, n. Flesh of calf as food, as *~ cutlet*. Hence *~'Y³* a., like *~*, ***(colloq.) immature. [ME, f. OF *veel* (mod. *veau*) f. L *vitellus* dim. of *vitulus* calf]

vĕc'tor, n., & v.t. 1. (In quaternions etc.) line conceived to have fixed length & direction but no fixed position, quantity determining position of one point in space relative to another (*~ quantity*, one that may be represented by a *~*); carrier of disease or infection; RADIUS *~*. Hence **vĕctōr'IAL** a. 2. v.t. Direct (aircraft in flight) to desired point. [L, = carrier (*vehere vect-* convey, see -OR)]

Ve'da (vā-), n. (Also in pl.) ancient Hindu scriptures written in old form of Sanskrit (*Rig, Sama, Yajur, Atharva, ~*, four collections of hymns etc. composing the *~*). Hence **Ve'dic** (vā-) a. [Skr., lit. knowledge]

Vedān't|a (vā-), n. Hindu philosophy founded on the Veda. Hence *~IC* a., *~IST*(3) n. [Skr. (*vēda + anta* end)]

Vĕdd'a, n. Member of primitive race living in the Ceylon forests. [Sinhalese, = hunter]

vĕdĕtte', **vĭ-**, n. Mounted sentry placed in advance of an outpost. [F (ve-), f. It. vedetta]

veer[1], v.t. (naut.). Slacken, let out, (rope, cable, etc.); ~ & haul, tighten & slacken (rope etc.) alternately. [ME, f. MDu. vieren]

veer[2], v.i. & t., & n. 1. Change direction esp. (of wind, cf. BACK[2]) clockwise; (naut.) = WEAR[3]; (fig.) change one's mind, turn round in opinion or conduct or language. Hence ~**ingly**[2] adv. 2. n. Change of direction, shifting round. [f. F. virer f. Rom. *virare, alt. f. gyrare GYRATE]

ve'ga[1] (vā-), n. Low moist tract in Spain or Cuba; Cuban tobacco-field. [Sp.]

Vĕg'a[2], n. The brightest star in the constellation Lyra. [Sp. or med. L, f. Arab. wāqi' falling]

vĕ'gĕtable, a. & n. 1. Of (the nature of), derived from, concerned with, comprising, plants, as ~ colic (caused by use of unripe fruit), IVORY, jelly (= PECTIN), KINGDOM, MARROW, naphtha, oyster (= SALSIFY), physiology, SPONGE[1]. Hence vĕgĕtabil'ity n. 2. n. Plant, esp. herbaceous plant or part of one used for food, e.g. cabbage, potato, turnip, bean, (freq. attrib., as ~ diet, soup). [ME adj. f. OF. or f. LL vegetabilis vivifying (as VEGETATE, see -BLE); n.f. adj.]

vĕ'gĕt|al, a. & n. 1. Of (the nature of) plants, so ~o- comb. form; common to animals & plants, as the ~al functions (of growth, circulation, generation, etc.). 2. n. Plant, vegetable. Hence ~āl'ity n. [f. med. L *vegetalis f. L vegetare VEGETATE +-AL]

vĕgĕtār'ian, n. One who abstains from the use of flesh, fish, and fowl as food, with or without the addition of eggs and dairy produce, and whose diet includes roots, leafy vegetables, cereals, seeds, fruit, and nuts; attrib., as ~ diet, principles. Hence~ISM n. [irreg. f. VEGETABLE +-ARIAN]

vĕ'gĕtāt|e, v.i. Grow as plants do, fulfil vegetable functions; (fig.) live an idle or monotonous life. So ~IVE a., ~IVELY[2] adv., ~IVENESS n. [f. L vegetare enliven (vegetus f. vegēre move, quicken), see -ATE[3]]

vĕgĕtā'tion, n. Vegetating (lit. & fig.); plants collectively, plant life, as luxuriant ~, no sign of ~ for miles round; (path.) excrescence of surface of body. [f. med. L vegetatio growth (as prec., see -ATION)]

vĕ'hement (vēīm-), a. Showing or caused by strong feeling, impetuous, ardent, passionate, as a ~ desire, protest, man of ~ character; acting with great force, violent, as a ~ wind, onset. Hence or cogn. **vĕ'hemENCE** (vēīm-) n., ~**LY**[2] adv. [F, or f. L vehement-, nom. -ns]

ve'hicle (vēī-), n. Carriage, conveyance, of any kind used on land; liquid etc. used as a medium for pigments, drugs, etc.; thing, person, used as a medium for thought or feeling or action, as used the pulpit, the press, as a ~ for his political opinions, will not be used as the ~ of your resentment. So **vĕhic'ulAR**[1] a. [f. F véhicule or L vehiculum (vehere carry, see -CULE)]

vehmgericht (fām'geriҳt), n. German system of irregular tribunals prevailing esp. in Westphalia in 14th & 15th cc. & trying the more serious crimes in secret night sessions; such tribunal. Hence **veh'mic** (fām-) a. [G, also f-, f. feme punishment, tribunal, + gericht judgement, law]

veil (vāl), n., & v.t. 1. Piece of usu. more or less transparent material attached to woman's bonnet or hat or otherwise forming part of head-dress, esp. one serving to conceal the face or as protection against sun, dust, etc., as raised, dropped, her ~ (so as to uncover, cover, face), took the ~, became nun; curtain (the ~ of the temple; beyond the ~, in the unknown state of after death); (fig.) disguise, pretext, as under the ~ of religion; draw a ~ over, avoid discussing or calling attention to; scarf on pastoral staff; (bot., zool.)= VELUM; slight huskiness of voice, natural or due to a cold etc. Hence ~**ING**[1](3) n., ~'**LESS** a. 2. v.t. Cover (one's face, oneself, or abs. in same sense) with ~; (fig.) partly conceal, disguise, mask, as ~ed resentment. [ME, f. AF veile (OF voile) f. L vela pl. of velum]

vein (vān), n., & v.t. 1. Each of the membranous tubes that convey blood to the heart (cf. ARTERY; pulmonary ~s, returning oxygenated blood from lungs to left side, systemic ~s, returning venous blood from all parts to right side); (pop.) any blood-vessel; (entom., bot.) rib of insect's wing or of leaf; (geol., mining) fissure in rock filled with deposited matter (~'stone, = GANGUE); streak, stripe, of different colour in wood, marble, etc.; distinctive character or tendency, cast of mind or disposition, mood, as was of an imaginative ~, said in a humorous ~, other remarks in the same ~, am in the ~ for high play, am not in (the) ~ just now. Hence ~'**LESS**, ~'**LIKE**, ~'**Y**[2], aa., ~'**LET** n. 2. v.t. Fill or cover (as) with ~ or ~s (esp. in p.p.). Hence ~'**AGE**(1), ~'**ING**[1](6), nn. [ME, f. OF veine f. L vena]

vēlām'en (pl. -mina), **vĕlamĕn'tum** (pl. -ta), nn. Enveloping membrane esp. of brain. [L, f. velare (VELUM)]

vēl'ar, a. Of a veil or velum, as ~ gutturals, sounds produced by aid of soft palate (e.g. gw, kw). [f. L velaris (VELUM, see -AR[1])]

veld (fĕlt), n. S.-Afr. open country neither cultivated nor true forest. [Du.,=FIELD]

vēlitā'tion, n. (arch.). Slight skirmish, controversy. [f. L velitatio (velitari skirmish, as foll., see -ATION)]

vĕl′īte, n. (Rom. ant.). Light-armed soldier. [f. L *veles -itis*]

vĕllē′itў, n. Low degree of volition not prompting to action. [f. med. L *velleitas* (L *velle* vb wish, see -TY)]

vĕll′ic|āte, v.t. & i. (rare). Twitch. Hence or cogn. ~A′TION n., ~ātive a. [f. L *vellicare* (*vellere* pluck), see -ATE³]

vĕll′um, n. Fine parchment orig. from skin of calf; manuscript written on this; ~ *paper* (imitating ~). Hence~Y²a. [ME *relym, -um* f. OF *velin* (*veel* VEAL, -INE¹)]

vĕlō′ce (-chā), adv. (mus.). With great rapidity. [It.]

vĕlō′cipēd|e, n. Kinds of light vehicle impelled by rider (now chiefly hist. of obs. types e.g. hobby). Hence ~IST(3) n. [f. F *vélocipède* f. L *velox -ocis* swift + *pes pedis* foot]

vĕlō′citў, n. Quickness, rate, of motion usu. of inanimate things, as *uniform* ~; (mech.) speed in a given direction; *initial* ~, ~ of a body at starting, esp. (also *muzzle* ~) of projectile issuing from fire-arm. Hence **vĕlocĭM′ETER** n. [f. F *vélocité* or L *velocitas* (as prec., -TY)]

velours′ (-oor), n. Kinds of plush used for hats etc. [F (OF *-our, -ous*), as VELVET]

vĕloutine′ (-ōōtēn), n. Kinds of corded fabric & of toilet-powder. [F]

vĕl′um, n. (anat., bot., zool.; pl. *-la*). Kinds of membrane or membranous covering, esp. the soft palate. [L, = sail, curtain, covering, veil]

vĕl′ure, n., & v.t. Velvet or similar fabric; velvet or other pad for smoothing silk hat; (vb) smooth with ~. [f. OF *velour*, see VELOURS]

vĕlūt′inous, a. (bot., entom.). Velvety. [f. med. L as VELVET + -INE¹ + -OUS]

vĕl′verĕt, n. Bad kind of velvet. [irreg. dim. of foll.]

vĕl′vĕt, n. & a. 1. Closely woven fabric wholly (also *silk* ~) or partly (*cotton* ~) of silk with thick short pile on one side (*terry* ~, with pile uncut); furry skin covering a growing antler; (transf.) profit, gain; *on* ~, in an advantageous or prosperous position; ~ *pile*, fabric with pile like that of ~. 2. adj. Of, soft as, ~ (often in names of animals & plants, as ~ *ant, osier*); ~ *glove*, outward gentleness cloaking inflexibility (*with an iron hand in a* ~ *glove*); ~ *paw*, of cat, fig. of cruelty etc. veiled under suave manner; ~ *tread*, soft. Hence ~ED², ~Y³, aa. [ME, f. med. L *velvel(t)um*, also *vel(l)utum*, ult. f. L *villus* shaggy hair]

vĕlvĕteen′, n. Cotton fabric with pile like velvet; kind of velvet made of silk & cotton; ‖ (pl., transf.) gamekeeper. [prec. + *-een* -INE⁴]

vĕl′vĕting, n. Velvet goods collectively; pile, nap, of velvet. [-ING¹]

vĕn′al, a. (Of person) that may be bought, ready to sell influence or services or to sacrifice principles from sordid motive; (of conduct etc.) characteristic of ~

---

person. Hence or cogn. **vĕnăl′ITY** n., ~LY² adv. [f. L *venalis* (*venum*, sale, see -AL)]

vēnā′tion, n. Arrangement of veins on leaf, insect's wing, etc. Hence ~AL a. [f. L *vena* VEIN + -ATION]

vĕnd, v.t. Sell (now chiefly legal, whence or cogn. ~EE′, vĕn′dOR, nn.); offer (small wares) for sale, so (-)vĕn′dER¹ n.; *~ing machine*, SLOT¹-machine. Hence or cogn. ~ĭBIL′ITY n., ~IBLE a., ~′ĭBLY² adv. [f. F *vendre* or L *vendere* sell]

vĕn′dāce, n. Small & delicate fish found in some British & Continental lakes. [app. f. OF *vendese, -oise* dace]

Vĕndē′an, a. & n. (Native) of Vendée, department of W. France; (member) of ~ royalist party in 1793–5. [f. F *Vendéen* (*Vendée*, see -AN)]

vĕndĕtt′a, n. Blood-feud in which family of injured or murdered man seeks vengeance on offender or his family; this practice as prevalent in Corsica etc. [It., f. L *vindicta*, see VINDICTIVE]

vēneer′, v.t., & n. 1. Cover (wood, furniture, etc.) with thin coating of finer wood; cover (pottery etc.) with thin coat of finer substance; (fig.) disguise (character etc.) under superficial polish of manner etc. 2. n. Thin outer coating, ~ing (lit. & fig.); ~*moth*, kinds whose colouring suggests ~. [later form of (obs.) *fineer* f. G *furni(e)r, furni(e)ren* f. F *fournir* FURNISH]

vĕn′epŭnc′ture, n. (med.). Puncture of vein esp. with hypodermic needle to draw blood or for intravenous injection. [f. L *vena* vein + PUNCTURE]

vĕn′er|able, a. Entitled to veneration on account of character, age, associations, etc., as ~*able priest, relics, beard, ruins, Bede* (also in Ch. of Eng. as title of archdeacons, abbr. *Ven.*; in R.-C. Ch. as title of one who has attained first of three degrees of sanctity but is not canonized). Hence ~ABIL′ITY n., ~ABLENESS, nn., ~ABLY³ adv. [ME, f. OF, or L *venerabilis* (as foll., see -ABLE)]

vĕn′erāt|e, v.t. Consider worthy of & regard with deep respect or warm approbation; revere. So ~OR n. [f. L *venerari* -ATE³]

vĕnerā′tion, n. Profound respect, reverence; (phren., often joc.) faculty of feeling reverence, as *organ, bump*, of ~. [ME, f. L *veneratio* (as prec., see -ATION)]

vĕnēr′e|al, a. Of sexual intercourse, as ~*al desire*; ~*al disease*, communicated by sexual intercourse; ~*al remedies* (for ~al disease). Hence ~ŌL′OGIST, ~ŌL′OGY, nn. [f. L *Venereus* of VENUS + -AL]

vĕn′erў¹, n. (arch.). Hunting. [ME, f. OF *venerie* (*vener* hunt f. L *venari*, see -ERY)]

vĕn′erў², n. (arch.). Sexual indulgence. [VENUS, -Y¹]

vĕn′ĕsĕct, v.t. & i., **vĕnĕsĕc′tion**, n. = PHLEBOTOMIZE, PHLEBOTOMY. [vb f. n., f. mod. L *venae sectio* cutting of vein]

Vĕnē'tian (-shn), a. & n. **1.** Of Venice; ~ **blind**, window blind of slats of wood that may be turned so as to admit or exclude light; ~ **carpet** (of worsted, usu. with striped pattern); ~ (=FRENCH) **chalk**; ~ **glass**, glassware made at or near Venice, (also *Venice glass*) cup of this said to be destroyed by contact with poison; ~ **lace**, kind of point lace; ~ **mast**, spirally painted pole for use in street decorations; ~ (solid artificial) **pearl**; ~ **window** (with three separate openings). **2.** n. Native of Venice; (usu. v~) ~ **blind**, whence **vĕnē'tian**ED[2] (-sha-) a., (pl.) kind of tape for holding slats of this. [ME, f. OF *Venicien* or med. L *Venetianus* f. *Venetia* Venice, see -AN]

vĕn'geance (-jans), n. Punishment inflicted, retribution exacted, for wrong to oneself or to person etc. whose cause one espouses, as *will exact ample* ~, *took a bloody* ~ *on the murderer* or *for the murder of his children, you lay yourself open to his* ~; *with a* ~, in a higher degree than was expected or desired, in the fullest sense of the word(s), & no mistake, as *this is punctuality with a* ~. [ME, f. OF *(venger* avenge f. L as VINDICATE, see -ANCE)]

vĕnge'ful (-jf-), a. Disposed to revenge, vindictive. Hence ~LY[2] adv., ~NESS n. [f. obs. *venge* vb (as prec.)+-FUL]

vĕn'ial, a. (Of sin or fault) pardonable, excusable, not very wrong, (theol.) not mortal. Hence **vĕniăl'ITY**, ~NESS, nn., ~LY[2] adv. [ME, f. OF *venial*, *-el*, or LL *venialis (venia* pardon, see -AL)]

Vĕn'ice, n. (attrib.). ~ (= VENETIAN) *glass*; ~ *treacle*, = THERIAC.

vĕnī̆r'é (*fǎ'cĭǎs*) (-sh-), n. (law). Writ directing sheriff to summon jury. [L, = make or cause to come]

vĕn'ison (-nzon), n. Deer's flesh as food. [ME, f. OF *veneisun* f. L *venationem* hunting *(venari* hunt, see -ATION)]

Vĕnī̆t'é, n. (Musical setting of) *Ps.* xcv. [L, = Come ye, first word of psalm]

vĕn'om, n. Poisonous fluid secreted by serpents, scorpions, etc., & introduced into system of victim by bite or sting; (fig.) malignity, virulence, of feeling or language or conduct. Hence or cogn. ~ED[2] (-md), ~OUS, aa., ~OUSLY[2] adv., ~OUSNESS n. [ME, f. AF, OF *venim*, var. of *venin* f. Gallo-Rom. *venimen* f. L *venenum* poison]

vĕnŏs' itŷ, n. Excess of venous blood in organ etc.; deficient aeration of venous blood in lungs with afflux of venous blood into arteries. [as foll., see -OSITY]

vĕn'ous, -ōse, aa. (anat., zool., bot.). Of, full of, contained in, veins, as ~ (opp. to arterial) *blood*, ~ *congestion*, accumulation of ~ blood in organ etc. Hence **vĕn'ous**LY[2] adv. [f. L *venosus*, or f. L *vena*+-OSE[1], -OUS]

vĕnt[1], n., & v.t. & i. **1.** Hole or opening allowing passage out of or into confined space, e.g. touch-hole of gun, hole in top of barrel to admit air while liquid is being drawn out, finger-hole in musical instrument (also **vĕn'tAGE** n.), flue of chimney; = ~*faucet*; anus esp. of animals below mammals; (fig.) outlet, free passage, free play, as *gave* ~ *to his indignation*, *impatience found a* ~; ‖ ~ing of otter etc. (see vb); ~*faucet*, hollow gimlet for making ~ in cask etc.; ~*hole*, ~; ~*peg*, peg for stopping ~ of barrel, also = ~*faucet*; ~*plug*, plug for ~ of gun, also = ~*peg* (1st sense). Hence ~'LESS a. **2.** vb. Make ~ in (gun, cask, etc.); give ~ to, as ~*ed his disgust in an epigram, with a snort, on the office-boy*; ‖ (of otter or beaver) come to surface for breath. [n. partly f. F *vent* f. L *ventus* wind, partly f. F *évent (éventer* f. EX-+*vent* wind); vb f. n., & F *éventer*]

vĕnt[2], n. Slit in garment now esp. in back of coat; (obs.) = CRENEL. [ME, var. of *fent* f. OF *fente* f. L *findere* cleave]

vĕn'ter, n. (Anat.) belly, also, protuberant or concave part of muscle or bone; (law) womb, mother, as *a son by, the son of, another* ~. [f. AF *ventre, venter*, or L *venter* paunch, womb]

vĕn'tidŭct, n. (archit.). Air-passage, esp. subterranean one. [f. L *ventus* wind+DUCT]

vĕn'til, n. Valve in musical instrument; shutter for regulating air in organ. [G, f. med. L *ventile* shutter f. L *ventus* wind]

vĕn'til|āte, v.t. Cause air to circulate freely in (room etc.); purify by air, oxygenate, (blood); submit (question, subject, grievance, etc.) to public consideration & discussion. Hence or cogn. ~A'TION, ~ātOR (esp., appliance for~ating room), nn., ~ātIVE a. [f. L *ventilare* blow, winnow *(ventus* wind), see -ATE[3]]

vĕn'tral, a. & n. (zool., bot.). Of the venter; on the belly (opp. DORSAL); ~ (*fin*), either of the abdominal fins. Hence ~LY[2] adv. [F, or f. L *ventralis* (VENTER, see -AL)]

ventre à terre (see Ap.), adv. At full speed (lit. with belly to ground). [F]

vĕn'tricle, n. (anat.). Any cavity of the body, hollow part or organ, as ~*s of the brain, right, left,* ~ (*of the heart*). Hence **vĕntric'ūlAR**[1], **vĕntric'ūl**ous, aa. [ME, f. L *ventriculus* dim. of VENTER]

vĕn'tricōse, -ous, aa. Having a protruding belly; (bot.) distended, inflated. [f. VENTER+-IC-+-OSE[1], -OUS]

vĕntril'oqu|ism, n. Act, art, of speaking, or uttering sounds in such a manner that the voice appears to come from some other source than the speaker. So ~IST(1), ~Y[1], nn., **vĕntrilŏ'quIAL**, ~is'tIC, ~ous, aa., ~IZE(2) v.i. [all ult. f. LL *ventriloquus* ventriloquist (VENTER + *loqui* locut- speak)]

vĕn'tro-, comb. form of VENTER, as ~*dors'al*, extending from belly to back.

věn′ture, n., & v.t. & i. **1.** Undertaking of a risky, risky undertaking, as *declined the* ~, *ready for any* ~; commercial speculation, as *one lucky* ~ *made his fortune, failed in all his* ~s; (the thing at stake, property risked; *at a* ~, at random. **2.** vb. Dare, not be afraid, make bold, as *did not* ~ *to stop him, I* ~ *to differ from you*; dare to make or advance or put forward, hazard, as *would not* ~ *an opinion, a guess, a step*; expose to risk, stake, as *men who* ~ *their lives for the cause, will* ~ *five shillings on it*; (abs.) undertake risk; ~ (*up*)*on*, dare to engage in or grapple with or make, as *shall* ~ *on a mild protest, will you* ~ *on a slice of cucumber?* Hence věn′turER[1] n., (esp. hist.) one who undertakes or shares in a trading ~, ~SOME (-chers-) a., ~SOMELY[2] adv., ~SOMENESS n. [aphetic f. ADVENTURE]

věn′ūe, n. (law). Country within which jury must be gathered & cause tried (orig. neighbourhood of crime etc.), as *change the* ~ (to avoid riot, prejudiced jury, etc.); statement in indictment etc. indicating this; (pop.) rendezvous. [F, = coming, f. *venir* come f. L *venire*]

Věn′us, n. (Rom. myth.) goddess of love; a PLANET[1]; sexual love, amorous influences or desires, (*uranian, pandemian,* ~, spiritual, sensual, sex love); a beautiful woman; *Mount of* ~ (palmistry), base of thumb; ~'s *basin, bath*, common teazel; ~'s *comb*, plant of parsley family with comblike fruit; ~'s *fly-trap*, herb with leaves that close on insects etc.; ~'s *slipper,* = LADY'S-*slipper*. [L, gen. *-eris*]

vera′cious (-shus), a. Speaking, disposed to speak, the truth; (of statement etc.) true, not (meant to be) false. Hence or cogn. ~LY[2] adv., verA′CITY n. [f. L *verax* (*verus* true, see -ACIOUS)]

veran′da(h) (-da), n. Open portico or gallery along side of house with roof supported on pillars. [f. Port. *varanda*]

vě′ratr|ine, n. Poisonous compound from hellebore used esp. as local irritant in neuralgia & rheumatism. So ~ATE[1](3) n., verăt′riC a. ~IZE(5) v.t. [F (*vé-*), f. L *veratrum* hellebore +-INE[5]]

věrb, n. (gram.). Part of speech that predicates, word whose function is predication (e.g. italicized words in Time *flies*, Salt is good, You *surprise* me); *copulative* or *substantive* ~, be; AUXILIARY, DEPONENT, IMPERSONAL, (IN)TRANSITIVE, NEUTER, REFLEXIVE, ~. [ME, f. OF *verbe* or L *verbum* WORD, verb]

věrb′al, a. & n. **1.** Of, concerned with, words, as ~ *distinctions, subtleties, critic(ism), accuracy,* INSPIRATION ; (loosely) oral, not written, as *a* ~ *communication, contract,* ~ *evidence*; (of translation) literal, word for word; ~ *note* (diplomacy), unsigned memorandum on matter that is not urgent but must not be overlooked; (gram.) of (the nature of) a verb, as ~

inflexions, used in all the ~ *senses* (of the verb), ~ *noun*, noun derived from verb & partly sharing its constructions (e.g. E nouns in -ING[1]). **2.** n. ~ noun. Hence ~LY[2] adv. [F, or f. LL *verbalis* (as prec., see -AL)]

věrb′alism, n. Minute attention to words, verbal criticism. [-ISM]

věrb′alist, n. Person concerned with words only, verbal critic. [-IST]

věrb′aliz|e, -is|e (-iz), v.t. & i. Make (noun etc.) into a verb, so věrb′IFY v.t.; be verbose. Hence ~A′TION n. [f. F *verbaliser*, or f. VERBAL +-IZE]

verbāt′im, adv. & a. Word for word, as *copied it* ~, *a* ~ *reprint.* [med. L (adv.), f. L *verbum* VERB, cf. LITERATIM]

verběn′a, n. Kinds of plant of vervain family, as *lemon(-scented)* ~. [L, = sacred bough of olive etc., VERVAIN]

věrb′iage, n. Needless accumulation of words, verbosity. [F (as VERB, see -AGE)]

věrb′icīde, n. (joc.). Word-butcher(y). [as VERB +-CIDE]

verbōse′, a. Using, containing, more words than are wanted, prolix. Hence ~LY[2] adv., ~NESS, verbōs′ITY, nn. [f. L *verbosus* (as VERB, see -OSE[1])]

verb′um (sǎt) sǎpǐěn′tǐ, sent. (abbr. *verb. sap.*). A word is enough to the wise. [L]

věrd′ant, a. (Of grass etc.) green, fresh-coloured; (of field etc.) covered with ~ grass etc.; (of person) unsophisticated, raw, green. Hence věrd′ANCY n., ~LY[2] adv. [f. *verd-* (as in *verdure*), perh. partly after L *viridans -ant-* green]

věrd-ăntīque′ (-ēk), n. Ornamental usu. green building-stone formed chiefly of serpentine; green incrustation on ancient bronze. [older F = antique green]

věrd′erer, -or, n. (hist.). Judicial officer of royal forests. [AF *verderer*, f. *verder* (verd f. L *viridis* green) +-ER[1], -OR]

věrd′ict, n. Decision of jury on issue of fact in civil or criminal cause, as *brought in a* ~ *of not guilty, a* ~ *for the plaintiff, open* ~ (reporting commission of crime but not specifying criminal, also, open as between accident and suicide), *partial* ~ (finding person guilty of part of the charge), *privy or sealed* ~ (written = delivered to clerk of court when court has adjourned during deliberation of jury), *special* ~ (stating facts as proved but leaving court to draw conclusion from them); decision, judgement, as *the* ~ *of the public was in its favour, does not dispute your* ~. [ME & AF *verdit* (= OF *voirdit*) f. *ver, veir* true + *dit* p.p. of *dire* say]

věrd′igris (or -ēs), n. Green crystallized substance formed on copper by action of acetic acid & used in medicine & as pigment etc.; green rust on copper. [ME, f. AF, OF *vert de Grece* green of Greece]

věrd′iter, n. Blue, *green*, ~, pigments got from copper nitrate. [f. OF *vert de terre* green of earth]

vĕrd′ur|e (-dyer), n. Greenness of vegeta-
tion, green vegetation, whence ~ED[2]
(-dyerd), ~ELESS, vĕrd′ūrous, aa.; (fig.)
freshness. [ME, f. OF, f. *vert* f. L *viridis*
green+-URE]

verein (ferīn′), n. Association of persons
or parties, organized body. [G]

Verey. Var. of VERY[2].

vĕrge[1], n. Extreme edge, brink, border,
(usu. fig.), as *drew near to the very ~ of the
stream, on the ~ of 70, destruction, betraying his secret*; grass edging of flower-bed
etc.; wand, rod, carried before bishop,
dean, etc., as emblem of office; kinds of
shaft or spindle in various mechanisms;
(archit.) shaft of column, edge of tiles
projecting over gable, ~-*board*, = BARGE-
-*board*; (hist.) area of jurisdiction of
Marshalsea. [ME, f. OF, f. L *virga*
rod]

vĕrge[2], v.i. Incline downwards or in
specified direction (*the now verging sun*;
~ *towards old age, to a close*); ~ *on*, border
on, approach closely, as *path ~s on the
edge of a precipice, a solemnity verging on
the tragic*. [f. L *vergere* bend, incline]

vĕr′ger, n. Official in a church who shows
persons to their seats etc.; ‖ officer
who bears staff before bishop, (vice-)
chancellor of university, etc. Hence
~SHIP n. [15th c., prob. f. AF *verger* f.
verge VERGE[1], see -ER[2]; cf. med. L *virgarius*
rod-bearer]

vĕrid′ic|al, a. Truthful (usu. iron.);
(psych., spirit.; of visions etc.) coinciding
with realities. Hence or cogn. ~ALLY[3]
adv.,~OUS a. [f. L *veridicus* (*verus* true +
dicere say)+-AL]

vĕ′ri|fȳ, v.t. Establish the truth of, exam-
ine for this purpose, as *must ~fy the statement,· his figures, am now ~fying the
items, ~fy your references*; (of event,
action, etc.) bear out, make good, fulfil,
(prediction, promise); (law) append
affidavit to (pleadings), support (statement) by proofs. Hence or cogn. ~fīa-
BIL′ITY, ~FICA′TION, ~fiER[1], nn., ~fīABLE
a. [ME, f. OF *verifier* f. med. L *veri-
ficare* (*verus* true, see -FY)]

vĕ′rily, adv. (arch.). Really, truly, in
very truth (freq. ~ ~). [ME, f. VERY[1]
+-LY[2]]

vĕrisimil′itūde, n. Air of being true,
semblance of actuality, (*the ~ of the tale*;
~ *is not proof*); a thing that seems true.
So **vĕrisim′ilāR[1]** a. [f. obs. F, or L
verisimilitudo f. *verisimilis* probable (*veri*
gen. of *verus* true + *similis* like), see
-TUDE]

vĕ′ritab|le, a. Real, rightly so called, as
a ~le boon. Hence ~LY[2] adv. [OF (as
VERITY, see -ABLE)]

vĕ′ritäs, n. (Also *bureau véritas*) French
ship register like Lloyd's. [F (*vé-*), f. L as
foll.]

vĕ′rit|ȳ, n. Truth (*of* statement etc.); true
statement; really existent thing, as *these
things, alas! are ~ics*; *of a ~y* (arch.), in

truth, really. [ME, f. OF *verite* f. L
veritalem (*verus* true, see -TY)]

vĕr′juic|e (-ōos), n. Acid liquor got from
crab-apples, sour grapes, etc., & used in
cooking. Hence ~ED[2] (-st) a. [ME, f. OF
vertjus (*vert*, see VERDURE, +*jus* JUICE)]

vĕrm′eil (-mil), n. Silver gilt; varnish
used to give lustre to gilding; orange-red
garnet; (poet.) vermilion. [ME, f. OF, see
VERMILION]

vĕrm′|i-, comb. form of L *vermis* worm,
as: ~*icide*, drug that kills worms, so
~*icīd′al* a.; ~*iform*, worm-shaped (~*iform*
APPENDIX), structurally allied to worms;
~*ifuge*, drug that expels intestinal worms,
so ~*if′ugal* a.; ~*igrade*, moving like worm,
wriggling along; ~*iv′orous*, feeding on
worms.

vĕrm′ian, a. Of worms, wormlike. [f. L
vermis worm+-AN]

vĕrmicĕll′i, n. Paste of same materials as
macaroni made in slender threads. [It.,
pl. of *vermicello* dim. f. L *vermis* worm]

vermic′ūlar, a. Like a worm in form or
movements, as~(=VERMIform)*appendix*;
of worm-eaten appearance; marked
with close wavy lines. [f. med. L *vermi-
cularis* (L *vermiculus* dim. of *vermis* worm,
see -AR[1])]

vermic′ūlate, a. = prec. (rare, usu. fig.).
[f. L *vermiculari* be full of worms (prec.),
-ATE[2,3]]

vermiculā′tion, n. Being eaten or infested by or converted into worms;
vermicular marking; worm-eaten state.
[f. L *vermiculatio* (prec., -ATION)]

vermic′ūlite, n. (min.). Any of a number
of hydrous silicates, chiefly resulting from
alterations of mica. [as VERMICULATE,
-ITE[1] (2)]

vermil′ion (-yon), n., a., & v.t. 1. Cinnabar; brilliant red pigment made by
grinding this or artificially; (of) this
colour. 2. v.t. Colour (as) with ~. [ME,
f. OF *verm*(e)*illon* (*vermeil* f. L *vermiculus*
little worm (LL also ~ scarlet) dim. of
vermis worm, see -OON)]

vĕrm′in, n. (usu. treated as pl.). Mammals & birds injurious to game, crops,
etc., e.g. foxes, weasels, rats, mice, moles,
owls, etc.; noxious insects, e.g. fleas,
bugs, lice; parasitic worms or insects;
(fig.) vile persons, as *the ~ that infest race-
-courses*. So ~OUS a.,~OUSLY[2] adv. [ME,
f. OF *vermin, -ine* f. Rom. **verminum,
-ina* f. L *vermis* worm]

vĕrm′in|āte v.i. Breed vermin, become
infested with parasites. So ~A′TION n.
[f. L *verminare* (*vermis* worm), see -ATE[3]]

vĕrm′(o)uth (-ooth; *or* vărm′ŏŏt), n.
White wine flavoured with wormwood;
French, Italian, ~, dry, sweet, kind. [f.
F *vermout* f. G *wermuth* wormwood]

vernăc′ūlar, a. & n. 1. (Of language,
idiom, word) of one's native country,
native, indigenous, not of foreign origin
or of learned formation. 2. n. The
language or dialect of the country, as

Latin gave place to the ~. Hence ~ISM(4), ~ITY (-á'r-), ~ĪZA'TION, nn., ~IZE(3) v.t, ~LY² adv. [f. L *vernaculus* native (*verna* home-born slave, see -CULE)+-AR¹]

vẽrn'al, a. Of, appearing or occurring or done in, spring, as ~ *breezes, flowers,* EQUINOX, *migration,* ~ (malarial) *fever;* ~ *grass,* sweet-scented grass grown among hay. Hence ~LY² adv. [f. L *vernalis* (*vernus* f. *ver* spring, see -AL)]

vernā'tion, n. (bot.). Arrangement of leaves (cf. AESTIVATION) within leaf-bud. [f. L *vernare* bloom (as prec., see -ATION)]

Verner's law. See LAW¹.

vẽrn'ier, n. Small movable scale for obtaining fractional parts of the subdivisions on fixed scale of barometer, sextant, etc. [F, f. P. *V*~, inventor, d. 1637]

vẽ'ronal, n. Sedative drug. [P]

Vĕronēse' (-z), a., & n. (pl. the same). (Inhabitant) of Verona. [-ESE]

verŏn'ica, n. 1. Kinds of herb or shrub with blue, purple, pink or white flowers. 2. Cloth with respresentation of Christ's face, esp. one miraculously so impressed after being used by St V~ to wipe sweat from Christ's face. [*V*~, woman's name]

vẽrruc'|a (-rōō-), n. (path., zool., bot. ; pl. ~*ae* pr. -sē). Wart, wartlike elevation. Hence or cogn. ~ĪFORM (-rōō-), vẽ'rru-COSE¹ (-rōō-), vẽ'rrucOUS (-rōō-), ~ūlOSE¹ (-rōō-), aa. [L]

vẽrs'ant, n. Extent of land sloping in one direction, general slope of land. [F, f. L *versare* frequent. of *vertere vers-* turn]

vẽrs'atile, a. Turning readily from one subject or occupation to another, capable of dealing with many subjects, as ~ *author, genius, disposition, mind;* capable of being moved or turned as on hinge, as ~ *spindle;* (bot., zool.) moving freely about or up & down on a support, as ~ *anther, head, antennae;* changeable, inconstant. Hence or cogn. ~LY² adv., vẽrsatil'ITY n. [F, or f. L *versatilis* (as prec., see -ATILE)]

vers de société (vãr de sosiātá'), n. SOCIETY verse. [F]

vẽrse, n., & v.t. & i. 1. Metrical line containing definite number of feet, as *quoted some* ~s *of the Iliad, had a good* ~ *here & there,* CAP² ~s; group of definite number of ~s, stanza; metrical composition in general, particular type of this, as *wrote pages of* ~, *expressed in indifferent* ~, *what is not prose is* ~, *a prize for Latin* ~, BLANK¹, SOCIETY, *elegiac, iambic, trochaic,* etc., ~; each of the short divisions of chapter in Bible (CHAPTER *&* ~); short sentence as part of liturgy; solo part of anthem etc.; ~-*monger(ing),* maker, making, of bad ~s. Hence ~'LET (-sl-) n. 2. vb. Express in ~, make ~s. [OE *fers* (OHG, ON *vers*) f. L *versus* (*vertere vers-* turn); in ME reinforced by AF, OF *vers*]

vẽrsed (-st), a. Experienced, skilled, proficient, (*in* subject, occupation, etc.); reversed (now only in ~ SINE¹). [f. L

versatus p.p. of *versari* be engaged in, see VERSANT; trig. sense f. L *versus* p.p. as prec.]

vẽrs'ĕt, n. (mus.). Short prelude or interlude for organ. [F, dim. of *vers* VERSE]

vẽrs'icle, n. Short verse, esp. of each series of short verses in liturgy said or sung alternately by minister & people. [ME, f. OF *versicule* or L *versiculus* (as VERSE, see -CULE)]

vẽrs'ícolour(ed) (-ŭlerd), aa. Variegated; changing from one colour to another in different lights. [f. L *versicolor* (*vertere vers-* turn+*color* COLOUR)]

versic'ular, a. ~ *division* (into verses). [as VERSICLE+-ULAR]

vẽrs'i|fȳ, v.t. & i. Turn (prose) into verse; express in verse; make verses. Hence or cogn. ~FICA'TION, ~fiER¹, nn. [ME, f. OF *versifier* f. L *versificare* (as VERSE, see -FY)]

vẽr'sion (-shn), n. 1. Book etc. translated into another language, as *Authorized, Revised, V*~ (of the Bible, made 1604–11, 1870–84; abbr. *A.V., R.V.*). 2. Piece of translation, esp. into foreign language, as school exercise. 3. Account of a matter from particular person's point of view, as *now let me have your own* ~ *of the affair.* 4. Turning of child awkwardly placed for delivery so that head or feet may be first presented. Hence ~AL (-sho-) a. [F, or f. med. L *versio* (L *vertere vers-* turn, see -ION]

vers libre (vãrlĕb're), n. Versification or verses in which different metres are mingled, or prosodical restrictions disregarded, or variable rhythm substituted for definite metre. Hence **versli'brist** (vãrlĕ-) n., writer of ~. [F]

vẽrs'ō, n. (pl. ~s). Any left-hand page of book (cf. RECTO); reverse of coin. [L, abl. p.p. as VERSE]

verst, n. Russian measure of length, 3,500 feet. [f. Russ. *verstá*).

vẽrs'us, prep. (abbr. *v.*). Against, as (law) *Jones v. Smith,* (crick. etc.) *Surrey v. Kent.* [L, = towards, against]

vẽrt¹, n. (Law, hist.) all that bears green leaves in forest, right to cut this; (her.) the tincture green. [ME, f. OF, f. L *viridis* green]

‖ **vẽrt²,** n., & v.i. (colloq.). Convert or pervert; (vb) leave one Church for another. [short for CONVERT n., PERVERT n.]

vẽrt'ĕbr|a, n. (pl. ~*ae*). Each segment of backbone (*false* ~*a,* fixed, as os sacrum & coccyx in man, *true* ~*a,* movable; neither expression now used in human anat.). Hence ~AL a., ~àLY² adv., ~O- comb. form. [L (*vertere* turn)]

vẽrt'ĕbr|ate, a. & n. (Animal) having a spinal column or a notochord, esp. (member) of the division *Vertebrāt'a,* including mammals, birds, reptiles, amphibians, & fishes. Hence ~ātĕd [-ATE²] a. [f. L *vertebratus* jointed (as prec., see -ATE²)]

vértebra'tion, n. Formation of, division into, vertebrae or similar segments. [·ATION]

vert'ex, n. (pl. usu. *-ices*). Highest point, top, apex; (anat.) crown of head; (geom.) each angular point of triangle, polygon, etc., ~ *of an angle,* meeting-point of lines that form it. [L, gen. *-icis,* = whirlpool, head, vertex, (*vertere* turn)]

vert'ical, a. & n. 1. Of, at, the vertex or highest point; at the zenith; perpendicular to plane of horizon; (anat.) of the crown of the head; ~ *angles,* each pair of opposite angles made by two intersecting lines; ~ (= AZIMUTH-) *circle;* ~ *fins* (dorsal, anal, & caudal); ~ *plane,* plane perpendicular to the horizon. Hence~ITY (-ǎl⁴-), ~LY² adv. 2. n., ~ line, plane, or circle; *out of the* ~, not ~. [F, or f. LL *verticalis* (prec., see ·AL)]

vert'icil, n. (bot., zool.). Whorl, set of parts radiating from axis. Hence **verti⁴ ciILATE²** a., **verti'cillately²** adv. [f. L *verticillus* whorl of spindle, dim. of VERTEX]

vert'igo (or **verti⁴,** -tē²), n. (pl. ~*s*). Giddiness, dizziness, as *subjective, objective,* ~ (in which patient feels as if he, as if surrounding objects, were turning round), *essential* ~ (without apparent cause). Hence **verti'ginous** a., **verti'ginously²** adv., **verti'ginousness** n. [L, gen. *-ginis,* = whirling (*vertere* turn)]

vertu. See VIRTU.

vérv'ain, n. Kinds of weedy plant with small blue, white, or purple flowers, formerly believed to have various virtues & used as amulet etc. [ME, f. OF *verveine* f. L VERBENA]

verve (vārv), n. Enthusiasm, energy, vigour, in artistic or literary work. [F]

vérv'ét, n. A small S.-Afr. monkey freq. carried by organ-grinders. [F]

ve'rý¹, a. & adv. 1. Real, true, genuine, that is such in the truest or fullest sense, as ~ *God or* ~ *God, has shown himself a* ~ *knave, the veriest simpleton knows that, must consent from* ~ *shame,* (somewhat arch., exc. in foll. uses); (with *the, this, that,* or possessive adj., emphasizing identity, coincidence, significance, or extreme degree) *this is the* ~ *spot I found it on, speaking in this* ~ *room, the* ~ *fact of his presence is enough, you are the* ~ *man I am looking for, a needle is the* ~ *thing (for our purpose), come here this* ~ *minute, grieves me to the* ~ *heart, the* ~ *stones cry out, his* ~ *servants bully him, drank it to the* ~ *dregs;* (with *a*) *a* ~ *little more will do, give me only a* ~ *little.* 2. adv. (Perh. orig. adj., with superl. adj. often abs., or with *my* etc. *own*) in the fullest sense, as *drank it to the* ~ *last drop, the* ~ *last thing I expected, did the* ~ *best I could, did my* ~ *utmost, may keep it for your* ~ *own;* (used with advv. & the positive of non-verbal adjj.; with partt. established as independent adjj., as *a* ~ *dazzling effect,*

effect was ~ *dazzling, a* ~ *trying time;* with p.pp. in attrib. use applied to what is not the real object of the vbl action, as *wore a* ~ *pained, pleased, puzzled, troubled, vexed, annoyed, surprised,* etc., *expression,* but not *his expression was* ~ *pained* etc.; & colloq. with the same p.pp. in pred. use applied to the true object & fulfilling purely vbl function, as *I was* ~ *pleased, surprised, annoyed,* etc.; not otherwise used with vbs) in a high degree, as *that is* ~ *easily done,* ~ *often fails,* ~ *easy, not* ~ *much use, find* ~ *few instances, gives* ~ *little trouble,* but not ~ *better* etc. 3. ~ *well* (or, more respectfully, ~ *good*), formula of consent or approval. [ME, f. OF *verai,* f. Gallo-Rom. **veraius,* f. L *verus* true]

Ve'rý², n. (attrib.). ~ *light* (projected from ~ *pistol* for signalling or temporarily illuminating part of battlefield etc.). [S. W. ~, inventor (1877)]

vesic'a, n. (anat., bot.). 1. Bladder, cyst, sac, esp. (whence **vēs'icocele, vésicōt⁴ omy,** nn.) urinary bladder. 2. ~ (*piscis* or *piscium* = fish's or fishes'), the pointed oval (◊) used as an aureole in medieval sculpture & painting. Hence **vēs'icaL** a., **vēs'ico-** comb. form. [L]

vēs'ic|āte, v.t. Raise blisters on. Hence ~ANT(2), ~ātORY, aa. & nn., ~A'TION n. [f. mod. L *vesicare* (prec., -ATE³)]

vēs'icle, n. (anat., bot., geol.). Small bladder, cell, bubble, or hollow structure. Hence **vesic'ulaR¹, vesic'ulate²,** **vēsi⁴ culif'erous, vesic'uliform, vesic'ulose¹, vesic'ulous,** aa., **vesicūlā'tion** n., **vēsic⁴ ūlo-** comb. form. [f. F *vésicule,* or L *vesicula* dim. of VESICA]

vēs'per, n. (V~). Venus as evening-star. (poet.) evening; (pl.) sixth of the seven canonical hours of the breviary, EVEN¹- song; ~(-*bell*), bell that calls to ~s; *Sicilian V~s,* massacre of French residents in Sicily in 1282, begun at stroke of ~-bell. [(1) f. L *vesper;* (2) f. F *vespres* (mod. *vêpres*)]

vēs'pertine, a. Of, done in, the evening; (bot., of flowers) opening, (zool.) flying, in the evening; (astron.) descending towards horizon at sunset. [f. L *vespertinus* (VESPER)]

vēs'piary, n. Nest of wasps. [irreg. f. L *vespa* wasp, after *apiary*]

vēs'pine, a. Of wasps. So **vēs'piform** a. [f. L *vespa* wasp +-INE¹]

vēss'el, n. 1. Hollow receptacle esp. for liquid, e.g. cask, cup, pot, bottle, dish. 2. Ship, boat, esp. large one. 3. (Anat.) duct, canal, holding or conveying blood or other fluid, esp. *blood*~; (bot.) chain of cells that have lost intervening partitions, duct. 4. (bibl. or allus. esp. joc.). Person viewed as recipient or exponent, as *chosen* ~ (*Acts* ix. 15), *weaker* ~, woman (1 *Pet.* iii. 7), ~*s of wrath* (*Rom.* ix. 22). Hence ~FUL n. [ME, f. OF *vessel, -elle,* f. LL *vascellum,* (pl.) *-ella,* dim. of VAS]

vĕst¹, n. (Esp. U.S.) waistcoat; (also *under~*)‖knitted or woven undergarment; piece, usu. V-shaped, on front of body of woman's gown; (arch.) clothing, dress; *~-pocket*, (attrib. of small articles, esp. hand-cameras) of a size suitable for the pocket (as a size of plate or film, 6 × 4·5 cm.). Hence *~*'ING¹(3) n. [f. F f. It. *veste* f. L *vestis* garment]

vĕst², v.t. & i. Furnish (person *with* authority, powers, property, etc.); *~* (property, power) *in* (person), confer formally on him an immediate fixed right of present or future possession of it (*~ed rights, interests, estate,* etc., possession of which is determinately fixed in a person & is subject to no contingency); (of property, right, etc.) *~ in* (person), come to him; (poet.) clothe. [ME, f. OF *vestir* f. L *vestire* *-it-* clothe (as prec.)]

vĕs'ta, n. (Rom. myth., *V~*) goddess of the hearth; (astron., *V~*) an asteroid; short wooden or (*wax ~*) wax match. [L, = Gk *Hestia*]

vĕs'tal, a. & n. Of the goddess Vesta or the *~* virgins; *~* (*virgin*), virgin consecrated to Vesta, vowed to chastity, & charged with care of sacred fire perpetually burning on her altar, hence, woman of spotless chastity, esp. one who devotes her life to religion, nun. [ME, f. L *Vestalis* a. & n. (as prec., see *-AL*)]

vĕs'tiarȳ, n. (rare or obs.), & a. A vestry, robing-room, or cloakroom; (adj.) relating to clothes or dress. [ME, f. OF *vestiarie,* see VESTRY]

vĕs'tĭbŭl|e, n. Ante-chamber, hall, lobby, next to outer door of house & from which doors open into various rooms; porch of church etc.; **~e* (= CORRIDOR) *train*; (anat.) chamber or channel communicating with others, esp. *~e of the ear,* central cavity of labyrinth of internal ear. Hence **vĕstĭb'ūlAR¹, vĕstĭb'ūlATE²**(anat.),*~*ED² (-ld), aa. [F, or f. L *vestibulum*]

vĕs'tĭge, n. Footprint (now only fig.), track, trace, evidence, sign, as *~s of an earlier civilization, found no ~s of his presence*; (loosely, w. neg.) atom, particle, as *without a ~ of clothing, has not a ~ of evidence for this assertion*; (biol.) part, organ, now degenerate & of little or no utility but ancestrally well developed. Hence **vĕstĭ'gĭAL** (esp. biol.), **vĕstĭ'gĭARY¹**, aa. [F, f. L *vestigium* footstep]

vĕs'tĭture, n. (zool.). Hair, scales, etc., covering a surface. [f. med. L *vestitura* f. L as VEST², -URE]

vĕst'ment, n. Garment, esp. official or state robe; any of the official garments of clergy, choristers, etc., worn during divine service, esp. chasuble; altar-cloth. [ME, f. OF *vestement* f. L *vestimentum* (as VEST², see -MENT)]

vĕs'trȳ, n. Room, building, attached to church & in which vestments are kept & put on; chapel attached to non-liturgical church & used for prayer meetings etc.; ‖(also *common, general, ordinary, ~*) ratepayers of a parish, (also *select ~*) representatives of these, assembled for dispatch of parochial business; ‖(room used for) meeting of either of these bodies; ‖*~-clerk,* officer chosen by *~* to keep parish accounts etc.; *~man,* member of a *~*. [ME, f. AF **vest(e)rie* (f. VEST² + -ERY), repl. OF *vestiarie, vestiaire,* f. L *vestiarium* (VEST¹, -ARIUM)]

‖**vĕs'trȳdom**, n. (Corrupt, inefficient) government by vestry. [-DOM]

vĕs'ture, n., & v.t. (poet., rhet.). **1.** Garments, dress, clothes; covering. **2.** v.t. Clothe. [ME, f. OF f. med. L *vest(it)ura,* as VEST²; see -URE]

‖**vĕs'turer** (-cher-), n. Church official in charge of vestments; sub-treasurer of cathedral or church. [f. prec. + -ER¹]

vĕsūv'ian, a. & n. **1.** (*V~*). Of Vesuvius; volcanic. **2.** n. (Also *~*ITE¹ n.) brown or green mineral first found on Vesuvius. [f. L *Vesuvius* + -AN]

vĕt, n., & v.t. (colloq.; -tt-). **1.** = VETERINARY. **2.** v.t. Examine & pass fit, treat, (beast); (fig.) check & correct. [abbr.]

vĕtch, n. Kinds of plant of pea family largely used, wild or cultivated, for forage, esp. *common~,* tare; *kidney-~,* perennial herb with red or yellow flowers. Hence *~*'Y² a. [ME, f. ONF *veche* f. L *vicia*]

vĕtch'ling, n. Plant allied to vetch. [-LING¹]

vĕt'eran, n. & a. Person who has grown old in or had long experience of (esp. military) service or occupation, as *Wellington's ~s, a ~ golfer*; **ex-service man*; (adj.) of a *~*, composed of *~s,* as *~ service, troops.* Hence *~*IZE(3) v.t. [F, or f. L *veteranus* a. & n. (*vetus -eris* old, see -AN)]

vĕt'erinarȳ, a. & n. **1.** Of, for, (the treatment of) diseases & injuries of domestic animals, as *~ surgeon, science, college.* **2.** n. (abbr. *vet*). A *~* surgeon; also **vĕterinar'iAN** n. [f. L *veterinarius* f. *veterinae* cattle]

vĕt'ō, n. (pl. *~es*), & v.t. **1.** Constitutional right of sovereign, president, governor, upper house of legislature, etc., to reject a legislative enactment (*suspensory ~,* suspending but not necessarily preventing completion of measure), whence *~*IST(2) n.; (official message conveying) such rejection; prohibition, as *interposed his ~, put a* or *his ~ on the proposal.* **2.** v.t. Exercise *~* against (bill etc.), forbid authoritatively. [L, = I forbid, w. ref. to its use by tribune of the people in nullifying measures]

vĕx, v.t. Anger by slight or petty annoyance, irritate, as *this would ~ a saint, how ~ing!,* whence*~*'ÉDLY², *~*'ingLY², advv.; (arch.) grieve, afflict; (poet., rhet.) put (sea etc.) into state of commotion; *a ~ed* (much discussed) *question.* [ME, f. OF *vexer* f. L *vexare*]

vĕxā'tion, n. Vexing, being vexed; harassing by means of malicious or trivial litigation; state of irritation or distress, as *conceive my ~, in ~ of spirit*; annoying or distressing thing, as *subjected to many ~s.* Hence **věxā′tious** (-shus) a., **věxā′tious-**LY² adv., **věxā′tious**NESS n. [ME, f. OF. or f. L *vexatio*]

věxill′um, n. (pl. *-illa*). (Rom. ant.) military standard esp. of maniple, body of troops under this; (bot., also **věx′il** n.) large upper petal of papilionaceous flower; web of a feather, whence **věx′il**-IATE² a.; (eccl.) flag on or wound round bishop's staff, processional banner or cross. Hence or cogn. **věx′il**lAR(Y)¹ aa. [L (*vehere vect-* carry)]

vī′a, n. & prep. **1.** *Via Lăc′těa,* Milky Way; ~ *měd′ĭa,* mean between extremes (esp. of Anglican church as placed between Romanism & extreme Protestantism). **2.** prep. (Also *vid*) by way of, through, as *from Exeter to York ~ London* (also joc. of connected subjects etc.). [L, =way, road]

vī′able, a. (Of foetus or new-born child) capable of maintaining life; (of plant, animal, etc.) able to live or exist in particular climate etc., (of seed) able to germinate. So **vīabil′ity** n. [F (*vie* life f. L *vita,* see -ABLE)]

vī′aduct, n. Long bridgelike structure, esp. series of arches, for carrying road or railway over valley or dip in ground; such road or railway. [f. L *via* way, after AQUEDUCT]

vī′al, n. Small (usu. cylindrical glass) vessel for holding liquid medicines etc.; LEYDEN ~ (= *jar*); *pour out ~s of wrath,* take vengeance (*Rev.* xv. 7), (colloq.) give vent to anger. Hence ~FUL n. [ME, var. of *fiol, fiall,* etc., see PHIAL]

vīăm′eter, n. = HODOMETER. [L *via* way +-METER]

vī′and, n. (usu. in pl.). Article(s) of food, victual(s). [ME, f. OF *viande* food f. Rom. **vivanda* for L *vivenda,* neut. pl. gerundive of L *vivere* live]

vīăt′icum, n. (Rom. ant.) supplies or sum of money allowed to officer for journey on State service; provisions for journey; Eucharist as given to dying person; portable altar. [L (*via* way, see -ATIC); cf. VOYAGE]

vībrăc′ūlum, n. (pl. *~a*). Filamentous appendage of some polyzoa serving to bring food within reach by lashing movements. Hence ~AR¹ a. [mod. L as foll., see -CULE]

vīb′rant, a. Vibrating; thrilling *with* something; (of sound) resonant. [f. L *vibrare* (foll.), -ANT]

vībrāte′, v.i. & t. Move to & fro like pendulum, oscillate; (of sound) throb (on ear, in memory, etc.); (phys.) move unceasingly to & fro, esp. rapidly; thrill, quiver, (*with* passion etc.); cause to oscillate; (of pendulum) measure (seconds etc.) by vibrating. Hence **vīb′rative,** **vīb′ratory** aa. [f. L *vibrare* shake, swing, see -ATE²]

vīb′ratile, a. Capable of vibrating. Hence **vībratil′ity** n. [-ILE]

vībrā′tion, n. Vibrating, oscillation; (phys.) rapid motion to & fro esp. of the parts of a fluid or an elastic solid whose equilibrium has been disturbed (*amplitude of ~,* maximum departure of vibrating body from position of rest; *forced, free, ~,* whose period is, is not, modified by an outside force). Hence ~AL a., **vībrāt′iuncle** n. dim. [f. L *vibratio* (as VIBRATE, see -ATION)]

vībra′tō (vēbrah-), n. Effect like TREMOLO in singing & playing stringed instruments. [It.]

vībrāt′or, n. Person, thing, that vibrates, esp. (electr., teleg.) kinds of vibrating reed, (mus.) reed in reed-organ, (print.) inking-roller with vibrating & rotary movements, (med.) electric or other instrument used in massage. [-OR]

vībriss′ae, n. pl. Stiff coarse hair about mouth of most mammals & in nostrils of man; bristle-like feathers about mouth of some birds. [L (as VIBRATE)]

vīb′roscōpe, n. Instrument for observing vibrations. [-SCOPE]

vībūrn′um, n. Kinds of shrub of honeysuckle family. [L]

vic′ar, n. ‖ Incumbent of a parish the tithes of which belong to chapter or religious house or layman (cf. RECTOR); ~ *of Bray,* systematic turncoat, w. ref. to 17th-c. song; *lay ~,* cathedral officer singing some parts of service; ‖ ~ *choral,* clerical or lay assistant in some (esp. musical) parts of cathedral service; ‖ ~ *general,* (Ch. of Eng.) official assisting (arch)bishop in ecclesiastical causes etc. (usu. his chancellor), (R.-C. Ch.) bishop's assistant in matters of jurisdiction etc.; (R.-C. Ch.) *cardinal ~,* Pope's delegate acting as bishop of diocese of Rome, ~ *apostolic,* missionary or titular bishop (whence **vīcar′iate¹**(1) n.), ~ *fō′rane,* dignitary appointed by bishop to exercise limited local jurisdiction, *V~ of (Jesus) Christ,* Pope. Hence ~SHIP n. [ME, f. AF *viker(e),* OF *vicaire* f. L *vicarius* substitute f. *vicis* (VICE⁴, -ARY¹)]

vic′arage, n. Benefice, residence, of vicar. [-AGE]

vīcar′ial, a. Of, serving as, a vicar. [-AL]

vīcar′ious, a. Deputed, delegated, as ~ *authority*; acting, done, for another, as ~ *work, suffering,* ~ *sacrifice* (of Christ in place of sinner). Hence ~LY² adv., ~NESS n. [f. L as VICARIUS +-OUS]

vīce¹, n. Evil esp. grossly immoral habit or conduct, (particular form of) depravity, serious fault, as *has the ~ of gluttony, drunkenness is not among his~s, ~is duly punished & virtue rewarded in fifth act, has no redeeming ~* (to relieve overpowering rectitude); defect, blemish, (of character, literary style, etc.); fault, bad trick, in horse etc., as *has no ~s, is free from ~, has one ~*; (now rare) morbid state of physical system, as *inherited ~s of consti-tution*; (*V~*) buffoon in a MORALITY. [ME, f. OF, f. L *vitium*]

vice², ***vise**, n., & *v.t.* **1.** Instrument with two jaws between which thing may be gripped usu. by operation of screw so as to leave the hands free for working upon it, as *bench ~* (attached to carpenter's or machinist's bench), *instantaneous-grip ~*, *grips like a ~*. **2.** *v.t.* Secure (material to be worked upon, or fig.) in *~*. [ME, = winding-stair, screw, f. OF *vis* f. L *vitis* vine]

vice³, n. (colloq.). ■ VICE-*president* etc.

vi′cé, prep. In the place of, as *gazetted as captain ~ Captain Jones promoted*. [L, abl. of *vix vicis* change]

vice-, pref. (= prec.) forming nn. w. sense 'person acting or qualified to act in place of or next in rank to', w. their derivv., as: *~-ad′miral*, ADMIRAL of third grade; *~-ad′miralty*, office of *~-admiral* ‖ (*~-admiralty courts*, tribunals with admiralty jurisdiction in British colonial possessions); *~-a′gent*; *~-chair′man(ship)*; ‖ *~-cham′berlain* (esp. deputy of lord chamberlain); *~-chan′cellor*, (univ.) deputy chancellor discharging most administrative duties, (law, formerly) judge in chancery division of High Court of Justice, (R.-C. Ch.) cardinal at head of the branch of chancery in charge of bulls etc.; *~-chan′cellorship*; *~-con′sul(ship)*; *~-dean′*, subdean; *~-go′vernor*; *~-king′*, = VICEROY; *~-pres′ident(ship)*, *~-pres′i-dency*; *~-prin′cipal*; *~-queen′* (rare), woman acting as viceroy, viceroy's wife; *~-re′gent*; *~-reine* (-srān), viceroy's wife; *~-she′riff*; *~-trea′surer(ship)*; *~-war′den*.

vicegē′ren|t (-sj-; *also* -ēī²-), a. & n. (Person) exercising delegated power, deputy, as *regard the Pope as God's V~t*. Hence *~cy* n. [f. med. L *vicegerent-* nom. *-ens* (prec. + L *gerere* carry on, see -ENT)]

vicenn′ial, a. Lasting, happening every, twenty years. [f. LL *vicennium* period of 20 years (*viginti* 20 + *annus* year) + -AL]

vice′roy (-sr-), n. Ruler exercising royal authority in colony, province, etc., as (hist.) *V~ of India*. Hence *viceregˈAL*, *viceroyAL*, aa., *viceroy′alTY*, *~SHIP*, nn., (-sr-). [16th c., f. older F (VICE- + *roy* king f. L *regem* nom. *rex*)]

vi′cé vers′a, adv. or ellipt. sent. (The same is true, on the corresponding sup-position, etc.) with the order of terms changed, the other way round, as *the man blames his wife & ~* (she him), *cot stole the dog's dinner & ~* (he hers), *calls black white & ~* (white black). [L, (VICE⁴, *versa* abl. fem. p.p. of *vertere* turn)]

Vichy (water) (vē′shē), n. A mineral water. [*Vichy* in France]

vi′cinage, n. Neighbourhood, surround-ing district; relation of neighbours. [ME, f. OF *visenage* w. assim. to the L source *vicinus* f. *vicus* (WICK²)]

vicin′itÿ, n. Surrounding district; near-ness in place (*to*); close relationship (*to*). [f. L *vicinitas* (as prec., see -TY)]

vi′cious (-shus), a. Of the nature of vice, morally evil or injurious, as *~ tendencies, courses, life*; addicted to vice, as *~ com-panions*; (of horse etc.) having vices; (of language, reasoning, etc.) incorrect, faulty, unsound, corrupt, as *a ~ style, a notoriously ~ manuscript*, *~ CIRCLE¹*; *~ union* (surg.), faulty joining of frac-tured ends of bone, resulting deformity; bad-tempered, spiteful, as *~ dog, mood, remarks*. Hence *~LY²* adv., *~NESS* n. [ME, f. OF or f. L *vitiosus* (as VICE¹, see -OUS)]

viciss′itūde, n. Change of circumstances esp. of fortune, as *a life marked by ~s*. (arch., poet.) regular change, alterna-tion. Hence vicissitūd′inous a. [F, or f. L *vicissitudo -dinis* (as VICE⁴, see -TUDE)]

vic′tim, n. Living being sacrificed to a deity or in performance of religious rite; person, thing, injured or destroyed in pursuit of an object, in gratification of a passion etc., or as result of event or cir-cumstance, as *the ~s of his relentless am-bition, fell a ~ to his own avarice, the ~s of disease, of a railway accident*; prey, dupe, as *held the ~ in his talons, the numerous ~s of the confidence trick*. [f. L *victima*]

vic′timiz|e, *-is|e* (-īz), *v.t.* Make (person etc.) the victim of a swindle etc. or of one's ambition, loquacity, etc.; make (striker etc.) suffer by dismissal or other excep-tional treatment. Hence *~A′TION* n. [-IZE]

vic′tor, n. (rhet.). Conqueror in battle or contest (also attrib., as *~ troops, sword*). Hence vic′trESS¹ n. [ME, f. AF *victo(u)r* or L *victor* (*vincere vict-* conquer, -OR)]

victōr′ia, n. **1.** Low light four-wheeled carriage with seat for two & raised driver's seat & with falling top. **2.** Kinds of gigantic water-lily. **3.** Kinds of domestic pigeon. **4.** *V~ Cross* (abbr. *V.C.*), decora-tion awarded to members of the armed services for conspicuous act of bravery founded by Queen V~ in 1856. [L, = victory (as prec., see -Y¹)]

Victōr′ian, a. & n. Of, (person esp. author) living in, the reign of Queen Victoria (1837–1901); *~ Order* (founded by Queen Victoria in 1896 & conferred usu. for great service rendered to sovereign). [-AN]

victōr′ious, a. Conquering, triumphant; marked by victory (*~ day* etc.). Hence *~LY²* adv., *~NESS* n. [ME, f. AF f. L *victoriosus* (VICTORIA, -OUS)]

vic′tory, n. Defeat of enemy in battle or opponent in contest, as *battle ended in a decisive ~, fought hard for ~, hero of many victories*, (fig.) *gained a ~ over his passions*, *Cadmean* or PYRRHIC² *~*, MORAL *~*; (*V~*), (statue of) goddess of *~ (winged etc. V~*). [ME, f. AF *victorie*, ■ OF *victoire*, f. L VICTORIA, see -Y¹]

victual (vĭ′tl), n., & *v.t.* & *i.* (-ll-). **1.** (Usu.

pl.) food, provisions. **2. vb.** Supply with ~s, obtain stores, eat ~s. Hence ~LESS a. [ME, f. OF *vitaile*, *-aille*, f. LL *victualia*, neut. pl. of L *victualis* f. *victus* food, see -AL; vb f. OF *vitailler*]

victualler (vit'ler), n. One who furnishes victuals, || esp. *licensed* ~, innkeeper licensed to sell spirits etc.; ship employed to carry stores for other ships. [ME, f. OF *vitaill(i)er* (prec., -OR)]

victualling (vit'ling), n. In vbl senses; ||~-*bill*, custom-house warrant for shipment of bonded stores; ||~-*note* (nav.), order authorizing ship's steward to victual a seaman; ||~-*office* (for supplying provisions to navy); ||~-*yard* (adjoining dockyard, for naval stores). [-ING[1]]

vicu'gna, **-u'ña**, (-kōonya), n. S.-Amer. mammal allied to llama & hunted for its flesh & wool; ~ *wool* (commerc.), mixture of wool & cotton, also wool of the~. [Sp. f. Peruv.]

vid'e (or -ē), vb imperat. (abbr. *v.*). (In formal or joc. reference to passage in book etc.) see, as ~ *supra*, *infra*, see above, below, QUOD[2]~,~ *the press passim.* [L, imperat. of *vidēre*]

vidĕl'icet, adv. (abbr. viz, usu. spoken as *namely*). That is to say, in other words, namely, (usu. following words that promise or more or less clearly require explanation etc. as: *under the following conditions, viz that* etc.; *a permanent board of three, viz*, etc.; opp. to *i.e.*, which explains or elaborates a statement). [L (*vidēre licet* one may see)]

•vid'eō, a. & n. Of or used in the transmission or reception of television; (n.) television. [L, = I see]

|| **vidette**. See VEDETTE.

vid'imus, n. (pl. ~es). Inspection of accounts etc.; abstract of document etc. [L, = we have seen (*vidēre*)]

vie, v.i. (*vying*). Strive for superiority, carry on rivalry, (*with* another in quality, *in* doing). [ult. aphetic f. F *envier* increase the stake, f. L *invitare* INVITE]

Viennēse' (-z), a. & n. (pl. same). (Inhabitant) of Vienna. [-ESE]

vi et arm'is, adv. (law). With force & arms, with violence. [L]

view (vū), n., & v.t. **1.** Inspection by eye, survey, (*of* surroundings etc.); (law) inspection by jury of place, property, etc., concerned in a case, or of dead body. **2.** Power of seeing, range of vision, as *stood in full* ~ *of* (visible to) *the crowd, came in* ~ *of* (where one could be seen from or see) *the castle, passed from our* ~ (sight); what is seen, scene, prospect, as *a superb* ~; picture etc. representing this. **3.** Mental survey, as *take a general* ~ *of the subject*; manner of considering a subject, opinion, mental attitude, as *takes a different* ~, *his* ~ *is that we are the aggressors, takes a favourable* ~ *of her conduct, holds extreme* ~s (in politics etc.). **4.** Intention, design, as *will this meet your* ~*s?*, *cannot fall in with your* ~*s, cat has* ~*s upon the larder.* **5.** *In* ~ *of*, having regard to, considering, as *in* ~ *of recent developments we do not think this step advisable,* (vulg.) = *with a* ~ *to* (1); *on* ~, open to inspection; *with a* ~ *to*, (1; also *with the* ~ *of*; vulg. *with a* ~ *of*) for the purpose of, as a step towards, as *with a* ~ *to extending* (vulg. *extend*) *our trade, with a* ~ *to further hostilities*, (2) in the hope or on the chance of getting, with an eye to, as *said this with a* ~ *to the vacant secretaryship*, (3, vulg.) = *in* ~ *of*; *to the* ~, openly, in public. **6.** BIRD'S-*eye* ~; *dissolving* ~s (see DISSOLVE); *have in* ~, have as one's object, also, bear (circumstance) in mind in forming judgement etc.; POINT[1] *of* ~; *private* ~ (of picture etc. exhibition, open only to exhibitors' friends, critics, etc.); ~-*finder*, part of camera showing limits of picture; ~ *halloo'*, huntsman's shout on seeing fox break cover; ~'*point*, point of ~, standpoint. **7.** v.t. Survey with the eyes; survey mentally, form mental impression or judgment of, as *subject may be* ~ed *in different ways, does not* ~ *the matter in the right light*, he or the proposal is ~ed *unfavourably*. Hence ~ABLE (vū'abl) a., ~ER[1] (vū'er) n., (esp.) television watcher. [ME & AF *vewe*, *viewe*, OF *veue* p.p. as n. f. *veoir* see f. L *vidēre*; vb f. n.]

view'less (vū-), a. (poet., rhet.). Invisible. [-LESS]

view'y (vū-), a. (colloq.). Given to odd or fanciful views, faddy. Hence ~iNESS n. [-Y[2]]

vi'gil, n. Keeping awake during the time usually given to sleep, watchfulness, as *keep* ~; (usu. pl.) nocturnal devotions; eve of a festival, esp. eve that is a fast. [ME, f. OF *vigile* f. L *vigilia* (*vigil* awake)]

vi'gil|ance, n. Watchfulness, caution, circumspection, so~ANT a.,~antLY[2] adv.; (med.) insomnia; ~*ance committee*, self-organized body for maintenance of order etc. in imperfectly organized community. [F, or f. L *vigilantia* (*vigilare* watch, as prec., -ANCE)]

•vigilän'te, n. Member of a vigilance committee. [Sp.]

vignett|e (věnyět'), n., & v.t. **1.** (Archit.) ornament of leaves & tendrils; flourishes round capital letter in MS.; engraved illustration, esp. on title-page of book, not enclosed in definite border; photograph or portrait showing only head & shoulders with background gradually shaded off; (fig.) character sketch. **2.** v.t. Make portrait of (person) in ~e style, shade off (portrait) thus, whence~'ER[2](2), ~'IST, nn. [F, dim. as VINE]

vigoros'o, adv. (mus.). With vigour. [It.]

vig'our (-ger), n. Active physical strength or energy; flourishing physical condition; healthy growth, vitality, vital force; mental strength or activity as shown in thought or speech or literary style, forcibleness, trenchancy, animation. Hence or cogn. **vig′orous**, ~LESS (-ger-), aa., **vig′orousLY**² adv., **vig′orousNESS** n. [ME, f. OF, f. L *vigorem* (*vigēre* be lively, see -OR)]

vik′ing, n. Northern sea robber of 8th to 10th c. Hence ~ISM(2) n. [f. ON *vikingr*, perh. f. OE *wīcing* (*wīc* camp, -ING³)]

vila′yet (-lahyĕt), n. Province of Turkey. [Turk., f. Arab. *welāyet* district]

vile, a. Worthless; morally base, depraved, shameful, abject, as *the* ~ *trade of an informer*, *sycophant's* ~ *practices*, *the* ~*st of mankind*; (colloq.) abominably bad, as *a* ~ *pen*, ~ *pastry*. Hence ~′LY² adv., ~′NESS n. [ME, f. OF (*vil vile*), f. L *vilis*]

vil′i|fy, v.t. Defame, traduce, speak ill of; (rare) degrade, debase. Hence ~FICA′TION, ~fiER¹, nn. [ME, f. LL *vilificare* (prec., -FY)]

vil′ipend, v.t. (literary). Treat contemptuously, disparage. [ME, f. OF *vilipender* or L *vilipendere* (as VILE + *pendere* weigh)]

vill′a, n. Country residence; detached suburban house. Hence ~DOM n., suburban society. [L & It. *villa*]

vill′age, n. Assemblage of houses etc. larger than hamlet & smaller than town. [ME, f. OF, f. Rom. *villaticum* neut. sing. as n. f. L *-icus* f. VILLA, see -AGE]

vill′ager, n. Inhabitant of a village (usu. implying rusticity). [-ER¹]

vill′ain (-ăn), n. & a. **1.** Person guilty or capable of great wickedness, scoundrel, as *has played the* ~, *plays the* ~*s in melodramas*, (colloq., playful) *you little* etc. ~ (rascal); ‖ (arch.) rustic, boor; (hist., also *villein* a. & n.) feudal serf, tenant holding by menial services, so **vill′a(i)nAGE**(-lan-), **-e(i)nage**(-lĭn-), n. **2.** adj. Of, done by, a ~, as ~ *services*. [ME, f. OF *vilein*, *vil(l)ain* f. Rom. *villanus* f. VILLA, see -AN]

vill′ainous (-lan-), a. Worthy of a villain, vile, wicked, so **vill′ainy**² (-lan-) n.; (colloq.) abominably bad, as *a* ~ *scrawl*, *style*, *hotel*. Hence ~LY² adv., ~NESS n. [ME; -OUS]

villanelle′, n. Form of (esp. French) poem of 19 lines on two rhymes. [F, f. It. *villanella*]

villeggiatur′a (-jatoora), n. Stay, retirement, in the country. [It.]

vill′ein (-lĭn), a. & n. See VILLAIN.

vill′|us, n. (pl. ~i). (Anat.) each of the short hairlike processes on some membranes esp. on mucous membrane of intestine; (bot., pl.) long soft hair covering fruit, flower, etc. Hence or cogn. ~iFORM, ~OID, ~OSE¹, ~OUS, aa., ~ŏs′ITY n. [L, = shaggy hair]

vim, n. (colloq.). Vigour. [L, acc. of VIS]

vim′inal, a. (bot.). Of, producing, twigs or shoots. So **vimin′EOUS** a. [f. L *viminalis* (*vimen -minis* osier)]

vi′na (vē-), n. Indian seven-stringed musical instrument with fretted finger-board & a gourd at each end. [Hind.]

vinā′ceous (-shŭs), a. Of wine or grapes; wine-red. [f. L *vinaceus* (*vinum* wine, -ACEOUS)]

vinaigrette′ (-nĭg-), n. Bottle for holding aromatic vinegar etc., smelling-bottle. [F, dim. of *vinaigre* VINEGAR]

vin′cible, a. (rare). Not invincible. [f. L *vincibilis* (*vincere* conquer, see -BLE)]

vin′culum, n. (pl. *-la*). (Alg.) line drawn over several terms to show that they have a common relation to what follows or precedes (e.g. $a+b \times c = ac+bc$, but $a+b \times c = a+bc$; $\overline{a-b+c} = a-b-c$); (print.) = BRACE¹; (anat.) = FRAENUM. [L, = bond (*vincire* bind)]

vin′dic|ate, v.t. Maintain the cause of (person, religion, etc.) successfully; establish the existence or merits or justice of (one's veracity, courage, conduct, character, assertion). Hence or cogn. ~ABIL′ITY, ~A′TION, ~ātOR, ~ātRESS¹, nn., ~ABLE, ~ATIVE, aa. [f. L *vindicare* lay claim to, see -ATE³]

vin′dicatory, a. Tending to vindicate; (of laws) punitive. [-ORY]

vindic′tive, a. Revengeful, given to revenge; ~ (or *exemplary*) *damages* (awarded as punishment to defendant). Hence ~LY² adv., ~NESS n. [f. L *vindicta* vengeance (VINDICATE) + -IVE]

vine, n. Climbing woody-stemmed plant whose fruit is the grape (*under* one's ~ *& FIG¹-tree*); any plant with slender stem that trails or climbs, as *hop*, *melon*, ~; ~*-borer*, kinds of insect destroying ~; ~*-disease*, due to PHYLLOXERA etc. Hence **vin′Y²** a. [ME & OF *vigne*, *vine*, f. L *vinea* vineyard (*vinum* wine)]

vin′egar, n. & v.t. **1.** Acid liquid got from wine, cider, etc., by acetous fermentation & used as condiment or for pickling (fig., often attrib., as type of sourness, as *a* ~ *countenance*); *aromatic* ~ (holding camphor etc. in solution); *toilet* ~, aromatic ~ used for mixing with washing-water etc.; MOTHER³ *of* ~; *V*~ *Bible*, 1717 ed. with *parable of the* ~ (for *vineyard*) above *Luke* XX; ~*-eel*; ~*-plant*, microscopic fungus producing fermentation. Hence ~ISH¹, ~Y², aa. **2.** v.t. Apply ~ to, make sour like ~ (lit. & fig.). [ME, f. OF *vinegre* (*vin* wine f. L *vinum* + *egre*, see EAGER)]

vin′ery, n. Vine greenhouse. [f. med. L *vinarium* or f. VINE + -ERY]

vine′yard (-ny-), n. Plantation of grape-vines. [ME; VINE + YARD]

vingt-et-un (see Ap.), n. Card game in which the object is to reach the number of 21 pips without exceeding it. [F, = 21]

vini-, comb. form of L *vinum* wine, as: ~*cul′ture*, cultivation of vines, so ~*culturist*; *vinif′erous*, (of district) wine-producing; ~*ficāt′or*, apparatus for collecting alcoholic vapours in wine-making.

vinom′eter, n. Apparatus for measuring alcohol in wine. [f. L *vinum* wine + -METER]

vin ordinaire (see Ap.), n. Cheap (usu.

red) wine as drunk in France mixed with water. [F]

vin′ous, a. Of, like, due to, wine, as ~ *flavour, fermentation, eloquence*. So **vīnōs**-ITY n. [f. L *vinosus* (*vinum* wine, see -OUS)]

∥ **vint**[1], v.t. Make (wine). [f. VINTAGE]

vint[2], n. A Russian card-game. [Russ., = screw]

vin′tage, n. Season of gathering grapes; (wine made from) season's produce of grapes; ~ *wines* (of well-known ~s); (poet., rhet.) wine; (attrib.) of a past season, as *a* ~ *motor-car*. [alt. (after *vintner*) f. ME *vendage, vindage* f. OF *vendange* f. L *vindemia*]

vin′tager, n. Grape-gatherer. [prec., -ER[1]]

vint′ner, n. Wine-merchant. [alt. f. ME, AF *vinter* = OF *vinetier* f. L *vinum* wine]

vī′ol, n. Medieval (usu. 6-)stringed musical instrument, predecessor of violin etc. (*treble, tenor, bass,* ~); *bass* ~ (mod.), = VIOLONCELLO. [ME *viel* f. OF *viel(l)e*, alt. f. *viole* (whence mod. E sp.) f. pop L **vitula* f. L *vitulari* be joyful; see FIDDLE]

viŏl′a[1], n. 1. Kind of large violin, alto or tenor violin. 2. (hist.). = prec.; ~ *da braccio,* ~, (alto) violin; ~ *da gamba,* bass viol. [It. & Sp., = F *viole* (prec.)]

vī′ola[2], n. Kinds of plant including pansy, esp. of single colour, & violet. [L, = violet]

violā′ceous (-shŭs), a. Of violet colour; of violet family. [f. L *violaceus* (prec., -ACEOUS)]

vī′ol|āte, v.t. Transgress, infringe, act against the dictates or requirements of (oath, treaty, law, terms, conscience); treat profanely or with disrespect (sanctuary etc.); break in upon, disturb, (person's privacy etc.); commit rape upon, ravish. So ~ABLE a., ~A′TION, ~ātOR, nn. [ME, f. L *violare* (VIS), see -ATE[3]]

vī′olence, n. Quality of being violent; violent conduct or treatment, outrage, injury, as *was compelled to use* ~, *did* ~ *to* (outraged, acted contrary to) *his feelings, our principles*; (law) unlawful exercise of physical force, intimidation by exhibition of this. [ME, f. OF, f. L *violentia* (as foll., see -ENCE)]

vī′olent, a. Marked by great physical force, as *a* ~ *storm, came into* ~ *collision,* ~ *blows*; ~ *death* (resulting from external force or from poison, cf. NATURAL); marked by unlawful exercise of force, as *laid* ~ *hands on him*; intense, vehement, passionate, furious, impetuous, as ~ *pain, sickness, abuse, controversy, discrepancy, revulsion, contrast, dislike, shock, apt to form* ~ *attachments, is of* or *was in a* ~ *temper*; ~ *presumption* (law), one resting on almost conclusive evidence. Hence ~LY[2] adv [ME, f. OF, f. L *violentus* (VIS, -LENT)]

vī′olět, n. & a. 1. Kinds of plant chiefly of genus VIOLA, with blue, purple, white, or other flowers, as *common blue* ~, *sweet* ~, *dog-*~ 2. (Of) the colour seen at end of

spectrum opposite red, produced by slight admixture of red with blue, so **violěs**-CENT a. 3. Kinds of ~ *butterfly*. 4. ~-*powder*, toilet powder scented with orris or other perfume; ~-*wood*, myall & other kinds. [ME, f. OF *violette, -et,* dim. of *viole* f. L VIOLA[2]]

violin′[1], n. Musical instrument with 4 strings of treble pitch played with bow; (also ~IST n.) player on ~, as *first, second,* ~ (playing separate parts in orchestra etc.). [f. It. *violino* dim. of VIOLA[1]]

vī′olin[2], -ine, n. Emetic substance contained in sweet violet. [f. F *violine* (VIOLA[2], -IN, -INE[5])]

vī′olist, n. Performer on viol(a). [-IST]

violoncell′|ō (vē-, -chě-), n. (usu. abbr. *'cello*: pl. ~os). Bass violin, 4-stringed instrument held between player's knees. Hence ~IST(3) n. [It., dim. of *violone* large viol (VIOLA[1], see -OON)]

vip′er, n. Kinds of venomous snake esp. *common* ~, adder, the only poisonous snake in Gt Britain; (fig.) malignant or treacherous person; ~*'s bugloss,* stiff bristly blue-flowered plant; ~*'s grass,* black salsify. Hence or cogn. ~iFORM, ~INE[1], ~ISH[1] (fig.), ~OID, ~OUS (fig.), aa. [f. F *vipère* or L *vipera*]

virāg′ō, n. (pl. ~s). Turbulent woman, termagant; ∥ (arch.) woman of masculine strength or spirit. [OE & ME, f. L, = female warrior (*vir* man)]

vī′rėlay, n. Kinds of (esp. old French) poem with two rhymes to a stanza variously arranged. [ME, f. OF *virelai, -li*]

virement (vēr′mahń), n. Power to transfer items from one account to another. [F]

vī′rėō, n. (Kinds of) small greenish-coloured American singing bird (also *greenlet*). [L, perh. = greenfinch]

virěs′c|ence, n. Greenness; (bot.) abnormal greenness in petals etc. normally of some bright colour. So ~ENT a. [f. L *virescere,* see -ESCENT, -ENCE]

vīrg′ate[1], a. (nat. hist.). Slim, straight, & erect. [f. L *virgatus* (*virga* rod, -ATE[2])]

vīrg′ate[2], n. (hist.). A varying measure of land. [f. med. L *virgata* (*terrae*), rendering OE *gierd-land* yard-land, f. L *virga* rod + -ATE[1]]

Vīrgil′ian, a. Of, in the style of, the Roman poet Virgil (d. 19 B.C.). [f. L *Virgilianus* (*Virgilius* Virgil, -AN)]

vīr′gin, n. & a. 1. Person esp. woman who has had no sexual intercourse, whence or cogn. ~HOOD, **vīrg′in′**ITY, nn.; member of any order of women under a vow to remain ~s; *the* (*Blessed*) *V*~ (*Mary*) (abbr. *B.V.M.*), mother of Christ; picture, statue, of the B.V.M.; female insect producing eggs without impregnation; (astron., *V*~) = VIRGO; ~*'s bower,* = TRAVELLER'S *joy.* 2. adj. That is a ~; of, befitting, a ~, as ~ *modesty*; undefiled, spotless; not yet used or tried, as ~ *soil,* ~ *clay* (not fired); (of insect) producing eggs without impregnation; ~ *comb* (that has been used only once for honey & never for brood); ~ *honey* (taken from ~ comb, also, drained from comb without heat or pressure); ~ *queen*, unfertilized queen bee; *the V~ Queen*, Queen Elizabeth I. [ME, f. OF *virgine* f. L *virginem*, nom. *-go*]

vir′ginal, a. & n. **1.** That is or befits or belongs to a virgin, whence ~LY[2] adv. **2.** n. (hist.). (Also ~*s*, *pair of* ~s) square legless spinet used in 16th–17th cc. [(adj., ME) f. OF, or L *virginalis* (as prec., see -AL); origin of n. use unknown]

Vir′gin′i|a, n. One of the U.S.; tobacco from ~*a*; ~*a creeper*, a vine cultivated for ornament. Hence ~AN a. & n. [f. VIRGIN (Queen) + -IA[1]]

vir′gin′ibus pueris′que, L phr. (Addressed, suited) to girls & boys (i.e. respecting innocence).

Vir′g′o, n. **1.** Sixth zodiacal sign; a constellation. **2.** v~ *intāc′ta* (law), virgin with hymen intact. [L, = virgin]

virides′c|ent, a. Greenish, tending to become green. Hence ~ENCE n. [f. LL *viridescere* (*viridis* green, see -ESCENT)]

virid′itȳ, n. Greenness, esp. of oysters etc. after feeding on certain vegetable organisms. [ME, f. OF *viridite* or L *viriditas* (*viridis* green, see -TY)]

vi′rile (*also* vir′il-), a. Of man as opp. to woman or child; of, having, procreative power; (of mind, character, literary style, etc.) having masculine vigour or strength. So viril′ITY n. [f. F *viril* or L *virilis* (*vir* man, see -ILE)]

viriles′c|ent, a. (Of female animal) assuming in advanced age some male characteristics. So ~ENCE n. [f. L as prec., -ESCENT]

virol′og|ȳ, n. Science or study of viruses. So ~IST n. [VIR(US), -O-, -LOGY]

vir′|ōse, a. Poisonous, full of virus, so ~OUS a.; (bot.) having fetid smell. [f. L *virosus* (VIRUS, see -OSE[1])]

virtu′ (-ōō), n. Love of fine arts; *articles of* ~ (interesting from workmanship, antiquity, rarity, etc.). [f. It. *virtu* VIRTUE, virtu]

vir′t′ual, a. That is such for practical purposes though not in name or according to strict definition, as *is the* ~ *manager of the business, take this as a* ~ *promise, constitutes a* ~ *exculpation*; ~ *focus* (opt.), point at which the lines of a pencil of rays would meet if produced; ~ *velocity* or *displacement*, infinitesimal displacement of the point of application of a force measured in the direction of that force. Hence ~ITY (-ăl[2]) n., ~LY[2] adv. [ME, f. med. L *virtualis* f. L *virtus* after LL *virtuosus*, see -AL]

vir′t′ūe, n. Moral excellence, uprightness, goodness, as ~ *is its own reward, make a* ~ *of necessity*, feign alacrity or sense of duty while acting under compulsion; particular moral excellence, *as patience is a* ~, *she has every* ~, *the*

(*seven*) *cardinal* ~s (*natural* ~s, justice, prudence, temperance, fortitude; *theological* ~s, faith, hope, charity); chastity esp. of women, as *a woman of* ~; good quality, as *has the* ~ *of being adjustable, of resisting temperature*; inherent power, efficacy, as *no* ~ *in such drugs*; (pl.) seventh ORDER[1] of angels; *by* or *in* ~ *of*, on the strength of, on the ground of, as *claims it in* ~ *of his long service, is entitled to it by* ~ *of his prerogative*. Hence ~LESS (-ŭl-) a. [ME, f. OF *vertu* f. L *virtutem* nom. *-tus* f. *vir* man]

virtŭōs′ō, n. (pl. *-si* pr. *-sē*). Person with special knowledge of or taste for works of art or virtu; person skilled in the mechanical part of a fine art. Hence virtŭōs′ITY, ~SHIP, nn. [It., as foll.]

vir′t′uous, a. Possessing, showing, moral rectitude; chaste. Hence ~LY[2] adv., ~NESS n. [ME, f. OF *vertuous* f. LL *virtuosus* f. *virtus* VIRTUE, see -OUS]

vi′rŭl|ent (*or* -rōō-), a. Poisonous; caused by or containing virus, as ~*ent ulcer*, so [irreg.] ~IF′EROUS a. (med.); malignant, bitter, as ~*ent animosity, tone, abuse*. Hence or cogn. ~ENCE n., ~entLY[2] adv. [f. L *virulentus* (foll., see -LENT)]

vir′us, n. Morbid poison, poison of contagious disease, as *smallpox* ~; (fig.) moral poison; (fig.) malignity, acrimony. [L, = poison]

vis, n. (mech.). ~ INERTIAE; ~ *mōr′t′ŭa*, force that does no work, dead force; ~ *viv′a*, living force (= mass × square of velocity) of moving body. [L, = force]

visa (vēz′a; -sa′d), (obs.) visé (vēz′ā; -sēd, -sē′d), n., & v.t. **1.** Indorsement on passport etc. showing that it has been found correct. **2.** v.t. Mark with ~. [L *visa* fem. p.p. of *videre* to see; F *visé* p.p. of *viser* to examine]

vis′ag|e (-z-), n. (now chiefly literary). Face, countenance. Hence (-)~ED[2] (-zĭjd) a. [ME, f. OF, f. L *visus* face, see -AGE]

visard. See VISOR.

vis-à-vis (vēz′ahvē′), adv. & n. **1.** In a position facing one another; opposite *to*. **2.** n. Person facing another esp. in some dances; kinds of carriage & couch in or on which persons sit facing each other. [F, =face to face (*vis* face f. L as VISAGE)]

viscăch′a, viz-, n. S.-Amer. burrowing rodent with valuable fur. [of native orig.]

vis′cer|a, n. pl. The interior organs in the great cavities of the body (e.g. brain, heart, liver), esp. in the abdomen (e.g. the intestines). Hence ~AL a., ~I-, ~O-, comb. forms. [L, pl. of *viscus -eris*]

vis′cerāte, v.t. Disembowel. [f. prec. + -ATE[3], after *eviscerate*]

vis′cid, a. Sticky; semifluid. So ~ITY (-ĭd[2]) n. [f. LL *viscidus* (L *viscum* mistletoe, birdlime, see -ID[1])]

vis′cin, n. Sticky substance got from mistletoe & used in birdlime. [F, f. *viscum*, prec., -IN]

vis′cōse, n. (In the manufacture of rayon) cellulose reduced to a viscous state (suitable for drawing into yarn) by treatment with sodium hydroxide solution & carbon disulphide. [f. L *viscum* birdlime +-OSE²]

viscŏs′ity, n. Stickiness; (phys., of fluids, semifluids, & gases) internal friction, power of resisting a change in the arrangement of the molecules, whence **viscŏm′eter, viscŏm′etry, viscŏsim′eter, nn.** [ME, f. OF *viscosite* or med. L *vis-cositas* (as VISCOUS, see -TY)]

visc′ount (vīk-), n. Noble ranking between earl & baron. Hence or cogn. ~CY, ~ESS¹, ~SHIP or ~Y⁴, nn., (vīk-). [ME, f. AF *viscounte*, OF *vi(s)conte* (VICE-+*counte* COUNT³)]

vis′cous, a. Sticky; (phys.) having viscosity. Hence ~NESS n. [ME, f. AF, or f. LL *viscosus* (as VISCID, see -OUS)]

visé. See VISA.

***vise.** See VICE².

vis′ible (-z-), a. That can be seen by the eye; that can be perceived or ascertained, apparent, open, as *has no ~ means of support*, *spoke with ~ impatience*; prepared to receive callers (*is she ~?*); *the ~ church*, whole body of professed believers; *~ horizon*, the line that bounds sight; *~ speech*, system of alphabetical characters designed to represent all possible articulate utterances. Hence or cogn. **visibil′ity** (in adj. senses, & esp., meteorol., naut., conditions of light & atmosphere as regards distinguishing of objects by sight), ~NESS, nn., **vis′ibly³ adv., (-z-).** [ME, f. OF, or f. L *visibilis* (*vidēre vis-* see, see -BLE)]

vi′sion (-zhn), n., & v.t. 1. Act or faculty of seeing, sight, as *beyond our ~*, *has impaired his ~*, *the field of ~*, all that comes into view when the eyes are turned in some direction, *reflected, refracted, ~* (as affected by reflected, refracted, rays of light); thing seen in dream or trance; supernatural or prophetic apparition, phantom; thing seen in the imagination, as *romantic ~s of youth*, *had ~s of roast beef & plum pudding*; (without article) imaginative insight, statesmanlike foresight, political sagacity. 2. v.t. See, present, (as) in a ~. [ME, f. OF, or f. L *visio* (as prec., see -ION)]

vi′sion|ary (-zho-), a. & n. 1. Given to seeing visions or to indulging in fanciful theories; existing only in a vision or in the imagination, imaginary, fanciful, unpractical. 2. n. (Also ~IST n.) ~ary person. Hence or cogn. ~AL a., ~allY³ adv., ~arINESS n., (-zho-). [-ARY¹]

vis′it (-z-), v.t., & n. 1. Go, come, to see (person, place, etc., or abs.) as act of friendship or ceremony, on business, or from curiosity, as *have never ~ed us*, *had no time to ~ the Tower*, *hope to ~ Rome*; go, come, to see for purpose of official inspection or supervision or correction;

(of disease, calamity, etc.) come upon, attack; (bibl.) punish (person, sin), avenge (his *sins* etc.) *upon* person, comfort, bless, (person *with* salvation etc.). 2. n. Call on a person or at a place, temporary residence with person or at place, as *was on a ~ to some friends, paid him a long ~, during his second ~ to the East*; formal or official call for purpose of inspection etc., as DOMICILIARY ~, *right of ~* (see VISITATION). Hence ~ABLE a. [ME, f. OF *visiter* or L *visitare* frequent. of *visare* f. *vidēre vis-* see; n.f. F *visite* or f. Engl. vb]

vis′itant (-z-), a. & n. 1. (poet.). Visiting. 2. n. Migratory bird; (poet., rhet.) visitor; (V~) member of an order of nuns concerned with education of young girls. [F, or f. L *visitare* (as prec., see -ANT)]

visita′tion (-z-), n. Official visit of inspection or the like esp. bishop's examination of the churches of his diocese; (colloq.) unduly protracted visit or social call; boarding of vessel belonging to another State to learn her character & purpose (*right of ~* or *visit*, right to do this, not including right of search); divine dispensation of punishment or reward, notable experience compared to this; (eccl.) festival in honour of visit of B.V.M. to Elizabeth (*Luke* i. 39); (zool.) unusual & large migration of animals; *Nuns of the V~*, = VISITANTS; *V~ of the Sick*, office of Anglican Church. [ME, f. OF, or f. LL *visitatio*; as VISIT, see -ATION]

vis′iting (-z-), n. Paying visits, making calls; *have a ~ acquaintance with*, *be on ~ terms with*, know well enough to visit; ~*-book* (for names of persons to be called upon); ∥~*-card*, small card with one's name, address, etc., left in making call etc. [-ING¹]

vis′itor (-z-), n. One who visits a person or place; ∥ (in colleges etc.) official with the right or duty of occasionally inspecting & reporting, whence or cogn. **visit-(at)ōr′ial aa.**; ∥~*s′ book*, book in hotel, boarding-house, etc., in which ~s write their names and addresses and occas. remarks. [ME, f. AF *visitour*, OF *visiteur* (as VISIT, -OR)]

vis′or (-z-), -zor, vis′ard (-z-), -zard, n. (Hist.) movable part of helmet covering face; projecting front part of cap; (hist.) mask. Hence **vīs′orED³ (-zerd), vīs′or-LESS (-z-), aa.** [ME & AF *viser* f. *vis* face (L *visus*)]

vis′ta, n. Long narrow view as between rows of trees; long succession of remembered or anticipated events etc., mental prospect or retrospect, as *opened up new ~s* or *a new ~ to his ambition*, *searched the dim ~ of his childhood*. Hence ~′d [-ED²] a. [It., p.p. of *vedere* see (L *vidēre vis-*)]

vis′ual (-zhy̆ŏŏ- or -zū-), a. Of, concerned with, used in, seeing, as ~ *nerve, organ*; ~ *angle* (formed at the eye by rays from the extremities of an object viewed); ~

field (of VISION); ~ *rays*, lines of light supposed to come from object to eye; ~ *point*, point in the horizontal line in which the ~ rays unite. Hence ~ITY (-ăl⁻) n., ~LY² adv. [f. LL *visualis* (*visus -ūs* sight f. *vidēre* see, -AL)]

vis'ualiz|e (-zhyŏŏ- *or* -zū-), **-is|e** (-īz), v.t. Make visible to the eye, give outward & visible form to, (mental image, idea, etc.); call up distinct mental picture of (thing imagined or formerly seen, or abs.). Hence ~A'TION n. [-IZE]

vit'a glass (-ah-), n. Kind of glass by which the ultra-violet vitalizing rays of sunlight are not excluded as by ordinary glass. [P]

vit'al, a. & n. **1.** Of, concerned with or essential to, organic life, as ~ *energies*, *functions*, ~ *power* (to sustain life), *wounded in a* ~ *part*; essential to existence or to the matter in hand, as *a* ~ *question*, *question of* ~ *importance*, *secrecy is* ~ *to the success of the scheme*; affecting life, fatal to life or to success etc., as *a* ~ *wound*, *error*; ~ *centre* (med.), part in which wound appears to be instantly fatal, esp. respiratory nerve-centre in medulla oblongata; ~ *force* or *principle* (assumed to account for organic life); ~ *statistics* (of birth, marriage, death, etc.; also, colloq., feminine measurements of bust, waist, and hips). Hence ~LY² adv. **2.** n. pl. ~ parts, e.g. lungs, heart, brain. [ME, f. OF, or f. L *vitalis* (*vita* life, see -AL)]

vit'al|ism, n. (biol.). Doctrine that life originates in a vital principle distinct from chemical & other physical forces. So ~IST n., ~is'TIC a. [F -*isme*, or f. prec. +-ISM]

vităl'itў, n. Vital power, ability to sustain life; (fig., of institution, language, etc.) ability to endure & to perform its functions. [f. L *vitalis* (as VITAL, see -TY)]

vit'alize, **-ise** (-īz), v.t. Endow with life. [-IZE]

vit'amĭn, n. Any of a number of accessory food factors chiefly of very complex chemical composition, present in many food-stuffs esp. in the raw state, & essential to the health of man & other animals; their absence from the diet is associated with malnutrition in various parts of the body or deficiency diseases. [f. G -*ine*, f. L *vita* life +AMINE]

vitĕll'in, n. (chem.). Chief protein constituent of yolk of egg. [f. foll. +-IN]

vitĕll'|us, n. (pl. ~i). Yolk of egg, protoplasmic contents of ovum. Hence **vit'ell**ARY¹, ~INE¹, aa., ~I-, ~O-, comb. forms. [L, = yolk]

vi'ti-, comb. form of L *vitis* vine, as : ~*cide*, insect etc. destructive to vines; ~*culture*, grape-growing, so ~*cul'tural* a., ~*cul'tur(al)ist* nn.

vi'tiăt|e (-shĭ-), v.t. Impair the quality of, corrupt, debase, contaminate, as *constitution* ~*ed by excess*, ~*ed air*, *blood*, *mind*,

judgement; make invalid or ineffectual, as *a word may* ~*e a contract*. So **vitia'TION**, ~OR, nn., (-shĭ-). [f. L *vitiare* f. *vitium* (VICE¹), see -ATE³]

vit'rĕous, a. Of (the nature of) glass; like glass in hardness, brittleness, transparency, structure, etc.; ~ *body* or *humour*, transparent jellylike tissue filling ball of eye; ~ ELECTRICITY. Hence or cogn. **vitrĕos'ITY**, ~NESS, **vitrĕs'CENCE**, nn., **vitres'CENT**, **vit'riFORM(1)**, aa. [f. L *vitreus* (*vitrum* glass) +-OUS]

vit'ri|fý, v.t. & i. Convert, be converted, into glass or glasslike substance. Hence or cogn. ~FAC'TION, ~fiaBIL'ITY, ~FICA⁻TION, nn., ~fiABLE a. [f. F *vitrifier* (as prec., see -FY)]

vit'riol, n. Sulphuric acid or any of its salts; (fig.) caustic speech, criticism, etc.; *blue* or *copper* ~, copper sulphate; *white* ~, zinc sulphate; *oil of* ~, concentrated sulphuric acid; ~*-throwing*, throwing ~ in person's face as act of vengeance etc. Hence **vitriŏl'IC**, ~INE¹, aa. [ME, f. OF, or f. med. L *vitriolum* f. *vitrum* glass]

vit'riol|ize, **-ise** (-īz), v.t. Convert into a sulphate, so ~ATE³ v.t., ~A'TION n.; poison, burn, with vitriol. Hence ~īZABLE a., ~īZA'TION n. [-IZE]

Vĭtru'vĭan (-ōō-), a. Of Vitruvius, Roman architect of the Augustan age; ~ *scroll*, scroll pattern in frieze decorations etc. [-AN]

vitt'|a, n. (pl. ~ae). (Rom. ant.) fillet, garland, as decoration of priest, victim, statue, etc.; lappet of mitre; (bot.) oil-tube in fruit of some plants; (zool.) strips of colour. So ~ATE² a. [L]

vitūp'er|āte, v.t. Revile, abuse. Hence or cogn. ~A'TION, ~ātOR, nn., ~ative a., ~ativeLY² adv. [f. L *vituperare*, see -ATE³]

vi'va¹ (vē-), int. & n. (The cry) long live —. [It., 3rd pers. subj. of *vivere* live, cf. VIVAT, VIVE]

viva². See VIVA VOCE.

vivace (vēvah'chā), adv. (mus.). In a lively manner. [It.]

vivā'cious (-shus), a. Lively, sprightly, animated, whence or cogn. ~LY² adv., **vivă'cITY** n.; (bot.) tenacious of life, surviving winter, perennial. [f. L *vivax* (*vivere* live, -ACIOUS)]

vivandière (vēvahndyār'), n. (hist.). Woman attached to continental esp. French regiment & selling provisions & liquor. [F]

vivār'ĭum, n. (pl. -ia). Place artificially prepared for keeping animals in their natural state, zoological garden or the like. [L (*vivus*, see VIVIFY & -ARIUM)]

viv'ăt, int. & n. (The cry) long live, as ~ *rex*, *regina*, long live the king, queen. [L, 3rd sing. subj. of *vivere* live]

viv'a vō'cè, adv., a., & n. **1.** Oral(ly). **2.** n. (abbr. *viva*). Oral examination. Hence **viv'a**(-vō'cè) v.t., examine ~. [L, = with the living voice]

vive (vēv), int. Long live, as ~ *le roi* (the

king), QUI VIVE. [F, 3rd sing. subj. of *vivre* live f. L *vivere*]

‖ **viv′ers** (-z), n. pl. (Sc.). Food, victuals. [f. F *vivres* (*vivre* live f. L *vivere*)]

vīves (-vz), n. Hard swellings of the submaxillary glands of a horse. [apheitic f. obs. *avives* f. F *avives* f. Sp. *avivas* f. Arab. *addhibah* (*al* the +*dhibah* she-wolf)]

viv′id, a. (Of light or colour) bright, intense, glaring, as ~ *flash of lightning*, *of a ~ green*; (of person) full of life; (of mental faculty or impression) clear, vigorous, strongly marked, as *has a ~ imagination*, *gave a ~ description*, *have a ~ recollection of the scene*. Hence ~LY² adv., ~NESS n. [f. L *vividus* (*vivere* live, see -ID¹)]

viv′ifȳ, v.t. Give life to, enliven, animate, (chiefly fig.). [f. F *vivifier* f. LL *vivificare* (*vivus* living f. *vivere* live, see -FY)]

vivip′arous, a. (Zool.) bringing forth young alive, not hatching by means of egg, (cf. OVIPArous); (bot.) producing bulbs or seeds that germinate while still attached to parent plant. Hence vivi-pā′RITY, ~NESS, nn., ~LY² adv. [f. L *viviparus* (*vivus*, see prec., +*parēre* bring forth)+-OUS]

viv′isĕct, v.t. Dissect (animal, or abs.) while living. [f. foll.]

vivisĕc′tion, n. Dissection of or (loosely) inoculation etc. tried upon living animals. Hence ~AL a., ~IST(2, 3), viv′isector, nn. [f. L *vivi-*, comb. form of *vivus* living +*sectio* cutting]

vi′vŏ (vē-), adv. (mus.). = VIVACE. [It.]

vix′en, n. She-fox; quarrelsome woman, termagant. Hence ~ISH¹, ~LY¹, aa. [ME *fixen* f. OE *fyxen* (= MHG *vühsinne*, G *füchsin*), fem. of FOX; see -EN³]

viz. See VIDELICET.

vizard. See VISOR.

vizcacha. See VISCACHA.

vizi(e)r (-zēr), n. High official, esp. State minister, in Mohammedan countries; *grand ~*, prime minister in Turkish empire & other countries. Hence ~ATE¹(1), ~SHIP, nn., ~IAL a. [f. Turk. *vezir* f. Arab. *wazir* counsellor, orig. porter (*wazara* bear burden); cf. F, Sp. *visir*]

Vlach (-ăk), a. & n. Member of a SE. European Latin-speaking people, Walachian or Romanian, Wal(l)ach. [Slav., ult. f. Gmc *Walh* foreigner, Celt, Italian, Latin]

vlei (flā), n. (S. Afr.). Hollow in which water collects during rainy season. [Du. dial., f. Du. *vallei* valley]

vŏc′able, n. Word, esp. w. ref. to form rather than meaning. [F, or f. L *vocabulum* (*vocare* call)]

vocăb′ūlarȳ, n. (List, arranged alphabetically with definitions, of) the (principal) words used in a language or usu. in a particular book or branch of science etc., or by a particular author, as *a Livy with notes & ~*, *a word not found in the Chaucerian ~*, *the ever-increasing scientific*

~, *his ~* (range of language) *is limited*. [f. med. L *vocabularius*, -*um* (prec., -ARY¹)]

vŏc′al, a. & n. 1. Of, concerned with, uttered by, the voice, as *a ~ communication*, ~ *auscultation* (of the sounds of the voice as heard through walls of chest), ~ *cords*, folds of lining membrane of larynx about the opening of the glottis, ~ *music* (written for or produced by the voice with or without accompaniment), ~ *thrill*, vibration of wall of chest in audible speech; (poet., of trees, water, etc.) endowed (as) with a voice; (phonet.) voiced, sonant, (also) of vowel character. Hence or cogn. vŏc′al′ITY n., ~LY² adv. 2. n. Vowel, whence vŏc′al′IC a.; (R.-C. Ch.) person entitled to vote in certain elections. [f. L *vocalis* (as VOICE, see -AL)]

vŏc′alism, n. Use of voice in speaking or singing; vowel sound. [-ISM]

vŏc′alist, n. Singer (opp. to *instrumentalist*) [-IST]

vŏc′aliz|e, -**is|e** (-īz), v.t. & i. Form (sound), utter (word), with the voice, esp. make sonant, as *t is ~ed into* v; write (Hebrew etc.) with vowel points; (joc.) speak, sing, hum, shout, etc.; (mus.) sing florid passage to a vowel. So ~A′TION n. [-IZE]

vocā′tion, n. Divine call to, sense of fitness for, a career or occupation, as *fell no ~ (for the ministry)*, *has never had the sense of ~*, *little or no ~ to literature*; employment, trade, profession, as *mechanical ~s*, *all ~s are overcrowded*, *mistook his* (chose the wrong) ~. Hence ~AL (-sho-) a., ~alLY² adv. [ME, f. OF, or f. L *vocatio* f. *vocare* call, see -ATION]

vŏc′ative, a. & n. (gram.). (Case) employed in addressing person or thing. [ME, f. OF (-*if*, -*ive*) or L *vocativus* (*vocare*, see VOCABLE & -ATIVE)]

vŏcif′er|āte, v.t. Utter (words etc., or abs.) noisily, shout, bawl. Hence or cogn. ~ANCE (rare), ~A′TION, ~ātoR, nn., ~ANT(1) a. & n. [f. L *vociferari* (as VOICE +*ferre* bear)]

vŏcif′erous, a. (Of person, speech, etc.) noisy, clamorous. Hence ~LY² adv., ~NESS n. [as prec. +-OUS]

vŏd′ka, n. Kind of fiery brandy made esp. in Russia by distillation of rye etc. [Russ.]

‖ **vŏe**, n. (Shetland). Small bay, creek. [f. Norw. *vaag*, ON *vōgr*]

vogue (vōg), n. & v.i. 1. (Now chiefly literary) *the* prevailing fashion, as *the ~ of large hats*, *large hats are the ~*; popular use or reception, as *has had a great ~*; *in ~*, in fashion, generally current. 2. v.i. ~ *la galère* (-ĕr), here goes (lit. let the galley set forth). [F, orig. = course, f. *voguer* f. It. *vogare* row in galley]

voice, n., & v.t. 1. Sound uttered by the mouth, esp. human utterance in speaking, shouting, singing, etc., as *heard a ~*, *did not recognize his ~*, *cried out in a loud ~*, *has lost her* (esp. singing-) ~, *is not in ~* (proper vocal condition for singing or speaking), CHEST, HEAD², ~, *the ~ of the cuckoo*, *veiled* ~ (due to malformation etc.), (fig.) *sea, storm, lifts up its* ~, whence -VOICED² (-st) a. 2. Use of the ~, utterance esp. in spoken or (fig.) written words, opinion so expressed, right to express opinion, as *gave* ~ *to his indignation in a pamphlet, dog gave* ~ *to his joy, took it* (natural phenomenon, calamity, popular outcry, etc.) *for the* ~ (expression of the will, resentment, etc.) *of God, I count on your* ~ (spoken or written support), *I have no* ~ *in the matter, refused with one* ~ (unanimously), (arch., rhet.) *my* ~ *is for peace*. 3. (phonet.). Sound uttered with resonance of vocal cords, not with mere breath. 4. (gram.). Set of forms of a verb showing relation of the subject to the action, as ACTIVE, PASSIVE, MIDDLE¹, ~. 5. v.t. Give utterance to, express, as *was chosen to* ~ *their grievance, believe I am voicing the general sentiment when I say*; (mus.) regulate tone-quality of (organ pipes); (phonet.) utter with ~, make sonant, (esp. in p.p.). [ME, f. OF *vois* f. L *vocem*, nom. *vox*]

voice'ful (-sf-), a. (poet.). Sonorous. [-FUL]

voice'less (-sl-), a. Speechless, dumb, mute; (phonet.) not voiced. Hence ~NESS n. [-LESS]

void, a., n., & v.t. 1. Empty, vacant, as *a* ~ *space, interval*; (of office) vacant, as *bishopric fell* ~; (esp. law, of deed, promise, contract, etc.) invalid, not binding, as *null & ~*; (poet., rhet.) ineffectual, useless; ~ *of*, lacking, free from, as *a proposal wholly* ~ *of sense, his style is* ~ *of affectation*. Hence ~LY³ adv., ~'NESS n. 2. n. Empty space, as *vanished into the* ~, (fig.) *the aching* ~ *of his heart, cannot fill the* ~ *made by death*. 3. v.t. Render invalid; emit (excrement etc.); (arch.) quit, evacuate. Hence ~'ABLE a. [ME, f. OF *voide*, fem. of *voit, vuit* (mod. *vide*) f. Rom. *vocitus* repl. L *vacuus*; vb partly f. *voider*, partly aphetic f. AVOID]

void'ance, n. Ejection from benefice; vacancy in benefice; voiding. [ME, f. OF (prec., -ANCE), or aphetic f. AVOIDANCE]

void'ed, a. In vbl senses, also (her., of bearing) having the central area cut away so as to show the field. [-ED¹]

voile (vwahl, voil), n. A thin semi-transparent cotton, woollen, or silken dress material. [F, = VEIL]

vol'ant, a. (Zool.) flying, able to fly; (her.) represented as flying; (poet.) nimble, rapid. [F, f. L *volare* fly, see -ANT]

Volapük' (-ōōk), **Vōl'apuk** (-ōōk), n. Artificial international language invented about 1879 by J. M. Schleyer. Hence ~IST(2, 3) n. [Volapük (*vol* world + -*a*- + *pük* speech)]

vol'ar, a. (anat.). Of the palm or sole. [f. L *vola* palm, sole, + -AR¹]

vol'atile, a. Evaporating rapidly, as ~ *salts,* ~ (= ESSENTIAL) *oil*; (fig.) lively,

gay, changeable, as ~ *wit, writer, disposition*. Hence or cogn. ~NESS, vŏlatil'ITY, nn. [F (-*il*, -*ile*), or f. L *volatilis* (*volare* -*at*- fly, -ILE)]

volăt'iliz|e, -is|e (-īz), v.t. & i. (Cause to) evaporate. Hence or cogn. ~ABLE a., ~A'TION n. [-IZE]

vol-au-vent (see Ap.), n. Kind of rich raised pie. [F]

vŏlcān'|ic, a. Of, like, produced by, a volcano; ~*ic bomb*, mass of lava usually rounded & sometimes hollow; ~*ic glass*, obsidian. Hence ~ICALLY adv., vŏlcani-CITY n. [f. F -*ique*, or f. VOLCANO + -IC]

vŏlcān'o, n. (pl. ~es). Mountain, hill, having opening(s) in earth's crust through which lava, cinders, water, gases, etc., are expelled continuously or at intervals (*active, dormant, extinct*, ~; *submarine* ~, originating beneath sea & rising above surface by accumulation). Hence vŏl-canism(2), vŏl'canist(3), vŏlcanŏl'ogy, nn., vŏlcanolo'gical a. [It., f. L as VULCAN]

vōle¹, n., & v.i. (In some card-games) winning of all the tricks in a deal; (vb) win all the tricks. [(vb f. n.) F, f. *voler* fly f. L *volare*]

vōle², n. Kinds of mouselike rodent; *water-*~, large kind. [orig. ~*-mouse* f. Norw. *vollmus* (Icel. *vallarmús*) f. *voll* field + *mús* mouse]

vŏl'et (-lā), n. Panel, wing, of triptych. [F, f. *voler* f. L *volare* to fly]

vŏl'itant, a. (zool.). = VOLANT. [f. L *volitare* frequent. of *volare* fly, see -ANT]

voli'tion, n. Exercise of the will; power of willing. Hence ~AL, ~ARY¹, ~LESS, (-sho-), vŏl'itive, aa., ~aliTY² adv. [F, or f. med. L *volitio* (*velle* wish, pres. *volo*, see -ITION)]

vŏlks'lied (f-, -lēt), n. Folk-song. [G]

vŏlks'raad (f-, -raht), n. (hist.). Legislative assembly of Transvaal & Orange Free State. [Afrikaans]

vŏll'ey, n. (pl. ~s), & v.t. & i. 1. Simultaneous discharge of missiles, missiles so discharged; (fig.) noisy emission (*of* oaths etc.) in quick succession; (tennis, lawn tennis) return of ball in play before it touches ground; (crick.) pitching of ball, ball pitched, right up to batsman or wicket without bouncing; *half-*~, (lawn tennis) return of ball as soon as it touches ground, (crick.) ball so pitched that batsman may hit it as it bounces, hit so made, (v.t.) return, send, (ball, or abs.) thus; ~*-gun*, machine-gun discharging~. 2. vb. Discharge (missiles, abuse, etc., or abs.) in ~; (tennis, crick.) return, send, (ball, or abs.) in ~; (of missiles) fly in a ~; (of guns etc.) sound together. [f. F *volée* f. Rom. *volata* fem. p.p. as n. f. L *volare* fly, see -Y⁴]

vŏl'plāne, n., & v.i. (Of aeroplane or its pilot) descent, descend, by gliding without use of engine. [f. F *vol plané* (*vol* flight, *planer* hover)]

vŏlt[1], v.i., & n. Make a volte (n., var. of) VOLTE. [VOLTE]

vŏlt[2], n. Unit of electromotive force, the force that would carry one ampere of current against one ohm resistance. Hence ~'METER n., instrument for measuring electric currents in ~s. [as VOLTAIC]

vŏl'ta, n. (mus.; pl. *-te* pr. -tā). *Una* ~, *due* etc. *volte*, once, twice etc.; *prima* etc. ~, first etc. time. [It.]

vōl'tage, n. Electromotive force expressed in volts. [-AGE]

vŏltā'ĭc, a. (chiefly hist.). Of electricity produced by chemical action, galvanic, as ~ *battery, cell,* PILE[2]. [f. A. *Volta*, Italian physicist (d. 1827), -IC]

Vŏltair'(ian)ism, nn. Principles of Voltaire (d. 1778), scepticism. [-IAN, -ISM]

vŏltăm'ēter, n. Instrument for measuring electric currents by their electrolytic effects. [as VOLTAIC, -METER]

vŏlte, n. (Fenc.) quick movement to escape thrust; circular tread of horse. [F, f. It. *volta* turn]

vŏlte-face' (-tfahs), n. Turning round, esp. (fig.) complete change of front in argument, politics, etc. [F]

vŏl'ŭb|le, a. (Of speech or speaker) fluent, glib, whence or cogn. **vŏlŭBIL'ITY**, ~le-NESS, nn., ~LY[2] adv.; (arch.) revolving, rotating; (bot.) twisting round a support, twining. [F, or f. L *volubilis* (*volvere* roll, see -BLE]

vŏl'ūme, n. 1. Set of (usu. printed) sheets of paper bound together & forming part or the whole of a work or comprising several works (abbr. *vol.*), as *is now issued in* 3 ~s, *an odd* ~ *of* Punch, *library of* 12,000 ~s, SPEAK ~s (for); (hist.) scroll of papyrus etc., ancient form of book (cf. CODEX). 2. (usu. pl.). Wreath, coil, rounded mass, of smoke etc. 3. Solid content, bulk, whence **volu'minAL** (-lōō-) a.; (mus.) fullness of tone. Hence (-)**vŏlūmED**[2] (-md) a. [ME, f. OF, f. L *volumen -minis* roll (*volvere*, see prec.)]

volumen|ŏm'ēter (-lōō-), n. Instrument for measuring volume of a solid body by quantity of liquid etc. displaced. Hence ~ŏM'ETRY n. [f. L (prec.) + -O- + -METER]

volu'mēter (-lōō-), n. Kinds of instrument for measuring volume of gas or liquid. Hence **vŏlumĕt'rĭc(AL)** aa., **vŏlumĕt'rĭcaLLY**[2] adv. [f. VOLUME + -METER]

volūm'ĭnous (*or* -lōō-), a. Having coils or convolutions (of snakes, the brain, etc.; now rare); consisting of many volumes, as *a* ~ *work*; (of writer) producing many books; of great volume, bulky, (of drapery etc.) loose or ample. Hence **volūmĭnOS'ITY**, ~NESS, nn., ~LY[2] adv. [f. LL *voluminosus* (as VOLUME, see -OUS)]

vŏl'untarў, a. & n. **1.** Done, acting, able to act, of one's own free will, not constrained, purposed, intentional, as *a* ~ *gift, there was no* ~ *mis-statement, was a* ~ *agent in the matter,* ~ (opp. to *compulsory*) *service, army,* ~ *confession* (of criminal, not prompted by promise or threat); brought about, produced, etc., by ~ action, as ||~ *school* (supported by ~ contributions), ~ *waste* (of property by tenant's deliberate act or order); (of limb, muscle, movement) controlled by the will; (law) ~ *conveyance* (made without valuable consideration), ~ *grantee* (in ~ *conveyance*), ~ *partition* (by mutual agreement, not by judgement of court). Hence **vŏl'untarĭ**[2] adv., **vŏl'untarĭ-NESS** n. **2.** n. Organ solo played before, during, or after service; one who holds that the Church or the schools should be independent of the State & supported by ~ contributions, whence ~ISM (3) n., reliance on ~ subscriptions & not on State aid for the maintenance of education, reliance on ~ enlisting & not on compulsion for raising military etc. forces, ~IST(2)n.; (in competitions) special performance left to performer's choice. [ME, f. OF *volontaire* or f. L *voluntarius* (*voluntas* will, see -ARY[1])]

vŏlunteer', n., & v.t. & i. **1.** Spontaneous undertaker of task etc.; person who voluntarily enters military or other service, esp. member of any of the corps of voluntary soldiers formerly organized in U.K. & provided with instructors, arms, etc., by government (often attrib., as ~ *corps, manœuvres*); (attrib., of vegetation) growing spontaneously. **2.** vb. Undertake, offer, (one's services, remark, explanation, etc., *to do*) voluntarily; make voluntary offer of one's services (*for* campaign, purpose), be a ~. [f. F *volontaire* (obs. *-un-*), as prec., w. assim. to -EER]

volŭp'tuarў, a. & n. Concerned with, (person) given up to, luxury & sensual gratifications. [f. L *volupt(u)arius* (as foll., see -ARY[1])]

volŭp'tūous, a. Of, tending to, occupied with, sensuous or sensual gratification, as ~ *life, liver, music, beauty.* Whence ~LY[2] adv., ~NESS n. [ME, f. OF *voluptueux* or L *voluptuosus* f. *voluptas* pleasure, see -OUS]

volŭt|e', n. & a. **1.** Spiral scroll characteristic of Ionic, Corinthian, & Composite capitals, whence ~'ED[3] a.; kinds of (chiefly tropical) gasteropod often with beautiful shell, whence **vŏl'ūtOID** a. & n. **2.** adj. (bot.). Rolled up. [f. L *voluta* (*volvee volut-* roll), or f. F *volute*]

volu'tion (-lōō-), n. Spiral turn; whorl(s) of spiral shell; (anat.) convolution. [as prec., -ION, after *revolution*]

vŏm'er, n. (anat.). The small thin bone partitioning the nostrils in man and most vertebrates. [L, = ploughshare]

vŏm'ĭt, v.t. & i., & n. **1.** Eject from stomach through mouth; puke, spew; (fig., of volcano, chimney, etc.) eject violently, belch forth. **2.** n. Matter

~ed from stomach; emetic; *black* ~, (black substance ~ed in) yellow fever; ~ *-nut*, = NUX VOMICA. [ME; n. f. AF *vomit*(e), OF *-ite*, or f. L *vomitus* (*-ūs*) f. *vomere, -it-*; vb f. L *vomere* or frequent. *vomitare*]

vŏm'itorў, a. & n. 1. Emetic (a. & n.), so vŏm'itive a. 2. n. (Rom. ant.). Each of a series of passages for entrance & exit in (amphi)theatre. [f. L *vomitorius* a., *-um* n., (as prec., see -ORY)]

vŏmĭtŭri'tion, n. Ineffectual attempt to vomit, retching; repeated vomiting. [F, or mod. L *vomituritio*]

vōō'dōō, n., & v.t. 1. Use of, belief in, witchcraft & the like prevalent among W.-Ind. & U.S. creoles & Negroes; (also ~ *doctor*, ~ *priest*) person skilled in this. Hence ~ISM, ~IST(2, 3), nn. 2. v.t. Affect by~, bewitch. [(vb f. n.) Afr. *vodu*]

-vora. See -VOROUS.

vorā'cious (-shus), a. Greedy in eating, ravenous, (lit. & fig.), as *party of* ~ *trippers, a* ~ *appetite for scandal, a* ~ *whirlpool*. Hence or cogn. ~LY² adv., ~NESS, vorā'CITY, nn. [f. L *vorax* (*vorare* swallow, see -ACIOUS)]

-vore. See foll.

-vorous, suf. f. L *-vorus* (*vorare* devour, eat) + -OUS, forming adjj. w. sense ' feeding on ', as *carni-, gramini-*; also *-vora*, in L neut. pl. names of animals classified by their food, as *herbivora*; also F & E *-vore* forming name of individual of such class, as *carnivore*.

vŏr'tĕx, n. (pl. *-ĭcēs, ~exes*). Mass of whirling fluid, esp. whirlpool; (phys.) portion of fluid whose particles have rotatory motion; any whirling motion or mass, esp. (fig.) system, pursuit, etc., viewed as swallowing up or engrossing those who approach it, as *the ~ex of society, ~ex* (spiral arrangement of fibres at apex) *of the heart; ~ex-ring, ~ex* whose axis is a closed curve, e.g. smoke-ring puffed from smoker's lips or pipe. Hence ~ICAL, ~ICOSE¹, ~ic'ŭlAR¹ [-UL-], aa., ~icalLY² adv. [L, var. of VERTEX]

vŏr'ticĕl, n. Bell-shaped animalcule found in stagnant water etc. [f. mod. L *vorticella*, dim. of prec.]

vŏr'ticĭst, n. (Metaphys.) person regarding the universe, with Descartes, as a plenum in which motion propagates itself in circles; (art) painter of school using vortices as the CUBIST uses cubes etc. So ~ISM n. [f. *vortic-* st. of L VORTEX + -IST]

vŏrti'ginous, a. Whirling, vortical. [f. L *vortigo*, var. of VERTIGO, + -OUS]

vŏt'arȳ, n. Person vowed to the service of (God etc.); ardent follower, devoted adherent or advocate, (*of* system, pursuit, etc.). Hence ~ESS¹ n. [f. L *vot-* (see foll.) + -ARY¹]

vōte, n., & v.i. & t. 1. Formal expression of will or opinion in regard to election of officer etc., sanctioning law, passing resolution, etc., signified by ballot, show of hands, voice, or otherwise, as *shall give my* ~ *to* or *for the Labour candidate, passed without a dissentient* ~, CAST¹ ~, SPLIT¹ one's ~, CASTING-VOTE, TRANSFER-ABLE ~; opinion expressed, money granted, by majority of ~s, as *Government received a* ~ *of confidence, the army* ~; *the* collective ~s given or to be given by a party etc., as *will lose the Labour, Conservative,* ~, *the floating* ~ (of persons not attached to a party); *the right to* ~, as *women now have the* ~; ticket etc. used for recording ~. Hence ~'LESS a. 2. vb. Give a ~ (*for, against,* person or measure); enact, resolve, (*that*), grant (sum), by majority of ~s; (colloq.) pronounce, declare, by general consent, as *was* ~*d a failure*; (colloq.) propose (*that*); ~ *down*, defeat (measure) by ~s; ~ *in*, elect by ~s. Hence vōt'ABLE a., vōt'ER¹ n. [ME, n. f. L *votum*; vb f. same p.p. st. *vot-* of L *vovēre* vow, or f. LL *votare*]

vōt'ing, n. In vbl senses; ~*-paper* (used in ~ by ballot in election of M.P. etc.); CUMULATIVE ~. [-ING¹]

vōt'ive, a. Offered, consecrated, in fulfilment of a vow, as ~ *offering, tablet, picture*. [f. L *votivus* (as VOTE, see -IVE)]

vouch, v.t. & i. 1. Confirm, uphold, (statement) by evidence or assertion; answer *for*, be surety *for*, as *will* ~ *for the truth of this, for him or his honesty, can* ~ *for it that no step was taken*. [ME, f. OF *vo(u)cher* call etc., obsc. f. L *vocare* call]

vouch'er, n. In vbl senses, esp.: document, receipt, etc., establishing the payment of money or the truth of accounts; document which can be exchanged for goods or services as token of payment made or promised. [AF (prec., -ER⁴)]

vouchsafe', v.t. Condescend to grant, as ~ *d me no answer,* ~ *me a visit*; condescend (*to* do). [ME, f. VOUCH in sense 'warrant' + SAFE²]

voussoir (vōō'swär), n. Each of the wedge-shaped stones forming an arch. [f. OF *vossoir*, ult. f. L *volvere* roll]

vow, n., & v.t. 1. Solemn promise or engagement esp. in the form of an oath to God, as *baptismal* ~s (given at baptism by baptized person or by sponsors), *monastic* ~ (by which monk binds himself to poverty, celibacy, & obedience), *lovers' ~s* (promises of fidelity), *am under* (have taken) *a* ~ *to drink no wine*; action, conduct, etc., promised by ~, as *is this your* ~? 2. v.t. Promise solemnly (thing, conduct), as ~*ed a temple to Apollo,* ~ *obedience, vengeance against the oppressor*; (arch.) utter, make, *a* ~; declare solemnly (*that*); (arch.) declare, as *I* ~ *you are most obliging*. [ME, f. OF *vou, veu*, f. L as VOTE; vb f. OF *vouer*]

vow'el, n. Each of the more open sounds uttered in speaking, sound capable of forming a syllable, (opp. to, but not sharply divided from, *consonant*); letter representing this, as a, e, ĭ, o, u; *neutral* ~ (heard in second syllable of *cousin*, *reason*, *haddock*); ~ *gradation*, = ABLAUT; ~ *mutation*, = UMLAUT; ~ *point*, each of a set of marks indicating ~s in Hebrew & other Oriental languages. Hence (-)~ ĬED² (-ld), ~LESS, ~LY², aa. [ME, f. OF *vouel* f. L *vocalis* (*littera*) VOCAL (letter)]

vow′ēlīze, -ise (-īz), v.t. Insert the vowels in (Hebrew etc., shorthand). [-IZE]

vox, n. ~ *barb′ara* (anat., bot., etc.), hybrid or incorrectly formed word; ~ *ĕt praetĕ′rĕa ni′hĭl*, a voice & nothing more (i.e. esp. an empty word); ~ *hūma′na* (-mā-, -mah-), organ-stop with tones supposed to resemble human voice; ~ *pŏp′ŭlĭ*, the people's voice (i.e. public opinion, the general verdict, popular belief, or rumour). [see VOICE]

voy′ag|e, n., & v.i. & t. 1. Journey, esp. long one, by sea or water; *broken* ~*e*, unsuccessful whaling etc. ~e. 2. vb. Travel, traverse, by water. Hence ~EABLE (-ĭja-) a., ~ER¹ n. [ME, f. AF, OF *veage*, *veiage*, *voiage* f. L *viaticum*, see -AGE; vb f. F *voyager*, or f. the n.]

voyageur (vwahyahzhẽr′), n. Man employed in transportation of goods & passengers between trading posts in the Hudson's Bay territory; Canadian boatman. [F]

‖ vraic (vrăk), n. A seaweed found in the Channel Islands, used for fuel and manure. [F dial.; cf. VAREC]

vraisemblance (vrăsahŭblahⁿs′), n. Appearance of truth, plausible appearance, verisimilitude. [F]

Vŭl′can, n. (Rom. myth.) god of fire & metal-working; ~ *powder*, an explosive. [f. L *Volcanus*, *Vu*-]

vulcanic etc. See **vol-**.

Vŭl′canist, n. (geol.). Holder of PLUTONIC theory. [f. F *vulcaniste* (VULCAN, -IST)]

vŭl′canīte, n. Hard vulcanized rubber, ebonite. [-ITE¹]

vŭl′canīz|e, -is|e (-īz), v.t. Treat (rubber) with sulphur at high temperature to increase elasticity & strength & yield hard or soft flexible rubber. Hence ~ABLE a., ~A′TION, ~ER¹(1, 2), nn. [-IZE]

vŭl′gar, a. Of, characteristic of, the common people, plebeian, coarse, low, as ~ *expressions, mind, tastes, finery, an air of* ~ *prosperity, the* ~ HERD¹, (abs.) *the* ~, the common people; in common use, generally prevalent, as ~ *errors, superstitions, the* ~ (national, esp. formerly as opp. to Latin) *tongue*, ~ FRACTION, *the* ~ (Christian) *era*. Hence or cogn.~ISM(4, 2), vŭlgä′rĬTY, nn., ~LY² adv. [ME, f. L *vulgaris* f. *vulgus* common people, see -AR¹]

vŭlgār′ian, n. Vulgar (esp. rich) person. [-IAN]

vŭl′garĭz|e, -is|e (-īz), v.t. Make (person, manners, etc.) vulgar, infect with vulgarity; spoil (scene, sentiment, etc.) by making too common or frequented or well

known. Hence ~A′TION n. [VULGAR + -IZE (3)]

Vŭl′gate, n. Latin version of the Bible prepared by Jerome late in the 4th c.; (v~) traditionally accepted text of any author. [f. L *vulgata* (*editio* edition), fem. p.p. of *vulgare* make public (*vulgus*, see VULGAR)]

‖ vŭl′gus, n. (school sl.). Greek or Latin verse-exercise in some schools. [prob. alt. f. 16th-c. *vulgars* = vulgar-tongue (i.e. English) passages for rendering into Latin]

vŭl′ner|able, a. That may be wounded (lit. & fig.), susceptible of injury, not proof against weapon, criticism, etc.; (contract bridge) having won one game towards rubber & therefore being liable to higher penalties. Hence ~ABĬL′ITY, ~ableNESS, nn. [f. LL *vulnerabilis* (*vulnerare* wound f. *vulnus -eris* wound, see -BLE)]

vŭl′nerary, a. & n. (Drug, unguent, etc.) useful or used for healing wounds. [f. L *vulnerarius* (*vulnus*, see prec. & -ARY¹)]

vŭl′p|ine, a. Of (the nature of) a fox, so ~ĬCIDE(1, 2) n.; crafty, cunning. [f. L *vulpīnus* (*vulpes* fox, see -INE¹)]

vŭl′tur|e, n. Kinds of large bird of prey with head & neck more or less bare of feathers feeding chiefly on carrion; (fig.) rapacious person. Hence or cogn. ~INE¹, ~ISH¹, ~OUS, aa., (-cher-). [ME, f. AF *vultur*, OF *voltour* etc., or L *vultur*, or L *vulturius*]

vŭl′v|a, n. (anat.). Opening, orifice, esp. of female genitals. Hence ~AR¹, ~ATE², ~ĬFORM, aa., ~IT′IS n., ~O- comb. form. [L]

vying. See VIE.

W

W (dŭb′ĕlyŏŏ), letter (pl. *W*s, W's).

‖ Waac (wăk), n. (colloq.). Member of the *Women's Army Auxiliary Corps* (organized in 1917). [f. initials]

‖ Waaf (wăf), n. (colloq.). Member of the *Women's Auxiliary Air Force* (organized in 1939). [f. initials]

wabble. See WOBBLE.

wăc′ke (-ke), n. Kind of greyish-green or brownish clay resulting from decomposition of volcanic rock. [G, f. MHG *wacke* large stone]

wad (wŏd), n., & v.t. (-dd-). 1. Small lump of soft material used to keep things apart or in place or to stuff up opening, esp. disc of felt etc. keeping powder or shot compact in gun; *roll of notes, money. 2. v.t. Press (cotton etc.) into ~ or wadding; line (garment, coverlet), protect (person, walls, etc.), with wadding (also fig., as *well* ~*ded with conceit*); stop up (aperture, gun-barrel), keep (powder etc.) in place, with ~; ram (~) home. [16th c., of unkn. orig.]

wa'dding (wŏd-), n. Spongy material usu. of cotton or wool used to stuff garments, quilts, etc., or to pack fragile articles in, cotton wool; material from which gun--wads are made. [-ING¹]

waddl|e (wŏ'dl), v.i., & n. **1.** Walk with the rocking motion natural to fat short--legged person or to bird with short legs set far apart as duck or goose; hence ~**ingly**² adv. **2.** n. ~ing gait. [WADE + -LE(3)]

wa'ddy (wŏ-), n. Australian war-club. [native]

wade, v.i. & t., & n. **1.** Walk through water or other impeding medium as snow, mud, sand (also fig., as ~ *through slaughter* or *blood*, make one's way by massacre etc.; ~ *through book*, read it in spite of dullness etc.; ~ *in*, colloq., intervene, make vigorous attack on one's opponent; ~ *into*, colloq., attack energetically); ford (stream) on foot, whence **wad'able** a.; *wading bird*, long-legged water-bird that ~s (opp. short-legged web-footed swimmers). **2.** n. Spell of wading. [OE *wadan*, OHG *watan*, ON *vatha* f. Gmc *wadhan* cogn. w. L *vadere* go]

wad'er, n. In vbl senses; esp.: wading bird (see prec.); (pl.) high waterproof boots worn in fishing. [-ER¹]

wa'di, -ȳ, (wah-), n. Rocky watercourse dry except in rainy season (chiefly of Eastern countries). [Arab. *wādī*]

Wafd (-ah-), n. The extreme Nationalist party in Egypt. Hence ~'**ist** a. & n. [Arab.]

wāf'er, n., & v.t. **1.** Kind of very thin sweet honeycomb-faced biscuit now chiefly eaten with ices (*thin as a* ~, whence ~**y**² a.); thin disc of unleavened bread used in Eucharist; small disc of dried paste formerly used for fastening letters, holding papers together, etc.; disc of red paper stuck on law papers instead of seal. **2.** v.t. Attach or seal with ~. [ME & AF *wafre* (= ONF *waufre*, F *gaufre* whence GOF(F)ER), f. MLG *wāfel*, see foll.]

wa'ffle¹ (wŏ-), n. Small batter cake baked in ~-*iron*, special utensil. [f. Du. *wafel*, see prec.]

wa'ffle² (wŏ-), v.i., & n. (Indulge in) continual rapid chatter, twaddle. [orig. unkn.]

waft (wah-, wŏ-), v.t., & n. **1.** Convey (as) through air or over water, sweep smoothly & lightly along. **2.** n. Single sweep of bird's wing; whiff of odour; fugitive sensation of peace, joy, etc.; (naut., also *weft*) distress signal, e.g. ensign rolled or knotted or garment flown in rigging. [c. 1500 ' convoy (ship etc.) ' back form. f. obs. *waughter*, *wafter* armed convoy--ship, f. Du. or LG *wachter* f. *wachten* to guard]

wăg¹, v.t. & i. (-gg-), & n. **1.** Shake (t. & i., of thing attached by one end, as tail) to & fro, oscillate, (*dog* ~s *his tail*, in sign of pleasure; *tail was* ~*ging*; *tail* ~s *dog*,

least important member of society or section of party has control; ~ *one's finger at*, in reproof etc.; ~ *one's head*, in derision or amusement; *beards, chins, jaws, tongues, are* ~*ging*, talk going on); (arch., of the world, times, etc.) go along with varied fortune or characteristics (*how* ~s *the world?*); ~'*tail*, kinds of small bird (*grey, pied, yellow*, etc., ~*tail*) with long tail in constant motion. **2.** n. Single ~ging motion (*with a* ~ *of his tail, head*, etc.). [ME *wagge* f. root of OE *wagian*]

wăg², n. Facetious person, one given to jesting or practical jokes; || (sl.) truant (esp. *play* ~ or *the* ~). Hence ~**g'ery** (4) n., ~**g'ish**¹ a., ~**g'ishly**² adv., ~**g'ish-ness** n., (-g-). [prob. f. prec.]

wāge¹, n. Amount paid periodically, esp. by the day or week or month, for time during which workman or servant is at employer's disposal (usu. pl. exc. in certain phrr.; *gets good* ~s; *brings his* ~s *home*; *at a* ~ or ~s *of £10 a week*; *living* ~, ~s that allow earner to live without fear of starvation; *a fair day's work for a fair day's* ~); requital (usu. pl.; *the* ~s *of sin is death*); ~ FREEZE; ~(s)-*fund* in pol. econ., part of community's capital devoted to paying ~s & salaries. [ME, f. AF *vage*, OF *g(u)age*, see GAGE¹, WED]

wāge², v.t. Carry on (war, conflict). [ME pledge, gage, f. ONF *wagier* f. *wage* (prec.)]

wā'ger, n., & v.t. **1.** = BET n. & v.t. **2.** (hist.). ~ *of battle*, ancient form of trial by personal combat between parties or champions; ~ *of law*, COMPURGATION. [f. AF *wageure* f. *wager* WAGE² + -URE² (3)]

wăg'gle, v.i. & t., & n. = WAG¹ (but in more familiar use); esp. (golf) of swinging club-head to & fro over ball before playing shot. Hence **wăgg'ly**² a., unsteady. [f. WAG¹ + -LE(3)]

wăg(g)'on, n. Four-wheeled vehicle for drawing heavy loads, often with removable semicylindrical tilt or cover, usu. drawn by two or more horses (*hitch* one's ~ *to a star*, utilize powers higher than one's own); || open railway truck; ~-*boiler, -ceiling, -roof, -vault*, shaped like ~-tilt. [early 16th c. *wagan, waghen*, f. Du. *wag(h)en*, cogn. w. OE *wægn* WAIN]

wăg(g)'oner, n. Driver of wagon; *the W*~, constellation Auriga. [-ER¹]

wăg(g)onëtte', n. Four-wheeled open pleasure vehicle (or with removable cover) for one or more horses & with facing side seats. [-ETTE]

wagon-lit (văgawnlē'), n. Sleeping-car on continental railway. [F]

Waha'bi, -ee, (-hahbē), n. One of a sect of Mohammedan puritans following the letter of the Koran. [Abd-el-*Wahhab*, founder c. 1700]

waif, n. Ownerless object or animal, thing cast up by or drifting in sea or brought by unknown agency; homeless & helpless person, esp. unowned or abandoned child;

~s & strays, odds & ends, unowned or neglected children. [ME, f. AF waif=OF gaif, prob. of Scand. orig., cf. ON veif something flapping or waving; see WAIVE]

wail, v.i. & t., & n. (Lament, i. & t., with) prolonged plaintive inarticulate usu. high--pitched cry; (fig.) lament(ation) in words (often over); (of wind etc.) sound (v. & n.) like person ~ing; ~ing wall, place, part of the Solomonic wall at Jerusalem where the Jews assemble to bewail the destruction of the Temple. Hence ~'FUL a. (poet.), ~'ingLY² adv. [ME; prob. f. ON *veila f. vei int., see WOE]

wain, n. Wagon (chiefly poet. or agricultural); Charles's, Arthur's, or the W~, CHARLES'S WAIN. [OE wægen, wæn, OS, OHG wagan, ON vagn f. Gmc *wagnaz; cf. WAY, WEIGH]

wain'scot, n., & v.t. 1. Wooden panelling or boarding on room-wall from floor to a limited height. 2. v.t. Line with ~, whence ~ING(3) n. [ME, kind of imported oak-wood, f. MLG wagenschot, app. f. wagen WAGON + schot of uncert. meaning]

waist, n. 1. Part of human body below ribs & above hips (large, small, ~, of such circumference; long, short, ~, of such vertical extent). 2. Contraction marking this in normal figure (has no ~, of stout person); analogous contraction in middle of long object, e.g. fiddle or hour-glass. 3. Part of ship between forecastle & quarter-deck. 4. Part of garment encircling ~, band round ~ from which petticoats etc. may be suspended; *bodice. 5. ~-band, -belt, worn round ~; ~-cloth, = LOIN-cloth; ‖ ~coat (wǎs(t)'kŏt, wěs'kot), garment reaching down to ~ with front showing when coat is open & usu. without sleeves (sleeved ~coat, with sleeves for extra warmth or for use without coat by workmen); ~-deep or -high aa. & advv., up to ~. Hence (-)~'ED² a. [ME wast, perh. repr. OE *wæst, *weahst (= Goth. wahstus growth), f. root of WAX²]

wait¹, v.i. & t. 1. Abstain from action or departure till some expected event occurs, pause, tarry, stay, kick one's heels, be expectant or on the watch, (often for, till; ~ a minute; shall not ~ here any longer; kept me ~ing or made me ~; have a month to ~ yet; ~ till I come, for high water or a fine day; everything comes to those who ~; always has to be ~ed for, is unpunctual). 2. Await, bide, (is ~ing his opportunity; you must ~ my convenience; am only ~ing the signal). 3. Act as waiter, as servant shifting plates etc. at table, (are you accustomed to ~ing?; often at table), or as attendant (LORD¹, GROOM, in ~ing). 4. Defer (meal) till someone arrives (don't ~ dinner for me). 5. ~-a-bit [tr. Afrikaans wag-'n-bietjie], kinds of S.-Afr. shrub with hooked thorns; ~ (up)on, watch (arch.), await convenience of, serve as attendant esp. at table, pay visit to (person regarded

as superior), escort (arch.), (in race) purposely keep close behind (competitor), follow as result; ~ing-room, provided for persons to ~ in esp. at railway-station or house of doctor, dentist, etc. [ME, f. AF, ONF waitier = OF guaitier, f. WG *wahta watch, f. Gmc *wak- see WAKE¹]

wait², n. 1. pl. Official bands of musicians maintained by a city or town (hist.); street singers of Christmas carols. 2. Act or time of waiting (had a long ~ for the train); watching for enemy, ambush, (lie in or lay ~ usu. for). [sense 1 f. ONF *wait, wet (= OF guail, guet) sentinel f. waitier (prec.); sense 2 f. prec.]

wait'er, n. In vbl senses; also or esp.: man who takes & executes orders, shifts plates, etc., at hotel or restaurant tables, whence wait'RESS¹ n.; tray, salver; DUMB¹~; TIDE-~. [-ER¹]

waive, v.t. Forbear to insist on or use, tacitly or implicitly relinquish or forgo, (right, claim, opportunity, legitimate plea, etc.). Hence waiv'ER³ n. (legal). [f. AF weyver allow to become a ' waif ', abandon, f. weyf WAIF]

wake¹, v.i. & t. (past wŏke, ~d; p.p. ~d, wŏken, wŏke). 1. Cease to sleep, rouse from sleep, (often up; also fig., as spring ~s all nature, nature ~s); be awake (arch. exc. in part. or gerund, as in his waking hours, waking or sleeping; waking dream, day-dream, reverie); cease or rouse from sloth, torpidity, inactivity, or inattention (usu. up; ~ up there!; wants something to ~ him up; the insult ~d his dull spirit); rise or raise from the dead. 2. (chiefly Ir.) Hold wake over. 3. Disturb (silence, place) with noise, make re-echo. 4. ~-robin, wild arum, lords-&-ladies. [goes back to two OE forms: (a) strong vb *wacan; wōc; *wacen; (b) weak vb wacian (cf. OS wakōn, OHG wachēn, -ōn, ON vaka, Goth. wakan), f. Gmc *wak-; see WATCH²]

wake², n. 1. Vigil commemorating church dedication, merry-making or fair on the occasion, (hist.); ‖ (usu. pl.) annual holiday in northern England. 2. (Ir.) ‖ Watch by corpse before burial, lamentations & merry-making in connexion with it. [partly f. OE *wacu = OHG wacha, ON vaka, rel. to prec.; in ME partly f. prec.; sense 'vigil' perh. f. ON]

wake³, n. Strip of smooth water left behind moving ship (in the ~ of, behind; following, after the example of). [f. ON *vaku, vǫk, hole or opening in ice]

wake'ful (-kf-), a. Unable to sleep, (of person's night etc.) passed with little or no sleep; vigilant. Hence ~LY² adv., ~NESS n. [WAKE¹, -FUL]

wak'en, v.t. & i. Cause to be, become, awake (usu. = wake up, but conveying less of abruptness). [OE wæcnan = ON vakna, Goth. -waknan f. Gmc *wak-WAKE¹]

Walach, Wall-, (wŏl'ak), n. = VLACH.

Hence **Wal(l)achian** (wŏlăk′ĭan) a. (of the ~s or of Walachia, a principality now forming part of Romania) & n. (= ~, also the language of the ~s). [see VLACH]

Waldén′s|es (wŏ-, -z), n. pl. Puritan sect in valleys of Piedmont, Dauphiné, & Provence, started c. 1170 & much persecuted in 16th & 17th cc. Hence ~IAN a. & n. [Peter *Waldo* of Lyons, founder]

wāle, weal, n., & v.t. 1. Ridge raised on flesh by stroke of rod or whip; ‖ *wale-knot* or *wall-knot*, made at end of rope by intertwining strands to prevent unravelling or act as stopper. 2. v.t. Raise ~ on; (mil., *vale*) weave (a hurdle or gabion). Hence wāl′ING[1] n.. hurdlework used as revetment. [OE *walu* stripe, ridge; sp. *weal* is mod. var., by assoc. w. obs. *wheal* pustule, suppurate, whence the misspelling *wheal*]

Wāl′er, n. (hist.). Horse imported for Indian army from New South Wales. [N.S. *Wales*, -ER[1]]

Wāles (-lz), n. Principality inhabited by the Welsh (*Prince of* ~, title usu. conferred on heir-apparent of Great Britain). [OE *Wealas* pl. of *wealh* see WELSH[1]]

Walhalla. See VALHALLA.

walk[1] (wawk), v.i. & t. 1. (Of men) progress by advancing each foot alternately never having both off ground at once (*heel-&-toe* ~*ing*, in which both heel & toe are used, as required in ~*ing*-races; ~ *backwards*, *sideways*, go in those directions with analogous motions; ~ *over course* or ~ *over*, win easily, see WALK[2]-*over*; ~ *away from*, easily out-distance), go with the gait usual except when speed is desired (~*ing* DICTIONARY); (of animals) go with slowest gait corresponding to human walk. 2. Travel or go on foot (~ *into shop*, *up to* person, *down hill*, etc.; *please* ~ *in*, invitation to enter; ~ *up*, showman's invitation to circus etc.; ~ *out with*, have as sweetheart; ~ *about*, stroll; ~*s two hours*, *ten miles*, *a day*; *ghost* ~*s*, shows itself (see also GHOST); ~ *into*, sl., thrash, abuse, eat heartily of; ~ *off*, depart, esp. abruptly; ~ *off* or *away with*, carry off, steal; *~ out on* person, leave him). 3. (arch.). Live with or in specified principle or manner, conduct oneself, (~ *in love*, *humbly*, *honestly*, *after the flesh*, *by faith*, *with God*, etc.). 4. Perambulate, tread floor or surface of, (~ *the streets*, in gen. sense, also be prostitute; ~ *the hospitals*, be medical student; ~ *the boards*, be actor; ~ *the* PLANK[1]; ~ *the chalk*, prove sobriety to police etc. by ~*ing* straight between chalked lines), whence ~′ABLE (wawk-) a. 5. Cause to ~ with one, have ~*ing*-race with, (~ *horse*, when riding or driving or leading it; *policeman* ~*ed the man off*; *Smith will* ~ *Jones for* £100 *a side*; *you have* ~*ed me off my legs*, tired out). 6. (Of farmer etc.) take charge of (hound puppy). 7. ~*ie-talkie* (wawk′I-ˌtawk′I) n., small transmitting and receiv-

ing radio set carried on the person; ~ING[1] *chair*, = GO[1]-*cart*; ~ING[2] *delegate*, trade-union official who visits sick members, interviews employers, etc.; ~ING[1]-*dress*, for outdoor wear; ~ING[2]-*fern*, N.-Amer. kind with slender-tipped fronds that bow down to ground & take root; ~ING[1] *gentleman*, *lady*, actor, actress, of part requiring good presence but no skill; ~ING[2]-*leaf*, insect imitating leaf; ~ING[1]-*papers* or -*ticket*, sl., dismissal; ‖~ING[1]-*stick*, carried in ~*ing*; ~ING[1]-*tour*, pleasure journey on foot. [OE *wealcan* roll, toss, wander, *wealcian* muffle up, corresp. to OHG *walchan*, (M)Du., (M)LG *walken* to full, cudgel, ON *valka* drag about]

walk[2] (wawk), n. Walking gait, person's action in walking, (see prec.; *go at*, *never gets beyond*, *a* ~; *know him a mile off by his* ~); excursion on foot, stroll, constitutional, (*go for*, *take*, *a* ~; *across the hills from X to Z is a good* ~; ~-*over*, race in which from absence or inferiority of competitors winner can go at a ~ if he chooses, easy victory); person's favourite walking ground, round of hawker etc., place or track intended or suitable for strollers or foot-passengers, promenade, colonnade, footpath, (ROPE-~; SHEEP-~; ~ *of life*, calling, profession, occupation); *~-out*, workmen's strike; *~′way*; passage for walking along, esp. one connecting different sections of a building; wide path in garden etc. [ME, f. prec.]

wa′lker (wawk-), n. In vbl senses; esp.: ‖ SHOP-~; STREET-~; (class-name for) bird such as common fowl that neither flies nor swims, also bird that does not hop but walks on alternate feet. [-ER[1]]

Walkyrie. See VALKYR.

wall (wawl), n., & v.t. 1. Continuous & usu. vertical & solid structure of stones, bricks, concrete, timber, etc., narrow in proportion to length & height serving to enclose (partly) or protect or divide off town, house, room, field, etc., surface of inner side(s) of room, (*party* or *partition* ~, separating two rooms, houses, fields, etc.; ~ *of partition*, fig., line of division, gulf; *blank* ~, without door or gate or window, also without decoration; *run* one's *head against a* ~, attempt impossibilities; *see through brick* ~, have miraculous insight; ~*s have ears*, eavesdroppers are or may be about; *with* one's *back to the* ~, brought to bay, fighting alone against odds; RETAIN*ing* ~). 2. Something resembling ~ in appearance or effect (*mountain* ~, line of steep hills; ~ *of armed men*, *fire*, *bayonets*, protection or obstacle consisting of these; *cell* ~, ~*s of the chest* etc., enclosing tissue or framework in bot. or anat.; *hanging*, *foot-*, ~, in mining, upper, lower, rock enclosing lode). 3. (Position next) ~ as opp. gutter side of street footpath (*give one the* ~, allow him cleaner and safer part in passing; *take* *the ~ of*, refuse this courtesy to). **4.** Side as opp. centre of road (*the weakest goes to the ~*, is pushed aside, gets the worst in competition). **5.** ~*-creeper*, kinds of bird; ~*-cress*, kinds of plant growing in stony places; ~*-fern*, common polypody; ~*-flower*, yellow-flowered plant growing wild on old ~s, fragrant spring garden--plant with usu. orange or brown clustered flowers, (colloq.) woman sitting out dances for lack of partners; ~*-fruit*, of trees fastened against ~ for protection & warmth; ‖ ~ *game*, an Eton form of football; ~*-painting*, on ~ usu. of room, esp. fresco; ~*-paper*, for pasting over room~s, freq. with decorative printed patterns; ~*-pepper*, kind of stonecrop; ~*-plate*, timber laid in or on ~ to distribute pressure of girder etc.; ~*-rue*, small fern growing on ~s & rocks; ~*-washer*, plate used with tie-rod in supporting shaky ~; hence ~*LESS* (wawl-l) a. **6.** v.t. Provide or protect with ~ (esp. in p.p., as ~*ed towns*); block *up* aperture etc. with ~. [OE *wall* = OFris. *wal*, OS *wal(l)*, f. L *vallum* rampart.]

walla(h) (wŏl'a), n. (Anglo-Ind.). Person or thing employed about or concerned with something, -man, (BOX[2]~; *competition-*~, Indian civilian appointed by competitive examination; *punkah-*~, servant who works punkah). [f. Hind. *-wālā* suf. = -ER[1](3)]

wa'llaby (wŏ-), n. Kinds of smaller kangaroo; *on the ~ (track)*, on tramp, unemployed; (pl., colloq.) Australians. [Austral.]

Wallach. See WALACH.

wallaroō' (wŏ-), n. Kinds of larger kangaroo. [Austral.]

wa'llet (wŏ-), n. (Arch.) bag for carrying personal necessaries, food, etc., on journey, esp. pilgrim's or beggar's scrip; small leather case holding repairing tools for bicycle etc., fishing-kit, papers, or other small articles; flat case for holding bank-notes etc. [ME *walet*, of unkn. orig.]

wall-eye (wawl'ī), n. Appearance of whitish opacity of eye caused by injury or disease; (loosely) eye showing abnormal amount of white owing to squint etc., or large & glaring as in some fishes. [back formation f. foll.]

wall-eyed (wawl'īd), a. Having wall-eye. [f. ON *vagl-eygr* (*vagl* unexpl., *auga* eye)]

‖ **wall-knot.** See WALE.

Walloon', n. & a. **1.** Member, language (a French dialect), of people scattered in Belgium & neighbouring parts of France. **2.** adj. Of the ~s or in their language. [f. F *Wallon* f. med. L *Wallonem* f. Gmc *walh*, see WELSH[1]; cf. VLACH]

wa'llop (wŏ-), v.t., & n. (sl.). **1.** Thrash, beat, hide; (part.) big, strapping, thumping. **2.** n. A heavy blow; (sl.) beer. Hence ~ING[1](1) n. [earlier senses *gallop, boil*, f. ONF *waloper*, f. Frank. *wola lōpan*; see GALLOP]

wallow (wŏl'ō), v.i., & n. **1.** Roll about in mud, sand, water, etc. (*~ in money*, be very rich); take swinish or gross delight *in* sensuality etc. **2.** n. Place to which buffaloes etc. resort to ~. [OE *wealwian* roll, cf. Goth. *walwjan*; cogn. w. L *volvere*]

Wa'llsend (wawlz-), n. Kind of superior house-coal orig. from ~ on Tyne.

Wall Street (wawl), n. (Used for) the New York money-market. [street in New York]

wa'lnut (wawl-), n. (Kinds of tree yielding) delicate-flavoured nut in pair of similar boat-shaped shells (*over the ~s & the wine*, at dessert); timber of ~-tree used in cabinet-making & for gunstocks. [OE *walhhnutu* f. *wealh* foreign + NUT; cf. WELSH[1]]

Walpur'gis-night (vahlpoorgis-nīt), n. Eve of 1st May, when witches meet at the Brocken or elsewhere & hold revels with the devil. [*Walpurgis*, female saint of 8th c.]

wa'lrus (wawl-, wŏl-), n. Kinds of large amphibious arctic long-tusked mammal related to seal, morse, sea-horse. [prob. f. Du. *walrus, -ros*, perh. w. metath., after *walvisch*, f. wd repr. by OE *horshwæl*, ON *hross hvalr*]

waltz (wawlts, wawls), n., & v.i. **1.** (Music for) dance in triple time with graceful flowing melody & (usu.) one harmony to each bar. **2.** v.i. Dance ~; dance *in, out, round*, etc., in joy etc.; hence ~*ER*[1] (wawls-) n. [f. G *walzer* (*walzen* revolve)]

wampee' (wŏ-), n. (Tree yielding) grape-like fruit grown in China & E. Indies. [Chin. (*hwang* yellow, *pī* skin)]

wa'mpum (wŏ-), n. Beads made from shells & strung for money or decoration by N.-Amer. Indians. [f. N.-Amer. Ind. *wampumpeag* (*wompi* white, *-ampi* string)]

wan (wŏn), a. Pale, colourless, bloodless, looking worn or exhausted, (chiefly of persons or their complexion or look, or of sky or light); (arch., of night, water, etc.) dark, black. Hence ~*LY*[2] adv., ~*NESS* (-n-n-) n. [OE *wann, wonn*, dark, black, of unkn. orig.]

wand (wŏ-), n. Slender rod for carrying in hand or setting in ground as temporary mark (chiefly now of conjurer's or music conductor's baton, or of staff symbolizing some officials' authority). [ME, f. ON *vandur, vǫndr*, = Goth. *wandus*, prob. f. *wend-, wand-*, see WEND[1], WIND[3]]

wa'nder (wŏ-), v.i. & t. **1.** Rove, stroll, go from country to country or from place to place without settled route or destination, (~*ing Jew*, supposed to be still living from when Christ said 'Thou shalt ~ on the earth till I return' as punishment for an insult, also person who never settles down, also kinds of climbing plant; ~*ing cell, abscess, kidney*, etc., moving about, normally or abnormally attached to place in body; ~*ing sailor*, kinds of climbing plant), whence ~ER¹ (wŏ-) n. **2.** Stray, diverge from the right way lit. or fig., get lost, depart from home. **3.** Talk or think irrelevantly or disconnectedly or incoherently, stray from subject in hand, be inattentive or delirious, (*his wits are ~ing*; *~s in his talk*). **4.** Traverse desultorily (*you may ~ the world*, or usu. *the world through, & not find such another*). Hence ~ING¹(1) n. (usu. pl.), ~ingly² adv., (wŏ-). [OE *wandrian* f. Gmc *wand-+-ER⁵, see prec.; cf. MHG *wandern*]

wanderlust (vahn'derlŏŏst), n. Eager desire or fondness for travelling or wandering. [G]

wanderoo' (wŏ-), n. Kind of Ceylon monkey. [Sinhalese *wanderu*]

wāne, v.i., & n. **1.** Decrease in size or splendour like moon after the full, lose power or vigour or importance or repute, decline. **2.** n. Process of waning (esp. *is on the ~*, declining). [OE *wanian* = OS *wanon*, OHG *-ōn*, *-ēn*, ON *vana* f. Gmc *wano-* lacking, see WANT¹]

‖ **wangl|e** (wăng'gl), v.t., & n. (sl.). **1.** Secure (favour, desired result) by plausibility or management or other dubious means; show in the desired light, cook, fake, (report etc.). **2.** n. Act of ~ing. [orig. unkn.; first recorded (1888) as printers' sl.]

‖ **wanion** (wŏn'yon), n. *With a ~* (to), imprecation (arch.). [var. of *waniand* part. of WANE (waning moon = unlucky hour)]

want¹ (wŏ-, wah-), n. Lack, absence, deficiency, *of* (*ship rotting for ~ of paint*; *shows great ~ of thought, care, sense, judgement*); need *of*, need of sustenance, poverty, (*is in ~ of money, a servant*, etc.; *living in the direst ~*; *~ is a severe but efficient teacher*); desire for thing as necessary to life or happiness or success or completion (whence *~'LESS* a.), thing so desired, (*a man of few ~s*; *superfluities soon become ~s*; *it, supplies, a felt ~*; *can supply your ~s*). [ME, f. ON *vant* neut. of *vanr* lacking = ON *wan*, Goth. *wans*, f. Gmc *wana-*, see WANE]

want² (wŏ-, wah-), v.i. & t. **1.** Be without or deficiently supplied with, fall short *of*, fall short by (specified amount) *of* specified limit, (part.) lacking *in* quality or unequal *to* requirements or absent or deficient or (orig. dial.) lacking in intelligence, (*~s, is ~ing in, judgement*; *fortunately ~s the power to do it*; *what was ~ing, what we unfortunately ~ed, was the will*; *~s something of perfection*; *be found ~ing*, or *~ing to the occasion*, one's duty, etc.; *head of statue is ~ing*; *statue ~s the head*; *infinitive ~ing*, verb has none; *~s half a minute of the hour, an inch of the regulation measurement*). **2.** Be in want (*for*; *let him ~ for nothing*; *must not be allowed to ~*). **3.** Require (thing, *-ing*, *to be -ed*, *to do*; *boy ~s the whip, whipping, to be whipped, to feel the whip*; *it

~s careful handling*). **4.** Desire, wish for possession or presence of, (*to do, thing, person*; *don't ~ to go*; *I ~ some sugar, it done, you to try*; *call me if I am ~ed*; *is ~ed by the police*, of suspected criminal etc.; *tell Jones I ~ him*, send him to me). [ME, f. ON *vanta* (prec.)]

wa'nting (wŏ-, wah-), quasi-prep. Without, minus, less, (*~ common honesty, nothing can be done*; *made a century ~ one run*). [-ING²; use of part. either abs., cf. NOTWITHSTANDING, or in ordinary agreement]

wa'nton (wŏ-), a., n., & v.i. **1.** Sportive, gambolling, playful, irresponsible, capricious, (*~ child, kid, wind, mood*); luxuriant, unrestrained, wild, (*~ growth, ringlets, profusion*); licentious, unchaste, lewd, (*a ~ woman*; *~ thoughts*); motiveless, serving no purpose, random, arbitrary, (*~ mischief, destruction*); hence~LY⁵ adv., ~NESS n. **2.** n. Unchaste woman or rarely man; (rare) playful child. **3.** v.i. Sport, gambol, move capriciously; (rare) act lasciviously. [ME *wantowen* f. WAN+*towen* (cf. obs. *wanhope* despair), f. OE *togen* p.p. of *tēon* draw, educate; cf. G *ungezogen*]

wap. See WHOP.

wa'pentāke (wŏ-), n. (Old name in Yorkshire and some other shires for) hundred or division of shire. [OE *wǣpengetǣc* f. ON *vdpnatak* (*vdpn* weapon, *tac* taking f. *taka* TAKE)]

wa'pĭti (wŏ-), n. N.-Amer. stag resembling red deer but larger. [f. Amer.-Ind. *wapitik* white deer]

‖ **Wappen(c)haw** (wah'penshaw), n. (Sc.). (Hist.) periodical muster & inspection of men under arms in a particular district; (mod.) rifle-meeting. [f. *wapen* obs. form of *weapon*+*schaw* show (n.)]

war¹ (wôr), n. **1.** Quarrel usu. between nations conducted by force, state of open hostility, & suspension of ordinary international law, prevalent during such quarrel, military or naval attack or series of attacks, (fig.) hostility or contention between persons, (*civil ~*, between parts of one nation for supremacy; *cold ~*, unfriendly relations between nations characterized by hostile propaganda & attempted economic sabotage; *~ of nerves*, attempt to wear down opponent by gradual destruction of morale, opp. SHOOT¹ing *~*; *private ~*, feud between persons or families carried on in defiance of laws of murder etc., or armed attack made by members of one State without government sanction upon another; *holy ~*, waged in support of some religious cause; *TOTAL ~*); *make* or *wage ~*, begin or carry on hostile operations; *declare ~*, announce that hostilities may be expected, often *upon* another nation, also fig. *upon* institution, party, custom, etc.; so *declaration of ~*; *drift into ~*; *be at ~*, engaged in hostilities *with* enemy or abs., also fig.; *roll back tide of* ∼, repel invasion; *go to the* ∼s, arch., serve as soldier; *carry the* ∼ *into the enemy's country*, (fig.) make counter-accusations etc., not confine oneself to defence; *has been in the* ∼s, usu. fig. of person who has been mauled physically or otherwise; *on a* ∼ *footing*, of army, fleet, etc., with full establishment; ∼ *to the knife*, struggle to the bitter end usu. between persons; *Secretary of State for War*, also *Secretary for War*, *War Secretary*, ‖ parliamentary head of War Office; *art of* ∼, strategy & tactics; *trade of* ∼, soldier's profession; *sinews of* ∼, money etc. for waging ∼ or for effecting any object; TUG, CONTRABAND, COUNCIL, HONOUR[1]S, *of* ∼; MAN[1]-*of*-∼; *laws of* ∼, those recognized by civilized nations as limiting belligerents' action; *rights of* ∼, those similarly permitting to belligerents certain acts illegitimate in peace; *the dogs of* ∼, poet., havoc attending ∼; ∼s & *rumours of* ∼s, prevalence of the appeal to force among nations; ∼ *of the elements*, storms & catastrophes in nature; *all's* FAIR[2] *in love & ∼*). 2. ∼ *baby*, illegitimate child attributable to ∼ conditions; ∼*cloud*, position of international affairs that threatens ∼; ∼*cry*, phrase or name formerly shouted in charging or rallying to attack, party catchword, savages' battle-shout; ∼*dance*, indulged in by savages before ∼; ∼*game*, = KRIEGSPIEL; ∼*god*, one worshipped as giving victory in ∼, esp. the Greek Ares or Roman Mars; ∼*head*, explosive head of torpedo or similar weapon; ∼*horse*, charger (arch. & poet. exc. in phr. *like an old* ∼*horse*, of person excited by memories of abandoned pursuit or controversy); ∼*lord* (derog.), military commander (esp. of William II of Germany, & of Chinese civil-war generals); ∼*monger*, one who seeks to bring about ∼; ‖ *War Office*, State department in charge of army; ∼*paint*, put on body by savages before battle, (fig.) ceremonial costume, full fig; ∼*path*, (route of) warlike expedition of Amer. Indians (*be, go, on the* ∼*path*, fig., be engaged in, enter upon, any conflict, have taken, take, up the cudgels); ∼*ship*, for use in ∼; ∼*song*, sung by savages before battle, also any song on martial theme; ∼*whoop*, yell esp. of Amer. Indians in charging; ∼*worn*, experienced in or damaged or exhausted by ∼. [late OE *werre* f. AF, ONF *werre* (OF *guerre*) f. WG *werra* (cf. OHG *werra* confusion, strife, OS, OHG *werran* embroil), f. Gmc *werz-*, *wers-* (WORSE)]

war[2] (wŏr), v.i. & t. (-rr-). Make war (arch.); bring or beat *down* by war; (part.) rival, competing, inconsistent, (∼*ring creeds, principles*). [ME, f. prec.]

war'bl|e[1] (wŏr-), v.i. & t., & n. **1.** Sing (i. & t.) in gentle continuous trilling manner (esp. of birds, also of person or sound); speak, utter, in manner sug-

gestive of bird's song; relate in verse. **2. n.** ∼ed song etc.; ∼ing voice (*spoke in a* ∼*e*). [ME, f. ONF *werble*(r) f. WG f. Gmc *hwerbh-* revolve, see WHIRL]

war'ble[2] (wŏr-), n. Hard lump on horse's back from galling of saddle; (tumour produced by) larva of gadfly. [orig. obsc.; cf. MSw. *varbulde* boil (*var* pus, *bulde* tumour)]

war'bler (wŏr-), n. In vbl senses: esp., many kinds of small bird including nightingale, whitethroat, and chiff-chaff, some not remarkable for song. [-ER[1]]

ward[1] (wŏrd), n. **1.** Act of guarding or defending place etc. (now only in *keep watch &* ∼). **2.** Guard or parry in fencing (arch.). **3.** Confinement, custody, guardian's control, (arch.; *is under* ∼; *put him in* ∼; *to whom the child is in* ∼). **4.** Minor under care of guardian or Court of Chancery. **5.** Administrative division of city. **6.** Separate room or division in prison (*condemned* etc. ∼) or hospital (*isolation* etc. ∼) ‖ or workhouse (*casual* etc. ∼). **7.** pl. Notches & projections in key and lock designed to prevent opening by wrong key. **8.** ∼*mote* (hist.), meeting of city ∼ [OE *mōt* meeting]; ∼*room*, in warship for commissioned officers below commanding officer. [OE *weard*, OS *ward*, OHG *wart*, ON *vorthr*, Goth. ∼*wards*, f. Gmc *wardh-* extended form of *war-* WARE[2,3]; cf. GUARD[1]]

ward[2] (wŏrd), v.t. Have in keeping, protect, (chiefly now of God); parry (blow, often *off*), keep *off* (danger, poverty, etc.). [OE *weardian*, OS *-on*, OHG *wartēn*, ON *vartha*, f. Gmc *wardh-* (prec.)]

-ward(s) (-ward, -dz), suf. repr. OE *-weard*, primarily forming adjj., w. sense 'having a specified direction', corresp. to OS *-ward*, OHG *-wart*, f. Gmc *-wardha-* f. *wardh-*, *werth-* to turn, cogn. w. L *vertere* (cf. *versus*). OE adjj. in *-weard* usu. denoted direction of movement. They could be used adv. in the acc., or in the gen. case (*-weardes* (now *-wards*): see -ES). The suf. was occas. attached to a phr. consisting of a n. or pron. governed by a prep., e.g. *tō Lundene weard* 'to Londonward(s)', wh. survives in arch. use, as in *'to us-ward'.* On the anal. of such compds after loss of *to* (e.g. *heavenward*, *for to heavenward*) the suf. has been added to nn. (*Godward*, *earthward*) esp. in lit. use. *-ward* & *-wards* are so nearly syn. that no hard & fast rules can be given for their use; it is largely a matter of idiom & euphony; e.g. *-wards* is required when manner is indicated as well as direction of movement, as *to walk backwards*; we say *a forward* (adj.) *movement*, *to come forward* (adv.) but *it is moving forwards, not backwards*. As living suff., *-ward* & *-wards* form extempore adjj. & advv., freq. more or less *joc.*, *as bankwards, bedward, Perth-wards.*

war′den[1] (wôr-), n. Watchman, sentinel, (arch.); member of civilian organization for assisting the civil population in air raids; guardian, president, governor, of (in obs. or existent titles, as *W~ of the Marches, Merton College* etc., *the Cinque Ports*), whence ~SHIP n. [ME, f. AF, ONF *wardein*, var. of OF *guarden(e)* GUARDIAN]

war′den[2] (wôr-), n. Kind of cooking pear. [ME, of unkn. orig.]

war′der (wôr-), n. ‖ Sentinel (arch.); ‖ gaoler, whence **war′dress**[1] (wôr-), n. (hist.) staff of authority carried by king or commander & occas. used to give signals. [ME, f. AF *wardere*, *-our* f. *warder* =.OF *guarder* GUARD[2], see ·ER]

War′dour Street (wôr′der), n. A London street formerly noted for antique & imitation-antique furniture (~ *English*, affectedly archaic) but now given over esp. to the film trade; (used for) the film trade.

ward′robe (wôr-), n. Place where clothes are kept, esp. large cabinet or movable cupboard with pegs, shelves, etc.; person's stock of clothes; ~ *dealer*, dealer in second-hand clothes; ~ *mistress*, one who has charge of the professional ~ of an actor or actress, or of a theatrical company; ~ *trunk* (fitted with drawers, coat-hangers, etc., & designed to stand on end, serving as ~). [ME, f. *warderobe*, ONF var. of OF *garderobe* (GUARD[2], ROBE)]

war′dship (wôr-), n. Tutelage, guardian's care, (*under* ~; *has the* ~ *of*). [WARD[1], ·SHIP]

ware[1], n. 1. Things manufactured for sale, esp. pottery of any kind (otherwise usu. in comb., as HARD~, TIN~); (pl.) articles that person etc. has for sale (usu. *his* etc. ~s); (with distinctive epithet) kind of manufactured material esp. pottery, named from inventor, place of manufacture, or some characteristic (*Wedgwood, Delft* or *Delf, black*, etc., ~, kinds of pottery; *Tunbridge* ~, inlaid wood). 2. ~*house* (-s) n., building in which goods are stored, bonded, or displayed for sale, repository, wholesale or large retail store; ~*house* (-z) v.t., store (esp. furniture or bonded goods) temporarily in respository; ~*houseman*, owner of repository. [OE *waru*, MDu., MLG, MHG *ware*, ON *vara*]

ware[2], pred. a. (poet.). Aware. [OE *wær*, OS *war*, ON *varr*, Goth *wars* f. Gmc *war-*, cf. WARD[1]]

ware[3] (wôr, wâr), v.t. (Imperat.) look out for, be cautious about, (~ *hounds, wire, traps!*; esp. in hunting-field); (colloq. usu. imperat.) decline to have anything to do with, bar, avoid, fight shy of. [OE *warian*, OS *-on*, OHG *-ōn* f. Gmc *war-* (prec.)]

war′fare (wôr-), n. State of war, campaigning, being engaged in war, (*after long* ~; *his* ~ *is over*). [f. WAR[1] + FARE[2]]

war′like (wôr-), a. Martial, fond of or skilful in war; military, of or for war, (~ *preparations*); bellicose, threatening war. [ME; ·LIKE]

war′lock (wôr-), n. (arch.). Sorcerer, wizard. [OE *wǣr-loga* = OS *wār-logo*, prob. f. *wǣr* covenant (OHG *wāra* truth) + *loga* liar]

warm[1] (wôrm), a. & n. 1. Hottish, of or at rather high temperature, (*hot*, ~, *tepid, cool, cold*; ~ *water, weather, countries*; ~ *blood*, that of mammals & birds ranging from 98° to 112° F., also fig. passionate or amorous or emotional disposition, whence ~-blood**ED**[2] (·lŭd-) a.; (of persons etc.) having temperature of skin raised by exercise or excitement or external heat. 2. (Of clothes etc.) serving to keep one ~. 3. (Of friendly relations or actions or agents) enthusiastic, hearty, zealous, (*a* ~ *partisan, friend, welcome*, RECEPTION; ~ *thanks*). 4. Animated, heated, exciting or excited, in or resulting from sanguine or offended or indignant or unreserved mood, (*when* ~ *with wine; the dispute or disputants grew* ~; ~ *work*, keen or dangerous conflict). 5. (Of position etc.) difficult or dangerous to maintain or meet (*a* ~ *corner*, hot part of battle etc.; *so* ~ RECEPTION; *make it* or *things* ~ *for* one, create strong feeling against him). 6. (Of feelings etc.) sympathetic, emotional, affectionate, susceptible, (*has a* ~ *heart*, whence ~-heart**ED**[2] (·hârt-) a., ~-heart′**ed**ly[2] adv., ~-heart′**ed**ness n.; *a* ~ *temperament*, susceptible esp. to amorous impressions; ~ *descriptions* etc., intended to appeal to amorous feelings, indelicate). 7. (Of colour) suggestive of ~th, esp. containing rich reds or yellows. 8. (Of scent in hunting) fresh & strong, indicating recent passage of quarry; (of seeker in children's hiding games etc.) near the object sought, on verge of finding. 9. (colloq.). (Of person) comfortably off, rich. 10. (Of official etc.) no longer strange, comfortably established, *in* office. 11. n. Something ~, esp. BRITISH ~. Hence ~′**ly**[2] adv., ~**th**[1] n., (wôr-). [OE *wearm*, OS, OHG *warm*, ON *varmr* f. Gmc *warmaz*, prob. cogn. w. L *formus*, Gk *thermos*, Skr. *gharma*]

warm[2] (wôrm), v.t. & i., & n. 1. Make warm, excite, (*fire* ~*s room, person*, etc.; *wine to* ~ *the heart*; ~ *oneself at fire* etc.; ~ *person* or *his jacket*, thrash him, whence ~′**ing**[1] n., sl.); ~ *oneself at fire* etc.; become warm or animated or sympathetic (often *up*; *room is* ~*ing up*; *he* ~*ed up* or ~*ed as he got into his subject; my heart* ~*s to him*); ~*ing-pan*, flat closed long-handled usu. brass vessel holding live coals formerly used for ~*ing* inside of bed before it was occupied, (fig.) person holding office temporarily to keep it for another not yet of age etc.; hence (·)~**ER**[1] (2) n. 2. n. Act of ~*ing* oneself or something (*must have, give it, another* ~ *first*).

[OE *werman* (= OS *wermian*, OHG *-en*, Goth. *-jan*), f. Gmc *warm- (prec.)]

warn (wŏrn), v.t. Give notice to, put on guard, caution, admonish, (person *of* danger or consequences or future or unknown present circumstance, *against* person or thing or do*ing, that* something impends or must be reckoned with, *that* he is neglecting or has neglected to do something, *to* do, or abs.). Hence ~² **ingLY²** adv. [OE *war(e)nian, wearnian*, OHG *warnōn*, f. Gmc *war- WARE²]

war'ning (wŏr-), n. In vbl senses (*take* ~, have one's caution excited, mentally register danger etc., act on a ~); also or esp.: thing that serves to warn (*palpitation is a* ~ *of heart trouble; let this be a* ~ *to you*); *give* (master, servant) ~, announce that employment is to terminate in specified (e.g. *a month's*) time. [-ING¹]

warp¹ (wŏrp), v.t. & i. **1.** Make or become crooked or perverted, change from straight or right or natural state, bias, (*sun had* ~*ed the boards; seasoned timber does not* ~; *hardship* ~*ed his disposition; judgement* ~*ed by self-interest*). **2.** (naut.). Haul (ship) in some direction by rope attached to fixed point, progress thus. **3.** Fertilize by inundating with WARP². [OE *weorpan* throw, OS *werpan*, OHG *werfan*, ON *verpa*, Goth. *wairpan*, f. Gmc *werp-, *warp-, *wurp-]

warp² (wŏrp), n. **1.** Threads stretched lengthwise in loom to be crossed by weft. **2.** Rope used in towing or warping. **3.** Crooked state produced in timber etc. by uneven shrinking or expansion; (fig.) perversion or perverse inclination in mind. **4.** Sediment or alluvial deposit, esp. that left by turbid water kept standing on poor land. [OE *wearp*, OHG *warf*, ON *varp*, f. Gmc *warp- (prec.)]

wa'rrant (wŏ-), n. **1.** Thing that bears person out in or authorizes action (*have no* ~ *for what you do; his promise or order, our strength, is our* ~; *I will be your* ~; *with the* ~ *of a good conscience*). **2.** Voucher, written authorization to receive money (*dividend*, TREASURY, ~), carry out arrest or distress (*a* ~ *is out against him*), represent principal in lawsuit (~ *of attorney*), etc. **3.** Certificate from War Office or Admiralty or Air Ministry (cf. COMMISSION) held by ~-*officer* (between commissioned officers & N.C.O.s, as gunner, boatswain, sergeant-major). [ME, f. ONF *warant, -and*, var. of OF *g(u)arant, -and*, f. subst. use of part of WG *waren* to warrant]

wa'rrant² (wŏ-), v.t. Serve as warrant for, justify, (*nothing can* ~ *such insolence*), whence ~ABLE a., (also, of a stag) of an age to be hunted (5 or 6 years); = GUARANTEE v., esp. in sense *answer for genuineness* etc. *of* (goods; ~*ed pure* etc., to be so), & in *I* or *I'll* ~ (*you*) usu. parenthet. = no doubt, whence ~ER¹, ~OR, ~EE¹ (one to whom warranty is given), nn., (wŏ-). [ME,

f. *warantir, -dir*, dial. var. of OF *g(u)arantir, -dir*, f. com.-Rom. f. prec.]

wa'rranty (wŏ-), n. Authority or justification (usu. *for* doing or saying or supposing); (law) express or implied undertaking on vendor's part that thing sold is vendor's & is fit for use or fulfils specified conditions. [f. AF (OF) *warantie*, dial. var. of *guarantie* (GUARANTY), f. *warant* WARRANT¹]

wa'rren (wŏ-), n. Piece of ground in which rabbits are preserved or abound (*like rabbits in a* ~, of thick population). [ME, f. AF, ONF *warenne* (OF *garenne*), f. Gmc *war- (WARE³)]

wa'rrior (wŏ-), n. Distinguished or veteran soldier (rhet., poet.); member of any of the fighting services (*the Unknown W~*, or *Soldier*, unidentified body of one killed in the 1914–18 war selected for public burial as symbolizing his country's sacrifice); (attrib., of nation etc.) martial; (of savages) fighting man; ~ *ant*, of kinds that make slaves of other species. [ME, f. *werreior* etc., ONF var. of OF *guerreior* etc., f. *werreier, guerreier*, f. com. Rom. f. WG *werra* WAR¹]

wart (wŏrt), n. Small hardish excrescence on skin caused by abnormal growth of papillae (*paint* one *with his* ~s, without concealment of blemishes), similar lump on stem etc. of plant; ~-*grass*, *-weed*, *-wort*, kind of spurge with juice used to cure ~s; ~-*hog*, kinds of African large-headed swine with ~y lumps on face. Hence ~'Y² a. [OE *wearte*, OS *warla*, OHG *warza*, ON *varla* f. Gmc *wartōn*]

war'|ly, a. Given to caution, habitually on the look-out, circumspect; cautious *of* do*ing*; showing, done with, caution. Hence ~iLY² adv., ~iNESS n. [f. WARE³ +-Y²]

was. See BE.

wash¹ (wŏ-), v.t. & i. **1.** Cleanse with liquid (~ one's *face* etc., one*self*, or any object; ~ thing *out*, clean its inside; ~ one's *dirty* LINEN; ~ one's *hands*, fig., decline responsibility usu. *of*), (fig.) purify (~ *me throughly from mine iniquity*); take (stain, dirt, etc.) *out* or *off* or *away* by ~*ing*; ~ *up* (plates etc., or usu. abs.), clean table utensils after use; (abs.) ~ oneself or esp. one's (face &) hands (*must* ~ *before dinner*), ~ clothes (~*es for a living*). **2.** (Of coloured material or dye) bear ~ing without loss of colour (*won't* ~, fig. of argument etc., stand examination), whence ~'ING² (wŏ-) a.; ~*ed out*, (fig.) enfeebled, limp, demoralized, esp. as effect of dissipation. **3.** Moisten (*roses* ~*ed with dew*); (of river, sea, etc.) touch (coast, bank, country) with its waters. **4.** (Of moving liquid) carry along in specified direction (chiefly in pass.; *a wave* ~*ed him overboard; was* ~*ed up by the sea; beef* ~*ed down with ale*); denude (*sea-*~*ed cliffs*); scoop out (*water had* ~*ed a channel*); go splashing or sweeping *over*, along, out, in, or into. 5. Sift (ore) by action of water. 6. Brush thin coating of watery colour over (paper in water-colour or sepia painting, wall), coat (inferior metal) thinly with gold etc. Hence ~ABLE (wŏ-) a. [OE wæscan, OS, OHG wascan, ON vaska, f. Gmc *waskan f. *watskan f. root *wat- as in WATER]

wash² (wŏ-), n. 1. Washing or being washed (give it a good ~; must get a ~; the ~, treatment at laundry, as send the linen to the ~); quantity of clothes just (to be, being) washed. 2. Visible or audible motion of agitated water, esp. waves caused by passage of vessel. 3. Soil swept off by water, alluvium. 4. Kitchen water & scraps given to pigs. 5. Thin or weak or inferior liquid food (this soup, tea, claret, is mere ~); (fig.) twaddle, wishwash. 6. Liquid for spreading over surface to cleanse or heal or colour, lotion, cosmetic; thin coating of water-colour, wall-colouring, or metal. [f. prec.]

wash- (wŏ-), comb. form of WASH¹, ², often =& used as substitute for washING; ‖ ~-basin; ~-board, of ribbed wood for use in scrubbing clothes at wash, also board attached to gunwale, port, etc., to prevent water from washing in, also board skirting bottom of room-wall; ~-boiler, clothes-washing cauldron; ~-bottle, apparatus for purifying gases etc. by passage through liquid; ~-bowl; ~-cloth, piece of linen etc. used in washing dishes etc.; ~-day, on which clothes are washed; ‖ ~-hand-basin; ‖ ~-hand-stand, piece of furniture with toilet utensils; ~-house, laundry; ~-leather, chamois or similar leather; ~-out, breach in railway or road track caused by flood, heavy rainfall, etc., (sl.) complete failure, fiasco, (sl.) useless or inefficient person; ~-pot (arch. exc. of pot with melted tin for final dipping of tinplate); *~-rag, ~-cloth; *~-room, lavatory; ~-stand, = ~-hand-stand; ~-tub, esp. for clothes.

wa'sher (wŏ-), n. In vbl senses; also, flat ring or perforated piece of leather, rubber, metal, etc., used to give tightness to joint, nut, fastening, etc.; BOTTLE¹-~; ‖ ~-woman, laundress. [-ER¹]

wa'shing (wŏ-), n. In vbl senses (& see WASH-); esp., linen etc. sent to the wash; BRAIN-~; ~ machine, for the ~ of clothes etc.; ~ soda, sodium carbonate, used dissolved in water for ~ & cleaning; ~-stand, = WASH-stand; ~-up, ~ of table utensils after a meal. [-ING¹]

Wa'shington (wŏ-), n. (Used for) the U.S. Government. [capital of U.S.]

Washingtōn'ia (wŏ-), n. Californian palm-tree named after George Washington. [-IA¹]

wa'sh|y (wŏ-), a. (Of liquid food etc.) too watery, weak, thin, insipid; (of colour) faded-looking, thin; (of style, sentiment, etc.) diffuse, feeble, lacking vigour or compression. Hence~ILY² adv.,~INESS n. [-Y²]

wasn't (wŏznt). See BE.

wasp (wŏ-), n. Kinds of hymenopterous social or solitary insect of which the common kind has black & yellow transverse stripes, very slender waist, taste for fruit & sweets, & powerfully venomous sting (has a waist like a ~'s, whence ~-waistED² a.); ~-bee, -beetle, -fly, kinds having some resemblance to ~. [OE wæfs, wæps, wæsp, OS wepsia, OHG wafsa, wefsa, f. Gmc *wabhis-, *waps-, cogn. w. L vespa & WEAVE, w. ref. to nests]

wa'spish (wŏ-), a. Irritable, petulant, ill-tempered, sharp in retort. Hence ~LY² adv., ~NESS n. [-ISH¹]

wassail (wŏ'sl, wǎ'sl), n., & v.i. (arch.). 1. Festive occasion, drinking-bout; kind of liquor drunk on such occasion; ~-bowl, -cup, -horn, etc. 2. v.i. Make merry, hold festivities. [ME wæs hæil etc., f. ON ves heill, corresp. to OE wes hāl 'be in good health' (hāl=WHOLE), form of salutation]

wast. See BE.

wäst'age, n. Amount wasted or that runs to waste, loss by waste. [-AGE]

wäste¹, a. (Of district etc.) desolate, desert, uninhabited, uncultivated, as result of natural barrenness etc. or of ravages or catastrophe (lay ~, ravage; lie ~, be uncultivated; ~ land, not occupied for any purpose); (fig.) monotonous or presenting no features of interest (the ~ periods of history); superfluous, refuse, no longer serving a purpose, left over after use, (~ products, useless by-products of manufacture; ~ energy, steam, etc.; ~ paper, esp. books or documents that fail or are valueless). [ME, f. AF, ONF wast, var. of OF g(u)ast f. Rom. *wasto f. L vastus infl. by cogn. WG, as OS wōsti]

wäst|e², v.t. & i. Lay WASTE¹; (law) bring (estate) into bad condition by damage or neglect; expend to no purpose or for inadequate result, use extravagantly, squander, (~e money, time, food, etc., or abs. as ~e not, want not; ~e breath or words, talk uselessly; wear (t. & i.) gradually away, wither, (arch., of time) pass t. & i., (his resources were ~ed, were rapidly ~ing; day ~es, draws to a close; sorcerer ~ed his arm; a ~ing disease; is ~ing away for lack of food); run to waste (that water is ~ing). [ME, f. AF, ONF waster, var. of OF g(u)aster f. Rom. *wastare f. L vastare infl. by cogn. WG *wōstjan, see prec.]

wäste³, n. 1. Desert, waste region, dreary scene, (a ~ of waters, unbroken expanse of sea or floods). 2. Being used up, diminution by wear & tear, (the ~ of tissue is continuous; ~ & repair balance each other). 3. Waste material or food, useless remains, refuse, scraps, shreds; = COTTON ~. 4. Act of wasting, throwing away or extravagant or ineffectual use of time, money, food, etc., (wilful ~ makes woeful want; it is ~ of time to argue further; run *to* ~, of liquid or fig. of affection etc., be wasted). **5.** (law). Injury to estate caused by act or neglect esp. of life-tenant. [ME, f. AF, ONF *wast*(e), var. of OF *g*(*u*)*ast*(e), partly f. L *vastum* (WASTE[1]), partly f. *waster* (prec.)]

wäste-, comb. form of WASTE[1] [2] [3]; ~-*basket*, for waste odds & ends esp. of paper; || ~-*book* in book-keeping, book in which rough preliminary entries of transactions are made; **wäste′FUL** (-tf-) a., extravagant, given to or exhibiting waste, whence **wäste′fuLLY** adv., **wäste′ful-NESS** n.; **wäste′LESS** (-tl-) a.; || ~-*pap′er-basket*, receptacle for used paper etc.; ~-*pipe*, for carrying off used or superfluous water.

wäst′er, n. In vbl senses; also, article spoilt or flawed in manufacture; (sl.) good-for-nothing person. [ME; -ER[1]]

wäst′rel, n. Thing spoilt in making; stray child, street arab, waif; good-for-nothing fellow; wasteful person. [f. WASTE[2] + -REL]

watch[1] (wŏ-), n. **1.** Wakefulness at night (now rare; *in the* ~*es of the night*, while one lies awake; *pass as a* ~ *in the night*, be soon forgotten). **2.** Alert state, being on the look-out, vigilance, constant observation, attention to what may come, (*keep* ~, *a* ~, *good* or *a good* ~; ~ *& ward*, orig. guard by night & day, now emphatic reduplication of ~; *on the* ~, waiting usu. for expected or desired or feared occurrence, whence ~'FUL a., ~'fuLY[2] adv., ~'fulNESS n. **3.** (hist.). Man or body of men charged with patrolling streets at night, guard (BLACK[1] ~, orig. an armed company). **4.** (hist.). One of three or of four parts into which night was anciently divided (*first* etc. or *evening* etc. ~). **5.** Four-hour spell of duty on board ship (DOG-~, 2-hr; one of the halves (*starboard & port* ~ from position of men's bunks) into which ship's crew is divided to take alternate duty. **6.** Small timepiece worked by coiled spring for carrying on person (STOP-~). **7.** ~-*case*, outer metal case enclosing ~-*works*; ~-*chain*, metal ~-*guard*; || *W*~ *Committee*, committee of a (county) borough council dealing with (policing &) lighting etc.; ~-*fire*, at night in camps etc.; || ~-*glass*, disc covering face of ~; ~-*guard*, chain for securing ~ on person; ~-*key*, instrument for winding up ~-*works*; ~-*maker*; ~-*man*, (formerly, & still poet.) sentinel or member of street patrol, (now) man employed to look after empty building etc. at night; ~-*night*, last night of year esp. as celebrated by religious services; ~ *oil*, fine thin kind for lubricating ~-*works* etc.; ~-*pocket*, in garment esp. waistcoat, or separate for attachment to bed etc., holding ~; ~-*spring*, kind used in ~-*works*, also mainspring of ~ (cf. HAIR*spring*); ~-*stand*, small pillar etc. for hanging ~ on; ~-*tower*, post of observation usu. fortified;

~-*word*, (formerly) military password, (now) phrase expressing briefly the principles of a party etc. (e.g. *Equal pay for equal work*). [OE *wæcce* (*wæccan*, see foll.); cf. WAKE[2]]

watch[2] (wŏ-), v.i. & t. Remain awake for a purpose (now rare; ~*ed all night by his side*; ~ *& pray*); be on the watch, keep watch, be vigilant, look out for opportunity etc., exercise protecting care *over*; keep eyes fixed on, keep under observation, follow observantly, (*had him* ~*ed by detectives*; *if you don't* ~ *it*, colloq., take care or precautions; ~*ed pot never boils*, strained expectation makes time seem long); look out for, bide, await, (opportunity; ~ *one's time*, wait for right moment). Hence ~'ER[1] n. [OE *wæccan*, doublet of *wacian* (WAKE[1]), f. Gmc *wakæjan* (OHG *wahhēn*)]

wa′ter[1] (waw-), n. **1.** Colourless transparent tasteless scentless compound of oxygen & hydrogen in liquid state convertible by heat into steam & by cold into ice, kinds of liquid consisting chiefly of this seen in sea, lake, stream, spring, rain, tears, sweat, saliva, urine, serum, etc., body of ~ as sea or lake or river, (*hot & cold*, *salt & fresh* or *sweet*, *smooth* or *still & rough* or *troubled*, HARD or SOFT, *aerated*, *saline*, *chalybeate*, *thermal*, BLUE[1], HEAVY, HOLY, MINERAL, etc., ~; *the upper* ~*s of the Thames*; *strong* ~*s*, arch., distilled spirits; *table* ~*s*, esp. mineral ~s bottled for use at meals; *red* ~, bloody urine; *in smooth* ~, going easily, past one's troubles; *on the* ~, in boat or ship; *by* ~, using ships, barges, etc., for travel or transport; *in deep* ~ or ~*s*, floundering, in great difficulties, in affliction; *still* ~*s run deep*, quiet manner may cover depths of emotion, knowledge, or cunning; FISH[2] *in troubled* ~*s*; *cup of cold* ~, symbol of charitable intent; *get into*, *be in*, *hot* ~, bring or have brought trouble or rebuke on oneself by indiscretion etc.; *throw cold* ~ *on* scheme etc., discourage or poohpooh it; *written in* ~, of name, achievements, etc., transient; *keep one's head above* ~, chiefly fig., avoid financial ruin; *the* ~*s*, rhet., the sea, as *cross the* ~*s*; *cast one's bread upon the* ~*s*, do good without looking for gratitude or immediate or definite return; *drink the* ~*s*, attend spa for health; *brings the* ~ *to* one's *mouth*, makes it water; FISH[2] *out of* ~; BETWEEN *wind & * ~; *pour* OIL[1] *on the* ~*s*; *spend money*, *shed blood*, *like* ~, lavishly or recklessly; *go through* FIRE[1] *& * ~; *fire & * ~, arch., symbol of necessaries of life not to be supplied to outlaw; HOLD[1] ~; *make*, *pass*, ~, void urine; *tread* ~, maintain position in deep ~ by action of marking time; ~ *on the brain*, *knee*, etc., morbid accumulation of fluid; ~ *bewitched*, very weak tea etc. or spirit-&~; ~ *of life*, spiritual enlightenment; ~*s of forgetfulness*, Lethe, oblivion, death). **2.** State of tide (*high*, *low*, ~;

in low ~, fig., in depressed condition, esp. badly off for money; *high, low,* ~ *mark,* highest, lowest, point reached by tidal ~, also fig. of best & worst results of fluctuating process). **3.** Solution of specified substance in ~ (*lavender, rose,* etc., ~*,* scents; *soda, lithia, dill,* etc., ~*,* beverages or medicines). **4.** Transparency & brilliance of gem esp. diamond (*of the first*~, of finest quality, often also transf. as *a genius, blunder, of the first* ~). **5.** (finance). Amount of nominal capital added by watering, see WATER². **6.** ~· (in compounds of which those especially that distinguish varieties of plants & animals are too numerous to be given separately), haunting, growing in, used or employed on, etc., the~; of, for, worked or effected by, made with, containing, using, yielding, etc., ~. **7.** || ~·*anchor,* = DRAG²·*anchor;* ~ AVENS; || ~·*bailiff,* customhouse officer at port (hist.), official who prevents poaching of fish in protected ~s; ~·*bed,* rubber mattress filled with ~ for invalid to avoid bed-sores; ~·*bellows,* blower made by suspension in ~ of inverted valved vessel by raising & lowering of which air is drawn in & expelled; ~·*bird;* ~·*biscuit;* ~·*blister,* containing colourless fluid, not blood; ~·*boatman,* kind of aquatic bug; ~·*borne,* (of goods) conveyed by ~, (of diseases) communicated or propagated by use of contaminated drinking~; ~·*bottle,* esp. of glass for wash-hand-stand or dining table, also of metal etc. for soldier's kit; ~·*brash,* form of indigestion with eructation of watery fluid; ~·BREAKER²; ~·*buffalo,* the common domestic Indian buffalo; || ~ *bus,* river craft carrying passengers on regular run; ~·*butt;* ~·*carriage,* conveyance of goods by ~; *W*~·*carrier,* Aquarius; ~·*cart,* esp. with ~ for sale or for watering roads; ~·*chute,* slope of boards slippery with running ~ for tobogganing down; ~·*closet,* place for evacuation of bladder or bowels with arrangement for flushing pan with ~; ~·*colour,* pigment mixed with ~ & not oil, picture painted with such colours, (pl. or sing.) art of painting such pictures; ~ COMPRESS²; ~·*course,* brook, stream; ~·*cracker,* kind of biscuit; ~·*cress,* creeping ~·plant, eaten as salad; ~·*cure,* hydropathy; ~·*diviner,* dowser (see DOWSING); ~·*drinker,* (esp.) abstainer from alcohol; ~·*fall,* stream falling over precipice or down steep hillside; ~·*finder,* dowser (DOWSING); ~·*fowl* (usu. collect. as pl.), birds haunting~, esp. as objects of sport; ~·*gas,* got by decomposing ~ & used after treatment with carbon as illuminant; ~·*gate,* flood-gate, also gate giving access to river etc.; ~·*gauge,* glass tube etc. indicating height of ~ inside reservoir, boiler, etc.; ~·*glass,* tube with glass bottom enabling objects under ~ to be observed, also solution of silicate of soda used as a vehicle for fresco-painting, or

used for preserving eggs; ~·*gruel;* || ~·*guard,* (member of) Customs and Excise marine anti-smuggling service; ~·*hammer,* percussion made by ~ in pipe when tap is turned off, or by ~ in steam-pipe when live steam is admitted; ~·*hen,* = MOOR¹·*hen;* ~·*hole,* shallow depression or cavity in which ~ collects (esp. in the bed of a river otherwise dry); ~·*ice,* flavoured & frozen ~ & sugar; ~·*inch,* quantity discharged in 24 hrs through 1 in. pipe under least pressure; ~·*jacket,* case filled with ~ & enclosing part of machine that is to be kept cool; ~·*joint,* proof against leakage; || ~·*junket,* sandpiper; ~·*laid,* (of rope) = CABLE¹·*laid;* ~·*lens,* magnifying lens made of glass-bottomed brass cell filled with ~; ~·*level,* surface of ~ in reservoir etc., also plane below which ground is saturated with~, also levelling-instrument made of glass tube to be held horizontal with two upturned graduated open ends in which the contained ~ must be at same height; ~·*lily,* kinds of plant with broad leaves & white or blue or yellow or red flowers floating on surface of ~; ~·*line,* along which surface of ~ touches ship's side (when loaded, *load*-~·*line,* when empty, *light*-~·*line*), also one of the semi-transparent parallel lines formed in some papers in manufacture; ~*logged,* (of wood) so saturated, (of vessel) so filled, with~ as barely to float; ~·*main,* main pipe in ~·supplying system; ~·*man,* boatman plying for hire, also oarsman *good, bad,* etc., at keeping boat truly balanced etc., whence ~ MANSHIP(3) n.; ~*mark,* (n.) faint design seen in some paper when held against light indicating maker, size, etc., (v.t.) impress such mark on in making; ~·*meadow,* kept fertile by being flooded; ~·*melon,* one of two divisions of melon (the other being *musk*-*melon*) with ellipse shape, smooth skin, & watery juice; ~·*meter;* ~·*mill,* worked by ~·wheel; ~·*monkey,* jar with long narrow neck for ~ used in hot countries; ~·*motor,* ~·wheel, turbine, small motor using ~ under pressure; ~·*nymph,* naiad; ~ OUZEL; ~·*pepper,* acrid plant found in wet places; ~·*pillar,* upright with revolving head for feeding steam-engines etc.; ~·*pipe;* ~·*plane,* plane passing through ship's~·line; ~·*plate,* with double bottom to hold hot ~ for keeping food warm; ~·*platter,* kind of~·lily with upturned edges to leaves; *W*~ *Poet* (the), John Taylor (d. 1653); ~ *polo,* hand-ball game with goals played by swimmers; ~·*power,* mechanical force got from weight or motion of ~, fall in stream capable of being utilized as force; ~·*proof,* (adj.) impervious to ~, (n.) ~·proof garment or material, (v.t.) make ~·proof with rubber etc., whence ~·proofER¹ n.; ~·*ram,* hydraulic ram; ~·*rat,* = ~ *vole;* ~·*rate,* || charge made for use of public ~·supply; ~·*sail,* below lower studding-sail close over ~; ~-*seal*, body of ~ used in bent pipe or about mouth of pipe to prevent passage or escape of gas; ~-*shed*, line of separation between~s flowing to different rivers or basins or seas [cogn. w. SHED¹], (pop.) slope down which ~ flows, (pop.) river basin; ~-*shoot*, pipe or trough throwing off ~ from house etc.; ~-*side*, margin of sea, lake, or river; ~-*skiing*, sport of being towed on skis behind a motor-boat; ~-*skin*, skin bag for carrying ~; ~-*soldier*, aquatic plant with flowers above surface; ~ *souchy* (sōō'shi), fish boiled & served in its own liquor; ~-*splash*, part of road submerged by stream or pool; ~-*spout*, phenomenon in which whirling cloud forms a funnel-shaped pendant, which descends towards sea & draws up corresponding volume of whirling ~, the whole forming a pillar uniting sea & cloud; ~-*sprite*; ~-*supply*, providing & storing of ~, amount of ~ stored, for use of town, house, etc.; ~-*table*, string-course arranged to throw ~ off building, plane below which the soil or rock is saturated with ~; ~-*tiger*, larva of certain ~-beetles; ~-*tight*, (of joint, boots, cask, compartment in ship, etc.) tightly enough fastened or fitted to prevent ingress or egress of ~ (~-*tight compartments*, fig., keeping of subjects etc. entirely separate); ~-*tower*, supporting elevated tank to secure pressure for distributing ~-supply; ~-*tube boiler*, in which ~ circulates in tubes exposed to flames & hot gases; ~-*vole*, large vole haunting ~; ~-*wag(g)on*, =~-*cart* (*on the* ~-*waggon*, sl., abstaining from alcohol); ~ *wagtail*, common pied wagtail; ~-*wave*, wave in the hair produced by ~-*waving*, a method of waving hair with the use of ~; ~-*way*, navigable channel, also thick planks at outer edge of deck along which channel is hollowed for ~ to run off by; ~-*wheel*, kinds of wheel (*overshot, undershot, breast, & turbine, wheel*) worked by ~ & working machinery; ~-*wings*, floats fixed behind shoulders of persons learning to swim; ~-*witch*, = ~-*finder*, also kinds of bird; ~-*withe*, W.-Ind. vine so full of sap that branch broken off yields draught of ~; ~-*works*, establishment for managing ~-supply, also ornamental fountain (*turn on the* ~-*works*, sl., shed tears). Hence ~LESS a. [OE *wæter*, OS *watar*, OHG *wazzar* (cf. ON *vatn*, Goth. *wato*), f. Gmc **wat-*, cogn. w. WET, L *unda*, Gk *hudōr*]

wa'ter² (waw-), v.t. & i. 1. Sprinkle (road, plants, etc.), adulterate (milk, beer, etc.), with water. 2. Give drink of water to (horse etc.), (of animals) go to pool etc. to drink. 3. (Of ship, engine, etc., or persons in charge) take in supply of water. 4. (Of smarting eyes, or of mouth when food is seen or food or pleasure eagerly anticipated) secrete or run with water (*makes* one's *mouth* ~, excites

desire or envy). 5. (Chiefly in p.p., as ~*ed silk*) produce irregular wavy damask--like markings on (material) by moistening & pressing in manufacture. 6. (finance). Increase (company's debt or nominal capital) by issue of new shares without corresponding addition to assets. 7. ~ *down*, make (details of story etc.) less vivid or horrifying; ~*ing-cart*, with perforated pipe or other device for ~ing road; ~*ing-place*, pool etc. at which animals ~, also spa, also seaside place frequented at certain seasons by holiday--makers & invalids; ~*ing-pot*, with perforated nozzle or rose for ~ing plants. [OE *wæterian* f. *wæter*, see prec.]

Waterloo' (waw-), n. The battle in which Napoleon was finally defeated in 1815; (with *a* or *his*) crushing blow, decisive contest, chiefly in phr. *meet* one's ~.

wa'ter|ỹ (waw-), a. Containing too much water, over-moist, sodden, (esp. of cooked vegetables or fish); (of eyes or lips) suffused or running with water; (of liquids) too thin, actually or apparently diluted, resembling water, (fig., of expression, talk, style, etc.) vapid, insipid, uninteresting, feeble, (of colour) pale, washed- out; indicative of rain (*a* ~*y moon, sky*). Hence ~INESS n. [OE, -Y²]

watt (wŏt), n. Unit of electric power, rate of working in circuit when electromotive force is one volt & intensity of current one ampere. Hence ~'AGE n, amount of electrical power expressed in ~s, ~t METER n. [J. *W*~, engineer (d. 1819)]

Watteau (wŏt'ō), n. French painter d. 1721 (~ *back*, arrangement of woman's dress-back with broad pleat falling from neck to ground without girdle; ~ *bodice*, with square opening at neck & short ruffled sleeves).

wa'ttle¹ (wŏ-), n., & v.t. 1. Interlaced rods & twigs as material of fences, walls, or roofs (~ *& daub*, plastered with mud or clay); (sing. or pl.) rods & twigs for such use; kinds of Australian acacia supplying such twigs, having bark used in tanning, & bearing golden flowers adopted as national emblem; (dial.) a wicker hurdle. 2. v.t. Construct of ~; interlace (twigs etc.); enclose or fill up with ~-work. [OE *watul*, of unkn. orig.]

wa'ttle² (wŏ-), n. Fleshy appendage on head or throat of turkey & other birds; BARB¹ of fish. Hence ~ED³ (wŏt'ld) a. [orig. unkn.]

waul, v.i. Squall, cry like cat. [imit.]

wāve¹, v.i. & t. 1. Vibrate or be stirred with sinuous or sweeping motions like those of flag or tree or field of corn in wind, flutter, undulate; impart waving motion to (~ *sword*, brandish it as encouragement to followers etc.; ~ one's *hand* often *to* person, in greeting or as signal); ~ hand or thing held in it usu. *to* person, give direction thus *to* person *to* do, send (person *away* thus, summon

(person) *nearer* thus, direct (person) thus
to do, express *farewell* etc. thus; ~ *aside*,
dismiss as intrusive or irrelevant. **2.** Give
undulating surface or course or appearance to (hair of head, lines in drawing,
etc.), make wavy, (of hair, line, etc.)
have such appearance, be wavy. [OE
wafian, MHG *waben*, f. Gmc *wabh- move
to and fro; cf. WAVER]

wāve², n. **1.** Ridge of water between two
depressions or (also *breaker*) long body of
water curling into arched form & breaking on shore (*the* ~s or ~, poet. & rhet.,
the sea, water; *attack in* ~s, mil., in
successive lines advancing like sea-~s).
2. Disturbance of the particles of a fluid
medium e.g. water, air, ether, into a
ridge-&-trough oscillation by which motion is propagated & heat, light, sound,
electricity, etc., conveyed in some direction without corresponding advance or
without any advance of the particles in
the same direction; single curve in the
course of such motion. **3.** Temporary
heightening of some influence or condition
or feeling (*a* ~ *of enthusiasm, prosperity,
depression; heat, cold,* ~, rise or fall of
temperature travelling over large area).
4. Undulating line or outline or surface,
waviness. **5.** Gesture of waving. **6.** ~
length, distance in any undulation from
one crest to the next; corresponding
distance between points in the same
phase in sound ~s or electromagnetic
radiation, i.e. the speed of light divided
by the frequency. Hence ~'LESS a.,
~'LET n., (-vĭ-). [f. prec.; in sense 1 repl.
ME *wawe*]

wāv'er, v.i. Oscillate unsteadily, flicker,
quiver, (rare; chiefly of flame); (of troops)
falter, become unsteady, begin to give
way; be irresolute or undecided between
different courses or opinions, be shaken
in resolution or belief. Hence ~ER¹ n.,
~ĭnġLY² adv. [ME, f. ON *vafra* corresp.
to MHG *waberen*, f. Gmc *wabh- WAVE¹]

wāv'y̆¹, a. Undulating, (of line or surface)
consisting of or showing alternate con-
trary curves, (~ *hair*); || *W*~ *Navy*
(colloq., hist.), R.N.V.R. (from ~ line of
insignia on sleeve). Hence **wāv'ĭLY²**
adv., **wāv'ĭNESS** n. [-Y²]

wāv'y̆², -ey, n. The snow-goose. [f.
Amer.-Ind. *wawa*]

wawl, v. = WAUL.

wăx¹, n., & v.t. **1.** Sticky plastic yellowish
substance secreted by bees as material of
honeycomb cells, bees~, white translucent scentless tasteless material got
from this by bleaching & purifying &
used for candles, in modelling, & for
other purposes, (*mould* one *like* ~, form
his character, on desired lines or induce
him to act just as desired); substance
resembling ~ in some respect, as the
secretion of some other insects esp.
Chinese ~, *ear*~ or cerumen, *mineral* ~,
esp. ozocerite, bee-bread, *paraffin* ~,

obtained from shale or petroleum,
vegetable ~ or exudation of certain plants,
SEAL²*ing*-~, COBBLERS'-~; (attrib., now
usu. preferred to *waxen*) made of ~.
2. ~*'bill*, kinds of small bird with translucent bill; ~ *candle*; ~-*chandler*, maker
or seller of ~ candles; ~'*cloth*, floor-cloth;
~ *doll*, with face etc. of ~, also person esp.
woman with pretty but unexpressive
face; ~-*flower*, HOYA; ~-*insect*, kinds that
secrete ~, esp. that collected as Chinese
~ from which superior candles are made;
~-*light*, taper or candle of ~; ~-*myrtle*,
candleberry; ~-*painting*, encaustic; ~-
-*palm*, S.-Amer. palm with stem coated in
mixture of resin & ~; ~-*paper*, waterproofed with layer of ~; ~-*pink*, kind of
garden-plant; ~-*pocket*, one of bee's ~-
-exuding apertures; ~-*pod*, = BUTTER-
-*bean*; ~-*tree*, kinds exuding ~ or encrusted with it by insects; ~'*wing*, kinds
of bird with small horny tips like red
sealing-~ to some feathers; ~'*work*,
modelling-work, objects modelled, in ~,
esp. dummies of persons with face &
hands of coloured ~ clothed to look like
life & be exhibited. **3.** v.t. Smear, polish,
encrust, treat surface of, with ~. [OE
weax, OS, OHG *wahs*, ON *vax*, f. Gmc
wahsam]

wăx², v.i. (Of moon between new & full)
have progressively larger part of surface
illuminated (cf. *wane*; ~ & *wane* also
transf. of influence etc.), undergo alternations of increase & decrease); (arch. &
poet.) grow or increase; (with adj. compl.)
pass into specified condition or esp. mood
or tone (~ *fat, old, merry, facetious, indignant, pathetic, angry*). [OE *weaxan*,
OS, OHG *wahsan*, ON *vaxa*, Goth.
wahsjan f. Gmc *wahs- cogn. w. L
augēre, Gk *auxanō*]

wăx³, n. (sl.). Fit of anger (*is in, got into,
put him in, a* ~). [orig. unkn.]

wăx'en, a. Made of wax (being ousted by
attrib. use of *wax*); presenting surface as
of wax (esp. of complexion, used with less
of depreciation than *waxy*); impressible
as wax, plastic. [OE; -EN³]

wăx'|y̆, a. Resembling wax in some way,
esp. easily moulded or presenting smooth
pale translucent surface; (of tissue) having degenerated into consistency resem-
bling wax (so ~*y liver* etc.); || (sl.) angry,
quick-tempered. Hence ~ĭLY² adv.,
~ĭNESS n. [WAX¹, ³, -Y²]

way, n. **1.** Road or track lit. or fig.
provided for passing along (HIGH~; OVER
the ~; || *permanent* ~, complete piece of
regular railroad track; || *six-foot* ~, space
left between each pair of rails & the next
on railway; *covered* ~, roofed or in fortif.
screened passage; *Appian, Latin*, etc.,
Way, great Roman roads in Italy; MILKY
~; *the* ~ *of the Cross*, series of paintings
in church etc., to receive successive attention in certain services, illustrating
Christ's progress to Calvary; *go the* ~ *of*

all the earth, of all flesh, of nature, die; *pave the ~ for,* take steps that will facilitate or prepare people's minds to accept some change); (pl.) structure of timber etc. on which new ship is slid down at launch. **2.** Best route or route taken or contemplated between two places or to place, method or plan for attaining object, person's desired or chosen course of action, *(ask the* or *one's ~; farthest~ about is nearest ~ home,* short cuts are delusive; *find* one's or *the ~,* reach destination; *lose* one's or *the ~,* go astray; *parting of the ~s,* usu. fig., time for momentous decision; *take* one's *~,* go in some direction, usu. *to* or *towards; go* one's *~* or *~s,* depart; *came by ~ of London,* via; *lead the ~,* act as guide or leader, show by example how thing can be done; *put oneself out of the ~,* inconvenience oneself to serve another; *is nothing out of the ~,* not uncommon or remarkable; *an out-of-the-~ corner,* remote, inaccessible; *go out of the* or *one's ~ to be rude,* show gratuitous rudeness; *right & wrong ~s of doing a thing; that is the ~ to do it; don't like the ~ she smiles; where there's a will there's a ~; you will never manage it that ~; will find* or *make a ~; will do it one ~* or *another; ~s & means,* methods esp. of providing money as in parliamentary *Committee of Ways & Means; go, take,* one's *own ~,* act independently esp. against others' advice; *have* one's *own* or *one's ~,* get what one wants, see one's orders carried out or desires gratified). **3.** Travelling-distance, length of road etc. (to be) traversed, *(India is a long ~ off; went a little, a good, a long, some, ~ with* or *to meet him;* ONCE *in a ~; is still a long ~ off perfection).* **4.** Unimpeded opportunity of advance, room free of obstacles, ground over which advance is desired or would naturally take place, (GIVE[1], MAKE[1], *~;* LION *in the ~; stand, be, in the ~ of, in* one's *~,* or *in the ~,* be obstacle to, be obstacle; *get out of, in, the ~,* cease, begin, to be impediment; *get* thing *out of the ~,* dispose of, get rid of, settle; *put* person *out of the ~,* confine or secretly kill him; *clear the ~,* remove obstacles, stand aside; RIGHT *of ~; put* one *in the ~ of a good bargain, of doing,* give him opportunity). **5.** Being engaged, time spent, in locomotion lit. or fig. *(with songs to clear the ~; met him on the ~ out* or *home; is on the ~,* travelling or approaching; *by the ~,* during journey, (fig.) incidentally, often used by speaker to introduce more or less irrelevant remark). **6.** Specified direction (usu. in adv. phrr. without prep.; *which ~ is he looking, going?; look the other ~,* avoid meeting person's eye, cut him; appended colloq. to names of places, as *lives somewhere London~).* **7.** Custom, manner of behaving, personal peculiarity, *(the good old~s,* old fashions; *the ~ of a man with a maid;*

the ~ of the world, conduct no worse than is justified by custom; *it is not my ~ to desert people in misfortune; has a little ~ of leaving his bills unpaid; it is only his ~,* piece of rudeness etc. from him has no special significance, so *pretty Fanny's ~);* specific manner of life *(I soon got into his ~s).* **8.** Scope, sphere, range, line of occupation, branch of business, *(hunting is not, does not lie* or *come or fall, in my ~; is in the grocery ~,* a grocer; *want a few things in the stationery ~).* **9.** Advance in some direction, impetus, progress, *(make* one's *~ home, into a shop,* etc.; *make* one's or one's *own ~,* prosper; *make the best of* one's *~,* go as fast as one can; *make ~,* advance lit. or fig.; *gather, lose, ~,* gain or lose speed; *give~,* of oarsmen, row hard; *~ enough!,* call to boat's crew to complete their stroke & then cease rowing; *ship has ~ on, is under ~,* moves through water). **10.** Respect *(not a bad fellow in some ~s; is satisfactory in one* or *a ~; in a ~,* to a limited extent, not altogether; *no ~ inferior,* not at all). **11.** Ordinary course *(did it in the~ of business).* **12.** Condition, assumption, hypothesis, state, train, degree, *(things are in a bad ~; have it* BOTH *~s;* ‖ *each ~, both ~s,* in backing horse etc., to win, to be placed; *any ~,* in either or any case or event; *we are all in the same ~, live in a* SMALL *~; is an author, builds ships, in a small ~,* on small scale; ‖ *be in a ~* or *a great~,* colloq., be agitated; ‖ *be in the family ~,* with child). **13.** *By ~ of,* as substitute for or form of, with intention of, *(carries a stick by ~ of weapon; did it by ~ of apology, of discovering the truth; is by ~ of making an effort,* represents himself to himself or others to be doing so). **14.** *~-bill,* list of passengers or parcels on conveyance; ‖ *~-board,* thin layer separating thicker strata; *~'farer,~'faring,* traveller, travelling, esp. on foot; *~'faring-tree,* white-flowered shrub common along roadsides, species of viburnum; *~lay'* v.t., lie in wait for, wait about for to rob or interview; *~-leave,* right of ~ rented by mine-owners etc.; *~-shaft* in steam-engine, rocking shaft for working slide-valve from eccentric; *~'side,* side of road (esp. attrib., as *~side flowers, inn); ~-worn,* tired with travel. [OE, OS, OHG *weg,* ON *vegr,* Goth. *wigs,* f. Gmc **wegaz* f. **weg-;* cogn. w. WAIN, WEIGH, L *vehere*]

-way, orig. adv. acc. of WAY, = foll.; most advv. in *-way* have synonyms in *-ways: alway(s), crossway(s),* etc.

-ways (-z), orig. adv. gen. of WAY (see -ES), now terminal element of advv., as *length~, side~, al~;* freq. used indifferently w. -WISE; see prec.

way'ward, a. Childishly self-willed or perverse, capricious, unaccountable, freakish. Hence ~LY[2] adv., ~NESS n. [aphetic f. *away*WARD, cf. *froward*]

‖ **wayz'gŏōse,** n. Printing-house's annual

festivity. [1683 *waygoose* (also from 1731 *wayzgoose*), of unkn. orig.]

wĕ, pl. subj. of *I*² (used, besides the ordinary pron. use, by royal person in proclamations etc. instead of *I*, by writer in unsigned article of newspaper etc., & as collective name for speaker & all others of the class that context shows him to be representing for the moment). [OE *wē*, OS *wī*, *wē*, OHG *wir*, ON *vér*, Goth. *weis*, f. Gmc **wiz*, cogn. w. Skr. *vayam*]

weak, a. **1.** Wanting in strength or power or number, fragile, easily broken or bent or defeated, (~ *barrier, rope*, etc.; ~ AS a *rat, water*; a ~ *eleven*, of poor players; *offer but a* ~ *resistance*; ~ *vessel*, usu. fig., unreliable person; a ~ *crew*, short-handed; ~ *hand*, deficient in high cards; *the* ~*er sex*, women; *the* ~*est goes to the* WALL; ~ *knees*, usu. fig., inability to stand firm, want of resolution, whence ~-kneED² (-nēd) a.; ~*ending* in blank verse, unaccented or proclitic word such as *if* at end). **2.** Wanting in vigour, not acting strongly, sickly, feeble, (~ *constitution*, want of power to resist disease etc.; ~ *stomach*, easily upset; ~ *eyes, sight*, easily tired or not seeing well, whence ~-eyED² (-id), ~-sightED², aa.; ~ *heart*, acting feebly; ~ *mind, head*, below average in intelligence, verging on idiocy, whence ~-mindED², ~-headED², aa.; so ~ *intellect*; ~ *imagination*; ~ *voice*, easily tired or not reaching far; ~ *demand* for goods or stocks, slack; so *the market was* ~). **3.** Wanting in resolution or power of resisting temptation, easily led, (~ *character, man*; person's ~ *side* or *point*, at which he is open to temptation); (of action) indicating want of resolution in agent (a ~ *surrender, compliance*). **4.** Unconvincing, logically deficient, (~ *logic, evidence*; a ~ *argument*). **5.** (Of mixed liquid or solution) watery, thin, (~ *tea, brandy-&-water, brine*). **6.** (Of style etc.) not nervous or well-knit, diffuse, slipshod. **7.** (gram.). Inflected by consonantal additions to, not vowel change in, stem (in English esp. of verbs making past & p.p. by addition of -*ed*). Hence ~'EN⁴ v.t. & i., ~'ISH¹(2) a., ~'lỹ¹ [-LY²] adv. [ME, f. ON *veikr*, corresp. to OE *wāc* pliant, OS *wēk*, OHG *weih*]

weak'ling, n. Feeble person etc. [-LING¹]

weak'lỹ², a. Sickly, not robust, ailing. [-LY¹]

weak'ness, n. In adj. senses; also or esp.: weak point or defect; inability to resist a particular temptation; foolish liking or inclination *for*. [ME; -NESS]

weal¹, n. Welfare, prosperity, good fortune, (chiefly now in ~ *& woe*, ~ *or woe*, in COMMONWEAL, & in *for the public* or *general* ~). [OE *wela*, OS *welo*, f. Gmc **wel-* WELL³]

weal², n. Ridge raised on flesh by stroke of rod or whip, WALE. [var. of WALE]

‖ **weald**, n. District including parts of

Kent, Surrey, Hants, & Sussex, with geologically interesting characteristics; ~-*clay*, beds of clay, sandstone, limestone, & iron-stone, forming top of ~ strata, with abundant fossil remains. [OE *weald* forest, the WS equivalent of Anglian *wald* WOLD]

‖ **weal'den**, a. & n. **1.** Of the weald, resembling the weald geologically. **2.** n. Series of lower-cretaceous freshwater strata above oolite & below chalk best exemplified in the weald. [-EN²]

wealth (wĕl-), n. Welfare, prosperity, (arch.; *in health & ~ long to live*); riches, large possessions, opulence, being rich; the rich; abundance, a profusion or great quantity or display, *of* (a ~ *of illustration, wit, fruit*; ~ *of words is not eloquence*). Hence ~'Y² a., ~'ILY² adv. ~'INESS n. [ME *welthe*, f. WELL³ or WEAL¹ +-TH, after *health*; cf. MDu. *we(e)lde*, OHG *welida*]

wean¹, v.t. Teach (sucking child or animal) to feed otherwise than from the breast (often *from* mother or breast); disengage or cure *from* or rarely *of* habit, specified company, etc., by enforced abstinence or counter-attractions. [OE *wenian* accustom, OS *wennian*, OHG *wennen*, ON *venja*, f. Gmc **wanjan* f. **wan-*; cf. WONT]

‖ **wean²**, n. (Sc.). Child. [= *wee ane* little one]

wean'ling, n. New-weaned child etc. [-LING¹]

wea'pon (wĕp-), n. Material thing designed or used or usable as an instrument for inflicting bodily harm, e.g. gun, bomb, rifle, sword, spear, stick, hammer, poker, horn, claw; action or procedure or means used to get the better in a conflict (*irony is a double-edged* ~; *use the* ~ *of a general strike; tears, the woman's* ~). Hence ~LESS a. [OE *wæpen*, OS *wāpan*, OHG *wāfan*, ON *vápn*, Goth. **wepn*, f. Gmc **wæpnam*]

wear¹ (wār), v.t. & i. (*wōre, wórn*). **1.** Be dressed habitually in, have on, carry or exhibit on one's person or some part of it, (~s *green, serge, shorts*, etc., as usual colour etc.; *is* ~*ing diamonds*, on this occasion; *worn clothes*, that have been put on at least once; ~ *the crown, sword, gown, willow, breeches* or *trousers*, be a monarch or martyr, soldier, lawyer, desolate lover, husband-ruling wife; ~ *one's hair long, short*, etc.; ~ *a face of joy, sour look*, etc.; ~ *one's* HEART (*up*)*on one's sleeve*; ~ *person* or *principle in one's heart*, be devoted to; ~ *one's years well*, remain young-looking, whence ~ER¹ n.; (of ship) fly (flag). **2.** Injure surface of, partly consume or obliterate, damage, attenuate, or alter, by rubbing or use, suffer such injury or consumption or change, come or bring into specified state by use, rub (t. & i.) *off* or *out* or *away* or *down*, (*step worn with pilgrims' knees; worn clothes*, the worse for wear; *inscription has been worn,*

or *has worn, away*; ~ *the freshness, the nap,
off*; *impression soon* ~*s off*; *clothes* ~ *to
one's shape*, fit better with use; ~ *one's
trousers, trousers have worn, into holes or
bagginess*; *seams* ~ *white, ragged, threadbare*; *is worn to a shadow with care*; *stick
*~*s down to a stump*; *a worn or well-worn
joke*, stale; ~ *out*, use or be used till usable
no longer). **3.** Exhaust, tire or be tired
out, put *down* by persistence, (*worn with
travel*; *a* ~*ing occupation, companion*, etc.;
~ *out one's welcome*, go too often or stay
too long as visitor etc.; *his patience wore,
or was worn, out at last*; *succeeded in* ~*ing
down opposition*). **4.** Endure continued
use *well, badly*, etc., remain specified time
in working order or presentable state, last
long, (*won't* ~, of inferior material, transitory impression, etc.; ~*s for years*;
person ~*s well*, retains youthful strength
or esp. look). **5.** (Of time) go slowly
or tediously *on*, pass (t. & i. of time)
gradually *away*, (*winter, time, day*, ~*s
on or away*; ~ *away or out one's life or
time or youth in trifles*; ~ *through the day*,
get through it somehow). **6.** Make (hole,
groove, channel) by attrition (usu. of incidental or undesigned action, cf. BORE¹;
often of water). **7.** ~*ing-apparel*, clothes;
~*ing-iron or -plate*, piece of metal attached
to protect surface exposed to friction.
Hence ~'ABLE a. [OE *werian*, = OHG
werien, ON *verga*, Goth. *wasjan* to clothe,
f. Gmc **was-*, cogn. w. L *vestis*]

wear² (wār), n. **1.** Wearing or being worn
on person, use as clothes, (*the best materials
for Sunday, working, spring, seaside*, etc.,
~; *tweeds were in general* ~, fashionable;
the coat I have in ~, am regularly wearing). **2.** Thing to wear, fashionable or
suitable apparel, (in phrr. on type or
motley's the only ~; also in *foot* etc. ~,
chiefly in trade use as collective for things
worn on feet etc.). **3.** Damage sustained
as result of ordinary use (esp. ~ *& tear*;
will stand any amount of ~; *is the worse
for* ~, damaged by use). **4.** Capacity for
resisting ~ & tear (*there is a great deal of,
no*, ~ *in it*). [f. prec.]

wear³ (wār), v.t. & i. (naut.; past & p.p.
wore). Bring (ship), (of ship) come, about
by putting up of helm (cf. *tack*). [orig.
obsc.; perh. f. VEER by confusion w.
WEAR¹]

wear⁴. = WEIR.

wear'|y̆, a., & v.t. & i. **1.** Tired, with
energy abated, dispirited (~ *Willie*, sl.,
habitually ~ person, tramp); sick or
impatient of; tiring, tedious, irksome;
hence ~ILY adv., ~INESS n. **2.** vb. Make
~y (esp. of or with importunity or monotony), whence ~ISOME a., ~ISOMELY²
adv., ~ISOMENESS n.; grow ~y (esp.
of importunity or importunate person),
whence ~ILESS a.; (chiefly Sc.) long to do
or *for*. [OE *wērig*, OS *wōrig*, OHG *wuarag*
(drunk), f. WG **wōrīga, -aga*; vb f. OE
wēr(i)gian]

weas'and (wēz-), n. Windpipe, gullet,
throat; (pl.) sausage skins made from the
windpipes of cows. [OE (OS) *wāsend*,
OHG *weisant*, of unkn. orig.]

weas'el¹ (-zl), n., & v.i. **1.** Small nimble
reddish-brown white-bellied slender
-bodied carnivorous quadruped allied to
stoat & ferret (*catch a* ~ *asleep*, deceive
wide-awake person); ~*-faced*, with thin
sharp features. **2.** *v.i.* Equivocate,
quibble. [OE *wes(u)le*, OHG *wisula*, f.
WG **wisulōn* of unkn. orig.]

weas'el² (-zl), n. Tracked amphibious
vehicle, snow tractor. [official designation WSL (water, snow, land)]

wea'ther¹ (wĕdh-), n. & a. **1.** Atmospheric conditions prevailing at a place &
time, combination produced by heat or
cold, clearness or cloudiness, dryness
or moisture, wind or calm, high or low
pressure, & electrical state, of local air &
sky, (*April* ~, showers alternating with
sunshine, fig. smiles & tears; FAIR³,
FOUL¹, DIRTY, FINE, SOFT, ~; || *King's or
Queen's or royal* ~, fine on ceremonial
occasion; *favourable, seasonable, good,
bad*, etc., ~; *under stress of* ~, owing to
storms etc.; CLERK *of the* ~; *make good or
bad* ~, naut., meet with; *make heavy* ~ *of*,
fig., find trying; *under the* ~, colloq.,
indisposed, out of sorts). **2.** ~*-beaten*,
seasoned by or bearing the marks of
exposure to storms; ~*-board*, (n.) sloping
board attached at bottom of door to keep
out rain, (vb) supply with ~*-boarding,
-boards*, horizontal boards of which each
overlaps the next below to throw off rain
as protective casing to wall etc.; ~*-
bound*, unable to proceed owing to bad~;
~*-box*, ~*-indicator* with figures of man
& woman, one issuing to foreshow rain,
the other fine~; ~*-bureau*, meteorological
office; ~*-chart*, diagram showing details
of ~ over wide area; ~*-cock*, revolving
pointer often in shape of cock mounted
in high place esp. on church spire to show
whence wind blows, (fig.) inconstant
person; ~*-contact* or *-cross*, leakage from
one telegraph wire to another due to wet
~; ~*-forecast*, prophecy of the day's ~;
~*-glass*, barometer; ~*-map*, = ~*-chart*;
~*-moulding*, dripstone; ~*-PROOF²*; ~*-
prophet*, person who foretells ~; ~*-
service, -ship*, organization, ship, for
meteorological observations; ~*-stain*,
discoloration of wall etc. by exposure;
so ~*-stained*; ~*-station*, post of observation in connexion with ~*-service*; ~*-strip*,
piece of material used to make door or
window proof against rain or wind; ~*-
tiles*, arranged to overlap like ~*-board-
ing*; ~*-vane*, = ~*-cock*; ~*-wise*, able to
forecast ~; ~*-worn*, marked by storms
etc. **3.** adj. (naut.). Windward (*on the* ~
quarter, beam, bow, etc.; *have the* ~ *gage
or* GAUGE¹ *of*; *keep one's* ~ *eye open*, fig.,
be on the look-out); hence ~MOST a.
[OE *weder*, OS *-ar*, OHG *wetar*, ON *vethr*

f. Gmc *wedhram*, prob. f. root *wē- to blow (WIND[1])]

wea'ther[2] (wědh-), v.t. & i. **1.** Expose to atmospheric changes; (usu. in pass.) discolour or partly disintegrate (rock, stones) by exposure to air (esp. in geol.); be discoloured or worn thus. **2.** (Of ship or its crew) get to windward of (cape etc.); come safely through (storm lit. or fig.). **3.** Make (boards, tiles) overlap downwards, whence ~ING[2] n. [ME, f. prec.]

wea'therl|y (wědh-), a. (naut.). (Of ship) making little leeway, capable of keeping close to wind. Hence ~iNESS n. [-LY[1]]

weave, v.t. & i. (*wŏve, wŏv'en* &, chiefly in some trade phrr., *wove*), & n. **1.** Form (thread etc.) into fabric, (fabric) out of thread etc., by interlacing, make fabric thus, work at loom; work up (facts etc.) introduce (details), *into* a story or connected whole, fashion (tale, poem, etc.); contrive (plot); move to & fro or from side to side; (R.A.F. sl.) dodge, take evasive action; *wove(n) paper*, with uniform unlined surface given by making in frame of crossed wire-gauze. **2.** n. Style of weaving. [OE *wefan*, OHG *weban*, ON *vefa*, f. Gmc *webh-*]

weav'er, n. In vbl senses; esp.: artisan who lives by weaving (~*'s knot*, kind used esp. for joining cords of different size); (also ~*-bird*) kinds of bird remarkable for elaborate or dextrously made textile nests. [ME; -ER[1]]

weazen. See WIZENED.

wěb, n. **1.** Woven fabric, amount woven in one piece, (also fig., as *a ~ of lies*). **2.** Cob~ (with help of context only; often *spider's* ~), similar product of any spinning creature, gossamer, etc. **3.** Membrane filling spaces between toes esp. of swimming bird or bat; connective tissue. **4.** Vane of feather. **5.** Large roll of paper used esp. in newspaper-printing. **6.** Thin flat part connecting more solid parts in machinery etc., e.g. part of railway-carriage wheel between nave & rim. **7.** ~*-eye*, disease of eye with film or excrescence, whence ~*-*eyED[2] (-ĭd) a.; ~*-fingers, -toes*, abnormally or normally connected with ~, whence ~*-*fingerED[2], ~*-*toED[2] (-tōd), aa.; ~*-foot*, with ~*-*toes, whence ~*-*footED[2] a.; ~*-wheel*, with plate or ~ instead of spokes, or with rim, spokes, & centre, in one piece as in watch-wheels; ~*-worm*, kinds of gregarious larvae spinning large ~s to sleep or to feed on enclosed foliage in. Hence ~bED[2] (-bd) a. [OE *web(b)*, OS *webbi*, OHG *weppi*, ON *vefr* f. Gmc *wabjam* f. *wabh-* var. of *webh-* WEAVE]

wěbb'ing, n. Strong narrow fabric such as is used for horse-girths, gymnastic belts, etc.; stronger edging of more delicate fabric. [-ING[1]]

wěd, v.t. & i. (~*ded, ~ded* or rarely & not in adj. use *wed*). (Of party, priest, or parent etc.) MARRY[1] (t. & i., rhet. exc. in

p.p. ~*ded* in adj. use, as *a ~ded pair*; ~*ded life, bliss*, etc., in matrimony; *newly-*~s n., newly-~ded pair); unite (qualities·often separated; ~ *efficiency to economy*); (p.p.) devoted *to* opinions, pursuits, etc., so as to be unable to abandon them. [OE *weddian* to pledge, OHG *wettōn*, ON *vethja*, Goth. *gawadjōn*, f. Gmc *wadhjam* pledge (whence Goth. *wadi*, OE (now dial.) *wed*); cf. GAGE[1]]

wědd'ing, n. Marriage ceremony (& festivities); *silver, ruby, golden, diamond,* ~, 25th, 40th, 50th, 60th or 75th, anniversary of ~; ‖ *penny* ~, with money contributions from guests; ~ *breakfast*, entertainment usual between~ ceremony & departure for honeymoon; ~*-cake*, distributed to ~-guests & sent in portions to absent friends; ~*-cards*, with names of pair sent to friends as announcement of ~; ~*-day*, day or anniversary of ~; ~*-favour*, white rosette or knot of ribbons worn in honour of ~; ~ *garment*, qualification for participating in feast of some kind (ref. to *Matt.* xxii. 11); ~*-ring*, that put on bride's finger at ~-ceremony & freq. worn constantly as distinctive mark of married woman. [ME; -ING[1]]

wědge, n., & v.t. **1.** Piece of wood or metal of which one end is an acute-angled edge formed by two converging planes used to split wood or rock or widen opening or exert force in various ways, one of the MECHANICAL powers (or a special application of the INCLINE[1]d plane), (*thin end of the* ~, change, measure, action, etc., that will lead to further changes or developments & is therefore of more importance than it seems); anything resembling a ~ in being chiefly outlined by two radial planes or lines converging at acute angle (*a ~ of cake* etc.; *the seats are disposed in* ~s; *drew up his men in a* ~); golf-club with ~-shaped head used for approaching; ~*-shaped*, like solid ~, also V-shaped; ~*-tailed*, of birds having middle tail-feathers longest; hence ~ WISE adv. **2.** v.t. Split with ~ (rare); fasten by use of ~; thrust or pack (usu. *in*) tightly between other things or persons; push *off* or *away* like a ~. [OE *wecg*, OS *weggi*, OHG *wecki*, ON *veggr*, f. Gmc *wagjaz*]

Wědg'wŏod, n. Kind of superior (semi-) vitrified pottery or ware made by Josiah ~ (d. 1795) and his successors; (attrib.) of the blue colour characteristic of ~. [P]

wěd'lŏck, n. The married state (*born in lawful* ~, legitimately, of married parents). [OE *wedlāc* (*wed* pledge, *lāc* n. of action suf.) marriage vow]

Wednesday (wěnz'dĭ), n. Fourth day of week (ASH[3] ~). [OE *wōdnes dæg* day of (the god) Woden, transl. of LL *Mercurii dies*]

wee, a. (~*er*, ~*est*). Little, very small, (esp. in nursery, Sc., & Ir. use); *Wee Frees*, nickname for part of Free Church of

Scotland that refused inclusion in the United Free Church in 1900. [f. north. ME *wei* f. Anglian *wēg(e)* = West Saxon *wǣg(e)*, whence WEIGH rel. to WEY]

weed, n., & v.t. & i. **1.** Wild herb springing where it is not wanted (*ill* ~*s grow apace,* gibe at tall or fast-growing child); *the* (*Indian, soothing,* etc.) ~, tobacco; lanky & weakly horse or person; ~-*grown,* ~y or overgrown with ~s; hence ~'LESS, ~'Y², aa., ~'INESS n. **2.** vb. Clear (ground) of ~s (also fig.), cut off or uproot ~s, whence ~'ER¹(1, 2) n.; sort *out* (inferior parts or members of a quantity or company) for riddance, rid (quantity or company) of inferior members etc. [OE *wēod,* OS *wiod,* of unkn. orig.; vb f. OE *wēodian* = OS *wiodon*]

weeds (-z), n. pl. Mourning worn by widow (usu. *widow's* ~). [OE *wǣd* garment, = OS *wād,* OHG *wāt,* ON *vāth,* f. Gmc **wǣdhiz*]

week, n. **1.** Period of seven days reckoned from midnight on Saturday-Sunday (*what day of the* ~ *is it?,* is it Sunday, Monday, Tuesday, Wednesday, Thursday, Friday, or Saturday?; HOLY, PASSION, EASTER, ~; ~ *of Sundays* or ~*s,* seven ~s; *feast of* ~s, Jewish PENTECOST; *middle of next* ~, see KNOCK¹). **2.** Period of seven days reckoned from any point (*can you come to us for a* ~?; *today* ~, 7 days hence; *tomorrow, yesterday, Friday,* etc., ~, day later, earlier, than such future, past, day by a ~; *have not seen you for* ~s; *did it* ~s *ago*). **3.** The six days between Sundays. **4.** ~-day, any day other than Sunday; ~-*end,* Sunday & parts of Saturday & Monday (occas. from Friday to Tuesday) as time for holiday or visit, (v.i.) make ~-end visit etc., whence ~-*ĕn'DER¹* n. [OE *wice,* OS *-wika,* OHG *wehha, wohha,* ON *vika,* (cf. Goth. *wikō*), f. Gmc **wikōn*]

week'lỹ, a., adv., & n. **1.** (Occurring, issuing, done, etc.) once a week, every week; of or for or lasting a week. **2.** n. ~ newspaper or periodical. [-LY¹·²]

ween, v.t. (poet.). Be of opinion (usu. *I* ~ abs. & parenthet. also with *that* expressed or omitted), expect *to* get etc. [OE *wēnan,* OS *wānian,* OHG *wānen,* ON *vǣna,* Goth *wēnjan,* f. Gmc **wǣnjan*]

weep, v.i. & t. (*wĕpt*). **1.** Shed tears (*for* person; *for* pain, rage, joy, etc.); shed tears for, lament over, bewail. **2.** Send forth or be covered with drops, come or send forth in drops, exude, sweat, drip, (~*ing eczema,* with exudation; ~*ing pipe,* designed to drip at intervals); *W*~*ing Cross* (hist.), wayside cross for penitents to pray at (*come home by W*~*ing Cross,* be made to repent one's conduct etc.). **3.** (Of tree) have drooping branches (chiefly in part. as distinctive epithet of variety, ~*ing birch, willow,* etc.). **4.** ~ *out,* utter with tears; ~ *oneself out,* ~ one's fill; ~ *away,* consume (time) in ~ing.

[OE *wēpan,* OS *wōpian,* OHG *wuofan,* ON *ōpa,* Goth. *wōpjan* f. Gmc **wōp-* lamentation]

weep'er, n. In vbl senses; also or esp.: hired mourner at funeral; crape hat-sash worn by men at funerals; widow's black crape veil; (pl.) widow's white cuffs. [ME; -ER¹]

weev'er, n. Kinds of fish (*dragon & lesser* ~) with sharp dorsal spines inflicting wound that often festers. [f. OF *vivre* weever, orig. = serpent, see WIVERN]

weev'il, n. Kinds of beetle with head extended into a proboscis feeding on grain, nuts, fruit, & leaves; any insect damaging stored grain similarly to corn-~. Hence (of grain) ~LED² (-vld), ~Y² (-vll), aa. [OE *wifel,* OS *-wivil,* OHG *wibil,* ON *vifill* f. Gmc **webhilaz* f. **webh-* (**wabh-* WAVE) move about briskly]

wĕft¹, n. Cross-threads woven into warp to make web; (loosely) web. [OE *wefta, weft,* = ON *veptr, vipta,* MHG *wift,* f. Gmc **weft-* f. **webh-* WEAVE]

wĕft², Var. of WAFT n. (naut.).

Wehrmacht (vār'mahχt), n. German armed forces. [G, = defensive force]

weigh (wā), v.t. & i., & n. **1.** Find weight of with scales or other machine, whence ~AGE(4) (wā'ĭj) n., balance in hands (as if) to guess weight of, (~ *sugar, luggage;* meditatively ~*ed his stick in his hand;* ~ *out,* take definite weight of, take specified weight from larger quantity, distribute, in definite quantities, by aid of scales, as ~ *out butter, portions* or *3 lb. of butter*); ascertain one's own weight (*when did you* ~ *last?; ~ out, in,* of jockey before & after race, & transf. ~ *in,* enter an appearance; ~ *in with* argument etc., produce it triumphantly). **2.** Estimate relative value or importance of, compare *with* or *against* or abs., consider with a view to choice or rejection or preference, (~ *consequences, pros & cons, oath* or *argument with* or *against* another; ~ *one's words,* select such as express neither more nor less than one means; ~ *the claims, merits,* etc., *of rival candidates*). **3.** Be equal to or balance (specified weight) in the scales, (fig.) have specified importance, exercise pressure or influence, have weight or importance, be heavy or burdensome, (~*s a ton, 6 oz, little, nothing, light, heavy, heavily;* ~ *heavy* etc., or abs., *upon,* be burdensome or depressing to; *the point that* ~*s with me*). **4.** Bring *down* by weight lit. or fig., (of counterweight) force *up,* (*fruit* ~*s down branch; one good argument* ~*s down six bad ones;* ~*ed down with ~ares; bucket is* ~*ed up by mass of iron at end of lever*). **5.** Raise from below water (~ *anchor,* start for voyage); ~ *ship* (rare), refloat it when sunk). **6.** ~-*beam,* portable steelyard suspended in frame; ~'*bridge,* ~ing-machine with plate on to which vehicles etc. can be driven to be ~ed;

~-*house*, building in which goods can be ~ed officially; ~-*lock*, canal lock with provision for ~ing barges; ~*ing-machine*, usu. for great weights or of more complicated mechanism than simple balance. **7.** n. Process or occasion of ~ing; *under* ~, by erron. assoc. with (*under*) WAY. [OE, OS, OHG *wegan*, ON *vega* lift, weigh, Goth. *gawigan* shake, f. Gmc *weg-*, *wag-*, *wæg-*; cf. WAG[1], WAIN, WAY; n. f. OE *wæg(e)*, see WEY]

weight[1] (wāt), n. **1.** Force with which body tends to centre of attraction (*the ~s of the planets*); (of terrestrial things) degree of downward tendency in body produced as resultant of earth's gravitation & centrifugal force (*the ~ of a body varies with latitude & altitude, its mass does not*). **2.** Relative mass or quantity of matter contained, downward force, heaviness, regarded as a property of bodies (*superior both in size & in ~; he is twice your ~;* DEAD ~; ~ *of metal*, total amount that can be thrown by ship's gun at one discharge). **3.** Body's mass numerically expressed in some recognized scale (*what is your ~?; reached the ~ of 12 st.*); scale or notation for expressing ~s (TROY, AVOIRDUPOIS, ~); BOX[5]*ing* ~s. **4.** Heavy body (*keep papers down with a ~; clock is worked by ~s; must not lift ~s*); piece of metal etc. of known mass used in scales for weighing articles (*where is the ounce ~?*). **5.** Load to be supported (*the pillars have a great ~ to bear*), heavy burden of care, responsibility, etc. **6.** Importance, convincing effect, influence, preponderance, (*considerations of no ~; men of ~; has great ~ with me; the ~ of evidence is against him*). Hence ~'LESS a. [OE *wiht*, (M)Du., (M)LG *wicht*, ON *vétt* f. Gmc *wehtiz* f. *weg-* WEIGH]

weight[2] (wāt), v.t. Attach a weight to, hold down with a weight or weights; impede or burden with load lit. or fig.; treat (fabric) with mineral etc. to make it seem stouter; (statistics) multiply components of (average) by compensating factors. Hence ~'ING[1] (wāt-) n., extra pay or allowances given in special cases. [f. prec.]

weight'/y̆ (wāt-), a. Weighing much, heavy; momentous, important; well-weighed, evidencing thought, deserving of consideration; influential, authoritative. Hence ~iLY[2] adv., ~iNESS n. [-Y[2]]

weir, wear (wēr), n. Dam across river to raise level of water above it; enclosure of stakes etc. set in stream as trap for fish. [OE (= MLG, MHG) *wer*, f. st. of *werian* dam up f. Gmc *war-*, cf. WARE[3]]

‖ **weird[1]** (wērd), n. Fate, destiny, (chiefly Sc.; DREE one's ~). [OE *wyrd* destiny, = OS *wurd*, OHG *wurt*, ON *urthr*, f. Gmc *werth-*, *warth-*, *wurth-* become, see WORTH[2]]

weird[2] (wērd), a. Connected with fate (*the ~ sisters*, the fates, witches); super-

natural, uncanny, unearthly; (colloq.) queer, odd, old-fashioned, strange, incomprehensible. Hence ~'LY[2] adv., ~'NESS n. [ME, attrib. use of prec., in ~ *sister(s)*]

Weis'mannism (vīs-), n. A theory of heredity, in which transmission of acquired characters is denied. [A. *Weismann*, German biologist (d. 1914), +-ISM]

Welch[1], a. Obs. var. of WELSH[1] surviving in names of regiments (~ *Regiment, Royal ~ Fusiliers*; but *Welsh Guards*).

welch[2](er). See WELSH[2].

wel'come, int., n., v.t., & a. **1.** Hail, know that your coming gives pleasure (often with adv. addition, as ~ *home, to Edinburgh!*). **2.** n. Saying ~ to person, kind or glad reception or entertainment of person or acceptance of offer, gift, etc., (*bid one ~*, assure him he is ~; WEAR[1] *out or outstay* one's ~; *give warm ~*, show great joy at arrival, also make vigorous resistance). **3.** v.t. Say ~ to, greet on arrival, receive (guest, arrival, news, opportunity, event) with pleasure or signs of it. **4.** adj. Gladly received (*a ~ guest, interruption, gift, rest, denial, sight, etc.; ~ as snow in harvest,* un~; *make one ~,* let him feel so); (pred. only) ungrudgingly permitted to do or given right to thing, absolved of thanking or recompensing, (*you are ~ to take what steps you please; any one is ~ to my share, to any service I can do; you are ~,* or ellipt. ~, no thanks required); hence ~NESS n. [orig. OE *wilcuma* (*wil-* desire, pleasure, + *cuma* comer) one whose coming is pleasing, w. later change to *wel-* = WELL[3] after OF *bien venu* (or ON *velkominn*)]

weld[1], n. Dyer's-weed, plant formerly used to dye yellow. [OE *wealde* = MDu. *woude*, MLG *walde*]

weld[2], v.t. & i., & n. **1.** Unite (pieces of metal, esp. iron) into homogeneous mass by hammering or pressure (usu. when iron is softened by heat but not melted), make by ~ing, (of iron etc.) admit of being ~ed *easily* etc.; (fig.) bring (recruits, parts, arguments, etc.) into homogeneous whole (usu. *into*); hence ~'ABLE a., ~abil'ity n. **2.** n. ~ed junction. [alt. f. WELL[2] in obs. (exc. dial.) sense *weld* (heated metal), prob. infl. by p.p.]

wel'fare, n. Satisfactory state, health & prosperity, well-being, (usu. *of* person, society, etc., or with *my* etc.); ~ *State*, one having national health, insurance, & other social services; ~ *work*, efforts to make life worth living for employees etc. [ME; WELL[3], FARE[1]]

welk, v.i. (arch.). Fade, wither. [ME, prob. of Continental orig.; cf. (M)Du., LG *welken*]

wel'kin, n. (poet.). Sky. [OE *wolcen* cloud, sky, = OS *wolcan*, OHG *wolkan*]

well[1], n. **1.** Spring or fountain, (fig.) source, (poet. or arch.; ~ *of English undefiled,* Chaucer). **2.** Shaft sunk in ground

& lined with stone or other protection for obtaining subterranean water, oil, etc. (ARTESIAN ~). **3.** Enclosed space more or less resembling ~-shaft, space in middle of house from floor to roof containing stairs (also ~ *staircase*) or lift or surrounded by stairs (also ~-*hole*) or open for light & ventilation; || railed space for counsel etc. in court; receptacle for ink in inkstand. **4.** ~-*deck*, space on main deck enclosed by bulwarks & higher decks; ~-*dish*, with hollow for gravy to collect in; ~-*grate*, in which fire burns on hearth, receiving its air supply from below; ~-*head*, source, fountain-head; ~-*room*, where spa water is dispensed; ~-*-sinker*, person whose occupation is sinking ~s; ~-*spring*, = ~-*head*. [Anglian *wella* = West Saxon *wielle* etc. f. st. of *weallan* to boil, bubble up, cf. OHG *wella* wave]

wĕll², v.i. Spring (as) from fountain (often *up*, *out*, *forth*). [Anglian *wellan* (West Saxon *wiellan*) causative of *weallan* (prec.)]

wĕll³, adv. (BETTER, BEST), pred. a. (*better, best*), attrib. a. (no comp.), & n. **1.** In good manner or style, satisfactorily, rightly, (*the work is* ~ *done*; *that is* ~ *said*; *a* ~ *situated house*; ~ *begun is half done*; ~ *done!, run!*, etc., cry of commendation; ~ *met!*, greeting to person one has been wanting to see; *come off* ~, have good luck, distinguish oneself; *wish I was* ~ *out of it*, without disaster etc.; *you did* ~, *it was* ~ *done of you, to come*). **2.** Thoroughly, with care or completeness, sufficiently, to a considerable distance or extent, with margin enough to justify description, quite, (*look* ~ *to yourself; judge* ~ & *truly; smack him, polish it,* ~; *is* ~ *up in the list,* ~ *on in life,* ~ *advanced or stricken in years,* ~ *past forty,* ~ *among the leaders of thought; as* ~, in addition, to an equal extent, not less truly, as *but he is a Christian as* ~, *he gave me clothes as* ~ *as food*). **3.** Heartily, kindly, laudatorily, approvingly, on good terms, (*love, like*, person ~; *treat* person ~; *think or speak* ~ *of; it speaks* ~ *for his discipline that he never punishes*, serves as commendation; *stand* ~ *with* one, be in his good graces). **4.** Probably, not incredibly, easily, with reason, wisely, advisably, (*it may* ~ *be that* —; *can, cannot,* ~ *manage it; you may* ~ *ask, say, that; we might* ~ *make the experiment; as* ~, with equal reason, preferably, without worse consequences, as *you might as* ~ *throw your money into the sea as lend it to him, as* ~ *be hanged for a sheep as a lamb, we may as* ~ *begin at once; that is just as* ~, need not be regretted; *you might as* ~, nursery formula of request). **5.** pred. adj. (often indistinguishable from adv.). In good health (*is she* ~ *or ill?; will soon be better; is best in the winter; quite* ~, *thank you; am perfectly* ~); in satisfactory state or posi-

tion, satisfactory, advisable, (*am very* ~ *where I am; all's* ~; *it is all very* ~, ironical expression of discontent, or rejection of comfort, arguments, etc.; *it is* ~ *with him; it would have been, were,* ~ *for him if; it would be* ~ *to inquire;* ~ *enough*, tolerably good or good-looking; *as* ~, not unadvisable, as *it may be as* ~ *to explain;* ~ & *good*, formula of dispassionate acceptance of decision, as *if you choose to take my advice,* ~ & *good;* VERY ~). **6.** attrib. adj. (rare). In good health (*a* ~ *man should not be dawdling in bed; the* ~ *are impatient of the sick*). **7.** n. Good things (*I wish him* ~); what is satisfactory (*let* ~ *alone*, do not meddle needlessly). [OE *wel*(l), OS, OHG *wela, wola,* ON *vel,* Goth *waila,* f. same st. as WILL¹]

wĕll⁴, int. expressing great astonishment (~, *who would have thought it?;* ~ *!;* ~ *to be sure!*), relief (~, *here we are at last*), concession (~, *come if you like;* ~, *perhaps you are right;* ~ *then, say no more about it*), resumption of talk (~, *who was it?;* ~, *he says he must see you*), qualified recognition of point (~, *but what about Jones?*), expectation (~ *then?*), resignation (~, *it can't be helped*), etc. [ellipt. uses of prec. adv.]

wĕll-. **1.** In a few words *well-* or *well* is an inseparable pref.: ~-*being,* welfare; ~-*doer, -doing,* virtuous person, conduct; ~-*nigh,* rhet., almost; ~-*wisher,* person who wishes well to one. **2.** *Well* may precede any participle or word in -ED²; when the combination is used attrib. with n. following, it is usu. hyphened (*he is a* ~-*known person*); this is done in the pred. use also when the combination ends in -ING² or -ED², but not usu. when it ends in -ED¹ (*the stroke was well timed,* cf. *a* ~-*timed stroke*) unless it has acquired a sense or use other or more restricted than that of the separate elements (*my watch is well regulated; I do not think his action was* ~-*advised,* cf. *he is not well advised by his friends*); a list of the commoner combinations follows with special senses or contexts noted; ~-*advised,* prudent, wise, (chiefly of action taken); ~ *aimed;* ~-*appointed,* having all necessary equipment (esp. of expedition fleet, etc.); ~ *armed;* ~ *attested;* ~ *authenticated;* ~-*balanced,* sane, sensible, (esp. of mind); ~-*behaved;* ~ *beloved;* ~-*born,* of good family; ~-*bred,* having good breeding or manners, (of horse etc.) of good or pure stock; ~ *chosen,* esp. of words or phrases; ~-*conditioned,* not querulous; ~-*conducted,* characterized by good conduct; ~-*connected,* connected by blood etc. with good families; ~ *contented;* ~ *contested;* ~ *defined;* ~ *directed,* esp. of blow or shot; ~-*disposed,* having good disposition or kindly feeling (*towards*); || ~ *done,* (of meat) cooked through; ~ *dressed;* ~ *drilled;* ~ *earned;* ~ *educated;* ~-*favoured,* good-looking; ~ *fed;* ~ *fought;* ~-*found,*

= ~-*appointed*; ~ *founded*, having foundation in fact (of suspicion or other belief or sentiment); ~ *furnished*; ~-*graced*, possessed of attractive qualities; ~ *grounded*, = ~ *founded*, also ~ trained in rudiments; ~-*informed*, having ~-stored mind or access to best information; ~-*intentioned*, aiming or aimed (usu. unsuccessfully) at good results; ~-*judged*, showing good judgement or tact or good aim (of action taken); ~-*knit*, compact, not loose-made or sprawling, (esp. of person or his frame); ~ *known*; || ~-*liking*, with ~-fed prosperous look (usu. *fat & ~-liking*); ~-*looking*, of attractive appearance; ~ *loved*; ~ *made*, (esp.) of symmetrical bodily make; ~-*mannered*, with good manners; ~ *marked*, distinct, easy to detect; ~-*meaning*, = ~-*intentioned* (of person or attempt); ~ *meant*, = ~-*intentioned* (of attempt); ~ *oiled*, (fig., of expression) complimentary; ~ *ordered*, arranged in orderly manner; ~ *paid*; ~ *painted*; ~ *pleased*; ~-*pleasing*; ~-*proportioned*; ~-*read*, having read much [cf. -ED¹(2)], with mind ~ stored by reading; ~ *regulated*, under proper control, not undisciplined; ~ *remembered*; ~-*reputed*, of good repute; ~-*rounded*, complete & symmetrical; ~-*seeming*, apparently satisfactory or good; || ~-*seen* (arch.), accomplished *in*; ~ *set*, compact, firmly knit, (esp., also ~ *set up*, of bodily frame); ~ *sifted* (esp. of facts or evidence); ~ *spent* (esp. of time or effort); ~-*spoken*, refined in speech; ~-*timbered*; ~ *timed*, opportune; ~ *trained*; ~-*tried*, often tested with good result; ~-*trod(den)*, frequented; ~ *tuned*; ~ *turned*, happily expressed (of compliment, phrase, verse); ~-*worn*, (esp.) trite, stale. **3.** ~ *off*, = fortunately situated (*does not know when he is ~ off*), sufficiently rich, is two words when used pred., but hyphened when attrib. (~-*off people*); ~-*to-do*, = sufficiently rich, is hyphened when attrib. & usu. when pred. also.

wel'laday', -*away'*, int. of grief (arch. or joc.). [OE *wei lā wei* alt. f. *vā lā wā* (woe, lo! woe) after OScand. *wei*; *welladay* 16th c. alt. after *lackaday*]

Wel'lington'ia, n. Kinds of sequoia. [named after Duke of Wellington, -IA¹]

Well'ingtons (-z), n. pl. Boots coming up or nearly up to knees. [as prec.]

Welsh¹ (& see WELCH¹), a. & n. (Language, *the* people) of Wales (~ *mutton*, from small ~ mountain sheep; ~ *rabbit* or by pop. etym. *rarebit*, dish of toasted cheese); ~ *man*, ~ *woman*, native of Wales. [OE (Anglian & Kentish) *welisc, wælisc* f. *wealh, walh* Celt, Briton, +-ISH¹]

welsh², welch, v.t. & i. Decamp without paying (winner of bet on horse-race etc., or abs.). Hence ~'ER¹ n. [orig. unkn.]

welt¹, n., & v.t. **1.** Strip of leather sewn round edge of boot or shoe uppers to serve as attachment to sole; wale; border or edging of garment etc., trimming. **2.** v.t. Provide with ~; raise wales on, beat, flog. [ME *welte, walt*, of unkn. orig.]

Welt² (v-), n. (German for) world; ~*anschau'üng* (-show⁴), philosophical survey of the world as a whole; ~'*politik'* (-ēk), foreign policy on the grand scale; ~'*schmerz* (-shmèrts), vague yearning & discontent with regard to the constitution of things. [G]

wel'ter¹, v.i. & n. **1.** Roll, wallow, be washed about, be soaked or steeped or dabbled *in* blood etc. **2.** n. General confusion, disorderly mixture or aimless conflict of creeds, policies, vices, etc. [ME, f. MDu., MLG *welteren*]

wel'ter², n. **1.** Heavy rider (now rare); (attrib.) ~ *race, cup, stakes, handicap*, etc., horse-races for heavy-weight riders (also ellipt., =~-race); ~-*weight*, heavy-weight rider, also weight carried apart from weight for age as test, (boxing) see BOX³*ing-weights*. **2.** (colloq.). Heavy blow, big person or thing. [orig. unkn.]

wen¹, n. More or less permanent tumour of benign character on scalp or other part of body; goitre; (fig.) abnormally large or congested city (*the great ~*, London). [OE *wen(n), wæn(n)*, of unkn. orig.; cf. Du. *wen*, MLG *wene*, LG *wehne* tumour, wart]

wen², n. The Old English and early Middle English letter ƿ (w). [OE, var. of *wyn* joy (see WINSOME) used as beginning with the letter, cf. THORN]

wench, n., & v.i. & t. **1.** Girl or young woman, lass, (esp. of rustics or servants, or joc. & colloq.; *a strapping, buxom*, etc., ~); || (arch.) strumpet. **2.** vb. Court (dial.); whore, whence ~'ER¹ n. (arch.). [shortened f. ME *wenchel*, f. OE *wencel* child (*wancol* weak, tottering)]

wend¹, v.t. & i. Direct one's *way*; (arch.) go. [OE *wendan*, OS -*ian*, OHG *wentan*, ON *venda*, Goth. *wandjan*, causative of Gmc *wendan* WIND³]

Wend², n. One of a Slavic people formerly spread over N. Germany, & now inhabiting E. Saxony. Hence ~'IC, ~'ISH, aa. [f. G *Wende, Winde*]

Wens'leydale (-zli-), n. Kind of cheese. [~ in Yorks.]

went. See GO¹, WEND¹ etym.

wen'tletrăp (-tel-), n. Shellfish with spiral shell of many whorls. [f. Du. *wenteltrap* winding stair, spiral shell]

wept. See WEEP.

were, weren't (wèrnt). See BE.

were'wolf, wer'wolf, (wēr'wŏŏlf), n. (myth.; pl. -*ves*). Human being turned into wolf. [OE *werewulf*, = (M)Du. *weer-wolf*, MHG *werwolf* (G *wer-, wehr-*); the first element is usu., but doubtfully, identified w. OE *wer* man]

wert. See BE.

Wer'therism (vàrter-), n. Morbid sentimentality as of Werther in Goethe's *Sorrows of Werther* (1774). [-ISM(3)]

Wesleyan (wĕz'lĭan, wĕs², wĕzlō'an), a. & n. (hist.). (Member) of the denomination founded by John Wesley (d. 1791). Hence ~ISM(3) n. [-AN]

wĕst, adv., n., & a. (abbr. W.). **1.** Towards or in the region in front of observer on equator at equinox who faces setting sun (~ BY[1] *north* or *south*; ~ *of*, farther ~ than; DUE[1] ~; *lies* etc. *east & ~*, lengthwise along line between east & ~; *go*, *gone*, ~, sl., die, dead); ~*-north-~*, ~*-south-~*, advv., nn., & aa., (regions) midway between ~ & north-~, south-~ (with uses & derivatives corresponding to those of ~, as ~*-north-~erly*, ~*-north-~ern*, ~*-north-~wardly*; see WESTERLY etc.); hence ~'WARD adv., n., & a., ~² WARDS adv. & n. **2.** n. Cardinal point lying ~; western part of England, Scotland, Ireland, or Europe, part of U.S. beyond earlier settled States or ~ of Mississippi; = OCCIDENT (*Empire of the W~*, WESTERN *Empire*); western part of any country; ~ *wind*. **3.** adj. Situated, dwelling, in or more towards the ~; ~ *longitude*; || ~ *central*, abbr. W.C., London postal district; || ~ *country*, part of England ~ of line from Southampton to mouth of Severn; *W~* INDIES, whence *W~-Indian* a.; *W~ End*, richer & more fashionable district in ~ of London; (of wind) coming from the ~; || ~*-country*, of or from or characteristic of the~ country; || ~*-countryman* (or *-woman*), native of it; *W~-end*, in or characteristic of W~ End. [OE, OS, OHG *west*, ON *vestr* f. Gmc **wes-t-*, cogn. w. L *vesper*, Gk *hesperos*]

wĕs'tering, a. & part. Tending towards the west (usu. of sun). [f. *wester* vb f. WEST adv. +-ER⁵]

wĕs'terlў, a. & adv. = foll. (rare); (of direction) towards the west; (of wind) blowing from the west or thereabouts. [f. WEST as EASTERLY]

wĕs'tern, a. & n. **1.** Living or situated in, coming from, the west (*W~ Empire*, one of two parts, with Rome as capital, cf. *Eastern Empire* with Constantinople, into which Theodosius divided Roman Empire 395; *W~* or *Latin Church*, part of Christian church that continued to acknowledge the popes at the Greek schism, see GREEK); = OCCIDENTA*l*; (of wind) westerly (rare); hence ~ER[1](4) n., ~IZE(3) v.t., make (oriental people or country) ~ in ideas, institutions, etc., ~MOST a. **2.** n. ~er; a film or novel dealing with American cowboys, rustlers, sheriffs, etc. [OE *westerne* (-ERN)]

wĕst'ing, n. Westward progress or deviation esp. in sailing (cf. NORTHING). [-ING¹]

Wĕst'minster, n. City forming part of London (~ *Abbey*, **fig.**, glorious death such as would entitle one to place among celebrities there buried); (the Houses of) Parliament, the political arena; member of ~ School; STATUTE *of ~*.

wĕt, a., v.t. (-tt-), & n. **1.** Soaked, covered, dabbled, moistened, or supplied, with or *with* water or other liquid (~ *sponge*, *land*, *road*, *table*, *eyes*, *cheeks*, *clothes*, *feet*; *am ~ to the skin*, with clothes soaked through); *not prohibiting or opposing use of alcohol; (sl.) crazy, futile; ~ BLANKET[1]; ~ *bargain*, closed with drink; ~ BOB⁵; ~ *bulb*, see DRY¹*-bulb thermometer*; ~ *dock*, in which ship can float; ~ *pack*, wrapping of body in ~ cloths enclosed in dry blankets etc.; ~ *plate* in photog., sensitized collodion plate exposed while ~; *rainy* (~ *day*, *weather*); ~*-nurse*, (n.) woman employed to suckle another's child, (v.t.) act as ~*-nurse* to (child); hence ~'NESS n., ~t'ISH¹(2) a. **2.** v.t. Make ~ (~ *bargain*, close it with drink; ~ *one's whistle*, drink); hence ~t'ING¹(1) n. **3.** n. Moisture, liquid that ~s something, rainy weather; (sl.) a drink; *opponent of prohibition. [OE *wæt* adj. = ON *vátr*, superseded in ME (*wet*) by p.p. of the vb; n. (OE *wæt*) & vb (OE *wǣtan*) f. adj.; rel. to WATER]

wĕth'er (-dh-), n. Castrated ram. [OE *wether*, OS *withar*, OHG *widar*, ON *vethr*, Goth. *withrus*]

wey (wā), n. Unit of weight varying from 2 cwt to 3 cwt with different kinds of goods. [orig. identical w. *weigh* n., OE *wǣg(e)*, balance, weight, OS, OHG *wāga*, ON *vág* f. Gmc **wǣg-* WEIGH]

wh-. In a few of the words beginning thus the w is, as indicated in the pronunc. brackets, not sounded; in all others the h is silent in ordinary modern usage, but the earlier sound, = hw, is retained by the Scots, Irish, Welsh, & northern English, & by some purists in pronunciation, as well as for the nonce in unfamiliar wds or such as might be confused with commoner wds having no -h- (*whet*, *whey*).

whăck, v.t., & n. **1.** Strike heavily with stick etc., thwack, whence ~'ING¹(1) n.; (sl.) go shares in, distribute. **2.** n. Heavy blow esp. with stick; (sl.) share (*have had my~ of pleasure*). [imit., or alt. f. THWACK]

whăck'er, n. (sl.). Thing or person big of its kind. [-ER¹; cf. *thumper*, *whopper*, etc.]

whăck'ing, a. (sl.). Big of its kind. [-ING²; see prec.]

whāle, n. & v.i. **1.** Kinds of large fishlike marine mammal some of which are hunted for their oil, spermaceti, ~bone, ambergris, etc. (*right*, *arctic*, *Greenland*, or *bowhead* ~, kind yielding best ~bone; SPERM², *humpback*, *bottle-nosed*, etc., ~; *bull*, *cow*, ~, adult male, female, ~; *very like a* ~, ironical assent to absurd statement, see *Hamlet* III. ii. 399). **2.** *A* ~ *of* (colloq.), no end of; *a* ~ *on*, *at*, *for*, very good at or keen on (something); ~*-boat*, (double-bowed like those) used in whaling; ~'bone, elastic horny substance growing in thin parallel plates in upper jaw of certain ~s, & used in many kinds of manufacture; ~-calf, young ~; ~-fin, commerc. name for ~bone; ~-head, African bird allied to herons & storks; ~-line, superior rope 2 in. round used in whaling; ~'man, seaman engaged in whaling; ~-oil, train oil or sperm oil got from ~s. 3. v.i. Be engaged in ~-fishing; whaling-gun, for firing harpoon etc. at ~s; whaling-master, captain of a whaler. [OE hwæl, = OHG wal, ON hvalr]

whāl'er, n. Whaling ship or man; kind of clinker-built seaboat with pointed stern, carried by some warships. [-ER¹]

whǎng, v.t. & i:, & n. (colloq.). 1. Strike heavily & loudly, whack; (of drum etc.) sound (as) under blow. 2. n. ~ing sound or blow. [imit.]

whǎngee' (-ngg-), n. Cane made from a kind of Chinese bamboo. [Chin. huang]

wharf (wôrf), n. (pl. -fs, -ves), & v.t. 1. Wooden or stone platform beside which ship may be moored for (un)loading etc.; hence ~'AGE(1, 4) n. 2. v.t. Moor (ship) at, store (goods) on, ~. [OE hwearf, = MLG warf, werf]

whar'finger (wôrfinjer), n. Wharf-owner. [app. f. earlier *wharfager, f. wharfage +-ER¹; cf. messenger]

what (wŏt), a. & pron. interrog., excl., & rel. 1. adj.: (a) interrog., asking for selection from indefinite number (cf. which from definite number; ~ books have you read?; don't know ~ plan he will try) or for specification of amount or number or kind (~ money, men, abilities, has he?; ~ news?; ~ matter?, = does it matter?; ~ good, use, is it?, = purpose will it serve?; ~ manner of man is he?; I know ~ difficulties there are, cf. c); (b) excl., = how great or strange or otherwise remarkable for good or ill (~ a fool you are!; ~ impudence!; ~ an idea!; ~ genius he has!) or, before adj. & n., = how (~ partial judges we are!); (c) rel., = the — that, any — that, as much or many — as, (dispose of ~ difficulties there are, cf. a; lend me ~ money or men you can; will give you ~ help is possible; ~ time, arch., when, while). 2. pron.: (a) interrog., = ~ thing(s)?, with many modifications given by context, & often in ellipt. uses for sentence, some of which are here illustrated (so ~?, colloq., freq. implying that one is at a loss ~ to do or think; ~ will people say?, is it respectable to do it?; W~?, i.e. did you say; ~ ho!, excl. of greeting or hailing; ~ is he?, i.e. in respect of occupation; ~, do you really mean it?, i.e. I must have heard wrongly; ~ if we vers to try?, i.e. would result; ~ for?, for ~ reason or purpose?; ~-for n. (sl.), severe punishment, reprimand, etc., as he gave him ~-for; ~ though we are

poor?, i.e. does it matter; ~ next?, no absurdity can outdo this; ~ of or about ~?, i.e. ~ news?, or how can you dispose of this point?; well, ~ of it?, formula admitting fact but not inference etc. from it; ~ is he the better for it?, in ~ way or to ~ extent; ~ is your name?; ~ not usu. without interrog. mark, many other things of the same kind, anything; ~-not, piece of furniture with shelves for knick-knacks; ~ like is he?, provincial for ~ is he like? or what sort of man is he?, ~-d'ye--call-him, -her, -it, -'em, ~'s-his (or -her, -its)-name, substitutes for name that has slipped memory; I wonder ~ you are; don't know ~ he said; ~ followed is doubtful, cf. c; cannot guess ~ he was attempting, cf. c; *~ have you (sl.), anything else of that sort; I know ~, have a new idea; I'll tell you ~, i.e. the truth or right course is; know ~'s ~, i.e. a good thing etc. from a bad etc.); (b) excl., = ~ thing(s)!, how much!, etc. (~ he has suffered!); (c) rel., = that or those which, the thing(s) that, anything that, a thing that, (~ followed was unpleasant, cf. a; did ~ he was attempting, cf. a; ~ I have written I have written; ~ I know not is not knowledge; give me ~ you can; ~ is called the general reader; come ~ will or may, in spite of any results etc.; tell me ~ you remember of it; but, ~ even you must condemn, he was lying; will do ~ I can for you; use no arguments but ~ you believe in yourself; so also various more or less incorrect colloq. uses of but ~ for but, as not a day comes but ~ makes a change, not a man but ~ likes her, not a day but ~ it rains, I never see him but ~ I think, I don't know but ~ I will, NOT but ~; ~ with ~ with —, between various causes etc., as ~ with drink & ~ with fright, he did not know much about the facts). [OE hwæt, OHG (h)waz, ON hvat, Goth. hwa f. Gmc *hwat f. Aryan q^wod (cf. L quod) neut. sing. of q^wos WHO]

whatev'er (wŏt-), what'e'er(poet.;wŏtār'), a. & pron. indef. rel. used (1) = prec. in rel. uses with addition of or emphasis on indefinite sense (~ I have is yours; ~ measures are considered best; do ~ you like); (2) in indef. concessive clauses where what is not possible, = though any- (thing), as ~ results follow, ~ happens, ~ friends we may offend, we shall have done our duty); (3) ellipt. for ~ it, he, etc., may be, = at all after noun in negative context (never whate'er), as there is no doubt ~, is there any chance~?, no one ~ would accept, cannot see any one ~; (4) colloq. for what EVER. [ME; WHAT +EVER]

What'man (-ŏt-), n. (attrib.). ~ (paper), brand of paper used for drawing, water--colours, engraving, & photography. [maker's name]

what'sō (arch.; -ŏt-), whatsoev'er (emphatic), **whatsoe'er'** (poet.; wŏtsōǒr'), aa. & pronn. = WHATEVER (1, 2), & *whatsoever* = also WHATEVER (3). [ME, reduced f. OE *swā hwæt swā*]

‖ **whaup**, n. Curlew (chiefly Sc.). [imit. of cry]

wheal[1], mis-spelling of WALE, WEAL.

‖ **wheal**[2], n. (Cornwall). Mine (esp. tin-mine). [Cornish *huel*]

wheat, n. (Highly nutritious seeds of) kinds of corn-plant bearing dense four-sided spike of grain (esp. *winter* or *unbearded* ~, *summer* or *bearded* ~, & *German* ~ or *spelt*); ~-*grass*, couch-grass. Hence ~'EN[5] a. [OE *hwǣte*, OS *hweti*, OHG *weizzi*, ON *hveiti*, Goth. *hwaiteis* f. Gmc **hwaitjaz* f. **hwīt-* WHITE]

wheat'ear, n. Small bird with white belly & rump. [earlier *wheatears* (WHITE, ARSE)]

Wheat'stone bridge, n. Apparatus for measuring electrical resistances. [C. *Wheatstone*, English physicist (d. 1875)]

whee'dl|e, v.t. Coax *into* doing or *into* good temper etc., persuade by flattery or endearments, cajole, humour for one's own ends; get (thing) by ~ing *out of* person; cheat (person) *out of* thing by ~ing. Hence ~ER[1] n., ~ING[2] a., ~INGLY[2] adv. [orig. obsc.; perh. f. OE *wǣdlian* beg (*wǣdl* poverty)]

wheel[1], n. 1. Circular frame or disc arranged to revolve on axis & used to facilitate motion of vehicle or for various mechanical purposes, machine etc. of which a ~ is an essential part, object resembling a ~, (BALANCE, CATHERINE, COG[1], FLY[3], MILL[1], OVERSHOT, PADDLE, POTTER'S, RATCHET, SPINning, STEERing, SUN-&-planet, UNDERSHOT, ~; *eccentric* ~, turning on axis not at its centre; *fifth* ~, apparatus enabling front ~s etc. of four-wheeled conveyance to be slewed, also see FIFTH ~; ~s *within* ~s, intricate machinery, indirect or secret agencies; *the* ~s *of life*, the vital processes etc.; ~ *of life* (obs.), scientific toy converting series of pictures of successive attitudes into semblance of continuous motion; *Fortune's* ~, ~ with which Fortune is depicted as symbol of ups & downs, also fig. vicissitudes; *break on the* ~, maim & kill on medieval instrument of torture that revolved with victim bound on it; BREAK[1] *butterfly on* ~; *a* FLY[1] *on the* ~; *put* SPOKE[1] *in* one's ~, one's SHOULDER *to the* ~; ~ *& axle*, utilization of leverage given by difference in circumference between ~ & its axle, called one of the MECHANICAL *powers*; *go on* ~s, smoothly); Fortune's ~ (*we may be rich at the next turn of the* ~); steering-~ (*don't speak to the man at the* ~). 2. Motion as of ~, circular motion, motion of line as on pivoted end esp. as military evolution, (*street arab turning* ~s *in the gutter*; *the* ~s *& somersaults of the gulls*; *right, left,* etc., ~, words of command to company etc. in line to swing round on right, left, flank as pivot). 3. ~'BARROW[2];

~ *base*, distance between front & rear axles of vehicle; ~ *chair*, invalid's on ~s; ~-*horse*, wheeler; ~-*house*, steersman's shelter; ~-*lock*, (gun with) antiquated lock having steel ~ to rub against flint etc.; ~-*seat*, part of axle fitting into hub; ~-*tread*, part of carriage etc. ~ that touches ground; ~ *window*, circular with spokelike tracery; ~'*wright*, maker of ~s. Hence (-)~ED[2] (-ld), ~'LESS, aa. [OE *hweogol, hwēol*, MDu. *wiel*, MLG *wēl*, ON *hjól, hvél*, f. Gmc **hwe(g)ula*, cogn. w. Gk *kuklos* CYCLE]

wheel[2], v.t. & i. Swing (t. & i. of line of men etc.) round in line on one flank as pivot, (loosely) change direction lit. or fig., face another way, (often *round*); push or pull (wheeled thing esp. wheelbarrow or Bath chair or its load or occupant, or furniture on castors) in some direction; go in circles or curves; ride on bicycle. [ME, f. prec.]

wheel'er, n. In vbl senses; also: rear horse in four-in-hand, tandem, etc. (cf. LEADER); FOUR-~; ‖ wheelwright. [WHEEL[1,2], -ER[1]]

wheez|e, v.i. & t., & n. 1. Breathe with audible friction; ~e *out*, utter with ~ing. 2. n. Sound of ~ing, whence ~'Y[2] a., ~'ILY[2] adv., ~'INESS n.; (theatr. sl.) joke, anecdote, etc., interpolated by actor during performance; (sl.) scheme, plan. [prob. f. ON *hvǣsa* to hiss]

whelk[1], n. Kinds of marine spiral-shelled mollusc, some used as food. [ME *wilke, welke* f. OE *wioloc, weoloc*, of unkn. orig.]

whelk[2], n. Pimple. Hence ~ED[2] (-kt) a. [OE *hwylca* (*hwelian* suppurate), see WALE]

whelm, v.t. (poet., rhet.). Engulf, submerge, overwhelm. [perh. f. OE **hwelman* = *hwylfan* overturn, whence dial. *whelve*]

whelp, n., & v.i. & t. 1. Young dog, pup; young lion, tiger, bear, wolf, etc., cub; disagreeable or ill-bred child or youth. 2. vb. Produce pups or cubs or (derog.) child, give birth to (esp. derog. of human mother); originate (evil scheme etc.). [OE, OS *hwelp*, OHG *(h)welf*, ON *hvelpr*]

when, adv. interrog. & rel., pron., & n. 1. adv. interrog. At what time ?, on what occasion ?, how soon ?, how long ago ?, (~ *did, shall, you see him*? *don't know* ~ *it was*; *say* ~, ellipt., i.e. process is to begin or stop; in rhet. questions equivalent to neg. statement, as ~ *shall we see his like again*?, ~ *did I suggest such a thing*?). 2. adv. rel. (With *time* etc. as antecedent) at which (*the time* ~ *such things could happen is gone*; *there are occasions, conjunctures,* etc., ~); at the or any time that, on the or any occasion that, at whatever time, as soon as, (*he exclaimed* ~ *he saw me*; ~ *Greek meets Greek*; ~ *it rains he stays at home*; *shall have it* ~ *you ask politely*); also ellipt. like WHILE[2], as *he looked in* ~ *passing,* ~

found make a note of; also introducing exclamatory clause with ellipse of apodosis, as ~ *I think what I have done for that man!*); although, considering that, (*walks* ~ *he might ride; how could you,* ~ *you knew it might kill him?; how convince him* ~ *he will not listen?*); after or upon which, but just then, & then, (*the conflict began,* ~ *it soon appeared which was stronger; we were just coming to the point* ~ *the bell interrupted us*). **3.** pron. What (interrog.) or which (rel.) time (*till* ~ *can you stay?, from* ~ *does it date?; since* ~ *things have been better*). **4.** n. Time, date, occasion, (*told me the* ~ *& the how of it*). [OE *hwanne* etc., = OS *hwan,* OHG *wanne,* Goth. *hwan,* f. interrog. st. *hwa-* (WHO, WHAT), as *then* is of *tha-* (THE, THAT)]

whĕnce, adv. interrog. & rel., pron., & n. (now poet., literary, etc.). **1.** From what place or source? (being ousted by *where* — *from* in lit. sense & *how, why,* etc., in fig.; ~ *comes it that,* how is it that; *no one knows* ~ *she comes*); (with *place* etc. as antecedent) from which (*the source* ~ *these evils spring*; now usu. *from which*); to or rarely at or from the place from which (*return* ~ *you came; abides* ~ *he sent me; comes* ~ *he came*; now usu. *where — from, from where —*); ~*soev'er,* from whatever place or source. **2.** pron. What (interrog.) or which (rel.) starting-place (*from* ~ *is he?; the source from* ~ *it springs*). **3.** n. Source (*we know neither our* ~ *nor our whither*). [ME *whannes, whennes,* f. *whanne* (OE *hwanone* whence, f. st. *hwa-,* see prec.) +-ES; cf. THENCE]

whĕnĕv'er, whĕne'er (poet.; -âr), **whĕn- sŏĕv'er** (emphatic), adv. rel. indef. (cf. *when* EVER). At whatever time, on whatever occasion, as soon as, every time that. [SO, EVER]

where (wâr), adv. interrog. & rel., pron., & n. **1.** adv. interrog. In or to what place or position lit. or fig., in what direction, at what part, in what respect, (~ *is Heaven?*; ~ *did you read that?*, in what book; ~ *are you going?,* now usu. preferred to *whither; showed me* ~ *they were;* ~ *does it touch our interests?;* ~ *are you looking?,* ~ *shall we be if prices fall now?,* how situated; *don't know* ~ *to have him,* said of person of elusive character; often in rhet. questions = neg. statements, as ~ *is the sense of it?,* ~ *is the use of trying?*). **2.** adv. rel. (see also WHERE-). (With *place* etc. as antecedent) in which (*places* ~ *they sing;* also with ellipse of noun, as ~ *he is weakest is in his facts*); in or to the or any place, in the direction or part or respect, in which (~ *your treasure is; go* ~ *you like; is, send him,* ~ *he will be taken care of;* ~ *the ancients knew nothing we know a little; that's* ~ *it is,* colloq., that **is** the real reason for it or point of it).

3. pron. What (interrog.) or which (rel.) place (~ *do you come from, are you going to?*; vulg. in rel. use, as *the place* ~ *he comes from*). **4.** n. Place, scene of something, (*the* ~*s & whens are important*; cf. *any*~, *no*~, *every*~). [OE *hwær, hwār,* OS *hwār,* OHG (*h*)*wār, wā,* cf. also ON *hvar,* Goth. *hwar*; f. st. *hwa-* (see WHEN); cf. HERE, THERE]

where- (wâr). **1.** ~ is written in one word with appended prep. as substitute for the prep. preceding or following *what* interrog. pron. or *which* rel. pron. (~*by shall we know him?; the signs* ~*by he shall be known;* ~*by I saw that he was angry*), cf. corresp. compounds of *there;* the use is becoming rare exc. either in formal or poet. or in joc. or uneducated writing or in special uses as noted : ~*'about'* (& see 2); ~*at'*; ~*by'*; ~*'fore* (for what reason?, why?, on what account, on which account: also as n. pl. = reasons as *the whys & ~fores*); ~*from'*; ~*in'* (also ~*inso- ev'er*); ~*in'to*; ~*of'*; ~*on'*; ~*out'*; ~*through'*; ~*to'*; ~*un'der*; ~*un'to*; ~*upon'* (still common introducing new sentence in narrative); ~*with'* (or ~*withal'*; the longer form common as n.= money etc. needed for a purpose; *has not the* ~*withal to do it,* oŕ *the* ~*withal*). **2.** ~ in its proper local use is qualified in sense by additions: ~*abouts'* adv. interrog., where within considerable limits or vaguely (~*abouts is he?; don't know even* ~*abouts to look*), (n., ~*'abouts*) person's or thing's locality roughly defined; ~*as'* conj., taking into consideration or having as premiss the fact that (esp. in legal preambles), in contrast or comparison with the fact that, but in contrast with what has been said; **wherev'er, where'er** (poet.; -âr), ~*soev'er* (emphat.), advv. rel. indef., in or to whatever place etc.

whe'rry̆, n. Light shallow rowing-boat usu. for carrying passengers. [orig. unkn.]

whĕt, v.t. (-tt-), & n. **1.** Sharpen by rubbing on or with stone etc.; stimulate (appetite, stomach, desire); ~*stone,* shaped stone for tool-sharpening, thing that sharpens the wits. **2.** n. Sharpening; small quantity taken to create or creating appetite for more; dram. [OE *hwettan,* OHG *wezzan,* ON *hvetja,* f. *hwæt* bold, cf. OHG *hwaz* sharp]

wheth'er[1] (wĕdh-), a. & pron. interrog. & rel. (arch.). Which of the two. [OE *hwæther, hwe-,* = OS *hwethar,* OHG *hwedar,* ON *hvatharr,* Goth. *hwathar* f. Gmc **hwa-,* **hwe-* (see WHEN) +-THER; cf. OTHER]

wheth'er[2] (wĕdh-), conj. **1.** Introducing indirect questions of which the direct form would be answerable with *yes* or *no* (*don't know* ~ *he will be here*); such questions involve an alternative, which may be unexpressed as above, expressed precisely

(~ *he is here or* ~ *he is in London*, or more usu. ellipt. *or in London*), or expressed comprehensively by the negative (~ *he is here or* ~ *he is not here*, or more usu. ellipt. *or not*); i.e., the alternative if expressed has always *or*, after which ~ is usu. repeated if subj. & vb are expressed; ~-clauses may be appended directly to many adjj. & nn. as well as to vbs (*doubtful, uncertain, anxious*, etc., ~; *the question* etc. ~), though *as to* is often needlessly inserted; DOUBT² ~; ~ *or* NO²; formerly also with direct questions (~ *shall we live or die?*). **2.** Used with following *or* or *or*~ (according as second alternative has its subj. & vb expressed, as in 1) to introduce the protasis having alternatives corresponding to a single conditional apodosis (~ *we stay or* ~ *we go*, ~ *we go to him or he comes to us*, ~ *we go or not, the result will be bad*); ~ *or* NO²; formerly also when each alternative had apodosis (~ *we live, we live unto the Lord, & ~ we die, we die* etc.). [f. prec.]

whew (hwū), int. expressing (usu. joc.) consternation.

whey (wā), n. Part of milk that remains liquid when the rest forms curds; ~-*faced* (arch.), pale esp. with fear. [OE *hwæg, hweg*, MDu. *wey*, f. Gmc **hwaja-*]

which, a. & pron. interrog. & rel. **1.** adj. interrog. Asking for selection from alternatives conceived as limited in number or known (cf. WHAT; ~ *way shall we go?*; *say* ~ *chapter you prefer*). **2.** adj. rel. And, now, although, since, etc., this or these (now rare exc. with n. serving to sum up details of a compound or vague antecedent; *a smile & a shilling*, ~ *equipment is within most people's reach, will suffice*; ~ *things are an allegory*); *the* ~, arch. for~. **3.** pron. interrog. ~ *person(s)*, ~ *thing(s)*, (~ *of you am I to have for this?*; *say* ~ *you would like best*; ~ *is* ~*?*, ~ of two etc. given persons etc. corresponds to one of given descriptions etc., & ~ to another*?*). **4.** pron. rel. (cf. THAT). Used to convert what would in the simplest grammar be an independent sentence into a subordinate clause by being substituted for a noun expressed in it after being expressed or implied in the sentence to which it is to be subordinated, = ~ person or persons (arch.), ~ thing(s) as modified by context, (*Our Father*, ~ *art in heaven*; *the river* ~, or better *that, flows through London*; *the meeting*, ~ *was held in the Park, was a failure*; *he said he saw me there*, ~ *was a lie*; occas. in clause preceding antecedent, *as moreover*, ~ *you will hardly credit, he was not there himself*; *the* ~, arch. for ~; in the possessive case *whose* is occas. for convenience preferred to the usual of ~, as *the only place whose supply of baths is adequate*). [OE *hwelc, hwilc*, = OS *hwilic*, OHG (*h)welih*, Goth. *hwaleiks* f. Gmc **hwa-, *hwi-+*liko-body* (LIKE¹, -LY¹); cf. SUCH]

whichev′er, whichsoev′er (emphat.), aa. & pronn. rel. indef. used correspondingly to WHATEVER, WHATSOEVER, but with the restricted area of choice that distinguishes WHICH from WHAT (cf. *which* EVER). [SO, EVER]

whid′ah-bĭrd (-da-), n. Small W.-Afr. bird, male of which has tail-feathers of enormous length. [orig. WIDOW-*bird*, altered f. assoc. w. *Whidah* in Dahomey]

whiff¹, n., & v.i. & t. **1.** Puff of air, smoke, odour, etc. (~ *of grape-shot*, a few discharges; *want a* ~ *of fresh air*); (commerc.) small cigar; ‖ light uncovered outrigged sculling-boat. **2.** vb. Blow or puff (t. & i.) lightly. [imit.; perh. partly alt. of ME *weffe* foul smell]

whiff², n. Kind of flatfish. [perh.=prec.]

whiff³, v.i. Fish with line towing bait near surface. [orig. unkn.]

whif′fle, v.i. & t., & n. **1.** (Of wind) blow lightly, shift about, drive (ship) in varying directions; (of flame, leaves, & fig. of thought etc.) flicker, flutter, wander; make the sound of a light wind in breathing etc. **2.** n. Slight movement of air. [f. WHIFF¹+-LE(3)]

whig, n. & a. (Member) of the political party that, after the Revolution of 1688, aimed at subordinating the power of the crown to that of Parliament & the upper classes, passed the Reform Bill, & in the 19th c. was succeeded by the Liberals (opp. TORY; DISH² *the~s*). Hence ~g′ERY (4), ~g′ISM(3), nn., ~g′ISH¹ a., ~g′ishLY adv., ~g′ishNESS n., (-g-). [*c.* 1648 of Scottish Covenanters, prob. short for *whiggamer, -more*, of unascertained orig.]

while¹, n., & v.t. **1.** Space of time, time occupied by or given to some action etc., (*have been waiting all this* ~; *go away for a* ~; *in a little* ~, soon; MEAN²~; *once in a* ~, occasionally, at long intervals; *have not seen him for a long* ~, *this long* ~ *past*; *happened a long* ~ *ago*; *that is enough for one* ~, for some time; *worth* ~ or *my* etc. ~, repaying the time spent in doing it etc.; *looked in her eyes the* ~ or *whilst*, during some other process; *the* ~ or *whilst*, poet., during the time that). **2.** v.t. Pass (time, hour, etc.) *away* in leisurely manner. [OE *hwil*, OS, OHG *hwil(a)*, ON *hvila*, Goth. *hweila*, f. Gmc **hwilō*, cogn. w. L *quies* QUIET]

while², conj. **1.** During the time that, for as long as, at the same time as, (*please write* ~ *I dictate*; *Jones got 98* ~ *his partner was making 15*; ~ *there is life there is hope*; also with ellipse of pronominal subject & *am, is, was*, etc., as ~ *reading I fell asleep, we are safe* ~ *in his care, he retained the consciousness of it* ~ *asleep*). **2.** In contrast more or less marked with the fact that simultaneously, although, whereas, (chiefly journalistic) and, (*Nero fiddling* ~ *Rome burns*; ~ *I have no money to spend, you have nothing to spend money on*; ~ *I admit his good* *points I can see his bad*; also erron. ~ *admitting* etc., cf. the correct ellipses above; *Jones lost an arm, Brown a leg,* ~ *Robinson had both amputated*). [short for OE *thā hwile the*, ME *the while that*]

whiles. See WHILST.

whil′om, adv. & a. **1.** (arch.). Once, formerly. **2.** adj. Quondam (*his* ~ *friend*). [OE *hwilum*, dat. pl. of WHILE¹; cf. OS, OHG *hwilom*]

whilst, whiles (arch.; wīlz), conj. & n. = WHILE²; (n.) *the* ~, = *the* WHILE. [ME, orig. in comb., as *sumehwiles* etc., (WHILE¹ +-ES), +-*t* as in *amongst, amidst*]

whim, n. Sudden fancy, caprice, crotchet; kind of windlass for raising ore from mine; ~′*wham*, arch. [redupl. of ~], plaything, toy, ~. [orig. unkn.; perh. symbolic]

whim′brel, n. Kind of curlew. [perh. f. foll., f. the bird's cry]

whim′per, v.i. & t., & n. **1.** Make feeble querulous or frightened sounds, cry & whine softly; utter ~ingly; hence ~ER¹ n., ~ingLY² adv. **2.** n. Sound of ~ing. [imit., f. earlier dial. *whimp* +-ER⁵]

whim′sical (-z-), a. Capricious; oddlooking, fantastic. Hence ~ITY (-zīkăl⁴) n., ~LY² adv. [foll., -ICAL]

whim′sy (-zĭ), n. Crotchet, whim. [see WHIM]

whin¹, n. Gorse, furze, (used in pl. also); ~′*chat*, kind of small bird. [prob. Scand., cf. Norw. *hvine, hvēn*, Sw. *hven*]

whin², whin′sill, whin′stone, nn. Kinds of basaltic rock or hard sandstone. [orig. unkn.]

whin|e, v.i. & t., & n. (Make) long-drawn complaining cry (as) of dog; (utter) querulous talk; utter ~ingly (often *out*). Hence ~ER¹ n., ~ingLY² adv. [OE *hwinan*, ON *hvina*]

|| **whing′er,** n. Short sword, dirk, or long knife. [app. rel. to 15th c. *whinyard*, of unkn. orig.]

whinn′y, v.i., & n. **1.** Neigh gently or joyfully. **2.** n. ~ing sound. [imit., cf. WHINE]

whip¹, v.t. & i. (-pp-). **1.** Move (t. & i.) with sudden motion, snatch, dart, (always with adv. or prep.; ~ *behind the cupboard*; ~*ped away to France*; ~*ped up her toy terrier*; ~ *out sword, knife*; ~ *off one's coat*). **2.** Bind (cord, stick) with close covering of twine, sew (seam) with overhand stitches. **3.** Flog, lash, (horse, boy, etc.; ~ *in, off, together*, of managing hounds with ~, & transf. followers esp. in Parliament; ~ *stream*, fish it with ~ping motion; ~ *horses on*, urge with whip; ~ *fault out of* person; ~ *eggs, cream*, beat into froth); (sl.) excel, defeat, (~ *creation*, beat all). **4.** Hoist (coal etc.) with rope passed through pulley. **5.** ~*ping-boy*, (hist.) boy educated with & chastised for young prince, (fig.) scapegoat; ~*ping-post*, to which persons were tied to be

~ped; ~*ping-top*, kept spinning by blows of lash. Hence ~p′ING¹(1, 4) n. [ME; early hist. uncert.; f. (M)Du., (M)LG *wippen* swing, leap, dance, = MHG *wipfen* dance]

whip², n. **1.** Instrument for urging on or punishing with lash attached to short or long stick; *good, poor*, etc., coachman (esp. of four-in-hand or tandem driver). **2.** (Also *whipper-in*) hunt official subordinate to huntsman charged with management of hounds; || (transf.) official appointed to maintain discipline among, secure attendance of, & give necessary information to, members of his party in House of Parliament, also written notice (variously underscored with number of lines representing degrees of urgency, as *three-line* ~) requesting attendance on particular occasion. **3.** (Also ~-*&-derry*) rope-&-pulley hoisting apparatus. **4.** ~*cord*, tightly twisted cord such as is used for making ~-lashes (*his veins stood out like* ~*cord*); ~*crane*, light derrick with tackle for hoisting; ~*fish*, kind with dorsal fin produced into filament like ~-lash; ~*gin*, tackle-block with hoisting rope with several ends each to be simultaneously hauled on; ~ *hand*, hand that holds ~ (esp. in *have the* ~ *hand of*, be in position to control); ~*ray*, ray-fish with long slender tail; ~*round*, appeal circulated among friends, members of a club or society, etc., for contributions (usu. for some charitable object); ~*saw*, narrow saw-blade with ends held by frame; ~*snake*, slender kinds. Hence ~p′Y³ a., flexible, springy, ~p′INESS n. [ME; partly f. prec., partly f. (M)LG *wippe, wip*, quick movement, leap, etc.]

whipp′er, n. In vbl senses; esp.: ~-*in*, (now usu. shortened to) WHIP²; ~-*snapper*, small child, young & insignificant but presuming or intrusive person [perh. for *whipsnapper*, implying noise & unimportance]. [-ER¹]

whipp′et, n. Cross-bred dog of modified greyhound type used for racing; (mil.) fast light tank. [perh. f. WHIP¹+-ET]

whip′poorwill, n. American bird allied to goatsucker. [imit. of cry]

Whip′snāde, n. (Used for) ~ Park, in the Chilterns, a reserve for the breeding & exhibition of wild animals. [place]

whip′ster, n. Small child; || trifling frivolous person such as should still be subject to the whip. [-STER]

whir̂(r), v.i. (part. *whir′ring*), & n. (Make) continuous buzzing or softly clicking sound as of bird's wings quickly flapped or cogwheels in rapid action. [ME, prob. Scand., cf. Da. *hvirre*, Norw. *kvirra*]

whirl, v.t. & i., & n. **1.** Swing (t. & i.) round & round, revolve (t. & i.) rapidly (~*ing* DERVISH); send (missile etc.), (of moving body) travel, swiftly in orbit or curve; convey or go rapidly *away* etc. in wheeled conveyance; (of brain, senses, etc.) be giddy, seem to spin round, (of thoughts etc.) follow each other in bewildering succession. **2.** n. ~ing movement (*my thoughts are in a* ~). **3.** ~'*pool*, circular eddy in sea etc.; ~'*wind*, mass of air ~ing rapidly round & round in cylindrical or funnel shape (*sow wind & reap* ~*wind*, suffer worse results of bad action). [ME; prob. f. ON *hvirfla* f. Gmo *hwerbh-* rotate]

whirl'igig (-g-), n. Kinds of spinning toy, (fig.) revolving motion (~ *of time*, changes of fortune); merry-go-round; kinds of water beetle that circle about on surface. [f. prec.+obs. *gig* whipping-top]

whisht. See WHIST[1].

whisk, n., & v.t. & i. **1.** Bunch of grass, hair, etc., to flap dust off, flies away, etc., with; instrument for beating up eggs or cream; quick movement (as) of ~ or of animal's tail. **2.** vb. Flap (dust, fly, etc.) *away* or *off*; beat up (eggs etc.); take *away* or *off* with sudden motion (*waiter* ~*ed my plate off*); convey or go lightly & quickly esp. out of sight (*was* ~*ed across channel in aeroplane*; *mouse* ~*s into its hole*); brandish lightly or flip or wave about (*went* ~*ing a cane, her tail*). [ME *wisk*, prob. Scand., cf. ON *visk* wisp, Sw. *viska* besom, Sw. *viska* to whisk]

whis'ker, n. Hair of man's cheek (cf. *moustache, beard*; usu. in pl.); bristle growing from upper lip of cat etc., set of such bristles on one side. Hence (·)~ED[5] (-*erd*) a. [f. WHISK vb+-ER[1]]

whis'ky[1], -key, n. Spirit distilled from malted barley, other grains, or sugar etc.; *whiskified* (joc.), affected by ~-drinking; ~-*liver*, liver-complaint from alcoholic poisoning. [short for *whiskybae*, var. of USQUEBAUGH]

whis'ky[2], n. Kind of light gig or chaise. [f. WHISK, w. ref. to lightness of motion]

whis'per, v.i. & t., & n. **1.** Speak without vibration of vocal cords; talk with intention of being audible only close at hand or to confidant; inform or bid (person) thus *that* or *to* do; converse privately, indulge in slander or plotting; put secretly in circulation (tale, *that*; esp. *it is* ~*ed that*); (of leaves, stream, etc.) rustle; ~*ing-gallery*, gallery, cave, etc., in which some acoustic peculiarity causes least sound made at a particular point to be audible at another far off; hence ~ER[1], ~ING[1] (1), nn., ~ingLY[2] adv. **2.** n. ~ing speech (*always talks in a* ~ or ~s); ~ed remark; STAGE[1]~; rumour of unknown origin, mysterious hint; rustling sound. [O Northumb. *hwisprian*; cf. early Flem. *wisperen*, OHG (*h*)*wispalōn* (G *wispeln*)]

‖ **whist**[1], whisht (hw-), int. enjoining silence (now rare exc. in representations of Irish talk, -*sht*). [ME, cf. HIST, HUSH]

‖ **whist**[2], a. (arch.). Silent. [ME, f. prec.]

whist[3], n. Card game of mingled skill &

chance for four or exceptionally three or two persons (*long, short,* ~, with ten, five, points to game; DUMMY, *double* DUMMY, ~; RUBBER[2] *of* ~; ~ *drive*, PROGRESSIVE ~ party. [alt. f. (1621) *whisk* (perh. f. WHISK vb), w. ref. to the silence usual in the game]

whistl|e (wi'sl), v.i. & t., & n. **1.** Make with the lips or with instrument for the purpose, or, (of birds etc.) with the voice, or (of missile, wind, etc.) by rapid motion, the shrill sound of breath forced through small orifice formed with lips (*boy, bird, steam-engine, driver, wind, bullet,* ~*es*; ~*e for a wind*, of becalmed sailors, whence *may* ~*e for it*, vainly wish; *let one go* ~*e*, disregard his wishes; ~*ing*, in names of kinds of bird & animal, as ~*ing eagle, marmot*); (obs.) act as informer, peach; summon or give signal to (dog, attendant) by ~ing (~*e down the wind* metaph. f. hawking, let go, abandon); give (tune etc.) by ~ing. **2.** n. ~ing sound or note; instrument for producing such sound (*penny* ~*e*, tin pipe with six holes giving notes; *steam* ~*e*, sounded by jet of steam; *pay for* one's ~*e* (of anecdotic orig.), pay high for some caprice); throat (WET one's ~*e*); *~e-stop*, small unimportant town on railway (~*e-stop speech*, electioneering speech made on tour at railway stations). [OE *hwis(t)lian, wistlian* (also *hwistle* n.), of imit. orig.; cf. ON *hvisla* whisper, MSw. *hvisla* whistle]

whistler (wis'ler), n. In vbl senses; esp.; kind of marmot; kinds of bird. [-ER[1]]

whit[1], n. Particle, least possible amount, (usu. in *no* ~, *not* or *never a* ~, not at all). [early mod. E *whyt, wyt*, app. alt. f. WIGHT in phr. *no wight* etc.]

Whit[2], a., **Whit'**|sun, a. & n. ~ *Sunday*, seventh Sunday after Easter, commemorating day of Pentecost; ~ *Monday, Tuesday*, those following, ~ *week*, that containing, ~ Sunday; ~'*suntide* (also ~*sun* as n.), ~ Sunday & following days; ~'*sun week*, ~ week. [late OE *Hwita Sunnandæg* White Sunday, app. w. ref. to white baptismal robes; from ME analysed as *Whit Sunday* or *Whitsun Day*, both used attrib. in same sense, & *Whitsun* as n. (ME *w(h)itsone(n)*)]

white[1], a., & v.t. **1.** Resembling a surface reflecting sunlight without absorbing any of the visible rays, of the colour of fresh snow- or common salt or the common swan's plumage, having some approach to such colour, pale (~ *as a sheet*), less dark than other things of the same kind (*bleed* ~, fig., drain of wealth etc., w. ref. to hanging of calf to ~*n* veal), characterized by presence of some white, (~ in many -ED[2] compounds used esp. in naming animals etc., as ~-*backed*, -*beaked*, -*bearded*, -*bellied*, -*breasted*, -*crested*, -*crowned*, -*eyed*, -*faced*, -*footed*, -*fronted*, -*headed*, -*necked*, -*rumped*, -*tailed*, -*throated*, -*winged*). **2.** (Of water, air, light) transparent, colourless. **3.** (fig.). Innocent, unstained, of harmless kind. **4.** Of ~ men (see ~ *man* below); ~ *culture, civilization,* etc.). **5.** (pol.). Of royalist or counter-revolutionary or reactionary tendency (opp. RED, & cf. TERROR). **6.** ~ *alloy*, any of the cheap imitations of silver; ~ ANT; ~'*bait*, small fish prob. the fry of several kinds eaten fried in quantities when about 2 in. long; ~'*beam*, tree with silvery underleaf; ~ *bear*, polar bear; W~'*boy*, member of 18th-c. illegal agrarian association in Ireland wearing ~ frocks at nightly meetings & outrages; ~-*caps*, breakers out at sea; ~ *coal*, water power [F *houille blanche*]; ~ (snowy) *Christmas*; ~ *coffee* (with milk); ~-*collar worker*, one not engaged in manual labour; ~ *corpuscle*, = LEUCOcyte; ~ CROW¹, CURRANT; W~ *Czar* (hist.), (Asian phr. for) Czar of Russia; ~ ELEPHANT; || ~ ENSIGN, flown by ships of British navy, cf. RED *ensign*; ~ FEATHER¹; ~ *fish*, any kind of sea-fish except herring, salmon, and sea-trout; ~ FLAG⁴, FRIAR, FROST; || ~ *gloves* (presented to assize judge who finds no criminal cases to try); ~ GROUSE¹; ~-*gum*, eruption on infant's neck & arms; ~ *hands*, (lit.) as sign of exemption from labour, (fig.) innocency or integrity; so ~-*handed*; ~ *heart-cherry*, pale heart-shaped kind; ~ HEAT¹ (lit., & fig. of passion etc.; so ~-*hot*); ~ *horses*, waves with ~ crests at sea; W~ *House*, official residence of U.S. president; ~ LEAD¹, LIB¹; ~ *light*, colourless, e.g. ordinary daylight, also fig. of unprejudiced judgement; ~-*lipped*, esp. with fear; ~-*livered*, cowardly; ~ MAGIC; ~ *man*, member of one of the paler races chiefly inhabiting or having inhabited Europe, & characterized by a certain type of civilization (cf. *black, brown, red, yellow, man*; *the* ~ *man's burden*, task of leading the world forward), (colloq.) person of honourable character, good breeding, etc.; ~ *meat*, poultry, veal, rabbits, pork; ~ *metal*, = ~ *alloy*; ~ (sleepless) *night* [F *nuit blanche*]; ~-*out* n., atmospheric condition, esp. in polar regions, marked by dense snow-cloud & total obscuration of physical features [after BLACK²-*out*]; || ~ *paper*, report issued by Government to give information; W~ (western) *Russia*(n); ~ *sale* (of house- & body-linen); ~ SCOURGE; ~ *sheet*, penitent's garb (usu. *stand in a* ~ *sheet*, confess sin etc.); ~ *slave*, girl entrapped (& exported) for purpose of prostitution (*the* ~-*slave traffic*, ~ *slavery*); ~'*smith*, worker in tin, also polisher or galvanizer of iron; ~ *squall*, sudden tropical storm at sea announced only by line of ~ water approaching; ~'*thorn*, hawthorn (cf. BLACK¹-*thorn*); ~ (counter-revolutionary) *terror*; ~-*throat*, kinds of small songbird; ~ *war*,

war without bloodshed, economic warfare; ~'*wash*, (n.) solution of quicklime or of whiting & size for brushing over walls, ceilings, etc., to give clean appearance, also fig. means employed to clear person or his memory of imputations, (v.t.) cover with ~wash, attempt to clear reputation of, (pass., of insolvent) get fresh start by passage through bankruptcy court; ~ *wine*, of amber or golden colour (opp. *red*); ~ *witch* (using power for beneficent purposes only); hence ~LY² adv. (rare), whit'EN⁵ v.t. & i., ~'NESS (-tn-) n., whit'ISH¹(2) a. **7.** v.t. (arch.). Make ~. [OE, (OS) *hwit*, OHG (*h*)*wiz*, ON *hvitr*, Goth. *hweits* f. Gmc *hwitaz]

white², n. White or nearly white colour; kinds of white pigment (*Chinese* etc. ~); white clothes or material (*dressed in* ~); albuminous part round yolk of egg; visible part round iris of eye; = *whiteman* (MEAN³ ~); kinds of butterfly; (med.; pl.) LEUCOrrhoea. [OE; f. prec.]

|| **White'chapel** (-t-ch-), n., & v.i. **1.** ~ *cart*, light two-wheeled spring-cart used by shopkeepers for sending goods round. **2.** (whist). Lead from one-card suit with a view to subsequent trumping. [~ in London]

|| **White'hall** (-t-hawl), n. (Used for) the Civil Service, the Government offices. [street in London]

white'ning (-tn-), n. = WHITING¹. [*whiten* (WHITE¹), -ING¹]

whith'er (-dh-), adv. interrog. & rel. (chiefly arch.), & n. **1.** To what place or point? (now usu. *where?*, *where* — *to?*, *how far?*, etc., but cf. *I see* ~ *your question tends*), whence ~WARD adv.; (rel.), with antecedent *place* etc.) to which (now usu. *to which, where*), (without antecedent) to the or (also ~*soever*) any place to which (now usu. *where*); = & thither. **2.** n. Destination (*our whence & our* ~; *no* ~, arch., to no place). [OE *hwider*, f. Gmc *hwi-, cf. WHICH, + -THER (b)]

whit'ing¹, n. Chalk prepared by drying, grinding, etc., for use in whitewashing, plate-cleaning, etc. [WHITE¹ vb, -ING¹(4)]

whit'ing², n. Kind of sea-fish much used as food; ~'*pout*, fish with some resemblance to ~ & an inflatable membrane over part of head. [ME, f. (M)Du. *wijting*, app. f. WHITE¹ a. +-ING³]

whit'leather (-lĕdh-), n. White leather dressed with alum instead of being tanned. [WHITE¹]

|| **Whit'ley Coun'cil**, n. A council of representatives of employers & workers for discussion & settlement of industrial relations & conditions. Hence Whit'ley-ISM n., use of such methods for dealing with industrial problems. [J. H. *Whitley*, Speaker 1921–8]

whit'low (-ō), n. Inflammatory tumour on finger esp. about the nail. [ME *whit*flaw, -*flow*, app. = WHITE + FLAW[1], but perh. of LG orig.; cf. early mod. Du. *vijt, fijt*, LG *fit* whitlow]

Whitsun. See WHIT².

whit′tle¹, n. (arch.). Long knife, esp. such as is used by butchers. [var. of ME *thwitel* f. OE *thwitan* to cut +-LE(1)]

whit′tle², v.t. & i. Trim, carve, slice off pieces from, (wood) with knife; shape, thin down, cut repeatedly *at*, piece of wood with knife; reduce amount or effect of by repeated subtraction (usu. *down*, *away*). [f. prec.]

Whit′worth thread (-wer-, -red), n. Standard screw-thread for metal. [Sir Joseph *Whitworth*, English engineer (d. 1887)]

whit′ÿ, a. Inclining to white (usu. in comb. with other colour-name, esp. ~-*brown*). [-Y²]

whiz, whizz, v.i. (-zz-), & n. (Make) sound given by friction of body moving at great speed through air; ~-*bang* (army sl.), shell from a small-calibre high--velocity gun. [imit.]

who (hōō), pron. pers. interrog. & rel. (obj. *whom* pr. hōōm; poss. WHOSE pr. hōōz). **1.** interrog. What person(s)?, which person(s)?, what sort of person(s) in regard to position or authority?, (~ *said so?*; ~*m* or colloq. ~ *do you mean?*, *told him* ~ *they were*, ~*m* or colloq. ~ *to look out for*; ~*se son is he?*; ~ *would have thought it?*, no one would; ~ *are the Joneses, I should like to know?*; ~ *am I that I should object?*; *know* ~ *'s* ~, ~ or what each person is; *a* ~ *'s* ~, list with description of notables; ~-*does-what dispute* or *strike*, one about which trade union is to do a particular job). **2.** rel. (Person or persons) that (*the man* ~*m you saw; those for* ~*se benefit it was done; any-one* ~ *chooses can apply*; *there is no one* ~ *we can believe is competent*, often incorrectly ~*m*); (arch.) the or any person(s) that (~ *breaks pays*; ~*m the gods love die young*; *as* ~ *should say*, like a person ~ said, as though one said); and, but, though, since, if, etc., he, him, they, etc. (*sent it to Jones*, ~ *passed it on to Smith*; *is flirting with Dick*, ~*m she detests*). [OE *hwā*, OS *hwe*, OHG (*h*)*wer*, Goth. *hwas*, f. Gmc **hwaz, *hwez* f. Aryan *qʷos, qʷes*, cogn. w. L *quis*, Gk *tis*; cf. WHAT]

whoa. See wo.

who′dŭ(n)nit (hōō-), n. (sl.). Detective or mystery story. [= *who done* (illiterate for *did*) *it?*]

whoëv′er, who′sō (arch.), **whosoëv′er** (emphat.), **whoe′er′** & **whosōe′er** (poet.; -âr), (hōō-), pronn. pers. indef. rel. (cases as with WHO; *whomsoever* or the incorrect *whoever* is usu. substituted without special emphasis for *whomever*, & *whosoever* occas. for *whose-ever*), used (1) as mod. equivalent of arch. *who* in indef. rel. sense (*whoever comes will be welcome*; *stopped whomsoever* or *whoever* or *whom-*

ever he saw; *return it to whose-ever* or *whosesoever address is on it*); (2) in indef. concessive clauses=though any one (*who-ever else objects, I do not*; *whose-ever it is, I mean to have it*; *whomsoever* or *who-ever* or *whomever I quote, you retain your opinion*); (3) vulg. for *who* EVER. [WHO, SO, EVER]

whole (hōl), a. & n. **1.** (arch.). In good health, well (*they that be* ~ *need not a physician*). **2.** In sound condition, uninjured, not broken, intact, (*hope you will come back* ~; *got off with a* ~ *skin*; *there is not a plate left* ~; *has swallowed a raisin* ~). **3.** Integral, consisting of one or more units, without fractions, (~ *numbers*, integers). **4.** Undiminished, without subtraction, (*bread made of* ~ *meal*, not deprived by bolting of some constituents). **5.** (With *a* in sing.) not less than (*spent* ~ *years of misery*; *went up a* ~ *tone*; *lasted three* ~ *days*; ~ *regiments were cut down*; *talked a* ~ *lot of nonsense*); (with *the, his*, etc.) all that there is of (*the* ~ *truth, world, duty of man*; *do thing with one's* ~ *heart*, heartily, with concentrated effort etc., without doubts etc., whence ~-*heart*ED² a., ~-*heart′*EDLY² adv., ~-*heart′*EDNESS n.; *the* ~ *priesthood*, *city*, etc., all members or inhabitants of it; COMMITTEE *of the* ~ *House*; *go the* ~ HOG¹, whence ~-*hŏgğ′*ER¹ (-g-) n.). **6.** ~-*coloured*, all of one colour; ~-*hoofed*, with undivided hoofs; ~-*length′*, (portrait) representing person from head to foot; ²~ *note*, semibreve; ~′*sale*, (n., chiefly attrib.) selling of articles in large quantities to be retailed by others(*a* ~*sale dealer*; *sells by* ~*sale*; ~*sale prices*), (adj. & adv.) on the ~sale plan, (transf.) on large scale, (*our business is* ~*sale only*; *sells* ~*sale*; *a* ~*sale slaughter took place*; *sends out begging letters* ~*sale*); ~′*saler*, ~sale dealer; hence ~′NESS (hōln-) n. **7.** n. Thing complete in itself; all that there is of something (often *of*; *the golden rule contains the* ~ *of morality*; *on* or *upon the* ~, taking into consideration everything that bears on the question, after weighing pros & cons etc.); organic unity, complete system, total made up of parts, (*nature is a* ~; *the* ~ *& the parts*). [OE *hāl*, OS *hēl*, OHG *heil*, ON *heill*, Goth *hails* f. Gmc **hailaz*, cf. HALE; for *wh-* cf. WHORE]

whole′some (hōls-), a. Promoting physical or moral health, salubrious, salutary, not morbid, (~ *food, air, exercise, advice, neglect, excitement*). Hence ~LY² adv., ~NESS n. [ME; prec., -SOME]

wholly (hōl·li), adv. Entirely, without abatement, (*I am* ~ *yours*); exclusively, without admixture, (*a* ~ *bad example*). [WHOLE, -LY²]

whom. See WHO. [formally repr. OE *hwām*, dat. of *hnā* WHO & *hwæt* WHAT]

whoop (hōōp). Var. of HOOP²; ~*ing cough*, infectious disease, esp. of children, with short violent cough followed by long sonorous inspiration. Hence ~'ER[1] n., in vbl senses; esp. (also ~er or ~ing swan) the wild or whistling swan.

whoo'pee (wōō-), n. (colloq.). *Make ~*, rejoice noisily, have a roaring time. [f. prec.]

whŏp, v.t. (sl.; -pp-). Thrash, (fig.) defeat, overcome, whence ~p'ING[1](1) n.; (part.) very large of its kind (esp. *a ~ping lie*), whence ~p'ER[1] n. [orig. unkn.; var. of (dial.) *wap*]

whore (hōr), n., & v.i. **1.** Prostitute, strumpet, (*the* SCARLET *W~*); ~*-master*, -*monger*, fornicator; hence ~'DOM (hŏrd-) n. **2.** v.i. (Of man) practise fornication; (fig., arch., esp. *go a-whoring after strange gods* etc.) practise idolatry or iniquity. [late OE *hōre*, OHG *huora*, ON *hóra*, f. Gmc *hōr-* (whence ON *hórr*, Goth. *hors*) cogn. w. L *carus* dear; for *wh-* cf. WHOLE]

whŏrl, n. Ring of leaves or other organs round stem etc. of plant; one turn of a spiral; disc on spindle steadying its motion. Hence ~ED[2] (-ld) a. [ME *wharwyl, whorwil*, app. var. of WHIRL, infl. by *wharve* n., whorl of spindle]

whor'tleberrў (wér̄telb-), n. = BILBERRY. [16th c., south-western dial. form of *hurtleberry* (c. 1450, of unkn. orig.); so *whort, whortle* for *hurt, hurtle*]

whose (hōōz). Possessive case of WHO, used also as case of WHICH 4; ~-*ever*, ~*soever*, see WHOEVER. [ME *hwās*, later *hwōs, whōs*, alt. f. *hwas, hwes*, OE *hwæs*, gen. of *hwā* WHO & *hwæt* WHAT, infl. by *hwā, hwō* WHO & *hwǣm, hwōm* WHOM]

whoso, whosoever. See WHOEVER.

whȳ[1], adv. interrog. & rel., & n. (pl. ~s). **1.** On what ground ?, for what reason ?, with what purpose ?, (~ *did you do it?*; *cannot think ~ you came*; often ellipt., as *You are late; ~?*, esp. in ~ *so?*, demand for grounds of statement or view); (rel.) on account of which (*the reasons ~ he did it are obscure*). **2.** n. Reason, explanation, (*cannot go into the ~s & wherefores now*). [OE *hwī, hwȳ* instr. of *hwæt* WHAT, f. Gmc *hwī*, Aryan *qwei*, locative of *qwo-* WHO]

whȳ[2], int. expr. surprised discovery or recognition (~, *it is surely Jones!*; ~, *what a bruise you have got!*; ~, *of course, that was it*), protest at simplicity of question etc. (*'What is twice two?' ' ~, four.'* ~, *a child could answer that*), pause for reflection (*'Is it true?' ' ~, yes, I think so'*), objection (~, *what is the harm?*), introduction of apodosis (*if silver will not do, ~, we must try gold*), etc. [ellipt. uses of prec. interrog.]

wick[1], n. (Piece of) fibrous or spongy material by which lamp or candle flame is kept supplied with melted grease or oil; (surg.) gauze strip inserted in wound

to drain it. [OE *wēoce, wēoc*, ~ MDu. *wiecke*, MLG *wēke*, OHG *wioh* (G *wieche*)]

wick[2], n. Town, hamlet, district, (rare exc. in place-names as *Hampton W~* or other compounds as *baili~*). [OE *wīc*, OS *wīk*, OHG *wīch*, app. f. L *vicus*, cogn. w. Gk *oikos*, Goth. *weihs*]

wick'ĕd, a. Sinful, iniquitous, vicious, given to or involving immorality, (~ *Bible*, edition of 1632 with *not* omitted in seventh commandment), offending intentionally against the right; spiteful, ill-tempered, intending or intended to give pain, playfully mischievous, roguish. Hence ~LY[2] adv., ~NESS n. [ME, f. obs. *wick* of same sense (perh. adj. use of OE *wicca* wizard) + -ED[1] as in WRETCHED]

wick'er, n. Plaited twigs or osiers as material of baskets, chairs, mats, protective covers, etc. (usu. attrib., as ~ *chair*), whence ~ED[2] (-erd) a.; ~*-work*, (things made of) ~. [ME, f. east Scand., cf. MSw. *viker*, early Da. *vigger* willow, f. root of Sw. *vika* bend]

wick'ĕt, n. **1.** Small door or gate, esp. one beside or in the compass of a larger one for use when the latter is not open (also ~*-door*, *-gate*); turnstile entrance; aperture in door or wall usu. closed with sliding panel; door closing only lower half of doorway. **2.** (crick.). One set of three stumps & two bails (*keep ~*, be ~-*keeper*, fieldsman stationed close behind batsman's ~; *keep one's ~ up*, succeed in not being put out); the ~s as defended by one batsman (*5 ~s down*, five men out; *match won by 2 ~s*, with three of winning side still not out); *good* etc. state of the pitch (*play began on a perfect ~*); *be on a good, sticky, ~*, (fig.) be in an advantageous, unfavourable, position. [ME, f. AF = ONF *wiket*, = OF *guichet*, of uncert. orig.]

widdershins. Var. of WITHERSHINS.

wide, a., adv., & n. **1.** Measuring much or more than other things of same kind across or from side to side, broad, not narrow, (~ *door, road, river, brim, margin, cloth, interval*; ~ *margin*, fig., a good deal more allowed than is likely to be needed). **2.** (Appended to measurement) in width (*a strip 3 ft ~*). **3.** Extending far, embracing much, of great extent, (*has a ~ range*; ~ *fame*, known to many; *the ~ world*, all the world great as it is; *a ~ domain*, large; *is of ~ distribution*, occurs in many places; *a ~ generalization*, covering many particulars; *there is a ~ difference between*; also adv., as *the principle ranges ~*, & esp. in *far & ~*), whence ~LY[2] adv. **4.** Not tight or close or restricted, loose, free, liberal, unprejudiced, general, (~ *knickerbockers*; ~ *culture*, not specialized; *takes ~ views*; *hazard a ~ guess*, one allowing margin for errors of detail; *give ~ berth to*, not go too near, keep clear of, avoid). **5.** Open to full extent (*staring with* ~ *eyes*; also adv. or pred. a., as *yawned* ~, *open your mouth* ~, *window is* ~ *open, person is* ~ *awake*). **6.** At considerable distance from a point or mark, not within reasonable distance *of*, (~ *ball* in cricket, ball judged by umpire to pass wicket beyond batsman's reach & counting one to his side; *gave an answer quite* ~ *of the mark or purpose*; also adv. or pred. a., as *is bowling, shooting,* ~; *arrow fell* ~ *of target*). **7.** (sl.), Crafty (*a* ~ *boy*). **8.** n. A ~ ball; *the* ~, *the* ~ *world* (*broke to the* ~, sl., completely broke). **9.** ~ *awake* a. (colloq.), wary, knowing; ~*-awake* n., soft ~*-brimmed felt hat*; ~*'spread'*, ~ly disseminated (esp. of beliefs or impressions). Hence **wid'EN⁶** v.t. & i., **wid'ISH¹** (2) a. [OE *wid*, OS *wid*, OHG *wit*, ON *vithr*, f. Gmc *•widaz*]

wi(d)geon (wi'jn), n. Kinds of wild duck. [early 16th c., of F form, but unkn. orig.; cf. 17th c. F *vigeon, vingeon* kind of duck]

wid'ow (-ō), n., & v.t. **1.** Woman who has lost her husband by death & not married again (GRASS ~; ~*'s weeds*; ~*'s cruse*, supply that looks small, but proves inexhaustible, see 1 *Kings* xvii. 10–16; ~*'s mite*, see *Mark* xii. 42; ~*'s peak*, V-shaped growth of hair in centre of forehead; also attrib., as ~ *lady, woman*); BLACK¹~; *the* ~ (sl.), champagne [f. the *Veuve* (F=~) Cliquot brand]; ~*-bird*, black-plumaged African bird of genus *Vidua* (L = ~); hence ~HOOD (-dōh-) n. **2.** v.t. Kill husband or mate of, deprive of husband or wife or mate, make into ~ or widower, (usu. in p.p.; *the* ~*ed father, mother, etc.*); (poet.) bereave *of* friend etc. [OE *widewe* etc., OS *widowa*, OHG *wituwa*, Goth. *widuwō*, cogn. w. L *vidua*, Skr. *vidhavā*]

wid'ower (-ōer), n. Man who has lost his wife by death & not married again. [ME, f. prec. + -ER¹]

width, n. Distance or measurement from side to side; comprehensiveness or liberality *of* mind, views, etc.; piece of material of certain ~ (*shall want three* ~s *of it*). [17th c. (WIDE, -TH¹), repl. *wideness*]

wield, v.t. Control, sway, hold & use, manage with the hands or otherwise, (~ *power, the sceptre, a kingdom* etc. chiefly poet., *weapon* lit. or fig.). [OE *wealdan* (-*wieldan*), OS, Goth. *waldan*, OHG *waltan*, ON *valda* f. Gmc *•waldh-*]

wife, n. (pl. *-ves*). **1.** Woman, esp. one who is old & rustic or uneducated (now rare exc. in *old wives' tale*, foolish or superstitious tradition, & in comb. as FISH¹~, HOUSEWIFE, MIDWIFE). **2.** Married woman esp. in relation to her husband (usu. *my* etc. ~, *the* ~ *of*, or with epithet as-*will make a good* ~; *the* ~, joc or vulg., = *my* ~; *wedded, lawful,* ~, emphatic phrr. in contrast w. *mistress, concubine,* etc.; *all the* WORLD *& his* ~; *have, take, to* ~, = as

~). Hence ~'HOOD (-fh-), **wif'ie** [-ʏ³], nn., ~'LESS, ~'LIKE, ~'LY¹, (-fi-), aa. [OE *wif*, OS *wif*, OHG *wip*, ON *vif*; ult. orig. unkn.]

wig¹, n. Artificial head of hair formerly much worn as ornament, & still to conceal baldness or disguise appearance ‖ or as part of official dress esp. of judge or lawyer or of servant's livery (*there will be* ~s *on the green*, a free fight). Hence (-)~GED³ (-gd), ~'LESS, aa. [short for PERIWIG; cf. WINKLE]

wig², v.t. (-gg-). Rebuke sharply, rate, (chiefly in·the vbl n.). Hence ~g'ING¹(1) (-g-) n. [app. f. *wig* n. rebuke (1804), in sl. or colloq. use]

wig'an, n. Stiff canvas-like material used for stiffening. [*Wigan* in Lancashire]

wigeon. See WI(D)GEON.

wig'gle, v.t. (colloq. or dial). Cause (something) to move from side to side; ‖ scull (a boat) with single oar over stern. [ME, cogn. w. or f. MDu., (M)LG *wiggelen*; cf. WAG¹ & WAGGLE]

wight (wīt), n. (arch. or joc.). Person, being, (esp. *luckless, wretched*, etc., ~). [OE (= OS, OHG) *wiht*, ON *vættr*, Goth. *waihi(s)*; ult. orig. unkn.]

wig'wăm (or -ŏm), n. N.-Amer. Indian's tent or hut of skins or mats or bark; *•the W*~, Tammany Hall. [native]

wild, a., adv., & n. **1.** Not domesticated or cultivated (chiefly of animals & plants, & esp. of species allied to others that are not ~; in the commoner combinations ~ & the n. are hyphened, or treated as one wd with accent on ~; ~ *beast, plant*; ~ *man*, savage; ~ *ass*; ~*-boar*; ~*-duck*; ~*'fowl*; ~ *vine*; ~*'cat* lit., also fig. as a. or attrib. of finance or commercial speculations or strikes etc., reckless, unsound; ~*-goose* lit., also in ~*-goose chase*, absurdly impossible enterprise; ~ *horse*, also in *be drawn by* ~ *horses*, form of torture & death; ~ *hyacinth*, bluebell; ~ OATS; ~ *scenery* etc., of conspicuously desolate appearance; *woodnotes* ~, spontaneous & artless poetry). **2.** (Of horses, game-birds, etc.) shy, given to shying, easily startled, hard to get near. **3.** Unrestrained, wayward, disorderly, irregular, out of control, unconventional, (*a* ~ *fellow; settled down after a* ~ *youth*; ~ *work*, lawless doings; *hair hanging in* ~ *locks; living in* ~ *times; room is in* ~ *disorder; run* ~, grow unchecked or undisciplined or untrained). **4.** Tempestuous, violent, (*a* ~ *wind, night*, etc.). **5.** Intensely eager, excited, frantic, passionate, distracted, mad, (*is* ~ *with excitement, to try it; the* ~ *men*, extremists of a party etc.; ~ *about* person or subject, enthusiastically devoted to; ~ *delight, excitement, enthusiasm, grief, rage*; ~ *looks, appearance,* etc., indicating distraction; *drive* ~, madden). **6.** Haphazard, rash, ill-considered, ill--aimed, disturbed by excitement, (*a* ~ *guess, shot, blow, venture*; ~ *opinions,*

bowling; also as adv., as *shoot, talk,* ~).
7. ~*fire,* = Greek FIRE[1] (*report spreads like* ~*fire,* very fast). Hence ~ISH[1](2) a.,
~'LY[2] adv., ~'NESS n. **8.** n. Desert, ~
tract. [OE *wilde,* OHG *wildi,* ON *villr,*
Goth. *wiltheis,* also OE, OHG *wild* n., f.
Gmc *wilth-*]

wil′debēest (v-), n. The gnu. [Afrikaans
(now *wildebees,* pl. *wildebeeste*); (prec.,
BEAST)]

∥ **wil′der,** v.t. (poet.). Bewilder. [orig.
obsc.; prob. extracted f. foll.]

wil′derness, n. Desert, uncultivated &
uninhabited tract, (*voice in the* ~ etc., unregarded advocate of some reform, w. ref.
to *Matt.* iii. 3 etc.; *wandering* etc. *in the* ~,
of political party out of office, w. ref. to
Num. xiv. 33 etc.); part of garden left
wild; unlimited number or quantity of.
[OE *wild*(d)*ēornes,* f. *wil*(d)*dēor* WILD DEER,
see -NESS]

wild′ing, n. Plant sown by natural
agency, esp. wild crab-apple, or fruit of
such plant (also attrib.). [-ING[3]]

wile, n., & v.t. **1.** Trick, cunning procedure, artifice, (usu. in pl.). **2.** v.t. Lure,
entice, *away, into,* etc. (also incorrectly
for WHILE[1] vb). [ME *wil,* perh. f. Scand.
(ON *vél* craft)]

wil′ful, a. For which compulsion or ignorance or accident cannot be pleaded as
excuse, intentional, deliberate, due to
perversity or self-will, (~ *murder, waste,
ignorance, disobedience*); obstinate, self-
-willed, headstrong, refractory. Hence
~LY[2] adv., ~NESS n. [ME; WILL[2], -FUL]

Wilhelmstrasse (vil′helmshtrahse), n.
(Used for) the German Foreign Office.
[Berlin street]

will[1], v.t. & aux. (pres. *I, he, we, you, they,*
~ or *'ll, thou will* or *'ll;* past & condit.
I, he, we, you, they, would pr. wŏŏd or *'d,
thou wouldst* pr. wŏŏdst or *wouldest* or
'dst; neg. forms ~ *not* or *wŏn't,* would
not or *wouldn't,* or *'d not;* no other forms
or parts used). **1.** (used irrespective of
person with more or less of orig. sense
of volition). Desire (thing; arch.; *what
will thou?; what would they?*); want or
desire or choose to (*the haven where I
would be; come when you* ~); wish that,
rarely *that* (usu. in condit. with optative
effect; *I* often omitted; *it shall be as
you* ~; *said it should be as we would*;
would or *I would I were a bird!; would it
were otherwise!; would God I had died!,*
i.e. if only God had wished, or perh. ellipt.
for *I would to God; I would to heaven I was
dead; would-be,* prefixed as adj. or adv.
to wd describing character that person
vainly aspires to or that thing is meant to
have, as *a would-be gentleman, smart saying*); consent or be prevailed on to (~ *or
would not go any farther; wound would not
heal; would you pass the salt?; would not
do it for £100*); refuse to be prevailed on
not to (*boys* ~ *be boys; accidents* ~ *happen; you* ~ *have your way; he* ~, *would,*

get in my light); be accustomed or observed from time to time to (~ *sit there
for hours; now & then a blackbird would
call;* ~ *succeed once in ten times*); be
likely to turn out to (*this* ~ *be Waterloo,
I suppose; I don't know who it would be*).
2. As tense & mood auxiliaries ~ &
would are used (a) in 2nd & 3rd person
(1st having *shall, should*) to form a plain
future or conditional statement or question (*you* ~ *hear soon enough; they would
have been killed if they had let go;* ~ *or
would you, they,* be able to hear at such a
distance?, but cf. SHALL 5); (b) in 1st person (others having *shall, should*) to form
a future or conditional statement expressing speaker's will or intention (*I* ~
*not be caught again; we would have come if
you had given us longer notice*); (c) alternatively with *shall, should,* in sentences of
type *a* changed in reporting to 1st from
other person (*you say I* ~, *said I would,
never manage it,* reporting 'You ~
never'; now more usu. *shall, should*) or
from first to other person (*he said he
would never manage it,* reporting 'I shall
never'); (d) in reporting 1st pers.
sentences of type *b* (*you promised you
would not be caught again*). [OE *willan,*
OS *-ian,* ON *vilja,* Goth *wiljan,* f. Gmc
wel(l)*jan* f. *wel-, wal-,* cogn. w. L
velle wish]

will[2], n. **1.** Faculty by which person decides or conceives himself as deciding
upon & initiating action (*mind consists of
the understanding & the* ~; *freedom of the*
~, *free* ~, power of determining one's
choice of action independently of causation). **2.** (Also ~*-power*) control exercised
by deliberate purpose over impulse, self-
-control, (*has a strong, weak,* etc., ~).
3. Deliberate or fixed intention (*the* ~ *to
live in a patient is the surgeon's best ally;
the* ~ *to power* etc., Germanisms for
determination to win power etc.; *did it
against my* ~, *of my own free* ~; *where
there's a* ~ *there's a way; my poverty but
not my* ~ *consents*). **4.** Energy of intention, power of effecting one's intentions
or dominating other persons, (*do thing
with a* ~, energetically; *has a* ~ *that over-
bears all opposition*). **5.** Contents of the
~, what is desired or ordained by person,
(*thy* ~ *be done; what is your* ~?, what do
you wish done?; *have one's* ~, get thing
desired; *worked his wicked* ~ *upon them*).
6. Arbitrary discretion (esp. *at* ~, whenever one pleases; *tenant at* ~, who can be
turned out without notice; ~*-worship,*
arch., religion constructed to suit oneself).
7. Disposition towards others, wishing of
good or ill, (*good, ill,* ~, usu. as compd
wds, & see GOODWILL). **8.** Directions
written in legal form for disposition to be
made of person's property & minor children after his death (often *last* ~ *& testament; nuncupative* ~, see NUNCUPATE;
make one's ~). Hence (·)~ED[2] (-ld),

~´LESS, aa. [OE *willa*, OS *willio*, OHG *willo*, Goth *wilja* f. Gmc *wel- (prec.)]

will³, v.t. 1. Have as contents of one's will, intend unconditionally, (*God* ~s, ~*eth*, ~*ed, that man should be happy*; *can we* ~ *what we are told to* ~?; *he who* ~s *success is half way to it*); (abs.) exercise will-power (*has no power to* ~; ~*ing & wishing are not the same*). 2. Instigate or impel or compel by exercise of will-power (*you can* ~ *yourself into contentment*; *mesmerist* ~s *patient to think himself well*; ~*ed the genie into his presence*). 3. Bequeath by will (*shall* ~ *my money to a hospital*). [OE *willian*, f. prec.]

will'ét, n. N.-Amer. snipe. [imit. of cry]

will'ing, a. Not reluctant, cheerfully ready, (*to do*, or abs.; *do not spur a* ~ *horse*); of, given etc. by, ~ person (~ *hands, help*, etc.). Hence ~LY² adv., ~NESS n. [WILL¹, -ING²]

will-o'-the-wisp' (-dh-), n. = IGNIS FATUUS, JACK¹-o'-*lantern*; also, person of uncertain whereabouts or appearances. [orig. *Will with the wisp*; *wisp* = handful of (lighted) tow etc.]

will'ow¹ (-ō), n. 1. Kinds of tree & shrub with pliant branches growing usu. near water in temperate climates, many of which yield osiers & some timber used for cricket bats & other purposes (*wear the* ~, mourn loss or absence of one's beloved, formerly indicated by garland of ~ *leaves*; ~-*pattern*, conventional design of Chinese type done in blue on white china etc. introduced in England 1780). 2. Cricket-bat (*handle the* ~, bat). 3. ~´-*herb*, kinds of plant, the commonest with leaves like ~ & pale purple flowers. [OE *welig*, OS *wilgia*, MDu. *wilghe*, MHG *wilge*, f. Gmc *walg-, *welg-]

will'|ow² (-ō), v.t. & n., will'|ỹ, n. 1. Clean (fibrous material) by beating, picking, etc., with machinery. 2. n. (Also ~*ow*, ~*owing*, -*machine*) machine for ~owing. [*willow* for *willy* f. OE *wilige* wicker basket, rel. to *welig* (prec.)]

will'owy (-ōi), a. Abounding in willows; lithe & slender. [-Y²]

villỹ-nill'ỹ. See NILL.

wilt¹. See WILL¹.

wilt², v.t. & i. Wither (t. & i. of plant, leaf, flower), (make) droop. [of dial. orig., perh. alt. f. *wilk* WELK]

Wil'ton, n. (Also ~ *carpet*) kind of Brussels carpet with loops cut open into thick pile made at town of ~ in Wilts.

vil'|ỹ, a. Full of wiles, crafty, cunning. Hence ~ILY² adv., ~INESS n. [ME; WILE, -Y²]

Wim'bledon (-beld-), n. (Used for) the lawn-tennis tournaments with championship matches etc. held at ~.

vim'ple, n., & v.t. & i. 1. Covering of linen etc. worn by nuns & formerly by other women arranged in folds about head, cheeks, chin, & neck; (vb) put ~ upon, veil, arrange in folds. 2. Winding,

twist, turn, ripple; (vb) fall in folds, (of stream) twist about, meander, ripple. [OE *wimpel*, OHG -*al* (G -*el* pennon), ON *vimpill*]

win, v.t. & i. (won pr. wŭn), & n. 1. Secure as result of fighting or competition or (often of person, also colloq. off person) betting & gaming or of effort (~ *victory, fortress, prize, honour, fame, fortune*, one's BLUE², *wife*; ~ one's *spurs*, be knighted, (fig.) get recognition as expert at something; *won £5 of him at cards*, whence ~*n'ings* n. pl., see -ING¹(2); ~ one's *way*, progress by struggle etc.; ~ one's *bread*, earn livelihood, chiefly now in BREAD-~*ner*; ~ *ore* etc., get it from mine). 2. Be victorious in (~ *battle, game, bet, race*; ~ *the field*, arch., be victorious in battle or fig.; ~ *the* TOSS); (abs.) ~ *race, contest, money*, etc. (~ *by a* HEAD¹, *in a* CANTER, HAND¹s *down, by two* etc. *lengths, easily*, etc.; ~*ning*¹-*post*, marking end of race; *the* ~*ning horse, side*, etc.; ~ *at cards*; *let those laugh who* ~); (part.) determining victory (*the* ~*ning hit, goal, card*, etc.). 3. Make one's way to (~ *the shore, summit*, etc.). 4. Make one's way, or (with compl.) become by successful effort, (~ *home*; ~ *through the day, through all difficulties*; ~ *free, clear*, etc.). 5. Persuade, induce to do, gain over, (*you have won me*; *won him to consent*; *soon won his audience over*). 6. Exercise increasing attraction *upon* (*a theory that* ~s *upon one by degrees*); (part. as adj.) charming, attractive, (*a* ~*ning smile*, ~*ning manners, personality*, etc.), whence ~*n'ingLY*² adv. 7. ~*ning* HAZARD¹. Hence (-)~*neR*¹ n. 8. n. A success or victory in a game (*has had three* ~s & *no defeats*). [OE, OS, OHG, Goth. *winnan*, ON *vinna*]

wince, v.i., & n. 1. Show bodily or mental pain or distress by slight start or loss of composure, flinch, (often *under pain, the knife, at allusion*, etc.). 2. n. Act of wincing. [f. AF *wencir = OF *guencir, guenchir*, f. WG *wenkjan (= OHG *wenken*); cf. WINCH, WINK]

win'cey, n. (pl. ~s). Strong material of wool & cotton or wool used for shirts etc. Hence ~ETTE²(2) (-sï-) n. [perh. corrupt. of LINSEY-WOOLSEY]

winch, n. Crank of wheel or axle; hoisting-machine, windlass. [OE *wince* f. Gmc *wenk-, see WINCE]

Win'chéster¹, n. ~ (*rifle*), type of repeating rifle used esp. by big-game hunters. [O. F. ~, Amer. maker (d. 1880)]

Win'chéster², n. ~ (*quart*), (bottle holding) half a gallon. [~ in Hants, where standard measures were orig. deposited]

wind¹ (*poet. also* wī-), n. 1. Air in more or less rapid natural motion, breeze or gale or blast, (*north* etc. ~, coming from N. etc.; *fair, contrary*, ~, helping, hindering, ship's course; *hot, cold, whistling, variable*, etc., ~s; *constant* ~, that always blows in same direction at same place; *periodical*

~, recurring at known periods; ~ *rises*, begins to blow or gets stronger; *sound, scent, is carried by, comes on, the* ~; CAP- FUL, SLANT, *of* ~; ILL ~; *before, down, the* ~, helped by its force; WHISTLE *down the* ~; BETWEEN ~ *& water*; *sail, be, close to or near the* ~, as nearly against it as is con- sistent with using its force, (fig.) venture very near indecency or dishonesty; *in the* ~*'s eye, in the teeth of the* ~, directly against it; *on a* ~, naut., sailing against a ~ on either bow; *off the* ~, naut., sailing with the ~ on either quarter; *fling* or *cast prudence* etc. *to the* ~*s*, aban- don, neglect, take no thought of; PUT[1] *the* ~ *up* one; *have* or *get the* ~ *up*, sl., be or become frightened; *go like the* ~, swiftly; *there is something in the* ~, there are signs that some step is being secretly prepared; *find out how the* ~ *blows* or *lies*, what developments are likely or what.is the state of public opinion; *take the* ~ *out of* one's *sails*, frustrate him by anticipat- ing his arguments, using his material, etc.; *sow* ~, *& reap* WHIRL~; *raise the* ~, fig., obtain money needed). 2.~ward position or *weather*-GAUGE[1] (*take* or *get the* ~ *of*). 3. pl. The four cardinal points (*came from the four* ~*s*, from all directions; *scatter to the four* ~*s of heaven*). 4. Mere empty words, unmeaning rhetoric. 5. Artifi- cially produced air-current, air stored for use or used as current, (collect.) part of band consisting of ~-instruments, (*organ stops when the* ~ *is exhausted*; *was knocked down by the* ~ *of the blow*; *the strings were drowned by the* ~, *the wood*-~, i.e. flutes etc., *by the brass*). 6. Smell, conveyed on ~, indication of thing's whereabouts or existence, commencing publicity, (*get* ~ *of*, smell out, begin to suspect, hear rumour of; *take* or *get* ~, be rumoured). 7. Gas generated in bowels etc. by indigestion, flatulence, (*break*~, release it by anus; *baby* etc. *is troubled with* ~). 8. Breath as needed in exertion, power of fetching breath without difficulty while running or making similar continuous effort, spot below centre of chest blow on which temporarily paralyses breathing, (*have lost, let me recover* or *get, my* ~; *has a good, bad,* ~; *broken* ~, see BROKEN- -*winded*; *second*~, recovery of ~ in course of exercise after initial breathlessness; *have* one's ~ *taken*, be paralysed by blow in the ~; *hit him in the* ~). 9. ~'*bag*, wordy orator; ~-*bound*, unable to sail for contrary ~s; ~-*break*, fence, shrubs, etc., serving to break force of ~; ~-*cheater*, garment for protecting person from ~; ~-*chest*, box for compressed air in organ; ~-*colic*, pain caused by flatulence; ~- -*cutter*, upper lip of mouth of flue-pipe in organ; ~-*egg*, unfertilized egg incapable of producing chicken; ~'*fall*, fruit blown down, (fig.) unexpected good fortune, esp. legacy; || ~ -*fanner*, = ~*hover*; ~-*flower* (poet.), the plant anemone; ~-*gall*, soft

tumour on horse's fetlock-joint; ~-*gauge*, anemometer, also instrument showing amount of ~ in organ, also apparatus attached to sights enabling allowance to be made for ~ in shooting; || ~'*hover*, kestrel; ~-*instrument*, musical instrument in which sound is produced by current of air, as organ, flute; ~-*jammer*, merchant sailing-ship; ~'*mill*, mill worked by action of ~ on sails (*fight* ~*mills*, tilt at imaginary foe or grievance, w. ref. to Don Quixote); ~-*pipe*, breathing-tube, tra- chea; ~-*row*, line of raked hay, corn- -sheaves, peats, etc., made to allow of drying by ~; ~-*sail*, canvas funnel con- veying air to lower parts of ship; || ~- -*screen*, *~-*shield*, (of glass in front of motor-car driver); ~-*sock*, canvas cylin- der or cone flying from masthead to show direction of ~; ~-*spout*, waterspout, tornado, or whirl~; ~-*sucker, -sucking*, (horse with) the vice of noisily drawing in & swallowing breath; ~-*swept*, exposed; ~-TIGHT; ~-*tunnel*, tunnel-like apparatus for producing air-stream of known velocity past model aircraft etc. to in- vestigate effect of ~ pressure on structure; ~-*ward* a. & n., (region) lying in the direction from which the ~ blows, ex- posed to the ~, (*look to* ~*ward*; *the* ~- *ward side*; *get to* ~*ward of*, avoid smell of, also get weather GAUGE[1] of or fig. advan- tage over). Hence ~'LESS a. [OE, OS *wind*, OHG *wint*, ON *vindr*, Goth. *winds* f. Gmc *windaz* cogn. w. L *ventus*, f. root *wĕ*- blow, cf. WEATHER[1]]

wind[2], v.t. 1. Sound (horn, bugle, blast, call) by blowing (wī-; *winded* or by con- fusion w. foll. *wound*). 2. Detect presence of by scent (wī-; *winded*; *hounds, deer,* ~ *the fox, stalkers*; ~*ed his tobacco half a mile off*). 3. Breathe, make breathe quick & deep by exercise, exhaust wind of, renew wind of by rest, (wī-; *winded*; *give horse a gallop to* ~ *him*; *am quite* ~*ed by the climb*; *rested to* ~ *the horses*). [f. prec.]

wind[3], v.i. & t. (*wound*), & n. 1. Go in circular, spiral, curved, or crooked course, meander, (*path, river,* ~*s*; *herd* ~*s o'er the lea*; *creeper* ~*s round pole*; ~*ing staircase*, spiral; *in* ~*ing*, out of truth, askew); make one's or its *way* etc. circuitously, insinuate one*self into*, (*brook* ~*s its way*; *wound himself* or *his way into my affections*). 2. Coil (t. & i.), wrap closely (t. & i.), surround with coil, em- brace, (~ *cotton on reel, wool into ball*, etc.; also with *off* adv. or prep. = unwind; ~ *person round* one's *fingers*, exercise com- plete domination over; *wound the blanket round him, her arms round the child, the child in her arms*; ~ING[1]-*sheet*, in which corpse is wound; ~ *pegtop*, coil string round it; *serpent* ~s *itself* or ~s *round victim*); hoist or draw by use of windlass etc. (~ *ship out of harbour, ore up from mine*). 3. = ~ *up* (clock etc.). 4. ~ *ship*, reverse positions of bow & stern. 5. ~ *up*, coil the whole of (~ *up piece of string*), tighten coiling or coiled spring or fig. tension or intensity or efficiency of (~ *up strings of fiddle*; ~ *up clock etc.*); ~ *ing himself up for an effort or to do it; the administration needs ~ing up*, is slack; *person is wound up to fury; expectation was wound up to a high pitch*); bring to a conclusion, conclude t. & i., (*wound up his speech, or wound up, by declaring; shot his wife & child & wound up by stabbing himself; ~ up company*, arrange its affairs & dissolve it; *company ~s up*, ceases business, goes into liquidation, whence ~'ING¹-up n.); hence ~'ER¹(1, 2) n., ~'inGLY² adv. 6. n. Bend or turn in course; single turn in ~ing clock, string, etc.; ~-*up*, conclusion, finish. [OE, OS, OHG (-*lan*), Goth. *windan*, ON *vinda*, f. Gmc *wend-, *wand-, cf. WANDER, WEND¹]

win'dage, n. Difference between projectile's & gun-bore's diameter allowing escape of gas; (allowance for) influence of wind in deflecting missile. [-AGE]

wind'lass, n., & v.t. 1. Machine for hauling or hoisting on wheel-&-axle principle. 2. v.t. Hoist or haul with ~. [alt. (by assoc. w. dial. *windle* to wind) f. obs. (f. AF) *windas*, = OF *guindas* f. ON *vinddss* (*vinde* wind + *dss* pole)]

win'dlestraw (-del-), n. Old stalk of kinds of grass. [OE *windelstrēaw* grass for plaiting (WIND³, STRAW)]

win'dow (-ō), n. 1. Opening in wall or roof of building, ship, carriage, etc., usu. filled with glass in fixed or sliding or hinged frames to admit light & sometimes air to room etc. (*look out of ~ or the ~; have all one's goods in the ~*, be superficial; *blank, blind, false, ~*, mouldings or recess as for ~ without aperture; BOW WINDOW; BAY³; CASEMENT, DORMER, FRENCH, LATTICE, ORIEL, SASH², ~). 2. Opening in envelope to show address written on letter. 3. ~-*box*, slide for weights in sash-~, also box on ~-sill in which flowers are grown; ~-*dressing*, art of arranging goods attractively in shop-~, often fig. of adroit presentation of statistics etc.; ~ *envelope* (with opening or transparent part allowing address inside to show); ~-*shopping*, feasting one's eyes on the goods displayed in the shop-~s. Hence (·)~ED² (-ōd), ~LESS (-ŏl-), aa. [ME, f. ON *vindauga* (WIND¹, EYE²)]

Wind'sor (-z-), n. Town in Berks. (*House of* ~, style of British Royal Family assumed 1917; ~ *chair*, all of wood with curved support for back (& arms); *brown* ~ *soap*, brown scented kind; ∥ ~ *uniform*, blue coat with red collar & cuffs worn at ~ by the royal family, & by others having royal grant).

vind'|ỹ, a. Wind-swept (~*y hill-top, plain, situation*); in which wind is high (~*y night, weather, crossing*); wordy, verbose, empty, (~*y eloquence, logic, speaker*); generating or characterized by flatulence; (arch.)

windward (*on the ~y side of the law*, safely out of its reach); (sl.) frightened. Hence ~ILY² adv., ~INESS n. [-Y²]

wine, n., & v.i. & t. 1. (Kinds of) fermented grape-juice (*is a sound* ~; DRY¹ or *sweet*, STILL¹ or *sparkling*, WHITE¹ or *red*, ~; *green* ~, in first year; *port* ~, port; COMET ~; *Adam's* ~, water; *good* ~ *needs no* BUSH¹; *new ~ in old bottles*, new principle too powerful to be restrained by ancient forms; *take* ~ *with*, pledge & be pledged by at table; SPIRIT *of* ~; TEAR²s *of strong* ~; *over the* WALNUTS *& the* ~; ~ *whey*, beverage of ~ & curdled milk; *in* ~, exhilarated or drunk with ~). 2. ∥ (At universities) party for ~-drinking after dinner (~*s have gone out of fashion*). 3. Fermented drink resembling ~ made from specified fruit etc. (*cowslip, currant, gooseberry, orange, palm,* ~). 4. Solution of drug in ~ (*quinine* ~; ~ *of opium*). 5. A dark-red tint. 6. ~'*bag*, ~skin, or ~bibber; ~'*bibber*, tippler, drunkard; so ~'*bibbing* a. & n.; ~'*bottle*, glass bottle for ~, also ~skin; ~'*bowl*, lit., also drinking habits etc.; ~-*carriage*, wheeled utensil for circulating ~ at table; ~-*cooler*, vessel in which ~bottles are cooled with ice; ~'*cup*, as ~bowl; ∥~'*fat*, arch., ~*press*; ~'*glass*, any glass for drinking ~ from, esp. of size used for sherry, often as measure (also ~'*glassful*) of medicine to be taken, = four tablespoons; ~-MARC; ~ *of Scotland*, whisky; ~'*palm*, kind from which ~ is made; ~'*press*, in which grapes are squeezed; ~'*sap*, large red American winter apple; ~'*skin*, whole skin of goat etc. sewn up & used to hold ~; ~-*stone*, tartaric deposit in ~-casks; ~'*vault*, cellar in which ~ is kept, also bar etc. where it is retailed; hence ~'LESS, wīn'Y², aa. 7. vb. Drink ~; entertain to ~; often *dine & ~*. [OE *wīn*, OS, OHG *win*, ON *vin*, Goth *wein* f. L *vinum*]

wing, n., & v.t. & i. 1. One of the limbs or organs by which the flight of a bird, bat, insect, angel, etc., is effected, part in non-flying bird or insect corresponding to ~, supporting part of flying-machine, (*clip one's ~s*, limit his movements or ambitions or expenditure; *come on the ~s of the wind*, swiftly; *lend, add, ~s to*, accelerate; *take under* one's ~, treat as protégé; *his ~s are sprouting* etc., his virtues are too great for a being below the degree of an angel; *money takes to itself ~s*, disappears; *high-, low-, mid-~*, aa., (of monoplane) having the ~s set near the top, near the bottom, in the middle, of the fuselage. 2. (Esp. of wounding) arm. 3. More or less separate projecting part of something, esp. of building or battle array (*the north ~ was added in the 17th century; cavalry were massed on left* ~; ~*s* in theatre, sides of stage, pieces of side scenery; mudguard of motor vehicle. 4. (footb., hockey, etc.). Forward etc. whose place is either side of the centre

(also attrib., as ~ *three-quarter*). **5.**
‖ R.A.F. formation of two or more
squadrons. **6.** pl. Pilot's badge in R.A.F.
etc. **7.** ~ed flight, ~s, (on the ~), flying,
travelling, in motion; *take*~, start flying).
8. ~*beat*, one complete set of motions
with ~ in flying; ~*case*, horny cover,
a modified fore-~, protecting some insects' flying ~; ‖ ~ *commander*, officer
of AIR[1]*-force*; ~*covert*, one of small
feathers covering insertion of bird's flying feathers; ~*footed*, poet., swift; ~-
-sheath, = ~*case*; ~*spread*, measurement across~s when extended, surface or
area of aircraft's ~s; ~*stroke*, = ~*beat*;
hence ~ED[2](*winged*, wing'ĭd), ~'LESS, aa.,
~'LET n. **9.** vb. Equip with ~s, enable to
fly or mount, send in flight, lend speed to,
(~ *arrow with eagle's feathers or at the
mark*; *vengeance* ~*ed the shaft*; ~*ed words*,
going like arrows to mark, significant;
ambition ~*s his spirit*; *fear* ~*ed his steps*;
~*ed horse*, Pegasus, poetry; ~*ed god*,
Mercury; ~*ed Victory*, statue of goddess
of victory with ~s). **10.** Travel, traverse,
on ~s (*bird* ~*s its way*, ~*s to its mate*, ~*s
the air*). **11.** Wound (bird) in ~, (person)
in arm. [ME pl. *wenge*, *-en*, *-es* f. ON
vængir, pl. of *vængr*]

wink, v.i. & t., & n. **1.** Close & open eyes,
blink, close & open (eyes or eye), (of eye)
close & open, (*like* ~*ing*, sl., very quickly
or vigorously); momentarily close one
eye to awaken attention of or convey
private intimation to person (usu. *at*
person); (of light, star, etc.) twinkle,
shine intermittently; ~ *at*, shut one's
eyes to, purposely avoid seeing, affect not
to notice, connive at, (abuse, transgression, etc.). **2.** n. Act of ~*ing*, esp. as
signal etc. (*nod is as good as* ~ *to blind
horse*; *tip* one *the* ~, sl., give him signal
or intimation: *could not get a* ~ *of sleep*;
did not sleep a ~ *all night*; *forty* ~*s*, nap).
[OE *wincian*, OS *wincon*, f. Gmc *wenk*-,
cf. WINCE, WINCH]

winkle (wing'kl), n., & v.t. **1.** Edible sea
snail, periwinkle. **2.** ~*out*, extract or
eject (as a ~ from its shell with a pin).
[abbr. PERIWINKLE[2], cf. WIG[1]]

winn'ow (-ō), v.t. Fan (grain) free of chaff
etc., fan (chaff etc.) *away* or *out* or *from*;
sift, separate, clear of refuse or inferior
specimens or falsehood, clear (refuse etc.)
out or *away*, examine, sort, weed out;
(poet.) fan (air with wings), flap (wings),
stir (hair etc.). Hence ~ER[1](1, 2) (-ōer) n.
[OE *windwian* (WIND[1])]

win'some, a: (Of person or his or her
appearance, manner, smile, etc.) charming, winning, attractive, engaging, bright.
Hence ~LY[2] adv., ~NESS n. [OE *wynsum*,
OS *wunsam*, OHG *wunnisam*, f. *wyn(n)*
joy + -SOME]

win'ter, n., & v.i. & t. **1.** Fourth season
of the year, Dec.–Feb. (astron., from
winter solstice to vernal equinox);
hard, mild, ~, with, without, much frost;

(attrib.) occurring, used, etc., in or lasting
for the ~ (~ *apple, cough, solstice*, etc.;
~ *sleep*, hibernation; ~ *quarters*, esp. to
which troops retire for ~; ~ *garden*,
glass-covered space with plants etc. used
as lounge). **2.** (rhet., poet.). Year of life
(*a man of 50* ~*s*, 50 years old). **3.** ~*cress*,
cruciferous plant formerly cultivated for
~ salad; ~*green*, kinds of plant green
through ~; ~*lodge* (bot.), bud or bulb
protecting plant's embryo through ~;
~*tide* (poet.), ~; hence ~LESS, ~LY[2], aa.
4. vb. Spend the ~ *at, in*, etc.; keep or
feed (plants, cattle) during~. [OE *winter*,
OS, OHG *wintar*, ON *vetr*, Goth. *wintrus*
f. Gmc *went-*, prob. rel. to WET]

win'tr|ỹ, a. Having the temperature,
storminess, or aspect appropriate to
winter, cold, windy, cheerless, (~*y weather,
day, sun, scene*); (of smile, greeting, etc.)
lacking warmth or interest or vivacity.
Hence ~INESS n. [-Y[2]]

wipe, v.t. & i., & n. **1.** Clean or dry
surface of by rubbing with cloth, paper,
hand, etc. (~ *table, dish, face, hands*, etc.;
~ *one's eyes*, dry tears, cease weeping; ~
one's eye, sl., steal march on him, get
advantage by anticipating him; ~ *out
bath* or other hollow utensil); get rid of,
clear *away* or *off*, take *up*, wash *out*, by
wiping (~ *away* or ~ *your tears*; ~ *up
slops*; ~ *out stain*, or fig. *disgrace, insult,*
etc., esp. by vengeance); ~ *out*, utterly
destroy, annihilate, (*their very name, the
whole army, was* ~*d out*); ~ *the floor with*
(sl.), inflict humiliating defeat or correction on (person); (sl.) take or aim sweeping
blow or stroke *at* (~*d at me with his stick*).
2. n. Act of wiping (*give this plate a* ~);
(sl.) sweeping blow (*fetched* or *took a* ~ *at
him*; *fetched him a* ~); (sl.) handkerchief.
[OE *wīpian* (cf. OHG *wīfan* wind round,
Goth. *weipan*), rel. to WHIP]

wire, n., & v.t. & i. **1.** (Piece of) metal
drawn out into form of thread or slender
round or square or tapelike flexible rod
(*platinum, silver, copper*, etc., ~; BARB[1]*ed*,
LIVE[1], ~; *telegraph* etc. ~*s*; *private* ~,
telegraph ~ reserved for person's exclusive use; *was sent for, sent congratulations, by* ~, telegraph); *pull the* ~*s*,
control puppets by ~s or usu., fig.,
manage political party or movement by
secret influence). **2.** Telegraphic message
(*sent me a* ~). **3.** ~*cloth*, ~ *gauze, netting*,
fabrics woven or twisted of ~; ~*cutter*,
tool for cutting ~; ~*dancer*, person
performing on stretched ~; ~*draw*,
draw (metal) out into ~, (fig.) refine or
apply or press (argument, point, etc.)
with idle or excessive subtlety (esp. in
p.p.); ~*edge*, false edge that turns back
when blade is over-sharpened; ~ *entanglement*, arrangement of barbed or
other ~ set up to prevent rapid attack
of enemy; ~*gun*, one made by coiling
flat ~ round tube; ~*haired*, with stiff or
wiry hair (esp. of dogs); ~*heel*, disease

of horse's foot; ~*puller*, politician etc. who pulls the ~s; ~ *rope*, made by twisting ~s together as strands; ~-*tapping*, eavesdropping on telephone conversation; ~-*worm*, kinds of destructive larva; ~-*wove*, (of paper) = wove (WEAVE). **4.** vb. Provide, fasten, etc., with ~(s); string (beads) on~; snare (bird) with~; (electr.) install circuits for lighting in (a house etc.); (croquet) obstruct (ball, shot, player) by~ of hoop (chiefly pass.); telegraph (~ *me the result*; ~*d to him*; *was* ~*d for*); ‖ (sl.) ~ *in*, operate vigorously, put all one's force into some continuous effort. [OE *wīr*, MLG *wīre*, ON *vírr*]

wire′less (wīr'l-), a., n., & v.i. & t. **1.** Without wire(s), esp. in ~ TELEGRAPHY. **2.** n. ~ telegraphy or telegram; ‖ ~ receiving set or broadcast or programme, radio, (also attrib.). **3.** vb. Send ~, send (message) or inform (person) by~. [-LESS]

wīr′|y̆, -ĭ. Made of wire (poet.); tough & flexible as wire, (of persons) sinewy, untiring, whence ~ILY² adv., ~INESS n. [-Y²]

wis, v.i. pres. 1st sing. (pseudo-arch.). *I* know well (parenth.). [orig. in *I wis* = obs. *iwis* certainly, erron. taken as 'I know' & as pres. tense of *wist* WIT¹]

wis′dom (-z-), n. Being wise, (possession of) experience & knowledge together with the power of applying them critically or practically, sagacity, prudence, common sense; wise sayings (*pour forth* ~; *W~ of Solomon*, abbr. *Wisd.*, *W~ of Jesus the Son of Sirach* or *Ecclesiasticus*, books of Apocrypha); ~*tooth*, molar usu. cut after 20 years of age (*cut one's* ~*-teeth*, gain discretion). [OE (OS) *wīsdōm*, OHG *wīstuom*, ON *vísdómr* (WISE¹, -DOM)]

wīse¹ (-z), a., & v.t. & i. **1.** (Of persons) having, (of action, course, speech, opinion, etc.) dictated by or in harmony with or showing, experience & knowledge judiciously applied, sagacious, prudent, sensible, discreet; having knowledge (~ *after the event*, of person who has failed to foresee; *came away none the* ~*r* or *as* ~ *as he went*, knowing no more than before; *where ignorance is bliss 'tis folly to be* ~); ‖ (arch.) having occult power or knowledge of mysterious things (~ *man*, wizard; ‖ ~ *woman*, witch, fortune-teller, also midwife); suggestive of wisdom, oracular, (*with a* ~ *shake of the head*; ~ *saw*, proverbial saying); *(sl.) *be* or *get* ~ *to*, be or become aware of; *(sl.) *put* one ~ (*to*), inform one (of), enlighten one (concerning); *(sl.) ~ *crack*, smart pithy remark (so ~*-crack* v.i.). **2.** vb. *~ up* (sl.), put or get ~. Hence ~LY² (-zl-) adv. [OE *wīs*, OS, OHG *wīs*, ON *víss*, Goth. *weis*, f. Gmc *wīsaz* f. *wittos* cogn. w. WIT¹]

wīse² (-z), n. Way, manner, guise, (*in solemn etc.* ~, arch.; *pres. in some, no, any,* ~, *on this* ~). [OE *wīse*, OS, OHG *wīsa*, ON *vísa* f. Gmc *wīsōn*, *wīsō* f. *wit*-WIT¹]

-**wīse** (-z), suf. = prec., forming advv. of manner as in *clock*~ with motion in direction of clock hands, *cross*~ with cross arrangement, *length*~ with length arranged in given direction, with regard to length, *no*~ in no way, not at all.

wise′acre (-zāker), n. Sententious dullard. [16th c., f. MDu. *wijsseggher* soothsayer, app. f. OHG *wīzago*, w. assim. to *wijs* WISE¹ & *seggher* sayer]

wish, v.t. & i., & n. **1.** Have as a desire or aspiration (*that*-clause with *that* usu. omitted, or obj. & compl.; ~ *I had never been born*, *were* or *was a bird*, *may live to see it*; ~ *you would be quiet*; *it is to be* ~*ed that*, is desirable that; *I ~ it may not prove*; fear it will; *could not* ~ *it better*; ~ *oneself dead*, *home*, *at home*, etc.; ~ *person happy*, *away*; ~ *one at the devil* or *further*, ~ *he were away*). **2.** Want with the kind of desire that tends to affect result (*to do*, person or thing *to do*, person or thing *-ed*, or rarely with simple obj. esp. pronoun; *I ~ to go*, *you to do it*, *it finished* or *to be finished*; *what do you* ~?; *they say they* ~ *peace*, *an interview*). **3.** Be *well* or *ill* inclined to or to (~*es me well*, *well to all men*, ~*es nobody ill*), whence (-)~ER¹ n. **4.** Say one hopes for (joy, luck, pleasant journey, sorrow, etc.) in person's favour or against him (ind. obj. or *to*; *I ~ you joy*, ~ *success to each & all*); ~ person *joy of*, (iron.) hope he will enjoy; express desire *for* (*has nothing left to* ~ *for*; *would not* ~ *for anything better*); (colloq.) foist (*up*)on person. **5.** ~(*ing*)*-bone*, merrythought (longer part of it when broken between two persons entitling holder to magic fulfilment of any ~); ~*ing-cap*, magic cap securing to wearer fulfilment of any ~. **6.** n. (Expression of) desire or aspiration, request, implied command, (*the* ~ *is father to the thought*, we believe thing because we~ it true; *if* ~*es were horses beggars might ride*; *has a great* ~ *to go to sea*, whence ~'FUL a., desirous (*to do*; ~*ful thinking*, belief founded on ~es rather than facts); *good* ~*es*, hopes felt or expressed for another's happiness etc.; *cannot grant your* ~; *he disregarded* or *disobeyed my* ~*es*); thing desired (*have got my* ~). [OE *wȳscan*, OHG *wunsken*, ON *œskja*, f. Gmc *wunskjan*, ult. cogn. w. WEEN]

wish′-wash (-ŏsh), n. Washy drink or talk. [redupl. of WASH²]

wish′y̆-washy̆ (-wŏ-), a. Thin, sloppy, (of soup, tea, talk, etc.). [redupl. of WASHY]

wisp, n. **1.** Small bundle or twist of straw etc. **2.** Flock (of snipe). [ME, of uncert. orig.; cf. WFris. *wisp*]

wist. See WIT¹.

Wistā′r′ia, -tēr′, n. Genus of pale-purple-flowered climbing plant. [C. *Wistar* (or -*ter*), Amer. anatomist (d. 1818), -IA¹]

wist′ful, a. Affected with or betraying vague yearnings or unsatisfied desire to understand (of persons or usu. of eyes, look, voice, mood, etc.). Hence ~LY² adv., ~NESS n. [app. assim. of obs. *wisly* adv. intently (cf. WHIST¹, ²) to WISH*ful*, w. corresp. change of sense]

wit¹, v.t. & i. (arch.); pres. *I, he, wot, thou wottest*; past *wist*; inf. *wit*; part. ~*ting*; other parts not used). Know (*God wot*, knows; *I wot*, know well; *to* ~, that is to say, namely; ~*ting*, not unconscious or unintentional, whence ~t'*ing*LY³ adv.). [OE, OS *witan*, OHG *wizzan*, ON *vita*, Goth. *witan*, f. Gmc *wait-*, *wit-*, cogn. w. L *vidēre*, Gk (*w*)*oida*, (*w*)*eidon*, Skr. VEDA]

wit², n. 1. (Sing. or pl.) intelligence, understanding, (*has not the* ~, *the* ~s, ~ *enough, to see*; *remedy is past the* ~ *of man to devise*; *out of* one's ~s, mad, distracted; *has his* ~s *about him*, is observant or of lively intelligence; *has quick, slow*, etc., ~s, *a nimble* ~, whence (-)~tED³ a.; *at* one's ~'s *end*, utterly at a loss; *live by* one's ~s, by ingenious hand-to-mouth shifts; *the five* ~s, arch., the senses or the mind), whence ~'LESS a., ~'lÉssLY² adv., ~'lÉssNESS n. 2. (Power of giving sudden intellectual pleasure by) unexpected combining or contrasting of previously unconnected ideas or expressions (*possessed of both* ~ & HUMOUR; *pages sparkling with* ~), whence ~t'Y² a., ~t'ILY³ adv., ~t'INESS n. [OE *wit, gewit*(*t*), OS *wit*, OHG *wizzi*, ON *vit*, Goth. *witi* f. *wit-* (prec.)]

wit³, n. Wise man (arch.); witty person (see prec.), person who talks wittily, whence ~'LING¹(2) n. [uses of prec.; 1st sense f. 15th, 2nd f. 17th, c.]

witch, n., & v.t. 1. Woman or (now rarely) man practising sorcery (*white* ~, using powers . for beneficent purposes only; ~*es'* SABBATH), (fig.) fascinating or bewitching woman; ugly old woman, hag; (local) flat-fish resembling the lemon sole. 2. ~'*craft*, sorcery, use of magic; ~*doctor*, = MEDICINE¹-*man*; ~*hunt*, (fig.) search for suspected Communists, spies, etc.; ~*meal*, pollen of CLUB¹-*moss*. 3. v.t. Bewitch (*the* ~*ing time of night*, Ham. III. ii. 406, time when ~es are active, midnight), esp. fig., fascinate, charm, whence ~'ERY(4, 5) n., ~'ING² a., ~'ingLY² adv. [OE *wicca* masc., *wicce* fem. f. *wiccian* vb, later prob. aphetic f. BEWITCH]

witch-. See WYCH-.

wit'enagĕmōt' (-g-), n. (hist.). Anglo-Saxon national council or parliament. [OE *witena* gen. pl. of *wita* wise man, *gemōt* meeting; cf. MOOT]

with (-dh, -th), prep. 1. In antagonism to, against, (*fight, quarrel, struggle, dispute, argue, compete, vie*, ~). 2. In or into company of or relation to, among, beside, (*come, go, walk, eat, live, spend the day, mix* t. & i., *meet*; ~; *king is expected* ~ or *together* ~ *queen & court*; *numbered* ~ *the transgressors*; *compare* ~; *have nothing to do* ~; *deal* ~; ~ *God*, dead & in heaven; *have* ~ *you*, arch., I accept your offer or challenge; so *done* ~ *you*). 3. Agreeably or in harmonious relations to (*I feel, think, sympathize*, ~ *you*; also with neg. wds in opp. sense, as *I disagree* ~ *you*; *that is not* ~ *me is against me*; *vote* ~ *the Liberals*; *blue does not go* ~ *green*; *one* ~, part of same whole as). 4. Having, carrying, possessed of, characterized by, (*vase* ~ *handles, man* ~ *sinister expression*; *walking* ~ *a gun*; *went out* ~ *no hat on*; ~ *child* or *young*, pregnant). 5. In the care or charge or possession of (*have no money* ~ *me*; *leave child, parcel*, ~ *nurse, porter*; *it rests* ~ *you to decide*; *the deal, decanter, next move, is* ~ *you*). 6. By use of as instrument or means (*cut it* ~ *a knife*; *have no pen to write* ~; *walks* ~ *a crutch*; *damn* ~ *faint praise*). 7. By addition or supply or acquisition or possession of as material (*fill it, overflowing*, ~ *water*; *laden* ~ *baggage*; *blessed* ~ *beauty*; *adorn* ~ *frescoes*). 8. In same way or direction or degree or at the same time as (*changes* ~ *the seasons*; *varies directly* or *inversely, increases*, ~; *rise* ~ *the sun*; ~ *that*, thereupon, simultaneously; *begin* ~, take as starting-point). 9. Because or by operation of, owing to, (*trembles* ~ *fear*; *it down* ~ *fear*; *stiff, silent*, ~ *cold, shame*). 10. Displaying or so as to display, under favourable or unfavourable circumstances of, (*heard it* ~ *calmness*; *fought* ~ *courage*; *won* ~ *ease, difficulty, a good deal to spare*; *shot well* ~ *a good, wretched, light*). 11. In regard to, concerning, in the sphere of, in the mind or view of, (*be patient* ~ *him*; *bear, do*, or *put up*, ~, tolerate, be indulgent to; *my dealings* ~ *the natives*; *what do you want* ~ *me*?; *away, down, up, to the devil*, etc., ~ *him*, take or send or put him, he may go, away etc.; *can do anything, nothing*, ~ *him*, influence or utilize him in any, no, direction; ~ *God all things are possible*; *is it well* ~ *thee*?; *it is holiday time* ~ *us*; *the first object* ~ *him is*; *has great influence* ~ *theHouse*). 12. So as to be separated from (*part, break, dispense*, ~). 13. Despite, notwithstanding, the presence of (~ *all his learning, he is the simplest of men*; ~ *many admirable qualities, the best of intentions, he failed completely*). [OE, OS *with*, ON *vith*, app. shortened f. Gmc *withrō* = OE *wither*, OHG *widar* (G *wider*) against, ON *vithr*, Goth. *withra*]

withal' (-dhawl), adv. & prep. (arch.). 1. With it, in addition, moreover, as well, at the same time. 2. prep. (always after its expressed or omitted obj.). With (*what shall he fill his belly* ~?). [ME; prec., ALL]

withdraw' (-dh-), v.t. & i. Pull aside or back (~ *curtain*, one's *hand*); take away, remove, (boy from school, coins from circulation, horse from race, troops from position, favour etc. from person); retract (offer, statement, promise; *cries of* ' ~ ', demands that speaker shall unsay something as unparliamentary etc.); retire from presence or place, go aside or apart; ‖ ~*-ing-room* (arch.), DRAWING-ROOM. Hence ~AL(2) n. [ME; WITH, DRAW[1]]

with'e (-dhī, *or* widh), **with'y** (-dhī), n. (pl. *-thes* pr. -dhīz, *or* -ths). Tough flexible branch esp. of willow or osier used for binding bundles etc. [OE *withthe* (also *withig*, mod. *withy*), OHG *wida*, f. Gmc *withjōn*]

with'er (-dh-), v.t. & i. Make or become dry & shrivelled (often *up*), deprive of or lose vigour or vitality or freshness or importance (often *away*), decline, languish, decay, (*has a ~ed arm; flowers & beauty ~; age cannot ~ her; the individual ~s*, ceases to be important); blight with scorn etc. (~ one *with a look*, usu. joc.), whence ~ING[2] a., ~INGLY[2] adv. [ME, app. var. of WEATHER[2], different. for certain senses]

with'ers (-dherz), n. pl. Ridge between horse's shoulder-blades (*my ~ are unwrung*, imputation etc. does not touch me). [app. reduced f. (16th c.) *widersome* or *-sone*, f. *wither* (see WITH), as the part that resists strain of collar; second element obsc.]

‖ **with'ershins** (-dhershĭnz), **widd'er-**, adv. (Sc.). In a direction contrary to apparent course of sun (considered as unlucky), counter-clockwise. [f. MLG *weddersins* f. MHG *widersinnes* (MHG *wider* against, *sin, sint* direction)]

withhōld' (-dh-h-), v.t. (*-held*). Refrain from putting in action, refuse to grant, (~ one's *hand*, arch. for *hold*, not take action; ~ one's *consent, support, the light of* one's *countenance*, etc.). [ME; WITH, HOLD[1]]

within' (-dh-), adv., n., & prep. **1.** Inside, to or at or on the inside, indoors, internally, (chiefly arch.; *clean~ & without; go* ~, into house or room; *stay* ~, not go out of doors; *is Mr Jones* ~*?*, at home; *beauty without & foulness* ~*; make me pure* ~, in spirit; *Bishopsgate* ~, inside the walls). **2.** n. The inside (*as seen from* ~). **3.** prep. To or on or in the inside of, enclosed by, (~ *doors*, in or into house; *safe* ~ *the walls*; WHEEL[1]s ~ *wheels*); not beyond, not too far for, not transgressing, so as not to pass or exceed, subject to, (*live, keep*, ~ one's *income*; ~ *the meaning of the Act* etc., covered by it; *immortality* ~ *the law*, not illegal; *keep it* ~ *bounds*; *a task well* ~ *his powers*; *running* ~ *himself*, without putting forth whole power; *is true* ~ *limits*); not too far for, near enough to affect or be affected by, not farther off than (*of* with sense *from*, or abs.), (*is* ~ *reach, sight, call*, near enough to reach or be reached etc.; often *of*, as ~ *sight of port; is* ~ *three miles of a station; was* ~ *an ace of destruction*); in a time no longer than, before expiration

or since beginning of, (*of* with sense *from*, or abs.; *shall have it* ~ *an hour;* ~ *a year of his death*, ~ *a year, all was changed; have seen him* ~ *these three days*). [OE *withinnan* on the inside (WITH, *innan* adv.; ME *inne* in)]

without' (-dh-), adv., n., prep., & conj. **1.** Outside, to or at or on the outside, out-of-doors, externally, (chiefly arch.; *white within &* ~*; stands disconsolate* ~, outside the house etc.; *listening to the wind* ~). **2.** n. The outside, external sources, (*as seen from* ~; *the suggestion came from* ~). **3.** prep. Outside of (arch.; *met us* ~ *the gates; negotiations within &* ~ *the House; is* ~ *the pale of civilization; things* ~ *us*, all that is not ourselves); not having, not with, with no, devoid of, lacking, in want of, free from, with freedom from, not feeling or showing, in or with absence of, less, (*came* ~ *a hat; a rose* ~ *a thorn; am* ~ *friends or money; did it* ~ *difficulty or being discovered; act* ~ *hesitation; cannot live* ~ *her, go away* ~ *thanking you; is absolutely* ~ *fear, anxiety; cannot make an* OMELETTE ~ *breaking eggs;* ~ *health happiness is impossible; do, go*, ~, dispense with, also ellipt. dispense with something implied; COLD ~; ~ *doubt*, admittedly, certainly; ~ FAIL[1], PREJUDICE, RESERVE[2]; ~ *end*, infinite, eternal; *goes* ~ *saying*, is too well known or obvious to need mention). **4.** conj. (arch., vulg.). Unless. [OE *withūtan* (WITH, *ūtan* adv.; ME *ute(n)* out)]

withstānd' (-dh-), v.t. & i. (*-stood*). Resist, oppose, (person, force, hardship, wear, etc.); make opposition (poet.). [OE *withstandan* (= ON *vithstanda*), see WITH, STAND]

withy. See WITHE.

wit'ness, n., & v.t. & i. **1.** Testimony, evidence, (*bear* ~ *to* or *of*, state one's belief in, state facts tending to establish; thing stated by way of evidence (*my* ~ *is not true*; arch.), confirmation (*stands there in* ~ *of the event; call to* ~, appeal to for confirmation); thing or person whose existence, position, state, etc., serves as testimony to or proof of (*is a living* ~ *to my clemency*); (also EYE~) spectator of incident, bystander, person present at event; person giving sworn testimony in law-court or for legal purpose (~ often used for *the* ~); person attesting genuineness of signature to document by adding his signature; ‖ ~*-box*, *-stand*, enclosure in law-court reserved for ~es. **2.** vb. State in evidence (noun, *that*, etc.; arch.); give evidence (*against, for*), serve as evidence (usu. *against, for, to*; ~ or *as* ~ *my poverty*, of which let my poverty be the proof); be a or the ~ (arch.; ~ *Heaven!*, I call Heaven to ~); indicate, serve as evidence of, (*a deathly pallor ~ed his agitation*); see, be spectator of; act as ~ of (document, signature, etc.). [OE *witnes* (WIT[2], -NESS)]

witt'icism, n. Witty remark, jest, (usu. in disparaging sense). [coined by Dryden f. WIT[1]*ly*, after *criticism*]

wittingly. See WIT[1].

|| **witt'ol**, n. (arch.). Man who winks at wife's infidelity, acquiescent cuckold. [ME *wetewold*, app. formed by substitution of WIT[1] for first syllable of *cokewold* CUCKOLD]

wive, v.t. & i. (now rare). Provide with, take, wife. [OE *wīfian* (WIFE)]

wīv′ern, **wȳv-**, n. (her.). Winged two-legged dragon with barbed tail. [f. ME *wyver*, f. OF *wivre* (*guivre*), var. of *vivre* f. L VIPERA+*n*; cf. BITTERN]

wives. See WIFE.

wiz′ard, n. & a. **1.** Magician, sorcerer, male witch; person who effects seeming impossibilities; conjurer. **2.** adj. (sl.). Wonderful. Hence ~RY(4, 5) n. [ME *wysard* (WISE[1], -ARD)]

wiz′ened (-nd), **wiz′en**, **weaz′en**, a. Of shrivelled or dried-up appearance (chiefly of person or his face or look). [OE *wisnian*, OHG *wesanēn*, ON *visna*]

wizier. See VIZIR.

wō, whoa (wō'a), int. Stop (chiefly to horses); GEE-*wo*; *wo-back′*, int. used in backing horses.

woad, n., & v.t. **1.** (Plant yielding) kind of blue dye. **2.** v.t. Dye with ~. [OE *wād*, OHG *weit*, f. Gmc **waida-*, **waizda-*]

wŏb′ble, **wa′bble** (wŏ-), v.i., & n. **1.** (Of top or revolving body) revolve with changing inclinations, rock; (of person, missile, etc.) go unsteadily, vibrate from side to side, swerve, stagger; (fig.) vacillate, waver, act inconsistently, be inconstant, whence **wŏbb′lER**[1] n.; (of voice or sound) quaver, pulsate. **2.** n. Rocking movement, change of direction or policy, swerve, piece of vacillation. [corresp. to LG *wab*(*b*)*eln*, MHG *wabelen*, f. Gmc **wabh-*, cf. WAVER]

|| **wŏdge**, n. (colloq.). Chunk. [alt. f. WEDGE]

wŏe, n. (chiefly poet. or joc.). Affliction, bitter grief, distress, (*weal & ~*, prosperity & adversity; ~ *is me*, alas; ~ *be to*, a curse upon; ~ WORTH[2] *the day*); (pl.) calamities, troubles; ~*begone* (-awn, -ōn), dismal-looking [p.p. of OE *began* (BY, GO) surround]. Hence ~*′FUL*(wŏf-)a., ~*′fulLY*[2] adv., (often joc., as ~*ful ignorance*, ~*fully disappointed*). [OE *wā*, *wǣ*, OS, OHG *wē*, ON *vei*, *vǣ*, Goth. *wai*, f. Gmc *wai cogn. w. L *vae*]

wŏg, n. (sl.). Native of a Middle Eastern country, esp. Egypt. [orig. unkn.]

woke. See WAKE[1].

wōld, n. Piece of open uncultivated country, down or moor land. [OE (Anglian) *wald*, OS, OHG *wald*, ON *vǫllr* f. Gmc *wallhuz; see WEALD]

wolf (wŏŏ-), n. (pl. -*ves*), & v.t. **1.** Erect-eared straight-tailed harsh-furred tawny-grey wild gregarious carnivorous quadruped allied to dog, preying on sheep etc.

or combining in packs to hunt larger animals (*cry* ~ *too often*, raise false alarms till genuine ones are disregarded; *have, hold*, ~ *by the ears*, be in a precarious situation; *keep* ~ *from door*, avert starvation; ~ *in sheep's clothing*, hypocrite). **2.** Rapacious or greedy person, whence ~*′ISH*[1] a., ~*′ishLY*[2] adv., ~*′ishNESS* n., (wŏŏ-). **3.** (mus.). Jarring sound from some notes in a bowed instrument; out-of-tune effect when playing in extremer keys on old organs (before present 'equal temperament' was in use). **4.** ~*-cub*, young~, || junior boy scout; ~*-dog*, kinds of dog kept to guard sheep from wolves, also dog-&~ hybrid; ~*-fish*, large voracious kind; ~*-hound*, Russian breed of dog, (also) Alsatian breed popular in U.K.; ~*′s-bane*, monk's-hood, aconite; ~*′s-claws*, *-foot*, club-moss; || ~*′s-fist*, puff-ball [OE *fist* fart]; ~*′skin*, (mat, cloak, etc., made of) ~'s skin; ~*′s-milk*, kind of spurge; ~ *spider*, tarantula, also kinds that chase instead of netting prey; ~*-tooth*, supernumerary pre-molar in horse; ~*-whistle*, whistle of a male interested in and trying to attract the attention of a woman. **5.** v.t. Devour or swallow greedily (freq. *down*). [OE, OS *wulf*, OHG *wolf*, ON *ulfr*, Goth. *wulfs*, f. Gmc *wulfaz, cogn. w. L *lupus*, Gk *lukos*]

wo′lfram (wŏŏ-), n. (Also ~*ite*) ore yielding tungsten, native tungstate of iron & manganese; (now usu. for) tungsten. [G, perh. f. WOLF+*rahm* cream, or MHG *rām* dirt, soot]

wo′lverēne (wŏŏ-), **-ine** (-ēn), n. American carnivorous mammal called also GLUTTON & *carcajou*. [obsc. f. *wolv-*, st. of WOLF]

wolves. See WOLF.

wo′man (wŏŏ-), n. (pl. *women* pr. wĭm′ĭn), & v.t. **1.** Adult human female (*every* ~ *is to him a lady*; ~*'s* or *women's rights*, position of legal equality with men demanded for women; *there's a* ~ *in it*, way of accounting for man's inexplicable conduct; ~ *with a past*, with some scandal attaching to her past life; ~ *of the world*, experienced in society, not raw & innocent; *play the* ~, weep or show fear; *make an honest* ~ *of*, marry after seducing; *tied to* ~*'s apron-strings*, controlled like child by her; *single* ~, spinster; *the* SCARLET ~; WISE[1]~). **2.** (Without article) the average or typical ~, the female sex, any ~, (*how does* ~ *differ from man?*; *man born of* ~, mortal man; *is an excellent thing in* ~; ~*'s wit*, instinctive insight or resource; ~*'s* REASON[1]; *O W*~, in apostrophes). **3.** Queen's or great lady's female attendant, lady in waiting, (arch.; *sent one of her women to ask*). **4.** Man with feminine characteristics (*is a* ~ *in tenderness*; *the old women in the Cabinet*; *all the old women of both sexes*). **5.** The feminine emotions (*all the* ~ *in her rose in rebellion*; *stirred the* ~ *in him*; *has much of the* ~ *in his*

composition). **6.** attrib. Female (~ *doctor,
friend, counsellor, councillor*; ~ *suffrage,*
extension or possession of political
suffrage to or by women). **7.** (As suf.;
chiefly in terms correl. to compounds
in -*man*) ~ concerned or dealing or skilful
with (*country*~, *shop*~, *horse*~, *church*~,
chair~, *ferry*~, *apple*~, *needle*~, etc.; also
by close comb. with adj., as *gentle*~).
8. ~-*hater*, misogynist; ~*kind*, women
(one's ~*kind*, *wo'menkind*, the women of
one's family); *wo'menfolk*, women, one's
~kind; hence ~HOOD n. (=female maturity, womanly instincts, ~kind), ~LESS,
~LIKE, aa. **9.** v.t. Make behave like a ~,
cause to weep etc.; address as '~', 'my
good ~', etc., speak of as '~' (not
'lady'). [OE *wífmon(n)*, -*man(n)* (WIFE,
MAN), a formation peculiar to English, the
ancient wd being WIFE]

wo'manish (woŏ-), a. (Of man or his
feelings, conduct, looks, etc.) like women' or their ways etc. (usu. derog.),
effeminate. Hence ~LY² adv., ~NESS n.
[ME; -ISH¹]

wo'manize (woŏ-), -**ise** (-īz), v.t. & i.
Make womanish; (of men) be licentious,
frequent prostitutes. [-IZE]

wo'manl|y (woŏ-), a. (Of woman or her
feelings, conduct, etc.) having or showing
the qualities befitting a woman, not masculine or girlish, (*a truly* ~*y woman*; ~*y
modesty*, *compassion*, *tact*, etc.). Hence
~iNESS n. [ME; -LY¹]

womb (woŏm), n. Organ in woman &
other female mammals in which child or
young is conceived & nourished till birth,
uterus, (*falling of the* ~, PROLAPSUS; *fruit
of the* ~, children; also fig., as *in the* ~ *of
time*, of future events etc.). [OE *wamb*,
womb, OHG *wamba*, ON *vǫmb*, Goth.
wamba]

wŏm'băt, n. Australian marsupial mammal about size of badger. [f. native *wom-
back*, -*at*]

women. See WOMAN.

won. See WIN.

wo'nder¹ (wŭ-), n. **1.** Miracle, prodigy,
strange or remarkable thing or specimen
or performance or event, (*signs & ~s*,
miracles; *work* ~s, do miracles, succeed
remarkably; whence ~-WORKER¹ n.; *the
child is a* ~, marvellously precocious etc.;
did ~s, had remarkable success; *seven* ~*s
of the world*, sights, so called in antiquity;
a nine-days' ~, event of passing interest;
for a ~, esp. by way of welcome exception,
as *you are punctual for a* ~; *what* ~, *it is
no* ~, *no* ~, *that*, naturally, inevitably, of
course, one cannot be surprised or might
have guessed that, *that* usu. omitted; so
he refused, & no ~; *is a* ~ *of delicate workmanship*). **2.** Emotion excited by what
surpasses expectation or experience or
seems inexplicable, surprise mingled with
admiration or curiosity or bewilderment,
(*were filled with* ~; *looked at him in silent
or open-mouthed* ~). **3.** ~*land*, fairyland,

a country of surprising fertility etc.; ~-
-*struck*, -*stricken*, filled or dumb with ~.
[OE *wundor*, OS -*ar*, OHG *wuntar*, ON
undr, of unkn. orig.]

wo'nder² (wŭ-), v.i. & t. Be filled with
wonder, feel surprise, (usu. *at*, rarely *to*
see etc., or abs.; *shall never cease to* ~ *at
it*; *can you* ~ *at it?*; *I* ~ *at you* to child
etc., am shocked by your conduct; ~*ed to
hear your voice*; *the kind of person that
never* ~*s*), whence ~INGLY² adv., ~MENT
n., (wŭ-); be surprised to find *that* (*that*
usu. omitted; *I* ~ *he didn't kill you*); be
curious, desire, to know (~ *why pain exists,
who invented gas-lamps, what the time is,
how to proceed*, etc.). [OE *wundrian*
(prec.)]

wo'nderful (wŭ-), a. Marvellous, surprising, exceeding what was expected,
remarkable, admirable. Hence ~LY² adv.
[ME; -FUL]

wo'ndrous (wŭ-), a. & adv. (poet., rhet.).
1. Wonderful; hence ~LY² adv., ~NESS n.
2. adv. (qualifying adjj. only). Wonder-
fully (~ *kind* etc.). [alt. f. obs. *wonders*
adv. (genit. of WONDER¹, cf. -ES), after
marvellous]

‖ **wŏnk'y̆**, a. (sl.). Shaky, groggy; unreliable. [fanciful]

wont¹ (wō-, wŭ-), pred. a. Accustomed *to*
do (usu. after *is*, *was*, *are*, etc.; *as he was
~ to say*). [OE *gewunod* p.p. of *gewunian*
(*wunian* dwell)]

wont² (wō-, wŭ-), v. aux. (poet.; pres.
ind., ~, ~*est*, ~s or ~, pl. ~; past ind.,
~, ~*est*, ~, pl. ~, or ~*ed* for ~). Be
accustomed (usu. *to* do). [ME, f. prec., or
back form. f. WONTED]

wont³ (wō-, wŭ-), n. What is customary
in general or habitual to a person (*use
& ~*, established custom; *according to
his* ~; *it is my* ~ *to*). [16th c., of doubtful
orig.]

won't. See WILL¹.

wont'ed (wō-, wŭ-), attrib. a. Habitual to
person, (rarely) usual, (*heard me with his
~ courtesy*; *met with the* ~ *obstacles*).
[either f. WONT² +-ED, or an extension of
WONT¹]

woo, v.t. (rhet.). Ask in marriage, pay
amorous court to, ask the love of, whence
~'ER¹ n.; pursue, seek to win, (fame,
fortune, etc.); (abs.) go courting, conduct
oneself as ~er; coax, importune, try to
persuade, (person usu. *to* do or *to* compliance etc.). Hence ~'INGLY² adv. [late
OE *wōgian* intr., *āwōgian* trans., of unkn.
orig.]

woo'but, ou'bĭt (oō-), n. = WOOLLY-*bear*.
[ME *wolbode* (WOOL, +OE *budda* beetle)]

wood, n. **1.** Growing trees occupying considerable tract of ground, forest, (also pl.
in same sense, as *came upon a clearing in
the* ~*s*; *cannot see the* ~ *for trees*, details
impede general view; *out of the* ~, out of
danger etc.; *don't halloo till you are out of
the* ~, assume too soon that difficulties
are over), whence (·)~ED² a. **2.** Fibrous

substance between pith & bark of tree, whether growing or cut for timber or fuel. 3. *The* cask or unbottled storage of wine etc. (*in, from, the* ~). 4. (mus.). (Also ~*-wind*) *the* wooden wind-instruments of a band etc. 5. (Bowls) a BOWL² (first sense); (golf) a wooden club. 6. ~*-agate*, showing grain of ~; ~ *anemone*, the wild flowering ANEMONE; ~*'bine* or *-bind*, honeysuckle; ~*-block*, die usu. of box-from which ~cuts are taken; ~*'cock*, kinds of game bird related to snipe; ~*'craft*, knowledge of forest conditions esp. as applied in hunting etc.; ~*'cut*, (print, usu. as illustration in book, taken from) engraving made on ~; ~*'cutter*, man who cuts ~, engraver of ~cuts; ~*-engraver*, maker of ~cuts, kinds of boring insect; ~*-fibre*, fibre got from ~ esp. as material for paper; ~*-gas*, carburetted hydrogen got from ~; ~ *ibis*, kind of N.-Amer. stork; ~*'land*, ~ed country, ~s, (often attrib., as ~*land scenery*; *the* ~*land choir*, birds); ~ *leopard*, kind of moth; ~*-louse*, kinds of small isopod land crustacean; ‖~*'man*, forester, ~cutter; ~*-notes*, spontaneous poetry; ~*-nymph*, dryad, kinds of humming-bird & moth; ~*-opal*, silicified ~; ~ *paper*, made of ~pulp; ~ *pavement*, wooden blocks used as paving of road; ~*'pecker*, kinds of bird that cling to tree-stems & tap them to discover insects; ~*-pie*, great spotted ~-pecker; ~*-pigeon*, ringdove; ~*-pulp*, ~fibre reduced to pulp as material for paper; ~*'ruff*, kinds of white-flowered plant, *sweet* ~*ruff* grown esp. for fragrance of leaves when dried or crushed; ~*s'man*, dweller in or frequenter of ~s; ~*-sorrel*, kinds of acid-juiced plant; ~ *spirit*, crude methyl alcohol got from ~; ~*-tar*, got from ~; ~*-warbler*, kind of bird; ~*-wasp*, kinds that hang nest in tree or burrow in rotten ~; ~*-wool*, fine pine shavings used as surgical dressing or for packing; ~*'work*, things made of ~, esp. the wooden part of a house etc. Hence ~*'LESS* a. [OE *widu, wiodu, vudu,* OHG *witu,* ON *vithr,* f. Gmc **widhuz*]

wood'chuck, n. Kind of N.-Amer. marmot. [f. Amer.-Ind. name, cf. Cree *wuchak, otchock*]

wood'en, a. Made of wood (~ *head,* stupidity, whence ~*-head*ED² a., ~*-head'ÉDNESS* (-hĕd-) n.; ~ *horse,* by use of which Troy was taken; ~ SPOON; ~ *walls,* warships); stiff, clumsy, without animation, inexpressive, (~ *motions, manners, stare, face,* etc.), whence ~*-LY²* adv., ~*-NESS* n. [-EN⁵]

wood'ly̆, a. (Of region) abounding in woods, well-wooded; of the nature, consisting, of wood (*the* ~*y parts of a plant;* ~*y stem, tissue*); (rare) found in woods (~*y* NIGHTSHADE). Hence ~*INESS* n. [ME; -Y²]

woof, n. = WEFT¹. [ME *oof* f. OE *ōwef* (A- 1, *wef*=WEB)=that which is woven on

(to the warp); cf. ABB; *woof* by assoc. w. WARP² (in *warp and (w)oof*) or WEFT¹]

wŏŏl, n. 1. Kind of hair distinguished by fineness & wavy structure & scaly surface forming fleece of sheep, goat, alpaca, etc., & occurring mixed with ordinary hair in coat of some other animals (*carding* or *short, combing* or *long,* ~, less, more, than 4 in. long & prepared by different processes for spinning; *dyed in the* ~, dyed before spinning or weaving, (fig.) thorough-going, out-&-out; *much cry & little* ~, disappointing result, fiasco; *go for* ~ & *come home shorn,* have tables turned on one), whence ~ED¹ (-ld) a. 2. Woollen yarn, worsted, (*spent an hour matching* ~*s; Berlin* ~, fine dyed ~ for knitting etc.); woollen garments or cloth (*safest to wear* ~). 3. Soft short under-fur or down. 4. Negro's hair, (joc.) any person's hair (*lose one's* ~, sl., show anger). 5. Kinds of ~-like substance (COTTON¹~; LEAD¹~; *mineral* ~, made from molten slag subjected to strong blast & used for packing walls etc.). 6. ~*-ball,* esp. lump of concreted ~ occas. formed in stomach of sheep etc.; ~*-carding, -combing,* processes by which short, long, ~ is prepared for spinning; ~*-dyed,* dyed in the ~, see above; ~*-fat, -oil,* lanolin; ~*-fell,* skin of sheep etc. with fleece still on; ~*-gathering,* absent-minded(ness), inattentive (mood); ‖~*-hall,* ~*-merchants'* exchange or market; ~*-pack,* (formerly) 240-lb. bale of ~, also fleecy cloud; ‖~*-sack,* ~-stuffed cushion on which Lord Chancellor sits in House of Lords (*reach* etc. *the* ~*sack,* become Lord Chancellor; *take seat on the* ~ *sack,* open proceedings in House of Lords); ~*-sorters' disease,* anthrax; ~*-stapler,* one who grades producer's ~ & sells to manufacturer; ~*-work,* embroidery with Berlin ~s imitating tapestry. [OE *wull,* OHG *wolla,* ON *ull,* Goth. *wulla* f. Gmc **wullō*]

wŏŏll'en, a. & n. 1. Made of wool. 2. n. ~ fabric, as blanket, flannel, cloth; ~*-draper,* retailer of ~s; hence ~ETTE'(2) n. [-EN⁵]

wŏŏll'ly̆, a. & n. 1. Bearing or naturally covered with wool or wool-like hair (*the* ~ *flock*; ~*-bear,* kinds of hairy caterpillar; *a* ~ *puppy, head*); resembling or suggesting wool (~ *hair, clouds*; ~ *voice,* husky); (paint.) lacking in definition or luminosity or incisiveness (~ *texture, style,* etc.); (fig., of the mind) confused & hazy; (bot.) downy, pubescent. 2. n. Woollen garment, esp. sweater. Hence wŏŏll'INESS n. [-Y²]

Wŏŏl'wich (-lĭj), n. (Used for) ~ Arsenal with magazines for naval & military stores; (formerly used for) the Royal Military Academy, ~, for cadets of Royal Engineers & Artillery. [~ in Kent]

woora'lĭ (-ah-), **woorär'a**. = CURARE.

wop¹. See WHOP.

*Wŏp², n. (sl.). Mid- or South-European

(esp. Italian) immigrant in U.S. (cf. DAGO, SQUARE*head*). [orig. unkn.]

word[1] (wěrd), n. **1.** Any sound or combination of sounds (or its written or printed symbol) recognized as a PART[1] of speech, conveying an idea or alternative ideas, & capable of serving as a member of, the whole of, or a substitute for, a sentence (*coin, play upon, torture, ~s; is not the ~ for it,* not an adequate description; *have no ~s to express my gratitude* etc.; *takes ~s for things; ~s are the wise man's counters & the fool's money; in a or one ~,* briefly, to sum up; *translate or repeat ~ for ~,* literally or verbatim). **2.** Speech (*honest in ~ & deed; bold in ~ only; by ~ of mouth,* orally). **3.** Thing said, saying, conversation, (usu. in pl.) *take one at his ~,* act on assumption that he means what he says; *fair or good ~s,* complimentary, conciliatory, flattering, etc.; *high, hard, warm, hot, sharp,* etc., *~s,* angry talk; *big ~s,* boasting, bluff; *burning ~s,* enthusiastic, inspiring, excited, etc.; *wild & whirling ~s,* not well weighed; *hard ~s break no bones, fine ~s butter no parsnips, ~s are but wind,* depreciations of talk as compared with action; *so ~s or things, ~s & deeds;* HOUSEHOLD *~; in so many ~s,* bluntly, explicitly; *have ~s with,* quarrel with; *they had ~s,* quarrelled; *have a ~ with,* converse briefly with; *so a ~ with you* as demand for interview; *suit the action to the ~,* do at once what one has threatened etc.; *on or with the ~,* as soon as something has been said; *a ~ & a blow,* impetuous person's procedure; *proceed from ~s to blows; waste ~s,* talk vainly; *a ~ in, out of, season,* well, ill, timed advice or interference; *have the last ~,* not let opponent in altercation speak last; *the last ~ on a subject,* pronouncement including latest views & likely to be definitive; *a truer ~ was never spoken; have a ~ to say,* something worth hearing; *man of few ~s,* taciturn; *hasn't a ~ to throw at a dog,* is unsociably or superciliously taciturn; *say a good ~ for,* commend, defend; *give person one's good ~,* recommend him for post etc.; *eat one's ~s,* retract, apologize under compulsion; *~ of command, ~ or phrase giving direction* esp. to soldiers being drilled; *a ~ to the wise,* transl. of VERBUM SAPIENTI; *God's W~,* the scriptures; so *the W~ of God,* & see below). **4.** News, intelligence, a message, (*send ~ of; send ~; ~ came that* or *of*). **5.** One's promise, assurance, or responsible statement (*give person, give, pledge, pass,* one's ~, make promise or rarely statement; *keep, break,* one's ~; *I give you my ~ for it,* promise it shall be or state that it is so; so ellipt. *my ~! upon it; upon my ~,* on my honour, also as excl. at something that shocks; *~ of honour,* promise or statement made upon one's HONOUR[1]; *a man of his ~,* a promise-

-keeper; *be as good as* one's ~, fulfil or exceed what one has promised; *his ~ is as good as his bond,* may be relied on). **6.** Command, order, password, motto, (*his ~ is law; give the ~ to* do or *for; act promptly at the ~; must give the ~ before you can pass; sharp's the ~,* exhortation to hurry). **7.** *The W~* (*of God*), Christ as mediator or manifestation of God to man. **8.** *~-blind, -deaf,* incapacitated by kinds of brain trouble from attaching meaning to *~s* seen or heard; *~-book,* vocabulary; *~-painter, -painting,* graphic or picturesque writer, writing; *~-perfect,* knowing part, piece, etc., by heart; *~-picture,* piece of *~-painting; ~-play,* verbal fencing, also play on *~s,* pun, etc.; *~-splitter, -splitting,* (maker of) oversubtle verbal distinctions; *~-square,* set of *~s* so chosen that when they are written under each other the letters read downward in columns give same *~s,* e.g. *rat, ado, too.* Hence *~'LESS* a. [OE, OS *word,* OHG *wort,* ON *orth,* Goth. *waurd,* f. Gmc **wordam*]

word[2] (wěrd), v.t. Put into words, phrase, select words to express. Hence *~'ING*[1] n. [ME, f. prec.]

wor'dý̆ (wěr-), a. Verbose, given to or expressed in many words, diffuse; in, consisting of, words (*~y warfare*). Hence *~ILY*[2] adv., *~INESS* n. [ME; -Y[2]]

wore. See WEAR[1,3].

work (wěrk), n. **1.** Expenditure of energy, striving, application of effort to some purpose, (*set to ~,* begin or make begin operations; *has got to, is at, ~ at last; all ~ & no play; never does a stroke of ~; never liked, will do no, ~*); (phys.) exertion of force in overcoming resistance or producing molecular change (*convert heat into ~; unit of ~,* lifting of 1 lb. for 1 ft; *internal ~,* exerted on molecules of a body). **2.** Task (to be) undertaken, materials (to be) used in task, (*the ~ of converting the heathen; have* one's *~ cut out for* one, no light task, as much as one can do; *all in the day's ~,* normal; *bring your ~ downstairs,* i.e. sewing-materials, lesson-books, etc.). **3.** Thing done, achievement, thing made, book or piece of literary or musical composition, literary or other product *of,* specimen *of,* (theol., usu. in pl.) meritorious act as opposed to faith or grace, (*mighty ~s,* miracles; *a good day's ~,* much accomplished; *the ~s of God,* nature; *honest man the noblest ~ of God; the ~s of Cicero,* his writings; *a learned, historical, ~,* book; *a ~ of art,* fine picture, building, poem, etc.; *is the ~ of the devil; ~s of mercy,* charitable actions; *covenant of ~s,* O.-T. dispensation; *~s of* SUPER*erogation*). **4.** Doings or experiences of specified kind (*sharp, bloody, wild, ~; thirsty, dry, ~; make short ~ of,* quickly accomplish or get rid of or overcome). **5.** Employment, esp. the opportunity of earning money by labour, laborious

B b

occupation, (*is out of, is in regular, wants, is looking for, ~; many hands make light ~; do you want the ~ or the wages?; rich men's luxury makes ~ for the poor*). **6.** (Usu. in pl., & in comb. or with adj.) piece of fortification, structure for defence, (*the ~s are impregnable; advanced, detached, defensive, ~s or ~; out~s, earth-~*). **7.** pl. Operations in building etc. (*public ~s*, such operations done by or for the State; RELIEF¹ *~s*; ‖ *Ministry of W~s*; CLERK *of the ~s*). **8.** pl. Acting or operative part of machine (usu. *of; the ~s of a watch* etc.; *something must be wrong with the ~s*). **9.** pl. (Often with sing. constr., usu. in comb. with attrib. n.) manufactory (*the owner of an iron, a glass, ~s; the ~s will be closed from 1st Oct.*). **10.** (Articles having) ornamentation of kind specified by adj. or by usu. hyphened attrib. n., things or parts made of material or with tools etc. so specified, (*covered with elaborate ~; rustic, embossed, beaten, frosted,* etc., ~; *wood~, iron~, stone~; fancy, needle, stucco, relief, poker, ~~*); (naut.) UPPER *~s*. **11.** *~'aday*, fit for or used or seen on ~days, ordinary, practical, (now chiefly in *this ~aday world*); *~-bag, -basket, -box*, holding materials & implements for ~. esp. for sewing; *~'day*, day other than Sunday or festival; *~: house*, ‖ public institution for reception of paupers in parish or union of parishes (hist.), *house of correction for petty offenders; *~'man*, operative, man hired to do manual labour, person *good, bad, skilled*, etc., at his job (*an ill ~man quarrels with his tools*); *~'manlike*, characteristic of a good ~man; *~'manship*, person's relative skill in doing task, relative finish or execution seen in manufactured article or ~ of art, one's making (*we are God's or of God's ~manship*); *~people, ~men* or *~women*; *~'piece*, thing worked on with tool or machine; *~-room*, in which ~ is done; *~'shop*, room or building in which manufacture is carried on; *~-shy,* (adj.) disinclined to work, (n.) lazy wastrel; *~ study*, system of measuring jobs so that they can produce the best results for employees and employers; *~-table*, with drawers for sewing-materials etc., ; *~'woman*, female operative. Hence *~'LESS* a. [OE *weorc*, OS *werk*, OHG *werc*, ON *verk*, f. Gmc *werkam, cogn. w. Gk (w)*ergon*]

work² (wẽrk), v.t. & i. (*~ed*; also *wrought* pr. rawt, arch. exc. as specified below). **1.** Engage or be engaged in bodily or mental work, carry on operations, make efforts, be a craftsman *in* some material, (*men must ~; ~ away* or *on,* continue to ~; *~ double* TIDES; *~ to rule,* make efficiency impossible by keeping every rule in & out of season, as substitute for open strike; *is ~ing at Greek, history, social reform; ~s, ~ed* or *wrought, in brass, leather, oils, distemper*; person is *hard to*

~ with, impracticable; *is ~ing for, against, the cause*). **2.** (Of machine, plan, etc.) operate, act, do its appointed work, (of person) put or keep (machine etc.) in operation, keep (person, horse, machine, etc.) going or at work, exact toil from, (*charm, drug, pump, scheme, ~s* or *will not ~; ~ ship, typewriter; ~s his men* etc. *too hard, to death*); (of wheel etc.) run, revolve, go through regular motions, (*strap, handle, wheel, ~s on a wheel, pivot, axle; ~ freely, stiffly,* etc.). **3.** Carry on, manage, control, (*~ mine, scheme; ~s the coach from London to Brighton,* has charge of it; *my partner ~s the Liverpool district; is ~ed by wires, electricity,* etc.). **4.** Have influence or effect, exercise influence on, (often *wrought; now let it ~,* leave it to produce its effect; *~ upon person* or his *mind* etc.; *all these things have ~ed together for good; the appeal wrought powerfully upon him; ~ the* ORACLE). **5.** Bring about, effect, accomplish, produce as result, (often *wrought; ~ wonders, cures, mischief, a change; ~ one's will,* accomplish one's purpose often *upon* person or thing; *will ~ it if I can,* sl., bring it about). **6.** Be in motion, be agitated, cause agitation, ferment lit. & fig., (*face, features, ~ed violently; waves ~ to & fro; thoughts, conscience, ~ing within him; yeast began to ~; to be wroth with one we love doth ~ like madness in the brain*). **7.** Make way or make (way etc.) or cause to make way slowly or with difficulty or by shifting motions (usu. with adv. or prep.), gradually become (loose, free, tight, etc.) by motion, (*stockings, shirt, ~ down, up; needle ~ed out eventually from her arm; ferrule has ~ed off, loose; ~ your knife through the card, your point in; grub ~s its way into or out of; wind has ~ed round; ship is ~ing eastwards; some influences ~ upwards, some downwards, in society; angler ~s up stream*). **8.** Knead, hammer, fashion, into shape or desired consistence (*~ dough, clay,* etc.; *butter should be thoroughly ~ed; wrought iron,* forged or rolled, not cast). **9.** Artificially & gradually excite *into* (*~ed his audience, himself, into enthusiasm, a rage*). **10.** Do, make by, needlework or the like (*reads to them while they ~; ~ pattern, initials,* etc., *on linen* etc.; *is ~ing a shawl*). **11.** Solve (sum) by mathematical processes. **12.** Purchase (one's *passage*) with labour instead of money, also transf. **13.** *~ in,* find place for (illustration, subject, etc.), admit of being introduced. **14.** *~ off,* get rid of get over, find customers etc. for, (*~s off his bad temper on his servants; has ~ed off his debauch; ~ off 3000 copies; ~s off old joke on us*). **15.** *~ out,* find (amount etc. or solve (sum) by calculation, (of amount etc.) be calculated *at* (*~s out at £6 10s.*), (of sum) give definite result (*will not ~ out*), exhaust with work (*person, mine,* etc.

is quite ~ed out), accomplish or attain with difficulty (*~ out one's salvation*), provide for or plan all details of (*has ~ed out a scheme of invasion*); *~-out* n. (esp. boxing, sports, etc.), a practice or test. **16.**~ *up*, bring gradually to efficient state, elaborate in description (often *wrought*), advance gradually *to* (climax), excite (persons, expectations, etc.) by degrees (often *wrought*; *his wrought-up nerves*; *is in a highly wrought-up state*, nervous, hysterical), mingle (materials) into whole, acquire familiarity with (subject) by study. [OE *wyrcan* (Gmc *wurkjan*), *wircan* (Gmc *werkjan*), *we(o)rcan* (f. *we(o)rc* n.); Gmc *werk-, *wurk-*, see prec.]

wor′k|able (wĕr-), a. That can be worked, that will work, that is worth working, practicable, feasible. Hence ~ABIL′ITY, ~ableNESS, nn., ~abLY² adv. [-ABLE]

wor′ker (wĕr-), n. In vbl senses; esp., (also ~ *bee, ant*, etc.) undeveloped female of various social insects. [ME; -ER¹]

wor′king¹ (wĕr-), n. In vbl senses; also or esp.: way thing works or result of its ~ (*the ~s of his face, conscience, fancy*); mine, quarry, etc., or part of it in which work is being or has been done (*was found in a disused ~*); ~ *day*, = WORK¹-*day*, also hours of the twenty-four devoted to work; ~ *capital, expenses*, those required by or devoted to actual carrying on of business; ~ *drawing, plan* (serving as guide for building or construction); ~ *lunch* etc., meal at which business, policy, etc. are discussed; *~-out*, calculation of results, elaboration of details; ~ *party*, (esp.) committee etc. appointed to secure efficiency in an industry etc. or to investigate & report on some question. [ME; -ING¹]

wor′king² (wĕr-), a. In vbl senses; esp., engaged in manual labour (*~ man; the ~ class*). [-ING²]

world (wĕr-), n. **1.** Time or state or scene of existence (*the* or *this ~*, mortal life; *the other* or *next ~*, *the ~ to come*, life after death; *the lower ~*, hell, Earth; *Prince of this ~*, the devil; *we bring nothing into the ~*, at birth; *bring child into the ~*, beget or bear it; *make the best of both ~s*, reconcile secular & spiritual interests; *the end of the ~*, cessation of all mortal life by destruction of universe or otherwise; ~ *without end*, for ever). **2.** Secular interests & occupations (*the ~, the flesh, & the devil*, kinds of temptation; *forsake the ~*). **3.** The universe, all creation, everything, (*the creation of the ~; the best of all possible ~s; in the ~*, at all, that exists, etc., as *who, how, what, in the ~ was it?, nothing in the ~*; *for all the ~ like*, precisely like; *carry the ~ before* one, have rapid & complete success). **4.** Everything that exists outside oneself (*the external ~*, all phenomena; *the ~ of dreams*, things as they seem in dreams; *would not do it for*

the, *to gain the whole*, ~; *she is all the ~ to me*; *would give the ~ to know*). **5.** The earth, heavenly body supposed to resemble it, its countries & their inhabitants, all people, the earth as known or in some respect limited, (*go round the ~*; *to the ~'s end*, to farthest attainable distance; *a universe of ~s*; *are there other ~s than ours?*; *citizen of the ~*, cosmopolitan; *all the ~'s a stage*; *make a noise in the ~*, be widely talked of; *all the ~ knows*, it is generally known; *makes the whole ~ kin*; *the wise old ~*, general experience & custom; ~ *politics, movement, tendency*, affecting or seen among many peoples; *the Old W~*, Europe, Asia, & Africa, part known by ancients to exist; *the New W~*, America; *the Roman* etc. ~, as much of the ~ as concerned Rome etc.; *the Anglo-Saxon, English-speaking*, etc., ~). **6.** Human affairs, their course & conditions, active life, (*so wags the ~; how goes the ~ with you?; know, see, the ~*, have, acquire, experience; *man of the ~*, experienced practical tolerant person; *begin the ~*, start one's career; *all 's right with the ~*, expression of optimism; *take the ~ as it is, as one finds it*, be adaptable; *let the ~ slide*, not try to influence events, also disregard convention & public opinion). **7.** Average or respectable or fashionable society or people or their customs or opinions (*the great ~*, fashionable society; *all the ~ & his wife*, all with pretensions to fashion; *what will the ~ say?*, dare we defy opinion?; *live out of the ~*, avoid society). **8.** All that concerns or all who belong to specified department or class, sphere, domain, (*the literary, scientific, sporting, animal, ancient, ~; the ~ of letters, art, sport*). **9.** A vast or infinite number or amount or extent (*a ~ of meaning, trouble, faults; a ~ of waters*, expanse of sea; *a ~ too wide* etc., by far). **10.** *To the ~* (sl.), utterly (*tired, drunk*, etc., *to the ~*, perh. by misapplication of *dead to the ~*); ~ *language*, that was or will be or is meant to be universal, also spoken in more than one part of ~; *~-old*, (usu. by exag.) old as creation; *~-power*, powerful State whose policy etc. may affect the ~ at large; *~-weary*, tired of existence; *~-wide*, spread over the ~, known or found everywhere. [OE *w(e)orold, world*, OS *werold*, OHG *weralt*, ON *verǫld*, f. Gmc *wer-* man + *aldh-* age, ELD]

wor′ldling (wĕr-), n. Worldly person. [-LING¹]

wor′ldly (wĕr-), a. Temporal, earthly, (*~ goods*, property); exclusively or preponderantly concerned with or devoted to the affairs of this life, esp. to pursuit of wealth or pleasure (*~ wisdom*, esp. prudence in advancing one's own interests; ~ *people, life*, etc.); OTHER~; *~-minded*, intent on ~ things, whence *~-mind′ed*NESS n.; *~-wise*, having ~

wisdom. Hence **wor'ldliness** (wẽr-) n. [-LY¹]

worm¹ (wẽrm), n. **1.** Kinds of invertebrate limbless or apparently limbless creeping animal, esp. such as are segmented in rings or are parasitic in the intestines or tissues (also in compd names of larvae, insects, lizards, etc., with some resemblance to ~s, as *silk, glow, slow,* ~; *dog, child, has*~s, internal parasites; *food for*~s, of person when dead; *a*~ *will turn,* the meekest will resist or retaliate if pushed too far; *the* ~ *of conscience,* gnawing pain of remorse; so *where their* ~ *dieth not; am a* ~ *today,* out of sorts & spiritless, w. ref. to *Ps.* xxii. 6). **2.** Insignificant or contemptible person. **3.** Spiral part of screw, spiral cartridge--extractor, spiral pipe of still in which vapour is cooled & condensed. **4.** Ligament under dog's tongue. **5.** ~-*cast,* tubular mass of earth voided by earth~; ~'*eaten,* gnawn by ~s, full of ~-holes, (fig.) antiquated; ~-*fishing,* with ~ for bait; ~-*gear,* arrangement of toothed wheel worked by revolving spiral; ~-*hole,* left in wood, fruit, etc., by passage of ~; ~-*holed,* ~eaten (lit.); ~-*seed,* (Levantine plant bearing) seed used to expel intestinal ~s; ~'*s-eye view* (joc.), as seen from below (opp. *bird's-eye view*); ~-*wheel,* wheel of ~-gear. Hence ~'y² a., ~'iness n. [OE *wyrm,* OS, OHG *wurm,* ON *ormr,* Goth. *waurms,* cogn. w. L *vermis*]

worm² (wẽrm), v.t. & i. **1.** Insinuate one*self into* (*favour,* person's *confidence,* etc.); convey one*self, progress,* make one's *way,* with crawling motion (~*ed himself* or *his way* or ~*ed through the bushes*). **2.** Draw (secret etc.) by crafty persistence *out* (*of* person). **3.** Cut worm of (dog's tongue). **4.** Rid (garden-bed etc.) of worms. [f. prec.]

worm'wood (wẽr-), n. Kinds of perennial herb with bitter, tonic, & stimulating qualities used in preparation of vermouth & absinth & in medicine; bitter mortification or its cause. [alt. f. obs. *wermod* (OE *wermod,* OS -*mōde,* OHG -*muot,* of unkn. orig.), after WORM, WOOD; cf. VERMOUTH]

worn. See WEAR¹.

wo'rrit (wŭ-), v.t. & i., & n. = foll. (vulg.).

wo'rr|y (wŭ-), v.t. & i., & n. **1.** (Of dogs) bite (rat, sheep, dog) repeatedly, shake or pull about with the teeth (~ *problem* etc. *out,* assail it again & again till it is solved; ~*y the sword* in fencing, try to fluster opponent by small movements in quick succession); tease, harass, importune, be continuously or intermittently troublesome to, allow no rest or peace of mind to (~*y* one*self,* take needless trouble; *is much* ~*ied,* full of uneasiness; *wears a* ~*ied look,* looks anxious or troubled); give way to anxiety, let the mind dwell on troubles, fret; **I should* ~*y* (colloq.), it doesn't trouble me at all; ~*y along,* manage to advance in spite of obstacles;

hence ~iment n., ~ying³ adv. **2.** n. Hound's ~ying of quarry; (usu. in pl.) care(s), thing(s) ~ying person; cares, ~ied state, over-anxiety; hence ~iless a. [OE *wyrgan* kill, OHG *wurgan,* f. Gmc **wurgjan*]

worse (wẽrs), a. & adv. comp., & n. **1.** More BAD or BADLY; (as pred. a.) in or into less good health (*is* ~ *today, is getting* ~), in less good condition or circumstances (*is none the* ~ *for it*). **2.** n. ~ thing(s) (*have* ~ *to tell; but* ~ *followed, remains*); *the* ~, defeat in contest (*have, put to, the* ~, be defeated, defeat), ~ condition (*a change for the* ~). Hence **wor'sen⁵** (wẽr-) v.t. & i. [OE *wyrsa, wiersa,* OS *wirsa,* OHG *wirsiro,* ON *verri,* Goth. *wairsiza* f. Gmc **wers-,* cf. WAR¹]

wor'ship (wẽr-), n., & v.t. & i. (-pp-). **1.** (arch.). Worthiness, merit, recognition given or due to these, honour & respect, (*men of* ~, worthies: *win, have,* ~, reach, enjoy, high repute; ‖ so still in *your, his, W*~, used to or of certain magistrates, or to show respect for person of higher station or ironical pretence of this), whence ~FUL a., ~fuLY² adv., ~fulness n. **2.** Reverent homage or service paid to God (*public* ~, *the hours of* ~, *forms of* ~, etc., church services; *place of* ~, church); adoration or devotion comparable to this felt or shown towards person or principle (*an object of* ~; *regarding her with* ~ *in his eyes; the* ~ *of rank, wealth, intellect, athletics*). **3.** vb. Adore as divine, pay religious homage to; idolize, regard with adoration, (~*s the ground she treads on*); attend public ~ (*where does he* ~?), whence ~per¹ n.; be full of adoration. [OE *weorthscipe* (WORTH¹, -SHIP)]

worst (wẽr-), a. & adv. sup., n., & v.t. **1.** Most BAD, BADLY. **2.** n. ~ part, feature, state, possible assumption, event, possible issue, or action (*the* ~ *of the storm is over; the* ~ *of it is that* —; *saw him at his* ~; *when things are at the* or *their* ~; *at* ~, *at the* ~, *our lives are safe; get the* ~ *of it,* be ~ed; *have, put to, the* ~, be defeated, defeat; *the* ~ *has happened; be prepared for the* ~; *if the* ~ *comes to the* ~, if the ~ happens; *do your, let him* etc. *do his* etc., ~, expression of defiance). **3.** v.t. Get the better of, defeat, outdo, best. [OE *wyrsta* etc., adj., *wyrst* adv., f. Gmc **wersistaz* (**wers-* WORSE + -EST)]

wor'sted (wŏŏs-), n. Woollen yarn (often attrib., as ~ *sock*). [*Worste(a)d* in Norfolk]

wort (wẽrt), n. **1.** Plant, herb, (rare exc. in comb., as *spleen, stitch,* ~). **2.** Infusion of malt before it is fermented into beer. [sense 1 f. OE *wyrt* = OS *wurt,* OHG, G *wurz,* ON *urt,* Goth. *waurts,* cogn. w. ROOT, L *radix*; sense 2 f. OE *wyrt* = OS *wurtja,* MHG, G *würze,* derivative f. same st.]

worth¹ (wẽrth), pred. a. (governing noun like trans. part.), & n. **1.** Of value equivalent to (*is* ~ *much, little, nothing, about 2/6; is little* ~, poet., ~ *little*; BIRD *in the hand is* ~ *two in bush; what is the house* ~*?; the rarer it is the more it is* ~). **2.** Deserving, worthy of, bringing compensation for, (~ *one's salt*, earning one's keep by good service; ~ *doing, hearing, notice, the trouble,* WHILE¹, an effort, troubling oneself about, etc.; ~ *it*, colloq., ~ *while*; *to reign is* ~ *ambition; game not* ~ *the* CANDLE; *I give you, you must take, this for what it is* ~, I do not guarantee its truth, wisdom, etc.). **3.** Possessed of, having property amounting to, (*is, died,* ~ *a million; spent all he was* ~ *on it; for all one is* ~, colloq., with one's utmost efforts, without reserve). **4.** ~-*while,* that is ~ while (*a* ~-*while experiment*). **5. n.** What a person or thing is ~, value, merit, high merit or excellence, (*of great, little, no,* ~; *persons of* ~; *true* ~ *often goes unrecognized*), whence ~'LESS a., ~'lĕssLY² adv., ~'lĕssNESS n. **6.** Coin's equivalent of commodity (*give me a shilling's, half a crown's,* ~ *of stamps*); also in comb. as *penny*~, *two-penny*~ or -*pennorth, three-ha'porth* etc.). [OE *wcorth* etc. a. & n., = OS *werth,* OHG *werd,* ON *verth*(r), Goth. *wairth*(s)]

worth² (wẽrth), **v.t.** 3rd sing. subjunct. (arch.). Befall (only in *woe* ~ *the day* = cursed be). [OE *weorthan* become, = OHG *werdan,* Goth. *wairthan*]

worthy (wẽr'dhǐ), **a. & n. 1.** Estimable, having some moral worth, of a fair degree of merit, respectable, (*a* ~ *man; has lived a* ~ *life;* often with patronizing effect, cf. HONEST, as *I asked the* ~ *rustic whether*); deserving of or deserving of or deserving *to* be or do (*is* ~ *of* or rarely ~ *remembrance* or *being remembered; is* ~ *to be remembered, take the lead;* also in comb. as *praise*~, *blame*~); corresponding to the worth of or of, adequate, appropriate, of sufficient worth or merit, (*in words* ~ *of* or ~ *the occasion; is not* ~ *of* or ~ *my sword, steel; has found a* ~ *adversary, received a* ~ *reward*); hence wor'thiLY² adv., wor'thiNESS n., (wẽr'dhǐ-). **2. n.** ~ person, person of some distinction in his country, time, etc., (esp. in pl., as *the Worthies of England; an Elizabethan* etc.~). [ME *wurthi* etc., f. WORTH¹ n. +-Y²]

wot. See WIT¹.

would. See WILL¹.

would'-be (wŏŏd-), **a. & adv.** prefixed to n. or adj. expressing a quality aspired to or intended (~ *gentleman, facetious*). [WILL¹, BE]

wound¹ (wŏŏ-), **n., & v.t. 1.** Injury done by cut or stab or blow or tear to animal or vegetable tissues including & usu. going beyond the cutting or piercing or breaking or tearing of the skin or bark or other integument, (fig.) injury done to person's

reputation etc. or pain inflicted on his feelings, (poet.) pangs of love, (*receive, inflict, make, heal, a* ~; *incised, punctured, contused, lacerated,* ~; *open, incurable, festering, mortal,* ~); ~-*wort,* kinds of plant supposed to have healing properties; hence ~'LESS a. **2. v.t.** Inflict ~ on (often fig., esp. ~ed *vanity, feelings; willing to* ~, spiteful). [OE *wund,* OS -*da,* OHG -*ta,* ON *und;* vb f. OE *wundian*]

wound². See WIND², ³.

woura'li. See CURARE.

wove(n). See WEAVE.

***wow,** int. expr. astonishment & admiration; (n., sl.) a sensational success. [16th c., orig. Sc.]

wows'er (-z-), **n.** (Austral.). Puritanical fanatic. [orig. unkn.]

wr-. In all words beginning thus *w* is silent.

wrăck, n. Wreckage; sea-weed cast up & used for manure etc. [ME *wrak* f. MDu. *wrak* or MLG *wra*(*c*)*k,* a parallel form. to OE *wræc,* rel. to *wrecan* WREAK; cf. WRECK, RACK¹]

wraith, n. Person's double or apparition seen shortly before or after his death; ghost. [orig. Sc., of unkn. orig.]

wrangle (răng'gl), **v.i., & n.** Brawl, (engage in) loud or vulgar or confused argument or altercation or quarrel. [ME; cf. LG *wrangelen,* MHG *rangelen,* frequent. of *rangen* to struggle; cogn. w. WRING]

wrăng'ler (-ngg-), **n.** In vbl senses; || also, (Camb. Univ.) person placed in first class of mathematical tripos (person in 2nd, 3rd, class being called *senior, junior, ŏp'tǐmē; senior* ~, first in first class when it was arranged in order of merit), whence ~SHIP n. [-ER¹; spec. sense f. obs. sense of vb *dispute publicly on a thesis*]

wrăp, v.t. & i. (-pp-), **& n. 1.** Enfold, enclose or pack or conceal in folded or soft encircling material, (often *up; ~ it in paper, cotton wool;* ~ *up parcel; mountain, affair, is* ~*ped in mist, mystery;* ~*s up his meaning in tortuous sentences, allegory*); (p.p. with *up*) engrossed or included (*mother, country's prosperity, is* ~*ped up in her child, its shipping*); ~ *up,* put on ~*s* (*mind you* ~ *up well if you go out*); arrange or draw (pliant covering) *round* or *about* person or thing (~*ped her shawl closer about her*), whence ~p'ING¹(3) n.; overlap (intr.; *the edges should, do not,* ~). **2. n.** (Usu. in pl.) shawl(s), rug(s), cloak(s), neckerchief(s), etc., as addition to ordinary clothes. [ME, of unkn. orig.]

wrăpp'age, n. Wrapping(s). [-AGE]

wrăpp'er, n. In vbl senses: esp.: (garment resembling) dressing-gown; paper enclosing newspaper or similar packet for posting; (freq. detachable) paper cover of book, outer tobacco-leaf of superior quality enclosing cigar. [-ER¹]

In words beginning with *wr-, w* is silent.

wrapt. = RAPT.

wrässe, n. Kinds of thick-lipped strong-toothed bright-coloured rock-haunting sea-fish. [f. Corn. *wrach,* mutated f. *gwrach,* = W *gwrach*]

wrath (raw-), n. Anger, indignation, (poet., rhet., or joc.; *vessels, children, of* ~, persons destined to divine chastisement; *slow to* ~, not irascible). Hence ~'FUL a., ~'fuLLY² adv. [OE *wrǣththu* f. *wrǣth* WROTH + -*thu* -TH¹]

wreak, v.t. Avenge (wrong, wronged person; arch.); give play or satisfaction to, put in operation, (*vengeance, rage,* etc., usu. *upon* enemy etc.; rarely *desire* etc., as ~ one's *thoughts upon expression,* find adequate words). [OE *wrecan* drive, avenge, etc., OS *wrekan,* OHG *rechan,* ON *reka,* Goth. *wrikan* f. Gmc *⁕wrekan,* cogn. w. L *urgēre*; cf. WRACK, WRECK]

wreath, n. (*pl. pr.* -dhz). Flowers or leaves strung or woven or wound together into ring for wearing on head or for decorating statue, building, coffin, etc., carved imitation of such ~; similar ring of soft twisted material such as silk; curl *of* smoke, circular or curved band *of* cloud, (poet.) circle *of* dancers or spectators. [OE *writha* f. wk grade of *writhan* WRITHE]

wreathe (-dh), v.t. & i. Encircle as or with or as with a wreath (*face* ~*d in smiles*); form (flowers, silk, etc.) into wreath; wind one's *arms* etc. or (of snake etc.) *itself round* person etc.; make (garland); (of smoke etc.) move in shape of wreaths. [16th c., partly back form. f. *wrethen,* p.p. of WRITHE, partly f. prec.]

wrĕck, n., & v.t. & i. 1. Ruin, destruction, disablement, esp., of ship (*save ship,* one's *fortunes, from* ~; *gale caused many* ~*s; the* ~ *of the Hesperus, of his life*); ship that has suffered ~, greatly damaged or disabled building or person, disorganized remains or sorry remnant *of,* (*shores are strewn with* ~*s; person, building, is a* ~; *is but a* or *the* ~ *of his former self*); goods etc. cast up by the sea (~ *of the sea belongs to the Crown*); ~*-master,* officer appointed to take charge of goods etc. cast up from ~ed ship. 2. vb. Cause ~ of (ship, train, hopes, undertaking, person or his fortunes), (p.p.) involved in ship-~ (~*ed sailors, goods*); ||~*ing amendment* (pol.), alteration designed to frustrate the whole purpose of a bill; suffer ~ (rare; *this is the obstacle your hopes will* ~ *on*). [ME, f. AF *wrec, wrech* (cf. VAREC), f. ON *⁕wrek,* f. Gmc *⁕wrecan* to drive, see WREAK, WRACK; vb f. n.]

wrĕck'age, n. Wrecked material, remnants, fragments. [-AGE]

wrĕck'er, n. In vbl senses; also: man who tries from shore to bring about shipwreck with a view to profiting by wreckage or who steals such wreckage; person employed in recovering wrecked ship or its contents; man who demolishes buildings etc. [-ER¹]

wrĕn¹, n. Kinds of very small cock-tailed short-winged European songbird (often *Jenny W*~). [OE *wrenna,* obsc. rel. to OHG *wrendo,* -*ilo,* Icel. *rindill*]

|| **Wrĕn²,** n. Member of the Women's Royal Naval Service, organized in 1917.

wrĕnch, n., & v.t. 1. Violent twist or oblique pull or tearing off, (fig.) pain caused by parting, (*gave a* ~ *to his ankle, at the door-handle; leaving home was a great* ~). 2. Implement made to grip & turn nuts, bolts, etc. 3. v.t. Twist or pull violently round or sideways, injure or pull *off* or *away* by twisting, (~*ed the door open, his horse's head round, his ankle, fowl's head off, opponent's sword from him*); pervert, wrest, (*facts* etc.). [OE *wrencan* twist, OHG *rencken*]

wrĕst, v.t., & n. 1. Twist, deflect, distort, pervert, (~*s the law to suit himself;* ~ *the facts, sense* or *words of a passage,* etc.); force or wrench away from person's grasp (~*ed his sword from him*). 2. n. Key for tuning harp etc.; ~*-block,* part of piano holding ~*-pins,* to which strings are attached. [OE *wrǣstan,* = ON *reisla,* f. Gmc *⁕wraistjan,* rel. to WRIST]

wrĕ'stle (-sl), v.i. & t., & n. 1. Grapple with & try to throw adversary esp. in sporting contest under code of rules (*with,* or abs.); have ~ing-match with; contend, grapple, do one's utmost to deal, *with* evil, temptation, duty, task, problem, etc.; ~*e with God* or *in prayer,* pray fervently; hence ~ER¹, ~ING¹, nn., (rĕs'l-). 2. n. ~ing-match; hard struggle. [OE *⁕wrǣstlian,* f. prec. + -LE(3)]

wrĕtch, n. Very unfortunate or miserable person; despicable person, person without conscience or shame (often as term of playful abuse). [OE *wrecca* = OHG *reccho* exile, adventurer (G *recke*) f. Gmc *⁕wrak-,* *⁕wrek-,* see WREAK]

wrĕtch'ĕd, a. Miserable, unhappy, afflicted; inferior, of bad quality or no merit, contemptible, unsatisfactory, causing discontent or discomfort or nuisance, confounded, (~ *weather, health, horse, inn, accommodation, poetry, poet,* etc.); (with nn. of condemnation) great, severe, excessive, (~ *insufficiency, stupidity,* etc.). Hence ~LY² adv., ~NESS n. [irreg. f. prec. + -ED¹, cf. WICKED]

wrick, rick, v.t., & n. 1. Slightly sprain or strain (neck, back, joint). 2. n. Sprain or strain (*have a* ~ *in my neck; gave my back a* ~). [earlier (18th c.) *rick*; cf. MLG *vorwricken* sprain; dial. *wrig* sprain, WRIGGLE]

wrig'gl|e, v.i. & t., & n. 1. (Of worm etc.) move body with short twistings, (of animals or persons) make wormlike motions, (fig.) be slippery, practise evasion; make way *along, through, out, in*, etc., by ~ing (often fig., as ~*e out of a difficulty*); move one*self*, one's *body, tail, hand*, etc., with ~ing motion; make one's *way* by ~ing. 2. n. ~ing movement. [f. (M)LG *wriggeln* frequent. of *wriggen*, whence E dial. *wrig* to twist]

wright (rīt), n. Workman, maker, (now rare exc. in comb. as *ship, wheel, play*, ~, or with help of context as *the wheel must go to the ~ for repair*). [OE *wryhta, wyrhta* f. *wurh-*, var. of *wurk-* WORK²]

wring, v.t. (*wrŭng*), & n. **1.** Squeeze, squeeze & twist, twist forcibly, break by twisting, pervert sense of, torture, (~ *person's hand*, press it with emotion; ~ one's *hands*, squeeze them together in sign of great distress; ~ *out* or ~ *clothes*, press water from them by twisting; ~*ing wet*, or colloq. ~*ing*, so wet as to need ~ing; ~ *neck of*, kill *chicken* etc.; *has wrung the words from their true meaning; soul was wrung with agony*); extract by squeezing, get *out* by pressure or importunity, extort, (~ *water, groan, consent, money, from* or *out of* or *out*); hence (-)~ER¹(2) n. **2.** n. Squeeze (*gave my hand, give those clothes, a ~*). [OE (OS) *wringan*, OHG *ringan*, rel. to WRANGLE, WRONG]

wrinkle (rǐng'kl), n., & v.t. & i. **1.** Furrow-like crease or depression or ridge in the skin (esp. of the kind produced by age) or other flexible surface; hence **wrink'ly²** a.; (colloq.) piece of serviceable information not generally known, tip, dodge, (*is full of ~s*; *gave me, put me up to, a ~* or *two*). **2.** vb. Produce ~s in (often *up*; *he* ~*d his forehead*; ~*d with age*); assume ~s, show ~d appearance. [orig. obsc.; n. & vb app. back form. f. *wrinkled*, repr. OE *gewrinclod* sinuous]

wrist, n. Joint connecting hand with forearm; (effect dot in fencing, ball-games, sleight-of-hand, etc., by) working of the hand from the ~ alone (*his wonderful ~; that was all ~*); (mech., also ~*-pin*) stud projecting from crank etc. as attachment for connecting-rod; ~*bānd*, band usu. of folded & starched linen forming or concealing end of shirt-sleeve, cuff; ~*-drop*, paralysis of forearm muscles from lead-poisoning; ~ *watch* (attached to ~). [OE *wrist* (= MHG, ON *rist*), prob. f. *writh-* wk grade of *writhan* WRITHE]

wrist'let, n. Band or ring worn on wrist to strengthen or guard it or as ornament, bracelet, handcuff, etc. (~ *watch*, attached to ~). [-LET]

writ¹, n. *Holy, sacred*, ~, the Bible; form of written command in name of sovereign, State, court, etc., issued to official or other person & directing him to act or abstain from acting in some way (~ *of attachment, habeas corpus, subpoena*, etc.; *serve* ~ *on* one, deliver it to him; ~ *runs* in district etc., is theoretically valid or is actually respected). [OE *writ*, ON *rit*, Goth. *writs* f. wk grade of *writan* WRITE]

writ². See foll.

write, v.i. & t. (*wrōte*, arch. **writ**; **written**, arch. **writ**). **1.** Trace symbols representing word(s) esp. with pen or pencil or typewriter on paper or parchment, trace (such symbols), trace the symbols that represent or constitute (word, special script, etc.), (fig.) stamp marks indicating (quality or conditions) *on* or *in* or *over* person's face etc., (~ *well, legibly, disgracefully*, etc.; ~ *in ink, in pencil*; ~*s a good, niggling*, etc., *hand*, produces good etc. writing; *cannot read* or ~; *can* ~ *his alphabet, the Greek letters, Greek*; ~ *your letters separate*; ~ *one's name*; *has honesty written in his face*; *a paper written all over*, covered with writing; *a notice is written up on the wall*; *what I have written I have written*, of refusal to correct, see *John* xix. 22; ~ *thing down*, record or take note of it in writing; ~ *off*, ~ & dispatch letter; ~ *out*, ~ the whole of, ~ in full; ~ *out fair*, make fair copy of; *name is written in book of life*, included in the list of the saved; *written in* or *on water*, transient; *writ large*, on a large scale, in a magnified form). **2.** Fill, draw up or fill in, with writing (*has written three sheets*; ~ *cheque, certificate, application*, etc.; ~ *up the books, reports*, etc., make entries bringing them up to date). **3.** Compose for written or printed reproduction or publication, put into literary form & set down in writing, be engaged temporarily or permanently in such composition, compose books etc. well etc., (*is writing a book, article, his life, poetry, a novel, report, letter*, etc.; ~ *off*, compose with facility; ~*s cleverly, like an angel*; ~*s a little, in* or *for the papers, for a living*, etc.). **4.** ~ & send letter (*to* person or abs., also commerc. or colloq. without *to*; ~*s home once a week; have written to him; we wrote you last week; will* ~ *off*, or ~, *for a fresh supply*). **5.** Send or convey (person or *to* person news, *that, how*, etc.) by letter (~ *me all the news, the result, how you got home; wrote to his mother that he was bullied*). **6.** State in writing or print (*Herodotus* ~*s, it is written, that*). **7.** Describe, put *down*, in writing as (~*s himself esquire*; ~ *me down an ass*). **8.** ~ *down*, disparage in writing, (also) reduce nominal value of (stock); ~ *off*, cancel, recognize in writing the non-existence or annulment of, (bad debts, sums absorbed by depreciation, etc.); ~ *out*, refl., exhaust by writing (*has written himself out*, has no ideas etc. left); ~ *up*, praise in writing, also elaborate account of (incident etc.), bring (diary etc.) up to date. [OE *writan* score, write, OS *writan* cut, write, OHG *rizan* tear, draw, ON *rita* score, write]

writ'er, n. In vbl senses; esp.: ‖ clerk in certain offices, whence ~SHIP n.; author; manual teaching how to write specified language (*French* etc.~); ‖ ~ *to the signet*, abbr. *W.S.*, Scots solicitor conducting cases before Court of SESSION; ~*'s cramp* or *palsy*, muscular affection incapacitating for writing. [OE; -ER[1]]

writhe (rīdh), v.i. & t., & n. **1.** Twist or roll oneself about (as) in acute pain, squirm; twist (one's *body* etc.) about; shrink mentally, be stung or bitterly annoyed, (*under, at,* insult etc.; *with* shame etc.). **2.** n. Act of writhing. [OE *wrīthan,* OHG *rīdan,* ON *rītha,* rel. to WREATH(E), WREST, WRIST]

writ'ing, n. In vbl senses; also: written document; piece of literary work done, book, article, etc., (*the ~s of Plato*); *put thing in ~,* write it down; ~-*case,* holding ~-materials; ~-*desk,* desk; ~-*ink,* opp. *printing-ink; the ~ on the wall,* ominously significant event etc. (see *Dan.* v); ~-*paper,* paper for ~ on esp. cut to size usual for letters; ~-*table,* KNEE[1]-hole or other table kept for ~ at. [ME; -ING[1]]

written. See WRITE.

wrŏng, a. (*more, most*), n., adv. (no comp.), & v.t. **1.** Out of order, in(to) bad condition, (*something is ~ with him; my liver is or has gone or has got ~; what's ~ with —?,* colloq., surely no substitute is wanted); contrary to law or morality, wicked, (*knows the right from the ~; lying is ~*); other than the right or the more or most desirable (*always does the ~ thing; took the ~ way; the ~ answer, move; in the ~ box,* awkwardly placed, in a difficulty, at a disadvantage; *is ~ side out,* inside out; *has hold of the ~ end of the stick,* has inverted a theory, position, etc.; *on the ~ side of 40* etc., older than; *~ side of the* BLANKET; ~'*un,* crick., GOOGLY; *~ fount,* abbr. *w.f.,* notice to compositor that letter or word is not of right FOUNT[2]); mistaken, in error, (*a ~ opinion, guess, decision, hypothesis; I think you are, can prove you, ~*); ~-*headed,* perverse & obstinate; hence~'LY[1] adv. **2.** n. What is morally ~,~ action, (*the difference between right & ~; can two ~s make a right?; do ~,* sin, offend, transgress, whence ~'DOER[1], ~'DOING[1], nn., (-dōō-); *king can do no ~,* maxim expressing principle of ministerial responsibility in constitutional monarchy; injustice, unjust action or treatment, (*do ~ to; suffer~; has done me a great~; you do me ~,* malign me; *complains of her ~s*); position or responsibility for having caused quarrel, made the mistake, been the offender, etc. (*you were, they are both, in the ~; put one in the ~,* show or make it appear that he was the offender); hence (of actions)~'FUL a.,~'fulLY[2] adv.,~'fulNESS n. **3.** adv. (usu. placed last). Amiss, in~ direction, with incorrect result, (*aim, guess, answer, do sum, sort things, ~; you told, led, me ~; go ~,* take ~ path, esp. fig.); *(colloq.) get in ~ with* person, incur his dislike, *get* person *in ~,* bring him into disfavour. **4.** v.t. Treat unjustly,

do ~ to, (*his deeply ~ed wife*); mistakenly attribute bad motives etc. to (*I assure you you~ me*). [late OE *wrang* f. ON **wrangr, rangr,* rel. to WRING]

∥ **wrŏng'ous,** a. (Sc. law). Illegal, unjust. [alt. f. ME *wrangwis* f. *wrang* WRONG+ -*wis,* after *rihtwis* RIGHTEOUS]

wrote. See WRITE.

wroth (rō-, rŏ-), pred. a. (rhet., poet., or joc.). Angry. [OE *wrāth,* f. var. st. of *wrīthan* WRITHE; cf. OS *wrēth,* OHG *reid,* ON *reithr*]

wrought. See WORK[2].

wrung. See WRING.

wrȳ, a. (-*ier, -iest,* or -*yer, -yest*). Distorted, turned to one side, skew, (*~ face, mouth,* grimace expressing disgust; *has a ~ nose*); ~'*bill,* kind of plover; ~'*mouth,* kinds of fish; ~-*mouthed,* ironically flattering etc.; ~'*neck,* bird allied to woodpeckers able to turn head over shoulder. Hence ~'NESS n. [f. obs. *wrigian* tend, incline, in ME deviate, swerve, contort]

wy'andŏtte, n. American breed of fowl. [name of Amer.-Ind. tribe]

wych-, wich-, witch-, preff. in names of trees, as ~-*alder, -elm, -hazel.* [OE *wice, wic,* app. f. Gmc **wik-* bend., cogn. w. WEAK]

wye, n. Letter Y; thing so shaped.

Wyke'hamist (-kam-), a. & n. (Past or present member) of Winchester college. [f. mod. L *Wykehamista* (16th c.), William of *Wykeham,* founder (d. 1404), -IST]

∥ **wȳnd,** n. (Sc.). Alley in Scots town. [app. f. st. of WIND[3] n.]

wyvern. See WIVERN.

X

X (ĕks), letter (pl. Xs, X's). (As Rom. numeral) 10, as IX 9, xv 15, lx 60, XC 90, MX 1010, DXL 540; (alg.; *x*) first unknown quantity (cf. A, Y), (transf.) incalculable or mysterious factor or influence (*X-RAY*[1]s).

Xanthipp'e (zăntĭ-), n. Shrewish wife. [wife of Socrates]

xăn'th|(o)- (z-), comb. form of Gk *xanthos* yellow: ~*ate,* a salt of ~*ic* acid; ~*ĕin(e),* soluble part of yellow colouring-matter in flowers; ~*ic,* yellowish (~*ic acid,* ethyl- -disulpho-carbonic acid with yellow salts; ~*ic flowers,* typically yellow & never passing into blue but only into red or white, opp. *cyanic flowers* with blue as typical & red or white as alternative colours); ~*ŏch'rŏi* (-k-) n. pl. (ethnol.), blonds or fair whites (cf. MELANOCHROI); ~*omĕl'anous* (ethnol.), with black hair & yellow or brown or olive skin; ~*ophyll,* yellow colouring-matter occurring with chlorophyll in plants; ~*ous* (ethnol.), yellow or Mongoloid.

xĕb'ĕc (z-), n. Small three-masted Medi-

In words beginning with wr-, w is silent.

terranean vessel with some square & some lateen sails. [alt. f. F *chebec* after Sp. *xabeque*]

xĕn|(o)- (z-), comb. form of Gk *xenos* strange(r); ~*'ial*, of hospitality or relations between host & guest; ~*ŏg'amy* (bot.), cross-fertilization; ~*'olith* (geol.), stone or rock occurring in a system of rock to which it does not belong; so ~*ophŏb'ia*, morbid dislike of foreigners, so ~*'ophobe*.

xĕn'ŏn (z-), n. (chem.). Heavy inert gaseous element. [Gk, neut. of *xenos* strange]

xēr|(o)- (z-), comb. form of Gk *xēros* dry: ~*ăn'sis* [Gk, f. *xērainō* dry up], desiccation, drying up; ~*ăn'themum*, kinds of annual with everlasting composite flowers; ~*ŏg'raphy*, process of electrostatic printing or dry photography in which negatively-charged powder is sprinkled on a positively-charged surface, so ~*ogrăph'ic* a.; ~*ŏph'ilous* (bot.), adapted to hot & dry climate; ~*ŏphthăl'mia*, ophthalmia without discharge.

xī, n. Greek letter (*Ξ, ξ*) = x. [Gk]

xiph|(ĭ, -o)- (z-), comb. form of Gk *xiphos* sword; ~*'oid*, sword-shaped (~*oid appendage, cartilage,* or *process,* or ~*oid* as n., lower end of sternum); ~*ĭstern'um*, ~oid appendage.

Xmas (kris'mas), n. Abbr. for CHRISTMAS.

xŏ'anŏn (z-), n. (Gk ant.; pl. *-ana*). Primitive usu. wooden image of deity supposed to have fallen from heaven. [Gk (*xuō* scrape)]

X'-rays, n. pl. (Now usu. term for) *Röntgen* RAY[1]s; attrib. in sing., as *X-ray examination, photograph.* Hence **X-ray'** v.t., examine or treat or photograph with ~. [see x]

xȳl'ĕm (z-), n. (bot.). Woody tissue (opp. PHLOEM). [f. Gk *xulon*, cf. PHLOEM]

xȳl|(o)- (z-), comb. form of Gk *xulon* wood: ~*obal'samum*, (decoction of) dried twigs of balm-of-Gilead tree; ~*'ocarp*, (tree with) hard woody fruit, so ~*ocarp'ous* a.; ~*'ograph*, a (esp. 15th-c.) wood-engraving, also a decorative pattern got by mechanical reproduction of wood-grain, so ~*ŏg'raphy*, ~*ŏg'rapher*, ~*ograph'ic*; ~*'onite*, = CELLULOID n.; ~*ŏph'agous*, (of insects) feeding on wood [-PHAGOUS]; ~*'ophone*, musical instrument of wooden bars graduated in length & vibrating when struck.

xȳs'ter (z-), n. (surg.). Instrument for scraping bones. [f. Gk *xustēr* (*xuō* scrape)]

xȳs'tus, n. (pl. *-tī*). Covered portico used by athletes for exercise in classical antiquity; garden walk or terrace. [L, f. Gk *xustos* smooth (*xuō* scrape)]

Y

Y (wī), letter, (pl. *Ys*, *Y's*). (Alg.; *y*) second unknown quantity (cf. X, B); Y--shaped arrangement of lines, piping, roads, etc., forked clamp or support,

(often attrib., as *Y-branch, -cartilage, -joint, -ligament*); *Y-cross*, Y-shaped cross esp. on chasubles suggesting figure of crucified Christ; *Y-gun*, gun with two firing-arms for discharging depth-bombs (usu. mounted aft in destroyers); *Y-level*, surveying-level mounted on Ys; *Y-moth*, kind called also *gamma* with mark like Y or gamma on wings; *Y-track*, Y of railway-line with two branches running into main track enabling engine to reverse direction by running down one branch into stem & returning up the other.

y̆-, pref. common in ME & still found in a few arch. forms (*yclad* clad, YCLEPT, *ywis* surely), repr. OE, Du., & G *ge-* as pref. of p.pp., collective nn., & other wds; the same element is seen under different forms in ALIKE, AMONG, AWARE, EITHER, ENOUGH, HANDIWORK.

-y[1], suf. (a) repr., thr. (O)F *-ie*, Rom. *-ia* (forming nn. of state or condition) = L *-īa* (Gk *-ia, -eia*). E wds in *-y* repr. (i) AF learned adoptives, f. L, in *-ie*, as *glory, victory* (AF *glorie,* OF *gloire*), (ii) similar forms in (O)F, as *fury* (OF *furie*, besides organic *fuire*), (iii) OF formations on OF adjj., as *courtesy* (OF *corteisie* f. *corteis* courteous), (iv) L wds dir., as *family, irony*; so (v) in names of countries, as *Brittany, Italy, Normandy.* The corresp. of adjj. in *-ic* & *-ous* to nn. in *-y* makes possible the form., after Gk types, of such wds as *brachycephaly, synchrony* f. *brachycephalic, synchronous.* Meanings: (1) state, condition, quality; (2) an activity or its result; (3) concrete meanings from these (*company, library*): cf. *-IA*[1]. (b) repr., first thr. AF *-ie*, later by dir. adaptation, L *-ium* appended to vbl roots to denote an act, as *remedy* (AF *-ie*, L *-ium*), *colloquy* (L *colloquium*).

-y[2], suf. forming adjj., repr. OE *-ig*; when the n. ends in *-y*, the suf. is spelt *-ey*, as in *skyey, clayey*; in nn. ending in vowel *+-e*, this is retained, as in *gluey*; occas. there is variation, as in *hom(e)y, nos(e)y.* The general sense is 'full of', 'having the qualities of', as in *bony, thorny, angry, slangy*, in later use freq. colloq. or trivial, as *mousy, hammy, messy, oniony, &c,* w. sense 'addicted to', *booky, doggy, horsy.* From 15th c. appended to adjj., as *dusky, hugy, vasty, slippery*; so w. adjj. of colour, w. sense of *-ISH*[1](2), as *yellowy*, & esp. in comb., as *pinky-white.* Added to vb stems w. meaning 'inclined or apt to' (do something), as *blowy, drowsy, sticky, runny.*

-y[3], *-ie*, suf. w. dim. sense, earliest (1400) in Sc. proper names; of unkn. orig. Appears in proper names, as *Annie, Betty, Sally, Micky*; in names of tools etc., as *jemmy, jenny*; added to common nn., as *laddie, lassie, granny, doggie, slavey*; mod. colloq. uses are *bookie, nightie, undies, talkies, movies.*

-y[4], suf. repr. AF, OF *-e, -ee*, F *-é, -ée*, f.

L *-atu-*, *-ala*; see -ATE¹, ², -ADE, -ADO, -EE. (a) in nn. (= -ATE¹), as *county*, *army*; this suf. appears in other forms, as in *assignee*, *journey*, *attorney*, *valley*; (b) in adjj. (= -ATE²), as in *easy*, *tawny*, & chiefly in heraldic terms, as *barry*, *lozengy*, occas. w. var. in *-é*, as *tenny*, *tenné* (= *tawny*).

yacht (yŏt), n., & v.i. **1.** Light sailing--vessel kept, & usu. specially built & rigged, for racing; vessel propelled by sails, steam, electricity, or motive power other than oars, & used for private pleasure excursions, cruising, travel, etc.; ~*club*, esp. for ~-racing; ~*s'man*, person who ~s. **2.** v.i. Race or cruise in ~; hence ~ING¹ (yŏt-) n. [f. early mod. Du. *jaghl(e)* = *jaghlschip*, f. *jag(h)t* chase + *jagen* to hunt]

|| **yaf'fle, yäff'il**, n. The green wood-pecker. [imit. of laughing cry]

yäg'er (-g-), n. Member of certain German military corps esp. of riflemen. [f. G *jäger* orig. = hunter (*jagen* hunt)]

yah, int. of derision.

yahoo' (*-a*-h-), n. Brute in human shape (*Gulliver's Travels*); coarse person of bestial passions & habits. [made by Swift]

Yahveh' (-vä) n., **Yahweh'** (-wä) n., **Yah'vist** n., **Yahvis'tic** a. = JEHOVAH, JEHOVIST(ic).

yăk, n. Long-haired humped grunting wild or domesticated ox of Tibet; ~ *lace*, heavy kind made from ~'s hair. [f. Tibetan *gyak*]

Yăle lŏck, n. Cylinder lock for doors etc. invented by L. Yale (d. 1868). [P]

yăm, n. (Edible tuber of) kinds of tropical climbing plant. [f. Port. *inhame* or Sp. *igname*, of unkn. orig.]

Ya'ma (yah-), n. Hindu god of departed spirits & judge of the dead. [Skr.]

ya'men, -un, (yah-), n. Chinese mandarin's official residence (*the Tsung li* ~, Chinese Foreign Office). [Chin. (*ya* general's marquee, *mun* gate)]

yămm'er, v.i., & n. (colloq. & dial.). Lament, wail, grumble. [f. OE *geōmrian* f. *geōmor* sorrowful]

yănk¹, v.t. & i., & n. (colloq.). **1.** Pull (lever etc., or abs.) with a jerk. **2.** n. Sudden hard pull. [orig. unkn.]

Yănk², n. (colloq.). Yankee. [abbr.]

Yănk'ee (-kĭ), n. Inhabitant of New England; Federal soldier or inhabitant of northern States in American civil war; || inhabitant of U.S., American; (attrib.) of or as of the ~s (~ *notions*, American appliances etc.); ~ *Doodle*, American tune & song regarded as a national air; *y*~*fied*, of acquired ~ character [-FY]. Hence ~DOM, ~ISM(2, 4), nn. [source unascert.; perh. f. Du. *Janke* dim. of *Jan* John used derisively (1683); a widely accepted conjecture derives *Jankees* pl. f. *Jengees*, Ind. pronunc. of *English*]

yaourt (yah'oort), n. Curd-like food prepared from milk fermented by action of certain cultures. [f. Turk. *yŏghurt*]

yăp, v.i. (-pp-), & n. **1.** Bark shrilly or fussily; (colloq.) chatter, talk idly. **2.** n. Shrill or fussy bark. [imit.]

yăp'ŏck, n. S.-American water-opossum, with webbed hind feet. [f. *Oyapok*, S.-Amer. river]

yăpp, n. Kind of bookbinding with limp leather cover projecting considerably. [name of London bookseller (c. 1860)]

yărb'orough (-ru), n. Whist or bridge hand with no card above a 9. [f. an Earl of Y~ who betted against its occurrence]

yärd¹, n. **1.** The unit of long measure, = 3 ft, 36 in., or 1/1760 mile (abbr. *yd*; *100* ~s, esp. flat-race distance; *square*, *cubic*, ~); ~-length *of* material (*5* ~s, a ~ & a half, of cloth). **2.** Cylindrical spar tapering to each end slung horizontally (*square* ~) or slantwise (*lateen* ~) across mast to support sail (*lower*, *topsail*, *topgallant*, *royal*, ~, according to sail supported; *man the* ~s, place men, stand, along ~s as form of salute). **3.** ~*-arm*, either end of sail-~; ~ *measure*, rod, tape, etc., a ~ long & usu. divided into feet, inches, & quarters or fifths; ~'*stick*, *-wand*, rigid ~-measure; ~*stick*, (fig.) standard of comparison. [OE *gierd*, *gyrd*, OS *gerdia*, OHG *gerla* f. Gmc *gazdjō*; cf. GAD-FLY]

yärd², n., & v.t. **1.** Piece of enclosed ground, especially one surrounded by or attached to building(s) or used for some manufacturing or other purpose often specified by combination with another word (CHURCH¹, COURT¹, DOCK⁴, FARM¹, KALE, RICK¹, TIMBER, -~, VINEYARD; *brick*-~, where bricks are made); *railway*-~, space near station where rolling-stock is kept, trains made up, etc.; *stock*-~, where cattle are penned; *tan*-~, tanning--ground); || *the Y*~, SCOTLAND YARD; ~-*man*, *-master*, man working in, manager of, railway-~. **2.** v.t. Put (cattle) into stock-~, so ~'AGE(4) n. [OE *geard*, OS *gard*, OHG *gart*, ON *garthr* (GARTH), Goth. *gards*; cf. GARDEN]

yärn, n., & v.i. **1.** Any spun thread esp. of kinds prepared for weaving, knitting, or rope-making (~*-beam* or *roll*, on which warp-threads are wound for weaving). **2.** (colloq.). Story, traveller's tale, anecdote, rambling discourse, (*spin a* ~, ~*s*, tell ~s). **3.** v.i. (colloq.). Tell ~s. [OE *gearn*, OHG, ON *garn*]

yă'rrow (-ō), n. Common perennial herb with pungent smell & astringent taste, milfoil. [OE *gearwe*, OHG *gar(a)wa* (G *garbe*), of unkn. orig.]

yăsh'măk, n. Veil worn by Moslem women in public. [Arab.]

yăt'aghan (-găn), n. Mohammedan sword without guard or cross-piece. [Turk.]

yaw, v.i., & n. (naut., aeron.). **1.** (Of ship or aircraft) fail to hold straight course, fall off, go unsteadily. **2.** n. Deviation of ship etc. from course. [cf. ON *jaga* swing]

‖ **yawl**[1], v.i., & n. (rare). Howl, yell. [ME, imit.]

yawl[2], n. Kinds of small boat, esp. ship's jolly-boat with four or six oars; two-masted fore-&-aft sailing-boat with mizzen-mast stepped abaft the rudder post; kind of fishing-boat. [17th c., app. f. MLG *jolle* or Du. *jol*, of unkn. orig.]

yawn, v.i. & i., & n. **1.** (Of chasm etc.) gape, be wide open, (*a~ing gulf, rent*, etc.; *hell ~s for him*), (of person or animal) open the mouth wide as effect of drowsiness, boredom, etc.; utter or say with a ~ (*~ed goodnight*; '*What is the use?*' he *~ed*). **2.** n. Act of *~ing*. Hence *~*'**ingLY**[2] adv. [OE *ginian*, *geonian*, OHG *ginôn*; rel. to OE *gānian*, *ginan*, ON *gina*]

yaws(-z), n. pl. Framboesia. [orig. unkn.]

y̆clĕpt[1], a. (arch., joc.). Called (so-&-so). [Y-, obs. *clepe* call, OE *clipian*, -ED[1]]

ye (yĕ *or* yī *acc. to emphasis*), 2nd pers. pron. pl. (cf. THOU, YOU) now only poet., arch., religious, or joc. or colloq., & almost exclusively (after confusion in 15th–18th cc.) as subjective case (*blessed are ye when men shall hate you*; *ye zephyrs gay*; *ye gods!*, int.; *ye gods & little fishes!* joc.; *go it, ye cripples!*, joc. encouragement; also written or spoken for *you* in some familiar phrr., as *How d'ye do?*, *What d'ye think?*, *Thank ye, I tell ye*). [OE *ge*, *gē*, *gīe*, = OS *gi*, *ge*, OHG *ir*, ON *ér*, ult. f. Gmc *jūs*, *juz* (= Goth. *jus*), cf. Skr. *yū-yám*]

yea (yā), particle & n. (arch.; pl. *~s*). Yes (*let your communication be ~, ~*, *nay, yes & no without oaths*; *~s & nays*, arch., ayes & noes, affirmative & negative votes; *~ &*, & moreover); indeed, nay, (*ready, ~ eager*). [OE *gēa*, *gē*, OS, OHG, ON *jd*, Goth. *ja*, *jai* f. Gmc *ja*, *je*]

yean, v.t. & i. Bring forth (lamb, kid), bring forth lamb or kid. [perh. OE *geēanian* (Y-+*ēanian*, obs. *ean*)]

yean'ling, n. Young lamb or kid. [-LING[1]]

year, n. **1.** Time occupied by the earth in one revolution round the sun (also *astronomical, equinoctial, natural, solar, tropical, ~*; 365d. 5h. 48′ 46″ in length) or (*astral* or *sidereal ~*, longer by 20′ 23″) by the sun in recovering its previous apparent relation to the fixed stars or (*Platonic* or *Great* or *Perfect ~*, estimated by ancient astronomers at about 26000 *~s*) by the celestial bodies in recovering their relative positions at the Creation. **2.** Period of days (esp. *common ~* of 365 or *leap-~* or *bissextile ~* of 366 reckoned from 1st Jan.) used by community for dating or other purposes commencing on a certain day & corresponding more or less exactly in length to the astronomical *~* (also *legal, civil, calendar, ~*; *lunar ~*, of 12 lunar months; LUNI-SOLAR *~*; NEW[1], OLD, *~*; *Gregorian, Julian, ~*, as fixed by GREGORIAN, JULIAN, calendars; SABBATICAL *~*; *~ of* GRACE, *of our* LORD; *in the ~ 1963*; *in the ~ 1*, lit., & = very long ago; *from*

~ to ~, *~ by ~*, as *~s* go by, each *~*; *~ in ~ out*, right through the *~*, continuously). **3.** Period of the same length as a civil *~* commencing at any day (*Christian, Church, ecclesiastical, ~*; round of sacred seasons reckoned from & to Advent; *the fiscal ~*, reckoned from 1st April for taxing purposes; *the school ~*, *~*'s school terms usu. reckoned from beginning of autumn term; *a ~ & a day*, period specified in some legal matters; *was away for two ~s*; *it is ~s since we met*). **4.** pl. Age, time of life, (*young for his ~s*, bearing age lightly; *in ~s*, old). **5.** *~-book*, annual publication bringing information on some subject up to date; *~-long*, lasting a *~*. [OE *gēar*, OS, OHG *jār*, ON *ár*, Goth. *jēr* f. Gmc *jæram*, cogn. w. Gk *hōros* year, *hōra* season]

year'ling, n. & a. **1.** Animal more than one & less than two years old; (racing) colt a year old dating from 1st Jan. of year of foaling. **2.** adj. A year old, having existed or been so-&-so for a year, (*~ heifer, bride*). [-LING[1]]

year'lў, a. & adv. (Occurring etc.) once a year or every year or by or for the year, annual(ly). [OE; -LY[1, 2]]

yearn (yĕrn), v.i. & (impers., arch.) t. Be filled with longing or compassion or tenderness (*for* or *after* rest, home, affection, etc.; *to do*; *towards* or *to* person etc.), whence *~*'**ING**[1] n., *~*'**ING**[2] a., *~*'**ingLY**[2] adv.; ‖ *it~s me*, arch., I*~* or am troubled. [OE *giernan*, OS *girnean*, ON *girna*, Goth. *gairnjan*]

yeast, n. Yellowish frothy viscous substance consisting of fungous cells developed by germination in contact with saccharine liquids & producing alcoholic fermentation, used in brewing beer, making wine, distilling spirit, & raising bread etc.; *~-powder*, substitute for *~* used in bread-making. [OE *gist*, MDu. *ghist*, MHG *jest*, OHG *jast*, f. Gmc *jes-* boil, ferment, cogn. w. Gk *zeō* boil]

yeast'|ў, a. Frothy like yeast (*~y waves* etc.); in a ferment, working like yeast, (*a ~y conscience, turmoil, imaginings*); wordy, superficial, (*a ~y fellow*; *~y talk, professions*). Hence *~*iNESS n. [-Y[2]]

***yĕgg**, n. (sl.). (Also *~'man*) travelling burglar or safe-breaker. [said to be a surname]

yelk. See YOLK.

yĕll, v.i. & t., & n. (Make, utter with) shrill cry of pain or anger or fright, high-pitched shout, or uncontrollable burst of laughter (*~ed with pain, fury, delight, laughter*; *~ out an oath, orders*; *~ed curses, my name*, a refusal, defiance; *with ~s of horror* etc.); (U.S. Univv.) organized cry used by students e.g. in encouraging their representatives in athletic contests. [OE, OHG *gellan*, ON *gjalla*, rel. to *galan* (cf. NIGHTINGALE)]

yĕll'ow (-ō), a. (*~er, ~est*) & n., & v.t. & i. **1.** Of the colour between green & orange in the spectrum, coloured like buttercup or primrose or lemon or sulphur or gold, (with many names of plants, animals, etc., as ~ rattle, wagtail, ochre, jaundice; often also in comb. with parts of body etc., as ~-bill, -head, -legs, -root, -rump, -seed, -shank, -tail, -throat, -top, -wood, forming animal & plant names; ‖ ~ boy, obs. sl., gold coin; ~ cartilage, elastic kind forming artery-walls etc.; ~ fever, or Jack, tropical fever with jaundice & black vomit; ~ jacket, state garment in China for royal persons & subjects selected for high honour; the SERE & ~ leaf; ~ men, races, etc., Chinese, Japanese, Mongols, etc.; ~ metal, brass of 60 parts copper & 40 parts zinc; the ~ peril, the danger that the ~ races may overwhelm the white or overrun the world; the ~ press, sensational newspapers esp. of chauvinistic tendencies, orig. of U.S. newspapers urging war with Spain 1898; ~ spot, point of acutest vision in retina. 2. (fig.). (Of looks, mood, feelings, etc.) jealous, envious, suspicious; (colloq.) cowardly. 3. ‖ ~back, cheap novel in ~ paper boards common in 19th c., also French novel in ~ paper cover; ~-gum, infants' black jaundice; ~-(h)ammer, bunting with ~ head & neck & breast [hammer prob. not a corruption, but of separate orig.]; hence ~ISH¹(2) (-ŏī-), ~Y² (-ŏī), aa., ~NESS (-ŏn-) n. 4. n. ~ colour; kinds of ~ pigment; (colloq.) cowardice; kinds of moth & butterfly; the~s, jaundice, (arch.) jealousy, * a peach-disease. 5. vb. Turn ~ (paper ~ed with age; the ~ing leaves). [OE geolu, OS, OHG gelo, f. Gmc *gelwaz, cf. GOLD]

yelp, v.i. & n. (Utter) cry (as) of dog in pain or in eager anticipation. [f. OE gielpan = MDu. gelfen f. Gmc *galpjan]

yen¹, n. (pl. yen). Japanese monetary unit. [Jap., f. Chin. yüan round, dollar]

*yen², n., & v.i. (sl.). 1. Longing, yearning. 2. v.i. Yearn. [Chin., ~ craving as for opium]

yeo'man (yō-), n. (pl. -men). 1. (hist.). Person qualified by possessing free land of 40/- annual value to serve on juries, vote for knight of shire, etc. 2. ‖ Small landowner, farmer, person of middle class engaged in agriculture; ‖ member of the yeomanry force. 3. (nav.). ‖ ~ of signals, petty officer in branch concerned with visual signalling; *petty officer performing clerical duties on board ship. 4. ~('s) service, help in need; ~ of the guard, BEEFeater. Hence ~LY¹ a. [ME yoman, yeman, prob. = YOUNG+MAN]

yeo'manry (yō-), n. Yeomen; ‖ volunteer cavalry force raised from farmers etc. [-RY]

-yer, suf. var. of -IER, esp. after w, as bowyer, lawyer, sawyer.

yer'cum. See MUDAR. [Tamil]

yes, particle equivalent to affirmative sentence, & n. (pl. ~es). 1. The answer to

your question is affirmative, it is as you say or as I have said, your request or command will be complied with, the statement made or course intended is correct or satisfactory; (~ &, ~ or, forms for substituting stronger phr., as I could endure, ~, & enjoy it; he would beat me, ~, and you too; ~?, indeed?, is that so?); (in answer to summons or address) I am here, I hear or am attending to you, (~?, what more have you to say?). 2. n. The word or answer ~ (say ~, consent; confine yourself to ~ & no or ~es & noes); ~-man (colloq.), characterless, obedient, weakly acquiescent person. [OE gēse, gīse, prob. f. gēa YEA+sī 3 sing. pres. subj. of bēon BE]

yes'ter- in comb. (1) in ~day n. & adv., (on) the day before today (he arrived ~day; is but of ~day, of recent origin; the day before ~day, n. & adv.; often attrib. as ~day morning); (2) chiefly poet. with sense of ~day, in compds serving as nn. & advv. for which ordinary usage prefers ~day — or last —; so ~morn(ing) (usu. ~day morning), ~eve, ~even(ing), (Sc.) yestreen', (usu. ~day evening), ~night (usu. last night); (3) poet. w. sense last past in ~-year n. & adv. (usu: last year). [OE geostran,gystran dæg(cf. Goth.gistradagis); cf. (without ' day ') MDu. gisteren, OHG gestaron]

yet, adv. & conj. 1. As late as now or then, with continuance to this or to that time, still, (there is ~ time; is he ~ alive? there is life in the old dog ~; much ~ remains to be done; there is one ~ missing; his hands were ~ red with blood; his ~ unfinished task; I seem to see him ~; while it was ~ morning). 2. (With neg. context) so soon as now or then, by this or by that time, so far, in the immediate future, (it is not time ~; is he dead ~? they have not ~ heard; I have never ~ lied; the largest ~ found; haven't you learnt ~ that fire burns? need you go ~? it will not happen just ~; these things are not ~). 3. Again, in addition, (~ once more or ~ once; another & ~ another; ~ again; more & ~ more); (with nor) either (won't listen to me nor~ to her). 4. Before the matter is done with, before all is over, in the time that still remains, (he will win, I will be even with you, ~). 5. (With compar.) even (a ~more difficult, easier, task). 6. Nevertheless, and in spite of that, but for all that, (though they curse, ~ bless thou; &, having nothing, ~ hath all; it is strange, & ~ it is true; strange & ~ true; the logic seems sound, but ~ it does not convince me). 7. As ~, up to now or then (esp. w. suggestion that the statement would not be true of later time; it has worked well as ~; a conscience as ~ clear). 8. conj. But at the same time, & ~, (~ what is the use of it all?; faint ~ pursuing; a rough ~ ready helper). [OE giet(a), ~ OFris. ieta, of unkn. orig.]

yet′i (yă-), n. Native (Sherpa) name for the *Abominable* SNOWman.

yew, n. (Wood of) kinds of slow-growing dark-leaved evergreen tree (also ~*-tree*) often planted in graveyards & used formerly for making bows & still in cabinet--making. [OE *īw*, *ēow*, OS *īh*, OHG *īw*, *īwa* (G *eibe*), f. Gmc *ihw-*, *igw-*]

Yg(g)′drasil (ĭg-), n. (Scand. myth.). Tree whose roots & branches bind together heaven & earth & hell. [ON *yg(g)drasill* app. f. *Yggr* name of Odin + *drasill* horse]

Yid, n. (sl., contempt.). Jew. [back form. f. foll.]

Yidd′ish, a. & n. (In) a form of old German (with words borrowed from many modern languages) spoken by Jews in or from central and eastern Europe. [f. G *jüdisch* Jewish]

yield, v.t. & i., & n. 1. Produce or give or bring as fruit or result (*earth ~s her increase*; *land ~s good crops*; *investment ~s 5%*; *tax ~s a handsome revenue, little*; *sin ~s bitter fruit*); (abs., of land etc.) repay cultivation etc. *well, poorly*, etc. 2. Give up, deliver over, surrender (trans.), resign (trans.), comply with demand for, concede, (~ *fortress* etc.; ~ one*self prisoner*; ~ *possession*, one's *pride of place*; ~ *precedence to*; ~ *the palm*, be surpassed; ~ *submission, consent*, submit, consent; ~ *up the ghost*, die; ~ *the point*, concede it in argument); surrender (intr.), make submission *to*, give consent or change one's course in deference *to*, comply with demand (whence ~*ING³* a., ~*′ingly²* adv.), be inferior or confess inferiority *to*, (*town ~ed without awaiting assault*; ~ *to superior force, persuasion*; *courage never to submit or ~*; *I ~ to none in appreciation of his merits*). 3. n. Amount ~ed or produced, output, return. [OE *gieldan*, OS *geldan*, OHG *geltan*, ON *gjalda*, Goth. *-gildan*, f. Gmc *geldhan*]

-yl, suf. (chem.) used to form wds denoting a RADICAL, as *amyl, ethyl*, f. F *-yle* f. Gk *hulē* wood, substance.

yl′äng-yl′äng (ēl⁴, -ēl⁴), n. Malayan tree from the flowers of which a perfume is distilled; the perfume itself. [Tagalog *dlang-ilang*]

yŏd′el, v.t. & i. (-ll-), & n. 1. Sing (t. & i.), make melodious inarticulate sounds, with frequent changes between falsetto & normal voice in the manner of Swiss & Tyrolese mountaineers. 2. n. ~ling cry, match of ~ling. [f. G dial. *jodeln*]

yŏg′a, n. Hindu system of philosophic meditation & asceticism designed to effect the reunion of the devotee's soul with the universal spirit. [Hind. f. Skr., = union]

yogh (yŏχ), n. The Middle-English letter ȝ used for certain values of g & y. [prob. f. ME *ȝoc* yoke, as beginning with the sound]

yog(h)urt (yŏg′oort), n. Var. of YAOURT.

yōg′i (-gī), n. Devotee of yoga. Hence **yōg′ism(3)** (-g-) n. [Hind. (YOGA)]

yō′heave-hō′, yohō′, intt. used by sailors in heaving together.

yoicks, int. & n., **yoick**, v.i. & t. Fox-hunter's halloo; (vb) cry yoicks, urge (hounds) *on* etc. with it. [orig. unkn.; also *hoicks, hoik, hyke*]

yōke, n., & v.t. & i. 1. Wooden cross-piece fastened over necks of two oxen etc. & attached to the plough or waggon that they are to (help to) draw; (Rom. hist.) uplifted ~ or arch of three spears symbolizing it under which defeated enemy was made to march (*send, pass* intr., *under the ~*); (fig.) sway or dominion or servitude (*submitted to his ~*; *the heavy ~ of opinion*; *had never endured the ~*); (fig.) bond of union esp. the marriage tie. 2. Pair of oxen etc. (‖ ~ *of land*, arch., as much as one ~ of oxen can plough in a day). 3. Piece of timber shaped to fit person's shoulders & support pail etc. at each end. 4. Separately made shoulder--piece of shirt or coat or blouse, or waist--piece of skirt, from which the rest is suspended. 5. Cross-bar on which bell swings; cross-bar of rudder to whose ends ropes are fastened; coupling-piece of two pipes discharging into one; kinds of coupling or controlling piece in machinery. 6. ~*bone*, cheek-bone connecting bones of head & face; ~*fellow*, ~*mate*, partner in marriage, work, etc.; ~*lines*, *-ropes*, with which rudder~ is worked. 7. vb. Put ~ upon; couple or unite (esp. pair) in marriage or otherwise, link (one to another); (intr.) match or work together (*together, with*, or abs.; *do not ~ well*). [OE *geoc*, OHG *joh*, OS, Goth. *juk*, ON *ok*, cogn. w. L *jugum*]

yōk′el, n. Rustic, country bumpkin. [orig. obsc.]

yolk (yōk), (now rare) **yĕlk**, n. Yellow part of egg; sebaceous secretion from skin of sheep, wool-oil; ~*bag, -sac*, membrane enclosing ~ of egg. Hence (-)~ED² (yōkt), ~Y² (yōk′ĭ), aa. [OE *geolca* (YELLOW)]

yŏn, a., adv., & pron. 1. Yonder (a. & adv.; arch. or poet. or provincial). 2. pron. (arch. etc.). Yonder person or thing. [OE *geon*, OHG *jener*, ON *enn*, Goth. *jains*]

yŏn′der, a. & adv. (Situated) over there, in the direction towards which I am looking or pointing, within or conceived as within view but distant. [ME, cf. OS *gendra*, Goth. *jaindrē*]

yōre, n. Old times (now only in *of ~*, formerly, in or of old days). [OE *gēara*, of obsc. orig.]

Yŏrk¹, n. ~ *& Lancaster*, rival royal houses & parties in the Wars of the Roses (~*-&-Lancaster rose*, parti-coloured kind); *House of ~*, kings Edw. IV-Rich. III; ~ *stone*, kind used in building.

yŏrk², v.t. Bowl with yorker. [back form.]

yŏrk'er, n. Ball so bowled as to pitch immediately in front of batsman's block (also *tice*). [prob. f. *York*, as introduced in Yorkshire, -ER¹]

Yŏrk'ist, a. & n. (Adherent) of family descended from Edmund Duke of York son of Edward III, or of the White-rose party fighting for it in Wars of the Roses. [-IST]

Yŏrk'shire (-er), n. County (~ *flannel*, undyed; ~ *grit*, stone used in polishing marble; ~ *pudding*, batter baked under & eaten with meat esp. beef; ~ *stone*, kind used in building; ~ *terrier*, small shaggy toy kind).

you (ū *or* yŏŏ *acc. to emphasis*), 2nd pers. pron. sing. (w. pl. vb) & pl. (arch. etc. subj. pl. YE; arch. etc. sing. THOU, *thee*; possess. YOUR, YOURS). **1.** The person(s) or thing(s) addressed (~ *are mad, an angel, all fools*; *who sent* ~?; *I choose* ~ *three*; *the rest of* ~ *can stay here*; ~ & *I or me*; ~'*re another*, vulg., retort to one who calls names; occas. expressed w. imperat., as *don't* ~ *go away*, *begin* ~ *or* ~ *begin*; as voc. w. n. in apposition = exclamatory statement, as ~ *fool!*, ~ *darling!*, occas. w. ~ appended also, as ~ *idiot* ~ *!*; as voc. calling attention, as ~ *there, what is your name?*). **2.** (arch.). Yourself (*get* ~ *gone*, begone; ~ *should find* ~ *a wife*; *sit* ~ *down*). **3.** (In general statements) one, any one, all concerned, every one, a person, (~ *never can tell*; *what are* ~ *to do with a child like this?*; *it is bad at first, but* ~ *soon get used to it*; *there's a shot for* ~ *!*). [OE *ēow* acc. & dat. of *gē* YE, supplanting *ye* f. more frequent use of obj. case, & *thou* & *thee* (cf. similar substitutes in F, G, It.) as more courteous form]

young (yŭ-), a. (~*er*, ~*est*, pr. -ngg-), & n. (only in collect. sing). **1.** Not far advanced in life or growth or development, of recent birth or origin or formation, not yet old, still vigorous, immature, youthful, inexperienced, (*a* ~ *child, man, animal, plant, nation, institution*; *a* ~ *family*, of ~ *children*; *a* ~ *person*, servants' phr. for unknown ~ woman of lower classes; *the* ~ *person*, those whose innocence must be shielded from the indecent in talk & literature; ~ *people*, esp. the marriageable; *my* etc. ~ *man or woman*, sweetheart; *the night, year, century, is yet* ~, still near its beginning; OLD *head on* ~ *shoulders*; ~ & OLD; *you* ~ *rascal* etc., usu. in playful address to child; *a* ~ *man in a hurry*, esp. ardent reformer; ~ *for his* YEARS; *men are now* ~ *at fifty*; *an old man but a* ~ *convert*; ~ BLOOD¹; ~*er son*, esp. member of noble family poor owing to primogeniture; ~ *things*, often indulgently etc. of persons; *is* ~ *in crime*, unpractised; ~ *Jones*, esp. Jones the son; ~ '*un*, youngster, often as voc.; *in my* ~ *days*, while I was ~; ~ *love, ambition*, etc., felt in or characteristic of youth; *the* ~*er* before or after name of person to be distinguished from another, as *the* ~*er Pitt, Teniers the* ~*er*; so *the* ~ PRETENDER; ~ *England, Ireland, Italy*, etc., especially as names of political parties claiming to speak for the rising generation; *Y*~ *Turks*, esp. the party that in 1908 forced the Sultan to restore the constitution; ~*ers* occas. as n. pl. opp. *elders*, as *is kind to his* ~*ers*). Hence ~'ISH¹(2) a., ~'LING¹ n. (poet.). **2.** n. Offspring esp. of animals before or soon after birth (*with* ~, pregnant; *cares for, deserts, its* ~). [OE *geong*, OS *jung*, OHG *junc*, ON *ungr*, Goth. *juggs*, f. Gmc *ju(wu)ngaz*, cogn. w. L *juvencus, juvenis*]

you'nger (yŭ-), n. Child, esp. active or lively boy. [-STER]

you'nker (yŭ-), n. Youngster (arch. or colloq.); = JUNKER. [f. MDu. *jonckher* (*jonc* young, *hēre* lord)]

your (ūr, yŏr, yer, *acc. to emphasis*), attrib. a. Of, belonging to, spoken of by, done to or by, you (~ *danger, hat, expectations*; *so this is* ~ *immaculate saint!*; ~ *dismissal of him, by him*; ~ *father* & *mine*; ~ & *my father, fathers*; cf. foll.); (colloq. & chiefly arch., now usu. w. depreciatory implication) much talked of, well known, familiar, (*no one so fallible as* ~ *expert in handwriting*; ~ *facetious bore is the worst of all*). [(1) OE *ēower* gen. pl. of *gē* YE; (2) OE *ēower, -ru, -er* possess. adj.]

yours (ūrz, yŏrz), pron. & pred. a. **1.** The one(s) belonging to or of you (*my father* & ~; ~ & *my father*, erron. for *your* &; *my father is not* ~; *I like* ~ *better*; ~ *is the only way*; *am no child of* ~; *that cough of* ~; *some friends of* ~; *you* & ~, you & your family, property, etc.; ~ *is to hand, your letter has come*; so ~ *of the 11th* etc.). **2.** adj. Belonging to you, at your service, (*it is* ~ *if you will accept it*; *ever* ~, ~ *truly*, FAITHFULLY, OBEDIENTLY, etc., epistolary formulae preceding signature; ~ *truly*, joc., I, as *but* ~ *truly was not taking any*, I refused etc.); *what's* ~? (colloq.), what will you drink? [prec., -ES, see OURS]

yourse'lf' (ūr- etc., as in YOUR), pron. (pl. -*ves*). (Emphat.) you in person, in particular, in your normal state, & not another or others, or alone (usu. in apposition w. *you* except in commands, & either next after it or later, rarely substituted for it; *please see to it* ~ *or yourselves*; *you* ~ *said so* *or you said so* ~; ~ *have said it*, arch., poet., etc.; *by* ~, alone, as *why are you sitting by* ~?, also unaided, as *you cannot do it by yourselves*; *it is* ~ *I want, not your money*; *how's* ~?, sl., how are you?, esp. after answering similar inquiry; *be* ~, colloq., pull ~ *together*; *you are not quite* ~ *tonight*, are out of humour etc.); (refl.) the person(s) previously described as *you*, or to whom a command is addressed (*have you hurt* ~?; *you seemed pleased with yourselves*; *ask* ~ *whether it is not true*). [YOUR, SELF]

youth (ūth), n. (*pl. pr.* ūdhz). Being young, adolescence, (the vigour or enthusiasm or weakness or inexperience or other characteristic of) the period between childhood & full manhood or womanhood, (*has all the appearance of extreme* ~; *in my hot, raw, vigorous*, etc. ~; *from* ~ *onwards*; ~'s *a stuff will not endure*; *the secret of perpetual, of keeping one's*, ~; *the* ~ *of the world*, early times), whence ~'FUL (ūth-) a., ~'FULLY[2] adv., ~'FULNESS n.; young man (*as a* ~ *of 20*; *promising, lanky*, etc., ~s); young men & women (*the* ~ *of the country*; *loves to be surrounded by* ~; *our* ~ *are infected with commerciality*); ~ *centre, club*, place or organization provided for leisure-time activities of young people; ~ *hostel*, place where hikers etc. can put up for the night. [OE *geoguth*, OS *juguth*, OHG *jugund*, f. WG **jugunthi-* f. **juwunthi-* (YOUNG, -TH[1])]

yowl. Var. of YAWL[1].

ytterb'|ium, n. (chem.). Rare-earth metallic element. Hence ~IC a. [*Ytterby* in Sweden, -IUM]

ytt'r|ium, n. (chem.). Rare-earth metallic element. Hence ~IC, ~IOUS, aa., ~o- comb. form. [as prec.]

yucc'a, n. Kinds of American white-flowered liliaceous plant. [Carib]

Yugoslav. See JUGOSLAV.

yule (ūl), n. The Christmas festival (also ~-*tide*; ~-*log*, burnt on Christmas Eve). [OE *geol(a)*, cf. ON *jól*, ult. orig. obsc.]

Z

Z (zĕd; *zē), letter (pl. Zs, Z's, *zeds*); (Alg.; *z*) third unknown quantity (cf. C, X).

Zăd'kiĕl, n. (Used for) a popular astrological almanac founded by R. J. Morrison (d. 1874), who adopted this pseudonym.

zăf'fre (-er), **zăff'er**, n. Impure oxide of cobalt used in making cobalt-blue & as blue pigment in enamelling & porcelain-painting. [f. It. *zaffera* or F *zafre*, f. Arab. *sofre*]

Zăm'bō. Var. of SAMBO (in first sense).

zăn'y̆, n. (Hist.) attendant clown awkwardly mimicking chief clown in shows, merry andrew; (mod.) person given to buffoonery, foolish jester, half-witted person. [f. F *zani*, or It. *zan(n)i*, Venetian form of *Gianni, Giovanni* John]

Zănzibăr'ĭ, n. & a. (Native) of Zanzibar.

zăp'tieh (-ā), n. Turkish policeman. [f. Turk. *ḍabtiyeh* f. Arab. *ḍabt* administration]

Zarathustr-. See ZOROASTRIAN.

zari'ba (-rē-), **-rēb'a**, n. Hedged or palisaded enclosure for protection of camp or village in the Sudan etc. [f. Arab. *zarība* pen]

zax. Var. of SAX.

zeal, n. Earnestness or fervour in advancing a cause or rendering service, hearty & persistent endeavour. So ~'OUS (zĕl-) a., ~'OUSLY[2] adv. [ME *zele* f. LL f. Gk *zēlos*]

zeal'ot (zĕl-), n. Uncompromising or extreme partisan, fanatic, (Z~, one of a Jewish sect resisting the Romans A.D. 6-70). Hence ~RY(4) n. [f. eccl. L f. Gk *zēlōtēs* (prec., -OT[2])]

zebec(k). Var. of XEBEC.

zĕb'ra, n. Kinds of striped quadruped (true or mountain ~, Burchell's ~, quagga) allied to ass or horse; (attrib., & in comb. w. names of animals etc.) striped like ~ (~ *markings*, ~ *caterpillar*, ~ *woodpecker*, ~-*wood*, etc.); ~ *crossing*, striped street-crossing where pedestrians have precedence over other traffic. Hence **zĕb'rINE**[1] a. [It. or Pg., f. Congolese]

zĕb'ū, n. The E.-Ind. humped ox. [F *zébu*]

zĕd, n. Letter Z. [f. F *zède* f. L f. Gk *zēta*]

zĕd'oary̆, n. Kinds (*long, round*, ~) of aromatic gingerlike substance made from rootstock of E.-Ind. plants & used in medicine, perfumery, & dyeing. [f. med. L *zedoarium* f. Arab. *zedwār*]

zeit'geist (tsītgī-), n. Spirit of the times, drift of thought & feeling in a period. [G]

zĕlōs'ō, mus. direction. With fervour. [It.]

zĕmin'dăr, n. (Anglo-Ind.). (Hist.) district governor & revenue-farmer under Mogul empire; (later) Indian landed proprietor paying land-tax to British government. [Hind., f. Pers. *zamīndār* (*zamīn* earth, *dār* holder)]

zĕmst'vŏ, n. (hist.; pl. ~s). Local elective assembly regulating affairs of district in Russia. [Russ., f. *zemlya* land]

zĕna'na (-ah-), n. Part of house in which women of high-caste families are secluded in India (~ *mission*, of women visiting ~s to spread medical & other reform among inmates); ~ (*cloth*), a light fabric for women's dresses. [Hind., f. Pers. *zanāna* (*zan* woman)]

Zĕnd, n. Ancient language of the Iranian family, allied to Sanskrit, named from the Zend-Avesta (Avesta or text & Zend or commentary) or Zoroastrian scriptures.

zĕn'ith (or zēn-), n. Point of heavens directly above observer (opp. NADIR); (transf.) highest point, time or place of greatest power or prosperity or happiness (*is at his, its, the*, ~); ~-*distance*, arc intercepted between any body & ~, complement of body's altitude. Hence ~AL a. [ME, f. OF *cenit(h)* or med. L *cenit* f. Arab. *samt* (*ar-rās*) way (over the head)]

zĕ'olite, n. Any one of a number of minerals consisting mainly of hydrous silicates of lime, soda, & alumina, commonly found in the cavities of igneous rocks. [f. Gk *zeō* boil + -LITE; from their characteristic swelling & fusing before the blowpipe]

zĕph'yr (-er), n. **1.** The west wind personified (Z~); balmy breeze, light wind.

2. Athlete's thin gauzy jersey for running, rowing, boxing, etc. in; kinds of dress-material. [f. L f. Gk *zephuros* west wind]

Zĕpp'elĭn, n. (colloq. *Zĕpp*). Large dirigible airship of type built (*c.* 1900), orig. for military use in Germany. [Count ~, inventor]

zēr'ō, n. (pl. ~*s*). Figure 0, cipher; no quantity or number, nil; starting-point in scales from which positive & negative quantity is reckoned (~ in thermometers, freezing-point of water or other point selected to reckon from; *absolute* ~ in temperature, point at which the particles whose motion constitutes heat would be at rest, estimated at −273.16° C.); (mil.) point of time from which the start of each movement in a timed programme is at a specified interval; lowest point, bottom of scale, nullity, nadir; *fly at* ~ (under 1,000 ft). [f. F *zéro* or It. *zero* f. Arab. *çifr* CIPHER]

zĕst, n. Piquancy, stimulating flavour, (esp. fig.; *adds a* ~ *to*); keen enjoyment or interest, relish, gusto, (*entered into it with* ~). [17th c., f. F *zeste* orange or lemon peel, of unkn. orig.]

zēt'a, n. Greek letter (*Z*, *ζ*) = z. [Gk (*zē-*)]

zětĕt'ic, a. (rare). Proceeding by inquiry. [f. Gk *zētētikos* (*zēteō* seek, -IC)]

zeug'ma, n. (gram.). Figure of speech in which a verb or adjective does duty with two nouns to one of which it is strictly applicable while the word appropriate to the other is not used (e.g. *kill the boys & sc.* destroy *the luggage, with weeping eyes & sc.* grieving *hearts*; cf. SYLLEPSIS). Hence **zeugmăt'ic** a. [L f. Gk (genit. *-atos*), f. *zeugnumi* yoke]

Zeus, n. (Gk ant.). King of the Olympian gods. [Gk]

zib'ĕt, n. The Asian or Indian civet. [f. med. L *zibethum* as CIVET]

zĭg'zăg, a., n., adv., & v.i. (-gg-). **1.** With abrupt alternate right & left turns, with alternating salient & re-entrant angles, with motion as of tacking ship, (*a* ~ *line, course, road, fence, trench, flash of lightning*). **2.** n. ~ line or (esp. for mounting steep hill) road or (in sieges) set of trenches. **3.** adv. With ~ course. **4.** v.i. Go ~. [F, f. G *zickzack*]

zĭll'ah (-*a*), n. Administrative district in India. [Hind. *zilah* f. Arab. *ḍilah*]

zĭnc, n., & v.t. **1.** A white metallic element much used in the arts esp. as component of brass & German silver, as roofing material, as coating for sheet iron (cf. GALVANIZE), in electric batteries, & in relief-printing blocks (*flowers of* ~ or ~ *oxide*, powder used as white pigment & in kinds of ointment & cement); hence (spelt, before -i-, with -c- or -k- or -ck-) ~'IC, ~'IF'EROUS, ~'OID, aa., ~'IFY v.t.; ~IFICA'TION n., ~'OUS (esp. of negative pole of voltaic battery), **zĭnk'Y²**, aa.,

~o- comb. form. **2.** v.t. (-*k*- or -*ck*-). Coat with ~. [f. G *zink*, of obsc. orig.]

zĭnc'ō, n. (pl. ~*s*), & vb. = ZINCOGRAPH. [abbr.]

zĭnc'|ŏgraph (-ahf), n., & v.i. & t. **1.** Zinc plate with design etched in relief on it for printing from, picture taken from it. **2.** vb. Etch (t. & i.) on zinc, reproduce (design) thus. So ~ŏG'RAPHY, ~ŏG'RAPHER nn., ~ŏGRAPH'IC a. [ZINCO-, -GRAPH]

zĭnc'ŏtȳpe, n. = prec. n. [as prec., TYPE]

Zĭng'arō (-ngg-), n. (pl. *-rī*). Gipsy. [It.]

zĭnn'ĭa, n. Kinds of composite plant with showy rayed flowers of deep red & other colours. [J. G. *Zinn* German botanist (d. 1759), -IA¹]

Zī'on, n. (Holy hill of) ancient Jerusalem; the Hebrew theocracy; the Christian Church; the Heavenly Jerusalem or kingdom of heaven, whence ~WARDS adv.; ‖ (name for) nonconformist chapel. [f. eccl. L *Sion* f. Heb. *Tsiyōn* orig. hill]

Zī'onǐsm, n. A movement resulting in the re-establishment of a Jewish nation in Palestine. So ~IST. [-ISM(3)]

zǐp, n. Light sharp sound, as of bullet passing through air, the sudden tearing of cloth, etc.; (fig.) energy, ' pep '; ~-*fastener*, (also *zipp'er*) fastening device consisting of two flexible stringers operated by means of the constriction of a sliding clip pulled between them. [imit.]

zǐr'con, n. A silicate of zirconium of which some varieties (HYACINTH, JARGON²) are cut into gems. [f. F *zircone* f. Arab. *zarqūn*]

zǐrcōn'ium, n. A metallic element found chiefly in zircon & used to alloy iron. Hence **zǐrcŏn'ic** a., **zǐrc'ŏnATE¹(3)** n. [-IUM]

zĭth'er|(n), n. Simple flat many-stringed instrument placed on table or knees & played partly with fingers of left hand & partly with plectrum in right hand. Hence ~IST(1) n. [G (as CITHER)]

zlŏt'ȳ, n. Polish coin. [Pol.]

Zō'ar, n. Place of refuge, sanctuary. [*Gen.* xix]

zōd'iac, n. A belt of the heavens limited by lines about 8° from the ecliptic on each side, including all apparent positions of the sun & planets as known to the ancients, & divided into 12 equal parts called *signs of the* ~ (Aries, Taurus, Gemini, Cancer, Leo, Virgo, Libra, Scorpio, Sagittarius, Capricorn(us), Aquarius, Pisces) each formerly containing the similarly named *zodiacal constellation* but now by precession of equinoxes coinciding with the constellation that bears the name of the preceding sign (e.g. the constellations Pisces, Aries, are now in the signs Aries, Taurus), (transf., now rare) complete course, circuit, or compass. [ME, f. OF *zodiaque* f. L f. late Gk *zōdiakos* f. *zō(i)dion* dim. of *zō(i)on* animal]

zodī'acal, a. Of, in, the zodiac (~ *light*, luminous tract of sky shaped like tall triangle occas. seen in east before sunrise or in west after sunset esp. in tropics). [f. LL *zodiacus* adj. (as prec.) + -AL]

zo'ĕtrŏpe, n. WHEEL¹ of life. [irreg. f. Gk *zōē* life, *tropos* turn]

zŏ'hăr, n. A cabalistic textbook prob. of 14th c. called Bible of the Mystics. [Heb., = brightness]

zŏ'ic, a. Of animals; (geol., of rocks etc.) containing fossils, with traces of animal or plant life. [f. Gk *zōikos* (*zōon* see ZODIAC, -IC)]

Zŏl'a|ism, n. Absence of reserve, detailed realism, in describing the gross or immoral. So ~IST(2) n., ~ESQUE' (-ĕsk), ~is'tic, aa. [*Zola*, French novelist d. 1902, -ISM]

zollverein (tsŏl'fĕrīn), n. Union of States having a common customs-tariff against outsiders & usu. free trade with each other. [G]

zŏm'bi(e), n. A corpse said to be revived by witchcraft. [orig. unkn.]

zōne, n., & v.t. 1. Belt or girdle worn round the body (chiefly arch. & poet.; *maiden* or *virgin* ~, symbol of virginity; *loose the maiden* ~ *of*, deprive of virginity). 2. Encircling band or stripe distinguishable in colour or texture or character from the rest of the object encircled. 3. (Geog.) any of five divisions of the earth bounded by circles parallel to the equator (*frigid* ~s, N. of arctic, S. of antarctic, circle; *torrid* ~, between the tropics; *North*, *South*, *temperate* ~, between frigid & torrid ~s); area enclosed between two exact or approximate concentric circles; part of surface of sphere enclosed between two parallel planes, or of cone or cylinder between such planes cutting it perpendicularly to axis; any well-defined tract of more or less beltlike form; ~ *time*, local time for any longitude as opposed to Greenwich time; hence zōn'AL, zōn'ARY¹, zōn'ŪlAR¹ [-UL-], zōn'ATE² (bot., zool.), aa., zōn'alLY² adv. 4. v.t. Encircle as or with ~; arrange or distribute by ~s. [F, or f. L f. Gk *zōnē* girdle (*zōnnumi* gird)]

Zōō, n. (colloq.). Zoological garden, esp. that in London. [abbr.]

zōo-, comb. form of Gk *zōos* living, *zōon* an animal (see ZODIAC), = of animals, of animal life, (occas. as opp. vegetables & minerals, occas. excluding man also or especially); *zōōg'amy*, sexual reproduction; ~*geŏg'raphy*, zoology dealing with local distribution of animals, so ~*geŏg'rapher*, ~*geograph'ic(al)*; *zōōg'raphy*, descriptive zoology, so *zōōg'rapher*, ~*graph'ic(al)*, *zōōg'raphist*; *zōōl'atry*, religious worship of animals; *zō'olite*, fossil animal, fossilized animal substance; *zō'omancy*, divination from appearances or behaviour of animals; ~*morph'ic*, dealing with or represented under animal forms, having gods of beastlike form (cf. *anthropomorphic*), so ~*morph'ism*; *zō'o-*

phȳte, kinds of plantlike animal, esp. holothurians, starfishes, jelly-fishes, sea-anemones, & sponges, so ~*phȳt'ic*, ~*phȳtŏl'ogy*, ~*phȳtolo'gical*, ~*phȳtŏl'ogist*; *zō'osperm*, spermatozoon, also ~spore; *zō'ospore*, spore capable of motion, so ~*spŏ'ric*; *zōŏt'omy*, dissection or anatomy of animals other than man.

zŏ'oid, a. & n. 1. Of incompletely animal nature. 2. n. Organic body or cell resembling but not being animal or plant; more or less independent organism given by gemmation or fission; member of compound organism. [prec., -OID]

zōŏl'og|ў, n. Natural history of animals, science of their structure, physiology, classification, habits, & distribution. So zōōlo'GICAL a. (~*ical garden*, public garden or park with collection of animals kept for exhibition), zōōlo'gicalLY² adv., ~IST(3) n. [f. mod. L *zoologia* (ZOO-, -LOGY)]

zōōm, v.i., & n. 1. Force aeroplane to mount at high speed & steep angle. 2. n. Aeroplane's steep climb; ~ *lens* (cinemat. etc.), lens which by variation of focal length enables quick transmission from long shot to close-up. [imit.]

zŏ'ril, n. Carnivorous quadruped of Africa & Asia Minor allied to skunk & weasel. [f. F *zorille* f. Sp. *zorrilla* (*zorra* fox)]

Zŏrŏăs'trĭan, Zărathus'tr- (-thŏŏ-), nn. & aa. (Follower) of Zoroaster, Zarathustra, or Zerduscht, (adherent) of the religious system taught by him & his followers in the Zend-Avesta based on the conflict between Ormuzd god of light & good & Ahriman god of darkness & evil, the religion of the magi & ancient Persia still held by Parsees & occas. called *fire-worship*. Hence **Zŏrŏăs'trĭan**-ISM(3), **Zărathus'tr(ian)ism,** nn. [f. L f. Gk *Zoroastrēs* f. Zend *Zarathustra*, -IAN]

zouave (zŏŏ'ahv), n. 1. Member of French light-infantry corps orig. formed of Algerians & retaining Oriental uniform. 2. Woman's short jacket like that of ~ uniform. [name of tribe]

‖ **zounds** (-z), int. (arch.) of indignation. [= (*God*)*'s wounds* (i.e. Christ's on the cross)]

zucchĕtt'a, -ĕtt'ō, (tsŏŏk-), n. R.-C. ecclesiastic's skull-cap, black for priest, purple for bishop, red for cardinal, & white for Pope. [It. (-*a*), dim. of *zucca* gourd]

Zulu (zŏŏl'ŏŏ), n. Member, language, of a S.-Afr. Kaffir people. [native]

zwieback (tswĕb'ahk), n. Kind of biscuit rusk or sweet cake toasted in slices. [G]

Zwing'lian (tswĭngg-), a. & n. (Follower) of the Swiss religious reformer Zwingli (1484–1531). [-IAN]

zȳg'al, a. H-shaped (esp. of brain-fissures). [as foll., -AL]

zȳg(o)-, comb. form of Gk *zugon* yoke: *zygapŏph'ysis*, one of the processes on a vertebra serving as articulation with another; **zygodac'tyl** a. & n., **-ylous** a., (bird) with toes disposed in pairs, two toes pointing forward & two backward; **zygomorph'ous**, (of flower) divisible into similar halves only in one plane; **zyg'ospore**, spore formed by conjugation of two similar gametes.

zygōm'a, n. (pl. **~ta**). Bony arch of cheek, yoke-bone. Hence **zȳgōmăt'ıc** a. [f. Gk *zugōma* f. *zugon* yoke]

zȳgōs'ıs, n. (biol.). = CONJUGATION. [f. Gk *zugōsis* joining (prec.)]

zȳg'ōte, n. Product of the fusion of two gametes, e.g. zygospore. [f. Gk *zugoō* yoke (*zugon*)]

zymōs'ıs, n. Fermentation; zymotic disease in general or any form of it. [f. Gk *zumōsis* f. *zumoō* ferment f. *zumē* leaven, see -OSIS]

zymŏt'ıc, a. Of fermentation (~ *diseases*, epidemic, endemic, contagious, or sporadic diseases regarded as caused by multiplication of germs introduced from without). [f. Gk *zumōtikos* (prec., -OTIC)]

ADDENDA

NOTE

THESE addenda consist of (1) words not recorded in the body of the dictionary, and (2) further senses and constructions of words already treated. Additions of the latter kind, being arranged as appendages to existing articles, are readily distinguished by the absence of pronunciation, grammatical description, and etymology from the independent articles dealing with new words.

References to other entries in this Dictionary are in SMALL CAPITALS, preceded by ‡ for entries in these Addenda.

ăb'seil (-zīl), n., & v.i. **1.** Climber's method of letting himself down steep face with doubled rope. **2.** v.i. Use ~. [f. G *abseilen* (f. *ab* down, *seil* rope)]

acrȳl'ic, a. (Chem.). ~ *acid*, unsaturated organic acid, $C_2H_3.COOH$, from which synthetic substances are derived (~ *plastic, resin*, etc.); ~ *(fibre)*, wool-like synthetic fibre. [f. *acrolein* (f. L *acer -cris* pungent + *olēre* smell + -IN) + -YL + -IC]

ăc'ūpŭncture, n. (Med.). Puncture of tissues with needles as treatment for various conditions. [f. L *acu* with a needle + PUNCTURE]

addic'tive, a. Causing addiction & dependence. [f. ADDICT + -IVE]

aero-. ~*space*, earth's atmosphere & outer space.

ăfrŏrmōs'ia (-zĭa), n. African wood like teak, used for furniture. [f. AFRO- + mod. L *Ormosia* genus of trees]

age². Hence **age(e)ING** [1] (āj'ĭng), n., change of properties occurring in some metals after heat treatment or cold working.

air¹. ~*'space*, air above country etc., esp. considered as subject to its jurisdiction.

Al'gŏl, ALGOL, (ă-), n. Algebraic computer language. [f. ‡ALGO(RITHMIC) + L(ANGUAGE)]

ăl'gorĭthm (-dhm), n. **1.** = ALGORISM. **2.** Process or rules for (esp. machine-) calculation etc. Hence **ălgorĭth'mic** a.

ălmŭcăn'tar, -mac-, n. Line of constant altitude above the horizon. [f. F *almucantarat* f. Arab. (AL-², *qanṭarah* a bridge)]

ămphĕt'amine (*or* -ēn), n. Synthetic stimulant drug. [f. *alpha-methyl-phenethylamine*]

ăm'ȳtal, n. White crystalline powder used as sedative & hypnotic, esp. as sodium salt. [P]

anaemia. (Also) deficiency of red blood-corpuscles or their haemoglobin.

analogue. ~ (*analog) *computer*, one using physical quantities (voltage, weight, length, etc.) to represent numbers.

ăn'ti-freeze, n. Substance (usu. ethylene glycol) added to water to lower its freezing-point. [ANTI- (2)]

ăn'ti-mătter, n. Hypothetical matter composed solely of ‡ANTI-PARTICLES. [ANTI- (1)]

ăn'ti-pắrticle, n. Elementary particle of same mass as given particle but having opposite electric charge or differing in direction of its magnetic moment. [ANTI- (1)]

ắrcane', a. Mysterious, secret. [f. L *arcanus* (*arca* chest, see -ANE)]

arrĕs'table, a. ~ *disease*, that can be prevented from getting worse; ~ *offence* (Law), for which person can be arrested without a warrant. [f. OF (ARREST¹, -ABLE)]

articulate². ~*d lorry*, one made up of vehicles jointed together (abbr. ắrt'ic).

astro-. ~*naut*, (also) space traveller.

aud'io, a. Relating to (the reproduction of) sound. Also abs. as n. [f. foll.]

aud'io-, comb. form, f. L *audire* hear: ~*-typist*, one typing direct from tape or other recording; ~*-visual* a., making use of both hearing & sight.

back³. ~*'lash*, (also, fig.) after-effects; excessive or violent reaction, esp. against racial integration.

band¹. ~*'width* (Electr. etc.), range of frequencies.

băng'er, n. In vbl senses: (esp., sl.) noisy old car; (also, sl.) sausage. [-ER¹]

băr⁴, n. **1.** (Meteor.). Unit of barometric pressure equivalent to a pressure of 29·53 in. or 750·1 mm. of mercury at 0 °C in latitude 45°. **2.** (Chem.). Unit of pressure equivalent to one dyne per square centimetre. [f. Gk *baros* weight]

beat². (Also) strongly marked rhythm of jazz & popular music.

beat³, n. & a. (Also ~*'nĭk*) (one) of the ~ *generation*, young people adopting unconventional dress, manners, habits, etc., as a means of self-expression & social protest. [~*nik* after *sputnik*, perh. reinforced by U.S. use of Yiddish *-nik*]

beatific. (Also, colloq.) blissful.

black. ~ *box*, box containing electronic equipment, esp. one on aircraft recording details of flight; any complex apparatus of undisclosed structure.

blast². ~ *off* v.i., (of rocket etc.) take off; so ~-*off* n.

bleed. (Also, Print.) cut into printed area when trimming margin; be thus cut.

bŏn'gō² (-ngg-), n. (pl. *bongo(e)s*). One of pair of small drums played with fingers. Also ~ *drum*. [Amer. Sp. *bongó*]

boost. ~*er*, (also) auxiliary rocket used"to give initial acceleration; (Med.) dose increasing or renewing effect of earlier one.

bouclé (bŏŏk'lā), n. & a. **1.** Yarn of looped or curled ply; fabric of this. **2.** adj. Woven of such yarn; having looped or curled surface. [F]

boutique (bŏŏtēk'), n. Small shop or department selling ready-made fashionable clothes etc. [F]

box². ~-*spring* (*mattress*), mattress of vertical springs in cloth-covered frame.

break'-through (-āk-; -ōō), n. Act of breaking through obstacle, enemy's line, etc.; major advance in science etc.

breath'alȳser, *-ȳzer* (brĕ-; -zer), n. Instrument measuring amount of alcohol in breath. [f. BREATH + ANALYSE + -ER¹]

broil. ~*er house*, building for rearing ~*er* chickens in close confinement.

buffer¹. ~ *stock*, reserve of commodity used to offset price fluctuations.

bug. (Also, colloq.) concealed microphone; (v.t.) install ~ in, listen to by means of ~.

bŭtt'ȳ³, n. (Dial.) slice of bread & butter. [f. BUTTER¹ + -Y³]

Caerphill'ȳ (kār-, kär-, ker-), n. Kind of cheese. [~ in Wales]

caftan, k-. (Also) woman's long loose-hanging dress.

cămp³, a., & v.i. & t. **1.** Affected, effeminate; exaggerated. **2.** v.i. & t. Behave, do, in a ~ way. [orig. unkn.]

candle. ~*wick*, thick soft cotton or other yarn used for raised usu. tufted embroidery; material so embroidered.

cănn'abis, n. Kinds of hemp plant; preparation of hemp smoked as intoxicant. [L]

caption. (Also) wording under illustration; (v.t.) provide with ~.

catamaran. (Also) boat with two hulls side by side.

cĕrm'ĕt, n. Alloy of ceramic substance & metal. [f. CERAMIC + METAL]

chăl'ōne (k-), n. Kinds of internal secretion that reduce or inhibit action of organs & tissues. [f. Gk *khalōn* part. of *khalaō* slacken, after *hormone*]

charis'm|a (k-; -z-), n. Divine gift or talent; capacity to inspire followers with devotion & enthusiasm. Hence ~AT'IC a. [f. Gk *kharisma*]

chicane (n.). (Also) barrier or obstacle on (motor) racecourse.

chipola'ta (-lah-), n. Small (spicy) sausage. [F, f. It. *cipollata* dish of onions (f. *cipolla* onion)]

chromat|o-, ~*ŏg'raphy* (Chem.), separation of substances by allowing them to pass slowly through or over adsorbing material so that the different substances are separately adsorbed (e.g. in coloured layers) to form a *chrŏmăt'ogram* (k-).

clip¹. ~*'board*, small board with spring-clip for holding papers etc.

coast¹. ~*'guard*, (also) body of men orig. formed to prevent smuggling, now chiefly a life-saving service; member of this body.

Cŏb'ol, COBOL, n. Computer language using standardized English terms, designed for business operations. [f. initial letters of *Common Business-Oriented Language*]

cō'itus, n. Sexual intercourse; ~ *interrŭp'tus*, with withdrawal of penis before ejaculation. [L]

cologne' (-ōn), n. = EAU-*de-Cologne*.

commissioner. *C*~ *for Oaths*, solicitor authorized to administer oaths to persons making affidavits.

common¹. ~ *market*, customs union, esp. (w. caps.) the European Economic Community.

consortium (now commonly pron. -tǐ-) (pl. -*ia*). (Esp.) association of business, banking or manufacturing organizations.

contain. ~*er*, (also) large (metal) box of standard size for transporting goods. Hence ~ERIZE v.t., pack in, transport by, ~, ~*eriza'tion* n.

continental (a.). ~ *shelf*, bed of shallow sea area bordering continent.

contin'uō, n. (Mus.). Figured BASS², hence accompaniment (usu. keyboard) based on it; instrument(s) playing this. [It. *basso* ~ continuous bass]

cōol'abah, cōol'ibah, n. Kinds of Australian gum-tree. [Aboriginal wd]

cosmetic (a.). (Also, of surgery or prosthetic devices) re-creating normal appearance.

cŏs'monaut (-z-), n. Astronaut, esp. Russian. [f. Russ. *kosmonavt* (COSMO-, Gk *nautēs* sailor)]

crash¹. (Also, v.t. & i., of vehicle) (cause to) collide violently with other vehicle or obstacle (~ *into* wall); so ~ n.

credit¹. (Also, pl.) acknowledgements of contributors' services to film, book, etc.; ~ *titles*, ~s at beginning or end of film or of television broadcast.

crew¹. (Also, v.t. & i.) supply, act as, (member of) ~ (for).

crook (a.). (Also, Austral. & New Zealand, colloq.) ailing, out of sorts; (of things) out of order, unsatisfactory; angry; *go* ~ (*at*), become angry (with), speak angrily (to).

crush[2]. ~*-barrier*, (temporary) barrier for restraining crowd.

cry'o- (*or* -ŏ), comb. form of Gk *kruos* frost, as : ~*stăt*, apparatus for maintaining low temperature; ~*sur'gery*, done at low temperature.

culotte', n. (*usu. pl., pr.* -ŏt). Women's trousers cut to resemble skirt. [F, = breeches]

cutting. (Also) piece cut from plant for propagation.

debrief'ing, n. Interrogation, discussion, after completion of mission etc. [f. DE- (3) + BRIEF[2] + -ING[1]]

decarbonize. (Esp.) remove carbon deposit from (engine of car etc.).

decăth'lon, n. Athletic contest comprising ten different events. [f. DECA- + Gk *athlon* contest]

decŏke', v.t. (colloq.). Decarbonize (car engine); so ~ n. (colloq.). [f. DE- (3) + COKE]

deep[1]. ~*-freeze* n., refrigerator in which food etc. can be frozen rapidly & kept for long periods at very low temperatures. [P]

deŏxÿrībonŭcle'ic ă'cid, DNA, n. Substance with long-chain molecules present in cell nuclei & some viruses which stores genetic information required for synthesis of more ~ & of ribonucleic acid. [f. DE- (3) + OXY- (2) + ‡RIBONUCLEIC]

deplāne', v.i. Descend from aeroplane. [f. DE- (3) + PLANE[3]]

desălina'tion, n. Removal of salt (from sea-water etc.). [f. DE- (3) + SALINE + -ATION]

die[1]. ~(-)*casting*, casting produced from metal mould(s); process of making such castings.

digit. ~*al computer*, one making calculations with data represented by ~s.

dipole. (Also) type of radio aerial.

dis'cothèque (-tĕk), n. Café, bar, etc. with dancing to records. [F, = record library]

dive (n.). (Also, Boxing sl.) *take a* ~, pretend to be knocked out.

dodeca-. ~*phŏn'ic* a., ‡TWELVE-NOTE.

dŏ'dgem, n. One of set of small imitation motor-cars running on electricity within ring and colliding with others as fun-fair amusement. [DODGE[1] + 'EM; P]

Dŏpp'ler ĕffĕct, n. Apparent increase (decrease) in frequency of sound or other waves when source moves towards (away from) observer. [f. C. *Doppler*, Austrian physicist, d. 1853]

drăg[2]. (Also, sl.) women's clothes worn by man; a bore.

drip[1]. ~*-drÿ* a., that can be hung to ~ and dry without wringing or ironing.

drive[1]. ~*-in* n. & a., (cinema etc.) that may be used without alighting from car.

drop[3]. ~ *out* (v.i.), abandon course or career embarked on, way of life, etc.; so ~*-out* n., one who ~s out.

dÿslĕx'|ia, n. Word-blindness. Hence ~IC a. [f. DYS- + Gk *lexis* speech + -IA[1]]

ĕcŏnomĕt'r|ics, n. Branch of economics concerned with constructing mathematical models & testing them by statistical methods. So ~IC(AL) aa., ~icalLY[2] adv., ĕcŏnomĕtrī'CIAN n. [f. ECONOMY + *metric* (= METRICAL)]

ĕlăs'to|mer (*or* -lah-), n. Synthetic rubber or rubber-like plastic. Hence ~mĕ'rIC a. [f. ELASTIC + -*omer* as in *isomer*]

electro-. ~*phŏrēs'is*, movement of suspended colloidal particles under the influence of an electric field; ~*phorĕt'ic* a.

élite. (Also) select group or class.

ĕph'edrin(e), n. Drug used to relieve hay fever etc. [f. *Ephedra* plant from which extracted + -INE[5]]

ĕpŏx'ĭde, n. Chemical compound containing oxygen atom & two carbon atoms forming ring. [f. EPI- + OXIDE]

ĕpŏx'ÿ, a. & pref. Pertaining to, deriving from, an ‡EPOXIDE; ~ *resins*, chemically resistant synthetic resins with good adhesive & insulating properties. [f. EPI- + OXY-(2)]

ĕrgonŏm'ic|s, n. Study of efficiency of man in his working environment. So~ a., ~alLY[2] adv., ĕrgŏ'nomIST (3) n. [f. Gk *ergon* work (see ECONOMICS)]

ĕs'cal|āte, v.t. & i. Increase to new level or step by step. So ~A'TION n. [Back form. f. ESCALATOR]

eschatology. (Also, esp. *realized* ~) present significance of ~ in Christian life.

establishment. *the E~*, (also) those with (official or unofficial) authority or influence, regarded as having joint interest in resisting change.

estate. (Also) residential, industrial, etc. district planned by one owner or local council.

ethic. ~*al*, (also, of proprietary products) ‡advertised only in the medical press & not to the general public.

ĕth'ÿlēne, n. First member of olefine series of hydrocarbons, C_2H_4, inflammable gas with faint sweet smell; ~ *glycol*, colourless slightly viscous liquid used as anti-freeze etc. [f. ETHYL + -ENE]

ĕxtra-sĕn'sorÿ, a. Derived by means other than the five senses; ~ *perception*, of objects, events, etc. not present to the senses. [f. EXTRA- + SENSORY]

fāce'less (-sl-), a. Purposely not identifiable. [f. FACE[1] + -LESS]

fade. (Also, v.i., of brake) gradually lose power; hence ~ n., such loss.

fantastic. (Also, colloq.) excellent, extraordinary.

Fĕst'schrift (-stshr-), n. (pl. ~*en*, ~*s*). Collection of papers produced in honour of scholar reaching certain age etc. [G, = festival-writing]

fibre. ~*glass*, glass in fibrous form, used for packing, insulation, textiles, etc.; plastic reinforced with this.

film. ~*-setting*, photographic composing of matter to be printed.

*****finā′gle**, v.i. & t. (colloq.). Use trickery (to get), wangle. [orig. unkn.]

fix¹. (Also, sl.) addict's dose of drug.

flat². ~ *spin*, (Aeron.) nearly horizontal SPIN², in which controls are almost useless; (colloq.) state of panic or excitement.

flip¹ (n.). ~ *side*, reverse side (of gramophone record).

flu′orid|āte (floō-), v.t. Add fluoride to (water, as tooth-decay preventive). Hence ~A′TION n. [f. FLUORIDE + -ATE³]

flying. ~ *squad*, (also) motorized unit for medical emergencies.

folder. (Also) cover or holder, for loose papers.

Fŏr′trän, FORTRAN, n. Computer language using combination of algebraic formulae & standardized English terms. [f. *formula translation*]

franchise. (Also)***** right to market company's goods or services in particular area.

fringe (n.). ~ *benefits*, perquisites, benefits of various kinds provided by employers to supplement money wages and salaries.

fun. ~*-fair*, (part of) fair (sometimes permanent) devoted to amusements such as roundabouts, Ferris wheels, etc. & side-shows.

fusion. (Also) union of atomic nuclei to form heavier nuclei, with release of energy.

gō³, n. Japanese game played with pieces on board. [Jap.]

gross². ~ *national product*, annual total of goods produced & services provided in a country.

G-string (jē′-),¹n. Covering for genitals, attached to string round waist. [orig. unkn.]

guide¹. ~*-dog*, dog trained to guide blind person.

gym. ~*-slip*, ~*-tunic*, schoolgirl's sleeveless usu. belted garment reaching from shoulder to thigh.

hallu′cino|gen (-loō-), n. Drug causing hallucinations. Hence ~gĕn′IC a. [f. HALLUCINATION + -GEN (1)]

happen. ~*ing*, (also) dramatic performance consisting of impromptu events having no logical connection, with visual & sound effects, etc., & often with audience participation.

hard. (Also, of drugs) potent & addictive; ~*back* n. & a., (book) bound in durable covers; ~ *sell*, aggressive salesmanship; ~*ware*, (also, colloq.) (parts of) machine(s), items of equipment, etc. made of metal or opp. to men; (esp., of computer) machine, opp. ‡SOFTWARE.

haute couture (ōt koōtūr′), n. High-class dressmaking, esp. Parisian. [F]

hi′jäck, v.t., & n. Seize, seizure *of*, (means of transport, esp. aircraft in flight) by (threat of) violence. Hence ~ER¹, ~ING¹ nn. [orig. unkn.]

hipp′y̆, hipp′ie, n. Person rejecting conventional standards & organized society in favour of unconstrained living. [f. *hip* (U.S. sl.) aware + -Y³]

hŏm′inid, n. & a. (Member) of the human zoological family (incl. existing & fossil man). [f. mod. L *Hominidae*]

hood. (Also) separate ~like garment worn over academic gown etc. to indicate degree; (waterproof) folding top of motor-car, perambulator, etc.

hōōd² (or hŏōd), n. HOODLUM; gangster, gunman. [f. HOODLUM]

Hŏpp′us (cūb′ic) fŏŏt, n. Unit of volume measurement based on the square of the quarter-girth, still used in British Commonwealth forestry for the cubic content of round logs or trees. [f. E. *Hoppus*, surveyor and compiler of calculating tables, d. *c.* 1758]

hŏrrĕn′dous, a. (colloq.). Horrifying. [f. L *horrendus* (*horrēre* bristle, shudder at) + -OUS]

hot¹. ~ *line*, permanently open telephone line, esp. for diplomatic emergencies; ~*-plate*, heated metal plate, portable heater, for cooking food or keeping it hot.

hous′ing² (-z-), n. In vbl senses, esp.: (provision of) accommodation, houses collectively; shelter, covering; socket, casing; ~ *estate*, = residential ‡ESTATE.

hŏv′ercraft (-ahft), n. Craft supported just above surface of water or land by air driven downwards. [f. HOVER + CRAFT; P]

hy̆d′rofoil, n. Device under hull of craft which forces it out of water at speed; craft equipped with this. [f. HYDRO- (1) + FOIL¹]

hy̆sterĕc′tomy̆, n. Excision of womb. [f. HYSTERO- + -ECTOMY]

image¹. (Also) character of thing or person as perceived by the public.

implō′sion (-zhn), n. (Phonet.). Compression of air between simultaneous closures in glottis & mouth. So **implōs′-IVE** a. & n. [f. L IM-¹(*plodere plos- = plaudere* clap), see -ION]

in′put (-ŏŏt), n. What is put in, esp. in economic, electrical & industrial processes. [f. IN adv. + PUT¹]

instant¹. (Also) that can be prepared or produced immediately, e.g. ~ (soluble) *coffee*.

integrate². (Also, v.t. & i.) cease to segregate (racially), end (racial) segregation at (place).

ïnterfēr′ŏn, n. Protein preventing development of virus in cell. [f. INTERFERE + Gk -*on*]

In'terpŏl (I-), n. International police organization, with headquarters in Paris. [f. di*methyl*amino + *diphenyl* + *hepta-none*]

interpolate. (Also) interpose orally.

jigger[1]. (Also) small MEASURE[1](3), esp. for spirits.

kaftan. See ‡CAFTAN.

kangaroo. ∼ *court*, self-constituted court held by strikers, mutineers, etc.

kara'tè (-rah-), n. Japanese system of unarmed combat. [Jap.]

kerfŭf'fle, n. (colloq.). Fuss, commotion. [orig. unkn.]

king[1]. ∼*-crab*, (also) * large edible spider--crab; ∼*-size*(d), of larger than standard size.

la'hăr (lah-), n. Flow of volcanic mud. [Jav.]

landscape. (Also, v.t. & i.) improve by ∼-gardening etc., engage in ∼-gardening.

lās'er (-z-), n. Amplifying device producing strong narrow beam of light. [light amplification by stimulated emission of radiation]

light[1]. ∼*-year*, distance ∼ travels in one year (approx. 6 million million miles).

ma'na (mah-), n. Power, authority, prestige; supernatural power. [Maori]

mantle[1]. (Also) region between earth's crust & core.

marăc'a, n. Dried gourd etc. with stones or seeds inside, shaken as percussion instrument. [Port., prob. f. Tupi]

marin'a (-rē-), n. Pleasure-boat harbour. [fem. of It. & Sp. *marino* marine]

măs'cŏn, n. Concentration of dense matter with strong gravitational pull below moon's surface. [f. *mass concentration*]

măs'er (-z-), n. Device for amplifying microwaves; *optical* ∼ = ‡LASER. [*micro*wave *a*mplification by *s*timulated *e*mission of *r*adiation]

master[1]. (Also, *M*∼) courtesy title usu. given to eldest son of Scottish viscount or baron, as *the M∼ of Falkland*.

mĕg'a-[2], **mĕg-** (etym. as MEGA-), prefixed in physics to unit-names = one million units: *megawatt, megohm*.

merge. (Also) join or blend gradually, without abrupt change (*into, with*).

mĕritŏc'racў, n. (*Elite* of) system in which position is determined by academic ability. [f. MERIT + -O- + -CRACY]

mĕs'căl, n. 1. Strong spirit distilled from fermented sap of wild agave. 2. ‡PEYOTE. [Sp.]

mĕs'calin, n. Active principle in peyote. [f. ‡MESCAL(2) + -IN]

metamorphosis. (Also, Zool.) change, usu. rapid, between immature form & adult.

mĕth'adōne, n. Narcotic analgesic drug. [f. di*methyl*amino + *diphenyl* + *hepta-none*]

mĕthămphĕt'amine (*or* -ēn), n. Euphoria-inducing stimulant drug. [f. METHYL + ‡AMPHETAMINE]

Mĕth'edrine, n. Methamphetamine. [P]

mĕths, n. (colloq.). Methylated spirits. [abbr.]

mĕtrica'tion, n. Conversion to metric system. [f. METRIC + -ATION]

mick'eу, n. *Take the* ∼ *out of*, (sl.) make fun of, 'get at'. Also abs. [orig. unkn.]

micro-[1]. ∼*dot*, photograph reduced to the size of a dot or a very small spot.

minèstrōn'è, n. Soup of vegetables, pasta, etc. [It.]

min'i, n. (colloq.). ∼*car*, ∼*skirt*, etc. [abbr.]

min'i-, comb. form of *miniature* = very small, as: ∼*bus*, van-sized, ∼*skirt*, ending well above the knee, ∼*-State*, with population numbered in thousands.

mint[2]. (Also) pepper∼ lozenge.

mobile. (Also, n.) piece of sculpture with parts free to move in currents of air; similar object of cardboard etc.

modul|e. (Also) standardized part or unit, esp. independent unit in space craft. Hence ∼AR[1] a.

mō'hŏ, n. Mohorovicic discontinuity. [abbr.]

Mŏhorŏ'vicic discontinuity (-chĭch), n. Discontinuity between earth's crust & mantle. [f. A. *Mohorovičić*, Yugoslav geophysicist, d. 1936]

mŏn'ō, a. & n. Monophonic (recording). [abbr.]

mŏnophŏn'ic, a. (Of recording) sounding as from a single source, opp. STEREOPHONIC. [f. MONO- + PHONIC]

moon[1]. ∼*light*, (also, *v.i.*, colloq.) have two occupations; so ∼*lighting* n.

moral. ∼ *pressure*, acting through the moral sense; ∼ *support*, having psychological rather than physical effect.

muscular. ∼ *dўs'trophў*, wasting disease of muscles.

mutation. So **mūt'**ANT a. & n. (Biol.), (individual) differing from its parents as a result of ∼.

neutri'nō (-rē-), n. Elementary particle having no charge & negligible mass. [It. (*neutrone* neutron + *-ino* dim. suf.)]

night. ∼*-life*, entertainments open at ∼.

note[1]. ∼*-row* (-rō) (Mus.), SEQUENCE (1) of (usu. all twelve) different notes in chromatic scale, none to be repeated before the rest have sounded in melody or harmony, though row as a whole may be reversed & inverted.

nōv'a, n. (pl. *-vae*). Star showing sudden & great increase of light & energy & then subsiding, formerly mistaken for new star. [fem. of L *novus* new]

nūm'er|ate, n. & a. (Person) familiar with

basic principles of mathematics & science. Hence ~ACY n. [f. L *numerus* number, after *literate*]

nŭmĕrŏl'ŏgў, n. Study of occult significance of numbers. [f. L *numerus* number + -OLOGY]

ōl'ĕfīne, n. (Chem.). Any of the series of hydrocarbons C_nH_{2n}. [f. F *oléfiant* oil-making + -INE⁵]

ŏlĭgŏ'polў, n. Possession of trade in a commodity by only a few sellers. [f. OLIGO- + *-poly* after MONOPOLY]

ŏm'budsman (-bŏŏdz-), n. Official who investigates private individuals' grievances against State authorities (in Britain = Parliamentary Commissioner for Administration). [Scand.]

ŏp, a. (Of art) giving illusions of movement based on optical effects. [f. OPTICAL]

ŏrgăn'za, n. Thin stiff transparent fabric of silk or synthetic fibre. [prob. f. *Lorganza* P]

ōrienteer'|ing (or ŏr-), n. Cross-country racing on foot, using map & compass. Hence~ n., person who engages in~ing. [f. Sw. *orientering*]

output. (Also) what is produced, esp. in economic, electrical & industrial processes.

over. ~*kill* n., greater (capacity for) destruction than necessary; (fig.) any use of disproportionate means; ~*pass* (also, n.) (ō'-), road-bridge over another road.

pad³. (Also) flat surface for helicopter take-off, launching of rockets, etc.; (sl.) house, dwelling.

pallet². (Also) portable platform for transporting & storing loads.

păn⁵, v.i., & n. **1.** Pivot (camera), usu. horizontally. **2.** n.~ning movement. [f. PANORAMA]

paper¹. ~*back* n. & a., (book) bound in paper (freq. cheap reprint).

para-¹. ~*psycho'logy* n., study of mental phenomena outside sphere of ordinary psychology (hypnosis, telepathy, etc.).

parliamentary. P~ *Commissioner for Administration,* official who investigates private individuals' grievances against government authorities, ombudsman.

păs'ta (or pah-), n. Dried flour paste used in Italian cooking, in various shapes such as macaroni, spaghetti, vermicelli, etc. [It.]

pastel. (Also, attrib., of light colour) soft, subdued.

pĕrm'afrost (-ŏs-, -aws-), n. Permanently frozen subsoil etc. in arctic regions. [f. PERMANENT+FROST]

petro-. ~*chem'ical* n. & a., substance obtained from petroleum or natural gas; (a.) of ~chemicals or ~chemistry; ~*chem'istry* n., chemistry of rocks or petroleum.

peyote (pāyōt'I), n. (Hallucinogenic drug produced from tops of) a Mexican cactus. [Amer. Sp.]

photo-. ~*copy* n., & v.t., (make) ~graphic copy (of).

phŏt'ŏn, n. Discrete indivisible quantity of electromagnetic energy, sometimes viewed as particle. [f. PHOTO-, after ELECTRON]

phras|e. (Also, v.t. & i.) divide (music) into, shape in, ~es. Hence ~ING n.

pill¹. (Also, colloq.) *the* ~, contraceptive ~.

pit'ŏn (pē-), n. Peg or spike driven into rock or crack to hold climber or rope. [F]

ploy. (Also) stratagem, manœuvre, esp. in personal relations.

pocket¹. ~*-book*, (also) *book of size to be carried in ~; *handbag.

pollen. ~ *count*, index of amount of ~ in air published as warning to sufferers from respiratory ailments.

poly-. ~*ester*, ~*ethylene*, ~*styr'ēne*, ~*thēne* P, ~*ūr'ethāne* (or *ūrĕth'āne*), ~*vinyl chloride*, kinds of synthetic resin.

pony. ~*tail*, hair drawn back, gathered at crown & hanging loose behind.

pop³. (Also, a.) of ~s, popular; akin to ~ art in style; ~ *art*, movement dealing with objects characteristic of modern industrial culture in manner of commercial art.

pŏt³, n. (sl.). ‡CANNABIS. [orig. unkn.]

pre-. ~*strĕssed* (-st) a., (of concrete) strengthened by compression with steel rods under tension.

print². ~*-out* n., computer output in ~ed form.

prĭss'ў, a. Prim, over-decorous. [prob. f. PRIM + CISSY]

private. ~ *enterprise*, economic activity under ~ control; (fig.) individual initiative.

programme, -am. (Also, usu. *-am*) set of instructions & data enabling computer to perform task; (v.t.) express (problem) in this way, feed ~ into (computer).

progressive. ~ *education*, stressing individualism & unconventional methods rather than formal instruction & discipline; ~ *taxation*, at rates increasing with sum taxed; ~ *tense*, formed from part of *be* & present participle of verb & having continuous meaning, as *I am doing.*

prototype. (Also) trial model, preliminary version, esp. of aeroplane.

psўchĕdĕl'ic (sĭk-), a. (Of certain hallucinogenic drugs & their effects) expanding the mind's awareness; suggesting experience or effect of such drugs. [irreg. f. Gk *psukhē* mind + *dēlos* clear + -IC]

psychological. ~ *warfare*, achieving aims by acting on enemy's minds.

pull¹. ~ *in* v.i., (also) (cause vehicle to) leave traffic lane for roadside etc., so ~*-in* n., place to pull in at, esp. lorry-drivers' café; ~ *out* v.i., (also) (cause vehicle to) move out (further) from road-side, (v.i. & t.) (cause aeroplane to) come out of dive, (esp. of troops) withdraw.

pulp. ~ *magazine*, trashy magazine.

pŭl'sâr, n. Cosmic source of pulsating radio signal. [f. PULSE¹, after ‡QUASAR]

puppy. ~ *fat*, fatness in childhood & adolescence which disappears later.

quârk (*or* -ôr-), n. (One of three kinds of) hypothetical component of sub-atomic particles. [arbitrarily f. 'Three quarks for Muster Mark' in J. Joyce, *Finnegans Wake*]

quäs'âr (*or* -z-), n. Very small star-like cosmic source of light & radio waves. [f. *quasi*-stellar object etc.]

rachĕl' (-sh-), n. & a. (Of the) colour of light-fawn face-powder. [R~, Fr. actress, d. 1858]

rag¹. ~ *trade* (sl.), fashion industry.

rag³ (n.). (Also) students' annual parade accompanied by horseplay.

ra'ga (rah-), n. One of sets of scales & melodies used as basis for improvisation in Indian music; piece in a certain ~. [Skr., = colour, musical tone]

rand. (Also, *pr.* rahnt) unit of S.-Afr. decimal currency (= 100 cents), adopted 1961.

rǎvio̐l'ĭ, n. (Italian dish of) small pasta cases containing meat etc. [It.]

reader. ~ship, (also) (number of) readers of magazine etc.

real². ~ *income*, *wages*, valued by purchasing power, adjusted for changes in value of money.

rĕdiffu'sion (-zhn), n. Relaying of broadcasts by wires from central receiver.

relegate. (Also) transfer (football team etc.) to lower division of league.

resin. (*Synthetic*) ~, any of various synthetic plastic & other ~-like materials produced by polymerization etc.

rĕs'onate (-z-), v.i. Produce or show resonance, resound. [f. L *resonare* resound]

retard. ~ed *child*, one whose mental or physical development is behind what is normal at his age.

rĕtsin'a (-tsē-), n. Resinated Greek wine. [mod. Gk]

rĕvămp', v.t. (colloq.). Give new look to, renovate, revive. [f. RE- 8 + VAMP¹]

rhythm. ~ *& blues*, (Jazz) form of blues with ~ic accompaniment.

ribonŭclē'ic ǎ'cid, RNA, n. Substance with long-chain molecules present in cells & some viruses which participates in synthesis of proteins. [f. *ribose* a sugar + *nucleic* (NUCLEUS + -IC)]

riffle. (Also, *v.t.*) flick, leaf *through*; ruffle; shuffle cards rapidly, esp. by flexing & combining two halves of pack.

ring¹. ~ *main*, electric circuit forming ~, so providing alternative paths for current

to power points; ~ *road*, bypass encircling town.

road¹. ~ *block*, traffic BLOCK¹ (7); barrier to stop traffic while search or check is made.

rocket². ~eer' n., person engaged in space- -~ work.

rō'ger, int. indicating receipt & understanding of message, hence (sl.) expressing agreement. [= *R* (for *received*) in wireless communication etc.]

roll³. ~ing *mill*, mill which ~s metal into various shapes.

rubber¹. ~-*stamp'* v.t., (fig.) approve automatically without considering substance; ~ *stamp* n., one who does so, (sign of) such approval.

sacred. ~ *cow*, (fig.) person or thing (unjustifiably) held to be sacrosanct.

salon. (Also) dressmaker's, hairdresser's, etc. establishment.

sanction. (Also) (non-military) measure intended to make State comply with norms of international conduct.

saun'a (sow- *or* saw-), n. Steam bath. [Finnish]

scăm'pi, n. pl. (Dish of) kind of large prawns. [It.]

scat. (Also, n., Jazz) (quasi-instrumental) singing of meaningless syllables.

Schnorkel. (Also) breathing-tube for swimmer with head under water.

screen. ~ *printing*, method of printing fabrics etc. through silk ~.

scub'a (-ōō-), n. Self-contained underwater breathing apparatus; ~ *diver*, one using ~. [acronym]

segreg|ate¹. (Also) separate; ~ateD¹ a., subjected to, characterized by, (racial) ~ation; *racial* ~*ation*, enforced separation of racial groups within community or institution.

self-. ~-*employed'*, running own business etc.

sĕll'otǎpe, S-, n., & v.t. (Seal with) adhesive usu. transparent cellulose tape. [P]

semi-. ~-*conduc'tor*, a solid, non-conducting when pure or at low temperatures, which when impure or at higher temperatures has a conductivity between that of insulators and that of most metals.

send¹. ~ *up*, mock, parody. Hence ~-*up* n.

serial. (Also, Mus.) formed out of a ‡SERIES; often = ‡TWELVE-NOTE. Hence ~ISM, ~IST nn.

series. (Also, Mus.) a constantly repeated SEQUENCE (1) of notes which differ mainly as to pitch, sometimes also as to duration, volume, etc.

sĕrv'o-|mĕch'anism (-k-), n. Power- -assisted device usu. for effecting movement (e.g. of brake). So ~-*control* n. [f. L *servus* slave]

shalōm' ('-ah-), int. of greeting etc. [Heb., = peace]

shock[1]. ~ *wave*, sharp change of pressure etc. produced by body moving through air or other medium at speed exceeding that of transmission of sound through the medium, or by explosion.

side[1]. ~*-road*, minor or subsidiary road, road joining or diverging from main road; ~*-street*, street lying aside from main streets or roads.

sign[1]. ~*post*, (also, v.t.) provide with ~posts; indicate; direct.

sil'icône, n. One of group of synthetic resins containing silicon which resist effects of water & high temperatures. [f. SILICON + -ONE]

sit. ~*-in* n., ~ting in a place contrary to law or custom as a public protest.

sit'ǎr (or -ǎr'), n. Plucked stringed instrument used in Indian music. [Hind.]

skid. ~*-pan*, (also) surface artificially prepared to induce ~ding, for practice in control of ~ding vehicles.

sky'jǎck, v.t. (colloq.). Hijack (aircraft). [f. SKY + ‡HIJACK]

sleeve. (Also) gramophone-record cover.

slick. (Also, n.) smooth patch on surface of water, usu. caused by oil etc.; oil etc. causing ~.

slip-. ~*-road*, (also) road giving access to or exit from motorway etc.

snŏrk'el, n. = SCHNORKEL. [Anglicized form]

sŏ'cio- (-shǐ-, -sǐ-), comb. form of *social*, as; ~*-economic*, social & economic.

soft. ~*'ware*, general-purpose programs & procedures associated with computer, opp. machine itself (‡HARDWARE).

sŏnde, n. = RADIO~. [F]

son et lumière (sŏn ǎ lōōm'yǎr), n. Entertainment recounting history connected with building etc. & using recorded sound & lighting effects. [F, = sound & light]

sophisticate. (Also, n.) ~d person; (p.p., also) not simple or natural; experienced, free of naïvety; subtle, refined; appealing to ~d taste; (of machinery, systems, etc.) advanced, complicated, versatile.

sound[2]. ~ *barrier* = SONIC *barrier*.

space[1]. (Also) the universe beyond the earth's atmosphere.

spinner. (Also) kinds of (artificial) trout-fly.

sponge[1]. ~*-bag*, waterproof bag for toilet articles; (a., of trousers) of checked material.

spring[1]. *sprung rhythm*, poetic metre approximating to speech in which each foot has one stressed syllable & up to four (occasionally more) unstressed.

standard. ~ *English*, the form of English used, with local variations, by the majority of cultured English-speaking people; so ~ *pronunciation*.

starch (n.). ~*-reduced*, containing less than normal proportion of ~.

statesman. *Elder S~*, (also) distinguished

retired ~ whose advice is available.

storage. ~ *heater*, electric heater storing in bricks etc. heat accumulated outside peak hours.

sub-. ~*atomic*, ~*nuclear*, occurring in or smaller than atom, nucleus; relating to ~atomic, ~nuclear, particles or phenomena; ~*standard*, of less than required or normal quality or size, inferior.

summary. (Also, Law) done rapidly without certain formalities required by common law; ~ *conviction*, before magistrates, opp. conviction by jury; *court of* ~ *jurisdiction*, that can itself judge or convict.

super-. ~*nova* n., 3b, ‡NOVA of very great brightness.

swag. (Also) ornamental festoon of flowers, fruit, etc.; representation of this in plaster or carved wood; drapery of similar appearance.

swing. ~*-wing* a., (of aircraft) having wings that can be swung back.

tǎch'ograph (-k-; -ahf), n. Device on vehicle recording speeds & travel-times. [f. Gk *takhos* speed + -GRAPH (2)]

talent. ~*-scout*, seeker-out of ~, esp. for entertainment industry.

tape (v.t.). (Also) record on magnetic ~.

tea. ~*-bag*, small permeable bag of ~-leaves for infusion.

team. ~ *up* v.i. & t., join, put together in a ~ (*with*).

tele-. *tĕl'ecamera*, television camera.

tĕllǔr'ic, a. 1. Of the earth or soil. 2. See TELLURIUM.

tĕrotĕchnŏl'ogў (-k-), n. Maintenance engineering. [f. Gk *tēreō* watch over, take care of + TECHNOLOGY]

tĕrrǎzz'o (-tsŏ), n. Flooring material of stone chips set in concrete & given smooth surface. [It., = terrace; P]

thalid'omide, n. Sedative drug, taking of which by pregnant women was followed *c.* 1960 by birth of malformed babies. [f. ph*thalimidoglutarimide*; P]

thermo-. ~*plas'tic* n. & a., (substance) that becomes plastic when heated, hardens when cooled, & can do this repeatedly.

three. ~*-point turn*, forward-reverse-forward manœuvre to turn vehicle.

toe. ~*-hold*, minimal foothold (also fig.).

tone[1]. ~*-row* (-rŏ) = ‡NOTE-ROW. [f. G *tonreihe*]

tonne (tŭn), n. Metric TON[1].

top[1]. ~ *secret*, most secret (esp. as security classification).

topŏl'ogў, n. Branch of mathematics dealing with the properties of spaces (sets of points) esp. in respect of their being one connected piece & forming a boundary, independently of shape & size. Hence tŏpolŏ'GICAL a., tŏpolŏ'gicalLY adv., topŏl'ogIST n. [f. G *topologie* (Gk *topos* place, -LOGY)]

tracker. ~ *dog*, police dog tracking by scent.

trăd, a. & n. (sl.). Tⁱaditional (jazz). [abbr.]

trade. *trading-stamp*, COUPON given by retailer.

traffic (n.). ~ *warden*, official supervising & regulating traffic & parking.

transfer[1]. (Also, v.t.&i.) reassign (person), change, to new duties or organization.

transfer[2]. (Also) reassignment, change, to new duties or organization; ~*-fee*, fee for ~ (esp. of professional footballer to new club).

transistor. Hence ~IZED a., equipped with ~s.

transplant. (Also, trăns'-, n.) ~ing of tissue or organ; tissue or organ ~ed.

trap[1]. (Also, pl.) percussion instruments in jazz-, dance-band, etc.; ~*-drummer*, one who plays ~s.

trĭb|ŏl'ogў, n. Study of friction, wear, lubrication, & bearing design. Hence ~olŏ'gICAL a., ~ŏl'ogIST n. [f. Gk *tribos* rubbing + -LOGY]

trī'marăn, n. Boat with three hulls side by side. [f. TRI- + ‡CATAMARAN]

trip. ~*-wire*, wire setting off explosive or warning device etc. when ~ped over.

trompe-l'œil (tromp lŭ'ĕ), n. & a. (Painting) designed to make the spectator think the objects represented are real. [F, = deceives the eye]

trŏp'ism, n. (Biol.). Turning of (part of) organism in particular direction in response to external stimulus. [second element of GEOTROPISM etc.]

trouble. ~*-maker*, one who stirs up ~, agitator.

T-shĭrt (tē'-), n. Collarless short-sleeved cotton (under)shirt. [f. shape of letter T]

Turkish. ~ *coffee*, strong usu. sweet black coffee made with very finely ground beans.

twelve. ~*-note, -tone* aa., (Mus.) using the twelve notes of the chromatic scale equally, without regard to diatonic key relationships, on basis of a ‡NOTE-ROW.

type[1]. ~*-cast* v., cast (actor) in certain type of role because of predisposing characteristics.

ŭnscrĭp'tĕd, a. Not made or read from prepared script. [UN-[2] 1 + SCRIPT + -ED[2]]

ŭnzĭp', v.t. & i. Undo (zippered garment, person wearing one); (v.i.) admit of being ~ped. [UN-[1] + ZIP]

up-. ~*stage*, (also, a., & adv. pr. -stāj') nearer back of stage; ~*stage left*, left of person at back of stage facing audience (so ~*stage right*); (v.t.) (-stāj') move ~ of (another actor), thus making him face away from audience; (fig.) draw attention away from (someone) to oneself; *up'-swept* a., (of hair) combed up & arranged on top of head; curved or sloped upwards.

văc, n. (colloq.). Vacation; vacuum cleaner. [abbr.]

veteran. ~ *(motor-)car*, early motor-car, sometimes limited to those built up to 1904.

video. ~*-recording*, ~*-tape*, recording, record, of television programme on magnetic tape.

vĭn'ўl, n. 1. Radical, CH₂CH, forming basis of many plastics etc. 2. = ‡POLY-VINYL CHLORIDE. [f. L *vinum* wine + -YL]

virus. (Also) kinds of ultramicroscopic organic particle that can grow & reproduce only in living cells, & esp. that can cause disease.

web. ~*-offset*, offset process using continuous roll of paper.

weight.[1] ~*-lifter*, one who does ~*-lifting*; ~*-lifting*, lifting heavy objects as athletic sport or exercise.

wil'cō, int. used in signalling etc. to indicate that directions received will be carried out. [abbr. of *will comply*]

wire. ~ *wool*, very fine ~ massed together, used esp. for cleaning pots & pans.

write. ~ *off*, (also) reckon as lost or worthless; ~*-off* n., something to be written off as total loss or wreck, failure; ~*-up* n., (favourable) review or report.

yield (v.i.). (Also) give right of way (*to* other traffic).

APPENDIX I

GENERAL ABBREVIATIONS

(For list of special abbreviations used in text see pp. xiv–xvi)

ABBREVIATIONS are made chiefly in two ways. (1) The beginning of the word is given, and at any point (after one letter, after all but one letter, or anywhere between) it is cut short with a full stop; so N. = North, Liv. = Livy, syn. = synonym; the full stop serves to announce that it is needless to go further with the word. (The mathematical abbreviations for cosecant, cosine, cotangent, secant, sine, and tangent, namely cosec, cos, cot, sec, sin, and tan, are used without the full stop. Sometimes, as in ENSA and SCAPA, the full stop is omitted between the letters.) (2) Some portion of the middle of the word is dropped out, the first and last letters being retained with or without others between; so wt = weight, hrs = hours, exrx = executrix, Abp = Archbishop; the writing of a full stop at the end of these on the analogy of that in (1), though now usual, is to be deprecated; it is not a natural device (as in (1)), but artificial; it has very rarely the merit of announcing that the letters printed are not a full word, since that is nearly always clear without it (*caps* for *capitals* is one of the few exceptions); and it has always the demerit of failing to let the reader know that in the riddle he is called upon to read the last as well as the first letter is given him. There is also a mixed class in which the full stop at the end does convey that the end of the word is missing, but without implying (as in (1)) that all the letters up to that point are present; such are cg. = c(enti)g(ram), cf. = c(on)f(er), avdp. = av(oir)d(u)p(ois); the first two of these consist of the initial letters of their words' etymological elements, the last gives the first letter followed by such of the consonants as may suggest the general sound.

The method adopted in the following list is to omit the otiose full stop in accordance with the view expressed above; it is, however, to be understood that all abbreviations here given without the full stop may also be, and more frequently are, used with it. The U.S. State names and those of British counties should be mentioned; in the former we give the full stop or omit it as explained above (Vt, Va, Ky, for Vermont, Virginia, Kentucky; Mass., O., Oreg., for Massachusetts, Ohio, Oregon); in the latter we write the full stop after the 's' (Yorks., Leics., Berks., etc.) as representing *shire*. Viz and oz are preferred to viz. and oz. on the ground that the z itself represents a written terminal flourish.

A., adult (i.e. for adults only, referring to cinema picture); air; alto; *avancer* (on timepiece regulator, = to accelerate).

A.A., anti-aircraft; Automobile Association.

A.A.A., Agricultural Adjustment Administration; Amateur Athletic Association.

A.A.F., Auxiliary Air Force.

A.A.G., Assistant Adjutant-General.

A.A.I., Associate of the Chartered Auctioneers' & Estate Agents' Institute.

A. and M., Ancient and Modern (Hymns).

A.A.Q.M.G., Assistant Adjutant and Quartermaster-General.

A.B., able-bodied seaman.

A.B.C., the alphabet; alphabetical train time-table; Aerated Bread Company('s Shop).

ab init., ab initio (= from the beginning).

Abp, Archbishop.

A.C., aircraftman; Alpine Club; alternating current; *ante Christum* (= before Christ).

a/c, account.

A.C.A., Associate of the Institute of Chartered Accountants.

acc., account.

A.C.F., Army Cadet Force.

A.C.G.B., Arts Council of Great Britain.

A.C.I., Army Council Instruction.

A.C.I.I., Associate of the Chartered Insurance Institute.

A.C.I.S., Associate of the Chartered Institute of Secretaries.

A.C.W., aircraftwoman.

A.C.W.A., Associate of the Institute of Cost & Works Accountants.

A.D., *anno Domini* (= in the year of our Lord).

A.D.C., aide-de-camp; Amateur Dramatic Club.

ad fin., *ad finem* (= towards the end).

ad init., *ad initium* (= at the beginning).

Adjt, Adjutant.

Adm., Admiral.

advt, advertisement.

Æ (see A in dictionary).

A.E.A., Atomic Energy Authority.

A.E.F., Amalgamated Union of Engineering & Foundry Workers.

A.F., Admiral of the Fleet.

A.F.A., Amateur Football Alliance.

A.F.A.S., Associate of the Faculty of Architects & Surveyors.

A.F.C., Air Force Cross.

A.F.L., American Federation of Labour.

A.F.M., Air Force Medal.

A.F.O., Admiralty Fleet Order.

A.F.S., Army Fire Service; Auxiliary Fire Service.

A.F.V., Armoured Fighting Vehicle.

A.G., Adjutant-General; air gunner.

A.H., *anno Hegirae* (= in the year of the Hegira).

A.I., Admiralty Instruction.

A.I.A., Associate of the Institute of Actuaries.

A.I.B., Associate of the Institute of Bankers.

A.I.D., A.I.H., artificial insemination by donor, by husband.

A.I.M.T.A., Associate of the Institute of Municipal Treasurers & Accountants.

A.Inst.P., Associate of the Institute of Physics.

a.l., autograph letter.

A.L.A., American Library Association.

Ala, Alabama.

Alas., Alaska.

Alban, (Bp) of St Albans (see Cantuar.).

Ald., Alderman.

a.l.s., autograph letter signed.

A.M., Air Ministry; Albert Medal; = M.A.

a.m., *anno mundi* (= in the year of the world); *ante meridiem* (= before noon).

A.M.D.G., *ad majorem Dei gloriam* (= to the greater glory of God).

A.M.G.(O.T.), Allied Military Government (of Occupied Territory).

A.M.I.C.E., A.M.I.E.E., A.M.I.Mech. E., A.M.I.Mun.E., Associate Member of Institution of Civil, Electrical, Mechanical, Municipal, Engineers.

A.M.S., Army Medical Staff (*or* Service).

A.M.S.E., Associate Member of the Society of Engineers.

A.M.T.P.I., Associate Member of the Town Planning Institute.

A.O., Army Order.

A.O.C.(-in-C.), Air Officer Commanding (-in-Chief).

A. of F., Admiral of the Fleet.

A.P., Associated Press.

A.P.M., Assistant Provost-Marshal.

Apocr., Apocrypha.

Apr., April.

A.Q.M.G., Assistant Quartermaster-General.

A.R., advice of receipt; annual return.

A.R.A., Associate of the Royal Academy.

A.R.A.D., Associate of the Royal Academy of Dancing.

A.R.A.M., Associate of the Royal Academy of Music.

A.R.C.A., A.R.C.M., A.R.C.O., A.R.C.S., Associate of the Royal College of Art, of Music, of Organists, of Science.

Argyl., Argyllshire.

A.R.I.B.A., Associate of the Royal Institute of British Architects.

A.R.I.C., Associate of the Royal Institute of Chemistry.

A.R.I.C.S., Associate of the Royal Institution of Chartered Surveyors.

Ariz., Arizona.

Ark., Arkansas.

A.R.P., air-raid precautions.

arr., arrives etc.

A.R.S.H., Associate of the Royal Society for the Promotion of Health.

A.R.W.S., Associate of the Royal Society of Painters in Water Colours.

A.S., Anglo-Saxon.

A/S, anti-submarine.

Asaph., (Bishop) of St Asaph (see Cantuar.).

A.S.C., American Society of Cinematographers.

A.S.E., Amalgamated Society (*or* Associate of the Society) of Engineers.

A.S.L.E.F., Associated Society of Locomotive Engineers & Firemen.

A.S.L.I.B., Association of Special Libraries & Information Bureaux.

A.S.R.S., Amalgamated Society of Railway Servants.

A.S.W., anti-submarine warfare.

Asst, Assistant.

A.T.A.(S.), Air Transport Auxiliary (Service).

A.T.C., Air Training Corps.

A.T.S., Auxiliary Territorial Service.

Å.U., Ångström unit.

A.U.C., *ab urbe condita* or *anno urbis conditae* (= from, in the year of, the founding of the city, i.e. Rome).

Aug., August.

a.u.n., *absque ulla nota* (= unmarked).

A.V., Authorized Version (of the Bible).

avdp., avoirdupois.

A.V.M., Air Vice-Marshal.

*A.W.O.L., absent without leave.

B, black (of pencil lead).

B., *Beatus, -a* (= Blessed).

b., born; (in cricket) bowled, bye.

B.A., Bachelor of Arts; British Academy.

B.Agr(ic)., Bachelor of Agriculture.

B.A.O.R., British Army of the Rhine.

Bart, Baronet.

Bart's, St Bartholomew's Hospital.

Bath: & Well:, (Bishop) of Bath & Wells (see Cantuar.).

B.B., Boys' Brigade.

BB, BBB, double-, treble-, black (of pencil-lead).

B.B.C., British Broadcasting Corporation.

B.C., Battery Commander; before Christ; British Columbia.

B.C.A., Bureau of Current Affairs.

B.Ch., = Ch.B.

B.C.L., Bachelor of Civil Law.

B.Com., Bachelor of Commerce.

B.D., Bachelor of Divinity.

Bdr, Bombardier.

B.D.S., Bachelor of Dental Surgery.

bds, boards (in bookbinding).

B.D.S.T., British double summer time.

B.E., (Order of the) British Empire.

B.E.A., British European Airways.

B.Ed., Bachelor of Education.

Beds., Bedfordshire.

B.E.F., British Expeditionary Force.

B.E.M., British Empire Medal.

B.Eng., Bachelor of Engineering.

Berks., Berkshire.

b.f., bloody fool; bold face (type); brought forward.

B.F.B.S., British & Foreign Bible Society.

b.h.p., brake horse-power.

B.I.F., British Industries Fair.

B.L., Bachelor of Law.

B.Litt., Bachelor of Letters.

B.M., Bachelor of Medicine.

B.M.A., British Medical Association.

B.Mus., Bachelor of Music.

B.N.C., Brasenose College, Oxford.

B.O., body odour.

B.O.A., British Optical Association.

B.O.A.C., British Overseas Airways Corporation.

B.O.T., Board of Trade.

bot, bought.

B.P., British Pharmacopoeia; British Public.

Bp, Bishop.

B.Q.M.S., Battery Quartermaster-Sergeant.

B.R., British Railways.

B.R.C.S., British Red Cross Society.

brev., brevet.

Brig.(-Gen.), Brigadier(-General).

Brit., Britain; British.

Britt., *Brit(t)an(n)iarum* (= of the Britains, on coins).

Bros, brothers.

B.S.A., Birmingham Small Arms (Co.); British South Africa.

B.S.A.A.C., British South American Airways Corporation.

B.Sc., Bachelor of Science.

b.s.g.d.g., *breveté sans garantie du gou-* *vernement* (= patented without government guarantee).

B.S.M., Battery Sergeant-Major.

B.S.I., British Standards Institution.

B.S.T., British summer time.

Bt, Baronet.

B.T.C., British Transport Commission.

B.Th.U., Btu, British thermal unit.

Bucks., Buckinghamshire.

B.U.P., British United Press.

B.V.M., *Beata Virgo Maria* (= the Blessed Virgin Mary).

B.W.I., British West Indies.

B.W.T.A., British Women's Temperance Association.

C, centum (= 100); coulomb.

C., Centigrade.

c., caught; cent(s); century; chapter; (c.) *circa*; *circiter*; colt; cubic.

C.A., Chartered Accountant (Sc.).

C.A.B., citizens' advice bureau; *Civil Aeronautics Board.

Cal(if)., California.

Cambs., Cambridgeshire.

Can., Canada.

c. & b., caught & bowled.

Cant., Canticles.

Cantab., Cantabrigian.

Cantuar., of Canterbury. (The signature of certain bishops consists of their Christian name(s) or initial(s) followed by an abbreviation of the Latin adj. of place; thus Dr Ramsey signs *Michael Cantuar.*).

cap., *caput* (= chapter).

caps, capital letters.

Capt., Captain.

Card., Cardinal.

Carliol, (Bishop) of Carlisle (see Cantuar.).

C.B., Companion of the Bath; confinement etc. to barracks; counter bombardment.

C.B.E., Commander of (the Order of) the British Empire.

C.C., Consular Corps; County Council(lor); cricket club.

c.c., cubic centimetre.

C.C.C., *Civilian Conservation Corps; || Corpus Christi College.

C.C.S., casualty clearing station; Ceylon Civil Service.

C.D., Civil Defence; Contagious Diseases (Acts).

c.d., c.div., cum dividend.

Cdr, Commander.

c.d.v., *carte de visite* (= visiting-card).

C.E., Church of England; Civil Engineer.

C.E.A., Central Electricity Authority.

Cels., Celsius.

C.E.M.A., Council for the Encouragement of Music & the Arts (now Arts Council of Great Britain).

C.E.M.S., Church of England Men's Society.

Cent., Centigrade.

cent., century.

Cestr., (Bishop) of Chester (see Cantuar.).

C.E.T.S., Church of England Temperance Society.

C.F., Chaplain to the Forces.

cf., *confer* (= compare).

cg., centigram.

C.G.M., Conspicuous Gallantry Medal.

C.G.S., centimetre, gram, second (as elements in a system of scientific measurement); Chief of the General Staff.

C.G.T., *Confédération Générale du Travail* (F, = General Confederation of Labour).

C.H., Companion of Honour.

ch., chap., chapter.

Chas, Charles.

Ch.B., *Chirurgiae Baccalaureus* (= Bachelor of Surgery).

Ch. Ch., Christ Church, Oxford.

C.H.E.L., Cambridge History of English Literature.

Ches., Cheshire.

Ch.M., *Chirurgiae Magister* (= Master of Surgery).

Chron., Chronicles (O.T.).

C.I., Channel Islands; (Order of the) Crown of India.

Cicestr., (Bishop) of Chichester (see Cantuar.).

C.I.D., Committee for Imperial Defence; Criminal Investigation Department.

C.I.E., Companion of (the Order of) the Indian Empire.

c.i.f., cost, insurance, freight.

C.I.G.S., Chief of the Imperial General Staff.

C.-in-C., Commander-in-Chief.

C.I.O., Congress of Industrial Organizations.

circ., *circa; circiter.*

C.J., Chief Justice.

cl., centilitre; class; classical.

Clar., Clarendon (type).

cm, cm., centimetre.

C.M.A.S., Clergy Mutual Assurance Society.

C.M.B., (certificated by) Central Midwives' Board; coastal motor-boat.

Cmd, command paper (with series number, as *Cmd 7957*).

Cmdre, Commodore.

C.M.G., Companion of (the Order of) St Michael & St George.

Cmnd, = Cmd.

C.M.S., Church Missionary Society.

C.N.D., CND, Campaign for Nuclear Disarmament.

C.O., Colonial Office; commanding officer; conscientious objector.

Co., company; county.

c/o, care of.

C.O.D., cash on delivery; Concise Oxford Dictionary.

C. of E., Church of England.

C.O.I., Central Office of Information.

Col., Colonel; Colossians (N.T.).

col., column.

Coll., College.

Colo., Colorado.

Col.-S(er)gt, Colour-Sergeant.

Conn., Connecticut.

Cons., Conservative; Consul.

Co-op., Co-operative Society.

C.O.P.E.C., COPEC, Conference on Politics, Economics, & Citizenship.

Cor., Corinthians (N.T.).

Corn., Cornwall.

Corp., Corporal.

cos, cosine.

cosec, cosecant.

cot, cotangent.

Coy, Company.

c.p., candle-power.

cp., compare.

Cpl, Corporal.

C.P.O., Chief Petty Officer.

C.P.R., Canadian Pacific Railway.

C.P.R.E., Council for the Preservation of Rural England.

C.Q.M.S., Company Quartermaster-Sergeant.

Cr, Creditor.

C.R.A., C.R.E., Commander, Royal Artillery, Royal Engineers.

cres., *crescendo.*

crim. con., criminal conversation.

C.R.O., Commonwealth Relations Office.

C.S.C., Conspicuous Service Cross.

C.S.C.S., Civil Service Co-operative Stores.

C.S.I., Companion of (the Order of) the Star of India.

C.S.M., Company Sergeant-Major.

C.T.C., Cyclists' Touring Club.

cu., cub., cubic.

C.U.A.C., C.U.A.F.C., Cambridge University Athletic Club, Association Football Club.

C.U.B.C., C.U.C.C., C.U.D.S., C.U.G.C., C.U.H.C., C.U.L.T.C., Cambridge University Boat Club, Cricket Club, Dramatic Society, Golf Club, Hockey Club, Lawn Tennis Club.

cum., cumulative.

Cumb., Cumberland.

cum d., cum div., cum dividend.

C.U.P., Cambridge University Press.

C.U.R.U.F.C., Cambridge University Rugby Union Football Club.

C.V.O., Commander of the Royal Victorian Order.

C.W.S., Co-operative Wholesale Society.

cwt, hundredweight.

d., date; daughter; *dele* (= expunge); *denarius* (= penny); departs etc.; died.

d—, damn.

D.A., District Attorney.

D.A.A.G., Deputy Assistant Adjutant-General.

D.A.B., Dictionary of American Biography.

D.A.D.M.S., D.A.D.O.S., Deputy Assistant Director of Medical, Ordnance, Services.

D.A.G., Deputy Adjutant-General.

dag., decagram.
Dak., Dakota.
dal., decalitre.
dam., decametre.
Dan., Daniel (also O.T.).
D.A.Q.M.G., Deputy Assistant Quartermaster-General.
D.B.E., Dame Commander of (the Order of) the British Empire.
D.C., *da capo* (= repeat from the beginning; also **d.c.**); direct current; District of Columbia.
D.C.L., Doctor of Civil Law.
D.C.L.I., Duke of Cornwall's Light Infantry.
D.C.M., Distinguished Conduct Medal; District Court Martial.
D.D., Doctor of Divinity; *dono dedit* (= gave as a gift; also **d.d.**).
d—d, damned.
D.D.D., *dat, dicat, dedicat* (= gives, devotes, & dedicates; also **d.d.d.**).
D.D.S., Doctor of Dental Surgery.
D.D.T., dichlor-diphenyl-trichlorethane (an insecticide).
Dec., December.
deg., degree.
Del., Delaware.
del., *delineavit* (= drew this).
dep., departs etc.
dept, department.
Des. R.C.A., Designer of the Royal College of Art.
Deut., Deuteronomy (O.T.).
D.F., direction-finder (*or* -finding).
D.F.C., D.F.M., Distinguished Flying Cross, Medal.
D.G., *Dei gratia* (= by the grace of God); Dragoon Guards.
dg., decigram.
dim., *diminuendo*; (dim.) diminutive etc.
dkg., dkl., dkm., decagram, decalitre, decametre.
D.L., Deputy Lieutenant.
dl., decilitre.
D.L.I., Durham Light Infantry.
D.Lit., Doctor of Literature.
D.Litt., Doctor of Letters.
D.M., Doctor of Medicine.
dm., decimetre.
D.M.I., Director of Military Intelligence.
D.Mus., Doctor of Music.
d—n, damn.
D.N.B., Dictionary of National Biography.
do, ditto.
dol., dollar(s).
D.O.M., *Deo optimo maximo* (= to God the best & greatest).
D.O.R.A., Defence of the Realm Act.
doz., dozen.
D.P., displaced person.
D.P.H., Diploma in Public Health.
D.Ph(il)., Doctor of Philosophy.
D.P.I., Director of Public Instruction.
D.R., dead reckoning; dispatch rider.
Dr, Debtor; Doctor.
dr., drachm.

dram. pers., *dramatis personae* (= characters of the play).
D.S., *dal segno* (= repeat from the mark).
D.S.C., Distinguished Service Cross.
D.Sc., Doctor of Science.
D.S.M., D.S.O., Distinguished Service Medal, Order.
d.t(s)., **D.T.**, delirium tremens.
Dunelm., (Bishop) of Durham (see Cantuar.).
D.Th(eol)., Doctor of Theology.
D.V., *Deo volente* (= God willing).
dwt, pennyweight.
dyn(am)., dynamics.

E., East (as compass point, & as London postal district); Egyptian (in £E); Engineering.
E. & O. E., errors & omissions excepted.
E.B., Encyclopaedia Britannica.
E. by N., E by N, East by North.
Ebor., (Archbishop) of York (see Cantuar.).
E. by S., E by S, East by South.
E.C., East Central (London postal district).
E.C.A., Economic Co-operation Administration (now **M.S.A.**).
Eccles., Ecclesiastes (O.T.).
Ecclus., Ecclesiasticus (Apocr.).
E.C.U., English Church Union.
Ed., Edward.
ed., editor etc.
E.D.C., European Defence Community.
E.D.D., English Dialect Dictionary.
Edin., Edinburgh.
Edm., Edmund.
E.D.S., English Dialect Society.
Edw., Edward.
E.E.C., European Economic Community.
E.E.T.S., Early English Text Society.
E.F.T.A., Ef'ta, European Free Trade Association.
e.g., *exempli gratia* (= for example).
E.I.S., Educational Institute of Scotland.
E. long., East longitude.
E.M.F., electromotive force.
E.N.E., ENE, East-north-east.
ENSA, Entertainments National Service Association; also **En'sa.**
E.P., electroplate.
Eph., Ephesians (N.T.).
E.P.N.S., electroplated nickel silver.
E.P.T., excess profits tax.
E.R., *Elizabeth Regina* (= Queen Elizabeth); East Riding (of Yorkshire).
E.R.P., European Recovery Programme.
E.S.E., ESE, East-south-east.
Esq., Esquire.
Esth., Esther (O.T.).
E.T.A., estimated time of arrival.
etc., et cetera.
et seq., et seqq., et sq., et sqq., *et sequentia* (= and what follows).
E.T.U., Electrical Trades Union.
E.W.O., Essential Work Order.
exc., except; *excudit* (= engraved this).
ex div., ex dividend.

Exod., Exodus (O.T.).

Exon., (Bishop) of Exeter (see Cantuar.).

exor(s), executor(s).

exrx, executrix.

Ezek., Ezekiel (O.T.).

F, fine (of pencil-lead); French.

F., Fahrenheit.

f., feet; feminine; filly; folio; foot; franc(s); free; from.

f, forte (= loud).

F.A., Football Association.

F.A.A., Fleet Air Arm.

f.a.a., free of all average.

Fahr., Fahrenheit.

F.A.I., Fellow of the Chartered Auctioneers' & Estate Agents' Institute.

F.A.N.Y., First Aid Nursing Yeomanry.

F.A.O., Food & Agriculture Organization.

f.a.s., free alongside ship.

F.B.A., Fellow of the British Academy.

F.B.I., *Federal Bureau of Investigation; || Federation of British Industries.

F.B.O.A., Fellow of the British Optical Association.

F.C., Football Club.

F.C.A., Fellow of the Institute of Chartered Accountants.

fcap, fcp, foolscap.

F.C.I.I., Fellow of the Chartered Insurance Institute.

F.C.I.S., Fellow of the Chartered Institute of Secretaries.

F.C.W.A., Fellow of the Institute of Cost & Works Accountants.

F.D., *Fidei Defensor* (= Defender of the Faith).

Feb., February.

fec., *fecit* or *fecerunt* (= made).

F.E.I.S., Fellow of the Educational Institute of Scotland.

*F.E.R.A., Federal Emergency Relief Administration.

ff, fortissimo (= very loud).

F.F.A.S., Fellow of the Faculty of Architects & Surveyors.

f.g.a., free of general average.

F.G.C.M., field general court-martial.

F.G.S., Fellow of the Geological Society.

F.H., fire hydrant.

F.I.A., Fellow of the Institute of Actuaries.

F.I.A.T., *Fabbrica Italiana Automobili Torino* (= Italian automobile factory, Turin).

F.I.B., Fellow of the Institute of Bankers.

Fid. Def., = F.D.

fi. fa., fieri facias (= see it is done).

fig., figure.

F.I.J., Fellow of the Institute of Journalists.

F.I.M.T.A., Fellow of the Institute of Municipal Treasurers & Accountants.

fin., ad finem (= towards the end).

F.Inst.P., Fellow of the Institute of Physics.

f.l., falsa lectio (= false reading).

fl., florin(s); *floruit* (= flourished).

Fla, Florida.

flor., floruit (= flourished).

F.L.S., Fellow of the Linnean Society.

Flt-Lt, -Sgt, Flight-Lieutenant, -Sergeant.

F.M., Field-Marshal.

F.O., Flying Officer; Foreign Office.

fo, folio.

f.o.b., free on board.

f.o.r., free on rail.

F.P., field punishment; fire plug; former pupil.

fp, forte-piano (= loud, then soft).

F.P.S., Fellow of the Pharmaceutical Society.

Fr, Father.

Fr., French.

fr., franc(s).

F.R.A.D., Fellow of the Royal Academy of Dancing.

F.R.A.M., Fellow of the Royal Academy of Music.

F.R.A.S., Fellow of the Royal Astronomical Society.

F.R.C.M., F.R.C.O., F.R.C.P.(E.), Fellow of the Royal College of Music, of Organists, of Physicians (of Edinburgh).

F.R.C.S.(E.), Fellow of the Royal College of Surgeons (of Edinburgh).

F.R.G.S., Fellow of the Royal Geographical Society.

Fri., Friday.

F.R.I.B.A., Fellow of the Royal Institute of British Architects.

F.R.I.C., Fellow of the Royal Institute of Chemistry.

F.R.I.C.S., Fellow of the Royal Institution of Chartered Surveyors.

Frl., *Fräulein* (= Miss).

F.R.P.S., Fellow of the Royal Photographic Society.

F.R.S., Fellow of the Royal Society.

F.R.S.A., F.R.S.E., Fellow of the Royal Society of Arts, of Edinburgh.

F.R.S.G.S., Fellow of the Royal Scottish Geographical Society.

F.R.S.H., Fellow of the Royal Society for the Promotion of Health.

F.R.S.L., F.R.S.S., Fellow of the Royal Society of Literature, of the Royal Statistical Society.

F.S., Fleet Surgeon.

F.S.A., Fellow of the Society of Antiquaries, of Arts.

F.S.E., Fellow of the Society of Engineers.

F.S.M.C., Freeman of the Spectacle Makers' Company.

F.S.R., Field Service Regulations.

F.S.S., Fellow of the Statistical Society.

F.S.S.U., Federated Superannuation System for Universities.

ft, feet; foot.

fur., furlong.

F.W.A., Family Welfare Association.

F.Z.S., Fellow of the Zoological Society.

G, gram(me).

Ga, Georgia.

Gal., Galatians (N.T.).

gal., gallon(s).

G.A.T.T., General Agreement on Tariffs & Trade.

G.B., Great Britain.

G.B.E., Knight (or Dame) Grand Cross (of the Order) of the British Empire.

G.B.S., George Bernard Shaw.

G.C., George Cross.

G.C.A., ground-control(led) approach (of aircraft).

G.C.B., Knight Grand Cross of the Bath.

G.C.E., General Certificate of Education.

G.C.F., greatest common factor.

G.C.I.E., Knight Grand Commander (of the Order) of the Indian Empire.

G.C.M., general court-martial; greatest common measure.

G.C.M.G., Knight Grand Cross (of the Order) of St Michael & St George.

G.C.S.I., Knight Grand Commander (of the Order) of the Star of India.

G.C.V.O., Knight Grand Cross of the (Royal) Victorian Order.

Gen., General; Genesis (O.T.).

Geo., George.

Ger., German.

G.G., Grenadier Guards.

G.H.Q., General Headquarters.

•G.I., government issue; (colloq.) enlisted man.

Gib., Gibraltar.

Glam., Glamorganshire.

Glos., Gloucestershire.

G.M., George Medal.

gm., gram(s).

G.M.C., General Medical Council.

G.M.T., Greenwich mean time.

G.O.C.(-in-C.), General Officer Commanding(-in-Chief).

G.O.M., grand old man.

G.P., general practitioner (doctor).

G.P.I., general paralysis of the insane.

G.P.O., General Post Office.

G.R., general reserve; *Georgius Rex* (= King George).

gr., grain(s); grammar.

Grad. Inst. P., Graduate of the Institute of Physics.

G.S., general service.

gs, guineas.

G.S.O., General Staff Officer.

gym., gymnasium; gymnastics.

H, hard (of pencil-lead).

h., hour(s).

H.A.A., heavy anti-aircraft.

Hab., Habakkuk (O.T.).

H.A.C., Honourable Artillery Company.

Hag., Haggai (O.T.).

h. & c., hot & cold (water).

Hants, Hampshire.

HB, hard black (of pencil-lead).

H.B.M., Her (or His) Britannic Majesty.

H.C. (B.), House of Commons (Bill).

H.C.F., highest common factor.

H.C.S., Home Civil Service.

H.E., high explosive; His Excellency.

Heb., Hebrew; Hebrews (N.T.).

hectog., hectol., hectom., hectogram, hectolitre, hectometre.

Herts., Hertfordshire.

hf bd, half-bound.

hf cf, half-calf.

H.G., High German (also HG); His (or Her) Grace; Holy Ghost; Home Guard; Horse Guards.

hg., hectogram.

H.H., His (or Her) Highness; His Holiness (the Pope).

HH, double-hard (of pencil-lead).

hhd, hogshead.

HHH, treble-hard (of pencil-lead).

H.I.H., H.I.M., His (or Her) Imperial Highness, Majesty.

H.K., House of Keys (Isle of Man).

H.L., House of Lords.

hl., hectolitre.

H.L.I., Highland Light Infantry.

H.M., Her (or His) Majesty.

hm., hectometre.

H.M.A.S., H.M.C.S., Her (or His) Majesty's Australian, Canadian, Ship.

H.M.I.(S.), Her (or His) Majesty's Inspector (of Schools).

H.M.S., H.M.T., Her (or His) Majesty's Ship, Trawler.

H.O., Home Office; hostilities only.

ho., house.

Hon., Honorary; Honourable.

Hon. Sec., Honorary Secretary.

Hos., Hosea (O.T.).

h.p., half-pay; high pressure; hire purchase; horse-power.

H.Q., Headquarters.

hr, hour.

H.R.H., His (or Her) Royal Highness.

hrs, hours.

H.S.E., *hic sepultus est* (= here is buried).

H.S.H., His (or Her) Serene Highness.

h.t., high tension.

ht wt, hit wicket.

Hunts., Huntingdonshire.

h.w., hit wicket.

H.W.M., high-water mark.

Hy, Henry.

I., Idaho; Island(s).

I.A., Indian Army.

Ia, Iowa.

I.A.T.A., International Air Transport Association.

ib., ibid., *ibidem.*

i/c, in charge.

I.C.B.M., inter-continental ballistic missile.

I.C.I., Imperial Chemical Industries.

I.C.S., Indian Civil Service.

id., *idem.*

I.D.B., illicit diamond-buying.

I.E., (Order of the) Indian Empire.

i.e., *id est.*

i.h.p., indicated horse-power.

IHS (see dictionary).

Ill., Illinois.

I.L.O., International Labour Organization.

I.L.P., Independent Labour Party.

I.M.S., Indian Medical Service.

in., inch(es).

Inc., Incorporated.

incog., incognito.

Ind., India(n); Indiana.

inf., infra.

init., initio.

I.N.R.I., *Iesus Nazarenus Rex Iudaeorum* (= Jesus of Nazareth, King of the Jews).

inst., instant (= of the current month).

int. comb., internal combustion.

internat., international.

inv., *invenit, invenerunt.*

I. of M., I. of W., Isle of Man, of Wight.

I.O.G.T., International Order of Good Templars.

I.O.M., Isle of Man.

IOU (see dictionary).

I.O.W., Isle of Wight.

I.Q., intelligence quotient.

i.q., *idem quod.*

I.R.A., I.R.B., Irish Republican Army, Brotherhood.

I.R.B.M., intermediate-range ballistic missile.

I.R.O., International Refugee Organization.

Is., Isaiah (also Isa.); Island.

I.S.O., Imperial Service Order.

I.T.A., Independent Television Authority.

it(al)., italic (type).

I.W., Isle of Wight.

I.W.T.(D.), Inland Water Transport (Department).

I.W.W., Industrial Workers of the World.

J., Judge; Justice.

J.A., Judge Advocate.

J.A.G., Judge Advocate-General.

Jam., Jamaica; James (N.T.).

Jan., January.

Jas, James.

J.C., Justice Clerk.

Jer., Jeremiah.

jn, junction.

Jno., John.

Jon., Jonathan.

Jos., Joseph.

Josh., Joshua (also O.T.).

J.P., Justice of the Peace.

Jr, junior.

J.T.C., Junior Training Corps (in schools).

Jud., Judith (Apocr.).

Judg., Judges (O.T.).

jun., junior.

Kan., Kansas.

K.B., King's Bench.

K.B.E., Knight Commander (of the Order) of the British Empire.

K.C., King's College; King's Counsel; Knight(s) of Columbus.

kc., kilocycle(s).

K.C.B., K.C.I.E., K.C.M.G., K.C.S.I., K.C.V.O., Knight Commander of the Bath, (of the Order) of the Indian Empire, (of ¦the Order) of St Michael & St George, of the Star of India, of the (Royal) Victorian Order.

K.G., Knight (of the Order) of the Garter.

kg., kilogram.

K.H.C., K.H.P., K.H.S., Honorary Chaplain, Physician, Surgeon, to the King.

*K.K.K., Ku Klux Klan.

kl., kilolitre.

km., kilometre.

Knt, Knight.

K.O., knock-out.

K.O.S.B., K.O.Y.L.I., King's Own Scottish Borderers, Yorkshire Light Infantry.

K.P., Knight (of the Order) of St Patrick.

K.R., King's Regulations.

K.R.R.C., King's Royal Rifle Corps.

K.S., King's Scholar.

K.S.L.I., King's Shropshire Light Infantry.

K.T., Knight (of the Order) of the Thistle; Knight Templar.

Kt, Knight.

kv., kilovolt.

kw., kW., kilowatt.

Ky, Kentucky.

L, Latin; learner (on motor vehicle); Roman numeral = 50.

L., Liberal.

l., left; *libra(e)* = pound(s); line; lira; lire; litre(s).

La, Louisiana.

L.A.A., light anti-aircraft.

Lab., Labour; Labrador.

L.A.C., leading aircraftman; London Athletic Club.

Lam., Lamentations (O.T.).

Lancs., Lancashire.

Lat., Latin.

lat., latitude.

l.b., leg-bye.

lb., *libra(e)* = pound(s) in weight.

L.-Bdr, Lance-Bombardier.

l.b.w., leg before wicket.

L.C., left centre (of stage).

l.c., *loco citato*; lower case (of print).

L.C.C., London County Council.

L.C.J., Lord Chief Justice.

L.C.M., lowest common multiple.

L.C.P., Licentiate of the College of Preceptors.

L.-Cpl, Lance-Corporal.

Ld, limited; Lord.

L.D.S., Licentiate in Dental Surgery.

L.E.A., Local Education Authority.

Leics., Leicestershire.

Lev., Leviticus (O.T.).

L.F.A.S., Licentiate of the Faculty of Architects & Surveyors.

L.G., Life Guards.

L.G.U., Ladies' Golf Union.

Lib., Liberal.

Lieut., Lieutenant.

Lieut.-Col., -Gen., -Gov., Lieutenant- -Colonel, -General, -Governor.

L.I.F.O., L.I.L.O., last in first out, last in last out (stock valuation).

Lincs., Lincolnshire.

Linn., Linnaeus.

Lit. Hum., *literae humaniores.*

Litt.D., *literarum doctor.*

Liv., Livy.

L.J., Lord Justice.

L.JJ., Lords Justices.

ll., lines.

LL.B., *legum baccalaureus* (= Bachelor of Laws).

LL.D., *legum doctor* (= Doctor of Laws).

L.M.S., London Missionary Society.

loc. cit., *loco citato.*

log., logarithm; logic.

Londin., London., (Bishop) of London (see Cantuar.).

long., longitude.

loq., *loquitur.*

l.p., large paper; long-playing (record; also L.P.); long primer; low pressure.

L.R.A.D., Licentiate of the Royal Academy of Dancing.

L.R.A.M., Licentiate of the Royal Academy of Music.

L.R.C., Leander, London, Rowing Club.

L.R.C.P., L.R.C.S., Licentiate of the Royal College of Physicians, Surgeons.

l.s., *locus sigilli* (= the place of the seal).

L.S.D., = £. s. d.; Lightermen, Stevedores, & Dockers; lysergic acid diethylamide.

L.S.O., London Symphony Orchestra.

Lt, Lieutenant.

l.t., landed terms; low tension.

L.T.A., Lawn Tennis Association; London Teachers' Association.

L.T.C., Lawn Tennis Club.

Lt-Col., Lt-Cdr, Lieutenant-Colonel, -Commander.

Ltd, Limited.

Lt-Gen., Lt-Gov., Lieutenant-General, -Governor.

L.W.M., low-water mark.

LXX, Septuagint.

£, *libra(e)* (= pounds sterling).

£E, pounds Egyptian.

£. s. d. (see dictionary).

£T, pounds Turkish.

M., Monsieur.

m., maiden (over); male; mark(s) (coin); married; masculine; metre(s); mile(s); million(s); minute(s).

M.A., Master of Arts; Military Academy.

M.A.B., Metropolitan Asylums Board.

Macc., Maccabees (Apocr.).

Maj., Major; Maj.-Gen., Major-General.

Mal., Malachi (O.T.).

Man., Manitoba (also Manit.).

Mancun., (Bishop) of Manchester (see Cantuar.).

M. & B., initials of manufacturers (May & Baker) used as name of therapeutic drug (also M. & B. 693).

Mar., March.

Mass., Massachusetts.

matric., matriculation.

Matt., Matthew.

M.B., *medicinae baccalaureus* (= Bachelor of Medicine).

M.B.E., Member (of the Order) of the British Empire.

M.Brit.I.R.E., Member of the British Institution of Radio Engineers.

M.C., Master of Ceremonies; Member of Congress (*or* Council); Military Cross.

M.C.C., Marylebone Cricket Club.

M.Ch., *magister chirurgiae* (= Master of Surgery).

M.D., *medicinae doctor* (= Doctor of Medicine); mentally deficient.

Md, Maryland.

Me, Maine; *Maître* (French advocate's title).

mem., *memento* (= remember).

memo., memorandum.

Messrs (see MESSIEURS).

met., meteorology etc.

Met.R., Metropolitan Railway (London).

Metro., Metropolitan Railway (Paris).

mf, mezzo forte (= half loud).

M.F.H., Master of Foxhounds.

m.g., machine gun.

mg., milligram(s).

Mgr, Monseigneur; Monsignor (pl. Mgri).

M.I., Military Intelligence (*M.I.5*, branch dealing with security & counter-espionage in Britain); Mounted Infantry.

Mic., Micah (O.T.).

M.I.C.E., Member of the Institution of Civil Engineers.

Mich., Michaelmas; Michigan.

Milt., Milton.

M.I.Mech.E., M.I.Mun.E., Member of the Institution of Mechanical, Municipal, Engineers.

Minn., Minnesota.

misc., miscellaneous; miscellany.

Miss., Mississippi.

M.I.T., Massachusetts Institute of Technology.

M.J.I., Member of the Institute of Journalists.

mk, mark (coin).

ml., millilitre(s).

M.L.A., Member of the Legislative Assembly; Modern Languages Association.

M.L.F., multilateral (nuclear) force.

Mlle, Mademoiselle (pl. Mlles).

M.L.N.S., Ministry of Labour & National Service.

M.M., Military Medal.

MM., Messieurs.

mm., millimetre(s).

Mme, Madame (pl. Mmes).

M.Mus., Master of Music.

M.N., Merchant Navy.

M.N.I., Ministry of National Insurance.

M.O., mass observation; Medical Officer; money order.

Mo., Missouri.

Mods., Moderations (Oxf. Univ.).

M.O.H., Medical Officer of Health; Ministry of Health.

Mon., Monday; Monmouthshire.

Mont., Montana.

M.P., Member of Parliament; military police.

mp, mezzo piano (= half soft).

M.P.B.W., Ministry of Public Building & Works.

m.p.g., m.p.h., miles per gallon, per hour.

M.P.N.I., MPNI, Ministry of Pensions and National Insurance.

M.P.S., Member of the Pharmaceutical (*or* Philological *or* Physical) Society.

M.R., Master of the Rolls; municipal reform(er).

Mr (see MISTER).

M.R.B.M., medium-range ballistic missile.

M.R.C.P. (E., I.), Member of the Royal College of Physicians (of Edinburgh, of Ireland).

M.R.C.S. (E., I.), Member of the Royal College of Surgeons (of Edinburgh, of Ireland).

M.R.C.V.S., Member of the Royal College of Veterinary Surgeons.

M.R.G.S., Member of the Royal Geographical Society.

Mrs (see dictionary).

M.R.S.H., Member of the Royal Society for the Promotion of Health.

MS., manuscript.

M.S.A., Mutual Security Agency (replacing E.C.A.).

M.Sc., Master of Science.

M.S.E., Member of the Society of Engineers.

M.S.L., mean sea-level.

M.S.M., Meritorious Service Medal.

MSS., manuscripts.

M.T., Mechanical (*or* Motor) Transport.

Mt, Mount.

M.T.B., motor torpedo-boat.

M.T.P.I., Member of the Town Planning Institute.

Mus.B(ac).,   Mus.D(oc).,   Mus.M., *musicae baccalaureus, doctor, magister* (= Bachelor, Doctor, Master, of Music).

M.V., motor vessel; (also **m.v.**) muzzle velocity.

M.V.O., Member of the (Royal) Victorian Order.

M.W.B., Metropolitan Water Board.

Mx, Middlesex.

N., Nationalist; Navigator; New; North (as compass point, & as London postal district).

n., neuter; nominative; noon; noun.

N.A.A.F.I., Navy, Army, & Air Force Institute(s) (also **Naafi**, pr. năf'ĭ).

Nah., Nahum (O.T.).

N.A.L.G.O., National & Local Government Officers' Association (also Năl'gō).

N.A.S., National Association of Schoolmasters.

N.A.S.D., National Amalgamated Stevedores & Dockers.

Nat., Nathaniel; National(ist).

N.A.T.O., North Atlantic Treaty Organization (also Nāt'ō).

NATSOPA, National Association of Operative Printers & Assistants (now merged with others to form S.O.G.A.T.)

N.B., New Brunswick; North Britain; *nota bene.*

n.b., no ball (Cricket).

N. by E., N by E, North by East.

N.B.G., n.b.g., no bloody good.

N. by W., N by W, North by West.

N.C., North Carolina.

N.C.B., National Coal Board.

N.C.C.V.D., National Council for Combating Venereal Diseases.

N.C.O., non-commissioned officer.

n.d., no date; not dated.

N.Dak., North Dakota.

N.D.C., National Defence Contribution.

N.E., NE, North-east(ern).

N.E. by E., NE by E, N.E. by N., NE by N, North-east by East, by North.

Neb(r)., Nebraska.

N.E.D., New English Dictionary (= O.E.D.).

N.E.D.C., National Economic Development Council (colloq. Nědd'ў).

Neh., Nehemiah (O.T.).

nem. con., nem. dis(s)., nemine contradicente, dissentiente.

Nev., Nevada.

N.F., Newfoundland; Norman French.

N.F.S., National Fire Service.

N.F.U., National Farmers' Union.

N.H., New Hampshire.

N.H.I., National Health Insurance.

n.h.p., nominal horse-power.

N.H.S., National Health Service.

N.I.C., National Incomes Commission (colloq. Nick'ў).

N.J., New Jersey.

N.L., National Liberal; north latitude (also **N.lat.**).

N.L.C., N.L.F., National Liberal Club, Federation.

N.Mex., New Mexico.

N.N.E., NNE, North-north-east.

N.N.W., NNW, North-north-west.

N.O., natural order.

n.o., not out (Cricket).

N°, *numero* (= in number); number.

N.O.D., Naval Ordnance Department.

N.O.I.C., Naval Officer in charge.

nom., nominal.

non-com., non-commissioned officer.

non-U, not upper-class.

Northants., Northamptonshire.

Northumb., Northumberland.

Norvic., (Bishop) of Norwich (see Cantuar.).

N°ˢ, nos, numbers.

Notts., Nottinghamshire.

Nov., November.

N.P., Notary Public.

n.p., net personalty; new paragraph.

n.p. or d., no place or date.

N.R., Northern Rhodesia; North Riding (of Yorkshire).

nr, near.

N.R.A., *National Recovery Administration; National Rifle Association.

N.S., new series; new style; Nova Scotia.

n.s., not sufficient (funds to meet cheque).

N.S.A., National Skating Association.

N.S.P.C.C., National Society for the Prevention of Cruelty to Children.

N.S.W., New South Wales.

N.T., New Testament; Northern Territory (Australia).

N.U.G.M.W., National Union of General & Municipal Workers.

N.U.M., National Union of Mineworkers.

Num., Numbers (O.T.).

N.U.R., N.U.S.E.C., N.U.T., National Union of Railwaymen, of Societies for Equal Citizenship, of Teachers.

N.W., NW, North-west; North-western (London postal district).

N.W. by N., NW by N, N.W. by W., NW by W, North-west by North, by West.

N.W. Prov., North-west Provinces (India).

N.W.T., North-west Territories (Canada).

N.Y.(C.), New York (City).

N.Z., New Zealand.

O., observer; Ohio.

O.A.S., on active service; Organization of American States.

ob., *obiit.*

Obad., Obadiah (O.T.).

obdt, obedient.

O.B.E., Officer of the (Order of the) British Empire.

ob.s.p., *obiit sine prole* (= died without issue).

O.C., Officer Commanding.

Oct., October.

oct., octavo.

O.C.T.U., Officer Cadets Training Unit (also Oc'tu).

O.E.C.D., Organization for Economic Co-operation & Development (formerly O.E.E.C.).

O.E.D., Oxford English Dictionary.

O.E.E.C., Organization for European Economic Co-operation.

O.F.C., Overseas Food Corporation.

O.F.M., Order of Friars Minor.

O.F.S., Orange Free State.

O.H.M.S., on Her (or His) Majesty's Service.

O.K., all correct.

Okla, Oklahoma.

Ol., Olympiad.

O.M., Order of Merit.

Ont., Ontario.

O.P., observation post; (also o.p.)

opposite prompt (side, in theatre); *Ordinis Praedicatorum* (= of the Order of Preachers, i.e. Dominicans).

o.p., out of print; over proof.

op., opus.

op. cit., *opere citato* (= in the work quoted).

opp., opposite.

O.R., other ranks.

ord., ordained; order; ordinary.

Ore(g)., Oregon.

O.S., old series; old style; ordinary seaman; Ordnance Survey; outsize.

O.S.A., O.S.B., O.S.D., O.S.F., of the Order of St Augustine, Benedict, Dominic, Francis.

O.T., Old Testament.

O.T.C., Officers' Training Corps.

O.U.A.C., O.U.A.F.C., O.U.B.C., O.U.C.C., Oxford University Athletic, Association Football, Boat, Cricket, Club.

O.U.D.S., Oxford University Dramatic Society.

O.U.G.C., O.U.H.C., O.U.L.T.C., Oxford University Golf, Hockey, Lawn Tennis, Club.

O.U.P., Oxford University Press.

O.U.R.F.C., Oxford University Rugby Football Club.

Oxf., Oxford.

Oxon., (Bishop) of Oxford (see Cantuar.); Oxfordshire; Oxford University.

oz, ounce(s).

P., (car) park; pawn (Chess); pedestrian (crossing).

p., page; particle; past; perch.

p, *piano.*

P.A., Press Association.

p.a., per annum.

Pa, Pennsylvania.

P. & O., Peninsular & Oriental (Steamship Co.).

par., paragraph.

P.A.Y.E., pay as you earn.

Paym.(-Gen.), Paymaster(-General).

P.B., Prayer Book.

P.B.I., poor bloody infantry.

P.C., police constable; postcard; Privy Council(lor).

p.c., per cent; postcard.

pd, paid.

pdr, -pounder (of fish, gun, etc.).

P.D.S.A., People's Dispensary for Sick Animals.

p.e., personal estate.

P.E.N., (International Association of) Poets, Playwrights, Editors, Essayists, & Novelists.

pen(in)., peninsula.

Penn., Penna, Pennsylvania.

P.E.P., Political & Economic Planning.

per pro., *per procurationem* (= by proxy).

Pet., Peter (N.T.).

Petriburg., (Bishop) of Peterborough (see Cantuar.).

P.F., Procurator Fiscal.

pf, piano forte (= soft, then loud).

p.f.c., private first class.

P.G., paying guest.

P.G.A., Professional Golfers' Association.

Ph.B., Ph.D., *philosophiae baccalaureus, doctor* (= Bachelor, Doctor, of Philosophy).

Phil., Philippians (N.T.).

phot., photograph.

pinx., pinxit.

pizz., pizzicato.

pl., place; plate; plural.

P.L.A., Port of London Authority.

P.M., Prime Minister; Provost-Marshal.

p.m., *post meridiem*; post mortem.

P.M.G., Paymaster-General; Postmaster-General.

p.m.h., production per man-hour.

P.M.O., Principal Medical Officer.

pnxt, pinxit.

P.O., Petty Officer; Pilot Officer; postal order; Post Office.

pop., population.

P.O.S.B., Post Office Savings Bank.

P.O.W., prisoner of war.

P.P., parcel post; Parish Priest.

p.p., past participle; = *per pro.*

pp., pages.

pp, pianissimo.

P.P.C., *pour prendre congé* (= to take leave).

P.P.S., Parliamentary Private Secretary; *post postscriptum* (= further postscript).

P.R., proportional representation.

pr, pair; -pounder.

P.R.A., President of the Royal Academy.

P.R.B., Pre-Raphaelite Brotherhood.

Preb., Prebendary.

Pref., Preface.

pref., preference etc.; prefix.

prep., preparation; preposition.

Pres., President.

P.R.O., Public Relations Officer.

Prof., Professor.

Prol., Prologue.

prop., proposition.

pro tem., pro tempore (= for the time).

Prov., Proverbs (O.T.).

prox., proximo.

prox. acc., proxime accessit.

P.S., police sergeant; postscript; (also p.s.) prompt side.

Ps., Psalms (O.T.).

P.S.A., Pleasant Sunday Afternoon.

P.T., physical training.

pt, part; pint; port.

Pte, Private (soldier).

P.T.O., please turn over.

pty, proprietary.

Pty Co., Proprietary Company.

P.W.D., Public Works Department.

pxt, pinxit.

Q., Queen.

q., query.

Q.A.I.M.N.S., Queen Alexandra's Imperial Military Nursing Service.

Q.B., Q.C., Queen's Bench, Counsel.

Q.E.D., Q.E.F., Q.E.I., see QUOD.

Q.F., quick-firing (gun).

q.l., quantum libet.

Q.M., Quartermaster.

Q.M.G., Q.M.S., Quartermaster-General, -Sergeant.

q.p., quantum placet.

qr, quarter.

Q.S., Quarter Sessions.

q.s., quantum sufficit.

q.t. (sl.), quiet (*on the strict q.t.,* privately, avoiding notice).

qt, quart(s).

qu., quasi; query.

quant. suff., quantum sufficit.

Que., Quebec.

quot., quotation etc.

q.v., *quantum vis* (= as much as you wish); QUOD[2] *vide.*

qy, query.

R., Réaumur; *Regina; retarder* (on timepiece regulator, = to retard); *Rex;* River.

R., railway; right; run(s); rupee.

R.A., Royal Academy (*or* Academician); Royal Artillery.

R.A.A.F., Royal Australian Air Force; Royal Auxiliary Air Force.

R.A.C., Royal Armoured Corps; Royal Automobile Club.

rad., radical.

R.A.D.A., Royal Academy of Dramatic Art.

R.A.D.C., R.A.E.C., Royal Army Dental, Educational, Corps.

R.A.F.(V.R.), Royal Air Force (Volunteer Reserve).

R.A.G.C., Royal & Ancient Golf Club, St Andrews; also R. & A.

rall., rallentando.

R.A.M., Royal Academy of Music.

R.A.M.C., Royal Army Medical Corps.

R.A.N., Royal Australian Navy.

R.A.O.C., R.A.P.C., R.A.S.C., R.A.V.C., Royal Army Ordnance, Pay, Service, Veterinary, Corps.

R.B., Rifle Brigade.

R.B.A., R.B.S., Royal (Society of) British Artists, Sculptors.

R.C., Red Cross; right centre (of stage); Roman Catholic.

R.C.A.F., Royal Canadian Air Force.

R.C.M., Royal College of Music.

R.C.M.P., Royal Canadian Mounted Police.

R.C.N., Royal Canadian Navy; Royal College of Nursing.

R.C.N.C., Royal Corps of Naval Constructors.

R.C.O., Royal College of Organists.

R.C. of Sig., Royal Corps of Signals.

R.C.P., R.C.S., Royal College of Physicians, of Surgeons.

R.D., refer to drawer; Royal (Naval Reserve) Decoration.

rd, road.

R.D.C., Rural District Council.

R.E., Royal Engineers.

recd, received.

regt, regiment.

R.E.M.E., Royal Electrical & Mechanical Engineers.

repr., represent etc.; reprinted.

R. (et) I., *Regina (et) Imperatrix* (= Queen & Empress); *Rex (et) Imperator* (= King & Emperor).

Rev., Revelation (N.T.); Reverend.

rev., revolution.

Revd, Reverend.

R.F., Royal Fusiliers.

R.F.C., *Reconstruction Finance Corporation; Rugby Football Club.

R.G.S., Royal Geographical Society.

R.H., Royal Highlanders; Royal Highness.

R.H.A., R.H.G., Royal Horse Artillery, Guards.

R.H.S., Royal Horticultural, Humane, Society.

R.I., = R. et I.; Rhode Island; Royal Institute (of Painters in Water Colours); Royal Institution.

R.I.A., Royal Irish Academy.

R.I.B.A., Royal Institute of British Architects.

R.I.C., Royal Irish Constabulary.

R.I.I.A., Royal Institute of International Affairs.

R.I.P., *requiesca(n)t in pace.*

R.M., Resident Magistrate; Royal Mail; Royal Marines.

R.M.A., Royal Military Academy (Sandhurst; formerly Woolwich).

R.M.C., Royal Military College (Sandhurst; now R.M.A.).

R.M.L., Royal Mail Lines Ltd..

R.M.S., Royal Mail Steamer.

R.N., Royal Navy.

R.N.C., R.N.D., Royal Naval College, Division.

R.N.L.I., Royal National Lifeboat Institution.

R.N.(V.)R., Royal Naval (Volunteer) Reserve.

R.N.Z.A.F., R.N.Z.N., Royal New Zealand Air Force, Navy.

Robt, Robert.

R.O.C., Royal Observer Corps.

Roffen., (Bishop) of Rochester (see Cantuar.).

Rom., Romans (N.T.).

rom., roman (type).

R.P.S., Royal Photographic Society.

R.Q.M.S., Regimental Quartermaster-Sergeant.

R.R.C., (Lady of the) Royal Red Cross.

R.S., Royal Scots; Royal Society.

Rs, rupees.

R.S.A., Royal Scottish Academy; Royal Society of Arts.

R.S.D., R.S.E., Royal Society of Dublin, of Edinburgh.

R.S.F., Royal Scots Fusiliers.

R.S.M., Regimental Sergeant-Major.

R.S.O., railway sub-office.

R.S.P.C.A., Royal Society for the Prevention of Cruelty to Animals.

R.S.V.P., *répondez s'il vous plaît.*

R.S.W., Royal Scottish Society of Painters in Water Colours.

R.T., R/T, radio-telegraphy, -telephony.

Rt Hon., Right Honourable.

R.T.O., Railway Transport Officer.

R.T.R., Royal Tank Regiment.

Rt Rev., Right Reverend.

R.T.S., Religious Tract Society.

R.U., Rugby Union.

R.U.R., Royal Ulster Rifles.

R.V., Revised Version (of Bible).

R.W.S., Royal Society of Painters in Water Colours.

Ry, railway.

R.Y.S., Royal Yacht Squadron.

Ŕ, recipe.

Ŕ, rupee.

Ŕs, rupees.

Ŕx, tens of rupees.

S., Saint; Signor; soprano; South(ern); Submarines.

s., second; shilling; singular; *solidus*; son.

S.A., Salvation Army; South Africa; (also SA.) *Sturmabteilung* (= storm detachment; Nazi party army).

S.A.A., small arms ammunition.

Salop, Shropshire.

Sam., Samuel (O.T.).

S. & M., (Bishop) of Sodor & Man (see Cantuar.).

Sarum., (Bishop) of Salisbury (see Cantuar.).

Sask., Saskatchewan.

Sat., Saturday.

S.A.T.B., soprano, alto, tenor, bass.

S. by E., S by E, S. by W., S by W, South by East, by West.

S.C., South Carolina; Special Constable.

sc, *scilicet; sculpsit.*

SCAPA, Society for Checking the Abuses of Public Advertising.

s. caps, small capital letters.

S.C.C., Sea Cadet Corps.

sch., scholar; school.

scil., *scilicet.*

S.C.M., State Certified Midwife.

sculps., *sculpsit.*

s.d., several dates.

S.Dak., South Dakota.

S.E., SE, South-east; South-eastern (London postal district).

S.E.A.T.O., South-east Asia Treaty Organization (also Seat'ō).

S.E. by E., SE by E, S.E. by S., SE by S, South-east by East, by South.

Sec., Secretary.

sec., second.

sect., section.

Sen., Senate; Senator; Senior (also Senr).

S.E.N., State Enrolled Nurse.

Sept., September; Septuagint.

seq(q)., *sequentes, sequentia.*

Sergt, Sergeant.

s.f., *sub finem.*

sf, *sforzando.*

S.F.A., Scottish Football Association.

s.g., specific gravity.

s.g.d.g., *sans garantie du gouvernement* (= without government guarantee).

Sgt, Sergeant.

sh., shilling(s).

S.H.A.P.E., Supreme Headquarters Allied Powers in Europe (also Shape).

s.h.p., shaft horse-power.

S.I., (Order of the) Star of India.

S.J., Society of Jesus.

S.J.A., St. John Ambulance (Association & Brigade).

•S.J.C., Supreme Judicial Court.

S. lat., South latitude.

S.M., Sergeant-Major; short metre.

S.M.O., Senior Medical Officer.

s.m.p., *sine mascula prole* (= without male issue).

S.N.O., Senior Naval Officer.

S.O., Staff Officer; Stationery Office; sub-office.

Soc., Socialist; Society.

S.O.E.D., Shorter Oxford English Dictionary.

S.O.G.A.T., Society of Graphical & Allied Trades.

Sol.-Gen., Solicitor-General.

Som., Somerset.

Song of Sol., Song of Solomon (O.T.).

S.O.S. (see dictionary).

sov., sovs, sovereign(s) (coin).

S.P., starting price (Betting); stirrup pump.

s.p., *sine prole* (= without issue).

S.P.C.K., Society for Promoting Christian Knowledge.

S.P.E., Society for Pure English.

S.P.G., Society for the Propagation of the Gospel.

sp. gr., specific gravity.

S.P.Q.R., *senatus populusque Romanus* (= the senate & people of Rome); small profits & quick returns.

S.P.R., Society for Psychical Research.

s.p.s., *sine prole superstite* (= without surviving issue).

sq., square.

sq(q)., *sequentes, sequentia.*

Sqn. Ldr., Squadron Leader.

S.R., Scottish Rifles.

Sr, Senior.

S.R.N., State Registered Nurse.

S.R.O., Statutory Rules & Orders.

SS., Saints.

S.S., *Schutzstaffel* (= protection patrol; Nazi police force; also SS.); screw steamer; (also s.s.) steamship.

S.S.A.F.A., Soldiers', Sailors', & Airmen's Families Association.

S.S.C., Solicitor to the Supreme Court (Scotland).

S.S.E., SSE, South-south-east.

S.S.J.E., Society of St John the Evangelist.

S.S.W., SSW, South-south-west.

St, Saint; Strait; Street.

st., stem; stone (weight); stumped.

Staffs., Staffordshire.

S.T.C., Senior Training Corps (at universities).

S.T.D., subscriber trunk dialling (telephony).

St. Ex(ch)., Stock Exchange.

stg, sterling.

S.T.P., *sanctae theologiae professor* (= Professor of Sacred Theology).

str., stroke (oar).

S.T.S., Scottish Text Society.

Sts, Saints.

Sun., Sunday.

sup., superlative; *supra* (= above).

suppl., supplement.

Supt, Superintendent.

surg., surgeon; surgery.

sus. per coll. (see dictionary).

s.v., *sub voce.*

S.W., SW, South-west; South-western (London postal district).

S.W. by S., SW by S, S.W. by W., SW by W, South-west by South, by West.

S.Y., steam yacht.

T., tenor; Turkish (pounds).

t., taken (Betting); ton(s).

T.A., Territorial Army.

t. & o., taken & offered.

T.B., torpedo-boat; tubercle bacillus; tuberculosis.

T.B.D., torpedo-boat destroyer.

T.C., Town Council(lor).

T.C.D., Trinity College, Dublin.

T.D., *Teachta Dála* (= Deputy of Dail); Territorial (Officer's) Decoration.

t.e.g., top edge(s) gilt.

temp. (see dictionary).

Tenn., Tennessee.

Tex., Texas.

T.F., Territorial Force.

T.G.W.U., Transport & General Workers' Union.

Thess., Thessalonians (N.T.).

Thos, Thomas.

Thurs., Thursday.

T.H.W.M., Trinity high-water mark.

T.I.H., Their Imperial Highnesses.

Tim., Timothy (N.T.).

Tit., Titus (N.T.).

T.N.T., trinitrotoluene.

T.O., Transport Officer; turn over.

Toc H (see dictionary).

T.R.C., Thames Rowing Club.

Treas., Treasurer.

T.R.H., Their Royal Highnesses.

trs., transpose.

Truron,, (Bishop) of Truro (see Cantuar.).

T.S.H., Their Serene Highnesses.

T.S.O., town sub-office.

T.S.S.A., Transport Salaried Staffs Association.

T.T., teetotaller; Tourist Trophy; tuberculin tested.

T.U., Trade Union.

T.U.C., Trades Union Congress.
Tues., Tuesday.
TV, T.V., television.
T.V.A., Tennessee Valley Authority.
T.W.A., Trans World Airlines.
12mo, duodecimo.
T.Y.C., Thames Yacht Club.

U., universal (i.e. for everyone, referring to cinema picture); upper-class.
U.A.R., United Arab Republic.
u.c., upper case (of print).
U.C.C.A., Universities Central Council on Admissions.
U.D.C., Urban District Council.
U.K.(A.), United Kingdom (Alliance).
***ult.**, ultimo.*
U.N., United Nations.
U.N.E.S.C.O., United Nations Educational, Scientific, & Cultural Organization (also Unes'co).
Univ., University.
U.N.O., United Nations Organization (also Uno).
U.N.R.R.A., United Nations Relief & Rehabilitation Administration (also UNRRA, Unrra, pr. ŭn'rah).
U.P., United Presbyterian; United Press.
u.p., under proof.
U.S., United States (of America).
U.S.A., United States of America; United States Army.
U.S.(A.)A.F., United States (Army) Air Force.
U.S.N., United States Navy.
U.S.S., United States Senate; United States Ship (or Steamer).
U.S.S.C., United States Supreme Court.
U.S.S.R., Union of Soviet Socialist Republics.
Ut., Utah.

V, *Vergeltungswaffe* (= reprisal weapon; **V 1**, flying bomb; **V 2**, long-range rocket projectile).
v., verse; versus; *vide*; volt.
V.A., Vice-Admiral; (Order of) Victoria & Albert.
Va, Virginia.
V.A.D., Voluntary Aid Detachment.
V.C., Vice-Chancellor; Victoria Cross.
V.D., venereal disease; Volunteer (Officer's) Decoration.
v.d., various dates.
V.D.H., valvular disease of the heart.
VE, victory in Europe (*VE day*, 8/5/45).
Ven., Venerable.
v.f., very fair.
V.G., Vicar-General.
v.g., very good.
V.H.F., VHF, very high frequency.
Vic., Victoria.
V.I.P., very important person.
Vis., Visct, Viscount.
viz, *videlicet*.
VJ, victory in Japan (*VJ day*, 15/8/45 or in U.S. 2/9/45).
***v.l.**, varia lectio.*

V.O., Victorian Order.
vol., volume.
V.R., *Victoria Regina* (= Queen Victoria); Volunteer Reserve.
V.S., Veterinary Surgeon.
Vt, Vermont.
V.T.O.L., VTOL, vertical take-off & landing.
Vulg., Vulgate.
vv., verses.

W., Welsh; West (as compass point, & as London postal district).
w., watt; wicket; wide; wife; with.
W.A.A.C., Women's Army Auxiliary Corps (in 1914–18 war.)
W.A.A.F., Women's Auxiliary Air Force.
w.a.f., with all faults.
War., Warwickshire.
Wash., Washington.
W. by N., W by N, W. by S., W by S, West by North, by South.
W.C., West Central (London postal district).
w.c., water closet.
W.C.A., Women's Christian Association.
W.D., War Department.
W.D.A., W.D.C., War Damage Act, Contribution.
W.E.A., Workers' Educational Association.
Wed., Wednesday.
w.f., wrong fount.
W.F.T.U., World Federation of Trade Unions.
W.I., West Indies; Women's Institute.
Wigorn., (Bishop) of Worcester (see Cantuar.).
Wilts., Wiltshire.
Winton., (Bishop) of Winchester (see Cantuar.).
Wisc., Wisconsin.
Wisd., Wisdom (of Solomon; Apocr.).
W/L, wave-length.
W.L.A., Women's Land Army.
W. long., West longitude.
Wm, William.
W.N.W., WNW, West-north-west.
W.O., War Office; Warrant Officer.
Worcs., Worcestershire.
W.P., weather permitting.
W.P.B., waste-paper basket.
W.R., West Riding (of Yorkshire).
W.R.A.C., W.R.A.F., Women's Royal Army Corps, Air Force.
W.R.I., War Risk Insurance; Women's Rural Institute.
W.R.N.S., Women's Royal Naval Service.
W.S., Writer to the Signet.
W.S.P.U., Women's Social & Political Union.
W.S.W., WSW, West-south-west.
W/T, wireless telegraphy, telephony.
wt, weight.
W. Va, West Virginia.
W.V.S., Women's Voluntary Service(s).
Wyo., Wyoming.

x-cp., ex coupon.
xd, x-d., x-div., ex dividend.
x-i., ex interest.
Xmas, Christmas.
x-n., ex new shares.
Xt(ian), Christ(ian), (prop. χ = Gk letter chi, formed like English X).

Y., Yeomanry.
ye (pr. as *the*), the (*y* a survival in corrupt form of obs. þ, symbol for th; still used as archaism).
Yeo(m)., Yeomanry.

Y.H.A., Youth Hostels Association.
Y.L.I., Yorkshire Light Infantry.
Y.M.C.A., Young Men's Christian Association.
Yorks., Yorkshire.
yr(s), year(s); your(s).
yt (pr. as *that*), that (conj.; as *y*e).
Y.W.C.A., Young Women's Christian Association.

Zech., Zechariah (O.T.).
Zeph., Zephaniah (O.T.).

ADDENDA

A, ampere.
A & R, artists & recording.
A.C.C., Army Catering Corps.

c, centi-.
CERN, *Conseil Européen pour la Recherche Nucléaire* (= European Nuclear Research Council).
Cert. Ed., Certificate in Education.

d, deci-.
da, deca-.
Dip. Ed., Diploma in Education.
D.J., disc jockey.
DNA, deoxyribonucleic acid.

E.S.P., extra-sensory perception.
EURATOM, Eurä'tom, European Atomic Energy Community.

F, (Also) farad.

g, gram.
G.L.C., Greater London Council.
G.N.P., g.n.p., gross national product.

h, hecto-.
H.N.C., Higher National Certificate.
H.N.D., Higher National Diploma.

IAEA, International Atomic Energy Agency.
IBRD, International Bank for Reconstruction and Development (colloq. World Bank).
ICAO, International Civil Aviation Organization.
IDA, International Development Association.
IFC, International Finance Corporation.
IMCO, Intergovernmental Maritime Consultative Organization.
IMF, International Monetary Fund.
ITU, International Telecommunication Union.

J, joule.

k, kilo-.

M, mega-.
m, milli-.
M.O.T., Ministry of Transport.

*NASA (năs'ă), National Aeronautics & Space Administration.
N.U.S., National Union of Students.

O & M, organization & methods.
O.A.U., Organization of African Unity.
O.N.C., Ordinary National Certificate.
O.N.D., Ordinary National Diploma.

PVC, polyvinyl chloride.

R & B, rhythm & blues.
R.C.T., Royal Corps of Transport.
RNA, ribonucleic acid.
R.P.C., Royal Pioneer Corps.

SF, science fiction.
SI, *Système International d'Unités* (= International System of Units).
SST, supersonic transport.
STOL, short take-off & landing.

TAB, typhoid, paratyphoid A & paratyphoid B (vaccine).

U.D.I., unilateral declaration of independence.
UHF, ultra-high frequency.
UNICEF, Un'icĕf (ū-), United Nations International Children's Emergency Fund.
UNIDO (ūnĕd'ō), United Nations Industrial Development Organization.
UNRWA (ŭn'rah), United Nations Relief and Works Agency.
UPU, Universal Postal Union.

V, volt.

W, watt.
WHO, World Health Organization.
WMO, World Meteorological Organization.

APPENDIX II
PRONUNCIATION OF NON-ENGLISH WORDS

THE words in the following Appendix list are those containing sounds that (like the French nasals and the Scottish ch) are non-English and therefore not covered by our notation. In this appendix they are arranged in three lists: the words in their ordinary form; the anglicized pronunciation, denoted by the same symbols as those used throughout the dictionary, but with extra symbols to represent the unEnglish sounds; and the foreign pronunciation in the alphabet of the Société Phonétique Internationale.

CONSONANTS

In the anglicized pronunciation the new symbol to be noted is CH, which is used here to represent a soft guttural sound between sh and k, heard in Scottish words like *loch* and common in German.

In the International Phonetic alphabet the consonants have their usual values, except the following:

j is the sound in Eng. *young*			ʒ is the sound in Eng. *vision*		
ɲ	,,	,, Fr. *digne*	x	,,	,, Scottish and German *loch*.
ʃ	,,	,, Eng. *shout*			

VOWELS

The nasal vowels characteristic of French are pronounced 'through the nose', that is, with the soft palate at the back of the mouth lowered so that the breath passes through the nasal passages. The nasal vowels are four; and are approximately the nasalized forms of the vowels in English *at, art, all, earl*. In the anglicized pronunciation they are denoted by ăṅ, ahṅ, awṅ, ẽrṅ, in the phonetic alphabet by ɛ̃ ã ɔ̃ œ̃. These vowels are all heard in the phrase 'un bon vin blanc' (œ̃ bɔ̃ vɛ̃ blã).

The vowels in the International Phonetic alphabet are as follows:

a as in Fr. patte			o as in Fr. note		
ɑ	,,	pas	ɔ	,,	bon (= nasalized aw)
ã	,,	ban (= nasalized ah)	ø	,,	peu
e	,,	dé	œ	,,	seul
ɛ	,,	fait	œ̃	,,	brun (= nasalized ẽr)
ɛ̃	,,	fin (= nasalized ă)	u	,,	tout
ə	,,	de (obscure)	y	,,	pu
i	,,	ni	ɥ	,,	buis
o	,,	beau			

· denotes that the preceding syllable is long.

Ordinary Form	Anglicized Pronunciation	Foreign Pronunciation
abandon	ăbahṅ'dawṅ	abãdɔ̃
abattoir	ăbat'wahr	abatwa·r
accouchement	ăkōō'shmahṅ	akuʃmã
accoucheur	ăkōō'shẽr	akuʃœ·r
accoucheuse	ăkōō'shẽrz	akuʃø·z
acharnement	ăshaȓn'mahṅ	aʃarnemã
à deux	ah dẽr'	a də
affaire de cœur	ăfāȓ' de kẽr'	afɛ·r də kœ·r

Ordinary Form	*Anglicized Pronunciation*	*Foreign Pronunciation*
à fond	ah fawn′	a fɔ̃
agent provocateur	ah′zhahn prŏvŏkahtĕr′	aʒɑ̃ provokatœ·r
aide-de-camp	ā′ de kahn′	ɛ·dəkɑ̃
âme damnée	ahm dahn′ā	a·m da·ne
amende honorable	ămahnd′ ŏnŏrah′bl	amã·d ɔnorabl
ancien régime	ahn′syan răzhēm′	ɑ̃sjɛ̃ reʒim
à outrance	ah ōō′trahns	a utrã·s
aperçu	ahp′ärsōō	apersy
aplomb	ah′plawn	aplɔ̃
arme blanche	ärm blahn′sh	arm blã·ʃ
arrière-pensée	a′riär pahn′sā	arjɛ·r pã·se
arrondissement	ărondĕs′mahn	arɔ̃disma
atelier	ăt′elyā	atəljɛ
au fond	ō fawn′	o fɔ̃
au grand sérieux	ō grahn sĕrēĕr′	o grã serjø
au naturel	ō·nătūrĕl′	o natyrɛl
ausgleich	ows′glich	ausglaix
avion	ăv′yawn	avjɔ̃

B

ballon d'essai	băl′awn dĕsă′	balɔ̃ dese
bas bleu	bah blĕr	ba blø
battue	bătōō′	baty
beau monde	bō mawnd	bo mɔ̃·d
bêche-de-mer	bāsh′ də mār	bɛ·ʃ də mɛ·r
bersaglieri	bŭrsahlyär′ē	bersalje·ri
bon	bawn	bo
bon-bon	bŏn′bŏn	bɔ̃bɔ̃
bonne bouche	bŏn bōō′sh	bon buʃ
bonnes fortunes	bŏn fôrtūn′	bon fortyn
bon ton	bawn tawn	bɔ̃ tɔ̃
bon vivant	bawn vē′vahn	bɔ̃ vi·vã
bouillon	bōōl′yawn	bujɔ̃

C

café chantant	kăf′ā shō′ntahn	kafe ʃã·tã
cancan	kahn′kahn	kãkã
carte blanche	kärt blahnsh	kart blã·ʃ
char-à-bancs	shä′rabăng	ʃarabã
charlotte russe	shär′lŏt rōōs′	ʃarlot rys
chartreuse	shär′trĕrz′	ʃartrø·z
chassé-croisé	shăs′ā krwah′zā	ʃase krwaze
chevalier d'industrie	shĕvălĕr′ dăn′dōōstrē	ʃ(ə)valje dɛ̃dystri
chiffon	shif′ŏn	ʃifɔ̃
chignon	shĭnŏn′, shĕn′yŏn	ʃiɲɔ̃
chose jugée	shŏz zhōō′zhā	ʃo·z ʒy·ʒe
chronique scandaleuse	krŏn′ĕk skahndălĕrz′	kronik skãdalø·z
ci-devant	sē devahn′	sidvã
coiffeur	kwah′fĕr	kwafœ·r
coiffure	kwah′fūr	kwafy·r
communiqué	komū′nĭkā	komynike
concierge	kawn′siärzh	kõsjɛrʒ
confrère	kŏn′frär	kɔ̃frɛ·r
congé	kawn′zhā	kɔ̃ʒe
consommé	konsŏ′mā	kɔ̃some
contretemps	kawn′tretahn	kɔ̃·trətã
convenances	kawn′venahns	kɔ̃vnã·s
cordon bleu	kôr′dawn blĕr	kordɔ̃ blø
corps de ballet	kôr de băl′ā	ko·r də bale
coup-de-main	kōō′ de măn	kudmɛ̃
cul-de-sac	kōōl′ de săk	kydsak
curé	kū′rā	kyre

Ordinary Form	Anglicized Pronunciation	Foreign Pronunciation

D

début	dã′bŏŏ	deby
débutant	dã′bŏŏtahñ	debytã
débutante	dã′bŏŏtahǐt	debytã·t
dégagé	dāgah′zhā	degaʒe
de haut en bas	de ōtahñ bah′	de ho tã ba
démenti	dāmahñ′tē	demã·ti
dénouement	dānŏŏ′mahñ	denumã
déshabillé	dāzahbē′yā	dezabije
détente	dātŏ′nt	detã·t
deux-temps	dĕr tahñ	de tã
distingué	distē′nggā	distĕ·ge
double entendre	dŏŏbl ahñtahñ′dr	dubl ātã·dr
douceur	dŏŏ′sĕr	dusœ·r
doyen	doi′yen	dwajẽ
duvet	dŏŏ′vā	dyve

E

eau sucrée	ō sŏŏ′krā	o sykre
éclaircissement	ěklărsēs′mahñ	eklersismã
édition de luxe	edish′on de lŏŏks	edisjɔ̃ d(ə)lyks
élan	ā′lahñ	elã
embonpoint	ahñbawñpwäñ′	ãbɔ̃pwẽ
embouchure	ahñbŏŏshŏŏr′	ãbuʃy·r
émeute	īmū′t	emœ·t
empressement	ahñprĕs′mahñ	ãpresmã
enceinte	ahñsäñt′	ãsẽ·t
encore	ŏngkōr′	ãko·r
enfant terrible	ahñ′fahñ tĕrĕbl′	ãfã teri·bl
en garçon	ahñ gär′sawñ	ã garsɔ̃
ennui	ŏn′wē	ãnɥi
ennuyé	ŏnwē′yā	ãnɥije
en passant	ahñ päs′ahñ	ã pasã
ensemble	ahñsahñbl′	ãsã·bl
entente cordiale	ŏntŏ′nt kôrdiahl′	ãtã·t kordjal
entourage	ŏntŏŏrah′zh	ãtura·ʒ
entr'acte	ŏ′ntrăkt	ã·trakt
entrée	ŏ′ntrā	ã·tre
entremets	ŏ′ntremā	ã·trəme
entre nous	ŏ′ntre nŏŏ	ã·trə nu
entrepôt	ŏ′ntrepō	ã·trəpo
entresol	ŏ′ntresōl	ã·tresɔl
espièglerie	ěsplā′glerē	espjɛɡlərı

F

faïence	fah′yahñs	fajã·s
fainéant	fā′nāahñ	feneã
fait accompli	fāt ahkawñ′plē	fetakɔ̃pli
fanfare	fán′fār	fãfa·r
fauteuil	fōtĕr′ŏ	fotœ·j
femme de chambre	fäm de shahñ′br	fam də ʃã·br
fête champêtre	fāt shahñpātr′	fɛt ʃãpɛ·tr
feuilleton	fĕr′yetawñ	fœjtɔ̃
fiancé(e)	fēahñ′sā	fjã·se
fin-de-siècle	fáñ de syākl′	fẽ de sjɛkl
fine champagne	fēn shahñpin′	fin′ ʃãpaɲ
franc-tireur	frahñ tērĕr′	frã tirœ·r

G

gamin	gǎm′áñ	gamẽ
garçon	gär′sawñ	garsɔ̃
gendarme	zhŏn′därm	ʒãdarm
gendarmerie	zhŏndärm′erē	ʒãdarməri

Ordinary Form	Anglicized Pronunciation	Foreign Pronunciation
genre	zhahńr	ʒã·r
gourmand	gōōr'mahń	gurmã
gourmandise	gōōr'mahńdēz	gurmãdiz
grande	grahńd	grã·d
grand seigneur	grahń sĕnyĕ̀r'	grã sɛɲœ·r
gratin	grăt'ăń	gratɛ̃
grisaille	grĕzĭl'	griza·j
guilloche	gĕyŏsh'	gijoʃ
guipure	gĕ'pūr	gipy·r

H

hauteur	ōtĕr'	ho·tœ·r
hors concours	ŏrr kawńkōōr'	hor kõku·r
hors de combat	ŏrdekawm'bah	hor d(ə)kõba
hors-d'œuvre	ŏrdĕ̀r'vr	hordœ·vr

I-K

ingénue	ăń'zhänōō	ɛ̃geny
insouciance	ăńsōōs'yahńs	ɛ̃susjã·s
insouciant	ăńsōōs'yahń	ɛ̃susjã
instantané	ăństăntah'nă	ɛ̃stãtane
jeu	zhĕr	ʒø
jeu d'esprit	zhĕr dĕsprē'	ʒø dɛspri
jeunesse dorée	zhĕr'nĕs dŏr'ă	ʒœnɛs do·re
jongleur	zhawń'glĕr	ʒɔ̃·glœ·r
julienne	zhōōlyĕn'	ʒyljɛn
kümmel	kōōm'el	kümɛl

L

langue-d'oc	lahńge dŏk'	lã·gdok
langue-d'oïl	lahńge doil'	lã·gdoil
le roi le veult	le rwah le vĕr	lə rwa lə vø
le roi s'avisera	le rwah sahvĕ'zerah	lə rwa savizəra
liaison	liă'zn	ljɛzõ
lingerie	lă'ńzherē	lɛ̃·ʒri
littérateur	lĕtĕrahtĕr'	literatœ·r
loch	lŏcн	lox
lough	lŏcн	lɔx

M

mademoiselle	mădemwazĕ'l.	madmwazɛl, mamzɛl
manqué	mahń'kă	mã·ke
mariage de convenance	mă'riahzh ɗe kawń'venahńs	marja·ʒ də kõvnã·s
marron glacé	mă'rŏn glah'să	marõ glase
marseillaise	marselăz'	masɛjɛz
masseur	măsĕr'	masœ·r
masseuse	măsĕrz'	maso·z
mauvaise honte	mōvăz ŏńt'	move·z hõ·t
mauvais quart d'heure	mŏ'vă kărdĕr'	move kardœ·r
mauvais sujet	mŏ'vă sōō'zhă	move syʒe
mélange	măl'ahńzh	melã·ʒ
menu	mĕnōō', mĕn'ū	m(ə)ny
mésalliance	măzăl'Iahńs	mezaljã·s
mignon	mĕ'nyawń	miɲõ
milieu	mĕ'lyĕr	miljø
mise en scène	mĕzahńsăn'	mi·z ã sɛ·n
mitrailleuse	mĕtralyĕrz'	mitrajø·z
moire antique	mwahr ŏntĕ'k	mwa·r ãtik
monseigneur	mawńsĕnyĕ̀r'	mõsɛɲœ·r
monsieur	mesyĕ̀r'	m(ə)sjø
morgue anglaise	mŏrg ahńglăz'	morg ãglɛ·z
mot juste	mŏ zhōōst'	mo ʒyst

Ordinary Form	*Anglicized Pronunciation*	*Foreign Pronunciation*

N–O

nom-de-guerre	nŏm de găr′	nɔ̃ də gɛ·r
nom-de-plume	nŏm de ploom′	nɔ̃ də plym
nuance	nū′ahns	nyã·s
och	ŏCH	ox
ombre	awn′br	ɔ̃·br
on dit	ŏn dē′	ɔ̃ di

P

par excellence	păr ĕ′kselahns	par ɛksɛlã·s
parvenu	păr′venoo	parvəny
pas-de-deux	pah de dẽr′	pɑ də də
passé	pă′sā	pɑse
passementerie	păs′mentrĭ	pɑsmã·tri
pas seul	pah sũl′	pɑ sœl
pâté	pă′tā	pɑ·te
patois	pă′twah	patwa
peignoir	pā′nwăr	pɛɲwa·r
penchant	pahn′shahn	pã·ʃã
père	păr	pɛ·r
petits soins	pĕtē swăn′	p(ə)ti swɛ̃
pibroch	pē′brŏCH	pibrox
pièce-de-résistance	pē′ăs de rāzēs′tahns	pjɛs də rezistã·s
pince-nez	păns′nā	pɛ̃·sne
pis aller	pēzăl′ā	pizale
planchette	plahn′shĕt′	plã·ʃɛt
poilu	pwah′loo	pwaly
pompon	pŏm′pŏn	pɔ̃·pɔ̃
poseur	pōzẽr′	po·zœ·r
poste restante	pōst rĕ′stahnt	post restã·t
prie-dieu	prēdyẽr′	pridjə
Provençal	prŏvahnsah′l	provã·sal
purée	pūr′ā	py·re
pur sang	pūr sahn′	pyrsã

Q–R

quand même	kahn măm′	kã mɛ·m
raconteur	răkŏntẽr′	rakɔ̃tœ·r
raconteuse	răkŏntẽrz′	rakɔ̃tø·z
raison d'être	rā′zawn dā′tr	rezɔ̃ dɛ·tr
ranz des vaches	rahns dā vahsh′	rã·s də vaʃ
rapprochement	răprŏsh′mahn	raproʃmã
Réaumur	rā′ōmūr	reomyr
réchauffé	răshō′fā	reʃo·fe
recherché	reshăr′shā	rəʃɛrʃe
réclame	rā′klahm	rekla·m
renaissance	rĕnā′sahns	rənɛsã·s
rencontre	rahnkawn′tr	rãkɔ̃·tr
répondez s'il vous plaît	răpawn′dā sĭ voo plă	repɔ̃de si vu plɛ
restaurant	rĕ′storahn	restorã
résumé	rā′zōōmā	rezyme
robe-de-chambre	rŏb de shahn′br	rob də ʃã·br
roturier	rŏtū′rēă	rotyrje
ruche	roosh	ryʃ
ruse	rooz	ryz
rusé	roo′zā	ryze

S

salle-à-manger	săl *a* mahn′zhă	salamãʒe
salle d'attente	săl dătahn′t	saldatã·t
salon	săl′awn	salɔ̃
sang-froid	sahn′frwah′	sã frwa

Ordinary Form	Anglicized Pronunciation	Foreign Pronunciation
sans cérémonie	sahṅ sĕ'rĕmŏnē	sã seremoni
sansculotte	sahṅ'kŏōlŏt	sã kylot
sans façon	sahṅ fäs'awṅ	sã fasõ
sans gêne	sahṅ zhã'n	sã ʒe·n
sans peur et sans reproche	sahṅ pĕrr' ã sahṅ rĕprŏsh'	sã pœ·r e sã rəproʃ
sans phrase	sahṅ frahz'	sã fra·z
sans souci	sahṅ sŏō'sē	sã susi
Sassenach	säs'enahcк	sasənax
savant	säv'ahṅ	savã
séance	sã'ahṅs	seãs
Sèvres	sã'vr	sɛ·vr
soi-disant	swah dĕ'zahṅ	swadizã
soixante-quinze	swah'zahṅt kăṅz'	swasã·t kɛ·z
soupçon	sŏō'psawṅ	supsõ
succès d'estime	sŏōksă dĕstē'm	sykse dɛstim
succès fou	sŏōksă fŏō'	sykse fu

T

tableau vivant	tăb'lŏ vĕ'vahṅ	tablo vivã
tic douloureux	tĭk dŏlerŏō'	tik dulurə
timbre	tăm'ber	tɛ̃br
tirailleur	tĕrahyĕr'	tirajœ·r
torchon	tŏr'shŏn	torʃõ
tout ensemble	tŏōt ahṅsahṅ'bl	tutãsã·bl
train de luxe	trăṅ de lŏōks'	trɛ̃ dlyks
trente-et-quarante	trahṅt ã kă'rahṅt	trã·t e karã·t
trois-temps	trwah tahṅ	trwa tã
trouvaille	trŏō'vil	tru·vaj
tulle	tŏōl, tūl	tyl

V

Valenciennes	vălănsĕnz'	valã·sjen
ventre à terre	vahṅ'trahtăr	vã·trate·r
vingt-et-un	văṅt ã ĕrṅ	vɛ̃te õ
vin ordinaire	văṅ ŏrdĭnăr'	vɛ̃ ordinɛ·r
vol-au-vent	vŏl'ŏvahṅ	volovã

APPENDIX III

PRONUNCIATION OF PROPER NAMES

THIS list is intended as a guide to the pronunciation of some difficult proper names frequently met with. It makes no claim to completeness, and many geographical names in particular have had to be omitted.

One or two general points may perhaps be noted here: Classical names ending in -*es* are usually pronounced (-ēz). In New Zealand and in many other overseas countries native names are normally pronounced with all vowels sounded (and pronounced as Italian vowels, i.e. *a* = ah, *e* = ā or ě, *i* = ē or ĭ, *u* = oo). The U.S. pronunciation of some American place-names differs from the usual English pronunciation; in the following list such specifically U.S. pronunciations are preceded by an asterisk. There are many proper names (e.g. Kerr, Smyth) the pronunciation of which varies according to the family or individual referred to; such names have usually been omitted.

The following symbols have been employed in indicating pronunciation, in addition to those in the body of the work:

χ = *ch* in the Scottish pronunciation of *loch*.
ğ = 'soft' *g* in *ginger*.
ñ indicates that the preceding vowel is nasalized.

Aar'on (ār'-)
Abbeville (ăb'vēl)
Abĕd'nĕgō
A'bel (ā-)
Ab'ēlărd (ă-)
Abi'jah (-*a*)
Aboukir (ahbōōkēr')
About (ah'bōō)
A'brahăm (ā-)
Abruz'zi (-brōōtsĭ)
Abyd'ŏs
Accra (ăk'ra *or* akrah')
Acĕl'dama (-k- *or* -s-)
Ach'erŏn (ăk-)
Achĭt'ŏphĕl (ak-)
Ad'ĕlaide (ă-)
A'den (ā-)
Adĭrŏn'dăck (ă-)
Adonā'ĭs (ă-)
Adrĭăt'ĭc (ā-)
Aegē'an
Aegī'na
Æl'frĭc (ă-)
Aenē'ăs
Aen'ĕĭd
Ae'olus
Aes'chȳlus (-k-)
Aes'ŏp
Afghăn'ĭstăn (ăfg-; *or* -ahn; *or* ăfgănĭstăn')
A'găg (ā-)
Agincourt (ăğ'ĭnkôrt)
Ag'ra (ah- *or* ă-)
Aï'da (ah-ē-)
Aix-la-Chapelle (ā'ks-lah-shăpĕl')
Aix-les-Bains (ā'ks-lā-băñ)
Ajmēr' (ah-)
Alabama (ălabah'ma;* -bă-)

Albani (ălbah'nĭ)
Al'banȳ (awl-)
Alcan'tara (ălcahn-)
Alcēs'tĭs (ă-)
Alcĭbī'adēs (ă-; -z)
Aldĕb'aran (ă-)
Alğĕcī'r'as (ă-)
Alğēr'ĭa (ă-)
Algiers (ălğērz')
Allahabad (ăla-habăd')
Alleghany (ălĕgăn'ĭ; *or* -ănĭ)
Almerī'a (ă-)
Alsace (ăl'săs; *or* -ăs)
Amiens [French city] (ăm'ĭăñ)
Amiens [in Shakespeare] (ăm'ĭens)
A'mŏs (ā-)
Anăc'rĕon
An'ăm (ă-)
Anani'as (ă٠)
Anchises (ăngkī'sēz)
Andes (ăn'dēz)
An'droclēs (ă-; -z)
Andrŏm'ache (ă-; -ăkĭ)
Andrŏm'ĕda (ă-)
Andrŏn'ĭcus [in Shakespeare] (ă-)
Anğĕl'ĭcō (ă-)
An'ğĕvĭn (ă-)
Angōr'a (ăngg-; *or* ăng'gora)
Antæ'us (ă٠)
Anthæa (ăn'thĭa)
Antĭg'onĕ (ă-)
Antigua (ăntē'gwa)
Antĭn'ŏus (ă-)
Antonĭn'us (ă-)
Apĕll'ĕs (-z)
Aphrŏdī't'ĕ (ă٠)
Apŏllinār'ĭs

Appalách'ian (ă-; or -ăch-)
Aquin'ās
Arăch'nē (-kn-)
Aravalli (arah'vall)
Archimedes (ărkĭmēd'ēz)
Areōpagĭt'ica (ă-; or -g-)
Arēthūs'a (ă-; -za)
Ar'gentine (ār-)
Argyll (ārgīl')
Arĭăd'nē (ă-)
Ar'iel (ār-)
Aristid'ēs (ă-; -z)
Aristoph'anēs (ă-; -z)
A'rĭstōtle (ă-)
Arizōn'a (ă-)
Arkansas (ār'kansaw)
Artaxerxes (ārtagzer'ksēz)
Ar'tĕmĭs (ār-)
Ar'un (ār-)
A'rundel (ă-)
Asia (ā'sha)
Assi'sĭ (ăsē-)
Assouan (ăsōōăn')
Astār'tē (ă-)
Astrakhan (ăstrakăn')
Atalăn'ta (ă-)
A'tē (ă- or ah-)
Athēn'ē
Ath'ens (ă-; -z)
At'ropŏs (ă-)
Auch'ĭnlĕck (awk'-, Scottish ŏx'-)
Augē'as
Augŭs'tĭne
Aurēl'ius
Autŏl'ўcus
Av'alon (ă-)
Avignon (ăv'ēnyawn)
A'von (ă-)
Azores' (-ōrz)
Az'rāel (ă-)
Bach (bahx)
Ba'den (bah-)
Bā'den-Pow'ell (-ŏel)
Bagehot (băg'et)
Bahamas (ba-hah'maz)
Baiæ (bī'ē)
Bălĕá'rĭc (or balĕr'ĭc)
Băll'ĭol
Bălmō'ral
Bălthazār' [in Shakespeare]
Balu'chistăn (-lŏŏk-; or balŏŏkĭstăn')
Bantu (bah'ntŏŏ; or băn-)
Barăbb'as
Bārbăd'os (-ōz)
Bār'mecīde
Barŏd'a
Bărŏt'sĕland
Bās'ăn
Băsh'ăn
Băs'ra (-z-; or bŭs-)
Bassan'ĭŏ (-ahn-)
Băstille' (-tēl)
Basut'ōland (-ŏŏ-)
Batāv'ĭa
Băt'on Rouge (rŏŏzh)
Bau'cĭs
Bayeux (bă-yŏŏ')
Bayreuth (bī'roit)

Bea'consfield (bĕ- or bē-)
Beauchamp (bē'cham)
Beaulieu (bū'lĭ)
Beaune (bōn)
Bĕchua'na (-kŭahna; or bĕch-)
Bĕĕl'zĕbŭb (or bēĕl-)
Beethoven (bāt'ōven)
Behr'ĭng (bĕ-; or bār-)
Beira (bī'ra)
Beirut (bā'rŏŏt)
Bĕl'gĭum (-um)
Bĕl'ĭal
Bĕllāgg'ĭŏ (-j-)
Belle'rophon
Bĕlli'nĭ (-lē-)
Belvoir (bēv'er)
Bēnăr'ēs (-z; or bĕ-)
Berkeley (bār'lĭ)
Bĕrk'ley [America]
Berkshire (bārk'sher)
Berlioz (bār'lĭŏs)
Bĕrmūd'as (-z)
Berwick (bĕ'rĭk)
Bethune [English surname] (bē'ten)
Bicester (bĭs'ter)
Bĭd'éford
Bĭg'ĕlow (-g-; -ō)
Bĭhăr'
Bĭkanir' (-ēr)
Bĭlbā'ō
Blanc (-ahṅ)
Bleriot (blĕ'rĭŏ)
Bloem'fŏntein (-ōō-; -ăn)
Blücher (blŏŏk'er)
Bōadĭcĕ'a
Bŏcca'ccĭŏ (-kahch-)
Bŏd'iham (-dĭam)
Bŏdleian (-lē'an)
Bōēth'ĭus
Bohun (bŏōn)
Boleyn (bŏŏl'ĭn)
Bom'pas (-ŭm-)
Boŏtes (bō-ō'tēz)
Bŏrdeaux' (-dō)
Bŏrdōn'ē
Bō'tha (-ta)
Bŏttĭcĕll'ĭ (-chĕl-)
Boulogne (bŏŏlōn')
Bourchier (bow'cher)
Bow (bō)
Bŏz (or -ō-)
Braemār' (brā-)
Brāse'nōse (-zn-; -z)
Breadal'bane (ĕdawl-)
Brougham (brŏŏm or brŏō'am)
Bruges (brŏŏzh)
Buccleuch (buklŏō')
Būch'arĕst (-ker-)
Bŭd'apĕst'
Buenos Aires (bwĕn'ozăr'ĭz; or bŏō'ĭn-)
Bulawayo (bŏŏlawī'ō)
Būr'leigh (-lĭ)
Bўr'on
Bysshe (bĭsh)
Bўzăn'tĭum
Căb'ot
Căd'ĭz

Cadog'an (-ŭg-)
Cæd'mon (kă-)
Caen (kahń)
Cagliostro (kăllŏs'trŏ)
Cai'aphãs (kī-)
Cairo (kīr'ŏ)
Caius [Roman name] (kī'us)
Caius [Cambridge college] (kēz)
Căl'ais (-īs or -ā or -ī)
Călédōn'ĭa
Calĭg'ŭla
Callĭ'opē
Cămbȳs'ēs (-z)
Cămpa'gna (-ahnya)
Campbell (kăm'bl)
Căn'berra
Căndă'cē
Canōp'us
Carăc'tacus
Carew' (-ŏŏ)
Carew [Thomas, 1589–1639] (kăr'ĭ)
Căr'ey
Cărlisle' (-lĭl)
Carmăr'then (-dh-)
Carnăr'von
Cărněg'ie (-gĭ; or -ăgĭ)
Cărolĭn'a
Căsabiăn'ca
Căssĭopei'a (-ĕa)
Căstile' (-ēl)
Căthay
Catrī'ona (or kătrĭō'na)
Catŭll'us
Căv'ell
Cavour' (-oor)
Cecil (sĕsl or sĭsl)
Cĕcĭl'ĭa
Cellini (chĕlē'nĭ)
Cenci (chĕn'chĭ)
Cĕr'ēs (-z)
Cĕrvăn'tēs (-z)
Ceylön' (sĭ-)
Cézănne' (sā-)
Chăl'kĭs (k-)
Chamonix (shăm'onĭ)
Chapultĕpĕo' (chahpŏŏl-)
Chă'rĭng Cross (-aws; or chăr-)
Charlemagne (shărl'emăn)
Chăr'teris (-terz)
Chăt'ham (-tam)
Chautau'qua (sha-; -kwa)
Cherbourg (shĕr'boorg)
Cher'wĕll (chăr-)
Chicago (shĭkah'gŏ, •shĭkaw'gŏ)
Chĭl'ē
Chiswick (chĭz'ĭk)
Chloe (klŏ'ĭ)
Cholmondeley (chŭm'lĭ)
Chopin (shŏp'ăň or shŏ-)
Cicero (sĭs'erŏ)
Cimabu'e (chē-; -ŏŏ-ĭ)
Cimarŏs'a (chē-; -z-)
Cĭncĭnnăt'ĭ (or -ah-)
Cĭr'encĕster (or sĭs'ĭster)
Clăv'erhouse (or klăv'erz)
Clerk'enwell (klăr-)
Clough (klŭf, klŏŏ)
Clovĕll'ȳ

Cŏch'ĭn-Chĭn'a
Cŏckaigne' (-kān)
Cœur de Lion (kĕrdelē'awń)
Colbourne (kŏb'en)
Cŏl'chĭs (-k-)
Cologne' (-ōn)
Colom'bŏ (-ŭm-)
Colōn'
Cōlora'dŏ (-ah-; •-ă-)
Colquhoun (ko-hŏŏn')
Cŏm'ŏ
Comte (kauńt)
Connect'icut (-nĕt-)
Con'stable (kŭn-)
Cophĕt'ŭa
Cŏrdĭller'a (-lyăra)
Cŏrneille' (-nă)
Cŏr'rot (-rŏ)
Cŏrrĕgg'ĭŏ (-j-)
Cŏr'tĕs (-z; or -ĭz)
Cow'per (kŏŏ-)
Creusa (krĕŏŏ'za)
Crichton (krīt'on)
Crĭmē'a
Crŏ'cē (-ch-)
Cullŏd'en
Cȳm'bĕline (-lēn)
Cȳn'ewulf (k-; -ŏŏlf)
Cȳrĕn'ē
Cȳthĕr'a
Czech (chĕk)
Dæd'alus
Dahōm'ey (da-h-)
Dakōt'a
Dăn'ăē (-ĭ)
Dăn'tē
Dăph'nē
Dăr'ēs (-z)
Darī'us
Daudet (dŏ'dā)
Dăv'entry (or dăn'trĭ)
Da'vŏs (dah-; or davŏs')
Debuss'y (-ŏ)
De Crespigny (dekrĕp'ĭnĭ; or krĕs-)
De'găs (dā-)
Dehra Dun (dā'ra-dŏŏn')
Dĕlagō'a
De la Mare (dĕlamăr')
Delhi (dĕl'ĭ)
Dĕl'ĭus
Dĕl'phĭ
Dĕmĕt'er
Dĕmĕt'rĭus (or -mĕt-)
Dĕmŏs'thenĕs (-z)
Dĕr'went
Descartes (dăk'ărt)
Desdĕmŏn'a (dĕz-)
Des Moines (dĭmoin')
Dĕtroit'
Deutsch'lănd (doich-)
Diderot (dĕd'erŏ)
Dĭd'ŏ
Dieppe (dē-ĕp')
Dijon (dē'zhawń)
Dĭŏclē'tian (-shĭan)

Diŏġ′énēs (-z)
Diomēd′ēs (-z)
Dionȳs′ius
Dionȳs′us
Disrael′I (-zrāl-)
Domi′tian (-shǐan)
Dŏn Giova′nnI (ġŏvah-)
Dŏn Ju′an (jōōan)
Dŏnne
Donne [John, 1573-1631] (dŭn)
Dŏn Quǐx′ōte (or kwǐk′set)
Do′theboys (dōōdhe-)
Doug′las (dǔg-)
Drey′fus (drā-)
Dǔb′lǐn
Dǔl′wich (-lǐj)
Dǔ′mas (-mah)
Dū Maurier (mŏr′lā)
Dǔmfries′ (-ēs)
Dǔnēd′ǐn
Dǔr′ban
Durham (dǔ′ram)
Dvořák (dvŏr′zhák)
Ebbw (ĕb′ōō)
Ed′ǐnburgh (ĕ-; -bure)
Eiff′el tower (ǐf-)
Einstein (īn′stīn)
Eire (ār′ĕ)
El′I (ē-)
El′ǐa (ē-)
El′ȳ (ē-)
Empĕd′oclēs (ĕ-; -z)
Endȳm′iŏn (ĕ-)
Eng′land (ǐngg-)
Entŏbb′ĕ (ĕ-)
Eph′ésus (ĕf-)
Epǐcūr′us (ĕ-)
E′rĕwhŏn (ĕ-)
Erie (ēr′I)
Erin (ĕ′rǐn or ēr′-)
Es′tĕ (ĕ-)
Estŏn′ia (ĕ-)
Etherege (ĕth′erǐj)
Eubœa (ūbǐ′a)
Euphrāt′ēs (-z)
Euph′ūēs (-z)
Eurǐp′ǐdēs (ūr-; -z)
Europe (ūr′op)
Eurȳd′Icē (ūr-)
Evélin′a (ĕ-; -ēna)
Ev′elȳn (ĕ- or ĕ-)
Eyck (īk)
Ezĕk′iel (I-)
Fäġ′ǐn (-g-)
Fâll′odon
Fâr′quhar (-kwer)
Fät′ǐma
Fa(u)lk′land (fawk-)
Faust (fowst)
Featherstonehaugh (fǎn′shaw)
Fǐde′liō (-dā-)
Fiennes (fǐnz)
Fie′solé (fē-āz-)
Fǐg′arō
Fiji (fē′jē)
Finǐsterre′ (-âr)
Flŏr′ēs (-z)
Flŏ′rida

Foch (fŏsh)
Fŏlk′estone (fōks-)
Fŏrtūnāt′us
Frăncĕs′ca (or -chĕs-)
Freud (froid)
Frö′bel (frēr-)
Frŏb′isher
Froude (frōōd)
Frowde (-owd; or -ōōd)
Gala′pagōs (gahlah-)
Gäl′ĕn
Gălǐle′o (-āō)
Galle (gawl)
Galsworthy (gaw′lzwerdhǐ)
Gamäl′iel
Găn′ġēs (-z)
Gĕdd′ēs (g-)
Geoff′rey (ġĕf-)
Ghats (gawts)
Ghǐrländai′o (ġĕr-; -dǐ′yō)
Giaour (ġowr)
Gǐbral′tar (ġ-; -awl-)
Gǐd′ĕa (g-)
Gǐl′ĕăd (g-)
Gǐllĕtte′ (ġ-)
Giŏrġiŏ′nè (ġ-; -ġ-)
Giŏtt′ō (ġ-)
Giovanni (ġŏvah′nǐ)
Glamis (glahmz)
Glás′gow (-zgō)
Gloucester (glŏs′ter)
Gluck (-ōōk)
Gŏ′a
Gŏd′alming
Gŏda′varǐ (-dah-)
Godǐv′a
Goethe (gĕr′te)
Gounod (gōōn′ō)
Gracchus (grăk′us)
Grātia′nō (-shǐah-)
Greuse (grērz)
Grieg (grēg)
Grǐn′delwald (-vahld)
Groote Schoor (grōt′skoor)
Gros′venor (grŏv-)
Guadeloupe (gwahdĕlōōp′)
Guatemala (gwätǐmah′la)
Gudrun (gŏōd′rōōn)
Guelph (gwĕlf)
Guiana (gǐ-ah′na)
Gǔsta′vus (-tah-)
Haar′lem (hâr-)
Hăg′âr
Hägg′āi
Hague (hāg)
Haifa (hǐf′a)
Hain′ault (-awt)
Hait′I (or hī-)
Hǎk′luyt (-ōōt)
Hare′wŏŏd (hâr-; locally hâr-)
Hǎr′lĕch (-χ)
Hǎ′run-ăl-Rǎsch′id (-rōō-; -shǐd)
Harwich (hǎ′rǐj)
Hǎr′wǐch [America]
Hausa (hou′za)
Havre (hah′vr)
Hawai′i (-wǐ-I)
Haw′arden (-erd-; or hârd-)

Haw'orth (or how'erth)
Hay'dn (hī-)
Hĕb'rĭdĕs (-z)
Hŏc'atē
He'gel (hāg-)
Hei'delbĕrg (hī-)
Heine (hī'ne)
Hĕll'ĕspŏnt
Hĕm'ans
Hŏn'gĭst (-ngg-)
Hĕ'raclēs (-z)
Hĕraclīt'us
Hĕrcūlān'ĕum
Hĕ'rĕford
Hĕ'rĕward
Hĕrmī'onē
Hĕrŏd'ĭās
Hĕrŏd'otus
Hert'ford [England] (hârf-)
Hârt'ford [America]
Herts (hârts)
Hĕspŏ'rĭdĕs (-z)
Hīawath'a (-wŏ-)
Hil'dĕbränd
Hĭmalay'a (or hĭmah'lĭa)
Hĭn'du-Kush (-dōō kŏŏsh)
Hĭppŏc'ratēs (-z)
Hĭppŏl'ўta
Hŏbb'ĕma
Hō'bōken
Hoh'enlĭn'den (hōen-)
Hŏl'bein (-bīn)
Hŏl'born (hōben)
Hŏlŏfĕr'nēs (-z)
Hŏl'ўrōod
Hŏl'ўwĕll
Hŏm'er
Hŏndūr'ās
Hŏnolu'lu (-lŏŏlŏŏ)
Hous'ton (hōōs-)
Hūd'Ibrās
Hun'yadĭ (hŏŏn-yah-)
Hūr'on
Hўd'erabād
Hўgei'a (-ĭa)
Hўmĕtt'us
Hўpā'tia (-shĭa)
Hўpēr'ĭon
Iago (I-ah'gō)
Iăn'thē (I-)
Ic'arus (I-)
Idaho (I'da-hō)
Id'ō (ē-)
Idūmē'a (I-)
Illinois' (ĭ-; -noi)
Illў'rĭa (I-)
Indiăn'a (I-)
Indiănăp'olis (I-)
Inge (Ing or Ĭng)
Ingelow (ĭn'gĭlō)
In'ĭgō (I-)
In'terlaken (I-; -lah-)
Iŏlän'thē (I-)
Iŏl'chus (I-; -k-)
Iŏn'a (I-)
I'owa (I-)
Iphĭgĕnī'a (I-)
Iquique (Ikē'kĭ)

Irawad'ī (I-; -wŏd-)
I'roquois (I-; -kwoi or -kwah)
Isaac (iz'ac)
Isaiah (Izī'a)
Is'Is (I-)
Is'leworth (izelw-)
Ismailia (Izmah-ē'lĭa)
Isŏc'ratēs (I-; -z)
Isolde (Izŏl'da)
Ispahan (Ispa-hahn')
Ith'aca (I-)
Ixī'on (I-)
Jă'ĕl
Jaipur (jīpoor')
Jăn'us (or jīn'us)
Janeir'ō (-ēr-)
Jăph'ĕt
Jă'ques [in Shakespeare] (-kwĭz)
Ja'va (jah-)
Je'na (yā-)
Jĕ'rome (or Jĕrōm')
Jĕr'vaulx (-vō)
Jŏhänn'ésbûrg
Jŏl'lĕt
Jungfrau (yŏŏng'frou)
Kaap'stadt (kah-; -t)
Kabul' (-ōōl; or kaw'bŏŏl)
Kalahâr'ī (kah-; -ee)
Kălamazōō'
Kăndahâr' (-da-h-)
Kăn'sas [state] (-nz-)
Kăn'sas [city] (-ns-)
Kara'chĭ (-rah-)
Kăttégăt'
Kĕ'ble
Kĕd'âr
Kĕntŭck'ў
Kĕ'nya
Kĕr'guelén (-gĭl-)
Keswick (kĕz'ĭk)
Keynes (kānz)
Khârtoum' (k-; -ōōm)
Khayyám (kĭ-ahm')
Khўb'er (k-)
Kiel (kēl)
Kiev (kēĕf')
Kĭl'ĭmanjâr'ō
Kirkcud'bright (kerkŏō'brī)
Knollys (nōlz)
Kōb'ĕ
Kreisler (krīs'ler)
Kreutzer (kroit'ser)
Lăbouchère' (-bōōshâr)
Lăch'ĕsĭs (-k-)
Laĕr'tēs (-z)
Lafitte (lahfēt')
Lăg'ŏs
La Junta (lah hŏŏn'ta)
L'Alle'grō (lălā-)
Lancelot (lahn'slet)
Lăŏc'ōŏn
Lascelles (lăs'els)
Las Pal'mas (lahs pahl-)
Lausănne' (lōz-)
Lăv'ĕngrō
Lăv'erў (or lă-)
Lăvoi'sier (-vwahzyā)

Leam'ington (lĕm-)
Leăn'der (or lĕ-)
Lĕd'a
Le Feuvre (fĕv'er)
Leicester (lĕs'ter)
Leigh (lē)
Lein'ster (lĕn-)
Leip'zĭg (līp-)
Leith (lē-)
Lĕl'and
Lĕl'ў
Lĕn'ĭn
Leominster (lĕm'ster)
Leonắrd'ŏ (lā-on-)
Le Queux (lekū')
Leveson-Gower (lōō'sen-gŏr')
Lhăs'a (lä-)
Liège (llăzh')
Li'ma (lē-)
Līmoges' (-ozh)
Līszt (-st)
Llan- [as the first element in Welsh names] (hlän-)
Llewĕll'ўn (hlōō-)
Loh'ĕngrĭn (lō-)
Lŏngĭn'us (-nj-)
Lŏr'ĕlci (-ī)
Lŏs An'gĕlĕs (-ăngg-, also -ang-; -z)
Louĭsiăn'a (lōō-ĕz-)
Lou'ĭsville (lōō-)
Lourdes (loord)
Lourĕn'çŏ Márques' (-sŏ; -ks)
Luga'nŏ (lōōgah-)
Lў'cĭdăs
Lўcŭr'gus
Lў'lў
Lўm'ĭngton
Lympne (līm)
Lўsăn'der
Mắ'cĕdon
Mackay (makī')
Macleod (maklowd')
Madrăs' (or -ahs)
Madrĭd'
Măd'ūra
Mae'terlĭnck (mah- or mä-)
Mắf'ĕkĭng
Magĕll'an (-g-)
Măggĭŏr'ĕ (-j-)
Mahŏn' (ma-h-; or -ōōn)
Mahony (mah'nĭ)
Mainwaring (măn'erĭng)
Măl'achī (-k-)
Măl'herbe (-lărb)
Măl'orў
Mal'ta (mawl-)
Mal'vern (mawl-)
Măn'et (-ā)
Măr'ĭon (or mă-)
Marjoribănks (măr'chb-)
Márque'săs (-kä-)
Măr'tĭneau (-nō)
Mártĭnique' (-ĕk)
Măr'ўlănd (*mĕ-)
Mắ'rylebone (-eleben; or mắ'rĭben)
Masai' (-sī; or mah'sī)
Măssachus'ĕtts (-ōō-)
Măss'enet (enā)

Mătabĕl'ĕ
Maurī'tius (-shyes)
Mazzini (mădzĕn'ĭ)
Mĕch'lĭn (-kl-)
Mĕdĕ'a
Mĕd'ĭci (-chĭ)
Mĕdĭn'a (-ē-)
Mĕdĭn'a [America]
Meis'tersĭnger (mi-)
Mĕn'ai (-nī)
Mĕn'delssohn (-son; or -sōn)
Mĕnĕlā'us
Menzies (mĕn'zĭz, mĕng'ĭs, mĭng'ĭs)
Mĕrcĕd'ĕs (-z)
Mĕrcū'tĭŏ (-shĭ-)
Mĕ'rĕdĭth (in Wales mĕrĕd'ĭth)
Mĕ'rope
Mĕssĭn'a (-sē-)
Mĕtt'ernĭch (-k)
Mey'nell (mĕ- or mă-)
Mĭăm'ĭ
Mĭch'igan (-shĭ-)
Mĭd'ăs
Mĭlăn' (or mĭl'an)
Mĭll'ais (-ā)
Milngavie (mĭlgī')
Mĭnnĕăp'olĭs
Mĭnnĕsŏt'a
Mĭrăn'da
Mĭssour'Ĭ (-oor-; *mĭz-)
Mĭthrĭdăt'ĕs (-z)
Mĭtўlĕn'ĕ (or -ē)
Mŏbile' (-ĕl)
Moh'īcan (mŏ-; properly mŏ-hē'-)
Mohun (mōōn)
Mŏl'ière (-lĭăr)
Mŏna'cŏ (-ah-)
Mŏntaigne' (-ăn)
Mŏnta'na (-ah-; *-ă-)
Mŏntrĕal' (-awl)
Mŏrŏn'ĕ
Mŏs'cow (-ŏ; *-ow)
Moul'main
Mŏzambique' (-bĕk)
Müller (mŭl'er)
Mŭn'ich (-ĭk)
Mŭrĭll'ŏ
Mўcĕ'næ
Mўtĭlĕn'ĕ (or -ē)
Nairŏb'Ĭ (nīr-)
Nă'omĭ
Năp'ĭer (or napĕr')
Natăl'
Năv'ajo (-a-hŏ)
Nĕpal' (-awl)
Nĕva'da (-vah; *-ă-)
Newfoundland' (-fend-)
Nĭăg'ara
Nibelung (nĕb'elŏŏng)
Nietzsche (nē'che)
Nī'ğer
Nĭğĕr'ĭa
Nĭl'gĭrĭ (-g-)
Nĭn'ĕveh (-vĭ)
Norwich (nŏ'rĭj)
Nўăs(s)'a
Ob'an (ŏ-)
Ober-ămm'ergau (ŏ-; -gow)

Ob'eron (ŏ-)
Odyss'eus (-ŭs)
Oenōn'ê (ē-)
Ohī'ō (ŏ-h-)
Oklahōm'a (ŏ-)
Omaha (ŏma-hah'; •-aw)
Oman (ōmahn')
Ontār'iō (ŏ-)
Ophēl'ia (ŏ-)
Orēs'tēs (ŏ-; -z)
Orī'on (ŏ-)
Orlê'ans (ôr-; -z)
Orleans [America] (ôrlēnz')
Orpheus (ôr'fŭs)
Orsino (ôrsēn'ō)
Osī'rīs (ŏ-)
Os'ler (ŏ-)
Ota'gō (ōtah-,
Othēll'ō (ŏ-)
Ottawa (ŏt'a-wa)
Ottŭm'wa (ŏ-)
Ouida (wē'da)
Ouse (ōōz)
Ov'id (ŏ-)
Pach'mann (pahk-)
Păderew'skī (-ĕvskĭ)
Păgani'nī (-ēn-)
Pagliacci (pălliăch'ī)
Pălamēd'ēs (-z)
Păl'amon
Pălěstri'na (-ēn-)
Păll'ăs
Păll Măll' (or pĕl'mĕl')
Pănama' (-ah)
Păph'ōs
Pă'raguay (-gwă or -gwĭ)
Părnăss'us
Parŏll'ès
Pās'teur (-êr)
Patrŏc'lus
Pau (pō)
Pausān'iăs
Paví'a
Pēkĭn'
Pēl'eus (-lŭs)
Pěloponnēs'us
Pěl'ŏps
Pěnnsylvăn'ia
Pěnthěsilē'a
Pepys (pēps or pĕps or pĕp'ĭs)
Pêr'dĭta
Pêrgole'sê (-lăz-)
Pě'rĭclēs (-z)
Pě'rrault (-rō)
Pěrsěph'onê
Pěrsěp'olĭs
Pêr'seus (-ŭs)
Peru' (-ōō)
Pěrugi'nō (-ōōğĕ-)
Peshawar (peshŏr')
Pěstalŏzz'i (-tsĭ)
Pěsth (-st)
Pět'ra
Pět'rărch (-k)
Pětru'chio (-ōōk- or -ōōch-)
Phæd'ra
Phā'ěthōn
Phărsāl'ia

Philěm'ŏn
Phō'cĭs
Phœb'ê (fē-)
Phœnīc'ia (fē-)
Phrȳn'ê
Pie'dmont (pē- or pyĕ- or pyă-)
Pietermā'rĭtzbŭrg (pē-; or -rĭtz'-)
Pila'tus (-ah-)
Pīněr'ō
Piræ'us
Plăt'ō
Plin'ȳ
Plotin'us
Plu'tărch (-ōō-; -k)
Pole Carew (pōōl kăr'ī)
Pŏllaiuo'lō (-lĭ-ŏō-ō-)
Pŏlȳb'ius
Pŏlȳc'ratēs (-z)
Pŏlȳphēm'us
Pŏlȳx'ěna
Pom'frět (pŭm-)
Pŏmpei'ï (-ĕī or -āĕ)
Pŏrt Said (sah'ĭd or săd)
Pŏsei'don (-sī-)
Potōm'ăc
Poughkeep'sie (pokĭp-)
Poussin (pōō'săn)
Pŏ'wȳs
Prăxĭt'elēs (-z)
Prětōr'ia
Prī'am
Promēth'eus (-ŭs)
Prŏs'erpine
Proust (prōost)
Ptŏl'emȳ (t-)
Puccini (pōōchē'nĭ)
Pŭnjab' (-ahb)
Pȳ'ramus
Pȳtch'ley
Pȳthăg'orăs
Quêbĕc'
Răb'elais (-elă)
Răc'ine (-sěn)
Rae'bŭrn (rā-)
Rajputana (rahjpōōtah'na)
Raleigh (raw'lĭ or rah- or rá-)
Răm'ēsēs (-z)
Răn'ělagh (-le)
Răph'ăel
Ra'walpĭndī (rah-w-)
Read'ĭng (rĕd-)
Reger (rāg'er)
Reu'ter (roi-)
Reyk'javĭk (rěkya-)
Rheims (rēms)
Rhōdē'sia (rō-; -z- or -s-; also -zha, -sha)
Rī'ca (rē-)
Rĭch'elieu (-shelŭ)
Rio (rē'ō)
Rĭvier'a (-āīa)
Robespierre (rŏbz'pyär)
Rŏcke'fěller (-kf-, •-kĭf-)
Rŏm'ney (or rŭm-)
Rōntgen (rĕrn'tyen)
Rōō'sevĕlt (-sv-, •-sĭv-)
Rossětt'ī (rŏz-)
Rŏtoru'a (-ōōa)
Rouen (rōō'ahṅ)

Röx'burgh (-brĕ)
Ruy Blas (rwē blahs)
Sachĕv'erell (-sh-)
Ság'ĭnaw
Sainte-Beuve (sănt bĕrv)
Saint-Saenṡ (săṅ'sahṅs)
Salis'burў (sawlzb-)
Salōm'ĕ
Salōn'ĭca (or sălonĕ⁴)
Săn'chō (-ngk-)
Săn Diego (dĕ-ā'gō)
Săn Jacin'tō
Săn Joaquin (wahkĕn')
Săn Jose (hōsā')
Săn Juan' (hwahn)
Săn Re'mō (rā-)
Săn'ta Fé (fā)
Săntia'gō (-ah-)
Sărasa'tĕ (-ah-)
Sara'wak (-rah-)
Săskătch'ĕwan
Săskatōōn'
Sault Sainte Marie (sōō sănt măr'Ĭ; or sănt)
Săvonarōl'a
Sca'fĕll' (scaw-)
Scăl'ĭgĕr
Schĕhĕreza'dĕ (sh-; -ezah-)
Schĕnĕc'tadў (sk-)
Schu'bĕrt (shōō-)
Schuy'ler (skī-)
Schuy'lkĭll (skōōl-)
Scĭll'ў (s-)
Scĭp'ĭō (s-)
Scrĭ'abĭn
Scone (skōōn)
Sĕátt'le
Sĕdăn'
Sĕd'bergh [school] (-ber; -bĕrg)
Sĕd'bergh [town] (-ber)
Seine (sān)
Sĕm'ĕlĕ
Sĕmĭ'ramĭs
Sĕn'ĕca
Sĕnĕgal' (-awl)
Sĕnnāch'erĭb (-k-)
Sĕt'ĕbōs
Shrews'burў (-ōōz- or -ōz-)
Sĭăm'
Sĭerr'a Lĕone' (-ăr-; -ōn-)
Sĭm'ĕon
Sĭm'on
Simplon (săṅ'plawṅ)
Sī'nai (-nlī)
Sĭs'ўphus
Sĭ'va (shĕ-)
Skĭdd'aw (or skĭddaw')
Slough (slow)
Smĕth'wick (-dhĭk)
Sŏc'ratēs (-z)
Sŏfi'a
Sōma'll (-ah-)
Som'ersĕt (sŭm-)
Sŏph'oclēs (-z)
Southey (sow'dhĭ)
Southwark (sŭdh'ark)
Sou'za (-ōō-)
Srīna'gar (-ah-)

St Al'bans (awl-)
Stendhal (stahṅ'dahl)
St John (sĭn'jon)
St Lou'ĭs (sănt lōō-)
St Ma'lō (-ah-)
Stōke Pō'gĕs
Strachan (strawn or strah'ҳan)
Streath'am (strĕt-)
Stuy'vĕsant (stī-)
Sudăn' (sōō- or sōō-)
Su'ĕz (-ōō-)
Suma'tra (sōōmah-)
Sumurun (sōōmōōrōōn')
Surăt' (sōō-)
Sŭsquĕhănn'a (-kw-)
Swa'zĭländ (swah-)
Sўnge (-ng)
Sўr'acŭse (-z)
Sў'racŭse [America]
Tăg'us
Tahi'tĭ (tah-hē-)
Taj Mahal (tahj mahahl')
Tănganyi'ka (-ngg-; -yĕ-)
Tăngier' (-jĕr)
Tănnhäu'ser (-hoiz-)
Tărragŏn'a
Tchaikovsky (chīkŏv'skĭ)
Tecŭm'seh (-sĕ)
Teh'răn (tăer-)
Teignmouth (tĭn'meth)
Tĕlĕm'achus (-kus)
Tĕnerif(f)e' (-ĕf)
Tĕrpsĭch'orĕ (-k-)
Tĭĕ'rra dĕl Fuego (fōōā'gō)
Tĕrtŭll'ian
Thame (tām)
Thames (tĕmz)
Thăn'ĕt
Thēbes (-bz)
Thĕmĭst'oclēs (-z)
Thĕ'obald (-awld; or tĭb'ald)
Thĕŏd'orĭc
Thĕrmŏp'ўlae
Thĕrsīt'ĕs (-z)
Thĕs'eus (-ŭs)
Thĕs'pĭs
Thĕssaloni'ca
Thĕss'alў
Thĭs'bĕ (-z-)
Thom'as (tŏm-)
Thomas [Ambroise] (tō'mah)
Thŏr'eau (-ō)
Thŭcўd'Ĭdĕs (-z)
Tĭbĕr'Ĭus
Tĭbĕt'
Tĭbŭll'us
Tĭci'nō (-chĕ-)
Tĭt'lĭs
Tĭg'rĭs
Tĭm'ŏa
Tĭtăg'el
Tĭtăn'Ĭa
Tĭt'ian (-shĭ-)
Tĭt'us
Tĭv'oll
Tōbĭ'as
Tō'kўō
Tŏlĕ'dŏ (or -ā'dŏ)

Tŏ'rrĕs
Tŏt'nĕs
Toulon (tōŏlawñ')
Toulouse (tōŏlōōz')
Touraine' (tōŏ-)
Tours (toor)
Tow'cester (tŏ'ster)
Trafăl'gar (or trăfalgăr')
Trāj'an
Trăn'skei (-kī)
Transvaal (trah'nsvahl)
Trévi'so (-vēz-)
Trĭchĭnŏp'olĭ
Trĭĕste'
Trĭnc'ōmalee'
Trŏll'ope (-ep)
Trŏss'ăchs (-ks)
Trou'ville (-ōō-)
Tucson (tōŏ'sawñ; or -ăn)
Tuileries (twēl'erē)
Tūrĭn' (or tūr'ĭn)
Tûrkĕstăn'
Tŭskĕ'gee
Tussaud's' (-sōz)
Tў'chō (-k-)
Tўn'dale (-dl)
Tў'rol (or tĭrōl' or tĭrŏl')
Tў'rwhitt (-rĭt)
Ugăn'da (ū- or ōō-)
Uh'land (ōō-)
U'ĭst (ū-)
Ulўss'ēs (ū-; -z)
Uphăr'sĭn (ū-)
Urī'ah (ūr-)
Ur'ĭel (ūr-)
Urquhart (ûr'kert)
Uruguay (ōŏ'rōŏgway'; or -ĭ)
Ush'ant (ū-)
Utah (ū'tah, *ū'taw)
U Thant (ōŏ thŭnt)
Utrecht (ūtrĕkt')
Văl'kўrie
Văl'ois (-wah)
Vălparais'ō (-z-)
Văn'burgh (-brē)
Văsăr'ĭ
Văs'cō da Ga'ma (gah·)
Văthĕk
Vaughan (vawn)
Vauxhall (vŏks'hawl')
Vĕlăs'quez (-kwĭz or -kĭz)
Vĕn'ĕzūĕ'la
Vĕrde
Ver'dĭ (vār-)
Vĕr'dun (or vār·)
Vĕr'gĭl
Verne (vārn)
Vĕrone'se (-ăzl)
Vĕ'rulam (-ōō-)
Vĕsūv'ĭus
Vichy (vē'shē)
Vĭĕnn'a

Vĭg'ō
Vĭll'iers (-lerz)
Vĭn'ci (-chĭ)
Vi'ola
Vĭr'gĭl
Vosges (vōzh)
Wa'băsh (waw-)
Wadham (wŏd'am)
Wag'ner (vah-)
Waldegrāve (wawl'g·)
Wantage (wŏn'tĭj)
Wapp'ing (wŏ-)
Wār'ing
Warwick (wŏ'rĭk)
Watteau (wŏt'ō)
Wazir'ĭstan (-ēr-; -ahn)
Wear [river] (wēr)
We'ber (vā-)
Wednes'bury (wĕnzb-)
Wei'măr (vī-)
Weiss'hŏrn (vīs-h-)
Welwyn (wĕl'ĭn)
Wemyss (wēmz)
We'ser (văz- or wēz-)
Whewell (hūl)
Wies'baden (vēzbah-)
Wĭs'bĕch (-z-)
Wĭscŏn'sĭn
Wŏŏl'wĭch (-lĭj)
Wŏŏtt'on
Worcester (wŏŏs'ter)
Wŏrms (v-; -z)
Wrĕk'ĭn (r-)
Wўch'erley
Wўc'lĭf
Wўc'ombe (-om)
Wўk'eham (-kam)
Wymondham [Norfolk] (wĭnd'am)
Wўō'mĭng
Xăv'ĭer (z-)
Xĕn'ophon (z-)
Xĕr'xēs (z-; -z)
Xhosa (kaw'sa)
Yeats (yāts)
Ye'men (yă-)
Yeo'vil (yō-)
Yŏkōha'ma (-hah-)
Yŏsĕm'ĭtĕ
Ypres (ēpr, wĭ'perz)
Ysaye (ĭsī'ĭ)
Yucatan' (ū-; -ahn)
Zăcharī'ah (-a)
Zeiss (zīs)
Zĕlŏt'ēs (-z)
Zĕn'ō
Zĭmba'bwĕ (-bah-)
Zō'ĕ
Zŏl'a
Zŏrōăs'ter
Zürich (zūr'ĭk)
Zuĭ'der Zee' (zī-)

APPENDIX IV

WEIGHTS AND MEASURES

(a) ENGLISH AND METRIC EQUIVALENTS

Linear Measure:

English to Metric

1 inch	= 25·3999 millimetres.
1 foot (12 inches)	= 0·30480 metre.
1 yard (3 feet)	= 0·9144 metre.
1 pole (5½ yards)	= 5·02919 metres.
1 chain (22 yards)	= 20·11678 metres.
1 furlong (220 yards)	= 201·16778 metres.
1 mile (1,760 yards)	= 1·60934 kilometres.

Square Measure:

1 square inch	= 6·45159 sq. centimetres.
1 square foot (144 sq. in.)	= 9·29028 sq. decimetres.
1 square yard (9 sq. ft.)	= 0·836126 sq. metre.
1 perch (30¼ sq. yards)	= 25·29280 sq. metres.
1 rood (40 perches)	= 10·11712 ares.
1 acre (4,840 sq. yards)	= 0·40468 hectare.
1 square mile (640 acres)	= 258·99824 hectares.

Cubic Measure:

1 cubic inch	= 16·3870 cubic centimetres.
1 cubic foot (1,728 cub. in.)	= 0·02832 cubic metre.
1 cubic yard (27 cub. ft.)	= 0·764553 cubic metre.

Measure of Capacity:

1 gill	= 1·42058 decilitres.
1 pint (4 gills)	= 0·56823 litre.
1 quart (2 pints)	= 1·13646 litres.
1 gallon (4 quarts)	= 4·5459631 litres.
1 peck (2 gallons)	= 9·0917 litres.
1 bushel (8 gallons)	= 3·6366 dekalitres.
1 quarter (8 bushels)	= 2·90935 hectolitres.

Apothecaries' Measure:

1 fluid drachm (60 minims)	= 3·55145 millilitres.
1 fluid ounce (8 drachms)	= 2·84123 centilitres.
1 gal. (8 pints or 160 fluid ounces)	= 4·54596 litres.

Avoirdupois Weight:

1 grain	= 0·0648 gram.
1 dram (27·34 grains)	= 1·77185 grams.
1 ounce (16 drams)	= 28·34953 grams.
1 pound (16 ounces)	= 0·45359237 kilogram.
1 stone (14 lb.)	= 6·35029 kilograms.
1 quarter (28 lb.)	= 12·70059 kilograms.
1 hundredweight (cwt. = 112 lb.)	= 50·80235 kilograms.
1 ton (20 cwt.)	= 1·01604 metric tons.

Troy Weight:

1 pennyweight (24 grains)	= 1·55517 grams.
1 ounce (480 grains avdp.)	= 31·10348 grams.

Apothecaries' Weight:

1 scruple (20 grains)	= 1·29598 grams.
1 drachm (3 scruples)	= 3·88794 grams.
1 ounce (8 drachms)	= 31·10348 grams.

The Apothecaries' ounce is the Troy ounce of 480 Avoirdupois grains.

(b) METRIC AND ENGLISH EQUIVALENTS

Linear Measure:

Metric to English

1 millimetre (1/1000 m.)	= 0·03937 inch.
1 centimetre (1/100 m.)	= 0·39370 inch.
1 decimetre (1/10 m.)	= 3·93701 inches.
1 metre (m.)	= 1·0936143 yards.
1 decametre (10 m.)	= 10·93614 yards.
1 hectometre (100 m.)	= 109·3614 yards.
1 kilometre (1,000 m.)	= 0·62137 mile.
1 myriametre (10,000 m.)	= 6·21372 miles.

Square Measure:

1 sq. centimetre	= 0·15500 sq. inch.
1 sq. decimetre (100 sq. centimetres)	= 15·50006 sq. inches.
1 sq. metre or centiare (100 sq. decimetres)	} = { 10·76393 sq. feet. / 1·19599 sq. yards.
1 are (100 sq. metres)	= 119·59926 sq. yards.
1 hectare (100 ares or 10,000 sq. metres)	= 2·47106 acres.

Cubic Measurement:

1 cubic centimetre (1,000 cub. millimetres)	= 0·06102 cubic inch.
1 cubic decimetre (1,000 cub. centimetres)	= 61·02394 cubic inches.
1 cubic metre or stere (1,000 cub. decimetres)	} = { 35·31477 cubic feet. / 1·307954 cubic yards.

Measure of Capacity:

1 millilitre (1/1000 litre)	= 0·00704 gill.
1 centilitre (1/100 litre)	= 0·07039 gill.
1 decilitre (1/10 litre)	= 0·17598 pint.
1 litre	= 1·75985 pints.
1 decalitre (10 litres)	= 2·19981 gallons.
1 hectolitre (100 litres)	= 2·74976 bushels.
1 kilolitre (1,000 litres)	= 3·43720 quarters.

Weight:

1 milligram (1/1000 gm.)	= 0·01543 grain.
1 centigram (1/100 gm.)	= 0·15432 grain.
1 decigram (1/10 gm.)	= 1·54324 grains.
1 gram	= 15·43236 grains.
1 decagram (10 gm.)	= 5·64383 drams.
1 hectogram (100 gm.)	= 3·52740 ounces.
1 kilogram (1,000 gm.)	= 2·2046223 lb.
1 myriagram (10 kg.)	= 22·04622 lb.
1 quintal (100 kg.)	= 1·96841 cwt.
1 tonne (1,000 kg.)	= 0·98420 ton.

	Troy	0·03215 ounce.
	,,	15·43236 grains.
1 gram = {	Apothecaries'	0·25721 drachm.
	,,	0·77162 scruple.
	,,	15·43236 grains.